MW00714919

PERMANENT VOLUMES

Book Review Digest
Annual volumes 1905 to date

Book Review Digest Author/Title Index, 1905-1974
Book Review Digest Author/Title Index, 1975-1984
Book Review Digest Author/Title Index, 1985-1994

Book Review Digest, 2014, published by Grey House Publishing, Inc., Amenia, NY, under exclusive license from EBSCO Information Services, Inc.

International Standard Serial Number 0006-7326

International Standard Book Number 978-1-61925-279-0

Library of Congress Control Number 6-24490

Printed in Canada

BOOK REVIEW DIGEST

One-Hundred-Tenth Annual Cumulation

DECEMBER 2013 TO OCTOBER 2014 INCLUSIVE

H. W. Wilson
A Division of EBSCO Information Services
Ipswich, Massachusetts
2014
GREY HOUSE PUBLISHING

EXPLANATORY NOTES

Book Review Digest consists of the review listings and the Subject and Title Index.

CONTENT OF THE DIGEST

Review Listings

The main body of the Digest lists the books reviewed in alphabetical order by the last name of the author or by title, when the title is the main entry. The book citation includes the title, authorship responsibility, edition, series, pagination, illustration note, binding, year of publication, and publisher. Subject headings are derived from *Library of Congress Subject Headings*. The International Standard Book Number and Library of Congress Control Number are given when available.

A descriptive note, which is labeled SUMMARY, follows the book citation. It provides information about the content of the work and indicates the age or grade level for juvenile books. The source of the note is given in parentheses.

The review citations are labeled REVIEW. They are arranged alphabetically by periodical title abbreviation, which is printed in italic type. The full name of the periodical and other information pertaining to it are given in the List of Periodicals. The review citation also includes the volume number, page, and date of the periodical and the name of the reviewer. When an excerpt of the review is provided, the excerpt follows the citation.

Brackets and ellipsis points are used in the summaries and review excerpts to indicate interpolations and omissions from quoted texts.

Added entries for co-authors, editors, illustrators, and variant titles send the user to the main entry. *See* references guide the reader from variant forms of an author's name to the form that is used.

Subject and Title Index

The Subject and Title Index follows the main body of the Digest. Each book is listed under title (which is printed in lightface type) and under the subject headings that appear in the book citation. Additional access by genre is provided using headings for biographies, plays, poetry, and short stories.

Collections of short stories or novels for adults are entered under the heading for a topic, place name, personal name or corporate name with the subdivision *Fiction*, e.g., Ghosts—Fiction.

See references in the Subject and Title Index guide the user from terms not used as headings to those under which entries are to be found. When subject headings are changed to reflect new terminology, a see reference is made from the earlier form of the heading to the new form. *See* references are also provided from variant forms of book titles when appropriate

See also references guide the user from terms used as headings to related or more specific headings under which additional material may be found.

FILING

Alphabetization is based on *Library of Congress Filing Rules.* Numbers file before the letter A and are arranged according to their numerical value. When initials are separated by periods, other punctuation marks or spaces, each initial is treated as a separate word. Acronyms and initialisms in which the characters are not separated are treated as complete words. Initial articles in titles are disregarded. If a surname that includes an article or preposition is not found under the prefix, it should also be searched for under the part of the name following the prefix.

In the Subject and Title Index, subjects and titles are interfiled alphabetically. Subjects with subdivisions are treated as separate headings and filed alphabetically.

SAMPLE ENTRY

CLARK, DANIEL A. Creating the college man; American mass magazines and middle-class manhood, 1890-1915. 256p il 2010 University of Wisconsin Press

1. Middle class men—United States—History 2. Male college students 3. Education, Higher—United States—History 4. American periodicals—History
ISBN 978-0-299-23534-5 (pa); 0-299-23534-3 (pa)
LC 2009-40636

The book under review is entitled *Creating the college man; American mass magazines and middle-class manhood, 1890-1915* by Daniel A. Clark. It contains 256 pages and was published by University of Wisconsin Press in 2010. The subject headings assigned to this book are the topical subjects "Middle class men—United States—History," "Male college students," "Education, Higher—United States—History," and "American periodicals—History." The 13-digit International Standard Book Number for this item is 978-0-299-23534-5, and the 10-digit International Standard Book Number is 0-299-23534-3. The book is published in paperback. The Library of Congress Control Number is 2009-40636.

SUMMARY: Clark argues that early twentieth-century "popular magazines such as Cosmopolitan and the Saturday Evening Post . . . depicted the college man as simultaneously cultured and scientific, genteel and athletic, polished and tough." (Publisher's note). Index.

The summary is a description of the contents of the book. It is not a review, although it may be quoted from the descriptive, non-evaluative part of a review. In this case it is taken from the publisher's note.

REVIEW: *Am Hist Rev* v115 no5 p1482-3 D 2010. Clifford Putney

REVIEW: *Bookforum* v17 no2 p50 Je/Jl 2010. Isaiah Wilner
"Magazines were the first national news medium. They arrived before the radio and newsreels, backed by techniques and technologies . . . that spread a sensational brand of reporting that challenged governments, put pressure on trusts, and stimulated reform. . . . [This book is] an engaging contribution to the history of the mass media that provides evidence of the power of magazines to shape our mental lives."

The first review, by Clifford Putney, appeared in the December 2010 issue of *The American Historical Review*, volume 115, number 5, on pages 1482-3. The second review, by Isaiah Wilner, appeared in *Bookforum*, volume 17, number 2, June-July 2010, on page 50. Following the second review citation is an excerpt of the review, a quotation of the reviewer's own words.

ABBREVIATIONS

Ag	August
Ap	April
Aut	Autumn
bdg	binding
bk,-s	book, -s
comp	compiler
D	December
distr	distributed
ed	edited, -or
Engl	English
enl	enlarged
F	February
il	illustrations, -or
Ja	January
Je	June
Jl	July
lib	library
Mr	March
My	May
N	November
O	October
p	pages
pa	paper
pl	plates
pt	part
rev	revised
S	September
Spr	Spring
Summ	Summer
tr	translator
v; vol; vols	volume, -s
w	words
Wint	Winter

PERIODICALS INDEXED

A

AAAS Science Books and Films. See Science Books & Films

AJS. See American Journal of Sociology

America. w (except occasional bi-w issues) ISSN (0002-7049) America Press Inc., 106 W. 56th St., New York, NY 10019

American Academy of Political and Social Science Annals. See The Annals of the American Academy of Political and Social Science

American Academy of Religion Journal. See Journal of the American Academy of Religion

American Book Review. bi-m ISSN (0149-9408) School of Arts and Sciences, American Book Review, 3007 N. Ben Wilson, Victoria, TX 77901-5731

The American Historical Review. 5 times a yr ISSN (0002-8762) American Historical Assn., 400 A St., S.E., Washington, DC 20003

American Journal of Sociology. bi-m ISSN (0002-9602) University of Chicago Press, Journals Div., Subscription Fulfillment Dept., P.O. Box 37005, Chicago, IL 60637

American Literature. q ISSN (0002-9831) Duke University Press, Box 90660, College Station, Durham, NC 27708-0660

American Quarterly. q ISSN (0003-0678) Johns Hopkins University Press, 2715 N. Charles St., Baltimore, MD 21218-4319

The American Scholar. q ISSN (0003-0937) The American Scholar, Editorial and Circulation Offices, 1606 New Hampshire Ave., NW, Washington, DC 20009

The Annals of the American Academy of Political and Social Science. bi-m ISSN (0002-7162) Sage Publications, Inc., 2455 Teller Rd., Thousand Oaks, CA 91320

The Antioch Review. q ISSN (0003-5769) Antioch Review, Subscriptions, P.O. Box 148, Yellow Springs, OH 45387

Apollo (London, England). m ISSN (0003-6536) Apollo, c/o Speedimpex USA Inc., 35-02 Forty-Eighth Ave., Long Island City, New York 11101-2421

Archaeology. bi-m ISSN (0003-8113) Archaeology Subscription Service, P.O. Box 469025, Escondido, CA 92046-9025

Art in America. m ISSN (0004-3214) Art in America, P.O. Box 37003, Boone, IA 50037-0003

Atlantic Monthly (1993). m (bi-m Ja/F and Jl/Ag) ISSN (1072-7825) Atlantic Subscription Processing Center, Box 52661, Boulder, CO 80322

Audubon. q ISSN (0097-7136) National Audubon Society, Membership Data Center, P.O. Box 52529, Boulder, CO 80322

B

Bookforum. bi-m ISSN (1098-3376) Artforum International Magazine, 350 Seventh Avenue, New York, NY 10001

Booklist. semi-m (m Jl, Ag) ISSN (0006-7385) Booklist, P.O. Box 607, Mt. Morris, IL 61054-7564 Incorporating: Reference Books Bulletin

The British Journal of Sociology. q ISSN (0007-1315) The British Journal of Sociology, Routledge Journals Subscriptions, PO Box 362 Abingdon, Oxon, OX14 3WB England

The Bulletin of the Atomic Scientists. bi-m ISSN (0096-3402) Bulletin of the Atomic Scientists, Circulation Dept., 6042 S. Kimbark Ave., Chicago, IL 60637

Bulletin of the Center for Children's Books. m (except Ag) ISSN (0008-9036) Johns Hopkins University Press, Journals Publishing Div., 2715 N. Charles St., Baltimore, MD 21218

The Burlington Magazine. m ISSN (0007-6287) Royal Mail Intl., P.O. Box 618000, Dallas, TX 72561-8009

Business History Review. q ISSN (0007-6805) Business History Review, c/o Denise Rubino, Harvard Business School, 60 Harvard Way, Boston, MA 02163

Business Horizons. bi-m ISSN (0007-6813) JAI Press Inc., Subscription Dept., P.O. Box 1678, 55 Old Post Rd. No-2, Greenwich, CT 06830-7602

C

Canadian Historical Review. q ISSN (0008-3755) University of Toronto Press, Journals Dept., 5201 Dufferin St., Downsview, Ont. M3H 5T8, Canada

Canadian Literature. q ISSN (0008-4360) Canadian Literature, Buchanan E158, 1866 Main Mall, Vancouver, B.C. V6T 1Z1, Canada

Choice. m (bi-m Jl/Ag) ISSN (0009-4978) Association of College and Research Libraries, 100 Riverview Center, Middletown, CT 06457

The Christian Century. bi-w ISSN (0009-5281) Christian Century Subscription Service, 407 S. Dearborn St., Chicago, IL 60605-1150

The Christian Science Monitor (Eastern edition). daily (except Sat., Sun., & holidays) ISSN (0882-7729) The Christian Science Monitor, P.O. Box 37124, Boone, IA 50037-0124

Christianity Today. m (semi-m Ap, O) ISSN (0009-5753) Christianity Today Subscription Services, P.O. Box 37059, Boone, IA 50037-0059

The Classical Review. 2 times a yr ISSN (0009-840X) Cambridge University Press, The Edinburgh Bldg, Shaftesbury Rd, Cambridge CB2 2RU United Kingdom

The Classical World. q ISSN (0009-8418) The Classical World, Dept. of Classics, Duquesne University, Pittsburgh, PA 15282-1704

Columbia Journalism Review. bi-m ISSN (0010-194X) Columbia Journalism Review, Subscription Service Dept., P.O. Box 578, Mt. Morris, IL 61054

Commentary. m ISSN (0010-2601) American Jewish Committee, 165 E. 56th St., New York, NY 10022

Commonweal. bi-w (except Christmas/New Year's; m in Jl, Ag) ISSN (0010-3330) Commonweal Foundation, 475 Riverside Dr., Room 405, New York, NY 10115

Contemporary Sociology. bi-m ISSN (0094-3061) American Sociological Assn., Executive Office, 1722 N St., N.W., Washington, DC 20036

Current Anthropology. 5 times a yr ISSN (0011-3204) University of Chicago Press, Journals Div., Subscriptions Fulfillment Dept., P.O. Box 37005, Chicago, Illinois 60637

E

The Economist. w ISSN (0013-0613) Economist, Subscription Dept., P.O. Box 58524, Boulder, CO 80322-8524

Educational Studies (American Educational Studies Association). 6 times a yr ISSN (0013-1946) Erlbaum Associates, Inc., 10 Industrial Ave., Mahwah, NJ 07430-2262

Endeavour (Oxford, England). q ISSN (0160-9327) Pergamon Press Inc., 660 White Plains Rd., Tarrytown, NY 10591-5153

The English Historical Review. 5 times a yr ISSN (0013-8266) Oxford University Press, 2001 Evans Road, Cary, NC 27513 USA

Ethics. q ISSN (0014-1704) University of Chicago Press, Journals Div., Subscription Fulfillment Dept., P.O. Box 37005, Chicago, IL 60637

Ethnic and Racial Studies. bi-m ISSN (0141-9870) Routledge Journals, Subscription Dept., 29 W. 35th St., New York, NY 10001-2299

F

Film Quarterly. q ISSN (0015-1386) University of California Press, 2120 Berkeley Way, Berkeley, CA 94720

H

Harper's. m ISSN (0017-789X) Harper's Magazine, P.O. Box 7511, Red Oak, IA 51591-0511

Harvard Educational Review. q ISSN (0017-8055) Harvard Educational Review, Subscriber Service Dept., Gutman Library, Ste. 349, 6 Appian Way, Cambridge, MA 02138-3752

Harvard Review (1992). semi-ann ISSN (1077-2901) Houghton Library of the Harvard College Library, Lamont Library, Harvard University, Cambridge, MA 02138

History. q ISSN (0018-2648) Historical Assn., 59A Kennington Park Rd., London SE11 4JH, England

History Today. m ISSN (0018-2753) History Today, 20 Old Compton St., London W1V 5PE, England

The Horn Book. 6 times a yr ISSN (0018-5078) Horn Book Inc., 56 Roland St., Ste. 200, Boston, MA 02129

J

The Journal of American History. q ISSN (0021-8723) Organization of American Historians, 112 N. Bryan St., Bloomington, IN 47408-4199

The Journal of Economic Literature. q ISSN (0022-0515) American Economic Association, 2014 Broadway, Ste. 305, Nashville, TN 37203

Journal of Marriage and Family. 5 times a yr ISSN (0022-2445) National Council on Family Relations, 3989 Central Ave. NE, Ste. 550, Minneapolis, MN 55421

The Journal of Religion. q ISSN (0022-4189) University of Chicago Press, Journals Div., Subscription Fulfillment Dept., P.O. Box 37005, Chicago, IL 60637

Journal of the American Academy of Religion. q ISSN (0002-7189) Oxford University Press, Journals Customer Service, 2001 Evans Rd., Cary, NC 27513-2009

K

The Kenyon Review. q ISSN (0163-075X) The Kenyon Review, Kenyon College, Gambier, OH 43022

Kirkus Reviews (New York, N.Y.: 1991). semi-m Kirkus Service Inc., 200 Park Ave. South, New York, N.Y. 10003

L

Lancet (North American edition). w ISSN (0099-5355) Williams & Wilkins, 655 Avenue of the Americas, New York, NY 10010

Library Journal (1976). 20 times a yr ISSN (0363-0277) Reed Business Information, 8878 S. Barrons Blvd., Highlands Ranch, CO 80129-2345

London Review of Books. 24 times a yr ISSN (0260-9592) London Review of Books, P.O. Box 1953, Marion, OH 43305-1953

M

The Middle East Journal. q ISSN (0026-3141) Middle East Journal, 1761 N St., N.W., Washington, DC 20036-2882

Monthly Labor Review. m ISSN (0098-1818) Superintendent of Documents, U.S. Government Printing Office, Available from: http://www.bls.gov/opub/mlr/mlrhome.htm eased publication in print form with Vol. 130, No. 12 (December 2007) Electronic resource

Ms. q ISSN (0047-8318) Ms. Magazine, P.O. Box 5299, Harlan, IA 51593

MultiCultural Review. q ISSN (1058-9236) Greenwood Publishing Group, Inc., 88 Post Rd. W., P.O. Box 5007, Westport, CT 06881-5007

Music Library Association Notes. See Notes

N

The Nation. w (except 2nd week in Ja & bi-w 3rd week of Jl through 3rd week of S) ISSN (0027-8378) The Nation, P.O. Box 55149, Boulder, CO 80322-5149

National Review. bi-w (except 1st issue in Ja) ISSN (0028-0038) National Review, P.O. Box 668, Mt. Morris, IL 61054-0668

Natural History. m (bi-m Jl/Ag, D/Ja) ISSN (0028-0712) Natural History, Box 5000, Harlan, IA 51537-5000

The New England Quarterly. q ISSN (0028-4866) MIT Press Journals, 238 Main St., Suite 500, Cambridge, MA USA 02142-1406

The New Leader. bi-m ISSN (0028-6044) American Labor Conference on International Affairs, Inc., 275 Seventh Ave, New York, NY 1000, United States Publication suspended with Vol. 89, No. ½ (January/April 2006); resumed publication in electronic format with January/February 2007.

The New Republic. semi-m ISSN (0028-6583) Subscription Dept., New Republic, 1220 19th St, NW, Washington, DC 20036

New Scientist. w ISSN (0262-4079) New Scientist Publications, New Science Publications, Reed Business Information Ltd.,151 Wardour St., London W1F 8WE England

New Statesman (London, England: 1996). w ISSN (1364-7431) New Statesman & Society, C and C Mailers Int'l, 900 Lincoln Blvd., P.O. Box 177, Middlesex, NJ 08846

The New York Review of Books. bi-w (m Ja, Jl, Ag, S) ISSN (0028-7504) New York Review of Books, P.O. Box 420384, Palm Coast, FL 32142-0384

New York Times (Late New York Edition). daily ISSN (0362-4331) New York Times, Times Bldg., 229 W. 43rd St., New York, NY 10036

The New York Times Book Review. w ISSN (0028-7806) New York Times Co., Times Bldg., 229 W. 43rd St., New York, NY 10036

The New Yorker. w (except 6 combined issues) ISSN (0028-792X) The New Yorker, Box 56447, Boulder, CO 80328-6447

Newsweek. w ISSN (0028-9604) Newsweek, P.O. Box 59967, Boulder, CO 80322-9967

Notes. q ISSN (0027-4380) Music Library Association, Business Office, P.O. Box 487, Canton, MA 02021

O

Orion. bi-m ISSN (1058-3130) Orion, Subscription Dept., 136 E. 64th St., New York, NY 10021

P

Parameters (Carlisle Barracks, Pa.). q ISSN (0031-1723) Superintendent of Documents, U.S. Government Printing

Office, New Orders, P.O. Box 371954, Pittsburgh, PA 15250-7954

Poetry (Modern Poetry Association). m ISSN (0032-2032) Modern Poetry Assn., 60 W. Walton St., Chicago, IL 60610

Political Science Quarterly. q ISSN (0032-3195) Academy of Political Science, 475 Riverside Dr., Ste. 1274, New York, NY 10115-1274

Publishers Weekly. w (except last week in D) ISSN (0000-0019) Reed Business Information, 8878 S. Barrons Blvd., Highlands Ranch, CO 80129-2345

Q

Quill & Quire. m ISSN (0033-6491) Quill & Quire Customer Service, 35 Riviera Dr., Unit 17, Markham, Ont. L3R 8N4, Canada: Includes: Books for Young People (August 1989-)

R

Reference Books Bulletin. See Booklist

Religious Education. q ISSN (0034-4087) Publications Expediting, Inc., 200 Meacham Ave., Elmont NY 11003

Reviews in American History. q ISSN (0048-7511) Johns Hopkins University Press, Journals Publishing Div., 2715 N. Charles St., Baltimore, MD 21218-4319

S

School Library Journal. m ISSN (0362-8930) Reed Business Information, 8878 S. Barrons Blvd., Highlands Ranch, CO 80129-2345

Science. w (except last week in D) ISSN (0036-8075) American Association for the Advancement of Science, P.O. Box 1811, Danbury, CT 06813-1811

Science Books & Films. bi-m ISSN (0098-342X) Science Books & Films, P.O. Box 3000, Dept. SBF, Denville, NJ 07834

Scientific American. m ISSN (0036-8733) Scientific American, P.O. Box 3187, Harlan, IA 51593-2377

The Sewanee Review. q ISSN (0037-3052) The Johns Hopkins University Press, 2715 North Charles Street, Baltimore, Maryland 21218-4363

Sight & Sound. m ISSN (0037-4806) Mercury Airfreight International Ltd., Inc., 2323 Randolph Ave., Avenel, NJ 07001

Smithsonian. m ISSN (0037-7333) Smithsonian, P.O. Box 420311, Palm Coast, FL 32142-0311

Society. bi-m ISSN (0147-2011) Society, Box A, Rutgers-The State University, New Brunswick, NJ 08903

T

Time. w ISSN (0040-781X) Time, P.O. Box 30601, Tampa, FL 33630-0601

The Times Literary Supplement. w ISSN (0307-661X) TLS Subscriptions, P.O. Box 3000, Denville, NJ 07834

TLS. See The Times Literary Supplement

V

The Virginia Quarterly Review. q ISSN (0042-675X) The University of Virginia, One West Range, Charlottesville, VA 22903

VQR. See The Virginia Quarterly Review

W

Women's Review of Books. m (except Ag) ISSN (0738-1433) Old City Publishing, Inc., 628 North 2nd Street, Philadelphia, PA 19123 Temporarily suspended after December 2004

World Literature Today. q ISSN (0196-3570) University of Oklahoma Press, Editorial Office, 110 Monnet Hall, Univ. of Oklahoma, Norman, OK 73069

Y

The Yale Review. q ISSN (0044-0124) Blackwell Publishers, Yale Review, Subscriber Services Coordinator, 238 Main St., Cambridge, MA 02142

BOOK REVIEW DIGEST

2014

(Subject and Title index follows the review listings)

1001 IDEAS THAT CHANGED THE WAY WE THINK; 960 p. 2013 Pocket Books
1. Historical literature 2. Idea (Philosophy) 3. Intellectual life—History 4. Philosophy—History 5. Thought & thinking
ISBN 1476705720; 9781476705729

SUMMARY: This book, edited by Robert Arp, traces notable ideas throughout history. "The inspirational ideas explored here range from [Mahatma] Gandhi's theory of civil disobedience to Henry David Thoreau's praise of the simple life and Mary Wollstonecraft's groundbreaking advocacy of women's rights. The book also covers a wide variety of lifestyle concepts, such as 'rational dress' and naturism, and cultural movements including Neoclassicism, Surrealism, and Postmodernism." (Publisher's note)

REVIEW: *Booklist* v110 no11 p45 F 1 2014 Rachael Elrod

"1001 Ideas That Changed the Way We Think." "As the title reveals, this work covers ideas that have inspired humankind and changed our lives. Entries are listed chronologically, and the first is 'Human Control of Fire,' estimated to have occurred around 1,600,000 BCE, while the last entry is 'Not-Junk DNA,' regarding the human genome work done in 2012. . . . Colorful illustrations and photographs are found throughout the book--at least one and often more on every other page. This entertaining and informative book is recommended for both public and academic libraries."

REVIEW: *Libr J* v138 no21 p122 D 1 2013 Rosanne Cordell

100 ENTERTAINERS WHO CHANGED AMERICA; an encyclopedia of pop culture luminaries; 738 p. 2013 Greenwood, An Imprint of ABC-CLIO, LLC
1. Celebrities—United States—Biography Dictionaries 2. Encyclopedias & dictionaries 3. Entertainers—United States—Biography—Dictionaries 4. Fame 5. United States—Biography—Dictionaries
ISBN 9781598848304 (cloth : alk. paper)
LC 2013-000306

SUMMARY: This biographical encyclopedia of entertainers was edited by Robert C. Sickels. "Each article covers the subject's early life, career, and impact over the duration of his or her career (and after, in the case of those who are deceased). Articles run generally between 5 and 10 pages, include a clear black-and-white photo of the subject, and conclude with a bibliography of print works for more in-depth research." (Booklist)

REVIEW: *Booklist* v110 no5 p41 N 1 2013 Ann Welton

"100 Entertainers Who Changed America: An Encyclopedia of Pop Culture Luminaries." "Editor [Robert C.] Sickels notes that the deciding factor in inclusion was the question of influence over the times in which a person lived; and this method of determination seems to have been used relatively faithfully. . . .Unfortunately, the writing is extremely uneven. Most contributors have some university affiliation. . . and a significant percent of them are independent scholars; accordingly, the writing style runs the gamut between informed and readable and nearly unbearable, peppered with unclear sentences and in need of serious editing. Some of the articles are practically hagiographic--a poor practice when the subjects are still living and clearly less than perfect."

REVIEW: *Choice* v51 no6 p980 F 2014 G. M. Hermann

100 FIRST WORDS; 12 p. 2013 Tiger Tales
1. Bedtime 2. Clothing & dress—Juvenile literature 3. Picture books for children 4. Toys 5. Vocabulary—Juvenile literature
ISBN 1589256077; 9781589256071

SUMMARY: "This oversized lift-the-flap word book presents 100 terms that toddlers can relate to. Each large page is devoted to a category central to a toddler's life: toys, party time, bed and bath, clothes, fruit and vegetables, food, at the zoo, at the beach, on the farm, pets, out and about, and things that go. The individual words presented within each category are items that youngsters will be familiar with and interested by." (Kirkus Reviews)

REVIEW: *Kirkus Rev* v82 no1 p36 Ja 1 2014

"100 First Words". "Every page consists of a set of square and rectangular flaps bearing images—many of which incorporate photographs of babies and toddlers, most Caucasian—on bright, bold backgrounds. When the flaps are lifted, the word is revealed, along with another picture that represents it. It's not for babies and toddlers to explore on their own—the book is hefty, and the flaps are difficult to grasp and manipulate (they lift in different directions)—but suitable for guided exploration. . . . The engaging images and familiar terms presented will appeal to little ones and help them to add to their quickly expanding vocabularies."

REVIEW: *Kirkus Rev* v81 no19 p359 O 1 2013

1990; Russians remember a turning point; xvii, 521 p. 2013 MacLehose Press, Quercus
1. Historical literature 2. History—Sources
ISBN 9780857052001
LC 2013-376793

SUMMARY: This book examines "the aspirations of the Russian people in the days before Communism finally fell. It charts--among many other social developments--the appearance of new political parties and independent trade unions, the rapid evolution of mass media, the emergence of a new class of entrepreneurs, a new openness about sex and pornography and a sudden craze for hot-air ballooning, banned under the Communist regime." (Publisher's note)

REVIEW: *TLS* no5765 p8-9 S 27 2013 STEPHEN LOVELL

"1990: Russians Remember a Turning Point." "This enormously absorbing work shows us that the collapse of the Soviet Union, so extensively described by contemporaries and analysed by economists and political scientists, is ripe for appropriation by historians. . . . [It] contains chapters on a fascinating diversity of topics. . . . Its primary achievement is to plunge readers back into that turbulent moment and to make strange an era that has perhaps come to seem too familiar after all those telescoped accounts of the fall of Communism. Not only does the book range widely in its subject matter, it also offers instructive interplay between retrospective analysis and contemporary perception."

THE 2011 LIBYAN UPRISINGS AND THE STRUGGLE FOR THE POST-QADHAFI FUTURE; 2013 Palgrave Macmillan
ISBN 9781137308085 (hardback)
LC 2012-049574

SUMMARY: This book, by Jason Pack, "analyzes the 2011 Libyan uprisings thematically--focusing on the roles of economics, outside actors, tribes, ethnic minoritics, and Islamists. This volume's contributors include the British Ambassador to Libya during the uprisings, the President of the American University of Cairo, a former commander of the Libyan Islamic Fighting Group, and the world's leading academic and security specialists in Libyan affairs." (Publisher's note)

REVIEW: *Middle East J* v68 no1 p166-9 Wint 2014 Jacques Roumani

"The 2011 Libyan Uprising and the Struggle for the Post-Qadhafi Future." "They provide in-depth analyses of hte key dimensions of the uprising and its continuing sociopolitical and economic dynamics. This is an indispensable book for understanding Libya's renewed search for political community today and for the foreseeable future. Its appearance soon after the uprising began is a tribute to the editor and the authors. . . . Center-periphery relations . . . is an intriguing hypothesis about today's Libya, and it may be a way to reformulate the traditional power structure. . . . The problem is that after the collapse of the center, occupied solely by Qadhafi, there is no alternative institutional framework to define center-periphery relations."

THE 50 STATES; In Depth, Comprehensive Profiles of 50 Great States; 1210 p. 2013 Salem Press
1. Reference books 2. U.S. states 3. U.S. states—Charts, diagrams, etc. 4. U.S. states—Politics & government 5. U.S. states—Population
ISBN 1619252082 (hbk.); 9781619252080 (hbk.)

SUMMARY: This reference book on the 50 U.S. states, in its third edition, "comprises two volumes," including "facts regarding the state profile, state ranking for 30 topics, and 46 statistical tables from 'Educational Attainment,' to 'State Government Cash and Debt' and 'Public Road Length.' Facts from sources including the U.S. Department of Commerce, KIDS COUNT Data Center's Data Bank, and U.S. News and World Report can be read in the 'Survey Says' section." (Library Journal)

REVIEW: *Choice* v51 no7 p1188 Mr 2014 S. L. Pham

"The 50 States." "This third edition . . . of this two-volume work, arranged alphabetically by state, offers readers a wealth of interesting information. Each state has its own chapter, and includes a state profile, an essay on the state's history, and a time line of events. . . . Volume 2 includes state comparative ranking tables, along with an entry for the District of Columbia. Lastly, the set features photographs of each state capitol building and other points of interest. Overall, this is a straightforward, useful, and pleasing resource for all readers."

A

AAL, GHADA ABDEL. I want to get married!; one wannabe bride's misadventures with handsome Houdinis, technicolor grooms, morality police, and other Mr. not-quite-rights; [by] Ghada Abdel Aal xiv, 160 p. 2010 Center for Middle Eastern Studies at the University of Texas at Austin
1. Arranged marriage—Egypt—Blogs 2. Courtship—Egypt—Blogs 3. Memoirs 4. Women—Egypt—Social conditions—Blogs
ISBN 9780292723979 (paper : alk. paper)
LC 2010-934842

SUMMARY: "After years of searching for Mr. Right in living-room meetings arranged by family or friends, Ghada Abdel Aal, a young Egyptian professional, decided to take to the blogosphere to share her experiences and vent her frustrations at being young, single, and female in Egypt. . . . 'I Want to Get Married!' has since become a best-selling book in Egypt and the inspiration for a television series." (Publisher's note)

REVIEW: *World Lit Today* v88 no1 p6 Ja/F 2014 M. Lynx Qualey

"The Servant," I Want to Get Married!," and "Life Is More Beautiful Than Paradise." "'The Servant'--originally titled Faten, after its main character--is a beautiful coming-of-age story that follows a young teenager from rural Lebanon to her new life in Beirut. . . . ['I Want to Get Married'] began as a series of blog posts by author Ghada Abdel Aal, chronicling absurd family meetings and other woes on the path to searching for a suitable husband. . . . It's funny, sharp and engaging. . . . Khaled al-Berry's story begins in Asyut, a midsized upper Egyptian city, when he is thirteen years old. . . . This is not just the story of al-Berry's journey toward and away from religious conservatism but also his struggles with many ordinary adolescent concerns."

AARONOVITCH, BEN. Broken Homes; A Rivers of London Novel; [by] Ben Aaronovitch 320 p. 2014 Penguin Group USA
1. Magic—Fiction 2. Magicians—Fiction 3. Murder investigation—Fiction 4. Police—Fiction 5. Urban fantasy fiction
ISBN 0756409608; 9780756409609

SUMMARY: In this book, part of Ben Aaronovitch's "Rivers of London" series, "a mutilated body in Crawley means another murderer is on the loose. The prime suspect is one Robert Weil, who may either be a common serial killer or an associate of the twisted magician known as the Faceless Man." There is also a "case about a town planner going under a tube train and another about a stolen grimoire. . . . Just the typical day for a magician constable." (Publisher's note)

REVIEW: *Booklist* v110 no11 p34 F 1 2014 David Pitt

REVIEW: *Kirkus Rev* v82 no1 p250 Ja 1 2014

"Broken Homes". "Another entry in the Rivers of London urban fantasy series. . . . All this is even more shapeless than the summary indicates—a phenomenon mystery fans will be familiar with—and it's only in the last 50 pages or so that the plot coheres and the title's significance becomes apparent. Still, you've got to like a book where the city itself is the main character—literally. And there are plenty of surprises for alert readers. Worth a try for series fans, although, since [Ben] Aaronovitch provides no catch-up help, newcomers are best advised to begin at the beginning."

REVIEW: *Libr J* v139 no3 p78 F 15 2014 Megan M. McArdle

REVIEW: *Libr J* v139 no9 p38 My 15 2014 Dob West

ABANI, CHRIS. Song for night; a novella; [by] Chris Abani 164 2007 Akashic Books

1. Child soldiers—Fiction 2. Children—Africa 3. Children and war—Fiction 4. Novellas (Literary form)
ISBN 1933354313; 9781933354316
LC 2007--926049

SUMMARY: Written by Chris Abani, this novella "is the story of a West African boy soldier's . . . [journey] in search of his lost platoon. . . . The reader is led by the voiceless protagonist who, as part of a land mine-clearing platoon, had his vocal chords cut, a move to keep these children from screaming when blown up, and thereby distracting the other minesweepers."(Publisher's note)

REVIEW: *World Lit Today* v88 no2 p6 Mr/Ap 2014 J. L. Powers

"Song for Night," "Between Shades of Gray," and "Mali Under the Night Sky: A Lao Story of Home." "In this lyrical novella ['Song for Night'] narrated by a child soldier, we travel across a West African country as fifteen-year-old 'My Luck' searches for his platoon. . . . Fifteen-year-old Lina loves boys, drawing, her cousin, and her father, a professor in Soviet-occupied Lithuania. . . . [Author Ruta] Sepetys paints Lina's experiences in delicate, layered strokes, revealing the humanity of both prisoner and prison guard in unique and subtle ways. . . . In 'Mali under the Night Sky,' a true story, a young girl named Mali flees her beloved home in Laos, seeking safety on foreign soil."

ABANI, CHRISTOPHER, 1966-. The secret history of Las Vegas; a novel; [by] Christopher Abani 336 p. 2014 Penguin Books

1. Detective & mystery stories 2. Murder—Fiction 3. Secrets—Fiction 4. Twins—Fiction
ISBN 0143124951; 9780143124955
LC 2013-033496

SUMMARY: In this book, by Chris Abani, "Las Vegas detective Salazar is determined to solve a recent spate of murders. When he encounters a pair of conjoined twins with a container of blood near their car, he's sure he has apprehended the killers, and enlists the help of Dr. Sunil Singh, a South African transplant who specializes in the study of psychopaths. As Sunil tries to crack the twins, the implications of his research grow darker." (Publisher's note)

REVIEW: *Booklist* v110 no7 p29-30 D 1 2013 Stephanie Zvirin

REVIEW: *Kirkus Rev* v82 no1 p186 Ja 1 2014

"The Secret History of Las Vegas". "A detective on the brink of retirement and a psychiatrist with a guilty burden are brought together by a series of deaths in Las Vegas in this grim but beautifully written tale. . . . [Chris] Abani . . . creates vivid metaphors not just with his characters, but also with a drowned town emerging from the waters of Lake Mead, a ghost town that hosts the Carnival of Lost Souls, and the city of Las Vegas, which celebrates the dark, the hidden and the grotesque."

REVIEW: *Libr J* v139 no1 p1 Ja 2014

REVIEW: *Libr J* v139 no6 p55 Ap 1 2014 Cliff Glaviano

REVIEW: *N Y Times Book Rev* p17 Ja 26 2014 MARCEL THEROUX

REVIEW: *Publ Wkly* v260 no48 p35 N 25 2013

ABBOTT, PHILIP. Bad presidents; failure in the White House; [by] Philip Abbott x, 260 p. 2013 Palgrave Macmillan

1. Kings & rulers in literature 2. Political leadership—United States—Case studies 3. Political science literature 4. Presidents—United States—History 5. Shakespeare, William, 1564-1616—Characters
ISBN 9781137306586 (alk. paper)
LC 2012-037740

SUMMARY: In this book, "based on the insights found in [William] Shakespeare's treatment of two bad kings, [Philip] Abbott identifies two kinds of bad presidents and examines the case for including eleven in this category. In each case study, from John Tyler to Richard Nixon . . . he finds a tipping point that places them in this unenviable category. Abbott concludes by discussing why we elected these bad presidents . . . and how we might avoid adding future bad presidents to the list." (Publisher's note)

REVIEW: *Choice* v51 no6 p1093 F 2014 D. P. Franklin

"Bad Presidents: Failure in the White House." "There is much speculation as to who were the best presidents and why. But there is very little thought given to who were not the best and why not. This fascinating book attempts to fill that gap. . . . Ultimately, the success of this book depends on its classification scheme, the author's ingenious attempt to use a literary analogy to rate presidents. . . . Although literature tells a lot about the human character, [Philip] Abbott . . . ultimately fails because actual historical precedents are as difficult to buttonhole as are the best fictional characters. However, he should be applauded for the attempt. This entertaining book is worth the read for its thoughtful insights into why presidents fail."

ABBOTT, STACEY. TV horror; investigating the dark side of the small screen; [by] Stacey Abbott xv, 270 p. 2013 I.B. Tauris

1. Historical literature 2. Horror television programs 3. Horror television programs—History and criticism 4. Television programs—Great Britain 5. Television programs—History 6. Television programs—United States
ISBN 1848856172 (hbk.); 1848856180 (pbk.); 9781848856172 (hbk.); 9781848856189 (pbk.)
LC 2012-533815

SUMMARY: In this book, authors Lorna Jowett and Stace Abbott show "how TV Horror continues to provoke and terrify audiences by bringing the monstrous and the supernatural into the home, whether through adaptations of Stephen King and classic horror novels, or by reworking the gothic and surrealism in 'Twin Peaks' and 'Carnivale.' They uncover horror in mainstream television from procedural dramas to children's television and, through close analysis of landmark TV auteurs . . ." (Publisher's note)

REVIEW: *Choice* v51 no2 p252-3 O 2013 K. Hatch

"TV Horror: Investigating the Dark Side of the Small Screen." "[Authors Lorna] Jowett . . . and [Stacey] Abbott . . . demonstrate that horror has constituted a substantial portion of British and American television programming from the 1950s to the present, challenging the view that horror is antithetical to TV. The authors closely analyze episodes of shows ranging from 'Dark Shadows' and 'Night Gallery to Twin Peaks' and 'Dexter' to understand how the genre has been shaped by the medium of television. The book is clearly written, and the authors succinctly summarize the scholarship they cite. . . . In tackling such a broad subject, however, they tend toward generalizations rather than nuanced analysis, which may make the book of limited appeal to scholars."

A'BECKETT, JOHN.ed. Ljubljana Tales. See Ljubljana Tales

ABI-RACHED, JOELLE M. Neuro. See Rose, N.

ABLEY, MARK. Conversations With a Dead Man; The Legacy of Duncan Campbell Scott; [by] Mark Abley 256 p. 2014 Pgw

1. Canada. Dept. of Indian Affairs 2. Canadian poets 3. Historical literature 4. Imaginary conversations 5. Scott, Duncan Campbell, 1862-1947

ISBN 1553656091

SUMMARY: This book examines Canadian poet Duncan Campbell Scott. "In his nearly two decades as the head of the Department of Indian Affairs, Scott worked to force the people of First Nations to assimilate, suppressing their traditions, presiding over the charnel house residential school system. . . . The author attempts to humanize this great monster in a series of imagined conversations . . . in the process underlining how Scott's essentially racist views inform some of his lauded poems." (Publishers Weekly)

REVIEW: *Quill Quire* v80 no1 p38 Ja/F 2014 Paul Gessell

"Conversations With a Dead Man: The Legacy of Duncan Campbell Scott". "Should Scott's poetry be overshadowed by his role as a racist bureaucrat? . . . Should historical figures be judged according to today's mores or those of their own time, or by some other yardstick? Montreal author Mark Abley wades into these thorny issues in his new book, which is cast as a spirited debate between Abley and Scott's ghost, who ohas appeared to try to rehabilitate his reputation. Though unforgiving of Scott's various transgressions, Abley presents a very nuanced portrait of a man's troubled soul. . . . Far too little is said about his poetry, which is also part of his legacy. . . . Nevertheless, this disturbing page-turner is an insightful contribution to the debate."

ABLIN, RICHARD J. The great prostate hoax. See Piana, R.

ABORIGINAL PEOPLES AND FOREST LANDS IN CANADA; xi, 352 p. 2013 UBC Press

1. Aboriginal title—Canada 2. Forest management—Canada 3. Forest policy—Canada 4. Forestry literature 5. Forests and forestry—Canada 6. Human ecology—Canada 7. Indian business enterprises—Canada 8. Indians of North America—Canada—Economic conditions 9. Indians of North America—Land tenure—Canada 10. Native peoples—Ecology—Canada 11. Native peoples—Land tenure—Canada 12. Traditional ecological knowledge—Canada

ISBN 0774823348; 0774823356; 9780774823340; 9780774823357

LC 2012-554411

SUMMARY: Editors D.B. Tindall, Ronald L. Trosper, and Pamela Perreault "bring together the diverse perspectives of Aboriginal and non-Aboriginal scholars to address the political, cultural, environmental, and economic implications of forest use. This book discusses the need for professionals working in forestry and conservation to understand the context of Aboriginal participation in resource management." (Publisher's note)

REVIEW: *Choice* v51 no2 p292-3 O 2013 J. L. Rhoades

"Aboriginal Peoples and Forest Lands in Canada." "[Editors D. B.] Tindall . . . , [Ronald L.] Trosper . . . , and [Pamela] Perreault . . . have compiled and edited contributions from both 'Aboriginal and non- Aboriginal scholars' to produce this volume. Advocating for increased aboriginal co-management of forest lands, the book explores topics ranging from the historical impacts of colonialism and treaty negotiation to conflicts over forest use and the complexities of present-day policy formation. Many chapters ground these subjects in specific historical and contemporary case studies from British Columbia. Overall, the book presents a meaningful contribution to the subject of aboriginal participation in Canadian forest management."

ABORIGINAL PEOPLES AND SPORT IN CANADA; historical foundations and contemporary issues; x, 254 p. 2013 UBC Press

1. Historical literature 2. Indigenous peoples—Sports—Canada 3. Native peoples—Canada—Social conditions 4. Native peoples—Sports—Canada 5. Native peoples—Sports—Social aspects—Canada

ISBN 0774824204; 9780774824200

LC 2013-409291

SUMMARY: This book "is an interdisciplinary anthology that brings together fourteen leading scholars to offer an ethnographic study of Aboriginal people's involvement in sport in Canada. It was the authors' intent to "demonstrate the value of positioning sport studies alongside the larger literature on Aboriginal peoples, while revealing 'the extent to which sport plays an integral role in understandings of Aboriginal history, culture, identity, politics, and health.'" (Canadian Historical Review)

REVIEW: *Can Hist Rev* v95 no1 p101-42 Mr 2014

"Settling and Unsettling Memories: Essays in Canadian Public History," "Prophetic Identities: Indigenous Missionaries on British Colonial Frontiers," and "Aboriginal Peoples and Sport in Canada: Historical Foundations and Contemporary Issues". "This important collection maps the rapidly expanding field of collective memory in Canada, presenting a sampling of articles that usefully balances older pioneering studies by established practitioners with more recent work by emerging scholars. . . . In comparative work at its best, [Tolly] Bradford argues that these two, admittedly exceptional Indigenous missionaries created for themselves "new" Indigenous identities. What makes this study noteworthy is its framing of these men within empire and the processes of modernity. . . . 'Aboriginal Peoples and Sport in Canada' stands as an exceptional collection that demonstrates the ways in which sport studies can make Aboriginal world views accessible to a non-Aboriginal audience."

REVIEW: *Choice* v50 no11 p2058 Jl 2013 E. Smith

ABRAMS, DOUGLAS CARLTON.ed. The book of forgiving. See Tutu, D.

ABRAMS, JEANNE E. Revolutionary medicine; the Founding Fathers and mothers in sickness and in health; [by] Jeanne E. Abrams 304 p. 2013 New York University Press

1. Founding Fathers of the United States 2. Historical literature 3. Medical care—United States—History—18th century 4. Medical care—United States—History—19th century 5. Public health—Philosophy 6. Public health—United States—History—18th century 7. Public health—United States—History—19th century
ISBN 9780814789193 (cl: alk. paper)
LC 2013-010673

SUMMARY: In this book on early American medicine by Jeanne E. Abrams, "five case studies demonstrate the new nation's state of medical practice, the founders' bouts of illness and the republican ideal that individual and national health were connected—the roots, Abrams argues, of repeated attempts to rationalize our national health-care system." (American History)

REVIEW: *Choice* v51 no8 p1436 Ap 2014 I. Richman
"Revolutionary Medicine: The Founding Fathers and Mothers in Sickness and in Health". "There's nothing 'revolutionary' in this spiritedly written, intensively researched book by historian [Jeanne E.] Abrams. . . . However, readers learn that Thomas Jefferson was the healthiest of the Founding Fathers. He, along with Benjamin Franklin, also took informed scientific interest in health issues. . . . Magnificently indexed, this is not a specialist's book, but rather one of special value to undergraduates. It also deserves a wide audience of general readers."

REVIEW: *N Y Rev Books* v61 no12 p43-5 Jl 10 2014 Gordon S. Wood

REVIEW: *Publ Wkly* v260 no26 p81 Jl 1 2013

ABRAMS, ROGER I. Playing tough; the world of sports and politics; [by] Roger I. Abrams xii, 258 p. 2013 Northeastern University Press

1. Social science literature 2. Sports—History 3. Sports—Political aspects 4. Sports and society 5. Sports and state
ISBN 9781555537531 (cloth : alk. paper); 9781555538156 (ebook)
LC 2012-042100

SUMMARY: This book by Roger I. Abrams "focuses on the historical relationship between sports and politics, primarily from the late 19th century onward. He approaches the subject through eight test cases, ranging from sports and machine politics during the Gilded Age, the 1936 Olympics, and the Central American 'fútbol war' to Muhammad Ali, Olympic boycotts, the use and misuse of sports in South Africa, and financing modern stadiums." (Choice: Current Reviews for Academic Libraries)

REVIEW: *Choice* v51 no6 p1050 F 2014 R. W. Roberts
"Playing Tough: The World of Sports and Politics." "Each chapter tells a distinct, compelling story of the relationship between sports and politics, and the whole strips away any illusion that sports can exist without political implications. [Roger I.] Abrams writes for a general audience, and the book will be welcome by anyone interested in sports history. Some may suggest certain other political/sports episodes, but few can argue with the legitimacy of Abrams's claim. . . Highly recommended."

ABRAMSKY, SASHA. The American way of poverty; how the other half still lives; [by] Sasha Abramsky 368 p. 2013 Nation Books

1. Equality—United States 2. Poor—United States 3. Poverty—United States 4. Social science literature
ISBN 1568587260; 9781568587264 (hardback)
LC 2013-018771

SUMMARY: In this book author Sasha Abramsky "explores poverty in America 50 years after Michael Harrington's groundbreaking book, The Other America. Abramsky offers historical perspective, detailing how poverty as well as social attitudes and public policy regarding poverty have changed. He points to the antitax policies of conservatives that have contributed to growing income inequality in the U.S." (Publisher's note)

REVIEW: *Booklist* v110 no1 p5-6 S 1 2013 Vanessa Bush
"The American Way of Poverty: How the Other Half Still Lives." "[Sasha] Abramsky's portraits of the poor illustrate three striking points: the isolation, diversity--people with no jobs and people with multiple jobs--and resilience of the poor. Drawing on ideas from a broad array of equality advocates, Abramsky offers detailed policies to address poverty, including reform in education, immigration, energy, taxation, criminal justice, housing, Social Security, and Medicaid, as well as analysis of tax and spending policies that could reduce inequities."

REVIEW: *Choice* v51 no6 p1059 F 2014 R. S. Rycroft

REVIEW: *Kirkus Rev* v81 no13 p174 Jl 1 2013

REVIEW: *N Y Times Book Rev* p21 S 22 2013 DAVID K. SHIPLER

REVIEW: *N Y Times Book Rev* p26-8 D 8 2013
"The Accursed," "Children Are Diamonds: An African Apocalypse," "The American Way of Poverty: How the Other Half Still Lives." "['The Accursed' is Joyce Carol] Oates's extravagantly horrifying, funny prolix postmodern Gothic novel. . . . The adventure-seeking protagonist of [Edward] Hoagland's novel ['Children Are Diamonds: An African Apocalypse'] is swept up in the chaos of southern Sudan. . . . ['The American Way of Poverty'], based on [author Sasha] Abramsky's travels around the country meeting the poor, both describes and prescribes."

REVIEW: *Publ Wkly* v260 no27 p1-1/2 Jl 8 2013

ABU-ZAHRA, NADIA. Unfree in Palestine; registration, documentation and movement restriction; [by] Nadia Abu-Zahra x, 222 p. 2013 Pluto Press Distributed in the U.S. by Palgrave Macmillan

1. Identification cards—Law and legislation—Palestine 2. Palestinian Arabs—Palestine—Social conditions 3. Privacy, Right of—Palestine 4. Race discrimination—Palestine 5. Social science literature
ISBN 0745325270 (Paperback); 0745325289 (Hardback); 9780745325279 (Paperback); 9780745325286 (Hardback)
LC 2012-474336

SUMMARY: Written by Nadia Abu-Zahra and Adah Kay, this book "reveals the role played by identity documents in Israel's apartheid policies towards the Palestinians, from the red passes of the 1950s to the orange, green and blue passes of today. The authors chronicle how millions of Palestinians have been denationalised through the bureaucratic tools of census, population registration, blacklisting and a discriminatory legal framework." (Publisher's note)

REVIEW: *Choice* v51 no2 p344 O 2013 G. E. Perry

"Unfree in Palestine: Registration, Documentation, and Movement Restriction." "Although much of the material in this excellent book by [Nadia] Abu-Zahra . . . and [Adah] Kay . . . is hardly new to scholars, the authors provide unique, well-researched analysis of the dynamics of oppression. They put this under the overall rubric of 'denationalization' of those who were Palestinian nationals under the British mandate and stress the roles of population registration, identity documents, and restrictions on movement. . . . 'Unfree in Palestine' should interest Middle East specialists and those from a variety of disciplines, notably comparative politics, dealing broadly with settler colonialism, human rights, and techniques for keeping populations subordinated."

ABUL-MAGD, ZEINAB. Imagined empires; a history of revolt in Egypt; [by] Zeinab Abul-Magd 201 p. 2013 University of California Press

1. Elite (Social sciences)—Egypt—History 2. Government, Resistance to—Egypt—History 3. Historical literature 4. Imperialism—History 5. Peasants—Political activity—Egypt—History 6. Postcolonial analysis 7. Revolutions—Egypt—History 8. Working class—Political activity—Egypt—History

ISBN 9780520275522 (cloth: acid-free paper); 9780520275539 (paper: acid-free paper)

LC 2013-003749

SUMMARY: "Through a microhistory of a small province in Upper Egypt, this book investigates the history of five world empires that assumed hegemony in Qina province over the last five centuries." Written by Zeinab Abul-Magd, "'Imagined Empires' charts modes of subaltern rebellion against the destructive policies of colonial intruders and collaborating local elites in the south of Egypt." (Publisher's note)

REVIEW: *Choice* v51 no5 p899 Ja 2014 B. Harris Jr.

REVIEW: *Middle East J* v68 no3 p470-2 Summ 2014 Terence Walz

"Imagined Empires: A History of Revolt in Egypt." "Zeinab Abul-Magd's history of Upper Egypt covers the 1750-1950 period, and is centered on the idea that this region has always been suppressed by the governments of Cairo and the north, regardless of the dynasty or empire in control. . . . Abul-Magd's style is rousing and deliberate—this is not a subtle historical study. . . . Students will read 'Imagined Empires' for its postcolonial recasting of a people's history and appreciate the immense research that went into it. Historians of the period and of Upper Egypt will be grateful for the spotlight on this long-neglected region, but might have hoped for more facts about people and events from the voluminous archives she consulted."

ACAMPORA, PAUL. I kill the mockingbird; [by] Paul Acampora 176 p. 2014 Roaring Brook Press

1. Books and reading—Fiction 2. Friendship—Fiction 3. Psychological fiction

ISBN 9781596437425 (hardback)

LC 2013-044998

SUMMARY: In this book, "Lucy and her bibliophile best friends Elena and Michael embark on a campaign of literary rebellion in an attempt to compel fellow students to read To Kill a Mockingbird over the summer. Their plan? Hide copies of Harper Lee's classic novel in local bookstores and libraries, which will promote a false sense of scarcity and increase demand. . . . Before long the friends' brand of 'literary terrorism' has grown out of their control." (Publishers Weekly)

REVIEW: *Booklist* v110 no17 p96 My 1 2014 Michael Cart

REVIEW: *Bull Cent Child Books* v67 no10 p494 Je 2014 K. Q. G.

"I Kill the Mockingbird". "The plot is breezily amiable, and it provides a lighthearted focal point for an otherwise emotionally challenging summer for young Lucy. . . . The banter among the three whip-smart friends would make John Green proud, and they manage to come off as intelligent but not precocious, witty without being unrealistic. Lucy is very much a young fourteen in some ways (a chaste kiss with Michael seems awfully daring in her eyes), but her sharp observations regarding her Catholic faith, her mother's mortality, and the shifting dynamics of adolescent friendships reveal an age-appropriate wisdom. You won't have to hide any copies of this to create demand."

REVIEW: *Horn Book Magazine* v90 no4 p87 Jl/Ag 2014 ELISSA GERSHOWITZ

REVIEW: *Kirkus Rev* v82 no5 p197 Mr 1 2014

REVIEW: *Publ Wkly* v261 no13 p66 Mr 31 2014

REVIEW: *SLJ* v60 no4 p138 Ap 2014 Kathy Kirchoefer

REVIEW: *Voice of Youth Advocates* v37 no1 p58 Ap 2014 Jennifer M. Miskec

ACHTERBERG, PETER.ed. The transformation of solidarity. See The transformation of solidarity

ACKERMAN, BRUCE. We the people; the civil rights revolution; [by] Bruce Ackerman 432 p. 2014 The Belknap Press of Harvard University Press

1. African Americans—Civil rights 2. Civil rights—United States 3. Constitutional history—United States 4. Constitutional law—United States 5. Historical literature

ISBN 0674050290; 9780674050297 (alk. paper)

LC 2013-031132

SUMMARY: This book by Bruce Ackerman is a "sweeping reinterpretation of constitutional history . . . beginning with Brown v. Board of Education. From Rosa Parks's courageous defiance . . . to the Supreme Court's decisions . . . the movement to end racial discrimination decisively changed our understanding of the Constitution. Ackerman anchors his discussion in the landmark statutes of the 1960s: the Civil Rights Act of 1964, the Voting Rights Act of 1965, and the Fair Housing Act of 1968." (Publisher's note)

REVIEW: *Atlantic* v313 no3 p88-98 Ap 2014 MICHAEL O'DONNELL

"We the People: The Civil Rights Revolution," "An Idea Whose Time Has Come: Two Presidents, Two Parties, and the Battle for the Civil Rights Act of 1964," and "The Years of Lyndon Johnson: The Passage of Power". "[Bruce] Ackerman's is the most ambitious; it is the third volume in an ongoing series on American constitutional history called 'We the People'. . . . [Todd S.] Purdum's . . . book is an astute, well-paced, and highly readable play-by-play of the bill's journey to become a law. . . . Purdum's version of this story is excellent, but he cannot surpass the masterful Robert A. Caro, who offers a peerless and truly mesmerizing account of Johnson's assumption of the presidency in 'The Passage of Power'."

REVIEW: *Kirkus Rev* v82 no1 p193 Ja 1 2014

REVIEW: *Libr J* v139 no5 p128 Mr 15 2014 Becky Kennedy

REVIEW: *Publ Wkly* v260 no51 p50 D 16 2013

ACKROYD, PETER, 1949-. Three brothers; a novel; [by] Peter Ackroyd 256 p. 2014 Nan A. Talese, Doubleday

1. Brothers—Fiction 2. City and town life—England—London—Fiction 3. FICTION—Historical 4. FICTION—Literary 5. FICTION—Sagas 6. Reporters & reporting—Fiction
ISBN 9780385538619
LC 2013-033737

SUMMARY: This book "follows the fortunes of Harry, Daniel, and Sam Hanway, a trio of brothers born on a postwar council estate in Camden Town. Marked from the start by curious coincidence, each boy is forced to make his own way in the world—a world of dodgy deals and big business, of criminal gangs and crooked landlords, of newspaper magnates, backbiters, and petty thieves. London is the backdrop and the connecting fabric of these three lives." (Publisher's note)

REVIEW: *Booklist* v110 no11 p31 F 1 2014 Adam Morgan

REVIEW: *Kirkus Rev* v82 no1 p254 Ja 1 2014

REVIEW: *Kirkus Rev* v82 no1 p254 Ja 1 2014

"Three Brothers". "[An] intriguing if inconsistent . . . stew of family saga, murder mystery, political conspiracy and tableau of London's history. . . . With its echoes of Charles Dickens and the angry young men of the 1950s, and its population of caricatures and ghosts, Ackroyd's short novel maintains a patchy course, passing through gothic flourishes to reach an open-ended conclusion. At times humdrum and perfunctory, at others fantastical, this genre-spanning novel offers lightweight bookish entertainment."

REVIEW: *N Y Times Book Rev* p13 Ap 20 2014 GARY KRIST

REVIEW: *Publ Wkly* v261 no2 p48-9 Ja 13 2014

REVIEW: *TLS* no5769 p22 O 25 2013 EDMUND GORDON

"Three Brothers." "The London literary world . . . is expressively drawn. . . . The most consistent presence in 'Three Brothers' is that of London itself: grand, shadowy, seedy, influencing the mood of the novel and lives of its protagonists. In spite of these connecting threads, the three brothers often seem to belong to three different books: . . . The discord between the stories is only partially harmonized by the patter of an omniscient narrator. . . . 'Three Brothers' is consistently intriguing and intermittently gripping, but it is a strangely unfocused performance."

ACKROYD, PETER, 1949-. Tudors; The History of England from Henry VIII to Elizabeth I; [by] Peter Ackroyd 512 p. 2013 Thomas Dunne Books

1. Historical literature 2. Reformation 3. Religion & state
ISBN 1250003628; 9781250003621
LC 2013-024573

SUMMARY: This book, the "second title in [Peter Ackroyd's] projected six-volume history of England," focuses on "the 16th-century religious reformation that began, as a dynastic matter, with Henry VIII's divorce from Katherine of Aragon in 1533. . . . The Reformation in England was marked by upheaval and bloodshed, as the Tudors imposed religious changes upon an initially reluctant populace." (Publishers Weekly)

REVIEW: *Booklist* v110 no1 p29 S 1 2013 Brad Hooper

"Tudors: The History of England From Henry VIII to Elizabeth I." "The Tudor era was pivotal in English history and remains of perennial interest to the general reader. [Peter] Ackroyd takes on this much-written-about family history in his new, highly engaging book. His bona fides as an author to trust and enjoy rest on many well-appreciated nonfiction titles. . . . Ackroyd presents in rich prose and careful explanations how the English Reformation was not a movement of the people but a personal project of King Henry, who, Ackroyd insists, remained, despite his removal of papal authority over the English church, an orthodox Catholic."

REVIEW: *Choice* v51 no9 p1667-8 My 2014 M. Frasier-Robinson

REVIEW: *Choice* v51 no9 p1667-8 My 2014 M. Frasier-Robinson

"Tudors: The History of England From Henry VIII to Elizabeth I". "In this study, the second of a planned six-volume history of England . . . [Peter] Ackroyd recounts the reigns of four Tudor monarchs from the accession of Henry VIII in 1509 to the death of Elizabeth I in 1603. The author successfully illustrates how Tudor England left the medieval world behind and embraced the early modern era. . . . Ackroyd's thoroughly researched narrative of the notorious Tudors is colorful, engaging, and highly accessible to general readers."

REVIEW: *Libr J* v138 no15 p84 S 15 2013 Kathleen McCallister

REVIEW: *Kirkus Rev* v81 no17 p41 S 1 2013

REVIEW: *Libr J* v138 no8 p61 My 1 2013

REVIEW: *Publ Wkly* v260 no31 p60 Ag 5 2013

ACOSTA, KATIE L. Amigas y amantes; sexually nonconforming Latinas negotiate family; [by] Katie L. Acosta xi, 167 p. 2013 Rutgers University Press

1. Hispanic American bisexual women 2. Hispanic American lesbians 3. Hispanic American women—Family relationships 4. Lesbian mothers 5. Social science literature
ISBN 9780813561950 (pbk.: alk. paper); 9780813561967 (hardcover: alk. paper)
LC 2013-000430

SUMMARY: This book by Katie L. Acosta "examines how Latinas manage the multiple relationships in their lives—with their families, friends, children, and partners. Social status, education, immigration, and the Latino/a culture all play a role in how these women negotiate, or fail to negotiate, their lives with a same-sex partner. Quite often, those who lack familial acknowledgment and support find themselves in either abusive or failed relationships." (Choice: Current Reviews for Academic Libraries)

REVIEW: *Choice* v51 no9 p1686-7 My 2014 M. Martinez

"Amigas y Amantes: Sexually Nonconforming Latinas Negotiate Family". "This book fills a large gap in social science research on same-sex relationships; oftentimes. Latinas and other minorities are subsumed by scholarship on white lesbians. Furthermore, [Katie L.] Acosta addresses unique struggles of same-sex relationships among Latinas, such as interracial/interethnic same-sex couples, and struggles faced by poor and undocumented LBQ mothers and women. A well-written, deeply engaging sociological work that discusses and promotes thought on gender conformity and femininity within the Latina culture. All academic libraries with sociology or women's studies programs absolutely must own this book."

ACQUISTO, JOSEPH.ed. Thinking poetry. See Thinking poetry

ADAMOVICH, ALES. Khatyn; [by] Ales Adamovich 332 p. 2012 Glagoslav Publications Ltd.

1. Khatyn War Memorial (Belarus) 2. War stories 3. World War, 1939-1945—Atrocities—Belarus 4. World War, 1939-1945—Belarus 5. World War, 1939-1945—Underground movements—Belarus

ISBN 1909156086; 9781909156081

SUMMARY: In this World War II novel, which follows "Flyora--a boy who matures during the war--author Ales Adamovich beholds genocide and horrific crimes against humanity. The former teen partisan goes back in time and remembers atrocities of 1943. The novel's pages become the stage where perished people come to life for one last time, get to say their last word, all at the backdrop of blood chilling cries of women and children being burned alive by a Nazi death squad." (Publisher's note)

REVIEW: *TLS* no5755 p10-1 Jl 19 2013 TIMOTHY SNYDER

"Khatyn." "In 'Khatyn' the authorial power arises not from the time and skill needed to describe a setting, but rather from [Ales] Adamovich's startling capacity to make us see a swamp, a forest, a village or a corpse among the associations they provoke in Florian's mind. . . . The extraordinary depiction of an extraordinary war, the achieved rendering of unachieved Florian, and in general the mastered modernism of the prose all place 'Khatyn' on the shortlist of the great novels of the twentieth century."

ADAMS, GEOFF W. Marcus Aurelius in the Historia Augusta and beyond; [by] Geoff W. Adams ix, 333 p. 2013 Lexington Books

1. Emperors—Rome 2. Emperors—Rome—Biography—History and criticism 3. Historical literature 4. History & biography

ISBN 0739176382; 9780739176382 (cloth : alkaline paper)

LC 2012-028547

SUMMARY: This book "examines the biography of the Roman Emperor Marcus Aurelius. It seeks to further understand the author of the 'Historia Augusta' alongside the reminiscences of the Emperor Marcus Aurelius. Geoff W. Adams arrives at this understanding through a study of a wide range of literary texts. Marcus Aurelius was a very important ruler of the Roman Empire, who has had an impact symbolically, philosophically, and historically upon how the Roman Empire has been envisioned." (Publisher's note)

REVIEW: *Choice* v51 no1 p72 S 2013 J. S. Louzonis

"Marcus Aurelius in the 'Historia Augusta' and Beyond." "[Author Geoff W.] Adams . . . provides a welcome précis of his biographical-literary methods that reveal the intensely aretalogical aspect (narrating the mythical or miraculous deeds of a hero or god) in the 'Vita Marci Antonini Philosophi', set within the larger context of the historically and textually problematic 'Historia Augusta'. . . . Adams presents a trenchantly detailed literary dissection of the 'Vita' using a distinctive approach (complete with graphs) that focuses on the biographical elevation of thematic progression over historical fact."

REVIEW: *Classical Rev* v64 no1 p159-61 Ap 2014 J.S. Ward

ADAMS, J. N. Social variation and the Latin language; [by] J. N. Adams xxi, 933 p. 2013 Cambridge University Press

1. Historical literature 2. Latin language—Grammar 3. Latin language—Grammar, Comparative—Romance 4. Latin language—History 5. Latin language—Influence on Romance 6. Latin language—Orthography and spelling 7. Latin language—Social aspects 8. Latin language—Variation 9. Latin language, Vulgar 10. Latin philology 11. Romance languages—Grammar, Comparative—Latin

ISBN 9780521886147

LC 2012-035052

SUMMARY: Written by J. N. Adams, "This book is a history of many of the developments undergone by the Latin language as it changed into Romance, demonstrating the varying social levels at which change was initiated. About thirty topics are dealt with, many of them more systematically than ever before. Discussions often start in the early Republic with Plautus, and the book is as much about the literary language as about informal varieties." (Publisher's note)

REVIEW: *Classical Rev* v64 no2 p439-41 O 2014 Philip Baldi Paul B. Harvey

REVIEW: *TLS* no5791 p10 Mr 28 2014 ROY GIBSON

"Social Variation and the Latin Language." "In J. N. Adams's monumental new work 'Social Variation and the Latin Language,' the Latin grammarians of late antiquity—vigilantes on the look-out for perceived abuses of the language—emerge as the counterparts of the enraged centurion who compels a redrafting of Brian's graffito. What these authorities on the language disliked above all was change. . . . In effect, the book is a history of the Latin language, with particular stress on questions of social variation. It is also surprisingly accessible. . . . If 'Social Variation' has one disappointment, it is that the overall conclusion is a little underwhelming."

ADAMS, JACQUELINE. Surviving dictatorship; a work of visual sociology; [by] Jacqueline Adams xiv, 302 p. 2012 Routledge

1. Dictatorship—Chile—History—20th century 2. Poor women—Chile—Social conditions—20th century 3. Poor women—Political activity—Chile—History—20th century 4. Sociology literature 5. Squatter settlements—Chile—History—20th century 6. Visual sociology

ISBN 0203137396 (ebook); 0415998034; 0415998042 (pbk.); 9780203137390 (ebook); 9780415998031; 9780415998048 (pbk.)

LC 2011-039699

SUMMARY: This book by Jacqueline Adams " focuses on shantytown women, examining how they join groups to cope with exacerbated impoverishment and targeted repression and how this leads them into very varied forms of resistance aimed at self-protection, community-building, and mounting an offensive. Drawing on a visual database of shantytown photographs. . . as well as on interviews . . . the book is an example of how multiple methods might be successfully employed to examine dictatorship." (Publisher's note)

REVIEW: *Contemp Sociol* v43 no1 p62-3 Ja 2014 Rik Scarce

"Surviving Dictatorship: A Work of Visual Sociology". "Through her extensive qualitative research, including interviews with women who endured shantytown life and careful use of an array of visual materials, Jacqueline Adams takes us inside those women's worlds. . . . Hers is a work appropriate for its target undergraduate audience, including introductory classes and those in visual sociology and gender—'Surviving Dictatorship' also will be relevant to diverse graduate courses and to scholars of repression and resistance as well. . . . However, the image-interview connections that Adams make are almost all too subtle, and one longs for explicit bridge building between the two data sources."

ADAMS, RACHEL. Raising Henry; a memoir of motherhood, disability, and discovery; [by] Rachel Adams 272 p. 2013 Yale University Press

1. Memoirs
ISBN 0300180004; 9780300180008 (cloth: alk. paper)
LC 2013-002096

SUMMARY: In this memoir on her experiences raising a child with Down syndrome, author Rachel Adams "chronicles the first three years of Henry's life and her own transformative experience of unexpectedly becoming the mother of a disabled child. . . . Adams untangles the contradictions of living in a society that is more enlightened and supportive of people with disabilities than ever before, yet is racing to perfect prenatal tests to prevent children like Henry from being born." (Publisher's note)

REVIEW: *Kirkus Rev* v81 no17 p42 S 1 2013

REVIEW: *N Y Rev Books* v60 no15 p16-8 O 10 2013 Jerome Groopman

"Raising Henry: A Memoir of Motherhood, Disability, and Discovery". "'Raising Henry' is written as an unfolding personal history. For such an account to succeed, the reader should be emotionally engaged with the narrator and be not only intellectually informed but elevated by her insights. Rachel Adams succeeds in all these respects, in part by writing with stark honesty. . . . We learn from Adams what it means to have a son very different from most others in mind and body, whose future is uncertain, but whose life is infused with love and so worth living."

REVIEW: *New York Times* v163 no56353 pD5 D 17 2013 SUSANNAH MEADOWS

"Raising Henry". "[Rachel Adam's] book is less a memoir about mothering a child with Down syndrome than it is her attempt to set people straight. The syndrome is a disability, as she makes clear, not an illness and certainly not a tragedy. 'Raising Henry' is an important, hopeful book for that reason alone, and it's easy to be on Ms. Adam's team. Sometimes, though, you wish she were a more effective captain. . . . While she makes many good points, she leaves her most compelling evidence, her case-closer, largely out of the picture: Henry himself. She writs that her son is separate from his diagnosis, but barely offers a sense of who he is."

ADAMS, RICK A.ed. Bat evolution, ecology, and conservation. See Bat evolution, ecology, and conservation

ADAMS, ROBERT, 1946-. Langland and the Rokele family; the gentry background to Piers Plowman; [by] Robert Adams 147 p. 2013 Four Courts Press

1. English literature—Middle English, 1100-1500—History and criticism 2. Historical literature 3. Literature—History & criticism
ISBN 1846823811; 9781846823817
LC 2013-431476

SUMMARY: This book by Robert Adams examines "hitherto neglected facts about [William] Langland's extended family, the Rokeles, and their prominent public role in his own time, as well as in the generations that preceded his birth." It is suggested that the "social and political opinions" expressed in 'Piers Plowman' "derive from, and reflect, a personal background significantly different from that of [Geoffrey] Chaucer, [John] Gower, or the Pearl-poet." (Publisher's note)

REVIEW: *TLS* no5772 p24 N 15 2013 TOM SHIPPEY

"Langland and the Rokele Family: The Gentry Background to Piers Plowman." "Provocative. . . . The weak point of [Robert] Adams's study, for many, will be the reluctance to engage with the connections to 1381, mistaken though they may have been, or with the C-text autobiography. . . . The strong point is the claim that many of the opinions expressed in the poem are just what one might expect from a member of a 'proud gentry family'. . . . Whatever the deductions, one has to admire the dedication with which Robert Adams has tried to find out the facts, and trace the outline of a man to fit them."

ADAMSON, GLENN. The invention of craft; [by] Glenn Adamson 272 p. 2013 Bloomsbury

1. DESIGN—History & Criticism 2. Great Britain—Social life & customs—History 3. Handicraft—History 4. Handicraft—Political aspects 5. Historical literature 6. Industrial revolution
ISBN 9780857850645 (hardback); 9780857850669 (pbk.)
LC 2012-049664

SUMMARY: In this book, author Glenn "Adamson searches out the origins of modern craft, locating its emergence in the period of the industrial revolution. He demonstrates how craft was invented as industry's 'other', a necessary counterpart to ideas of progress and upheaval. In the process, the magical and secretive culture of artisans was gradually dominated through division and explication." (Publisher's note)

REVIEW: *Choice* v51 no2 p243-4 O 2013 K. L. Ames

"The Invention of Craft." "[Author Glenn] Adamson here offers an impressive, authoritative revisionist historical analysis of the origins of craft. As the title implies, Adamson understands the concept of craft as a modern invention, a response to the 'trauma' of modernity and industrialization. In his account, canonical figures long associated with reigning interpretations (Pugin, Ruskin, Morris, et al.), for reasons personal, political, and other, misunderstood material production and misdefined craft. For them, craft was a fragile and endangered vestige of a largely imaginary past. Adamson argues that their romanticizing or Utopian visions blinded them to the continued presence, even prominence, of craft in the material culture of Victorian Britain."

ADDERSON, CAROLINE. Jasper John Dooley; Not in Love; [by] Caroline Adderson 132 p. 2014 Kids Can Pr

1. Friendship—Fiction 2. Humorous stories 3. Infatuation 4. Playdates for children 5. Trampolines
ISBN 1554538033; 9781554538034

SUMMARY: In this book, by Caroline Adderson, "Jasper struggles to deal with the excessive attentions of his classmate Isabel, who just won't leave him alone. . . . After school, she invites him over for a playdate! When Jasper complains to his parents that he's too sick to go to her house. . . . However, once he arrives, Jasper is thrilled to discover Isabel has a trampoline. . . . Can Jasper find a way to keep using her trampoline and get her to stop being in love with him?" (Publisher's note)

REVIEW: *Kirkus Rev* v82 no3 p140 F 1 2014

"Not in Love". "[Caroline] Adderson perfectly captures the trials of early childhood, and with brief text and a simple vocabulary, she breathes full life into her cast of characters, from Paul C., new to the school and hiding behind a library book at recess, to Ori, Jasper's best friend, whose common-sense approach is hilarious, and even to Isabel, a bit wild but fully recognizable. Another chapter book that will readily brighten the day of emergent readers—or adults offering an extended read-aloud."

ADDONIZIO, MICHAEL F. Education reform and the limits of policy; lessons from Michigan; [by] Michael F. Addonizio xi, 297 p. 2012 W.E. Upjohn Institute for Employment Research

1. Education—Economic aspects—United States 2. Education and state—Michigan—Case studies 3. Education and state—United States 4. Educational change—Michigan—Case studies 5. Educational change—United States 6. Educational literature 7. Public schools—Michigan—Case studies 8. School improvement programs—Michigan—Case studies 9. School improvement programs—United States
ISBN 0880993871 (pbk. : alk. paper); 0880993898 (hardcover : alk. paper); 9780880993876 (pbk. : alk. paper); 9780880993890 (hardcover : alk. paper)
LC 2012-001332

SUMMARY: In this book, authors "Michael F. Addonizio and C. Philip Kearney use Michigan as a laboratory to examine a set of commonly implemented reforms in an attempt to answer three key questions: 1) What is the nature of these reforms? 2) What do they hope to accomplish? and 3) How successful have they been? The authors begin by examining one of the most contentious issues facing education money and schools." (Publisher's note)

REVIEW: *Contemp Sociol* v42 no6 p824-5 N 2013 JANET F. ALPERSTEIN

"Education Reform and the Limits of Policy: Lessons From Michigan." "In summary, high-quality and substantive data sources cannot make-up for an incomplete review of the literature; the lack of hypotheses; the lack of methodology, analysis, and conclusions based on the hypothesis; and the lack of well-organized chapters built around thesis statements. 'Education Reform and the Limits of Policy: Lessons from Michigan' was a good start to what eventually could become a significant research study."

ADELBERG, MICHAEL. Saving the hooker; [by] Michael Adelberg 192 p. 2014 The Permanent Press

1. Academics—Fiction 2. Escort services—New York (State)—New York—Fiction 3. Humorous stories 4. Man-woman relationships—Fiction 5. Prostitutes—Rehabilitation—New York (State)—New York—Fiction
ISBN 9781579623685
LC 2013-043539

SUMMARY: In this novel by Michael Adelberg, protagonist "Matthew wins a post-doc to see if real fallen women can be saved by a good man. He casts himself as Prince Charming and sets out to study and rehabilitate real New York City prostitutes, at least until he meets a fiery auburn-haired prostitute who calls herself Julia Roberts." (Publisher's note)

REVIEW: *Kirkus Rev* v82 no1 p256 Ja 1 2014

"Saving the Hooker". "A mostly funny first-person tale of a lazy and unprincipled postdoc whose brain resides firmly in his crotch. . . . Most novels give the reader a protagonist to like and root for; this isn't one of those. Only Matthew's father, portrayed as a bumpkin from the Midwest, seems truly decent. All he wants is for his misbegotten son to come home to Illinois and find a nice girl to marry. There is plenty to like in [Michael] Adelberg's comic romp, which also has a serious undercurrent: Who says a hooker needs saving, anyway? And what business is it of a man? This one's well-crafted and enjoyable if you're up for a rather raunchy read."

ADELMAN, JEREMY. Worldly philosopher; the odyssey of Albert O. Hirschman; [by] Jeremy Adelman 758 p. 2013 Princeton University Press

1. BIOGRAPHY & AUTOBIOGRAPHY—Business 2. BIOGRAPHY & AUTOBIOGRAPHY—Political 3. BUSINESS & ECONOMICS—Economics—General 4. Biographies 5. Economic development 6. Economics 7. Economists—Biography 8. HISTORY—Modern—20th Century 9. SOCIAL SCIENCE—General
ISBN 0691155674 (hardcover); 9780691155678 (hardcover)
LC 2012-046072

SUMMARY: This book, by Jeremy Adelman, "chronicles the times and writings of Albert O. Hirschman. . . . His intellectual career led him to Paris, London, and Trieste, and to academic appointments at Columbia, Harvard, and . . . Princeton. He was an influential adviser to governments in the United States, Latin America, and Europe. . . . Along the way, he wrote some of the most innovative and important books in economics, the social sciences, and the history of ideas." (Publisher's note)

REVIEW: *Choice* v51 no2 p315 O 2013 M. Perelman

"Worldly Philosopher: The Odyssey of Albert O. Hirschman." "[Author Jeremy] Adelman . . . provides a masterful biography of one of the most remarkable economists of the 20th century, Albert O. Hirschman. Any one of Hirschman's many lives would provide ample fodder for an interesting book. . . . Although Hirschman won worldwide acclaim for his pioneering work in development economics, he was largely dismissive of the field for overestimating its ability to succeed with top-down plans without paying close attention to the people who were the ultimate subjects of those plans. . . . Instead, his work transcended numerous academic boundaries. This book is obviously a labor of love, in which Adelman painstakingly reconstructs Hirschman's private and intellectual life."

REVIEW: *J Econ Lit* v51 no4 p1185-7 D 2013

REVIEW: *N Y Rev Books* v60 no9 p14-7 My 23 2013 Cass R. Sunstein

REVIEW: *TLS* no5775 p12-3 D 6 2013 RAY MONK

ADI, HAKIM. Pan-Africanism and Communism; the Communist International, Africa and the diaspora, 1919-1939; [by] Hakim Adi xxvi, 445 p. 2013 Africa World Press

1. Communism—History—20th century 2. Historical literature 3. Pan-Africanism—History—20th century
ISBN 9781592219155 (hard cover); 9781592219162 (pbk.)
LC 2012-049798

SUMMARY: This book by Hakim Adi "explains the history and activities of The International Trade Union Committee of Negro Workers (ITUCNW) in relation to the attainment of black emancipation, the role of such leading figures as George Padmore, the nuanced discussions within the communist movement on Pan Africanism and how to attain liberation from colonial domination." (Publisher's note)

REVIEW: *Choice* v51 no5 p893-4 Ja 2014 C. Pinto

"Pan-Africanism and Communism: The Communist International, Africa and the Diaspora." "[Hakim] Adi . . . has written a sweeping history of the activities of the Comintern through the lens of the 'Negro Question' during the 1930s. . . Adi succeeds in his strong effort to 'research the history of the ITUCNW and to present a more accurate account of the Comintern's attempts to find answers to "the Negro Question."' The depth of research . . . is impressive. The author skillfully explores his topic through a series of case studies in France, Great Britain, South and West Africa, and the Caribbean. While this comprehensive volume provides readers with an understanding of communism and race, the book struggles toward synthesis and cohesion."

ADKINS, LESLEY. Jane Austen's England; [by] Lesley Adkins 422 p. 2013 Viking

1. Historical literature
ISBN 0670785849; 9780670785841
LC 2013-016959

SUMMARY: This book, by Roy and Lesley Adkins, "explores the customs and culture of the real England of [Jane Austen's] everyday existence depicted in her classic novels as well as those by Byron, Keats, and Shelley. Drawing upon a . . . array of contemporary sources, . . . [they] vividly portray the daily lives of ordinary people, discussing topics as diverse as birth, marriage, religion, sexual practices, hygiene, highwaymen, and superstitions." (Publisher's note)

REVIEW: *Kirkus Rev* v81 no17 p42 S 1 2013

REVIEW: *New Yorker* v89 no30 p1 S 30 2013

"Traveling Sprinkler," "Night Film," and "Jane Austen's England." " This tender novel finds Paul Chowder, the poet narrator of [Nicholson] Baker's previous novel 'The Anthologist,' driving around Portsmouth, New Hampshire, and speaking into a handheld recorder. . . .[Marisha] Pessl has fun elaborating the backstory . . . but the foreground isn't always sufficiently compelling. The effect is that of a finely wrought diorama, brilliantly detailed but static. . . . This enjoyable history enlarges on themes that permeate Austen's evocations of the social customs of early-nineteenth-century England."

REVIEW: *Publ Wkly* v260 no25 p165 Je 24 2013

ADKINS, ROY (ROY A.) Jane Austen's England. See Adkins, L.

ADLER-OLSEN, JUSSI. The purity of vengeance; a Department Q novel; [by] Jussi Adler-Olsen 512 p. 2014 Dutton Adult

1. Cold cases (Criminal investigation) 2. FICTION—Mystery & Detective—General 3. FICTION—Mystery & Detective—Police Procedural 4. Missing persons—Fiction 5. Prostitutes—Fiction
ISBN 0525954015; 9780525954019 (hardback)
LC 2013-033253

SUMMARY: This book, by Jussi Alder-Olsen, is "another cold case for . . . Copenhagen's Department Q. . . . Except for the prostitute who reported her missing, no one much cared when brothel keeper Rita Nielsen vanished back in 1987. . . . Now, however, the mystery assumes new urgency with the news that she wasn't the only one to disappear. The very same day, attorney Philip Nørvig, fisherman Viggo Mogensen, women's asylum guard Gitte Charles and do-nothing Tage Hermansen also went AWOL." (Kirkus Reviews)

REVIEW: *Booklist* v110 no5 p32 N 1 2013 Keir Graff

REVIEW: *Booklist* v110 no17 p62-4 My 1 2014 Candace Smith

REVIEW: *Kirkus Rev* v81 no24 p107 D 15 2013

"The Purity of Vengeance". "[Jussi] Adler-Olsen . . . cuts back and forth between the fatal day in 1987 when Nete decided to avenge herself on the people who had ruined her life and the present day, when Carl's investigation of both Nete and Wad is complicated by rumors that Carl helped his cousin Ronny kill Ronny's father many years ago and further hints of the horrific fatality that first sent Carl to Department Q. Fans can rest assured that neither of these lesser subplots comes anywhere near closure. Another accomplished exercise in three-decker suspense, though the climactic twist would be harder to predict if the story had ended 100 pages earlier."

REVIEW: *Libr J* v139 no7 p46 Ap 15 2014 Sandra C. Clariday

REVIEW: *N Y Times Book Rev* p19 Ja 19 2014 MARILYN STASIO

REVIEW: *Publ Wkly* v261 no8 p177-8 F 24 2014

REVIEW: *Publ Wkly* v260 no42 p35 O 21 2013

ADLER, DAVID A., 1947-.il. Danny's doodles. See Adler, D. A.

ADLER, DAVID A., 1947-. Danny's doodles; the jelly bean experiment; [by] David A. Adler 112 p. 2013 Sourcebooks Jabberwocky

1. Baseball—Fiction 2. Eccentrics and eccentricity—Fiction 3. Friendship—Fiction 4. Intellect—Fiction 5. School stories 6. Schools—Fiction
ISBN 9781402287213 (tp : alk. paper)
LC 2013-011802

SUMMARY: In this book, by David A. Adler, "Danny Cohen and Calvin Waffle are two very different kids. Danny likes playing baseball; Calvin enjoys strange experiments. Danny follows the rules at school; Calvin tries to drive his teacher crazy. Danny and Calvin decide to team up for the big jelly bean experiment. Will it lead to trouble? Maybe." (Publisher's note)

REVIEW: *Bull Cent Child Books* v67 no2 p70-1 O 2013 T. A.

"Danny's Doodles: The Jellybean Experiment." "[Author David A.] Adler adds some depth to the befriend-the-new-kid story with inventive phrasing, humorous characterization, and a gentle backstory about Calvin's absent father. Although some more complex vocabulary might push this toward stronger readers or reading aloud, moderately oversized text and manageable, chunky chapters enhance readability, and the doodles that lend this series its name pepper the text in the form of cleverly captioned squiggles and stick figures. Danny and Calvin are classic non-superhero chapter book protagonists, and they're remarkably easy to relate to; the factual information about experimentation might also make this an interesting literature complement to a classroom study of the scientific method."

REVIEW: *Kirkus Rev* v81 no15 p280 Ag 1 2013

REVIEW: *Publ Wkly* v260 no30 p68 Jl 29 2013

REVIEW: *SLJ* v60 no1 p63 Ja 2014 Erica Thorsen Payne

ADLER, DAVID A., 1947-. Things that float and things that don't; [by] David A. Adler 32 p. 2013 Holiday House

1. Buoyant ascent (Hydrodynamics)—Juvenile literature 2. Children's nonfiction 3. Density 4. Floating bodies—Juvenile literature 5. Hydrostatics—Juvenile literature

ISBN 0823428621; 9780823428625 (hardcover)

LC 2012-045827

SUMMARY: This book by David A. Adler is an "introduction to density." The "examples provide extension activities that can be done at home or in the classroom. . . . Readers meet a boy, a girl, and their dog as they embark on an adventure to discover what will float and what won't. For example, a spread . . . shows the dog looking over a kitchen sink full of water as a piece of aluminum foil floats as a loose ball and sinks as a tight one." (School Library Journal)

REVIEW: *Booklist* v110 no1 p105 S 1 2013 Carolyn Phelan

"Things That Float and Things That Don't". "In this engaging book on density, [David A.] Adler explains the concept in terms a child can understand; he does so through straightforward text and basic density-related activities. The brief explanation that something's density is 'its weight relative to its size' is useful, but the varied ways of demonstrating the concept are even better. . . . The section on 'guessing which things float and which things don't' is particularly fine, not only because it's challenging and fun but also because it leads kids to use elements of the scientific method without mentioning the term. . . . It's rare to find a picture book that uses simple hands-on activities so successfully."

REVIEW: *Horn Book Magazine* v89 no6 p113 N/D 2013 DANIELLE J. FORD

"Things That Float and Things That Don't". "[David A.] Adler expertly teaches the concept of density, moving beyond the classic floating and sinking experiments to a carefully constructed lesson that helps young thinkers appreciate both scientific explanations and practices. The treatment of density is masterful: Adler introduces the fundamental physical relationship with terms familiar to readers (weight relative to size), then gradually builds to the scientific definition through examples and ideas that draw on intuitive, everyday experiences. . . . This takes readers well beyond vocabulary memorization into true science comprehension."

REVIEW: *Kirkus Rev* v81 no15 p122 Ag 1 2013

REVIEW: *Publ Wkly* p31 Children's starred review annual 2013

REVIEW: *Publ Wkly* v260 no25 p173 Je 24 2013

REVIEW: *Science* v342 no6162 p1043 N 29 2013 Marc Lavine

REVIEW: *SLJ* v59 no8 p118 Ag 2013 Melissa Smith

ADLER, DAVID A., 1947-. Triangles; [by] David A. Adler 32 p. 2014 Holiday House

1. Angles (Geometry) 2. Children's nonfiction 3. Mathematics—Juvenile literature 4. Robots—Juvenile literature 5. Triangle—Juvenile literature

ISBN 0823423786; 9780823423781 (hardcover)

LC 2012-037371

SUMMARY: This children's book, written by David A. Adler and illustrated by Edward Miller, "tackle[s] questions about different kinds of triangles with . . . text and . . . illustrations starring two friendly kids and one savvy robot." (Publisher's note) "Beginning with the definition of a triangle and a breakdown of its parts—sides, angles, vertices—[David A.] Adler quickly launches into a discussion of angles, even teaching kids how they are named, measured and classified." (Kirkus Reviews)

REVIEW: *Booklist* v110 no14 p70 Mr 15 2014 Carolyn Phelan

REVIEW: *Kirkus Rev* v82 no4 p199 F 15 2014

"Triangles". "Everything kids need to know about triangles-vocabulary, explanations and all. . . . A clever activity instructs readers to cut out a triangle, any triangle. By tearing off the corners and lining them up so the vertices touch, kids can see that the angles of a triangle always sum 180 degrees. . . . Labels and diagrams make the learning easy, while the endpapers show several examples of each type of triangle presented. . . . With lots of layers of information, this is a book that can grow with kids; new information will be accessible with each repeat reading."

REVIEW: *SLJ* v60 no5 p146 My 2014 Jasmine L. Precopio

ADLER, THOMAS. Bean Blossom; the Brown County Jamboree and Bill Monroe's bluegrass festivals; xxii, 239 p. 2011 University of Illinois Press

1. Bluegrass music—Indiana—Beanblossom—History and criticism

ISBN 0252036158; 0252078101 (trade pbk.); 9780252036156; 9780252078101 (trade pbk.)

LC 2010-051968

SUMMARY: In this "monograph on [the] Bean Blossom [bluegrass festival] and its predecessor, the Brown County Jamboree, folklorist Thomas Adler draws upon his own long history with Bill Monroe's festivals, . . . archival study, and oral history to document the important place that this Indiana community has played in the bluegrass community. . . .

Perhaps more important than the onstage activities, . . . Adler argues, were the informal communities that were formed in campgrounds and parking lots across the festival grounds." (Notes)

REVIEW: *Notes* v68 no4 p772-4 Je 2012 Travis D. Stimeling Stephen Luttmann

"Bean Blossom: The Brown County Jamboree and Bill Monroe's Bluegrass Festivals." "In his meticulously researched monograph on Bean Blossom and its predecessor, the Brown County Jamboree, folklorist Thomas Adler draws upon his own long history with Bill Monroe's festivals, detailed archival study, and oral history to document the important place that this Indiana community has played in the bluegrass community. . . . Perhaps more important than the onstage activities that took place during the annual festivals, Adler argues [in this volume of the Music in American Life series], were the informal communities that were formed in campgrounds and parking lots across the festival grounds."

AENEAS OF GAZA; Theophrastus With Zacharias of Mytilene: Ammonius; 216 p. 2013 Bloomsbury USA Academic

1. Christian philosophy 2. Creation 3. Neoplatonism 4. Philosophical literature 5. Resurrection
ISBN 178093209X; 9781780932095

SUMMARY: This book is part of the "Ancient Commentators on Aristotle" series. "50 years before Philoponus, two Christians from Gaza, seeking to influence Alexandrian Christians, defended the Christian belief in resurrection and the finite duration of the world, and attacked rival Neoplatonist views. Aeneas addresses an unusual version of the food chain argument against resurrection, that our bodies will get eaten by other creatures. Zacharias attacks the Platonist examples of synchronous creation." (Publisher's note)

REVIEW: *TLS* no5751 p7-8 Je 21 2013 DAVID SEDLEY

"The Ancient Commentators on Aristotle: Aeneas of Gaza, Theophrastus, With Zacharias of Mytilene, Ammonius." "A volume that has won attention by the accident of coming in at number 99 in the series adds yet another layer to the wealth of materials. It rescues from relative obscurity a pair of Christian dialogues, by Aeneas of Gaza and Zacharias of Mytilene--the latter too a native of Gaza, though later Bishop of Mytilene. Neither of these Gazans is known as the author of a commentary on Aristotle or anyone else, but their dialogues nevertheless play an integral role in the overall economy of the Commentators series, by representing one phase of a particular long-running debate among its protagonists."

AESOP'S FABLES; 76 p. 2013 Scholastic Inc.

1. Aesop's fables 2. Conduct of life—Juvenile fiction 3. Fables 4. Folklore 5. Illustrated books
ISBN 9780545467223 (pbk.)
LC 2013-012383

SUMMARY: "This collection contains 61 of Aesop's Fables, including both well-known titles like 'The Tortoise and the Hare' and 'The Boy Who Cried Wolf' and the less familiar 'The Wizard' and 'Jupiter, Neptune, Minerva, and Momus.' All are told in two pages or less, most with stylized black-and-white illustrations, and each story contains a moral appearing in boldface print at the end." (Booklist)

REVIEW: *Booklist* v110 no5 p50-3 N 1 2013 Suanne Roush

"Aesop's Fables." "All are told in two pages or less, most with stylized black-and-white illustrations, and each story contains a moral appearing in boldface print at the end. In addition to the table of contents, there is an alphabetical index that will be helpful for teachers or readers looking for a specific fable. The interior design of this slim volume has an old-fashioned feel, and it is possible that the gray background panels on which the stories appear may make it difficult for use by students with visual impairments. Even so, these fables would be well utilized in a classroom setting in support of the Common Core standards and may lead students to seek out further Aesop retellings."

AESTHETICS, EMPATHY AND EDUCATION; vi, 252 p. 2013 Peter Lang Publishing

1. Aesthetics 2. Affective education 3. Arts in education 4. Educational literature 5. Empathy
ISBN 9781433120107 (pbk. : alk. paper); 9781433120114 (alk. paper)
LC 2012-046916

SUMMARY: This book explores the relationship between aesthetics, empathy, and education. "The book is organized in four sections; one sets forth several 'differing perspectives' of research methodology; a second focuses on 'the self as research subject'; in the third, two contributors develop more explicit philosophical underpinnings; and a final section examines approaches to classroom practice." (Choice: Current Reviews for Academic Libraries)

REVIEW: *Choice* v51 no7 p1274 Mr 2014 R. R. Sherman

"Aesthetics, Empathy, and Education." "These contributions are insightful. The final section might interest undergraduate students, while the earlier sections would interest graduate students and researchers. [Boyd] White . . . and [Tracie] Costantino . . . think of the sections more as 'emphases rather than boundaries,' not 'divisions' but 'links' to each other. Given that, it is unfortunate that no final, concluding chapter attempts to summarize a general understanding from the various perspectives."

AETIA; introduction, text, translation, and commentary; 2012 Oxford University Press

1. Ancient poetry 2. Callimachus 3. Greek poetry 4. Historical literature 5. Poetry (Literary form)—History & criticism
ISBN 0198144911 (v. 1); 019814492X (v. 2); 0199581010 (set); 9780198144915 (v. 1); 9780198144922 (v. 2); 9780199581016 (set)
LC 2011-501386

SUMMARY: Edited by Annette Harder, "The aim of the present volumes is to make the 'Aetia' newly accessible to readers. Volume 1 comprises an introduction dealing with matters such as the work's composition, contents, date, literary aspects, and its function in the cultural and historical context of third-century BC Alexandria, . . . while Volume 2 presents a detailed commentary, including introductions to the separate aetiological stories." (Publisher's note)

REVIEW: *Classical Rev* v63 no2 p373-5 O 2013 Jeffrey Hunt

"Callimachus: Aetia: Introduction, Text, and Translation" and "Callimachus: Aetia: Commentary." "Despite negotiating a somewhat crowded field since she began her edition of the Aetia in the late 1980s, [author Annette Harder] has succeeded in crafting a magnificent work of scholarship that will surely become a standard tool for Callimachean and Hellenistic scholars. [Harder's] commentary comprises two volumes: the first contains the introduction, text and translation, and the second consists entirely of commentary. . . . In all her analyses [Harder] is meticulous with bibliography. . . . Beyond the expected bibliography on the 'Aetia,' however, [Harder] has also filled her commentary with countless gems, complete with bibliography, on a dizzyingly wide array of subjects."

AFRICAN AMERICAN WOMEN'S LIFE ISSUES TODAY; vital health and social matters; xxxvi, 168 p. 2013 Praeger, an imprint of ABC-CLIO, LLC

1. African American women—Diseases 2. African American women—Health and hygiene 3. African American women—Social conditions 4. Medical literature 5. Mental illness
ISBN 1440802971 (hbk. : acid-free paper); 9781440802973 (hardcopy : alk. paper)
LC 2013-006761

SUMMARY: This book presents an "overview of health-related topics pertaining to African American women. The edited collection, organized into three parts, includes nine chapters authored by nurses, educators, and psychologists." The three titled sections are "Physical Health," "Mental Health," and "Environmental Factors." Topics discussed include "breast cancer . . . depression and dementia . . . [and] interpersonal and community violence." (Choice: Current Reviews for Academic Libraries)

REVIEW: *Choice* v51 no5 p872 Ja 2014 H. Aquino

"African American Women's Life Issues Today: Vital Health and Social Matters." "This book provides a good overview of health-related topics pertaining to African American women. . . . The chapter on breast cancer is framed within the story of how this disease affected the author's grandmother; this personal account is very accessible and informative and presents a wide variety of factors related to the disease. . . . While the book is uneven in terms of accessibility, readability, and the number of topics covered in each section, the individual chapters offer strategies for innovation and are enhanced by graphs and figures as well as references for further investigation."

AFRICAN LIVES; an anthology of memoirs and autobiographies; xii, 401 p. 2013 Lynne Rienner Publishers, Inc.

1. Africa—History 2. Africans—Biography 3. Anthologies 4. Autobiography—Africa
ISBN 9781588268624 (hc : alk. paper); 9781588268877 (paperback : alk. paper)
LC 2012-044240

SUMMARY: This book, edited by Geoff Wisner, presents a "selection of memoirs (inclusive of an interview, a speech, and court testimony) and autobiographical works" by Africans. "The anthology contains forty-eight works of nonfiction that span the continent during various times in its turbulent history." Authors include Chimamanda Ngozi Adichie, Emily Ruete, and Ngugi wa Thiong'o. (World Literature Today)

REVIEW: *Choice* v51 no2 p255 O 2013 E. A. Blakesley

REVIEW: *World Lit Today* v87 no6 p74-5 N/D 2013 Adele Newson-Horst

"African Lives: An Anthology of Memoirs and Autobiographies." "Geoff Wisner's selection of memoirs (inclusive of an interview, a speech, and court testimony) and autobiographical works answers the need for a collection of 'true-life narratives' about the people of Africa. The anthology contains forty-eight works of nonfiction that span the continent during various times in its turbulent history. It is an amazing anthology--a cacophony of African voices in splendid diversity as vast as the continent itself. . . . Geoff Wisner has made a wonderful contribution to the emerging tradition."

AGAMBEN, GIORGIO, 1942-. The highest poverty; monastic rules and form-of-life; [by] Giorgio Agamben xiii, 157 p. 2013 Stanford University Press

1. Franciscans 2. Monastic and religious life—History—Middle Ages, 600-1500 3. Monasticism and religious orders—Rules 4. Philosophical literature 5. Vow of poverty
ISBN 9780804784054 (cloth: alk. paper); 9780804784061 (pbk.: alk. paper)
LC 2012-041964

SUMMARY: This book by Giorgio Agamben "is a study of the Franciscan monastic life, particularly around the Franciscans' relation to property and how this influenced the dialectic between the rules they set down and the life that the rules regulated. Form-of-life refers to a life that is inseparable from its form and within which rules and life coincide without remainder." (Griffith Law Review)

REVIEW: *Choice* v51 no3 p477 N 2013 A. W. Klink

REVIEW: *Commonweal* v141 no1 p26-7 Ja 10 2014 Paul J. Griffiths

"The Highest Poverty: Monastic Rules and Form-of-Life". "It's the great strength of this book to show, by careful analysis of the arguments surrounding central features of the Franciscan life, what the difference between the two ways of thinking comes to. . . . [Giorgio] Agamben's book is an intellectual delight. It's analytically sharp and profoundly illuminating in its treatment of the rules of religious communities, materials too often left to canonists who are so close to the material that they cannot think about its meaning."

AGAR, MARY.ed. Illuminated shadows. See Illuminated shadows

AGARD, JOHN, 1949-. Travel light travel dark; [by] John Agard 95 p. 2013 Bloodaxe Books Ltd

1. English poetry 2. Great Britain—Colonies 3. Historical poetry 4. Imperialism 5. Poems—Collections
ISBN 1852249919 (pbk.); 9781852249915 (pbk.)
LC 2013-409736

SUMMARY: In this poetry collection, John Agard examines "the intermingling strands of British history, and leads us into metaphysical and political waters. Cross-cultural connections are played out in a variety of voices and cadences. Prospero and Caliban have a cricket match recounted in calypso-inspired rhythms, and in the long poem, 'Water Music of a Different Kind,' the incantatory orchestration of the Atlantic's middle passage, becomes a moving counterpoint to Handel's Water Music." (Publisher's note)

REVIEW: *TLS* no5770 p29 N 1 2013 RORY WATERMAN

"Travel Light Travel Dark." "Many of these poems are also typically playful. In some, the metre jerks around violently and the rhymes flail for one another, and the poet embraces their flailing. . . . This can add lustre to . . . original and entertaining poems. . . . Often it is less successful. . . . But readers--especially schoolteachers and their pupils--tend to love his work, perhaps not noticing . . . that the rhyme is firmly in the driving seat, or that the phrasing is stiff . . . but relishing the boldly mischievous conceits, the ease with which [John] Agard shows them things they wouldn't have imagined and enables them to talk about anything but poetry. This thought-provoking, puckish, tender book will not disappoint them."

AGER, DEBORAH.ed. The Bloomsbury anthology of contemporary Jewish American poetry. See The Bloomsbury anthology of contemporary Jewish American poetry

AGNEW, JEREMY. Alcohol and opium in the Old West; use, abuse, and influence; [by] Jeremy Agnew vii, 252 p. 2014 McFarland & Company, Inc., Publishers

1. Alcoholism—West (U.S.)—History—19th century 2. Drinking of alcoholic beverages—United States—History 3. Historical literature 4. Opium abuse—West (U.S.)—History—19th century 5. Social problems—United States—History

ISBN 9780786476299 (softcover : alk. paper)

LC 2013-036296

SUMMARY: "This book explores the role and influence of drink and drugs (primarily opium) in the Old West, which for this book is considered to be America west of the Mississippi from the California gold rush of the 1840s to the closing of the Western Frontier in roughly 1900. This period was the first time in American history that heavy drinking and drug abuse became a major social concern." (Publisher's note)

REVIEW: *Choice* v51 no7 p1287-8 Mr 2014 D. M. Fahey

"Alcohol and Opium in the Old West: Use, Abuse, and Influence." "Intended for general readers, this book is a reliable introduction to a large subject. It is clearly written, rich in anecdote, and amply illustrated. . . . [Jeremy] Agnew has written prolifically about the Old West. His earlier books about prostitution . . . and medicine . . . help him in this new volume. It is a useful synthesis of the books listed in his four-page bibliography, supplemented by contemporary magazines. There are, however, limits to Agnew's research, especially in scholarly journals. . . . Recommended."

AGRARIAN CHANGE AND CRISIS IN EUROPE, 1200-1500; x, 364 p. 2012 Routledge

1. Agriculture—Economic aspects—Europe—History—To 1500 2. Agriculture—Social aspects—Europe—History—To 1500 3. Crises—Europe—History—To 1500 4. Historical literature 5. Social change—Europe—History—To 1500

ISBN 0415895782 (alk. paper); 9780415895781 (alk. paper)

LC 2011-004621

SUMMARY: Edited by Harry Kitsikopoulos "'Agrarian Change and Crisis in Europe, 1200-1500' addresses one of the classic subjects on economic history: the process of aggregate economic growth and the crisis that engulfed the European continent during the late Middle Ages. . . . This book offers an empirical synthesis on a host of economic, demographic, and technological developments which characterized the period 1200-1500." (Publisher's note)

REVIEW: *Engl Hist Rev* v128 no534 p1201-2 O 2013 Christopher Dyer

"Agrarian Change and Crisis in Europe, 1200-1500." "This book is based on the proceedings of a conference held in 2008. The contributors have provided papers on the economic and social history of eight areas of Europe: England and France in the west, Italy, Spain and Byzantium in the south, Russia and Central Europe (Czech lands, Hungary and Poland) in the east, and Scandinavia in the north. . . . The key question however, is the explanation of the late medieval crisis, which in its most extreme form led to a halving of the population, caused the abandonment of numerous farms and large areas of cultivated land, and resulted in profound economic changes across the continent. . . . Much learning is deployed by this team of authors."

AGUILAR, DAVID A.il. Space encyclopedia. See Aguilar, D. A.

AGUILAR, DAVID A. Space encyclopedia; a tour of our solar system and beyond; [by] David A. Aguilar 191 p. 2013 National Geographic

1. Astronomy 2. Cosmology 3. Planets 4. Scientific literature

ISBN 1426309481 (reinforced library binding); 1426315600 (hbk.); 1426316291 (Scholastic); 9781426309489 (reinforced library binding); 9781426315602 (hbk.); 9781426316296 (Scholastic)

LC 2013-444119

SUMMARY: This book on outer space by David A. Aguilar is "broken up into five sections. . . . Aguilar moves from the origins of the universe, to the planets and bodies of our Solar System, and then to the impressive phenomena from all corners of the universe. Everything from black holes to dark matter and theories about multiple universes is touched upon." (Children's Literature)

REVIEW: *Booklist* v110 no4 p42 O 15 2013 Carolyn Phelan

AGUIRRE, A. ALONSO.ed. New directions in conservation medicine. See New directions in conservation medicine

AHMAD, AHRAR. Government and politics in South Asia. See Kapur, A.

AHMED, AKBAR. The thistle and the drone; how America's War on Terror became a global war on tribal Islam; [by] Akbar Ahmed xi, 424 p. 2013 Brookings Institution Press

1. Afghan War, 2001- 2. Islamic sociology 3. Political science literature 4. Tribes—Islamic countries 5. War on Terrorism, 2001-2009

ISBN 9780815723783 (hardcover : alkaline paper)

LC 2013-003952

SUMMARY: This book by Akbar Ahmed "is the third and final book of a trilogy that examines the relationships between the United States and the Muslim world. This books specifically assesses Muslim tribal groupsw, which, in many cases, live in border areas and represent the periphery of their nations. . . . The real 'clash,' according to Ahmed, 'is not between civilizations based on religion; rather, it is between central governments and the tribal [honor] communities of the periphery.'" (Middle East Journal)

REVIEW: *Middle East J* v68 no1 p181-2 Wint 2014 Thomas H. Johnson

"The Thistle and the Drone: How America's War on Terror Became a Global War on Tribal Islam." "This is an important book that deserves the attention of scholars as well as policy makers. . . . I suspect that many readers of this book will charge [Akbar] Ahmed with having adopted an orientalist perspective, claiming that he believes that he societies of his focus are static in their evolution. For the most part, however, Ahmed avoids this pitfall by letting the tribal societies define themselves. . . . While he believes that negotiation might be a way out, the disarray of the tribes has resulted in a situation where there are not clearly recognized and regarded leaders to negotiate on the tribal side."

REVIEW: *N Y Rev Books* v60 no16 p20-4 O 24 2013 Malise Ruthven

AHMED, MOHAMMED M. A.ed. The Kurdish spring. See The Kurdish spring

AHMED, SAFDAR. Reform and modernity in Islam; the philosophical, cultural and political discourses among Muslim reformers; [by] Safdar Ahmed vii, 296 p. 2013 I.B. Tauris distrib. in the US & Canada exclusively by Palgrave Macmillan

1. Islam—21st century 2. Islamic civilization 3. Islamic renewal 4. Muslims—Attitudes 5. Social science literature
ISBN 1848857357 (hbk.); 9781848857353 (hbk.)
LC 2013-415575

SUMMARY: This book by Safdar Ahmed critiques " the idea that Muslim reformers have either reproduced or reacted against Western ideas. Rather, Ahmed argues, they have reconstructed and appropriated these ideas, and so the thread of Western influence runs through modern Islamic thought on nationalism and sovereignty, femininity and gender." (Publisher's note)

REVIEW: *Choice* v51 no7 p1306 Mr 2014 A. T. Kuru

REVIEW: *Middle East J* v68 no1 p184-5 Wint 2014 Bettina Koch

"Reform and Modernity in Islam: The Philosophical, Cultural and Political Discourses Among Muslim Reformers." "A very welcome book. It is a worthwhile and original read for both experts in contemporary and modern Islamic thought, as well as students interested in a sound and thoughtful introduction to the complexity of Islamic discourses on modernity. [Safdar] Ahmed avoids the oversimplification one encounters far too often in works on Islamic discourses and their relationship to the West. . . . An original, thoughtful, and well-argued book that should be of interest to a wide readership."

AHMED, SHARBARI ZOHRA. The Ocean of Mrs Nagai; [by] Sharbari Zohra Ahmed 157 p. 2013 Daily Star Books

1. Bangladeshi Americans 2. Bangladeshis 3. Ethiopia—Fiction 4. New York (N.Y.)—Fiction 5. Short stories—Collections
ISBN 9789849027188; 9849027185

SUMMARY: "Sharbari Zohra Ahmed's stories are spread across continents, involving characters from an old Japanese woman to a Bangladeshi child making friends with downtrodden kids in Ethiopia, to an adopted American woman of Bangladeshi origin. In other words, these are stories of cultural encounters. . . . What makes these stories stand out from the very beginning is their tonality, which is fresh and challenges agreed-upon perceptions of the world." (Publisher's note)

REVIEW: *World Lit Today* v88 no2 p55-6 Mr/Ap 2014 Shilpa Kameswaran

"The Ocean of Mrs. Nagai: Stories." "Sharbari Ahmed's debut collection of short fiction, 'The Ocean of Mrs. Nagai: Stories,' took her fifteen years to complete. . . . The long execution of this collection of eight stories is reflected in the fact that there is never a tone of repetition or a sense of similarity in the plots or the protagonists of each of the pieces. Sharbari's literary profile spreads over performance, film direction, scriptwriting, and teaching creative writing, but it seems as if the only task Sharbari was perfectly poised to do was write short fiction. Sharbari sets out to deconstruct the subtlest of shades that make up the myriad experiences of South Asians."

AI WEIWEI, 1957-. Ai Weiwei's blog; writings, interviews, and digital rants, 2006-2009; [by] 1957- Ai Weiwei 307 2011 MIT Press

1. Architects 2. Artists 3. China—Politics & government 4. Dissenters, Artistic 5. Essays
ISBN 0262015218 pa; 9780262015219 pa
LC 2010--24293

SUMMARY: The Chinese artist Ai Weiwei "began blogging in 2005. . . . Over the ensuing three and a half years, he wrote more than twenty-seven hundred posts. . . . [In this book] about one hundred of his writings have been translated and collected." (Bookforum) Topics include "social commentary, criticism of government policy, thoughts on art and architecture, and autobiographical writings." (Publisher's note)The Chinese artist Ai Weiwei "began blogging in 2005. . . . Over the ensuing three and a half years, he wrote more than twenty-seven hundred posts. . . . [In this book] about one hundred of his writings have been translated and collected." (Bookforum) Index.

REVIEW: *N Y Rev Books* v60 no16 p49-51 O 24 2013 Perry Link

"For a Song and a Hundred Songs: A Poet's Journey Through a Chinese Prison," "This Generation: Dispatches From China's Most Popular Literary Star (and Race Car Driver)," and "Ai Weiwei's Blog: Writings, Interviews, and Digital Rants, 2006-2009." "A great virtue of Liao Yiwu's new book . . . is that it suggests what we have to look at before crediting the regime with efficiency. It shows that not only cleverness but a beastly ruthlessness undergirds the resilience. . . . Many of Han Han's views, although artfully put, are unsurprising versions of what other critics of the regime have been saying for years. . . . But Han Han does more than just put well-known complaints into clever form. On some topics he is uniquely astute. . . . Ai [Weiwei's] creativity seems to come in bursts. He lacks the reflective mood that allows Han Han to achieve analytic depth, and his essays are not as carefully written as Han Han's. But his intuitive eruptions sometimes yield stark, profound perceptions."

AIDEN, EREZ. Uncharted. See Michel, J- B.

AIDI, HISHAM D. Rebel music; race, empire, and the new Muslim youth culture; [by] Hisham D. Aidi 432 p. 2013 Pantheon
1. Music and youth—Western countries 2. Muslim youth—Western countries—Social conditions 3. Popular music—Political aspects 4. Protest movements—Western countries 5. Social science literature
ISBN 0375424903; 9780375424908 (hardback)
LC 2013-028800

SUMMARY: This "book on the connection between music and political activism among Muslim youth around the world looks at how hip-hop, jazz, and reggae . . . have become a means of building community and expressing protest in the face of the West's policies in the War on Terror. [Author] Hisham Aidi interviews musicians and activists, and reports from music festivals and concerts . . . to give us an up-close sense of the identities and art forms of urban Muslim youth." (Publisher's note)

REVIEW: *Booklist* v110 no11 p18 F 1 2014 June Sawyers

REVIEW: *Kirkus Rev* v82 no1 p172 Ja 1 2014

"Rebel Music: Race, Empire, and the New Muslim Youth Culture". " In this intriguing study, [Hisham D.] Aidi . . . demonstrates the immense and widespread appeal to transnational, disgruntled Muslims of black music such as hip-hop, drawing its roots from Muslim influences since the 1970s—e.g., in the form of the Nation of Islam. . . . Aidi shows how the Western 'soundtrack of struggle' inspires the world in surprising ways. Moving from jazz to the late Moroccan pop star Salim Halali, Aidi's wide-ranging, dense work persuades by its passionate accretion of detail."

REVIEW: *New York Times* v163 no56481 pC1-4 Ap 24 2014 JANET MASLIN

REVIEW: *Publ Wkly* v260 no51 p46-7 D 16 2013

AIKINS, DAVE.il. Baby loves colors. See Baby loves colors

AIMÉE RAY'S SWEET & SIMPLE JEWELRY; 131 p. 2013 Lark Crafts
1. Do-it-yourself literature 2. Embroidery 3. Jewelry—Equipment & supplies 4. Jewelry design 5. Jewelry making
ISBN 1454707925; 9781454707929
LC 2012-042166

SUMMARY: This book on jewelry making was written by Aimee Ray and Kathy Sheldon. "The text begins with an introduction and basics covering the embroidery stitches and other techniques used throughout the projects. . . . Each design features a list of needed materials and tools at the beginning and presents numbered directions." (Booklist)

REVIEW: *Booklist* v110 no2 p14 S 15 2013 Rebecca Pfenning

"Aimee Ray's Sweet & Simple Jewelry: 17 Designers, 10 Techniques & 32 Projects to Make." "Adorable and sweet. . . . As a former graphic designer, she has an eye for simple beauty. Her book focuses on inspiration and ideas to delight beginners and experienced crafters with unique materials and techniques. . . . Although the book lacks diagrams and assumes some prior knowledge of technique and basic skills, the jewelry featured is trendy, so the book will definitely be a popular title with young-adult crafters."

AIN, BETH Starring Jules (super-secret spy girl); [by] Beth Ain 176 p. 2014 Scholastic Press
1. Acting—Fiction 2. Families—Juvenile fiction 3. Family life—Fiction 4. Friendship—Fiction 5. Friendship—Juvenile fiction 6. Motion picture acting—Juvenile fiction 7. Psychological fiction 8. Spy films—Fiction 9. Spy films—Juvenile fiction
ISBN 9780545443562
LC 2013-018127

SUMMARY: In this book, part of a series by Beth Ain, "even though she'll be spending it in Quebec filming a movie, child actress Jules' summer is not off to a good start. First, Charlotte gets to go to acting camp, and Elinor is returning to England, leaving Jules feeling lonely. Next, a birthday week with her father is replaced by a road trip with her annoying family friend, Teddy. Finally, teen star Emma Saxony proves to be a rude introduction to the world of celebrities." (Kirkus Reviews)

REVIEW: *Kirkus Rev* v82 no1 p184 Ja 1 2014

"Starring Jules (Super-Secret Spy Girl)". "Each chapter is full of diverting and dramatic plot twists, making the pacing of the book somewhat breathless, as many problems are given the same urgency. It is obvious that Jules is out of her comfort zone. Luckily, through the help of Elinor's emails, the support of megastar Rick Hinkley and the love of her family, Jules is able to keep an even keel. Fans of Jules' previous books will enjoy seeing the soon-to-be-third-grader back in action as she exuberantly experiences the busy life of a budding television and film star."

AINSWORTH, KIMBERLY. Moustache Up!; A Playful Game of Opposites; [by] Kimberly Ainsworth 16 p. 2013 Simon & Schuster Merchandise
1. Guessing games 2. Mustaches 3. Picture books for children 4. Polarity 5. Toy & movable books
ISBN 1442475269; 9781442475267

SUMMARY: This picture book includes "twelve cardboard mustaches—thin and wide, straight and curly" which "can be inserted into slots in a guessing game for readers: 'Moustache up and moustache down./ Which 'stache covers up a frown?' [Daniel] Roode's wiry illustrations reveal weightlifters and pirates, businessmen and dour gents, adding to the book's hipster vibe." (Publishers Weekly)

REVIEW: *Kirkus Rev* v82 no1 p12 Ja 1 2014

"Moustache Up! A Playful Game of Opposites". "The verse and art seem to point to a correct mustache for each face, but youngsters will likely enjoy experimenting with various facial-hair arrangements. Some of the interchangeable mustaches, the backs of which sport a descriptive word (straight, curly, smooth, rough, etc.) to help with matching, are sturdier than others, and a couple of the thinner ones will be easily torn and the smaller ones easily lost. These multiple, small accessories make it inappropriate for the typical board-book audience or for library circulation, but this offering will likely appeal to readers who appreciate a quirky and stylized design aesthetic and books with interactive features."

REVIEW: *Publ Wkly* v260 no18 p58 My 6 2013

AITKEN, JONATHAN. Margaret Thatcher; Power and Personality; [by] Jonathan Aitken 784 p. 2013 St. Martin's Press

1. Biographies 2. Conservative Party (Great Britain) 3. Great Britain—Politics & government—1979-1997 4. Thatcher, Margaret, 1925-2013 5. Women prime ministers
ISBN 1620403420; 9781620403426

SUMMARY: In this biography of Margaret Thatcher, author Jonathan Aitken "chronicles her strict childhood, marriage, political rise, and relationships with figures including Presidents Reagan and George H.W. Bush and Soviet leader Mikhail Gorbachev. A woman of steely discipline and determination, powerful on the international stage, she eventually ran afoul of local politics in a dispute within her party." (Booklist)

REVIEW: *Booklist* v110 no4 p13 O 15 2013 Vanessa Bush

"Margaret Thatcher: Power and Personality." "[Jonathan] Aitken, a former member of Parliament, served for a time with Thatcher but also dated her daughter and knew the PM on a more personal level. That mixture of professional and personal relationships with Thatcher affords him a close-up, long-term perspective on one of the most powerful women in recent history, with a hand in major economic and geopolitical changes. . . . Aitken admits to a complex admiration of Thatcher, having seen her at her best and her worst, in this thoroughly insightful and compelling look at a remarkable world figure."

REVIEW: *Choice* v51 no10 p1877 Je 2014 G. M. Stearns

REVIEW: *Kirkus Rev* v81 no20 p121 O 15 2013

AITKEN, MARTIN.tr. The purity of vengeance. See Adler-Olsen, J.

AITKEN, ROBIN. Can we trust the BBC?; [by] Robin Aitken xl, 213 p. 2008 Continuum

1. Journalism 2. Savile, Jimmy, 1926-2011 3. Television & politics 4. Television—Social aspects—Great Britain
ISBN 9780826498847 (pbk.)
LC 2009-286050

SUMMARY: This book on the British Broadcasting Corporation was originally published "in 2008, when, after twenty-five years employed by the Corporation as a reporter, Robin Aitken concluded that an unacceptable left-wing bias was at work. . . . The new material focuses on the revelations about Jimmy Savile. . . . Aitken's central argument . . . is that the BBC's output mirrors the views of its staff, who are mostly left-leaning metropolitan graduates." (Times Literary Supplement)

REVIEW: *TLS* no5753 p26-7 Jl 5 2013 ED CUMMING

"Can We Still Trust the BBC?" "Most of 'Can We Still Trust the BBC?' was published in 2008. . . . Inevitably, the new material focuses on the revelations about Jimmy Savile. [Robin] Aitken reminds us of the facts with a veteran's eye for the process of programme-making. . . Most of the book is a concise reminder of the BBC's failures, particularly in comparison to the 'golden age' of the mid-twentieth century. Aitken's central argument, which is difficult to dismiss, is that the BBC's output mirrors the views of its staff, who are mostly left-leaning metropolitan graduates. . . . On balance we probably can still trust the BBC, but only as long as writers like Aitken are prepared to hold it to the standard it claims for itself."

AJMERA, MAYA. Music everywhere!; [by] Maya Ajmera 32 p. 2013 Random House Distribution Childrens

1. Child musicians 2. Children's nonfiction 3. Music & culture 4. Music & society 5. Music appreciation—Juvenile literature
ISBN 1570919364; 9781570919367 (reinforced for library use); 9781570919374 (softcover); 9781607346708 (ebook)
LC 2012-027113

SUMMARY: In this book, by Maya Ajmera, Elise Hofer Derstine, and Cynthia Pon, "photographs from around the world celebrate the universal joy that kids get from making music, whether they're playing instruments, clapping their hands, stomping their feet, or singing." According to the book "music can . . . bring a whole community together." (Publisher's note)

REVIEW: *Booklist* v110 no9/10 p92 Ja 1 2014 Annie Miller

REVIEW: *Bull Cent Child Books* v67 no8 p392 Ap 2014 H. M.

REVIEW: *Kirkus Rev* v82 no2 p106 Ja 15 2014

"Music Everywhere!". "A collection of charming photographs showing children enjoying music in 35 countries around the world. . . . The selection of images is wide-ranging, and the underlying message, inclusive. On each spread, well-chosen and crisply reproduced photographs that vary in size are set against solid, colored backgrounds with a single sentence of text and identifying captions. The variety of musical instruments, traditional and improvised, will gladden the hearts of teachers and those who want to encourage their children's appreciation for music. The backmatter includes a map, glossary and suggestions for readers' own music-making. A medley perfectly tuned. "

REVIEW: *SLJ* v60 no4 p178 Ap 2014 Elaine Lesh Morgan

AJVIDE LINDQVIST, JOHN. Let the old dreams die; [by] John Ajvide Lindqvist 416 p. 2013 St. Martin's Press

1. Horror tales 2. Paranormal fiction 3. Short story (Literary form) 4. Swedish fiction 5. Vampires—Fiction
ISBN 0312620535; 9780312620530 (hardcover)
LC 2013-016555

SUMMARY: This short story collection offers sequel stories to John Ajvide Lindqvist's "Handling the Undead" and "Let the Right One In." In "Final Processing," the "psychically gifted Flora, aided by musician/hauler Kalle, seeks final peace for the zombies imprisoned in a government facility." In "The Border," an "ugly, lonely customs agent who can literally smell deceit finally discovers where she fits." (Kirkus Reviews)

REVIEW: *Booklist* v109 no22 p52 Ag 1 2013 Regina Schroeder

REVIEW: *Kirkus Rev* v81 no16 p243 Ag 15 2013

"Let the Old Dreams Die." "Swedish author [John Ajvide Lindqvist] offers sequel stories to 'Handling the Undead' . . . and 'Let the Right One In.' . . . The spare, poetic quality of Lindqvist's translated prose and the inexplicable dream logic that drives so many of his stories recall the work of Jonathan Carroll or Ray Bradbury in his less baroque moments. Even at its darkest, the collection affirms the importance of love: Its presence and its lack cause people to do strange things, terrible things, heroic things, with horrible and/or exultantly beautiful consequences. Gripping, cerebral, intriguing, enigmatic--like a puzzle you enjoy working on but may never solve."

REVIEW: *N Y Times Book Rev* p30 O 20 2013 Terrence Rafferty

REVIEW: *Publ Wkly* v260 no32 p40 Ag 12 2013

AKASS, KIM.ed. TV's Betty goes global. See TV's Betty goes global

AKTURK, SENER. Regimes of ethnicity and nationhood in Germany, Russia, and Turkey; [by] Sener Akturk xxii, 304 p. 2012 Cambridge University Press

1. Ethnic groups—Government policy—Germany 2. Ethnic groups—Government policy—Russia (Federation) 3. Ethnic groups—Government policy—Turkey 4. Ethnicity—Political aspects—Germany 5. Ethnicity—Political aspects—Russia (Federation) 6. Ethnicity—Political aspects—Turkey 7. Historical literature
ISBN 9781107021433 (hbk.); 9781107614253 (pbk.)
LC 2012-011975

SUMMARY: "In this . . . comparative study of change in state policies regarding ethnic diversity, Şener Aktürk proposes a tripartite typology of ethnic regimes [monoethnic, antiethnic,

and multiethnic regimes] that he describes as 'exhaustive and coherent . . . [and] theoretically applicable to every country in the world'. . . .His ideal types permit him to compare the three different different states he examines [Germany, Russia, and Turkey] and to chart change over time." (American Historical Review)

REVIEW: *Am Hist Rev* v119 no1 p158-9 F 2014 Eli Nathans

"Regimes of Ethnicity and Nationhood in Germany, Russia, and Turkey". "One must recognize [Şener] Aktürk's extraordinary skills, not least linguistic, and the care he has taken, through extensive interviews and research in primary and secondary sources, to cast light on a central question of the modern age. However, his ambitious effort to create a common framework to explain complex realities in three different societies necessarily simplifies. In the view of this reviewer, the degree of simplification involved makes his categories significantly less useful as heuristic devices. Nonetheless, Aktürk has produced a fascinating study from which the reader can learn a great deal."

AL-BERRY, KHALED. Life is more beautiful than paradise; a jihadist's own story; [by] Khaled Al-Berry 189 p. 2009 American University in Cairo Press

1. Islamists 2. Jamiyat al-Ikhwan al-Muslimin (Egypt) 3. Memoirs 4. Mujahideen 5. Youth—Egypt
ISBN 9774162943; 9789774162947

SUMMARY: Written by Khaled al-Berry, "This book opens a window onto the mind of an extremist who turns out to be disarmingly like many other clever adolescents, and bears witness to a history with whose reverberations we continue to live. It also serves as an intelligent and critical guide for the reader to the movement's unfamiliar debates and preoccupations, motives and intentions." (Publisher's note)

REVIEW: *Libr J* v139 no8 p38 My 1 2014 Victoria Caplinger

REVIEW: *World Lit Today* v88 no1 p6 Ja/F 2014 M. Lynx Qualey

"The Servant," I Want to Get Married!," and "Life Is More Beautiful Than Paradise." "'The Servant' originally titled Faten, after its main character--is a beautiful coming-of-age story that follows a young teenager from rural Lebanon to her new life in Beirut. . . . ['I Want to Get Married'] began as a series of blog posts by author Ghada Abdel Aal, chronicling absurd family meetings and other woes on the path to searching for a suitable husband. . . . It's funny, sharp and engaging. . . . Khaled al-Berry's story begins in Asyut, a midsized upper Egyptian city, when he is thirteen years old. . . . This is not just the story of al-Berry's journey toward and away from religious conservatism but also his struggles with many ordinary adolescent concerns."

AL-FARSI, SULAIMAN H. Democracy and youth in the Middle East; Islam, tribalism and the rentier state in Oman; [by] Sulaiman H. Al-Farsi xii, 265 p. 2013 I.B. Tauris Distrib. in the U.S. & Canada exclusively by Palgrave Macmillan

1. Democracy—Middle East 2. Democracy—Religious aspects—Islam 3. Islam & politics 4. Oman—Politics & government 5. Political science literature
ISBN 9781780760902
LC 2013-443784

SUMMARY: In this book, "Sulaiman Al-Farsi looks at the impact the rentier nature of the Gulf States has on political participation, focusing on the nexus between tribe, religion and a new generation of young, highly educated citizens that is present in Oman." Particular focus is given to " the concept of shura (consultation), and how nascent concepts of democracy in the practice of shura have impacted and shaped the process of democratization." (Publisher's note)

REVIEW: *Choice* v51 no8 p1481-2 Ap 2014 C. H. Allen

"Democracy and Youth in the Middle East: Islam, Tribalism and the Rentier State in Oman". "Independent scholar al-Farsi presents Oman as a case study of democratization in rentier states in the Arab world, arguing that declining oil revenues (rents) combined with globalization and a better-educated population will force authoritarian regimes to allow greater political participation. . . . The analysis suffers from a small pool of respondents (only 10 in each group) of questionable representation, a very uncritical view of the shura tradition, and an unresolved contradiction that democratization has been the result of pressures from the young educated class that, at the same time, is characterized as lacking any real power to change the system."

REVIEW: *Middle East J* v68 no2 p327-8 Spr 2014 Calvin H. Allen Jr.

AL-MUTANABBI STREET STARTS HERE; poets and writers respond to the march 5th, 2007, bombing of baghdad's street of the booksellers; 300 p. 2012 PM Press

1. Anthologies 2. Baghdad (Iraq) 3. Bombings 4. Booksellers & bookselling 5. Terrorism—Iraq
ISBN 1604865903; 9781604865905 (pbk. : alk. paper)
LC 2011-939672

SUMMARY: This anthology was created in response to the March 5, 2007 car bombing of "al-Mutanabbi Street in Baghdad--the historic center of Baghdad bookselling." It "begins with a historical introduction to al-Mutanabbi Street and includes the writing of Iraqis as well as a wide swath of international poets and writers who were outraged by this attack." (Publisher's note)

REVIEW: *World Lit Today* v87 no5 p72 S/O 2013 Issa J. Boullata

"Al-Mutanabbi Street Starts Here." "On March 5, 2007, a car bomb was exploded on [Al-Mutanabbi Street in Baghdad, Iraq], perhaps to intimidate intellectuals.The pieces are of different lengths and moods. Some describe the street and decry the horrible event, others commemorate the innocent victims, and others still exult defiantly in the eventual triumph of freedom and truth. . . . The anthology begins with an impressive five-page essay by Anthony Shadid. . . . This anthology is recommended, not only for its literary merits, but also for its testimony."

AL-RASHEED, MADAWI. A most masculine state; gender, politics and religion in Saudi Arabia; [by] Madawi Al-Rasheed xii, 333 p. 2013 Cambridge University Press

1. Feminism—Religious aspects—Islam 2. Feminism—Saudi Arabia 3. Muslim women—Saudi Arabia—Social conditions 4. Political science literature 5. Sex role—Saudi Arabia 6. Women—Saudi Arabia—Social conditions 7. Women and religion—Saudi Arabia 8. Women's rights—Saudi Arabia

ISBN 9780521122528 (pbk.); 9780521761048 (hbk.)
LC 2012-028649

SUMMARY: This book by Madawi Al-Rasheed "examines the Saudi 'woman question' through analysis of different categories of Saudi women and their varied modes of expression: education, consumption, literature, demonstrations, and religious interpretation (and reinterpretation). The book provides an overview of both the challenges and opportunities Saudi women have experienced since 9/11 and highlights the complex interplays between gender, religion, tradition, and the state." (Middle East Journal)

REVIEW: *Choice* v51 no4 p707 D 2013 M. Lazreg

REVIEW: *Middle East J* v67 no4 p651-2 Aut 2013 Natana J. DeLong-Bas

"A Most Masculine State: Gender, Politics, and Religion in Saudi Arabia." "[Madawi] Al-Rasheed delivers some insightful analyses, insisting that Saudi women be viewed not only through the standard lens of 'religion' . . . but also through their interactions with contemporary capitalism, the state as both patron and patriarch, and social media. . . . At times, the analysis is brilliant and creative such as her discussion of the impact of consumerism on changing images of Saudi women. . . . At others, many details and summaries of events or writings are provided, yet analysis of what they mean is limited to critique of the worldview as overly theoretical and idealized."

AL-SHAYKH, HANAN.tr. One thousand and one nights. See One thousand and one nights

AL-TURK, AKRAM. The Arab awakening. See Pollack, K. M.

ALAGONA, PETER S. After the grizzly; endangered species and the politics of place in California; [by] Peter S. Alagona viii, 323 p. 2013 University of California Press

1. Endangered species—California 2. Endangered species—United States 3. Grizzly bear—California 4. Historical literature 5. Wildlife conservation—California 6. Wildlife conservation—United States

ISBN 0520275063 (cloth : alk. paper); 0520275071 (pbk. : alk. paper); 9780520275065 (cloth : alk. paper); 9780520275072 (pbk. : alk. paper)
LC 2012-038183

SUMMARY: This book "traces the history of endangered species and habitat in California, from the time of the Gold Rush to the present. . . . Focusing on the stories of four high-profile endangered species . . . [Peter S.] Alagona offers an . . . account of how Americans developed a political system capable of producing and sustaining debates in which imperiled species serve as proxies for broader conflicts about the politics of place." (Publisher's note)

REVIEW: *Choice* v51 no4 p666-7 D 2013 R. L. Smith

"After the Grizzly: Endangered Species and the Politics of Place in California." "This well-researched book focuses on the evolution of a politically charged habitat approach to endangered species protection, intertwined with a history of the roles of ecological science, natural resource management, ethics, environmental law, and politics in its development. . . . 'After the Grizzly' emphasizes the need to redefine habitat conservation beyond protecting wildlands, since nature reserves alone will not protect endangered species. A critical resource for current/future conservation and wildlife biologists and environmentalists."

REVIEW: *Science* v341 no6148 p843 Ag 23 2013 Stephen Redpath

"After the Grizzly: Endangered Species and the Politics of Place in California." "[Peter S.] Alagona . . . offers absorbing accounts of the changing fortunes of five species in the Golden State. . . . He presents each of these stories in its rich historical and political context, amid evocative descriptions of the landscapes and habitats where the species live. . . . Alagona, a gifted writer, skillfully brings to life the people involved in each of these case studies. . . . Although I thoroughly enjoyed reading the book, I have to question the assertion that we have not moved on from solely focusing on protected areas as the way to conserve biological diversity. . . . Despite this oversight, I highly recommend 'After the Grizzly'."

ALAHMADY, RYADH KHALAF. Code Name Johnny Walker. See DeFelice, J.

ALAMEDDINE, RABIH. An Unnecessary Woman; [by] Rabih Alameddine 320 p. 2014 Grove Press

1. Beirut (Lebanon) 2. Friendship—Fiction 3. Psychological fiction 4. Recluses—Fiction 5. Translators

ISBN 9780802122148 hc; 0802122140

SUMMARY: This book, by Rabih Alameddine, follows "seventy-two-year-old Beirut native Aaliya Sobhi. . . . Divorced at 20 after a negligible marriage, she lived alone and began her life's work of translating the novels she most loved into Arabic from other translations, then simply storing them, unread, in her apartment. Sustained by her 'blind lust for the written word' and surrounded by piles of books, she anticipates beginning a new translation project each year until disaster appears to upend her life." (Booklist)

REVIEW: *Booklist* v110 no5 p26 N 1 2013 Michele Leber

"An Unnecessary Woman". "Seventy-two-year-old Beirut

native Aaliya Sobhi, living a solitary life, has always felt herself unnecessary. . . . The richness here is in Aaliya's first-person narration, which veers from moments in her life to literature to the wars that have wracked her beloved native city during her lifetime. Studded with quotations and succinct observations, this remarkable novel by [Rabih] Alameddine . . . is a paean to fiction, poetry, and female friendship. Dip into it, make a reading list from it, or simply bask in its sharp, smart prose."

REVIEW: *Kirkus Rev* v81 no21 p143 N 1 2013

REVIEW: *Libr J* v138 no14 p82 S 1 2013

REVIEW: *New York Times* v163 no56425 pC6 F 27 2014 Carmela Ciuraru

REVIEW: *Publ Wkly* v260 no41 p30 O 14 2013

REVIEW: *World Lit Today* v88 no5 p95 S/O 2014 Jen Rickard Blair

ALARCÃO, RENATO.il. Soccer star. See Javaherbin, M.

ALBEE, SARAH. Bugged; How Insects Changed History; [by] Sarah Albee 176 p. 2014 Bloomsbury/Walker

1. Epidemics 2. Historical literature 3. Human-animal relationships—History—Juvenile literature 4. Insects—History—Juvenile literature 5. Insects as carriers of disease

ISBN 0802734227; 0802734235; 9780802734228 (pbk.); 9780802734235 (library edition)

LC 2013-025968

SUMMARY: This book, by Sarah Albee, illustrated by Robert Leighton, focuses on the impact of insects on the world throughout history. According to the book, "beneficial bugs have built empires. Bad bugs have toppled them." The book is a "combination of world history, social history, natural science, epidemiology, public health, conservation, and microbiology." (Publisher's note)

REVIEW: *Booklist* v110 no11 p51 F 1 2014 Sarah Hunter

REVIEW: *Bull Cent Child Books* v67 no10 p495 Je 2014 E. B.

"Bugged! How Insects Changed History". "[Sarah] Albee takes a humorous but informed look at the "collision of the insect world with the human world," demonstrating that any number of pivotal episodes in world history were directly or indirectly influenced by insects acting as serious annoyances or disease vectors. . . . Albee is a gleeful punster, playing with inset boxes labeled 'Insect Aside,' and goofy section titles such as 'The Reign of Spain is Plainly on the Wane,' and 'Let Us Spray.' Photographs (like the text, in rich purple tones accented with teal) are chosen for jokeyness as often as information, and they mingle cheerfully with cartoons and spot art."

REVIEW: *Kirkus Rev* v82 no2 p286 Ja 15 2014

"Bugged: How Insects Changed History". ". Setting readers up for major 'ick' moments, the introduction includes a disingenuous warning that squeamish readers should skip the explicit "TMI" side boxes (as if!). . . . Along with the aforementioned TMI features, the pages are liberally endowed with side profiles of 'Bug Thugs' and human notables, quick quotes and other tidbits, as well as maps, photos, period images and [Robert] Leighton's lighthearted cartoon vignettes. Ominous observations toward the end that pesticide-resistant bugs and microbes are on the rise don't entirely spoil the fun. Tailor-made for epidemiologists-in-the-making and connoisseurs of the gross."

REVIEW: *Publ Wkly* v261 no19 p60 My 12 2014

REVIEW: *SLJ* v60 no4 p184 Ap 2014 Heather Acerro

ALBER, LISA. Kilmoon; A County Clare Mystery; [by] Lisa Alber 358 p. 2014 Muskrat Press, LLC

1. Detective & mystery stories 2. Family secrets—Fiction 3. Ireland—Fiction 4. Marriage brokerage 5. Murder investigation—Fiction

ISBN 0989544605; 9780989544603

SUMMARY: In this book, part of Lisa Alber's "County Clare Mysteries" series, "Californian Merrit Chase travels to Ireland to meet her father, a celebrated matchmaker, in hopes that she can mend her troubled past. Instead, her arrival triggers a rising tide of violence, and Merrit finds herself both suspect and victim, accomplice and pawn, in a manipulative game that began thirty years previously." (Publisher's note)

REVIEW: *Kirkus Rev* v82 no2 p104 Ja 15 2014

"Kilmoon". "A woman hoping to meet her biological father is embroiled in village scandal and murder. . . . Lonnie O'Brien, heir to a prominent local family, is found dead in his Internet Café, and Merrit is one of the suspects. . . . Blackmail schemes, a second murder, and odd clues like a cake and a bloody afghan point to heartbreak, revenge, and past and present betrayal near the ruins of Our Lady of the Kilmoon. In her moody debut, Alber skillfully uses many shades of gray to draw complex characters who discover how cruel love can be."

REVIEW: *Libr J* v139 no2 p57 F 1 2014 Teresa L. Jacobsen

ALBERT, BRUCE. The falling sky; words of a Yanomami shaman; [by] Bruce Albert 648 p. 2013 The Belknap Press of Harvard University Press

1. Autobiographies 2. Shamanism—Brazil—History—20th century 3. Women shamans—Brazil—Biography 4. Yanomamo Indians—History—20th century 5. Yanomamo women—Brazil—Biography

ISBN 9780674724686 (alk. paper)

LC 2013-008942

SUMMARY: This book presents an autobiography by Davi Kopenawa, an "indigenous lowland Amazonian. It is the result of a collaboration between French anthropologist Bruce Albert . . . and Davi Kopenawa, a shaman who became spokesman for all Amazonians through his work with indigenous-rights organisation Survival International. . . . Each offers his perspective, but the central story is Kopenawa's." Particular focus is given to Kopenawa's views of white people. (New Scientist)

REVIEW: *Choice* v51 no9 p1640 My 2014 C. J. MacKenzie

"The Falling Sky: Words of a Yanomami Shaman". "This engaging text, the autobiography of Yanomami shaman and activist Davi Kopenawa, translated with some prefatory remarks, appendixes, notes, and additional biographical comments by anthropologist [Bruce] Albert . . . offers a valuable insider perspective on a much-studied Amazonian society, with rich details on myth and religious practices, including shamanic initiation. . . . The text offers a trenchant critique of the characterization of the Yanomami as humanity's primordial 'fierce people,' highlighting the beauty and virtues of these people while reminding readers of Western cultural and ecological destruction in the Amazon (an exceptionally virulent brand of fierceness)."

REVIEW: *Libr J* v138 no16 p81 O 1 2013 Elizabeth Salt

REVIEW: *N Y Rev Books* v61 no17 p50-2 N 6 2014 Glenn H. Shepard Jr.

REVIEW: *TLS* no5806 p11 Jl 11 2014 LAURA RIVAL

ALBERT, SUSAN WITTIG. A Wilder Rose; [by] Susan Wittig Albert 302 p. 2013 Persevero Press

1. Biographical fiction, American 2. Lane, Rose Wilder, 1886-1968 3. Little House on the Prairie book series 4. Wilder, Laura Ingalls, 1867-1957 5. Women authors—Fiction

ISBN 0989203506; 9780989203500

SUMMARY: "Based on the unpublished diaries of Rose Wilder Lane and other documentary evidence, 'A Wilder Rose' tells the surprising true story of the often strained collaboration that produced the Little House books--a collaboration that Rose and her mother, Laura Ingalls Wilder, concealed from their agent, editors, reviewers, and readers. . . . Author Susan Wittig Albert follows the clues that take us straight to the heart of this fascinating literary mystery." (Publisher's note)

REVIEW: *Kirkus Rev* v81 no16 p151 Ag 15 2013

"A Wilder Rose." "This pitch-perfect novel reimagines the life of Rose Wilder Lane, co-author of 'Little House on the Prairie.' [Author Susan Wittig] Albert . . . has discovered an endlessly fascinating protagonist. Lane, the libertarian and rumored lesbian, was an established, award-winning writer in her own right, but she may be best remembered today as the uncredited co-author of the Little House books written by her mother, Laura Ingalls Wilder. Albert's well-researched novel draws from the letters and journal entries of both women to offer a fictionalized account of the years spanning 1928-1939. . . . With all of the charm of the Little House series--and the benefit of a sophisticated, adult world-view--Albert's novel is an absolute pleasure."

REVIEW: *Kirkus Rev* p3 D 15 2013 supplemet best books 2013

ALBERTINE.il. Little bird. See Zullo, G.

ALBERTS, JOHN R. Playing Until Dark; Selected Poems 1995-2013; [by] John R. Alberts 100 p. 2013 Authorhouse

1. American poetry 2. Human sexuality 3. Jazz 4. Play 5. Poems—Collections

ISBN 1491811552; 9781491811559

SUMMARY: "This free verse collection" by John R. Alberts contains poems written between 1995 and 2013. Topics discussed include death, sexuality, the Biblical characters Adam and Eve, war, jazz music, and baseball. "His narrators play with form, with sounds and with the boundaries of time and space." (Kirkus Reviews)

REVIEW: *Kirkus Rev* v82 no2 p72 Ja 15 2014

"Playing Until Dark: Selected Poems 1995-2013". "Free-wheeling yet carefully wrought, this free verse collection is a joyful reminder that, at its best, poetry is music. [John R.] Alberts' jazz-soaked debut jukes and jives in unfettered celebration of the musicality of poetry. . . . The sheer fun of Alberts' poetry, coupled with its virtuosity, may occasionally distract readers from the poetry's deeper currents, but they'll have no problem catching the rhythm. Remarkable poetry, good for the body and mind."

ALBON, DEBORAH. Negotiating adult-child relationships in early childhood research. See Rosen, R.

ALBRECHT, GARY L.ed. Assistive technology and science. See Assistive technology and science

ALBRIGHT, LEN. Climbing Mount Laurel. See Massey, D. S.

ALCOHOL AND DRUGS IN NORTH AMERICA; a historical encyclopedia; 919 p. 2013 ABC-CLIO, LLC

1. Alcohol—North America—Encyclopedias 2. Alcoholic beverage industry—Encyclopedias 3. Alcoholism—North America—Encyclopedias 4. Drinking of alcoholic beverages—North America—Encyclopedias 5. Drug abuse—North America—Encyclopedias 6. Drugs—North America—Encyclopedias 7. Reference books 8. Temperance—Encyclopedias

ISBN 1598844784; 9781598844788 (cloth: alk. paper)

LC 2012-051495

SUMMARY: "This reference covers the social, political, and cultural aspects of drug and alcohol use in North America, with a focus on the last 200 years. The two-volume set begins with a chronology providing the reader with a context and time frame for major events, developments, and laws related to drugs and alcohol in the U.S., Canada, and Mexico. . . . This encyclopedia not only includes illegal drugs but also regulated legal substances . . . as well as unregulated legal substances." (Booklist)

REVIEW: *Booklist* v110 no8 p31 D 15 2013 Janet Pinkley

"Alcohol and Drugs in North America: A Historical Encyclopedia". "The set offers more than 250 entries. . . . Each entry is comprehensive in its treatment of the topic and concludes with a high-quality list of references. Although the encyclopedia is comprehensive, the work could benefit from identifying slang terminology in relation to specific drugs. . . There are several pages of bibliographical tools, including a section on Internet resources. The index is highly detailed, which makes navigation of the two volumes extremely easy and user-friendly. . . . This resource would be a valuable addition to high-school, public, and undergraduate academic libraries. Its breadth and depth of substances make it a great starting point for undergraduate students."

REVIEW: *Choice* v51 no6 p980-1 F 2014 L. M. McMain

ALDERSON, KEVIN.ed. Letters home to Sarah. See Taylor, Guy C.

ALDERSON, PATSY.ed. Letters home to Sarah. Taylor, Guy C.

ALDRICH, DANIEL P. Building resilience; social capital in post-disaster recovery; [by] Daniel P. Aldrich 232 p. 2012 The University of Chicago Press

1. Disaster relief—Citizen participation 2. Disaster relief—Social aspects 3. Disaster victims—Social net-

works 4. Social action 5. Social capital (Sociology) 6. Social science literature
ISBN 0226012875 (cloth: alkaline paper); 0226012883 (paperback: alkaline paper); 9780226012872 (cloth: alkaline paper); 9780226012889 (paperback: alkaline paper)
LC 2011-050821

SUMMARY: This book, by Daniel P. Aldrich, presents a" mixed methods analysis of the role of social capital in disaster recovery. More specifically, the book explores four case studies: the 1923 Tokyo earthquake, the 1995 Kobe earthquake, the 2004 Indian Ocean Tsunami, and Hurricane Katrina, which hit New Orleans in late August 2005." (British Journal of Sociology)

REVIEW: *Br J Sociol* v65 no1 p192-3 Mr 2014 Daniel Béland

"Building Resilience: Social Capital in Post-Disaster Recovery". "A compact and dense book grounded in serious research and an impressive knowledge of the relevant social science literature. The first two chapters are clear and well organized but the case studies are sometimes repetitive and do not always flow well. . . . Another limitation concerns the relative lack of attention to the perceptions of the actors involved in post-disaster recovery and reconstruction. . . . . Despite its limitations, this book is indispensable reading for students of disaster relief and reconstruction. More important, sociologists interested in social capital and in public policy would gain from reading this well-researched book."

REVIEW: *Choice* v50 no7 p1339 Mr 2013 E. L. Hirsch

REVIEW: *J Econ Lit* v51 no2 p576-8 Je 2013

ALEX-ASSENSOH, YVETTE M. Malcolm X; a biography; [by] Yvette M. Alex-Assensoh xxii, 162 p. 2014 Greenwood
1. African Americans—Biography 2. Biography (Literary form) 3. Black Muslims—Biography 4. Civil rights movements—United States—History—20th century
ISBN 9780313378492 (hardcopy: alk. paper); 0313378495
LC 2013-029454

SUMMARY: This biography of Malcolm X, part of the Greenwood Biographies series, "depicts the civil rights leader's tumultuous journey from serving a stint in prison to becoming a Nation of Islam leader and the subsequent events that led to his assassination. The text notes Malcolm X's comparisons and contrasts to Martin Luther King Jr. and his lasting legacy in the civil rights movement and the ongoing struggle for racial equality." (Booklist)

REVIEW: *Booklist* v110 no14 p71 Mr 15 2014 Angela Leeper

"Elena Kagan: A Biography" and "Malcolm X: A Biography". "Biographies are a staple of any school library, and, luckily, these titles in the Greenwood Biographies series make it easier for teens to discover noteworthy Americans, whether for academic or personal research. The thorough coverage begins with a look at each individual's formative years . . . and shows how these events shaped personal and career paths. . . . Black-and-white photos, time lines, and extensive bibliographies round out these solid bios."

ALEXANDER, KWAME. The crossover; a basketball novel; [by] Kwame Alexander 240 p. 2014 Houghton Mifflin Harcourt
1. African Americans—Fiction 2. Basketball—Fiction 3. Brothers—Fiction 4. Fathers and sons—Fiction 5. Novels in verse 6. Sports stories 7. Twins—Fiction
ISBN 0544107713; 9780544107717
LC 2013-013810

SUMMARY: In this novel, by Kwame Alexander, "12 year old Josh Bell . . . and his twin brother Jordan are awesome on the court. But Josh has more than basketball in his blood, he's got mad beats, too, that tell his family's story in verse. . . . Josh and Jordan must come to grips with growing up on and off the court to realize breaking the rules comes at a terrible price, as their story's . . . climax proves a game-changer for the entire family." (Publisher's note)

REVIEW: *Booklist* v110 no14 p74 Mr 15 2014 Gail Bush

REVIEW: *Bull Cent Child Books* v67 no6 p303 F 2014 Karen Coats

"The Crossover". "[Kwame] Alexander fully captures Josh's athletic finesse and coming-of-age angst in a mix of free verse and hip-hop poetry that will have broad appeal. The lively basketball poems in particular beg for energetic oral performance, while the free verse shows the multidimensionality of a teen wordsmith figuring out the shifting conditions of life on and off the court. The book draws additional strength from the portrait of Josh's father, a strong but flawed role model who's so haunted by his own father's early death that he won't take steps to guard his health."

REVIEW: *Horn Book Magazine* v90 no3 p79 My/Je 2014 KATRINA HEDEEN

REVIEW: *Kirkus Rev* v82 no2 p124 Ja 15 2014

"The Crossover". "Basketball-playing twins find challenges to their relationship on and off the court as they cope with changes in their lives. . . .This novel in verse is rich in character and relationships. Most interesting is the family dynamic that informs so much of the narrative, which always reveals, never tells. While Josh relates the story, readers get a full picture of major and minor players. The basketball action provides energy and rhythm for a moving story. Poet [Kwame] Alexander deftly reveals the power of the format to pack an emotional punch."

REVIEW: *N Y Times Book Rev* p21 My 11 2014 CORNELIUS EADY

REVIEW: *Publ Wkly* v261 no3 p56 Ja 20 2014

REVIEW: *SLJ* v60 no3 p132 Mr 2014 Kiera Parrott

REVIEW: *SLJ* v60 no10 p53 O 2014 Kira Moody

REVIEW: *Voice of Youth Advocates* v37 no3 p56 Ag 2014 Ann Reddy Damon

ALEXANDER, SIMONE A. JAMES.ed. Feminist and critical perspectives on Caribbean mothering. See Feminist and critical perspectives on Caribbean mothering

ALEXANDROV, VLADIMIR. The Black Russian; [by] Vladimir Alexandrov 304 p. 2013 Pgw
1. African American businesspeople—Biography 2. African Americans—History 3. Americans—Russia 4. Biographies 5. Thomas, Frederick Bruce
ISBN 0802120695 (hardcover); 9780802120694 (hardcover)

SUMMARY: This book, by Vladimir Alexandrov, offers the "story of Frederick Bruce Thomas, born . . . in Mississippi . . . , Frederick . . . went to Russia in 1899. . . . He became one of the city's . . . most famous owners of variety theaters and restaurants. The Bolshevik Revolution ruined him, and he barely escaped with his life and family to Constantinople in 1919. Starting from scratch, he made a second fortune by opening celebrated nightclubs that introduced jazz to Turkey." (Publisher's note)

REVIEW: *Booklist* v109 no19/20 p24 Je 1 2013 Donna Seaman

REVIEW: *Booklist* v109 no11 p16 F 1 2013 Donna Seaman

REVIEW: *Kirkus Rev* v81 no3 p171 F 1 2013

REVIEW: *Libr J* v137 no17 p57-9 O 15 2012 Barbara Hoffert

REVIEW: *Libr J* v138 no5 p113 Mr 15 2013 Maria Bagshaw

REVIEW: *N Y Rev Books* v60 no15 p39-41 O 10 2013 Darryl Pinckney

"The Black Russian." "In 'The Black Russian,' Vladimir Alexandrov tells the extraordinary story of how Frederick Bruce Thomas fled the post-Reconstruction American South and became Fyodor Fydorovich Tomas, a millionaire entrepreneur of Moscow's nightlife to whom Nicholas II granted citizenship in 1915. . . . The remaining records are biased against him, but Alexandrov interprets them with great sensitivity. Thomas's personal solution to the problem of being black in America was to get away. It worked for a while, until what had been the right place for someone like him got torn apart."

REVIEW: *Publ Wkly* v260 no3 p58 Ja 21 2013

REVIEW: *TLS* no5767 p32 O 11 2013 DONALD RAYFIELD

"The Black Russian." "Until this fascinating account of Frederick Bruce Thomas (1872-1928), the son of ex-slaves fi-om Mississippi, the only famous black Russian was Gannibal, [Alexander] Pushkin's great-grandfather. . . . This is a life that presents major problems. . . . Thomas committed little to paper, and what he did write or say was not always true. . . . The biographer has to rely on dozens of casual remarks made after chance encounters with Thomas. . . . But Vladimir Alexandrov manages his narrative superbly. He has combed the French, American and Russian press thoroughly and has filled in the background, particularly hedonistic Moscow of the 1900s, with such skill that not for a moment do we feel the narrative has been padded."

ALEXIE, SHERMAN, 1966-. Blasphemy; [by] Sherman Alexie viii, 465 p. 2012 "Grove Press Publishers Group West"

1. Fathers & sons—Fiction 2. Indians of North America—Fiction 3. Loneliness—Fiction 4. Proofs (Printing)—Specimens 5. Race relations—Fiction 6. Short stories, American
ISBN 0802120393; 9780802120397
LC 2012-286407

SUMMARY: Author Sherman Alexie presents a short story collection. "A son envisions his dead father's 'impossibly small corpse' peering out of his morning omelet in the page-long 'Breakfast.' In 'Gentrification,' a white narrator's do-gooder intentions go predictably awry in his all-black neighborhood. 'Night People' finds a sex-starved insomniac and a connection-hungry manicurist at a 24-hour New York City salon finding common ground in their loneliness and lack of sleep." (Publishers Weekly)

REVIEW: *N Y Times Book Rev* p30 N 17 2013

"Blasephemy," "The Story of Ain't: America, Its Language and the Most Controversial Dictionary Ever Published," and "Ike and Dick: Portrait of a Strange Political Marriage." "[Sherman] Alexie has carved out a space in American literature as an audacious observer of the Native American experience in the Pacific Northwest. . . . [David] Skinner's spry cultural history revisits the brouhaha that greeted Webster's Third and describes the societal metamorphoses that have shaped our language. . . . [Jeffrey] Frank skillfully examines the embittering relationship that shaped the American agenda for decades: President Dwight Eisenhower . . . and his two-term vice president, Richard Nixon."

ALEXIS, ANDRÉ, 1957-. A; [by] André Alexis 96 p. 2013 Litdistco

1. Creative ability 2. Creative writing—Fiction 3. Critics 4. Inspiration 5. Psychological fiction
ISBN 1927040795; 9781927040799

SUMMARY: This book by André Alexis presents the story of "Alexander Baddeley, a Toronto book reviewer obsessed with the work of the elusive and mythical poet Avery Andrews. Baddeley is in awe of Andrews's ability as a poet—more than anything he wants to understand the inspiration behind his work—so much so that, following in the footsteps of countless pilgrims throughout literary history, Baddeley tracks Andrews down thinking that meeting his literary hero will provide some answers." (Publisher's note)

REVIEW: *Quill Quire* v80 no1 p33-4 Ja/F 2014 George Fetherling

"A". "A wondrous piece (long story? novella?) that deftly plays with the conventions of satire, polemic, and magic realism. . . . Sophisticated readers will enjoy watching the author perform incredible linguistic feats that perfectly convey his view that Toronto's literary scene is more of a literary screen, imposing itself between serious writing and serious reading. Of Baddeley he writes 'How could a man who had for so long studied the ends of creativity (books and paintings and such) be anything but thrilled by his (admittedly strange) experience of creativity's origin?' How indeed."

REVIEW: *Quill Quire* v79 no7 p11 S 2013 Vit Wagner

ALFONEH, ALI. Iran unveiled; how the revolutionary guards Is turning theocracy into military dictatorship; [by] Ali Alfoneh xii, 266 p. 2013 AEI Press

1. Civil-military relations—Iran 2. Iran—Politics and government—1997- 3. Political science literature
ISBN 9780844772530 (cloth); 9780844772547 (pbk.); 9780844772554 (ebook)
LC 2012-050830

SUMMARY: In this book, Ali Alfoneh "contends that the Pasdaran, Iran's Revolutionary Guard Corps (IRGC), which has suppressed ideological heresy alongside its security operations, expanded its power and influence in the country. As a state within a state, he argues, the IRGC could hold the clerics hostage. The book explains the IRGC's origins and outlines its destruction of governmental oversight, its enhanced economic power, and ways it foiled political foes." (Choice: Current Reviews for Academic Libraries)

REVIEW: *Choice* v51 no5 p914 Ja 2014 S. Zuhur

REVIEW: *Middle East J* v68 no1 p163-5 Wint 2014 Kevan Harris

"Iran Unveiled: How the Revolutionary Guards Is Transforming Iran From Theocracy Into Military Dictatorship." "In the regrettably titled 'Iran Unveiled,' Ali Alfoneh portrays a single military organization in Iran, the Islamic Revolutionary Guards Corps (IRGC), as a praetorian juggernaut that has determinedly pushed out the sole other competitor for postrevolutionary power: the Shi'i revolutionary clergy. . . . Alfoneh, to his credit, relies on Persian source material for his allegations. Unfortunately, the sources he use tell a different story. . . . The book suffers from a striking retrospective determinism: the fallacy that because something happened, it was bound to happen. The author began with a policy conclusion and worked backwards for an analysis to support it."

ALIANO, DAVID. Mussolini's national project in Argentina; [by] David Aliano x, 209 p. 2012 Fairleigh Dickinson University Press

1. Fascism—Italy—History—20th century 2. Historical literature 3. Immigrants—Argentina—History—20th century 4. Italians—Argentina—Ethnic identity—History—20th century 5. Italians—Argentina—History—20th century 6. Nationalism—Argentina—History—20th century

ISBN 9781611475760 (cloth: alk. paper); 9781611475777 (electronic)

LC 2012-022836

SUMMARY: This book presents an "analysis of fascist Italy's project to promote the political and ideological construction of transnational Italian nationhood among Italian immigrants in Argentina. . . . [David] Aliano documents the multifaceted fascist project to win political converts among Italian immigrants in Argentina, which included offers of service from the renowned playwright Luigi Pirandello during two Argentine tours (1927 and 1936)." (American Historical Review)

REVIEW: *Am Hist Rev* v119 no1 p227-8 F 2014 David M. K. Sheinin

"Mussolini's National Project in Argentina". "This is a thoughtful analysis of fascist Italy's project to promote the political and ideological construction of transnational Italian nationhood among Italian immigrants in Argentina. The author draws effectively on government archival material in Italy and Argentina, as well as on newspaper and other sources. . . . This book excels in illustrating Italian fascist policymaking and propaganda, the links between [Benito] Mussolini's national project and both pro- and anti-fascist political and institutional responses in Argentina . . . and the Argentine government responses in the 1930s. However, by framing his book more amply the author falls short on some stated objectives."

ALL MEN FREE AND BRETHREN; essays on the history of African American freemasonry; 280 p. 2013 Cornell University Press

1. African American freemasonry—History 2. African American freemasons 3. African American freemasons—History 4. Freedmen—United States 5. Freemasons—United States—History 6. Historical literature

ISBN 0801450306; 9780801450303 (alk. paper)

LC 2012-033412

SUMMARY: This book, edited by Peter P. Hinks and Stephen Kantrowitz, provides "historical consideration of [African American] freemasonry from the Revolutionary era to the early decades of the twentieth century. Through a growing network of lodges, African American Masons together promoted fellowship, Christianity, and social respectability, while standing against slavery and white supremacy." (Publisher's note)

REVIEW: *Am Hist Rev* v118 no5 p1540-1 D 2013 Joy Porter

REVIEW: *Choice* v51 no2 p332 O 2013 J. M. B. Porter

"All Men Free and Brethren: Essays on the History of African American Freemasonry." "In this slim volume of eight essays examining the contribution of black freemasons from the Revolutionary era to the early 20th century, readers see how Prince Hall brethren promoted brotherhood, fellowship, and social respectability. Questions over jurisdiction and legitimacy plagued the Prince Hall Affiliation, but in the aftermath of the Civil War it is clear that freemasonry was a crucial means for those born in slavery to 'throw off the mental shackles of slaveholders' white supremacy' During the Jim Crow era. . . . This remarkably useful book explores an aspect of US history long overlooked by historians of both historical freemasonry and the African American experience.

ALLAN RAMSAY; Portraits of the Enlightenment; 200 p. 2013 Prestel Pub

1. Art literature 2. Bluestockings (Literary societies) 3. British portrait painting 4. Enlightenment 5. Ramsay, Allan, 1686-1758

ISBN 3791348787; 9783791348780

SUMMARY: This book "brings together [Allan] Ramsay's most celebrated sitters, such as [Jean-Jaques] Rousseau, [David] Hume, and William Hunter, along with numerous drawings and prints to consider his critical role in the British Enlightenment. Many of the artist's rarely seen portraits of women are included." Essays by various contributors examine "the unique sensitivity of Ramsay's painting, the development of his technique, and familial influences on his work." (Publisher's note)

REVIEW: *Burlington Mag* v156 no1337 p539 Ag 2014 MARTIN POSTLE

REVIEW: *Choice* v51 no9 p1580 My 2014 L. R. Matteson

"Allan Ramsay: Portraits of the Enlightenment". "Recent studies of the Scottish portraitist Allan Ramsay tend to consider him as an active participant in the Enlightenment. . . . The contributors to the current book continue this vein of inquiry. . . . [Anne] Dulau's fascinating chapter discusses Ramsay's portraiture of and correspondence with the Bluestockings—high-born women who used their salons to promote progressive social, literary, and artistic ideas. Two other chapters deal with Ramsay's attraction to Italian classical landscape and technical matters regarding his use of pigments. Well illustrated."

ALLAWI, ALI A. Faisal I of Iraq; [by] Ali A. Allawi 672 p. 2014 Yale University Press

1. BIOGRAPHY & AUTOBIOGRAPHY—Royalty 2. Biography (Literary form) 3. HISTORY—Middle East—General 4. HISTORY—Modern—20th Century

ISBN 0300127324; 9780300127324 (hardback)

LC 2013-021873

SUMMARY: This book, by Ali A. Allawi, is a biography of King Faisal I of Iraq. "A battle-hardened military leader who, with the help of Lawrence of Arabia, organized the Arab Revolt against the Ottoman Empire . . . a founding father and king of the first independent state of Syria; the first king of Iraq--in his many roles Faisal overcame innumerable crises and opposing currents while striving to build the structures of a modern state." (Publisher's note)

REVIEW: *Economist* v410 no8873 p79 F 8 2014

"Faisal I of Iraq." "An impressive biography. . . . Through his skilful use of Arabic as well as British sources, [Ali A. Allawi] portrays Faisal as a convincing multi-dimensional figure. . . . As Mr. Allawi concedes, he became more autocratic as he remained in power. . . . Mr. Allawi's book would have benefited from more thorough editing and proof-reading. The decision to open the narrative with Faisal's death and funeral gives it a good beginning but deprives it of a strong ending. These are minor complaints. This is the fullest portrait yet of a fascinating figure who played a significant role in the making of the modern Middle East."

REVIEW: *Kirkus Rev* v82 no1 p253 Ja 1 2014

ALLEGREZZA, WILLIAM.ed. The Salt companion to Charles Bernstein. See The Salt companion to Charles Bernstein

ALLEN, DAVID. Powerful teacher learning; what the theatre arts teach about collaboration; [by] David Allen 154 p. 2013 Rowman & Littlefield Publishers, Inc.

1. Drama in education—United States 2. Educational literature 3. Professional learning communities—United States 4. Teachers—In-service training—United States 5. Teachers—Professional relationships—United States 6. Theater—Study and teaching—United States
ISBN 9781610486811 (cloth: alk. paper); 9781610486828 (pbk.: alk. paper)
LC 2013-012115

SUMMARY: This book by David Allen "takes the reader outside traditional sites of professional development for teachers and into the black box theatres and rehearsal studios of contemporary theatre companies. It investigates the methods and specific tools these theatre artists use to collectively create new works for performance. Drawing on these methods and tools, it provides a model for understanding and improving the practices of teacher learning groups." (Publisher's note)

REVIEW: *Choice* v51 no9 p1650 My 2014 D. Pellegrino

"Powerful Teacher Learning: What the Theatre Arts Teach About Collaboration". "[David] Allen . . . uses a cross-domain methodology and extends it from teachers' preservice experiences to practicing teachers as they work together in teacher learning groups (TLG) in K-12 schools. . . . The lessons learned from the theater companies offer inquiry groups and critical-friends groups in schools specific tools for meaningful professional learning and instruction improvement. This book is highly recommended for practicing teachers."

ALLEN, JONATHAN (JONATHAN J. M.) HRC. See Parnes, A.

ALLEN, JULIA M. Passionate commitments; the lives of Anna Rochester and Grace Hutchins; [by] Julia M. Allen xiv, 364 p. 2013 State University of New York Press

1. Historical literature 2. Women communists—United States—Biography 3. Women labor leaders—United States—Biography 4. Women social reformers—United States—Biography
ISBN 9781438446875 (hardcover : alk. paper)
LC 2012-025921

SUMMARY: This book presents "a story of two women whose love for each other sustained their political work. [Julia M.] Allen examines the personal and public writings of [Anna] Rochester and [Grace] Hutchins to reveal under-reported challenges to capitalism as well as little-known efforts to strengthen feminism during their time." (Publisher's note)

REVIEW: *Choice* v51 no5 p825 Ja 2014 F. Alaya

"Passionate Commitments: The Lives of Anna Rochester and Grace Hutchins." "[Julia M.] Allen . . . a specialist in deconstruction of political rhetoric, is at home with the rich body of sources surrounding the two women. She lets FBI files and correspondence from/to them create the story, weaving sympathy and dispassion into her scrutiny of the muted drama of their private lives. Set against a backdrop of semi-secret, supportive love, this account becomes exhilaratingly, complexly cinematic. . . . Highly recommended."

REVIEW: *Women's Review of Books* v31 no1 p7-9 Ja/F 2014 Bettina Aptheker

ALLEN, LORI. The rise and fall of human rights; cynicism and politics in occupied Palestine; [by] Lori Allen xviii, 258 p. 2013 Stanford University Press

1. Arab-Israeli conflict—1973-1993 2. Arab-Israeli conflict—1993- 3. Human rights—Palestine—History 4. Human rights advocacy—Political aspects—Palestine—History 5. Palestinian Arabs—Civil rights—Gaza Strip—History 6. Palestinian Arabs—Civil rights—West Bank—History 7. Political science literature
ISBN 9780804784702 (cloth : alk. paper); 9780804784719 (pbk. : alk. paper)
LC 2013-005079

SUMMARY: This book by Lori Allen "ethnographic investigation of the Palestinian human rights world--its NGOs, activists, and 'victims,' as well as their politics, training, and discourse--since 1979. Though human rights activity began as a means of struggle against the Israeli occupation, it has since been professionalized and politicized, transformed into a public relations tool for political legitimization and state-making." (Publisher's note)

REVIEW: *Choice* v51 no6 p1089 F 2014 P. Rowe

REVIEW: *Middle East J* v68 no1 p173-5 Wint 2014 Deena R. Hurwitz

"The Rise and Fall of Human Rights: Cynicism and Politics in Occupied Palestine." "In her exceptional book . . . anthropologist Lori Allen explores a complex set of interlocking themes about the role of human rights in the Palestinian nationalist agenda, viewed through the prism of cynicism. . . . Allen's ethnography of the professionalization of human rights activism is astute and applies to many other sites of international 'democratization' and 'development'. . . . The book is a must read--with relevance far wider than the case of Palestine."

ALLEN, MARTIN. Mints and money in medieval England; [by] Martin Allen xvii, 576 p. 2012 Cambridge University Press

1. Coinage—England—History 2. England—Eco-

nomic conditions—1066-1485 3. Historical literature 4. Mints (Finance) 5. Money—England—History
ISBN 1107014948; 9781107014947
LC 2011-049741

SUMMARY: This "study of mints and money" in medieval England by Martin Allen "eschews the wider issues of monetary history . . .in order to present detailed evidence about how minting was organised and how the quantity and composition of the coinage changed over time. The book discusses, with new detail, the changing output of English mints and the revenue they generated." (English Historical Review)

REVIEW: *Choice* v50 no6 p1125 F 2013 K. W. Harl

REVIEW: *Engl Hist Rev* v129 no536 p179-81 F 2014 Richard Britnell

"Money in the Medieval English Economy, 973-1489" and "Mints and Money in Medieval England". "The survey of monetary history throughout the book is both well informed and much fuller and more richly elaborated than it would be in a survey aiming to give due weight to all the variables in play. Both in general, and in much of the detailed discussion about minting, monetary circulation and credit, the book will serve as an excellent introduction to an extensive literature. . . . Martin Allen's full and authoritative study of mints and money . . . makes an outstanding contribution to our knowledge of minting as a productive activity. . . . Allen's book, in short, is a primary reference work for the history of medieval English coinage."

ALLEN, NANCY. Winning by giving; [by] Nancy Allen 24 p. 2013 Rourke Educational Media
1. Charities 2. Children—Conduct of life—Juvenile literature 3. Children's nonfiction 4. Communities 5. Generosity
ISBN 9781621699101
LC 2013-937305

SUMMARY: This book on philanthropy by Nancy Kelly Allen is part of the Social Skills series, which "takes one aspect of a winning attitude and explains why it might be a worthy goal. 'Winning by Giving' defines philanthropy and then suggests that readers give their kindness, talents, and time to family, friends, and the community." (Booklist)

REVIEW: *Booklist* v110 no5 p56 N 1 2013 Daniel Kraus

"Winning By Giving," "Winning By Teamwork," and "Winning By Waiting." "Each cheerful title in the Social Skills series takes one aspect of a winning attitude and explains why it might be a worthy goal. 'Winning by Giving' defines philanthropy and then suggests that readers give their kindness, talents, and time to family, friends, and the community. 'Winning by Teamwork' is the series standout, alternating modern examples of good sportsmanship with photos of a U.S. Olympics team, Babe Ruth, and a famous college basketball handshake between a white and black player. 'Winning by Waiting' teaches a lesson well suited to impatient children to appreciate the strategy of the tortoise. . . . Though the text can be a bit cornball, the clean design and bright full-bleed photos of giddy kids make these books suitable and approachable tools in addressing those, shall we say, character quirks out there."

ALLEN, TOM, 1945-. Dangerous convictions; what's really wrong with the U.S. Congress; [by] Tom Allen p. cm. 2013 Oxford University Press, USA
1. POLITICAL SCIENCE—Government—Legislative Branch 2. Partisanship 3. Political science literature 4. United States. Congress
ISBN 9780199931989 (hardback)
LC 2012-028783

SUMMARY: In this book, former U.S. Congressman Tom Allen "argues that what's really wrong with Congress is the widening, hardening conflict in worldviews that leaves the two parties unable to understand how the other thinks about what people should do on their own and what we should do together. Members of Congress don't just disagree, they think the other side makes no sense." (Publisher's note)

REVIEW: *Choice* v51 no1 p162 S 2013 S. E. Frantzich

"Dangerous Convictions: What's Really Wrong With the U.S. Congress." "Former [U.S.] Representative [Tom] Allen (D-ME) promises an intriguing book about his former colleagues and argues that 'All of us--Right or Left--are potentially subject to adopting convictions that are not true ... worldviews lead us to reject evidence that conflicts with our pre-existing convictions.' He points out that deeply held, contradictory, and seldom-examined convictions caused many of his colleagues to reach erroneous conclusions. . . . The argument makes sense and is bolstered by many examples but loses some of its power when conservatives, much more than liberals, feel the brunt of his frustration. At times, the author seems just as hidebound as those he criticizes."

REVIEW: *Libr J* v138 no3 p112 F 15 2013 Robert Nardini

REVIEW: *Publ Wkly* v259 no43 p49 O 22 2012

ALLEN, TONY, 1940-. Tony Allen; an autobiography of the master drummer of afrobeat; [by] Michael E. Veal 199 p. 2013 Duke University Press
1. Africa 70 (Performer) 2. Afrobeat—Biography 3. Autobiography 4. Drummers (Musicians)—Nigeria—Biography 5. Fela, 1938-1997
ISBN 9780822355779 (cloth: alk. paper); 9780822355915 (pbk.: alk. paper)
LC 2013-013821

SUMMARY: This book presents an "autobiography of legendary Nigerian drummer Tony Allen, the rhythmic engine of Fela Kuti's Afrobeat. . . . Allen's memoir is based on hundreds of hours of interviews with the musician and scholar Michael E. Veal. It spans Allen's early years and career playing highlife music in Lagos; his fifteen years with Fela, from 1964 until 1979; his struggles to form his own bands in Nigeria; and his emigration to France." (Publisher's note)

REVIEW: *Choice* v51 no8 p1408 Ap 2014 D. J. Sehmalenberger

"Tony Allen: An Autobiography of the Master Drummer of Afrobeat". "This book is both a fascinating memoir and a compelling historical snapshot of West African culture and politics seen through the lens of Nigerian popular music. . . . The most significant thread throughout this autobiography is Allen's personal and musical relationship with Fela Kuti, multi-instrumentalist, composer, and leader of Africa 70, a musical group in which Allen drummed. . . . The book features an extensive bibliography and discography. Numerous black-and-white photos also help weave the tapestry of Allen's career."

ALLENBY, VICTORIA. Nat the Cat Can Sleep Like That; [by] Victoria Allenby 32 p. 2014 Orca Book Pub
1. Bedtime—Juvenile fiction 2. Cats—Juvenile fiction

3. Children's stories 4. Human-animal relationships—Fiction 5. Sleep
ISBN 1927485525; 9781927485521

SUMMARY: In this picture book, written in verse by Victoria Allenby and illustrated by Tara Anderson, "Nat has a talent for sleeping all day long. Name any place in the house, and Nat can sleep in, on, under or sprawled over it. In fact, Nat is so devoted to slumber that the imaginative antics of a crazy kitten don't seem to bother him one bit, until. . . ." (Publisher's note)

REVIEW: *Kirkus Rev* v81 no24 p298 D 15 2013

"Nat the Cat Can Sleep Like That". " Canadians [Victoria] Allenby and [Tara] Anderson have captured a cat any young ailurophile will recognize. The simple rhyming text listing the odd (yet realistic) places Nat can sleep during the daytime and all the silly mischief he and his black-and-white kitten sidekick get up to at night will hook young listeners. The watercolor, acrylic and pencil illustrations of floppy, goggle-eyed Nat and his buddy are a just-right pairing. Good kitty fun that will demand repeated reads."

REVIEW: *SLJ* v60 no3 p99 Mr 2014 Marianne Saccardi

ALLEYNE, MARK D., 1961-.ed. Anti-racism and multiculturalism. See Anti-racism and multiculturalism

ALLISON, JOHN. Bad Machinery 2; The Case of the Good Boy; [by] John Allison 136 p. 2014 Oni Press
1. Detective & mystery stories 2. Dogs—Fiction 3. Graphic novels 4. Missing children—Fiction 5. Teenagers—Fiction
ISBN 1620101149; 9781620101148

SUMMARY: In this book, by John Allison, "everyone's favorite pre-teen British detectives are back for another case! With toddlers disappearing and rumors of a large, beast-like creature roaming the woods, Tackleford is in serious danger. And then there's Mildred's new dog Archibald . . . if you can even call it a dog. . . . Everything comes to a head once the boys get a picture of the beast and Archibald goes missing. Is there a connection?" (Publisher's note)

REVIEW: *Booklist* v110 no13 p48-50 Mr 1 2014 Snow Wildsmith

"Bad Machinery: The Case of the Good Boy." "[John] Allison's series begins to hit its stride in this second volume, after 'The Case of the Team Spirit' (2013). Though the characters don't get much of an introduction, even new fans will quickly pick up on who's who, thanks to Allison's distinctive drawing style. The story veers between realism and fantasy, with just a touch of absurdism to keep things fun. Teens will likely admire Sonny's stubborn uniqueness, laugh at Shauna's reluctant love of her baby brother, and appreciate Mildred's ability to skirt her parents' sillier rules. The bright, colorful art and snarky dialogue are icing on a delightful cake."

REVIEW: *Voice of Youth Advocates* v36 no6 p52-3 F 2014 KAT KAN

ALLITT, PATRICK. A Climate of Crisis; America in the Age of Environmentalism; [by] Patrick Allitt 336 p. 2014 Penguin Group USA
1. Climatic changes 2. Environmental policy 3. Environmentalism—United States—History 4. Historical literature 5. Overpopulation
ISBN 1594204667; 9781594204661

SUMMARY: In this book, Patrick Allitt "examines contemporary American environmentalism historically, from his 'counter-environmentalist' and pro-industrialist stance, in order to allay fears of a real crisis. He structures his work chronologically. . . . His initial chapter on the 1950s describes 'nuclear anxieties' and worries about overpopulation, eventually making his way through discussions of biofuels, invasive species, and alternative energy." (Publishers Weekly)

REVIEW: *Bookforum* v20 no5 p19-20 F/Mr 2014 AMANDA LITTLE

"A Climate of Crisis: America in the Age of Environmentalism" and "Bloomberg's Hidden Legacy: Climate Change and the Future of New York City." "I've become impatient, at best, with books that question the existence of climate change. . . . That's why found it vexing (if at times unexpectedly entertaining) to slog through Patrick Allitt 'A Climate of Crisis' . . . . A supercilious air . . . . wafts through much of his narration. . . Allitt completely fails to recognize the enormous chasm that sets climate change apart from previous environmental concerns. . . . [Katherine] Bagley and [Maria] Gallucci's book is a short and in some ways rushed treatment of its vital and underreported subject. It clocks in at around twenty-five thousand words, and reads more like a magazine feature than a book in the traditional sense. But for all its weaknesses of format and style. 'Hidden Legacy' represents a vital, paradigm shifting turn in the sprawling climate literature."

REVIEW: *Booklist* v110 no12 p18-9 F 15 2014 Vanessa Bush

REVIEW: *Kirkus Rev* v82 no3 p131 F 1 2014

REVIEW: *Publ Wkly* v261 no7 p88 F 17 2014

ALLMAN, GALADRIELLE. Please be with me; a song for my father, Duane Allman; [by] Galadrielle Allman 400 p. 2014 Spiegel & Grau
1. Biography (Literary form) 2. Rock musicians—United States—Biography
ISBN 1400068940; 9781400068944; 9781588369604 (ebook)
LC 2013-046247

SUMMARY: This memoir, by Galadrielle Allman, is a "portrait of Duane Allman, founder of the legendary Allman Brothers Band, . . . [who] was killed in a motorcycle accident at the age of twenty-four. . . . Galadrielle was raised in the shadow of his loss and his fame. . . . [She] listened intently to his music, read articles about him, steeped herself in the mythic stories, and yet the spotlight rendered him too simple and too perfect to know." (Publisher's note)

REVIEW: *Kirkus Rev* v82 no4 p299 F 15 2014

"Please Be With Me: A Song for My Father, Duane Allman". "The author tries to connect with the famous father she never knew in an account that is most illuminating when she's telling her story and that of her mother. . . . The vast majority of this narrative covers decades when the author wasn't even alive, which doesn't prevent her from re-creating situations and dialogue and even asserting what her father was thinking long before he was her father. She had help, of course—access to her mother and other family, friends and members of the band, as well as interviews with those whose recordings Allman's guitar had graced."

REVIEW: *Newsweek Global* v162 no9 p123-8 F 28 2014

Barbara Herman

REVIEW: *Publ Wkly* v261 no17 p132 Ap 28 2014

ALMHJELL, TONE. The Twistrose Key; [by] Tone Almhjell 336 p. 2013 Dial

1. Animals—Fiction 2. Fantasy 3. Missing persons—Fiction 4. Pets—Fiction 5. Princes—Fiction 6. Riddles—Fiction 7. Winter—Fiction
ISBN 0803738951; 9780803738959 (hardcover)
LC 2012-050173

SUMMARY: In this book by Tone Almhjell, "something is wrong in the house that Lin's family has rented; Lin is sure of it. When a secret key marked 'Twistrose' arrives for her, Lin finds a crack in the cellar, a gate to the world of Sylver. This frozen realm is the home of every dead animal who ever loved a child. Lin is overjoyed to be reunited with Rufus, the pet she buried. Together they must find the missing Winter Prince in order to save Sylver from destruction." (Publisher's note)

REVIEW: *Booklist* v110 no8 p50 D 15 2013 Sarah Hunter

REVIEW: *Kirkus Rev* p69-70 N 15 2013 Best Books

REVIEW: *Kirkus Rev* v81 no18 p301 S 15 2013

REVIEW: *N Y Times Book Rev* p25 N 10 2013 BRAD LEITHAUSER

"The Twistrose Key." "A fanciful tale for children. . . . Those readers who like their magical domains rimmed with hoarfrost should find 'The Twistrose Key' particularly congenial. . . . [Tone] Almhjell makes bustling Sylveros seem sufficiently beguiling--with its polycolored domes and tradesmen's signposts, its rabbit tailor, its hamster baker--that its potential destruction creates genuine foreboding. . . . Elsewhere, though, 'The Twistrose Key' feels overstuffed, almost as though Almhjell had contemplated a multi-volume series and then chose to cram all her inventions into a single book. . . . Lin makes an appealing, stalwart heroine. I cared less than I would have liked about Rufus, however, whose character never emerged as anything beyond that of a trusty servant."

REVIEW: *Publ Wkly* v260 no36 p57-8 S 9 2013

ALMOND, DAVID, 1951-. The true tale of the monster Billy Dean; [by] David Almond 255 p. 2011 Viking

1. Dystopias—Fiction
ISBN 0763663093; 9780763663094
LC 2012-358384

SUMMARY: This novel, by David Almond, is "about a hidden-away child who emerges into a broken world. Billy Dean is a secret child. . . . His father fills his mind and his dreams with mysterious tales and memories and dreadful warnings. But then his father disappears, and Billy's mother brings him out into the world at last. He learns the horrifying story of what was saved and what was destroyed on the day he was born, the day the bombers came to Blinkbonny." (Publisher's note)

REVIEW: *Booklist* v110 no7 p51 D 1 2013 Daniel Kraus

REVIEW: *Horn Book Magazine* v90 no2 p108 Mr/Ap 2014 DEIRDRE F. BAKER

REVIEW: *Kirkus Rev* v81 no22 p140 N 15 2013

REVIEW: *Publ Wkly* v260 no43 p62 O 28 2013

REVIEW: *SLJ* v60 no4 p62 Ap 2014 Rebecca James

REVIEW: *SLJ* v60 no2 p99 F 2014 Nancy Silverrod

REVIEW: *TLS* no5669 p21 N 25 2011 SHEENA JOUGHIN

"What I Did" and "The True Tale of the Monster Billy Dean." "Something is 'not right' about ['What I Did'] as a convincing piece of fiction. Like many contemporary child narrators, Billy seems afflicted with some syndrome. This renders him obsessed with facts about the animal kingdom and prey to feelings of 'electricity' in his limbs . . . Wakling seems not to differentiate between writing about a child and writing as if he were one. Like everyone in the book, he imposes himself on Billy, which is a pity for the character, and for us. . . . David Almond's narrator is a very different 'Billy'. . . . born in the ruins of Blinkbonny . . . he spells life as he hears it and tells a fantastical tale of his journey from a locked room . . . into the wreck of his war-tom world. . . . Almond creates a luminous world where 'the living and the dead are all mixed up'. There are passages of great lyricism."

ALPERS, EDWARD A. The Indian Ocean in world history; [by] Edward A. Alpers 172 p. 2014 Oxford University Press

1. Cultural relations 2. Historical literature 3. Indian Ocean Region—Commerce
ISBN 9780195165937 (alk. paper); 9780195337877 (alk. paper)
LC 2013-020136

SUMMARY: In this book, "Edward A. Alpers explores the complex issues involved in cultural exchange in the Indian Ocean Rim region . . . by combining a historical approach with the insights of anthropology, art history, ethnomusicology, and geography. . . . [He] also discusses issues of trade and production that show the long history of exchange throughout the Indian Ocean world; politics and empire-building by both regional and European powers; and the role of religion." (Publisher's note)

REVIEW: *Choice* v51 no9 p1652-3 My 2014 I. Iumi

"The Indian Ocean in World History". "[Edward A.] Alpers . . . marshals his formidable pedagogical and authorial skills to integrate a plethora of human experiences from Eastern Africa to the South China Sea over 7,000 years. Convincingly making the case that the many disparate regions across half the globe warrant study collectively, this text aimed at world history students is peppered with appropriate quotes from primary sources, helpful maps locating all the disparate locales discussed, and illustrative photographs. . . . And yet, for as much as the case is made, the book reads densely. Students will need to consult other works for details about the complexities of varied intersections between peoples and processes in this newest addition to the OUP series on world history.'"

ALPINE, RACHELE. Canary; [by] Rachele Alpine 400 p. 2013 Medallion Press

1. School sports 2. School stories 3. Sexual assault 4. Teenage girls—Fiction 5. Young adult fiction
ISBN 1605425877; 9781605425870

SUMMARY: "In this debut novel . . . Kate Franklin's . . . . dad is hired to coach at Beacon Prep, home of one of the best basketball teams in the state. In a blog of prose and poetry, Kate chronicles her new world--dating a basketball player, being caught up in a world of idolatry and entitlement, and discovering the perks the inner circle enjoys. Then Kate's fragile life shatters once again when one of her boyfriend's teammates assaults her at a party." (Publisher's note)

REVIEW: *Kirkus Rev* v81 no12 p78 Je 15 2013

REVIEW: *SLJ* v59 no10 p1 O 2013 Suanne B. Roush

REVIEW: *Voice of Youth Advocates* v36 no4 p56 O 2013 Jan Chapman

"Canary." "Kate is a high school student who has had more than her fair share of loss. . . . But when Kate is assaulted by a member of the basketball team, her decision to speak out will test the limits of her friendships and even her relationship with her father. This is a contemporary novel that will resonate with many teens and is especially topical considering a recent high profile case of rape involving high school football players. Along with Kate, the reader experiences her gradual and horrified realization of the school's complicity in covering up the abuses that have gone unchallenged for years. . . . Teens will also like the format of the novel, told in blog posts and verse reminiscent of Ellen Hopkins's popular 'problem' novels."

REVIEW: *Voice of Youth Advocates* v37 no1 p13-5 Ap 2014

ALS, HILTON, 1960-. Kara Walker; Dust jackets for the niggerati; [by] Hilton Als 144 p. 2013 Gregory R. Miller & Co.

1. African Americans in popular culture 2. Art literature 3. Popular culture—United States 4. Power (Social sciences)
ISBN 9780982681367 (alk. paper)
LC 2012-046908

SUMMARY: This art book by Kara Walker presents "a major series of graphite drawings and hand printed texts on paper that grew out of Walker's attempts to understand how interpersonal and geopolitical powers are asserted through the lives of individuals. . . . The accompanying essays take us through Walker's saga of American experience." (Publisher's note)

REVIEW: *Bookforum* v20 no4 p20-1 D 2013/Ja 2014 CHRISTOPHER LYON

"Kara Walker: Dust Jackets for the N##gerati," "Great War: July 1, 1916: The First Day of the Battle of the Somme," and "Wall: Israeli & Palestinian Landscape 20008-2012." "The artist, assisted by the design firm CoMa, has cleverly folded the dust jacket into a large artwork that includes her entire foreword and a full-scale detail of a large text piece. The fine reproductions include these boldly graphic works as well as her powerfully kinetic figurative drawings. . . . Sacco conveys an eloquent, convincing, entirely wordless story. . . . [There is an] accompanying booklet with an affecting, brief account . . . by Adam Hochschild. . . . Josef Koudelka's book of purposely ugly photos--from which we cannot turn away."

ALS, HILTON, 1960-. White Girls; [by] Hilton Als 300 p. 2013 McSweeney's

1. African American gay men 2. Gender identity 3. Masculinity 4. Racial identity of whites 5. Social commentary
ISBN 1936365812; 9781936365814

SUMMARY: This book by Hilton Als presents a collection of essays. "His eponymous 'white girls' include Louise Brooks, Flannery O'Connor, Truman Capote, Richard Pryor, Malcolm X, Michael Jackson, Eminem, and others. Using his subjects as a springboard to analyze literature, photography, films, music, television, performance, race, gender, sexual orientation, and history, Als offers wry insights throughout." (Publishers Weekly)

REVIEW: *Bookforum* v20 no4 p48 D 2013/Ja 2014 MELISSA ANDERSON

"White Girls". "The thirteen essays collected in 'White Girls' . . . all jump off spectacularly. . . . Yet even these audacious introductions aren't as attention grabbing as the title of the volume itself, which is more provocative than that of its predecessor. . . . 'White Girls' . . . suggests an epithet, a diminishment, a marker of privilege, a pariah status—us, them, nobody, everybody. [Hilton] Als's always nimble, sometimes outrageous, complicating of alleged binaries—white or black, male or female, gay or straight—makes him one of our most vital, vibrant cultural critics. . . . In this destabilizing, exhilarating blur of fact and fiction. Als assumes the place of the performers he extols, making a habit of not only disjunction but also brilliant lunacy."

REVIEW: *Booklist* v110 no3 p16-7 O 1 2013 Donna Seaman

REVIEW: *Kirkus Rev* v81 no14 p317 Jl 15 2013

REVIEW: *Kirkus Rev* p19 Ag 15 2013 Fall Preview

REVIEW: *Libr J* v138 no18 p105 N 1 2013 Molly McArdle

REVIEW: *Libr J* v138 no14 p107 S 1 2013 Molly McArdle

REVIEW: *N Y Rev Books* v61 no2 p4-6 F 6 2014 Elaine Blair

"White Girls". "Hilton [Als's] characteristic form is a kind of essay in which biography, memoir, and literary criticism flow into one another as if it were perfectly natural that they should. . . . In all of his essays, the life gets as much scrutiny as the work, with an eye to one particular question: How do artists come alive to their ambitions and then proceed to realize them? How does the work get made? . . . Als will seem to be breaking some essential rule of first-person essay-writing in disastrous fashion and then turn the passage inside-out, revealing it to have a different rhetorical function than you originally thought."

REVIEW: *N Y Times Book Rev* p16 N 10 2013 RICH BENJAMIN

"White Girls". "Hilton Als, in the fierce style of street reading and the formal tradition of critical inquiry, reads culture, race and gender in his new essay collection, 'White Girls.' Here, reading becomes psychoanalytic self-exhibition, complete with insights on identity, sexuality, voice and the attainment of knowledge. . . . His resulting critique of whiteness is effortless, honest and fearless. He doesn't afford whites any reverence, nor any hip, posturing, disdain. Some of his remarks on race and sexuality—so original and mordant—may offend the mullahs of pious multicultural liberalism (and will certainly offend conservatives). Als floats outside political and cultural orthodoxies, and this independence, this integrity, gives 'White Girls' much of its charm."

REVIEW: *N Y Times Book Rev* p32 S 28 2014 IHSAN TAYLOR

REVIEW: *Nation* v297 no24 p44-5 D 16 2013 AARON THIER

REVIEW: *New Statesman* v142 no5184 p53-5 N 15 2013 Olivia Laing

REVIEW: *Publ Wkly* v260 no30 p52 Jl 29 2013

ALTER, ADAM. Drunk tank pink; and other unexpected forces that shape how we think, feel, and behave; [by] Adam Alter 272 p. 2013 The Penguin Press

1. Environmental psychology 2. Mental suggestion 3. Psychological literature 4. Psychology, Applied 5. Social psychology

ISBN 1594204543 (hardcover); 9781594204548 (hardcover)

LC 2012-046810

SUMMARY: This book by Adam Alter explores "how words, symbols, culture, and our surroundings inevitably and imperceptibly shape how we think and behave. He points to research showing that children who grow up in noisy apartments take longer to learn to read, that warm weather seems to spark more road rage, and that bystanders can shape our inclination to help someone in need." (Psychology Today)

REVIEW: *Choice* v51 no1 p167 S 2013 I. I. Katzarska-Miller

"Drunk Tank Pink: And Other Unexpected Forces That Shape How We Think, Feel, and Behave." "Most people perceive themselves as agents in control of their environments and behaving in ways consistent with their thoughts. [Author Adam] Alter . . . , using empirically based research findings, challenges these notions, and illustrates the environmental affordances that shape individuals' thoughts and behaviors. Human perceptions and decisions are based partially on hidden contextual cues that influence not only immediate thoughts and actions but also long-term life outcomes. . . . Alter does an impressive job in translating social psychological research into an accessible, engaging, and exciting read."

REVIEW: *Publ Wkly* v260 no1 p49-50 Ja 7 2013

REVIEW: *Smithsonian* v43 no11 p100-1 Mr 2013 Chloë Schama

ALTER, JONATHAN. The Center Holds; Obama and His Enemies; [by] Jonathan Alter 448 p. 2013 Simon & Schuster

1. Obama, Barack, 1961- 2. Political science literature 3. Presidents—United States—Election—2012 4. United States—Economic conditions—21st century 5. United States—Politics & government—2009- 6. United States—Social conditions—21st century

ISBN 1451646070; 9781451646078

SUMMARY: This book by Jonathan Alter "chronicles the campaign that assured President Barack Obama a second term. . . . The 2012 election was neither the referendum on the president and the ailing economy as the GOP had hoped, nor simply a choice between the president and his opponent as Obama had wished. Rather, . . . Alter . . . insists, it was a judgment on the Republicans and their mean-spirited billionaire backers." (Kirkus Reviews)

REVIEW: *America* v209 no13 p33-4 N 4 2013 PETER REICHARD

REVIEW: *Bookforum* v20 no3 p8-59 S-N 2013 THOMAS FRANK

REVIEW: *Christ Century* v130 no15 p35 Jl 24 2013

REVIEW: *Commentary* v136 no4 p47-8 N 2013 PHILIP TERZIAN

"The Center Holds: Obama and His Enemies." "Jonathan Alter's 'The Center Holds' is the second installment of a likely three-volume account of the Obama presidency. Now, if the second of three books about an incumbent politician by an admiring journalist sounds appealing to readers, then 'The Center Holds' might be worth the cost and time. Otherwise, the student of contemporary history might wish to refrain from investing. Strictly speaking, there is nothing to be learned here--almost nothing whatsoever--not known already to the faithful consumer of newspapers and magazines."

REVIEW: *Kirkus Rev* v81 no2 p43 Je 1 2013

REVIEW: *N Y Times Book Rev* p19 Ag 18 2013 Jeffrey Frank

"The Center Holds: Obama and His Enemies." "The Yeatsian title reflects President Obama's view that the real struggle of the 2012 election wasn't between conservatives and liberals but between 'right-wing extremism' and 'pragmatic centrism'. . . . [Jonathan Alter] is very good at describing the intimidating power of those close to the president. . . . Although his focus is [Barack] Obama, he doesn't neglect the opposition. . . . Obama rightly regarded his re-election as a pivotal event. This well-reported account of how he won, though, can only hint at what lies ahead in an age whose poisonous politics, Alter seems to suggest, may bring out the inner derangement in anyone."

REVIEW: *New York Times* v162 no56156 pC1-4 Je 3 2013 MICHIKO KAKUTANI

REVIEW: *Publ Wkly* v260 no4 p115-21 Ja 28 2013 JESSAMINE CHAN

ALTINYELKEN, HÜLYA KOSAR.ed. Global education policy and international development. See Global education policy and international development

ALTMAN, IDA. The war for Mexico's west; Indians and Spaniards in New Galicia, 1524-1550; [by] Ida Altman xx, 340 p. 2010 University of New Mexico Press

1. Historical literature 2. Imperialism—History 3. Indians of Mexico—History 4. Mexico—History—Conquest, 1519-1540 5. Nueva Galicia

ISBN 9780826344939; 0826344933

LC 2010-005576

SUMMARY: This book by Ida Altman "examines a dramatic, complex episode in the early history of New Spain that stands as an instructive counterpoint to the much more familiar, triumphalist narrative of . . . the conquest of central Mexico. As Spaniards consolidated their hold over central Mexico they fanned out in several directions, first entering western Mexico--the future New Galicia--in 1524. A full-fledged expedition of conquest followed several years later." (Publisher's note)

REVIEW: *Am Hist Rev* v118 no4 p1228-9 O 2013 David Tavárez

"The War for Mexico's West: Indians and Spaniards in New Galicia, 1524-1550." "The book has a compelling narrative structure. Ida Altman begins with an account of Cortés's failed campaign, which was followed by Guzmán's notoriously ruthless establishment of a permanent Spanish colonial presence in what would become Nueva Galicia. . . . This book provides an accessible and judiciously documented overview of a crucial conquest event that complements the historiography of military encounters in Mesoamerica. In particular, Altman joins forces with an emerging literature on the essential role of indigenous allies in conquest events, which in turn is part of a new conquest history for early Spanish America."

ALTSHUL, VICTOR. Stumblings; [by] Victor Altshul 62 p. 2013 CreateSpace Independent Publishing Platform

1. Communication 2. Odin (Norse deity) 3. Parent & child 4. Poems—Collections 5. Ring of the Nibelung, The (Theatrical production)

ISBN 148189756X; 9781481897563

SUMMARY: This book presents a collection of poetry by Victor Altshul. "In 'Wotan,' a tongue-in-cheek ode to a character from Richard Wagner's operatic Ring cycle, he reflects on the god's vexed relationship with his daughter while also exploring the nature of parenthood. . . . 'Standpipe' . . . turns a drainage tube into a metaphor for missed communications." (Kirkus Reviews)

REVIEW: *Kirkus Rev* v81 no24 p31 D 15 2013

"Stumblings". "A sensitive, precise and moving first offering from a poet of real promise. For 50 years, Altshul has practiced psychiatry in New Haven, Conn., and now, in the autumn of his life, he's published his first book of poetry. If he's half as good a therapist as he is a poet, he must have some extremely healthy patients, for this is as accomplished a debut collection as readers are likely to find. . . . There's so much for readers to enjoy here. . . . A mature poetic effort from a sure-handed rookie."

REVIEW: *Kirkus Rev* v81 no22 p265 N 15 2013

ALUMINUM ORE; The Political Economy of the Global Bauxite Industry; 388 p. 2013 University of Washington Press

1. Aluminum mines & mining—Economic aspects 2. Economics literature 3. Globalization 4. Mineral industries 5. Mining machinery industry

ISBN 0774825324; 9780774825320

SUMMARY: This book, edited by Robin S. Gendron, Mats Ingulstad, and Espen Storli, "explores the history of bauxite in the twentieth century and the global forces that this history represents, from its strategic development in the First World War to its role in the globalization of markets as companies from the northern hemisphere vied for the resources of the south." (Publisher's note)

REVIEW: *Choice* v51 no8 p1435 Ap 2014 T. S. Reynolds

"Aluminum Ore: The Political Economy of the Global Bauxite Industry". "Collected works often suffer from uneven scholarship and lack of integration. Neither criticism applies here. Virtually all the papers are solid, well-documented scholarship, and all share a basic theme: the history of bauxite reflects the history of economic globalization in the 20th century. . . . This and the authors' practice of referring to companion essays provide a feeling of integration often absent in compilations. Some essays needed maps, and a contribution dealing with American bauxite production would have rounded out the volume."

ALUN-JONES, DEBORAH. The wry romance of the literary rectory; [by] Deborah Alun-Jones 208 p. 2013 Thames & Hudson

1. Clergy as authors 2. English authors—Homes & haunts—Great Britain 3. English literature—History & criticism 4. Historical literature 5. Parsonages

ISBN 9780500516775 (hardcover)

LC 2012-944892

SUMMARY: "The case studies, which range chronologically from the Revd Sydney Smith . . . in the early 1800s, to Vikram Seth's present cohabitation with the spirit of George Herbert at Bemerton, Wiltshire, illustrate the claim that in the rectory 'the creative life takes on sacramental importance'." (Times Literary Supplement)

REVIEW: *TLS* no5747 p9-10 My 24 2013 SAMANTHA MATTHEWS

"The Wry Romance of the Literary Rectory." "An engaging, eclectic account of eight British writers' personal and literary 'romance' with the rectory--her generic term for parsonages, vicarages and other domestic buildings associated with Church of England livings. . . . The book's strongest suit is its evocation of non-literary domestic and familial arts. . . . 'The Wry Romance of the Literary Rectory' evinces the author's humour and relish of eccentricities, but has an underlying melancholy. This is partly due to its historical focus on the past 200 years, when clergymen found it increasingly difficult to maintain their homes on a church income, and the Church Commissioners sold many clerical homes on the open market."

AMANO, YOSHITAKA. The Sky; The Art of Final Fantasy; [by] Yoshitaka Amano 576 p. 2013 Dark Horse

1. Art literature 2. Dragons in art 3. Fantastic art 4. Final Fantasy games 5. Video game design

ISBN 1616551607 (hbk.); 9781616551605 (hbk.)

SUMMARY: "This book focuses on [Yoshitaka] Amano's art for the first 10 Final Fantasy video games, from 1987 to 2001. These 570-plus pages of dreamscapes and nightmarelands are populated by demons and monsters, by expert swordsmen and women aside dragons." (New York Times) " Volume 1 contains Amano's work for Final Fantasy I-III, Volume 2 his contributions for Final Fantasy IV-VI, and Volume 3 features his art for Final Fantasy VII-X." (Publisher's note)

REVIEW: *New York Times* v163 no56286 pC32 O 11 2013 Dana Jennings

"The Sky: The Art of Final Fantasy," "Conan: Red Nails," and "Gil Kane's the Amazing Spider-Man." "With his elegant and sinuous line, the Japanese artist Yoshitaka Amano understands the power of pen and ink. . . . Mr. Amano's light, deft touch defies genre conventions in a fantasy world where blood and beauty twine, where the ethereal has bite. . . . Mr. [Barry] Windsor-Smith shows his skill at creating a world on just one textured black-and-white page. The heroes in this lush, oversize book . . . are clearly Conan--and Mr. Windsor-Smith. . . . Gil Kane was one of the best unsung comic artists of the 1960s and '70s. . . . His muscular line and cinematic sense of page design served well superheroes like Green Lantern, Batman and especially Spider-Man."

AMATO, MARY. Missing monkey!; [by] Mary Amato 128 p. 2014 Egmont USA

1. Brothers and sisters—Fiction 2. Conduct of life—Fiction 3. Family life—Fiction 4. Humorous stories 5. Robbers and outlaws—Fiction 6. Twins—Fiction

ISBN 1606845098; 9781606843963 (hardcover); 9781606845097 (digest pbk.)

LC 2013-018251

SUMMARY: This book, by Mary Amato, is part of the Good

Crooks series. "When their parents steal a monkey from the zoo to help them pick pockets, our heroes rush into action and return the wily animal using disguises, inventions, and old-fashioned shoe leather. They also learn what a monkey can do in 11 minutes." (Publisher's note)

REVIEW: *Bull Cent Child Books* v67 no10 p496 Je 2014 J. H.

"Missing Monkey!". "Zany, lightweight middle-grade series, in which character development and believable plotting take a back seat to milk-snorting entertainment, are a dime a dozen. However, [Mary] Amato's playful, genuinely funny writing . . . and her keen understanding of the middle-grade audience make this a solid winner. Quick pacing, plentiful humor, a large font, and the numerous illustrations will reassure reluctant readers. [Ward] Jenkins' lively, monochromatic art has a cartoonish flavor that successfully partners with the wackiness of the book's events."

REVIEW: *Kirkus Rev* v82 no1 p135 Ja 1 2014

REVIEW: *Publ Wkly* v260 no45 p71-2 N 11 2013

REVIEW: *SLJ* v60 no3 p99 Mr 2014 Sarah Polace

AMBROSE, JONATHAN. The natural communities of Georgia. See Edwards, L.

AMBROZY, LEE.ed. Ai Weiwei's blog. See Ai Weiwei,

AMERICAN CIVIL WAR; the definitive encyclopedia and document collection; 2778 p. 2013 ABC-CLIO, LLC

1. Encyclopedias & dictionaries 2. History—Sources 3. United States—Military history

ISBN 1851096779; 9781851096770 (hardcover : alk. paper)

LC 2013-016414

SUMMARY: This book "provides a broad, multidisciplinary examination" of the American Civil War with "the aim of being a 'definitive' set. . . . Historian [Spencer C.] Tucker and his editorial team have assembled nearly 3,000 entries as well as a collection of 172 primary documents. Coverage includes all significant battles, people, places, and weapons; and the work encompasses the social, political, cultural, and economic issues of the time." (Booklist)

REVIEW: *Booklist* v110 no1 p60 S 1 2013 Rebecca Vnuk

"American Civil War: The Definitive Encyclopedia and Document Collection." "There seems to be no shortage of books on the Civil War, but this work provides a broad, multidisciplinary examination of the time period and fulfills the aim of being a 'definitive' set. . . . The alphabetically arranged entries are signed and tend to be brief but thorough, ranging from a half-page or less. . . . The entries, across the board, are succinct and well written. . . . This remarkably thorough yet easy-to-digest encyclopedia is highly recommended for high-school, public, and academic libraries where budget allows."

REVIEW: *Choice* v51 no7 p1188 Mr 2014 T. S. Hefner-Babb

REVIEW: *Libr J* v139 no3 p127 F 15 2014 Brian Odom

REVIEW: *SLJ* v60 no2 p62 F 2014 Eldon Younce

THE AMERICAN HERITAGE DICTIONARY OF THE ENGLISH LANGUAGE; xxvii, 2084 2011 Houghton Mifflin Harcourt

1. Definitions 2. Encyclopedias & dictionaries 3. English language 4. English language—Dictionaries 5. English language—Usage 6. English language—Usage—Dictionaries 7. Reference books

ISBN 9780547041018

LC 2011-004777

SUMMARY: This book, "the fifth edition of "The American Heritage Dictionary of the English Language" (AHD)" includes 10,000 new words, with "color photos in the margin to illustrate the definitions. Countries all have a small map with their location and major cities. . . . [U]sage notes . . . . have been updated . . . AHD also includes example sentences, and many of these have been lengthened with the addition of quotations from writers . . . Synonyms for words have been added . . . The purchase of this print edition contains a passkey for a free app version, and there is a free online version at www.ahdictionary.com." (Booklist)

REVIEW: *Booklist* v108 no12 p33 F 15 2012 Christine Bulson

The American Heritage Dictionary of the English Language. 5th ed. "[The American Heritage Dictionary of the English Language] is known for its usage notes, which are based on the opinions of a panel of respected authors, scholars, journalists, politicians, and even the cartoonist Ed Koren. Many of these notes have been updated, including one for unique, which admits that the word—being an absolute term with no comparison or modification by an adverb—is waning. . . . The New Oxford American Dictionary (3rd ed., 2010) and [The American Heritage Dictionary of the English Language] are considered comprehensive dictionaries in the middle between college dictionaries and those that are unabridged."

REVIEW: *Libr J* v136 no19 p97 N 15 2011 Marilyn S. Lary

AMERICAN IMMIGRATION; an encyclopedia of political, social, and cultural change; 1272 p. 2013 M.E. Sharpe

1. Encyclopedias & dictionaries 2. Immigrants—United States—Encyclopedias 3. United States—Emigration & immigration—Government policy 4. United States—Emigration & immigration—History

ISBN 9780765682123 (hardcover)

LC 2013-010015

SUMMARY: This book, edited by James Ciment and John Radzilowski, provides an "assessment of the legacy of immigration and of the upcoming debate on immigration reform" It covers "all aspects of US immigration, including causes, processes, patterns, history, society, culture, and politics, as well as nations of origin and US destinations." (Choice: Current Reviews for Academic Libraries)

REVIEW: *Booklist* v110 no16 p33 Ap 15 2014 Rebecca Vnuk

REVIEW: *Choice* v51 no8 p1374 Ap 2014 T. G. Walch

"American Immigration: An Encyclopedia of Political, Social, and Cultural Change". "This new edition . . . provides an enhanced and updated assessment of the legacy of immigration and of the upcoming debate on immigration reform. . . . This edition also includes more than 80 documents from the 18th century to the present, 60 tables and charts, a thorough bibliography, and a detailed index. The two editors enlisted more than 125 immigration scholars to write and revise each of the entries. Collectively, the editors, contributors, and publisher have produced an admirable work on a timely, important topic. . . . Highly recommended."

REVIEW: *Libr J* v139 no5 p138 Mr 15 2014 Carol Fazioli

AMIRSADEGHI, HOSSEIN.ed. Art studio America. See Art studio America

AMODIO, MARK C. The Anglo-Saxon literature handbook; [by] Mark C. Amodio xvi, 412 p. 2014 Wiley-Blackwell, A John Wiley & Sons Ltd., Publication

1. Anglo-Saxon civilization 2. Anglo-Saxon mythology 3. Civilization, Anglo-Saxon—Handbooks, manuals, etc 4. English literature—Old English, ca. 450-1100—History and criticism—Handbooks, manuals, etc 5. Illumination of books & manuscripts, Anglo-Saxon 6. Literature—History & criticism

ISBN 9780631226970 (cloth); 9780631226987 (pbk.)

LC 2012-050143

SUMMARY: "Released in the new 'Blackwell Literature Handbooks' series, this volume offers an overview of Anglo-Saxon literature, including its political, historical, and cultural contexts. Following an . . . introductory section, [Mark C.] Amodio . . . discusses prose and poetry, . . . surveying the corpus of important Anglo-Saxon works. Discussion of each work opens with a description of the manuscript containing it, including current location and physical condition." (Choice: Current Reviews for Academic Libraries

REVIEW: *Choice* v51 no7 p1210-1 Mr 2014 C. P. Jamison

REVIEW: *Choice* v51 no5 p882 Ja 2014 C. P. Jamison

"The Anglo-Saxon Literature Handbook." "Following a thorough introductory section, [Mark C.] Amodio . . . discusses prose and poetry, successfully surveying the corpus of important Anglo-Saxon works. . . . Although he does not include a detailed discussion of language, numerous passages in Old English will serve as illustration for beginning students. By nature, such an ambitious endeavor must be selective, and this is most noticeable in Amodio's presentations of critical perspectives. Nonetheless, the discussions are well informed, and readers will benefit from them. . . . The handbook concludes with sections on critical approaches and recurring themes, and these additions broaden the perspective of this accessible, invaluable book."

AMSTER, ELLEN J. Medicine and the saints; science, Islam, and the colonial encounter in Morocco, 1877-1956; [by] Ellen J. Amster xiv, 334 p. 2013 University of Texas Press

1. Health—Religious aspects—Islam 2. Historical literature 3. Islam and science—History 4. Medicine—Morocco—History 5. Muslim saints—Cult—Morocco 6. Sufism—Morocco—History

ISBN 9780292745445 (cloth : alk. paper)

LC 2012-046686

SUMMARY: This book "traces a history of colonial embodiment in Morocco through a series of medical encounters between the Islamic sultanate of Morocco and the Republic of France from 1877 to 1956." Author Ellen Amster "investigates the positivist ambitions of French colonial doctors, sociologists, philologists, and historians . . . [and] the social history of the encounters and transformations occasioned by French medical interventions." (Publisher's note)

REVIEW: *Am Hist Rev* v119 no2 p647-8 Ap 2014 Sahar Bazzaz

REVIEW: *Middle East J* v68 no1 p170-2 Wint 2014 Hannah-Louise Clark

"Medicine and the Saints: Science, Islam, and the Colonial Encounter in Morocco, 1877-1956." "An ambitious, path-breaking interdisciplinary study of the politics of health in Morocco. . . . [Ellen J. Amster's] major contribution lies in connecting two historiographies that until now have largely operated in isolation. Amster brings methods and analytical techniques familiar to Africanist historians, particularly oral narratives, to the attention of historians of the Middle East and North Africa. Conversely, historians of health and healing in sub-Saharan Africa will gain rich comparative insights from this study of science, Islam, and colonialism. . . . Amster has written a tremendous book, which will appeal to a wide range of specialists."

ANASTASIO, ANDREA. Alone in the forest. See Alone in the forest

ANCIENT ANIMALS; terror bird; 32 p. 2013 Charlesbridge

1. Animals—Juvenile literature 2. Cenozoic paleontology 3. Children's nonfiction 4. Extinct birds 5. Phorusrhacidae—Juvenile literature

ISBN 1580893988; 9781580893985 (reinforced for library use); 9781580893992 (softcover); 9781607346104 (ebook)

LC 2012-029366

SUMMARY: This book looks at the terror bird called the "Kelenken guillermoi, a seven-foot-tall predator that lived about fifteen million years ago. . . . The text intersperses facts within imagined hunting scenes. . . . The accompanying picture shows two prehistoric birds labeled Brontornis and Psilopterus." Another "spread compares the role of these top predators with those that exist today, such as sharks, wolves and tigers." (Kirkus Reviews)

REVIEW: *Booklist* v110 no7 p58 D 1 2013 Sarah Hunter

REVIEW: *Bull Cent Child Books* v67 no1 p57 S 2013 E. B.

"Ancient Animals: Terror Bird." "Meet the terror birds, flightless apex predators that once feasted on their Cenozoic neighbors in South America and now posthumously delight primary students cutting their own teeth on easy readers. This debut entry in a new Ancient Animals series mainly highlights size and predation, with a nod to migration to North America, relegating even the name of the featured bird, Kelenken guillermoi, to a sentence on the title page verso. No mention is made of the fossil discoveries that inform our understanding of terror birds, an omission that fans of extinct beasties are sure to notice."

REVIEW: *Kirkus Rev* v81 no14 p123 Jl 15 2013

REVIEW: *SLJ* v59 no9 p180 S 2013 Maggie Chase

ANCIENT EGYPTIAN LITERATURE; Theory and practice; 2013 Oxford University Press

1. Ancient literature 2. Egypt—Civilization 3. Egyptian literature 4. Literary critiques 5. Literature—History & criticism—Theory, etc.

ISBN 9780197265420 hardcover

SUMMARY: Edited by Roland Enmarch and Verena M.

Lepper, "the book covers a wide range of Ancient Egyptian uses of written culture, with contributions covering the Middle Egyptian, Late Egyptian, and Demotic language stages. There are also contributions touching on genre, performance, intertextuality, biography, monumental context, and reception." (Publisher's note)

REVIEW: *Choice* v51 no4 p632 D 2013 S. M. Burstein

"Ancient Egyptian Literature: Theory and Practice." "This interesting volume comprises the proceedings of a 2006 conference held at All Souls College, Oxford, UK, to consider the potential value of literary theory for the study of Egyptian literature. . . . Especially valuable are Christopher Eyre's consideration of the relationship between performance and audience in Egypt, Elizabeth Frood's analysis of modes of self representation in Third Intermediate Period biographies, and Ludwig Morenz's study of the role of the reader in Egyptian literary texts. A useful introduction to a significant area of current scholarship."

ANCIENT LIBRARIES; xx, 479 p. 2013 Cambridge University Press

1. Books & reading—History 2. HISTORY—General 3. Historical literature 4. Libraries—History—To 400 5. Library architecture

ISBN 9781107012561 (cloth)

LC 2012-032869

SUMMARY: This book, edited by Jason König, Katerina Oikonomopoulou, and Greg Woolf, "presents a fundamental reassessment of how ancient libraries came into being, how they were organized and how they were used. Drawing on papyrology and archaeology, and on accounts written by those who read and wrote in them, it presents new research on reading cultures, on book collecting and on the origins of monumental library buildings." (Publisher's note)

REVIEW: *TLS* no5767 p25-6 O 11 2013 GLEN BOWERSOCK

"Ancient Libraries." "[An] important contribution to ancient cultural history. . . . The editors of the present volume might have considered looking beyond the early third century AD, where their story suddenly breaks off. . . . They might also have exercised a little more restraint on some of their contributors, such as Pier Luigi Tucci, whose polemic against critics of his views on the libraries mentioned by Galen is both tiresome and out of place. . . . Ancient libraries, whether sacred, royal, private or public, not only deserve a lucid prose that is worthy of the books they contained, but also some account of the process whereby texts moved out of libraries with book rolls and into libraries with bookshelves."

THE ANCIENT WORLD IN SILENT CINEMA; xxi, 379 p. 2013 Cambridge University Press

1. Civilization, Ancient, in motion pictures 2. Historical films—History and criticism 3. Motion picture literature 4. Silent films—History and criticism 5. Ten Commandments, The (Film)

ISBN 9781107016101 (hardback)

LC 2013-000786

SUMMARY: This book looks at silent film depictions of ancient civilizations. "In the first half of the volume, contributors examine topics from archival cataloging of the films and the role of these films in shaping national self-conceptions to revival of Egyptian culture and the exotic spectacle of dance. The second half comprises readings of individual films, for example, the 1907 'Ben Hur' and the issues of copyright infringement surrounding it." (Choice: Current Reviews for Academic Libraries)

REVIEW: *Choice* v51 no9 p1598-9 My 2014 T. Lindvall

"The Ancient World in Silent Cinema". "Encompassing both classical and biblical emphases of Mediterranean epics, the contributors offer pithy, precisely focused, cogent perspectives in this exquisitely illustrated publication. . . . The essays take the reader on a fascinating odyssey through this kingdom of shadows, with each offering a remarkably lucid analysis. . . . Of particular note are David Shepherd's study of DeMille's 'Ten Commandments' (1923) and [Maria] Wyke's perspicacious, playful study of the comic depictions in the genre, which keys in on Buster Keaton's 'Three Ages'. This stellar book is itself a dazzling, exceptional classic."

ANDERMANN, JENS.ed. New Argentine and Brazilian cinema. See New Argentine and Brazilian cinema

ANDERSEN, BENNY. The Contract Killer; [by] Benny Andersen 54 p. 2013 Dufour Editions

1. Comedy 2. Detective & mystery plays 3. Murder for hire 4. Private investigators 5. Unemployed

ISBN 187004178X; 9781870041782

SUMMARY: This play by Benny Andersen follows "Karlsen . . . a down-on-his-luck private investigator looking for work. When the only job on offer is a contract killing, Karlsen agrees despite his lack of experience. Things don't go to plan and it seems the contract is open to negotiation. This play follows the twists and turns of an inexperienced contract killer with a weakness for turquoise dresses and wide-eyed women." (Publisher's note)

REVIEW: *World Lit Today* v87 no5 p55-79 S/O 2013

"The Contract Killer," "Nazim Hikmet: The Life and Times of Turkey's World Poet," and "The People of Forever Are Not Afraid." "[Benny] Andersen presents absurdist approaches to questions of life and death, never losing his sense of humor or his lighthearted turn of phrase. . . . [Mutlu Konuk] Blasing is a prolific translator of Hikmet's work, and she incorporates elements of literary scholarship into her investigation of his life. . . . Shani Boianjiu's gripping debut novel illustrates the lives of three Israeli girls who grow up together after they are conscripted into the army."

ANDERSEN, CHRIS.ed. Indigenous in the city. See Indigenous in the city

ANDERSEN, HANS CHRISTIAN, 1805-1875. The Snow Queen; a retelling of the fairy tale; [by] Hans Christian Andersen 40 p. 2013 HarperCollins

1. Fairy tales 2. Fairy tales—Adaptations 3. Friendship—Juvenile fiction 4. Magic—Juvenile fiction 5. Queens—Fiction

ISBN 0062209507; 9780062209504 (hardcover)

LC 2012-011533

SUMMARY: Author Hans Christian Andersen and illustrator Bagram Ibatoulline present a story of "friendship, love, and bravery. Best friends Kai and Gerda would do anything for each other. When Kai starts to behave cruelly and disappears, Gerda sets out on an epic quest to save Kai from the evil Snow Queen. But can Gerda break the Snow Queen's enchantment and complete the final task?" (Publisher's note)

REVIEW: *Kirkus Rev* v81 no16 p163 Ag 15 2013

"The Snow Queen." "One of the great illustrators of our time takes on one of the knottier Andersen fairy tales, producing a gorgeous and winning result. [Adaptor Allison Grace] MacDonald's retelling hews closely to [author Hans Christian] Andersen's original in all its complexity but without its Christian allusions. . . . [illustrator Bagram] Ibatoulline renders the northern lights more exquisitely than any photograph. A deep subtext of love and loss, childhood and awakening, power and trust resonate through these pages at least as strongly as the magnificent images."

REVIEW: *SLJ* v59 no9 p111 S 2013 Marilyn Taniguchi

ANDERSON, AARON D. Builders of a New South; merchants, capital, and the remaking of Natchez, 1865-1914; [by] Aaron D. Anderson viii, 279 p. 2013 University Press of Mississippi

1. Historical literature 2. Merchants—Mississippi—Natchez—Case studies 3. Merchants—United States
ISBN 9781617036675 (cloth : alk. paper); 9781617036682 (ebook)
LC 2012-020574

SUMMARY: This book by Aaron D. Anderson "describes how, between 1865 and 1914, ten Natchez mercantile families emerged as leading purveyors in the wholesale plantation supply and cotton handling business, and soon became a dominant force in the social and economic Reconstruction of the Natchez District. They were able to take advantage of postwar conditions in Natchez to gain mercantile prominence." (Publisher's note)

REVIEW: *Am Hist Rev* v118 no4 p1181-2 O 2013 Jonathan Daniel Wells

"Builders of a New South: Merchants, Capital, and the Remaking of Natchez, 1865-1914." "Aaron D. Anderson's fine analysis of postbellum Natchez is a welcome addition to this growing historiography. Natchez, Mississippi, long known among historians of the early republic for its sprawling plantations and significant wealth, is a promising place in which to study the rapid decline of the Old South. . . . The ten merchant families Anderson studies are remarkable for their diversity. . . . Anderson has produced a careful and well-researched study that continues the new work on the political economy of the nineteenth-century South, while the press is to be commended for producing a handsome volume containing fascinating and illuminating photograph."

REVIEW: *Choice* v51 no1 p146 S 2013 S. A. Jacobe

"Builders of a New South: Merchants, Capital, and the Remaking of Natchez, 1865-1914." "[Author Aaron D.] Anderson . . . has prepared an important addition to the scholarship of the New South by focusing his attention on the merchant families of the Natchez district. He argues that the Civil War allowed merchants in Natchez to create a new economic system through crop liens. . . . As destructive as it was, the crop lien system could not last in the boom and bust economy of the late 19th century. Crop failures combined with the plummeting price of cotton caused the demise of many of the merchant firms by the first decade of the 20th century."

ANDERSON, BRIAN, 1974-. Monster chefs; [by] Brian Anderson 32 p. 2014 Roaring Brook Press

1. Cooks—Fiction 2. Diet—Fiction 3. Humorous stories 4. Kings, queens, rulers, etc.—Fiction 5. Monsters—Fiction
ISBN 1596438088; 9781596438088 (hardcover: alk. paper)
LC 2012-046930

SUMMARY: In this book, by Brian and Liam Anderson, "the horribly horrible monster king summoned his four equally horrible chefs. . . . Trembling with fear, they each set off in a different direction to look for something truly scrumptious. But what, besides eyeballs and ketchup, could a monster king possibly want to eat? A rabbit? A fish? A snake? What one finally brings back may change dinnertime in the kingdom forever." (Publisher's note)

REVIEW: *Bull Cent Child Books* v67 no8 p392-3 Ap 2014 T. A.

"Monster Chefs". "The repeated story elements lend a folkloric tinge to this gently goofy tale, and while there are a few glitches in the concept (would the pastry chef agree to stick around a smelly castle to help churn out rows of eyeball-decorated cupcakes?), they're likely to be overlooked in the service of an otherwise entertaining story. The mixed-media illustrations, scratchy and thin ink outlines with mottled watercolor hues on bright white paper, have a soft cloudiness of pigment that provides a pleasing balance to the zany humor."

ANDERSON, CHRIS. The numbers game; why everything you know about soccer is wrong; [by] Chris Anderson 384 p. 2013 Penguin Books

1. Soccer—Mathematical models 2. Soccer—Statistical methods 3. Soccer—Statistics 4. Sports literature 5. Sports statistics
ISBN 0143124560; 9780143124566
LC 2013-011448

SUMMARY: This book from Chris Anderson and David Sally is "about the use of analytics in soccer." Topics include "what percentage of possession determines victory," "whether it is best to focus on scoring goals or not conceding them," "how much coaches matter to a team's success," among others. (Kirkus Reviews)

REVIEW: *Booklist* v109 no19/20 p14 Je 1 2013 Keir Graff

REVIEW: *Choice* v51 no6 p1050 F 2014 J. Walker

REVIEW: *Kirkus Rev* v81 no12 p40 Je 15 2013

REVIEW: *Libr J* v138 no14 p116 S 1 2013 Boyd Childress

REVIEW: *New York Times* v162 no56210 pB11 Jl 27 2013 JACK BELL

REVIEW: *TLS* no5762 p30 S 6 2013 DAVID GOLDBLATT

"The Numbers Game: Why Everything You Know About Football is Wrong." "There is much in the book that is pleasingly counter-intuitive. I learnt a lot, and it's hard not to applaud a project that is bent on the disenchantment of football's internal conversations and archaic practices, while simultaneously acknowledging an ineradicable core of the unpredictable and random at its heart. However, the embrace of the numerical should not come at the cost of the word. The dismally inappropriate hyperbole of the subtitle gives a warning of what is coming. I found the book's endless gee-whizzery and boyish enthusiasm soon grated to the point of unreadability."

ANDERSON, ELIJAH. The cosmopolitan canopy; race

and civility in everyday life; [by] Elijah Anderson p. cm. 2011 W. W. Norton

1. African Americans—Social conditions 2. City and town life 3. Gentrification 4. Sociology literature
ISBN 978-0-393-07163-4
LC 2010--44411

SUMMARY: In this book, author Elijah Anderson "takes the reader on an ethnographic walking tour of Philadelphia to observe how city dwellers interact across racial lines. He attends particularly to the 'cosmopolitan canopy'--public settings like parks, malls, town squares that maintain civil and comfortable interactions between diverse populations. Anderson moves then to those areas where the canopy breaks down (the workplace, public transportation)." (Publisher's note)

REVIEW: *Am J Sociol* v118 no5 p1445-7 Mr 2013 John R. Logan

REVIEW: *Contemp Sociol* v42 no6 p809-14 N 2013 MITCHELL DUNEIER

"The Cosmopolitan Canopy: Race and Civility in Everyday Life." "At his best in this book, [author Elijah] Anderson writes with the authority and wisdom of a Jane Jacobs. He even adopts a similar anecdotal style, which is different from the voice and fieldwork for which he became well known earlier in his career. . . . The final picture we get is very compelling, but his departure from the more professionalized style of fieldwork has its costs. Because he is frequently gathering his data by participating in his own life rather than that of others, he ends up making some key inferences about people and situations on the basis of their appearances, much as all of us do in our own lives."

ANDERSON, EMMA. The death and afterlife of the North American martyrs; [by] Emma Anderson 480 p. 2013 Harvard University Press

1. Christian martyrs—North America 2. Christian shrines 3. Historical literature 4. North America—Religion
ISBN 9780674051188 (alk. paper)
LC 2013-009723

SUMMARY: "In 'The Death and Afterlife of the North American Martyrs,' Emma Anderson untangles the complexities of these seminal acts of violence and their ever-changing legacy across the centuries. . . . In tracing the creation and evolution of the cult of the martyrs across the centuries, Anderson reveals the ways in which both believers and detractors have honored and preserved the memory of the martyrs in this 'afterlife.'" (Publisher's note)

REVIEW: *America* v211 no8 p33-4 S 29 2014 MICHAEL STOGRE

REVIEW: *Choice* v51 no9 p1660 My 2014 R. Berleant-Schiller

REVIEW: *TLS* no5793 p27 Ap 11 2014 NATHAN M. GREENFIELD

"The Death and Afterlife of the North American Martyrs." "In this fascinating book, Emma Anderson shows that the black robes sought out painful and terrible deaths, believing each quantum of suffering would buy them time from the more terrible pain of Purgatory. . . . While the Canadian Jesuits did not, as the Americans did, explicitly link les religieux's deaths at the hands of the 'red men' to the Red Menace of the 1950s, the Canadians too, fairly revelled in the gore of the martyrs' deaths. Until the 1980s, both shrines staged re-enactments in which the 'natives' were often played by whites and were all but silent and always menacing."

ANDERSON, JAYNIE. ed. The Cambridge companion to Australian art. See The Cambridge companion to Australian art

ANDERSON, LARRY. Inspiration to Live Your MAGIC!; 75 Inspiring Biographies; [by] Larry Anderson 256 p. 2011 LIAP Media Corp.

1. Biography (Literary form) 2. Lincoln, Abraham, 1809-1865 3. Mandela, Nelson, 1918-2013 4. Resilience (Personality trait) 5. Winfrey, Oprah, 1954-
ISBN 0986941700; 9780986941702

SUMMARY: In this, one of three books in the 'Live Your Magic' series, [Larry] Anderson . . . tells the stories of 75 people who achieved greatness, largely in the face of adversity. He profiles a significant number of well-known personalities (including Abraham Lincoln, Nelson Mandela and Oprah Winfrey) but focuses on their resilience rather than their fame." (Kirkus Reviews)

REVIEW: *Kirkus Rev* v82 no2 p386 Ja 15 2014

"Inspiration to Live Your Magic! 75 Inspiring Biographies". "A compendium of artfully written capsule biographies intended to inspire. In this, one of three books in the 'Live Your Magic' series, [Larry] Anderson . . . follows a winning formula. . . . The Canadian author apparently scoured the world for these profiles, although for some readers, it may skew a bit too much toward Canadians. However, this doesn't detract from the collection's value. The brevity of these illustrated biographies, and the simple elegance of the prose, may particularly appeal to middle and high school students, as well as adults in need of spiritual renewal. An upbeat, inspiring celebration of mankind's ability to challenge the odds."

REVIEW: *Kirkus Rev* v82 no4 p89 F 15 2014

ANDERSON, LAURIE HALSE, 1961-. The impossible knife of memory; [by] Laurie Halse Anderson 400 p. 2014 Viking, published by Penguin Group

1. Family problems—Fiction 2. Fathers and daughters—Fiction 3. Post-traumatic stress disorder—Fiction 4. Veterans—Fiction 5. Young adult fiction
ISBN 0670012092; 9780670012091 (hardback)
LC 2013-031267

SUMMARY: In this book, by Laurie Halse Anderson, "Hayley Kincaid and her father, Andy, have been on the road, never staying long in one place as he struggles to escape the demons that have tortured him since his return from Iraq. Now they are back in the town where he grew up so Hayley can attend school. Perhaps, for the first time, Hayley can have a normal life. . . . Will being back home help Andy's PTSD, or will his terrible memories drag him to the edge of hell, and drugs push him over?" (Publisher's note)

REVIEW: *Booklist* v110 no6 p39-40 N 15 2013 Ann Kelley

REVIEW: *Booklist* v110 no5 p50 N 1 2013 Gillian Engberg

REVIEW: *Bull Cent Child Books* v67 no5 p255-6 Ja 2014 D. S.

"The Impossible Knife of Memory." "[Laurie Halse] Anderson depicts with lacerating clarity Hayley's secondhand

PTSD, with threat assessment a part of her daily life; Hayley's lucid yet emotional narration ensures the experience is immersive rather than didactic (the book never actually diagnoses her), so readers will begin to share her defensive reactions and self-protective thinking. Her father is both infuriating and fearfully broken, making Hayley's blend of frustration and hypervigilance absolutely plausible, while interspersed flashbacks to her father's wartime experience add a further dimension. Anderson never limits her characters to being merely a type, and the growth of Hayley's romance with Finn takes its own interesting path."

REVIEW: *Horn Book Magazine* v90 no2 p108-9 Mr/Ap 2014 LAUREN ADAMS

"The Impossible Knife of Memory." "Hayley's caustic observations about the 'fully assimilated zombies' who swarm the halls and the oxymoronic 'required volunteer community service' are trademark [Laurie Halse] Anderson. . . . As ever, Anderson has the inside track on the emotional lives of adolescents; she plays high school clichés for laughs but compassionately depicts Hayley's suffering as well as the hurts of Finn and Gracie, whose families are struggling with their own demons. The novel's theme is woven artfully throughout as both Hayley and her dad fight the flashes of memory that are sure to tear them apart unless they confront them once and for all."

REVIEW: *Kirkus Rev* v81 no21 p211 N 1 2013

REVIEW: *Libr J* v139 no5 p83 Mr 15 2014 Erin Cataldi

REVIEW: *N Y Times Book Rev* p16 Ja 12 2014 JO KNOWLES

REVIEW: *Publ Wkly* v260 no42 p52-3 O 21 2013

REVIEW: *SLJ* v60 no3 p73 Mr 2014 Amanda Rollins

REVIEW: *SLJ* v60 no1 p92 Ja 2014 Allison Tran

REVIEW: *Voice of Youth Advocates* v36 no6 p54 F 2014 Blake Norby

ANDERSON, LIAM. Monster chefs. See Anderson, B.

ANDERSON, NATE.ed. The internet police. See The internet police

ANDERSON, RAY C.ed. Energy industries and sustainability. See Energy industries and sustainability

ANDERSON, SCOTT, 1959-. Lawrence in Arabia; war, deceit, imperial folly and the making of the modern Middle East; [by] Scott Anderson 592 p. 2013 Doubleday

1. Historical literature 2. Soldiers—Great Britain—Biography 3. World War, 1914-1918—Campaigns—Middle East 4. World War, 1914-1918—Campaigns—Turkey

ISBN 038553292X; 9780385532921

LC 2012-049719

SUMMARY: In this biography of Lawrence of Arabia, Scott Anderson "reasons that 'Lawrence was both eyewitness to and participant in some of the most pivotal events leading to the creation of the modern Middle East . . . a corner of the earth where even the simplest assertion is dissected and parsed and argued over.' Too many biographers of Lawrence, he suggests, have let political biases and academic hobbyhorses overshadow their work." (Publishers Weekly)

REVIEW: *Bookforum* v20 no3 p20-1 S-N 2013 SUZY HANSEN

"Lawrence in Arabia: War, Deceit, Imperial Folly and the Making of the Modern Middle East." "The pleasure and heartache of books like [Scott] Anderson's are in the connections we can make between the past and the present--especially when they concern the Middle East. We all know that the Western powers made (and continue to make) the same mistakes over and over in the twentieth and twenty-first centuries, but a skilled and perceptive writer like Anderson . . . can provoke a kind of intellectual astonishment, a feeling of revelation. In fact, his more analytical and sweeping passages often surpass the book's intricate rehashings of battles and field strategy. Yet Anderson is first and foremost a storyteller."

REVIEW: *Booklist* v109 no22 p22 Ag 1 2013 Gilbert Taylor

REVIEW: *Kirkus Rev* v81 no2 p44 Je 1 2013

REVIEW: *Libr J* v138 no11 p100 Je 15 2013 Elizabeth Hayford

REVIEW: *Libr J* v138 no18 p54 N 1 2013 Edwin B. Burgess Margaret Heilbrun

REVIEW: *Libr J* v139 no8 p37 My 1 2014 Victoria Caplinger

REVIEW: *Libr J* v138 no5 p93 Mr 15 2013 Barbara Hoffert

REVIEW: *Libr J* v139 no1 p1 Ja 2014

REVIEW: *London Rev Books* v36 no7 p23-4 Ap 3 2014 Bernard Porter

REVIEW: *N Y Times Book Rev* p16 Ag 11 2013 ALEX VON TUNZELMANN

REVIEW: *Natl Rev* v65 no16 p37-9 S 2 2013 DAVID PRYCE-JONES

REVIEW: *New Statesman* v143 no12 p44-5 Mr 28 2014 William Dalrymple

REVIEW: *New York Times* v162 no56254 pC4 S 9 2013 JANET MASLIN

"Lawrence in Arabia: War, Deceit, Imperial Folly and the Making of the Modern Middle East." "Scott Anderson's fine, sophisticated, richly detailed 'Lawrence in Arabia' is filled with invaluably complex and fine-tuned information. This demanding but eminently readable account of the Middle East is certainly no hagiographic T. E. Lawrence biography. . . . That does not make Mr. Anderson's account a debunking. For those already fascinated by Lawrence's exploits and familiar with his written accounts of them, Mr. Anderson's thoughtful, big-picture version only enriches the story it tells. . . . Beyond having a keen ear for memorable wording, Mr. Anderson has a gift for piecing together the conflicting interests of warring parties."

REVIEW: *New York Times* v163 no56356 pC23-9 D 20 2013 JANET MASLIN

REVIEW: *Publ Wkly* v260 no20 p44 My 20 2013

ANDERSON, T. NEILL. Horrors of history; ocean of fire; [by] T. Neill Anderson 176 p. 2014 Charlesbridge

1. Family life—South Carolina—Fiction 2. Historical fiction 3. Refugees—Fiction 4. Slavery—Fiction 5. Survival—Fiction

ISBN 9781580895163 (reinforced for library use)

LC 2013-004291

SUMMARY: In this book, "when Union soldiers marched into Columbia [S.C.] in 1865, the city was a potential tinderbox of strong winds and loose bales of cotton. After drunken Yankee soldiers started fires both accidentally and intentionally, the wind kept them going. This fictionalized third-person narrative tells of Emma LeConte, a real young woman who left a diary. She watches from her family's home as other houses burn up and the local hospital . . . is evacuated." (Kirkus Reviews)

REVIEW: *Kirkus Rev* v82 no2 p110 Ja 15 2014

"Ocean of Fire: The Burning of Columbia, 1865". "Only readers with a strong knowledge of and interest in the Civil War will persist in reading this grim, stilted novel about the burning of Columbia, S.C. . . . Unfortunately, neither characters nor relationships are developed; readers are simply told what characters feel, especially how much Emma despises Yankees. The focus is on events, but [T. Neill] Anderson provides too little context to explain the level of hatred between Southerners and Union soldiers after so many years of war and loss. The awkward combination of facts and fiction fails to adequately inform or engage readers, despite the dramatic topic."

REVIEW: *SLJ* v60 no2 p81 F 2014 Tammy Turner

ANDERSON, TARA.il. Nat the Cat Can Sleep Like That. See Allenby, V.

ANDREAE, CHRISTOPHER. Joan Eardley; [by] Christopher Andreae 198 p. 2013 Lund Humphries

1. Art literature 2. Eardley, Joan 3. Landscapes in art 4. Scottish art 5. Scottish painting
ISBN 9781848221147 (hardcover : alk. paper)
LC 2012-947514

SUMMARY: In this book on artist Joan Eardley, author Christopher Anddreae "provides . . . [an] assessment of her work & its relative Scottishness or universality." He "also looks at her relationships, quotes from letters previously embargoed, & discusses published & unpublished assessments of her work both during her life & posthumously." (Publisher's note)

REVIEW: *TLS* no5746 p27 My 17 2013 FRANCES SPALDING

"Joan Eardley." "The problems here are multiple. Christopher Andreae's text is disorganized and repetitive, with facts appearing long after the information is needed. His use of footnotes is inadequate and his convivial tone permits lazy thinking. He has been permitted to publish a few of Eardley's hitherto unpublished love letters to Audrey Walker, but he has ignored other available letters, parts of which have been quoted elsewhere. Nor does he engage properly with existing scholarship on Eardley until the end of the book. . . . The illustrations receive scant analysis and often have only tangential relation to the text. . . . Yet, anyone interested in Eardley cannot ignore this book."

ANDREWS, CHRIS.tr. The insufferable gaucho. See Bolaño, R

ANDREWS, EDWARD E. Native apostles; Black and Indian missionaries in the British Atlantic world; [by] Edward E. Andrews 336 p. 2013 Harvard University Press

1. African American missionaries 2. British—Atlantic Ocean Region—History 3. Historical literature 4. Indigenous peoples 5. Missionaries 6. Missions—History
ISBN 9780674072466
LC 2012-034736

SUMMARY: This book by Edward E. Andrews "offers one of the most significant untold stories in the history of early modern religious encounters, marshalling wide-ranging research to shed light on the crucial role of Native Americans, Africans, and black slaves in Protestant missionary work. The result is a pioneering view of religion's spread through the colonial world." (Publisher's note)

REVIEW: *Am Hist Rev* v119 no3 p853 Je 2014 Bonnie Sue Lewis

REVIEW: *Choice* v51 no2 p279 O 2013 C. T. Vecsey

REVIEW: *J Am Hist* v101 no1 p242-3 Je 2014

REVIEW: *Libr J* v138 no5 p115 Mr 15 2013 John R. Burch

REVIEW: *N Engl Q* v87 no1 p160-3 Mr 2014 Kelly Wisecup

REVIEW: *Rev Am Hist* v42 no2 p213-8 Je 2014 Joshua Piker

"Native Apostles: Black and Indian Missionaries in the British Atlantic World." "While other scholars have made similar points about the ability of native peoples to domesticate Christianity, Andrews demonstrates that native missionaries played a critical role in carving out a space for themselves and their people within Europe's dominant religious system and an ever more European-inflected Atlantic world. Native Apostles, then, achieves a great deal. It is, for example, impossible to read this book and not be struck by the sheer number of native missionaries working in the British Atlantic world."

ANDREWS, JOHN A. Y.tr. The view of life. See Simmel, G.

ANDREWS, RICHARD.ed. The Tempest. See The Tempest

ANGELL, STEPHEN W.ed. The Oxford handbook of Quaker studies . See The Oxford handbook of Quaker studies

ANGLEBERGER, TOM. The surprise attack of Jabba the Puppett; an Origami Yoda book; [by] Tom Angleberger 224 p. 2013 Harry N. Abrams

1. Eccentrics and eccentricities—Fiction 2. Finger puppets—Fiction 3. Interpersonal relations—Fiction 4. Middle schools—Fiction 5. Origami—Fiction 6. School stories 7. Schools—Fiction
ISBN 1419708589; 9781419708589
LC 2013-020765

SUMMARY: In this book by Tom Angleberger "dark times have fallen on McQuarrie Middle School. Dwight's back . . . as the gang faces the FunTime Menace: a new educational program. When Principal Rabbski cancels the students' field trip . . . to make time for FunTime, the students turn to Origami Yoda for help. United, can they defeat the FunTime Menace and . . . a surprise attack from Jabba the Puppett?" (Publisher's note)

REVIEW: *Booklist* v110 no16 p64 Ap 15 2014 Amanda Blau

REVIEW: *Kirkus Rev* v81 no16 p308 Ag 15 2013

"The Surprise Attack of Jabba the Puppett." "The seventh-graders of MMS have little time to celebrate Dwight and Origami Yoda's return from Tippett Academy before Principal Rabbski holds a special assembly to announce that since the school's standardized test scores were so low, new classes for all students will begin immediately. . . . Tommy's case file grows in [author Tom] Angleberger's fourth doodle-filled paean to individuality, friendship and all things Star Wars. This book may not win any fans among school administrators, but those who have delighted in Tommy and his friends' previous case files will be pleased. . . . Origami instructions are included (of course), and it's otherwise chock-full of customarily quirky fun."

REVIEW: *SLJ* v60 no2 p51 F 2014 Debbie Whitbeck

ANGLES, JEFFREY.tr. Twelve views from the distance. See Twelve views from the distance

ANIMAL PERSONALITIES; behavior, physiology, and evolution; 507 p. 2013 University of Chicago Press

1. Animal behavior 2. Molecular genetics 3. Parental behavior in animals 4. Personality 5. Scientific literature

ISBN 0226922057 (cloth : alk. paper); 9780226922058 (cloth : alk. paper)

LC 2012-022902

SUMMARY: This book, edited by Claudio Carere and Dario Maestripieri, presents "research on animal personality. Grouped into thematic sections, chapters approach the topic with empirical and theoretical material and show that to fully understand why personality exists, we must consider the evolutionary processes that give rise to personality, the ecological correlates of personality differences, and the physiological mechanisms underlying personality variation." (Publisher's note)

REVIEW: *Choice* v51 no1 p107 S 2013 B. E. Fleury

"Animal Personalities: Behavior, Physiology, and Evolution." "This collection of 15 papers is divided into four parts, beginning with 'Personalities across Taxa.' The next three parts discuss genetics, ecology and evolution; developmental mechanisms; and implications for conservation and animal welfare. The first part surveys personality research in invertebrates, fish, birds, and nonhuman primates. . . . Part 2 examines the molecular genetics of personality, and the variation and natural selection of such traits. Part 3 reviews parental influence on personality and neuroendocrine mechanisms involved in its development. The final part examines ways in which personality research can be applied in conservation biology, fish farming, and public health."

THE ANIMALS; Love Letters Between Christopher Isherwood and Don Bachard; 528 p. 2014 Farrar, Straus and Giroux

1. Authors—Correspondence 2. Bachardy, Don 3. Gay men 4. Isherwood, Christopher, 1904-1986 5. Love letters

ISBN 0374105170; 9780374105174

SUMMARY: "This collection of letters between famed writer Christopher Isherwood (1902–1986, author of Goodbye to Berlin), and his partner of over three decades, Don Bachardy, a 30-years younger portrait painter, offers . . . insight into the life of this extraordinary couple. . . . Bachardy often wrote to Isherwood to discuss insecurities, doubts, and despair; both men gave each other much-needed support." (Publishers Weekly)

REVIEW: *London Rev Books* v36 no3 p21-3 F 6 2014 Andrew O'Hagan

"Becoming a Londoner: A Diary and "The Animals: Love Letters Between Christopher Isherwod and Don Bachardy". "Early in David Plante's diaries, we find him tinkling away, dropping names in basso profundo, as if knowing people and knowing what they do in private can be the thing that makes one special. . . . Let's applaud him, though. . . . His diaries are good because they are true to his own narcissism. . . . A taste for silliness is a capital virtue when it comes to considering the Isherwoods. . . . Their letters to each other must be the silliest in modern literature and none the less entertaining for that. For five hundred pages, it's like watching two pre-adolescent girls in full spate, giving vent to an OMGfest involving sparkles, super-furry animals and lots of pink, while occasionally dropping bombshells about the teachers."

REVIEW: *N Y Times Book Rev* p18 Ag 31 2014 HENRY GIARDINA

REVIEW: *New Statesman* v142 no5177 p65 S 27 2013 Olivia Laing

REVIEW: *Publ Wkly* v261 no12 p72 Mr 24 2014

REVIEW: *TLS* no5779 p8 Ja 3 2014 DAVID COLLARD

ANSWERABLE STYLE; the idea of the literary in medieval England; 2013 Ohio State University Press

1. Literary critiques 2. Literary style 3. Manuscripts 4. Medieval aesthetics in literature 5. Medieval literature

ISBN 9780814212073

SUMMARY: The essays in this book, edited by Andrew Galloway and Frank Grady, "address the medieval idea of the literary, with special focus on the poetry of [Geoffrey] Chaucer, [William]Langland, and [John] Gower. The essays . . . range from the 'contact zones' between clerical culture and vernacular writing, to manuscript study and its effects on the modalities of "persona" and voicing, to the history of emotion as a basis for new literary ideals." (Publisher's note)

REVIEW: *Choice* v51 no4 p634 D 2013 M. Aaij

"Answerable Style: The Idea of the Literary in Medieval England." "Taking the work of Anne Middleton--influential scholar of [William] Langland, [John] Gower, and [Geoffrey] Chaucer--as a 'touchstone,' these 13 essays, by established scholars, explore the ways in which 14th-century English authors developed 'the literary' as a style, a language, and a mode of expression. . . . Katherine Zieman offers an astute case study of Chaucer's 'meddling' toward a vernacular authorial voice. . . . There are two essays on the Troilus--one by Lee Patterson, another by Steven Justice, a tour de force discussing aposiopesis as used by the characters and by Chaucer himself to create (the illusion of) character depth and history. . . . Highly recommended."

ANTARCTIC PENINSULA; A Visitor's Guide; 128 p. 2013 Trafalgar Square

1. Animals—Antarctica 2. Antarctic Peninsula (Antarctica) 3. Guidebooks 4. Physical geography—Antarctica 5. Plants—Antarctica

ISBN 0565093088; 9780565093082

SUMMARY: This travel guide to the Antarctica Peninsula provides information on the region's "geographical and geological conditions, indigenous flora and fauna, international governance, and history of place names and explorations." (Booklist) Particular focus is given to "the geographical setting, climate and weather, geology, [and] glaciology." (Publisher's note)

REVIEW: *Booklist* v110 no2 p23 S 15 2013

"World's Ultimate Cycling Races," "A Field Guide to Gettysburg: Experiencing the Battlefield Through Its History, Places, and People," and "Antarctic Peninsula: A Visitor's Guide." "These exciting, beautifully presented guides present pertinent--and inspirational--information on a wealth of places to test one's mettle on foot or bike. . . . An attractive presentation--beautiful color photos and handsomely laid-out text--partners with a wealth of information on individuals, troop movements, and skirmishes, amounting to an indispensable guide to a major event in American history. . . . This guide will inform you of the geographical and geological conditions, indigenous flora and fauna, international governance, and history of place-names and explorations that will be necessary background for a worthwhile trip."

ANTI-RACISM AND MULTICULTURALISM; studies in international communication; 253 p. 2010 Transaction Publishers

1. Anti-racism 2. Communication, International 3. Conflict management 4. International relations—Social aspects 5. Multiculturalism 6. Sociology literature
ISBN 9781412813211
LC 2010-017608

SUMMARY: Edited by Mark D. Alleyne, this volume addresses "five questions: How does the literature on anti-racism improve our understanding of conflict resolution? How does the analysis of the media's role . . . improve . . . theorizing on hate and war propaganda? How can research . . . improve UN peacekeeping? What implications does this subject have for theory-building and cultural diversity? How and why should the literature on anti-racism expand research in international relations?" (Publisher's note)

REVIEW: *Contemp Sociol* v42 no5 p760 S 2013

"Anti-Racism and Multiculturalism: Studies in International Communication." "'Anti-Racism and Multiculturalism: Studies in International Communication,' edited by the late Mark D. Alleyne, is a timely collection that analyzes anti-racism within the context of global communications. Alleyne's volume not only explores the role of anti-racist discourse in international affairs, but also, as he stresses in the introduction, 'facilitate[s] the scrutiny of anti-racism discourse via more methods than discourse analysis.' . . . 'Anti-Racism and Multiculturalism' is an exceptional transdisciplinary project that offers a sophisticated approach to the study of mass communications and racist and anti-racist media campaigns."

ANTONETTA, SUSANNE. Make me a mother; a memoir; [by] Susanne Antonetta 256 p. 2014 W.W. Norton & Co. Inc

1. Adoptive parents—United States—Biography 2. Child rearing—United States 3. Intercountry adoption—Korea (South) 4. Intercountry adoption—United States 5. Interracial adoption—United States 6. Memoirs 7. Mothers—United States—Biography 8. Parenting—United States
ISBN 039306817X; 9780393068177 (hardcover: alkaline paper)
LC 2013-049526

SUMMARY: In this memoir, Susanne Antonetta "adopts an infant from Seoul, South Korea. After meeting their six-month-old son, Jin, . . . Susanne and her husband learn lessons common to all parents. . . . They also learn lessons particular to their own family: not just how another being can take over your life but how to let an entire culture in, how to discuss birth parents who gave up a child, and the tricky steps required to navigate race in America." (Publisher's note)

REVIEW: *Booklist* v110 no11 p6 F 1 2014 Donna Chavez

REVIEW: *Kirkus Rev* v82 no2 p48 Ja 15 2014

"Make Me A Mother: A Memoir". "An award-winning memoirist's moving account of how adopting a South Korean baby taught her about motherhood and love. . . . With both anxiety and joy, [Susanne] Antonetta plunged into motherhood knowing that it would remake her as a woman, wife and daughter. Though fear of rejection by Jin dogged her, she overcame it and learned to navigate the murky waters of transracial parent-child relationships in the process. As she felt him 'grow into [her], ounce by ounce,' Antonetta's notion of family also evolved."

REVIEW: *Publ Wkly* v260 no51 p48 D 16 2013

ANTOSA, SILVIA. Richard Francis Burton; Victorian Explorer and Translator; [by] Silvia Antosa 219 p. 2013 Peter Lang

1. Biographies 2. Explorers—Great Britain—Biography 3. Scholars—Great Britain—Biography 4. Translators—Great Britain—Biography
ISBN 9783034313605
LC 2012-045341

SUMMARY: This book presents a biography of explorer and translator Richard Francis Burton. "A first chapter outlines the social, political and cultural discourses pervading the nineteenth century with reference to colonialism and the emergence of Orientalism. The second contends that Burton's unconventional attitudes . . . and often contradictory stances reveal instabilities inherent in the British identity. The last examines Burton's contribution to contemporary debates on sexuality." (Times Literary Supplement)

REVIEW: *TLS* no5754 p27 Jl 12 2013 CHRISTOPHER STACE

"Richard Francis Burton: Victorian Explorer and Translator." "Silvia Antosa's new book concentrates on the two factors that shaped his reputation . . . and, if one can weather the critical jargon, makes important points. . . . There are a few misleading emphases and the odd factual error . . . but this is a useful addition to Burton studies, especially perhaps in its examination of Burton's marginality, and his attitude towards the 'colonial other'. . . . As to his translations of erotica, Silvia Antosa limits herself to an account of their impact and the controversies they engendered."

ANTRIM, ZAYDE. Routes and realms; the power of place in the early Islamic world; [by] Zayde Antrim xviii, 212 p. 2012 Oxford University Press

1. Geography—Philosophy 2. Geography—Religious aspects—Islam 3. Geography, Arab 4. Historical litera-

ture
ISBN 9780199913879 (hardcover: alk. paper)
LC 2012-003180

SUMMARY: This book "explores the ways in which Muslims expressed attachment to land from the ninth through the eleventh centuries, the earliest period of intensive written production in Arabic." Author "Zayde Antrim develops a 'discourse of place,' a framework for approaching formal texts devoted to the representation of territory across genres" including "topographical histories, literary anthologies, religious treatises, world geographies, poetry, travel literature, and maps." (Publisher's note)

REVIEW: *Am Hist Rev* v119 no1 p281 F 2014 Ahmed El Shamsy

"Routes and Realms: The Power of Place in the Early Islamic World". "A reader who picks up [Zayde] Antrim's book expecting to find out what the Muslim attitude to place is will come away unsatisfied: the author refuses to provide a simple, pat answer. The discourses that she identifies and analyzes are too rich and varied to yield a single unifying theme. . . . The book contains a very useful bibliography of classical texts and—where available—their translations, and it includes several handsome historical maps. Calling it an easy read, however, would be a stretch. Instead of foregrounding the rich texture of poetry and travelers' accounts, Antrim has opted for a lean analytical essay that classifies the various approaches to place and weighs their uses."

APPEL, ANNE MILANO.tr. The art of joy. See Sapienza, G.

APPEL, ANNETTE.tr. Little Naomi, Little Chick. See Little Naomi, Little Chick

APPELBAUM, PETER C. Loyalty Betrayed; Jewish Chaplains in the German Army During the First World War; [by] Peter C. Appelbaum 398 p. 2013 Vallentine Mitchell

1. Historical literature 2. Jews—Germany—History—1800-1933 3. Military chaplains—History—20th century 4. Rabbis—History 5. World War, 1914-1918—Germany
ISBN 0853038473; 9780853038474

SUMMARY: This book by Peter C. Appelbaum tells how "Around 30 Jewish chaplains served . . . in the German army during World War I, providing spiritual care for about 100,000 Jewish, as well as non-Jewish, soldiers, and also Jewish refugees made homeless by the Tsarist army. This is the first book in English to detail the writings of these Jewish chaplains, and it includes original translations of memoirs and diaries, annotated with historical, religious, and literary notes." (Publisher's note)

REVIEW: *TLS* no5791 p24 Mr 28 2014 EDWARD TIMMS

"Loyalty Betrayed: Jewish Chaplains in the German Army During the First World War." "The documentation presented in [author Peter C.] Appelbaum's book, introduced by Michael Meyer with a foreword by Jonathan Wittenberg, shows that during the First World War those rabbis, like the majority of German citizens of Jewish faith, were loyal supporters of the Fatherland. . . . The most gripping section of the book is devoted to the writings of Aron Tänzer, . . . a rabbi from Württemberg who served on the Eastern Front. . . . Peter Appelbaum, with his passionate interest in Jewish writing of the First World War, sets a shining example for mainstream scholars in the field. He has produced a landmark publication that transforms our understanding of German-Jewish relations."

APPELHANS, CHRIS.il. Sparky. See Offill, J.

APUZZO, MATT. Enemies Within. See Goldman, A.

THE ARAB SPRING; change and resistance in the Middle East; xii, 274 p. 2012 Westview Press

1. Arab Spring, 2010- 2. Political science literature 3. Revolutions—Arab countries—History—21st century
ISBN 9780813348193 (pbk. : alk. paper); 9780813348209 (e-book)
LC 2012-028568

SUMMARY: This book on the Arab Spring uprisings of 2010 and 2011 was edited by David W. Lesch and Mark L. Haas. The editors "devote half the book to specific explanations of protests in Arab countries and the other half to analyses of their impact on countries either within the region or powers such as the United States and Russia." (Middle East Journal)

REVIEW: *Middle East J* v67 no4 p633-43 Aut 2013 Charles D. Smith

"Democracy Prevention: The Politics of the U.S.-Egyptian Alliance," The Arab Spring: Change and Resistance in the Middle East," and "The Arab Spring: Will It Lead to Democratic Transitions?." "The [Mark L.] Haas and [David W.] Lesch coedited volume . . . devotes half the book to specific explanations of protests in Arab countries and the other half to analyses of their impact on countries either within the region or powers such as the United States and Russia. . . . The [Clement] Henry and [Jang] Ji-Hyang coedited 'Arab Spring' contains substantive chapters on Algeria, American policies in the Middle East, the economies of uprising-affected societies, but some chapters are extremely brief and could have been excluded. . . . Only [Jason] Brownlee's 'Democracy Prevention' can be considered the product of a long-term research project whose timing of publication was most opportune."

ARASSE, DANIEL. Take a closer look; [by] Daniel Arasse 167 p. 2013 Princeton University Press

1. Art criticism 2. Art literature 3. Meaning (Philosophy)—In art 4. Painting—Appreciation 5. Painting—Themes, motives
ISBN 9780691151540 (hardcover : alk. paper)
LC 2012-050981

SUMMARY: "In this publication of work by . . . art historian [Daniel] Arasse . . . the author searches for the meaning of master paintings. . . . In his analysis of depictions of Mary Magdalene and of seminal work by Tintoretto, Francesco del Cossa, Pieter Bruegel the Elder, Titian, and Diego Rodriguez Velazquez, Arasse mentions the limitations of conventional approaches for analyzing art." (Choice: Current Reviews for Academic Libraries)

REVIEW: *Choice* v51 no6 p990 F 2014 D. H. Cibelli

"Take a Closer Look." "[Daniel Arrase] favors a keen discernment of form and subject matter that allows him to speculate on the original meaning of each work. He discusses patronage, human perception, humanism, and sexuality as these issues become relevant to understanding an artwork. Arasse's comments can be playful and provocative, and he examines issues with humor and wit. Each one of the six essays in this collection, including a letter, an interview, and a dialogue among academics, is creative and original. Throughout, Arasse explores the significance of images in ways that provide enormous insight into Renaissance and Baroque art and culture."

ARBER, CAROLINE.il. Virginia Woolf's garden. See Zoob, C.

THE ARCHAEOLOGY OF FRENCH AND INDIAN WAR FRONTIER FORTS; 304 p. 2013 University Press of Florida

1. Archaeological literature 2. Excavations (Archaeology)—United States 3. Fortification—United States—History 4. Historic sites—United States

ISBN 9780813049069 (alk. paper)

LC 2013-024206

SUMMARY: "This collection of essays presents an overview of the fortifications that guarded the frontiers and borderlands between Native Americans, French settlers, and Anglo-American settlers. Civilian, provincial, or imperial, the fortifications examined here range from South Carolina's Fort Prince George to Fort Frontenac in Ontario and Fort de Chartres in Illinois." (Publisher's note)

REVIEW: *Choice* v51 no9 p1660 My 2014 J. B. Richardson III

"The Archaeology of French and Indian War Frontier Forts". "The first chapter in this survey of frontier forts provides background to the French and Indian War that consumed all of North America east of the Mississippi from 1754 to 1760, and was fought by French and British forces and their ever-shifting Indian allies. Chapter 2 provides the French military engineering principles that guided the construction of French and British fortifications. The remaining 11 chapters provide the history and archaeology of the forts and their significance to the war effort. . . . Included are a chronology of the French and Indian War and a glossary of fortification terms. A must read for those with an interest in fortifications and military history."

ARCHER, IAN W.ed. English historical documents. See English historical documents

ARCHITECTS OF THE INFORMATION AGE; xviii, 156 p. 2012 Rosen Pub. Group

1. Biographies 2. Computer scientists—Biography 3. Computers—History 4. High technology industries—History 5. Telecommunications engineers—Biography

ISBN 1615306617; 9781615306619 (library binding)

LC 2011-015174

SUMMARY: Editor Robert Curley presents a book on modern inventors and the "rapid development of computer technology since the mid-20th century . . . As far back as the eighteenth century, inventors began setting the stage for future minds to advance hardware and software that would change our world forever. This engaging volume introduces readers to the titans of the technology industry, including Bill Gates, Steve Jobs, and Mark Zuckerberg, among many others." (Publisher's note)

REVIEW: *Voice of Youth Advocates* v36 no4 p94-5 O 2013 Heather Christensen

"Architects of the Information Age," "Gaming: From Atari to Xbox 3," "Breakthroughs in Telephone Technology." "Britannica gives readers a chronological perspective of computer and information technology in this five book series. Each book introduces a particular topic and then more fully explores it from its historic roots to the most recent innovations and developments. . . . 'Architects of the Information Age' provides biographical information on over fifty movers and shakers in the history of computers. Although illustrated with both black-and-white and color photographs, readers may be disappointed to discover that few of the entries include portraits of the subjects. . . . Overall, this is a well-developed series on an ever-changing topic."

REVIEW: *Voice of Youth Advocates* v35 no3 p292 Ag 2012 Meghann Meeusen

THE ARCHITECTURE OF CHANGE; building a better world; 2013 University of New Mexico Press

ISBN 9780826353856

SUMMARY: This book, edited by Jerilou Hammett, Maggie Wrigley, Michael Sorkin, "explores communal architecture produced not by specialists but by people, drawing on their common lives and experiences, who have a unique insight into their particular needs and environments. These unsung heroes are teachers and artists, immigrants and activists, grandmothers in the projects, students and planners, architects and residents of some of our poorest places." (Publisher's note)

REVIEW: *Choice* v51 no8 p1445 Ap 2014 J. F. Bauman

"The Architecture of Change: Building a Better World". "Collectively, the articles convey the message that ordinary people, young and old, despite obstacles (mainly poverty), can effectively design neighborhoods, build houses and playgrounds, and in other ways shape sustainable communities. . . . The book's narrow chronological framework (1999-2008) begs a longer opening chapter to provide context. For its progressive perspective, the book is most useful in upper-level planning courses at both graduate and undergraduate levels."

ARDEN, ALYS. The Casquette Girls; [by] Alys Arden 432 p. 2013 fortheARTofit Publishing

1. American paranormal romance stories 2. Hurricane Katrina, 2005—Reconstruction 3. New Orleans (La.)—Fiction 4. Vampires—Fiction 5. Witches—Fiction

ISBN 0989757706; 9780989757706

SUMMARY: In this book, "after the Storm of the Century rips apart New Orleans, Adele Le Moyne and her father are among the first to return to the city following the mandatory evacuation. Adele wants nothing more than for life to return to normal, but with the silent city resembling a mold-infested war zone, a parish-wide curfew, and mysterious new faces lurking in the abandoned French Quarter, normal will have to be redefined." (Publisher's note)

REVIEW: *Kirkus Rev* v82 no1 p344 Ja 1 2014

"The Casquette Girls". " Debut author [Alys] Arden offers readers a full plate of Southern gothic atmospherics and sparkling teen romance in a patiently crafted tale that will best reward careful readers. Adele is a strong, sensible protagonist who's just vulnerable enough. . . . Her winning characterization is topped off with subtly drawn superpowers. . . . Best of all, Arden's insights regarding her fragile city color the narrative with tragic realism: 'Everything we drove past—an abandoned supermarket, a dilapidated bank, a gym, a hamburger chain, a laundry mat, a pizza joint, a housing project—everything had that same distinct mark of the Storm left on it: the water line.' Satisfying teen entertainment but also a cathartic, uncompromising tribute to New Orleans."

REVIEW: *Kirkus Rev* v82 no3 p54 F 1 2014

"The Casquette Girls". " Debut author [Alys] Arden offers readers a full plate of Southern gothic atmospherics and sparkling teen romance in a patiently crafted tale that will best reward careful readers. Adele is a strong, sensible protagonist who's just vulnerable enough. . . . Her winning characterization is topped off with subtly drawn superpowers. . . . Best of all, Arden's insights regarding her fragile city color the narrative with tragic realism: 'Everything we drove past—an abandoned supermarket, a dilapidated bank, a gym, a hamburger chain, a laundry mat, a pizza joint, a housing project—everything had that same distinct mark of the Storm left on it: the water line.' Satisfying teen entertainment but also a cathartic, uncompromising tribute to New Orleans."

REVIEW: *Publ Wkly* v261 no21 p24 My 26 2014

ARDIZZONE, EDWARD.il. The warden. See Trollope, A.

ARIYUKI KONDO. Robert and James Adam, architects of the Age of Enlightenment; [by] Ariyuki Kondo xii, 209 p. 2012 Pickering & Chatto

1. Architects—Scotland—Biography 2. Architectural literature 3. Architecture—Great Britain—History—18th century 4. Architecture—Philosophie—Grande-Bretagne—18e siècle 5. Architecture and philosophy—Great Britain—History—18th century 6. Architecture, Modern—18th century 7. Enlightenment—Great Britain

ISBN 1848931794 (hbk.); 9781848931794 (hbk.)

LC 2011-534698

SUMMARY: "While previous studies on the Adam brothers have focused on describing their style and their inspirations, [author Ariyuki] Kondo's work places them within the context of eighteenth-century intellectual thought. Only by examining the Adams' work in this context can the full extent of their contribution to Enlightenment development be understood." (Publisher's note)

REVIEW: *Engl Hist Rev* v128 no534 p1254-6 O 2013 Geoffrey Tyack

"Robert and James Adam, Architects of the Enlightenment." "Ariyuki Kondo's book (part of a series entitled 'The Enlightenment World') sets out to reinterpret the Adam brothers' work in the light of their architectural theory. . . . It is one thing to relate the Adams' architecture to the Zeitgeist in a general way, but quite another to point to specific examples of how Enlightenment philosophy influenced their work. Kondo's book, which started life as a doctoral thesis, performs a useful service in explaining the intellectual and cultural context in which the Adam brothers moved, but it adds little of real significance to our understanding of their varied and fascinating oeuvre. For this it is still necessary to refer to other writers and, above all, to the buildings themselves."

ARLON, PENELOPE. Reptiles; [by] Penelope Arlon 80 p. 2013 Scholastic Press

1. Children's reference books 2. Crocodiles—Juvenile literature 3. Lizards—Juvenile literature 4. Reptiles—Juvenile literature 5. Snakes—Juvenile literature

ISBN 0545505097; 9780545505093

SUMMARY: This book, by Penelope Arlon, is part of the Scholastic Discover More series. It "includes three . . . collection spreads featuring hundreds of snakes, and an interview with a snake expert about these misunderstood and essential creatures. The digital book focuses on reptile hunting techniques. Structured layouts, age-appropriate vocabulary, and infographics [are included]." (Publisher's note)

REVIEW: *Booklist* v110 no1 p100 S 1 2013 Carolyn Phelan

"Reptiles" and "Weather." "Each large-format book in the Discover More series offers hundreds of colorful illustrations and small parcels of information related to a range of broad topics. . . . The illustrations (mainly photos) are often quite good, though some are too small to be useful. The heavy, glossy pages allow for excellent clarity. . . . The back matter, which includes a glossary but no sources, is disappointing in a book for this grade level. . . . The photo of a snake skeleton and the cross-sectional illustration of a turtle's innards are very effective in showing what cannot normally be seen. . . . 'Weather' offers plenty of factoids for browsers as well as some dramatic photos. However, the spreads that are crowded with several types of text and overlapping look cluttered."

REVIEW: *Publ Wkly* v260 no22 p62 Je 3 2013

ARLON, PENELOPE. Weather; [by] Penelope Arlon 19 p. 2013 Scholastic Reference

1. Children's nonfiction 2. Meteorologists 3. Natural disasters—Juvenile literature 4. Storms—Juvenile literature 5. Weather 6. Weather—Juvenile literature

ISBN 054550516X; 0756625319 (hbk.); 9780545505161; 9780756625313 (hbk.)

LC 2007-296464

SUMMARY: This book, by Penelope Arlon, is part of the Scholastic Discover More series. It "informs children about different types of weather [and] helps them understand how weather systems are connected. Case studies that run throughout the book give eyewitness accounts of weather disasters and a final section includes weather heroes from meteorologists to storm chasers." (Publisher's note)

REVIEW: *Booklist* v110 no1 p100 S 1 2013 Carolyn Phelan

"Reptiles" and "Weather." "Each large-format book in the Discover More series offers hundreds of colorful illustrations and small parcels of information related to a range of broad topics. . . . The illustrations (mainly photos) are often quite good, though some are too small to be useful. The heavy, glossy pages allow for excellent clarity. . . . The back matter, which includes a glossary but no sources, is disappointing in a book for this grade level. . . . The photo of a snake skeleton and the cross-sectional illustration of a turtle's innards are very effective in showing what cannot normally be seen. . . . 'Weather' offers plenty of factoids for browsers as well as some dramatic photos. However, the spreads that are crowded with several types of text and overlapping look cluttered."

ARMANET, FRANÇOIS. The killer detail; defining moments in fashion: sartorial icons from Cary Grant to Kate Moss; [by] François Armanet 262 p. 2013 Random House Inc

1. Appearance (Philosophy) 2. Celebrities—History 3. Clothing & dress—History 4. Fashion—History 5. Photobooks

ISBN 2080201530; 9782080201539

SUMMARY: In this book on personal style, François Armanet and Élisabeth Quin present "a photographic and psychological study of the allure of 126 male and female writers, artists, performers and fashion figures of the 20th century. . . . They focus on the gestures, poses and sartorial choices of the famous through the camera lenses of some of the world's best-known photographers. In their view, it is the offbeat, dissonant, original, flamboyant detail that creates the illusion of perfection." (New York Times)

REVIEW: *Libr J* v139 no3 p102 F 15 2014 Lindsay King

REVIEW: *New York Times* v163 no56344 p12-3 D 8 2013 ELAINE SCIOLINO

"The Killer Detail". "A photographic and psychological study of the allure of 126 male and female writers, artists, performers and fashion figures of the 20th century. . . . This is not just a book of beautifully posed photographs. Mr. [François] Armanet . . . and Ms. [Élisabeth] Quin . . . have accompanied each photograph with text analyzing the connection between outer appearance and inner spirit. . . . The authors offer the historical origins of some of the most ordinary articles of clothing."

ARMANTROUT, RAE, 1947-. Just saying; [by] Rae Armantrout 112 p. 2013 Wesleyan University Press

1. Aging—Poetry 2. American poetry 3. Death—Poetry 4. Motherhood—Poetry 5. Poems—Collections

ISBN 0819572993; 9780819572998 (cloth : alk. paper); 9780819573001 (eBook)

LC 2012-024671

SUMMARY: Author Rae Armantrout discusses "familiar yet challenging laconic modes, alert to the hypocrisies of daily life, the stresses and fears of adulthood, and the contradictions within our own desires." She presents a "poem about motherhood, flowers, cold weather and firewood." The book "often turns outward into the shared facts of age and death, or at the oddities of our shared culture, with its superhero movies" and politics. (Publisher's note)

REVIEW: *Booklist* v109 no11 p12 F 1 2013 Carolyn Alessio

REVIEW: *Libr J* v137 no20 p88 D 1 2012 Barbara Hoffert

REVIEW: *Publ Wkly* v259 no52 p31-2 D 24 2012

REVIEW: *World Lit Today* v87 no6 p71-2 N/D 2013 Michael Leddy

"Just Saying." "The sixty-seven poems of 'Just Saying' tend toward short titles (often announcing a field of inquiry), short lines, and short, fragmentary sections that form (to borrow from George Oppen) discrete series, inviting the reader to consider oblique relations among parts. . . . 'Just Saying' is attuned to the facts of life in this twenty-first century. . . . These details are present in Armantrout's poems not as occasions of easy irony, not as objects of angry indictment, but as elements in 'a permanent tizzy' of stimulus and response."

ARMENTEROS, CAROLINA. The French idea of history; Joseph de Maistre and his heirs, 1794-1854; [by] Carolina Armenteros xiii, 361 p. 2011 Cornell University Press

1. France—Historiography 2. Historical literature 3. Philosophy & history 4. Philosophy—History

ISBN 080144943X (alk. paper); 9780801449437 (alk. paper)

LC 2011-011636

SUMMARY: In this book, "Carolina Armenteros attempts to demonstrate in this book that [Joseph de] Maistre was more of moderate than has been alleged, that he drew on some of the leading Enlightenment thinkers, and that his influence on a variety of approaches to the philosophy of history was enormous, at least until the mid-nineteenth century. The book is in two parts: Maistre in his time and place, and his influence on, and legacy for, historical thought in France." (Canadian Journal of History)

REVIEW: *Am Hist Rev* v119 no1 p153-4 F 2014 Cara Camcastle

"The French Idea of History: Joseph de Maistre and His Heirs, 1794-1854". "[Carolina] Armenteros argues convincingly that Maistre believed that a pope, possessing spiritual authority and special powers, could use his influence to prevent a king from taking actions not in accordance with the traditions of a country. But Armenteros also incorrectly claims that Du Pape represented a change from what Maistre had argued in earlier essays. . . . Armenteros expertly recovers Maistre's sometimes implicit historical thought and argues that historians and philosophers of history need to take his insightful reflections into account."

REVIEW: *Engl Hist Rev* v128 no533 p978-80 Ag 2013 Michael Drolet

ARMENTROUT, JENNIFER L. Don't look back; [by] Jennifer L. Armentrout 369 p. 2014 Hyperion

1. Amnesia—Fiction 2. Dating (Social customs)—Fiction 3. Family life—Fiction 4. Identity—Fiction 5. Interpersonal relations—Fiction 6. Missing persons—Fiction 7. Mystery and detective stories

ISBN 1423175123; 9781423175124 (hardback)

LC 2013-047574

SUMMARY: In this young adult novel by Jennifer L. Armentrout, "Samantha is a stranger in her own life. Until the night she disappeared with her best friend, Cassie, everyone said Sam had it all—popularity, wealth, and a dream boyfriend. Sam has resurfaced, but she has no recollection of who she was or what happened to her that night. As she tries to piece together her life from before, she realizes it's one she no longer wants any part of." (Publisher's note)

REVIEW: *Booklist* v110 no17 p52-3 My 1 2014 Krista Hutley

REVIEW: *Bull Cent Child Books* v67 no10 p497 Je 2014 K. C.

"Don't Look Back". "While Sam sifts through clues and half-formed memories to solve the mystery of her own personality conversion as well as Cassie's disappearance, the posh school setting with a serious mean-girl problem provides an entertaining if familiar context. Cassie's brother and his girlfriend stabilize the ground under Sam's newly insecure social feet, narratively speaking, and her growing romance with Carson rounds out the genre blend as murder mystery merges with prom fisticuffs, and family tragedy with mean-girl melodrama. Recommend this to readers who prefer their soap operas set in high school."

REVIEW: *Kirkus Rev* v82 no5 p94 Mr 1 2014

REVIEW: *SLJ* v60 no4 p156 Ap 2014 Joanna Sondheim

REVIEW: *Voice of Youth Advocates* v37 no1 p58 Ap 2014 Richard Vigdor

ARMENTROUT, JENNIFER L. White Hot Kiss; [by] Jennifer L. Armentrout 400 p. 2014 Paw Prints

1. Demonology 2. Gargoyles 3. Man-woman relationships—Fiction 4. Paranormal fiction 5. Paranormal romance stories

ISBN 0373211104; 1480638528; 9780373211104; 9781480638525

SUMMARY: In this book, "seventeen-year-old Layla just wants to be normal. But with a kiss that kills anything with a soul, she's anything but normal. Half demon, half gargoyle, Layla has abilities no one else possesses.Layla tries to fit in, but that means hiding her own dark side from those she loves the most. Especially Zayne, the . . . completely off-limits Warden she's crushed on since forever. Then she meets Roth—a tattooed, sinfully hot demon who claims to know all her secrets." (Publisher's note)

REVIEW: *Booklist* v110 no8 p48 D 15 2013 Julie Trevelyan

REVIEW: *Kirkus Rev* v81 no24 p278 D 15 2013

"White Hot Kiss". " Yes, it's another novel about exotic paranormal hybrids, but this one's written with wry humor that seeps into nearly every sentence, making it constantly entertaining no matter its subject. . . . Layla's problem with divided loyalties doesn't interfere with the stopping-Armageddon plot, and the narrative sizzles with as much tension as romance. [Jennifer L.] Armentrout's sophisticated, layered humor keeps the narrative bubbling all the way through, and she delivers a terrific character in Roth, the unrepentant demon. Of course, both Zayne and Roth fit the chiseled-abs, drop-dead-gorgeous mold, but this is a romance. Totally entertaining."

REVIEW: *Publ Wkly* v260 no51 p63 D 16 2013

REVIEW: *Voice of Youth Advocates* v36 no5 p69-70 D 2013 Lucy Schall

ARMESTO, SEBASTIAN. Moby-Dick; [by] Sebastian Armesto 2013 Oberon Books

ISBN 9781849435109

SUMMARY: This book is Sebastien Armesto's theatrical adaptation of Herman Melville's novel. "Nantucket. 1851. Centre of a whaling industry that transformed blubber into the oils and candles that lit the world. It's there that a schoolmaster called Ishmael arrives to ship on a whale-boat. He enrols under Ahab, Captain of the Pequod—a man bent on destroying the white whale that lost him his leg." (Publisher's note)

REVIEW: *Natl Rev* v66 no2 p36-8 F 10 2014 RICHARD LOWRY

"Moby-Dick". "Moby-Dick outstrips its ponderous reputation in almost every way. Outside the occasional treatises on marine biology, it is a crackling good read. I marveled at the wit and whimsy; the lush descriptive language; the Shakespearean soliloquies; the haunting sense of foreboding that builds from the first pages. . . . The major—and many of the not-so-major—episodes of Moby-Dick had stuck with me for a couple of decades, such is their vividness and power. . . . And with that, back 'Moby Dick' goes on the shelf, with awe and enduring admiration."

ARMITAGE, JOHN.ed. The Virilio dictionary. See The Virilio dictionary

ARMSTRONG-TOTTEN, JULIA. A dynasty of dealers; John Smith and successors 1801-1924: a study of the art market in nineteenth-century London; [by] Julia Armstrong-Totten 464 p. 2013 The Roxburghe Club Maggs Bros. Ltd

1. Art—Collectors and collecting—England—London—History—19th century 2. Art dealers—England—London—Correspondence 3. Letters

ISBN 1901902102; 9781901902105

LC 2013-455374

SUMMARY: In this book, authors Charles Sebag-Montefiore and Julia I. Armstrong Totten "transcribe and publish in full 564 letters from and to [art dealer John] Smith and his sons. . . . Tbe letters are presented in eighteen sections, each prefaced by an introductory essay. They are mosty arranged chronologically." (Burlington Magazine)

REVIEW: *Burlington Mag* v156 no1332 p177-8 Mr 2014 CHRISTOPHER BROWN

"A Dynasty of Dealers: John Smith and Successors 1801-1924: A Study of the Art Market in Nineteenth-Century London". "It is an exemplary edition with very careful transcriptions, excellent notes that identify bis correspondents and individual paintings, and a superb index. [Charles] Sebag-Montefiore is a member of the Roxburghe Club and this is his Roxburghe volume, produced with the lavishness characteristic of those volumes. . . . The personal detail that has been so evidently lacking in earlier accounts of Smith is all here."

ARMSTRONG, CORY L.ed. Media disparity. See Media disparity

ARMSTRONG, KELLEY, 1968-. Omens; a Cainsville novel; [by] Kelley Armstrong 416 p. 2013 Dutton

1. Adopted children—Fiction 2. Birthparents—Identification—Fiction 3. Fantasy fiction 4. Serial murder investigation—Fiction 5. Serial murderers—Fiction

ISBN 9780525953043

LC 2013-013203

SUMMARY: Written by Kelley Armstrong, this novel between the Cainsville series. "Twenty-four-year-old Olivia Taylor Jones has the perfect life. . . . But Olivia's world is shattered when she learns that she's adopted. Her real parents? Todd and Pamela Larsen, notorious serial killers serving a life sentence. . . . Olivia ends up in the small town of Cainsville, Illinois . . . to uncover her birth parents' past." (Publisher's note)

REVIEW: *Booklist* v109 no21 p50 Jl 1 2013 Margaret Flanagan

REVIEW: *Kirkus Rev* v81 no12 p6 Je 15 2013

REVIEW: *Libr J* v138 no10 p104 Je 1 2013 Crystal Renfro

REVIEW: *Libr J* v138 no4 p55 Mr 1 2013 Barbara Hoffert

REVIEW: *Publ Wkly* v260 no19 p48 My 13 2013

REVIEW: *Quill Quire* v79 no7 p28 S 2013 Suzanne Gardner

"Omens." "Twenty-four-year-old socialite Olivia Taylor Jones seems to have a perfect life. . . . In the opening chapters of this new series, best-selling author Kelley Armstrong seems to be venturing into dark thriller territory, but the story soon cedes ground to the author's usual supernatural fare, when Olivia begins having premonitions. . . . Armstrong . . . does an excellent job of writing her heroine. . . . Armstrong transforms her into someone the reader wants to root for. . . . The novel's strengths are the characters . . . , but it's difficult to care about whether Olivia's parents have been wrongly convicted."

ARNAL, WILLIAM E.ed. Failure and nerve in the academic study of religion. See Failure and nerve in the academic study of religion

ARNDT, INGO. Best foot forward; exploring feet, flippers, and claws; [by] Ingo Arndt 31 p. 2013 Holiday House

1. Animals—Adaptation 2. Animals—Juvenile literature 3. Children's nonfiction 4. Foot—Juvenile literature 5. Nature photography
ISBN 0823428575; 9780823428571 (hardcover)
LC 2012-039295

SUMMARY: Author Ingo Arndt's book features photos "and a brief description of how the foot is used. A tiger stalks its prey on velvet paws. A gecko's ribbed feet enable it to climb walls as smooth as glass. The mole uses its feet for digging. The webbed feet of a duck help it swim. Rabbits and kangaroos have feet adapted for jumping fast and far. Caterpillars, starfish, and octopuses all use their feet to grab hold. The guessing-game format makes learning about natural adaptation fun." (Publisher's note)

REVIEW: *Booklist* v110 no2 p63 S 15 2013 Ann Kelley

REVIEW: *Bull Cent Child Books* v67 no2 p73 O 2013 D. S.

"Best Foot Forward: Exploring Feet, Flippers, and Claws." "This introductory nature-study photoessay takes a look at feet from a literally different perspective--most of the feet are photographed from the underside, showing the characteristics of the foot that really make it valuable to its owner. . . . The text in this German import is streamlined and focused, acting mainly as captions for the photographs, which are the real stars of the show. The photos typically feature the limb in question isolated against an inky black background for maximum focus, and the details--the prickly spininess of a lobster's foot, the almost botanical purity of the gecko's foot, the leathery delicacy of the pink pads of the tiger--are visually arresting."

REVIEW: *Kirkus Rev* v81 no17 p77 S 1 2013

REVIEW: *Nat Hist* v121 no9 p43 N 2013 Dolly Setton

REVIEW: *Publ Wkly* v260 no32 p57 Ag 12 2013

REVIEW: *SLJ* v59 no10 p1 O 2013 Susan E. Murray

ARNDT, MICHAEL. Cat says meow; and other animalopoeia; [by] Michael Arndt 36 p. 2014 Chronicle Books LLC

1. Alphabet 2. Animal sounds—Fiction 3. Animal sounds—Juvenile fiction 4. Animals—Juvenile fiction 5. Picture books for children
ISBN 1452112347; 9781452112343 (alk. paper)
LC 2013-003270

SUMMARY: In this book by Michael Arndt, "animals and the sounds they make are paired up in playfully compelling ways . . . featuring bold colors and an engaging use of onomatopoeia. Kids and parents [can discover] the ways in which the letters that spell out each animal's sound are key elements of that animal's illustration." (Publisher's note)

REVIEW: *Kirkus Rev* v82 no1 p264 Ja 1 2014

"Cat Says Meow: And Other Animalopeia". "No other book of simple sentences about animal sounds also boasts eye-catching, often humorous graphics that show the letters of the sound forming the animal's head or body. For beginning readers, the cover invites a long perusal, a preparation for how to "read" the pictures inside. . . . Each page turn reveals a new graphic in a bold color, with a pleasing variety of single- and double-page spreads, as well as subtle changes in composition. This is one of those rare picture books with something for everyone to enjoy, beginning with colors, sounds and shapes for the youngest."

REVIEW: *Publ Wkly* v260 no51 p58 D 16 2013

REVIEW: *SLJ* v60 no3 p100 Mr 2014 Jess deCourcy Hinds

ARNDT, RICHARD J. Horror comics in black and white; a history and catalog, 1964-2004; [by] Richard J. Arndt vii, 289 p. 2013 McFarland & Co.

1. Comic books, strips, etc.—History & criticism 2. Horror comic books, strips, etc. 3. Horror comic books, strips, etc.—United States—History and criticism 4. Horror tales, American—History and criticism 5. Literature—History & criticism
ISBN 9780786470259 (softcover : alk. paper)
LC 2012-049772

SUMMARY: This book, by Richard J. Arndt, "offers a comprehensive history and retrospective of the black-and-white horror comics that flourished on the newsstands from 1964 to 2004. In 1954, the comic book industry instituted the Comics Code, a set of self-regulatory guidelines imposed to placate public concern over gory and horrific comic book content. . . . Many artists and writers turned to black and white to circumvent the Code's narrow confines." (Publisher's note)

REVIEW: *Choice* v50 no11 p1982 Jl 2013 A. Ellis

"Horror Comics in Black and White: A History and Catalog, 1964-2004." "Black-and-white horror comics in magazine format were created to circumvent the strictures of the Comics Code Authority (CCA), which gripped the comic book medium beginning in 1954. . . . Veteran comics fan/historian [Richard J.] Arndt chronicles the history of this black-and-white genre within the overall medium. . . . Arndt's value judgments may become tiresome. . . . The true strength of this work is the historical information it presents on a little-explored publishing phenomenon."

ARNETT, MINDEE. The Nightmare dilemma; [by] Mindee Arnett 384 p. 2014 Tor Teen

1. Boarding schools—Fiction 2. Dreams—Fiction 3. Magic—Fiction 4. Mystery and detective stories 5. Schools—Fiction 6. Supernatural—Fiction
ISBN 9780765333346 (hardback)

LC 2013-039498

SUMMARY: In this book, part of a series by Mindee Arnett, "Dusty Everhart might be able to predict the future through the dreams of her crush, Eli Booker, but that doesn't make her life even remotely easy. When one of her mermaid friends is viciously assaulted and left for dead, and the school's jokester, Lance Rathbone, is accused of the crime, Dusty's as shocked as everybody else. Lance needs Dusty to prove his innocence by finding the real attacker." (Publisher's note)

REVIEW: *Kirkus Rev* v82 no3 p78 F 1 2014

"The Nightmare Dilemma". " In a fast-moving and easily digestible magical school story, Destiny 'Dusty' Everhart, a teen who can enter others' dreams, investigates an attack on a mermaid classmate. . . . There's plenty of action to keep readers engaged, and frequent exposition—in the form of narrative asides and dialogue—helps readers keep track of the many characters and rules of magic. The prose is more serviceable than artful, and some lines are downright clunky. . . . Nothing too deep, but good fun for fans of romance, fantasy and magical boarding school escapades."

REVIEW: *SLJ* v60 no4 p156 Ap 2014 Pete Smith

ARNN, JOHN WESLEY. Land of the Tejas; native American identity and interaction in Texas, a.d. 1300 to 1700; [by] John Wesley Arnn xiii, 300 p. 2012 University of Texas Press

1. Archaeological literature 2. Excavations (Archaeology)—Texas 3. Historical literature 4. Indians of North America—Antiquities 5. Indians of North America—Texas 6. Indians of North America—Texas—Antiquities 7. Indians of North America—Texas—Ethnic identity 8. Indians of North America—Texas—History 9. Social archaeology—Texas 10. Toyah culture

ISBN 9780292728738 (cloth : alk. paper); 9780292734999 (e-book)

LC 2011-014840

SUMMARY: This book by John Wesley Arnn is "a sweeping, interdisciplinary look at Texas during the late prehistoric and early historic periods. . . . Drawing heavily on a detailed analysis of Toyah (a Late Prehistoric II material culture), as well as early European documentary records, an investigation of the regional environment, and comparisons of these data with similar regions around the world, 'Land of the Tejas' examines a full scope of previously overlooked details." (Publisher's note)

REVIEW: *Am Hist Rev* v118 no4 p1172-3 O 2013 Juliana Barr

"Land of the Tejas: Native American Identity and Interaction in Texas, A.D. 1300 to 1700." "In this book, John Wesley Arnn III seeks a 'holistic approach'--combining ethnographic, environmental, and historical data with that of archaeology--'in order to support a model of prehistoric hunter-gatherer social interaction and identity' . . . as well as to trace 'continuity in Native American prehistory and history.' . . . The missteps here may lie in the fact that despite the book's avowed desire to utilize historical sources, it evinces little recognition of the vast historiography regarding the region, its native residents, the Spanish intruders, or even, for that matter, identity formation."

REVIEW: *Choice* v49 no11 p2106 Jl 2012 P. J. O'Brien

ARNOLD, DAVID. Everyday technology; machines and the making of India's modernity; [by] David Arnold 223 p. 2013 University of Chicago Press

1. Historical literature 2. Modernity—History 3. Technology—India—History 4. Technology transfer—India

ISBN 9780226922027 (cloth : alk. paper)

LC 2012-050734

SUMMARY: "Few would question the dominant role that technology plays in modern life, but to fully understand how India first advanced into technological modernity, argues David Arnold, we must consider the technology of the everyday. 'Everyday Technology' is a pioneering account of how small machines and consumer goods that originated in Europe and North America became objects of everyday use in India in the late nineteenth and early twentieth centuries." (Publisher's note)

REVIEW: *Choice* v51 no4 p658 D 2013 V. V. Raman

REVIEW: *TLS* no5788 p30 Mr 7 2014 DAVID WASHBROOK

"Everyday Technology: Machines and the Making of India's Modernity." "In this fascinating study, David Arnold casts his eye over a range of much smaller and humbler machines which, nonetheless, have transformed the 'everyday' lives of the people using them. He explores the histories of the bicycle, the sewing machine, the typewriter, the gramophone and the rice mill in the context of colonial India. . . . If David Arnold's study lacks anything, it is perhaps a fuller appreciation of the extraordinary artisanal creativity demonstrated at [the] 'everyday' end of the technology spectrum."

ARNOLD, ELLEN F. Negotiating the landscape; environment and monastic identity in the medieval Ardennes; [by] Ellen F. Arnold 301 p. 2013 University of Pennsylvania Press

1. Benedictine monasteries—Belgium—Stavelot—History—To 1500 2. Historical literature 3. Human ecology—Ardennes—History—To 1500 4. Human ecology—Religious aspects—Catholic Church—History—To 1500 5. Landscapes—Ardennes—History—To 1500 6. Landscapes—Religious aspects—History—To 1500

ISBN 9780812244632 (hardcover: alk. paper)

LC 2012-023964

SUMMARY: This book "explores the question of how medieval religious identities were shaped and modified by interaction with the natural environment. Focusing on the Benedictine monastic community of Stavelot-Malmedy in the Ardennes, Ellen F. Arnold . . . explore[s] the contexts in which the monks' intense engagement with the natural world was generated and refined." (Publisher's note)

REVIEW: *Am Hist Rev* v119 no1 p231 F 2014 Steven A. Epstein

"Negotiating the Landscape: Environment and Monastic Identity in the Medieval Ardennes". "Ellen F. Arnold has made an imaginative and entirely original contribution to the massive amount of scholarship on medieval monasticism as well as to the new and still small field of medieval environmental history. Neither endeavor is easy. . . . What is most impressive about the scope of this book is how it goes beyond the confines of its genre to apply a well-grounded understanding of modern environmental history to this unexpected place and time."

ARP, ROBERT.ed. 1001 ideas that changed the way we think. See 1001 ideas that changed the way we think

ARRINGTON, LAUREN.ed. Beauty. See Beauty

ARROWSMITH, WILLIAM.tr. Poetic notebook, 1974-1977. See Montale, E.

ARROWSMITH, WILLIAM.tr. Poetic diaries 1971 and 1972. See Montale, E.

ARSENAULT, ISABELLE.il. Jane, the fox & me. See Britt. F.

ART & PLACE; Site-Specific Art of the Americas; 373 p. 2013 Phaidon Inc Ltd

1. Art—Themes, motives 2. Art literature 3. North American art 4. Site-specific art 5. South American art
ISBN 0714865516; 9780714865515
LC 2013-474154

SUMMARY: This book, edited by the artistic publisher Phaidon Press, "celebrates the most . . . outstanding examples of site-specific art in the Americas . . . , whether created for indoor spaces, or urban, desert or mountainous settings. . . . Over 500 artworks from all periods, arranged geographically across fifteen countries that span the Americas, from Canada to Argentina, have been specially selected by a panel of experts." (Publisher's note)

REVIEW: *Libr J* v138 no21 p100 D 1 2013 Michael Dashkin

REVIEW: *Publ Wkly* v260 no43 p18-23 O 28 2013

REVIEW: *Time* v182 no20 p56 N 11 2013 Richard Lacayo

"Art & Place: Site-Specific Art of the Americas." "Among the sculptures, murals, earthworks and architectural carvings in this enjoyable page-turner of a book, the Easter Island heads coexist with a Picasso. . . . 'Art & Place' has its flaws, none of them fatal. It's not true that the Rothko Chapel in Houston can be visited only on prearranged tours. It's a stretch to use site-specific to describe some of these works, like Mark di Suvero's wonderful Joie de Vivre, which touched down at several spots before coming to rest on Wall Street. And how could this book fail to include Mount Rushmore? Problems with securing photo rights? Unlikely. Sheer art-world snobbery? Could be. But no matter. Long after every coffee-table book has crumbled, those boys will still be on-site."

ART IN OCEANIA; a new history; 536 p. 2012 Yale University Press

1. Art—Oceania 2. Art history 3. Art literature 4. Pacific Island art 5. Visual culture
ISBN 9780300190281 (cloth : alk. paper)
LC 2012-026213

SUMMARY: This book, edited by Peter Brunt and Nicholas Thomas, examines the visual culture of Oceania. "Covering works discovered in earliest archaeological evidence through those created in the last 50 years, the book pays credence to the impact of changing relations among Pacific peoples as well as their resilience and creativity in the face of globalization. The result is a portrait of Oceanic art as both traditional and innovative." (Publisher's note)

REVIEW: *Burlington Mag* v155 no1329 p836-7 D 2013 PETER STUPPLES

REVIEW: *Choice* v50 no10 p1899 Je 2013 A. J. Stone

REVIEW: *Libr J* v138 no5 p125 Mr 15 2013 Julia A. Watson

REVIEW: *TLS* no5741 p7-9 Ap 12 2013 ANDREW SHARP

"Art in Oceania: A New History." "The 'art' that is the subject of this large, multiauthored volume is so diverse as not to be easily characterized; and in any case 'art' is treated by the book's authors as a category of human activity and production best not defined very precisely at all. All the authors, however, do believe that it is desirable to historicize what it is they deal with. . . . Since they intend a comprehensive account of 'art in Oceania', these are wise positions for the authors and editors to take. They wish above all to inform rather than to make any contentious cases, and they do so from several institutional, disciplinary and cultural standpoints."

THE ART OF RUBE GOLDBERG; a) inventive b) cartoon c) genius; 192 p. 2013 Abrams ComicArts

1. Art literature 2. Caricatures & cartoons—United States—History—20th century 3. Cartoonists 4. Goldberg, Rube, 1883-1970 5. Inventions in art
ISBN 9781419708527
LC 2013-940525

SUMMARY: In this book on cartoonist Rube Goldberg, "author Jennifer George celebrates all aspects of her grandfather's career, from his very first published drawings in his high school newspaper and college yearbook to his iconic inventions, his comic strips and advertising work, and his later sculpture and Pulitzer Prize-winning political cartoons. Also included are essays by noted comics historians, rare photographs, letters, memorabilia, and patents, many reproduced here for the first time." (Publisher's note)

REVIEW: *N Y Times Book Rev* p30-1 D 15 2013 Steven Heller

REVIEW: *New York Times* v163 no56346 pD2 D 10 2013 DANA JENNINGS

"The Art of Rube Goldberg: (A) Inventive (B) Cartoon (C) Genius". "This generously illustrated and well-designed appreciation captures all those facets of his career and more, and includes essays by the New Yorker writer Adam Gopnik, Jennifer George . . . the Mad Magazine cartoonist Al Jaffee and a range of comic strip historians. . . . At heart, Goldberg . . . was an ideas guy. . . . And through his labyrinthine thingamajigs, he invented a way to blunt America's 20th-century lust for efficiency and hyper-rationalism, even if only on the funny pages, and maybe even make his readers crack a smile."

ART STUDIO AMERICA; 600 p. 2013 Thames & Hudson

1. American art—21st century 2. Art literature 3. Artists—United States 4. Artists' studios 5. Los Angeles (Calif.) art scene 6. New York (N.Y.) art scene
ISBN 9780500970539 (hardcover)
LC 2013-934843

SUMMARY: This book "focuses on personal sites of artistic production in the U.S. and highlights interviews with and photographs of contemporary artists in and around their studios. . . . Introduced by a sequence of brief essays that consider geopolitical movements within the modern art world, the roles of the studio in artistic practice, and individualized artistic responses to space and place, this peripatetic guide hovers . . . around New York City and Los Angeles." (Choice: Current Reviews for Academic Libraries)

REVIEW: *Choice* v51 no8 p1384 Ap 2014 E. Baden

"Art Studio America: Contemporary Artist Spaces". "The book is a lavish compendium both trendy and archival, offering a snapshot glimpse and encyclopedic breadth. Its production resources—logistical, financial, and natural—were clearly considerable, and it flaunts an exuberance outweighed only, perhaps, by its carbon footprint. Nonetheless, this is a rich and useful resource—a privileged glimpse into ranges of personal artistic practice by a bevy of successful artists. And it offers, of course, stunning views of real estate."

ARTHUR, SHAWN. Early Daoist dietary practices; examining ways to health and longevity; [by] Shawn Arthur 416 p. 2013 Lexington Books

1. Diet—China 2. Diet Therapy—China 3. Health Behavior—China 4. Longevity—China 5. Medical literature 6. Religion and Medicine—China 7. Religious Philosophies—China
ISBN 9780739178928 (cloth : alk. paper)
LC 2013-010278

SUMMARY: In this book, "focusing on a fifth-century manual of herbal-based, immortality-oriented recipes--the Lingbao Wufuxu. . . . Shawn Arthur investigates the diets, their ingredients, and their expected range of natural and supernatural benefits. Analyzing the ways that early Daoists systematically synthesized religion, Chinese medicine, and cosmological correlative logic, this study" examines "Daoist ideas regarding the body's composition and mutability, health and disease." (Publisher's note)

REVIEW: *Choice* v51 no6 p1042-3 F 2014 J. Saxton

"Early Daoist Dietary Practices: Examining Ways to Health and Longevity." "Centering body movement practices, such as qigong and taiji, are widely known, but information from ancient texts on the relationship between diet and optimal health is harder to come by. This book discusses historical and cultural contexts for a selection of ancient Chinese 'recipes' utilizing various food and herbal ingredients. [Shawn] Arthur . . . who specializes in Chinese religions and 'the intersection of religion, culture, medicine, and the body,' then evaluates the recipes' potential therapeutic value from a modern scientific perspective. . . . Useful for researchers specializing in Daoist traditions relating to health and longevity."

ARTIÈRES, PHILIPPE, 1968-.ed. Speech begins after death. See Speech begins after death

ARTS AND CRAFTS OF THE ISLAMIC LANDS; 288 p. 2013 Thames & Hudson

1. Art literature 2. Art technique 3. Handicraft 4. Islam & art 5. Islamic art & symbolism
ISBN 0500517029; 9780500517024 (hardcover)
LC 2012-955177

SUMMARY: This book, edited by Khaled Azzam, discusses Islamic arts and crafts, covering "a range of artworks and media from intricate geometric drawing, decorative Kufic calligraphy, and Persian miniature painting to ceramics, wood parquetry, mosaics, and glassblowing. Common tools and materials, such as gesso panels, gilding, and brush and wasli paper are presented along with information on their historical significance." (Publisher's note)

REVIEW: *Choice* v51 no5 p798 Ja 2014 K. E. Staab

"Arts & Crafts of the Islamic Lands: Principles, Materials, Practice." "Overall, this is a practical, modern, how-to volume, chock-full of photos. It is an excellent resource for art students and those interested in learning how to select the necessary tools and how to create traditional Islamic art. This work will be less useful for researchers, though short paragraphs in each chapter connect the techniques to history. Images of both modern and historic examples are featured within the text. A limited, nonalphabetical, but very useful glossary is included."

REVIEW: *Libr J* v139 no2 p71 F 1 2014 Jennifer Naimzadeh

ASBURY, NICK. White Hart, Red Lion; The England of Shakespeare's Histories; [by] Nick Asbury 198 p. 2013 Oberon Books

1. Great Britain—Description & travel 2. Great Britain—History—Wars of the Roses, 1455-1485 3. Royal Shakespeare Co. 4. Shakespeare, William, 1564-1616—Histories 5. Social commentary
ISBN 1849432414; 9781849432412

SUMMARY: "[Author] Nick Asbury acted in the Royal Shakespeare Company's famed Histories cycle. . . . With fellow RSC actors for company, Nick travels the country visiting the buildings, landscapes and former sites of war and intrigue that feature in the plays, and asks the question: what is it about the England of Shakespeare's Histories that continues to fascinate? . . . This is his snapshot of England and its people, then and now." (Publisher's note)

REVIEW: *TLS* no5786 p27 F 21 2014 MICHAEL THOMAS

"White Hart, Red Lion: The England of Shakespeare's Histories." "From 2007 onwards, Nick Asbury appeared the RSC cycle of Shakespeare's Histories, and his emotional connection with those plays has given rise, via an RSC blog, to White Hart, Red Lion, a blend of travelogue, actor's memoir and historical meditation, the last principally on the Houses of York and Lancaster, politics and blood. . . . Several places prompt Asbury to put passages from Shakespeare in their historical and topographical context. . . . This book is not intended for a scholarly audience, but a bibliography would not have gone amiss."

ASCHER, ABRAHAM. Was Hitler a riddle?; western democracies and national socialism; [by] Abraham Ascher x, 243 p. 2012 Stanford University Press

1. Diplomacy—History—20th century 2. Diplomats—Germany—Attitudes 3. Germany—Foreign relations—History 4. Historical literature 5. National socialism 6. National socialism—Public opinion 7. World War, 1939-1945—Causes
ISBN 9780804783552 (cloth : alk. paper); 9780804783569 (pbk. : alk. paper)
LC 2012-014297

SUMMARY: This book by Abraham Ascher "is the first comparative study of how British, French, and American diplomats serving in Germany assessed Hitler and the Nazi movement. These assessments provided the governments in London, Paris, and Washington with ample information about the ruthlessness of the authorities in Germany and of their determination to conquer vast stretches of Europe." (Publisher's note)

REVIEW: *Am Hist Rev* v118 no4 p1243-4 O 2013 Peter Hayes

"Was Hitler a Riddle? Western Democracies and National Socialism." "This smoothly written but ultimately unconvincing book contends that the answer to its title question is a resounding 'no.'... Abraham Ascher tells readers a good deal that is new about what Western diplomats were saying to their governments during the 1930s, but he provides few fresh insights into why their superiors at home discounted their harsher commentaries and engaged in wishful thinking about taming or satisfying the Nazi regime.... The book contains several telling errors and omissions.... But nothing that he says in these regards is original, and the portrait of diplomatic perspicacity that he presents is considerably overstated."

REVIEW: *Choice* v50 no9 p1685 My 2013 P. Scherer

ASHBURN, BONI. The fort that Jack built; [by] Boni Ashburn 32 p. 2013 Abrams Books for Young Readers

1. Building—Fiction 2. Children's stories 3. Family life—Fiction 4. Grandparent & child 5. Play 6. Stories in rhyme
ISBN 9781419707957 (alk. paper)
LC 2012-036739

SUMMARY: In this children's book by Boni Ashubrn, "Jack assembles a fort out of household items without asking permission. One by one, his family members reclaim their possessions, taking down the fort. Luckily Grandma is willing to share, helping Jack see a more effective approach to building." (Horn Book Magazine)

REVIEW: *Booklist* v110 no2 p72 S 15 2013 Lolly Gepson

REVIEW: *Horn Book Magazine* v90 no1 p121-2 Ja/F 2014

"The Fort That Jack Built," "Rosie Revere, Engineer," and "My Dream Playground." "The cumulative 'House That Jack Built' rhymes are peppy, and [Brett] Helquist's homey oil paintings in muted tones capture the action of imaginative play.... [Andrea] Beaty's rhymes are cleverly constructed, and [David] Roberts's meticulous illustrations, some on drafting paper, capture the quirkiness of the girl and her gizmos.... The author's note explains that the uplifting (if idealized) story is based on a real project by KaBOOM!, a national nonprofit organization. Sunny digital illustrations underscore the sense of community."

REVIEW: *Kirkus Rev* v81 no16 p106 Ag 15 2013

REVIEW: *Publ Wkly* v260 no29 p68 Jl 22 2013

THE ASHGATE RESEARCH COMPANION TO THE COUNTER-REFORMATION; 2013 Ashgate Publishing

1. Catholic Church & science 2. Catholic Church—History 3. Christianity & art—Catholic Church 4. Counter-Reformation 5. Historical literature
ISBN 9781409423737 hardcover

SUMMARY: Edited by Alexandra Bamji, Geert H. Janssen, and Mary Laven, this book "presents a comprehensive examination of recent scholarship on early modern Catholicism in its many guises." It "incorporates topics as diverse as life cycle and community, science and the senses, the performing and visual arts, material objects and print culture, war and the state, sacred landscapes and urban structures." (Publisher's note)

REVIEW: *Choice* v51 no5 p852 Ja 2014 G. J. Miller

"The Ashgate research companion to the Counter-Reformation." "This handbook is an excellent survey of current research trends in early modern Catholicism.... The scholarship of Eamon Duffy and John Bossy influences almost every essay. Of the 24 chapters, no single one is dedicated to the Council of Trent or the Jesuits.... Contributors argue that seeing Rome as overseeing a loose federation of national and regional churches, rather than as a monolithic force, makes sense. A third theme is the treatment of global Catholicism on equal terms to European Catholicism, rather than its inclusion only in regard to missionary activity.... Recommended."

ASHTON, BRODI. Evertrue; an Everneath novel; [by] Brodi Ashton 368 p. 2014 Balzer + Bray, an imprint of HarperCollinsPublishers

1. Fantasy fiction 2. Future life—Fiction 3. Hell—Fiction 4. Love—Fiction 5. Supernatural—Fiction
ISBN 9780062071194 (hardcover bdg. : alk. paper)
LC 2013-014513

SUMMARY: This book is the third installment of Brodi Ashton's Everneath trilogy. It "focuses on Nikki, who is determined to destroy the Everneath. Even though, thanks to Cole's trickery, she is now an Everliving, Nikki is adamant that she would rather die than live at the expense of human forfeits. But her plans are in direct conflict with Cole's, who still hopes to persuade her to join him in overthrowing the current queen of the Everneath and ruling it herself." (Booklist)

REVIEW: *Booklist* v110 no5 p72-4 N 1 2013 Kara Dean

"Evertrue." "Picking up two weeks after the events of 'Everbound' (2013), this book focuses on Nikki, who is determined to destroy the Everneath.... Fans of the series will not be disappointed as the story heads toward the inevitable showdown; although, as is often the case with a story that takes three books to build, it all seems over rather quickly. Fittingly, the resolution of the love triangle is the finest moment of the book, as it unflinchingly embraces the only solution that can plausibly bring this Persephone tale to a close."

REVIEW: *Kirkus Rev* v81 no23 p93 D 1 2013

REVIEW: *SLJ* v60 no4 p176 Ap 2014

REVIEW: *Voice of Youth Advocates* v36 no6 p67-8 F 2014 Nancy K. Wallace

ASHTON, DIANNE. Hanukkah in America; a history; [by] Dianne Ashton 368 p. 2013 New York University Press

1. Antisemitism—United States—History 2. Hanukkah—United States 3. Historical literature 4. Jews—United States—History 5. Judaism—United States—History—21st century
ISBN 0814707394; 9780814707395 (cl: alk. paper)
LC 2013-014009

SUMMARY: In this history of Hanukkah in the U.S. author Diane Ashton argues that the holiday "has been a vehicle for asserting solidarity among a never-large American minority and establishing that minority's credentials as faithful Americans as well as faithful Jews. Further, Ashton asserts, Hanukkah has always played a role in response to the successive challenges American Jews have faced over the course of the last century and a half." (Booklist)

REVIEW: *Commentary* v137 no3 p52-3 Mr 2014 JEREMY DAUBER

"Hanukkah in America: A History". "In many ways, [Diane] Ashton persuasively argues, the history of American Hanukkah is the history of the American Jewish experience. . . . Those familiar with the contours of the American Jewish story won't find much surprising here in the way of grand narrative. But the devil—or in this case, the delight—is in the details. . . . Ashton, who has written before on Jewish women's spirituality, is particularly adept at showing the blurred and blurry lines between the centrality of the domestic sphere and the role played by family networks, communal institutions, and religious leaders and opinion-makers."

REVIEW: *J Am Hist* v101 no1 p299-300 Je 2014

REVIEW: *Kirkus Rev* v81 no19 p24 O 1 2013

REVIEW: *Libr J* v138 no13 p103 Ag 1 2013 Matt Rice

REVIEW: *Publ Wkly* v260 no28 p156 Jl 15 2013

ASHTON, TIMOTHY J. Soccer in Spain; politics, literature, and film; [by] Timothy J. Ashton xviii, 217 p. 2013 the Scarecrow Press, Inc.

1. Soccer—Political aspects—Spain 2. Soccer—Social aspects—Spain 3. Soccer—Spain 4. Soccer in motion pictures 5. Sports literature
ISBN 9780810891739 (cloth: alk. paper)
LC 2013-019542

SUMMARY: In this book on soccer, author Timothy J. Ashton "examines the sport's association with Spanish culture and society. In this volume, Ashton demonstrates how Spain's soccer clubs reflected the politics of the region they represented and continue to reflect them today. The author also explores the often-tenuous relationship between the intellectual classes and the soccer community in Spain." (Publisher's note)

REVIEW: *Choice* v51 no8 p1443-4 Ap 2014 E. A. Sanabria

"Soccer in Spain: Politics, Literature, and Film". "Though the first part, 'Tackling Spain's National Identity Crisis,' is based on a dated, shallow historiography and is unsatisfactory, the subsequent two parts offer much of merit. At times, however, the martyred tone of one who is trying to salvage 'kick-lit' and 'kick-flicks' (witty though poignant terms devised by the author) can be off-putting. By creating a straw man out of intellectual titans like Jorge Luis Borges, who was unabashed in his soccer antipathies, [Timothy J.] Ashton seeks to proclaim the legitimacy of kick-lit and kick-flicks as modern genres while also demonstrating how soccer has long been a subject of enthusiasm in the writings of some of Spain's cultural elite."

ASHURA, DAVIS. A Warrior's Path; [by] Davis Ashura 586 p. 2014 DuSum Publishing, LLC

1. Caste 2. Fantasy fiction 3. Goddesses 4. Imaginary wars & battles 5. Warriors
ISBN 0991127617; 9780991127610

SUMMARY: In this book, "Rukh Shekton—a dedicated young member of his world's warrior caste—fights for the survival of his people. . . . His devotion to the traditions of his culture sustains him, but he's tested when he learns the real character of the Chimeras' leaders, the dark plans of Suwraith and how the two are not as aligned as he'd once thought. And when Rukh begins to question the way things have always been, he changes his destiny forever." (Kirkus Reviews)

REVIEW: *Kirkus Rev* v82 no1 p332 Ja 1 2014

"A Warrior's Path". "The characters, dialogue and action are mature enough to satisfy readers at the older end of the YA range, and the author weaves them all into an attention-sustaining tale. Pacing and description are also strong in what is clearly the opening novel of a series. . . . The somewhat racially based nature of the castes is a little troubling at first glance, though the castes are also focused on innate talents, personality traits and abilities. . . . Although the set bears enough resemblance to J.R.R. Tolkien's universe . . . the milieu is markedly original. And with a full-color map and an eight-page glossary, the novel offers readers easy references to answer any questions that might arise. Good fantasy fiction with first-rate worldbuilding."

ASIAN TIGERS, AFRICAN LIONS; comparing the development performance of Southeast Asia and Africa; 524 p. 2013 Brill

1. Economic development—Africa 2. Economic development—Southeast Asia 3. Economics literature
ISBN 9789004256538 (pbk.: alk. paper)
LC 2013-033845

SUMMARY: This book reports on a research project which "compared the performance of growth and development of four pairs of countries in Southeast Asia and Sub-Sahara Africa during the last sixty years. It tried to answer the question how two regions with comparable levels of income per capita in the 1950s could diverge so rapidly. Why are there so many Asian tigers and not yet so many African lions? What could Africa learn from Southeast Asian development trajectories?" (Publisher's note)

REVIEW: *Choice* v51 no9 p1645 My 2014 J. H. Cobbe

"Asian Tigers, African Lions: Comparing the Development Performance of Southeast Asia and Africa". "There was a clear policy orientation in all the studies, and ministry officials participated throughout. The case studies are preceded by four introductory and overview chapters, and followed by a concluding chapter helpfully titled 'Policy and Governance . . . Firm Findings and Remaining Questions.' In a capsule, governance matters for good policy and outcomes, but the details of how and why are not always clear. As a one-volume, evidence-based response to why Asia has done so well and Africa so poorly, this book has no peer."

ASKEW, RILLA. Kind of Kin; [by] Rilla Askew 432 p. 2013 Ecco

1. Domestic fiction 2. Families—Fiction 3. Illegal aliens—Fiction 4. Oklahoma—Fiction 5. Runaway children—Fiction
ISBN 0062198793; 9780062198792

SUMMARY: In this book by Rilla Askew, "[w]hen Oklahoma passes a tough new law making harboring 'illegals' a felony, Robert John Brown refuses to defend himself and is sent to prison for hiding a barn full of undocumented migrant workers. Brown's daughter Sweet is left to manage a family (including a troublesome son and an orphaned nephew) that is coming apart at the seams as her marriage collapses under the stress." (Library Journal)

REVIEW: *N Y Times Book Rev* p28 F 16 2014 IHSAN TAYLOR

"The Marlowe Papers," "Coolidge," and "Kind of Kind."

"[Ros] Barber's novel isn't the first to reimagine the life (and mysterious death) of the Elizabethan playwright Christopher Marlowe, but it may be the first to do so in verse. . . . With a deft finger on today's conservative pulse, [Amity] Shlaes . . . portrays Calvin Coolidge (1872-1933) as a paragon of a president by virtue of his small-government policies. . . . The fraught issue of illegal immigration divides an Oklahoma clan and their town in [Rilla] Askew's heartfelt novel ['Kind of Kin']."

ASPE, PIETER. The Midas Murders; An Inspector Van In Mystery; [by] Pieter Aspe 336 p. 2013 W W Norton & Co Inc

1. Bruges (Belgium) 2. Counterterrorism—Fiction 3. Detective & mystery stories 4. Murder—Fiction 5. Terrorism—Fiction

ISBN 1605984876; 9781605984872

SUMMARY: "In the second novel by . . . Pieter Aspe, Inspector [Pieter] Van In races against the clock to thwart a series of terrorist plots. . . . Aided by the spunky and beautiful assistant DA Hannelore Maartens, Inspector Van In finds himself enmeshed in the case that threatens not just the lives of countless of innocent people, but the heart of the city he loves," Bruges, Belgium. (Publisher's note)

REVIEW: *Booklist* v110 no5 p29 N 1 2013 Connie Fletcher

REVIEW: *Kirkus Rev* v81 no24 p15 D 15 2013

"The Midas Murders". " As the police focus on the links to the Mouvement Wallon Révolutionnaire, . . . [Pieter] Van In, a hard-bitten, hard-drinking, hard-wenching cop whose couplings with the whore Véronique are so inveterate that he doesn't even think he's cheating on his prosecutor, closes in on a plot that links the Nazi hoarding of Old Masters half a century ago to a fiendishly modern scheme to manipulate the real estate market in historic Bruges. Only Van In's intuition and his knack for noticing important details can explain how this raffish cop could possibly keep his job in this jokey, down-and-dirty tour of a town that can't make up its mind whether it's a museum for tourists or a haven for crooks."

REVIEW: *N Y Times Book Rev* p19 Ja 5 2014 MARLIYN STASIO

"Dark Times in the City," "The Invisible Code," and "The Midas Murders." "In Gene Kerrigan's novel 'Dark Times in the City' . . . Kerrigan writes with a grim elegance that takes the edge off the blunt language and brutal deeds of his underworld villains and spares some grace for their hapless victims. . . . There are witches on Fleet Street in 'The Invisible Code.' . . . There are also devils and demons and ladies who lunch in Christopher Fowler's latest madcap mystery about the strange police detectives in London's Peculiar Crimes Unit. . . . In 'The Midas Murders' . . . , a new police procedural (its rhetorical excesses intact in Brian Doyle's translation) from Pieter Aspe. . . . It's all intricately plotted by Aspe."

REVIEW: *Publ Wkly* v260 no35 p32 S 2 2013

ASPINWALL, MARK. Side effects; Mexican governance under NAFTA's labor and environmental agreements; [by] Mark Aspinwall xviii, 209 p. 2013 Stanford University Press

1. Administrative agencies—Mexico 2. Environmental law—Mexico 3. Environmental policy—Mexico 4. Labor laws and legislation—Mexico 5. Labor policy—Mexico 6. Political science literature

ISBN 0804782296; 9780804782296 (cloth : alk. paper); 9780804782302 (pbk. : alk. paper)

LC 2012-022089

SUMMARY: This book, by Mark Aspinwall, examines "governance in Mexico after the labor and environmental accords—called 'side agreements'—that accompanied the NAFTA treaty went into effect. [It] explores how differences in institutional design (of the side agreements) and domestic capacity (between the labor and environment sectors) influenced norm socialization in Mexico." (Publisher's note)

REVIEW: *Choice* v51 no1 p155 S 2013 M. A. Morris

"Side Effects: Mexican Governance Under NAFTA's Labor and Environmental Agreements." "This is an important book about how North American free-trade side agreements on labor and the environment have impacted Mexican governance. The 1994 NAFTA treaty among the US, Mexico, and Canada included, at US behest, side agreements on labor and the environment. These side agreements required all three member states to enforce their labor and environmental laws, with the US concern being that Mexico had a problem with law enforcement in these areas. . . . Assessment and comparison of multiple variables leads to a sophisticated explanation of differences in the two selected policy areas as well as implications for other policy areas."

ASSENSOH, A. B. Malcolm X. See Alex-Assensoh, Y. M.

ASTILL, JAMES. The great tamasha; cricket, corruption and the turbulent rise of modern India; [by] James Astill 304 p. 2013 Bloomsbury USA

1. Caste—India 2. Cricket—India—History 3. Historical literature 4. India—History 5. Sports business

ISBN 9781608199174 (alk. paper)

LC 2013-011749

SUMMARY: In this book, author James Astill "finds the game of cricket a telling metaphor for what ails and heals the new India. Cricket has functioned as a tool to both institutionalize India's caste system and break it. From a quintessentially Victorian gentleman's game, cricket was first adopted by the Brahmin class . . . and prosperous merchants. . . . Astill sees cricket's subsequent growth across India as 'unplanned, organic and almost exclusively on sectarian lines.'" (Kirkus Reviews)

REVIEW: *Booklist* v109 no19/20 p14-5 Je 1 2013 Alan Moores

REVIEW: *Choice* v51 no6 p1050 F 2014 R. D. Long

REVIEW: *Kirkus Rev* v81 no10 p42 My 15 2013

REVIEW: *N Y Times Book Rev* p10 Ag 18 2013 RAHUL BHATTACHARYA

"The Great Tamasha: Cricket, Corruption, and the Spectacular Rise of Modern India." " 'The Great Tamasha' is a series of excursions into a cricket-fixated society. . . . [James Astill] devotes much of the book to recounting how Indian cricket went from colonial recreation to national addiction, and while treading this familiar ground, the narrative lacks the propulsion of discovery. . . . Astill attempts to make the big themes contemporary, not always with conviction. His grasp of caste does not inspire confidence. . . . Astill's excursions, however, give the book its spice. . . . 'The Great Tamasha' is a book of breadth rather than depth. It buzzes with field trips and brisk interviews that sometimes bring insight, and more often momentum and freshness."

REVIEW: *N Y Times Book Rev* p34 Ag 25 2013

REVIEW: *New Statesman* v142 no5167 p42 Jl 19 2013 Philip Maughan

REVIEW: *New Statesman* v142 no5185 p42-7 N 22 2013

REVIEW: *Publ Wkly* v260 no21 p50 My 27 2013

REVIEW: *TLS* no5756 p5 Jl 26 2013 STEPHEN FAY

ASTOLFO, CATHERINE. Sweet Karoline; [by] Catherine Astolfo 224 p. 2013 Imajin Books

1. Detective & mystery stories 2. Family secrets 3. Friendship—Fiction 4. Love stories 5. Murder—Fiction

ISBN 192779207X; 9781927792070

SUMMARY: In this novel by Catherine Astolfo, protagonist "Anne Williams says she killed her best friend, Karoline. . . . Anne embarks on a compelling journey to discover her past and exposes an unusual history, horrific crimes and appalling betrayals. Through unexpected turns and revelations, Anne learns about love, family and who she really is. Can she survive the truth?" (Publisher's note)

REVIEW: *Kirkus Rev* v81 no16 p3 Ag 15 2013

"Sweet Karoline." " In her latest novel, [author Catherine] Astolfo . . . takes what at first glance appears to be a straightforward story of murder and guilt to an unexpected place where love is discovered. . . . Astolfo adeptly makes vast leaps of character transformation completely believable, even for a murderer. Anne goes on a treasure hunt for her real family's secrets related to the fate of freed slaves, interracial relationships, incest and a fortune. . . . A deliciously vibrant portrait that realistically muddles good and evil."

AT THE TOP OF THE GRAND STAIRCASE; the late Cretaceous of Southern Utah; xvi, 634 p. 2013 Indiana University Press

1. Animals, Fossil—Utah 2. Geology—Utah 3. Geology, Stratigraphic—Cretaceous 4. Paleontology—Cretaceous 5. Scientific literature

ISBN 9780253008831 (hbk: alk. paper)

LC 2013-005859

SUMMARY: This book, edited by Alan L. Titus and Mark A. Loewen, looks at "the diverse fossils and the complex geology" of the region surrounding "southern Utah's Grand Staircase-Escalante National Monument. . . . There are chapters on flora, macroinvertebrates, fish, amphibians, snakes, crocodilians, and mammals, and eight chapters on dinosaur." (Choice: Current Reviews for Academic Libraries)

REVIEW: *Choice* v51 no8 p1431 Ap 2014 D. Bardack

"At the Top of the Grant Staircase: The Late Cretaceous of Southern Utah". "While the geology of southern Utah and some of its fossils have been known for more than 125 years, this is the first time that more than 50 researchers have contributed 28 articles focusing on this region. Most of the papers have numerous excellent photographs and drawings of specimens as well as photographs and maps of specific geologic areas. Appropriate comparisons are made with similar fossils in other regions of the US. . . . Since there are few comprehensive studies of the fossils, geology, and environment of large areas, this work will be an important resource for library collections. It will be valuable to paleontologists and geologists who are working throughout the US and the world."

ATHANS, SANDRA K. Secrets of the sky caves; danger and discovery on Nepal's Mustang Cliffs; [by] Sandra K. Athans 64 p. 2014 Millbrook Press

1. Archaeological literature 2. Caves—Nepal—Mustang (District) 3. Mountaineering—Nepal—Mustang (District)

ISBN 1467700169; 9781467700160 (lib. bdg.: alk. paper)

LC 2013-017736

SUMMARY: This children's book by Sandra K. Athans asks "What's more dangerous than scaling Mount Everest? For mountaineer Pete Athans, the answer lies in the ancient kingdom of Mustang, a remote part of the Asian nation of Nepal. . . From 2007 to 2012, Pete explored Mustang's sky caves with a team that included scientists, mountain climbers, and even two children. They found mummies, murals, manuscripts, and other priceless artifacts." (Publisher's note)

REVIEW: *Bull Cent Child Books* v67 no10 p498 Je 2014 E. B.

"Secrets of the Sky Caves: Danger and Discovery on Nepal's Mustang Cliffs". "Discussion of caving techniques and the team's relationship with Nepalese government and religious leaders opens a window to the more knotty technical and bureaucratic aspects of archaeology. Meanwhile, the informal color photographs are particularly effective in conveying the scale of the terrain and blend of tradition and modernity throughout the region. Often, though, the text is marred by missed opportunities (description of grave gods is unspecific) and unexplained incongruities (e.g., few plants are present, but farmers raise wheat and barley)."

REVIEW: *Kirkus Rev* v82 no5 p112 Mr 1 2014

REVIEW: *SLJ* v60 no3 p178 Mr 2014 Helen Foster James

ATKINS, TONY. A dictionary of mechanical engineering; [by] Tony Atkins 428 p. 2013 Oxford University Press

1. Encyclopedias & dictionaries 2. Fluid mechanics 3. Machinery 4. Mechanical engineering—Dictionaries 5. Technical literature

ISBN 0199587434 (pbk.); 9780199587438 (pbk.)

LC 2012-554924

SUMMARY: This dictionary of mechanical engineering was compiled by Tony Atkins and Marcel Escudier. "Focusing on the fundamental areas of mechanical engineering, such as fluid mechanics, stress analysis, dynamics, and design, it also includes numerous terms from electronics, bioengineering, acoustics, materials science, and other areas as they relate to mechanical engineering." (Choice: Current Reviews for Academic Libraries)

REVIEW: *Choice* v51 no5 p804-6 Ja 2014 M. A. Manion

"A Dictionary of Mechanical Engineering." "The outstanding feature of this handy mechanical engineering dictionary is the clarity and conciseness of its 8,500-plus entries. Given the central role of mechanical engineering in manufacturing and design, and the interdisciplinary nature of engineering, this dictionary will be useful to those in other engineering disciplines as well as lawyers, journalists, and others needing definitions of engineering terms. . . . Included are numerous cross-references and an excellent companion website. . . . Clearly drawn illustrations accompany the volume and about 20 percent of the entries. . . . It is well worth the price."

ATKINSON, ANDREW.ed. Running the Whale's Back. See Running the Whale's Back

ATLANTIC BIOGRAPHIES; individuals and peoples in the Atlantic world; xvi, 356 p. 2014 Brill
1. Atlantic studies 2. Biography (Literary form) 3. Slavery—History
ISBN 9789004258976 (hardback: alk. paper)
LC 2013-030104

SUMMARY: This collection of biographies, edited by Jeffrey A. Fortin and Mark Meuwese, "highlights the tensions and contradictions within the Atlantic world to demonstrate how individuals navigated, confronted, and shaped this world. The 13 essays are organized into three overarching categories: Atlantic Sojourners, Slavery and Freedom on the Edges of the Atlantic World, and Forging Atlantic Identities." (Choice: Current Reviews for Academic Libraries)

REVIEW: *Choice* v51 no8 p1461-2 Ap 2014 J. Rankin
"Atlantic Biographies: Individuals and Peoples in the Atlantic World". "The subject matter is diverse, and readers are presented with a wide range of interesting stories, including Alexander von Humboldt and his scientific investigations in the Americas; an Irishman sent to Africa as punishment for his crimes; indigenous and Maroon leaders in the Atlantic world; the story of Pierre Biard, a priest accused of piracy. By including such a wide array of topics, the book is certain to be of value to a broad range of scholars. Taken as a whole, this thought-provoking work demonstrates the value of biography as a tool for understanding Atlantic history."

ATTLEE, HELENA. The Land Where Lemons Grow; The Story of Italy and its Citrus Fruit; [by] Helena Attlee 272 p. 2014 Particular Books
1. Agriculture—Italy—History 2. Citrus—Varieties 3. Citrus fruit growing 4. Citrus fruit industry 5. Historical literature 6. Italy—Description & travel 7. Lemon
ISBN 1846144302; 9781846144301

SUMMARY: "In 'The Land Where Lemons Grow,' Helena Attlee sets out to explore its curious past and its enduring resonance in Italian culture. . . . The book is a celebration of the unique qualities of Italy's citrus fruit, from bergamot that will thrive only on a short stretch of coastline, to Calabria's Diamante citrons, vital to Jews all over the world during the celebration of Sukkoth." (Publisher's note)

REVIEW: *Booklist* v111 no3 p24-5 O 1 2014 Barbara Jacobs

REVIEW: *TLS* no5794 p30 Ap 18 2014 CLARISSA HYMAN
"The Land Where Lemons Grow: The Story of Italy and Its Citrus Fruit." "Helena Attlee acknowledges the complexities of international trade in 'The Land Where Lemons Grow: The story of Italy and its citrus fruit,' her fascinating grand tour of the citrus-growing regions of Italy. Her focus is . . . on the history of the fruit in its adopted home, and the migration of waves of citrons, sour oranges, lemons, sweet oranges and mandarins to . . . Mediterranean Europe. . . . One gripe persists: the publishers have selected perfunctory maps. . . . Nonetheless, Helena Attlee's elegant, absorbing prose and sure-footed ability to combine the academic with the anecdotal, make 'The Land Where Lemons Grow' a welcome addition to the library of citrologists and Italophiles alike."

ATWOOD, MARGARET, 1939-. Maddaddam; a novel; [by] Margaret Atwood 416 p. 2013 Nan A. Talese
1. Communal living—Fiction 2. FICTION—Humorous 3. FICTION—Science Fiction—Adventure 4. Genetic engineering—Fiction 5. Science fiction
ISBN 0385528787; 9780385528788 (hardback)
LC 2013-018715

SUMMARY: In this book by Margaret Atwood, "after the Waterless Flood pandemic has wiped out most of humanity, Toby and Ren have rescued their friend Amanda from the vicious Painballers. They return to the MaddAddamite cob house, newly fortified against man and giant pigoon alike. Accompanying them are the Crakers, the gentle, quasi-human species engineered by the brilliant but deceased Crake." (Publisher's note)

REVIEW: *Booklist* v109 no19/20 p30 Je 1 2013 Donna Seaman

REVIEW: *Kirkus Rev* v81 no14 p98 Jl 15 2013

REVIEW: *Libr J* v138 no7 p54 Ap 15 2013 Barbara Hoffert

REVIEW: *N Y Times Book Rev* p11 S 8 2013 ANDREW SEAN GREER

REVIEW: *New Statesman* v142 no5171 p42-3 Ag 23 2013 Sarah Churchwell

REVIEW: *New Yorker* v89 no32 p113-1 O 14 2013

REVIEW: *Orion Magazine* v33 no3 p100-1 My/Ag 2014 Kristen Hewitt

REVIEW: *Publ Wkly* v260 no23 p50 Je 10 2013

REVIEW: *Publ Wkly* v260 no37 p12 S 16 2013 Louis Ermelino

REVIEW: *Quill Quire* v79 no8 p28 O 2013 Jan Dutkiewicz

REVIEW: *Science* v343 no6167 p139 Ja 10 2014 Michael A. Goldman

REVIEW: *TLS* no5759 p3-4 Ag 16 2013 RUTH SCURR
"Maddaddam." "The third volume of a dystopian sequence, so far including 'Oryx and Crake' . . . and 'The Year of the Flood'. . . . There is much that is bleak and terrifying in [Margaret] Atwood's fiction, but it is leavened by her humour. . . . 'MaddAddam' opens with Atwood's leaden summary of the previous two volumes, 'The Story so Far'. Readers are advised to skip it. Writers are rarely the best summarizers of their own work, and Atwood is one of the worst. . . . In this novel, her ear for dialogue is unsteady, frequently falling back on dated or strange colloquialisms and vocabulary. . . . Beyond these glitches, 'MaddAddam' is remarkable for enacting the transition from oral to written history within a fictional universe --one complete with myths and false gods."

ATWOOD, MEGAN. Leaping at shadows; [by] Megan Atwood 100 p. 2013 Darby Creek
1. Dance—Fiction 2. Dance schools 3. Haunted places—Fiction 4. Horror tales 5. Supernatural—Fiction
ISBN 1467709301; 9781467709309 (lib. bdg. : alk. paper)
LC 2012-046156

SUMMARY: In this book, part of the Dario Quincy Academy of Dance series, Madeline is "determined to succeed as a scholarship student at the country's most prestigious residential dance academy. . . . She gradually makes some friends, and when her grandmother's necklace disappears along with jewelry with sentimental value to other students . . . The friends explore the sinister stone tunnels beneath the building . . . and fall prey to a cultish group of masked people who want the girls' blood." (Booklist)

REVIEW: *Booklist* v110 no2 p68-9 S 15 2013 Carolyn Phelan

"Leaping at Shadows." "Determined to succeed as a scholarship student at the country's most prestigious residential dance academy, Madeleine suppresses her feeling of foreboding upon entering the massive old building. . . . The encounters with the strange 'cult' are less than convincing, and the portrayals of secondary characters are a bit thin. Still, the idea of horror lurking beneath a ballet school has its appeal. Older readers looking for short, accessible books are the target audience for the Dario Quincy Academy of Dance series. The first ' volume may end in rescue, but clearly 'something is very wrong,' and further volumes are likely to explore the ongoing mystery."

REVIEW: *Publ Wkly* v260 no32 p59 Ag 12 2013

REVIEW: *SLJ* v59 no8 p95 Ag 2013 Maralita L. Freeny

AUGUSSEAU, STÉPHANIE.il. Celia. See Vallat, C.

AUGUST, MARILYN J. To catch a virus. See Booss, J.

AUGUSTAVE, ELSIE. The roving tree; [by] Elsie Augustave 300 p. 2013 Akashic Books

1. Adoptees—Fiction 2. Haiti—Fiction 3. Haitians—United States 4. International adoption 5. Psychological fiction

ISBN 9781617751653 (trade pbk. original)

LC 2012-954507

SUMMARY: This book by Elsie Augustave follows "Iris Odys . . . the offspring of Hagathe, a Haitian maid, and a French-educated mulatto father, Brahami, who cares little about his child. Hagathe, who had always dreamed of a better life for her child, is presented with the perfect opportunity when Iris is five years old. Adopted by a white American couple, Iris is transported from her tiny remote Haitian village, Monn Neg, to an American suburb." (Publisher's note)

REVIEW: *Kirkus Rev* v81 no5 p302 Mr 1 2013

REVIEW: *World Lit Today* v87 no6 p61 N/D 2013

"The Roving Tree." "Iris Odys is caught between two worlds: the politically oppressive Haiti of her birth and the culturally uninviting America into which she was adopted. Iris's ensuing cultural identity crisis causes her to write a letter to her own newborn daughter. This personally addressed autobiography makes up the bulk of" the book. "[Elsie] Augustave ultimately illustrates the devastating rootlessness of cultural disaffiliation."

AUGUSTEIJN, JOOST.ed. Region and state in nineteenth-century Europe. See Region and state in nineteenth-century Europe

AUGUSTINE, NONNIE. One Day Tells Its Tale to Another; [by] Nonnie Augustine 104 p. 2013 CreateSpace Independent Publishing Platform

1. Autobiographical poetry 2. Dancers 3. Disillusionment 4. Poems—Collections 5. Women—Poetry

ISBN 1482730995; 9781482730999

SUMMARY: This book by Nonnie Augustine presents "many seemingly autobiographical poems. . . . Compromise and disillusionment are frequent themes here but so are resilience and learning, although the narrators are often too busy navigating their lives to recognize their growing wisdom. . . . She reimagines fairy tales, evokes foreign lands through bodily sensation, valorizes women's perseverance, and revels in the rollicking pleasures of sex, even when they come with risk." (Kirkus Reviews)

REVIEW: *Kirkus Rev* p4 D 15 2013 supplemet best books 2013

"One Day Tells Its Tale to Another". "[Nonnie] Augustine often layers the perspectives of the narrator, author and reader to bolster the poems' realism and emotional sincerity, and it's a technique she hones to near perfection. On rare occasions, the poet usurps the narrator and lapses into bathos. . . . On the whole, however, Augustine demonstrates much greater control and precision as she works through multiple iterations of love and loss, employing to great effect forms as varied as the prose poem, the concrete poem, the villanelle, the sestina, the sonnet and the ballad. . . . Poetry that often transcends its own bounds, spilling over into readers' lives and forcing them to confront their own narratives."

REVIEW: *Kirkus Rev* v81 no21 p280 N 1 2013

REVIEW: *Kirkus Rev* v81 no23 p27 D 1 2013

AUSTIN, ALLAN W. Quaker brotherhood; interracial activism and the American Friends Service Committee, 1917-1950; [by] Allan W. Austin xi, 257 p. 2012 University of Illinois Press

1. American Friends Service Committee 2. Historical literature 3. Quakers—United States 4. Race relations—Religious aspects 5. Race relations—Religious aspects—Society of Friends—History 6. United States—Race relations—History

ISBN 9780252037047 (cloth : acid-free paper)

LC 2012-022675

SUMMARY: Written by Allan W. Austin, this book "is the first extensive study of the AFSC's [American Friends Service Committee's] interracial activism in the first half of the twentieth century, filling a major gap in scholarship on the Quakers' race relations work from the AFSC's founding in 1917 to the beginnings of the civil rights movement in the early 1950s." (Publisher's note)

REVIEW: *Am Hist Rev* v118 no4 p1197 O 2013 Alan Scot Willis

"Quaker Brotherhood: Interracial Activism and the American Friends Service Committee, 1917-1950." "Allan W. Austin offers an institutional history of the American Friends Service Committee's (AFSC) racial activism. He argues that, by 1950, Quakers in the AFSC had 'developed an indirect, Friendly approach to interracial relations that while still working to correct individual ignorance now saw the need to reform society as well.' . . . Austin's work fills a gap in Quaker historiography. . . . Austin does not take advantage of opportunities to explore what was specifically Quaker about the 'Friendly activism' of the AFSC. . . . Despite these drawbacks, Quaker Brotherhood is a detailed, well-researched study that will prove valuable to those who are interested in . . . Quaker history."

REVIEW: *Choice* v50 no8 p1502 Ap 2013 J. Kleiman

REVIEW: *J Am Hist* v100 no1 p243-4 Je 2013 James Emmett Ryan

REVIEW: *J Relig* v93 no3 p389-91 Jl 2013 TOBIN MILLER SHEARER

REVIEW: *Rev Am Hist* v41 no4 p592-9 D 2013 Michael Birkel

AUXIER, JONATHAN. The Night Gardener; [by] Jonathan Auxier 368 p. 2014 Amulet Books

1. Blessing and cursing—Fiction 2. Brothers and sisters—Fiction 3. Dwellings—Fiction 4. Ghosts—Fiction 5. Horror stories 6. Household employees—Fiction 7. Orphans—Fiction 8. Storytelling—Fiction
ISBN 141971144X; 9781419711442 (hardback)
LC 2013-047655

SUMMARY: Written by Jonathan Auxier, "'The Night Gardener' follows two abandoned Irish siblings who travel to work as servants at a creepy, crumbling English manor house. But the house and its family are not quite what they seem. Soon the children are confronted by a mysterious spectre and an ancient curse that threatens their very lives." (Publisher's note)

REVIEW: *Booklist* v110 no19/20 p95 Je 1 2014 Debbie Carton

REVIEW: *Bull Cent Child Books* v67 no9 p441 My 2014 A. S.

"The Night Gardener". "Molly is staunch and defiant, a sturdy protagonist who is loyal if not always wise in her efforts to protect those she cares for. . . . [Jonathan] Auxier achieves an ideal mix of adventure and horror, offering all of it in elegant, atmospheric language that forces the reader to slow down a bit and revel in both the high-quality plot and the storytelling itself. An informative author's note offers a bit of background into the Great Famine in Ireland, and how kids like Kip and Molly might have found themselves as orphans in England at such young ages."

AUYERO, JAVIER. Patients of the state; the politics of waiting in Argentina; [by] Javier Auyero xii, 196 p. 2012 Duke University Press

1. Marginality, Social—Argentina 2. Poor—Government policy—Argentina 3. Poor—Services for—Argentina 4. Poverty—Argentina 5. Social science literature
ISBN 9780822352334 (pbk. : alk. paper); 9780822352594 (cloth : alk. paper)
LC 2011-035892

SUMMARY: Written by Javier Auyero, "'Patients of the State' is a sociological account of the extended waiting that poor people seeking state social and administrative services must endure. It is based on ethnographic research in the waiting area of the main welfare office in Buenos Aires, in the line . . . where legal aliens apply for identification cards, and among people who live in a polluted shantytown on the capital's outskirts, while waiting to be allocated better housing." (Publisher's note)

REVIEW: *Am J Sociol* v118 no6 p1704-5 My 2013 Gianpaolo Baiocchi

REVIEW: *Contemp Sociol* v42 no5 p736-7 S 2013 Claudio E. Benzecry

"Patients of the State: The Politics of Waiting in Argentina." "How do you write sociology when confronted with the urgent situation of those who cannot wait any longer? In 'Patients of the State,' a short yet powerfully moving ethnographical text, Javier Auyero and his collaborators intend to answer this question by conducting in situ research with poor people in Argentina to explore the many different faces and locales under which temporality and domination go hand in hand. . . . There are of course disadvantages to the book's writing cum analytical strategy--at times the text feels rushed. . . . Nevertheless, these criticisms should not detract from our valuation of a very fine and original piece of ethnographic work."

AVAGYAN, SHUSHAN.tr. Bowstring. See Shklovskii, V.

AVAGYAN, SHUSHAN.tr. A hunt for optimism. See Shklovskii, V.

AVASTHI, SWATI. Chasing Shadows; [by] Swati Avasthi 320 p. 2013 Random House Childrens Books

1. Friendship—Fiction 2. Grief—Fiction 3. Murder—Fiction 4. Speculative fiction 5. Superheroes
ISBN 0375863427; 9780375863424

SUMMARY: Author Swati Avasthi's book looks "at the impact of one random act of violence." The book offers a "portrait of two girls teetering on the edge of grief and insanity. Two girls who will find out just how many ways there are to lose a friend . . . and how many ways to be lost." Holly and Savitri cope with the death of their friend Corey as they look for Corey's killer. (Publisher's note)

REVIEW: *Booklist* v110 no1 p112-3 S 1 2013 Daniel Kraus

"Chasing Shadows." "[Swati] Avasthi pulls a dramatic 180 from her gritty debut, 'Split' (2010), with this hyperstylized, graphic-novel-infused superhero-origin story--though even that doesn't suffice for this genre-bender. . . . The continual stylistic grace notes in the dual point-of-view voices often prevent a smooth narrative flow. But [Craig]Phillips' graphic interludes make for visceral thrills when words, or reality, fail the characters, adding further interest to this rate avenger story that takes mental illness seriously. It's a lot to mesh, and it doesn't always work, but it's undoubtedly bold and unique. Avasthi continues to impress."

REVIEW: *Horn Book Magazine* v90 no1 p83-4 Ja/F 2014 JONATHAN HUNT

"Chasing Shadows." "The narrative alternates among Savitri's voice, the voice of a second-person narrator . . . and Holly's perspective, told through both first-person text and dramatic graphic novel-style interludes interspersed throughout the story. [Swati] Avasthi delves deeply into the pysche of both girls, and in less capable hands the juggling of the magical realism of the comic panels, the adrenaline rush of the plot, and the staccato cadence of the second-person narration would be too gimmicky. It not only works here but seems like a natural fit for this visceral story of love, grief, and madness that is both action-packed and psychologically acute."

REVIEW: *Publ Wkly* p128 Children's starred review annual 2013

AVILES, MARTHA.il. Don't sneeze at the wedding. See Mayer, P.

AVINERI, SHLOMO. Herzl; Theodor Herzl and the Foundation of the Jewish State; [by] Shlomo Avineri 224 p. 2014 Phoenix

1. Biography (Literary form) 2. Herzl, Theodor, 1860-1904 3. Jewish nationalism 4. Zionism—History 5. Zionists—Biography

ISBN 1780224559; 9781780224558

SUMMARY: This biography of politician and activist Theodor Herzl " follows Herzl's transformation from a private person into the founder and leader of a political movement which made the quest for a Jewish state into a player in international politics." Author Shlomo Avineri "shows how it was the political crisis of the Austro-Hungarian Habsburg Empire, torn apart by contending national movements, which convinced Herzl of the need for a Jewish polity." (Publisher's note)

REVIEW: *Hist Today* v64 no3 p62 Mr 2014 Colin Shindler

"Herzl: Theodor Herzl and the Foundation of the Jewish State" and "The Idea of Israel: A History of Power and Knowledge." "Herzl emerges from his diaries as a dreamer and a realist. . . . In this book [Shlomo] Avineri has reclaimed Herzl from the propagandists. . . . While [Ilan] Pappe argues that there had been a quasi-official plan, based on Zionist beliefs, to expel the Palestinian Arabs, others believe that this is not revealed by the documentation. . . . While this book gives numerous insights into the subject, Pappe also conducts a megaphone war with his Israeli academic opponents, which mars an otherwise interesting account."

REVIEW: *TLS* no5789 p28 Mr 14 2014 DUNCAN KELLY

AYDIN, ANDREW. March. See Lewis, J. R.

AYERS, AMANDA CONLEY.ed. The Oxford handbook of happiness. See The Oxford handbook of happiness

AYERS, BILL. Public enemy; confessions of an American dissident; [by] Bill Ayers 240 p. 2013 Beacon Press

1. BIOGRAPHY & AUTOBIOGRAPHY—Personal Memoirs 2. Left-wing extremists—United States—Biography 3. Memoirs 4. POLITICAL SCIENCE—Political Ideologies—General 5. Radicalism—United States—History—20th century 6. Vietnam War, 1961-1975—Protest movements—United States

ISBN 080703276X; 9780807032763 (hardback)

LC 2013-023310

SUMMARY: In this memoir, "Weather Underground cofounder [Bill] Ayers chronicles his return to society after years on the lam as well as life after being branded a 'terrorist' by Sarah Palin during Barack Obama's 2008 presidential campaign, an accusation that led to rampant death threats." Topics include "his experiences as an early education specialist, professor, husband (to former Weather Underground leader Bernardine Dohrn), father of three, author, and activist." (Publishers Weekly)

REVIEW: *Booklist* v110 no2 p8 S 15 2013 June Sawyers

"Public Enemy: Confessions of an American Dissident." "This compelling sequel to [Bill] Ayers' 'Fugitive Days' . . . describes the author's chaotic life after he and his wife, Bernadette Dohrn, became the topic and target of conversation during Barack Obama's first run for the presidency. . . . Demonized and blacklisted, Ayers maintains not only his sanity but also his humor. When a reporter notes that he doesn't look like a real Weatherman, Ayers laughs and asks her what a real Weatherman looks like. A wonderful homage to free speech."

REVIEW: *Kirkus Rev* v81 no21 p4 N 1 2013

REVIEW: *Publ Wkly* v260 no27 p75 Jl 8 2013

AYLOTT, NICHOLAS. Political parties in multi-level polities; the Nordic countries compared; [by] Nicholas Aylott x, 251 p. 2013 Palgrave Macmillan

1. Political accountability 2. Political parties—Scandinavia 3. Political science literature 4. Power (Social sciences)

ISBN 9780230243736

LC 2012-048091

SUMMARY: In this book, the authors "examine the four largest Nordic countries--Denmark, Finland, Norway, and Sweden--in terms of the internal organization and distribution of power within individual political parties. Using a principal-agent analytical framework, the book assesses the extent to which members of parliament and cabinet ministers are controlled and/or held accountable by political parties and their members." (Choice)

REVIEW: *Choice* v51 no4 p718 D 2013 A. Siaroff

"Political Parties in Multi-Level Polities: The Nordic Countries Compared." "In this detailed, well-written book, Swedish scholars [Nicholas] Aylott and [Magnus] Bergman . . . and [Torbjörn] Blomgren . . . examine the four largest Nordic countries--Denmark, Finland, Norway, and Sweden--in terms of the internal organization and distribution of power within individual political parties. . . . The book provides excellent case studies, not least because precise background information is given for each country. . . . Clear contrasts are made both across the countries and with regard to individual parties. The book is essential reading not just for students of Nordic politics, but for all those interested in political parties in parliamentary systems."

AZIMOVA, SHAKHNOZA S.ed. Natural Compounds. See Natural Compounds

AZZAM, KHALED.ed. Arts and crafts of the Islamic lands. See Arts and crafts of the Islamic lands

B

BAARSEN, REINIER. Paris 1650-1900; decorative arts in the Rijksmuseum; [by] Reinier Baarsen 608 p. 2013 Yale University Press

1. Art literature 2. Decorative arts—France—Paris—Catalogs 3. Decorative arts—Netherlands—Amsterdam—Catalogs 4. French art—History 5. French decorative arts 6. Paris (France) art scene 7. Rijksmuseum (Netherlands)

ISBN 0300191294; 9780300191295

LC 2012-038656

SUMMARY: Written by Reinier Baarsen, "This book traces the wonderful story of Parisian decorative arts from the reign of Louis XIV to the triumph of art nouveau, through a selection of 150 . . . masterpieces from the collection of the Rijksmuseum in Amsterdam. It features an exhilarating mixture of furniture, gilt bronze, tapestries, silver, watches, snuff-boxes, jewellery, Sèvres porcelain, and other ceramics, as well as some design drawings and engravings." (Publisher's note)

REVIEW: *Apollo: The International Magazine for Collec-*

tors v178 no612 p120-2 S 2013 Bertrand Rondot

"Paris 1650-1900: Decorative Arts in the Rijksmuseum." "Published to coincide with the much acclaimed reopening of the Rijksmuseum, this opulent book of over 600 pages presents a fascinating selection of the museum's collections of more than 250 years of French decorative arts. Through detailed new research, Reinier Baarsen, senior curator of furniture at the Rijksmuseum and--amazingly--sole author here, reveals the masterpieces of one of the finest, if lesser known, collections of such objects."

REVIEW: *Apollo: The International Magazine for Collectors* v178 no615 p46 D 2013

REVIEW: *Burlington Mag* v156 no1333 p244 Ap 2014 HELEN JACOBSEN

REVIEW: *Choice* v51 no3 p442 N 2013 A. Luxenberg

REVIEW: *Libr J* v138 no14 p106 S 1 2013 Stephen Allan Patrick

BABA YAGA; the wild witch of the East in Russian fairy tales; 202 p. 2013 University Press of Mississippi Jackson

1. Baba Yaga (Legendary character) 2. Folklore—Russia (Federation) 3. Tales 4. Tales—Russia 5. Witches in literature

ISBN 9781617035968 (cloth : alkaline paper)

LC 2013-003373

SUMMARY: This book on the mythical figure Baba Yaga presents "a selection of tales that draws from the famous collection of Aleksandr Afanas'ev, but also includes some tales from the lesser-known nineteenth-century collection of Ivan Khudiakov. This new collection includes beloved classics such as 'Vasilisa the Beautiful' and 'The Frog Princess,' as well as a version of the tale that is the basis for the ballet 'The Firebird.'" (Publisher's note)

REVIEW: *Choice* v51 no7 p1219-20 Mr 2014 B. K. Beynen

"Baba Yaga: The Wild Witch of the East in Russian Fairy Tales." "In his foreword. Jack Zipes points out Baba Yaga's powerful, ambiguous, and protean nature. Most countries have similar tales, but Baba Yaga is uniquely Russian probably because she is so 'amply described' in Russian tales. The book is very attractive, thanks to the superb illustrations [Martin] selected by Skoro; [Helena] Goscilo provided informative captions. Forrester's folkloric and linguistic notes, which accompany her detailed, instructive introduction, and her superb, smooth translations are scholarly and make the tales easy to understand. The volume will be useful to those interested in Russian studies, children's literature, and folklore."

BABBITT, NATALIE. The moon over High Street; [by] Natalie Babbitt 148 p. 2012 Scholastic

1. Adoption—Fiction 2. Children in literature 3. Families—Juvenile fiction 4. Family relations 5. Family-owned business enterprises—Succession 6. Orphans—Juvenile fiction

ISBN 054537636X; 9780545376365 (alk. paper)

LC 2011-926886

SUMMARY: This children's novel by Natalie Babbitt "presents 12-year-old Joe. . . . Orphaned shortly after his birth, Joe, who loves the moon, has been raised by his Gran, but after she breaks a hip, he's sent to spend some of the summer with his father's cousin. . . . In nearly idyllic Midville, . . . he inadvertently comes to the attention of the very wealthy factory owner Mr. Boulderwall . . . who decides that he will adopt Joe and raise him to take over his company." (Kirkus)

REVIEW: *Booklist* v108 no14 p62 Mr 15 2012 Carolyn Phelan

REVIEW: *Horn Book Magazine* v88 no3 p74-5 My/Je 2012 Deirdre F. Baker

"The Moon over High Street." "Anson Boulderwall, a Polish American millionaire who has made it big with his 'swervit' factory, is looking for someone to groom to be the business's next president. And when Joe arrives in Boulderwall's little Ohio town, Midville, to stay with his aunt in the summer of 1965, Boulderwall decides that Joe will be the one. . . . [Natalie] Babbitt's subtle prose cloaks and deepens this brief moral fable of American ambition, ranging from the bald 'Here in America, we like things to be big and beautiful' to the atmospheric 'in the dimness the little farms had settled quietly behind rail fences, where cowsheds and hay barns were turning into comfortable shapes resting in their own shadows.'"

REVIEW: *Kirkus Rev* v80 no1 p2426 Ja 1 2012

REVIEW: *Publ Wkly* v259 no1 p84 Ja 2 2012

REVIEW: *SLJ* v58 no4 p154 Ap 2012 Caroline Ward

REVIEW: *Voice of Youth Advocates* v35 no2 p151 Je 2012 Shana Morales

BABINEAUX, RYAN. Fail fast, fail often. See Krumboltz, J.

BABITS, LAWRENCE E.ed. The archaeology of French and Indian War frontier forts. See The archaeology of French and Indian War frontier forts

BABY LOVES COLORS; 12 p. 2013 Penguin Group USA

1. Board books 2. Colors—Juvenile literature 3. Green 4. Red 5. Yellow

ISBN 0448477904; 9780448477909

SUMMARY: This is a "board book designed for babies 6 months or older about all the colors they can see: red, yellow, orange, green and blue!" (Publisher's note)

REVIEW: *Kirkus Rev* v81 no21 p316 N 1 2013

REVIEW: *Kirkus Rev* v82 no1 p86 Ja 1 2014

"Baby Loves Colors". "A baby's introduction to red, green, yellow, orange and blue from Sassy, a well-known manufacturer of baby toys. Each spread presents a full page of the color in question on the left with a bold caption in white and a selection of five objects in the featured hue on the right. The orange pages, for example, depict cartoon illustrations, with subtle tactile embossing, of a butterfly, a goldfish, an orange, a pumpkin and a couple of carrots. Some of the art incorporates the black-and-white stripes and checkerboard patterns often found on Sassy toys. . . . It is simple and direct enough to catch the eyes of the very, very young."

BACA, JIMMY SANTIAGO, 1952-. Singing at the Gates; Selected Poems; [by] Jimmy Santiago Baca 254 p. 2014 Pgw

1. Environmentalism 2. Families—Poetry 3. Oppression (Psychology) 4. Poems—Collections 5. Prisoners'

writings
ISBN 0802122108; 9780802122100

SUMMARY: This book "is a collection of new and previously published poems that reflect back over four decades of [Jimmy Santiago] Baca's life . . . raging against war and imprisonment, celebrating family and the bonds of friendship, heightening appreciation for and consciousness of the environment. . . . It includes his early work . . . written while serving a five-year prison sentence . . . and recent pieces meditating on the significance of breaking through oppression." (Publisher's note)

REVIEW: *Booklist* v110 no9/10 p34-6 Ja 1 2014 Donna Seaman

"Singing at the Gates." "[A] fiery retrospective collection. . . . The surge and embrace of his narrative poetry never ceases, nor does his cosmic admiration and love for women, nor his profound camaraderie with other men who have known poverty, prejudice, injustice, and incarceration. [Jimmy Santiago] Baca's earliest works are torrents of erotic longing and political awakening. . . . . Baca's poems are warm and furious, feathered and drumming, plowed and tattooed, righteous and prayerful. His is a clarion and necessary voice, and this standout volume belongs in every library."

BACCALARIO, PIERDOMENICO D. Suitcase of stars; [by] Pierdomenico D. Baccalario 240 p. 2014 Stone Arch Books

1. Adventure and adventurers—Fiction 2. Adventure stories 3. Friendship—Fiction 4. Friendship—Juvenile fiction 5. Magic—Fiction 6. Magic—Juvenile fiction
ISBN 9781434265166 (library binding); 9781434265197 (pbk.); 9781623700393 (paper-over-board)
LC 2013-036657

SUMMARY: In this book, "Finley's duties as a substitute mail carrier bring him to the [Enchanted] Emporium, where he meets the shop owners, the Lilys, and their lovely teenaged daughter Aiby, with whom Finley quickly is smitten. When a crazed Dutchman wakes a giant in the nearby castle ruins and it threatens to destroy the store, Finley must help Aiby save the family business—preferably without being killed in the process." (Bulletin of the Center for Children's Books)

REVIEW: *Bull Cent Child Books* v67 no8 p394 Ap 2014 J. H.

"Suitcase of Stars". "This Italian import, the first in a series, is slow to start, and there are a few incongruities in the plot. . . . Furthermore, the titular Suitcase of Stars, discovered in the Dutchman's hotel room, is merely mentioned once and then never referred to again. The magical action, however, is enjoyable, Finley and Aiby are an engaging and intrepid pair, and the interspersed illustrations and descriptions of various magical items (pages from the Lilys' Big Book of Magical Objects) are intriguing. Kids willing to skim the slower bits may find plenty to entertain them in the scenes of magic gone awry."

REVIEW: *Kirkus Rev* v82 no2 p145 Ja 15 2014

REVIEW: *SLJ* v60 no4 p138 Ap 2014 Lisa Nabel

BACEVICH, ANDREW J., 1947-. Breach of trust; how Americans failed their soldiers and their country; [by] Andrew J. Bacevich 256 p. 2013 Metropolitan Books, Henry Holt and Company

1. Citizenship—Social—United States 2. Military service, Voluntary—United States 3. National security—Social aspects—United States 4. Political science literature 5. Sacrifice—Social aspects—United States 6. War and society—United States
ISBN 0805082964; 9780805082968
LC 2013-004885

SUMMARY: In this book, professor and U.S. Army veteran Andrew C. Bacevich criticizes the way the U.S. uses its military. Bacevich "asserts bluntly that a disengaged and compliant citizenry has reduced military service from a universal duty to a matter of individual choice, allowing our leaders to wage war whenever (and for however long) they choose--with little to fear from an electorate who are neither paying nor perishing." (Publishers Weekly)

REVIEW: *America* v210 no5 p36-7 F 17 2014 BILL WILLIAMS

"Breach of Trust: How Americans Failed Their Soldiers and Their Country". "[A] passionate new book about military policy in the post-Vietnam era. [Andrew] Bacevich has excellent credentials, having served for 23 years as an officer in the U.S. Army. . . . The most provocative argument in this new book involves Bacevich's assertion that the United States now embraces Israel's aggressive policy of military superiority and a strike-first mentality. . . . Although Bacevich generally makes a persuasive case that Congress should bring back the draft, he occasionally engages in rhetorical overkill. . . . Overall, Bacevich has written a bracing call for Americans to 'revert to a concept of citizenship in which privileges entail responsibilities.'"

REVIEW: *Bookforum* v20 no3 p7 S-N 2013 JEFF STEIN

"Breach of Trust: How Americans Failed Their Soldiers and Their Country: and "Thank You for Your Service." "[Andrew] Bacevich, a West Point graduate . . . now writes perceptive, bristling essays and books from his perch at Boston University. . . . If [David] Finkel weren't such a vivid, compelling, heartrending writer, you'd never get through his agonizing weave of battles, from the bomb-strewn highways of Iraq to the psycho clinics of VA hospitals and many ruined homes in between. . . . ['Breach of Trust' is a] gripping, appropriately lacerating book."

REVIEW: *Booklist* v109 no22 p6 Ag 1 2013 Jay Freeman

REVIEW: *Christ Century* v130 no21 p36-7 O 16 2013 Timothy Renick

REVIEW: *Commonweal* v140 no17 p33-5 O 25 2013 David M. Kennedy

REVIEW: *Kirkus Rev* v81 no13 p203 Jl 1 2013

REVIEW: *N Y Times Book Rev* p15-6 S 8 2013 RACHEL MADDOW

REVIEW: *Parameters: U.S. Army War College* v44 no2 p114-6 Summ 2014 Dennis Laich Andrew J. Bacevich

REVIEW: *Publ Wkly* v260 no24 p52-3 Je 17 2013

BACON, ELLIS. World's Ultimate Cycling Races; 300 of the Greatest Cycling Events; [by] Ellis Bacon 512 p. 2013 HarperCollins UK

1. Bicycle racing 2. Mountain biking 3. Race Across America 4. Sports literature 5. Tour de France (Bicycle race)
ISBN 0007482817; 9780007482818

SUMMARY: "This book [by Ellis Bacon] highlights the must-ride races and gran fondos where riders can really test their legs against both the terrain and their fellow riders. Options include cheering on the world's top professionals from the roadside as they take on the Tour Down Under, heading into the Alps to watch the sport's greatest riders tackle the Tour de France, conquering the U.S. on the Race Across America, or mountain biking one's way through South Africa on the Cape Epic." (Publisher's note)

REVIEW: *Booklist* v110 no2 p23 S 15 2013

"World's Ultimate Cycling Races," "A Field Guide to Gettysburg: Experiencing the Battlefield Through Its History, Places, and People," and "Antarctic Peninsula: A Visitor's Guide." "These exciting, beautifully presented guides present pertinent--and inspirational--information on a wealth of places to test one's mettle on foot or bike. . . . An attractive presentation--beautiful color photos and handsomely laid-out text--partners with a wealth of information on individuals, troop movements, and skirmishes, amounting to an indispensable guide to a major event in American history. . . . This guide will inform you of the geographical and geological conditions, indigenous flora and fauna, international governance, and history of place-names and explorations that will be necessary background for a worthwhile trip."

BADARACCO, JOSEPH, 1948-. The good struggle; responsible leadership in an unforgiving world; [by] Joseph Badaracco 224 p. 2013 Harvard Business Review Press

1. Business ethics 2. Business literature 3. Decision making 4. Leadership 5. Social responsibility of business

ISBN 9781422191644 (alk. paper)

LC 2013-018295

SUMMARY: In this book on leadership, Joseph Badaracco "poses five questions thoughtful leaders need to ask: Am I really grappling with the fundamentals? What am I really accountable for? How do I make critical decisions? Do we have the right core values? Why have I chosen this life? His conclusion is that responsible leadership requires commitment that, while difficult . . . is absolutely necessary for leaders . . . to reach their personal and corporate goals." (Choice: Current Reviews for Academic Libraries)

REVIEW: *Choice* v51 no6 p1056 F 2014 T. R. Gillespie

"The Good Struggle: Responsible Leadership in an Unforgiving World. "Well-known author [Joseph] Badaracco (Harvard Business School) has written another insightful reflection on the nature of leadership. 'The Good Struggle' is practical and provocative. . . . His conclusion is that responsible leadership requires commitment that, while difficult . . . is absolutely necessary in order for leaders to develop the patience, courage, determination, and confidence that will allow them to reach their personal and corporate goals. As in his previous books . . . this volume is well researched and includes extensive endnotes and numerous examples."

BADDELEY, ELIZABETH.il. A woman in the House and Senate. See Cooper, I.

BADIOU AND THE PHILOSOPHERS; interrogating 1960s French Philosophy; 2013 Bloomsbury Academic

ISBN 9781441184856

SUMMARY: This book, edited and translated by Giuseppe Bianco and Tzuchien Tho, presents English-language translations of "a televised series in which . . . philosopher Alain Badiou . . . interviewed some of the most influential contemporary philosophers of the period, including Michel Foucault, Paul Ricoeur, Michel Henry and Michel Serres. . . . [The] interviews provide a snapshot of French philosophy in the 1960s." (Publisher's note)

REVIEW: *Choice* v51 no8 p1411-2 Ap 2014 A. D. Schrift

"Badiou and the Philosophers: Interrogating 1960s French Philosophy". "[Alain] Badiou's contributions also vary widely: only with [Michel] Henry and [Michel] Serres does he offer more than respectful and insightful questions to his interlocutor. As the editors indicate, these interviews provide a glimpse into the state of 'French philosophy' prior to the emergence of 'French theory' and poststructuralism. In that regard, they will interest those wanting to learn what was happening in French philosophy prior to the appearance of the major works of [Gilles] Deleuze, [Jacques] Derrida, [Michel] Foucault, and related philosophers."

BAER, MARC. The rise and fall of radical Westminster, 1780-1890; [by] Marc Baer xvi, 363 p. 2012 Palgrave Macmillan

1. Great Britain—Politics & government—19th century 2. Historical literature 3. Radicalism—History 4. Westminster (London, England)—History 5. Westminster (London, England)—Politics & government

ISBN 9780230349315

LC 2012-012275

SUMMARY: Written by Marc Baer, this book "explores a critical chapter in the story of Britain's transition to democracy. Utilizing the remarkably rich documentation generated by Westminster elections, Baer reveals how the most radical political space in the age of oligarchy became the most conservative and tranquil in an age of democracy." (Publisher's note)

REVIEW: *Am Hist Rev* v118 no4 p1250 O 2013 Edward Royle

"The Rise and Fall of Radical Westminster, 1780-1890." "Marc Baer seeks to explore the changing nature of politics as Britain evolved, between 1780 and 1890, toward a democratic system of representation, but he is at all times careful not to fall back on easy generalizations. . . . Within such a richly suggestive book there are nevertheless lost opportunities. . . . Local history permits depth, but comparative history lends strength to historical analysis. These cavils, though, are diminished by the rich and thought-provoking nature of this excellent study, which many students of other places and subjects will read with great profit."

REVIEW: *Choice* v50 no9 p1703 My 2013 J. R. Breihan

REVIEW: *History* v98 no331 p465-7 Jl 2013 David S. Karr

BAERT, PATRICK.ed. The politics of knowledge. See The politics of knowledge

BAEV, PAVEL K. The Arab awakening. See Pollack, K. M.

BAGGE, PETER. The Woman Rebel; The Margaret Sanger Story; [by] Peter Bagge 104 p. 2013 Farrar Straus & Giroux

1. Birth control—History 2. Feminists—United States—Biography 3. Graphic novels 4. Sanger, Margaret, 1879-1966 5. Women's rights—History

ISBN 1770461264; 9781770461260

SUMMARY: "Peter Bagge's 'Woman Rebel: The Margaret Sanger Story' is a dazzling and accessible biography of the social and political maverick, jam-packed with fact and fun. In his signature cartoony, rubbery style, Bagge presents the life of the birth-control activist, educator, nurse, mother, and protofeminist from her birth in the late nineteenth century to her death after the invention of the birth control pill." (Publisher's note)

REVIEW: *Libr J* v138 no20 p1 N 15 2013 Martha Cornog Steve Raiteri

REVIEW: *N Y Times Book Rev* p20-1 D 15 2013 Douglas Wolk

"Nowhere Men, Vol. 1: Fates Worse Than Death," "Blue Is the Warmest Color," "Woman Rebel: The Margaret Sanger Story." "Thanks to the imminent 50th anniversary of the British Invasion, we're seeing a small wave comics inspired by the Beatles, none more inventive than Eric Stephenson and Nate Bellegarde's 'Nowhere Men, Vol. 1: Fates Worse Than Death.' . . . Julie Maroh's first graphic novel, 'Blue Is the Warmest Color,' was published in France in 2010. . . . Her delicate linework and ink-wash effects illuminate the story's quiet pauses and the characters' fraught silences and wordless longing. . . . 'Woman Rebel: The Margaret Sanger Story' . . . , a biography of the birth-control activist . . . , is an unlikely but inspired pairing of author and subject."

REVIEW: *Publ Wkly* v260 no25 p34-8 Je 24 2013 HEIDI MACDONALD

BAGGETT, DAVID. Good God; the theistic foundations of morality; [by] David Baggett xv, 283 p. 2011 Oxford University Press

1. God—Proof 2. Good & evil—Religious aspects 3. Religion & ethics 4. Religious ethics 5. Religious literature

ISBN 9780199751808; 9780199751815

LC 2010-020028

SUMMARY: It was the authors' intent to demonstrate "how strides in answering the problem of evil, the Euthyphro Dilemma, and epistemic vacuity and arbitrariness challenges to theistic ethics make possible a compelling cumulative moral argument that can greatly contribute to the rational case for God's existence--and God's goodness." (Publisher's note)

REVIEW: *TLS* no5759 p28 Ag 16 2013 JOHN COTTINGHAM

"From Morality to Metaphysics: The Theistic Implications of Our Ethical Commitments," "God and Moral Obligation," and "Good God: The Theistic Foundations of Morality." "In . . . a powerful and carefully organized study, Angus Ritchie goes systematically through the main options available to the secularist, and finds them all wanting. . . . Stephen Evans's superbly lucid book . . . provides one of the best overviews of the current debate on this matter that one could hope for. . . . David Baggett and Jerry Walls . . . work carefully and conscientiously through some of the manoeuvres in the recent literature on the Euthyphro debate. . . . The overall impression left by all four books is of a rich and fertile area of research."

BAGGOTT, JIM. Farewell to Reality; How Modern Physics Has Betrayed the Search for Scientific Truth; [by] Jim Baggott 336 p. 2013 W W Norton & Co Inc

1. Dark matter (Astronomy) 2. Philosophy of physics 3. Physics literature 4. Quantum theory 5. Theoretical particle physics

ISBN 1605984728; 9781605984728

SUMMARY: Author Jim Baggott's book focuses on modern theoretical physics. "Quantum theory led scientists to create a Standard Model of physics in the mid-20th century, but that model is really an amalgam of distinct individual quantum theories necessary to describe a diverse array of forces and particles. Meanwhile, astronomical observations have revealed that 90% of our universe is made of something we can't see (dark matter)." (Publishers Weekly)

REVIEW: *Booklist* v109 no21 p9 Jl 1 2013 Bryce Christensen

REVIEW: *Choice* v51 no6 p1049 F 2014 K. D. Fisher

"Farewell to Reality: How Modern Physics Has Betrayed the Search for Scientific Truth." "A broad and detailed examination of the current state of theoretical physics. . . . a . . . comprehensive indictment. . . . The book ends with a warning about the damage done to science by a wide program of speculation untethered to experiment and observation. Whether or not one agrees with his view of contemporary theoretical physics, readers will be treated to very clear explications of the topics considered."

REVIEW: *Economist* v407 no8837 p84-5 My 25 2013

REVIEW: *Kirkus Rev* v81 no14 p12 Jl 15 2013

REVIEW: *Publ Wkly* v260 no15 p51 Ap 15 2013

BAGGOTT, JULIANNA. Burn; [by] Julianna Baggott 432 p. 2014 Grand Central Publishing, Hachette Book Group

1. FICTION—Science Fiction—Adventure 2. FICTION—Thrillers 3. Kings & rulers—Fiction 4. Power (Social sciences) 5. Science fiction

ISBN 1455502995; 9781455502998 (hardback)

LC 2013-017792

SUMMARY: This book, by Julianna Baggott, is the final installment in the post-apocalyptic Pure Trilogy. "Inside the Dome Patridge has taken his father's place as leader of the Pures. His intent had been to bring down the Dome from the inside, . . . but from his new position of power, things don't seem quite as clear. . . . Outside the Dome Pressia and Bradwell continue piecing together the clues left to them by their parents from the time before the detonations." (Publisher's note)

REVIEW: *Booklist* v110 no8 p29 D 15 2013 Michael Cart

REVIEW: *Kirkus Rev* v82 no1 p62 Ja 1 2014

"Burn". "Fantasist [Julianna] Baggott . . . wraps up her post-apocalyptic Pure Trilogy with an installment that will leave fans wanting more. Baggott is a worldbuilder; she imagines settings on a grand scale, and it's not pretty. . . . t's a hallmark of good fantasy writing that all the elements of the imagined world are at once believable and not quite like the world in which we live, and Baggott eminently succeeds. She also writes arrestingly, and if her story drags a little as she ties together the many loose ends, it's worth the longueurs."

REVIEW: *Libr J* v138 no14 p86 S 1 2013

REVIEW: *Publ Wkly* v260 no42 p36 O 21 2013

BAHNSON, FRED. Soil & sacrament; a spiritual memoir of food and faith; [by] Fred Bahnson 288 p. 2013 Simon & Schuster

1. Gardeners—Religious life 2. Gardening—Religious aspects—Christianity 3. Gardens—Religious aspects—Christianity 4. Interfaith dialogue 5. Memoirs
ISBN 9781451663303
LC 2013-007992

SUMMARY: This memoir "tells the story of how [Fred] Bahnson and people of faith all over America are re-rooting themselves in the land, reconnecting with their food and each other. . . . Through his journeys to four different faith communities—Catholic, Protestant, Pentecostal, and Jewish—Bahnson explores the connections between spiritual nourishment and the way we feed our bodies with the sensitivity, personal knowledge." (Publisher's note)

REVIEW: *Christ Century* v131 no4 p38-40 F 19 2014 Richard Gilbert

REVIEW: *Commonweal* v140 no19 p34-6 D 6 2013 Paul Elie

"Soil and Sacrament: A Spiritual Memoir of Food and Faith" and "Unapologetic". "The book, about [Fred] Bahnson's efforts to open new portals in the soil, also becomes a soil of sorts where the reader's interior life can find space and light and nourishment with which to grow. . . . I've been describing ['Unapologetic'] to people as an account of Christian belief as David Foster Wallace might have written it, but that's not quite right. It's probably closer to Julian Barnes. . . . Spufford's attention to emotion is original and remarkable. . . . Spufford asks these questions—asks them colorfully and dramatically. I would say his book, beautifully written as it is, reads like a novel, but it doesn't. It is unapologetically not a fiction."

REVIEW: *Kirkus Rev* v81 no12 p40 Je 15 2013

REVIEW: *Publ Wkly* v260 no27 p84 Jl 8 2013

BAHR, ARTHUR. Fragments and assemblages; forming compilations of medieval London; [by] Arthur Bahr x, 285 p. 2013 University of Chicago Press
1. English literature—Middle English, 1100-1500—History and criticism 2. English literature—Middle English, 1100-1500—Manuscripts 3. Historical literature 4. Manuscripts, Medieval—England—London
ISBN 9780226924915 (cloth)
LC 2012-027389

SUMMARY: "In this study of what he terms the poetics of assemblage, Arthur Bahr examines various kinds of relationship between form and meaning in a group of works compiled in and around London over the course of the fourteenth century. . . . He considers the significance of his chosen assemblages not only from the viewpoint of their earliest readers but also as historical artefacts with meanings liable to reformulation over time." (Times Literary Supplement)

REVIEW: *TLS* no5755 p26 Jl 19 2013 JULIA BOFFEY

"Fragments and Assemblages: Forming Compilations of Medieval London." "[Arthur] Bahr's analysis of the collocation of items in the manuscripts he examines is directed by an overarching interest in tensions between city and crown, especially between mercantile and knightly factions whose distinctness he sees as part of a wider urban tendency to social fragmentation. . . . Bahr is not especially interested in the textual relationships of the works he explores, nor indeed in any wider contextualizing of his selected manuscripts. But his attractively written, often witty book, informed by a wide range of scholarship, elegantly demonstrates one way of using material form in the service of critical analysis."

BAILEY, BLAKE. Farther and Wilder; the lost weekends and literary dreams of Charles Jackson; [by] Blake Bailey 496 p. 2013 Alfred A. Knopf
1. Alcoholics—Biography 2. Authors—Biography 3. Authors, American—Biography 4. Biographies
ISBN 030727358X (hardcover); 9780307273581 (hardcover); 9780307475527 (paperback); 9780307962201 (ebook)
LC 2012-036685

SUMMARY: This biography, by Blake Bailey, follows "Charles Jackson, . . . a writer whose life and work encapsulated what it meant to be an addict and a closeted gay man in mid-century America, and what one had to do with the other. Charles Jackson . . . was published widely . . . and knew everyone from Judy Garland and Billy Wilder. . . . Yet he ultimately found it nearly impossible to write without the stimulus of pills or alcohol and felt his devotion to his work was worth the price." (Publisher's note)

REVIEW: *Bookforum* v20 no1 p4 Ap/My 2013 CHOIRE SICHA

REVIEW: *Booklist* v109 no12 p17 F 15 2013 Ray Olson

REVIEW: *Choice* v51 no1 p73-4 S 2013 R. Blackwood

"Farther & Wilder: The Lost Weekends and Literary Dreams of Charles Jackson." "'Farther and Wilder' offers an exhaustive, thoroughly documented literary study and biography of Charles Jackson, author of 'The Lost Weekend'--a successful novel about an alcoholic, and an even better-known motion picture directed by Billy Wilder. [Author Blake] Bailey . . . explores how Jackson's gifts as a writer were usually squandered in his maddening lifestyle. . . . Bailey's encyclopedic knowledge of the publications and unpublished works of Jackson and his almost day-by-day retelling of periods in Jackson's life are admirable."

REVIEW: *Kirkus Rev* v81 no2 p284 Ja 15 2013

REVIEW: *Libr J* v138 no3 p99-100 F 15 2013 William Gargan

REVIEW: *N Y Times Book Rev* p26 Ap 28 2013

REVIEW: *N Y Times Book Rev* p14 Ap 21 2013 DONNA RIFKIND

REVIEW: *New Yorker* v89 no14 p117 My 20 2013

REVIEW: *Publ Wkly* v260 no4 p169 Ja 28 2013

BAILEY, BLAKE. The Splendid Things We Planned; A Family Portrait; [by] Blake Bailey 288 p. 2014 W.W. Norton & Co. Inc
1. Alcoholism 2. Authors, American—Biography 3. Biographers—United States—Biography 4. Memoirs 5. Mental illness 6. Schizophrenia
ISBN 0393239578; 9780393239577
LC 2013-039720

SUMMARY: In this book, "biographer [Blake] Bailey tells the story of his own life by chronicling his brother Scott's alcoholism and drug addiction, which causes him to descend into violence and madness. Told in chronological order, starting with the marriage of his straight-laced lawyer father to his bohemian, German-immigrant mother, Bailey's story captures the contradictions and tensions that simmer just below the surface of the family, as they try to live a normal suburban life in Oklahoma." (Publishers Weekly)

REVIEW: *Booklist* v110 no9/10 p26 Ja 1 2014 Brendan Driscoll

REVIEW: *Kirkus Rev* v81 no24 p69 D 15 2013

"The Splendid Things We Planned: A Family Portrait". "An award-winning biographer reveals his troubled past . . . [in a] bleak, repetitious memoir. . . . Bailey chronicles Scott's descent, but also notes that he, too, was an alcoholic. Scott, however, supplemented alcohol with various other drugs, including heroin. . . . Some of Scott's escapades seem like plots from a [John] Cheever story. . . . . Bailey gives no evidence of his or his brother's splendid plans, only decades of depression, isolation and insidious self-absorption."

REVIEW: *Libr J* v139 no4 p88 Mr 1 2014 Patrick A. Smith

REVIEW: *N Y Times Book Rev* p17 Mr 9 2014 DAVE ITZKOFF

REVIEW: *New York Times* v163 no56422 pC1-4 F 24 2014 JANET MASLIN

REVIEW: *New Yorker* v90 no10 p77-1 Ap 28 2014

"The Splendid Things We Planned: A Family Portrait." "In this captivating memoir about his troubled family in Oklahoma, the author recounts his parents' failings and his own. But the dark heart of the book is his brother Scott—mentally unstable, drug-addicted, and often dangerous—whose story is harrowing. After one of many blowups, Bailey's father kicks Scott out of the house. . . . Bailey maintains a lacerating tone, and examines with the coolness of a detective the staggering things that we can do to the people we love."

REVIEW: *Publ Wkly* v260 no48 p41 N 25 2013

BAILEY, JOANNE. Parenting in England, 1760-1830; emotion, identity, and generation; [by] Joanne Bailey 304 p. 2012 Oxford University Press

1. Great Britain—Social conditions—History 2. Great Britain—Social life & customs—History 3. Historical literature 4. Parenting—Great Britain—History—18th century 5. Parenting—Great Britain—History—19th century

ISBN 0199565198 (hbk.); 9780199565191 (hbk.)

LC 2012-930322

SUMMARY: This book "sets out to document the 'ideals, representations and experiences' . . . of parenting between 1760 and 1830. Hence it poses questions on how men and women felt and thought about parenthood during these years; on their memories of their own parents; and on the ways in which they interacted with contemporary understandings of parenthood." (English Historical Review)

REVIEW: *Am Hist Rev* v118 no3 p928-9 Je 2013 H. R. French

REVIEW: *Choice* v50 no5 p950 Ja 2013 E. J. Jenkins

REVIEW: *Engl Hist Rev* v129 no536 p224-6 F 2014 Colin Heywood

"Parenting in England, 1760-1830: Emotion, Identity, and Generation". "It proposes a judicious balance between continuity and change, with the biological bonds involved in parenting pointing to the former, the construction of maternal and paternal identities to the latter. What is new in the approach to this work are insights from recent developments in the study of the past, notably a growing interest in the history of emotions and 'emotionology', subjectivities, memory, the body, and materiality. . . . She has assembled an impressive array of primary sources to do so. . . . In sum, this is an excellent contribution to our knowledge of parent–child relations, which should appeal to students as well as specialist historians of childhood."

REVIEW: *Hist Today* v63 no7 p58 Jl 2013 PAT THANE

REVIEW: *History* v98 no331 p459-61 Jl 2013 Hannah Newton

BAILEY, KEVIN M. Billion-dollar fish; the untold story of Alaska pollock; [by] Kevin M. Bailey 288 p. 2013 University of Chicago Press

1. Fishing—Economic aspects 2. Natural history literature 3. Overfishing 4. Pollock fisheries—History—20th century 5. Walleye pollock—Effect of fishing on

ISBN 022602234X; 9780226022345 (cloth : alkaline paper)

LC 2012-044795

SUMMARY: This book, by Kevin M. Bailey, presents a "natural history of Alaska pollock. Crucial to understanding the pollock fishery, he shows, is recognizing what aspects of its natural history make pollock so very desirable to fish, while at the same time making it resilient, yet highly vulnerable to overfishing. Bailey delves into the science, politics, and economics surrounding Alaska pollock in the Bering Sea." (Publisher's note)

REVIEW: *Booklist* v109 no16 p9 Ap 15 2013 Mark Knoblauch

REVIEW: *Choice* v51 no3 p490 N 2013 F. T. Manheim

REVIEW: *Science* v341 no6144 p345-6 Jl 26 2013 Elizabeth Lester

REVIEW: *TLS* no5767 p28 O 11 2013 RICHARD SHELTON

"Billion-Dollar Fish: The Untold Story of the Alaska Pollock." "The background to this economic and ecological 'tragedy of the commons' and the remaining problems suffered by some of the national home water fisheries are carefully explored by [Kevin M.] Bailey. He paints a revealing picture of the colourful personalities at sea and ashore whose economic imperatives raised rates of fishing mortality to levels which, experience was to show, made little long-term biological or even economic sense. How the American fishery authorities met the management challenge is well covered in 'Billion-Dollar Fish'."

BAILEY, MARTHA J.ed. Legacies of the War on Poverty. See Legacies of the War on Poverty

BAILEY, PAUL. The Prince's Boy; [by] Paul Bailey 160 p. 2014 St. Martin's Press

1. Bildungsromans 2. Gay men—Fiction 3. Paris (France)—Fiction 4. Romanians—France 5. Young gay men

ISBN 1620407191; 9781620407196

SUMMARY: In this novel by Paul Bailey' "In May 1927, nineteen-year-old Dinu Grigorescu, a skinny boy with literary ambitions, is newly arrived in Paris. He has been sent from Bucharest, the city of his childhood, by his wealthy father to embark upon a bohemian adventure and relish the unique pleasures of Parisian life." (Publisher's note)

REVIEW: *Kirkus Rev* v82 no16 p83 Ag 15 2014

REVIEW: *Libr J* v139 no11 p82 Je 15 2014 Barbara Love

REVIEW: *New Statesman* v143 no5205 p49 Ap 11 2014 Leo Robson

REVIEW: *Publ Wkly* v261 no28 p45-6 Jl 14 2014

REVIEW: *TLS* no5795 p20-1 Ap 25 2014 DAVID COLLARD

"The Prince's Boy" and "A Room In Chelsea Square." "Paul Bailey's slim novella 'The Prince's Boy' is set in the summer of 1927 when Dinu Grigorescu, a callow nineteen-year old, arrives in Paris from Bucharest in search of adventure and literary fame. . . . Bailey opts throughout for a style both formal and florid. . . . This might work well on the stage but it wears thin on the page, however true it may be to the period, and however expertly done. . . . Michael Nelson's 'A Room in Chelsea Square' is an intermittently amusing roman-à-clef first published, anonymously, in 1958. . . . 'A Room in Chelsea Square' has value as a portrait of a transitional moment in our culture."

BAIR, JULENE. The Ogallala road; a memoir of love and reckoning; [by] Julene Bair 288 p. 2014 Viking

1. Agricultural conservation—Kansas 2. Agriculture—Environmental aspects—Kansas 3. Family farms—Kansas 4. Farm life—Kansas

ISBN 0670786047; 9780670786046 (hardback)

LC 2013-036969

SUMMARY: In this memoir by Julene Bair, "nostalgia for the family farm in arid western Kansas vies with a deep consternation about the draining of the Ogallala Aquifer by crop irrigation." The book focuses on the "fateful events in the year preceding the reluctant, yet seemingly inevitable, selling of Bair's parents' farm in 2006: then in her early 50s, Bair was raising her teenaged son, Jake, by herself in Laramie, Wyo." (Publishers Weekly)

REVIEW: *Booklist* v110 no13 p8 Mr 1 2014 Colleen Mondor

"The Ogallala Road: A Memoir of Love and Reckoning." "In this thoughtful consideration of life at a crossroads, [Julene] Bair tackles questions about single parenthood, romance, and the monumental task of determining the future of the family farm. . . . Bair's measured approach to her family's ultimate decision about the farm provides readers in a nonrural setting with a thoughtful look into America's heartland. Book groups should find much to discuss here, from love to family to the big questions we all must face about how we live now."

REVIEW: *Kirkus Rev* v82 no2 p75 Ja 15 2014

REVIEW: *N Y Times Book Rev* p10 Ap 27 2014 MARK BITTMAN

REVIEW: *Publ Wkly* v260 no49 p70 D 2 2013

REVIEW: *World Lit Today* v88 no3/4 p118-9 My-Ag 2014 Nancy Cook

BAJAJ, VARSHA. Abby Spencer Goes to Bollywood; [by] Varsha Bajaj 256 p. 2014 Albert Whitman & Co

1. Fathers & daughters—Fiction 2. India—Fiction 3. Motion picture actors & actresses—Fiction 4. Motion picture industry—India—Mumbai 5. Psychological fiction

ISBN 0807563633; 9780807563632

SUMMARY: In this book, "thirteen-year-old Abby Spencer learns that the father she's never met is a Bollywood superstar and travels from Houston to Mumbai to meet him. . . ." Besides the establishment of . . . Abby's mostly smooth relationship with Kumar's household and entourage, the rest of the story involves Abby's reaction to India, her nascent romantic relationship with handsome Shaan and her difficulty remaining mum about the fact that she's Kumar's daughter." (Kirkus Reviews)

REVIEW: *Bull Cent Child Books* v67 no8 p394 Ap 2014 A. A.

REVIEW: *Kirkus Rev* v82 no3 p202 F 1 2014

"Abby Spencer Goes to Bollywood". "Unfortunately, nice is great in a girlfriend, but for characters in a novel, spice is necessary, and there's not enough of it in [Varsha] Bajaj's pleasant but bland first-person cross-cultural tale. Nevertheless, readers will want for Abby what she wants for herself—to find her place in her two families—and should be touched and satisfied by the story's ending. Culturally intriguing but dramatically dry, this story showcases the glamour and grit of Mumbai and gives readers an entertaining glimpse of backstage Bollywood."

REVIEW: *Publ Wkly* v261 no2 p67 Ja 13 2014

REVIEW: *SLJ* v60 no4 p139 Ap 2014 Leigh Collazo

REVIEW: *Voice of Youth Advocates* v36 no6 p54 F 2014 Kim Carter

BAJNOK, BÉLA. An invitation to abstract mathematics; [by] Béla Bajnok 432 p. 2013 Springer

1. Abstract algebra 2. Mathematical literature 3. Problem solving 4. Symbolic & mathematical logic 5. Textbooks

ISBN 9781461466352

LC 2013-935711

SUMMARY: "This undergraduate textbook is intended primarily for a transition course into higher mathematics, although it is written with a broader audience in mind. The heart and soul of this book is problem solving, where each problem is carefully chosen to clarify a concept, demonstrate a technique, or to enthuse. The exercises require relatively extensive arguments, creative approaches, or both, thus providing motivation for the reader. " (Publisher's note)

REVIEW: *Choice* v51 no5 p876-7 Ja 2014 D. S. Larson

"An Invitation to Abstract Mathematics" "The book . . . includes very complete and rigorous treatments of number systems and the cardinality of sets as well as sections devoted to famous problems and mathematical conjectures. . . . [An] extensive collection of interesting and imaginative problems [is] contained within the text. The author claims that the approximately 280 problems presented are the 'heart and soul' of the book. That is a difficult claim with which to argue. Few routine exercises make an appearance. The bulk of the problems are substantial and aimed at getting the reader to think mathematically. Students may find the problems taxing, but any reader able to complete this work and its problems will be suitably prepared for further studies in mathematics."

BAK, HANS.ed. The long voyage. See The long voyage

BAKER, JOSIAH R. Religion, politics, and polarization. See D'Antonio, W. V.

BAKER, KYLE.il. The Fifth Beatle. See Tiwary, V.

BAKER, NICHOLSON, 1957-. House of holes; a book of raunch; [by] Nicholson Baker 262 2011 Simon & Schuster
1. Erotic stories 2. Fantasies 3. Imaginary places 4. Sex 5. Speculative fiction
ISBN 978-1-4391-8951-1; 1-4391-8951-X
LC 2010--47433

SUMMARY: In this book, author Nicholson Baker "uses an alternative reality, the house of holes, as a playground of latent desires in which characters experience their most erotic fantasies. The characters travel to this place, drawn with a touch of the magical, through portals such as washing machines and wooden sculptures. A world seemingly constructed from sexual energy, the house of holes encourages individuals to indulge rather than repress their sexual desire." (Library Journal)

REVIEW: *Harper's Magazine* v325 no1947 p74-8 Ag 2012

REVIEW: *London Rev Books* v33 no21 p21-2 N 3 2011 Christopher Tayler

REVIEW: *N Y Rev Books* v60 no18 p47-50 N 21 2013 Michael Dirda
"Traveling Sprinkler," "The Way the World Works: Essays," and "House of Holes: A Book of Raunch." "While Nicholson Baker may have started out as a somewhat lighthearted literary microscopist, genially teasing out the overlooked yet fetching particularities of the world around us . . . over the years he's increasingly assumed a far more iconoclastic and contentious presence on the cultural scene. . . . His latest novel, 'Traveling Sprinkler,' isn't just a further report from the sad sack poet Paul Chowder . . . it's also a political jeremiad and a plea for what the book calls 'loving-kindness.' . . . He has continued to criticize the technocratic mind-set, notably in the scathing 'Truckin' for the Future,' included in his 2012 essay collection 'The Way the World Works'. . . . 'House of Holes' exults throughout in a spring-like air of innocence and glad animal spirits."

REVIEW: *New Yorker* v87 no35 p82-4 N 7 2011 Joan Acocella

BAKER, NICHOLSON, 1957-. Traveling Sprinkler; A Novel; [by] Nicholson Baker 288 p. 2013 Blue Rider Press
1. Humorous stories 2. Man-woman relationships—Fiction 3. Poets—Fiction 4. Quakers—Fiction 5. Singer-songwriters
ISBN 0399160965; 9780399160967 (hardcover)
LC 2013-019296

SUMMARY: This book, by Nicholson Baker, follows the protagonist of his previous novel, "The Anthologist." "Although Paul Chowder's life is not exactly coming apart, it's also not what it could be. His girlfriend, Roz, has taken up with someone else, he's become less committed to writing poetry, and to make a little extra money, he shrink-wraps boats. . . . On the other hand, he enjoys going to Quaker meetings, and he's really getting into music." (Kirkus Reviews)

REVIEW: *Booklist* v109 no22 p33 Ag 1 2013 Donna Seaman

REVIEW: *Kirkus Rev* p3 Ag 15 2013 Fall Preview

REVIEW: *Kirkus Rev* p5 N 15 2013 Best Books

REVIEW: *Kirkus Rev* v81 no14 p325 Jl 15 2013

REVIEW: *Libr J* v138 no7 p56 Ap 15 2013 Barbara Hoffert

REVIEW: *Libr J* v139 no3 p59 F 15 2014 Joanna Burkhardt

REVIEW: *N Y Rev Books* v60 no18 p47-50 N 21 2013 Michael Dirda
"Traveling Sprinkler," "The Way the World Works: Essays," and "House of Holes: A Book of Raunch." "While Nicholson Baker may have started out as a somewhat lighthearted literary microscopist, genially teasing out the overlooked yet fetching particularities of the world around us . . . over the years he's increasingly assumed a far more iconoclastic and contentious presence on the cultural scene. . . . His latest novel, 'Traveling Sprinkler,' isn't just a further report from the sad sack poet Paul Chowder . . . it's also a political jeremiad and a plea for what the book calls 'loving-kindness.' . . . He has continued to criticize the technocratic mind-set, notably in the scathing 'Truckin' for the Future,' included in his 2012 essay collection 'The Way the World Works'. . . . 'House of Holes' exults throughout in a spring-like air of innocence and glad animal spirits."

REVIEW: *N Y Times Book Rev* p23 O 6 2013 JONATHAN MILES
"Traveling Sprinkler." "[Paul] Chowder is back, in the awkwardly titled 'Traveling Sprinkler,' but without nearly so much to say. . . . He does what characters tend to do, often to exquisitely sublime effect, in Nicholson Baker novels: not much. . . . It would be unjust to bemoan poetry's absence; . . . the more palpable loss is tonal: Chowder's authority. . . . This demotion manifests itself in Baker's language, which is less alert and less frisky than we've come to expect from him. . . . The lessons Chowder transmits drift toward the elementary , , , and, as with all students, the regurgitative. . . . 'Traveling Sprinkler' can be read as a curious coming-of-age novel. And a funny, abundantly textured, warmhearted one, at that."

REVIEW: *New York Times* v162 no56255 pC1-8 S 10 2013 DWIGHT GARNER

REVIEW: *New Yorker* v89 no30 p1 S 30 2013
"Traveling Sprinkler," "Night Film," and "Jane Austen's England." " This tender novel finds Paul Chowder, the poet narrator of [Nicholson] Baker's previous novel 'The Anthologist,' driving around Portsmouth, New Hampshire, and speaking into a handheld recorder. . . .[Marisha] Pessl has fun elaborating the backstory . . . but the foreground isn't always sufficiently compelling. The effect is that of a finely wrought diorama, brilliantly detailed but static. . . . This enjoyable history enlarges on themes that permeate Austen's evocations of the social customs of early-nineteenth-century England."

REVIEW: *Publ Wkly* v260 no29 p36-7 Jl 22 2013

BAKER, PETER. Days of fire; Bush and Cheney in the White House; [by] Peter Baker 816 p. 2013 Doubleday
1. BIOGRAPHY & AUTOBIOGRAPHY—Presidents & Heads of State 2. HISTORY—United States—21st Century 3. Historical literature 4. POLITICAL SCIENCE—Government—Executive Branch
ISBN 0385525184; 9780385525183 (hardback)
LC 2013-018745

SUMMARY: Author Peter Baker presents a "study of the inner workings, conflicts, and critical policy decisions made during the eight years of [George W.] Bush and [Dick] Cheney['s] governance. Baker sees [Bush] as a man trapped by events, whose hopes for a more 'modest' foreign policy and a 'compassionate conservatism' domestic affairs were frustrated by the vast shadows cast by 9/11." (Booklist)

REVIEW: *Booklist* v110 no2 p18 S 15 2013 Jay Freeman

REVIEW: *Commentary* v136 no5 p37-9 D 2013 ABE GREENWALD

REVIEW: *Kirkus Rev* v81 no19 p158 O 1 2013

REVIEW: *Libr J* v139 no2 p45 F 1 2014 Kelly Sinclair

REVIEW: *N Y Times Book Rev* p12 O 20 2013 DAVID FRUM

"Days of Fire: Bush and Cheney in the White House." "The story of those eight years would seem far too vast to contain inside a single volume. Yet here that volume is. Peter Baker . . . neither accuses nor excuses. He writes with a measure and balance that seem transported backward in time from some more dispassionate future. Yet 'Days of Fire' is not a dispassionate book. Its mood might rather be described as poignant: sympathetic to its subjects, generous to their accomplishments and extenuating none of their errors. . . . Baker's book is informed by remarkable access to its main characters. . . . Yet 'Days of Fire' is something more than the reporter's 'first rough draft of history'."

REVIEW: *New York Times* v163 no56297 pC4 O 22 2013 JIM KELLY

"Days of Fire: Bush and Cheney in the White House." "Mr. [Peter] Baker demolishes any lingering myth that Mr. [Dick] Cheney engineered his own selection for what he once called 'a cruddy job'. . . . Mr. Baker's main thesis is not exactly groundbreaking: that Mr. [George W.] Bush and Mr. Cheney created the most influential White Hosue partnership since Richard M. Nixon and Henry A. Kissinger. . . . Filled with enlivening detail and judicious analysis, 'Days of Fire' is the most reliable, comprehensive history of the Bush years yet."

BAKER, PETER.ed. The selected letters of Robert Creeley. See The selected letters of Robert Creeley

BAKER, S. JOSEPHINE (SARA JOSEPHINE), 1873-1945. Fighting for life; [by] S. Josephine (Sara Josephine) Baker 264 p. 2013 New York Review Books

1. Autobiographies 2. Child Mortality—history—New York City 3. Child Welfare—history—New York City 4. History, 19th Century—New York City 5. History, 20th Century—New York City 6. Physicians—New York City—Autobiography 7. Public Health—history—New York City

ISBN 9781590177068 (paperback : alk. paper)

LC 2013-020026

SUMMARY: This book presents an autobiography of "public health crusader Dr. S. Josephine Baker. . . . By the time she retired in 1923, Baker was famous worldwide for saving the lives of 90,000 children. The programs she developed, many still in use today, have saved the lives of millions more. She fought for women's suffrage, toured Russia in the 1930s, and captured 'Typhoid' Mary Mallon, twice." (Publisher's note)

REVIEW: *New York Times* v163 no56304 pD6 O 29 2013 ABIGAIL ZUGER

"Fighting For Life." "Josephine Baker was a wise woman, a graceful writer and a visionary whose insights remain intensely relevant today. . . . Her just-reissued 1939 autobiography proves to be one of those magical books that reaches effortlessly through time, as engaging and as thought-provoking as if it were written now. . . . Baker was a creature of her time when it came to some prejudices against the ethnic groups inhabiting the city's tenements. Otherwise, especially in her thoughtful reflections on women's rights (they are hard won, then often undervalued), she speaks with a startlingly modern voice."

BAKER, SHANNON. Broken trust; a Nora Abbott mystery; [by] Shannon Baker 360 p. 2014 Midnight Ink

1. Detective & mystery stories 2. Embezzlement investigation—Fiction 3. Hopi indians—Fiction 4. Murder—Investigation—Fiction 5. Women environmentalists—Fiction

ISBN 9780738734255

LC 2013-027484

SUMMARY: In this book, part of Shannon Baker's Nora Abbott Mysteries series, "the heroine finds a new job that appears safer than her previous stint running a ski resort: she becomes the financial director for the Living Earth Trust, a Boulder, Colo.–based nonprofit. So why is she having ominous visions of a 'Kachina,' a spirit from Hopi folklore? And what happened to the previous financial director?" (Publishers Weekly)

REVIEW: *Kirkus Rev* v82 no3 p262 F 1 2014

"Broken Trust". "While Nora tries to make sense of Sylvia's project and the role of a father-and-son team from Ecuador, she has to keep haunting memories, her overbearing mother, and a handsome, overprotective rancher at arm's length. A Hopi friend is receiving warnings from a man who supposedly died 150 years ago. Will they come too late to save Nora? No wonder the hapless heroine is so overwhelmed that she makes decisions she knows are bad: Baker throws her into a vortex of corporate greed, Hopi mythology, speculative science, exaggerated characters, muddled flashbacks and one preposterous incident after another. Overstuffed."

REVIEW: *Publ Wkly* v261 no4 p173 Ja 27 2014

BAKKER, GERBRAND. Ten white geese; a novel; [by] Gerbrand Bakker 240 p. 2012 Penguin Books

1. Dickinson, Emily, 1830-1886 2. Dutch—Wales—Fiction 3. Psychological fiction 4. Terminally ill—Fiction 5. Translators

ISBN 0143122673 (paperback); 9780143122678 (paperback)

LC 2012-034808

SUMMARY: This novel from Gerbrand Bakker "begins with an unnamed middle-aged woman settling into a remote farmhouse in Wales. She is a professor of translation and an Emily Dickinson scholar who has recently had an affair with one of her students, lost her job, and left her husband. It becomes clear as well that she has a serious, perhaps terminal, illness. During the novel, she becomes increasingly troubled and attempts to translate one of Dickinson's most famous poems about death." (Library Journal)

REVIEW: *Kirkus Rev* v81 no4 p305 F 15 2013

REVIEW: *Libr J* v138 no7 p71 Ap 15 2013 Patrick Sullivan

REVIEW: *N Y Rev Books* v60 no13 p40-1 Ag 15 2013 Christopher Benfey

"Ten White Geese." "Gerbrand Baker's evocative and unsettling short novel . . . has the laconic texture and angular plotting of a thriller, with shifting points of view that keep the reader guessing about what surprise is lurking around the corner. . . . The decision of the estimable translator, David Colmer, to change the title from 'The Detour' to the faintly japoniste-sounding Ten White Geese confers added weight and menace to the vanishing geese, as though the solution to that mystery . . . might also reveal the many other things we want to know about the enigmatic Emilie. . . . But it becomes increasingly clear that Bakker's interests lie elsewhere, and involve deeper, more existential mysteries."

REVIEW: *New Yorker* v89 no4 p75 Mr 11 2013

REVIEW: *Publ Wkly* v260 no6 p2 F 11 2013

REVIEW: *World Lit Today* v87 no3 p59-79 My/Je 2013

BALCERZAK, SCOTT. Buffoon men; classic Hollywood comedians and queered masculinity; [by] Scott Balcerzak x, 258 p. 2013 Wayne State University Press

1. Comedy films—United States—History and criticism 2. Masculinity in motion pictures 3. Motion picture literature 4. Motion pictures—Social aspects—United States 5. Queer theory

ISBN 9780814339657 (pbk. : alk. paper)

LC 2013-006169

SUMMARY: In this book, "while examining the buffoonish masculinity of W. C. Fields, Eddie Cantor, [and] Jack Benny . . . the author re-historicizes these figures within the gender history of the 20th century and demonstrates how they reacted to masculine ideals. [Scott] Balcerzak focuses on the early sound period. . . . As national anxiety challenged concepts of traditional masculinity, these comedians challenged hegemonic masculinity." (Choice: Current Reviews for Academic Libraries)

REVIEW: *Choice* v51 no6 p1011-2 F 2014 G. R. Butters Jr.

"Buffoon Men: Classic Hollywood Comedians and Queered Masculinity.""The notion of 'queerness' . . . has gone from meaning 'gay' to 'non-normative' to simply 'different,' and this is problematic when the radical origin of the term loses all its meaning. Unfortunately, [Scott] Balcerzak . . . also falls into this trap. Still, this well-written, thought-provoking book is on the cutting edge of cinematic masculinity studies. . . . Balcerzak's analyses and close readings are rich and nuanced, his use of theory is substantial though never unreadable, and his perceptions about contemporary on-screen comedians are dynamic. Comedy is one of the least written about film genres, and Balcerzak's work serves as a landmark in the field."

BALDACCI, DAVID. The finisher; [by] David Baldacci 512 p. 2014 Scholastic Press

1. Brothers & sisters—Fiction 2. Fantasy fiction 3. Forests & forestry—Fiction 4. Missing persons—Fiction 5. Secrecy—Fiction

ISBN 0545652200; 9780545652209 (jacketed hardcover)

LC 2013-951103

SUMMARY: In this book, by David Baldacci, "fourteen-year-old Vega Jane works as a 'Finisher,' creating goods she'll never be able to afford and leading a hardscrabble life with her little brother. Like all other 'Wugmorts,' they have never left the town of Wormwood, trapped there by the deadly Quag surrounding it. When Vega discovers a map leading through the Quag, she suspects there's more to Wormwood than believed." (Publishers Weekly)

REVIEW: *Booklist* v110 no12 p73 F 15 2014 Ilene Cooper

"The Finisher." "What happens when an international best-selling crime novelist tries his hand at a youth fantasy? Well, in this case, success. [David] Baldacci, best known for writing thrillers, also has a talent for creating magical worlds. . . . Baldacci gets several things just right. He offers readers a smart, tough heroine worth rooting for; provides enough hints of a mysterious backstory to keep them wondering; and builds each chapter to a cliff-hanger that pushes them to turn the page. There is also head-spinning action, which is sometimes a bit too repetitious. How often can Vega be chased by a monster and run faster than she has ever run in her life? The ending is predictable, but it leads seamlessly into the next book, where, perhaps, some of Vega's answers await."

REVIEW: *Bull Cent Child Books* v67 no8 p395 Ap 2014 A. S.

"The Finisher". "Vega Jane is an angry teen, and the reader may be able to spot that she is an occasionally unreliable narrator, commenting from her assumptions rather than her observations. This insider perspective heightens sympathy for the beleaguered protagonist while also offering further glimpses into what drives characters in the carefully built world [David] Baldacci has created. The book's choice to overrely on 'wug' as a wordstem is distracting, but this is a minor issue in what is otherwise a clever, intriguing, and refreshingly different world populated with flawed characters who respond to their environment with a unique set of moral guidelines, just as they should given their sheltered, intensely controlled lives."

REVIEW: *Kirkus Rev* v82 no4 p244 F 15 2014

REVIEW: *Publ Wkly* v261 no21 p56 My 26 2014

REVIEW: *SLJ* v60 no6 p62 Je 2014 Michaela Schied

REVIEW: *Voice of Youth Advocates* v37 no2 p70 Je 2014 Jan Chapman

BALDWIN, KATHLEEN.tr. Zibaldone. See Leopardi, G.

BALDWIN, LEWIS V.ed. In an Inescapable Network of Mutuality. See In an Inescapable Network of Mutuality

BALL, EDWARD. The inventor and the tycoon; a Gilded Age murder and the birth of moving pictures; xiv, 447 p. 2013 Doubleday

1. Businesspeople—California—Biography 2. Cinematographers—California—Biography 3. Cinematography—United States—History 4. Motion pictures—United States—History 5. Trials (Murder)—California—San Francisco

ISBN 9780385525756 (hardcover: alk. paper); 9780385535496 (electronic); 9780767929400 (pbk.)

LC 2012-019977

SUMMARY: This book by Edward Ball "interweaves [Eadweard] Muybridge's quest to unlock the secrets of motion through photography, an obsessive murder plot, and the peculiar partnership of an eccentric inventor and a driven entrepreneur. . . The artist and inventor Muybridge was also a murderer who killed coolly and meticulously, and his trial is one of the early instances of a media sensation. His patron was railroad tycoon (and former California governor) Leland Stanford." (Publisher's note)

REVIEW: *N Y Times Book Rev* p82 D 8 2013 IHSAN

TAYLOR

"The Inventor and the Tycoon: The Murderer Eadweard Muybridge, the Entrepreneur Leland Stanford, and the Birth of Moving Pictures," "Middle C," and "Magnificence." "[Author Edward] Ball weaves an account of . . . crime . . into the larger story of Muybridge's complicated relationship with his patron, the railroad magnate Leland Stanford. . . . [Author William H.] Gass's unquiet bildungsroman about a family of Austrian emigrants . . . is arranged in a variety of rhythms, forms and tones. . . . A new widow inherits a peculiar Southern California estate in the final installment of [author Lydia] Millet's lyrical trilogy."

BALL, HOWARD, 1937-. At liberty to die; the battle for death with dignity in America; [by] Howard Ball ix, 229 p. 2012 New York University Press

1. Assisted suicide 2. Assisted suicide—Law and legislation—United States 3. Euthanasia—Law and legislation—United States 4. Right to die—Law and legislation—United States 5. Social science literature

ISBN 081474527X (ebook); 0814769756 (ebook); 0814791042 (alk. paper); 9780814745274 (ebook); 9780814769751 (ebook); 9780814791042 (alk. paper)

LC 2011-052258

SUMMARY: In this book, political scientist Howard Ball offers a "legal history of the right to die in America. He starts with the case of Nancy Cruzan, who was left in a persistent vegetative state after a car accident, and the Supreme Court's ruling that the state had the right to require 'clear and convincing evidence' of Cruzan's intentions before removing her from life support. He then traces battles to legalize physician-assisted death (PAD) in Oregon, Washington State, Montana, Vermont, and Hawaii." (Library Journal)

REVIEW: *Choice* v50 no5 p964 Ja 2013 J. S. Taylor

REVIEW: *Contemp Sociol* v43 no2 p191-2 Mr 2014 Amy C. Krull

"At Liberty to Die: The Battle for Death With Dignity in America". "Howard Ball has written a good reference book about the efforts in the United States to legalize physician-assisted death. . . . While the description of historical events is greatly detailed, his analysis is limited and simplified to terms of conservative versus liberal politics and the disproportionate spending by the Catholic Church in anti-PAD legislative efforts. . . . The strength of this text is its thoroughness of description. To the individual who is new to understanding the case law and legislative action around the PAD issue, this text could prove invaluable in establishing one's foundation of knowledge about this issue."

REVIEW: *Libr J* v137 no12 p93 Jl 1 2012 Aaron Klink

REVIEW: *Polit Sci Q (Wiley-Blackwell)* v128 no4 p765-6 Wint 2013/2014 JAMES M. HOEFLER

BALL, JESSE, 1978-. Silence once begun; [by] Jesse Ball 256 p. 2013 Pantheon Books

1. Americans—Japan—Fiction 2. Crime—Fiction 3. Journalists—Fiction 4. Murder—Investigation—Fiction 5. Secrets—Fiction

ISBN 9780307908483

LC 2013-005948

SUMMARY: In this novel by Jesse Ball, "Over the course of several months, eight people vanish from their homes in the same Japanese town, a single playing card found on each door. . . . Our narrator, a journalist named Jesse Ball, is grappling with mysteries of his own when he becomes fascinated by the case. . . .As Ball interviews Sotatsu's family, friends, and jailers, he uncovers a complex story of heartbreak, deceit, honor, and chance." (Publisher's note)

REVIEW: *Booklist* v110 no9/10 p46 Ja 1 2014 Donna Seaman

REVIEW: *Kirkus Rev* v81 no21 p72 N 1 2013

REVIEW: *N Y Times Book Rev* p12 Mr 23 2014 HELEN OYEYEMI

"Silence Once Begun." "In Jesse Ball's absorbing, finely wrought fourth novel, 'Silence Once Begun,' a journalist also named Jesse Ball tells the story of a thread salesman who makes a wager with two people in a bar. Upon losing that wager, he signs an extremely detailed confession to a crime he didn't commit—the kidnapping of eight people from a Japanese town called Narito over the course of four months. . . . In this book Ball the poet and novelist joins forces with 'Ball' the lovelorn journalist to relate a piercing tragedy in a language that combines subtlety and simplicity in such a way that it causes a reader to go carefully, not wanting to miss a word."

REVIEW: *New Yorker* v89 no48 p77-1 F 10 2014

"Silence Once Begun." "Like his earlier work, Jesse Ball's strange, brief, beguiling fourth novel, 'Silence Once Begun' . . . , flirts with the hermetic. Laid out as a series of Q. & A. interviews (and a small collection of photographs), the book sometimes resembles a film script; the pages bloom with whiteness. . . . Ball tells the story, or stories, of Oda Sotatsu, a twenty-nine-year-old Japanese man of no great distinction or education. . . . Ball's talents, as both a storyteller and a writer of prose, tend to burst the borders of his structures."

REVIEW: *Publ Wkly* v260 no35 p28 S 2 2013

BALL, PHILIP. Serving the Reich; The Struggle for the Soul of Physics under Hitler; [by] Philip Ball 320 p. 2013 Bodley Head

1. Debye, Peter J. W. (Peter Josef William), 1884-1966 2. Heisenberg, Werner, 1901-1976 3. Historical literature 4. National socialism & science 5. Physicists—Germany—Biography 6. Planck, Max, 1858-1947 7. Science—Germany—History—20th century 8. Science—Political aspects

ISBN 1847922481; 9781847922489

SUMMARY: "After World War II, most scientists in Germany maintained that they had been apolitical or actively resisted the Nazi regime, but the true story is much more complicated. In 'Serving the Reich,' Philip Ball takes a fresh look at that controversial history, contrasting the career of Peter Debye, director of the Kaiser Wilhelm Institute for Physics in Berlin, with those of two other leading physicists in Germany during the Third Reich: Max Planck . . . and Werner Heisenberg." (Publisher's note)

REVIEW: *Hist Today* v64 no1 p60-2 Ja 2014 Andrew Robinson

REVIEW: *New Sci* v220 no2938 p48-9 O 12 2013 Steve Fuller

REVIEW: *New Statesman* v142 no5179 p45 O 11 2013 Philip Maughan

REVIEW: *TLS* no5781 p12 Ja 17 2014 CHRISTOPHER COKER

"Serving the Reich: The Struggle for the Soul of Physics Under Hitler" and "Churchill's Bomb: A Hidden History of

Science, War, and Politics." "The subtitle to Philip Ball's fine book is 'The struggle for the soul of physics under Hitler.' . . . Many German scientists stood by as the Jews were purged from institutions and university departments, including Göttingen. . . . Despite his voracious interest in science, Churchill was always personally impatient and suspicious of boffins, with the exception of his not particularly talented scientific adviser, Frederick Lindemann. And yet as Graham Farmelo shows in 'Churchill's Bomb,' Churchill floundered when it actually came to building the bomb after the United States entered the war and a year later began the Manhattan Project."

BALLARD, MIGNON F. Miss Dimple picks a peck of trouble; [by] Mignon F. Ballard 272 p. 2014 Minotaur Books

1. Elementary school teachers—Fiction 2. FICTION—Mystery & Detective—Historical 3. Teenage girls—Crimes against—Fiction 4. Women teachers—Fiction 5. World War, 1939-1945—Georgia—Fiction

ISBN 9781250035622 (hardback)

LC 2013-032597

SUMMARY: In this book, "respected teacher and part-time sleuth Miss Dimple Kilpatrick is picking peaches with her fellow teachers . . . when Miss Dimple hears a scream. Only later do they learn that the lovely Prentice Blair has vanished from her job selling produce at the Peach Shed. . . . When her body is found, her longtime boyfriend, Clay Jarrett, whose family owns the peach farm, is immediately suspected." (Kirkus Reviews)

REVIEW: *Booklist* v110 no11 p27 F 1 2014 Amy Alessio

REVIEW: *Kirkus Rev* v81 no24 p254 D 15 2013

"Miss Dimple Picks a Peck of Trouble". "A murder horrifies the residents of a small Georgia town already coping with the deprivations of wartime living. The blazing hot summer of 1944 is taking a toll on the hardy citizens of Elderberry, who consider themselves lucky to be living in a rural area where they can grow and can their own food. Respected teacher and part-time sleuth Miss Dimple Kilpatrick is picking peaches with her fellow teachers, Charlie Carr and Annie Gardner, when Miss Dimple hears a scream. Only later do they learn that the lovely Prentice Blair has vanished from her job selling produce at the Peach Shed . . . [Mignon F.] Ballard's latest exercise in nostalgia . . . presents more delightful characters tangled in a solid mystery."

REVIEW: *Publ Wkly* v260 no52 p36 D 23 2013

BALLIF-SPANVILL, BONNIE. Sex and world peace. See Hudson, V. M.

BALYI, ISTVAN. Long-term athlete development; [by] Istvan Balyi ix, 286 p. 2013 Human Kinetics

1. Athletes—education 2. Athletic Performance—physiology 3. Athletic Performance—psychology 4. Physical education 5. Sports—Philosophy 6. Sports literature

ISBN 0736092188 (print); 9780736092180 (print)

LC 2013-008554

SUMMARY: In this book, authors Istvan Baiyi, Richard Way, and Colin Higgs "propose that a program of systematic athlete preparation, geared toward a lifetime of activity, will benefit both the 'athlete' and the 'citizen,' if the program includes elements that they elaborate, e.g., inclusion rather than exclusion and developmentally appropriate progressions rather than one-size-fits-all training." (Choice: Current Reviews for Academic Libraries)

REVIEW: *Choice* v51 no9 p1636 My 2014 D. W. Hill

"Long-term Athlete Development". "The authors' questions are provocative: who is actually teaching/coaching kids? What are kids being prepared for? The book provides a comprehensive road map and is a valuable resource for parents, educators, administrators, and coaches. Although the reference list includes sources such as lay articles and coaching bulletins, which may not be based directly on research evidence, the volume is appropriate for everyone interested in physical education and sport."

BALZ, DAN. Collision 2012; Obama Vs. Romney and the Future of Elections in America; [by] Dan Balz 400 p. 2013 Penguin Group USA

1. Obama, Barack, 1961- 2. Political science literature 3. Presidents—United States—Election—2012 4. Romney, Mitt, 1947- 5. United States—Politics & government—2009-

ISBN 0670025941; 9780670025947

SUMMARY: This book by Dan Balz "traces the 2012 Democratic and Republican presidential campaigns. He discusses the 2010 mid-term election results . . . as well as the Democratic Party's resurrection in 2012, when it was able to cast itself as the responsible choice for the middle class, owing to the Obama reelection committee's reinvented message on spending cuts and modest tax increases. The section on the Republican Party begins with its response to the rise of the Tea Party." (Library Journal)

REVIEW: *Bookforum* v20 no3 p8-59 S-N 2013 THOMAS FRANK

REVIEW: *Choice* v51 no9 p1681 My 2014 B. E. Altschuler

REVIEW: *Kirkus Rev* v81 no12 p40-1 Je 15 2013

REVIEW: *Libr J* v138 no5 p92 Mr 15 2013 Barbara Hoffert

REVIEW: *N Y Times Book Rev* p19 Ag 18 2013 Jeffrey Frank

"Collision 2012: Obama vs. Romney and the Future of Elections in America." "It's a challenge for even a first-rate political reporter like . . . [Dan] Balz to make the 2012 election seem fresh. . . . Balz seems a little bored by some of it, and a little mournful that some colorful Republican contenders . . . sat it out, but he still finds interesting material in a race that 'big stakes but not always a campaign to do them justice. . . . Balz was present for many of the year's weird moments. . . . The Republicans provided an entertaining spectacle, Balz observes, but at a cost."

REVIEW: *New York Times* v162 no56207 pA17 Jl 24 2013 JONATHAN MARTIN

REVIEW: *Publ Wkly* v260 no25 p164-5 Je 24 2013

BAMJI, ALEXANDRA.ed. The Ashgate research companion to the Counter-Reformation. See The Ashgate research companion to the Counter-Reformation

BANKER, JAMES R. Piero Della Francesca; artist and man; [by] James R. Banker 304 p. 2014 Oxford University Press

1. Art literature 2. Biography (Literary form) 3. Italian

art 4. Painters—Italy—Biography 5. Piero, della Francesca, ca. 1416-1492
ISBN 9780199609314 (hardback)
LC 2013-938929

SUMMARY: This book on artist Piero della Francesca "integrates the story of Piero's artistic and mathematical achievements with the full chronicle of his life. . . . The book presents us with Piero's friends, family, and collaborators, all set against the social background of the various cities and courts in which he lived." (Publisher's note)

REVIEW: *Apollo: The International Magazine for Collectors* v179 no617 p85 F 2014

"Dumfries House: An Architectural Story," "Piero della Francesca: Artist and Man," and "Whistler: A Life for Art's Sake". "This study, which draws on previously unpublished archival material, opens up the house and its history as never before—apt for a building and collection that has recently been saved for the public. . . . James Banker couches the Tuscan painter's achievements carefully within the social and artistic contexts of his time, making compelling claims about the dating of certain works, and offering a new interpretation of the enigmatic Flagellation of Christ. . . . This is the first full biography of [James] Whistler for more than 20 years. Making use of the painter's private correspondence, historian Daniel Sutherland presents a more introspective figure than the truculent eccentric who has entered the public consciousness."

REVIEW: *Apollo: The International Magazine for Collectors* v179 no619 p106-7 Ap 2014 Charles Hope

REVIEW: *N Y Rev Books* v61 no11 p53-6 Je 19 2014 Julian Bell

BANKS, JOHN. Co-Creating Videogames; [by] John Banks 200 p. 2013 Bloomsbury USA Academic
1. Artistic collaboration 2. Computer science literature 3. Computer software developers 4. User-generated content 5. Video game design
ISBN 184966496X; 9781849664967

SUMMARY: This book by John Banks presents "an explanation and analysis of the relatively new phenomenon of user-generated content integrated into professional video game development." It focuses on a case study of the game Trainz and "outlines the overall issues and problems with this practice. These include determining how player-developers can be recognized and remunerated for their contributions to a game." (Choice: Current Reviews for Academic Libraries)

REVIEW: *Choice* v51 no7 p1255 Mr 2014 E. Bertozzi

"Co-Creating Videogames." "This well-researched, informative volume provides readers with an explanation and analysis of the relatively new phenomenon of user-generated content integrated into professional video game development. [John] Banks . . . describes an individual case study (Trainz) in great detail, offers more general perspectives of other companies and other games, and outlines the overall issues and problems with this practice. . . . The content is supported by citations from player-developers, descriptions of meetings that the author attended in person, and insights from industry professionals that validate and explicate the author's points. . . . Recommended."

BANKS, MILENA. Riding the Tiger; [by] Milena Banks 532 p. 2013 iUniverse.com
1. Betrayal—Fiction 2. Forgiveness—Fiction 3. Historical fiction 4. Hong Kong (China)—Fiction 5. Orphans—Fiction
ISBN 147595638X; 9781475956382

SUMMARY: This novel "focuses on Jardine, a young Chinese orphan who knows little of her past. In 1997, Jack Morgan, an elderly, dying Kentuckian who has lived in China for decades, summons Jardine to his apartment and tells her, 'The woman who kept you from knowing who you are has recently died.' That woman, Violet Summerhays Morgan, was Jack's long-suffering, infertile wife and the daughter of Percival Summerhays, Jack's benefactor and boss." (Kirkus Reviews)

REVIEW: *Kirkus Rev* p5 D 15 2013 supplemet best books 2013

"Riding the Tiger". "This novel draws on the shared, complicated colonial history between the British and Chinese peoples and spans six decades, starting in 1937 when fighting between Japanese and Chinese troops led to the Second Sino-Japanese War. . . . [Milena] Banks' evocative prose is impressive throughout. . . . The plot twists like ginkgoes in the wind as the characters cruelly betray one another. . . . In the end, Banks delivers an engaging tale of forgiveness and the strength of familial ties, even when those ties have been frayed almost to extinction. . . . A spectacular novel of colonial China that should put this first-time author on the map."

REVIEW: *Kirkus Rev* v81 no7 p45 Ap 1 2013

BANKSTON, CARL L.ed. The 50 States. See The 50 States

BANKSTON, JOHN. Leif Erikson; [by] John Bankston 48 p. 2013 Mitchell Lane Publishers
1. Biographies 2. Explorers—America—Biography—Juvenile literature 3. Explorers—Scandinavia—Biography—Juvenile literature 4. Vikings—Juvenile literature
ISBN 9781612284309 (library bound)
LC 2013-012556

SUMMARY: This book on Leif Erikson by John Bankston is part of the Junior Biographies From Ancient Civilizations series. "Leif Erikson, the Viking explorer, was a hero in his own lifetime. The focus here is on Erikson's voyage to Canada, where he became one of the first white men to see the new land." The book also includes "lengthy, illustrated sidebars" on Viking society. (Booklist)

REVIEW: *Booklist* v110 no5 p54 N 1 2013 Ilene Cooper

"Archimedes," "Leif Erikson," and "Nero." "The Junior Biographies from Ancient Civilizations series brings its subjects to life by focusing on some of history's most famous (and infamous) names. . . . The story of Archimedes begins with his famous 'Eureka!' moment and then goes back to look at his boyhood, mathematical training, and the impact he had on ancient Greek civilization. . . . The focus here is on [Leif] Erikson's voyage to Canada, where he became one of the first white men to see the new land. Roman emperor Nero was trouble almost from the beginning. . . . The books are a solid blending of art and text, with lengthy, illustrated sidebars doing the heavy lifting when it comes to explaining societies' mores."

BANVILLE, JOHN, 1945-. The black-eyed blonde; a Philip Marlowe novel; [by] John Banville 304 p. 2014 Henry Holt and Co.
1. Detective & mystery stories 2. FICTION—Mystery

& Detective—General 3. Marlowe, Philip (Fictitious character)—Fiction 4. Missing persons—Fiction 5. Social classes—Fiction
ISBN 0805098143; 9780805098143 (hardback)
LC 2013-026790

SUMMARY: This book, by Benjamin Black, features private detective Philip Marlowe–a character originally created by Raymond Chandler. "It is the early 1950s, Marlowe is as restless and lonely as ever. Then a new client is shown in: young, beautiful, and expensively dressed, she wants Marlowe to find her former lover, a man named Nico Peterson. Marlowe sets off on his search, but almost immediately discovers that Peterson's disappearance is merely the first in a series of bewildering events." (Publisher's note)

REVIEW: *Booklist* v110 no12 p28-30 F 15 2014 Bill Ott

REVIEW: *Booklist* v111 no1 p136 S 1 2014 David Pitt

REVIEW: *Harper's Magazine* v328 no1967 p83-5 Ap 2014 Joshua Cohen

REVIEW: *Kirkus Rev* v82 no4 p44 F 15 2014

"The Black-Eyed Blonde". "Man Booker Prize-winning novelist John Banville, already disguised as mystery writer [Benjamin] Black . . . goes under even deeper cover to imitate Raymond Chandler in this flavorsome pastiche. . . . [Benjamin] Black's plotting is no better than Chandler's, but he has Marlowe's voice down to a fault. Both the dialogue and the narration crawl with overblown, Chandler-esque similes . . . and devotees will recognize borrowings. . . . The portrait of 1950s LA is less precise than Chandler's, but the aging, reflective Marlowe is appropriately sententious. A treat for fans, even if they end up throwing it across the room."

REVIEW: *London Rev Books* v36 no7 p3-6 Ap 3 2014 Christopher Tayler

REVIEW: *N Y Times Book Rev* p25 Mr 23 2014

REVIEW: *N Y Times Book Rev* p18 Mr 16 2014 OLEN STEINHAUER

REVIEW: *Nation* v298 no19 p31-6 My 12 2014 SARAH WEINMAN

"The Black-Eyed Blonde: A Philip Marlowe Novel." "Benjamin Black [author John Banville's pseudonym] had no . . . poignant emotional issues to mine when writing 'The Black-Eyed Blonde.' If it reads like a literary challenged conceived during National Novel-Writing Month, at least it's of a superior quality. . . . Unfortunately, the wheels come loose. . . . By the time 'The Black-Eyed Blonde' gets around to its big reveal . . . it's hard to tell whether this is ersatz Chandler or ersatz Black."

REVIEW: *New Statesman* v143 no5202 p46 Mr 21 2014 Ian Sansom

REVIEW: *New York Times* v163 no56433 pC34 Mr 7 2014 JANET MASLIN

REVIEW: *Publ Wkly* v261 no4 p56-61 Ja 27 2014

REVIEW: *Publ Wkly* v261 no2 p52 Ja 13 2014

REVIEW: *Publ Wkly* v261 no17 p132 Ap 28 2014

BANVILLE, JOHN, 1945-.ed. The old devils . See Amis, K.

BARAK, GREGG. Theft of a nation; Wall Street looting and federal regulatory colluding; [by] Gregg Barak 226 p. 2012 Rowman & Littlefield Publishers, Inc.
1. Commercial crimes—United States 2. Law enforcement—United States 3. Ponzi schemes—United States 4. Social science literature 5. White collar crimes—United States
ISBN 1442207787; 9781442207783 (cloth : alk. paper); 9781442207790 (pbk. : alk. paper); 9781442207806 (electronic)
LC 2012-024450

SUMMARY: This book, by Gregg Barak, "presents a powerful criminological examination of Wall Street's recent financial meltdown and its profound impact on the rest of the country. This provocative book asks why, if the actions of key players on Wall Street and in the government resulted in an economic downturn that harmed millions of Americans and destroyed capital worldwide, no one was held criminally liable for these actions." (Publisher's note)

REVIEW: *Choice* v50 no10 p1888 Je 2013 H. Mayo

REVIEW: *Contemp Sociol* v42 no5 p674-6 S 2013 Sally S. Simpson

REVIEW: *Contemp Sociol* v42 no5 p671-3 S 2013 Henry N. Pontell

"Theft of a Nation: Wall Street Looting and Federal Regulatory Colluding." "In 'Theft of a Nation,' Gregg Barak effectively argues that fraud was central to the current meltdown. . . . Using detailed historical analysis and major case studies he exposes how and why the American public was victimized by deregulatory policies designed to benefit large private firms and which simultaneously created a criminogenic environment in the housing and financial industries. . . . Overall, the most important contribution of this book is that it provides a significant blow against the 'trivialization of fraud'' in both academic and policy circles."

BARAKIVA, MICHAEL. One man guy; [by] Michael Barakiva 272 p. 2014 Farrar, Straus & Giroux
1. Armenian Americans—Fiction 2. Coming out (Sexual orientation)—Fiction 3. Gays—Fiction 4. Love—Fiction 5. Young adult fiction
ISBN 9780374356453 (hardcover)
LC 2013-033518

SUMMARY: In this book, "being forced to attend summer school becomes a blessing in disguise for 14-year-old Alek Khederian when it sparks a romance with an older boy named Ethan, who runs with a crowd of skateboarders and perceived burnouts. Alek's Armenian heritage is the ever-present frame for the boys' budding relationship in suburban New Jersey. . . . [Michael] Barakiva draws sharp parallels between homophobia and the ongoing enmity between Armenians and Turks due to the Armenian genocide." (Publishers Weekly)

REVIEW: *Booklist* v110 no17 p98 My 1 2014 Michael Cart

REVIEW: *Bull Cent Child Books* v67 no10 p499 Je 2014 T. A.

"One Man Guy". "The tension between the responsibilities of heritage for a second-generation kid and a budding sense of teenage rebellion is expertly manifested in Alek's wanting to do the right thing. His bewilderment at falling for a guy presents a realistic picture of developing sexuality, and the non-event of his coming out is eclipsed by a family drama involving the bad blood between Turks (Alek's brother's girlfriend is half-Turkish) and Armenians. . . . The ending does rely on contrivances that are little too perfect, but what feel-good, bubblegum romance doesn't?"

REVIEW: *Kirkus Rev* v82 no5 p199 Mr 1 2014

REVIEW: *Publ Wkly* v261 no9 p66 Mr 3 2014

REVIEW: *SLJ* v60 no5 p124 My 2014 Sarah Allen

BARAM, GILAD. Wall. See Dolphin, R.

BARATON, ALAIN. The Gardener of Versailles; my life in the world's grandest garden; [by] Alain Baraton 304 p. 2014 Rizzoli Ex Libris

1. Château de Versailles (Versailles, France) 2. Gardening 3. Gardens, French 4. Horticultural literature 5. Memoirs

ISBN 0847842681; 9780847842681 (alk. paper)

LC 2013-943445

SUMMARY: Translated by Christopher Brent Murray, this book is "for gardening aficionados and Francophiles, a love letter to the Versailles Palace and grounds, from the man who knows them best. In Alain Baraton's Versailles, every grove tells a story. As the gardener-in-chief, Baraton lives on its grounds. . . . His memoir captures the essence of the connection between gardeners and the earth they tend, no matter how humble or grand." (Publisher's note)

REVIEW: *Kirkus Rev* v82 no1 p128 Ja 1 2014

"The Gardener of Versailles: My Life in the World's Grandest Garden". "The author philosophizes about the ability of gardens to provide space for deep reflection, and he writes poetically about the beautiful power of the grounds he tends. He also provides some practical advice. . . . In addition to paying tribute to the work of these innovators, [Alain] Baraton also looks at the various films that have been filmed on the grounds, storms that have battered them, and the effects of each season on the flora and fauna. The descriptions of the various sites on the grounds could only come from a man fortunate enough to have lived on and loved the site for almost 40 years."

REVIEW: *Libr J* v138 no21 p116 D 1 2013 Bonnie Poquette

REVIEW: *N Y Times Book Rev* p34 Ap 27 2014 Dominique Browning

REVIEW: *Publ Wkly* v261 no3 p49 Ja 20 2014

BARBARA WRIGHT; translation as art; 400 p. 2013 Dalkey Archive Press

1. French language—Translating 2. Literature—History & criticism 3. Translating and interpreting 4. Translators—Great Britain—Biography

ISBN 9781564788863 (pbk.: acid-free paper)

LC 2013-007424

SUMMARY: Edited by Madeleine Renouard and Debra Kelly, "This . . . collection of texts about and by Barbara Wright—including work by David Bellos, Breon Mitchell, and Nick Wadley, as well as a previously unpublished screenplay written and translated by Wright in collaboration with Robert Pinget—begins the work of properly commemorating a figure toward whom all of English letters owes an unpayable debt." (Publisher's note)

REVIEW: *TLS* no5794 p27 Ap 18 2014 DENNIS DUNCAN

"Barbara Wright: Translation As Art." "The bulk of Madeleine Renouard and Debra Kelly's tribute is taken up with a previously unpublished translation by Wright—the script of an unmade film by Pinget, '15 Rue des Lilas.' The rest of the book consists of a number of essays on Wright's landmark translations. . . . There are also a number of reminiscences from those who knew Wright, of which Breon Mitchell's is both touching and illuminating about her working practice. . . . For scholars in this field, 'Barbara Wright: Translation as art,' with its bibliography and its catalogue of Wright's materials in archives in Europe and the US, is both a useful resource and a fitting memorial to one of translation's modem virtuosos."

BARBER, BENJAMIN R., 1939-. If mayors ruled the world; dysfunctional nations, rising cities; [by] Benjamin R. Barber 432 p. 2013 Yale University Press

1. Comparative government 2. Leadership 3. Mayors—Case studies 4. Municipal government 5. POLITICAL SCIENCE—Government—Comparative 6. POLITICAL SCIENCE—History & Theory 7. POLITICAL SCIENCE—Public Affairs & Administration 8. Political science literature

ISBN 030016467X; 9780300164671 (hardback)

LC 2013-016680

SUMMARY: In this book, author Benjamin R. Barber "cheers the decline of the nation-state and anticipates the rise of the city-state. He asserts that modern cities with pragmatic mayors are the political institutions that hold the most promise for reducing poverty, fighting terrorism, mitigating climate change, and building global connections. The volume is divided into 12 chapters, each cataloging the policy and civic innovations that have been engineered by cities." (Library Journal)

REVIEW: *Kirkus Rev* v81 no20 p59 O 15 2013

REVIEW: *N Y Times Book Rev* p29 N 24 2013 SAM ROBERTS

"If Mayors Ruled the World: Dysfunctional Nations, Rising Cities" and "A Mayor's Life: Governing New York's Gorgeous Mosaic." "[Benjamin R.] Barber's book is the most audacious--even messianic--of a torrent of recently advanced urban manifestoes. . . . Barber builds a strong case for an informal parliament of cities . . . which would in effect ratify a shift in power and political reality that, he argues, has already taken place. . . . He persuasively builds his case with capsule profiles of visionary mayors from around the world. . . . Barber's book should be required reading for New York's new mayor, Bill de Blasio. So should 'A Mayor's Life: Governing New York's Gorgeous Mosaic,' by David N. Dinkins, a moving memoir."

REVIEW: *Publ Wkly* v260 no38 p69-70 S 23 2013

BARBER, ELIZABETH WAYLAND. Resplendent dress from Southeastern Europe; a history in layers; [by] Elizabeth Wayland Barber 276 p. 2013 Fowler Museum at UCLA

1. Art literature 2. Clothing and dress—Balkan Peninsula—History 3. Clothing and dress—Social aspects—Balkan Peninsula 4. Historical literature

ISBN 9780984755035 (soft cover); 9780984755042 (hard cover)

LC 2012-047633

SUMMARY: This book looks at "more than fifty ensembles and accessories drawn from . . . twelve represented countries of Southeastern Europe. . . . This region has developed some of the most elaborate and diverse traditions of dress. . . . Dating from the nineteenth- to twentieth centuries, the book discusses the weaving, sewing and embroidering of festive dress, codifying a woman's marital status, religion, wealth, and textile skills." (Ornament)

REVIEW: *Choice* v51 no5 p818 Ja 2014 M. Tulokas

"Resplendent Dress From Southeastern Europe: A History in Layers." "In this catalogue for an exhibition at UCLA's Fowler Museum, renowned textile historian [Elizabeth Wayland] Barber, [Barbara Belle] Sloan (Fowler Museum), and others trace the European clothing tradition from the string skirt of the Paleolithic era, and its significance as an indicator of the wearer's childbearing age, to the 20th century. . . . This well-researched volume is richly illustrated with high-quality color photographs from the Fowler Museum's collections. A time line, an appendix, and notes complement this valuable record. . . . Recommended."

BARBER, MALCOLM.tr. Letters from the East. See Letters from the East

BARBER, RICHARD. Edward III and the Triumph of England; The Battle of Crecy and the Company of the Garter; [by] Richard Barber 672 p. 2013 Allen Lane

1. Battle of Crecy, Crecy-en-Ponthieu, France, 1346 2. Edward III, King of England, 1312-1377 3. Great Britain—Military history—1066-1485 4. Historical literature 5. Order of the Garter

ISBN 0713998385; 9780713998382

SUMMARY: In this book of King Richard III of England and his chivalric order the Order of the Garter, Richard Barber "argues that English successes in France between 1346 and 1349 owed much to the monarch's shrewd leadership. The king combined innovative tactics and new technologies to overcome larger, if more fractious, armies under the command of Philip VI of France." (The Guardian)

REVIEW: *Choice* v51 no6 p1080 F 2014 A. C. Reeves

REVIEW: *Economist* v408 no8850 p75-6 Ag 24 2013

"Edward III and the Triumph of England." "[A] scholarly examination of the [Order of the Garter]. . . . If Mr. [Richard] Barber is right, then the motto has several meanings. It is not simply a challenge to those who denied Edward's right to the French crown over that of Philip VI. It is also a reference to Edward's shamed French opponents in the wake of Crécy, and a riposte to parliamentary critics of the wartime taxes that Edward had raised to finance his ambitious campaign. . . . [The Order of the garter] wad intended to be a religious society more than a military one, Mr. Barber argues. Their chief duty was to attend an annual service in a private chapel in Windsor on St. George's Day."

REVIEW: *History* v99 no335 p313-4 Ap 2014 Nigel Saul

BARBER, ROS, 1964-. The Marlowe papers; a novel; [by] Ros Barber 464 p. 2013 St. Martin's Press

1. FICTION—Historical 2. FICTION—Literary 3. Historical fiction

ISBN 1250017173; 9781250017178 (hardback)

LC 2012-037986

SUMMARY: In this novel by Ros Barber "Christopher Marlowe reveals . . . that his 'death' was an elaborate ruse to avoid a conviction of heresy; . . . that he continued to write plays and poetry, hiding behind the name of a colorless man from Stratford--one William Shakespeare. This novel . . . in verse gives voice to . . . a cobbler's son who counted nobles among his friends, a spy in the Queen's service, a fickle lover and a declared religious skeptic." (Publisher's note)

REVIEW: *Booklist* v109 no9/10 p51 Ja 1 2013 Ray Olson

REVIEW: *Kirkus Rev* v80 no20 p183 O 15 2012

REVIEW: *N Y Times Book Rev* p15 Ja 27 2013 CHARLES NICHOLL

REVIEW: *N Y Times Book Rev* p22 F 3 2013

REVIEW: *N Y Times Book Rev* p28 F 16 2014 IHSAN TAYLOR

"The Marlowe Papers," "Coolidge," and "Kind of Kind." "[Ros] Barber's novel isn't the first to reimagine the life (and mysterious death) of the Elizabethan playwright Christopher Marlowe, but it may be the first to do so in verse. . . . With a deft finger on today's conservative pulse, [Amity] Shlaes . . . portrays Calvin Coolidge (1872-1933) as a paragon of a president by virtue of his small-government policies. . . . The fraught issue of illegal immigration divides an Oklahoma clan and their town in [Rilla] Askew's heartfelt novel ['Kind of Kin']."

REVIEW: *Publ Wkly* v259 no46 p41 N 12 2012

REVIEW: *TLS* no5709 p21 Ag 31 2012 Jackie Watson

BARBIERI, MAGGIE. Once upon a lie; [by] Maggie Barbieri 304 p. 2013 Minotaur Books

1. Bakers—Fiction 2. Cousins—Crimes against—Fiction 3. FICTION—Mystery & Detective—General 4. FICTION—Mystery & Detective—Women Sleuths 5. Family secrets 6. Women—Fiction

ISBN 1250011671; 9781250011671 (hardback)

LC 2013-025294

SUMMARY: In this book, by Maggie Barbieri, "Maeve Conlon's life is coming apart at the seams. Her bakery is barely making ends meet, and one of her daughters spends as much time grounded as the other does studying. Her ex-husband has a new wife [and] a new baby. . . . Her father insists he's still independent, but he's slowly and obviously succumbing to Alzheimer's. And now, her cousin Sean Donovan has been found dead." (Publisher's note)

REVIEW: *Kirkus Rev* v81 no24 p111 D 15 2013

"Once Upon a Lie". " The creator of the college-themed cozies in the Murder 101 series . . . goes big in her first standalone. Maeve Conlon's life is finally back on track after her husband, Cal, left her for her beautiful Brazilian best friend, Gabriela. A Culinary Institute grad, she's made a success of the Comfort Zone, the gourmet shop she owns in Westchester County. And she's making progress toward mastering single parenting. . . . Grace and humor mark this tale of a woman trying to protect her family without losing herself."

BARCLAY, ERIC. Hiding Phil; [by] Eric Barclay 32 p. 2013 Scholastic Press

1. Brothers and sisters—Fiction 2. Brothers and sisters—Juvenile fiction 3. Children's stories 4. Elephants—Fiction 5. Elephants—Juvenile fiction

ISBN 0545464773; 9780545464772

LC 2012-049321

SUMMARY: Author and Illustrator Eric Barclay's book focuses on three children's adventure hiding an elephant named Phil. "In this story, three siblings come upon an elephant named Phil and decide to bring him home" until they realize that their parents will be mad. "They try to stuff him into their doghouse--but he's too big. . . . Can the kids convince their parents to keep Phil, or will they have to bring him back where he belongs?" (Publisher's note)

REVIEW: *Bull Cent Child Books* v67 no2 p74 O 2013 T. A.

"Hiding Phil." "Three siblings are playing outside one fine day when they discover an affable turquoise elephant on a park bench, whose luggage tags proudly proclaim that his name is 'Phil'. . . . The fuzzy pencil outlines and muted but lively palette of the oil illustrations soften the cartoonishness of Phil's big, round eyes and rounded rectangular body to make him a comically cuddly pal, while the siblings quietly evoke the Peanuts gang with their emotive gesturing and slightly oversized heads. The sparseness of the text, with only a few lines of dialogue on most pages, makes the paintings do most of the work here, a task they accomplish with both their friendly straightforwardness and amusing attention to detail."

REVIEW: *Kirkus Rev* v81 no16 p38 Ag 15 2013

REVIEW: *Publ Wkly* v260 no31 p68 Ag 5 2013

REVIEW: *SLJ* v59 no9 p112 S 2013 Janene Corbin

BARCLAY, ERIC.il. Hiding Phil. See Barclay, E.

BARCLAY, JENNIFER. Falling in Honey; How a Tiny Greek Island Stole My Heart; [by] Jennifer Barclay 352 p. 2014 Sourcebooks

1. English—Greece—Telos Island—Biography 2. Man-woman relationships 3. Memoirs 4. Self-realization
ISBN 9781402285103 (pbk.: alk. paper)
LC 2013-031146

SUMMARY: This book presents a memoir by Jennifer Barclay, who " first visited the tiny Greek island of Tilos with friends, including a lover with promising prospects. In her mid-thirties when those prospects fell apart, she never forgot the appeal of the island. . . . Emotionally adrift, she makes herself three pledges, gifts to herself: cut back on work, take a six-month hiatus from relationships to reconnect with herself, and spend a month in Tilos." (Booklist)

REVIEW: *Booklist* v110 no14 p44 Mr 15 2014 Vanessa Bush

REVIEW: *Kirkus Rev* v82 no2 p202 Ja 15 2014

"Falling in Honey: Life and Love on a Greek Island". "A peripatetic 30-something Englishwoman's account of how a Greek island "got under [her] skin" and showed her the way to contented self-direction. . . . . [Jennifer] Barclay remained unfazed by romantic disappointment. In the end, she realized that 'it was always meant to be all about [her] and Tilos,' not about the fragile romantic relationships that too often undermined her hopes and dreams. Light and lively reading with an understated edge."

BARCLAY, LINWOOD. A tap on the window; [by] Linwood Barclay 512 p. 2013 New American Library

1. FICTION—Suspense 2. Missing persons—Fiction 3. Private investigators—Fiction 4. Runaway children—Fiction
ISBN 9780451414182 (hardback)
LC 2012-050861

SUMMARY: In this book, "middle-aged PI Cal Weaver hesitates to pick up a teenage girl hitchhiking one evening. . . . He decides to give her a ride after she says she was a friend of Cal's teenage son, Scott, who died a few months earlier. . . . He pulls over at a burger place he knows. The girl who returns to his car resembles Claire, but is not Claire. When confronted, the second teen demands to be let out. The next day both girls are missing, and Cal feels honor bound to find them." (Publishers Weekly)

REVIEW: *Booklist* v110 no5 p40 N 1 2013 Candace Smith

REVIEW: *Booklist* v109 no22 p43 Ag 1 2013 Christire Tran

REVIEW: *Kirkus Rev* v81 no17 p27-8 S 1 2013

REVIEW: *N Y Times Book Rev* p31 Ag 25 2013 Marilyn Stasio

"A Tap on the Window," "The Wicked Girls," and "The Crooked Maid: A Novel." "[Linwood] Barclay's convoluted 'now you see me, now you don't' plot opens on such a low-key note that it's a shock when it takes off for the narrative badlands. But even when he's tending to the gruesome details of the bad stuff, he never loses touch with the fundamental fear of people who live in nice communities like Griffon--that their children are beyond their control. . . . Alex Marwood . . . demonstrat[es] a deep, warm feeling for the shabby seaside town where she sets her harrowing first novel. . . . [In 'The Crooked Maid' the lives of . . . two strangers become intricately (if much too expediently) entwined in a complicated but gracefully executed narrative."

REVIEW: *Publ Wkly* v260 no26 p69 Jl 1 2013

REVIEW: *Quill Quire* v79 no7 p32 S 2013 Chadwick Ginther

BARDHAN-QUALLEN, SUDIPTA. Tyrannosaurus wrecks!; [by] Sudipta Bardhan-Quallen 32 p. 2014 Abrams Books for Young Readers

1. Behavior—Fiction 2. Children's stories 3. Dinosaurs—Fiction 4. Stories in rhyme 5. Tyrannosaurus rex—Fiction
ISBN 1419710354; 9781419710353
LC 2013-022197

SUMMARY: Written by Sudipta Bardhan-Quallen and illustrated by Zachariah O'Hora, "in this read-along picture book, a classroom full of young dinosaurs plays with toys, does art projects, and reads books. But each activity is another opportunity for the over-enthusiastic Tyrannosaurus Rex to wreak havoc. . . . The format is extra vertical in order to accommodate T. Rex's biggest messes." (Publisher's note)

REVIEW: *Booklist* v110 no16 p55 Ap 15 2014 Jesse Karp

REVIEW: *Bull Cent Child Books* v67 no9 p442 My 2014 T. A.

"Tyrannosaurus Wrecks!" "The message in this rhyming story is cheery, and it's enhanced by a bouncy rhythm well suited for reading aloud, while the set-up for a (possibly participatory) shout at the page turn adds some suspense. . . . The shapely dinos, whose rough charcoal-style outlines and strong colors vividly contrast with the white or sometimes black backgrounds, are chunky and friendly in an eight-crayon-box color scheme and snazzy Peanuts-reminiscent outfits. Tyrannosaurus is particularly well captured as a non-threatening but mischievous reptile, with his orange skin, rounded teeth, bumpy tail, black cargo shorts, and green sneaker. Lower elementary classrooms will especially want to add this one."

REVIEW: *Horn Book Magazine* v90 no4 p72 Jl/Ag 2014 JULIE ROACH

REVIEW: *Kirkus Rev* v82 no5 p258 Mr 1 2014

REVIEW: *Publ Wkly* v261 no5 p57 F 3 2014

REVIEW: *SLJ* v60 no10 p52 O 2014 Jessica Gilcreast

REVIEW: *SLJ* v60 no5 p73 My 2014 Maralita L. Freeny

BARDI, LINA BO. Stones Against Diamonds; [by] Lina Bo Bardi 160 p. 2012 Architectural Association Publications

1. Anthologies 2. Architectural literature 3. Architecture—Brazil 4. Essay (Literary form) 5. Women architects

ISBN 1907896201; 9781907896200

SUMMARY: Written by Lina Bo Bardi, "This collection of essays is the first-ever English anthology of her writings. It includes texts written when she was still living in Italy as well as later contributions to a number of Brazilian newspapers, journals and magazines." It "proposes a series of new parameters for design thinking and practice, such as the notions of 'historical present,' 'roughness' and 'tolerance to imperfection.'" (Publisher's note)

REVIEW: *N Y Rev Books* v61 no9 p12-5 My 22 2014 Martin Filler

"Lina Bo Bardi," "Lina Bo Bardi: The Theory of Architectural Practice," and "Stones Against Diamonds." "'Lina Bo Bardi,' the first full-length life-and-works, by Zeuler R. M. de A. Lima . . . is a feat of primary-source scholarship and thoughtful analysis. Lima does a masterful job of candidly assessing his brilliant, somewhat erratic, and not always truthful subject. . . . Cathrine Veikos's 'Lina Bo Bardi: The Theory of Architectural Practice' [is] the first English translation of . . . Bo Bardi's fullest exposition of a design philosophy. . . . 'Stones Against Diamonds,' a collection of Bo Bardi's writings, was recently issued by London's Architectural Association, part of its commendable Architecture Words series."

BARDOE, CHERYL. Behold the beautiful dung beetle; [by] Cheryl Bardoe 32 p. 2014 Charlesbridge

1. Children's nonfiction 2. Dung beetles 3. Insect behavior 4. Insects—Physiology 5. Picture books for children

ISBN 9781580895545 (reinforced for library use); 9781607346203 (ebook)

LC 2012-038692

SUMMARY: This children's picture book looks at dung beetles. "When an animal lightens its load, dung beetles race to the scene. They battle over, devour, hoard, and lay their eggs in the precious poop. Dung is food, drink, and fuel for new life—as crucial to these beetles as the beetles are to many habitats, including our own." (Publisher's note)

REVIEW: *Bull Cent Child Books* v67 no9 p442 My 2014 D. S.

REVIEW: *Kirkus Rev* v82 no3 p92 F 1 2014

"Behold the Beautiful Dung Beetle". "Each double-page spread contains text in two fonts: The larger-type text is chatty and informative, while the smaller provides more detail. Both sets are immensely readable. Golden watercolor sunsets and vast open plains surround the text. Compelling close-ups show deep tunnels and every part of the beetle. The exalted tone of the title and cover illustration of a dung beetle in a triumphant, legs-to-the-heavens stance may seem a bit excessive at first. But no doubt by the end, readers will find it difficult not to join in the adulation. An excrement—er, excellent—read."

REVIEW: *SLJ* v60 no3 p170 Mr 2014 Frances E. Millhouser

BARDOS, MAGALI. 100 Bears; 104 p. 2014 Flying Eye Books

1. Bears—Juvenile fiction 2. Counting 3. Forests & forestry—Juvenile literature 4. Hunting stories 5. Picture books for children

ISBN 190926315X; 9781909263154

SUMMARY: This illustrated children's counting book, written and illustrated by Magali Bardos is a "real bear caper." The book presents "a a wacky, . . . anarchic tale of hunters, feasts, and marauding beasts, [in which] we chase the numbers 1-100 through mountains, forests, and cities." (Publisher's note)

REVIEW: *Bull Cent Child Books* v67 no9 p442-3 My 2014 J. H.

"100 Bears". "The narrative structured around the bears combines with a lighthearted tone to make this inventive take on the traditional counting book effective. Bardos' stunning art—in fluorescent tones of red, orange, fuchsia, purple, and turquoise and highlighted by white, black, and brown—is reminiscent of retro graphic design, and the bold compositions allow for group sharing. . . . Those examples that do entice kids to count require some focus for the higher number and busier spreads, but the items are all honestly visible. Between its usefulness and its inviting illustrations, this will be a helpful title."

REVIEW: *Kirkus Rev* v82 no4 p334 F 15 2014

REVIEW: *Publ Wkly* v261 no9 p64 Mr 3 2014

REVIEW: *SLJ* v60 no7 p61 Jl 2014 Marge Loch-Wouters

BARISH, EVELYN. The Double Life of Paul De Man; [by] Evelyn Barish 564 p. 2014 W.W. Norton & Co. Inc.

1. Biography (Literary form) 2. College teachers—United States—Biography 3. Critics—United States—Biography 4. Impostors & imposture 5. United States—Intellectual life—20th century

ISBN 0871403269; 9780871403261

LC 2013-041488

SUMMARY: In this biography of Paul de Man, Evelyn Barish "concentrates on the . . . upbringing of this charismatic character who eluded justice from Nazi-occupied Belgium and later fabricated his academic reputation at Harvard. . . The tale of de Man is not only the tangled trajectory of a . . . young man . . . who saw an opportunity to advance himself through Nazi collaboration, but also the story of the striking gullibility of an American elitist intellectual milieu." (Kirkus Reviews)

REVIEW: *Am Sch* v83 no2 p109-11 Spr 2014 ROBERT ZARETSKY

REVIEW: *Booklist* v110 no8 p8 D 15 2013 Bryce Christensen

REVIEW: *Choice* v51 no12 p2175 Ag 2014 N. Lukacher

REVIEW: *Harper's Magazine* v328 no1966 p77-80 Mr 2014 Christine Smallwood

REVIEW: *Kirkus Rev* v82 no1 p65 Ja 1 2014

REVIEW: *N Y Rev Books* v61 no6 p44-7 Ap 3 2014 Peter Brooks

REVIEW: *N Y Times Book Rev* p14 Mr 9 2014 SUSAN RUBIN SULEIMAN

REVIEW: *Nation* v298 no17 p37 Ap 28 2014 DAVID MIKICS

"The Double Life of Paul de Man." "[Author Evelyn] Barish did many years of research, interviewing de Man's widows as well as dozens of his acquaintances, and what she discovered beggars the imagination: de Man was not just a collaborator but a world-class con artist, an embezzler, forger and bigamist who repeatedly falsified the details of his personal history in the most brazen ways. . . . Barish makes the case that de Man's con-artistry had deep and disturbing roots. . . . Barish skillfully takes us inside the enigma of de Man's strange life story."

REVIEW: *New Repub* v244 no25 p34-9 Ap 7 2014 Robert Alter

"The Double Life of Paul de Man." "In all that pertains to the facts of [Paul] de Man's life, [author Evelyn] Barish seems entirely reliable, and for this readers should be grateful to her. Unearthing buried facts and sifting through others about which contradictory views have been proposed are Barish's long suit. Her psychological interpretation of her subject is less impressive. . . . The writing is by and large serviceable, but sprinkled through the text is usage in which Barish appears to have an uncertain relationship with the English language."

REVIEW: *New Yorker* v90 no5 p87-1 Mr 24 2014

"The Double Life of Paul de Man." "Evelyn Barish's new biography, 'The Double Life of Paul de Man' (Liveright), is an important update on the story. Barish worked in Belgian archives, and she interviewed many people who knew de Man, including both of his wives. She's not a hundred per cent reliable on the historical background; she is a little over her head with the theoretical issues; and she sometimes characterizes as manipulative or deceptive behavior that might have a more benign explanation. Her book is a brief for the prosecution. But it is not a hatchet job, and she has an amazing tale to tell. In her account, all guns are smoking. There are enough to stock a miniseries."

REVIEW: *Publ Wkly* v260 no47 p46 N 18 2013

REVIEW: *TLS* no5818 p3-4 O 3 2014 ANN JEFFERSON

BARKHAM, PATRICK. Badgerlands; The Twilight World of Britain's Most Enigmatic Animal; [by] Patrick Barkham 380 p. 2013 Granta

1. Animals—Government policy 2. Animals—Great Britain 3. Badgers 4. Journalism 5. Wildlife management—Great Britain

ISBN 1847085040; 9781847085047

SUMMARY: "Accompanied by the eccentrics and scientists who feed and study badgers, [author Patrick] Barkham explores Badgerland; a nocturnal world in which sounds and scents are amplified, and Britain seems a much stranger place, one in which these low slung, snuffling, distinctively striped creatures gambol and dig, and live out their complex social lives." (Publisher's note)

REVIEW: *TLS* no5784 p30 F 7 2014 PATRICK EVANS

"Badgerlands: The Twilight World of Britain's Most Enigmatic Animals." "Part of the reason why badgers find themselves the subject of such fierce debate is that nobody can decide whether, as the author Patrick Barkham considers, they are a pest or a national treasure. . . . Partly in homage to his grandmother's achievements, and partly applying journalistic rigour to the question of why badgers are again under attack in the British countryside, Barkham sets off on a wild travelogue. . . . The timeliness of Barkham's book is vital, as the British badger cull is about to reach is peak. . . . 'Badgerlands' will give generations of interested parties much fascinating information to ponder just as tens of thousands of these tanks of the woods suffer untimely deaths."

BARKS, CARL. Walt Disney's Donald Duck; Christmas on Bear Mountain; [by] Carl Barks 210 p. 2013 W W Norton & Co Inc

1. Christmas stories for children 2. Comic books, strips, etc. 3. Disney characters 4. Donald Duck (Fictitious character) 5. McDuck, Scrooge (Fictitious character)

ISBN 1606996975; 9781606996973

SUMMARY: This collection of Carl Barks' world-famous Disney comics includes Uncle Scrooge's first appearance, a Christmas tale and many other adventure yarns. . . . In 'Volcano Valley' Donald and the Nephews end up stuck in Volcania, a south-of-the-border country inhabited by sombrero-wearing, siesta-addicted Volcanians. Other long-form adventures include the self explanatory 'Adventure Down Under,' as well as . . . the West Indies-based 'Ghost of the Grotto'." (Publisher's note)

REVIEW: *Booklist* v110 no8 p33-4 D 15 2013 Gordan Flagg

"Walt Disney's Donald Duck: 'Christmas on Bear Mountain'." "This volume in the ambitious project collecting [Carl] Barks' entire Duck-Family oeuvre introduces Donald's skinflint uncle, Scrooge McDuck, who would go on to become the most enduring of the original characters Barks created to expand into the world of the animated cartoons. . . . These tales from 1947 exemplify Barks' strengths: vivid yet precise cartooning; brilliant comedic dialogue and timing; and incisive characterizations (of ducks, no less). The pristine, full-color restoration of the vintage pages and the insightful historical notes do justice to these timeless tales, which remain as enthralling and delightful today as when they first appeared, nearly seven decades ago.

BARLEY, SARAH DOTTS.ed. Don't call me baby. See Don't call me baby

BARNARD, ALAN. Genesis of symbolic thought; [by] Alan Barnard xiii, 194 p. 2012 Cambridge University Press

1. Anthropology literature 2. Human evolution 3. Language and languages—Origin 4. Symbolic anthropology 5. Thought and thinking

ISBN 9781107025691 (hardback); 9781107651098 (pbk.)

LC 2011-052551

SUMMARY: In this book, Alan Barnard "attempts to answer the question of when and how human symbolic thought originated. To answer this question, he looks at early expressions of art and religion as evidenced in the archaeological record and examines speculations on the origin of language and ctilture. Although the author is well-known as a social anthropologist, in this book he draws together information from diverse fields." (Choice: Current Reviews for Academic Libraries)

REVIEW: *Choice* v51 no6 p1054-5 F 2014 C. L. Thompson

"Genesis of Symbolic Thought." "Although the author is well-known as a social anthropologist, in this book he draws together information from diverse fields, including linguistics, genetics, and neuroscience. Because of the nature of the subject matter, the book is highly speculative and therefore potentially controversial. However, [Alan] Barnard does carefully discuss the data that support his claims and discusses alternative explanations. The book is written in a way that should make it easily understood by nonspecialists, but it should be of value and interest to specialists as well."

BARNES, DIANA G. Epistolary community in print, 1580-1664; [by] Diana G. Barnes xii, 250 p. 2013 Ashgate

1. English letters—History and criticism 2. English prose literature—Early modern, 1500-1700—History and criticism 3. Historical literature 4. Letter writing—Great Britain—History—16th century 5. Letter writing—Great Britain—History—17th century
ISBN 9781409445357 (hardcover)
LC 2012-021797

SUMMARY: "Focusing on six examples of printed letters from the period, in this study Diana Barnes develops a genealogy of epistolary discourse in early modern England. She considers how the examples--from the writings of Gabriel Harvey and Edmund Spencer, Angel Day, Michael Drayton, Jacques du Bosque and Margaret Cavendish--manipulate this generic tradition to articulate ideas of community under specific historical and political circumstances." (Publisher's note)

REVIEW: *TLS* no5780 p28 Ja 10 2014 H. R. WOUDHUYSEN

"Epistolary Community in Print, 1580-1664," "By the eighteenth century, letters ('epistolae') were certainly the common currency of the republic of literature. Diana G. Barnes's book 'Epistolary Community in Print,' in which she examines familiar letters in print between 1580 and 1664, examines how this eventually came about. Her argument is that the genre is an 'implicitly democratic' one which was 'crucial to the expansion of public political discourse to permit broader enfranchisement and participation in the public sphere.'... Barnes has evidently read widely in the epistolary literature of the time and has interesting things to say about letter writers other than her six main ones, such as Edmund Spenser and Gabriel Harvey, Edmund Gayton and James Howell."

BARNES, JULIAN, 1946-. Levels of life; [by] Julian Barnes 144 p. 2013 Alfred A. Knopf

1. Ballooning 2. Bereavement 3. Burnaby, Fred 4. Experimental literature 5. Grief
ISBN 0385350775; 9780345806581 (trade pbk.); 9780385350778 (hardcover)
LC 2013-004601

SUMMARY: "It is divided into three . . . parts: a . . . discussion of ballooning; a . . . short story about the fictional romance of a real English adventurer named Fred Burnaby and the celebrated actress Sarah Bernhardt; and a . . .consideration of grief." (New York Review of Books)

REVIEW: *Booklist* v110 no1 p25-6 S 1 2013 Donna Seaman

REVIEW: *Christ Century* v131 no5 p30-3 Mr 5 2014 Richard Lischer

REVIEW: *Commonweal* v141 no3 p32-4 F 7 2014 Denis Donoghue

"Levels of Life". "'The Loss of Depth,' an elegy on the death of [Julian] Barnes's wife Pat, is the best part of the book. . . . Barnes finds it an outrage that his wife died at sixty- eight. Or perhaps that she would ever die. If Barnes believed in God—he doesn't—he would denounce Him for the injustice. As it is, Barnes foists his denunciation on something he calls Life or 'the universe,' finding it guilty of 'stuff.' This word, repeated more often than necessary, comes to sound like Donald Rumsfeld's famous explanation for looting in Baghdad: 'Stuff happens.' . . . Mostly these broodings are intelligent, often eloquent, and just to the elegiac occasion. But Barnes is sometimes hard."

REVIEW: *Economist* v407 no8830 p97-8 Ap 6 2013

REVIEW: *Kirkus Rev* p21 Ag 15 2013 Fall Preview

REVIEW: *Kirkus Rev* v81 no14 p335 Jl 15 2013

REVIEW: *Libr J* v138 no7 p54 Ap 15 2013 Barbara Hoffert

REVIEW: *London Rev Books* v35 no9 p20-1 My 9 2013 Michael Wood

REVIEW: *N Y Rev Books* v60 no20 p8-12 D 19 2013 Cathleen Schine

"Levels of Life." "The book is short, crisp, measured, and deeply felt. Not a grief memoir so much as a grief meditation, it is divided into three improbable parts: an appealing discussion of ballooning; a touching short story about the fictional romance of a real English adventurer named Fred Burnaby and the celebrated actress Sarah Bernhardt; and a thoughtful consideration of grief. . . . It is, not surprisingly, a marvel of flickering Barnesian leitmotifs, none of them subtle, all of them subtly and unexpectedly intertwined. [Julian] Barnes's language is even more disciplined than usual. He has managed to tenderly expose the grief of mourning in all its naked, writhing confusion, without exposing himself, something of a miracle of restraint."

REVIEW: *N Y Times Book Rev* p20 S 22 2013 SARAH MANGUSO

REVIEW: *New Statesman* v142 no5156 p44-5 My 3 2013 Leo Robson

REVIEW: *Publ Wkly* v260 no29 p61 Jl 22 2013

REVIEW: *TLS* no5744 p5-7 My 3 2013 JOYCE CAROL OATES

BARNES, LINDA. The Perfect Ghost; [by] Linda Barnes 304 p. 2013 St Martins Pr

1. Agoraphobia 2. Authors—Fiction 3. Detective & mystery stories 4. Ghostwriters 5. Murder—Fiction
ISBN 1250023637 (hardcover); 9781250023636 (hardcover)
LC 2013-002519

SUMMARY: This novel from Anthony Award-winner Linda Barnes focuses on "Em Moore, an agoraphobe who ghostwrites celebrity biographies under the joint pseudonym T.E. Blakemore, [who] worries whether she can complete her current project--an 'autobiography' of famed actor-director

Garrett Malcolm--without her writing partner, Teddy Blake, after his death in a car crash." (Publishers Weekly)

REVIEW: *Booklist* v110 no1 p55-6 S 1 2013 Laurie Hartshorn

"The Perfect Ghost." "[Hillary] Huber portrays Em with the right combination of anxiety-ridden shyness and plucky determination, complete with a Boston accent. She adeptly voices Garrett and Teddy in confident and cocky tones and is particularly effective narrating taped interviews between suave and skillful Teddy and a variety of actors, relatives, and associates familiar with Garrett's life. Huber shines expressing the comments of a washed-up, alcoholic actor who is by turns combative, whiny, breezy, and pathetic."

REVIEW: *Booklist* v109 no12 p34 F 15 2013 Stephanie Zvirin

REVIEW: *Kirkus Rev* v81 no4 p202 F 15 2013

REVIEW: *Libr J* v138 no6 p65 Ap 1 2013 Charli Osborne

REVIEW: *Publ Wkly* v260 no4 p152 Ja 28 2013

BARNES, SANDRA L. Live long and prosper; how Black megachurches address HIV/AIDS and poverty in the age of prosperity theology; [by] Sandra L. Barnes 242 p. 2013 Fordham University Press

1. AIDS (Disease)—Religious aspects—Christianity 2. African American churches 3. African Americans—Religion 4. Big churches 5. Black theology 6. Church work with the poor 7. Church work with the sick 8. Faith movement (Hagin) 9. Poverty—Religious aspects—Christianity 10. Religious literature

ISBN 0823249565; 9780823249565 (cloth : alk. paper); 9780823249572 (pbk. : alk. paper)

LC 2012-022301

SUMMARY: This book, by Sandra L. Barnes presents a "study that reaches beyond superficial understandings of the Black megachurch phenomenon in a piercing interrogation of how powerful megachurches address (or fail to address) two social crises in the Black community: HIV/AIDS and poverty. Professor Barnes makes the case that the Black megachurch is a complex, contemporary model of the historic Black church in response to globalism, consumerism, secularism, religious syncretism, and the realities of race." (Publisher's note)

REVIEW: *Choice* v51 no1 p94-5 S 2013 J. M. Robinson

"Live Long and Prosper: How Black Megachurches Address HIV/AIDS and Poverty in the Age of Prosperity Theology." "[Author Sandra L.] Barnes . . . offers a provocative, thoughtful treatise on black megachurches in the US, with particular emphasis on how these religious centers have responded to issues of poverty and HIV/AIDS. With a striking interrogation of black church culture and . . . how black megachurch ministers use . . . liberation theology, womanism, black uplift, and the social gospel, Barnes weaves an interesting tapestry of . . . black megachurch culture. A key component of her work explores the ideological impact of prosperity theology on black megachurches and argues for a continuum of perspectives that lie within its application among black clergy."

BARNETT, CORRELLI. The Lords of War; From Lincoln to Churchill, Supreme Command 1861-1945; [by] Correlli Barnett 336 p. 2013 Casemate Pub & Book Dist Llc

1. Historical literature 2. Leadership 3. Lincoln, Abraham, 1809-1865 4. Military art & science 5. Military history

ISBN 1781590931; 9781781590935

SUMMARY: In this "study of leadership, Correlli Barnett examines the strengths and weaknesses of twenty leaders in the nineteenth and early twentieth centuries. He examines how the difficulties they faced and the political and strategic backgrounds of their days and analyses how they performed and what they achieved. " Subjects include "Abraham Lincoln, David Lloyd George, Winston Churchill, Adolf Hitler and Joseph Stalin." (Publisher's note)

REVIEW: *TLS* no5765 p28 S 27 2013 BRIAN HOLDEN REID

"The Lords of War: From Lincoln to Churchill, Supreme Command, 1861-1945." " [Correlli] Bamett's introductory survey of the sources . . . is one of the best short statements I have read on the subject . . . Bamett is one of the few British historians who has gauged Eisenhower's great abilities accurately. . . . The chapters on the nineteenth century are more derivative than those on the twentieth. Bamett is a lively and provocative historian who writes in a wonderfully readable and trenchant style, sprinkled with arresting metaphors and apt judgements, as he does here. But his views also provoke dissent. . . . He has also not been well served by his editor, for there is much overlap and repetition. . . . Yet there is much to admire here."

BARNETT, MAC. Battle Bunny; 32 p. 2013 Simon & Schuster Books for Young Readers

1. Birthdays—Fiction 2. Forest animals—Fiction 3. Humorous stories 4. Parties—Fiction 5. Rabbits—Fiction 6. Supervillains—Fiction

ISBN 1442446730; 9781442446731 (hardcover); 9781442446748 (e-book)

LC 2012-025515

SUMMARY: In this book, by Jon Scieszka, "Alex has been given a saccharine, sappy, silly-sweet picture book about Birthday Bunny that his grandma found at a garage sale. Alex isn't interested--until he decides to make the book something he'd actually like to read. So he takes out his pencil, sharpens his creativity, and totally transforms the story!" (Publisher's note)

REVIEW: *Booklist* v110 no3 p52 O 1 2013 Thom Barthelmess

"Battle Bunny." "This deliciously subversive piece of metafiction skewers--with a sharp wit and a sharper pencil—the earnest, purposeful literature so popular in the middle of the last century. The fun begins with a facsimile of something akin to an antique Little Golden Book, Birthday Bunny, complete with worn cover, yellowed pages, and wholesome message. But the book has been 'improved' in story and pictures by a child named Alex wielding his trusty no. 2. The cover, retitled Battle Bunny, now features rockets, planes, bombs, and a general promise of mayhem."

REVIEW: *Bull Cent Child Books* v67 no4 p239 D 2013 K. C.

REVIEW: *Horn Book Magazine* v89 no6 p82 N/D 2013 ROGER SUTTON

REVIEW: *Kirkus Rev* v81 no17 p116 S 1 2013

REVIEW: *Publ Wkly* p41-2 Children's starred review annual 2013

REVIEW: *Publ Wkly* v260 no31 p69 Ag 5 2013

BARNETT, MAC. President Taft is stuck in the bath; [by] Mac Barnett 32 p. 2014 Candlewick Press

1. Bathtubs 2. Cabinet officers 3. Children's stories 4 Presidents—United States—Juvenile literature 5. Taft, William H. (William Howard), 1857-1930
ISBN 0763663174; 9780763663179
LC 2013-943103

SUMMARY: Written by Mac Barnett and illustrated by Chris Van Dusen and "inspired by a true anecdote, this larger-than-life tale of a presidential mishap is brimming with humor and over-the-top illustrations." It portrays "a parade of clueless cabinet members advising the exasperated" U.S. President William Howard Taft" on how to extricate himself from his bathtub. (Publisher's note)

REVIEW: *Booklist* v110 no14 p84 Mr 15 2014 Angela Leeper

REVIEW: *Bull Cent Child Books* v67 no8 p395 Ap 2014 A. A.

REVIEW: *Kirkus Rev* v81 no24 p314 D 15 2013

"President Taft is Stuck in the Bath". "[Marc] Barnett spins a probably apocryphal but nonetheless hilarious incident into a Cabinet-level crisis. . . . [Chris] Van Dusen goes for a humorous, rather than mean, caricature. He depicts the porky president as a corpulent, bare figure sporting artfully placed suds, plus a fierce glower and a bristling handlebar mustache over multiple chins. Eventually, the luxuriously appointed White House bathroom fills up with likewise caricatured officials. At the suggestion of the (petite) first lady, they pull together so effectively that they send their lardy leader rocketing out the window."

REVIEW: *Publ Wkly* v260 no52 p51 D 23 2013

REVIEW: *SLJ* v60 no3 p100 Mr 2014 Wendy Lukehart

BARNEY, JAMES. The Joshua Stone; [by] James Barney 416 p. 2013 William Morrow

1. Conspiracies—Fiction 2. FICTION—General 3. FICTION—Suspense 4. FICTION—Thrillers 5. Government investigators—Fiction 6. Religion and science—Fiction
ISBN 0062021397; 9780062021397 (pbk.)
LC 2013-033188

SUMMARY: In this book, by James Barney, "scientists working in a top-secret lab in 1959 have disappeared; what they found before the disappearance, we learn, has the potential to destroy the modern world. Government agents Mike Califano and Ana Thorne investigate, but what they discover seems . . . unbelievable. Then, in the small town where the scientists disappeared, an out-of-place man arrives in a diner with clothing and money from an earlier era. Could he be one of the missing scientists?" (Booklist)

REVIEW: *Booklist* v110 no3 p35 O 1 2013 Jeff Ayers

"The Joshua Stone." "[James] Barney mixes the political thriller, technology gone awry, religion, and even some elements of science fiction in this page-turning adventure spectacle. . . . Barney does a phenomenal job juggling all of the elements, creating a thriller unlike any other. Imagine a mix of Michael Crichton, Dan Brown, and Dean Koontz, with a sprinkle of Brad Thor--and maybe a touch of Stephen King's '11/22/63'. 'The Joshua Stone' is completely original and totally terrific. Readers will quickly be looking for Barney's previous novel, 'The Genesis Key' (201 I),and will likely become a fan of his writing for life."

REVIEW: *Kirkus Rev* v81 no19 p235 O 1 2013

REVIEW: *Publ Wkly* v260 no35 p36 S 2 2013

BARNEY, JO. Graffiti Grandma; [by] Jo Barney 338 p 2013 Encore Press

1. Detective & mystery stories 2. Graffiti 3. Homeless persons—Fiction 4. Intergenerational relations 5. Runaway teenagers—Fiction
ISBN 0615726453; 9780615726458

SUMMARY: In this book, "grouchy old Ellie Miller, the 'graffiti grandma,' is on a quixotic mission to scrub the graffiti off the mailboxes in her neighborhood. With solvent and rags, she does it at least once a week. One day, she encounters Sarah, a homeless teenage goth girl who offers to help. But they're wary of each other. In the first chapter, they discover, under a pile of leaves, the body of Peter, a homeless boy who was Sarah's friend and protector." (Kirkus Reviews)

REVIEW: *Kirkus Rev* p6 D 15 2013 supplemet best books 2013

"Graffiti Grandma". "[Jo] Barney is an agile writer with an uncanny ability to tie the plot strings together. . . . Each chapter has its own appropriate point of view, with Ellie and Sarah in first person and Matt and Jeffrey in third. As such, it's easy to get to know Ellie and Sarah and their wary dance around each other; Matt and Jeffrey, less so. Key to the plot is the camp in the nearby dense woods, where young runaways make up a ragtag family. But runaways are turning up dead. Who's the killer? Fortunately, Barney's narrative nimbleness helps wrangle the storylines as they race to a satisfying conclusion. . . . A gripping book with compelling characters who don't want your pity."

REVIEW: *Kirkus Rev* v81 no13 p81 Jl 1 2013

REVIEW: *Publ Wkly* v260 no47 p23 N 18 2013

BARONE, MICHAEL. The almanac of American politics 2012; [by] Michael Barone xviii, 1838 p. 2011 University of Chicago Press

1. Almanacs, American 2. Politicians—United States 3. Reference books 4. United States—Politics & government—2009- 5. United States. Congress—Biography
ISBN 0226038076 (hardcover); 0226038084 (paperback); 9780226038070 (hardcover); 9780226038087 (paperback)
LC 2011-929193

SUMMARY: This book, by Michael Barone and Chuck McCutcheon, is a 2012 edition almanac on U.S. politics. It "includes profiles of every member of Congress and every governor. It offers in-depth and completely up-to-date narrative profiles of all 50 states and 435 House districts, covering everything from economics to history to, of course, politics." (Publisher's note)

REVIEW: *N Y Rev Books* v59 no7 p12-5 Ap 26 2012 Joseph Lelyveld

"The Almanac of American Politics 2012." "The 2012 edition of 'The Almanac of American Politics,' . . . makes it possible to look at . . . [U.S. Congress'] least-known Republican subspecies, the House freshmen, on a district-by-district basis. . . . 'The Almanac' typically offers up three small-print pages on each district, packed with statistics and sidelights on the local economy, demography, recent elections, chatty bios of the incumbents, their embarrassing missteps, boundary changes due to reapportionment, and campaign spending. . . . [Michael] Barone's invaluable compendium stays close to the ground. It isn't easily faulted for slapdash or one-sided commentary. What it offers is a mosaic, not a landscape."

BARONE, MICHAEL. Shaping Our Nation; How Surges of Migration Transformed America and Its Politics; [by] Michael Barone 320 p. 2013 Random House Inc

1. Historical literature 2. Immigrants—United States—History 3. Internal migration—United States 4. United States—Emigration & immigration 5. United States—Politics & government

ISBN 0307461513; 9780307461513

SUMMARY: This book by Michael Barone "examines the internal and immigrant migrations that have 'peopled' America. . . . He emphasizes two recurring themes: the unanticipated beginnings and the rather abrupt endings of these mass migrations and the widespread unease, even fear, each development engendered. . . . Barone . . . demonstrates . . . how sturdy our constitutional framework has proven, at accommodating the religious, economic and cultural diversities." (Kirkus Reviews)

REVIEW: *Kirkus Rev* v81 no17 p44 S 1 2013

REVIEW: *Natl Rev* v65 no21 p39-40 N 11 2013 VICTOR DAVIS HANSON

"Shaping Our Nation: How Surges of Migration Transformed America and Its Politics." "In this brief but fascinating study of both immigration to the United States and mass migrations within it, Michael Barone traces the peopling of America, from the original British Protestants of the 17th century to the present influxes of millions of Mexican nationals and Asians. . . . Barone adroitly charts the early stages of America's path toward the Civil War in a story of parallel migrations. . . . Barone's masterly account of our demographic history could be reassuring in our present chaos, but only if we have not broken with our own precedents. The problem with historical adjudication is that different inputs can often result in quite different outcomes."

REVIEW: *Publ Wkly* v260 no34 p63 Ag 26 2013

BARONE, TOM.ed. Culturally relevant arts education for social justice. See Culturally relevant arts education for social justice

BARR, ALLAN H.tr. Boy in the twilight. See Yu Hua

BARR, DAMIAN. Maggie and Me; [by] Damian Barr 256 p. 2013 Bloomsbury Publishing PLC

1. Bullying 2. Gay men—Great Britain—Biography 3. Memoirs 4. Scotland—Politics & government—20th century 5. Thatcher, Margaret, 1925-2013

ISBN 1408838060; 9781408838068

SUMMARY: This book by Damian Barr presents a "memoir of the difficulties of growing up poor and gay in Margaret Thatcher's Scotland. . . . The collapse of his parents' marriage when he was 8 threw him into a difficult situation with Logan, the 'wicked stepfather.' . . . Ultimately, school became his saving grace, even with the taunting of schoolmates. . . . In addition to his personal story, the author follows the effects of Thatcher's economic policies." (Kirkus Reviews)

REVIEW: *Booklist* v110 no13 p13 Mr 1 2014 Michael Cart

REVIEW: *Kirkus Rev* v82 no4 p74 F 15 2014

"Maggie & Me: Coming Out and Coming of Age in 1980s Scotland". "In addition to his personal story, the author follows the effects of [Margaret] Thatcher's economic policies, as she canceled the free school milk, beat back the coal miners and closed the steel mill where his father worked. If ever a prime minister was hated, it was in the council houses of Britain; her name couldn't be uttered without an expletive. Few readers will blame the author or anyone else angered by her methods; she massively cut social programs and suggested taxing the poor due to the fact that there were more of them. While it should be heartbreaking, [Damian] Barr tells a wonderful story, demonstrating the remarkable resilience of a child not only surviving, but succeeding in such a grand way."

REVIEW: *Libr J* v139 no4 p47 Mr 1 2014 Lisa N. Johnston

REVIEW: *New Statesman* v142 no5156 p42 My 3 2013 Stuart Maconie

BARRERA, ALBINO. Biblical economic ethics; sacred scripture's teachings on economic life; [by] Albino Barrera xv, 351 p. 2013 Lexington Books

1. Economics—Moral & ethical aspects 2. Economics—Religious aspects—Christianity 3. Economics in the Bible 4. Providence & government of God 5. Religious literature

ISBN 9780739182291 (cloth: alk. paper)

LC 2013-016951

SUMMARY: Written by Albino Barrera, "this book is a theological synthesis of the findings of scripture scholars and ethicists on what the Bible teaches about economic life. . . . This book finds that the Bible's economic norms are, in fact, an invitation to participate in God's providence. . . Thus, biblical economic ethics is best characterized as a chronicle of how God provides for humanity through people's mutual solicitude and hard work." (Publisher's note)

REVIEW: *Choice* v51 no8 p1415-6 Ap 2014 L. J. Greenspoon

"Biblical Economic Ethics: Sacred Scripture's Teachings on Economic Life". "[Albino] Barrera . . . offers an account of biblical teachings on the economy that is characterized by thorough and clear presentation of the ancient texts, fair and thoughtful analysis of passages within their biblical context, and sensible and reasonable discussions of how to apply this material to the contemporary world. He begins forthrightly with a well-conceived presentation of methodological issues . . . This book should be required reading for everyone who takes seriously the role of the Bible in the assessment of current economic policies that, for better or worse, are determinative in how people live their lives at the micro- and the macro-level."

BARRERA, MAGDA.ed. Ensuring a sustainable future. See Ensuring a sustainable future

BARRETT, A. IGONI. Love is power, or something like that; [by] A. Igoni Barrett 176 p. 2013 Farrar Straus & Giroux

1. Bad breath 2. Nigeria—Fiction 3. Police—Fiction 4. Rich people—Fiction 5. Short story (Literary form)

ISBN 1555976409 (paperback); 9781555976408 (paperback)
LC 2012-956123

SUMMARY: This collection of short stories, by A. Igoni Barrett, centers on Nigeria. "In these wide-ranging stories, A. Igoni Barrett roams the streets with people from all stations of life. A man with acute halitosis navigates the chaos of the Lagos bus system. A minor policeman, full of the authority and corruption of his uniform, beats his wife. A family's fortunes fall from love and wealth to infidelity and poverty as poor choices unfurl over three generations." (Publisher's note)

REVIEW: *Booklist* v109 no18 p15-6 My 15 2013 Leak Strauss

REVIEW: *Kirkus Rev* v81 no5 p107 Mr 1 2013

REVIEW: *Publ Wkly* v260 no9 p44 Mr 4 2013

REVIEW: *World Lit Today* v87 no5 p8 S/O 2013

"Love is Power, or Something Like That," "The Planets," and "The Mortiloquist." "A. Igoni Barrett presents several stories, all about the absurdity that undoubtedly comes with love. . . . [Sergio] Chejfec tells a compelling story of human loss, how people continue with their lives after tragedy, and how they deal with grief, privately and publicly. First published in English in 2012 and a finalist for the 2013 Best Translated Book Award, 'The Planets' is now available in a digital edition. . . . [Reza] Negarestani's book combines speculative theory, drama, and philosophy with elements of absurdity, tragedy, and horror. . . . Structured in the style of a play, the narrative is both disturbing and captivating for readers interested in challenging what they think they know."

REVIEW: *World Lit Today* v87 no6 p59-60 N/D 2013 Jim Hannan

"Love is Power, or Something Like That." "The egoism, cruelty, and cynicism expressed here fittingly bring to a close a book that strives to capture an edgy, dangerous, volatile society struggling under corruption and, frequently, disregard for the well-being of other people. . . . Whether such acts are prevalent in Lagos (the setting of most of the stories), [A. Igoni] Barrett could do more to convey why he wants to write about them. Too frequently his stories lack self-reflection or insight into what makes his characters act the way they do. . . . Barrett is at his best when he allows himself to move from caricature, a problem that plagues other stories, to more fully developed characters."

BARRETT, ANDREA. Archangel; Fiction; [by] Andrea Barrett 238 p. 2013 W W Norton & Co Inc

1. Evolution (Biology) 2. Science—Social aspects—History—19th century—Fiction 3. Science—Social aspects—History—20th century—Fiction 4. Short stories 5. Women scientists—Fiction
ISBN 0393240002 (hardcover); 9780393240009 (hardcover)
LC 2013-016958

SUMMARY: This is a collection of science-focused stories from National Book Award winner Andrea Barrett. "In 'The Ether of Space,' set in 1920, astronomer Phoebe Wells struggles with the implications of Einstein's theories; in 'The Island,' set in 1873, young biologist Henrietta Atkins, initially worshipful of a creationist professor, succumbs to Darwinism. (Publishers Weekly)

REVIEW: *Booklist* v109 no21 p43 Jl 1 2013 Donna Seaman

REVIEW. *Kirkus Rev* p6 N 15 2013 Best Books

REVIEW: *Kirkus Rev* v81 no2 p6 Je 1 2013

REVIEW: *Libr J* v138 no4 p55 Mr 1 2013 Barbara Hoffert

REVIEW: *Libr J* v138 no10 p104 Je 1 2013 Susanne Wells

REVIEW: *N Y Rev Books* v60 no18 p54-6 N 21 2013 April Bernard

"The Signature of All Things" and "Archangel." "Andrea Barrett is a splendid writer of what, for lack of any better term, we call literary fiction; Elizabeth Gilbert . . . is an energetic scribbler. Barrett writes of science and scientists from profound understanding and passion, exploring how scientific reason and human feeling collide and illuminate one another. Gilbert's novel is another matter. . . .Inside this big sloppy novel, there is a good short story longing to get out. . . . Like [Charles] Darwin, and [Albert] Einstein, and all her other heroes, Barrett the storyteller pulls us relentlessly away from false comforts, into the dazzling, often chaotic, world as it really is."

REVIEW: *N Y Times Book Rev* p24 S 29 2013 Andrea Barrett

"Archangel." "This is the essence of [Andrea] Barrett's method: where we expect a moment of high drama or forceful resolution, we get a tiny, resonant detail, a shade of melancholy, a small satisfaction. . . . There are the experiments themselves, which Barrett describes in rich and nuanced detail, and, likewise, the feelings of the characters. But the characters themselves are bit players, whose insights seem almost intentionally modest and limited. . . . Andrea Barrett is a consummate literary artist, but in 'Archangel' she's trying to superimpose order and decorum on an era that tolerated neither."

REVIEW: *New York Times* v162 no56248 pC1-4 S 3 2013 JANET MASLIN

REVIEW: *Publ Wkly* v260 no24 p38 Je 17 2013

BARRETT, CATHERINE ANNE. Dictionary of computer and internet terms. See Covington, M.

BARRETT, DAVID M. (DAVID MARTIN), 1937-2014. Blind over Cuba. See Holland, M.

BARRON, ASHLEY.il. Shaping Up Summer. See Flatt, L.

BARROWS, ANNIE. Ivy + Bean take the case; [by] Annie Barrows 128 p. 2013 Chronicle Books

1. Bean (Fictitious character: Barrows)—Juvenile fiction 2. Best friends—Fiction 3. Best friends—Juvenile fiction 4. Friendship—Fiction 5. Humorous stories 6. Ivy (Fictitious character: Barrows)—Juvenile fiction 7. Mystery and detective stories 8. Private investigators—Fiction 9. Private investigators—Juvenile fiction
ISBN 1452106991; 9781452106991 (alk. paper)
LC 2012-046876

SUMMARY: In this children's book by Annie Barrows, "inspired by a black-and-white movie . . . Bean goes into the PI business. Donning an old fedora, in no time she attracts the attention of the other neighborhood children, including best friend Ivy. Bean solves a couple of mysteries . . . but the kids are not particularly impressed. Then a real mystery arises: A bright yellow rope appears, tied around Dino's chimney and trailing onto his lawn." (Kirkus Reviews)

REVIEW: *Horn Book Magazine* v89 no6 p86-7 N/D 2013 JENNIFER M. BRABANDER

"Ivy + Bean Take the Case". "The intrepid girls are ultimately unable to solve the case but decide they like having a mystery in their midst. Ivy and Bean enjoy imagining that an alien (or a gnome or a rabbit) is behind the rope tricks, as will many young readers. For those kids dissatisfied with the open ending, adults might nudge them toward the likely culprit—Jake the teenager, whose large shopping bag and slight smile as he walks past Bean's front-lawn 'office' are more than a little mysterious. It's no mystery, though, why these early chapter books continue to please: cleverly entertaining stories, and illustrations to match."

BARRY, DAVE, 1947-. You can date boys when you're forty; Dave Barry on parenting and other topics he knows very little about; [by] Dave Barry 240 p. 2014 G.P. Putnam's Sons

1. Aging—Humor 2. American wit & humor 3. Family—Humor 4. Men—Humor 5. Parenting—Humor
ISBN 0399165940; 9780399165948 (hardback)
LC 2013-037714

SUMMARY: This book, by humorist Dave Barry "includes nine never-before-published essays. . . Though not only about parenting (Viagra commercials, horseback riding, cremation and grammar are just a few of the topics addressed), Barry . . . [focuses on] describing his role as the 65-year-old dad of a 13-year-old daughter." (Publishers Weekly)

REVIEW: *Booklist* v111 no2 p67 S 15 2014 Candace Smith

REVIEW: *Booklist* v110 no8 p4-5 D 15 2013 Vanessa Bush

"You Can Date Boys When You're Forty: Dave Barry on Parenting and Other Topics He Knows Very Little About". "Parenting is one of many topics Barry treats to his humorous take on life. . . . Barry laments the current lack of manliness and offers detailed instructions on a host of activities a manly man should be capable of doing, such as barbecuing a steak, jump-starting a dead battery, riding a horse, and performing emergency first aid, and offers hilarious musings on the popularity among women of 'Fifty Shades of Grey' (2011). Barry fans will appreciate this latest collection by the Pulitzer Prize-winning humorist."

REVIEW: *Kirkus Rev* v82 no1 p182 Ja 1 2014

"You Can Date Boys When You're Forty". " Another wide-ranging collection of funny essays about parenting . . . by best-selling humorist [Dave] Barry. . . . Although parenting is well-worn fodder for comedians, only Barry would coolly share his idea to install traps around his home to capture any teenage boys who would dare watch TV from the same sofa as his daughter and release the boys . . . into the Everglades. . . . A mishmash, but even those who don't have children and have never lived in Miami or searched for a Wi-Fi connection in the Israeli desert will appreciate Barry's lighthearted absurdity."

REVIEW: *Publ Wkly* v260 no50 p57-8 D 9 2013

BARRY GOLDWATER AND THE REMAKING OF THE AMERICAN POLITICAL LANDSCAPE; viii, 281 p. 2013 University of Arizona Press

1. Conservatism—United States—History—20th century 2. Legislators—United States—Biography 3. Political culture—United States—History—20th century 4. Political science literature 5. Presidential candidates—United States—Biography
ISBN 9780816521098 (cloth : alk. paper)
LC 2012-029636

SUMMARY: "The twelve essays in this volume thoroughly examine the life, times, and impact of" U.S. politician Barry Goldwater. Scrutinizing the transformation of a Phoenix department store owner into a politician, de facto political philosopher, and five-time US senator, contributors highlight the importance of power, showcasing the relationship between the nascent conservative movement's cadre of elite businessmen, newsmen, and intellectuals and their followers at the grassroots . . . level." (Publisher's note)

REVIEW: *Choice* v51 no5 p921-2 Ja 2014 R. J. Meagher

"Barry Goldwater and the Remaking of the American Political Landscape." "Particularly perceptive chapters include Brian Allen Drake on the tension between Goldwater's distrust of 'big government' and his longstanding support for environmental conservation, and Joseph Crespino's account of Goldwater's complicated relationship with South Carolina Senator Strom Thurmond. Other chapters wander further away from Goldwater than might be useful; Michael Bowen's description of the resistance of liberal Republicans to conservative supporters of Ohio Senator Robert A. Taft, while well argued, offers more prologue than insight into Goldwater's politics. Taken as a whole, however, this book offers valuable scholarship that further cements Goldwater's central place in the rise of American conservatism."

BARRY, JOHN.ed. Great Deeds in Ireland. See Great Deeds in Ireland

BARSHAM, DIANA. William Hayley (1745-1820), Poet, Biographer and Libertarian; A Reassessment; [by] Diana Barsham 208 p. 2013 University of Chichester

1. Authorship 2. Biographers 3. English poetry—History & criticism 4. Hayley, William, 1745-1820 5. Literature—History & criticism 6. Poets
ISBN 1907852158; 9781907852152

SUMMARY: "Containing essays by eleven scholars, the book demonstrates the continued relevance of [William] Hayley's kind of poetry--which was lauded in his time, his most successful poem, 'The Triumphs of Temper,' achieving sixteen British editions between 1781 and 1817 which is far more, in the period, than any work by his 'Romantic' successors." (Publisher's note)

REVIEW: *TLS* no5767 p22 O 11 2013 MIN WILD

"William Hayley (1745-1820): Poet, Biographer, and Libertarian: A Reassessment" and "William Hayley (1745-1820): England's Lost Laureate: Selected Poetry." "Hayley's own fatal facility has often compromised him for later audiences, and even though these two volumes contain much of use and interest, nobody's heart seems to have been in the making of them, just as Hayley's heart did not always suffuse his written words with the feeling he claimed. . . .Readers may leave these volumes grieving for two missed opportunities. One concerns production values, which are poor in both, though 'Selected Poetry' is atrocious. . . . The second missed opportunity, then, is . . . any book reassessing him needed to align itself firmly alongside current scholarly work on pre-Romantic and Romantic networks of friendship and patronage."

BARSLUND, CHARLOTTE.tr. A fairy tale. See Bengtsson, J. T.

BARSS, BILL.il. The hour. See De Voto, B. A.

BARSTOW, STAN, 1928-2011. The Likes of Us; Stories of Five Decades; [by] Stan Barstow 697 p. 2013 Parthian Books

1. Death—Fiction 2. Great Britain—Fiction 3. Marriage—Fiction 4. Murder—Fiction 5. Short stories
ISBN 1908069678; 9781908069672

SUMMARY: This collection of short stories by Stan Barstow "covers the last five decades of British life." Topics include "a group of young tearaways on a night out that begins with horseplay and ends in tragedy; the loneliness of a drunken miner's wife; a war-shocked ex-sailor forced beyond endurance; and a factory worker finding his way through his marriage." (Publisher's note)

REVIEW: *TLS* no5754 p19 Jl 12 2013 DAVID COLLARD

"The Likes of Us: Stories of Five Decades." "[Stan] Barstow's strength lies in characterization and situation, and he is brilliantly concise in his set-ups--who, what, where, when--before exploring the whys and hows. . . . Barstow's years as an engineering draughtsman are reflected in the hand-finished feel of his precise, persuasive prose. He paces dialogue very well (many of the stories consist of little else), has a good ear for everyday speech, and a feel for the social nuances and inequalities within classes. There is an occasional whiff of O. Henry hokum in the weaker yarns, usually involving poetic justice or comeuppance."

BARTFAI, TAMAS. The future of drug discovery; who decides which diseases to treat?; [by] Tamas Bartfai xxx, 346 p. 2013 Academic Press

1. Drug Discovery—trends 2. Drug Industry—economics 3. Drug development 4. Drugs—Design 5. Social science literature
ISBN 0124071805 (pbk.); 9780124071803 (pbk.)
LC 2012-277814

SUMMARY: This book examines "the efforts of the pharmaceutical industry and how they relate, or should relate, to societal needs. The authors posit that as a result of increasing risk aversion and accelerated savings in research and development, the industry is not developing drugs for increasingly prevalent diseases, such as Alzheimer's disease, untreatable pain, antibiotics and more." (Publisher's note)

REVIEW: *Choice* v51 no4 p674 D 2013 D. C. Eustice

"The Future of Drug Discovery: Who Decides Which Diseases to Treat?." "[Tamas] Bartfai . . . and [Graham V.] Lees . . . provide a critical, much-needed review of the pharmaceutical industry, worldwide. . . . This book reviews in exquisite detail the drug development process from the initial inception of an idea through the life cycle of a new drug entity. The authors also spend an appropriate amount of time on the role of government-funded research programs along with the role of medium and small biotechnology companies in the drug treatment of diseases. . . . The excellent indexing will allow readers to use the book as a reference source without having to read it cover to cover."

BARTHEL-BOUCHIER, DIANE. Cultural heritage and the challenge of sustainability; [by] Diane Barthel-Bouchier 235 p. 2012 Left Coast Press, Inc.

1. Cultural landscapes 2. Cultural property—Environmental aspects 3. Heritage tourism 4. Social science literature 5. Sustainability 6. Sustainable tourism 7. World heritage areas—Environmental aspects
ISBN 9781611322378 (hardback: alk. paper); 9781611322385 (pbk.: alk. paper); 9781611322392 (institutional ebook); 9781611326789 (consumer ebook)
LC 2012-020774

SUMMARY: In this book on the cultural heritage industry, Diane Barthel-Bouchier "argues that programmatic commitments to sustainability arose both from direct environmental threats to tangible and intangible heritage, and from social and economic contradictions as heritage developed into a truly global organizational field. . . . She examines key international organizations . . . and national trust organizations of Great Britain, the United States, Australia, and many others." (Publisher's note)

REVIEW: *Choice* v50 no12 p2273 Ag 2013 J. F. Kovacs

REVIEW: *Contemp Sociol* v43 no1 p130 Ja 2014

"Cultural Heritage and the Challenge of Sustainability". "The author maintains a sociological narrative throughout the book and utilizes many quotes from familiar thinkers. Relying on interviews and conversations with heritage representatives and conference delegates, she provides plentiful real-life examples from around the globe to illustrate the progressing relationship between heritage conservation and sustainability. This book would be especially useful to environmental sociologists, but could also appeal to anyone interested in collective memory, cultural heritage, globalization, organizations, or the construction of social problems."

BARTLETT, DON.tr. Before I burn. See Gaute H. I.

BARTLETT, DON.tr. Boyhood Island. See Knausgaard, K. O.

BARTLETT, DON.tr. Cold Hearts. See Staalesen, G.

BARTLETT, DON.tr. My struggle. See Knausgaard, K.O.

BARTLETT, MYKE. Fire in the Sea; [by] Myke Bartlett 320 p. 2014 Text Publishing Company

1. Australia—Fiction 2. Demonology 3. Fantasy fiction 4. Gods 5. War stories
ISBN 1921922745; 9781921922749

SUMMARY: In this novel by Myke Bartlett "Sadie is sixteen and bored with life. It's summer, and lazing on the beach in the stifling heat with her cousins and Tom is a drag. Then something comes out of the sea. Sadie soon finds herself caught in the middle of an ancient conflict that is nearing its final battle, a showdown that threatens to engulf her city and all those she loves in a furious tsunami." (Publisher's note)

REVIEW: *Kirkus Rev* v81 no24 p258 D 15 2013

"Fire in the Sea". "Immortality, a sunken city, a violent Minotaur and a cult join in contemporary Australia for adventure that's haphazard but fast-paced. . . . Despite deft handling of Sadie's grief over her parents' deaths years ago, [Myke] Bartlett neglects Jake's crucial emotional back story: Supposedly, fear and shame prevented Jake from solving the demon/Gods crisis ages ago, but the text gives barely a nod to Jake's emotions, so that explanation seems empty. Narrative perspective wanders; careless slams ('lezzo'; the Drowners 'look . . . Japanese') rankle. Aussie-flavored excitement with ancient Greek tidbits, underdeveloped in places."

REVIEW: *Publ Wkly* v260 no49 p86 D 2 2013

REVIEW: *Voice of Youth Advocates* v37 no1 p77 Ap 2014 Hilary Crew

BARTON, BYRON. My bus; [by] Byron Barton 40 p. 2014 Greenwillow Books, an imprint of HarperCollinsPublishers

1. Buses—Fiction 2. Children's stories 3. Mathematics—Fiction 4. Pets—Fiction 5. Transportation—Fiction

ISBN 0062287362; 9780062287366 (trade ed.)

LC 2013-007869

SUMMARY: This book, by Byron Barton, "is a lively celebration of vehicles and transportation, occupations, pets, and basic math concepts. The busy bus driver . . . has a job to do. He drives his bus along his route, picks up the cat and dog passengers waiting at the bus stops, and delivers them to their destinations--which in this case include the airport, the harbor, and the train station. Along the way, children are introduced to the concepts of addition, subtraction, and sets." (Publisher's note)

REVIEW: *Booklist* v110 no14 p82 Mr 15 2014 Daniel Kraus

REVIEW: *Horn Book Magazine* v90 no2 p95-6 Mr/Ap 2014 KATHLEEN T. HORNING

"My Bus." "Beyond the initial excitement many young children will feel as they share Joe's journey and see the departing animals through the windows of their various vehicles, there is so much here for repeated readings (and there will be repeated readings). [Byron] Barton ingeniously introduces the basic concepts of cardinal and ordinal numbers, addition, subtraction, and sets, but he does it all so subtly that even parents may not realize they're getting a math lesson. And yet it's all there for little brains to absorb and work out on their own as they 'sail, ride, and fly away' again and again. Illustrated in [Byron] Barton's signature style, with bold, flat colors and with only the most important visual details included, this is a welcome companion to 'My Car'."

REVIEW: *Kirkus Rev* v82 no3 p209 F 1 2014

REVIEW: *Publ Wkly* v261 no11 p83 Mr 17 2014

REVIEW: *SLJ* v60 no3 p102 Mr 2014 Diane McCabe

BARTON, BYRON.il. My bus. See Barton, B.

BASBANES, NICHOLAS A. On paper; the everything of its two-thousand-year history; [by] Nicholas A. Basbanes 448 p. 2013 Alfred A. Knopf

1. Historical literature 2. Paper—History 3. Paper—Social aspects 4. Paper industry—History 5. Papermaking—History

ISBN 0307266427; 9780307266422

LC 2012-050267

SUMMARY: This book, by Nicholas A. Basbanes, presents "a consideration of all things paper: its invention that revolutionized human civilization; its thousand-fold uses (and misuses), proliferation, and sweeping influence on society; its makers, shapers, collectors, and pulpers. Basbanes writes about the ways in which paper has been used to record history, make laws, conduct business, and establish identities." (Publisher's note)

REVIEW: *Choice* v51 no7 p1177 Mr 2014 D. G. Davis Jr.

"On Paper: The Everything of Its Two-Thousand-Year History." "Noteworthy for his written works on books and their readers, journalist [Nicholas] Basbanes has produced a significant treatment of paper as a phenomenon. Its subtitle notwithstanding, the book is a pleasant, personal survey and travelogue treating the history of paper. . . . In most chapters the author and his wife's encounters with crafts folk, entrepreneurs, forensic specialists, and scholars enrich the work, drawing general readers into an appreciation of the role of paper in the past two millennia. Like the illustrations and case studies, the arrangement of the chapters seems a bit idiosyncratic, if entertaining."

REVIEW: *Kirkus Rev* v81 no17 p45-6 S 1 2013

REVIEW: *Libr J* v138 no21 p108 D 1 2013 Stewart Desmond

REVIEW: *Libr J* v138 no9 p54 My 15 2013 Barbara Hoffert

REVIEW: *New Yorker* v89 no36 p83-1 N 11 2013

REVIEW: *Publ Wkly* v260 no31 p60 Ag 5 2013

REVIEW: *TLS* no5790 p25 Mr 21 2014 LEAH PRICE

"On Paper: The Everything of Its Two-Thousand-Year History." "'On Paper's' 448 pages are weighed down by quotations from mission statements (Kimberly-Clark's, the Digital Public Library of America's), posed portraits of CEOs and library directors, and [author Nicholas A.] Basbanes's tic of introducing his sources as 'eminent,' 'noted,' or 'highly respected.' But a slimmer volume might not have done justice to paper's travels from its beginnings in China sometime before the first century BC. . . . In the decade since then, Silicon Valley has touted the paperless office as the answer to deforestation. Basbanes's rejoinder is that paper, made for centuries from old clothes, was one of the first industrial products to incorporate recycled materials."

BASHOR, WILL. Marie Antoinette's head; the royal hairdresser, the queen, and the revolution; [by] Will Bashor 320 p. 2013 Lyons Press

1. BIOGRAPHY & AUTOBIOGRAPHY—Royalty 2. HISTORY—Europe—France 3. Historical literature

ISBN 9780762791538 (hardback)

LC 2013-019803

SUMMARY: This "biography . . . looks at the French Revolution through the eyes of the queen's hairdresser and confidant. When Léonard Autié first arrived as a young man in Paris in 1769 . . . his possessions consisted of little more than a few coins, a tortoiseshell comb and 'an ample supply of confidence.' Ten years later, after he created the famous "pouf" hairstyle, he was the hairdresser to the queen of France." (Kirkus Reviews)

REVIEW: *Kirkus Rev* v81 no24 p393 D 15 2013

"Marie Antoinette's Head: The Royal Hairdresser, the Queen, and the Revolution". "Fortunately . . . [Will] Bashor liberally quotes from the Souvenirs de Léonard [Autié], giving his own account a gossipy, entertaining directness, similar to a historical novel. . . . Bashor doesn't clearly explain the specifics of hair powdering and wig making or how Autié arranged his fantastic poufs (although he does include illustrations), but his depiction of Autié's fascinating fly-on-the wall role as confidant to doomed royalty makes up for it. Overall, he delivers an informative examination of a little-known player on a great stage. An entertaining, well-researched work that will particularly interest students of cultural history and the French Revolution."

REVIEW: *Kirkus Rev* v82 no1 p165 Ja 1 2014

REVIEW: *Libr J* v138 no16 p81 O 1 2013 Linda Frederiksen

BASKIN, NORA RALEIGH. Runt; [by] Nora Raleigh Baskin 208 p. 2013 Simon & Schuster Books for Young Readers

1. Bullying—Fiction 2. Dogs—Fiction 3. JUVENILE FICTION—Social Issues—Bullying 4. JUVENILE FICTION—Social Issues—Emotions & Feelings 5. JUVENILE FICTION—Social Issues—Friendship 6. Middle schools—Fiction 7. Online social networks—Fiction 8. Popularity—Fiction 9. School stories 10. Schools—Fiction
ISBN 1442458070; 9781442458079 (hardback); 9781442458086 (paperback)
LC 2012-049461

SUMMARY: This book shows "the day-to-day torments of students in a sixth-grade class. In a series of brief vignettes, [Nora Raleigh Baskin] moves between classmates including 'Smelly-Girl' Elizabeth, who can't shake the lingering scent (or shed hair) of her mother's dog-sitting business; Elizabeth's nemesis, Maggie, who . . . hasn't been able to repair her fallout with her artistically talented former best friend Freida; and Stewart and Matthew, two athletes whose rivalry leads to a fight." (Publishers Weekly)

REVIEW: *Booklist* v109 no21 p75 Jl 1 2013 Carolyn Phelan

REVIEW: *Bull Cent Child Books* v67 no1 p6-7 S 2013 D. S.

REVIEW: *Kirkus Rev* v81 no12 p80 Je 15 2013

REVIEW: *N Y Times Book Rev* p18 Ag 25 2013 JESSICA GROSE

"Runt" and "Trash Can Days: A Middle School Saga." "'Runt' has a straightforward message to impart: Don't sink to the level of the mean girl. 'Trash Can Days' has a more nuanced, more entertaining take on the socially powerful--one that doesn't fit into the tidy parameters of an 'After-school Special'-style lesson. . . . [Nora Raleigh] Baskin uses the animals Elizabeth's mother looks after to make a heavy-handed, book-long metaphor about alpha dogs . . . and submissive dogs. . . . [Teddy] Steinkellner has a sharp grasp of the insult-laden dialogue middle schoolers use with obnoxious abandon. Just as he doesn't sugarcoat the way his characters express themselves, the relationship between Danny and Jake doesn't resolve itself neatly or painlessly."

REVIEW: *Publ Wkly* v260 no22 p61 Je 3 2013

REVIEW: *SLJ* v59 no8 p95 Ag 2013 Kathy Cherniavsky

BASKIN, NORA RALEIGH, 1961-. Subway love; [by] Nora Raleigh Baskin 224 p. 2014 Candlewick Press

1. Child abuse—Fiction 2. Families—Fiction 3. Love stories 4. Subways—New York (State)—New York 5. Time travel—Fiction
ISBN 9780763668457
LC 2013-946617

SUMMARY: In this book, by Nora Raleigh Baskin, "the whole peace and love movement seems to have been lost on Laura's mom's latest boyfriend . . . who beats Laura with an alarming regularity. Meanwhile, sixteen-year-old Jonas is dealing with his own family issues. . . . The two teenagers are drawn to each other on a New York City subway car, but it's Jonas who realizes their connection transcends time, with Laura existing in 1973 and Jonas living in modern day NYC." (Bulletin of the Center for Children's Books)

REVIEW: *Booklist* v110 no17 p98 My 1 2014 Francisca Goldsmith

REVIEW: *Bull Cent Child Books* v67 no10 p500 Je 2014 K. Q. G.

"Subway Love". "This is a quiet, heartfelt love story that is not only about two kids falling for each other but also about their healing from painful events and learning to take charge of their own fate, despite the failures of the adults in their lives. Although she's shadowed by her abuse, Laura's not defined by it, and [Nora Raleigh] Baskin paints her as an active and eager partner in her emotional and physical relationship with Jonas, not just a girl needing to be saved. A subplot involving a subway graffiti artist further contextualizes their romance and leaves readers with the message that this love story, like any love story, is both singularly important and also just one of many human narratives."

REVIEW: *Kirkus Rev* v82 no7 p125 Ap 1 2014

REVIEW: *Publ Wkly* v261 no11 p87 Mr 17 2014

REVIEW: *SLJ* v60 no4 p156 Ap 2014 Karen Alexander

REVIEW: *Voice of Youth Advocates* v37 no1 p77 Ap 2014 Matthew Weaver

BASL, JOHN.ed. Designer biology. See Designer biology

BASS, GARY JONATHAN, 1969-. The Blood telegram; Nixon, Kissinger, and a forgotten genocide; [by] Gary Jonathan Bass 528 p. 2013 Alfred A. Knopf

1. Genocide—Bangladesh 2. Historical literature
ISBN 0307700208; 9780307700209
LC 2013-014788

SUMMARY: This book by Gary J. Bass examines "humanitarian crisis that propelled the creation of Bangladesh." Particular focus is given to how "[Richard] Nixon's deep distrust of India--which he viewed as an ungovernable cauldron of Soviet-leaning liberals, lefties and hippies--and his long-time support of the military in Pakistan disastrously steered his and [Henry] Kissinger's resolve not to stay the hand of Gen. Agha Mohammad Yahya Khan against a dissenting East Pakistan in March 1971." (Kirkus Reviews)

REVIEW: *Bookforum* v20 no3 p55 S-N 2013 LLOYD GARDNER

"The Blood Telegram: Nixon, Kissinger, and a Forgotten Genocide." "[An] impressively researched book about a 'forgotten genocide'. . . . It might not have been possible to avoid the partition that produced Bangladesh, but [Gary J.] Bass makes a powerful argument that [Richard] Nixon and Henry] Kissinger were responsible for the conflict veering into a full-scale genocide. They dismissed [Archer] Blood's telegram for both political and personal reasons, yet the document still stands as a powerful historical indictment of what happened--not simply in the 1971 crisis in South Asia, but also over the next two decades of the Cold War."

REVIEW: *Booklist* v110 no2 p17 S 15 2013 Brendan Driscoll

REVIEW: *Choice* v51 no10 p1884 Je 2014 W. R. Pruitt

REVIEW: *Economist* v408 no8854 p90-1 S 21 2013

"The Blood Telegram: Nixon, Kissinger and a Forgotten Genocide." "The centrepiece of Mr. [Gary] Bass's gripping and well-researched book is the story of how America's most senior diplomat in East Pakistan, Archer Blood, the consul-general in Dhaka, sent regular, detailed and accurate reports of the bloodshed. . . . Mr. Bass does a good job of explaining [Richard] Nixon's willful support of Pakistan. . . . He sets out with admirable clarity what else was at stake. . . . Could things have been different if America, having listened to Blood, had pressed Pakistan not to slaughter its own people in 1971? Mr. Bass does not speculate directly."

REVIEW: *Kirkus Rev* v81 no16 p270 Ag 15 2013

REVIEW: *N Y Times Book Rev* p15 S 29 2013 Gary J. Bass

"The Blood Telegram: Nixon, Kissinger, and a Forgotten Genocide." "This is a dark and amazing tale, an essential reminder of the devastation wrought by the hardhearted policy and outright bigotry that typified much of the diplomacy of the cold war. . . . The voices of [Henry] Kissinger and [Richard] Nixon are the book's most shocking aspects. [Gary J.] Bass has unearthed a series of conversations, most of them from the White House's secret tapes, that reveal Nixon and ?Kissinger as breathtakingly vulgar and hateful. . . . Nixon and Kissinger spent the decades after leaving office burnishing their image as great statesmen. This book goes a long way in showing just how undeserved those reputations are."

REVIEW: *Nation* v297 no23 p36-40 D 9 2013 THOMAS MEANEY

REVIEW: *New Repub* v244 no19 p44-9 N 25 2013 Sunil Khilnani

"The Blood Telegram: Nixon, Kissinger, and a Forgotten Genocide" and "1971: A Global History of the Creation of Bangladesh." "Now we have two excellent and uncannily complementary books about the crucible of 1971. [Gary J.] Bass . . . has written an account--learned, riveting, and eviscerating--of the delusions and the deceptions of [Richard] Nixon and [Henry] Kissinger. Steeped in the forensic skills of a professional academic historian, he also possesses the imaginative energies of a classical moralist, and he tells the story of the choices and the decisions that led to the slaughter in Bengal . . . appropriately as a moral saga. Srinath Raghavan, a former Indian army officer who researches and teaches in Delhi and in London, takes a more dispassionate approach. His superb analysis of the global intricacies of 1971 uses that wider lens with great precision to explain the breakup of Pakistan more convincingly than any preceding account."

REVIEW: *New Yorker* v89 no29 p109-14 S 23 2013 Pankaj Mishra

"1971: A Global History of the Creation of Bangladesh" and "The Blood Telegram: Nixon, Kissinger, and a Forgotten Genocide." "Two absorbing new books . . . describe, from different perspectives, this strangely neglected episode of the Cold War. [Srinath] Raghavan covers a range of mentalities, choices, and decisions in Islamabad, Moscow, Beijing, Washington, New Delhi, and other capitals. [Gary J.] Bass focusses mainly on American actions and inaction. . . . Bass describes the devious way that [Richard] Nixon and [Henry] Kissinger managed to bury their role in the debacle."

REVIEW: *TLS* no5780 p11 Ja 10 2014 ISAAC CHOTINER

"The Blood Telegram: Nixon, Kissinger, and a Forgotten Genocide" and "1971: A Global History of the Creation of Bangladesh." "As Gary J. Bass so astutely argues in his superb book 'The Blood Telegram,' in 1971 the Bangladesh Liberation War did not raise the question of whether Americans should try to prevent or cut short a genocide. The Nixon administration, in violation of American law, had been giving moral and material aid to Pakistan's junta as it slaughtered its own citizens. The United States was already involved--on the wrong side. . . . [Srinath] Raghavan's book focuses on the world's reaction to the crisis. . . . Raghavan generally refrains from moral judgements . . . and describes the ways in which the crisis could have been prevented."

BASS, KAREN, 1962-. Graffiti knight; [by] Karen Bass 272 p. 2014 Orca Book Publishers

1. Communist countries 2. Germany (East) 3. Graffiti 4. Historical fiction 5. Resistance to government

ISBN 1927485533; 9781927485538

SUMMARY: In this book, "after a childhood cut short by war and the harsh strictures of Nazi Germany, sixteen-year-old Wilm is finally tasting freedom. . . . It's dangerous, of course, to be sneaking out at night to leave messages on police buildings. But it's exciting, too, and Wilm feels justified, considering his family's suffering. Until one mission goes too far, and Wilm finds he's endangered the very people he most wants to protect." (Publisher's note)

REVIEW: *Booklist* v110 no14 p74 Mr 15 2014 Angela Leeper

REVIEW: *Bull Cent Child Books* v67 no8 p395-6 Ap 2014 E. B.

"Graffiti Knight". "[Karen] Bass positions her protagonist at a creditably vulnerable point in his life—old enough for an intellectually mature understanding of the injustices around him, but young enough to rush headlong into action with adolescent impulsiveness. So many World War II stories come to an abrupt halt on VE or VA Day, or segue awkwardly straight into the Cold War; this is a rare and effective exception that pauses to look at the aftermath for vanquished Germans, and to puzzle out who the post-war bad guys really are."

REVIEW: *Kirkus Rev* v82 no1 p218 Ja 1 2014

"Graffiti Knight". "This gripping page-turner set in 1947 East Germany explores the aftereffects of war and occupation. . . . Risk-taking proves energizing and deeply satisfying—also addictive and eventually desensitizing. . . . The authentic setting, compelling characters, and taut, suspenseful plot claim attention throughout. Bass refuses to oversimplify human beings. When motivations are tangled and complex, actions, even the best-intended, have unforeseen consequences. A different kind of war story, highly recommended."

REVIEW: *Quill Quire* v79 no7 p38 S 2013 John Wilson

REVIEW: *SLJ* v60 no5 p124 My 2014 Kim Dare

REVIEW: *Voice of Youth Advocates* v37 no1 p59 Ap 2014 Shanna Miles

BASS, MELISSA. The politics and civics of national service; lessons from the Civilian Conservation Corps, Vista, and AmeriCorps; [by] Melissa Bass xi, 304 p. 2013 Brookings Institution Press

1. Historical literature 2. National service—United States 3. Voluntarism—United States 4. Volunteer service—History

ISBN 0815723806; 9780815723806 (hardcover : alk. paper)

LC 2012-045776

SUMMARY: In this book author Melissa Bass "focuses on the history, current relevance, and impact of domestic national service. She argues that only by examining programs over time can we understand national service's successes and limitations, both in terms of its political support and its civic lessons." (Publisher's note)

REVIEW: *Choice* v51 no1 p163 S 2013 W. C. Johnson

"The Politics and Civics of National Service: Lessons From the Civilian Conservation Corps, VISTA, and AmeriCorps." "The history of national citizen service in the US is spotty, asserts [author Melissa] Bass . . . in an analysis of the Civilian Conservation Corps (CCC), VISTA, and AmeriCorps. She explores how each program was established, its political status, and its major accomplishments. . . . Bass concludes that AmeriCorps offers the best prospect for educating volunteers in the often-gritty work of public service and the deeper meanings of citizenship. A thorough study in assessing political costs and benefits and in projecting future policy directions."

REVIEW: *Contemp Sociol* v42 no6 p884 N 2013

BASSELIN, TIMOTHY J. Flannery O'Connor; writing a theology of disabled humanity; [by] Timothy J. Basselin xi, 146 p. 2013 Baylor University Press

1. Christianity in literature 2. Literature—History & criticism 3. People with disabilities in literature 4. Theology in literature

ISBN 9781602587656 (hardback : acid-free paper)

LC 2012-028957

SUMMARY: In this book, "literature critic and theologian Timothy J. Basselin consults [Flannery] O'Connor's life and work to illustrate the profound connections existing between the theme of the grotesque and Christian theology. O'Connor's own disability, Basselin argues, inspired a theology that leads readers toward greater recognition of God's activity in a sinfully grotesque world." (Publisher's note)

REVIEW: *Choice* v51 no5 p831 Ja 2014 R. Alibegic

"Flannery O'Connor: Writing a Theology of Disabled Humanity." "As appealing as his premise sounds, it is not new, though [Timothy J.] Basselin attempts to present it as such by substituting 'grotesque' with 'disabled' throughout his book. Regardless, his analysis is solid. But his prose is confusing, e.g., 'relating disability to the grotesque is not problematic; rather, it is a view of disability that does not perceive disability negatively'. . . . In addition, it is overly explanatory and unnecessarily repetitive."

BASSOFF, LEAH. Lost Girl Found; [by] Leah Bassoff 192 p. 2014 Pgw

1. Historical fiction 2. Refugee camps 3. Refugees—Fiction 4. Sudan—History—Civil War, 1983-2005 5. Women refugees

ISBN 1554984165; 9781554984169

SUMMARY: In this book, by Leah Bassoff and Laura DeLuca, "Poni . . . [lives in a] small village in southern Sudan. . . . Then the war comes and there is only one thing for Poni to do. Run. . . . [She is] driven by the sheer will to survive and the hope that she can . . . make it to the Kakuma refugee camp in Kenya. . . . In Kakuma she is almost overwhelmed by the misery that surrounds her. Poni realizes that she must leave the camp at any cost. Her destination is a compound in Nairobi." (Publisher's note)

REVIEW: *Bull Cent Child Books* v67 no9 p443 My 2014 H. M.

REVIEW: *Horn Book Magazine* v90 no4 p88 Jl/Ag 2014 KATHLEEN T. HORNING

REVIEW: *Kirkus Rev* v82 no4 p333 F 15 2014

"Lost Girl Found". "Relating her tale in present tense in a distinct, spirited voice . . . Poni goes on to describe her narrow escape . . . and a forced marriage in the wake of a United Nations worker's failure to honor a promise of help. . . . Readers will come away with clear pictures of gender roles in Poni's culture as well as the South Sudan conflict's devastating physical and psychological effects. Two afterwords and a substantial bibliography (largely on the Lost Boys, perforce) will serve those who want to know more. Moving and necessary."

REVIEW: *SLJ* v60 no4 p157 Ap 2014 Candyce Pruitt-Goddard

BASTIANICH, LIDIA MATTICCHIO. Lidia's commonsense Italian cooking; 150 delicious and simple recipes everyone can master; [by] Lidia Matticchio Bastianich 304 p. 2013 Alfred A. Knopf

1. Cookbooks 2. Cooking (Eggplant) 3. Cooking (Pasta) 4. Cooking (Potatoes) 5. Cooking, Italian

ISBN 0385349440; 9780385349444 (alkaline paper)

LC 2013-005067

SUMMARY: In this cookbook, it was the authors' intent to "creat[e] a new sort of Italian cooking for American kitchens that crosses time-honored boundaries and looks to fashion a more relaxed . . . cuisine." Recipes include "potatoes baked in beer, eggplant and rice parmigiana, and veggie 'meatballs.' Traditionally unadorned pasta carbonara gets some sliced artichokes in its cream-and-egg sauce. Desserts include an apple cake, cookies, and several variations of rice pudding." (Booklist)

REVIEW: *Booklist* v110 no4 p8-9 O 15 2013 Mark Knoblauch

"Lidia's Commonsense Italian Cooking: 150 Delicious and Simple Recipes Anyone Can Master." "Having extensively surveyed the world of Italian and Italian American cooking in previous books and television series, indefatigable and entrepreneurial [Lidia Matticchio] Bastianich seems bent on creating a new sort of Italian cooking for American kitchens that crosses time-honored boundaries and looks to fashion a more relaxed but no-less-appealing cuisine. . . . Most dishes can be readily reproduced, but acquiring razor clams away from the Atlantic coast may be daunting. The authors' celebrity and their upcoming public-television series mark this a cookbook sure to be in great demand."

BASU, ARJUN. Waiting for the Man; [by] Arjun Basu 296 p. 2014 Pgw

1. American Dream 2. Copy writers 3. Fame—Fiction 4. Psychological fiction 5. Self-realization—Fiction

ISBN 1770411771; 9781770411777

SUMMARY: In this book by Arjun Basu, "Joe, a lauded

copywriter for a prestigious Manhattan firm, is confronted by the grim truth that material success is no guarantor of personal happiness. Jaded, deeply unhappy with his shallow life, Joe begins to dream of a mysterious figure, the Man. On the advice of the Man, Joe abandons his career in search of a life poorer but with meaning. Thanks to a reporter named Dan, Joe's personal quest will become the focus of a growing media frenzy." (Publishers Weekly)

REVIEW: *Quill Quire* v80 no2 p29-30 Mr 2014 Heather Cromarty

"Waiting for the Man". "Toronto writer Arjun Basu's debut novel ponders the possibility of escaping the ennui of modern life, where the safe, corporate dream jobs of our parents don't offer the expected fulfillment. . . . Perhaps the dark subtext to this entertaining novel is that movement is impossible, even for many seemingly privileged boys. . . . Joe is a manifestation of the modern American Dream, and 'Waiting for the Man' hides a chilling truth under its lighthearted surface: the American Dream is a trap."

BASU, SANJAY. The body economic; why austerity kills : recessions, budget battles, and the politics of life and death; [by] Sanjay Basu xxi, 216 p. 2013 Basic Books

1. Economics—Sociological aspects 2. Economics literature 3. Financial crises—Social aspects 4. Public health 5. Social justice

ISBN 0465063985; 9780465063987

LC 2012-474394

SUMMARY: In this book, authors David Stuckler and Sanjay Basu "offer insight into the economic crisis--including the Great Recession--and its effect on public health, arguing that countries attempt to fix recessions by balancing budgets, but have failed to protect public well-being. They demonstrate how maintaining a healthy populace is intimately entwined with the health of the social environment." (Publishers Weekly)

REVIEW: *Bookforum* v20 no2 p8 Je-Ag 2013 KIM PHILLIPS-FEIN

REVIEW: *Booklist* v109 no21 p17 Jl 1 2013 Mary Whaley

REVIEW: *Choice* v51 no4 p694 D 2013 K. J. Buhr

REVIEW: *Kirkus Rev* v81 no9 p67 My 1 2013

REVIEW: *Science* v341 no6151 p1176-7 S 13 2013 José A. Tapia Granados

"The Body Economic: Why Austerity Kills: Recessions, Budget Battles, and the Politics of Life and Death." "In a journalistic style, the engaging and ambitious 'The Body Economic' jumps from economic to political to health issues, intermingling academic discussions with plenty of human-interest anecdotes. Overall, David Stuckler and Sanjay Basu present a picture in which Keynesian economics is the magic wand that fixes the economy and promotes health. . . . Unfortunately, things are a little bit more complex. . . . Although recessions and austerity policies may have many adverse social consequences, their effects on health are likely much more nuanced and complex than Stuckler and Basu suggest."

BAT EVOLUTION, ECOLOGY, AND CONSERVATION; xvi, 547 p. 2013 Springer

1. Bats—Conservation 2. Bats—Ecology 3. Bats—Evolution 4. Echolocation (Physiology) 5. Natural history literature

ISBN 1461473969 (alk. paper); 9781461473961 (alk. paper)

LC 2013-943698

SUMMARY: This book on bats was edited by Rick A. Adams and Scott C. Pederson. "Areas covered include evolution of flight, echolocation, and the application of molecular biology to scientific understanding of evolutionary relationships among bats. Contributors also explore several fascinating aspects of bat ecology and behavior, including migration, habitat disturbance, colonization, learning/memory, group dynamics, and aeroecology." (Choice: Current Reviews for Academic Libraries)

REVIEW: *Choice* v51 no8 p1428-9 Ap 2014 D. A. Brass

"Bat Evolution, Ecology, and Conservation". "The book is generally quite interesting, but this reviewer was somewhat dismayed by one chapter about establishing conservation role models for children, in which readers are cautioned about the 'sick people from natural history museums.' This text provides a close look at the many challenges facing bat biologists/conservationists and the various tools that future research may bring to bear on solving pressing problems in biology and conservation. It will interest students of evolutionary biology, conservation, and bat ecology."

BATCHELOR, JOHN. Tennyson; To Strive, To Seek, To Find; [by] John Batchelor 448 p. 2012 Chatto & Windus

1. Biographies 2. English poetry—19th century 3. Fame 4. Poets—Biography 5. Tennyson, Alfred Tennyson, Baron, 1809-1892

ISBN 0701180587; 9780701180584

SUMMARY: This book by John Batchelor is a biography of the poet Alfred Lord Tennyson. "Rising from provincial roots, he strived for acceptance by the upper class but never felt comfortable among them. . . . Even when he became indisputably famous, lauded by [William] Wordsworth, Thomas Carlyle and Robert Browning, 'he needed constantly the reassurance of being feted by the rich and the great.'" (Kirkus Reviews)

REVIEW: *Booklist* v110 no5 p12 N 1 2013 Bryce Christensen

"Tennyson: To Strive, To Seek, to Find." "In the poet who consoles Queen Victoria when Prince Albert dies, [John] Batchelor recognizes the quintessential Victorian. Yet in a poet whose lyricism preserves the Romantic daring of [John] Keats and whose personal life as a 'dirty monk' makes him a social curiosity, Batchelor sees a man who transcends his age. Drawing on sources and scholarship not available when [Robert Bernard] Martin published 'Tennyson: The Unquiet Heart' (1980) and offering a broader perspective than [Leonee] Ormond gives in 'Alfred Tennyson: A Literary Life' (1999), Batchelor develops a surprisingly complex portrait of an iconic writer. . . . A trove of insights into the personality and literary vision of an exceptional poet."

REVIEW: *Choice* v51 no10 p1799 Je 2014 T. Hoagwood

REVIEW: *Kirkus Rev* v81 no20 p94 O 15 2013

REVIEW: *N Y Times Book Rev* p30 Ap 20 2014 Daisy Fried

REVIEW: *New Statesman* v141 no5131 p40-1 N 9 2012 Emma Hogan

REVIEW: *TLS* no5723 p5 D 7 2012 GREGORY TATE

BATE, KEITH.tr. Letters from the East. See Letters from

the East

BATES, IVAN.il. There, there. See McBratney, S.

BATESON, PATRICK. Play, playfulness, creativity and innovation; [by] Patrick Bateson 162 p. 2013 Cambridge University Press

1. Creative ability 2. Creative thinking 3. MEDICAL—Veterinary Medicine—General 4. Play—Psychological aspects 5. Social science literature

ISBN 1107015138; 9781107015135 (hardback)

LC 2013-001078

SUMMARY: In this book on play, "the authors emphasise its significance for development and evolution, before examining the importance of playfulness in creativity. This discussion sheds new light on the links between creativity and innovation, distinguishing between the generation of novel behaviour and ideas on the one hand, and the implementation of these novelties on the other." (Publisher's note)

REVIEW: *Choice* v51 no10 p1860 Je 2014 S. Sugarman

REVIEW: *New Sci* v219 no2933 p44 S 7 2013 Jonathon Keats

"Play, Playfulness, Creativity and Innovation." "Patrick Bateson and Paul Martin advance a theory so compelling as to seem obvious: 'We argue that play is an important form of behaviour that facilitates creativity, and hence innovation, in the natural world and human society.' As keen observers of animal and human behaviour, the authors approach their theory through an issue familiar to engineers: how do you let go of easy fixes in pursuit of better solutions that are less immediately accessible? . . . Sadly, the authors' academic style is unlikely to reach the right people to foment a revolution in child-rearing or education. Maybe they should heed their own advice: there's no reason why scholarship can't be as seriously playful as bubble-blowing."

REVIEW: *Science* v342 no6159 p694 N 8 2013 Gillian R. Brown

BAUER, A. C. E. Gil Marsh; [by] A. C. E. Bauer 183 p. 2012 Random House

1. Best friends—Fiction 2. Death—FIction 3. Fiction 4. Friendship—Fiction 5. Track and field—Fiction 6. Voyages and travels—Fiction

ISBN 9780375869334 (hardcover); 9780375969331 (hardcover library binding); 9780375983115 (e-book)

LC 2011-024113

SUMMARY: This book, "a contemporary treatment of the "Epic of Gilgamesh,"" follows "Smart, athletic, and well liked Gil . . . [who] forms a deep friendship with an equally talented and good-natured newcomer, Enko. Soon Enko is diagnosed with an aggressive form of leukemia that takes his life; before he dies, he gives Gil a garnet ring, a family heirloom made by a supposedly immortal blacksmith in the countryside north of Quebec. A griefstricken Gil is wounded further by learning that Enko will be buried at home in Quebec and that Gil's parents won't be taking him to visit his friend's grave for a final goodbye. Gil sets off alone for Quebec on his own on a quest to find the grave and the maker of the ring, hoping that perhaps the man's immortality is real, and that he will have the secret to bringing Enko back." (Bulletin of the Center for Children's Books)

REVIEW: *Booklist* v108 no12 p55 F 15 2012 Daniel Kraus

REVIEW: *Bull Cent Child Books* v65 no6 p294 F 2012 K. C.

"Gil Marsh." "As a contemporary treatment of the 'Epic of Gilgamesh,' this has the right bones, but as a piece of young adult literature, the bones are disappointingly bare. Gil and Enko's fierce closeness develops rapidly and the book tells more than shows the relationship's significance. Gil's open talk of the deep love he bears his friend is couched in terms that more often signal a love affair in contemporary literature, so readers may misunderstand the boys' relationship as one based on homosexual feelings rather than the deeply homosocial sensibilities of the original epic. There's still reward in following his journey, however, even if it ends in closure rather than success."

REVIEW: *Kirkus Rev* v80 no1 p2426 Ja 1 2012

REVIEW: *SLJ* v58 no2 p108 F 2012 Patricia N. McClune

REVIEW: *Voice of Youth Advocates* v34 no6 p585-6 F 2012 Barbara Allen Devin Johnson

BAUER, CARLENE. Frances and Bernard; [by] Carlene Bauer 195 p. 2013 Houghton Mifflin Harcourt

1. Authors—Fiction 2. FICTION—General 3. FICTION—Historical 4. FICTION—Literary 5. Religious fiction, American

ISBN 0547858248 (hardcover); 9780547858241 (hardcover)

LC 2012-014028

SUMMARY: In this book, set in the late 1950s, "over the course of one long lunch at a writer's workshop, Frances and Bernard begin a journey of love and loss. They banter about writing and the workshop's limitations, and, while falling in love, they struggle with the meaning of religion and the nature of friendship. In the end, their relationship is tested to the limits when Bernard suffers a manic episode." (Library Journal)

REVIEW: *Booklist* v109 no4 p28 O 15 2012 Donna Seaman

REVIEW: *Christ Century* v130 no8 p41 Ap 17 2013

REVIEW: *Christ Century* v130 no23 p34-5 N 13 2013 Amy Frykholm

REVIEW: *Kirkus Rev* v80 no22 p85 N 15 2012

REVIEW: *Libr J* v137 no14 p88 S 1 2012 Joanna M. Burkhardt

REVIEW: *Libr J* v138 no12 p40 Jl 1 2013 Suanne B. Roush

REVIEW: *N Y Times Book Rev* p13 Mr 24 2013 CHRISTOPHER BENFEY

REVIEW: *N Y Times Book Rev* p24 F 23 2014 IHSAN TAYLOR

""The Hour of Peril: The Secret Plot to Murder Lincoln Before the Civil War," "Frances and Bernard," and "Ghana Must Go." "['The Hour of Peril'] is a swift and detailed rendering of the little-known Baltimore-based plot to assassinate Abraham Lincoln in February 1861. . . . Inspired by the lives of Flannery O'Connor and Robert Lowell, Bauer's epistolary novel concerns kindred spirits who meet at an artists' colony in 1957. . . . In [Taiye] Selasi's daring first novel, the of Kweku Sai, a renowned Ghanaian surgeon and failed husband, sends a ripple around the world.

REVIEW: *New York Times* v162 no56092 p26 Mr 31 2013

REVIEW: *New York Times* v162 no56065 pC4 Mr 4 2013

CLAUDIA LA ROCCO

REVIEW: *Publ Wkly* v259 no36 p41 S 3 2012

BAUER, DOUGLAS. What happens next?; matters of life and death; [by] Douglas Bauer 160 p. 2013 University of Iowa Press

1. Families 2. Farmers—United States 3. Food 4. Iowa—Social life & customs 5. Marriage 6. Memoirs
ISBN 1609381831 (pbk. : alk. paper); 160938203X (ebk.); 9781609381837 (pbk. : alk. paper); 9781609382032 (ebk.)
LC 2013-934854

SUMMARY: "In these highly evocative personal essays, Douglas Bauer weaves together the stories of his own and his parents' lives, the meals they ate, the work and rewards and regrets that defined them, and the inevitable betrayal by their bodies as they aged. His collection features at its center a long and memory-rich piece seasoned with sensory descriptions of the midday dinners his mother cooked for her farmer husband and father-in-law every noon for many years." (Publisher's note)

REVIEW: *Kirkus Rev* v81 no16 p115 Ag 15 2013

"What Happens Next? Matters of Life and Death." "[Author Douglas] Bauer, a Boston-based writer and teacher . . . , was once an Iowa farm boy. In these deeply personal essays, he celebrates his family's life in the Hawkeye State. Age-related ailments are the author's evocative madeleine in his search for times past in the American heartland. . . . With his narrative artistry, Bauer renders the commonplace uncommon. He ably brings to life his forebear farmers and their diligent wives, the mean-tempered coal-miner grandfather in his bib overalls and his wife, and the corpulent grandmother."

BAUER, KAREN TILLOTSON. The essentials of beautiful singing; a three-step kinesthetic approach; [by] Karen Tillotson Bauer xviii, 149 p. 2013 Scarecrow Press

1. Do-it-yourself literature 2. Music literature 3. Singing—Breath control 4. Singing—Instruction and study 5. Vocal music
ISBN 9780810886872 (cloth: alk. paper); 9780810886889 (pbk.: alk. paper); 9780810886896 (ebook)
LC 2013-013994

SUMMARY: In this book, vocal instructor Karen Tillotson Bauer "eschews the technical information and jargon currently found in most vocal pedagogy books and concentrates instead on the physical experience of singing. Her kinesthetic approach espouses a mind-body coordination supported by sound technical principles imparted and recalled by simple language prompts." (Choice: Current Reviews for Academic Libraries)

REVIEW: *Choice* v51 no8 p1409 Ap 2014 S. C. Champagne

"The Essentials of Beautiful Singing: A Three-Step Kinesthetic Approach". "The explanations provided for each of the three steps of her method are uncomplicated and adaptable to a wide variety of teaching styles. Though she cultivates simplicity in style and terminology, the author reveals a keen understanding of the vocal mechanism and also familiarity with modern advances in vocal science and pedagogy. The omission of any extended discussion of phonation as one of the key elements of classical vocal technique, however, may well lead to charges of oversimplification. The opposite is true when Bauer addresses musical skills. . . . Experienced singers and novices should still find the vast majority of the book enlightening and refreshing in its ease of use and practicality."

BAUER, LAURIE. The Oxford reference guide to English morphology. See Plag, I.

BAUER, SHANE. A sliver of light; three Americans imprisoned in Iran; [by] Shane Bauer 352 p. 2014 Houghton Mifflin Harcourt

1. Americans—Iran—Biography 2. Hikers—Iran—Biography 3. Memoirs 4. Political prisoners—Iran—Biography
ISBN 0547985533; 9780547985534 (hardback)
LC 2013-049037

SUMMARY: This book tells the story of authors Shane Bauer, Josh Fattal, and Sarah Shourd, the "three young Americans captured by Iranian forces [in 2009] and held in captivity for two years. . . . They recount the deception that lured them into Iran in the first place and describe the psychological torment of interrogation and solitary confinement. We follow them as they make surprising alliances with their fellow prisoners and even some of their captors, while their own bonds . . . are tested." (Publisher's note)

REVIEW: *Booklist* v110 no11 p7 F 1 2014 Steve Uhrich

REVIEW: *Kirkus Rev* v82 no2 p74 Ja 15 2014

"A Sliver of Light: Three Americans Imprisoned in Iran". "In their well-developed and detailed accounts, told in alternate first-person voices, the three remind the world how human, vulnerable and terribly isolated they were during their months of incarceration, when they knew little of what was going on in the outside world and existed day by day in an entrenched survival mode. . . . All were critical of American government policy before their incarceration and emerged from their ordeal unbowed and outspoken. An unsugared account that demonstrates the admirable, unbreakable bond of friends, parents and countrymen."

REVIEW: *Publ Wkly* v260 no50 p58 D 9 2013

BAUERDICK, ROLF. The madonna on the moon; [by] Rolf Bauerdick 401 p. 2013 Alfred A. Knopf

1. Detective & mystery stories 2. Historical fiction 3. Romania—History—1944-1989 4. Space race
ISBN 0307594122; 9780307594129
LC 2012-033299

SUMMARY: This novel, the winner of the 2012 European Book Prize, "opens in 1957, as young narrator Pavel observes his family and neighbors dispute the meaning of the second Sputnik launch." Communism is drawing "closer: The local priest is found murdered, and Pavel's teacher is discovered hanged. What ensues is largely a detective story, led by Pavel, involving the sexual peccadillos of Communist Party functionaries, complete with sordid photos and anguished diary entries." (Kirkus Reviews)

REVIEW: *Booklist* v109 no21 p29 Jl 1 2013 Brendan Driscoll

REVIEW: *Kirkus Rev* v81 no13 p185 Jl 1 2013

REVIEW: *TLS* no5780 p21 Ja 10 2014 REBECCA K. MORRISON

"The Madonna on the Moon." "It is 1957 in a lightly fictionalized Romania, and the fifteen-year-old narrator Pavel Botev is about to leave childhood behind. . . . Rolf Bauerdick's storytelling is first-rate and underpinned by his intimate knowledge of the region and its inhabitants. 'The Madonna on the Moon' fizzes with the gusto of an Emir Kusturica film, sharp dialogue, a delicious sense of the absurdity of the self-serving schemes of local and national politicians, the alluring lunar leitmotif. David Dollenmayer's translation of this winner of the 2012 European Book Prize is convincing and light-footed."

BAUSUM, ANN. Marching to the mountaintop; how poverty, labor fights, and civil rights set the stage for Martin Luther King, Jr.'s final hours; [by] Ann Bausum 104 p. 2012 National Geographic

1. African Americans—Economic conditions 2. African Americans—Tennessee—Memphis—Social conditions—20th century 3. African Americans—Tennessee—Memphis—Social conditions—20th century—Juvenile literature 4. Civil rights—United States—History 5. Historical literature 6. King, Martin Luther, Jr., 1929-1968 7. Labor movement—Tennessee—Memphis—History—20th century 8. Labor movement—Tennessee—Memphis—History—20th century—Juvenile literature 9. Memphis (Tenn.) 10. Public sector—Economic aspects 11. Sanitation Workers Strike, Memphis, Tenn., 1968 12. Sanitation Workers Strike, Memphis, Tenn., 1968—Juvenile literature
ISBN 1426309392 (hbk. : alk. paper); 1426309406 (library binding : alk. paper); 9781426309397 (hbk. : alk. paper); 9781426309403 (library binding : alk. paper)
LC 2011-024661

SUMMARY: "In this . . . [book about] the 1968 Memphis Sanitation Workers Strike, [author Ann] Bausum . . . handles both the labor action itself--born of institutionalized racial injustice within the public works system and the tragic deaths of two African-American workers in a faulty compactor--and what would be the final civil rights action of Dr. King's storied career. . . . She . . . [covers] the African-American workers who accepted . . . dangerous sanitation jobs, and . . . the ploys to cut back their already minimal pay. . . . [T]he focus shifts to follow King's involvement, as he hoped the national focus on labor injustice would draw attention to his broader plans for an attack on poverty itself as the next great civil rights issue." (Bulletin of the Center for Children's Books)

REVIEW: *Booklist* v108 no11 p81 F 1 2012 Erin Anderson

REVIEW: *Bull Cent Child Books* v65 no7 p339-40 Mr 2012 E. B.

"Marching to the Mountaintop: How Poverty, Labor Fights, and Civil Rights Set the Stage for Martin Luther King, Jr.'s Final Hours." "In this riveting account of the 1968 Memphis Sanitation Workers Strike, Bausum adroitly handles both the labor action itself—born of institutionalized racial injustice within the public works system and the tragic deaths of two African-American workers in a faulty compactor—and what would be the final civil rights action of Dr. King's storied career. . . . Clearly organized and densely illustrated, this title includes features such as an introductory 'cast of characters,' an annotated timeline of the strike, and a list of King's campaigns from 1955 through 1968 to help untangle a complex set of intertwined events."

REVIEW: *SLJ* v58 no3 p181-2 Mr 2012 Ann Welton

REVIEW: *SLJ* v58 no8 p16 Ag 2012 Kathleen Baxter

BAXTER, JEANNETTE.ed. A literature of restitution . See A literature of restitution

BAYLESS, MARTHA. Sin and filth in medieval culture; the devil in the latrine; [by] Martha Bayless xxi, 242 p. 2012 Routledge

1. Civilization, Medieval 2. Historical literature 3. Literature, Medieval—History and criticism 4. Middle Ages 5. Sin in literature 6. Sins—Folklore
ISBN 9780415897808 (acid-free paper)
LC 2011-051394

SUMMARY: In this book, "Martha Bayless focuses on the theological and moral meanings of excrement across the long medieval period. Bayless argues that scatology is less comic than readers of [Geoffrey] Chaucer might think. Using conceptual metaphor theory, which asserts that 'down' (the lower half of the body and its products) can be mapped onto 'evil,' . . . Bayless makes a . . . case for the equation of her title: excrement is inextricably associated with sinfulness in medieval thought." (American Historical Review)

REVIEW: *Am Hist Rev* v119 no1 p232-3 F 2014 Carolyne Larrington

"Sin and Filth in Medieval Culture: The Devil in the Latrine". "[Martha] Bayless's book achieves two valuable objectives: it offers a representative overview of medieval Western European practices in the management of human and animal waste, and it establishes the association between . . . sin and excrement within medieval culture. . . . 'Sin and Filth' is thoroughgoing in its exploration of theological, moral, and exegetical instances of the excrement-evil nexus. . . . But Bayless is right to insist on the identity of sin and filth as crucial to understanding medieval mentalités, and her book is to be welcomed as both insightful and highly readable."

BAYLEY, STEPHEN. Ugly; [by] Stephen Bayley 272 p. 2012 Innovative Logistics Llc

1. Aesthetics—Social aspects 2. Aesthetics literature 3. Popular culture 4. Ugliness 5. Ugliness in art
ISBN 1906863474; 9781906863470

SUMMARY: This book by Stephen Bayley presents a "history of white people's thoughts on the beautiful and the tacky. Bayley plumbs the shallowest depths of white culture of the last few hundred years, from high kitsch (snow-globe collections, the infamous Madonna Inn), to the compelling ugliness of plants, animals, disfigurement, and racism, to the reactionary pro-ugliness movements of punk and modernist architecture." (Bookforum)

REVIEW: *Bookforum* v20 no3 p4 S-N 2013 CHOIRE SICHA

"Ugly: The Aesthetics of Everything." "a terrific history of white people's thoughts on the beautiful and the tacky. [Stephen] Bayley plumbs the shallowest depths of white culture of the last few hundred years, from high kitsch . . . to the compelling ugliness of plants, animals, disfigurement, and racism, to the reactionary pro-ugliness movements of punk and modernist architecture. . . . Bayley never takes us beyond Europe and America, with the exception of a wee excursion to Australia and a brief discussion of a Turkish town. . . . Still, this is a very good coffee-table book for white people and admirers of their culture, particularly because you can eventually read the words if you get terribly bored in your beach house."

BEAH, ISHMAEL, 1980-. Radiance of tomorrow; a novel; [by] Ishmael Beah 256 p. 2014 Sarah Crichton Books, Farrar, Straus and Giroux

1. FICTION—Cultural Heritage 2. FICTION—Literary 3. Villages—Sierra Leone—Fiction 4. West African fiction (English)

ISBN 0374246025; 9780374246020 (hardback)

LC 2013-036856

SUMMARY: This novel, by Ishmael Beah, is "about postwar life in Sierra Leone. . . . Benjamin and Bockarie . . . return to their hometown, Imperi, after the civil war. . . . [They] try to forge a new community by taking up their former posts as teachers, but they're beset by obstacles . . . and the depredations of a foreign mining company. . . . As Benjamin and Bockarie search for a way to restore order, they're forced to reckon with the uncertainty of their past and future alike." (Publisher's note)

REVIEW: *Booklist* v110 no5 p26 N 1 2013 Hazel Rochman

REVIEW: *Kirkus Rev* v81 no20 p189 O 15 2013

REVIEW: *Libr J* v138 no20 p1 N 15 2013

REVIEW: *N Y Times Book Rev* p7 Ja 19 2014 SARA CORBETT

REVIEW: *New York Times* v163 no56384 pC37 Ja 17 2014 JENNIFER SCHUESSLER

REVIEW: *New Yorker* v89 no47 p79-1 F 3 2014

REVIEW: *Publ Wkly* v260 no43 p30 O 28 2013

REVIEW: *Publ Wkly* v261 no13 p60 Mr 31 2014

REVIEW: *Time* v183 no2 p54 Ja 20 2014 Belinda Luscombe

"Radiance of Tomorrow." "In Sierra Leonean culture, respect is usually directed the way of old people. What made the civil war that knifed through his country from 1991 to 2002 so destructive, says [author Ishmael] Beah, was that boys, enlisted by both sides, killed elders. . . . This is the territory that Beah's new book, 'Radiance of Tomorrow,' explores: how communities knit together after such an unraveling. . . . The villagers' biggest obstacles, however, are not one another but forces beyond their control."

BEAL, MARJORIE.il. The flea. See Cohen, L.

BEAM, ALEX. American crucifixion; the murder of Joseph Smith and the fate of the Mormon church; [by] Alex Beam 352 p. 2014 PublicAffairs

1. Historical literature 2. Mormon Church—History 3. Polygamy—Religious aspects—Mormon Church

ISBN 1610393139; 9781610393133 (hardcover); 9781610393140 (pbk.)

LC 2014-004063

SUMMARY: This book, by Alex Beam, focuses on "founding prophet of Mormonism, Joseph Smith. . . . Beam tells how Smith went from charismatic leader to public enemy: How his most seismic revelation—the doctrine of polygamy—created a rift among his people; how that schism turned to violence; and how, ultimately, Smith could not escape the consequences of his ambition and pride . . . Smith's brutal assassination propelled the Mormons to colonize the American West." (Publisher's note)

REVIEW: *Booklist* v110 no13 p4 Mr 1 2014 Vanessa Bush

REVIEW: *Kirkus Rev* v82 no5 p39 Mr 1 2014

"American Crucifixion: The Murder of Joseph Smith and the Fate of the Mormon Church". "[Alex] Beam is the consummate journalist, precise about his research and offering judgment only where there is ample proof of wrongdoing. He treats Smith with journalistic objectivity but doesn't hesitate to point out that 'Joseph received so many revelations that they inevitably conflicted.' With so much history to tackle, from the roots of Mormonism to the economic, political and moral climates in which hatred of the new religion developed, it is impressive that Beam maintains narrative tension and excitement while injecting personality. . . . A fascinating history that, while particularly appealing to those interested in religion, is sure to inform a far wider audience."

REVIEW: *Libr J* v139 no15 p37 S 15 2014 Pam Kingsbury

REVIEW: *Libr J* v139 no5 p124 Mr 15 2014 David Azzolina

REVIEW: *N Y Times Book Rev* p17 Jl 6 2014 BENJAMIN MOSER

REVIEW: *Publ Wkly* v261 no3 p42 Ja 20 2014

BEAN, JONATHAN. Big snow; [by] Jonathan Bean 32 p. 2013 Farrar, Straus and Giroux

1. Helpfulness—Fiction 2. JUVENILE FICTION—Concepts—Seasons 3. JUVENILE FICTION—Family—Parents 4. JUVENILE FICTION—Holidays & Celebrations—Christmas & Advent 5. Mothers and sons—Fiction 6. Picture books for children 7. Snow—Fiction

ISBN 0374306966 (reinforced); 9780374306960 (reinforced)

LC 2013-000499

SUMMARY: In this book by Jonathan Bean "a 'big snow' can't arrive soon enough for a boy named David. Mom tries to keep him occupied with household tasks, but everything he does only makes him think about what's happening outside. When it's clear that David's help is actually creating more mess. Mom suggests a nap--and David, in turn, dreams that the snow has turned into a vengeful, invasive blizzard." (Publisher's note)

REVIEW: *Booklist* v110 no3 p98 O 1 2013 Lolly Gepson

REVIEW: *Bull Cent Child Books* v67 no3 p135-6 N 2013 Deborah Stevenson Jonathan Bean

REVIEW: *Horn Book Magazine* v89 no6 p72 N/D 2013 KATHLEEN T. HORNING

"Big Snow". [Jonathan] Bean's superbly patterned text builds anticipation, and his pen-and-ink and watercolor illustrations make clear links between what is going on in David's imagination and what is happening out in the real world. The warm illustrations showing brown-skinned David's cozy home provide a nice contrast to the occasional wordless double-page spread showing the outdoors, with an ever-increasing amount of snow. Young readers are sure to identify with David's longing and excitement."

REVIEW: *Kirkus Rev* v81 no17 p128 S 1 2013

REVIEW: *N Y Times Book Rev* p14 D 22 2013 NELL CASEY

"Big Snow," "When It Snows," and "Winter Is for Snow." "In 'Big Snow,' written and illustrated by Jonathan Bean, another child anxious to see a winter wonderland asks his mother again and again about the impending blizzard. . . . In his first picture book, 'When It Snows,' . . . illustrator Richard Collingridge dives headlong into a fantasy of the season, showing it to be a vast and mountainous expanse of white, both eerie and enchanting. . . . 'Winter Is for Snow' is a tale of two siblings--a brother who loves the icy flakes pouring down outside their apartment window and a sister who is cranky about it all--by the prolific children's book author and illustrator Robert Neubecker."

REVIEW: *Publ Wkly* v260 no24 p61 Je 17 2013

REVIEW: *Publ Wkly* p34 Children's starred review annual 2013

REVIEW: *SLJ* v59 no9 p112 S 2013 Marilyn Taniguchi

BEARD, MARY, 1955-. Confronting the classics; traditions, adventures, and innovations; [by] Mary Beard 320 p. 2013 Liveright Publishing Corporation, a Division of W. W. Norton & Company

1. Books—Reviews 2. Civilization, Classical 3. Classical antiquities 4. Classical education 5. Educational literature 6. Humanistic education

ISBN 0871407167; 9780871407160 (hardcover)

LC 2013-016133

SUMMARY: "This collection comprises a decade's worth of [Mary] Beard's . . . book reviews, mostly from the 'Times Literary Supplement' and the 'New York Review of Books,' plus one lecture not previously published. . . . The work follows a chronological arrangement, with the first section on ancient Greece, the next on early Rome, the third on Imperial Rome, and so forth, with later pieces focusing on the classicists themselves across the subsequent centuries." (Library Journal)

REVIEW: *Am Sch* v82 no4 p113-5 Aut 2013 A. E. Stallings

"Confronting the Classics: Traditions, Adventures, and Innovations." "in September 1948, Terence Rattigan's play, "The Browning Version," debuted. It concerns a crusty old classics teacher named Andrew Crocker-Harris . . . , an endangered species in a losing battle with modernity. It is through the lens of this play and its anxiety about the future of the classics that Mary Beard addresses the perennial question, 'Are classics dying?' in the opening essay of her new collection of book reviews, 'Confronting the Classics.' . . . Beard conveys in her survey of the subject and the people who study it the excitement and romance of that tradition."

REVIEW: *Booklist* v109 no22 p22 Ag 1 2013 Bryce Christensen

REVIEW: *Kirkus Rev* v81 no12 p42 Je 15 2013

REVIEW: *Libr J* v138 no12 p80 Jl 1 2013 Margaret Heller

REVIEW: *Publ Wkly* v260 no24 p49-50 Je 17 2013

BEARDSON, TIMOTHY. Stumbling giant; the threats to China's future; [by] Timothy Beardson 528 p. 2013 Yale University Press

1. China—Social conditions 2. Political science literature

ISBN 9780300165425 (cl : alk. paper)

LC 2013-002119

SUMMARY: In this book, Timothy Beardson "spells out China's situation: an inexorable demographic future of a shrinking labor force, relentless aging, extreme gender disparity, and even a falling population. Also, the nation faces social instability, a devastated environment, a predominantly low-tech economy with inadequate innovation, the absence of an effective welfare safety net, an ossified governance structure, and radical Islam lurking at the borders." (Publisher's note)

REVIEW: *Kirkus Rev* v81 no8 p42-3 Ap 15 2013

REVIEW: *Libr J* v138 no10 p124 Je 1 2013 Joshua Wallace

REVIEW: *N Y Rev Books* v60 no18 p59-61 N 21 2013 Ian Johnson

"Wealth and Power: China's Long March to the 21st Century," "Stumbling Giant: The Threats to China's Future," and "The China Choice: Why America Should Share Power." "[Orville] Schell and [John] Delury describe a series of eleven thinkers, activists, and leaders in their stylishly written, provocative book. . . . Identifying [wealth and power]--correctly, I think--as the dominant discourse over the past nearly two hundred years allows the authors to make several important points. . . . [Timothy] Beardson's thesis is clear and succinct. . . . Perhaps the least interesting part of the book is the chapter on serious issues that need fixing, but that are not unfixable. . . . Hugh White . . . writes . . . that the United States must find a way to coexist with China. In my view, however. White constructs something of a straw man by arguing that Barack Obama's 'pivot' to Asia means the United States has chosen to confront China."

BEATTIE, JAMES, 1977-. Empire and environmental anxiety; health, science, art and conservation in South Asia and Australasia, 1800-1920; [by] James Beattie xv, 320 p. 2011 Palgrave Macmillan

1. Australasia—History 2. Environmental policy—Australasia—History—19th century 3. Environmental policy—South Asia—History—19th century 4. HISTORY—Asia—India & South Asia 5. HISTORY—Australia & New Zealand 6. HISTORY—Modern—19th Century 7. HISTORY—Modern—20th Century 8. Historical literature 9. Imperialism—Australasia—History—19th century 10. Imperialism—Environmental aspects 11. Imperialism—History—19th century 12. Imperialism—South Asia—History—19th century 13. Public health administration—Australasia—History—19th century 14. Public health administration—South Asia—History—19th century 15. Science and state—Australasia—History—19th century 16. Science and state—South Asia—History—19th century 17. South Asia—History

ISBN 9780230553200 (hardback)

LC 2011-004888

SUMMARY: This book by James Beattie offers "A new interpretation of imperialism and environmental change, and the anxieties imperialism generated through environmental transformation and interaction with unknown landscapes. Tying together South Asia and Australasia, this book demonstrates how environmental anxieties led to increasing state resource management, conservation, and urban reform." (Publisher's note)

REVIEW: *Am Hist Rev* v118 no4 p1151-2 O 2013 Mark Harrison

"Empire and Environmental Anxiety: Health, Science, Art, and Conservation in South Asia and Australasia, 1800-1920." "Other historians . . . have examined particular aspects of environmental anxiety in some detail, especially in relation to health. Beattie's wide-ranging book weaves together these threads and demonstrates their interconnectedness. Another important feature of Beattie's monograph is its focus on British India and Australasia--colonial possessions that are not normally considered in the same frame of reference. . . . The book is clearly written and the move from one territory to another accomplished without confusing the reader. What is lost in the process, perhaps, is a sense of place and . . . finely grained portraits of conservators."

BEATY, ANDREA. Rosie Revere, engineer; [by] Andrea Beaty 32 p. 2013 Abrams Books for Young Readers
1. Children's stories 2. Engineers—Fiction 3. Failure (Psychology)—Fiction 4. Inventions—Fiction 5. Perseverance (Ethics)—Fiction 6. Stories in rhyme
ISBN 1419708457; 9781419708459 (alk. paper)
LC 2012-048268

SUMMARY: This children's picture book conveys "the story of a girl who likes to build things but is shy about it. . . . Rosie picks up trash and oddments where she finds them, stashing them in her attic room to work on at night. Once, she made a hat for her favorite zookeeper uncle to keep pythons away, and he laughed so hard that she never made anything publicly again. But when her great-great-aunt Rose comes to visit and reminds Rosie of her own past building airplanes," Rosie is inspired. (Kirkus Reviews)

REVIEW: *Booklist* v110 no2 p73 S 15 2013 Edie Ching

REVIEW: *Horn Book Magazine* v90 no1 p121-2 Ja/F 2014
"The Fort That Jack Built," "Rosie Revere, Engineer," and "My Dream Playground." "The cumulative 'House That Jack Built' rhymes are peppy, and [Brett] Helquist's homey oil paintings in muted tones capture the action of imaginative play. . . . [Andrea] Beaty's rhymes are cleverly constructed, and [David] Roberts's meticulous illustrations, some on drafting paper, capture the quirkiness of the girl and her gizmos. . . . The author's note explains that the uplifting (if idealized) story is based on a real project by KaBOOM!, a national nonprofit organization. Sunny digital illustrations underscore the sense of community."

REVIEW: *Kirkus Rev* v81 no15 p134 Ag 1 2013

REVIEW: *Publ Wkly* v260 no27 p87 Jl 8 2013

REVIEW: *Science* v342 no6162 p1048 N 29 2013

REVIEW: *SLJ* v59 no9 p114 S 2013 Maggie Chase

BEATY, DANIEL. Knock knock; my dad's dream for me; [by] Daniel Beaty 40 p. 2014 Little, Brown and Company
1. Absentee fathers 2. African Americans—Fiction 3. Children's stories 4. Fathers and sons—Fiction 5. Separation (Psychology)—Fiction
ISBN 0316209171; 9780316209175
LC 2012-043088

SUMMARY: In this book, by Daniel Beaty, a father and son play knock knock every morning. "But what happens when, one day, that 'knock knock' doesn't come? This . . . book shows the love that an absent parent can leave behind, and the strength that children find in themselves as they grow up and follow their dreams." (Publisher's note)

REVIEW: *Booklist* v110 no5 p84-5 N 1 2013 Lolly Gepson

REVIEW: *Bull Cent Child Books* v67 no5 p256 Ja 2014 T. A.

REVIEW: *Horn Book Magazine* v89 no6 p73 N/D 2013 ROBIN L. SMITH

REVIEW: *Kirkus Rev* v81 no21 p184 N 1 2013

REVIEW: *N Y Times Book Rev* p16 F 16 2014 GLENDA R. CARPIO
"Mumbet's Declaration of Independence," "Under the Same Sun," and "Knock Knock: My Dad's Dream for Me." "Gretchen Woelfle's 'Mumbet's Declaration of Independence' . . . tells the story of . . . Bett or Betty [who] successfully sued her owner . . . for her emancipation, and once liberated chose to name herself Elizabeth Freeman. . . . In 'Under the Same Sun,' Sharon Robinson, the daughter of the baseball legend Jackie Robinson, also deals with the history of slavery but folds it into a story about a modern-day family reunion. . . . [In] Daniel Beaty's 'Knock Knock: My Dad's Dream for Me,' . . . a letter from the father finally arrives explaining that he will not be coming home."

REVIEW: *Publ Wkly* v260 no41 p58 O 14 2013

REVIEW: *Publ Wkly* p36-7 Children's starred review annual 2013

REVIEW: *SLJ* v59 no10 p1 O 2013 Yelena Alekseyeva-Popova

BEAUDOIN, SEAN. Wise Young Fool; [by] Sean Beaudoin 448 p. 2013 Little, Brown and Co.
1. Bands (Music)—Fiction 2. Delinquent youths 3. Juvenile detention homes—Fiction 4. Male juvenile delinquents 5. Musicians—Fiction 6. Young adult fiction
ISBN 0316203793; 9780316203791
LC 2012-032472

SUMMARY: In this book by Sean Beaudoin, protagonist "Ritchie grabs readers by the throat before (politely) inviting them along for the (max-speed) ride. A battle of the bands looms. Dad split about five minutes before Mom's girlfriend moved in. There's the matter of trying to score with the dangerously hot Ravenna Woods while avoiding the dangerously huge Spence Proffer--not to mention just trying to forget what his sister, Beth, said the week before she died." (Publisher's note)

REVIEW: *Booklist* v109 no22 p75 Ag 1 2013 Daniel Kraus

REVIEW: *Bull Cent Child Books* v67 no2 p75 O 2013 K. C.
"Wise Young Fool." "Just as the plot summary suggests, this hits all of the expected plot points of the Angry Young Man genre, hewing so close to the line Frank Portman traced in 'King Dork' . . . that the two are almost indistinguishable in tone and conceit (there's even a chapter devoted entirely to band names, as well as an appendix devoted to a snarky hipster critique of existing band names). Such imitation is unusual for [author Sean] Beaudoin, who has proven nothing if not starkly original in his previous works, . . . but he nonetheless plays language like Hendrix plays a guitar, so what might seem stale in conception makes up many thousand bonus points in linguistic style, inventiveness, and dexterity."

REVIEW: *Kirkus Rev* v81 no13 p149 Jl 1 2013

REVIEW: *Voice of Youth Advocates* v36 no3 p56 Ag 2013 Heather Christensen

BEAUSOLEIL, BEAU.ed. Al-mutanabbi street starts here. See Al-mutanabbi street starts here

BEAUTY; 2013 Cambridge University Press

ISBN 9781107693432 paperback

SUMMARY: Edited by Lauren Arrington, Zoe Leinhardt, and Philip Dawid, "This collection arises from the Darwin College Lecture Series of 2011 and includes essays from eight distinguished scholars. . . . Classical, conventional aspects of beauty are addressed in subtle, unexpected ways: symmetry in mathematics, attraction in the animal world and beauty in the cosmos." (Publisher's note)

REVIEW: *Kirkus Rev* v82 no2 p250 Ja 15 2014

"Beauty". "There are strong echoes of Jimmy Stewart rallying the townspeople in 'It's A Wonderful Life'. Carol has Anna Rose, redoubtable organizer of the Wives of the Sea, on her side; the town is thrilled; Carol is a hero. All this happens at improbable breakneck speed, but [Frederick] Dillen presents the business choices so clearly that we cut him some slack. While the way forward will not be problem-free, the story's sentimental populism has its own momentum. Kudos to Dillen for his unusual premise. The workplace drama that follows is rousing, if predictable."

BEBAWI, SABRI. God on Trial; [by] Sabri Bebawi 212 p. 2013 Createspace Independent Pub

1. Crimes against humanity 2. Faith 3. God—Fiction 4. Psychological fiction 5. Trials (Crimes against humanity)

ISBN 1491212039; 9781491212035

SUMMARY: In this book by Sabri Bebabwi, "while watching and reading news of a world seemingly falling apart . . . and in his nervous, hyperstressed, 'semi dream state,'" the protagonist 'feels the need to impeach God.' Specifically, he'll try God in absentia before the Human Rights Council for crimes against humanity. . . . . As the man's obsession picks up momentum, his wife, friends and colleagues understandably become worried for his sanity." (Kirkus Reviews)

REVIEW: *Kirkus Rev* v82 no3 p173 F 1 2014

REVIEW: *Kirkus Rev* v82 no2 p392 Ja 15 2014

"God on Trial: A Short Fiction". " Distressed by the state of the world, a man decides to prosecute God. . . . While watching and reading news of a world seemingly falling apart . . . and in his nervous, hyperstressed, 'semi dream state, he feels the need to impeach God.' Specifically, he'll try God in absentia before the Human Rights Council for crimes against humanity. Through mysteries and well-laid legal wrangles, the novel accelerates toward a fascinating, surprisingly spiritual climax. There's a great deal of food for thought here, for believers and nonbelievers alike, and it's all presented in a fluid, gripping narrative. A man's arraignment of God for crimes against humanity becomes a passionate investigation of faith."

BEBOUT, LEE. Mythohistorical interventions; the Chicano movement and its legacies; [by] Lee Bebout 248 p. 2011 University of Minnesota Press

1. Chicano movement 2. Feminism—United States 3. Historical literature 4. Mexican American lesbians—Social conditions 5. Mexican American women—Ethnic identity 6. Mexican Americans—Ethnic identity 7. Mexican Americans—Study and teaching

ISBN 0816670862 (hc : alk. paper); 0816670870 (pb : alk. paper); 9780816670864 (hc : alk. paper); 9780816670871 (pb : alk. paper)

LC 2010-032722

SUMMARY: This book "explores how myth and history impacted the social struggle of the Chicano movement and the postmovement years. Drawing on archival materials and political speeches as well as music and protest poetry, Lee Bebout scrutinizes the ideas that emerged from the effort to organize and legitimize the Chicano movement's aims." (Publisher's note)

REVIEW: *Am Lit* v85 no3 p598-600 S 2013 José E. Limón

"Mythohistorical Interventions: The Chicano Movement and Its Legacies" and "Of Space and Mind: Cognitive Mappings of a Contemporary Chicano/a Fiction." "These books offer competent close readings of their chosen texts in the service of their respective arguments. However, each argument is questionable on a sociological scale but in a way not necessarily of the author's own making. . . . Rather than reflective, this cultural production is better seen as refractive; rather than producing a collective counter-consensus among US Mexicans, it should be viewed, at best, as vanguardist."

REVIEW: *J Am Hist* v98 no4 p1202-3 Ja 2012 Rodolfo F. Acuña

BECCALOSSI, CHIARA. Female sexual inversion; same-sex desires in Italian and British sexology, c. 1870-1920; [by] Chiara Beccalossi xiv, 304 p. 2012 Palgrave Macmillan

1. HISTORY—Europe—Great Britain 2. HISTORY—Europe—Italy 3. HISTORY—Modern—19th Century 4. HISTORY—Modern—20th Century 5. HISTORY—Social History 6. Historical literature 7. Lesbianism—Great Britain—History 8. Lesbianism—Italy—History 9. Lesbians—History 10. Medicine—Italy 11. Sex research—History 12. Sexology—History

ISBN 9780230234987

LC 2011-029570

SUMMARY: Written by Chiara Beccalossi, this book presents "An examination of how female same-sex desires were represented in a wide range of Italian and British medical writings, 1870-1920. It shows how the psychiatric category of sexual inversion was positioned alongside other medical ideas of same-sex desires, such as the virago, tribade-prostitute, fiamma and gynaecological explanations." (Publisher's note)

REVIEW: *Am Hist Rev* v118 no4 p1242-3 O 2013 Vernon A. Rosario

"Female Sexual Inversion: Same-Sex Desires in Italian and British Sexology, c. 1870-1920." "Chiara Beccalossi's monograph addresses a huge lacuna in the history of European sexuality: Italian sexology in general, particularly the conceptualization of female same-sex desire. . . . Whatever the reasons for the differential handling of female same-sex desires, Beccalossi has provided a cogent and engaging historical review and analysis of the medical literature. Scholars are particularly indebted to her for shining a light on Italian material that I hope she, or other researchers, will mine further."

BECK-CLARK, DENISE. The Zen of Forgetting; Poems; [by] Denise Beck-Clark 66 p. 2013 CreateSpace Independent Publishing Platform

1. Aging—Poetry 2. Death—Poetry 3. Marriage—Poetry 4. Parents of children with disabilities 5. Poems—Collections

ISBN 1484961846; 9781484961841

SUMMARY: "In this collection of narrative poems, [Denise] Beck-Clark produces a visual array of life moments, turning points and wisdom. . . . Beginning the collection with a graphic narrative of a bicycle accident, Beck-Clark introduces the theme of death and the temporary nature of all life, a thread that runs throughout the book. Whether speaking about health, friends' unwise marriages, dreams or childhood memories, the author addresses aging and the grace of wisdom." (Kirkus Reviews)

REVIEW: *Kirkus Rev* v81 no24 p394 D 15 2013

REVIEW: *Kirkus Rev* v82 no2 p78 Ja 15 2014

"The Zen of Forgetting: Poems". "[Denise] Beck-Clark's use of imagery delivers poignant verses with sharp alliteration and soundplay to awaken readers' senses. . . . The color drawings are similar in theme and motif but markedly different, serving as breaks between the often poignant poems. The author concludes the collection with a poem about her son and the lifelong struggle between nature and nurture, between protection and empowerment. This last poem, 'Special Needs Mom,' succinctly ties together the collection, ending on a universal and positive theme of love. Overall, with its conversational tone, stimulating images and sounds, the collection succeeds in depicting universal themes within particular, personal moments. A short, confessional collection of imagery-driven poems."

BECK, PETER J. Presenting history; past and present; [by] Peter J. Beck p. cm. 2012 Palgrave Macmillan

1. Audiences 2. Communication 3. Historians—Biography 4. Historical literature 5. Historiography 6. Historiography—Social aspects 7. History—Methodology 8. History—Philosophy 9. Public history

ISBN 9780230242074 (hbk.); 9780230242081 (pbk.)

LC 2011-049926

SUMMARY: This book "surveys the various media through which 'history presenters,' as Peter J. Beck calls them, have aimed to inform a wider public about the past. He chastises his fellow historians for producing books designed only for disciplinary specialists." Particular focus is given to "the challenge that 'history-presenters' face in reaching a wider public without 'dumbing down' the difficulties attending the interpretation of the past." (American Historical Review)

REVIEW: *Am Hist Rev* v119 no1 p154 F 2014 Elizabeth A. Clark

"Presenting History: Past and Present". "[Peter J.] Beck offers a number of case studies to illustrate how some historians (and writers interested in history) have deployed public history. Throughout, he registers clearly (often through citing other historians' critiques) the challenge that 'history-presenters' face in reaching a wider public without 'dumbing down' the difficulties attending the interpretation of the past. Beck seems to waver, however, between his critique of 'old-fashioned,' 'male-oriented,' political and military history, and his selection of authors who primarily engage that very type of scholarship. . . . All in all, this work seems written for a more elementary audience than presumably its 'real' readers (i.e., historians)."

BECKER, AARON.il. Journey. See Becker, A.

BECKER, HELAINE. Zoobots; Wild Robots Inspired by Real Animals; [by] Helaine Becker 32 p. 2014 Kids Can Pr

1. Animal behavior 2. Children's nonfiction 3. Mechatronics 4. Robotics 5. Robots

ISBN 1554539714; 9781554539710

SUMMARY: This book by Helaine Becker introduces readers to "the world of robo-animals, or zoobots. In an attempt to design robots that can solve problems or perform tasks that humans can't, or just can't do easily, roboticists have been looking at the unique skills some animals have. Using something called mechatronics—mechanical and electrical engineering combined with computer science—they are finding ways to closely mirror those skills in robot form." (Publisher's note)

REVIEW: *Booklist* v110 no17 p90 My 1 2014 J. B. Petty

REVIEW: *Kirkus Rev* v82 no2 p269 Ja 15 2014

REVIEW: *Quill Quire* v80 no2 p38-7 Mr 2014 Cori Dusmann

"Zoobots: Wild Robots Inspired By Real Animals". "Helaine Becker . . . shares a marvellous selection of robots, including the human-like Geminoied F, microscopic nanobots, and the heavyweight Ole Pill Bug—a 200-pound firefighting machine. . . . The text is supported beautifully by [Alex] Ries's bright, graphic artwork and a handy glossary. 'Zoobots' will intrigue many children, but is better suited to younger or high interest/low vocabulary readers. While the text serves as a great introduction, older readers may be left wanting more."

REVIEW: *SLJ* v60 no4 p178 Ap 2014 Anne Chapman Callaghan

BECKER, KATE M. My dream playground; [by] Kate M. Becker 32 p. 2013 Candlewick Press

1. Children's stories 2. Communities 3. KaBoom! Inc. 4. Playgrounds 5. Volunteer service

ISBN 0763655317; 9780763655310

LC 2012-947706

SUMMARY: In this children's picture book, "an unnamed young girl tells readers how the empty lot down the street from her urban apartment became her dream playground--and the part she played in its unfolding. . . . She is unsurprised but thrilled to see a man arrive at the lot with a measuring tape and clipboard. . . . After months of planning, the whole community, the young girl included, comes together as volunteers to make the dream playground a reality." (Kirkus Reviews)

REVIEW: *Horn Book Magazine* v90 no1 p121-2 Ja/F 2014

"The Fort That Jack Built," "Rosie Revere, Engineer," and "My Dream Playground." "The cumulative 'House That Jack Built' rhymes are peppy, and [Brett] Helquist's homey oil paintings in muted tones capture the action of imaginative play. . . . [Andrea] Beaty's rhymes are cleverly constructed, and [David] Roberts's meticulous illustrations, some on drafting paper, capture the quirkiness of the girl and her gizmos. . . . The author's note explains that the uplifting (if idealized) story is based on a real project by KaBOOM!, a national nonprofit organization. Sunny digital illustrations underscore the sense of community."

REVIEW: *Kirkus Rev* v81 no12 p80 Je 15 2013

REVIEW: *SLJ* v59 no8 p65 Ag 2013 Linda Ludke

BECKERMAN, STEPHEN. The ecology of the Bari; rainforest horticulturalists of South America; [by] Stephen Beckerman xv, 273 p. 2013 University of Texas Press

1. Anthropology literature 2. Indigenous peoples—

Ecology—Venezuela—Maracaibo Basin 3. Motilon Indians—Agriculture—Venezuela—Maracaibo Basin 4. Motilon Indians—Venezuela—Maracaibo Basin—Social conditions 5. Rain forest ecology—Venezuela—Maracaibo Basin 6. Traditional ecological knowledge—Venezuela—Maracaibo Basin
ISBN 9780292748194 (cl.: alk. paper)
LC 2013-000152

SUMMARY: This anthropological study of the Barí people by Stehen Beckerman and Roberto Lizarralde "illustrates its quantitative findings with an in-depth biographical sketch of the remarkable life of an individual Barí woman and a history of Barí relations with outsiders, as well as a description of the rainforest environment that has informed all aspects of Barí history for the past five hundred years." (Publisher's note)

REVIEW: *Choice* v51 no8 p1448 Ap 2014 E. N. Anderson

"The Ecology of the Barí: Rainforest Horticulturalists of South America". "The Barí inhabit the tropical, forested border country between Venezuela and Colombia, west of Lake Maracaibo. They grow manioc and bananas, hunt and fish, and live in longhouses, which are moved fairly frequently according to needs for new fields and for security from enemies. . . . Anthropologists [Stephen] Beckerman . . . and [Roberto] Lizarralde . . . provide a superb account, excellently written and compelling. Essential for anyone interested in survival and reproduction in tropical forest conditions."

BECKETT, CHRIS. Dark Eden; [by] Chris Beckett 404 p. 2012 Corvus

1. Communities 2. Exile (Punishment) 3. Extraterrestrial life 4. Space colonies—Fiction 5. Speculative fiction
ISBN 9781848874633
LC 2012-358389

SUMMARY: This novel by Chris Beckett is set in "a world called Eden populated by a mere 532 inhabitants, all descended from two common ancestors,Tommy and Angela, who came to the planet 163 years earlier by spaceship and stayed to populate a world. . . . Its protagonist is 15-year-old John Redlantern, whose act of rebellion defies sacred tradition and changes his world forever, resulting in his being banished from his rudimentary hunter-gatherer community." (Booklist)

REVIEW: *Booklist* v110 no12 p38 F 15 2014 Michael Cart

"Dark Eden." "[A] superb novel of speculative fiction.. Its protagonist is 15-year-old John Redlantern, whose act of rebellion defies sacred tradition and changes his world forever, resulting in his being banished from his rudimentary hunter-gatherer community. He will be joined in exile by three young friends, and theirs becomes a compelling story of both survival and discovery. It is told in a number of distinctive first-person voices that beautifully define character and reveal the fact that Eden's language has become corrupted. . . . [Chris] Beckett has done a brilliantly imaginative job of world building in both global concepts and quotidian details. . . .The book is a superb entertainment, a happy combination of speculative and literary fiction. And it is not to be missed."

REVIEW: *Kirkus Rev* v82 no3 p248 F 1 2014

"Dark Eden". "The stage is set for a parting of ways, exploration, conflict, murder and the erasure of accepted truths. The narrative unfolds via several first-person accounts, which allows [Chris] Beckett to develop a perspective on his archetypal main characters. Absorbing if often familiar, inventive and linguistically adept but less than fully satisfying—there's no climax, and a sequel seems assured. Despite all this, the book was extravagantly praised in Beckett's native U.K. Enjoyable but no blockbuster."

REVIEW: *Libr J* v139 no5 p99 Mr 15 2014 Megan M. McArdle

REVIEW: *N Y Times Book Rev* p14-5 Je 1 2014 N . K. JEMISIN

REVIEW: *Publ Wkly* v261 no5 p42 F 3 2014

BECKETT, SANDRA L. Revisioning Red Riding Hood around the world; an anthology of international retellings; [by] Sandra L. Beckett xiv, 401 p. 2014 Wayne State University Press

1. Anthologies 2. Children in literature 3. Fairy tales—Social aspects 4. Little Red Riding Hood (Tale) 5. Little Red Riding Hood (Tale)—History and criticism
ISBN 0814334792; 9780814334799
LC 2013-942573

SUMMARY: In this anthology of interpretations of the Little Red Riding Hood story, "rather than looking at the stories chronologically or geographically, [Sandra L.] Beckett groups the titles around seven themes, moving from the more traditional interpretation of the story as a cautionary tale about the vulnerability of children (specifically girls) to more exploratory retellings that address the perspective of the wolf or the agency of the child." (Bulletin of the Center for Children's Books)

REVIEW: *Bull Cent Child Books* v67 no9 p486 My 2014 K. Q. G.

"Revisioning Red Riding Hood Around the World: An Anthology of International Retellings". "This scholarly exploration of the classic folktale also serves as a fascinating primer in children's literature published outside the U.S., both historically and currently. . . . The selected stories represent a good chunk of the globe, from Chile to France to Korea and much in between. . . . The result is an academic exercise that fulfills two significant purposes: it offers a critical lens through which to view the stories, and it provides an opportunity to engage with international works that a U.S. audience might otherwise not see. This has obvious value to children's literature and folktale scholars, but the stories might also make for excellent storytelling fodder."

REVIEW: *Choice* v51 no10 p1796 Je 2014 E. R. Baer

REVIEW: *SLJ* v60 no4 p193 Ap 2014 Jackie Gropman

BEDFORD, DAVID. Two tough crocs; [by] David Bedford 24 p. 2014 Holiday House

1. Animal stories 2. Bullying—Juvenile fiction 3. Crocodiles—Fiction 4. Friendship—Fiction 5. Swamps—Fiction
ISBN 9780823430482 (hardcover)
LC 2013-023666

SUMMARY: In this children's book, a "smackdown between . . . two rival crocs is derailed when they're one-upped by a bigger and even tougher croc named Betty. . . . The cowed Sylvester and Arnold first escape and then befriend Betty (getting dunked in brown swamp mud proves to be the great equalizer), and when last seen, the once-terrible trio is enjoying some well-behaved jungle gym time with the smaller animals they used to terrorize." (Publishers Weekly)

REVIEW: *Booklist* v110 no16 p55 Ap 15 2014 Maryann Owen

REVIEW: *Bull Cent Child Books* v67 no10 p500-1 Je 2014 T. A.

REVIEW: *Kirkus Rev* v82 no2 p308 Ja 15 2014

'Two Tough Crocs". " Two tough crocs learn that there is always a bigger, tougher croc in the swamp. [Tom] Jellett's two saurian bullies, Sylvester and Arnold, live in a big swamp. They have never even met. They both wear tough-croc shorts, so what else is there to say? . . . This is all tamely farcical as drawn in fruity colors by [David] Bedford, though with just enough menace in the crocs' eyes to keep things from unadulterated silliness. . . . Despite its modest charms, there is not much of a story here, nor is the twist memorable enough to withstand many exposures. Good for one time around the block, though probably not for two."

REVIEW: *SLJ* v60 no4 p112 Ap 2014 Kathleen Kelly MacMillan

BEDFORD, MARTYN. Never ending; [by] Martyn Bedford 304 p. 2014 Wendy Lamb Books

1. Family problems—Fiction 2. Grief—Fiction 3. Guilt—Fiction 4. Psychological fiction 5. Psychotherapy—Fiction

ISBN 0385908091; 9780375865534 (pbk.); 9780385739917 (trade); 9780385908092 (lib. bdg.)

LC 2012-047731

SUMMARY: In this book, by Martyn Bedford, "Shiv's best mate, her brother Declan, is dead. It's been all over the news. Consumed by grief and guilt, she agrees to become an inpatient at the Korsakoff Clinic. There she meets Mikey. Caron. The others. They share a similar torment. And there, subjected to the clinic's unconventional therapy, they must face what they can't bear to see. Shiv is flooded with memories of Nikos, the beautiful young man on the tour boat. It started there, with him." (Publisher's note)

REVIEW: *Booklist* v110 no12 p74 F 15 2014 Jeanne Fredriksen

REVIEW: *Bull Cent Child Books* v67 no8 p396 Ap 2014 D. S.

REVIEW: *Horn Book Magazine* v90 no2 p109-10 Mr/Ap 2014 DEIRDRE F. BAKER

REVIEW: *Kirkus Rev* v82 no2 p150 Ja 15 2014

"Never Ending". " An English teen can't stop blaming herself for her brother's death. . . . The characters and the scenery are rendered with such photographic precision that readers will feel as though they're watching a film. They'll also find [Martyn] Bedford's compellingly blunt, sharply drawn narrative (laced with [J. D.] Salinger references) sometimes too painful to read as they experience the harsh treatments right alongside Shiv. The results, however, are absolutely worth it. Beautiful and illuminating but as hard as therapy."

REVIEW: *Publ Wkly* v261 no3 p59 Ja 20 2014

REVIEW: *SLJ* v60 no3 p151 Mr 2014 Miriam Lang Budin

REVIEW: *Voice of Youth Advocates* v36 no6 p55 F 2014 Rebecca O'Neil

BEDRICK, CLAUDIA ZOE.tr. The day I lost my superpowers. See Escoffier, M.

BEDRICK, CLAUDIA ZOE.tr. Ghosts. See Goldie, S.

A BEDTIME PRAYER; 24 p. 2013 Tiger Tales

1. Bedtime 2. God—Juvenile literature 3. Gratitude 4. Picture books for children 5. Prayer—Juvenile literature

ISBN 1589256069; 9781589256064

SUMMARY: This children's picture book presents "a long nighttime prayer in verse offering thanks to God for everything good in a child's world. This includes the bright blue skies and songbirds of a new day. . . . The illustrations depict cuddly baby animals—a dog, kitty, bear and lamb—and, in a few instances, a caregiver or two joining in the fun." (Kirkus Reviews)

REVIEW: *Kirkus Rev* v82 no1 p32 Ja 1 2014

"A Bedtime Prayer". "The lengthy, singsong (and occasionally clunky) verse isn't likely to keep children engaged, but it might successfully help ease them into peaceful sleep. The illustrations depict cuddly baby animals—a dog, kitty, bear and lamb—and, in a few instances, a caregiver or two joining in the fun. The cheerful scenes have a soft, quiet quality that contributes to the offering's overall soporific effect, as does the padded cover reminiscent of a cushy blanket. Best for parents looking for a sweet nighttime prayer ritual to share with toddlers and preschoolers."

REVIEW: *Kirkus Rev* v81 no19 p357 O 1 2013

BEE, WILLIAM. And the cars go...; [by] William Bee 32 p. 2013 Candlewick Press

1. Automobiles—Juvenile literature 2. Children's stories 3. Police—Juvenile literature 4. Sheep 5. Traffic congestion

ISBN 0763665800; 9780763665807

LC 2012-947829

SUMMARY: This children's book by William Bee centers around a traffic jam where "everyone's in a hurry! There's the family in the paneled station wagon . . . packed to the roof rack with gear for the beach. There's the be-hatted Duke and Duchess, out for a drive in their ornate Rolls Royce. Not to mention a yellow school bus . . . an overheating race car . . . and other vehicles revving to go." (Publisher's note)

REVIEW: *Horn Book Magazine* v90 no1 p68 Ja/F 2014 KITTY FLYNN

"And the Cars Go. . ." "The vehicles may be at a standstill, but [William] Bee's rhythmic text motors along as the officer investigates the problem. Each double-page spread is devoted to one fancifully detailed auto and its idiosyncratic occupants. . . . Although digitally created, Bee's stylish compositions have a distinctly sixties vibe. The pages practically vibrate with eye-popping colors held in place with a lively, sure-handed line. . . . This is a nifty companion to Bee's previous transportation ode, 'And the Train Goes. . .'"

BEESON, TREVOR. Priests and Politics; The Church Speaks Out; [by] Trevor Beeson 256 p. 2013 Presbyterian Pub Corp

1. Church of England 2. Church of England—Bishops—Political activity 3. England—Church history—1485- 4. Great Britain—Politics & government—1485- 5. Historical literature

ISBN 0334046572; 9780334046578

SUMMARY: This book by Trevor Beeson is a "study of how the Church of England's leaders responded to the radical social changes that transformed life in Britain during the nineteenth and twentieth centuries. Their response was never prompt and rarely enthusiastic,and all too often the bishops resisted change in society as well as in the church. Nonetheless there were always a few prophets who recognised the need for reform and sometimes led the way to its realisation." (Publisher's note)

REVIEW: *TLS* no5779 p22 Ja 3 2014 JONATHAN BENTHALL

"Priests and Politics: The Church Speaks Out." "The Church of England, Trevor Beeson concludes, is now 'less influential in public life than at any time during the past two centuries.' A prolific author and consummate ecclesiastical insider (formerly Rector of St Margaret's, Westminster, and Chaplain to the Speaker of the House of Commons), he presents a view of political history in Britain since the eighteenth century seen through the lens of its principal Church. . . . 'Priests and Politics' is basically a series of linked obituaries of Anglican luminaries (a few of whom are still alive and working), structured by themes including Ireland, women's suffrage, the nuclear deterrent, inner city renewal, and sex. Many readers would hope for more contextualization."

BEGLEY, ADAM. Updike; [by] Adam Begley 576 p. 2014 Harper

1. Authors—Biography 2. Authors, American—20th century—Biography 3. Biography (Literary form) 4. New England 5. Updike, John, 1932-2009
ISBN 0061896454; 9780061896453 (hardback)
LC 2013-039246

SUMMARY: This biography of John Updike "explores the stages of the writer's pilgrim's progress: his beloved home turf of Berks County, Pennsylvania; his escape to Harvard; his brief, busy working life as the golden boy at The New Yorker; his family years in suburban Ipswich, Massachusetts; his extensive travel abroad; and his retreat to another Massachusetts town, Beverly Farms, where he remained until his death in 2009." (Publisher's note)

REVIEW: *Am Sch* v83 no2 p100-2 Spr 2014 ROBERT WILSON

REVIEW: *Booklist* v110 no14 p41-4 Mr 15 2014 Brad Hooper

"Updike". "A keen appreciation for literary criticism is a prerequisite for reader interest in this thoroughly researched and rigorously presented biography of one of the most honored and respected American writers of the twentieth century. . . . It is [Adom] Begley's primary goal to stitch [John] Updike's writing to the realities of his existence. He does so meaningfully but too often intrusively, at the expense of a smoothly flowing pursuit of the events in Updike's life. Nevertheless, this is an important view of a giant literary figure."

REVIEW: *Choice* v52 no1 p73 St 2014 S. Miller

REVIEW: *Christ Century* v131 no13 p37-9 Je 25 2014 Jon M. Sweeney

REVIEW: *Harper's Magazine* v328 no1969 p86-90 Je 2014 Jonathan Dee

REVIEW: *Kirkus Rev* v82 no3 p318 F 1 2014

REVIEW: *Libr J* v139 no5 p118 Mr 15 2014 Lonnie Weatherby

REVIEW: *Libr J* v138 no20 p1 N 15 2013 Barbara Hoffert

REVIEW: *London Rev Books* v36 no11 p11-2 Je 5 2014 Christian Lorentzen

REVIEW: *N Y Rev Books* v61 no8 p6-8 My 8 2014 Hermione Lee

"Updike" and "The Collected Stories: Collected Early Stories," and "The Collected Stories: Collected Later Stories." "[Author Adam] Begley is quiet, careful, self-effacing, and steady. He is especially good and revealing on how others see Updike: friends, fellow writers, mother, first wife, children, lovers, editors. . . . The childhood stories—stories of 'family, family without end'—shine out of the two-volume Library of America 'Collected Stories.' This has been excellently edited by Christopher Carduff, whose very full chronology makes a useful aid to set alongside the biography, which has no family tree, timeline, or bibliography."

REVIEW: *N Y Times Book Rev* p30 Ap 27 2014

REVIEW: *N Y Times Book Rev* p10-1 Ap 20 2014 ORHAN PAMUK

REVIEW: *New Repub* v245 no15 p38-43 S 15 2014 William Deresiewicz

REVIEW: *New Statesman* v143 no5207 p42-4 My 2 2014 David Baddiel

REVIEW: *New Statesman* v143 no5207 p44-5 My 2 2014 Jeffrey Meyers

REVIEW: *New York Times* v163 no46466 pC1-6 Ap 9 2014 DWIGHT GARNER

REVIEW: *New Yorker* v90 no10 p70-1 Ap 28 2014

REVIEW: *Publ Wkly* v261 no7 p89-90 F 17 2014

REVIEW: *TLS* no5802 p3-4 Je 13 2014 JAMES CAMPBELL

REVIEW: *Va Q Rev* v90 no2 p216-21 Spr 2014 John Freeman

BEHR, EDWARD. 50 foods; the essentials of good taste; [by] Edward Behr 432 p. 2013 The Penguin Press

1. Cooking 2. Flavor 3. Food 4. Food & wine pairing 5. Food habits 6. Gastronomy 7. Reference books
ISBN 1594204519; 9781594204517
LC 2013-007774

SUMMARY: In this book, a "primer on the most tasty ingredients in good cooking," author Edward Behr "shares . . . of growing, choosing, and pairing foods with other foods and, especially, wines." (Publishers Weekly) "Using the guideposts of aroma, appearance, flavor and texture, Behr hones in on what . . . 'the best' means for each of the highlighted foods. . . . Behr proposes using the least amount of industrial processing possible, which results in foods closer to nature." (Kirkus Reviews)

REVIEW: *Booklist* v110 no4 p7-8 O 15 2013 Mark Knoblauch

"50 Foods: The Essentials of Good Taste." "Compacting the world's myriad foods to an inventory of just 50 may prove a formidable task. But [Edward] Behr is up to the challenge and makes compelling and intelligent arguments for each of his selections. . . . Behr's tastes are particular but not fussy, although some of his prescriptions, such as avoiding combining oysters with lemon juice, fly in the face of convention. Behr chooses the best wines, where appropriate, to accompany each item on his list. Some favored wines will be familiar to connoisseurs only, but plenty abound on the shelves of any decently stocked wine merchant. This is equally a reference text and a book for foodies to savor."

REVIEW: *Kirkus Rev* v81 no18 p106 S 15 2013

REVIEW: *Libr J* v138 no14 p136 S 1 2013 Jane Hebert

REVIEW: *Publ Wkly* v260 no34 p61 Ag 26 2013

BEHRENS, PETER, 1954-. The O'Briens; [by] Peter Behrens 552 2011 House of Anansi Press

1. Canada—History 2. Family—Fiction 3. Historical fiction 4. Irish—Canada—Fiction 5. Married people—Fiction

ISBN 978-0-88784-229-0

SUMMARY: "This novel follows the descendants of the Irish immigrant family from The Law of Dreams (2006) two generations later. Joe O'Brien is coming of age in a new century in remote Pontiac County, Quebec, with his two brothers and two sisters by his side. Their father has abandoned the family and died in the South African war; their frail mother has remarried the abusive and lecherous Mick Heaney. Joe and his siblings escape the poverty and violence of the Pontiac, but as Joe travels the continent, building a business and a . . . family with his wife, Iseult, he is never quite able to leave his past behind. [The story is] told from the perspectives of Joe, Iseult, and their children and spans the construction of the Canadian railroad as well as both world wars." (Publisher's note)

REVIEW: *Booklist* v108 no11 p40 F 1 2012 Bridget Thoreson

REVIEW: *Kirkus Rev* v80 no4 p329 F 15 2012

"The O'Briens." " So far, so good; there are glimpses of the elemental in human nature. But then [Peter] Behrens stops digging, becoming an observer of a marriage with the usual personal and historical markers. Babies: they lose one, keep three. Business booms, more construction projects after the railroad. Returning East, to Montreal. World War I. Grattan, a fighter pilot and decorated hero. Prohibition. Grattan bootlegging. Marital crisis; Iseult bolts. Reconciliation. World War II. Letters from the front. A son dies; a son-in-law survives. The jerky forward motion begs some profound questions, left unanswered. Behrens is an effective storyteller, but his idiosyncratic vision is not yet fully formed."

REVIEW: *Libr J* v137 no1 p88 Ja 1 2012 Joy Humphrey

REVIEW: *N Y Times Book Rev* p28 Ap 28 2013

REVIEW: *New Yorker* v88 no10 p79 Ap 23 2012

REVIEW: *Publ Wkly* v259 no1 p56 Ja 2 2012

BEHRENS, REBECCA. When Audrey met Alice; [by] Rebecca Behrens 304 p. 2014 Sourcebooks Jabberwocky

1. Friendship—Fiction 2. Presidents—Family—Fiction 3. Young adult fiction

ISBN 1402286422; 9781402286421 (hc: alk. paper)

LC 2013-023325

SUMMARY: In this children's novel, by Rebecca Behrens, "Audrey finds the White House to be more like a prison than a privilege, especially since her mom, the president, and her dad, a cancer researcher, find little time for her. Security concerns ruin her first party, and she has difficulty making friends at school. Poking around in a White House closet, Audrey finds a long-hidden diary that belonged to Alice Roosevelt, Theodore Roosevelt's spirited oldest daughter." (Kirkus Reviews)

REVIEW: *Booklist* v110 no12 p83 F 15 2014 Carolyn Phelan

REVIEW: *Kirkus Rev* v81 no24 p324 D 15 2013

"When Audrey Met Alice". "This charming debut brings Alice Roosevelt to life when 13-year-old "first daughter" Audrey finds Alice's century-old diary and turns to it for advice. . . . [Rebecca] Behrens invents a fictional Alice, as she reveals in her author's note, and writes the diary entries in credible period prose that's still accessible to modern readers. Audrey knows that she's just a normal girl for all that she lives in the White House, making Audrey and the story nicely accessible. An appealing journey and a fascinating life."

REVIEW: *Publ Wkly* v260 no51 p61 D 16 2013

REVIEW: *SLJ* v60 no3 p132 Mr 2014 Mary-Brook J. Townsend

REVIEW: *Voice of Youth Advocates* v37 no1 p59 Ap 2014 Debbie Kirchoff

BEI LYNN.il. Gus, the dinosaur bus. See Liu, J.

BEIL, MICHAEL D. Lantern Sam and the Blue Streak bandits; [by] Michael D. Beil 288 p. 2014 Alfred A. Knopf

1. Cats—Fiction 2. Human-animal communication—Fiction 3. Kidnapping—Fiction 4. Mystery and detective stories 5. Railroad trains—Fiction

ISBN 9780385753173 (hardcover); 9780385753180 (hardcover library binding); 9780385753203 (pbk.)

LC 2013-013509

SUMMARY: In this book by Michael D. Beil, "Henry Shipley and his family are going home to meet his father, a ship captain returning from his latest journey at sea. While aboard the train, Henry meets Ellie Strasbourg, who disappears shortly thereafter. With the help of Clarence Nockwood, the head train conductor, and Lantern Sam, a talking cat touted as the world's greatest detective since Sherlock Holmes, Henry sets out to discover what has happened to Ellie." (School Library Journal)

REVIEW: *Booklist* v110 no17 p56 My 1 2014 Carolyn Phelan

REVIEW: *Bull Cent Child Books* v67 no8 p396-7 Ap 2014 E. B.

"Lantern Sam and the Blue Streak Bandits". "Much of the tension deflates . . . when Ellie is found bound up but safe with plenty of chapters still to go, and identifying the baddies isn't quite as fun as searching the train. However, alternating chapters that chronicle Lantern Sam's previous cat lives are consistently amusing, and an action climax at the 1937 inaugural run of the real life Blue Streak toilet coaster in Conneaut Lake, Pennsylvania is a satisfying payoff. [Michael D.] Beil scatters clues broadly enough for a challenge, yet makes them transparent enough for tyro 'tecs to whiff out, assuring that most middle-graders will happily reach the mystery's solution a stop or two ahead of Henry."

REVIEW: *Kirkus Rev* v82 no6 p72 Mr 15 2014

REVIEW: *SLJ* v60 no3 p134 Mr 2014 Stephanie Charlefour

BEISER, FREDERICK C. Late German idealism; [by] Frederick C. Beiser 352 p. 2013 Oxford University Press

1. German philosophy—19th century 2. Idealism, German 3. Lotze, Hermann 4. Philosophical literature 5. Trendelenburg, Adolf

ISBN 9780199682959 (hardback)

LC 2013-939027

SUMMARY: In this book, "Frederick C. Beiser presents a study of the two most important idealist philosophers in Germany after Hegel: Adolf Trendelenburg and Rudolf Lotze. Trendelenburg and Lotze dominated philosophy in Germany in the second half of the nineteenth century. They were important influences on the generation after them." (Publisher's note)

REVIEW: *Choice* v51 no12 p2194 Ag 2014 J. M. Fritzman

REVIEW: *TLS* no5794 p7 Ap 18 2014 MICHAEL INWOOD

"Late German Idealism: Trendelenburg and Lotze." "In the present work [author Frederick C.] Beiser turns to the backwash of classical German idealism. In line with his purpose of historical restitution he avoids the fashionable and well-explored outsiders, such as Schopenhauer, Nietzsche and Marx, and focuses on two staid academic philosophers, who were influential in their day, hut are now all but forgotten: Adolf Trendelenburg (1802-72) and Hermann Lotze (1817-81). . . . Beiser expounds Trendelenburg's and Lotze's philosophy with impeccable scholarship, immense learning and judicious philosophical commentary."

BELFIORE, ELIZABETH S. Socrates' daimonic art; love for wisdom in four platonic dialogues; [by] Elizabeth S. Belfiore xvii, 304 p. 2012 Cambridge University Press

1. Dialogues (Book : Plato) 2. Friendship—Philosophy 3. PHILOSOPHY—History & Surveys—Ancient & Classical 4. Philosophical literature 5. Platonic love
ISBN 9781107007581
LC 2011-049196

SUMMARY: This book by Elizabeth S. Belfiore responds to the fact that "Despite increasing interest in the figure of Socrates and in love in ancient Greece, no recent monograph studies these topics in all four of Plato's dialogues on love and friendship. This book provides important new insights into these subjects by examining Plato's characterization of Socrates in 'Symposium,' 'Phaedrus,' 'Lysis' and the often neglected 'Alcibiades I.'" (Publisher's note)

REVIEW: *Choice* v50 no3 p490 N 2012 J. Bussanich

REVIEW: *Classical Rev* v63 no2 p358-60 O 2013 Andrea Tschemplik

"Socrates' Daimonic Art: Love for Wisdom in Four Platonic Dialogues." "A great virtue of this work is that [author Elizabeth S. Belfiore] is particularly detailed and thorough in tracing the themes under consideration--the daimonic, erôs, poetry, education and their relation to one another--though this sometimes results in repetition. Despite this, [Belfiore] never clearly defines what she (or Plato) means by 'wisdom'; she regularly has it as the object of erôs or philia, suggesting that philosophy is a philia of wisdom, but why not an erôs? [Belfiore] is thorough and eminently fair in her utilisation of secondary sources, drawn from a wide array of scholarship. The book is a mine of reliable information for scholars working on any of the relevant themes."

BELL, ANTHEA.tr. The Collected Stories of Stefan Zweig. See Zweig, S.

BELL, ANTHEA.tr. In times of fading light. See Ruge, E.

BELL, ANTHEA.tr. My wish list. See Delacourt, G.

BELL, ANTHEA.tr. Tales from the Brothers Grimm. See Zwerger, L.

BELL, ANTHEA.tr. Winters in the south. See Gstrein, N.

BELL, IAN. Once upon a time; the lives of Bob Dylan; [by] Ian Bell 590 p. 2013 Pegasus

1. Biographies 2. Jewish musicians 3. Self-realization 4. Singers—United States—Biography
ISBN 1605984817; 1780574568 (ebook); 1780575734 (hbk.); 9781605984810; 9781780574561 (ebook); 9781780575735 (hbk.)
LC 2012-545195

SUMMARY: This book by Ian Bell on musician Bob Dylan focuses on Dylan's self-reinvention "from his upbringing within a tiny Jewish community in northern, gentile Minnesota . . . to his early days in Greenwich Village as a fabulist folksinger. . . . It is a partial biography in terms of covering the arc of Dylan's long career; Bell ends with Dylan's masterful Blood on the Tracks in 1975, followed by a nod to his artistic resurrection in the 1990s and up to the present day." (Booklist)

REVIEW: *Booklist* v110 no1 p25 S 1 2013 June Sawyers

"Once Upon a Time: The Lives of Bob Dylan." "Less a full-fledged biography than an often insightful attempt to understand, as the title indicates, the many lives of this singular and frustratingly mysterious figure. . . . It is a partial biography in terms of covering the arc of Dylan's long career; Bell ends with Dylan's masterful Blood on the Tracks in 1975, followed by a nod to his artistic resurrection in the 1990s and up to the present day. . . This is best described as a fully formed emotional biography, a fascinating read about an artist who, to this day, defends his right of 'artistic autonomy,' refusing to be anyone but himself, whoever that may be."

REVIEW: *Kirkus Rev* v81 no17 p46 S 1 2013

REVIEW: *Publ Wkly* v260 no30 p57-8 Jl 29 2013

REVIEW: *TLS* no5777/8 p12-3 D 20 2013 DANIEL KARLIN

BELL, JENNIFER A.il. Miss you like crazy. See Hall, P.

BELL, JONAS.il. Hands On! Math Projects. See King, A.

BELL, LESLIE C. Hard to get; twenty-something women and the paradox of sexual freedom; [by] Leslie C. Bell 274 p. 2013 University of California Press

1. Man-woman relationships 2. Sexual ethics 3. Sexual freedom 4. Social science literature 5. Women—Identity 6. Young women—Sexual behavior
ISBN 0520261496; 9780520261495 (cloth : alk. paper)
LC 2012-028369

SUMMARY: Author Leslie Bell's book presents an "examination of the sex and love lives of the most liberated women in history--twenty-something American women who have had more opportunities, more positive role models, and more information than any previous generation. . . . Bell takes us directly into the lives of young women who struggle to negotiate the complexities of sexual desire and pleasure, and to make sense of their historically unique but contradictory constellation of opportunities and challenges." (Publisher's note)

REVIEW: *Choice* v51 no1 p170-1 S 2013 J. M. Irvine

"Hard to Get: Twenty-Something Women and the Paradox of Sexual Freedom." "This new work joins the myriad academic and popular books that explore the sex lives of US women of all ages. Sociologist and psychotherapist [Leslie C.] Bell examines what she calls the "twenty-somethings," a post-Title IX generation in a liminal stage of early adulthood. Like earlier scholars, she describes paradoxes women confront in an increasingly expansive sexual culture, nonetheless replete with contradiction and sexism. . . . The author describes her sample as 'ordinary' women, although they were 60 multiracial, college-educated, childless women between 24 and 29 who lived in Northern California. Critics may fault Bell on this narrow sample, but the stories will resonate with many."

REVIEW: *Kirkus Rev* v81 no2 p132 Ja 15 2013

REVIEW: *Publ Wkly* v259 no52 p46 D 24 2012

BELL, MACALESTER. Hard feelings; the moral psychology of contempt; [by] MacAlester Bell 320 p. 2013 Oxford University Press

1. Contempt (Attitude) 2. Emotions (Philosophy) 3. Ethics—Psychological aspects 4. Philosophical literature 5. Psychology & ethics

ISBN 0199794146; 9780199794140 (alk. paper)

LC 2012-037390

SUMMARY: Author "Macalester Bell argues that we must reconsider contempt's role in our moral lives. . . . Bell provides an account of the nature of contempt and its virtues and vices. While some insist that contempt is always unfitting because of its globalism, Bell argues that this objection mischaracterizes the person assessments at the heart of contempt. . . . The book concludes with a discussion of overcoming contempt through forgiveness." (Publisher's note)

REVIEW: *Choice* v51 no1 p90-1 S 2013 S. J. Shaw

"Hard Feelings: The Moral Psychology of Contempt." "In the debate regarding emotions, contempt has not received its due attention. [Author Macalester] Bell . . . rectifies this with tight, incisive arguments about the benefits and potential pitfalls concerning contempt. Bell argues that contempt is valuable as a fitting reaction to 'superbia'--the vices of superiority, especially regarding moral status. The hope is that contempt is able to cause in the target a sense of shame that leads to character change. . . . Taking this 'bottom-up' approach to morality allows Bell to adroitly separate contempt from other hard emotions such as disgust and hatred, and to see what possible moral value it may have."

BELLAIR, JORDIE.il. Nowhere men. See Stephenson, E.

BELLATIN, MARIO. Shiki Nagaoka; A Nose for Fiction; [by] Mario Bellatin 82 p. 2013 Phoneme Books

1. Alienation (Social psychology)—Fiction 2. Authors—Fiction 3. Japan—Fiction 4. Nose 5. Novellas (Literary form)

ISBN 1939419026; 9781939419026

SUMMARY: This novella by Mario Bellatin "purport[s] to be a Life of Shiki Nagaoka--a Japanese wdter whose nose was so large it impaired his ability to eat--is the only suitably sized aspect of the story. Shiki, we leam, is born in early twentieth-century Japan, when the upper echelons of society are still largely isolationist. His nose dooms him to be an outsider from the start." (Times Literary Supplement)

REVIEW: *TLS* no5766 p21 O 4 2013 ANDRÉ NAFFIS-SAHELY

"Shiki Nagoka; A Nose for Fiction." "Impeccably translated from the Spanish by David Shook, 'Shiki Nagaoka' is the latest of [Mario] Bellatin's books to appear in English. . . . The chronicle of Shiki's life is merely a pretext for Bellatin to voice his opinions on literature, philosophy and photography, and, despite the narrator's quasi-academic tone, the reader breezes through it as though it were a thriller, partly thanks to its tongue-in- cheek assault on the validity of its own protagonist."

BELLEGARDE, NATE.il. Nowhere men. See Stephenson, E.

BELLER, STEVEN. Democracy; All That Matters; [by] Steven Beller 160 p. 2014 McGraw-Hill

1. Democracy—History 2. Democracy—Philosophy 3. Political science—History 4. Political science literature 5. Political systems

ISBN 1444178873; 9781444178876

SUMMARY: "We can no longer take democracy for granted, if we ever could, because it is both more powerful and widespread than it has ever been, and more under threat." Written by Steven Beller, "This short book, of about 25,000 words, spells out the basic characteristics of modern-day democracy, its origins, its history, its current practice and problems, and its potential future." (Publisher's note)

REVIEW: *TLS* no5794 p22 Ap 18 2014 ANDREW GAMBLE

"The Confidence Trap: A History of Democracy in Crisis From World War I to the Present" and "Democracy: All That Matters." "Why does democracy everywhere seem to be in crisis, unable to deliver what its citizens want? In 'The Confidence Trap,' David Runciman argues this is because democracy has always been like that. It invariably disappoints. . . . From Runciman's perspective, [author Steven] Beller is claiming that democracy can still bring a moment of truth, when the people gain control of their fate, decide who they are, and what they should do collectively. For Runciman, this is an illusion."

BELLOW, GREG. Saul Bellow's heart; a son's memoir; [by] Greg Bellow 240 p. 2013 Bloomsbury

1. Authors—Family relationships 2. Fathers and sons—Biography 3. Memoirs 4. Novelists, American—20th century—Biography

ISBN 9781608199952

LC 2012-035407

SUMMARY: This memoir by Greg Bellow traces his father Saul Bellow's gradual shift from "'Young Saul'--emotionally accessible, often soft, with a set of egalitarian social values and the ability to laugh at the world's folly and at himself" to "Old Saul," whose "accessibility and lightheartedness waned as he aged. . . . These changes taxed the relationship between Bellow and his son . . . so sorely that Greg often worried whether it would survive." (Publisher's note)

REVIEW: *Booklist* v109 no14 p43 Mr 15 2013 Donna Seaman

REVIEW: *Kirkus Rev* v81 no3 p158 F 1 2013

REVIEW: *Libr J* v138 no5 p107 Mr 15 2013 Patrick A. Smith

REVIEW: *N Y Rev Books* v60 no14 p64-5 S 26 2013 Edward Mendelson

"Saul Bellow's Heart: A Son's Memoir." "In outline form, Greg Bellow's memoir of his father Saul tells a familiar twentieth-century story: a young Jewish left-wing idealist becomes an overbearing middle-aged reactionary, driven in part by sexual anxieties obvious to everyone but himself. In detail, the story is nuanced, moving, and idiosyncratic, with an unpredictable ending. . . . 'Saul Bellow's Heart' is persuasive but artless, making it an easy target for reviewers who didn't want to hear what it has to say. Greg Bellow writes as if he were speaking aloud, shifting unguardedly between nostalgia and rage. He . . . slips now and then into a fog of pop-psych clichés, but emerges with telling anecdotes that make their point without commentary."

REVIEW: *TLS* no5747 p21 My 24 2013 CLIVE SINCLAIR

"Saul Bellow's Heart: A Son's Memoir." "'Saul Bellow's Heart' is his ambitious riposte. But it is a project beset with a fundamental problem. On the one hand he wants to prove his father's heart, as a jeweller tests gold, and thereby reveal its flaws; on the other he wishes to proclaim its twenty-two-carat greatness, and furnish proof that he is now its legitimate custodian. How to accommodate the latter with the story of rejection he cannot help telling? . . . For a psychotherapist . . . Greg seems touchingly naive about the perils of unconscious self-exposure."

BELLOW, SAUL, 1915-2005. Collected Stories; [by] Saul Bellow 2013 Penguin Group (USA), Inc.

1. Bellow, Janis

ISBN 9780143107255

SUMMARY: In this short story collection, by Saul Bellows, edited by Janis Bellows, "chosen by the author himself, are favorites such as 'What Kind of Day Did You Have?', 'Leaving the Yellow House,' and a previously uncollected piece, 'By the St. Lawrence.' With his larger-than-life characters, irony, wisdom, and unique humor, Bellow presents a sharp, rich, and funny world that is infinitely surprising." (Publisher's note)

REVIEW: *London Rev Books* v35 no12 p3-6 Je 20 2013 James Meek

REVIEW: *TLS* no5748 p19-20 My 31 2013 MICHAEL SALER

"All That Is" and "Collected Stories." "Such extravaganzas more commonly serve as a novel's climax, but here they are merely the prologue to a narrative of everyday experience, which appears as no less significant than global conflict. Since the beginning of his literary career in the 1950s, Salter's genius has been to invoke the ancient muses to chant about modern existence making the ordinary revelatory of heroism, tragedy and mystery in a secular world. . . . The often dark tales in his 'Collected Stories,' also gesture towards an occult dimension while never departing from a naturalistic register."

BELTRAMINI, GUIDO. The Private Palladio; [by] Guido Beltramini 120 p. 2012 Prestel Pub

1. Architects—Italy—Biography 2. Biographies 3. Italy—History—16th century 4. Palladio, Andrea, 1508-1580 5. Renaissance architecture—Italy

ISBN 3037782994; 9783037782996

SUMMARY: This book on architect Andrea Palladio " follows his career, his rise from being the ordinary miller's son Pietro della Gondola to become the architect Andrea Palladio. [Guido] Beltramini . . . explore[s] Palladio's origins, his training as a stonemason, and his complex relationship with powerful clients and scholars . . . his life as a married man with five children, and not least his profound conviction that architecture can and must enrich life." (Publisher's note)

REVIEW: *TLS* no5749 p8 Je 7 2013 RODERICK CONWAY MORRIS

"The Private Palladio." "This short but enlightening monograph, based on a judicious re-examination of the original documents relating to the architect's life, and drawing on new discoveries and on many years of research into the artistic, intellectual and social world in which [Andrea] Palladio rose to prominence, has been felicitously translated by Irena Murray and Eric Ormsby. . . . [Guido] Beltramini argues convincingly that Giangiorgio Trissino was the most likely originator of Palladio's assumed classical-sounding name, with its echoes of the goddess Pallas Athene."

BELZUNCE, PHILIP R. Eight Pathways of Healing Love; Your Journey of Transformation (Volume 1); [by] Philip R. Belzunce 276 p. 2013 Bella-Tierra International

1. Awareness 2. Couples 3. Love 4. Marital communication 5. Self-help materials

ISBN 0985766603; 9780985766603

SUMMARY: In this book, "drawing on decades of client counseling, as well as their own experience as a couple, [Philip R.] Belzunce and [Lalei E.] Gutierrez have created a road map for exploring eight areas of human existence and interaction, which they call pathways. . . . Each discussion of pathways includes explanations, illustrative case histories, questionnaires and worksheets." (Kirkus Reviews)

REVIEW: *Kirkus Rev* v81 no10 p119 My 15 2013

REVIEW: *Kirkus Rev* p8 D 15 2013 supplemet best books 2013

"Eight Pathways of Healing Love". " From the first pages, this treatise diverges from the surface-skating norm. . . . Such idiosyncratic terminology—and the unapologetically heart-centered language, which belies an inherent, worldly wisdom—is easy to resist at first brush. Familiarity, however, breeds understanding and acceptance. . . . . Exposure alone has value, even to the reader who foregoes completing the exercises (or who would balk at couples' therapy). Any relationship, post-divorce included, stands to benefit from exploring all of the pathways, as do the individuals involved. A valuable addition to the self-help genre, for skimmers and divers alike."

BEMIS, MAX, 1984-. Polarity; [by] Max Bemis 112 p. 2013 Simon & Schuster

1. Artists—Fiction 2. Graphic novels 3. Hipsters (Subculture) 4. People with bipolar disorder 5. Superheroes

ISBN 1608863468; 9781608863464

SUMMARY: In this graphic novel, "Timothy Woods is a bipolar artist stuck in the world of hipsters, meaningless sex, and vain art. . . . But after he survives a near fatal car accident, Timothy discovers that his mental instability is more than just a disorder, and that his bipolar medication . . . [has] been suppressing his super powers! Now it's time for Timothy to stand up to his disease alongside an onslaught of wretched human villainy as he finally finds his place in the world." (Publisher's note)

REVIEW: *Booklist* v110 no11 p49-50 F 1 2014 Sarah Hunter

"Polarity." "[Max] Bemis' tongue-in-cheek dialogue is insouciantly self-aware--'I'm the guy reluctantly making it safe to be a douchey indie rocker in a gentrified former ghetto, you big ugly mammoth'--but [Jorge] Coelho's gorgeous full-color art saves it from being a mere joke by bringing vivid life to Tim's mania and adding a much-needed touch of pathos in delicately rendered facial expressions. Though the plot is nothing new, the hipster-bashing trappings and entrancing art certainly make up for it."

BENATAR, DAVID. The second sexism; discrimination against men and boys; [by] David Benatar xi, 288 p. 2012 Wiley-Blackwell

1. Men—Psychology 2. Men—Social conditions 3. Sex discrimination against men 4. Social science literature 5. Violence

ISBN 9780470674512 (pbk.: alk. paper)

LC 2011-038087

SUMMARY: This book by David Benatar "aims to show how men are victims of sexism, and then attempts to disprove feminist critiques that argue the opposite. . . . The book focuses on men's mandatory enrollment in the military, experiences with violent crime, corporal punishment, child custody, and rape. Benatar asserts that these forms of male disadvantage speak to the devaluing of male bodies compared to female bodies." (Contemporary Sociology)

REVIEW: *Choice* v50 no4 p764 D 2012 P. K. Steinfeld

REVIEW: *Contemp Sociol* v43 no2 p194-6 Mr 2014 Rashawn Ray

"The Second Sexism: Discrimination Against Men and Boys". "David Benatar is a philosopher who attempts to include literature on gender and sexism from an array of disciplines. With this said, sociological research on gender, sexism, and masculinity (which has much to say on this topic) was lacking. . . . From the opening pages of 'The Second Sexism,' sociologists will read statements which they may find pejorative and that might preclude one from discerning the main contribution of the book. . . . These controversial claims could possibly distract readers from an intriguing discussion about how best to conceptualize discrimination, disadvantage, and sexism. Based on how a scholar defines these terms will influence how one interprets the book's analysis."

BENDER, AIMEE. The color master; stories; [by] Aimee Bender 240 p. 2013 Doubleday

1. Families—Fiction 2. Ghouls & ogres 3. Marriage—Fiction 4. Sexual fantasies 5. Short stories

ISBN 9780385534895

LC 2013-001489

SUMMARY: This short story collection, by Aimee Bender, features "stories about people searching for connection through love, sex, and family—while navigating the often painful realities of their lives. A traumatic event unfolds when a girl with flowing hair of golden wheat appears in an apple orchard. . . . A woman plays out a prostitution fantasy with her husband and finds she cannot go back. . . . An ugly woman marries an ogre and struggles to decide if she should stay with him." (Publisher's note)

REVIEW: *Booklist* v109 no22 p26-8 Ag 1 2013 Kristine Huntley

REVIEW: *Kirkus Rev* v81 no13 p295 Jl 1 2013

REVIEW: *Libr J* v138 no5 p90 Mr 15 2013 Barbara Hoffert

REVIEW: *N Y Times Book Rev* p11 S 1 2013 SCOTT BRADFIELD

"The Color Master: Stories." "[Aimee] Bender is best known for the fabulist elements of her stories, and this new book features many deliberately nondescript characters referred to simply as 'the woman' or 'the new teacher'. . . . But some of the most successful stories here (the ones that don't suffer from an excess of peripeteia or whimsy) are those that explore less fabulist locations and people, like the college roommates divided by radically different tastes in boyfriends in 'Bad Return'."

REVIEW: *New York Times* v162 no56243 pC6 Ag 29 2013 John Williams

REVIEW: *Publ Wkly* v260 no19 p42 My 13 2013

BENDING, STEPHEN. Green retreats; women, gardens, and eighteenth-century culture; [by] Stephen Bending 319 p. 2013 Cambridge University Press

1. Gardeners—Great Britain—Biography 2. Gardeners—Great Britain—Correspondence 3. Gardening—Great Britain—History—18th century 4. Historical literature 5. LITERARY CRITICISM—European—English, Irish, Scottish, Welsh 6. Women—Great Britain—Social conditions—18th century 7. Women gardeners—Great Britain—Biography 8. Women gardeners—Great Britain—Correspondence

ISBN 1107040027; 9781107040021 (hardback)

LC 2013-005956

SUMMARY: This book by Stephen Bending presents an "account of eighteenth-century women in their gardens, in the context of the larger history of their retirement from the world--whether willed or enforced--and of their engagement with the literature of gardening." Subjects include "Elizabeth Montagu . . . Lady Caroline Holand and Lady Mary Coke." (Publisher's note)

REVIEW: *Choice* v51 no10 p1826 Je 2014 S. E. Brazer

REVIEW: *Hist Today* v63 no9 p62-3 S 2013 ROSIE ATKINS

"Green Retreats: Women, Gardens and Eighteenth-Century Culture." "Don't be misled by the title of Stephen Bending's new book. . . .This well-researched work explores the cultural significance of the garden to well-heeled women living in the 18th century, although there are descriptions of their own gardens. 'Garden Retreats' is divided into three parts, a wordy introduction followed by a section questioning the meaning of retirement--a search for solitude for some or a banishment from polite society for others? For me the revelations came at the end with the case histories that explained how the garden shaped the identities and occupied the time of four intelligent women."

BENDIX, JOHN.tr. Seduction and desire. See Quindeau, I.

BENGTSSON, JONAS T. A fairy tale; 336 p. 2014 Other Press

1. Adult child abuse victims—Fiction 2. FICTION—Coming of Age 3. FICTION—Literary 4. Family secrets—Fiction 5. Fathers and sons—Fiction
ISBN 9781590516942 (pbk.)
LC 2013-042499

SUMMARY: In this book, "a young boy bounces around Copenhagen with his father, a loving but seemingly unstable man who moves restlessly from apartment to apartment and job to job. The boy, who shows a talent and love for drawing, is homeschooled and nourished on elaborate fairy tales. . . . After his father's fixations turn violent, the boy is shuttled off to his mother and her new husband. Only as a young man does he begin asking questions about what led to his father's actions." (Publishers Weekly)

REVIEW: *Booklist* v110 no14 p47-8 Mr 15 2014 Michael Cart

REVIEW: *Kirkus Rev* v82 no4 p297 F 15 2014

"A Fairy Tale". "A boy's unconventional upbringing skews his worldview in this Danish author's third novel (but first U.S. publication). Dad is upset. He's sobbing. He is reacting to the news that a progressive Swedish politician has been murdered. This is how we first see the young father with the shoulder-length hair-through the eyes of his 6-year-old son, the narrator. (Neither father nor son is named.) The politics, the violence, the emotional vulnerability, they all presage the novel's key moment. . . . Is this the father's story or the son's? [Jonas T.] Bengtsson's ambivalence proves fatal, yielding a broken-backed narrative."

REVIEW: *Publ Wkly* v261 no2 p45-6 Ja 13 2014

REVIEW: *TLS* no5796 p20 My 2 2014 PAUL BINDING

BENINCASA, SARA. Great; [by] Sara Benincasa 272 p. 2014 HarperTeen, an imprint of HarperCollinsPublishers

1. Blogs—Fiction 2. Celebrities—Fiction 3. Conduct of life—Fiction 4. Fashion—Fiction 5. Lesbians—Fiction 6. Wealth—Fiction 7. Young adult fiction
ISBN 9780062222695 (hardcover bdg.)
LC 2013-008047

SUMMARY: In this book, Naomi is "friendly with Delilah Fairweather, senator's daughter and up-and-coming model. She's got her first boyfriend, the dorky yet popular Jeff. Things are good with her mother. And then there's Jacinta Trimalchio, fashion blogger and Naomi's next-door neighbor. She's mysterious and different, and Naomi likes her. But Jacinta has many secrets and one obsession: Delilah Fairweather. And that obsession will lead to scandal, an accident and death." (Kirkus Reviews)

REVIEW: *Booklist* v110 no15 p86 Ap 1 2014 Gail Bush

REVIEW: *Bull Cent Child Books* v67 no10 p501 Je 2014 K. C.

"Great". "For readers familiar with 'The Great Gatsby,' there are no surprises as to how this ends, but [Sara] Benincasa's overlay of contemporary media and social structures onto that source text is ingenious, making this a savvy and believable remake. Even readers who don't recognize the parallels will be drawn into the tragedy of a young woman willing to risk everything to reclaim a lost love. . . . Delilah's unworthiness and Jacinta's need are explored critically but without overly harsh judgment, as Naomi's evolving understanding of her mother expands her capacity for compassion. The guys, though, remain despicably serene in their lack of accountability for any wrongdoing, reminding us that the lessons of Gatsby are, unfortunately, still current."

REVIEW: *Kirkus Rev* v82 no4 p177 F 15 2014

"Great". "Alas, this debut is anything but the titular great, though it could have been pretty good. . . . This retelling of The Great Gatsby-especially with the 'edgy' twist of a lesbian relationship between Jacinta/Gatsby and Delilah/Daisy-disappoints, as the story's original elements are good enough that riding Fitzgerald's coattails isn't necessary. Naomi's voice and character are engaging, and her relationships with Jeff and her mother provide plenty of fodder for a coming-of-age novel. The Gatsby elements are the weakest, from the character types to the plot. Read this for Naomi and try to forget The Great Gatsby."

REVIEW: *Publ Wkly* v261 no4 p195 Ja 27 2014

REVIEW: *SLJ* v60 no4 p157 Ap 2014 Elizabeth Kahn

REVIEW: *Voice of Youth Advocates* v37 no1 p59 Ap 2014 Judith A. Hayn

BENJAMIN, RUHA. People's science; bodies and rights on the stem cell frontier; [by] Ruha Benjamin 272 p. 2013 Stanford University Press

1. Embryonic stem cells—Research—Government policy—California 2. Embryonic stem cells—Research—Social aspects—California 3. Medical policy—Social aspects—California 4. Scientific literature 5. Stem cells—Research—Government policy—California 6. Stem cells—Research—Social aspects—California
ISBN 9780804782968 (cloth : alk. paper); 9780804782975 (pbk. : alk. paper)
LC 2013-006484

SUMMARY: This book on stem cell research "uncovers the tension between scientific innovation and social equality, taking the reader inside California's 2004 stem cell initiative, the first of many state referenda on scientific research, to consider the lives it has affected. [ruha] Benjamin reveals the promise and peril of public participation in science, illuminating issues of race, disability, gender, and socio-economic class." (Publisher's note)

REVIEW: *Choice* v51 no7 p1252-3 Mr 2014 M. D. Lagerwey

"People's Science: Bodies and Rights on the Stem Cell Frontier." "[Ruha] Benjamin . . . problematizes this easy dichotomy, writing persuasively of the complex divides between support versus critique and advancement versus opposition to this branch of scientific research. Although some of these divisions fall along expected lines, the author focuses on race and privilege. . . . Benjamin is refreshingly forthcoming in positioning herself in relationship to stem cell controversies, but her book's arguments, unfortunately, are clouded by extensive use of lengthy quotes and attempts to thoroughly illustrate the intricacies of related issues."

REVIEW: *Publ Wkly* v260 no17 p125-6 Ap 29 2013

BENN, GOTTFRIED, 1886-1956. Impromptus; selected poems and some prose; [by] Gottfried Benn 416 p. 2013 Farrar, Straus and Giroux

1. Experimental poetry 2. German authors—20th century 3. German poetry—20th century 4. Poems—Collections 5. Poetry (Literary form)—Translations
ISBN 9780374175375
LC 2013-021683

SUMMARY: Translated and edited by Michael Hofmann, this poetry and prose collection contains works by poet Gottfried Benn. "Over the decades, as Benn suffered the vicissitudes of fate . . . , the harsh voice of the poems relented and mellowed. His later poetry—from which 'Impromptus' is chiefly drawn, many of the poems translated into English for the first time—is deeply affecting." (Publisher's note)

REVIEW: *Antioch Rev* v72 no1 p192 Wint 2014 Alex M. Frankel

REVIEW: *Booklist* v110 no5 p12 N 1 2013 Michael Autrey

REVIEW: *New Repub* v244 no25 p46-51 Ap 7 2014 Adam Thirlwell

"Impromptus: Selected Poems and Some Prose." "The career of Gottfried Benn is a case study in disgrace. And now the international reader, whose acquaintance with Benn might have otherwise been as fragmentary as a mention in an essay by T.S. Eliot or in a poem by Frank O'Hara, can finally examine this case study with voracious comprehensiveness, owing to the virtuosic, acidic selection of translations by the poet Michael Hofmann. Benn's late style is one of literature's great inventions, and the composition of this selection conditions its reader to concentrate on that phenomenon."

REVIEW: *TLS* no5804 p21-2 Je 27 2014 ANTHONY PHELAN

BENN, TONY, 1925-2014. A Blaze of Autumn Sunshine; The Last Diaries; [by] Tony Benn 320 p. 2014 Trafalgar Square

1. English diaries 2. Great Britain—Politics & government—1945- 3. Labour Party (Great Britain) 4. Politicians—Diaries 5. Politicians—Great Britain

ISBN 0099564955; 9780099564959

SUMMARY: A diary collection by Tony Benn, edited by Ruth Winstone, "'A Blaze of Autumn Sunshine' chronicles both the public and the personal events of the last decade of his life in Westminster and his 'retirement' thereafter. Covering the rise and fall of New Labour, Tony's tireless campaigning against the wars in Iraq and Afghanistan and his passionate commitment to encouraging public debate and demonstrations, this volume also gives us an insight into . . . growing older." (Publisher's note)

REVIEW: *TLS* no5790 p30 Mr 21 2014 JAD ADAMS

"A Blaze of Autumn Sunshine: The Last Diaries." "'The Diaries of Tony Benn,' who died last week, are one of the longest records of public and private life ever published in Britain. They stretch from 1940 to 2009, and encompass fifty years in parliament. . . . Taken as a whole, the series is a model of diary writing: sharply observed, readable, informative and often indiscreet, though much of the credit for that can be taken by the editor Ruth Winstone, who has worked on the diaries for twenty-eight years. . . . Inevitably this ninth volume, clearly subtitled 'The last diaries' is something of a recessional with elements previously prominent now faded or absent. Benn is no longer an MP so the day-to-day business of the Houses of Parliament has gone from this volume."

BENNETT, ANDY.ed. Pop Pagans. See Pop Pagans

BENNETT, JEFFREY. What is relativity?; an intuitive introduction to einstein's ideas, and why they matter; [by] Jeffrey Bennett 208 p. 2014 Columbia University Press

1. Black holes (Astronomy) 2. Einstein, Albert, 1879-1955 3. Relativity (Physics)—Popular works 4. Scientific literature 5. Thought experiments

ISBN 0231167261; 9780231167260 (cloth : alk. paper)

LC 2013-026801

SUMMARY: In this introduction to Albert Einstein's theory of relativity for lay readers, Jeffrey Bennett "relies heavily on thought experiments. Einstein himself used thought experiments to understand how to make sense of the shortcoming of Newtonian physics. Bennett takes the reader step by step from the special theory of relativity through the broader general theory of relativity." (Library Journal)

REVIEW: *Booklist* v110 no11 p7 F 1 2014 Bryce Christensen

"What Is Relativity? An Intuitive Introduction to Einstein's Ideas, and Why They Matter." "In its relatively few pages, [Jeffrey] Bennett explains relativity to ordinary readers. Applying two simple principles--the uniformity of natural law and the invariance of the speed of light--readers conduct thought experiments that fuse time and space into a single concept. . . . In the very fact that one man could formulate a theory as powerful as relativity, Bennett sees reason to hope that the entire human species can ultimately conquer stubborn nonscientific problems--social, political, even metaphysical. An impressively accessible distillation of epoch-making science."

REVIEW: *Choice* v52 no2 p300 O 2014 F. Potter

REVIEW: *Kirkus Rev* v82 no2 p58 Ja 15 2014

"What Is Relativity? An Intuitive Introduction to Einstein's Ideas, and Why They Matter". "Understanding the universe requires understanding relativity, and this slim volume does an admirable job without resorting to the gimmicks or magic show common in the [Albert] Einstein-for-laymen genre. . . . What's relative in relativity, [Jeffrey Bennett writes, is motion. Its foundation rests on two absolutes: 1) The laws of physics are the same for everyone and, 2) the speed of light is the same for everyone. Readers will share Bennett's amazement at the weird consequences of the latter. . . . A sober, comprehensible account of what every intelligent layman should know about space and time."

REVIEW: *Libr J* v139 no4 p108 Mr 1 2014 William Baer

REVIEW: *Publ Wkly* v260 no49 p72 D 2 2013

BENNETT, JENN. Bitter Spirits; [by] Jenn Bennett 336 p. 2014 Berkley Pub Group1. Blessing & cursing—Fiction 2. Historical fiction 3. Love stories 4. Magic—Fiction 5. Mediums

ISBN 0425269574; 9780425269572

SUMMARY: In this book by Jenn Bennett "Aida Palmer performs a spirit medium show onstage at Chinatown's illustrious Gris-Gris speakeasy. Winter Magnusson is a notorious bootlegger [and] the recent target of a malevolent hex that renders him a magnet for hauntings. After Aida's supernatural assistance is enlisted to banish the ghosts [they] hunt for the curseworker responsible for the hex . . . and the closer they become." (Publisher's note)

REVIEW: *Booklist* v110 no9/10 p58 Ja 1 2014 Pat Henshaw

"Bitter Spirits." "[Jenn] Bennett's absolutely delightful first in a new series stirs intrigue, paranormal activity, and romance into a wonderfully refreshing brew. . . . In 1927 San Francisco, spirit medium Aida Palmer is working speakeasies, reuniting customers with their loved ones, when she meets rugged bootlegger Winter Magnusson, who's been poisoned and put under a spell he hopes she can cure. Bennett's fast-paced dialogue, often witty and sharp, as well as her charming characters and detailed setting, will truly captivate romance readers."

REVIEW: *Publ Wkly* v260 no45 p1 N 11 2013

BENNETT, JONATHAN. The Colonial Hotel; [by] Jonathan Bennett 218 p. 2014 Pgw

1. Adventure stories 2. Man-woman relationships—Fiction 3. Physicians—Fiction 4. Volunteers 5. War stories
ISBN 177041178X; 9781770411784

SUMMARY: This book follows Helen and Paris, "humanitarian volunteers in an unnamed nation on the brink of civil war. . . . Pregnant Helen is able to escape; the unfortunate Paris is captured and imprisoned by the Colonel. . . . Paris is dragged across a nation torn by war towards a fate as uncertain as it seems likely to be unpleasant, but even in a land bent on self-destruction the possibility of unexpected love exists." (Publisher's note)

REVIEW: *Quill Quire* v80 no2 p28 Mr 2014 Alex Good

"The Colonial Hotel". "'The Colonial Hotel' takes a classic tale and recasts it in a form both episodic and abstract. . . . Just as the names suggest elemental types rather than conventionally realistic characters, the setting is left deliberately generic and vague: it's never specified where or when the action is taking place. . . . Adding to the sense of storybook indeterminacy is the elevated language, which seems at times as though it is being translated from some ancient text. . . . Originally conceived as a poetic sequence, the writing is also frequently pitched at a stilted rhetorical level. . . . One can understand [Jonathan] Bennett's desire to write a political fable both contemporary and timeless, but his intensity and moral earnestness can be burdensome."

BENNETT, KELLY. Vampire baby; [by] Kelly Bennett 32 p. 2013 Candlewick Press

1. Brothers & sisters 2. Illustrated children's books 3. Infants—Juvenile fiction 4. Mythical animals—Juvenile fiction 5. Vampires—Fiction
ISBN 9780763646912
LC 2012-943658

SUMMARY: Author Kelly Bennett and illustrator Paul Meisel have created this children's book about a "vampire baby" and her older brother. "Although his baby sister, Tootie, used to be sweet, cuddly, and toothless, she's suddenly grown fangs! The unnamed little boy narrator joins his mom and baby sister at the doctor's office, where the doctor assures them that she's no vampire--Tootie's canines have just grown in before her incisors." (Booklist)

REVIEW: *Bull Cent Child Books* v67 no1 p7 S 2013 H. M.

"Vampire Baby." "'Kids may not catch the clues that the 'vampire' family who approaches Tootie in the store are actually in costume, but they'll recognize the shift from annoyance to ownership, familiar from titles such as 'Young's Don't Eat the Baby' . . . and from life experience. [Illustrator Paul] Meisel's mixed-media illustrations are predominately line and watercolor, with acrylics providing extra oomph and touches of collage and hatchwork detailing adding texture to the compositions. Vampire or not, this baby's got bite, and the ultimate message about sibling love carries the day in this comic treatment of a common phase."

REVIEW: *Horn Book Magazine* v89 no5 p63 S/O 2013 ELISSA GERSHOWITZ

REVIEW: *Kirkus Rev* v81 no15 p20 Ag 1 2013

REVIEW: *Publ Wkly* v260 no29 p67 Jl 22 2013

REVIEW: *SLJ* v59 no6 p75 Je 2013 Lindsay Persohn

BENNETT, MICHAEL.ed. Sicily. See Sicily

BENNETTS, MARC. Kicking the Kremlin; Russia's New Dissidents and the Battle to Topple Putin; [by] Marc Bennetts 320 p. 2014 Pgw

1. Journalism 2. Pussy Riot (Performer) 3. Putin, Vladimir Vladimirovich, 1952- 4. Resistance to government 5. Russia (Federation)—Politics & government
ISBN 1780743483; 9781780743486

SUMMARY: In this book on anti-government movemments in Russia, "journalist and long-time Moscow resident Marc Bennetts introduces a new generation of Russian dissidents, united by their hatred of Putin and his bid to silence all political adversaries. We meet a bustling cast of urban youth working to expose the injustices of the regime and a disjointed bunch of dissenters – from 'It Girl' hipsters to 21st-century socialists." (Publisher's note)

REVIEW: *Booklist* v110 no13 p6 Mr 1 2014 Eloise Kinney

REVIEW: *Kirkus Rev* v82 no2 p296 Ja 15 2014

"Kicking the Kremlin: Russia's New Dissidents and the Battle to Topple Putin". "Engagingly grim, frequently absurdist portrait of Vladimir Putin and the popular protests against him, which are gaining steam. . . . Journalist [Marc] Bennetts . . . maintains a cool, even tone throughout these portraits of the Putin oligarchs, who are determined to keep power, and the leaders of the dissident movements aiming to oust them. . . . Bennetts insightfully portrays a Russia on the cusp of popular revolt."

REVIEW: *New Statesman* v143 no5197 p44-5 F 14 2014 Daniel Trilling

REVIEW: *TLS* no5790 p11 Mr 21 2014 JOHN LLOYD

BENNY, MIKE.il. Just as good. See Crowe, C.

BENSON, RAYMOND. The Black Stiletto; Secrets & Lies; [by] Raymond Benson 336 p. 2014 Midpoint Trade Books Inc

1. Adventure stories 2. Alzheimer's disease 3. Organized crime—Fiction 4. Revenge—Fiction 5. Vigilantes—Fiction
ISBN 1608091015; 9781608091010

SUMMARY: In this fourth installement of the Black Stiletto series, "Judy, the Stiletto, meets Leo, a charismatic man who convinces her to move to Los Angeles when she is run out of New York by increasingly hazardous police heat. But soon Judy suspects that Leo is not the white knight she first thought. . . . Meanwhile, in the present, Alzheimer's-stricken Judy takes a turn for the worse as Martin comes to grips with the imminent end of his mother's life." (Publisher's note)

REVIEW: *Booklist* v110 no9/10 p52-3 Ja 1 2014 Michele Leber

"Secrets & Lies: The Fourth Diary--1961." "Desire for revenge lives on for decades, threatening middle-age accountant Martin Talbot as it threatened his mother, Judy, the internationally known vigilante called the Black Stiletto, in the early 1960s. . . .This fourth entry in the Black Stiletto series is darker than earlier ones, given the escalating violence in both past and present story lines. But it's no less entertaining, as fast-paced action leads to a cliff-hanger; closure is likely in the next entry, and there's potential for a spinoff. Addictive escapism."

BENT, TIMOTHY.tr. The Conversation. See D'Ormesson, J.

BENTLEY, DANA FRANTZ. Everyday artists; inquiry and creativity in the early childhood classroom; [by] Dana Frantz Bentley 144 p. 2013 College Press

1. Art—Study and teaching (Preschool) 2. Creative activities and seat work 3. Early childhood education 4. Education, Preschool—Activity programs 5. Educational literature

ISBN 9780807754405 (pbk. : alk. paper); 9780807754412 (hardcover : alk. paper)

LC 2013-003857

SUMMARY: In this book, "the author addresses the disconnect that exists between the teaching of art and the way young children actually experience art. In doing so, this book . . . opens up . . . possibilities for art education in the early childhood classroom. . . . [Dana Frantz] Bentley uses vignettes of children's everyday activities from block building to clean-up to outdoor play to help teachers identify and scaffold the genuine artistic practice of young children." (Publisher's note)

REVIEW: *Choice* v51 no6 p1064 F 2014 S. Sugarman

"Everyday Artists: Inquiry and Creativity in the Early Childhood Classroom." "[Dana Frantz] Bentley, an early-childhood teacher in child centered emerging curriculum classrooms, has an advantage over most teachers in the US--she can listen to children and follow up on their interests. She offers a model of a teacher learning along with and from the children whom she teaches. There are vivid anecdotes of the children's thinking and of her responses to their ideas. . . . This short book has much to offer, as Bentley considers art a way of thinking, not a separate part of the curriculum. . . . Recommended."

BENTLY, PETER. Twin Trouble; [by] Peter Bently 20 p. 2013 Natl Geographic Soc Childrens books

1. Accidents—Fiction 2. Bears—Juvenile fiction 3. Children's stories 4. Families—Juvenile fiction 5. Toy & movable books

ISBN 1426313616; 9781426313615

SUMMARY: In this children's story by Peter Bently, part of the Wild Tales series, "two bear cubs get themselves in a jam. . . . Bobby and Bella go off to meet relatives, and Bobby ends up taking a tumble into the river. Their aunt and cousins arrive just in the nick of time to rescue the cub and bring him home." (Kirkus Reviews)

REVIEW: *Kirkus Rev* v81 no21 p271 N 1 2013

REVIEW: *Kirkus Rev* v82 no1 p38 Ja 1 2014

"Twin Trouble: A Lift-the-Flap Story About Bears". "Two bear cubs get themselves in a jam in this ineffective lift-the-flap story. . . . The flaps, which are unfinished brown cardboard on the verso, are a big distraction, and there is little rhyme or reason to their presence. They often block the view of the characters and rarely reveal anything new or surprising on their interiors. . . . A note to parents on the back cover . . . encourages interaction between youngster and grown-up. National Geographic, known for its nonfiction publishing, provides little information to tots in this slight tale."

BENTON, JIM, 1960-. The end (almost); [by] Jim Benton 40 p. 2014 Scholastic Press

1. Bears—Fiction 2. Bears—Juvenile fiction 3. Books and reading—Fiction 4. Books and reading—Juvenile fiction 5. Children's stories 6. Humorous stories 7. Storytelling—Fiction 8. Storytelling—Juvenile fiction

ISBN 9780545177313

LC 2013-009268

SUMMARY: In this book, author Jim Benton "introduces readers to a rotund blue bear who is alarmed that the narrator has declared, 'The end' after only two pages. Donut is incredulous, defiant, and dejected by turns, conversing with the narrator via speech bubbles. Finally, the narrator agrees to continue the story; however, the next page turn reveals that the book is out of pages. Donut is crestfallen until the narrator offers to read the story again." (School Library Journal)

REVIEW: *Booklist* v110 no13 p75-6 Mr 1 2014 Jesse Karp

REVIEW: *Bull Cent Child Books* v67 no7 p349 Mr 2014 T. A.

"The End (Almost)." "The book's design is sharp, with minimal figures against goldenrod pages in the bold, digitally created art. Postmodern, breaking-the-fourth-wall picture books have become an established genre by now, though, and there's not much to this one to distinguish it. . . . Additionally, the humor often overly relies on gags like burps rather than the cleverness of the construction. Still, Donut stealthily tip-toeing across the page in red-sneakered feet going 'SNEAK SNEAK' is going to garner giggles, and this would have plenty of possible pairings for a disruptive storytime, especially for audiences who can't bear a story to end."

REVIEW: *Kirkus Rev* v81 no24 p141 D 15 2013

"The End (Almost)". "An unimpressive addition to the plethora of metafictive picture books flooding the market. . . . Donut does not want his story to end, and so begins a tedious back and forth between the two characters as the narrator attempts to convince Donut that the story is indeed over. Donut, in his turn, tries excuses, disguises and a tantrum—none of which is particularly clever—to augment his story, finally achieving success only to be thwarted when the book runs out of pages. The story ends with the narrator suggesting a reread, which Donut joyously encourages, but it may leave readers wondering why they would want to spend even more time with such an uninspired book."

REVIEW: *Publ Wkly* v260 no52 p49 D 23 2013

REVIEW: *SLJ* v60 no2 p66 F 2014 Anna Haase Krueger

BENTON, TIM.ed. Le corbusier and the power of photography. See Le corbusier and the power of photography

BENWAY, ROBIN. Going rogue; an Also Known As novel; [by] Robin Benway 320 p. 2014 Bloomsbury/Walker Walker Books, an imprint of Bloomsbury

1. Adventure and adventurers—Fiction 2. Adventure stories 3. High schools—Fiction 4. Schools—Fiction 5. Spies—Fiction

ISBN 0802736041; 9780802736048 (hardback)

LC 2013-024934

SUMMARY: In this book, by Robin Benway, "safecracker Maggie Silver, now 17, discovers that her beloved parents have been accused by the international but unsanctioned spy ring, 'The Collective,' of stealing priceless gold coins. Once members of the criminal crew, the 'The Collective' has viciously turned against the Silvers. They are forced to go rogue—that is, act on their own, against expectation or instruction-to determine the truth." (School Library Journal)

REVIEW: *Bull Cent Child Books* v67 no5 p256-7 Ja 2014 E. B.

"Going Rogue". "The spy-caper plotting is a bit thinner than that of [Robin] Benway's series debut, but what it lacks in intricacy it makes up for in strengthened relationships among and characterizations of Maggie, Rotix, and Jesse. Maggie continues to be a self-deprecatingly funny heroine, and her two besties rise well beyond their status as sidekicks to strong, loving friends with plausible episodes of balking at involvement with Maggie's perilous life. Teens who appreciate the old school romantic capers in the tradition of Charade and the Pink Panther movies will happily nuke a bag of microwave popcorn and settle in for an entertaining, kissing-intensive romp."

REVIEW: *Kirkus Rev* v81 no24 p262 D 15 2013

"Going Rogue". " High shenanigans and chases through the streets of New York erupt, with stolen Fabergé eggs, gold coins, bomb blasts and sniper attacks adding to the confusion. . . . Various muddled plots unravel, culminating in a denouement in the Louvre, as spies and agents try to entrap the evil Collective member. While the spy story is good fun and Maggie's quandaries will resonate with readers, the action at times slows to a crawl with her lengthy internal monologues, and characters tend to be flat. A fluffy romp with authentic teen dialogue, cardboard characters and a plot gone rogue."

REVIEW: *SLJ* v60 no3 p151 Mr 2014 Susan Riley

REVIEW: *SLJ* v60 no5 p65 My 2014 Nicole Martin

REVIEW: *Voice of Youth Advocates* v36 no5 p54 D 2013 Mary Kusluch

REVIEW: *Voice of Youth Advocates* v36 no5 p53-4 D 2013 Nancy Wallace

BENZ, JENNIFER K. Interest groups and health care reform across the United States. See Lowery, D.

BERENDSEN, BERNARD.ed. Asian tigers, African lions. See Asian tigers, African lions

BERENSON, LAURIEN. Gone with the woof; [by] Laurien Berenson 288 p. 2013 Kensington Pub Corp

1. Detective & mystery stories 2. Dog shows 3. Dogs—Fiction 4. Murder—Fiction 5. Promiscuity
ISBN 0758284527; 9780758284525
LC 2013-940649

SUMMARY: In this novel by Laurien Berenson, "Despite Melanie's domestic demands--a toddler and a house full of Standard Poodles--helping Edward March pen his life story is an opportunity she can't pass up. . . . . It's juicy gossip, but not dangerous . . . until Andrew, Edward's son, pays Melanie an angry visit to stop her from working on the book. When Andrew suddenly turns up very dead, the victim of a seemingly intentional hit-and-run, the police are looking at Edward." (Publisher's note)

REVIEW: *Kirkus Rev* v81 no16 p191 Ag 15 2013

"Gone With the Woof." "Melanie Travis' offer to render professional assistance to a retiring dog-show judge turns into much more for a mother returning to work. When Melanie agrees to help Edward March write his memoir, she assumes that Edward will be highlighting his life as a judge of dog shows. . . . Andrew, Edward's adult son, is struck and killed by a car while jogging, and Edward insists that Melanie take responsibility for investigating whatever the police might have missed. . . . [Author Laurien] Berenson . . . , who has a nose for balancing fun and fright, devises another story that will appeal to dog aficionados and cozy lovers alike."

REVIEW: *Libr J* v138 no14 p94 S 1 2013

REVIEW: *Publ Wkly* v260 no27 p68 Jl 8 2013

BERG, A. SCOTT. Wilson; [by] A. Scott Berg 832 p. 2013 G.P. Putnam's Sons

1. Biographies 2. Presidents—United States—Biography 3. United States—History—1913-1921
ISBN 0399159215; 9780399159213
LC 2013-009339

SUMMARY: This book is a biography of the United States' 28th president, Woodrow Wilson. Author A. Scott Berg "is generally sympathetic to the man (he puts much emphasis on Wilson's love for his two wives and characterizes him as a passionate lover as well as a determined leader), while taking a more critical stand against his racial views and policies, his handling of the League of Nations, and of the secrecy that surrounded his late-presidency illness." (Publishers Weekly)

REVIEW: *America* v210 no15 p34-6 Ap 28 2014 NICHOLAS P. CAFARDI

REVIEW: *Booklist* v110 no7 p38 D 1 2013 Alan Moores

REVIEW: *Booklist* v109 no19/20 p22 Je 1 2013 Brad Hooper

REVIEW: *Booklist* v110 no9/10 p8-11 Ja 1 2014

REVIEW: *Kirkus Rev* v81 no12 p43 Je 15 2013

REVIEW: *Libr J* v138 no7 p54 Ap 15 2013 Barbara Hoffert

REVIEW: *Libr J* v138 no21 p58 D 1 2013 Pam Kingsbury

REVIEW: *Libr J* v138 no10 p116 Je 1 2013 Robert B. Slater

REVIEW: *N Y Times Book Rev* p14 S 22 2013 KEVIN BAKER

REVIEW: *Natl Rev* v65 no20 p54-6 O 28 2013 MICHAEL KNOX BERAN

"Wilson." "An entertaining study of one of the more extraordinary instances of the messianic temperament in American politics. . . . What stands out most sharply in [A. Scott] Berg's account is the rhetorical cast of [Woodrow] Wilson's mind. Naturally his speeches are rhetorical, but what is curious is that his literary prose is no less so--is as rigid as the poor man's own hardening arteries. . . .One comes to see that not only Wilson's writing, but his thought, is rhetorical. His policies are as sclerotic as his rhetoric, and serve the same bureaucratic purpose: to overmaster the crowd and compel it to submit to the will of the lawgiver."

REVIEW: *New Yorker* v89 no27 p81-5 S 9 2013 Jill Lepore

REVIEW: *N Y Rev Books* v61 no11 p34-6 Je 19 2014 Mar-

garet MacMillan
"Wilson." "[Author] Scott Berg is adept at probing beneath the public image. He has made good use of the available primary sources, including recently discovered family letters that were in the possession of one of Wilson's grandsons, to show us the man. . . . What the reader will not get, sadly, is any coherent sense of progressivism, that great wave of reform directed against entrenched power, monopoly, and inequality that convulsed American politics from the city to the national level at the turn of the century. . . . Berg's biography, for all its flaws, leaves us with a vivid picture of an intensely ambitious and idealistic man."

REVIEW: *Publ Wkly* v260 no27 p77-8 Jl 8 2013

BERG, MANFRED.ed. The U.S. South and Europe. See The U.S. South and Europe

BERGER, DAVID.ed. Bohemians. See Bohemians

BERGER, GLEN. The Song of Spider-man; The Inside Story of the Most Controversial Musical in Broadway History; [by] Glen Berger 416 p. 2013 Simon & Schuster

1. Memoirs 2. Musical theater—Production & direction 3. Musical theater producers & directors 4. Spider-Man: Turn off the Dark (Theatrical production) 5. Taymor, Julie, 1952-

ISBN 1451684568; 9781451684568

SUMMARY: In this book, "When the renowned director Julie Taymor picked [Glen] Berger to co-write the musical 'Spider-Man: Turn Off the Dark' he joined a dream team of Taymor and U2's Bono and Edge. Berger's book offers a behind-the scenes- look into that collaboration--the making of a musical that went on to become both hugely successful and the ultimate source for backstage gossip and tales of theatrical hubris." (Publishers Weekly)

REVIEW: *Libr J* v138 no18 p88 N 1 2013 Maggie Knapp

REVIEW: *Libr J* v138 no11 p58 Je 15 2013 Barbara Hoffert

REVIEW: *New York Times* v162 no56244 pC1-3 Ag 30 2013 PATRICK HEALY

REVIEW: *New York Times* v163 no56310 pC4 N 4 2013 MARK HARRIS

"Song of Spider-Man: The Inside Story of the Most Controversial Musical in Broadway History." "[This is] Glen Berger's dishy, entertaining-up-to-a-point account of the continuing Broadway disaster 'Spider-Man: Turn Off the Dark'. . . . Mr. Berger himself was, as he admits with strategically disarming bluntness, one of the parties responsible for the mess that is now in its third enfeebled year at the Foxwoods Theater. . . . This makes 'Song of the Spider-Man' less akin to a standard anatomy of a disaster than to a post-Watergate memoir. . . . Part sigh, part shrug, part snicker, Mr. Berger's book is a coroner's report signed, sealed and delivered by one of the parties responsible for the victim's demise."

BERGER, JOE.il. Dot. See Zuckerberg, R.

BERGER, LEE R., 1965-. The skull in the rock. See Aronson, M.

BERGER, LOU. Dream dog; [by] Lou Berger 40 p. 2013 Schwartz & Wade Books

1. Children's stories 2. Dogs—Fiction 3. Fathers and sons—Fiction 4. Imaginary companions 5. Imagination—Fiction

ISBN 0375866558 (hardcover); 9780375866555 (hardcover); 9780375966552 (library)

LC 2011-048582

SUMMARY: In this children's picture book, "Harry wants a dog, but Dad has allergies. So Harry puts on his X-35 Infra-Rocket Imagination Helmet and conjures up his own perfect pet, a dream dog named Waffle. This new pet is huge and fuzzy, all light blue and white like cumulous clouds, and only Harry can see him. Waffle and Harry become best pals, with Harry's dad playing along with the idea of the imaginary dog. . . . When Dad's allergies suddenly improve, he brings home a real dog." (Kirkus Reviews)

REVIEW: *Booklist* v110 no5 p83 N 1 2013 Jesse Karp

REVIEW: *Kirkus Rev* v81 no24 p3 D 15 2013

"Dream Dog". "The common developmental stage of imaginary friendship is creatively and charmingly addressed in this bittersweet tale of a boy and his dogs—one real and one pretend (or maybe not). . . . An imaginative, humorous text is well-complemented by large-format illustrations in gouache, pencil and ink. The busy illustrations are filled with fanciful details and funny peripheral characters, but Waffle is a captivating star with a real personality all his own. This delightful story waffles irresistibly between reality and fantasy, and young readers will find Waffle the dream dog a tasty treat."

REVIEW: *Kirkus Rev* p40 2013 Guide to BookExpo America

REVIEW: *Publ Wkly* v260 no49 p81-2 D 2 2013

REVIEW: *SLJ* v60 no1 p64 Ja 2014 Marge Loch-Wouters

BERGER, SAMANTHA. Crankenstein; [by] Samantha Berger 40 p. 2013 Little, Brown and Co.

1. Behavior—Fiction 2. Children's stories 3. Emotions (Psychology)—Juvenile literature 4. Monsters—Juvenile fiction 5. Temper tantrums in children

ISBN 031612656X (reinforced); 9780316126564 (reinforced)

LC 2012-029480

SUMMARY: This book, written by Samantha Berger and illustrated by Dan Santat, features Crankenstein, "a monster of grumpiness. He may look like any ordinary boy, but when faced with a rainy day, a melting popsicle, or an early bedtime, one little boy transforms into a mumbling, grumbling Crankenstein! When Crankenstein meets his match in a fellow Crankenstein, the results could be catastrophic--or they could be just what he needs to brighten his day." (Publisher's note)

REVIEW: *Bull Cent Child Books* v67 no2 p76 O 2013 T. A.

"Crankenstein." "A run-down of all those situations--rainy days, long lines, and bedtime--when Crankenstein might show up will be recognizable to most kids, and the implicit lesson that we all have bad days is effectively carried out by the matter-of-fact, personable narration. . . . The oversized, full-bleed digital illustrations and easy-to-follow wobbly hand-lettering make this exceptionally conducive to sharing, and the pale green-skinned protagonist with black hair plastered to his forehead is easy to relate to with his everyday clothes and tight close-ups of his face as he over-expresses his emotions. Soft lines and friendly colors make the monster snuggly in spite of his disposition, and the impressive use of contrast lighting helps keep the tone of the book warm."

REVIEW: *Horn Book Magazine* v89 no5 p63 S/O 2013 ROGER SUTTON

"Crankenstein." "Sometimes . . . all there is to say is 'MEHHRRRR!' The life of the little guy depicted here seems to be one unfortunate event after another, and he responds accordingly, if repetitively. This is a 'No, David!' for slightly older kids, with intense but comical closeups of a toddler's enraged face, turned Frankenstein-green for that festive Halloween touch. The ending is a sop to parents, as the boy meets a friend and his rage (and green skin) turns peaceable-- but never fear, the monster still lurks within."

REVIEW: *Kirkus Rev* v81 no15 p18 Ag 1 2013

REVIEW: *Publ Wkly* v260 no20 p56-7 My 20 2013

REVIEW: *SLJ* v59 no7 p55 Jl 2013 Susan Weitz

BERGER, TAMARA FAITH. Maidenhead; [by] Tamara Faith Berger 171 p. 2012 Coach House Books

1. Fiction 2. High school students—Canada 3. Race identity 4. Sexual intercourse 5. Summer vacations
ISBN 155245259X; 9781552452592
LC 2012-397934

SUMMARY: The book features "[s]ixteen-year-old Myra and her family . . . [who] are attempting a vacation in a down-market Key West beachfront motel overrun with college kids on spring break. . . . Myra . . . soon meets Elijah, an older Tanzanian musician who charms her on the beach, and later, in his motel room. . . . Myra discovers her sexuality. . . . Returning home to Toronto, . . . Myra trades in her 'toxic and naïve' high school friends for an older, intellectual crowd." (Quill & Quire)

REVIEW: *Am Book Rev* v34 no6 p10 S/O 2013 Elisabeth Sheffield

BERGER, WARREN. A more beautiful question; the power of inquiry to spark breakthrough ideas; [by] Warren Berger 272 p. 2014 Bloomsbury USA

1. BUSINESS & ECONOMICS—Entrepreneurship 2. Business literature 3. Creative ability in business 4. Entrepreneurship 5. Inquiry-based learning 6. PHILOSOPHY—General 7. SCIENCE—Life Sciences—Neuroscience 8. SELF-HELP—General
ISBN 9781620401453 (hardback)
LC 2013-036021

SUMMARY: This book by Warren Berger "examines the science of questioning and the ways in which the world's top innovators have used it to their advantage. Establishing a 'culture of inquiry' is a prudent move for both producer and consumer, writes the author, who . . . examines the impact the 'Whys, What Ifs, and Hows' have on the development of products like snow shovels, baby carrots and Crackerjack, among many others." (Kirkus Reviews)

REVIEW: *Booklist* v110 no12 p6-8 F 15 2014 Mary Whaley

"A More Beautiful Question: The Power of Inquiry to Spark Breakthrough Ideas." "[Warren] Berger emphasizes the power of inquiry as he challenges us to see things with a fresh eye. He concentrates on game-changing questions, those that can result in actions that lead to real results. . . . Asking the right questions will help us discover what matters, what opportunities exist, and how to find them. This thought-provoking book offers important insights to executives, and to those aspiring to leadership, for their business and personal use."

REVIEW: *Kirkus Rev* v82 no1 p183 Ja 1 2014

REVIEW: *N Y Times Book Rev* p30 Ap 13 2014 Nancy Koehn

REVIEW: *Publ Wkly* v261 no3 p44 Ja 20 2014

BERGERON, ANNE. Magnetic. See Tuttle, B.

BERGMAN, TERESA. Exhibiting patriotism; creating and contesting interpretations of American historic sites; [by] Teresa Bergman 251 p. 2013 Left Coast Press

1. Historic sites—Interpretive programs—United States 2. Historiography—Social aspects—United States 3. Lincoln Memorial (Washington, D.C.) 4. Museum studies literature 5. USS Arizona Memorial (Hawaii) 6. Visitors' centers—United States
ISBN 1598745964; 9781598745962 (hardback : alk. paper); 9781598745979 (pbk. : alk. paper)
LC 2012-032797

SUMMARY: Author Teresa "Bergman analyzes exhibits, interpretive materials, and orientation films at major US sites, from Mt. Rushmore and to the USS Arizona Memorial, where controversy has erupted over the stories they tell about the past. She shows how historic narratives are the result of dynamic relationships between institutions and the public, and how these relationships are changing in an era when museums are becoming more visitor-centered, seeing visitors as partners in historical interpretation." (Publisher's note)

REVIEW: *Choice* v51 no1 p146 S 2013 S. Ferentinos

"Exhibiting Patriotism: Creating and Contesting Interpretations of American Historic Sites." "In the past decade, museum interpretation has undergone a paradigm shift from an emphasis on collections to an emphasis on visitors. . . . [Author Teresa] Bergman . . . further develops understanding of this transition by examining shifting interpretation at five historic sites. Using the USS Arizona Memorial, the California State Railroad Museum, the Alamo, the Lincoln Memorial, and Mount Rushmore as case studies, the author considers how the meanings of patriotism and citizenship have expanded (or failed to expand). . . . Taken together, the case studies offer a rich portrayal of the issues involved in reconceptualizing patriotism."

BERGMAN, TORBJÖRN. Political parties in multi-level polities. See Aylott, N.

BERGMANN, DANIEL. How to Take over the World!; Of Monopoly; [by] Daniel Bergmann 136 p. 2013 Createspace Independent Pub

1. Board games—Psychological aspects 2. Do-it-yourself literature 3. Monopoly (Game) 4. Strategy games 5. Success
ISBN 1481900102; 9781481900102

SUMMARY: In this book on the game of Monopoly, Daniel Bergmann "divulges ruthless strategies and sneaky advice for winning the classic board game. . . . He says that too many competitors rely on simple luck . . . in a game that can only be mastered as a battle of cold, calculating, thought-out strategy, like chess. . . . Bergmann advises that aspiring Monopoly conquerors sabotage other players' attempts at achieving a monopoly." (Kirkus Reviews)

REVIEW: *Kirkus Rev* v82 no2 p394 Ja 15 2014

"How to Take Over the World! (of Monopoly). "[Daniel] Bergmann doesn't spare the exclamation points in his passionate guide for how to emerge gloriously triumphant in Monopoly. In a Gen. Patton-like voice, he declares, 'Everything you know about Monopoly is probably wrong.' He says that too many competitors rely on simple luck—i.e., wherever the dice take them—in a game that can only be mastered as a battle of cold, calculating, thought-out strategy, like chess. Some of his well-argued advice is counter-intuitive. . . . Quick-reference appendices help summarize the short book in bullet points and break down various risk and reward factors. A sharp-eyed guide to dominating the playing board."

REVIEW: *Kirkus Rev* v82 no4 p105 F 15 2014

"How to Take Over the World! (of Monopoly). "[Daniel] Bergmann doesn't spare the exclamation points in his passionate guide for how to emerge gloriously triumphant in Monopoly. In a Gen. Patton-like voice, he declares, 'Everything you know about Monopoly is probably wrong.' He says that too many competitors rely on simple luck—i.e., wherever the dice take them—in a game that can only be mastered as a battle of cold, calculating, thought-out strategy, like chess. Some of his well-argued advice is counter-intuitive. . . . Quick-reference appendices help summarize the short book in bullet points and break down various risk and reward factors. A sharp-eyed guide to dominating the playing board."

BERGTHOLD, LEE. There Must Have Been an Angel; The Cross-Country Odyssey from Badwater, Death Valley, to the Summit of Mount Whitney; [by] Lee Bergthold 262 p. 2012 Createspace Independent Pub

1. California—Description & travel 2. Death Valley (Calif. & Nev.) 3. Memoirs 4. Whitney, Mount (Calif.) 5. Wilderness survival

ISBN 1463765118; 9781463765118

SUMMARY: In this memoir, "former Marine and survival expert [Lee] Bergthold . . . documents his grueling trek from Death Valley to Mt. Whitney. In October 1989, Bergthold and a longtime adventure companion set out on a 14-day odyssey through the most extreme climates and barren regions of North America. Armed with carefully selected gear and food, the men arranged to pick up water at checkpoints as their only form of outside aid." (Kirkus Reviews)

REVIEW: *Kirkus Rev* v82 no2 p356 Ja 15 2014

"There Must Have Been an Angel: The Cross-Country Odyssey From Badwater, Death Valley, to the Summit of Mount Whitney". "[Lee] Bergthold shines when explaining the internal motivations that impelled his Frodo-like quest as well as the nirvana attained during the final ascent. . . . A few issues prevent this otherwise exciting narrative from unfolding with maximum dramatic impact. For one thing, the lack of details about the men's 'real lives' prior to the trek limits the reader's emotional investment in their journey. Second, the author considerably undercuts the climactic effect of reaching the summit of Mt. Whitney by frequently overusing exclamation points, italics and sensational adjectives throughout earlier chapters."

BERING, JESSE. Perv; The Sexual Deviant in All of Us; [by] Jesse Bering 288 p. 2013 Farrar Straus & Giroux

1. Human sexuality 2. Human sexuality—Psychological aspects 3. Human sexuality—Social aspects 4. Paraphilias 5. Social science literature

ISBN 0374230897; 9780374230890

SUMMARY: In this book, Jesse Bering " makes the claim that, deep down, we are all sexual deviants in one form or another--and that sexual deviancy is, in fact, not deviant at all. From the beginning of human history, people have engaged in antiheteronormative behaviors, from bestiality to pedophilia. Furthermore, Bering shows how most sexual deviancy isn't a choice, but rather is the result of a genetic predisposition over which the individual has no control." (Publishers Weekly)

REVIEW: *Booklist* v110 no1 p18 S 1 2013 David Pitt

REVIEW: *Choice* v51 no9 p1685 My 2014 W. P. Anderson

REVIEW: *Kirkus Rev* v81 no9 p39 My 1 2013

REVIEW: *Kirkus Rev* p22 2013 Guide 20to BookExpo America

REVIEW: *N Y Times Book Rev* p34 O 13 2013

REVIEW: *N Y Times Book Rev* p9 O 6 2013 DANIEL BERGNER

"Perv: The Sexual Deviant in All of Us." "[Jesse] Bering's book, written in mostly comic prose, is infused with noble intention. . . . This is a humanizing book--although unfortunately, it's a book mostly devoid of humans. Aside from his own brief memories, Bering gives us few stories of anyone among the different. No person is profiled for more than a paragraph or two. As a result, the reader sometimes feels inundated buy a catalog of oddities . . . rather than moved to empathy. The compensation for this impersonal approach should be intellectual illumination. And Bering does lead us to confront the reality that we all have a bit, or more than a bit, of sexual aberration within us. . . . The disappointment is that 'Perv' is less than the sum of its provocative parts."

REVIEW: *New Statesman* v142 no5189 p50-1 D 13 2013 Frances Wilson

REVIEW: *Publ Wkly* v260 no30 p54 Jl 29 2013

REVIEW: *Sci Am* v310 no1 p80 Ja 2014 Steve Mirsky

BERK, JOSH. Say it ain't so; [by] Josh Berk 288 p. 2014 Alfred A. Knopf Books for Young Readers

1. Baseball—Fiction 2. Best friends—Fiction 3. Friendship—Fiction 4. Mystery and detective stories 5. Sports—Corrupt practices—Fiction

ISBN 0375870091; 9780307930071 (trade pbk.); 9780375870095 (hardcover); 9780375970092 (library binding)

LC 2013-015225

SUMMARY: "The second installment in the Lenny & the Mikes mysteries finds Lenny Norbeck and his friends Mike and Other Mike in seventh grade with a new case to solve. Though starting catcher Davis Gannett has been kicked off the team for stealing a cellphone, and Mike has taken his place, Davis keeps showing up at games. As the season goes on, Lenny discovers that another team, Griffith Middle School, is stealing the catcher's signs, allowing their hitters to know what pitches to expect." (Kirkus Reviews)

REVIEW: *Bull Cent Child Books* v67 no10 p502 Je 2014 E. B.

"Once again, Lenny's on the case, and with a bit of assistance from the local librarian (who, as in the debut title, gets major props for excellent patron service), tracks down the thieves and saves the season. The trio is just as endearing this time around, bantering, arguing, forgiving and readily forgetting their way through new configurations of seventh-grade life that put pressure on their friendship. Lenny's narrative flights play out as well-crafted stand-up comedy routines, making this series as attractive to humor fans as to baseball and mystery lovers."

REVIEW: *Kirkus Rev* v82 no2 p142 Ja 15 2014

"Say It Ain't So". "It's not as dramatic as the murder mystery of the series opener, 'Strike Three, You're Dead' (2013), but [Josh] Berk delivers important life lessons wrapped up in a satisfying story of baseball and friendship. . . . These common middle school moral dilemmas are treated realistically in the believable context of baseball as a metaphor for life. Lenny is thrown several curves as he solves the mystery and finds a deeper appreciation of what it means to be a friend in this satisfying caper."

REVIEW: *SLJ* v60 no4 p140 Ap 2014 Jane Henriksen Baird

BERKOWITZ, PETER. Constitutional conservatism; liberty, self-government, and political moderation; [by] Peter Berkowitz 140 p. 2013 Hoover Institution Press

1. Conservatism—United States 2. Constitutional law—United States 3. Libertarianism 4. Liberty 5. Political science literature

ISBN 9780817916046 (cloth : alk. paper)

LC 2012-045831

SUMMARY: This book, written by Peter Berkowitz, "identifies the political principles social conservatives and libertarians share . . . and sketches . . . common ground on which they can . . . join forces. Drawing on the writings of Edmund Burke, 'The Federalist,' and the high points of post-World War II American conservatism, he argues that the top political priority for social conservatives and libertarians should be to rally around the principles of liberty embodied in the US Constitution." (Publisher's note)

REVIEW: *Choice* v51 no2 p352 O 2013 J. Simeone

"Constitutional Conservatism: Liberty, Self-Government, and Political Moderation." "American conservatives searching for a usable past will find much to ponder in this . . . volume. [Author Peter] Berkowitz . . . argues that libertarians, social conservatives, and Tea Party followers can and should unify behind 'the conservative side of the liberal tradition.' He surveys the writings of Edmund Burke, 'The Federalist,' modern day classical liberals such as Friedrich Hayek, Goldwater-era writers such as William F. Buckley, and neoconservatives such as Irving Kristol to reorient conservative thought around the ideal of political moderation. . . . Those of like mind, as well as those with views across the political spectrum, will find this book challenging and thought provoking."

REVIEW: *Commentary* v135 no5 p41-2 2013 PAUL O. CARRESE

REVIEW: *Natl Rev* v65 no4 p42-3 Mr 11 2013 MATTHEW J. FRANCK

REVIEW: *Society* v50 no6 p649-50 D 2013 Daniel DiSalvo

BERLIN, DELIA. Tales of Eva and Lucas / Cuentos De Eva Y Lucas; [by] Delia Berlin 38 p. 2013 CreateSpace Independent Publishing Platform

1. Bilingual books 2. Chickens—Juvenile fiction 3. Friendship—Juvenile fiction 4. Imagination 5. Sharing

ISBN 1491097833; 9781491097830

SUMMARY: "This Spanish-English picture book" presents three stories "about the day-to-day adventures of two avian friends. "Eva is a young hen with a great imagination," and "Lucas, her neighbor and best friends" is "a thoughtful, empathetic chicken." Topics include fear, sharing, and generosity. (Kirkus Reviews)

REVIEW: *Kirkus Rev* v82 no1 p96 Ja 1 2014

"Tales of Eva and Lucas/Cuentos de Eva y Lucas". "This Spanish-English picture book soars with three charming tales about the day-to-day adventures of two avian friends. . . . Whimsical black-and-white illustrations bring to life these endearing characters and the world they share with dogs, ducks and other types of birds. As a bonus, little ones may enjoy coloring in the drawings. Both the English and Spanish texts flow smoothly, and the book as a whole offers early readers and preschoolers great lessons in friendship, sharing and creative thinking. An absorbing, educational book for adults to read to their children or for young readers to peruse on their own."

REVIEW: *Kirkus Rev* v81 no24 p362 D 15 2013

BERLINER, CHARLES. I Want Much More Than a Dinosaur; [by] Charles Berliner 50 p. 2006 Xlibris Corp

1. Animals—Juvenile fiction 2. Children's stories 3. Imagination 4. Mythical animals 5. Platypus

ISBN 1425711928; 9781425711924

SUMMARY: In this children's book, by Charles Berliner, " a little imagination goes a long way when a boy envisions combinations of different animals." Illustrations "show a boy envisioning a combination of an octopus and a monkey. . . He then pictures a rabbit and an owl merging. . . . The . . . book continues through other unusual pairings, until the boy finally imagines a combination that produces a real-life platypus." (Kirkus Reviews)

REVIEW: *Kirkus Rev* v82 no2 p34 Ja 15 2014

"I Want Much More Than a Dinosaur". "[Charles] Berliner, who designs scenery and costumes for plays, musicals, and film, television and dance productions, knows the importance of visuals, and here, the illustrations are just as important as the text. Each animal gets a page of its own; the true-life animal portraits are realistic, and the fictional, combined animals are fanciful and fun. The rhyming text has a singsong quality that fits with the lighthearted premise. The book creates a game that's easy to replicate, which may make it suitable for an elementary school classroom. . . . A well-illustrated story that encourages kids to use their imaginations."

REVIEW: *Kirkus Rev* v81 no24 p369 D 15 2013

"I Want Much More Than a Dinosaur". "[Charles] Berliner, who designs scenery and costumes for plays, musicals, and film, television and dance productions, knows the importance of visuals, and here, the illustrations are just as important as the text. Each animal gets a page of its own; the true-life animal portraits are realistic, and the fictional, combined animals are fanciful and fun. The rhyming text has a singsong quality that fits with the lighthearted premise. The book creates a game that's easy to replicate, which may make it suitable for an elementary school classroom. . . . A well-illustrated story that encourages kids to use their imaginations."

BERMAN, NINA. German literature on the Middle East; discourses and practices, 1000-1989; [by] Nina Berman ix, 324 p. 2011 University of Michigan Press

1. German literature 2. German literature—History and criticism—Theory, etc. 3. Historical literature 4. Literature—History & criticism 5. Middle East—History 6. Middle East—In literature

ISBN 0472117513 (cloth : alk. paper); 9780472117512 (cloth : alk. paper)

LC 2010-030240

SUMMARY: Written by Nina Berman, "'German Literature on the Middle East' explores the dynamic between German-speaking and Middle Eastern states and empires from the time of the Crusades to the end of the Cold War. This insightful study illuminates the complex relationships among literary and other writings on the one hand, and economic, social, and political processes and material dimensions on the other." (Publisher's note)

REVIEW: *Am Hist Rev* v117 no4 p1307-8 O 2012 Nicholas A. Germana

REVIEW: *Choice* v49 no9 p1651 My 2012 C. L. Dolmetsch

REVIEW: *TLS* no5787 p27 F 28 2014 LYDIA WILSON

"German Literature on the Middle East: Discourses and Practices, 1000-1989." "The title alone is ambitious, but the true scope of 'German Literature on the Middle East' is yet greater: to situate a thousand years of literature, Nina Berman argues, requires the political, economic, social and material backgrounds of each era, area and empire of both the German-speaking and Middle Eastern peoples in question, as well as their complex, shifting relations. Her study marshals extraordinary amounts of diverse information to deploy a narrative of enduring and evolving tropes of the Middle East, presenting genres from grisly newspaper reports to travelogues, opera to ethnographies, showing continuities and discontinuities of the attitudes of elites and masses alike."

BERNARD, G. W. The late medieval English church; vitality and vulnerability before the break with Rome; [by] G. W. Bernard pages cm 2012 Yale University Press

1. HISTORY—Europe—Great Britain 2. HISTORY—Medieval 3. Historical literature 4. RELIGION—Christian Church—History

ISBN 9780300179972 (hardback)

LC 2012-000106

SUMMARY: In this book on the late medieval English church, author G. W. Bernard "emphasizes royal control over the church. He examines the challenges facing bishops and clergy, and assesses the depth of lay knowledge and understanding of the teachings of the church, highlighting the practice of pilgrimage. He reconsiders anti-clerical sentiment and the extent and significance of heresy. He shows that the Reformation was not inevitable: the late medieval church was much too full of vitality." (Publisher's note)

REVIEW: *Am Hist Rev* v119 no1 p236-7 F 2014 Katherine L. French

"The Late Medieval English Church: Vitality and Vulnerability Before the Break With Rome". "Many will undoubtedly disagree with [G. W.] Bernard's characterization of the late medieval English church as monarchical, which does follow on his earlier scholarship on the Reformation. Yet, at the same time, his vision of the pre-Reformation church is very static. . . . Bernard's selective use of sources, largely documents from the king's state papers and episcopal registers, and how he employs them contribute to his vision of the late medieval church as static. Even when he does venture into locally produced sources, he still reads them for what they 'say,' not questioning why and how they were written and the power dynamics that lie below their reported information."

REVIEW: *Choice* v50 no5 p951 Ja 2013 J. P. Huffman

REVIEW: *Engl Hist Rev* v128 no535 p1550-2 D 2013 L. Sangha

BERNHEIMER, KATE. The girl who wouldn't brush her hair; [by] Kate Bernheimer 40 p. 2013 Schwartz & Wade Books

1. Children's stories 2. Cleanliness—Fiction 3. Girls—Fiction 4. Hair—Care and hygiene—Fiction 5. Mice—Fiction

ISBN 037586878X; 9780375868788; 9780375968785 (glb)

LC 2012-006440

SUMMARY: This book, by Kate Bernheimer, asks "what happens when one little girl refuses to brush her long, beautiful hair? Well, one day a mouse comes to live in a particularly tangled lock. Soon after, more mice move in, and the girl's unruly mop is transformed into a marvelous mouse palace complete with secret passageways and a cheese cellar! But as the girl comes to find out, living with more than a hundred mice atop your head isn't always easy." (Publisher's note)

REVIEW: *Booklist* v110 no2 p72 S 15 2013 Jeanne McDermott

REVIEW: *Bull Cent Child Books* v67 no3 p137-8 N 2013 J. H.

"The Girl Who Wouldn't Brush Her Hair." "Many an adult will recognize this little girl who loves her long, long hair but does not love to brush it. . . . The vocabulary and the tone of the narration are more suited to an adult audience, but the kid-friendly premise will maintain reader interest, and animal fans in particular may be entranced with the notion of having so many live-in furry friends. [Illustrator Jake] Parker's illustrations, drawn in pencil and colored digitally, are smoothly stylized, and the little girl, with her increasingly towering heap of brunette hair, is a pleasant point of focus; the dreamy haze that uniformly overlays the scenes, however, is distracting."

REVIEW: *Kirkus Rev* v81 no15 p117 Ag 1 2013

REVIEW: *N Y Times Book Rev* p18 Ag 25 2013 SARAH HARRISON SMITH

REVIEW: *SLJ* v59 no9 p114 S 2013 Linda L. Walkins

BERNHEIMER, KATE. The lonely book; [by] Kate Bernheimer 40 p. 2012 Random

1. Books 2. Books & reading 3. Books and reading—Fiction 4. Children's literature 5. Fathers & daughters 6. Libraries—Fiction 7. Library bookstores 8. Loneliness—Fiction

ISBN 9780375862267; 9780375962264 (glb)

LC 2010-005283

SUMMARY: This children's book tells the story of how "[o]ne day young Alice discovers the book and falls in love with it, reading it every night with her father; she's distracted at the library when she means to renew the book, and it accidentally ends up with the book-sale titles. Fortunately, a distraught Alice attends the book sale and finally recovers her beloved book: ""I knew I'd find you!" Alice cried, gently touching the frayed yellow ribbon." . . . [Chris] Sheban's . . . illustrations . . . [are] rendered in watercolor, graphite, and colored pencil." (Bulletin of the Center for Children's Books)

REVIEW: *Booklist* v108 no12 p61 F 15 2012 Kristen McKulski

REVIEW: *Bull Cent Child Books* v65 no7 p340 Mr 2012 J. H.

"The Lonely Book." "This emotionally affecting story will resonate with young (and old) readers who have already experienced book love firsthand, and it may prompt reluctant readers to keep searching for that special book that will hook them as well. Bernheimer's clear, direct language possesses a slightly formal tone that keeps the story's emotion from tipping over into sloppy sentiment, and the titular book is wisely anthropomorphized just enough to evoke sincere sympathy. [Chris] Sheban's softly textured illustrations . . . are both dreamy and substantive, and his striking compositions and deft use of light and shadow add dramatic emphasis to the contemplative text. . . . This quiet title would make an excellent prompt for a heartfelt discussion about favorite books."

REVIEW: *Kirkus Rev* v80 no1 p2427 Ja 1 2012

REVIEW: *Publ Wkly* v259 no7 p55-6 F 13 2012

REVIEW: *SLJ* v58 no3 p114 Mr 2012 Kathleen Kelly MacMillan

BERNHEIMER, KATE.ed. xo Orpheus. See xo Orpheus

BERNOFSKY, SUSAN.tr. Microscripts. See Walser, R.

BERNSTEIN, ALAN. Mastering the art of quitting; why it matters in life, love, and work; [by] Alan Bernstein 272 p. 2013 Da Capo Press

1. BUSINESS & ECONOMICS—Careers—General 2. Change (Psychology) 3. Failure (Psychology) 4. Motivation (Psychology) 5. PSYCHOLOGY—Applied Psychology 6. Perseverance (Ethics) 7. SELF-HELP—Personal Growth—General 8. Self-help materials

ISBN 9780738216546 (hardback)

LC 2013-022265

SUMMARY: In this book, authors Peg Streep and Alan Bernstein "argue that the national tendency to stay the course, however off-track, is misguided. They urge Americans afflicted by the 'myth of persistence' to abandon 'the hopeless pursuit of the unattainable' and build better goals . . . Their book breaks down obstacles to quitting, illustrated by exemplary stories of men and women who had the courage to gracefully quit jobs that did not satisfy them," (New York Times)

REVIEW: *New York Times* v163 no56365 p7 D 29 2013 LIESL SCHILLINGER

"Mastering the Art of Quitting: Why It Matters in Life, Love, and Work," "Reset: How to Beat the Job-Loss Blues and Get Ready For Your Next Act," and "Fail Fast, Fail Often: How Losing Can Help You Win". "Shrewd, detailed, and exhortatory, ['Mastering the Art of Quitting'] breaks down obstacles to quitting, illustrated by exemplary stories of men and women who had the courage to gracefully quit jobs that did not satisfy them. . . . 'Reset' . . . is [Dwain Schenk's] blow-by-blow memoir of his struggle to restore his fortunes. . . . 'Fail Fast, Fail Often' . . . argues for an even more proactive approach to self-invention, encouraging those who are contemplating a new beginning to kick-start their dreams."

BERNSTEIN, CHARLES, 1950-. Recalculating; [by] Charles Bernstein 208 p. 2013 The University of Chicago Press

1. Bereavement—Poetry 2. Historical poetry 3. Language poetry 4. Poems—Collections 5. Political poetry

ISBN 9780226925288 (cloth : alk. paper)

LC 2012-026200

SUMMARY: This poetry collection by Charles Bernstein "take readers on a journey through the history and poetics of the decades since the end of the Cold War as seen through the lens of social and personal turbulence and tragedy." Bernstein suggests "the idea that radically new structures, appropriated forms, an aversion to received ideas and conventions, political engagement, and syntactic novelty will open the doors of perception to exuberance and resonance." (Publisher's note)

REVIEW: *Booklist* v109 no14 p42 Mr 15 2013 Diego Báez

REVIEW: *TLS* no5773 p21 N 22 2013 MARK FORD

"All the Whiskey in Heaven: Selected Poems," "Recalculating," and "The Salt Companion to Charles Bernstein." "That's not to say that there is no fun to be had from this 'Selected Poems,' which offers a smorgasbord of disruptive techniques, verbal distortion and extravagant pastiche, as well as much literary knockabout. . . . The essays gathered in 'The Salt Companion to Charles Bernstein' tend towards a celebration of the guerrilla tactics with which he attempts to undermine linguistic conventions rather than antithetical readings, or evaluative assessments of particular poems or books. . . . 'Recalculating' includes inventive versions of poems by Baudelaire, Mandelstam, Apollinaire, Celan and Catullus, but the finest of Bernstein's translations is a ravishingly simple rendition of Victor Hugo's elegy for his daughter Léopoldine."

BERNSTEIN, KEI. Horsey Up and Down; A Book of Opposites; [by] Kei Bernstein 12 p. 2013 Scholastic

1. Children's stories 2. Horse racing 3. Horses—Juvenile fiction 4. Polarity 5. Toy & movable books

ISBN 0545512042; 9780545512046

SUMMARY: In this board book, "the first of several movable components appears on the cover, which features a Caucasian toddler on a carousel horse that can move up and down via a sliding panel. Most of the consecutive pages present relatively sturdy tactile or interactive elements, all relating to horses. . . . Readers follow a toddler duo, a boy and girl pair with dark hair who could likely be fraternal twins, through a whole range of equine-related settings." (Kirkus Reviews)

REVIEW: *Kirkus Rev* v82 no1 p4 Ja 1 2014

"Horsey Up and Down". "A highly interactive, lightly conceptual board book. . . . [Caroline Jayne] Church's cartoons, drawn with black lines over lightly textured backgrounds, present the scenes with crystal clarity. The rhyming text is minimal, but it frames each scene nicely and is just enough for the youngest readers. . . . While the subtitle claims this work is 'A Book of Opposites,' with only three opposite concepts presented in 12 pages, it hardly qualifies as a concept book. The playful gimmicks will keep readers turning the pages and asking for it again and again."

REVIEW: *Publ Wkly* v260 no18 p58 My 6 2013

BERNSTEIN, MICHÈLE. The Night; [by] Michèle Bernstein 160 p. 2013 Book Works

1. Couples—Fiction 2. Experimental literature 3. London (England)—Fiction 4. Paris (France)—Fiction 5. Translators in literature
ISBN 1906012520; 9781906012526

SUMMARY: This book presents "two slim volumes published as one. . . . 'The Night' is a translation of 'La Nuit' by the Situationist author Michèle Bernstein. . . . It is a Parisian perambulation, set in and around the Latin Quarter. . . . The twin volume, 'After the Night,' comes with photographs and transcriptions of email exchanges. It is set in London, in the present." (Times Literary Supplement)

REVIEW: *TLS* no5750 p36 Je 14 2013 J. C.

"The Night," "After the Night," and "The Breakfast Book." "It was with pleasure . . . that we encountered 'The Night/After the Night,' two slim volumes published as one by Book Works of East London. . . . The desire to leap back and forth between the original and its upstart English doppelgänger becomes compulsive. . . . The image comes from 'The Breakfast Book' by Andrew Dalby. . . In case all that brain and brawn should prove too tempting, Mr Dalby inserts a cautionary follow-up from 'Jane Eyre'."

BERNSTEIN, NEIL W. Ethics, identity, and community in later Roman declamation; [by] Neil W. Bernstein 2013 Oxford University Press

1. Ethics 2. Identity (Psychology) 3. Literature—History & criticism 4. Oratory, Ancient 5. Speeches, addresses, etc., Latin—History & criticism
ISBN 9780199964116

SUMMARY: This book, by Neil W. Bernstein, discusses "Major Declamations," "a collection of nineteen full-length Latin speeches attributed in antiquity to Quintilian but most likely composed by a group of authors in the second and third centuries CE. . . . It argues that the fictional scenarios of the Major Declamations enable the conceptual exploration of a variety of ethical and social issues." (Publisher's note)

REVIEW: *Choice* v51 no6 p1000-1 F 2014 M. L. Goldman

"Ethics, Identity, and Community in Later Roman Declamation." "Declamation has been criticized since antiquity for its unreality, but [Neil W.] Bernstein shows that declamations allowed speakers to explore key ethical and social fissures in Rome's elite cultural code. . . . Bernstein rightly insists on the ethical value practitioners could find in composing and performing such legal fictions and on the value they have for scholars interested in the Roman mentality. In counterpoint to the wildly dramatic orations, Bernstein's own prose is clear, concrete, and not without a dry scholarly wit."

BERNSTEIN, SUSAN DAVID. Roomscape; [by] Susan David Bernstein 272 p. 2013 Columbia Univ Pr

1. British Museum 2. English literature—History & criticism 3. English women authors 4. Historical literature 5. Reading rooms
ISBN 0748640657; 9780748640652

SUMMARY: This book by Susan David Bernstein examines women's activities in the Reading Room of the British Museum. "As Bernstein stresses, the Reading Room, which opened in 1857, was particularly significant in allowing women access not only to intellectually productive books but also to each other. Friendships crucial to the flowering of feminism towards the fin de siècle formed there." (Times Literary Supplement)

REVIEW: *Choice* v51 no3 p454 N 2013 J. Mills

REVIEW: *TLS* no5750 p22 Je 14 2013 MATTHEW INGLEBY

"Roomscape: Women Writers in the British Museum From George Eliot to Virginia Woolf." "[Susan David] Bernstein persuasively argues that the social aspect or 'exteriority' of working in a public space led to the consolidation of communities through which individuals were able to navigate a competitive literary field. Bernstein's inclusive focus on the social . . . aspects of libraries is the book's strength. . . . Unfortunately, the theoretical framework of 'Roomscape' is too heterogeneous and, subsequently, rather thin. . . . Despite these drawbacks, 'Roomscape' deserves to find a readership, for its original pursuit of a rich topic and the possibilities it suggests for further study."

BERRA, TIM M. Darwin and his children; his other legacy; [by] Tim M. Berra xii, 248 p. 2013 Oxford University Press

1. Evolution (Biology) 2. Historical literature 3. Naturalists—England—Biography
ISBN 9780199309443 (alk. paper)
LC 2013-003193

SUMMARY: This book on the family of Charles Darwin traces the "lives of his children from their birth to their death, each in his or her own chapter." It "explores Darwin's marriage to his first cousin, Emma Wedgwood, a devout Unitarian, who worried that her husband's lack of faith would keep them apart in eternity, and describes the early death of three children of this consanguineous marriage. Many of the other children rose to prominence in their own fields." (Publisher's note)

REVIEW: *Choice* v51 no8 p1423 Ap 2014 J. S. Schwartz

"Darwin and His Children: His Other Legacy". "This work focuses on [Charles] Darwin's children and his consanguineous marriage to his first cousin, Emma Wedgwood, and discusses the early deaths of three of his ten children—often ascribed to a lack of vigor from inbreeding. Berra . . . includes a brief biography of Darwin and his relationship with Emma, but the book is primarily devoted to biographical profiles of his children as well as frequent digressions about how they may have been connected with key episodes in Darwin's life. . . . Excellent photographs and illustrations support the text."

BERRY, EMILY. Dear Boy; [by] Emily Berry 64 p. 2013 Faber and Faber

1. Long-distance relationships 2. Love poetry 3. Parent & child 4. Physician & patient 5. Poems—Collections

ISBN 0571284051; 9780571284054

SUMMARY: This book presents a collection of poems by Emily Berry. Its "undercurrent" concerns "the anguish and energy brought about by a long-distance love affair." In other poems, "an ingenue masquerades as a femme fatale, a doctor appears more disturbed than his patient, and parents seem more unruly than their children." (Publisher's note)

REVIEW: *TLS* no5748 p21 My 31 2013 LAURA MARSH

"Dear Boy." "In these poems, [Emily] Berry has developed a voice that sounds as though it cannot be rattled, even in untoward circumstances. . . . Sometimes this unfazed attitude leads Berry into a self-consciously casual register that recalls the New York School. She launches one poem with 'Anyway,' and in another finds herself 'contemplating stuff.' These are not the strongest moments in this collection, since Berry can be flippant with more precision and with her own distinctiveness. It is refreshing when she sends the earlier style up. . . . This aptness to listen to herself and change tack is what makes 'Dear Boy' such a bracing first collection, and one that addresses its reader with unusual freshness."

BERRY, JULIE. All the truth that's in me; [by] Julie Berry 288 p. 2013 Viking

1. Community life—Fiction 2. Historical fiction 3. Selective mutism—Fiction 4. War—Fiction 5. Young adult fiction

ISBN 0670786152; 9780670786152 (hardcover : alk. paper)

LC 2012-043218

SUMMARY: In this book by Julie Berry, "sixteen-year-old Judith is still in love with Lucas, even after his father held her prisoner for two years and violently silenced her by cutting out part of her tongue. Another girl went missing at the same time and her body was found washed down a stream. Only Judith knows the truth of what happened to Lottie, but her muteness leaves her an outcast in the village, even from her own mother, and the truth stays bottled up inside her." (School Library Journal)

REVIEW: *Booklist* v109 no22 p76 Ag 1 2013 Daniel Kraus

REVIEW: *Booklist* v110 no12 p95 F 15 2014 Chery Ward

"All the Truth That's in Me." "In a seamless, almost musical narration, [Kathleen] McInerney slowly builds tempo as she peels off the layers of this fine listening experience with appropriate pacing, artfully propelling this mysterious and powerful read to a satisfying conclusion. Pitch-perfect in her depiction of this gentle, memorable protagonist, who has been silenced in many ways, she deftly exposes Judith's inner turmoil to tell the truth, the shame associated with her condition, and her profound loneliness. In addition, by McInerney's convincingly creating distinctive voices--regardless of age or gender--all characters are totally fleshed out with easily recognizable personalities. A clean and absorbing production."

REVIEW: *Bull Cent Child Books* v67 no2 p76-7 O 2013 A. M.

REVIEW: *Horn Book Magazine* v89 no6 p87-8 N/D 2013 JENNIFER M. BRABANDER

REVIEW: *Kirkus Rev* p49 Ag 15 2013 Fall Preview

REVIEW: *Kirkus Rev* v81 no13 p286 Jl 1 2013

REVIEW: *N Y Times Book Rev* p41 N 10 2013 JENNIFER HUBERT SWAN

REVIEW: *Publ Wkly* v260 no29 p70 Jl 22 2013

REVIEW: *Publ Wkly* v261 no1 p53 Ja 6 2014

REVIEW: *Publ Wkly* p126 Children's starred review annual 2013

REVIEW: *SLJ* v59 no8 p109 Ag 2013 Susan Riley

REVIEW: *SLJ* v60 no2 p56 F 2014 Katie Llera

REVIEW: *SLJ* v59 no12 p1 D 2013

BERSANI, SHENNEN.il. Butterfly colors and counting. See Pallotta, J.

BERTI, BENEDETTA. Hezbollah and Hamas. See Gleis, J. L.

BERTRAND, CARA. Lost in Thought; [by] Cara Bertrand 288 p. 2014 Luminis Books, Inc.

1. Boarding school stories 2. Paranormal romance stories 3. Psychics—Fiction 4. Psychokinesis 5. Teenagers—Fiction

ISBN 1935462938; 9781935462934

SUMMARY: In this book, the first in Cara Bertrand's Sententia series, "Lainey learns that she is one of the Sententia and can use Thought to affect the physical world. As she deals with her quickly developing powers, Lainey falls for Carter, the handsome boy who works in his family's bookstore and is involved with the secret society of Sententia all over the world." (Kirkus Reviews)

REVIEW: *Kirkus Rev* v82 no5 p125 Mr 1 2014

"Lost In Thought". "This debut sends a paranormally afflicted teen to a posh school with a secret in this familiar-feeling series opener. . . . Lainey falls for Carter, the handsome boy who works in his family's bookstore and is involved with the secret society of Sententia all over the world. Alas, several other female students also covet Carter's attentions, and when he seems to fall for Lainey, jealousies arise. . . . [Cara] Bertrand focuses mostly on the romance between Carter and Lainey, though the plot broadens a bit toward the end. She takes some potshots at science, favoring the metaphysical instead. Characterizations skew toward genre norms, and the book ends with a whopper of a premonition to propel readers into the sequel. For genre fans only."

REVIEW: *SLJ* v60 no4 p157 Ap 2014 Danielle Serra

REVIEW: *Voice of Youth Advocates* v37 no2 p70 Je 2014 Beth Green

BESH, JOHN. Cooking from the heart; my favorite lessons learned along the way; [by] John Besh 320 p. 2013 Andrews McMeel Pub., LLC

1. Celebrity chefs 2. Cookbooks 3. Cooking 4. European cooking 5. Photography of food

ISBN 1449430562; 9781449430566

LC 2013-936654

SUMMARY: In this book "James Beard Award-winning chef John Besh shares the lessons he learned from his mentors through 140 accessible recipes and cooking lessons. . . . From Germany's Black Forest to the mountains of Provence, each chapter highlights . . . memories and . . . recipes—the framework for his love of food." (Publisher's note)

REVIEW: *N Y Times Book Rev* p20-1 D 8 2013 WILLIAM GRIMES

"Cooking From the Heart: My Favorite Lessons Learned

Along the Way," "Pok Pok: Food and Stories From the Streets, Homes, and Roadside Restaurants of Thailand," and "Daniel: My French Cuisine." "John Best has an interesting life story to tell in 'John Besh: Cooking From the Heart.' . . . There are a few too many usual-suspect recipes, but Besh makes an engaging guide. . . . By Andy Ricker with J.J. Goode, . . . As a tutorial on Thai cuisine and its principal regional styles, 'Pok Pok' can't be beat. . . . In 'Daniel: My French Cuisine' . . . , Daniel Boulud . . . conducts a guided tour of his life and the parts of France he know best. . . . From there it's a giant leap to the . . . drop-dead elegant dishes from Daniel that take up about half the book."

REVIEW: *Publ Wkly* v260 no29 p22-32 Jl 22 2013 NATALIE DANFORD

BEST CARE AT LOWER COST; the path to continuously learning health care in America; xix, 416 p. 2012 National Academies Press

1. Costs and Cost Analysis—United States 2. Delivery of Health Care—economics—United States 3. Efficiency, Organizational—economics—United States 4. Medical literature 5. Quality of Health Care—economics—United States

ISBN 9780309260732 (pbk.); 9780309260749 (pdf)

LC 2012-040484

SUMMARY: This book "explains that inefficiencies, an overwhelming amount of data, and other economic and quality barriers hinder progress in improving health and threaten the nation's economic stability and global competitiveness. According to this report, the knowledge and tools exist to put the health system on the right course to achieve continuous improvement and better quality care at a lower cost." (Publisher's note)

REVIEW: *Choice* v51 no6 p1043 F 2014 T. P. Gariepy

"Best Care at Lower Cost: The Path to Continuously Learning Health Care in America." "The material is intricate and difficult, but because of the provenance of the idea, continuously learning systems will frame policy debates. However, these systems are not always congruent with other strong policy models, such as Donald Berwick's 'triple aim' of better care, better health, and lower cost. . . . The committee claims that a learning health system leads to best care at lower cost. Where is better health? Overall, a thought-provoking read."

BEST CUSTOMERS; demographics of consumer demand; 795 p. 2013 New Strategist Press

1. Consumer surveys 2. Consumers—United States 3. Marketing—United States 4. Marketing literature 5. United States. Bureau of Labor Statistics

ISBN 1937737101; 193773711X; 9781937737108; 9781937737115

SUMMARY: This book, from New Strategist Publications, "analyzes household spending [in the U.S.] on more than 300 products and services by age of householder, household income, household type, race and Hispanic origin of householder, region of residence, and educational attainment of householder. [Readers will] find out how the American marketplace has been transformed by the Great Recession." (Publisher's note)

REVIEW: *Choice* v51 no1 p50-1 S 2013 L. Hickey

"Best Customers: Demographics of Consumer Demand." "The 2010 Consumer Expenditure Survey from the Bureau of Labor Statistics is the source for the raw data used in this survey. . . . This ninth edition offers information on more than 300 products and services in 21 chapters. . . . The layout of the data contributes to ease of use. Chapters cover broad categories of consumer spending in alphabetical order. . . . Each table shows average household spending, best customers (indexed spending), and biggest customers (market share of spending), with the data categorized by age of householder, household income, household type, race and Hispanic origin, region, and education."

BEUMERS, BIRGIT.ed. The cinema of Alexander Sokurov. See The cinema of Alexander Sokurov

BEVAN, ANDREW.ed. Computational approaches to archaeological spaces. See Computational approaches to archaeological spaces

BEVINGTON, DAVID.ed. The Cambridge edition of the works of Ben Jonson. See The Cambridge edition of the works of Ben Jonson

BEW, JOHN. Castlereagh; a life; [by] John Bew p. cm. 2012 Oxford University Press

1. Biography (Literary form) 2. Statesmen—Great Britain—Biography

ISBN 9780199931590 (acid-free paper)

LC 2012-008785

SUMMARY: This book presents a biography of Robert Stewart, who "stood at the center of the most momentous events in Irish, British, European, and world history during the Age of Revolutions, the Napoleonic Wars, and their aftermath. He was the engineer of the Irish union with Britain in 1801. As war secretary and foreign secretary, he implemented William Pitt the Younger's strategic plans, and then became the architect . . . of a peace settlement that lasted for a century." (American Historical Review)

REVIEW: *Am Hist Rev* v119 no1 p252-3 F 2014 Ellis Wasson

"Castlereagh: A Life". "It is hard to see what John Bew has added to our understanding of Castlereagh's career that was not already addressed by previous biographers. . . . We learn more about the statesman's intellectual hinterland here, and the Irish elements of his character are sketched in more fully. But these gains hardly justify nearly six hundred pages. Bew's assertion that there are still those who see Castlereagh as a knee-jerk reactionary . . . is unsubstantiated. . . . Bew provides enormous amounts of detail. Unfortunately, too often, material is introduced simply because the information is available and not because it moves the story forward. . . . more serious is Bew's insecure grasp of the practices and personalities of Castlereagh's world."

REVIEW: *Libr J* v137 no16 p83 O 1 2012 Hanna Clutterbuck

BEYOND THE ASTERISK; understanding Native students in higher education; xvi, 189 p. 2013 Stylus

1. Indian college students 2. Indian students—United States 3. Indians of North America—Education (Higher)—United States 4. Minorities—Education (Higher) 5. Social science literature

ISBN 157922623X; 9781579226237 (cloth : alk. paper); 9781579226244 (pbk. : alk. paper)
LC 2012-040238

SUMMARY: Editor Heather J. Shotton's book discusses Native American students in higher education. "The purpose of this book is to move beyond the asterisk in an effort to better understand Native students, challenge the status quo, and provide an informed base for leaders in student and academic affairs, and administrators concerned with the success of students on their campuses." (Publisher's note)

REVIEW: *Choice* v51 no1 p134-5 S 2013 A. A. Hodge

"Beyond the Asterisk: Understanding Native Students in Higher Education." "Editors [Heather J.] Shotton, [Shelly C.] Lowe, and [Stephanie J.] Waterman accomplish their goal of moving Native American college students 'beyond the asterisk.' This must-read text challenges academicians to go beyond the 'American Indian research asterisk': exclusion from institutional data and reporting, omission from the curriculum, and nonexistence in research and literature. . . . Topics are varied and include first-year experiences. Native culture, the Native fraternity and sorority movement. Native American affairs, tribal college collaborations, indigenous faculty role models, and support from national organizations."

BHANEJA, BALWANT. Troubled Pilgrimage; Passage to Pakistan; [by] Balwant Bhaneja 240 p. 2013 TSAR Publications

1. India—Foreign relations—Pakistan 2. Memoirs 3. Pakistan—Description & travel 4. Pakistan—History 5. Sindhi (South Asian people)
ISBN 1927494265; 9781927494264

SUMMARY: In this memoir, Balwant Bhaneja, "a retired Canadian diplomat raised in India . . . decides to search for the roots of an ancestral homeland he once visited as a child—the Sindhi towns of his parents' youth that now fall on the other side of the India-Pakistan border. The itinerary is a whistle-stop tour of subcontinental history. . . . Bhaneja records his impressions of the places he visits and people he meets." (Quill & Quire)

REVIEW: *Quill Quire* v80 no1 p40 Ja/F 2014 Piali Roy

"Troubled Pilgrimage: Passage to Pakistan". "The descriptions are sometimes too sparse, the transitions too abrupt, but the author is honest about his inability to overcome his own prejudices: he flees a group of young Muslims on a train only to realize the missed opportunity for dialogue. [Balwant] Baneja points out that his book is not a work of journalism but an homage to roots, ancestors, and parents. Nor is it a traditional travelogue, but an honest reflection on the importance of identity, culture, and heritage, from a childhood visit to Mahatma Gandhi to the influence of Sufi and Sikh traditions on Sindhi Hindu culture. In the end, the book is a celebration of pluralism where the author least expects to find it."

BHATTACHARYA, NANDINI. Contagion and Enclaves; Tropical Medicine in Colonial India; [by] Nandini Bhattacharya 219 p. 2013 University of Chicago Press

1. Diseases & history 2. Historical literature 3. Imperialism 4. Medical care—India—History 5. Segregation—History
ISBN 1846318297; 9781846318290

SUMMARY: This book "studies the social history of medicine within two intersecting enclaves in colonial India; the hill station of Darjeeling which incorporated the sanitarian and racial norms of the British Raj; and in the adjacent tea plantations of North Bengal, which produced tea for the global market. This book . . . examines how the threat of epidemics and riots informed the conflictual relationship between the plantations with the adjacent agricultural villages and district towns." (Publisher's note)

REVIEW: *Am Hist Rev* v119 no1 p162-3 F 2014 Sarah Hodges

"Contagion and Enclaves: Tropical Medicine in Colonial America". "Nandini Bhattacharya serves up a devastating critique of the brutal logic of place, health, and labor under colonial rule. . . . In this impressive book, Bhattacharya . . . lays open the brutal ties that bound the health of laboring bodies to wider strategic aims of the Indian economy and polity. In the final analysis, Bhattacharya's book suggests that capitalism's growth story in India—that is, the seemingly endless supply of cheap and 'replaceable' labor—remains much the same today as it was a century ago."

BIANCO, GIUSEPPE.ed. Badiou and the philosophers . See Badiou and the philosophers

BICK, ILSA J. Monsters; [by] Ilsa J. Bick 680 p. 2013 Egmont USA

1. Adventure stories 2. Apocalyptic literature (Christian literature) 3. Science fiction 4. Survival—Fiction 5. Zombies—Fiction
ISBN 9781606841778 (hardcover)
LC 2012-045750

SUMMARY: This book is the final installment of Ilsa J. Bick's Ashes Trilogy. "Indomitable heroine Alex again claws her way out of one danger and into another. Rescued from a cave-in by Wolf, she rejoins the Changed, despite the risk of ending up on the menu, and gradually learns Wolf's and Peter's secrets. Meanwhile, other familiar faces reappear, each belonging to one of various other small groups scrapping for survival." (Kirkus Reviews)

REVIEW: *Booklist* v109 no22 p90 Ag 1 2013 Cindy Welch

REVIEW: *Bull Cent Child Books* v66 no11 p499-500 Jl/Ag 2013 K. C.

"Monsters." "Weighing in at more than 800 pages, this conclusion to the Ashes trilogy is pretty monstrous itself. Readers who have followed the fates of Alex, Tom, and Ellie since the first book will know to expect gore, but this finale amps up the horrific violence and bodily degradation, with plot almost falling by the wayside in favor of yet another desperate chase followed by a fight scene that ends in dismemberments, puncture wounds . . . , and pain explosions. . . . Old hostilities collide as the groups converge in Rule, where Tom, Ellie, and Alex finally find one another only to play out one final climax that almost claims Alex as she unleashes the monster within. This is a somewhat disappointing conclusion."

REVIEW: *Horn Book Magazine* v89 no5 p85-6 S/O 2013 APRIL SPISAK

"Monsters." "A brutal, stunning, and compellingly written trilogy [the Ashes Trilogy] . . . comes to a close as Alex, who had been destined to die of a brain tumor just before the world effectively ended, is still battling nature, herself, the humans who have turned into monsters, and the other 'normal' humans whose ethics seem rather monstrous as well. . .

. The frequent cliffhangers created by chapters that focus on different characters wear a bit thin but are a logical choice given the division of the three protagonists around whom the first book was focused. Fans may initially find the length daunting, but there are few wasted scenes and ample chances to say goodbye to these beleaguered characters."

REVIEW: *Kirkus Rev* v81 no16 p66 Ag 15 2013

REVIEW: *Voice of Youth Advocates* v36 no4 p76-7 O 2013 Matthew Weaver

BICK, ILSA J. White space; [by] Ilsa J. Bick 560 p. 2014 Egmont USA

1. Authors—Fiction 2. Characters & characteristics in literature—Fiction 3. Horror stories 4. Mystery and detective stories 5. Science fiction

ISBN 9781606844199 (hardback)

LC 2013-033060

SUMMARY: This book is the first in Ilsa J. Bick's "Dark Passages" series. "A brilliant five-year-old watches her novelist father call horrors from a powerful mirror. A high school junior with static-filled gaps in her memory pens a horror tale, one that had already been written decades ago. A psychically gifted girl accepts a ride from a troubled but sweet boy. . . . Fleeing their separate nightmares, the cast assembles in a fog-bound, snow-filled valley from which there seems to be no escape." (Publishers Weekly)

REVIEW: *Booklist* v110 no11 p66-7 F 1 2014 Frances Bradburn

"White Space." "It's an interesting premise. . . . With allusions to The Matrix, The Bell Jar, and The Shining, to name a few, [Ilsa J.] Bick forces readers to face a complex question: Are Emma and others in the story simply characters in one or more books who somehow got trapped together in the white spaces between pages? Or are they real people? This is hardly an easy read, Bick pushes readers, moving between story lines and points of view with little uniting the disparate threads except Emma herself. With incessant violence and gore, this series starter is for the most hard-core connoisseurs of horror or world-shifting fiction."

REVIEW: *Bull Cent Child Books* v67 no7 p350 Mr 2014 K. C.

"White Space." "The premise of this formidable brick of a book is soundly intriguing, and the details are clever in their literary conceits and originality. The plot, however, is marred by gratuitous and attenuated horror scenarios whose excess makes them unintentionally comic and squanders the adrenaline. Bick's fecund imagination and insatiable rage for the macabre make the book read like a textbook for phantasmagoria artists and effects designers, giving relatively short shrift to the promising plot development even as the events grow more elaborate. However, the concept allows her the luxury of cramming four or five horror novels into one, so readers who think they can't get enough may well find that they have met their match here."

REVIEW: *Kirkus Rev* v81 no23 p188 D 1 2013

REVIEW: *Publ Wkly* v260 no50 p71 D 9 2013

REVIEW: *SLJ* v60 no2 p100 F 2014 Katya Schapiro

BIDINI, DAVE. Keon and Me; My Search for the Lost Soul of the Leafs; [by] Dave Bidini 304 p. 2013 Viking Canada

1. Hockey—Canada 2. Hockey players 3. Keon, Dave 4. Memoirs 5. Toronto Maple Leafs (Hockey team)

ISBN 0670066478; 9780670066476

SUMMARY: Written by Dave Bidini, this book is "Told in two narratives--one from the point of view of the young Bidini growing up in Toronto in the early 70s and one from the perspective of the man looking for his absent hero--Keon and Me tells not only the story of a hockey icon who has haunted Toronto for decades, but of a life lived in parallel to Keon's. . . . Part ode to a legendary hockey player, part memoir, Keon and Me captures what we all cherish in the game we love." (Publisher's note)

REVIEW: *Quill Quire* v79 no9 p28 N 2013 Vit Wagner

"Keon and Me: My Search for the Lost Soul of the Leafs" and "The Lonely End of the Rink: Confessions of a Reluctant Goalie." "The author of a dozen books--all of which have been autobiographical at least to some extent, and many of which have probed our irrepressible national fixation with shinny--[Author Dave] Bidini has written a thoughtful, amusing, coming-of-age meditation on what it means, as both a child and an adult, to be a fan. 'Keon and Me' also has the virtue of dividing its focus between two subjects. . . . There is a sense that [hockey player Dave] Keon isn't much interested in reliving or revisiting the past; would that [author] Grant Lawrence shared some of Keon's reticence. . . . Lawrence leans on pop culture references to the point that it quickly feels like a lazy alternative to actual writing."

BIEHI, JOÃO.ed. When people come first. See When people come first

BIEHLER, DAWN DAY. Pests in the city; flies, bedbugs, cockroaches, and rats; [by] Dawn Day Biehler 336 p. 2013 University of Washington Press

1. Discrimination in housing—United States 2. Historical literature 3. Pests—Control 4. Race discrimination in housing 5. Social marginality 6. Urban ecology (Biology) 7. Urban pests 8. Urban policy—United States—History

ISBN 9780295993010 (cloth : alk. paper)

LC 2013-019967

SUMMARY: "In 'Pests in the City,' Dawn Day Biehler argues that the urban ecologies that supported pests were shaped not only by the physical features of cities but also by social inequalities, housing policies, and ideas about domestic space. . . . This story of flies, bedbugs, cockroaches, and rats reveals that such creatures thrived on lax code enforcement and the marginalization of the poor, immigrants, and people of color." (Publisher's note)

REVIEW: *Choice* v51 no7 p1235 Mr 2014 S. Hammer

REVIEW: *Libr J* v138 no21 p120 D 1 2013 Scott Vieira

REVIEW: *Publ Wkly* v260 no33 p60 Ag 19 2013

REVIEW: *Science* v343 no6174 p971 F 28 2014 Frederick R. Davis

"Pests in the City: Flies, Bedbugs, Cockroaches, and Rats." "In laying out her history of urban ecology, [author Dawn Day] Biehler . . . develops the notion of 'ecologies of social injustice.' In case after case, she reveals how wealthier urban residents drew on domestic help to combat pests while impoverished minorities, especially African Americans, remained vulnerable to the incessant onslaught of those unwanted co-inhabitants of our cities. . . . 'Pests in the City' demonstrates that wonderful studies can emerge from extremely mundane origins. . . . In her meticulous and thoughtful analysis of urban environmental injustice, Biehler deftly illustrates how these pests continue to undermine aspirations for modern and healthy living conditions for all."

BIESTY, STEPHEN.il. The Story of buildings. See Dillon, P.

BIG GIPP (PERFORMER) Everybody's brother. See Wild, D.

THE BIG NEW YORKER BOOK OF CATS; 352 p. 2013 Random House Inc

1. Anthologies 2. Cats—Anecdotes 3. Cats—Fiction 4. Cats—Humor 5. Cats—Poetry 6. Cats in art
ISBN 0679644776; 9780679644774
LC 2013-013345

SUMMARY: "Look what 'The New Yorker' dragged in! It's . . . celebrating our feline companions. This . . . collection, . . . illustrated in full color, features articles, fiction, humor, poems, cartoons, cover art, drafts, and drawings from the magazine's archives. Among the contributors are Margaret Atwood, . . . Roald Dahl, . . . Robert Graves, . . . Ted Hughes, . . . Haruki Murakami, . . . Robert Pinsky, . . . James Thurber, John Updike, . . . and E. B. White." (Publisher's note)

REVIEW: *Kirkus Rev* v81 no17 p72 S 1 2013

REVIEW: *Libr J* v138 no18 p111 N 1 2013 Eva Lautemann

REVIEW: *N Y Times Book Rev* p56 D 8 2013 JENNIFER B. MCDONALD

"Balthus: Cats and Girls" and "The Big New Yorker Book of Cats." "A great strength of [author Sabine] Rewald's catalog is its informed (if brief) reading of Balthus's confrères in the portrayal of un-self-conscious eroticism. . . . 'The Big New Yorker Book of Cats' . . . comes a year after 'The Big New Yorker Book of Dogs.' . . . Comprising 57 works of prose and poetry (with pictures!), it assembles quite a cast, both feline and human. We meet cats loitering at wine shops and book shops, a cat that stops at Sardi's on book tour, cats prone to vice."

BIG TENT; The Story of the Conservative Revolution - As Told by the Thinkers and Doers Who Made It Happen; 464 p. 2014 HarperCollins

1. Conservatism—United States—History 2. Neoconservatism 3. Political science literature 4. Reagan, Ronald, 1911-2004 5. United States—Politics & government
ISBN 006229069X; 9780062290694

SUMMARY: This book, by Mallory Factor and Elizabeth Factor, "is a panoramic portrait of the intellectual history of the conservative movement. Some of the leading lights of the right offer an . . . introduction to conservative figures and ideas, from the Revolution to William F. Buckley; Barry Goldwater to the Reagan Revolution; Libertarianism to the War on Terror." (Publisher's note)

REVIEW: *Kirkus Rev* v82 no4 p253 F 15 2014

"Big Tent: The Story of the Conservative Revolution-as Told by the Thinkers and Doers Who Made It Happen". "A few of these essays transition awkwardly to the page—e.g., Newt Gingrich's too-colloquial remarks on the American Revolution, Rand Paul's tossed-off observations on bending conservatism in a libertarian direction, and a gassy afterword by Haley Barbour on party-building and winning elections. On the other hand, there are some gems. . . . An uneven but useful handbook for those looking to understand the roots of conservatism and the contours of the contemporary movement."

BIGAR, SYLVIE. Daniel. See Boulud, D.

BIGGAR, NIGEL. In defence of war; [by] Nigel Biggar x, 361 p. 2013 Oxford University Press

1. Christian ethics 2. Just war doctrine 3. Religious literature 4. War & ethics 5. War—Religious aspects—Christianity
ISBN 019967261X (hbk); 9780199672615 (hardback)
LC 2013-454121

SUMMARY: In this book, author Nigel Biggar argues that "Western Christians . . . have succumbed to the virus of wishful thinking, willfully ignoring the fact that soldiers and military action, like police officers and law enforcement, are essential to social peace and justice. Military power guarantees what Americans too often take for granted: a high standard of living and civil liberties. War can sometimes help us extend these blessings to peoples who suffer under tyrannous regimes." (Christian Century)

REVIEW: *Choice* v51 no11 p1993-4 Jl 2014 J. H. Sniegocki

REVIEW: *Christ Century* v131 no8 p40-1 Ap 16 2014 John P. Burgess

REVIEW: *J Am Acad Relig* v82 no3 p883-6 S 2014 Darrell Cole

REVIEW: *Natl Rev* v66 no1 p44-5 Ja 27 2014 VICTOR LEE AUSTIN

"In Defence of War". "This book, which is hands-down the most ambitious and consequential defense of the Christian just-war tradition we've seen in decades, is, first of all, an argument 'against the virus of wishful thinking.' . . . [Nigel Biggar's] thought is careful and exact—he really does mean, for instance, that Christian pacifism is 'wishful thinking' for the precise reason that it is not grounded in realism and imports into its Biblical exegesis unwarranted assumptions. . . . I linger over the first chapter because, for a moral theologian today, it is an impressive achievement. But it is only the first of many refreshingly clear chapters."

REVIEW: *TLS* no5776 p9 D 13 2013 DAVID MARTIN

BIGGINS, MICHAEL.tr. The master of insomnia. See The master of insomnia

BIGGS, BRIAN.il. Santa goes everywhere! See Biggs, B.

BIGGS, BRIAN. Santa goes everywhere!; 24 p. 2013 Balzer + Bray

1. Boats & boating—Juvenile literature 2. Christmas stories for children 3. Motor vehicles—Juvenile literature 4. Santa Claus—Juvenile fiction 5. Transportation—Juvenile literature
ISBN 9780061958175 (board bk.)
LC 2013-930092

SUMMARY: This book, part of Brian Biggs' "Everything

Goes" series, "finds Santa Claus delivering presents by land, sea, and air. Accompanied by a single reindeer, he hauls around a huge round bag of presents in vehicles that are common and those that are a bit unconventional. Each one is identified in a single word on the page, such as 'snowmobile,' 'canoe,' 'bus,' 'bicycle,' 'helicopter,' 'sailboat,' 'truck,' 'motorcycle,' 'airplane,' and 'speedboat.'" (School Library Journal)

REVIEW: *Horn Book Magazine* v89 no6 p61-2 N/D 2013 KITTY FLYNN

"Everything Goes: Santa Goes Everywhere!" "The latest board book in [Brian] Biggs's transportation-celebration series features a winning formula: Santa, vehicles, and silly preschool humor. . . . The old standards are here: bus, bicycle, helicopter, sailboat, truck, motorcycle, airplane. Santa also branches out, speeding across the pages on a snowmobile, in a canoe, and on water skis. The pictures pop with color, the animated scenes are detailed but not too busy for the intended audience, who will delight in the visual jokes. This stocking stuffer will get a lot of mileage."

BIGGS, BRIAN. What flies in the air; 24 p. 2013 Balzer + Bray

1. Airplanes—Juvenile literature 2. Birds—Juvenile literature 3. Counting 4. Helicopters—Juvenile literature 5. Picture books for children
ISBN 9780061958168 (board bk.)
LC 2012-956561

SUMMARY: This children's book on flying machines, part of the "Everything Goes" series, doubles as a counting book. "On the opening double-page spread, '10 birds' fly across a bright blue sky. On subsequent pages, a seaplane, a balloon, a helicopter and more appear on the scene, and as they do, one bird leaves the flock to hitch a ride on the vehicle in question. The text is simple, describing the number of birds still left to count and labeling the flying apparatus." (Kirkus Reviews)

REVIEW: *Kirkus Rev* v81 no22 p314 N 15 2013

REVIEW: *Kirkus Rev* v82 no1 p78 Ja 1 2014

"Everything Goes: What Flies in the Air?". " A compelling collection of things that fly and a counting book all rolled into one. . . . The text is simple, describing the number of birds still left to count and labeling the flying apparatus. . . . While the end is a little anticlimactic, [Brian] Biggs' thick-lined cartoons in bright colors provide a clear counting experience for little ones and are playfully droll as goggled and wide-eyed pilots and passengers are visible inside the various contraptions. A delightful addition to the Everything Goes book series; here's hoping more vessels are not too far behind."

BILDNER, PHIL. The soccer fence; a story of friendship, hope, and apartheid in South Africa; [by] Phil Bildner 40 p. 2014 G. P. Putnam's Sons, an imprint of Penguin Group (USA) Inc.

1. Apartheid—Fiction 2. Blacks—South Africa—Fiction 3. Children's stories 4. Race relations—Fiction 5. Soccer—Fiction
ISBN 0399247904; 9780399247903
LC 2013-014675

SUMMARY: In this book, by Phil Bildner, "Hector loved playing soccer in his small Johannesburg township. He dreamed of playing on a real pitch with the boys from another part of the city, but apartheid made that impossible. Then, in 1990, Nelson Mandela was released from prison, and apartheid began to crumble. . . When the beloved Bafana Bafana national soccer team won the African Cup of Nations, Hector realized that dreams once impossible could now come true." (Publisher's note)

REVIEW: *Booklist* v110 no11 p62 F 1 2014 Carolyn Phelan

REVIEW: *Bull Cent Child Books* v67 no8 p397 Ap 2014 T. A.

REVIEW: *Kirkus Rev* v82 no4 p50 F 15 2014

"The Soccer Fence: A Story of Friendship, Hope, and Apartheid in South Africa". "The stark color contrasts throughout the book alternate between the rich greens and blues of the white boys' lush lawn and purple and orange scenes, in which democracy begins. . . . When the boys and the country unite to cheer on their mixed-race soccer team . . . and celebrate their victory over Tunisia in the African Cup of Nations, [Jesse Joshua] Watson creates a jubilant scene awash in yellow. The wordless final page hints at a brighter future for a South Africa positively influenced by the people's passion for sports. [Phil] Bildner and Watson offer young readers an informative snapshot of a divided land through the lens of boys who just want to play."

REVIEW: *Publ Wkly* v260 no52 p51 D 23 2013

REVIEW: *SLJ* v60 no6 p73 Je 2014 Kristine M. Casper

BILLINGS, LEE. Five billion years of solitude; the search for life among the stars; [by] Lee Billings 304 p. 2013 Current

1. Astronomers 2. Exobiology 3. Extrasolar planets 4. Journalism 5. Life on other planets
ISBN 1617230065; 9781617230066
LC 2013-017672

SUMMARY: This book presents an "overview of the still-evolving field of 'exoplanetary' research (discovery and characterization of planets orbiting other stars). Early dreams that we would locate and visit intelligent, technologically sophisticated beings elsewhere in space have been tempered as declining governmental funding has restricted our planet hunting." (Library Journal)

REVIEW: *Booklist* v110 no3 p8-10 O 1 2013 Carl Hays

REVIEW: *Choice* v51 no9 p1617 My 2014 D. E. Hogg

REVIEW: *Economist* v409 no8856 p88 O 5 2013

"Five Billion Years of Solitude: The Search for Life Among the Stars." "Lee Billings, an American science journalist, has written a definitive guide to astronomy's hottest field. 'Five Billion Years of Solitude' is, in equal parts, a primer on the search for alien worlds, a biography of Earth and the life that inhabits it, and a story about how exoplanetology grew, and how, with the hour of its greatest triumph approaching, it fell short. . . .The various disciplines that make up planetary science--astronomy, biology, and geology, offer a wonderful, immense perspective."

REVIEW: *Kirkus Rev* v81 no16 p201 Ag 15 2013

REVIEW: *N Y Times Book Rev* p18 N 10 2013 DENNIS OVERBYE

"Five Billion Years of Solitude: The Search for Life Among the Stars." "[A] graceful new book on the history, meaning and personalities behind the search for life among the stars. . . [Lee] Billings sketches this history ably, though he is light on the exploits of Kepler, which has driven the news of late.

His main interest is less in chasing Goldilocks planets than in exploring the deeper issues involved, including just how hard it will be to learn anything about these planets once we find them. . . . Reading this book is like peering over Billings's shoulder. . . . The story may meander at times, but this is the best book I have read about exoplanets, and one of the few whose language approaches the grandeur of a quest that is practically as old as our genes."

REVIEW: *Nat Hist* v122 no3 p46 Ap 2014 LAURENCE A. MARSCHALL

REVIEW: *New York Times* v163 no56306 pC2 O 31 2013 John Williams

REVIEW: *Sci Am* v309 no4 p94 O 2013 Michael Lemonick

"Five Billion Years of Solitude: The Search for Life Among the Stars." "In his compelling, wide-ranging survey, [Lee] Billings steps back to look at this broader picture, largely through richly textured portraits of some of the giants of the field, including Frank Drake, inventor of SETI; Geoff Marcy, the world's most accomplished planet hunter; Jim Kasting, who literally wrote the book on what makes a world habitable; and Sara Seager, whose thinking is firmly rooted in the exoplanetology of the future. That's just the smallest sampling, however, of where Billings's extraordinary tale of scientific discovery will take you."

BILLONE, AMY. The Light Changes; [by] Amy Billone 78 p. 2013 Hope Street Press

1. American poetry 2. Fathers & daughters 3. Mother & child 4. Poems—Collections 5. Suicide
ISBN 0989074005; 9780989074001

SUMMARY: In this poetry collection by Amy Billone, the narrator describes being struck by a train in a failed suicide attempt. "Billone revisits again and again this vivid moment of loss, of clarity and of new beginnings. For all the isolation this act of surrender implies, Billone's narrator seems as concerned about the repercussions for her father as for herself. Recently emerged from a coma, she peers from the buzzing confines of her damaged skull and notices his small discomforts." (Kirkus Reviews)

REVIEW: *Kirkus Rev* p9 D 15 2013 supplemet best books 2013

"The Light Changes". "The rattle of crushing bones reverberates through this volume as [Amy] Billone revisits again and again this vivid moment of loss, of clarity and of new beginnings. . . . Though headed by epigraphs drawn from Virginia Woolf and Elizabeth Barrett Browning—their influences here are undeniable —this volume's insistent attention to self-violence, suffused with a complex longing for, and yet wariness of, paternal blessing begs for comparison to Sylvia Plath, a comparison in which Billone more than holds her own. Poems such as 'Invitation from a Carnival after a Storm,' 'Paris to London' and 'If Nothing Else' demonstrate her ability to convey a rich, fraught sensuality with sharply lucid verse."

REVIEW: *Kirkus Rev* v81 no20 p83 O 15 2013

REVIEW: *Publ Wkly* v260 no41 p25 O 14 2013

BILTON, NICK. Hatching Twitter; a true story of money, power, friendship, and betrayal; [by] Nick Bilton 304 p. 2013 Portfolio Hardcover

1. BUSINESS & ECONOMICS—Corporate & Business History 2. BUSINESS & ECONOMICS—General 3. BUSINESS & ECONOMICS—Industries—Media & Communications Industries 4. Businesspeople—United States—Biography 5. Internet industry—United States 6. Journalism 7. Online social networks—United States
ISBN 9781591846017 (hardback)
LC 2013-037924

SUMMARY: This book examines "Twitter's contentious origins in the techie subculture of San Francisco." Author Nick Bilton "reconstructed this history from interviews and the digital trails . . . of his four principals: blogger, founder and chief investor Evan 'Ev' Williams and his friends and employees Noah Glass, Christopher 'Biz' Stone and Jack Dorsey. Each contributed an important share in the invention of the platform that . . . would revolutionize the way the world communicates and interrelates." (Kirkus Reviews)

REVIEW: *Economist* v409 no8862 p84-5 N 16 2013

"Hatching Twitter: A True Story of Money, Power, Friendship, and Betrayal" and "The Everything Store: Jeff Bezos and the Age of Amazon." "'Hatching Twitter' by Nick Bilton . . . is a made-for-the-movies account of the personal rivalries that fuelled several epic boardroom battles at the fast-growing startup. . . . Mr. Bilton is at his best when describing the turmoil at the top of Twitter. He also captures the thrill of being at a startup whose 140-character messages captivate high-profile people. . . . There is little boardroom drama to liven up Mr. [Brad] Stone's pages. But his book has triggered a bust-up online. . . . Such controversy will do doubt be good for sales of a tome that paints a fascinating picture of a remarkable tech entrepreneur."

REVIEW: *Kirkus Rev* v81 no22 p219 N 15 2013

REVIEW: *N Y Times Book Rev* p20 N 3 2013 MAUD NEWTON

REVIEW: *New Yorker* v89 no38 p68-1 N 25 2013

BINGHAM, HARRY. Love story, with murders; a novel; [by] Harry Bingham 400 p. 2013 Delacorte Press

1. Cotard syndrome 2. Detective & mystery stories 3. Murder investigation—Fiction 4. Policewomen—Fiction
ISBN 0345533763; 9780345533760 (acid-free paper)
LC 2013-001316

SUMMARY: In this murder mystery by Harry Bingham, "D.C. Fiona Griffiths is facing the prospect of a dull weekend when the call comes in, something about illegal dumping in a Cardiff suburb. But when she arrives on the scene she finds, in a garage freezer, a severed human leg, complete with a pink suede high-heeled shoe. . . . Still in recovery from a devastating psychotic breakdown, Fiona is wary of exploring a path that might end at her father's door." (Publisher's note)

REVIEW: *Kirkus Rev* v82 no3 p2 F 1 2014

"Love Story, With Murders". "A pair of murders five years apart forms the basis of a fact-based sophomore case for DC Fiona Griffiths, of the South Wales CID, that's just as intense as her first. . . . It's Fiona, whose Cotard's syndrome prevents her from feeling all kinds of emotions and sometimes even sensing feelings in her own body, who has what it takes to close the case and deliver some of the most memorably staccato narration in the genre. Not as surprising or carefully structured as [Harry] Bingham's striking debut, but his remote, unquenchable heroine makes her stand apart from every one of her procedural brothers and sisters."

REVIEW: *N Y Times Book Rev* p15 F 16 2014 MARILYN

STASIO

REVIEW: *Publ Wkly* v260 no50 p49-50 D 9 2013

BINGHAM, KELLY. Formerly shark girl; [by] Kelly Bingham 352 p. 2013 Candlewick Press

1. Amputees—Rehabilitation 2. Children's stories 3. Dating (Social customs)—Fiction 4. Girls—Fiction 5. Medical rehabilitation
ISBN 0763653624 (reinforced); 9780763653620 (reinforced)
LC 2012-952049

SUMMARY: This book is the sequel to Kelly Bingham's "Shark Girl" and "chronicles Jane's recovery from her injuries." Jane struggles with boyfriends and with her future: Will she become a nurse or continue as an artist even though she has lost her drawing hand? Her artwork continues to improve, but she feels obligated to give back to others what she received from the doctors and nurses who saved her life when she lost her right arm to a shark." (Kirkus)

REVIEW: *Bull Cent Child Books* v67 no1 p8 S 2013 K. C.

"Formerly Shark Girl." "This next chapter in Jane's recovery is as solid as the first, relating the fears, hopes, and agonies of adjusting to her new circumstances with realistic waves of emotion that, while intense, never tip into the sentimental or maudlin. . . . The lyrical free verse is an especially apt choice for Jane's narrative voice; internal rhyme, assonance, and alliteration reflect the mental boxes that close around Jane's small daily decisions, decisions that she then second-guesses and revises as she goes along. Though a young woman recovering from a life-altering trauma, Jane is also experiencing the transitions common to senior year, and her careful working through of her decisions will resonate strongly with readers."

REVIEW: *Kirkus Rev* v81 no8 p76 Ap 15 2013

REVIEW: *SLJ* v59 no7 p88 Jl 2013 Madigan McGillicuddy

BIOFUEL CROPS; production, physiology, and genetics; xii, 525 p. 2013 CAB International

1. Biomass energy 2. Energy crops 3. Energy crops—Breeding 4. Energy crops—Genetics 5. Scientific literature
ISBN 9781845938857 (hbk)
LC 2013-008421

SUMMARY: This book on biofuel crops, edited by Bharat P. Singh, "includes detailed coverage on crops of current importance or with high future prospects, including sections on algae, sugar crops and grass, oil and forestry species. The chapters focus on the genetics, breeding, cultivation, harvesting and handling of each crop." (Publisher's note)

REVIEW: *Choice* v51 no9 p1620-1 My 2014 V. G. Kakani

"Biofuel Crops: Production, Physiology and Genetics". "For each of the biofuel crops presented, [Bharat P.] Singh . . . has brought together worldwide experts, providing a much-needed holistic understanding of the various species. The book is well organized into three parts, and each of the 23 chapters presents up-to-date information on production, physiological, and genetic aspects of the crops. . . . Each chapter is followed by a list of references used in developing the chapter, which will he helpful for readers seeking more information. The book will be a valuable resource for faculty training the next generation of scientists in agronomy and biofuel crop improvement as well as students in these areas."

BIRD, JOAN CAROL. Nightmare and Nostalgia; Fifteen Wicked Little Ghost Stories; [by] Joan Carol Bird 238 p. 2013 Createspace Independent Pub

1. Death—Fiction 2. Future life—Fiction 3. Ghost stories 4. Haunted houses (Amusements) 5. Short story (Literary form)
ISBN 1492847607; 9781492847601

SUMMARY: "These 15 short stories take place in Great Britain, Peru and the United States, many in Arizona. . . . Each story examines encounters between the living and the dead. . . . In the second story, 'Dreamscape,' the narrator clings to life while visiting places with his deceased wife, Nell, and others who have predeceased him. . . . 'A Subtle Something Extra' [is] the story of Franny, a 12-year-old girl who haunts her father's seasonal haunted house." (Kirkus Reviews)

REVIEW: *Kirkus Rev* v82 no2 p352 Ja 15 2014

"Nightmare and Nostaliga: Fifteen Wicked Little Ghost Stories". "An eerie, debut assortment of short stories that explores the tenuous link between the land of the living and that of the dead. . . . Due to the similarities between the stories, the element of surprise dissipates early in the collection. . . . However, the tales are nonetheless enjoyable since [Joan Carol] Bird writes so skillfully. She has compiled a delightful collection of ghost stories, most of which are only slightly scary or, more likely, thought-provoking. You could share this collection with your grandmother. . . . A provocative short story collection that may leave readers re-evaluating their understandings of the afterlife."

BIRD, SARAH. Above the East China Sea; A Novel; [by] Sarah Bird 336 p. 2014 Alfred A. Knopf

1. Daughters—Fiction 2. Historical fiction 3. Orphans—Fiction 4. World War, 1939-1945—Japan
ISBN 0385350112; 9780385350112 (Hardcover)
LC 2013-024336

SUMMARY: This novel, by Sarah Bird, "tells the entwined stories of two teenaged girls, an American and an Okinawan, whose lives are connected across seventy years by the shared experience of profound loss, the enduring strength of an ancient culture, and the redeeming power of family love." (Publisher's note)

REVIEW: *Booklist* v110 no14 p47 Mr 15 2014 Mary Ellen Quinn

REVIEW: *Kirkus Rev* v82 no4 p285 F 15 2014

"Above the East China Sea". "[Sarah Bird's] novel is rich with detail on Okinawan religious lore about lost souls. Tamiko's and Luz's narratives make for interesting tonal counterpoints to each other. Tamiko's story is foursquare and mordant, focused as it is on war's devastation; Bird writes potently of her being thrust into the role of a Princess Lily girl, a young nursing assistant helping the demoralized Japanese soldiers. Luz's story is no less concerned with loss, but it's lighter on its feet, making room for her comic banter with friends and a growing crush on one of her new Okinawan acquaintances. Though the novel occasionally feels bogged down by Bird's research, she sensitively connects her two sharp narrators."

REVIEW: *Libr J* v139 no4 p78 Mr 1 2014 Jennifer B. Stidham

REVIEW: *N Y Times Book Rev* p30 Ag 10 2014 Barbara Fisher

BIRNEY, EARLE, 1904-1995. We Go Far Back in Time; The Letters of Earle Birney and Al Purdy, 1947-1984; [by] Earle Birney 480 p. 2013 Partners Pub Group

1. Authors—Correspondence 2. Authorship 3. Canadian poetry—20th century—History & criticism 4. Canadian poets 5. Letters
ISBN 1550176102; 9781550176100

SUMMARY: "This collection of letters illustrates the long friendship between two of Canada's most highly regarded poets, Earle Birney and Al Purdy. . . . It captures the changing relationship between the writers, each of whom was fiercely committed to the other's work. The letters are full of mutual praise and stern criticism, as Purdy and Birney, relentless in their pursuit of poetic success, look to each other for advice and share their many dissatisfactions with the literary life." (Publisher's note)

REVIEW: *Libr J* v139 no12 p90 Jl 1 2014 Victoria Frerichs

REVIEW: *Quill Quire* v80 no2 p32 Mr 2014 George Fetherling

"We Go Far Back in Time: The Letters of Earle Birney and Al Purdy, 1947-1984". "Al Purdy was a voluminous and candid letter-writer who, during his lifetime, saw publication of his correspondence/ . . . A general collected letters appeared in 2004 . . . but there is little overlap between its contents and this new book of his exchanges with fellow poet Earle Birney, himself no slouch in epistolary matters. . . . 'We Go Far Back in Time' is especially revealing in light of the men's posthumous reputations. . . . This splendid collection, expertly edited and richly annotated, is indeed an important contribution not only to the available output of these two individuals, but also to the story of Canadian writing in the second half of the 20th century."

BIRTCHNELL, THOMAS.ed. Elite mobilities. See Elite mobilities

BISHOP, ANNE. Murder of crows; a novel of the Others; [by] Anne Bishop 368 p. 2014 ROC

1. Fantasy fiction 2. Slavery—Fiction 3. Vampires—Fiction 4. Werewolves—Fiction 5. Women prophets—Fiction
ISBN 0451465261; 9780451465269
LC 2013-033927

SUMMARY: This book, by Anne Bishop, is "set on an Earth-like world, Namid, populated by a panoply of supernatural Others—and the humans who are their natural prey, On the continent of Thaisia, in the city of Lakeside, a delicate balance has been struck between humans and the terra indigene—shape-shifting wolves, raptors, bears, vampires and worse—thanks to Meg Corbyn, a cassandra sangue, or blood prophet, who sees the future when her skin is cut." (Kirkus Reviews)

REVIEW: *Booklist* v110 no11 p35 F 1 2014 Rebecca Gerber

REVIEW: *Kirkus Rev* v82 no1 p258 Ja 1 2014

"Murder of Crows". "Second in the series . . . set on an Earth-like world, Namid, populated by a panoply of supernatural Others—and the humans who are their natural prey. . . . This one is less exquisitely controlled than the previous book, with a plot that functions only intermittently; despite this, it delves more deeply into characters' motivations, interactions and emotions, with the outcome even more compelling and wrenching. Technically less accomplished but nonetheless fully satisfying."

REVIEW: *Libr J* v139 no13 p46 Ag 1 2014 Janet Martin

REVIEW: *Libr J* v139 no3 p75 F 15 2014 Nicole R. Steeves

REVIEW: *Publ Wkly* v261 no2 p54 Ja 13 2014

BISHOP, JULIA. New Penguin Book of English Folk Songs; [by] Julia Bishop 608 p. 2012 Penguin Press/Classics

1. Anthologies 2. English folk songs 3. Folk literature 4. Folk music—England 5. Folk music—History & criticism
ISBN 0141194618; 9780141194615

SUMMARY: This collection of popular English folk songs, edited by Steve Roud and Julia Bishop, "brings together all the classic folk songs as well as many lesser-known discoveries, complete with music and annotations on their original sources and meaning." (Publisher's note). Songs include "The Seeds of Love," "The Barley Mow," and "Geordie." (Times Literary Supplement)

REVIEW: *TLS* no5769 p19-20 O 25 2013 PADDY BULLARD

"The New Penguin Book of English Folk Songs." "Those indications of popularity have now been adopted as the basic criteria for selection in this indispensable anthology. The rarest of the 151 songs included by [Steve] Roud and [Julia] Bishop has fifteen unique entries in the Index. . . . Roud and Bishop aim to present the 'core tradition' of English popular singing. . . . The centre of gravity in Roud and Bishop's anthology, however, lies to one side of these well-known pieces. Their most characteristic choices come from the class of minor lyrics that includes 'The Seeds of Love'."

BISHOP, NIC, 1955-.il. Chasing cheetahs. See Montgomery, S.

BISHOP, NIC, 1955-.il. The tapir scientist. See The tapir scientist

BISKIND, PETER.ed. My Lunches With Orson. See Biskind, P.

BISSELL, TOM. The disaster artist; my life inside the room, the greatest bad movie ever made; [by] Tom Bissell 288 p. 2013 Simon & Schuster

1. Friendship 2. Memoirs 3. Motion picture industry 4. Wiseau, Tommy
ISBN 9781451661194 (hardback); 9781476730400 (trade paperback)
LC 2013-008798

SUMMARY: This book presents a "first-person account of the making of The Room (2003), 'the Citizen Kane of bad movies.'" Greg Sestero's memoir is as "concerned with the romantic American obsession with celebrity as with his trying involvement with The Room and its notorious producer/director/writer/star, Tommy Wiseau." (Kirkus Reviews)

REVIEW: *Bookforum* v20 no3 p48 S-N 2013 LOUIS BAYARD

"The Disaster Artist: My Life Inside 'The Room,' The Greatest Bad Movie Ever Made." "[Greg] Sestero started as the film's line producer, when filming began in San Francisco, but stepped into the role of the hero's faithless pal, a perch that gave him a clear view of the surrounding maelstrom. . . . 'The Disaster Artist is cowritten (or probably, judging by its wit and literacy, written) by journalist Tom Bissell, and with its allusions to Ripley and Sunset Boulevard, it understands the story it wants to tell. Tommy is a middle-aged man of some means and cloudy provenance, desperately lonely, waiting for the world to take notice. Greg is the beautiful young man who notices."

REVIEW: *Booklist* v110 no1 p24 S 1 2013 David Pitt

REVIEW: *Kirkus Rev* v81 no16 p121 Ag 15 2013

REVIEW: *N Y Times Book Rev* p18 O 6 2013 MICHAEL IAN BLACK

BITTNER, AMANDA.ed. Parties, elections, and the future of Canadian politics. See Parties, elections, and the future of Canadian politics

BLACK, BARBARA J. A room of his own; a literary-cultural study of Victorian clubland; [by] Barbara J. Black x, 301 p. 2012 Ohio University Press

1. Clubs—England—London—History 2. English literature—19th century—History and criticism 3. Historical literature 4. Literature and society—England—History—19th century 5. Men—Books and reading—England—History—19th century
ISBN 9780821420164 (hc : acid-free paper); 9780821444351 (electronic book)
LC 2012-033506

SUMMARY: This book by Barbara Black addresses "the gentlemen's clubs that formed the exclusive preserve known as 'clubland' in Victorian London." It "sheds light on the mysterious ways of male associational culture as it examines such topics as fraternity, sophistication, nostalgia, social capital, celebrity, gossip, and male professionalism." (Publisher's note)

REVIEW: *Choice* v51 no2 p256-7 O 2013 M. S. Vogeler

"A Room of His Own: A Literary-Cultural Study of Victorian Clubland." "Memoirs and academic studies of the Victorian period have not neglected its clubs, but the density of theorizing and plethora of detail provided by [author Barbara] Black . . . justify her return to the subject. . . . Victorian middle- and upper-class men often . . . sought to escape their family demands in a club's well-appointed rooms, where they could converse, dine, drink, smoke, and perhaps gamble with men of likely compatibility. Black . . . covers the depiction of clubs by Victorian novelists and journalists, their importance to imperialists and military men, explorers and other travelers. . . . The . . . detailed endnotes, bibliography, and index testify to the author's erudition."

REVIEW: *TLS* no5776 p25 D 13 2013 MARY L. SHANNON

BLACK, DAN. Old enough to fight. See Boileau, J.

BLACK, HOLLY, 1971-. The coldest girl in Coldtown; [by] Holly Black 432 p. 2013 Little Brown & Co

1. Dystopias 2. Love—Fiction 3. Quarantine 4. Vampires—Fiction 5. Young adult fiction
ISBN 0316213101 (hardcover); 9780316213103 (hardcover)
LC 2012-043790

SUMMARY: In this book by Holly Black, the vampires live in government-created ghettos called Coldtowns. "Seventeen-year-old Tana wakes up after a wild night of partying to discover that almost everyone in attendance has been killed by vampires. . . . Wandering through the carnage, she finds her infected ex-boyfriend, Aiden, and a mysterious, half-mad vampire named Gavriel chained in a bedroom. Escaping the massacre, Tana drives them to the nearest Coldtown," risking her life. (Publishers Weekly)

REVIEW: *Booklist* v110 no18 p72 My 15 2014

REVIEW: *Booklist* v110 no14 p5-33 Mr 15 2014

"Animal Wise: The Thoughts and Emotions of Our Fellow Creatures," "Any Duchess Will Do," and "The Coldest Girl in Coldtown." "No critters were harmed in the making of this book. . . . Desperate for grandchildren, the Duchess of Halford strikes a bargain with her only son,Griff: pick a woman--any woman. If she can transform her son's choice into duchess material, he must marry the girl. Griff picks the least likely candidate in bluestocking barmaid Pauline, only to quickly realize he has no idea who he is dealing with. A humorous and clever historical romance. . . . Welcome to Coldtown, a quarantined city for vampires, the infected, and humans. The price for residence, however, is that you can never leave."

REVIEW: *Booklist* v110 no8 p55 D 15 2013 Pam Spencer Holley

REVIEW: *Booklist* v109 no22 p72 Ag 1 2013 Candice Mack

REVIEW: *Bull Cent Child Books* v67 no3 p138-9 N 2013 K. Q. G.

"The Coldest Girl in Coldtown." "As a child, Tana watched her mother go Cold, i.e., turn into a bloodthirsty, flesh-crazed monster and succumb to the infection that turned much of the world's population into vampires. A teenager now, Tana wakes up after a drunken night to the massacre of her fellow partygoers by vampires; fleeing with her infected ex-boyfriend and another mysterious boy, Tana is bitten herself. Refusing to put her family through more grief, Tana decides to go to Coldtown--a glamorous, quarantined city where vampires and their prey mingle in a seductive dance that is televised live to the rest of the world. {Author Holly] Black has already revamped fairies . . . and sorcerers . . . and she attacks the vampire genre with the same creativity and morbidity. . . ."

REVIEW: *Horn Book Magazine* v89 no6 p88 N/D 2013 LAUREN ADAMS

"The Coldest Girl in Coldtown." "In an alternate here-and-now, vampires are sequestered in 'Coldtowns' guarded by barbed wire and Homeland Security. . . . [Holly] Black's compelling prose, descriptive yet direct, conjures a modern gothic world populated by cruel immortals, desperate humans offering themselves as food, and a few hardscrabble survivors. Tana is a winning heroine, by turns staking killer vampires and giving herself over to Gavriel's deep, smoldering kisses. As in previous works . . . Black displays her gift for channeling the dark side, seeming to wake the very shadows around us."

REVIEW: *Kirkus Rev* p49-51 Ag 15 2013 Fall Preview

REVIEW: *Kirkus Rev* v81 no14 p26 Jl 15 2013

REVIEW: *Kirkus Rev* p60 2013 Guide 20to BookExpo America

REVIEW: *Libr J* v138 no20 p1 N 15 2013

REVIEW: *Publ Wkly* v260 no26 p91 Jl 1 2013

REVIEW: *Publ Wkly* p122 Children's starred review annual 2013

REVIEW: *SLJ* v59 no8 p109 Ag 2013 Jennifer Furuyama

BLACK, JENNA. Resistance; [by] Jenna Black 368 p. 2014 St Martins Pr

1. Conspiracies—Fiction 2. Friendship—Fiction 3. Gays—Fiction 4. Memory—Fiction 5. Science fiction
ISBN 0765333724; 9780765333728 (pbk.)
LC 2013-025954

SUMMARY: In this book, by Jenna Black, "Nate Hayes is a Replica. The real Nate was viciously murdered, but thanks to Paxco's groundbreaking human replication technology, a duplicate was created that holds all of the personality and the memories of the original. Or...almost all. Nate's backup didn't extend to the days preceding his murder, leaving him searching for answers about who would kill him, and why." (Publisher's note)

REVIEW: *Booklist* v110 no13 p71 Mr 1 2014 Stacey Comfort

REVIEW: *Kirkus Rev* v82 no2 p134 Ja 15 2014

"Resistance". "Histrionic characters overpower the action in this dystopian-political-thriller sequel to 'Replica' (2013). . . . Dante's and Bishop's practical skills are not enough to save the plot from an overreliance on convenience—Nadia's escape from confinement, in particular, stretches the limits of believability. Also unconvincing are the characters' continual emotional vacillations, which make them simply unpredictable rather than complex, particularly in the novel's final moments. Only for fans of the first book."

BLACK WORKERS' STRUGGLE FOR EQUALITY IN BIRMINGHAM; p. cm 2004 University of Illinois Press

1. Blacks—Alabama—History 2. Blue collar workers—History 3. Civil rights—Alabama—History 4. Historical literature 5. Labor unions—Alabama—History 6. Unions—Alabama—History 7. Working class—History
ISBN 0-252-02952-6
LC 2004--7253

SUMMARY: In this book, "editors Horace Huntley and David Montgomery transform annotated interviews of participants in the 1960s Civil Rights Movement into a book that tells the story of the struggles and triumphs of those who stood up for justice and equality in Birmingham, Alabama. These men and women, Black and White . . . recount their experiences in overcoming a number of different kinds of prejudice and discrimination, including sharecropping . . . police brutality, and hate crimes." (Monthly Labor Review)

REVIEW: *Mon Labor Rev* p1-3 2014 Sidney W. Samuel

"Black Workers' Struggle for Equality in Birmingham." "Editors Horace Huntley and David Montgomery transform annotated interviews of participants in the 1960s Civil Rights Movement into a book that tells the story of the struggles and triumphs of those who stood up for justice and equality in Birmingham, Alabama. . . . Not only do the interviews presented in this book capture the importance of the many struggles of African Americans and provide new insights into the civil rights demonstrations of the 1960s, but they also recount decades of struggle before and after in the ever-present fight for equality. . . . This book is a must-read for anyone searching for firsthand knowledge of how hard minorities had to fight for equality in a land of opportunity."

BLACKALL, SOPHIE.il. The 9 lives of Alexander Baddenfield. See Marciano, J. B.

BLACKALL, SOPHIE.il. Ivy + Bean take the case. See Barrows, A.

BLACKALL, SOPHIE.il. Lord and Lady Bunny—almost royalty! See Lord and Lady Bunny—almost royalty!

BLACKSTONE, MATT. Sorry you're lost; [by] Matt Blackstone 320 p. 2014 Farrar Straus & Giroux

1. Conduct of life—Fiction 2. Dating (Social customs)—Fiction 3. Fathers and sons—Fiction 4. Grief—Fiction 5. Middle schools—Fiction 6. Popularity—Fiction 7. Psychological fiction 8. Schools—Fiction
ISBN 0374380651; 9780374380656 (hardback)
LC 2013-021215

SUMMARY: In this book, by Matt Blackstone, "Denny "Donuts" Murphy's mother dies [and] he becomes the world's biggest class clown. But deep down, Donuts just wants a normal life. . . . And so Donuts tries to get back into the groove by helping his best friend with their plan to get dates for the end-of-the-year school dance. When their scheme backfires, he learns that laughter is not the best medicine for all of his problems. Sometimes it's just as important to be true to yourself." (Publisher's note)

REVIEW: *Booklist* v110 no9/10 p110 Ja 1 2014 Sarah Hunter

REVIEW: *Bull Cent Child Books* v67 no6 p303-4 F 2014 Karen Coats

REVIEW: *Horn Book Magazine* v90 no2 p110 Mr/Ap 2014 DEAN SCHNEIDER

"Sorry You're Lost." "Ever since his mother died, seventh grader Denny 'Donuts' Murphy has felt alone and small. . . . So he intentionally develops a big persona: clowning in the classroom, making everything into a joke, doing robot dances and 'surfing' on a desk(before falling into the trash can). But inside, Donuts is hurting. . . . The first-person narrative is a perfect vehicle to reveal Donuts's inner self, and what might have been just a series of clichéd middle-school antics turns out to be a story of substance and hope."

REVIEW: *Kirkus Rev* v81 no23 p167 D 1 2013

REVIEW: *Publ Wkly* v260 no44 p67-8 N 4 2013

REVIEW: *SLJ* v60 no2 p81 F 2014 Colleen S. Banick

REVIEW: *Voice of Youth Advocates* v36 no6 p55 F 2014 Stacy Holbrook

BLACKWELL, ELIZABETH. While beauty slept; [by] Elizabeth Blackwell 432 p. 2014 Amy Einhorn Books

1. Courts & courtiers—Fiction 2. Fairy tales 3. Kings & rulers—Fiction 4. Sleeping Beauty (Tale) 5. Women—Fiction
ISBN 0399166238; 9780399166235 (hardback)
LC 2013-030337

SUMMARY: This novel, by Elizabeth Canning Blackwell, offers a "retelling of 'Sleeping Beauty' in the once-upon-a-time past but makes the standard version's reliance on magic subservient to a more psychological/sociological interpretation. When aged Elise overhears her granddaughter telling the popular legend about a sleeping princess brought back to life by a kiss, she feels compelled to tell the real events she witnessed 50 years earlier." (Kirkus Reviews)

REVIEW: *Booklist* v110 no8 p27 D 15 2013 Cortney Ophoff

REVIEW: *Kirkus Rev* v82 no2 p246 Ja 15 2014

"While Beauty Slept". "In her first novel, [Elizabeth] Blackwell keeps her retelling of 'Sleeping Beauty' in the once-upon-a-time past but makes the standard version's reliance on magic subservient to a more psychological/sociological interpretation. When aged Elise overhears her granddaughter telling the popular legend about a sleeping princess brought back to life by a kiss, she feels compelled to tell the real events she witnessed 50 years earlier while a beloved servant of King Ranolf and Queen Lenore. . . . Intelligent escapism that should please Brothers Grimm lovers more than Disney fans."

REVIEW: *Libr J* v138 no21 p87 D 1 2013 Katie Lawrence

REVIEW: *Libr J* v139 no15 p138 S 15 2014 Mary Knapp

REVIEW: *Publ Wkly* v260 no47 p30 N 18 2013

BLACKWELL, PAUL. Undercurrent; [by] Paul Blackwell 320 p. 2013 HarperTeen, an imprint of HarperCollins Publishers

1. Conduct of life—Fiction 2. Family life—Fiction 3. High schools—Fiction 4. Identity—Fiction 5. JUVENILE FICTION—Horror & Ghost Stories 6. JUVENILE FICTION—Mysteries & Detective Stories 7. JUVENILE FICTION—Social Issues—New Experience 8. Schools—Fiction 9. Speculative fiction 10. Supernatural—Fiction

ISBN 0062123505; 9780062123503 (hardback)

LC 2012-025504

SUMMARY: In this book, by Paul Blackwell, "Callum Harris . . . has miraculously survived a trip over [a] waterfall. . . . He wakes up from his coma into a life that is very different than the one he remembers. Nerdy Cal finds himself a star athlete with more than one person who wants him dead in a grimier, bleaker version of the town he hates. He must now undo what has happened or accept his new reality." (Booklist)

REVIEW: *Booklist* v110 no4 p61-2 O 15 2013 Magan Szwarek

"Undercurrent." "In his first novel for young adults, [Paul e.] Blackwell . . . has fashioned a menacing, suspenseful thriller. . . . The ending is a little rushed and tidy, but Cal's reactions are everything one would expect from an average teen boy who finds himself in a world that looks similar to his but is infinitely more dangerous. Hand this to fans of Mary Pearson's 'The Adoration of Jenna Fox' (2008), Michael Grant and Katherine Applegate's 'Eve and Adam' (2012), and the novels of Neal Shusterman."

REVIEW: *Bull Cent Child Books* v67 no3 p139 N 2013 A. M.

REVIEW: *Kirkus Rev* v81 no2 p76-7 Je 1 2013

REVIEW: *Voice of Youth Advocates* v36 no4 p77 O 2013 Margaret Capobianco

BLACKWOOD, GARY. Curiosity; [by] Gary Blackwood 320 p. 2014 Dial Books for Young Readers, an imprint of Penguin Group (USA) Inc.

1. Apprentices—Fiction 2. Chess—Fiction 3. Historical fiction 4. Poverty—Fiction 5. Robots—Fiction

ISBN 0803739249; 9780803739246 (hardcover)

LC 2013-013438

SUMMARY: This novel, by Gary Blackwood, begins in "Philadelphia, PA, 1835. Rufus, a twelve-year-old chess prodigy, is recruited by a shady showman named Maelzel to secretly operate a mechanical chess player called the Turk. . . . But Rufus's job working the automaton must be kept secret, and he fears he may never be able to escape his unscrupulous master. And what has happened to the previous operators of the Turk, who seem to disappear as soon as Maelzel no longer needs them?" (Publisher's note)

REVIEW: *Booklist* v110 no16 p61 Ap 15 2014 Sarah Hunter

REVIEW: *Bull Cent Child Books* v67 no9 p443-4 My 2014 E. B.

"Curiosity". "[Gary] Blackwood constructs a plot with appeal to several readerships: the gearheads who enjoy the mechanical workings of these robotic oddities . . . those who shiver at the possibility of life force within the machine . . . those who gravitate toward plucky orphan stories; and of course, those who appreciate a solid historical fiction riff on a real-life invention, the Turk itself. Rufus' self-effacing narration is thoroughly engaging; acknowledging that not all of his listeners will be equally intrigued with the game of chess, he handily brings the ignorant up to speed and then moves briskly along with the details of his precarious employment, and the bittersweet climax to his family drama."

REVIEW: *Horn Book Magazine* v90 no2 p110-1 Mr/Ap 2014 JONATHAN HUNT

REVIEW: *Kirkus Rev* v82 no4 p165 F 15 2014

"Curiosity". "The suspenseful narrative unfolds through the first-person voice of the fictional Rufus, a sickly, stooped yet strong-spirited boy who never loses his insatiable curiosity or his passion for chess even through bouts of abuse, near-starvation, deceit and, alas, unrequited love. A thrilling look at the 19th-century age of automata—'a time of curiosity-seekers'—and the riveting story of a likable Philadelphia boy whose life of the mind helps him transcend his extraordinary, oft-cruel circumstances."

REVIEW: *SLJ* v60 no3 p134 Mr 2014 Erinn Black Salge

REVIEW: *Voice of Youth Advocates* v37 no1 p60 Ap 2014 Deena Viviani

REVIEW: *Voice of Youth Advocates* v37 no1 p60 Ap 2014 Maia Raynor

BLAIN, MICHAEL. Power, discourse, and victimage ritual in the war on terror; [by] Michael Blain 157 p. 2012 Ashgate

1. Political violence—Social aspects 2. Power (Social sciences) 3. Social science literature 4. Terrorism—Social aspects 5. War on Terrorism, 2001-2009

ISBN 9781409436058 (marketing: alk. paper); 9781409436065 (ebook)

LC 2012-005212

SUMMARY: In this book, "focusing on the sources of media and news discourse through the duration of the [War on Terror], [Michael] Blain analyzes methods in which American elites legitimate social control by creating culprits through the victimage ritual process as a way of amplifying their own power and control within the United States, as well as in foreign territories." (Contemporary Sociology)

REVIEW: *Contemp Sociol* v43 no2 p284-5 Mr 2014

"Power, Discourse, and Victimage Ritual in the War on Terror". "Michael Blain offers a thorough analysis of political and news discourse on terrorism, while implementing theoretical perspectives which critically assess the war on terror led by the United States. This book can easily be of interest to a large audience ranging from political scientists, to sociologists, and to theorists whose areas focus on social control, paranoia, surveillance, and foreign policy. . . . Blain does a marvelous job of organizing the chapters, and offers a thorough discussion of ritual rhetoric and political violence throughout his assessment."

BLAINEY, GEOFFREY. A short history of Christianity; [by] Geoffrey Blainey 636 p. 2013 Rowman & Littlefield

1. Christianity & history 2. Christianity & other religions 3. Christians—History 4. Church history 5. Historical literature

ISBN 9781442225893 (cloth: alk. paper)

LC 2013-029361

SUMMARY: This history of Christianity by Geoffrey A. Blainey "describes many of the significant players in the religion's rise and fall through the ages, from Jesus himself to Francis of Assisi, Martin Luther, Francis Xavier, John Wesley, and even the Beatles, who claimed to be 'more popular than Jesus.' Blainey takes us into the world of Christian worshipers through the ages—from housewives to stonemasons—and traces the rise of the critics of Christ and his followers." (Publisher's note)

REVIEW: *Choice* v51 no9 p1609-10 My 2014 M. Y. Spomer

"A Short History of Christianity". "Written in a very accessible, narrative style. All the major events, movements, and people in 2,000 years of Christian history are included, but [Geoffrey A.] Blainey also provides connections with politics . . . other religions . . . literature . . . historical events . . . and popular culture. . . . The maps and index are excellent, and the chapter notes provide ample opportunities for further research. . . . Given its brevity and readability, this book would be an ideal introduction for those unfamiliar with Christianity, and for undergraduate students in history and religion courses."

REVIEW: *Libr J* v138 no18 p93 N 1 2013 Kathleen Dupré

BLAIR, JAMIE. Leap of Faith; [by] Jamie Blair 240 p. 2013 Simon & Schuster

1. Fugitives from justice—Fiction 2. Kidnapping—Fiction 3. Parenting—Fiction 4. Runaways—Fiction 5. Young adult fiction

ISBN 1442447133; 1442447168; 9781442447134 (hardcover); 9781442447165 (pbk.)

LC 2012-043125

SUMMARY: In this book, "17-year old Faith recounts her grim life with her abusive, drug-addicted mother and the circumstances that motivate her to flee. Although inured to her mother's frequent male visitors, Faith longs to save the baby her mother is carrying (for pay) for a guy that Faith considers 'drug-dealing scum.' Kidnapping the newborn from the hospital, Faith drives from Ohio to Florida, determined to start a new life with baby Addy." (Publishers Weekly)

REVIEW: *Bull Cent Child Books* v67 no3 p139-40 N 2013 E. B.

"Leap of Faith." "Faith is disgusted by her drug-dependent mother's agreement to carry a child to term for a pair of her junkie acquaintances. Determined that this baby won't fall into the family's cycle of poverty and neglect, Faith stockpiles baby supplies and, as soon as the baby is born, swipes Mom's money and car and makes a run for Florida with newborn Addy carefully strapped into a rear-facing car seat. The care and feeding of an infant is especially hard for a seventeen-year-old with limited funds, no childcare experience, and the likelihood that the police are hot on her trail. YA literature has been known, however, to shower improbable blessings on its heroines. . . ."

REVIEW: *Kirkus Rev* v81 no14 p251 Jl 15 2013

REVIEW: *Publ Wkly* v260 no32 p63 Ag 12 2013

BLAIR, PEGGY. The Poisoned Pawn; [by] Peggy Blair 336 p. 2014 Pintail

1. Child pornography 2. Child sexual abuse by clergy 3. Detective & mystery stories 4. Havana (Cuba)—Fiction 5. Jurisdiction

ISBN 014318976X (pbk.); 9780143189763 (pbk.)

LC 2012-545758

SUMMARY: This book by Peggy Blair is the sequel to "The Beggar's Opera." "Detective Mike Ellis returns home after he is cleared in the death of a young boy while on vacation in Cuba, only to discover that his estranged wife, Hilary, is dead, and that he's the main suspect. Meanwhile, Inspector Ramirez, head of the Havana Major Crimes Unit, is dispatched to Ottawa to take custody of a Cuban priest apprehended by authorities while in possession of a laptop full of child pornography." (Publisher's note)

REVIEW: *Booklist* v110 no12 p33 F 15 2014 Bill Ott

"The Poisoned Pawn." "[Peggy] Blair follows up her outstanding debut, 'The Beggar's Opera' (2013), with another superb crime novel starring Inspector Ricardo Ramirez, head of Havana's Major Crimes Unit, who sees and communicates with the dead bodies whose murders he is investigating. . . . Blair brilliantly unspools her tightly wound plot, revealing more than one shocker in the process. This Is a fine series with a thoroughly outstanding cast. . . . Expect to hear much more about this series; it's just waiting to be discovered in the big way it deserves."

BLANK, ROBERT H. Intervention in the brain; politics, policy, and ethics; [by] Robert H. Blank 370 p. 2013 MIT Press

1. Bioethical Issues 2. Brain 3. Drugs—Moral & ethical aspects 4. Neurosciences—ethics 5. Scientific literature

ISBN 9780262018913 (hardcover : alk. paper)

LC 2012-036419

SUMMARY: "In this book, Robert Blank examines the complex ethical and policy issues raised by our new capabilities of intervention in the brain. After surveying current knowledge about the brain and describing a wide range of experimental and clinical interventions--from behavior-modifying drugs to neural implants to virtual reality--Blank discusses the political and philosophical implications of these scientific advances." (Publisher's note)

REVIEW: *Choice* v51 no4 p662-3 D 2013 K. C. Michael

"Intervention in the Brain: Politics, Policy, and Ethics." "This book aims to be more practical than philosophical. Using language easily understandable to a lay audience, [Robert H.] Blank . . . provides a basic overview of neuroscience and the existing methods of manipulating the brain and behavior, and then applies these principles to a number of provocative contemporary ethical and policy issues. Some sections of the work are problematic. The author dismisses epigenetics as unimportant. . . . On some topics, he presents only one branch of research and neglects the body of published work that contradicts his conclusion. . . . Later chapters, however, are more comprehensive in their scope and address a variety of compelling ethical topics."

BLANK, TREVOR J. The last laugh; folk humor, celebrity culture, and mass-mediated disasters in the digital age; [by] Trevor J. Blank xxix, 156 p. 2013 University of Wisconsin Press

1. Folklore and the Internet 2. Gossip in mass media 3. Mass media & celebrities 4. Social science literature 5. Wit & humor

ISBN 9780299292034 (e-book); 9780299292041 (pbk. : alk. paper)

LC 2012-032669

SUMMARY: In this book, Trevor J. Blank argues that "'folk humor' allows virtual communities to offer critical commentary on the ways that 'disasters' . . . are portrayed in the mass media. . . . The author traces continuities from predigital culture; the transition from photocopy lore to photoshop lore, or from the 'folksy' emotionality of nineteenth-century journalism . . . to the rumour-mongering and gossipy exchanges of forums and chat rooms." (Times Literary Supplement)

REVIEW: *Choice* v51 no6 p995-6 F 2014 C. J. Lamb

REVIEW: *TLS* no5766 p27 O 4 2013 FRANK BRUCE

"The Last Laugh: Folk Humor, Celebrity Culture, and Mass-Mediated Disasters in the Digital Age." "'The Last Laugh' . . . advances Trevor J. Blank's thesis that 'folk humor' allows virtual communities to offer critical commentary on the ways that 'disasters' (ranging from the truly catastrophic to celebrity meltdowns) are portrayed in the mass media. . . . Some of Blank's points are tangled and hard to prove given the difficulty in defining exactly what is a community in the first place, or what jokes might really mean to audiences. His suggestion that jokes made in poor taste are a symbolic way of relieving anxiety about death lets the tellers off lightly. Nevertheless, 'The Last Laugh' provides a useful map for a changing landscape."

BLASER, MARTIN J. Missing microbes; how the overuse of antibiotics is fueling our modern plagues; [by] Martin J. Blaser 288 p. 2014 Henry Holt & Co.

1. Antibiotics 2. Drug resistance in microorganisms 3. Human biology 4. Science—Popular works

ISBN 0805098100; 9780805098105 (hardback); 9780805098112 (electronic copy)

LC 2013-042578

SUMMARY: "In 'Missing Microbes,' Dr. Martin Blaser invites us into the wilds of the human microbiome where for hundreds of thousands of years bacterial and human cells have existed in a peaceful symbiosis that is responsible for the health and equilibrium of our body. . . . Taking us into both the lab and deep into the fields where these troubling effects can be witnessed firsthand, Blaser . . . provides cutting edge evidence for the adverse effects of antibiotics." (Publisher's note)

REVIEW: *Booklist* v110 no15 p8 Ap 1 2014 Tony Miksanek

REVIEW: *Kirkus Rev* v82 no5 p152 Mr 1 2014

REVIEW: *Libr J* v139 no10 p126 Je 1 2014 Marianne Stowell Bracke

REVIEW: *Libr J* v138 no20 p1 N 15 2013 Barbara Hoffert

REVIEW: *New Sci* v222 no2970 p49 My 24 2014 Debora MacKenzie

"Missing Microbes: How the Overuse of Antibiotics Is Fueling Our Modern Plagues." "Antibiotics have ended untold human misery by curing bacterial infections, yet we are in danger of losing these wonder drugs. . . . 'Missing Microbes' is partly about that. But it is mainly a story you may not know, about the damage antibiotics do when they actually do work. . . . The great thing about this very readable account is that [author Martin J. Blaser] tells us why he thinks so, enthusiastically describing how the research was done. . . . It's all frighteningly convincing. . . . What we have overlooked in our cavalier treatment of our bacterial guests is their complexity."

REVIEW: *New York Times* v163 no56486 pD5 Ap 29 2014 ABIGAIL ZUGER

REVIEW: *Publ Wkly* v261 no7 p88 F 17 2014

REVIEW: *Science* v344 no6183 p472 My 2 2014 Alison E. Mather

BLASHFIELD, JEAN F. Ireland; [by] Jean F. Blashfield 144 p. 2014 Children's Press ; an imprint of Scholastic Inc.

1. Children's nonfiction 2. Ireland—History 3. Ireland—Politics & government 4. Ireland—Social life & customs

ISBN 0531236765; 9780531236765 (library binding)

LC 2013-002015

SUMMARY: This book, by Jean F. Blashfield, focuses on Ireland. The book focuses on "country's culture, history, and geography are explored in detail. . . . Sidebars highlight especially interesting people, places, and events. . . . Recipes give readers the opportunity to experience foreign cuisine." (Publisher's note)

REVIEW: *Booklist* v110 no9/10 p94 Ja 1 2014 Susan Dove Lempke

"Brazil," "Ireland," "North Korea." "For reliably accurate, attractively presented and well-calibrated information, the longstanding 'Enchantment of the World' series remains a superior choice. . . . Although the basic structure holds true to past versions, the updated photographs are truly eye-popping and take care to portray the countries as modern. . . . 'Brazil' . . . conveys an excitement about the country and its people as well as its plentiful animals and plants. It might not be necessary for libraries to replace 'Ireland,' since it hasn't changed radically, but this is a solid offering with updated statistics. 'North Korea' has a new author and a strong political focus, discussing life under the new leader, Kim Jong-un."

BLASIM, HASSAN. The corpse exhibition and other stories of Iraq; [by] Hassan Blasim 208 p. 2014 Penguin Books

1. American short stories 2. Iraq War, 2003-2011—Fic-

tion 3. Terrorism—Fiction 4. War stories
ISBN 0143123262; 9780143123262 (pbk.)
LC 2013-043633

SUMMARY: This book, by Hassan Blasim, presents several short stories featuring "the [Iraq] war as we have never seen it before. Here is a world not only of soldiers and assassins, hostages and car bombers, refugees and terrorists, but also of madmen and prophets, angels and djinni, sorcerers and spirits." (Publisher's note)

REVIEW: *Bookforum* v21 no2 p17-9 Je-Ag 2014 WILLIAM T. VOLLMANN

REVIEW: *Booklist* v110 no9/10 p39 Ja 1 2014 John Mort

REVIEW: *Kirkus Rev* v81 no24 p332 D 15 2013

"The Corpse Exhibition and Other Stories of Iraq". " Expect nothing but the impressionistic here—magical realism, bloody allegories and macabre parables—elusive tales, each one a different window into modern Iraq's tragic history. . . . In each piece, there's no happy ending, but [Hassan] Blasim's language is powerful, moving and deeply descriptive, thanks to [Jonathan] Wright's translation. . . . All the stories share a complexity and depth that will appeal to readers of literary fiction, while some focus more plainly on evil's abyss, much like biblical parables. A collection of fractured-mirror reality stories for fans of Günter Grass, Gabriel García Márquez or Jorge Luis Borges."

REVIEW: *Libr J* v139 no4 p86 Mr 1 2014 James Coan

REVIEW: *New York Times* v163 no56396 pC4 Ja 29 2014 DAVID KIPEN

"The Corpse Exhibition & Other Stories of Iraq". "There are no sides and no front in the Iraqi exile Hassan Blasim's arresting, auspicious story collection . . . only paranoid top dogs and desperate bottom feeders. . . . Culled from Mr. Blasim's two award-winning collections published in Britain, . . . 'The Corpse Exhibition' heralds a writer whose promise deepens as the book progresses. . . . The prose here, at least in Jonathan Wright's translation from the Arabic, is fine but not world-beating. . . . It's unclear in what order he wrote these stories, but their sequence imparts a mounting novelistic power."

REVIEW: *Publ Wkly* v260 no51 p1 D 16 2013

BLASING, MUTLU KONUK. Nâzım Hikmet; the life and times of Turkey's world poet; [by] Mutlu Konuk Blasing 288 p. 2013 Persea Books

1. Biographies 2. Poets, Turkish—Biography 3. Turkey—History—20th century 4. Turkish poetry—History & criticism
ISBN 0892554177; 9780892554171 (hardcover : alk. paper)
LC 2012-043694

SUMMARY: Author Mutlu Konuk Blasing presents "an authoritative biography of [Nâzim Hikmet] Turkey's most important and most popular poet. [Hikmet] lived through a turbulent era—the end of the Ottoman Empire, the rise of Communist Russia, and the birth of the Turkish Republic. His stirring free verse in simple words, praising his country, his women, and the common man, was considered 'subversive' and banned for decades. Today it is available in more than fifty languages." (Publisher's note)

REVIEW: *Booklist* v109 no17 p59 My 1 2013 Ray Olson

REVIEW: *Choice* v51 no1 p71 S 2013 W. L. Hanaway

REVIEW: *TLS* no5752 p13 Je 28 2013 WILLIAM ARMSTRONG

"Nazim Hikmet: The Life and Times of Turkey's World Poet." "This excellent new biography . . . [was] written by an award-winning translator of Hikmet's poems into English. . . . While Mutlu Konuk Biasing admits that Hikmet's silence on Soviet cruelty was a critical blot in his copybook, she perhaps lets him off the hook a little too lightly, all the same. Indeed, her biography at times veers towards the reverential, but if there is a modem Turkish poet who deserves attention outside his native country it is probably Hikmet. . . . This is a valuable biography of a vital twentieth-century figure."

REVIEW: *World Lit Today* v87 no5 p55-79 S/O 2013

"The Contract Killer," "Nazim Hikmet: The Life and Times of Turkey's World Poet," and "The People of Forever Are Not Afraid." "[Benny] Andersen presents absurdist approaches to questions of life and death, never losing his sense of humor or his lighthearted turn of phrase. . . . [Mutlu Konuk] Blasing is a prolific translator of Hikmet's work, and she incorporates elements of literary scholarship into her investigation of his life. . . . Shani Boianjiu's gripping debut novel illustrates the lives of three Israeli girls who grow up together after they are conscripted into the army."

BLECHMAN, NICHOLAS.il. Information graphics animal kingdom. See Rogers. S.

BLEGVAD, ERIK, 1923-2014.il. The tenth good thing about Barney. See Viorst, Judith.

BLENKINSOPP, JOSEPH. David remembered; kingship and national identity in ancient Israel; [by] Joseph Blenkinsopp xii, 219 p. 2013 William B. Eerdmans Publishing Company

1. Historical literature 2. Jews—History—586 B.C.-70 A.D 3. Judaism—History—Post-exilic period, 586 B.C.-210 A.D 4. Monarchy
ISBN 9780802869586 (pbk. : alk. paper)
LC 2012-045983

SUMMARY: In this book, author Joseph Blenkinsopp "traces how the idea and ideal of a Davidic ruler developed in new, often messianic ways once the last reigning Davidic king was deposed. Beginning in late-7th-century-BCE Judah just before the Babylonian exile, he analyzes the history and relevant biblical and allied ancient Near Eastern texts, concluding his survey in the first century CE." (Choice: Current Reviews for Academic Libraries)

REVIEW: *Choice* v51 no5 p852 Ja 2014 J. S. Kaminsky

"David Remembered: Kingship and National Identity in Ancient Israel." "In this well-researched monograph [Joseph] Blenkinsopp . . . traces how the idea and ideal of a Davidic ruler developed in new, often messianic ways once the last reigning Davidic king was deposed. . . . Blenkinsopp is excellent at evoking the many historical traumas experienced by the Judean populace during this period of foreign domination, and at showing how various texts often reveal reactions to particular historical stresses. The author presents a nuanced and rich portrait of the movement . .. While he writes clearly and concisely, Blenkinsopp's arguments are quite detailed."

A BLESSING IN DISGUISE; War and Town Planning in Europe 1940-1945; 416 p. 2013 Lakewood Art & Architecture

1. Buildings—War damage 2. Cities & towns—Europe—History 3. Historical literature 4. Reconstruction (1939-1951)—Europe 5. Urban planning—History
ISBN 3869222956; 9783869222950

SUMMARY: In this book, "a number of architectural historians have come together to explore the relationship between aerial warfare and town planning in Europe in the 1930s and 1940s. The maps and plans reprinted in colour in the book, many of them never previously published, testify to the enthusiasm with which planners went about their work. Their Utopian schemes stand in a long tradition of planning in the wake of urban catastrophe." (London Review of Books)

REVIEW: *London Rev Books* v35 no23 p27-9 D 5 2013 Richard J. Evans

"A Blessing in Disguise: War and Town Planning in Europe, 1940-45". "'A Blessing in Disguise' can be read as a critique of the Utopian planners like Le Corbusier or Fritz Schumacher, but it's hard to extract any consistent argument from its pages, partly because the authors often ramble on, repeat themselves, digress and get stuck on side issues, and partly because of the execrable standard of much of the English. . . . This is all very unfortunate in an otherwise highly instructive volume with some arresting contemporary quotes and a very large number of beautifully reproduced illustrations."

BLISS, HARRY.il. Diary of a worm. See Cronin. D.

BLOCK, FRANCESCA LIA. Love in the time of global warming; [by] Francesca Lia Block 240 p. 2013 Henry Holt and Co.

1. Earthquakes—Fiction 2. Families—Fiction 3. Love—Fiction 4. Science fiction 5. Survival—Fiction 6. Voyages and travels—Fiction
ISBN 0805096272; 9780805096279 (hardcover)
LC 2012-047808

SUMMARY: In this book, after "an earthquake and tidal wave destroy much of Los Angeles, Penelope—now going by Pen—sets out to find her family. In the course of a journey that explicitly parallels the one described in Homer's Odyssey, Pen navigates the blighted landscape with a crew of three other searchers. . . . Eventually they arrive in Las Vegas (the contemporary stand-in for the land of the dead) where Pen confronts the evil genius behind her world's destruction." (Publishers Weekly)

REVIEW: *Booklist* v109 no21 p68 Jl 1 2013 Michael Cart

REVIEW: *Booklist* v110 no14 p24 Mr 15 2014

REVIEW: *Bull Cent Child Books* v67 no2 p77 O 2013 K. C.

"Love in the Time of Global Warming." "After a massive earthquake and tsunami devastate Los Angeles and possibly the entire U.S., Penelope is alone in her seaside home when looters come, one of them a mysterious man named Merk, who insists that she take his van and go find her parents with a map he has provided. The map launches Pen on a journey that loosely follows the exploits of Odysseus, re-imagined, in [author Francesca Lia] Block's familiar dreamlike fashion, in the ruined locales of her beloved city. . . . Block's self-conscious efforts to fuse multiple mythologies and genres has the logical weakness common to dreams: the plot is disjointed and often unsatisfying, with . . . the completely unrealistic and wish-fulfilling conclusion."

REVIEW: *Horn Book Magazine* v89 no5 p86 S/O 2013 KATRINA HEDEEN

REVIEW: *Kirkus Rev* v81 no2 p77 Je 1 2013

REVIEW: *Publ Wkly* v260 no21 p63 My 27 2013

REVIEW: *Publ Wkly* p124 Children's starred review annual 2013

REVIEW: *SLJ* v59 no8 p109 Ag 2013 Kelly Jo Lasher

BLOCK, FRANCESCA LIA. Teen spirit; [by] Francesca Lia Block 240 p. 2014 HarperTeen, an imprint of HarperCollinsPublishers

1. Dating (Social customs)—Fiction 2. Dead—Fiction 3. Grandmothers—Fiction 4. Paranormal fiction 5. Single-parent families—Fiction 6. Spirits—Fiction 7. Supernatural—Fiction
ISBN 0062008099; 9780062008091 (hardcover bdg.)
LC 2013-008057

SUMMARY: In this novel, by Francesca Lia Block, when Julie's grandmother Miriam dies, "Julie's entire world is beginning to unravel. . . . [Then] she meets sweetly eccentric Clark, who is also mourning a loss. . . . One night, the two use a Ouija board . . . , believing it's a chance to reach out to her grandmother. But when they get a response, it isn't from Miriam. And Julie discovers that while she has been eager to regain her past, Clark is haunted by his." (Publisher's Note)

REVIEW: *Booklist* v110 no5 p78-9 N 1 2013 Daniel Kraus

"Teen Spirit." "It may sound like standard paranormal romantic stuff, but if we've learned anything from [Francesca Lia] Block's takes on vampires . . . and dystopia . . . it's that nothing she does is standard. Classic Blockian traits are in place: a kitschy, palm-tree-decked California wonderland; a guileless sweetness spiked with moments of grittiness and sexuality; and characters steeped in time-sensitive pop culture in a way that feels timeless. All that said, this coasts on charm a bit while the plot works itself out along expected lines. But readers who are already grooving to Block's tune will love it."

REVIEW: *Bull Cent Child Books* v67 no5 p257-8 Ja 2014 K. C.

"Teen Spirit." "[Francesca Lia] Block's sensual language and strong evocation of place embroider this tale of unresolved grief with an overlay of subtle and delicate creepiness. This is less agonizing than some of Block's recent work and less horrific than some evil twin stories, but it's nonetheless haunted with familiar sinister character types, thereby coloring reader expectations with a quiet dread. The substantive emotional trajectory, though, is that of a person working through profound loss; neither Julie nor Clark is strong or resolute on his or her own, but together they help each other past the emotional deadlock that has them in its grip. Block has a knack for composing supportive friendships that draw on complementary qualities."

REVIEW: *SLJ* v60 no1 p95 Ja 2014 Kimberly Garnick Giarratano

BLOMGREN, MAGNUS. Political parties in multi-level polities. See Aylott, N.

BLOODWORTH, JEFFREY. Losing the center; the decline of American liberalism, 1968-1992; [by] Jeffrey Bloodworth 345 p. 2013 University Press of Kentucky

1. Democratic Party (U.S.)—History 2. Historical literature 3. Liberalism—United States—History—20th century 4. Political science literature 5. United States—Politics & government—20th century
ISBN 9780813142296 (hardcover : alk. paper)
LC 2013-015478

SUMMARY: In this book, author "Jeffrey Bloodworth demonstrates how and why the once-dominant ideology began its steep decline, . . . through the biographies of some of the Democratic Party's most important leaders, including Daniel Patrick Moynihan, Henry 'Scoop' Jackson, Bella Abzug, Harold Ford Sr., and Jimmy Carter. . . . Bloodworth sheds new light on topics such as feminism, the environment, the liberal abandonment of the working class, and civil rights legislation." (Publisher's note)

REVIEW: *Choice* v51 no7 p1307 Mr 2014 P. F. Campbell

REVIEW: *Commentary* v136 no3 p56-7 O 2013 JAMES ROSEN

"Losing the Center: The Decline of American Liberalism, 1968-1992." "In his unusual multi-disciplinary effort, . . . [author Jeffrey Bloodworth] does more than serve up . . . trivia. Combining political science, biography, and sociology, Bloodworth expertly traces the evolution of the Democratic Party and its attendant electoral woes. . . . The rest of the book is given over, less profitably, to 11 short biographies of politicians, pollsters, activists, and others who played (mostly) unheralded roles in liberalism's Great Marginalization. . . . Still, there isn't an important political event or trend of the fractious quarter-century of history assayed . . . that escapes Bloodworth's keen eye, and his book will serve as a useful, if not exhaustive, primer on the era."

BLOOM, CLIVE. Victoria's Madmen; Revolution and Alienation; [by] Clive Bloom 320 p. 2013 Palgrave Macmillan

1. Dissenters—Great Britain 2. Great Britain—History—Victoria, 1837-1901 3. Great Britain—Social conditions—19th century 4. Historical literature 5. Radicals—Great Britain—History 6. Revolutionaries—History—19th century
ISBN 0230313825; 9780230313828

SUMMARY: "'Victoria's Madmen' tells the stories of a host of figures who came to exemplify a contradictory history of the Victorian age: not one of Dickensian London and smoking factories, but one of little known revolutionaries and radicals. . . . This is the story of those who were outcasts by temperament and choice; the non-conformists of the age. Clive Bloom's . . . account . . . captures the unrest bubbling under the surface of strait-laced society." (Publisher's note)

REVIEW: *Choice* v51 no10 p1786 Je 2014 F. Alaya

REVIEW: *New Statesman* v142 no5170 p41-2 Ag 16 2013 Hannah Rosefield

REVIEW: *TLS* no5785 p22-3 F 14 2014 CLARE PETTITT

"High Minds: The Victorians and the Birth of Modern Britain" and "Victoria's Madmen: Revolution and Alienation." "Both [Simon] Heffer's and [Clive] Bloom's histories . . . get the dragnets out, gathering great tankloads of Victorian specimens. . . . Rather than setting up a question that needs an answer, both these authors start their books by telling us off. . . . Heffer makes use of archives that are familiar to nineteenth-century historians, but what he does with them is disappointing. . . . Bloom undoubtedly has an instinct for juicy quotations, and 'Victoria's Madmen' is perhaps best approached as a sort of common-place book, but . . . there are no footnotes. . . . Many of Bloom's sentences are improbably long, grammatically challenged and disorientating to read."

BLOOM, PATIENCE. Romance is my day job; a memoir of finding love at last; [by] Patience Bloom 320 p. 2014 Dutton Adult

1. BIOGRAPHY & AUTOBIOGRAPHY—Editors, Journalists, Publishers 2. BIOGRAPHY & AUTOBIOGRAPHY—Personal Memoirs 3. BIOGRAPHY & AUTOBIOGRAPHY—Women 4. Book editors—United States—Biography 5. Editors—United States—Biography 6. Love stories—Publishing—United States 7. Memoirs
ISBN 9780525954385 (hardback)
LC 2013-024050

SUMMARY: This book is a memoir by Patience Bloom, "an editor [of romance novels] at Harlequin. . . . She jumps from one short-lived relationship to another. . . . When she reaches her 40s, fresh out of another unfulfilling relationship, she finally concludes that 'romance doesn't exist.' Then, via Facebook, Bloom reconnects with Sam, a high school acquaintance with whom she shared one dance at a winter formal back in 1984." (Publishers Weekly)

REVIEW: *Booklist* v110 no9/10 p20 Ja 1 2014 Pat Henshaw

REVIEW: *Kirkus Rev* v81 no24 p71 D 15 2013

"Romance Is My Day Job: A Memoir of Finding Love at Last". "A veteran editor of romance novels at Harlequin delivers a witty memoir of her history with romance. Unlike the novels she edits, her real-life relationships have been messy and the happy endings elusive. . . . She cleverly juxtaposes the conventions of romantic novels and movies with the challenges of maintaining a real relationship, avoiding maudlin territory. . . . This is classic girls'-night-out dishing. Though the men in her memoir, with the exception of one, are more typecast than fully formed, the deeper thread here is the idea of self-evaluation and betterment."

REVIEW: *Libr J* v139 no2 p75 F 1 2014 Audrey Snowden

REVIEW: *Publ Wkly* v260 no48 p41-2 N 25 2013

BLOOM, PAUL. Just babies; the origins of good and evil; [by] Paul Bloom 288 p. 2013 Crown Publishers

1. Child development 2. Ethics—Psychological aspects 3. Good and evil 4. PHILOSOPHY—Ethics & Moral Philosophy 5. PSYCHOLOGY—Developmental—Child 6. PSYCHOLOGY—Neuropsychology 7. Psychological literature 8. Values
ISBN 0307886840; 9780307886842 (hardback); 9780307886859 (trade paperback)
LC 2013-012697

SUMMARY: In this book author Paul Bloom "argues that humans are in fact hardwired with a sense of morality. Drawing on groundbreaking research at Yale, Bloom demonstrates that, even before they can speak or walk, babies judge the goodness and badness of others' actions; feel empathy and compassion; act to soothe those in distress; and have a rudimentary sense of justice." (Publisher's note)

REVIEW: *Atlantic* v312 no4 p102-18 N 2013 ROBERT WRIGHT

"Moral Tribes: Emotion, Reason, and the Gap Between Us and Them" and "Just Babies: The Origins of Good and Evil." "[Joshua] Greene writes that his book is about 'the central tragedy of modern life.' He's not alone in thinking this is high-gravitas stuff. The Yale psychologist Paul Bloom, who also studies the biological basis of morality, has a new book called 'Just Babies', about the emergence of moral inclinations in infants and toddlers. . . . Anyone who doubts that basic moral impulses are innate will have Paul Bloom's book to contend with. . . . If Greene thinks that getting people to couch their moral arguments in a highly reasonable language will make them highly reasonable, I think he's underestimating the cleverness and ruthlessness with which our inner animals pursue natural selection's agenda."

REVIEW: *Booklist* v110 no4 p3 O 15 2013 Bridget Thoreson

REVIEW: *Choice* v51 no10 p1893 Je 2014 R. E. Osborne

REVIEW: *Kirkus Rev* v81 no19 p88 O 1 2013

REVIEW: *Libr J* v138 no11 p62 Je 15 2013 Barbara Hoffert

REVIEW: *N Y Times Book Rev* p15 D 29 2013 SIMON BARON-COHEN

REVIEW: *N Y Times Book Rev* p21 Ja 5 2014

REVIEW: *New Sci* v220 no2940 p50 O 26 2013 Shaoni Bhattacharya

REVIEW: *Publ Wkly* v260 no32 p44 Ag 12 2013

REVIEW: *Sci Am* v310 no5 p78 My 2014 Michael Shermer

BLOOM, TOM.il. While You Were Sleeping. See Murrie, S.

THE BLOOMSBURY ANTHOLOGY OF CONTEMPORARY JEWISH AMERICAN POETRY; xii, 329 p. 2013 Bloomsbury

1. American poetry—20th century 2. American poetry—21st century 3. American poetry—Jewish authors 4. American poetry—Jewish authors—History and criticism 5. Jewish religious poetry, American 6. Poems—Collections 7. Poets, American—Biography

ISBN 9781441125576 (hbk.); 9781441136022 (epub); 9781441183040 (epdf); 9781441188793 (pbk.)

LC 2013-024853

SUMMARY: "This anthology brings together poets whose writings offer . . . insight into Jewish cultural and religious topics and Jewish identity. Featuring established poets as well as representatives of the next generation of Jewish voices, it includes poems by Ellen Bass, Charles Bernstein, Carol V. Davis, Edward Hirsch, Jane Hirshfield, David Lehman, Jacqueline Osherow, Ira Sadoff, Philip Schultz, Alan Shapiro, Jane Shore, Judith Skillman, Melissa Stein, Matthew Zapruder, and many others." (Publisher's note)

REVIEW: *Choice* v51 no8 p1398 Ap 2014 S. L. Kremer

"The Bloomsbury Anthology of Contemporary Jewish American Poetry". "Alphabetically organized and wide-ranging, the collection offers distinctive voices that, the editors write, 'include second-generation Jews, converts, those on the path to conversion, secular Jews, a rabbi, those who have made Aliya . . . poems that both do and do not focus on Jewish themes.'. . . . Helpful to the reader are the biographic-bibliographic head notes for each poet. . . . Unfortunately and inexplicably, the volume lacks a good critical introduction or even 'further reflections' by the editors addressing the thematic and stylistic diversity and complexity of contemporary Jewish American poetry."

BLUEMLE, ELIZABETH. Tap tap boom boom; [by] Elizabeth Bluemle 32 p. 2014 Candlewick Press

1. Children's stories 2. Cities & towns—Juvenile literature 3. Rainbows 4. Thunderstorms 5. Urban life—Juvenile literature

ISBN 0763656968; 9780763656966

LC 2013-943093

SUMMARY: In this children's picture book, by Elizabeth Bluemle and illustrated by G. Brian Karas, "as a thunderstorm rolls in, people of all stripes race down to the subway to get away from the crackling rain and wind. With quirky wordplay and . . . rhymes, Elizabeth Bluemle crystallizes an unexpected moment of community." (Publisher's note)

REVIEW: *Booklist* v110 no14 p84 Mr 15 2014 Lolly Gepson

REVIEW: *Bull Cent Child Books* v67 no7 p350-1 Mr 2014 J. H.

REVIEW: *Horn Book Magazine* v90 no2 p97-8 Mr/Ap 2014 SUSAN DOVE LEMPKE

"Tap Tap Boom Boom." "People of all ethnicities, ages, and sizes (along with their dogs) wait out the storm, while musicians play and pizza and umbrellas are shared. The emphasis here is not on a child's fear of storms but on the excitement of the experience, all finished with 'a surprise in the sky' of a rainbow. [G. Brian] Karas's pictures combine painting, drawing, and photographs to show the grit, energy, and beauty of the urban scene and its amusingly quirky people. This would make a great pair with John Rocco's 'Blackout,' with both books celebrating the urban experience of community."

REVIEW: *Kirkus Rev* v82 no2 p158 Ja 15 2014

REVIEW: *N Y Times Book Rev* p20 Mr 16 2014 BRUCE HANDY

REVIEW: *Publ Wkly* v260 no50 p67 D 9 2013

REVIEW: *SLJ* v60 no4 p112 Ap 2014 Wendy Lukehart

BLUM, HOWARD. Dark invasion; the secret war against the Kaiser's spies; [by] Howard Blum 496 p. 2014 Harper

1. Espionage, German—United States—History—20th century 2. Historical literature 3. Intelligence service 4. Sabotage—United States—History—20th century 5. World War, 1914-1918—Secret service—Germany 6. World War, 1914-1918—Secret service—United States

ISBN 006230755X; 9780062307552 (hardback); 9780062307569 (paperback)

LC 2013-026760

SUMMARY: This book, by Howard Blum, is the "true-life tale of German espionage and terror on American soil during World War I, and the NYPD Inspector who helped uncover the plot. . . . When a 'neutral' United States becomes a trading partner for the Allies, . . . a team of [German] saboteurs . . . devise a series of 'mysterious accidents' using explosives and biological weapons. . . . Police Inspector Tom Tunney, head of the department's Bomb Squad, is assigned the difficult mission of stopping them." (Publisher's note)

REVIEW: *Booklist* v110 no9/10 p37 Ja 1 2014 Connie Fletcher

REVIEW: *Kirkus Rev* v81 no24 p99 D 15 2013

"Dark Invasion 1915: Germany's Secret War Against America". "Terrifically engaging and pertinent tale of the New York City bomb squad that foiled German terrorist plots against the United States at the outbreak of World War I. . . . [Howard Blum] masterly retrieves this largely forgotten, haunting history of Germany's subversive attempts to halt the U.S. ability to send munitions to the Allies fighting against it in Europe. . . . Blum creates some memorable portraits, accompanied by a lively gallery of photos, and keeps the heroic good-versus-evil plot simmering along in a nicely calibrated work of popular narrative history. Instructive, yes, but also as engrossing as good detective fiction."

REVIEW: *Libr J* v139 no3 p117 F 15 2014 Brian Odom

REVIEW: *Publ Wkly* v260 no47 p41-2 N 18 2013

BLUMENTHAL-BARBY, MARTIN. Inconceivable effects; ethics through twentieth-century German literature, thought, and film; [by] Martin Blumenthal-Barby 188 p. 2013 Cornell University Press Cornell University Library

1. Ethics—Germany—History—20th century 2. Ethics in literature 3. Ethics in motion pictures 4. German literature—20th century—History and criticism 5. Philosophical literature

ISBN 9780801478123 (pbk. : alk. paper)

LC 2013-013210

SUMMARY: In this book, Martin Blumenthal-Barby "explores literary and scholarly discussions of overtly negative topics such as doubt, lying, death (by torture), paradoxical justice, violence, terrorism, and enmity in 20th-century German texts (including one film), all in the context of an ethics of literary representation. Authors treated include Hannah Arendt . . . Franz Kafka, [and] Walter Benjamin." (Choice: Current Reviews for Academic Libraries)

REVIEW: *Choice* v51 no5 p837 Ja 2014 J. M. Jeep

"Inconceivable Effects: Ethics Through Twentieth-Century German Literature, Thought, and Film." "The narrative stance responds in surprising, sometimes seemingly illogical ways, especially when the cultural artifacts considered attempt to grasp the 'inconceivable.' . . . . The space created by the distance between narrator and material allows for an 'other' form. The author provides footnotes and helpful, on occasion critically reflective, English translations of quotations throughout. Four of the seven chapters evolved from previously published articles. Specialists familiar with the texts will be able to absorb the layered analysis."

BLUSTEIN, DAVID L.ed. The Oxford handbook of the psychology of working. See The Oxford handbook of the psychology of working

BLYTHE, RONALD. The Time by the Sea; Aldeburgh, 1955-1958; [by] Ronald Blythe 272 p. 2013 Faber & Faber

1. Aldeburgh (England) 2. Britten, Benjamin, 1913-1976 3. English authors 4. Forster, E. M. (Edward Morgan), 1879-1970 5. Memoirs

ISBN 0571290949; 9780571290949

SUMMARY: This book "is about Ronald Blythe's life in Aldeburgh during the 1950s. He had originally come to the Suffolk coast as an aspiring young writer, but found himself drawn into Benjamin Britten's circle and began working for the Aldeburgh Festival. Although befriended by Imogen Holst and by E M Forster, part of him remained essentially solitary, alone in the landscape while surrounded by a stormy cultural sea." (Publisher's note)

REVIEW: *TLS* no5761 p26 Ag 30 2013 PETER J. CONRADI

"The Time By the Sea: Aldeburgh 1955-58." "This short book reads like a much bigger one: each of its eighteen brief chapters chronicles a rich aspect of the time that he lived near the Suffolk coast. . . . [Ronald Blythe's] lyrical gift is never ostentatious or facile. He can be elliptical when this serves his sense of truth. . . . Thus he writes as if you (the reader) were his friend, an insider with the patience to elicit his meaning, and discover a satisfying whole emerging from kaleidoscopic shards and fragments. His style mimes the movement of thought. . . . He is a writer whom we feel we know from his work, and an English institution."

BLYTHE, RONALD. Under a Broad Sky; [by] Ronald Blythe 160 p. 2013 Presbyterian Pub Corp

1. Church year meditations 2. Country life 3. Essay (Literary form) 4. Stour Valley (Cambridgeshire, Essex, & Suffolk, England) 5. Stour Valley (Kent, England)

ISBN 1848254741; 9781848254749

SUMMARY: In this book by Ronald Blythe, "Britain's most admired rural writer chronicles daily life in the Stour valley village, finding beauty and significance in its sheer ordinariness as well as in its many literary, artistic and historic associations. The year takes its shape from the seasons of nature and the feasts and festivals of the Christian year. . . . Literature, poetry, spirituality and memory all merge to create an exquisite series of stories of our times." (Publisher's note)

REVIEW: *TLS* no5777/8 p34 D 20 2013 ROGER CALDWELL

"Under a Broad Sky." "A book consisting of selections from a column called 'Words from Wormington' in the Church Times, written by an elderly Anglican lay canon with a penchant for cats, may not seem to offer the most inviting of prospects. But when you add that the man in question is Ronald Blythe, the renowned author of 'Akenfield,' and one of the best prose stylists in the language, then it becomes another matter. The texts in 'Under a Broad Sky' are arranged by month, and follow the natural seasons, the cycles of agricultural life, and the liturgical year of the Church. . . . The poet that the youthful Blythe once aspired to be resurfaces in a prose that almost demands to be spoken aloud."

BOATRIGHT, TRAVIS ALEXANDRA.ed. The Dollies. See The Dollies

BOAZ, RACHEL E. In search of "Aryan blood"; serology in interwar and National Socialist Germany; [by] Rachel E. Boaz 245 p. 2011 Central European University Press

1. Anthropology—Political aspects—Germany—History—20th century 2. Antisemitism—Germany—History—20th century 3. Biopolitics—Germany—History—20th century 4. Blood groups 5. Historical literature 6. National socialism & science 7. National socialism and medicine—History 8. Racism—History 9. Racism in anthropology—Germany—History—20th century 10. Racism in medicine—Germany—History—20th century 11. Serology—History—20th century 12. Serology—Political aspects—Germany—History—20th century

ISBN 9789639776500 (hardbound)
LC 2011-037678

SUMMARY: This book by Rachel E. Boaz "demonstrates how ambiguous the relationship between eugenics, sero-anthropology and anti-Semitism was in Germany, not least because proeminent German eugenicists and race scientists were Jewish or of Jewish origin." It "Gives an all encompassing interpretation of how the discovery of blood groups in around 1900 galvanised not only old mythologies of blood and origin but also new developments in anthropology and eugenics in the 1920s and 1930s." (Publisher's note)

REVIEW: *Am Hist Rev* v118 no4 p1268-9 O 2013 Mark Walker

"In Search of 'Aryan Blood': Serology in Interwar and National Socialist Germany." "Seroanthropology was a branch of science that sought to identify race through blood. Paradoxically, it was neglected during the Third Reich by the Nazi government, which was keenly interested in being able to identify an individual's race. Rachel E. Boaz's book explains why. . . . Boaz's book begs the question: is this an example of science and medicine trumping ideology? Did Nazi officials, despite being obsessed with the racial sorting of people under their control, reject blood type research because it was not rigorous science? Perhaps a simpler explanation is that seroanthropology failed to win acceptance in the Third Reich because it did not prove useful for Nazi racial policy."

REVIEW: *Choice* v50 no2 p353 O 2012 J. D. Smith

BOBBITT, PHILIP. The Garments of Court and Palace; Machiavelli and the World That He Made; [by] Philip Bobbitt 240 p. 2013 Pgw

1. Historical literature 2. Italian philosophy—History 3. Machiavelli, Niccolò, 1469-1527 4. Political philosophy—History—16th century 5. Political science—Italy—History

ISBN 0802120741; 9780802120748

SUMMARY: "'The Prince,' a political treatise by the Florentine public servant and political theorist Niccolo Machiavelli is widely regarded as the single most influential book on politics—and in particular on the the politics of power—ever written. In this . . . book, [author] Philip Bobbitt explores this often misunderstood work in the context of the time. He describes 'The Prince' as one half of a masterpiece . . . along with Machiavelli's often neglected 'Discourses.'" (Publisher's note)

REVIEW: *Atlantic* v312 no5 p1 D 2013 Michael Ignatieff

REVIEW: *Booklist* v109 no14 p41 Mr 15 2013 Bryce Christensen

REVIEW: *Kirkus Rev* v81 no4 p214 F 15 2013

REVIEW: *Libr J* v137 no17 p59 O 15 2012 Barbara Hoffert

REVIEW: *N Y Rev Books* v61 no10 p50-1 Je 5 2014 Quentin Skinner

"The Garments of Court and Palace: Machiavelli and the World That He Made." "[Author Philip] Bobbitt's contention that Machiavelli has a single great truth to impart to us is carried to somewhat bizarre lengths. . . . One could quibble at Bobbitt's vague remarks about the dying feudal age. . . . Nevertheless, Bobbitt's central thesis about 'The Prince' seems to me to embody a valuable corrective. . . . Most important, Bobbitt is right to emphasize what he describes as Machiavelli's reification of the state as an entity with its own reality that is not to be identified with the personal power of the prince."

REVIEW: *N Y Times Book Rev* p12 Ag 4 2013 GARRY WILLS

BOCK, CAROLINE. Before my eyes; [by] Caroline Bock 320 p. 2014 St. Martin's Griffin

1. Family problems—Fiction 2. Mental illness—Fiction 3. Politics, Practical—Fiction 4. Schizophrenia—Fiction 5. Young adult fiction

ISBN 125003566X; 9781250035660; 9781250045584 (hardback)

LC 2013-032019

SUMMARY: In this book, by Caroline Bock, "Claire has spent the last few months taking care of her six-year-old sister, Izzy, as their mother lies in a hospital bed. Claire believes she has everything under control until she meets a guy online who appears to be a kindred spirit. Claire is initially flattered by the attention but when she meets Max, the shy state senator's son, her feelings become complicated. . . . Lonely and obsessive, Barkley has been hearing a voice in his head." (Publisher's note)

REVIEW: *Booklist* v110 no9/10 p103 Ja 1 2014 Daniel Kraus

REVIEW: *Bull Cent Child Books* v67 no7 p351 Mr 2014 K. C.

"Before My Eyes." "While Barkley and Max are distinctly unlikable in their coarse treatment of others, their intense sadness makes their actions comprehensible in sympathetic ways, particularly when balanced against their responses to Claire. . . . From a narrative standpoint, a near drowning acts as an obvious metaphor for these teens who feel suffocated by their lives; the depressive angst and helplessness felt by the characters are relentless to the point of needing the climactic release of Barkley's mass shooting, which serves to release Max and Claire from their inward focus. . . . Readers who enjoy diving into such deep waters will appreciate the way [Caroline] Bock both pulls them under the waves of depression and mental illness and lifts them out again."

REVIEW: *Kirkus Rev* v81 no24 p151 D 15 2013

"Before My Eyes". "Grim but intelligent. . . . Alternating narratives in the first person by each of the three at times seem to go on a bit too long, given that it's clear from the beginning what the outcome will be. Claire is the most likable, and readers will appreciate her lack of cookie-cutter edges, both in her physical description and in her emotional ups and downs as she takes care of her younger sister largely on her own. Max is less sympathetic, at times frustratingly self-absorbed, but is also clearly struggling. And Barkley, adrift in an increasingly violent storm of mental illness, is deeply troubling. Gripping, disturbing and nuanced."

REVIEW: *Publ Wkly* v260 no45 p73 N 11 2013

REVIEW: *SLJ* v60 no2 p100 F 2014 Elizabeth Jakubowski

REVIEW: *Voice of Youth Advocates* v36 no6 p56 F 2014 Kate Neff

BOCK, DENNIS. Going home again; [by] Dennis Bock 272 p. 2013 Alfred A. Knopf

1. Brothers—Fiction 2. Divorced men—Fiction 3. FICTION—Family Life 4. FICTION—Literary 5. FICTION—Psychological

ISBN 1400044634; 9781400044634 (hardback); 9781400096107 (paperback)
LC 2012-050903

SUMMARY: Author Dennis Bock's book is a "story of a man studying the suddenly confusing shape his life has taken, and why, and what his responsibilities—as a husband, a father, a brother, and an uncle—truly are. . . . But two tragic events (one long past, the other very much in the present) finally threaten to destroy everything he's ever believed in." (Publisher's note)

REVIEW: *Kirkus Rev* v81 no14 p103 Jl 15 2013

REVIEW: *N Y Times Book Rev* p13 S 1 2013 ELLIOTT HOLT

"Going Home Again." "[Dennis] Bock's prose in 'Going Home Again' is looser and less precise. . . . The bland sentences prevent these characters from coming fully to life. Bock can be equally vague in his descriptions of Charlie's inner life. . . . Charlie's colloquial voice is appealing, but it often saps his story of urgency. And the structure of the book undermines its power and narrative momentum. . . . The landscape of memory and regret is fertile ground for Bock, even if he mined it more successfully in his first two novels."

REVIEW: *Publ Wkly* v260 no23 p49 Je 10 2013

REVIEW: *Quill Quire* v79 no7 p26 S 2013 Emily Donaldson

"Going Home Again." "The novel is narrated retrospectively by Charlie, who after almost two decades in Spain has come home to Toronto, where he hopes to expand the chain of language schools he runs and gain perspective on his foundering marriage. The move is bittersweet: Charlies's tween daughter, Ava, still in Madrid with her mother, deeply resents his departure. Returning home also necessitates a reckoning with his older brother, Nate. . . . [Author Dennis] Bock's writing is what's generally referred to as 'transparent.' . . . 'Going Home Again' consistently hits the sweet spot between understatement and intense readability."

BOD, RENS.ed. The making of the humanities. See The making of the humanities

BODDEN, VALERIE. Bryce Harper; [by] Valerie Bodden 21 p. 2014 Creative Education

1. Athletes—Education 2. Baseball players—United States—Biography—Juvenile literature 3. Biographies
ISBN 9781608184743 (hardcover : alk. paper)
LC 2013-014551

SUMMARY: This book on baseball player Bryce Harper by Valerie Bodden is part of the Big Time book series. Harper "was so good at baseball that he got his GED instead of finishing school so that he could jump to the pros by age 19. However, his team, the Washington Nationals, continue to pay for his college classes." (Booklist)

REVIEW: *Booklist* v110 no4 p44 O 15 2013 Daniel Kraus

"Bryce Harper," "Carrie Underwood," and "Rihanna." "The Big Time series offers celebrity bios to early middle-grade students but delivers them in a package with enough visual sophistication for somewhat older reluctant readers as well. Bright, oversize photos dominate the spare, glossy layout, while just a few lines of uninflected (though fawning) text move along the seven short chapters. . . . Though Rihanna's parents' domestic violence is mentioned, oddly her own well-publicized bouts with Chris Brown are ignored in favor of sales figures, awards, and semi-provocative photos. . . . A map of each subject's home state is always featured, as is a closing page of quotes. A very appealing celeb series."

BODDEN, VALERIE. Carrie Underwood; [by] Valerie Bodden 21 p. 2014 Creative Education

1. Biographies 2. Children's nonfiction 3. Country musicians—United States—Biography—Juvenile literature 4. Music industry
ISBN 9781608184767 (hardcover : alk. paper)
LC 2013-014552

SUMMARY: This book on performer Carrie Underwood, by Valerie Bodden, is part of the Big Time book series. "After winning 'American Idol' in 2005," Underwood "became a country-music icon, despite her dream of working in TV news." The book features "a map of [Underwood's] home state" as well as "a closing page of quotes." (Booklist)

REVIEW: *Booklist* v110 no4 p44 O 15 2013 Daniel Kraus

"Bryce Harper," "Carrie Underwood," and "Rihanna." "The Big Time series offers celebrity bios to early middle-grade students but delivers them in a package with enough visual sophistication for somewhat older reluctant readers as well. Bright, oversize photos dominate the spare, glossy layout, while just a few lines of uninflected (though fawning) text move along the seven short chapters. . . . Though Rihanna's parents' domestic violence is mentioned, oddly her own well-publicized bouts with Chris Brown are ignored in favor of sales figures, awards, and semi-provocative photos. . . . A map of each subject's home state is always featured, as is a closing page of quotes. A very appealing celeb series."

BODDEN, VALERIE. Dragonflies; [by] Valerie Bodden 2013 Creative Education

1. Children's nonfiction 2. Damselflies 3. Dragonflies—Juvenile literature 4. Insect anatomy 5. Insects—Juvenile literature
ISBN 9781608183548
LC 2013-010464

SUMMARY: This book on dragonflies by Valerie Bodden is part of the "Creepy Creatures" series. "Each introduction includes where the insect or arachnid might be found; a general description of size, shape, and body parts; and an overview of its life cycle; and every book concludes with a simple craft project. 'Dragonflies' illustrates the wide variety of these flying insects." (Booklist)

REVIEW: *Booklist* v110 no11 p54 F 1 2014 Kathleen Isaacs

"Dragonflies," "Fleas," "Mites." "Striking photographs distinguish the well-named 'Creepy Creatures' series. On each spread, a page of simple text and cutout pictures against a white background sits opposite a full-bleed photograph. These enlarged close-ups give readers a good look at details of the animals' body parts or eggs. (These images aren't usually identified further, and no scale is given.) . . . For the youngest readers, these titles offer an appealing combination of high-interest subjects and very basic information."

BODDEN, VALERIE. Fleas; [by] Valerie Bodden 2014 Creative Education

1. Children's nonfiction 2. Flea circuses 3. Fleas—Behavior 4. Fleas—Juvenile literature 5. Insect anatomy
ISBN 9781608183555 (hardcover : alk. paper)

LC 2013-009795

SUMMARY: This book on fleas by Valerie Bodden is part of the "Creepy Creatures" series. "Each introduction includes where the insect or arachnid might be found; a general description of size, shape, and body parts; and an overview of its life cycle; and every book concludes with a simple craft project. . . . Bodden makes a strong connection to humans through mentions of the plague and flea circuses." (Booklist)

REVIEW: *Booklist* v110 no11 p54 F 1 2014 Kathleen Isaacs

"Dragonflies," "Fleas," "Mites." "Striking photographs distinguish the well-named 'Creepy Creatures' series. On each spread, a page of simple text and cutout pictures against a white background sits opposite a full-bleed photograph. These enlarged close-ups give readers a good look at details of the animals' body parts or eggs. (These images aren't usually identified further, and no scale is given.) . . . For the youngest readers, these titles offer an appealing combination of high-interest subjects and very basic information."

BODDEN, VALERIE. Mites; [by] Valerie Bodden 24 p. 2014 Creative Education

1. Children's nonfiction 2. Insect anatomy 3. Insects—Juvenile literature 4. Mites—Behavior 5. Mites—Juvenile literature

ISBN 9781608183579 (hardcover : alk. paper)

LC 2013-009754

SUMMARY: This book on mites by Valerie Bodden is part of the "Creepy Creatures" series. "Each introduction includes where the insect or arachnid might be found; a general description of size, shape, and body parts; and an overview of its life cycle; and every book concludes with a simple craft project. . . . 'Mites' features microscope images and emphasizes the abundance of these common but typically invisible neighbors." (Booklist)

REVIEW: *Booklist* v110 no11 p54 F 1 2014 Kathleen Isaacs

"Dragonflies," "Fleas," "Mites." "Striking photographs distinguish the well-named 'Creepy Creatures' series. On each spread, a page of simple text and cutout pictures against a white background sits opposite a full-bleed photograph. These enlarged close-ups give readers a good look at details of the animals' body parts or eggs. (These images aren't usually identified further, and no scale is given.) . . . For the youngest readers, these titles offer an appealing combination of high-interest subjects and very basic information."

REVIEW: *SLJ* v60 no4 p179 Ap 2014 Denise Moore

BODDEN, VALERIE. Rihanna; [by] Valerie Bodden 21 p. 2014 Creative Education

1. Biographies 2. Family violence 3. Music industry 4. Singers—Biography—Juvenile literature

ISBN 9781608184798 (hardcover : alk. paper)

LC 2013-014411

SUMMARY: This book on performer Rihanna, by Valerie Bodden, is part of the Big Time book series. "Though Rihanna' parents' domestic violence is mentioned, . . . her own well publicized bouts with Chris Brown are ignored in favor of sales figures, awards, and semi-provocative photos." The book includes "a closing page of quotes." (Booklist)

REVIEW: *Booklist* v110 no4 p44 O 15 2013 Daniel Kraus

"Bryce Harper," "Carrie Underwood," and "Rihanna." "The Big Time series offers celebrity bios to early middle-grade students but delivers them in a package with enough visual sophistication for somewhat older reluctant readers as well. Bright, oversize photos dominate the spare, glossy layout, while just a few lines of uninflected (though fawning) text move along the seven short chapters. . . . Though Rihanna's parents' domestic violence is mentioned, oddly her own well-publicized bouts with Chris Brown are ignored in favor of sales figures, awards, and semi-provocative photos. . . . A map of each subject's home state is always featured, as is a closing page of quotes. A very appealing celeb series."

REVIEW: *Voice of Youth Advocates* v37 no1 p95 Ap 2014 Brenna Shanks

BODEEN, S. A. The Fallout; [by] S. A. Bodeen 336 p. 2013 Feiwel & Friends

1. Brothers—Fiction 2. Corporations—Corrupt practices—Fiction 3. Genetic engineering—Fiction 4. Kidnapping—Fiction 5. Young adult fiction

ISBN 0312650116; 9780312650117

SUMMARY: This book by is a sequel to author S. A. Bodeen's novel "The Compound." "Eli and his family lived in an underground shelter they called the Compound for six years. They thought they were the only survivors of a nuclear attack, but when Eli learned that it was all a twisted experiment orchestrated by his tech-visionary father, he broke the family out. His father died trying to keep them imprisoned. Now, the family must readjust to life in the real world." (Publisher's note)

REVIEW: *Booklist* v110 no1 p114 S 1 2013 Cindy Welch

REVIEW: *Horn Book Magazine* v89 no5 p87 S/O 2013 CLAIRE E. GROSS

"The Fallout." "As in the first book, [S. A.] Bodeen excels at\ using complex and deeply uneasy family dynamics to escalate the corporate and psychological intrigue, driving tensions higher as the story unfolds. Unfortunately, the medical conspiracy subplot that fuels the latter half of the book hinges on several contrived twists and is ultimately far less compelling than the family drama. Nevertheless, the family members' respective reactions to the disorientation of re-entering the real world are distinct and realistic. . . . Crisp, atmospheric first-person narration never wavers from Eli's blunt, anxious perspective, allowing the book to sustain immediacy and draw empathy, even in its less successful plot twists."

REVIEW: *Voice of Youth Advocates* v36 no4 p77 O 2013 Ann McDuffie

BODINE, CATHY. Assistive technology and science; 304 p. 2013 SAGE Publications, Inc.

1. Access technologies 2. Assistive computer technology 3. Computerized self-help devices for people with disabilities 4. Disability studies 5. Reference books 6. Self-help devices for people with disabilities

ISBN 1412987989; 9781412987981 (cloth)

LC 2012-035564

SUMMARY: Author Cathy Bodine's book "explores issues involving assistive technology engineering and science." The book "incorporates links from varied fields making up Disability Studies as volumes examine topics central to the lives of individuals with disabilities and their families. With a balance of history, theory, research, and application, specialists set out the findings and implications of research and practice for others whose current or future work involves the care and/or study of those with disabilities, as well as for the disabled themselves." (Publisher's note)

REVIEW: *Booklist* v109 no15 p37 Ap 1 2013 Ken Black

REVIEW: *Choice* v51 no1 p48-9 S 2013 P. E. Reese

"Assistive Technology and Science." "[Author Cathy] Bodine (Univ. of Colorado) has had a distinguished career in the assistive technology field, and is thus well qualified to author this work. Part of the eight-volume 'SAGE Reference Series on Disability', it is an excellent introduction to this ever-evolving field. . . . Throughout the text, the author provides understandable descriptions of the numerous acronyms at their first usage. She also clearly explains the responsibility of all parties involved in the field, and the best ways to navigate the assessment and health care bureaucratic systems. . . . Overall, the book is a good resource for students interested in the disability field, and might influence some to redirect their studies to this area."

BODOR, ÁDÁM. The sinistra zone; [by] Ádám Bodor 200 p. 2013 New Directions Publishing Corporation

1. Fathers & sons—Fiction 2. Political fiction 3. Runaway teenagers—Fiction 4. Speculative fiction 5. Totalitarianism—Fiction

ISBN 081121978X; 9780811219785 (alk. paper)

LC 2012-050353

SUMMARY: In this book, "when Andrei, a wayfarer and 'simple harvester of fruit,' arrives in the Ukrainian border town of Dobrin in search of his runaway adopted son he becomes entangled in the bizarre social and political world of the isolated village. Dobrin borders the Sinistra military zone (a pun on 'sinister' and the real breakaway territory of Transnistria) where Andrei's son supposedly lives." (Publishers Weekly)

REVIEW: *N Y Times Book Rev* p30 S 1 2013 Alison McCulloch

"Through the Night," "The Matchmaker, the Apprentice, and the Football Fan," and "The Sinistra Zone." "[Stig] Saeterbakken entices the reader along some dark paths from which, in the end, there is no easy escape. . . . Even in this grim tale, Zhu [Wen] manages to inject some of the sly humor that suffuses these stories, which, unlike some of the lives he describes, are never dreary. . . . Like everything else in this cryptic novel, its main character is a bit of a mystery. . . . Adding to its perplexity is the book's structure: 15 overlapping chapters that could double as independent short stories."

BOGDAN, RADU J. Mindvaults; sociocultural grounds for pretending and imagining; [by] Radu J. Bogdan xxi, 236 p. 2013 MIT Press

1. Imagination 2. Imagination in children 3. Scientific literature 4. Social cognitive theory 5. Social perception 6. Social psychology

ISBN 9780262019118 (hardcover: alk. paper)

LC 2012-036428

SUMMARY: "This book explores the uniquely human capacity to escape current perceptions, actions, and emotions into the realm of past, future, or even impossible worlds. The author's use of the term 'mindvaulting' thus highlights not only the nature of this mental process, but the heights in cognition that it confers upon humans in relation to other primates. [Radu J.] Bogdan considers why such a remarkable ability exists and how it evolved." (Quarterly Review of Biology)

REVIEW: *Choice* v51 no2 p357 O 2013 J. Bailey

BOGIN, NINA.tr. The Illiterate. See Kristof, A.

BOHEMIANS; a Graphic Anthology; 304 p. 2014 Verso

1. Bohemianism—United States—Comic books, strips, etc 2. Bohemianism in literature 3. Counterculture—United States—Comic books, strips, etc 4. Graphic nonfiction 5. Modern art

ISBN 1781682615; 9781781682616 (pbk.)

LC 2013-047893

SUMMARY: This book, edited by Paul Buhle and David Berger "is the graphic history of . . . the nineteenth-century countercultures that came to define the bohemian lifestyle." It "spanned both sides of the Atlantic, ranging from Walt Whitman to Josephine Baker, and from Gertrude Stein to Thelonius Monk." The book covers "the rise of Greenwich Village, the multiracial and radical jazz world, and West Coast and Midwest bohemians, among other scenes." (Publisher's note)

REVIEW: *Booklist* v110 no16 p39 Ap 15 2014 Ray Olson

REVIEW: *Kirkus Rev* v82 no4 p233 F 15 2014

"Bohemians: A Graphic History". "Brooklyn-based writer [David] Berger and prolific graphic-arts editor [Paul] Buhle . . . make fine selections in this thoughtful successor to Harvey Pekar's 'The Beats: A Graphic History' (2009). . . . All of the art is bold and visually distinct; fittingly, many of the artists have deep roots in the underground comics scene. . . . A terrific appraisal of culture's gypsies, tramps and thieves, worthy of the editors' judgment: 'Obituaries for bohemia have, in short, always been premature.'"

BOIANJIU, SHANI. The people of forever are not afraid; a novel; [by] Shani Boianjiu 338 p. 2012 Hogarth

1. Arab-Israeli conflict—Fiction 2. Friendship—Fiction 3. Military education—Israel—Fiction 4. Psychological fiction 5. Women soldiers—Israel—Fiction

ISBN 0307955958 (hardcover); 9780307955951 (hardcover); 9780307955968 (ebook)

LC 2012-008962

SUMMARY: This novel, by Shani Boianjiu, follows three Israeli women soldiers. "Yael, Avishag, and Lea grow up together in a tiny, dusty Israeli village. . . . When they are conscripted into the army, their lives change in unpredictable ways, influencing the women they become and the friendship that they struggle to sustain. . . . They drill, constantly, for a moment that may never come. They live inside that single, intense second just before danger erupts." (Publisher's note)

REVIEW: *Booklist* v109 no1 p44 S 1 2012 Leah Strauss

REVIEW: *Kirkus Rev* v80 no14 p1424 Jl 15 2012

REVIEW: *Kirkus Rev* v80 no10 p6 My 15 2012

REVIEW: *Libr J* v137 no15 p60-1 S 15 2012 Gwen Vredevoogd

REVIEW: *Publ Wkly* v259 no28 p34 Jl 9 2012

REVIEW: *World Lit Today* v87 no5 p55-79 S/O 2013

"The Contract Killer," "Nazim Hikmet: The Life and Times of Turkey's World Poet," and "The People of Forever Are Not Afraid." "[Benny] Andersen presents absurdist approaches to questions of life and death, never losing his sense of humor or his lighthearted turn of phrase. . . . [Mutlu Konuk] Blasing is a prolific translator of Hikmet's work, and she incorporates elements of literary scholarship into her investigation of his life. . . . Shani Boianjiu's gripping debut novel illustrates the lives of three Israeli girls who grow up together after they are conscripted into the army."

BOIGER, ALEXANDRA.il. Poor Doreen. See Lloyd-Jones, S.

BOIGER, ALEXANDRA.il. Tallulah's Nutcracker. See Singer, M.

BOILEAU, JOHN. Old enough to fight; Canada's boy soldiers in the First World War; [by] John Boileau 448 p. 2013 James Lorimer & Company

1. Child soldiers—Canada—Biography 2. Historical literature 3. World War, 1914-1918—Participation, Juvenile 4. World War, 1914-1918—Personal narratives, Canadian 5. World War, 1914-1918—Sources
ISBN 1459405412 (bound); 9781459405417 (bound)
LC 2012-517799

SUMMARY: This book by Dan Black and John Boileau describes how "Between 15,000 and 20,000 underage youths, some as young as ten, signed up to fight in Canada's armed forces in the First World War. They served in the trenches alongside their elders, and fought in all the major battles; Ypres, the Somme, Passchendaele, Vimy Ridge, and the rest. Many were injured or suffered psychological wounds. Many died." (Publisher's note)

REVIEW: *TLS* no5780 p27 Ja 10 2014 NATHAN M. GREENFIELD

"Old Enough to Fight: Canada's Boy Soldiers in the First World War." "An unknown number of under-eighteen-year-olds joined the Canadian army during the First World War, primed by the 'Boy's Own' annual and youth's feeling of invincibility. However, as Dan Black and John Boileau show in this examination of the war from a unique angle, several of the boys explained their reasons for joining up in political and high patriotic terms. . . . Our revulsion at the thought of child soldiers aside, this book raises a vexed question. Given these youths' prowess in battle, . . . is our conception of what might be called 'late childhood' relevant to those who fought the Great War?"

BOISSEAU, TRACEY JEAN.ed. Gendering the fair. See Gendering the fair

BOK, DEREK. Higher education in America; [by] Derek Bok x, 479 p. 2013 Princeton University Press

1. Education, Higher—Aims and objectives—United States—History 2. Education, Higher—United States—History 3. Educational literature 4. Professional education—United States—History 5. Universities and colleges—United States—History
ISBN 9780691159140 (hardcover: alk. paper)
LC 2013-013887

SUMMARY: In this book, former Harvard University president Derek Bok discusses various issues related to U.S. higher education. These include "'stagnating graduation rates'; attrition in graduate school; the increased importance of research in the sciences; and "the hazards of commercialization." His purview extends from the historic roots of the American college to the impact of technology and expansion to overseas locations." (Publishers Weekly)

REVIEW: *Choice* v51 no9 p1650 My 2014 D. Yalof

"Higher Education in America". "With more than two decades of service as president of Harvard University behind him, Derek Bok has views on higher education that must be taken seriously. . . . In what should be characterized as 'part reference work, part polemic,' no aspect of modern colleges and universities escapes his criticism, including more recent developments such as massive open online courses and for-profit colleges. While issues in undergraduate education encompass more than half the book, Bok directs frustration at the state of affairs in medical schools, law schools, and business schools as well."

BOLAÑO, ROBERTO, 1953-2003. The insufferable gaucho; 164 2010 New Directions

1. Literature—History & criticism 2. Short stories—By individual authors 3. Short stories—Collections 4. Spanish fiction—Translations into English 5. Spanish short stories—Translations into English
ISBN 0-8112-1716-7; 978-0-8112-1716-3
LC 2010—21112

SUMMARY: Written by Roberto Bolaño, "The stories in 'The Insufferable Gaucho'—unpredictable and daring, highly controlled yet somehow haywire—might concern a stalwart rat police detective investigating terrible rodent crimes, or an elusive plagiarist, or an elderly Argentine lawyer giving up city life for an improbable return to the family estate on the Pampas, now gone to wrack and ruin." (Publisher's note)

REVIEW: *New Statesman* v143 no5205 p51 Ap 11 2014 Ollie Brock

REVIEW: *TLS* no5792 p20 Ap 4 2014 MICHAEL GORRA

"The Insufferable Gaucho." "Roberto Bolaño's stories appear at first glance to share almost nothing with each other. 'The Insufferable Gaucho' was the final book he put together before his death in 2003, and its five tales and two essays offer little consistency of subject or theme, character or setting. What holds his work together is instead the pace and structure of his sentences. . . . 'The Insufferable Gaucho' concludes with two essays. One concerns the limitations of literature itself, its inability to provide any sense of healing in the face of physical failure; the other is an enraged account of the world of the bestseller. They earn their anger."

BOLLETER, JULIAN.ed. Made in Australia. See Made in Australia

BOLLIG, MICHAEL.ed. Pastoralism in Africa. See Pastoralism in Africa

BOLTON, J. L. Money in the medieval English economy 973-1489; [by] J. L. Bolton xv, 317 p. 2012 Manchester University Press

1. Coinage 2. Credit 3. Historical literature 4. Mon-

ey—England—History—To 1500
ISBN 0719050391 (hbk.); 0719050405 (pbk.); 9780719050398 (hbk.); 9780719050404 (pbk.)
LC 2012-406809

SUMMARY: This book by J. L. Bolton "integrates information about the medieval English monetary system, both coinage and credit, into a broader study of medieval economic transformations, and the author's conclusions concerning the money supply are . . . framed in the context of current debates." (English Historical Review)

REVIEW: *Engl Hist Rev* v129 no536 p179-81 F 2014 Richard Britnell

"Money in the Medieval English Economy, 973-1489" and "Mints and Money in Medieval England". "The survey of monetary history throughout the book is both well informed and much fuller and more richly elaborated than it would be in a survey aiming to give due weight to all the variables in play. Both in general, and in much of the detailed discussion about minting, monetary circulation and credit, the book will serve as an excellent introduction to an extensive literature. . . . Martin Allen's full and authoritative study of mints and money . . . makes an outstanding contribution to our knowledge of minting as a productive activity. . . . Allen's book, in short, is a primary reference work for the history of medieval English coinage."

REVIEW: *History* v99 no337 p679-80 O 2014 Philip Slavin

BOND, CYNTHIA. Ruby; a novel; [by] Cynthia Bond 336 p. 2014 Hogarth
1. African Americans—Fiction 2. First loves—Fiction
ISBN 0804139091; 9780804139090 (hardback)
LC 2013-033049

SUMMARY: In this book, "the citizens of Liberty, TX, have always watched Ruby Bell, first as a small child playing in the Piney Woods . . . then as a beautiful young woman on her way to a new life in New York City . . . and finally as she wanders aimlessly down the red dirt roads upon her return . . muttering incoherently. . . . Childhood friend Ephram Jennings decides to reach out to Ruby, but his doing so angers his sister Celia and mobilizes his church brethren to intervene." (Library Journal)

REVIEW: *Booklist* v110 no12 p30 F 15 2014 Joanne Wilkinson

"Ruby." "Ephraim Jennings . . . has been in love with the beautiful Ruby Bell ever since childhood. But Ruby has been so badly used by the men in her small African American town of Liberty,Texas, that she flees for New York City as soon as she is able, in search of the mother who abandoned her. When Ruby's best friend dies, Ruby returns home, only to succumb to the bad memories that haunt her still. . . . In her first novel, [Cynthia] Bond immerses readers in a fully realized world, one scarred by virulent racism and perverted rituals but also redeemed by love. Graphic in its descriptions of sexual violence and suffering, this powerful, explosive novel is, at times, difficult to read, presenting a stark, unflinching portrait of dark deeds and dark psyches."

REVIEW: *Kirkus Rev* v82 no4 p227 F 15 2014

"Ruby". "The echoes of Alice Walker and Toni Morrison are clear, but [Cynthia] Bond is an accomplished enough writer to work in a variety of modes with skill and insight. . . . Some of the more intense passages of the novel lapse into purple prose, and the horror of Ruby's experience (which intensifies as the novel moves along) makes her closing redemption feel somewhat pat. But the force of Ruby's character, and Bond's capacity to describe it, is undeniable. A very strong first novel that blends tough realism with the appealing strangeness of a fever dream."

REVIEW: *Libr J* v138 no18 p67 N 1 2013 Barbara Hoffert

REVIEW: *Libr J* v139 no6 p78 Ap 1 2014 Jennifer B. Stidham

REVIEW: *Publ Wkly* v261 no4 p164 Ja 27 2014

BOND, GEOFFREY. Lord Byron's Best Friends; From Bulldogs to Boatswain and Beyond; [by] Geoffrey Bond 120 p. 2013 Nick McCann Associates Ltd
1. Byron, George Gordon Byron, Baron, 1788-1824 2. Dogs 3. English poets—19th century—Biography 4. Historical literature 5. Pets—History
ISBN 0951689118; 9780951689110

SUMMARY: "It is not widely known that man's best friend held a precious place in Byron's affections. This book by renowned Byron enthusiast, Geoffrey Bond, sheds new light on the poet's canine love affairs: from bulldogs to Boatswain and beyond. There are Newfoundlands, Mastiffs, Terriers, Greyhounds, and even a Poodle!" (Publisher's note)

REVIEW: *TLS* no5796 p22 My 2 2014 MIKA ROSS-SOUTHALL

"The Vampyre Family: Passion, Envy, and the Curse of Byron" and "Lord Byron's Best Friends: From Bulldogs to Boatswain and Beyond." "The effect of Byron was not just felt by women; the Romantic age was feverishly obsessed with him. But those who came closest to the poet and his fame discovered that what they had hoped would improve their own lives turned out to destroy them, as Andrew McConnell Stott shows us in his biography, 'The Vampyre Family: Passion, envy and the curse of Byron.' . . 'Lord Byron's Best Friends: From bulldogs to Boatswain and beyond' also concentrates on peripheral characters in Byron's life. . . . [Author Geoffrey] Bond narrates the story of Byron's life plainly, with help from paintings."

BONE, KEVIN. Lessons from modernism; environmental design considerations in 20th century architecture, 1925-1970; [by] Kevin Bone 224 p. 2014 Monacelli Press
1. Architectural literature 2. Le Corbusier, 1887-1965 3. Modern architecture—20th century 4. Niemeyer, Oscar, 1907-2012 5. Sustainable architecture
ISBN 9781580933841
LC 2013-955485

SUMMARY: This book "examines twentieth-century modern architecture, including buildings by Le Corbusier and Oscar Niemeyer, through the lens of sustainability." It "demonstrates how these architects integrated environmental concerns into their designs. Buildings are located across the United States, Central and South America, Cuba, Japan and more--and includes houses, art centers, commercial buildings, and civic buildings." (Publisher's note)

REVIEW: *Art Am* v102 no1 p51 Ja 2014

"Lessons From Modernism: Environmental Design Strategies in Architecture, 1925-1970," "The Filming of Modern Life: European Avant-Garde Film of the 1920s," and "Anywhere or Not at All: Philosophy of Contemporary Art." "Twenty-five buildings completed between 1925 and 1970 provide insight into how architects like Oscar Niemeyer and

Le Corbusier dealt with environmental issues and influenced green building today. . . . Five classic experimental films by artists such as Hans Richter and Salvador Dalí offer contrasting--and sometimes self-contradictory--views of modernity. . . . Drawing from philosophers like [Immanuel] Kant and the German Romantics and artists like Sol Le Witt and the Atlas Group, [Peter] Osborne critically redefines what's 'contemporary' about contemporary art."

BONER, PATRICK J. Kepler's cosmological synthesis; astrology, mechanism and the soul; [by] Patrick J. Boner 224 p. 2013 Brill

1. Astronomy—History 2. Biography (Literary form) 3. Cosmology—History 4. Scientists—Biography

ISBN 9789004246089 (hardback : alk. paper); 9789004246096 (e-book)
LC 2013-013707

SUMMARY: This book by Patrick J. Boner presents a biography of scientist Johannes Kepler. "Spanning the course of his career, this book" examines "Kepler's vitalistic views and their central place in his world picture. It challenges our view of Kepler as a nascent mechanical philosopher who fell back on an older form of physics." (Publisher's note)

REVIEW: *Choice* v51 no6 p1030 F 2014 K. L. Schick

"Kepler's Cosmological Synthesis: Astrology, Mechanism and the Soul." "It is well documented with an enormous bibliography and is rich with detail, presenting a man whose thinking and interaction with fellow workers reflected a then-popular view of the universe as being analogous to a living object, yet also analogous to a machine. . . . Even astrology found its way into [Johannes] Kepler's thinking and was easily absorbed. This is a fascinating, unusually well-done biography, although the details sometimes become a bit heavy. It both illuminates Kepler as a man and helps readers understand the scientific and philosophic perspectives of the period in which he lived."

BONIKOWSKI, WYATT. Shell shock and the modernist imagination; the death drive in post-World War I British fiction; [by] Wyatt Bonikowski 192 p. 2012 Ashgate

1. Death instinct in literature 2. English fiction—20th century—History and criticism 3. Historical literature 4. Modernism (Literature)—Great Britain 5. Psychic trauma in literature 6. World War, 1914-1918—Literature and the war

ISBN 9781409444176 (hardcover : alk. paper); 9781409444183 (ebook)
LC 2012-035217

SUMMARY: This book on post-WWI British fiction examines "the representation of war trauma through the techniques of narration and figurative language that are used in the autobiographies of combatants and in medical case studies. The relationship between the narratives of physicians and those of novelists is . . . essential to the cohesion of this study, which focuses on Ford Madox Ford, Rebecca West and Virginia Woolf." (Times Literary Supplement)

REVIEW: *TLS* no5756 p26 Jl 26 2013 LAUREN ARRINGTON

"Shell Shock and the Modernist Imagination: The Death Drive in Post-World War I British Fiction." "The boundary between literature and history, fiction and non-fiction is blurred by Wyatt Bonikowski's attention to the representation of war trauma through the techniques of narration and figurative language that are used in the autobiographies of combatants and in medical case studies. The relationship between the narratives of physicians and those of novelists is implicit but is nonetheless essential to the cohesion of this study. . . . As 'Shell Shock and the Modernist Imagination' progresses, Bonikowski's arguments gain momentum, coalescing in his powerful point that in the aesthetic sublimation of the death drive, modernist fiction can 'sustain the pleasures of life'."

BONIWELL, ILONA.ed. The Oxford handbook of happiness. See The Oxford handbook of happiness

BONNEFOY, YVES. The Arriere-pays; [by] Yves Bonnefoy 165 p. 2012 Univ of Chicago Pr

1. Art—Psychological aspects 2. Authorship 3. Books & reading 4. Illustrated books 5. Travel

ISBN 0857420267; 9780857420268

SUMMARY: This illustrated book was written by Yves Bonnefoy. "The essay's five chapters, accompanied by forty or so illustrations, weave together recollections of particular places--in Italy and Greece, but also India and Japan--and memories of artistic or literary works that seem imbued with a similar atmosphere and promise." It "moves from the origins and lineaments of the writer's obsession within elsewheres to the stratagems he devised to free himself from their grip." (Times Literary Supplement)

REVIEW: *Choice* v50 no5 p880 Ja 2013 M. Gaddis Rose

REVIEW: *TLS* no5767 p12 O 11 2013 MICHAEL SHERINGHAM

"The Arrière-Pays." "A magnificent English translation of [Yves Bonnefoy's] crucial prose work, 'L'Arrière-pays,' dating from 1972 when the poet was approaching fifty. The translation is the work of another poet, Stephen Romer. . . . 'L'Arrière-pays' . . . is an unclassifiable combination of autobiographical self-questioning, travel narrative and metaphysical rumination. But it is also a picture book, and the numerous reproductions of Renaissance, Baroque, and some modem paintings, as well as photographs of sites, monuments and landscapes, are not simply illustrative, but the work's very core. . . . Bonnefoy's prose style in 'L'Arrière-pays' sets a challenge that Romer's translation meets with resounding success."

BONNER, C. D. I Talk Slower Than I Think; An Antidote to Helicopter Parenting; [by] C. D. Bonner 138 p. 2012 C. D. Bonner

1. Alabama—Social life & customs 2. Children 3. Georgia—Social life & customs 4. Memoirs 5. Southern States—Social life & customs

ISBN 098579500X; 9780985795009

SUMMARY: This memoir by C. D. Bonner "is made up of 52 true short stories" relating incidents from his childhood in Alabama and Georgia in the 1960s and 1970s. "In just a few of his tales, a child must dodge bobcats on the way to the bathroom; he has a biscuit that is so hard firemen must remove it, and he wades through a treasure of Confederate money. Listen to tales of his second cousin, twice (forcibly) removed." (Publisher's note)

REVIEW: *Kirkus Rev* v81 no20 p311 O 15 2013

REVIEW: *Kirkus Rev* v81 no24 p17 D 15 2013

"I Talk Slower Than I Think". "A debut memoir that bursts

with Southern flavor and charm. Bonner recounts the lively antics of his rural Georgia childhood in the 1960s and '70s in this pleasant book. . . . Throughout, the author captures the slow, easy pace of Southern living, dwelling on the day-to-day activities of a young boy who's encouraged to find adventure all around him. . . . Overall, these brief anecdotes are candid, humorous and enjoyable. The author's ability to see the bright side of any situation makes for a pleasant, undemanding read, and he recreates these stories of his siblings and extended family with loving detail, in straightforward, precise prose."

BONNETT, ALASTAIR. Off the Map; [by] Alastair Bonnett 320 p. 2014 Aurum Press Ltd

1. Curiosities & wonders 2. Extinct cities 3. Islands 4. Journalism 5. Travelers' writings

ISBN 1781312575; 9781781312575

SUMMARY: In this book, author "Alastair Bonnett goes to some of the most unexpected, offbeat places in the world to reinspire our geographical imagination. Bonnett's remarkable tour includes moving villages, secret cities, no man's lands, and floating islands. He explores places as disorienting as Sandy Island, an island included on maps until just two years ago despite the fact that it never existed." (Publisher's note)

REVIEW: *New Sci* v222 no2967 p49 My 3 2014 Bob Holmes

"Off the Map." "In his latest book, 'Off the Map,' [author Alastair Bonnett] makes a compelling case for the role of a sense of place through an exploration of its absence. His shtick is to take us on a tour of 47 geographical aberrations, most of which lack some element that helps create a complete locality. . . . Now and then Bonnett's scattershot structure coalesces into a more obvious thematic progression. . . . Over the course of the book, Bonnett's 'failed' places gradually make a powerful point about the ways today's society . . . falls short of building an authentic sense of place."

REVIEW: *TLS* no5808 p3-4 Jl 25 2014 NICHOLAS CRANE

BONONNO, ROBERT.tr. Speech begins after death. See Speech begins after death

THE BOOK OF JEZEBEL; an illustrated encyclopedia of lady things; 300 p. 2013 Grand Central Pub.

1. Encyclopedias & dictionaries 2. Satire 3. Women in popular culture 4. Women's encyclopedias & dictionaries 5. Women's history

ISBN 9781455502806 (hardcover)

LC 2013-939252

SUMMARY: Edited by Anna Holmes, "With contributions from the writers and creatives who give the site its distinctive tone and broad influence, 'The Book of Jezebel' is an encyclopedia of everything important to the modern woman. Running the gamut from Abzug, Bella and Baby-sitters Club, The to Xena, Yogurt, and Zits, and filled with entertaining sidebars and arresting images, this is a must-read for the modern woman." (Publisher's note)

REVIEW: *N Y Times Book Rev* p19 D 22 2013 MOIGNON FOGARTY

"The Book of Jezebel: An Illustrated Encyclopedia of Lady Things," "The Horologicon: A Day's Jaunt Through the Lost Words of the English Language," "Wordbirds: An Irreverent Lexicon for the 21st Century." "'The Book of Jezebel' is drawn from the energetic contributors to the Jezebel.com blog, and its editor, Anna Holmes . . . takes care to note that what appears to be a colorful encyclopedia is actually a work fo both fact and opinion. . . . Once you pick up 'The Horologicon' it's hard to put down. As a devotee of useful tips, I approached Mark Forsyth's book with skepticism. . . . Liesl Schillinger's 'Wordbirds' embraces the theme of birds. . . . While 'The Horologicon' shines a light on the past, 'Wordbirds' does the same for our times."

BOOKER, MATTHEW MORSE. Down by the bay; San Francisco's history between the tides; [by] Matthew Morse Booker 278 p. 2013 University of California Press

1. Historical literature 2. Human ecology—California—San Francisco—History 3. Human ecology—California—San Francisco Bay Area—History 4. Land use—California—San Francisco—History 5. Land use—California—San Francisco Bay Area—History 6. Nature—Effect of human beings on—California—San Francisco—History 7. Nature—Effect of human beings on—California—San Francisco Bay Area—History

ISBN 9780520273207 (cloth : acid-free paper)

LC 2013-000528

SUMMARY: This book, "focusing on human inhabitation of [San Francisco Bay] since Ohlone times . . . reveals the ongoing role of nature in shaping that history. From birds to oyster pirates, from gold miners to farmers, from salt ponds to ports, this is the first history of the San Francisco Bay and Delta as both a human and natural landscape. It offers . . . context for current discussions over the best management and use of the Bay in the face of sea level rise." (Publisher's note)

REVIEW: *Choice* v51 no4 p707-8 D 2013 K. Edgerton

"Down by the Bay: San Francisco's History Between the Tides." "San Francisco Bay is the most ecologically and culturally important estuary on the West coast. Historian [Matthew Morse] Booker . . . seeks to uncover the many layers of environmental manipulation of the mudflats and salt marshes surrounding the region. . . . No matter how hard humans have tried to eradicate the natural inconveniences of building a major city on shifting tidal flats and salt marshes, nature has proven stubborn. The author concludes optimistically that 'the bay is more accessible and cleaner than it has been for nearly a century' as a result of more aggressive environmental regulations and imaginative public policy."

BOONE, BOB. Write Through Chicago; Learn About a City by Writing About a City; [by] Bob Boone 180 p. 2013 Amika Press

1. Authorship 2. Chicago (Ill.)—History 3. Common Core State Standards 4. Revision (Writing process) 5. Textbooks

ISBN 1937484157; 9781937484156

SUMMARY: This book by Mark Henry Larson and Bob Boone presents "a writing manual based on the city of Chicago. . . . Their guide covers nearly a dozen of the nationwide Common Core State Standards for writing, including orienting students to the rhetorical forms of argument, exposition and narrative, and to disciplines like planning, revising and rewriting. The authors approach their task by presenting students with a series of archived headlines from different pivotal points in Chicago history." (Kirkus Reviews)

REVIEW: *Kirkus Rev* v82 no1 p91 Ja 1 2014

REVIEW: *Kirkus Rev* v81 no24 p355 D 15 2013

"Write Through Chicago: Learn About a City By Writing About A City". "Students are carefully guided through the use of educator Benjamin Bloom's Taxonomy of Learning Objectives, first using so-called lower-level thinking (knowledge, comprehension and application) and then higher-level thinking (analysis, synthesis and evaluation). The headlines are well-chosen to represent a wide range of interests—everything from the social reforms of Jane Addams and Hull House to the poetry of Carl Sandburg and the prose of Studs Terkel—and the concept of making writing exercises come alive through local history is an inspired one. A stimulating, well-presented approach to getting students interested in writing."

BOOSS, JOHN. To catch a virus; [by] John Booss 350 p. 2013 ASM Press

1. Historical literature 2. History, 19th Century 3. History, 20th Century 4. History, 21st Century 5. Virology—history 6. Virology—methods 7. Virus Diseases—diagnosis 8. Virus Diseases—history

ISBN 1555815073; 9781555815073 (pbk. : alk. paper)

LC 2012-035227

SUMMARY: This book, by John Booss and Marilyn J. August, addresses "historical discoveries that defined viruses and their roles in infectious diseases over a century of developments, epidemics, and molecular advances, and continuing into the 21st century." It "describes how scientists applied revolutionary technologies, studying viruses, first in animal models and tissue culture and progressing to molecular and genetic techniques." (Publisher's note)

REVIEW: *Choice* v51 no2 p289 O 2013 M. S. Kainz

"To Catch a Virus." "'To Catch a Virus' by [authors John] Booss . . . and [Marilyn J.] August . . . is a thorough history of the development of diagnostic virology. Each chapter focuses on a particular group of viruses or a particular research technique as the basis for a discussion of an aspect of virology. The readable text successfully describes how advances in laboratory techniques aided in scientific understanding of particular viruses and how study of a particular virus was key in the development of an important laboratory technique. . . . A strong point of the book is its rich descriptions of the people involved in the advancement of virology."

BOOTH, LAWRENCE.ed. Wisden Cricketers' Almanack 2013. See Wisden Cricketers' Almanack 2013

BOOTH, MICHAEL. Eating dangerously; why the government can't keep your food safe— and how you can; [by] Michael Booth 200 p. 2013 Rowman & Littlefield Publishers, Inc.

1. Food—Safety measures 2. Food adulteration and inspection—Government policy—United States

ISBN 1442222662; 9781442222663 (cloth: alk. paper)

LC 2013-037125

SUMMARY: This book, by Michael Booth and Jennifer Brown, "explains to the American consumer how their food system works—and more importantly how it doesn't work. It also dishes up course after course of useful, friendly advice gleaned from the cutting-edge laboratories, kitchens and courtrooms where the national food system is taking new shape. Anyone interested in knowing more about how their food makes it from field and farm to store and table will want the inside scoop." (Publisher's note)

REVIEW: *Booklist* v110 no11 p8 F 1 2014 Barbara Jacobs

"Eating Dangerously: Why the Government Can't Keep Your Food Safe . . . and How You Can". "More than a little Michael Moore-type scary is this eye-opening exposé of foods, grocery shopping, and government oversight in America. Two Denver Post journalists, who investigated the 2011 deadly listeria outbreak (32 killed by eating cantaloupes), use those same skills of inquiry in preparing an account that every U.S. consumer should read. . . . Most important . . . is the diagnostic and prevention section, keeping families safe (and, yes, sane)."

REVIEW: *Choice* v52 no2 p294 O 2014 M. Kroger

REVIEW: *Libr J* v139 no7 p109 Ap 15 2014 Janet Crum

BORDEN, LOUISE, 1949-. Baseball is...; [by] Louise Borden 48 p. 2013 Margaret K. McElderry Books, an imprint of Simon & Schuster Children's Pub. Division

1. Baseball—Juvenile literature 2. Baseball—United States—History—Juvenile literature 3. Children's poetry 4. Picture books for children 5. Women baseball players

ISBN 141695502X; 9781416955023 (hardcover)

LC 2013-008621

SUMMARY: This picture book presents a free-verse tribute to baseball. Author Louise Borden "enumerates the elements of the game, including ballparks and fans, plays and players. . . . A fold-out page gives special attention to Babe Ruth, Jackie Robinson, and Roberto Clemente. The author also mentions the 'long ago' Negro leagues and the women's league; and notes baseball's ability to bring diverse people together. Emphasis is placed on patriotic elements." (School Library Journal)

REVIEW: *Bull Cent Child Books* v67 no6 p304 F 2014 Elizabeth Bush

"Baseball Is. . ." "Unfortunately, the title amounts to little more than lists of definitions, observations and descriptions. . . . Occasionally, though, a verse rises well above the quotidian with a genuine flash of poetic power hitting: 'Baseball is a crescendo of joy that fills the stands./ And baseball is/ sudden silence./ The hush of error.' [Raúl] Colón's grainy, atmospheric paintings, though often prone to chaotic composition, manage to capture more of the passion of the game, particularly as experienced by fans and stadium staff."

REVIEW: *Kirkus Rev* v82 no3 p155 F 1 2014

REVIEW: *Publ Wkly* v261 no6 p88 F 10 2014

REVIEW: *SLJ* v60 no1 p111 Ja 2014 Marilyn Taniguchi

BORDERLINE SLAVERY; Mexico, United States, and the human trade; xxi, 275 p. 2012 Ashgate

1. Foreign workers—Mexican-American Border Region 2. Human smuggling—Mexican-American Border Region 3. Human trafficking—Mexican-American Border Region 4. Illegal aliens—Mexican-American Border Region 5. Slave labor—Mexican-American Border Region 6. Sociology literature

ISBN 9781409439684 (hbk. : alk. paper); 9781409439691 (ebook)

LC 2012-012823

SUMMARY: Edited by Susan Tiano and Moira Murphy-Aguilar, this book addresses "human trafficking in the US-Mexico borderlands as a regional expression of a pressing global problem, 'Borderline Slavery' sheds light on the contexts and causes of trafficking, offering policy recommendations for addressing it that do justice to border communities' complex circumstances. This book focuses on both sexual and labor trafficking." (Publisher's note)

REVIEW: *Contemp Sociol* v42 no5 p765 S 2013

"Borderline Slavery: Mexico, the United States, and the Human Trade." "'In Borderline Slavery: Mexico, United States, and the Human Trade,' Susan Tiano and Moira Murphy-Anguilar compile an excellent collection of essays that explore human trafficking between the United States and the Mexican border. . . . 'Borderline Slavery' presents an impressive collection that sheds light on one of the most pressing human rights tragedies of the twenty-first century. This book poses important challenges surrounding the modern human slave trade, yet still manages to offer cogent policy suggestions that may prevent and mitigate human trafficking."

BORG, TODD. Tahoe chase; an Owen Mckenna mystery thriller; [by] Todd Borg 351 p. 2013 Thriller Press

1. Detective & mystery stories 2. Serial murder investigation 3. Ski resorts 4. Skis & skiing 5. Wilderness areas—Fiction
ISBN 9781931296212 (alk. paper)
LC 2013-938829

SUMMARY: In this book, part of the Owen McKenna Mystery Thriller series, "while McKenna scrambles to find the killer and bring some peace to Joe and the other victims, he discovers that Cynthia has one remaining friend, Simone Bonnaire. . . . Thinking he's helping her escape, McKenna convinces Simone to take a grueling ski trip through the desolate wilderness, only to realize he's put her squarely in the path of the murderer, and he has no way to warn her. From that point forward, the chase is on." (Kirkus Reviews)

REVIEW: *Kirkus Rev* v81 no24 p59 D 15 2013

"Tahoe Chase: An Owen McKenna Mystery Thriller". "This is the 11th installment of the Owen McKenna thriller series, so at this stage, [Todd] Borg has solid command of his character and a fully realized sense of his personality, which readers will enjoy. The landscape is also beautifully crafted, perhaps leading readers to feel like they're curled by the fire as the snow comes down. The prose can be clunky at times, though, with bits of cliché—'Cynthia's heart beat so bad that it hurt'—but the pace builds nicely and doesn't let up once it gathers steam. A worthy follow-up in the long, enjoyable series of McKenna mysteries."

BORMAN, TRACY. Witches; A Tale of Sorcery, Scandal & Seduction; [by] Tracy Borman 320 p. 2013 Jonathan Cape

1. Flowers, Margaret 2. Great Britain—History—Stuarts, 1603-1714 3. Historical literature 4. Trials (Witchcraft)—History—17th century 5. Witchcraft—History
ISBN 0224090569; 9780224090568

SUMMARY: This book by Tracy Borman focuses on the 17th-century witchcraft trial of "Margaret and Phillippa Flower and their mother Joan." (History Today) "The case is among those which constitute the European witch craze of the 15th-18th centuries, when suspected witches were burned, hanged, or tortured by the thousand." (Publisher's note)

REVIEW: *Hist Today* v63 no10 p62 O 2013 MALCOLM GASKILL

"Witches: A Tale of Sorcery, Scandal and Seduction in Jacobean England." "[An] engaging yet flawed account of the witches of Belvoir Castle. . . . [Tracy] Borman guides us through their social and political world with brio, tracing ambitions and intrigues. . . . Borman, a royal curator whose other books are about English queens, has done some proper research. . . . Borman also writes elegantly and confidently and tells a good story, even if her contextualising digressions are distracting and sometimes look like padding. . . . The real problem with this book is that the author is not an expert in the history of witchcraft. . . . Too often she plays emotively to readers' assumptions, when the truth, widely available in the secondary literature she cites, was infinitely more complex."

BORNSTEIN, MARC H.ed. The infant mind. See The infant mind

BOROUJERDI, MEHRZAD.ed. Mirror for the Muslim prince. See Mirror for the Muslim prince

BOSLAUGH, SARAH. Health care systems around the world; a comparative guide; [by] Sarah Boslaugh 608 p. 2013 Sage Publications

1. Cross-Cultural Comparison 2. Delivery of Health Care—organization & administration 3. Health Policy 4. Health Status 5. Medical literature 6. World Health
ISBN 9781452203126 (cloth)
LC 2013-009279

SUMMARY: This book compares health care data "from 193 countries. Each country is objectively analyzed in two- to three-page country profiles using standardized categories including major health issues, access to health care, insurance, governments' roles in health care, and costs of hospitalization. Content comes from agencies such as the World Health Organization, Doctors without Borders and the United Nations Development Programme." (Choice: Current Reviews for Academic Libraries)

REVIEW: *Choice* v51 no6 p979 F 2014 S. Leslie

"Health Care Systems Around the World: A Comparative Guide." "[Sarah] Boslaugh . . . a statistical analyst and journalist, takes on the challenging task of compiling health care data from 193 countries. . . . The author acknowledges the difficulty in making comparisons between countries of vastly differing populations and economic resources; however, with a standardized template, the comparisons are credible. . . . Although the book has a bibliography, it lacks footnotes. Sources may be cited in-text as, 'According to . . .'; however, occasionally readers will not be able to ascertain the original source for the data. A very useful and informative book."

BOSSLER, BEVERLY. Courtesans, concubines, and the cult of female fidelity; gender and social change in China, 1000-1400; [by] Beverly Bossler ix, 464 p. 2013 Harvard University Asia Center

1. Concubinage—China—History—To 1500 2. Courtesans—China—History—To 1500 3. Historical literature 4. Man-woman relationships—China—History—To 1500 5. Sex role—China—History—To 1500 6.

Wives—China—History—To 1500 7. Women—China—Social conditions
ISBN 9780674066694
LC 2012-031807

SUMMARY: Written by Beverly Bossler, "This book traces changing gender relations in China from the tenth to fourteenth centuries by examining three critical categories of women: courtesans, concubines, and faithful wives. . . . Courtesan culture profoundly affected Song social and family life, as entertainment skills became a defining feature of a new model of concubinage and entertainer-concubines increasingly became mothers of literati sons." (Publisher's note)

REVIEW: *Choice* v51 no2 p327-8 O 2013 B. A. Elman

"Courtesans, Concubines, and the Cult of Female Fidelity: Gender and Social Change in China, 1000-1400." "[Author Beverly] Bossler . . . describes how Chinese men and women carved out space for themselves in a political world that Song dynasty literati both made and ruined. The limits on the social mobility of women, and the social mobility of men, were decisively loosened and redeployed outside the framework of medieval Chinese aristocratic ideals. . . . The regularization and moralization of concubinage, for example, reflected a growing concern for elite women whose status precipitously declined as Song family values faced an unprecedented revaluation in Mongol rimes."

BOSTRIDGE, MARK. The Fateful Year; England 1914; [by] Mark Bostridge 432 p. 2014 Viking

1. Great Britain—Social conditions—20th century 2. Historical literature 3. Nineteen fourteen, A.D. 4. Women—Great Britain—History 5. World War, 1914-1918—Great Britain
ISBN 0670919217; 9780670919215

SUMMARY: "'The Fateful Year' by Mark Bostridge is the story of England in 1914. War with Germany, so often imagined and predicted, finally broke out when people were least prepared for it. . . . With the coming of war, England is beset by rumour and foreboding. There is hysteria about German spies, fears of invasion, while patriotic women hand out white feathers to men who have failed to rush to their country's defence." (Publisher's note)

REVIEW: *New Statesman* v143 no1 p52-3 Ja 10 2014 Tom Gatti

REVIEW: *TLS* no5782 p24 Ja 24 2014 MARTIN PUGH

"The Fateful Year: England 1914." "[Author Mark] Bostridge tackles his subject not by means of a narrative, though the book proceeds by chronological stages, but thematically. Each chapter opens a fresh theme usually by means of an episode or case study. . . . Bostridge's treatment makes for a readable and often illuminating picture of England in 1914. . . . 'The Fateful Year' very effectively captures popular expectations and reactions as the country moved from peace into war, especially in those chapters dealing with recruitment, the wartime hysteria about German spies and the impact of the early casualties."

BOTTUM, JOSEPH. An anxious age; The post-Protestant ethic and the spirit of America; [by] Joseph Bottum 2014 Image

1. Liberals 2. Puritans 3. Social commentary 4. United States—Politics & government 5. United States—Social life & customs

SUMMARY: This book by Joseph Bottum argues that "We live in a profoundly spiritual age. . . . Huge swaths of American culture are driven by manic spiritual anxiety and relentless supernatural worry. Radicals and traditionalists, liberals and conservatives, together with politicians, artists, environmentalists, followers of food fads, and . . . television commentators: America is filled with people frantically seeking confirmation of their own essential goodness." (Publisher's note)

REVIEW: *Commonweal* v141 no12 p35-6 Jl 11 2014 Martin E. Marty

REVIEW: *Natl Rev* v65 no7 p38-9 Ap 21 2014 MARY EBERSTADT

"An Anxious Age: The Post-Protestant Ethic and the Spirit of America." "A strikingly original diagnosis of the national moral conditions, 'An Anxious Age' bears comparison for significance and scope to only a handful of recent seminal works. Deftly analytical and also beautifully written, it has the head of Christopher Lasch and the heart of Flannery O'Connor. Anyone wishing to chart the deeper intellectual and religious currents of this American time, let along anyone who purports to navigate them for the rest of the public, must first read and reckon with 'An Anxious Age.'"

BOUCHA, HENRY CHARLES. Henry Boucha, Ojibwa, Native American Olympian; [by] Henry Charles Boucha 482 p. 2013 Henry Boucha, Ojibwa, Native American Olympian

1. Detroit Red Wings (Hockey team) 2. Memoirs 3. National Hockey League 4. Native American hockey players 5. Olympic athletes
ISBN 0615717446; 9780615717449

SUMMARY: This book by Henry Charles Boucha, Sr. presents an "account of what it was like reaching for the highest echelons of professional hockey and what he found once he arrived. . . . He was often . . . made to feel inferior because of his proud heritage. . . Nevertheless, he persevered . . . [and] went on to win a spot on the 1972 Silver Medal U.S. Olympic hockey team. After that, it didn't take long for the NHL to come calling." (Kirkus Reviews)

REVIEW: *Kirkus Rev* v82 no3 p50 F 1 2014

"Henry Boucha, Ojibwa, Native American, Olympian"."This is Boucha's personal, affecting story of stuffing oversized ice skates with newspaper and using homemade hockey sticks to bat around crushed soda cans until his young ears literally almost fell off from frostbite. . . . The purity of such transcendental moments is rendered all the more sublime when juxtaposed with the ugly racism and personal tragedies that also profoundly impacted Boucha, a Native American. . . . A compelling sports memoir from an intriguing athlete with a lot on his mind and even more in his heart."

BOUCHER, GEOFF. Adorno reframed; interpreting key thinkers for the arts; [by] Geoff Boucher x, 163 p. 2012 I.B. Tauris

1. Art and philosophy 2. Modernism (Aesthetics)—Sweden 3. Music—Sweden—20th century—History and criticism 4. Philosophical literature 5. Postmodernism—Sweden
ISBN 1848859473; 9781848859470
LC 2012-277300

SUMMARY: In this book, Geoff Boucher "attempts to reconfigure [Theodor] Adorno's austere image by presenting a reading of his aesthetic theory that allows space for the expressive human subject, political critique, and a limited form of unrealized (and ultimately unrealizable) utopianism. . . . Boucher's situates Adorno within the context of Expressionism, explicates his aesthetic theory, and then shows how Adorno's thought can be helpful." (Choice)

REVIEW: *Choice* v51 no4 p725 D 2013 J. L. Miller

"Adorno Reframed: Interpreting Key Thinkers for the Arts." "Concisely, if sometimes a bit densely, [Geoff] Boucher situates [Theodor] Adorno within the context of Expressionism, explicates his aesthetic theory, and then shows how Adorno's thought can be helpful when considering thinkers like Jürgen Habermas, artists like Anselm Kiefer, as well as postmodernism and feminism. Boucher is at his best explaining Adorno's understanding of how progressive art avoids explicit political commitment while simultaneously rejecting previous forms of artistic expression. . . . Much here is commendable, especially if the reader is disinclined to wade through Adorno's own formidable writings, and Boucher does a good job of situating his reading of Adorno in the context of the literature."

BOUDREAU, JAMES H. Exporting Prosperity; Why the U.S. Economy May Never Recover...; [by] James H. Boudreau 102 p. 2013 NanoShoppes com

1. Balance of trade 2. Economics literature 3. Solar energy—Economic aspects 4. United States—Economic conditions 5. United States—Economic policy
ISBN 0989897303; 9780989897303

SUMMARY: In this book, "a frustrated business owner offers his analysis of the problems facing the United States economy and a range of possible solutions. In this overview of the American political economy, [James H.] Boudreau's debut work targets the trade deficit as one of the primary drivers of recent economic downturns, though government inefficiency, unreasonable consumer expectations and other factors share the blame." (Kirkus Reviews)

REVIEW: *Kirkus Rev* v82 no2 p382 Ja 15 2014

"Exporting Prosperity: Why the U.S. Economy May Never Recover". "While the author often notes in textual asides that he wants to avoid political discussions in his book, libertarians will appreciate many of his recommendations. Boudreau introduces interesting concepts and ideas, like refocusing on local manufacturing, but readers may have trouble following the arguments through their unpolished presentation. . . . The author is clearly passionate about his subject, but his enthusiasm often inhibits the creation of a logical and well-written argument. An unpolished economic prescription for the United States based on data, speculation and anecdotes."

BOUDRY, MAARTEN.ed. Philosophy of pseudoscience. See Philosophy of pseudoscience

BOUIS, ANTONINA W.tr. Definitely maybe. See Strugatskiĭ, A. N.

BOULUD, DANIEL. Daniel; my french cuisine; [by] Daniel Boulud 416 p. 2013 Grand Central Life & Style

1. Celebrity chefs 2. Cookbooks 3. French cooking 4. Lyonnais (France) 5. Photography of food
ISBN 145551392X; 9781455513925 (hardcover)
LC 2013-939294

SUMMARY: In this cookbook, chef Daniel Boulud focuses on "his love of French food. From coming of age as a young chef to adapting French cuisine to American ingredients and tastes, Daniel Boulud reveals how he expresses his culinary artistry at Restaurant Daniel." The book includes "more than 75 signature recipes, plus an additional 12 recipes Boulud prepares at home for his friends on more casual occasions." (Publisher's note)

REVIEW: *N Y Times Book Rev* p20-1 D 8 2013 WILLIAM GRIMES

"Cooking From the Heart: My Favorite Lessons Learned Along the Way," "Pok Pok: Food and Stories From the Streets, Homes, and Roadside Restaurants of Thailand," and "Daniel: My French Cuisine." "John Best has an interesting life story to tell in 'John Besh: Cooking From the Heart.' . . . There are a few too many usual-suspect recipes, but Besh makes an engaging guide. . . . By Andy Ricker with J.J. Goode, . . . As a tutorial on Thai cuisine and its principal regional styles, 'Pok Pok' can't be beat. . . . In 'Daniel: My French Cuisine' . . . , Daniel Boulud . . . conducts a guided tour of his life and the parts of France he know best. . . . From there it's a giant leap to the . . . drop-dead elegant dishes from Daniel that take up about half the book."

REVIEW: *Publ Wkly* v260 no29 p22-32 Jl 22 2013 NATALIE DANFORD

REVIEW: *Publ Wkly* v260 no28 p164 Jl 15 2013

BOURKE, JOANNA. The story of pain; from prayer to painkillers; [by] Joanna Bourke 416 p. 2014 Oxford University Press

1. Historical literature 2. Medical history 3. Pain—History 4. Pain management 5. Pain measurement
ISBN 9780199689422 (hardback)
LC 2013-948402

SUMMARY: Written by Joanna Bourke, "Focusing on the English-speaking world, this book tells the story of pain since the eighteenth century, addressing fundamental questions about the experience and nature of suffering over the last three centuries. How have those in pain interpreted their suffering—and how have these interpretations changed over time? How have people learnt to conduct themselves when suffering?" (Publisher's note)

REVIEW: *Kirkus Rev* v82 no15 p43-4 Ag 1 2014

REVIEW: *Libr J* v139 no12 p98 Jl 1 2014 Talea Anderson

REVIEW: *London Rev Books* v36 no16 p6-9 Ag 21 2014 Gavin Francis

REVIEW: *New Sci* v222 no2973 p49 Je 14 2014 Simon Ings

"The Story of Pain: From Prayer to Painkillers." "Joanna Bourke's 'The Story of Pain' conveys sensations with wincing precision and an admirable humanity. But her real business is to show us how we 'handle' pain, and how doctors acquired the controversial habit [of tending] . . . to treat ailments, not patients. . . . To get rid of [pain] would be to get rid of sensation altogether. It is to Bourke's credit that she offers us this consolation. . . . Her study of how we think and talk about pain also reminds us that science is not all experiment. There is real knowledge to be gained in close sympathetic observation."

REVIEW: *TLS* no5812/5813 p26-7 Ag 22 2014 ANDREW

SCULL

BOUTAVANT, MARC.il. Ghosts. See Goldie, S.

BOVA, BEN. Transhuman; [by] Ben Bova 368 p. 2014 Tor Books

1. Biologists—Fiction 2. Cancer—Patients—Fiction 3. Genetic engineering—Fiction 4. Grandparent and child—Fiction 5. Suspense fiction

ISBN 9780765332936 (hardback)

LC 2013-026346

SUMMARY: In this book, "iconoclastic cellular biologist Luke Abramson is determined to save his dying eight-year-old granddaughter, Angela, with his cutting-edge treatment for cancer. Inconveniently, his process is not yet approved for use on humans, and he's stymied by the objections of Angela's parents. When Luke and Angela vanish, FBI special agent Jerry Hightower is assigned to recover them." (Publishers Weekly)

REVIEW: *Booklist* v110 no14 p57 Mr 15 2014 Rebecca Gerber

"Transhuman." "When [Luke's] granddaughter Angela, is diagnosed with an aggressive and fatal brain cancer, he kidnaps her, convinced that he can save her with his new therapy. He takes her and her attending physician across the country to a private lab, where Angela can be treated, all the while dodging the FBI. . . . An exciting and action-packed book from start to finish, this could easily be turned into a movie. Plausible twenty-first-century medical research, the bond between a grandfather and his granddaughter, and political power all serve to make this book a must-read for those who enjoyed 'The Fugitive.' A combination of thriller, adventure, and drama will enthrall."

REVIEW: *Kirkus Rev* v82 no5 p227 Mr 1 2014

REVIEW: *Libr J* v139 no5 p99 Mr 15 2014 Megan M. McArdle

REVIEW: *Publ Wkly* v261 no5 p41 F 3 2014

BOVE, LORELAY.il. No slurping, no burping! See LaReau, K.

BOW, ERIN. Sorrow's knot; [by] Erin Bow 368 p. 2013 Arthur A. Levine Books

1. Fate and fatalism—Fiction 2. Fate and fatalism—Juvenile fiction 3. Identity (Philosophical concept)—Juvenile fiction 4. Identity (Psychology)—Juvenile fiction 5. Identity—Fiction 6. Knots and splices—Juvenile fiction 7. Magic—Fiction 8. Magic—Juvenile fiction 9. Speculative fiction

ISBN 0545166667; 9780545166669 (hardcover : alk. paper); 9780545166676 (pbk. : alk. paper); 9780545578004 (ebook)

LC 2013-007855

SUMMARY: In this book, by Erin Bow, "the dead do not rest easy. Every patch of shadow might be home to something hungry, something deadly. Most of the people of this world live on the sunlit, treeless prairies. But a few carve out an uneasy living in the forest towns, keeping the dead at bay with wards made from magically knotted cords. The women who tie these knots are called binders. And Otter's mother, Willow, is one of the greatest binders her people have ever known." (Publisher's note)

REVIEW: *Booklist* v110 no4 p49 O 15 2013 Cindy Welch

REVIEW: *Bull Cent Child Books* v67 no4 p203-4 D 2013 K. Q. G.

REVIEW: *Horn Book Magazine* v90 no2 p111 Mr/Ap 2014 ANITA L. BURKAM

"Sorrow's Knot." "The spirits of the dead are sketched with tactical vagueness, heightening the hair-raising sensation of being surrounded by unknown dangers. The magic of yarn and knots mixes the familiar and exotic to good effect, while the setting gestures toward Native American culture without caricaturing it. As Otter and Kestrel set out to find Cricket in defiance of their elders' rules, their journey takes them to Mad Spider's own territory, where, face-to-face with the oldest of the White Hands, they will either appease her--or be turned into White Hands themselves."

REVIEW: *Kirkus Rev* v81 no19 p101 O 1 2013

REVIEW: *Publ Wkly* v260 no41 p62 O 14 2013

REVIEW: *Quill Quire* v79 no7 p35 S 2013 Shannon Ozirny

REVIEW: *Quill Quire* v79 no5 p19 Je 2013 Dory Cerny

REVIEW: *SLJ* v60 no1 p79 Ja 2014 Sabrina Carnesi

REVIEW: *Voice of Youth Advocates* v36 no6 p68 F 2014 Sarah Cofer

BOWEN, BETSY.il. Plant a pocket of prairie. See Plant a pocket of prairie

BOWER, JOE.ed. De-testing and de-grading schools. See De-testing and de-grading schools

BOWERS, TIM.il. Snow Dog, Go Dog. See Heiligman, D.

BOWERSOCK, G. W. Throne of Adulis; Red Sea wars on the eve of Islam; [by] G. W. Bowersock xix, 181 p. 2013 Oxford University Press

1. Christianity and other religions—Judaism—History—6th century 2. Historical literature 3. Jews—Yemen (Republic)—Himyar—History—6th century 4. Judaism—Relations—Christianity—History—6th century

ISBN 0199739323; 9780199739325

LC 2012-023593

SUMMARY: This book by G. W. Bowersock describes how "just prior to the rise of Islam in the sixth century AD, southern Arabia was embroiled in a violent conflict between Christian Ethiopians and Jewish Arabs. Though little known today, this was an international war that involved both the Byzantine Empire, which had established Christian churches in Ethiopia, and the Sasanian Empire in Persia, which supported the Jews in what became a proxy war against its long-time foe Byzantium." (Publisher's note)

REVIEW: *Choice* v51 no2 p332 O 2013 M. Rautman

REVIEW: *Hist Today* v64 no1 p62-3 Ja 2014 Peter Frankopan

"The Throne of Adulis: Red Sea Wars on the Eve of Islam." "This remarkable book tells the astonishing story of how rising tensions in this region were sparked by the mass persecution of the Christian community in Najran and across the kingdom of Himyar . . . in the 520s. . . . The display of scholarship is formidable, backed up by command of recent research in this region and field. . . . This slender volume is an important work. It does not always do itself justice--there are sections . . . that are rather turgid to all but the specialist reader. It is also somewhat understated, delivering its argument with little fanfare, which might make the significance of the conclusions easy to overlook."

REVIEW: *N Y Rev Books* v60 no12 p35-7 Jl 11 2013 Peter Brown

REVIEW: *TLS* no5775 p9-10 D 6 2013 PETER THONEMANN

BOWLES, NORMA.ed. Staging social justice. See Staging social justice

BOYD, DANAH. It's complicated; the social lives of networked teens; [by] Danah Boyd 296 p. 2014 Yale University Press

1. Information technology—Social aspects 2. Internet and teenagers 3. Online social networks 4. Social commentary 5. Teenagers—Social life and customs—21st century

ISBN 0300166311; 9780300166316 (clothbound: alk. paper)

LC 2013-031950

SUMMARY: Author Danah Boyd "uncovers some of the major myths regarding teens' use of social media. She explores tropes about identity, privacy, safety, danger, and bullying. Ultimately, Boyd argues that society fails young people when paternalism and protectionism hinder teenagers' ability to become informed, thoughtful, and engaged citizens through their online interactions. Yet despite an environment of rampant fear-mongering, Boyd finds that teens often find ways to engage and to develop a sense of identity." (Publisher's note)

REVIEW: *Choice* v51 no12 p2276 Ag 2014 Y. Kiuchi

REVIEW: *Kirkus Rev* v82 no1 p137 Ja 1 2014

REVIEW: *Libr J* v139 no3 p120 F 15 2014 Janet Ingraham Dwyer

REVIEW: *N Y Times Book Rev* p25 Ap 27 2014 ALISSA QUART

REVIEW: *New Sci* v221 no2961 p51 Mr 22 2014 Simon Ings

"Parentology: Everything You Wanted to Know About the Science of Raising Children But Were Too Exhausted to Ask" and "It's Complicated: The Social Lives of Networked Teens." "For all its insightful, funny, fully researched, conscientiously cited, . . . approach to science and statistics, what really powers 'Parentology' is a species of loving rage. The numbers teach us a great deal. . . . However, . . . Love, care, interest and empathy . . . render most of the measures discussed in this book profoundly unimportant. . . . [Author Danah] Boyd has little time for technological determinism. Her fieldwork with . . . parents and their kids reveals the fault is not in our computers but in ourselves. . . . And she marshals a huge body of sociological evidence."

REVIEW: *New Statesman* v143 no5205 p44-5 Ap 11 2014 Helen Lewis

REVIEW: *Publ Wkly* v260 no50 p59-60 D 9 2013

BOYD, HILARY. Thursdays in the park; [by] Hilary Boyd 336 p. 2013 Quercus

1. Grandparents—Fiction 2. Infidelity (Couples) 3. Love stories 4. Marriage—Fiction 5. Older women—Fiction

ISBN 1623650968; 9781623650957 (ebk.); 9781623650964 (pbk.)

LC 2013-937918

SUMMARY: In this book, by Hilary Boyd, "the year Jeanie turns 60 marks a decade since her reliable but controlling husband, George, started sleeping in a separate room and refused to tell her why. Adrift in a marriage that is now more comfortable routine than partnership, she focuses instead on the health foods store she owns . . . [and] her granddaughter Ellie, whom she takes to the park on Thursdays. It's there that Jeanie and Ellie meet Ray and his grandson Dylan." (Kirkus Reviews)

REVIEW: *Booklist* v110 no4 p30-2 O 15 2013 Susan Maguire

"Thursdays in the Park." "Jeanie Lawson runs a modestly successful health food store in London and has been married for more than 30 years. Her husband, George, is looking forward to retiring to the country, but as Jeanie turns 60, she's not quite ready to be put out to pasture. . . . This first novel is heartfelt without being angst-ridden and full of likable characters (even the unlikable ones warm up), and readers of women's fiction will relate to Jeanie. A warm, tender novel about a woman finally finding a place of her own."

REVIEW: *Kirkus Rev* v81 no18 p257 S 15 2013

REVIEW: *Libr J* v138 no14 p95 S 1 2013 Jane Jorgenson

BOYD, WILLIAM, 1952-. Solo; a James Bond novel; [by] William Boyd 336 p. 2013 HarperCollins

1. Africa—Fiction 2. Assassins—Fiction 3. Bond, James (Fictitious character) 4. Civil war 5. Spy stories

ISBN 0062223127; 9780062223128

SUMMARY: In this continuation of Ian Fleming's James Bond series, written by William Boyd, "Bond's mission takes him to a fictional West African nation called Zanzarim. With the discovery of oil deposits in the Zanza River Delta, the local Fakassa tribe has demanded the profits for itself, leading to the proclamation of the Democratic Republic of Dahum and a devastating civil war and humanitarian disaster." Bond's mission is to assassinate a villanous warlord. (New York Times Book Review)

REVIEW: *London Rev Books* v35 no24 p33 D 19 2013 Colin Burrow

REVIEW: *N Y Rev Books* v61 no10 p48-9 Je 5 2014 James Walton

REVIEW: *N Y Times Book Rev* p13 O 13 2013 OLEN STEINHAUER

"Solo." "There's a neat metafictional trick during the relaxed opening chapters. . . . Given William Boyd's deep familiarity with Africa . . . it's no surprise that [James] Bond's mission takes him to a fictional West African nation. . . . In true Bond form, he traverses the world, heading from England to Africa and then to America, but it's the fictional Zanzarim that feels most real. . . . The Zanzarim civil war gives 'Solo' its greatest power, at times raising it to the heights of . . . the best of [Ian] Fleming's own novels. . . . More than half a century on, Boyd proves that there are plenty of pages left in 007's passport. . . . I doubt his creator could have done it better."

REVIEW: *New Statesman* v142 no5181 p68-70 O 25 2013 Leo Robson

REVIEW: *New York Times* v162 no56290 pC1-6 O 15 2013 MICHIKO KAKUTANI

BOYDEN, JOSEPH. The orenda; a novel; [by] Joseph Boyden 384 p. 2014 Knopf

1. Canadian historical fiction 2. Indians—Wars—Fiction 3. Iroquois Indians—Fiction 4. Jesuits—Fiction 5. Whites—Relations with Indians—Fiction 6. Wyandot Indians—Fiction

ISBN 0385350732; 9780345806451 (trade paperback); 9780385350730 (hardback); 9780385350747 (ebook)

LC 2013-030392

SUMMARY: This historical novel by Joseph Boyden "traces a story of blood and hope, suspicion and trust, hatred and love, that comes to a head when Jesuit and Huron join together against the stupendous wrath of the Iroquois, when everything that any of them has ever known or believed faces nothing less than annihilation. A saga nearly four hundred years old, it is also timeless and eternal." (Publisher's note)

REVIEW: *Booklist* v110 no16 p29 Ap 15 2014 Brad Hooper

REVIEW: *Booklist* v110 no13 p24 Mr 1 2014 Sarah Johnson

REVIEW: *Kirkus Rev* v82 no4 p298 F 15 2014

REVIEW: *Libr J* v138 no21 p68 D 1 2013 Barbara Hoffert

REVIEW: *Quill Quire* v79 no7 p29 S 2013 Kamal Al-Solaylee

"The Orenda." "Now that 'The Orenda' has arrived, it's hard not to think of [author] Joseph Boyden's first two novels . . . as preludes to this magnificent literary beast. . . . How do you revere native life while also exposing its violent, sadistic past? Can the demonization of European colonial powers (the French in this instance) and the cultural genocide they were responsible for exist alongside the possibility that their motives were in essence compassionate? . . . The history may be complicated, but the novel's narrative is relatively simple: three characters take the reins and the story, set in the early 17th century, unfolds more or less chronologically."

REVIEW: *Quill Quire* v79 no10 p12-8 D 2013

BOYLE, BOB. Rosie & Rex; a nose for fun!; [by] Bob Boyle 40 p. 2014 Harper, an imprint of HarperCollinsPublishers

1. Animals—Fiction 2. Children's stories 3. Friendship—Fiction 4. Play—Fiction 5. Robots—Fiction

ISBN 9780062211316 (hardcover bdg.)

LC 2013-021367

SUMMARY: In this children's book by Bob Boyle, "two very different friends have a bit of trouble deciding what to do. . . . Rex wants to play with robots. Rosie wants to play 'princess ballerina tea party'. . . .When they find a mysterious discarded object . . . Rosie becomes disconsolate upon discovering that it is the nose of a giant, jovial, animate robot. Then, much to her delight, the robot suggests that the trio have a 'PRINCESS BALLERINA ROBOT TEA PARTY!'" (Kirkus Reviews)

REVIEW: *Kirkus Rev* v82 no2 p112 Ja 15 2014

"Rosie & Rex: A Nose for Fun!". "This punch line comes a few pages before the conclusion, leading to something of an anticlimax that may leave readers wishing it had ended with the threesome at tea. Minimal background detail and tidy speech balloons present an uncluttered design, and [Bob] Boyle's background in television animation is apparent throughout the colorful, digitally illustrated story. Rosie, Rex and the robot even bear stylistic resemblances to the characters populating his Emmy-winning television series, Wow! Wow! Wubbzy! But despite this common ground, the final product doesn't have much of a wow factor. In the end, this is a simple friendship story with pictures that will likely grab attention but won't stand up well to multiple readings. "

REVIEW: *Publ Wkly* v261 no2 p66 Ja 13 2014

REVIEW: *SLJ* v60 no3 p102 Mr 2014 Amy Seto Musser

BOYLE, BOB.il. Rosie & Rex. See Boyle, B.

BOYNE, JOHN. Stay where you are & then leave; [by] John Boyne 256 p. 2014 Henry Holt & Company

1. Fathers and sons—Fiction 2. Mental illness—Fiction 3. War stories 4. World War, 1914-1918—England—Fiction 5. World War, 1914-1918—England—Juvenile fiction

ISBN 1627790314; 9781627790314 (hardback)

LC 2013-043620

SUMMARY: In this book, by John Boyne, "Alfie Summerfield's father . . . go[es] away to fight [in the First World War]. . . . Four years later, Alfie doesn't know where his father might be, other than that he's away on a special, secret mission. Then, . . . Alfie unexpectedly sees his father's name on a sheaf of papers belonging to a military doctor. Bewildered and confused, Alfie realizes his father is in a hospital close by—a hospital treating soldiers with shell shock." (Publisher's note)

REVIEW: *Booklist* v110 no13 p74 Mr 1 2014 Carolyn Phelan

REVIEW: *Bull Cent Child Books* v67 no8 p397-8 Ap 2014 A. A.

"Stay Where You Are & Then Leave". "[John] Boyne takes on the war to end all wars with a sure but gentle touch, surrounding the believable and endearing Alfie with compelling side characters, especially his father's best friend, conscientious objector Joe Patience. Through Joe and other figures Alfie encounters, Boyne touches on important aspects of the war and its effects on the homefront. . . . As much about familial love as about war, this novel tugs at the heartstrings, creating a sentimental but sound story that would shine as a classroom readaloud."

REVIEW: *Horn Book Magazine* v90 no3 p80-1 My/Je 2014 MARTHA V. PARRAVANO

REVIEW: *Kirkus Rev* v82 no2 p136 Ja 15 2014

"Stay Where You Are and Then Leave". "Another child's-eye view of war from the author of 'The Boy in the Striped Pajamas' (2006). . . . Alfie's the novel's strong suit: self-centered, altruistic, schooled by years of war, yet clinging to the belief that he can control the uncontrollable. His authenticity lends credibility to the sometimes-far-fetched, coincidence-heavy plot. (Conversely, a didactic tone creeps in when the viewpoint shifts from Alfie.) A vivid, accessible tale of the staggering price war exacts from those who had no voice in waging it."

REVIEW: *Publ Wkly* v261 no1 p57 Ja 6 2014

REVIEW: *SLJ* v60 no7 p50 Jl 2014 C. A. Fehmel

REVIEW: *SLJ* v60 no3 p135 Mr 2014 Kristyn Dorfman

REVIEW: *Voice of Youth Advocates* v36 no6 p56 F 2014 Jennifer McIntosh

BOYNTON, SANDRA, 1953-. Frog Trouble; . . . and Eleven Other Pretty Serious Songs; [by] Sandra Boynton 70 p. 2013 Workman Pub Co

1. Animals—Juvenile literature 2. Animals—Songs & music 3. Children's songs 4. Music—Juvenile 5. Songbooks

ISBN 0761171762; 9780761171768

SUMMARY: This book is author Sandra Boynton's "fifth . . . CD-and-illustrated-songbook collaboration. This time, she embraces country music. . . . With longtime songwriting and producing partner Mike Ford and . . . musicians including Alison Krauss, Ryan Adams, Dwight Yoakam, and Fountains of Wayne, Boynton presents 12 tunes with some familiar country themes (trucks, dogs, heartache) as seen through a child's or parent's eyes." (Publishers Weekly)

REVIEW: *Booklist* v110 no5 p70 N 1 2013 J. B. Petty

REVIEW: *Kirkus Rev* p40-1 2013 Guide 20to BookExpo America

REVIEW: *Kirkus Rev* v81 no14 p48 Jl 15 2013

REVIEW: *N Y Times Book Rev* p15 D 22 2013 SARAH HARRISON SMITH

"Herman and Rosie," "Frog Trouble: Deluxe Songbook," "Never Play Music Right Next to the Zoo." "Music is the food of love for Herman, a crocodile who plays oboe, and his neighbor Rosie, a doe who sings jazz at the Mangy Hound. . . . You might have been so distracted by [author Sandra] Boynton's prolific literary production that you missed her musical endeavors . . . In 'Frog Trouble,' she illustrates 12 witty children's country songs with pictures of the adorably smiley animals who ostensibly sing them. . . . In [author John] Lithgow's zany and toe-tapping song, illustrated with comic abandon by [illustrated by Leeza] Hernandez, all sorts of unexpected things happen when a boy and his family attend an outdoor concert at a city zoo."

REVIEW: *Publ Wkly* p44 Children's starred review annual 2013

REVIEW: *Publ Wkly* v260 no30 p67 Jl 29 2013

BOYNTON, SANDRA, 1953-.il. Frog Trouble. See Boynton, S.

BRACE, ERIC.il. Who stole New Year's Eve? See Freeman, M.

BRADBURY, JENNIFER. A moment comes; [by] Jennifer Bradbury 288 p. 2013 Atheneum Books for Young Readers

1. Family life—India—Fiction 2. Historical fiction 3. Household employees—Fiction 4. India—History—British occupation, 1765-1947—Fiction 5. Interpersonal relations—Fiction 6. Muslims—Fiction 7. Sikhs—Fiction 8. Toleration—Fiction 9. Young adult fiction

ISBN 1416978763 (hardcover); 9781416978763 (hardcover); 9781416983026 (ebook)

LC 2012-028331

SUMMARY: This book is a fictionalized "account of the final days before the line between the countries [of India and Pakistan] was announced, recounting it in the voices of three teens." English girl Margaret is the main narrator. "Much of Margaret's . . . relationship with India plays out through her growing friendship with Sikh Anupreet, who has been caught in the violence between Sikhs and Muslims already, and Muslim Tariq," who wants to go to Oxford. (Kirkus)

REVIEW: *Booklist* v109 no16 p65 Ap 15 2013 Michael Cart

REVIEW: *Bull Cent Child Books* v67 no2 p77-8 O 2013 E. B.

"A Moment Comes." "Three culturally disparate teens, caught in the perilous political drama of the 1947 partition of India, find their destinies irrevocably interlocked as they temporarily reside in the same household. . . . Bradbury is equally adept at limning characters ill at ease with their own motivations and at infusing historical background smoothly into the interlocking teen mini-dramas. An historical note is appended, but most necessary background is seamlessly incorporated into the alternating chapters in the three teens' voices, and readers who pick this up for the romantic triangle will come away with a surprising grasp of Britain's withdrawal from the mighty flagship of its empire, and the tragic cost of the 'population exchange' that accompanied independence."

REVIEW: *Kirkus Rev* v81 no2 p86 Je 1 2013

REVIEW: *Kirkus Rev* v81 no9 p72-3 My 1 2013

REVIEW: *SLJ* v59 no7 p88 Jl 2013 Jennifer Schultz

REVIEW: *Voice of Youth Advocates* v36 no3 p57 Ag 2013 Jane Gov

BRADBURY, RAY, 1920-2012. Something wicked this way comes; a novel; [by] Ray Bradbury 317 1962 Simon & Schuster

1. Aging 2. Carnivals—Fiction 3. Fantasy fiction 4. Horror tales 5. Occultism

LC 62-9-604

SUMMARY: For his first full-length novel of fantasy, the author turns back to the vein of his very earliest stories . . . whose mood is suggested in the titles of his collections, 'Dark Carnival' and 'The October Country' [BRD 1947 and 1955]. It is October in this novel when the visiting carnival brings dark terror to the sleepy little town, where two small boys and a library janitor stand between the townsfolk and the deadly sweet allure of damnation." (N Y Her Trib Books)

REVIEW: *Booklist* v110 no18 p25 My 15 2014 Brad Hooper

REVIEW: *Horn Book Magazine* v89 no2 p71 Mr/Ap 2013 Christine Taylor-Butler

"Something Wicked This Way Comes." "In this tale of good versus evil, the mood is bleak. Danger is foreshadowed by the arrival of a man selling lightning rods covered in strange symbols. . . . Posters announcing Cooger & Dark's Pandemonium Shadow Show appear. . . . And when the carnival finally arrives, the descriptions are ominous. The slithering train's grieving sounds, a wailing calliope, and the skeletal poles of the tent drew me into the weird landscape and held me captive. The book was odd, and not what my friends were reading, but I was hooked."

BRADFORD, TOLLY.ed. Prophetic identities. See Prophetic identities

BRADLEE, BENJAMIN C., 1921-2014. The kid; the immortal life of Ted Williams; [by] Benjamin C. Bradlee 864 p. 2013 Little Brown & Co

1. Baseball—United States 2. Baseball players—United States—Biography 3. Biography (Literary form) 4. Boston Red Sox (Baseball team)
ISBN 0316614351; 9780316614351
LC 2013-028253

SUMMARY: This book, by Ben Bradlee, Jr., offers a biography of the baseball player Ted Williams. "Born in 1918 in San Diego, Ted would spend most of his life disguising his Mexican heritage. During his 22 years with the Boston Red Sox, Williams electrified crowds across America—and shocked them, too: His notorious clashes with the press and fans threatened his reputation. Yet while he was a God in the batter's box, he was profoundly human once he stepped away from the plate." (Publisher's note)

REVIEW: *Choice* v51 no12 p2226 Ag 2014 C. M. Smith

REVIEW: *Kirkus Rev* v81 no24 p328 D 15 2013

"The Kid: The Immortal Life of Ted Williams". " Sprawling, entertaining life of the baseball great, renowned as a sports hero while leading a life as checkered as Babe Ruth's or Ty Cobb's. . . . The author dishes plenty—one of the kindest things he says about Williams as a human being was that he was "self-absorbed"—but the repeated demonstrations of flawed character do nothing to diminish Williams' outsized stature as a player. Bradlee is as enthusiastic as Vin Scully or Harry Caray when it comes to describing Williams on the field. . . . " An outstanding addition to the literature of baseball."

REVIEW: *Libr J* v138 no12 p55 Jl 1 2013

REVIEW: *N Y Times Book Rev* p54-5 D 8 2013 CHARLES McGRATH

REVIEW: *New York Times* v163 no56341 pC9 D 5 2013 BRUCE WEBER

"The Kid: The Immortal Life of Ted Williams". "Strikingly precise and colorful reporting. . . . A work of obvious journalistic muscle and diligence, 'The Kid' provides documentary evidence on every page to bolster the books' presumption that Williams was, to use the cliché, larger than life. Maybe he was. But Mr. [Ben] Bradlee is hampered by the incontrovertible fact that Williams was a significant person because of his batting feats. And though he hardly ignores Williams's years as a player, Mr. Bradlee is not an especially astute baseball writer. . . . Mr. Bradlee . . . writes a graceful sentence and crafts a cogent paragraph. . . . But Mr. Bradlee's evenhanded thoroughness ultimately does his subject . . . no favors."

REVIEW: *New York Times* v163 no56330 p8 N 24 2013 ALEX WILLIAMS

BRADLEY, ELIZABETH H. The American health care paradox; why spending more is getting us less; [by] Elizabeth H. Bradley 272 p. 2013 PublicAffairs

1. Delivery of Health Care—United States 2. Health Care Reform—United States 3. Health Expenditures—United States 4. Social Conditions—United States 5. Social Work—United States 6. Social science literature
ISBN 9781610392099 (hbk.: alk. paper)
LC 2013-030237

SUMMARY: It was the authors' intent to demonstrate that "the US, compared to other countries, manifests exorbitant health spending but 'poor health outcomes.' . . . This book suggests that improving American health while containing costs requires increasing social expenditure relative to health expenditure." (Choice: Current Reviews for Academic Libraries)

REVIEW: *Booklist* v110 no3 p10 O 1 2013 Donna Chavez

REVIEW: *Choice* v51 no9 p1646 My 2014 J. P. Burkett

"The American Health Care Paradox; Why Spending More Is Getting Us Less". "The article, acknowledging its limitations, emphasizes correlation, not causation. Yet this book suggests that improving American health while containing costs requires increasing social expenditure relative to health expenditure. While possibly correct, this suggestion does not follow from the data analysis. As models for American reformers, the authors examine Denmark, Norway, and Sweden. The comparisons are informative but should include Australia, Italy, and Japan, which all surpass the Scandinavians in LE and the ratio of LE to per capita health expenditure. The book makes interesting ideas accessible to undergraduates but should be supplemented hy readings on causal inference in health research."

REVIEW: *Christ Century* v130 no23 p36-8 N 13 2013 LaVonne Neff

REVIEW: *Kirkus Rev* v81 no19 p69 O 1 2013

REVIEW: *Libr J* v138 no21 p116 D 1 2013 Martha Stone

REVIEW: *Publ Wkly* v260 no38 p69 S 23 2013

BRADLEY, MARK A. A very principled boy; the life of Duncan Lee, Red spy and cold warrior; [by] Mark A. Bradley 384 p. 2014 Basic Books, a member of the Perseus Books Group

1. Biography (Literary form) 2. Cold War—Biography 3. Communists—United States—Biography 4. Espionage, Soviet—United States—History 5. Intelligence officers—United States—Biography 6. Moles (Spies)—United States—Biography 7. World War, 1939-1945—Secret service
ISBN 9780465030095 (hardback)
LC 2013-045461

SUMMARY: This book by Mark A. Bradley recounts how "during World War II, Duncan Lee (1913–88) served in the U.S. Office of Strategic Services (OSS, predecessor to the CIA) and spied for the USSR. . . . Although he was exposed by a flipped Soviet spy at a House Un-American Activities Committee hearing in 1948, Lee escaped punishment through a combination of deft strategy, bureaucratic bumbling, and sheer luck." (Library Journal)

REVIEW: *Kirkus Rev* v82 no5 p151 Mr 1 2014

"A Very Principled Boy: The Life of Duncan Lee, Red Spy and Cold Warrior". "An obscure wartime spy working for the OSS, the wartime precursor to the CIA, gets a thorough exposé by a government lawyer and former CIA officer. [Mark A.] Bradley's sense of frustration at how this arrogant, dissembling underling of William Donovan got away with passing information to the Soviet spy network is partly explained by the general atmosphere of fear raging after the war and the fact that the American government had bigger fish to net-e.g., Alger Hiss. . . A murky effort exacerbated by myriad shadowy agencies and a deeply unsympathetic protagonist."

REVIEW: *Libr J* v139 no10 p116 Je 1 2014 Joshua Wallace

REVIEW: *Publ Wkly* v261 no7 p89 F 17 2014

BRADLEY, NICHOLAS.ed. We Go Far Back in Time. See Birney, E.

BRADLEY, RICHARD. The idea of order; the circular archetype in prehistoric Europe; [by] Richard Bradley xv, 242 p. 2012 Oxford University Press

1. Antiquities, Prehistoric—Europe 2. Archaeological literature 3. Architectural literature 4. Earthworks (Archaeology) 5. Round buildings—Europe

ISBN 0199608091 (hbk.); 9780199608096 (hbk.)

LC 2012-532761

SUMMARY: This book "uses archaeological evidence, combined with insights from anthropology, to investigate the creation, use, and ultimate demise of circular architecture in prehistoric Europe. Concerned mainly with the prehistoric period from the origins of farming to the early first millennium AD, but extending to the medieval period, the volume considers the role of circular features from Turkey to the Iberian Peninsula and from Sardinia through Central Europe to Sweden." (Publisher's note)

REVIEW: *Choice* v50 no9 p1671 My 2013 A. F. Roberts

REVIEW: *TLS* no5753 p7-8 Jl 5 2013 PETER THONEMANN

"The Idea of Order: The Circular Archetype in Prehistoric Europe," "Prehistoric Materialities: Becoming Material in Prehistoric Britain and Ireland" and "How Ancient Europeans Saw the World: Vision, Patterns, and the Shaping of the Mind in Prehistoric Times." "Richard Bradley argues in his absorbing new book . . . that we are dealing not solely, or even primarily, with a practical choice, but with a particular way of seeing the world. . . . representation." . . . [Andrew Meirion] Jones's 'performative' approach to material culture has a lot going for it, and it is a pity that his prose is so hard going. . . . Jones could learn a thing or two from Peter Wells, whose 'How Ancient Europeans Saw the World' covers much of the same ground (and a lot more besides) in beautifully crisp and elegant English."

BRADSHAW, JOHN, 1950-. Cat sense; how the new feline science can make you a better friend to your pet; [by] John Bradshaw 336 p. 2013 Basic Books

1. Cat owners 2. Cats—Behavior 3. Cats—Psychology 4. Human-animal relationships 5. Veterinary literature

ISBN 0465031013; 9780465031016 (hardcover)

LC 2013-020749

SUMMARY: In this book, author John Bradshaw takes readers "further into the mind of the domestic cat . . . using cutting-edge scientific research to dispel the myths and explain the true nature of our feline friends. Tracing the cat's evolution from lone predator to domesticated companion, Bradshaw shows that although cats and humans have been living together for at least eight thousand years, cats remain independent, predatory, and wary of contact with their own kind." (Publisher's note)

REVIEW: *Booklist* v109 no22 p15 Ag 1 2013 Nancy Bent

REVIEW: *Kirkus Rev* v81 no14 p136 Jl 15 2013

REVIEW: *Libr J* v138 no18 p110 N 1 2013 Edell Marie Schaefer

REVIEW: *Nat Hist* v121 no7 p42-3 S 2013 LAURENCE A. MARSCHALL

REVIEW: *New Statesman* v142 no5173 p44 S 6 2013 Andrew Harrison

REVIEW: *New York Times* v163 no56374 pD6 Ja 7 2014 NICHOLAS WADE

"Cat Sense: How the New Feline Science Can Make You A Better Friend To Your Pet". "For any who may wonder what their feline companions are really thinking, 'Cat Sense,' by John Bradshaw, provides the best answers that science can give for the time being. . . . I found the book's sections on the evolution and archaeology of cats a little long-winded, and the writing in general is clear but stodgy in places. That aside, 'Cat Sense' will teach you much about the biology of cats that you never suspected."

REVIEW: *Publ Wkly* v260 no26 p78 Jl 1 2013

REVIEW: *Smithsonian* v44 no6 p111 O 2013 Chloë Schama

BRADY, EMILY. Humboldt; life on america's marijuana frontier; [by] Emily Brady 272 p. 2013 Grand Central Pub.

1. Drug legalization 2. Humboldt County (Calif.) 3. Journalism 4. Marijuana—Law & legislation—California 5. Marijuana industry

ISBN 9781455506767 (hardcover)

LC 2013-932822

SUMMARY: This book by Emily presents "a narrative exploration of an insular community in Northern California, which for nearly 40 years has existed primarily on the cultivation and sale of marijuana. . . . In Humboldt County, marijuana supports everything from fire departments to schools, but it comes with a heavy price. As legalization looms, the community stands at a crossroads and its inhabitants are deeply divided on the issue." (Publisher's note)

REVIEW: *Kirkus Rev* v81 no8 p43-4 Ap 15 2013

REVIEW: *Nation* v297 no20 p44 N 18 2013 KATE MURPHY

"Humboldt: Life on America's Marijuana Frontier." "Excellent. . . . The most interesting dynamic that [Emily] Brady explores is how the residents of Humboldt County view the seemingly inevitable legalization of marijuana. . . . 'Humboldt,' while fascinating, is a story without a real ending. The county's shadowy one-crop economy continues to thrive, and the government continues its futile efforts to eradicate it. . . . Reflecting on the people who continue to flock to Southern Humboldt looking for seasonal work--jobs that no grower would entrust to an outsider--Brady wonders if they've come for 'their last chance to experience the marijuana heartland before everything changed. . . . It was like the end of the gold rush."

REVIEW: *Publ Wkly* v260 no14 p50-1 Ap 8 2013 Larry Weissman

BRADY, LINZY.ed. The Tempest. See The Tempest

BRAIDOTTI, ROSI. The posthuman; [by] Rosi Braidotti 180 p. 2013 Polity

1. Biotechnology 2. Human body (Philosophy) 3. Philosophical literature 4. Philosophy of medicine 5. Technology & civilization

ISBN 0745641571; 9780745641577

SUMMARY: It was the author's intent to demonstrate "that medical science and biotechnology are fast remaking how we view our bodies, that they are becoming commodities to be traded. This matters greatly because it affects what we think is possible and reasonable to do to a person/body, and therefore has deep consequences for the moral and ethical dimensions of our choices in life." (New Scientist)

REVIEW: *Choice* v51 no5 p815-6 Ja 2014 T. J. Welsh

"The Posthuman." "In this argumentative survey, [Rosi] Braidotti . . . offers herself as 'a tracker and a cartographer,' mapping a course through the cluster of subjects bound up in the posthuman. Her discussion shows remarkable clarity and concision even as it lays out highly technical, complexly theoretical, and deeply interdisciplinary concepts. Given the breadth and intricacy of the material she covers, the signposts of Braidotti's argument may prove difficult for the uninitiated to follow. Still, this study has great value as an entry point for anyone engaged with the humanities and looking to its posthuman human future. . . . Recommended."

BRAKE, MARK. Alien life imagined; communicating the science and culture of Astrobiology; [by] Mark Brake 276 p. 2013 Cambridge University Press

1. Cosmology—History 2. Exobiology 3. Life on other planets 4. Science—Popular works 5. Unidentified flying object literature 6. Unidentified flying objects 7. Voyages, Imaginary
ISBN 0521491290; 9780521491297 (hardback)
LC 2012-022018

SUMMARY: Author Mark Brake's book focuses on the possibility of alien life. "As space agencies continue to search for life in our Universe, fundamental questions are raised: are we awake to the revolutionary effects on human science, society and culture that alien contact will bring? And how is it possible to imagine the unknown? In this book, Mark Brake tells . . . how the portrayal of extraterrestrial life has developed over the last two and a half thousand years." (Publisher's note)

REVIEW: *Choice* v51 no1 p102 S 2013 K. L. Schick

"Alien Life Imagined: Communicating the Science and Culture of Astrobiology." "The title will lead readers to expect a book largely about astrobiology. However, it seems that it raises and addresses, in the main, more fundamental issues related to the conception of humankind's place and role in the universe. . . . [Author Mark] Brake . . . starts with the Greeks and a cosmology that is dominated by geocentricism. . . . These philosophic musings have gradually given way to modern scientific considerations with a much more sophisticated picture of the structure and evolution of the universe. In addition, current understanding of the nature of life and its environmental requirements allows people to raise issues that were out of the realm of science not too long ago."

BRAKEFIELD, JAY. Deep Ellum. See Govenar, A.

BRAM STOKER; Centenary Essays; 206 p. 2014 Four Courts Press

1. Dracula, Count (Fictitious character) 2. Essay (Literary form) 3. Gothic fiction (Literary genre) 4. Irish authors 5. Literature—History & criticism
ISBN 1846824079; 9781846824074

SUMMARY: "Despite his vampire creation, Dracula, being world-famous, and in spite of a host of academic studies of the novel in which this vampire first appeared, Bram Stoker himself remains a figure shrouded in darkness, and his other writings are virtually unknown and ignored. This collection addresses this large gap. The main aim of the collection is to read Stoker in the round, . . . taking account of the full extent of Stoker's writing." (Publisher's note)

REVIEW: *TLS* no5796 p27 My 2 2014 SINÉAD STURGEON

"Bram Stoker: Centenary Essays." "Seldom has a writer been so eclipsed by the superstardom of his literary progeny as was Bram Stoker by 'Dracula.' Yet what emerges most compellingly from this volume, the proceedings of a conference at Trinity College Dublin, is the impression of a man who rarely stopped writing. . . . Worldly, intelligent, good-humoured. Stoker the man is attractively served in this collection. . . . The life and work of 'the least-known author of the best-known book in the world,' as Christopher Frayling phrases it in his account of Stoker's holiday in Whitby, in 1890, are reclaimed from the shadows in this restorative collection."

BRANDMAN, MICHAEL. Robert B. Parker's Damned if you do; [by] Michael Brandman 288 p. 2013 Putnam Adult

1. City and town life—Massachusetts—Fiction 2. FICTION—Crime 3. FICTION—Mystery & Detective—General 4. FICTION—Suspense 5. Murder—Fiction 6. Older people—Abuse of 7. Police chiefs—Massachusetts—Fiction 8. Stone, Jesse (Fictitious character)—Fiction
ISBN 9780399159503 (hardback)
LC 2013-019293

SUMMARY: In this book, "Ornery Jesse Stone again puts justice ahead of the law." This is "[Michael] Brandman's . . . third continuation of [Robert B.] Parker's series featuring the Massachusetts smalltown police chief. . . . Stone has two serious matters on his plate: endemic patient abuse at a nursing home and the stabbing murder of an unidentified prostitute at a motel." (Publishers Weekly)

REVIEW: *Booklist* v110 no2 p35-6 S 15 2013 Wes Lukowsky

"Robert B. Parker's Damned If You Do." "The girl is young, pretty, and looks vaguely familiar to Paradise Police Chief Jesse Stone. She's also dead. . . . She checked into the decaying bungalow resort with cash and an alias; undoubtedly, a working girl. Jesse feels he at least needs to determine her identity to avoid the indignity of an unmarked Jane Doe grave. . . . [Michael] Brandman, who worked closely with Parker on the Jesse Stone television movies, does a fine job moving the Jesse Stone series forward. He continues to be the gold standard for mystery writers attempting to preserve the Parker brand."

REVIEW: *Kirkus Rev* v81 no16 p312 Ag 15 2013

REVIEW: *Libr J* v138 no14 p94 S 1 2013

REVIEW: *Publ Wkly* v260 no28 p149-50 Jl 15 2013

BRANDT, WILLY, 1913-1992. My road to Berlin; [by] Willy Brandt 287 p. 1960 Doubleday

1. Autobiographies 2. Berlin (Germany)—Politics & government 3. Mayors 4. Norway—Politics & government—1905-

LC 6001-0666

SUMMARY: In this biography by Willy Brandt, as told to Leo Lania, "the Mayor of Berlin tells of his earlier activities in the Socialist underground, his years in Norway and of the vicissitudes of Berlin in recent years." (Foreign Affairs)

REVIEW: *TLS* no5763 p16 S 13 2013

"My Road to Berlin." "A free city in the heart of a hostile country cannot afford to be neutralist. Herr Brandt is,to all appearances, a high-minded realist. And yet a realist would never have undertaken the apparently hopeless task of keeping Berlin's head above water. If there is any need for evidence that Herr Brandt is still a Social Democrat at heart, it can be found in this: he is Governing Mayor of Berlin. Only an obstinate, old-fashioned, bloody-minded idealist would take on a job like that."

BRANNEN, SARAH S.il. Feathers. See Stewart, M.

BRANTLEY-NEWTON, VANESSA.il. We Shall Overcome. See Levy. D.

BRANTLEY, RICHARD E. Emily Dickinson's rich conversation; poetry, philosophy, science; [by] Richard E. Brantley x, 272 p. 2013 Palgrave Macmillan

1. Influence (Literary, artistic, etc.) 2. Literature & science 3. Literature—History & criticism 4. Philosophy in literature

ISBN 9780230340633 (hardcover : alk. paper)

LC 2012-050197

SUMMARY: This book presents an "account of Emily Dickinson's aesthetic and intellectual life. Through her letters and poems, Richard E. Brantley identifies Dickinson's dialogue with John Locke's rational empiricism . . . Ralph Waldo Emerson's idealism, and European and American intellectual traditions. Contrary to the image of the isolated poet, this ambitious study reveals Dickinson's agile mind developing through conversation with a community of contemporaries." (Publisher's note)

REVIEW: *Choice* v51 no7 p1211 Mr 2014 D. D. Kummings

"Emily Dickinson's Rich Conversation: Poetry, Philosophy, Science." "[Richard E.] Brantley's emphasis on [Emily] Dickinson's "dialogical aesthetic" makes this book a significant contribution to scholarship. Other valuable aspects of the book include situating the poet in an Anglo-American rather than a strictly New England context . . . and revealing her as a poet who is less an eccentric recluse than she is an individual mentally interacting with a community of authors and intellectuals. Although his focus is on the history of ideas, Brantley also comments on numerous poems, most interestingly, to this reviewer, those displaying the poet's knowledge of astronomy, geology, evolutionary biology, and steam technology."

BRASHARES, ANN. The here and now; [by] Ann Brashares 256 p. 2014 Delacorte Press

1. Community life—New York (State)—New York—Fiction 2. High schools—Fiction 3. Interpersonal relations—Fiction 4. Refugees—Fiction 5. Schools—Fiction 6. Science fiction 7. Time travel—Fiction

ISBN 0385736800; 9780385736800 (hc: alk. paper); 9780385906296 (glb. alk. paper)

LC 2013-018683

SUMMARY: This book, by Ann Brashares, "is the story of seventeen-year-old Prenna James, who immigrated to New York when she was twelve. Except Prenna didn't come from a different country. She came from a different time—a future where a mosquito-borne illness has mutated into a pandemic, killing millions and leaving the world in ruins. Prenna . . . must follow a strict set of rules. . . . But everything changes when Prenna falls for Ethan Jarves. " (Publisher's note)

REVIEW: *Booklist* v111 no2 p68 S 15 2014 Shari Fesko

REVIEW: *Bull Cent Child Books* v67 no8 p398 Ap 2014 K. Q. G.

REVIEW: *Kirkus Rev* v82 no3 p250 F 1 2014

"The Here and Now". "A lightning-paced sci-fi time-travel romp that, much like a cinematic blockbuster, offers intrigue, romance and a healthy dose of implausibility. . . . [Ann] Brashares' worldbuilding is solid, and she handles the time-travel elements with a fluid, cinematic ease. Unfortunately, she relies too much on dei ex machina to propel Ethan and Prenna forward. . . . Those willing to overlook such shortcuts will surely be swept into the whirlwind romance and breathlessly turn pages to discover if there truly is a possibility for a better future. This quirky tale of love and time travel demands that readers totally suspend disbelief to enjoy some of the more contrived plot elements."

REVIEW: *Libr J* v139 no3 p78 F 15 2014 Nicole R. Steeves

REVIEW: *N Y Times Book Rev* p24 Ap 6 2014 CASSANDRA CLARE

REVIEW: *Publ Wkly* v261 no4 p194 Ja 27 2014

BRAUN, SEBASTIEN. I love you more; [by] Sebastien Braun 18 p. 2013 Tiger Tales

1. Bears—Fiction 2. Board books 3. Love—Fiction 4. Parent and child—Fiction 5. Stories in rhyme

ISBN 1589256204 (board book); 9781589256200 (board book)

LC 2013-009972

SUMMARY: In this children's picture book by Sebastien Braun, "a bear cub express its love for its grown-up as they play together in an inviting woodland. One or two lines of verse are meted out on each double-page spread: 'I love you more than sunshine. // I love you more than rain. // I love it when you swoop me high, / Then twirl me back again.'" (Kirkus Reviews)

REVIEW: *Kirkus Rev* v81 no19 p356 O 1 2013

REVIEW: *Kirkus Rev* v82 no1 p30 Ja 1 2014

"I Love You More". "A bear cub express its love for its grown-up as they play together in an inviting woodland. One or two lines of verse are meted out on each double-page spread. . . . Some of the scenes, typical of the baby/parent love-story trope, resonate well enough, but a few of the lines feel forced to fit the rhyme scheme. . . . [Sebastien] Braun collages loose sketches on lightly corrugated papers and captures the cozy and playful scenes beautifully. . . . Here's hoping Braun can find a talented versifier to mesh with his loving and lovable bears."

BRAUN, WILLI.ed. Failure and nerve in the academic study of religion. See Failure and nerve in the academic study of religion

BRAVIN, JESS 1966-. The terror courts; rough justice at Guantanamo Bay; [by] Jess 1966- Bravin 448 p.

1. Military courts—Cuba—Guantánamo Bay Naval Base 2. Political science literature 3. United States—Politics & government 4. War crime trials—United States
ISBN 9780300189209 (clothbound)
LC 2012-034913

SUMMARY: In this book, author Jess Bravin "exposes the post-9/11 legal morass resulting in the detention of alleged terrorists at Guantanamo Bay. Bravin . . . explains why the administration of George W. Bush felt it could round up the terrorists from nations around the world, transport them in secret to Guantanamo, deny them basic legal safeguards, torture some of them and establish military commissions of questionable legality to mete out punishment." (Kirkus Reviews)

REVIEW: *America* v209 no14 p36-7 N 11 2013 LUKE HANSEN

REVIEW: *Commonweal* v140 no8 p32-5 My 3 2013 Tom Durkin

REVIEW: *Kirkus Rev* v80 no24 p278 D 15 2012

REVIEW: *New York Times* v162 no56096 pC4 Ap 4 2013 CHARLIE SAVAGE

REVIEW: *TLS* no5746 p7 My 17 2013 LAWRENCE R. DOUGLAS

"The Terror Courts: Rough Justice at Guantánamo Bay." "Admittedly, much of the material contained in 'The Terror Courts' will be familiar to a small group of concerned citizens and human rights monitors who have spent the past decade closely following the goings-on at Guantánamo Bay. Still, we owe a debt of gratitude to [Jess] Bravin, first for breaking many of these stories as a legal correspondent for the Wall Street Journal, and now for assembling them into a gripping narrative told with superb journalistic thoroughness, great legal sensitivity, and impressive moral clarity."

BRAY, BARBARA.tr. The bridge of beyond. See Schwarz-Bart, S.

BRAY, DONNA.ed. Santa goes everywhere! See Biggs, B.

BRAY, DONNA.ed. What flies in the air. See Biggs, B.

BRAY, HIAWATHA. You are here; from the compass to GPS, the history and future of how we find ourselves; [by] Hiawatha Bray 272 p. 2014 Basic Books

1. Electronics in navigation—History 2. Geographic information systems—History 3. Geospatial data 4. Global Positioning System 5. Journalism
ISBN 0465032850; 9780465032853 (hardback)
LC 2014-002731

SUMMARY: This book, by Hiawatha Bray, "examines the rise of our technologically aided era of navigational omniscience—or how we came to know exactly where we are at all times. In a sweeping history of the development of location technology in the past century, Bray shows how . . . humankind ingeniously solved one of its oldest and toughest problems—only to herald a new era in which it's impossible to hide." (Publisher's note)

REVIEW: *Choice* v52 no2 p278 O 2014 R. A. Kolvoord

REVIEW: *Kirkus Rev* v82 no7 p32 Ap 1 2014

REVIEW: *Libr J* v139 no10 p128 Je 1 2014 Wade M. Lee

REVIEW: *Sci Am* v310 no4 p86 Ap 2014 Clara Moskowitz

"You Are Here: From the Compass to GPS, the History and Future of How We Find Ourselves." "Now many people carry in their pockets the technology to pinpoint their exact geographic coordinates from nearly anywhere on the earth. 'Few technological marvels have been as marvelous as humanity's victory over the mysteries of location,' writes journalist [Hiawatha] Bray. In this history of navigation, he tells the story of how we learned to find our way around the planet ever more accurately and explores the implications of our 'locational transparency.'"

THE BREAD WE EAT IN DREAMS; 344 p. 2013 Subterranean

1. American short stories 2. Fairies—Fiction 3. Fantasy fiction 4. Imaginary places 5. Magic—Fiction
ISBN 1596065826; 9781596065826

SUMMARY: This book presents short fiction by Catherynne M. Valente. "In the Locus Award-winning novelette 'White Lines on a Green Field,' an old story plays out against a high school backdrop as Coyote is quarterback and king for a season. A girl named Mallow embarks on an adventure of memorable and magical politicks in 'The Girl Who Ruled Fairyland—For a Little While.' The award-winning . . . novella 'Silently and Very Fast' is an ancient epic set in a far-flung future." (Publisher's note)

REVIEW: *New York Times* v163 no56349 pC30 D 13 2013 DANA JENNINGS

"Horses of a Different Color" and "The Bread We Eat in Dreams". "Two fine collections of short stories. . . . Mr. [Howard] Waldrop, 67, is the sly old pro here, while Ms. [Catherynne M.] Valente, 34, is the incandescent young star, but both are steeped in American pop-cultural myth. . . . And they leaven these legends with the off-kilter literary shrewdness of writers like [Jorge Luis] Borges . . . and Donald Barthelme to forge a dark Americana where life tends to suddenly skid sideways. . . . At least half the 10 tales in his new collection are prime eccentric Waldrop, though some feel more like extended jokes than fully realized stories. . . . Ms. Valente, too, is adept at updating the tall tale, but also writes with grace and power. She was a poet first, and her precise and lyrical ear is apparent thoughout."

REVIEW: *Publ Wkly* v260 no35 p37 S 2 2013

BREAKTHROUGHS IN TELEPHONE TECHNOLOGY; from Bell to smartphones; xvi, 127 p. 2012 Britannica Educational Pub. in association with Rosen Educational Services

1. Electronics—History 2. Historical literature 3. Technological innovations 4. Telecommunication—History 5. Telephone—History
ISBN 9781615306787 (library binding)
LC 2011-032955

SUMMARY: Edited by Robert Curley, this detailed volume examines the development of the telephone and related technologies, including everything from the transistor to fax machines, smart phones, and VoIP technology." (Publisher's note)

REVIEW: *Voice of Youth Advocates* v36 no4 p94-5 O 2013 Heather Christensen

"Architects of the Information Age," "Gaming: From Atari to Xbox 3," "Breakthroughs in Telephone Technology." "Britannica gives readers a chronological perspective of computer and information technology in this five book series. Each book introduces a particular topic and then more fully explores it from its historic roots to the most recent innovations and developments. . . . 'Architects of the Information Age' provides biographical information on over fifty movers and shakers in the history of computers. Although illustrated with both black-and-white and color photographs, readers may be disappointed to discover that few of the entries include portraits of the subjects. . . . Overall, this is a well-developed series on an ever-changing topic."

BREDEHOFT, JOHN M. Democracy's Missing Arsenal. See King, M. B.

BREHONY, NOEL. Yemen divided; the story of a failed state in South Arabia; [by] Noel Brehony 2011 I. B. Tauris

1. Failed states 2. Historical literature 3. Yemen (Republic)—History 4. Yemen (Republic)—Politics & government 5. Yemen, South

ISBN 1848856350; 9781848856356

SUMMARY: This book looks at " history of the People's Democratic Republic of Yemen (PDRY)." Author Noel Brehony "explains the power politics that came to form a communist republic a few hundred miles from the holiest site in Islam, and the process and conflicts that led to Yemeni unification in 1990. The impact of the PDRY is still felt today as Saudi and government armed forces engage with Houthis in the North and unrest continues to simmer across the South." (Publisher's note)

REVIEW: *TLS* no5759 p16 Ag 16 2013 DANIEL MARTIN VARISCO

"Yemen Divided: The Story of a Failed State in South Arabia." "With such a politically lush plotline, how could a book on the recent history of Yemen go wrong? Noel Brehony . . . succeeds in detailing the political intrigue that played out in the South before and after unification, aided in part by his knowledge of regime sources only available in Arabic. Despite adding his own reflections based on first-hand knowledge of some of the main politicians, the overall result is a dry chronological accounting of who was who and what happened where that reads at times like a nineteenth-century governor general's report back to London. . . . Brehony is not an apologist for British involvement, but his text fails to provide the historical and cultural context that others do."

BREMER, KRISTA. My accidental jihad; a love story; [by] Krista Bremer 304 p. 2014 Algonquin Books of Chapel Hill

1. Interethnic marriage 2. Interfaith marriage 3. Memoirs 4. Parenting

ISBN 9781616200688

LC 2013-043143

SUMMARY: In this memoir, the author "explores the points of connection—and potential conflict—in her marriage to Libyan-born Ismail. [Krista] Bremer, a surfing aficionado, feminist, avid traveler, and aspiring journalist, was not looking for a commitment when she began dating the older Ismail and shortly thereafter became unexpectedly pregnant. Her eventual surrender to a different kind of imagined future forms one of the memoir's central themes." (Publishers Weekly)

REVIEW: *Kirkus Rev* v82 no5 p11 Mr 1 2014

"My Accidental Jihad: A Love Story". "A moving, lyrical memoir about how an American essayist fell in love with a Libyan-born Muslim man and learned to embrace the life she made with him. Sun associate publisher [Krista] Bremer was a wayward former California surfer girl just starting to build her life in North Carolina when she met Ismail. . . . As she gradually came to accept a different way of living-and eventually, worshipping-in middle-class America, Bremer grew to appreciate Ismail, her extended family and the struggle they brought into her life more than she even imagined possible. A sweet and rewarding journey of a book."

REVIEW: *Libr J* v139 no2 p76 F 1 2014 Joyce Sparrow

REVIEW: *Libr J* v139 no14 p63 S 1 2014 Nancy R. Ives

REVIEW: *N Y Times Book Rev* p23 My 25 2014 PAMELA DRUCKERMAN

REVIEW: *Publ Wkly* v260 no52 p41 D 23 2013

BRENNAN-NELSON, DENISE. Willow. See Brennan, R.

BRENNAN, ALLISON. Notorious; [by] Allison Brennan 336 p. 2014 Minotaur Books

1. Cold cases (Criminal investigation) 2. FICTION—Mystery & Detective—Women Sleuths 3. FICTION—Suspense 4. FICTION—Thrillers 5. Murder—Investigation—Fiction 6. Women journalists—Fiction

ISBN 9781250035059 (hardback)

LC 2013-032878

SUMMARY: In this book, "New York City journalist Maxine "Max" Revere, famed for her interest in cold cases . . . is driven by the one case she never solved years before: the one that left Lindy Ames dead and Kevin O'Neal destroyed by the shadow of unproven suspicion. When Kevin commits suicide, Max returns home to Atherton, Calif., where she finds an insular community whose wealthy families--including hers--will close ranks rather than betray their own to the law." (Publishers Weekly)

REVIEW: *Booklist* v110 no12 p32 F 15 2014 Stacy Alesi

"Notorious." "Working with ex-special forces turned detective Nick Santini, in charge of the homicide, Max finds that she shares a work ethic and a strong mutual attraction with the young, good-looking, and smart Nick. But Max is able to go outside the law on occasion, and Nick finds her reckless streak both maddening and endearing. Fireworks erupt on more than one occasion, and it seems like the beginning of an interesting relationship--a terrific new series. Sandra Brown and Hank Phillippi Ryan fans will feel right at home."

REVIEW: *Kirkus Rev* v82 no3 p188 F 1 2014

"Notorious". "New York Times best-selling author [Allison] Brennan . . . explores murder among the rich and arrogant in an exclusive California enclave. . . .The first few chapters of this book will either draw readers in or send them packing: Brennan introduces more than 15 characters by name in the prologue and first two chapters alone. Brennan's infodump style and tendency to linger over the perks of being Max Revere will do little for readers who demand substance over window dressing. A story that probably won't attract any new Brennan converts but will likely find favor with her hard-core fan base."

REVIEW: *Publ Wkly* v261 no1 p35 Ja 6 2014

BRENNAN, MARIE. The tropic of serpents; A Memoir by Lady Trent; [by] Marie Brennan 336 p. 2014 Tor

1. Dragons—Fiction 2. Fantasy fiction 3. Sexism 4. Women scientists—Fiction 5. Women travelers—Fiction

ISBN 0765331977; 9780765331977 (hardback)

LC 2013-026345

SUMMARY: This book is the sequel to "A Natural History of Dragons," by Marie Brennan. It is an "account of a woman's field work on dragons, which in this imagined 19th-century world are natural creatures. Isabella, Lady Trent, has even determined the six criteria for classifying an animal as a dragon, which include 'wings capable of flight,' 'a ruff or fan behind the skull,' and 'extraordinary breath.'" (Publishers Weekly)

REVIEW: *Booklist* v110 no15 p34 Ap 1 2014 David Pitt

REVIEW: *Kirkus Rev* v82 no4 p342 F 15 2014

"The Tropic of Serpents: A Memoir By Lady Trent". "During her adventures in the Green Hell—the book's finest section—Isabella will find sociology as important as natural history and the key to preventing a brutal war. This, the second of Isabella's retrospective memoirs, is as uncompromisingly honest and forthright as the first, narrated in [Marie] Brennan's usual crisp, vivid style, with a heroine at once admirable, formidable and captivating. Reader, lose no time in making Isabella's acquaintance."

REVIEW: *N Y Times Book Rev* p14-5 Je 1 2014 N . K. JEMISIN

REVIEW: *Publ Wkly* v261 no4 p174 Ja 27 2014

BRENNAN, ROSEMARIE. Willow; [by] Rosemarie Brennan un 2008 Sleeping Bear Press

1. Art—Fiction 2. Imagination—Fiction 3. Painting—Fiction

ISBN 978-1-58536-342-1; 1-58536-342-1

LC 2007-034588

SUMMARY: In art class, neatness, conformity, and imitation are encouraged, but when Willow brings imagination and creativity to her projects, even straight-laced Miss Hawthorn is influenced

REVIEW: *Booklist* v110 no11 p58-9 F 1 2014 Courtney Jones

"Willow." "Willow is the daughter of Knotwild Plantation's manager and the favored slave of Reverend Jeffers, a plantation owner known to be 'soft with the whip.' . . . With an unflinching eye, [Tonya Cherie] Hegamin explores the complicated relationships created by slavery and the horrors specific to being a female slave. While the slow reveal of Willow's family secrets require patient readers, the final exploration of those secrets creates a beautiful parallel to Willow's current dilemma. Duty, love, and the freedom to be a fully realized human being make up the crux of this stirring tale."

REVIEW: *Bull Cent Child Books* v67 no7 p360-1 Mr 2014 K. C.

REVIEW: *Kirkus Rev* v81 no23 p261 D 1 2013

REVIEW: *Publ Wkly* v260 no45 p74 N 11 2013

REVIEW: *SLJ* v60 no1 p99 Ja 2014 Tiffany Davis

REVIEW: *SLJ* v60 no5 p66 My 2014 Toby Rajput

REVIEW: *Voice of Youth Advocates* v36 no6 p60 F 2014 Amy Cummins

BRETT, JEANNIE.il. Wild about bears. See Brett, J.

BRETT, JEANNIE. Wild about bears; [by] Jeannie Brett 32 p. 2013 Charlesbridge

1. Bears—Behavior 2. Bears—Juvenile literature 3. Bears—Physiology 4. Children's nonfiction 5. Habitat (Ecology)

ISBN 1580894194; 9781580894180 (reinforced for library use); 9781580894197 (softcover); 9781607346364 (ebook)

LC 2012-038700

SUMMARY: This children's book, written and illustrated by Jeannie Brett, offers a "comprehensive look at the world's eight bear species focuses first on common physical traits and behaviors before profiling each bear. [Topics include] the habits and habitats of the polar bear, brown bear, American black bear, spectacled bear, Asiatic black bear, sloth bear, sun bear, and giant panda." (Publisher's note)

REVIEW: *Booklist* v110 no13 p64 Mr 1 2014 Abby Nolan

REVIEW: *Kirkus Rev* v82 no1 p222 Ja 1 2014

"Wild About Bears". " Both text and artwork support this book's title: full of facts, but only those emphasizing endearing bear habits; full of gentle watercolors that show peaceful bear-family scenes. The book is laid out logically. . . . There's plenty of new, gracefully defined vocabulary. . . . Despite the scientific, almost dry text, the bears' faces and body language border on anthropomorphism, with several bears gazing winsomely at readers. This helps to reinforce the author's assertion that humans need to protect bears and their habitats for everyone's mutual benefit. However, the older the reader, the less likely their acceptance of perpetually well-behaved bears."

REVIEW: *Publ Wkly* v260 no51 p58 D 16 2013

REVIEW: *SLJ* v60 no3 p171 Mr 2014 Susan E. Murray

BRETT, MICHAEL. Approaching African history; [by] Michael Brett xi, 356 p. 2013 James Currey

1. Historical literature

ISBN 1847010636; 9781847010636

LC 2012-462764

SUMMARY: It was the author's intent "to provide a narrative history of Africa over the past 10,000 years (the Holocene Era) as it has been presented in the discipline's sixty years of existence; to describe the growth of the concept of Africa; and to show the ways in which the narrative itself has been constructed and its context understood. He does this by treating the continent as a single unit of analysis." (Times Literary Supplement)

REVIEW: *Choice* v50 no12 p2292 Ag 2013 A. S. MacKinnon

REVIEW: *TLS* no5765 p24 S 27 2013 EMMANUEL AKYEAMPONG

"Approaching African History." "Structured in five parts, this is a lucid and very accessible study. In well-crafted short chapters, 'Approaching African History' can be digested in instalments, but it certainly rewards a reading from cover to cover. Its seamlessness, inter-regional connections, and integration into the Mediterranean, Indian Ocean and Atlantic worlds, underscore the artificiality of this division into Africa north and south of the Sahara, and the shortcomings of a regional focus. . . . I would have liked the book to end not just by pointing to a continent unable to feed its growing population, but also by acknowledging that in the past decade, six out of the ten fastest-growing countries in the world have been in Africa."

BREWSHIP, JAMES. Heaven's Tablet; Four Friends Search for a Beautiful Woman in Heaven; [by] James Brewship 244 p. 2013 Createspace Independent Pub

1. Angels—Fiction 2. Christian fiction 3. Future life—Fiction 4. Revelation 5. Tablets (Paleography)
ISBN 1481907387; 9781481907385

SUMMARY: In this book, "Michael Steele, senior employee of the Department of Fish and Game," is killed in a road accident. "He travels to heaven. . . . He meets his two guardian angels . . . who cheerfully handle his religious questions. . . . Eventually, Michael's wife, SarahAnn, and their friends Zach and Barbara Arnold join him in heaven, and they discover an ancient, jewel-encrusted tablet that had been brought from Earth to heaven centuries before, apparently by mistake." (Kirkus Reviews)

REVIEW: *Kirkus Rev* v82 no2 p316 Ja 15 2014

"Heaven's Tablet: Adventurers in Paradise Find a Way to Send a First-of-its-Kind Story From Heaven to Earth". "To put it mildly, there's no reason for a Muslim or a Jew to exist—to say nothing of an atheist; [James] Brewship's book is a fantasy solely for the Christian faithful. . . . Brewship's simple, brightly optimistic narration, in the vein of the most popular Christian fundamentalist fiction, will appeal to readers of Beverly Lewis and Ted Dekker who like their characters wholesome and the conclusions happy and faith-affirming. A sunny, fast-paced Christian afterlife-adventure story."

BRIANT, BONNIE.il. Mapping Manhattan. See Schwarz-Bart, Simone

BRIANT, ED.il. Petal and Poppy. See Clough, L.

BRIANT, ED.il. Petal and Poppy and the penguin. See Clough, L.

BRIGGS, CRAIG E. Our Lives As Caterpillars; [by] Craig E. Briggs 26 p. 2013 Createspace Independent Pub

1. Animal stories 2. Butterflies—Juvenile literature 3. Caterpillars—Juvenile literature 4. Children & death—Juvenile literature 5. Children's stories
ISBN 1484179293; 9781484179291

SUMMARY: "This book presents a framework for adults to discuss with children the death of a loved one, friend or pet without imposing any particular religious belief regarding life after death or even using the word death at all." It tells the story of a caterpillar mother and grandmother who must leave her family to become a butterfly. (Publisher's note)

REVIEW: *Kirkus Rev* v82 no1 p328 Ja 1 2014

"Our Lives As Caterpillars". "A comfortably homespun children's tale about caterpillars. . . . The author and illustrator—a former public school teacher and his 8-year-old granddaughter, respectively—touchingly address the loss of a beloved spouse and grandmother in their debut book. The book's strong specificity in its use of children's names, dates and actual locations, and its drawings from its young illustrator, encompass the reader in a unique world. Ten percent of the book's proceeds will support hospice centers, according to the book's cover, which shows that its heart beats even louder than its heartfelt words. An affecting children's book that accessibly addresses an uncomfortable issue for both children and adults."

BRIGGS, LAURA. Somebody's children; the politics of transracial and transnational adoption; [by] Laura Briggs xi, 360 p. 2012 Duke University Press

1. Adoption—United States 2. Child welfare—United States 3. Intercountry adoption—United States 4. Interracial adoption—United States 5. Social science literature
ISBN 9780822351474 (alk. paper); 9780822351610 (pbk. : alk. paper)
LC 2011-035893

SUMMARY: This book "examines the social and cultural forces--poverty, racism, economic inequality, and political violence--that have shaped transracial and transnational adoption in the United States during the second half of the twentieth century and the first decade of the twenty-first. . . . [Laura] Briggs analyzes the circumstances under which African American and Native mothers . . . have felt pressed to give up their children for adoption or have lost them involuntarily." (Publisher's note)

REVIEW: *Contemp Sociol* v42 no6 p829-30 N 2013 HEATHER JACOBSON

"Somebody's Children: The Politics of Transracial and Transnational Adoption." "In Somebody's Children: The Politics of Transracial and Transnational Adoption, Laura Briggs forcefully offers an alternative history focused on the various political, social, and cultural events that have shaped the processes through which vulnerable populations lose their children to adoption. . . . 'Somebody's Children' would be best read by those not only interested in adoption but who also have a knowledge of (or interest in) a range of historical and political events: domestic racial politics involving both African Americans and Native Americans; the various political figures and movements, wars, and uprisings in Latin America; Guatemalan politics; neoliberalism; fascism; and the Christian Right."

REVIEW: *Ethn Racial Stud* v37 no5 p857-9 My 2014 Ravinder Barn

REVIEW: *Women's Review of Books* v30 no1 p18-20 Ja/F 2013 Martha Nichols

BRIGGS, STEPHEN. Turtle Recall. See Pratchett, T.

BRIGGS, WARD.ed. The complete poems of James Dickey. See The complete poems of James Dickey

BRITISH ANTARCTIC SURVEY (COMPANY)comp. Antarctic Peninsula. See Antarctic Peninsula

BRITT, FANNY. Jane, the fox & me; 101 p. 2013 Pgw
1. Alienation (Social psychology)—Fiction 2. Bullying—Juvenile fiction 3. Eyre, Jane (Fictitious character) 4. Foxes 5. Graphic novels
ISBN 1554983606; 9781554983605

SUMMARY: Written by Fanny Britt, illustrated by Isabelle Arsentault, and translated by Christine Morelli and Susan Ouriou, this "graphic novel reveals the casual brutality of which children are capable, but also assures readers that redemption can be found through connecting with another, whether the other is a friend, a fictional character or even, amazingly, a fox." (Publisher's note)

REVIEW: *Booklist* v110 no4 p39 O 15 2013 Francisca Goldsmith

REVIEW: *Bull Cent Child Books* v67 no3 p140 N 2013 K. C.

REVIEW: *Horn Book Magazine* v90 no1 p84 Ja/F 2014 CYNTHIA K. RITTER

"Jane, the Fox & Me." "[Fanny] Britt and [Isabelle] Arsenault's powerful picture book–sized graphic novel about bullying, self-image, imagination, and (ultimately) hope centers on Hélène, ostracized by her former friends and now a loner at school. . . . Arsenault uses varied page layouts and a mix of illustrative techniques to pace the story and express emotion; monochromatic sketches depict Hélène's unhappy existence as well as surreal scenes that reflect her feelings, while pages in warm colors relate Jane's story. . . . she makes a new friend, the ebullient and compassionate Géraldine. This relationship transforms Hélène's world, as color begins to appear on the final spreads, highlighting her road to recovery. It's a profound ending to a brutally beautiful story."

REVIEW: *Kirkus Rev* v81 no15 p296 Ag 1 2013

REVIEW: *N Y Times Book Rev* p15 Ag 25 2013 TAFFY BRODESSER-AKNER

REVIEW: *Publ Wkly* v260 no28 p174 Jl 15 2013

REVIEW: *Quill Quire* v79 no7 p36 S 2013 Emily Donaldson

REVIEW: *Quill Quire* v79 no10 p18 D 2013 Kyo Maclear

REVIEW: *SLJ* v59 no11 p1 N 2013

BRITTAIN, DAVID. Eduardo Paolozzi at New Worlds; Science fiction and art in the sixties; [by] David Brittain 2013 Savoy Books
1. Ballard, J. G., 1930-2009 2. Historical literature 3. Moorcock, Michael 4. Paolozzi, Eduardo 5. Science fiction—Periodicals
ISBN 9780861301287 softcover

SUMMARY: "In 'Eduardo Paolozzi at New Worlds: Science Fiction and Art in the Sixties,' David Brittain examines the magazine during its prime period, throwing light on the interactions of the art of the time with what Judith Merril and Harlan Ellison called 'the new wave of science fiction.' The work of artist Eduardo Paolozzi was showcased in the magazine along with that of Pop Art colleague Richard Hamilton." (Publisher's note)

REVIEW: *TLS* no5785 p26 F 14 2014 PHIL BAKER

"Eduardo Paolozzi at 'New Worlds': Science Fiction and Art in the Sixties." "Founded in 1946, in the 'Golden Age' of mainstream science fiction, 'New Worlds' was a genre-bound publication featuring rocket ships and aliens. . . . David Brittain's book encompasses more than the title might suggest. As well as Eduardo Paolozzi's involvement with the magazine . . . , it details the role of [editor Michael] Moorcock himself, and that of [author J. G.] Ballard. . . . The tensions and contradictions at 'New Worlds' are among the book's most interesting aspects. . . . This solidly researched and sympathetically designed book shows 'New Worlds' to be as central to its era as the more celebrated underground press."

BROADLEY, ROSIE. Laura Knight Portraits; [by] Rosie Broadley 128 p. 2013 Antique Collectors Club Ltd
1. Art catalogs 2. British painting 3. British portrait painting 4. Knight, Laura, 1877-1970 5. Women painters
ISBN 1855144638; 9781855144637

SUMMARY: This catalogue of portraits by painter Laura Knight "features over 35 of her finest works from across her long and prolific career, demonstrating both the variety of her subjects and her consummate skills as an artist. During the course of an extraordinarily productive career that spanned over 70 years, Knight's work reflected her commitment to depicting modern life and her fascination with the human figure." (Publisher's note)

REVIEW: *Burlington Mag* v156 no1330 p39 Ja 2014 R.S.

"Sir Alfred Munnings: An Artist's Life," "Laura Knight Portraits," and "Sickert: From Life". "The works range from the painter's early East Anglian years and his visits to Newlyn—his most energetic and bravura period. Later paintings are for the most part smoothly equestrian but there are some good landscapes, a lesser-known aspect of Munnings's output, especially the sensitive Exmoor snow from the 1940s. . . . Knight's portraits and figure pieces are well catalogued here for the touring exhibition. . . . The Fine Art Society has a long connection with the work of Walter Sickert, particularly, in recent years, his prints. The exhibition it mounted in the summer of 2013 included fine prints from the Bromberg collection as well as paintings, drawings and watercolours."

BROCK-BROIDO, LUCIE. Stay, Illusion; Poems; [by] Lucie Brock-Broido 112 p. 2013 Random House Inc
1. Families—Poetry 2. Fathers & daughters 3. Grief 4. Poems—Collections 5. Self
ISBN 0307962024; 9780307962027 (Hardcover)
LC 2013-023978

SUMMARY: Author Lucie Brock-Broido presents a poetry collection designed to "spin, drape, and sculpt its virtuosic figures around the ideas and emotions of mourning. Often Brock-Broido commemorates her father, remembering him on his own, in her family, in conjunction with her own past selves." (Publishers Weekly)

REVIEW: *Antioch Rev* v72 no1 p192-3 Wint 2014 Alex M. Frankel

"Stay, Illusion". "[Lucie Brock-Broido's] love of words and her genius for manipulating them in order to explore their virtually limitless possibilities fill every page of this collection. In her art, language is foregrounded to an extent rarely seen even in poetry. . . . 'Stay, Illusion' is, for all the 'over-the-topness' of the writing, a very accessible book. Her mind may be bouncing in every direction, like a Baroque altarpiece in motion, but she is seldom obscure. Her only fault (if it can be called that) may be that she tends to focus on collecting brilliant individual lines at the expense of the unity of poems, so that the reader is often hyper-conscious of reading 'a poem' rather than experiencing the heat and heartbeat of life."

REVIEW: *Booklist* v110 no4 p11 O 15 2013 Donna Seaman

REVIEW: *Libr J* v138 no15 p76 S 15 2013 Barbara Hoffert

REVIEW: *New Yorker* v89 no34 p78-1 O 28 2013

"Stay, Illusion." "[Lucie] Brock-Broido's poems, haunted by old words and meanings, full of occult spells and curses, nearly Pre-Raphaelite in their taste for gilt and gaud, have much to say to the dead. Her work offers autobiography not as memoir--the chosen mode of so many American poets--but, rather, as grimoire. Brock-Broido's poems can be baffling, but because of their stylish spookiness (some combination of Poe and Stevie Nicks) they are never boring. Their aesthetic saturates every single word, so you can start out in her work almost anywhere. . . . I don't like everything in Brock-Broido's work, but, to steer clear of tour de force, a style like this one has to fail some of the time; it has to find some subject that suits it badly."

REVIEW: *Publ Wkly* v260 no34 p48 Ag 26 2013

REVIEW: *Va Q Rev* v90 no4 p214-21 Fall 2014 Lisa Russ Spaar

BROCKET, JANE.il. Cold, crunchy, colorful. See Brocket, J.

BROCKET, JANE. Cold, crunchy, colorful; using our senses; [by] Jane Brocket 32 p. 2014 Millbrook Press

1. Children's nonfiction 2. Senses and sensation—Juvenile literature 3. Smell—Juvenile literature 4. Taste—Juvenile literature 5. Touch—Juvenile literature

ISBN 1467702331; 9781467702331 (lib. bdg.: alk. paper)

LC 2013-020010

SUMMARY: This children's book, written and featuring photographs by Jane Brocket, part of Jane Brocket's Clever Concepts series focuses on the senses of sight, touch, taste, smell, and sound. According to the book, "seeing brightly colored flowers, hearing nuts go 'crunch,' and feeling cold ice cream on your tongue—we use our senses to explore the world." (Publisher's note)

REVIEW: *Booklist* v110 no11 p53 F 1 2014 J. B. Petty

REVIEW: *Kirkus Rev* v82 no2 p172 Ja 15 2014

"Cold, Crunchy, Colorful: Using Our Senses". "[Jane] Brocket's latest in the Clever Concepts series uses photographs to explore the five senses. The text explains the five senses in a way even the youngest of readers can understand, and it's paired with simple photos that highlight just what the text is mentioning but that are also full of patterns, shapes, colors and textures. . . . Teachers and parents eager for their children to experience the world in a different way will be thrilled."

REVIEW: *SLJ* v60 no2 p117 F 2014 Alyson Low

BROCKMAN, JOHN.ed. What Should We Be Worried About? See What Should We Be Worried About?

BROCKMANN, SUZANNE. Do or die; Reluctant Heroes; [by] Suzanne Brockmann 576 p. 2014 Ballantine Books

1. FICTION—Romance—Contemporary 2. FICTION—Romance—General 3. FICTION—Romance—Suspense 4. Kidnapping—Fiction 5. Private investigators—Fiction

ISBN 0345543793; 9780345543790 (hardback)

LC 2013-045806

SUMMARY: This novel by Suzanne Brockmann is part of the Reluctant Heroes series and describes how protagonist Ian Dunn is chosen to "breach a heavily guarded embassy and rescue a pair of children kidnapped by their own father, a sinister foreign national willing to turn his kids into casualties. Shockingly, Ian passes on the mission for reasons he will not—or cannot—reveal. But saying no is not an option. Especially not for Phoebe Kruger, Ian's beautiful . . . attorney." (Publisher's note)

REVIEW: *Kirkus Rev* v81 no24 p312 D 15 2013

"Do or Die". "Attorney Phoebe Kruger is tasked with negotiating client Ian Dunn's prison release, against his will, so he can rescue two kidnapped children, not realizing that doing so will set events in motion that will threaten dozens of lives—and a few hearts. . . . As outlandish as the plot sounds on paper, [Suzanne] Brockmann effortlessly and expertly tosses hundreds of details into the air and juggles them with brilliance. The first in her Reluctant Heroes series, the novel will captivate readers with its intense, action-filled plot, alpha-and-a-half hero, and his smart, perfect-for-him heroine, as well as secondary characters who contribute pathos and humor. Enthralling and breathtaking."

BRODY, FRANCES. Murder in the afternoon; [by] Frances Brody 400 p. 2014 Minotaur Books

1. FICTION—Mystery & Detective—Historical 2. FICTION—Mystery & Detective—Traditional British 3. FICTION—Mystery & Detective—Women Sleuths 4. Murder—Investigation—Fiction 5. Women private investigators—England—Fiction

ISBN 9781250037022 (hardback)

LC 2013-039454

SUMMARY: In Frances Brody's "third Kate Shackleton mystery set in post-WWI England . . . Harriet Armstrong and her younger brother, Austin, find the body of their stone mason father, Ethan, lying in a hut by the quarry where he works. Harriet goes to a nearby farm for help, but the body is gone by the time she returns. Ethan's wife, Mary Jane, later asks Kate, who is a private detective, to investigate; she also gives Kate news of her family that changes her life." (Publishers Weekly)

REVIEW: *Kirkus Rev* v82 no1 p298 Ja 1 2014

"Murder in the Afternoon". "The death of a radical stonemason changes the life of a sleuth forever. Kate Shackleton is a World War I widow who still hasn't given up hope that her MIA husband is alive. Adopted as a baby by a high-ranking police officer and his aristocratic wife, she's never had any interest in her birth family. When a woman pounds on her door in the middle of the night and announces that she's Kate's sister, Mary Jane Armstrong, Kate takes up the case of her missing husband. . . . [Frances] Brody's third in the series . . . is a perfect fit for lovers of classic British mysteries who'd like to watch a clever, introspective, delightful heroine solve a tricky puzzle."

REVIEW: *Libr J* v139 no2 p59 F 1 2014 Teresa L. Jacobsen

REVIEW: *Publ Wkly* v260 no51 p41 D 16 2013

BROICH, JOHN. London; water and the making of the

modern city; [by] John Broich xiii, 214 p. 2013 Univ of Pittsburgh Pr
1. Historical literature 2. London (England)—History—19th century 3. Water resources development—England—London—History 4. Water supply—Great Britain 5. Water supply—History 6. Water-supply—England—London—History
ISBN 0822944278; 9780822944270 (hardcover : alk. paper)
LC 2012-047752

SUMMARY: This book, by John Broich, examines how "the debate over how to supply London with water came to a head when the climate itself forced the endgame near the end of the nineteenth century. At that decisive moment, the Conservative party succeeded in dictating the relationship between water, power, and society in London for many decades to come." (Publisher's note)

REVIEW: *Choice* v51 no1 p151 S 2013 W. S. Rodner
"London: Water and the Making of the Modern City." "Supplying London with clean water in the 19th century became a major concern for reformers and leaders of the rapidly expanding city. The exploding population of Britain's commercial and political capital necessitated the introduction of vast public services to make the metropolis livable. Yet progress could be slowed by clashes between private interests and government. In this clearly written study, [author John] Broich . . . shifts from the customary emphasis on sewers and waste disposal to the acquisition of pure water for drinking and washing."

BROMFIELD, ANDREW.tr. A displaced person. Voinovich, V.

BROOKER, KYRSTEN.il. Dinner with the Highbrows. See Holt, K. W.

BROOKER, PETER. The Oxford critical and cultural history of modernist magazines; [by] Peter Brooker xvii, 955 2009 Oxford University Press
1. English literature—History & criticism 2. Historical literature 3. Literature and society 4. Little magazines—History 5. Modernism (Literature)
ISBN 9780199211159; 0199211159
LC 2009-280149

SUMMARY: This book looks at " the wide and varied range of 'little magazines' which were so instrumental in introducing the new writing and ideas that came to constitute literary and artistic modernism in the UK and Ireland. n thirty-seven chapters covering over eighty magazines . . . contributors investigate the inner dynamics and economic and intellectual conditions that governed the life of these fugitive but vibrant publications. " (Publisher's note)

REVIEW: *London Rev Books* v36 no2 p33-5 Ja 23 2014 Evan Kindley
"The Oxford Critical and Cultural History of Modernist Magazines: Britain & Ireland 1880-1955," "The Oxford Critical and Cultural History of Modernist Magazines: North America 1894-1955," "The Oxford Critical and Cultural History of Modernist Magazines: Europe 1880-1940". "A synoptic view of the modernist little magazine is very hard to come by, especially given that, on top of the sheer volume of the material, there are problems of definition. . . . 'The origins of the small review are lost in obscurity,' Ezra Pound wrote in his 1930 essay 'Small Magazines', but [Peter] Brooker and [Andrew] Thacker do their best to reconstruct them."

BROOKMYRE, CHRISTOPHER. Bred in the Bone; A Jasmine Sharp and Catherine Mcleod Novel; [by] Christopher Brookmyre 416 p. 2014 Pgw
1. Detective & mystery stories 2. Glasgow (Scotland)—Fiction 3. Murder investigation—Fiction 4. Organized crime—Fiction 5. Women detectives—Fiction
ISBN 0802122477; 9780802122476

SUMMARY: This book, by Christopher Brookmyre, is the third book in a series about Scottish "private investigator Jasmine Sharp and Detective Superintendent Catherine McLeod. . . . Sharp's father was murdered before she was born. . . . Since her mother's death, all she has been able to learn is his first name—and that only through . . . the man who killed him: Glen Fallan. But . . . Fallan is arrested for the murder of a criminal her mother knew since childhood." (Publisher's note)

REVIEW: *Booklist* v110 no14 p52 Mr 15 2014 Thomas Gaughan

REVIEW: *Kirkus Rev* v82 no4 p191 F 15 2014
"Bred in the Bone". "Jasmine Sharp and Catherine McLeod return in the third book of their series, this time to investigate the gangland execution of a Glasgow crime boss and its links to much-older murders. . . . [Christopher] Brookmyre . . . spares no detail in his account of Glasgow's violent underworld. Although his characters are satisfyingly multidimensional, the uninitiated will find the long, slow exposition that relies on previous cases even more challenging than the Scottish slang."

REVIEW: *Libr J* v138 no21 p66 D 1 2013 Barbara Hoffert

REVIEW: *Libr J* v139 no6 p73 Ap 1 2014 Roland Person

REVIEW: *Publ Wkly* v261 no9 p46 Mr 3 2014

BROOKS, DEBORAH JORDAN. He runs, she runs; why gender stereotypes do not harm women candidates; [by] Deborah Jordan Brooks xii, 221 p. 2013 Princeton University Press
1. Gender stereotypes 2. Political campaigns—United States 3. Political science literature 4. Women—Political activity—United States 5. Women political candidates—United States
ISBN 9780691153414 (hardcover: alk. paper); 9780691153421 (pbk.: alk. paper)
LC 2012-045252

SUMMARY: In this book, "Deborah Jordan Brooks examines whether various behaviors—such as crying, acting tough, displays of anger, or knowledge gaffes—by male and female political candidates are regarded differently by the public. Refuting the idea of double standards in campaigns, Brooks's overall analysis indicates that female candidates do not get penalized disproportionately for various behaviors, nor do they face any double bind regarding femininity and toughness. " (Publisher's note)

REVIEW: *Choice* v51 no8 p1491-2 Ap 2014 J. D. Rausch
"He Runs, She Runs: Why Gender Stereotypes Do Not Harm Women Candidates". "[Deborah Jordan] Brooks . . . argues that women candidates are not harmed by gender stereotypes, a position that challenges much of the conven-

tional wisdom explaining why women candidates lose to male opponents. The book begins by outlining the accepted theories on why gender matters in political campaigns. The concise review is a nice summary of this body of research. Chapter 2 presents the theoretical foundation of the book and introduces the reader to the impact of gender stereotypes on political campaigns. Brooks critiques this research as focusing only on descriptive stereotypes without considering prescriptive stereotypes, or how people should act."

REVIEW: *Women's Review of Books* v31 no4 p12-3 Jl/Ag 2014 Joanna Weiss

BROOKS, JEANICE. The musical work of Nadia Boulanger; performing past and future between the wars; [by] Jeanice Brooks xvi, 289 p. 2013 Cambridge University Press

1. Conductors (Music)—France—Biography 2. Music—History & criticism—Study & teaching 3. Music literature 4. Music teachers—France—Biography
ISBN 1107009146; 9781107009141
LC 2012-027495

SUMMARY: This book on musician Nadia Boulanger, by Jeanice Brooks, "considers how gender shaped the possibilities that marked Boulanger's performing career, tracing her meteoric rise as a conductor in the 1930s to origins in the classroom and the salon. Brooks investigates Boulanger's promotion of structurally motivated performance styles, showing how her ideas on performance of historical repertory and new music relate to her teaching of music analysis and music history." (Publisher's note)

REVIEW: *Choice* v51 no8 p1409-10 Ap 2014 J. M. Edwards

"The Musical Work of Nadia Boulanger: Performing Past and Future Between the Wars". "Grounded in broad cultural understanding and detailed research, this book presents a fascinating account of Boulanger's teaching and performing lives. Focusing on the interwar years, [Jeanice] Brooks . . . utilizes Boulanger's many published reviews of major performers, letters, score annotations, reviews of her performances as conductor and at the keyboard, and extensive analysis of Boulanger's recordings to show the unity of Boulanger's approach to performance and teaching."

BROOKS, RICHARD R. W. Saving the neighborhood; racially restrictive covenants, law, and social norms; [by] Richard R. W. Brooks 294 p. 2013 Harvard University Press

1. Discrimination in housing—Law and legislation—United States 2. Historical literature 3. Housing—Law & legislation—United States 4. Real covenants—United States 5. Social norms
ISBN 9780674072541
LC 2012-034463

SUMMARY: In this book, Richard R. W. Brooks and Carol M. Rose "uncover how loosely knit urban and suburban communities, fearing ethnic mixing or even 'tipping,' were fair game to a new class of entrepreneurs who catered to their fears while exacerbating the message encoded in covenants: that black residents threatened white property values. Legal racial covenants expressed and bestowed an aura of legitimacy upon the wish of many white neighborhoods to exclude minorities." (Publisher's note)

REVIEW: *Choice* v51 no9 p1681 My 2014 M. E. Ethridge

"Saving the Neighborhood: Racially Restrictive Covenants, Law, and Social Norms". "Beginning in the early 20th century, real estate developers, banking institutions, and many homeowners began adding racially restrictive covenants to deeds to preserve racial segregation in housing. . . . The book presents no original empirical research, but it provides a solid overview of the relevant court cases, statutes, and legal and political commentary. 'Saving the Neighborhood' makes a convincing case for the proposition that the effect of legal provisions can he fully understood only in the context of relevant social norms, economic incentives, and informal influences."

REVIEW: *J Am Hist* v101 no2 p639-40 S 2014

REVIEW: *Rev Am Hist* v42 no3 p536-40 S 2014 Gail Williams O'Brien

BROOM, JENNY. The Lion and the mouse; turn-and-tell tales; [by] Jenny Broom 32 p. 2013 Candlewick Press

1. Children's stories 2. Fables 3. Friendship—Fiction 4. Lions—Juvenile literature 5. Mice—Juvenile fiction
ISBN 9780763666194
LC 2013-934309

SUMMARY: In this children's book, "rather than playing along with the mouse's attempt at negotiation, the lion refrains from eating the hungry mouse and helps him to get the juicy berries he desires. The mouse's promise to return the favor materializes when hunters come in the night and trap the unsuspecting lion in a net. Naturally, the mouse frees the lion by gnawing away the strings of the net. . . . Lion and mouse become BFFs." (Kirkus Reviews)

REVIEW: *Bull Cent Child Books* v67 no10 p503-4 Je 2014 H. M.

REVIEW: *Kirkus Rev* v82 no4 p121 F 15 2014

"The Lion and the Mouse". "A lackluster take on the well-worn Aesop's fable that does not stand up as well as other picture-book interpretations. . . . [Nahta] Nój's textured cut-paper collage with some subtle die cuts enliven the rather ho-hum text and are cleanly executed. However, the highly stylized nature of the collage makes the lion's shape more than a little odd in some of the illustrations. The style is so tight and formal that some of the shapes are hard to read, particularly when presented in silhouette. . . . Paper collage need not be as unforgiving as it is here; some of the figures have the look of Lego blocks and may be hard for young children to interpret. Almost too squeaky-clean to be much fun."

REVIEW: *SLJ* v60 no3 p171 Mr 2014 Janene Corbin

BROWN, ALISON. Eddie and Dog; [by] Alison Brown 32 p. 2014 Capstone Pr Inc

1. Children's stories 2. Dogs—Juvenile fiction 3. Friendship—Juvenile fiction 4. Human-animal relationships—Fiction 5. Parent & child—Juvenile literature
ISBN 1623701147; 9781623701147

SUMMARY: This children's book "begins at the airport, where Eddie dreams of adventure. A white dog emerges from the carrier on the luggage carousel and introduces himself, and the adventures begin. . . . Eddie's mother, being a more practical type, decides the dog cannot stay as they don't have a big yard. Three times she sends the dog away, and three times he returns, riding up on a motor scooter, snorkeling along the shore and parachuting from an airplane." (Kirkus

Reviews)

REVIEW: *Kirkus Rev* v82 no1 p196 Ja 1 2014

"Eddie and Dog". "This effervescent boy-and-dog tale is worth making some room on the shelf. . . . Children will see a warm story of a great dog and a red-haired little boy who have found a perfect friendship. Adults, if they listen closely, may see beyond the inconvenient realities of having a creative, active and persistent child. Unexpected adventures have their own unique rewards, like the glow of true happiness on an imaginative boy's face. A sweet choice for dog lovers, active children or anyone searching for a friend. "

REVIEW: *Publ Wkly* v260 no48 p53 N 25 2013

REVIEW: *SLJ* v60 no3 p104 Mr 2014 Laura J. Giunta

BROWN, ANDREW.tr. A journey around my room. See De Maistre, X.

BROWN, ANDY.tr. Why Hell Stinks of Sulfur. See Kroonenberg, S.

BROWN, BARBARA. Hanukkah in Alaska; [by] Barbara Brown 32 p. 2013 Henry Holt and Company

1. Auroras—Fiction 2. Children's stories 3. Hanukkah—Fiction 4. Jews—United States—Fiction 5. Moose—Fiction 6. Winter—Fiction

ISBN 0805097481; 9780805097481 (hardcover)

LC 2013-003166

SUMMARY: In this children's picture book set in Alaska, a girl and her family want to watch the aurora borealis, or northern lights. Things are complicated by the fact that in their backyard, "a moose has taken up residence. . . . While beautiful, the moose can also be dangerous. Luring him away with apples and carrots does not work, but . . . a trail of latkes on the snow tempts the moose away from the swing," and the family can watch the lights on the last night of Hanukkah. (Kirkus Reviews)

REVIEW: *Bull Cent Child Books* v67 no3 p140-1 N 2013 D. S.

"Hanukkah in Alaska." "Winter in Alaska is a different experience, marked by limited daylight and fearlessly marauding moose, who enjoy the convenience of human-plowed streets and driveways. Even the promise of Hanukkah isn't enough to cheer up the narrator, a young girl who's worried that the moose hanging around her family's backyard will wreck her beloved blue swing. . . . The text (adapted from a previously published short story) is an inviting combination of matter-of-factness and vivid local detail. . . . [Illustrator Stacey] Schuett's softly rounded and rosy-faced figures are particularly suited to the story, and the acrylic and gouache illustrations give the snow-mounded scenery a cozy domesticity with occasional comic touches. . . ."

REVIEW: *Horn Book Magazine* v89 no6 p62 N/D 2013 LISSA GERSHOWITZ

REVIEW: *Kirkus Rev* v81 no17 p128 S 1 2013

REVIEW: *Publ Wkly* v260 no37 p50-2 S 16 2013

REVIEW: *SLJ* v59 no10 p1 O 2013 Teri Markson

BROWN, BARRY.ed. The Sage Handbook of Digital Technology Research. See The Sage Handbook of Digital Technology Research

BROWN, CANDY GUNTHER. The healing gods; complementary and alternative medicine in Christian America; [by] Candy Gunther Brown xii, 322 p. 2013 Oxford University Press

1. Alternative medicine—Religious aspects—Christianity 2. Alternative medicine—United States 3. Christianity & medicine 4. Medical literature 5. Mind and body therapies—United States

ISBN 9780199985784 (cloth: alk. paper)

LC 2012-050010

SUMMARY: In this book on complementary and alternative medicine (CAM), author Candy Gunther Brown "explains how and why CAM entered the American biomedical mainstream and won cultural acceptance, even among evangelical and other theologically conservative Christians, despite its ties to non-Christian religions and the lack of scientific evidence of its efficacy and safety." (Publisher's note)

REVIEW: *Choice* v51 no8 p1437 Ap 2014 C. L. Mejta

"The Healing Gods: Complementary and Alternative Medicine in Christian America". "The author raises an interesting albeit controversial argument that CAM [complementary and alternative medicine] practices should be placed in the same category as other religious healing practices because of their theological underpinnings. Thus, CAM should be subjected to the same legal, constitutional, and medical-ethical regulations as other religions. . . . The author's arguments, while informed and logical, do have a conspiratorial edge to them at times. In targeting CAM, [Candy Gunther] Brown fails to note that many of today's medical paradigms have evolved from philosophical, theological, and sociological tenets of disease."

BROWN, CARRON. On the farm; [by] Carron Brown 18 p. 2013 Kingfisher

1. Agricultural equipment 2. Children's stories 3. Domestic animals—Juvenile literature 4. Farm life—Juvenile literature 5. Farmers

ISBN 0753469405; 9780753469408

SUMMARY: This children's book is an "introduction to farm life [and] includes a cover of layered, bubble-shaped pages of various sizes, each with an image of a farm animal peeking through. Once a page is turned, bright stock photos of livestock, working animals and even the farmer appear in the inside. A heading introduces them . . . and one or two simple facts are shared. . . . One section of each spread still retains the image that is visible from the cover and hints at what is coming next on the verso." (Kirkus Reviews)

REVIEW: *Kirkus Rev* v82 no1 p6 Ja 1 2014

"On the Farm". "This iteration of the Seek and Peek gimmick of shaped pages is more successful than others in the series such At the Zoo, In the Rainforest and Dinosaurs, with their confusing layouts. Here, the strong background color of each spread helps differentiate the information in question from the images of things to come. The last double-page spread shows a tractor and a combine harvester and shares a couple of tidbits about farmyard machinery. The novel format will make it difficult for spine-out shelving in libraries and elsewhere. With short facts about pigs, chickens, cattle, horses and more, there is just enough to be of interest to the youngest animal enthusiast."

BROWN, CARRON. Secrets of the apple tree; [by] Carron Brown 2014 Kane Miller, A Division of EDC Pub.

1. Apples 2. Birds—Juvenile literature 3. Earthworms 4. Habitat (Ecology) 5. Picture books for children
ISBN 9781610672436 (hardcover)
LC 2013-939410

SUMMARY: This children's book was written by Carron Brown. "Secret life under, in and around an apple tree can be revealed when light shines through the pages of this interactive . . . book. . . . The bird takes one of the earthworms to her chicks in a leaf-covered nest. A toad hides in the leaves, a lizard shelters under stones, and a moth is camouflaged on the trunk. . . . A paragraph of further information about each animal described is provided at the end." (Kirkus Reviews)

REVIEW: *Kirkus Rev* v82 no3 p292 F 1 2014

"Secrets of the Apple Tree: A Shine-a-Light Book". "Secret life under, in and around an apple tree can be revealed when light shines through the pages of this interactive, flawed book. . . . The author suggests that readers use a flashlight or hold the page up to a light to discern what might occupy the plain green area in the middle of the page. Luckily, if this proves awkward, or the right-sized light isn't available, the answers to the questions posed on each colorful right-hand page are revealed in the black-and-white silhouettes on the next page. . . . Very young book lovers might be intrigued by the peekaboo game but will be better served by a more accurate representation of the natural world."

BROWN, DAN, 1964-. Inferno; a novel; [by] Dan Brown x, 461 p. 2013 Doubleday

1. Adventure stories 2. Cryptographers—Fiction 3. Langdon, Robert (Fictitious character)—Fiction
ISBN 0385537859 (hardback); 9780385537858 (hardback)
LC 2012-533166

SUMMARY: In this book, Dan Brown's Robert Langdon "wakes up in a Florence hospital unable to remember the last several days. A bullet has grazed his head, and some bad people are after him, but with the help of the lovely Dr. Sienna Brooks, he's able to escape--and escape and escape, as he slowly comprehends that a plague is quite deliberately about to be released, and it's his job to figure out the puzzles and symbols that lead to its location." (Booklist)

REVIEW: *Booklist* v110 no1 p58 S 1 2013 Joyce Saricks

REVIEW: *Christ Century* v130 no19 p36-8 S 18 2013 Harold K. Bush

REVIEW: *N Y Rev Books* v60 no16 p41-3 O 24 2013 Robert Pogue Harrison

"Inferno," "Inferno," and "The Divine Comedy." "Like everything else in this astonishingly bad novel, [Robert] Langdon's lecture lacks verisimilitude. . . . Mary Jo Bang preserves the tercet form without attempting to reproduce Dante's rhyme scheme. Being an excellent poet in her own right, she succeeds in giving the Inferno's narrative drama an energetic idiom that gets the poem moving, and at times even dancing, on the page. . . . Clive James's translation has no such élan. His decision to dispense with explanatory notes altogether and to lift the relevant information 'out of the basement and put . . . it on display in the text' comes at a high price with minimal payoff, not only because it obliges him to import into the body of the poem much material that does not properly belong there, but because it invariably blunts the narrative impact of the original."

BROWN, DANIEL JAMES. The Boys in the Boat; Nine Americans and Their Epic Quest for Gold at the 1936 Berlin Olympics; [by] Daniel James Brown 432 p. 2013 Penguin Group USA

1. Historical literature 2. Olympic Games (11th : 1936 : Berlin, Germany) 3. Rowers—United States—Biography 4. Rowing—United States—History
ISBN 067002581X (hardcover); 9780670025817 (hardcover)
LC 2013-001560

SUMMARY: This book, by Daniel James Brown, "tells the story of the University of Washington's 1936 eight-oar crew and their . . . quest for an Olympic gold medal, a team that transformed the sport and grabbed the attention of millions of Americans. The sons of loggers, shipyard workers, and farmers, the boys defeated elite rivals first from eastern and British universities and finally the German crew rowing for Adolf Hitler in the Olympic games in Berlin, 1936." (Publisher's note)

REVIEW: *Booklist* v110 no1 p55 S 1 2013 Sue-Ellen Beauregard

REVIEW: *Booklist* v109 no17 p58 My 1 2013 Alan Moores

REVIEW: *Booklist* v110 no1 p32 S 1 2013 Bill Ott

"The Boys in the Boat," "A Chance to Win," and "Color Blind: The Forgotten Team That Broke Baseball's Color Line." "The Jesse Owens story will always be the big event of the 1936 Berlin Olympics, but the triumph of the University of Washington's crew team in those same games comes in a close second. [Daniel James] Brown retells the little-known story with verve. . . . [Jonathan] Schuppe follows the remarkable life story of Rodney Mason, a New Jersey baseball star and gang member who was confined to a wheelchair after a shooting and rebuilt his life around drawing young people at risk to baseball. . . . [Tom] Dunkel tells the story of a North Dakota car dealer who, more than a decade before Jackie Robinson, formed an integrated baseball team that captured the hearts of the region."

REVIEW: *Kirkus Rev* v81 no2 p58 Je 1 2013

REVIEW: *Kirkus Rev* v81 no7 p225 Ap 1 2013

REVIEW: *Libr J* v138 no7 p90 Ap 15 2013 Jerry P. Miller

REVIEW: *Libr J* v138 no1 p62 Ja 1 2013

REVIEW: *Publ Wkly* v260 no21 p9 My 27 2013

REVIEW: *Publ Wkly* v260 no15 p58 Ap 15 2013

REVIEW: *Smithsonian* v44 no3 p102 Je 2013 Chloë Schama

BROWN, DANNY. Influence marketing; how to create, manage, and measure brand influencers in social media marketing; [by] Danny Brown xii, 227 p. 2013 Que

1. Business literature 2. Influence (Psychology) 3. Internet marketing 4. Relationship marketing 5. Social media
ISBN 0789751046; 9780789751041
LC 2013-935189

SUMMARY: In this book on influence marketing, "the authors discuss the impact of social media on consumer decision making and the factors that affect purchase decisions in this new media environment. They point out that the challenge for marketers in this new world is to 'identify and manage influence paths' in a way that resonates with potential customers to build brand awareness and brand loyalty." (Choice: Current Reviews for Academic Libraries)

REVIEW: *Choice* v51 no5 p884 Ja 2014 P. G. Kishel

"Influence Marketing: How to Create, Manage, and Measure Brand Influencers in Social Media Marketing." "While the Internet makes it easier to expand one's reach, at the same time information overload and communication clutter can cause messages to get lost or shut out. [Danny] Brown and [Sam] Fiorella present a practical strategy to harness the power of influencers, the '4 Ms,' enabling marketers to 'make, manage, monitor, measure' the influencers critical to a brand's success. . . . Recommended."

BROWN, DON.il. The great American dust bowl. See Brown, D.

BROWN, DON. The great American dust bowl; [by] Don Brown 80 p. 2013 Houghton Mifflin Harcourt

1. Depressions—1929 2. Droughts—United States—History 3. Dust Bowl Era, 1931-1939 4. Dust storms—History 5. Graphic nonfiction
ISBN 0547815506; 9780547815503

SUMMARY: Author Don Brown presents a "graphic novel of one of America's most catastrophic natural events: the Dust Bowl. On a clear, warm Sunday, April 14, 1935, a wild wind whipped up millions upon millions of these specks of dust to form a duster, a savage storm on America's high southern plains." (Publisher's note)

REVIEW: *Booklist* v110 no4 p39 O 15 2013 Francisco Goldsmith

REVIEW: *Bull Cent Child Books* v67 no5 p292-5 Ja 2014 Deborah Stevenson

REVIEW: *Bull Cent Child Books* v67 no2 p69-70 O 2013 Elizabeth Bush Don Brown

REVIEW: *Bull Cent Child Books* v67 no2 p78 O 2013 T. A.

REVIEW: *Horn Book Magazine* v89 no6 p113-4 N/D 2013 SAM BLOOM

REVIEW: *Kirkus Rev* p72 N 15 2013 Best Books

REVIEW: *Kirkus Rev* v81 no15 p304 Ag 1 2013

REVIEW: *N Y Times Book Rev* p38 N 10 2013 BETSY BIRD

"The Great American Dust Bowl" and "Donner Dinner Party." "Don Brown and Nathan Hale use impressive artistry to recount two of the American West's most infamous tragedies in graphic-novel form. . . . Yet while Brown's narrative focuses on extreme woe's, there's something curiously undramatic about his illustrations. It's as if he wants to rein in the atrocious elements of his story even as he bring them to light. You come to wonder if his reluctance to heighten the action with more exciting pictures is part of a refusal to sensationalize. . . 'Donner Dinner Party' is, as it boats, 'dire and disgusting, but a testament to the human will to survive. . . . Most children will probably prefer Hale's blood-soaked adventures over Brown's careful and grim account of an environmental catastrophe."

REVIEW: *Publ Wkly* v260 no35 p63 S 2 2013

REVIEW: *SLJ* v59 no9 p168 S 2013 Peter Blenski

BROWN, DON, 1949-. He has shot the president!; April 14, 1865: the day John Wilkes Booth killed President Lincoln; [by] Don Brown 64 p. 2014 Roaring Brook Press

1. Children's nonfiction 2. Johnson, Andrew, 1808-1875 3. Seward, William Henry, 1801-1872
ISBN 1596432241; 9781596432246 (hardcover)
LC 2013-016334

SUMMARY: This book, by Don Brown, "is . . . [an] account of the assassination of President Lincoln. [John Wilkes] Booth 'believed that robbing the Union of the president's leadership would cripple the North and save the South.' . . . The assassination takes place early on, and the brunt of the book follows Booth's attempted flight, Lincoln's death, and the 'relentless, sweeping investigation' to find Booth and his conspirators." (Publishers Weekly)

REVIEW: *Booklist* v110 no14 p69 Mr 15 2014 Jesse Karp

REVIEW: *Bull Cent Child Books* v67 no9 p444-5 My 2014 E. B.

"He Has Shot the President!: April 14, 1865: The Day John Wilkes Booth Killed President Lincoln". "This new entry in [Don] Brown's Actual Times series revisits April 14,1863, when actor John Wilkes Booth fired the bullet that killed Abraham Lincoln. The constraint of sixty-four heavily illustrated pages naturally means that the events surrounding the fatal shot are condensed, but Brown uses that compression to his advantage in capturing the urgency in which the frantic manhunt for Lincoln's killer proceeded alongside the solemnities of Lincoln's funeral rites and how concurrent assassination plots against Vice-President [Andrew] Johnson and [William H.] Secretary of State Seward played (or failed to play) out."

REVIEW: *Horn Book Magazine* v90 no2 p136 Mr/Ap 2014 BETTY CARTER

REVIEW: *Kirkus Rev* v82 no4 p118 F 15 2014

REVIEW: *Publ Wkly* v261 no4 p192 Ja 27 2014

REVIEW: *SLJ* v60 no3 p171 Mr 2014 Misti Tidman

BROWN, DON, 1949-. Ruth Law thrills a nation. See Ruth Law thrills a nation

BROWN, ERICA. Comedy and the feminine middlebrow novel; Elizabeth von Arnim and Elizabeth Taylor; [by] Erica Brown ix, 164 p. 2013 Pickering & Chatto

1. English fiction—Women authors—History and criticism 2. Humor in literature 3. Humorous stories, English—History and criticism 4. Literary critiques 5. Middle class in literature 6. Women in literature
ISBN 184893338X (hbk.); 1848933398 (ebook); 9781848933385 (hbk.); 9781848933392 (ebook)
LC 2012-532345

SUMMARY: This book by Erica Brown on women's middlebrow writing focuses on authors Elizabeth von Arnim and Elizabeth Taylor. "First, she considers how comedy facilitates an ironic '"response" to war' without disruption of form. Her second discussion investigates intertextual narratives, And finally Brown considers the 'comedy of age,' demonstrating that sophistication is both at work in novels . . . and required in the reader." (Times Literary Supplement)

REVIEW: *TLS* no5753 p27 Jl 5 2013 LUCY CARLYLE

"Comedy and the Feminine Middlebrow Novel: Elizabeth von Arnim and Elizabeth Taylor." "[Erica Brown] display[s] . . . clarity and boldness in exploring narrative pleasure. She also engages assertively with 'middlebrow' itself--a slippery term--and with critical precedent regarding not only her primary authors but also fiction and humour more generally. . .

. This study goes some way towards redressing the balance. And although the argument feels a little repetitive at times, it is frequently enlivened by the comedy of the original material . . . while Brown's own style is lucid and engaging. As a result, this book is itself an entertaining piece of scholarship as well as a valuable one."

BROWN, FLEDA. No need of sympathy; poems; [by] Fleda Brown 88 p. 2013 BOA Editions, Ltd.
1. American poetry 2. American sonnets 3. Grandchildren 4. Literature & science 5. Poems—Collections
ISBN 9781938160189 (pbk); 9781938160196 (ebook)
LC 2013-013076

SUMMARY: "Any one poem in Fleda Brown's eighth collection may touch on contemporary science, physics, family, politics, the nature of poetry, and the nature of reality. There are sonnets for all ten grandchildren written by a grandmother, poems about the Big Bang, about child labor, the moon over Paris, and tent caterpillars, all written with humility, humor, curiosity, and a deep love of life." (Publisher's note)

REVIEW: *World Lit Today* v88 no2 p66-7 Mr/Ap 2014 Fred Dings

"No Need of Sympathy." "Reading a poem by [Fleda] Brown is a lesson in how to read one's life, how each small thing, each seemingly casual detail, is in fact connected to perceptions and understandings of profound significance that we can all divine if only we calm our vision enough to fully experience the perishing present. Her verses do not paraphrase, do not 'boil down,' precisely because of their fullness of connection and capaciousness of metaphor. The poems are marked by a naturalness of voice . . . that keeps a balance among opposites such as levity/gravity, micro/macro, informal/formal, and generosity/restraint, and one clearly senses the influence of Buddhist meditation on this poet both in terms of poise and in terms of a vision of the interconnectedness of all things."

BROWN, FREDERICK. The embrace of unreason; France, 1914-1940; [by] Frederick Brown 368 p. 2014 Alfred A. Knopf
1. Antisemitism—France—History—20th century 2. Art and society—France—History—20th century 3. Fascism—France—History—20th century 4. Historical literature 5. World War, 1914-1918—France—Influence
ISBN 0307595153; 9780307595157 (hardback); 9780307742360 (paperback)
LC 2013-026942

SUMMARY: It was the author's intent to demonstrate that "the physical and human destruction of the Great War, the failed diplomacy of the interwar years, the rapid military collapse in WWII, and the shame of the Vichy regime . . . were directly linked to a political and cultural rot that permeated all levels of French society." Frederick Brown "describes a retreat from the rationalism of the Enlightenment and an embrace of emotionalism and romantic nostalgia among French elites." (Booklist)

REVIEW: *Bookforum* v21 no1 p44-5 Ap/My 2014 ARTHUR GOLDHAMMER

REVIEW: *Booklist* v110 no13 p15 Mr 1 2014 Jay Freeman

"The Embrace of Unreason: France, 1914-1940." "As this superb study reveals, these disasters were directly linked to a political and cultural rot that permeated all levels of French society. . . . On a more fundamental level, [Frederick] Brown describes a retreat from the rationalism of the Enlightenment and an embrace of emotionalism and romantic nostalgia among French elites. This was manifested in an exclusionary nationalism, virulent anti-Semitism, and a general distrust of pluralistic democracy. This is a riveting portrait of a society weakened by internal decay."

REVIEW: *Choice* v51 no12 p2259 Ag 2014 D. A. Harvey

REVIEW: *Economist* v411 no8884 p83-4 Ap 26 2014

REVIEW: *Kirkus Rev* v82 no3 p32 F 1 2014

"The Embrace of Unreason: France, 1914-1940". "[Frederick Brown] once again demonstrates his profound knowledge of French history, its people and their psyche. . . . Brown explores all the great and complicated minds of this period, including socialists, communists, fascists, royalists and radicals. Francophiles will love this book, but the roiling currents of philosophical and political ideas may daunt some readers. Read this illuminating book to see frightening similarities to the early years of the 21st century. The lies, innuendo, invented evidence and baseless arguments are all too familiar."

REVIEW: *Libr J* v138 no18 p67 N 1 2013 Barbara Hoffert

REVIEW: *New Repub* v244 no29 p62-5 Je 9 2014 David A. Bell

"The Embrace of Unreason: France, 1914-1940." "Frederick Brown, an accomplished literary biographer, has emerged as the leading English-language chronicler of this appalling but fascinating French story. . . . In 'The Embrace of Unreason,' he has taken the story through the interwar period. . . . The specter of Vichy looms on the horizon, as the final destination at which so many of those who 'embraced unreason' eventually arrived. . . . Occasionally Brown's method becomes needlessly distracting. . . . Brown never provides an overview of the period's history, and uninitiated readers will find themselves having to flick back continually to a timeline that he provides at the end."

REVIEW: *New Yorker* v90 no26 p83-1 S 8 2014

REVIEW: *Publ Wkly* v260 no51 p46 D 16 2013

BROWN, IAN. Scottish theatre; diversity, language, continuity ; [by] Ian Brown 2014 Editions Rodopi BV
1. Drama—History & criticism 2. Scotland—History 3. Scotland—Social life & customs—History 4. Scottish drama 5. Theater—Political aspects
ISBN 9789042037434

SUMMARY: This book, by Ian Brown, "challenges the dominant view of a broken and discontinuous dramatic culture in Scotland." Brown "describes the ways in which politically and religiously divisive moments in Scottish history, such as the Reformation or political Union, surprisingly fostered alternative dramatic modes and means of expression." His "revisionist history also analyses the changing relationships between drama, culture, and political change in Scotland in the 20th and 21st centuries." (Publisher's note)

REVIEW: *TLS* no5782 p22 Ja 24 2014 MARGERY PALMER McCULLOCH

"Scottish Theatre: Diversity, Language, Continuity." "Ian Brown's 'Scottish Theatre: Diversity, language, continuity' is the latest book to appear on the subject. . . . It is not until Chapter Four . . . that we make extended contact with the theatre of the title, and even here contact is on the whole related to the contextual situation of the work discussed, as opposed to giving the reader a sense of its specific formal and thematic nature. . . . 'Scottish Theatre' does not lead its readers into previously uncharted territories, but it makes a useful contribution to recent literature on the history of Scottish drama, nonetheless."

BROWN, JEFFREY. Star Wars; Jedi Academy; [by] Jeffrey Brown 160 p. 2013 Scholastic, Inc
ISBN 0545505178; 9780545505178 (paper over board); 9780545609999 (pbk.)
LC 2013-931939

SUMMARY: In this book, by Jeffrey Brown, "Roan Novachez thought he was destined to attend Pilot Academy Middle School, just as his older brother and father did. His dreams are crushed when he is rejected by Pilot Academy and accepted into a sketchy new school called Coruscant Jedi Academy. . . . Confused and struggling to keep up, Roan tries to fly under the radar and passes the time drawing comics of his daily life at his strange boarding school." (Booklist)

REVIEW: *Booklist* v110 no2 p60 S 15 2013 Candice Mack
"Star Wars: Jedi Academy". "This fantastic chapter book by[Jeffrey] Brown will satisfy those who loved his previous Star Wars works. . . . With its mix of comics and text, it will also appeal to fans of Jeff Kinney's 'Diary of a Wimpy Kid' and Dav Pilkey's 'Captain Underpants' hybrid books. On a deeper level, this book tackles serious issues like failure, bullying, friendship, determination, and starting a new school In a fun and funny way. Perhaps best of all, it encourages readers to practice creativity and to start their own journals."

REVIEW: *Kirkus Rev* v81 no14 p145 Jl 15 2013

REVIEW: *SLJ* v60 no1 p107 Ja 2014 J. M. Poole

BROWN, JENNIFER. Eating dangerously. See Booth, M.

BROWN, JONATHON.il. Cook Au Vin. See Brown, J.

BROWN, JONATHON. Cook Au Vin; Notes on Entertaining by Cooking With Wine; [by] Jonathon Brown 192 p. 2012 Createspace Independent Pub
1. Cookbooks 2. Cooking 3. Cooking (Liquors) 4. Cooking (Wine) 5. Entertaining
ISBN 1480223727; 9781480223721

SUMMARY: This book by Jonathon Brown about cooking with wine and other alcoholic beverages "is heavily influenced by [Henri de] Toulouse-Lautrec's recipe book cum memoir 'The Art of the Cuisine' and the eccentricity of many of the artist's ideas. . . . He revels in a judicious use of booze, not only wine, but cider, beer, sherry and spirits." (Times Literary Supplement)

REVIEW: *TLS* no5768 p27 O 18 2013 COLIN SPENCER
"Cook Au Vin." "Even experienced cooks can be both daunted and vague about cooking with wine. There is, however, universal agreement on never using plonk; only a drinkable quality wine will do. That advice may not go far, but Jonathon Brown does. . . . If you can overcome the fact that the book looks as if it has been cobbled together from rough notes with gauche, adolescent sketches that fail either to elucidate or entertain, the author's gusto, wedded to his brisk and breezy manner, reveals a love and knowledge of cooking. He revels in a judicious use of booze, not only wine, but cider, beer, sherry and spirits. One must be prepared for imprecision and lunatic moments."

BROWN, KATE. Plutopia; nuclear families, atomic cities, and the great Soviet and American plutonium disasters; [by] Kate Brown 416 p. 2013 Oxford University Press
1. Historical literature 2. Industrial safety—Government policy—Soviet Union—Case studies 3. Industrial safety—Government policy—United States—Case studies 4. Plutonium industry—Accidents—Russia (Federation)—Ozërsk (Cheliabinskaia oblast)—History—20th century 5. Plutonium industry—Accidents—Washington (State)—Richland—History—20th century
ISBN 0199855765; 9780199855766 (acid-free paper)
LC 2012-041758

SUMMARY: This book, written by Kate Brown, "draws on official records and dozens of interviews to tell the extraordinary stories of Richland, Washington and Ozersk, Russia-the first two cities in the world to produce plutonium. An untold . . . piece of Cold War history, Plutopia invites readers to consider the nuclear footprint left by the arms race and the enormous price of paying for it." (Publisher's note)

REVIEW: *Am Hist Rev* v118 no5 p1479-81 D 2013 Jon Wiener

REVIEW: *Choice* v51 no4 p697-8 D 2013 A. O. Edmond
"Plutopia: Nuclear Families, Atomic Cities, and the Great Soviet and American Plutonium Disasters." "Using an impressive array of US and Soviet archival sources and a series of profoundly effective and affecting interviews, the author focuses on how the two plants and communities actually mirrored each other: regimentation, separation of scientists and managers from workers, secrecy, and a conscious attempt to downplay or deny safety hazards that clearly existed. Although this judicious history examines all sides of a controversial issue. Brown concludes that many of the higher-ups involved were culpable, but she makes her case fairly. Most impressive is how Brown involves readers in the interview process."

REVIEW: *Kirkus Rev* v81 no2 p181 Ja 15 2013

REVIEW: *New Sci* v217 no2908 p50 Mr 16 2013 Rob Edwards

BROWN, KENDALL H. Quiet beauty; Japanese gardens of North America; [by] Kendall H. Brown 176 p. 2013 Tuttle Pub.
1. Gardens—North America 2. Gardens, Japanese—North America 3. Gardens, Japanese—North America—Pictorial works 4. Horticultural literature 5. Photography of gardens
ISBN 4805311959 (hardcover); 9784805311950 (hardcover)
LC 2012-036548

SUMMARY: This book, by Kendall H. Brown, with photographs by David M. Cobb, presents images and information on Japanese "gardens of the United States and Canada. . . . Featuring an intimate look at twenty-six gardens, with numerous . . . color photographs of each, that detail their style, history, and special functions, this book explores the ingenuity and range of Japanese landscaping." (Publisher's note)

REVIEW: *N Y Times Book Rev* p53 D 8 2013 ALIDA BECKER
"City Parks: Public Places, Private Thoughts," "Private

Gardens of the Hudson Valley," and "Quiet Beauty: The Japanese Gardens of North America." "The 18 contributors to Catie Marron's 'City Parks: Public Places, Private Thoughts' have . . . [created] an eloquent reminder of the way shard landscapes can provide intimate inspiration. . . . In 'Private Gardens of the Hudson Valley,' Jane Garmey and John M. Hall's follow-up . . . There's also some interesting whimsy. . . . Just flipping through the pages of 'Quiet Beauty: The Japanese Gardens of North America' will instantly lower your blood pressure."

REVIEW: *Publ Wkly* v260 no10 p51 Mr 11 2013

BROWN, LISA.il. 29 Myths on the Swinster Pharmacy. See Snicket, L.

BROWN, LOIS. Pauline Elizabeth Hopkins; Black daughter of the Revolution; [by] Lois Brown 690 2008 University of North Carolina Press

1. African American women—Intellectual life 2. African Americans—Biography 3. African Americans—History 4. African Americans—Intellectual life—19th century 5. Authors 6. Biographers 7. Biography (Literary form) 8. Biography, Individual 9. Dramatists 10. Essayists 11. Journalists 12. Novelists 13. Short story writers

ISBN 0807831662; 9780807831663; 978-0-8078-3166-3; 0-8078-3166-2

LC 2007-048985

SUMMARY: This book by Lois Brown presents a biography of "Pauline Elizabeth Hopkins . . . a . . . playwright, journalist, novelist, feminist, and public intellectual, best known for her 1900 novel 'Contending Forces: A Romance of Negro Life North and South' In this critical biography, Lois Brown [aims to] document . . . Hopkins's early family life and her ancestral connections to eighteenth-century New England, the African slave trade, and twentieth-century race activism in the North. (Publisher's note)

REVIEW: *Choice* v51 no10 p1738 Je 2014 L. J. Parascandola

"Pauline Elizabeth Hopkins: Black Daughter of the Revolution". "The present biography is much fuller than [Hanna] Wallinger's: [Lois] Brown . . . includes not only excellent readings of her novels . . . but also much new information about Hopkins's ancestry and her later years. . . . Appendixes, particularly one on Hopkins's correspondence, provide useful insights into the writer's thinking. The major problem with the book is its omissions; e.g.. Brown seems unaware of Wallinger's biography and does not cite pioneering work by Ann Allen Shockley and Mary Helen Washington in her bibliography. These oversights aside, this biography includes much new material and, coupled with Wallinger's book, provides a solid base for future study."

BROWN, LUKE. My Biggest Lie; [by] Luke Brown 288 p. 2014 Canongate Books Ltd

1. Buenos Aires (Argentina) 2. Editors—Fiction 3. English fiction 4. Humorous stories 5. Love letters

ISBN 1782110372; 9781782110378

SUMMARY: In this novel by Luke Brown, "Liam has it all. In front of him glitters an exciting career and a life with the woman he has loved from the moment he saw her. But on a feverish night out he loses his job, his home and his girlfriend. He is lucky to escape with his life. Trying to leave his shame behind in London, he flees to Argentina to live honestly, and to write the world's longest and truest love letter." (Publisher's note)

REVIEW: *TLS* no5796 p19 My 2 2014 HANNAH PHILLIPS

"My Biggest Lie." "'My Biggest Lie' is the story of a disorderly but well-meaning London publisher, who loses everything—job, girlfriend, home. Escaping in shame to Buenos Aires to live an honest life and write the love letter to top them all, Liam finds his search for an epiphany is plagued by new, formidable temptations, and a past that refuses to lie still. . . . Largely rewarding and ambitious, the plot becomes increasingly intricate and inward-facing, folding in on itself continually until by the end the reader is left holding something very small. . . . The ending may leave the reader feeling cheated, but simultaneously entertained. 'My Biggest Lie' is similar to any fantasy or falsehood in this way: its effectiveness relies on the extent to which you are willing to indulge it."

BROWN, MARC. Marc Brown's playtime rhymes; a treasury for families to learn and play together; [by] Marc Brown 48 p. 2013 Little, Brown and Co.

1. Children's poetry 2. Finger play 3. Nursery rhymes 4. School buses 5. Snowmen

ISBN 0316207357; 9780316207355 (hc)

LC 2012-048542

SUMMARY: This book presents "a treasury of twenty favorite finger rhymes compiled and illustrated by . . . artist Marc Brown. These are rhymes to say and sing aloud, each with pictorial instructions for the correlating finger movements. 'Playtime Rhymes' [is designed to] get little hands wiggling, jiggling, pointing, pounding, bending, stretching, and dancing as children animate the rhymes, pore over the vibrant pictures, and share the fun with family and friends." (Publisher's note)

REVIEW: *Horn Book Magazine* v89 no6 p111-2 N/D 2013 SUSAN DOVE LEMPKE

"Marc Brown's Playtime Rhymes: A Treasury for Families to Learn and Play Together". "[A] very appealing collection. Most of the rhymes and songs will be familiar to many parents and children. . . . Others, like 'The Snowman' . . . will bring new pleasures. . . . [Marc] Brown's gouache and colored-pencil illustrations jump with joyful energy, with lots of little jokes for children to spot amongst the many kids, dogs, and other animals that appear. A must-purchase for storytimes, this is also a great gift book that will help parents remember their own childhood rhymes."

BROWN, MARC. In New York; [by] Marc Brown 40 p. 2014 Alfred A. Knopf

1. New York (N.Y.)—History 2. Picture books for children 3. Statue of Liberty (New York, N.Y.) 4. Urban life—Juvenile literature

ISBN 0375864547; 9780375864544 (hardcover); 9780375964541 (hardcover library binding)

LC 2013-020158

SUMMARY: In this book, author Marc Brown "shares his love for all that the city [of New York] has to offer and all that it stands for, including the way it's always changing and evolving. From its earliest days as New Amsterdam to the contemporary wonders of Central Park, the Statue of Liberty, and the Empire State Building, to the kid-appealing subway, High Line, and so much more, Marc's . . . text and . . . illustrations showcase what he's come to adore about New York." (Publisher's note)

REVIEW: *Booklist* v110 no11 p70 F 1 2014 Thom Barthelmess

REVIEW: *Horn Book Magazine* v90 no2 p98-9 Mr/Ap 2014 ROGER SUTTON

"In New York." "Just about all of Manhattan's child-pleasing sites get a place in [Marc] Brown's stupendously detailed gouache-and-watercolor pictures, from the top of the Empire State Building at sunset to Rockefeller Center at Christmas, and what a double-page spread that makes for, the tree lights glowing amidst a snowstorm. . . . The text is minimal but inviting ('wherever you walk in New York, you'll see a great parade of people passing by'), and the endpapers offer additional child-friendly vignettes and facts. Appended info includes phone numbers and websites for all the highlights. Book your trip now!"

REVIEW: *Kirkus Rev* v82 no4 p58 F 15 2014

In New York. "A very personal tour of New York takes readers eastside, westside, uptown and down. Although there is a hint of homage to Miroslav Sasek's classic This Is New York, [Marc] Brown makes it fresh and new and gets it just right, with a little history, a little geography, some mind-boggling statistics and the familiar iconic sights. It's not orderly in its approach, as New York is essentially an eclectic mix of people, sights, sounds, smells and tastes. . . . He employs breezy, conversational language, speaking directly to his audience. . . . An exuberant and heartfelt travelogue extraordinaire."

REVIEW: *N Y Times Book Rev* p20 Mr 16 2014 BRUCE HANDY

REVIEW: *Publ Wkly* v260 no51 p63 D 16 2013

REVIEW: *SLJ* v60 no2 p66 F 2014 Marian McLeod

BROWN, MIKE. A pedagogy of place; outdoor education for a changing world; [by] Mike Brown xxix, 214 p. 2011 Monash University Publishing

1. Education—Philosophy 2. Educational literature 3. Outdoor education 4. Place (Philosophy) 5. Place-based education
ISBN 9780980651249 (pb); 9780980651256 (web)
LC 2010-681558

SUMMARY: This book by Brian Wattchow and Mike Brown "calls into question some of the underlying assumptions and 'truths' about outdoor education, putting forward alternatives to current practice that are responsive to local conditions and cultural traditions. In this renewal of outdoor education philosophy and practice, the emphasis is upon responding to--and empathizing with--the outdoors as particular places rich in local meaning and significance." (Publisher's note)

REVIEW: *Educ Stud* v49 no5 p451-64 S/O 2013 David A. Greenwood

"A Pedagogy of Place: Outdoor Education for a Changing World." "Although it does not significantly address the local/global tensions inherent in contemporary place study, this book represents a major contribution to the place-conscious educational literature. . . . In 'A Pedagogy of Place,' [authors Brian] Wattchow and [Mike] Brown . . . attempt bridging experience on land and water with socially critical perspectives toward place. . . . In 'A Pedagogy of Place,' Wattchow and Brown . . . have created a compelling meeting ground for place-responsive stories and theories."

BROWN, PETE. Three sheets to the wind; one man's quest for the meaning of beer; [by] Pete Brown 457, [1] p. 2007 Pan

1. Bars (Drinking establishments)—History 2. Bars (Drinking establishments)—Social aspects 3. Beer—History 4. Beer—Social aspects 5. Beer industry—History 6. Travelers' writings
ISBN 0330442473 (pbk.); 9780330442473 (pbk.)
LC 2008-383276

SUMMARY: In this book, Pete Brown "discovers several countries produce, consume, and celebrate beer far more than the British do. The Germans claim they make the best beer in the world, the Australians consider its consumption a patriotic duty, the Spanish regard lager as a trendy youth drink. . . . At home, meanwhile, people seem to be turning their backs on the great British pint." Brown visits "more than 300 bars in 27 towns, through 13 different countries" in search of an explanation. (Publisher's note)

REVIEW: *Booklist* v110 no3 p20 O 1 2013 DAVID WRIGHT

"Boozehound: On the Trail of the Rare, the Obscure, and the Overrated in Spirits," "The Hour: A Cocktail Manifesto, and "Three Sheets to the Wind: One Man's Quest for the Meaning of Beer." "Bernard DeVoto's beloved and recently reprinted 'The Hour: A Cocktail Manifesto' is perhaps ounce for ounce a purer delight, with its deft, hilarious homage to the sweet transports of drink. . . . In 'Boozehound,' spirits columnist Jason Wilson travels the globe scaring up interesting liquors. . . . Wilson's style is friendly and down to earth as he pokes fun at fads and deflates the mystical malarkey of the spirits trade. . . . Pete Brown's 'Three Sheets to the Wind' does a similar job for beer, consisting of an epic pub crawl across the globe, exploring the sociability of beer."

BROWN, PETER. Mr. Tiger goes wild; [by] Peter Brown 48 p. 2013 Little Brown & Co

1. CIty and town life—Fiction 2. Etiquette—Fiction 3. Picture books for children 4. Self-actualization (Psychology)—Fiction 5. Tigers—Fiction
ISBN 0316200638 (reinforced); 9780316200639 (reinforced)
LC 2012-048429

SUMMARY: In this children's picture book, "Mr. Tiger lives a peaceable, if repressed, life alongside other anthropomorphic animals in a monochromatic, dreadfully formal little town." He finally gets tired of being respectable and starts embracing "a quadruped stance." Then he "sheds his clothing, runs away to the wilderness, roars and generally runs amok. But" he "comes to miss his friends, his city and his home, and so he returns to find 'that things were beginning to change.'" (Kirkus Reviews)

REVIEW: *Booklist* v110 no1 p104 S 1 2013 Thom Barthelmess

REVIEW: *Bull Cent Child Books* v67 no2 p78 O 2013 T. A.

REVIEW: *Horn Book Magazine* v90 no4 p14-20 Jl/Ag 2014 Martha V. Parravano

REVIEW: *Horn Book Magazine* v89 no6 p74 N/D 2013 DOVE LEMPKE

"Mr. Tiger Goes Wild". "This is a book made for storytime, with its bold mixed-media illustrations that work almost like a storyboard moving left to right, and a plot with a clear beginning, middle, and end. Children, who get tired of grownups and their requests for proper behavior, will relate to the proud joy Mr. Tiger clearly feels when he is free to be wild, and also to his eventual feelings of loneliness. The happy ending, almost a reverse of 'Where the Wild Things Are,' includes everyone discovering the fun of being at least a little bit wild."

REVIEW: *Kirkus Rev* p41 2013 Guide to BookExpo America

REVIEW: *Kirkus Rev* p46 N 15 2013 Best Books

REVIEW: *Kirkus Rev* v81 no14 p37 Jl 15 2013

REVIEW: *N Y Times Book Rev* p34 N 10 2013 CAROLYN JURIS

REVIEW: *Publ Wkly* v260 no45 p22-30 N 11 2013

REVIEW: *Publ Wkly* v260 no28 p167 Jl 15 2013

REVIEW: *Publ Wkly* p47 Children's starred review annual 2013

REVIEW: *SLJ* v59 no8 p66 Ag 2013 Kiera Parrott

BROWN, SAMUEL MORRIS. In heaven as it is on earth; [by] Samuel Morris Brown xii, 392 p 2012 Oxford University Press

1. Death—Religious aspects—Christianity 2. Historical literature 3. Mormon Church—Doctrines 4. Mormon Church—History—19th century 5. Smith, Joseph, 1805-1844

ISBN 9780199793570

LC 2011-002848

SUMMARY: 'This book examines Mormonism "through the lens of founder Joseph Smith's profound preoccupation with the specter of death. Revisiting historical documents and scripture from this . . . perspective, Brown offers . . . insight into the origin and meaning of some of Mormonism's earliest beliefs and practices. The world of early Mormonism was besieged by death--infant mortality, violence, and disease were rampant. A prolonged battle with typhoid fever, punctuated by painful surgeries including a threatened leg amputation, and the sudden loss of his beloved brother Alvin cast a long shadow over Smith's own life. Smith embraced and was deeply influenced by the culture of 'holy dying'--with its emphasis on deathbed salvation, melodramatic bereavement, and belief in the Providential nature of untimely death--that sought to cope with the widespread mortality of the period." (Publisher's note)

REVIEW: *Am Hist Rev* v118 no1 p185-6 F 2013 RICHARD E. BENNETT

REVIEW: *Booklist* v108 no6 p20 N 15 2011 Bryce Christensen

REVIEW: *Choice* v49 no11 p2075 Jl 2012 T. G. Alexander

REVIEW: *J Am Hist* v100 no2 p509-10 S 2013 Jan Shipps

REVIEW: *Publ Wkly* v258 no50 p63 D 12 2011

REVIEW: *Rev Am Hist* v42 no1 p65-70 Mr 2014 Susanna Morrill

"In Heaven As It Is on Earth: Joseph Smith and the Early Mormon Conquest of Death." "In this clearly written and brilliantly conceived work, Samuel Brown mines nineteenth-century North American death culture to uncover a new, contextualized view of the origins and early development of Mormonism. . . . Brown gives a new, interdisciplinary view of how and why Mormonism developed, and he does this with a tone that is objective and respectful of Smith and his followers as humans sincerely trying to make sense of their lives in the face of great difficulties. . . . It more fully integrates the subfield of Mormon studies and scholarship on American religious history."

BROWN, SARAH ANNES. A Familiar Compound Ghost; Allusion and the Uncanny; [by] Sarah Annes Brown 240 p. 2013 Palgrave Macmillan

1. Allusions in literature 2. Doppelgängers in literature 3. Intertextuality 4. Literary critiques 5. Uncanny, The (Psychoanalysis), in literature

ISBN 0719085152; 9780719085154

SUMMARY: This book "explores the relationship between allusion and the uncanny in literature. An unexpected echo or quotation in a new text can be compared to the sudden appearance of a ghost or mysterious double, the reanimation of a corpse, or the discovery of an ancient ruin hidden in a modern city." Author Sarah Annes Brown "identifies moments where this affinity between allusion and the uncanny is used by writers to generate a particular textual charge." (Publisher's note)

REVIEW: *TLS* no5747 p30-1 My 24 2013 YASMINE SHAMMA

"A Familiar Compound Ghost: Allusion and the Uncanny." "[Sarah Annes] Brown's book studies and solicits a mode of reading that depends on an unnatural anticipation of the uncanny, of connections between books. Throughout her well-written, persuasive and interesting introduction, Brown acknowledges that hers is a creative reading and that it is potentially misleading in the way it forces links and parallels. Is it enough merely to warn of these dangers and carry on? This is the book's major and unanswered theoretical problem; its frame (or framelessness) provides a second. . . . At the same time, she offers fascinating insights and unexpected and enlightening connections."

BROWN, SKILA. Caminar; [by] Skila Brown 208 p. 2014 Candlewick Press

1. Courage 2. Guatemala—History—Civil War, 1960-1996 3. Guerrillas—Guatemala 4. Historical fiction 5. Novels in verse

ISBN 0763665169; 9780763665166

LC 2013-946611

SUMMARY: This book, by Skila Brown, is "set in 1981 Guatemala. . . . Carlos knows that when the soldiers arrive with warnings about the Communist rebels, it is time to be a man and defend the village, keep everyone safe. But Mama tells him not yet. . . . Numb and alone, he must join a band of guerillas as they trek to the top of the mountain where Carlos's abuela lives. Will he be in time, and brave enough, to warn them about the soldiers? What will he do then?" (Publisher's note)

REVIEW: *Booklist* v110 no14 p79 Mr 15 2014 Sarah Bean Thompson

REVIEW: *Bull Cent Child Books* v67 no8 p397-8 Ap 2014 K. C.

"Caminar". "The free-verse poetry in this verse novel is tightly crafted to evoke Carlos' confusion and emotional turmoil both prior to and after the massacre, employing both shape and resonant language to pull readers into his hesitations, sadness, and terror. . . . The narrative arc is a bit tidy (his quick actions save both his new friends and his abuela's entire village), but the accessible imagery in the poetry will engage readers on a visceral level, ably communicating the limitations of Carlos' understanding, both in terms of his youth and his inability to comprehend the full scope of the conflict."

REVIEW: *Horn Book Magazine* v90 no2 p112 Mr/Ap 2014 KATHLEEN T. HORNING

REVIEW: *Kirkus Rev* v82 no2 p131 Ja 15 2014

REVIEW: *Publ Wkly* v261 no2 p70 Ja 13 2014

REVIEW: *SLJ* v60 no3 p135 Mr 2014 Denise Ryan

BROWN, TRACY. Facebook safety and privacy; [by] Tracy Brown 64 p. 2014 Rosen Central

1. Children's nonfiction 2. Cyberbullying 3. Facebook (Web resource) 4. Internet & privacy 5. Online social networks—Security measures—Juvenile literature
ISBN 1448895693 (Library Binding); 1448895804 (Paperback); 9781448895694 (Library Binding); 9781448895809 (Paperback)
LC 2012-277796

SUMMARY: This book on the social media website Facebook is part of the "21st Century Safety and Privacy" series, which "focuses on safe use of the Internet and social media, explaining each activity, noting pleasures as well as perils, and offering suggestions for minimizing risk. The information is organized into short chapters." The book discusses "cyberbullying" and "stresses the frequency of changes in site settings." (Booklist)

REVIEW: *Booklist* v110 no12 p71 F 15 2014 Kathleen Isaacs

"Downloading and Online Shopping Safety and Privacy," "Facebook Safety and Privacy," and "Twitter Safety and Privacy: A Guide to Microblogging." "This timely series focuses on safe use of the Internet and social media, explaining each activity, noting pleasures as well as perils, and offering suggestions for minimizing risk. The information is organized into short chapters liberally laced with appropriate subheadings, photographs of young users, and boxes to break up the text and presented in an oversize, easy-to-read font. . . . In spite of similarities across the titles, there is enough specific information in each to justify purchasing the full series. There are older teen faces on the covers, but this would be most useful for middle-schoolers just entering the social media world."

BROWN, TRACY L. Pueblo Indians and Spanish colonial authority in eighteenth-century New Mexico; [by] Tracy L. Brown viii, 235 p. 2013 University of Arizona Press

1. Historical literature 2. Pueblo Indians—Colonization 3. Pueblo Indians—Government relations 4. Pueblo Indians—Social conditions
ISBN 9780816530274 (hardcover: alk. paper)
LC 2013-009663

SUMMARY: This book "examines the multiple approaches Pueblo individuals and villages adopted to mitigate and manage the demands that Spanish colonial authorities made upon them. In doing so, author Tracy L. Brown counters the prevailing argument that Pueblo individuals and communities' only response to Spanish colonialism was to compartmentalize—and thus freeze in time and space—their traditions behind a cultural 'iron curtain.'" (Publisher's note)

REVIEW: *Choice* v51 no8 p1471 Ap 2014 R. G. Mendoza

"Pueblo Indians and Spanish Colonial Authority in Eighteenth-Century New Mexico". "Anthropologist [Tracy L.] Brown . . . offers a distinctive approach and problem-oriented historiography of the sort necessary for the identification of Pueblo Indian agents and indigenous voices in the formulation of a new history of 18th-century New Mexico. The author thereby challenges the otherwise problematic master narratives that continue to dominate the US Mexico borderlands, while systematically articulating the challenges of resurrecting indigenous voices from colonial documents framed within indigenous contexts. . . . Brown ultimately succeeds in formulating a nonlinear model for articulating a refreshing new perspective on the specifics of Puebloan responses to Spanish colonialism."

BROWN, VAHID. Fountainhead of jihad, the Haqqani nexus, 1973/2012; [by] Vahid Brown 320 p. 2012 Columbia University Press

1. Historical literature 2. Jihad 3. Terrorism—Religious aspects—Islam 4. Terrorists—Pakistan—History
ISBN 9780231704380 (alk. paper)
LC 2012-039143

SUMMARY: This book by Vahid Brown and Dan Rassler examines the Haqqani network, "a group frequently described as the most lethal actor in the current Afghan insurgency, and shown here to have been for decades at the centre of a nexus of transnational Islamist militancy, fostering the development of jihadi organisations from Southeast Asia to East Africa." (Publisher's note)

REVIEW: *Middle East J* v68 no1 p159 Wint 2014 Antonio Giustozzi

"Fountainhead of Jihad: The Haqqani Nexus, 1973-2012." "The interpretation provided by the authors of this volume is coherent. . . . The main criticism which could be extended to the authors' interpretation is that their main source, the Haqqani literature, might well have been intended for the purpose of mobilizing funding and therefore might have purposely overstated the influence and role of the international jihadis. . . . In their defense, [Vahid] Brown and [Dan] Rassler also use other sources such as memoirs of Arab and other volunteers, or interrogation files, to support their analysis, but inevitably, a shadow of doubt remains. . . . The volume should . . . be considered a useful contribution to the history of the 1980s jihad against the Soviet army and the leftist regime."

REVIEW: *N Y Rev Books* v60 no6 p24-30 Ap 4 2013 Anatol Lieven

BROWNE, JOHN, 1948-. Seven Elements That Changed the World; An Adventure of Ingenuity and Discovery; [by] John Browne 288 p. 2014 W W Norton & Co Inc

1. Carbon 2. Chemical elements 3. Historical literature 4. Iron 5. Technology & civilization
ISBN 1605985406; 9781605985404

SUMMARY: In this book, "the author has selected seven elements he believes have been prime contributors to the building of the modern world: iron, carbon, gold, silver, uranium, titanium and silicon. Regarding each element, he reaches back to its use in the ancient world or more recent discovery and then examines the changes each has wrought throughout history." (Kirkus Reviews)

REVIEW: *Booklist* v110 no7 p17 D 1 2013 Carl Hays

REVIEW: *Choice* v51 no12 p2214 Ag 2014 B. M. Simonson

REVIEW: *Kirkus Rev* v82 no2 p16 Ja 15 2014

"Seven Elements That Changed the World: An Adventure of Ingenuity and Discovery". "Any such selection will be arbitrary; for example, some may puzzle over his choice of titanium as one of the seven instead of copper, which gave us developments from the Bronze Age to telegraphy and telephony. . . . Such quirks aside, the topics the author chooses to cover, ranging from the use of coal in ancient China to the Bessemer converter and silver photography, unfold in thoughtful detail, and the ample footnotes accompanying the text are as diverting as they are helpful. Somewhat entertaining but lightweight stroll through some of the chemical underpinnings of the modern world."

REVIEW: *Libr J* v138 no21 p120 D 1 2013 Carla H. Lee

REVIEW: *Publ Wkly* v260 no42 p40 O 21 2013

BROWNING, ROBERT, 1812-1889. The complete works of Robert Browning; with variant readings & annotations; [by] Robert Browning 520 p. 1969 Ohio University Press

1. Anthologies 2. Authors & publishers 3. Poems—Collections 4. Strafford, Thomas Wentworth, Earl of, 1593-1641 5. Unpublished materials

ISBN 0821402307 (v. 7); 082141111X (v. 13); 0821411373 (v. 6); 0821412515 (v. 16); 0821413007 (v. 10); 0821413597 (v. 12); 0821414739 (v. 14 : acid-free paper); 0821417274 (v. 15 : acid-free paper); 9780821417270 (v. 15 : acid-free paper); 9780821418390 (v. 11); 9780821419816 (v. 17 : acid-free paper)

LC 6801-8389

SUMMARY: This book is Volume 17 in a series collecting the complete works of Robert Browning, edited by Ashby Bland Crowder and Allan C. Dooley. It "begins with Browning's last collection of poems, 'Asolando: Fancies and Facts'. . . . Also in this final volume are ninety-nine fugitive pieces, either unpublished or uncollected during the poet's lifetime." (Publisher's note)

REVIEW: *TLS* no5770 p3-5 N 1 2013 DANIEL KARLIN

"The Complete Works of Robert Browning: Volume Seventeen." "At the time of writing, Ohio/Baylor holds the field, but there are problems in designating it, as it would wish, as the standard reference work for students and scholars. . . . The variegated contents of the volume suggest some of the difficulties which all editions of Browning face, and others with which this edition in particular has struggled. There are also larger, and perhaps more unsettling questions as to what we are doing in editing Browning at all. . . . The textual apparatus itself, bristling with symbols and brackets, is ugly and unhelpful. . . . But the real problem is not with Ohio/Baylor's textual scholarship, but with its editorial principles."

BROWNLEE, JASON. Democracy prevention; the politics of the U.S.-Egyptian alliance; [by] Jason Brownlee xv, 279 p. 2012 Cambridge University Press

1. POLITICAL SCIENCE—Government—International 2. Political science literature

ISBN 9781107025714 (hardback); 9781107677869 (paperback)

LC 2012-004673

SUMMARY: In this book, "looking at the American-Egyptian relationship over more than three decades," author Jason Brownlee argues "that the military alliance between the two countries . . . did not just cause Washington to overlook the absence of democracy in Egypt, they also required it to ensure the survival of the autocrats in Cairo. . . . Any democratically elected alternative . . . would likely take Egyptian foreign and security policy in an unwanted new direction." (International Affairs)

REVIEW: *Choice* v50 no9 p1706-7 My 2013 G. E. Perry

REVIEW: *Middle East J* v67 no4 p633-43 Aut 2013 Charles D. Smith

"Democracy Prevention: The Politics of the U.S.-Egyptian Alliance," The Arab Spring: Change and Resistance in the Middle East," and "The Arab Spring: Will It Lead to Democratic Transitions?." "The [Mark L.] Haas and [David W.] Lesch coedited volume . . . devotes half the book to specific explanations of protests in Arab countries and the other half to analyses of their impact on countries either within the region or powers such as the United States and Russia. . . . The [Clement] Henry and [Jang] Ji-Hyang coedited 'Arab Spring' contains substantive chapters on Algeria, American policies in the Middle East, the economies of uprising-affected societies, but some chapters are extremely brief and could have been excluded. . . . Only [Jason] Brownlee's 'Democracy Prevention' can be considered the product of a long-term research project whose timing of publication was most opportune."

REVIEW: *Polit Sci Q (Wiley-Blackwell)* v128 no4 p760-2 Wint 2013/2014 ROBERT SPRINGBORG

BRU, SASCHA.ed. The Oxford critical and cultural history of modernist magazines. See Brooker, P.

BRUCE, IAIN.tr. Narcoland. See Hernandez, A.

BRUCE, TERESA. The Other Mother; A Rememoir; [by] Teresa Bruce 416 p. 2013 Joggling Board Pr

1. Dancers 2. Friendship 3. Marriage 4. Memoirs 5. Miller, Byrne

ISBN 0984107398; 9780984107391

SUMMARY: In this book, author Teresa Bruce is "assigned to interview the formidable modern-dance maven Byrne Miller. Soon she is swept up in Miller's story, which she presents alongside her own." The book "charts the intersections of the two women's lives and reveals their failures and triumphs. Bruce's own relationship with an abusive surfer is impacted by her reflections on Miller's time-tested marriage." (Booklist)

REVIEW: *Booklist* v110 no3 p12-3 O 1 2013 Bridget Thoreson

"The Other Mother." "This novel-like 'rememoir' . . . charts the intersections of the two women's lives and reveals their failures and triumphs. . . . The story is more potent than [Byrne] Miller's lighthearted 'womenisms' would suggest, as she confronts the damage caused by a diseased mind. Miller is a tower of strength and resolution, believing in someone unflinchingly even when that person no longer deserves such belief. [Teresa] Bruce's writing, laden with meaning and allegory, bestows an almost mythical quality on Miller's life. Poignant and eloquent, this is a graceful exploration of relationships and the independence afforded by self-expression."

BRUCK, PETER A.ed. Global mobile. See Global mobile

BRUCKMEIER, KARL. Natural resource use and global change; new interdisciplinary perspectives in social ecology; [by] Karl Bruckmeier x, 290 p. 2013 Palgrave Macmillan

1. Natural resources—Management 2. POLITICAL SCIENCE—Public Policy—Environmental Policy 3. SCIENCE—Environmental Science 4. SCIENCE—Life Sciences—Ecology 5. SOCIAL SCIENCE—Sociology—General 6. Scientific literature 7. Social ecology 8. Sustainable development

ISBN 9780230300606 (hardback)

LC 2012-045201

SUMMARY: "This book advances a new critical theory of society and nature, exploring social metabolism and global resource flows in contemporary society. Charting the historical development of social ecology in the context of environmental research, the book examines the interactions between society and nature and identifies both the barriers to global sustainability and the conditions and best practice for transforming industrial economies towards new sustainable resource use." (Publisher's note)

REVIEW: *Choice* v51 no4 p731-2 D 2013 C. M. Hand

"Natural Resource Use and Global Change: New Interdisciplinary Perspectives in Social Ecology." "[Karl Bruckmeier . . . indicates that social ecology seeks to organize interdisciplinary approaches to understanding the relationship between society and nature that accounts for global social and ecological complexity in an open and pluralistic theoretical framework. Social ecology theorizing springs up from such social science fields as philosophical and ecological anthropology, environmental sociology, human ecology, ecological modernization, [and] rural sociology. . . . Bruckmeier examines links between these fields and the natural science roots of social ecology . . . demonstrating shared theoretical resonance as well as barriers to interdisciplinary conversation."

BRUNO, IACOPO.il. Suitcase of stars. See Baccalario, P. D.

BRUNT, PETER. Art in Oceania. See Art in Oceania

BRYAN, CHRISTOPHER. Siding Star; [by] Christopher Bryan 406 p. 2012 The Diamond Press

1. Anglican priests 2. Astronomers—Fiction 3. Paranormal fiction 4. Secret societies—Fiction 5. Suspense fiction

ISBN 0985391103; 9780985391102

SUMMARY: In this book, "in England's Exeter Cathedral, a man with a strange black book is found dead in front of the altar, with occult signs spray-painted on the floor and a crucifix overturned. In Australia's Siding Springs Observatory, a young astronomer named Charlie Brown discovers a supernova that's sending 'a hail of high-energy particles and electromagnetic radiation' straight toward Earth. Linking these events are the machinations of a secret society bent on power and destruction." (Kirkus Reviews)

REVIEW: *Kirkus Rev* p10 D 15 2013 supplemet best books 2013

"Siding Star". "In this entertaining, thought-provoking novel, [Christopher] Bryan . . .—himself an Anglican priest—highlights the imaginative sweep and power of Christianity. . . . Bryan's heroes aren't just likable but lovable: intelligent, amusing, hardworking, even kind to animals. In contrast, the novel's villains are truly spooky and disturbing; readers are always aware of the urgency of stopping their evil plans. An enjoyable novel of spiritual mystery and adventure—well-plotted, intelligent and deeply moving."

REVIEW: *Kirkus Rev* v81 no2 p59 Ja 15 2013

BRYANT, LAURA J.il. Jo Macdonald hiked in the woods. See Jo Macdonald hiked in the woods

BRYNJOLFSSON, ERIK. The second machine age; work, progress, and prosperity in a time of brilliant technologies; [by] Erik Brynjolfsson 320 p. 2014 W W Norton & Co Inc

1. Economic development—Technological innovations 2. Economics literature 3. Information technology—Economic aspects 4. Progress—Social aspects 5. Social stratification

ISBN 9780393239355 (hardcover)

LC 2013-041204

SUMMARY: In this book, "the authors describe the forces driving the emerging age, notably the digitization of nearly everything . . . . and an amazing exponential growth in improvements. . . . Along with benefits . . . technological progress will bring economic disruption, leaving some people behind. . . . The authors describe the large differences that are already apparent . . . in both income and wealth and explain how individuals can improve their skills to maintain healthy wage and job prospects." (Kirkus Reviews)

REVIEW: *Economist* v410 no8871 p71 Ja 25 2014

"The Second Machine Age: Work, Progress, and Prosperity in a Time of Brilliant Technologies". "An ambitious, engaging and at times terrifying vision of where modern technology is taking the human race. . . . [Erik Brynjolfsson and Andrew McAfee] offer prescriptions. People should develop skills that complement, rather than compete with computers. . . . Policymakers should improve basic education. . . . This is sensible, but unsatisfying: it may expand the circle of winners and reshuffle its membership, though it seems unlikely that it will fundamentally alter the growing gap between them and the losers. The authors may not have the solution to growing inequality, but their book marks one of the most effective explanations yet for the origins of the gap."

REVIEW: *Kirkus Rev* v82 no1 p158 Ja 1 2014

"The Second Machine Age: Work, Progress, and Prosperity in a Time of Brilliant Technologies". "The authors describe the large differences that are already apparent among people in both income and wealth and explain how individuals can improve their skills to maintain healthy wage and job prospects. 'Our generation has inherited more opportunities to transform the world than any other,' they write. 'That's a cause for optimism, but only if we're mindful of our choices.' Valuable reading for policymakers."

REVIEW: *New Repub* v245 no12 p36-41 Jl 14 2014 Paul Starr

REVIEW: *New York Times* v163 no56413 pA17 F 15 2014 JOE NOCERA

BRYSON, BILL, 1951-. The life and times of the thunderbolt kid; a memoir; [by] Bill Bryson 270 2006 Broadway Books

1. Authors 2. Biography, Individual 3. Essayists 4. Journalists 5. Lexicographers 6. Linguists 7. Nonfiction writers 8. Travel writers

ISBN 0-7679-1936-X; 978-0-7679-1936-4

LC 2006--43859

SUMMARY: In this book, Bill Bryson "recounts his childhood and teen years. When he was very young, he ran about his town with a towel for a cape, declaring himself the superhero, Thunderbolt Kid. His father wrote for the local paper, his mother worked there as well, leaving their home rather free from 'the domestic arts' (i.e. rather dirty). As he grew up, some of his friends were demonically destructive, while others were skilled at liberating boxcar loads of beer." (Voice of Youth Advocates)"Bill Bryson remembers [his] 1950's childhood in the middle of America." (N Y Times Book Rev)

REVIEW: *Voice of Youth Advocates* v36 no2 p8-9 Je 2013 GERI DIORIO

"The Life and Times of the Thunderbolt Kid," "Brain on Fire: My Month of Madness," and "Blood, Bones & Butter." "[Bill] Bryson may not seem like an author in whom teens would be interested, but his wonderful humor and his bright, clear writing make him a delight to read. Here, he recounts his childhood and teen years. When he was very young, he ran about his town with a towel for a cape, declaring himself the superhero, Thunderbolt Kid. . . . When she was twenty-four years old, [Susannah] Cahalan had a seizure that was accompanied by delusions, paranoia, hallucinations, and violent mood swings. . . . She remembers almost nothing of this month, but after healing and being released from the hospital, she began researching what happened to her. . . . This book is an amazing chronicle of not only what happened to Cahalan, but also who she is: a survivor who is a talented reporter. . . . When [Gabrielle] Hamilton was growing up, her parents would throw enormous parties for their friends and neighbors. . . . As she grew up, she sought to recreate the challenge and joy of feeding all those people and, unsurprisingly, she became a world-class chef. . . . Hamilton is honest about her rough start and the rocky road she travelled to owning her own business, and foodie teens will enjoy her frankness and grit."

BRYSON, BILL, 1951-. One summer; America, 1927; [by] Bill Bryson 448 p. 2013 Doubleday

1. Historical literature 2. Popular culture—United States—History—20th century

ISBN 0767919408; 9780767919401 (alk. paper)

LC 2013-016041

SUMMARY: In this book, author Bill Bryson "reanimates the events and principal players across five key months in 1927. He establishes an early-20th-century, trial-and-error chronology of aviation evolution cresting with Charles Lindbergh. . . . Braided into Lindbergh's saga are profiles of cultural icons like . . . Herbert Hoover, famed gangster Al Capone, and baseball players Lou Gehrig and Babe Ruth, whose domination of America's 'National Game' captured the country's attention." (Kirkus Reviews)

REVIEW: *Booklist* v109 no22 p23 Ag 1 2013 Vanessa Bush

REVIEW: *Booklist* v110 no13 p29-30 Mr 1 2014 Joyce Saricks

"One Summer: America, 1927." "In this oddly compelling microhistory, [Bill] Bryson rambles through the summer of 1927, highlighting personalities and events in aviation . . . sports (baseball, with [Babe] Ruth's homerun record and [Lou] Gehrig's feats); Prohibition; politics (Hoover's politicking is amusingly skewered); and much more. . . . He's no professional, and his mid-Atlantic voice takes some getting used to. However, his idiosyncratic style perfectly matches this quirky history, which is a trivia addict's dream, filled with fascinating facts and warts-and-all glimpses of the famous and infamous."

REVIEW: *Kirkus Rev* v81 no10 p46 My 15 2013

REVIEW: *Kirkus Rev* p23 2013 Guide 20to BookExpo America

REVIEW: *Libr J* v138 no9 p54 My 15 2013 Barbara Hoffert

REVIEW: *Libr J* v138 no14 p123 S 1 2013 Charles K. Piehl

REVIEW: *N Y Times Book Rev* p25 N 24 2013 KEVIN BAKER

REVIEW: *Publ Wkly* v260 no31 p62 Ag 5 2013

REVIEW: *TLS* no5773 p12 N 22 2013 ELAINE SHOWALTER

BRZEZINSKI, ZBIGNIEW, 1928-. Strategic vision; America and the crisis of global power; [by] Zbigniew Brzezinski viii, 208 p. 2012 Basic Books

1. Balance of power—Forecasting 2. Developing countries—Foreign relations 3. Geopolitics—History—21st century—Forecasting 4. International relations—History—21st century—Forecasting 5. Political science literature 6. World politics—21st century—Forecasting

ISBN 046502954X (hbk.); 0465029558 (ebk.); 9780465029549 (hbk.); 9780465029556 (ebk.)

LC 2011-033312

SUMMARY: This book, by Zbigniew Brzezinski, "argues that without an America that is economically vital, socially appealing, responsibly powerful, and capable of sustaining an intelligent foreign engagement, the geopolitical prospects for the West could become increasingly grave. The ongoing changes in the distribution of global power and mounting global strife make it all the more essential that America does not retreat into an ignorant garrison-state mentality or wallow in cultural hedonism." (Publisher's note)

REVIEW: *Choice* v51 no1 p158 S 2013 M. Amstutz

REVIEW: *Kirkus Rev* v79 no23 p2188-9 D 1 2011

REVIEW: *New Repub* v243 no10 p47-51 Je 28 2012 James P. Rubin

"Strategic Vision: America and the Crisis of Global Power." "When it comes to offering a vision to guide American foreign policy, Zbigniew Brzezinski's latest book, unlike so much other literature of this type, refuses to lament or exaggerate the alleged decline in American power and influence. Instead 'Strategic Vision' offers a kind of blueprint --a path that Washington must take, in Brzezinski's view, to ensure a secure international order, in which free markets and democratic principles can thrive. . . . Unfortunately, important parts of the book's analysis seem overtaken by events, and Brzezinski's overarching idea --he has a weakness for overarching ideas --is divorced from the realities that Washington policymakers will confront in the coming years."

REVIEW: *New Statesman* v141 no5104 p40-2 My 7 2012

Mark Leonard

"Every Nation for Itself: Winners and Losers in a G-Zero World;" "Strategic Vision: America and the Crisis of Global Power;" "The World America Made." "Starting from the assumption that decline is a choice, [Robert] Kagan's elegant and perceptive essay 'The World America Made' aims to convince his compatriots not to commit what he calls 'superpower suicide' by laying out a dystopian vision of a world without the U.S. . . . The genius of [Zbigniew Brzezinski's] latest book ['Strategic Vision: America and the Crisis of Global Power'] is to show that it is the combination of these two trends – the power shift from west to east and the political awakening – that makes western dominance much more difficult to sustain. . . . [Ian] Bremmer's smart and snappy 'Every Nation for Itself' provides the most cogent prediction of how the politics of a post-American world will play out."

BUCAY, JORGE. Let me tell you a story; tales along the road to happiness; [by] Jorge Bucay 220 p. 2013 Penguin Group USA

1. Drama therapy 2. Fables—Psychological aspects 3. Happiness 4. Psychoanalysts 5. Psychological literature 6. Storytelling

ISBN 1609451236; 9781609451233

SUMMARY: In this book, "Demián desires happiness but is unable to face the problems in his life, from work to relationships with his lover, family, and friends. To learn more about himself and how to live life to the fullest, Demián goes to Jorge, a psychoanalyst who is known for his unorthodox treatments. At every session, Jorge tells Demián a tale from classic fables, folktales, or modern sagas, which help Demián better understand himself and find happiness." (World Literature Today)

REVIEW: *World Lit Today* v87 no6 p8 N/D 2013

"Let Me Tell You a Story: A New Approach to Healing Through the Art of Storytelling," "The Silence of the Wave," and "Helter Skelter: Fashion Unfriendly." "At every session, Jorge tells Demián a tale from classic fables, folktales, or modern sagas, which help Demián better understand himself and find happiness. The author is a gestalt psychotherapist and psychodramatist. . . . 'The Silence of the Wave' tells the story of Roberto Marías and the repressed memories he must conquer. . . . In this graphic novel, Liliko has been on top of the modeling world in Japan, representing the biggest brands. But she's not getting any younger, and the cutthroat world of modeling is constantly overthrowing the reigning queen with a new, younger model."

REVIEW: *World Lit Today* v87 no6 p81-2 N/D 2013

BUCHANAN, TOM. East wind; China and the British left, 1925-1976; [by] Tom Buchanan xx, 250 p. 2012 Oxford University Press

1. Historical literature 2. Liberalism—Great Britain—History—20th century 3. Right and left (Political science)—Great Britain—History—20th century 4. Socialism—Great Britain—History—20th century

ISBN 9780199570331 (hbk.)

LC 2012-002808

SUMMARY: This book presents an "account of the relationship between China and the British Left, from the rise of modern Chinese nationalism to the death of Mao Tse tung. Beginning with the "Hands Off China" movement of the mid-1920s, Tom Buchanan charts the mobilisation of British opinion in defence of China against Japanese aggression, 1931-1945, and the role of the British left in relations with the People's Republic of China after 1949." (Publisher's note)

REVIEW: *Am Hist Rev* v118 no3 p935 Je 2013 Ariane Knüsel

REVIEW: *Engl Hist Rev* v129 no536 p249-51 F 2014 Kevin Morgan

"East Wind: China and the British Left, 1925-1976". "Impressive . . . topical, scholarly and illuminating. . . . In some respects, the book is almost too conscientious in its coverage. In seemingly aspiring to be as comprehensive as a short research monograph permits, [Tom] Buchanan introduces a formidable cast of characters of whom some hundreds are noted in the index. Even the most profoundly implicated of these have to be dealt with somewhat perfunctorily, and inclusion of a more focused treatment, though necessarily selective, might have made for a greater depth of analysis even at the expense of some of its breadth."

BUCHOLZ, ROBERT O. London. See Ward, J. P.

BUCHWALD, JED Z. Newton and the origin of civilization. See Feingold, M.

BUCKLEY, CARLA. The deepest secret; a novel; [by] Carla Buckley 448 p. 2013 Bantam Books

1. Mothers—Fiction 2. Neighborhoods—Fiction 3. Secrets—Fiction 4. Sick children—Fiction 5. Suspense fiction

ISBN 9780345535245

LC 2013-020477

SUMMARY: In this book, "Eve Lattimore's every waking moment is consumed with care for her teenage son, Tyler, who suffers from Xeroderma pigmentosa (XP), a rare condition that makes sunlight deadly. Eve is vigilant in keeping Tyler under wraps 24/7. But how far should a mother's protection go? And at what cost? When a horrific accident is covered up, family lies are revealed, and Eve's safe haven and conscience start to disintegrate." (Library Journal)

REVIEW: *Booklist* v110 no11 p26-7 F 1 2014 Stephanie Turza

"The Deepest Secret." "Every family is vulnerable, but Eve's might be more fragile than most. Her son's incredibly rare medical condition means any exposure to UV light could be fatal, forcing Eve to change the way her son lives, learns, and plays. . . . [Carla] Buckley highlights the power of community in 'The Deepest Secret,' the story of a mother's desire to protect her child from the dangers of the outside world at any cost. Eve, her husband, and Tyler narrate the story in turn, weaving personal bias and suspicion into the overarching drama. Fans of Lisa Scottoline and Lisa Gardner will appreciate Buckley's unique blend of poignant emotion and thrilling suspense."

REVIEW: *Kirkus Rev* v81 no24 p179 D 15 2013

"The Deepest Secret". "Yes, everybody has secrets in [Carla] Buckley's third novel . . . about an Ohio woman who will go to any lengths to protect her impaired son, but some secrets are uglier than others. . . . The dialogue between [Eve and Charlotte]—and between Eve and David when they're not at each other's throats—is often blandly chirpy. As for Eve's neighbors' secrets, they are pretty low-grade as secrets go. Despite its high concept, the plot never rises to a temperature above lukewarm."

REVIEW: *Publ Wkly* v260 no49 p57 D 2 2013

BUCKLEY, CHRISTOPHER, 1952-. But enough about you; Essays; [by] Christopher Buckley 2014 Simon & Schuster

1. Essay (Literary form) 2. Satire 3. Social criticism 4. Travelers' writings, American 5. Wit & humor
ISBN 9781476749525 paperback; 978-1476749518 hardcover

SUMMARY: "In his first book of essays since his 1997 bestseller, 'Wry Martinis,' [author Christopher] Buckley delivers a rare combination of big ideas and truly fun writing. Tackling subjects ranging from 'How to Teach Your Four-Year-Old to Ski' to 'A Short History of the Bug Zapper,' and 'The Art of Sacking' to literary friendships with Joseph Heller and Christopher Hitchens, he is at once a humorous storyteller, astute cultural critic, adventurous traveler, and irreverent historian." (Publisher's note)

REVIEW: *Booklist* v110 no15 p13 Ap 1 2014 Donna Chavez

REVIEW: *Kirkus Rev* v82 no7 p42 Ap 1 2014

REVIEW: *Libr J* v139 no7 p83-4 Ap 15 2014 David Keymer

REVIEW: *N Y Times Book Rev* p55 Je 1 2014 MERYL GORDON

REVIEW: *Natl Rev* v65 no10 p43-4 Je 2 2014 ROGER KIMBALL

"But Enough About You: Essays." "There is something Wodehousean about large swaths of 'But Enough About You.' Many of the nearly 90 pieces that compose the book are allegro little divertissements, guaranteed to put a smile on your face, a song in your heart, and a spring in your step. . . . 'But Enough About You' belongs to that most exigent genre, the literary miscellany. There is a bit of this, a bit of that. Most of the pieces are quite short. Most are comic. But there are serious currents here, too."

REVIEW: *Publ Wkly* v261 no6 p76 F 10 2014

BUCKLEY, FIONA. A Traitor's Tears; [by] Fiona Buckley 240 p. 2014 Severn House Pub Ltd

1. Detective & mystery stories 2. Great Britain—History—Elizabeth, 1558-1603 3. Murder investigation—Fiction 4. Treason 5. Widows—Fiction
ISBN 1780290578; 9781780290577

SUMMARY: In this book, by Fiona Buckley, "recently widowed Ursula Blanchard is living a quiet life on her Surrey estate, caring for her infant son. But her peaceful existence is shattered when Ursula's neighbour Jane Cobbold is found dead in her own flowerbed, stabbed through the heart with a silver dagger - and Ursula's manservant Brockley is arrested for the crime. Determined to prove Brockley's innocence, Ursula seeks help from her old mentor Lord Burghley." (Publisher's note)

REVIEW: *Booklist* v110 no13 p23 Mr 1 2014 Margaret Flanagan

REVIEW: *Kirkus Rev* v82 no2 p266 Ja 15 2014

"A Traitor's Tears". "Queen Elizabeth's half sister tries to prove a loyal servant innocent of murder. Ursula Blanchard is doing her best to live quietly in Surrey with her young son Harry, the offspring of a liaison with the first husband she had thought dead but met on her last perilous mission on the Continent. Since Ursula's second husband passed away too early to have been Harry's father, she must live with nasty gossip, especially from her neighbor Jane Cobbold, whom she is nonetheless visiting when Jane is found stabbed to death in her garden. . . . Not the best of Ursula's 12 mysteries . . . but still as historically rich as ever."

REVIEW: *Libr J* v139 no4 p72 Mr 1 2014 Teresa L. Jacobsen

REVIEW: *Publ Wkly* v261 no1 p37 Ja 6 2014

BUCKNELL, KATHERINE.ed. The Animals. See The Animals

BUDIANSKY, STEPHEN. Mad music; Charles Ives, the nostalgic rebel; [by] Stephen Budiansky 306 p. 2014 University Press of New England

1. Biography (Literary form) 2. Composers—United States—Biography 3. Historical literature 4. Music—United States—History & criticism
ISBN 9781611683998 (cloth: alk. paper); 9781611685145 (ebook)
LC 2013-028737

SUMMARY: "'Mad Music' is the story of Charles Edward Ives (1874-1954), the innovative American composer who achieved international recognition, but only after he'd stopped making music. . . . To [author] Stephen Budiansky, Ives's life story is a personification of America emerging as a world power: confident and successful, yet unsure of the role of art and culture in a modernizing nation." (Publisher's note)

REVIEW: *Choice* v52 no1 p85 St 2014 J. E. Wickell

REVIEW: *N Y Rev Books* v61 no11 p37-8 Je 19 2014 Jeremy Denk

"Mad Music: Charles Ives, the Nostalgic Rebel." "At the outset of his excellent new biography, Stephen Budiansky summons up [the] confrontational [Charles] Ives. . . . It is upsetting to read about the wave of mockery and misunderstanding that washed back on the composer. . . . Budiansky, citing these insults, makes you despise America's conservative musical establishment of the time almost as much as Ives did. . . . There are basically two kinds of Ives pieces: serious pieces and satires. Budiansky has a perceptive section on Ives's satirical vein."

BUELL, LAWRENCE. The dream of the great American novel; [by] Lawrence Buell 500 p. 2014 Belknap Press of Harvard University Press

1. American fiction—19th century—History and criticism 2. American fiction—20th century—History and criticism 3. Literature—History & criticism 4. Literature and society—United States—History—19th century 5. Literature and society—United States—History—20th century 6. National characteristics, American, in literature
ISBN 0674051157; 9780674051157 (alk. paper)
LC 2013-032745

SUMMARY: "The idea of 'the great American novel' continues to thrive almost as vigorously as in its nineteenth-century heyday, defying 150 years of attempts to dismiss it as amateurish or obsolete." In this book, author Lawrence

Buell "reanimates this supposedly antiquated idea, demonstrating that its history is a key to the dynamics of national literature and national identity itself." (Publisher's note)

REVIEW: *Atlantic* v313 no5 p88-99 Je 2014 William Deresiewicz

"The Novel: A Biography" and "The Dream of the Great American Novel". "Michael Schmidt's 'The Novel: A Biography' . . . [contains] 45 brisk, brilliant, intimate, assured, and almost unfaggingly interesting chapters. . . . If anyone's up for the job, it would seem to be him. . . . Take a breath, clear the week, turn off the WiFi, and throw yourself in. . . . [Lawrence] Buell seems less interested in the 'dream,' the concept as a cultural phenomenon, than in constructing a taxonomy of GAN contenders—and thus, in large measure, of American fiction as a whole. This is where the ambition comes in, as well as Buell's enormous erudition. . . . Buell's book tells us a great deal about American fiction. What it also tells us, in its every line, is much of what is wrong with academic criticism. . . . The book does so much posturing, you think it's going to throw its back out."

REVIEW: *Booklist* v110 no9/10 p34 Ja 1 2014 Bryce Christensen

REVIEW: *Choice* v51 no12 p2178 Ag 2014 J. W. Miller

REVIEW: *Kirkus Rev* v81 no21 p123 N 1 2013

REVIEW: *N Engl Q* v87 no3 p538-40 S 2014 Nina Baym

REVIEW: *New Yorker* v90 no9 p102-1 Ap 21 2014

REVIEW: *Publ Wkly* v260 no45 p58 N 11 2013

REVIEW: *TLS* no5788 p27 Mr 7 2014

REVIEW: *TLS* no5807 p23 Jl 18 2014 SARAH GRAHAM

REVIEW: *Va Q Rev* v90 no1 p203-6 Wint 2014 Michael Dirda

BUHLE, PAUL.ed. Bohemians. See Bohemians

BUI, DIEM-MY T.ed. Monster culture in the 21st century. See Monster culture in the 21st century

BUILDING STORIES; p. cm. 2012 Pantheon Books
ISBN 9780375424335
LC 2012-007946

SUMMARY: This comic-book novel by Chris Ware "centers on a rundown Chicago apartment building, whose three floors form a kind of triptych of loneliness. The 'old woman'. . . on the ground floor . . . doesn't dream of companionship, but remembers the dreams of it she used to have. . . . The 'married couple' on the second floor are lonely together, trapped in a cycle of fighting and apologizing. . . And the 'girl' on the third floor . . . is lonely with a youthful, frenzied desperation." (New York Review of Books)

REVIEW: *Booklist* v109 no13 p43 Mr 1 2013

REVIEW: *Booklist* v109 no2 p58 S 15 2012

REVIEW: *Kirkus Rev* p41 N 15 2012 Best Fiction & Children's Books

REVIEW: *Kirkus Rev* v80 no15 p438 Ag 1 2012

REVIEW: *London Rev Books* v34 no23 p19-20 D 6 2012 Nick Richardson

REVIEW: *N Y Rev Books* v59 no20 p66-9 D 20 2012 Gabriel Winslow-Yost

"Building Stories." "[Chris] Ware's drawings are meticulous, even chilly, with flat, muted colors and the straight lines and perfect curves of an architectural rendering. The panels follow an orderly horizontal grid, but have a discomfiting tendency to occasionally shrink to near illegibility; or they might suddenly demand to be read from right to left, or even disappear entirely, to be replaced by pretty but unhelpful typography . . . complicated diagrams, or plans for a paper model of one of the stories' locations. . . . Throughout 'Building Stories,' Ware's attention to the awkward physicality, the constant humiliations and cruelties of human existence is as precise and as brutally funny as it is in his previous work."

REVIEW: *N Y Times Book Rev* p11 D 9 2012

REVIEW: *N Y Times Book Rev* p22 O 28 2012

REVIEW: *N Y Times Book Rev* p1 O 21 2012 DOUGLAS WOLK

REVIEW: *New York Times* p34 N 23 2012 THE NEW YORK TIMES

REVIEW: *Publ Wkly* v259 no26 p158 Je 25 2012

REVIEW: *Publ Wkly* v259 no25 p27 Je 18 2012

REVIEW: *Time* v180 no16 p52 O 15 2012 LEV GROSSMAN DOUGLAS WOLK

REVIEW: *Yale Rev* v101 no4 p148-59 O 2013 AMY HUNGERFORD

"Building Stories." "Upon raising the lid, the reader becomes ambitious to move beyond delighted curiosity (everyone who sees the box wants to open it) to serious reading. This takes commitment: the fourteen elements entice with color and shape, but 'Building Stories' requires the same number of hours demanded by a regular novel. Readers who can't make the time to read it may find it all too easy to give the beautiful thing away. But they shouldn't be too quick to give up or give away. The rewards of reading 'Building Stories,' and reading it in a way that attends to its special form, are significant."

BUILDING, T. H. The Story of Six According to Claire; [by] T. H. Building 334 p. 2013 CreateSpace Independent Publishing Platform

1. Child abuse—Fiction 2. Erotic stories 3. School stories 4. Sexual dominance & submission 5. Teenagers—Sexual behavior
ISBN 1492958794; 9781492958796

SUMMARY: This book is set in "Repeater's College, where [students] are taught discipline and respect via a deeply visceral method: caning. . . .Teenage Claire almost made it through her time at Repeater's without a caning, but when she's caught with a cigarette, it's off to the office. She expects pain and terror—not the sexual feelings that arise in anticipation of the beating and during the beating itself." (Kirkus Reviews)

REVIEW: *Kirkus Rev* v82 no1 p314 Ja 1 2014

"The Story of Six According to Claire". " [T. H.] Building attempts to turn a horrifying practice and a chronicle of psychological harm into erotic fiction for adults, even going so far as to describe both the beatings and sexual acts in similarly graphic detail. The problem with this endeavor is that, despite Building's many disclaimers, readers are placed in the position of the sadistic tormentors and encouraged to draw erotic pleasure from descriptions of abuse. . . some of which are rather poorly written . . . that, though they might turn on the characters, shouldn't titillate readers. An ultimately unsuccessful attempt to eroticize abuse."

BUKIET, MELVIN JULES. Naked Came the Post-Postmodernist; [by] Melvin Jules Bukiet 231 p. 2013 Arcade Publishing

1. College stories 2. College students—Fiction 3. College teachers—Crimes against—Fiction 4. Murder investigation—Fiction 5. Teacher-student relationships—Fiction
ISBN 9781611459098 (alk. paper)
LC 2013-030536

SUMMARY: In this book, written in a round-format by students at Sarah Lawrence College, "a senior mathematics professor at Underhill College has been found dead in his office, the victim of murder. At Underhill, a small liberal arts college with a pricy tuition and a pampered student body, all of the students are close to their professors. But at least one loved Eric Davenport in a deeply inappropriate fashion." (Publisher's note)

REVIEW: *Kirkus Rev* v82 no2 p70 Ja 15 2014

"Naked Came the Post-Postmodernist". "Thirteen members of a Sarah Lawrence writing workshop directed by [Melvin Jules] Bukiet . . . team up for this serial whodunit, with predictably episodic results. . . . There's no momentum, no sustained investigation, no characters worthy of the name since few of the contributors are interested in following up any of the clues, or even any of the developments, laid down by their predecessors. . . . If the continuity is weak, however, several individual episodes . . . are likely to provoke guffaws, or at least smirks."

BULAWAYO, NOVIOLET, 1981-. We need new names; a novel; [by] NoViolet Bulawayo 304 p. 2014 Back Bay Books

1. Emigration and immigration—Fiction 2. Families—Zimbabwe—Fiction 3. Girls—Zimbabwe—Fiction 4. Political violence—Zimbabwe—Fiction 5. Psychological fiction 6. Zimbabweans—United States—Fiction
ISBN 0316230812 (hbk.); 0316230847 (pbk.); 9780316230810 (hbk.); 9780316230841 (pbk.)
LC 2012-038068

SUMMARY: In this novel, by NoViolet Bulawayo, "Darling is only ten years old, and yet she must navigate a fragile and violent world . . . in Zimbabwe. But Darling has a chance to escape: she has an aunt in America. She travels to this new land in search of America's famous abundance only to find that her options as an immigrant are perilously few." (Publisher's note)

REVIEW: *Booklist* v109 no18 p17 My 15 2013 Donna Chavez

REVIEW: *Booklist* v110 no1 p58 S 1 2013 Laurie Hartshorn

REVIEW: *Kirkus Rev* p8 N 15 2013 Best Books

REVIEW: *Kirkus Rev* v81 no7 p317 Ap 1 2013

REVIEW: *Libr J* v137 no20 p60 D 1 2012 Barbara Hoffert

REVIEW: *Libr J* v138 no14 p70 S 1 2013 J. Sara Paulk

REVIEW: *Libr J* v138 no9 p68 My 15 2013 Sally Bissell

REVIEW: *Ms* v23 no4 p23 Fall 2013 ALICE DRIVER

REVIEW: *N Y Times Book Rev* p12 Je 9 2013 UZODINMA IWEALA

REVIEW: *New York Times* v162 no56162 p12 Je 9 2013 UZODINMA IWEALA

REVIEW: *New York Times* v162 no56138 pC1-6 My 16 2013 MICHIKO KAKUTANI

REVIEW: *Publ Wkly* v260 no14 p39 Ap 8 2013

REVIEW: *TLS* no5763 p21 S 13 2013 LUCY SCHOLES

"We Need New Names." "Narrated in the lyrical voice of the ten-year-old Darling, the escapades of childhood rough-and-tumble, guava stealing and the game of 'Find bin Laden' sit uneasily alongside the realities of daily existence. . . . [NoViolet] Bulawayo was born in Zimbabwe and moved to the US when she was eighteen, suggesting that her own complicated sense of identity has seeped into the fabric of these pages. . . . A novel that deals with the immigrant experience and tom identity is nothing new; what justifies the inclusion of 'We Need New Names' on the shortlist for the Man Booker Prize is NoViolet Bulawayo's command of Darling's captivating voice."

REVIEW: *World Lit Today* v88 no1 p55-6 Ja/F 2014 Jim Hannan

"We Need New Names." "Written with kinetic energy that crackles with life, NoViolet Bulawayo's debut novel should be read by anyone interested in emerging voices in world literature. At times joyful, funny, melancholic, ferocious, and defiant, Bulawayo's first-person narrator, Darling, is a trenchant observer of the human condition. After meeting a wealthy visitor from England near her home in Zimbabwe, a young Darling takes note of the visitor's 'smooth skin that doesn't even have a scar to show she is a living person.'"

BULLA, DAVID W.ed. Sensationalism. See Sensationalism

BULLARD, PADDY. Edmund Burke and the Art of Rhetoric; [by] Paddy Bullard xi, 272 p. 2011 Cambridge University Press

1. English language—18th century—Rhetoric 2. Historical literature 3. Political oratory—Great Britain—History—18th century 4. Political philosophy
ISBN 1107006570; 9781107006577
LC 2010-045700

SUMMARY: In this book, author Paddy Bullard "argues that [Edmund] Burke's ideas about civil society, and particularly about the process of political deliberation, are, for better or worse, shaped by the expressiveness of his language. Above all, Burke's eloquence is designed to express ethos or character. This rhetorical imperative is itself informed by Burke's argument that the competency of every political system can be judged by the ethical knowledge that the governors have." (Publisher's note)

REVIEW: *TLS* no5747 p7-8 My 24 2013 DANIEL HITCHENS

"The Cambridge Companion to Edmund Burke," "Edmund Burke and the Art of Rhetoric," and "Patriotism and Public Spirit: Edmund Burke and the Role of the Critic in Mid-18th-Century Britain." "'The Cambridge Companion to Edmund Burke' aims to disentangle Burke from his many contexts, and for the most part it succeeds impressively. . . . The collection is generally crisp, broad-minded and clearly written. . . . This is a fresh and immediately illuminating thesis, and [Paddy] Bullard's digressive erudition adds to the book's charm. My one complaint is that, as so often, the flesh-and-blood Burke begins to disappear into his own ideas. . . . [Ian] Crowe has hit on a valuable approach of some importance, simply by taking seriously the vibrant intellectual culture of mid-century London."

BULLOCH, JAMIE.tr. The taste of apple seeds. See Hagena, K.

BULLOUGH, OLIVER. The last man in russia; the struggle to save a dying nation; [by] Oliver Bullough 296 p. 2013 Basic Books

1. Alcoholism—Russia (Federation) 2. Dissenters—Soviet Union—Biography 3. Historical literature 4. Journalism 5. Russia (Federation)—Social conditions 6. Social problems—Russia (Federation) 7. Soviet Union—Church history
ISBN 9780465074983 (hardcover)
LC 2013-936486

SUMMARY: "Faced with staggering population decline--and near-certain economic collapse--driven by toxic levels of alcohol abuse, Russia is also battling a deeper sickness: a spiritual one. . . . In 'The Last Man in Russia,' award-winning journalist Oliver Bullough uses the tale of a lone priest to give life to this national crisis. Father Dmitry Dudko, a dissident Orthodox Christian, was thrown into a Stalinist labor camp for writing poetry." (Publisher's note)

REVIEW: *Booklist* v109 no15 p6-8 Ap 1 2013 Gilbert Taylor

REVIEW: *Economist* v407 no8838 p82-3 Je 1 2013

REVIEW: *Kirkus Rev* v81 no7 p46 Ap 1 2013

REVIEW: *Libr J* v138 no6 p94 Ap 1 2013 Elizabeth Zeitz

REVIEW: *N Y Times Book Rev* p10 Je 9 2013 ELLEN BARRY

REVIEW: *New Statesman* v142 no5151/5152 p82 Mr 29 2013

REVIEW: *New York Times* v162 no56162 p10 Je 9 2013 ELLEN BARRY

REVIEW: *Newsweek Global* v161 no15 p1 Ap 19 2013 Peter Pomerantsev

REVIEW: *Publ Wkly* v260 no12 p55-6 Mr 25 2013 Karolina Sutton

REVIEW: *TLS* no5779 p11 Ja 3 2014 WENDY SLATER

"The Last Man in Russia: And the Struggle to Save a Dying Nation." "The culture of mistrust and betrayal that defined Dmitry Dudko's fate is a central theme of Oliver Bullough's new book, 'The Last Man in Russia.' That this culture was a legacy of the Stalinist terror can hardly be doubted, but whether it can be blamed for the national decline that, Bullough claims, set in during the 1960s is more questionable. . . . This investigation of the Russian hinterland beyond Moscow and St Petersburg is all too rare in British journalism, though Bullough's research methods are disarmingly haphazard."

BUNTING, EVE, 1928-. Big Bear's big boat; [by] Eve Bunting 32 p. 2013 Clarion Books

1. Bears—Fiction 2. Boats & boating—Design & construction 3. Boats & boating—Juvenile literature 4. Boats and boating—Fiction 5. Children's stories 6. Friendship—Juvenile fiction
ISBN 0618585370 (hardcover); 9780618585373 (hardcover)
LC 2012-003974

SUMMARY: In this book by Eve Bunting "Big Bear outgrew his little boat, so he is building himself a big boat and can't wait till he's rowing, fishing, and relaxing in it. When his friends start suggesting improvements, Big Bear obligingly follows their advice. To his dismay, his big boat is turning out all wrong. It's because he hasn't followed his own dream, and he knows exactly how to fix it." (Publisher's note)

REVIEW: *Booklist* v109 no22 p86 Ag 1 2013 Ann Kelley

REVIEW: *Bull Cent Child Books* v67 no3 p141-2 N 2013 J. H.

"Big Bear's Big Boat." "After growing into Big Bear and giving away his beloved little boat in 'Little Bear's Little Boat', Big Bear decides its time to build himself a new boat to accommodate his new size. . . . The gentle, simply worded text and childlike bear will appeal to fans of Minarik's Little Bear series, and the short sentences and uncomplicated vocabulary may put this within range of the easy-reader crowd as well. [Illustrator Nancy] Carpenter's pen and ink and digital art have an appropriately casual, slightly rustic feel to them and the woodsy browns and greens and pale lake-blues are effectively highlighted by the brighter cerulean of Big Bear's boat and by touches of red in Little Bear's boat."

REVIEW: *Kirkus Rev* v81 no12 p82 Je 15 2013

REVIEW: *SLJ* v59 no8 p68 Ag 2013 Marian McLeod

BUNTING, EVE, 1928-. The Cart that carried Martin; [by] Eve Bunting 32 p. 2013 Charlesbridge

1. African Americans—Civil rights—History—20th century—Juvenile literature 2. African Americans—History—Juvenile literature 3. Children's stories 4. Civil rights movements—United States—History—20th century—Juvenile literature
ISBN 1580893872; 9781580893879 (reinforced for library use)
LC 2012-026688

SUMMARY: This book, by Eve Bunting, is "about the funeral of Dr. [Martin Luther] King in Atlanta, Georgia, in 1968. Bunting focuses on the funeral procession of Dr. King, beginning with the two men who found the cart to carry him through the streets of Atlanta. Back matter includes a brief introduction to Dr. Martin Luther King, Jr. s work, assassination, and funeral, accompanied by a full-color historical photograph of the real cart. (Publisher's note)

REVIEW: *Booklist* v110 no5 p58 N 1 2013 Erin Anderson

REVIEW: *Booklist* v110 no11 p60 F 1 2014 Ilene Cooper

REVIEW: *Bull Cent Child Books* v67 no4 p204-5 D 2013 E. B.

REVIEW: *Kirkus Rev* p37 Ag 15 2013 Fall Preview

REVIEW: *Kirkus Rev* v81 no16 p215 Ag 15 2013

"The Cart That Carried Martin." "An old, unwanted cart becomes part of Dr. Martin Luther King's funeral procession. . . . [Author Eve] Bunting uses simple declarative sentences to capture the sorrow of the day and the message that King's followers were intent upon proclaiming--his greatness came from humble beginnings. The mules, Belle and Ada, were a reminder that upon freedom, slaves were given forty acres and a mule. Tate's pencil-and-gouache artwork plays up the details of the cart and the two mules while depicting the crowds of mourners less distinctly. Adults looking for a title to share with young readers will find this helpful in imparting the emotions raised by King's assassination."

BUNTING, EVE, 1928-. Washday; [by] Eve Bunting 32 p. 2014 Holiday House

1. Children's stories 2. Frontier and pioneer life—Fiction 3. Grandmothers—Fiction 4. Laundry—Fiction 5. Parties—Fiction

ISBN 0823428680; 9780823428687 (hardcover)

LC 2012-040347

SUMMARY: "Lizzie helps her grandma on washday and gets rewarded with a tea party in this historical story celebrating family tradition and hard work," written by Eve Bunting and illustrated by Brad Sneed. (Publisher's note) "Their frontier life means this is a hard day's work: there is water to haul and to boil, homemade soap to shave, and stained clothes to run up and down the washboard before putting them through the wringer and hanging them to dry." (Bulletin of the Center for Children's Books)

REVIEW: *Booklist* v110 no16 p61 Ap 15 2014 Jeanne McDermott

REVIEW: *Bull Cent Child Books* v67 no10 p504 Je 2014 A. A.

"Washday". "[Eve] Bunting and [Brad] Sneed temper the tedious details of the washday process with quiet prose and gentle pencil and watercolor drawings, and the soft lines of the illustrations, hued in blues and greens, make the arduousness of the task more palatable. Lizzie's Blythe-doll eyes, however, render her woebegone and even unnerving, and the faces are occasionally strained; the story's pacing verges on the languorous, resulting in a rather unmemorable, though not unpleasant, audience experience. Still, the portrayal of frontier life and sweet details may fare well among those young audiences on the threshold of 'Little House in the Big Woods' and other pioneering tales."

REVIEW: *Kirkus Rev* v82 no4 p200 F 15 2014

REVIEW: *SLJ* v60 no4 p114 Ap 2014 Marianne Saccardi

BURG, ANN E. Serafina's promise; [by] Ann E. Burg 304 p. 2013 Scholastic Press

1. Brothers and sisters—Fiction 2. Brothers and sisters—Juvenile fiction 3. Earthquakes—Fiction 4. Families—Haiti—Juvenile fiction 5. Family life—Haiti—Fiction 6. Haiti Earthquake, Haiti, 2010—Fiction 7. Haiti Earthquake, Haiti, 2010—Juvenile fiction 8. Novels in verse

ISBN 0545535646; 9780545535649 (alk. paper)

LC 2012-045609

SUMMARY: In this book, by Ann E. Burg, "Serafina is an 11-year-old Haitian struggling to keep her dream of becoming a doctor alive. Living in a desolate mountain village, Serafina toils at her daily chores while planning to attend school . Serafina has a warm family . . . who all come to support her vision. Then a flood washes away the family home, and the roaring stampede of an earthquake devastates the city of Port-au-Prince, where Serafina's father works." (Publisher's note)

REVIEW: *Booklist* v110 no4 p52-3 O 15 2013 Gail Bush

REVIEW: *Bull Cent Child Books* v67 no3 p142 N 2013 H. M.

REVIEW: *Horn Book Magazine* v89 no5 p88 S/O 2013 ROBIN L. SMITH

"Serafina's Promise." "Woven into the spare first-person free-verse poems is the history of Haiti and Serafina's family. One night Gogo, Serafina's grandmother, tells the story of her husband, who had taught himself to read and was beginning to teach his family when the dreaded Tonton Macoutes took him away. Serafina determines to fulfill Granpe's dream of an education. . . . Rather than the sad story Americans often hear about Haiti, [Ann E.] Burg captures the lives of hard-working people who praise God and move forward, even when difficulties conspire against them. Rich details of everyday life add texture to this emotional, fast-moving tale. A glossary and a pronunciation guide are included."

REVIEW: *Kirkus Rev* v81 no16 p146 Ag 15 2013

REVIEW: *Kirkus Rev* p72 N 15 2013 Best Books

REVIEW: *Publ Wkly* v260 no36 p57 S 9 2013

REVIEW: *Voice of Youth Advocates* v37 no1 p13-5 Ap 2014

REVIEW: *Voice of Youth Advocates* v36 no5 p54 D 2013 Courtney M. Krieger

BURGER, JEFF.ed. Leonard Cohen on Leonard Cohen. See Leonard Cohen on Leonard Cohen

BURGESS, COLIN. Freedom 7; the historic flight of Alan B. Shepard, Jr.; [by] Colin Burgess 220 p. 2013 Springer

1. Aerospace technology 2. Historical literature 3. Manned space flight—History 4. Project Mercury (U.S.) 5. Shepard, Alan B., 1923-1998

ISBN 9783319011554

LC 2013-944297

SUMMARY: This book on "Alan Shepard's May 1961 flight" by Colin Burgess "considers all aspects of the preparation for Shepard's space flight in the Mercury capsule, including the development of the rocket, the precursor flight by Ham the chimpanzee in January 1961, and the training for the mission." (Choice: Current Reviews for Academic Libraries)

REVIEW: *Choice* v51 no9 p1617-8 My 2014 J. Z. Kiss

"Freedom 7: The Historic Flight of Alan B. Shepard, Jr.". "The chapter on the chimpanzee program is one of the most interesting, and the lessons learned paved the way for human space flight. The book contains many fascinating photographs and several appendixes, including Shepard's post-flight report, transcripts of voice communications, and more. While this volume will interest space flight enthusiasts, it covers little ground that has not been extensively considered by other works. . . . Recommended."

BURGESS, MELVIN. The hit; [by] Melvin Burgess 304 p. 2014 Chicken House/Scholastic Inc.

1. Death—Fiction 2. Death—Juvenile fiction 3. Designer drugs—Juvenile fiction 4. Drugs—Fiction 5. Families—England—Manchester—Juvenile fiction 6. Family life—England—Fiction 7. Teenagers—England—Manchester—Juvenile fiction 8. Young adult fiction

ISBN 0545556996; 9780545556996; 9780545557009

LC 2013-013792

SUMMARY: In this novel, by Melvin Burgess, "a new drug is on the street. Everyone's buzzing about it. Take the hit. Live the most intense week of your life. Then die. . . . Adam thinks it over. He's poor, and doesn't see that changing. . .

. His brother Jess is missing. And Manchester is in chaos, controlled by drug dealers and besieged by a group of home-grown terrorists who call themselves the Zealots. . . . Adam downs one of the Death pills." (Publisher's note)

REVIEW: *Booklist* v110 no9/10 p98 Ja 1 2014 Michael Cart

"The Hit". "[Melvin] Burgess, a master of YA literature, has written a novel of white knuckle suspense that has considerable violence and ambitious philosophical underpinnings. How does one deal with socioeconomic inequity? Is revolution a viable strategy? Is death? If this ambitious novel has flaws, it may be a lack of attention to these very questions. In addition, the villains—though terrifying—are over the top. But all that said, the novel is viscerally exciting and emotionally engaging. Best of all, it is sure to excite both thoughtful analysis and heated discussion among its readers. A clear winner from Burgess."

REVIEW: *Bull Cent Child Books* v67 no8 p399 Ap 2014 K. C.

REVIEW: *Horn Book Magazine* v90 no2 p112-3 Mr/Ap 2014 JONATHAN HUNT

"The Hit". "It's a decision that allows [Melvin] Burgess to hang some compelling ethical questions on a plot that will see Adam and Lizzie sort out their hormones from their true feelings, cope with their own mortality, and outwit menacing gangsters, particularly one with a disturbing penchant for making quadriplegics of those who cross him. Burgess is in fine form here: entertaining, provocative, vulgar, clever, and amoral. Some readers may wish that he had delved more deeply into the psyche of his characters or the civil unrest in the political landscape, but what this novel delivers—and delivers splendidly—is a gripping thriller with some food for thought."

REVIEW: *Kirkus Rev* v81 no24 p128 D 15 2013

REVIEW: *Publ Wkly* v260 no52 p53 D 23 2013

REVIEW: *SLJ* v60 no2 p100 F 2014 Ryan F. Paulsen

REVIEW: *Voice of Youth Advocates* v36 no6 p56 F 2014 Kimberly Bower

BURGESS, TONY. The N-Body Problem; [by] Tony Burgess 200 p. 2013 Chizine Publications

1. Apocalyptic literature (Christian literature) 2. Dystopias 3. Horror tales 4. Speculative fiction 5. Zombies
ISBN 1771481633; 9781771481632

SUMMARY: In this apocalyptic novel by Tony Burgess, "In the end, the zombie apocalypse was nothing more than a waste disposal problem. . . . The acceptable answer is to jettison the millions of immortal automatons into orbit. . . . Soon, earth's near space is a mesh of bodies interfering with the sunlight, having an effect on our minds that we never saw coming. . . . Life on earth slowly became not worth living." (Publisher's note)

REVIEW: *Quill Quire* v79 no9 p30 N 2013 Emily Donaldson

"The n-Body Problem." "The n-Body Problem is a gory, sometimes poetic, often confounding stream-of-consciousness nightmare, more post-apocalyptic fiction than zombie novel. . . . Around the midpoint, the novel takes a bizarre and extremely grotesque turn that is both perplexing and isolating. This frankly baffling twist, and its narrative fallout, leaves readers wondering where the plot might have gone had [author Tony] Burgess decided not to confine his grand premise to one unfortunate character's perspective."

BURGUNDY, RON. Let me off at the top!; my classy life and other musings; [by] Ron Burgundy 224 p. 2013 Crown Archetype

1. HUMOR—Form—Parodies 2. Humorous stories 3. Television broadcasting of news—Humor 4. Television news anchors
ISBN 0804139571; 9780804139571
LC 2013-037001

SUMMARY: This humorous book is purportedly a memoir by the fictitious news anchor Ron Burgundy, a native of a little town in Iowa named for a sectarian murderer and full of people who just didn't quite have the gumption to head further west, [who] has made himself an enduring star of the small screen, a jazz flautist, dog lover and collector of 'authentic replications of Spanish broadswords.'" (Kirkus Reviews)

REVIEW: *Kirkus Rev* v81 no24 p256 D 15 2013

"Let Me Off at the Top! My Classy Life and Other Musings". "A paean to silly self-regard from the master of the genre, TV anchor [Ron] Burgundy. Burgundy is, of course, a fictitious character, the product of comedian Will Ferrell. . . . The satire is broad to the point of micrometer-thinness, the targets all the usual suspects, the put-on chauvinism and arrogance just more of the same for anyone who's seen the films—and who besides the films' fans would plunk down the money for this book? Stephen Colbert has done wonders with his similarly broad-brushed character, but this is second-tier stuff."

REVIEW: *Publ Wkly* v260 no49 p14 D 2 2013

BURKE, DAVID ALLEN. Atomic testing in Mississippi; Project Dribble and the quest for nuclear weapons treaty verification in the Cold War era; [by] David Allen Burke ix, 194 p. 2012 Louisiana State University Press

1. Lamar County, Mississippi—History—20th century 2. Nuclear arms control—Verification—History 3. Nuclear weapons—Testing—Detection—Research—History 4. Underground nuclear explosions—Detection—Research—History 5. Underground nuclear explosions—Mississippi—History
ISBN 9780807145838 (cloth: alk. paper); 9780807145845 (pdf); 9780807145852 (epub); 9780807145869 (mobi)
LC 2012-006530

SUMMARY: In this book, author david Allen Burke seeks "to connect the atomic testing that took place in Mississippi to a range of developments, including the overall history of the region, the importance of atomic technology as a modernizer of the South, civil rights, the Cold War, and the public health aspects of radiation. By keeping his focus on one site, Burke gives readers a micro-history of a single set of nuclear tests while using the topic to look at larger issues." (American Historical Review)

REVIEW: *Am Hist Rev* v119 no1 p200-1 F 2014 Russell Olwell

"Atomic Testing in Mississippi: Project Dribble and the Quest for Nuclear Weapons Verification in the Cold War Era". "The great strength of the book is the sheer depth and relentlessness of [David Allen] Burke's research. He has uncovered every document possible about the testing program and has spoken to as many local residents as will talk about the events. He has dug into the politics of the tests as well as the ways in which local landowners tried to use the program for their own financial gain. . . . He weaves documents, maps, photos, and interviews together into a coherent narrative, and this history is brief, clear, and to the point."

REVIEW: *Choice* v50 no10 p1856-7 Je 2013 D. A. Johnson

BURKETT-CADENA, NATHAN D. Mosquitoes of the southeastern United States; [by] Nathan D. Burkett-Cadena xiii, 188 p. 2013 University of Alabama Press

1. Mosquitoes—Anatomy 2. Mosquitoes—Larvae 3. Mosquitoes—Physiology 4. Mosquitoes—Southern States—Identification 5. Natural history literature

ISBN 9780817317812 (hardcover : alk. paper); 9780817386481 (ebook)

LC 2012-024177

SUMMARY: "This work by [Nathan D.] Burkett-Cadena . . . is organized in two main sections; an illustrated dichotomous key to the identification of mosquitoes ofthe southeastern US and a concise account of individual species. . . . The volume actually contains two sets of identification keys, one to the genera of adult mosquitoes and one to the genera of fourth-instar larvae." (Choice)

REVIEW: *Choice* v51 no4 p667 D 2013 D. A. Brass

"Mosquitoes of the Southeastern United States." "A brief, but disappointingly short, introduction provides fundamental information on mosquito biology and natural history. The volume actually contains two sets of identification keys, one to the genera of adult mosquitoes and one to the genera of fourth-instar larvae. They feature stylized illustrations of all characteristics used, making them more user friendly than similar keys without accompanying illustrations or those with more simplistic black-and-white diagrams. One drawback to the keys, however, is a lack of reference from one couplet to the next. . . . This book will interest a wide range of readers, including students, entomologists, and mosquito-control workers."

BURLEIGH, MICHAEL. Small wars, faraway places; global insurrection and the making of the modern world, 1945-1965; [by] Michael Burleigh 608 p. 2013 Viking

1. Cold War 2. Historical literature 3. Imperialism 4. Low-intensity conflicts (Military science)—History—20th century 5. Military history, Modern—20th century 6. World politics—20th century

ISBN 0670025453; 9780670025459

LC 2013-017207

SUMMARY: In this book, Michael Burleigh looks at the "hot conflicts that erupted across the globe" following World War II, as the U.S. and the Soviet Union were engaged in the Cold War. Burleigh "surveys these forgotten wars and the people that fought them, ranging in his tale from Southeast Asia to the Middle East, Africa, and the Caribbean." (Publishers Weekly)

REVIEW: *Booklist* v110 no3 p18 O 1 2013 Gilbert Taylor

REVIEW: *Choice* v51 no6 p1065 F 2014 B. T. Browne

REVIEW: *Kirkus Rev* v81 no16 p122 Ag 15 2013

REVIEW: *N Y Times Book Rev* p7 D 29 2013 DANIEL LARISON

"Small Wars, Faraway Places: Global Insurrection and the Making of the Modern World, 1945-1965." "In 'Small Wars, Faraway Places,' Michael Burleigh recounts the violent end of the British and French empires in Africa and Asia, and their partial replacement by the United States in its often ill-informed and costly efforts to combat Communism during the early stages of the Cold War. . . . Burleigh proceeds episodically, jumping from one conflict to the next with each new chapter. Though this has the potential to be disorienting, he keeps the narrative moving along. He capably introduces each new subject without assuming too much prior knowledge, and uses brief biographical sketches of the key political and military actors to illustrate the experiences that informed their decisions."

REVIEW: *Natl Rev* v65 no18 p49-50 S 30 2013 MAX BOOT

"Small Wars, Faraway Places: Global Insurrection and the Making of the Modern World, 1945-1965." "There is a great story to be told here, and Michael Burleigh . . . captures some of the excitement and tumult of those heady years in this book. . . . This is an enjoyable, breezy read--perfect for a lazy afternoon at the beach--and it is full of nicely evocative descriptions. . . . But the book suffers from a glaring defect: it is riddled with errors. Some of Burleigh's mistakes are small and harmless. . . the kind of niggling error that any author can commit and I would not bother mentioning it, were this book not filled with many more significant mistakes that will lead the unwary reader astray."

REVIEW: *New Statesman* v142 no5156 p43 My 3 2013 David Herman

REVIEW: *Publ Wkly* v260 no26 p74 Jl 1 2013

BURNEY, NATHANIEL.il. The Illustrated Guide to Criminal Law. See Burney, N.

BURNEY, NATHANIEL. The Illustrated Guide to Criminal Law; [by] Nathaniel Burney 260 p. 2012 Jones McClure Publishing

1. Criminal law 2. Defense (Administrative procedure) 3. Graphic novels 4. Guilt (Law) 5. Punishment

ISBN 1598391836; 9781598391831

SUMMARY: This book, written by Nathaniel Burney, "is a complete law school course that keeps the laughter in manslaughter. You start with the absolute basics (what is crime?) and are soon deep in complex concepts like conspiracy, self-defense, and yes, entrapment--all explained with clarity, humor, and passion." (Publisher's note)

REVIEW: *Choice* v51 no2 p353-4 O 2013 J. E. Walsh

"The Illustrated Guide to Criminal Law." "'The Illustrated Guide to Criminal Law' by [Nathaniel] Burney is an irreverent cross between graphic novel and legal text, combining conceptual discourse with visual illustrations. The content is similar to what one might find in an introductory undergraduate text, although the information is presented in a narrative fashion and does not include many standard textbook functions such as definitions, case references, or scholarly support. Despite these missing materials, the narrative explanation is accurate and current. Readers are likely to find the explanation of some concepts to be quite helpful, especially those that relate to inchoate crimes (e.g., attempt, solicitation, and conspiracy), culpability, and responsibility."

REVIEW: *Voice of Youth Advocates* v36 no3 p87 Ag 2013 Jennifer Miskec

BURNS, ALLAN.ed. Haiku in English. See Haiku in English

BURNS, DAVID. The life and death of the radical historical Jesus; [by] David Burns xii, 275 p. 2013 Oxford University Press

1. Debs, Eugene V. (Eugene Victor), 1855-1926 2. Historical literature 3. Radicals—United States 4. Socialism—United States

ISBN 9780199929504 (hardcover : alk. paper)

LC 2012-024532

SUMMARY: This book by David Burns "contends that the influence of biblical criticism in America was more widespread than has been thought. Burns proves this point by uncovering the hidden history of the radical historical Jesus, a construct created and sustained by freethinkers, feminists, socialists, and anarchists during the Gilded Age and Progressive Era." (Publisher's note)

REVIEW: *Am Hist Rev* v118 no4 p1189-90 O 2013 Dan McKanan

"The Life and Death of the Radical Historical Jesus." "At the turn of the twentieth century, American socialists, anarchists, and labor activists assumed that Jesus of Nazareth was on their side. . . . For Burns, the pre-eminent expressions of the radical historical Jesus were Cyrenus Osborne Ward's 'The Ancient Lowly: A History of the Ancient Working People from the Earliest Known Period to the Adoption of Christianity by Constantine' (1889), Bouck White's 'The Call of the Carpenter (1911), and shorter writings by Socialist Party leaders George Herron and Eugene Debs. . . . In short, there is more to be said about the radical historical Jesus. But David Burns deserves our deepest thanks for starting the conversation with this fascinating and ably executed study."

REVIEW: *Choice* v51 no5 p900-1 Ja 2014 P. D. Travis

"The Life and Death of the Radical Historical Jesus." "[David] Burns . . . has written a notable social and cultural labor history of the US working-class movement of the late 19th and early 20th centuries. Those who adhere to the consensus idea of US history--little class conflict--will be shaken by Burns's thesis that labor uprisings (and socialism) were at least partly dependent upon the teachings of a secular Jesus as a model for attacking wealth and privilege. . . . Labor historians will gain much from Burns."

REVIEW: *J Am Hist* v100 no3 p848 D 2013 Paul Harvey

BURNS, E. JANE.ed. From beasts to souls. See From beasts to souls

BURNS, LOREE GRIFFIN. Handle with care; an unusual butterfly journey; [by] Loree Griffin Burns 33 p. 2014 Millbrook Press

1. Butterflies—Juvenile literature 2. Butterflies—Metamorphosis 3. Butterflies—Physiology 4. Butterfly farming—Costa Rica—Juvenile literature 5. Children's nonfiction

ISBN 0761393420; 9780761393429 (lib. bdg.: alk. paper)

LC 2013-018086

SUMMARY: In this book, author Loree Griffin Burns "focuses first on the life of the blue morpho butterfly at the El Bosque Nuevo butterfly farm in Costa Rica and concludes with its a final destination, the Museum of Science in Boston. . . . Factual back matter further supports the story. Additional information appears in the section 'Insects and Their Life Cycles,' which discusses the process of metamorphosis." (School Library Journal)

REVIEW: *Booklist* v110 no12 p69 F 15 2014 Carolyn Phelan

REVIEW: *Horn Book Magazine* v90 no3 p106-7 My/Je 2014 DANIELLE J. FORD

REVIEW: *Kirkus Rev* v82 no3 p108 F 1 2014

"Handle With Care: An Unusual Butterfly Journey". " This large, square album perfectly complements primary-grade butterfly studies. Crisply reproduced photographs show butterflies in all their stages, the greenhouse and other farm buildings where they are bred and grown, farm workers tending the caterpillars and collecting and packing the pupae, and finally, a child in Boston watching an adult butterfly emergc. A relatively simple text explains the insect's life cycle and the production process. . . . Sadly, the intriguing photographs of pupae on the front endpapers and adults on the back aren't labeled. Despite this miscalculation, an otherwise valuable addition to any classroom library."

REVIEW: *SLJ* v60 no2 p117 F 2014 Meg Smith

BURNS, TIMOTHY W. Shakespeare's political wisdom; [by] Timothy W. Burns x, 234 p. 2013 Palgrave Macmillan

1. Justice in literature 2. Kings & rulers in literature 3. Nobility in literature 4. Philosophical literature

ISBN 9781137320858 (alk. paper)

LC 2012-041570

SUMMARY: This book "offers. . . interpretations of five Shakespearean plays . . . with a view to the enduring guidance those plays can provide to human, political life. The plays have been chosen for their relentless attention to the questions that, for [William] Shakespeare, form the heart and soul of politics: Who should rule, and what is justice?" Author Timothy W. Burns "provides an original reading of the plays through the lens of political philosophy." (Publisher's note)

REVIEW: *Choice* v51 no9 p1679-80 My 2014 C. A. Colmo

"Shakespeare's Political Wisdom". "That [Timothy W.] Burns's ambitious book intends to engage not only poetry and politics but also theology is confirmed by the discussion of divine justice in 'King Lear'. All of these themes are skillfully integrated into the architectonic question of the book: 'Who should rule?' Burns's direct engagement with [William] Shakespeare's texts makes his essays highly accessible while at the same time engaging fundamental issues of politics and philosophy. This clearly written, deeply thoughtful volume addresses readers at all levels."

BURRIS, CAROL CORBETT. On the same track; how schools can join the twenty-first-century struggle against resegregation; [by] Carol Corbett Burris 208 p. 2013 Beacon Press

1. EDUCATION—Educational Policy & Reform—General 2. EDUCATION—Multicultural Education 3. EDUCATION—Testing & Measurement 4. Educational equalization—United States 5. Educational literature 6. Track system (Education)—United States

ISBN 9780807032978 (hardback)

LC 2013-039594

SUMMARY: This book presents a "critique of tracking, the practice of sorting students within schools or districts that gives them different access to learning. Drawing on numerous studies and her own experiences and interviews, Burris concludes that tracking causes segregation of those black, Latino and poor students who are identified as low achievers with limited intellectual prospects. . . . Moreover, high-achieving students do not lose their advantages when taught in heterogeneous groups." (Kirkus Reviews)

REVIEW: *Booklist* v110 no11 p14 F 1 2014 Vanessa Bush

REVIEW: *Kirkus Rev* v82 no2 p90 Ja 15 2014

"On the Same Track: How Schools Can Join the Twenty-First-Century Struggle Against Resegregation". "An educator offers a bold prescription to promote equality in America's public schools. High school principal and educational researcher [Carol Corbett] Burris . . . delivers a strong critique of tracking, the practice of sorting students within schools or districts that gives them different access to learning. . . . Burris offers concrete advice for school leaders trying to counter such assumptions, and she argues persuasively that tracking undermines real educational achievement for all students. An important book that should be required reading for educators, parents and school boards."

REVIEW: *Publ Wkly* v260 no52 p44 D 23 2013

BURT, JOHN. Lincoln's tragic pragmatism; Lincoln, Douglas, and moral conflict; [by] John Burt 814 p. 2013 Belknap Press of Harvard University Press

1. Democracy—Moral and ethical aspects—United States 2. Historical literature 3. Lincoln-Douglas Debates, Ill., 1858 4. Slavery—Moral and ethical aspects—United States—History—19th century
ISBN 9780674050181 (alk. paper)
LC 2012-011267

SUMMARY: This book by John Burt examines "the moral compasses of Abraham Lincoln, Stephen A. Douglas, and democracy itself, as revealed especially in the speeches of Lincoln and Douglas during the 1850s, when the slavery issue tore apart the old party system and led to secession and civil war." According to Burt, "Lincoln imagined black citizenship and equality even before he comprehended it." (Library Journal)

REVIEW: *Am Hist Rev* v119 no1 p177-8 F 2014 John Channing Briggs

"Lincoln's Tragic Pragmatism: Lincoln, Douglas, and Moral Conflict". "John Burt's ambitious book attempts to address several large questions at once. . . . Although the general outline of Burt's thesis is not new, his industrious adaptation of an imaginative, almost relentless dialectical argument is. . . . For all of his book's emphasis upon [Abraham] Lincoln's political and moral heroism, Burt invokes Lincoln to favor history: neither human agency nor Providence could have created the astounding, tragically disappointing, yet somehow promising results of the war. For Lincoln, however, there was arguably a much different mechanism in the process."

REVIEW: *America* v208 no16 p32-4 My 13 2013 LARRY MADARAS

REVIEW: *Choice* v51 no2 p352 O 2013 E. C. Sands

REVIEW: *J Am Hist* v100 no3 p837-8 D 2013 Douglas L. Wilson

REVIEW: *N Y Rev Books* v60 no5 p56 Mr 21 2013 Steven B. Smith

REVIEW: *N Y Rev Books* v60 no4 p2 Mr 7 2013 John Stauffer

REVIEW: *N Y Times Book Rev* p1-15 F 17 2013 Steven B. Smith

REVIEW: *Rev Am Hist* v42 no1 p1-6 Mr 2014 Harry S. Stout

BURTON, JOHANNA. Sarah Sze; Triple Point; [by] Johanna Burton 160 p. 2013 Gregory R. Miller & Co.

1. Art catalogs 2. Conceptual art—United States—Exhibitions 3. Site-specific installations (Art)—Italy—Venice—Exhibitions 4. Tools in art
ISBN 9780982681381
LC 2013-014944

SUMMARY: This book "documents Triple Point, [artist Sarah Sze's] commission for the US pavilion at the 2013 Venice Biennale, which conjures a series of vocational arenas . . . and references observational tools like pendulums, compasses, and weather vanes. An introduction by Carey Lovelace and Holly Block discusses how Sze reimagined the pavilion's neoclassical architecture. . . . Critic and art historian Johanna Burton focuses on gesture, production, and value across Sze's oeuvre." (Bookforum)

REVIEW: *Bookforum* v20 no3 p44 S-N 2013 JULIA BRYAN-WILSON

"Sarah Sze: Triple Point." "At the forefront of contemporary-art explorations of stuff-after-stuff-after-stuff, Sarah Sze creates exquisitely conceived and executed installations. Utilizing the ordinary things of everyday life (toothpicks, Q-tips, ladders), she produces great gravity-defying masses and immersive site-specific environments that wholly reconfigure their locations. . . . Lovely photographs by Tom Powel give a sense of the overall work as well as intimate access to its meticulous details. In a well-written essay, critic and art historian Johanna Burton focuses on gesture, production, and value across Sze's oeuvre. . . . The book also includes an illuminating conversation between novelist Jennifer Egan and Sze that emphasizes the role of narrative in Sze's sequencing."

BURTON, RICHARD. A Strong Song Tows Us; The Life of Basil Bunting; [by] Richard Burton 608 p. 2013 Prospecta Press

1. Biography (Literary form) 2. Bunting, Basil, 1900-1985 3. Poets—Biography 4. Poets—Travel 5. Pound, Ezra, 1885-1972
ISBN 1935212508; 9781935212508

SUMMARY: This book presents a biography of poet Basil Bunting. "For the decade or so 1942 to 1952 he was an esteemed man-manager, diplomat, journalist and spy. Richard Burton's book focuses mainly on Bunting as a wordsmith . . . but he also tells of his Second World War story, much of it spent in Persia." (Asian Affairs)

REVIEW: *London Rev Books* v36 no1 p3-6 Ja 9 2014 Michael Hofmann

"A Strong Song Tows Us: The Life of Basil Bunting". "It's a tremendously diligent and feisty and energetic biography, but has done little to change or educate my sense of Bunting, beyond the work of [Richard] Burton's much slighter predecessors, Victoria Forde, Richard Caddel and Carroll Terrell. An ideal biography, a deliriously wonderful biography as I hoped this might be, is somehow of a piece. This one seems to use back-projection: our hero is kept dimly in the foreground, while things are described happening behind him. . . . It means we are left short of real interaction, presence, behaviour, sense of lived life."

REVIEW: *TLS* no5803 p3-4 Je 20 2014 PAUL BATCHELOR

BURTON, ROBERT. On Melancholy; [by] Robert Burton 2014 Hesperus Press

1. Commonplace-books 2. England—Social life & customs—17th century 3. Melancholy 4. Philosophical literature 5. Social criticism

ISBN 9781843916222

SUMMARY: In this book, by Robert Burton, the author, "frustrated at the stagnant, disorderly society in which he found himself, became convinced that the problems of England lay in its inclination to melancholy. This is the starting-point, or pretext, for a hugely wide-ranging survey of the causes, descriptions (and cures) of melancholy." (Publisher's note)

REVIEW: *TLS* no5788 p31 Mr 7 2014 MARY ANN LUND

"On Melancholy." "Apart from some sparse marginalia in his library of over 1,700 books, Robert Burton left no records of how his lifetime's reading became his life's work. 'The Anatomy of Melancholy' (1621-51). . . . 'On Melancholy' compresses the 516,384 words of Burton's text into 108 pages of extracts, each under a heading. . . . Hesperus Press's On... series aims to provide accessible books for the general reader, and Nicholas Robins's edition makes for an enjoyable read. . . . Without marginal annotations, Latin, or many of the quotations. 'On Melancholy' is a tidy but flat version of Burton's book. . . . Although the introduction promises that translated phrases are indicated by italics, many are not, and there are many silent omissions."

BURTON, ROBERT A. A skeptic's guide to the mind; what neuroscience can and cannot tell us about ourselves; [by] Robert A. Burton 272 p. 2013 St. Martin's Press

1. Brain—Physiology 2. Human behavior 3. Mind and body 4. Neurosciences 5. Scientific literature

ISBN 1250001854; 9781250001856 (hardback)

LC 2012-041265

SUMMARY: In this book, "neurologist [Robert A.] Burton . . . focuses on new, key aspects of human behavior, specifically the control and lack of control humans have over their minds, treading a fine line of conscious and unconscious actions, thoughts, and decisions." (Library Journal) The book "provid[es] a critical overview of recent advances . . . in neuroscience" and "examines the inherent difficulties and flaws of the field." (Publishers Weekly)

REVIEW: *Choice* v51 no5 p861 Ja 2014 R. Borchardt

REVIEW: *Kirkus Rev* v81 no4 p242 F 15 2013

REVIEW: *Libr J* v138 no11 p105 Je 15 2013 Jill Morningstar

REVIEW: *New Sci* v218 no2919 p44-5 Je 1 2013 David Robson

REVIEW: *New Yorker* v89 no27 p86-8 S 9 2013 Adam Gopnik

"A Skeptic's Guide to the Mind: What Neuroscience Can and Cannot Tell Us About Ourselves," "Brainwashed: The Seductive Appeal of Neuroscience," and "Neuro: The New Brain Sciences and the Management of the Mind." "A series of new books all present watch-and-ward arguments designed to show that brain science promises much and delivers little. . . . Each author, though, has a polemical project, something to put in place of mere Bumpology. . . . [Sally Satel] and [Scott O.] Lilienfeld are worried that neuroscience will shift wrongdoing from the responsible individual to his irresponsible brain, allowing crooks to cite neuroscience in order to get away with crimes. This concern seems overwrought. . . . [Robert A.] Burton, a retired medical neurologist, seems anxious to prove himself a philosopher. . . . [Nikolas] Rose and [Joelle M.] Abi-Rached see the real problem: neuroscience can often answer the obvious questions but rarely the interesting ones."

REVIEW: *Publ Wkly* v260 no5 p58 F 4 2013

BURTT, EDWARD H. Alexander Wilson. See Davis, W. E.

BURUMA, IAN. Year zero; 1945 and the aftermath of war; [by] Ian Buruma 384 p. 2013 Penguin Press

1. Historical literature 2. World War, 1939-1945—Influence 3. World War, 1939-1945—Peace 4. World politics

ISBN 1594204365; 9781594204364

LC 2013-007702

SUMMARY: This book by Ian Buruma "explores the nascent social and political forces that later influenced the Cold War and post-colonial movements. . . . Starting with a world ruined by war, Buruma moves . . . from describing the elation of victory and the desire for revenge to the Allies' attempts to reform societies by eliminating all traces of militarism or fascism and establishing a European welfare state, as destroyed cities are rebuilt and fallen nations reimagined." (Publishers Weekly)

REVIEW: *Booklist* v110 no2 p19 S 15 2013 Brendan Driscoll

REVIEW: *Choice* v51 no6 p1065-6 F 2014 B. M. Puaca

REVIEW: *Economist* v405 no8855 p80 S 28 2013

REVIEW: *Kirkus Rev* v81 no18 p177 S 15 2013

REVIEW: *N Y Rev Books* v60 no15 p21-3 O 10 2013 Charles Simic

"Year Zero: A History of 1945." "'Year Zero' is a relatively short book that covers a great deal of history without minimizing the complexity of the events and the issues. It is well written and researched, full of little-known facts and incisive political analysis. What makes it unique among hundreds of other works written about this period is that it gives an overview of the effects of the war and liberation, not only in Europe, but also in Asia. . . . Unlike many recent books about World War II, [Ian] Buruma's doesn't have a revisionist interpretation of history to advance. What he has here, instead, is a stirring account of the year in which the world woke up to the horror of what had just occurred and . . . began to reflect on how to make sure that it never happens again."

REVIEW: *N Y Times Book Rev* p18 S 29 2013 Ian Buruma

REVIEW: *N Y Times Book Rev* p26 O 6 2013

REVIEW: *New Statesman* v142 no5180 p40-1 O 18 2013 Richard J. Evans

REVIEW: *New Yorker* v89 no29 p115 S 23 2013

REVIEW: *Smithsonian* v44 no5 p98 S 2013 Chloë Schama

REVIEW: *TLS* no5791 p24 Mr 28 2014 RODERICK BAILEY

BUSCH, FREDERICK, 1941-2006. The Stories of Frederick Busch; [by] Frederick Busch 512 p. 2014 W.W. Norton & Company

1. American fiction 2. Anthologies 3. Families—Fiction 4. Minimalism (Literature) 5. Short story (Literary form)

ISBN 0393239543; 9780393239546 (hardcover : alk. paper)

LC 2013-041070

SUMMARY: In this short story collection, by Frederick Busch, tales "selected by . . . Elizabeth Strout, are . . . of families trying to heal their wounds, save their marriages, and rescue their children. . . . A security guard struggles to hang on to his marriage. . . . A traveling teacher attends to students outside the school, including his own son, locked in a country jail. In Busch's work, we are reminded that we have no idea what goes on behind closed doors or in the mind of another." (Publisher's note)

REVIEW: *Booklist* v110 no8 p20 D 15 2013 Carol Haggas

REVIEW: *Kirkus Rev* v81 no23 p20 D 1 2013

REVIEW: *N Y Times Book Rev* p9 D 29 2013 KATIE ARNOLD-RATLIFE

"The Stories of Frederick Busch." "(Even champions of simplicity don't enjoy being oversimplified.) Which might explain why, in her introduction to 'The Stories of Frederick Busch,' Elizabeth Strout mentions the designation with a twinge of defensiveness. . . . His stories hum with sorrow, quake with wit, exude a rare magnitude of compassion even as they force his readers to face unsettling truths. . . . With luck, this collection will make more people see Frederick Busch for the master he was, one whose talent for subtle impact was downright maximal."

BUSH, AUSTIN.il. Pok Pok. See Ricker, A.

BUSH, PETER.tr. The Gray Notebook. See Pla, J.

BUSH, PETER.tr. In diamond square. See Rodoreda, M.

BUSHNELL, JEREMY P. The weirdness; a novel; [by] Jeremy P. Bushnell 288 p. 2014 Melville House

1. Authors—Fiction 2. Devil—Fiction 3. FICTION—Fantasy—Contemporary 4. FICTION—Fantasy—Paranormal 5. FICTION—Literary 6. Witches—Fiction

ISBN 9781612193151 (pbk.)

LC 2013-041263

SUMMARY: In this book by Jeremy P. Bushnell, "sad-sack aspiring Brooklyn-based writer Billy Ridgeway seems to have hit a rut: he's lost his girl, a local literary critic just panned his writing, and his roommate has suddenly disappeared. Bantering with Anil, his best bud and a coworker at the sandwich counter where he works, seems to be Billy's only solace throughout the day. But everything changes when the Devil shows up at Billy's apartment with a seemingly benign request." (Publishers Weekly)

REVIEW: *Kirkus Rev* v82 no3 p236 F 1 2014

"The Weirdness". "In a story that can't decide at all whether it wants to be parody or horror, this debut novel by Bushnell shudders to an unpredictable end. . . . This is all played for arch comedy in the vein of Christopher Moore or S.G. Browne, but there's something off-putting about the execution of Billy's deity-riddled adventure. . . . It's imaginative in some ways, but a plethora of deus ex machina tricks reveal that there's not much heavy lifting going on behind the curtain. Exactly the sort of novel a literary blogger would write. Proceed with caution."

REVIEW: *Publ Wkly* v261 no3 p30 Ja 20 2014

BUSWELL, ROBERT E. The Princeton dictionary of Buddhism. See Lopez, D. S.

BUTLER, JOHN.il. Where is baby? See Where is baby?

BUTLER, KATY. Knocking on Heaven's Door; Our Parents, Their Doctors, and a Better Way of Death; [by] Katy Butler 336 p. 2013 Simon & Schuster

1. Adult children of aging parents 2. Adult children of aging parents—Family relationships 3. Euthanasia—Moral & ethical aspects 4. Euthanasia—Moral and ethical aspects 5. Memoirs 6. Older people—Health 7. Terminal care 8. Terminal care—Decision making

ISBN 1451641974; 9781451641974

LC 2013-017659

SUMMARY: In this book, "when doctors refused to disable the pacemaker that caused her eighty-four-year-old father's heart to outlive his brain, Katy Butler . . . embarked on a quest to understand why modern medicine was depriving him of a humane, timely death. After his lingering death, Katy's mother, nearly broken by years of nonstop caregiving, defied her doctors, refused open-heart surgery, and insisted on facing death the old-fashioned way: bravely, lucidly, and head on." (Publisher's note)

REVIEW: *Kirkus Rev* v81 no13 p126 Jl 1 2013

REVIEW: *Libr J* v138 no6 p60 Ap 1 2013 Barbara Hoffert

REVIEW: *N Y Times Book Rev* p21-2 S 8 2013 ABRAHAM VERGHESE

"Knocking on Heaven's Door: The Path to a Better Way of Death." "A thoroughly researched and compelling mix of personal narrative and hard-nosed reporting that captures just how flawed care at the end of life has become. My hope is that this book might goad the public into pressuring their elected representatives to further transform health care from its present crisis-driven, reimbursement-driven model to one that truly cares for the patient and the family. And since life is, after all, a fatal illness and none of us are spared, there is an urgent need for us in America to reclaim death from medicine."

REVIEW: *New York Times* v162 no56269 pD6 S 24 2013 ABIGAIL ZUGER

"Knocking on Heaven's Door: The Path to a Better Way of Death." "A triumph, distinguished by the beauty of Ms. [Katy] Butler's prose and her saber-sharp indictment of certain medical habits. . . . In the 2010 New York Times Magazine article on which her book is based, Ms. Butler's attention never wavered from the message contained in that bitter passage. In the book her anguish is cushioned a bit by a broader context: she has the space to detail the difficult dynamics of the Butler family and, as a practicing Buddhist, to muse at length on the meaning of a 'good death'. But underlying all this commentary simmers her articulate challenge to the medical profession: to reconsider its reflexive postponement of death."

REVIEW: *Publ Wkly* v260 no21 p43 My 27 2013

BUTLER, MARTIN.ed. The Cambridge edition of the works of Ben Jonson. See The Cambridge edition of the works of Ben Jonson

BUTLER, NICKOLAS. Shotgun lovesongs; a novel; [by] Nickolas Butler 320 p. 2014 Thomas Dunne Books

1. Brothers—Fiction 2. Change (Psychology)—Fiction 3. Families—Fiction 4. Homecoming—Fiction 5. Maturation (Psychology)—Fiction 6. Psychological fiction 7. Sibling rivalry—Fiction

ISBN 1250039819; 9781250039811 (hardback)

LC 2013-031435

SUMMARY: This novel, by Nickolas Butler, is set in the Wisconsin town of Little Wing. "For four friends . . . it is home. . . . Now all four are brought together for a wedding. Little Wing seems even smaller than before. While lifelong bonds are still strong, there are stresses—between the friends, between husbands and wives. There will be heartbreak, but there will also be hope, healing, even heroism as these memorable people learn the true meaning of adult friendship and love." (Publisher's note)

REVIEW: *Booklist* v110 no4 p30 O 15 2013 Annie Bostrom

REVIEW: *Booklist* v111 no1 p138-40 S 1 2014 Mary Burkey

REVIEW: *Kirkus Rev* v82 no2 p253 Ja 15 2014

REVIEW: *Libr J* v138 no16 p57 O 1 2013 Barbara Hoffert

REVIEW: *Libr J* v138 no21 p87 D 1 2013 Christine DeZelar-Tiedman

REVIEW: *N Y Times Book Rev* p13 Ap 6 2014 JONATHAN EVISON

REVIEW: *New York Times* v163 no56436 pC4 Mr 10 2014 JANET MASLIN

"Shotgun Lovesongs". "The most lyrical parts of this big-hearted book are about how all the characters, including the star, are almost physically drawn to the town and one another. . . . Mr. [Nickolas] Bulter makes his character sufficiently different to create all sorts of memorable interactions when their paths cross. . . . Mr. Butler's instincts for how the two men's friendship would withstand this blow are quite keen. . . . There are a lot of big egos and mulish tempers in this small place, and they have all emerged by the time this impressively original debut is over."

REVIEW: *Publ Wkly* v260 no49 p55-6 D 2 2013

REVIEW: *World Lit Today* v88 no5 p8 S/O 2014

BUTLER, ROBERT OLEN. The Hot Country; [by] Robert Olen Butler 440 p. 2012 Mysterious Press

1. Americans—Mexico—Fiction 2. Historical fiction 3. Journalists—Fiction 4. Love stories 5. Mexico—History—Revolution, 1910-1920—Fiction

ISBN 0802120466; 9780802120465

SUMMARY: In Robert Olen Butler's novel "'The Hot Country,' Christopher Marlowe Cobb ('Kit'), the . . . early 20th century American newspaper war correspondent travels to Mexico in April and May of 1914, during that country's civil war, the American invasion of Vera Cruz and the controversial presidency of Victoriano Huerta, El Chacal (The Jackal). Covering the war in enemy territory . . . , Cobb falls in love with Luisa, a young Mexican laundress, who is not as innocent as she seems." (Publisher's note)

REVIEW: *Booklist* v109 no6 p24 N 15 2012 Bill Ott

REVIEW: *Kirkus Rev* v80 no17 p79 S 1 2012

REVIEW: *Libr J* v137 no13 p81 Ag 1 2012 David Keymer

REVIEW: *N Y Times Book Rev* p20 D 29 2013 IHSAN TAYLOR

"The Generals: American Military Command From World War II to Today," "The Hot Country," and "A Man of Misconceptions: The Life of an Eccentric in an Age of Change." "History has been kind to the American generals of World War II. . . . But today's Army is an entrenched bureaucracy . . . , [author Thomas E.] Ricks argues in ['The Generals']. . . . [Author Robert Olen] Butler's crime fiction debut ['The Hot Country'] is a high-spirited adventure set during the Mexican Revolution. . . . ['A Man of Misconceptions'] is told through the life of the 17th-century Jesuit priest and polymath Athanasius Kircher, who wrote sweeping (and error-filled) studies on alchemy, astronomy, optics, hieroglyphics, medicine and music."

REVIEW: *Publ Wkly* v259 no34 p40-1 Ag 20 2012

BUTLER, ROBERT OLEN. The star of Istanbul; [by] Robert Olen Butler 369 p. 2013 Pgw

1. Actresses—Fiction 2. Historical fiction 3. Lusitania (Steamship) 4. Spy stories 5. World War, 1914-1918—Fiction

ISBN 0802121551; 9780802121554

SUMMARY: This book by Robert Olen Butler is part of a series following "Christopher Marlowe ('Kit') Cobb, war correspondent, secret agent,a nd all-around soldier of fortune. . . . He's aboard the doomed Lusitania, tracking a German American who may be a secret-service agent and falling under the spell of a famous actress, Selene Bourgani, who has secrets of her own. . . . Meanwhile, there's a German assassin out there somewhere called Der Wolf, whose eyes may be on both Selene and Kit." (Booklist)

REVIEW: *Booklist* v110 no15 p37 Ap 1 2014 Mary McCay

REVIEW: *Booklist* v110 no6 p25 N 15 2013 Bill Ott

"The Star of Istanbul." "[Robert Olen] Butler juggles a lot of elements here, in terms of both plotting, as double and triple crosses merge like lanes in a traffic roundabout, and tone, as the novel commingles character-driven historical fiction with melodrama and swashbuckling action. Somehow, though, it all works; on one level, Butler is playing with genre conventions in an almost mad-scientist manner, but at the same time, he holds the reader transfixed, like a kid at a Saturday matinee."

BUTTAR, PRIT. Between giants; the battle for the Baltics in World War II; [by] Prit Buttar 400 p. 2013 Osprey Publishing

1. HISTORY—Military—World War II 2. Historical literature 3. World War, 1939-1945—Campaigns—Baltic States 4. World War, 1939-1945—Soviet Union

ISBN 1780961634; 9781780961637

LC 2012-277493

SUMMARY: This book by Prit Buttar recounts "what happened when Nazi Germany and Soviet Russia carved up northeastern Europe between them before turning on each other. . . . There's plenty here on weaponry, on tactics and strategy, on the movement of units. . . . Mr. Buttar takes his story through the postwar periods." (Wall Street Journal)

REVIEW: *TLS* no5773 p27 N 22 2013 IAN THOMSON

"Between Giants: The Battle for the Baltics in World War II." "As Prit Buttar points out in . . . his lucid history of the Baltics during the Second World War, it was only with German aid that Latvians and Estonians in particular felt they could hold back [Joseph] Stalin in the autumn of 1944. . . . In Buttar's analysis, the war brought no freedom to the Baltics, but merely substituted one form of tyranny for another: [Adolf] Hitler's for Stalin's. Estonia was liberated from Hitler in the autumn of 1944; but Estonia was immediately afterwards occupied by Stalin. Both these words are accurate; and in their juncture lies one small nation's sad fate."

BUTTERWORTH, CHRIS. See what a seal can do!; [by] Chris Butterworth 32 p. 2013 Candlewick Press

1. Children's nonfiction 2. Marine animals 3. Picture books for children 4. Seals (Animals) 5. Seals (Animals)—Behavior
ISBN 0763665746; 9780763665746
LC 2012-947729

SUMMARY: This book, by Chris Butterworth and illustrated by Kate Nelms, features illustrations that "portray the seal's transformation from awkward land dweller to sinuous and powerful denizen of the deep. The below-water scenes . . . evoke the murky ocean habitat and the singular seal's steep descent to the bottom." (School Library Journal)

REVIEW: *Horn Book Magazine* v90 no1 p108 Ja/F 2014 ELISSA GERSHOWITZ

"See What a Seal Can Do." "Facts about seals appear in smaller italicized type throughout the conversational main text. Textured, realistic-looking mixed-media illustrations in aqua or sandy hues show the creature at home in both of its natural habitats, gracefully shooting through the water and 'flumping' along on land. . . . An author's note on the copyright page tells more about wild seals; illustrations of the eighteen types of 'true seals' appear on the front and back endpapers. Two websites and an index are appended."

REVIEW: *Nat Hist* v121 no9 p44 N 2013 Dolly Setton

REVIEW: *Publ Wkly* v260 no32 p57 Ag 12 2013

REVIEW: *SLJ* v59 no9 p175 S 2013 Carol S. Surges

BYATT, LUCINDA.tr. Tumult and Order. See Tumult and Order

BYNAM, DANIEL L. The Arab awakening. See Pollack, K. M.

BYNUM, HELEN.ed. Great discoveries in medicine. See Great discoveries in medicine

BYNUM, WILLIAM.ed. Great discoveries in medicine. See Great discoveries in medicine

BYNUM, WILLIAM. A little history of science. See Bynum, W. F.

BYRD, JAMES P. Sacred scripture, sacred war; the Bible and the American Revolution; [by] James P. Byrd 256 p. 2013 Oxford University Press

1. Historical literature 2. War—Biblical teaching 3. War—Religious aspects—Christianity
ISBN 9780199843497
LC 2012-038604

SUMMARY: In this book, "James Byrd offers the first comprehensive analysis of how American revolutionaries defended their patriotic convictions through scripture. Byrd shows that the Bible was a key text of the American Revolution. Indeed, many colonists saw the Bible as primarily a book about war." It provides "a detailed analysis of specific biblical texts and how they were used, especially in making the patriotic case for war." (Publisher's note)

REVIEW: *Am Hist Rev* v119 no2 p517-8 Ap 2014 Amanda Porterfield

REVIEW: *Choice* v51 no2 p279-80 O 2013 P. S. Spalding

"Sacred Scripture, Sacred War: The Bible and the American Revolution." "Drawing on 17,148 biblical citations in 543 sources ranging from King Philip's War to the early Federal period (1674-1800), Byrd . . . offers a convincing, first systematic analysis of how early American preachers and authors used the Bible to interpret Americans' engagement in war. He concludes that among the most important Old Testament passages cited for political purposes were those portraying God as warrior and inspirer of Israelites against such oppressors as Pharaoh, Sisera, Goliath, and Rehoboam. . . . In citing New Testament admonitions to practice peace and obey rulers (Matthew 5, Romans 13, 1 Peter 2), colonial interpreters frequently denied their application in cases of oppression."

REVIEW: *Christ Century* v130 no21 p44-6 O 16 2013 Randall Balmer

REVIEW: *Publ Wkly* v260 no19 p65 My 13 2013

BYRD, ROBERT.il. Africa is my home. See Edinger, M.

BYRNE, ANGELA. Geographies of the romantic north; science, antiquarianism, and travel, 1790-1830; [by] Angela Byrne xiv, 265 p. 2013 Palgrave Macmillan

1. British—Arctic regions—History—19th century 2. Clarke, Edward Daniel, 1769-1822 3. Fidler, Peter 4. Historical literature 5. Romanticism—Great Britain—History—19th century
ISBN 9781137311313
LC 2013-014876

SUMMARY: This book "concentrates largely on the writings of . . . Edward Daniel Clarke, a gentleman traveler in Scandinavia, and Peter Fidler, who traveled widely in the northern regions of present-day Canada. . . . Their journal entries on landscapes and inhabitants of these regions are used to illustrate [Angela] Byrne's thesis that Romanticism and science played complementary roles in British experiences and imaginings of the North." (Choice: Current Reviews for Academic Libraries)

REVIEW: *Choice* v51 no9 p1575-6 My 2014 R. M. Bryce

"Geographies of the Romantic North: Science, Antiquarianism, and Travel, 1790-1830". "In this concise yet wide-ranging study, [Angela] Byrne . . . examines British scientific and antiquarian perceptions of 'the North,' defined broadly as including northern Europe and North America, between the years 1790 and 1830. . . . Byrne concentrates largely on the writings of two polymaths, Edward Daniel Clarke, a gentleman traveler in Scandinavia, and Peter Fidler, who traveled widely in the northern regions of present-day Canada as a factor for the Hudson's Bay Company."

C

CABIN, ROBERT J. Restoring paradise; rethinking and rebuilding nature in Hawaii; [by] Robert J. Cabin xiii, 236 p. 2013 University of Hawai'i Press

1. Environmental literature 2. Extinction (Biology) 3. Human ecology 4. Nature conservation—Hawaii 5. Restoration ecology—Hawaii

ISBN 0824836936 (pbk. : alk. paper); 9780824836931 (pbk. : alk. paper)

LC 2012-044810

SUMMARY: In this book, author Robert J. Cabin "shows why current attempts to preserve Hawaii's native fauna and flora require embracing the emerging paradigm of ecological restoration--the science and art of assisting the recovery of degraded species and ecosystems and creating more meaningful and sustainable relationships between people and nature." (Publisher's note)

REVIEW: *Choice* v51 no7 p1241-2 Mr 2014 K. B. Sterling

"Restoring Paradise: Rethinking and Rebuilding Nature in Hawai'i." "Hawaii claims a tiny amount of total US land area, but 'three quarters of the United States' bird and plant extinctions have occurred in Hawaii.' Using his field experiences in Limahuli Garden, Auwahi Dry Forest, and other natural areas, [Robert J.] Cabin . . . raises knotty questions about conservation efforts. . . . The book is informative and anecdotal, illustrated by photos, some in color. Of interest to conservationists and readers sympathetic to the cause."

CABRERA, JANE. The 12 days of Christmas; [by] Jane Cabrera 32 p. 2013 Holiday House

1. Christmas music 2. Christmas music—Texts 3. Folk songs—England 4. Folk songs, English—England—Texts 5. Picture books for children

ISBN 9780823428700 (hardcover)

LC 2012-045824

SUMMARY: This children's book by Jane Cabrera presents a "version of 'The Twelve Days of Christmas' featuring groups of cheerful animals and other cute characters getting ready for Christmas. The little girl in this version of the folk song is surprised by her 'true love' (or, more likely, her best pal), who gives her a flock of tiny birds partying in the pear tree. That gift is followed by two drumming dogs, three cute cats and four magic mice." (Kirkus Reviews)

REVIEW: *Horn Book Magazine* v89 no6 p62 N/D 2013 CYNTHIA K. RITTER

"The 12 Days of Christmas". "On the first day of Christmas my true love gave to me . . . / a party in a pear tree.' A page turn reveals a tree full of reveling birds, thus beginning this festive and playful rendition of the traditional carol. Here, a boy gives a girl twelve days of presents, including four magic mice, seven skiing squirrels, and ten singing snowmen. The vibrancy and warmth of [Jane] Cabrera's textured acrylic paintings and the jovial rhyming lines make this a welcome picture book adaptation of the classic song."

CADGE, WENDY. Paging God; religion in the halls of medicine; [by] Wendy Cadge xii, 293 p. 2013 University of Chicago Press

1. Academic medical centers 2. Chaplains, Hospital—United States 3. Hospitals—Sociological aspects 4. Medicine—Religious aspects 5. Sociology literature 6. Spirituality

ISBN 0226922103 (cloth : alkaline paper); 0226922111 (paperback : alkaline paper); 9780226922102 (cloth : alkaline paper); 9780226922119 (paperback : alkaline paper)

LC 2012-021906

SUMMARY: This book, by Wendy Cadge, "takes readers inside major academic medical institutions to explore how today's doctors and hospitals address prayer and other forms of religion and spirituality. From chapels to intensive care units to the morgue, hospital caregivers speak directly in these pages about how religion is part of their daily work in visible and invisible ways." (Publisher's note)

REVIEW: *Choice* v51 no1 p113-4 S 2013 A. W. Klink

"Paging God: Religion in the Halls of Medicine." "[Author Wendy] Cadge . . . explores religion's role in contemporary American hospitals by combining ethnography, sociology, and history. The author drew from interviews with staff at various hospitals and also became part of the chaplaincy staff at one hospital for a year in order to gain a deeper understanding of her topic. . . . Cadge . . . explores the design of hospital chapels, richly illustrating her case with photographs from around the country. From these physical spaces, she turns to the world of chaplains, using interviews to explore how they see their role in health care in a pluralistic society. . . . This book will interest students of medicine, nursing, and theology for its grounded analysis rooted in real-world contexts."

REVIEW: *Christ Century* v131 no10 p37-9 My 14 2014 R. Stephen Warner

CAESAR, MICHAEL. ed. Zibaldone. See Zibaldone

ÇAĞAPTAY, SONER. The rise of Turkey; the twenty-first century's first Muslim power; [by] Soner Çağaptay xvi, 168 p. 2014 Potomac Books, An imprint of the University of Nebraska Press

1. Islam and state—Turkey 2. Political science literature 3. World politics—21st century

ISBN 9781612346502 (cloth: alk. paper); 9781612346519 (pdf: alk. paper)

LC 2013-034280

SUMMARY: This book by Soner Cagaptay describes how "Based on a dynamic economy and energetic foreign policy, Turkey's growing engagement with other countries has made it a key player in the newly emerging multidirectional world order. Turkey's trade patterns and societal interaction with other nations have broadened and deepened dramatically in the past decade, transforming Turkey from a Cold War outpost into a significant player internationally." (Publisher's note)

REVIEW: *N Y Rev Books* v61 no6 p18-22 Ap 3 2014

Christopher de Bellaigue

"The Rise of Turkey: The Twenty-First Century's First Muslim Power," "Gülen: The Ambiguous Politics of Market Islam in Turkey and the World," and "İmamin Ordusu." "'The Rise of Turkey: The Twenty-First Century's First Muslim Power' . . . might have struck one as triumphal. . . . 'Gülen: The Ambiguous Politics of Market Islam in Turkey and the World' is . . . a helpful and detailed account of a movement that is defined . . . by obfuscation. . . . In 2011, a journalist called Ahmet Şik brought out a book . . . that shows how the Gülenists took control of the police force over a period of two decades. 'The Imam's Army' is full of fascinating details."

CAHILL, KEVIN. Physical mathematics; [by] Kevin Cahill xvii, 666 p. 2013 Cambridge University Press

1. Fourier analysis 2. Lie algebras 3. Mathematical literature 4. Mathematical physics 5. SCIENCE—Mathematical Physics

ISBN 9781107005211 (hardback)

LC 2012-036027

SUMMARY: This book covers "the mathematics that graduate students and professional physicists need in their courses and research. The author illustrates the mathematics with numerous physical examples drawn from contemporary research. In addition to basic subjects such as linear algebra, Fourier analysis . . . and Bessel functions, this textbook covers topics such as the singular-value decomposition, Lie algebras, [and] the tensors and forms of general relativity." (Publisher's note)

REVIEW: *Choice* v51 no4 p679-80 D 2013 D. V. Feldman

"Physical Mathematics." "This book's title fixes the standard misnomer that labels similar material, despite only tangential physical content, as mathematical physics. . . . Covering basic linear algebra, Fourier analysis, Lie theory (the avant-garde mathematics of 40-year-old particle physics), and differential geometry (for relativity), this book delivers the student mathematically prepared with string theory fundamentals and ready for a presumably physical treatment. . . . Though the book is streamlined to get so far so fast, [Kevin] Cahill gets the mathematics right and even slips in some physics freebies as well. . . . Highly recommended."

CAHILL, THOMAS, 1940-. Heretics and heroes; the exaltation of ego in the Renaissance and the Reformation; [by] Thomas Cahill 368 p. 2013 Nan A. Talese/Doubleday

1. Ego (Psychology)—History 2. Historical literature 3. Reformation 4. Renaissance

ISBN 0385495579; 9780385495578 (alk. paper)

LC 2013-006241

SUMMARY: This is the sixth installment in Thomas Cahill's Hinges of History series. In this book, "Cahill covers the startling artistic and scientific advances, power struggles and religious schism, and exploration and emerging individualism that defined the late 14th to early 17th centuries." (Library Journal)

REVIEW: *Booklist* v110 no3 p18 O 1 2013 Brett Beasley

REVIEW: *Choice* v51 no10 p1862 Je 2014 D. C. Kierdotf

REVIEW: *Commonweal* v141 no2 p24-6 Ja 24 2014 Thomas F. X. Noble

"Heretics and Heroes: How Renaissance Artists and Reformation Priests Created Our World". "This is a very difficult book to review because, as Gertrude Stein famously said about Oakland, 'There is no there there.' [Thomas] Cahill's newest installment in his 'Hinges of History' series . . . is a long series of vignettes organized more or less chronologically. The volume does not present a coherent argument or thesis, although on careful inspection it does reveal a few basic perspectives and emphases. . . . Those words are not easy to understand but they point to a persistent presentism, a tendency to view the past through the lens of the present. . . . His treatment of religious figures is sprightly hut often leaves much to he desired."

REVIEW: *Kirkus Rev* v81 no18 p134 S 15 2013

REVIEW: *Libr J* v138 no9 p54 My 15 2013 Barbara Hoffert

REVIEW: *Libr J* v139 no3 p61 F 15 2014 Stephen L. Hupp

REVIEW: *Publ Wkly* v260 no31 p56-7 Ag 5 2013

CAIANI, FABIO. The Iraqi novel. See Cobham, C.

CAINE, RACHEL. Prince of Shadows; a novel of Romeo and Juliet; [by] Rachel Caine 368 p. 2014 NAL, New American Library

1. Families—Fiction 2. Historical fiction 3. Love—Fiction 4. Vendetta—Fiction

ISBN 0451414411; 9780451414410 (hardback)

LC 2013-033482

SUMMARY: This book, by Rachel Caine, is a "retelling of the star-crossed tale of Romeo and Juliet. . . . In the Houses of Montague and Capulet, there is only one goal: power. The boys are born to fight and die for honor. . . . Benvolio Montague, cousin to Romeo, knows all this. He expects to die . . . for his house, but a spark of rebellion still lives inside him. At night, he is the Prince of Shadows, the greatest thief in Verona—and he risks all as he steals from House Capulet." (Publisher's note)

REVIEW: *Bull Cent Child Books* v67 no9 p445-6 My 2014 K. C.

"Prince of Shadows: A Novel of Romeo and Juliet". "Benvolio Montague takes center stage in this utterly irresistible reconceptualization of Romeo and Juliet. . . . [Rachel] Caine's exquisite attention to detail in plot, scene-setting, character, and language make this a book-lover's dream, correcting in some ways the implausibilities . . . and replacing them with period superstitions and prejudices that seat more comfortably within contemporary readers' expectations. . . . Her prose integrates both direct quotations and paraphrases seamlessly while creating moments of stylistic pleasure. Even the many fight scenes possess an elegant narrative grace amid the gore, serving to ennoble and vilify character and motive by turns."

REVIEW: *Kirkus Rev* v82 no1 p240 Ja 1 2014

"Prince of Shadows". "Should a successful author of vampire novels . . . attempt to write an alternative [William] Shakespeare? Thankfully this one did, as the results are delicious. . . . While Shakespeare's plot clearly anchors Caine's, the novel focuses on providing context for the well-known story rather than embellishing it. . . . Most impressive is the author's simulation of Shakespeare's language in her prose. Never too obscure for modern readers, it retains the flavor of Shakespearean dialogue throughout, lending an atmosphere of verisimilitude that's reinforced by the detailed city setting. Simply superb. "

REVIEW: *SLJ* v60 no3 p152 Mr 2014 Geri Diorio

REVIEW: *SLJ* v60 no6 p66 Je 2014 Julie Paladino

REVIEW: *Voice of Youth Advocates* v37 no2 p70-1 Je 2014 Kaitlin Connors

CAIRNCROSS, FRANCES. Exeter College; The First 700 Years; [by] Frances Cairncross 192 p. 2014 Antique Collectors Club Ltd

1. Anniversaries 2. Exeter College (University of Oxford) 3. Historical literature 4. Universities & colleges—Great Britain—History 5. University of Oxford—History

ISBN 1906507880; 9781906507886

SUMMARY: "Exeter College is working with Third Millennium to publish 'Exeter College: The First 700 Years,'" edited by Frances Cairncross. "The past seven centuries will be brought to life with historical insight, personal reminiscences, and a large collection of photographs and illustrations. The book will most of all reflect the College that you knew and hold dear to this day." (Publisher's note)

REVIEW: *TLS* no5788 p30 Mr 7 2014 GRAHAM CHAINEY

Title:"Exeter College: The First 700 Years." "Fourth oldest of the Oxford colleges, Exeter celebrates its imminent 700th birthday with this sumptuously illustrated compilation, edited and largely written by its Rector [Frances Cairncross]. The College's founder, Walter de Stapeldon, Bishop of Exeter, a 'visionary, flawed, tragic medieval figure,' murdered in 1326 by a London mob, receives his due. A Devon farmer's son, risen via Oxford to power and wealth, he intended Exeter for the education of students from the West Country, a connection that has continued to this day. . . . The positive note of the subtitle underscores the fact that Exeter is currently one of the most popular and diverse of Oxford colleges, and clearly going from strength to strength."

CALARGÉ, CARLA.ed. Haiti and the Americas. See Haiti and the Americas

CALETRÍO, JAVIER.ed. Elite mobilities. See Elite mobilities

CALETTI, DEB. The last forever; [by] Deb Caletti 336 p. 2014 Simon Pulse

1. Death—Fiction 2. Friendship—Fiction 3. Grief—Fiction 4. Love—Fiction 5. Love stories

ISBN 1442450002; 9781442450004 (hardback)

LC 2013-031010

SUMMARY: This book, by Deb Caletti, is a "novel of love and loss. . . . Nothing lasts forever, and no one gets that more than Tessa. After her mother died, it's all she can do to keep her friends, her boyfriend, her happiness from slipping away. And then there's her dad. He's stuck in his own daze, and it's hard to feel like a family when their house no longer seems like a home. Her father's solution? An impromptu road trip that lands them in a small coastal town." (Publisher's note)

REVIEW: *Booklist* v110 no9/10 p82 Ja 1 2014 Gillian Engberg

"The Hangman's Revolution," "The Here and Now," and "The Last Forever." "New York Times best-selling author [Eoin] Colfer continues his W.A.R.P. series with another time-traveling adventure. This time, young FBI agent Chevie Savano returns to contemporary London, which is under threat trom a Fascist European government. . . . The author of the blockbuster Traveling Pants books moves into brand-new territory with this sf novel about a time-traveling teen who carries a terrifying secret about the future. . . . A grieving teen finds romance and hope during a summer spent in a small coastal town in the latest from [Deb] Caletti, a National Book Award finalist and perennially bestselling author."

REVIEW: *Booklist* v110 no11 p56 F 1 2014 Ann Kelley

"The Last Forever." "[Tess is] forced to make sense of how to adjust to her new surroundings, while her heart remains very much at home and with her mother. Along for the ride is a rare plant--a pixiebell--which may be the last of its kind. . . . The start of each chapter is a short, explanatory chapter about a seed, which ties into the novel's theme of rebirth, healing, and growth. [Deb] Caletti writes movingly here, particularly as Tess reflects on her mother's final days, and offers up a surprising story about love, loss, and putting down roots in a world that's constantly changing. . . . Caletti has a sizable fan base--and they'll all be waiting for this latest effort."

REVIEW: *Bull Cent Child Books* v67 no8 p399-400 Ap 2014 D. S.

"The Last Forever". "This is classic [Deb] Caletti, with comradely travel, extended families, flawed parents, and quirky coastal communities . . . key elements in a girl's self-defining growth, and the author's lucid, thoughtful prose and effective portraiture is on full display here. The reveal that Henry is gay is a little overhistrionic (and the book's oddly silent about the possibility of his bisexuality, despite the fact he seems pretty happy to date Tess). . . . Caletti fans and other aficionadoes of solid drama will warm to this satisfying tale of a bittersweet summer that changes things, breaks hearts, and heals them in new configurations."

REVIEW: *Horn Book Magazine* v90 no3 p81-2 My/Je 2014 JENNIFER M. BRABANDER

REVIEW: *Kirkus Rev* v82 no5 p92 Mr 1 2014

REVIEW: *Publ Wkly* v261 no4 p194-5 Ja 27 2014

REVIEW: *SLJ* v60 no3 p152 Mr 2014 Stephanie DeVincentis

REVIEW: *Voice of Youth Advocates* v37 no1 p60-2 Ap 2014 Morgan Brickey

CALLAGHAN, MADELEINE.ed. The Oxford handbook of Percy Bysshe Shelley. See The Oxford handbook of Percy Bysshe Shelley

CALLAHAN, REBECCA M. Coming of political age. See Muller, C.

CALO, MARCOS.il. The mystery of the gold coin. See Paris, H.

CALOMIRIS, CHARLES W. Fragile by design; the political origins of banking crises and scarce credit; [by] Charles W. Calomiris 624 p. 2014 Princeton University Press

1. Bank failures—History 2. Banks and banking—History 3. Credit—History 4. Economics literature 5. Historical literature

ISBN 9780691155241 (hardcover: alk. paper)

LC 2013-033110

SUMMARY: Written by Charles W. Calomiris and Stephen H. Haber, "Analyzing the political and banking history of the United Kingdom, the United States, Canada, Mexico, and Brazil through several centuries, 'Fragile by Design' demonstrates that chronic banking crises and scarce credit are not accidents due to unforeseen circumstances. Rather, these fluctuations result from the complex bargains made between politicians, bankers, bank shareholders, depositors, debtors, and taxpayers." (Publisher's note)

REVIEW: *Choice* v51 no12 p2234-5 Ag 2014 E. C. Erickson

REVIEW: *N Y Times Book Rev* p22 Ap 13 2014 LIAQUAT AHAMED

REVIEW: *Natl Rev* v65 no8 p36-7 My 5 2014 DIANA FURCHTGOTT-ROTH

"Fragile by Design: The Political Origins of Banking Crises and Scarce Credit." "If you have time to read only one book about the causes of the 2008 financial collapse, read this one. . . . [Authors] Charles W. Calomiris and Stephen H. Haber . . . have written an exhaustively researched and readable volume. It compares banking systems and five countries and shows why some are more stable than others. . . . It is really six books in one—the banking histories of Britain, the United States, Canada, Mexico, and Brazil, and an analysis of how banks operate."

REVIEW: *Publ Wkly* v260 no52 p44 D 23 2013

CALVERT, JANE. Synthetic aesthetics. See Schyfter, P.

THE CAMBRIDGE COMPANION TO AUSTRALIAN ART; xx, 377 p. 2011 Cambridge University Press

1. Art & culture 2. Art history 3. Art literature 4. Art, Aboriginal Australian 5. Art, Australian
ISBN 9780521197007; 9781107601581 (pbk)
LC 2011-507600

SUMMARY: This book, edited by Jaynie Anderson, "provides a wide-ranging overview of the movements, themes and media found in Australian art. This Companion features essays that explore the influence of different cultures on Australian art, written by some of the leading scholars and professionals working in the field." (Publisher's note)

REVIEW: *TLS* no5754 p22 Jl 12 2013 PATRICK McCAUGHEY

"The Cambridge Companion to Australian Art." "Such a weighting in favour of Aboriginal art projects am radical shift in perspective for the study of Australian art. . . . There are, however, casualties in this concentration on indigenous art. Many major figures in twentieth-century Australian art are omitted or treated so cursorily that they hardly dent the consciousness of the reader. . . . There is a whiff of political and aesthetic correctness here. . . . The overriding merit of 'The Cambridge Companion to Australian Art' is that it initiates new ways of seeing one of the finest, least known national schools of art."

THE CAMBRIDGE COMPANION TO CICERO; xvi, 422 p. 2013 Cambridge University Press

1. Historical literature 2. LITERARY COLLECTIONS—Ancient, Classical & Medieval
ISBN 0521509939 (hardback); 0521729807 (paperback); 9780521509930 (hardback); 9780521729802 (paperback)
LC 2012-035051

SUMMARY: This book, edited by Catherine Steel, as part of the "Cambridge Companions to Literature" series, focuses on the life and works of Cicero. [He] "was one of classical antiquity's most prolific, varied and self-revealing authors. . . . This Companion discusses the whole range of Cicero's writings, with particular emphasis on their links with the literary culture of the late Republic, their significance to Cicero's public career and their reception in later periods." (Publisher's note)

REVIEW: *TLS* no5762 p8-9 S 6 2013 MARY BEARD

"Community and Communication: Oratory and Politics in Republican Rome," "The Cambridge Companion to Cicero," and "Pro Marco Caelio." "All the main players . . . have contributed essays discussing contiones to 'Community and Communication,' and, despite the wealth of expertise on show, it is hard to resist the conclusion that the law of diminishing returns is beginning to apply. Taken together, these essays show all the signs of a debate whose groundbreaking phase is over. . . . For those starting out to explore Cicero, 'The Cambridge Companion' is a brisk and business-like guide; though I was disappointed that the final chapter is a rather plodding piece on Cicero's role in modern film, fiction and popular history. . . . I suspect that [Robert Symes] might have admired the austerity of [Andrew R.] Dyck's Pro Caelio, and its undoubted philological expertise. But as a way to introduce twenty-first-century readers to Cicero's unusually engaging speech? No."

THE CAMBRIDGE COMPANION TO EDMUND BURKE; xxvi, 254 p. 2012 Cambridge University Press

1. Historical literature 2. POLITICAL SCIENCE—History & Theory 3. Political science—Great Britain—History—18th century 4. Politics and literature—Great Britain—History—18th century 5. Speeches, addresses, etc., English—History and criticism
ISBN 9780521183314 (pbk.); 9781107005594 (hbk.)
LC 2012-002708

SUMMARY: This book " provides a comprehensive assessment of [Edmund] Burke's thought, examining the intellectual traditions that shaped it and the concrete issues to which it was addressed. The volume explores all his major writings from his early treatise on aesthetics to his famous polemic, Reflections on the Revolution in France. It also examines the vexed question of Burke's Irishness and seeks to determine how his cultural origins may have influenced his political views." (Publisher's note)

REVIEW: *TLS* no5747 p7-8 My 24 2013 DANIEL HITCHENS

"The Cambridge Companion to Edmund Burke," "Edmund Burke and the Art of Rhetoric," and "Patriotism and Public Spirit: Edmund Burke and the Role of the Critic in Mid-18th-Century Britain." "'The Cambridge Companion to Edmund Burke' aims to disentangle Burke from his many contexts, and for the most part it succeeds impressively. . . . The collection is generally crisp, broad-minded and clearly written. . . . This is a fresh and immediately illuminating thesis, and [Paddy] Bullard's digressive erudition adds to the book's charm. My one complaint is that, as so often, the flesh-and-blood Burke begins to disappear into his own ideas. . . . [Ian] Crowe has hit on a valuable approach of some importance, simply by taking seriously the vibrant intellectual culture of mid-century London."

THE CAMBRIDGE COMPANION TO HUMAN RIGHTS LAW; xv, 355 p. 2012 Cambridge University Press

1. Human rights—Congresses 2. Human rights—International cooperation 3. International law & human rights 4. Political science literature 5. Quality of life
ISBN 9781107016248 (hardback); 9781107602359 (paperback)
LC 2012-023178

SUMMARY: Edited by Conor Gearty and Costas Douzinas, this book "presents . . . the variety of platforms on which human rights law is practiced today, reflecting also on the dynamic inter-relationships that exist between these various levels. The collection has a critical edge. The chapters engage with how human rights law has developed in its various subfields, what (if anything) has been achieved and at what cost, in terms of expected or produced unexpected side-effects. (Publisher's note)

REVIEW: *Choice* v51 no1 p158-9 S 2013 D. P. Forsythe

"The Cambridge Companion to Human Rights Law." "[Conor] Gearcy . . . and [Costas] Douzinas . . . have edited a book by and for law professors (3 of the 18 contributors are from other fields). Specific topics covered vary widely (e.g., foundational considerations, the UN Disabilities Convention, humanitarian intervention, interdisciplinary studies, biopolitics and reproductive rights, British internal law, treaties, ill treatment, etc.). . . . More than one contributor to this compendium is critical of the ability of human rights law to make a progressive difference in the lives of people around the world."

THE CAMBRIDGE COMPANION TO MICHAEL TIPPETT; xxxi, 299 p. 2013 Cambridge University Press

1. Composers—England 2. Composition (Musical composition) 3. Music—20th century 4. Music literature
ISBN 1107021979; 9781107021976
LC 2012-025549

SUMMARY: This book, edited by Kenneth Gloag and Nicholas Jones, "provides a wide ranging and accessible study of [composer Michael] Tippett and his works. It discusses the contexts and concepts of modernism, tradition, politics, sexuality and creativity that shaped Tippett's music and ideas, engaging with archive materials, relevant literature and models of interpretation." (Publisher's note)

REVIEW: *Choice* v51 no1 p86 S 2013 J. E. Wickell
REVIEW: *TLS* no5776 p23 D 13 2013 DAVID MATTHEWS

"The Cambridge Companion to Michael Tippett." "One of the questionable features of this 'Cambridge Companion' is the reluctance of its twelve contributors to make value judgements of Tippett's works. Tippett is a very uneven composer, and if he is ever to regain the reputation he once held--for in the past fifteen years he has seriously fallen from grace--an attempt must first be made to sort out the wheat from the chaff. . . . This 'Companion' includes essays on a wide range of topics. . . . The 'Companion' also deals analytically with almost every work (the only serious omission is the 'Corelli Fantasia'), but only occasionally are any doubts raised about the quality of the music."

THE CAMBRIDGE COMPANION TO PRIDE AND PREJUDICE; xxi, 209 p. 2013 Cambridge University Press

1. Literary critiques
ISBN 9780521279581 (hbk.); 9781107010154 (hbk.)
LC 2012-027117

SUMMARY: This book, edited by Janet Todd, as part of the "Cambridge Companions to Literature" series, presents literary criticism of "Pride and Prejudice" by Jane Austen. "With a combination of original readings and factual background information, this Companion investigates some of the sources of the novel's power. . . . The history of the book's composition and first publication is set out, both in individual essays and in the section of chronology." (Publisher's note)

REVIEW: *TLS* no5761 p11 Ag 30 2013 ALICIA RIX

"Happily Ever After: Celebrating Jane Austen's 'Pride and Prejudice,'" and "The Cambridge Companion to 'Pride and Prejudice'." "An enjoyable and loyally enthusiastic tribute to 'Pride and Prejudice,' written largely for, and often about, die-hard Janeites. . . . The book contains thoughtful plot and character summaries useful for orienting the school student, and is full of trivia for Austen enthusiasts. . . . It is also delightfully illustrated. . . . The last four essays of the intelligent and accessible 'Cambridge Companion to "Pride and Prejudice"' consider the novel's afterlife as a cultural industry. . . . The Companion's heady journey through the novel's 'proliferation' and expansion . . . is balanced; however, by essays addressing the novel's style, topography, and literary and historical contexts."

THE CAMBRIDGE COMPANION TO VIRTUE ETHICS; xiv, 365 p. 2013 Cambridge University Press

1. Character 2. Ethics 3. Philosophical literature 4. Virtue 5. Virtue ethics
ISBN 9781107001169 (hardback)
LC 2012-024122

SUMMARY: "In this volume of newly commissioned essays, leading moral philosophers offer a comprehensive overview of virtue ethics. They examine the theoretical structure of virtue ethics and its place in contemporary moral theory and other topics discussed include the history of virtue-based approaches to ethics, what makes these approaches distinctive, what they can say about specific practical issues and where we can expect them to go in the future." (Publisher's note)

REVIEW: *Choice* v51 no4 p648-9 D 2013 R. White

"The Cambridge Companion to Virtue Ethics." "None of the essays has appeared before in print, and each is of a high intellectual caliber. . . . Refreshingly, a number of the essays show how the focus on virtue and character also can illuminate features of one's own contemporary life: hence, the discussion of virtue ethics and business; virtue ethics in politics, and in bioethics; and environmental virtue ethics. Some essays deal with objections to virtue ethics, while others speculate on the reasons for its initial decline and consequent resurgence in contemporary philosophy. Every philosophy research library should own a copy of this book."

THE CAMBRIDGE EDITION OF THE WORKS OF BEN JONSON; 7 v. 2012 Cambridge University Press

1. Anthologies 2. Drama—Collections 3. English drama 4. English dramatists—Early modern, 1500-1700 5.

Jonson, Ben, 1573?-1637
ISBN 9780521782463 (set); 9781107096462 (v. 1); 9781107096479 (v. 3); 9781107096486 (v. 2); 9781107096493 (v. 4); 9781107096509 (v. 5); 9781107096516 (v. 6); 9781107096523 (v. 7)
LC 2012-021559

SUMMARY: "'The Cambridge Edition of the Works of Ben Jonson' presents Jonson's complete writings in the light of current editorial thinking and recent scholarly interpretation and discovery. It provides a clear sense of the shape, scale, and variety of the entire Jonsonian canon, including plays, court masques and entertainments, poems, prose works and letters. The texts, which are edited in modern spelling, appear in chronological sequence." (Publisher's note)

REVIEW: *London Rev Books* v34 no19 p17-20 O 11 2012 Blair Worden

REVIEW: *TLS* no5782 p3-5 Ja 24 2014 BRIAN VICKERS
"The Cambridge Edition of the Works of Ben Jonson." "The seven handsome volumes of "The Cambridge Edition of the Works of Ben Jonson" mark a departure from previous Cambridge editions of English drama. . . . Compared with the seventy years Percy Simpson took, to produce this comprehensive edition in a mere two decades, meeting higher bibliographical standards and evaluating a far wider range of primary texts, is a masterpiece of logistics and scholarly cooperation, aided by generous grants from funding bodies around the world. . . . Using the "Cambridge Jonson" will surely inspire creative engagement across the whole of his massive body of work. It can be welcomed as the outstanding edition of any English dramatist in our time."

CAMMUSO, FRANK. The Misadventures of Salem Hyde; Spelling Trouble; [by] Frank Cammuso 96 p. 2013 Harry N Abrams Inc
1. Cats—Juvenile fiction 2. Children's stories 3. Graphic novels 4. Human-animal relationships—Fiction 5. Magic—Juvenile fiction 6. Witches—Juvenile fiction
ISBN 1419708031; 9781419708039

SUMMARY: This is the first book in Frank Cammuso's Salem Hyde series. Here, "Salem Hyde just wants a friend. After a misguided attempt to use her magic lands her in the principal's office, Salem's family decides she needs an animal companion. One well-placed call later, she meets knowledgeable and talkative feline Percival J. Whamsford III, otherwise known as Whammy. Whammy isn't just a chatty kitty; he is a Magical Animal Companion and will help Salem learn how to use her magic properly." (Kirkus Reviews)

REVIEW: *Booklist* v110 no6 p33 N 15 2013 Kat Kan

REVIEW: *Bull Cent Child Books* v67 no3 p142-3 N 2013 K. Q. G.
"The Misadventures of Salem Hyde: Spelling Trouble." "In the opening pages of this graphic-novel-styled easy reader, young witch Salem Hyde accidentally turns a crossing guard into a dinosaur, unleashing terror at her school and almost blowing her cover as a normal (albeit mischievous) girl. The incident spurs her grandmother to get Salem an animal companion to guide the young girl's budding magical powers and keep her propensity for troublemaking in check. . . . [Author Frank] Cammuso evokes both the sarcastic spunk and gentle warmth of 'Calvin and Hobbes' in this humorous tale of unlikely pals, and the simple black and white illustrations reaffirm the parallel with their wide-eyed, big-headed figures and frantic energy."

REVIEW: *Publ Wkly* p96 Children's starred review annual 2013

REVIEW: *Publ Wkly* v260 no38 p83 S 23 2013

REVIEW: *SLJ* v60 no1 p107 Ja 2014 Kristine M. Casper

CAMP, KATHRYN PAGE. Writers in Wonderland; Keeping Your Words Legal; [by] Kathryn Page Camp 342 p. 2013 KP PK Publishing
1. Advice literature 2. Authorship 3. Copyright 4. Plagiarism 5. Public domain
ISBN 0989250415; 9780989250412

SUMMARY: This book presents "a guide to the rights and responsibilities of writers, whether they are not yet published, self-published or traditionally published. In this handbook for writers, [Kathryn Page] Camp . . . draws on her legal background and Lewis Carroll's Alice's Adventures in Wonderland to cover a broad range of issues of which every writer subject to U.S. law should be aware." (Kirkus Reviews)

REVIEW: *Kirkus Rev* v82 no3 p120 F 1 2014
"Writers in Wonderland: Keeping Your Words Legal". "[Kathryn Page] Camp cogently explains the difference between copyright infringement and plagiarism, an often confusing topic, with samples of several works involved in recent accusations of plagiarism; she cites case law in nontechnical language to demonstrate the definition of fair use that courts have come to accept. . . . With its clear explanations of complex topics supported by easy-to-follow actual and hypothetical examples, this book has the potential to be a useful reference tool for writers who want to understand both their own rights and their responsibilities to other content creators. A comprehensive, usable explanation of contracts, copyright and other key legal concepts that all writers need to understand."

CAMP, LAUREN. The Dailiness; [by] Lauren Camp 68 p. 2013 Edwin E. Smith Publishing
1. American poetry 2. Interpersonal relations 3. Lyric poetry 4. Poems—Collections 5. Poetry (Literary form)
ISBN 1619275562; 9781619275560

SUMMARY: "The volatile compounds at the core of Lauren Camp's second book are poems of the coiled environment and tremendous loss. . . . As she writes, perhaps wryly, perhaps optimistically, either we're standing in disordered light before the disappointment, or it's after. The Dailiness offers precision paired with undeviating attention to all the human senses." (Publisher's note)

REVIEW: *World Lit Today* v88 no1 p25 Ja/F 2014 Daniel Simon
"The Dailiness." "Many of the themes in 'The Dailiness' reprise earlier preoccupations threaded through [author Lauren] Camp's first collection, 'This Business of Wisdom' (2010): the autobiographical voice of the writer who looks back at herself. . . . In 'The Dailiness,' we encounter both the quotidian pleasures implied by the title (especially in poems like 'The uh-huh of Desire') as well as many of the deeper themes encountered in Camp's earlier work. . . . For a poet who is still 'learning to embrace,' we are glad to accept the bounty of arms laden with such treasure."

CAMPBELL, ALASTAIR V. Bioethics: the basics; [by] Alastair V. Campbell x, 188 p. 2013 Routledge
1. Bioethics 2. Medical ethics 3. Medical laws & legislation 4. Medical literature 5. Social medicine
ISBN 9780415504089 (pbk); 9780415504096 (hardback)
LC 2013-005003

SUMMARY: This book by Alastair V. Campbell, part of the book series "The Basics," presents "an introduction to the foundational principles, theories and issues in the study of medical and biological ethics. Readers are introduced to bioethics from the ground up before being invited to consider some of the most controversial but important questions facing us today." (Publisher's note)

REVIEW: *Choice* v51 no8 p1437 Ap 2014 M. M. Gillis

"Bioethics: The Basics". "This work is part of Routledge's 'The Basics' series, a growing collection of titles on a range of topics. Before this reviewer finished reading it, she had already decided to recommend it to a team developing her university's first interprofessional graduate ethics course in the health sciences as a way to focus curriculum design and to serve as a student textbook. This concise, precise, and inexpensive book contains a trove of information useful for both general health sciences audiences and laypersons wanting a clear introduction to ethical issues in health."

CAMPBELL, COLIN. Montecito heights; a Resurrection Man novel; [by] Colin Campbell 384 p. 2014 Midnight Ink
1. British—California—Fiction 2. Detective & mystery stories 3. Police—England—Yorkshire—Fiction 4. Pornography 5. Reality television programs
ISBN 9780738736327
LC 2013-042073

SUMMARY: In this book, "California Sen. Dick Richards needs rescuing when a porn video featuring his teen daughter surfaces. Jim Grant, a British cop who now works on assignment in the States, has been brought in to resolve the problem. . . . Grant has a rock-star notoriety. Among his many admirers is beautiful Robin Citrin, a reality TV show producer, who wants to hire Grant. But not everyone loves Grant; his old nemesis, Rodrigo Dominguez, and his drug cartel are still pursuing him." (Library Journal)

REVIEW: *Kirkus Rev* v82 no4 p171 F 15 2014

"Montecito Heights". "In [Colin] Campbell's . . . second book in his Resurrection Man series, a gritty detective steps through the looking glass of Los Angeles' porn industry and nearly loses his way. Grant seems more bemused by the incongruity of a drug cartel moonlighting as kidnappers than intimidated by Dominguez's threats. And the deeper Grant digs, the more irregularities he finds in the Richards home. Prolific Campbell layers an abundance of interesting movie trivia into the tale, and while the plot is shaggy, wry maverick Grant never fails to entertain."

REVIEW: *Libr J* v139 no4 p72 Mr 1 2014 Teresa L. Jacobsen

CAMPBELL, GORDON. The Hermit in the Garden; From Imperial Rome to Ornamental Gnome; [by] Gordon Campbell 304 p. 2013 Oxford University Press
1. Gardens—History 2. Gardens, English 3. Hermitages 4. Hermits 5. Historical literature
ISBN 0199696993; 9780199696994

SUMMARY: This book looks at the history of "the fad for ornamental hermitages and hermits. [Gordon] Campbell . . . briefly touches on the early religious and contemplative origins of true hermits but mainly focuses on the British Isles in the Georgian era, when the hermitage became a fashionable part of a rambling garden, with hermits a sought-after accessory." (Library Journal)

REVIEW: *Choice* v51 no4 p619 D 2013 A. H. Widder

REVIEW: *Libr J* v138 no10 p120 Je 1 2013 Kathleen McCallister

REVIEW: *TLS* no5759 p31 Ag 16 2013 JENNIFER POTTER

"The Hermit in the Garden: From Imperial Rome to Ornamental Gnome." "[Gordon] Campbell's thread becomes clearer when he explores the strands in Georgian culture (horticultural, antiquarian, philosophical, literary and architectural) that engendered the fad for ornamental hermits. . . . More tenuous is the connection Campbell makes between ornamental hermits and garden gnomes. . . . Campbell's train-spotting approach at times obscures . . . deeper meanings. A simpler format might have served him better. . . . [The book is] commendable nonetheless for Campbell's dogged enthusiasm in assembling the first work devoted solely to ornamental hermits and their habitations."

CAMPBELL, JAMES W. P. The library; a world history; [by] James W. P. Campbell 320 p. 2013 University of Chicago Press
1. Historical literature 2. Illustrated books 3. Libraries—History 4. Library architecture 5. Library buildings
ISBN 9780226092812 (cloth : alkaline paper)
LC 2013-019928

SUMMARY: This illustrated book "tell[s] the story of library architecture around the world . . . from ancient Mesopotamia to modern China and from the beginnings of writing to the present day. . . . Each age and culture has reinvented the library, molding it to reflect their priorities and preoccupations. . . . [James W. O.] Campbell's . . . text recounts the history of these libraries, while [Will] Pryce's . . . photographs . . . capture each building's structure and atmosphere." (Publisher's note)

REVIEW: *TLS* no5769 p8 O 25 2013 J. MORDAUNT CROOK

"The Library: A World History." "This is Thames and Hudson's third attempt in a decade to get to grips with this theme. And it is by far the best. . . . On every count--scholarship, production, readability--'The Library: A World History' is way ahead of its predecessors, particularly with regards to production and design. The photographs by Will Pryce are technically flawless, and they give point and purpose to a text which is not only informative but persuasive. The message is clear: of the making of libraries there can be no end."

CAMPBELL, K. G.il. Flora and Ulysses. See DiCamillo, K.

CAMPBELL, K. G.il. Tea party rules. See Dyckman, A.

CAMPBELL, MUNGO.ed. Allan Ramsay. See Allan Ramsay

CAMPBELL, T. COLIN. Whole; rethinking the science of nutrition; [by] T. Colin Campbell 352 p. 2013 DanBella Books, Inc.

1. Diet 2. Longevity—Nutritional aspects 3. Medical literature 4. Nutrition 5. Vegetarianism
ISBN 1937856240; 9781937856243 (hardback); 9781937856250 (e-book)
LC 2012-051561

SUMMARY: This book, by T. Colin Campbell and Howard Jacobson, explores nutrition. "Nutritional science, long stuck in a reductionist mindset, is at the cusp of a revolution. . . . He explains . . . the ways our current scientific paradigm ignores the fascinating complexity of the human body, and why, if we have such overwhelming evidence that everything we think we know about nutrition is wrong, our eating habits haven't changed." (Publisher's note)

REVIEW: *Choice* v51 no2 p301 O 2013 R. A. Hoots

"Whole: Rethinking the Science of Nutrition." "According to [author T. Colin] Campbell . . . , plant-based whole food is the nutritional elixir for maintaining health. The noted nutrition researcher criticizes the current scientific reductionist mind-set, along with the medical system that focuses on disease rather than health, and provides evidence that proper nutrition is basic to fitness. A diet that excludes fats and sugars and is low in meat-based proteins is the holistic recipe to avoid cancer, diabetes, obesity, and heart disease. . . . Campbell emphatically and emotionally argues for a shift from the reductionist paradigm of science to a broader, holistic view of how food affects the body."

REVIEW: *Kirkus Rev* v81 no6 p126 Mr 15 2013

CAMPBELL, TRACY. The Gateway Arch; a biography; [by] Tracy Campbell 232 p. 2013 Yale University Press

1. Arches—Missouri—Saint Louis—Design and construction 2. Architectural literature 3. Gateway Arch (Saint Louis, Mo.) 4. Gateway Arch (Saint Louis, Mo.)—History 5. Historical literature 6. Saarinen, Eero, 1910-1961
ISBN 9780300169492 (cloth : alkaline paper)
LC 2012-045255

SUMMARY: This book addresses the history of the Gateway Arch in Saint Louis, Missouri. "By weaving together social, political, and cultural history, historian Tracy Campbell uncovers the complicated and troubling history of the beloved structure. This compelling book explores how a medley of players with widely divergent motivations (civic pride, ambition, greed, among others) brought the Gateway Arch to fruition, but at a price the city continues to pay." (Publisher's note)

REVIEW: *Booklist* v109 no16 p17 Ap 15 2013 Jay Freeman

REVIEW: *Choice* v51 no2 p248-9 O 2013 D. Sachs

"The Gateway Arch: A Biography." "[Author Tracy] Campbell . . . provides revealing insights into the forces behind the creation of the Gateway Arch/Jefferson National Expansion Memorial in St. Louis, beginning with its inception in the late 1920s and ending after the completion of its construction in the late 1960s. The story unfolds through a series of discrete chapters covering the unique history of St. Louis; the political motivations and machinations behind the memorial; the obstacles to realizing its development; the design competition; a brief biography of Eero Saarinen, winner of the competition. . . . The book is thoroughly researched and appropriately documented. It is also well written."

CAMUS, ALBERT, 1913-1960. Algerian chronicles; [by] Albert Camus 240 p. 2013 Harvard University Press

1. French—Algeria 2. Journalism
ISBN 0674072588 (hardcover); 9780674072589 (hardcover)
LC 2012-036100

SUMMARY: This book is "the first English translation of [Albert Camus'] 'Chroniques Algériennes' (1958)." It includes his "reportage of the 1939 famine in Kabylia" as well as other observations "fixed historically in the French-Algerian war." Camus' struggles "with the concept and conflicts of colonialism" are shared. (Publishers Weekly)

REVIEW: *America* v209 no11 p34-5 O 21 2013 MARK HENNINGER

"Algerian Chronicles." "This short book makes available for the first time in English a series of articles in French compiled in 1958 by Albert Camus from his writings on Algeria from 1939 to 1958. . . . These articles chronicle his attempts over 20 years to influence the powerful forces at play, and his anguish at being powerless in the face of intransigence is palpable. It comes as some surprise that Camus was not in favor of Algerian independence, as were so many in France, as Jean-Paul Sartre and others. . . . Neither side listened to Camus then, but that does not mean that we should not listen to him today: engaged, informed, humane and anguished."

REVIEW: *Bookforum* v20 no1 p39 Ap/My 2013 GEORGE SCIALABBA

REVIEW: *Choice* v51 no2 p255 O 2013 T. L. Jackson

REVIEW: *Commonweal* v140 no20 p26-7 D 20 2013 Gerald Russello

REVIEW: *Kirkus Rev* v81 no7 p47 Ap 1 2013

REVIEW: *N Y Rev Books* v60 no17 p56-8 N 7 2013 Claire Messud

REVIEW: *N Y Times Book Rev* p32 My 12 2013 SUSAN RUBIN SULEIMAN

REVIEW: *Publ Wkly* v260 no7 p50-1 F 18 2013

REVIEW: *Society* v50 no6 p636-40 D 2013 Juana Pita

REVIEW: *TLS* no5767 p11 O 11 2013 ROBERT ZARETSKY

CAMUS, ALBERT, 1913-1960. Outsider; [by] Albert Camus 144 p. 2012 Penguin Press/Classics

1. Existentialism 2. Fiction—Male authors 3. French fiction—20th century 4. French fiction—Translations into English 5. Psychological fiction
ISBN 0141389583; 9780141389585

SUMMARY: "Sandra Smith's new translation, based on close listening to a recording of [author Albert] Camus reading his work aloud on French radio in 1954, sensitively renders the subtleties and dream-like atmosphere of 'L'Etranger.' In 'The Outsider' (1942), his classic existentialist novel, Camus explores the alienation of an individual who refuses to conform to social norms. Meursault, his antihero, will not lie." (Publisher's note)

REVIEW: *N Y Rev Books* v61 no10 p6 Je 5 2014

"The Outsider." "One of the most widely read French novels of the twentieth century, Albert Camus's 'L'Étranger,' carries, for American readers, enormous significance in our cultural understanding of midcentury French identity. . . . [Translator Sandra] Smith is throughout attuned to . . . subtleties. She has a precise literary understanding of Camus's creations, and her Meursault emerges, in the crisp clarity of her prose, emphatically not as a monster, but as a man who will not embellish or elaborate. . . . Sandra Smith is a very fine translator indeed."

REVIEW: *TLS* no5725/5726 p36-7 D 21 2012

CANDER, CHRIS. 11 stories; [by] Chris Cander 234 p. 2013 Rubber Tree Press

1. Apartment buildings—Fiction 2. Compulsive hoarding 3. Couples 4. Musicians—Fiction 5. Psychological fiction
ISBN 9780988946507
LC 2013-934292

SUMMARY: In this book, "as a teenage trumpet prodigy, Roscoe lost a finger in the gate of his apartment building's elevator. His trumpet dream shattered, he became superintendent of that same building, where he's lived all his life. On a fateful autumn evening, he ascends to the roof of the building . . . but loses his balance and begins his fatal plunge. Then the frame story launches: Time slows as Roscoe descends 11 floors, remembering a story about someone who lived on each floor he passes." (Kirkus Reviews)

REVIEW: *Kirkus Rev* v81 no14 p375 Jl 15 2013

REVIEW: *Kirkus Rev* p11 D 15 2013 supplemet best books 2013

"11 Stories". "The superintendent of an 11-story apartment building in Chicago falls from the roof, remembering stories of the tenants on his way down. . . . [Chris] Cander's book isn't quite Sherwood Anderson's 'Winesburg, Ohio' (1919), though. Some stories, like the perennially clogged toilet on eight, are playful anecdotes. Yet many of the tenants show heartbreaking spiritual damage; some of them are admirable, some not so much. Quiet, diffident Roscoe, who's spent half a century supporting them all in one way or another, just as admirably supports these stories. A wonderfully clever compilation."

REVIEW: *Kirkus Rev* v81 no15 p38 Ag 1 2013

REVIEW: *Kirkus Rev* p3 D 15 2013 supplemet best books 2013 Karen Schechner

REVIEW: *Publ Wkly* v260 no27 p47 Jl 8 2013

CANDLEWICK PRESS (COMPANY)comp. Fizzy's lunch lab. See Fizzy's lunch lab

CANNON, EOIN F. The saloon and the mission; addiction, conversion, and the politics of redemption in American culture; [by] Eoin F. Cannon xv, 321 p. 2013 University of Massachusetts Press

1. Alcoholics—Rehabilitation—United States—History 2. Alcoholism—Social aspects—United States—History 3. Alcoholism—Treatment—United States—History 4. Alcoholism in literature 5. Historical literature 6. Recovery movement—United States—History 7. Rescue missions (Church work)—United States—History 8. Temperance in literature
ISBN 155849992X (hardcover : alk. paper); 1558499938 (pbk. : alk. paper); 9781558499928 (hardcover : alk. paper); 9781558499935 (pbk. : alk. paper)
LC 2013-001343

SUMMARY: "This book traces the evolution of the drunkard's conversion narrative--which was central to the work of the evangelical rescue missions of the 19th century--into Alcoholics Anonymous recovery narratives. The missions wanted to save souls, whereas AA seeks to cure a disease, but both employ the same structural narrative of redemption." (Choice: Current Reviews of Academic Libraries)

REVIEW: *Choice* v51 no5 p880 Ja 2014 G. Grieve-Carlson

"The Saloon and the Mission: Addiction, Conversion, and the Politics of Redemption in American Culture." "In a careful and cogent argument, [Eoin F.] Cannon . . . shows that the logic and conventions of that narrative were used by [Franklin Delano] Roosevelt to justify his New Deal recovery programs, and that this narrative has always been open to ideological appropriation by both Right and Left (the founders of AA were opponents of FDR). . . . This is a fresh approach to familiar concepts--evangelical Christianity, alcoholism, individualism, and liberalism."

CANTOR, JAY. Forgiving the Angel; Four Stories for Franz Kafka; [by] Jay Cantor 224 p. 2014 Knopf

1. FICTION—Historical 2. FICTION—Literary 3. FICTION—Short Stories (single author) 4. Historical fiction
ISBN 9780385350341 (Hardcover); 0385350341
LC 2013-016747

SUMMARY: Author Jay Cantor presents a collection of short stories that act as a "tribute to Franz Kafka, one of the twentieth century's most revolutionary voices. In four by-turns bayoneting and tender stories, Cantor imagines the profound impact Kafka had on those closest to him, including Max Brod, his trusted friend . . . his last lover, the exiled Dora Diamant; her husband, German Communist zealot Lusk Lask [and] . . . translator and journalist Milena Jesenská." (Booklist)

REVIEW: *Booklist* v110 no8 p26 D 15 2013 Donna Seaman

REVIEW: *Kirkus Rev* v81 no24 p236 D 15 2013

"Forgiving the Angel: Four Stories for Franz Kafka". "A quartet of somber fictions on the surprising influence of Franz Kafka's work and life on those around him. . . . The whole book thrives on the tension between the liberating honesty of Kafka's writing and the existential suffering it depicted, most effectively in the novella-length 'Lusk and Marianne.' . . . The tone of these stories is inevitably dour, but [Jay] Cantor's prose is never ponderous; in Brod, Lusk and Eva, he uncovers three different varieties of emotional pain, depicting each with intelligence and depth. Shot through with black comedy, unsparing honesty and robust intellect—in short, a fitting Kafka tribute."

REVIEW: *N Y Times Book Rev* p19 F 23 2014 TOM LECLAIR

REVIEW: *New York Times* v163 no56388 pC1-4 Ja 21 2014 MICHIKO KAKUTANI

"Forgiving the Angel: Four Stories for Franz Kafka." "With his erratic new book, 'Forgiving the Angel,' the novelist Jay Cantor has given us four--er, Kafkaesque--stories based on real people from Kafka's real life. The stories are written in a style that tries to echo Kafka's idiosyncratic voice. . . . This group of Kafka-inspired tales . . . are well carpentered--and, at times, emotionally affecting--but ultimately less compelling than the real-life stories on which they are based. . . . They also tip over into melodrama and sentimentality: two decidedly un-Kafkaesque qualities."

CANTOR, JILLIAN. Searching for Sky; [by] Jillian Cantor 288 p. 2014 Bloomsbury

1. Acculturation—Fiction 2. Friendship—Fiction 3. Grandmothers—Fiction 4. Islands of the Pacific—Fiction 5. Survival—Fiction 6. Young adult fiction

ISBN 1619633515; 9781619633513 (hardback)

LC 2013-039234

SUMMARY: In this book, by Jillian Cantor, "Sky and River have always lived on Island, the only world they've ever known. Until the day River spots a boat. Across Ocean, in a place called California, Sky is separated from River and forced to live with a grandmother she's just met. Here the rules for survival are different. People rely on strange things like cars and cell phones. They keep secrets from one another. And without River, nothing makes sense." (Publisher's note)

REVIEW: *Booklist* v110 no17 p98 My 1 2014 Lexi Walters Wright

REVIEW: *Bull Cent Child Books* v67 no10 p505 Je 2014 A. S.

"Searching for Sky". "Sky's absolute bewilderment and the concurrent misery are palpable at times, and it makes the small victories she achieves all the more relieving. The glimpses of how horrifying the world would appear to someone who doesn't know about school shootings or cults are mostly well employed to further sympathy for Sky, and readers will likely be firmly on her side from the first moment of terror when she spots the incoming boat. Survival fans may wish initially that Sky had stayed on the wild island, but they will likely readily admit that this twist on the usual survival scenario demands just as much grit, savvy, and determination from her."

REVIEW: *Kirkus Rev* v82 no7 p101 Ap 1 2014

REVIEW: *SLJ* v60 no5 p125 My 2014 Janet Hilbun

REVIEW: *Voice of Youth Advocates* v37 no1 p62 Ap 2014 Mary Kusluch

REVIEW: *Voice of Youth Advocates* v37 no1 p62 Ap 2014 Nancy K. Wallace

CANTOR, RACHEL. A highly unlikely scenario, or a Neetsa Pizza employee's guide to saving the world; a novel; [by] Rachel Cantor 256 p. 2014 Melville House

1. Dystopias 2. Fast food restaurants—Officials & employees 3. Philosophy 4. Pizzerias 5. Satire

ISBN 9781612192642

LC 2013-024566

SUMMARY: This novel by Rachel Cantor discusses how "In the not-too-distant future, competing giant fast food factions rule the world. Leonard works for Neetsa Pizza, the Pythagorean pizza chain, in a lonely but highly surveilled home office, answering calls on his complaints hotline." In this book, "medieval Kabbalists, rare book librarians, and Latter-Day Baconians skirmish for control over secret mystical knowledge." (Publisher's note)

REVIEW: *Booklist* v110 no9/10 p40-2 Ja 1 2014 Donna Seaman

REVIEW: *Kirkus Rev* v82 no1 p249 Ja 1 2014

REVIEW: *N Y Times Book Rev* p19 Ja 12 2014 LYDIA NETZER

"A Highly Unlikely Scenario: Or, A Neetsa Pizza Employee's Guide to Saving the World." "In [this] world, fast-food chains and political philosophies are one. . . . Quirkiness abounds in [author] Rachel Cantor's alternate universe. . . . While Cantor delights in strangeness and demonstrates a rakish disregard for sense, she's not wallowing in nonsense, nor is she dishing up whimsy just for whimsy's sake. At the center of the book, her hero is real, and his problems feel urgent. . . . A dystopian satire; a story about storytelling, believing and listening--'A Highly Unlikely Scenarios' is ultimately a history of our own strange world."

CANTRILL, DAVID J. The vegetation of Antarctica through geological time; [by] David J. Cantrill viii, 480 p. 2012 Cambridge University Press

1. Geological time 2. Paleobotany—Devonian 3. Paleoecology—Devonian 4. Paleontology—Devonian 5. Plants—Evolution—Antarctica 6. Plants, Fossil—Antarctica 7. SCIENCE—Paleontology 8. Scientific literature

ISBN 0521855985; 9780521855983 (hardback)

LC 2012-001241

SUMMARY: This book by David J. Cantrill and Imogen Poole "provides the only detailed overview of the development of Antarctic vegetation from the Devonian period to the present day. Details of specific floras and ecosystems are provided within the context of changing geological, geographical and environmental conditions, alongside comparisons with contemporaneous and modern ecosystems. The authors demonstrate how palaeobotany contributes to our understanding of the palaeoenvironmental changes." (Publisher's note)

REVIEW: *Choice* v51 no1 p105-6 S 2013 M. S. Zavada

"The Vegetation of Antarctica Through Geological Time." "It was a pleasant surprise to see that this book on Antarctica by [David J.] Cantrill . . . and [Imogen] Poole . . . is a thoughtful synthesis of the current research on the evolutionary history of a continent that spent much of its past history in high latitudes. The work spans the paleobotanical history of the continent from the Paleozoic to the Holocene, and focuses on ecological and climatic changes through time. The synthesis and discussion often have direct application to contemporary topics in ecology and climatology. The well-written, well-illustrated book contains instructive figures and tables, and has a comprehensive bibliography."

CAPETTA, AMY ROSE. Entangled; [by] Amy Rose Capetta 336 p. 2013 Houghton Mifflin Books for Children, Houghton Mifflin Harcourt

1. Adventure and adventurers—Fiction 2. Friendship—Fiction 3. Guitar—Fiction 4. JUVENILE FICTION—Action & Adventure—General 5. JUVENILE FICTION—Fairy Tales & Folklore—Adaptations 6. JUVENILE FICTION—Family—Alternative Family 7. JUVENILE FICTION—Girls & Women 8. JUVENILE FICTION—Performing Arts—Music 9. JUVENILE FICTION—Robots 10. JUVENILE FICTION—Science Fiction 11. JUVENILE FICTION—Social Issues—Runaways 12. Life on other planets—Fiction 13. Musicians—Fiction 14. Robots—Fiction 15. Science fiction

ISBN 0544087445; 9780544087446 (hardback)

LC 2013-003937

SUMMARY: In this novel, "the scattered remains of the human race live as second-class citizens on alien worlds, plagued by the 'spacesick' that comes from space travel. Seventeen-year-old Cade survives on the desert planet Andana." She learns that she "is the product of an experiment and has been entangled on a quantum level since babyhood with a boy named Xan. Xan is being held captive in Hades, an area of space infested with black holes, and" she must find him. (Publishers Weekly)

REVIEW: *Booklist* v110 no6 p46 N 15 2013 Stacey Comfort

REVIEW: *Bull Cent Child Books* v67 no5 p258-9 Ja 2014 A. M.

"Entangled." "This first entry in a new series applies an intriguing scientific premise to one girl's emotional journey, and the result is a rollicking space adventure. . . . The science is light (and sometimes specious) but it works serviceably enough as a pretext for the plot. The focus here is on action, which picks up early and never slows down, and on Cade's gradual shift from self-defensive loner to interconnected friend and compatriot. The slang-heavy writing style is at times awkward, but the sense of a space-based vernacular strengthens the world building and adds spice to the narrative palette. The strongest draw is the ensemble cast, a quirky, friendly, memorable crew that readers will happily follow into further adventures in expected sequels."

REVIEW: *Kirkus Rev* v81 no18 p26 S 15 2013

REVIEW: *Publ Wkly* v260 no37 p58 S 16 2013

REVIEW: *Publ Wkly* p112-3 Children's starred review annual 2013

REVIEW: *Voice of Youth Advocates* v36 no5 p71 D 2013 Bonnie Kunzel

CAPLE, NATALEE. In Calamity's Wake; A Novel; [by] Natalee Caple 224 p. 2013 Bloomsbury USA

1. Calamity Jane, 1852-1903 2. Calamity Jane, 1852-1903—Fiction 3. Frontier & pioneer life—West (U.S.)—Fiction 4. Historical fiction 5. Mothers & daughters—Fiction 6. Mothers and daughters—Fiction 7. Travelers—Fiction 8. Voyages and travels—Fiction
ISBN 1620401851; 9781620401859
LC 2013-009056

SUMMARY: In this book, "Miette has no desire to meet the mother who abandoned her, a woman she knows only as an infamous soldier, drinker, and exhibition shooter: Martha Canary, made notorious as Calamity Jane. But Miette's beloved adoptive father makes a deathbed request that the two be reunited." Author Natalee Caple "tells the story of Miette's quest across a landscape occupied by strangers, ghosts, and animals." (Publisher's note)

REVIEW: *Booklist* v110 no1 p49-50 S 1 2013 John Mort

"In Calamity's Wake." "Into Miette's odyssey, [Natalee] Caple interjects lore about Calamity Jane in the form of poems and songs, as well as narrative, and she emerges as a drunk, a sharpshooter, a great show-woman, and even a sort of Florence Nightingale when she ministers to friends down with smallpox. There are some marvelous scenes. . . . Some scenes, such as the account of President McKinley's assassination, don't seem to belong. 'In Calamity's Wake' is beautifully written, reminiscent of Karen Fisher's lyrical 'A Sudden Country,' except for its lack of focus. The novel is likely to appeal to readers of women's fiction or experimental novels."

REVIEW: *Kirkus Rev* v81 no17 p7-8 S 1 2013

REVIEW: *Publ Wkly* v260 no35 p32 S 2 2013

REVIEW: *Quill Quire* v79 no1 p12-5 Ja/F 2013

REVIEW: *Quill Quire* v79 no4 p21 My 2013 Dory Cerny

CAPLES, GARRETT.ed. The collected poems of Philip Lamantia. See The collected poems of Philip Lamantia

CAPP, BERNARD. England's culture wars; Puritan reformation and its enemies in the Interregnum, 1649-1660; [by] Bernard Capp xiii, 274 p. 2012 Oxford University Press

1. Historical literature 2. Puritan movements—Great Britain—History—17th century
ISBN 0199641781 (acid-free paper); 9780199641789 (acid-free paper)
LC 2012-450106

SUMMARY: This book by Bernard Capp looks at "the struggle for the reformation of English religion and society between the execution of Charles I and the Restoration. . . . The first [part] assesses Puritan aims, [and] describes the political and institutional frameworks . . . in which they were pursued. The second examines the campaigns to . . . root out sexual misconduct , and terminate . . . the social pleasures of music and drama. . . The third looks at . . . local contexts." (English Historical Review)

REVIEW: *Am Hist Rev* v119 no2 p597-8 Ap 2014 John Spurr

REVIEW: *Choice* v50 no7 p1321 Mr 2013 B. R. Burg

REVIEW: *Engl Hist Rev* v129 no536 p210-2 F 2014 Blair Worden

"England's Culture Wars: Puritan Reformation and Its Enemies in the Interregnum, 1649-1660". "Through his command of a remarkable range of evidence . . . [Bernard] Capp gives us by far our fullest and most rounded account of the topic. The evidence is not always generous, and some of its limitations seem insuperable. No one could handle it more judiciously or authoritatively than Capp, but even in his hands many an incident or initiative or opinion can be glimpsed only dimly and will sustain no more than a sentence or two of exposition. . . . Even if this is not the most ambitious or originally conceived of Capp's books, his scholarly standards and versatility, and his capacity for the lucid exposition of complexity, are as imposing as ever."

REVIEW: *History* v99 no334 p141-2 Ja 2014 Anthony Fletcher

CAPRIOLI, MARY. Sex and world peace. See Hudson, V. M.

CAPUTI, MARY. Feminism and power; the need for critical theory; [by] Mary Caputi xxi, 195 p. 2013 Lexington Books

1. Feminism 2. Feminist literature 3. Feminist theory 4. Power (Social sciences)
ISBN 9780739175798 (cloth : alk. paper)
LC 2012-051421

SUMMARY: This book "argues that the critical theories of Theodor Adorno and Jacques Derrida have much to offer feminism, and a feminist understanding of female empowerment. Its pages rely on Adorno's assertion that it is only by allowing the sufferer to speak that we can unveil social truth rather than be duped by the bravado of victory culture. Similarly, it demonstrates how Derrida's insistence on the trace . . . lead[s] feminism away from the perils of contented triumphalism." (Publisher's note)

REVIEW: *Choice* v51 no6 p1092 F 2014 E. R. Gill
"Feminism and Power: The Need for Critical Theory." "[Mary] Caputi . . . uses critical theory as a lens through which to assess third-wave feminism. Where second-wave feminism emphasized ways that women are victimized, what Caputi terms 'power feminism' celebrates women's victories and newfound status. Simultaneously, however, it is often characterized by a triumphal self-aggrandizement and toughness that ignores the importance of care and the needs of those who are neither listened to nor understood."

CAPUTO, JOHN D. Truth; Philosophy in transit; [by] John D. Caputo 2014 Penguin
1. Continental philosophy 2. Philosophical literature 3. Postmodernism (Philosophy) 4. Transportation—Social aspects 5. Truth
ISBN 9781846146008 paperback

SUMMARY: "Arguing that transport is an important metaphor for our uncertain, freewheeling postmodernism age, where any reality is possible, [author] John D. Caputo explores the ways in which science, ethics, politics, art and religion all claim to offer us the 'truth,' and posits his own surprising theory of the many notions of truth." (Publisher's note)

REVIEW: *TLS* no5785 p12 F 14 2014 TIM CRANE
"Truth: Philosophy in Transit." "John D. Caputo's book is one in a new series from Penguin called 'Philosophy in Transit'." . . . The transit metaphor is . . . not a good way of illustrating Caputo's central themes. . . . Caputo's postmodernists are not so interested in clarification and categorization. . . . His readable and eloquent book is an excellent guide to the outlook common in a certain strain of Continental European philosophy. His neglect of other areas of philosophy is disappointing. . . . 'Truth' is also strikingly parochial. . . . If postmodernism is supposed to demonstrate how parochial all our concerns and commitments are, then it should not be surprising that postmodernism itself is as parochial as all other philosophies."

CARDI, ANNIE. The Chance you won't return; [by] Annie Cardi 352 p. 2014 Candlewick Press
1. Delusions 2. Families of the mentally ill 3. Mentally ill women—Fiction 4. Mothers & daughters—Fiction 5. Young adult fiction
ISBN 0763662925; 9780763662929
LC 2013-946619

SUMMARY: In this book, protagonist Alex's "mother believes herself to be Amelia Earhart. As Alex's mother's delusion becomes more persistent, she is hospitalized, but Alex's father's insurance isn't enough, and the family has to take care of her at home. . . .When she realizes that her mother is working on a timeline that will eventually lead to her disappearance . . . her confession closes the distance she has been maintaining between herself and her friends." (Bulletin of the Center for Children's Books)

REVIEW: *Booklist* v110 no15 p80-2 Ap 1 2014 Daniel Kraus

REVIEW: *Bull Cent Child Books* v67 no9 p446-7 My 2014 K. C.
"The Chance You Won't Return". "Alex's mom's delusion works as both metaphor and real problem in this double-edged story of a girl coming of age. Character development through the rendering of small detail is strong here, particularly with respect to Alex's younger siblings, Katy and Teddy, who emerge in realistic response to their mother's withdrawal from their lives. The result is a solidly crafted family story that sensitively explores the ripple effects of the temporary brokenness of one member."

REVIEW: *Kirkus Rev* v82 no5 p114 Mr 1 2014

REVIEW: *SLJ* v60 no9 p140 S 2014 Geri Diorio

REVIEW: *SLJ* v60 no7 p53 Jl 2014 Karen Alexander

REVIEW: *Voice of Youth Advocates* v37 no1 p62 Ap 2014 Jennifer Rummel

CARDUFF, CHRISTOPHER.ed. Collected early stories. See Updike, J.

CARDUFF, CHRISTOPHER.ed. Collected later stories. See Updike, J.

CARERE, CLAUDIO.ed. Animal personalities. See Animal personalities

CAREY, JOHN, 1934-. The Unexpected Professor; an Oxford Life; [by] John Carey 384 p. 2014 Faber & Faber
1. Books & reading 2. College teachers 3. Critics 4. Memoirs 5. University of Oxford
ISBN 0571310923; 9780571310920

SUMMARY: This book by Oxford University literature professor John Carey "is an autobiography (postwar austerity, grammar school, national service, Oxford, Oxford, Oxford) that doubles as a 'selective and opinionated' history of English literature, and a glories-of-reading memoir." (New Statesman)

REVIEW: *Economist* v410 no8878 p78-9 Mr 15 2014
"The Unexpected Professor: An Oxford Life in Books". "In his blog, . . . John Carey . . . states that he writes to 'stimulate and involve the general reader'. This autobiography, written with sympathy, a light touch and a sardonic sense of humour, amply fulfills that aim. It suggests that this well-known book reviewer and author retains strong opinions and a love of controversy . . . but also portrays a sensitive man dedicated to academic study and to reading. He admits that 'courage matters more than understanding poetry' but, having read almost everything there is to read, he is unapologetic about trying to convey just what an enjoyable activity reading is."

REVIEW: *New Statesman* v143 no5201 p44-7 Mr 14 2014 Leo Robson

REVIEW: *TLS* no5790 p10 Mr 21 2014 D. J. TAYLOR
"The Unexpected Professor: An Oxford Life in Books." "The book is at its best, and also its funniest, when . . . three elements coalesce, when [author John] Carey's invincible sense of who he is and where he comes from, not to mention the books he likes, collides head-on with an environment designed to call these affiliations sharply into question. . . . One of Carey's charms as a critic, it goes without saying,

is his ability to have it both ways without seeming to notice that the trick is being played. Another is his prodigious self-confidence. . . . If this apologia . . . is rather light on relative values, then it is strong on sympathy, particularly for those whom Carey believes to have been conspired against or otherwise let down."

CARLE, DAVID. Traveling the 38th Parallel; a water line around the world; [by] David Carle 278 p. 2013 University of California Press

1. Environmental literature 2. Human geography 3. Hydrology 4. Korean Demilitarized Zone (Korea) 5. Oceanography
ISBN 0520266544 (cloth : alk. paper); 9780520266544 (cloth : alk. paper)
LC 2012-030001

SUMMARY: In this book, by David Carle and Janet Carle, "the authors set out on an around-the-world journey in search of water-related environmental and cultural intersections along the 38th parallel. This book is a chronicle of their adventures as they meet people confronting challenges in water supply, pollution, wetlands loss, and habitat protection." (Publisher's note)

REVIEW: *Choice* v51 no2 p297 O 2013 R. C. Hedreen

"Traveling the 38th Parallel: A Water Line Around the World." "Environmental activists and former California park rangers David Carle and Janet Carle document their journeys along the 38th parallel to explore environmental projects around the world. While the most famous location at 38 degrees north is probably the Korean DMZ, the first stop in the book, the authors travel through regions where the environment has been modified for millennia by human civilization, including China, Turkey, and Greece. They also investigate more recent issues such as raptor poaching in Sicily and mountaintop removal in West Virginia. . . . The stories are inspiring, sometimes heartbreaking, and should whet the appetite for more information about the history and environment of the areas."

CARLE, JANET. Traveling the 38th Parallel. See Carle, D.

CARLIN, LAURA.il. The Promise. See Davies, N.

CARLISLE, RODNEY.ed. The 50 States. See The 50 States

CARLSON, CAROLINE. Magic marks the spot; [by] Caroline Carlson 344 p. 2013 Harper, an imprint of HarperCollinsPublishers

1. Adventure and adventurers—Fiction 2. Adventure stories 3. Magic—Fiction 4. Pirates—Fiction 5. Sex role—Fiction
ISBN 9780062194343 (trade bdg.); 9780062314673 (international edition)
LC 2013-021822

SUMMARY: This book is the first in the Very Honorable League of Pirates series. It follows " headstrong Hilary Westfield," who "longs to be a pirate but is sent to finishing school, where embroidery, etiquette, and fainting are mainstays of the curriculum; accompanying her is a wisecracking gargoyle carved centuries before by an enchantress. Hilary runs away from school to join the crew of a 'freelance' pirate, Jasper Fletcher." (Publishers Weekly)

REVIEW: *Bull Cent Child Books* v67 no3 p143 N 2013 J. H.

REVIEW: *N Y Times Book Rev* p37 N 10 2013 MARJORIE INGALL

"Treasure Hunters" and "The Very Nearly Honorable League of Pirates: Magic Marks the Spot." "['Treasure Hunters'] is pretty jam-packed. . . . This wild ride is narrated by Bick, 12, whose rat-a-tat descriptions of the siblings' adventures are accompanied by drawings by his twin sister, Beck. These black-and-white illustrations are delightful. . . . There isn't a lot of emotional heft, jazzy writing or deep characterization here, and the broad humor often falls flat. . . . Caroline Carlson's 'Very Nearly Honorable League of Pirates' is a more langurously paced seafaring adventure. . . . Basically, this is a drawing-room comedy set on the high seas. . . . The book is deliciously feminist but wears its politics lightly."

CARLSON, W. BERNARD. Tesla; inventor of the electrical age; [by] W. Bernard Carlson xiii, 500 p. 2013 Princeton University Press

1. Biographies 2. Electrical engineers—United States—Biography 3. Inventors—United States—Biography
ISBN 0691057761 (hardcover); 9780691057767 (hardcover)
LC 2012-049608

SUMMARY: This book, by W. Bernard Carlson, presents a biography of the inventor Nikola Tesla, "a major contributor to the electrical revolution . . . at the turn of the twentieth century. His inventions, patents, and theoretical work formed the basis of modern AC electricity, and contributed to the development of radio and television. . . . An astute self-promoter and gifted showman, he cultivated a public image of the eccentric genius." (Publisher's note)

REVIEW: *Booklist* v109 no17 p56 My 1 2013 Bryce Christensen

REVIEW: *Choice* v51 no2 p286 O 2013 K. D. Stephan

REVIEW: *Kirkus Rev* p23 2013 Guide 20to BookExpo America

REVIEW: *Kirkus Rev* v81 no9 p40 My 1 2013

REVIEW: *Libr J* v138 no9 p99 My 15 2013 Brian Odom

REVIEW: *Nat Hist* v121 no7 p42 S 2013 LAURENCE A. MARSCHALL

REVIEW: *Publ Wkly* v260 no14 p54-5 Ap 8 2013

REVIEW: *Science* v341 no6147 p715-6 Ag 16 2013 Thomas J. Misa

"Tesla: Inventor of the Electrical Age." "Carefully researched and thoughtfully written. . . . A generally sympathetic portrait of [Nikola] Tesla as the most colorful inventor of his generation. . . . As Carlson sees it, Tesla careened uneasily between 'ideal and illusion.' . . . Carlson also admirably surveys the clashes among [Thomas] Edison, Tesla, and [George] Westinghouse covered by Jill Jonnes. . . . Clearly surpassing earlier accounts . . . his will be the gold standard for Tesla biography."

CARLTON, KAT. Two lies and a spy; [by] Kat Carlton 2013 Simon & Schuster

1. Brothers & sisters—Fiction 2. High school stu-

dents—Fiction 3. Spy stories 4. Twins—Fiction 5. Young adult fiction
ISBN 9781442481725 paperback; 9781442481749 ebook

SUMMARY: In this young adult spy novel by Kat Carlton, "Kari plunges into the world of espionage on a mission to save her parents while trying to impress the guy she's been in love with forever. . . . Kari soon discovers that her parents have been disavowed and declared traitors, and she's determined to clear their names. Breaking into the Agency seems like a reasonable plan, especially with the help of a team that includes her longtime crush, Luke. . . . (Publisher's note)

REVIEW: *Bull Cent Child Books* v67 no3 p143-4 N 2013 E. B.

"Two Lies and a Spy." "The cardboard ensemble cast comprises the predictable vamp, hacker, fighter, and pair of rival hunks, plus one truly adorable little savant brother who calms himself with online research when things get tense. And they do get tense, as the team is lured into a maximum-security detention facility, and the Andrews parents prove to be not what they seem. Double-entendre-laced flirtation, devoid of finesse, makes the teen relationships sound steamier than they actually are, but it does add a dash of spice to the action fare. By tale's end, the Andrews family is in shambles, Kari and Charlie are off to train with a youth division of Interpol, and Kari's love life is up in the air--a sure recipe for a sequel."

REVIEW: *Kirkus Rev* v81 no15 p84 Ag 1 2013

REVIEW: *SLJ* v59 no9 p141 S 2013 Elizabeth Kahn

REVIEW: *Voice of Youth Advocates* v36 no4 p57-8 O 2013 Lauri J. Vaughan

CARMACK, ROBERT M. Anthropology and global history; from tribes to the modern world-system; [by] Robert M. Carmack vi, 399 p. 2013 AltaMira Press, a division of Rowman & Littlefield Publishers, Inc.
1. Anthropology—History 2. Anthropology literature 3. Ethnohistory 4. World history 5. World politics
ISBN 0759123896 (cloth: alk. paper); 9780759123892 (cloth: alk. paper)
LC 2013-023068

SUMMARY: This book by Robert M. Carmack "provides an overview of global history intertwined with a discussion of scholarly attempts to conceptualize historical change. He employs what he calls a 'global-oriented world-system and civilization framework.'" Particular focus is given to "liberal developmentalist or radical revolutionary agendas." (Choice: Current Reviews for Academic Libraries)

REVIEW: *Choice* v51 no9 p1637-8 My 2014 M. A. Soderstrom

"Anthropology and Global History: From Tribes to the Modern World-System". "There is nothing exactly new here, but the book provides a helpful introduction to many critical ideas. It is less successful as an overview of global history. Coverage of individual countries and regions is reliant on a small number of textbooks, is marred by occasional inaccuracies, and is sometimes overly reductionist and redundant. Readers seeking such an overview will be better served by turning to more standard global or world history texts. That said, those trying to grapple with and conceptualize the 'big picture' will find much of value in the book's theoretical summaries, definitions, and vignettes."

CARMAIN, EMILY.ed. Unit 400. See Unit 400

CARNEY, CHARITY R. Ministers and masters; Methodism, manhood, and honor in the old South; [by] Charity R. Carney xi, 188 p. 2011 Louisiana State University Press
1. Historical literature 2. Honor—Religious aspects—Methodist Episcopal Church, South 3. Masculinity—Religious aspects 4. Masculinity—Religious aspects—Methodist Episcopal Church, South 5. Methodists—United States 6. Slavery and the church—Methodist Episcopal Church, South 7. Southern States—Religion 8. Southern States—Social life & customs—1775-1865
ISBN 9780807138861 (cloth : alk. paper); 9780807138878 (pdf); 9780807138885 (epub); 9780807138892 (mobi)
LC 2011-011948

SUMMARY: This book by Charity R. Carney "presents a thorough account of the way in which Methodist preachers constructed their own concept of masculinity within--and at times in defiance of--the constraints of southern honor culture of the early nineteenth century. By focusing on this unique subgroup of southern men, the book explores often-debated concepts like southern honor and patriarchy in a new way." (Publisher's note)

REVIEW: *Am Hist Rev* v118 no4 p1179-80 O 2013 Ted Ownby

"Ministers and Masters: Methodism, Manhood, and Honor in the Old South." "'Ministers and Masters' joins a small body of scholarship on the antebellum South that sees white evangelicals as standing outside some of the norms of southern society, either as critics or as awkward participants. Analyzing tensions especially evident in the lives of white Methodist men, Charity R. Carney studies both church and household politics. . . . As religious history, getting inside tensions specific to Methodism in the antebellum South, the book makes considerable and unique contributions. Based on personal papers and Methodist publications, the work takes a personal approach to understanding gender and religion."

REVIEW: *J Am Hist* v99 no4 p1240 Mr 2013 Anna M. Lawrence

CARNIE, ETHEL. Miss Nobody; [by] Ethel Carnie vii, 300 p. 2013 Kennedy & Boyd
1. Country life—England—Fiction 2. English fiction—20th century 3. English fiction—Women authors 4. Great Britain—Fiction 5. Marriage—Fiction
LC 1302-0486

SUMMARY: "A centenary edition of the 1913 novel, 'Miss Nobody,' by Ethel Carnie (later Ethel Carnie Holdsworth), widely believed to be the first published novel written by a working-class woman in Britain. 'Miss Nobody' charts the fortunes of the independent Carrie Brown, a former 'scullery drudge' turned oyster shop owner from Ardwick, Greater Manchester." (Publisher's note)

REVIEW: *TLS* no5788 p28 Mr 7 2014 DAVID MALCOLM

"Miss Nobody," "Weep Not My Wanton: Selected Short Stories," and "Mr. Bazalgette's Agent." "[Author Ethel] Carnie's 'Miss Nobody,' her first published novel, came out in 1913. . . . The novel's rich material involves the conflict between the two women. . . . [Leonard] Merrick's Mr Bazalgette's Agent marks an important text in the evolution of detective fiction. As the editor of this new edition, Mike Ashley, notes, 'this book is almost certainly the first ever British novel to feature a professional female detective.' . . . The seven stories republished in 'Weep Not My Wanton' are among [A. E.] Coppard's best known and provide a good, if fragmentary, introduction to his work. They are mostly about the rural poor sometime in the early twentieth century."

CARPENTER, DON, 1931-1995. Fridays at Enrico's; a novel; [by] Don Carpenter 352 p. 2014 Counterpoint

1. Authors, American—20th century—Fiction 2. Beat generation—Fiction 3. Psychological fiction
ISBN 9781619023017 (hardback)
LC 2013-043960

SUMMARY: This book by Don Carpenter "is the story of four writers living in Northern California and Portland during the early, heady days of the Beat scene, a time of youth and opportunity. This story mixes the excitement of beginning with the melancholy of ambition, often thwarted and never satisfied. Loss of innocence is only the first price you pay." (Publisher's note)

REVIEW: *Kirkus Rev* v82 no4 p231 F 15 2014

"Fridays At Enrico's". "Do we need another work about the struggles of writers? Sure, we do—if it has the warmth and charm and sexy vibe of [Don] Carpenter's . . . novel. This recently discovered, not-quite-final draft has been lovingly shaped for publication by author Jonathan Lethem. . . . Both Stan and Charlie gravitate to Hollywood, which Carpenter treats with surprising generosity as he takes his story up to 1975, when the future still beckons invitingly. This publication is an important event: Welcome back, Don Carpenter."

REVIEW: *Libr J* v139 no10 p94 Je 1 2014 Barbara Hoffert

REVIEW: *N Y Times Book Rev* p14 Jl 6 2014 DOUGLAS BRINKLEY

REVIEW: *New York Times* v163 no56560 p22 Jl 12 2014

CARPENTER, JULIET WINTERS.tr. A true novel. See Mizumura Mi.

CARPENTER, LEA. Eleven Days; [by] Lea Carpenter 288 p. 2013 Random House Inc

1. Afghan War, 2001- 2. Bin Laden, Osama, 1957-2011 3. Families of military personnel 4. Mothers & sons—Fiction 5. United States. Army. Special Forces
ISBN 0307960706; 9780307960702

SUMMARY: This book by Lea Carpenter "opens in May 2011, when Sara's son, Jason, has been missing for nine days following a Special Operations Forces mission that took place the same night as the bin Laden raid. Knowing nothing more about Jason's fate than the reporters camped out in front of her Pennsylvania farmhouse, Sara--an editor who immersed herself in all things military after her son became a Naval officer--is determined to discover what's happened." (Publisher's note)

REVIEW: *Booklist* v109 no19/20 p30 Je 1 2013 Donna Chavez

REVIEW: *Kirkus Rev* v81 no2 p8 Je 1 2013

REVIEW: *Libr J* v138 no1 p64 Ja 1 2013

REVIEW: *Libr J* v138 no12 p70 Jl 1 2013 Leslie Patterson

REVIEW: *N Y Times Book Rev* p18 Ag 11 2013 ELIZABETH D. SAMET

REVIEW: *New York Times* v162 no56166 pC1-8 Je 13 2013 MICHIKO KAKUTANI

REVIEW: *New Yorker* v89 no34 p79-1 O 28 2013

"Eleven Days." "In this début novel . . . a mother awaits news of her son, a soldier who has gone missing from an overseas mission. Her plight has made her a local celebrity and a symbol for a mourning nation, and she abhors the attention as if it were the cause of her misfortune. The narrative includes the son's perspective, revealed through flashbacks and through his letters home. Carpenter's writing is graceful and assured. The grieving protagonist imagines a future of smart wars, 'where we touch and swipe the places we want to destroy, or make circles around the places we want to protect.'"

REVIEW: *Newsweek Global* v161 no19 p1 My 22 2013 Jimmy So

CARPENTER, MURRAY. Caffeinated; how our daily habit helps, hurts, and hooks us; [by] Murray Carpenter 288 p. 2014 Hudson Street Press

1. Caffeine—Health aspects 2. Caffeine habit 3. Coffee drinking 4. Drug abuse—Government policy 5. Journalism
ISBN 9781594631382 (hardcover)
LC 2013-044492

SUMMARY: Written by Murray Carpenter, "'Caffeinated' reveals the little-known truth about this addictive, largely unregulated drug found in coffee, energy drinks, teas, colas, chocolate, and even pain relievers." It addresses "why caffeine has such a powerful effect on everything from boosting our mood to improving our athletic performance as well as how--and why--brands such as Coca-Cola have ducked regulatory efforts for decades." (Publisher's note)

REVIEW: *Kirkus Rev* v82 no3 p169 F 1 2014

REVIEW: *New York Times* v163 no56451 pD5 Mr 25 2014 ABIGAIL ZUGER

REVIEW: *Sci Am* v310 no3 p80 Mr 2014 Rachel Feltman

"Caffeinated: How Our Daily Habit Helps, Hurts, and Hooks Us." "[Author Murray Carpenter's] book examines the caffeine industry, the coffee and other products it churns out, and the complex effects the chemical has on our bodies. The book is anything but preachy, yet along with acknowledging caffeine's benefits, Carpenter bluntly addresses its dangers, which can include anxiety, panic attacks, disrupted sleep and, if taken in large doses, even death. 'Caffeinated' highlights not just the physiological downsides of caffeine but the problems that regulators face."

CARPENTER, NANCY.il. Big Bear's big boat. See Bunting, E.

CARPENTER, NANCY.il. Queen Victoria's Bathing Machine. See Whelan, G.

CARPENTER, TAD. I say, you say feelings!; [by] Tad Carpenter 18 p. 2013 Little, Brown and Co.

1. Animals—Juvenile literature 2. Emotions (Psychology)—Juvenile literature 3. Lift-the-flap books 4. Picture

books for children 5. Vocabulary—Juvenile literature
ISBN 9780316200745
LC 2012-950948

SUMMARY: This children's book by Tad Carpenter presents a "lift-the-flap introduction to eight emotions and the facial and verbal actions that often accompany them. [Tad] Carpenter uses a cast of . . . cartoon animals to showcase each emotion: "I say grumpy, you say..." reads one scene as an orange cat stands scowling by the side of the road in the rain. That scowl deepens when, after opening a large flap, the cat gets splashed by a passing car ('FROWN!')." (Publishers Weekly)

REVIEW: *Kirkus Rev* v81 no24 p203 D 15 2013

"Feelings!". "Quickly falling into a predictable and comforting pattern, the left-hand page introduces a feeling—'I say happy, you say. . .'—and the gatefold flap on the right-hand page lifts to reveal a corresponding response: 'SMILE!'. . . The bright, busy pages, which star wide-eyed, cartoon-style animal characters in situations typically associated with the emotions featured, will appeal to little ones and help them to understand the concepts presented. . . . [Tad] Carpenter's predicable, interactive titles in the I Say, You Say series offer appealing introductions to basic concepts just right for toddlers and preschoolers."

CARPENTER, TAD.il. Trick-or-treat! See Leppanen, D.

CARR, AARON. The school; [by] Aaron Carr 2013 AV2 by Weigl

1. Children's nonfiction 2. School facilities 3. Schools—Juvenile literature 4. Student activities 5. Teaching aids & devices
ISBN 9781621273486 (hardcover : alk. paper); 9781621273530 (softcover : alk. paper)
LC 2013-006841

SUMMARY: This book by Aaron Carr, part of the "My Neighborhood" series, "introduces young ones" to school. "A single sentence per page reiterates the actions being conducted by happy, multicultural kids. . . . Kids will learn about what they'll study in school; the tools they'll use (yes, a tablet computer makes a cameo); and the activities they'll take part in, both during and after school hours, from athletics to plays to bake sales." (Booklist)

REVIEW: *Booklist* v110 no3 p84-6 O 1 2013 Daniel Kraus

"The School." "The My Neighborhood series introduces young ones to the places they may often see--and what will they see more often than school? A single sentence per page reiterates the actions being conducted by happy, multicultural kids. . . . The sharp photographs are saturated with rich color--even the text is centered atop bright blue boxes outlined in yellow--and the horizontal trim size will settle this easily upon laps. A code in the books leads to additional multimedia contact via the AV2 website."

CARR, AARON. Spring; [by] Aaron Carr 2013 AV2 by Weigl

1. Children's nonfiction 2. Picture books for children 3. Plants—Juvenile literature 4. Seasons—Juvenile literature 5. Spring—Juvenile literature
ISBN 9781621274933 (hardcover : alk. paper); 9781621274995 (softcover : alk. paper); 9781621278207 (ebk.)
LC 2013-934646

SUMMARY: This book on spring by Aaron Carr is part of the "Science Kids: Seasons" series, which "presents basic information about the four seasons." It features "photos . . . full of soft green trees and plants." It "concludes with a quiz question related to six photos from the book" and provides Internet links to "additional activities such as simple word finds and crossword puzzles." (Booklist)

REVIEW: *Booklist* v110 no6 p38 N 15 2013 Miriam Aronin

"Fall," "Spring," and "Summer." "The Science Kids: Seasons series presents basic information about the four seasons in a way that is perfect for beginning readers or prereaders. Each book begins with a simple, clear diagram of the seasonal cycle. The rest of the book includes large, beautiful photos that are a treat for both adult and child readers. . . . It is worth keeping in mind, though, that not all readers will live in climates like the ones described in the books. . . . This quibble aside, the books are effective. Each one concludes with a quiz question related to six photos from the book. These open-ended questions can provoke discussion with prereaders or help keep beginning readers engaged."

CARR, AARON. Summer; [by] Aaron Carr 2013 AV2 by Weigl

1. Animals—Juvenile literature 2. Children's nonfiction 3. Picture books for children 4. Seasons—Juvenile literature 5. Summer—Juvenile literature
ISBN 9781621274940 (hardcover : alk. paper); 9781621275008 (softcover : alk. paper); 9781621278214 (ebk.)
LC 2013-934644

SUMMARY: This book on summer by Aaron Carr is part of the "Science Kids: Seasons" series, which "presents basic information about the four seasons." It features photos of "landscapes, skyscapes, and animals." It "concludes with a quiz question related to six photos from the book" and provides Internet links to "additional activities such as simple word finds and crossword puzzles." (Booklist)

REVIEW: *Booklist* v110 no6 p38 N 15 2013 Miriam Aronin

"Fall," "Spring," and "Summer." "The Science Kids: Seasons series presents basic information about the four seasons in a way that is perfect for beginning readers or prereaders. Each book begins with a simple, clear diagram of the seasonal cycle. The rest of the book includes large, beautiful photos that are a treat for both adult and child readers. . . . It is worth keeping in mind, though, that not all readers will live in climates like the ones described in the books. . . . This quibble aside, the books are effective. Each one concludes with a quiz question related to six photos from the book. These open-ended questions can provoke discussion with prereaders or help keep beginning readers engaged."

CARR, ALISTAIR. The Nomad's path; travels in the Sahel; [by] Alistair Carr 256 p. 2014 I.B. Tauris

1. Africa, North—Description & travel 2. Memoirs 3. Nomads 4. Sahel 5. Travelers' writings
ISBN 9781780766898
LC 2013-388031

SUMMARY: "'The Nomad's Path' is [an] . . . account of a journey across this inhospitable region at a time of Tuareg insurgency in 2004 and 2008. [Author Alistair] Carr sets out to explore the centuries-old link between the Barbary Coast and the Sahel along the Old Salt Road, while conjuring to life a lost wilderness and those who survive within it. At its heart is the story of a daring journey across the Sahel with the Tubu nomads." (Publisher's note)

REVIEW: *TLS* no5791 p26 Mr 28 2014 JOHN URE

"The Nomad's Path: Travels in the Sahel." "This book is, at once, a history of a troubled and virtually unknown part of the Sahara desert, and an account of a brave and possibly unique journey by a European across the Manga—a barren and unforgiving landscape in southern Niger, bordering both Chad and northern Nigeria, and only fleetingly inhabited by nomads. . . . Against this background it was remarkable that [author] Alistair Carr felt himself to be so safe when travelling with the Tubu, a nomadic people who are obliged to move with their herds in search of meagre and widely interspersed pastures. . . . This is a classic desert travel book, in the best English tradition of Doughty and Wilfrid Thesiger."

CARREIRA DA SILVA, FILIPE.ed. G.H. Mead. See G.H. Mead

CARRIGER, GAIL. Curtsies & conspiracies; [by] Gail Carriger 320 p. 2013 Little, Brown and Co.

1. Boarding schools—Fiction 2. Espionage—Fiction 3. Etiquette—Fiction 4. Robots—Fiction 5. Schools—Fiction 6. Science fiction 7. Steampunk fiction
ISBN 031619011X; 9780316190114
LC 2012-048520

SUMMARY: In this book, by Gail Carriger, "Sophronia's first year at Mademoiselle Geraldine's Finishing Academy for Young Ladies of Quality . . . is training her to be a spy. A conspiracy is afoot--one with dire implications for both supernaturals and humans. Sophronia must rely on her training to discover who is behind the dangerous plot-and survive the London Season with a full dance card." (Publisher's note)

REVIEW: *Booklist* v109 no22 p72 Ag 1 2013 Krista Hutley

REVIEW: *Horn Book Magazine* v90 no1 p86-7 Ja/F 2014 KATIE BIRCHER

"Curtsies & Conspiracies." "[Gail] Carriger relies a bit heavily on exposition to communicate the rival groups' complex political machinations, and the action occasionally lacks clear context. But Sophronia, availing herself of every opportunity to hone her skills in intelligence and social manipulation (the boys from an evil genius academy provide good practice), is a charismatic heroine whose faults--including a nonchalant disregard for consequences--make her all the more engaging. Like the first installment, this is a witty and suspenseful steampunk romp."

REVIEW: *Kirkus Rev* v81 no19 p128 O 1 2013

REVIEW: *Publ Wkly* p112 Children's starred review annual 2013

REVIEW: *Publ Wkly* v260 no41 p61 O 14 2013

CARROLL, ABIGAIL. Three squares; the invention of the American meal; [by] Abigail Carroll 344 p. 2013 Basic Books, a member of the Perseus Books Group

1. Breakfasts—United States—History 2. Diet—United States—History 3. Dinners and dining—United States—History 4. Food habits—United States—History 5. Historical literature 6. Luncheons—United States—History 7. National characteristics, American
ISBN 9780465025527 (hardcover)
LC 2013-008929

SUMMARY: "In 'Three Squares,' food historian Abigail Carroll upends the popular understanding of our most cherished mealtime traditions, revealing that our eating habits have never been stable--far from it, in fact. . . . The story of how the simple gruel of our forefathers gave way to snack fixes and fast food, 'Three Squares' also explains how Americans' eating habits may change in the years to come." (Publisher's note)

REVIEW: *Booklist* v109 no22 p13-4 Ag 1 2013 Mark Knoblauch

REVIEW: *Choice* v51 no6 p1074-5 F 2014 A. B. Audant

"Three Squares: The Invention of the American Meal." "Meals in the US were once messy, unstructured, and repetitive affairs. Food historian [Abigail] Carroll explores the evolution of the American meal from the colonial era to the present by focusing on the emergence and ongoing evolution of breakfast, lunch, and dinner as distinct events. . . . Wise use of primary sources livens up historical sections, and the index illustrates Carroll's deep dive into the literature. Individual chapters are plumped full of information; more attentive editing would have ensured a smoother flow. . . . It is a timely and optimistic reminder that as people eat, they define and redefine their 'three squares.'"

REVIEW: *Kirkus Rev* v81 no13 p221 Jl 1 2013

REVIEW: *N Y Times Book Rev* p25 D 15 2013 JENNY ROSENSTRACH

"Biting Through the Skin: An Indian Kitchen in America's Heartland," "Three Squares: The Invention of the American Meal," and "Fried Walleye and Cherry Pie: Midwestern Writers on Food." "In Nine Mukerjee Furstenau's memoir, 'Biting Through the Skin: An Indian Kitchen in America's Heartland' . . . , the author uses family recipes to bridge two worlds. . . . In the engrossing 'Three Squares: The Invention of the American Meal' . . . , Abigail Carroll lays down some historical context, reminding us dinner became a signifier of class. . . . In Peggy Wolff's 'Fried Walleye and Cherry Pie' . . . the quality of the writing is uneven, but Heartland natives will embrace the recipes."

REVIEW: *Publ Wkly* v260 no27 p80 Jl 8 2013

CARROLL, MICHAEL. Stronger; a Super human clash; [by] Michael Carroll 378 p. 2012 Philomel Books

1. Adventure and adventurers—Fiction 2. Monsters—Fiction 3. Science fiction 4. Superheroes
ISBN 0399257616; 9780399257612
LC 2011-022436

SUMMARY: In this book, "Gethin Rao is a 12-year-old choir boy who suffers a sudden inexplicable transformation during church service one Sunday, becoming a blue-skinned giant who is almost impervious. Twenty-seven years into the future, he is a prisoner known as 'Brawn,' made to mine platinum with others like him in a secure domed facility in an unknown location. . . . The novel switches back and forth between these two time periods." (School Library Journal)

REVIEW: *SLJ* v58 no6 p114-6 Je 2012 Eric Norton

"Stronger: A Super Human Crash." "Gethin Rao is a 12-year-old choir boy who suffers a sudden inexplicable transformation during church service one Sunday, becoming a blue-skinned giant who is almost impervious. . . . Eventually the kindhearted monster is recruited by two powerful groups and must make a choice between them. Like a single graphic novel from a superhero universe, 'Stronger' can be appreciated by itself but it is certainly part of a larger whole; there are links to other books in the series that may take place before, after, or at the same time as this one. Carroll fans or hero comics readers will snap this up but others may wish to start with the two earlier volumes."

REVIEW: *Voice of Youth Advocates* v35 no2 p172 Je 2012 Iain McCormick

REVIEW: *Voice of Youth Advocates* v35 no2 p172 Je 2012 Nancy Wallace

CARROLL, NOËL, 1947-. Humour; a very short introduction; [by] Noël Carroll 144 p. 2014 Oxford University Press

1. Evolutionary psychology 2. Philosophical literature 3. Philosophy & humor 4. Wit & humor—Moral & ethical aspects 5. Wit & humor—Psychological aspects
ISBN 9780199552221 (pbk.)
LC 2013-947882

SUMMARY: "Humour is a universal feature of human life. It has been discovered in every known human culture, and thinkers have discussed it for over two thousand years. In this 'Very Short Introduction' [author] Noel Carroll considers the nature and value of humour: from its leading theories and its relation to emotion and cognition, to ethical questions of its morality and its significance in shaping society." (Publisher's note)

REVIEW: *TLS* no5794 p26 Ap 18 2014 FRANK BRUCE

"Humour: A Very Short Introduction." "As Noël Carroll notes in 'Humour: A very short introduction,' his subject has been discussed for over 2,000 years and the literature on it is vast. . . . As a philosopher, Carroll surveys the main theoretical approaches and brings clarity and concision to a confused field. . . . The incongruity theory also offers the best way to explore the relationship between humour, emotion and cognition. This is controversial terrain, but Carroll believes it is worth going over because if, as he argues, humour is an emotion, then the most recent research in that field could offer new insight into the question of why humour evolved at all."

CARROLL, SEAN B. Brave genius; two remarkable friends and their unlikely journey from the French resistance to the Nobel prize; [by] Sean B. Carroll 576 p. 2013 Crown Publishers

1. Authors, Algerian—20th century—Biography 2. Authors, French—20th century—Biography 3. Historical literature 4. Molecular biologists—France—Biography 5. Nobel Prize winners—France—Biography 6. Politics and culture—France—History—20th century 7. World War, 1939-1945—Underground movements—France
ISBN 0307952339; 9780307952332; 9780307952349
LC 2012-050707

SUMMARY: Author Sean B. Carroll tells how "writer Albert Camus and budding scientist Jacques Monod were quietly pursuing ordinary, separate lives in Paris. After the German invasion and occupation of France, each joined the Resistance to help liberate the country [and] after the war . . . they became friends. [He] tells the story of how each man endured the most terrible episode of the twentieth century and then blossomed into extraordinarily creative and engaged individuals." (Publisher's note)

REVIEW: *Am Sch* v82 no4 p115-7 Aut 2013 David Brown

REVIEW: *Booklist* v109 no22 p14 Ag 1 2013 Bryce Christensen

REVIEW: *Choice* v51 no10 p1878-9 Je 2014 A. H. Pasco

REVIEW: *Kirkus Rev* v81 no14 p85 Jl 15 2013

REVIEW: *Libr J* v138 no12 p87 Jl 1 2013 David Keymer

REVIEW: *Libr J* v138 no7 p54 Ap 15 2013 Barbara Hoffert

REVIEW: *New York Times* v163 no56297 pD3 O 22 2013 JENNIFER SCHUESSLER

REVIEW: *Publ Wkly* v260 no25 p163 Je 24 2013

REVIEW: *Sci Am* v309 no3 p90 S 2013 Arielle Duhaime-Ross

"Brave Genius: A Scientist, A Philosopher, and Their Daring Adventures From the French Resistance to the Nobel Prize." "The surprising tale of how two of France's most extraordinary 20th-century minds, biologist Jacques Monod and writer Albert Camus, each survived and rebelled against the Nazi occupation of France only to become close friends in the years leading up to their fame and receipt of Nobel Prizes. (Monod's Nobel was in medicine; Camus's was in literature.) Using a wealth of newly discovered letters and other documentation, Carroll beautifully encapsulates how two men seemingly so far apart in their philosophies and achievements both ended up sharing 'exceptional lives' transformed by 'exceptional events.'"

CARSON, CIARÁN, 1948-. In the light of; after Illuminations by Arthur Rimbaud; [by] Ciarán Carson 62 p. 2012 Gallery Books

1. Alexandrine verse 2. English poetry—Irish authors—21st century 3. Poems—Collections
ISBN 1852355417 (pbk.); 1852355425 (hbk.); 9781852355418 (pbk.); 9781852355425 (hbk.)
LC 2012-954305

SUMMARY: This poetry collection, translated by Ciaran Carson, presents "prose poems from [Arthur Rimbaud's] 'Les Iluminations' that have been reworked as rhyming couplets." They are rendered in "an Alexandrine format of twelve-syllable rhyming couplets. . . . The poems in 'Les Illuminations 'are probably Rimbaud's last, before—barely twenty—he renounced poetry to seek work abroad." (Times Literary Supplement)

REVIEW: *Antioch Rev* v72 no1 p193-200 Wint 2014 Jordan Smith

"In the Light Of: after Illuminations by arthur rimbaud". "Ciaran Carson has arranged and re-arranged Rimbaud's 'Illuminations' in musically virtuosic and tonally varied rhyming couplets. If it is difficult to read Rimbaud now without thinking of the voices of musical prophecy that he's enabled—Bob Dylan, Patti Smith—it is useful to be reminded by Carson's translation of how intimately the visionary (the sort that recognizes the brutal theme underlying all of the cacophony of modernity) is associated with the shifting music of language."

REVIEW: *TLS* no5770 p28 N 1 2013 BEVERLEY BIE BRAHIC

CARSON, PETER.tr. The death of Ivan Ilyich and Confession. See Tolstoi, L.

CARSON, SUSANNAH.ed. Shakespeare and Me. See Shakespeare and Me

CARTER, CAELA. Me, him, them, and it; [by] Caela Carter 320 p. 2013 Bloomsbury Distributed to the trade by Macmillan
1. Emotional problems—Fiction 2. Family problems—Fiction 3. Pregnancy—Fiction 4. Teenage pregnancy—Fiction 5. Young adult fiction
ISBN 1599909588 (hardcover); 9781599909585 (hardcover)
LC 2012-014331

SUMMARY: In this novel, by Caela Carter, "when Evelyn . . . [upset] her parents with a bad reputation, she wasn't planning to ruin her valedictorian status. She also wasn't planning to fall for Todd—the guy she was just using for sex. And she definitely wasn't planning on getting pregnant. When Todd turns his back on her, Evelyn's not sure where to go." (Publisher's note)

REVIEW: *Horn Book Magazine* v89 no6 p125-6 N/D 2013 Katrina Hedeen

"Revenge of a Not-So-Pretty Girl," "Me, Him, Them and It," and "The Alliance". [In 'Revenge of a Not-So-Pretty Girl,] abused fourteen-year-old Faye hates her Brooklyn Catholic school. . . . Characters and place ring true in a story about learning what (and who) is really important in life. . . . The difficult decision [in 'Me, Him, Them, and It] becomes whether to keep the baby or give it up, and the narrative's ongoing debate will keep readers guessing. This is a compelling pregnant-teen story, and the topic is given sensitive treatment by [Caela] Carter. . . . [In 'The Alliance', part of the Surviving Southside series,] out-and proud Carmen teams up with oblivious jock Scott to start a gay-straight alliance group after his best friend Jamie is bullied into suicide. The issue is given formulaic packaging, but this hi-lo problem novel is a gap-filler."

CARTER, GRAYDON, 1949-.ed. Vanity fair 100 years. See Vanity fair 100 years

CARTER, GREG. The United States of the united races; a utopian history of racial mixing; [by] Greg Carter ix, 265 p. 2013 New York University Press
1. Historical literature 2. Miscegenation—United States—History 3. Post-racialism—United States 4. Racially mixed people—United States—History 5. United States—Race relations—History
ISBN 0814772498; 9780814772492 (cl: alk. paper); 9780814772508 (pb: alk. paper)
LC 2012-045598

SUMMARY: In this book, Greg Carter looks into "the long historical roots of racial mixing as the way to reconfigure race itself, a means of disrupting hierarchical racial categorization and creating a new, truly American, people to fulfill the nation's destiny with human equality. Moving chronologically in seven chapters from the early republic to the present, Carter explores signs, symbols, social conflicts, and, especially, tensions in the intellectual history of American racial thinking." (Library Journal)

REVIEW: *Am Hist Rev* v119 no1 p166-7 F 2014 Elise Lemire

"The United States of the United Races: A Utopian History of Racial Mixing". "While his approach initially seems radically new, [Greg] Carter is ultimately forced to retread much of the usual ground. . . . Because he covers so much ground, Carter is often forced to skim along more quickly than specialists in respective areas will like. That is not to say that there is no new material here. . . . Efforts to follow such leads may be hampered, however, by Carter's lack of clear citations or the visual images in his book."

REVIEW: *Ethn Racial Stud* v37 no10 p1839-46 O 2014 Peter Aspinall

REVIEW: *Ethn Racial Stud* v37 no10 p1847-51 O 2014 C. Matthew Snipp

REVIEW: *J Am Hist* v101 no2 p610 S 2014

REVIEW: *Libr J* v138 no9 p86 My 15 2013 Thomas J. Davis

CARTLEDGE, PAUL. After Thermopylae; the oath of Plataea and the end of the Graeco-Persian Wars; [by] Paul Cartledge 240 p. 2013 Oxford University Press
1. Greece—History—Persian Wars, 500-449 B.C. 2. Historical literature 3. Oaths—History 4. Plataea, Battle of, Plataiai, Greece, 479 B.C 5. Plataea, Battle of, Plataiai, Greece, 479 B.C. 6. Thermopylae, Battle of, Greece, 480 B.C.
ISBN 9780199747320
LC 2013-010296

SUMMARY: "In 'After Thermopylae,' Paul Cartledge masterfully reopens one of the great puzzles of ancient Greece to discover, as much as possible, what happened on the field of battle and, just as important, what happened to its memory. Part of the answer to these questions, Cartledge argues, can be found in a little-known oath reputedly sworn by the leaders of Athens, Sparta, and several other Greek city-states prior to the battle--the Oath of Plataea." (Publisher's note)

REVIEW: *Choice* v51 no3 p524 N 2013 S. M. Burstein

REVIEW: *Libr J* v138 no7 p93 Ap 15 2013 Evan M. Anderson

REVIEW: *TLS* no5782 p28 Ja 24 2014 NICK ROMEO

"After Thermopylae: The Oath of Plataea and the End of the Graeco-Persian Wars." "In 'After Thermopylae: The oath of Plataea and the end of the Graeco-Persian Wars,' Paul Cartledge examines the Battle of Plataea, often neglected by comparison with those earlier battles; and he complicates the received wisdom that the united Greeks repelled the invading forces in the Persian Wars. . . . Cartledge provides an engaging and nuanced picture of the politics of commemoration that followed the Battle of Plataea."

CARTWRIGHT, JUSTIN. Lion Heart; [by] Justin Cartwright 352 p. 2014 St. Martin's Press Bloomsbury Pub. Plc
1. Crusades—Third, 1189-1192—Fiction 2. Historical fiction 3. Historiography—Fiction
ISBN 1620401835; 9781620401835
LC 2013-036199

SUMMARY: In this novel by Justin Cartwright, "Richie, thirty-something, is in search of his own role. . . . Following his father's trail to the Holy Land to research the Art of the Medieval Latin Kingdom, Richie's quest--to uncover the fate of Christianity's most sacred relic and the truth about his father--takes him from the high-table intrigue of Oxford to the imposing Crusader castles of Jordan and into a passionate love affair with Noor, a Canadian-Arab journalist." (Publisher's note)

REVIEW: *Booklist* v110 no8 p19 D 15 2013 Julie Trevelyan

REVIEW: *Kirkus Rev* v81 no21 p191 N 1 2013

REVIEW: *New Statesman* v142 no5175 p57-8 S 13 2013 John Sutherland

REVIEW: *Publ Wkly* v260 no49 p55 D 2 2013

REVIEW: *TLS* no5776 p20 D 13 2013 JANE JAKEMAN

"Lion Heart." "Justin Cartwright's previous books have mainly been about the modem world, so it is surprising to find him smitten by that questing beast, Richard the Lionheart, whose name reverberates through the tripartite structure of Cartwright's latest novel. Following recent convention, the author interweaves the present with the past, though Richie, Cartwright's contemporary narrator, seems to have little in common with his medieval namesake. . . . Cartwright's lively style carries much of the book along but there are two serious disjunctions. One is almost inevitable: probably the only people nowadays who can empathize with the mentality of Crusading are Jihadists. . . . The other problem is the modem narrative, which becomes disjointed."

CARWARDINE, MARK. Natural History Museum Book of Animal Records; [by] Mark Carwardine 256 p. 2013 Firefly Books Ltd

1. Animal behavior 2. Animals 3. Animals—Classification 4. Natural history literature 5. World records

ISBN 1770852697; 9781770852693

SUMMARY: This book by Mark Carwardine "provides facts about the animal record holders from each of the main animal groups: mammals, birds, reptiles, amphibians, fishes, and invertebrates. . . . Each animal group has its own section. Where appropriate, the sections are further divided into orders, families, and species. There are different records for the different groupings." (Booklist)

REVIEW: *Booklist* v110 no9/10 p74 Ja 1 2014 Anne Hoffman

"Natural History Museum Book of Animal Records." "This attractive volume provides facts about the animal record holders from each of the main animal groups: mammals, birds, reptiles, amphibians, fishes, and invertebrates. There are thousands of facts and stunning photographs of many of the animals discussed. . . . The records are not comprehensive but are what the author considers the most relevant and interesting for each type of animal. . . . With the index, it is fairly simple to locate the animal record holders. But the lack of sources for the records and the arbitrary decisions about what records to include for each grouping limit its usefulness for reference collections. However, this is truly a book made for browsing, and it is suitable for public and school libraries."

REVIEW: *Kirkus Rev* v81 no22 p170 N 15 2013

REVIEW: *SLJ* v60 no1 p119 Ja 2014 Anne Barreca

CASCIANO, REBECCA. Climbing Mount Laurel. See Massey, D. S.

CASE, CHRIS.il. Jacob's new dress. See Hoffman, S.

CASEY, MAUD. The man who walked away; a novel; [by] Maud Casey 240 p. 2014 Bloomsbury USA

1. Dadas, Albert 2. Historical fiction 3. Mentally ill—Fiction 4. Psychotherapy patients—Fiction 5. Veterans—Mental health

ISBN 1620403110; 9781620403112 (hardback)
LC 2013-044905

SUMMARY: In this novel, by Maud Casey, "in a trance-like state, Albert walks—from Bordeaux to Poitiers, . . . and farther afield . . . all over Europe. . . . When the reverie of his walking ends, he's left wondering where he is, with no memory of how he got there. . . . Loosely based on the case history of Albert Dadas, a psychiatric patient in the hospital of St. André in Bordeaux in the nineteenth century." (Publisher's note)

REVIEW: *Kirkus Rev* v81 no24 p330 D 15 2013

"The Man Who Walked Away". "[Maud] Casey . . . fictionalizes a story based on the real-life figure of Albert Dadas, a man from the late 19th century whose strange pathology dictated to him that he walk continually, though he temporarily ends up in an asylum—and eventually walks away from that as well. . . . While Dadas vaguely recalls having deserted the army with his friend Baptiste and also alludes to a difficult and problematic relationship with his father, his story ultimately remains cryptic and inexplicable. Lyrical in its style and fascinating in its psychology, Casey's narrative provokes a host of intriguing questions beyond those the Doctor raises, and Casey is wise enough as an author not to provide easy answers."

REVIEW: *Libr J* v139 no10 p94 Je 1 2014 Barbara Hoffert

REVIEW: *N Y Times Book Rev* p9 My 18 2014 GERALDINE BROOKS

REVIEW: *Publ Wkly* v261 no4 p168 Ja 27 2014

CASSELLA, CAROL. Gemini; a novel; [by] Carol Cassella 352 p. 2014 Simon & Schuster

1. FICTION—General 2. FICTION—Literary 3. FICTION—Medical 4. Friendship—Fiction 5. Man-woman relationships—Fiction 6. Medical fiction 7. Women physicians—Fiction

ISBN 9781451627930 (hardback); 9781451627947 (trade paper)
LC 2013-027386

SUMMARY: In this book, an "intensive-care doctor in Seattle grappling with her stagnant relationship and ticking biological clock, Charlotte Reese becomes engrossed in the case of a Jane Doe delivered to her hospital comatose after a highway hit-and-run. After no one comes to the hospital looking for the new patient, Charlotte take a special interest in the case, and with the help of her boyfriend, Eric Bryson, begins to dig into Jane Doe's past." (Publishers Weekly)

REVIEW: *Kirkus Rev* v82 no3 p180 F 1 2014

"Gemini". "In a new mystery from [Carol] Cassella . . . the lives of a doctor and her critically injured patient intertwine in unexpected ways. . . . Despite the potential ruination of her own future with Eric, Dr. Charlotte embarks on a determined quest to solve the puzzle of how this Jane Doe found herself in her present condition. Readers may well overlook Cassella's frequently interjected bromides about love ('Is it a room inside your soul that opens when your lover enters?') since this engaging medical mystery makes far more compelling points about economics and sociology."

REVIEW: *Libr J* v139 no2 p61 F 1 2014 Sheila M. Riley

REVIEW: *Publ Wkly* v261 no1 p31 Ja 6 2014

CASSON, CATHERINE. The entrepreneur in history. See Casson, M.

CASSON, MARK. The entrepreneur in history; from medieval merchant to modern business leader; [by] Mark Casson vii, 139 p. 2013 Palgrave Macmillan

1. Businesswomen—History 2. Capitalists and financiers—History 3. Entrepreneurship—History 4. Historical literature 5. Merchants

ISBN 1137305819 (Hardback); 9781137305817 (Hardback)

LC 2013-478053

SUMMARY: This book, "Covering the period c.1200-c.2000, . . . examines entrepreneurship in a long-run historical perspective, investigating the characteristics of successful entrepreneurs and identifying the conditions which encourage entrepreneurship. The multiple case studies, spanning many sectors, highlight the achievements of a range of individuals, including media moguls, female investors and Quaker chocolate manufacturers." (Publisher's note)

REVIEW: *Choice* v51 no5 p884-5 Ja 2014 C. J. Munson

"The Entrepreneur in History: From Medieval Merchant to Modern Business Leader." "The fourth chapter contains interesting case studies of the entrepreneur throughout recorded history. The early entrepreneurs lent money and facilitated financial transactions for royalty. Their role permutated with historical changes, and now entrepreneurs are seen associated with charities, technologies, and politics. The authors show how at all times the entrepreneur is embedded in the fabric of society. Each chapter ends with a comprehensive bibliography for further study. The book has a complete index but few footnotes. It would work well as supplementary reading for upper-division business classes and as a sourcebook for research."

CASTELLUCCI, CECIL. Tin Star; [by] Cecil Castellucci 240 p. 2013 Roaring Brook Press

1. Human-alien encounters—Fiction 2. JUVENILE FICTION—Social Issues—Adolescence 3. JUVENILE FICTION --Science Fiction 4. Science fiction 5. Space stations—Fiction

ISBN 1596437758; 9781596439146 (ebook); 9781596437753 (hardback)

LC 2013-002600

SUMMARY: In this book by Cecil Castellucci "Tula and her family travel on . . . a colony ship headed to a planet in the outer reaches of the galaxy. All is going well until the ship [stops] at a remote space station . . . and the colonist's leader, Brother Blue, beats Tula. An alien, Heckleck, saves her and teaches her the ways of life on the space station. But just as Tula begins to concoct a plan to get off the space station and kill Brother Blue, everything goes awry." (Publisher's note)

REVIEW: *Booklist* v110 no9/10 p110 Ja 1 2014 Daniel Kraus

REVIEW: *Bull Cent Child Books* v67 no7 p351-2 Mr 2014 A. M.

REVIEW: *Horn Book Magazine* v90 no2 p114 Mr/Ap 2014 TANYA D. AUGER

"Tin Star." "Light years from Earth, on the isolated space station Yertina Feray, fourteen-year-old Tula Bane is beaten to a pulp and abandoned by the charismatic cult leader Brother Blue. After a lengthy stint in the space station's medical bay, Tula must fend for herself. . . . [Cecil] Castellucci's distant future setting is cleverly conceived and satisfyingly consistent. At times, the writing is wonderfully understated and eloquent ('Betrayal and grief have a certain color no matter what the species is'), but then it can veer to clunky and clichéd ('I felt like I'd plunged a knife into my own heart'). Still, it's an imperfection teen readers will easily overlook as they race through the riveting page-turner."

REVIEW: *Kirkus Rev* v81 no23 p193 D 1 2013

REVIEW: *Publ Wkly* v260 no47 p54 N 18 2013

REVIEW: *Quill Quire* v80 no2 p36 Mr 2014 Robert J. Wiersema

"Tin Star". "Cecil Castellucci . . . takes readers to the boundless realm of outer space for a novel that tells not only of aliens and intrigue, but of our fundamental humanity. . . . The multi-talented Castellucci . . . writes with a straightforwardness that belies the complexities of her ideas and world-building. The alien species Tula encounters are never merely set dressing; they are as richly and completely drawn as the human characters. The complications in Tula's life, and the situations in which she finds herself, are also briskly but thoroughly rendered (though the romantic elements in the second half of the book aren't entirely welcome and occasionally edge toward pro forma)."

REVIEW: *SLJ* v60 no2 p101 F 2014 Sunnie Lovelace

REVIEW: *Voice of Youth Advocates* v36 no6 p69 F 2014 Walter Hogan

CASTLE, M. E. Game of clones; [by] M. E. Castle 256 p. 2014 Egmont USA

1. Bullies—Fiction 2. Cloning—Fiction 3. Middle schools—Fiction 4. Reality television programs—Fiction 5. Schools—Fiction 6. Science fiction 7. Scientists—Fiction

ISBN 9781606842348 (hardcover)

LC 2013-018266

SUMMARY: In this installment of the Clone Chronicles series, "Fisher Bas and his much cooler clone, Two, return to life at Wampalog Middle School. . . . Fisher and Two aren't the only Fisher Bas-es in town anymore. Before the boys even have one middle school dance under their belts to revel in their shiny, new, fresh-from-saving-the-world-in-Los-Angeles-hero status, Three turns up in all of his evil, power-hungry glory." (Kirkus Reviews)

REVIEW: *Kirkus Rev* v81 no24 p157 D 15 2013

"Game of Clones". "This third series installment, true to form, teems with goofy gadgetry that will delight young readers and presents a continuingly charming, nerdy protagonist who remains worthy of the special place he's likely earned in the hearts of the series' fans. In a nice turn of events, Two is allowed to really come into his own in this novel, as Fisher is finally forced to introduce him to his parents. . . . Once again, this Clone Chronicles novel strikes just the right balance between over-the-top adventure and real-life middle school drama. A character-driven, action-packed success."

CASTOR, H. M. VIII; [by] H. M. Castor 399 p. 2013 Simon & Schuster Books for Young Readers

1. Hallucinations & illusions 2. Historical fiction 3.

Kings, queens, rulers, etc.—Fiction
ISBN 1442474181; 9781442474185 (hardcover); 9781442474208 (ebook)
LC 2012-021550

SUMMARY: This book is a biography of Henry VIII of England. As a second son, Henry's youth is full of "fighting, jousting and gambling. When his elder brother, Arthur, unexpectedly dies, Hal realizes that . . . he now has a straight line to the throne. However . . . the difficulties of producing a royal heir, together with the thwarting of his overweening military ambition against the French by Spanish Catherine's family and his own . . . advisers cause Henry to become increasingly cynical and desperate." (Kirkus Reviews)

REVIEW: *Bull Cent Child Books* v67 no1 p9 S 2013 E. B.

"VIII." "Adhering closely to historical fact, [author H. M.] Castor explores the life of Henry VIII, imaginatively supplying the personal demons and political exigencies that transformed the historical figure from neglected second son to arrogant, relentless despot. She begins her tale with Henry as a young child, accidentally privy to his indulgent mother's anxieties concerning the death of her two brothers and prophecies that suggest that another claimant threatens her husband's throne. . . . That Castor can bring this fictionalized life to a soul-shaking moment of tragic justice without succumbing to cheesy melodrama is remarkable indeed."

REVIEW: *Kirkus Rev* v81 no12 p83 Je 15 2013

REVIEW: *Voice of Youth Advocates* v36 no5 p54 D 2013 Laura Perenic

CASTRO, ADAM-TROY. Gustav Gloom and The Nightmare Vault; [by] Adam-Troy Castro 232 p. 2013 Grosset & Dunlap

1. Haunted houses—Fiction 2. Horror stories 3. Neighborhoods—Fiction 4. Shadows—Fiction 5. Supernatural—Fiction
ISBN 9780448458342 (pob)
LC 2012-012898

SUMMARY: In this second installment of Adam troy Castro's "Gustav Gloom" series, "Fernie and Gustav find themselves battling another shadowy foe--The Shadow Eater. He is after one thing, The Nightmare Vault, which his master, the evil Lord Obsidian will use to unleash the most terrifying and threatening shadows into the world. As Fernie and Gustav race to stop the Shadow Eater, Fernie learns about Gustav's mysterious past and just what happened to his missing parents." (Publisher's note)

REVIEW: *Horn Book Magazine* v89 no5 p126-7 S/O 2013 Katrina Hedeen

"Gustav Gloom and the Nightmare Vault," "The Sinister Sweetness of Splendid Academy," and "How to Scare the Pants Off Your Pets." "In 'Nightmare,' Fernie discovers more oddities in the spooky house, and she and Gustav go up against a new foe. The enjoyably weird and eerie stories are accompanied by suitably somber drawings. . . . This creepy modern 'Hansel and Gretel' story [The Sinister Sweetness of Splendid Academy] succeeds thanks to a well-paced plot and fluid writing. . . . ['How to Scare the Pants Off Your Pets' is part of Henry Winkler and Lin Oliver's]Ghost Buddy series. . . . There's a lesson here, but it's nicely camouflaged by this third series installment's humorous spirit and witty banter."

REVIEW: *Kirkus Rev* v81 no3 p204 F 1 2013

REVIEW: *SLJ* v59 no7 p78 Jl 2013 Wayne R. Cherry Jr.

CASTRO, JOY.ed. Family trouble. See Family trouble

CASTRO, LIZ.ed. What's up with Catalonia? See What's up with Catalonia?

CATALANOTTO, PETER. Monkey and Robot; [by] Peter Catalanotto 64 p. 2013 Atheneum Books for Young Readers

1. Friendship—Fiction 2. Monkeys—Fiction 3. Robots—Fiction
ISBN 144242978X (hardcover); 9781442429789 (hardcover); 9781442430600 (paperback)
LC 2012-003044

SUMMARY: This children's chapter book, by Peter Catalanotto, presents four stories which follow a monkey and robot who are friends. "They simply belong together, and it never matters that silly Monkey is furry, or that kind Robot can rust. What matters is their sharing: movies and popcorn, games of hide-and-seek, a fish tank for . . . a hippopotamus?" (Publisher's note)

REVIEW: *Kirkus Rev* v82 no1 p206 Ja 1 2014

"More of Monkey & Robot". " Odd-couple friends find the best in each another. . . . Graphite-and-ink illustrations lend a classic feel to the book while supporting characterization by underscoring the winning qualities of Monkey's sweet nature. . . . The collection concludes with a story quietly reminiscent of Laura Vaccaro Seeger's 'Dog and Bear: Two's Company' (2009) as Robot wears himself out trying to gather things needed for breakfast. A strong second outing in this new series for new readers."

CATHER, WILLA, 1873-1947. The selected letters of Willa Cather; [by] Willa Cather 752 p. 2013 Alfred A. Knopf

1. Authors—Correspondence 2. Authors—Family relationships 3. Letters 4. Novelists, American—20th century—Correspondence
ISBN 0307959309 (hardcover); 9780307959300 (hardcover); 9780307959317 (ebook)
LC 2012-036882

SUMMARY: This book is a collection of some of author Willa Cather's personal correspondence. "Beginning with a witty missive written in 1888 when she was only 14, the volume continues through her early years as a successful magazine editor for McLure's, into the 1910s and '20s, when she experienced success as a novelist, all the way through to her death in 1947." (Publishers Weekly)

REVIEW: *America* v210 no6 p33-5 F 24 2014 JON M. SWEENEY

REVIEW: *London Rev Books* v36 no4 p29-30 F 20 2014 Benjamin Lytal

REVIEW: *New Repub* v244 no17 p56-9 O 21 2013 Christopher Benfey

"The Selected Letters of Willa Cather." "Nothing in Cather's letters, frank and readable and (at their bracing best) angry and indignant as they often are, is likely to inspire readers not already so inclined to turn to Cather's sparkling and still arresting novels. . . . It seems likely that Cather wanted her letters, mostly written in haste and on the fly, to remain unpublished for the same reason that she avoided . . . lecturing, reviewing, and interviews: she simply didn't have time. . . .If her letters weren't up to the standard of [Gustav] Flaubert . . . she preferred to keep them secret. The letters do provide a pleasurable meander through Cather's interesting childhood, her very long literary apprenticeship, and her early forays into writing."

CATLING, JO.tr. A place in the country. See A place in the country

CATROW, DAVID.il. Dream dog. See Berger, L.

CATTON, ELEANOR, 1985-. The luminaries; [by] Eleanor Catton 848 p. 2013 Little, Brown and Co.

1. Detective & mystery stories 2. Gold mines & mining—New Zealand 3. Historical fiction 4. New Zealand—History 5. Prostitutes—Fiction

ISBN 0316074314; 9780316074315

LC 2013-941814

SUMMARY: In this book by Eleanor Catton, winner of the 2013 Man Booker Prize, "it is 1866, and Walter Moody has come to make his fortune upon the New Zealand goldfields. He stumbles across a tense gathering of twelve local men, who have met in secret to discuss a series of unsolved crimes. A wealthy man has vanished, a prostitute has tried to end her life, and an enormous fortune has been discovered in the home of a luckless drunk. Moody is soon drawn into the mystery: a network of fates and fortunes." (Publisher's note)

REVIEW: *Kirkus Rev* p10 N 15 2013 Best Books

REVIEW: *Kirkus Rev* v81 no19 p286 O 1 2013

REVIEW: *Libr J* v138 no21 p87 D 1 2013 Shaunna E. Hunter

REVIEW: *N Y Times Book Rev* p17 N 10 2013 BILL ROORBACH

REVIEW: *New York Times* v162 no56299 pC1-6 O 24 2013 JANET MASLIN

REVIEW: *Quill Quire* v79 no10 p12-8 D 2013

REVIEW: *Quill Quire* v79 no8 p24 O 2013 Vit Wagner

"The Luminaries." "It's easy to toss around words like 'potential' and 'promising' when a young author forges the kind of impression made by Eleanor Catton with her 2009 debut, 'The Rehearsal.' . . . 'The Luminaries,' which has already been longlisted for the 2013 Man Booker Prize, would rank as a remarkable achievement for a writer of any age, let alone one still several years shy of her 30th birthday. . . . Catton . . . has surpassed the daring and assurance of her previous effort with a massive, intricate, painstakingly detailed and deliriously readable historical yarn set amid the scrabbling greed of the mid-1860s Hokitika gold rush on New Zealand's South Island."

REVIEW: *TLS* no5759 p23 Ag 16 2013 KATE WEBB

CAUCHON, ANNE MARIE WIRTH. Nothing; [by] Anne Marie Wirth Cauchon 2013 Two Dollar Radio

1. Apocalyptic literature (Christian literature) 2. Internal migrants 3. Montana—Fiction 4. Wildfires 5. Youth & alcohol—Fiction

ISBN 9781937512118 paperback

SUMMARY: "'Nothing,' an edgy debut from [Anne Marie Wirth] Cauchon, follows Bridget and Ruth . . . as they stumble in and out of parties under the influence of booze and pills, not enough food or self-respect, and a vicious anger that manifests in Ruth as something more like desire. Oppressive smoke from nearby wildfires grows ever denser, the story's ticking bomb. . . . Cauchon's characters have serrated edges; they're impossible to like, but they'll get under the reader's skin." (Publisher's note)

REVIEW: *N Y Times Book Rev* p10 D 22 2013 TAO LIN

"Nothing." "Anne Marie Wirth Cauchon's bluntly apocalyptic and psychologically attentive first novel . . . doesn't seem interested in maintaining the illusion that Ruth and James are people, rather than characters. . . . But the distractions resolve, with graceful directness, partly via what appear to be authorial clues. . . . Ruth and James, who take turns narrating the book's brisk chapters . . . , are young drifters who seem to be in their early 20s and have separately left Minneapolis for the valley town of Missoula, Mont."

REVIEW: *Publ Wkly* v260 no34 p41 Ag 26 2013

CAVAFY, CONSTANTINE, 1863-1933. Complete Plus; The Poems of C.P. Cavafy in English; [by] Constantine Cavafy 228 p. 2013 Shearsman Books

1. Literature—Translations 2. Love poetry 3. Modern Greek poetry—Translations into English 4. Poems—Collections 5. Unfinished poems

ISBN 1848612664; 9781848612662

SUMMARY: This collection of poems by C. P. Cavafy, translated by George Economou, "contains 162 poems: the 154 canonical Collected Poems, presented by year and within each year's order of composition and/or first printing, plus seven of the Uncollected Poems interspersed chronologically among them. Only one of his rejected, early poems has been included, 'Ode and Elegy of the Street," used here as a kind of overture to the collection." (Publisher's note)

REVIEW: *World Lit Today* v87 no5 p68 S/O 2013 Richard Beck

"Complete Plus: The Poems of C. P. Cavafy in English." "George Economou, with Stavros Deligiorgis, has translated all the poems Cavafy himself considered canonical, plus eight others, arranged chronologically with brief but helpful notes. The introduction, which culminates decades of thinking about Cavafy, is a worthy companion to the translation. . . . His discussion of 'Cavafy's wide and deep appreciation of the Second Sophistic's devotion to culture and art' is particularly engaging. . . . Economou's imaginative, energetic translation casts plenty of light on Cavafy's Greek. The English of the poems he creates from Cavafy's is so smooth and natural that it is easy to forget that you are reading a translation."

CAWS, MARY ANN. The Modern Art Cookbook; [by] Mary Ann Caws 300 p. 2013 University of Chicago Press

1. Art literature 2. Cookbooks 3. Dinners & dining in art 4. Food in art 5. Food in literature

ISBN 1780231741; 9781780231747

SUMMARY: Written by Mary Ann Caws, "Exploring a panoply of artworks of food, cooking, and eating from Europe and the Americas, 'The Modern Art Cookbook' opens a window into the lives of artists, writers, and poets in the kitchen and the studio throughout the twentieth century and beyond. From the early moderns to the impressionists; from symbolists to cubists and surrealists . . . Mary Ann Caws surveys how artists and writers have eaten, cooked, and depicted food." (Publisher's note)

REVIEW: *TLS* no5777/8 p15-6 D 20 2013 ALEX DANCHEV

"The Modern Art Cookbook" and "Modern Art Desserts." "Connecting the senses is what 'The Modern Art Cookbook' is all about. For Mary Ann Caws, the larger purpose of this delectable anthology is the association of reading, looking and cooking. It is a potpourri (or perhaps a bouillabaisse) of literary texts in verse and prose, recipes and images. . . . 'Modern Art Desserts' is a different kettle of fish--more rambunctious, more delirious, more ingenious; in the end, perhaps, more scrumptious. But only if you like cake. . . . The design of the book is intricate. Each dessert has its own entry: at its headman illustration of the relevant artwork, with a kind of potted biography."

CAYUELA VALENCIA, RAFAEL. The future of the chemical industry by 2050; [by] Rafael Cayuela Valencia xiv, 322 p. 2013 Wiley-VCH

1. Business literature 2. Chemical industry—Environmental aspects 3. Chemical industry—Forecasting 4. Chemical industry—Social aspects 5. Climatic changes
ISBN 352733257X (hd.bd.); 9783527332571 (hd.bd.)
LC 2013-427365

SUMMARY: This book on the chemical industry 'focuses on six megatrends shaping the world: "social, economic, political, energy, climate change, and wild cards" (e.g., war and pandemics). . . . The core chapters are the first one, on megatrends; the third, on the current status of the chemical industry; and the fifth, on the chemical industry in 2050. A sixth chapter draws conclusions." (Choice: Current Reviews for Academic Libraries)

REVIEW: *Choice* v51 no5 p868 Ja 2014 L. W. Fine

"The Future of the Chemical Industry." "[Rafael] Cayuela Valencia's investigation is timely and important for business and industry. . . . Understanding megatrends serves global economic strategies and also defines the lives of individuals because of the reach of the chemical industry, at four trillion dollars in 2011. . . . Written in a comfortable style with fun epigraphs scattered about, the book is unblemished but for the scaled-down graphs and charts that are too hard to read. Offering them online would be helpful. Valuable for those who need to know, now and in the future. . . . Highly recommended."

CECCARELLI, LEAH. On the frontier of science; an American rhetoric of exploration and exploitation; [by] Leah Ceccarelli viii, 210 p. 2013 Michigan State University Press

1. Communication in science 2. Historical literature 3. Research—Social aspects—United States 4. Research—United States 5. Rhetoric 6. Science & rhetoric 7. Scientists—United States
ISBN 9781611861006 (pbk. : alk. paper)
LC 2012-049442

SUMMARY: "'The frontier of science' is a metaphor that has become ubiquitous in American rhetoric, from . . . early twentieth-century American intellectuals and politicians . . . to its more recent use in scientists' arguments in favor of increased research funding. Here, Leah Ceccarelli explores what is selected and what is deflected when this metaphor is deployed, its effects on those who use it, and what rhetorical moves are made by those who try to counter its appeal." (Publisher's note)

REVIEW: *Choice* v51 no8 p1420-1 Ap 2014 R. A. Logan

"On the Frontier of Science: An American Rhetoric of Exploration and Exploitation". "[Leah] Ceccarelli . . . suggests that scientists often present the goals of research using rhetoric similar to that used to justify taming the American West. The author details how competitive scientists and science policy makers want to be the first to 'claim the riches' of a new frontier and often depict research support as a 'manifest destiny.' . . . Ceccarelli's findings are based on a qualitative rhetorical analysis. Helpful footnotes support the text. Part of the 'Rhetoric and Public Affairs' series, the book is a good companion to 'And No Birds Sing: Rhetorical Analyses of Rachel Carson's Silent Spring,' edited by Craig Waddell."

REVIEW: *Science* v343 no6173 p841 F 21 2014 Catherine L. Newell

"On the Frontier of Science: An American Rhetoric of Exploration and Exploitation." "[Author Leah] Ceccarelli . . . explores how the metaphor of the frontier (with its close cousin, the pioneer) has become rooted in American scientific rhetoric. . . . Ceccarelli argues that the frontier metaphor in science changes 'what is selected and what is deflected' in scientific practice--the type of science funded by the government or industry and the sort disdained as too safe. . . . While Ceccarelli limits the scope of her inquiry to the biological sciences, 'On the Frontiers of Science' prompts questions of broader relevance."

CEE-LO (PERFORMER) Everybody's brother; 288 p. 2013 Grand Central Pub.

ISBN 9781455516674 (hardcover); 9781619696358 (audiobk.)
LC 2013-942951

SUMMARY: Author CeeLo Green presents an autobiography. "This story begins in The Dirty South, where South Atlanta's native son transformed himself into the Abominable SHOWman. Along the way, innocence was lost; farther down the path, his parents passed on. Yet he still found family at the Dungeon with the likes of Goodie Mob, Outkast, L.A. Reid, and Lauryn Hill. Then one day he teamed up with Danger Mouse and everything went 'Crazy.' The book "is the untold story of CeeLo Green's rise from the streets of Atlanta to the top of the charts." (Publisher's note)

REVIEW: *Kirkus Rev* v81 no16 p280 Ag 15 2013

"Everybody's Brother." "An entertaining memoir that captures the voice of an artist who hasn't necessarily accomplished enough to warrant the telling of his life story. . . . He made his breakthrough as the singer of Gnarls Barkley's 'Crazy,' which he followed with the viral solo hit known to some as 'Forget You.' He then parlayed that into TV exposure on The Voice. . . . But if the ebullient entertainer born Thomas DeCarlo Burton is mainly a legend in his own mind, he seasons that legend with plenty of spice. . . . For all his grandiosity, CeeLo (who seems to be moving toward single-name status) is a funny guy with a colorful story to share, from his proto-gangster days as a petty criminal in his native Atlanta through his musical redemption."

CEPEDA, JOE.il. Cub's big world. See Cub's big world

CEPEDA, JOE.il. Two bunny buddies. See Galbraith, K. O.

CHABOT, JACOB.il. Hello Kitty; here we go! See Chabot, J.

CHABOT, JACOB. Hello Kitty; delicious!; [by] Jacob Chabot 62 p. 2014 Paw Prints

1. Comic books, strips, etc. 2. Dinners & dining 3. Extraterrestrial life—Fiction 4. Food 5. Hello Kitty (Fictitious character)

ISBN 1480646296; 9781480646292

SUMMARY: This comic book featuring the character Hello Kitty presents "many a food-related escapade. . . . Kicking off with a spicy adventure, Kitty and Thomas find many practical uses for the flames spewing from Thomas' mouth after ingesting a hot chili. . . . One notable tale features an alien abduction send-up, wherein Kitty and her new Martian pal bake a pie that bites back." (Booklist)

REVIEW: *Booklist* v110 no13 p54-5 Mr 1 2014 Courtney Jones

"Hello Kitty: Delicious!." "Kitty and friends have many a food-related escapade in this funny, wordless (excluding well-placed onomatopoeia) follow-up to 'Hello Kitty: Here We Go!' (2013). . . . Endearing interstitials featuring ice cream purchases, jelly-bean counting, and cake-baking forays break up the longer stories. . . . The cleverness of the execution and the bright cheeriness of the design leave plenty more to gush over. Some of the youngest readers might need a little help picking up on background clues and punch lines that might run right past them, but the sweet surprises will entertain everyone following along."

CHABOT, JACOB. Hello Kitty; here we go!; 62 p. 2013 Paw Prints

1. Comic books, strips, etc. 2. Hello Kitty (Fictitious character) 3. Himalaya Mountains 4. Spies 5. Time travel—Fiction

ISBN 1480632635; 9781480632639

SUMMARY: In this comic book, by Jacob Chabot and Jorge Monlongo, the character Hello Kitty "explores an underground realm, moonlights as an international superspy, climbs the Himalayas, travels back in time, and discovers that sometimes, the best place to get away from it all is between the pages of a good book." (Publisher's note)

REVIEW: *Booklist* v110 no11 p50 F 1 2014 Sarah Hunter

REVIEW: *Booklist* v110 no13 p46 Mr 1 2014 SARAH HUNTER

"Hello Kitty: Here We Go!," "Little Lit: Folklore & Fairy Tale Funnies," and "Nursery Rhyme Comics: 50 Timeless Rhymes From 50 Celebrated Cartoonists." "Hello Kitty is cute, cute, cute! And in this collection of short, wordless comics, she spoofs everything from James Bond flicks to Chandleresque noir. Kids won't be able to resist the cheerful, bubbly art, and parents will chuckle over the artists' clever visual jokes. . . . [Art] Spiegelman and his wife, Françoise Mouly . . . invited 15 stellar talents to create original graphic stories that poke often ironic fun at tales. . . . It's an extravagant treat for readers of all ages. . . . Having 50 of the finest cartoonists draw simple nursery rhymes, each no more than two or three pages long, is such a crazy move that it's borderline genius."

CHAD, JON. Leo Geo and his miraculous journey through the center of the earth; [by] Jon Chad 40 p. 2012 Roaring Brook Press

1. Adventure and adventurers—Fiction 2. Geology—Fiction 3. Graphic novels 4. Illustrated children's books 5. Kings, queens, rulers, etc.—Fiction 6. Magic—Fiction

ISBN 9781596436619

LC 2011-017353

SUMMARY: In this book, "the featureless protagonist, an enthusiastic scientist named Leo, sets off on a journey to the center of the Earth through the book's tall pages, and readers are encouraged to turn the book vertically to follow his trek downward. Leo spouts real science facts, but also encounters fantastic creatures in the Earth's mantle at temperatures where nothing ought to be able to survive. Leo uses some big scientific words and even a few wicked-looking math equations, although he is careful to clarify most of what he says for younger audiences." (Publishers Weekly)

REVIEW: *Booklist* v108 no12 p37 F 15 2012 Ian Chipman

REVIEW: *Bull Cent Child Books* v65 no8 p391-2 Ap 2012 E. B.

"Leo Geo: And His Miraculous Journey Through the Center of the Earth." "Just when readers settle in to Leo Geo's adventure as a quirky lesson in geology, [Jon] Chad jolts them abruptly into the realm of sci-fi. . . . Neither evil mantle-dwelling creatures nor fussy Rube Goldbergian devices keep the intrepid Leo Geo from completing his mission. . . . This blend of genre-busting text and richly detailed black-line cartoons, smarty-pants scientific rambling and bizarre adventure, will appeal to kids who wear their nerdiness as a badge of honor."

REVIEW: *Kirkus Rev* v79 no23 p2219 D 1 2011

REVIEW: *Publ Wkly* v258 no45 p71 N 7 2011

REVIEW: *SLJ* v58 no2 p140 F 2012 Catherine Brenner

CHAI, JEAN JULIA.ed. Idea of the temple of painting. See Idea of the temple of painting

CHAIM POTOK; Confronting modernity through the lens of tradition; 2013 Penn State University Press

1. American literature—Jewish authors—History & criticism 2. Jewish authors 3. Jews in literature 4. Literature—History & criticism 5. Potok, Chaim

ISBN 9780271059815 hardcover

SUMMARY: Edited by Daniel Walden, "This collection aims to widen the lens through which we read Chaim Potok and to establish him as an authentic American writer who created unforgettable characters forging American identities for themselves while retaining their Jewish nature. The essays illuminate the central struggle in Potok's novels, which results from a profound desire to reconcile the appeal of modernity with the pull of traditional Judaism." (Publisher's note)

REVIEW: *Choice* v51 no6 p1001-2 F 2014 B. Adler

"Chaim Potok: Confronting Modernity Through the Lens of Tradition." "These critical essays and personal reflections on Potok's work and life will go far in solidifying his reputation as a leading American writer of fiction. . . . Potok's entire oeuvre is covered here, with a particular focus on the novels. . . . The concept of covenant, in its many problematic guises, receives much attention. The last third of the volume comprises personal reflections, eulogies, and interviews (with Potok, in 1982, and with his wife, Adema Potok). . . . Highly recommended."

CHALMERS, MARTIN.tr. Not I. See Fest, J.

CHAMBERS, JOHN. From dust to life. See Mitton, J.

CHAMBERS, MARK.il. Captain of the toilet. See Inserra, R.

CHAMBERS, THOMAS A. Memories of war; visiting battlegrounds and bonefields in the early American republic; [by] Thomas A. Chambers xvi, 232 p. 2012 Cornell University Press

1. Battlefields—United States—History—18th century 2. Battlefields—United States—History—19th century 3. Cemeteries—United States—History—19th century 4. Collective memory—United States—History—19th century 5. Heritage tourism—United States—History—19th century 6. Historical literature 7. Memorialization—United States—History—19th century

ISBN 0801448670 (hardcover); 9780801448676 (hardcover)

LC 2012-013902

SUMMARY: In this book, Thomas A. Chambers "critically describes the development of battlefield tourism over three conflicts, dozens of battlefields, and a century of US history from the Seven Years War to the onset of the 'bloody' Civil War. The centennial of the Revolution countered recent bloody memories by recalling the martial sacrifice of founding conflicts that were to be the basis for a shared nationalism." (Choice)

REVIEW: *Choice* v50 no8 p1503-4 Ap 2013 B. Osborne

REVIEW: *J Am Hist* v100 no1 p192-3 Je 2013 Robert E. Cray

REVIEW: *N Engl Q* v86 no3 p517-9 S 2013 Elise Lemire

REVIEW: *Rev Am Hist* v42 no2 p296-302 Je 2014 Gaines M. Foster

"Memories of War: Visiting Battlegrounds and Bonefields in the Early American Republic" and "Conflicting Memories on the 'River of Death': The Chickamauga Battlefield and the Spanish-American War, 1863-1933." "'Memories of War' and 'Conflicting Memories on the "River of Death"' . . . help historicize current American reverence for battlefields. . . . Despite their differing conceptualizations and time frames, the two books have much in common. Both are well written and solidly researched. They address some of the same issues and put the story of battlefields in larger historic and historiographical contexts, though [author Bradley S.] Keefer does a better job of that than [author Thomas A.] Chambers."

CHAN, CRYSTAL. Bird; [by] Crystal Chan 304 p. 2014 Atheneum Books for Young Readers

1. Family problems—Fiction 2. Grief—Fiction 3. Psychological fiction 4. Racially-mixed people—Fiction 5. Selective mutism—Fiction 6. Superstition—Fiction

ISBN 9781442450899 (hardcover); 9781442450912 (pbk.)

LC 2013-002377

SUMMARY: In this book by Crystal Chan, "Jewel never met her brother. On the day she was born, he tried to fly off a cliff and died. Her parents believe that Grandpa's nickname for his grandson, Bird, caused a bad spirit, a duppy, to trick the boy into believing he could fly. Twelve years later, Grandpa has still not spoken a word." Jewel "meets a boy who calls himself John, her brother's real name. . . . Grandpa thinks John is a duppy in disguise." (School Library Journal)

REVIEW: *Booklist* v110 no7 p66 D 1 2013 Ann Kelley

REVIEW: *Booklist* v110 no18 p69 My 15 2014 Lolly Gepson

REVIEW: *Bull Cent Child Books* v67 no7 p352 Mr 2014 K. C.

"Bird." "[Crystal] Chan has carefully crafted John and Jewel as effective foils for each other; their shared interest in science propels multiple metaphors that help Jewel figure out what is solid and knowable versus what must be taken on faith or intuited. John's family situation also provides an inverted mirror for Jewel's, offering both of them a chance for reflection and growth as they start to assert themselves and insist that their parents stop taking them for granted. Their process is realistically fumbled yet ultimately successful; both character arcs show a deep respect for readers' abilities to negotiate the complexities of belief and doubt, and to find meaning via character reflection."

REVIEW: *Kirkus Rev* v81 no22 p141 N 15 2013

REVIEW: *Publ Wkly* v261 no8 p178-9 F 24 2014

REVIEW: *SLJ* v60 no1 p79 Ja 2014 Clare A. Dombrowski

REVIEW: *SLJ* v60 no5 p64 My 2014 Anne Bozievich

CHAN, EVANS.tr. Angel Island. See Freedman, R.

CHANAN, NOEL. The Photographer of Penllergare; A Life of John Dillwyn Llewelyn 1810-1882; [by] Noel Chanan 276 p. 2013 Impress

1. Art literature 2. Historical literature 3. Llewelyn, John Dillwyn 4. Nobility (Social class)—History 5. Photography—History

ISBN 0957540507; 9780957540507

SUMMARY: This book presents photographs and other artwork by "John Dillwyn Llewelyn, an amateur scientist and pioneering British photographer". Author Noel Chanan has also included "histories . . . of Llewelyn, his extended family, the life of the landed gentry, early photographic processes, and More." (New York Times)

REVIEW: *New York Times* v163 no56407 p22-2 F 9 2014 VICKI GOLDBERG

"The Photographer of Penllergare: A Life of John Dillwyn Llewelyn 1810-1882". "[The book] is graced with an uncommonly generous supply of histories—of Llewelyn, his extended family, the life of the landed gentry, early photographic processes, and more. Photographs, too, are generously supplied, many never seen before, and while Llewelyn's best images impress themselves on eye and mind, the book reproduces a host of family watercolors, drawings, and ephemera that write history in another visual language. . . . On one or two occasions, Noel Chanan's meticulous research may seem like a surfeit of information. Still, the life of this family is instructive on several levels."

CHANDRA, VIKRAM. Geek Sublime; [by] Vikram Chandra 272 p. 2014 Faber & Faber

1. Authorship 2. Computer programming 3. Indic philosophy 4. Literature & technology 5. Philosophical literature

ISBN 0571310303; 9780571310302

SUMMARY: In this book, author "draws . . . parallels between the process of writing computer code and some of the Indian philosophical systems that have profoundly influenced art, literature and poetry in the subcontinent, but which remain largely unknown in the West. . . . It ranges from the intricacies of machine code and the history of logic, to an ancient Indian theorist of poetry, Anandavardhana, and the remarkable algorithmic rules of the Ashtadhyayi." (New Scientist)

REVIEW: *Economist* v410 no8873 p80-1 F 8 2014

"Geek Sublime: Writing Fiction, Coding Software." "The result is partly aesthetic analysis, partly an investigation of linguistic theory, partly a history of programming--and an entirely original work. . . . It takes a while for 'Geek Sublime' to get to its argument. But the wait is worth it. Mr. [Vikram] Chandra's description of how computers work is masterly. . . . The proposition in 'Geek Sublime' is simple, even if the lengthy explanations required to get there are not. If it is possible to write and appreciate poetry and literature in as rule-bound a language as Sanskrit, surely it is possible to do so in code. Alas, concludes Mr. Chandra, it is not. . . . It may not be the conclusion he hoped to reach, but the pleasure of reading repays the effort."

REVIEW: *New Sci* v221 no2957 p52 F 22 2014 Justin Mullins

"Geek Sublime: Writing Fiction, Coding Software". "The book is broad and idiosyncratically engaging. . . The parallels between the Ashtadhyayi and programming today are remarkable and worth exploring. But [Vikram] Chandra's frequent self-indulgent forays into his own writing process are less engaging. His comparisons are fascinating, but his fundamental thesis—that computer code shares the same aesthetic qualities as Sanskrit poetry and literature—is ultimately unconvincing. . . . 'Geek Sublime' may garner a cult following . . . perhaps among the increasingly influential cultural group of Indian programmers. But, while it may inspire, 'Geek Sublime' will frustrate in equal measure."

REVIEW: *New Statesman* v143 no9 p45 Mr 7 2014 Vikram Chandra

REVIEW: *New Yorker* v90 no31 p116-1 O 13 2014

REVIEW: *TLS* no5820 p3-4 O 17 2014 JENNIFER HOWARD

CHANG, JANIE. Three souls; a novel; [by] Janie Chang 496 p. 2014 William Morrow Paperbacks

1. China—History—Civil War, 1945-1949—Fiction 2. Ghost stories 3. Historical fiction 4. Marriage—Fiction 5. Women—China—Social conditions

ISBN 9780062293190 (pbk.)

LC 2013-031946

SUMMARY: In this book by Janie Chang, "set against the Chinese civil war, . . . a young woman's consciousness awakens at her own funeral, surrounded by her three souls: her yin, manifesting as a dancing schoolgirl; her yang, manifesting as an elderly scholar; and her han, manifesting as a silhouette of light. Until she can remember her sins, she cannot ascend to the afterlife. . . . To help her remember, Song Leiyin's souls make her watch her own life unfold again." (Kirkus Reviews)

REVIEW: *Booklist* v110 no9/10 p46 Ja 1 2014 Cortney Ophoff

REVIEW: *Kirkus Rev* v82 no4 p195 F 15 2014

"Three Souls". " Revolutionary and domestic politics collide in this tale of a woman's ghost attempting to understand her life decisions and make amends for her transgressions. Set against the Chinese civil war, [Janie] Chang's debut novel explores the frustrations of intelligent women valued only for beauty and obedience. A young woman's consciousness awakens at her own funeral, surrounded by her three souls. . . . Until she can remember her sins, she cannot ascend to the afterlife and reincarnation; she runs the risk of becoming a hungry ghost, roaming the Earth for eternity. To help her remember, Song Leiyin's souls make her watch her own life unfold again. . . . Historically and politically compelling, yet the three-soul plot device is contrived."

REVIEW: *Publ Wkly* v260 no49 p55 D 2 2013

CHANIN, CLIFFORD.ed. The stories they tell. See The stories they tell

THE CHANSON D'ANTIOCHE; an old French account of the First Crusade; viii, 428 p. 2011 Ashgate

1. Chansons de geste—History and criticism 2. Chansons de geste—Translations into English 3. Crusades—First, 1096-1099—Poetry 4. Crusades in literature 5. Epic poetry, French—History and criticism 6. Epic poetry, French—Translations into English 7. French literature—History & criticism

ISBN 9780754654896 (hbk.); 9781409435709 (ebk.)

LC 2011-015236

SUMMARY: This edition of the "Chanson d'Antioche" offers an "introduction which, firstly, examines the textual history of the poem from its possible oral beginnings through several re-workings to its present form, achieved early in the thirteenth century. A second chapter assesses the 'Chanson's' value as a source for the crusade, and a third considers its status as a literary text. A complete prose translation follows, the first in English and based on the definitive edition." (Publisher's note)

REVIEW: *Engl Hist Rev* v129 no536 p176-8 F 2014 Kevin Lewis

"Letters From the East: Crusaders, Pilgrims and Settlers in the 12th-13th Centuries" and "The chanson d'Antioche: An Old French Account of the First Crusade". "Ashgate's flourishing Crusade Texts in Translation series grows with two very different volumes. . . . The translations are readable without compromising on accuracy and, where potential ambiguity or controversy exists, original terms are supplied in parentheses. . . . The introduction outlines concisely how the letters should, and could, be read. . . . As the translators [of The Chanson d'Antioche] admit, their conclusions often cannot go beyond informed guesswork, but their hypotheses are nonetheless convincing. . . . A structural problem with the book is that the three introductory chapters often tread similar ground, albeit with differing nuances. . . . Nevertheless, this accomplished translation and its thoughtful introduction will certainly prove useful to researchers and undergraduates alike."

REVIEW: *History* v99 no334 p126-8 Ja 2014 Nicholas Vincent

CHANTLER, SCOTT.il. The king's dragon. See Chantler, S.

CHANTLER, SCOTT. The king's dragon; [by] Scott

Chantler 112 p. 2014 Kids Can Press
1. Circus performers—Fiction 2. Courts & courtiers—Fiction 3. Graphic novels 4. Kidnapping—Fiction 5. Knights & knighthood—Fiction
ISBN 1554537797; 9781554537792

SUMMARY: In this graphic novel, written and illustrated by Scott Chantler, part of the "Three Thieves" graphic novel series, "royal knight Capt. Drake . . . briefly catches up with his quarry, Dessa, a young circus acrobat hobbled (but not much) by a broken leg, and also looks back on his early days as a member of the elite but corrupt Dragons." (Kirkus Reviews)

REVIEW: *Booklist* v110 no13 p50-1 Mr 1 2014 Jesse Karp

REVIEW: *Kirkus Rev* v82 no5 p147 Mr 1 2014
"The King's Dragon". "[Scott] Chantler puts his ongoing tale of magic, treachery, kidnapping and hot pursuit largely on pause to fill in some back story on the chief pursuer. . . . In his cleanly drawn action sequences, Chantler ingeniously links present and past with parallel acts or dialogue. . . . The author barely advances his main storyline about Dessa, but he does throw in several new clues and twists while giving readers even more reason to admire this scarred, intelligent, fundamentally decent character. Just a quick side jaunt in the journey, but it's a diversion that adds further depth to a particularly well-wrought tale."

REVIEW: *SLJ* v60 no5 p120 My 2014 Sarah Knutson

CHAPPELL, DAVID. The Kanak awakening; the rise of nationalism in New Caledonia; [by] David Chappell xx, 289 p. 2013 Ctr. for Pacific Islands Stud., School of Pacific & Asian Stud., Univ. of Hawai'i, Mānoa
1. Group identity 2. Historical literature 3. Kanaka (New Caledonian people)—Politics and government 4. Nationalism—New Caledonia
ISBN 0824838181 (cloth: alk. paper); 9780824838188 (cloth: alk. paper)
LC 2013-016765

SUMMARY: This book "covers the emergence of New Caledonian cultural nationalism from the 1960s to the 2010s, although the primary focus is on the 1960s and 1970s. . . . [David] Chappell's study is an analysis of the manner in which indigenous leadership grew, covering its internal tensions and the French reaction. . . . It shows how French colonisation helped unify the Kanaks' indigenous self-identity." (Australian Journal of Politics & History)

REVIEW: *Choice* v51 no9 p1656 My 2014 L. Lindstrom
"The Kanak Awakening: The Rise of Nationalism in New Caledonia". "[David] Chappell's timely history, which draws on archival material and interviews with survivors (Kanaks, long-term French colonists, and new immigrants), updates other accounts of the independence movement, including John Connell's 'New Caledonia or Kanaky?' (1986) and Myriam Dornoy's 'Politics in New Caledonia' (1984). Chappell is particularly useful in teasing out the numerous organizations and parties that the pro- and anti-independence blocs established during these years."

CHAPPELL, DAVID L. Waking from the Dream; The Struggle for Civil Rights in the Shadow of Martin Luther King, Jr.; [by] David L. Chappell 256 p. 2013 Random House Inc
1. African Americans—Civil rights 2. Civil rights movements—United States—History 3. Historical literature 4. King, Martin Luther, Jr., 1929-1968 5. United States—Race relations—History—20th century
ISBN 1400065461; 9781400065462

SUMMARY: In this book on the U.S. Civil rights movement, author David L. Chappell "chronicles the fits and starts of continued efforts at civil rights that are uncelebrated but nonetheless pushed forward [Martin Luther] King's agenda" following his 1968 assassination. "Among those efforts are the campaign for a national holiday to honor King, fair housing legislation and the Humphrey-Hawkins full employment bill . . . and Jesse Jackson's two presidential campaigns." (Booklist)

REVIEW: *Bookforum* v20 no4 p41 D 2013/Ja 2014 JAMELLE BOUIE
"Waking From the Dream: The Struggle for Civil Rights in the Shadow of Martin Luther King, Jr." "It should be said that the subject of [David L.] Chappell's book is something of a challenge to the popular narrative, which holds that the civil rights movement was unable to weather the trauma of King's assassination. In reality, the organizational structure of the movement remained intact after King's death in 1968, with various individuals fighting for prominence and leadership, from Ralph Abernathy--King's designated successor--to King's widow, Coretta Scott King, to young activists such as the Reverend Jesse Jackson."

REVIEW: *Booklist* v110 no4 p5-6 O 15 2013 Vanessa Bush
"Waking From the Dream: The Struggle for Civil Rights in the Shadow of Martin Luther King, Jr." "The assassination of Martin Luther King Jr. in 1968 left the civil rights movement in search of a strong leader and lively debate about how his legacy would be remembered. Civil rights scholar [David L.] Chappell chronicles the fits and starts of continued efforts at civil rights that are uncelebrated but nonetheless pushed forward King's agenda. . . . Chappell details the failed efforts as much as the successes, highlighting the valuable lessons learned as groups and individuals renewed their strategies and determination to move forward."

REVIEW: *Kirkus Rev* v81 no21 p111 N 1 2013

REVIEW: *Libr J* v138 no4 p56 Mr 1 2013 Barbara Hoffert

REVIEW: *Publ Wkly* v260 no45 p62 N 11 2013

CHAPPELL, LAURA. Germany, Poland and the Common Security and Defence Policy; converging security and defence perspectives in an enlarged EU; [by] Laura Chappell xi, 232 p. 2012 Palgrave Macmillan
1. POLITICAL SCIENCE—Government—Comparative 2. POLITICAL SCIENCE—International Relations—General 3. POLITICAL SCIENCE—Political Freedom & Security—General 4. Political science literature
ISBN 9780230292017 (hardback)
LC 2012-022924

SUMMARY: This book, written by Laura Chappell, "offers a comprehensive comparative analysis of an old and a new EU Member State's perceptions of . . . EU security and defence at the beginning of the 21st Century. Utilising a distinct theoretical framework intertwining strategic culture and role theory, this book focuses on change and continuity in Poland and Germany's defence policies . . . through two case studies on the EU Battlegroup Concept and the European Security Strategy." (Publisher's note)

REVIEW: *Choice* v51 no2 p348-9 O 2013 D. N. Nelson
"Germany, Poland, and the Common Security and De-

fence Policy: Converging Security and Defence Perspectives in an Enlarged EU." "Looking back on the history of the Common Security and Defense Policy of the EU, [author Laura] Chappell . . . focuses on two key players--the reunited Germany and the new EU/NATO post-communist member, Poland. Although the book reads rather like a dissertation and does not tell readers much that they would not glean from firsthand literature and reporting, the author tries to set these states' relations within an intellectual framework she calls foreign security policy analysis. . . . However, the book is not for undergraduates, and professionals already understand its points."

CHAPPELL, SHARON VERNER. The arts and emergent bilingual youth. See Faltis, C. J.

CHARBONNEAU, DIANE.ed. Chihuly. See Chihuly

CHARTERS, ANN. Brother-souls; John Clellon Holmes, Jack Kerouac, and the Beat generation; [by] Ann Charters 441 2010 University Press of Mississippi

1. Authors 2. Authors, American 3. Beat generation 4. Essayists 5. Historical literature 6. Novelists 7. Poets
ISBN 978-1-60473-579-6; 1-60473-579-1; 978-1-60473-580-2; 1-60473-580-5
LC 2010--10192

SUMMARY: This book by Ann Charters and Samuel Charters explores the friendship between Jack Kerouac and John Clellon Holmes. "These two ambitious writers . . . shared days and nights arguing over what writing should be, wandering from one explosive party to the next, and hanging on the new sounds of bebop." Topics include "Neal Cassady, Allen Ginsberg, William Burroughs, Gregory Corso, and their friends and lovers." (Publisher's note)

REVIEW: *Am Lit* v83 no4 p878-80 D 2011 Tony Trigilio

REVIEW: *Rev Am Hist* v41 no3 p525-32 S 2013 Ann Douglas

"The Typewriter is Holy: The Complete, Uncensored History of the Beat Generation," "Brother Souls: John Clellon Holmes, Jack Kerouac, and the Beat Generation," and "The Voice is All: The Lonely Victory of Jack Kerouac." "[Bill Morgan's] presentation is mainly chronological; at times he's inattentive to the demands of thematic coherence and pedestrian in style, neutering rather than demythologizing his subjects. . . . Morgan, whatever his shortcomings, is still the most trustworthy, as well as the most profoundly good-natured, of Beat scholars. . . . 'Brother Souls' is strangely, punitively, lopsided--a deliberately partial picture of one man, not two. . . . The hostility is out in the open as never before, and it diminishes an otherwise remarkable achievement. . . . [Joyce] Johnson has turned for the first time to biography, and the result is by far the best book on Kerouac to date."

CHARTERS, SAMUEL. Brother-souls. See Charters, A.

CHARYN, JEROME. I Am Abraham; A Novel of Lincoln and the Civil War; [by] Jerome Charyn 464 p. 2014 W.W. Norton & Co. Inc.

1. American historical fiction 2. Interior monologue 3. Presidents—United States—Fiction
ISBN 0871404273; 9780871404275
LC 2013-041287

SUMMARY: In this book, author Jerome Charyn presents sixteenth U.S. President Abraham Lincoln's story in first person narrative. The book covers ". . . Lincoln's life from his days as a . . . lawyer in Sangamon County, Illinois, through his . . . marriage to . . . Mary Todd, to his 1865 visit to . . . Richmond [Virginia] only days before his assassination." The author mixes historical and fictional characters with Lincoln's own letters and speeches to present his story. (Publisher's note)

REVIEW: *Booklist* v110 no8 p25-6 D 15 2013 Margaret Flanagan

REVIEW: *Kirkus Rev* v81 no23 p169 D 1 2013

REVIEW: *Libr J* v138 no14 p82 S 1 2013

REVIEW: *Libr J* v138 no21 p90 D 1 2013 David Keymer

REVIEW: *N Y Rev Books* v61 no4 p34-5 Mr 6 2014 Andrew Delbanco

REVIEW: *N Y Times Book Rev* p11 F 23 2014 RICHARD BROOKHISER

"I Am Abraham: A Novel of Lincoln and the Civil War." "Jerome Charyn takes the approach of fiction. 'I Am Abraham' is an interior monologue, with Lincoln surveying his own live. . . . Charyn's best touch is Lincoln's voice: thoughtful, observant and droll, good for the long narrative haul. . . . Readers may be surprised by how lewd this Lincoln can be. . . . Charyn's Lincoln is a man of sorrows. . . . What's missing? Lincoln seems to think hardly at all about his writing. . . . Still less credible is the near absence of politics. . . . Where, finally, is God? Lincoln thought about him, off and on, all his adult life, more and more as the war ground on."

REVIEW: *New Yorker* v90 no4 p73-1 Mr 17 2014

REVIEW: *Publ Wkly* v260 no43 p29 O 28 2013

CHASE, ELLA MARCH. The queen's dwarf; a novel; [by] Ella March Chase 384 p. 2014 Thomas Dunne Books

1. Courts and courtiers—Fiction 2. Dwarfs—Great Britain—Fiction 3. FICTION—Historical
ISBN 1250006295; 9781250006295 (hardback)
LC 2013-030262

SUMMARY: This book, by Ella March Chase, is a "historical novel set in the Stuart court featuring . . . Jeffrey Hudson, a dwarf tasked with spying on the . . . queen. It's 1629, and King Charles I and his French queen Henrietta Maria have reigned in England for less than three years. . . . Desperately homesick in a country that hates her for her nationality and Catholic faith, Henrietta Maria surrounds herself with her 'Royal Menagerie of Freaks and Curiosities of Nature.'" (Publisher's note)

REVIEW: *Kirkus Rev* v81 no24 p183 D 15 2013

"The Queen's Dwarf". "Jeffrey witnesses a pageantry of splendor and excess, majesty and corruption, love and betrayal. Yet his own affairs remain restricted to the bonds of family and friends. As tensions rise between Protestants and Catholics, Buckingham and Henrietta Maria vie for Charles' allegiance, and Jeffrey soon finds his own loyalty challenged. Rich in detail and brimming with intriguing characters, Chase's novel will please fans of historical fiction, although the lack of romance may disappoint some."

CHASE, FREDERICK I.ed. The Encyclopedia of Caribbean Religions. See The Encyclopedia of Caribbean Religions

CHAST, ROZ. Can't We Talk About Something More Pleasant?; A Memoir; [by] Roz Chast 240 p. 2014 St. Martin's Press

1. Adult children of aging parents 2. Graphic nonfiction 3. Memoirs 4. Parent & adult child 5. Parents—Death
ISBN 1608198065; 9781608198061

SUMMARY: In this memoir, author Roz Chast "brings her signature wit to the topic of aging parents. Spanning the last several years of their lives and told through four-color cartoons, family photos, and documents, and a narrative as rife with laughs as it is with tears, Chast's memoir is both comfort and comic relief for anyone experiencing the life-altering loss of elderly parents." (Publisher's note)

REVIEW: *Booklist* v110 no18 p43 My 15 2014 Francisca Goldsmith

REVIEW: *Kirkus Rev* v82 no3 p192 F 1 2014

"Can't We Talk About Something More Pleasant? A Memoir". "A revelatory and occasionally hilarious memoir by the New Yorker cartoonist on helping her parents through their old age. Few graphic memoirs are as engaging and powerful as this or strike a more responsive chord. [Roz] Chast . . . retains her signature style and wry tone throughout this long-form blend of text and drawings, but nothing she's done previously hits home as hard as this account of her family life. . . . Chast rarely lapses into sentimentality and can often be quite funny. . . . a series of 12 largely wordless drawings of her mother's final days represents the most intimate and emotionally devastating art that Chast has created."

REVIEW: *Libr J* v139 no5 p103 Mr 15 2014 Martha Cornog

REVIEW: *N Y Times Book Rev* p17 Je 1 2014 ALEX WITCHEL

REVIEW: *New Repub* v245 no13 p60-3 Ag 4 2014 David Hajud

REVIEW: *New York Times* v163 no56493 pC1-6 My 6 2014 MICHIKO KAKUTANI

REVIEW: *Publ Wkly* v261 no4 p34-40 Ja 27 2014

REVIEW: *Publ Wkly* v261 no10 p50 Mr 10 2014

CHATTERJEE, PARTHA. The black hole of empire; history of a global practice of power; [by] Partha Chatterjee xiv, 425 p. 2012 Princeton University Press

1. Black Hole Incident, Calcutta, India, 1756 2. Historical literature 3. Imperialism—History
ISBN 9780691152004 (hardcover : alk. paper); 9780691152011 (pbk. : alk. paper)
LC 2011-028355

SUMMARY: This book "follows the ever-changing representations of this historical event and founding myth of the British Empire in India, from the eighteenth century to the present. [Author] Partha Chatterjee explores how a supposed tragedy paved the ideological foundations for the 'civilizing' force of British imperial rule and territorial control in India." (Publisher's note)

REVIEW: *Choice* v50 no2 p337 O 2012 R. D. Long

REVIEW: *Current Anthropology* v54 no5 p650-3 O 2013 Peter Pels

"The Black Hole of Empire: History of a Global Practice of Power." "'The Black Hole of Empire' is at once a testimony to Partha Chatterjee's love for the city of Calcutta, and its drama and its histories, and a continuation of his path-breaking empirical investigations of political theory. . . . There are . . . indications that the project outlined in Chatterjee's preface became unwieldy. . . . 'The Black Hole of Empire' is, in all its richness or argument and historical detail, a book that no anthropologist, historian, or political theorist of empire can afford to miss."

REVIEW: *History* v99 no335 p299-301 Ap 2014 Catherine Hall

REVIEW: *London Rev Books* v34 no24 p29-30 D 20 2012 Ramachandra Guha

REVIEW: *TLS* no5714 p24 O 5 2012 David Washbrook

CHAUD, BENJAMIN.il. The bear's song. See Chaud, B.

CHAUD, BENJAMIN. The bear's song; 32 p. 2013 Chronicle Books

1. Bears—Fiction 2. Bears—Juvenile fiction 3. Children's stories 4. Fathers and sons—Fiction 5. Fathers and sons—Juvenile fiction
ISBN 1452114242; 9781452114248 (alk. paper)
LC 2012-046877

SUMMARY: Author Benjamin Chaud presents a "immersive picture book about two bears on a big-city adventure. Papa Bear is searching for Little Bear, who has escaped the den. Little Bear is following a bee, because where there are bees, there is honey! When the quest leads both bears into the bustling city and a humming opera house, theatrical hijinks ensue." (Publisher's note)

REVIEW: *Booklist* v110 no8 p41 D 15 2013 Ann Kelley

REVIEW: *Kirkus Rev* p48 N 15 2013 Best Books

REVIEW: *Kirkus Rev* v81 no17 p81 S 1 2013

REVIEW: *Kirkus Rev* p53 N 15 2013 Best Books

REVIEW: *N Y Times Book Rev* p35 D 8 2013

"Boxers and Saints," "Eleanor & Park," and "The Bear's Song." "In ['Boxers' and 'Saints,'] companion graphic novels, [author Gene Luen] Yang . . . tackles the complicated history of China's Boxer Rebellion, using characters with opposing perspectives to explore the era's politics and religion. . . . [In 'Eleanor & Park,' written by Rainbow Rowell,] a misfit girl from an abusive home and a Korean-American boy from a happy one bond over music and comic books on the school bus. . . . [In 'The Bear's Song,' written and illustrated by Benjamin Chaud,] a bear cub chases a bee into the Paris opera house while his father struggles to find him amid the amusing distractions of Chaud's busy scenes."

REVIEW: *Publ Wkly* v260 no35 p57 S 2 2013

REVIEW: *Publ Wkly* p20 Children's starred review annual 2013

REVIEW: *SLJ* v59 no9 p117 S 2013 Teri Markson

REVIEW: *SLJ* v60 no2 p30 F 2014 Brenda Dales

CHAUDHURI, AMIT, 1962-. Calcutta; two years in the city; [by] Amit Chaudhuri 320 p. 2013 Alfred A. Knopf

1. Indic literature 2. Kolkata (India)—History 3. Urban life 4. West Bengal (India)—Politics & government
ISBN 9780307270245

LC 2013-005865

SUMMARY: Author Amit "Chaudhuri guides us through the city where he was born, the home he loved as a child, the setting of his acclaimed novels. . . . He takes us along vibrant avenues and derelict alleyways; introduces us to intellectuals, Marxists, members of the declining haute bourgeoisie, street vendors, domestic workers; brings to life the city's sounds and smells, its architecture, its traditional shops and restaurants, new malls and hotels." (Publisher's note)

REVIEW: *Booklist* v110 no1 p25 S 1 2013 Michael Autrey

REVIEW: *Kirkus Rev* v81 no12 p45 Je 15 2013

REVIEW: *Libr J* v138 no5 p93 Mr 15 2013 Barbara Hoffert

REVIEW: *London Rev Books* v35 no10 p23-4 My 23 2013 Deborah Baker

REVIEW: *N Y Rev Books* v60 no14 p52-3 S 26 2013

REVIEW: *New Yorker* v89 no31 p1 O 7 2013

REVIEW: *Publ Wkly* v260 no21 p45 My 27 2013

REVIEW: *TLS* no5786 p3-4 F 21 2014 SIDDHARTHA DEB

"Calcutta: Two Years in the City." "As Amit Chaudhud writes in his first fully fledged work of non-fiction, 'Calcutta: Two years in the city': 'This city--Kolkata--is neither a shadow of Calcutta, nor a reinvention of it, nor even the same city.' . . . it is his refusal to embrace the change as well as his considered nostalgia for aspects of the old city that gives his book its subject as well as its particular shape and texture. . . . Chaudhuri conducts an elliptical investigation of the city's transformation through a series of loosely linked essays."

REVIEW: *World Lit Today* v87 no6 p75-6 N/D 2013 Graziano Krätli

CHAZDON, ROBIN L. Second growth; the promise of tropical forest regeneration in an age of deforestation; [by] Robin L. Chazdon 472 p. 2014 University of Chicago Press

1. Deforestation 2. Forest conservation 3. Forest ecology 4. Forestry literature 5. Reforestation
ISBN 9780226117911 (cloth: alk. paper); 9780226118079 (pbk.: alk. paper)
LC 2013-033834

SUMMARY: "For decades, conservation and research initiatives in tropical forests have focused almost exclusively on old-growth forests because scientists believed that these 'pristine' ecosystems housed superior levels of biodiversity. With 'Second Growth,' Robin L. Chazdon reveals those assumptions to be largely false, bringing to the fore the previously overlooked counterpart to old-growth forest: second growth." (Publisher's note)

REVIEW: *Science* v344 no6190 p1349 Je 20 2014 Valerie Kapos

"Second Growth: The Promise of Tropical Forest Regeneration in an Age of Deforestation." "In 'Second Growth,' Robin Chazdon expands comprehensively on the question and the answers for a scientific audience and presents a well-argued case for why they matter. . . . The book reflects Chazdon's impressive record of research on, and encyclopedic knowledge of, regenerating tropical forests. It pulls together a huge literature (the references occupy more than 110 pages) on topics ranging from the history of human impacts, through pathways of primary and secondary succession and the factors that influence them, to the drivers of reforestation and the importance of landscape in affecting the course of regeneration."

CHEESMAN, TOM.ed. German text crimes. See German text crimes

CHEEVER, SUSAN. E.E. Cummings; a poet's life; [by] Susan Cheever 240 p. 2014 Pantheon

1. American poetry—20th century—History & criticism 2. Biography (Literary form) 3. Poets, American—20th century—Biography 4. Pound, Ezra, 1885-1972
ISBN 9780307379979
LC 2013-004225

SUMMARY: This book presents a biography of poet e. e. cummings. "Cummings's innovations in poetic form and syntax made him a true original, and his kinship to Ezra Pound placed him in league with a variety of modernists. However, his career moved in fits and starts, ultimately succeeding late in life with the 1938 publication of his Collected Poems, and as a touring reader and lecturer in the '50s and '60s." (Publishers Weekly)

REVIEW: *Booklist* v110 no11 p11 F 1 2014 Donna Seaman

"E. E. Cummings." "[Susan] Cheever incisively dissects Cummings' two disastrous marriages and the shocking abduction of his adored only child, Nancy Thayer, who became an artist and poet unaware of who her father actually was. With Ezra Pound as friend and mentor, Cummings deftly created 'wild, expressive syntax' and wielded his signature lower-case 'i' as critical response ran hot and cold, and ardent fans left flowers on his doorstep. Cheever's reconsideration of Cummings and his work charms, rattles, and enlightens in emulation of Cummings' radically disarming, tender, sexy, plangent, and furious poems."

REVIEW: *Economist* v410 no8875 p1 F 20 2014

REVIEW: *Kirkus Rev* v81 no22 p156 N 15 2013

REVIEW: *Libr J* v138 no14 p86 S 1 2013

REVIEW: *New Yorker* v90 no2 p70-1 Mr 3 2014

REVIEW: *Publ Wkly* v260 no43 p46-7 O 28 2013

CHEMICAL ECOLOGY OF INSECT PARASITOIDS; xv, 312 p. 2013 John Wiley & Sons Inc.

1. Insect-plant relationships 2. Parasitoids 3. Plant chemical ecology 4. Plant parasites 5. Scientific literature 6. Semiochemicals
ISBN 9781118409527 (cloth)
LC 2012-049864

SUMMARY: This book on insect parasitoids examines their use of "intra-- and interspecific chemical production and recognition systems to cue behaviors that aid their survival. . . . Part 2, 'Applied Concepts' (based on the chemical ecology of parasitoids), contains five chapters representing a range of agricultural systems in which prospects for economic impact in the next decade or two appear bleak." (Choice: Current Reviews for Academic Libraries)

REVIEW: *Choice* v51 no5 p865 Ja 2014 M. K. Harris

"Chemical Ecology of Insect Parasitoids." "Recent research shows that insect parasitoids rely heavily on intra- and interspecific chemical production and recognition systems to cue behaviors that aid their survival. This two-part work, with contributions from worldwide experts, provides good coverage of this research. . . . Tabulations and graphics help focus various concepts and aid readers in understanding each chapter. Many cited works were published in the last decade, commensurate with this subject being an emerging field of study. This volume will contribute to future syntheses and help integrate insect parasitoids within chemical and community ecology and, hopefully, eventual strategic applications in pest management programs."

CHEN-MORRIS, RAZ. Baroque science; [by] Raz Chen-Morris xiv, 333 p. 2013 University of Chicago Press

1. Discoveries in science—History—17th century 2. Historical literature 3. Mathematics—History—17th century 4. Optics—History—17th century 5. Science—History—17th century 6. Science—Philosophy—History—17th century

ISBN 9780226923987 (cloth : alk. paper)

LC 2012-043141

SUMMARY: In this book, the authors "examine science in the context of the baroque, analyzing the tensions, paradoxes, and compromises that shaped the New Science of the seventeenth century and enabled its spectacular success. [Ofer] Gal and [Raz] Chen-Morris show how scientists during the seventeenth century turned away from the trust in the acquisition of knowledge through the senses towards a growing reliance on the mediation of artificial instruments." (Publisher's note)

REVIEW: *Choice* v51 no2 p286 O 2013 G. D. Oberle III

REVIEW: *TLS* no5755 p29 Jl 19 2013 NICOLA K. S. DAVIS

"Baroque Science." "[Ofer] Gal and [Raz] Chen-Morris's book shows with some originality how scientists unpicked entrenched beliefs and replaced them with a new science and a new world view. . . . Unfortunately, 'Baroque Science' suffers from a lack of lucidity. Many of the conundrums tackled by these scholars are explained with the help of the original diagrams of their experiments. But the impromptu drawings . . . complete with cryptic notations, are rarely illuminating. For those not deeply familiar with . . . Christiaan Huygens's doodles of cycloids, it requires some impressive mental acrobatics to fathom exactly what they were up to. The result is that the authors dampen the excitement of discovery, turmoil of doubt and fervour of intellectual conviction."

CHEN, ANTHONY S. The fifth freedom; jobs, politics, and civil rights in the United States, 1941-1972; [by] Anthony S. Chen 395 2009 Princeton University Press

1. Affirmative action programs—United States—History—20th century 2. African Americans—Employment—History—20th century 3. Civil rights movements—United States 4. Discrimination in employment—Government policy—United States 5. Historical literature

ISBN 069113457X; 0691139539; 9780691134574; 9780691139531

LC 2009-003503

SUMMARY: The author traces the roots of the policy of affirmative action in employment "to partisan conflicts over fair employment practices (FEP) legislation from the 1940s to the 1970s. . . . Millions of Americans across the country debated whether government could and should regulate job discrimination. Conservatives ultimately prevailed, but their obstruction of FEP legislation unintentionally facilitated the rise of affirmative action." (Publisher's note)

REVIEW: *Contemp Sociol* v43 no1 p16-29 Ja 2014 Edwin Amenta

"The Fifth Freedom:Jobs, Politics, and Civil Rights in the United States, 1941-1972," "Doctors and Demonstrators: How Political Institutions Shape Abortion Law in the United States, Britain, and Canada," and "The Civil Rights Movement and the Logic of Social Change". "[Joseph E.] Luders analyzes a series of civil rights campaigns and policy debates, with business as well as government targets. His cost perspective yields insights about the influence of protest generally. . . With its combination of historical sophistication, astute political analysis, and quantitative examinations of lower-level political battles, this study's venal sins are mainly of omission. . . . [Drew] Halfmann demonstrates his arguments by comparative analyses, process tracing, and within-case analyses across three countries and several decades with meticulous and impressive archival research. His comparative approach cries out for imitation."

CHENEY, RICHARD B., 1941-. Heart; an American medical odyssey; [by] Jonathan Reiner vii, 344 p. 2013 Scribner

1. BIOGRAPHY & AUTOBIOGRAPHY—Medical 2. BIOGRAPHY & AUTOBIOGRAPHY—Presidents & Heads of State 3. Heart—Diseases—Patients—United States—Biography 4. Heart—Transplantation—Patients—United States—Biography 5. MEDICAL—Cardiology 6. Medical literature 7. Myocardial infarction—Patients—United States—Biography 8. Vice-Presidents—United States—Biography

ISBN 9781476725390 (hardcover)

LC 2013-030129

SUMMARY: This book looks at the history of cardiac health care in the U.S. In 1978, when [Vice President Dick Cheney] suffered his first heart attack, he received essentially the same treatment President Eisenhower had had in 1955. Since then, cardiac medicine has been revolutionized, and Cheney has benefitted from nearly every medical breakthrough. At each juncture . . . the technology was one step ahead of his disease. Cheney's story is in many ways the story of the evolution of modern cardiac care." (Publisher's note)

REVIEW: *Kirkus Rev* v81 no22 p247 N 15 2013

REVIEW: *Natl Rev* v66 no4 p46-7 Mr 10 2014 MICHAEL WALSH

"Heart: An American Medical Odyssey". "[A] riveting true-life medical thriller . . . [written] in collaboration with the country's most famous heart patient, former vice president Dick Cheney, and with Liz Cheney, the ex-veep's daughter. . . . 'Heart' is written in alternating sections, taking us through Cheney's entire cardio history, as seen through the eyes of both the patient and the doctor. Much of Cheney's personal story will be familiar to those who read his 2011 memoir. . . . The real interest here is [Jonathan] Reiner's contribution, a lucid and jargon-free recounting of the history of heart surgery."

CHERNESKY, FELICIA SANZARI. Cheers for a dozen ears; a summer crop of counting; [by] Felicia Sanzari Chernesky 32 p. 2014 Albert Whitman & Company

1. Counting 2. Farm produce—Fiction 3. Picture books for children 4. Stories in rhyme 5. Summer—Juvenile literature

ISBN 9780807511305 (hardcover)
LC 2013-027327

SUMMARY: In this children's book, "a mom and two siblings visit a farm stand on a hot summer day. The boy and girl count their way through Mom's list, from 1 watermelon to 12 ears of corn." (Kirkus Reviews)

REVIEW: *Kirkus Rev* v82 no2 p178 Ja 15 2014

"Cheers for a Dozen Ears: A Summer Crop of Counting". " Chernesky's rhymed couplets are uneven, with spry ones undercut by others that employ tired rhymes or sacrifice kid appeal for rhythm. . . . [Susan] Swan's digital-and-cut-paper collages elevate the piece, presenting a riotous harvest of brilliant produce against an azure sky and green fields. The light-brown-skinned children (perhaps Latino) exude good spirits, but Swan—an extraordinary colorist, highly skilled at capturing texture by combining painted, cut paper and digital elements—is not at her best depicting humans. The cheerful but banal faces of people are static and cartoonish throughout. But those onions and peaches? Gorgeous. Nails its seasonal and counting concepts, with both flair and flaws."

REVIEW: *Publ Wkly* v261 no1 p56 Ja 6 2014

REVIEW: *SLJ* v60 no3 p106 Mr 2014 Julie Roach

CHERNILO, DANIEL. The natural law foundations of modern social theory; a quest for universalism; [by] Daniel Chernilo vii, 248 p. 2013 Cambridge University Press

1. Historical literature 2. Natural law—History 3. Natural law—Social aspects 4. Philosophical literature 5. Social theory
ISBN 1107009804; 9781107009806 (hardback)
LC 2012-027742

SUMMARY: This book by Daniel Chernilo "reassesses the universalistic orientation of social theory and explains its origins in natural law theory, using an impressive array of classical and contemporary sources that include, among others, Jürgen Habermas, Karl Löwith, Leo Strauss, Weber, Marx, Hegel, Rousseau and Hobbes." (Publisher's note)

REVIEW: *Choice* v51 no1 p171 S 2013 Y. R. Magrass

"The Natural Law Foundations of Modern Social Theory: A Quest for Universalism." "Is the theorist's vision of how people should live simply a personal choice or part of something dictated by nature or god? Although this debate may appear modern, especially when put in scientific language, it is old, and [author Daniel] Chernilo . . . traces it from the Judeo-Christian Bible through Plato and Aristotle to Hobbes, Rousseau, Kant, Hegel, Marx, Weber, Durkheim, and post-WW II social theorists. The author does not really take a clear position of his own, but his purpose is to elucidate the issues, providing a context for examining classical and contemporary social theorists helpful to both experts and novices."

CHEVAILLIER, FLORE. The body of writing; an erotics of contemporary American fiction; [by] Flore Chevaillier x, 161 p. 2013 Ohio State University Press

1. American fiction—History and criticism—Theory, etc 2. English language—Style 3. Literature—History & criticism 4. Reading 5. Semiotics and literature
ISBN 0814212174 (cloth : alk. paper); 9780814212172 (cloth : alk. paper); 9780814293188 (cd)
LC 2012-041520

SUMMARY: This book "examines four postmodern texts whose authors play with the material conventions of 'the book': Joseph McElroy's 'Plus' (1977), Carole Maso's 'AVA' (1993), Theresa Hak Kyung Cha's 'DICTEE' (1982), and Steve Tomasula's 'VA' (2003). By demonstrating how each of these works calls for an affirmative engagement with literature, Flore Chevaillier explores a centrally important issue in the criticism of contemporary fiction." (Publisher's note)

REVIEW: *Choice* v51 no5 p831-2 Ja 2014 E. L. Battistella

"The body of Writing: An Erotics of Contemporary American Fiction." "In this compact revision of her PhD dissertation, [Flore] Chevaillier . . . examines the rhetorical apparatus of experimental fiction by analyzing four books that play with their own materiality. . . . Along the way, Chevaillier demystifies experimental texts and their relationship to pleasure; she makes especially fine use of 27 illustrations from the texts, showing authors' uses of image, print, sound, page, orthography, and syntax. Well argued and clearly written, the book will be of most interest to literary scholars, creative writers, and poets."

CHEW, ELIZABETH V. Thomas Jefferson; a day at Monticello; [by] Elizabeth V. Chew 56 p. 2013 Abrams Books For Young Readers Thomas Jefferson Foundation

1. Historical literature 2. Jefferson, Thomas, 1743-1826 3. Slavery—United States
ISBN 9781419705410
LC 2012-010023

SUMMARY: This book "reconstructs the septuagenarian [Thomas] Jefferson's active daily round" at his estate, Monticello. "Jefferson's fixed routine begins with a faithful recording of temperature and weather at first rising and ends with a final period of solitary reading by candlelight in his unusual alcove bed. In between, the author describes . . . the range of his interests and enterprises." (Kirkus Reviews)

REVIEW: *Booklist* v110 no13 p62-3 Mr 1 2014 Carolyn Phelan

REVIEW: *Kirkus Rev* v82 no2 p268 Ja 15 2014

"Thomas Jefferson: A Day at Monticello". "Stepping carefully around the controversies, a former curator at Monticello reconstructs the septuagenarian Jefferson's active daily round. . . . The author describes in often fussy detail the range of his interests and enterprises. . . . Like the dialogue, which mixes inventions with historical utterances, the generous suite of visuals includes photos of furnishings and artifacts as well as stodgy full-page tableaux and vignettes painted by [Mark] Elliott."

REVIEW: *SLJ* v60 no4 p185 Ap 2014 Maggie Chase

CHIANTORE, OSCAR. Conserving contemporary art; issues, methods, materials, and research; [by] Oscar Chiantore 327 p. 2012 Getty Conservation Institute

1. Art—Conservation & restoration 2. Art deterioration 3. Art, Modern—20th century—Conservation and restoration 4. Art, Modern—21st century—Conservation and restoration 5. Modern art museums 6. Museum conservation methods 7. Museum studies literature
ISBN 1606061046; 9781606061046 (pbk.)
LC 2012-020854

SUMMARY: Author Oscar Chiantore's book provides "a comprehensive overview of the many considerations faced by the conservator of modern and contemporary art. The book takes into account both the material and ethical aspects of contemporary art, focusing on the enormous variety of techniques and materials used by contemporary artists, as well as on their deterioration. It also emphasizes the need to understand the meaning of these works when devising an appropriate conservation strategy." (Publisher's note)

REVIEW: *Choice* v51 no1 p62 S 2013 E. K. Mix

"Conserving Contemporary Art: Issues, Methods, Materials, and Research." "Since the 1960s, artists have increasingly worked with ephemeral materials (including food, polyurethane foam, and plastics); have mixed materials that create chemical instabilities; and also have continued the traditional application of multiple layers of varnish, which discolor over time. . . . This volume by [Oscar] Chiantore . . . and conservator [Antonio] Rava has short chapters dedicated to pertinent issues (new materials, methodological problems, degradation), techniques (cleaning, inpainting, visual reintegration), and conservation of installation art, conceptual art, and Internet art."

CHIARENZA, CARL. Transmutation; Photographic Works by Carl Chiarenza; [by] Carl Chiarenza 62 p. 2012 Ub Art Gallery

1. Abstract art 2. Abstract photography 3. Art & philosophy 4. Photographs 5. Photography—Philosophy

ISBN 0984251847; 9780984251841

SUMMARY: This book, featuring photography by Carl Chiarenza and an essay by Robert Hirsch, documents "the evolution of the artist's photography, exploring how his tightly framed, documentary-style images from the 1960s and 70s present a vocabulary of abstraction that would be further developed in his ongoing series of photographed collages, started in the 1979, constructed from scrap materials." (Publisher's note)

REVIEW: *Choice* v51 no1 p66-7 S 2013 J. Natal

"Transmutation: Photographic Works by Carl Chiarenza." "In light of the recent resurgence of interest in abstraction in photography, Chiarenza's catalogue is particularly timely and worthy of celebration. . . . Chiarenza . . . builds visual metaphors that allude to the great mysteries of life, and psychological states of being, reminding viewers that photography is always open to a multiplicity of meanings. . . . The exhibition was organized by photographer and writer [Robert] Hirsch, who wrote the exceptionally informative essay shining light on Chiarenza's creative process and metaphysical concepts."

CHICO, BEVERLY. Hats and headwear around the world; a cultural encyclopedia; [by] Beverly Chico xxiii, 531 p. 2013 ABC-CLIO

1. Encyclopedias & dictionaries 2. Hats—Encyclopedias 3. Hats—Social aspects 4. Headgear—Encyclopedias 5. Headgear—History

ISBN 9781610690621 (hardcopy: alk. paper)

LC 2013-011508

SUMMARY: This reference book on hats and headwear, by Beverly Chico, "examines topics from ancient times to the modern era, providing not only detailed physical descriptions and historical facts but also information that addresses cultural significance, religion, historical events, geography, demographic and ethnic issues, fashion, and contemporary trends." (Publisher's note)

REVIEW: *Booklist* v110 no13 p32 Mr 1 2014 Asia Gross

REVIEW: *Choice* v51 no9 p1570 My 2014 C. Stevens

"Hats and Headwear Around the World: A Cultural Encyclopedia". This book on headwear by [Beverly] Chico . . . presents the author's highly personal and idiosyncratic examination of the subject of hats and head coverings. . . . Given this book's subtitle, it is puzzling that popular culture did not make the list. The audience for this book is not clear. Encyclopedias should be arranged in highly logical ways or have excellent indexes. . . . There are enough gaps here to give one pause, and the index is very poorly arranged."

REVIEW: *Libr J* v139 no2 p96 F 1 2014 Judy Quinn

CHIEN, CATIA.il. My blue is happy. See Young, J.

CHIHULY; 230 p. 2013 Montreal Museum of Fine Arts; DelMonico Books, an imprint of Prestel

1. Art literature 2. Artistic collaboration 3. Glass art—20th century—Exhibitions 4. Glass art—21st century—Exhibitions

ISBN 2891923685; 3791353241; 9782891923682 (Montreal Museum of Fine Arts); 9783791353241 (Del Monico Books/Prestel)

LC 2012-277913

SUMMARY: In this book on artist Dale Chihuly, the authors "examine Chihuly's personal and artistic development, working environment and collections, and collaborative working methods, in addition to recognizing Chihuly's important achievements and contributions to craft and art history." Particular focus is given to his studio glass artwork. "Also included are Chihuly's energetic acrylic paintings and innovative burned drawings." (Choice)

REVIEW: *Choice* v51 no5 p819 Ja 2014 C. A. Ventura

"Chihuly". "The full-page color photographs of vibrant blown and fabricated studio glass in this oversized book . . . are mesmerizing. Captivating essays by editor [Diane] Charbonneau . . . Nathalie Bondil . . ., and three invited curators (Davira Taragin, Timothy Anglin Burgard, and Gerald W. R. Ward) provide visual relief and critical context. . . . [Dale] Chihuly's own words lend authenticity to the engaging text and provide insight into the man behind the persona. This volume effectively presents the Neon, Cylinders, Baskets, Seaforms, Macchia, Persians, Venetians, Putti, Ikebana, Floats, Chandeliers, Towers, and Mille Fiori series, revealing the inspiration and evolution of the brilliantly hued, bold organic forms."

CHILDERS, JAY P. Political tone. See Hart, R. P.

CHIN, CARL.il. Inside and out. See Vermond, K.

CHIN, JASON. Gravity; [by] Jason Chin 32 p. 2014 Roaring Brook Press

1. Distances 2. Earth (Planet)—Gravity 3. Gravity—Juvenile literature 4. Mass (Physics) 5. Picture books for children

ISBN 1596437170; 9781596437173 (hardcover)

LC 2013-001634

SUMMARY: This children's book, by Jason Chin, focuses on gravity. The book will answer children's questions such as: "What keeps objects from floating out of your hand? What if your feet drifted away from the ground? What stops everything from floating into space?" It is aimed at children from age 5 to 8. (Publisher's note)

REVIEW: *Booklist* v110 no16 p45 Ap 15 2014 Carolyn Phelan

REVIEW: *Bull Cent Child Books* v67 no9 p439-40 My 2014 Elizabeth Bush

"Gravity". "So far this sounds like the sort of mind-bending fantasy that will appeal to fans of David Wiesner. And it is, but [Jason] Chin is also a dab hand at blending imagination with information. . . . It will come as no surprise that his universe-disturbing 'Gravity' . . . delivers a solid science lesson. . . . Kids ready for a more traditional scientific treatment can share with an adult reader the double-page spread of brief paragraphs that pursue the relationship between mass, distance, and gravitational force, as well as how weight becomes 'the measure of Earth's gravity pulling on objects.' Concise diagrams and tongue-in-cheek pictures that accompany the instruction are as entertaining as they are effective."

REVIEW: *Horn Book Magazine* v90 no3 p107-8 My/Je 2014 ROGER SUTTON

REVIEW: *Kirkus Rev* v82 no4 p116 F 15 2014

REVIEW: *Publ Wkly* v261 no4 p195 Ja 27 2014

REVIEW: *SLJ* v60 no3 p171 Mr 2014 Katy Charles

CHISHOLM, P. F. An air of treason, an; [by] P. F. Chisholm 250 p. 2014 Poisoned Pen Press

1. Detective & mystery stories 2. Elizabeth I, Queen of England, 1533-1603 3. Great Britain—Politics & government—1485-1603 4. Monmouth, Robert Carey, 1st Earl of, 1560?-1639 5. Murder investigation—Fiction
ISBN 9781464202209 (hardcover: alk. paper); 9781464202223 (trade pbk: alk. paper)
LC 2013-941236

SUMMARY: In this book, "Sir Robert Carey has finally tracked down Queen Elizabeth, who is about to make a state visit to Oxford. But instead of giving the Courtier his much-needed warrant and fee for being Deputy Warden of the West March with Scotland, Her Majesty orders him to investigate the most dangerous cold case of her reign—the mysterious 1560 death of Amy Dudley (née Robsart), unloved wife of Robert Dudley, Earl of Leicester." (Publisher's note)

REVIEW: *Kirkus Rev* v82 no2 p270 Ja 15 2014

"An Air of Treason". "A most difficult and dangerous murder inquiry is forced upon a flamboyant nobleman. Sir Robert Carey, the son of Lord Chamberlain Hunsdon, illegitimate half brother of Elizabeth I, is seeking out the queen to obtain his warrant and fee for serving as deputy warden of the West March. Elizabeth's royal progress has taken her to Oxford, and when Carey arrives there, the queen orders him to investigate the death of Amy Robsart Dudley, wife of the love of Elizabeth's life, Robert Dudley, Earl of Leicester. . . . Carey's sixth adventure . . . is packed with historical detail, dangerous exploits and humor. The fact-based mystery moves along at a fairly quick pace to a complicated denouement."

REVIEW: *Libr J* v139 no4 p73 Mr 1 2014 Teresa L. Jacobsen

CHIU, MONICA.ed. Diversity in diaspora. See Diversity in diaspora

CHOMSKY, NOAM, 1928-. Power systems; conversations on global democratic uprisings and the new challenges to U.S. empire; [by] Noam Chomsky 224 p. 2013 Henry Holt & Co

1. Arab Spring, 2010- 2. Democratization—Arab countries—History—21st century 3. HISTORY—Modern—21st Century 4. Occupy movement—History—21st century 5. POLITICAL SCIENCE—International Relations—General 6. Political science literature 7. Protest movements—History—21st century 8. Revolution—History—21st century
ISBN 0805096159; 9780805096156 (pbk.)
LC 2012-035686

SUMMARY: This book by Noam Chomsky is a "collection of conversations [with David Barsamian], conducted from 2010 to 2012, [in which] Chomsky explores the most immediate and urgent concerns: the future of democracy in the Arab world, the implications of the Fukushima nuclear disaster, the European financial crisis, the breakdown of American mainstream political institutions, and the rise of the Occupy movement." (Publisher's note)

REVIEW: *Kirkus Rev* v80 no20 p207 O 15 2012

REVIEW: *Publ Wkly* v260 no12 p64 Mr 25 2013

REVIEW: *Publ Wkly* v259 no45 p60 N 5 2012

REVIEW: *TLS* no5754 p25 Jl 12 2013 TOBY LICHTIG

"Power Systems: Conversations With David Barsamian on Global Democratic Uprisings and the New Challenges to US Empire." "[David] Barsamian is a prompter rather than an interrogator, his style staccato and taciturn. He keeps his voice out of the dialogue and his name off the front cover. This may suit [Noam] Chomsky, whose capacity for diatribe remains undimmed; but it can also be a drag on the reader. There are times when you wish the interviewer would challenge his interlocutor. . . . He notes the importance of oil to the 2003 invasion of Iraq, though his belief that 'Saddam Hussein would have been overthrown from within' is debatable at best."

CHORAO, KAY.il. Ed and Kip. See Chorao, K.

CHORAO, KAY. Ed and Kip; [by] Kay Chorao 32 p. 2014 Holiday House

1. Animal stories 2. Elephants—Fiction 3. Jungle animals—Fiction 4. Play—Fiction 5. Rocks—Fiction
ISBN 0823429032; 9780823429035 (hardcover)
LC 2012-045920

SUMMARY: This children's book, written and illustrated by Kay Chorao, focuses on the adventures of two elephants and their insect friend. "When elephants Ed and Kip get into mischief, their friend Bug uses some quick thinking [and] . . . big brains . . . to get them out of Crocodile's pond . . . [and] save the day!" (Publisher's note)

REVIEW: *Kirkus Rev* v82 no2 p264 Ja 15 2014

"Ed and Kip". "[Kay] Chorao's charming watercolor illustrations depict the appealing pachyderm pair as they frolic and stroll through a colorful rain forest, while simple text, closely tied to the pictures, gives just the right amount of repetition for young readers and succinctly describes the elephants' adventures. . . . The format works well as an early reader or a picture book for the very young, and the comic-book-type panels and dialogue bubbles will attract fans of that genre as well. . . . An engaging tale of friendship, play and cooperation, replete with mild suspense and gentle humor."

REVIEW: *SLJ* v60 no3 p106 Mr 2014 Mary Jean Smith

CHOYCE, LESLEY. Jeremy Stone; [by] Lesley Choyce 216 p. 2014 Red Deer Press

1. Friendship—Fiction 2. Native American teenagers 3. Novels in verse 4. School bullying 5. Spirits

ISBN 0889955042; 9780889955042

SUMMARY: "In this novel-in-verse, sixteen-year-old troubled loner Jeremy Stone is a First Nations teenager whose ties to the spirit world guide him through his real-world hostile academic environment and broken home. In a Caucasian school, Jeremy confronts racist bullies and is befriended by the intense Caitlin, who cuts herself and mourns her previous boyfriend whom she claims bullies drove to suicide." (VOYA Reviews)

REVIEW: *Bull Cent Child Books* v67 no9 p447 My 2014 K. C.

REVIEW: *Kirkus Rev* v82 no3 p301 F 1 2014

"Jeremy Stone". "[Lesley] Choyce's novel traverses the difficult landscapes of identity, depression, violence, parental struggles, substance abuse, bullying, cutting and suicide with the brilliant accessibility of free verse, which may have particular appeal to reluctant readers. Jeremy's shamanlike gift to navigate between real and spirit worlds leads him to conclude that 'what is real to us / is what we believe is real.' Few would disagree, though readers' journeys to that conclusion become difficult in the final third of the book, as the account loses focus and begins to meander. Despite a disappointing ending, an intricate story that opens up the universe of troubled silence."

REVIEW: *Voice of Youth Advocates* v37 no1 p62-3 Ap 2014 Lucy Schall

CHRISMAN, SARAH A. Victorian secrets; what a corset taught me about the past, the present, and myself; [by] Sarah A. Chrisman 264 p. 2013 Skyhorse Pub., Inc.

1. Corsets—History 2. Corsets—Social aspects 3. Historical literature 4. Women's clothing—History 5. Women's clothing—Symbolic aspects

ISBN 9781626361751 (alk. paper)

LC 2013-030246

SUMMARY: In this book on corsets, author Sarah A. Chrisman "explains how a garment from the past led to a change in not only the way she viewed herself, but also the ways she understood the major differences between the cultures of twenty-first-century and nineteenth-century America. The desire to delve further into the Victorian lifestyle provided Chrisman with new insight into issues of body image and how women, past and present, have seen and continue to see themselves." (Publisher's note)

REVIEW: *New York Times* v163 no56330 p12 N 24 2013 LAREN STOVER

"Victorian Secrets: What A Corset Taught Me About the Past, the Present, and Myself." "Nothing about [the book] is racy. The most suggestive phrase the author uses to describe her newfound silhouette is 'showed off my figure to full advantage.' . . . Opinions [on corsets] are mixed, and Ms. Chrisman seeks to debunk the taboos. . . . She emphasized, again, that the corset to her is 'strictly underwear' and that she sees herself as 'a lady and not a vixen'. Not that there would be anything wrong with that, of course. 'The vibrator was invented in the Victorian era,' Ms. Chrisman said. 'People forget that.'"

CHRISTELOW, EILEEN. Five little monkeys trick-or-treat; [by] Eileen Christelow 40 p. 2013 Clarion Books

1. Babysitters—Fiction 2. Behavior—Fiction 3. Costume—Fiction 4. Halloween—Fiction 5. Monkeys—Fiction 6. Picture books for children

ISBN 9780547858937 (hardcover)

LC 2012-025208

SUMMARY: In this children's picture book by Eileen Christelow, "it's Halloween, and the five little monkeys are eager to trick-or-treat. With Lulu, the babysitter, as the group's chaperone, the monkeys venture into the night and encounter several costumed friends. Mischief ensues as the trick-or-treaters swap outfits in a furtive masquerade. The little monkeys' mother, however, has the last laugh." (Horn Book Magazine)

REVIEW: *Booklist* v109 no22 p87 Ag 1 2013 Edie Ching

REVIEW: *Horn Book Magazine* v89 no5 p64 S/O 2013 LILY ROTHMAN

"Five Little Monkeys Trick-or-Treat." "It's Halloween, and the five little monkeys are eager to trick-or-treat. With Lulu, the babysitter, as the group's chaperone, the monkeys venture into the night and encounter several costumed friends. . . . Playfully illustrated with a colorful parade of animals and disguises, [Eileen] Christelow's latest Five Little Monkeys volume has none of Halloween's horror and gloom. Instead, the book is a lighthearted farce, and bonus recipes for 'Lulu's Eyeball Cookies' and 'Worm Juice' should put readers in a festive mood."

REVIEW: *Kirkus Rev* v81 no15 p14 Ag 1 2013

REVIEW: *Publ Wkly* v260 no29 p66 Jl 22 2013

REVIEW: *SLJ* v59 no6 p78 Je 2013 Maryann H. Owen

CHRISTENSEN, MARK Z. Nahua and Maya Catholicisms; texts and religion in colonial central Mexico and Yucatan; [by] Mark Z. Christensen 318 p. 2013 Stanford University Press and The Academy of American Franciscan History, Berkeley, California

1. Aztecs—Religion 2. Christianity and culture—Mexico—History 3. Christianity and other religions—Mexico—History 4. Historical literature 5. Imperialism & religion 6. Indian Catholics—Mexico—History 7. Mayas—Religion 8. Nahuas—Religion 9. Religious literature, Spanish—Translations into Maya 10. Religious literature, Spanish—Translations into Nahuatl

ISBN 9780804785280 (alk. paper)

LC 2012-043584

SUMMARY: This book, by Mark Z. Christensen, "examines ecclesiastical texts written in Nahuatl and Yucatec Maya to illustrate the role of these texts in conveying and reflecting various Catholic messages--and thus Catholicisms--throughout colonial Central Mexico and Yucatan. . . . The book's study of these texts also allows for a better appreciation of the negotiations that occurred during the evangelization process between native and Spanish cultures." (Publisher's note)

REVIEW: *Choice* v51 no2 p330-1 O 2013 V. H. Cummins

"Nahua and Maya Catholicisms: Texts and Religion in Colonial Central Mexico and Yucatan." "This well-written, well-documented book adds to the contributions of scholars like Louise Burkhart . . . and David Tavárez . . . to help in understanding the origins and nature of indigenous religious beliefs and practices in colonial Mexico. Historian [Mark Z.] Christensen . . . takes a comparative approach, analyzing published and unpublished religious texts written in Nahuatl and Maya over a 300-year period. He emphasizes the differences not only between indigenous Catholicism in central Mexico and the Yucatan, but also within Nahuatl and Maya-speaking populations across place and time."

CHRISTIANSEN, RUPERT. I Know You're Going to be Happy; The Story of a Sixties Family; [by] Rupert Christiansen 176 p. 2013 Short Books Ltd

1. Children of divorced parents 2. Divorce 3. Memoirs 4. Runaway husbands 5. Single mothers

ISBN 1780721242; 9781780721248

SUMMARY: This memoir by Rupert Christiansen tells the story of his parents' divorce. "Two rising joumalists fall in love, marry, and soon after their second child is bom, the husband announces he is in love with his secretary and moves out. The ensuing gladiatorial engagement inflicts permanent wounds on both mother and son. . . . To recapture his father's voice and personality he tums to the trove of letters his father wrote as a young man to his own father." (Times Literary Supplement)

REVIEW: *TLS* no5749 p27 Je 7 2013 TERRI APTER

"I Know You're Going to Be Happy: A Story of Love and Betrayal." "This memoir offers a sharp and atmospheric social history alongside a haunting, original account of the enduring puzzlement of parental betrayal; but the portrayal of the primary players in the drama is pocked and disjointed. [Rupert] Christiansen describes his mother as a furious Medea, yet offers no evidence of any harmful intent to her children. He exposes his raw need to forge links to his father, yet claims that he is devoid of feeling for, or interest in him. What is missing from this superb short book is a final section in which Christiansen might bravely puzzle over such fissures."

CHRISTIE, DOUGLAS E. The blue sapphire of the mind; notes for a contemplative ecology; [by] Douglas E. Christie p. cm. 2013 Oxford University Press

1. Contemplation 2. Ecotheology 3. Nature—Religious aspects—Christianity 4. Religious literature 5. Spiritual life—Christianity

ISBN 9780199812325 (alk. paper)

LC 2012-019801

SUMMARY: In this book, "Douglas E. Christie proposes a distinctively contemplative approach to ecological thought and practice. . . . Drawing on the insights of the early Christian monastics as well as the ecological writings of Henry David Thoreau, Aldo Leopold, [and] Annie Dillard . . . Christie argues that . . . it is the quality of our attention to the natural world that must change if we are to learn how to live in a sustainable relationship with other living organisms and with one another." (Publisher's note)

REVIEW: *Christ Century* v130 no8 p38-9 Ap 17 2013 Mark S. Burrows

REVIEW: *J Am Acad Relig* v82 no1 p248-50 Mr 2014 Colleen Mary Carpenter

"The Blue Sapphire of the Mind: Notes for a Contemplative Ecology". "Douglas Christie has written a book that is at once beautiful and scholarly, both lyrical in its prose and impressive in its erudition. He joins together a deep knowledge of the ancient Christian monastic tradition and a wide-ranging command of modern/contemporary literature on ecology, nature, and the human place in creation to create a powerful argument that we will not escape our current ecological crisis without confronting our need for spiritual transformation. . . . 'The Blue Sapphire of the Mind' is a book to savor, a book full of surprising connections and beautiful images, and absolutely a book that leaves the reader with newfound hope about the future of our broken, beloved Earth."

REVIEW: *Publ Wkly* v259 no46 p58 N 12 2012

CHRISTIE, R. GREGORY.il. Philip Reid saves the statue of freedom. See Lapham, S. S.

CHRISTIE, R. GREGORY.il. Sugar Hill. See Weatherford, C. B.

CHRISTMAS, JANE. And Then There Were Nuns; Adventures in a Cloistered Life; [by] Jane Christmas 304 p. 2013 Pgw

1. Church of England 2. Convents 3. Memoirs 4. Nuns 5. Vocation (in religious orders, congregations, etc.)

ISBN 1553657993; 9781553657996

SUMMARY: In this memoir, "just as Jane Christmas decides to enter a convent in mid-life to find out whether she is 'nun material,' her long-term partner Colin, suddenly springs a marriage proposal on her. Determined not to let her monastic dreams be sidelined, Christmas puts her engagement on hold and embarks on an extraordinary year long adventure to four convents--one in Canada and three in the UK." (Publisher's note)

REVIEW: *Booklist* v110 no6 p18 N 15 2013

REVIEW: *Booklist* v110 no2 p6 S 15 2013 Hene Cooper

"And Then There Were Nuns: Adventures in a Cloistered Life." "[Jane] Christmas takes readers along on a thought-provoking (and often amusing) journey to four . . . cloistered communities in Great Britain, as she tries to make her life-changing decision over the course of many months. . . . Although she writes with a light touch, Christmas girds the narrative with solid questions. . . . This is the best kind of memoir, revealing, refreshing, and reflective enough to make readers turn many of the questions on themselves. A delightful trip down the road less traveled."

REVIEW: *Quill Quire* v79 no8 p33 O 2013 Suzanne Gardner

CHRISTOFF, PETER. Globalization and the environment; [by] Peter Christoff 256 p. 2013 Rowman & Littlefield Pub Inc

1. Climatic changes 2. Environmental literature 3. Environmental protection 4. Global environmental change 5. Globalization

ISBN 9780742556584 (cloth: alk. paper); 9780742556591 (pbk.: alk. paper)

LC 2013-012112

SUMMARY: This book presents a "systematic analysis of the relationship between globalization and the environment from the early Modern period to the present. Peter Christoff and Robyn Eckersley develop a broad conceptual framework for understanding the globalization of environmental problems and the highly uneven, often faltering, international political response." (Publisher's note)

REVIEW: *Choice* v51 no8 p1432 Ap 2014 F. T. Manheim

"Globalization and the Environment". "Noted environmental politics scholars [Peter] Christoff and [Robyn] Eckersley . . . seek to investigate the 'claims and counter-claims' associated with the effects of the globalization of trade, production, and consumption on the intensification of climate change. The authors draw on many sources, ranging from intellectual history and social science to the history of global climate change and international policy debates. . . . The writing is skilled but includes conceptual complexity potentially difficult for undergraduates or nonprofessionals."

CHRISTOPHER, ADAM. Hang Wire; [by] Adam Christopher 384 p. 2014 Osprey Pub Co

1. Circus—Fiction 2. Good & evil—Fiction 3. Serial murderers—Fiction 4. Sleepwalking 5. Speculative fiction

ISBN 0857663178; 9780857663177

SUMMARY: In this book, "San Francisco blogger Ted Hall is enjoying a birthday dinner in Chinatown with friends when he gets a fortune cookie that will change his life. Suffering from blackouts since the party, Ted comes to fear that there is some connection between him and a serial killer known as Hangwire who has been stringing up victims all over town. Powers are stirring in San Francisco, and they all seem connected somehow to the circus that has come to town and to Ted." (Library Journal)

REVIEW: *Booklist* v110 no9/10 p62 Ja 1 2014 David Pitt

"Hang Wire." "There's a lot going on in this genre-bender. . . . It's only natural to approach a new novel by the author of 'Empire State' . . . 'Seven Wonders' . . . and 'The Age Atomic' . . . with wide-eyed enthusiasm and a child-like sense of eager anticipation, and [Adam] Christopher fulfills our expectations and more: just when we think the story couldn't get any weirder, he adds a whole new layer of weird, bouncing from one unexpected moment of goofiness to another, keeping us stuck to our chairs until we think it'll take an industrial strength solvent to pry us loose. Days after finishing the book, you'll still have a grin on your face."

REVIEW: *Libr J* v139 no3 p75 F 15 2014 Megan M. McArdle

CHRISTOPHER, LUCY. The killing woods; [by] Lucy Christopher 384 p. 2014 Chicken House/Scholastic

1. Fathers & daughters—Fiction 2. Games—Fiction 3. Murder—Fiction 4. Mystery and detective stories 5. Post-traumatic stress disorder

ISBN 0545461006; 9780545461009; 9780545461016; 9780545576710

LC 2013-022566

SUMMARY: In this young adult novel, by Lucy Christopher, winner of the Michael L. Printz Honour and ALA Best Fiction for Young Adults awards, "Ashlee Parker is dead, and Emily Shepherd's dad is accused of the crime. . . . What really happened that night? Before he's convicted, Emily must find out the truth. Mina and Joe . . . warn Emily against it, but she feels herself strongly drawn to Damon, Ashlee's charismatic boyfriend. Together they explore the dark woods." (Publisher's note)

REVIEW: *Booklist* v110 no22 p86 Ag 1 2014 Lynette Pitrak

REVIEW: *Booklist* v110 no8 p45 D 15 2013 Daniel Kraus

REVIEW: *Bull Cent Child Books* v67 no5 p259-60 Ja 2014 D. S.

"The Killing Woods". "The technical side of the mystery is murky and implausible (and occasionally preachy), but when the story moves into the secrets of the Game (which Damon dubs their 'own private Fight Club in the woods') and the shame and doubt of the protagonists, it takes off into a creepy and atmospheric psychological puzzler. Ashlee is a tantalizing figure, and her sexually charged take on the Game amplifies the uneasy and disturbing tone of what's already a feral pastime. While not as taut as the author's 'Stolen' . . . the book offers plenty of tension and secrecy, making it a satisfyingly escapist piece of realism."

REVIEW: *Kirkus Rev* v81 no24 p207 D 15 2013

"The Killing Woods". "This taut, psychologically realistic murder mystery knits trauma, danger, tragedy and hope into one cohesive tale. . . . Darkwood's thick forest, high peak and leftover war bunker make a vivid setting. Readers will be riveted by slow, potent reveals about the rough nature of the Game, Ashlee's insistence on danger and adrenaline, and what happened that night. The answers hurt, but they feel right and they make sense. A sprout of hope at the end is fragile and unforced. A gripping, heartbreaking, emotionally substantial look at war wounds and the allure of danger. "

REVIEW: *SLJ* v60 no5 p65 My 2014 Maggie Knapp

REVIEW: *SLJ* v60 no3 p154 Mr 2014 Laura Lutz

CHRISTOPHER, NICHOLAS, 1951-. The true adventures of Nicolo Zen; a novel; [by] Nicholas Christopher 288 p. 2014 Alfred A. Knopf

1. Adventure stories 2. Clarinet—Fiction 3. Love—Fiction 4. Magic—Fiction 5. Musicians—Fiction

ISBN 9780375864926 (pbk.); 9780375867385 (hardcover); 9780375967382 (hardcover library binding)

LC 2013-012853

SUMMARY: In this book, "orphan Nicolò Zen's most prized possession is an ivory clarinet, a new instrument in the early 18th century. However, this clarinet is even more unusual because he believes it's enchanted. . . . Nicolò's desperation and his love of music lead him to . . . a girls' orphanage which is the home of a renowned orchestra led by Antonio Vivaldi. Nicolò disguises himself as a girl in order to become a member of the orchestra. However, life in the orphanage proves to be dangerous." (School Library Journal)

REVIEW: *Booklist* v110 no9/10 p110 Ja 1 2014 Sarah Hunter

REVIEW: *Bull Cent Child Books* v67 no5 p260-1 Ja 2014 K. Q. G.

"The True Adventures of Nicolò Zen." "Decadent with period detail as it is, this is still a surprisingly speedy read, and [Nicholas] Christopher manages to capture both the beauty and the bawdiness of eighteenth-century Venice while moving his protagonist through a satisfyingly folkloric talc of gender-bending and supernatural music. . . . Nicolò's decision to eventually lose the enchanted clarinet and make a name by his own skills, unassisted by magic, is admirable but not overwrought, while his happy reunion with his first love provides a tidily romantic conclusion. History buffs, aspiring musicians, and armchair travelers will find Nicolò's adventures just to their liking."

REVIEW: *Kirkus Rev* v81 no21 p186 N 1 2013

REVIEW: *Voice of Youth Advocates* v36 no6 p69 F 2014 Stephanie Wilkes

CHU, WESLEY. The Deaths of Tao; [by] Wesley Chu 464 p. 2013 Osprey Pub Co

1. Extraterrestrial life—Fiction 2. Heroes—Fiction 3. Imaginary wars & battles—Fiction 4. Science fiction 5. Space flight—Fiction
ISBN 0857663321; 9780857663320

SUMMARY: In this book by Wesley Chu, "the Prophus and the Genjix are at war. For centuries they have sought a way off-planet, guiding humanity's social and technological development to the stage where space travel is possible. The end is now in sight, and both factions have plans to leave the Earth, but the Genjix method will mean the destruction of the human race. . . . It's up to Roen and Tao to save the world." (Publisher's note)

REVIEW: *Booklist* v110 no6 p28 N 15 2013 David Pitt

"The Deaths of Tao." "In this follow-up to 'The Lives of Tao' (2013), the Prophus and the Genjix are close to finding a way to extricate themselves from their symbiotic relationship with humanity and finally, after countless millennia, leave Earth and get back to their homeworld. . . . At times treading close to outright comedy, this is a fast-paced sf adventure that is, if you look at it from the right angle, more accurately a political thriller posing as an sf adventure. Fans of the first novel will have a great time, and newcomers should have no trouble picking up the plot's various threads as the story moves along. Great stuff."

CHUA, AMY. The Triple Package. See Rubenfeld, J.

CHURCH, CAROLINE JAYNE.il. Horsey Up and Down. See Bernstein, K.

CHURCH, CLIVE H. A concise history of Switzerland; [by] Clive H. Church xvi, 324 p. 2013 Cambridge University Press

1. HISTORY—Europe—General 2. Historical literature 3. Switzerland—Economic conditions 4. Switzerland—Politics & government
ISBN 0521143829; 052119444X; 9780521143820 (Paperback); 9780521194440 (Hardback)
LC 2012-031494

SUMMARY: This book by Clive H. Church and Randolph C. Head presents an "overview of Swiss history from the 13th century to the present. Focusing primarily on political and economic developments, the central question structuring the narrative is how a distinctive Swiss identity emerged and sustained itself, transforming a loose urban confederation into a modern nation." (Choice)

REVIEW: *Choice* v51 no4 p716 D 2013 J. W. McCormack

"A Concise History of Switzerland." "[Randolph C.] Head . . . and [Clive H.] Church . . . present a brisk overview of Swiss history from the 13th century to the present. . . . The last chapter successfully lays out how Swiss national identity absorbed challenges from economic downturn and gradual reentry into the larger European community, giving birth to a populist, often reactionary strain in contemporary politics. The authors' complementary specialties in early modern and contemporary European history make the book unusually well balanced between the remote and recent past for an overview of this kind. A clear, engaging synthesis appropriate for a wide variety of readers."

CHURCHLAND, PATRICIA S. Touching a nerve; the self as brain; [by] Patricia S. Churchland 304 p. 2013 W.W. Norton & Company

1. Brain 2. Cognitive science—Philosophy 3. Materialism 4. Mind & body 5. Neuropsychology—Philosophy 6. Philosophical literature 7. Philosophy of mind
ISBN 0393058328; 9780393058321 (hardcover)
LC 2013-007208

SUMMARY: In this book author Patricia S. Churchland "grounds the philosophy of mind in the essential ingredients of biology. She reflects with humor on how she came to harmonize science and philosophy, the mind and the brain, abstract ideals and daily life. She reveals how the latest research into consciousness, memory, and free will can help us reexamine enduring philosophical, ethical, and spiritual questions." (Publisher's note)

REVIEW: *Choice* v51 no8 p1412 Ap 2014 H. Storl

"Touching a Nerve: The Self As Brain". "'Touching a Nerve' continues the themes of [Patricia S.] Churchland's previous work, but with a twist. Churchland embeds weighty neuroscientific issues in personal stories. Her aim 'to interweave the science with the stories' has the effect of providing high-level discussions of traditional neuroscientific topics that are accessible to a much broader audience. None of her usual rigor is diminished, but the field itself opens up to all readers with an interest in the nature of neurophilosophy and its implications for living."

REVIEW: *Kirkus Rev* v81 no10 p50 My 15 2013

REVIEW: *Libr J* v138 no12 p100 Jl 1 2013 Beth Dalton

REVIEW: *N Y Rev Books* v51 no7 p62 Ap 24 2014 Colin McGinn

"Touching a Nerve: The Self As Brain." "Patricia Churchland's 'Touching a Nerve' belongs to . . . the . . . genre . . . neuroscience cheerleading, to put it crudely, Churchland is avowedly a big fan of the brain. . . . And her book well conveys her enthusiasm, being generally well written, informative, and readable. . . . It is when she approaches a philosophical issue that the wheels tend to come off the tracks. . . . Though there is very little philosophy in 'Touching a Nerve,' Churchland does at one point address herself to certain philosophers she calls 'naysayers.'"

REVIEW: *New York Times* v162 no56213 pD2 Jl 30 2013 ABIGAIL ZUGER

REVIEW: *Publ Wkly* v260 no19 p59 My 13 2013

CHURCHWELL, SARAH. Careless People; Murder, Mayhem, and the Invention of The Great Gatsby; [by] Sarah Churchwell 368 p. 2014 Penguin Press HC, The

1. Fitzgerald, F. Scott (Francis Scott), 1896-1940 2. Fitzgerald, Zelda, 1900-1948 3. Historical literature 4. Murder—History 5. Murder—New Jersey—New Brunswick Region—History—20th century 6. New York (N.Y.)—History—20th century
ISBN 1594204748; 9781594204746
LC 2013-028116

SUMMARY: This book on author F. Scott Fitzgerald, his milieu, and his novel "The Great Gatsby" "weaves together a variety of strands: a summary of the novel (including its earlier drafts), a biographical account of the years Fitzgerald was working on the novel . . . and an account of a sensational New Jersey murder case in 1922 (the year that Gatsby takes place), an investigation that resulted in arrests and a trial but no convictions." (Kirkus Reviews)

REVIEW: *Kirkus Rev* v81 no21 p138 N 1 2013

REVIEW: *Libr J* v139 no8 p45 My 1 2014 Nancy R. Ives

REVIEW: *London Rev Books* v35 no13 p9-11 Jl 4 2013 Thomas Powers

REVIEW: *N Y Times Book Rev* p11 F 16 2014 JESSICA KERWIN JENKINS

REVIEW: *New Statesman* v142 no5161 p41 Je 7 2013 Alexandra Harris

REVIEW: *New Yorker* p69-1 Ja 27 2014

REVIEW: *Publ Wkly* v260 no41 p45-6 O 14 2013

REVIEW: *TLS* no5752 p5 Je 28 2013 FRANCES WILSON

"Careless People: Murder, Mayhem and the Invention of The Great Gatsby" and "Flappers: Six Women of a Dangerous Generation." "A handful of [F. Scott] Fitzgerald scholars. . . have explored the connections between the once-famous murders and the meanings of Gatsby, but [Sarah] Churchwell takes the ball and runs with it. . . . what makes 'Careless People' so suggestive is that Churchwell . . . avoids drawing what she calls 'literal-minded, simplistic equations between fiction and reality'. . . . Re-invention is the subject of Judith Mackrell's 'Flappers,' a sober and sure-footed picture of six women, Zelda Fitzgerald, Diana Cooper, Nancy Cunard, Tallulah Bankhead, Josephine Baker and Tamara de Lempicka, whose careers as drinking, smoking, jazzing party creatures reached their critical mass in 1925."

CHWE, MICHAEL SUK-YOUNG. Jane Austen, game theorist. See Suk-Young Chwe, M.

CHÖNAM, LAMA, 1964-.tr. The epic of Gesar of Ling. See The epic of Gesar of Ling

CICIONI, MIRNA.tr. Of Jewish race. See Modiano, R.

CIMENT, JAMES.ed. American immigration. See American immigration

THE CINEMA OF ALEXANDER SOKUROV; xix, 262 p. 2011 "I.B. Tauris Distributed in the U.S. and Canada exclusively by Palgrave Macmillan"

1. Film criticism 2. Motion picture producers and directors—Russia (Federation) 3. Motion pictures & history 4. Motion pictures—Russia (Federation)

ISBN 1848853432 (pbk.); 1848859066; 9781848853430 (pbk.); 9781848859067

LC 2012-397626

SUMMARY: This book analyzes the work of Russian film director Alexander Sokurov. It presents "12 . . . essays and nine reprinted 'Russian responses.' . . . [M]ost of the exegesis on hand tends towards nuts-and-bolts discussion of Sokurov's cultural contexts, his political realities, . . . and his complex (that is, often inexplicable) lyricism, particularly as it colours portraits of historical figures often imagined during life passages in which nothing much is happening at all. . . . Less formalist, the political portrait films are analysed for their defiant refusal to be political, and for their sometimes bizarre narrative idiosyncrasies." (Sight & Sound)

REVIEW: *Choice* v49 no10 p1878 Je 2012 S. Liebman

CINOTTO, LAURIE. The Itty Bitty Kitty Committee; [by] Laurie Cinotto 128 p. 2014 Roaring Brook Press

1. Cat adoption—Juvenile literature 2. Children's nonfiction 3. Foster care of animals—Juvenile literature 4. Kittens—Juvenile literature 5. Kittens—Pictorial works—Juvenile literature

ISBN 9781596439375 (paperback)

LC 2013-023155

SUMMARY: In this book, "through . . . profiles and numerous, adorable photos, kitten fosterer and blogger [Laurie] Cinotto introduces readers to many of her feline charges and also gives suggestions to youngsters interested in fostering, covering a range of topics from basic cat care to making inexpensive kitten toys to photo-taking tips." (Bulletin of the Center for Children's Books)

REVIEW: *Bull Cent Child Books* v67 no10 p506 Je 2014 J. H.

"The Itty Bitty Kitty Committee". "This is a cat-loving browsers' paradise, with multi-photo sections such as 'Belly Stripes and Spots' and 'Kittens Grooming' interspersed with the text along with individual shots of kittens in full-on cuteness mode. [Laurie] Cinotto writes with obvious affection for her cats, and the information is chunked into blocks that make it easy for readers to dip in and out of the book. The photos, taken by Ginotto, are generally clear and attractively composed, and the three DJY projects included (a fleece cat blanket, a cardboard cat playhouse, and a cardboard tube toy) are clearly outlined, kid-friendly crafts (although one does require an adult wielding a utility knife)."

REVIEW: *SLJ* v60 no6 p136 Je 2014 Nancy Call

CINOTTO, SIMONE. Soft soil, black grapes; the birth of Italian winemaking in California; [by] Simone Cinotto 267 p. 2012 New York University Press

1. Historical literature 2. Italian Americans—California—History 3. Italians—California—History 4. Vintners—California—History 5. Vintners—Italy—Piedmont—History 6. Viticulture—California—History 7. Wine and wine making—California—History 8. Wine and wine making—Italy—Piedmont—History 9. Wine and wine making—Social aspects—California—History

ISBN 0814717381; 9780814717387 (cloth: acid-free paper); 9780814717394 (ebook); 9780814790311 (ebook)

LC 2012-016870

SUMMARY: This book by Simone Cinotto, translated by Michelle Tarnopolski, is an "account of the ethnic origins of California wine. . . . Cinotto argues that it was the [Italian] wine-makers' access to 'social capital,' or the ethnic and familial ties that bound them to their rich wine-growing heritage, and not financial leverage or direct enological experience, that enabled them to develop such a successful and influential wine business." (Publisher's note)

REVIEW: *Am Hist Rev* v119 no1 p193-4 F 2014 Mark I. Choate

"Soft Soil, Black Grapes: The Birth of Italian Winemaking in California". "This beautifully typeset book, with well-chosen black and white illustrations, draws the reader into the entrepreneurial spirit and immigrant group dynamics behind the success of California Italian wines. Engagingly written, Simone Cinotto's account deserves a wide distribution among economic, cultural, and migration historians and all who love wine. The book blends rich and colorful descriptions of food history with business intrigues and family passions. It is a story of high-stakes risks and economic rewards."

REVIEW: *Booklist* v109 no3 p25-7 O 1 2012 Mark Knoblauch

REVIEW: *J Am Hist* v100 no3 p884-5 D 2013 David Vaught

REVIEW: *Libr J* v137 no20 p104 D 1 2012 Ginny Wolter

CIRIBASSI, JOHN.ed. Decoding Your Dog. See Decoding Your Dog

CITY AS CANVAS; New York City graffiti from the Martin Wong Collection; 240 p. 2013 Skira Rizzoli Publications

1. Art literature 2. Graffiti 3. New York (N.Y.) art scene—History 4. Street art 5. Wong, Martin
ISBN 9780847839865 (hardcover : alk. paper)
LC 2013-937103

SUMMARY: Edited by Carlo McCormick and Sean Corcoran, this is "A visual account of the birth of graffiti and street art, showcasing as-yet-unseen works collected by preeminent artist Martin Wong. Referred to by the 'New York Times' as an artist 'whose meticulous visionary realism is among the lasting legacies of New York's East Village art scene of the 1980s,' Martin Wong (1946-1999) was firmly entrenched in the NYC street art world of the late '70s and '80s." (Publisher's note)

REVIEW: *N Y Times Book Rev* p57 D 8 2013 RAILLAN BROOKS

"City As Canvas: New York City Graffiti From the Martin Wong Collection" and "The World Atlas of Street Art and Graffiti." "Dwelling int he resplendent squalor of [Martin] Wong's apartment is precisely the experience the curators Sean Corcoran and Carlo McCormick recreate in 'City as Canvas: New York City Graffiti From the Martin Wong Collection,' an accounting of Wong's huge personal trove and its in history, with reflections on the man by his artist friends. . . . 'The World Atlas of Street Art and Graffiti' is broader in scale and scope. . . . Rafael Schacter . . . has bundled into the book's 400 pages a range of styles and modes offering a rare and pleasant encounter with at in which the critic stays (mostly) out of the way."

THE CIVIL WAR; The Third Year Told by Those Who Lived It; xxv, 814 p. 2011 The Library of America

1. Grant, Ulysses S. (Ulysses Simpson), 1822-1885 2. Historical literature 3. History—Sources 4. United States—History—Civil War, 1861-1865—African American participation
ISBN 9781598530889 (alk. paper)
LC 2010-931718

SUMMARY: This book, "the third in a four-volume series," presents primary-source documents about the third year of the U.S. Civil War. Topics include "near-universal male conscription; the North's decision to send black soldiers into front-line combat; the battles of Chancellorville, Gettysburg and Chattanooga, with their terrible casualties . . . and the emergence of Ulysses S. Grant as the North's commander-in-chief." (Times Literary Supplement)

REVIEW: *TLS* no5759 p35 Ag 16 2013 MICK GIDLEY

"The Civil War: The Third Year Told By Those Who Lived It." "This book conveys experiences of the American Civil War with intense immediacy. . . . These letters, speeches, sermons, journals, newspaper articles, government decrees, judicial testimonies--and even a 'petition from the colored citizens of Beaufort, North Carolina' (seeking proper payment for requisitioned labour on military installations)--reach us with the urgency of their moment. Arranged chronologically, from January 1863 to the spring of 1864, each offers insight as the war takes its mounting toll. . . . It does the Library of America proud."

CLANTON, BEN.il. Jasper John Dooley. See Adderson, C.

CLAPSON, MARK. Anglo-American Crossroads; Urban Research and Planning in Britain, 1940-2010; [by] Mark Clapson 208 p. 2013 Bloomsbury USA Academic

1. Historical literature 2. New urbanism 3. Urban planning—Great Britain 4. Urban planning—United States 5. Urban sociology
ISBN 1441141499; 9781441141491

SUMMARY: This book, by Mark Clapson, "beginning with debates about reconstruction during the Second World War, . . . explores how Americanisation influenced key approaches to town planning, from reconstruction after 1945 to the New Urbanism of the 1990s. Clapson pays particular attention to the relationship between urban sociological research and planning issues since the 1950s." (Publisher's note)

REVIEW: *Choice* v51 no2 p359-60 O 2013 J. R. Breiban

"Anglo-American Crossroads: Urban Research and Planning in Britain, 1940-2010." "The transatlantic exchange of city planning ideas has long been thought of as flowing from Britain to the US, with the greenbelt and the garden city, in particular, crossing the ocean to inspire the layout of US suburbs. [Author Mark] Clapson . . . examines a reciprocal flow eastward, as British planners took up such US ideas as the street grid, the 'neighborhood unit,' the 'Radburn plan' for separating pedestrian and vehicular traffic, 'the new urbanism,' and, of course, the motorway/expressway system. . . . In this book, he adds the Ford and Rockefeller Foundations' support for British sociological research as a basis for postwar planning."

CLARE, ALYS. Winter King, the; [by] Alys Clare 240 p. 2014 Severn House Pub Ltd

1. Great Britain—History—John, 1199-1216 2. Historical fiction 3. Murder—Fiction 4. Nobility (Social class)—Fiction 5. Women healers
ISBN 0727883496; 9780727883490

SUMMARY: In this book, part of Alys Clare's Hawkenlye series, "Lord Benedict de Vitré of Medley Hall, an obese nobleman suspected of lining his pockets with his sovereign's money, dies. . . . Sabin fears that the medications she secretly supplied to make procreation less likely may have contributed to de Vitré's death. Evidence of murder soon emerges, and de Vitré isn't the last to die, giving Sabin and her fellow healer, Meggie d'Acquin, several crimes to solve." (Publishers Weekly)

REVIEW: *Booklist* v110 no13 p23-4 Mr 1 2014 Emily Melton

"The Winter King." "When the sheriff determines that Benedict was murdered, a bizarre string of circumstantial evidence leads not to Benedict's wife or servants but to renowned healer Meggie, daughter of Sir Josse d'Aquin. Desperate to prove her innocence, Meggie begs her father to help. Attention is temporarily diverted from the murder when two young men who were apparently headed to visit the reclusive Lord Wimarc are discovered brutally murdered. Were their murders linked in any way to Lord Benedict's? Outstanding period detail, an intriguing plot, engaging characters and suspenseful twists make for an excellent read."

REVIEW: *Kirkus Rev* v82 no5 p300 Mr 1 2014

CLARK, BRIDIE. Maybe tonight?; [by] Bridie Clark 224 p. 2013 Roaring Brook Press

1. Boarding schools—Fiction 2. Dating (Social customs)—Fiction 3. Interpersonal relations—Fiction 4. JUVENILE FICTION—Humorous Stories 5. JUVENILE FICTION—Interactive Adventures 6. JUVENILE FICTION—Love & Romance 7. JUVENILE FICTION—Social Issues—Dating & Sex 8. Plot-your-own stories 9. Schools—Fiction

ISBN 9781596438163 (pbk.); 9781596438187 (ebook)

LC 2012-040908

SUMMARY: This book by Bridie Clark "opens as the reader is getting ready for the most exciting party of the year--Midwinter's Night Dream, set in the frosty woods just off campus--with her roommates and best friends Annabel Snow, Spider Harris, and Libby Monroe. Choices unfold quickly and the reader must decide which risks to take in pursuit of social status, adventure, success, and love." (Publisher's note)

REVIEW: *Booklist* v110 no2 p74-5 S 15 2013 Bethany Fort

REVIEW: *Kirkus Rev* v81 no13 p144 Jl 1 2013

REVIEW: *N Y Times Book Rev* p19 Ag 25 2013 JEN DOLL

"Confessions of a Hater" and "Snap Decision: Maybe Tonight?" "The perspective of these novels is subtle enough to be engrossing for both teenagers and adults for whom high school's intense friendships and antipathies still resonate. . . . Both novels are polished to a gleam, and their savvy, self-aware references to fashion and music and other timely cultural touchstones would meet the standards of any mean girl worth her salt. . . . These are great subjects for young adult readers, and both books do what they do well. . . . The questions [Caprice] Crane and [Bridie] Clark address don't' get answered neatly and tied up with a bow upon graduation, and perhaps that's why both novels are so enjoyable even to those who've crossed that threshold."

REVIEW: *Voice of Youth Advocates* v36 no4 p58-60 O 2013 Vikki Terrile

CLARK, BRIDIE. You only live once; [by] Bridie Clark 224 p. 2014 Roaring Brook Press

1. Boarding schools—Fiction 2. Dating (Social customs)—Fiction 3. Interpersonal relations—Fiction 4. Plot-your-own stories 5. Schools—Fiction

ISBN 9781596438170 (pbk.)

LC 2013-023160

SUMMARY: This "Choose Your Own Adventure" style book by Bridie Clark is set at an "elite boarding school" during the protagonist's "sophomore year of high school. . . . unlike the physical challenges of many Choose Your Own Adventure stories, this novel tends to provide moral dilemmas" such as "flirting with a married employer" and "assisting a bullying victim". (Kirkus Reviews)

REVIEW: *Kirkus Rev* v82 no5 p139 Mr 1 2014

"You Only Live Once". "This type of 'interactive' story often engages readers by forcing them to choose between two unfamiliar physical hazards for survival. . . . But unlike the physical challenges of many Choose Your Own Adventure stories, this novel tends to provide moral dilemmas that too often have a clearly 'right" and "wrong' answer. . . . . Though some readers will enjoy exploring various scenarios, others will quickly find the predictable results tiresome. This format, which rarely devotes more than a few pages to any particular character or topic, results in a novel that skims, rather than explores, the pressures many high school students face daily."

REVIEW: *SLJ* v60 no6 p116 Je 2014 Morgan Brickey

CLARK, DAVID.il. Fractions in disguise. See Einhorn, E.

CLARK, GREGORY, 1957-. The son also rises; surnames and the history of social mobility; [by] Gregory Clark 384 p. 2014 Princeton University Press

1. Ability 2. Personal names 3. Social classes 4. Social mobility—History 5. Social science literature

ISBN 9780691162546 (hardcover : alk. paper)

LC 2013-042815

SUMMARY: It was the author's intent to "prove that movement on the social ladder has changed little over eight centuries." By "tracking family names over generations . . . economic historian Gregory Clark reveals that mobility rates are lower than conventionally estimated, do not vary across societies, and are resistant to social policies. The good news is that these patterns are driven by strong inheritance of abilities and lineage does not beget unwarranted advantage." (Publisher's note)

REVIEW: *Economist* v410 no8872 p72-3 F 1 2014

"The Son Also Rises: Surnames and the History of Social Mobility." "Most of the text is given over to methodical presentation of research, with the uniting theme that optimistic assessments of mobility are badly wrong. . . . Oddly, Mr. [Gregory] Clark judges the world to be 'a much fairer place than we intuit.' He explains this by stating that the rich acquire their wealth because they are clever and work hard, and not because the system is rigged. . . . This conclusion gives the book a cheery tone,, but there are also plenty of nasty conclusions to be drawn. . . . 'The Son Also Rises' may not be a racist book, but it certainly traffics in genetic determinism. That is a weakness. Mr. Clark is too quick to write off the promise of recent social changes."

REVIEW: *Libr J* v139 no8 p86 My 1 2014 Carol Elsen

CLARK, KEITH. The radical fiction of Ann Petry; [by] Keith Clark xi, 257 p. 2013 Louisiana State University Press

1. Gender in literature 2. Gothic fiction (Literary genre) 3. Literature—History & criticism 4. Masculinity in literature

ISBN 9780807150665 (cloth: alk. paper)
LC 2012-039922

SUMMARY: In this "analysis of the works of Ann Petry (1908 1997), a major mid-twentieth-century African American author, Keith Clark moves beyond assessments of Petry as the sole female member of the Wright School of Social Protest to acclaim her innovative approaches to gender performance, sexuality, and literary technique." (Publisher's note)

REVIEW: *Choice* v51 no8 p1398-9 Ap 2014 L. J. Parascandola

"The Radical Fiction of Ann Petry". "[Keith] Clark . . . attempts to expand understanding and appreciation of Petry's entire oeuvre. He discusses not only the two canonical works . . . but also her other two novels, 'Country Place' and 'The Narrows,' and her collection 'Miss Muriel and Other Stories'. Perhaps most interesting is Clark's use of gothic critical theory to analyze the less-known 'Country Place' and the short stories 'The Bones of Louella Brown,' 'The Witness,' and 'In Darkness and Confusion.' A valuable study of African American literature."

REVIEW: *Women's Review of Books* v31 no2 p10-2 Mr/Ap 2014 Cheryl Wall

CLARK, KRISTIN ELIZABETH. Freakboy; [by] Kristin Elizabeth Clark 448 p. 2013 Farrar, Straus and Giroux

1. Family life—Fiction 2. High schools—Fiction 3. Novels in verse 4. Schools—Fiction 5. Sexual orientation—Fiction 6. Transgender people—Fiction 7. Wrestling—Fiction
ISBN 0374324727; 9780374324728 (hardcover)
LC 2012-050407

SUMMARY: In this book, by Kristin Elizabeth Clark, "Brendan . . . seems to have it pretty easy. He's a star wrestler . . . and a loving boyfriend to . . . Vanessa. But on the inside, Brendan struggles to understand why his body feels so wrong. Clark folds three narratives into one powerful story: Brendan trying to understand his sexual identity, Vanessa fighting to keep her and Brendan's relationship alive, and Angel struggling to confront her demons." (Publisher's note)

REVIEW: *Booklist* v110 no4 p58 O 15 2013 Ann Kelley

"Freakboy." "When Brendan Chase types 'Wants to be a girl' into his Mac's search engine, one word pops up: transsexual. . . . In [Kristin Elizabeth] Clark's raw, honest debut novel, told in verse, three voices capture a few experiences of teens on the transgender spectrum. . . . Unlike many novels that deal with one transgender character, this movingly explores so many gender identities, from the three main characters (each appears in a different font) to Angel's roommates. A must have for library shelves, this will be popular with fans of Ellen Hopkins. Resources and further reading conclude."

REVIEW: *Bull Cent Child Books* v67 no3 p144-5 N 2013 K. C.

"Freakboy." "Three perspectives-- Brendan's, Angel's, and Vanessa's--braid the story of Brendan's frustration into a moving portrayal of two very different ways gender dysphoria can manifest itself. . . . Each voice finds a distinct register in the well-made poetry of this verse novel that plays with font and shape on the page as lithely and effectively as it does with the language itself; the result is an effective visual and verbal echo of the poignant emotions that play out as Vanessa and Brendan, with Angel's help, square their shoulders to face their new reality."

REVIEW: *Horn Book Magazine* v89 no6 p88-9 N/D 2013 SIÂN GAETANO

REVIEW: *Kirkus Rev* v81 no18 p54 S 15 2013

REVIEW: *Publ Wkly* p100-2 Children's starred review annual 2013

REVIEW: *Publ Wkly* v260 no37 p57 S 16 2013

REVIEW: *SLJ* v59 no10 p1 O 2013 Teresa Pfeifer

REVIEW: *Voice of Youth Advocates* v36 no5 p54 D 2013 Alicia Abdul

CLARK, T. J. Lowry and the Painting of Modern Life; [by] T. J. Clark 224 p. 2014 Tate Publishing

1. Art catalogs 2. British art 3. Cities & towns in art 4. England—In art 5. English painting—20th century 6. Lowry, Laurence Stephen, 1887-1976
ISBN 1849760918; 9781849760911

SUMMARY: "This book, published to accompany a retrospective at Tate Britain, shows how [L.S.] Lowry depicted the public rituals of working-class urban life: football matches and protest marches; evictions and fistfights; workers going to and from the mill. He was also a landscape painter, and he sought to show the effects of the industrial revolution." (Publisher's note)

REVIEW: *N Y Rev Books* v60 no14 p26-9 S 26 2013 Sanford Schwartz

"Lowry and the Painting of Modern Life" and "L. S. Lowry: The Art and the Artist." "T. J. Clark and Anne M. Wagner, while writing as admirers, imply what many viewers have no doubt felt: that in the sheer volume of his work Lowry was something of an industrial producer himself. . . . When Clark writes that in some of Lowry's paintings 'the real energy, obduracy and confinement of working-class England are visible,' his carefully chosen words enliven our sense of the paintings and of the North West of the time. But his and Wagner's exhibition shortchanges Lowry."

CLARK, T. J. Picasso and truth; from cubism to Guernica; [by] T. J. Clark 352 p. 2013 Princeton University Press

1. Art literature 2. Cubism 3. Human sexuality in art 4. Painting—History—20th century 5. Violence in art
ISBN 9780691157412 (hardcover : alk. paper)
LC 2012-039423

SUMMARY: This book "reproduces six lectures that . . . [T. J.] Clark . . gave at the National Gallery of Art in Washington, D.C., in 2009. . . . The renowned scholar . . . tracks [Pablo] Picasso's work from the 1920s through the '30s . . . culminating in a close look at the 1937 masterpiece, Guernica. . . . Clark argues that a ubiquitous 'grimness' underlies the exuberant sex and violence Picasso portrayed during these years." (Publishers Weekly)

REVIEW: *Apollo: The International Magazine for Collectors* v177 no610 p119 Je 2013

REVIEW: *Apollo: The International Magazine for Collectors* v178 no615 p46 D 2013

REVIEW: *Apollo: The International Magazine for Collectors* v178 no611 p98-9 Jl/Ag 2013 Michael Prodger

REVIEW: *Choice* v51 no3 p445-6 N 2013 A. Verplaetse

REVIEW: *London Rev Books* v36 no4 p21-3 F 20 2014

Malcolm Bull

REVIEW: *Publ Wkly* v260 no19 p62 My 13 2013

REVIEW: *TLS* no5769 p3-5 O 25 2013 JACK FLAM

"Picasso and Truth: From Cubism to Guernica." "Ambitious but sometimes exasperating. . . . [T. J.] Clark's book sets out to explore just how radical and how strange these paintings are, and the new kind of moral universe that they embody. . . . The way in which Clark resists allowing the conventions of modernism to serve as a kind of apologia for the pathological elements in [Pablo] Picasso's work is refreshing. . . . What is unconvincing, and often annoying, are Clark's repeated assertions that most of the vast body of writing about Picasso is irrelevant because it strives to keep the wild and disturbing spirit of the artist at bay."

CLARKE, AUSTIN, 1934-. They Never Told Me; And Other Stories; [by] Austin Clarke 216 p. 2013 Exile Editions

1. Aging 2. Blacks—History 3. Historians—Fiction 4. Immigrants—Fiction 5. Short stories—Collections
ISBN 1550963597; 9781550963595

SUMMARY: This short story collection by Austin Clarke depicts "a sweet longing for youth and an anxiety-stricken rage at old age; an immigrant's longing for a placid, lost home and his lust for a new high-speed motorcar life; and an intellectual's sense of empowerment by black history even as he watches what little he knows about such history engulf him." (Publisher's note)

REVIEW: *Quill Quire* v80 no1 p36 Ja/F 2014 Safa Jinje

"They Never Told Me and Other Stories". "The choice between adopting the language of the colonizer and writing in the dialect of one's own people becomes especially problematic in the case of a Canadian immigrant hailing from the Caribbean, but it's a problem that [Austin] Clarke solves nicely. . . . The story's narrative style may shock unseasoned ears and those unfamiliar with the nuances of Caribbean-English dialects. Yet the choice to write in this voice serves to boost the authenticity of the experience. . . . 'They Never Told Me' is much more than a collection of stories; it's a howl of dissidence. . . . Each piece is a confrontation; together they form a series of pleas for acknowledgement, for recognition of lives lived, hopes thwarted, pain suffered."

CLARKE, FRANCES M. War stories; suffering and sacrifice in the Civil War North; [by] Frances M. Clarke xiv, 251 p. 2011 University of Chicago Press

1. Historical literature 2. Sacrifice—Social aspects—Northeastern States—History—19th century 3. Soldiers' writings, American—Northeastern States—History—19th century 4. Suffering—Social aspects—Northeastern States—History—19th century
ISBN 0226108627 (cloth : alk. paper); 9780226108629 (cloth : alk. paper)
LC 2010-048794

SUMMARY: "The American Civil War is often seen as the first modern war, not least because of its immense suffering. . . . While scholars typically dismiss . . . everyday writing as simplistic or naïve, [author] Frances M. Clarke argues that we need to reconsider the letters, diaries, songs, and journalism penned by Union soldiers and their caregivers to fully understand the war's impact and meaning." (Publisher's note)

REVIEW: *Am Hist Rev* v117 no2 p529-30 Ap 2012 James Marten

REVIEW: *Choice* v49 no6 p1130-1 F 2012 P. D. Travis

REVIEW: *J Am Hist* v99 no3 p925-6 D 2012 Cheryl A. Wells

REVIEW: *Rev Am Hist* v42 no1 p104-9 Mr 2014 Jamie Pietruska

"War Stories: Suffering and Sacrifice in the Civil War North." "Rejecting the paradigm of the war as historical discontinuity, [author Frances M.] Clarke demonstrates the persistence of idealized narratives of suffering and asks why sentimental stories of patriotic sacrifice endured in the face of unimaginable . . . casualties. . . . Nineteenth-century Americans understood suffering . . . on multiple registers, as Clarke illustrates with a wide-ranging introductory discussion of contexts including medicine, abolitionism and reform, philosophy, liberal Protestantism and evangelicalism, and Victorian literature. . . . Prodigiously researched, meticulously argued, and elegantly written, 'War Stories' deserves a wide readership and makes important contributions to a range of fields."

CLARKE, ROBERT C. Cannabis; evolution and ethnobotany; [by] Robert C. Clarke 434 p. 2013 University of California Press

1. Botanical literature 2. Cannabis 3. Cannabis—Evolution 4. Cannabis—Utilization 5. Human-plant relationships
ISBN 9780520270480 (cloth : alk. paper)
LC 2012-036385

SUMMARY: In this book, authors Robert C. Clarke and Mark D. Merlin "begin with a discussion of the pros and cons of Cannabis production. A multifaceted look at Cannabis in human history follows, unraveling the complex tale of domestication and global distribution through time, cultures and their religions, medicine, and economic change." (Choice: Current Reviews for Academic Libraries)

REVIEW: *Choice* v51 no7 p1244-5 Mr 2014 L. Swatzell

"Cannabis: Evolution and Ethnobotany." "This is a true ethnobotanical work. Authors of other botanical-related publications frequently omit key aspects of a plant's history, but here [Robert C.] Clarke . . . and [Mark D.] Merlin . . . capture a 'high resolution' picture of this complicated plant. . . . The authors tell the whole story of the plant so that the book is more than a report; it is interesting reading, filled with fascinating information. Glossy color plates show the movement of cannabis and the change in its use, which makes the scientific evidence more palatable and easy to understand. . . . This well-written work will be useful for freshmen through seniors in higher education. . . . It will intrigue even casual readers."

CLASSEN, CONSTANCE. The deepest sense; a cultural history of touch; [by] Constance Classen p. cm. 2012 University of Illinois Press

1. Historical literature 2. Senses & sensation—History 3. Senses and sensation—History 4. Social history 5. Touch—History
ISBN 9780252034930 (hardcover: alk. paper); 9780252078590 (pbk.); 9780252094408 (e-book)
LC 2011-034118

SUMMARY: In this book, author Constance Classen "focuses on various kinds of touch in medieval and early modern Europe while also grappling with how these meanings evolved in later periods. She charts how they were denigrated in the Enlightenment, drilled into new forms during the industrial revolution, and displayed and marketed in modernity." (American Historical Review)

REVIEW: *Am Hist Rev* v119 no1 p155 F 2014 Holly Dugan

"The Deepest Sense: A Cultural History of Touch". "Although framed as a cultural history, [Constance] Classen's study also offers a thoughtful meditation on the value of sensing history. . . . Although it is not always an easy history to read . . . it is one many scholars should undertake. To touch is to be touched, and in embracing this paradox, Classen shows that the history of touch is itself reflexive: although they can only be inferred from sources, these once palpable embraces tell the history of the very deepest connections between us."

REVIEW: *Choice* v50 no4 p728 D 2012 C. Apt

REVIEW: *Libr J* v137 no11 p89 Je 15 2012 Kathleen McCallister

CLAVIN, PATRICIA. Securing the world economy; the reinvention of the League of Nations, 1920-1946; [by] Patricia Clavin xii, 400 p. 2013 Oxford University Press

1. Economic development—International cooperation—History—20th century 2. Historical literature 3. International economic relations—History—20th century 4. International organization—History

ISBN 0199577935; 9780199577934

LC 2012-277624

SUMMARY: Written by Patricia Clavin, this book "explains how efforts to support global capitalism became a core objective of the League of Nations. Based on new research drawn together from archives on three continents, it explores how the world's first ever inter-governmental organization sought to understand and shape the powerful forces that influenced the global economy, and the prospects for peace." (Publisher's note)

REVIEW: *Am Hist Rev* v119 no2 p481-2 Ap 2014 Daniel Laqua

REVIEW: *Choice* v51 no1 p130-1 S 2013 S. Prisco III

"Securing the World Economy: The Reinvention of the League of Nations, 1920-1946." "[Author Patricia] Clavin offers a detailed analysis of the transformation of the League of Nations from an institution dedicated to maintaining peace after the Great War to one focused on a variety of economic policies beyond the initial scope of Wilsonian free trade. Postwar stagnation, high inflation, and war reparations played havoc with the international economy such that the league became heavily involved in global economics and finance. . . . A significant aspect of the study is its thorough examination of the league's Economic and Financial Organization (EFO). . . . Dry prose and print errors aside, the book is appropriate for advanced readers."

CLAYTON, ELAINE.il. Pie in the Sky. See Pie in the Sky

CLAYTON, EWAN. The Golden Thread; The Story of Writing; [by] Ewan Clayton 400 p. 2014 Pgw

1. Alphabet—History 2. Historical literature 3. Publishers & publishing—History 4. Writing—History 5. Writing materials & instruments

ISBN 1619022427; 9781619022423

SUMMARY: In this book, author Ewan Clayton "traces the history of [writing]. . . . He explores the social and cultural impact of, among other stages, the invention of the alphabet; the replacement of the papyrus scroll with the codex in the late Roman period; the perfecting of printing using moveable type in the fifteenth century and the ensuing spread of literacy; [and] the industrialization of printing during the Industrial Revolution." (Publisher's note)

REVIEW: *Booklist* v110 no12 p4 F 15 2014 Donna Seaman

"The Golden Thread: The Story of Writing". "[Ewan] Clayton builds on his far-reaching experiences in this avidly researched and enthusiastically told history of writing in the West, in which he pairs exacting analysis of the materials, technology, and skills involved in the ever-evolving craft of writing, from papyrus scrolls to scrolling down a computer screen, and fresh perspectives on the social contexts. . . . Along the way, Clayton, who will delight fans of Simon Garfield and Nicholas Basbanes, profiles calligraphers and typographers, assesses the impacts of various forms of correspondence and publishing, and discusses in eye-opening detail the expressiveness of diverse styles of handwriting."

REVIEW: *Kirkus Rev* v81 no23 p196 D 1 2013

REVIEW: *Publ Wkly* v260 no48 p42 N 25 2013

CLAYTON, PAUL. Strange Worlds; [by] Paul Clayton 208 p. 2012 Createspace Independent Pub

1. Cats—Fiction 2. Death—Fiction 3. Science fiction 4. Short story (Literary form) 5. Zombies

ISBN 1475233930; 9781475233933

SUMMARY: This book by Paul Clayton "delivers 14 sci-fi tales." These "include 'Dog Man,' about Steve 'Cap' Crowley and the other residents of Penn's Village Nursing Home, plagued by a cat with a sense for who will die next; [and] 'Day, or Two, of The Dead'" in which benign zombies visit from another dimension to bond with loved ones (or failing that, annoy former acquaintances)." (Kirkus Reviews)

REVIEW: *Kirkus Rev* v82 no2 p368 Ja 15 2014

"Strange Worlds". "These eclectic stories feature many of the political riffs and future-shock themes found throughout classic sci-fi; they're also loaded with enough tragic irony to satisfy die-hard Twilight Zone fans. . . . Clayton's cybernetic humans, enfeebled outcasts and future societies parade maniacally from his fertile imagination. . . . Shorter tales, like 'The Triumph,' 'The Thing in the Box' and 'About Our Cats,' are stunningly compact, envisioning fascinating scenarios readers will want to explore further. Overall, a cutting wit drives commentary on everything from race and religion to father-son relationships and the elderly. One too many portrayals of young people as texting-happy dolts, however, might date this volume in years to come. Hot, glowing sci-fi nuggets."

CLEAGE, PEARL. Things I Should Have Told My Daughter; Lies, Lessons & Love Affairs; [by] Pearl Cleage 320 p. 2014 Atria Books

1. Self-realization in women 2. Women authors, American—Biography

ISBN 1451664699; 9781451664690 (hardback); 9781451664706 (paperback)

LC 2013-034164

SUMMARY: This book, by Pearl Cleage, "reprints journal entries chronicling her tumultuous life in the 1970s and '80s . . . the decades in which she discovered her vocation as a playwright, poet and novelist while remaining deeply engaged in political activism, as a speechwriter for the first black mayor of Atlanta, and as a feminist grappling with marriage, motherhood, divorce and subsequent sexual freedom." (Kirkus Reviews)

REVIEW: *Booklist* v110 no11 p16 F 1 2014 Donna Seaman

REVIEW: *Kirkus Rev* v82 no3 p112 F 1 2014

"Things I Should Have Told My Daughter: Lies, Lessons and Love Affairs". "The great virtue of this seemingly unedited journal is that it gives a vivid sense of a real life's varied nature, with an entry about how women can serve the revolution followed by the author's comments on the film Women in Love. . . . The drawback is that there are absolutely no notes in the text to do anything as basic as identify Daddy' . . . or the last name of her first husband, Michael (Lomax). [Pearl] Cleage apparently thinks everybody knows all about her public life, and she comes across as self-involved, even within the context of a journal. (The solipsism is leavened by some poignant letters from her dying mother and a couple of tough professional memos to Atlanta mayor Maynard Jackson.)"

REVIEW: *Libr J* v139 no2 p76 F 1 2014 Kathryn Bartelt

REVIEW: *Publ Wkly* v261 no6 p82 F 10 2014

CLEAR, TODD R. The punishment imperative; the rise and failure of mass incarceration in America; [by] Todd R. Clear 272 p. 2014 New York University Press

1. Corrections—United States 2. Criminal justice, Administration of—United States 3. Imprisonment—United States 4. Prisons—United States 5. Sociology literature

ISBN 0814717195; 9780814717196 (cl: alk. paper)

LC 2013-017727

SUMMARY: In this book "criminologists Todd R. Clear and Natasha A. Frost argue that America's move to mass incarceration from the 1960s to the early 2000s was more than just a response to crime or a collection of policies adopted in isolation; it was a grand social experiment. Tracing a wide array of trends related to the criminal justice system, [it] charts the rise of penal severity in America." (Publisher's note)

REVIEW: *Choice* v51 no8 p1495-6 Ap 2014 P. Horne

"The Punishment Imperative: The Rise and Failure of Mass Incarceration in America". "Criminal justice professors [Todd R.] Clear . . . and [Natasha A.] Frost . . . clearly examine the history and politics of punishment over the last four decades. . . . The book points out that it will be difficult to move away from the legacy of the past 40 years. But the authors feel that the US is on the threshold of a new era of penal philosophy, and they offer some practical policy solutions to enable the country to move away from a reliance on mass incarceration. It is too soon to tell if a sea change is upon the US penal system, but the authors make their cogent argument in this well-written book."

REVIEW: *Publ Wkly* v260 no41 p51 O 14 2013

CLEARY, BRIAN P., 1959-. Pre- and re-, mis- and dis; what is a prefix?; [by] Brian P. Cleary 31 p. 2013 Millbrook Press

1. Cats—Juvenile literature 2. Children's nonfiction 3. English grammar 4. English language—Suffixes and prefixes—Juvenile literature 5. Language arts (Primary)

ISBN 0761390316; 9780761390312 (lib. bdg. : alk. paper)

LC 2013-001050

SUMMARY: This book, by Brian P. Cleary and illustrated by Martin Goneau, is part of the Words are CATegorical series. It "presents the concept of prefixes for young readers. For easy identification, key prefixes appear in color and comical cats reinforce each idea. [It] turns traditional grammar lessons on end!" (Publisher's note)

REVIEW: *Booklist* v110 no4 p40-2 O 15 2013 John Peters

"Pre- and Re-, Mis- and Dis-: What Is a Prefix?." "[Brian P.] Cleary's latest entry in the Words are CATegorical series pairs a rhymed introduction to common prefixes and how they change the meanings of words, with freewheeling cartoon illustrations of clothed cats in diverse colors modeling or acting out those changes. Though he avoids bringing up messy complications like contronyms . . . and prefixes that look the same but have different meanings . . . he does tuck sufficient qualifiers into the discourse. . . . Budding wordsmiths in particular will benefit from this lively look at one of language's most versatile transformative tools."

REVIEW: *Kirkus Rev* v81 no18 p72 S 15 2013

CLEEVES, ANN. Dead Water; a Shetland mystery; [by] Ann Cleeves 400 p. 2014 Minotaur Books

1. Communities 2. FICTION—Mystery & Detective—General 3. Journalists—Fiction 4. Murder investigation—Fiction

ISBN 9781250036605 (hardback)

LC 2013-038928

SUMMARY: In this book by Ann Cleeves, "when the body of a journalist is found, Detective Inspector Willow Reeves is drafted from outside to head up the investigation. Inspector Jimmy Perez has been out of the loop, but his local knowledge is needed in this case, and he decides to help Willow. The dead journalist had left the islands years before to pursue his writing career. In his wake, he left a scandal involving a young girl." (Publisher's note)

REVIEW: *Booklist* v110 no9/10 p49 Ja 1 2014 Connie Fletcher

"Dead Water." "In the sixth of [Ann] Cleeves' Shetland Island series starring Inspector Jimmy Perez, a very controlled Scottish public prosecutor who seems passionate only about team-rowing, makes a discovery that threatens to tumble the Jenga-like structure of her life. . . . Cleeves has an unusually deft hand with characters; not one of them seems purely plot-functional, and Perez's character keeps deepening with each book. The rough islands cresting the Atlantic fit the bleakness of the murders depicted here. This series is one of two that Cleeves has going; the other stars Northumberland detective Vera Stanhope and is a hit BBC series."

REVIEW: *Kirkus Rev* v82 no2 p274 Ja 15 2014

"Dead Water". "A grieving detective clashes with an incoming supervisor to solve a pair of murders on the main island of Shetland. Not long after photojournalist Jerry Markham has returned to Shetland after years in the south, someone runs his car off the foggy road from the oil terminal in Sullom Voe. . . . [Ann] Cleeves . . . returns to a sea-bound land of crofters' cottages, barren rocks and fog, especially the fog surrounding the murders. Although some of the characters are sketchier than the setting itself, the well-constructed procedural gains another dimension from Jimmy's re-engagement with his work and his life."

REVIEW: *Libr J* v139 no2 p60 F 1 2014 Teresa L. Jacobsen

REVIEW: *N Y Times Book Rev* p19 Mr 2 2014 MARILYN STASIO

REVIEW: *Publ Wkly* v260 no52 p35 D 23 2013

CLEMENT, JENNIFER. Prayers for the stolen; a novel; [by] Jennifer Clement 224 p. 2014 Hogarth

1. Girls—Mexico 2. Kidnapping—Fiction 3. Mexican fiction 4. Mexico—Fiction 5. Young women—Mexico—Fiction

ISBN 0804138788; 9780804138789

LC 2013-025756

SUMMARY: In this novel, by Jennifer Clement, "Ladydi Garcia Martínez is fierce, funny and smart. She was born into a world where being a girl is a dangerous thing. . . . Here in the shadow of the drug war, bodies turn up on the outskirts of the village to be taken back to the earth by scorpions and snakes. . . . Despite the odds against her, this spirited heroine's resilience and resolve bring hope to otherwise heartbreaking conditions." (Publisher's note)

REVIEW: *Booklist* v110 no9/10 p44 Ja 1 2014 Donna Chavez

REVIEW: *Kirkus Rev* v81 no23 p258 D 1 2013

REVIEW: *Ms* v24 no1 p58-9 Wint/Spr 2014

REVIEW: *N Y Times Book Rev* p14 Mr 2 2014 FRANCISCO GOLDMAN

"Prayers for the Stolen." "Every day in contemporary Mexico adolescent girls and young women are abducted. . . . Some do become the slave-mistresses of drug lords and their armies of assassins. . . . This is the horrific reality behind 'Prayers for the Stolen.' . . . [Author Jennifer] Clement has produced a novel that is not a work of verisimilitude, but something else. 'Prayers for the Stolen' is as harrowing as you would expect, but it's also beguiling, and even crazily enchanting. . . . The novel is an ebullient yet deeply stirring paean to its female characters' resiliency and capacity for loyalty, friendship, compassion and love, but also to the power of fiction and poetry to transform such a dark reality into a parallel one that can engage and move us."

REVIEW: *Publ Wkly* v260 no48 p30 N 25 2013

REVIEW: *TLS* no5796 p19 My 2 2014 SOPHIE BAGGOTT

CLEVELAND, CUTLER J.ed. Handbook of Energy, Volume I. See Handbook of Energy, Volume I

CLIFF, TONY. Delilah Dirk and the Turkish Lieutenant; [by] Tony Cliff 176 p. 2013 First Second

1. Historical fiction 2. Military personnel—Fiction 3. Turkey—Fiction 4. Turkey—History—1683-1829

ISBN 1596438134 (paperback); 9781596438132 (paperback)

LC 2013-947230

SUMMARY: In this book, "Delilah Dirk has abandoned conventional court life and become a globe-trotting soldier of fortune. She is captured and held prisoner in 1800s Constantinople. Eventually she escapes, taking along the astonished Turkish Lieutenant Erdemogul Selim, whose quiet life centers around a proper cup of tea. This unlikely pair embarks on a wild journey that includes flying a ship, outwitting the Evil Pirate Captain Zakul, and escaping burning buildings." (School Library Journal)

REVIEW: *Booklist* v110 no13 p54 Mr 1 2014 Sarah Hunter

REVIEW: *Booklist* v109 no19/20 p57 Je 1 2013 Snow Wildsmith

REVIEW: *Bull Cent Child Books* v67 no1 p10 S 2013 E. B.

"Delilah Dirk and the Turkish Lieutenant." "This graphic novel of mismatched road buddies, set in 1807 Asia Minor, has all the right components of an action-adventure tale, but there's little chemistry between the protagonists, who seem to play out their roles side by side rather than together. . . . The transfer of Cliff's concept from web comic to print ultimately may leave readers with the sense that Delilah and Mr. Selim's story is wrapped up before it ever really took off, but the tidily boxed action sequences are ably choreographed and will satisfy readers who like their swordplay laced with humor."

REVIEW: *Kirkus Rev* v81 no12 p84 Je 15 2013

REVIEW: *Publ Wkly* p134 Children's starred review annual 2013

REVIEW: *Publ Wkly* v260 no24 p66 Je 17 2013

REVIEW: *Publ Wkly* v260 no45 p22-30 N 11 2013

REVIEW: *SLJ* v59 no7 p103 Jl 2013 Barbara M. Moon

REVIEW: *Voice of Youth Advocates* v37 no1 p28-9 Ap 2014 AMANDA FOUST JACK BAUR

REVIEW: *Voice of Youth Advocates* v36 no3 p72 Ag 2013 Cynthia Winfield

CLIKEMAN, PAUL M. Called to account; financial frauds that shaped the accounting profession; [by] Paul M. Clikeman ix, 371 p. 2013 Routledge

1. Accounting—Standards—United States 2. Accounting fraud—United States 3. Business literature 4. Corporations—Corrupt practices—United States—Accounting 5. Fraud

ISBN 9780203097946 (ebook : alk. paper); 9780415630245 (hardback : alk. paper); 9780415630252 (pbk. : alk. paper)

LC 2012-041544

SUMMARY: This book "takes a broad perspective on how financial frauds have shaped the public accounting profession by focusing on cases of fraud around the globe. . . . The book traces the development of the accounting standards and legislation put in place as a direct consequence of these epic scandals. The new edition offers updated chapters on ZZZZ Best and Arthur Andersen, plus new chapters devoted to Parmalat, Satyam, and The Great Recession." (Publisher's note)

REVIEW: *Choice* v51 no6 p1057 F 2014 F. A. Marino

"Called to Account: Financial Frauds That Shaped the Accounting Profession." "[Paul M.] Clikeman has done a superb job of presenting this evolution through the masterfully told accounts of 16 of the most famous financial frauds. Starting with the Ivar Kreuger matchstick fraud of the early 20th century, Clikeman takes the reader through the major eras of the profession's history, revealing how specific financial scandals provided the stimulus for many key professional, legislative, and regulatory developments. This second edition . . . includes a new section dealing with recent events, including Parmalat, Satyam, and the recession. The book is extensively documented and includes suggested discussion questions and a full index. . . . Essential."

CLIMATE CHANGE IN THE MIDWEST; impacts, risks, vulnerability, and adaptation; xvi, 266 p. 2013 Indiana University Press

1. Climatic changes—Environmental aspects—Middle West 2. Climatic changes—Middle West 3. Climatic changes—Risk assessment—Middle West 4. Plants—Effect of global warming on—Middle West 5. Scientific literature 6. Vegetation and climate 7. Water levels—Great Lakes (North America)

ISBN 9780253006820 (cloth : alk. paper); 9780253007742 (ebk.)

LC 2012-017798

SUMMARY: This book "focuses on identifying and quantifying the major vulnerabilities to climate change in the Midwestern United States. . . . The contributors assess the risks and susceptibility of the critical socio-economic and environmental systems. Key sectors discussed are agriculture, human health, water, energy and infrastructure, and the vulnerabilities that may be amplified under current climate trajectories." (Publisher's note)

REVIEW: *Choice* v50 no11 p2047 Jl 2013 T. N. Chase

CLINE-RANSOME, LESA. Benny Goodman & Teddy Wilson; taking the stage as the first black and white jazz band in history; [by] Lesa Cline-Ransome 32 p. 2014 Holiday House

1. Children's nonfiction 2. Jazz musicians—United States—Biography—Juvenile literature 3. Race relations—History—20th century—Juvenile literature

ISBN 082342362X; 9780823423620 (hardcover)

LC 2010-048154

SUMMARY: "In 1936, the Benny Goodman Trio became the first interracial band to perform in public, with Benny Goodman (the son of Jewish immigrants) on clarinet and African-American Teddy Wilson on piano (Gene Krupa, on drums, completed the trio). Writing in punchy free verse that echoes the bounce of both men's music," author Lesa Cline-Ransome, "traces Goodman and Wilson's parallel--but separate--paths to jazz fame, before eventually meeting in 1935." (Publishers Weekly)

REVIEW: *Bull Cent Child Books* v67 no8 p400 Ap 2014 E. B.

REVIEW: *Horn Book Magazine* v90 no2 p136-7 Mr/Ap 2014 KATHLEEN T. HORNING

"Benny Goodman & Teddy Wilson: Taking the Stage as the First Black-and-White Jazz Band in History. "In 1936 the Trio 'ma[de] history as the first interracial band to perform publicly.' The story is recounted here in short bursts of text, almost like jazz riffs, accompanied by pencil and watercolor illustrations that capture distinctive moments in the subjects' lives. An informative author's note gives more information on both men, a timeline, and capsule biographies of other significant jazz musicians of the time."

REVIEW: *Kirkus Rev* v82 no6 p62 Mr 15 2014

REVIEW: *Publ Wkly* v261 no4 p192 Ja 27 2014

REVIEW: *SLJ* v60 no3 p171 Mr 2014 Krishna Grady

CLINE-RANSOME, LESA. Words set me free; the story of young Frederick Douglass; [by] Lesa Cline-Ransome 32 p. 2012 Simon & Schuster Books for Young Readers

1. Abolitionists—United States—Biography—Juvenile literature 2. African American abolitionists Biography—Juvenile literature 3. Antislavery movements—United States—History—19th century—Juvenile literature 4. Biographies 5. JUVENILE NONFICTION—Biography & Autobiography—Cultural Heritage 6. JUVENILE NONFICTION—History—United States—Civil War Period (1850-1877) 7. JUVENILE NONFICTION—People & Places—United States—African American 8. Slaves—United States—Biography—Juvenile literature

ISBN 9781416959038 (hardback)

LC 2011-013323

SUMMARY: In this book, the historical character Frederick Douglass "relates his early years, from first vague memories of his mother . . . through his childhood, with his service leased to the Auld family of Baltimore; to his first attempt to make an escape from Talbot County, Maryland. The narration is . . . focused on the way learning to read both inspired and enabled young Frederick to plan for a life of freedom in the North . . . This chapter in Douglass' story concludes with his forgery of a pass, written 'in a firm and steady hand,' which would allow him to 'walk right out of Talbot County and into freedom up north.'" (Bulletin of the Center for Children's Books)

REVIEW: *Booklist* v108 no14 p55 Mr 15 2012 Linda Perkins

REVIEW: *Bull Cent Child Books* v65 no6 p300-1 F 2012 E. B.

"Words Set Me Free: The Story of Young Frederick Douglass." "The narration is dignified and tightly focused on the way learning to read both inspired and enabled young Frederick to plan for a life of freedom in the North. The depiction of the risk involved for a slave to achieve literacy is particularly well handled for a picture-book audience. . . . James Ransome's oil and acrylic paintings underscore young Frederick's determination and independent spirit, and their interplay with the text leaves readers with the strong impression that, once he had mastered the written word, Frederick's labors in town and fields were only going to be unfortunate layovers on his unstoppable journey to freedom."

REVIEW: *Kirkus Rev* v80 no1 p2459-60 Ja 1 2012

REVIEW: *Publ Wkly* v258 no48 p56 N 28 2011

REVIEW: *SLJ* v58 no1 p91 Ja 2012 Barbara Auerbach

CLINE, ERIN M. Confucius, Rawls, and the sense of justice; [by] Erin M. Cline xiii, 354 p. 2013 Fordham University Press

1. Analects of Confucius (Chinese text) 2. Justice (Philosophy) 3. Philosophical literature

ISBN 9780823245086 (cloth: alk. paper)

LC 2012-029099

SUMMARY: "This book compares the role of a sense of justice in the ethical and political thought of Confucius and John Rawls. Erin Cline demonstrates that the Analects (the most influential record of Confucius' thought) and Rawls's work intersect in an emphasis on the importance of developing a sense of justice. Despite deep and important differences between the two accounts, this intersection is a source of significant philosophical agreement." (Publisher's note)

REVIEW: *Ethics* v124 no2 p388-92 Ja 2014 SOR-HOON TAN

"Confucius, Rawls, and the Sense of Justice". "Erin Cline achieves these objectives with fluent and clear textual analyses and arguments, contextualized within sophisticated reflections on why comparative philosophy is a worthwhile activity and discussions of the methodological issues it raises. . . . Cline's examination of Rawls's psychological construction of its development process shows convincingly that the sense of justice is developed in the family, community, and larger society. . . . My skepticism about some of Cline's arguments does not diminish my admiration for this comparative study."

CLOSE, JOHN WEIR. A giant cow-tipping by savages; the boom, bust, and boom culture of M&A; [by] John Weir Close 320 p. 2013 Palgrave Macmillan

1. Big business—United States—History 2. Business—History—20th century 3. Business literature 4. Consolidation and merger of corporations—United States—History 5. Turner, Ted, 1938-

ISBN 0230341810; 9780230341814 (alk. paper)

LC 2013-014658

SUMMARY: Author John Weir Close's book "starts at the origin and moves through to the present and next wave of Mergers & Acquisitions. Modern mergers and acquisitions, or M&A as it's more commonly known, is a new phenomenon. . . . Discrete stories have been pulled from the annals of M&A, both true and fictionalized, that have become touchstones for wealth and excess. But while there have been a few iconic characters and tales to emerge, no one has told the rich history of M&A, until now." (Publisher's note)

REVIEW: *Economist* v409 no8866 p89-90 D 14 2013

"A Giant Cow-Tipping by Savages: The Boom, Bust and Boom Culture of M&A." "John Weir Close . . . has written an entertaining history of the American merger-and-acquisition scene since the mid-1980s. Rather oddly, he omits the best-known deal of all: the takeover of RJR Nabisco. . . . Despite the poor results of many of these mergers, Mr. Close sees the raiders of the 1980s as iconoclasts who brought down the managerial elite. . . . But the reality is that these merger waves did not necessarily prove beneficial. . . . The outsized personalities, and the way they behaved, make for eminently readable stories. Perhaps the book's main fault is that it focuses on these entertaining anecdotes, rather than the bigger picture of how takeovers affect the economy."

REVIEW: *Kirkus Rev* v81 no17 p50 S 1 2013

REVIEW: *Publ Wkly* v260 no33 p60 Ag 19 2013

CLOUGH, LISA. Petal and Poppy; 32 p. 2014 Houghton Mifflin Harcourt

1. Best friends—Fiction 2. Children's stories 3. Elephants—Fiction 4. Friendship—Fiction 5. Rhinoceroses—Fiction

ISBN 9780544113800; 9780544114777

LC 2013-020667

SUMMARY: In this children's book, "Petal . . . is thrilled her friend Poppy is not around so she can practice her tuba. Little does she know that Poppy . . . is sitting nearby, quietly reading. Disrupted by the music, Poppy declares it an opportune time to scuba dive. . . . After her dive, when Poppy returns to the surface, she discovers the fog has rolled in, obscuring her boat. Happily, Petal's resonant tuba serves as a foghorn and helps reunite the friends." (Kirkus Reviews)

REVIEW: *Booklist* v110 no14 p84 Mr 15 2014 Annie Miller

REVIEW: *Bull Cent Child Books* v67 no9 p448 My 2014 J. H.

"Petal and Poppy" and "Petal and Poppy and the Penguin". "Smaller, comic-like panels alternate with larger illustrations in these graphic novel/easy reader mash-ups, and dialogue and sound effects, presented in speech bubbles, comprise the minimal text. The digital art, though cheery, is flat and sometimes overloud and busy compositions bury the all-important dialogue balloons. Kids who can tackle [Mo] Willems' Elephant and Piggie series may nonetheless embrace a new appealing easy-reader duo in Petal and Poppy."

REVIEW: *Kirkus Rev* v82 no5 p65 Mr 1 2014

"Petal and Poppy". "The simple story with clear, bright art demonstrates that friends do not always need to agree and bobs along as buoyantly as sun across the water. Although a sweet and cheery pair, Petal and Poppy may not have enough oomph-be it laughs, silliness or a winning combination of the two-to stand out in an already glutted market of early-reader buddy stories. Still, readers beguiled by the elephant-rhino pals may want to check out their second tale, 'Petal and Poppy and the Penguin,' publishing simultaneously. A blithe and breezy charmer."

REVIEW: *Publ Wkly* v261 no3 p55 Ja 20 2014

REVIEW: *SLJ* v60 no5 p76 My 2014 Joy Poynor

CLOUGH, LISA. Petal and Poppy and the penguin; 32 p. 2014 Houghton Mifflin Harcourt

1. Best friends—Fiction 2. Children's stories 3. Elephants—Fiction 4. Friendship—Fiction 5. Penguins—Fiction 6. Rhinoceroses—Fiction

ISBN 9780544133303; 9780544137707

LC 2013-020668

SUMMARY: In this children's book, part of Lisa Clough's "Petal and Poppy" series, "a storm brings an unexpected guest to the lighthouse: a penguin. After Poppy brings the little guy inside, the penguin quickly endears himself to both friends, fixing a meal, doing dishes, dancing to Petal's tuba music, and falling asleep in Petal's lap, and the duo decides that he can stay." (Bulletin of the Center for Children's Books)

REVIEW: *Bull Cent Child Books* v67 no9 p448 My 2014 J. H.

"Petal and Poppy" and "Petal and Poppy and the Penguin". "Smaller, comic-like panels alternate with larger illustrations in these graphic novel/easy reader mash-ups, and dialogue and sound effects, presented in speech bubbles, comprise the minimal text. The digital art, though cheery, is flat and sometimes overloud and busy compositions bury the all-important dialogue balloons. Kids who can tackle [Mo] Willems' Elephant and Piggie series may nonetheless embrace a new appealing easy-reader duo in Petal and Poppy."

REVIEW: *SLJ* v60 no5 p78 My 2014 Melissa Smith

COAKLEY, SARAH, 1951-.ed. Evolution, games, and God. See Evolution, games, and God

COATES, JOHN.ed. Decolonizing social work. See Decolonizing social work

COBB, DARYL K. Baseball, Bullies & Angels; [by] Daryl K. Cobb 288 p. 2013 10 To 2 Children's Books

1. Baseball stories 2. Bullying 3. Friendship—Fiction 4. School stories 5. Young adult fiction

ISBN 0615879233; 9780615879239

SUMMARY: In this book, "when a group of students make Stephen the target of their merciless bullying he struggles even more to make sense of his life. With all the pressure and pain he feels each day, he still searches for hope. He finds some in his best friend Charlie who tries to show him the humor in it all. And a kind gesture from Megan, the new girl in class, helps to spark a connection between two kindred spirits. But when everything is at its worst he always finds hope in baseball." (Publisher's note)

REVIEW: *Kirkus Rev* v81 no22 p331 N 15 2013

REVIEW: *Kirkus Rev* v81 no24 p81 D 15 2013

"Baseball, Bullies and Angels". "Author [Daryl K.] Cobb brings home the supposed simplicity of small-town life with a patient eye. . . . Stephen is a charming, funny narrator, and once he starts describing baseball games, this tale's versatility begins to shine. . . . Cobb's long stretches of naturally engaging dialogue also help deliver characters and twists that positively outstrip stories merely about athletic glory. 'I'm a nice guy,' says Stephen, 'and that is who I want to be.' Rather than sounding trite, this statement is a rallying cry for those who must deal with bullies and don't want to sink to their level. Always sincere, occasionally shocking, this tale is required reading for kids and parents."

COBB, DAVID M.il. Quiet beauty. See Brown, K. H.

COBHAM, CATHERINE. The Iraqi novel; key writers, key texts; [by] Catherine Cobham xiv, 264 p. 2013 Edinburgh University Press

1. Arabic fiction—20th century—History and criticism 2. Arabic fiction—21st century—History and criticism 3. Arabic fiction—Iraq—History and criticism 4. Iraq—History—20th century 5. Literature—History & criticism

ISBN 0748641416; 9780748641413 (hardback)

LC 2013-362064

SUMMARY: This book on Iraqi literature "focus[es] on four male writers at the centre of the mid-twentieth century literary revival in Iraq. 'Abd al-Malik Nuri, Gha'ib Tu'ma Farman, Mahdi 'Isa al-Saqr and Fu'ad al-Takarli were all born in the 1920s and their lives and work were marked by foreign occupation, dictatorship, war and exile. . . . Fabio Caiani and Catherine Cobham's monograph provides detailed textual analyses of selected works." (Times Literary Supplement)

REVIEW: *TLS* no5771 p26 N 8 2013 ELEANOR KILROY

"The Iraqi Novel: Key Writers, Key Texts." "Part of a series on modern Arabic literature aimed at a wider readership, Fabio Caiani and Catherine Cobham's monograph provides detailed textual analyses of selected works. . . . Cobham and Caiani offer the reader--particularly the non-Arabic speaker--a rare insight into the cultural life of Iraq, drawing on a large body of work by Arab critics, as well as memoirs and private correspondence. The book deftly places the texts in their historical and political contexts, while capturing the defiant nonconformity of a literary generation that insisted that in fiction 'truth is not enough'."

COCCA-LEFFLER, MARYANN.il. Theo's mood. See Cocca-Leffler, M.

COCCA-LEFFLER, MARYANN. Theo's mood; 24 p. 2013 Albert Whitman & Company

1. Babies—Fiction 2. Brothers and sisters—Fiction 3. Emotions—Fiction 4. School stories 5. Schools—Fiction

ISBN 9780807577783 (alk. paper)

LC 2012-049834

SUMMARY: In this book, written and illustrated by Maryann Cocca-Leffler, "It's Mood Monday and Miss Cady's class is sharing how they feel after the weekend. But Theo doesn't know whether he's in a good mood or a bad mood. He has a new baby sister and he isn't just happy like Eric who got a new bike or sad like April who lost her dog. As Theo's classmates discuss all their feelings, he realizes he's not in a good mood or a bad mood--he's all those things!"

REVIEW: *Bull Cent Child Books* v67 no2 p79 O 2013 H. M.

"Theo's mood." "On Mondays in Miss Cady's class, students share their 'mood news,' but Theo, who became a big brother over the weekend, isn't exactly sure what he feels. . . . This is a useful resource for talking about emotions, and the narrative partners effectively with the mixed-media art, with a clean page design that enhances focus on the theme: an image of the student making the suggestion faces a scrapbook-style snapshot of the described event. The simple emotions and kid-oriented examples make this accessible for young listeners, and there are plenty of springboard activities about feelings that could follow a sharing of Theo's tale."

REVIEW: *Kirkus Rev* v81 no15 p155 Ag 1 2013

REVIEW: *Publ Wkly* v260 no25 p173 Je 24 2013

REVIEW: *SLJ* v59 no9 p118 S 2013 Grace Oliff

COCCA-LEFFLER, MARYANN. Time to say bye-bye; [by] Maryann Cocca-Leffler 32 p. 2012 Viking Children's Books

1. Change in literature 2. Day—Fiction 3. Fiction 4. Picture books for children 5. Toddlers—Fiction

ISBN 9780670013098 (hardcover)

LC 2011-016082

SUMMARY: This "picture book addresses the challenge of transitioning between activities for the toddler set, focusing on a kid who must move from park to Grandma's to home to bath and finally to bed . . . for each place, a few featured activities are mentioned . . . the tyke's reluctance to depart is noted . . . then there's an audible farewell to a handful of the key objects for that setting." (Bulletin of the Center for Children's Books) The protagonist's "day full of simple pleasures" includes "playing at the park, baking cookies with Grandma, and splashing in the tub. The hard part comes when each good time ends, but when it's time to let go, this child knows the formula that makes it easier: "Bye-bye swing," "Bye-bye Grandma," and so on through the day, until bedtime." (Booklist)

REVIEW: *Booklist* v108 no12 p61 F 15 2012 Carolyn Phelan

REVIEW: *Bull Cent Child Books* v65 no6 p301 F 2012 H. M.

"Time to Say Bye-Bye." "This very accessible picture book addresses the challenge of transitioning between activities for the toddler set, focusing on a kid who must move from park to Grandma's to home to bath and finally to bed. . . . [Maryann] Cocca-Leffler's illustrations enhance watercolor and pencil with patterned fabric elements . . . that add visual interest to the cheerful scenes. This would be a great addition to a babies' laptime, particularly if the little ones were encouraged to say/wave bye-bye along with the story. While parents are likely to be impressed with (and perhaps a bit skeptical about) the smoothness of the transitions, tots will just enjoy the description of this little kid's happy, busy day."

REVIEW: *Kirkus Rev* v79 no24 p2317 D 15 2011

REVIEW: *SLJ* v58 no2 p84 F 2012 Debbie Lewis

COCHRAN, SHERMAN. The Lius of Shanghai; [by] Sherman Cochran 472 p. 2013 Harvard University Press

1. China—Economic conditions—1912-1949 2. China—Social conditions—1912-1949 3. Family-owned business enterprises—China—History—20th century 4. Historical literature

ISBN 9780674072596 (alk. paper)

LC 2012-039399

SUMMARY: This book presents "a study of the family correspondence of Liu Hongsheng (1888–1956), one of modern China's most famous entrepreneurs. The work is animated by questions of business history, especially the issue of how the internal dynamics of a Chinese family enterprise worked, but it is written as a family history in which we get to know Liu, his wife, and their twelve children during the crucial period of the 1930s and 1940s when the family was at the height of its power." (American Historical Review)

REVIEW: *Am Hist Rev* v119 no1 p161-2 F 2014 Henrietta Harrison

"The Lius of Shanghai". "This unusual but immensely readable book by Sherman Cochran and Andrew Hsieh is a study of the family correspondence of Liu Hongsheng (1888–1956), one of modern China's most famous entrepreneurs. . . . . Overall the book is quite hard to put down. Although there are many idealistic descriptions of this kind of modernized family relationships in China during this period, to see how one such family worked in practice is fascinating. The book is also very well written. Its accessibility means that it would work excellently for teaching, although it would benefit from being used alongside other materials that gave students more general context."

REVIEW: *Choice* v51 no3 p524-5 N 2013 A. Cho

REVIEW: *Libr J* v138 no6 p87 Ap 1 2013 Charles Hayford

REVIEW: *Publ Wkly* v260 no7 p54-5 F 18 2013

COCKER, MARK. Birds & People; [by] Mark Cocker 704 p. 2013 Trafalgar Square

1. Birds 2. Birds—Folklore 3. Birds—Religious aspects 4. Human-animal relationships 5. Natural history in literature

ISBN 0224081748; 9780224081740

SUMMARY: Author Mark Cocker presents a "book on the relationship between birds and humankind, with contributions from more than 600 bird enthusiasts from all over the world. Part natural history and part cultural study, this book describes and maps the entire spectrum of human engagements with birds, drawing in themes of history, literature, art, cuisine, language, lore, politics, and the environment." (Publisher's note)

REVIEW: *Booklist* v110 no3 p47 O 1 2013 Linda Scarth

REVIEW: *Nat Hist* v121 no9 p40 N 2013 LAURENCE A. MARSCHALL

REVIEW: *New Statesman* v142 no5168 p70-2 Jl 26 2013 John Burnside

REVIEW: *Science* v342 no6165 p1449 D 20 2013 Henry T. Armistead

REVIEW: *TLS* no5766 p12 O 4 2013 JEREMY MYNOTT

"Birds and People." "Mark Cocker's magnificent and extraordinary book . . . is surely the ne plus ultra of the genre. It weighs in at 8 pounds (about the weight of a flamingo or two and a half ostrich eggs), has 592 pages of tightly set double-column text, containing over 430,000 words. . . . It is also beautifully illustrated. . . . The book is driven by the text, which represents an extraordinary feat of comprehension, disciplined passion and literary skill. Cocker has sifted through a mass of printed and anecdotal material and subjected it to serious critical scrutiny. . . . Cocker adds to this research from his own extensive first-hand experience in the field. . . . This gives many of the individual entries a fresh and authentic force."

CODY, MATTHEW. Will in scarlet; [by] Matthew Cody 272 p. 2013 Alfred A. Knopf Books for Young Readers

1. Historical fiction 2. Inheritance and succession—Fiction 3. Middle Ages—Fiction 4. Robbers and outlaws—Fiction 5. Robin Hood (Legendary character)—Fiction

ISBN 037586895X; 9780375868955 (hardcover); 9780375872921 (pbk.); 9780375899805 (ebook); 9780375968952 (library binding)

LC 2012-042503

SUMMARY: In this book, by Matthew Cody, "Will Scarlet is on the run. Once the sheltered son of nobility, Will has become an exile. While his father, Lord Shackley, has been on the Crusades with King Richard, a . . . plot to unseat Richard has swept across England, and Shackley House has fallen. Will flees the only home he's ever known into neighboring Sherwood Forest, where he joins the elusive gang of bandits known as the Merry Men." (Publisher's note)

REVIEW: *Booklist* v110 no4 p54 O 15 2013 Carolyn Phelan

REVIEW: *Bull Cent Child Books* v67 no3 p145 N 2013 K. Q. G.

REVIEW: *Horn Book Magazine* v90 no1 p87-8 Ja/F 2014 SAM BLOOM

"Will in Scarlet". "[Matthew] Cody does a serviceable job slotting Will and Much in with Robin Hood, Little John, and the rest, all the while adding depth and realism to these classic characters. Fans of John Flanagan's Ranger's Apprentice series will find plenty to like here: lots of action, witty repartee, and an immediate style that will draw readers into the story. However, one of the problems with Flanagan's popular series—a tendency to overshare characters' thought processes, which hinders the pacing despite cracking action scenes—also crops up in Cody's writing from time to time. Other than the occasional slog, this should be a popular choice. A cast of characters and a map are included."

REVIEW: *Kirkus Rev* v81 no17 p82 S 1 2013

REVIEW: *SLJ* v60 no1 p60 Ja 2014 C.A. Fehmel

REVIEW: *SLJ* v59 no10 p1 O 2013 Devin Burritt

COELHO, JORGE.il. Polarity. See Bemis, M.

COETZEE, J. M., 1940-. The Childhood of Jesus; [by] J. M. Coetzee 288 p. 2013 Viking Adult
1. FICTION—Literary 2. Future life—Fiction 3. Guardian and ward—Fiction 4. Immigrants—Fiction 5. Parent & child—Fiction
ISBN 0670014656; 9780670014651
LC 2013-016960

SUMMARY: In this book, by J.M. Coetzee, David is "separated from his mother as a passenger on a boat bound for a new land. The piece of paper explaining his situation is lost, but a fellow passenger, Simón, vows to look after the boy. When the boat docks, David and Simón are issued . . . virtually a whole new life. Strangers in a strange land, knowing nothing of their surroundings, nor the language or customs, they are determined to find David's mother." (Publisher's note)

REVIEW: *Bookforum* v20 no3 p28-9 S-N 2013 ALEX ABRAMOVICH

"The Childhood of Jesus." "The book is a riddle, but not an impossible one, and, in any case, its chancy title gives little away. . . . As always, [J.M. Coetzee's sentences are economical and surgically precise. . . . But leviathans swim just below the novel's surface. . . . 'The Childhood of Jesus' is one of Coetzee's longest works; it's full of incident, and gripping from the very first page. But the book's setting is dreamlike, and defined not so much by the things it contains as by the things it seems to lack. . . . Among other things, the novel is also a brilliant, blistering description of what it means to seek refuge."

REVIEW: *Booklist* v109 no19/20 p4 Je 1 2013

REVIEW: *Booklist* v109 no22 p28 Ag 1 2013 Brendan Driscoll

REVIEW: *Christ Century* v130 no25 p22-3 D 11 2013

REVIEW: *Commonweal* v140 no17 p43-4 O 25 2013 Gabriel Brownstein

REVIEW: *Kirkus Rev* v81 no14 p192 Jl 15 2013

REVIEW: *Libr J* v138 no7 p54 Ap 15 2013 Barbara Hoffert

REVIEW: *London Rev Books* v35 no6 p13-6 Mr 21 2013 Christopher Tayler

REVIEW: *N Y Rev Books* v60 no14 p58-60 S 26 2013 Fintan O'Toole

REVIEW: *N Y Times Book Rev* p1-15 S 1 2013 Joyce Carol Oates

"The Childhood of Jesus." "Starkly narrated . . . in uniformly plain, flat, unadorned prose, in which nothing so luxurious as a metaphor emerges, or a striking employment of syntax, or a word of more than a few syllables. . . . Not a very convincing child, David would seem to be a symbol in the author's imagination of 'childness' is the Romantic, Wordsworthian sense--that is, the child as close to God. . . . Consequently, the author has difficulty forming a coherent picture of him. . . . 'The Childhood of Jesus' is clearly an allegory--but it isn't an allegory with the transparency of Plato's allegory of the cave. . . . Nor is it an allegory of the emotional, psychological and visceral density of 'Waiting for the Barbarians'."

REVIEW: *Nation* v297 no15 p33-5 O 14 2013 LAILA LALAMI

"The Childhood of Jesus." "It is a fascinating premise, though not a particularly dramatic one. [J. M.] Coetzee is known for his spare prose, which highlights beautifully all the excesses of power about which he writes so often and so intensely. But in this new novel, his brief, clinically precise sentences only draw more attention to the tediousness of a peaceful, but inefficient, vegetarian and sexless world. Still, his great talent has always been to make the reader (or this reader, at least) feel as though he is writing for her alone, challenging her to ask herself the same questions he puts to his characters."

REVIEW: *New Statesman* v142 no5147 p44-5 Mr 1 2013 Leo Robson

REVIEW: *New York Times* v162 no56243 pC1-6 Ag 29 2013 DWIGHT GARNER

REVIEW: *New Yorker* v89 no31 p1 O 7 2013

REVIEW: *Newsweek Global* v161 no11 p1 Mr 15 2013 Benjamin Lytal

REVIEW: *Publ Wkly* v260 no24 p39 Je 17 2013

REVIEW: *TLS* no5738 p20 Mr 22 2013 EDMUND GORDON

COHEN-COLE, JAMIE. The open mind; cold war politics and the sciences of human nature; [by] Jamie Cohen-Cole 368 p. 2014 University of Chicago Press
1. Cognitive science—Political aspects—United States 2. Historical literature 3. Human behavior models—Political aspects—United States 4. Social sciences—Political aspects—United States 5. Social sciences—United States—History—20th century
ISBN 9780226092164 (cloth: alkaline paper)
LC 2013-020551

SUMMARY: This book "chronicles the development and promulgation of a scientific vision of the rational, creative, and autonomous self, demonstrating how this self became a defining feature of Cold War culture. [Author] Jamie Cohen-Cole illustrates how from 1945 to 1965 policy makers and social critics used the idea of an open-minded human nature to advance centrist politics." (Publisher's note)

REVIEW: *Choice* v51 no11 p2051 Jl 2014 R. Muccigrosso

REVIEW: *Nation* v298 no22 p36-9 Je 2 2014

"The Open Mind: Cold War Politics and the Sciences of Human Nature." "Jamie Cohen-Cole's fascinating new book 'The Open Mind' tells the story of liberal tolerance since World War II, examining how an ideal of open-mindedness was deliberately cultivated in psychology, pedagogy and social science. Exposing all the contradictions of liberalism, Cohen-Cole has written and highly illuminating prehistory of the muddles and riddles of contemporary political rhetoric. He shows how specific prescriptions for the ideal type of citizen—unprejudiced, intellectually flexible and tolerant of ambiguity, with tastes running from Abstract Impressionism to strong coffee—crystallized around the fight against totalitarianism at home and abroad."

REVIEW: *Science* v345 no6192 p40 Jl 4 2014 Joel Isaac

COHEN, JARED. The new digital age. See Schmidt, E. E.

COHEN, JESSICA.tr. Falling out of time. See Grossman, D.

COHEN, LAURIE. The flea; 32 p. 2014 Owlkids Books, Inc.
1. Animal stories 2. Body size—Juvenile literature 3. Children's stories 4. Fleas 5. Size perception—Juvenile literature
ISBN 9781771470568
LC 2013-949119

SUMMARY: This children's picture book by Laurie Cohen centers on a flea, depicted by illustrator Marjorie Béal as "just a black circle with two white dots for eyes . . . as shown by the opening illustration of a ruler, he's just one millimeter tall. To counter this, he climbs a series of objects of increasing size. First, a pea. Then, an apple. And on it goes, with each object growing larger while the flea, to the reader's perspective, grows tinier." (Booklist)

REVIEW: *Booklist* v110 no14 p80-1 Mr 15 2014 Daniel Kraus

"The Flea." "The flea, as drawn by [Marjorie] Béal, is just a black circle with two white dots for eyes, and as shown by the opening illustration of a ruler, he's just one millimeter tall. To counter this, he climbs a series of objects of increasing size. . . .[Laurie] Cohen keeps the text clear and clean, and both qualities are reiterated by the generous white space across each page. Béal's art looks like colored-paper cutouts--big, bold, geometric, and without any inner detail. It's a great fit for the story, giving young readers a chance to interpret the rather abstract shapes as actual objects. Fleas are rarely this welcome."

REVIEW: *Kirkus Rev* v82 no3 p208 F 1 2014

"The Flea". " A tiny flea with size issues gets mad rather than wiser in this terse and unsatisfying fable. . . . Like the minimal text, [Marjorie] Béal's illustrations are stripped down to essentials. The pea is a green dot floating on the white page, and successive perches are likewise portrayed as very simple geometric or organic shapes. Even readers willing to go with the flow may wonder how the flea, a chubby black oval topping out at (a magnified) 1 mm. in the first picture, can still be a visible dot on a huge skyscraper and then a remote cloud. Not to mention what became of any moral. Too rudimentary to be more than a joke with a mildly amusing punch line."

REVIEW: *SLJ* v60 no3 p106 Mr 2014 Joy Poynor

COHEN, LEAH HAGER. No book but the world; a novel; [by] Leah Hager Cohen 320 p. 2014 Riverhead Hardcover
1. Autism—Fiction 2. Brothers and Sisters—Fiction 3. FICTION—Contemporary Women 4. FICTION—Family Life 5. FICTION—Literary 6. Family life—Fiction 7. Murderers—Fiction
ISBN 9781594486036 (hardback)
LC 2013-025052

SUMMARY: In this book, "Ava's placid domestic life is severely disrupted when she finds out that [her brother] Fred has been arrested on several charges involving the disappearance and death of a 12-year-old boy named James Ferebee. . . . Growing up, Fred had always been strange and alienating, exhibiting symptoms of Asperger's or perhaps something further on the autism spectrum, though Ava can hardly imagine him as a killer." (Kirkus Reviews)

REVIEW: *Booklist* v110 no13 p19 Mr 1 2014 Kristine Huntley

REVIEW: *Kirkus Rev* v82 no4 p225 F 15 2014

"No Book But The World". "A brother and sister with unconventional childhoods grow into adulthood, with predictably quirky results. . . . Through substantial flashbacks to their childhoods, adolescences and early adult lives, Ava is always looking to put the family narrative into some kind of meaningful whole, though Fred's arrest and incarceration severely challenge this attempt to find coherence. [Leah Hager] Cohen is finely attuned to family dynamics here, both the quiet inner workings of Ava's successful marriage and her genuine bewilderment about Fred's fall from grace."

REVIEW: *N Y Times Book Rev* p30 Ap 27 2014

REVIEW: *N Y Times Book Rev* p14 Ap 20 2014 JULIE MYERSON

REVIEW: *New Yorker* v90 no13 p91-1 My 19 2014

REVIEW: *Publ Wkly* v261 no4 p165 Ja 27 2014

COHEN, LISA. All we know; three lives; [by] Lisa Cohen 429 p. 2012 Farrar, Straus and Giroux
1. Biographies 2. Biography—20th century 3. Modernism (Aesthetics)—History—20th century 4. Socialites—United States—Biography 5. Women—Biography 6. Women authors, American—19th century—Biography 7. Women fashion designers—England—Biography 8. Women intellectuals—Biography
ISBN 0374176493; 9780374176495 (alk. paper)
LC 2011-041055

SUMMARY: This collective biography examines the lives of "Esther Murphy (1897-1962) . . . Mercedes de Acosta (1893-1968) . . . and feminist Madge Garland (1898-1990). . . .They knew each other well from social circles, and none of them had simple lives. [Lisa] Cohen . . . delineates the . . . biographical matters of ancestry, parents, schooling, marriages, affairs, friendships, breakups, work, and death. . . . [A] three-part inquiry into the meaning of failure, style, and sexual identity." (Publishers Weekly)

REVIEW: *N Y Times Book Rev* p32 S 22 2013 IHSAN TAYLOR

"The Scientists: A Family Romance," "Some Kind of Fairy Tale," and "All We Know: Three Lives." "In this memoir [Marco] Roth . . . investigates his father's troubled life through the novels he cherished. . . . Drawing faithfully on English folklore, [Graham] Joyce's novel of disruption and grief concerns Tara, who vanished from a forest when she was a teenager. . . . This group biography plunges readers into the milieu of midcentury upper-class lesbians, portraying it as a beguiling, exclusive club."

REVIEW: *Women's Review of Books* v30 no2 p27-9 Mr/Ap 2013 Emily Toth

COHEN, MICHAEL DAVID. Reconstructing the campus; higher education and the American Civil War; [by] Michael David Cohen xi, 273 p. 2012 University of Virginia Press
1. Education (Higher)—United States—History—19th century 2. Educational change—United States—History—19th century 3. Historical literature 4. Universities and colleges—Curricula—United States—History—19th century 5. Universities and colleges—United States—Admission—History—19th century 6. Universities and colleges—United States—History—19th century
ISBN 9780813933177 (cloth: alk. paper); 9780813933184 (e-book)

LC 2012-000870

SUMMARY: In this book, author Michael David Cohen "argues that the Civil War and the political and social conditions the war created prompted major reforms, including the establishment of a new federal role in education. Reminded by the war of the importance of a well-trained military, Congress began providing resources to colleges that offered military courses and other practical curricula. . . . For the first time, the U.S. government both influenced curricula and monitored institutions." (Publisher's note)

REVIEW: *Am Hist Rev* v119 no1 p178-9 F 2014 Nancy Beadie

"Reconstructing the Campus: Higher Education and the American Civil War". "By judiciously selecting his sample to represent both regional diversity and a range of institutional types, and by thoroughly grounding his description and analysis in archival sources, [Michael David] Cohen provides a rich and nuanced account of the character of higher education in the United States during a critical period. In the process he also highlights significant regional variations that have previously been insufficiently explored. . . . In some ways Cohen may overstate the impact of the war. . . . By abstracting institutions currently recognized as colleges and universities from this broader institutional context, Cohen may overestimate discontinuities between prewar and postwar higher education."

REVIEW: *Choice* v50 no7 p1315 Mr 2013 D. Steeples

REVIEW: *J Am Hist* v100 no2 p535-6 S 2013 W. Bruce Leslie

COHEN, NICK. You can't read this book; censorship in an age of freedom; [by] Nick Cohen xxii, 330 p. 2012 Fourth Estate

1. Censorship 2. Freedom of speech 3. Freedom of the press 4. Political science literature 5. Rushdie, Salman, 1947-
ISBN 0007308906 (pbk.); 9780007308903 (pbk.)
LC 2012-397627

SUMMARY: This book by Nick Cohen was the "winner of Polemic of the Year at the 2013 Political Book Awards." It was the author's intent to demonstrate that "from the revolution in Iran that wasn't, to the Great Firewall of China . . . the traditional opponents of freedom of speech--religious fanaticism, plutocratic power and dictatorial states--are thriving, and in many respects finding the world a more comfortable place in the early 21st century than they did in the late 20th." (Publisher's note)

REVIEW: *New Statesman* v141 no5090 p55 Ja 30 2012

REVIEW: *TLS* no5761 p23 Ag 30 2013 ALEX DANCHEV

"You Can't Read This Book: Censorship in an Age of Freedom." "Few escape Nick Cohen's bite. He is especially severe on those who should know better. He takes intellectuals seriously, even personally, and finds them wanting. . . . The insistent cultural critique is reminiscent of Robert Hughes. . . . The author is a contrarian. His book is dedicated to the late Christopher Hitchens. . . . At its coruscating best, it is indeed Hitchensonian; too often, however, it smacks of Nick Cohen's Observer column and lacks the terrifying erudition, the raking fire and mordant wit of Hitchens himself."

COHEN, RACHEL. Bernard Berenson; a life in the picture trade; [by] Rachel Cohen 344 p. 2013 Yale University Press

1. ART—History—Renaissance 2. Art historians—United States—Biography 3. BIOGRAPHY & AUTOBIOGRAPHY—Cultural Heritage 4. BIOGRAPHY & AUTOBIOGRAPHY—Religious
ISBN 0300149425; 9780300149425 (hardback)
LC 2013-022541

SUMMARY: Author Rachel Cohen presents a biography of art dealer Bernard Berenson and "draws on new archival materials that bring out the significance of his secret business dealings and the way his family and companions . . . helped to form his ideas and his legacy. Cohen explores Berenson's inner world and exceptional visual capacity while also illuminating the historical forces." (Publisher's note)

REVIEW: *Apollo: The International Magazine for Collectors* v179 no616 p89 Ja 2014

REVIEW: *Apollo: The International Magazine for Collectors* v179 no617 p88-9 F 2014 Charles Saumarez Smith

"Bernard Berenson: A Life in the Picture Trade". "Rachel Cohen . . . has written an extremely thoughtful and readable biography of Berenson. . . . In reading her account of him, it is not altogether clear why he was so much, and so internationally esteemed for more than just the range of his intellect and the conversational brilliance that already made him well known in the salons of Boston. . . . Where Cohen's book is deeply interesting is in her account of Berenson's Jewishness, which is not surprising since it is a volume in a series of Jewish Lives. . . . Cohen also documents the astonishing and constant infidelity of both Berenson himself and his wife Mary."

REVIEW: *Booklist* v110 no5 p20 N 1 2013 Donna Seaman

REVIEW: *Burlington Mag* v156 no1336 p472-3 Jl 2014 ROBERT B. SIMON

REVIEW: *Choice* v51 no8 p1385 Ap 2014 M. Miller

REVIEW: *Commentary* v137 no5 p82-3 My 2014 HENRIK BERING

REVIEW: *N Y Rev Books* v60 no18 p66-8 N 21 2013 Walter Kaiser

COHEN, YEHUDA. The Italians; family as a core; [by] Yehuda Cohen xii, 193 p. 2013 Sussex Academic Press

1. National characteristics, Italian 2. Social science literature
ISBN 1845193911 (h/b : alk. paper); 9781845193911 (h/b : alk. paper)
LC 2013-009289

SUMMARY: This book by Yehuda Cohen, "setting out the historical national and religious characteristics of the Italians as they impact on the integration within the European Union, . . . makes note of the two characteristics that have an adverse effect on Italian national identity: cleavages between north and south and the dominant role of family. It discusses how for Italians family loyalty is stronger than any other allegiance, including feelings towards their country, their nation, or the EU." (Publisher's note)

REVIEW: *Choice* v51 no6 p1082-3 F 2014 C. De Santi

"The Italians: Family as a Core." "[Yehuda] Cohen's derivative and informally written book is part of a series analyzing how well certain European countries fit within the European Union. His study about the Italians, which fails to take into consideration major historians, political scientists, or even sociologists of the Italian family, seeks to show how the family became Italy's central societal unit, creating structural problems in terms of politics, economics, and society in both the past and present. . . . Based largely on simplistic stereotypes, the book's insistence on the role of the family as the major explanation for why Italians cannot be loyal to the state or to Europe ends up producing something akin to an essay that is neither novel nor convincing.

COHN, LAWRENCE.ed. Nothing but the blues. See Nothing but the blues

COHN, SAMUEL K. Popular protest in late medieval English towns; [by] Samuel K. Cohn 375 p. 2012 Cambridge University Press

1. HISTORY—Europe—Great Britain 2. Historical literature 3. Protest movements—England—History—To 1500

ISBN 9781107027800 (hardback)

LC 2012-017173

SUMMARY: This book "refocuses attention on the varied nature of popular movements in towns from Carlisle to Dover and from the London tax revolt of Longbeard in 1196 to Jack Cade's Rebellion in 1450, exploring the leadership, social composition, organisation and motives of popular protest. The book charts patterns of urban revolt in times of strong and weak kingship, contrasting them with the broad sweep of ecological and economic change that inspired revolts on the continent." (Publisher's note)

REVIEW: *Am Hist Rev* v119 no1 p234-5 F 2014 David Rollison

REVIEW: *Choice* v50 no12 p2302 Ag 2013 C. L. Hamilton

REVIEW: *TLS* no5750 p26 Je 14 2013 JOHN HATCHER

"Popular Protest in Late Medieval English Towns." "The compilation of a database of English urban conflicts is most welcome, but producing valid generalizations from it is a formidable task. . . . Such is the ambition of the book that it frequently canters at a perilously fast pace over a multitude of hurdles. . . . Another difficulty is the bias in the main sources. . . . 'Popular Protest in Late Medieval English Towns' falls short of producing a definitive comprehensive summary of the manifold characteristics of disorder in this period, but it is a step forward and bound to stimulate and facilitate further study."

COKAL, SUSANN. The Kingdom of little wounds; [by] Susann Cokal 576 p. 2013 Candlewick Press

1. Fairy tales 2. Historical fiction 3. Kings & rulers—Fiction 4. Syphilis—Patients 5. Young adult fiction

ISBN 0763666947; 9780763666941

LC 2013-933162

SUMMARY: In this book, by Susann Cokal, it's "the eve of Princess Sophia's wedding [and] the Scandinavian city of Skyggehavn prepares to fete the occasion with a sumptuous display of riches. . . . Yet beneath the . . . celebration, a shiver of darkness creeps through the palace halls. . . . When [the] . . . prick of a needle sets off a series of events that will alter the course of history, the fates of seamstress Ava Bingen and mute nursemaid Midi Sorte become . . . intertwined with that of mad Queen Isabel." (Publisher's note)

REVIEW: *Booklist* v110 no5 p74-6 N 1 2013 Sarah Hunter

REVIEW: *Bull Cent Child Books* v67 no5 p261 Ja 2014 K. C.

REVIEW: *Kirkus Rev* v81 no18 p170 S 15 2013

REVIEW: *N Y Times Book Rev* p16 D 22 2013 DARCEY STEINKE

"The Kingdom of Little Wounds." "Like a fairy tale, 'The Kingdom of Little Wounds' starts with a pin's prick and a drop of blood. . . . It's a fitting start to this dark young adult novel by Susann Cokal. . . . 'The Kingdom fo Little Wounds' takes syphilis as its central metaphor. . . . This is lewd and raucous territory for a young adult novel, almost de Sadean in its rich, sumptuous details. . . . The sex here may be more conventional than in de Sade, but there is the same undercurrent of corruption. . . . There is also a lot of blood."

REVIEW: *Publ Wkly* v260 no38 p83 S 23 2013

REVIEW: *Publ Wkly* p130 Children's starred review annual 2013

REVIEW: *SLJ* v60 no3 p73 Mr 2014 Alissa Bach

REVIEW: *Voice of Youth Advocates* v36 no5 p54-5 D 2013 Heather Christensen

COKER, CHRISTOPHER. Warrior geeks; how 21st -century technology is changing the way we fight and think about war; [by] Christopher Coker 384 p. 2012 Columbia University Press

1. Drone aircraft pilots—Psychology 2. Military art and science—Technological innovations—History 3. Military ethics 4. Military weapons—Technological innovations—Moral and ethical aspects 5. Social science literature 6. Soldiers—Psychology 7. Soldiers in literature 8. Virtual reality—Psychological aspects 9. War in literature

ISBN 9780231704083 (alk. paper)

LC 2012-039145

SUMMARY: This by Christopher Coker "surveys the cybernetic technologies aiming to incorporate soldiers into a cybernetic system through which the military can read their thoughts and mold them accordingly. It considers the anticipated cooperation of men and robots on the battlefields of tomorrow, and it measures the extent to which armies may one day be able to reengineer warriors through pharmacological manipulation." (Publisher's note)

REVIEW: *TLS* no5755 p8-9 Jl 19 2013 VICTOR DAVIS HANSON

"Saltpeter: The Mother of Gunpowder," "Napalm: An American Biography," and "Warrior Geeks: How Twenty-First-Century Technology is Changing the Way We Fight and Think About War." "David Cressy offers a brief but fascinating history of saltpetre. . . . He has skilfully turned 200 pages on the collection of human and animal waste into a fascinating reflection on how civic liberties were often quashed by concerns for national security. . . . [Robert M.] Neer is often highly critical of the American m use of napalm; yet his narrative of its origins, production and use over the past seven decades is not a jeremiad, but learned, fair and historically accurate. . . . Do not let the almost flippant title of Christopher Coker's 'Warrior Geeks' fool you. . . . [It is] a masterly account from a very well-read humanist about the fearful advance of post-human technologies in war."

COLAZZA, STEFANO.ed. Chemical ecology of insect parasitoids. See Chemical ecology of insect parasitoids

COLBERT, BRANDY. Pointe; [by] Brandy Colbert 288 p. 2014 G. P. Putnams Sons, an imprint of Penguin Group (USA) Inc

1. African Americans—Fiction 2. Anexoria nervosa—Fiction 3. Ballet dancing—Fiction 4. Emotional problems—Fiction 5. Family life—Illinois—Fiction 6. High schools—Fiction 7. Kidnapping—Fiction 8. Schools—Fiction 9. Young adult fiction

ISBN 0399160345; 9780399160349 (hardcover)

LC 2013-020689

SUMMARY: In this novel, by Brandy Colbert, "Theo is better now. She's eating again, dating guys who are almost appropriate, and well on her way to becoming an elite ballet dancer. But when her oldest friend, Donovan, returns home after spending four long years with his kidnapper, Theo starts reliving memories about his abduction—and his abductor. . . . Theo knows she didn't do anything wrong, telling the truth would put everything she's been living for at risk. But keeping quiet might be worse." (Publisher's note)

REVIEW: *Booklist* v110 no16 p50 Ap 15 2014 Daniel Kraus

REVIEW: *Bull Cent Child Books* v67 no10 p506-7 Je 2014 K. C.

"Pointe". "While the plot is a bit raw for the typical ballet-book reader, the various elements here guarantee multiple interest points for fans of the problem novel, the most interesting being the way Theo ever so slowly comes to understand how naive she was at thirteen, how skewed her ideas of sex and love still are, and how the legacy of Trent's abuse continues to haunt her decision-making. . . . The book chooses Theo's understanding rather than Donovan's experience as a culminating moment, but since the story is focused on her recovery, that understanding is enough of a spur toward doing the right thing for both ethical validity and narrative closure."

REVIEW: *Horn Book Magazine* v90 no4 p88-9 Jl/Ag 2014 KATIE BIRCHER

REVIEW: *Kirkus Rev* v82 no5 p107 Mr 1 2014

"Pointe". " It's an intriguing premise, and debut author [Brandy] Colbert does a commendable job creating authentic teen characters that readers will recognize from the halls of their own high schools. Unfortunately, while there is enough here to entertain, the story never reaches its full potential. References to Theo's struggles with anorexia are surprisingly and disappointingly lacking in emotion. Ditto for her relationship with Donovan. Theo's a textbook anorexic, almost to the point of cliché, but never are readers given the opportunity to feel her desperation. And while there are flashbacks aplenty, there are surprisingly few that shed light on the deep connection Theo and Donovan presumably once shared. This is a novel that ultimately misses the . . . point."

REVIEW: *Publ Wkly* v261 no6 p91 F 10 2014

REVIEW: *SLJ* v60 no3 p154 Mr 2014 Jill Ratzan

REVIEW: *Voice of Youth Advocates* v37 no3 p36-7 Ag 2014 KELLY JENSEN

REVIEW: *Voice of Youth Advocates* v37 no1 p63 Ap 2014 Shana Morales

COLD WAR SOCIAL SCIENCE; knowledge production, liberal democracy, and human nature; xv, 270 p. 2012 Palgrave Macmillan

1. Cold War, 1945-1989 2. Social science literature 3. Social sciences—Research—United States—History 4. Theory of knowledge 5. World politics—1945-1989

ISBN 0230340504 (hardback); 9780230340503 (hardback)

LC 2011-047895

SUMMARY: In this book on the history of social science, editors "Mark Solovey and Hamilton Cravens . . . have chosen the Cold War era to highlight how long-term, low-level war planning and crises used different types of social science research to develop a knowledge base for all forms of contemporary life." (Contemporary Sociology)

REVIEW: *Contemp Sociol* v43 no2 p266-7 Mr 2014 Andrew D. Grossman

"Cold War Social Science: Knowledge Production, Liberal Democracy, and Human Nature". "'Cold War Social Science' is very well thought out and researched and there are no catastrophic flaws or tendentiousness in any of these collected essays. . . . The editors and the authors did a fine job of staying on point, writing fine pieces of analysis, and, most importantly, doing it in a cross-disciplinary fashion. I highly recommend this book for anyone interested in the social sciences and especially those who teach qualitative social science methods, which I do. It is real pleasure to find and read such a tightly written and well-researched piece of work."

REVIEW: *J Am Hist* v99 no4 p1319-20 Mr 2013 David Paul Haney

REVIEW: *Rev Am Hist* v41 no4 p742-7 D 2013 Audra J. Wolfe

COLE, HENRY.il. Bogart and Vinnie. See Vernick, A.

COLE, ISABEL FARGO.tr. The Jew Car. See Fühmann, FF,

COLE, PETER. The invention of influence; [by] Peter Cole 128 p. 2014 New Directions Publishing Corporation

1. American poetry 2. Freud, Sigmund, 1856-1939 3. Mysticism—Judaism 4. Poems—Collections 5. Tausk, Victor

ISBN 9780811221726 (acid-free paper)

LC 2013-039879

SUMMARY: This book of poetry by Peter Cole "retains tangible traces of his work as a translator of the poetry of Hebrew mystics. These poems extend the mystics' project, seeking the spiritual self and finding it, quite often, in the threshold between 'world' and 'word.' . . . The story of [Sigmund] Freud's under-appreciated and complicated disciple Victor Tausk . . . serves as a . . . backdrop against which Cole deeply explores wide ranging concerns." (Publishers Weekly)

REVIEW: *Booklist* v110 no12 p12 F 15 2014 Michael Autrey

"The Invention of Influence." "'The Invention of Influence' is [Peter Cole's] fourth collection, and it is masterful. Harold Bloom's introduction--an imprimatur of quality if there ever was one--combines fulsome praise with careful and welcome exposition of some of the countless allusions in this deeply profound, committed verse. The long narrative title poem examines the life and work of Victor Tausk, an early disciple of Freud who committed suicide. The variety of verse forms, the attention to and respect for Tausk's complex path, the pressure the poem contains and releases--it might be a masterpiece."

REVIEW: *Libr J* v139 no7 p85 Ap 15 2014 Annalisa Pesek

REVIEW: *Publ Wkly* v261 no5 p35 F 3 2014

COLE, SARAH. At the violet hour; Modernism and violence, in England and Ireland; [by] Sarah Cole xiv, 377 p. 2012 Oxford University Press

1. English literature—20th century—History and criticism 2. English literature—Irish authors—History and criticism 3. Historical literature 4. Modernism (Literature)—Great Britain 5. Violence in literature
ISBN 0195389611; 9780195389616 (hdbd)
LC 2012-005223

SUMMARY: Author Sarah Coles shows how "modernism emerged as an imaginative response to the devastating events that defined the period, including the chaos of anarchist bombings, World War I, the Irish uprising, and the Spanish Civil War. [It] explores the strange intimacy between modernist aesthetics and violence in the late nineteenth and early twentieth centuries." (Publisher's note)

REVIEW: *Choice* v51 no2 p257 O 2013 D. Stuber

REVIEW: *Kirkus Rev* v81 no19 p282 O 1 2013

REVIEW: *New York Times* v163 no56306 pC2 O 31 2013 John Williams

REVIEW: *TLS* no5762 p23 S 6 2013 LAUREN ARRINGTON

"At the Violet Hour: Modernism and Violence in England and Ireland." "[Sarah] Cole focuses almost exclusively on English and Irish literature . . . but her close readings of 'Portrait' and 'To the Lighthouse' resonate powerfully across Anglo-American modernism. . . . In Cole's dynamite reading of [Joseph] Conrad's 'The Secret Agent,' meanwhile, she playfully argues that the unfortunate Stevie's body is history. . . . Cole's close readings of violence in the work of some of the major modernists are superb. Yet in her long chapter 'The Irish Insurrection and the Limits of Enchantment', she loses purchase because of factual errors that compound superficial glosses."

COLE, TEJU. Every day is for the thief; a novel; [by] Teju Cole 162 p. 2014 Random House Inc

1. Homecoming—Nigeria—Lagos—Fiction 2. Identity (Psychology)—Fiction 3. Life change events—Fiction 4. Nigerian fiction (English) 5. Nigerians—New York (State)—New York—Fiction 6. Reunions—Nigeria—Lagos—Fiction
ISBN 0812995783; 9780812995787 (hardcover: acid-free paper)
LC 2014-004326

SUMMARY: In this book, by Teju Cole, "a young Nigerian living in New York City goes home to Lagos for a short visit, finding a city both familiar and strange. In a city dense with story, the unnamed narrator moves through a mosaic of life, hoping to find inspiration for his own. He witnesses . . . email frauds from an Internet café, longs after a mysterious woman reading on a public bus, . . . and recalls the tragic fate of an eleven-year-old boy accused of stealing at a local market." (Publisher's note)

REVIEW: *Bookforum* v21 no1 p32 Ap/My 2014 YASMINE EL RASHIDI

REVIEW: *Booklist* v110 no16 p14 Ap 15 2014 Michele Leber

REVIEW: *Kirkus Rev* v82 no6 p334 Mr 15 2014

REVIEW: *Libr J* v138 no16 p59 O 1 2013 Barbara Hoffert

REVIEW: *Libr J* v139 no13 p46 Ag 1 2014 Terry Ann Lawler

REVIEW: *London Rev Books* v36 no13 p21-3 Jl 3 2014 Adam Mars-Jones

REVIEW: *N Y Rev Books* v61 no12 p61-2 Jl 10 2014 Gideon Lewis-Kraus

REVIEW: *N Y Times Book Rev* p32 Ap 6 2014

REVIEW: *N Y Times Book Rev* p14 Mr 30 2014 HARI KUNZRU

REVIEW: *New Statesman* v143 no5214 p46-9 Je 13 2014 Hedley Twidle

REVIEW: *New York Times* v163 no56446 pC7 Mr 20 2014 JOHN WILLIAMS

REVIEW: *New York Times* v163 no56452 pC1-4 Mr 26 2014 DWIGHT GARNER

REVIEW: *New Yorker* v90 no6 p77-1 Mr 31 2014

"Every Day Is for the Thief." "In this slim novel, previously published in Nigeria, a man travels from the U.S., where he lives, to visit family and friends in Lagos, his childhood home. Accompanied by the author's photographs, the narrative consists of digressive accounts of random encounters around the city, which is viewed with both the curiosity of a foreigner and the intimacy of a native. The narrator is infuriated by local corruption, the threat it poses to everyday activity and to the serenity he needs to work. Yet he also feels pity for American writers, who 'must hoe the same arid patch for stories.'"

REVIEW: *TLS* no5808 p20 Jl 25 2014 KATE WEBB

REVIEW: *World Lit Today* v88 no5 p8 S/O 2014

COLEMAN, JON T. Here lies Hugh Glass; a mountain man, a bear, and the rise of the American nation; [by] Jon T. Coleman p. cm. 2012 Hill and Wang

1. Biographies 2. Frontier and pioneer life—West (U.S.) 3. Pioneers—West (U.S.)—Biography
ISBN 9780809054596 (cloth : alk. paper)
LC 2011-036617

SUMMARY: This book examines "[a]n inadvertent American archetype . . . Hugh Glass had no idea he'd be a figure in the history books. A sort of entry-level mountain man in the early days of American exploration in the West, he 'approached grizzly bears and bosses with the same disreputable grin.' One of those grizzly bears mutilated him so badly that it was highly unlikely he would survive. Andrew Henry, his boss on a trapping expedition along the Missouri River, left two men to bury Glass. The two men fled when a party of Indians approached, but Glass didn't die. Instead, he crawled and hobbled for 38 days eastward to the nearest American outpost, swearing to avenge himself on the men who had abandoned him. . . . But Glass, writes the author, turns up in countless other places in the larger story of the American West, an illustration of his staying power as a symbol of an ordinary guy who 'merely endured.'" (Kirkus Reviews)

REVIEW: *Rev Am Hist* v42 no1 p51-7 Mr 2014 Jared Farmer

"Here Lies Hugh Glass: A Mountain Man, a Bear, and the Rise of the American Nation." "Credit Jon Coleman with chutzpah. As a biographer, he chose . . . Hugh Glass, . . .

the mountain man who earned fame for being half-eaten by a grizzly bear in 1823. . . . Like so many book titles, this one misleads. Perhaps ten percent of the book is about Hugh Glass the biographical person (whose entire documentary record consists of a single letter). . . . The last phrase in the title comes closest to Coleman's two main subjects: the significance of the frontier in American culture, and literary nationalism in the era of humbuggery. . . . Coleman, like his anti-hero, possesses exemplary style."

COLEMAN, T. F. Deadly Provocation; A Year of Domestic Surveillance; [by] T. F. Coleman 228 p. 2013 Outskirts Press

1. Mass surveillance 2. Missing persons—Fiction 3. Private investigators—Fiction 4. Spy stories 5. Violence—Fiction

ISBN 1478703415; 9781478703419

SUMMARY: In this book, "a private investigator is recruited by a clandestine company that may be using questionable methods of surveillance. . . . The PI catches the attention of Alan Michaels of the Domestic Surveillance Consulting Company, who makes Jake an offer he gladly accepts. . . . But Jake quickly grows suspicious of the DSCC when he realizes that some monitored subjects, or 'targets,' don't seem to have done anything wrong." (Kirkus Reviews)

REVIEW: *Kirkus Rev* v82 no2 p366 Ja 15 2014

"Deadly Provocation: A Year of Domestic Surveillance". "Readers will empathize with a man in an unfamiliar new career, and he proves himself both proficient and honorable when he goes against his DSCC orders and makes direct contact with Dillon, a seemingly harmless man under scrutiny. But Jake's treatment of women is frivolous. . . .The novel concludes with Jake drafting a few friends, including retired detective Thomas Luck, for a rescue mission; it's well-done and undoubtedly enjoyable but also unfortunately signifies the close of the espionage plot. But, with Jake's future left open, he's definitely ripe for a sequel. At its best when the protagonist is surveilling; Jake Conley could use another book or two to work on his spying abilities."

COLES, ALEX.ed. EP Volume 1. See EP Volume 1

COLES, POLLY. The Politics of Washing; Real Life in Venice; [by] Polly Coles 192 p. 2013 Robert Hale Ltd

1. Foreign teachers—Italy 2. Memoirs 3. Tourism—Italy—Venice 4. Venice (Italy)—Description & travel 5. Venice (Italy)—Social life & customs

ISBN 0719808782; 9780719808784

SUMMARY: This book is the author's account of living in Venice, Italy for a year. "When Polly Coles and her family left England for Venice, they discovered a city caught between modern and ancient life . . . where schools are housed in renaissance palaces, and your new washing machine can only be delivered on foot. This is a city perilously under siege from tourism, but its people refuse to give it up--indeed they love it with a passion." (Publisher's note)

REVIEW: *Booklist* v110 no16 p13 Ap 15 2014 Mark Knoblauch

REVIEW: *Libr J* v139 no7 p96 Ap 15 2014 Benjamin Malczewski

REVIEW: *New York Times* v163 no56477 p2-5 Ap 20 2014 SUZANNE MacNEILLE

REVIEW: *TLS* no5751 p29 Je 21 2013 JONATHAN KEATES

"The Politics of Washing." "A resident population nevertheless contrives to endure in theme-park Venice. . . . Polly Coles evokes the dogged practicalities and quotidian rhythms of existence among this dedicated minority. An English teacher with an Italian violin-maker as her partner, she spent a year living in Venice, a short enough spell but one in which she and her surroundings developed a significant mutual sympathy. . . . Coles's Venice is emphatically unromantic, its beauties accidental. . . . No book as thoughtful, perceptive and humane on Venice considered simply in terms of a living community has appeared since William Dean Howells wrote his 'Venetian Life' in 1866."

COLFER, EOIN, 1965-. The hangman's revolution; [by] Eoin Colfer 384 p. 2014 Hyperion

1. Assassins—Fiction 2. Science fiction 3. Time travel—Fiction

ISBN 9781423161639 (hardback); 1423161637

LC 2014-001938

SUMMARY: In this book, "young FBI agent Chevie Savano arrives back in modern-day London after a time-trip to the Victorian age, to find the present very different from the one she left. Europe is being run by a Fascist movement known as the Boxites. . . . Chevie's memories come back to her in fragments, and just as she is learning about the WARP program from Professor Charles Smart, inventor of the time machine, he is killed by secret service police." (Publisher's note)

REVIEW: *Booklist* v110 no9/10 p82 Ja 1 2014 Gillian Engberg

"The Hangman's Revolution," "The Here and Now," and "The Last Forever". "New York Times best-selling author [Eoin] Colfer continues his W.A.R.P. series with another time-traveling adventure. This time, young FBI agent Chevie Savano returns to contemporary London, which is under threat from a Fascist European government. . . . The author of the blockbuster Traveling Pants books moves into brand-new territory with this sf novel about a time-traveling teen who carries a terrifying secret about the future. . . . A grieving teen finds romance and hope during a summer spent in a small coastal town in the latest from [Deb] Caletti, a National Book Award finalist and perennially bestselling author."

REVIEW: *Bull Cent Child Books* v68 no1 p16 S 2014 E. B.

REVIEW: *Kirkus Rev* v82 no10 p295 My 15 2014

REVIEW: *SLJ* v60 no8 p108 Ag 2014

REVIEW: *Voice of Youth Advocates* v37 no3 p79 Ag 2014 Sean Rapacki

COLLARD, SNEED B. The CIA and FBI; top secret; [by] Sneed B. Collard 32 p. 2013 Rourke Educational Media

1. Children's nonfiction 2. Intelligence service—United States—History 3. September 11 Terrorist Attacks, 2001—Influence 4. United States. Central Intelligence Agency 5. United States. Federal Bureau of Investigation

ISBN 9781621699255

LC 2013-938877

SUMMARY: In this book on the FBI and CIA, author Sneed B. Collard III "walks readers through the inception of each organization, from the FBI's small number of agents hired in 1908 to investigate federal crimes, to Harry Truman's signing of the law in 1947 to create the CIA as a way to gather intelligence after WWII. The author . . . places great emphasis on the 9/11 attacks and the changes it brought to both agencies." (Booklist)

REVIEW: *Booklist* v110 no3 p74-6 O 1 2013 Angela Leeper

"The CIA and FBI: Top Secret." "This title in the Freedom Forces series takes some of the mystery out of the clandestine activities in the FBI and the CIA. . . . The author highlights their similarities and differences, methods of gathering information, and roles in American history, and places great emphasis on the 9/11 attacks and the changes it brought to both agencies. The layout matches the book's focus with crisp full-color photos and high-tech images, while sidebars on such topics as J. Edgar Hoover, Osama bin Laden, unmanned aerial vehicles, and spy gadgets add to the already engaging information."

THE COLLECTED LETTERS OF THOMAS HARDY; Further Letters 1861-1927; 320 p. 2012 Oxford University Press

ISBN 0199607753; 9780199607754

LC 7703-0355

SUMMARY: This book, edited by Michael Millgate and Keith Wilson, "contains previously unpublished letters from all periods of [poet Thomas] Hardy's career, his earliest known letter among them. It introduces important new correspondents, throws fresh light on existing correspondences, and richly enhances the reader's understanding of both familiar and hitherto unfamiliar aspects of Hardy's life and work and of the times in which he lived." (Publisher's note)

REVIEW: *Choice* v51 no1 p76 S 2013 S. A. Parker

REVIEW: *Sewanee Rev* v122 no1 pix-xi Wint 2014 Floyd Skloot

REVIEW: *TLS* no5754 p3-4 Jl 12 2013 ANGELIQUE RICHARDSON

"The Collected Letters of Thomas Hardy: Further Letters 1861-1927." "The letter was the form of communication that best served this quiet, extraordinarily sympathetic, and most intently observant of Victorians. . . . Hardy's own letters were places for quiet reflection and deepening emotional ties, for occasional advice, details to visitors of the times of the Waterloo trains, and for public protests on the iniquity (and absurdity) of war and against cruelty to animals. . . . More than any other form, letters provide insight into Hardy's many-sidedness. . . . The editors have done some remarkable detective work, and the volume supplements almost a hundred 'additional letters' from the seventh volume, confidently assumed, a quarter of a century ago, to be the last."

THE COLLECTED POEMS OF PHILIP LAMANTIA; 512 p. 2013 University of California Press

1. American poetry 2. Drugs in literature 3. Mysticism in literature 4. Poems—Collections 5. Surrealism (Literature)

ISBN 0520269721; 9780520269729 (cloth : alk. paper)

LC 2012-050020

SUMMARY: This book presents poems by Philip Lamantia, who "sought to extend and renew the visionary tradition of Romanticism in a distinctly American vernacular, drawing on mystical lore and drug experience in the process. 'The Collected Poems' gathers not only his published work but also an extensive selection of unpublished or uncollected work; the editors have also provided a biographical introduction." (Publisher's note)

REVIEW: *Bookforum* v20 no3 p34 S-N 2013 ALBERT MOBILIO

"The Collected Poems of Philip Lamantia." "From the mid-1940s till his death in 2005, Lamantia produced verse rich in flourish and invention, every bit as intense as [Allen] Ginsberg's, even as it tunes in to abstruse and deeply interior frequencies. The 'Collected Poems' offers a wide-angle view on a career that waxed and waned--sometimes owing to the author's struggle with depression--over several decades. . . . He sought a poetry of transcendence via language designed to rise above mere meaning and chime at those higher spiritual elevations where emptiness and fullness are one and the same. . . . A great unevenness, though, marks the collection, and furnishes readers with insight into the emotional complexities of composition."

REVIEW: *Choice* v51 no8 p1401 Ap 2014 J. A. Zoller

COLLEY, LINDA. Acts of Union and Disunion; [by] Linda Colley 192 p. 2014 Profile Books Ltd

1. Great Britain—History 2. Great Britain—Politics & government 3. Historical literature 4. Ireland—History—Union, 1801 5. National characteristics, British 6. Scotland—History—Union, 1707

ISBN 1781251851; 9781781251850

SUMMARY: In this book, author Linda Colley "examines the mythology of Britishness, and how far--and why--it has faded. She discusses the Acts of Union with Wales, Scotland and Ireland, and their limitations, while scrutinizing England's own fractures. And she demonstrates how the UK has been shaped by movement: of British people to other countries and continents, and of people, ideas and influences arriving from elsewhere." (Publisher's note)

REVIEW: *Economist* v410 no8868 p66 Ja 4 2014

"Acts of Union and Disunion." "Linda Colley's short and fascinating study . . . centres on Britain's internal and external relations but the themes it explores are universal. . . . Ms. Colley, who has long studied the complexities of British national identities, purports to be neutral. Yet she is not, quite. For the prescriptions she offers are designed to maintain some kind of union. She calls for England to have its own parliament, for local governments to raise and collect more taxes and for Britain to have a written constitution. This last, she believes, 'might supply some fresh constitutive stories for a new kind of union'. Whether Britain's politicians could write this new magna carta is less clear."

REVIEW: *New Statesman* v143 no8 p46-8 F 28 2014 Andrew Marr

REVIEW: *TLS* no5792 p25-6 Ap 4 2014 VERNON BOGDANOR

"Acts of Union and Disunion: What Has Held the UK Together and What Is Dividing It?" "The historian Linda Colley is best known . . . for her book 'Britons: Forging the Nation 1707-1837,' first published in 1992, in which she argued that the notion of Britishness was, in large part, an artificial construct. . . . One implication was that . . . Britishness would be squeezed by a pincer movement—internally from a resurgent Celtic nationalism and externally from the pressures of European integration. 'Acts of Union and Disunion,' based on a recent fifteen-part Radio 4 series, may be seen as a series of reflections on this theme. . . . Colley offers much food for thought. 'Acts of Union and Disunion' is a miracle of compression based on wide reading and reflection over several decades."

COLLICUTT, PAUL.il. The Murder Mile; 128 p. 2012 SelfMadeHero

1. Bannister, Roger, 1929- 2. Graphic novels 3. Murder—Fiction 4. Murder investigation—Fiction 5. Running

ISBN 1906838623; 9781906838621

SUMMARY: In this graphic novel, "runner Todd . . . Naylor, is found dead and Private Detective Daniel Stone, himself a former miler, is called in to investigate. The prime suspect is Naylor's coach . . . thought to have been bribing athletes to throw races. . . . Stone is attacked by an unknown man who makes off\ with Naylor's training diary; the detective gives spirited chase. The murder plot develops in parallel with the race for the four-minute mile." (Times Literary Supplement)

REVIEW: *TLS* no5745 p26 My 10 2013 JOSH RAYMOND

"The Murder Mile." "The murder plot develops in parallel with the race for the four-minute mile, sprinting towards an effusively imagined climax at the contest between [Roger] Bannister and the Australian John Landy. . . . [Paul] Collicutt's artwork is exemplary. The watercolour shading both arrests and soothes the eye, runners convey pace, and occasional pain, and the correspondence between text and illustration is so precise that the speech bubbles feel like titles. But a detective novel invites forensic exactitude, and it is unfortunate that the late Todd Naylor, twice described as having been found 'face down in the desert', is later said (and depicted) to have fallen on his back. Nonetheless, 'The Murder Mile' remains a diverting and aesthetically pleasing American adventure."

COLLIER, BRYAN.il. Knock knock. See Beaty, D.

COLLIER, PAUL. Exodus; how migration is changing our world; [by] Paul Collier 320 p. 2014 Oxford University Press

1. Assimilation of immigrants 2. Economics literature 3. Emigration and immigration—History—21st century 4. Multiculturalism—History—21st century

ISBN 0195398653; 9780195398656

LC 2013-006809

SUMMARY: In this book, "Paul Collier . . . lays out the effects of encouraging or restricting migration. Drawing on original research and case studies, he explores this volatile issue from three perspectives: that of the migrants themselves, that of the people they leave behind, and that of the host societies where they relocate." (Publisher's note)

REVIEW: *Atlantic* v312 no4 p44-6 N 2013 JASON DePARLE PAUL COLLIER

"Exodus: How Migration Is Changing Our World." "[Paul] Collier drew attention a few years back with 'The Bottom Billion', which called for rescuing the global poor by unconventional means (including military intervention) that he cast as evidence of his tough-mindedness. In 'Exodus: How Migration Is Changing Our World', Collier is even more eager to present himself as an enemy of orthodoxy. Like most economists, he thinks the benefits of migration have generally exceeded the costs; unlike many, he sees cause for worry should migration significantly rise. . . . Collier warns that rapid ethnic change can threaten fragile social bonds and weaken support for the welfare state--imperiling the 'fruits of successful nationhood' that migrants seek."

REVIEW: *Choice* v51 no7 p1261 Mr 2014 D. W. Haines

REVIEW: *Economist* v405 no8855 p78-9 S 28 2013

"Exodus: How Migration is Changing Our World." "Paul Collier is one of the world's most thoughtful economists. His books consistently illuminate and provoke. 'Exodus' is no exception. . . . Mr. Collier's most arresting argument is that past waves of migration have created the conditions under which migration will henceforth accelerate. . . . Mr. Collier is plainly not a bigot and his arguments should be taken seriously. Nevertheless, he is far too gloomy. . . . His worries are mostly about the harm that immigration might do, rather than any it has already done. Indeed, the evidence he marshals suggests that so far it has been hugely beneficial. . . . Mr. Collier finds endless objections to a policy . . . that no country has adopted."

REVIEW: *Kirkus Rev* v81 no16 p11 Ag 15 2013

"Exodus: How Migration Is Changing Our World." "[Author Paul] Collier . . . considers migration from poor to rich nations and what immigration policies are most appropriate. . . . Collier writes at length about the critical roles of diasporas, which make the cost of migration fall and provide much-needed help to the newly arrived. . . . He notes that migrants are winners in the process. . . . The biggest losers are the people left behind in poor, mainly African nations, which lose their brightest and most talented, gaining somewhat from remittances. . . . Valuable reading for policymakers. "

COLLINGRIDGE, RICHARD.il. When It Snows. See Collingridge, R.

COLLINGRIDGE, RICHARD. When It Snows; [by] Richard Collingridge 32 p. 2013 Feiwel & Friends

1. Boys—Fiction 2. Children's stories 3. Snow—Juvenile literature 4. Teddy bears 5. Winter—Juvenile literature

ISBN 1250028310; 9781250028310

SUMMARY: In this children's book written and illustrated by Richard Collingridge, a boy takes a journey though the snow and sees various creatures. "When it snows, magic happens. Follow a boy and his teddy bear on a wondrous snowy adventure which will lead readers of all ages to a surprising place." (Publisher's note)

REVIEW: *N Y Times Book Rev* p14 D 22 2013 NELL CASEY

"Big Snow," "When It Snows," and "Winter Is for Snow." "In 'Big Snow,' written and illustrated by Jonathan Bean, another child anxious to see a winter wonderland asks his mother again and again about the impending blizzard. . . . In his first picture book, 'When It Snows,' . . . illustrator Richard Collingridge dives headlong into a fantasy of the season, showing it to be a vast and mountainous expanse of white, both eerie and enchanting. . . . 'Winter Is for Snow' is a tale of two siblings--a brother who loves the icy flakes pouring down outside their apartment window and a sister who is cranky about it all--by the prolific children's book author and illustrator Robert Neubecker."

REVIEW: *Publ Wkly* v260 no37 p46-7 S 16 2013

COLLINI, STEFAN, 1947-. Two cultures?; the significance of C.P. Snow; [by] Stefan Collini 121 p. 2013 Cambridge University Press
1. Literature & science 2. Science & the humanities 3. Science and the humanities 4. Snow, C. P. (Charles Percy), 1905-1980 5. Social criticism
ISBN 9781107617353 (pbk.)
LC 2013-017282

SUMMARY: "In this first annotated edition of F. R. Leavis's famous critique of C. P. Snow's influential argument about 'the two cultures', Stefan Collini reappraises both its literary tactics and its purpose as cultural criticism. . . . In his comprehensive introduction Collini situates Leavis's critique within the wider context of debates about 'modernity' and 'prosperity', not just the 'two cultures' of literature and science." (Publisher's note)

REVIEW: *London Rev Books* v35 no17 p10-2 S 12 2013 John Mullan
"Memoirs of a Leavisite: The Decline and Fall of Cambridge English," "English As a Vocation: The 'Scrutiny' Movement," and "The Two Cultures? The Significance of C. P. Snow." "[Author David] Ellis is well aware of Leavis's joyless reputation and tries to redeem it. . . . Christopher Hilliard's 'English as a Vocation' shows that applicants to Downing were expected already to have read large swathes of Shakespeare, 17th-century poetry, Romantic poetry and 19th-century fiction. . . . In the year of his retirement from his readership in the Cambridge English Faculty [author F. R. Leavis] achieved notoriety with his riposte to C.P. Snow's lecture 'The Two Cultures and the Scientific Revolution'. . . . The performance survives rather well."

COLLINS, CATHERINE FISHER.ed. African American women's life issues today. See African American women's life issues today

COLLINS, CIARÁN. The gamal; [by] Ciarán Collins 480 p. 2013 Bloomsbury USA
1. Bereavement in youth—Fiction 2. Friendship in youth—Fiction 3. Psychological fiction 4. Psychotherapy patients—Fiction 5. Youth—Psychology—Fiction 6. Youths' writings—Fiction
ISBN 1608198758; 9781608198757 (alk. paper)
LC 2012-046539

SUMMARY: In this novel by Ciarán Collins "Charlie has a story to tell, about his best friends Sinead and James and the bad things that happened. Charlie has promised Dr Quinn he'll write 1,000 words a day, but it's hard to know which words to write. And which secrets to tell. This is the story of the dark heart of an Irish village, of how daring to be different can be dangerous, and how there is nothing a person will not do for love." (Publisher's note)

REVIEW: *Booklist* v109 no18 p15 My 15 2013 Michael Cart

REVIEW: *Kirkus Rev* v81 no6 p151 Mr 15 2013

REVIEW: *Libr J* v138 no8 p68 My 1 2013 John G. Matthews

REVIEW: *N Y Times Book Rev* p22 S 1 2013 KATHARINE WEBER
"The Gamal." "The narrator of Ciaran Collins's remarkable first novel, 'The Gamal,' has been encouraged by a mental health professional to write his story for therapeutic purposes. . . . He is in fact a savant, a sensitive oddball whose cheeky, strange, defiant and witty monologue is as disturbing as it is dazzling. . . . We must wait for the rather diffuse ending before all is revealed. At times the narrative features a few too many dictionary definitions and self-indulgent, associative bits of wordplay, while at other moments drawings and photographs are unnecessarily scattered through the text. . . . The novel's greatest gift is the playful language that celebrates the thrill and desperation of living in this small country town."

REVIEW: *Publ Wkly* v260 no19 p40 My 13 2013

COLLINS, IRMA H. Dictionary of music education; [by] Irma H. Collins xxxiii, 339 p. 2013 The Scarecrow Press, Inc.
1. Encyclopedias & dictionaries 2. Music—Instruction & study—Societies, etc. 3. Music—Instruction and study—Bio-bibliography 4. Music—Instruction and study—Dictionaries 5. Music—Instruction and study—Encyclopedias
ISBN 9780810886513 (cloth: alk. paper)
LC 2013-012478

SUMMARY: This book by Irma H. Collins presents "an alphabetic dictionary of words utilized in the learning of music including important associations, people, words, and occurrences. . . . The dictionary contains a contents, foreword, preface, acknowledgments, list of acronyms and abbreviations, organizations and abbreviations, chronology, introduction, the A-Z dictionary, and four appendixes." (American Reference Books Annual)

REVIEW: *Booklist* v110 no15 p40 Ap 1 2014 Carolyn Mulac

REVIEW: *Choice* v51 no8 p1367-8 Ap 2014 D. Ossenkop
"Dictionary of Music Education". "Some biographies (e.g. Julia Crane, Charles Leonhard, Lilla Belle Pitts) are informative, and the brief commentaries on British, Canadian, and Australian organizations are useful. Regrettably, errors and omissions detract from the value of this dictionary. . . . Occasionally entries for terms contain erroneous information (e.g., the vocal concerto was established in the 17th century, not the 18th), and the decision to include people . . . who were not music educators is hard to comprehend. Students and faculty are better served by M. Ely and A. E. Rashkin's 'Dictionary of Music Education: A Handbook of Terminology' (2005), which presents accurate and detailed content."

COLLINS, JACKIE, 1937-. Confessions of a Wild Child; [by] Jackie Collins 304 p. 2014 St. Martin's Press
1. Boarding school stories 2. Children of the rich—Fiction 3. Human sexuality—Fiction 4. Organized crime—Fiction 5. Teenage girls—Fiction
ISBN 1250050936; 9781250050939

SUMMARY: In this book, "despite living in a palace replete with tennis courts and servants to attend to her every whim, Lucky realizes that she and her brother, Dario, are just prisoners in a posh jail. Certainly her mobster father, Gino, wants to keep his children safe . . . but at 15, Lucky is already champing at the bit to live a little more on the wild side. Ironically, being sent to an elite boarding school in Switzerland is her big chance." (Kirkus Reviews)

REVIEW: *Booklist* v110 no7 p20 D 1 2013 Pat Henshaw

REVIEW: *Kirkus Rev* v82 no3 p40 F 1 2014

"Confessions of a Wild Child". "Despite all the (not particularly explicit) action, Lucky's tale has a fairly flat plotline. Part of the trouble in building tension lies with Lucky's own gimlet-eyed stoicism. She is, indeed, her father's daughter, and nothing will distract her from her ultimate goal of becoming Gino's successor. Even the potentially catastrophic arranged marriage to a senator's son is met with bemused calculation rather than horror. Even the staunchest fans of the Santangelo family may be disappointed with this rather thin addition to the saga."

REVIEW: *Libr J* v138 no14 p82 S 1 2013 Barbara Hoffert

REVIEW: *Publ Wkly* v261 no8 p177 F 24 2014

COLLINS, KAREN. Playing with sound; a theory of interacting with sound and music in video games; [by] Karen Collins xii, 185 p. 2013 The MIT Press

1. Interactive multimedia 2. Music psychology 3. Psychological literature 4. Video game music 5. Video gamers—Psychology 6. Video games 7. Video games—Sound effects

ISBN 0262018675 (hardcover : alk. paper); 9780262018678 (hardcover : alk. paper)

LC 2012-025349

SUMMARY: In this book author Karen Collins "examines video game sound from the player's perspective. She explores the many ways that players interact with a game's sonic aspects—which include not only music but also sound effects, ambient sound, dialogue, and interface sounds—both within and outside of the game. She investigates the ways that meaning is found, embodied, created, evoked, hacked, remixed, negotiated, and renegotiated by players in the space of interactive sound in games." (Publisher's note)

REVIEW: *Choice* v51 no1 p116-7 S 2013 A. Chen

"Playing With Sounds: A Theory of Interacting With Sound and Music in Video Games." "'Playing with Sound' is a concise and densely researched study of game audio. It approaches sound from an active player-centric view and positions it apart from passively consumed audio. [Author Karen] Collins . . . highlights and explains the myriad opportunities for interactions presented through audio, such as dialogue, sound effects, ambience, and music. While not a history of video games, the work examines audio throughout gaming history and highlights its major contributions to interactive player experiences. . . . Overall, this is a significant step forward in game audio and game studies."

COLLINS, RENEE. Relic; [by] Renee Collins 2013 Paw Prints

1. Fantasy fiction 2. Orphans—Fiction 3. Teenage girls—Fiction 4. Western stories 5. Young adult fiction, American

ISBN 1480626724; 9781480626720

SUMMARY: In this young adult fantasy novel by Renee Collins, "After a raging fire consumes her town and kills her parents, Maggie Davis is on her own to protect her younger sister and survive the best she can in the Colorado town of Burning Mesa. In Maggie's world, the bones of long-extinct magical creatures such as dragons and sirens are mined and traded for their residual magical elements." (Publisher's note)

REVIEW: *Kirkus Rev* v81 no16 p103 Ag 15 2013

"Relic: Entangled Teen." "Plot trumps characterization in this Wild West fantasy. When mysterious attackers burn their hometown, survivors Maggie Davis and her younger sister, Ella, seek refuge in a nearby town. Local law enforcement assumes the burnings are Apache attacks against relic-mining communities, as the Apache culture views relic use as religious desecration. . . . The text often tells readers that Maggie is strong, yet more often than not, other characters must push her along through the plot. The ending demands a sequel, but only readers willing to forgive slipshod characterization for the innovative worldbuilding will look forward to it. Simplistic characters undermine an exciting, creative fantasy world."

COLLINS, SUZANNE, 1962-. Year of the jungle; [by] Suzanne Collins 40 p. 2013 Scholastic Press

1. Children of military personnel—Juvenile fiction 2. Children's stories 3. Fathers and daughters—Fiction 4. Separation (Psychology)—Fiction 5. Separation (Psychology)—Juvenile fiction 6. Soldiers—Fiction 7. Vietnam War, 1961-1975—Fiction 8. Vietnam War, 1961-1975—Juvenile fiction

ISBN 0545425166; 9780545425162 (hc)

LC 2012-015346

SUMMARY: This children's picture book "recounts, through the author's eyes as a child, the year of her father's military tour of duty in Viet Nam. The youngest of four kids growing up in a safe, loving family, Suzy is first seen listening to her dad read Ogden Nash's poem about Custard, the dragon who stays brave despite his inner fears. Thus the stage is set for her father's imminent deployment," a challenge for Suzy and her father alike. (School Library Journal)

REVIEW: *Booklist* v110 no1 p105 S 1 2013 Thom Barthelmess

REVIEW: *Bull Cent Child Books* v67 no2 p80 O 2013 E. B.

REVIEW: *Horn Book Magazine* v90 no1 p69-70 Ja/F 2014 MARTHA V. PARRAVANO

"Year of the Jungle." "The narrator's limited point of view is what allows a complex story to work as a picture book for young children. . . . Scenes of Suzy's everyday life (getting a new lunchbox, tracing her hand to make Thanksgiving turkeys, playing with her cat) alternate with wordless spreads from Suzy's imagination, as her benign picture of the Vietnam jungle begins to morph into something much more dark, dangerous, and realistic. . . . An understated, extremely effective home-front story."

REVIEW: *Kirkus Rev* v81 no15 p158 Ag 1 2013

REVIEW: *Kirkus Rev* p38 Ag 15 2013 Fall Preview

REVIEW: *Publ Wkly* v260 no33 p32-4 Ag 19 2013 SALLY LODGE

REVIEW: *Publ Wkly* p40 Children's starred review annual 2013

REVIEW: *Publ Wkly* v260 no21 p58 My 27 2013

REVIEW: *SLJ* v59 no9 p51 S 2013 Kathleen T. Isaacs

REVIEW: *SLJ* v59 no10 p1 O 2013 Barbara M. Moon

REVIEW: *SLJ* v59 no8 p69 Ag 2013 Kathleen Finn

COLMAN, DINA. Four quadrant living; making healthy living your new way of life; [by] Dina Colman 234 p. 2013 Wyatt-MacKenzie Pub., Inc.

1. Environmental health 2. Health 3. Mental health 4. Relationship quality 5. Self-help materials

ISBN 9781939288226 (pbk)
LC 2013-944717

SUMMARY: Author Dina Colman "rejects the idea that healthy living simply means eating well or getting enough exercise, instead choosing to see health as 'a state that emerges from four areas—four quadrants—Mind, Body, Relationships, and Environment.' By taking positive actions in each of these four areas, Colman says, the reader can improve his or her health, reduce the risk of serious disease and live a better life. The book's four sections discuss each quadrant in detail." (Kirkus Reviews)

REVIEW: *Kirkus Rev* v82 no6 p11 Mr 15 2014

REVIEW: *Kirkus Rev* v82 no2 p330 Ja 15 2014

"Four Quadrant Living: Making Healthy Living Your New Way of Life". "An easy approach to integrating different realms of your life and achieving a healthy lifestyle. . . . This small-step approach to improving life is notably appealing, since it's easy enough to follow suggestions such as striving to find humor in stressful situations or switching to nontoxic household cleaners. Other recommendations are more intensive and won't be as easy to put into action as [Dina] Colman sometimes makes them sound. . . . Nonetheless, Colman packs plenty of sensible suggestions into this slim book. What might come off as judgmental in less-deft hands is here more like gentle advice from a close friend. Useful tools for living a more balanced life."

REVIEW: *Publ Wkly* v261 no4 p158-9 Ja 27 2014

COLMAN, JOHN. Lucretius as theorist of political life; [by] John Colman x, 173 p. 2012 Palgrave Macmillan

1. Philosophy & politics 2. Philosophy, Ancient, in literature 3. Political science literature 4. Politics & literature 5. Rome—Politics & government

ISBN 1137292318; 9781137292315
LC 2012-277225

SUMMARY: This book by John Colman "is an interpretation of Lucretius' poem 'On the Nature of Things' as a defense of philosophy given the irremediable tension between the competing claims of the philosophic and political life. The central issue is the need for, and attempt by, philosophy to justify and defend its way of life to the political community." (Publisher's note)

REVIEW: *Choice* v51 no1 p161 S 2013 D. Schaefer

"Lucretius As Theorist of Political Life." "[Author John] Colman's study is only the second book-length analysis of Lucretius's 'On the Nature of Things,' the classic poetic exposition of ancient Epicureanism, that treats it primarily as a work of political philosophy rather than emphasizing the poet's atomistic physics. Through a close sequential reading of the poem's six books. Colman seeks to demonstrate that Lucretius's primary theme was 'the tension between philosophy and the city,' his aim being to introduce philosophy into Rome in a way that would overcome its rejection as impious, 'introduc[ing] rational deliberation into theological matters without undermining' religion's service to humanity. . . . A thoughtful, well-argued work."

COLMER, DAVID.tr. Ten white geese. See Bakker, G.

COLOR AND DESIGN; 228 p. 2013 Berg Publishers

1. ART—Color Theory 2. ART—Techniques—General 3. Color in design 4. DESIGN—Product 5. DESIGN—Textile & Costume 6. Design literature

ISBN 9781847889515 (pbk.); 9781847889522 (); 9781847889539 ()
LC 2012-027465

SUMMARY: Edited by Marilyn DeLong and Barbara Martinson, this book "addresses how we understand and experience colour, and through specific examples explores how colour is used in a spectrum of design-based disciplines including apparel design, graphic design, interior design, and product design. Through highly engaging contributions from a wide range of international scholars and practitioners, the book explores colour . . . as a valuable marketing tool." (Publisher's note)

REVIEW: *Choice* v51 no4 p619-20 D 2013 L. L. Kriner

"Color and Design." "The 20 essays in 'Color and Design' use philosophical and theoretical research to help students understand how people experience color, and the applications of color in design fields. The book is divided into three major parts: 'Experiencing and Responding to Color,' 'Color in Context, Culture, and Traditions,' and 'Markets and Trends.' Its short three- to eight-page essays are supported with 48 color plates, 37 black-and-white figures, case studies, examples, and ample notation. . . . Dedicated design libraries will find this book useful. However, the variety of subject matter precludes a tight focus, so the volume will best serve as supportive material rather as the main textbook for a class."

COLÓN, RAÚL, 1952-.il. Roberto Clemente. See Roberto Clemente

COLÓN, RAÚL, 1952-.il. Baseball is.... See Borden, L.

COMMUNITY AND COMMUNICATION; Oratory and Politics in Republican Rome; 2013 Oxford University Press

1. Cicero, Marcus Tullius, 106 B.C.-43 B.C. 2. Historical literature 3. Oratory, Ancient 4. Political oratory 5. Rome—Politics & government

ISBN 978-0199641895; 0199641897
LC 2012-532817

SUMMARY: In this book, "nineteeen international contributors . . . rethink the role of public speech in the Roman Republic. . . . This volume shines a light on orators other than Cicero, and considers the oratory of diplomatic exchanges and impromptu heckling and repartee alongside the more familiar genres of forensic and political speech. In doing so, it challenges the idea that Cicero was a normative figure." (Publisher's note)

REVIEW: *TLS* no5762 p8-9 S 6 2013 MARY BEARD

"Community and Communication: Oratory and Politics in Republican Rome," "The Cambridge Companion to Cicero," and "Pro Marco Caelio." "All the main players . . . have contributed essays discussing contiones to 'Community and Communication,' and, despite the wealth of expertise on show, it is hard to resist the conclusion that the law of diminishing returns is beginning to apply. Taken together, these essays show all the signs of a debate whose groundbreaking phase is over. . . . For those starting out to explore Cicero, 'The Cambridge Companion' is a brisk and business-like guide; though I was disappointed that the final chapter is a rather plodding piece on Cicero's role in modern film, fiction and popular history. . . . I suspect that [Robert Symes] might have admired the austerity of [Andrew R.] Dyck's Pro Caelio, and its undoubted philological expertise. But as a way to introduce twenty-first-century readers to Cicero's unusually engaging speech? No."

A COMPANION TO SOPHOCLES; xix, 598 p. 2012 Wiley-Blackwell

1. Drama—History & criticism 2. Greece—Intellectual life—To 146 B.C. 3. Greek drama 4. Historical literature 5. Sophocles, ca. 497 B.C.-406 B.C.
ISBN 1405187263 (alk. paper); 9781405187268 (alk. paper)
LC 2011-034659

SUMMARY: This book, edited by Kirk Ormand, "presents the first comprehensive collection of essays in decades to address all aspects of the life, works, and critical reception of Sophocles." It "features new essays on Sophoclean drama, presents readings that historicize Sophocles in relation to the social, cultural, and intellectual world of fifth century Athens, [and] seeks to place later interpretations and adaptations of Sophocles in their historical context." (Publisher's note)

REVIEW: *Choice* v50 no3 p476 N 2012 S. E. Goins

REVIEW: *Classical Rev* v63 no2 p342-4 O 2013 Josh Beer

"A Companion to Sophocles." "The 'Companion' contains one significant omission; there is no chapter on the gods in Sophocles. . . . Several contributions are . . . character driven. Although the question of how to read characterisation in Sophocles and Greek tragedy in general has been the subject of critical debate, this 'Companion' shows no evidence of this. . . . These things are plot rather than character driven. The understanding of Sophocles is not helped by applying modern, more 'realistic' criteria of characterisation. This 'Companion' has many strong points but also has limitations."

A COMPANION TO WORLD HISTORY; 2012 Wiley-Blackwell

1. Historical literature 2. Historiography 3. History—Methodology 4. History—Study & teaching 5. World history
ISBN 1444334182; 9781444334180

SUMMARY: This book, edited by Douglas Northrop, "presents over 30 essays from an international group of historians that both identify continuing areas of contention, disagreement, and divergence in world and global history, and point to directions for further debate." It "explores a wide range of topics and themes, including . . . the practice of world history, key ideas of world historians, the teaching of world history and how it has drawn upon and challenged "traditional" teaching approaches." (Publisher's note)

REVIEW: *Choice* v50 no12 p2289 Ag 2013 H. P. Langerbein

REVIEW: *Engl Hist Rev* v129 no536 p157-60 F 2014 Alan Strathern

"A Companion to World History". "An honest picture of the state of the field. . . . Particularly for readers outside the USA (which has been overwhelmingly dominant in the field), the Wiley-Blackwell volume will provide a useful guide to the way in which the subject has emerged from moral and pedagogical shifts of perspective. Indeed, the mildly politicised tone that surfaces in many chapters indicates the way in which world history has developed as a reflection of the liberal politics of inclusion in the last generation or two. . . . The focus in the Wiley-Blackwell volume on the practicalities of how to do world history probably gives it the edge. . . . Its most obvious drawback is the shocking price."

A COMPANION TO WORLD WAR II; 2 v. (xvi, 1030 p.) 2013 Wiley-Blackwell

1. Historical literature 2. Reference sources 3. World War, 1939-1945 4. World War, 1939-1945—Historiography 5. World War, 1939-1945—Social aspects
ISBN 1405196815; 9781405196819 (2 v. set : alk. paper)
LC 2012-017188

SUMMARY: Editor Thomas W. Zeiler's book "brings together a series of fresh academic perspectives on World War II, exploring the many cultural, social, and political contexts of the war. Essay topics range from American anti-Semitism to the experiences of French-African soldiers, providing nearly 60 new contributions to the genre arranged across two comprehensive volumes." (Publisher's note)

REVIEW: *Choice* v51 no1 p137-8 S 2013 C. C. Lovett

"A Companion to World War II." "Editors [Thomas W.] Zeiler and [Daniel M.] DuBois . . . have marshaled a blend of 58 seasoned and promising academics who review both the analytical and bibliographical components of the global war for readers seeking a handy reference. Using Gerhard Weinberg's masterful analysis of the war's origins as a guide, professionals now have the opportunity to grasp the diplomacy, strategic imperatives, and economics of the war, as well as the social forces that the conflict unleashed. For . . . a different approach, the contributors . . . provide the back story of the conflict in Asia and the environmental and civil rights issues dramatized by the war. . . . This companion is destined to become a valuable contribution to the historiography of the war."

COMPARATIVE MYSTICISM; an anthology of original sources; xxiii, 618 p. 2011 Oxford University Press

1. Anthologies 2. Mysticism—Christianity 3. Mysticism—History—Sources 4. Mysticism—Judaism 5. Religion
ISBN 9780195143799 (hardcover : acid-free paper)
LC 2010-020299

SUMMARY: This anthology, edited by Steven T. Katz, "comprises poetry, prayer, narrative, and other writings from Jewish, Christian, Muslim, Hindu, Buddhist, Taoist, Confucianist, and Native American traditions. This collection provides readers not only with the primary mystical texts from each religious tradition, but with an explanation of the context of the source and tradition." (Publisher's note)

REVIEW: *Choice* v51 no4 p654-5 D 2013 G. R. Thursby

"Comparative Mysticism: An Anthology of Original Sources." "In top form in this exemplary sourcebook are editor [Steven T.] Katz . . . and seven contributing editors--one for each major tradition (Jewish, Christian, Hindu, Buddhist) and composite category (Sufi, Confucian-Daoist, Native American) represented here. . . . Katz himself is an ideal coordinator for this kind of project. . . . He critiques 'convergence' or 'uniformity' models that suppose mystics to be exemplars of a higher wisdom common to all true religions and metaphysical systems."

COMPESTINE, VINSON. Secrets of the terra-cotta soldier. See Compestine, Y. C.

COMPESTINE, YING CHANG. Secrets of the terra-cotta soldier; [by] Ying Chang Compestine 240 p. 2014 Amulet Books

1. Historical fiction 2. Kings, queens, rulers, etc.—Fiction
ISBN 9781419705403
LC 2013-006284

SUMMARY: In this book, "thirteen-year-old Ming lives in a small village in Maoist China in the 1970s. His father is convinced that Emperor Qin's tomb . . . lies hidden in the hills around them. But if Ming's father doesn't prove it soon, the town's Political Officer will condemn him to the brutal labor camps. From the stories of a terra-cotta soldier who has survived through the centuries, Ming learns the history of Emperor Qin." (Publisher's note)

REVIEW: *Booklist* v110 no9/10 p114 Ja 1 2014 Courtney Jones

REVIEW: *Bull Cent Child Books* v67 no8 p401 Ap 2014 E. B.

"Secrets of the Terra-Cotta Soldier". "The Compestines have the demanding task of bringing readers up to speed simultaneously on the emperor, the archaeologically significant site of his burial, and the Cultural Revolution, and the strain of the effort shows in frequently awkward insertion of information into stiff dialogue and the relatively thin development of each of the individual themes. There's enough humor and action, however, to keep fiction readers' attention, and enough black and white photographs of artifacts and geographic settings to remind nonfiction fans that this is reality-based."

REVIEW: *Kirkus Rev* v82 no1 p280 Ja 1 2014

"Secrets of the Terra-Cotta Soldier". "Shi's brutal war stories tend to overshadow aspects of Ming's personal story, like Ming's relationship with his father, but they are compelling nonetheless. Although Ming's acceptance of a talking statue feels swift, their friendship is believable. They hail from different eras, but they share a common desire: to keep their parents safe. Historical photos and Indiana Jones-style adventure enrich this tale of an unusual meeting between the Qin Dynasty and the 20th century."

REVIEW: *SLJ* v60 no4 p142 Ap 2014 Jennifer Rothschild

THE COMPLETE DIRECTORY FOR PEOPLE WITH CHRONIC ILLNESS 2013/14; 864 p. 2013 Grey House Pub

1. Chronic diseases 2. Chronically ill—Care 3. Chronically ill—Services for 4. Directories 5. Medical care costs—United States
ISBN 1619251140; 9781619251144

SUMMARY: This book "provides . . . information on some 90 illnesses. . . . Arranged alphabetically by disorder, each section begins with a very brief description of the illness, probable causes, symptoms, and treatment options. Following are listings with contan information for national associations, state agencies, libraries and resource centers, publications for adults and children, research centers, support groups and hotlines . . . and websites." (Choice: Current Reviews for Academic Libraries)

REVIEW: *Choice* v51 no7 p1185 Mr 2014 T. R. Faust

"The Complete Directory for People With Chronic Illness: Condition Descriptions, Associations, Publications, Research Centers, Support Groups, Web Sites." "This volume is among the most useful of directories, with its goal of helping people with long-term medical conditions find helpful resources. It provides valuable information on some 90 illnesses, ranging from Addison's Disease to Wilsons Disease. . . . A directory like this is a Herculean effort, whose contents can only be as current as the responses to update requests make it. A few omissions and errors are evident. . . . Nevertheless, this directory is a good starting point for those seeking more information on particular conditions."

THE COMPLETE JOURNALS OF L.M. MONTGOMERY; The PEI Years, 1901-1911; 444 p. 2013 OUP Canada

1. Diary (Literary form) 2. Novelists, Canadian (English)—20th century—Diaries
ISBN 0199002118 (hbk.); 9780199002115 (hbk)
LC 2013-409795

SUMMARY: This book presents L. M. Montgomery's unabridged journals from 1901-1991. It "covers Montgomery's early adult years, including her work as a newspaper editor in Halifax, Nova Scotia; her publishing career taking flight; the death of her grandmother; and her forthcoming marriage to a local clergyman. It also documents her own reflections on writing, her increasingly problematic mood swings and feelings of isolation, and her changing relationship with the world around her." (Publisher's note)

REVIEW: *Can Lit* no217 p183-4 Summ 2013 Emily Aoife Somers

REVIEW: *TLS* no5768 p21 O 18 2013 FAYE HAMMILL

"The Complete Journals of L. M. Montgomery: The PEI Years, 1901-1911." "The first remarkable thing about L. M. Montgomery's journals is their darkness, their enormous distance from the sunny world of her novels. . . . The second remarkable thing about the journals is their silences. . . . . Montgomery's journal was much less a record of daily experience than a record of moods and thoughts. She makes two types of entry. In the longer ones, which are more like autobiographical essays, she explores her memories. . . . . These extended accounts illuminate her intellectual growth and creative processes. . . . . In the shorter entries . . . she tries to capture her rapturous response to the natural beauty of Prince Edward Island or . . . seeks release from present suffering."

COMPTON, ANN.ed. Garth Evans Sculpture. See Garth Evans Sculpture

COMPUTATIONAL APPROACHES TO ARCHAEOLOGICAL SPACES; 330 p. 2013 Left Coast Press

1. Archaeological literature 2. Archaeology—Computer simulation 3. Phenomenology 4. Spatial analysis (Statistics) in archaeology 5. Virtual reality in archaeology
ISBN 9781611323467 (hardback : alk. paper)
LC 2013-007682

SUMMARY: This book on computational archaeology is "organized around three broad themes: spatial analysis, spatial modeling, and spatial experience. Roughly one-third of the book is devoted to each topic. The first set of three papers represents inductive, exploratory approaches to archaeological spatial analysis. The second set comprises four chapters offering more deductive and model-driven approaches." (Choice: Current Reviews for Academic Libraries)

REVIEW: *Choice* v51 no7 p1263-4 Mr 2014 C. E. Peterson

"Computational Approaches to Archaeological Spaces." "These first seven chapters of the book are the most interesting and, arguably, the most useful to the majority of analysts. The final set of three articles concerns the analysis of viewsheds, visualscapes, and 3D architectural models. Some readers, particularly those based in North America, will find the emphasis on phenomenology in this latter section discomforting. A concluding chapter that does not fit neatly under any previous heading calls for archaeologists to embrace the open-source movement and to share their data more freely. None of the contributions represents truly novel approaches to analysis, but instead new takes on old techniques. Not for undergraduates or the quantitatively faint of heart."

COMPUTER TECHNOLOGY INNOVATORS; 414 p. 2013 Salem Press

1. Computer science—Technological innovations 2. Computer scientists—Biography 3. Gates, Bill, 1955- 4. Jobs, Steven, 1955-2011 5. Reference books
ISBN 9781429838054 (hardcover)
LC 2012-045266

SUMMARY: This book presents "biographies of individuals who contributed to the development and expansion of the Internet. Fields of specialization include mathematics and logic; physics and engineering; computer software, hardware, and programming; Internet management, marketing, commerce, and security; social media; applications; news and entertainment; and ethics and policy. 'Computer Technology Innovators' profiles many well-known icons, including Steve Wozniak, Bill Gates, and Steve Jobs." (Booklist)

REVIEW: *Booklist* v110 no1 p59 S 1 2013 Kathleen McBroom

"Computer Technology Innovators" and "Internet Innovators." "In most cases, the book's contributors are well matched to their subjects and provide detailed profiles and sufficient background information to establish the importance and relevance of their subjects, whether in technological, social, economic, or political context. . . . The preface indicates that selection criteria included each individual's significance, his or her relevance to academic curriculum, and the appeal to the intended audience: high-school and undergraduate students. These volumes should serve as authoritative resources and are recommended for high-school, large public, and academic libraries."

REVIEW: *Choice* v51 no2 p229-30 O 2013 J. W. Barnes

"Computer Technology Innovators" and "Internet Innovators." "Drawing on the work of over 40 contributors, these two volumes each feature biographical essays on more than 120 men and women noted for their contributions to the development of computer technology, or its myriad applications over the Internet. Alphabetically arranged essays, each about 2,000 words long, often feature a line drawing of the subject, and conclude with a 'Further Reading' section. . . . Good indexes provide access to the many topics covered in both books. Unfortunately, in these otherwise well-planned and attractively printed publications, numerous lapses in copy editing are evident throughout. Part of the 'Great Lives from History' series, these volumes provide online access with purchase of the print version."

REVIEW: *Libr J* v138 no10 p138 Je 1 2013 Jennifer Michaelson

REVIEW: *SLJ* v59 no10 p1 O 2013 Vicki Reutter

A CONCISE COMPANION TO CONTEMPORARY BRITISH AND IRISH DRAMA; 2013 Wiley-Blackwell

1. Irish drama 2. Theater—Great Britain 3. Theater—History 4. Theater—Ireland 5. Theater literature
ISBN 9781118492130; 1118492137

SUMMARY: This book, edited by Nadine Holdsworth and Mary Luckhurst, as part of the "Concise Companions to Literature and Culture" series, "focus[es] on major and emerging playwrights, institutions, and various theatre practices . . . [and] examines the key issues in British and Irish theatre since 1979. . . . This collection offers new ways of thinking about the social, political, and cultural contexts within which specific aspects of British and Irish theatre have emerged." (Publisher's note)

REVIEW: *Choice* v51 no5 p846 Ja 2014 J. S. Baggett

"A Concise Companion to Contemporary British and Irish Drama." "Most of the works discussed respond to the changes confronting Britain and the rest of Europe since the end of the Cold War, addressing the challenges related to such issues as national and ethnic tensions, migration, genocide, and globalization. But the collection also includes analyses of experimentations with form--including site-specific performance, verbatim theater, and tribunal and documentary plays--and investigations of the use of new technologies and the practice of physical theater. This volume provides valuable insight into the issues and practices of contemporary theater."

CONDEE, NANCY.ed. The cinema of Alexander Sokurov. See The cinema of Alexander Sokurov

CONDRA, JILL.ed. Encyclopedia of national dress. See Encyclopedia of national dress

CONFINO, ALON. A world without Jews; the Nazi imagination from persecution to genocide; [by] Alon Confino 304 p. 2014 Yale University Press

1. Historical literature 2. Holocaust, Jewish (1939-1945)—Germany 3. Jews—Germany—History—1933-1945 4. Jews—Persecutions—Germany
ISBN 0300188544; 9780300188547 (hardback)
LC 2013-041276

SUMMARY: In this book, Alon Confino explores "how Germans came to conceive of the idea of a Germany without Jews. He traces the stories the Nazis told themselves . . . and how those stories led to the conclusion that Jews must be eradicated. . . . The creation of this new empire required that Jews and Judaism be erased from Christian history. . . . As Germans imagined a future world without Jews, persecution and extermination became imaginable, and even justifiable." (Publisher's note)

REVIEW: *Choice* v52 no2 p334 O 2014 D. A. Meier

REVIEW: *Kirkus Rev* v82 no4 p235 F 15 2014

"A World Without Jews: The Nazi Imagination From Persecution to Genocide". "An insightful new study that develops the theme of Jewish annihilation as necessary to the Nazi myth of genesis. Using a wealth of standard historical sources . . . as well as evidence considered unique in the history of genocide . . . [Alon] Confino . . . pursues the chilling buildup to the Holocaust, from 1933 onward, in Germany as emotional, messianic and not at all secretive. . . . A thoughtful study that represents Nazism less as a 'banality of evil' and more as an 'intimate brutality.'"

REVIEW: *Libr J* v139 no5 p127 Mr 15 2014 Frederic Krome

CONFLICT IN THE EARLY AMERICAS; an encyclopedia of the Spanish Empire's Aztec, Incan, and Mayan conquests; xvi, 485 p. 2013 ABC-CLIO

1. Aztecs—History—16th century—Encyclopedias 2. Conquerors—America—History—Encyclopedias 3. Conquerors—Spain—History—Encyclopedias 4. Historical literature 5. Incas—History—16th century—Encyclopedias 6. Mayas—History—16th century—Encyclopedias 7. Mayas—History—17th century—Encyclopedias

ISBN 9781598847765 (hardcopy : alk. paper)

LC 2013-009363

SUMMARY: In this book, "editor [Rebecca M.] Seaman offers a one-volume encyclopedia with entries that summarize the conflict between the Spanish and the Aztec, Inca, and Maya civilizations during the 16th century. She also includes other indigenous peoples crucial to the narrative. Most entries are biographical and topical in scope, the latter often dealing with the nature of differing social groups or concepts that engendered conflict between groups." (Choice: Current Reviews for Academic Libraries)

REVIEW: *Booklist* v110 no7 p40 D 1 2013 Mary Ellen Snodgrass

REVIEW: *Choice* v51 no7 p1190 Mr 2014 J. A. Reuscher

"Conflict in the Early Americas: An Encyclopedia of the Spanish Empire's Aztec, Incan, and Mayan Conquests." "This reviewer would have liked to see more material on North America, since it is a significant part of the story of conflict between the Spanish and indigenous peoples. Entries on the struggles and ultimate failures of Juan Pardo, Francisco Vásquez de Coronado, and Juan Ponce de León--to name a few--along with an expanded entry on Hernando de Sotos failure and death in North America, would have revealed a more complex reality concerning conflict at this time (a reality that was not synonymous with successful Spanish conquest). Nevertheless, this encyclopedia lives up to its subtitle, and is a compact compendium on a broad topic of study."

CONLEY, DALTON. Parentology; everything you wanted to know about the science of raising children but were too exhausted to ask; [by] Dalton Conley 256 p. 2014 Simon & Schuster

1. Child rearing 2. Memoirs 3. Parenthood 4. Parenting

ISBN 1476712654 (hardback); 9781476712659 (hardback)

LC 2013-024320

SUMMARY: "'Parentology' hilariously reports the results of [author Dalton] Conley's experiments as a father, demonstrating that, ultimately, what matters most is love and engagement. He teaches you everything you need to know about the latest literature on parenting—with lessons that go down easy." (Publisher's note)

REVIEW: *Kirkus Rev* v82 no5 p2 Mr 1 2014

REVIEW: *N Y Times Book Rev* p19 Mr 16 2014 REBECCA TRAISTER

REVIEW: *New Sci* v221 no2961 p51 Mr 22 2014 Simon Ings

"Parentology: Everything You Wanted to Know About the Science of Raising Children But Were Too Exhausted to Ask" and "It's Complicated: The Social Lives of Networked Teens." "For all its insightful, funny, fully researched, conscientiously cited, . . . approach to science and statistics, what really powers 'Parentology' is a species of loving rage. The numbers teach us a great deal. . . . However, . . . Love, care, interest and empathy . . . render most of the measures discussed in this book profoundly unimportant. . . . [Author Danah] Boyd has little time for technological determinism. Her fieldwork with . . . parents and their kids reveals the fault is not in our computers but in ourselves. . . . And she marshals a huge body of sociological evidence."

REVIEW: *Publ Wkly* v260 no49 p79 D 2 2013

CONLY, SARAH. Against autonomy; justifying coercive paternalism; [by] Sarah Conly 206 p. 2012 Cambridge University Press

1. Autonomy (Philosophy) 2. Choice (Psychology) 3. Decision making—Philosophy 4. Decision making—Political aspects 5. PHILOSOPHY—Political 6. Paternalism 7. Philosophical literature

ISBN 9781107024847 (hardback)

LC 2012-021094

SUMMARY: In this book, Sarah Conly "advocates 'the permissibility of interference in personal lives, interference even in actions a person takes that will affect only himself'. . . .Indeed, she argues that 'we . . . are sometimes morally obligated to force people to refrain from certain actions and to engage in others'. . . . Conly contends that state-sponsored coercive paternalism can be justified for a range of self-regarding harms on moral grounds, as well as on prudential or instrumental grounds." (Ethics)

REVIEW: *Choice* v50 no12 p2313-4 Ag 2013 J. S. Taylor

REVIEW: *Ethics* v124 no2 p392-7 Ja 2014 MARINA OSHANA

"Against Autonomy: Justifying Coercive Paternalism". "Timely. . . . [Sarah] Conly defends the idea that coercing people to prevent their performing actions that will harm them is not just permissible but obligatory. Her defense is philosophically astute. But I am unconvinced that 'as we become more familiar with the concept of coercive paternalism, and understand the rationale for it, we will come to welcome it when it is indeed the most effective method of getting what we in fact want'."

REVIEW: *N Y Rev Books* v60 no4 p8-11 Mr 7 2013 Cass R. Sunstein

CONNELLY, JOAN BRETON. The Parthenon enigma; [by] Joan Breton Connelly 512 p. 2014 Alfred A. Knopf

1. Greek mythology 2. Historical literature 3. Symbolism in architecture—Greece—Athens

ISBN 030759338X; 9780307476593 (paperback); 9780307593382 (hardback)

LC 2013-024771

SUMMARY: In this book, author "Joan Breton Connelly challenges our most basic assumptions about the Parthenon and the ancient Athenians. . . . In particular, she probes the

Parthenon's legendary frieze: the 525-foot-long relief sculpture that originally encircled the upper reaches. . . . Connelly reveals . . . a world in which our modern secular conception of democracy would have been simply incomprehensible." (Publisher's note)

REVIEW: *Choice* v51 no11 p1971 Jl 2014 L. M. Bliss

REVIEW: *New Yorker* v90 no8 p34-1 Ap 14 2014

"The Parthenon Enigma: A New Understanding of the World's Most Iconic Building and the People Who Made It." "[Author Joan Breton] Connelly's sensational theory is, in fact, nearly two decades old. She first aired it in a 1996 scholarly article that has, over time, failed to persuade art historians and archeologists. In the book, she takes her case directly to the people. Like other popularizing tomes by specialists who, in promoting controversial theses, have done what amounts to an end-run around the academic establishment, this one has the defects of its virtues. The infectious enthusiasm, even emotionality, that the author displays toward her subject . . . cannot, in the end, compensate for questionable methods and wobbly evidence."

CONNELLY, MICHAEL, 1956-. The Gods of Guilt; [by] Michael Connelly 416 p. 2013 Little Brown & Co

1. Detective & mystery stories 2. FICTION—Crime 3. FICTION—Legal 4. FICTION—Mystery & Detective—General 5. FICTION—Suspense 6. FICTION—Thrillers 7. Lawyers 8. Murder—Fiction 9. Murder—Investigation—Fiction 10. Prostitutes—Fiction 11. Trials (Murder) 12. Trials (Murder)—Fiction

ISBN 0316069515; 9780316069519

LC 2013-032952

SUMMARY: This book is Michael Connelly's "fifth novel featuring Mickey Haller . . . the L.A. defense attorney who uses a Lincoln town car as a mobile office. . . . Andre La Cosse, a high-tech pimp, is charged with murdering one of his clients, Giselle Dallinger. . . . Haller's strategy is not to uncover the truth but to develop a credible alternative theory of the crime, and the investigation that follows is like a police procedural seen from the other side of the criminal justice world." (Publishers Weekly)

REVIEW: *Booklist* v110 no1 p4 S 1 2013 Brad Hooper

REVIEW: *Booklist* v110 no4 p19 O 15 2013 Bill Ott

"The Gods of Guilt." "As he's done throughout the Haller series, [Michael] Connelly shows a remarkable ability to bring the courtroom alive--not just the details of the case at hand and the procedural machinations but also the personal drama simmering below the surface of the thrust and counterthrust of legal strategy. . . . Connelly's Harry Bosch series has typically dug deeper into personal demons and questions of existential identity than the Haller novels, but this time the fast-talking attorney is forced to look inward, where his tricks of the trade do him little good. A gripping novel, both in the courtroom and outside of it, and a testament to the melancholy maturing of Mickey Haller."

REVIEW: *Kirkus Rev* v81 no22 p189 N 15 2013

REVIEW: *Libr J* v138 no12 p52 Jl 1 2013

REVIEW: *Libr J* v139 no6 p55 Ap 1 2014 Joyce Kessel

REVIEW: *N Y Times Book Rev* p27 D 1 2013 MARILYN STASIO

REVIEW: *New York Times* v163 no56345 pC4 D 9 2013 JANET MASLIN

REVIEW: *Publ Wkly* v260 no41 p1 O 14 2013

CONNIE, ELLIOTT. Solution-building in couples therapy; [by] Elliott Connie 115 p. 2013 Springer

1. Couples Therapy—methods 2. Couples therapy 3. Marital Therapy—methods 4. Psychological literature 5. Psychotherapy—Methodology

ISBN 0826109594; 9780826109590; 9780826109606 (E-book)

LC 2012-029942

SUMMARY: "In the first book written about solution focused therapy (SFT) with couples, author Elliott Connie describes how his use of SFT made working with couples a pleasure rather than a burden. The solution focused approach is one that facilitates cooperation between partners in the creation of an agreed-upon future, rather than merely focusing on the problems that have come to define the relationship." (Publisher's note)

REVIEW: *Choice* v51 no1 p167-8 S 2013 D. Sydiaha

"Solution-Building in Couples Therapy." "An unanticipated episode of successfully counseling a couple led [Author Elliott] Connie . . . to discover the power of solution-based counseling, as distinct from problem-based counseling. . . . The method is simple yet difficult because the counselor must be appropriately skillful in consistently directing conversation away from problems to solutions. This brief volume presents the basic premises of solution building, liberally enriched with examples. This is a remarkable book, the first of its kind, radical in its message, written about couples but also suitable for all manner of referrals."

CONNORS, LUCY. The lonesome young; [by] Lucy Connors 336 p. 2014 Razorbill, a division of Penguin Young Readers Group

1. Drug traffic—Fiction 2. Family life—Kentucky—Fiction 3. Family problems—Fiction 4. High schools—Fiction 5. Love—Fiction 6. Love stories 7. Schools—Fiction 8. Vendetta—Fiction

ISBN 9781595147097 (hardback)

LC 2013-030034

SUMMARY: In this book, "Victoria and Mickey's romance is doomed before it even begins. She is from the Whitfield family, well-established players in the horse business. He is a Rhodale, known for their drug ties and violent tempers. Though a deep-seated family feud usually keeps Whitfields and Rhodales in separate worlds, Victoria and Mickey cannot deny their instantaneous connection. Their feelings for each other and about their family situations are revealed through short chapters." (Kirkus Reviews)

REVIEW: *Booklist* v110 no15 p86 Ap 1 2014 Daniel Kraus

REVIEW: *Kirkus Rev* v82 no4 p167 F 15 2014

"The Lonesome Young". " Most of the plot centers around the hormone-addled Victoria and Mickey as they hem and haw over their relationship, while their families do everything in their power to keep them apart. However, several juicy subplots are interwoven throughout the storyline, including Victoria's sister Melinda's battle with addiction, the historical connection between the Whitfield and Rhodale families, and dangerous developments in Mickey's brother Ethan's drug business. The narrative suffers from the introduction of some superfluous characters and drags on a bit longer than necessary, but it also sets the stage for further titles. . . . Romance fans will be enthralled by the back-and-forth drama, though general readers may grow impatient with the protagonists."

REVIEW: *Publ Wkly* v261 no5 p59 F 3 2014

REVIEW: *SLJ* v60 no4 p160 Ap 2014 Liz Overberg

CONOR, LIZ.ed. A cultural history of women in the modern age. See A cultural history of women in the modern age

CONQUERGOOD, DWIGHT. Cultural struggles; performance, ethnography, praxis; [by] Dwight Conquergood 336 p. 2013 University of Michigan Press

1. Capital punishment 2. Ethnology—Philosophy 3. Performing arts—Social aspects 4. Praxis (Social sciences) 5. Social science literature 6. Theater & society
ISBN 9780472051953 (paper); 9780472071951 (hardback)
LC 2013-006637

SUMMARY: Editor E. Patrick Johnson divided "this compilation of 11 of [Dwight] Conquergood's essays into three areas of exploration: 'Performance,' 'Ethnography,' and 'Praxis.'" It includes "early works like 'Performing Cultures: Ethnography, Epistemology, and Ethics' and later pieces sucb as 'Lethal Theatre: Performance, Punishment, and the Death Penalty,'" as well as "'Critical Responses'" from other scholars in the field. (Choices)

REVIEW: *Choice* v51 no4 p643 D 2013 S. R. Irelan

"Cultural Struggles: Performance, Ethnography, Praxis." "This is the book the late [Dwight] Conquergood never got to write. Those who have in the last two decades searched through Theater Journal, Communication Monographs, TDR, or other academic journals . . . for Conquergood's paradigm-shifting works will be pleased with this book. And those just now being introduced to Conquergood's writing will find that this collection will open pathways of thought about interpreting cultural struggles with 'courage, ethics, and integrity,' as [E. Patrick] Johnson writes in the introduction."

CONROY, PAT. The Death of Santini; The Story of a Father and His Son; [by] Pat Conroy 352 p. 2013 Nan A. Talese/Doubleday

1. Conflict of generations—Fiction 2. Dysfunctional families—Fiction 3. Fathers and sons—Fiction 4. Life change events—Fiction 5. Memoirs 6. Teachers as authors—Fiction
ISBN 0385530900; 9780385530903 (alk. paper)
LC 2013-019095

SUMMARY: "In this memoir, [Pat] Conroy . . . reveals that his father, fighter pilot Donald Conroy, was actually much worse than the abusive Meechum in his novel. Telling the truth also forces the author to confront a number of difficult realizations about himself. . . . Although his father's fearsome persona never really changed, Conroy learned to forgive and even sympathize with his father, who would attend book signings with his son and good-naturedly satirize his own terrifying image." (Kirkus Reviews)

REVIEW: *Booklist* v110 no4 p12 O 15 2013 Jay Freeman

REVIEW: *Booklist* v110 no15 p35 Ap 1 2014 Sue-Ellen Beauregard

REVIEW: *Kirkus Rev* v81 no20 p161 O 15 2013

REVIEW: *Natl Rev* v65 no24 p46-7 D 31 2013 FLORENCE KING

"The Death of Santini: The Story of a Father and His Son". "[This] book, a nonfiction sequel to 'The Great Santini,' is such a prolix apologia for [Pat Conroy's] nonstop search for private demons that he has become the Great Explainer. . . . His present book is an overwritten mess crammed with so much purple prose that it resembles a bruise with pages. . . . I am not entirely convinced by any of it, including the extent of the childhood abuse, but it doesn't matter because it all led to the delightful final section of this sorry book. 'The Great Santini' may have been a tough customer and not a man to cross, but his political incorrectness is like a breath of fresh air."

REVIEW: *N Y Times Book Rev* p14 N 17 2013 FRANK BRUNI

"The Death of Santini: The Story of a Father and His Son." "The book assumes its reader has traveled to it via 'The Great Santini' and maybe also . . . [Pat] Conroy's other best-known novels. That's probably a safe guess, given how briskly they've sold, but it can come across as a self-flattering one, considering the way Conroy sometimes takes the measure of his oeuvre. . . . Conroy tends to paint in extravagant strokes, and 'The Death of Santini' instantly reminded me of the decadent pleasures of his language. . . . [It] makes for engrossing reading because the real-life Santini's shifting response to his son's public vivisection of him both conforms to and utterly contradicts what you'd expect."

REVIEW: *Publ Wkly* v261 no4 p189 Ja 27 2014

CONSTANTINOU, EUGENIA SCARVELIS. Guiding to a blessed end; Andrew of Caesarea and the Apocalypse; [by] Eugenia Scarvelis Constantinou xv, 350 p. 2013 Catholic University of America Press

1. Andrew, Archbishop of Caesarea 2. Bible—Commentaries 3. Bible. Revelation 4. Historical literature
ISBN 0813221145; 9780813221144 (cloth : alk. paper)
LC 2012-036759

SUMMARY: Author Eugenia Scarvelis Constantinou's book focuses on "Andrew, archbishop of Caesarea, [who] was tasked with writing what would become the first Greek patristic commentary on the Apocalypse. . . . She explains the direct correlation between Andrew of Caesarea and fluctuating status of the Book of Revelation in Eastern Christianity through the centuries." (Publisher's note)

REVIEW: *Choice* v51 no1 p96-7 S 2013 V. M. Ehret

REVIEW: *Choice* v51 no1 p96 S 2013 L. Turcescu

"Guiding to a Blessed End: Andrew of Caesarea and His Apocalypse Commentary in the Ancient Church." "[Author Eugenia Scarvelis] Constantinou . . . brings her expertise on Andrew of Caesarea to this new book on the late-sixth- to early-seventh-century bishop of Cappadocia. . . . In 17 chapters in the present volume, Constantinou convincingly traces the trajectory of early commentaries on the Apocalypse, arguing for the independence of Andrew's commentaries from Latin commentaries (e.g., by Victorinus-Jerome or Tyconius). . . . She detects a pastoral, liturgical, and sacramental orientation in the 'Commentary' while analyzing Andrew's technique, dogmatic theology, and eschatology and noting its lasting influence on Eastern eschatology."

CONWAY, DANIEL. Masculinities, militarisation and the End Conscription Campaign; war resistance in apartheid South Africa; [by] Daniel Conway x, 176 p. 2012 Manchester University Press

1. Conscientious objection 2. Conscientious objec-

tors 3. Historical literature 4. Masculinity—History 5. South Africa—Military history 6. South Africa. South African Defence Force
ISBN 9780719083204
LC 2012-533741

SUMMARY: This book by Daniel Conway "explores the gendered dynamics of apartheid-era South Africa's militarisation and analyses the defiance of compulsory military service by individual white men, and the anti-apartheid activism of the white men and women in the End Conscription Campaign (ECC), the most significant white anti-apartheid movement to happen in South Africa." (Publisher's note)

REVIEW: *Am Hist Rev* v118 no4 p1293 O 2013 William Kelleher Storey

"Masculinities, Militarisation, and the End Conscription Campaign: War Resistance in Apartheid South Africa." "Most white South African men went along with the draft. As Daniel Conway recounts in his excellent study, the state fostered notions of citizenship that were bound up with military service, often stressing the connections between fighting and manliness. These connections made it especially difficult for men who were inclined to resist conscription. Some persisted in their beliefs and joined the End Conscription Campaign (ECC), the nexus of organized resistance to the draft. . . . Conway skillfully integrates a variety of primary sources, including newspapers, journals, songs, and archival documents, plus twelve interviews that he conducted with ECC members."

COOGAN, PETER.ed. What is a superhero? See What is a superhero?

COOK, BRUCE. The Wishbone Express; [by] Bruce Cook 428 p. 2013 CreateSpace Independent Publishing Platform
1. Friendship—Fiction 2. Interplanetary voyages 3. Science fiction 4. Space vehicles 5. Witnesses—Fiction
ISBN 1484922999; 9781484922996

SUMMARY: This book follows "interstellar couriers Bill Jenkins and Randy Henson, two young, handsome, clever and daring pals self-employed in the galactic delivery business. They're known for taking especially risky assignments just for the thrill of it. . . . But the Wishbone's latest contract turns out to be more than they bargained for, as the boys must deliver a witness and a dossier of evidence about deep-space corporate violations to a tribunal on the corrupt world of Philcani-Tu." (Kirkus Reviews)

REVIEW: *Kirkus Rev* v81 no24 p356 D 15 2013

REVIEW: *Kirkus Rev* v82 no1 p92 Ja 1 2014

"The Wishbone Express". "In a narrative that is, essentially, one long space chase, the lead characters and relentless posse resemble the crux of Butch Cassidy and the Sundance Kid. Such is the forward momentum that even the predictable bits breeze past enjoyably, and the tale still takes a few eventful turns after it appears the finish line has been crossed. . . . The story avoids careening into camp. In dealing with malicious faster-than-light missiles and other menaces, some of the dynamic duo's problem-solving skills are worthy of Capt. [Han] Solo. A quicksilver, retro-style space opera packed with zero-gravity thrills."

COOK, EILEEN. Year of mistaken discoveries; [by] Eileen Cook 272 p. 2014 Simon Pulse
1. Adoption—Fiction 2. Birthmothers—Fiction 3. Dating (Social customs)—Fiction 4. Friendship—Fiction 5. Young adult fiction
ISBN 1442440228; 9781442440227 (hardback)
LC 2013-035459

SUMMARY: In this novel, by Eileen Cook, "as first graders, Avery and Nora bonded over a special trait they shared—they were both adopted. Years later, Avery is smart, popular, and on the cheerleading squad, while Nora spends her time on the fringes of school society. . . . Then Avery learns that Nora overdosed on pills. Left to cope with Nora's loss and questioning her own actions, Avery decides to honor her friend by launching a search for her own birth mother." (Publisher's note)

REVIEW: *Booklist* v110 no8 p48 D 15 2013 Ann Kelley

REVIEW: *Bull Cent Child Books* v67 no9 p449 My 2014 D. S.

"Year of Mistaken Discoveries". "[Eileen] Cook provides her usual fluid prose, and the search story is generally credibly constructed, with the internet allowing for progress based on small bits of information; Avery's mixed motivations for her search add complexity. The relationship and eventual romance with Brody are less successful, though, since Brody is a largely flat character, who's mostly there to identify and fulfill Avery's needs. Additionally, Avery's journey toward self-realization dives into sentimental corniness . . . that undermines the significance of her growth. Even readers living with their birth families will understand Avery's search for her own identity, though, and they'll wish they could have Avery's handsome loyal assistant as they define themselves."

REVIEW: *Kirkus Rev* v81 no24 p116 D 15 2013

REVIEW: *Publ Wkly* v260 no48 p59 N 25 2013

COOK, GLEN. Working God's mischief; [by] Glen Cook 432 p. 2014 Tor Books
1. Brothers and sisters—Fiction 2. FICTION—Fantasy—Epic 3. Gods 4. Good and evil—Fiction 5. Imaginary wars and battles—Fiction
ISBN 9780765334206 (hardback)
LC 2013-028356

SUMMARY: In author Glen Cook's "fourth Instrumentalities of the Night epic installment . . . Monarchs have fallen, clerical leaders have been deposed, and gods themselves have died. Now Godslayer Piper Hecht, a man of masks and nested identities, forces some of the remaining divinities to surrender to his will. But Hecht is not the only one determined to reshape the world in his image." (Publishers Weekly)

REVIEW: *Booklist* v110 no11 p35 F 1 2014 Roland Green

REVIEW: *Kirkus Rev* v82 no2 p200 Ja 15 2014

"Working God's Mischief". "[Glen] Cook disdains any explanations or even hints that might help ease newcomers into the flow. . . . All this, in Cook's capable hands, comes across as less derivative than it might appear in summary; his characters have substance, their conversations sparkle. What he doesn't convey are any senses of urgency, what it all means, why it matters or how it fits into the context of the series. Presumably, you have to start at the beginning, and readers looking for a lengthy, well-narrated, but rather shapeless immersion should do just that."

REVIEW: *Publ Wkly* v261 no1 p38 Ja 6 2014

COOK, JUDE. Byron Easy; a novel; [by] Jude Cook 512 p. 2014 W W Norton & Co Inc
1. Bildungsromans, English 2. Humorous stories 3. Marriage—Fiction 4. Poets—Fiction 5. Psychoses
ISBN 1605984914; 9781605984919

SUMMARY: This book, by Jude Cook, follows "one man's terminal train journey home. It's December 24th, 1999. Byron Easy, a poverty-stricken poet, half-drunk and suicidal, sits on a train at King's Cross Station waiting to depart. In his lap is a backpack containing his remaining worldly goods. . . . What has led him to this point? Where are his friends, his family, his wife? What has happened to his dreams? And what disturbing plan awaits him at the end of his journey?" (Publisher's note)

REVIEW: *Booklist* v110 no4 p26 O 15 2013 Donna Seaman

REVIEW: *Kirkus Rev* v81 no20 p190 O 15 2013

REVIEW: *N Y Times Book Rev* p8 F 2 2014 TOM SHONE

"Byron Easy." "Byron Easy, the young hero of Jude Cook's first novel, . . . is a poet of the self-published and permanently wine-stained variety. . . . Cook can clearly write but he can also overwrite, in prose studded with literary name-drops and triple-word-score winners. . . . It's wan, unconvincing stuff and the reader soon tires of it. . . . Cook has written something new: a bildungsroman that refuses to bilden. . . . One hopes that next time he'll cut back on the cleverness--an overrated quality in a novelist--and seek out the ley lines undergirding his fiction. The good news is, they are there."

REVIEW: *TLS* no5749 p21 Je 7 2013 CHRISTOPHER YOUNG

COOK, KEVIN. Kitty Genovese; the murder, the bystanders, the crime that changed America; [by] Kevin Cook 288 p. 2014 W.W. Norton & Co. Inc.
1. Murder—New York (State)—New York—Biography 2. Murder victims—New York (State)—New York—Biography 3. Police—New York (State)—New York 4. True crime stories 5. Witnesses—New York (State)—New York
ISBN 0393239284; 9780393239287 (hardcover)
LC 2013-041176

SUMMARY: This book, by Kevin Cook, is the "true story of a crime. New York City, 1964. A young woman is stabbed to death on her front stoop. . . . The victim, Catherine 'Kitty' Genovese, became an urban martyr, butchered by a sociopathic killer in plain sight of thirty-eight neighbors who 'didn't want to get involved.' Her sensational case provoked an anxious outcry and launched a sociological theory known as the 'Bystander Effect.'" (Publisher's note)

REVIEW: *Booklist* v110 no11 p4 F 1 2014 Carol Haggas

REVIEW: *Kirkus Rev* v82 no3 p14 F 1 2014

"Kitty Genovese: The Murder, the Bystanders, the Crime That Changed America". "[Kevin Cook] eventually arrives at some well-founded conclusions on this controversial subject. Cook's breathless pacing and painstaking research manage to make his minibio of Genovese sound more interesting that it should: He frames her own fairly quotidian existence (other than her attraction to women, which was definitely not quotidian in 1964) in the bigger picture of the important social changes that were taking place in New York City and in America as a whole in the early 1960s. The author's game-changing contribution to the Genovese case pushes past mere sensationalism into previously unexplored territory. An engrossing true-crime tour de force."

REVIEW: *Libr J* v139 no3 p119 F 15 2014 Mahnaz Dar

REVIEW: *N Y Times Book Rev* p30 Mr 16 2014 Amy Finnerty

REVIEW: *Nation* v298 no17 p27-31 Ap 28 2014 PETER C. BAKER

"Kitty Genovese: A True Account of a Public Murder and Its Private Consequences" and "Kitty Genovese: The Murder, the Bystanders, the Crime That Changed America." "In 'Kitty Genovese: The Murder, the Bystanders, the Crime That Changed America,' journalist Kevin Cook argues that the familiar version of the story doesn't conform to what actually happened. . . . In 'Kitty Genovese: A True Account of a Public Murder and Its Private Consequences,' Catherine Pelonero insists that this brand of revisionism is ludicrous. . . [Pelonero's] extreme irritation with the revisionists makes her a weak historian."

REVIEW: *New York Times* v163 no56435 p3 Mr 9 2014 SAM ROBERTS

REVIEW: *New Yorker* v90 no3 p73-1 Mr 10 2014

REVIEW: *Publ Wkly* v260 no45 p57 N 11 2013

COOK, THOMAS H. Sandrine's Case; [by] Thomas H. Cook 352 p. 2013 Pgw
1. College teachers—Fiction 2. Detective & mystery stories 3. Murder investigation—Fiction 4. Spouses—Fiction 5. Trials (Murder)—Fiction
ISBN 0802126081; 9780802126085

SUMMARY: In this novel, "Sam Madison and his wife, Sandrine, both professors at Georgia's Coburn College (he of literature, she of history) and parents of a grown daughter, appear to have a solid marriage. But below the surface there are problems, which culminate in Sandrine's death from a cocktail of Demerol and vodka. While the coroner rules the death a suicide, the police suspect foul play and soon zero in on Sam as his wife's killer." (Publishers Weekly)

REVIEW: *Booklist* v109 no17 p38 My 1 2013 Connie Fletcher

REVIEW: *Booklist* v109 no19/20 p40 Je 1 2013 Connie Fletcher

REVIEW: *Kirkus Rev* v81 no12 p12 Je 15 2013

REVIEW: *N Y Times Book Rev* p21 S 1 2013 Marilyn Stasio

"How the Light Gets In," "The Boy Who Could See Demons," and "Sandrine's Case." "The only way to thwart the dastardly schemes (too dastardly for credibility) of that monstrous villain (too monstrous to be true) is to set up a satellite link to the outside world. . . . Once met, the delightfully quirky inhabitants of Three Pines are the kind of people you can't wait to see again. . . . But they all seem better suited to the modestly scaled subplot. . . . [A] 10-year-old boy . . . shares narrative duties with his psychiatrist in Carolyn Jess-Cooke's startling novel. . . . Although Thomas H. Cook is often praised for the clarity of his prose and the sheer drive of his storytelling, he deserves a special citation for bravery. In 'Sandrine's Case,' he not only dares to write a novel with an unpleasant protagonist, but also makes him the narrator."

REVIEW: *Publ Wkly* v260 no24 p44 Je 17 2013

COOK, TRISH. A really awesome mess. See Halpin, B.

COOKE, LUCY.il. A little book of sloth. See Cooke, L.

COOKE, MERVYN.ed. Letter From a Life. See Letter From a Life

COOKE, RACHEL. Her Brilliant Career; Ten Extraordinary Women of the Fifties; [by] Rachel Cooke 368 p. 2013 Virago

1. Biography (Literary form) 2. Nineteen fifties 3. Women—Great Britain—Social conditions—20th century 4. Women employees 5. Women's history—20th century

ISBN 1844087409 (hbk.); 9781844087402 (hbk.)

SUMMARY: This book by Rachel Cooke "look[s] at ten women in the 1950s—pioneers whose professional careers and complicated private lives helped to create the opportunities available to today's women. These plucky and ambitious individuals—among them a film director, a cook, an architect, an editor, an archaeologist, a race car driver—left the house, discovered the bliss of work, and ushered in the era of the working woman." (Publisher's note)

REVIEW: *Economist* v409 no8861 p87 N 9 2013

REVIEW: *Libr J* v139 no12 p56 Jl 1 2014 Barbara Hoffert

REVIEW: *London Rev Books* v35 no24 p31-2 D 19 2013 Rosemary Hill

"Her Brilliant Career: Ten Extraordinary Women of the Fifties". "More women than is perhaps generally supposed managed to escape, and in this collection of lively and thought-provoking biographical essays Rachel Cooke considers the careers often who made their names in the decade. . . . Yet for all Cooke's justified satisfaction in finding so many possible subjects from which to make her selection, the cumulative effect is to emphasise how very bold and persistent these women had to be, what prejudice, sacrifice and discouragement they faced. She has chosen them as 'role models' and 'inspirational figures' but these are not exactly 'Stirring Stories for Girls' (published in 1960), more like cautionary tales, their moral, sadly often, women beware women."

REVIEW: *New Statesman* v142 no5181 p73 O 25 2013 Caroline Crampton

REVIEW: *Publ Wkly* v261 no35 p57 S 1 2014

COOLEY, ALISON E. Pompeii and Herculaneum; a sourcebook; [by] Alison E. Cooley 2013 Routledge

ISBN 9780415666794 (hardback: alk. paper); 9780415666800 (pbk.: alk. paper)

LC 2013-012886

SUMMARY: This book, by Alison E. Cooley and M. G. L. Cooley, explores the ancient extinct cities of Pompeii and Herculaneum. "Focusing upon inscriptions and ancient texts, it translates and sets into context . . . the . . . material uncovered in these towns. . . . The individual chapters explore the early history of Pompeii and Herculaneum, their destruction, leisure pursuits, politics, commerce, religion, the family and society." (Publisher's note)

REVIEW: *Choice* v51 no8 p1377 Ap 2014 M. C. Su

"Pompeii and Herculaneum: A Sourcebook". "The resource should have been noted as a revised rather than a second edition, since the original title did not include information on Herculaneum. The chapter on excavations has been removed and incorporated into the body of the short narrative on the two sites. A new chapter titled 'Law and Society' is included. The authors have added a few more visual examples, along with more details included in appendixes; a glossary; further readings (footnotes) for each chapter; a bibliography; and indexes by person, place, and theme. Geared toward secondary students in the UK, this sourcebook complements resources such as Mary Beard's 'The Fires of Vesuvius'."

COOLEY, M. G. L. Pompeii and Herculaneum. See Cooley, A. E.

COOLIDGE, W. A. B. Alpine studies; [by] W. A. B. Coolidge xiii, 307 p. 1912 Longmans, Green and co.

1. Historical literature 2. Mountaineering 3. Switzerland—Description & travel 4. Switzerland—History

LC 1202-5303

SUMMARY: This illustrated book by W. A. B. Coolidge "contains twelve chapters describing expeditions in the High Alps, four chapters on the history and nomenclature of the mountain region round Monte Rosa, and four 'subalpine' chapters on scenes in the lower parts of Switzerland." (Nation). The author "he treats not only of climbing . . . . but . . . of certain historical problems and of certain features of Swiss life . . . which do not come under the observation of ordinary travellers." (Times Literary Supplement)

REVIEW: *TLS* no5756 p15 Jl 26 2013

"Alpine Studies." "Now, as few people know more of the Alps than Mr [W. A. B.] Coolidge, so none can have a keener sense of joy among them, a larger vista of triumphs, or more stimulating and glorious memories.... Mr Coolidge has an encyclopaedic knowledge of the Alpine chain, and not only of its physical features. . . . Thus he approaches his subject as a scientific man and an accurate historian, and such an approach does not lead to the production of entertainment so much as to the imparting of information. . . . These papers will always be valuable so long as travellers visit the Alps and wish to know the story of their first conquest. But their publication in almost their original form betrays an uncertainty of aim."

COON, JAMES G.ed. Ljubljana Tales. See Ljubljana Tales

COOPER, ARTEMIS. Patrick Leigh Fermor; [by] Artemis Cooper 2012 John Murray

1. Biographies 2. Fermor, Patrick Leigh 3. Travel writers 4. Travelers 5. World War, 1939-1945—Campaigns—Greece—Crete

ISBN 0719554497; 9780719554490

SUMMARY: This book offers a biography of Sir Patrick Leigh Fermor, who "explored eastern Europe, fell in love with a Romanian princess and lived with her in a Balkan idyll until the outbreak of war. . . . He was commissioned in the intelligence corps and sent to the Middle East. After escaping from a defeated Greece he returned to Crete to help organise the resistance and made his name with the capture and evacuation to Egypt of a German general." (Economist)

REVIEW: *Commonweal* v141 no5 p22-5 Mr 7 2014 Jeffrey Meyers

REVIEW: *N Y Times Book Rev* p11 O 27 2013 CHRISTOPHER BENFEY

"Patrick Leigh Fermor: An Adventure." "An affectionately intimate, informative and forgiving biography. . . . [Artemis] Cooper doesn't shy away from what she gingerly calls 'the interplay of Paddy's memory and imagination'. Did he really cross the Great Hungarian Plain on horseback? Well he may, as she put it, have 'smudged the facts a little,' but he explained that he 'felt the reader might be getting bored of me just plodding along.' . . . If, as Cooper remarks, 'the magpie mind adds details freely' . . . Fermor mostly got the larger story right."

REVIEW: *New Yorker* p69-1 Ja 27 2014

COOPER, ARTEMIS.ed. The Broken Road. See Fermor, P. L.

COOPER, BECKY. Mapping Manhattan; a love (and sometimes hate) story in maps by 75 New Yorkers; 118 p. 2013 Abrams Image

1. Cartography

ISBN 9781419706721

LC 2012-033160

SUMMARY: Written by Becky Cooper, this "illustrated, PostSecret-style tribute to New York, 'Mapping Manhattan' includes 75 maps from both anonymous mapmakers and notable New Yorkers, including 'Man on Wire' aerialist Philippe Petit, 'New York Times' wine critic Eric Asimov, Tony award-winning actor Harvey Fierstein, and many more." (Publisher's note)

REVIEW: *N Y Times Book Rev* p85 D 8 2013 Clyde Haberman

"The Stories They Tell: Artifacts From the National September 11 Memorial Museum: A Journey of Remembrance," "The Nature of Urban Design: A New York Perspective on Resilience," and "Mapping Manhattan: A Love (and Sometimes Hate) Story in Maps by 75 New Yorkers." "Artifacts in this handsome 'journey of remembrance' are drawn from the museum that is part of New York's Sept. 11 memorial. The book matches photos with essays by museum staff members. . . . For [author Alexandros] Washburn . . . the ruination inflicted by Hurricane Sandy was intensely personal. . . . This book may appeal more to students of urban policy than to general readers. . . . [Author Becky] Cooper, a cartographer, takes us on an entertaining journey."

COOPER, DIANA, 1892-1986. See Norwich J.

COOPER, ELSPETH. The Raven's Shadow; [by] Elspeth Cooper 576 p. 2014 St. Martin's Press Tor

1. Fantasy fiction 2. Good & evil—Fiction 3. Imaginary wars and battles—Fiction 4. Magic—Fiction 5. Witches—Fiction

ISBN 0765331675; 9780765331670

LC 2014-009951

SUMMARY: "'The Raven's Shadow,' the third book of Elspeth Cooper's 'The Wild Hunt' series finds war brewing on both sides of the Veil between the worlds. . . . Wrestling with his failing grip on the power of the Song, and still trying to come to terms with the horrifying events he witnessed in El Maqqam, Gair returns to the mainland with only one thing on his mind: vengeance." (Publisher's note)

REVIEW: *Booklist* v110 no12 p38 F 15 2014 Regina Schroeder

REVIEW: *Kirkus Rev* v82 no4 p340 F 15 2014

"The Raven's Shadow". "The follow-up to 'Trinity Rising' (2013) is the third and largest entry in what has expanded from a fantasy trilogy into a series. . . . The stumbling block with this and other doomsday scenarios: What happens once the evil guys slaughter everyone? Do they just sit around waving their swords in triumph? . . . . This installment ramps up the tension, with plenty of gory action, [Elspeth] Cooper's usual high level of characterization, and controlled plotting that, while showing few original touches, rolls solidly along. An excellent addition to this superior epic."

REVIEW: *Publ Wkly* v261 no4 p174 Ja 27 2014

COOPER, FLOYD.il. A dance like starlight. See Dempsey, K.

COOPER, FLOYD.il. Queen of the track. See Lang, H.

COOPER, HELEN, 1947-.ed. Medieval Shakespeare. See Medieval Shakespeare

COOPER, ILENE. A woman in the House and Senate; how women came to the United States Congress, broke down barriers, and changed the country; 144 p. 2014 Abrams Books for Young Readers

1. Historical literature 2. Women—Political activity—United States—History—Juvenile literature 3. Women in politics—United States—History 4. Women legislators—United States—History—Juvenile literature

ISBN 9781419710360 (alk. paper)

LC 2013-022201

SUMMARY: In this book, "beginning with the women's suffrage movement and going all the way through the results of the 2012 election, Ilene Cooper . . . covers more than a century of U.S. history in order to highlight the influential and diverse group of female leaders who opened doors for women in politics as well as the nation as a whole. Featured women include Hattie Caraway (the first woman elected to the Senate) [and] Patsy Mink (the first woman of color to serve in Congress)." (Publisher's note)

REVIEW: *Bull Cent Child Books* v67 no10 p508 Je 2014 E. B.

"A Woman in the House (and Senate): How Women Came to the United States Congress, Broke Down Barriers, and Changed the Country". "[Ilene] Cooper goes beyond noting the women's arrivals and offers a brief overview of issues, committee work, successes, and disappointments that marked their stay. The layout is clear and generally attractive: cameo photographs accompany each entry, interspersed with slightly stilted art and set against pages bordered with patriotic motifs. Copious end matter includes a crash course on federal-level civics and women's suffrage; a complete list of women in Congress; citations, bibliography, and a particularly well-designed and helpful index."

REVIEW: *Kirkus Rev* v82 no2 p267 Ja 15 2014

REVIEW: *SLJ* v60 no3 p179 Mr 2014 Mary Mueller

REVIEW: *Voice of Youth Advocates* v37 no1 p92 Ap 2014 Julia Bowerson

COOPER, JOHN M. (JOHN MONTGOMERY), 1881-1949. Pursuits of wisdom; six ways of life in ancient philosophy from Socrates to Plotinus; [by] John M. (John Montgomery) Cooper xiv, 442 p. 2012 Princeton University Press

1. Conduct of life 2. Philosophical literature 3. Philosophy, Ancient 4. Plotinus 5. Socrates, ca. 469-399 B.C. 6. Wisdom
ISBN 9780691138602 (hardcover)
LC 2012-002204

SUMMARY: This book by John M. Cooper presents a "survey of six ancient Greek ethical theories, covering most of the main currents of ancient philosophical ethics, from Socrates to the Platonism of late antiquity, with Aristotle and the major Hellenistic schools (Stoics, Epicureans, and Skeptics) in between. Its focus is particularly on the idea of philosophy as a way of life." (Ethics)

REVIEW: *Choice* v50 no3 p491 N 2012 C. R. McCall

REVIEW: *Classical Rev* v64 no1 p52-4 Ap 2014 Michael J. Griffin

REVIEW: *Ethics* v124 no2 p397-402 Ja 2014 RAPHAEL WOOLF

"Pursuits of Wisdom: Six Ways of Life in Ancient Philosophy From Socrates to Plotinus". "John Cooper's book is a rich and stimulating survey of six ancient Greek ethical theories, covering most of the main currents of ancient philosophical ethics, from Socrates to the Platonism of late antiquity, with Aristotle and the major Hellenistic schools (Stoics, Epicureans, and Skeptics) in between. . . . Its four hundred close-packed pages are written with a combination of intellectual vigor and passionate seriousness of purpose that is characteristic of Cooper's work. Reading it through as a whole is an intense and commensurately rewarding experience."

REVIEW: *TLS* no5704 p5 Jl 27 2012

COOPER, KATE. Band of Angels; The Forgotten World of Early Christian Women; [by] Kate Cooper 320 p. 2013 Penguin Group USA

1. Christian women—History 2. Church history—Primitive & early church, ca. 30-600 3. Historical literature 4. Women—Religious aspects—Christianity—History 5. Women in Christianity—History
ISBN 1468307401; 9781468307405

SUMMARY: Author Kate Cooper's book focuses on "the triumphs and hardships of the first mothers of the infant church." The book tells the "story of how a new way of understanding relationships took root in the ancient world. As Cooper demonstrates, women from all walks of life played an invaluable role in Christianity's growth to become a world religion. Peasants, empresses, and independent businesswomen contributed what they could to an emotional revolution unlike anything the ancient world had ever seen." (Publisher's note)

REVIEW: *Kirkus Rev* v81 no16 p265 Ag 15 2013

REVIEW: *New Statesman* v142 no5170 p44 Ag 16 2013 Lucy Winkett

REVIEW: *TLS* no5787 p28 F 28 2014 LUCY BECKETT

"Band of Angels: The Forgotten World of Early Christian Women." "Kate Cooper's approach to her disparate material, assembled to persuade the reader that early Christianity was not misogynist, is enthusiastic and optimistic: if a woman is mentioned, she must be interesting even if it is impossible to discover anything about her beyond her name. . . . Much of Cooper's extrapolation is no more than plausible guesswork. . . . Her book is written, with frequent exaggeration and in sometimes woolly prose, for readers who know little about either Christianity or the ancient world. A firmer chronological structure, a few clear paragraphs of basic history and a more generously labelled map would help such readers. And she could have done with a good copy-editor."

COOPER, MICHAEL L., 1950-. Fighting fire!; ten of the deadliest fires in American history and how we fought them; [by] Michael L. Cooper 224 p. 2014 Henry Holt and Co.

1. Fire extinction—Equipment & supplies 2. Fire extinction—United States—History—Juvenile literature 3. Fires—History 4. Historical literature 5. Triangle Shirtwaist factory fire, New York (N.Y.), 1911
ISBN 0805097147; 9780805097146 (hardback)
LC 2013-043580

SUMMARY: This book, by Michael L. Cooper, "brings to life ten of the deadliest infernos . . . [the United States] has ever endured: the great fires of Boston, New York, Chicago, Baltimore, and San Francisco, the disasters of the Triangle Shirtwaist Factory, the General Slocum, and the Cocoanut Grove nightclub, the wildfire of Witch Creek in San Diego County, and the catastrophe of 9/11." (Publisher's note)

REVIEW: *Booklist* v110 no11 p52 F 1 2014 Carolyn Phelan

REVIEW: *Bull Cent Child Books* v67 no7 p353 Mr 2014 E. B.

"Fighting Fire!: Ten of the Deadliest Fires in American History and How We Fought Them." "Although each chapter stands as a self-contained episode, reading the title in its entirety leads the audience to a broader understanding of how human negligence and error and fire's deviousness and intensity collaborate in the infernos. Unfortunately, when it comes to the physics of fire and the engineering of firefighting equipment, this title comes up somewhat short, with only a scanty background on fire's behavior and little detail on the incremental improvements in the fire engines on display throughout the book and in an appended gallery. Illustrations are a mixed lot as well."

REVIEW: *Horn Book Magazine* v90 no3 p108-9 My/Je 2014 DEAN SCHNEIDER

REVIEW: *Kirkus Rev* v82 no2 p117 Ja 15 2014

REVIEW: *SLJ* v60 no4 p186 Ap 2014 Lisa Crandall

COOPER, MIKE. Clawback; [by] Mike Cooper 390 p. 2012 Viking

1. Adventure stories 2. Crime—Fiction 3. Finance—Fiction 4. Murder—Investigation—Fiction
ISBN 9780670023295
LC 2011-036310

SUMMARY: In this book, "ex-special ops Cade has earned his CPA, decided not to bean-count and decided to apply his skill set to become a one-man lost-funds recovery operation.

. . . Client Thomas Marlett is killed by a sniper, a murder happening at the same time Cade "claws back" Marlett's $10 million from an about-to-be-arrested fraud. In the Wall Street milieu where traders "have long ago left behind law, morality and the social compact," Cade doesn't lack clients. His next, Quint Ganderson, investment-fund managing partner, informs Cade that Marlett's fund was down 78 percent and two other CEOs of poorly performing funds are also recently dead. As Cade searches for the assassin, Clara Dawson inserts herself into his investigation." (Kirkus)

REVIEW: *Booklist* v108 no12 p22 F 15 2012 Thomas Gaughan

REVIEW: *Kirkus Rev* v80 no4 p331-2 F 15 2012

"Clawback." "In Cooper's debut thriller, ex-special ops Cade has earned his CPA, decided not to bean-count and decided to apply his skill set to become a one-man lost-funds recovery operation. . . . There's much snappy, half-cynical repartee reminiscent of 1930s Hollywood cinema, including snarks about the necessity of gun control, and a firefight aboard a mega-yacht followed by a jet ski-Zodiac water pursuit. Cooper sets the action in New York City, a locale he has down pat, from neighborhood diners to the only place it's legal to live on your boat. Arm a Hollywood hero with a Beretta and disposable cell, point him at a Gordon Gekko-type, and this book's big screen ready."

REVIEW: *Publ Wkly* v259 no4 p146 Ja 23 2012

COOPER, SUSAN. Ghost Hawk; [by] Susan Cooper 328 p. 2013 Margaret K. McElderry Books

1. Coming of age—Fiction 2. Ghosts—Fiction 3. Historical fiction 4. Indians of North America—Massachusetts—Fiction 5. Survival—Fiction 6. Wampanoag Indians—Fiction

ISBN 1442481412 (hardcover); 9781442481411 (hardcover); 9781442481435 (ebook)

LC 2012-039892

SUMMARY: This novel is "a story of adventure and friendship between a young Native American and a colonial New England settler. Little Hawk is sent into the woods alone [and] if [he] survives three moons by himself, he will be a man. John Wakely is only ten when his father dies. . . . John sees how quickly the relationships between settlers and natives are deteriorating. His friendship with Little Hawk will put both boys in grave danger." (Publisher's note)

REVIEW: *Booklist* v110 no9/10 p125 Ja 1 2014 Karen Cruze

REVIEW: *Booklist* v110 no9/10 p83 Ja 1 2014 MICHAEL CART

"Ghost Hawk," "Looks Like Daylight," and "If You Could Be Mine." "[Susan] Cooper's heartfelt historical fantasy about the magical relationship between two boys, Native American Little Hawk and trader's son John, is richly plotted, beautiful in tone, and serious in theme as it examines the injustices of early colonial life. . . . Canadian author [Deborah] Ellis has interviewed 45 young Native people from Canada and the U.S. The 9- to 18-year-olds tell her about the often appalling conditions of their lives, which are blighted by alcohol and drug abuse, poverty, suicide, broken families, and more. 'That they are here at all,' Ellis movingly writes, 'is a miracle.' . . . [Sara] Farizan's unusual first novel tells an important story about the stubbornness of love and offers an inside look at secret gay life in Iran."

REVIEW: *Booklist* v109 no21 p64 Jl 1 2013 Michael Cart

REVIEW: *Bull Cent Child Books* v67 no3 p145-6 N 2013 K. Q. G.

"Ghost Hawk." "After surviving three solitary months in a harsh Northeast winter to prove himself a man. Little Hawk, an eleven-year-old Wampanoag boy of the late seventeenth century, returns home to find his tribe decimated by plague. . . . The shift in focus after Little Hawk's death is frustrating, as the character goes from a solid, developing protagonist to merely a placid observer, a mostly impotent engine by which John's story is then told. The ghostly connection between the two, however, provides an opportunity for a cultural exchange that would likely not have otherwise happened, and [author Susan] Cooper explores the similarities and differences between the two communities. . . ."

REVIEW: *Horn Book Magazine* v89 no5 p89 S/O 2013 JONATHAN HUNT

Title:"Ghost Hawk." "A single fantasy element bridges the two parts and allows Little Hawk not only to narrate his own story but, omnisciently, to relate the entwined destinies of [John] Wakeley, the colonial settlers, and the Pokanoket tribe. The novel maintains an admirable sense of historical empathy, foreshadowed in the epigraphs (from Roger Williams and Woody Guthrie) and punctuated by an appended timeline that chronicles the demise of the native way of life in the face of hostile invaders. [Susan] Cooper here demonstrates that there's plenty of magic left in her pen, delivering a powerful and memorable novel."

REVIEW: *Kirkus Rev* v81 no12 p84-5 Je 15 2013

REVIEW: *Publ Wkly* v260 no24 p64 Je 17 2013

REVIEW: *Publ Wkly* p88 Children's starred review annual 2013

REVIEW: *Publ Wkly* v260 no43 p57 O 28 2013

REVIEW: *SLJ* v59 no9 p141 S 2013 Necia Blundy

COOPER, T. Changers book one; Drew; [by] T. Cooper 288 p. 2014 Akashic Books

1. Gender 2. High school students—Fiction 3. Identity (Psychology)—Fiction 4. Paranormal fiction 5. Urban fantasy fiction

ISBN 1617751952; 9781617751950 (trade pbk.); 9781617752070 (e-bk.); 9781617752117 (hardcover)

LC 2013-938807

SUMMARY: This book, by T Cooper and Allison Glock, "opens on the eve of Ethan Miller's freshman year of high school in a brand-new town. . . . everything is looking up in life. Until the next morning. When Ethan awakens as a girl. Ethan is a Changer, a little-known, ancient race of humans who live out each of their four years of high school as a different person. After graduation, Changers choose which version of themselves they will be forever." (Publisher's note)

REVIEW: *Bull Cent Child Books* v67 no10 p508-9 Je 2014 T. A.

REVIEW: *Kirkus Rev* v81 no24 p147 D 15 2013

"Changers: Drew". "Drew is a Changer, one of "an ancient race of humans" who wake up as a different person on the first day of each year of high school (how ancient Changers transformed before the existence of high schools is one of many questions left oddly unaddressed). . . . Drew's narrative voice is engaging, often sarcastic and sometimes poignant. Her outsider observations about how it feels to be a girl and how girls are treated are genuine, keenly observed and sometimes funny. . . . Two love interests develop for

Drew, a Changer boy and a Static girl, and their genders are, refreshingly, a nonissue. . . . A fresh and charmingly narrated look at teens and gender, but the worldbuilding is distractingly bizarre."

REVIEW: *N Y Times Book Rev* p22 Mr 16 2014 BENOIT DENIZET-LEWIS

REVIEW: *Publ Wkly* v260 no50 p70 D 9 2013

COPELAND, MISTY. Life in motion; an unlikely ballerina; [by] Misty Copeland 288 p. 2014 Touchstone Books

1. African American dancers—Biography 2. Ballerinas—United States—Biography 3. Ballet dancers—United States—Biography 4. Memoirs

ISBN 1476737983; 9781476737980 (hardcover)

LC 2014-002922

SUMMARY: This book presents a memoir by Misty Copeland, an African American soloist for the American Ballet Theatre. "When a teacher encouraged I 3-year-old Misty to take ballet at the Boys and Girls Club of Los Angeles, she discovered a hidden talent. Her natural flexibility and grace had her on pointe within two months, something other ballerinas work years to achieve. She was offered lead roles before finishing high school." (Booklist)

REVIEW: *Booklist* v110 no11 p17 F 1 2014 Amber Peckham

"Life in Motion: An Unlikely Ballerina." "Her professional success is impressive, but it's not what makes her memoir such an unexpected page-turner. After all, we already know [Misty] Copeland will overcome racial and socioeconomic bias to claim her spotlight. What keeps us reading is Copeland's intelligent, fair, and warm voice. She speaks with candor about having to lose her luscious curves and cover herself with white makeup to look more acceptable on stage, but she never places blame on those who asked her to do so. Her story is an inspiration to anyone--man or woman, black or white--who has ever chased a dream against the odds, and the grace with which she triumphs is an example for us all."

REVIEW: *Kirkus Rev* v82 no3 p73 F 1 2014

REVIEW: *New York Times* v163 no56421 p25 F 23 2014 ROSLYN SULCAS

COPLAND, AARON, 1900-1990. The complete Copland; [by] Aaron Copland vii, 374 p. 2012 Pendragon Press

1. Autobiographies 2. Composers—United States—Biography 3. Music—20th century 4. Music literature 5. Oral history

ISBN 157647190X; 9781576471906 (alk. paper)

LC 2012-013998

SUMMARY: This book, by Aaron Copland and Vivian Perlis, "is an updated edition of Copland's autobiography, originally published as 'Copland: 1900 through 1942' . . . and 'Copland: Since 1943.' . . . Copland's original narrative, primarily edited from oral history interviews that be gave in 1975-76, is interspersed with "interludes" by Perlis . . . that set the historical context." (Choice: Current Reviews for Academic Libraries)

REVIEW: *Choice* v51 no4 p645-6 D 2013 M. D. Jenkins II

"The Complete Copland." "This book is an updated edition of [Aaron] Copland's autobiography, originally published as 'Copland: 1900 through 1942' . . . and 'Copland: Since 1943'. . . . This book is valuable not only for the light it sheds on Copland's career but also for his personal comments on Nadia Boulanger, Serge Koussevitzky, Leonard Bernstein, and other important figures in 20th-century music with whom be came into contact. Curiously, in an apparent attempt to keep the book from being dauntingly thick, the publishers chose an oblong layout with two columns per page. This makes casual reading a bit awkward. . . . That minor complaint aside, having this important work in an updated, single-volume format is helpful."

COPPA, FRANK J. The life and pontificate of Pope Pius XII; between history and controversy; [by] Frank J. Coppa xxix, 306 p. 2013 The Catholic University of America Press

1. Biographies 2. Catholic Church & world politics 3. Popes—Biography 4. World War, 1939-1945—Religious aspects—Catholic Church

ISBN 0813220157; 9780813220154 (cloth : alk. paper); 9780813220161 (pbk. : alk. paper)

LC 2012-033239

SUMMARY: This book, by Frank J. Coppa, is a pigraphy of Eugenio Pacelli, who became Pope Pius XII. "It probes the roots of his traditionalism and legalism, his approach to modernity and reformism in Church and society, and the influences behind his policies and actions." (Publisher's note) Coppa argues that "the key to understanding Pacelli was his legal mindset and the diplomatic course established by the Holy See through the first third of the century." (Times Literary Supplement)

REVIEW: *Choice* v51 no1 p96 S 2013 W. L. Pitts Jr.

REVIEW: *London Rev Books* v35 no18 p13-5 S 26 2013 Eamon Duffy

"The Life and Pontificate of Pope Pius XII: Between History and Controversy," "The Pope's Jews: The Vatican's Secret Plan to Save Jews from the Nazis," and "Soldier of Christ: The Life of Pope Pius XII." "These welcome new biographies by Frank Coppa and Robert Ventresca make telling use of the newly available papers of Pius XI. The detailed picture that emerges of Pacelli's diplomatic career and years as secretary of state brings a new depth to our understanding of this austere and complicated man. . . . Gordon Thomas's account of Pacelli's response to the Final Solution, for instance, is a tendentious exercise in exculpation and hagiography that implausibly depicts Pacelli as a papal pimpernel, actively masterminding a campaign to save European Jewry."

REVIEW: *TLS* no5750 p7-8 Je 14 2013 JOHN CORNWELL

"Soldier of Christ: The Life of Pope Pius XII" and "The Life and Pontificate of Pope Pius XII: Between History and Controversy." "According to both [Frank J.] Coppa and [Robert A.] Ventresca, the key to understanding [Eugenio] Pacelli was his legal mindset and the diplomatic course established by the Holy See through the first third of the century. . . . It is clear from these new biographies that the Holy's See's concordat policy with Germany gave unintentional impetus to [Adolf] Hitler's plans. . . . These new studies amply illustrate the vexed entanglement of Pacelli's case. . . . Ventresca has more successfully captured Pacelli in the round, with telling, if meagre, details of human interest."

COPPARD, A. E. (ALFRED EDGAR), 1878-1957. Weep Not My Wanton; Selected Short Stories; [by] A. E. (Alfred Edgar) Coppard 112 p. 2013 Turnpike Books

1. Country life—England—Fiction 2. English ballads—England 3. English fiction—20th century 4. Folklore—England 5. Short stories—Collections
ISBN 0957233620; 9780957233621

SUMMARY: "A. E. Coppard's short stories capture a sensual rural England combining poetic description of its landscape with characters tied to a more elemental life, who experience passions of love, loss and regret. Drawing on traditional folklore and ballads, at a time when the countryside's traditional culture was dying out, Coppard's stories have a uniquely melancholic tone, an understanding of human nature and the secret desires of women with an individual vision of England." (Publisher's note)

REVIEW: *TLS* no5788 p28 Mr 7 2014 DAVID MALCOLM

"Miss Nobody," "Weep Not My Wanton: Selected Short Stories," and "Mr. Bazalgette's Agent." "[Author Ethel] Carnie's 'Miss Nobody,' her first published novel, came out in 1913. . . . The novel's rich material involves the conflict between the two women. . . . [Leonard] Merrick's Mr Bazalgette's Agent marks an important text in the evolution of detective fiction. As the editor of this new edition, Mike Ashley, notes, 'this book is almost certainly the first ever British novel to feature a professional female detective.' . . . The seven stories republished in 'Weep Not My Wanton' are among [A. E.] Coppard's best known and provide a good, if fragmentary, introduction to his work. They are mostly about the rural poor sometime in the early twentieth century."

COQUILLETTE, DANIEL R.ed. Portrait of a patriot. See Portrait of a patriot

CORACE, JEN.il. I hatched! See Esbaum, J.

CORCHADO, ALFREDO. Midnight in Mexico; a reporter's journey through a country's descent into the darkness; [by] Alfredo Corchado 304 p. 2013 The Penguin Press

1. Drug traffic—Mexico 2. Investigative reporting—Mexico 3. Journalism 4. Organized crime—Mexico
ISBN 9781101617830; 9781594204395
LC 2012-046885

SUMMARY: In this book, "Mexico-born U.S. journalist Corchado frames a portrait of a torn nation within an account of escaping his own murder." Particular focus is given to "the author's reflections on a Mexico that is malformed and crime-stricken largely due to American influences, unintended perhaps but real nonetheless, the drug cartels having filled an economic and political vacuum produced by neoliberal free trade." (Kirkus Reviews)

REVIEW: *Kirkus Rev* v81 no9 p41-2 My 1 2013

REVIEW: *London Rev Books* v36 no9 p21-3 My 8 2014 Álvaro Enrigue

REVIEW: *TLS* no5764 p24 S 20 2013 BENJAMIN SMITH

"Midnight in Mexico: A Reporter's Journey Through a Country's Descent into Darkness." "Few writers have managed to describe the emotional tenor of Mexico's recent past, except perhaps the existential terror of staring into the void. [Alfredo] Corchado' s book bucks the trend. By mixing the political with the personal, journalistic revelations with an aching sense of frustrated opportunity, paranoia and sadness, 'Midnight in Mexico' manages to capture both the rhythms of national politics and the everyday emotional fallout. Superbly structured, elegantly written and deeply felt, the book is the finest non-fictional account of the drug war and required reading for anyone interested in contemporary crime, politics or the media."

CORCORAN, SEAN.ed. City as canvas. See City as canvas

CORDELL, MATTHEW.il. Like carrot juice on a cupcake. See Sternberg, J.

CORDELL, MATTHEW.il. Rooting for you. See Hood, S.

CORKIN, SUZANNE. Permanent present tense; the unforgettable life of the amnesic patient, H.M.; [by] Suzanne Corkin 400 p. 2013 Basic Books

1. Amnesiacs—Biography 2. BIOGRAPHY & AUTOBIOGRAPHY—Medical 3. Epilepsy—Surgery—United States—History 4. SCIENCE—History 5. SCIENCE—Life Sciences—Neuroscience
ISBN 0465031595; 9780465031597 (hardback); 9780465031597
LC 2013-002391

SUMMARY: In this biography of amnesic patient Henry Gustav Molaison, author Suzanne Corkin "uses stories about his experiences and capabilities to illustrate some of the scientific principles underlying memory. She also offers a . . . historical sketch of the study of memory and the burgeoning field of neuroscience--from the dubious and gruesome practice of prefrontal lobotomy to the development of powerful brainimaging techniques." (Science)

REVIEW: *Choice* v51 no2 p357 O 2013 C. J. Jones

REVIEW: *Kirkus Rev* v81 no8 p47 Ap 15 2013

REVIEW: *Libr J* v138 no12 p95 Jl 1 2013 Kathleen Arsenault

REVIEW: *London Rev Books* v35 no10 p15-6 My 23 2013 Mike Jay

REVIEW: *Nation* v297 no18 p27-31 N 4 2013 CHARLES GROSS

"Permanent Present Tense: The Unforgettable Life of the Amnesic Patient, H. M." "[Suzanne Corkin's] accessible book places [Henry Gustav Molaison's] story in the context of past and present research on memory and describes many of the questions initiated by research on H.M. It is a scientifically exciting and personally moving portrait of a man whose life and brain ended up being devoted to the science of memory. . . . Corkin and her students made many of the important subsequent discoveries about H.M. . . . No one knew him better or longer, personally or scientifically, and no other person could have written 'Permanent Present Tense'.

REVIEW: *Newsweek Global* v161 no20 p1 My 29 2013 Robert Herritt

REVIEW: *Science* v341 no6145 p459 Ag 2 2013 Nicholette Zeliadt

CORMAN, JESSICA R.ed. Phosphorus, food, and our future. See Phosphorus, food, and our future

CORNELISON, SUE.il. You're wearing that to school?! See Plouchard, L.

CORNELL, KEVIN.il. Lulu's mysterious mission. See Viorst, J.

CORNELL, SAUL.ed. The Second Amendment on trial. See The Second Amendment on trial

CORNWALL, ANDREA.ed. Women, sexuality and the political power of pleasure. See Women, sexuality and the political power of pleasure

CORNWELL, JOHN, 1940-. The dark box; a secret history of confession; [by] John Cornwell 320 p. 2014 Basic Books, a member of the Perseus Books Group

1. Catholic Church—History—20th century 2. Child sexual abuse by clergy 3. Confession (Canon law) 4. Confession—History 5. Historical literature 6. Pius X, Pope, 1835-1914

ISBN 9780465039951 (hardcover: alk. paper)
LC 2013-042961

SUMMARY: In this book, "Drawing on extensive historical sources, contemporary reports, and first-hand accounts, [author John] Cornwell takes a hard look at the long evolution of confession. . . . [The] sweeping, inappropriately early imposition of the sacrament gave priests an unprecedented and privileged role in the lives of young boys and girls—a role that a significant number would exploit in the decades that followed." (Publisher's note)

REVIEW: *Booklist* v110 no9/10 p20-4 Ja 1 2014 Christopher McConnell

REVIEW: *Commonweal* v141 no8 p28-30 My 2 2014 Leslie Woodcock Tentler

REVIEW: *Kirkus Rev* v82 no2 p97 Ja 15 2014

REVIEW: *Libr J* v139 no2 p80 F 1 2014 Augustine J. Curley

REVIEW: *New Statesman* v143 no5204 p48 Ap 4 2014 Frank Cottrell Boyce

REVIEW: *Publ Wkly* v261 no9 p16-31 Mr 3 2014

REVIEW: *TLS* no5791 p3-4 Mr 28 2014 PETER MARSHALL

"The Dark Box: A Secret History of Confession." "As a young teenager at junior seminary—a type of institution now largely abolished in much of the Catholic world—[author John] Cornwell was sexually propositioned by a trusted priest hearing his confession. This painful personal reminiscence is the point of departure for a provocatively layered thesis. In the first instance, Cornwell proposes that, as it has developed historically, the practice of confession in the Catholic Church has tended to produce a psychologically unhealthy obsession with sin and guilt. . . . Cornwell's personal reflections on seminary life and values lend moral authority to his case, but may involve a lack of critical distance from it."

CORNWELL, PATRICIA DANIELS, 1956-. Dust; [by] Patricia Daniels Cornwell 480 p. 2013 Penguin Group USA

1. Detective & mystery stories 2. Massachusetts Institute of Technology 3. Medical examiners (Law)—Fiction 4. Murder—Fiction 5. Sandy Hook Elementary School Massacre, Newtown, Conn., 2012

ISBN 0399157573; 9780399157578

SUMMARY: In this novel by Patricia Cornwell, "Kay Scarpetta has just returned from working one of the worst mass murders in U.S. history when she's awakened at an early hour by Detective Pete Marino. . . . A body, oddly draped in an unusual cloth, has just been discovered inside the sheltered gates of MIT. . . .The murder of Gail Shipton soon leads deep into the dark world of designer drugs, drone technology, organized crime, and shocking corruption at the highest levels." (Publisher's note)

REVIEW: *Booklist* v110 no5 p22-4 N 1 2013 Mark Levine

REVIEW: *Kirkus Rev* v81 no21 p83 N 1 2013

REVIEW: *Kirkus Rev* v81 no23 p255 D 1 2013

REVIEW: *Libr J* v138 no10 p76 Je 1 2013

REVIEW: *Libr J* v139 no3 p59 F 15 2014 Lisa Youngblood

REVIEW: *N Y Times Book Rev* p27 D 15 2013 MARILYN STASIO

"Dust," Nowhere Nice," and "City of Lies." "[Author] Patricia Cornwell's imperious forensic scientist, Kay Scarpetta, shows uncharacteristic signs of vulnerability at the beginning of 'Dust.' . . . There's plenty going on at Scarpetta's bustling lab. . . . Buckle up for a rowdy ride with [author] Rick Gavin in 'Nowhere Nice' . . . , the latest in a riotous series set in the Mississippi Delta. . . . Calling these characters colorful doesn't begin to get at the rich regional nuances that Gavin mines at every pit stop from Arkansas to Alabama. . . . A sensitive hero is a good thing to have in a tough crime novel--up to a point. That point is passed in R. J. Ellory's 'City of Lies' . . . , when the doting author allows these tender feelings to soften his protagonists's brain."

REVIEW: *Publ Wkly* v260 no44 p45 N 4 2013

CORNWELL, SARAH. What I Had Before I Had You; [by] Sarah Cornwell 288 p. 2014 HarperCollins

1. Bipolar disorder 2. Family secrets—Fiction 3. Missing children—Fiction 4. Parent & child—Fiction 5. Psychological fiction

ISBN 0062237845; 9780062237842

SUMMARY: In this book by Sarah Cornwell, "Olivia was only fifteen the summer she left her hometown of Ocean Vista. Two decades later, on a visit with her children, her nine-year-old son Daniel, recently diagnosed with bipolar disorder, disappears. Olivia's search for him sparks tender and painful memories of her past—of her fiercely loving and secretive mother, Myla, an erratic and beautiful psychic, and the discovery of heartbreaking secrets." (Publisher's note)

REVIEW: *Booklist* v110 no7 p30 D 1 2013 Cortney Ophoff

REVIEW: *Kirkus Rev* v81 no24 p121 D 15 2013

"What I Had Before I Had You". " Twenty years ago, Olivia fled Ocean Vista, fled her psychic mother, fled her betrayed friends. Now recently divorced, she has come home with her teenage daughter, Carrie, and her 9-year-old son, Daniel, in tow. Like Olivia, Daniel struggles with bipolar disorder. Her husband could live with Olivia's battle but not Daniel's. But Daniel disappears, and as Olivia searches for him, she must confront the ghosts of her past. . . . Gorgeously crafted, [Sarah] Cornwell's tale shimmers and shimmies with nimble dialogue and poignantly flawed characters. Grafting magical thinking onto gimlet-eyed acceptance, Cornwell's debut novel enchants."

REVIEW: *Publ Wkly* v260 no41 p32 O 14 2013

CORONA, LAUREL. The Mapmaker's Daughter; [by] Laurel Corona 368 p. 2014 Sourcebooks Inc

1. Historical fiction 2. Identity (Psychology)—Fiction 3. Inquisition—Fiction 4. Jews—Portugal 5. Marranos
ISBN 140228649X; 9781402286490

SUMMARY: This novel "imagines the life of a Jewish woman in 15th-century Spain. Starting life as a converso publicly living as a Christian while being secretly taught Jewish practices by her mother and grandmother, Amalia longs to follow openly the faith that she loves. . . . Her life continues to be shaped by conflicts between religious belief and societal forces, first during a love affair with a Muslim man and then culminating in the Inquisition and expulsion of all Jews from Spain in 1492." (Library Journal)

REVIEW: *Booklist* v110 no12 p35-6 F 15 2014 Carol Gladstein

"The Mapmaker's Daughter." "As she contemplates her imminent departure, Amalia reviews her long and varied life as wife, mother, family matriarch, and converso, a Jew forced to hide her faith and live as a Christian. [Laurel] Corona . . . brings to life one of the most tumultuous periods in European history. Her Amalia is the perfect character through which readers will experience these turbulent times as she spends a lifetime struggling to honor her faith and survive. Vividly detailed and beautifully written, this is a pleasure to read, a thoughtful, deeply engaging story of the power of faith to navigate history's rough terrain."

REVIEW: *Kirkus Rev* v82 no6 p30 Mr 15 2014

REVIEW: *Publ Wkly* v261 no4 p167-8 Ja 27 2014

CORREA-CABRERA, GUADALUPE. Democracy in "two Mexicos"; political institutions in Oaxaca and Nuevo León; [by] Guadalupe Correa-Cabrera xvi, 219 p. 2013 Palgrave Macmillan

1. Mexico—Politics & government 2. Political science literature 3. Political violence
ISBN 9781137263025
LC 2012-033388

SUMMARY: "This book provides an explanation of some of the root causes of civil upheaval and violent political conflict in Mexico by examining the cases of Oaxaca and Nuevo León in the period from 2000 to 2006. Oaxaca and Nuevo León represent 'two Mexicos': the rich Mexico and the poor Mexico. The author assesses two main groups of explanatory factors . . . and examines some of the mechanisms through which these variables operate . . . to generate massive political turmoil." (Publisher's note)

REVIEW: *Choice* v51 no4 p719 D 2013 L. O. Imade

"Democracy in 'Two Mexicos': Political Institutions in Oaxaca and Nuevo León." "This book is different in many ways from the plethora of studies devoted to democracy in Mexico. For one, the study sheds new light on the confusion within much of the contemporary literature on democracy, factionalism, and inequality in Mexico. . . . This thought-provoking synthesis of the factors that facilitate and obstruct the development of democracy in Mexico in particular and Latin America in general would be an asset to any library."

THE CORRESPONDENCE OF HENRY D. THOREAU; 544 p. 2013 Princeton University Press

1. Authors, American—19th century—Correspondence 2. Intellectuals—United States—Correspondence 3. Letters 4. Naturalists—United States—Correspondence
ISBN 9780691158921 (v. 1)
LC 2012-043255

SUMMARY: This book, "the first of a projected three-volume edition of [Henry D.] Thoreau's correspondence . . . contains 163 letters, 96 written by Thoreau, 67 to him by his correspondents. Spanning the years 1834 through 1848, the letters chart Thoreau's progress frora Harvard student to fledgling professional author. Among his principal correspondents were his sisters . . . brother . . . parents . . . friends . . . and professional acquaintances." (Choice: Current Reviews for Academic Libraries)

REVIEW: *Choice* v51 no6 p1008 F 2014 D. D. Kummings

"The Correspondence of Henry D. Thoreau." "Illuminating the letters are a 'General Introduction,' 'Historical Introduction,' and 'Textual Introduction.' Equally informative are the detailed annotations on correspondents, persons and places mentioned, books cited, and current events that follow each letter. Thoreau's letters unquestionably enlarge understanding of his character. The personality who emerges is not just cold, impassive, and stoic but also witty, playful, and sociable, not just reclusive and idealistic but also engaged and practical."

REVIEW: *N Engl Q* v87 no2 p360-2 Je 2014 Kevin J. Hayes

CORRIGALL-BROWN, CATHERINE. Patterns of protest; trajectories of participation in social movements; [by] Catherine Corrigall-Brown xiii, 177 pages 2012 Stanford University Press

1. Political activists—United States 2. Political participation—United States 3. Social action—United States 4. Social movements—United States 5. Social reformers—United States 6. Social science literature
ISBN 9780804774109 (alk. paper)
LC 2011-007293

SUMMARY: In this book, author "[Catherine] Corrigall-Brown reveals how individual characteristics and life experiences impact the pathway of participation, illustrating that the context and period in which a person engages are critical. . . . This book challenges the current conceptualization of activism and pushes us to more systematically examine the varying ways that individuals participate in contentious politics over their lifetimes." (Publisher's note)

REVIEW: *Am J Sociol* v118 no5 p1456-8 Mr 2013 Kraig Beyerlein

REVIEW: *Choice* v49 no10 p1972 Je 2012 J. Li

REVIEW: *Contemp Sociol* v42 no6 p835-6 N 2013 KENNETH T. ANDREWS

"Patterns of Protest: Trajectories of Participation in Social Movements." "Catherine Corrigall-Brown's 'Patterns of Protest' shows that our attention and underlying models of activism are limited. . . . She notes that activists vary in their patterns of involvement over the life course, just as they vary in their commitment at any given point in time. . . . To explain these differential trajectories, Corrigall-Brown builds a synthetic model drawing on existing theory. The major explanatory factors are biographical availability . . . , resources . . . , and ideology. . . . 'Patterns of Protest' makes fundamental theoretical and empirical contributions to our understanding of social movements and should inspire further research on trajectories of participation."

CORRIGAN, ROSE. Up against a wall; rape reform and the failure of success; [by] Rose Corrigan x, 320 p. 2013 New York University Press

1. Anti-rape movement—United States 2. Feminist theory—United States 3. LAW—Criminal Law—General 4. LAW—Gender & the Law 5. Law reform—United States 6. Political science literature 7. Rape—United States 8. Rape victims—Legal status, laws, etc.—United States 9. SOCIAL SCIENCE—Women's Studies
ISBN 9780814707937 (hbk. : alk. paper); 9780814708231 (ebook); 9780814725214 (ebook)
LC 2012-028495

SUMMARY: This book "weaves together scholarship on law and social movements, feminist theory, policy formation and implementation, and criminal justice to show how the innovative legal strategies employed by anti-rape advocates actually undermined some of their central claims. But even as its more radical elements were thwarted, pieces of the rape law reform project were seized upon by conservative policy-makers." (Publisher's note)

REVIEW: *Choice* v51 no5 p923 Ja 2014 R. A. Cramer

"Up Against a Wall: Rape Reform and the Failure of Success." "[Rose] Corrigan's examination of the impact of rape law reform convincingly argues that such reform has often been weakened, modified, and co-opted, all in ways that dilute the impact promised by far-reaching, woman-centered policy. Drawing on deeply textured case studies, extensive interview data, and a clear reading of the laws in various US jurisdictions Corrigan . . . offers an analysis of legal implementation from the ground up. . . . Corrigan's comparative case study approach is an appropriate and useful way to examine the nuances between and within jurisdictions. . . . The interview data are particularly interesting and effective, though the dispassionate treatment of the topic, as a whole, is disappointing"

REVIEW: *Polit Sci Q (Wiley-Blackwell)* v128 no4 p791-2 Wint 2013/2014 CARRIE N. BAKER

REVIEW: *Women's Review of Books* v31 no1 p12-3 Ja/F 2014 Marianne Wesson

CORRIVEAU, ART. 13 hangmen; [by] Art Corriveau p. cm. 2012 Amulet Books

1. Brothers—Fiction 2. Family life—Massachusetts—Boston—Fiction 3. Fantasy fiction 4. JUVENILE FICTION—General 5. JUVENILE FICTION—Mysteries & Detective Stories 6. Moving, Household—Fiction 7. Mystery and detective stories 8. Paranormal fiction 9. Supernatural—Fiction 10. Twins—Fiction
ISBN 9781419701597 (hardback)
LC 2011-052137

SUMMARY: This book's protagonist was "willed [a house] by a great uncle, Zio Angelo . . . on his thirteenth birthday, on the condition that he doesn't sell the house and that he sleep in the attic bedroom. Along with the legacy comes another gift . . . a baseball cap. . . . The baseball cap is the first key to unlocking the mystery, as it puts Tony into contact with Angelo as a thirteen-year-old." (Bulletin of the Center for Children's Books)

REVIEW: *SLJ* v58 no9 p140 S 2012 Emma Burkhart

CORRY, OLAF. Constructing a global polity; theory, discourse and governance; [by] Olaf Corry 256 p. 2013 Palgrave Macmillan

1. Discourse theory (Communication) 2. Globalization 3. International agencies 4. International relations 5. Political science literature
ISBN 9780230238756
LC 2013-008165

SUMMARY: This book "offers a new model for understanding international relations that is not based on hierarchy or anarchy but on the object of governance itself. A variety of polities are possible in [Olaf] Corry's model, each determined by the identification of actors with the object of governance. . . . The second half of his book moves to an examination of three globalization discourses and what they mean for the creation of a global polity." (Choice: Current Reviews for Academic Libraries)

REVIEW: *Choice* v51 no6 p1089-90 F 2014 K. Buterbaugh

"Constructing a Global Polity: Theory, Discourse and Governance." "The model [Olaf] Corry created provides analysts with a new, and possibly fruitful, method for examining outcomes dealing with global governance objects. However, it is unclear whether the model differs that significantly from previous models like the theory of international regimes. Also, the examination of the discourses on globalization, while quite interesting, is not clearly connected to the model Corry created. For instance, the discussions are largely on the ways that different schools of thought have framed the issue of globalization and its governance."

CORVINO, JOHN. What's wrong with homosexuality?; [by] John Corvino 192 p. 2013 Oxford University Press

1. Homosexuality—Moral and ethical aspects 2. Homosexuality—Religious aspects 3. Philosophical literature 4. Same-sex marriage—Moral and ethical aspects 5. Sexual orientation
ISBN 0199856311 (hardcover); 9780199856312 (hardcover)
LC 2012-027319

SUMMARY: This book, by John Corvino, "address[es] the standard objections to homosexuality and offering insight into the culture wars more generally. Is homosexuality unnatural? Does the Bible condemn it? Are people born gay (and should it matter either way)? Corvino approaches such questions . . . [and] makes a fresh case for moral engagement, forcefully rejecting the idea that morality is a 'private matter.'" (Publisher's note)

REVIEW: *Booklist* v109 no11 p4 F 1 2013 Ray Olson

REVIEW: *Choice* v51 no1 p91 S 2013 D. Hurst

REVIEW: *Libr J* v138 no3 p107 F 15 2013 James F. DeRoche

REVIEW: *Publ Wkly* v260 no2 p47 Ja 14 2013

REVIEW: *TLS* no5762 p26 S 6 2013 MARK VERNO

"What's Wrong With Homosexuality?" "Whatever might he said to be wrong with homosexuality, John Corvino rebuts, in this concise, thorough and chatty book. A philosopher and religious sceptic, he makes the case for gay relationships as a public good, because they are of intrinsic human value, as well as tackling the opposing positions in chapters that cover religious views, natural law, and scientific insights on sexuality. . . . A particularly engaging element in the book is the account Corvino offers of his relationship with Glenn Stanton from the anti-gay marriage organization,

Focus on the Family."

CORY, AMY C.ed. Encyclopedia of school health. See Encyclopedia of school health

COSEI KAWA.il. Rifka takes a bow. See Rifka takes a bow

COSIMANO, ELLE. Nearly gone; [by] Elle Cosimano 400 p. 2014 Kathy Dawson Books, a imprint of Penguin Group (USA) Inc.

1. Criminal investigation—Fiction 2. Mathematics—Fiction 3. Mystery and detective stories 4. Paranormal fiction 5. Serial murderers—Fiction
ISBN 0803739265; 9780803739260 (hardcover)
LC 2013-010335

SUMMARY: In this novel, by Elle Cosimano, "Nearly Boswell . . . knows better than to share . . . the emotions she can taste when she brushes against someone's skin. But when a serial killer goes on a killing spree and starts attacking students, leaving cryptic ads in the newspaper that only Nearly can decipher, she confides in the . . . the new guy at school--a reformed bad boy working undercover for the police, doing surveillance. . . on her." (Publisher's note)

REVIEW: *Booklist* v110 no14 p75 Mr 15 2014 Paula Willey

REVIEW: *Bull Cent Child Books* v67 no8 p401 Ap 2014 A. S.

REVIEW: *Horn Book Magazine* v90 no2 p115-6 Mr/Ap 2014 RACHEL L. SMITH

"Nearly Gone." "With help from bad-boy Reece, Leigh has to figure out who framed her, and why. The plot moves at a breakneck pace, picking up along the way a first-rate romance between Leigh and Reece as well as a paranormal element (Leigh can taste people's emotions by touching them). And STEM enthusiasts can rejoice: the killer's riddles--including the puzzle of what the victims' numbers mean--involve algebra, geometry, chemistry, physics, even astronomy. This is an addictive and multilayered debut; Cosimano has established herself as a thriller writer to watch."

REVIEW: *Kirkus Rev* v82 no2 p146 Ja 15 2014

"Nearly Gone". "With regard to believability, the science-class conceits are as tricky to swallow as the idea that a teenager in 2014 browses print personals. But the point here isn't realism—it's puzzles. Cryptic missed-connections clues, a sequence of numbers left on the victims' bodies, and of course, the identity and motive of the murderer leave plenty for readers to contemplate as Leigh rushes to crime scenes and runs from the police. The story's single supernatural element—when Leigh touches people, she experiences their emotions—is woven deftly into the story, and the romance plot is compelling. Tense and engaging—well worth the effort of suspending one's disbelief."

REVIEW: *Publ Wkly* v261 no2 p71 Ja 13 2014

REVIEW: *SLJ* v60 no2 p101 F 2014 Candyce Pruitt-Goddard

REVIEW: *Voice of Youth Advocates* v36 no5 p55 D 2013 Erin Seareto

COSTA, MARGARET JULL.tr. Things look different in the light and other stories. See Fraile, M.

COSTANTINI, ROBERTO. Deliverance of evil; [by] Roberto Costantini 576 p. 2014 Quercus

1. Detective & mystery stories 2. FIFA World Cup 3. Italy—Fiction 4. Murder investigation—Fiction 5. Police—Fiction
ISBN 162365002X; 9781623650025 (hardcover); 9781623650032 (ebk.)
LC 2013-937742

SUMMARY: This book, by Roberto Costantini, was the winner of the Scerbanenco Prize for the best Italian crime thriller. It follows "police captain Michele Balistreri. . . . When, just after Italy wins the World Cup in 1982, a young woman turns up brutally murdered, he seems to regard it as an inconvenience. He takes his job infinitely more seriously when, a quarter-century later, Italy again returns to the championship and the bodies start popping up once more." (Kirkus Reviews)

REVIEW: *Booklist* v110 no12 p32 F 15 2014 Bill Ott

REVIEW: *Kirkus Rev* v82 no2 p162 Ja 15 2014

"The Deliverance of Evil". " A long, complex crime novel that moves from savage murder to the political and social realities of contemporary Italy. . . . Here, the story, already absorbing (though too long by 100 pages), picks up speed. . . . It helps to have a little knowledge of Italian politics to appreciate some of the subtleties of [Roberto] Costantini's story, as well as a nodding familiarity with the geography of Rome (and the fact, for instance, that the Hotel Hassler is the city's most elite). None of those things are necessary in order to understand the essential nastiness of the bad guy and the moral ambiguities of the supposedly good ones. A promising debut."

REVIEW: *Publ Wkly* v260 no49 p61 D 2 2013

REVIEW: *TLS* no5751 p19-20 Je 21 2013 SEAN O'BRIEN

COSTANTINO, TRACIE.ed. Aesthetics, empathy and education. See Aesthetics, empathy and education

COSTELLO, VICTORIA. A lethal inheritance; a mother uncovers the science behind three generations of mental illness; [by] Victoria Costello p. cm. 2012 Prometheus Books

1. Families of the mentally ill 2. Memoirs 3. Mental illness—Genetic aspects 4. Mentally ill—Family relationships 5. Parents of mentally ill children 6. Schizophrenia—Popular works
ISBN 9781616144661 (pbk. : alk. paper)
LC 2011-037539

SUMMARY: This book "is a cautionary tale about the price families pay for keeping mental illness secret. It is also a road map for identifying risk factors for and recognizing early signs of psychiatric issues, the better to preempt advanced disease. . . . At the point where it was almost too late to intervene in her eldest son's mental deterioration, [author Victoria] Costello embarked on a journey backward in time that moved her and both of her sons forward into a brighter future." (Publisher's note)

REVIEW: *Booklist* v108 no7 p18 D 1 2011 Donna Chavez

COSTIGLIOLA, FRANK.ed. The Kennan diaries. See The Kennan diaries

CÔTÉ, GENEVIÈVE, 1964-. Starring Me and You; [by] Geneviève Côté 32 p. 2014 Kids Can Press

1. Amateur plays 2. Animal stories 3. Children's stories 4. Emotions (Psychology)—Juvenile literature 5. Friendship—Juvenile fiction

ISBN 1894786394; 9781894786393

SUMMARY: In this children's story, "two animal friends, a bunny and a pig, explore the world of their emotions as they attempt to put on a play together. Along the way, they must face a few challenges, such as when the bunny wants them to 'be sunflowers and sing a duet,' while the pig would rather 'be pirates on a shipwreck.' As they work their way to a successful collaboration, they take turns describing the different ways they act when they are shy, scared, eager, angry and sad." (Publisher's note)

REVIEW: *Booklist* v110 no13 p78-9 Mr 1 2014 Tiffany Erickson

REVIEW: *Kirkus Rev* v82 no3 p143 F 1 2014

REVIEW: *Publ Wkly* v261 no2 p68 Ja 13 2014

REVIEW: *Quill Quire* v80 no1 p42-3 Ja/F 2014 Linda Ludke

"Starring Me and You". "Bunny and Piggy's conversation flows naturally with an engaging patter that is great fun to read aloud. Each character has a distinct voice enhanced by use of the varied typefaces. The minimalist text deftly conveys how the two friends experience the same emotions but express them differently. . . . [Geneviève] Côté's accomplished mixed-media illustrations also capture this dichotomy. . . . 'Starring Me and You' is an applause-worthy exploration of friendship and emotion. Here's hoping there's another encore for these two loveable characters."

REVIEW: *SLJ* v60 no3 p106 Mr 2014 John Trischitti

CÔTÉ, GENEVIÈVE, 1964-.il. Starring Me and You. See Côté, G.

COTLER, T. ZACHARY. Ghost at the Loom; [by] T. Zachary Cotler 224 p. 2014 Pgw

1. Americans—Europe—Fiction 2. Brothers & sisters—Fiction 3. Imagination 4. Poets—Fiction 5. Psychological fiction

ISBN 184982245X; 9781849822459

SUMMARY: In this book, by T. Zachary Cotler, "Rider Sonnenreich, a young poet, retrieves memories of wild acts of imagination that once bound his sister Leya and him together. Retracing the travels of long-dead poets in Europe, Rider looks for Leya, but can't be sure who or what he will find in the end. Among restless cosmopolitans and enigmatic wanderers, he tries to sort the real from the illusory and to protect the latter from the former." (Publisher's note)

REVIEW: *Kirkus Rev* v82 no1 p100 Ja 1 2014

"Ghost at the Loom". " Poet Cotler's (Sonnets to the Humans, 2012, etc.) affecting, lyric novel is a long letter from writer Rider Sonnenreich to his sister Leya, its subject nothing less than the mind of an artist. . . . Readers looking for a tidy travel narrative should look elsewhere. . . . . Featuring this kind of overt meditation that's often on a writer's mind can be risky, but Cotler pulls it off, injecting feeling into each image, each response, each gesture. It's no slight to call this a poet's novel—its narrative thrust is a lyrical one, its strengths are its precision of thought and image, variety of prose and the depth of its meditations."

REVIEW: *Publ Wkly* v261 no16 p46 Ap 21 2014

COTTROL, ROBERT J. The long, lingering shadow; slavery, race, and law in the American hemisphere; [by] Robert J. Cottrol xii, 370 p. 2013 The University of Georgia Press

1. Blacks—Legal status, laws, etc.—Western Hemisphere 2. Historical literature 3. Race relations—History—Western Hemisphere 4. Slavery—History—Western Hemisphere 5. Slavery—Law and legislation—America 6. Slavery—Law and legislation—Western Hemisphere

ISBN 0820344052 (hardcover : alk. paper); 0820344311 (pbk. : alk. paper); 9780820344058 (hardcover : alk. paper); 9780820344317 (pbk. : alk. paper)

LC 2012-029629

SUMMARY: This book "looks at the parallel legal histories of race relations in the United States, Brazil, and Spanish America. Robert J. Cottrol takes the reader on a journey from the origins of New World slavery in colonial Latin America to current debates and litigation over affirmative action in Brazil and the United States, as well as contemporary struggles against racial discrimination and Afro-Latin invisibility in the Spanish-speaking nations of the hemisphere." (Publisher's note)

REVIEW: *Choice* v51 no7 p1277-8 Mr 2014 L. Rosen

"The Long, Lingering Shadow: Slavery, Race, and Law in the American Hemisphere." "The author . . . shows that while racism was deeply ingrained in the US and less so in Latin America, the situation all but reversed itself in the last half of the 20th century. . . . In the course of his analysis, [Robert J.] Cottrol's thoughtful approach to legal history adds significantly to the understanding of activist movements in each country, the advisability of racial preference as a response to past inequities, and the reasons why simply ignoring race in the law fails to address its continuing importance in each national context. . . . Recommended."

COUCH, KENNETH.ed. Lifecycle events and their consequences. See Lifecycle events and their consequences

COULTON, BETH. Goldi Rocks and the three bears. See Schwartz, C. R.

COUPLAND, DOUGLAS, 1961-. Worst. person. ever; [by] Douglas Coupland 320 p. 2014 Blue Rider Press, a member of Penguin Group (USA)

1. Camera operators 2. FICTION—Humorous 3. Islands—Fiction 4. Male friendship—Fiction 5. Reality television programs—Fiction

ISBN 9780399168437 (hardback)

LC 2013-036985

SUMMARY: This book follows "an unlikable man named Ray on his way to a job as a cameraman on a well-known tropical island reality show. He provokes and is attacked by a homeless man, Neal, whom he then magnanimously employs as his personal assistant. The two bond in male fellowship largely interspersed with the hearty use of the f-word. . . .Their absurd escapades range from involvement in the impromptu dropping of an atomic bomb to casual philosophical musing on the merits of bestiality." (Library Journal)

REVIEW: *Kirkus Rev* v82 no7 p41 Ap 1 2014

REVIEW: *Quill Quire* v79 no9 p24-5 N 2013 Heather Cromarty

REVIEW: *TLS* no5770 p20 N 1 2013 CLAIRE LOWDON
"Worst. Person. Ever." "Naming unnamed things, particularly unnamed new things, is what [Douglas] Coupland does best. . . . Coupland's fourteenth novel deviates from this formula, with unhappy results. 'Worst. Person. Ever.' fatally rehashes not his own work but another writer's much older, better book. . . . Gunt is not even a name: it is a poor excuse for Gunt jokes. . . . No one speaks like this. These are not characters, just conglomerates of gags. . . . They don't feel fresh or hip, they feel dutiful: the mark of a tired author going through the motions, in thrall to the cult of himself."

COUSINEAU, THOMAS J. An unwritten novel; Fernando Pessoa's The book of disquiet; [by] Thomas J. Cousineau 200 p. 2013 Dalkey Archive Press
1. Literature—History & criticism 2. Modernism (Literature) 3. Pessoa, Fernando, 1888-1935 4. Unfinished books
ISBN 9781564788856 (pbk.: acid-free paper)
LC 2013-022017

SUMMARY: In this book, Thomas Cousineau "analyzes [Fernando] Pessoa's major prose work—the unfinished, unordered, and 'unwritten' 'Book of Disquiet,' attributed to heteronym Bernardo Soares, the self-confessed 'character of an unwritten novel.' Picking up on Soares's wry self-description, Cousineau fills a largely missing dimension in the existing anglophone criticism and commentary on Fernando Pessoa's famous 'Book.'" (Modernism/Modernity)

REVIEW: *Choice* v51 no8 p1404-5 Ap 2014 K. D. Jackson
"An Unwritten Novel: Fernando Pessoa's The Book of Disquiet". "In this clearly written, well-documented book, [Thomas J.] Cousineau . . . analyzes Pessoa's major work in prose—the unfinished, unordered, and 'unwritten' Book of Disquiet attributed to hetetonym Bernardo Soares, the self-confessed 'character of an unwritten novel.' . . . High points of the book include comparisons to Eliot and Borges and discussion of Ulysses's voyage, the Hamlet complex, presence of Shakespeare, Daedalus and the labyrinth, and surrogate forms of suffering. . . . This is required reading for those who wish to understand Pessoa."

COUSINS, LUCY. Maisy's first numbers; [by] Lucy Cousins 14 p. 2013 Candlewick Press
1. Animals—Juvenile fiction 2. Counting—Juvenile literature 3. Fishes—Juvenile literature 4. Mice—Juvenile fiction 5. Picture books for children
ISBN 9780763668051
LC 2012-950567

SUMMARY: In this counting book by Lucy Cousins, young readers "learn to count [. . . [by] exploring animals with Maisy," a young mouse/ "Three butterflies flutter, four fish swim along, five snails enjoy the rain—and everyone comes back on the final spread for a recount." (Publisher's note)

REVIEW: *Kirkus Rev* v81 no15 p351 Ag 1 2013
REVIEW: *Kirkus Rev* v82 no1 p8 Ja 1 2014
"Maisy's First Numbers". "Maisy counts up to five in the simplest of concept books. On the left page, each numeral and the written word for the number is presented starting with one. Across the gutter, Maisy interacts with one stripy tiger, two strolling tortoises, three spotted butterflies and so on. The oversized numeral is playfully presented with the markings of the animal in question; the number four, accompanied by four fish, is scaly and yellow, and the number five, shown with swirly snails, has spiral markings of similar hues. [Lucy] Cousins' childlike cartoons using bold outlines and bright colors are as delightful as ever against solid backgrounds. The last two pages review the numbers one through five, and the animals are clearly presented for easy counting."

COUSINS, LUCY. Peck, peck, peck; [by] Lucy Cousins 32 p. 2013 Candlewick Press
1. Assonance 2. Birds—Juvenile literature 3. Children's poetry 4. Fathers & sons—Fiction 5. Woodpeckers
ISBN 0763666211; 9780763666217
LC 2012-947728

SUMMARY: In this book written and illustrated by Lucy Cousins "little woodpecker has just learned to peck. He's having so much fun that he peck-peck-pecks right through a door and has a go at everything on the other side, from the hat to the mat, the racket to the jacket, the teddy bear to a book called 'Jane Eyre'. Children will be drawn to the young bird's exuberance at learning a new skill." (Publisher's note)

REVIEW: *Booklist* v109 no21 p65 Jl 1 2013 Ilene Cooper

REVIEW: *Bull Cent Child Books* v67 no2 p81-2 O 2013 H. M.
"Peck, Peck, Peck." "A daddy woodpecker teaches his young woodpecker how to peck a hole in a tree. . . . The young woodpecker heads off to a small house where he pecks a hole first in the gate, then the front door, then just about everything he can find within the home. . . . The playful repetition of the pecking is enhanced by die-cut apertures, with every woodpecker hole is literally hole-punched through the page. . . . The rhymed text is a little simplistic, relying on assonant lists, . . . and there is little plot to drive the pecking of objects. The draw here is therefore mostly visual, with [author Lucy] Cousins' signature expansive fields of bold, bright gouache outlined in thick black lines."

REVIEW: *Kirkus Rev* v81 no2 p79-82 Je 1 2013

REVIEW: *Publ Wkly* v260 no19 p66 My 13 2013

REVIEW: *SLJ* v59 no8 p70 Ag 2013 Brooke Rasche

COUTTS, ALEXANDRA. Tumble & fall; [by] Alexandra Coutts 384 p. 2013 Farrar Straus & Giroux (BYR)
1. Asteroids—Collisions with Earth—Fiction 2. Conduct of life—Fiction 3. Family life—Fiction 4. Interpersonal relations—Fiction 5. JUVENILE FICTION—Action & Adventure—Survival Stories 6. JUVENILE FICTION—Family—General (see also headings under Social Issues) 7. JUVENILE FICTION—Science Fiction 8. JUVENILE FICTION—Social Issues—Friendship 9. Science fiction
ISBN 0374378614; 9780374378615 (hardback)
LC 2013-012969

SUMMARY: In this book, as "the world faces a catastrophic collision with a giant asteroid, three teenagers spending the summer on Martha's Vineyard discover that their last week on Earth may be life-changing in good ways as well." Sienna "tries to relearn how to trust and love with help from a childhood friend; Zan wonders whether the dead boyfriend she has grieved for was faithful to her . . . ; and Caden has to decide whether he can forgive two parents who have abandoned him." (Publishers Weekly)

REVIEW: *Booklist* v110 no4 p61 O 15 2013 Courtney Jones

REVIEW: *Horn Book Magazine* v89 no6 p89 N/D 2013 RACHEL L. SMITH

"Tumble & Fall." "An asteroid will strike Earth in a week, potentially ending all human life. Like everyone else, three teens on Martha's Vineyard have trouble processing the news, but they live what could be their last few days as best they can. . . . Richly developed characters and a tight-knit island setting characterize this impressive novel, made more so by a restrained ending that resists sensationalism: neighbors forgive one another; a wedding takes place on a beach; a community stands together in solidarity, facing an uncertain future with bravery and love."

REVIEW: *Kirkus Rev* v81 no14 p43 Jl 15 2013

REVIEW: *Kirkus Rev* p63 2013 Guide 20to BookExpo America

REVIEW: *Publ Wkly* v260 no27 p90 Jl 8 2013

REVIEW: *SLJ* v59 no9 p154 S 2013 Jane Henriksen Baird

REVIEW: *Voice of Youth Advocates* v36 no4 p60 O 2013 Elaine Gass Hirsch

COVELL, KATHERINE. Education in the best interests of the child. See Howe, R. B.

COVERDALE, LINDA.tr. 1914. See Echenoz, J.

COVERLY, DAVE.il. The very inappropriate word. See The very inappropriate word

COVINGTON, MELODY MAULDIN. Dictionary of computer and internet terms. See Covington, M.

COVINGTON, MICHAEL. Dictionary of computer and internet terms; [by] Michael Covington v, 583 p. 2013 Barron's Educational Series

1. Computer science literature 2. Computers—Dictionaries 3. Encyclopedias & dictionaries 4. Internet—Dictionaries 5. Terms & phrases

ISBN 9780764147555 (pbk. : alk. paper)

LC 2012-021295

SUMMARY: "This dictionary, edited by [Douglas A.] Downing . . . , comprises over 3,200 entries ranging from '1G' to 'Mark Zuckerberg.'" It "is not intended for computer scientists, but offers a mix of . . . definitions for the average computer user, along with black-and-white illustrations. . . . This edition updates the previous one . . . with new and expanded entries on topics like tablet computers, smartphones. Twitter, and other social networking sites." (Choice: Current Reviews for Academic Libraries)

REVIEW: *Choice* v51 no6 p979-80 F 2014 M. Shores

"Dictionary of Computer and Internet Terms." "This compact little dictionary is not intended for computer scientists, but offers a mix of readable definitions for the average computer user, along with black-and-white illustrations. . . . This edition updates the previous one (10th ed., 2009) with new and expanded entries on topics like tablet computers, smartphones. Twitter, and other social networking sites. Appendixes include Greek letters, a visual dictionary of characters and symbols, and country codes for top-level domains. One minor quibble: the book would have benefitted from updated screenshots to enhance its currency. . . . This title benefits from a long track record of publication and a low price."

COVINGTON, SARAH. Dictionary of computer and internet terms. See Covington, M.

COWAN, ANDREW. Worthless Men; [by] Andrew Cowan 272 p. 2013 Sceptre

1. Emotional trauma 2. Historical fiction 3. World War, 1914-1918—England—Fiction 4. World War, 1914-1918—Veterans—Fiction

ISBN 144475940X; 9781444759402

SUMMARY: This book by Andrew Cowan is set in "an English provincial city in 1916. . . . Beneath the surface normality, the war has permeated high and low: the local mansion has become a temporary hospital, the netting factory now produces barbed wire and the women are doing the men's jobs. And on this day Walter Barley returns from the front--a ghostly presence watching as the girl he once loved is lured towards his former captain, the shell-shocked Montague Beckwith." (Publisher's note)

REVIEW: *TLS* no5766 p26 O 4 2013 KATE MCLOUGHLIN

"Worthless Men." "[Andrew] Cowan deserves credit for two pieces of bravery: he mentions the unmentionable wound and he records how horror can provoke hilarity. . . . To portray the returned soldier as invisible to the society on behalf of which he has been fighting conveys, at a stroke, more about the veteran's plight than pages of recollected trauma. In this, Cowan's first work of historical fiction, period detail is not only meticulously observed but actually moving. . . . Cowan not only conveys the real texture of life enjoyed, but the worth one human being attaches to another."

COWLEY, MALCOLM, 1898-1989 -- CORRESPONDENCE. The long voyage; selected letters of Malcolm Cowley, 1915-1987; 848 p. 2014 Harvard University Press

1. American poets 2. Critics 3. Letters 4. Periodical editors

ISBN 9780674051065 (alk. paper)

LC 2013-012605

SUMMARY: This book collects the correspondence of author Malcolm Cowley. "The book follows Cowley (1898–1989) from his 1920s salad days as a poet and critic in New York and Paris . . . through his 1930s reign as the New Republic's literary editor, when he discovered Marxism and drew (not unfounded) accusations of pushing a Stalinist line that dogged him during and after World War II; to his postwar efforts to champion old masters and newcomers." (Publishers Weekly)

REVIEW: *Bookforum* v20 no4 p15-6 D 2013/Ja 2014 GERALD HOWARD

"The Long Voyage: Selected Letters of Malcolm Cowley, 1915-1987." "[A] vast and rich omnium-gatherum of epistolary activity by Malcolm Cowley. . . .On the evidence of 'The Long Voyage,' the product of editorial acuity and old-school industrial-strength scholarship. Professor [Hans] Bak harbors in his capacious brain enough knowledge about twentieth-century American literature to match the English departments of any five Ivy League universities picked at random. Cowley sent letters the way today's teenagers thumb out text messages, and Bak had to carve this 850-page book from some twenty-five thousand items residing in the Newberry Library, as well as hunt down many more letters in collections around the country."

REVIEW: *New York Times* v163 no56410 pC1-4 F 12 2014 DWIGHT GARNER

REVIEW: *TLS* no5788 p9-10 Mr 7 2014 MARC ROBINSON

COX, JULIAN. Controversy and hope; the civil rights photographs of James Karales; [by] Julian Cox 176 p. 2013 University of South Carolina

1. African Americans—Civil rights—History—20th century—Pictorial works 2. Art literature 3. Civil rights movements—United States—History—20th century—Pictorial works 4. Selma to Montgomery Rights March (1965 : Selma, Ala.)—Pictorial works

ISBN 9781611171570 (hardbound : alk. paper); 9781611171587 (pbk. : alk. paper)

LC 2012-038659

SUMMARY: "This collection features 93 of veteran photojournalist James Karales's (1930–2002) images. . . . The book provides a timeline of Karales's life and career and delves into his work capturing Dr. Martin Luther King Jr.--including candid pictures of King relaxing at home with his family. The collection centers on Karales's coverage of the five-day, 54-mile, Selma-to Montgomery March for Voting Rights in 1965." (Publishers Weekly)

REVIEW: *Choice* v51 no6 p995 F 2014 P. C. Bunnell

"Controversy and Hope: The Civil Rights Photographs of James Karales." "Many of these photographs have never been published before. Karales befriended Martin Luther King Jr. early on, and through this association had unusual access to him, his family, and his colleagues. Andrew Young, one of the latter, contributes a foreword. Rebekah Jacob is a Charleston gallery owner who, together with the photographer's widow, selected the pictures. The critical and biographical text is by Julian Cox, curator of photography at the Fine Arts Museums of San Francisco. Included are reproductions of the proof sheet for Karales's most famous picture and a King essay from Look. This collection is an affecting and candid portrait without the forceful hype of news photography."

REVIEW: *Libr J* v138 no14 p106 S 1 2013 Eugene C. Burt

REVIEW: *Publ Wkly* v260 no15 p59 Ap 15 2013

COX, TREVOR. The sound book; the science of the sonic wonders of the world; [by] Trevor Cox 304 p. 2014 W.W. Norton & Co. Inc.

1. Concert halls 2. Noise—Popular works 3. Scientific literature 4. Sound design 5. Sounds—Popular works

ISBN 0393239799; 9780393239799 (hardcover)

LC 2013-034491

SUMMARY: Author Trevor Cox "explores how the psychological and physical worlds of sound come together. Using the design of concert halls to illustrate 'the fusion of the objectivity of physics with the subjectivity of perception,' [he] explains how, in the final analysis, it is the audience that judges the quality of the acoustics. The reverberation of sound as it bounces around a room determines how we hear a sound." (Kirkus Reviews)

REVIEW: *Booklist* v110 no7 p17 D 1 2013 Carl Hays

REVIEW: *Kirkus Rev* v82 no1 p60 Ja 1 2014

"The Sound Book: The Science of the Sonic Wonders of the World". "[Trevor] Cox . . . explores how the psychological and physical worlds of sound come together. Using the design of concert halls to illustrate 'the fusion of the objectivity of physics with the subjectivity of perception,' the author explains how, in the final analysis, it is the audience that judges the quality of the acoustics. . . . Cox has devoted much of his career to the design of concert halls and theaters that enhance sound quality or quiet spaces that reduce unwanted noise. . . . An intriguing tour d'horizon of the world of sound."

REVIEW: *Libr J* v139 no15 p38 S 15 2014 Kelly Sinclair

REVIEW: *New York Times* v163 no56481 pC1-7 Ap 24 2014 CORINNA da FONSECAWOLLHEIM

REVIEW: *Publ Wkly* v260 no44 p56 N 4 2013

COYLE, DANIEL. The Secret Race. See Hamilton, T.

COYLE, DIANE. GDP; a brief but affectionate history; [by] Diane Coyle 168 p. 2014 Princeton University Press

1. Econometrics—History 2. Economic history 3. Economics—History 4. Gross domestic product—History 5. Historical literature

ISBN 0691156794; 9780691156798 (hardcover: alk. paper)

LC 2013-022478

SUMMARY: "This . . . book tells the story of GDP, making sense of a statistic that appears constantly in the news, business, and politics, and that seems to rule our lives. . . . [Author] Diane Coyle traces the history of this artificial, abstract, complex, but exceedingly important statistic from its eighteenth- and nineteenth-century precursors through its invention in the 1940s and its postwar golden age, and then through the Great Crash up to today." (Publisher's note)

REVIEW: *Kirkus Rev* v82 no8 p273 Ap 15 2014

REVIEW: *New York Times* v163 no56463 p6 Ap 6 2014 FRED ANDREWS

REVIEW: *Science* v344 no6186 p811-2 My 23 2014 Nicholas Oulton

"GDP: A Brief But Affectionate History." "In six short chapters, [author Diane] Coyle (an economist at Oxford University) discusses how the concept of GDP was developed. . . . Coyle structures the book around epochs in economic history, seen from a Western perspective. She uses each epoch to illustrate how GDP was employed for policy purposes. . . . Anyone who wants to know how GDP and the SNA have come to play such important roles in economic policy-making will gain from reading Coyle's book. As will anyone who wants to gain more understanding of the concept's strengths and weaknesses."

COYLE, MARCIA. The Roberts court; the struggle for the constitution; [by] Marcia Coyle 352 p. 2013 Simon & Schuster

1. Constitutional law—United States 2. Political questions and judicial power—United States—History—21st century 3. Political science literature

ISBN 1451627513; 9781451627510 (hardcover);

9781451627527 (trade pbk.); 9781451627534 (ebook)
LC 2012-051637

SUMMARY: In this book, author Marcia Coycle "reveals the fault lines in the conservative-dominated [U.S. Supreme] Court led by Chief Justice John Roberts Jr." It "captures four landmark decisions--concerning health care, money in elections, guns at home, and race in schools. Her analysis shows how dedicated conservative lawyers and groups are strategizing to find cases and crafting them to bring up the judicial road to the Supreme Court with an eye on a receptive conservative majority." (Publisher's note)

REVIEW: *America* v209 no16 p25-6 N 25 2013 GREGORY A. KALSCHEUR

"The Roberts Court: The Struggle for the Constitution." "[Author Marcia] Coyle skillfully crafts engaging narratives that invite the reader to consider both what sort of justice John Roberts has been and what sort of court he has been striving to lead. . . . Coyle's presentation of the book's focal cases provokes questions about the extent to which judicial modesty actually can be said to characterize the work of the Roberts court. . . . Those who read Coyle's book will be well prepared to enter into the story of the coming term as it unfolds."

REVIEW: *Booklist* v109 no17 p54 My 1 2013 Vanessa Bush

REVIEW: *Kirkus Rev* v81 no8 p47 Ap 15 2013

REVIEW: *Nation* v297 no1/2 p35-7 Jl 8 2013 Double Issue MICHAEL O'DONNELL

REVIEW: *Publ Wkly* v260 no4 p115-21 Ja 28 2013 JESSAMINE CHAN

REVIEW: *Publ Wkly* v260 no11 p1 Mr 18 2013

CRACE, JOHN. Harrys Games; [by] John Crace 256 p. 2013 Constable & Robinson

1. Redknapp, Harry 2. Soccer—Great Britain 3. Soccer—Management 4. Soccer managers 5. Sports literature

ISBN 1780339119; 9781780339115

SUMMARY: This book on Harry Redknapp "tells the story of a good football manager who has harmed a series of English football clubs, all of which have had the misfortune to be in commuting distance of his home in Poole, Dorset. . . . Harry Redknapp has, according to John Crace, left fans and fellow professionals divided or undecided about how best to remember his time in charge." (Times Literary Supplement)

REVIEW: *New Statesman* v142 no5157 p44 My 10 2013 Sophie Elmhirst

REVIEW: *TLS* no5751 p26-7 Je 21 2013 MICHAEL CAINES

"Harry's Games: Inside the Mind of Harry Redknapp." "A dodgy dossier on Redknapp, serviceably written, yet confined largely to subjunctive speculation by its lack of direct access to the man himself. . . . It returns repeatedly to recent events: Redknapp and his former chairman Milan Mandaric appeared in court last spring, charged with tax evasion relating to the sale of an England international, Peter Crouch. (In fact, Redknapp bought and sold Crouch several times, making the most out of a relatively slender talent.) [John] Crace attended the trial, and watched Redknapp closely; he enjoys the show this supposedly ordinary geezer puts on for the media, while also noting his public solecisms, such as the notorious humiliating comments on members of his own team."

CRAFTS, NICHOLAS.ed. The Great Depression of 1930s. See The Great Depression of 1930s

CRAIG, DOUGLAS B. Progressives at war; William G. McAdoo and Newton D. Baker, 1863-1941; [by] Douglas B. Craig x, 525 p. 2013 Johns Hopkins University Press

1. Biographies 2. Cabinet officers—United States—Biography 3. Historical literature 4. Lawyers—United States—Biography 5. Progressivism (United States politics) 6. World War, 1914-1918—United States

ISBN 1421407183 (hdbk. : alk. paper); 1421408155 (electronic); 9781421407180 (hdbk. : alk. paper); 9781421408156 (electronic)
LC 2012-018229

SUMMARY: "In this dual biography, Douglas B. Craig examines the careers of two prominent American public figures, Newton Diehl Baker and William Gibbs McAdoo, whose lives spanned the era between the Civil War and World War II. . . . Both eventually became cabinet officers in the presidential administration of another southerner with personal memories of defeat and Reconstruction: Woodrow Wilson." (Publisher's note)

REVIEW: *Choice* v51 no2 p333-4 O 2013 T. Maxwell-Long

"Progressives at War: William G. McAdoo and Newton D. Baker, 1863-1941." "[Author Douglas B.] Craig . . . effectively manages to intertwine the greater significances of William McAdoo and Newton Baker as a tandem as well as provide insight into their separate lives. The author's central focus is the role these two played in government, their respective influences as progressives, and how they were shaped by the Progressive movement of the late 19th and early 20th centuries. As the title implies, Craig gives considerable attention to their roles in President Woodrow Wilson's cabinet during WW I. . . . Within this full context, Craig examines McAdoo and Baker in relationship to their views of the US role during WW I and its aftermath. Historians of the era will appreciate this compelling work."

CRAIG, HELEN.il. Amy's three best things. See Pearce, P.

CRAIG, SIENNA R. Healing elements; efficacy and the social ecologies of Tibetan medicine; [by] Sienna R. Craig 321 p. 2012 University of California Press

1. Asian Continental Ancestry Group—ethnology—Tibet 2. Holistic Health—Tibet 3. Medicine, Tibetan Traditional—Tibet

ISBN 9780520273238 (cloth: alk. paper); 9780520273245 (pbk.: alk. paper)
LC 2012-007775

SUMMARY: This book "explores how Tibetan medicine circulates through diverse settings in Nepal, China, and beyond as commercial goods and gifts, and as target therapies and panacea for biophysical and psychosocial ills. Through an exploration of efficacy—what does it mean to say Tibetan medicine 'works'?—this book illustrates a bio-politics of traditional medicine and the meaningful, if contested, translations of science and healing that occur across distinct social ecologies." (Publisher's note)

REVIEW: *Choice* v50 no8 p1469-70 Ap 2013 J. Saxton

REVIEW: *Current Anthropology* v55 no1 p123-4 F 2014 Geoffrey Samuel

"Healing Elements: Efficacy and the Social Ecologies of Tibetan Medicine". "In recent years, a small group of young scholars working on the medical anthropology of Tibetan societies have transformed our understanding of the Tibetan tradition of healing. . . . Sienna Craig is one of the most talented of this group. . . . Her first full-length book is a major contribution to this growing field of scholarship. Healing Elements is also a delight to read, both because of its accessible style and because of the subtlety and sensitivity with which Craig handles complex intercultural situations. . . . 'Healing Elements' is also a delight to read, both because of its accessible style and because of the subtlety and sensitivity with which Craig handles complex intercultural situations."

CRANE, CAPRICE. Confessions of a Hater; [by] Caprice Crane 368 p. 2013 Feiwel & Friends

1. Friendship—Fiction 2. High school students—Fiction 3. Popularity 4. School stories 5. Young adult fiction, American

ISBN 1250008468; 9781250008466

SUMMARY: In this book, "Life takes a dramatic turn for 15-year-old Hailey Harper, who is used to feeling 'ugly, uninformed and completely lost in a world where superficial bitches reigned supreme,' when her family's cross-country move to Hollywood coincides with the discovery of her 'perfect' older sister's diary. . . . Using its snarky advice as a 'roadmap to cool,' Hailey infiltrates her new school's popular clique, then ditches them to form her own group of quirky, artistic 'Invisibles.'" (Publishers Weekly)

REVIEW: *Booklist* v109 no22 p77 Ag 1 2013 Ann Kelley

REVIEW: *N Y Times Book Rev* p19 Ag 25 2013 JEN DOLL

"Confessions of a Hater" and "Snap Decision: Maybe Tonight?" "The perspective of these novels is subtle enough to be engrossing for both teenagers and adults for whom high school's intense friendships and antipathies still resonate. . . . Both novels are polished to a gleam, and their savvy, self-aware references to fashion and music and other timely cultural touchstones would meet the standards of any mean girl worth her salt. . . . These are great subjects for young adult readers, and both books do what they do well. . . . The questions [Caprice] Crane and [Bridie] Clark address don't get answered neatly and tied up with a bow upon graduation, and perhaps that's why both novels are so enjoyable even to those who've crossed that threshold."

REVIEW: *Publ Wkly* v260 no26 p91 Jl 1 2013

REVIEW: *SLJ* v59 no9 p154 S 2013 Traci Glass

CRANE, NICK. Barefoot Books World Atlas; [by] Nick Crane 56 p. 2011 Barefoot Books

1. Atlases 2. Children's atlases 3. Electronic books 4. Geography

ISBN 1846863333 (hbk.); 9781846863332 (hbk.)

SUMMARY: This interactive electronic book is '[b]ased on the 'Barefoot Books World Atlas'. . . . The illustrations represent various aspects of an area or country (wildlife, landmarks, recreation, transportation, etc.). . . . When a country is selected, the globe rotates to that location. Live data about each nation appears of the screen including the current time, temperature, and its distance in miles from the viewer's location." (School Library Journal)

REVIEW: *Kirkus Rev* v80 no10 p55 My 15 2012

REVIEW: *SLJ* v58 no5 p64-5 My 2012 Cathy Potter

"Barefoot World Atlas." "[T]his stunning title takes full advantage of the iPad's interactive capabilities. . . . Children won't be able to resist tapping the colorful animated images that rise above the landmasses and ocean surfaces as they circle the planet. . . . The illustrations represent various aspects of an area or country (wildlife, landmarks, recreation, transportation, etc.). . . . Older children will enjoy comparing country statistics in the scrollable list that opens upon tapping on a fact. . . . The 'Barefoot World Atlas' is a highly engaging, educational experience that warrants repeat visits."

CRANE, SUSAN. Animal encounters; contacts and concepts in medieval Britain; [by] Susan Crane 270 p. 2013 University of Pennsylvania Press

1. Animals in literature 2. Anthropomorphism in literature 3. British literature 4. English literature—Middle English, 1100-1500—History and criticism 5. Historical literature 6. Human-animal relationships in literature 7. Medieval literature

ISBN 9780812244588 (hardcover : alk. paper)

LC 2012-019532

SUMMARY: This book by Susan Crane discusses how "The grip of a certain humanism was strong in medieval Britain . . . : the humanism that conceives animals in diametrical opposition to humankind. . . . Crane brings . . . other ways of thinking to light in her readings of the beast fable, the hunting treatise, the saint's life, the bestiary, and other genres." (Publisher's note)

REVIEW: *Choice* v51 no1 p74-5 S 2013 R. D. Morrison

"Animal Encounters: Contacts and Concepts in Medieval Britain." "This study by [author Susan] Crane . . . represents a welcome and highly valuable contribution to the emerging field of animal studies. It is one of several recent books focused on the significance of animals to medieval literature and culture. Through an analysis of a variety of genres--romance, beast fable, bestiary, saint's life, and others, in Latin and in the vernacular--the author posits that many medieval works problematize the Western humanistic notion of an impenetrable boundary between humans and animals. . . . Despite her exhaustively thorough critical apparatus . . . , Crane offers admirably lucid prose as well as lively, appealing examples."

REVIEW: *TLS* no5788 p29 Mr 7 2014 ANNETTE VOLFING

CRANSHAW, WHITNEY. Bugs rule!; an introduction to the world of insects; [by] Whitney Cranshaw 496 p. 2013 Princeton University Press

1. Centipedes 2. Entomology 3. Insects 4. Scientific literature 5. Spiders

ISBN 9780691124957 (hardcover : alk. paper)

LC 2013-934688

SUMMARY: This book presents an "introduction to the biology and natural history of insects and their noninsect cousins, such as spiders, scorpions, and centipedes." It features "a concise overview of the basics of entomology, and numerous sidebars that highlight and explain key points. Detailed chapters cover each of the major insect groups, describing their physiology, behaviors, feeding habits, reproduction, human interactions, and more." (Publisher's note)

REVIEW: *Choice* v51 no7 p1246-7 Mr 2014 D. A. Brass

"Bugs Rule! An Introduction to the World of Insects." "This is an interesting, well-written introduction to entomology, providing a broad overview of the biology and natural history of insects and related arthropods. . . . Having developed out of a specific need to create an entomology text for nonscience majors, this book is readily accessible to a wide range of readers and will appeal to anyone interested in learning about insects and their kin. Terms are well defined, and the book also includes the etymology of insect order names. The use of jargon and discussions of difficult concepts are kept to a minimum. Nonscience majors or readers unfamiliar with insect biology will appreciate this discussion of the fascinating diversity of insect life."

REVIEW: *New Sci* v220 no2944 p54 N 23 2013

CRAVENS, CRAIG.tr. My Crazy Century. See My Crazy Century

CRAVENS, HAMILTON.ed. Cold War social science. See Cold War social science

CRAWFORD, DAVE. The Deadly Serious Republic; [by] Dave Crawford 288 p. 2013 Author Solutions

1. Capitalism 2. Privatization 3. Rich people—Fiction 4. Satire 5. Violence

ISBN 1483648958; 9781483648958

SUMMARY: This satire by Dave Crawford "begins in a depressing pocket of poverty reminiscent of Central America, from which the protagonist, Max, escapes to the U.S., aka 'the Deadly Serious Republic' or 'the DSR.' Once there, he searches for his hapless father, Dingle. Enter the other main character, Memie Benzlo, one of the richest young women in the DSR (and the world), who gravitates toward communism despite her suffocating wealth." (Kirkus Reviews)

REVIEW: *Kirkus Rev* v82 no2 p328 Ja 15 2014

"The Deadly Serious Republic". "An alternately playful and serious novel set in a vaguely limned dystopian future. . . . The early chapters are picaresque and relatively lighthearted, and [Dave] Crawford apparently enjoys taking potshots at easy targets such as runaway capitalism, casual violence, rampant privatization. . . . this is where the book turns into a genuine suspense thriller, and although aficionados of such novels may feel that Crawford has yet to master the genre, he certainly gives it a good try. . . . Those who agree with the author's left-leaning politics will most enjoy this novel, but those who don't may still enjoy its cleverness. A satirical thriller that offers witty observations in a sprawling framework."

CRAWFORD, DOROTHY H. The virus that causes cancer; the discovery of the Epstein-Barr virus; [by] Dorothy H. Crawford 256 p. 2014 Oxford University Press

1. Cancer research—History 2. Epstein-Barr virus—Research 3. Epstein-Barr virus diseases—Research 4. Historical literature 5. Science—Popular works

ISBN 9780199653119 (hardback)

LC 2013-948406

SUMMARY: This book by Dorothy H. Crawford, Ingolfur Johannessen, and Alan Rickinson, tells how "The Epstein-Barr virus (EBV) was discovered in 1964. At the time, the very idea of a virus underlying a cancer was revolutionary. . . . This book tells the story of the discovery of the virus, and the recognition of its connection with these various diseases—an account that spans the world and involves some remarkable characters and individual stories." (Publisher's note)

REVIEW: *New Sci* v221 no2962 p53 Mr 29 2014 Linda Geddes

"Cancer Virus: The Story of Epstein-Barr Virus." "The Epstein-Barr virus (EBV) is a curiosity, as well as a killer. . . . 'Cancer Virus' tells its story through the scientists who worked on it. It reads like a thriller. . . . The authors also offer a potted history of virology. . . . All three narrators were involved in EBV research and so occasionally veer into complex explanations—they do provide a helpful glossary, though. Overall, the book is compelling and colourful, capturing the romance of scientific discovery so well that it is exciting and accessible."

CRAWFORD, ROBERT. On Glasgow and Edinburgh; [by] Robert Crawford 345 p. 2013 Belknap Press of Harvard University Press

1. Historical literature 2. Scotland—History 3. Scotland—Social life & customs

ISBN 9780674048881 (alk. paper)

LC 2012-020952

SUMMARY: This book on the cities of Edinburgh and Glasgow, Scotland, "is animated by the one-upping that has been entrenched since the eighteenth century, when Edinburgh lost parliamentary sovereignty and took on its proud wistfulness, while Glasgow came into its industrial promise and defiance. Using landmarks and individuals as gateways to their character and past, this tale of two cities mixes novelty and familiarity just as Scotland's capital and its largest city do." (Publisher's note)

REVIEW: *Hist Today* v63 no9 p61-2 S 2013 OWEN DUDLEY EDWARDS

"On Glasgow and Edinburgh." "Anyone who loves either city can't fail to delight in the book, apart from the irritating intrusions of the obsession with rivalry. Even if uncle will insist the train is passing real ghosts, we can tolerate his folly since on all else he is incisive, if not necessarily accurate. And he writes beautifully. . . . But while [Robert] Crawford rightly knows nobody can compete with [Robert Louis] Stevenson, he himself is a great man and has written a learned and likeable book, where his obsession alone is an old wives' tale of two cities."

CRAWLEY, GERARD M.ed. The World Scientific handbook of energy. See The World Scientific handbook of energy

CREASMAN, ALLYSON F. Censorship and civic order in Reformation Germany, 1517-1648; 'printed poison & evil talk'; [by] Allyson F. Creasman xi, 282 p. 2012 Ashgate

1. Censorship—Germany—History—16th century 2. Censorship—Germany—History—17th century 3. Historical literature 4. Popular culture—Germany 5. Reformation—Germany

ISBN 9781409410010

LC 2012-006244

SUMMARY: This book by Allyson F. Creasman "reassesses the Reformation's spread by examining how censorship impacted upon public support for reform in the German cities. Drawing upon criminal court records, trial manuscripts and contemporary journals—mainly from the city of Augsburg—the study exposes the networks of rumour, gossip, cheap print and popular songs that spread the Reformation message and shows how ordinary Germans adapted these messages to their own purposes." (Publisher's note)

REVIEW: *Am Hist Rev* v119 no1 p263-4 F 2014 C. Scott Dixon

"Censorship and Civic Order in Reformation Germany, 1517-1648: Printed Poison and Evil Talk". "[Allyson F.] Creasman has some important things to say about the flow of ideas in the German Reformation. By adopting a notion of censorship that projects it as a dynamic force in dialogue rather than just a normative measure impressed from above, we get a sense of how it 'served as both a forum for negotiating competing demands and a vehicle for creating and enforcing new concepts of civic order'. . . . Similarly, due to Creasman's very careful, and very colorful, re-creation of the dynamics of communication in the Reformation city, we have a much better picture of how texts interacted with song, speech, and rumor."

CREATING AND CONTESTING CAROLINA; proprietary era histories; 2013 University of South Carolina Press

ISBN 9781611172720

SUMMARY: This book, edited by Michelle LeMaster and Bradford Wood, discusses "how the various peoples of the Carolinas responded to the tumultuous changes shaping the geographic space that the British called Carolina during the Proprietary period (1663-1719)." According to the book, "these years brought challenging and dramatic changes to the region, such as the violent warfare between British and Native Americans or British and Spanish, the . . . development of the plantation system, and the decline of proprietary authority." (Publisher's note)

REVIEW: *Choice* v51 no9 p1660-1 My 2014 M. Mulcahy

"Creating and Contesting Carolina: Proprietary Era Histories". "These 15 essays, mostly by younger and midcareer scholars, cover topics ranging from the process of mapping the new colony, to links to Barbados, the trade in enslaved Africans, revolt against the Proprietors in the Bahamas and South Carolina, and the rise and fall of colonists' support of piracy. . . . The volume's attention to the early history of Carolina and the focus on both Carolinas are welcome additions to the historiography, which the editors outline in a helpful introductory essay. Overall, a terrific collection, and required reading for anyone interested in the colonial Carolinas."

THE CREATIVE CLASS GOES GLOBAL; 336 p. 2013 Routledge

1. Creative ability—Economic aspects 2. Creative ability—Social aspects 3. Creative ability in technology 4. Economics literature 5. Human capital 6. Leisure 7. Social classes 8. Technology and civilization 9. Work ethic—United States

ISBN 9780415633604 (hardback); 9780415633611 (pbk.)

LC 2013-013909

SUMMARY: "This book brings together detailed studies of the creative class in cities across the globe, examining the impact of the creative class on growth and development. . . . Taken together, the contributions deepen our understanding of the creative class and the various factors that affect regional development, highlighting the similarities and differences between the creative class and economic development across countries." (Publisher's note)

REVIEW: *Choice* v51 no8 p1455 Ap 2014 P. K. Kresl

"The Creative Class Goes Global". "Richard Florida's 'The Rise of the Creative Class' . . . generated much response and further research on the creative class. This important new volume, to which Florida serves as a coeditor and contributor, reviews the creative class as it is manifested in 12 industrialized countries. The conclusions of the international group of contributors modify some of the understanding from the literature on urban development. . . . A must read for anyone interested in urban studies and economic development."

CREATIVE COMMUNITIES; art works in economic development; xi, 225 p. 2013 Brookings Institution Press

1. Art and state—Economic aspects 2. Artists and community—Economic aspects 3. Arts—Economic aspects 4. Economic development 5. Economics literature 6. Regional economics

ISBN 9780815724735 (pbk. : alk. paper)

LC 2013-005090

SUMMARY: "This collection of essays . . . investigat[es] how art can play a role as an engine of economic development. Some of the ten studies have a natural inclination toward considerations of new growth theory and the ties among human capital, the arts, scientific innovation, and economic growth. Others take a more traditional look at spending, manifest both in special cultural rax districts and the levels of per capita spending." (Choice)

REVIEW: *Choice* v51 no4 p691-2 D 2013 J. M. Nowakowski

"Creative communities: Art Works in Economic Development." "All chapters are data driven, with some relying on sophisticated econometric models to evaluate their models. This collection is diverse in its consideration of various synergies between artistic efforts and economic growth, and represents a step forward in understanding how culture and commerce interact. The issues it examines and the questions it raises that remain to be answered should make policy makers and voters pause when considering how best to allocate scarce resources intended to foster growth."

CREECH, SHARON. The Boy on the Porch; [by] Sharon Creech 160 p. 2013 Harpercollins Childrens Books

1. Abandoned children—Fiction 2. Children's stories 3. Foster parents 4. Foundlings—Fiction 5. Mute persons—Fiction

ISBN 0061892351; 9780061892356

SUMMARY: In this book by Sharon Creech, "When a young couple finds a boy asleep on their porch, their lives take a surprising turn. Unable to speak, the boy Jacob can't explain his history. All John and Marta know is that they have been chosen to care for him. And, as their connection and friendship with Jacob grow, they embrace his exuberant spirit and talents. The three of them blossom into an unlikely family and begin to see the world in brand-new way." (Publisher's note)

REVIEW: *Booklist* v109 no22 p84 Ag 1 2013 Kara Dean

REVIEW: *Booklist* v109 no19/20 p60 Je 1 2013

REVIEW: *Bull Cent Child Books* v67 no2 p82-3 O 2013 T. A.

The Boy on the Porch." "One summer day, young couple John and Marta find a young boy curled up asleep on the porch, in his pocket a note: 'Plees taik kair of Jacob' and a promise to return. . . . When a man proving his paternity with Jacob's birth certificate shows up, though, they're forced to turn the boy over to . . . him, and their house feels startlingly empty--until a friend suggests the two apply to be foster parents, sparking a new life course for the couple. [Author Sharon] Creech's signature voice . . . lyrical and quaint, without being inaccessible or contrived--reappears here . . . while slim chapters and easygoing folksy dialogue enhance readability.

REVIEW: *Horn Book Magazine* v89 no5 p90 S/O 2013 ELISSA GERSHOWITZ

REVIEW: *Kirkus Rev* v81 no15 p128 Ag 1 2013

REVIEW: *Publ Wkly* v260 no23 p78 Je 10 2013

REVIEW: *SLJ* v59 no8 p96 Ag 2013 Rhona Campbell

CREMER, ANDREA. The inventor's secret; [by] Andrea Cremer 336 p. 2014 Philomel Books, an imprint of Penguin Group (USA) Inc.

1. Amnesia—Fiction 2. Imaginary histories 3. Refugees—Fiction 4. Science fiction 5. Survival—Fiction
ISBN 9780399159626
LC 2013-018111

SUMMARY: In this alternate history novel, "the British have won the Revolutionary War, enslaved the Americans, and turned Boston into a prison and New York City into a socially stratified power center. Giant, robotic Imperial Labor Gatherers and man-eating rats terrorize the population. A colony of teenage resistance fighters are hiding in a remote maze of caves in the New York Wilderness." (Kirkus Reviews)

REVIEW: *Booklist* v110 no12 p80 F 15 2014 Ilene Cooper

REVIEW: *Bull Cent Child Books* v67 no10 p509 Je 2014 K. Q. G.

"The Inventor's Secret". "The premise and the world are intriguing, and there's a formality to the descriptions of shining floating cities, mechanized underwater submarines, and slightly creepy automatons that gives the steampunk setting a tarnished grandeur. Unfortunately, once the group gets to the city, the story shifts its focus abruptly from the mystery behind the boy to Charlotte's affair with Jack, which at first seems like a sure thing but is then jeopardized by both Jack's high-society fiancée and his handsome more attentive older brother. Readers who value romance over plot, however, may nonetheless be taken in by Charlotte and Jack's witty repartee and steamy encounters, and their estrangement at the book's close ensures a sequel."

REVIEW: *Horn Book Magazine* v90 no6 p134-5 N/D 2014

REVIEW: *Kirkus Rev* v82 no2 p282 Ja 15 2014

"The Inventor's Secret". "Paranormal-romance queen [Andrea] Cremer . . . tries her hand at writing steampunk with an alternative-history twist. The year is 1816. The British have won the Revolutionary War, enslaved the Americans, and turned Boston into a prison and New York City into a socially stratified power center. . . . Charlotte's steamy romantic intrigues with Jack and his Machiavellian brother dominate much of the action, leaving some plot details frustratingly opaque, including the titular secret itself. The cliffhanger at the conclusion of the novel clearly anticipates a sequel. On balance, it's an entertaining romp in a richly imaginative setting."

REVIEW: *Publ Wkly* v261 no3 p58 Ja 20 2014

REVIEW: *SLJ* v60 no9 p67 S 2014 Nicole Martin

REVIEW: *SLJ* v60 no3 p136 Mr 2014 Jane Henriksen Baird

REVIEW: *Voice of Youth Advocates* v37 no2 p72 Je 2014 Gwen Amborski

REVIEW: *Voice of Youth Advocates* v37 no2 p71-2 Je 2014 Adrienne Amborski

CREMER, ANDREA. Snakeroot; [by] Andrea Cremer 336 p. 2013 Philomel Books, an Imprint of Penguin Group (USA) Inc.

1. Fantasy fiction 2. JUVENILE FICTION—Action & Adventure—General 3. JUVENILE FICTION—Fantasy & Magic 4. JUVENILE FICTION—Love & Romance 5. Love—Fiction 6. Shapeshifting—Fiction 7. Supernatural—Fiction 8. Werewolves—Fiction
ISBN 9780399164224 (hardback)
LC 2013-011331

SUMMARY: In this book, author Andrea Cremer "Gremer combines the present-day world of her Nightshade novels with the backstory for the world she created in 'Rift'. . . . Gremer binds the two worlds together, with the powerful medieval priestess Eira present, in a magical necklace; evil Bosque Mar seduc[es] a new generation; and the complicated love lives of Galla, Shay, Ren, Adne, Logan, Sabine, and Ethan" are explored. (Booklist)

REVIEW: *Booklist* v110 no1 p115-6 S 1 2013 Debbie Carton

"Snakeroot." "[Andrea] Cremer combines the present-day world of her Nightshade novels with the backstory for the world she created in 'Rift'. . . . With so much history from very different times and a huge cast of primary characters, this title is not a good place to begin exploring Cremer's world of werewolves. Keepers, Guardians, and Searchers. But the series' many fans will be delighted to see how Cremer binds the two worlds together. . . . The first third of the book is heavily involved in plot exposition, which is both confusing for new readers and tiresome for devoted fans, but once she has laid out the basic history, the swift pace, romantic sensuality, and powerful magic will keep readers glued to the page."

REVIEW: *Kirkus Rev* v81 no18 p207 S 15 2013

REVIEW: *Voice of Youth Advocates* v36 no4 p78 O 2013 Liz Sundermann

CRESSY, DAVID. Saltpeter; the mother of gunpowder; [by] David Cressy xii, 237 p. 2013 Oxford University Press

1. Great Britain—History 2. Gunpowder—History 3. Gunpowder industry—History 4. Historical literature 5. Saltpeter—History
ISBN 019969575X (hdbk.); 9780199695751 (hdbk.)
LC 2013-370223

SUMMARY: This book, by David Cressy, explores "the history of saltpeter . . . craved by governments from the Tudors to the Victorians. . . . [It overviews] the many inter-connected stories--scientific, technological, political, and military-

-arising from this vital but mysterious substance . . . , [and] traces the central importance of saltpeter . . . over a period lasting several centuries." (Publisher's note)

REVIEW: *Choice* v51 no2 p286 O 2013 K. R. De Vries

REVIEW: *TLS* no5755 p8-9 Jl 19 2013 VICTOR DAVIS HANSON

"Saltpeter: The Mother of Gunpowder," "Napalm: An American Biography," and "Warrior Geeks: How Twenty-First-Century Technology is Changing the Way We Fight and Think About War." "David Cressy offers a brief but fascinating history of saltpetre. . . . He has skilfully turned 200 pages on the collection of human and animal waste into a fascinating reflection on how civic liberties were often quashed by concerns for national security. . . . [Robert M.] Neer is often highly critical of the American m use of napalm; yet his narrative of its origins, production and use over the past seven decades is not a jeremiad, but learned, fair and historically accurate. . . . Do not let the almost flippant title of Christopher Coker's 'Warrior Geeks' fool you. . . . [It is] a masterly account from a very well-read humanist about the fearful advance of post-human technologies in war."

CRIBB, VICTORIA.tr. Strange shores. See Indridason, A.

CRIMINAL PSYCHOLOGY; 1689 p. 2013 Praeger, an imprint of ABC-CLIO, LLC

1. Criminal behavior 2. Criminal justice administration 3. Criminal psychology 4. Forensic psychology 5. Psychological literature

ISBN 9780313396076 (hbk. 4 volume set : alk. paper)

LC 2012-051076

SUMMARY: This reference work examines "the history, developments, emerging and classic research issues, controversies, and victories in the expanding field of criminal psychology. The first volume examines the general theories in the study of criminal psychology. The second volume focuses more specifically on research of criminal behavior and crime types, while the last two volumes delve into criminal justice and forensic applications." (Publisher's note)

REVIEW: *Choice* v51 no4 p730 D 2013 T. Cottledge

"Criminal Psychology." "[Jacqueline B.] Helfgott . . . has done an extraordinary job with this four-volume set. The nature and extent of the relationship and interconnectivity between criminality and psychology is skillfully portrayed throughout in discussions of theoretical foundations, psychological typologies, disorders, profiles, policing, juvenile populations, and assessment. The 13 chapters are consistently relevant, current, and substantive, providing understanding of correlations between forensic assessment, policing, corrections, and treatment from a largely psychological perspective--though the set includes interdisciplinary discussions that extend the reach of the volumes across all the social sciences."

CRIMMINS, JAMES E.ed. Encyclopedia of utilitarianism. See Encyclopedia of utilitarianism

CRIST, CHARLIE, 1956-. The party's over; how the extreme right hijacked the GOP and I became a Democrat; [by] Charlie Crist 320 p. 2014 Dutton Adult

1. BIOGRAPHY & AUTOBIOGRAPHY—Political 2. Conservatism—United States 3. POLITICAL SCIENCE—Government—General 4. POLITICAL SCIENCE—Political Process—Political Parties 5. Radicalism—United States 6. Right and left (Political science)

ISBN 9780525954415 (hardback)

LC 2013-039612

SUMMARY: In this memoir, focused on polarization and partisanship in U.S. politics, Charlie Crist, "the former Republican governor of Florida explains why he became disenchanted with his party and ended up running for the Senate as an independent, endorsing [Barack] Obama, and finally becoming a Democrat." (Library Journal)

REVIEW: *Kirkus Rev* v81 no24 p268 D 15 2013

"The Party's Over: How the Extreme Right Hijacked the GOP and I Became a Democrat". "For [Charlie] Crist, this Republican 'tribalism' was 'silly—and wrong,' but his memoir gives evidence that he and his lifelong party had been diverging long before then. . . . Democrats, of course, will eat up Crist's self-presentation as common-sense populist, as well as his unflattering portraits of the Bushes, Karl Rove, Sarah Palin and many other GOP and tea party stars. Republicans will find little to cheer about here, but independent-minded readers might enjoy this front-row view of Florida politics at the turn of the millennium."

REVIEW: *Libr J* v138 no15 p48 S 15 2013

CRIST, ROBERT L.tr. Emily Dickinson. See Lala-Crist, D.

CRONIN, DOREEN. Diary of a worm; un 2003 HarperCollins Pubs.

1. Worms—Fiction

ISBN 0-06-000150-X; 0-06-000151-8 lib bdg

LC 2002--7949

SUMMARY: A young worm discovers, day by day, that there are some very good and some not so good things about being a worm in this great big worldA young woman discovers, day by day, that there are some very good and some not so good things about being a worm in this great big world. "Grades two to four." (Bull Cent Child Books)

REVIEW: *Bull Cent Child Books* v67 no1 p24-5 S 2013

"Diary of a Worm: Teacher's Pet." "This easy reader based on Cronin and Bliss' Diary of a Worm . . . follows the premise of the original, sharing the entries Worm writes in his diary that address the trials and tribulations of being a worm. In this offering, Worm is trying to come up with the perfect gift for his teacher's birthday. . . . As is often the case when picture books are adapted into easy reader format, there isn't much new here; the dynamics among characters, the humor, and the diary format are more or less repackaged with somewhat simpler text and more visual clues. . . . Still, Worm was entertaining the first time around and proves entertaining once again in this format."

CRONIN, EILEEN. Mermaid; a memoir of resilience; [by] Eileen Cronin 336 p. 2014 W W Norton & Co Inc

1. Memoirs 2. People with disabilities—United States—Biography 3. Thalidomide—Side effects 4. Women with disabilities—United States—Biography

ISBN 9780393089011 (hardcover)

LC 2013-036717

SUMMARY: In this memoir, author Eileen Cronin "writes

about growing up, as one of 11 children, without having legs, and trying to get her chain-smoking mom, who gets shock treatments and takes lithium for her 'nervous breakdowns,' to tell her whether she took thalidomide during her 1960 pregnancy. . . . . She attests to her many foolish choices, from riding a bike without a helmet to dumping seemingly sweet boyfriends and drinking too much until she chooses sobriety at age 27." (Booklist)

REVIEW: *Booklist* v110 no6 p5 N 15 2013 Karen Springen

REVIEW: *Kirkus Rev* v81 no24 p11 D 15 2013

"Mermaid: A Memoir of Resilience". "A clinical psychologist's memoir about how she uncovered the truth behind the family secret that surrounded her disability. . . . [Eileen] Cronin's confrontation with family secrets eventually allowed her to enjoy a successful career and marriage. Perhaps the greatest achievement with this book, which brings to light one of the great medical tragedies of the 20th century, is that she is able to tell her story with a winning combination of candor, grace and humor."

REVIEW: *Publ Wkly* v260 no36 p45 S 9 2013

CRONIN, GLORIA L.ed. A political companion to Saul Bellow . See A political companion to Saul Bellow

CRONIN, STEPHANIE. Armies and State-Building in the Modern Middle East; Politics, Nationalism and Military Reform; [by] Stephanie Cronin 320 p. 2014 Palgrave Macmillan

1. Historical literature 2. Middle East—Politics & government—1945- 3. Military reform 4. Nation building 5. Nationalism—Middle East

ISBN 1780767390; 9781780767390

SUMMARY: "By adding an historical understanding to a contemporary political analysis, [author] Stephanie Cronin examines the structures and activities of Middle Eastern armies and their role in state- and empire-building. Focusing on Iran, Afghanistan and Saudi Arabia, 'Armies, Tribes and States in the Middle East' presents a clear and concise analysis of the nature of armies and the differing guises military reform has taken throughout the region." (Publisher's note)

REVIEW: *Middle East J* v68 no3 p485-6 Summ 2014 Robert Springborg

"Armies and State-Building in the Modern Middle East: Politics, Nationalism and Military Reform." "Rarely can one characterize an historical study as timely, but 'Armies and State-Building in the Modern Middle East' is, and by design. . . . 'Armies and State-Building in the Modern Middle East' provides rich historical detail in support of themes embedded in a broader theoretical understanding of the vital roles played by Middle Eastern militaries in the building and management of state power. The book's one small short-coming is a considerable redundancy that no doubt results from it being compiled in part from material previously published. But the reader is well rewarded for persevering in the face of those redundancies."

CRONIN, STEPHANIE.ed. Iranian-Russian encounters. See Iranian-Russian encounters

CROSS, JULIE. Timestorm; a Tempest novel; [by] Julie Cross 368 p. 2014 St. Martin's Griffin

1. Adventure and adventurers—Fiction 2. Love—Fiction 3. Science fiction 4. Spies—Fiction 5. Time travel—Fiction

ISBN 0312568916; 9780312568917 (hardback)

LC 2013-039477

SUMMARY: "The battle between the Tempest Division and Eyewall comes to a shocking conclusion in 'Timestorm'—the final installment of Julie Cross's Tempest trilogy, where . . . the world Jackson Meyer once knew is a place forever marked by the detrimental effects of time travel. As Jackson recovers from his brush with death, he's surrounded not only by the people he loves most—his dad, Courtney, and Holly—he's also among a few of the original time travelers." (Publisher's note)

REVIEW: *Kirkus Rev* v82 no1 p204 Ja 1 2014

"Timestorm". "Here's hoping fans have had time to rest their brains before leaping into the final installment of the Tempest trilogy, as it will push them nearly to the breaking point. The mental gymnastics necessary to keep up with Jackson Meyer and his band of time-traveling "misfits" are not for out-of-shape readers. . . . . As in its predecessors, the best part of the novel lies in the emotional connections among the characters, particularly with respect to Jackson and his ill-fated twin sister, Courtney. . . . Unfortunately, the introduction of too many new characters and the relentless jumps back and forth in time make it nearly impossible to stay rooted in the story, no matter how endearing the cast might be. In a word: exhausting."

CROSSAN, SARAH. Resist; [by] Sarah Crossan 368 p. 2013 Greenwillow Books, an imprint of HarperCollins Publishers

1. Adventure and adventurers—Fiction 2. Environmental degradation—Fiction 3. Insurgency—Fiction 4. Science fiction 5. Survival—Fiction

ISBN 0062118722; 9780062118721 (hardback)

LC 2013-011914

SUMMARY: This novel, by Sarah Crossan, is "the sequel--and conclusion--to Sarah Crossan's 'Breathe.' Three teen outlaws must survive on their own in a world without air, exiled outside the glass dome that protects what's left of human civilization. . . . Bea has lost her family. Alina has lost her home. And Quinn has lost his privileged life. Can they survive in the perilous Outlands?" (Publisher's note)

REVIEW: *Horn Book Magazine* v90 no1 p88-9 Ja/F 2014 APRIL SPISAK

"Resist." "In this sequel (and conclusion) to 'Breathe,' . . . the world is still perilously low on oxygen, and the have-nots are still slowly dying. Alina, Quinn, and Bea, all of whose lives changed dramatically since Quinn and Bea were cast out of their protective dome dwellings, are still trying to save themselves--and perhaps the world if they can survive. . . . [Sarah] Crossan effectively portrays hope as a feral, desperate thing that keeps people fighting against oxygen depletion to remain alive and that fuels the book's romances, betrayals, alliances, and battles. The conclusion is tragic yet cathartic, a fitting end to a complex story set in a fraught world."

REVIEW: *Kirkus Rev* v81 no19 p257 O 1 2013

REVIEW: *SLJ* v60 no1 p96 Ja 2014 Cindy Wall

REVIEW: *Voice of Youth Advocates* v36 no5 p71-2 D 2013 Laura Lehner

CROSSAN, SARAH. The Weight of Water; [by] Sarah Crossan 224 p. 2013 Bloomsbury USA

1. Alienation (Social psychology)—Juvenile fiction 2. Immigrant children 3. Immigrants—England—Coventry—Juvenile fiction 4. Immigrants—England—Fiction 5. Immigrants—Fiction 6. Immigrants—Great Britain 7. Mothers and daughters—Fiction 8. Mothers and daughters—Juvenile fiction 9. Narrative poetry 10. Novels in verse 11. Polish people—Foreign countries 12. Race relations—Fiction 13. Swimming—Fiction 14. Swimming—Juvenile fiction

ISBN 1599909677; 9781599909677
LC 2012-038645

SUMMARY: In this book, "12-year-old Kasienka moves with Mama from Gdansk, Poland, to Coventry, England, to find Tata, her father. The adjustment is difficult. At school, Kasienka is ostracized. At home, she questions why they are searching for a man who ran from them. When Kasienka complains, Mama questions her love. Kasienka feels powerful only when she swims at the pool—something Tata taught her to do. That is also where William, a schoolmate, first notices her." (Kirkus Reviews)

REVIEW: *Booklist* v109 no21 p75 Jl 1 2013 Sarah Bean Thompson

REVIEW: *Bull Cent Child Books* v67 no1 p11 S 2013 K. C.

"The Weight of Water." "In this verse novel, Kasienka and her mother emigrate from Poland to England in search of Kasienka's father. Because of her weak English skills, Kasienka is put in sixth grade instead of seventh where she belongs, and because she is white among a community of brown and black immigrants, she is ostracized from the start and even actively bullied when she is moved to her rightful grade. . . . The verse form highlights Kasienka's emotional arc through the events that shape it; sharply observed, imagistic impressions of her first days in her new home and in school give way to more nuanced depictions of her feelings as she suffers her classmates' bullying and tramps through the streets looking for her father."

REVIEW: *Horn Book Magazine* v89 no4 p126-7 Jl/Ag 2013 SUSAN DOVE LEMPKE

REVIEW: *Kirkus Rev* v81 no2 p82 Je 1 2013

REVIEW: *Publ Wkly* v260 no23 p78 Je 10 2013

REVIEW: *Publ Wkly* p82 Children's starred review annual 2013

REVIEW: *SLJ* v59 no6 p118 Je 2013 Jill Heritage Maza

CROSSLEY-HOLLAND, KEVIN, 1941-. Bracelet of bones; [by] Kevin Crossley-Holland 313 p. 2014 Random House Inc

1. Europe—Fiction 2. Fathers & daughters—Fiction 3. Historical fiction 4. Vikings—Fiction 5. Young adult fiction

ISBN 1623651123; 9781623651121

SUMMARY: In this historical novel by Kevin Crossley-Holland, "Solveig is stunned that her father has left her behind to go and serve with another Viking in Constantinople, and she quickly decides that she would rather risk her life to follow him rather than live a safe, empty existence without him at home. The sharp fourteen-year-old has a lot of courage, but she has little life experience or knowledge of other cultures." (Bulletin of the Center for Children's Books)

REVIEW: *Bull Cent Child Books* v67 no8 p401-2 Ap 2014 A. S.

"Bracelet of Bones". "Solveig is a compelling protagonist, moving through the unknown with little more than her fierce grit, and the world through her eyes is at once terrifying and wildly exciting. [Kevin] Crossley-Holland's elegant, poetic language adds richness to the travelogue-meets-adventure plot, and his eye for authentic character development is strong. This is one of those rare books that will lure history buffs, those seeking strong girl characters, and Viking fans—and it will actually please all of them. An author's note, list of characters, map, and vocabulary list add background and context to the complex story."

CROUCH, JULIAN.il. Maggot moon. See Maggot moon

CROUCH, STANLEY, 1945-. Kansas City lightning; the rise and times of Charlie Parker; [by] Stanley Crouch 384 p. 2013 Harper

1. Biographies 2. Jazz musicians—United States—Biography 3. Kansas City (Mo.) 4. Nightlife

ISBN 0062005596; 9780062005595
LC 2013-015773

SUMMARY: This book, by Stanley Crouch, "is the first installment in . . . [a] portrait of one of the most talented and influential musicians of the twentieth century, from Stanley Crouch, one of the foremost authorities on jazz and culture in America. Drawing on interviews with peers, collaborators, and family members, 'Kansas City Lightning' recreates Parker's Depression-era childhood; his early days navigating the Kansas City nightlife." (Publisher's note)

REVIEW: *Booklist* v110 no5 p18 N 1 2013 Donna Seaman

"Anything Goes: A History of American Musical Theatre," "Furious Cool: Richard Pryor and the World That Made Him," and "Kansas City Lightning: The Rise and Times of Charlie Parker." "[Ethan] Mordden traces the evolution of the musical, a quintessential American art form, and analyzes dozens of standout examples in this comprehensive, witty, and sassy history. . . . Richard Pryor drew on his difficult life and ferocious energy to create his blazing comedy, and the brothers [David Henry and Joe] Henry detail every facet of his troubled life in this superbly written account of a manic genius. . . . [Stanley] Crouch captures with novelistic verve the early years of jazz master Charlie Parker's short life in Kansas City, capturing the excitement of his artistic daring."

REVIEW: *Booklist* v109 no22 p18 Ag 1 2013 Mark Levine

REVIEW: *Choice* v51 no10 p1811 Je 2014 K. R. Dietrich

REVIEW: *Commentary* v136 no2 p58-61 S 2013 TERRY TEACHOUT

REVIEW: *Kirkus Rev* v81 no16 p116 Ag 15 2013

REVIEW: *Kirkus Rev* p20 Ag 15 2013 Fall Preview

REVIEW: *London Rev Books* v36 no2 p26-9 Ja 23 2014 Ian Penman

REVIEW: *N Y Rev Books* v60 no17 p71-3 N 7 2013 Adam Shatz

REVIEW: *N Y Times Book Rev* p51 D 8 2013 DAVID HAJDU

"Kansas City Lightning: The Rise and Times of Charlie Parker" and "Bird: The Life and Music of Charlie Parker." "'Lightning: The Rise and Times of Charlie Parker' is . . . a virtuoso performance of musical-literary mimesis. . . . In jazz scholarship, few writers have been as devoted to their subjects as Crouch has been to Parker. . . . 'Bird,' by Chuck Haddix . . . has also recently been published, and its benign but bloodless presentation of the facts about Parker's life reminds one of the value of critical analysis and interpretation. . . . The information in Haddix's book is not always accurate, either."

REVIEW: *New York Times* v163 no56286 pC19-26 O 11 2013 DWIGHT GARNER

REVIEW: *New York Times* v163 no56286 pC19-26 O 11 2013 DWIGHT GARNER

REVIEW: *New Yorker* v89 no34 p79-1 O 28 2013

REVIEW: *Publ Wkly* v260 no30 p58 Jl 29 2013

REVIEW: *Publ Wkly* v260 no35 p26-7 S 2 2013 EUGENE HOLLEY JR.

CROWDER, ASHBY BLAND.ed. The complete works of Robert Browning. See Browning, R.

CROWE, CHRIS. Just as good; How Larry Doby changed America's game; 32 p. 2012 Candlewick Press

1. African Americans—Fiction 2. Baseball—Fiction 3. Fiction
ISBN 9780763650261
LC 2010-047678

SUMMARY: In this book "[a] young boy and his parents gather round their brand-new radio, purchased just for the occasion, to listen anxiously and, finally, exultantly as [baseball player] Larry Doby leads the 1948 Cleveland Indians to World Series victory. The boy, African-American, had been told that there was no future for him in baseball because of segregation, even though Jackie Robinson now played with the Brooklyn Dodgers and Doby had signed with the Indians. . . . Doby integrated the American League and was a brilliant hitter and fielder who got lost in the Robinson accolades." (Kirkus)

REVIEW: *Booklist* v108 no11 p84 F 1 2012 Ian Chipman

REVIEW: *Bull Cent Child Books* v65 no6 p303 F 2012 E. B.

"Just As Good: How Larry Doby Changed America's Game." "Satchel Paige would also make his appearance in that World Series, the spotlight here is strictly on [Larry] Doby and the photograph that would rattle segregationist fans. . . . However, the effort here is somewhat diluted by the fictional storyline and the distractingly awkward artwork, which focuses less on the play action and more on Homer's family, with their rigid poses, frozen smiles, and eyes that glare disconcertingly off into an indeterminate distance. There is nonetheless considerable appeal here for baseball fans, and kids who think that Jackie Robinson's entry into the majors signaled smooth sailing for his race will think again."

REVIEW: *Kirkus Rev* v80 no1 p2460 Ja 1 2012

REVIEW: *Publ Wkly* v258 no48 p56 N 28 2011

REVIEW: *SLJ* v58 no1 p92 Ja 2012 Kara Schaff Dean

CROWE, IAN. Patriotism and public spirit; Edmund Burke and the role of the critic in mid-eighteenth-century Britain; [by] Ian Crowe xiii, 288 p. 2012 Stanford University Press

1. Historical literature 2. Patriotism—Great Britain—History—18th century
ISBN 9780804781275 (cloth : alk. paper)
LC 2011-052150

SUMMARY: This book presents a "study of the formative influences shaping the early writings of the Irish-English statesman Edmund Burke and an early case-study of the relationship between the business of bookselling and the politics of criticism and persuasion. . . . The book argues that Burke saw Patriotism as the best way to combine public spirit with the reinforcement of civil order and to combat the use of coded partisan thinking." (Publisher's note)

REVIEW: *TLS* no5747 p7-8 My 24 2013 DANIEL HITCHENS

"The Cambridge Companion to Edmund Burke," "Edmund Burke and the Art of Rhetoric," and "Patriotism and Public Spirit: Edmund Burke and the Role of the Critic in Mid-18th-Century Britain." "'The Cambridge Companion to Edmund Burke' aims to disentangle Burke from his many contexts, and for the most part it succeeds impressively. . . . The collection is generally crisp, broad-minded and clearly written. . . . This is a fresh and immediately illuminating thesis, and [Paddy] Bullard's digressive erudition adds to the book's charm. My one complaint is that, as so often, the flesh-and-blood Burke begins to disappear into his own ideas. . . . [Ian] Crowe has hit on a valuable approach of some importance, simply by taking seriously the vibrant intellectual culture of mid-century London."

CROWELL, JENN. Etched on me; a novel; [by] Jenn Crowell 320 p. 2014 Washington Square Press

1. Adult child sexual abuse victims—Fiction 2. Cutting (Self-mutilation) 3. Psychological fiction 4. Survival—Fiction
ISBN 1476739064; 9781476739069
LC 2013-014712

SUMMARY: In this novel by Jenn Crowell, "Lesley . . . recently ran away from home, where her father had spent years sexually abusing her [and] she's secretly cutting herself as a coping mechanism. Lesley spends the next two years in and out of psychiatric facilities, where she . . . finds the support of a surrogate family. [When] she becomes unexpectedly pregnant in her early twenties . . . the same team that saved her as an adolescent will now question whether Lesley is fit to be a mother." (Publisher's note)

REVIEW: *Booklist* v110 no7 p20-2 D 1 2013 Ann Kelley

REVIEW: *Kirkus Rev* v82 no2 p224 Ja 15 2014

"Etched on Me". "A courageous survivor of sexual abuse, Lesley Holloway has always cooperated with social services. That is, until they take her newborn daughter away from her and she has to battle to win her back. After years of being dragged into the hall closet to be raped by her own father, Lesley runs away. From that moment, she is thrust into the world of child protective services, a world filled with tremendously helpful individuals but also riddled with the very bureaucracy that will rip away Lesley's hard-won independence again and again. . . . With its deft plotting, rich characterization and often hilariously poignant dialogue, [Jenn] Crowell's . . . latest is a gem."

REVIEW: *Publ Wkly* v260 no40 p27-8 O 7 2013

CROWELL, SAM. Emergent teaching; a path of creativity, significance, and transformation; [by] Sam Crowell 147 p. 2012 Rowman & Littlefield Education, a division of Rowman & Littlefield Publishers, Inc.

1. Creative teaching 2. Educational literature 3. Effective teaching 4. Emergence (Philosophy) 5. Teaching—Methodology 6. Teaching—Philosophy

ISBN 1475802544; 9781475802542 (cloth : alk. paper); 9781475802559 (pbk. : alk. paper)

LC 2012-041692

SUMMARY: Author Sam Crowell's book focuses on "how teachers can relate subject matter to students' lives and experience." The book illustrates "rituals and processes that help establish a caring learning community. Finally, the book applies the theories of complexity and chaos while reaffirming the natural wisdom that teachers possess within themselves." (Publisher's note)

REVIEW: *Choice* v51 no1 p135-6 S 2013 S. T. Schroth

"Emergent Teaching: A Path of Creativity, Significance, and Transformation." "[Authors Sam] Crowell and [David] Reid-Marr . . . assert that although teachers may anticipate certain patterns, classroom practice largely involves assisting learners to discover personal significance and creating a sense of belonging. Organized into ten chapters, the book defines emergent teaching and then examines some central tenets of the approach, including the experience of nonseparation, event-centric teaching, non-linear instruction, the emergence of understanding, and the roles of play and joy in the classroom. . . . Clearly written and full of useful examples of emergent teaching in action."

CRUMP, JAMES.ed. Elena Dorfman. See Elena Dorfman

CRUVELLIER, THIERRY. The Master of Confessions; The Making of a Khmer Rouge Torturer; [by] Thierry Cruvellier 352 p. 2014 HarperCollins

1. Cambodia—History—20th century 2. Journalism 3. Kang, Kech Ieu, 1943- 4. Parti communiste du Kampuchéa 5. Torture 6. Trials (Genocide)—Cambodia

ISBN 0062329545; 9780062329547

SUMMARY: This book, by Thierry Cruvellier, is an "account of a Chief Interrogator's trial for war crimes. On April 17, 1975, the communist Khmer Rouge, led by its secretive prime minister Pol Pot, took over Cambodia. Renaming the country Democratic Kampuchea, they cut the nation off from the world and began systematically killing and starving two million of their people. Thirty years after their fall, a man named Duch, . . . stood trial for war crimes and crimes against humanity." (Publisher's note)

REVIEW: *Kirkus Rev* v82 no4 p301 F 15 2014

"The Master of Confessions: The Trial of a Khmer Rouge Torturer". "With chilling clarity, a veteran international journalist delineates the totalitarian ideology and horrific crimes of the leaders of Cambodia's Khmer Rouge. . . . [Thierry] Cruvellier . . . attended the arduous eight-month Khmer Rouge Tribunal in 2009 of the notorious head of the S-21 'death mill' in Phnom Penh, Kaing Guek Eav, aka Duch.. . . The author's portrait of the cool, contrite and calculating Duch is superbly memorable. Cruvellier is an extremely articulate and compassionate observer to a country and its people plunged through the rings of hell."

REVIEW: *Libr J* v138 no18 p67 N 1 2013 Barbara Hoffert

CRYSTAL, BILLY, 1948-. Still foolin' 'em; where i've been, where i'm going, and where the hell are my keys?; [by] Billy Crystal 288 p. 2013 Henry Holt and Company

1. Aging 2. American wit & humor 3. BIOGRAPHY & AUTOBIOGRAPHY—Entertainment & Performing Arts 4. Comedians—United States—Biography

ISBN 0805098208; 9780805098204 (hardback)

LC 2013-012238

SUMMARY: Author and comedian Billy Crystal "outlines the absurdities and challenges that come with growing old, from insomnia to memory loss to leaving dinners with half your meal on your shirt. Crystal not only catalogues his physical gripes, but offers a road map to his 77 million fellow baby boomers who are arriving at this milestone age with him. He also looks back at the most powerful and memorable moments of his long and storied life." (Publisher's note)

REVIEW: *Booklist* v109 no22 p19 Ag 1 2013 David Pitt

REVIEW: *Kirkus Rev* v81 no13 p312 Jl 1 2013

REVIEW: *Kirkus Rev* p22 Ag 15 2013 Fall Preview

REVIEW: *Libr J* v139 no3 p63 F 15 2014 Theresa Horn

REVIEW: *N Y Times Book Rev* p58 N 10 2013 Anita Gates

"Jack Be Nimble: The Accidental Education of an Unintentional Director," "Room 1219: The Life of Fatty Arbuckle, the Mysterious Death of Virginia Rappe, and the Scandal That Changed Hollywood," and "Still Foolin' 'Em: Where I've Been, Where I'm Going, and Where the Hell Are My Keys? "Most of this gracefully written book is about [Jack O'Brien's] early days, and the influence of . . . Ellis Rabb and . . . Rosemary Harris. . . . Some scenes are quite personal, even invasive, but O'Brien's admiration for both comes through. . . . [Greg] Merritt's account of the crime . . . the three trials and the people involved is admirably evenhanded, meticulously researched and compelling. . . . [A] breezy memoir. . . . Sometimes the humor is bright. . . . Crystal is at his authorial finest when he switches into mean mode and mouths off about people and things that annoy him."

REVIEW: *Publ Wkly* v260 no32 p52-3 Ag 12 2013

REVIEW: *Publ Wkly* v260 no48 p52 N 25 2013

CRYSTAL, DAVID. Wordsmiths & warriors; the English-language tourist's guide to Britain; [by] David Crystal vii, 424 p. 2013 Oxford University Press

1. English language—History 2. Language & history 3. Travelers' writings, English

ISBN 0199668124 (hbk.); 9780199668120 (hbk.)

LC 2013-431538

SUMMARY: In this book, authors "David and Hilary Crystal take us on a journey through Britain to discover the people who gave our language its colour and character; Saxon invaders, medieval scholars, poets, reformers, dictionary writers. . . . They include a guide for anyone wanting to follow in their footsteps but arrange the book to reflect the chronology of the language." (Publisher's note)

REVIEW: *TLS* no5792 p32 Ap 4 2014 ELISABETH SALTER

"Wordsmiths and Warriors: The English-Language Tourist Guide to Britain." "Given the scope of the book, its tendency to travel rather rapidly through history is unsurprising. . . . It places an attractive emphasis on the non-canonical. . . . For those of us who spend a lot of time seeking to enthuse students about English literature and language or particular historical moments in Britain, or to instil in them a heightened sensitivity to language, 'Wordsmiths and Warriors' will also provide some of those nuggets of attention-grabbing trivia we seek out for introductory lectures."

CRYSTAL, HILARY.il. Wordsmiths & warriors. See Crystal, D.

CUCCO, GIULIANO, 1929-2006.il. Winston & George. See Miller, J.

CULLEN, LYNN. Mrs. Poe; [by] Lynn Cullen 320 p. 2013 Simon & Schuster

1. Authors—Fiction 2. Historical fiction 3. Osgood, Frances Sargent Locke, 1811-1850 4. Poe, Edgar Allan, 1809-1849 5. Poe, Virginia Clemm
ISBN 1476702918; 9781476702919

SUMMARY: This historical novel focuses on Edgar Allen Poe and "his relationship with fellow author Frances Sargent Locke Osgood. . . . At a gathering of New York elite, she meets Poe, who admires her talent. . . . They try to mask their attraction. . . . Even though she's uncomfortable with her situation, and suspects that Mrs. Poe's need to compete with her for Poe's attention is more ominous than mere jealousy suggests, Osgood is unable to break away." (Kirkus Reviews)

REVIEW: *Booklist* v110 no1 p50-1 S 1 2013 Laurie Borman

"Mrs. Poe." "Taking advantage of letters and published poems, imaginative historical novelist [Lynn] Cullen . . . cleverly spins a mysterious, dark tale told by Mrs. [Frances Sargent] Osgood about the long-ago intrigue, with just enough facts to make it believable. Celebrities like Louisa May Alcott, Walt Whitman, and John Jacob Astor make cameo appearances. Others . . . also step in for a fun romp through history. As the story unfolds, we're left to wonder if Mrs. Poe is Edgar's Mr. Hyde, or is Poe himself the villain? It's enough to make the teacups rattle."

REVIEW: *Kirkus Rev* v81 no8 p8-9 Ap 15 2013

REVIEW: *N Y Times Book Rev* p30 N 3 2013 Liesl Schillinger

REVIEW: *Publ Wkly* v260 no33 p41 Ag 19 2013

CULTURAL ENCOUNTERS DURING THE CRUSADES; 329 p. 2013 University Press of Southern Denmark

1. Civilization, Western—Islamic influences—Congresses 2. Crusades—Influence—Congresses 3. Cultural relations—History—Congresses 4. East and West—Congresses 5. Historical literature 6. Islamic civilization—Western influences—Congresses
ISBN 8776746593; 9788776746599
LC 2013-431778

SUMMARY: This book on the Crusades covers such topics as "the geo-strategies and historical perspectives of Pope Urban II and 'Ali ibn Tahir al-Sulami, the impact of crusading ideology on early 12th-century Denmark, the rationality behind Manuel I Domnenos' attempt to reform the abjuration formula for converts from Islam, the Armenian kingdom and the Mongol-Frankish encounter, and Baybars and the crusades in Arab film and television." (Reference & Research Book News)

REVIEW: *Choice* v51 no6 p1072-3 F 2014 J. W. Nesbitt

"Cultural Encounters During the Crusades." "Jerusalem fell to the Crusaders in 1099. The event provoked a reaction in Muslim lands that slowly gained momentum, and eventually resulted in Saladin's recapture of the city in 1187. Some essays in this collection deal with the fallout from these events:Books on the Crusades are common, but the inclusion of reflections on the evolution of Muslim holy war and Muslim thoughts about Christianity raises this volume to another level. . . . Recommended."

A CULTURAL HISTORY OF WOMEN IN THE AGE OF ENLIGHTENMENT; xi, 286 p. 2013 Bloomsbury

1. Historical literature 2. Women—History—17th century 3. Women—History—18th century 4. Women—United States—Social conditions—18th century
ISBN 9780857851000 (HB); 9781847884756 (set)
LC 2012-036398

SUMMARY: This book, part of the "Cultural History of Women" series, discusses women's lives during the Age of Enlightenment. It "begins with a detailed introduction that provides an overview of women's experiences during that period." Topics "include the areas of life cycle, women's bodies and sexuality, religion and popular beliefs, medicine and disease, public and private life, education and work, power, and artistic representation." (Booklist)

REVIEW: *Booklist* v110 no9/10 p74 Ja 1 2014 Lyndsie Robinson

Titles:"A Cultural History of Women in the Renaissance," "A Cultural History of Women in the Age of Enlightenment," "and "A Cultural History of Women in the Modern Age." "This impressive six-volume set surveys the cultural representation and varied experiences of women throughout history. Each volume focuses on a specific time period, ranging from antiquity (roughly 500 BCE) to the present. And though each volume can easily stand on its own, the consistency of format across the series allows the reader to easily compare and contrast the cultural representation and lives of women between each of the time periods. . . . The individual essays within each volume are extremely well written and informative throughout the set."

A CULTURAL HISTORY OF WOMEN IN THE MODERN AGE; vi, 249 p. 2013 Bloomsbury

1. Historical literature 2. Women & religion 3. Women—Health 4. Women—Sexual behavior 5. Women—Social conditions—20th century
ISBN 9780857851024 (hb); 9781847884756 (set)
LC 2012-036721

SUMMARY: This book, part of the "Cultural History of Women" series, discusses women's lives during the modern age. It "begins with a detailed introduction that provides an overview of women's experiences during that period." Topics "include the areas of life cycle, women's bodies and sexuality, religion and popular beliefs, medicine and disease, public and private life, education and work, power, and artistic representation." (Booklist)

REVIEW: *Booklist* v110 no9/10 p74 Ja 1 2014 Lyndsie Robinson

Titles:"A Cultural History of Women in the Renaissance," "A Cultural History of Women in the Age of Enlightenment," "and "A Cultural History of Women in the Modern Age." "This impressive six-volume set surveys the cultural representation and varied experiences of women throughout history. Each volume focuses on a specific time period, ranging from antiquity (roughly 500 BCE) to the present. And though each volume can easily stand on its own, the consistency of format across the series allows the reader to easily compare and contrast the cultural representation and lives of women between each of the time periods. . . . The individual essays within each volume are extremely well written and informative throughout the set."

A CULTURAL HISTORY OF WOMEN IN THE RENAISSANCE; 271 p. 2013 Berg

1. Historical literature 2. Women—Europe—Social conditions 3. Women—Health 4. Women—History—Renaissance, 1450-1600 5. Women—Sexual behavior
ISBN 9780857850997 (hbk.)
LC 2012-036399

SUMMARY: This book, part of the "Cultural History of Women" series, discusses women's lives during the Renaissance. It "begins with a detailed introduction that provides an overview of women's experiences during that period." Topics "include the areas of life cycle, women's bodies and sexuality, religion and popular beliefs, medicine and disease, public and private life, education and work, power, and artistic representation." (Booklist)

REVIEW: *Booklist* v110 no9/10 p74 Ja 1 2014 Lyndsie Robinson

Titles:"A Cultural History of Women in the Renaissance," "A Cultural History of Women in the Age of Enlightenment," "and "A Cultural History of Women in the Modern Age." "This impressive six-volume set surveys the cultural representation and varied experiences of women throughout history. Each volume focuses on a specific time period, ranging from antiquity (roughly 500 BCE) to the present. And though each volume can easily stand on its own, the consistency of format across the series allows the reader to easily compare and contrast the cultural representation and lives of women between each of the time periods. . . . The individual essays within each volume are extremely well written and informative throughout the set."

A CULTURAL HISTORY OF WOMEN; 1700 p. 2013 Bloomsbury

1. Civilization, Ancient 2. Historical literature 3. Women—Greece—Social conditions 4. Women—History—To 1500 5. Women—Rome—Social conditions
ISBN 184788475X; 9781847884756
LC 2012-036396

SUMMARY: This volume, by Linda Kalof, "presents an authoritative survey from ancient times to the present. With six volumes covering 2500 years, this is [an] authoritative history . . . of women in Western cultures. Each volume discusses the same themes in its chapters: the Life Cycle; Bodies and Sexuality; Religion and Popular Beliefs; Medicine and Disease; Public and Private Worlds; Education and Work; Power; and Artistic Representation." (Publisher's note)

REVIEW: *Choice* v51 no2 p323-4 O 2013 M. E. Snodgrass

"A Cultural History of Women." "In this tantalizing survey of female culture, general editor [Linda] Kalof's attractive six-volume set presents a keen-eyed evaluation of period obstacles, developments, and opportunities. . . . The eight-part organization of each volume balances a sampling of evidence from biological, physiological, religious, medical, personal, intellectual, political, and artistic spheres. . . . Omitted are questions of immigration, veiling, activism, and gender selection, the sources of the shrillest current commentary targeting women. . . . Impressive bibliographies specify avenues of research. Primary and secondary indexing simplifies detailed studies, such as women in Islam, the elite, industry, travel, witchcraft, and colonialism."

REVIEW: *Libr J* v138 no12 p102 Jl 1 2013 Diane Fulkerson

CULTURALLY RELEVANT ARTS EDUCATION FOR SOCIAL JUSTICE; a way out of no way; xiii, 243 p. 2013 Routledge

1. Arts—Study and teaching—United States 2. Arts education advocacy 3. Education—Social aspects—United States 4. Educational literature 5. Social justice—Study and teaching
ISBN 9780203077573 (alk. paper); 9780415656603 (alk. paper); 9780415656610 (alk. paper)
LC 2012-038682

SUMMARY: This book, "examining a range of efforts across different forms of art, various educational settings, and diverse contexts . . . foregrounds the assets of imagination, creativity, resilience, critique and cultural knowledge, working against prevailing understandings of marginalized groups as having deficits of knowledge, skills, or culture. . . . It explores and illustrates the elements of social justice arts education as "a way out of no way" imposed by dominance and ideology." (Publisher's note)

REVIEW: *Choice* v51 no5 p891-2 Ja 2014 G. A. Clark

"Culturally Relevant Arts Education for Social Justice: A Way Out of No Way." "The 35 contributors to this book explore different aspects on how to make the arts relevant for social justice. All, from different points of view, exhort readers to realize and incorporate the emotional content. . . . Obviously, with so many contributors, professional terms are variously defined and applied, although the various authors are careful to define their own particular aspects of social changes and activism. . . . It is vitally important for arts teachers to read the many articles contained here and to realize the importance of their various constituencies."

CUMMINGS, PAT.il. Beauty and the beast. See Beauty and the beast

CUMMINS, JULIE. Flying solo; how Ruth Elder soared into America's heart; [by] Julie Cummins 32 p. 2013 Roaring Brook Press

1. Air pilots—United States—Biography—Juvenile literature 2. Elder, Ruth 3. Historical literature 4. Women—United States—History—20th century 5. Women air pilots—United States—Biography—Juvenile literature
ISBN 1596435097; 9781596435094 (hardcover)
LC 2012-029743

SUMMARY: Written by Julie Cummins and illustrated by Malene R. Laugesen, this book describes how "Ruth Elder, a contemporary of Amelia Earhart, set her sights on becoming the first woman to fly across the Atlantic. At age 23, and after only a few flying lessons, she and her copilot set forth. Two-thirds of the way into their flight, the gas line sprung a leak, and they were forced to abandon the plane. Fortunately, they were rescued by a nearby ship." (Booklist)

REVIEW: *Booklist* v109 no19/20 p85 Je 1 2013 J. B. Petty

REVIEW: *Bull Cent Child Books* v67 no1 p12 S 2013 E. B.

"Flying Solo: How Ruth Elder Soared Into America's Heart." "From her beauty-queen wing poses to the flirty name of her plane, 'American Girl', pioneering aviatrix Ruth Elder was not only an able and ambitious pilot but also a savvy dame who evidently knew that glamour would do as much as raw achievement to promote the cause of women in American aviation. . . . While [author Julie] Cummins avoids discussion of the possibility that aviation was a publicity stunt for Elder's acting career, readers get the full flavor of a Roaring Twenties age of spectacle, through both the text and with [illustrator Malene R.] Laugesen's lightly textured pastel art, some based on period photographs."

REVIEW: *Horn Book Magazine* v89 no5 p120-1 S/O 2013 SUSAN DOVE LEMPKE

"Flying Solo: How Ruth Elder Soared Into America's Heart." "[Julie] Cummins captures the feel of the era by employing quaint vocabulary such as dillydally and gumption. [Malene R.] Laugesen's pastel illustrations capture the lofty feeling of the experience of flying in a small plane and landing in a field, and also pay careful attention to the clothes of the era. This makes a lively and well-researched addition to Women's History Month biographies, with a closing illustration showing little girls inspecting a wall of portraits of aviatrixes, from (according to the key) Elder and [Amelia] Earhart to the first female combat pilots to women astronauts."

REVIEW: *Publ Wkly* v260 no22 p59 Je 3 2013

REVIEW: *SLJ* v59 no7 p108 Jl 2013 Barbara Auerbach

CUNNANE, KELLY. Deep in the Sahara; [by] Kelly Cunnane 40 p. 2013 Schwartz & Wade Books

1. Clothing and dress—Fiction 2. Coming of age—Fiction 3. Muslims—Fiction 4. Picture books for children
ISBN 0375970347; 9780375870347 (trade); 9780375970344 (g.l.b.)
LC 2011-050245

SUMMARY: This book shows "a Mauritanian girl who's fascinated with the malafa, the veil the women in her family wear. The second-person narration . . . presents the veil as desirable rather than confining and describes the girl's wish to wear it so she can be beautiful . . . [and] mysterious. . . . Her relatives reject these superficial reasons. It's not until the girl shows she understands the malafa as a sign of Muslim belief . . . that Mama gives the girl one of her own." (Publishers Weekly)

REVIEW: *Booklist* v110 no6 p45 N 15 2013 Ilene Cooper

"Deep in the Sahara." "[Kelly] Cunnane explains in an author's note that when she first lived in Mauritania, she believed wearing the veil was repressive, but the people's 'relaxed and colorful expression of their faith and culture' changed her mind. She will certainly make readers think about their preconceived notions thanks to a text that is as thoughtful as it is charming. [Hoda] Hadadi, who is Iranian, creates paper collages with a whimsical beauty that work well with the story's sense of longing. The women, all individualized, exude true warmth, and readers will feel a quiet satisfaction when Lalla joins them. A special offering."

REVIEW: *Bull Cent Child Books* v67 no3 p146 N 2013 H. M.

REVIEW: *Kirkus Rev* v81 no17 p83-4 S 1 2013

REVIEW: *Kirkus Rev* p48 N 15 2013 Best Books

REVIEW: *Publ Wkly* v260 no36 p56 S 9 2013

REVIEW: *Publ Wkly* p34-5 Children's starred review annual 2013

CUNNINGHAM, MICHAEL, 1952-. The snow queen; [by] Michael Cunningham 272 p. 2014 Farrar, Straus & Giroux

1. Brothers—Fiction 2. Cancer—Patients—Fiction 3. Drug addiction—Fiction 4. Paranormal fiction 5. Psychological fiction
ISBN 0374266328; 9780374266325 (hardcover)
LC 2013-038712

SUMMARY: This book follows "Barrett Meeks, a poetically minded man in his late thirties who . . . shares a Brooklyn apartment with Tyler, his older musician-bartender brother, and Beth, Tyler's great love. . . . Beth is undergoing full-throttle treatment for cancer. Tyler is struggling to write the perfect love song for their wedding, and breaking [his] promise not to do drugs. Barrett . . . remains in an altered state after seeing a . . . 'celestial light' over dark and snowy Central Park." (Booklist)

REVIEW: *Booklist* v110 no14 p50 Mr 15 2014 Donna Seaman

"The Snow Queen". "[Michael] Cunningham's elegant and haunting new novel examines the complex dynamics among a couple and a brother. . . . As his characters try to reconcile exalted dreams and crushing reality, Cunningham orchestrates intensifying inner monologues addressing such ephemeral yet essential aspects of life as shifting perspectives, tides of desire and fear, 'rampancy' versus 'languidness,' and revelation and receptivity. Tender, funny, and sorrowful, Cunningham's beautiful novel is as radiant and shimmering as Barrett's mysterious light in the sky, gently illuminating the gossamer web of memories, feelings, and hopes that mysteriously connect us to each other as the planet spins its way round and round the sun."

REVIEW: *Kirkus Rev* v82 no6 p329 Mr 15 2014

REVIEW: *Libr J* v138 no21 p68 D 1 2013 Barbara Hoffert

REVIEW: *Libr J* v139 no11 p50 Je 15 2014 Heather Malcolm

REVIEW: *Libr J* v139 no5 p108 Mr 15 2014 Joshua Finnell

REVIEW: *N Y Times Book Rev* p13 My 11 2014 MARIA RUSSO

REVIEW: *New York Times* v163 no56485 pC1-4 Ap 28 2014 MICHIKO KAKUTANI

REVIEW: *New Yorker* v90 no15 p79-1 Je 2 2014

REVIEW: *Publ Wkly* v261 no7 p75 F 17 2014

REVIEW: *TLS* no5798 p20 My 16 2014 SAM SOLNICK

CUNNINGHAM, SCOTT. Bad for you; the truth behind the campaign against fun; [by] Scott Cunningham 192 p. 2013 Henry Holt and Co.

1. Comic books, strips, etc. 2. Pseudoscience 3. Social criticism 4. Technology & children—Social aspects 5. Youth culture
ISBN 0805092897; 9780805092899 (pbk.)
LC 2012-953810

SUMMARY: Written by Kevin C. Pyle and Scott Cunningham and illustrated by Pyle, this comic book addresses criticism of youth culture. "Covering topics such as comics, games, technology, and play, the chapters begin with a historical perspective on each subject. The authors then go on to explain how time after time, as new pastimes develop, they gain in popularity with youth until they enter the public limelight and are deemed potentially harmful to children." (School Library Journal)

REVIEW: *Booklist* v110 no2 p59 S 15 2013 Jesse Karp

REVIEW: *Bull Cent Child Books* v67 no3 p175-6 N 2013 E. B.

"Bad for You: Exposing the Campaign Against Fun: A Graphic Investigation." "Although the term ephebiphohia, fear of youth, doesn't appear until well into this title, it is the controlling idea behind [author and illustrator Kevin C.] Pyle's exploration of buzzkill, past and present. . . . Pyle acts as provocateur, encouraging readers to think critically about adult critiques of kid culture, and to be particularly aware of the trap of conflating correlation with causation. It's great advice, and it's best when packaged in Pyle's own comics-formatted arguments. Too often, though, clever and pithy discussion is interrupted by less effective prose rants, and Pyle even slips occasionally into the correlation mire as he sidesteps finesse."

REVIEW: *Kirkus Rev* v81 no18 p40 S 15 2013

REVIEW: *SLJ* v59 no9 p171 S 2013 Ragan O'Malley

REVIEW: *Voice of Youth Advocates* v36 no6 p82 F 2014 Laura Perenic

CUOCO, AL. Learning modern algebra; from early attempts to prove Fermat's last theorem; [by] Al Cuoco xix, 459 p. 2013 Mathematical Association of America

1. Abstract algebra 2. Algebra—Textbooks 3. Fermat's last theorem 4. Mathematical literature 5. Number theory

ISBN 1939512018; 9781939512017

LC 2013-940990

SUMMARY: "This book covers abstract algebra from a historical perspective by using mathematics from attempts to prove Fermat's last theorem. . . . [Al] Cuoco . . . and [Joseph J.] Rotman . . . begin with a discussion of number theory familiar to Diophantus and Euclid. The next seven chapters cover the details of induction, mathematics of the Renaissance, modular arithmetic, abstract algebra, polynomials, field theory, and cyclotomic integers." (Choice: Current Reviews for Academic Libraries)

REVIEW: *Choice* v51 no7 p1256-7 Mr 2014 D. P. Turner

"Learning Modern Algebra: From Early Attempts to Prove Fermat's Last Theorem." "This book covers abstract algebra from a historical perspective by using mathematics from attempts to prove Fermat's last theorem, as the title indicates. The target audience is high school mathematics teachers. However, typical undergraduate students will also derive great benefit by studying this text. The book is permeated with fascinating mathematical nuggets that are clearly explained. . . . The book contains more than 620 exercises without solutions. Readability is enhanced by 70-plus figures. A list of 39 references supports the text . . . Recommended."

CURDY, AVERILL. Song & error; [by] Averill Curdy 112 p. 2013 Farrar, Straus and Giroux

1. Núñez Cabeza de Vaca, Alvar, fl. 16th century 2. Persona (Literature) 3. Poems—Collections 4. Sandys, George 5. Woolson, Constance Fenimore, 1840-1894

ISBN 9780374280611 (hardcover: alk. paper)

LC 2012-021668

SUMMARY: This book presents poems by Avcrill Curdy. "Persona poems make up nearly half of this collection. Among those whose voices Curdy assumes are George Sandys, Alvar Nunez Cabeza da Vaca, Constance Fenimore Woolson, and John Audubon. . . . 'Dark Room,' the final poem in the collection, shifts the focus from human personae to the world itself as a kind of personality." (Commonweal)

REVIEW: *Commonweal* v141 no2 p28-9 Ja 24 2014 Nick Ripatrazone

"Song & Error". "[Averill] Curdy's language is soft: light flushes and touches; gardens seethe. . . . Curdy's personae work best as lenses rather than mirrors. We get stories told with a distinctive, self-revealing voice rather than outright self-portraiture. . . . While the personae poems give 'Song & Error' some of its breadth, the depth of Curdy's work is no less evident elsewhere in this collection—in poems such as 'Northwest Passage,' for example, where the range is narrow but not provincial, a fragment of history opening out into the actual. . . . What all the poems have in common is a sharp awareness of perspective. . . . Despite their deceptive modesty, they include multitudes."

REVIEW: *N Y Times Book Rev* p22 D 29 2013 Major Jackson

REVIEW: *Publ Wkly* v259 no52 p31 D 24 2012

CURLEY, ROBERT.ed. Architects of the information age. See Architects of the information age

CURLEY, ROBERT.ed. Breakthroughs in telephone technology. See Breakthroughs in telephone technology

CURRIE, PHILIP J.ed. Tyrannosaurid paleobiology. See Tyrannosaurid paleobiology

CURTIS, DEVON.ed. Peacebuilding, power, and politics in Africa. See Peacebuilding, power, and politics in Africa

CURTIS, VALERIE. Don't look, don't touch, don't eat; the science behind revulsion; [by] Valerie Curtis 184 p. 2013 University of Chicago Press

1. Aversion 2. Aversion—Social aspects 3. Evolutionary psychology 4. Hygiene—Psychological aspects 5. Science—Popular works 6. Subconsciousness

ISBN 9780226131337 (cloth: alkaline paper)

LC 2013-017713

SUMMARY: This book by Valerie Curtis describes how "There is a powerful subconscious reaction that influences a disturbingly wide range of our daily behaviour—our eating habits, our relationships, our values. The very same reaction that makes us draw back, lip curled, when we step on dog dirt is also constantly at play in our lives. . . . A raft of studies show it influences what we wear, what we eat, what products we buy, who we desire, and how we vote." (Publisher's note)

REVIEW: *TLS* no5791 p27 Mr 28 2014 NICOLA K. S.

DAVIS

"Don't Look, Don't Touch: The Science Behind Revulsion." "Much of our behaviour, Valerie Curtis points out in 'Don't Look, Don't Touch,' is devoted to the avoidance of parasites. . . . Yet for a book riddled with rancid and revolting things, 'Don't Look, Don't Touch' is surprisingly difficult to put down. . . . In a narrative peppered with revelations of how the animal kingdom copes with keeping clean . . . Curtis illustrates how disgust is not only a matter of nurture, but an emotion tied up in natural selection itself."

CUSHMAN, GREGORY T. Guano and the opening of the Pacific world; a global ecological history; [by] Gregory T. Cushman xxii, 392 p. 2013 Cambridge University Press

1. Guano—Environmental aspects—History 2. Guano—Peru—History 3. Guano—Social aspects—History 4. Guano industry—Pacific Area—History 5. Historical literature 6. Human ecology—History 7. Phosphate industry—History

ISBN 9781107004139 (hbk.)

LC 2012-010866

SUMMARY: "This book explores how the production and commodification of guano has shaped the modern Pacific Basin and the world's relationship to the region. Marrying traditional methods of historical analysis with a broad interdisciplinary approach, Gregory T. Cushman casts this once little-known commodity as an engine of Western industrialization offering new insight into uniquely modern developments such as environmental consciousness and conservation movements." (Publisher's note)

REVIEW: *Choice* v51 no5 p859 Ja 2014 R. Scaglion

REVIEW: *Science* v340 no6140 p1525-6 Je 28 2013 Frederick R. Davis

REVIEW: *TLS* no5775 p10-1 D 6 2013 DAVID ARMITAGE

"The Great Ocean: Pacific Worlds From Captain Cook to the Gold Rush" and "Guano and the Opening of the Pacific World." "David Igler's 'The Great Ocean' and Gregory T. Cushman's 'Guano and the Opening of the Pacific World' are some of the first waves of a gathering tsunami of scholarship on the Pacific world. . . . 'The Great Ocean' calculates the high price of proto-globalization in the Pacific. . . . Igler's topical approach can make the chronology of Pacific history hard to follow, but the pivotal periods are tolerably clear. . . . By turns illuminating and obsessive, Cushman's book traces every thread in the modem history of nitrates and phosphates from their origins in Peru, Chile and the Pacific islands outwards to Australasia, Britain and beyond."

CUSSLER, CLIVE. The bootlegger; an Isaac Bell adventure; [by] Clive Cussler 416 p. 2014 G.P. Putnam's Sons

1. Bell, Isaac (Fictitious character)—Fiction 2. Bootlegging 3. Detective & mystery stories 4. Private investigators—Fiction 5. Prohibition—Fiction

ISBN 0399167293; 9780399167294 (hardback)

LC 2013-044314

SUMMARY: In this book, by Clive Cussler and Justin Scott, "it is 1920, and both Prohibition and bootlegging are in full swing. When Isaac Bell's boss and lifelong friend Joseph Van Dorn is shot and nearly killed leading the high-speed chase of a rum-running vessel, Bell swears to him that he will hunt down the lawbreakers. . . . Bell is up against a team of Bolshevik assassins and saboteurs—and they are intent on overthrowing the government of the United States." (Publisher's note)

REVIEW: *Booklist* v110 no13 p20 Mr 1 2014 David Pitt

REVIEW: *Kirkus Rev* v82 no2 p304 Ja 15 2014

"The Bootlegger". "The seventh page-turner in the [Clive] Cussler series featuring indomitable detective Isaac Bell. . . . Cussler/[Justin] Scott do a bang-up job with characterizations in this historical action tale. . . . The plot's believable, and there are fistfights, knifings or a Lewis gun spitting bullets page after page. . . . Cussler and company love historical factoids—across the Long Island landscape, bootleggers and others prowl in Pierce-Arrows, Packards and Rolls Royces. . . . Great fun from one of the better Cussler series."

REVIEW: *Libr J* v138 no16 p56 O 1 2013 Barbara Hoffert

REVIEW: *Libr J* v139 no3 p94 F 15 2014 Cynde Suite

REVIEW: *Publ Wkly* v261 no2 p50-1 Ja 13 2014

CUTHBERTSON, GUY. Wilfred Owen; [by] Guy Cuthbertson 352 p. 2014 Yale University Press

1. Biography (Literary form) 2. Gay men—History—20th century 3. Poets, English—20th century—Biography 4. World War, 1914-1918—Great Britain—Literature and the war

ISBN 9780300153002 (hardback)

LC 2013-037642

SUMMARY: This biography of Wilfred Owen presents an "account of Owen's life and formative influences: the lower-middle-class childhood that he tried to escape; the places he lived in, from Birkenhead to Bordeaux; his class anxieties and his religious doubts; his sexuality and friendships; his close relationship with his mother and his childlike personality." (Publisher's note)

REVIEW: *Booklist* v110 no14 p45 Mr 15 2014 Ray Olson

"Wilfred Owen." "Granting that there are more thorough biographies of Owen, [Guy] Cuthbertson says he wishes to highlight Owen's life and character by focusing on the relationships of 'the child and the man,' 'the man and the poet-ry,' and 'the child and the western front.' . . . He accounts for why Owen could be initially dubious about the war yet join in it, be against it yet determined to fight and suffer with the troops under him. Most important for some, Cuthbertson argues that if, as gay advocates claim, Owen was homosexual, he wasn't what we now call a homosexual, whether open or closeted. Invaluable insight into a man whose words will be heard often during the upcoming WWI centennial."

REVIEW: *New Statesman* v143 no7 p42-4 F 21 2014 Rowan Williams

CUTLER, JUDITH. Double fault; [by] Judith Cutler 212 p. 2014 Severn House Pub Ltd

1. Detective & mystery stories 2. Marriage—Fiction 3. Missing children—Fiction 4. Murder investigation—Fiction 5. Policewomen—Fiction

ISBN 0727883399; 9780727883391

SUMMARY: In this book, part of Judth Cutler's Fran Harman series, "when a child goes missing at the local tennis club on the day when several skeletons are unearthed on an Ashford building site, Fran Harman finds her caseload heavier than ever at a time when the force is cripplingly short-staffed and she has a less than supportive new Chief Constable to contend with." (Publisher's note)

REVIEW: *Booklist* v110 no14 p52-3 Mr 15 2014 Barbara Bibel

"Double Fault." "Chief Superintendent Fran Harman is busy planning her wedding to her partner, Mark, who has retired from the force. Her load of cases is getting heavier due to budget cuts, and her chief constable is not at all supportive. While Mark is enjoying a tennis match with a group of seniors called the Golden Oldies, a young girl, the daughter of the tennis coach, disappears from the youth group on the adjacent court. . . . British-procedural fans will enjoy the latest installment in this series, which offers a nice blend of crime and domestic life."

REVIEW: *Kirkus Rev* v82 no4 p314 F 15 2014

CUTTER, NICK. The troop; [by] Nick Cutter 368 p. 2014 Gallery Books

1. Boy Scouts—Fiction 2. Genetic engineering—Fiction 3. Horror tales 4. Tapeworm infections 5. Transgenic animals

ISBN 9781476717715 (hardcover); 9781476717722 (mass market)

LC 2013-011673

SUMMARY: In this horror novel by Scotiabank Giller Prize monminee Craig Davidson, writing as Nick Cutter, "five teenage boy scouts and one adult scoutmaster [are] camping on a supposedly uninhabited island off of the edge of PEI. They encounter a man infected by a tapeworm that's been genetically modified into an ultra-fast weight-loss agent and killing machine." (Quill & Quire)

REVIEW: *Kirkus Rev* v81 no19 p42 O 1 2013

REVIEW: *Libr J* v138 no16 p71 O 1 2013 Matt Schirano

REVIEW: *Publ Wkly* v260 no43 p38 O 28 2013

REVIEW: *Quill Quire* v80 no1 p32 Ja/F 2014 Alex Good

"The Troop". "Scotiabank Giller Prize nominee Craig Davidson couldn't have come up with a less inspired pseudonym than Nick Cutter for this pure-genre outing, but that's the only knock against an otherwise outstanding tale of terror, full of chills, thrills, and very good kills. . . . Every horror novel has to operate within convention, and 'The Troop' is no different. . . . Familiarity comes with the territory; the only question is whether it all works. And in this case it does, marvellously. Cutter has crafted a story that plays to his strengths. . . . Strong characters, a snappy narrative, a wonderfully disgusting monster, and an obvious delight in going over the top with the gore all add up to one of the best horror novels of the decade."

CUYLER, MARGERY. Skeleton for Dinner; [by] Margery Cuyler 32 p. 2013 Albert Whitman & Co

1. Dinners & dining 2. Ghost stories 3. Halloween—Juvenile fiction 4. Picture books for children 5. Skeleton 6. Witches—Juvenile fiction

ISBN 0807573981; 9780807573983

SUMMARY: In this children's picture book, "Big Witch and Little Witch brew a stew and prepare a list of the guests to invite for dinner. What follows is a kind of Halloween version of Chicken Little, as timid Skeleton misunderstands, believing he's an ingredient, not a guest. He dashes off to warn two friends--Ghost, a wispy girl, and Ghoul, who resembles Quasimodo." (Publishers Weekly)

REVIEW: *Booklist* v110 no3 p102 O 1 2013 Kat Kan

REVIEW: *Horn Book Magazine* v89 no5 p65 S/O 2013 SIÂN GAETANO

"Skeleton For Dinner." "As the stew simmers, Big Witch--impressed by their tasty concoction--states that they simply 'must have Skeleton for dinner.' Skeleton, passing by, misinterprets her statement and fears the worst. What follows is a comedy of errors in which the childlike skeleton attempts to save itself (and its other friends on the invitation list) from being eaten. The occasionally rhyming verse, along with some changes in text size and font, creates a natural rhythm for Halloween-themed read-alouds."

REVIEW: *Kirkus Rev* v81 no15 p239 Ag 1 2013

REVIEW: *Publ Wkly* v260 no29 p64 Jl 22 2013

CYBERPSYCHOLOGY AND NEW MEDIA; a thematic reader; xviii, 242 p. 2014 Psychology Press

1. Cyberspace—Psychological aspects 2. Internet—Psychological aspects 3. Internet—Social aspects 4. Internet users—Psychology 5. Psychological literature 6. Psychology—Computer network resources

ISBN 9781848721654 (hb); 9781848721661 (pb)

LC 2013-012645

SUMMARY: "This volume collects various studies and theories associated with the study of cyberpsychology—which [Andrew] Power and [Gráinne] Kinvan . . . define as the study of 'how we interact with others using technology, how our behavior is influenced by technology, and how our psychological states can be affected by technologies." (Choice: Current Reviews for Academic Libraries)

REVIEW: *Choice* v51 no8 p1493-4 Ap 2014 N. D. Bowman

"Cyberpsychology and New Media: A Thematic Reader". "The literature reviews are solid; they are comprehensive and precise without being loaded down by extraneous citations. Indeed, any one of them would make excellent course material for students looking to orient themselves to the general field of cyberpsychology. However, a major drawback of the volume is the quality of the studies themselves: many suffer from convenience sampling, underpowered statistical models, and questionable data interpretation and seem to replicate rather than extend understanding of cyberpsychology. As a result, the reports of the studies tend to distract from rather than complement the theory in this reader."

CYRINO, MONICA S.ed. Screening love and sex in the ancient world. See Screening love and sex in the ancient world

CYRUS, KURT. Motor dog; [by] Kurt Cyrus 40 p. 2014 Disney-Hyperion Books

1. Cats—Fiction 2. Dogs—Fiction 3. Humorous stories 4. Robots—Fiction 5. Stories in rhyme

ISBN 1423168224; 9781423168225

LC 2013-010687

SUMMARY: Written by Kurt Cyrus and illustrated by David George Gordon, "This one's a tale of a boy and his robotic best (canine) friend. When Scoot the Cat comes on the scene, Motor Dog does what any normal dog would do: gives chase! Our boy Flip does everything he can to call him off, but no commands-verbal or electronic-can stop his new dog. When Flip runs after his malfunctioning pet, things go haywire!" (Publisher's note)

REVIEW: *Kirkus Rev* v82 no1 p124 Ja 1 2014

"Motor Dog". "A boy named Flip orders a robotic dog from the Internet in this cleverly rhymed story that manages to be both original in concept and conventional in portraying the bond between boy and dog. The snappy, effective text will grab readers with its bouncy rhythm and catchy rhymes, , like Motor Dog/catalog and extra stuff/ruff! ruff! . . . The bold illustrations are full of motion and varied perspectives, with sound-effect words set in red display type. An amusing fable for the techno-savvy and Luddites alike."

CZEKALSKI, TRAVIS.il. Summer at the Z House. See Zanville, H.

CZUKAS, LIZ. Ask again later; [by] Liz Czukas 336 p. 2014 HarperTeen, an imprint of HarperCollinsPublishers
1. Chance 2. Dating (Social customs)—Fiction 3. Gay teenagers 4. Proms—Fiction 5. Young adult fiction, American
ISBN 9780062272393 (pbk.)
LC 2013-005073

SUMMARY: In this book by Liz Czukas, "Heart LaCoeur had planned to go to prom with a group of friends—as the No Drama Prom-a Crew—but suddenly gets two other invitations. Heart's brother promises her to his recently dumped best friend, and her friend Ryan confesses that he's gay and asks her to be his platonic date. . . . She waffles and finally flips a coin. The remainder of the book alternates between the two paths." (Publishers Weekly)

REVIEW: *Booklist* v110 no11 p63 F 1 2014 Ann Kelley

REVIEW: *Bull Cent Child Books* v67 no7 p353-4 Mr 2014 A. A.

REVIEW: *Kirkus Rev* v82 no3 p68 F 1 2014

"Ask Again Later". " In her debut, [Liz] Czukas gives readers a glimpse of a genuine comedic voice and surprisingly well-developed characters, but much of the book's promise is lost, victim of its own contrivance, in a choose-your-own-prom adventure without actual choices. Some genuinely laugh-out-loud moments are scattered throughout the unevenly paced narrative. This may work for readers seeking a cute and frothy prom-night romp, but anyone looking for something more substantial will be disappointed. Great characters in search of a less gimmicky narrative."

REVIEW: *Publ Wkly* v261 no1 p58 Ja 6 2014

REVIEW: *SLJ* v60 no3 p156 Mr 2014 Nicole Knott

REVIEW: *Voice of Youth Advocates* v36 no6 p57 F 2014 Cynthia Winfield

D

DABIJA, VIOLETA.il. A leaf can be. See A leaf can be

DAGERMAN, STIG. Sleet; selected stories; [by] Stig Dagerman 176 p. 2013 David R. Godine
1. Automobiles—Fiction 2. Children—Fiction 3. Children—Sweden 4. Short story (Literary form) 5. Swedish fiction—Translations into English
ISBN 1567924468; 9781567924466
LC 2012-043446

SUMMARY: "This selection, containing a number of new translations [by Steven Hartman] of [author Stig] Dagerman's stories never before published in English, is unified by the theme of the loss of innocence. Often narrated from a child's perspective, the stories give voice to childhood's tender state of receptiveness and joy tinged with longing and loneliness." (Publisher's note)

REVIEW: *TLS* no5777/8 p26 D 20 2013

"Sleet." "Stig Dagerman's first collection of short stories, 'Nattens lekar' ('The Games of Night') was first published in 1947 when the author was twenty-four. Now, almost seventy years later, we have 'Sleet,' a collection of a dozen short stories, superbly translated by Steven Hartman. . . . Dagerman has a gift for expressing the horrors and humiliations of children, as well as the impact this has on their future lives. . . . Dagerman's beautifully understated tales show that the world children are subjected to can often be a disastrous product of the adults who created it."

REVIEW: *World Lit Today* v87 no6 p67 N/D 2013

DAHL, ERIK J. Intelligence and surprise attack; failure and success from Pearl Harbor to 9/11 and beyond; [by] Erik J. Dahl x, 277 p. 2013 Georgetown University Press
1. Human intelligence (Intelligence service) 2. Intelligence service—United States 3. Military literature 4. National security—United States 5. Surprise (Military science)
ISBN 9781589019980 (pbk.: alk. paper)
LC 2012-042488

SUMMARY: In this book on surprise attacks, "the author maintains that piecing together intelligence information rarely undermines surprise attacks, and too much information (known as 'noise') is not the cause of defensive intelligence failures. The most effective keys to defensive success, according to [Erik J.] Dahl, are the receptivity of policy makers to intelligence warnings and greater usage of human intelligence ('humint')." (Choice: Current Reviews for Academic Libraries)

REVIEW: *Choice* v51 no8 p1486 Ap 2014 A. Klinghoffer

"Intelligence and Surprise Attack: Failure and Successes From Pearl Harbor to 9/11 and Beyond". "This factual, organized, and well-argued account by [Erik J.] Dahl . . . a former naval intelligence officer, is a welcome contribution. . . . This volume is excellent, but includes two minor weaknesses. One is the meaning of 'success' or 'failure'; these terms are used in a confusing manner as they are applied to the perpetrators as well as the defenders. The other is too much emphasis on dichotomy, as states using conventional methods may also use terrorists as proxies. . . . Despite some problems, this book is highly recommended for both intelligence analysts and policy makers."

REVIEW: *Libr J* v138 no16 p88 O 1 2013 Mark Jones

DAHL, ROALD, 1916-1990. Boy; tales of childhood; [by] Roald Dahl 176 1988 Penguin Bks.
1. Authors 2. Authors—Education 3. Autobiographies 4. Children 5. Children's authors 6. Short story writers
ISBN 0-14-008917-9 pa

SUMMARY: Roald Dahl's "autobiography of his first 20 years of life begins with a brief description of his parents' backgrounds, including his father's death when Dahl was only three years old. Dahl then moves into short memories from his childhood and school days beginning with his year in kindergarten and then the move to Llandaff Cathedral

School. . . . The final section includes memories of his teen years at Repton School and his first job outside of school with the Shell Company." (Children's Literature)

REVIEW: *Booklist* v110 no12 p96 F 15 2014 Joyce Saricks

"Boy: Tales of Childhood" and "Going Solo." "Among Penguin Audio's fresh recordings of [Roald] Dahl's fiction are new releases of his autobiographical titles, 'Boy: Tales of Childhood' and 'Going Solo,' both enthusiastically narrated by [Dan] Stevens. Written for a middle-school audience, these are not autobiographies, which, according to Dahl's introduction, contain only boring details. He's correct: these are anything but boring. . . . 'Going Solo' offers more adventurous episodes, including encounters with deadly snakes in Africa and his exploits as a pilot during WWII. Stevens' companionable voice enlivens these anecdotes and draws listeners into the life of this consummate storyteller. His matter-of-fact narration matches Dahl's prose and sangfroid."

REVIEW: *SLJ* v60 no1 p55 Ja 2014 Michaela Schied

DAHL, ROALD, 1916-1990. Going solo; [by] Roald Dahl 207 1986 Farrar, Straus & Giroux

1. Authors 2. Authors, English 3. Autobiographies 4. Children's authors 5. Short story writers 6. World War, 1939-1945—Personal narratives

LC 86-1-2022

SUMMARY: In this book, author Roald Dahl "offers his impressions of Tanzania, where he sailed to work for the Shell Oil Company in 1938. At the outbreak of World War II, he volunteered for the RAF and trained as a fighter pilot. Posted to his squadron in Greece, Dahl was chagrined to learn he was one of only 14 pilots who made up the RAF in that theater. He describes the attempts of this small group of British pilots to survive both the Luftwaffe and their own superiors." (Library Journal)

REVIEW: *Booklist* v110 no12 p96 F 15 2014 Joyce Saricks

"Boy: Tales of Childhood" and "Going Solo." "Among Penguin Audio's fresh recordings of [Roald] Dahl's fiction are new releases of his autobiographical titles, 'Boy: Tales of Childhood' and 'Going Solo,' both enthusiastically narrated by [Dan] Stevens. Written for a middle-school audience, these are not autobiographies, which, according to Dahl's introduction, contain only boring details. He's correct: these are anything but boring. . . . 'Going Solo' offers more adventurous episodes, including encounters with deadly snakes in Africa and his exploits as a pilot during WWII. Stevens' companionable voice enlivens these anecdotes and draws listeners into the life of this consummate storyteller. His matter-of-fact narration matches Dahl's prose and sangfroid."

DAHL, VICTORIA. Turn Up the Heat. See Foster, L.

DAHLSTROM, DANIEL O. The Heidegger dictionary; [by] Daniel O. Dahlstrom xi, 312 p. 2013 Bloomsbury

1. Encyclopedias & dictionaries 2. Influence (Literary, artistic, etc.) 3. Phenomenology 4. Philosophical literature

ISBN 9781441171023 (epub); 9781847065131 (hardback); 9781847065148 (paperback)

LC 2012-021337

SUMMARY: This dictionary on philosopher Martin Heidegger "covers all his major works, ideas and influences and provides a firm grounding in the central themes of Heidegger's thought. . . . A-Z entries include . . .definitions of all the key terms used in Heidegger's writings and detailed synopses of his key works. The Dictionary also includes entries on Heidegger's major philosophical influences." (Publisher's note)

REVIEW: *Choice* v51 no5 p799 Ja 2014 R. E. Kraft

"The Heidegger Dictionary." "A much-needed beginners guide to [Martin] Heidegger that covers the thoughts, conventions, and linguistic terminology across the whole of his work. The individual entries, which are both accessible and cited, surely will be useful to someone struggling with a problematic term. On occasion Dahlstrom uses his own idiosyncratic translations, such as 'on-handness' for Vorhandenheit. . . . This will be a handy resource for those in the early or middle stages of work on Heidegger, but may end up being more frustrating than not for those who are further along."

DAILEY, PATRICIA. Promised bodies; time, language, and corporeality in medieval women's mystical texts; [by] Patricia Dailey 260 p. 2013 Columbia University Press

1. Christian literature—Women authors—History and criticism 2. Hadewijch, 13th century 3. Historical literature 4. Mysticism—History—Middle Ages, 600-1500 5. Women mystics

ISBN 9780231161206 (cloth : alk. paper)

LC 2012-050242

SUMMARY: In this book, "Patricia Dailey connects the embodied poetics of Hadewijch [of Brabant's] visions, writings, and letters to the work of Julian of Norwich, Hildegard of Bingen, Marguerite of Oingt, and other mystics and visionaries. . . . By underscoring the similarities between men's and women's writings of the time, [she] collapses traditional conceptions of gender as they relate to differences in style, language, interpretative practices, forms of literacy, and uses of textuality." (Publisher's note)

REVIEW: *Choice* v51 no6 p1021-2 F 2014 G. H. Shriver

"Promised Bodies: Time, Language and Corporeality in Medieval Women's Mystical Texts." "In this insightful book, [Patricia] Dailey . . . centers her attention on the Beguine Hadewijch Brabant and her writings, which reflect her theological context in the 12th and 13th centuries. . . . Hadewijch's mystical works express their meaning in the smaller community of Beguines as well as the larger social community. In this unique volume, Dailey successfully shows how 'letter and body are interconnected' in medieval mystical writings. Excellent and very full notes. . . . Highly recommended."

DALBY, ANDREW. The Breakfast Book; [by] Andrew Dalby 256 p. 2013 The University of Chicago Press

1. Breakfast cereals 2. Breakfasts 3. Food—Marketing 4. Food habits 5. Food in literature

ISBN 1780230869 (hardcover); 9781780230863 (hardcover)

SUMMARY: This book, by Andrew Dalby, discusses breakfast. "Breakfast is the most important meal of the day. It's also one of the most diverse, varying greatly from family to family and region to region, even while individuals tend to eat the same thing every day. . . . Taking a multifaceted approach to the story of the morning meal, [the book] collects narratives of breakfast in an attempt to pin down the mottled history of eating in the A.M." (Publisher's note)

REVIEW: *Booklist* v109 no14 p38 Mr 15 2013 Mark Knoblauch

REVIEW: *TLS* no5750 p36 Je 14 2013 J. C.

"The Night," "After the Night," and "The Breakfast Book." "It was with pleasure . . . that we encountered 'The Night/After the Night,' two slim volumes published as one by Book Works of East London. . . . The desire to leap back and forth between the original and its upstart English doppelgänger becomes compulsive. . . . The image comes from 'The Breakfast Book' by Andrew Dalby. . . In case all that brain and brawn should prove too tempting, Mr Dalby inserts a cautionary follow-up from 'Jane Eyre'."

DALE, PENNY. Dinosaur rescue; [by] Penny Dale 32 p. 2013 Nosy Crow

1. Dinosaurs—Juvenile fiction 2. Emergency vehicles 3. Picture books for children 4. Railroads—Juvenile literature 5. Rescue work—Fiction
ISBN 076366829X; 9780763668297
LC 2012-950617

SUMMARY: In this children's picture book, "a dinosaur passenger train is chugging along, but unbeknownst to the engineer, an orange pickup truck is stuck on the tracks up ahead. Dinos from the truck try pushing it off the tracks, but they have to hurriedly call Dinosaur Rescue for assistance. Emergency vehicles, including a fire truck, a police car, and a helicopter, quickly drive or fly in to help as the train bears down." (Booklist)

REVIEW: *Booklist* v110 no6 p51-3 N 15 2013 Maryann Owen

"Dinosaur Rescue!" "Bright endpapers with colorful illustrations of 10 labeled dinosaurs will immediately capture young dinosaur buffs and lead readers into a breath-stopping emergency. . . . Repetition in the text makes this story a great read-aloud, and the bold watercolor-and-pencil double-page-spread illustrations will catch and hold young children's attention. The concluding endpapers feature the five emergency vehicles plus the train and truck. An exciting tale that will be requested more than once."

REVIEW: *Kirkus Rev* v81 no17 p84 S 1 2013

REVIEW: *SLJ* v59 no10 p1 O 2013 Krista Welz

DALE, PENNY.il. Dinosaur rescue. See Dale, P.

DALE, STEVE.ed. Decoding Your Dog. See Decoding Your Dog

DALES, DOUGLAS. Alcuin; Theology and Thought; [by] Douglas Dales 360 p. 2013 David Brown Book Co

1. Alcuin, 735-804 2. Clergy—Great Britain 3. Historical literature 4. Poets—History 5. Theology—History
ISBN 0227173945; 9780227173947

SUMMARY: This book by Douglas Dales explores the theology of Alcuin, a "scholar, ecclesiastic, teacher and poet of the eighth century." (Publisher's note) It discusses "Alcuin's achievement in making the complexities of Augustine and much else intelligible in a different world, which was already under Viking attack as he wrote." (Times Literary Supplement)

REVIEW: *TLS* no5752 p26 Je 28 2013 LUCY BECKETT

"Alcuin: Theology and Thought." "[Alcuin's][major contribution was . . . the writing of scriptural commentaries, devotional books and textbooks . . . in all of which he clarified, shortened and simplified . . . the inheritance from the patristic and the classical past. . . . Douglas Dales's much-needed new book--he has already published 'Alcuin: His life and legacy' (2012)--gives a thorough and careful account of all this, with full scholarly apparatus and a warm appreciation of Alcuin's achievement in making the complexities of Augustine and much else intelligible in a different world, which was already under Viking attack as he wrote."

D'ALESSANDRO, STEPHANIE. Magritte. See Magritte

DALEY, MICHAEL J. Pinch and Dash make soup; [by] Michael J. Daley 48 p. 2012 Charlesbridge

1. Animals—Fiction 2. Animals—Juvenile fiction 3. Cooking 4. Cooking (Spices) 5. Cooking—Fiction 6. Cooking—Juvenile fiction 7. Cooperativeness—Fiction 8. Cooperativeness—Juvenile fiction 9. Friendship—Fiction 10. Friendship—Juvenile fiction 11. Illustrated children's books 12. Restaurants 13. Soups 14. Soups—Fiction 15. Soups—Juvenile fiction
ISBN 1580893465 (reinforced); 1580893473 (softcover); 9781580893466 (reinforced for library use); 9781580893473 (softcover)
LC 2011-003473

SUMMARY: In this book, "Pinch (an unidentified, vaguely gopher-ish critter) is hungry, and his fridge contains only a potato, spinach, and cheese. Too lazy to walk all the way to the Chat and Chew Café, he instead makes his way to friend Dash's house. . . . He prudently brings along some hot sauce and pepper, however, knowing that Dash doesn't share Pinch's love for spicy heat. Dash (another unidentified animal) is indeed cooking, but his soup is pretty thin, so Pinch offers his potato, and then, one by one, the rest of his stores. Both Pinch and Dash in turn secretly slip extra heat into the dish, and the resulting soup is so spicy as to be ruined, so the two end up amiably heading to the Chat and Chew after all." (Bulletin of the Center for Children's Books)

REVIEW: *Bull Cent Child Books* v65 no7 p345 Mr 2012 J. H.

"Pinch and Dash Make Soup." "Beginning readers who need a lot of flash and action will not find it here, but those youngsters who appreciate a quieter approach will find this enjoyable. Daley's effective use of repeated words and phrases, simple vocabulary, and grouping of events into four short chapters make this very accessible to novices, while the gentle situational humor will also help facilitate readers' digestion of this easy reader. Yezerski's line-and-watercolor illustrations are loosely low-key as well, with muted shades of golds, browns, blues, and greens punctuated with slightly scratchy thin black outlines. For instructional use, or for kids who like their entertainment on the mild side, this is a solid little title."

REVIEW: *Kirkus Rev* v80 no1 p2431 Ja 1 2012

REVIEW: *SLJ* v58 no2 p86 F 2012 Amy Commers

DALEY, MICHAEL P.ed. Enjoy The Experience. See Enjoy The Experience

DALLEO, RAPHAEL.ed. Haiti and the Americas. See Haiti and the Americas

DALTON, DAVID, 1945-. To hell and back; an autobiography; [by] David Dalton 285 p. 1999 Regan Books
1. Autobiographies 2. Drug abuse 3. Music industry 4. Rock musicians—United States—Biography
ISBN 0060392932 (hc.)
LC 9904-8892

SUMMARY: This book presents an autobiography of the rock musician Meat Loaf, born Marvin Lee Aday. Unflatteringly nicknamed 'Meat Loaf' by his alcoholic father . . . no one pegged this misfit kid to become a rock star. That is, until he recorded the third best-selling album of all time. . . . In a swirl of devious managers, drugs, lawyers, guns, money, nervous breakdowns (including the psychosomatic loss of his voice), and more lawsuits than he could count, Meat Loaf lost it all." (Publisher's note)

REVIEW: *Booklist* v110 no9/10 p42 Ja 1 2014 DAVID WRIGHT

"To Hell and Back," "The Wishbones," and "The Night Train." "Tom Perrotta captures my neighbor's vibe perfectly in his first novel, 'The Wishbones'. . . . Dave's stairway to purgatory is hilarious and familiar to pretty much everyone who isn't a rock star. . . . [James] Brown's gargantuan presence looms large over two novels that deal with the universality of music. In Clive Edgerton's 'The Night Train,' it is young Dwayne's all-consuming desire to be James Brown that lures him across the color line in 1963 North Carolina. . . . 'To Hell and Back' is truly irresistible. Imagine being stuck in an elevator with Mr. [Meat] Loaf while he tells you about the amazing, tragicomic train wreck that is his life. You can't look away. With 17 brain concussions to his name. Meat proves to be every bit the poster child for testosterone poisoning that you'd expect."

DALTON, PHILIP. Coarseness in U.S. public communication. See Kramer, E.

DALY, MARY.ed. Lifecycle events and their consequences. See Lifecycle events and their consequences

DAMAREN, CHRISTOPHER J. Spacecraft dynamics and control. See De Ruiter, A. H. J.

DAMICO, GINA. Croak; [by] Gina Damico 311 p. 2012 Houghton Mifflin Harcourt
1. Death 2. Death—Fiction 3. Future life—Fiction 4. Grim Reaper (Symbolic character) 5. Justice 6. Mystery in literature 7. Paranormal fiction 8. Young adult fiction
ISBN 9780547608327
LC 2011-017125

SUMMARY: This book tells the story of "sixteen-year-old bad girl Lex Bartleby [who] is shipped off to her uncle Mort's farm, supposedly to figure out her anger issues with the help of manual labor. Instead, she learns that "farmer" Mort is a reaper of another kind entirely and that, as mayor of Croak, a small collection of Grim Reapers, he will be teaching Lex the family business. Although she initially takes to ferrying souls into the Afterlife with aplomb, Lex begins to question the roles of Reapers as silent witnesses to the world's injustices, especially when their knowledge of people's deaths would allow them to wreak karmic justice upon the murderers and rapists that otherwise get away with their crimes." (Bulletin of the Center for Children's Books)

REVIEW: *Booklist* v108 no14 p58 Mr 15 2012 Lynn Rutan

REVIEW: *Bull Cent Child Books* v65 no7 p345-6 Mr 2012 K. Q. G.

"Croak." "Damico nicely balances the grim subject matter with a heavy dose of humor, and the third-person narration provides some deadpan perspective on Lex's absurd situation that gives the story an appealing tall-tale feel. The macabre comedy extends to the setting . . . and a host of eccentric, death-obsessed folk, but under all this dry wit lies an intricate and imaginative construction of the afterlife that is as amusing as it is unique. Both Lex and the reader are presented with a very real ethical dilemma . . . and the surprising conclusion will leave readers with plenty of questions while laying the groundwork for the second installment. Fans who thought McBride's 'Hold Me Closer, Necromancer' . . . was to die for will find this one equally croak-worthy."

REVIEW: *Kirkus Rev* v80 no4 p391 F 15 2012

"Croak." "A teen hellion realizes her calling as a grim reaper in this derivative but enjoyable novel set in an unusual town in upstate New York. . . . Many of the details here have a distinctly Potteresque feel--Lex is the most powerful Grim in a millennia, but bears similarity to a legendarily terrible villain. However, the central mystery is genuinely puzzling, and Lex's narrative voice is funny and fresh--'Maybe this was one of those things that people should keep to themselves, like a hatred of baby pandas or a passion for polka music.' An unexpectedly (and frustratingly) abrupt conclusion leaves no doubt that there will be a sequel. Fantasy fans who like their tales gritty and filled with irreverent humor will be eager for the follow-up."

REVIEW: *Publ Wkly* v259 no5 p57 Ja 30 2012

REVIEW: *SLJ* v58 no4 p158 Ap 2012 Gretchen Kolderup

REVIEW: *Voice of Youth Advocates* v34 no5 p508 D 2011 Taryn Bush

D'AMICO, STEFANO. Spanish Milan; a city within the empire, 1535-1706; [by] Stefano D'Amico xiv, 249 p. 2012 Palgrave Macmillan
1. Historical literature 2. Imperialism 3. Spaniards—Italy—Milan—History
ISBN 9781137003829 (alk. paper)
LC 2012-006116

SUMMARY: "This study reworks the traditional narrative depicting Spanish rule as the primary factor of decadence in seventeenth-century Italy: in reality the Spanish monarchy provided new opportunities for wealth and prosperity to Milan and its elites. The city took advantage of its new important strategic and financial functions within the Spanish empire and used its extended network to maintain a primary economic and political role in Europe." (Publisher's note)

REVIEW: *Am Hist Rev* v119 no1 p266-7 F 2014 Gabriel Guarino

"Spanish Milan: A City Within the Empire, 1535-1706". "Stefano D'Amico's book fills a gap within this literature by offering a much-needed revisionist account of Milan in the sixteenth and seventeenth centuries, when it was regarded as one of Spain's most cherished possessions. Indeed, D'Amico's study successfully debunks Milan's decadent and abject image. . . . The author skillfully employs an impressive variety of original documents, both archival and in print. . . . His careful handling of the secondary literature, in several European languages, is equally impressive. . . . The book is very well organized. . . . The book ultimately excels not only in locating Milan's place within the Spanish Empire but also in placing Milan into its wider Italian and European contexts."

REVIEW: *Choice* v50 no10 p1915 Je 2013 E. A. Sanabria

DAMROSCH, LEO. Jonathan Swift; his life and his world; [by] Leo Damrosch 573 p. 2013 Yale University Press

1. Authors, Irish—18th century—Biography 2. Historical literature 3. Ireland—Intellectual life 4. Satirists, Irish

ISBN 0300164998; 9780300164992 (clothbound: alk. paper)

LC 2013-013063

SUMMARY: "In this . . . biography, Leo Damrosch draws on discoveries made over the past thirty years to tell the story of [Jonathan] Swift's life anew. Probing holes in the existing evidence, he takes seriously some daring speculations about Swift's parentage, love life, and various personal relationships and shows how Swift's public version of his life—the one accepted until recently—was deliberately misleading." (Publisher's note)

REVIEW: *Am Sch* v83 no1 p125-7 Wint 2014 GEORGE O'BRIEN

"Jonathan Swift: His Life and His World". "[Leo] Damrosch happily pursues 'daring speculations about [Swift's] family and his relationships that differ radically from the official story.' . . . Such excursions into the unknowable are ultimately less interesting than the challenging openness of what Swift has to say, and perhaps more attention might have been given to masks in relation to outspokenness. . . . When the focus changes to Swift's public life, 'Jonathan Swift: His Life and His World' forgoes its speculative inclinations and gives a well-paced but somewhat unexceptional account."

REVIEW: *Choice* v51 no10 p1800 Je 2014 J. T. Lynch

REVIEW: *Kirkus Rev* v82 no1 p48 Ja 1 2014

"Jonathan Swift: His Life and His World". "A feisty, first-class life of the sage and scourge of English Literature. . . . [Leo] Damrosch . . . is bent on both correcting the record and adding to it, creating a fresh and vivid life even as he wrestles with previous biographers—namely Irvin Ehrenpreis—along the way. . . . Damrosch also amply scrutinizes Swift's inner life. . . . Damrosch gets close to Swift as both a talented author and a man, detailing his frustrations, habits and multiple physical torments from deafness, vertigo and a variety of odd ailments."

REVIEW: *Libr J* v138 no21 p101 D 1 2013 Elizabeth Heffington

REVIEW: *London Rev Books* v36 no8 p33-4 Ap 17 2014 Thomas Keymer

REVIEW: *N Y Rev Books* v60 no20 p55-7 D 19 2013 Fintan O'Toole

REVIEW: *N Y Times Book Rev* p22 D 1 2013 JOHN SIMON

REVIEW: *N Y Times Book Rev* p24 S 21 2014 IHSAN TAYLOR

REVIEW: *Natl Rev* v66 no2 p38-9 F 10 2014 JOHN J. MILLER

REVIEW: *New Statesman* v142 no5187 p40-1 D 6 2013 Jonathan Bate

REVIEW: *New Statesman* v142 no5188 p40-1 12/092013 Jonathan Bate

REVIEW: *New Yorker* v89 no47 p79-1 F 3 2014

"Jonathan Swift." "Swift 'liked to be mysterious toward everyone,' [author Leo] Damrosch writes, in a biography that aims at sweeping away misconceptions, many of which were encouraged by the man himself. The result might have made for tedious reading, but Damrosch writes with wit and constructs a compelling portrait of the Irish clergyman, whose satires delighted and scandalized eighteenth-century Britain. . . . Contradiction defined his character: he detested Ireland but did much to forge its national identity."

REVIEW: *Publ Wkly* v260 no39 p59 S 30 2013

DAN SMYER YU. The spread of Tibetan Buddhism in China; charisma, money, enlightenment; [by] Dan Smyer Yu xi, 193 p. 2012 Routledge

1. Buddhism—China—History—20th century 2. Buddhism—China—Tibet Autonomous Region 3. POLITICAL SCIENCE—General 4. Religion and sociology—China 5. SOCIAL SCIENCE—Ethnic Studies—General 6. Social science literature

ISBN 9780203803431 (ebook); 9780415575324 (alk. paper)

LC 2011-011730

SUMMARY: This book, "focusing on contemporary Tibetan Buddhist revivals in the Tibetan regions of the Sichuan and Qinghai Provinces in China . . . explores the intricate entanglements of the Buddhist revivals with cultural identity, state ideology, and popular imagination of Tibetan Buddhist spirituality in contemporary China. In turn, the author explores the broader socio-cultural implications of such revivals." (Publisher's note)

REVIEW: *Choice* v50 no2 p296 O 2012 F. J. Hoffman

REVIEW: *Current Anthropology* v55 no1 p128-9 F 2014 David A. Palmer

"The Spread of Tibetan Buddhism in China: Charisma, Money, Enlightenment". "Unbeknownst to most observers . . . has been the increasing popularity of Tibetan Buddhism among the Han Chinese. 'The Spread of Tibetan Buddhism in China' by Dan Smyer Yü is the first account of this phenomenon. It is based on fieldwork conducted in the mountains and grasslands of Eastern Tibet as well as in Han cities and in Chinese cyberspace. . . . More than a rich ethnographic account that complicates our stereotypes of Tibetan masters, Chinese tourists, and Western spiritual seekers, this book offers a treasure-trove of thought-provoking reflections on anthropological theories of charisma, landscape, money, spirituality, and globalization."

DANCE, JENNIFER. Red Wolf; [by] Jennifer Dance 256 p. 2014 Dundurn

ISBN 1459708105 (pbk.); 9781459708105 (pbk.)

SUMMARY: This book, "set in the mid-1880s, . . . is the story of an Anishnaabe boy who is taken to a residential school at the age of five and endures the evils of that system. His story runs parallel to, and occasionally intersects with, that of an orphaned young wolf named Crooked Ear. The tale is mostly told from the perspectives of these two main characters, though it occasionally strays into a minor participant's point of view." (Quill & Quire)

REVIEW: *Publ Wkly* v260 no48 p58 N 25 2013

REVIEW: *Quill Quire* v80 no2 p38 Mr 2014 John Wilson

"Red Wolf". "Red Wolf's experiences at the school, where he is forced to give up his own culture for one that will never accept him, are a good composite of the many horrors and abuses that tens of thousands of native children suffered. The portrayal of Crooked Ear, on the other hand, is overly anthropomorphized, and the descriptions of animal behaviour are flawed. . . . [Jennifer] Dance's fervently held beliefs and understandable disgust with residential schools overwhelm the story. The characters are either very good or very bad, and this oversimplification tends to make them clichéd ciphers who stand in for the wrongs of the school system or the doomed spirituality of the native way of life."

REVIEW: *SLJ* v60 no3 p137 Mr 2014 Elizabeth Nicolai

DANDELION, PINK.ed. The Oxford handbook of Quaker studies . See The Oxford handbook of Quaker studies

D'ANDRADE, HUGH.il. The Grimm conclusion. See The Grimm conclusion

DANISH FOLKTALES, LEGENDS, AND OTHER STORIES; 280 p. 2013 University of Washington Press

1. Denmark—Social life & customs 2. Folk literature 3. Kristensen, Evald Tang 4. Legends—Denmark 5. Tales—Denmark

ISBN 9780295992594 (cloth : alk. paper)

LC 2012-051593

SUMMARY: This book presents "a collection of translated and annotated Nordic folklore that presents full repertoires of five storytellers along with extensive archival material. The printed book presents some of the most compelling stories of these five important storytellers along with historical and biographical introductions. . . . The basis of the work is the collection of Evald Tang Kristensen (1843-1929)." (Publisher's note)

REVIEW: *Choice* v51 no10 p1805 Je 2014 J. Sundquist

REVIEW: *TLS* no5766 p5 O 4 2013 PAUL BINDING

"Danish Folktales, Legends and Other Stories." "Evald Tang Kristensen [is] the collector and folklore scholar at the centre of Timothy R. Tangherlini's fascinating, cohesive and timely book. . . . As Tangherlini shrewdly points out . . . the character of the collector plays a part in the way the narrative proceeds. . . . After a full, informative introduction, Tangherlini gives us generous selections from five of Tang Kristensen's most productive informants, three men and two women. . . . Many of the stories are essentially anecdotal . . . and some stories are ambitious, lengthy narratives, raising interesting questions about sources and kin."

DANNA, JEN J. A flame in the wind of death; Abott and Lowell Forensic Mysteries; [by] Jen J. Danna 2014 Five Star, a part of Gale, Cengage Learning

1. Detective & mystery stories 2. Forensic anthropologists—Fiction 3. Halloween—Salem (Mass.)—Fiction 4. Policewomen—Fiction 5. Serial murder investigation—Fiction

ISBN 1432828096 (hardcover); 9781432828097 (hardback)

LC 2013-041355

SUMMARY: In this book, "forensic anthropologist Matt Lowell and Massachusetts State Police Trooper Leigh Abbott are called in to investigate burned remains following a fire in a historic antique shop. As Matt, Leigh and their team of graduate students investigate the death, clues point to Salem's traditional Witchcraft community. . . . A second body is found in a similar fire and the team begins to suspect that coven members are being framed." (Publisher's note)

REVIEW: *Kirkus Rev* v82 no3 p274 F 1 2014

"A Flame in the Wind of Death". "Witches are suspected of murder in modern-day Salem, Mass. State Trooper Leigh Abbott and forensic anthropologist Matt Lowell have barely recovered from the horrors of their first case together . . . when they're called on to work an arson-cum-murder. Leigh, one of the few women in a man's world, infuriates a colleague when she lands a case involving badly burned remains in an antiques shop thanks to Matt's refusal to work with anyone else. . . . A tricky mystery rich in intriguing suspects and forensic detail."

D'ANNUNZIO, GABRIELE, 1863-1938. Pleasure; [by] Gabriele D'Annunzio 355 p. 2013 Penguin Books

1. Aristocracy (Social class)—Fiction 2. Degeneration 3. Erotic stories 4. Italian fiction—19th century 5. Italian fiction—Translations into English

ISBN 9780143106746

LC 2013-006549

SUMMARY: Edited and translated by Lara Gochin Raffaelli, "This new translation of [author Gabriele] D'Annunzio's masterpiece, the first in more than one hundred years, restores what was considered too offensive to be included in the 1898 translation--some of the very scenes that are key to the novel's status as a landmark of literary decadence." (Publisher's note)

REVIEW: *TLS* no5779 p19 Ja 3 2014 JOSEPH LUZZI

"Pleasure." "Gabriele D'Annunzio never met an adverb he didn't like. . . . These modifiers fill his sentences like the flowers and antiques that stuff the scented boudoirs of his writing. . . . The closer one looks at a novel like 'Pleasure,' the more one detects the irony and humour that balance the toe-curling pretensions of the prose and the protagonist, Andrea Sperelli. More importantly, a close reading reveals an astonishing streak of literary innovation that manages to preserve what is most valuable in those same traditions that it refashions. . . . Lara Gochin Raffaelli's superb new translation puts 'the sex back in Pleasure' (as the book's publicity announces), restoring . . . parts that the Victorian translator Georgina Harding had prudishly omitted."

DANTE ALIGHIERI, 1265-1321. Inferno; 352 p. 2012 Greywolf Press

1. Celebrities 2. Hell in literature 3. Literature—Translations 4. Poems 5. Popular culture in literature

ISBN 1555976190 (hbk.); 9781555976194 (hbk.)

LC 2012-936221

SUMMARY: For this book, "Mary Jo Bang has translated the 'Inferno,'" by Dante Alighieri. "Dante wrote his poem in the vernacular, rather than in literary Latin. Bang has similarly created a . . . contemporary version" that features modern idioms. She has "incorporat[ed] cultural references familiar to contemporary readers" such as psychologist Sigmund "Freud and [television show] 'South Park,' [philosopher Søren] Kierkegaard and [television host] Stephen Colbert." (Publisher's note)

REVIEW: *N Y Rev Books* v60 no16 p41-3 O 24 2013 Robert Pogue Harrison

"Inferno," "Inferno," and "The Divine Comedy." "Like everything else in this astonishingly bad novel, [Robert] Langdon's lecture lacks verisimilitude. . . . Mary Jo Bang preserves the tercet form without attempting to reproduce Dante's rhyme scheme. Being an excellent poet in her own right, she succeeds in giving the Inferno's narrative drama an energetic idiom that gets the poem moving, and at times even dancing, on the page. . . . Clive James's translation has no such élan. His decision to dispense with explanatory notes altogether and to lift the relevant information 'out of the basement and put . . . it on display in the text' comes at a high price with minimal payoff, not only because it obliges him to import into the body of the poem much material that does not properly belong there, but because it invariably blunts the narrative impact of the original."

DANTICAT, EDWIDGE. Claire of the sea light; [by] Edwidge Danticat 256 p. 2013 Alfred A. Knopf

1. City and town life—Haiti—Fiction 2. FICTION—Cultural Heritage 3. FICTION—Literary 4. FICTION—Sagas 5. Girls—Crimes against—Fiction 6. Missing children—Fiction 7. Secrets—Fiction
ISBN 030727179X; 9780307271792 (hardback)
LC 2012-043876

SUMMARY: In this novel, "Claire Limyè Lanmè ('Claire of the Sea Light'), whose mother died in childbirth and whose fisherman father has made the wrenching decision to give her a better life by relinquishing her, goes missing just before her seventh birthday. As the entire community searches for her, secrets emerge that clarify our relationships with one another and with the natural world, even as we see the beauty and heartbreak of Haiti." (Library Journal)

REVIEW: *Booklist* v109 no19/20 p28-30 Je 1 2013 Vanessa Bush

REVIEW: *Booklist* v110 no7 p36 D 1 2013 Laurie Hartshorn

REVIEW: *Christ Century* v130 no25 p22-3 D 11 2013

REVIEW: *Kirkus Rev* v81 no14 p223 Jl 15 2013

REVIEW: *Libr J* v138 no4 p55 Mr 1 2013 Barbara Hoffert

REVIEW: *Libr J* v138 no21 p26 D 1 2013 Mahnaz Dar Bette-Lee Fox Liz French Margaret Heilbrun Barbara Hoffert Stephanie Klose Annalisa Pesek Henrietta Thornton-Verma Wilda Williams

REVIEW: *Libr J* v138 no14 p97 S 1 2013 Susanne Wells

REVIEW: *Libr J* v138 no21 p54 D 1 2013 Judy Murray

REVIEW: *Ms* v23 no3 p56-7 Summ 2013 Gina Athena Ulysse

REVIEW: *N Y Rev Books* v60 no19 p23-4 D 5 2013 Pooja Bhatia

"Claire of the Sea Light." "Claire of the Sea Light' has a looming, end-times feel. . . . Happily, the book is wholly devoid of the fireworks that many English-language books set in Haiti feature. . . . [Edwidge] Danticat's prose is typically sensitive and precise, and as usual, it resists sentimentality, especially when describing traumas. . . . At the same time, Danticat's language here feels looser, possessed of a generosity and, at times, a playfulness that seem new. . . . The book is intensely patterned, its plot full of repetitions, resonances, and symmetries."

REVIEW: *N Y Times Book Rev* p11 S 1 2013 DEBORAH SONTAG

REVIEW: *New York Times* v162 no56251 pC21-6 S 6 2013 MICHIKO KAKUTANI

REVIEW: *Publ Wkly* v260 no21 p26 My 27 2013

REVIEW: *Va Q Rev* v89 no4 p249-51 Fall 2013 Lisa Page

REVIEW: *Women's Review of Books* v31 no2 p23-4 Mr/Ap 2014 Tiphanie Yanique

REVIEW: *World Lit Today* v88 no2 p56-7 Mr/Ap 2014 John Cussen

"Claire of the Sea Light." "Another way of looking at separation, Edwidge Danticat's signature theme, is the attitude expressed by the novel's titular 'Claire.' Early in the fiction, the seven-year-old disappears into hiding rather than let herself be given away by her hard-pressed, widowed fisherman father to a widow with space in her life for a daughter. . . . 'Claire of the Sea Light' is not Danticat's best work. Too many of the novel's pages roil in her characters' disconsolate ruminations. Still, the fiction holds because its chief suspense--concern for the runaway child and curiosity about what she will do--holds. Also, it ends brilliantly."

D'ANTONIO, PATRICIA.ed. Routledge handbook on the global history of nursing. See Routledge handbook on the global history of nursing

D'ANTONIO, WILLIAM V. American Catholics in transition. See Dillon, M.

D'ANTONIO, WILLIAM V. Religion, politics, and polarization; how religiopolitical conflict is changing Congress and American democracy; [by] William V. D'Antonio viii, 163 p. 2013 Rowman & Littlefield Publishers, Inc.

1. Church and state—United States 2. Legislators—United States 3. Political science literature 4. Religion and politics—United States
ISBN 9781442221079 (cloth: alk. paper)
LC 2012-044709

SUMMARY: It was the authors' intent to demonstrate "that the organizational cultures of the two major

parties in the United States draw from distinct religious traditions—a mainline Protestant tradition emphasizing personal autonomy and individualism in the case of the Republicans and an Abrahamic tradition of 'welcoming strangers' and showing compassion for the poor for Democrats." (America)

REVIEW: *America* v210 no7 p30-3 Mr 3 2014 JAMES A. MCCANN

"American Catholics in Transition" and "Religion, Politics, and Polarization: How Religiopolitical Conflict is Changing Congress and American Democracy". "'American Catholics in Transition' draws from this rich set of surveys to identify patterns of stability and change in the Catholic mind-set since the 1980s. Catholic leaders and rank-and-file members alike could learn much from this book about the internal life of the church. Readers who are not Catholic but wish to know more about the makeup and trajectory of the largest religious denomination in the country will also find the discussion accessible. . . . The central takeaway from 'Religion, Politics, and Polarization' is that the organizational cultures of the two major parties in the United States draw from distinct religious traditions. . . . These two books underscore the significance of religion as a central force in U.S. politics and society."

DANZIGER, SHELDON.ed. Legacies of the War on Poverty. See Legacies of the War on Poverty

DARE, TESSA. Any Duchess Will Do; [by] Tessa Dare 384 p. 2013 HarperCollins Publishers

1. Household employees—Fiction 2. Love stories 3. Man-woman relationships—Fiction 4. Nobility (Social class)—Fiction 5. Regency fiction

ISBN 0062240129 (paperback); 9780062240125 (paperback)

SUMMARY: This is Tessa Dare's fourth Spindle Cove romance novel. Here, "Griffin York, the marriage-shy eighth Duke of Halford, is dragged to the town by his mother, who orders him to pick a bride. He brashly selects Pauline Simms, a proud tavern serving girl. Griff's mother declares she can turn Pauline into duchess material; Griff retorts that if she fails, he'll be off the hook. He offers Pauline £1,000 to go to London and fail the training," but things become complicated when attraction arises. (Publishers Weekly)

REVIEW: *Booklist* v110 no2 p49 S 15 2013 Donna Seaman

"The Accidental Bride," "Any Duchess Will Do," and "Cowboy Take Me Away." "Jilly loves being a chef, but the stress is killing her. Off she goes to the Lost Creek Resort in Wyoming for a calming knitting retreat, but instead, she meets Walker Hale. . . . With just one day to select a bride, the future Duchess of Halford, Griffin chooses serving girl Pauline, as RITA Award-winning [Tessa] Dare continues her sparkling and sexy Spindle Cove series. . . . Graves launches a new series with this charming, emotionally rich novel about the return to Rainbow Valley, Texas, of champion bull rider Luke Dawson and Shannon North, who left her big-city career to run a no-kill animal shelter."

REVIEW: *Booklist* v110 no14 p5-33 Mr 15 2014

"Animal Wise: The Thoughts and Emotions of Our Fellow Creatures," "Any Duchess Will Do," and "The Coldest Girl in Coldtown." "No critters were harmed in the making of this book. . . . Desperate for grandchildren, the Duchess of Halford strikes a bargain with her only son,Griff: pick a woman--any woman. If she can transform her son's choice into duchess material, he must marry the girl. Griff picks the least likely candidate in bluestocking barmaid Pauline, only to quickly realize he has no idea who he is dealing with. A humorous and clever historical romance. . . . Welcome to Coldtown, a quarantined city for vampires, the infected, and humans. The price for residence, however, is that you can never leave."

REVIEW: *Booklist* v109 no17 p70 My 1 2013 John Charles

REVIEW: *Kirkus Rev* v81 no7 p278 Ap 1 2013

REVIEW: *Libr J* v138 no11 p70 Je 15 2013 Kristi Chadwick

REVIEW: *Publ Wkly* v260 no14 p46 Ap 8 2013

DARE, TESSA. Romancing the duke; [by] Tessa Dare 384 p. 2014 HarperCollins

1. Blind—Fiction 2. Castles—Fiction 3. Inheritance & succession—Fiction 4. Love stories 5. Nobility (Social class)—Fiction

ISBN 0062240196; 9780062240194

SUMMARY: In this book, by Tessa Dare, "Isolde Ophelia Goodnight grew up on tales of brave knights and fair maidens. She never doubted romance would be in her future, too. The storybooks offered endless possibilities. And as she grew older, Izzy crossed them off. One by one by one. . . . Now Izzy's given up yearning for romance. She'll settle for a roof over her head. What fairy tales are left over for an impoverished twenty-six year-old woman who's never even been kissed? This one." (Publisher's note)

REVIEW: *Booklist* v110 no9/10 p60 Ja 1 2014 John Charles

"Romancing the Duke". "Izzy discovers that she is now the proud owner of Gostley Castle, a rapidly crumbling pile of stones deep in the wilds of Northumberland. Much to Izzy's surprise, she also discovers that the castle comes complete with one unmentioned, additional feature: its previous owner, Ransome William Dacre Vane, the Duke of Rothbury. . . Splendidly talented [Tessa] Dare . . . creates cleverly written dialogue, exceptionally appealing characters, and an engaging plot that gives a wink toward Beauty and the Beast and a nod to fandom, all key components in this wickedly funny and soul-satisfyingly romantic novel, the perfect launch to Dare's new Castles Ever After series."

REVIEW: *Kirkus Rev* v82 no2 p95 Ja 15 2014

REVIEW: *Libr J* v139 no9 p72 My 15 2014 ALA Rusa-Codes

REVIEW: *Libr J* v139 no3 p79 F 15 2014 Kristin Ramsdell

REVIEW: *Publ Wkly* v260 no51 p44-5 D 16 2013

DARGAVEL, JOHN. Science and hope. See Johann, E.

DARRIEUSSECQ, MARIE. All the Way; [by] Marie Darrieussecq 248 p. 2014 The Text Publishing Company

1. Erotic stories 2. France—Social life & customs—Fiction 3. French fiction—Translations into English 4. Teenage girls—Fiction 5. Teenagers—Social life & customs

ISBN 1921922737; 9781921922732

SUMMARY: Written by Marie Darrieussecq, translated by Penny Hueston, this book is a "story about a young French girl discovering her sexuality. . . . She'd like to see more of her father, even though he's so embarrassing. As for her mother, she's too depressed. Something to do with the photo of the dead boy on the mantelpiece. . . . But who cares, Solange will get to do it, go all the way, whatever it takes." (Publisher's note)

REVIEW: *TLS* no5793 p21 Ap 11 2014 NATASHA LEHRER

"All the Way." "The rather banal title of the English translation of Marie Darrieussecq's novel 'All the Way' doesn't do justice to the wry subtleties that the French title, Clèves, hints at. . . . The text is peppered with the lyrics of 1980s French pop songs, dictionary definitions of sexual organs and positions, and the fake confidence and genuine cruelty of teenagers, all nicely rendered into English by Penny Hueston. . . . The most disturbing aspect of the novel is the relationship between Solange and her sometime babysitter Monsieur Bihotz, with whom she carries on a quasi-sexual relationship that isn't consummated until the very end of the novel."

DAS, AMRITA. Hope Is a Girl Selling Fruit; 28 p. 2014 Pgw

1. Caste—India 2. Children with disabilities 3. Picture books 4. Poor people—India 5. Railroad travel 6. Women—India

ISBN 9383145021; 9789383145027

SUMMARY: In this book by Amrita Das, "the author/artist describes a journey she once took and how that journey later became an inspiration for her art. Rather than focusing on the train's physical path, Das describes being emotionally moved by a poor girl traveling alone, heading toward what she imagines as a limited future. Is the girl limited by her caste, her gender, or both?" (School Library Journal)

REVIEW: *Kirkus Rev* v82 no3 p296 F 1 2014

"Hope Is A Girl Selling Fruit". "[Amrita] Das debuts with illustrations done in a distinctive Indian style paired to a brief meditative text—part memoir, part artist's statement, part rumination—on women's personal journeys. . . . Though strongly stylized, the activities in which these figures are engaged are easy to identify, and they range from traditional farm or domestic work to riding a scooter, painting, using a computer keyboard or just sitting in quiet thought. . . . Older, Western children and teens may well feel they've found an unexpected comrade."

REVIEW: *Publ Wkly* v261 no4 p191-3 Ja 27 2014

REVIEW: *SLJ* v60 no4 p186 Ap 2014 Heather Webb

DASCHUK, JAMES. Clearing the Plains; Disease, Politics of Starvation, and the Loss of Aboriginal Life; [by] James Daschuk 354 p. 2013 Canadian Plains Research Center

1. Genocide—History 2. Historical literature 3. Indians of North America—Canada 4. Indians of North America—Diseases 5. Indigenous peoples—Canada—Diseases 6. Indigenous peoples—Government relations

ISBN 0889772967; 9780889772960

SUMMARY: Written by James Daschuk, this book "examines the roles that Old World diseases, climate, and, most disturbingly, Canadian politics--the politics of ethnocide--played in the deaths and subjugation of thousands of aboriginal people" It "destroys the view that Canada has a special claim to humanity in its treatment of indigenous peoples. Daschuk shows how infectious disease and state-supported starvation combined to create a . . . catastrophe that persists to the present day." (Publisher's note)

REVIEW: *Quill Quire* v79 no7 p33 S 2013 Megan Moore Burns

"Clearing the Plains: Disease, Politics of Starvation, and the Loss of Aboriginal Life." "Examining Canada's natives through the lens of disease, [author James] Daschuk paints a disturbing portrait of an entire people perishing as a result of British and Canadian indifference. . . . 'Clearing the Plains' is not an easy book to read, both because of the subject matter and the style in which it is written; the language is academic and extremely dense, and prior knowledge of the history of the Canadian West is essential. This is a shame, because . . . Canadians need to read this book."

DASGUPTA, RANA. Capital; A Portrait of Twenty-First Century Delhi; [by] Rana Dasgupta 512 p. 2014 Canongate Books Ltd

1. Capitalism—India 2. Delhi (India) 3. Delhi (India)—Economic conditions 4. Delhi (India)—Social conditions 5. Social science literature

ISBN 085786002X; 9780857860026

SUMMARY: In this book, author Rana Dasgupta "conducts a series of interviews and personal explorations which reveal the history and evolution of the city of Delhi, examined through the attitudes and opinions of its inhabitants. He paints a picture of wealth and privilege, poverty and neglect, rampant corruption and boundless ambition, emphasizing the dichotomy which has transformed the landscape over the past few decades." (Publishers Weekly)

REVIEW: *Economist* v310 no8876 p84-6 Mr 1 2014

"Capital: A Portrait of Twenty-First Century Delhi." "It is crammed with the boasts and insecurities of the children of some of Delhi's richest and best-connected business families. . . . 'Capital' is formed largely of interviews with these twenty-something young men. . . . [Rana Dasgupta] lets them all talk; half of nearly every chapter is made up of conversation. . . . 'Capital' is just the latest book to examine the effects of globalisation on South Asia. Like those before it, it takes a dim view of Western capital's seductive appeal. But the book should have been taken more firmly in hand by its editor. 'Capital' shouts rather than persuades."

DASHNER, JAMES. The eye of minds; [by] James Dashner 336 p. 2013 Delacorte Press

1. Computer games—Fiction 2. Cyberterrorism—Fiction 3. Science fiction 4. Terrorism—Fiction 5. Virtual reality—Fiction

ISBN 9780375990014 (glb); 9780385741392 (hc)

LC 2012-050779

SUMMARY: In "this first book in the Mortality Doctrine series . . . three teens must track down a dangerous rogue player in a popular virtual game. Michael, Bryson, and Sarah live for their hours in the VirtNet, where they seek out the wildest adventures possible without any risk to their physical selves. Then Michael encounters a player so haunted by a gamer named Kaine that she disables her safety device in order to kill herself. Michael is drafted by VirtNet Security to root out Kaine." (Publishers Weekly)

REVIEW: *Booklist* v110 no12 p95 F 15 2014 Rachel Reinwald

REVIEW: *Booklist* v110 no1 p113 S 1 2013 J. B. Petty

REVIEW: *Bull Cent Child Books* v67 no5 p262 Ja 2014 A. M.

"The Eye of Minds." "This high-intensity science fiction adventure emphasizes suspense from its very first scene and never lets up. Fans of video games, especially quest and puzzle-platforms like Portal, will revel in the mission-based narrative, while readers enjoyed [Cory] Doctorow's 'Little Brother' . . . or [Brian] Falkner's 'Brain Jack' . . . will find themselves at home in the hacker-friendly cyber-setting. Characterization isn't deep, but the relationship between Michael and his friends provides plenty of playful banter. A last-minute twist subverts everything the reader knows about Michael, provides the perfect set-up for expected sequels, and makes for a bombshell ending that will have readers rereading and then coming back for more."

REVIEW: *Kirkus Rev* v81 no17 p84 S 1 2013

REVIEW: *Kirkus Rev* p63-4 2013 Guide 20to BookExpo America

REVIEW: *Publ Wkly* v261 no4 p188 Ja 27 2014

REVIEW: *SLJ* v59 no9 p155 S 2013 Maggie Knapp

REVIEW: *SLJ* v60 no1 p54 Ja 2014 MaryAnn Karre

REVIEW: *Voice of Youth Advocates* v36 no5 p72 D 2013 Jayme Home

REVIEW: *Voice of Youth Advocates* v36 no5 p72 D 2013 Etienne Vallee

DATLA, KAVITA SARASWATHI. The language of secular Islam; Urdu nationalism and colonial India; [by] Kavita Saraswathi Datla 234 p.

1. Historical literature 2. Language and education—India—Hyderabad (State)—History—20th century 3. Language policy—India—Hyderabad (State)—History—20th century 4. Muslim educators—Political activity—India—Hyderabad (State)—History—20th century 5. Urdu language—Political aspects—India—Hyderabad (State)—History—20th century
ISBN 9780824836092 (hardcover: alk. paper)
LC 2012-025444

SUMMARY: In this book, "through her discussion of language debates in the princely state of Hyderabad in the 1920s and 1930s, which focused on the revival of Urdu as a national language, Kavita Saraswathi Datla reveals the nuances of the negotiations for Muslim cultural and literary recognition in the decades before independence." (American Historical Review)

REVIEW: *Am Hist Rev* v119 no1 p163-4 F 2014 Chitralekha Zutshi

"The Language of Secular Islam: Urdu Nationalism and Colonial India". "This book is a refreshing contribution to the scholarship on Muslim politics, nationalism, and language in late colonial India. . . . [Kavita Saraswathi] Datla puts forward a noteworthy definition of secularism for this moment in colonial India. . . . Urdu nationalism, this book skillfully demonstrates, was a secular and national, not a communal, enterprise. . . . Overall, Datla argues persuasively that linguistic arguments were not simply about the position of Urdu but about the definition of the secular."

REVIEW: *Choice* v50 no12 p2293 Ag 2013 L. M. Proctor

DAUBER, JEREMY. The worlds of Sholem Aleichem; the remarkable life and afterlife of the man who created Tevye; [by] Jeremy Dauber 464 p. 2013 Schocken Books

1. Authors, Yiddish—19th century—Biography 2. Biography (Literary form) 3. Jews—Ukraine—Biography 4. Tevye (Fictitious character : Sholem Aleichem)
ISBN 0805242783; 9780805242782
LC 2013-009267

SUMMARY: This book, by Jeremy Dauber, presents a "comprehensive biography of . . . author [Sholem Aleichem]: the creator of 'Tevye the Dairyman,' the collection of stories that inspired 'Fiddler on the Roof.' Novelist, playwright, journalist, essayist, and editor, Sholem Aleichem was one of the founding giants of modern Yiddish literature." (Publisher's note)

REVIEW: *Kirkus Rev* v81 no15 p331 Ag 1 2013

REVIEW: *Nation* v298 no6 p41-4 F 10 2014 JULIA M. KLEIN

"The Worlds of Sholem Aleichem: The Remarkable Life and Afterlife of the Man Who Created Tevye" and "Wonder of Wonders: A Cultural History of 'Fiddler on the Roof'." "Two new books, complementary in their aims and conclusions, manage these daunting tasks with aplomb, even if they're nowhere near as much fun as reading the writer himself. In 'The Worlds of Sholem Aleichem,' Jeremy Dauber . . . offers a sometimes irreverent--but also deeply serious--literary biography that attempts to channel his subject's antic spirit. Episodic in feel, it is most effective as a work of criticism that identifies Sholem Aleichem's affinities with literary modernism and postmodernism. . . . [Alisa] Solomon . . . finds her footing with the wonderfully gossipy creation tale of the long-running Broadway musical."

REVIEW: *New Yorker* v89 no38 p127-1 N 25 2013

DAUDI, IMBESAT. Civilization & Violence; Islam, the West, and the Rest; [by] Imbesat Daudi 428 p. 2013 QED Books

1. Islam & politics 2. Islamic countries 3. Political violence 4. Religious literature 5. Violence—Religious aspects
ISBN 1938883160; 9781938883163

SUMMARY: This book presents a "defense of Islam in the face of Western propaganda. Author Imbesat Daudi argues that "the West and Muslim-majority nations are not destined to be at odds . . . in fact, they fought on the same side against Soviets and Communists. The religious right's unquestioning support for Israel and the fact that Islamic countries safeguard 75 percent of oil reserves may be major factors behind the recent demonization of Islam, he says." (Kirkus Reviews)

REVIEW: *Kirkus Rev* v82 no1 p340 Ja 1 2014

"Civilization and Violence: Islam, the West and the Rest". "[Imbesat] Daudi mounts a spirited, logical defense of Islam in the face of Western propaganda. . . . Daudi approaches Islam as a neutral, methodical observer. . . . Though sometimes verging on conspiratorial, his arguments are rational and supported with clearly presented statistics. However, his failures to discuss violence in the Quran or differing interpretations of the doctrine of jihad seem to be curious omissions. Anecdotal or journalistic elements would make this treatise more readable for lay readers, who might be interested in stories as well as facts. A dense secular defense that makes important points about how the West scapegoats Muslims."

DAUGHERTY, C. J. Night School; [by] C. J. Daugherty 432 p. 2013 Katherine Tegen Books

1. Boarding schools—Fiction 2. Conduct of life—Fiction 3. Interpersonal relations—Fiction 4. Paranormal fiction 5. Schools—Fiction 6. Supernatural—Fiction
ISBN 0062193856 (hardcover); 9780062193858 (hardcover)
LC 2012-022151

SUMMARY: In this book, "upset over the loss of her brother, Christopher, Allie's vandalism gets her expelled from school" and she is sent to the mysterious boarding school Cimmeria Academy. Students are "not to enter the woods after dark; computers and cellphones are forbidden. A few [students] . . . attend the mysterious Night School but refuse to discuss it. Even Allie's best friend, Jo, keeps secrets from her." (Kirkus)

REVIEW: *Booklist* v109 no19/20 p93-4 Je 1 2013 Peter Gutierrez

REVIEW: *Bull Cent Child Books* v67 no1 p13 S 2013 A. M.

"Night School." "A fast-paced read with solid plotting and plenty of intrigue, this novel provides a diverting, straightforward summertime thrill. Characterization and the love story are underexplored, hut this is all about suspense, and there the book delivers in spades. The boarding-school setting, with its spooky gothic atmosphere and the underlying elements of espionage and long-standing grudges, sets up a slow-burning tension that builds to an intense finale, with plenty of questions left unanswered as setup for a planned sequel."

REVIEW: *Kirkus Rev* v81 no8 p81 Ap 15 2013

REVIEW: *Voice of Youth Advocates* v36 no3 p60 Ag 2013 Suanne B. Roush

DAUPHIN, VAYA. The Turquoise Tattoo; [by] Vaya Dauphin 286 p. 2012 BookPal

1. Brothers—Fiction 2. Fantasy fiction 3. Mythology, Maori 4. New Zealand fiction 5. Telepathy—Fiction

ISBN 1742841902; 9781742841908

SUMMARY: In this book, "Scarlet Flint . . . can read the minds and feelings of others, causing her no shortage of trouble. Her unstable life gets more chaotic once she moves from her Australian home to New Zealand. She ends up in the middle of the feud between the mysterious Sterling and his menacing brother, Manu. Her involvement turns out to be greater than she ever imagined just as her telepathic abilities increase. Scarlet is an Elemental, a half-human with supernatural abilities." (Kirkus Reviews)

REVIEW: *Kirkus Rev* p14-5 D 15 2013 supplemet best books 2013

"The Turquoise Tattoo". "While fantasy books based on myth aren't uncommon, stories based specifically on Maori myth are, making this novel unusual. Detailed explanations of Maori myth provide solid context—[Vaya] Dauphin even includes a glossary—but do not slow the narrative. The characters also help set the book apart. Scarlet is a remarkably strong young woman who faces each new challenge bravely. She is loyal to her love interest but also allows herself to be frustrated with him when he deserves it, and she aims to walk beside him, rather than chase after him. . . . Skillful foreshadowing appears throughout, and most chapters end with a teaser that keeps the pages turning."

REVIEW: *Kirkus Rev* v80 no24 p41 D 15 2012

DAVENPORT-HINES, R. P. T. (RICHARD PETER TREADWELL), 1953-.ed. One hundred letters from Hugh Trevor-Roper. See One hundred letters from Hugh Trevor-Roper

DAVENPORT-HINES, R. P. T. (RICHARD PETER TREADWELL), 1953-.ed. The wartime journals. See The wartime journals

DAVENPORT, GUY, 1927-2005. A Guy Davenport reader; [by] Guy Davenport 421 p. 2013 Counterpoint Press

1. Anthologies 2. Authorship 3. Fathers & sons 4. Literary form 5. Modernism (Literature)

ISBN 161902103X; 9781619021037

LC 2013-014418

SUMMARY: This book, edited by Erik Reece, presents a collection of writings by American author Guy Davenport. It "is partitioned according to genre, with sections devoted to stories, essays, oems, translations, and excerpts rom his journals." A "postscript reminiscence" by Reece, "a former student and longtime friend of Davenport's." (Bookforum)

REVIEW: *Bookforum* v20 no3 p39 S-N 2013 JAMES GIBBONS

"The Guy Davenport Reader." "His stories, published in collections from the '70s to the '90s, are marvelous constructions intermingling fact and fiction, built from the biographies of artists and writers, philosophers and presidents. . . . Davenport was an exceedingly private man, unlikely to be the subject of a biography, so one of the reasons we should welcome 'The Guy Davenport Reader' is for its glimpses into a personality that was mostly subsumed in his work. [Erik] Reece's own contribution, a postscript reminiscence, gives a sense of Davenport's humor and charisma without papering over his flaws. . . . The autobiographical essays gathered here, pleasingly meandering and chatty, are among Davenport's most accessible writings."

DAVEY, OWEN. Laika; Astronaut dog; [by] Owen Davey 2013 Templar Publishing

1. Animal space flight—History 2. Dogs—Juvenile fiction 3. Historical fiction 4. Outer space—Exploration—Juvenile literature 5. Soviet Union—Fiction

ISBN 9781783700271 paperback; 9781848778788 hardcover

SUMMARY: "Laika is a homeless stray living on the streets of Moscow when she is picked by the Space Programme to be the first ever animal launched into orbit! But her rocket disappears and everyone thinks Laika is lost forever--no one knows what happened to her. Now you'll discover in Owen Davey's imaginative story that Laika was rescued by a loving new owner and found her true home on a planet far, far away." (Publisher's note)

REVIEW: *Booklist* v110 no4 p55-6 O 15 2013 J. B. Petty

REVIEW: *Bull Cent Child Books* v67 no3 p146-7 N 2013 E. B.

"Laika: Astronaut Dog." "In 1957 Russian scientists launched Sputnik 2 into Earth's orbit, and perhaps the best-known legacy of that particular mission is the story of its doomed passenger Laika, the stray terrier whose vital signs were monitored to shed light on the reaction of life forms to space travel. Here [author Owen] Davey pares down and anthropomorphizes the tale for a young audience, outlining Laika's experience from a little orphan longing for a family, to proud astronaut in training, to a space traveler who found her life in her capsule as lonely as life back on Earth, to the inevitable end. . . . This bizarre mash-up of history and fantasy comes attractively tricked out in a deftly composed homage to Soviet visual art design. . . ."

REVIEW: *Kirkus Rev* v81 no15 p302 Ag 1 2013

REVIEW: *Publ Wkly* v260 no33 p67 Ag 19 2013

DAVID, DEIRDRE, 1934-. Fanny Kemble; a performed life; [by] Deirdre David 384 2007 University of Pennsylvania Press

1. Actors 2. Biography, Individual 3. Memoirists 4. Novelists 5. Poets

ISBN 0-8122-4023-5; 9780812240238

LC 2007-017365

SUMMARY: This book by Deirdre David presents a biography of Fanny Kemble, an actor who was also known "as a fierce opponent of slavery despite her marriage to a wealthy slave owner, . . . and as the author of journals about her career and life on her husband's Georgia plantations."

REVIEW: *Choice* v51 no10 p1738 Je 2014 D. B. Wilmeth

"Fanny Kemble: A Performed Life". "This scholarly, erudite, and thorough study by [Deirdre] David . . . is the one to use. It is also the most thematically driven of the biographies, stressing Kemble's performance of self and her role playing—both on and off stage—in action and in her writing. . . . As superb as this biography is, [J.C.] Fumas remains definitive on Fanny's theatrical life; David's effort far exceeds all others in its balance and in its careful analysis of this complex and variegated life. Though it does not completely supersede its predecessors, this well-illustrated volume is a great addition to the literature on important women, the theater, and numerous aspects of the 19th century."

DAVID, SUSAN A.ed. The Oxford handbook of happiness. See The Oxford handbook of happiness

DAVIDI, SHI. Great Expectations. See Lott, J.

DAVIDSON, HILARY. Blood always tells; [by] Hilary Davidson 320 p. 2014 Forge Books

1. FICTION—Crime 2. FICTION—Mystery & Detective—Women Sleuths 3. Kidnapping—Fiction 4. Murder—Investigation—Fiction 5. Travel writers—Fiction
ISBN 9780765333544 (hardback)
LC 2013-025068

SUMMARY: In this book by Hilary Davidson, "Dominique Monaghan, Desmond Edgars, and Polly Brandov are all haunted by the events of their pasts—encounters with the law, family disappearances, abuse, and murder. Dominique's plot to embarrass and inconvenience her cheating ex-boyfriend sees her tumbling into a relentless downward spiral of kidnapping and, ultimately, murder." (Quill & Quire)

REVIEW: *Libr J* v139 no2 p62 F 1 2014 Amy Hoseth

REVIEW: *Publ Wkly* v261 no7 p79 F 17 2014

REVIEW: *Quill Quire* v80 no2 p28-9 Mr 2014 Chadwick Ginther

"Blood Always Tells". "The many intersecting plot threads involving a family fortune, a missing child, and multiple secrets could easily have become a tangled mess. Fortunately, [Hilary] Davidson knows how to handle a complicated story and also keep her reader turning the pages. Motivation, history, and plot twists are meted out in the novel's short, punchy chapters, building suspense and escalating the thrills quickly but logically. . . . Throughout, Davidson's prose is measured and effective. . . . Davidson also displays a great facility for evoking memorable characters, whether through physical description or a focus on their habits and obsessions."

DAVIDSON, IAN.ed. Placing poetry. See Placing poetry

DAVIES, DEBORAH KAY. Reasons She Goes to the Woods; [by] Deborah Kay Davies 256 p. 2014 Pgw

1. English fiction—Welsh authors 2. Girls—Fiction 3. Human sexuality—Fiction 4. Incest 5. Mothers & daughters—Fiction
ISBN 1780743769; 9781780743769

SUMMARY: "A mystery to all who know her; a little girl who has her own secret reasons for escaping to the nearby woods. . . . Told in vignettes across Pearl's childhood years, 'Reasons She Goes To The Woods' is a nervy and lyrical novel about a girl growing up who is trying to be normal, even though she doesn't know quite what normal is." (Publisher's note)

REVIEW: *TLS* no5787 p21 F 28 2014 DAISY HILDYARD

"Reasons She Goes to the Woods." "Pearl is a little girl. She is clever, brutal, brave, and highly sexualized from the first page of 'Reasons She Goes to the Woods.' . . . Pearl's childhood and adolescence are told in single-paragraph, page-long chapters. Each chapter focuses on one short scene and there are no speech marks to differentiate conversation from thought, action or description. The effect is laconic, and detail presses close. . . . The story is plotted across a series of incidents, some apparently unconnected, at least at first. . . . Pearl's hatred of her mother, and incestuous feelings for her father, become more emphatic. It is a child's story that Deborah Kay Davies is telling."

DAVIES, HUMPHREY.tr. Life is more beautiful than paradise. See Al-Berry, K.

DAVIES, JAMIE A. Life Unfolding; How the Human Body Creates Itself; [by] Jamie A. Davies 336 p. 2014 Oxford Univ Pr

1. Developmental biology 2. Human body 3. Human embryos 4. Scientific literature 5. Self-organizing systems
ISBN 0199673535; 9780199673537

SUMMARY: This book by Jamie Davies looks at human biology."Based on the central principle of 'adaptive self-organization,' it explains how the interactions of many cells, and of the tiny molecular machines that run them, can organize tissue structures vastly larger than themselves, correcting errors as they go along and creating new layers of complexity where there were none before." (Publisher's note)

REVIEW: *New Sci* v221 no2959 p48 Mr 8 2014 Claire Ainsworth

"Life Unfolding: How the Human Body Creates Itself". "[Jamie] Davies is a professor of experimental anatomy at the University of Edinburgh in the UK. He has spent years studying how organs form in embryos. It's an ideal perspective from which to describe our journey from fertilised egg to an adult formed of trillions of cells. . . . Far from unweaving the rainbow of development, Davies's lucid and eloquent story increases the reader's sense of wonder. The ideas and examples come thick and fast. Anyone without an A level in biology will find themselves on a steep learning curve. But reading a book that stretches your brain is no bad thing, particularly as the concepts here extend beyond development and even beyond biology."

REVIEW: *Publ Wkly* v261 no13 p55 Mr 31 2014

REVIEW: *Sci Am* v310 no4 p86 Ap 2014 Clara Moskowitz

"Life Unfolding: How the Human Body Creates Itself." "Scientists . . . are still trying to answer this question on its most basic levels. Human bodies, after all, are not built like bridges by external engineers—they build themselves. [Author Jamie A.] Davies describes what we know and what we do not know about how tiny individual components come together to create the complexity of life, laying out the major insights that have been gleaned over the past decade. 'The story that is being unearthed . . . is an astonishing one,' Davies writes."

DAVIES, MATTHEW I. J.ed. Humans and the environment . See Humans and the environment

DAVIES, NICOLA, 1958-. The Lion who stole my arm; [by] Nicola Davies 96 p. 2014 Candlewick Press

1. Adventure stories 2. Courage 3. Lions 4. Revenge—Fiction 5. Wildlife conservation

ISBN 0763666203; 9780763666200

LC 2013-943082

SUMMARY: This book, by Nicola Davies, is an "illustrated novel for young readers that proves you don't need two arms to be strong. Pedru has always wanted to be a great hunter like his father, but after a lion takes his arm, he worries that he'll always be the crippled boy instead. Pedru longs to kill the lion that mauled him and strengthens himself to be ready for the hunt. But when the opportunity arises, will Pedru have the strength to turn his back on revenge?" (Publisher's note)

REVIEW: *Booklist* v110 no11 p68 F 1 2014 Jeanne E. Fredriksen

REVIEW: *Bull Cent Child Books* v67 no6 p306-7 F 2014 Elizabeth Bush

REVIEW: *Horn Book Magazine* v90 no2 p116 Mr/Ap 2014 ROBIN L. SMITH

REVIEW: *Kirkus Rev* v81 no24 p165 D 15 2013

"The Lion Who Stole My Arm". "The pen-and-wash illustrations provide details on the people, animals and village life in this part of Africa. . . . Although the building of the tourist lodge (by an important soccer player related to one of the conservation-project staff members) seems a little far-fetched, this brief tale bridges the gap between the few picture books and longer novels set in this region. Though on the purposive side, the tale both provides adventure and fills a cultural niche for chapter-book readers."

REVIEW: *Publ Wkly* v260 no50 p69-70 D 9 2013

REVIEW: *SLJ* v60 no3 p108 Mr 2014 Carol A. Edwards

DAVIES, NICOLA, 1958-. The Promise; 40 p. 2014 Candlewick Press

1. Children's stories 2. Cities & towns—Juvenile literature 3. Promises 4. Theft 5. Tree planting

ISBN 0763666335; 9780763666330

LC 2013-934311

SUMMARY: In this children's book by Nicola Davies, illustrated by Laura Carlin, "on a mean street in a mean, broken city, a young girl tries to snatch an old woman's bag. But the frail old woman, holding on with the strength of heroes, says the thief can't have it without giving something in return: the promise. It is the beginning of a journey that will change the thieving girl's life—and a chance to change the world, for good." (Publisher's note)

REVIEW: *Booklist* v110 no17 p94 My 1 2014 Ilene Cooper

REVIEW: *Bull Cent Child Books* v67 no9 p450 My 2014 T. A.

"The Promise". "The striking mixed-media illustrations complement the text nicely. . . . Though the ideas of paying it forward and rejuvenating urban space are well intended, the allegory is unfortunately heavy-handed in its melodrama ('Nothing grew. Everything was broken. No one ever smiled'), and the text ends up preachy in its strongly purposive themes of patience, generosity, and eco-mindedness. Still, the book's lyricism does mean it's lovely when read aloud, making this a possible choice as a green-themed and sensitive bedtime story."

REVIEW: *Horn Book Magazine* v90 no3 p62-3 My/Je 2014 KATHLEEN T. HORNING

REVIEW: *Kirkus Rev* v82 no5 p275 Mr 1 2014

REVIEW: *SLJ* v60 no4 p118 Ap 2014 Janene Corbin

DAVIES, NORMAN. Vanished kingdoms; the History of Half-forgotten Europe; [by] Norman Davies 2012 Allen Lane

1. Comparative civilization 2. Europe—History 3. Geography & history 4. Historical literature 5. Regression (Civilization)

ISBN 1846143381; 9781846143380

SUMMARY: This book argues "that all living states [die and], . . . that the rude life of living states is often founded on an act of forgetting, on myths of continuity that feed contemporary identities by erasing or doing violence to the past. It's this process of occlusion and misremembering that engages Davies's attention . . . [through] his investigation of fifteen vanished European polities. . . . [T]he book is . . . attentive to landscape and place, from . . . Montagne d'Alaric, once a landmark of the Visigothic Kingdom of Tolosa, . . . to the . . . the Firth of Clyde that once washed the shores of the 'Kingdom of the Rock' in today's Scotland, to the 'jumble of rocky morainic ridges covered with lakes and dense forests' that was once the heartland of the Grand Duchy of Lithuania." (TLS)

REVIEW: *Engl Hist Rev* v128 no531 p401-3 Ap 2013 Pit Péporté

DAVIES, OWEN. America Bewitched; Witchcraft After Salem; [by] Owen Davies 384 p. 2013 Oxford University Press

1. Historical literature 2. Hysteria (Social psychology) 3. Immigrants—United States—History 4. United States—Social life & customs—History 5. Witch hunting

ISBN 0199578710; 9780199578719

SUMMARY: This book by Owen Davies "reveals how witchcraft in post-Salem America was not just a matter of scary fire-side tales, Halloween legends, and superstitions. . . . If anything, witchcraft disputes multiplied as hundreds of thousands of immigrants poured into North America, people for whom witchcraft was still a heinous crime." It presents "new insights into popular American beliefs, the immigrant experience, racial attitudes, and the development of modern society." (Publisher's note)

REVIEW: *Choice* v51 no1 p146-7 S 2013 L. B. Gimelli

"America Bewitched: The Story of Witchcraft After Salem." "[Author Owen] Davies . . . offers a broad view of witchcraft, witches, and folk belief in the US from the witch mania at Salem to the modern era. He focuses on the witch beliefs of Native Americans, African Americans, and Americans of European origin, whose views of witches have been quite similar and have influenced the popular concept of 'witch' in the US. . . . While the malicious witch has not disappeared, she has been joined by other witch types. For example, TV and Hollywood have produced the mischievous witch, the glamorous witch, and the teenage witch. . . . An informative, useful introduction to a fascinating aspect of American culture that clearly demonstrates that witch beliefs in the US did not end with Salem."

REVIEW: *Libr J* v138 no8 p89 My 1 2013 Margaret Kappanadze

REVIEW: *Publ Wkly* v260 no11 p73 Mr 18 2013

DAVIES, RAY, 1944-. Americana; the Kinks, the riff, the road : the story; [by] Ray Davies 311 p. 2013 Sterling Pub Co Inc

1. Autobiography 2. Kinks (Musical group) 3. Rock musicians—Biography 4. United States—Social life & customs—20th century 5. Victims of violent crimes
ISBN 1402778910; 9781402778919

SUMMARY: "Legendary Kinks' singer/songwriter Ray Davies fell in love with America. . . . Then, as part of the British Invasion, he toured the US with the Kinks during one of the most tumultuous eras in recent history. . . . Many tours and trips later, while living in New Orleans, he experienced . . . the shooting . . . that nearly took his life. In Americana, Davies tries to make sense of his long love-hate relationship with the country that both inspired and frustrated him." (Publisher's note)

REVIEW: *N Y Times Book Rev* p26 D 22 2013 Alan Light

"Americana: The Kinks, the Riff, the Road: The Story," "Simple Dreams: A Musical Memoir," and "Everybody's Brother." "Like some Kinks songs, 'Americana' can be overstuffed with distracting detail (especially the passages about the band's various record deals), but [author Ray] Davies is candid and honest about his personal and creative struggles. . . . In her slim, warmhearted memoir, 'Simple Dreams,' [author Linda Ronstadt] claims . . . that she is allergic to alcohol. . . . 'I am like a human lava lamp,' writer CeeLo Green in his affable autobiography, 'Everybody's Brother.' Moments like that are the highlights of the book."

DAVIS, AERON. Promotional cultures; the rise and spread of advertising, public relations, marketing and branding; [by] Aeron Davis xi, 247 p. 2013 Polity

1. Advertising—Social aspects 2. Communication and culture 3. Communication and culture—Case studies 4. Marketing—Social aspects 5. Mass media and culture 6. Public relations 7. Social science literature
ISBN 0745639828 (hbk.); 0745639836 (pbk.); 9780745639826 (hbk.); 9780745639833 (pbk.)
LC 2013-363976

SUMMARY: This book "documents how the professions and practices of promotion have interacted with and reshaped so much in our world, from commodities, celebrities and popular culture to politics, markets and civil society. It offers a mix of historical accounts, social theory and documented case studies, including haute couture fashion, Apple Inc., Hollywood film . . . and the 2008 financial crisis. Together, these show how promotional culture may be recorded, understood and interpreted." (Publisher's note)

REVIEW: *Choice* v51 no5 p825-6 Ja 2014 D. Aron

"Promotional Cultures: The Rise and Spread of Advertising, Public Relations, Marketing and Branding." "To promotional industries--which include public relations, advertising, and marketing--[Aeron] Davis adds related occupations such as pollster, speech writer, and agent in asserting that promotion has a substantial impact on society, in both direct and indirect ways. This, Davis concludes, is beneficial in leading to an informed society, yet it is still rife with danger: promotion can stifle creativity, which is constrained by the very resources dedicated to promotional projects or by blinding consumers to a communicator's true message. Davis blends political science, economics, and sociology with media and communications."

DAVIS, BRENDA. Becoming vegan express edition; [by] Brenda Davis 283 p. 2013 Book Publishing Company

1. Self-help materials 2. Vegan cooking 3. Veganism 4. Vegetarian cooking 5. Vegetarianism 6. Vegetarianism—Health aspects
ISBN 1570672954; 9781570672958 (pbk.)
LC 2013-023875

SUMMARY: In this book, "registered dietitians [Brenda] Davis and [Vesano] Melina cover every aspect of the vegan life, from its ethical foundation, based on the recognition that animals are sentient beings, to how very nutritious and delicious a well-planned, plant-based diet can be. . . . The authors explain how to maximize nutrition via preparation guidelines, meal plans, and menus for all ages." (Booklist)

REVIEW: *Booklist* v110 no3 p19-22 O 1 2013 Donna Seaman

"Becoming Vegan: Express Edition--The Everyday Guide to Plant-Based Nutrition." "Registered dietitians [Brenda] Davis and [Vesano] Melina cover every aspect of the vegan life, from its ethical foundation, based on the recognition that animals are sentient beings, to how very nutritious and delicious a well-planned, plant-based diet can be. Their clear, detailed, and practical coverage of the benefits of eating vegetables, fruits, grains, legumes, nuts, and seeds is supported by easy-to-use, remarkably informative charts, and propelled by expertise and enthusiasm. . . . This is the go-to book for understanding and practicing healthy and enjoyable veganism."

DAVIS, CAROLINE. Creating postcolonial literature; African writers and British publishers; [by] Caroline Davis x, 255 p. 2013 Palgrave Macmillan

1. African literature (English)—Publishing—History—20th century 2. Historical literature 3. Publishers and publishing—Africa—History—20th century 4. Publishers and publishing—Great Britain—History—20th century
ISBN 9780230369368
LC 2013-008160

SUMMARY: This book "examines the publishing of African literature in the postcolonial period. Its focus is the largely forgotten Three Crowns series by Oxford University Press (1962-1976). . . . It addresses the construction of literary value, the relationships between African writers and British publishers, and the critical importance of the African marketplace in the development of African literature during this period." (Publisher's note)

REVIEW: *Choice* v51 no5 p828-9 Ja 2014 E. R. Baer

"Creating Postcolonial Literature: African Writers and British Publishers." "[Caroline] Davis . . . makes a significant contribution to African studies, the history of book culture, and literacy studies with this volume. She documents, in fascinating detail, the often neocolonial relationship between Oxford University Press (OUP) and postcolonial African writers. . . . By virtue of meticulous research . . .along with interviews, she writes authoritatively about OUP's financial strategy in working with African writers; which authors are approved for publication and why . . . and what one can learn from paratextual material, e.g., exotic book covers, blurbs, publicity."

DAVIS, DANIEL M. (DANIEL MICHAEL), 1970-. The compatibility gene; how our bodies fight disease, attract others, and define our selves; [by] Daniel M. (Daniel Michael) Davis 248 p. 2014 Oxford University Press

1. Human molecular genetics 2. Immunogenetics 3. Infection—Immunological aspects 4. MEDICAL—Immunology 5. Medical genetics 6. Scientific literature

ISBN 9780199316410 (hardback)

LC 2013-020914

SUMMARY: This book by Daniel M. Davis looks at "compatibility genes . . . those that vary most from person to person and give each of us a unique molecular signature. These genes determine both the extent to which we are susceptible to a vast range of illnesses and the different ways each of us fights disease. . . . Davis proposes that . . . in the not-too-distant future vaccines and other medications may be tailored to match our compatibility genes." (Publisher's note)

REVIEW: *Choice* v51 no9 p1628 My 2014 R. K. Harris

REVIEW: *New Sci* v219 no2934 p48-9 S 14 2013 Mark Viney

"The Compatibility Gene." "[Daniel M.] Davis provides a well-written and easy-to-read account of the sometimes complicated biology behind the crucial genes that affect our lives so profoundly. . . . Although Davis gives an up-to-date account of the science, he steers clear of the wider societal implications that might lie ahead. . . . Davis covers human compatibility genes well but a larger nod to compatibility systems in other animals and plants would not have gone amiss. These ubiquitous codes for uniqueness are a good reminder that we are just another species of animal. It is clear that other animals' compatibility genes are involved in their choice of mate, perhaps to avoid inbreeding."

REVIEW: *New Statesman* v142 no5172 p50 Ag 30 2013 Michael Brooks

REVIEW: *New York Times* v163 no56290 pD5 O 15 2013 NICHOLAS WADE

"The Compatibility Gene: How Our Bodies Fight Disease, Attract Others and Define Our Selves." "'The Compatibility Gene' will enhance most readers' appreciation for the immune system's heroic daily struggles to prevent their body from being overrrun by alien life-forms. . . . Its author, Daniel M. Davis, is a scientist . . . who not only writes gracefully but has taken the trouble to interview the major players in his field about how they made their discoveries. His book is enlivened by many details one would not find in an immunology textbook. . . . Dr. Davis is a productive researcher, in midcareer, and an expert on the immune system's natural killer cells. The book is frequently informed by his insider's perspective."

REVIEW: *Publ Wkly* v260 no38 p65 S 23 2013

DAVIS, DAVID BRION, 1927-. The problem of slavery in the age of emancipation; [by] David Brion Davis 448 p. 2014 Knopf

1. Antislavery movements—Great Bri 2. Antislavery movements—United States—History—19th century 3. Free African Americans—History—19th century 4. Historical literature 5. Slavery—United States—History—19th century 6. Slaves—Emancipation—United States

ISBN 0307269094; 9780307269096 (hardback)

LC 2013-032893

SUMMARY: Author David Brion Davis "offers . . . insights into what slavery and emancipation meant to Americans. He explores how the Haitian Revolution respectively terrified and inspired white and black Americans, hovering over the antislavery debates like a bloodstained ghost, and he offers a surprising analysis of the complex and misunderstood significance of colonization. Davis presents the age of emancipation as a model for reform." (Publisher's note)

REVIEW: *Choice* v51 no11 p2052 Jl 2014 T. P. Johnson

REVIEW: *Christ Century* v131 no21 p42-4 O 15 2014 Edward J. Blum

REVIEW: *Kirkus Rev* v81 no24 p79 D 15 2013

"The Problem of Slavery in the Age of Emancipation". " A distinguished historian brings his monumental trilogy to a stirring conclusion. Throughout a lifetime of scholarship devoted to the subject, [David Brion] Davis . . . has more than established his bona fides as a leading authority on slavery. . . . The author's treatment of Britain's abolition of the slave trade and its emancipation act and America's grappling with the problem of slavery through the Emancipation Proclamation, the Civil War and the 13th Amendment rests on the impeccable scholarship we've come to expect, but the triumph here is the sympathetic imagination he brings to the topic. . . . Deeply researched, ingeniously argued."

REVIEW: *Libr J* v138 no15 p47 S 15 2013

REVIEW: *New Repub* v244 no28 p36-43 My 26 2014 Steven Hahn

"The Problem of Slavery in the Age of Emancipation." "Over the past half century, [author David Brion] Davis has come to be recognized not only as the leading authority on slavery in the Euro-Atlantic world, but also for his profound engagement with slavery's moral challenges. . . . Although 'The Problem of Slavery in the Age of Emancipation' is the most recent of Davis's many books, it is also the third and concluding volume of a remarkable trilogy that he began to contemplate as long ago as the 1950s. . . . To say that 'The Problem of Slavery in the Age of Emancipation' is less than we might have expected is not to say that it lacks for insights, new material, and a real sense of fulfilling the trilogy as a whole."

DAVIS, KATHRYN. Duplex; [by] Kathryn Davis 208 p. 2013 Graywolf Press

1. American speculative fiction 2. Magicians in literature 3. Robots—Fiction 4. Suburbs 5. Time—Fiction

ISBN 1555976530; 9781555976538 (alk. paper)

LC 2013-936988

SUMMARY: In this book, by Kathryn Davis, "Mary and Eddie are meant for each other--but love is no guarantee, not in these suburbs. Like all children, they exist in an eternal present; time is imminent, and the adults of the street live in their assorted houses like numbers on a clock. . . . Soon a sorcerer's car will speed down Mary's street, and as past and future fold into each other, the resonant parenthesis of her girlhood will close forever." (Publisher's note)

REVIEW: *Booklist* v109 no22 p29 Ag 1 2013 Donna Seaman

REVIEW: *Kirkus Rev* v81 no8 p9 Ap 15 2013

REVIEW: *N Y Times Book Rev* p11 S 22 2013 LYNDA BARRY

"Duplex." "The real and the unreal are laminated so tightly in 'Duplex' you find yourself suddenly lost; you don't know where or when this book takes place, you don't know what this book is about at all. And that is how it takes you in. When I finished 'Duplex' I had the unshakable feeling that I'd only read half of the book, and the other half was still in there and if I wanted to finish it, I'd need to read it again. I wasn't wrong. By then I'd fallen in love with Davis's writing, what it did to me, that combination of horror and excitement that spilled out of the book, into my past, into the now, into everything around me."

REVIEW: *Publ Wkly* v260 no23 p47 Je 10 2013

DAVIS, LYDIA. Can't and Won't; [by] Lydia Davis 304 p. 2014 Farrar, Straus and Giroux

1. Dreams—Fiction 2. Epistolary fiction 3. Flaubert, Gustave, 1821-1880 4. Short stories—Collections 5. Wit & humor
ISBN 0374118582; 9780374118587 (hardcover)
LC 2013-033909

SUMMARY: In this book, author Lydia Davis presents a collection of short stories that "may be literal one-liners . . . [or] they may be lengthier investigations of the havoc wreaked by the most mundane disruptions to routine. The stories may appear in the form of letters of complaint; they may be extracted from Flaubert's correspondence; or they may be inspired by the author's own dreams, or the dreams of friends." (Publisher's note)

REVIEW: *Bookforum* v21 no1 p29 Ap/My 2014 CHRISTINE SMALLWOOD

REVIEW: *Booklist* v110 no14 p47 Mr 15 2014 Donna Seaman

REVIEW: *Kirkus Rev* v82 no5 p250 Mr 1 2014

REVIEW: *Libr J* v139 no4 p86 Mr 1 2014 Evelyn Beck

REVIEW: *London Rev Books* v36 no8 p15-6 Ap 17 2014 Adam Mars-Jones

REVIEW: *N Y Times Book Rev* p17 Ap 6 2014 PETER ORNER

REVIEW: *New Statesman* v143 no5203 p50 Mr 28 2014 Erica Wagner

REVIEW: *New York Times* v163 no56459 pC1-4 Ap 2 2014 DWIGHT GARNER

REVIEW: *Publ Wkly* v261 no2 p48 Ja 13 2014

REVIEW: *TLS* no5780 p32 Ja 10 2014 J. C.

REVIEW: *TLS* no5793 p19 Ap 11 2014 JOHN COHEN

"Can't and Won't." "In Lydia Davis's world, there can be no act or perception that does not raise troubled questions about itself. The protagonists of her recent collection—her longest and most various to date—get caught in knotty dilemmas. . . . They are puzzled by anomalies, such as the appetizing green peas let down by the drab yellow ones pictured on the packaging, or the tin of peppermints that is only two-thirds full. Supposedly trivial problems are transformed by the intensity and clarity of Davis's attention, recasting them as fundamental kinks in the order of the world. . . . Davis's exploration of writing and absence doesn't diminish the psychological richness and frequent poignancy in her stories."

REVIEW: *Va Q Rev* v90 no2 p222-6 Spr 2014 Elliott Holt

REVIEW: *Yale Rev* v102 no4 p162-6 O 2014 CALEB SMITH

DAVIS, LYDIA. Two American Scenes; [by] Lydia Davis 56 p. 2013 New Direction Publishing

1. American poetry 2. Brooks, Sidney 3. Harwich (Mass.) 4. Poems—Collections 5. Powell, John Wesley, 1834-1902
ISBN 0811220419 (paperbook : acid-free paper); 9780811220415 (paperbook : acid-free paper)
LC 2012-040746

SUMMARY: This book "features a diptych of American poems unearthed and reassembled by Lydia Davis and Eliot Weinberger. Davis offers a retelling of the diary of Sidney Brooks, her great-great-great uncle, who lived in the village of Harwich on Cape Cod in the early 1800s. . . . Weinberger mines a different vein in the same historical era--John Wesley Powell's exploration of the American West in 1869, which included the first successful trip down the Colorado River through the Grand Canyon." (fictionadvocate.com)

REVIEW: *TLS* no5756 p32 Jl 26 2013 J. C.

"Two American Scenes," "Power to the People," and "Vagina: A Literary and Cultural History." "'Our Village'. . . is a 're-presentation' of an existing work, 'Our Village' by Sidney Brooks, Ms [Lydia] Davis's great-great-great-uncle, born in Harwich, MA, in 1837. . . . Brooks wrote in prose; Davis has intervened with line breaks. Together with her abridgements and the change of a word here and there, this is all she has done to create a companion to the original. . . . 'Our Village' appears in 'Two American Scenes'. . . . The browser leafing through 'Power to the People' . . . may expect to meet such genial old friends as Love, Peace, and Happiness. . . . But was there really such an eager interest in pubic hair?. . . Among the season's most coveted prizes is the Kate Adie Award for the year's most unoriginal book title. . . . On the longlist is sure to be 'The Vagina: A Literary and Cultural History' by Emma L. E. Rees."

DAVIS, WILLIAM E. Alexander Wilson; the Scot who founded American ornithology; [by] William E. Davis 464 p. 2013 The Belknap Press of Harvard University Press

1. Birds—United States—Pictorial works 2. Historical literature 3. Ornithologists—United States—Biography 4. Ornithology—United States—History
ISBN 9780674072558 (alk. paper)
LC 2012-036742

SUMMARY: This book looks at "Alexander Wilson and 'American Ornithology,' a nine-volume work published between 1808 and 1814 that single-handedly transformed the study of birds in the wild and presaged the field guides of today. In addition to being the first to adopt the Linnaean system of binomial nomenclature to classify North American birds, Wilson was also one of the first to base his findings primarily on the 'observation and description of live birds.'" (Publishers Weekly)

REVIEW: *Choice* v51 no6 p1036 F 2014 D. Flaspohler

"Alexander Wilson: The Scot Who Founded American Ornithology." "Here, [Edward H.] Burtt . . . and Davis . . . cover what is known of Wilson's early life. The book includes many letters to and from US naturalists and dozens of beautifully reproduced and previously unpublished line drawings and paintings of birds that contributed to Wilson's greatest tangible achievement, the encyclopedic nine-volume American Ornithology. . . . This book is full of delightful anecdotes and excellent detailed drawings; it will do much to elevate the reputation of Wilson among those with an interest in birds, illustration, and history."

REVIEW: *Libr J* v138 no12 p100 Jl 1 2013 Henry T. Armistead

REVIEW: *N Y Rev Books* v60 no15 p41-3 O 10 2013 Robert O. Paxton

REVIEW: *Publ Wkly* v260 no10 p54 Mr 11 2013

REVIEW: *TLS* no5756 p22 Jl 26 2013 JEREMY MYNOTT

DAVISON, PETER.ed. George Orwell. See Orwell, G.

DAWE, ALEXANDER.tr. The Time Regulation Institute. See Tanpınar, A. H.

DAWES, JAMES. Evil men; [by] James Dawes 280 p. 2013 Harvard University Press

1. Psychological literature 2. Sino-Japanese War, 1937-1945—Atrocities—Psychological aspects 3. Sino-Japanese War, 1937-1945—Personal narratives, Japanese 4. War crimes—Psychological aspects 5. War criminals—Japan—Interviews 6. War criminals—Psychology
ISBN 9780674072657 (alk. paper)
LC 2012-038236

SUMMARY: "In this complex examination of people's potential for cruelty, as well as the difficult ethics of discussing them, . . . [James] Dawes focuses on interviews with Japanese war criminals who committed torture and rape in occupied China during the Second Sino-Japanese War (1937–1945). He intersperses the stories of these now-elderly men with explorations into related issues." (Publishers Weekly)

REVIEW: *Publ Wkly* v260 no9 p62 Mr 4 2013

REVIEW: *TLS* no5768 p23-4 O 18 2013 ANDREW STARK

"Evil Men." "Between 1937 and 1945, Japanese soldiers murdered, raped and tortured millions of Chinese and Korean civilians. After serving post-war time in Chinese prisons, they returned to Japan and resumed normal family lives. In 2008 James Dawes interviewed fifteen of the surviving men, inviting them--over tea in their modest homes--to account for their roles in some of the most sickening atrocities in human history. 'Evil Men' documents their reflections. . . . As 'Evil Men' eloquently attests, describing atrocities does not make them any more comprehensible. Nor, in trying to understand them, do we make them any more forgivable."

DAWID, PHILIP.ed. Beauty. See Beauty

DAWID, RICHARD. String theory and the scientific method; [by] Richard Dawid x, 202 p. 2013 Cambridge University Press

1. Evidence 2. SCIENCE—Physics 3. Science—Methodology 4. Scientific literature 5. String models
ISBN 9781107029712 (hardback)
LC 2012-044103

SUMMARY: In this book on string theory and scientific principles of empirical proof, Richard Dawid "argues that string theory is just the most conspicuous example of a number of theories in high-energy physics where non-empirical theory assessment has an important part to play. Aimed at physicists and philosophers of science, the book does not use mathematical formalism and explains most technical terms." (Publisher's note)

REVIEW: *Choice* v51 no6 p1049 F 2014 M. Dickinson

REVIEW: *Science* v342 no6161 p934 N 22 2013 George Ellis

"String Theory and the Scientific Method." "Richard Dawid's timely 'String Theory and the Scientific Method' provides a carefully written consideration of what kinds of criteria can be used for nonempirical theory assessment, in the absence of direct or even indirect evidence for the theory's core features. . . . Dawid makes what is probably the best possible case that theoretical justification can succeed. The skeptic will remain unconvinced. . . . I applaud the fact that 'String Theory and the Scientific Method' explicitly raises these questions and addresses them in a clear and well-considered way."

DAWIDOFF, NICHOLAS. Collision Low Crossers; A Year Inside the Turbulent World of NFL Football; [by] Nicholas Dawidoff 352 p. 2013 Little Brown & Co

1. Football 2. Football—United States 3. Football teams 4. New York Jets (Football team) 5. Ryan, Rex, 1962- 6. Sports literature
ISBN 0316196797; 9780316196796
LC 2013-030013

SUMMARY: This book by Nicholas Dawidoff follows the football team the New York Jets throughout 2011, "operations, from the February scouting 'combine' of collegiate talent, through the May draft of college players, the torturous preseason of practices and games, and, finally, to the entire 16-game, regular season schedule and subsequent coaches' postmortem. Head coach Rex Ryan and his staff receive the primary focus." (Booklist)

REVIEW: *Booklist* v110 no5 p11 N 1 2013 Alan Moores

"Collision Low Crossers: A Year Inside the Turbulent World of NFL Football." "[Nicholas] Dawidoff, author of a fine biography of baseball catcher and international spy Moe Berg . . . here turns to the 201 I New York Jets, who gave him apparently unfettered access to virtually every aspect of the team's day-to-day operations. . . . This is a superlative insider's portrait of one NFL team (reminiscent of John Feinstein's similar 'Next Man Up: A Year behind the Lines,' 2005, about the Baltimore Ravens), and it's accessible to casual fans and irresistible to NFL geeks."

REVIEW: *Kirkus Rev* v81 no20 p175 O 15 2013

REVIEW: *Libr J* v138 no11 p64 Je 15 2013 Barbara Hoffert

REVIEW: *Libr J* v138 no21 p105 D 1 2013 John Maxymuk

REVIEW: *Libr J* v138 no21 p105 D 1 2013 Melissa Stearns

REVIEW: *N Y Times Book Rev* p60 D 8 2013 MARK LEIBOVICH

"Collision Low Crossers: A Year Inside the Turbulent World of NFL Football." "The allure of the N.F.L.--as Nicholas Dawidoff points out in his riveting new case study of the professional game, 'Collision Low Crossers'--resides in its mystery. . . . But the book is a triumph less of access than of immersion and portraiture. . . . Dawidoff's writing is rich and lucid if occasionally vulnerable to literary high-stepping. . . . There is, in places, the feel of the author emptying his notebooks, and the book's 485 pages could probably be pared down like a preseason roster."

DAWSON, MADDIE. The opposite of maybe; a novel; [by] Maddie Dawson 400 p. 2014 Broadway Books

1. City and town life—Fiction 2. FICTION—Contemporary Women 3. FICTION—Family Life 4. FICTION—Romance—Contemporary 5. Family life—Fiction 6. Triangles (Interpersonal relations)—Fiction 7. Women—Fiction

ISBN 9780770437688 (pbk.)

LC 2013-031824

SUMMARY: In this book, "when things suddenly unravel, Rosie sends Jonathan packing and moves back home with Soapie, the irascible, opinionated grandmother who raised her" and "Soapie's very unsuitable caregiver, a gardener named Tony It's meant to be a temporary break, of course—until Rosie realizes she's accidentally pregnant at 44, completely unequipped for motherhood, and worse, may be falling in love with Tony, whose life is even more muddled than hers." (Publishers Weekly)

REVIEW: *Kirkus Rev* v82 no3 p172 F 1 2014

"The Opposite of Maybe". "A delightfully witty story of a 44-year-old first-time mother-to-be. . . . Rosie plans for the move to San Diego (Jonathan is going with or without her) but at the last minute decides not to go: She's had enough of Jonathan's myopic selfishness. He drops her off at Soapie's on his way out, and two weeks later, Rosie discovers she is pregnant. Everything seems impossible to handle (including Jonathan, who insists on an abortion), and Rosie would implode if not for Tony, who is kind, goofy and the most sweetly optimistic person Rosie has ever met. . . . Then Jonathan calls from San Diego, begging her to join him so they can be a real family. A messy, funny, surprising story of second chances."

REVIEW: *Libr J* v139 no4 p80 Mr 1 2014 Amy Brozio-Andrews

REVIEW: *Publ Wkly* v261 no3 p31 Ja 20 2014

DAY, ELIZABETH. Home Fires; [by] Elizabeth Day 256 p. 2013 St Martins Pr

1. Child abuse—Fiction 2. Families of military personnel 3. Mothers-in-law—Fiction 4. Older women—Fiction 5. Psychological fiction

ISBN 1608199592; 9781608199594

SUMMARY: In this book, set "in modern-day England, Elsa Weston is 98, debilitated by a stroke, and furious at not being able to express herself or make her body follow orders. In 1920, she is a child trying to cope with a father she barely recalls, back from the war that has left him depressed, angry, and abusive. In between she is the elegant, contained, upper-class woman who intimidates her daughter-in-law, Caroline." (Publishers Weekly)

REVIEW: *Booklist* v110 no2 p28-30 S 15 2013 Michele Leber

"Home Fires." "War marks the lives of three generations of an English family in this finely wrought novel. 1920, when Elsa is just six, her father comes home from war a changed man and begins to physically abuse her. Ninety years later, war brings tragedy again. . . . [Elizabeth] Day . . . captures nuances in the relationships between her well-drawn, fallible characters, focusing on one after the other in nonchronological chapters that constitute a vivid mosaic of grief and aging. A moving family portrait."

REVIEW: *Kirkus Rev* v81 no19 p79 O 1 2013

REVIEW: *Publ Wkly* v260 no28 p143 Jl 15 2013

DAY, H. ALAN. The horse lover; a cowboy's quest to save the wild mustangs; [by] H. Alan Day 264 p. 2014 University of Nebraska Press

1. Cowboys—South Dakota—Biography 2. Memoirs 3. Mustang—Conservation—South Dakota 4. Mustang—Government policy—United States 5. Ranch life—South Dakota 6. Ranchers—South Dakota—Biography 7. Wild horses—Conservation—South Dakota 8. Wild horses—Government policy—United States 9. Wildlife conservationists—South Dakota—Biography

ISBN 0803253354; 9780803253353 (cloth: alkaline paper)

LC 2013-035591

SUMMARY: This book, co-authored with Lynn Wiese Sneyd, presents H. Alan Day's account of "establishing the first sanctuary for wild horses that were considered 'unadoptable' by the federal government—the untamed mustangs were previously warehoused by the Bureau of Land Management. Day persuaded the bureau to let him develop the refuge and tend to the horses. He even proposed using gentle methods to train the animals to be comfortable around humans." (Library Journal)

REVIEW: *Booklist* v110 no13 p10 Mr 1 2014 Nancy Bent

"The Horse Lover: A Cowboy's Quest to Save the Wild Mustangs". "The wonderful story of a cowboy rancher taking on the care and management of 1,500 wild horses. Along the way, we are treated to [H. Alan] Day's reminiscences of his ranching upbringing, stories of some of his favorite cow horses, and tidbits such as the time Kevin Costner came calling while looking to film a little movie called 'Dances with Wolves'. With coauthor [Lynn Wiese] Sneyd's expert assistance, Day's authentic western voice, coupled with his deep understanding of the nature of horses, makes for an instant classic."

REVIEW: *Kirkus Rev* v82 no3 p175 F 1 2014

REVIEW: *Libr J* v139 no6 p106 Ap 1 2014 Deborah Emerson

DAY, LARRY.il. Voices from the Oregon Trail. See Voices from the Oregon Trail

DAY, PETER. Franco's Friends; [by] Peter Day 2011 Biteback Publishing

1. Franco, Francisco, 1892-1975 2. Great Britain—Foreign relations—Spain 3. Nonfiction 4. Spain—History—Civil War, 1936-1939

ISBN 1849540985 (hbk.); 9781849540988 (hbk.)

LC 2011-507752

SUMMARY: This book investigates "how [Spanish leader Francisco] Franco's Spanish supporters in Britain, aided and abetted by MI6 agents, literally flew the future dictator to power. This was done by providing the . . . general with a pilot and a Dragon Rapide aircraft based at Croydon Airport

. . . to get him from the Canary Islands to Spanish North Africa, where he took command of the rebel army . . . touching off the Spanish Civil War. The second part of Day's book tells the . . . tale of how British agents—and British bribes of gold—Kept Franco's regime from joining his ideological ally Hitler in the Second World War." (History Today)

REVIEW: *Hist Today* v62 no2 p58-9 F 2012 Nigel Jones

"The Black & Tans: British Police and Auxiliaries in the Irish War of Independence;" "Franco's Friends: How British Intelligence Helped Bring Franco to Power in Spain;" and "Snow: The Double Life of a World War II Spy." "Like buses on a wet November night good books on Intelligence are rare - but to have three corkers like these arrive at once is a treat indeed. . . . The Black and Tans are so notorious - casting a shadow across Anglo-Irish relations to this day - that it is remarkable that Professor [D.M.] Leeson's book is the first full academic study of them and also notable that Leeson is Canadian. . . . Light on another such discreditable episode is shed by Peter Day in 'Franco's Friends,' which, for the first time in book form, tells the full story of how Franco's Spanish supporters in Britain, aided and abetted by MI6 agents, literally flew the future dictator to power. . . . Like Leeson, [Peter] Day's writing is rather dense and confusingly jumps around chronologically, but the research is impeccable and the subject matter fascinating - a real life Graham Greene thriller. 'Snow' is a remarkable tale of wartime double dealing, espionage and deception that has never been described in such detail before."

DAYWALT, DREW. The day the crayons quit; [by] Drew Daywalt 40 p. 2013 Philomel Books

1. Children's art 2. Color—Fiction 3. Crayons—Fiction 4. Letters—Fiction 5. Picture books for children
ISBN 0399255370; 9780399255373
LC 2012-030384

SUMMARY: In this children's picture book, by Drew Daywalt, illustrated by Oliver Jeffers, "a schoolboy finds a mysterious parcel of letters addressed to him in what looks just like a child's handwriting. The letters, it turns out, are from his crayons, who deeply resent being typecasst according to color. Red is tired of drawing apples and fire engines, Green is bored of coloring dinosaurs and frogs, and so on." (New York Times Book Review)

REVIEW: *Booklist* v109 no21 p77-8 Jl 1 2013 Thom Barthelmess

REVIEW: *Bull Cent Child Books* v67 no1 p13-4 S 2013 H. M.

REVIEW: *Horn Book Magazine* v89 no6 p74-5 N/D 2013 SHARA L. HARDESON

REVIEW: *Kirkus Rev* v81 no9 p78 My 1 2013

REVIEW: *Kirkus Rev* p43 2013 Guide 20to BookExpo America

REVIEW: *N Y Times Book Rev* p16 Ag 25 2013 DAN YACCARINO

"Brush of the Gods," "Ike's Incredible Ink," and "The Day the Crayons Quit." "Four new books on art and white inspires it are just right for children who dream of being artists. . . . 'Brush of the Gods' [is] written by the veteran author Lenore Look, with illustrations by Meilo So evoking sumi ink paintings. . . . A blot of ink creating its own ink to write a story? Although I found the illustrations endearing, the narrative's lack of internal logic was a stumbling block I had a hard time getting over. . . . Although the crayons' wacky voices are believably the kind of thing creative kids come up with when they're daydreaming, [Drew] Daywalt's clever conceit seems stretched to its limit."

REVIEW: *Publ Wkly* p44 Children's starred review annual 2013

REVIEW: *Publ Wkly* v260 no15 p61 Ap 15 2013

REVIEW: *SLJ* v59 no12 p1 D 2013

REVIEW: *SLJ* v59 no7 p59 Jl 2013 Amy Holland

DE-TESTING AND DE-GRADING SCHOOLS; Authentic alternatives to accountability and standardization; 2013 Peter Lang

1. Achievement tests 2. Educational accountability 3. Educational change 4. Educational literature 5. Grading & marking (Students)
ISBN 9781433122408 hardcover; 9781433122392 softcover

SUMMARY: Edited by Joe Bower and P. L. Thomas, "this edited volume brings together a collection of essays that confronts the failure of testing and grading and then offers practical and detailed examinations . . . of education teaching and learning free of the weight of testing and grading. The book explores the historical failure of testing and grading . . . the negative influence of testing and grading on social justice, race, class, and gender." (Publisher's note)

REVIEW: *Choice* v51 no7 p1274-5 Mr 2014 A. L. Hsu

"De-testing and De-grading Schools: Authentic Alternatives to Accountability and Standardization." "[Joe] Bower and [P. L.] Thomas have edited a powerful volume that criticizes testing and the quantification of education. A selection of contributors with wide-ranging experiences in both K-12 and higher education settings offer diverse perspectives on the dangers of standardized testing and the utilization of grades to sort, classify, and compare students. . . . A must read for anyone in the field of education, including parents, teachers, administrators, and policy makers. Recommended for general readers, undergraduates, graduate students, and professionals."

DE BEISTEGUI, MIGUEL. Proust as philosopher; the art of metaphor; 130 p. 2013 Routledge

1. Metaphor in literature 2. Ontology in literature 3. Philosophical literature
ISBN 9780415584319 (hardback : alk. paper); 9780415584326 (pbk. : alk. paper)
LC 2012-007041

SUMMARY: In this analysis of the book "In Search of Lost Time" by Marcel Proust, author Miguel De Beistegui "begins by noting that the disillusion and disappointment repeatedly experienced by Marcel point to 'an ontological deficiency,' a 'lack or want of being' that is 'original and structural.' His main thesis is that this ontology of absence is articulated by metaphor, wbich involves deviation and displacement." (Times Literary Supplement)

REVIEW: *TLS* no5747 p32 My 24 2013 CLARE CARLISLE

"Proust as Philosopher: The Art of Metaphor." "In identifying a convergence between ontology and style . . . this short but ambitious book shows that . . . [Marcel] Proust's literary achievement is inseparable from a philosophy. Whose philosophy this is remains unclear, but Beistegui's insights yield a productive account of the unity of Proust's sprawling masterpiece. . . . Beistegui's reading of Proust is supplemented by brief but illuminating discussions of the novelist's key philosophical influences. . . . Less helpful, though, is the frequent invocation of Gilles Deleuze . . . Dorothée Bonnigal Katz's translation, which was assisted by the author, nicely renders Beistegui's often elegant prose, while preserving some flavour of the French original."

DE BEISTEGUI, MIGUEL.tr. Proust as philosopher. See De Beistegui, M.

DE BOTTON, ALAIN, 1969-. The news; a user's manual; [by] Alain De Botton 272 p. 2014 Pantheon Books Pantheon Books

1. Journalism—Political aspects 2. Journalism—Social aspects 3. Mass media—Political aspects 4. Mass media—Social aspects 5. News audiences 6. Philosophical literature

ISBN 0307379124; 9780307379122

LC 2013-031206

SUMMARY: In this book, "Alain de Botton takes twenty-five archetypal news stories—including an airplane crash, a murder, a celebrity interview, and a political scandal—and submits them to intense analysis. Why are disaster stories often so uplifting? Why do we enjoy watching politicians being brought down? Why are upheavals in far-off lands often so boring? What makes the love lives of celebrities so interesting?" (Publisher's note)

REVIEW: *Booklist* v110 no9/10 p20 Ja 1 2014 Vanessa Bush

REVIEW: *Commonweal* v141 no17 p40-1 O 24 2014 Raymond A. Schroth

REVIEW: *Kirkus Rev* v81 no24 p306 D 15 2013

"The News: A User's Manual". "Unfortunately, [Alain] de Botton's agenda for newsgathering is too often didactic and naïve. . . . In the weakest chapters, the author asks why readers are captivated by celebrity and envious of the rich and famous. He ignores investigative journalism that churns out films, books and documentaries that do ask hard questions. In the end, he urges us to forego news as distraction—especially on the Internet—and master 'the art of being patient midwives to our own thoughts.' How does news shape our thoughts and lives? That's a significant question, but de Botton's musings fall short of a serious response."

REVIEW: *New Statesman* v143 no5196 p48-50 F 7 2014 Peter Wilby

REVIEW: *Publ Wkly* v261 no17 p133 Ap 28 2014

DE COURCY, ANNE. The Fishing Fleets; Husband-hunting in the Raj; [by] Anne De Courcy 352 p. 2012 Weidenfeld & Nicolson

1. British—India—History 2. Courtship—History 3. Historical literature 4. India—History—British occupation, 1765-1947 5. Marriage—History 6. Women—India—History

ISBN 006229007X; 0297863827; 9780062290076; 9780297863823

SUMMARY: In this book, Anne de Courcy examines "the Victorian women who traveled halfway around the world on the hunt for a husband. By the late nineteenth century, . . . many of Her Majesty's best and brightest young men departed for [India] to make their careers, and their fortunes, as bureaucrats, soldiers, and businessmen. But in their wake they left behind countless young ladies who, suddenly bereft of eligible bachelors, found themselves facing an uncertain future." (Publisher's note)

REVIEW: *Booklist* v110 no6 p11 N 15 2013 Bridget Thoreson

REVIEW: *Hist Today* v63 no1 p62-3 Ja 2013 ROSIE LLEWELLYN-JONES

"The Fishing Fleet: Husband Hunting in the Raj." "Anne de Courcy's entertaining book is mainly concerned with the upper echelons of British society. . . . De Courcy has interviewed those of the fishing fleet still alive, and their descendants, making good use of letters, diaries and reminiscences published during the last three decades. Perhaps inevitably the stories that they tell merge into a social history of the Raj itself. . . . Indians do not get much of a look in, unless they were maharajas or loyal servants. . . . This book is not one of them and does not set out to be, but it may prove perhaps the last of a kind, a nostalgic, non-judgemental look back."

REVIEW: *Kirkus Rev* v81 no21 p89 N 1 2013

REVIEW: *N Y Times Book Rev* p9 Mr 2 2014 ALIDA BECKER

"The Fishing Fleet: Husband-Hunting in the Raj." "[Author Anne] de Courcy has done a good deal of . . . trolling for stories in sources that early days . . . to the end of British rule after World War II. . . . For most of the women of the British Raj, life after the wedding turned out to be a precarious blend of luxury and hardship. Servants were so plentiful that the lady of the house was often left with nothing to do, marooned in sometimes crushing loneliness in her own home and yet never really alone."

REVIEW: *Publ Wkly* v260 no38 p66-7 S 23 2013

REVIEW: *TLS* no5720 p32 N 16 2012 DENIS JUDD

DE GELDER, LEEN S. P.ed. Handbook of water analysis. See Handbook of water analysis

DE GOLDI, KATE. The ACB with Honora Lee; [by] Kate De Goldi 124 p. 2012 Longacre

1. Alphabet—Children's fiction 2. Children's stories 3. Grandmothers—Children's fiction 4. Grandparent and child—Children's fiction 5. Rest homes—Children's fiction

ISBN 1770497226; 9781869799892; 9781770497221 (hardcover)

LC 2012-515235

SUMMARY: In this juvenile book, by Kate De Goldi, illustrated by Gregory O'Brien, "Perry's mother and father are busy people . . . they're impatient, they're tired, they get cross easily. And they think that only children, like Perry, should be kept busy. . . . Perry . . . discovers her Gran has an unconventional interest in the alphabet, so Perry decides to make an alphabet book. . . . Soon everyone is interested in Perry's book project." (Publisher's note)

REVIEW: *Booklist* v110 no14 p78-9 Mr 15 2014 Sarah Hunter

"The ACB With Honora Lee." "Hoping to find something she and her gran can bond over, Perry notices Honora's obsession with spelling and decides to illustrate an alphabet book using her help. Over the course of the next several months, smart and observant Perry narrates in a matter-of-fact tone as she gets to know her gran and the nursing home residents by writing down things about them for each letter of the alphabet--though thanks to the scatterbrained residents, her abecedary is fittingly all out of order. [Kate] De Goldi's . . . quiet story, illustrated with [Gregory] O'Brien's lovely full-color abstract drawings, tells a moving tale of patience, compassion, and family."

REVIEW: *Kirkus Rev* v82 no6 p119 Mr 15 2014

REVIEW: *Publ Wkly* v261 no4 p193 Ja 27 2014

REVIEW: *SLJ* v60 no5 p105 My 2014 Michelle Anderson

REVIEW: *Voice of Youth Advocates* v37 no1 p63-4 Ap 2014 Loryn Aman

DE GRAMONT, NINA. Meet me at the river; [by] Nina De Gramont 384 p. 2013 Atheneum Books for Young Readers

1. Death—Fiction 2. Family life—Colorado—Fiction 3. Family problems—Fiction 4. Love—Fiction 5. Love stories 6. Stepfamilies—Fiction
ISBN 1416980148; 9781416980148 (hardcover); 9781416982814 (ebook)
LC 2012-030307

SUMMARY: In this book, by Nina de Gramont, "stepsiblings Tressa and Luke have been close since they were little and when they become teenagers, they slip from being best friends to being something more. Luke is killed in a horrible, tragic accident, and Tressa is suddenly and desperately alone. Unable to outrun the waves of grief and guilt and longing, she is haunted by thoughts of suicide. And then she is haunted by Luke himself." (Publisher's note)

REVIEW: *Booklist* v110 no2 p75 S 15 2013 Lexi Walters Wright

REVIEW: *Bull Cent Child Books* v67 no5 p262 Ja 2014 K. C.

REVIEW: *Kirkus Rev* v81 no16 p143 Ag 15 2013

"Meet Me at the River." "With a deft hand, [author Nina] de Gramont easily convinces the most skeptical of readers that the depth of Tressa's and her boyfriend Luke's emotions can enable a few fleeting, and frustratingly incomplete, moments of connection for them during the year following his tragic death. One of this riveting novel's most astonishing qualities is that it features a spectral character but avoids the clichés of many modern paranormal romances; it is instead a largely realistic tale of grief and healing."

REVIEW: *Voice of Youth Advocates* v36 no6 p57 F 2014 Lisa Martincik

DE HEER, MARGREET. Science, a discovery in comics; [by] Margreet De Heer 192 p. 2013 NBM Publishing

1. Discoveries in science 2. Graphic nonfiction 3. Philosophy of science 4. Science—History 5. Scientists—History
ISBN 1561637505; 9781561637508 (hardcover)
LC 2013-939851

SUMMARY: "This history of scientific discovery, [by Margreet de Heer] is presented as a series of conversations about understanding the laws that govern the universe. . . . Beginning with the ideals of scientific observation and inquiry, the book moves to detailed chronologies of the evolutions of biology, physics, geology, etc. Much of the information is organized in time-line form, which is used to depict the gradual accumulation and transformation of concepts." (School Library Journal)

REVIEW: *Booklist* v110 no4 p37-8 O 15 2013 Ray Olson

"Science: A Discovery in Comics." "[Margaret] De Heer and her colorist husband, Yiri T. Kohl, proceed with science as they did with philosophy ('Philosophy: A Discovery in Comics,' 2012). Appearing as cheerfully animated presenters, de Heer and Kohl first define science and identify three kinds of scientists. . . . Although the information on any one topic is very basic, a great many topics are treated, thanks to the economy of de Heer's visual presentation, and they are all handled very well, thanks to the energy of her drawing style and the vividness of Kohl's coloring. If anything, 'Science' is an even more successful, attractive, and engaging work than Philosophy."

REVIEW: *Voice of Youth Advocates* v36 no5 p50-1 D 2013 KAT KAN

DE LA CRUZ, MELISSA. Frozen; [by] Melissa De la Cruz 336 p. 2013 G.P. Putnam's Sons

1. Environmental degradation—Fiction 2. Immortality—Fiction 3. Magic—Fiction 4. Science fiction 5. Voyages and travels—Fiction
ISBN 0399257543; 9780399257544
LC 2012-034138

SUMMARY: Author Melissa de la Cruz's book focuses on the city of New Vegas that is covered in ice. "Like much of the destroyed planet, the place knows only one temperature--freezing. But some things never change. The diamond in the ice desert is still a 24-hour hedonistic playground and nothing keeps the crowds away from the casino floors, never mind the rumors about sinister sorcery in its shadows." (Publisher's note)

REVIEW: *Booklist* v109 no22 p77-8 Ag 1 2013 Debbie Carton

REVIEW: *Bull Cent Child Books* v67 no5 p263 Ja 2014 K. Q. G.

"Frozen." "The vivid descriptions of a world gone awry and the threat of an all-watching government are familiar dystopic elements, but the appearances of sea monsters, the Fair Folk, and magical dwarves are a bit more surprising. The resulting mash-up of tropes gives this plenty of cross-genre appeal, and the fantasy element is carefully interwoven. . . . Nat and Wes, too, are more complex than they initially appear to be; their individual searches for redemption for past wrongdoings are moving, particularly when they find forgiveness in each other. The ending gets a bit chaotic with an all-out dragon vs. military fight, but a new quest points towards a sequel; readers will want to strap on their snowshoes to tag along."

REVIEW: *Kirkus Rev* v81 no16 p64 Ag 15 2013

REVIEW: *Publ Wkly* v261 no4 p188 Ja 27 2014

REVIEW: *Publ Wkly* v260 no32 p62 Ag 12 2013

REVIEW: *SLJ* v60 no2 p56 F 2014 Toby Rajput

REVIEW: *SLJ* v59 no10 p1 O 2013 Ryan P. Donovan

REVIEW: *Voice of Youth Advocates* v36 no5 p72 D 2013 Susan Hampe

DE LA CRUZ, MELISSA. The ring & the crown; [by] Melissa De la Cruz 384 p. 2014 Hyperion

1. Arranged marriage—Fiction 2. Fantasy 3. Identity—Fiction 4. Kings, queens, rulers, etc.—Fiction 5.

Love—Fiction 6. Magic—Fiction 7. Princesses—Fiction
ISBN 1423157427; 9781423157427 (hardback)
LC 2014-001288

SUMMARY: "In this alternative history" by Melissa de la Cruz, "the Franco-British Empire dominates the globe, backed by the Queen's Merlin, a formidable magician with a stranglehold on the world's magic. At the beginning of the nineteenth century, however, the small country of Prussia makes a move toward rebellion, and the Queen and her Merlin must arrange a marriage between the heirs of the two kingdoms for peace." (Bulletin of the Center for Children's Books)

REVIEW: *Bull Cent Child Books* v67 no10 p510 Je 2014 K. Q. G.

"The Ring and the Crown". "Political intrigue is the name of the game here, and as the focus shifts among the younger characters and their various schemes to get what they want . . . [Melissa] de la Cruz expertly lays out clues to alert the reader to the fact that for all their planning, these youngsters are nonetheless going to fall prey to the larger plans of their politically savvy elders. Unfortunately, any authorial restraint falls completely apart in the last thirty pages or so, as stunning revelation after stunning (and sometimes illogical) revelation is made in a cascade of overkill. Still, secrets, sex, and stylish clothes tend to be a winning combination, so hand this to readers who like their costume dramas really dramatic."

REVIEW: *Kirkus Rev* v82 no7 p301 Ap 1 2014

REVIEW: *SLJ* v60 no4 p161 Ap 2014 Marissa Lieberman

REVIEW: *SLJ* v60 no8 p53 Ag 2014 Amanda Spino

REVIEW: *Voice of Youth Advocates* v37 no3 p80 Ag 2014 Deborah L. Dubois

DE LA MOTTE, ANDERS. Bubble; a thriller; [by] Anders De la Motte 468 p. 2014 Pocket Books

1. Families—Fiction 2. Games 3. Internet—Security measures 4. Social media 5. Suspense fiction
ISBN 1476712948; 9781476712949

SUMMARY: This book is the third in a trilogy by Anders de la Motte. "HP could never have imagined he'd become entwined in a chaotic and dangerous game of life and death when he picked up a lost cell phone on a commuter train. . . . Now, his paranoia quickly grows to mania, as he is convinced that the Game Master and past characters are following him and that the police are watching him. . . . What he uncovers is a potential link between his own father's past and the Game." (Publisher's note)

REVIEW: *Booklist* v110 no11 p25-6 F 1 2014 David Pitt

REVIEW: *Kirkus Rev* v82 no4 p90 F 15 2014

"Bubble". "The finale of a trilogy that presents an unlikely sibling alliance against a mysterious social media game. . . . Building on an Orwellian theme of owning the future through control of the past, this mysterious game utilizes a host of seemingly sinister characters to gain access to the information supplied by an individual in the past as a means to control their decisions in the future. While HP uncovers the far-ranging capacity for control that this premise offers, Rebecca discovers that their father may have been involved with top-secret affairs within Sweden. Issues of family and unresolved emotions loom in the background as the story jumps from one endorphin-charged scene to another. An interesting concept developed into an exciting read."

REVIEW: *Publ Wkly* v260 no52 p34-5 D 23 2013

DE LA MOTTE, ANDERS. Buzz; A Thriller; [by] Anders De la Motte 496 p. 2014 Pocket Books

1. Bodyguards 2. Brothers & sisters—Fiction 3. Internet games 4. Murder—Fiction 5. Suspense fiction
ISBN 1476712913; 9781476712918

SUMMARY: In this book, by Anders de la Motte, "HP Pettersson is on the run. And with good reason. After he learned that the mysterious Game, a sort of real-world role-playing exercise, wasn't all it was cracked up to be, HP cleaned out the Game's bank account as payback for all the misery he'd been forced to inflict on innocent people. Now he's flitting around the world, living under various assumed names, trying to find someplace where the Game can't find him." (Booklist)

REVIEW: *Booklist* v110 no6 p22-3 N 15 2013 David Pitt

REVIEW: *Kirkus Rev* v82 no3 p150 F 1 2014

"Buzz". "The distinct challenges facing both siblings develop into an elaborate maze that coincidentally reunites brother and sister. Although HP and Rebecca must overcome individual trials, they also find that they share common enemies and that their highly specialized skills make them a formidable team against an increasingly amorphous technological leviathan. To complicate matters, an old family friend offers his services to help Rebecca in exchange for contacting HP about a covert task, thus setting the stage for a follow-up novel. Although the story suffers from some gaps, [Anders] de la Motte uses his industry knowledge to offer a believable story. A timely, realistic thriller about the governance of online information."

REVIEW: *Publ Wkly* v260 no42 p33 O 21 2013

DE LA PEDRAJA TOMÁN, RENÉ. Wars of Latin America, 1982-2013; the path to peace; [by] René De la Pedraja Tomán 292 p. 2013 McFarland & Company, Inc., Publishers

1. Guerrilla warfare—Latin America—History—20th century 2. Guerrilla warfare—Latin America—History—21st century 3. Historical literature
ISBN 9780786470167 (softcover: alk. paper)
LC 2013-024290

SUMMARY: "This study completes a trilogy examining the impact of local and international wars across Latin America since 1899. . . . The book is divided into three . . . parts: 'Leftist Revolutionaries on the Defensive,' 'Leftist Revolutionaries in Retreat,' and 'Peru and Colombia.'" Topics include "Colombia and its notorious FARC guerrilla group" and "Peru and its Shining Path and Tupac Amaru Revolutionary Movement". (Choice: Current Reviews for Academic Libraries)

REVIEW: *Choice* v51 no8 p1469 Ap 2014 F. W. Knight

"Wars of Latin America, 1982-2013: The Path to Peace". "This study completes a trilogy examining the impact of local and international wars across Latin America since 1899. . . . The coverage is comprehensive, and special attention is given to Colombia and its notorious FARC guerrilla group, and to Peru and its Shining Path and Tupac Amaru Revolutionary Movement. But the broad coverage is attractive. . . . The writing is consistently clear, and [René] De La Pedraja . . . enhances the text with useful maps and excellent references. . . . The detailed information on CIA support for insurgent forces throughout Central America . . . makes this an attractive source for upper-division and graduate collections focusing on 20th-century Latin America or the military history of the region."

DE LA PEÑA, MATT. The living; [by] Matt De la Peña 320 p. 2013 Delacorte Press

1. Adventure stories 2. Cruise ships—Fiction 3. Diseases—Fiction 4. Mexican Americans—Fiction 5. Natural disasters—Fiction 6. Survival—Fiction
ISBN 9780375989919 (glb); 9780385741200 (hc)
LC 2012-050778

SUMMARY: In this book, by Matt de la Peña, "Shy took [a] summer job to make some money. In a few months on a luxury cruise liner, he'll rake in the tips and be able to help his mom and sister out with the bills. . . . But everything changes when the Big One hits. Shy's only weeks out at sea when an earthquake more massive than ever before recorded hits California, and his life is forever changed. The earthquake is only the first disaster. Suddenly it's a fight to survive for those left living." (Publisher's note)

REVIEW: *Booklist* v110 no1 p114-5 S 1 2013 Daniel Kraus

REVIEW: *Bull Cent Child Books* v67 no3 p174-5 N 2013 E. B.

"The Living." "It sounded like a great summer gig for a rising senior--pool boy and water server aboard a luxury liner shuttling rich vacationers between California and Mexico and Hawaii--but Shy Espinoza is finding the job isn't as fun-filled as he'd thought. . . . There's an awful lot going on here, and the pile-up of tragedies and evil plots could strain the credulity of even hardcore thriller fans. [Author Matt de la] Peña takes the time to establish some solid rapport among his characters before unleashing the mayhem, though, and the central disease and drug scam is so viciously immoral that readers will probably hook passage on the upcoming sequel, to learn whether Shy and his two smokin'-hot love interests will bring the bad guys to their knees."

REVIEW: *Kirkus Rev* v81 no19 p124 O 1 2013

REVIEW: *Libr J* v139 no4 p52 Mr 1 2014 Denise Garofalo

REVIEW: *N Y Times Book Rev* p39 N 10 2013 MOTOKO RICH

REVIEW: *SLJ* v59 no10 p1 O 2013 Vicki Reutter

REVIEW: *SLJ* v60 no3 p62 Mr 2014 Tim Wadham

REVIEW: *Voice of Youth Advocates* v36 no5 p55 D 2013 Karen Jensen

DE LAURENTIIS, GIADA, 1970-. Naples!; [by] Giada De Laurentiis 144 p. 2013 Grosset & Dunlap, published by the Penguin Group

1. Brothers and sisters—Fiction 2. Children's stories 3. Cooking, Italian—Fiction 4. Food—Fiction 5. Magic—Fiction 6. Space and time—Fiction
ISBN 9780448462561 (pbk); 9780448478531 (hc)
LC 2013-021689

SUMMARY: In this children's book in the Recipe for Adventure series by Giada de Laurentiis, illustrated by Francesca Gambatesa, "When Zia Donatella comes to live with the Bertolizzi family, little do Alfie and his older sister Emilia know what's in store for them. . . . Alfie and Emilia find themselves transported to Naples, where they meet Marco, a young Italian boy on a very important mission to shop for the essential ingredients for his family's entry in the city's annual pizzafest contest." (Publisher's note)

REVIEW: *Kirkus Rev* v81 no16 p67 Ag 15 2013

"Naples!" "[Author Giada] De Laurentiis should be embarrassed to have her name on this trite, clichéd and overlong story, although it is not clear how much she had to do with the writing. Siblings Alfredo and Emilia are having takeout pizza, again, as their parents are too busy to cook. Appearing on their doorstep is their mother's aunt, Zia Donatella, who travels the world having adventures and who loves to cook. The children find her making zeppole in the kitchen that night, and then, after a bite, they find themselves in Naples, their family's hometown, alone! . . . The siblings' teasing relationship, their aunt's glamour and their parents' occasional use of Italian are all broadly drawn and border on caricature. This kicks off a series. Oh, dear."

REVIEW: *Publ Wkly* v260 no28 p171 Jl 15 2013

DE LINT, CHARLES, 1951-. Seven wild sisters; A Modern Fairy Tale; [by] Charles De Lint 272 p. 2013 Little, Brown and Co.

1. Adventure and adventurers—Fiction 2. Fairies—Fiction 3. Fantasy fiction 4. Kidnapping—Fiction 5. Magic—Fiction 6. Sisters—Fiction
ISBN 0316053562; 9780316053563
LC 2012-045328

SUMMARY: This book, by Charles de Lint, is a "companion novel to 'The Cats of Tanglewood Forest.' . . . When it comes to fairies, Sarah Jane Dillard must be careful what she wishes for. . . . When Sarah Jane discovers a tiny man wounded by a cluster of miniature poison arrows, she brings him to the reclusive Aunt Lillian for help. But the two quickly find themselves ensnared in a longtime war between rival fairy clans, and Sarah Jane's six sisters have been kidnapped to use as ransom." (Publisher's note)

REVIEW: *Bull Cent Child Books* v67 no9 p450 My 2014 A. S.

REVIEW: *Kirkus Rev* v82 no2 p240 Ja 15 2014

"Seven Wild Sisters: A Modern Fairy Tale". " Beautiful bookmaking, lovely storytelling and wondrous illustrations make for a splendid sequel-of-sorts to 'The Cats of Tanglewood Forest' (2013). . . . The language is as pretty on the page as it is in the speaking, with rich echoes of fantasy tropes. The story and the art are reworked from a limited edition of some time ago, described by [Charles] Vess in an artist's note. There is a promise of more stories at the ever-so-satisfying end, which comes with the tiniest hint of romance past and future—readers will be enchanted."

REVIEW: *SLJ* v60 no4 p142 Ap 2014 Michele Shaw

DE LISLE, LEANDA. Tudor; passion. manipulation. murder. the story of England's most notorious royal family; [by] Leanda De Lisle 576 p. 2013 PublicAffairs

1. Beaufort, Margaret, Countess of Richmond & Derby, 1443-1509 2. Elizabeth I, Queen of England, 1533-1603 3. Great Britain—History—Tudors, 1485-1603 4. Historical literature 5. Tudor, Owen
ISBN 9781610393638 (hardcover); 9781610393645 (electronic)
LC 2013-945411

SUMMARY: This book on the Tudor dynasty "cover[s]

everything from the Tudors' obscure beginnings, when a Welsh squire named Owen Tudor literally fell into the lap of Henry V's widow, Catherine of Valois, and later married her, to the death of the couple's great-great-granddaughter, Elizabeth I." Leanda de Lisle "notes the key roles played by often-overlooked female members of the extended family in the events that culminated in the accession of the first Tudor monarch." (Publishers Weekly)

REVIEW: *Booklist* v110 no2 p19 S 15 2013 Jay Freeman

"Tudor: The Family Story, 1437-1603." "The Tudor epoch in English history lends itself to the soap-opera treatment as well as serious historical study. This enjoyable, well-written account is a bit of both. . . . Bouncing between hard historical facts and sometimes-debatable speculations, [Leanda] De Lisle examines the key events and characters that make the Tudor story interesting. She offers a surprisingly sympathetic portrait of Margaret Beaufort, the mother of the first Tudor monarch, Henry VII. . . . This is a very well-done popular history ideal for general readers."

REVIEW: *Hist Today* v63 no11 p62-3 N 2013 DESMOND SEWARD

REVIEW: *Publ Wkly* v260 no29 p52 Jl 22 2013

DE LOS SANTOS, MARISA. Saving Lucas Biggs. See Teague, D.

DE MAISTRE, XAVIER. A journey around my room; 256 p. 2013 Alma Books

1. Memory (Philosophy) 2. Patriotism 3. Prisoners' writings 4. Satire 5. Time

ISBN 1847493084 (pbk.); 9781847493088 (pbk.)

SUMMARY: In this book, "confined in 1790 to his room for forty-two days for his part in a duel, Xavier de Maistre (1763-1852), a military man of conservative outlook, seized the opportunity to become an armchair traveller. He reports his discoveries with mock-serious, self-deprecating humour in forty-two short musings which show him with one foot in Shandy-land and the other in the nascen troman gai." (Times Literary Supplement)

REVIEW: *TLS* no5753 p26 Jl 5 2013 DAVID COWARD

"A Journey Around My Room." "[Xavier de Maistre] reports his discoveries with mock-serious, self-deprecating humour in forty-two short musings which show him with one foot in Shandy-land and the other in the nascent roman gai. As a mode of locomotion, armchair travel, being inexpensive and physically undemanding, is recommended for both sexes and all ages. . . . This new translation is exceptionally good, though [Andrew] Brown might have chosen to work from the texts published byn Pierre Dumas in 1984 rather than those issued by Laffont in 1959."

DE QUEIROZ, ALAN. The monkey's voyage; how improbable journeys shaped the history of life; [by] Alan De Queiroz 368 p. 2013 Basic Books

1. Animal dispersal 2. Animals—Dispersal 3. Biogeography 4. Biological literature 5. Plant dispersal 6. Plants—Dispersal 7. Species distribution

ISBN 0465020518; 9780465020515 (hardcover)

LC 2013-036248

SUMMARY: In this book, biologist Alan De Queiroz "describes the radical new view of how fragmented distributions came into being: frogs and mammals rode on rafts and icebergs, tiny spiders drifted on storm winds, and plant seeds were carried in the plumage of sea-going birds to create the map of life we see today. In other words, these organisms were not simply constrained by continental fate; they were the makers of their own geographic destiny." (Publisher's note)

REVIEW: *Booklist* v110 no8 p5 D 15 2013 Ray Olson

REVIEW: *Kirkus Rev* v81 no22 p160 N 15 2013

REVIEW: *Libr J* v139 no2 p93 F 1 2014 Cynthia Lee Knight

REVIEW: *N Y Times Book Rev* p17 Ja 19 2014 JONATHAN WEINER

"The Monkey's Voyage: How Improbable Journeys Shaped the History of Life." "The book's centerpiece is the incredible journey of the New World monkeys. . . . [Author Alan] De Queiroz writes in a pleasant, relaxed style. If anything, his book's organization is a little too relaxed . . . , with charts, maps, photographs and sidebars defining technical terms scattered throughout, and big blocks of anecdotes in italics tacked on at the end of each chapter. It reads like an eclectic scrapbook, full of interesting bits from hither and yon."

REVIEW: *Publ Wkly* v260 no43 p51 O 28 2013

REVIEW: *Science* v343 no6180 p153-4 Ap 11 2014 Ran Nathan Oz Nathan

"The Monkey's Voyage: How Improbable Journeys Shaped the History of Life." "In 'The Monkey's Voyage,' Alan de Queiroz argues that long-distance dispersals are necessary to explaining the evolutionary histories of many animals and plants across the world. . . . Although some readers may deem it too slow or too one-sided, we found 'The Monkey's Voyage' a joy to read and a great example of how a potentially dry scientific debate can be presented to attract a broad readership. . . . 'The Monkey's Voyage' lacks a basic quantitative treatment of the link between very low probabilities and big numbers. It provides only a short—but admittedly brilliant—glimpse into this core issue through a wonderful hypothetical present-day discussion among prominent biogeographers."

DE RUITER, ANTON H. J. Spacecraft dynamics and control; an introduction; [by] Anton H. J. De Ruiter xviii, 569 p. 2013 Wiley

1. Aeronautical literature 2. Artificial satellites—Attitude control systems 3. Space flight 4. Space vehicles—Attitude control systems 5. Space vehicles—Dynamics 6. TECHNOLOGY & ENGINEERING—Aeronautics & Astronautics

ISBN 9781118342367 (hardback)

LC 2012-033616

SUMMARY: Written by Anton H. de Ruiter, Christopher Damaren, James R. Forbes, this book "presents the fundamentals of classical control in the context of spacecraft attitude control. . . . The entire treatment of both orbital and attitude dynamics makes use of vectrix notation, which is a tool that allows the user to write down any vector equation of motion without consideration of a reference frame." (Publisher's note)

REVIEW: *Choice* v51 no1 p112 S 2013 D. B. Spencer

"Spacecraft Dynamics and Control: An Introduction." "This 26-chapter book starts with a review of kinematics and rigid body dynamics, covering the fundamentals readers need to know to proceed. [Authors Anton H. J.] De Ruiter .

. . , [Christopher J.] Damaren . . . , and [James R.] Forbes . . . then present orbital mechanics, which follows the derivation of important equations of motion from first principles. The authors also introduce modern topics such as the analysis and design of low-thrust trajectory and design as well as satellite formation flying. . . . Overall, this book provides a good, comprehensive examination of the fundamentals of translational and rotational dynamics, determination, and control of spacecraft."

DE SA, ANTHONY. Kicking the sky; a novel; [by] Anthony De Sa 336 p. 2014 Algonquin Books of Chapel Hill

1. Boys—Fiction 2. Canadian fiction 3. Murder—Fiction 4. Portuguese—Canada—Fiction

ISBN 9781565129276

LC 2013-038534

SUMMARY: In this novel by Anthony De Sa, "It was 1977 when a shoeshine boy, Emanuel Jaques, was brutally murdered in Toronto. In the aftermath of the crime, twelve-year-old Antonio Rebelo explores his neighborhood's dark garages and labyrinthine back alleys along with his rapscallion friends. As the media unravels the truth behind the Shoeshine Boy murder, Antonio sees his immigrant family--and his Portuguese neighborhood--with new eyes." (Publisher's note)

REVIEW: *Booklist* v110 no11 p23 F 1 2014 Michael Cart

REVIEW: *Kirkus Rev* v82 no2 p204 Ja 15 2014

"Kicking the Sky". "A scrappy immigrant community in Toronto in 1977 sinks deeper into superstition and violence after a child's murder; a pubescent boy struggles to comprehend the events in this gritty second book from Canadian [Anthony] De Sa . . . based on real events. . . . De Sa's novel, a feverish portrait of the impoverished but colorful Portuguese community, is sporadically sympathetic but more often spiky, laden with abusive childhoods, unreliable adults and dangerous sexuality. As the lies, disasters, disappointments and disillusionments accumulate, Antonio's group of friends and family fractures, and his childhood comes to an end. A largely bleak vision, top-heavy with angst and tragedy."

REVIEW: *Libr J* v139 no6 p80 Ap 1 2014 Lisa Rohrbaugh

REVIEW: *Publ Wkly* v260 no48 p28 N 25 2013

REVIEW: *Quill Quire* v79 no8 p25-7 O 2013 Angie Abdou

"Kicking the Sky." "Anthony De Sa's . . . long-awaited first novel . . . is set in a Portuguese neighbourhood in Toronto, and uses as its starting point the 1977 rape and murder of Emanuel Jaques, a young shoeshine boy originally from the Azores. The novel begins with Emanuel's disappearance and ends with his murderers being convicted, but the real-life tragedy forms the backdrop rather than the focus of De Sa's story. . . . At least initially, 'Kicking the Sky' does not boast the kind of amped-up drama that its background context might lead readers to expect. However, the confident narrative voice guides the reader into increasingly dark territory, and the Bildungsroman gradually morphs into full-fledged horror."

DE VERA, JEAN-PIERRE.ed. Habitability of other planets and satellites. See Habitability of other planets and satellites

DE VIGAN, DELPHINE. Nothing holds back the night; a novel; [by] Delphine De Vigan 352 p. 2014 St Martins Pr

1. Autobiographical fiction 2. Mentally ill women—Fiction 3. Mothers—Fiction

ISBN 1620400839; 9781620400838 (alk. paper)

LC 2013-021065

SUMMARY: In this autobiographical novel, by Delphine de Vigan, "only a teenager when Delphine was born, Lucile raised two daughters largely alone. She was a former child model from a Bohemian family, younger and more glamorous than the other mothers. . . . But as Delphine grew up, Lucile's occasional sadness gave way to overwhelming despair and delusion. She became convinced she was telepathic . . . she gave away all her money; she was hospitalized, medicated, and released in a kind of trance." (Publisher's note)

REVIEW: *Booklist* v110 no13 p19 Mr 1 2014 Leah Strauss

REVIEW: *Kirkus Rev* v81 no24 p61 D 15 2013

"Nothing Holds Back the Night". " Prompted by her mother's suicide, a French author delicately combines memoir, biography and fiction to explore her family's increasingly dark psychology. The book has sold an estimated half a million copies in France. . . . Constantly trying to separate truth from fable and family myth, the author treads carefully, conscious of sensitivities and her own uncertainties, while tracing events to their tragically preordained conclusion. Sympathy and sadness infuse this compelling investigation in which the author herself plays a difficult role."

REVIEW: *N Y Times Book Rev* p31 My 11 2014 NANCY KLINE

REVIEW: *New York Times* v163 no56453 pC4 Mr 27 2014 John Williams

REVIEW: *Publ Wkly* v260 no44 p42 N 4 2013

REVIEW: *Women's Review of Books* v31 no5 p14-5 S/O 2014 Carol Sternhell

DE VISE, DANIEL. I forgot to remember; a memoir of amnesia; [by] Daniel De Vise 288 p. 2014 Simon & Schuster

1. Amnesia—Patients—Biography 2. Brain—Concussion—Complications 3. Memoirs 4. People with mental disabilities—Family relationships

ISBN 0062237187; 9781451685817 (hardback); 9781451685824 (trade paperback)

LC 2013-034048

SUMMARY: This memoir describes how author "Su Meck was twenty-two and married with two children when a ceiling fan in her kitchen fell and struck her on the head, leaving her with a traumatic brain injury that erased all her memories of her life up to that point. . . . Yet after just three weeks in the hospital, Su was released and once again charged with the care of two toddlers and a busy household." (Publisher's note)

REVIEW: *Booklist* v110 no7 p18 D 1 2013 June Sawyers

REVIEW: *N Y Times Book Rev* p14 F 16 2014 SALLY SATEL

"The Answer to the Riddle Is Me: A Memoir of Amnesia" and "I Forgot to Remember: A Memoir of Amnesia." "David Stuart MacLean . . . wandered dazed and frightened on a train platform in Hyderabad, India. . . . 'The Answer to the Riddle Is Me' is his vivid reflection on the 10 years following the Lariam-induced break with reality and the memory problems that persisted in its wake. . . . Su Meck, who was 22 when she was hit by a kitchen fan that fell from her ceiling, has spent the last two decades trying to inhabit a completely new person. . . . Her understated book, 'I Forgot to Remember,' is more an account than a memoir. The matter-of-fact delivery makes the harrowing details of her ordeal stand out all the more."

REVIEW: *Publ Wkly* v260 no44 p57 N 4 2013

DE VOTO, BERNARD AUGUSTINE, 1897-1955. The hour; 127 p. 2010 Tin House Books

1. Alcoholic beverages 2. American wit & humor 3. Cocktails 4. Cocktails—Humor 5. Drinking customs
ISBN 9780982504802 (hbk.)
LC 2009-038327

SUMMARY: This humorous book by Bernard DeVoto, first published in 1948, is "one of the first attempts to formulate a philosophy of the cocktail." The author "lays down the law in words of fire, banishing all manner of mixed drinks to outer darkness, lamenting the perversion of national taste during Prohibition." (New York Times)

REVIEW: *Booklist* v110 no3 p20 O 1 2013 DAVID WRIGHT

"Boozehound: On the Trail of the Rare, the Obscure, and the Overrated in Spirits," "The Hour: A Cocktail Manifesto, and "Three Sheets to the Wind: One Man's Quest for the Meaning of Beer." "Bernard DeVoto's beloved and recently reprinted 'The Hour: A Cocktail Manifesto' is perhaps ounce for ounce a purer delight, with its deft, hilarious homage to the sweet transports of drink. . . . In 'Boozehound,' spirits columnist Jason Wilson travels the globe scaring up interesting liquors. . . . Wilson's style is friendly and down to earth as he pokes fun at fads and deflates the mystical malarkey of the spirits trade. . . . Pete Brown's 'Three Sheets to the Wind' does a similar job for beer, consisting of an epic pub crawl across the globe, exploring the sociability of beer."

DE WAAL, ELISABETH. The Exiles Return; A Novel; [by] Elisabeth De Waal 336 p. 2014 St. Martin's Press

1. Austria—History—20th century 2. Exiles 3. Historical fiction 4. Reconstruction (1939-1951) 5. Vienna (Austria)—History
ISBN 1250045789; 9781250045782

SUMMARY: This novel, by Elisabeth De Waal, tells the story of "post-Second World War Vienna. . . . [and] follows a number of exiles, each returning under very different circumstances. . . . There is Kuno Adler, a Jewish research scientist, who is tired of his unfulfilling existence in America; Theophil Kanakis, a wealthy Greek businessman; . . . Marie-Theres, a brooding teenager; . . . and Prince "Bimbo" Grein, a handsome young man with a title divested of all its social currency." (Publisher's note)

REVIEW: *Booklist* v110 no8 p18-9 D 15 2013 Donna Seaman

REVIEW: *Kirkus Rev* v81 no20 p178 O 15 2013

REVIEW: *Libr J* v138 no20 p1 N 15 2013

REVIEW: *Libr J* v138 no13 p53 Ag 1 2013 Barbara Hoffert

REVIEW: *N Y Rev Books* v51 no7 p35-6 Ap 24 2014 Leo Carey

"The Exiles Return." "'The Exiles Return,' now published for the first time, was written in the mid-1950s, after fraught years when [author] Elisabeth [de Waal] had taken on the burden of seeking restitution of the Ephrussis' property. . . . Elisabeth traveled to Vienna soon after the war and for five years wrote letters from England pressing her family's case. . . . In . . . interviews between exiles and natives, between those who have returned and those who never left, De Waal sees both sides and cannot decide which viewpoint to inhabit. The book, fascinating in its failure, is a testament to the dislocations it examines. It is a novel that doesn't know where it belongs."

REVIEW: *N Y Times Book Rev* p12 Ja 12 2014 ANDREW ERVIN

REVIEW: *New Yorker* v90 no4 p73-1 Mr 17 2014

REVIEW: *Publ Wkly* v260 no43 p31 O 28 2013

DE WIEL, JEROME AAN.ed. Ireland through European eyes. See Ireland through European eyes

DEAN, DAVID.il. Barefoot Books World Atlas. See Crane, N.

DEAR LIFE; stories; 2013 Vintage Books

1. Short stories 2. Huron, Lake (Mich. and Ont.) -- Fiction
ISBN 9780307743725

SUMMARY: This collection of short stories by Alice Munro, winner of the 2013 Nobel Prize in Literature, features "a soldier returning from war and avoiding his fiancee, a wealthy woman deciding whether to confront a blackmailer, an adulterous mother and her neglected children, a guilt-ridden father, a young teacher jilted by her employer. . . . Four autobiographical tales offers an unprecedented glimpse into Munro's own childhood." (Publisher's note)

REVIEW: *Atlantic* v310 no5 p108 D 2012

REVIEW: *Booklist* v109 no3 p31 O 1 2012 Brad Hooper

"Dear Life." "[Alice] Munro's latest collection brings to mind the expression, 'What is old is new again.' As curiously trite and hardly complimentary as that statement may sound, it is offered as unreserved praise for the continued wonderment provided by arguably the best short story writer in English today. . . . In every story she finds new ways to make the lives of ordinary people compelling. 'Amundsen' has a setting that will pique the interest of avid Munro followers, yet it is delivered with a tone surprising and even disturbing. A young woman ventures to a remote area to assume teaching duties in a TB sanitarium, soon entering into a dismal relationship with the head doctor."

REVIEW: *Christ Century* v130 no6 p40-1 Mr 20 2013 Amy Frykholm

REVIEW: *Commentary* v134 no4 p60-2 N 2012 D.G. MYERS

REVIEW: *Kirkus Rev* p30 N 15 2012 Best Fiction & Children's Books

REVIEW: *Kirkus Rev* v80 no20 p253 O 15 2012

REVIEW: *Libr J* v137 no18 p65 N 1 2012 Barbara Love

REVIEW: *N Y Rev Books* v60 no1 p24-6 Ja 10 2013 Cathleen Schine

"Dear Life." "With all their fullness of narrative and character, her stories are elegant and sharp, pared down--sometimes shockingly so. Her new collection. Dear Life, is as rich and astonishing as anything she has done before. . . . [Alice] Munro is eighty-one years old and claims that this will be her last book. 'Dear Life' is so full of momentum that this does not seem possible. . . . There is a surprising sense of possibility everywhere in 'Dear Life' that is almost optimistic. . . . In 'Dear Life,' the story and the collection named for it, there is everything we have come to recognize in an Alice Munro story and long to recognize as many more times as Alice Munro will grace us with one."

REVIEW: *N Y Times Book Rev* p11 N 18 2012 CHARLES McGRATH

REVIEW: *N Y Times Book Rev* p30 N 25 2012

REVIEW: *New Statesman* v141 no5132 p46-7 N 16 2012 Leo Robson

REVIEW: *New York Times* p1 D 11 2012 MICHIKO KAKUTANI

REVIEW: *Publ Wkly* v259 no39 p48 S 24 2012

REVIEW: *Publ Wkly* v260 no8 p161 F 25 2013

REVIEW: *Quill Quire* v78 no9 p25 N 2012 James Grainger

REVIEW: *Quill Quire* v78 no10 p16-22 D 2012

REVIEW: *TLS* no5721 p19 N 23 2012

DEATON, ANGUS. The great escape; health, wealth, and the origins of inequality; [by] Angus Deaton 376 p. 2013 Princeton University Press

1. Economic development 2. Economics literature 3. Equality 4. Income distribution 5. World health
ISBN 9780691153544 (hardcover : alk. paper)
LC 2013-941754

SUMMARY: This book "tells the . . . story of how, starting 250 years ago, some parts of the world began to experience sustained progress, opening up gaps and setting the stage for today's hugely unequal world. [Angus] Deaton takes an in-depth look at the historical and ongoing patterns behind the health and wealth of nations, and he addresses what needs to be done to help those left behind. . . . Deaton argues that international aid has been ineffective and even harmful." (Publisher's note)

REVIEW: *Choice* v51 no6 p1059-60 F 2014 J. P. Jacobsen

REVIEW: *Economist* v409 no8857 p100-1 O 12 2013

"The Great Escape: Health, Wealth, and the Origins of Inequality." "Is the world becoming a fairer as well as a richer place? Few economists are better equipped to answer this question than Angus Deaton of Princeton University, who has thought hard about measuring international well-being and is not afraid to roam through history. Refreshingly, Mr. Deaton also reaches beyond a purely economic narrative to encompass often neglected dimensions of progress such as better health. . . . 'The Great Escape' covers a lot of ground and there will be points that other scholars may dispute. . . . But the theme requires a big canvas and bold brushwork, and Mr. Deaton capably offers both."

REVIEW: *N Y Times Book Rev* p13 D 22 2013 DAVID LEONHARDT

REVIEW: *Nation* v297 no23 p43-7 D 9 2013 JENNIFER SZALAI

REVIEW: *New Sci* v220 no2937 p48-9 O 5 2013 Debora MacKenzie

REVIEW: *New York Times* v163 no56288 p4 O 13 2013 FRED ANDREWS

DEBELJAK, ERICA JOHNSON.tr. The master of insomnia. See Novak, B.A.

DECKER, JAMES K. Fallout; [by] James K. Decker 384 p. 2014 Penguin Group USA

1. Extraterrestrial life—Fiction 2. Human-alien encounters—Fiction 3. Missing persons—Fiction 4. Science fiction 5. Viruses
ISBN 0451413415; 9780451413413

SUMMARY: In this book, by James K. Decker, "Sam Shao has found out too much about the haan, by accident. All humans have to get along with them—we owe them our lives—and Sam even counts a haan among her best friends. But the more she learns, the less she trusts them. It doesn't help that the building of new haan colonies seems to be coinciding with a rash of missing persons cases. Sam and her hacker friends are determined to reveal the truth about the haan, before it's too late." (Publisher's note)

REVIEW: *Kirkus Rev* v82 no2 p290 Ja 15 2014

"Fallout". "With fast and furious action, hairsbreadth escapes and surprises on every page, it's eye-popping stuff, set against a gritty, grainy, visceral depiction of a city scarred by overpopulation, malnourishment and fear of the unknown. Yet it's impossible to ignore the gaping holes in the logical fabric. Earth, for instance, is now too radioactive to sustain human life in the long term; even the stars are different—and apparently nobody noticed. Readers who thrive on tension and excitement will feel themselves amply rewarded; those who tend to question underlying assumptions, not so much."

DECODING YOUR DOG; The Ultimate Experts Explain Common Dog Behaviors and Reveal How to Prevent or Change Unwanted Ones; 384 p. 2014 Houghton Mifflin Harcourt

1. Dog behavior 2. Dogs 3. Handbooks, vade-mecums, etc. 4. Human-animal communication 5. Training of dogs
ISBN 0547738919; 9780547738918

SUMMARY: This book, edited by Debra Horwitz, John Ciribassi, and Steve Dale, is a "dog behavior guide. . . . Experts analyze problem behaviors, decipher the latest studies, and correct common misconceptions and outmoded theories. The book includes: effective, veterinary-approved positive training methods [and] expert advice on socialization, housetraining, diet, and exercise." (Publisher's note)

REVIEW: *Booklist* v110 no12 p8 F 15 2014 Nancy Bent

"Decoding Your Dog: The Ultimate Experts Explain." "In 14 chapters, veterinary behaviorists walk dog owners through the stages of dog ownership. A basic chapter on learning to speak 'dog' starts us off, followed by essays on choosing a dog, house training, behavior training, and training tools. Chapters on common issues, such as separation anxiety, aggression, sound phobias, and compulsive behaviors, teach how to retrain the dog, and a final chapter on the aging canine rounds out the book. Boxes defining terms used in the chapter or containing in-depth coverage of a behavior fill many sections, and each chapter ends with a 'What Did We Say?' summary. Libraries and dog owners may have found the holy grail with this title."

REVIEW: *Libr J* v138 no18 p110 N 1 2013 Susan Riley

REVIEW: *Publ Wkly* v260 no41 p49 O 14 2013

DECOLONIZING SOCIAL WORK; xxiii,354 p. 2013

Ashgate
1. Decolonization 2. Social science literature 3. Social services & race relations 4. Social services—Philosophy 5. Social work with indigenous peoples
ISBN 9781409426318 (hardback : alk. paper)
LC 2012-041827

SUMMARY: In this book, "Indigenous and non-Indigenous social work scholars examine local cultures, beliefs, values, and practices as central to decolonization. Supported by a growing interest in spirituality and ecological awareness in international social work, they interrogate trends, issues, and debates in Indigenous social work theory, practice methods, and education models including a section on Indigenous research approaches." (Publisher's note)

REVIEW: *Choice* v51 no6 p1051-2 F 2014 J. C. Altman

"Decolonizing Social Work." "Improving on their fine 2008 book, Indigenous Social Work around the World . . . could not have been easy. Yet, [the] editors . . . do a serviceable job building on its foundation. This updated edition is a sturdy reminder of the vast social justice work still to do in the world. . . . The text benefits from clear writing and an excellent glossary of terms, but suffers some from uneven applications of the essential principles of decolonization. Some chapters offer more radical ideas than others, and some do a more poignant job of placing relevant examples within their narratives of oppression and subjugation. Overall, however, most readers will find this book meaningful and provocative."

DEE, TIM. Four Fields; [by] Tim Dee 288 p. 2013 Jonathan Cape
1. Grasses 2. Human beings—Effect of environment on 3. Human ecology 4. Meadows 5. Natural history literature
ISBN 0224090720; 9780224090728

SUMMARY: In this book, Tim Dee examines "the fen field at the bottom of his Cambridgeshire garden, a field in southern Zambia, a prairie field in Little Bighorn, Montana, USA, and a grass meadow in the exclusion zone at Chernobyl, Ukraine. Meditating on these four fields, Dee . . . argues that we must . . . look at and think about the way we have messed things up but also . . . notice how we have kept going alongside nature." (Publisher's note)

REVIEW: *Economist* v408 no8850 p74 Ag 24 2013

"Four Fields". "All fields are a life in waiting, writes Tim Dee in this mesmerising book. . . . Written in the same lyrical prose as 'The Running Sky,' . . . his new book tells the story of four fields around the world. . . . His home fenland provides the book's structure, much as a hedge or fence contains the promise of a field. Mr. Dee tanalisingly captures its seasonal flavours. . . . He describes the other fields with equal eloquence. . . . 'Four Fields' is about far more than pieces of earth; it is a summary of humanity's aspirations."

REVIEW: *New Statesman* v142 no5172 p51 Ag 30 2013 Olivia Laing

REVIEW: *Science* v344 no6187 p978 My 30 2014 Sandra Knapp

"Four Fields." "In a simple construct, writer and nature lover Tim Dee shows how our landscapes profoundly affect who and what we are. His at-times poetic paean to human-altered landscapes in Britain, Ukraine, Zambia, and the United States explores the meaning of the relationship between humans and the world they have altered, created, and in large part seemingly destroyed. . . . 'Four Fields' is an intensely personal book about our interactions with the world around us. . . . Above all, his book reminds us that there is much to celebrate in the seemingly ordinary."

REVIEW: *TLS* no5804 p28 Je 27 2014 IAIN BAMFORTH

DEFAZIO, ALBERT J.ed. The Letters of Ernest Hemingway. See Hemingway, E.

DEFELICE, JIM. Code Name Johnny Walker; The Extraordinary Story of the Iraqi Who Risked Everything to Fight With the U.S. Navy Seals; [by] Jim DeFelice 336 p. 2014 HarperCollins
1. Iraq—Politics & government 2. Iraq War, 2003-2011 3. Memoirs 4. Translators 5. United States. Navy. SEALs
ISBN 0062267558; 9780062267559

SUMMARY: In this memoir, Navy SEALs translator Ryadh Khalaf Alahmady, alias 'Johnny Walker,' "tells his inspiring story for the first time. . . . Over the course of eight years, the Iraqi native traveled around the country with nearly every SEAL and special operations unit deployed there. He went on thousands of missions, saved dozens of SEAL and other American lives, and risked his own daily. [He was] helped to the U.S. by the SEALs he protected." (Publisher's note)

REVIEW: *Kirkus Rev* v82 no2 p294 Ja 15 2014

"Code Name: Johnny Walker: The Extraordinary Story of the Iraqi Who Risked Everything to Fight With the U.S. Navy SEALS". " Fiery, insightful memoir from the former Iraqi translator who fought alongside U.S. Special Forces during the recent war in Iraq. With the assistance of [Jim] DeFelice . . . and writing as a first-time author under a protective pseudonym, 'Johnny Walker,' this Mosul-born, pro-American Muslim Iraqi relates a sometimes-biased but invaluable insider's perspective of Iraq after Saddam Hussein. . . . Throughout the book, the author gives a vivid sense of what it's like to be stuck geopolitically between a rock and a hard place. . . . A harrowing personal journey of courageous self-empowerment during wartime."

REVIEW: *Libr J* v138 no14 p87 S 1 2013

DEFORGE, MICHAEL. Ant Colony; [by] Michael DeForge 112 p. 2014 Farrar, Straus & Giroux
1. Animal stories 2. Ant colonies 3. Gay men—Fiction 4. Graphic novels 5. War stories
ISBN 177046137X; 9781770461376

SUMMARY: In this graphic novel, by Michael DeForge, "a colony of black ants serves as a vehicle to examine the human condition. . . . A cataclysmic clash with the red ants results in the destruction of both colonies, with the fate of their civilization resting on a handful of survivors—a homosexual couple, a youngster imbued with strange powers of prophecy from inhaling earthworm particles, a cowardly cop who dodged the battle, and a baby red ant." (Booklist)

REVIEW: *Booklist* v110 no13 p48 Mr 1 2014 Gordon Flagg

"Ant Colony". "A colony of black ants serves as a vehicle to examine the human condition in this stunningly accomplished graphic novel. . . . The story's conflation of the peculiar and the prosaic is reflected in [Michael] DeForge's artwork, which offsets a disturbingly bizarre drawing style, reminiscent of Mark Beyer but even more idiosyncratic, with straight-on camera angles and a nearly unvarying nine-panel grid. A quietly unsettling, masterfully realized work that marks DeForge . . .as a leading figure in the alternative-comics scene."

REVIEW: *Harper's Magazine* v328 no1964 p75-7 Ja 2014 Christine Smallwood

REVIEW: *Publ Wkly* v261 no9 p52 Mr 3 2014

DEIBERT, RONALD J. Black code; inside the battle for cyberspace; [by] Ronald J. Deibert 2014 McClelland & Stewart Ltd.

1. Computer crimes 2. Computer networks—Law & legislation 3. Computer security 4. Cyberspace 5. Political science literature
ISBN 9780771025358 (pbk.)
LC 2013-938866

SUMMARY: In this book, Ronald J. Deibert "lifts the lid on cyberspace and shows what's at stake for Internet users and citizens. As cyberspace develops in unprecedented ways, powerful agents are scrambling for control. Predatory cyber criminal gangs such as Koobface have made social media their stalking ground. The discovery of Stuxnet, a computer worm reportedly developed by Israel and the United States . . . showed that state cyberwar is now a very real possibility." (Publisher's note)

REVIEW: *Quill Quire* v79 no5 p28 Je 2013 Alex Good

REVIEW: *Science* v342 no6156 p313 O 18 2013 Laura DeNardis

"Black Code: Inside the Battle for Cyberspace." "Many readers will find 'Black Code' both illuminating and terrifying. . . . In a book researched and penned prior to Edward Snowden's whistleblowing on NSA surveillance, [Ronald J.] Deibert . . . cites a former NSA employee who estimated that 'billions' of phone calls and 'voluminous' quantities of e-mails are electronically processed every day. . . . One of Black Code's contributions is to illumine the privatized political architecture of the Internet's core technologies. . . . 'Black Code' ties together usually disparate subject matter . . . into a coherent exposé of what is at stake in how the Internet is designed, governed, and infiltrated."

DEITCH, KIM. The Amazing, Enlightening and Absolutely True Adventures of Katherine Whaley; [by] Kim Deitch 176 p. 2013 W W Norton & Co Inc

1. Animal experimentation—Fiction 2. Graphic novels 3. Motion picture producers & directors—Fiction 4. Paranormal fiction 5. Speculative fiction
ISBN 1606996312; 9781606996317

SUMMARY: This book, by Kim Deitch, follows "a girl, born at the beginning of the 20th century. Charles Varnay . . . comes to town, his sole companion a remarkably intelligent dog named Rousseau. Varnay wants to star Katherine in a movie serial. Varnay also claims that . . . Rousseau, is the product of experiments he has been making in advanced selective breeding. He's eager to continue these experiments with human subjects; Katherine realizes that he's expecting her to be a part of this." (Publisher's note)

REVIEW: *Booklist* v110 no6 p31 N 15 2013 Ray Olson

"The Amazing, Enlightening, and Absolutely True Adventures of Katherine Whaley". "Rich, eccentric [Charles] Varnay recruits Katherine to star in a serial he will make based on her resemblance (in the nude, no less) to the ancient statue of an original follower of Jesus that he found along with first-century recordings of the Messiah's voice that make his teachings much clearer than the Gospels do.The yarn [Kim] Deitch spins around that outrageous premise includes surprisingly less of the supernatural and many more words than usual, which wrap around the panels and are carefully chosen to project the heroine's personality—that of a smart but unpretentious woman who once had an utterly fantastic adventure. Even more riveting than Deitch's other spellbinders."

REVIEW: *Publ Wkly* v260 no32 p42 Ag 12 2013

DEKAR, PAUL R.ed. In an Inescapable Network of Mutuality. See In an Inescapable Network of Mutuality

DEL MONTE, LOUIS A. How to Time Travel; Explore the Science, Paradoxes, and Evidence; [by] Louis A. Del Monte 194 p. 2013 Louis A. Del Monte

1. Engineering 2. Physics 3. Scientific literature 4. Scientific method 5. Time travel
ISBN 0988171848; 9780988171848

SUMMARY: In this book, author Louis A. Del Monte " focuses on how time travel might be accomplished and the major issues that stand in the way of its realization. . . . He takes care to emphasize the scientific method, not just for time travel but in evaluating the theories and evidence behind it. By necessity, much of the book discusses various theories and speculations, beginning with Einstein's Theory of Relativity and extending forward to modern formulations." (Kirkus Reviews)

REVIEW: *Kirkus Rev* v82 no1 p103 Ja 1 2014

REVIEW: *Kirkus Rev* v81 no24 p371 D 15 2013

"How to Time Travel: Explore the Science, Paradoxes and Evidence". "Time travel—its possibilities, potential and primary obstacles—gets a levelheaded review from a physicist in this lucid, optimistic book. . . . While some of the ideas along the way are the stuff of conspiracy theorists and late-night talk radio. . . [Louis A.] Del Monte never condescends in his examinations, taking a rational, methodical approach to evaluating the possibilities and explaining why he thinks they do or don't merit further examination. In his refreshingly even-keeled, forthright approach—particularly in his discussion of scientific and anecdotal evidence and the place of both in any thought process—Del Monte does an excellent job of exemplifying the scientific method in action."

DELACOURT, GREGOIRE. My wish list; a novel; 176 p. 2014 Penguin Books

1. FICTION—Contemporary Women 2. FICTION—Literary 3. Lottery winners—Fiction 4. Married women—Fiction 5. Wealth
ISBN 9780143124658 (pbk.)
LC 2013-042843

SUMMARY: In this book, "Madame Jocelyn Guerbette is middle aged, stuck in a boring life, with a few friends, a business she likes, and a husband who's just okay. When her lottery ticket hits the big jackpot of 18 million Euro, the psychologist . . . warns Jocelyn about the perils of sudden wealth. Before cashing in her winning ticket, Jocelyn makes lists of her desires, which fluctuate with her moods." (Library Journal)

REVIEW: *Booklist* v110 no14 p61 Mr 15 2014 Stephanie

Turza

"My Wish List." "When Françoise and Daniele convince her to buy a lottery ticket, Jocelyn never expects her spur-of-the-moment purchase to pay off. But pay off it does, and Jocelyn quietly exchanges her winning ticket for a terrifyingly large check.'My Wish List' is about one woman's one-in-a-million response to a one-in-a-million chance. Jocelyn is an immensely likable narrator, and [Grégoire] Delacourt's fluid, elegant prose brings layers of depth to a relatively simple story. . . . An emotionally wrenching yet ultimately uplifting story of ambition, risk, and acceptance."

REVIEW: *Kirkus Rev* v82 no3 p312 F 1 2014

REVIEW: *Libr J* v139 no5 p108 Mr 15 2014 Mary K. Bird-Guilliams

REVIEW: *New York Times* v163 no56481 pC4 Ap 24 2014 Carmela Ciuraru

REVIEW: *Publ Wkly* v261 no4 p166 Ja 27 2014

DELANEY, ENDA. The curse of reason; the great Irish famine; [by] Enda Delaney x, 293 p. 2012 Gill & Macmillan

1. Historical literature 2. Ireland—History—Famine, 1845-1852 3. Nationalism—Ireland 4. Trevelyan, Charles E. (Charles Edward), 1807-1886
ISBN 0717154157 (hbk.); 9780717154159 (hbk.)
LC 2012-518948

SUMMARY: This book by Enda Delaney is "A survey history of The Great Irish Famine. In particular, the testimonies of four key contemporaries are used throughout to convey the immediacy of the unfolding disaster. They are: John MacHale, the Catholic Archbishop of Tuam; John Mitchel, the radical nationalist; Elizabeth Smith, the Scottish-born wife of a Wicklow landlord; and Charles E. Trevelyan, the assistant secretary to the Treasury." (Publisher's note)

REVIEW: *Choice* v51 no1 p152 S 2013 A. H. Plunkett

"The Curse of Reason: The Great Irish Famine." "[Author Enda] Delaney . . . bases his narrative history on many secondary and some original sources. Its novelty lies in its focus on the perspectives of four very different contemporaries. . . . The title refers to the ideology of [Charles] Trevelyan and other British leaders--a mixture of laissez-faire and providentialism--that severely limited government aid to the famine victims and sought to use the crisis to modernize the Irish economy and society. There is a good deal of biographical detail and scene setting, but Delaney offers an insightful, readable overview of this overwhelming disaster."

REVIEW: *Libr J* v138 no7 p93 Ap 15 2013 Hanna Clutterbuck

DELANEY, JOSEPH. The ghost prison; [by] Joseph Delaney 112 p. 2013 Sourcebooks Fire

1. Ghosts—Fiction 2. Horror stories 3. Orphans—Fiction 4. Prisons—Fiction 5. Supernatural—Fiction
ISBN 1402293186; 9781402293184 (hc : alk. paper)
LC 2013-017898

SUMMARY: This novella is set in the same universe as Joseph Delaney's Last Apprentice series. The story "is narrated by orphan Billy Calder, who is apprehensive about the new job he has landed: helping guard an infamously haunted prison on the night shift. The ghosts and dangers turn out to be all too real, as Billy learns about the prison's bloody history and has a life-altering encounter one night while on the job." (Publishers Weekly)

REVIEW: *Booklist* v110 no3 p94-5 O 1 2013 Carolyn Phelan

"The Ghost Prison." "Best known for the Last Apprentice series, [Joseph] Delaney takes a plucky, Dickensian orphan and places him in a story as deliciously horrifying as those of Edgar Allan Poe. His skillful writing creates an atmosphere of disquiet and a growing sense of dread that makes the story's climax a necessary release, though the worst horrors are left to the reader's imagination. The many black-and- white illustrations enhance the story's tone and its period setting. In appended notes, both Delaney and [Scott M.] Fischer reminisce about their own encounters with ghosts. A frightful pleasure for horror fans."

REVIEW: *Kirkus Rev* v81 no18 p292 S 15 2013

REVIEW: *Publ Wkly* v260 no35 p61 S 2 2013

REVIEW: *SLJ* v60 no1 p80 Ja 2014 Vicki Reutter

DELARGY, MARLAINE.tr. The Disappeared. See Ohlsson, K.

DELECKI, JACKI. An Inner Fire; [by] Jacki Delecki 316 p. 2013 Jacki Delecki

1. Detective & mystery stories 2. Fire fighters—Fiction 3. Human-animal communication—Fiction 4. Love stories 5. Veterinarians—Fiction
ISBN 0989939103; 9780989939102

SUMMARY: In this book, "a Seattle veterinary acupuncturist with an intuitive gift nearly gets in over her head when she gets mixed up in a fire investigation. Grayce Walters . . . has a secret: she's an empath who can communicate with animals—and with her dead sister. . . . Guarding her secret proves more difficult than she anticipated, however, when she falls for Fire Investigator Ewan Davis." (Kirkus Reviews)

REVIEW: *Kirkus Rev* v82 no3 p383 F 1 2014

"An Inner Fire". "In her debut novel, [Jacki] Delecki surprises readers with the fact that small, gentle Grayce doesn't need rescuing; instead, she repeatedly comes to alpha-male firefighter Davis' aid. Although the heavy-handed portrayal of Grayce's gay best friend James wavers between stereotypical and full-on caricature for much of the novel, the character ultimately subverts expectations while remaining true to himself. Overall, the novel is certain to delight romance fans and animal lovers alike. A fiery, engaging mystery."

DELINOIS, ALIX.il. Mumbet's Declaration of Independence. See Woelfle, G.

DELLAMORA, RICHARD. Radclyffe Hall; a life in the writing; [by] Richard Dellamora 319 2011 University of Pennsylvania Press

1. Biography (Literary form) 2. Gender identity 3. Hall, Radclyffe 4. Lesbianism in literature 5. Masculinity
ISBN 9780812243468
LC 2011-010285

SUMMARY: This biography of Radclyffe Hall examines "the entire range of Hall's published and unpublished works of fiction, poetry, and autobiography and reads through them to demonstrate how she continually played with the details of her own life to help fashion her own identity as well as to bring into existence a public lesbian culture. Along the way, [Richard] Dellamora revises many of the truisms about Hall that had their origins in the memoirs of her long-term partner, Una Troubridge." (Publisher's note)

REVIEW: *Choice* v51 no10 p1739-40 Je 2014 M. J. Emery

"Radclyffe Hall: A Life in the Writing". "This is perhaps the definitive book on Raddyfife Hall (1880-1943). [Richard] Dellamora . . . puts his background in Victorianism and queer studies to use in this readable treatment of Hall's body of work. . . . Dellamora reads Hall in terms more of female masculinity and transsexualism than of lesbianism. Identity is fluid in Hail's life and work: her 'I' is 'a continually varying performance of gender,' Dellamora writes. His challenging view of this author—whose greatest work of art may have been her life—is extraordinary."

DELOGU, C. JON.tr. The metamorphoses of fat. See Vigarello, G.

DELONG-BAS, NATANA J.ed. The Oxford encyclopedia of Islam and women. See The Oxford encyclopedia of Islam and women

DELONG, MARILYN.ed. Color and design. See Color and design

DELUCA, LAURA, 1963-. Lost Girl Found. See Bassoff, L.

DELURY, JOHN. Wealth and power. See Schell, O.

DEMAS, CORINNE. Returning to shore; [by] Corinne Demas 196 p. 2013 Carolrhoda Lab

1. Diamondback terrapin—Fiction 2. Fathers and daughters—Fiction 3. Psychological fiction 4. Remarriage—Fiction 5. Turtles—Fiction

ISBN 1467713287; 9781467713283 (trade hard cover: alk. paper)

LC 2013-018618

SUMMARY: In this book, by Corinne Demas, "a thoughtful teen reconnects with her nature-loving father on Cape Cod. Fourteen year-old Clare is less than thrilled with her mother's plan to have her spend three weeks on a remote island with her father, Richard: She hasn't seen him in twelve years, and they only speak on Christmas. Vera and her third husband are jetting off to honeymoon in France, though, so Blackfish Island, ho!" (Kirkus Reviews)

REVIEW: *Booklist* v110 no11 p65 F 1 2014 Angela Leeper

REVIEW: *Kirkus Rev* v82 no2 p144 Ja 15 2014

"Returning to Shore". "Some obnoxious neighbors, walking clichés whose every move embodies thoughtless entitlement and ignorance of the island's natural rhythms, are the one weak spot here. [Corinne] Demas' careful seeding of details about Richard's life in the years between his divorce from Vera and his re-emergence in Clare's life is subtle enough that the revelation of what held him back from maintaining any substantive relationship with her will be surprising and ring true to most readers. Their father-daughter bond feels both earned and earnest. A quiet, lovely story with a satisfyingly sentimental ending. "

REVIEW: *SLJ* v60 no9 p118 S 2014 L. Lee Butler

REVIEW: *Voice of Youth Advocates* v37 no1 p64 Ap 2014 Sarah Cofer

DEMBO, MARGOT BETTAUER.tr. Transit. See Seghers, A.

DEMOTTE, CHARLES. Bat, ball & bible; baseball and Sunday observance in New York; [by] Charles DeMotte xviii, 204 p. 2013 Potomac Books

1. Baseball—Law & legislation 2. Baseball—New York (State)—History 3. Baseball—Religious aspects 4. Baseball—Religious aspects—Christianity 5. Historical literature 6. New York (State)—Social life & customs 7. Sunday legislation 8. Sunday legislation—New Yorki (State)—History

ISBN 9781597979474 (hardcover : alk. paper); 9781597979481 (electronic)

LC 2012-034516

SUMMARY: This book by Charles DeMotte "chronicles the collision of moral and social forces in the argument over upholding New York State's blue laws, meant to restrict social activities and maintain Sunday's traditional standing as a day of religious observation. Baseball was at the center of this conflict, which led to upheaval in society at a time when New York, especially New York City, already was undergoing rapid changes." (Publisher's note)

REVIEW: *Am Hist Rev* v118 no4 p1185-6 O 2013 Alexis McCrossen

"Bat, Ball, and Bible: Baseball and Sunday Observance in New York." "Sociologist and historian Charles DeMotte chronicles the history of Sunday baseball in the Empire State in [this book]. Drawing largely on newspaper accounts, DeMotte describes illicit Sunday afternoon games of amateurs and professionals, periodic efforts of sheriffs and magistrates to enforce Sunday laws, moral crusaders' efforts to shore up restrictions against Sunday baseball, and legislative efforts to strike down Sunday laws. . . .DeMotte refers to social control and secularization as explanatory devices, but in each case the historical facts do not line up with the theory. . . . Despite these drawbacks, DeMotte has written an informative and useful book about Sunday baseball in New York."

DEMPSEY, KRISTY. A dance like starlight; one ballerina's dream; 32 p. 2014 Philomel Books

1. African Americans—Fiction 2. Ballet dancing—Fiction 3. Children's stories 4. Discrimination—Fiction

ISBN 0399252843; 9780399252846

LC 2013-009520

SUMMARY: This book, by Kristy Dempsey and illustrated by Floyd Cooper, "tell[s] the story of one little ballerina who was inspired by Janet Collins, [the first African-American prima ballerina] to make her own dreams come true." (Publisher's note) "When the Ballet Master at the ballet school where Mama works cleaning and sewing costumes notices the girl mimicking dancers backstage, he takes notice" and allows her to join lessons, though she is not allowed to perform with the white students. (Booklist)

REVIEW: *Booklist* v110 no12 p73 F 15 2014 Ann Kelley

"A Dance Like Starlight: One Ballerina's Dream." "It's hard to find stars in the sky over New York City, which means it's hard to wish on one. A young black girl living in Harlem in the 1950s has a big wish, though: to be a prima ballerina. Her mama says you don't need wishes to make a dream come true--you need hope. . . . [Kristy] Dempsey's lyrical prose soars as it depicts one girl's dream--and her efforts to make that dream a reality. [Floyd] Cooper's hazy mixed-media illustrations capture 1950s Harlem, from streetscapes to fashions, while also shining a spotlight on a girl's aspirations. An inspiring introduction to [Janet] Collins that will speak to little dreamers everywhere."

REVIEW: *Bull Cent Child Books* v67 no9 p451 My 2014 D. S.

REVIEW: *Kirkus Rev* v81 no21 p178 N 1 2013
"A Dance Like Starlight: One Ballerina's Dream". "The story is slow to start, focusing in abstract and sentimental terms on the narrator's dreams for too long before articulating the problem; the conclusion also will leave audiences wondering whether the girl's hope ever was fulfilled. More involving, however, is the girl's keen love of ballet and her joy at discovering a pioneer who proves her dream possible. . . . [Floyd] Cooper's smoky mixed-media artwork has a subtle and appropriate echo of Degas in scenes of dancers on stage and smartly dressed 1950s audience members, and the protagonist is vividly realistic, a talented down-to-earth girl rather than an ethereal sylph."

REVIEW: *Publ Wkly* v260 no44 p65-6 N 4 2013

REVIEW: *SLJ* v60 no1 p66 Ja 2014 Barbara Auerbach

DENMARK, FLORENCE L.ed. Violence against girls and women. See Violence against girls and women

DENTON, KADY MACDONALD.il. The Good-Pie Party. See Scanlon, L. G.

DÉON, MICHEL. The Foundling Boy; [by] Michel Déon 416 p. 2014 Gallic Books

1. Adoptees—Fiction 2. Adultery—Fiction 3. Families—Fiction 4. French fiction—Translations into English 5. French historical fiction

ISBN 1908313560; 9781908313560

SUMMARY: In this novel by Michel Déon, translated by Julian Evans, "When Jeanne and Albert Arnaud find an infant on their doorstep, they decide to raise him as their son. Born in 1919, Jean enters a world haunted by recent war. His adoptive parents are caretakers at La Sauveté, the du Courseau family's Normandy estate. The du Courseaus have their own struggles, for unfaithful husband Antoine and social-climbing wife Marie-Thérèse are the parents of three troubled children." (Booklist)

REVIEW: *Booklist* v110 no11 p29 F 1 2014 Jackie Thomas-Kennedy

REVIEW: *Kirkus Rev* v82 no5 p281 Mr 1 2014

REVIEW: *N Y Times Book Rev* p15 Je 15 2014 DIANE JOHNSON

REVIEW: *N Y Times Book Rev* p26 Je 22 2014

REVIEW: *New Statesman* v143 no5193 p53 Ja 17 2014 Jane Shilling

REVIEW: *TLS* no5796 p20 My 2 2014 NICHOLAS HEWITT
"The Foundling Boy." "'The Foundling Boy' begins in 1919, the year of Déon's own birth and, crucially, that of the Treaty of Versailles, with the discovery of an abandoned baby outside the caretakers' cottage on a declining Normandy estate owned by the du Courseau family. . . . In spite of some critics' reservations. The 'Foundling Boy' presents many of the characteristics associated with the Hussards' novels: the intervention of the author proclaiming the book's shortcomings, deliberate lacunae and a general playfulness."

DEPAOLA, TOMIE, 1934-.il. Nana Upstairs & Nana Downstairs. See dePaola, T.

DEPAOLA, TOMIE, 1934-. Nana Upstairs & Nana Downstairs; [by] Tomie dePaola 32 p. 1997 Putnam's

1. Death—Fiction 2. Grandmothers—Fiction 3. Great-grandmothers—Fiction 4. Old age—Fiction 5. Picture books for children

ISBN 0399231080 (hardcover)

LC 9603-1908

SUMMARY: This children's book presents a story about loss. "As a young boy, Tomie loved to visit his grandmother and great-grandmother. They lived in the same house and he called them Nana Upstairs and Nana Downstairs. During his Sunday visits with his great-grandmother, he . . . listen to her stories about the 'Little People.' Then she died, but for Tomie, she would always live in his memories. The same was true of his grandmother who died many years later when Tomie was grown up." (Children's Literature)

REVIEW: *Horn Book Magazine* v89 no5 p56-62 S/O 2013 Thom Barthelmess
"Nana Upstairs & Nana Downstairs," "The Tenth Good Thing About Barney," and "My Father's Arms Are A Boat." "[Tomie dePaola . . . fills the text and illustrations with fond, personal, sometimes humorous details . . . giving the story a tender immediacy that is perfectly suited to the nostalgic subject matter and establishing family love as life's central theme--and death as one of its necessary components. . . . Judith Viorst's 'The Tenth Good Thing About Barney . . . employs direct prose and spare etchings to recount the death of a boy's cat. . . . [In 'My Father's Arms Are A Boat'] only passing reference is made to the death of the boy's mother. Instead, the lyrical language and still, dioramic illustrations observe the evening's simple spectacle, with all the intimacy of warm detail."

DEPAOLA, TOMIE, 1934-.il. Little Poems for Tiny Ears. See Oliver, L.

DERANIYAGALA, SONALI. Wave; [by] Sonali Deraniyagala 240 p. 2013 Alfred A. Knopf

1. Bereavement 2. Children—Death 3. Disaster victims—Sri Lanka—Biography 4. Indian Ocean Tsunami, 2004 5. Memoirs 6. Parents—Death 7. Widows—Biography

ISBN 0307962695 (hardcover); 9780307962690 (hardcover)

LC 2012-040980

SUMMARY: This book offers author Sonali Deraniyagala's experience coping with the loss of her parents, husband, and two young sons, who perished in the "Indian Ocean tsunami that broke loose on December 26, 2004" and "killed something like 230,000 people." This is "an account of her coping with her grief while also celebrating the memories of those she loved. . . . She ranges over her childhood in Colombo, meeting her English husband at Cambridge, and the birth of her children." (Library Journal)

REVIEW: *Booklist* v109 no12 p18 F 15 2013 Donna Seaman

REVIEW: *Booklist* v109 no19/20 p120 Je 1 2013 Laurie Hartshorn

REVIEW: *Kirkus Rev* v81 no3 p298 F 1 2013

REVIEW: *Kirkus Rev* v81 no3 p282 F 1 2013

REVIEW: *Libr J* v137 no17 p58 O 15 2012 Barbara Hoffert

REVIEW: *N Y Times Book Rev* p28 Ja 26 2014 IHSAN TAYLOR

"Love Is a Canoe," "James Joyce: A New Biography," and "Wave." "Her marriage in trouble, the heroine of [Ben] Schrank's novel--a crackling sendup of the New York publishing industry . . . turns for help to the author of . . . a classic self-help book. . . . [Author Gordon] Bowker . . . intimately binds together the life and work of [writer James] Joyce . . . providing nuanced accounts. . . . ['Wave'] is an unforgettable memoir of [author Sonali] Deraniyagala's struggle to carry on living after her husband, sons and parents were killed in the tsunami that struck the southern coast of Sri Lanka on Dec. 26, 2004."

REVIEW: *N Y Times Book Rev* p11 Mr 24 2013 CHERYL STRAYED

REVIEW: *New York Times* v162 no56067 pC1-6 Mr 6 2013 DWIGHT GARNER

REVIEW: *New York Times* v162 no56092 p26 Mr 31 2013

REVIEW: *New Yorker* v89 no8 p1-83 Ap 8 2013

D'ERASMO, STACEY. Wonderland; [by] Stacey D'Erasmo 256 p. 2014 Houghton Mifflin Harcourt

1. Alternative rock music 2. Concert tours 3. Musical fiction 4. Rock musicians—Fiction 5. Women rock musicians
ISBN 0544074815; 9780544074811
LC 2013-019523

SUMMARY: In this novel by Stacey D'Erasmo, "Anna Brundage is a rock star. She is tall and sexy, with a powerhouse voice and an unforgettable mane of red hair. She came out of nowhere, an immediate indie sensation. And then, life happened. Anna went down as fast as she went up, and then walked off the scene for seven years. Without a record deal or clamoring fans, she sells a piece of her famous father's art to finance just one more album and a European comeback tour." (Publisher's note)

REVIEW: *Bookforum* v21 no2 p45 Je-Ag 2014 LINDSAY ZOLADZ

REVIEW: *Booklist* v110 no16 p17 Ap 15 2014 Donna Seaman

REVIEW: *Kirkus Rev* v82 no9 p4 My 1 2014

REVIEW: *Kirkus Rev* v82 no7 p245 Ap 1 2014

REVIEW: *Libr J* v138 no21 p68 D 1 2013 Barbara Hoffert

REVIEW: *Libr J* v139 no4 p80 Mr 1 2014 Kate Gray

REVIEW: *N Y Times Book Rev* p11 My 25 2014 LIONEL SHRIVER

REVIEW: *New Yorker* v90 no14 p72-1 My 26 2014

"Wonderland." "[Author Stacey] D'Erasmo's fourth novel charts the European comeback tour of Anna Brundage, a forty-four-year-old American indie rocker, who was briefly famous among 'people who pride themselves on being smart' and then flamed out. Brundage funds a new album, her first in seven years, by selling a rare work by her father, a renowned sculptor. Her story reads like an unusually lucid travel journal. Short chapters juxtapose memories . . . with sharply drawn scenes from the tour. In Brundage, D'Erasmo has created a wry, questioning, sensual artist."

REVIEW: *Publ Wkly* v261 no7 p75 F 17 2014

DERICKSON, ALAN. Dangerously sleepy; overworked Americans and the cult of manly wakefulness; [by] Alan Derickson xiii, 224 p. 2014 University of Pennsylvania Press

1. Historical literature 2. Hours of labor—United States—History 3. Men—Employment—United States 4. Men—United States—Attitudes 5. Shift systems—United States—History 6. Sleep deprivation—Health aspects—United States 7. Sleep deprivation—Social aspects—United States
ISBN 9780812245530 (hardcover: alk. paper)
LC 2013-011243

SUMMARY: "'Dangerously Sleepy' is the first book to track the longtime association of overwork and sleep deprivation from the nineteenth century to the present. Health and labor historian Alan Derickson charts the cultural and political forces behind the overvaluation—and masculinization—of wakefulness in the United States." (Publisher's note)

REVIEW: *Choice* v51 no9 p1642 My 2014 J. A. Young

REVIEW: *TLS* no5793 p29 Ap 11 2014 JIM HORNE

"Dangerously Sleepy: Overworked Americans and the Cult of Manly Wakefulness." "'Dangerously Sleepy' is a historical account of our relationship with sleep, beginning with the mixed blessings of Thomas Edison's invention of the electric light and the accompanying belief that sleep was a waste of otherwise valuable work time. Thereafter, much of the book is concerned with the evolution of the generally poor work practices and sleep loss inherent in three well-documented occupations from the early 1900s: those of steelworkers, railway stewards and . . . long-haul truck drivers. . . . Yet, a more critical examination of the hard evidence behind these assertions makes it highly doubtful that we ever did sleep for longer, or that six hours' daily sleep really constitutes a health risk."

DERICKSON, ELIZABETH. Climbing Mount Laurel. See Massey, D. S.

DEROO, NEAL. Futurity in phenomenology; promise and method in Husserl, Lévinas, and Derrida; [by] Neal Deroo xvii, 212 p. 2013 Fordham University Press

1. Derrida, Jacques, 1930-2004 2. Forecasting 3. Future, The 4. Husserl, Edmund, 1859-1938 5. Lévinas, Emmanuel, 1906-1995 6. Phenomenology 7. Phenomenology—Methodology 8. Philosophical literature
ISBN 9780823244645 (cloth : alk. paper)
LC 2012-035753

SUMMARY: This book by Neal DeRoo "offers the first sustained reflection on the significance of futurity for the phenomenological method itself." It inquires "into the phenomenological provenance of the "theological" turn and the phenomenological conclusions of Husserl, Levinas, and Derrida. Closely examining the themes of protention, eschatology, and the messianic," it covers areas of interest in "phenomenology, philosophy of religion, deconstruction, or philosophical theology." (Publisher's note)

REVIEW: *Choice* v51 no2 p275-6 O 2013 J. A. Simmons

"Futurity in Phenomenology: Promise and Method in Husserl, Levinas, and Derrida." "Perhaps as something of a methodological continuation of Jacques Derrida's critique of the 'metaphysics of presence,' [Author Neal] DeRoo . . . argues that phenomenology is not bound to concerns about the past and the present, but instead is importantly able to consider the future. Through a careful analysis of Husserl's notion of protention . . . DeRoo offers a nuanced and rigorous account of the experience of anticipation. . . . The author then moves on to consider, at length, Levinasian subjectivity and the Derridean messianic as important resources. . . . An important contribution to the literature, this volume sees the future of phenomenology as bright indeed."

DERSHOWITZ, ALAN. Taking the stand; my life in the law; [by] Alan Dershowitz 528 p. 2013 Crown Publishers

1. Autobiographies 2. Capital punishment—United States—Cases 3. Freedom of speech—United States—Cases 4. Jewish lawyers—United States—Biography 5. Law teachers—United States—Biography 6. Lawyers—United States—Biography

ISBN 0307719278; 9780307719270

LC 2013-022762

SUMMARY: In this book, author Alan Dershowitz "recounts his legal autobiography, describing how he came to the law, as well as the cases that have changed American jurisprudence over the past 50 years, most of which he has personally been involved in. Dershowitz reveals the evolution of his own thinking on such fundamental issues as censorship and the First Amendment, Civil Rights, Abortion, homocide and the increasing role that science plays in a legal defense." (Publisher's note)

REVIEW: *Kirkus Rev* v81 no17 p51 S 1 2013

REVIEW: *Libr J* v139 no4 p55 Mr 1 2014 Kelly Sinclair

REVIEW: *N Y Times Book Rev* p12 N 10 2013 DAHLIA LITHWICK

"Taking the Stand: My Life in the Law." "Argumentative and uncompromising, celebrity-obsessed and self-promoting. [Alan] Dershowitz likes to quote his own favorable press. He likes to talk about his centrality in the lives of others. . . . At its high-water mark, the book might have been subtitled '6,259 Things I Was Right About' or, alternatively, 'Fancy People With Whom I Dine.' Readers who tend to find the 'Dersh character' maddening on television or in print will find much of the book maddening as well. Which is too bad. Because 'the real Alan' has an amazing story to tell. . . . Dershowitz is at his best in his terse, elegantly argued chapters on doctrine. . . . These are short master classes in how to teach law to ordinary Americans."

REVIEW: *Publ Wkly* v260 no35 p51 S 2 2013

DERSTINE, ELISE HOFER. Music everywhere! See Ajmera, M.

DESAI, TEJAS. Good Americans; The Human Tragedy; [by] Tejas Desai 370 p. 2013 New Wei LLC, The

1. American short stories 2. College teachers—Fiction 3. Families—Fiction 4. Immigrants—Fiction 5. Loneliness—Fiction

ISBN 0988351935; 9780988351936

SUMMARY: This collection of short stories is the first in the "Human Tragedy" series. "'Old Guido' tells of a prejudiced Italian immigrant and his accidental relationship with an underage Hispanic girl; the vignette 'Bridget's Brother' confronts loneliness and family ties; 'The Apprentice' describes the Dominican-descended Javier, his Asian masseuse and his struggle up the academic ladder toward a tenured professorship." (Kirkus Reviews)

REVIEW: *Kirkus Rev* v82 no1 p320 Ja 1 2014

Title" "Good Americans". "While 'Dhan's Debut' is something of a letdown with its out-of-left-field ending, the other stories speak volumes about the human condition and modern life in America. Best of all, despite their difficult subjects, each one achieves that level of consideration without any sense of judgment or moralizing to cloud the experience; it's left to readers to make up their own minds about what they just witnessed. . . . And therein lies the power of this first volume, which, while not as grandiose or revolutionary as the fictionalized introduction makes it out to be, is a solid collection of rare caliber. Difficult subjects portrayed for readers who want to be challenged as well as entertained."

DESBORDES, FRANÇOIS. Primates of the world. See Primates of the world

DESHAZER, MARY K. Mammographies; the cultural discourses of breast cancer narratives; [by] Mary K. DeShazer 239 p. 2013 The University of Michigan Press

1. Breast—Imaging—Cross-cultural studies 2. Breast—Radiography—Cross-cultural studies 3. Ethnicity—Health aspects 4. Medical literature 5. Transcultural medical care

ISBN 047211882X; 9780472118823 (cloth : alk. paper)

LC 2013-000021

SUMMARY: This book presents an "examination of the changes in the writing and illustrations related to breast cancer in the new millennium. Using narratives of those who have experienced breast cancer or have worked with those with breast cancer, the author presents various perspectives that explore the 'cultural discourses' associated with the disease and its prevention and treatment." (Choice: Current Reviews for Academic Libraries)

REVIEW: *Choice* v51 no5 p873 Ja 2014 M. P. Tarbox

"Mammographies: The Cultural Discourse of Breast Cancer Narratives." "[Mary K.] DeShazer . . . presents a scholarly examination of the changes in the writing and illustrations related to breast cancer in the new millennium. . . . In addition to recounting the narratives of nonsurvivors, the book examines new methods of relating the experience of cancer, including graphic tales, blogs, and end-of-life accounts. Using literary criticism, feminist perspectives, and an interdisciplinary approach, the author explores a range of theoretical perspectives to identify what the narratives signify and how audiences may respond. The book includes a useful appendix of resources and extensive reference notes."

REVIEW: *Libr J* v138 no14 p135 S 1 2013 Bette-Lee Fox

DESIGNER BIOLOGY; the ethics of intensively engineering biological and ecological systems; 304 p. 2013 Lexington Books

1. Bioengineering—Moral and ethical aspects 2. Bioethics 3. Biotic communities—Effect of human beings on—Moral and ethical aspects 4. Environmental engineering—Moral and ethical aspects 5. Genetic engineering—Moral and ethical aspects 6. Geotechnical engineering—Moral and ethical aspects 7. Scientific literature
ISBN 9780739178218 (cloth : alkaline paper); 9780739184875 (paperback : alkaline paper)
LC 2013-017850

SUMMARY: In this book, "contributors address topics such as the consideration of moral responsibility for using engineering methods to select the sex of human embryos; using molecular techniques to create 'designer' children; using implants and/or drugs to affect moral behavior; altering the Earth's atmosphere to combat climate change; and artificially designing and developing technologically cteated organisms." (Choice: Current Reviews for Academic Libraries)

REVIEW: *Choice* v51 no6 p1031 F 2014 K. M. Foos

"Designer Biology: The Ethics of Intensively Engineering Biological and Ecological Systems." "This work, edited by [John] Basl and [Ronald L.] Sandier . . . is a compilation of papers based on a workshop held at Northeastern. . . .the last chapter does a very nice job of providing conclusions and generalizations based on the other chapters. . . . Each chapter stands alone and would pique a reader's interest in moral issues associated with new and future use of biological engineering to manipulate biological entities. The chapters are provocative and are valuable as a basis for considerations of the ethics of human intervention into natural systems."

DESIMINI, LISA.il. The great big green. See Gifford, P.

DESMOND, JENNI. Eric, the boy who lost his gravity; [by] Jenni Desmond 40 p. 2014 Blue Apple Books

1. Anger in children—Juvenile literature 2. Behavior—Fiction 3. Brothers and sisters—Fiction 4. Gravity—Fiction 5. Humorous stories 6. JUVENILE FICTION—Humorous Stories
ISBN 9781609053482 (hardback)
LC 2013-043463

SUMMARY: In this book by Jenni Desmond, "when Eric gets angry at his younger sister, Alice—so angry that his mouth becomes a pencil scribble of fierceness—he loses his gravity and floats up to the ceiling, through the window, and out into the sky. Flying cheers Eric up immediately ('Wow! This is excellent,' he says), and with the lifting of his mood, his gravity returns; he lands in a tree, and his family sprints to his rescue." (Publishers Weekly)

REVIEW: *Kirkus Rev* v82 no5 p35 Mr 1 2014

"Eric, the Boy Who Lost His Gravity". "There are pleasing, unexpected touches: Their mom reads the newspaper while their dad irons; the paper has metafictive headlines referring to both this book and another by the author; there is an excellent aerial view of the room from Eric's new perspective. Throughout, a combination of watercolor, collage and stark pencil lines complement a text that combines simple sentences in a sans-serif typeface with additional penned-in words. . . . Although this book has much to offer, the darkly scrawled marks that represent facial expressions are often grotesque; furious, jagged mouths express the children's anger. Sturdy children, particularly those with siblings, will respond to the starkness of emotions expressed."

REVIEW: *Publ Wkly* v260 no51 p59 D 16 2013

DESPAIN, BREE. The shadow prince; [by] Bree Despain 496 p. 2014 Egmont USA

1. Fantasy fiction 2. Fate and fatalism—Fiction 3. Gods—Fiction 4. Love—Fiction 5. Mythology, Greek—Fiction 6. Princes—Fiction
ISBN 9781606842478 (hardback)
LC 2013-033192

SUMMARY: "In this first book in [Bree] Despain's 'Into the Dark' trilogy, Haden is . . . a disgraced son of the King of Hades, desperate to redeem himself. His mission is to . . . entice a girl to come to Hades willingly as a 'Boon,' breeding stock for the all-male Underrealm. Daphne Raines, gifted with a beautiful voice and the ability to hear the song inside all living things, and her mother live in small-town Utah until Daphne's rock-star father comes to claim her." (Publishers Weekly)

REVIEW: *Bull Cent Child Books* v67 no9 p451 My 2014 A. S.

REVIEW: *Kirkus Rev* v82 no2 p116 Ja 15 2014

"The Shadow Prince". "While their fish-out-of water experiences would have been sufficient material for a first installment, [Bree] Despain attempts to layer apocalyptic deadlines and a convoluted tale of the prophecied Cypher who can find the lost Key of Hades atop reinterpretations of the tales of Orpheus and Persephone. Daphne and Haden occasionally surprise, but they are ultimately a standard heroine and hero. Naturally and supernaturally attuned to the music of the world, Daphne is inexplicably and irritatingly special, while her counterpart, Haden, is darkly handsome as well as sensitive but scarred. An overcrowded modern romance equally inspired by ancient Greece and Glee."

REVIEW: *Publ Wkly* v261 no3 p58 Ja 20 2014

REVIEW: *SLJ* v60 no5 p127 My 2014 Shelley Diaz

DESPRÉS, GENEVIÈVE.il. The highest number in the world. See MacGregor, R.

DESSEN, SARAH. The moon and more; [by] Sarah Dessen 384 p. 2013 Viking

1. Beaches—Fiction 2. Bildungsromans 3. Coming of age—Fiction 4. Dating (Social customs)—Fiction 5. Documentary films—Production and direction—Fiction 6. Family-owned business enterprises—Fiction 7. Fathers and daughters—Fiction 8. Resorts—Fiction
ISBN 0670785601 (hardcover); 9780670785605 (hardcover)
LC 2012-035720

SUMMARY: In this novel, by Sarah Dessen, "Luke is the perfect boyfriend. . . . But now, in the summer before college, Emaline wonders if perfect is good enough. Enter Theo, a super-ambitious outsider. . . . Emaline's . . . father, too, thinks Emaline should have a bigger life. . . . Emaline is attracted to the bright future that Theo and her father promise. But she also clings to the deep roots of her loving mother, stepfather, and sisters." (Publisher's note)

REVIEW: *Booklist* v109 no19/20 p93 Je 1 2013 Ann Kelley

REVIEW: *Bull Cent Child Books* v67 no1 p14 S 2013 K. C.

"The Moon and More." "While the character constellation here is vintage [Sarah] Dessen, the struggling romance with barely likable Theo is a departure from the usual liaisons with perfect boys she creates for her characters (and readers) to swoon over. She makes it work, however, by keeping Theo little more than a convenient part of Emaline's character arc as she prepares to leave her high school life behind; he's a transition boy, a reminder that there will be another boy after the first one, and still others after that. . . . Prior fans of Dessen may balk at the lack of a perfect romance, but the gentle realism here may attract readers who find some of her other works too good to be true."

REVIEW: *Horn Book Magazine* v89 no5 p90-1 S/O 2013 LAUREN ADAMS

"The Moon and More." "Things get complicated after her estranged birth father inexplicably pulls his offer to pay for an Ivy League education and arrives in town with her little half-brother in tow. A sudden, unexpected breakup with Luke is immediately followed by the stirrings of a new romance, leaving Emaline simultaneously grieving for her past relationship and excited about a new one. Exploring both family and romantic relationships, this quintessential [Sarah] Dessen novel sets Emaline's time of self-discovery in a beach-town summer of sunny, sandy days and soft, warm nights filled with promise."

REVIEW: *Kirkus Rev* v81 no10 p89 My 15 2013

REVIEW: *N Y Times Book Rev* p15 Jl 14 2013 JENNIFER HUBERT SWAN

REVIEW: *Publ Wkly* v260 no14 p66 Ap 8 2013 Leigh Feldman

REVIEW: *SLJ* v59 no7 p91 Jl 2013 Suzanne Gordon

REVIEW: *SLJ* v59 no10 p1 O 2013 Shari Fesko

REVIEW: *Voice of Youth Advocates* v36 no3 p60 Ag 2013 Jennifer McIntosh

DESTEFANIS, RICK. The Gomorrah Principle; A Vietnam Sniper's Story; [by] Rick DeStefanis 432 p. 2013 Createspace Independent Pub

1. Friendship—Fiction 2. Historical fiction 3. Snipers 4. Vietnam War, 1961-1975—Fiction 5. War stories
ISBN 1481896806; 9781481896801

SUMMARY: In this book, "a young man in the Vietnam War confronts the differences between good and evil. Brady Nash . . . [has] enlisted in the Vietnam War as a sniper. He's no stranger to the perils of combat; his best friend, Duff Cowan, went away months ago and was tragically killed in action. . . . Brady infiltrates the secretive world of black ops to find answers about his dead friend, and he learns that in a deadly war, things aren't always as clear as they are back home." (Kirkus Reviews)

REVIEW: *Kirkus Rev* v82 no2 p68 Ja 15 2014

"The Gomorrah Principle: A Vietnam Sniper's Story". "This novel's prose evokes a simplicity and clarity evident in certain classics of American literature, raising it slightly above most conventional wartime psychological thrillers. . . . The opening section, for example, feels somewhat reminiscent of Sherwood Anderson's work. The conflicts that play out in Brady's psyche work well in the Vietnam War setting, which is always ripe for exploration of moral dilemmas. Fans of historical fiction will also find plenty to enjoy here. A rare Vietnam story that manages to draw power from its protagonist rather than from the bewildering tragedies of war."

DESTEFANO, LAUREN. Perfect ruin; [by] Lauren DeStefano 368 p. 2013 Simon and Schuster Books for Young Readers

1. Conspiracy 2. Curiosity 3. Murder—Fiction 4. Science fiction 5. Utopias—Fiction
ISBN 1442480610; 9781442480612 (hardcover : alk. paper)
LC 2013-014392

SUMMARY: In this book by Lauren DeStefano "Morgan Stockhour knows getting too close to the edge of Internment, the floating city in the clouds where she lives, can lead to madness.Then a murder, the first in a generation, rocks the city. With whispers swirling and fear on the wind, Morgan can no longer stop herself from investigating, especially once she meets Judas. Betrothed to the victim, he is the boy being blamed for the murder, but Morgan is convinced of his innocence." (Publisher's note)

REVIEW: *Booklist* v110 no2 p66 S 15 2013 Ilene Cooper

"Perfect Ruin." "[Lauren] DeStefano has created a perfect storm--intertwining plot, characters, and setting beautifully. From the first page, readers will be enticed by Morgan's voice, precise in its descriptions yet filled with curiosity. Internment becomes practically a character in itself, and what at first seems an almost magical! place, surrounded by stars, will eventually stifle readers, as it does Morgan. The story's framework is expandable!e enough to encompass tenderness, tension, and surprise. This is a page-turner, and waiting for the next book will be hard, hard, hard."

REVIEW: *Bull Cent Child Books* v67 no4 p208 D 2013 A. M.

REVIEW: *Kirkus Rev* v81 no17 p85 S 1 2013

REVIEW: *Publ Wkly* v260 no36 p58 S 9 2013

REVIEW: *SLJ* v60 no1 p97 Ja 2014 Eric Norton

DESTENO, DAVID. The truth about trust; how it determines success in life, love, learning, and more; [by] David Desteno 304 p. 2014 Hudson Street Press

1. Interpersonal relations 2. Psychological literature 3. Success 4. Trust 5. Trust—Social aspects
ISBN 9781594631238 (alk. paper)
LC 2013-045481

SUMMARY: In this book, author "David DeSteno brings together the latest research from diverse fields, including psychology, economics, biology, and robotics, to create a . . . narrative about the forces that have shaped the human mind's propensities to trust. He shows us how trust influences us at every level, from how we learn, to how we love, to how we spend, to how we take care of our own health and well-being." (Publisher's note)

REVIEW: *Kirkus Rev* v81 no24 p226 D 15 2013

"The Truth About Trust: How It Determines Success In Life, Love, Learning, and More". "In concise prose backed by engaging stories, the author addresses the pros and cons of common issues such as trusting a business transaction, using trust in learning situations and the need for trust in personal relationships. . . . [David] DeSteno ends with six powerful and easy-to-remember rules regarding trust with the hope that the overall effect will be for the greater good of all. Fresh insight into a necessary part of everyday life."

DETWEILER, CRAIG. IGods; how technology shapes our spiritual and social lives; [by] Craig Detweiler 246 p. 2014 Brazos Press

1. Jobs, Steven, 1955-2011 2. Religious literature 3. Social networks 4. Technology & civilization 5. Technology—Religious aspects—Christianity
ISBN 9781587433443 (pbk.)
LC 2013-025133

SUMMARY: In this book, Craig Detweiler "demonstrates his passion for technology by providing a historical context for several of its founders. . . . Throughout the book, the author outlines the contributions that each of these individuals has made to society. Detweiler also builds a case for parallels between Christian theology and technology development. He uses the latter part of the book to outline some possible future scenarios for technology and the human race." (Choice: Current Reviews for Academic Libraries)

REVIEW: *Booklist* v110 no6 p12-4 N 15 2013 Christopher McConnell

REVIEW: *Choice* v51 no8 p1416-7 Ap 2014 W. J. Hyndman

"iGods: How Technology Shapes Our Spiritual and Social Lives". "He uses the latter part of the book to outline some possible future scenarios for technology and the human race. Time will tell how accurate these predictions may be. Multiple possibilities exist, according to the book, and so nothing concrete is promoted in the concluding chapters. The one thing that is glaringly missing is Bill Gates's considerable contribution to this same technology evolution. Any mentions of Gates tend to have a negative context. The author clearly prefers Apple computers to PCs, and this book likely will be of particular interest to Macintosh/Apple users."

REVIEW: *Publ Wkly* v260 no40 p20 O 7 2013

DEVINE, ERIC. Dare me; [by] Eric Devine 336 p. 2013 Running Press Teens

1. At-risk behavior 2. Internet videos 3. Teenage boys—Fiction 4. YouTube (Web resource) 5. Young adult fiction
ISBN 0762450150; 9780762450152
LC 2013-937586

SUMMARY: In Eric Devine's book, "Ben, a perfectly normal high school senior, and his buddies Ricky and John pull an amazing stunt, which they post anonymously on YouTube, hoping for 'weblebrity.' What comes their way is a contract promising them money if they continue to do evermore-dangerous dares. When not filming dares, narrator Ben works as a pizza-delivery guy and longs for popular coworker Alexia, who's attached to a bad boy. His reflections on physics, English class and math become more penetrating as the ante ups with each completed dare." (Kirkus Reviews)

REVIEW: *Booklist* v110 no2 p68 S 15 2013 Daniel Kraus

REVIEW: *Bull Cent Child Books* v67 no4 p208-9 D 2013 E. B.

REVIEW: *Kirkus Rev* p52 Ag 15 2013 Fall Preview

REVIEW: *Kirkus Rev* v81 no16 p212 Ag 15 2013

REVIEW: *Publ Wkly* v260 no33 p69 Ag 19 2013

REVIEW: *Voice of Youth Advocates* v36 no4 p60 O 2013 Deena Viviani

"Dare Me." "With his dad laid off, broke, and selling their house, and his crush dating an abusive guy, high school senior Ben Candido figures he has nothing to lose when Ricky asks him and their friend John to complete ten dares over ten months. . . . 'Dare Me's' premise is compelling; however, some of the dares are odd. . . . Though sometimes the emotional intensity is discomforting, it has sweet parts that keep the reader smiling. Just like the author's other novels, the theme of truth and consequences definitely applies."

REVIEW: *Voice of Youth Advocates* v36 no4 p60 O 2013 Maia Raynor

DEVINE, ERIC. Tap out; [by] Eric Devine p. cm. 2012 Running Press Teens

1. Drug dealers—Fiction 2. Mixed martial arts 3. Poor people—Fiction 4. Sports stories 5. Teenagers—Conduct of life
ISBN 9780762445691
LC 2012-934247

SUMMARY: In this book by Eric Devine, "when Tony is coerced into joining his friend Rob's Mixed Martial Arts class, he is surprised to find that he has a talent that he actually wants to develop. But with a meth-dealing biker gang that is hungry for recruits and a vicious cycle of poverty and violence that precedes him, Tony is going to need a lot more than blood and guts to find a way out." (Publisher's note)

REVIEW: *Booklist* v109 no8 p50-1 D 15 2012 Daniel Kraus

REVIEW: *Booklist* v110 no1 p107 S 1 2013

"Becoming Babe Ruth," "I'm With Stupid," and "Tap Out." "This engaging rags-to-riches chronicle puts an emphasis on Ruth's early school years before vividly capturing his larger-than-life career, accomplishments, and charm. The art, like the Babe, is irrepressible. . . . The second sequel to 'Stupid Fast' (2011) loses no steam, as football phenom Felton suffers the pressures of college recruitment while dealing with long-distance romance, suicide, and alcoholism. . . . Gritty, bloody, and chilling, this is an unblinking look at 17-year-old Tony, who uses a local mixed-martial-arts gym as inspiration to disengage from the drug dealers running his trailer park."

REVIEW: *Kirkus Rev* v80 no10 p60 My 15 2012

REVIEW: *Kirkus Rev* v80 no15 p21 Ag 1 2012

REVIEW: *Publ Wkly* v259 no33 p71 Ag 13 2012

REVIEW: *Voice of Youth Advocates* v35 no4 p357 O 2012 Cassandra Rondinella

DEWDNEY, ANNA. Llama Llama and the bully goat; [by] Anna Dewdney 40 p. 2013 Viking Published by Penguin Group

1. Animals—Fiction 2. Bullies—Fiction 3. Goats—Fiction 4. Llamas—Fiction 5. Picture books for children 6. Schools—Fiction 7. Stories in rhyme
ISBN 9780670013951 (hardcover)
LC 2012-048415

SUMMARY: In this book, "Llama Llama and his friends cannot enjoy their school day because Gilroy Goat is being a bully. He laughs at the other animals during circle time, and he calls Llama Llama a 'not-nice name' when he tries to sing. Although Gilroy's teacher tries to correct his behavior, the bullying continues into recess . . . until the llama calls him a Bully Goat. Realizing he's hurt potential new companions, Gilroy is happy to accept Llama Llama's renewed offer of friendship." (School Library Journal)

REVIEW: *Kirkus Rev* v81 no14 p114 Jl 15 2013

REVIEW: *N Y Times Book Rev* p12 Ag 25 2013 BECCA ZERKIN

"Sea Monster and the Bossy Fish," "Lion vs. Rabbit," and "Llama Llama and the Bully Goat." "Though the text is heavy-handed, especially when Ernest is setting things right, [Kate] Messner . . . subtly implies that the new fish is behaving badly because he feels vulnerable. . . . Young readers will relate as they settle into the new school year. . . . Alex Latimer . . . doesn't hit us over the head with a message. . . . It's too bad that Latimer renders Lion's victims overly passive and the aggressor a changed man only because he lost a bet; it makes the resolution less satisfying. . . . Anna Dewdney . . . writes touchingly about the emotions of young children."

REVIEW: *Publ Wkly* v260 no28 p168 Jl 15 2013

DEWDNEY, ANNA.il. Llama Llama and the bully goat. See Dewdney, A.

DEX, SHIRLEY.ed. Gendered Lives. See Gendered Lives

DI CAPUA, MICHAEL.ed. My brother's book. See Sendak, M.

DI CESARE, DONATELLA. Gadamer; a philosophical portrait; [by] Donatella Di Cesare ix, 233 p. 2013 Indiana University Press

1. Heidegger, Martin, 1889-1976 2. Philosophical literature 3. Philosophy—20th century 4. Pragmatism
ISBN 9780253007636 (cloth : alk. paper)
LC 2012-049480

SUMMARY: In this book, "Donatella Di Cesare highlights the central place of Greek philosophy, particularly Plato, in [Hans-Georg] Gadamer's work, brings out differences between his thought and that of [Martin] Heidegger, and connects him with discussions and debates in pragmatism. This is a . . . philosophical portrait of one of the 20th century's most powerful thinkers." (Publisher's note)

REVIEW: *Choice* v51 no6 p1017-8 F 2014 P. Amato

"Gadamer: A Philosophical Portrait." "The author's portrait of her mentor, Hans-Georg Gadamer, offers English readers a masterful but intimate tour through the sprawling museum of Gadamer's work with a guide who is an artist in her own right. [Donatella] Di Cesare treats the full gamut of Gadamer's thinking, including his later works and directions. She presents a nuanced view of Gadamer's appropriations of [Georg Wilhelm Friedrich] Hegel, [Martin] Heidegger, and [Ludwig] Wittgenstein, and gives careful and sustained attention to Gadamer's involvement with Platonic philosophy. . . . The translation by [Niall] Keane . . . is sometimes stiff and opaque, yet mostly succeeds in capturing Di Cesare philosophizing along with her mentor."

DI GIACOMO, KRIS.il. The day I lost my superpowers. See Escoffier, M.

DI ROBILANT, ANDREA. Chasing the rose; a garden adventure in the Venetian countryside; [by] Andrea Di Robilant 224 p. 2014 Alfred A. Knopf

1. Gardens—Italy—Venice Region 2. Horticultural literature 3. Old roses—Italy—Venice Region 4. Roses—Identification
ISBN 030796292X; 9780307962928 (hardcover)
LC 2013-023994

SUMMARY: This book, by Andrea di Robilant, presents "a historian's account of how he uncovered the identity of a mysterious wild rose growing on the old farming estate of an illustrious Venetian ancestor. . . . His journey took him to historical archives in Paris and brought him into contact with rose collectors and specialists. . . . Yet it would be happy accident—this time in an Umbrian garden full of old Chinese roses—that would lead him to the answers he sought." (Kirkus Reviews)

REVIEW: *Booklist* v110 no14 p38-9 Mr 15 2014 Carol Haggas

"Chasing the Rose". "[Andrea] di Robilant attempts to identify an old rose that has a deep and profound family history. . . . As di Robilant describes his labyrinthine and frequently exasperating quest to determine the rose's roots and gain official recognition by registering its name, he charmingly uncovers the history of many of the rose kingdom's venerable stars, Di Robilant's tender memoir of his tenacious horticultural hunt is a treat for rose aficionados and historians as well as acquisitive gardeners of every variety."

REVIEW: *Kirkus Rev* v82 no4 p22 F 15 2014

"Chasing the Rose: An Adventure in the Venetian Countryside". "A historian's account of how he uncovered the identity of a mysterious wild rose growing on the old farming estate of an illustrious Venetian ancestor. . . . Captivated by the mystery surrounding this flower, [Andrea] di Robilant began an investigation into its possible origins. . . . Illustrated throughout with charming watercolors, Di Robilant's is a unique exploration of how human history often leaves its imprint in the most unexpected of places. A quiet country pleasure."

REVIEW: *Publ Wkly* v260 no49 p70 D 2 2013

DIAMANDIS, PETER, 1961-. Abundance. See Kotler, S.

DIAMOND, VALERIE L. Stilettos in Vegas; [by] Valerie L. Diamond 212 p. 2013 Author Solutions

1. Las Vegas (Nev.)—Fiction 2. Man-woman relationships—Fiction 3. Psychological fiction 4. Striptease clubs 5. Stripteasers—Fiction
ISBN 1493105477; 9781493105472

SUMMARY: In this book, "strong, sexy African-American stripper Melissa Masters, 23, works the Stilettos strip club patrons like a pro, but the dancing lifestyle is anything but glitzy. Now in her fourth year at the club, Masters . . . must contend with exhaustive hours spent lap-dancing rich, pushy, strange men while fending off the sexual advances of Stilettos' sleazy, arrogant general manager, Scott. Her personal life is also messy thanks to Spider, a smooth operator on the Vegas scene." (Kirkus Reviews)

REVIEW: *Kirkus Rev* v82 no2 p60 Ja 15 2014

"Stilettos in Vegas". "Complementing the fast-moving storyline are pages of fascinating insider industry secrets . . . all culled from co-author [Valerie L.] Diamond's seven years as a Vegas stripper. Toward the book's conclusion, Diamond's intentions to educate, not patronize, the women working within the lucrative strip club world and challenge the preconceived notions associated with it are discreetly communicated through Sapphire. Diamond and [Don] McGann compile a rousing, spicy brew of sex, love and intrigue with a cliffhanger ending foretelling more Sapphire adventures to come. A readable, highly charged amalgam of erotic action and suspense headlined by a likable, compassionate exotic performer with a heart of gold."

DIAS, ROSIE. Exhibiting Englishness; John Boydell's Shakespeare Gallery and the formation of a national aesthetic; [by] Rosie Dias 288 p. 2013 Yale University Press

1. Aesthetics, British—18th century 2. Historical literature 3. Nationalism and art—Great Britain—History—18th century

ISBN 9780300196689 (cl : alk. paper)

LC 2013-004809

SUMMARY: This book discusses an 18th-century English art gallery established by John Boydell. "The book analyzes the works of such artists as Joshua Reynolds, Henry Fuseli, [and] James Northcote, . . . laying out their diverse ways of expressing notions of individualism, humor, eccentricity, and naturalism. Exhibiting Englishness also argues that Boydell's gallery radically redefined the dynamics of display and cultural aesthetics at that time." (Publisher's note)

REVIEW: *Choice* v51 no5 p819-20 Ja 2014 W. S. Rodner

"Exhibiting Englishness: John Boydell's Shakespeare Gallery and the Formation of a National Aesthetic." "Building on the period's fascination with 'the Bard,' London print dealer John Boydell established a gallery dedicated to the display of specially commissioned paintings of subjects from Shakespeare's plays . . . that would be exhibited and reproduced as engravings.[Rosie] Dias . . . applies a clear, scholarly focus to the details of this 'new history painting' while considering wider issues such as patronage, profit, audience, display, and the role of the Royal Academy. Included are nearly 100 fine illustrations, many in color. . . . Recommended."

DIBLEY, GLIN.il. Joy in Mudville. See Raczka, B.

DICAMILLO, KATE, 1964-. Flora and Ulysses; The Illuminated Adventures; 240 p. 2013 Candlewick Press

1. Children of divorced parents—Fiction 2. Friendship—Juvenile fiction 3. Graphic novels 4. Squirrels 5. Superheroes

ISBN 076366040X (reinforced); 9780763660406 (reinforced)

LC 2012-947748

SUMMARY: In this book by Newbury Medalist Kate DiCamillo, "bitter about her parents' divorce. Flora Buckman has withdrawn into her favorite comic book The Amazing Incandesto! and memorized the advisories in its ongoing bonus feature, Terrible Things Can Happen to You! She puts those life-saving tips into action when a squirrel is swallowed whole by a neighbor's new vacuum cleaner. . . . Flora resuscitates the squirrel," who now has superpowers. (Publishers Weekly)

REVIEW: *Booklist* v110 no9/10 p125 Ja 1 2014 Sally Miculek

REVIEW: *Booklist* v110 no9/10 p112 Ja 1 2014 JULIE GREEN

REVIEW: *Booklist* v109 no19/20 p74 Je 1 2013 Ilene Cooper

REVIEW: *Bull Cent Child Books* v67 no3 p147-8 N 2013 J. H.

"Flora & Ulysses: The Illuminated Adventures." "Ten-year-old Flora is a fan of comic-book superheroes, so it seems perfectly natural to her when a squirrel vacuumed up by the neighbor and revived by Flora develops intellectual and physical powers. . . . The twee voice and excessively quirky characters, however, frequently threaten to upend the story while Flora's mother's speedy transformation from attempted squirrel-murderer to apologetic and loving mother also strains credulity. [Illustrator K. G.] Campbell's attractive, soft-focus pencil illustrations, often appearing in comic-like panels, add individuality and depth to the characters and carry some of the narrative. Despite the book's flaws, this may appeal to kids with a bent for graphic novels and comics. . . ."

REVIEW: *Horn Book Magazine* v89 no5 p91 S/O 2013 CYNTHIA K. RITTER

REVIEW: *Kirkus Rev* p73 N 15 2013 Best Books

REVIEW: *Kirkus Rev* p39 Ag 15 2013 Fall Preview

REVIEW: *Kirkus Rev* v81 no13 p220 Jl 1 2013

REVIEW: *Publ Wkly* v261 no4 p188 Ja 27 2014

REVIEW: *Publ Wkly* v260 no25 p174 Je 24 2013

REVIEW: *Publ Wkly* p76 Children's starred review annual 2013

REVIEW: *SLJ* v59 no8 p96 Ag 2013 Rhona Campbell

REVIEW: *SLJ* v60 no2 p52 F 2014 Jennifer Furuyama

DICKENSON, DONNA. Me medicine vs. we medicine; reclaiming biotechnology for the common good; [by] Donna Dickenson 296 p. 2013 Columbia University Press

1. Biotechnology—ethics 2. Individualized Medicine—ethics 3. Medical literature 4. Public Health Practice—ethics 5. Social Justice

ISBN 9780231159746 (cloth : alk. paper); 9780231534413 (e-book)

LC 2012-037582

SUMMARY: This book by Donna Dickenson "takes a critical look at the emerging technologies that are = grouped under the name of personalized medicine, or what she calls 'me medicine.' In concentrating on 'me medicine,' humans could lose both their individual and collective well-being that could be advanced by medical biotechnology--what Dickenson calls 'we medicine,' which is basically the public health paradigm." (Choice: Current Reviews for Academic Libraries)

REVIEW: *Choice* v51 no7 p1253 Mr 2014 M. M. Gillis

"Me Medicine vs. We Medicine: Reclaiming Biotechnology for the Common Good." "Award-winning bioethicist [Donna] Dickenson . . . takes a critical look at the emerging technologies that are grouped under the name of personalized medicine, or what she calls 'me medicine.' . . . With chapters on controlling genetic information, pharmacogenomics, umbilical cord banking, neuroenhancement technologies, and the vaccine debate, this is a timely, easy-to-read, and important book. . . . Highly recommended."

REVIEW: *Publ Wkly* v260 no16 p49 Ap 22 2013

DICKERSON, MELANIE. The Captive Maiden; [by] Melanie Dickerson 352 p. 2013 Harpercollins Christian Pub

1. Cinderella (Legendary character) 2. Fairy tales 3. Historical fiction 4. Love stories 5. Orphans—Fiction
ISBN 0310724414; 9780310724414

SUMMARY: In this fairy tale retold by author Melanie Dickerson, "when Gisela learns the duke's son, Valten--the boy she has daydreamed about for years--is throwing a ball in hopes of finding a wife, she vows to find a way to attend. . . . Though he is rough around the edges, Gisela finds Valten has completely captured her heart. But other forces are bent on keeping the two from falling further in love, putting Gisela in more danger than she ever imagined." (Publisher's note)

REVIEW: *Booklist* v110 no7 p59 D 1 2013 Anne O'Malley

REVIEW: *Kirkus Rev* v81 no16 p235 Ag 15 2013

"The Captive Maiden." "Weaving a heavy dose of romance into a familiar fairy tale, and revisiting the same family as in 'The Healer's Apprentice' . . . and 'The Fairest Beauty' . . . , [author Melanie] Dickerson has concocted another lavish medieval idyll. . . . While Valten and Gisela are attractive characters, others lack the spark of life. Though it gets off to a fine start, it gradually loses its way--at least partly through heavy-handed references to other tales in the series--needlessly extending an otherwise pleasant if uninspired romance. Nevertheless, meticulous period detail and the slightly steamy--though modestly chaste--evolving relationship between Gisela and Valten ultimately sustain this tale."

REVIEW: *Kirkus Rev* p52 Ag 15 2013 Fall Preview

REVIEW: *Publ Wkly* v260 no42 p55 O 21 2013

REVIEW: *SLJ* v60 no1 p80 Ja 2014 June Shimonishi

DICKEY, JAMES, 1923-1997. The complete poems of James Dickey; xlix, 920 p. 2013 University of South Carolina Press

1. American poetry 2. Human sexuality in poetry 3. Hunting in literature 4. Poems—Collections 5. War poetry
ISBN 9781611170979 (cloth ; alk. paper)
LC 2012-020573

SUMMARY: This book, edited by Ward Briggs, collects "all 331 poems published by" James Dickey. "Dickey's most-admired and most-anthologized poems--such as 'The Performance,' 'Cherrylog Road,' 'The Firebombing,' 'Falling,' and 'May Day Sermon'--along with his epic poem The Zodiac are placed in chronological order of publication, affording a poetic autobiography that reveals the intellectual development and the constant experimentation of an iconic American literary figure." (Publisher's note)

REVIEW: *TLS* no5769 p23 O 25 2013 JULES SMITH

"The Complete Poems." "[James] Dickey's poems share . . . a folksy, expansive machismo, capable of humour yet having an undercurrent of menace. . . . Animated by visceral sensory experience, filled with scenes of hunting, fishing, war, sports and sexual obsession. . . . What this weighty 'Complete Poems' convincingly shows is that Dickey's writing was always as much fictional as confessional, making emotive impact by rhetorical means, like the advertising copywriter he also was.. . . Ward Briggs's edition contains all 331 poems, in chronological order of publication. . . . Briggs meticulously lists publication data and textual variants and gives explanatory notes, incorporating Dickey's statements though also correcting them."

DICKEY, JENNIFER.ed. Museums in a global context. See Museums in a global context

DICKIE, JOHN. Mafia Republic; Italy's Criminal Curse. Cosa Nostra, 'ndrangheta and Camorra from 1946 to the Present; [by] John Dickie 544 p. 2013 Sceptre

1. 'Ndrangheta 2. Camorra 3. Historical literature 4. Mafia—Italy 5. Mafia—United States
ISBN 1444726404; 9781444726404

SUMMARY: This book "describes the rise and rise of the Cosa Nostra, Camorra and 'Ndrangheta from their southern Italian heartlands, spreading out into the industrialised north and on into criminal networks across Europe, the USA and Australia. An entire alternative economy and social organisation based on a mix of omertà and narrow-minded familial greed/revenge, this fundamentally primitive phenomenon is largely responsible for so much of the . . .mayhem at the heart of the dysfunctional Italian state." (Adelaide Review)

REVIEW: *London Rev Books* v35 no19 p29-30 O 10 2013 Edward Luttwak

REVIEW: *TLS* no5769 p27 O 25 2013 JOSEPH FARRELL

"Mafia Republic: Italy's Criminal Curse--Cosa Nostra, Camorra and 'Ndrangheta From 1946 to the Present." "[John Dickie] makes no pretence at the nonjudgemental approach, and the tone throughout 'Mafia Republic' is one of baffled indignation. . . . It is a dismal picture, but drawn with expertise and a mastery of detail by John Dickie. He combines narrative skills in his description of skulduggery with excellent pen portraits of striking individuals who may be far from admirable but are certainly colourful. His reader-friendly, racy style becomes more sober and reflective when he offers points of analysis, and now, no one anywhere writes with such authority on Italy's criminal gangs."

DICKSON, C.tr. The African. See Le Clézio, J.-M. G.

DICKSON, KARI.tr. The hole. See Torseter, Ø.

DICKSON, KARI.tr. My father's arms are a boat. See My father's arms are a boat

DICTIONARY OF ENVIRONMENTAL AND CLIMATE CHANGE LAW; xii, 293 p. 2013 Edward Elgar

1. Climate change mitigation—Dictionaries 2. Climatic changes—Law and legislation—Dictionaries 3. Environmental law—China 4. Environmental law—Dictionaries 5. Environmental law—United States 6. Environmental law, International—Dictionaries 7. Environmental policy—China 8. Environmental policy—United States 9. Legal literature
ISBN 0857935771 (cased); 9780857935779 (cased)
LC 2012-948843

SUMMARY: Edited by Nicholas A. Robinson, Wang Xi, Lin Harmon, and Sarah Wegmueller, this book "defines terms employed in international agreements, national legislation and scholarly legal studies related to comparative and international environmental law and the emerging law of climate change. . . . Jointly prepared by scholars in China and the US, the Dictionary provides a linguistic bridge between English and Chinese speakers." (Publisher's note)

REVIEW: *Choice* v51 no4 p610-2 D 2013 T. H. Koenig

"Dictionary of Environmental and Climate Change Law." "This book's four editors, legal scholars from the US and China, have compiled definitions for well over 1,000 terms commonly employed in the rapidly evolving field of environmental law. This dictionary's unique aspect is that the terms (but not the definitions) are translated into both Chinese characters and Mandarin Pinyin formats. This approach is beneficial for those negotiating, implementing, litigating, and/or coordinating solutions to globalized ecological problems such as climate change. . . . The editors perform a valuable service by helping to diminish the confusion that inevitably arises when representatives of very different legal cultures must work together."

DICTIONARY OF FOOD COMPOUNDS WITH CD-ROM; 2013 CRC Press

1. Chemical literature 2. Chemistry—Dictionaries 3. Encyclopedias & dictionaries 4. Food additives 5. Nutrition

ISBN 9781420083514

SUMMARY: Edited by Shmuel Yannai, this book "is presented in a user-friendly format in both hard copy and . . . CD-ROM. It contains entries describing natural components of food raw materials and products as well as compounds added to foods or formed in the course of storage or processing. Each entry contains the name of the component, the chemical and physical characteristics, a description of functional properties related to food use, and nutritional and toxicological data." (Publisher's note)

REVIEW: *Choice* v51 no4 p608 D 2013 J. M. Lacey

"Dictionary of Food Compounds With CD-ROM." "The second edition . . . of the 'Dictionary of Food Compounds' is an invaluable, up-to-date resource for anyone involved in the science of food and nutrition. . . . Listed alphabetically are concise descriptions of over 40,000 compounds . . . present in food throughout various stages of development, storage, and processing. Naturally occurring components, additives, contaminants, and nutraceuticals are described by unique properties such as chemical structure, appearance, general food/usage information, melting/boiling points, spectroscopic data, densities, and toxicity data. . . . This is a useful and important work, particularly given the ever-widening international interest in food for human health, safety, and adequacy."

DIEHL, DIGBY. Alone Together; My Life With J. Paul Getty. See Gaston, T. G.

DIEHN, GWEN. Journal your way; desigining & using handmade books; [by] Gwen Diehn 180 p. 2013 Lark Crafts

1. Book design 2. Bookbinding—Amateurs' manuals 3. Do-it-yourself literature 4. Journal writing 5. Scrapbook journaling

ISBN 145470411X; 9781454704119

LC 2012-042569

SUMMARY: This book offers "step-by-step illustrations and instructions for more than sixteen formats and 10 cover styles" of personal journals. Author "Gwen Diehn celebrates the art of making and using a personalized journal." Images "showcase a . . . variety of working journals, . . . sidebars introduce longtime journal keepers, and nine . . . recipients of customized, handcrafted journals from the author share their own pages." (Publisher's note)

REVIEW: *Booklist* v110 no8 p14 D 15 2013 Brad Hooper Donna Seaman

"The Complete Photo Guide to Making Metal Jewelry," "Connect the Shapes Crochet Motifs: Creative Techniques for Joining Motifs of All Shapes," and "Journal Your Way: Designing and Using Handmade Books." "If any crafter has reservations about learning to make metal jewelry, [John] Sartin knocks those reservations out of the water in a very savvy approach to the subject. . . . This is smart publishing: a spiral-bound pattern and instructional book that actually lies flat, so that avid needleworkers can practice while reading instructions. . . . [Gwen] Diehn teaches readers how to create the blank book most suited to one's needs through a series of questions and selections from eight different personal journals."

REVIEW: *Booklist* v110 no1 p27 S 1 2013 Barbara Jacobs

"Journal Your Way: Designing and Using Handmade Books." "What three-time author [Gwen] Diehn . . . has accomplished is that oh-so-important reader inspiration, which will lead to the 'I can do this' conviction. . . . Especially savvy is the actual design of her how-to, colored and illustrated professionally to resemble a journal. Even the instructions for 10 covers, 16 books, and other techniques are lovingly explained in a combination of line drawings, words, and color examples. Everything included inside is ready to take anyone on a personal journaling expedition. A seven-page gallery of actual hand-made books adds interest."

DIETZ, TON.ed. Asian tigers, African lions. See Asian tigers, African lions

DIFFERENT BODIES; essays on disability in film and television; 272 p. 2013 McFarland & Company, Inc., Publishers

1. Disability studies 2. Documentary films 3. People with disabilities in motion pictures 4. People with disabilities on television 5. Social science literature

ISBN 9780786465354 (softcover: alk. paper)

LC 2013-022270

SUMMARY: This essay collection "focuses on contemporary film and television (1989 to the present)" and their depictions of disability. The essays are divided into three sections" containing "critical readings of narrative film and television . . . [and] essays on documentaries, biopics and autobiographically-informed films, and an essay on audience reactions to a television series." (Publisher's note)

REVIEW: *Choice* v51 no8 p1406 Ap 2014 K. L. Cole

"Different Bodies: Essays on Disability in Film and Television". "Because disability studies is still a relatively new field of inquiry, many if not most new studies on the subject deliver original and significant contributions. Such is the case with 'Different Bodies,' the first treatment of disability in television and film. [Marja Evelyn] Mogk . . . dedicates the collection to those new to disability studies, but her introduction will be useful for the specialist as well as the undergraduate. This is also true of the essays, which in terms of style are accessible but in terms of content and theoretical application will appeal to specialists. The range of topics is impressive and intriguing."

DIKSHITH, T. S. S. Hazardous chemicals; safety management and global regulations; [by] T. S. S. Dikshith xli, 638 p. 2013 CRC Press, Taylor & Francis Group

1. Chemical literature 2. Hazardous substances—Health aspects 3. Hazardous substances—International cooperation 4. Hazardous substances—Law & legislation 5. Hazardous substances—Management 6. Hazardous substances—Safety measures—Standards
ISBN 9781439878200
LC 2012-036757

SUMMARY: This book "covers proper management, precautions, and related global regulations on the safety management of chemical substances. The book helps workers and safety personnel prevent and minimize the consequences of catastrophic releases of toxic, reactive, flammable, or explosive chemical substances, which often result in toxic or explosive hazards. It also details safety measures for transportation of chemical substances by different routes, such as by road, rail, air, and sea." (Publisher's note)

REVIEW: *Choice* v51 no6 p1037-8 F 2014 H. E. Pence

"Hazardous Chemicals: Safety Management and Global Regulations." "Toxicologist [T.S.S.] Dikshith . . . provides little quantitative information of the type that safety officials and other professionals would desire, such as allowed regulatory levels, flash points, and solubilities. However, the format appears to be quite useful to the general public and those who do not have much background on the topic, since the information is presented as readily understandable blocks of text, rather than just numeric values. At the end of the book, a brief section describes the regulatory environment in a number of foreign countries, and there is a glossary of common terms and abbreviations."

DIKÖTTER, FRANK. The tragedy of liberation; a history of the Chinese revolution, 1945-1957; [by] Frank Dikötter 400 p. 2013 Bloomsbury Press

1. China—History—Cultural Revolution, 1966-1976 2. China—Politics & government—1949-1976 3. HISTORY—General 4. Historical literature 5. Mao, Zedong, 1893-1976
ISBN 9781620403471 (hardback)
LC 2013-031044

SUMMARY: This book on the Chinese Communist Revolution, "draw[s] on hundreds of previously classified documents, secret police reports, unexpurgated versions of leadership speeches, eyewitness accounts of those who survived, and more. . . . Interweaving stories of ordinary citizens with tales of the brutal politics of Mao's court, Frank Dikötter illuminates those who shaped the 'liberation' and the horrific policies they implemented." (Publisher's note)

REVIEW: *Kirkus Rev* v81 no16 p78 Ag 15 2013

REVIEW: *N Y Rev Books* v61 no1 p39-41 Ja 9 2014 Ian Burunia

"The Tragedy of Liberation: A History of the Chinese Revolution, 1945-1957." "In his dogged attempt to make his case, [Frank] Dikötter is just as addicted to statistics as the Party hacks whose myths he wants to demolish. Since his statistics are not about progress but about death and destruction, they make grim reading. . . . Dikötter's prose has only one tone: righteous indignation. That is his style. . . . The great merit of Dikötter's book is that it goes beyond the horrific statistics. . . . He clearly explains the mechanics of the revolutionary state, how mass violence was orchestrated, why people took part in the killing, and what the purposes of the terror were."

REVIEW: *Publ Wkly* v260 no31 p62 Ag 5 2013

REVIEW: *TLS* no5787 p24 F 28 2014 JEREMY BROWN

"China's War With Japan 1937-1945: The Struggle for Survival" and "The Tragedy of Liberation: A History of the Chinese Revolution 1945-1957." "'China's War with Japan' aims to present a comprehensive narrative of the war from the perspective of the three main political forces in China: Chiang Kai-shek's Nationalists, Mao Zedong's Communists and Wang Jingwei's collaborationist regime. [Author Rana] Mitter achieves his three-pronged goal, but Chiang's voice dominates the book. . . . In 'The Tragedy of Liberation,' Frank Dikötter agrees that terror was the foundation of Mao's regime. . . . But the mostly nameless victims . . . have been reduced to caricatures. . . . Portraying only the most terrible stories . . . as the norm . . . gives a distorted picture of everyday life in 1950s China."

DILLARD, SARAH. Extraordinary Warren, a super chicken; [by] Sarah Dillard 64 p. 2014 Aladdin

1. Animal stories 2. Chickens—Fiction 3. Farm life—Fiction 4. Humorous stories 5. Superheroes—Fiction
ISBN 9781442453401 (alk. paper)
LC 2013-029892

SUMMARY: In this book, "life on the farm stifles Warren, who . . . and declares himself 'more than just an ordinary chicken!' His dreams are aided and abetted by sinister Millard the rat, who's licking his chops as he dubs Warren 'Chicken Supreme.' When Warren realizes that Millard's celebratory chicken barbecue is going to feature the coop members as entrees rather than guests, Warren tries to warn them and heroically--and accidentally--saves the day." (Bulletin of the Center for Children's Books)

REVIEW: *Booklist* v110 no13 p52-4 Mr 1 2014 Francisca Goldsmith

"Extraordinary Warren: A Super Chicken." "[Sarah] Dillard allows her clever tale to unfold in both sentences and cartoon panels. This combined approach amplifies Warren's wry observations of his surroundings and peers, such as the egg, the rat, a duck, and a hungry fox. The brightly hued illustrations depict a wide variety of emotion and clever props, like the fox's suspicious chicken cookbook and the duck's coaching whistle, which looks remarkably like his own hat. There's even a bilingual pun, along with a handful of silly food jokes. The simple text, usually only appearing in one or two sentences, is easy enough for beginning readers. Warren has all the imagination of Rebecca Purcell's 'Super Chicken!' (2013) but with some added sly sophistication, too."

REVIEW: *Bull Cent Child Books* v67 no6 p307 F 2014 Deborah Stevenson

"Extraordinary Warren: A Super Chicken." "[Sarah] Dillard has a light hand in this easy reader, touching with gentle absurdity on the desire to be extraordinary and adding in some amusing details. . . . Unfortunately, the plot meanders off into strange directions (chicken flying lessons suddenly appear) and loses momentum, and the dénouement involves too many devices and not enough punch. The digital illustrations have a tidy perkiness, with trim lines and simple backgrounds; with its frequent panel sequences and speech bubbles, the layout resembles an airy graphic novel. The easygoing layout and friendly charm of the dialogue may still appeal to early readers, who may appreciate the hint that subsequent adventures are to come."

REVIEW: *Kirkus Rev* v81 no24 p148 D 15 2013

REVIEW: *Publ Wkly* v260 no48 p57 N 25 2013

DILLARD, SARAH.il. Extraordinary Warren, a super chicken. See Dillard, S.

DILLEN, FREDERICK. Beauty; a novel; [by] Frederick Dillen 256 p. 2014 Simon & Schuster

1. Business—Fiction 2. Businesswomen—Fiction 3. Corporations—Massachuestts—Fiction 4. Factories 5. Psychological fiction
ISBN 9781476716923 (hardback); 9781476716930 (paperback)
LC 2013-028658

SUMMARY: In this book, "as a corporate 'undertaker' for a mergers and acquisitions firm in New York, Carol MacLean travels from factory to factory, firing blue-collar workers. . . . To save the town and herself, Carol becomes determined to rescue the factory she's under orders to shut down. With the help of the townspeople and a roughly charming local fisherman . . . Carol throws herself into transforming the company—but is soon faced with increasingly difficult decisions." (Publisher's note)

REVIEW: *Booklist* v110 no12 p23 F 15 2014 Michele Leber

REVIEW: *Kirkus Rev* v82 no2 p250 Ja 15 2014

"Beauty". "There are strong echoes of Jimmy Stewart rallying the townspeople in 'It's A Wonderful Life'. Carol has Anna Rose, redoubtable organizer of the Wives of the Sea, on her side; the town is thrilled; Carol is a hero. All this happens at improbable breakneck speed, but [Frederick] Dillen presents the business choices so clearly that we cut him some slack. While the way forward will not be problem-free, the story's sentimental populism has its own momentum. Kudos to Dillen for his unusual premise. The workplace drama that follows is rousing, if predictable."

REVIEW: *Libr J* v139 no2 p62 F 1 2014 Christine DeZelar-Tiedman

REVIEW: *Publ Wkly* v260 no52 p28 D 23 2013

DILLMAN, LISA.tr. Let me tell you a story. See Bucay, J.

DILLON, JOHN.tr. Aeneas of Gaza. See Aeneas of Gaza

DILLON, MICHELE. American Catholics in transition; persisting and changing; [by] Michele Dillon 202 p. 2013 Rowman & Littlefield Publishers

1. Attitudes toward religion 2. Catholics—Religious identity 3. Religious literature 4. Women in the Catholic Church
ISBN 9781442219915 (cloth: alk. paper); 9781442219922 (pbk.: alk. paper)
LC 2012-046948

SUMMARY: This book "reports on five surveys carried out . . . over a period of 25 years, from 1987 to 2011. The surveys are national probability samples of American Catholics, age 18 and older, now including four generations of Catholics. Over these twenty five years, the authors have found significant changes in Catholics' attitudes and behavior as well as many enduring trends in the explanation of Catholic identity. Generational change helps explain many of the differences." (Publisher's note)

REVIEW: *America* v210 no7 p30-3 Mr 3 2014 JAMES A. MCCANN

"American Catholics in Transition" and "Religion, Politics, and Polarization: How Religiopolitical Conflict is Changing Congress and American Democracy". "'American Catholics in Transition' draws from this rich set of surveys to identify patterns of stability and change in the Catholic mind-set since the 1980s. Catholic leaders and rank-and-file members alike could learn much from this book about the internal life of the church. Readers who are not Catholic but wish to know more about the makeup and trajectory of the largest religious denomination in the country will also find the discussion accessible. . . . The central takeaway from 'Religion, Politics, and Polarization' is that the organizational cultures of the two major parties in the United States draw from distinct religious traditions. . . . These two books underscore the significance of religion as a central force in U.S. politics and society."

REVIEW: *Choice* v51 no3 p479 N 2013 L. S. Creider

REVIEW: *Libr J* v138 no11 p96 Je 15 2013 Augustine J. Curley

DILLON, PATRICK. The Story of buildings; from the pyramids to the Sydney Opera House and beyond; 96 p. 2014 Candlewick Press

1. Architectural history 2. Building—Juvenile literature 3. Centre Georges Pompidou 4. Crystal Palace (London, England) 5. Picture books
ISBN 0763669903; 9780763669904
LC 2013-943096

SUMMARY: This book, by Patrick Dillon and illustrated by Stephen Biesty, is a "narrative history of buildings. . . . Why and how did people start making buildings? How did they learn to make them stronger, bigger, and more comfortable? Why did they start to decorate them in different ways? . . . Dillon's stories of remarkable buildings—and the remarkable people who made them—celebrates the ingenuity of human creation." (Publisher's note)

REVIEW: *Booklist* v110 no16 p43-4 Ap 15 2014 Carolyn Phelan

REVIEW: *Bull Cent Child Books* v67 no10 p511 Je 2014 E. B.

"The Story of Buildings From the Pyramids to the Sydney Opera House and Beyond". "In this ambitious overview of architectural history, Dillon discusses in chronological order dozens of significant buildings. . . . Although some brief attention is given to non-Western cultures, coverage is heavily slanted toward European developments. Dillon's text shines brightest when he focuses narrowly on architectural innovations and architects' quirks. . . . Too often, though, swaths of text commenting on world events bog the narrative down, and they seem less interested in providing context than in hustling readers abruptly from one architectural style to the next."

REVIEW: *Horn Book Magazine* v90 no4 p114-5 Jl/Ag 2014 ROGER SUTTON

REVIEW: *Kirkus Rev* v82 no4 p335 F 15 2014

"The Story of Buildings: From the Pyramids to the Sydney Opera House and Beyond". "[Stephen] Biesty's precisely drawn, finely detailed architectural views supply the highlights for this unfocused survey of homes and prominent buildings through the ages. . . . The author . . . shows a weakness for grand generalizations ('Skyscrapers were the first truly American buildings') and for repeating the notion that buildings are a kind of machine. With a few exceptions, his main choices reflect a distinctly Eurocentric outlook, and he neglects even to mention Frank Gehry or more than a spare handful of living architects. There is no bibliography or further reading. Broad of historical (if not international) scope and with illustrations that richly reward poring over-but unfocused."

REVIEW: *SLJ* v60 no4 p186 Ap 2014 Bob Hassett

DINERSTEIN, ERIC. The kingdom of rarities; [by] Eric Dinerstein 312 p. 2013 Island Press

1. Biology—Juvenile literature 2. Biology—Textbooks 3. Endangered species 4. Extinction (Biology) 5. Rare animals 6. Rare vertebrates

ISBN 1610911954 (cloth : alk. paper); 1610911962 (pbk. : alk. paper); 9781610911955 (cloth : alk. paper); 9781610911962 (pbk. : alk. paper)

LC 2012-025535

SUMMARY: In this book, Eric Dinerstein "demonstrates that while rarity is a phenomenon of nature, few scientists have sought to study the more 'uncommon' species in a given ecosystem, and therefore may be missing key issues to better understand the natural world. He has cumulated over 40 years of his studies and experiences to highlight how rare species have developed intricate and complex webs, and how their existence has profound impacts on the ecosystem(s) in which they live." (Choice)

REVIEW: *Choice* v51 no1 p103 S 2013 K. K. Goldbeck-DeBose

DINKINS, DAVID N., 1927-. A mayor's life; governing New York's gorgeous mosaic; [by] David N. Dinkins 408 p. 2013 PublicAffairs

1. African American mayors 2. Mayors—New York (State)—New York—Biography 3. Memoirs

ISBN 1610393015; 9781610393010 (hardcover)

LC 2013-000769

SUMMARY: This book traces David N. Dinkins' political career leading up to his time as mayor of New York City. "As the newly-elected mayor of a city in which crime had risen precipitously in the years prior to his taking office, Dinkins vowed to attack the problems and not the victims. Criticized by some for his handling of the Crown Heights riots in 1991, Dinkins describes in these pages a very different version of events." (Publisher's note)

REVIEW: *Booklist* v110 no2 p18 S 15 2013 Vanessa Bush

REVIEW: *Kirkus Rev* v81 no16 p307 Ag 15 2013

REVIEW: *N Y Times Book Rev* p29 N 24 2013 SAM ROBERTS

"If Mayors Ruled the World: Dysfunctional Nations, Rising Cities" and "A Mayor's Life: Governing New York's Gorgeous Mosaic." "[Benjamin R.] Barber's book is the most audacious--even messianic--of a torrent of recently advanced urban manifestoes. . . . Barber builds a strong case for an informal parliament of cities . . . which would in effect ratify a shift in power and political reality that, he argues, has already taken place. . . . He persuasively builds his case with capsule profiles of visionary mayors from around the world. . . . Barber's book should be required reading for New York's new mayor, Bill de Blasio. So should 'A Mayor's Life: Governing New York's Gorgeous Mosaic,' by David N. Dinkins, a moving memoir."

DINTINJANA, MIA.tr. The master of insomnia. See The master of insomnia

D'INTINO, FRANCO.ed. Zibaldone. See Zibaldone

DIOUF, SYLVIANE A. Slavery's exiles; the story of the American Maroons; [by] Sylviane A. Diouf 384 p. 2014 New York University Press

1. Historical literature 2. Maroons—Southern States—History

ISBN 081472437X; 9780814724378 (hardback); 9780814760284 (pb)

LC 2013-029821

SUMMARY: In this book, author Sylvaine A. Diouf "reconstructs the lives of blacks who sought freedom and self-determination on the margins of an American slave society. Whether newly arrived from Africa or already acculturated to the demands of servitude, whether they fled to the hinterlands to live in secluded swamps or in the mountains, or to the borderlands, close by farms, plantations or towns, the maroons ran away intending to stay away, seeking autonomy even at the price of unspeakable danger." (Kirkus Reviews)

REVIEW: *Choice* v51 no11 p2052 Jl 2014 M. A. Byron

REVIEW: *Kirkus Rev* v81 no24 p63 D 15 2013

"Slavery's Exiles: The Story of the American Maroons". "[Sylvaine A. Diouf] tells the story of a few large communities, most notably that of the Great Dismal Swamp, and briefly examines the marronage subgroups of bandits and insurrectionists, but the triumph here is the author's portrait of the day-to-day precariousness of maroon lives, the courage and resourcefulness required for survival, and the terrible price they paid for trying to recover their freedom. A neglected chapter of the American slave experience brought sensitively and vividly to life."

REVIEW: *Libr J* v139 no4 p98 Mr 1 2014 Sonnet Ireland

REVIEW: *Publ Wkly* v260 no44 p56 N 4 2013

DIPRIMIO, PETE. Nero; [by] Pete DiPrimio 48 p. 2013 Mitchell Lane Publishers

1. Biographies 2. Emperors—Rome—Biography—Juvenile literature 3. Rome—Civilization

ISBN 9781612284392 (library bound)

LC 2013-012560

SUMMARY: This book on Nero by Pete DiPrimio is part of the Junior Biographies From Ancient Civilizations series. "Nero was trouble almost from the beginning. His murderous mother, Agrippina, killed off his uncle Claudius, so that she could rule through his heir, Nero. That didn't happen, and as Nero descended into madness, he followed the family tradition of killing many of his relatives." (Booklist)

REVIEW: *Booklist* v110 no5 p54 N 1 2013 Ilene Cooper

"Archimedes," "Leif Erikson," and "Nero." "The Junior Biographies from Ancient Civilizations series brings its subjects to life by focusing on some of history's most famous (and infamous) names. . . . The story of Archimedes begins with his famous 'Eureka!' moment and then goes back to look at his boyhood, mathematical training, and the impact he had on ancient Greek civilization. . . . The focus here is on [Leif] Erikson's voyage to Canada, where he became one of the first white men to see the new land. Roman emperor Nero was trouble almost from the beginning. . . . The books are a solid blending of art and text, with lengthy, illustrated sidebars doing the heavy lifting when it comes to explaining societies' mores."

DISHONGH, BRYCE.il. Minerva Day. See Keele, C.

DISIENA, LAURA LYN. Hippos can't swim; and other fun facts; [by] Laura Lyn DiSiena 32 p. 2014 Little Simon

1. Animals—Miscellanea—Juvenile literature 2. Children's nonfiction 3. Children's questions and answers 4. Hippopotamidae—Miscellanea—Juvenile literature 5. Hippopotamus

ISBN 9781442493247 (pbk: alk. paper); 9781442493254 (ebook: alk. paper); 9781442493520 (hc: alk. paper)

LC 2013-009391

SUMMARY: This book, part of the "Did You Know?" series, explores the "unique habits and characteristics" of "hippos, kangaroos, bats, chipmunks, and an assortment of other animals. . . . Large comical illustrations along with brief text provide information such as that sea turtles can swim up to 35 miles per hour, and how jellyfish provide light in their bodies (called bioluminescence). The book also includes other facts about fireflies, zebras, raccoons, rabbits, and blue herons." (Children's Literature)

REVIEW: *Booklist* v110 no16 p45 Ap 15 2014 Annie Miller

REVIEW: *Kirkus Rev* v82 no3 p329 F 1 2014

"Hippo's Can't Swim and Other Fun Facts". "Smooth segues provide the cement for this high-wattage, if less-than-carefully illustrated, set of animal facts. [Pete] Oswald's cartoon images of popeyed, well-caffeinated creatures crank up the visual energy to frantic levels. Unfortunately, at the outset, they contradict the author's correct observation that hippos' noses are placed on the tops of their heads. . . . For the most part, though, DiSiena and Eliot's revelations are both accurate and just as detailed as they need to be to keep and hold attention. . . . The pictures are a weak link, but younger readers and listeners will happily take this quick dive into the sea of random knowledge."

REVIEW: *Publ Wkly* v260 no51 p58 D 16 2013

REVIEW: *SLJ* v60 no5 p147 My 2014 Jeanette Lambert

DISRAELI, BENJAMIN, EARL OF BEACONSFIELD, 1804-1881. Benjamin Disraeli Letters; 1865-1867; 576 p. 2013 University of Toronto Press

1. Disraeli, Benjamin, Earl of Beaconsfield, 1804-1881 2. Great Britain—Politics & government—1837-1901 3. Letters 4. Prime ministers—Great Britain 5. Suffrage—Great Britain

ISBN 1442645466; 9781442645462

SUMMARY: This book, the ninth volume in a serial publication of Benjamin Disraeli's correspondence, "covers 1865 to 1867, crucial years leading up to Disraeli's first ministry in 1868. During this period, the prime minister, Lord Derby, and Disraeli, chancellor of the exchequer, grappled with a number of challenges. Their greatest accomplishment, however, was the passage of a landmark franchise reform bill that expanded the electorate in England to an unprecedented extent." (Publisher's note)

REVIEW: *TLS* no5746 p13 My 17 2013 STANLEY WEINTRAUB

"Benjamin Disraeli Letters: 1865-1867." "Volume Nine of 'Benjamin Disraeli Letters' reveals the leader of his party in the Commons, attacked by his political enemies as 'the Mephistopheles of statesmanship', and consumed with worry that he might 'die in a ditch'. . . . Only two insignificant letters appear in this volume to [W. E.] Gladstone, and four to [Henry Edward] Manning. There are fifty-seven to [Queen] Victoria, and thirty-six to Mary Anne [Disraeli]: one from the Commons, requesting replacement boots, another asking for pills, and a number of doting messages exchanged, in that epistolary culture, from nearby sickbeds in Grosvenor Gate."

DIVERSITY IN DIASPORA; Hmong Americans in the twenty-first century; xviii, 296 p. 2013 University of Hawai'i Press

1. Diaspora 2. Hmong (Asian people)—United States 3. Hmong Americans 4. Social science literature 5. Southeast Asian Americans

ISBN 0824835972; 9780824835972 (hardcover : alk. paper)

LC 2012-025448

SUMMARY: Editor Mark Edward Pfeifer's book focuses on "Hmong Americans' inclusion into and contributions to Asian American studies, as well as to American history and culture and refugee, immigrant, and diasporic trajectories. It negotiates both Hmong American political and cultural citizenship. . . . The collection boldly moves Hmong American studies away from its usual groove of refugee recapitulation that entrenches Hmong Americans points-of-origin and acculturation studies rather than propelling the field into other exciting academic avenues." (Publisher's note)

REVIEW: *Choice* v51 no1 p171 S 2013 J. R. Wendland

"Diversity in Diaspora: Hmong Americans in the Twenty-First Century." "The editors and contributors have crafted a strong interdisciplinary collection with wide-ranging research, background materials, and proposals for future study in this exploration of the lives of the growing Hmong American community. Of particular note are the four essays that carefully examine the cultural production of Hmong Americans since their arrival in the US. A recurring theme is the unique appropriations by Hmong American cultural producers to explain, describe, and articulate their experiences and identities. Discussions of Hmong American political activism and civic engagement provide important insights into the impact Hmong Americans have had on their local political situations."

DOCKING, GIL. Two Hundred and Forty Years of New Zealand Painting. See Dunn, M.

DOCTOROW, E. L., 1931-. Andrew's Brain; a novel; [by] E. L. Doctorow 224 p. 2014 Random House Inc

1. Grief—Fiction 2. Identity (Psychology)—Fiction 3. Memory—Fiction 4. Neuroscientists 5. Psychological fiction
ISBN 1400068819; 9781400068814

SUMMARY: This book, by E. L. Doctorow, "is structured as an extended series of conversations between Andrew, a cognitive neuroscientist by training, and an unnamed man who initially appears to be his psychotherapist. The book opens with Andrew's description of leaving his infant daughter with an ex-wife. When the baby's mother dies, Andrew claims to be too incapacitated by grief and self-doubt to care for the child." (Publishers Weekly)

REVIEW: *Booklist* v110 no5 p22 N 1 2013 Donna Seaman

"Andrew's Brain". "In stunning command of every aspect of this taut, unnerving, riddling tale, virtuoso [E. L.] Doctorow confronts the persistent mysteries of the mind—trauma and memory, denial and culpability—as he brings us back to one deeply scarring time of shock and lies, war and crime. Writing in concert with [Mark] Twain, [Edgar Allan] Poe, and [Franz] Kafka, Doctorow distills his mastery of language, droll humor, well-primed imagination, and political outrage into an exquisitely disturbing, morally complex, tragic, yet darkly funny novel of the collective American unconscious and human nature in all its perplexing contrariness."

REVIEW: *Harper's Magazine* v328 no1964 p75-7 Ja 2014 Christine Smallwood

REVIEW: *Kirkus Rev* v81 no19 p80 O 1 2013

REVIEW: *Libr J* v139 no6 p55 Ap 1 2014 Heather Malcolm

REVIEW: *Libr J* v138 no13 p53 Ag 1 2013 Barbara Hoffert

REVIEW: *N Y Times Book Rev* p22 Ja 19 2014

REVIEW: *N Y Times Book Rev* p1-20 Ja 12 2014 Terrence Rafferty

REVIEW: *Nation* v298 no19 p36 My 12 2014 HANNAH K. GOLD

REVIEW: *New Statesman* v143 no5197 p49 F 14 2014 Randy Boyagoda

REVIEW: *New Yorker* v90 no5 p93-1 Mr 24 2014

REVIEW: *Publ Wkly* v261 no8 p177 F 24 2014

REVIEW: *Publ Wkly* v260 no31 p43 Ag 5 2013

REVIEW: *TLS* no5782 p19 Ja 24 2014 EDMUND GORDON

DODD, C. KENNETH. Frogs of the United States and Canada; [by] C. Kenneth Dodd 2 v. (xxvii, 982 p.) 2013 Johns Hopkins University Press

1. Frogs—Behavior 2. Frogs—Canada 3. Frogs—Ecology 4. Frogs—Physiology 5. Frogs—United States 6. Natural history literature
ISBN 1421406330 (hdbk. : alk. paper); 9781421406336 (hdbk. : alk. paper)
LC 2012-017648

SUMMARY: This book "summarizes and synthesizes the scientific literature through May 2011 on frogs occurring north of Mexico. Volume 1 contains introductory material, abbreviations, and species accounts for the families Ascaphidae, Bufonidae, Craugastoridae, Eleutherodactylidae, Leptodactylidae, Microhylidae, and Rhinophrynidae. Volume 2 contains species accounts for the families Ranidae and Scaphiopodidae, and established nonnative species." (Choice)

REVIEW: *Choice* v51 no4 p667 D 2013 E. D. Keiser

"Frogs of the United States and Canada." "This monumental work on the 100 frog species of the US/Canada is much more detailed than Ana Wright and Albert Wright's 'Handbook of Frogs and Toads of the United States and Canada'. . . and L. Elliott, H. Cerhardt, and C. Davidson's 'The Frogs and Toads of North America'. . . . Species range maps, one or more excellent color photographs, and occasional monochrome line drawings illustrate the accounts. Species descriptions are detailed, but identification keys are not used. Account length varies with the extent of available literature. These very well-written, indispensable volumes are exceptionally detailed, accurate, and up-to-date."

DOEDEN, MATT. The World Series; baseball's biggest stage; [by] Matt Doeden 64 p. 2014 Millbrook Press, A division of Lerner Publishing Group, Inc.

1. Baseball—History 2. Baseball players—History 3. Baseball teams—History 4. Sports literature 5. World Series (Baseball)—History—Juvenile literature
ISBN 1467718963; 9781467718967 (lib. bdg.: alk. paper)
LC 2013-018082

SUMMARY: This book describes how "when the top teams face off in the World Series each season, team legacies and fans' hearts are on the line. Author Matt Doeden covers the century-long history of the World Series, from its humble beginnings to becoming a worldwide sensation. Discover the drama behind the statistics and record books that keeps the crowd enthralled!" (Publisher's note)

REVIEW: *Booklist* v110 no16 p45 Ap 15 2014 John Peters

REVIEW: *Kirkus Rev* v82 no3 p162 F 1 2014

"The World Series: Baseball's Biggest Stage". "[Matt] Doeden presents the Fall Classic's basic history as well as chapters spotlighting special games, players and individual moments, balancing long-ago events and players with those of recent years. All of them are interesting and informative, but no criteria are given concerning the selections. . . . Text is composed in accessible, conversational language and carefully arranged with clear headings in red display type. . . . Endlessly fascinating and a sharing opportunity for children and adults who love the game."

REVIEW: *SLJ* v60 no6 p143 Je 2014 Blair Christolon

DOERR, ANTHONY. All the light we cannot see; a novel; [by] Anthony Doerr 448 p. 2014 Scribner

1. Blind—Fiction 2. World War, 1939-1945—Youth—France—Fiction 3. World War, 1939-1945—Youth—Germany—Fiction
ISBN 1476746583; 9781476746586 (hardback); 9781476746593 (paperback)
LC 2013-034107

SUMMARY: This book, by Anthony Doerr, is told from "multiple viewpoints but focus[es] mostly on blind French teenager Marie-Laure and Werner, a brilliant German soldier just a few years older than she. . . . They are on opposite sides of the horrors of World War II, and their fates ultimately collide in connection with the radio—a means of resistance for the Allies and just one more avenue of annihilation for the Nazis." (Library Journal)

REVIEW: *America* v211 no5 p38-40 S 2014 KELLY CHERRY

REVIEW: *Booklist* v110 no9/10 p20 Ja 1 2014 Brad Hooper

"All the Light We Cannot See," "And the Dark Sacred Night," and "Lovers at the Chameleon Club, Paris 1932". "[Anthony] Doerr's brilliance as a short story writer was established by the popular 'Shell Collector' (2001), but his work in the novel form has also been exceptional; his latest one, about a young couple in Europe, will attest to that. . . . [Julia] Glass won the National Book Award for 'Three Junes' (2002), and she has been on serious fiction readers' radar ever since; they will not be disappointed in her latest novel, about family secrets. . . . One of the finest current literary-fiction writers, [Francine] Prose presents a novel focused on a Paris jazz club and its fascinating clientele in the 1920s and 1930s."

REVIEW: *Booklist* v110 no16 p23 Ap 15 2014 Brad Hooper

REVIEW: *Kirkus Rev* v82 no9 p2 My 1 2014 CLAIBORNE SMITH

REVIEW: *Kirkus Rev* v82 no6 p150 Mr 15 2014

REVIEW: *Libr J* v139 no2 p62 F 1 2014 Evelyn Beck

REVIEW: *Libr J* v138 no21 p68 D 1 2013 Barbara Hoffert

REVIEW: *Libr J* v139 no13 p46 Ag 1 2014 Judy Murray

REVIEW: *N Y Times Book Rev* p16 My 11 2014 WILLIAM T. VOLLMANN

REVIEW: *New York Times* v163 no56486 pC1-4 Ap 29 2014 JANET MASLIN

REVIEW: *New Yorker* v90 no17 p85-1 Je 23 2014

REVIEW: *Publ Wkly* v261 no4 p48-54 Ja 27 2014

REVIEW: *Publ Wkly* v261 no7 p75 F 17 2014

REVIEW: *TLS* no5803 p20 Je 20 2014 DAVID COLLARD

REVIEW: *Voice of Youth Advocates* v37 no4 p63 O 2014 Katherine Noone

DOHERTY, MEGHAN. How not to be a dick; an everyday etiquette guide; [by] Meghan Doherty 192 p. 2013 Zest Books

1. Etiquette—Handbooks, manuals, etc. 2. Etiquette—Humor 3. Handbooks, vade-mecums, etc. 4. Teenagers—Conduct of life 5. Youth—Conduct of life
ISBN 9781936976027
LC 2013-937668

SUMMARY: In this etiquette guide for teens and young adults, "following an introduction that defines what makes a person seem like a dick, seven chapters address situations ranging from initiating romantic relationships to behaving responsibly at after-office get-togethers." (Kirkus Reviews)

REVIEW: *Booklist* v110 no5 p58-60 N 1 2013 Daniel Kraus

"How Not to Be a Dick: An Everyday Etiquette Guide." "The atmosphere is pure Dick-and-Jane: fussy early-reader prose married to bland clip-art-style illustrations starring a deadpan boy and girl. Through these oldfangled characters, [Meghan] Doherty fires absurd twenty-first-century zingers that happen to be really, really, really funny, (When was the last time you LOL'd at a nonfiction book?) Droll humor is one thing, but does Doherty deliver substance? Shockingly, she does, offering teens blunt, no-nonsense advice on the adult world that awaits them. . . . Given the emphasis on roommates, office parties, and alcohol, this is clearly the gift book for next year's high-school and college grads."

REVIEW: *Kirkus Rev* v81 no17 p85 S 1 2013

REVIEW: *Publ Wkly* v260 no28 p172 Jl 15 2013

DOHERTY, THOMAS. Hollywood and Hitler, 1933-1939; [by] Thomas Doherty 429 p. 2013 Columbia University Press

1. Historical literature 2. Motion picture industry—Germany—History—20th century 3. Motion picture industry—United States—History—20th century 4. Motion pictures—Political aspects—Germany—History—20th century 5. Motion pictures—Political aspects—United States—History—20th century 6. Motion pictures in propaganda—Germany—History—20th century 7. Motion pictures, American—Germany—History—20th century 8. Motion pictures, German—United States—History—20th century 9. National socialism and motion pictures 10. Nazis in motion pictures
ISBN 9780231163927 (cloth : alk. paper)
LC 2012-046863

SUMMARY: In this book, Thomas Doherty examines "how Hollywood adjusted to the onset of World War II. In the 1930s, the studios were forced not only to find ways to continue business in Germany, but also to prepare for the eventual loss of that business. Many studios refused to run newsreels of Hitler, as film stars petitioned for complete economic withdrawal from Germany, and Hays Code censors battled with filmmakers about how to portray the truth of German brutality." (Library Journal)

REVIEW: *Am Hist Rev* v119 no2 p545-7 Ap 2014 M. Todd Bennett

REVIEW: *Choice* v51 no6 p1075 F 2014 J. Fischel

REVIEW: *Film Q* v67 no1 p84-6 Fall 2013 HANNAH GRAVES

REVIEW: *Libr J* v138 no5 p110 Mr 15 2013 Rochelle LeMaster

REVIEW: *London Rev Books* v35 no24 p25-6 D 19 2013 J. Hoberman

"Hollywood and Hitler: 1933-39" and "The Collaboration: Hollywood's Pact With Hitler". "Thomas Doherty's 'Hollywood and Hitler' and Ben Urwand's 'The Collaboration' cover much the same ground while emphasising different aspects of the Hollywood-Hitler connection. Doherty sees the moguls who founded and ran most of the large movie studios as only one part of Hollywood and is sensitive to the pressures both on and within the industry. . . He concludes, with some generosity, that when it came to dealing with the Nazis, Hollywood was 'no worse than the rest of American culture in its failure of nerve and imagination, and often a good deal better in the exercise of both'. Urwand has dug deep in the German archives and found evidence that the Nazis' business dealings with some of the studios were much closer than previously realised.. . . Urwand . . . is far less interested than Doherty in the American cultural climate of the 1930s and far more accusatory."

REVIEW: *N Y Times Book Rev* p8 My 27 2013 DAVE KEHR

REVIEW: *New Yorker* v89 no28 p1 S 16 2013 David Denby

"The Collaboration: Hollywood's Pact With Hitler," and "Hollywood and Hitler 1933-1939." "[Thomas] Doherty's book is much the better of the two. A witty writer familiar with Hollywood history and manners, Doherty places the studios' craven behavior within a general account of the political culture of the movies in the thirties and forties. He finds both greed and fear in studio practice, but in a recent Times report on the controversy he strongly objects to [Ben] Urwand's use of the word 'collaboration.' Urwand, an Australian, and the grandson of Hungarian Jews who spent the war years in hiding, flings many accusations. He speaks of [Adolf] Hitler's victory 'on the other side of the globe,' by which he means Hollywood, and he claims to see 'the great mark that Hitler left on American culture.' Throughout the book, he gives the impression that the studios were merely doing the Nazis' bidding."

REVIEW: *Sight Sound* v23 no8 p105 Ag 2013 Philip French

REVIEW: *TLS* no5769 p24 O 25 2013 NOAH ISENBERG

"Hollywood and Hitler, 1933-1939." "As Thomas Doherty demonstrates in his meticulously researched and captivating new book . . . the battle over images began well before the outbreak of war. . . . Over the course of thirteen crisp, eloquently argued chapters, Doherty chronicles the tug of war--or, really, the delicate tango steps of accommodation and opposition--between the Germans and their American counterparts. . . . Among the greatest strengths of Thomas Doherty's wide-ranging book is the lack of sanctimonious finger-pointing that occasionally skews scholarship on the period."

DOING TIME FOR PEACE; resistance, family, and community; xviii, 387 p. 2013 Vanderbilt University Press

1. HISTORY—United States—General 2. POLITICAL SCIENCE—Peace 3. Pacifism—United States—Case studies 4. Pacifists—United States—Case studies 5. Passive resistance—United States—Case studies 6. Political prisoners—United States—Case studies 7. RELIGION—Religion, Politics & State 8. Religious literature

ISBN 0826518729 (paperback); 9780826518712 (hardcover); 9780826518729 (paperback)

LC 2012-029830

SUMMARY: For this book, Rosalie G. Riegle "interviewed 193 persons who risked imprisonment for resisting war; the book contains highly edited selections from 88 of those interviews. . . . Religious faith was the source of most of [the subjects'] resistance; Catholics were the majority. Most worked within activist networks; many lived in intentional communities with other war resisters. Riegle particularly focuses on the Plowshares Movement and Catholic Worker communities." (Choice)

REVIEW: *America* v210 no2 p25-6 Ja 20 2014 ANNA J. BROWN

"Crossing the Line: Nonviolent Resister Speak Out for Peace" and "Doing Time for Peace: Resistance, Family, and Community". "[A] rather stunning collection of resistance stories. . . . [Rosalie G.] Riegle, the steward of such noble stories, has done a work of great service. . . . The text [of 'Crossing the Line'] is both challenging and inviting. . . In 'Doing Time for Peace: Resistance, Family, and Community,' the reader has a chance, in its seven chapters, to become immersed in the stories and lives of peacemakers and of their families and communities. To have this opportunity is a delight and a gift."

REVIEW: *Choice* v50 no10 p1906 Je 2013 S. S. Arpad

DOLAN, ELYS.il. Weasels. See Dolan, E.

DOLAN, ELYS. Weasels; [by] Elys Dolan 32 p. 2014 Candlewick Press

1. Children's stories 2. Conspiracies—Fiction 3. Humorous stories 4. Machinery 5. Weasels

ISBN 0763671002; 9780763671006

LC 2013-943084

SUMMARY: In this children's picture book, by Elys Dolan, "ultracaffeinated weasels plotting world domination face a setback when their room-sized, Rube Goldberg-ian machine breaks down. They scurry to troubleshoot, many of them inappropriately insistent on deploying tools like a blow torch, saws and a large electric drill. Luckily, the Health and Safety officer prevails, and the gang repairs to the laboratory to tinker." (Kirkus Reviews)

REVIEW: *Booklist* v110 no12 p84 F 15 2014 Sarah Hunter

REVIEW: *Bull Cent Child Books* v67 no6 p301-2 F 2014 Deborah Stevenson Elys Dolan

"Weasels." "Droll. . . . The complex weasel domain resembles some of Arthur Geisert's elaborate piggy realms and technologies, while the goofy humor and text-spattered art hits some of the same notes as Mélanie Watts' 'Scaredy Squirrel'. . . . Compositions are cleverly rhythmic: an initial sequence of thumbnails builds up the pace to the packed scenes, and the blackout spread effectively counterpoints the frenetics of the surrounding visuals. . . . The result is an appealing combination of sophisticated yet goofy humor and undemanding text that will draw many youngsters, and the book's appeal to a wide age range makes it an excellent choice for older and younger kids to share and snort over together."

REVIEW: *Kirkus Rev* v82 no1 p118 Ja 1 2014

"Weasels". "Observant kids will discern that [Elys] Dolan cleverly employs a blue-eyed white weasel as both the cause and the solver of the machine's malfunction. Their parents will chuckle over the Blofeld-like weasel stroking a white mouse. The final twist bucks the banal, customary 'Good triumphs over evil' message in favor of something more akin to 'Try, try again.' Darned if those weaselly co-conspirators haven't conquered the world after all: A page turn reveals a new currency, freshly installed heads of state and a revisionist retrofit for an Egyptian sphinx. Amid sight gags, crossed wires and way too many espresso drinks, these weasels rule!"

REVIEW: *Publ Wkly* v260 no49 p82 D 2 2013

REVIEW: *SLJ* v60 no2 p70 F 2014 Susan Weitz

DOLAN, FRANCES E. True relations; reading, literature, and evidence in seventeenth-century England; [by] Frances E. Dolan vi, 331 p. 2013 University of Pennsylvania Press

1. History—Methodology 2. Literature—History & criticism 3. Reading—Social aspects 4. Truth—Social aspects

ISBN 9780812244854 (hardcover : alk. paper)

LC 2012-031342

SUMMARY: "What we take as evidence, Frances E. Dolan

argues, often raises more questions than it answers. Although historians have tracked dramatic changes in evidentiary standards and practices in the period, these changes did not solve the problem of how to interpret true relations or ease the reliance on them. . . . Dolan connects early modern debates about textual evidence to recent discussions of the value of seventeenth-century texts as historical evidence." (Publisher's note)

REVIEW: *Choice* v50 no12 p2228 Ag 2013 J. R. Griffin

REVIEW: *TLS* no5784 p27 F 7 2014 JAMES SHARPE

"True Relations: Reading, Literature, and Evidence in Seventeenth Century England." "This imaginative and innovative book raises a number of questions about how to approach various categories of early modern texts. Frances E. Dolan claims that 'literature' (on which literary scholars base their endeavours) and 'evidence' (which most historians would see as crucial to their project) are treated as rivals. . . . Dolan approaches these materials with a sharp critical eye and a sound grasp of theoretical positions. There are, however, some technical difficulties. . . . These reservations do not detract from the overall importance of the book. . . . Her insights amount to a major contribution to early modern studies and deserve widespread consideration."

DOLLENMAYER, DAVID.tr. The Catholic Rubens. See Sauerländer, W.

DOLLENMAYER, DAVID.tr. The madonna on the moon. See Bauerdick, R.

DOLLENMAYER, DAVID.tr. Survival of the nicest. See Klein, S.

DOLLER, TRISH. Where the stars still shine; [by] Trish Doller 352 p. 2013 Bloomsbury

1. Family life—Florida—Fiction 2. Identity—Fiction 3. JUVENILE FICTION—Family—Stepfamilies 4. JUVENILE FICTION—General 5. JUVENILE FICTION—Love & Romance 6. JUVENILE FICTION—Social Issues—Dating & Sex 7. JUVENILE FICTION—Social Issues—Physical & Emotional Abuse (see also Social Issues—Sexual Abuse) 8. Parent and child—Fiction 9. Parental kidnapping—Fiction 10. Young adult fiction

ISBN 161963144X; 9781619631441 (hardback)

LC 2013-009609

SUMMARY: In this young adult novel by Trish Doller, "when Callie's mom is finally arrested for kidnapping her, and Callie's real dad whisks her back to what would have been her life, in a small town in Florida, Callie must find a way to leave the past behind. She must learn to be part of a family. And she must believe that love--even with someone who seems an improbable choice--is more than just a possibility." (Publisher's note)

REVIEW: *Booklist* v110 no6 p48 N 15 2013 Kara Dean

REVIEW: *Bull Cent Child Books* v67 no3 p148-9 N 2013 E. B.

"Where the Stars Still Shine." "One moment Callie and her mom are pulled over by the police for a burned-out taillight, and the next moment Mom is in handcuffs. It's not really a surprise, since Mom absconded with her daughter over a decade ago when she feared her marital breakup would result in loss of custody. . . . Readers will be so involved in cheering Callie on toward the open arms of her recovered family that only after they've mopped away the final happy tears will they realize how carefully--dare we say manipulatively--[author Trish] Doller has orchestrated the drama."

REVIEW: *Kirkus Rev* v81 no15 p92 Ag 1 2013

REVIEW: *Publ Wkly* v260 no31 p75 Ag 5 2013

REVIEW: *SLJ* v59 no9 p155 S 2013 Lalitha Nataraj

REVIEW: *Voice of Youth Advocates* v36 no4 p60 O 2013 Sara Martin

REVIEW: *Voice of Youth Advocates* v36 no4 p61 O 2013 Raluca Topliceanu

DOLNICK, BEN. At the bottom of everything; a novel; [by] Ben Dolnick 256 p. 2013 Pantheon Books

1. Americans—India—Fiction 2. Boys—Fiction 3. Forgiveness—Fiction 4. Male friendship—Fiction 5. Psychological fiction

ISBN 0307907988; 9780307907981

LC 2012-042259

SUMMARY: This book, by Ben Dolnick, is about "two friends, torn apart by a terrible secret, and the dark adventure that neither of them could have ever conceived. It's been ten years since the 'incident,' and Adam has long since decided he's better off without his former best friend, Thomas. . . . When he receives an email from Thomas's mother begging for his help, he finds himself drawn back into his old friend's world, and into the past he's tried so desperately to forget." (Publisher's note)

REVIEW: *Booklist* v109 no22 p26 Ag 1 2013 Jonathan Fullmer

REVIEW: *Kirkus Rev* v81 no15 p287 Ag 1 2013

REVIEW: *N Y Times Book Rev* p15 S 22 2013 ADELLE WALDMAN

"At the Bottom of Everything." "Ben Dolnick's . . . third [book] . . . is far more sophisticated. Dolnick has retained his strength--his sensitive gauge for emotional states and his empathy--but his writing is more taut, more piquant, not only observant but wry in its depiction of human fallibility. The result is a lively, often funny book about being young and smart and confused, fumbling through life in a middle-class American sort of way. There is tragedy here, too, but it is dressed in such ordinary clothes that it feels less like tragedy as we are used to it in art and more like the heartbreak we know from experience."

REVIEW: *Publ Wkly* v260 no30 p41 Jl 29 2013

DOLPHIN, RAY. Wall; Israeli & Palestinian landscape 2008-2012; [by] Ray Dolphin 128 p. 2013 Aperture Foundation

1. Arab-Israeli conflict 2. Documentary photography 3. Israel—Boundaries 4. Photobooks 5. Walls—Israel

ISBN 9781597112413 (hardcover : alk. paper)

LC 2013-930145

SUMMARY: This book "comprises panoramic landscape photographs made from 2008-2012 in East Jerusalem, Hebron, Ramallah, Bethlehem and in various Israeli settlements along the route of the barrier separating Israel and Palestine. Whereas Israel calls it the 'security fence,' Palestinians call it the 'apartheid wall,' and groups like Human

Rights Watch use the term 'separation barrier,' Koudelka's project is metaphorical in nature--focused on the wall as a human fissure in the natural landscape." (Publisher's note)

REVIEW: *Bookforum* v20 no4 p20-1 D 2013/Ja 2014 CHRISTOPHER LYON

"Kara Walker: Dust Jackets for the N##gerati," "Great War: July 1, 1916: The First Day of the Battle of the Somme," and "Wall: Israeli & Palestinian Landscape 20008-2012." "The artist, assisted by the design firm CoMa, has cleverly folded the dust jacket into a large artwork that includes her entire foreword and a full-scale detail of a large text piece. The fine reproductions include these boldly graphic works as well as her powerfully kinetic figurative drawings. . . . Sacco conveys an eloquent, convincing, entirely wordless story. . . . [There is an] accompanying booklet with an affecting, brief account . . . by Adam Hochschild. . . . Josef Koudelka's book of purposely ugly photos--from which we cannot turn away."

REVIEW: *N Y Times Book Rev* p38-9 D 8 2013 LUC SANTE

"Wall," "Top Secret: Images From the Stasi Archives," and "George Hurrell's Hollywood: Glamour Portraits 1925-1992." "An appreciation of stony texture . . . marks 'Wall' . . . , by the veteran Czech photographer Josef Koudelka . . . a remarkable collection of panoramic photos . . . of the barrier that has been erected over the past decade in defiance of the internationally recognized border. . . . Simon Menner's 'Top Secret: Images From the Stasi Archives' . . . might be a primer on the banality of evil. . . . 'George Hurrell's Hollywood: Glamour Portraits 1925-1992' by Mark A. Vieira . . . presents rapture upon rapture."

DOMHOFF, G. WILLIAM. The new CEOs; women, African American, Latino and Asian American leaders of Fortune 500 companies; [by] G. William Domhoff 216 2010 Rowman & Littlefield Publishers

1. Elite (Social sciences)—United States 2. Fortune 500 companies 3. Minority chief executive officers 4. Sociology literature 5. Women chief executive officers
ISBN 9781442207653
LC 2011-002320

SUMMARY: Written by Richard L. Zweigenhaft and G. William Domhoff, this book "looks at the women and people of color leading Fortune 500 companies, exploring the factors that have helped them achieve success and their impact on the business world and society more broadly. . . . Now there have been more than 100 women, African American, Latino, and Asian-American CEOs of Fortune 500 companies." (Publisher's note)

REVIEW: *Am J Sociol* v117 no5 p1540-2 Mr 2012 Elizabeth Higginbotham

REVIEW: *Contemp Sociol* v42 no6 p881-3 N 2013 RAKESH KHURANA

"The New CEOs: Women, African American, Latino, and Asian American Leaders of Fortune 500 Companies." "[Authors Richard L.] Zweigenhaft and [G. William] Domhoff have done a meticulous job working with a small data set, comparing the career paths of this group with a larger sample of business leaders, generating hypotheses based on a careful analysis of field and archival data, and constructing a novel sociological model of careers for members of these groups. The book builds on the authors' earlier works on diversify among elites and the combined results are fascinating, the sociological processes even more so."

DOMINGUEZ, ANGELA. Maria had a little llama/ María tenía una llamita; 28 p. 2013 Henry Holt and Company

1. Bilingual books 2. Llamas 3. Llamas as pets—Fiction 4. Spanish language materials—Bilingual 5. Stories in rhyme
ISBN 9780805093339 (hardcover)
LC 2012-013530

SUMMARY: This book, by Angela Dominguez, is a "bilingual presentation of a classic children's rhyme, set in rural Peru. Dominguez presents a straightforward version of the familiar rhyme, adding just enough new elements to transform it into a story. The text flows rhythmically in both the English and the Spanish, which are placed together on the page with the English in bold and positioned above the Spanish." (Kirkus Reviews)

REVIEW: *Bull Cent Child Books* v67 no2 p83-4 O 2013 T. A.

"Maria Had a Little Llama/María tenía una llama pequeña." "The ever-popular Mary and her little lamb have been transplanted to Peru, becoming Maria and her mischievous llama in this bilingual adaptation. [Author and illustrator Angela] Dominguez maintains the nursery rhyme fairly intact in the English text, which is set in slightly bolder type than its Spanish counterpart, altering only the girl and her pet's names and changing just a few verbs. She also opts for a direct translation, so the Spanish text doesn't scan but definitely aids language learning in either direction. The gouache and ink illustrations add interest to an old standby by providing an authentic Andean mise-en-scène, complete with panflutes and village markets."

REVIEW: *Horn Book Magazine* v89 no6 p75-6 N/D 2013 JIM ST. CLAIR

"Maria Had a Little Llama/María Tenía una Llamita". "The bold ink and gouache illustrations include plentiful cultural cues: the market, the village, the traditional headwear, and the musical instruments all help to place readers in the setting. The text mirrors the traditional tale . . . and the limited amount of text allows both languages to appear on the same page or spread. Maria and her llama, though, are the stars of this book. Their personalities and their affection for each other shine through."

DOMINGUEZ, ANGELA.il. Santiago stays. See Dominguez, A.

DOMINGUEZ, ANGELA. Santiago stays; [by] Angela Dominguez 32 p. 2013 Abrams Books

1. Brothers & sisters—Juvenile fiction 2. Children's stories 3. Dogs—Fiction 4. Infants—Juvenile fiction 5. Pets—Juvenile literature
ISBN 141970821X; 9781419708213
LC 2012-041376

SUMMARY: In this children's book, written and illustrated by Angela Dominguez, "Santiago [the French bulldog] stays . . . , despite the growing disappointment of the little boy who is trying to engage him. After several futile attempts, the boy's frustration bubbles over into a yell, which wakes the baby, and the reader realizes whom Santiago has been resolutely guarding all along." (Publisher's note)

REVIEW: *Booklist* v110 no1 p126 S 1 2013 Ilene Cooper

REVIEW: *Horn Book Magazine* v90 no1 p70 Ja/F 2014 MARTHA V. PARRAVANO

"Santiago Stays." "Simple and satisfying, with a brief text

in a large font, this works well as a read-to for preschoolers and read-alone or very new readers (with, perhaps, a little initial help) A young boy wants to take his little French bulldog Santiago for a walk, but, confoundingly, Santiago refuses all enticements. . . . The reason for Santiago's stubbornness is revealed: he is watching over the baby. . . . The illustrations, in pencil, marker, ink, tissue paper, and digital color, capture the boy's persistence and the bulldog's dug-in resistance; the warm palette is perfect for this affection-filled family story."

REVIEW: *Kirkus Rev* v81 no16 p158 Ag 15 2013

REVIEW: *Publ Wkly* v260 no30 p66 Jl 29 2013

REVIEW: *SLJ* v59 no10 p1 O 2013 Martha Link Yesowitch

DOMINGUEZ, OLIVER.il. Electrical wizard. See Electrical wizard

DOMÍNGUEZ RUBIO, FERNANDO.ed. The politics of knowledge. See The politics of knowledge

DONALDSON, IAN.ed. The Cambridge edition of the works of Ben Jonson. See The Cambridge edition of the works of Ben Jonson

DONALDSON, JULIA, 1948-. Superworm; [by] Julia Donaldson 32 p. 2014 Arthur A. Levine Books

1. Heroes—Fiction 2. Insects—Fiction 3. Lizards—Fiction 4. Stories in rhyme 5. Wizards—Fiction 6. Worms—Fiction

ISBN 0545591767; 9780545591768 (hardcover: alk. paper)

LC 2013-001546

SUMMARY: This book, by Julia Donaldson, features a worm superhero who "rescues toads and beetles from peril and young bees from boredom. The insects clap and cheer for their very own invertebrate champion, inciting the ire of the Wizard Lizard and his henchman crow, who kidnap Superworm for their own sinister devices. The toads, slugs, earwigs, and other bugs band together to rescue the hero." (School Library Journal)

REVIEW: *Booklist* v110 no11 p71 F 1 2014 Maryann Owen

REVIEW: *Bull Cent Child Books* v67 no7 p354 Mr 2014 T. A.

"Superworm". "Though the text is a bit lengthy, the strong iambic tetrameter makes for a bouncy, rhythmic readaloud, and with a bit of preparation, kids can join in the repeated chant for Superworm. . . . The breezy illustrations, with their detailed pen work, have a pleasing balance of full-bleed pages and vignettes against white pages. The googly-eyed bugs are friendly and inviting, and the sinister, dark hues of Wizard Lizard and his crow contrast nicely with the full rainbow used for Superworm and his friends. A goofy addition to friendship-tale picture books, this wriggly tribute to dirt-crawling friends might also work as a unique addition classroom study of poetry."

REVIEW: *Horn Book Magazine* v90 no2 p100-1 Mr/Ap 2014 SUSAN DOVE LEMPKE

"Superworm". "Although Superworm's friends may be small, they successfully conspire to rescue their pal using their own honey-making and web-building skills plus a little ingenuity. It's some old-fashioned storytelling, with snappy rhyming couplets and a bad guy with threatening henchman, but [Julia] Donaldson spruces things up with the particulars of a heroic worm whose band of friends includes an earwig, a slug, and beetles. [Axel] Scheffler's pictures pop with strong lines and vibrant colors as well as sly small details to catch on subsequent readings."

REVIEW: *Kirkus Rev* v81 no21 p248 N 1 2013

REVIEW: *N Y Times Book Rev* p21 My 11 2014 SARAH HARRISON SMITH

REVIEW: *Publ Wkly* v260 no48 p53-6 N 25 2013

REVIEW: *SLJ* v60 no2 p70 F 2014 Martha Link Yesowitch

DONOGHUE, EMMA. Frog music; a novel; [by] Emma Donoghue 405 p. 2014 Little, Brown and Co.

1. American historical fiction 2. Murder—Investigation—Fiction 3. Transvestites 4. Women dancers—Fiction

ISBN 9780316404587 (large print); 9780316371452 (international); 9780316324687 (hardback)

LC 2014-000840

SUMMARY: This novel, by Emma Donoghue, is set in "Summer of 1876: San Francisco is in the fierce grip of a record-breaking heat wave and a smallpox epidemic. Through the window of a railroad saloon, a young woman named Jenny Bonnet is shot dead.The survivor, her friend Blanche Beunon, is a French burlesque dancer. Over the next three days, she will risk everything to bring Jenny's murderer to justice—if he doesn't track her down first." (Publisher's note)

REVIEW: *Booklist* v110 no16 p29 Ap 15 2014 Brad Hooper

REVIEW: *Booklist* v110 no11 p29 F 1 2014 Sarah Johnson

REVIEW: *Kirkus Rev* v81 no24 p233 D 15 2013

REVIEW: *Libr J* v139 no3 p24 F 15 2014 Mahnaz Dar Bette-Lee Fox Liz French Margaret Heilbrun Stephanie Klose Annalisa Pesek Henrietta Thornton-Verma Wilda Williams

REVIEW: *Libr J* v138 no18 p66 N 1 2013 Barbara Hoffert

REVIEW: *Libr J* v139 no11 p52 Je 15 2014 Wendy Galgan

REVIEW: *N Y Rev Books* v61 no9 p39-40 My 22 2014 Francine Prose

REVIEW: *N Y Times Book Rev* p14 My 4 2014 PATRICK MCGRATH

REVIEW: *New York Times* v163 no56465 pC1-6 Ap 8 2014 JANET MASLIN

REVIEW: *New Yorker* v90 no13 p91-1 My 19 2014

"Frog Music." "This murder mystery, based on a true story, is set in San Francisco in the summer of 1876, as smallpox and a heat wave plague the city. Jenny Bonnet, a puckish cross-dresser and frog-catcher, is shot dead through a window while getting ready for bed. Her closest friend, a French burlesque dancer named Blanche Beunon, believes that she was the intended target. . . . Blanche's thoughts sometimes come across as stilted, but the setting she inhabits is alive, brimming with sin and with music."

REVIEW: *Publ Wkly* v260 no51 p36 D 16 2013

REVIEW: *Quill Quire* v80 no3 p31 Ap 2014 JAMES GRAINGER

DONOHUE, NANETTE. Women's fiction. See Vnuk, R.

DONOVAN, GAIL, 1962-. The waffler; [by] Gail Donovan 224 p. 2013 Dial Books for Young Readers

1. Decision making in children 2. Problem children—Behavior modification 3. School principals 4. School stories 5. Teacher-student relationships—Fiction
ISBN 0803739206; 9780803739208 (hardcover)
LC 2012-031856

SUMMARY: In this book, making "up his mind has always been hard for Monty to do, but when the principal tags him with the label 'waffler,' it becomes a nickname the fourth grader desperately wants to lose. He knows that objecting to the hated nickname will make it stick, and he fears that if his mother calls the teacher about the Band-Aid 'decision-aids' he has to wear, the teacher will be angry." He also has to deal with kindergarten Reading Buddies and his divorced parents. (Kirkus Reviews)

REVIEW: *Bull Cent Child Books* v67 no2 p84 O 2013 H. M.

"The Waffler." "Fourth-grader Monty is a 'mind-changer' when everyone wants him to be a 'mindmaker-upper.' His inability to make quick choices on other people's timelines draws the unfortunate attention of the school principal, who dubs him a waffler and places Monty on a probationary system to help him be more decisive. . . . The everyday-life plots, following Monty's relationship with his family and his accidental adoption of not one but four kindergarten buddies, are comedic and enjoyable. Less effective, though, is the treatment of Monty's indecisiveness. . . . Characterization is strong, though, with Monty a wholly likable protagonist dealing with a frustrating trait."

REVIEW: *Horn Book Magazine* v89 no5 p91-2 S/O 2013 ROBIN L. SMITH

"The Waffler." "Fourth grader Monty (short for Montana) seems to be the only one in his family who's paralyzed by indecision. . . . Though the story takes a while to get going, Monty's good spirits come through in the third-person narrative. Thankfully, his parents come through, too, after finally realizing that Monty's 'waffling' can be a good thing. It's nice to see a blended family realistically portrayed as busy but loving and to see Monty stand up for himself in the end. A solidly realistic school and family story for fans of Louis Sachar and Claudia Mills."

REVIEW: *Kirkus Rev* v81 no12 p86 Je 15 2013

REVIEW: *SLJ* v59 no10 p1 O 2013 Kathy Cherniavsky

DONOVAN, SANDY. Does my voice count?; a book about citizenship; [by] Sandy Donovan 32 p. 2014 Lerner Publications Company

1. Children's nonfiction 2. Citizenship—Juvenile literature 3. Ethics 4. Moral education—Juvenile literature 5. Voting
ISBN 9781467713665 (lib. bdg. : alk. paper)
LC 2013-019161

SUMMARY: This book by Sandy Donovan is part of the Show Your Character series, which "emphasizes development traits such as responsibility, respect, honesty, and empathy and strives to help kids learn how to be good citizens and improve both their own lives and the lives of those around them." (School Library Journal) It "tackles citizenship: why it's important to vote, ways to be a good citizen, and returning found valuables." (Booklist)

REVIEW: *Booklist* v110 no8 p39 D 15 2013 Ilene Cooper

"Can People Count on Me? A Book About Responsibility," "Does My Voice Count? A Book About Citizenship," and "How Can I Deal With Bullying? A Book Book About Respect." "Even young children can learn to be helpful, responsible citizens, and the Show Your Character series gives them a way to begin. . . . Sometimes the issues in the books overlap, but this series is a good placc for children to start thinking about ways to make their world a better place. The suggestions are age appropriate, and kids are urged to talk to parents or an adult when things get to be more than they can handle (though parental discussion should be even more emphasized than it is). The book tries not to have the answers seem pat, and happily, sometimes scenarios are taken a step further."

REVIEW: *SLJ* v60 no4 p101 Ap 2014 Rita Meade

DONOVAN, SANDY. How can I deal with bullying?; a book about respect; [by] Sandy Donovan 32 p. 2014 Lerner Publications Company

1. Aggressiveness in children—Juvenile literature 2. Bullying—Juvenile literature 3. Children's nonfiction 4. Ethics 5. Respect
ISBN 9781467713627 (lib. bdg. : alk. paper)
LC 2013-010879

SUMMARY: This book by Sandy Donovan is part of the Show Your Character series, which "emphasizes development traits such as responsibility, respect, honesty, and empathy and strives to help kids learn how to be good citizens and improve both their own lives and the lives of those around them." (School Library Journal) It "offers the tried-and-true methods of standing up for yourself and others and acknowledges how hard this can be." (Booklist)

REVIEW: *Booklist* v110 no8 p39 D 15 2013 Ilene Cooper

"Can People Count on Me? A Book About Responsibility," "Does My Voice Count? A Book About Citizenship," and "How Can I Deal With Bullying? A Book Book About Respect." "Even young children can learn to be helpful, responsible citizens, and the Show Your Character series gives them a way to begin. . . . Sometimes the issues in the books overlap, but this series is a good place for children to start thinking about ways to make their world a better place. The suggestions are age appropriate, and kids are urged to talk to parents or an adult when things get to be more than they can handle (though parental discussion should be even more emphasized than it is). The book tries not to have the answers seem pat, and happily, sometimes scenarios are taken a step further."

REVIEW: *SLJ* v60 no4 p101 Ap 2014 Rita Meade

DOOLEY, ALLAN C.ed. The complete works of Robert Browning. See Browning, R.

DORAN, MICHAEL S. The Arab awakening. See Pollack, K. M.

DORFMAN, ELENA.il. Elena Dorfman; Empire Falling; 96 p. 2013 Damiani/Crump

1. Art literature 2. Artistic photography 3. Photobooks 4. Quarries & quarrying 5. Rocks in art
ISBN 8862082665; 9788862082662

SUMMARY: This book of photography by Elena Dorfman "presents American rock quarries as geologic phenomena, both conceptually and representationally. In Dorfman's epic tableaux, the ancient sedimentation and erosion found at these sites form the basis for her complex and highly layered compositions." (Publisher's note)

REVIEW: *New York Times* v162 no56237 pC24 Ag 23 2013 Dana Jennings

"Revolution," "Elena Dorfman: Empire Falling," and "After Hiroshima." "These nocturnal seascapes--photographs of the Arctic Ocean, Red Sea, North Pacific and elsewhere--are flensed to stark essences: an infinite palette of blacks and grays garnished by sprigs of light. Spectral, the images could be from the beginning of time--or its end. This is not our world, but Mr. [Hiroshi] Sugimoto's. . . . The quarries of the photographer Elena Dorfman . . . are haunting postindustrial abstractions. . . . This is a book of the earth's guts ripped open, exposing layer upon layer of antediluvian time and tide. . . . 'After Hiroshima' is a kind of archaeology of memory. . . . Ms. [Elin O'Hara] Slavick's work reminds us that radiation has a long half-life--but so, too, does memory."

D'ORMESSON, JEAN. The Conversation; the Night Napoleon Changed the World; 108 p. 2013 Arcade Publishing

1. Kings & rulers—Drama 2. One-act plays, French
ISBN 9781611459050 (alk. paper)
LC 2013-035218

SUMMARY: This book by Jean d'Ormesson presents "a conversation between Napoleon and a trusted political ally. On a winter evening in 1804, Napoleon seeks the advice of Second Consul Jean-Jacques Cambacérès at the general's Tuileries residence in Paris. The two men ponder the fate of the fledgling French republic, sapped by years of bloody revolution and foreign wars. D'Ormesson formats his story as a one-act play." (Kirkus Reviews)

REVIEW: *Kirkus Rev* v82 no2 p6 Ja 15 2014

"The Conversation: The Night Napoleon Changed the World". "A lauded titan of French letters plumbs the intersection between character and despotism in a slender, tendentious imagining of a conversation between Napoleon and a trusted political ally. . . . While [Timothy] Bent's translation is fluent, there's a larger problem: [Jean] d'Ormesson resists other options to Napoleon's Great Man of History theory. 'Successful men of letters think themselves the center of the world,' Napoleon audaciously claims; and it's easy to believe that d'Ormesson, too, espouses this view. A snobbish, claustrophobic work."

DORRA, MARY TONETTI. Demeter's Choice; A Portrait of My Grandmother as a Young Artist; [by] Mary Tonetti Dorra 288 p. 2013 CreateSpace Independent Publishing Platform

1. Americans—Europe—Fiction 2. Historical fiction 3. Sculptors—Fiction 4. Women artists—Fiction 5. World's Columbian Exposition (1893: Chicago, Ill.)
ISBN 1492731838; 9781492731832

SUMMARY: This book by Mary Tonetti Dorra presents the fictionalized "story of her grandmother Mary Lawrence. The tale opens in 1893 as Lawrence's statue of Christopher Columbus goes on display at the Columbian Exposition at the World's Fair in Chicago. . . . The book also traces her travels through Europe in the late 1800s, presenting them through the eyes of a well-bred young woman with artistic ambitions." (Kirkus Reviews)

REVIEW: *Kirkus Rev* v82 no4 p237 F 15 2014

"Demeter's Choice: A Portrait of My Grandmother". "An aspiring female sculptor pursues art lessons at home and abroad, carves a place in history and finds love along the way in this well-written historical novel. . . . Dorra does a terrific job of providing a sense of place as Lawrence explores each new city. We can taste the fresh baguettes in Paris and see the picturesque canals in Venice. The book needs tighter editing to catch punctuation errors and typos, and occasionally, the dialogue sounds cheesy. . . . An elegant tale of a female trailblazer whose remarkable story deserves a wide audience."

REVIEW: *Kirkus Rev* v82 no3 p404 F 1 2014

DORST, DOUG. S.; [by] Doug Dorst 456 p. 2013 Mulholland Books / Little, Brown and Co.

1. Abrams, Jeffrey, 1966- 2. Books & reading—Fiction 3. Detective & mystery stories 4. Epistolary fiction 5. Love stories 6. Sea stories
ISBN 9780316201643 (hardcover)
LC 2013-942888

SUMMARY: "A young woman picks up a book left behind by a stranger. Inside it are his margin notes, which reveal a reader entranced by the story and by its mysterious author. . . . 'S.,' conceived by filmmaker J. J. Abrams and written by award-winning novelist Doug Dorst, is the chronicle of two readers finding each other in the margins of a book and enmeshing themselves in a deadly struggle . . . , and it is also Abrams and Dorst's love letter to the written word." (Publisher's note)

REVIEW: *Kirkus Rev* v82 no1 p361 Ja 1 2014

REVIEW: *New Yorker* v89 no41 p87-1 D 16 2013

"S." "This elaborately designed work, a collaboration between a television producer and a novelist, is arresting as an object but frustrating to read. . . . The effect is lovingly achieved by means of various inserts (postcards, newspaper clippings, maps) and dense, handwritten marginalia. . . . An epistolary romance between them unfolds across their notes as they try to unravel the novel's codes and historical secrets. Sadly, the text they are annotating is a dull Conrad pastiche, designed to provide occasions for commentary."

REVIEW: *TLS* no5775 p21 D 6 2013 STUART KELLY

"S." "Conceived by the film producer and director J. J. Abrams and written by Doug Dorst, this is certainly one of the most intriguing textual artefacts (let alone novels) that I have seen since Mark Z. Danielewski's 'House of Leaves'. . . and 'Only Revolutions,' or Steven Hall's 'The Raw Shark Texts.' . . . Is this a revolutionary enterprise, or a postmodern labyrinth? The creators of the book cleverly refuse to come down on either side of the literary avant-garde's divergent trajectories, instead squeezing the reader into an uncomfortable impasse. . . . The book is, as one would expect from an Abrams project, a puzzle box, a set of deliberate enigmas, part Fabergé egg, part Rorschach blot. It is also a clever exploration of the nature of reading."

DORYUN CHONG.ed. From postwar to postmodern. See From postwar to postmodern

DOUGLAS, HELEN. After Eden; [by] Helen Douglas 288

p. 2013 Bloomsbury
1. Best friends—Fiction 2. Friendship—Fiction 3. JUVENILE FICTION—Fantasy & Magic 4. JUVENILE FICTION—Love & Romance 5. JUVENILE FICTION—Social Issues—Friendship 6. Love—Fiction 7. Science fiction 8. Time travel—Fiction
ISBN 9781619631304 (hardback)
LC 2013-011982

SUMMARY: In this book, teen time traveler Ryan reveals that "Eden's best friend Connor will discover a new planet--one where human life is possible. The discovery will make him famous. It will also ruin the world as we know it. When Ryan asks Eden for help, she must choose between saving the world and saving her best friend's greatest achievement. And a crush on Ryan complicates things more than she could have imagined." (Publisher's note)

REVIEW: *Bull Cent Child Books* v67 no5 p264 Ja 2014 A. M.

"After Eden." "What's on offer here is essentially a science fiction version of paranormal romance, as the story focuses on the burgeoning relationship between Eden and Ryan more than the underlying concept. Fans of the genre will recognize its conventions, including a super-average heroine, an extraordinary hero, a love triangle, and otherworldly obstacles for the couple to overcome, and they will likely delight in the time-travel take on a narrative they love. Those willing to suspend disbelief and scientific skepticism for the joy of the ride will find themselves swept up in Eden's adventure and excited for expected sequels."

REVIEW: *Kirkus Rev* v81 no19 p114 O 1 2013

REVIEW: *Voice of Youth Advocates* v36 no5 p73 D 2013 Ed Goldberg

REVIEW: *Voice of Youth Advocates* v36 no5 p73 D 2013 Will Sanchez

DOUZINAS, COSTAS.ed. The Cambridge companion to human rights law. See The Cambridge companion to human rights law

DOUZINAS, COSTAS. Philosophy and resistance in the crisis; Greece and the future of Europe; [by] Costas Douzinas v, 234 p. 2013 Polity
1. Democracy—Greece 2. Neoliberalism 3. Political science—Philosophy 4. Political science literature 5. Protest movements—Greece
ISBN 0745665438 (hardback); 0745665446 (paperback); 9780745665436 (hardback); 9780745665443 (paperback)
LC 2012-277439

SUMMARY: "This book is about the global crisis and the right to resistance, about neoliberal biopolitics and direct democracy, about the responsibility of intellectuals and the poetry of the multitude. Using Greece as an example, [Costas] Douzinas argues that the persistent sequence of protests, uprisings and revolutions has radically changed the political landscape." (Publisher's note)

REVIEW: *Choice* v51 no5 p915 Ja 2014 C. P. Waligorski

"Philosophy and Resistance in the Crisis: Greece and the Future of Europe." "In a partly successful antidote to conventional images of Greece and the widespread economic crises since 2007, [Costas] Douzinas . . . employs normative-historical political theory, particularly European critical theory, to understand and predict the outcome of public demonstrations and resistance in Greece's political-economic crisis, and similar resistance in other countries. Despite many virtues, there are important lacunae: adequate understanding of liberalism, deeper historical and comparative analysis of successful resistance, . . . concrete specification and instantiation of radical goals to distinguish 'Left' and 'Right' justifications of resistance, and explication of direct democracy's operation."

DOVLATOV, KATHERINE.tr. Pushkin hills. See Dovlatov, S

DOVLATOV, SERGEĬ. Pushkin hills; 160 p. 2014 Counterpoint Press
1. Alcoholics—Fiction 2. Authors—Fiction 3. FICTION—Literary 4. Soviet Union—Fiction 5. Tour guides (Persons)
ISBN 1619022451; 9781619022454 (hardback)
LC 2013-028859

SUMMARY: This novel by Sergei Dovlatov describes how "an unsuccessful writer and an inveterate alcoholic, Boris Alikhanov has recently divorced his wife Tatyana, and he is running out of money. The prospect of a summer job as a tour guide at the Pushkin Hills Preserve offers him hope of regaining some balance in life as his wife makes plans to emigrate to the West with their daughter Masha, but . . . his life continues to unravel." (Publisher's note)

REVIEW: *Kirkus Rev* v82 no4 p98 F 15 2014

"Pushkin Hills". "A lively, playful translation . . . of this brief, fabulous, partly autobiographical 1983 novel. . . . Told mainly in barbed, surprising dialogue—[Sergei] Dovlatov's trademark technical flourish was never to have two words in any sentence begin with the same letter, and the result here is a breezy, angular, associative style that seems almost Grace Paley-ish—this is an odd, dark, idiosyncratic little dazzler. A black comedy of eyes-wide-open excess. . . . And a fine rumination on being Russian, besides."

DOW, DAVID R. Things I've learned from dying; a book about life; [by] David R. Dow 288 p. 2014 Twelve
1. BIOGRAPHY & AUTOBIOGRAPHY—Personal Memoirs 2. Death row inmates 3. Fathers—Death 4. MEDICAL—Nursing—Oncology & Cancer 5. Memoirs 6. SOCIAL SCIENCE—Death & Dying
ISBN 1455575240; 9781455575244 (hardback); 9781478925309 (audio download)
LC 2013-032569

SUMMARY: In this book, when death-row journalist David "Dow's father-in-law receives his own death sentence in the form of terminal cancer, . . . the author is forced to reconcile with death . . . both as a son and as a father. Told through the disparate lenses of the legal battles he's spent a career fighting, and the intimate confrontations with death each family faces at home, [it] . . . offers a . . . lyrical account of how illness and loss can ravage a family." (Publisher's note)

REVIEW: *Christ Century* v131 no4 p51 F 19 2014

REVIEW: *Kirkus Rev* v81 no22 p157 N 15 2013

REVIEW: *N Y Times Book Rev* p21 Ja 26 2014 PAIGE WILLIAMS

"Things I've Learned From Dying: A Book About Life" and "The Death Class: A True Story About Life." "In the latest memoir by David R. Dow . . . three important figures in his life are in danger. . . . Dow tells the story of trying to save all three. Each narrative is in its own way gutting. . . . A warm and fluid writer, he is also often funny, and angry, and embraces his own imagination. . . . The extended deliberations . . . can feel a bit repetitive. . . . Erika Hayasaki . . . began following a course called Death in Perspective . . . , which was taught by Norma Bowe, a registered nurse. . . . The book's strength lies in the well-observed details of the lives portrayed, and in the recognition that the work Bowe and her students are doing is messy, necessary stuff."

REVIEW: *Publ Wkly* v260 no44 p58-9 N 4 2013

DOWDING, PHILIPPA. The Strange Gift of Gwendolyn Golden; [by] Philippa Dowding 200 p. 2014 Dundurn

1. Flight 2. Magic—Fiction 3. Missing persons—Fiction 4. Speculative fiction 5. Teenagers—Fiction
ISBN 1459707354; 9781459707351

SUMMARY: In this book, by Philippa Dowding, "thirteen-year-old Gwendolyn Golden" discovers that she "is a Night Flyer, a rare group of humans with the power of flight. . . . Gwen's ability comes with new responsibilities, but it also has a dark side, as powers often do. The euphoria of flying means that, like Icarus, there's a risk she'll fly too close to the sun, and Gwen discovers a nefarious force that has the potential to overwhelm her." (Quill & Quire)

REVIEW: *Quill Quire* v80 no1 p43 Ja/F 2014 Emily Donaldson

"The Strange Gift of Gwendolyn Golden". "This lively, fast-paced novel by Philippa Dowding . . . moves fluidly from the whimsical to the fantastical and takes an intriguing detour to some dark places in between. . . . Dowding knits together a variety of elements—puberty, hidden talent, independence, loss—with a satisfying balance between humour and seriousness. This is an accessible story that readily lends itself to both metaphorical and literal interpretations. The open ending suggests we might be hearing more from the Night Flyers, and that will be welcome news for many readers."

DOWLING, ANDREW. Catalonia since the Spanish Civil War; reconstructing the nation; [by] Andrew Dowling vii, 213 p. 2013 Sussex Academic Press

1. Historical literature 2. Nationalism—Spain—Catalonia—History—20th century 3. Spain—History—20th century
ISBN 9781845195304 (h/b : alk. paper)
LC 2012-010933

SUMMARY: This book, written by Andrew Dowling, "examines the transformation of the Catalan nation in socio-economic, political and historical terms, and offers an innovative interpretation of the determinants of its nationalist mobilisation." It "traces the Francoist repression and the nationalist response to it, demonstrating how new political actors reconfigured Catalan nationalism over the course of the Franco regime (1939-1975)." (Publisher's note)

REVIEW: *Choice* v51 no2 p341-2 O 2013 N. Greene

"Catalonia Since the Spanish Civil War: Reconstructing the Nation." "[Author Andrew] Dowling . . . offers a succinct history of the development of Catalan nationalism from the late 19th century to the present. The author embraces broad and arguable generalizations about European history, but nonetheless provides important insights about the recent history of Catalonia. . . . Perhaps most compelling in this study is Dowling's account of that nationalism since Franco's death in 1975 and how it has developed, in the author's view, into a 'serious political option' for independence in what he describes as the 'collective imagination of the Catalans.'"

DOWN, SUSAN BROPHY. Theodore Weld; architect of abolitionism; [by] Susan Brophy Down 64 p. 2013 Crabtree Publishing Company

1. Abolitionists—United States—Biography—Juvenile literature 2. Antislavery movements—United States—History—19th century—Juvenile literature 3. Historical literature 4. Social reformers—United States—Biography—Juvenile literature
ISBN 9780778710622 (reinforced library binding); 9780778710653 (pbk.)
LC 2013-004912

SUMMARY: This book on Theodore Weld, by Susan Brophy, is part of the "Voices for Freedom: Abolitionist Heroes" series. It "describes how this writer, editor, orator, and organizer, who often published under pen names (thus, becoming less recognizable today), became an architect of abolitionism. It gives considerable attention to Weld's influential compendium, 'American Slavery as It Is: Testimony of a Thousand Witnesses'." (Booklist)

REVIEW: *Booklist* v110 no1 p101-2 S 1 2013 Angela Leeper

"Abraham Lincoln: The Great Emancipator" and "Theodore Weld: Architect of Abolitionism." "Covering both well- and lesser-known abolitionists, these entries in the Voices for Freedom: Abolitionist Heroes series provide an extensive view of the nation's anti-slavery movement. While the books touch upon the subjects' childhood, education, and career successes and failures, they differ from traditional biographies as they focus on each individual's role as an abolitionist. . . . Each title concludes with the subject's legacy on race relations. Archival photos, reproductions, maps, and copious back matter add to the richness of this valuable series."

DOWNES, LARRY. Big bang disruption; strategy in the age of devastating innovation; [by] Larry Downes 259 p. 2014 Portfolio Hardcover

1. BUSINESS & ECONOMICS—General 2. BUSINESS & ECONOMICS—Management 3. BUSINESS & ECONOMICS—Strategic Planning 4. Business literature 5. New business enterprises 6. Strategic planning 7. Technological innovations
ISBN 9781591846901 (hardback)
LC 2013-039107

SUMMARY: In this book, "two leaders in the field of technological applications and business productivity present dramatic evidence for the emergence of a new model for economic innovation, which they call 'exponential technology,' and warn that 'every industry is now at risk' and must learn how to negotiate the new landscape." (Kirkus Reviews)

REVIEW: *Economist* v410 no8869 p74 Ja 11 2014

"Big Bang Disruption: Strategy in the Age of Devastating Innovation." "Larry Downes . . . and Paul Nunes . . . argue that if companies are to survive attacks by 'big-bang disrupters' they need to ditch the traditional way of thinking about new entrants. . . . The challenge facing incumbent firms is . . . to work out which threats are worth worrying about and how best to respond to them--a rich seam that 'Big Bang Disruption' fails to mine deeply enough. Messrs. Downes and Nunes are right that the competitive heat has been turned up by new technology. But cool heads are still needed when dealing with disrupters."

REVIEW: *Kirkus Rev* v81 no24 p177 D 15 2013

DOWNEY, JEN SWANN. The ninja librarians; the accidental keyhand; [by] Jen Swann Downey 384 p. 2014 Sourcebooks Jabberwocky

1. Adventure stories 2. Censorship—Fiction 3. Librarians—Fiction 4. Secret societies—Fiction 5. Space and time—Fiction

ISBN 1402287704; 9781402287701 (hc: alk. paper)

LC 2013-049956

SUMMARY: In this adventure story by Jen Swann Downey, "when Dorrie and her brother Marcus chase Moe—an unusually foul-tempered mongoose—into the janitor's closet of their local library, they make an astonishing discovery: the headquarters of a secret society of ninja librarians. Their mission: protect those whose words get them into trouble, anywhere in the world and at any time in history." (Publisher's note)

REVIEW: *Booklist* v110 no16 p52 Ap 15 2014 Stacey Comfort

REVIEW: *Bull Cent Child Books* v67 no10 p512 Je 2014 K. Q. G.

"The Ninja Librarians: The Accidental Keyhand". "The delightful premise will be an obvious hit with librarians and their fans, and the very specific library humor and inside jokes are perhaps most suited for those kids who spend their lunch hour hanging around the reference desk or shelving books for fun. The plot meanders down a few too many blind alleys, however, and several subplots, including Dorrie's rivalry with not one but two mean girls, detract from the main storyline. A host of memorable characters—especially a bitingly snarky Cyrano de Bergerac cast as Dorrie's mentor—compensate, though, and the multiple allusions to history's unsung heroes of intellectual freedom will likely send a few readers to the 900s."

REVIEW: *Kirkus Rev* v82 no6 p286 Mr 15 2014

REVIEW: *SLJ* v60 no4 p142 Ap 2014 Marian McLeod

DOWNING, DOUGLAS A. Dictionary of computer and internet terms. See Covington, M.

DOWNING, JULIE.il. Spooky friends. See Spooky friends

DOYLE, ARTHUR CONAN, SIR, 1859-1930. Memories and adventures; [by] Arthur Conan Doyle 408 p. 1924 Hodder and Stoughton

1. Adventure and adventurers—Great Britain—Biography 2. Authors, Scottish—19th century—Biography 3. Autobiographies 4. Occultists—Great Britain—Biography

LC 2402-8732

SUMMARY: In this book, writer Arthur Conan Doyle recounts his "literary success, his collaboration with playwright J. M. Barrie (whose Sherlock Holmes parody is included), and his involvement in the setting up of volunteer groups during the First World War. He describes how the methods of Sherlock Holmes helped him solve several real-life mysteries and . . . closes with a chapter on his belief in spiritualism." (Publisher's note)

REVIEW: *TLS* no5770 p16 N 1 2013

"Memories and Adventures." "If it is wisdom to map out a career and go forward on it with calculated steps, Sir Arthur Conan Doyle has not been wise. But that sort of rationality does not make lives which it is a pleasure to recall and fun for other people to hear about; just as detective stories worked out like Euclidean problems would not have made the books that we take care always to have somewhere in the house. . . . He has every right to be proud of the deductions about the character of land fighting in 'the next war' drawn in his history of the Boer campaigns, and his prevision of the submarine blockade has already given him his hour of rather rueful prophetic fame. Nevertheless, as he frankly owns, his inspiration comes from a tricksy spirit."

DOYLE, BRIAN. The plover; a novel; [by] Brian Doyle 320 p. 2014 Thomas Dunne Books

1. Boats & boating—Fiction 2. FICTION—General 3. FICTION—Literary 4. FICTION—Sea Stories 5. Ocean travel—Fiction

ISBN 1250034779; 9781250034779 (hardback)

LC 2013-032101

SUMMARY: In this novel, by Brian Doyle, "Declan O Donnell has sailed out of Oregon and deep into the vast, wild ocean, having had just finally enough of other people and their problems. He will go it alone, he will be his own country, he will be beholden to and beloved of no one. . . . But the galaxy soon presents him with a string of odd, entertaining, and dangerous passengers, who become companions of every sort and stripe." (Publisher's note)

REVIEW: *Booklist* v110 no12 p24 F 15 2014 Jonathan Fullmer

REVIEW: *Kirkus Rev* v82 no3 p8 F 1 2014

"The Plover". "In near stream of consciousness, wave upon wave of words tumbles out in long, beautifully rendered, description-packed sentences, running on and on, as Declan, captain of the Plover, 'a roomy coffin,' skims across water two miles deep and weighing 'about eighty quintillion tons.' . . . After a fiery confrontation with the Tanets, Declan and company sail '[f]ree as air' on '[t]he continent of the sea.' A rare and unusual book and a brilliant, mystical exploration of the human spirit."

REVIEW: *Libr J* v138 no18 p68 N 1 2013 Barbara Hoffert

REVIEW: *Publ Wkly* v260 no43 p29 O 28 2013

DOYLE, MALACHY, 1954-. The Snuggle Sandwich; [by] Malachy Doyle 32 p. 2013 Trafalgar Square Books

1. Families—Juvenile fiction 2. Hugging 3. Mother & child 4. Picture books for children 5. Teddy bears

ISBN 1849393907; 9781849393904

SUMMARY: "This bedtime book starts in the morning, when a tiny girl in green pajamas sneaks between her dozing parents for a 'snuggle sandwich.' After her noisy siblings and jovial father leave for school and work, 'there's only her and Mama. No more fuss and clutter!'--the perfect time for another snuggle." (New York Times Book Review)

REVIEW: *N Y Times Book Rev* p20 Ag 25 2013 SARAH HARRISON SMITH

"Lena's Sleep Sheep: A Going-To-Bed Book," "The Snuggle Sandwich," and "On My Way To Bed." "[Anita] Lobel . . . tells the sweet and funny story of a little girl who is helped to sleep by a flock of sheep. . . . Full of singsong rhymes and scenes of cheerfully chaotic family life, this bedtime book [by Malachy Doyle] starts in the morning. . . . Seen in [Michael] Paraskevas's bright, action-packed illustrations, Livi's high jinks include juggling toys, playing zoo dentist and piloting an imaginary rocket."

DOYLE, PETER. World War II in numbers; an infographic guide to the conflict, its conduct, and its casualties; [by] Peter Doyle 223 p. 2013 Firefly Books Ltd.

1. Historical literature 2. World War, 1939-1945 3. World War, 1939-1945—Campaigns 4. World War, 1939-1945—Casualties 5. World War, 1939-1945—Statistics

ISBN 177085195X; 9781770851955

LC 2013-474006

SUMMARY: Written by Peter Doyle, "'World War II in Numbers' uses color graphics and succinct text to tell the key stories of the battles that engulfed the globe and affected virtually everyone alive during the 1940s. To see the war set out in numbers tells the story with a new certainty. . . . The book sets out six chapters with topics discussed in two- and four-page infographics spreads" (Publisher's note)

REVIEW: *Booklist* v110 no9/10 p76 Ja 1 2014 Sylvia Ashwell

REVIEW: *Choice* v51 no8 p1377-8 Ap 2014 W. F. Bell

"World War II in Numbers: An Infographic Guide to the Conflict, Its Conduct, and Its Casualties". "This book's main drawback lies in the nature of the subject. For instance, estimates of total human losses vary widely and, given the chaotic nature of war itself, are very hard to measure accurately. Some major omissions are evident as well. For example, the Holocaust statistics provide no information on the number of Soviet Jews massacred by the German SS Einsatzgruppen killing squads during the 1941-42 phase of the Russo-German War. Nevertheless, this is an easy-to-use source and a good beginning for anybody doing statistical research on this conflict."

REVIEW: *Libr J* v139 no5 p138 Mr 15 2014 Rob Tench

DOYLE, RODDY. The Guts; [by] Roddy Doyle 336 p. 2014 Viking Adult

1. Cancer—Patients—Fiction 2. Cancer patients 3. FICTION—General 4. FICTION—Literary 5. Families—Fiction 6. Friendship—Fiction 7. Middle age—Fiction 8. Middle-aged men—Fiction 9. Music fans 10. Music fans—Fiction 11. Musical fiction 12. Parent & child—Fiction

ISBN 0670016438; 9780670016433

LC 2013-036812

SUMMARY: In this book by Roddy Doyle, "Jimmy Rabbitte--last seen as the brash, young manager of the Commitments--is now middle-aged. He's still kicking around Dublin, married, with four kids, and working as a reasonably successful promoter of nostalgia bands--one-hit wonders that have been generally forgotten. When Jimmy is diagnosed with bowel cancer, however, he finds himself suddenly reevaluating his life, his decisions, and his legacy." (Publishers Weekly)

REVIEW: *Booklist* v110 no5 p25 N 1 2013 Ben Segedin

"The Guts." "Booker Prize winner [Roddy] Doyle revisits the Rabbitte family of his Barrytown trilogy--now with 25 members attending Christmas--along with its at-times incomprehensible North Dublin dialogue. Doyle expertly evokes the generational confusion over new technologies (especially texting), the sentimentality of children growing up way too fast, and the sobering fear and anxiety of living with a potentially fatal disease--all this without being overly morbid or maudlin and while maintaining his trademark soft touch."

REVIEW: *Kirkus Rev* v81 no21 p130 N 1 2013

REVIEW: *N Y Times Book Rev* p18 Ja 26 2014 MATTHEW SPECKTOR

"The Guts." "Roddy Doyle's new novel, 'The Guts,' begins with a conversation about Facebook. . . . At 47, Jimmy Rabbitte . . . has colon cancer, and the mere act of telling those closest to him . . . has him twisted up in knots. . . . The plot here is simple, albeit hectic. . . . Doyle is particularly strong on the forgetfulness, the daze and discomfort of cancer treatment. . . . The effect is gorgeously understated, and lets the book's high comedy, as well as its melancholy, have its due."

REVIEW: *New Yorker* p69-1 Ja 27 2014

REVIEW: *Publ Wkly* v261 no13 p60 Mr 31 2014

REVIEW: *TLS* no5759 p24 Ag 16 2013 TIM SOUSTER

"The Guts." "Many readers will be delighted by the return of Jimmy Rabbitte, the most likeable character from Roddy Doyle's eminently likeable debut novel, 'The Commitments'. . . . If 'The Guts' is not a leap forward in the author's writing, it is a welcome reminder of his core strengths. . . . The perfectly pitched dialogue allows the bonds of familial love to emerge clearly and believably. . . . For a book about a man with cancer and financial concerns, 'The Guts' is extremely buoyant. Jimmy suffers, but he never seems likely to die. Doyle is too fond of him for that, and there are moments when it feels as though the author has indulged his leading man a little too much, or solved his problems too smoothly."

DRABBLE, MARGARET, 1939-. The pure gold baby; [by] Margaret Drabble 304 p. 2013 Houghton Mifflin Harcourt

1. Children with disabilities—Fiction 2. FICTION—Literary 3. Mother and child—Fiction 4. Single mothers—Fiction

ISBN 9780544158900 (hardback)

LC 2013-021736

SUMMARY: In this book, "Jessica Speight, a young anthropology student in 1960s London, is at the beginning of a promising academic career when an affair with her married professor turns her into a single mother. Anna is a pure gold baby with a delightful sunny nature. But as it becomes clear that Anna will not be a normal child, the book circles questions of responsibility, potential, even age." (Publisher's note)

REVIEW: *Booklist* v109 no22 p30 Ag 1 2013 Donna Seaman

REVIEW: *Kirkus Rev* v81 no18 p151 S 15 2013

REVIEW: *Libr J* v138 no9 p52 My 15 2013 Barbara Hoffert

REVIEW: *Libr J* v138 no14 p98 S 1 2013 Jennifer B. Stidham

REVIEW: *N Y Rev Books* v61 no2 p41-4 F 6 2014 April

Bernard

"The Pure Gold Baby." "It does seem that [Margaret] Drabble's frequent use of 'proleptic' to describe events and feelings in 'The Pure Gold Baby' has been planted by her as a clue to what her novel is, thematically, brooding over. . . . It is a testament to the intensity and skill of Drabble's writing that part of this novel's suspense has to do with our waiting for definitions, diagnoses, and certainties that are never offered; and that part of our satisfaction lies in our acceptance that they cannot be."

REVIEW: *New Yorker* v89 no36 p83-1 N 11 2013

REVIEW: *Publ Wkly* v260 no31 p47 Ag 5 2013

REVIEW: *TLS* no5769 p22 O 25 2013

DRAGUET, MICHEL. Magritte. See Magritte

DRESSER, MADGE.ed. Slavery and the British Country House. See Slavery and the British Country House

DRESSLER, MARKUS. Writing religion; the making of Turkish Alevi İslam; [by] Markus Dressler xviii, 323 p. 2013 Oxford University Press

1. Alevis 2. Historical literature 3. Islamic sects—Turkey—History 4. National characteristics, Alevi 5. Nosairians—Turkey—History
ISBN 9780199969401 (alk. paper)
LC 2012-042587

SUMMARY: This book examines "the ways in which Alevi identity in Turkey has been historically and politically constructed. . . . The main premise . . . is that the Alevi Question in Turkey is historically related to the formation of secular Turkish nationalism." Author Markus Dressler "concludes that Turkish Alevism is nothign but a construct, aiming at the incorporation of a heterogeneous group of people into the newly established Turkish nation from the remnants of the Ottoman Empire." (Middle East Journal)

REVIEW: *Middle East J* v68 no1 p177-8 Wint 2014 Ayhan Kaya

"Writing Religion: The Making of Turkish Alevi Islam." "Markus Dressler's work is absolutely brilliant in its critical and elaborate reading of the ways in which the Alevi identity in Turkey has been historically and politically constructed. . . . The book is also very rich in attempting, by referring to the memoirs of the Christian missionaries in the 19th century, to establish parallels between Christianity and Alevism. . . . However, I should also say a few words about my criticisms on the work. First, the book starts with a misleading introduction . . . second . . . it contains a disproportionate amount of material on the Kurdish Alevis . . . third, the author does not inform the reader about the sources of the syncretic nature of the Alevi-Bektashi belief system."

REVIEW: *Middle East J* v68 no1 p175-6 Wint 2014 W. Andrew Terrill

DREYER, EILEEN. Once a Rake; [by] Eileen Dreyer 416 p. 2013 Grand Central Pub

1. Fugitives from justice—Fiction 2. Historical fiction 3. Love stories 4. Man-woman relationships—Fiction 5. Nobility (Social class)—Fiction
ISBN 1455519324; 9781455519323

SUMMARY: In this book, by Eileen Dreyer, "Colonel Ian Ferguson may be a rake, but he's no traitor. Accused of trying to kill the Duke of Wellington, the disgraced Scotsman is now a fugitive-from the law, the army, and the cunning assassin who hunts him. Wounded and miles from his allies, Ian finds himself at the mercy of an impoverished country wife. The spirited woman is . . . beautiful . . . and hiding some dangerous secrets of her own." (Publisher's note)

REVIEW: *Booklist* v110 no2 p44 S 15 2013 John Charles

"Once a Rake." "Ian is accused of trying to assassinate Wellington, and if Sarah is caught with him, she could lose what little she has left in life. Despite overwhelming circumstantial evidence, Sarah intuitively knows Ian is no traitor, but is that enough for her to risk everything for the love of one man? In the fourth addition to her top-notch Drake's Rakes series, [Eileen] Dreyer dazzles readers with her incomparable gift for creating heartbreakingly real characters and her inimitable flair for fusing sexy passion and dangerous intrigue in a richly emotional, wickedly witty, and altogether enthralling historical romance."

DRNDIC, DAŠA. Trieste; [by] Daša Drndic 368 p. 2014 Houghton Mifflin Harcourt

1. FICTION—Historical 2. FICTION—Jewish 3. FICTION—Literary 4. HISTORY—Holocaust 5. Historical fiction
ISBN 0547725140; 9780547725147 (hardback)
LC 2013-044258

SUMMARY: This "novel of WWII and its aftermath is acclaimed Croatian author [Daša] Drndić's American debut. In 2006, elderly Haya Tedeschi is awaiting a reunion with her son, who disappeared as an infant during WWII. . . . Interspersed with [protagonist] Haya's account are photographs, interviews, and personal testimonies, and, in one case, pages listing the names of all 9,000 Jews deported from or murdered in northern Italy during the war." (Publishers Weekly)

REVIEW: *Booklist* v110 no5 p26-7 N 1 2013 Sarah Johnson

REVIEW: *Kirkus Rev* v81 no21 p77 N 1 2013

REVIEW: *N Y Times Book Rev* p9 F 2 2014 CRAIG SELIGMAN

REVIEW: *New Yorker* v90 no1 p104-1 F 17 2014

"Trieste." "In this fractured, experimental novel, an elderly Jewish woman in Gorizia waits to be reunited with her son, who was fathered by an S.S. officer and, sixty-two years earlier, stolen from her as part of Himmler's Lebensborn project. [Author Daša] Drndić intercuts this narrative with material adapted from documentary accounts of survivors. . . . Killings at the San Sabba and Treblinka camps are depicted in harrowing detail. The voluminous records of the missing and the dead--these 'mislaid lives'--produce a cumulative sense of grief and horror."

REVIEW: *Publ Wkly* v260 no37 p2 S 16 2013

REVIEW: *TLS* no5696 p19 Je 1 2012 Mark Thompson

"Trieste." "With Trieste, the Croatian novelist and playwright Daša Drndić has bridged the gap between Yugoslav and post-Yugoslav fiction . . . responding to the genocidal violence unleashed in the 1990s. The plot has the starkness of a fable. . . . That the novel rarely feels disjointed is due to Drndić's skill at patterning information and to the bitter urgency of her address, so compelling that this reader ignored bumps in the road. . . . At its best, Trieste achieves a factographical poetry, superbly rendered by Ellen Elias-Bursać, implying that no one in Axis-occupied Europe stood more than two degrees from atrocity."

DRURY, JOHN. Music at Midnight; The Life and Poetry of George Herbert; [by] John Drury 416 p. 2013 Allen Lane

1. Biographies 2. Clergy—England—Biography 3. Clergy as authors 4. Herbert, George, 1593-1633 5. Poets—Biography

ISBN 1846142482; 9781846142482

SUMMARY: In this biography of poet and minister George Herbert, John Drury "integrates Herbert's poems . . . into his life. . . . Drury follows Herbert from his academic success as a young man, seemingly destined for a career at court, through his abandonment of those hopes, his devotion to the restoration of a church in Huntingdonshire, and his final years as a country parson." (Publisher's note)

REVIEW: *Booklist* v110 no16 p11 Ap 15 2014 Ray Olson

REVIEW: *Economist* v408 no8851 p72-3 Ag 31 2013

"Music at Midnight: The Life and Poetry of George Herbert." "Few biographers are better qualified than John Drury to write on [George] Herbert. Mr. Drury is not only a scholar, but also a chaplain . . . who knows Herbert's day-to-day spiritual territory. Accordingly, this book is both deeply knowledgeable and deeply felt. It overflows with the poetry, reveling in its 'lightness' and 'alacrity'; that is how it should be, for Herbert's inner life is indescribable in other form. The poetry is dissected, both for meaning, and as vitally, for metre, as much as it needs to be for 21st-century readers."

REVIEW: *Libr J* v139 no6 p91 Ap 1 2014 Herman Sutter

REVIEW: *New Statesman* v142 no5177 p69-70 S 27 2013 Jonathan Bate

REVIEW: *TLS* no5787 p3-4 F 28 2014 STEPHEN PRICKETT

"Music at Midnight: The Life and Poetry of George Herbert." "Driving authorial passion to make Herbert's work better known . . . helps to give [John] Drury's biography its curious internal structure. Each stage of his life is illustrated by one or more of his poems, often accompanied by an extensive analysis. This is (as Drury admits) a somewhat hit-or-miss technique. . . . Once the reader is accustomed to what amounts to a series of poetic digressions from the bare biographical narrative, this technique works reasonably well--and often does indeed seem to give greater insight into Herbert's actual, and usually more conflicted, state of mind than any recitation of the outward events might imply. This is less a critical biography than a poetic biography."

DRÈZE, JEAN. An uncertain glory; India and its contradictions; [by] Jean Drèze 448 p. 2013 Princeton University Press

1. Economic development—India 2. India—Economic conditions 3. India—Politics & government 4. India—Social conditions 5. Political science literature

ISBN 9780691160795 (alk. paper)

LC 2013-942038

SUMMARY: In this book, authors Jean Drèze and Amartya Sen argue "that India cannot move forward without investing significantly--as every other major industrialized country has already done--in public services. . . . According to Drèze and Sen, even though the poor constitute a vast majority of Indian voters, they have been shut out of public discourse. . . . Discrimination against girls" is also discussed. (New York Times Book Review)

REVIEW: *Choice* v51 no7 p1270 Mr 2014 R. M. Ramazani

REVIEW: *Economist* v407 no8842 p74-5 Je 29 2013

REVIEW: *N Y Rev Books* v60 no18 p51-3 N 21 2013 Pankaj Mishra

REVIEW: *N Y Times Book Rev* p10 S 8 2013 JYOTI THOTTAM

"An Uncertain Glory: India and Its Contradictions." "It's an urgent, passionate, political work that makes the case that India cannot move forward without investing significantly . . . in public services. . . . It would be a mistake to read 'An Uncertain Glory' as a screed against liberalization. This book is something bigger, a heartfelt plea to rethink what progress in a poor country ought to look like. . . . In the interest of pragmatism, [Jean] Drèze and [Amartya] Sen might have devoted more thought to how to make India's existing social-welfare initiatives work better. . . . The section on discrimination against girls . . . also cries out for a more prescriptive analysis. . . . Still, the value of 'An Uncertain Glory' is its wide-angle view."

REVIEW: *New Statesman* v142 no5165 p44-6 Jl 5 2013 William Dalrymple

REVIEW: *Science* v341 no6150 p1066 S 6 2013 Andrew Robinson

DU MAURIER, DAPHNE, 1907-1989. Rebecca; [by] Daphne Du Maurier 457 1938 Doubleday

1. Cornwall (England : County)—Fiction 2. Death—Fiction 3. Love stories 4. Marriage—Fiction 5. Suspense fiction

LC (W) -38-27778

SUMMARY: This novel by Daphne Du Maurier won the Anthony Award for Best Novel of the Century. "The novel begins in Monte Carlo, where our heroine is swept off her feet by the dashing widower Maxim de Winter and his sudden proposal of marriage. . . . It is only when they arrive at his massive country estate that she realizes how large a shadow his late wife will cast over their lives--presenting her with a lingering evil that threatens to destroy their marriage from beyond the grave." (Publisher's note)The heroine and narrator of this story, after a brief courtship, becomes the wife of an English aristocrat, Maxim de Winter, owner of a fine old country seat in the south of England. These two are deeply in love but the memory of Max's first wife, Rebecca, still lingers on at Manderley; her beauty and charm contrasted in the minds of servants and neighbors with the shyness and gaucherie of the new wife. Little by little, however, the mystery of Rebecca's life and death is revealed and the burden Max has borne can finally be fully shared.

REVIEW: *TLS* no5755 p16 Jl 19 2013

"Rebecca." "'Rebecca' is a lowbrow story with a middle-brow finish. As such it squares with a formula for novel-writing that yields handsome results several times in the year. If one chooses to read the book in a critical fashion--but only a tiresome reviewer is likely to do that--it becomes an obligation to take off one's hat to Miss [Daphne] du Maurier for the skill and assurance with which she sustains a highly improbable fiction. Whatever else she may lack, it is not the story-teller's flow of fancy. . . . Miss du Maurier's feat in unfolding the whole course of events through the mind of a single character is not to be underrated."

DUBERMAN, MARTIN. Howard Zinn; a life on the left; [by] Martin Duberman 365 p. 2012 New Press Distributed by Perseus Distribution

1. Biography (Literary form) 2. Historians—United States—Biography 3. History & politics 4. Radicals—United States—Biography
ISBN 1595586784; 9781595586780
LC 2012-017592

SUMMARY: This biography of historian Howard Zinn by Martin Duberman, a "bestselling author . . . political activist . . . lecturer, and one of America's most recognizable and admired progressive voices," details Zinn's life "from the battlefields of World War II to the McCarthy era, the civil rights and the antiwar movements, and beyond." (Publisher's note)

REVIEW: *Booklist* v109 no2 p15 S 15 2012

REVIEW: *Christ Century* v130 no16 p36-7 Ag 7 2013 John Fea

REVIEW: *Libr J* v137 no17 p82 O 15 2012 Scott H. Silverman

REVIEW: *New Repub* v244 no4 p44-9 Mr 25 2013 David Greenberg

REVIEW: *Publ Wkly* v259 no32 p46-7 Ag 6 2012

REVIEW: *Rev Am Hist* v42 no1 p152-6 Mr 2014 Glenn C. Altschuler

"Howard Zinn: A Life on the Left." "In this biography, then, Duberman emphasizes--and celebrates--Zinn's political engagement and the 'much needed role' . . . he played in popularizing the ideas of others, including history 'from the bottom up' and skepticism about 'objective' accounts of the past. Although he is by no means uncritical of Zinn, Duberman makes clear that biographer and subject 'held common convictions on a wide range of public issues.' He weighs in on those issues early and often, inserting them even at the risk of displacing Zinn from center stage. . . . Self-evidently partisan, Duberman's account of Zinn's turbulent quarter century as a professor of history at Boston University is informative and insightful as well."

DUBIN, NATHANIEL E.tr. The fabliaux. See The fabliaux

DUBOIS, DANIEL M.ed. A companion to World War II. See A companion to World War II

DUBOIS, JENNIFER. Cartwheel; a novel; [by] Jennifer DuBois 384 p. 2013 Random House

1. Americans—Argentina—Fiction 2. FICTION—Psychological 3. Foreign students 4. Murder—Investigation—Fiction 5. Women college students—Fiction
ISBN 0812995864; 9780812995862 (hardback)
LC 2013-016952

SUMMARY: This book "follows American exchange student Lily Hayes, who has been accused of murdering her roommate, Katy Kellers, in Argentina. Like [real-life accused murderer Amanda] Knox, Lily's troublesome lack of anguish, as reportedly evidenced by canoodling with her boyfriend the day after the murder, causes an uproar in the media. Like Knox, Lily seems to have been completely normal--so normal, in fact, that her disbelief at her predicament leads to some bad choices." (Publishers Weekly)

REVIEW: *Booklist* v110 no1 p35 S 1 2013 Michael Cart

"Cartwheel." "In her skillful examination of these matters, the author does an excellent job of creating and maintaining a pervasive feeling of foreboding and suspense. Sometimes bleak, [Jennifer] duBois' ambitious second novel is an acute psychological study of character that rises to the level of the philosophical, specifically the existential. In this it may not be for every reader, but fans of character-driven literary fiction will welcome its challenges. Though inspired by the Amanda Knox case, 'Cartwheel' is very much its own individual work of the author's creative imagination."

REVIEW: *Kirkus Rev* v81 no18 p244 S 15 2013

REVIEW: *Libr J* v139 no3 p59 F 15 2014 Mary Knapp

REVIEW: *N Y Times Book Rev* p16 O 13 2013 AMITY GAIGE

REVIEW: *Publ Wkly* v260 no27 p62 Jl 8 2013

DUBOSARSKY, URSULA. The golden day; [by] Ursula Dubosarsky 160 p. 2013 Candlewick

1. Missing persons—Fiction 2. Secrecy—Fiction 3. Teacher-student relationships—Fiction 4. Teachers—Fiction 5. Young adult fiction
ISBN 0763663999; 9780763663995; 9781742374710 (pbk.)
LC 2012-452201

SUMMARY: In this novel by Ursula Dubosarsky "eleven schoolgirls embrace their own chilling history when their teacher abruptly goes missing on a field trip. Who was the mysterious poet they had met in the Garden? What actually happened in the seaside cave that day? And most important —who can they tell about it?" (Publisher's note)

REVIEW: *Booklist* v109 no21 p64 Jl 1 2013 Daniel Kraus

REVIEW: *Bull Cent Child Books* v67 no1 p15 S 2013 E. B.

"The Golden Day." "Long since sworn to secrecy by Miss Renshaw concerning their discussions and outings, the girls instinctively adhere to a code of silence when questioned by school authorities, but an investigation is launched, revealing Morgan's past and presuming Miss Renshaw murdered. . . . Delicate, atmospheric, and provocative, this bijou tale stirs young adult readers to remember vividly the beguilement in which teachers can hold their little charges, and to consider with mature vision the complex meanings of adult actions that are only half understood by child observers. With secrecy, elegant language, crime, a short page count, and a touch of the supernatural, here's a teen book-club selection that everyone is likely to finish."

REVIEW: *Kirkus Rev* v81 no12 p87 Je 15 2013

REVIEW: *Publ Wkly* v260 no23 p78-9 Je 10 2013

REVIEW: *Publ Wkly* p129 Children's starred review annual 2013

REVIEW: *Voice of Youth Advocates* v36 no4 p61 O 2013 Barbara Allen

DUDDEN, FAYE E. Fighting chance; the struggle over woman suffrage and Black suffrage in Reconstruction America; [by] Faye E. Dudden 296 2011 Oxford University Press

1. African Americans—Suffrage—History 2. Anthony, Susan B. (Susan Brownell), 1820-1906 3. Historical literature 4. Stanton, Elizabeth Cady, 1815-1902 5. Women's suffrage—History
ISBN 9780199772636; 0199772630

LC 2010-053188

SUMMARY: In this "account of the struggle for suffrage in the years before, during, and especially after the Civil War, [Faye E.] Dudden charts the gradual splintering of the initially united feminist and abolitionist movements. . . . Dudden, . . . addresses the ugly racism employed by some in the women's suffrage movement, in particular [Elizabeth Cady] Stanton, in a late bid for support of racist Democrats. Dudden finds the split's roots in a bitter fight over priorities and over money." (Publishers Weekly)

REVIEW: *Choice* v49 no4 p751 D 2011 A. K. Frisken

REVIEW: *J Am Hist* v99 no3 p936-7 D 2012 Rosalyn Terborg-Penn

REVIEW: *Rev Am Hist* v41 no3 p467-72 S 2013 Laura E. Free

"Fighting Chance: The Struggle Over Woman Suffrage and Black Suffrage in Reconstruction America." "Carefully researched and clearly written. . . . Bringing new insight to this controversial moment, [Faye E.] Dudden challenges the most fundamental assumption historians have made about [Elizabeth Cady] Stanton and [Susan B.] Anthony in this period. . . . Dudden offers a persuasive explanation for what caused this schism, as well as engaging in a truly important, focused analysis of Stanton's racism. . . . Here, Dudden's book shines. . . . Dudden demonstrates that the presence (and absence) of money changed everything for the early equality movements. . . . This insight notably enhances our knowledge of the nation's earliest feminist leaders."

REVIEW: *Women's Review of Books* v29 no3 p11-3 My/Je 2012 Lisa Tetrault

DUDECK, THERESA ROBBINS. Keith Johnstone; A Critical Biography; [by] Theresa Robbins Dudeck 232 p. 2013 Bloomsbury USA Academic

1. Acting teachers 2. Biography (Literary form) 3. English dramatists—20th century—Biography 4. Improvisation (Acting) 5. Johnstone, Keith

ISBN 1408185520; 9781408185520

SUMMARY: This book by Theresa Robbins Dudeck examines "the life and work of the enigmatic, yet influential originator of the pedagogically groundbreaking Impro System and widely recognized Theatresports brand name, Keith Johnstone." The author "connect[s] Johnstone's formative experiences and personality to his teaching methodologies and praxis." (Theatre Topics)

REVIEW: *Choice* v51 no9 p1604-5 My 2014 J. Tomalin

"Keith Johnstone: A Critical Biography". "In this scholarly, first biography of master of improvisation Keith Johnstone (b. 1933), [Theresa Robbins] Dudeck (Johnstone's literary executor) details his entire career. Though Johnstone has become renowned in recent decades as an influential international teacher and director of 'impro theatre,' his early career is less known. . . . Starting in chapter 1 with an introduction to Johnstone's Impro System,Dudeck expertly limns Johnstone's journey. . . . A book for those interested in any aspect of improv."

DUFFY, CHRIS.ed. Fairy Tale Comics. See Fairy Tale Comics

DUFFY, CHRIS. Nursery rhyme comics; 50 timeless rhymes by 50 celebrated cartoonists; [by] Chris Duffy 2011 First Second

1. Baa, Baa, Black Sheep (Poem : Mother Goose) 2. Babysitting 3. Graphic novels 4. Nursery rhymes 5. Wizards—Fiction

ISBN 978-1-59643-600-8, 1-59643 600-X

SUMMARY: In this anthology, "classic nursery rhymes get a contemporary spin from artists as varied as the New Yorker's Roz Chast and Hellboy creator Mike Mignola. . . . In Dave Roman's 'One, Two, Buckle My Shoe,' the numbers in the title refer to tiny clones created by a wizard inventor." In "Lucy Kinsley's . . . 'There Was an Old Woman Who Lived in a Shoe' . . . the titular woman lives in a funky boot and runs Ruth's Rock & Rock Babysitting." (Publishers Weekly)

REVIEW: *Booklist* v110 no13 p46 Mr 1 2014 SARAH HUNTER

"Hello Kitty: Here We Go!," "Little Lit: Folklore & Fairy Tale Funnies," and "Nursery Rhyme Comics: 50 Timeless Rhymes From 50 Celebrated Cartoonists." "Hello Kitty is cute, cute, cute! And in this collection of short, wordless comics, she spoofs everything from James Bond flicks to Chandleresque noir. Kids won't be able to resist the cheerful, bubbly art, and parents will chuckle over the artists' clever visual jokes. . . . [Art] Spiegelman and his wife, Françoise Mouly . . . invited 15 stellar talents to create original graphic stories that poke often ironic fun at tales. . . . It's an extravagant treat for readers of all ages. . . . Having 50 of the finest cartoonists draw simple nursery rhymes, each no more than two or three pages long, is such a crazy move that it's borderline genius."

REVIEW: *Booklist* v108 no6 p42 N 15 2011 Ian Chipman

DUFFY, JENNIFER NUGENT. Who's your Paddy?; racial expectations and the struggle for Irish American identity; [by] Jennifer Nugent Duffy viii, 301 p. 2014 New York University Press

1. African Americans—Relations with Irish Americans 2. Historical literature 3. Irish Americans—New York (State)—New York—History 4. Irish Americans—New York (State)—New York—Social conditions 5. Irish Americans—New York (State)—Yonkers—History 6. Irish Americans—New York (State)—Yonkers—Social conditions 7. Irish Americans—Race identity—New York (State)—New York

ISBN 9780814785027 (hardback: acid-free paper); 9780814785034 (paper: acid-free paper)

LC 2013-023711

SUMMARY: This book by Jennifer Nugent Duffy "provides a case-study analysis of the Irish and American Irish communities of Yonkers, New York, from the mid-19th century to the present, investigating 'how Irish immigrants have been, and continue to be, socialized around race and become race-conscious subjects in the United States.' The author argues that the Irish experienced 'racial hazing' in the US, ultimately facilitating their acceptance as white Americans." (Choice: Current Reviews for Academic Libraries)

REVIEW: *Choice* v51 no8 p1472 Ap 2014 J. M. O'Leary

"Who's Your Paddy?: Racial Expectations and the Struggle for Irish American Identity". "Of interest is the cultural discord between 'newer' Irish arrivals to Yonkers, who stringently adhere to notions of Irishness, and earlier Irish immigrants, who chose to assimilate, generally, to US cultural norms. [Jennifer Nugent] Duffy makes excellent use of Irish testimonials gathered from extensive ethnographic fieldwork that she intertwines throughout the book; the result is a compelling narrative."

DUFFY, MARGARET. Dark Side; [by] Margaret Duffy 224 p. 2014 Severn House Pub Ltd

1. Detective & mystery stories 2. Friendship—Fiction 3. Married people—Fiction 4. Murder investigation—Fiction 5. Organized crime—Fiction

ISBN 0727883402; 9780727883407

SUMMARY: This book is author Margaret Duffy's "18th Patrick Galliard and Ingrid Langley mystery. . . . The intrepid married couple, who work for England's Serious Organized Crime Agency, search for an extremely violent criminal with a powerful organization. When Det. Chief Insp. James Carrick, a friend of theirs, is framed for murder, Patrick goes off the grid to find the ringleader." (Publishers Weekly)

REVIEW: *Booklist* v110 no14 p51 Mr 15 2014 David Pitt

REVIEW: *Kirkus Rev* v82 no4 p315 F 15 2014

"Dark Side". "Although their boss wants them to stay on the case he is working, the duo are not about to desert a friend, and they do some dangerous snooping in a club reported to belong to the head gangster, who likes to be known as the Raptor. When Ingrid is attacked and nearly raped by some of his minions, she is afraid that Patrick, who has had to kill in the past, will go to the dark side and use any methods to track the gang down. An exciting combination of police procedural and thriller, [Margaret] Duffy again . . . provides the daring duo with plenty of cerebral and physical challenges."

REVIEW: *Publ Wkly* v261 no2 p53 Ja 13 2014

DUGGAN, TARA. Modern art desserts; recipes for cakes, cookies, confections, and frozen treats based on iconic works of art; [by] Tara Duggan 224 p. 2013 Ten Speed Press

1. Art, Modern 2. COOKING—Courses & Dishes—Cakes 3. COOKING—Courses & Dishes—Confectionery 4. COOKING—Methods—Baking 5. Cookbooks 6. Desserts 7. Sugar art

ISBN 1607743906 (hardcover); 9781607743903 (hardcover)

LC 2012-047905

SUMMARY: This book, by "pastry chef Caitlin Freeman, . . . [offers] a collection of uniquely delicious dessert recipes (with step-by-step assembly guides) that give readers all they need to make their own edible masterpieces. . . . This collection of uniquely delicious recipes for cookies, parfait, gelées, ice pops, ice cream, cakes, and inventive drinks has everything you need to astound friends, family, and guests with your own edible masterpieces." (Publisher's note)

REVIEW: *Booklist* v109 no11 p10 F 1 2013 Barbara Jacobs

REVIEW: *Libr J* v138 no3 p118 F 15 2013 Lisa Campbell

REVIEW: *Publ Wkly* v260 no1 p55 Ja 7 2013

REVIEW: *TLS* no5777/8 p15-6 D 20 2013 ALEX DANCHEV

"The Modern Art Cookbook" and "Modern Art Desserts." "Connecting the senses is what 'The Modern Art Cookbook' is all about. For Mary Ann Caws, the larger purpose of this delectable anthology is the association of reading, looking and cooking. It is a potpourri (or perhaps a bouillabaisse) of literary texts in verse and prose, recipes and images. . . . 'Modern Art Desserts' is a different kettle of fish--more rambunctious, more delirious, more ingenious; in the end, perhaps, more scrumptious. But only if you like cake. . . . The design of the book is intricate. Each dessert has its own entry: at its headman illustration of the relevant artwork, with a kind of potted biography."

DUHIGG, CHARLES. The power of habit; [by] Charles Duhigg xx, 371 p. 2012 Random House

1. Change (Psychology) 2. Habit 3. Habit—Social aspects 4. Habit breaking 5. Human behavior 6. Psychology 7. Scientific literature 8. Self-control

ISBN 9780679603856 (ebook); 9781400069286 (alk. paper)

LC 2011-029545

SUMMARY: In this book, "science writer Charles Duhigg explores the reasons why we find it so hard to change ingrained behaviour. . . . [H]abits usually start with a simple sensory cue . . . which sets up a craving in the brain's reward centres. . . . Habitual behaviours can propagate through an organisation or society, he argues, offering . . . anecdotes that cover everything from the success of Starbucks to the civil rights movement. . . . [Duhigg examines the] way advertising hijacks your brain's reward centres to set off a new, irresistible habit." (New Scientist)

REVIEW: *N Y Times Book Rev* p24 Ja 19 2014 IHSAN TAYLOR

"The Power of Habit: Why We Do What We Do in Life & Business," "Ways of Going Home," Farewell, Fred Voodoo: A Letter From Haiti." "In engrossing narratives that take us from corporate boardrooms to N.F.L. sidelines and the civil rights movement, he distills research from the fields of social psychology, clinical psychology and neuroscience. . . . [Alejandro] Zambra's third novel . . . explores themes of loss, oppression and the nature of writing. . . . In 'Farewell,' an empathetic yet sharply analytical guide to the land and its resilient people, [author Amy] Wilentz tries 'to put Haiti back together again for myself.'"

DULONG, TERRI. Secrets on Cedar Key; [by] Terri DuLong 320 p. 2013 Kensington Pub Corp

1. Children of unmarried parents—Fiction 2. Florida—Fiction 3. Infidelity (Couples) 4. Love stories 5. Paris (France)—Fiction 6. Widows—Fiction

ISBN 0758288131; 9780758288134

SUMMARY: In this book, by Terri DuLong, "after the death of her husband, Marin moves back to the Florida island of Cedar Key. . . . She learns that her husband had been unfaithful and left behind a 19-year-old daughter, Fiona. Marin decides to take a vacation to Paris to contemplate her options and decide how she might move forward and tell her grown sons about this new development. . . . Worth offers to let her use the apartment he owns in Paris and then decides to join her for part of her trip." (Kirkus Reviews)

REVIEW: *Booklist* v110 no4 p23 O 15 2013 Pat Henshaw

REVIEW: *Kirkus Rev* v81 no24 p49 D 15 2013

"Secrets on Cedar Key". "[Terri] DuLong's fifth installment of the Cedar Key series, low-key, small-town romances designed around a knitting theme, proceeds as expected. Not much new ground here, and the plot marches along with steadfast good cheer and serendipity. Everything turns out better than anyone could have expected, and the characters feel blessed and grateful for that fact. Life-altering conflicts handled in simplistic, unrealistic yet heartwarming ways;

more of the same for Cedar Key fans, who will love it."

DUMAS, ALEXANDRE, 1824-1895. The Lady of the Camellias; [by] Alexandre Dumas 206 p. 2013 Penguin Books

1. Autobiographical fiction 2. Courtesans 3. Duplessis, Marie, 1824-1847 4. Love stories 5. Paris (France)—Fiction

ISBN 9780143107026

LC 2013-005491

SUMMARY: This book by Alexandre Dumas follows "Marguerite Gautier, the most beautiful, brazen, and expensive courtesan in all of Paris," who "is never seen without her favorite flowers. . . . But despite having many lovers, she has never really loved--until she meets Armand Duval, young, handsome, and hopelessly in love with her." (Publisher's note)

REVIEW: *N Y Rev Books* v60 no14 p8-12 S 26 2013 Julie Kavanagh

"The Girl Who Loved Camellias: The Life and Legend of Marie Duplessis" and "The Lady of the Camellias." "Liesl Schillinger's translation is notable for the fact that it succeeds in dusting off and invigorating the text without slipping into the contemporary idiom. This story, which sounded a little dated in the previous translations, can now be read with an urgency that seems wholly modern. . . . [Alexandre] Dumas blends factual details with others invented out of whole cloth. . . . [Julie] Kavanagh isn't fooled, but how can anyone resist the persuasive influence of the character depicted by the novelist? In spite of herself, Kavanagh falls under the sway of her elusive subject's charm. To her credit, she makes up for the shortage of unassailable facts by placing Marie's story within the larger setting of French gallantry in the first half of the nineteenth century, and she does so with uncommon precision."

REVIEW: *TLS* no5773 p8 N 22 2013 DAVID COWARD

"The Girl Who Loved Camellias: The Life and Legend of Marie Duplessis" and "The Lady of the Camellias." "Julie Kavanagh moves us briskly through her brief life. At first, she struggles with the lack of information about Alphonsine's early years and fills in the blanks with asides and lecturettes on alcoholism, social conditions, the Latin Quarter and the like. But once Marie appears on the historical radar, Kavanagh gains control of the narrative and paints a sympathetic but not uncritical portrait of the woman behind the legend. . . . [Liesl] Schillinger gives [Alexandre] Dumas's 'timeless, relatable [sic] and fiery story' a twenty-first-century voice which avoids the 'antiquated,' 'quaint' tone of the previous translations that she has perused. The result reads well enough, but . . . it is at times an awkward mixture which may not suit all tastes."

DUNCAN, ALICE. Spirits revived; spirits, featuring Daisy Gumm Majesty; [by] Alice Duncan 2014 Five Star

1. FICTION—Mystery & Detective—General 2. Majesty, Daisy Gumm (Fictitious character)—Fiction 3. Motion pictures—Production and direction—Fiction 4. Spiritualists—Fiction

ISBN 1432827987 (hardcover); 9781432827984 (hardback)

LC 2013-041054

SUMMARY: This book is part of Alice Duncan's Daisy Gumm Majesty series. "Her heroine, a church choir member and medium living in 1923 Pasadena, Calif., is surprised when a séance she's leading attracts a real ghost. . . . Deceased attorney Eddie Hastings appears to proclaim that his death was not suicide, and that he was murdered." (Publishers Weekly)

REVIEW: *Kirkus Rev* v81 no24 p270 D 15 2013

"Spirits Revived". "A fake spiritualist is shocked when she has a real ghostly experience. . . . Despite the care the powerful elder Hastings took to hush up Eddie's death, however, Sam begins to investigate, thinking that it may be connected to a drug smuggling case he's already working on. Despite Sam's warnings, Daisy continues to poke into the case, only to find that a hornet's nest awaits her. A slight, simple mystery for readers who'd like to learn more about life on both sides of the tracks in California during the Jazz Age."

REVIEW: *Libr J* v139 no2 p60 F 1 2014 Teresa L. Jacobsen

REVIEW: *Publ Wkly* v261 no2 p53 Ja 13 2014

DUNCAN, ROBERT, 1919-1988. The collected early poems and plays; [by] Robert Duncan 875 p. 2012 University of California Press

1. American drama 2. American poetry 3. Anthologies 4. Gay male poets 5. Modernism (Literature)

ISBN 9780520259263 (cloth : alk. paper)

LC 2012-024993

SUMMARY: This book "gathers all of [Robert] Duncan's books and magazine publications up to and including 'Letters: Poems 1953-1956.' . . . . This volume includes the celebrated works 'Medieval Scenes' and 'The VeBérénice Poem,' all of Duncan's long unavailable major ventures into drama, his extensive 'imitations' of Gertrude Stein, and the . . . poems written in Majorca as responses to a series of collaged paste-ups by Duncan's life-long partner, the painter Jess." (Publisher's note)

REVIEW: *Choice* v51 no4 p635-6 D 2013 M. Willhardt

"The Collected Early Poems and Plays." "With this collection, [Peter] Quartermain . . . provides an important document of mid-century American experimentalism. . . . Quartermain faced a challenging editorial problem, arising from the fact that [Robert] Duncan frequently did not publish his work until years . . . after its writing. Quartermain chose to present Duncan's work in the order of composition. Thus, what reads here as a through line of poetic development is belied by the poet's own choice of publication order and timing. Though complete, the volume might have been better served by honoring the poet's choices and saving now interspersed, uncollected material for an appendix.. . . This remains an important collection, albeit hampered by difficult editorial choices."

REVIEW: *Publ Wkly* v259 no48 p29 N 26 2012

DUNCAN, THOMAS G.ed. Medieval English lyrics and carols. See Medieval English lyrics and carols

DUNDY, ALISON.tr. The falling sky. See Albert, B.

DUNKEL, TOM. Color Blind; The Forgotten Team That Broke Baseball's Color Line; [by] Tom Dunkel 368 p. 2013 Pgw

1. African American baseball players 2. Baseball—His-

tory 3. Historical literature 4. Paige, Satchel, 1906-1982 5. Race discrimination in sports
ISBN 0802120121; 9780802120120

SUMMARY: In this book by Tom Dunkel, "a decade before Jackie Robinson broke the Major League Baseball color line in 1947, an integrated team captured the imagination of Bismarck, N.Dak. by winning the national, semiprofessional baseball title." Team Manager Neil Churchill "looked to the Negro Leagues, 'cherry-picking players' who were prohibited from playing in the Major Leagues to reinforce his roster, with his prize being the great Satchel Paige." (Publishers Weekly)

REVIEW: *Booklist* v110 no1 p32 S 1 2013 Bill Ott
"The Boys in the Boat," "A Chance to Win," and "Color Blind: The Forgotten Team That Broke Baseball's Color Line." "The Jesse Owens story will always be the big event of the 1936 Berlin Olympics, but the triumph of the University of Washington's crew team in those same games comes in a close second. [Daniel James] Brown retells the little-known story with verve. . . . [Jonathan] Schuppe follows the remarkable life story of Rodney Mason, a New Jersey baseball star and gang member who was confined to a wheelchair after a shooting and rebuilt his life around drawing young people at risk to baseball. . . . [Tom] Dunkel tells the story of a North Dakota car dealer who, more than a decade before Jackie Robinson, formed an integrated baseball team that captured the hearts of the region."

REVIEW: *Booklist* v109 no11 p20 F 1 2013 Wes Lukowsky

REVIEW: *Kirkus Rev* v81 no7 p2 Ap 1 2013

REVIEW: *Libr J* v138 no7 p90 Ap 15 2013 Robert C. Cottrell

REVIEW: *Publ Wkly* v260 no1 p47 Ja 7 2013

DUNLAP, THOMAS.tr. Philosophical temperaments. See Philosophical temperaments

DUNMIRE, WILLIAM W. New Mexico's Spanish livestock heritage; four centuries of animals, land, and people; [by] William W. Dunmire xii, 233 p. 2013 University of New Mexico Press
1. Animals—New Mexico 2. Domestic animals—New Mexico—History 3. Historical literature 4. Livestock—New Mexico—History 5. Livestock—Spain—History 6. New Mexico—Environmental conditions
ISBN 9780826350893 (cloth : alk. paper)
LC 2012-034415

SUMMARY: Written by William W. Dunmire, "This survey of the history of domestic livestock in New Mexico is the first of its kind, going beyond cowboy culture to examine the ways Spaniards, Indians, and Anglos used animals and how those uses affected the region's landscapes and cultures. The author has mined the observations of travelers and the work of earlier historians and other scholars to provide a history of livestock in New Mexico from 1540 to the present." (Publisher's note)

REVIEW: *Choice* v51 no2 p286 O 2013 L. S. Cline
"New Mexico's Spanish Livestock Heritage: Four Centuries of Animals, Land, and People." "Early chapters discuss ganado mayor (horses, donkeys, mules, cattle, and oxen) and ganado menor (sheep, goats, and pigs). Chapters on the development of domestic livestock production in New Mexico follow. They illustrate a slightly pedestrian ebb-and-flow catalog of livestock varieties and numbers, although [author William W.] Dunmire . . . does weave the interesting dynamics of cultural phenomena and peoples, both native (Pueblo, Navajo, and Apache) and immigrant (Spanish, Mexican, and Anglo), with land and livestock."

DUNMORE, HELEN The lie; [by] Helen Dunmore 304 p. 2014 Pgw
1. Cornwall (England : County)—Fiction 2. English fiction 3. Historical fiction 4. World War, 1914-1918—England—Fiction 5. World War, 1914-1918—Veterans—Fiction
ISBN 080212254X; 9780802122544

SUMMARY: In this book, by Helen Dunmore, "Daniel Branwell has survived the First World War and returned to the small fishing town where he was born. Behind him lie the trenches and the most intense relationship of his life. As he works on the land, struggling to make a living in the aftermath of war, he is drawn deeper and deeper into the traumas of the past and memories of his dearest friend and his first love. . . . Daniel is haunted by the terrible, unforeseen consequences of a lie." (Publisher's note)

REVIEW: *Kirkus Rev* v82 no3 p288 F 1 2014
"The Lie". " Orange Prize winner . . . [Helen] Dunmore, whose prolific output ranges from grim realism . . . to spellbinding fantasy . . . offers the heartbreaking internal struggle of a young soldier adjusting to life at home after World War I. . . . From the first page, [Helen] Dunmore shares Daniel's inner life, building an increasing sense of dread while exposing the tragedy of great promise thwarted by forces beyond Daniel's control. Dunmore's crystalline prose is almost too good; the pain she describes is often unbearable to read, yet the emotional power resonates, and Daniel is impossible to forget."

REVIEW: *Libr J* v139 no2 p62 F 1 2014 Barbara Love
REVIEW: *Publ Wkly* v261 no7 p78 F 17 2014

REVIEW: *TLS* no5784 p20 F 7 2014 ALEX PEAKE-TOMKINSON
"The Lie" and "Wake." "The Orange Prize-winning author Helen Dunmore and the first-time novelist Anne Hope have both written novels that look back at the First World War from the vantage point of 1920. . . . Daniel Bramall, Dunmore's narrator in 'The Lie,' is a soldier who has returned to his native Cornwall from the trenches. . . . 'The Lie' is a substantial work, and Dunmore is able to crystallize tragedy in a simple sentence. . . . 'Wake' is unashamedly commercial fiction but not less affecting or skilful for that. Hope does make technical mistakes. . . . The novelist also occasionally resorts to banalities. . . . But given the breadth of Hope's ambition in this novel it seems churlish to dwell on them too long."

DUNN, GWENAVERE W.ed. State and Metropolitan Area Data Book 2013. See State and Metropolitan Area Data Book 2013

DUNN, MICHAEL. Two Hundred and Forty Years of New Zealand Painting; [by] Michael Dunn 279 p. 2012 David Bateman
1. Art—Biography 2. Art literature 3. New Zealand art 4. Painting—History 5. Painting, New Zealand
ISBN 9781869538040

SUMMARY: "This landmark book on New Zealand artists and their work was first published in 1971, extended to 1990 by art historian Michael Dunn and now again to 2010 by art historian, writer and lecturer Edward Hanfling. . . . This book is an . . . introduction to the development of New Zealand painting from its very beginning, and also the development of critical thinking about the work of New Zealand artists over the last 40 years." (Publisher's note)

REVIEW: *Burlington Mag* v155 no1326 p628 S 2013 MARK STOCKER

"240: Two Hundred and Forty Years of New Zealand Painting." "In the third edition, [author] Edward Hanfling examines developments between 1990 and 2010, hence '240' of the new title. [Previous editor authors Gil] Docking's and [Michael] Dunn's texts are unaltered, which necessarily compromises factual reliability and currency. . . . Hanfling's text, doubtless constrained by word limits, cannot explore individual artists in the same detail. . . . A point well made, yet excessive subjectivity potentially vitiates such a book as a reference or guide to the period."

DUNNE, EAMONN. Reading theory now; an ABC of good reading with J. Hillis Miller; [by] Eamonn Dunne xxxiii, 139 p. 2013 Bloomsbury

1. Criticism—United States 2. Critics 3. Derrida, Jacques, 1930-2004 4. LITERARY CRITICISM—Semiotics & Theory

ISBN 9781441115140 (paperback); 9781441174581 (hardback)

LC 2013-000140

SUMMARY: Written by Éamonn Dunne, this book "explores movements in critical thinking through a host of radical theorists, and to channel those movements through the work of one of the most influential proponents of critical interpretation in the world today, J. Hillis Miller. It enables its readers to see how and why theoretical models of reading are of use only in the practical event of reading literary and philosophical texts." (Publisher's note)

REVIEW: *Choice* v51 no4 p628-9 D 2013 C. E. O'Neill

"Reading Theory Now: An ABC of Good Reading With J. Hillis Miller." "[Author Éamonn] Dunne . . . presumes of his reader a broad knowledge of fiction and criticism atypical of that mastered by the average undergraduate English major. With a preface by Miller himself and an afterword by Julian Wolfreys, editor of 'The J. Hillis Miller Reader' (2005), Dunne's latest tribute to the writings of this friend and colleague of Jacques Derrida will be helpful to advanced scholars seeking an authoritative perspective on Miller's oeuvre. The annotated bibliography offers a concise summary of Miller's major works."

DUNO GOTTBERG, LUIS.ed. Haiti and the Americas. See Haiti and the Americas

DURAND, HALLIE. Mitchell goes bowling; [by] Hallie Durand 40 p. 2013 Candlewick Press

1. Bowling—Fiction 2. Bowling—Juvenile fiction 3. Bowling alleys—Fiction 4. Bowling alleys—Juvenile fiction 5. Fathers and sons—Fiction 6. Fathers and sons—Juvenile fiction 7. Picture books for children

ISBN 0763660493; 9780763660499

LC 2012-947730

SUMMARY: Written by Hallie Durand and illustrated by Tony Fucile, this children's book describes how "One Saturday, when Mitchell almost knocks down his dad, his dad catches him and puts him in the car. And when they step into the bowling alley, Mitchell feels right at home. Pizza! Giant crashing noises! Special shoes!" (Publisher's note)

REVIEW: *Bull Cent Child Books* v67 no1 p15-6 S 2013 E. B.

REVIEW: *Kirkus Rev* v81 no16 p31 Ag 15 2013

"Mitchell Goes Bowling." "Boisterous Mitchell and his resourceful dad are back in a hilarious father-and-son tale that celebrates working together with wit and warmth. . . . Here, the family is mixed-race; the mother works (possibly from home); and the dad is a full and actively engaged partner in the parenting process, showing patience, understanding, creativity and love. [Author Hallie] Durand and [illustrator Tony] Fucile are a winning combination, and their father/son bonding will leave readers in stitches."

REVIEW: *Publ Wkly* v260 no28 p168-9 Jl 15 2013

REVIEW: *SLJ* v59 no8 p72 Ag 2013 Janene Corbin

DURHAM, LESLIE ATKINS. Women's voices on American stages in the early twenty-first century; Sarah Ruhl and her contemporaries; [by] Leslie Atkins Durham 215 p. 2013 Palgrave Macmillan

1. American drama—21st century—History and criticism 2. American drama—Women authors—History and criticism 3. Dramatic criticism 4. Feminism and literature—United States—History—21st century

ISBN 1137287101; 9781137287106 (hbk.)

LC 2012-046506

SUMMARY: This book by Leslie Atkins Durham describes how playwright Sarah "Ruhl's popular, feminist plays are best appreciated when they are read in concert with the work of her contemporaries--Lisa Loomer, Diana Son, Joan Didion, Jenny Schwartz, Young Jean Lee, Kate Fodor, Yasmina Reza, Bathsheba Doran, Lynn Nottage, and Kia Corthron--whose writing also wrestles with the vexing issues facing Americans in the new century." (Publisher's note)

REVIEW: *Choice* v51 no1 p88-9 S 2013 J. Fisher

"Women's Voices on American Stages in the Early Twenty-First Century: Sarah Ruhl and Her Contemporaries." "In this well-focused, vividly written study focusing on the last decade, [Leslie Atkins] Durham . . . examines gender and sexuality, and the evolving nature of feminism. . . . Emphasizing as a touchstone the popular feminist plays of Sarah Ruhl--arguably the most critically acclaimed woman playwright of the new millennium--Durham broadens her view to reveal the achievements of such Ruhl peers as Lisa Loomer, Diana Son, Yasmina Reza, Lynn Nottage, and Kia Corthron. . . . The author has provided an essential analysis and opened the door for scholars to delve more deeply into the aesthetics and content arising within this latest movement in contemporary theater."

DURON, LORI. Raising my rainbow; adventures in raising a slightly effeminate, possibly gay,totally fabulous son; [by] Lori Duron 224 p. 2013 Crown Trade

1. Child psychology 2. Child rearing 3. Gender differences (Psychology) in children 4. Gender identity 5. Memoirs

ISBN 0770437729; 9780770437725

LC 2012-042444

SUMMARY: This book, by Lori Duron, is the author's "account of her and her family's adventures of distress and happiness raising a gender-creative son. . . . C.J. is gender variant or gender nonconforming, . . . whatever the term, Lori has a boy who likes girl stuff. . . . He floats on the gender-variation spectrum from super-macho-masculine on the left all the way to super-girly-feminine on the right." (Publisher's note)

REVIEW: *Kirkus Rev* v81 no13 p168 Jl 1 2013

REVIEW: *Libr J* v139 no4 p46 Mr 1 2014 Lisa N. Johnston

REVIEW: *N Y Times Book Rev* p26 F 2 2014 Lori Duron

"Raising My Rainbow: Adventures in Raising a Fabulous, Gender Creative Son." "[Author Lori Duron] has taken what started as a blog about raising a son who likes 'girl' things and turned it into a heartwarming, though wrenching, tale of slowly accepting her child's difference. . . . But what makes 'Raising My Rainbow' fresh and enjoyable is Duron's utter lack of pretension. . . . I did find myself wishing Duron, who lives in 'conservative and competitive Orange County, Calif.,' had dedicated more time to problems other than fashion."

REVIEW: *Publ Wkly* v260 no24 p58 Je 17 2013

DURS GRÜNBEIN; a companion; xiv, 259 p. 2013 De Gruyter

1. German poetry—History & criticism 2. German poets 3. Grünbein, Durs 4. Literature—History & criticism 5. Poets—Interviews

ISBN 9783110227949 (pbk. : acid-free paper)

LC 2012-050949

SUMMARY: Edited by Michael Eskin, Karen Leeder, Christopher Young and "Written by a line-up of international scholars, the volume presents highly readable and wide-ranging essays on Grünbein's substantial uvre, complemented by specially commissioned material and an interview with the poet. It covers the German and European traditions, memory and cityscapes, the natural sciences, death, love, the visual arts, and presence." (Publisher's note)

REVIEW: *TLS* no5781 p28 Ja 17 2014 BEN HUTCHINSON

"Durs Grünbein: A Companion." "Durs Grünbein is regularly cited as the most important contemporary German poet. . . . One of the many strengths of this 'Companion'--when did collections of essays become 'companions'?--is a due regard both for the historical context and for the particularity of Grünbein's oeuvre. . . . The companion concludes with an interview with the poet himself, in the course of which a theme implicit throughout the book becomes explicit: poems, Grünbein argues, create a kind of 'anti-time.' . . . However 'companionable' they may be, the essays gathered here offer consistently incisive insights into both the conditions and the creations of this exile."

DUTTA, SAURAV K. Statistical techniques for forensic accounting; understanding the theory and application of data analysis; [by] Saurav K. Dutta xix, 262 p. 2013 FT Press

1. Accounting literature 2. Correlation (Statistics) 3. Data analysis 4. Forensic accounting—United States 5. Statistics

ISBN 0133133818 (hbk.: alk. paper); 9780133133813 (hbk.: alk. paper)

LC 2013-009077

SUMMARY: This book on forensic accounting presents "statistical tools for identifying and evaluating potential fraud". Author Saurav K. Dutta "demonstrates how to explore data to identify red flags and discover knowledge in 'data rich, information poor' environments." Topics include "essential concepts of probability . . . how to sample data properly, and use regression to establish correlation." (Publisher's note)

REVIEW: *Choice* v51 no9 p1642-3 My 2014 R. Derstine

"Statistical Techniques for Forensic Accounting: Understanding the Theory and Application of Data Analysis". "Surprisingly, the first third . . . does not include a single formula, equation, or statistical graph. Instead, [Saurav K.] Dutta . . . presents an excellent review of the various types of financial frauds; offers numerous case examples; and discusses the roles played by government regulations, corporate governance, internal control, and professional organizations in dealing with financial fraud. The preface states practicing accountants will require no prior knowledge in probability and statistics. However, unless readers are well versed in the subject matter, they should be prepared to spend significant time studying the remainder of the book."

DÜWEL, JÖRN.ed. A Blessing in Disguise. See A Blessing in Disguise

DWAN, DAVID.ed. The Cambridge companion to Edmund Burke. See The Cambridge companion to Edmund Burke

DWORKIN, RONALD, 1931-2013. Religion without god; [by] Ronald Dworkin 192 p. 2013 Harvard University Press

1. Atheism 2. Freedom of religion 3. Philosophical literature 4. Religion—Philosophy

ISBN 9780674726826 (alk. paper)

LC 2013-020724

SUMMARY: In this book, author Richard Dworkin "argues that religious sentiment is pervasive and comes down to two things: wonder and meaning (the latter, he explains, is linked to morality) and that these aspects are objectively real and cannot be reduced to something more basic, whether that be the will of God or some sort of biological imperative. The third chapter . . . deals with freedom of religion from a constitutional point of view." (Library Journal)

REVIEW: *Booklist* v110 no3 p5 O 1 2013 Christopher McConnell

REVIEW: *Commonweal* v141 no3 p26-8 F 7 2014 Paul Horwitz

REVIEW: *Nation* v298 no9 p36-7 Mr 3 2014 MICHAEL ROSEN

"Religion Without God." "[A] marvelous little book. . . . [Ronald] Dworkin still wants to call his attitude 'religious' because, although he does not believe in the existence of God, he 'accepts the full, independent reality of value' and hence rejects the naturalistic view that nothing is real except what is revealed by the natural sciences or psychology. Yet if values exist as 'fully independent,' how can we have access to them? . . . Dworkin is always wonderfully clear and honest about what is involved in his position--it is part of what makes his book such a pleasure to read--and he concludes his discussion of the nature of value by explaining its limitations."

REVIEW: *New Repub* v244 no17 p60-3 O 21 2013 Moshe Halbertal

DYBEK, STUART, 1942-. Ecstatic cahoots; fifty short stories; [by] Stuart Dybek 208 p. 2014 Fararr, Straus & Giroux

1. American short stories 2. Nuns—Fiction 3. Short story (Literary form) 4. Supernatural 5. Trust
ISBN 0374280509; 9780374280505 (paperback)
LC 2013-033912

SUMMARY: This collection of short stories, by Stuart Dybek, "explores the human appetite for rapture and for trust. . . . There are crazed nuns hijacking streetcars, eerie adventures across frozen ponds, and a boy who is visited by a miniature bride and groom every night in his uncle's doomsday compound." The stories " target the friction between our need for ecstatic self-transcendence and our passionate longing for trust between lovers, friends, family, and even strangers." (Publisher's note)

REVIEW: *Atlantic* v313 no5 p42-4 Je 2014 Nathaniel Rich

"Ecstatic Cahoots: Fifty Short Stories" and "Paper Lantern: Love Stories". "A virtuosic and occasionally addling torrent of short fiction by one of the form's living masters. Technically these collections contain 59 short stories, but given the nature of [Stuart] Dybek's style, that number seems a gross understatement. . . . Dybek's general approach . . . is to string together distinct and apparently un related episodes under the heading of a single story, like a jeweler stringing a chain through different stones, some glittering and some dull, some exotic and some mundane, to create a necklace unlike any that has existed. Of the two new volumes, 'Paper Lantern' is the more substantial and more satisfying, with nearly every story longer than the stories collected in 'Ecstatic Cahoots'."

REVIEW: *Booklist* v110 no15 p22 Ap 1 2014 Donna Seaman

REVIEW: *Kirkus Rev* v82 no11 p104 Je 1 2014

REVIEW: *N Y Times Book Rev* p22 Ag 3 2014 DARIN STRAUSS

REVIEW: *Publ Wkly* v261 no17 p106 Ap 28 2014

DYBEK, STUART, 1942-. Paper lantern; love stories; [by] Stuart Dybek 207 p. 2014 Farrar, Straus and Giroux

1. American short stories 2. Infidelity (Couples) 3. Love stories 4. Short story (Literary form) 5. Social worker & client
ISBN 9780374146443 (hardcover)
LC 2013-034414

SUMMARY: This book, by Stuart Dybek, is a collection of short stories "with a common focus on the turmoils of romantic love. . . . An execution triggers the recollection of a theatrical romance; then a social worker falls for his own client; and lovers part as giddily, perhaps as hopelessly, as a kid trying to hang on to a boisterous kite. A flaming laboratory evokes a steamy midnight drive . . . and an eerily ringing phone becomes the telltale signature of a dark betrayal." (Publisher's note)

REVIEW: *Atlantic* v313 no5 p42-4 Je 2014 Nathaniel Rich

"Ecstatic Cahoots: Fifty Short Stories" and "Paper Lantern: Love Stories". "A virtuosic and occasionally addling torrent of short fiction by one of the form's living masters. Technically these collections contain 59 short stories, but given the nature of [Stuart] Dybek's style, that number seems a gross understatement. . . . Dybek's general approach . . . is to string together distinct and apparently un related episodes under the heading of a single story, like a jeweler stringing a chain through different stones, some glittering and some dull, some exotic and some mundane, to create a necklace unlike any that has existed. Of the two new volumes, 'Paper Lantern' is the more substantial and more satisfying, with nearly every story longer than the stories collected in 'Ecstatic Cahoots'."

REVIEW: *Booklist* v110 no15 p22 Ap 1 2014 Donna Seaman

REVIEW: *Kirkus Rev* v82 no11 p105 Je 1 2014

REVIEW: *N Y Times Book Rev* p22 Ag 3 2014 DARIN STRAUSS

REVIEW: *Publ Wkly* v261 no17 p106 Ap 28 2014

DYCK, ANDREW R.ed. Pro Marco Caelio. See Pro Marco Caelio

DYCKMAN, AME. Tea party rules; 40 p. 2013 Viking, published by Penguin Group

1. Animals—Infancy—Fiction 2. Bears—Fiction 3. Etiquette—Fiction 4. Parties—Fiction 5. Picture books for children 6. Tea—Fiction
ISBN 0670785016; 9780670785018 (hardcover)
LC 2012-046989

SUMMARY: In this children's picture book, by Ame Dyckman, illustrated by K. G. Campbell, "Cub discovers a backyard tea party--with cookies! He is just about to dig in when the hostess of the tea party shows up. And she has several strong opinions on how Tea Party must be played. Cub tries to follow her rules . . . but just how much can one bear take, even for cookies?" (Publisher's note)

REVIEW: *Booklist* v110 no4 p46 O 15 2013 Ann Kelley

"Tea Party Rules." "[Ame] Dyckman . . . and [K. G.] Campbell . . . are a winning pair, using their comedic chops to pace the story beautifully. Seeing Cub masquerading as stuffed, with feet sticking stiffly out and eyeballs wide, is laugh-out-loud funny. Campbell's soft sepia-marker-and-colored-pencil illustrations appear on creamy backgrounds, alternating humorous spots and detailed full-page spreads; the depictions of an unhappy bear ensure little ones are in on the joke. This battle of wills between two charmers hits just the right note."

REVIEW: *Kirkus Rev* v81 no18 p76 S 15 2013

REVIEW: *Publ Wkly* p48 Children's starred review annual 2013

REVIEW: *Publ Wkly* v260 no33 p64 Ag 19 2013

DYER, CHRISTOPHER, 1944-. A country merchant, 1495-1520; trading and farming at the end of the Middle Ages; [by] Christopher Dyer xiii, 256 p. 2012 Oxford University Press

1. Farmers—England—History—16th century—Case studies 2. Historical literature 3. Merchants—England—History—16th century—Case studies
ISBN 0199214247 (hbk.); 9780199214242 (hbk.)
LC 2012-006115

SUMMARY: This book "tells the story of John Heritage, a

wool merchant and grazier born about 1470 and . . . based mainly in Moreton on Marsh, a small town . . . in the English west midlands. Second, it reconstructs the contemporary landscape, economy, and society. . . . Lastly, it situates the evidence from Heritage's country within debates about the longer-term significance of the decades around 1500, often regarded as a crucial era of transition and change in England." (American Historical Review)

REVIEW: *Am Hist Rev* v119 no1 p235-6 F 2014 Chris Briggs

"A Country Merchant, 1495-1520: Trading and Farming at the End of the Middle Ages". "Remarkable. . . . [Christopher] Dyer draws from his painstaking and readable account of John Heritage and his world no simplistic or dramatic new thesis about the transition from feudalism to capitalism, or the causes of sixteenth-century economic dynamism. . . . Instead, he offers a multifaceted account of a set of complex changes that are interrelated in various ways and in which certain features demand emphasis, such as the importance of the peasantry's contribution and the resilience of community structures. This book is highly recommended to anyone interested in late medieval or early modern England, or indeed to anyone interested in why we make that traditional divide between period."

REVIEW: *Bus Hist Rev* v87 no2 p344-6 Summ 2013 Steven A. Epstein

REVIEW: *Choice* v50 no8 p1508 Ap 2013 J. J. Butt

REVIEW: *History* v98 no333 p777-8 D 2013 Paul Warde

REVIEW: *TLS* no5716 p24 O 19 2012 PAUL FREEDMAN

DYER, GEOFF. The Contest of the Century; The New Era of Competition With China—and How America Can Win; [by] Geoff Dyer 320 p. 2014 Random House Inc Knopf

1. Competition (Economics) 2. Political science literature 3. World politics—21st century

ISBN 0307960757; 9780307960757
LC 2013-037496

SUMMARY: This book, by Geoff A. Dyer, is an "analysis of the emerging competition between China and the United States. . . . This contest will take place in every arena: from control of the seas, where China's new navy is trying to ease the United States out of Asia and reassert its traditional leadership, to rewriting the rules of the global economy, with attempts to turn the renminbi into the predominant international currency, toppling the dominance of the U.S. dollar." (Publisher's note)

REVIEW: *Booklist* v110 no4 p3-4 O 15 2013 Vanessa Bush

REVIEW: *Choice* v51 no12 p2235 Ag 2014 D. Li

REVIEW: *Kirkus Rev* v82 no1 p50 Ja 1 2014

"The Contest of the Century: The New Era of Competition With China—and How America Can Win". "[Geoff] Dyer counsels that instead of reacting with the usual China-bashing, with all its thinly veiled racially tinged codes, the U.S. would do well to 'roll out the red carpet for Chinese investments that do not have clear national security implications,' becoming partners in a two-way economy rather than mere consumers. Somewhat more optimistic than Harry Dent Jr.'s 'The Demographic Cliff' (2013), insistent that the key to Western influence-shaping lies in economic housecleaning. All bets are on as to whether that can happen."

REVIEW: *N Y Rev Books* v61 no8 p34-6 My 8 2014 Ian Johnson

REVIEW: *Natl Rev* v65 no7 p43-4 Ap 21 2014 ARTHUR L. HERMAN

"The Contest of the Century: The New Era of Competition With China—And How America Can Win." "Geoff Dyer . . . aims to find a middle ground, and succeeds brilliantly. . . . Still, Dyer concludes convincingly, we can guide this rivalry to an end where the two countries respect each other's security interests and don't wreck the modern global system. . . . As Dyer skillfully shows, while growth has brought unprecedented prosperity and power, it has also exposed the Middle Kingdom to a new kind of vulnerability that comes with being part of a global system."

REVIEW: *New Yorker* v90 no5 p93-1 Mr 24 2014

"The Contest of the Century: The New Era of Competition With China and How America Can Win." "Assessing China's growing rivalry with the U.S., [author Geoff Dyer] does not subscribe to the idea of a 'linear transfer' power from the U.S. to China. Instead, he highlights three areas of competition: military superiority at sea, political influence in greater Asia, and the preferred global currency. . . . Dyer does not anticipate direct confrontation, but he thinks that the contest with China will come to define U.S. foreign policy, and that America's interests are best served by fiscal and military restraint."

REVIEW: *Publ Wkly* v260 no48 p46 N 25 2013

DYER, WAYNE W. I can see clearly now; [by] Wayne W. Dyer 2014 Hay House, Inc.

1. Counselors—United States—Biography 2. Memoirs 3. Motivation (Psychology) 4. Motivational speakers—United States—Biography

ISBN 9781401944032 (hardback)
LC 2013-022893

SUMMARY: In this memoir, "from some of his earliest childhood memories in the early 1940s to the present, [Wayne W.] Dyer takes readers on a nearly year-by-year trip through the events in his life that led him to write more than 40 books and undertake other projects related to self-development. Each action, he writes, often directed by a divine force, put him one step further on the path of becoming the man he knew he was meant to become." (Kirkus Reviews)

REVIEW: *Booklist* v110 no13 p3 Mr 1 2014 Ilene Cooper

REVIEW: *Kirkus Rev* v82 no1 p46 Ja 1 2014

"I Can See Clearly Now". "Self-empowerment is one key to success in life, and nowhere is this more evident than in [Wayne W.] Dyer's . . . rich unfolding of his life stories. . . . The author's reflections on the twists and turns of his authentic life reveal the power inherent in each of us to have the same joyful existence, though many of his pronouncements may be too far out there for many readers. . . . For devotees of both Dyer and self-help books, an inspirational account of the essence of the man behind Your Erroneous Zones and other self-help titles."

DZAMA, MARCEL.il. Momo. See Momo

DZINESA, GWINYAYI A.ed. Peacebuilding, power, and politics in Africa. See Peacebuilding, power, and politics in Africa

E

EAKIN, JAMIE CLOUD. Bead embroidery jewelry projects; design and construction, ideas and inspiration; [by] Jamie Cloud Eakin 160 p. 2013 Lark Crafts

1. Bead embroidery 2. Beadwork 3. Do-it-yourself literature 4. Jewelry design 5. Jewelry making

ISBN 9781454708155

LC 2013-009853

SUMMARY: This book by Jamie Cloud Eakin "begins with basics of design and construction and encourages the individual design process, including creative exercises. The designs are then grouped by necklace style, and the last three chapters cover earrings, pins, and bracelets. Each chapter begins with an explanation of the style of jewelry and basic\ techniques." (Booklist)

REVIEW: *Booklist* v110 no3 p13-4 O 1 2013 Rebecca Pfenning

"Bead Embroidery Jewelry Projects: Design and Construction, Ideas and Inspiration." "The book begins with basics of design and construction and encourages the individual design process, including creative exercises. The designs are then grouped by necklace style, and the last three chapters cover earrings, pins, and bracelets. . . . . Some of the projects are beautiful and elegant, like the classic 'super simplicity necklace,' pendant style, while some are fun and whimsical. Got a Vegas vacation coming up? There's a fun collar necklace just for that. There are plenty of diagrams and pictures, a techniques index, and tips scattered throughout. This book will be loved by jewelry makers looking to learn a new technique or try design."

EARLY AND MIDDLE WOODLAND LANDSCAPES OF THE SOUTHEAST; 336 p. 2013 University Press of Florida

1. Adena culture—Southern States 2. Anthropology literature 3. Excavations (Archaeology)—Southern States 4. Mound-builders—Southern States 5. Woodland culture—Southern States

ISBN 9780813044606 (alk. paper)

LC 2013-015098

SUMMARY: This essay collection, edited by Alice P. Wright and Edward R. Henry, "deals with the Early (1000-200 BCE) and Middle (200 BCE-600-800 CE) Woodland complexes of the American Southeast (a region south of the Ohio River and east of Arkansas and Louisiana), with an emphasis on their diverse physical landscapes." (Choice: Current Reviews for Academic Libraries)

REVIEW: *Choice* v51 no8 p1448-9 Ap 2014 P. J. O'Brien

"Early and Middle Woodland Landscapes of the Southeast". "The articles use both US and British views of landscape: the former focuses on rigorously empirical investigations of human-environment interaction, while the latter asks what are the myriad ways past people shaped, cognized, and dwelled in their worlds. . . . The book's specific audience is professional archaeologists or graduate students working east of the Rocky Mountains and, more generally, scholars interested in landscape studies."

EASTBERG, JOHN C. Layton's legacy. See Layton's legacy

EASTERLY, WILLIAM, 1957-. The Tyranny of Experts; Economists, Dictators, and the Forgotten Rights of the Poor; [by] William Easterly 416 p. 2014 Perseus Books Group

1. Development economics 2. Economic development 3. International economic assistance 4. Political science literature 5. Poverty reduction

ISBN 0465031250; 9780465031252

SUMMARY: In this book, William Easterly criticizes "the anti-poverty programs associated with both the United Nations and its political and private sector supporters. . . . He charges that to the extent anti-poverty programs intended for the developing sector rely on outside economic and technical expertise and top-down government action, they become authoritarian, anti-democratic and unlikely to succeed." He "offers the alternative of fostering greater human rights and increasing political freedom." (Kirkus Reviews)

REVIEW: *Choice* v51 no12 p2236 Ag 2014 E. P. Hoffman

REVIEW: *Economist* v411 no8884 p83 Ap 26 2014

REVIEW: *Kirkus Rev* v82 no2 p154 Ja 15 2014

"The Tyranny of Experts: Economists, Dictators, and the Forgotten Rights of the Poor". "a scathing assault on the anti-poverty programs associated with both the United Nations and its political and private sector supporters. a scathing assault on the anti-poverty programs associated with both the United Nations and its political and private sector supporters. . . . He provides a broader historical perspective on especially African countries, demonstrating how the history of slavery still influences current politics. The author offers the alternative of fostering greater human rights and increasing political freedom. A sharply written polemic intended to stir up debate about the aims of global anti-poverty campaigns."

REVIEW: *Libr J* v139 no4 p97 Mr 1 2014 Caroline Geck

REVIEW: *N Y Rev Books* v61 no11 p28-30 Je 19 2014 David Rieff

"The Tyranny of Experts: Economists, Dictators, and the Forgotten Rights of the Poor." "It is one of the great merits of [author William] Easterly's book that he documents in great and convincing detail the tyrannical and repressive record not just of Ethiopia but of other regimes that have long been and remain the darlings of the development world. . . . Easterly is a fine polemicist, but . . . his rhetoric gets the better of him. . . . Easterly may well be correct, but even assuming he is, this hardly justifies his claim that over the long term autocracy and successful economic growth and poverty reduction can never go hand in hand."

REVIEW: *N Y Times Book Rev* p20 Ap 20 2014 HOWARD W. FRENCH

REVIEW: *Publ Wkly* v261 no1 p46 Ja 6 2014

EATON, MAXWELL. Okay, Andy; [by] Maxwell Eaton 96 p. 2014 Blue Apple Books

1. Alligators—Fiction 2. Animals—Infancy—Fiction 3. Coyote—Fiction 4. Friendship—Fiction 5. Humorous stories 6. JUVENILE FICTION—Humorous Stories 7. JUVENILE FICTION—Social Issues—Friendship

ISBN 9781609053505 (hardback)

LC 2013-043465

SUMMARY: In this children's book, "Andy and Preston are friends; Andy, the lime-green alligator, is the straight man, sober and easily annoyed, while Preston, a beige animal (whose species is never quite defined), is buoyantly enthusiastic and energetic. Their friendship plays off the combination of these archetypal traits as the duo meander about in their forest home looking for a rogue rabbit, learning about patience and identifying other animals' sounds." (Kirkus Reviews)

REVIEW: *Kirkus Rev* v82 no2 p218 Ja 15 2014

"Okay, Andy". "A silly buddy story about Andy the alligator and his mammalian friend Preston plods somewhat aimlessly along through three chapters of gentle, simple adventures. . . . Simple heavy lines, oversized panels and word balloons make this easy for young readers to follow. The slow-moving pace, though dotted with some bursts of humor, doesn't quite do enough to propel the action, though. With most pages containing a single panel with fewer than a half-dozen words, this offering may help burgeoning readers gain confidence in finishing a book quickly; however with many other, similar series . . . this may be passed over for more recognizable and lively selections."

REVIEW: *Publ Wkly* v260 no49 p87 D 2 2013

EAVES, WILL. The absent therapist; [by] Will Eaves 2014 CB Editions

1. Conversation 2. Everyday life 3. Experimental literature 4. Monologue 5. Parents—Death
ISBN 9781909585003 paperback

SUMMARY: "Will Eaves has written novels--but also poetry. And here, with 'The Absent Therapist,' he seems to aim (and reside) somewhere between the two. These are short narratives, some just one line long, nothing over a page and a half; snapshots, overheard conversations, different voices huddling in around one another." (Off the Tracks)

REVIEW: *TLS* no5785 p20 F 14 2014 ALISON KELLY

"The Absent Therapist." "The first character we meet in this polyvocal work is a whippet fancier with a wry sense of humour and a sentimental streak. . . . In 'The Absent Therapist' [author Will] Eaves . . . moves into more experimental ground. The death of a parent here is addressed through snippets of monologue separated by fragments from many speakers. . . . The variety and interplay is entertaining, up to a point, but it takes a diligent reader to hold on to the threads of the discrete narratives. . . . Perhaps the ideal reader of Eaves's book is a sort of absent therapist, too: attentive, receptive, neutral."

EBBELER, JEFF.il. Arlo Rolled. See Pearson, S.

EBNER, MICHAEL. All the Talk Is Dead; [by] Michael Ebner 234 p. 2009 CreateSpace Independent Publishing Platform

1. Bands (Musical groups)—Fiction 2. Death—Fiction 3. Fame—Fiction 4. Humorous stories 5. Musicians—Fiction
ISBN 1448623847; 9781448623846

SUMMARY: In this book by Michael Ebner, "unable to get a recording contract, Joel and Wade hatch a scheme: They'll go to New York, where they'll fake Joel's death and turn that tragedy into a launch pad for their music. Once the deed is done, Joel travels to Montreal, where he takes on an assumed name. Time passes, and Joel hears nothing from Wade. Then, one day, he turns on the radio and hears one of his songs being played as part of a tribute album put together in his memory." (Kirkus Reviews)

REVIEW: *Kirkus Rev* v81 no14 p64 Jl 15 2013

REVIEW: *Kirkus Rev* p15-7 D 15 2013 supplemet best books 2013

"All the Talk Is Dead". " The ensuing complications . . . humorously expose the dark underbelly of fame in the music business. The premise isn't entirely original, and the machinations of how Joel and Wade pull off their scam are a little on the sketchy side, but Joel's misadventures in three different cities are hilariously rendered. He and Wade fit into the pantheon of great losers, the author having a Charles Portis-like gift for writing about dim bulbs without condescending to them. The book's filled with laugh-out-loud lines and dialogue, more than compensating for any flaws in terms of story logic or narrative cohesion, making for a memorable trip through the demimonde of wannabe rock stars."

REVIEW: *Kirkus Rev* v81 no13 p351 Jl 1 2013

ECHENOZ, JEAN. 1914; a novel; 128 p. 2013 The New Press

1. Brothers—Fiction 2. Love stories 3. War stories 4. World War, 1914-1918—France—Fiction 5. World War, 1914-1918—Veterans—Fiction
ISBN 9781595589118 (pbk. : alk. paper)
LC 2013-013990

SUMMARY: This book by Jean Echenoz is "about two brothers who go to war and the woman they leave behind. Young Anthime has previously only existed in the shadow of his charismatic older brother Charles, but the losses he sustains in the war permanently change how he views both himself and the life he's led. Meanwhile, Blanche, the woman both brothers love, waits to discover whether either will be coming home to her." (Library Journal)

REVIEW: *Bookforum* v20 no5 p33 F/Mr 2014 GARY INDIANA

"1914." "In several recent novels the succinct, startling prose of Jean Echenoz has achieved the condition of a highly durable, transparent membrane. . . . As a response to the brutal ugliness of the world's indifferent violence, however, the book is perfect. . . . Echenoz's nod to the powerlessness of ordinary people caught in the first great modern cataclysm is a veritable monument to human dignity. . . . For those about to be bombarded by a year of patriotic drivel, lachrymose valediction, and militaristic brainlessness, Echenoz's little novel should provide a refreshing mental douche."

REVIEW: *Kirkus Rev* v81 no19 p104 O 1 2013

REVIEW: *Libr J* v138 no18 p82 N 1 2013 Mara Bandy

REVIEW: *N Y Times Book Rev* p20 Ja 26 2014 MAX BYRD

REVIEW: *New Yorker* v90 no9 p105-1 Ap 21 2014

ECKERSLEY, ROBYN. Globalization and the environment. See Christoff, P.

ECKMAN, EDIE. Connect-the-shapes crochet motifs; [by] Edie Eckman 272 p. 2012 Storey Publishing

1. Crocheting 2. Crocheting—Patterns 3. Do-it-yourself literature 4. Handicraft 5. Shapes
ISBN 9781603429733 (hardcover with concealed wire-o : alk. paper)
LC 2012-013934

SUMMARY: Author Edie Eckman presents "a book that

teaches 100 original motif designs and a variety of techniques to join them. The emphasis is squarely on motifs; only a few patterns are included. Each motif, gathered in 'families' of grannies, chains, clusters, flowers, swirls, radials and more, is shown in written directions, charted, and in full-color illustrations." (Publishers Weekly)

REVIEW: *Booklist* v110 no8 p14 D 15 2013 Brad Hooper Donna Seaman

"The Complete Photo Guide to Making Metal Jewelry," "Connect the Shapes Crochet Motifs: Creative Techniques for Joining Motifs of All Shapes," and "Journal Your Way: Designing and Using Handmade Books." "If any crafter has reservations about learning to make metal jewelry, [John] Sartin knocks those reservations out of the water in a very savvy approach to the subject. . . . This is smart publishing: a spiral-bound pattern and instructional book that actually lies flat, so that avid needleworkers can practice while reading instructions. . . . [Gwen] Diehn teaches readers how to create the blank book most suited to one's needs through a series of questions and selections from eight different personal journals."

REVIEW: *Booklist* v109 no8 p15 D 15 2012 Barbara Jacobs

REVIEW: *Libr J* v137 no17 p78-9 O 15 2012 NANETTE DONOHUE

ECONOMICS AND YOUTH VIOLENCE; crime, disadvantage, and community; 2013 NYU Press

1. Crime—Economic aspects 2. Social science literature 3. Violence—Economic aspects 4. Violent crimes 5. Youth violence

ISBN 9780814760598 (pb); 9780814789308 (hardback)
LC 2013-001059

SUMMARY: This book, edited by Richard Rosenfeld, Mark Edberg, Xiangming Fang, and Curtis S. Florence, "provides a . . . new perspective on [youth violence.] . . . Pinpointing the economic factors that are most important, the editors and contributors in this volume explore how different kinds of economic issues impact children, adolescents, and their families, schools, and communities." (Publisher's note)

REVIEW: *Choice* v51 no6 p1060 F 2014 S. Chaudhuri

"Economics and Youth Violence: Crime, Disadvantage, and Community." "[The] editors revolutionize the economics of youth and violence literature by bringing together expertly written contributions that focus on the relationship between macroeconomic factors (inflation, unemployment, poverty rate, income inequality) and the propensity of youth for violent crime. . . . Apart from this major shift in thinking, this volume is also important in providing economic perspectives on why youth from racial minority backgrounds are unfairly profiled. . . . A timely, must-read volume for students, faculty, and policy makers whose focus is sociology, the economics of inequality, public policy, and related disciplines."

ECONOMOU, GEORGE.tr. Complete Plus. See Cavafy, C.

EDBERG, MARK.ed. Economics and youth violence. See Economics and youth violence

EDDLEMAN, PEGGY. Sky jumpers; [by] Peggy Eddleman 288 p. 2013 Random House

1. Children's stories 2. Dystopias 3. Inventions—Fiction 4. Science fiction 5. Technological innovations—Fiction

ISBN 9780307981271
LC 2012-027037

SUMMARY: In this children's book by Peggy Eddleman, "Twelve-year-old Hope lives in White Rock, a town of inventors struggling to recover from the green bombs of World War III. But Hope is terrible at inventing and would much rather sneak off to cliff dive into the Bomb's Breath--the deadly band of compressed air that covers the crater left by the bombs--than fail at yet another invention." (Publisher's note)

REVIEW: *Bull Cent Child Books* v67 no3 p149-50 N 2013 E. B.

"Sky Jumpers." " When bandits hold the community hostage for its supply of antibiotics, Hope and her friends sneak out and make their way through a snow storm to bring in an armed militia from nearby Browning and save the day. The politics behind the war and the science behind the bombs and toxic air are given fairly short shrift, and the title is notably stronger on action scenes than character development. Although this is the first entry in a projected series, the bandit problem is so tidily wrapped up by the story's end that, but for the escape of one villain, it seems complete in one volume."

REVIEW: *Kirkus Rev* v81 no13 p240 Jl 1 2013

REVIEW: *Publ Wkly* v260 no32 p60 Ag 12 2013

REVIEW: *SLJ* v60 no1 p59 Ja 2014 Joan Kindig

REVIEW: *SLJ* v59 no10 p1 O 2013 Sabrina Carnesi

EDGE, CHRISTOPHER. Twelve minutes to midnight; [by] Christopher Edge 256 p. 2014 Albert Whitman & Company

1. Authorship—Fiction 2. Mystery and detective stories 3. Orphans—Fiction 4. Psychiatric hospitals—Fiction 5. Publishers and publishing—Fiction 6. Supernatural—Fiction

ISBN 080758133X; 9780807581339
LC 2013-029481

SUMMARY: In this book, by Christopher Edge, "Penelope Tredwell is the . . . orphan heiress of Victorian Britain's best-selling magazine, the Penny Dreadful. Her . . . tales–concealed under the pen name Montgomery Finch–are gripping the public. One day she receives a letter from the governor of the Bedlam madhouse requesting Finch's help to investigate the asylum's strange goings-on. Every night at precisely twelve minutes to midnight, the inmates all begin feverishly writing-incoherent ramblings." (Publisher's note)

REVIEW: *Booklist* v110 no12 p75 F 15 2014 Francisca Goldsmith

REVIEW: *Bull Cent Child Books* v67 no8 p402-3 Ap 2014 K. Q. G.

"Twelve Minutes to Midnight". "Readers will catch on relatively quickly that the inmates are describing events from the modern era, but the mystery is still compelling. . . .Unfortunately, a dream sequence in the last few chapters moves the book jarringly from paranormal thriller to an almost meta-fantasy, and the ultimate solution of waking up a comatose, sleeping population of London by telling the sleepers to 'fight back' against the future seen in their dreams seems oddly pointless, especially when the future in this case has indeed been written. Still, the descriptions of Victorian London are vivid without being overwhelming, and the storytelling has a direct, focused clip, making this a possible candidate for readers just delving into historical mysteries."

REVIEW: *Kirkus Rev* v82 no2 p123 Ja 15 2014

REVIEW: *SLJ* v60 no8 p108 Ag 2014

REVIEW: *Voice of Youth Advocates* v36 no6 p57-8 F 2014 Ed Goldberg

THE EDGE OF THE PRECIPICE; why read literature in the digital age?; 232 p. 2013 McGill Queens Univ

1. Books & reading 2. Electronic books 3. Literature & the Internet 4. Social science literature 5. Technology & civilization

ISBN 0773541780; 9780773541788

SUMMARY: This book "addresses questions around the future of print literature in the electronic age. For instance, studies show that young people today have interests that compete with reading--immersing oneself in a novel seems old hat. They reveal also that digital reading is distracting and that readers spend less time investigating complex texts. While the Internet provides easy access to information, it offers essentially unfiltered knowledge rather than meaning." (Library Journal)

REVIEW: *Choice* v51 no7 p1206-7 Mr 2014 C. Johanningsmeier

"The Edge of the Precipice: Why Read Literature in the Digital Age?" "A collection of 15 essays by a somewhat diverse group of writers (only one appears to be a digital native) who address this general topic. Most contributors contend a great deal has been lost by the advent of non-paper texts and the Internet, and all assert that sustained reading of literature (never fully defined) has enormous benefits. Some essays, notably those by [Paul] Socken, Michael Austin, Drew Nelles, and Sven Birkerts, offer extremely thought-provoking analyses; a good number, though, are rather desultory and offer nothing new to the larger conversation."

REVIEW: *Libr J* v138 no18 p86 N 1 2013 David Keymer

REVIEW: *Quill Quire* v79 no7 p30-1 S 2013 Alex Good

EDGERTON, CLYDE. The night train; a novel; [by] Clyde Edgerton 215 2011 Little, Brown and Company

1. African Americans—North Carolina 2. Boys 3. Friendship 4. Historical fiction 5. Musicians

ISBN 978-0-316-11759-3; 0-316-11759-5

LC 2010--41546

SUMMARY: In this book set "in 1963, at the age of 17, Dwayne Hallston discovers James Brown and wants to perform just like him. His band, the Amazing Rumblers, studies and rehearses Brown's Live at the Apollo album in the storage room of his father's shop in their small North Carolina town. Meanwhile, Dwayne's forbidden black friend Larry--aspiring to play piano like Thelonius Monk--apprentices to a jazz musician called the Bleeder. His mother hopes music will allow him to escape the South." (Publisher's note)

REVIEW: *Booklist* v110 no9/10 p42 Ja 1 2014 DAVID WRIGHT

"To Hell and Back," "The Wishbones," and "The Night Train." "Tom Perrotta captures my neighbor's vibe perfectly in his first novel, 'The Wishbones'. . . . Dave's stairway to purgatory is hilarious and familiar to pretty much everyone who isn't a rock star. . . . [James] Brown's gargantuan presence looms large over two novels that deal with the universality of music. In Clive Edgerton's 'The Night Train,' it is young Dwayne's all-consuming desire to be James Brown that lures him across the color line in 1963 North Carolina. . . . 'To Hell and Back' is truly irresistible. Imagine being stuck in an elevator with Mr. [Meat] Loaf while he tells you about the amazing, tragicomic train wreck that is his life. You can't look away. With 17 brain concussions to his name. Meat proves to be every bit the poster child for testosterone poisoning that you'd expect."

REVIEW: *Libr J* v136 no19 p42 N 15 2011 Juleigh Muirhead Clark

EDGINGTON, SUSAN B.tr. The Chanson d'Antioche. See The Chanson d'Antioche

EDIN, KATHRYN. Doing the best I can; fatherhood in the inner city; [by] Kathryn Edin x, 284 p. 2013 University of California Press

1. Fatherhood—United States 2. Poor children—United States 3. Single fathers—United States 4. Social science literature 5. Unmarried fathers—United States

ISBN 0520274067 (cloth: alk. paper); 9780520274068 (cloth: alk. paper)

LC 2012-030147

SUMMARY: This book is "a study of unwed urban fathers. . . . Based on 110 interviews conducted in Camden, NJ, and Philadelphia, the book offers an . . . examination of how these men view children, families, romantic relationships, and the world around them. . . . The authors highlight patterns, set the interviews against trends, and contrast their subjects with two-dimensional portraits in the media." (Library Journal)

REVIEW: *Choice* v51 no3 p556 N 2013 B. Weston

REVIEW: *Commonweal* v141 no4 p37-8 F 21 2014 Eve Tushnet

"Doing the Best I Can: Fatherhood in the Inner City". "'Doing the Best I Can' sometimes conveys exasperation at the way the men it profiles stumble into parenthood and sacrifice their first-chance family for the sake of second chances elsewhere, but it's impossible to finish the book without feeling love, sympathy, and admiration for many of these men. In context, the title is harsher than it may appear: 'Doing the best I can' means helping out the woman, who remains the primary financial provider, the parent of first response and last resort. But the men interviewed here are struggling, with virtually no models and little support, to do better than they did before—and better than their own fathers."

THE EDINBURGH COMPANION TO SIR WALTER SCOTT; 240 p. 2012 Edinburgh University Press

1. English literature—Scottish authors 2. Literary critiques 3. Romanticism in literature 4. Scott, Walter, Sir, 1771-1832 5. Scottish literature—History & criticism

ISBN 0748641300; 9780748641307

SUMMARY: This book on Sir Walter Scott offers "12 chapters . . . thematically, chronologically, and sequentially arranged. Chapters on Scott's early antiquarianism, book culture, and border ballads prepare the way for considerations of narrative poems and the Jacobite novels. . . . Other chapters consider political economy, the underestimated later novels, and 'afterlives,' the last a . . . look at Scott's survival and the commercialization of the 'Scott brand.'" (Choice: Current Reviews for Academic Libraries)

REVIEW: *Choice* v50 no7 p1243-4 Mr 2013 J. Walker

"The Edinburgh Companion to Sir Walter Scott." "This fresh, important collection comprises 12 chapters (most by US and Scots critics), thematically, chronologically, and sequentially arranged. Chapters on Scott's early antiquarianism, book culture, and border ballads prepare the way for considerations of narrative poems and the Jacobite novels. . . . Other chapters consider political economy, the underestimated later novels, and 'afterlives,' the last an entertaining look at Scott's survival and the commercialization of the 'Scott brand,' especially through 'Ivanhoe.' Excellent notes and bibliography. Summing Up: Recommended."

THE EDINBURGH EDITION OF THE WAVERLEY NOVELS; 1995 Edinburgh University Press Columbia University Press

1. Charles Edward, Prince, grandson of James II, King of England, 1720-1788 2. Historical fiction 3. Jacobites 4. Monasteries 5. Scotland—Fiction

ISBN 0231103964 (Columbia ed. : v. 3); 0231103980 (Columbia ed. : v. 16); 023110572X (Columbia ed. : v. 7a); 023110720X (v. 17); 0748605355 (Edinburgh ed. : v. 16); 0748605371 (Edinburgh ed. : v. 3); 0748605681 (v. 2); 0748605711 (Edinburgh ed. : v. 7a); 0748605738 (v. 8); 0748605746 (v. 9); 0748605754 (v. 10); 0748605762 (v. 12); 0748605770 (v. 13 : acid-free paper); 0748605797 (v. 15); 0748605843 (v. 20); 0748605851 (v. 21); 074860586X (v. 22)

LC 9522-9429

SUMMARY: This thirty-volume edition of Walter Scott's "Waverley" novels, which also includes a volume of short stories, presents "a text based on a reconsideration of the first printed editions, as better serving the author's original conception. It reproduces for a new readership something like the version of each novel that captivated its first readers." (Times Literary Supplement)

REVIEW: *TLS* no5765 p3-5 S 27 2013 KATHRYN SUTHERLAND

"The Edinburgh Edition of the Waverly Novels." "The EEWN is a passionately argued edition that refuses to shy away from the critical work that defines editing at its best. Corporately and individually, the editors have set and achieved demanding standards. Their minute scrutiny of textual states does not lie inert in synoptic apparatus, but is woven into cogent expositions of [Walter] Scott's remarkable feats of composition. Shining steady light on the organic imagination at work within those mechanical relations, the Edinburgh Edition of the Waverley novels vigorously rebuts Thomas Carlyle' s verdict on the man who was a 'Novel-manufactory'. Scott emerges once again as a writer of heroic stature."

THE EDINBURGH HISTORY OF THE BOOK IN SCOTLAND; Enlightenment and Expansion 1707-1800; 2011 Columbia Univ Pr

1. Books & reading—History—18th century 2. Enlightenment—Scotland 3. Historical literature 4. Publishers & publishing—Scotland—History 5. Scotland—History—18th century

ISBN 0748619127; 9780748619122

SUMMARY: This book, the second in a "four-volume history of the book in Scotland," covers the period from 1707 to 1800. Particular focus is given to a "reappraisal of the publication and reception of les philosophes écossais in relation to the developing Scottish book trade. Literacy, reading, subscription and circulating libraries, the popular press, and a range of genres, from the novel . . . to writing on archaeology, medicine . . . and politics are all given attention." (Times Literary Supplement)

REVIEW: *TLS* no5743 p24 Ap 26 2013 JAMES RAVEN

"The Edinburgh History of the Book in Scotland: Enlightenment and Expansion 1707-1800." "The latest instalment of this four-volume history of the book in Scotland is a significant accomplishment. . . . [It] is full of benchmark essays by evident authorities. Like other multi-author national histories of the book, it is uneven in its structure, with an effective but somewhat eccentric telescoping from thematic accounts to short case studies. Forty contributors provide a varied collection of essays that together form a more generous and satisfying history than do many equivalent projects."

EDINGER, MONICA. Africa is my home; 64 p. 2013 Candlewick Press

1. Adams, John Quincy, 1767-1848 2. Amistad mutiny 3. Child slaves 4. Historical fiction 5. Middle passage (Slave trade)

ISBN 0763650382; 9780763650384

LC 2012-947752

SUMMARY: In author Monica Edinger's book, "when a drought hits her homeland in Sierra Leone, nine-year-old Magulu is sold as a pawn by her father. But before she can work off her debt, an unthinkable chain of events unfolds: a capture by slave traders . . . where she and three other children are sold and taken aboard the Amistad; a mutiny aboard ship; a trial in New Haven that eventually goes all the way to the Supreme Court and is argued in the Africans' favor by John Quincy Adams." (Publisher's note)

REVIEW: *Horn Book Magazine* v89 no6 p90-1 N/D 2013 ANITA L. BURKAM

"Africa Is My Home: A Child of the Amistad". "[Monica] Edinger avoids sensationalism without underselling the more disturbing parts of the story (the horrors of the Middle Passage, for instance, are evoked in six stark sentences on a black double-page spread). The uncertainty of Margru's situation and the peril faced by Cinque and the other mutineers keep tension high. [Robert] Byrd's pen-and-watercolor illustrations use detailed but informal lines to both embellish and extend the story. . . . An author's note describes Edinger's motivation in seeking out Margru's story and traces some of her research methods, but it is her skill in imagining Margru's life from those original sources that opens up this episode in history to young readers."

EDISON, DAVID. The waking engine; [by] David Edison 400 p. 2014 Tor Books

1. Death—Fiction 2. FICTION—Fantasy—General 3. Future life—Fiction 4. Reincarnation 5. Secrecy—Fiction

ISBN 9780765334862 (hardback)

LC 2013-028407

SUMMARY: In this book, "the late Cooper, once of New

York City, is surprised to find death a temporary condition, each life a brief stop in a nearly endless chain of existence. He awakens from his brief demise in the vast and ancient City Unspoken, a community dominated by cruel elites, where a fortunate few may perhaps find total oblivion. Marooned in the decaying city . . . Cooper, who has only died once, finds himself a curiosity in a realm where death itself rarely offers final release." (Publishers Weekly)

REVIEW: *Booklist* v110 no8 p30 D 15 2013 David Pitt

REVIEW: *Kirkus Rev* v81 no24 p181 D 15 2013

"The Waking Engine". "[David] Edison's debut is an extraordinary and bewildering fantasy. . . . Even a New Yorker like Cooper finds this bizarre; worse, he doesn't remember dying or any previous lives, and he seems to be the only one in the city with a navel. Edison puts an impressive imagination to work and writes with clarity and precision. But with almost uniformly secretive main characters, the narrative lacks cohesion and drive, and the result, while often dazzling, offers little by way of involvement. A magic carpet ride—but the carpet just hovers."

REVIEW: *Publ Wkly* v260 no51 p43 D 16 2013

EDLICH-MUTH, MIRIAM. Malory and his European contemporaries; adapting late medieval Arthurian romance collections; [by] Miriam Edlich-Muth 186 p. 2014 D.S. Brewer

1. Arthurian romances—Adaptations—History and criticism 2. Literature—History & criticism 3. Literature, Medieval—History and criticism
ISBN 1843843676; 9781843843672
LC 2014-381183

SUMMARY: Written by Miriam Edlich-Muth, "This study re-evaluates Malory's 'Morte Darthur' and four broadly contemporary European romance collections, including Jean Gonnot's French BN.fr.112 manuscript, Ulrich Fuetrer's 'German Buch der Abenteuer,' the Dutch 'Lancelot Compilation,' and the Italian 'Tavola Ritonda,' in the context of this adaptive process." (Publisher's note)

REVIEW: *Choice* v52 no2 p255 O 2014 A. L. Kaufman

REVIEW: *TLS* no5797 p13 My 9 2014 CAROLYNE LARRINGTON

"Le Morte Darthur" and "Malory and His European Contemporaries." "[Editor P. J. C.] Field has, in Volume One, produced a wonderfully clean reading text. All the manuscript and print variants, and his comments about editorial choices, are contained in the second volume. The discussion of the different witnesses to the text yields fascinating insights into compositors' practice at the very birth of English printing. . . . All over late medieval Europe—in the Netherlands, Italy, Germany and France—as Miriam Edlich-Muth's new study 'Malory and His European Contemporaries' shows, writers or teams of writers were putting together large Arthurian compendia for their patrons."

EDMONDS, ANTONY. Jane Austen's Worthing; The Real Sandition; [by] Antony Edmonds 128 p. 2014 Casemate Pub & Book Dist Llc

1. Austen, Jane, 1775-1817 2. Cities & towns in literature 3. English literature—19th century 4. Literature—History & criticism 5. Seaside resorts in literature 6. Worthing (England)
ISBN 1445619733; 9781445619736

SUMMARY: Written by Antony Edmonds, "This book gives a detailed account of the town Jane Austen knew in 1805, and explores in full the close links between Sanditon and early Worthing. . . . Taking the first twenty-five years of the nineteenth century as his time frame, the author explains how Worthing changed and developed during this period, and paints vivid pictures of some of the people associated with the town." (Publisher's note)

REVIEW: *TLS* no5780 p12 Ja 10 2014 E. J. CLERY

"Jane Austen's Worthing: The Real Sanditon." "Worthing is not the real Sanditon. Having made the claim, and shown that Jane Austen visited the place in the autumn of 1805, [author] Antony Edmonds is forced to confess problems and exceptions until the reader grows weary and fretful: 'we would, in any case, not expect resemblances to be exact.' Just so. . . . Our guide to Worthing has no feel either for Austen's writing or for the modernizing excitements of Regency England. We are in his debt, however, for he has disinterred from the archive two historical figures who really might have something to do with 'Sanditon.'"

EDMONDSON, JACQUELINE.ed. Music in American life. See Music in American life

EDMONDSON, PAUL.ed. Shakespeare beyond doubt. See Shakespeare beyond doubt

EDMUNDS, KIRSTIE.il. Bruno and Lulu's playground adventures. See Lakin, P.

EDWARDS, JANET. Earth star; [by] Janet Edwards 360 p. 2014 Pyr, an imprint of Prometheus Books

1. Children with disabilities—Abuse of—Fiction 2. Extraterrestrial life—Fiction 3. Love stories 4. Science fiction 5. Women archaeologists—Fiction
ISBN 1616148977; 9781616148973 (hardback)
LC 2013-040057

SUMMARY: In this sequel to Janet Edwards's "Earth Girl," "it's 2789. People portal between planets in seconds, often many times per day—except the Handicapped, like Jarra, whose immune systems can survive only on Earth. . . . She plans to continue studying prehistory by excavating sites of long-dead cities. But before the next dig begins, Jarra and boyfriend Fian are whisked off to a military base and inexplicably sworn in as officers. An unidentified alien sphere is hovering above Africa." (Kirkus Reviews)

REVIEW: *Booklist* v110 no15 p83 Ap 1 2014 Daniel Kraus

REVIEW: *Kirkus Rev* v82 no3 p254 F 1 2014

"Earth Star". "This far-future science-fiction sequel skips tired genre tropes to offer a fresh and thrilling adventure about hazardous archaeological excavation, a mystery in the sky and a potential threat to all of humanity. . . . Jarra's skills, intelligence and courage are both exciting and believable. . . . Explosions, serious injuries, death and suspense mesh with fizzy romance that includes some sparkling gender-role reversal. Nitty-gritty archaeology details are vivid, and easy slang creates color. . . . [Janet] Edwards shows that speculative fiction needn't be dystopic, conspiracy-filled or love-triangled to be riveting and satisfying."

REVIEW: *SLJ* v60 no5 p128 My 2014 Stephanie DeVincentis

EDWARDS, LESLIE. The natural communities of Georgia; [by] Leslie Edwards xvii, 675 p. 2013 University of Georgia Press

1. Biodiversity conservation—Georgia 2. Biotic communities—Georgia 3. Ecological regions—Georgia 4. Environmental literature 5. Landscape protection—Georgia 6. Natural history—Georgia 7. Nature conservation—Georgia
ISBN 0820330213 (hardcover : alk. paper); 9780820330211 (hardcover : alk. paper)
LC 2012-008402

SUMMARY: This book by Leslie Edwards, Jonathan Ambrose, and L. Katherine Kirkman "presents a comprehensive overview of the state's natural landscapes, providing an ecological context to enhance understanding of this region's natural history. . . . Within Georgia's five major ecoregions the editors identify and describe a total of sixty-six natural communities." (Publisher's note)

REVIEW: *Choice* v51 no2 p289-90 O 2013 C. S. McCoy

"The Natural Communities of Georgia." "[Authors Leslie] Edwards . . . , [Jonathan] Ambrose . . . , and [L. Katherine] Kirkman . . . wrote this book as a tribute to Charles Wharton, a noted naturalist/conservationist. . . . The work showcases Georgia's natural heritage by exploring the native plants and animals in the Blue Ridge, Cumberland Plateau, Piedmont, coastal plain, and maritime ecosystems. . . . Better understanding Georgia's biological diversity, the problems caused by population growth and climate change, and the effects of habitat disturbance prepares readers for their journey through the five major ecosystems. . . . Excellent color pictures give one the feeling of being part of a natural history tour through each area."

EDWARDS, MICHELLE. Max makes a cake; [by] Michelle Edwards 32 p. 2014 Random House

1. Cake—Fiction 2. Children's stories 3. Family life—Fiction 4. Matzos—Fiction 5. Passover—Fiction
ISBN 9780375971648 (library edition); 9780449814314 (jacketed hardcover)
LC 2012-043411

SUMMARY: In this children's book by Michelle Edwards, "it's Mama's birthday and the first night of Passover, and Max is intent on baking her a cake. Max's dad is busy with the new baby, and he doesn't have time to help. Max comes up with a novel solution: He stacks pieces of matzo into a huge pile and covers them with jam and cream cheese. He even finds a tiny candle and places it on top for his mother's birthday." (Kirkus Reviews)

REVIEW: *Booklist* v110 no9/10 p120 Ja 1 2014 Connie Fletcher

REVIEW: *Kirkus Rev* v81 no21 p177 N 1 2013

REVIEW: *Kirkus Rev* v82 no5 p5 Mr 1 2014

"Max Makes A Cake". "[Michelle] Edwards offers a story about Passover, but it might be a bad idea to read it during the holiday-particularly toward the end. . . . As inventive as Max's solution is, observant Jews may think: There is nothing less appetizing than a giant stack of matzo. Readers will admire Max's creativity, no matter how they feel about unleavened bread. They may be less happy with the stilted dialogue. . . . Max's zeal is charming, but readers may find themselves thinking, more than once: No child has ever said that sentence. . . . Well-intentioned but, alas, as dry as matzo."

REVIEW: *Publ Wkly* v261 no7 p96 F 17 2014

EDWARDSON, ÅKE. Sail of stone; [by] Åke Edwardson 402 p. 2012 Simon & Schuster

1. Detective & mystery stories 2. FICTION—Mystery & Detective—General 3. FICTION—Mystery & Detective—Police Procedural 4. FICTION—Suspense 5. Göteborg (Sweden) 6. Missing persons—Fiction
ISBN 1451608500 (pbk.); 9781451608502 (pbk.)
LC 2011-028497

SUMMARY: This book presents "a pair of fresh cases for Erik Winter and Aneta Djanali, of the Gothenburg Police. Though she hasn't made any complaints herself, her neighbors have repeatedly indicated that Anette Lindsten has been attacked. . . . Imagine her surprise when, on a return visit, she finds Anette's father and brother packing up her things--and then her even greater surprise when she learns that Anette has no brother and that the solicitous men were a pair of thieves. . . . Winter, meanwhile, is chasing his own will-o'-the-wisp at the urging of his old girlfriend Johanna Osvald, who's worried because her fisherman father Axel has vanished during a trip to Scotland. It soon becomes clear that Axel was investigating the disappearance of his own father, John Osvald, from a fishing trawler during the war." (Kirkus)

REVIEW: *Booklist* v108 no11 p37 F 1 2012 Allison Block

REVIEW: *Kirkus Rev* v80 no4 p334-5 F 15 2012

"Sail of Stone." "A pair of fresh cases for Erik Winter and Aneta Djanali, of the Gothenburg Police. . . . Though she hasn't made any complaints herself, her neighbors have repeatedly indicated that Anette Lindsten has been attacked. Responding to the latest report, Aneta gets barely a glimpse of the alleged victim before she's turned away. . . . Winter, meanwhile, is chasing his own will-o'-the-wisp at the urging of his old girlfriend Johanna Osvald, who's worried because her fisherman father Axel has vanished during a trip to Scotland. . . . The detection in both cases is as inexorable and tedious as water chipping away stone. Recommended for readers with a taste for cold climates and a lot of time on their hands."

REVIEW: *Libr J* v137 no2 p58 F 1 2012 Jean King

REVIEW: *Publ Wkly* v259 no1 p60 Ja 2 2012

EGAN, R. DANIELLE. Becoming Sexual; A Critical Appraisal of the Sexualization of Girls; [by] R. Danielle Egan 200 p. 2013 John Wiley & Sons

1. Girls in popular culture 2. Sex in popular culture 3. Social science literature 4. Teenage girls—Sexual behavior 5. Young women—Sexual behavior
ISBN 0745650724; 9780745650722
LC 2012-277460

SUMMARY: Author R. Danielle Egan's book focuses on the sexualization of girls. Egan "illuminates the implications of dominant thinking on sexualization. The sexualized girl functions as a metaphor for cultural decay and as a common enemy through which adult rage, discontent and anxiety regarding class, gender, sexuality, race and the future can be expressed. Egan argues that, ultimately, the popular literature on sexualization is more reflective of adult disquiet than it is about the lives and practices of girls." (Publisher's note)

REVIEW: *Choice* v51 no1 p171-2 S 2013 Y. Kiuchi

REVIEW: *Contemp Sociol* v43 no1 p132 Ja 2014

"Becoming Sexual: A Critical Appraisal of the Sexualization of Girls". "Themes presented in this book will enlighten readers who are interested in gender, race, class, and sexuality. . . . The author argues that in examining the psychoanalytic mechanisms going on in the realm of sexualization, we can work to understand why these ideas are seen as natural. [R. Danielle] Egan offers that, 'It is my hope that my analysis will complicate reductionist thinking on the sexual child and add to the important conversations taking place on the sexual citizenship of children.'"

EGERTON, DOUGLAS R. The wars of Reconstruction; the brief, violent history of America's most progressive era; [by] Douglas R. Egerton 464 p. 2013 Bloomsbury Press

1. Freedmen—United States—History 2. Historical literature 3. Reconstruction (U.S. history, 1865-1877)
ISBN 9781608195664 (alk. paper)
LC 2013-009595

SUMMARY: In this "history of former slaves' rising to political involvement in the American South after the Civil War," Douglas R. Egerton "recalls Reconstruction at the state and local levels, where thousands of black veterans, activists, ministers, assemblymen and others, with help from white allies, integrated streetcars and schools and ran for office in this 'first progressive era in the nation's history.'" (Kirkus Reviews)

REVIEW: *Bookforum* v20 no5 p38 F/Mr 2014 GENE SEYMOUR

"The Wars of Reconstruction: The Brief, Violent History of America's Most Progressive Era." "It's easy to share the exasperation filtering through Douglas R. Egerton's 'The Wars of Reconstruction'. . . . Egerton's narrative doesn't equivocate in naming Reconstruction's villains, victims, and heroes. . . . However, Egerton stops short of engaging the contemporary resonances of the Reconstruction wars. . . . That may be the only significant oversight in this impassioned and comprehensive history of an era that was for far too long subject to far too many rank distortions and racist fabrications minted by the official guardians of our political tradition."

REVIEW: *Choice* v51 no12 p2252-3 Ag 2014 T. P. Johnson

REVIEW: *Kirkus Rev* v81 no24 p75 D 15 2013

"The Wars of Reconstruction: The Brief, Violent History of America's Most Progressive Era". " A richly detailed history of former slaves' rising to political involvement in the American South after the Civil War. . . . [Douglas R.] Egerton offers sharp sketches of freedmen. . . . He suggests that popular culture (Gone with the Wind, etc.) has sentimentalized the Old South and inaccurately portrayed Reconstruction as a vindictive, undemocratic period. An illuminating view of an era whose reform spirit would live on in the 1960s civil rights movement."

REVIEW: *Libr J* v139 no2 p83 F 1 2014 Thomas J. Davis

REVIEW: *N Y Times Book Rev* p11 F 2 2014 ERIC FONER

REVIEW: *Publ Wkly* v260 no33 p24-30 Ag 19 2013 SARAH J. ROBBINS

REVIEW: *Publ Wkly* v260 no45 p65-6 N 11 2013

EGGERS, DAVE, 1970-. The Circle; a novel; [by] Dave Eggers 504 p. 2013 Knopf

1. FICTION—Literary 2. FICTION—Technological 3. Internet—Fiction 4. Social media 5. Technological innovations—Fiction
ISBN 0385351399; 9780385351393 (hardback)
LC 2013-032894

SUMMARY: In this book, by Dave Eggers, "Mae Holland is hired to work for the Circle, the world's most powerful internet company. . . . The Circle, run out of a sprawling California campus, links users' personal emails, social media, banking, and purchasing with their universal operating system, resulting in one online identity. . . . Mae can't believe her luck, . . . even as a strange encounter with a colleague leaves her shaken." (Publisher's note)

REVIEW: *Bookforum* v20 no4 p26 D 2013/Ja 2014 FIONA MAAZEL

REVIEW: *Booklist* v110 no11 p36 F 1 2014 Joyce Saricks

"The Circle." "[Dion] Graham, who customarily narrates [David] Eggers' books, establishes the mood in this cautionary tale from the beginning. His brisk, almost breathless reading of the first chapters perfectly mirrors Mae's excitement at her amazing luck to be working for the Circle, a powerful Internet company. . . . In Graham's masterful reading, the Circle takes on its own seductive luster. . . . Although some listeners may be surprised to hear Graham narrate a book clearly told from a young woman's point of view, they won't be disappointed. . . . Graham's assured narration intensifies Eggers' prose and offers a chilling glimpse into a future world in which social media is king, transparency is demanded everywhere, and neither privacy nor individualism exists."

REVIEW: *Booklist* v110 no4 p15 O 15 2013 Keir Graff

REVIEW: *Economist* v409 no8857 p100 O 12 2013

REVIEW: *Kirkus Rev* v81 no19 p280 O 1 2013

REVIEW: *N Y Rev Books* v60 no18 p6-8 N 21 2013 Margaret Atwood

REVIEW: *N Y Times Book Rev* p10 N 3 2013 ELLEN ULLMAN

REVIEW: *Nation* v298 no14 p37 Ap 7 2014

REVIEW: *New Statesman* v142 no5180 p44-5 O 18 2013 Talitha Stevenson

REVIEW: *New York Times* v163 no56279 pC23-6 O 4 2013 MICHIKO KAKUTANI

REVIEW: *New Yorker* v89 no34 p33-1 O 28 2013

REVIEW: *Newsweek Global* v161 no38 p1-5 O 25 2013 Alexander Nazaryan

REVIEW: *Publ Wkly* v260 no48 p49 N 25 2013

REVIEW: *Time* v182 no16 p53 O 14 2013 Lev Grossman

"The Circle." "[Dave] Eggers has set his style and pace to technothriller: the writing is brisk and spare and efficient, with occasional gratuitous sexy bits, and his characters have a calculated shallowness that's almost Grishamesque. It works. One doesn't get the sense that he's making a bid to be more commercial; it's more like he's got something urgent to say and no time for literary foofery. . . . It will be interesting to see how much traction a novel that critiques the Net can get. . . . It says something that when I finished The Circle, I felt a heightened awareness of social media and the way it's remaking our world into a living hell of constant and universal mutual observation. Then I picked up my phone and tweeted about it."

REVIEW: *TLS* no5774 p25 N 29 2013 KATE WEBB

REVIEW: *Voice of Youth Advocates* v37 no2 p49 Je 2014 CATHI DUNN MACRAE

EGGERS, WILLIAM D. The solution revolution; how business, government, and social enterprises are teaming up to solve society's toughest problems; [by] William D. Eggers 304 p. 2013 Harvard Business Review Press

1. BUSINESS & ECONOMICS—Entrepreneurship 2. BUSINESS & ECONOMICS—Leadership 3. BUSINESS & ECONOMICS—Strategic Planning 4. Business literature 5. Economics—Sociological aspects 6. Social entrepreneurship 7. Social problems—Economic aspects 8. Social responsibility of business

ISBN 9781422192191 (hardback)

LC 2013-018709

SUMMARY: In this book, "executives [William D.] Eggers and [Paul] Macmillan set out to explain the multitrillion dollar 'solution economy,' which is arising as governments partner with the private sector (citizens, businesses, entrepreneurs, and foundations) to address society's urgent and deep-seated problems locally and worldwide. This new approach replaces the historic government-dominated model for solving entrenched problems." (Booklist)

REVIEW: *Booklist* v110 no1 p20 S 1 2013 Mary Whaley

REVIEW: *Choice* v51 no7 p1267-8 Mr 2014 S. R. Kahn

"The Solution Revolution: How Business, Government, and Social Enterprises Are Teaming Up to Solve Society's Toughest Problems." "Throughout this well-written book, the authors persuasively describe ways in which organizations from Fortune 500 companies and large institutions to grassroots movements and social enterprises are creatively overcoming the traditional private-public barriers to address pressing social problems such as poverty, public health, education, housing, and environmental protection. A plethora of real-life examples are presented as evidence of such collaboration producing social good."

REVIEW: *Publ Wkly* v260 no26 p77-8 Jl 1 2013

EGYPT'S TAHRIR REVOLUTION; vii, 287 p. 2013 Lynne Rienner Publishers

1. Arab countries—History—Arab Spring Uprisings, 2011- 2. Political science literature 3. Revolutions—History

ISBN 1588268845; 9781588268846 (hbk. : alk. paper)

LC 2012-028226

SUMMARY: Editor Dan Tschirgi's book focuses on the Tahrir Revolution in Egypt. "The eighteen-day revolt that ended Hosni Mubarak's thirty years of rule marked a historic turning point in the political fortunes not only of Egypt, but of the entire Middle East. While the impact of that seminal event will continue to unfold for years, this volume . . . presents a timely and authoritative exploration of the circumstances and implications--both political and theoretical--that surrounded what has come to be known as the Tahrir Revolution." (Publisher's note)

REVIEW: *Choice* v51 no1 p155 S 2013 G. E. Perry

"Egypt's Tahrir Revolution." "This is a collection of 14 readable and generally enlightening essays relating to the overthrow of the Hosni Mubarak dictatorship, including introductory and concluding pieces by the editors, [Dan] Tschirgi, [Walid] Kazziha, and [Sean F.] McMahon . . . , that ask whether a revolution has occurred and speculate about the future in an attempt to provide some cohesion to the volume. . . . The first section of the book focuses on political, social, and economic aspects of the Mubarak period as well as on the role of youth, women, and Islamists in the revolt. Then come pieces dealing with the broader regional context, including challenges to patronage regimes in the Arab world."

REVIEW: *Middle East J* v67 no3 p496 Summ 2013 A. B. G.

EHRENREICH, BARBARA, 1941-. Living with a Wild God; a nonbeliever's search for the truth about everything; [by] Barbara Ehrenreich 256 p. 2014 Twelve

1. Memoirs 2. Self-actualization (Psychology)—Biography

ISBN 145550176X; 9781455501762 (hardback)

LC 2013-038766

SUMMARY: In this memoir, author Barbara Ehrenreich "recounts her quest–beginning in childhood–to find 'the Truth' about the universe and everything else: What's really going on? Why are we here? In middle age, she rediscovered the journal she had kept during her tumultuous adolescence, which records an event so strange, so cataclysmic, that she had never, in all the intervening years, written or spoken about it to anyone." (Publisher's note)

REVIEW: *Atlantic* v313 no3 p38 Ap 2014 Ann Hulbert

REVIEW: *Bookforum* v21 no1 p51 Ap/My 2014 ANN FRIEDMAN

REVIEW: *Commonweal* v141 no16 p32-6 D 10 2014 Sidney Callahan

REVIEW: *Commonweal* v141 no16 p32-6 O 10 2014 Sidney Callahan

REVIEW: *Kirkus Rev* v82 no2 p196 Ja 15 2014

"Living With a Wild God: A Nonbeliever's Search for the truth about Everything". "A coming-of-age story with an edge and a focus. . . . Of most interest, of course, is that 1959 experience in Lone Pine, Calif., where, after spending the night in a car, she went for a walk at dawn and saw 'the world [had] flamed into life.' A talented student (co-valedictorian in high school), especially in the sciences, [Barbara] Ehrenreich studied chemistry and physics in college and graduate school, a career path she abandoned during the era of Vietnam and civil rights. But ever resting like a splinter in her mind: that Lone Pine experience. A powerful, honest account of a lifelong attempt to understand that will please neither theists nor atheists."

REVIEW: *Libr J* v139 no7 p91 Ap 15 2014 Crystal Goldman

REVIEW: *N Y Times Book Rev* p4 Ap 27 2014 JOHN WILLIAMS

REVIEW: *N Y Times Book Rev* p11 Ap 27 2014 PARUL SEHGAL

REVIEW: *New York Times* v163 no56473 pC1-6 Ap 16 2014 DWIGHT GARNER

REVIEW: *New Yorker* v90 no11 p75-1 My 5 2014

REVIEW: *Publ Wkly* v261 no3 p42 Ja 20 2014

EHRET, ULRIKE. Church, Nation and Race; Catholics and Antisemitism in Germany and England, 1918-1945; [by] Ulrike Ehret 288 p. 2012 Palgrave Macmillan

1. Antisemitism—History 2. Catholic Church—Germany 3. Catholic Church—Great Britain 4. Catholic

Church—Relations—Judaism—History 5. Christianity & antisemitism 6. Historical literature
ISBN 0719079438; 9780719079436

SUMMARY: This book "compares the worldviews and factors that promoted or, indeed, opposed antisemitism amongst Catholics in Germany and England after the First World War. . . . The book turns towards ideas and attitudes that preceded and shaped the ideologies of the 1920s and 1940s. Apart from the long tradition of Catholic anti-Jewish prejudices, the book discusses new and old alternatives to European modernity offered by Catholics in Germany and England." (Publisher's note)

REVIEW: *Engl Hist Rev* v129 no536 p243-6 F 2014 John Connelly

"Church, Nation, and Race: Catholics and Antisemitism in Germany and England, 1918-1945". "In her superb study of English and German Catholicism in the inter-war years, Ulrike Ehret . . . puts forward important and compelling arguments. . . . One question that hovers unresolved is why German Catholics were more susceptible to modern anti-Semitism, and in particular to racist visions of Jews. . . . In sum, Ehret's book exemplifies the virtues of the rarely practised methods of comparative history. She manages to illuminate the specific contours of two national variants of Catholicism in their attitudes toward Jews, while provoking new questions. This is a major work that deserves careful study by all those interested in anti-Semitism and anti-Judaism."

EHRLICH, AMY, 1942-. With a mighty hand; the story of the Torah; [by] Amy Ehrlich 224 p. 2013 Candlewick Press

1. Bible—Children's use 2. Bible—Illustrations 3. Bible stories, English—O.T. 4. Bible. Pentateuch 5. Moses (Biblical leader)
ISBN 0763643955; 9780763643959
LC 2012-947723

SUMMARY: This book is an interpretation of the Torah for children. Amy Ehrlich has "changed the traditional phrasing" of the Bible's first five books. She "describes Moses' basket as "a little ark of papyrus," reminding readers of how much danger the baby was in, floating in the middle of the Nile. . . . Not every word of the Bible has been included, the text having been pared down to a series of interconnected stories." (Kirkus Reviews)

REVIEW: *Booklist* v110 no6 p45 N 15 2013 Ilene Cooper

REVIEW: *Bull Cent Child Books* v67 no2 p85-6 O 2013 E. B.

"With a Mighty Hand: The Story in the Torah." "Here [author Amy] Ehrlich succeeds admirably in an ambitious effort to 'write a version of the Torah' by teasing out the narrative thread of Yahweh's covenant with Israel and following it 'through thickets of genealogy, law, and ritual.' Organized by book and broken into Ehrlich's own chapter demarcations, the stumbling journey from Eden to the borders of Canaan, from a clan to a blossoming nation is retold with an unwavering balance of reverence and fluency. . . . [Illustrator Daniel] Nevins' paintings, spare in compositional elements but rich in visual rhythm, highlight scenes not generally selected for standard Bible story illustration."

REVIEW: *Kirkus Rev* p73 N 15 2013 Best Books

REVIEW: *Kirkus Rev* v81 no14 p175 Jl 15 2013

REVIEW: *Kirkus Rev* p86-7 N 15 2013 Best Books

REVIEW: *N Y Times Book Rev* p36 N 10 2013 TAFFY BRODESSER-AKNER

REVIEW: *SLJ* v59 no10 p1 O 2013 Susan Scheps

EICHLER-LEVINE, JODI. Suffer the little children; uses of the past in Jewish and African American children's literature; [by] Jodi Eichler-Levine xxvi, 227 p. 2013 New York University Press

1. African Americans in literature 2. American literature—African American authors—History and criticism 3. Children's literature, American—History and criticism 4. Children's literature, Jewish—History and criticism 5. History in literature 6. Jews in literature 7. Literature—History & criticism 8. Suffering in literature
ISBN 9780814722992 (hardcover : acid-free paper)
LC 2012-043769

SUMMARY: This book "examines classic and contemporary Jewish and African American children's literature. Through close readings of selected titles published since 1945, [author] Jodi Eichler-Levine analyzes what is at stake in portraying religious history for young people, particularly when the histories in question are traumatic ones." She "asks readers to alter their worldviews about children's literature as an 'innocent' enterprise." (Publisher's note)

REVIEW: *Choice* v51 no2 p242 O 2013 T. L. Stowell

"Suffer the Little Children: Uses of the Past in Jewish and African American Children's Literature." "In this startling analysis of children's literature written by African Americans, Jews, and African American Jews, [Author Jodi] Eichler-Levine . . . claims that 'redemptive' stories about victimization are a necessary part of these works in order to gain acceptance. She bases her claim partly on the idea that an audience of conservative religious whites expects stereotyped story lines that are often tied to biblical stories of (primarily) Old Testament Jews. Eichler-Levine comments on older texts as they influence more-contemporary pieces, but her reader-response analysis focuses mainly on works published in the last 30 years."

EILAND, HOWARD. Walter Benjamin; a critical life; [by] Howard Eiland 704 p. 2014 The Belknap Press of Harvard University Press

1. Authors, German—20th century—Biography 2. Biography (Literary form) 3. Europe—Intellectual life—20th century 4. Jewish authors
ISBN 9780674051867 (alk. paper)
LC 2013-012858

SUMMARY: In this biography, authors "Howard Eiland and Michael Jennings make available for the first time a rich store of information which augments and corrects the record of an extraordinary life. They offer a comprehensive portrait of Benjamin and his times as well as extensive commentaries on his major works." (Publisher's note)

REVIEW: *Libr J* v138 no18 p92 N 1 2013 William Simkulet

REVIEW: *N Y Rev Books* v61 no12 p34-6 Jl 10 2014 Adam Kirsch

REVIEW: *New Repub* v244 no24 p50-5 Mr 24 2014 Peter E. Gordon

"Walter Benjamin: A Critical Life." "In their superb new biography, Howard Eiland and Michael W. Jennings have given us a portrait of this elusive but paradigmatic thinker that deserves to be ranked among the few truly indispensable intellectual biographies of the modern era. . . . Nearly seven hundred pages in length, this is not only a study of Benjamin's life, it is also a guide to the bewildering mix of themes and preoccupations that populated this most prolific and unfamiliar of minds. . . . The result is not a mere chronicle of a life but also a reliable map into Benjamin's intellectual labyrinth."

REVIEW: *New Yorker* v90 no27 p88-1 S 15 2014

REVIEW: *Publ Wkly* v260 no45 p60 N 11 2013

REVIEW: *TLS* no5802 p10-2 Je 13 2014

EINHORN, EDWARD. Fractions in disguise; a math adventure; 32 p. 2013 Charlesbridge

1. Auctions 2. Collectors & collecting 3. Fractions—Juvenile literature 4. Mathematical literature 5. Mathematics—Juvenile literature

ISBN 1570917736; 9781570917738 (reinforced for library use); 9781570917745 (softcover); 9781607346043 (ebook)

LC 2012-024435

SUMMARY: In this children's book, by Edward Einhorn and illustrated by David Clark, "when a valuable fraction goes missing, George Cornelius Factor (a.k.a. GCF) vows to track it down. Knowing that the villainous Dr. Brok likes to disguise his ill-begotten fractions, GCF invents a Reducer—a tool that strips away the disguise, reducing the fraction and revealing its true form." (Publisher's note)

REVIEW: *Booklist* v110 no11 p52 F 1 2014 Carolyn Phelan

REVIEW: *Kirkus Rev* v82 no4 p60 F 15 2014

"Fractions in Disguise: A Math Adventure". " Not only tackling fractions, but simplifying them, this fills a need and thoroughly entertains. . . . Throughout, [Edward] Einhorn finds ways to humorously add fractions to his tale-the fraction lovers bid portions of $1 million, and Brok's mansion is 1/10 of a mile tall-and painlessly describes the process of reducing them to their lowest terms. Backmatter summarizes the learning, though not as simply as the text. [David] Clark's ink-and-watercolor illustrations truly make the characters' personalities shine. Dr. Brok looks something like professor Hinkle of Frosty the Snowman fame, while the pages simply ooze with the aura of a great mystery. No question—a large fraction of parents and teachers will be reaching for this."

REVIEW: *Publ Wkly* v260 no52 p54 D 23 2013

REVIEW: *SLJ* v60 no3 p172 Mr 2014 Meaghan Darling

EIRHEIM, JEANNE.tr. The voyage. See The voyage

EISLER, MARYAM HOMAYOUN.ed. Art studio America. See Art studio America

EL-ARISS, TAREK. Trials of Arab modernity; literary affects and the new political; [by] Tarek El-Ariss x, 233 p. 2013 Fordham University Press

1. Arabic literature—20th century—History and criticism 2. Arabic literature—21st century—History and criticism 3. Literature—History & criticism 4. Literature, Experimental—Arab countries—History and criticism 5. Modernism (Literature)—Arab countries

ISBN 9780823251711 (cloth : alk. paper); 9780823251728 (paperback : alk. paper)

LC 2012-050166

SUMMARY: Written by Tarek El-Ariss, "Challenging prevalent conceptualizations of modernity--which treat it either as a Western ideology imposed by colonialism or as a universal narrative of progress and innovation--this study instead offers close readings of the simultaneous performances and contestations of modernity staged in works by authors such as Rifa'a al-Tahtawi, Ahmad Faris al-Shidyaq, Tayeb Salih, Hanan al-Shaykh, Hamdi Abu Golayyel, and Ahmad Alaidy." (Publisher's note)

REVIEW: *Choice* v51 no3 p452 N 2013 M. Cooke

REVIEW: *TLS* no5781 p22 Ja 17 2014 MARILYN BOOTH

"Politics of Nostalgia in the Arabic Novel: Nation-State, Modernity and Tradition" and "Trials of Arab Modernity: Literary Affects and the New Political." "Tarek El-Ariss and Wen-chin Ouyang take nineteenth-century artistry seriously, linking writers from this period to the sweep of creative technologies and political articulations that are shaping Arabic literature today. 'Trials of Arab Modernity' and 'Politics of Nostalgia in the Arabic Novel' both offer intimate glimpses of important works from across Arab-speaking societies. . . . 'Politics of Nostalgia' is the second half of a project mapping the Arabic novel, following 'Poetics of Love in the Arabic Novel.' . . . In 'Trials of Arab Modemity,' Tarek El-Ariss traverses similar ground differently, . . . through symptom and affect."

EL-HUSSEINI, ROLA. Pax Syriana; elite politics in postwar Lebanon; [by] Rola El-Husseini xxiii, 319 p. 2012 Syracuse University Press

1. Elite (Social sciences)—Political activity—Lebanon—History—20th century 2. Elite (Social sciences)—Political activity—Lebanon—History—21st century 3. Historical literature

ISBN 9780815633044 (cloth : alkaline paper)

LC 2012-034802

SUMMARY: This book, written by Rola El-Husseini, "provides an in-depth account of how the political elite left an indelible mark on the Lebanese state and society. Through extensive field work and firsthand interviews, el-Husseini offers an intimate portrait of postwar Lebanon and shows how the Syrian influence brought a degree of stability to this fragmented nation and yet simultaneously undermined the development of a full constitutional democracy." (Publisher's note)

REVIEW: *Choice* v51 no2 p345-6 O 2013 R. W. Olson

"Pax Syriana: Elite Politics in Postwar Lebanon." "[Author Rola] El-Husseini . . . focuses on the politics of the Lebanese elite during two vital periods of Lebanon's recent history. She analyzes Lebanon under Syria's military occupation during the first (1976-89). During the second (1989-2005), Syria's military occupation ended, but its political domination remained. El-Husseini argues that in spite of the trauma of 30 years of civil war and the withdrawal of Syrian combat forces (2005), family-based sectarian patronage continues to rule Lebanon. . . . El-Husseini ended her research in 2010, but the outbreak of civil war in Syria in March 2011, ongoing as of this writing, credits her arguments even more strongly."

REVIEW: *Middle East J* v67 no3 p482-3 Summ 2013 Marie-Joëlle Zahar

EL-NAWAWY, MOHAMMED. Egyptian revolution 2.0; political blogging, civic engagement, and citizen journalism; [by] Mohammed El-Nawawy viii, 241 p. 2013 Palgrave Macmillan

1. Citizen journalism—Egypt 2. Internet—Political aspects—Egypt 3. Political activists—Egypt—Blogs 4. Political participation—Egypt 5. Political science literature 6. Protest movements—Egypt—Blogs 7. Social media—Political aspects—Egypt
ISBN 9781137020918 (hardback : alk. paper)
LC 2012-048015

SUMMARY: "This book sheds light on the growing phenomenon of cyberactivism in the Arab world, with a special focus on the Egyptian political blogosphere and its role in paving the way to democratization and socio-political change in Egypt. . . . In doing so, it examines the relevance and applicability of the concepts of citizen journalism and civic engagement to the discourses . . .in five of the most popular political blogs in Egypt." (Publisher's note)

REVIEW: *Choice* v51 no7 p1204-5 Mr 2014 A. R. Cannella

"Egyptian Revolution 2.0: Political Blogging, Civic Engagement, and Citizen Journalism." "Though this book predates the ouster of Mohamed Morsi, who was elected president after [Hosni] Mubarak fell, and the takeover by the military and the bloody turmoil of the summer of 2013, it is not a stale read. The authors conducted many interviews, and not just of 'Sandmonkey' and the other four bloggers whose postings they skillfully culled. . . . The authors' astute analysis complements the blog postings and interview material they mined."

EL AZHAR, SAMIR.ed. Museums in a global context. See Museums in a global context

ELBERSE, ANITA. Blockbusters; hit-making, risk-taking, and the big business of entertainment; [by] Anita Elberse 320 p. 2013 Henry Holt and Company

1. Business literature 2. Celebrities 3. Mass media—Economic aspects 4. Motion picture industry 5. Music trade
ISBN 9780805094336 (hardcover)
LC 2013-014320

SUMMARY: This book by Anita Elberse presents "the story of the entertainment blockbuster model and why it isn't going anywhere." It was the author's intent to "identify the strategies entertainment companies employ to maximize profits in a uniquely competitive and unpredictable market. Her . . . conclusion is that there is no surer bet than focusing the lion's share of resources on 'blockbusters,' products intended to make the biggest initial splash with the largest possible audience." (Kirkus Reviews)

REVIEW: *Booklist* v110 no1 p20 S 1 2013 Mary Whaley

REVIEW: *Economist* v410 no8869 p73-4 Ja 11 2014

"Blockbusters: Hit-making, Risk-taking, and the Big Business of Entertainment." "[Anita] Elberse writes a great deal about the role of marketing and advertising campaigns in launching products, but devotes hardly any attention to what determines whether a media property will take off. . . . Nowhere in her book does Ms. Elberse address the question of when paying becomes overpaying. As more and more media companies follow the crowd, the temptation to bid up the price of author manuscripts, celebrity talent, film scripts and sports rights becomes hard to resist. This makes it more likely that returns on investment will decline. It is hard to predict when a potential blockbuster is too expensive, but that is the one question every hit-hungry media executive needs answered."

REVIEW: *Kirkus Rev* v81 no18 p126 S 15 2013

REVIEW: *New Yorker* v89 no39 p70-1 D 2 2013

REVIEW: *TLS* no5792 p27 Ap 4 2014 ROZ KAVENEY

"Blockbusters." "Anita Elbersee's mostly well-informed book 'Blockbusters' is full of optimistic praise for the wisdom of great men (and it is still mostly men) who have found a winning formula for running the entertainment industry. Elbersee's view is reasonable up to a point. . . . It is not always to its advantage that 'Blockbusters' ranges so widely across the entertainment industry. When Elbersee talks about sport, she misses an obvious point, which is that it is not good enough for a team to have the most prestigious players—those players have to deliver high scores. . . . Elbersee quotes with approval the old bookshop maxim 'stack them high and watch them fly,' and her enthusiasm is part of the problem with this otherwise intelligent, informative and useful book."

ELECTRICAL WIZARD; how Nikola Tesla lit up the world; 40 p. 2013 Candlewick Press

1. Children's nonfiction 2. Edison, Thomas A. (Thomas Alva), 1847-1931 3. Electricity—History 4. Inventors 5. Tesla, Nikola, 1856-1943
ISBN 0763658553; 9780763658557
LC 2012-954334

SUMMARY: This picture book by Elizabeth Rusch is a biography of inventor Nikola Tesla. "From childhood experiments through college studies, Tesla exhibited an interest in electricity. By the time he designed his alternating current (AC) system, he had moved from Eastern Europe to Paris but could find no investors to fund his projects." Tesla's rivalry with Thomas Edison and his partnership with Westinghouse are noted. (School Library Journal)

REVIEW: *Booklist* v109 no22 p65 Ag 1 2013 John Peters

REVIEW: *Bull Cent Child Books* v67 no3 p178 N 2013 E. B.

REVIEW: *Horn Book Magazine* v90 no1 p118 Ja/F 2014 BETTY CARTER

REVIEW: *Kirkus Rev* v81 no16 p223 Ag 15 2013

"Electrical Wizard: How Nikola Tesla Lit Up the World." "Nikola Tesla's curiosity and passion for discovery are on full display in this picture-book biography. . . . This is a lively introduction to the life of an important figure in technology, someone whose ideas are still at the center of today's world. [Author Elizabeth] Rusch highlights key episodes in Tesla's creative life that will resonate with young readers. [Illustrator Oliver] Dominguez's graphite, gouache, ink and acrylic paintings capture both the inventor's focus and his exuberance, ably complementing the narrative."

REVIEW: *SLJ* v59 no9 p178 S 2013 Kathy Piehl

ELFGREN, SARA B. The Circle; [by] Sara B. Elfgren 596 p. 2013 Penguin Group USA

1. Fantasy fiction 2. Good & evil—Fiction 3. Magic—Fiction 4. Paranormal fiction 5. Witches—Fiction
ISBN 1468306588 (hardcover); 9781468306583 (hardcover)

SUMMARY: This novel, by Sara B. Elfgren and Mats Strandberg, begins "The Engelsfors Trilogy." One night "Minoo wakes up outside her house, . . . drawn by an invisible force to . . . the outskirts of town. Soon five of her classmates . . . arrive. . . . A mystical being . . . tells them they are fated to fight an ancient evil. . . . Each girl discovers she has a unique magical ability. . . . The six are wildly different and definitely not friends . . . but they are the Chosen Ones." (Publisher's note)

REVIEW: *Booklist* v109 no18 p63 My 15 2013 Sarah Hunter

REVIEW: *Horn Book Magazine* v89 no5 p92-3 S/O 2013 JESSICA TACKETT

"The Circle." "Without mystical guidance, the girls are skeptical and prone to intracoven personality disputes. In this lengthy book, the story is slow to unfold, allowing ample time for everyday teen angst amidst magical revelations, but also potentially trying readers' patience. However, the six protagonists are dynamic heroines with dark motivations, conflicting desires, and plenty of secrets. When the demons finally threaten to kill off the girls one by one, tension climbs sharply toward a suspenseful conclusion, leaving fans eager for the next book in the [Engelsfors Trilogy] series."

REVIEW: *Kirkus Rev* v81 no7 p341 Ap 1 2013

REVIEW: *Publ Wkly* v260 no14 p67 Ap 8 2013

REVIEW: *SLJ* v59 no10 p1 O 2013 Necia Blundy

ELFGREN, SARA B. Fire; [by] Sara B. Elfgren 704 p. 2014 The Overlook Press

1. Demonology 2. Fantasy 3. Good & evil—Fiction 4. Magic—Fiction 5. Teenagers—Fiction
ISBN 1468306723; 9781468306729 (hardback)
LC 2013-044050

SUMMARY: In this book, by Sara B. Elfgren and Mats Strandberg, "Minoo, Vanessa, Linnéa, Anna-Karin and Ida have been struggling with their own demons all summer long. Now school is back in session, and whether they like it or not, the five Chosen Ones must stick together stronger than ever before. Evil is back in Engelsfors and it threatens to engulf everyone and everything—and only if the five girls accept their strengths and trust each other unconditionally will they have any chance of defeating it." (Publisher's note)

REVIEW: *Horn Book Magazine* v90 no4 p90 Jl/Ag 2014 JESSICA TACKETT MACDONALD

REVIEW: *Kirkus Rev* v82 no2 p278 Ja 15 2014

"Fire". "The intricate relationship chess that sets the opener of this teens-vs.-demons import apart really takes over in the projected trilogy's middle volume. The five young Swedes previously given paranormal powers . . . are thoroughly enmeshed in emotional turmoil fostered by the sprawling cast of questionable boyfriends and ex-boyfriends, vicious bullies, troubled parents and hostile townsfolk. This so preoccupies them that both the arrival of an investigator bent on punishing any unauthorized magic working and the imminent prospect of the world's destruction by otherworld demons seem mere distractions. . . . The fantasy elements remain as murky as they are inessential to a story that is really more about high schoolers poised to emerge from tough adolescences than magic."

ELFICK, ALISTAIR. Synthetic aesthetics. See Schyfter, P.

ELFMAN, ERIC. Tesla's attic; [by] Eric Elfman 256 p. 2014 Disney-Hyperion Books

1. Inventions—Fiction 2. Meteors 3. Science fiction
ISBN 1423148037; 9781423148036
LC 2012-039773

SUMMARY: This children's novel, by Eric Elfman and Neal Shusterman, is the first book of "The Accelerati Trilogy." "After getting rid of . . . odd antiques in a garage sale, Nick befriends some local kids . . . and they discover that all of the objects have extraordinary properties. What's more, Nick figures out that the attic is a strange magnetic vortex, which attracts all sorts of trouble. It's as if the attic itself has an intelligence . . . and a purpose." (Publisher's note)

REVIEW: *Booklist* v110 no9/10 p114 Ja 1 2014 Magan Szwarek

REVIEW: *Bull Cent Child Books* v67 no6 p335-6 F 2014

REVIEW: *Horn Book Magazine* v90 no2 p129 Mr/Ap 2014 SAM BLOOM

"Tesla's Attic." "Now Nick and his friends are in a race to save humanity while avoiding the (nefarious) Accelerati. The strong narrative voice propels the well-paced story, and while the plotting is shaky at times, future installments may very well clear up the problem spots. Although they rely heavily on action and adventure, the authors don't skimp on character development: Nick is a likable protagonist; his friends are a varied and humorous bunch. With a dynamic mix of secret-society intrigue, quirky gadgetry, appealing teen characters, and humor, this series has the makings of a hit."

REVIEW: *Kirkus Rev* v81 no24 p152 D 15 2013

REVIEW: *Publ Wkly* v260 no49 p84 D 2 2013

REVIEW: *SLJ* v60 no3 p148 Mr 2014 Vicki Reutter

ELGAR, DIETMAR. Gerhard Richter Catalogue Raisonné; Nos. 1-198, 1962-1968; [by] Dietmar Elgar 2011 Staatliche Kunstsammlung

1. Artists—Germany 2. Catalogues raisonnés (Art) 3. German art—20th century 4. Painting—Catalogs 5. Richter, Gerhard, 1932-
ISBN 9783775719780

SUMMARY: "Edited by Dietmar Elger, director of the Gerhard Richter Archive at the Staatliche Kunstsammlungen Dresden, who has spent years researching and preparing the publication, this first volume encompasses the works [artist Gerhard] Richter assigned numbers 1 to 198, which span the years 1962 to 1968. A total of 385 paintings and sculptures are listed, more than 30 of which were previously unseen or even unknown." (Publisher's note)

REVIEW: *Burlington Mag* v155 no1326 p631-2 S 2013 JOHN-PAUL STONARD

"Gerhard Richter Catalogue Raisonné, Volume I: Nos. 1-198, 1962-1968." "Gerhard Richter is known for his assiduous record-keeping and habit of assigning a number to all works--painting, sculpture or otherwise--that are officially part of his oeuvre. . . . [Author Dietmar] Elger's catalogue raisonné, the first volume of which covers the years 1962-68, therefore fills the gap for a more objective survey of Richter's prolific output. Elger is undoubtedly the right person for the job. . . . The catalogue is both generous in its presentation of images . . . and information, and concise in the selection of supporting material. . . . Alongside an informative chronology, a list of exhibitions includes a number of hitherto un-noted early shows."

REVIEW: *Choice* v49 no8 p1430 Ap 2012 J. T. Paoletti

ELGINDY, KHALED. The Arab awakening. See Pollack, K. M.

ELIAS-BURSAC, ELLEN.tr. Trieste. See Drndic, D.

ELIOPOULOS, CHRISTOPHER.il. I am Abraham Lincoln. See Melter, B.

ELIOT, HANNAH. Hippos can't swim. See DiSiena, L. L.

ELISABETH FRINK CATALOGUE RAISONNE OF SCULPTURE, 1947-93; 207 p. 2013 Lund Humphries

1. Art literature 2. Catalogues raisonnés (Art) 3. Frink, Elisabeth 4. Modern sculpture—20th century—History 5. Sculpture—20th century

ISBN 9781848221130 (hardcover : alk. paper)

LC 2012-947515

SUMMARY: Edited by Annette Ratuszniak, this book shows how "Elisabeth Frink (1930-93) was a leading British sculptor and printmaker whose work is distinguished by her commitment to naturalistic forms and themes. This new edition of the catalogue raisonne of her sculpture documents her complete sculptural output in a single volume. . . . Frink's subjects included men, birds, dogs, horses and religious motifs, and she concentrated on bronze outdoor sculpture with a scarred surface." (Publisher's note)

REVIEW: *Burlington Mag* v155 no1328 p785-6 N 2013 NICHOLAS WATKINS

"Elisabeth Frink. Catalogue Raisonné of Sculpture 1947-93." "The twentieth anniversary of Elisabeth Frink's death in 1993 at the age of sixty-two was marked by a major retrospective exhibition at The Lightbox in Woking and by the publication here under review, launched by Beaux Arts, its co-publisher, with a small exhibition. . . . The unwillingness of the various contributors to consistently establish her work in broader artistic and cultural frameworks make it difficult to arrive at a fuller understanding of her position in a history of post-Second World War sculpture."

ELITE MOBILITIES; 288 p. 2013 Routledge

1. Elite (Social sciences) 2. Emigration and immigration 3. Globalization 4. Rich people—Travel 5. Sociology literature

ISBN 9780415655804 (hardback)

LC 2013-012025

SUMMARY: "This book argues that since the 1980s, a new class of super rich has emerged with globalization and a shift from traditional industrial production to just-in-time manufacturing and financial services. This new class and their resources have produced new lifestyles that are based on extreme mobility; their travel takes them across international borders and links them with elites elsewhere." (Choice: Current Reviews for Academic Libraries)

REVIEW: *Choice* v51 no8 p1496 Ap 2014 J. Borchert

"Elite Mobilities". "The 14 articles range from analyses of private business aviation to super-rich lifestyles and offshore tax dodging. . . . A concluding essay challenges the authors to be more critical of elites and the changes that have brought them massive wealth. Missing are the larger contexts for the new elite: their political and economic power and relations with older elites. The authors are international scholars from geography, sociology, and related fields. Despite some jargon, their essays are important and accessible for students of elites everywhere."

ELKINS, JAMES, 1955-. After Hiroshima; [by] James Elkins 128 p. 2013 Daylight Books

1. Art literature 2. Artistic photography 3. Hiroshima-shi (Japan)—History—Bombardment, 1945 4. Museums—Japan 5. Photobooks

ISBN 0983231656; 9780983231653

SUMMARY: This photo essay by Elin O'Hara Slavick is "an attempt to address--historically, poetically and visually--what disappeared as well as what remains in Hiroshima. Her photographs of the city and of artifacts from its Peace Memorial Museum collection are images of loss and survival, with the trope of exposure--to history, light, radiation, the sun--at their core." (Publisher's note)

REVIEW: *New York Times* v162 no56237 pC24 Ag 23 2013 Dana Jennings

"Revolution," "Elena Dorfman: Empire Falling," and "After Hiroshima." "These nocturnal seascapes--photographs of the Arctic Ocean, Red Sea, North Pacific and elsewhere--are flensed to stark essences: an infinite palette of blacks and grays garnished by sprigs of light. Spectral, the images could be from the beginning of time--or its end. This is not our world, but Mr. [Hiroshi] Sugimoto's. . . . The quarries of the photographer Elena Dorfman . . . are haunting postindustrial abstractions. . . . This is a book of the earth's guts ripped open, exposing layer upon layer of antediluvian time and tide. . . . 'After Hiroshima' is a kind of archaeology of memory. . . . Ms. [Elin O'Hara] Slavick's work reminds us that radiation has a long half-life--but so, too, does memory."

ELLEDGE, JIM. Henry Darger, throw away boy; the tragic life of an outsider artist; [by] Jim Elledge 396 p. 2013 Overlook Hardcover

1. Artists—United States—Biography 2. Gay artists—United States 3. Outsider artists—United States—Biography 4. Watercolorists—United States—Biography

ISBN 9781590208557 (hardback); 1590208552

LC 2013-022351

SUMMARY: "While some art historians tend to dismiss [artist Henry] Darger as possibly psychotic, [author] Jim Elledge cuts through the cloud of controversy and rediscovers Darger as a damaged and fearful gay man, raised in a world unaware of the consequences of child abuse or gay shame. This thoughtful, sympathetic biography tells the true story of a tragically misunderstood artist." (Publisher's note)

REVIEW: *Art Am* v102 no4 p43-5 Ap 2014 David Ebony

REVIEW: *Booklist* v110 no1 p25 S 1 2013 Donna Seaman

REVIEW: *Kirkus Rev* v81 no14 p296 Jl 15 2013

REVIEW: *New Yorker* v89 no43 p67-1 Ja 6 2014

REVIEW: *New Yorker* v89 no43 p67-1 Ja 6 2014

"Henry Darger." "This famous outsider artist was an anonymous janitor until his death, in 1973, when hundreds of watercolors of children in distress and thousands of unpublished manuscript pages were found in his Chicago apartment. [Jim] Elledge's biography presents him as a fragile gay man in a secret long-term relationship and argues that his work was a response to an abusive childhood spent in asylums, shelters, and the slums of early-twentieth-century Chicago. But this analysis relies on a lot of extrapolation (for instance, from gnomic diary entries), and doesn't really illuminate his prolific output."

ELLENS, J. HAROLD.ed. Heaven, hell, and the afterlife. See Heaven, hell, and the afterlife

ELLIOT, DAVID. Henry's map; 40 p. 2013 Philomel Books

1. Children's literature 2. Domestic animals—Fiction 3. Farm life—Fiction 4. Maps—Fiction 5. Pigs—Fiction
ISBN 0399160728 (reinforced); 9780399160721 (reinforced)
LC 2012-035391

SUMMARY: This children's picture book stars a very organized pig named Henry, who "decries the messy state of the farm. . . . Henry decides to draw a map to sort things out and, armed with pencil and paper, makes his way across the barnyard. All the animals are excited to be included, falling in line behind the earnest cartographer." His efforts are less than successful, however, and ultimately all the animals stay where they were originally, "to the relief of all concerned." (Publishers Weekly)

REVIEW: *Bull Cent Child Books* v67 no1 p16 S 2013 J. H.

"Henry's Map." "'Henry was a very organized sort of pig,' so organized that he decides to map his surroundings to make sure everyone and everything is in its proper place on the farm. . . . The story is simple, but kids will enjoy the moment of feeling smarter than the farm animals as the creatures puzzle out why they are on the map but not in their actual places. The text is crisp and brisk, and the animals' dialogue makes this a lively choice for a readaloud. The pencil and watercolor illustrations, done in subdued tones, are casually drawn, with slightly scribbly lines depicting the animals' fur, feathers, or wool. The sheep are particularly comical as they swing from the tree branch, ride on the horse's back, or hold hooves with each other."

REVIEW: *Kirkus Rev* v81 no9 p79-80 My 1 2013

REVIEW: *Publ Wkly* v260 no17 p132 Ap 29 2013

REVIEW: *SLJ* v59 no6 p82 Je 2013 Kathleen Kelly MacMillan

ELLIOT, DAVID.il. Henry's map. See Elliott, D.

ELLIOTT, GREGORY.tr. Left hemisphere. See Left hemisphere

ELLIOTT, LAURA MALONE. Thanksgiving day thanks; [by] Laura Malone Elliott 32 p. 2013 Katherine Tegen Books

1. Animals—Fiction 2. Gratitude—Fiction 3. School stories 4. Schools—Fiction 5. Thanksgiving Day—Fiction 6. Thanksgiving Day—Juvenile literature
ISBN 9780060002367 (hardcover bdgs)
LC 2012-030717

SUMMARY: In this book, author "Laura Malone Elliott and [illustrator] Lynn Munsinger have created another holiday story about the lovable characters from 'A String of Hearts'." It "tells the story of Sam trying to figure out what he's thankful for. Sam also works on a special project to share at the Thanksgiving feast--his own version of the Macy's Thanksgiving Day Parade!" (Publisher's note)

REVIEW: *Booklist* v110 no1 p126 S 1 2013 Connie Fletcher

REVIEW: *Bull Cent Child Books* v67 no3 p150-1 N 2013 J. H

"Thanksgiving Day Thanks." "To celebrate Thanksgiving, Sam's teacher asks her students to each write something they're thankful for on a paper feather, and she also asks them to come up with a project of their own. . . . Although much of the book's plot covers ground already well trodden by picture-book authors, [author Laura Malone] Elliott's focus on Sam's love for the Thanksgiving parade's balloons is a somewhat novel and entirely kid-friendly angle. The first Thanksgiving story is, as often is the case, oversimplified, and Mary Ann's project of dressing up like Squanto remains problematic despite her relating of various Wampanoag facts."

REVIEW: *Kirkus Rev* v81 no16 p35 Ag 15 2013

"Thanksgiving Day Thanks." "Sam has trouble thinking of what he is most grateful for when his class celebrates Thanksgiving, and [author Laura Malone] Elliott has trouble sustaining the focus on group relationships begun with Sam's first outing. . . . [Illustrator Lynn] Munsinger's sweet, enthusiastic and diverse anthropomorphized animal cast is quite busy with individual projects, which all turn out, rather unrealistically, spectacularly. With its wide variety of activities and crafts, this is sure to spark some classroom celebration ideas, though it otherwise doesn't stand out from other holiday titles."

REVIEW: *N Y Times Book Rev* p41 N 10 2013 SARAH HARRISON SMITH

"How Big Could Your Pumpkin Grow?," "The Apple Orchard Riddle," and "Thanksgiving Day Thanks." "While the pie's in the oven, savor [Wendell] Minor's mighty vocabulary, silly humor and intriguing facts. . . . [G. Brian Karas], who lives in the Hudson Valley, boosts the flavor of this sweet story with soft pencil line and rich, muted colors. . . . [Laura Malone] Elliott includes facts about the Pilgrims and their friends, the Wampanoag; [Lynn] Munsinger's adorable illustrations show little animals at work on holiday crafts that readers may want to try, too."

REVIEW: *Publ Wkly* v260 no36 p56 S 9 2013

REVIEW: *SLJ* v59 no8 p72 Ag 2013 Jasmine L. Precopio

ELLIOTT, MARK.il. Thomas Jefferson. See Chew, E. V.

ELLIOTT, NICHOLAS.tr. The falling sky. See Albert, B.

ELLIOTT, REBECCA.il. Kiss, kiss good night. See Nesbitt, K.

ELLIOTT, WILL. The pilgrims; [by] Will Elliott 512 p.

2014 Tor
1. FICTION—Fantasy—General 2. Magic—Fiction 3. Slackers—Fiction 4. Wizards—Fiction
ISBN 9780765331885 (hardback)
LC 2013-029756

SUMMARY: In this book by Will Elliott, "journalist Eric Albright doesn't have a lot going for him in his life, which might explain why, when a door suddenly appears in a train underpass, he ventures to the strange world that appears on the other side. Eric and Case, his homeless friend and underpass dweller, travel to Levaal, a pocket world between worlds, and become dangerously embroiled in the local conflict between a power-mad wannabe god and the free cities that are opposed to him." (Library Journal)

REVIEW: *Kirkus Rev* v82 no3 p246 F 1 2014

"The Pilgrims". "The first entry in the Pendulum fantasy trilogy, from the author of 'The Pilo Family Circus' (2006). . . . Where is this going, and does it all add up? Answers are uncertain; the characters talk the talk but don't have a real presence, and the narrative is mostly aimless. Still, it's inventive enough, not to say puzzling, and sets forth in prose of great clarity; this may be enough to tempt readers to return for future installments. Not altogether convincing but it has its charms."

REVIEW: *Libr J* v139 no3 p76 F 15 2014 Megan M. McArdle

ELLIS, CHRISTINA.il. The numberlys. See Joyce, W.

ELLIS, DANNY. The boy at the gate; a memoir; [by] Danny Ellis 376 p. 2013 Arcade Publishing
1. Ireland—History—20th century 2. Memoirs 3. Orphanages 4. Singers—Ireland—Biography
ISBN 9781611458923 (hardcover : alk. paper)
LC 2013-012320

SUMMARY: Written by singer/songwriter Danny Ellis, "this is a brutally honest, often harrowing, depiction of a young boy's struggle to survive orphanage life, and stands as an inspiring testament to the healing power of music and love. . . .Although unnerved by his experience, Danny begins an arduous journey that leads him back to the streets of Dublin, the tenement slums, and, ultimately, the malice and mischief of the Artane playground." (Publisher's note)

REVIEW: *Booklist* v110 no1 p24 S 1 2013 Bridget Thoreson

REVIEW: *Kirkus Rev* v81 no16 p119 Ag 15 2013

"The Boy at the Gate: A Memoir." "An Irish singer/songwriter's powerful debut memoir about growing up at the notorious Artane Industrial School for orphaned and abandoned boys in Dublin. . . . In a story that alternates between his successful present and harrowing past, [author Danny] Ellis details how he survived the years of savagery at the hands of the school's sadistic, whip-wielding priests to become a critically acclaimed musician. . . . That Ellis uses the narrative to unearth a deliberately forgotten past makes for compelling reading. But what makes his work even more affecting is the way he uses his story to liberate the voices of otherwise forgotten children who endured 'one of the most abusive and brutal institutions in Ireland.'"

ELLIS, DAVID. Memoirs of a Leavisite; The Decline and Fall of Cambridge English; [by] David Ellis 224 p. 2013 Liverpool University Press
1. English literature—History & criticism—Theory, etc. 2. English literature—Study & teaching 3. Leavis, F. R. (Frank Raymond), 1895-1978 4. Memoirs 5. University of Cambridge
ISBN 1846318890; 9781846318894

SUMMARY: This book is a memoir by David Ellis. "In the second half of the last century, the teaching of English literature was very much influenced and, in some places, entirely dominated by the ideas of F. R. Leavis. . . . Ellis takes himself as representative of that pool of lower middle class grammar school pupils from which Leavisites were largely recruited, and explores the beliefs of both the Leavises, their lasting impact on him and why ultimately they were doomed to failure." (Publisher's note)

REVIEW: *Choice* v51 no7 p1212-3 Mr 2014 W. Baker

"Memoirs of a Leavisite: The Decline and Fall of Cambridge English." "[David] Ellis wrote this memoir 'to consider the effect [Frank Raymond Leavis's] teaching had on me.' Ellis admits that 'for most of those now teaching English in [British] schools or universities, Leavis is an irrelevance.' The photograph on the dust wrapper--Leavis in a garden setting--is remarkable and should be preserved. This is an important resource for those interested in 20th-century British cultural life and in literary critics and their impact. . . . Recommended."

REVIEW: *London Rev Books* v35 no17 p10-2 S 12 2013 John Mullan

"Memoirs of a Leavisite: The Decline and Fall of Cambridge English," "English As a Vocation: The 'Scrutiny' Movement," and "The Two Cultures? The Significance of C. P. Snow." "[Author David] Ellis is well aware of Leavis's joyless reputation and tries to redeem it. . . . Christopher Hilliard's 'English as a Vocation' shows that applicants to Downing were expected already to have read large swathes of Shakespeare, 17th-century poetry, Romantic poetry and 19th-century fiction. . . . In the year of his retirement from his readership in the Cambridge English Faculty [author F. R. Leavis] achieved notoriety with his riposte to C.P. Snow's lecture 'The Two Cultures and the Scientific Revolution'. . . . The performance survives rather well."

REVIEW: *New Statesman* v142 no5155 p46 Ap 26 2013

REVIEW: *TLS* no5768 p13 O 18 2013 NORA CROOK

"Memoirs of a Leavisite: The Decline and Fall of Cambridge English." "The dominant tone of this memoir is reflective, sometimes Wordsworthian in its attempt to paint what then he was, and to trace the modifications that views espoused with passion in youth have undergone in the light of experience, and what of them remains unchanged. . . . It is what it says it is: a retrospective on one man's experience and aspects of his career. . . . Underlying this book is another story about the difficulty of telling the truth, and about whether his experience is typical or idiosyncratic. . . . Contemporaries at Cambridge, and near-contemporaries like myself, will recognize the general truth of Ellis's recollections. . . . [A] brief, tactful and deceptively quiet book"

ELLIS, DEBORAH. Kids of Kabul; living bravely through a never-ending war; [by] Deborah Ellis 143 p. 2012 Groundwood Books
1. Afghan War, 2001- & children 2. Children & war 3. Children—Afghanistan 4. Interviews 5. Nonfiction
ISBN 1554981816; 9781554981816

SUMMARY: This book is a collection of interviews with Afghani children who "mostly don't remember the Taliban's fall more than a decade ago, but they can't help but be shaped by the damage the Taliban did to their country. . . . One girl is imprisoned for fleeing a forced child marriage, while another's mother is a member of Parliament; one boy's damaged by a landmine, and another's proud to be a Scout. . . . [I]ntroductions to each young person provide historical, legal and social context." (Kirkus Reviews)

REVIEW: *Booklist* v108 no18 p45 My 15 2012 Mary Russell

REVIEW: *Bull Cent Child Books* v65 no11 p557 Jl/Ag 2012 K. C.

"Kids of Kabul: Living Bravely Through a Never-Ending War." "[Deborah] Ellis . . . provides context for the interview[s] in a brief introduction that describes the larger cultural and historical reasons behind the particular situation the person finds him or herself in; these introductions are extremely useful in helping readers see the big picture of how the prolonged war has proven devastating to domestic life. A subtle but informative contrast then emerges as the interviewees describe how much better their lives are now than when they lived under the Taliban, and most credit the value of the education they are now able to receive for the hope they have for their futures."

REVIEW: *Kirkus Rev* v80 no7 p730 Ap 1 2012

"Kids of Kabul: Living Bravely Through a Never-Ending War." "The author of the Breadwinner trilogy turns from fictional Afghani children to real ones. The 10- to 17-year-olds interviewed for this collection mostly don't remember the Taliban's fall more than a decade ago, but they can't help but be shaped by the damage the Taliban did to their country. In a country that's been at war for more than 30 years, childhood is very different--or is it? . . . Clear introductions to each young person provide historical, legal and social context. This nuanced portrayal of adolescence in a struggling nation refrains, refreshingly, from wallowing in tragedy tourism and overwrought handwringing. Necessary."

REVIEW: *Quill Quire* v78 no5 p39 Je 2012 Paul Challen

REVIEW: *SLJ* v58 no6 p141 Je 2012 Gerry Larson

ELLIS, DEBORAH. Looks Like Daylight; Voices of Indigenous Kids; [by] Deborah Ellis 256 p. 2013 Pgw

1. Indian children 2. Indian families 3. Indians of North America—Alcohol use 4. Indians of North America—Social conditions 5. Young adult literature

ISBN 1554981204; 9781554981205

SUMMARY: This book, by Deborah Ellis, "is a . . . collection of interviews with [native] children aged nine to eighteen. They come from all over the continent, from Iqaluit to Texas, Haida Gwaai to North Carolina. . . . Many of these children are living with the legacy of the residential schools; many have lived through the cycle of foster care. Many others have found something in their roots that sustains them, have found their place in the arts, the sciences, athletics." (Publisher's note)

REVIEW: *Booklist* v110 no9/10 p83 Ja 1 2014 MICHAEL CART

"Ghost Hawk," "Looks Like Daylight," and "If You Could Be Mine." "[Susan] Cooper's heartfelt historical fantasy about the magical relationship between two boys, Native American Little Hawk and trader's son John, is richly plotted, beautiful in tone, and serious in theme as it examines the injustices of early colonial life. . . . Canadian author [Deborah] Ellis has interviewed 45 young Native people from Canada and the U.S. The 9- to 18-year-olds tell her about the often appalling conditions of their lives, which are blighted by alcohol and drug abuse, poverty, suicide, broken families, and more. 'That they are here at all,' Ellis movingly writes, 'is a miracle.' . . . [Sara] Farizan's unusual first novel tells an important story about the stubbornness of love and offers an inside look at secret gay life in Iran."

REVIEW: *Booklist* v110 no5 p60 N 1 2013 Michael Cart

REVIEW: *Bull Cent Child Books* v67 no3 p151 N 2013 T. A.

REVIEW: *Kirkus Rev* v81 no16 p302 Ag 15 2013

REVIEW: *SLJ* v59 no10 p1 O 2013 Jody Kopple

REVIEW: *Voice of Youth Advocates* v36 no4 p92 O 2013 Diane Colson

ELLIS, DEBORAH. My name is Parvana; [by] Deborah Ellis 201 p. 2012 Groundwood Books/House of Anansi Press

1. Afghan War, 2001- & women 2. Afghanistan—Social conditions—21st century 3. Military interrogation 4. Women—Social life & customs—Fiction 5. Young adult fiction

ISBN 1554982979 (hardcover); 9781554982974 (hardcover)

SUMMARY: In this novel by Deborah Ellis "15-year-old Parvana is imprisoned and interrogated as a suspected terrorist in Afghanistan. . . . Parvana's captors" read "aloud the words in her notebook to decide if the angry written sentiments of a teenage girl can be evidence of guilt. . . . The interrogation, the words of the notebook and the effective third-person narration combine for a . . . portrait of a girl and her country." (Kirkus Reviews)

REVIEW: *Booklist* v109 no4 p51 O 15 2012 Kathleen Issacs

REVIEW: *Bull Cent Child Books* v66 no5 p243 Ja 2013 K. C.

"My Name Is Parvana." "In this follow-up to the Breadwinner trilogy, readers are brought up to date on the fate of Parvana, who has struggled all her life to survive against the Taliban. Now a teenager, Parvana has been detained by American forces after being found wandering amidst the rubble of her school in Afghanistan. . . . Parvana here is shown to be a remarkably resourceful and highly intelligent young woman who maintains her optimism even through her anger at her circumstances. . . . Like the rest of [Deborah] Ellis' work, this is purposive but effective; leavened with a likable character for whom readers will feel compassion and energized with breathtaking action and suspense that keeps pages turning, it will inspire readers toward outrage and perhaps even social action."

REVIEW: *Kirkus Rev* p57 D 2 2012 Best NonFiction & Teen

REVIEW: *Kirkus Rev* v80 no17 p272 S 1 2012

REVIEW: *Publ Wkly* v259 no35 p78 Ag 27 2012

REVIEW: *SLJ* v58 no10 p130 O 2012 Rhona Campbell

REVIEW: *Voice of Youth Advocates* v36 no1 p658-9 Ap 2013 Deborah L. Dubois

ELLIS, M. HENDERSON. Petra K and the Blackhearts; [by] M. Henderson Ellis 208 p. 2014 Random House Inc
1. Dragons—Fiction 2. Fantasy fiction 3. Magic—Fiction 4. Orphans—Fiction 5. Revolutions—Fiction
ISBN 098506238X; 9780985062385

SUMMARY: This novel, by M. Henderson Ellis, is an "adventure [that] pits a poor, fatherless girl against all sides in a battle for a dragon's heart and a city's freedom. Petra . . . receive[s] a vial of perfume distilled from the mystical song of a dragonka (a descendent of ancient dragons)—launching events that culminate in revolution. . . . As the city falls under oppression, Petra . . . and a ragtag gang of orphans, the Blackhearts, must free the city from an ancient curse revived." (Kirkus Reviews)

REVIEW: *Bull Cent Child Books* v67 no6 p307-8 F 2014 Kate Quealy-Gainer

"Petra K and the Blackhearts". "The blend of magic and machinery is eerily intriguing. . . . Petra K is a stalwart but accessible heroine—her struggles with her friends and her mother give her immediate appeal while her transformation from schoolgirl to revolutionary is authentically bumpy, occurring in fits and starts as she is plagued by doubts and miscalculations. Her simple, direct narration doesn't do much scene-setting (more description of the dragonka would have been welcome), but it also provides moments of poignancy. . . . The ending makes this a bit of a tearjerker for pet lovers—Luma does indeed die—but sharing this as a classroom or family readaloud may soften the blow and spur some thoughtful discussion about love, loss, and loyalty."

REVIEW: *Kirkus Rev* v82 no2 p193 Ja 15 2014

REVIEW: *SLJ* v60 no5 p106 My 2014 Necia Blundy

REVIEW: *Voice of Youth Advocates* v36 no6 p69 F 2014 Lucy Schall

ELLIS, SARAH. Outside in; [by] Sarah Ellis 206 p. 2014 Pgw
1. Friendship—Fiction 2. Homeless persons—Fiction 3. Mothers & daughters—Fiction 4. Teenage girls—Fiction 5. Young adult fiction
ISBN 1554983673; 9781554983674

SUMMARY: In this book, by Sarah Ellis, "Lynn is a typical 13-year-old Canadian, navigating through life. . . . Things start to fall apart when her mom wrecks her relationship with the only man who has ever stuck around and Lynn's passport doesn't come in time for her to take the choir trip with the rest of her friends, who leave for Portland. . . Then a mysterious girl named Blossom is thrust into her life and introduces her to a wonderful world within their city called the Underland." (Publisher's note)

REVIEW: *Booklist* v110 no17 p94 My 1 2014 Kathleen Isaacs

REVIEW: *Bull Cent Child Books* v67 no10 p513 Je 2014 D. S.

"Outside In". "[Sarah] Ellis is simultaneously a knotty and substantive writer and one with a light, conversational style, so the third-person narration makes Lynn a relatable protagonist even amid a highly unusual situation. . . . The book nonetheless remains aware of its real-life issues, with Lynn consciously squelching some of her reservations about Blossom's lifestyle (her lack of schooling, her unorthodox entry into the family as an abandoned baby) even as she loves the romantic creativity of the Underlanders' world. As a result, this will be an excellent book for discussion, eliciting lively partisanship on the question of what's right and wrong here; readers' take on the ethics will determine just how happily ever after they think the characters end up living."

REVIEW: *Horn Book Magazine* v90 no3 p84 My/Je 2014

REVIEW: *Kirkus Rev* v82 no7 p244 Ap 1 2014

REVIEW: *Quill Quire* v80 no5 p43-4 Je 2014 Emily Donaldson

REVIEW: *SLJ* v60 no5 p106 My 2014 Ellen Norton

REVIEW: *Voice of Youth Advocates* v37 no2 p56 Je 2014 Gwen Amborski

REVIEW: *Voice of Youth Advocates* v37 no2 p56 Je 2014 Adrienne Amborski

ELLIS, SYLVIA. Freedom's pragmatist; Lyndon Johnson and civil rights; [by] Sylvia Ellis xii, 328 p. 2013 University Press of Florida
1. African Americans—Civil rights 2. Civil rights—United States—History 3. Civil rights movements—United States—History—20th century 4. Historical literature
ISBN 9780813044569 (alk. paper)
LC 2013-015083

SUMMARY: "This examination of [Lyndon B.] Johnson's life from childhood through his lengthy career in politics argues that place, historical context, and personal ambition are the keys to understanding his stance on civil rights. Johnson's viewpoint, in turn, is essential to understanding the history of civil rights in the United States." (Publisher's note)

REVIEW: *Choice* v51 no7 p1289-90 Mr 2014 R. L. Saunders

"Freedom's Pragmatist: Lyndon Johnson and Civil Rights." "This comprehensive reassessment of one facet of Lyndon Johnson's political career reasserts the central-figure narrative, providing a counterbalance to the grassroots school of scholars like Charles Payne, Aldon Morris, and John Dittmer. . . . [Sylvia] Ellis is clearly aware not only of what Johnson said, but also to whom and under what circumstances. She fairly clearly challenges Robert Caro's plain facts view of Johnson. Providing a measure of rhetorical analysis to understand motives and intentions, she asks why LBJ acted, spoke, and voted the way he did at various points in his political career. . . . Recommended."

ELLIS, WARREN.ed. Red Phone Box. See Red Phone Box

ELLISON, J. T. When shadows fall; [by] J. T. Ellison 416 p. 2014 Harlequin Books
1. Cold cases (Criminal investigation) 2. Criminal evidence 3. Detective & mystery stories 4. Forensic pathology 5. Murder investigation—Fiction
ISBN 0778316041; 9780778316046

SUMMARY: In J. T, Ellison's "third Samantha Owens novel . . . when Sam, now head of Georgetown University Medical School's forensic pathology department in Washington, D.C., receives a letter from a stranger named Timothy Savage asking her to solve his murder, she gets drawn back into her former career in law enforcement. Sam performs an autopsy on Savage, who recently died in Lynchburg, Va., and the examination shows he did not commit suicide, as the police ruled, but was indeed murdered." (Publishers Weekly)

REVIEW: *Booklist* v110 no12 p35 F 15 2014 Jeff Ayers

"When Shadows Fall." "What at first appears to be a suicide propels Dr. Samantha Owens into a case that will test her resolve and sanity in [J. T.] Ellison's third novel to feature the forensic pathologist. . . . The mystery only intensifies as the narrative unfolds, and it's a guarantee that readers will not figure out all of the details before the end. Ellison has crafted a terrific thriller, and fans of forensic mysteries, such as those by Patricia Cornwell, should immediately add this series to their A-lists. Familiarity with the prior books is not necessary to enjoy this one."

REVIEW: *Kirkus Rev* v82 no5 p229 Mr 1 2014

REVIEW: *Libr J* v139 no3 p94 F 15 2014 Mary Todd Chesnut

REVIEW: *Publ Wkly* v261 no4 p171 Ja 27 2014

ELLISON, KEITH. My country 'tis of thee; [by] Keith Ellison 304 p. 2013 Gallery Books/Karen Hunter Books

1. African American legislators—Biography 2. Legislators—United States—Biography 3. Multiculturalism—United States 4. Muslims—United States—Biography 5. Political science literature 6. Social change—United States

ISBN 145166687X (alkaline paper); 9781451666878 (alkaline paper); 9781451666892 (alkaline paper)

LC 2012-051565

SUMMARY: This book on race, religion, and U.S. Politics was written by Keith Ellison. "Elected U.S. Representative to Minnesota's 5th congressional district in 2007, Ellison is the first Black Muslim in the U.S. Congress and the first African American elected to the House from Minnesota. Not a memoir, though it contains personal anecdotes, his work decries the current political polarization and argues for an America that truly embraces all peoples and beliefs." (Library Journal)

REVIEW: *Kirkus Rev* v81 no24 p250 D 15 2013

"My Country, 'Tis of Thee: My Faith, My Family, Our Future". "An engaging memoir on what it means to be a black Muslim in American government. . . . With insights into the famous leaders who have influenced him, [Keith] Ellison passionately details the concepts that still divide America and offers suggestions on how the country can move beyond the color of a person's skin or religious belief to create a nation of the people, for the people. The empowering words of an insightful American who has risen to a place in government where his actions can really make a difference."

REVIEW: *Libr J* v138 no6 p59 Ap 1 2013 Barbara Hoffert

REVIEW: *Publ Wkly* v261 no3 p52 Ja 20 2014

ELLORY, R. J. City of lies; a thriller; [by] R. J. Ellory 464 p. 2013 Overlook Hardcover

1. Conspiracy—Fiction 2. Crime—Fiction 3. Deception—Fiction 4. FICTION—Thrillers 5. Organized crime—Fiction

ISBN 1590204654; 9781590204658 (hardback)

LC 2013-027469

SUMMARY: This book, by R. J. Ellory, is a "thriller about [a] . . . writer lured back to New York City to learn that there is more . . . to his past than he thought. . . . John Harper [works for the] Miami Herald. . . . Evelyn Sawyer, the aunt who raised him, calls to tell him his father has been shot. . . . He flies to the Big Apple, and Aunt Evelyn starts the 'everything you know is wrong' story. Turns out, John's absent father is the underworld big shot Edward 'Lenny' Bernstein." (Kirkus Reviews)

REVIEW: *Booklist* v110 no1 p43 S 1 2013 Christine Tran

REVIEW: *Kirkus Rev* v81 no18 p193 S 15 2013

REVIEW: *N Y Times Book Rev* p27 D 15 2013 MARILYN STASIO

"Dust," Nowhere Nice," and "City of Lies." "[Author] Patricia Cornwell's imperious forensic scientist, Kay Scarpetta, shows uncharacteristic signs of vulnerability at the beginning of 'Dust.' . . . There's plenty going on at Scarpetta's bustling lab. . . . Buckle up for a rowdy ride with [author] Rick Gavin in 'Nowhere Nice' . . . , the latest in a riotous series set in the Mississippi Delta. . . . Calling these characters colorful doesn't begin to get at the rich regional nuances that Gavin mines at every pit stop from Arkansas to Alabama. . . . A sensitive hero is a good thing to have in a tough crime novel--up to a point. That point is passed in R. J. Ellory's 'City of Lies' . . . , when the doting author allows these tender feelings to soften his protagonists's brain."

ELLWOOD, MARK. Bargain fever; the new shopping rules of getting more and paying less; [by] Mark Ellwood 288 p. 2013 Portfolio/Penguin

1. Consumer behavior 2. Consumer education 3. Discount 4. Journalism 5. Shopping

ISBN 9781591845805

LC 2013-019045

SUMMARY: This book by Mark Ellwood "offers an in-depth account of how American consumer culture has become permanently discount-driven. . . . He claims that this phase in retail shopping stems from oversupply and underdemand. . . . He touches on subjects ranging from sample sales of high-end fashion, both in person as well as online, to what paved the way for Groupon's e-commerce success and the company's effects on small businesses." (Kirkus Reviews)

REVIEW: *Booklist* v110 no1 p19-20 S 1 2013 David Pitt

"Bargain Fever: How to Shop in a Discounted World." "This is a highly informative and entertainingly written book about a radical shift in the relationship between consumers and sellers. . . . What we have now is an environment in which consumers demand bargains all the time, and sellers are always looking for new ways to convince consumers they're getting a deal, even when they're not. . . . [Mark] Ellwood helps us understand our own frame of mind as consumers while also providing insight into the point of view of the people whose products we buy."

REVIEW: *Kirkus Rev* v81 no21 p13 N 1 2013

REVIEW: *Publ Wkly* v260 no32 p52 Ag 12 2013

ELSE, BARBARA. The traveling restaurant; Jasper's voyage in three parts : a novel for children; [by] Barbara Else 295 p. 2012 Gecko Press

ISBN 1877579033; 9781877579035

SUMMARY: In this book by Barbara Else, set "on he mysterious sailing ship The Traveling Restaurant, twelve-year-old Jasper Ludlow . . . embarks on an adventure across Old Ocean and Lake Riversea in search of his baby sister. Jasper faces whirlpools, troublesome monkeys, and hungry pirates in this . . . tale of treachery, courage, and magic." (Publisher's note)

REVIEW: *Bull Cent Child Books* v65 no8 p394-5 Ap 2012 K. Q. G.

"The Traveling Restaurant: Jasper's Voyage in Three Parts." "Adventure fans with a taste for fine cuisine will delight in the mouthwatering descriptions that accompany the ship's maritime mealtimes, while Jasper and company's various run-ins with hot-tempered pirates, duplicitous journalists, and hat-loving monkeys make up the entertainment portion of this charming dinner and a show. The false monarch, the mysteriously missing heir, and the plucky boy at the center of it are all elements we've seen before, but here they come together in a unique way that may surprise even more sophisticated readers."

REVIEW: *Horn Book Magazine* v88 no3 p81-2 My/Je 2012 Anita L. Burkam

"The Traveling Restaurant: Jasper's Voyage in Three Parts." "When Lady Gall, the evil Provisional Monarch of Fontania, tries to poison Jasper's little sister, he and his family flee by ship. . . . [Another ship called] 'Restaurant' rescues a castaway Uncle Trump who reports that his ship sank in a storm and Jasper's family is missing. Devastated, Jasper hopes they were rescued but fears they were captured by Lady Gall. . . . Constant action, lively language, and a Mahy-esque sense of whimsy carry the narrative as the mysteries unfold. Jasper's startling ability to think on his feet will endear him to readers, as will his sister Sibilla's authentic toddler personality, while hidden relationships revealed at the end make for a satisfying conclusion."

REVIEW: *Kirkus Rev* v80 no4 p393 F 15 2012

"The Traveling Restaurant: Jasper's Voyage in Three Parts." "A seemingly ordinary lad boards a seagoing eatery and is swept up in a series of flights and pursuits that lead him to a higher destiny than he expects (or even wants, particularly). . . . Else arranges her narrative into short chapters . . . and strews it with pirates, wild waters, sudden twists of fortune, family revelations and scrumptious tucker . . . . She sets her quick-witted protagonist on a course that not only sharpens his already-considerable culinary skills but gives him a central role in rescuing his shipwrecked family, decisively scotching Lady Gall's schemes and restoring magic to the land."

REVIEW: *SLJ* v58 no3 p154 Mr 2012 Alissa LeMerise

ELSER, JAMES J.ed. Phosphorus, food, and our future. See Phosphorus, food, and our future

ELTAHAWY, NORA.tr. I want to get married! See Aal, G. A.

ELTIS, SOS. Acts of desire; women and sex on stage, 1800-1930; [by] Sos Eltis viii, 268 p. 2013 Oxford University Press

1. Drama—History & criticism 2. English drama—History and criticism 3. Sex differences in literature 4. Sex in literature 5. Women in literature

ISBN 0199691355 (hbk.); 9780199691357 (hbk.)

LC 2013-431430

SUMMARY: This book, edited by Sos Eltis, "traces the theatrical representation of illicit female sexuality from early nineteenth-century melodramas, through sensation dramas, Ibsenite sex-problem plays and suffrage dramas, to early social realism and the well-made plays of Pinero, Jones, Maugham, and Coward. This study reveals and analyses enduring plot lines and tropes that continue to influence contemporary theatre and film." (Publisher's note)

REVIEW: *Choice* v51 no5 p846 Ja 2014 M. D. Whitlatch

REVIEW: *TLS* no5779 p21 Ja 3 2014 ANNA-MARIA SSEMUYABA

"Acts of Desire: Women and Sex on Stage 1800-1930." "In 'Acts of Desire: Women and sex on stage 1800-1930,' Sos Eltis examines not only the plays themselves (by a broad range of playwrights), but also changing social attitudes to love and desire, allowing us to see how particular tropes and conventions dominated the period, and why. . . . 'Acts of Desire' looks beyond the depiction of women on stage to address the surrounding social, political and economic issues which affected the theatre. While she notes the intellectual roots of the 'fallen woman' stereotype and its many different cultural manifestations. Sos Eltis also considers playwrights who dared to challenge stereotypes."

ELVGREN, JENNIFER. The whispering town; [by] Jennifer Elvgren 32 p. 2014 Kar-Ben Publishing

1. Historical fiction 2. Jews—Denmark—Fiction 3. Jews—Denmark—Juvenile fiction 4. World War, 1939-1945—Denmark—Fiction 5. World War, 1939-1945—Denmark—Juvenile fiction

ISBN 1467711942; 9781467711944 (lib. bdg.: alk. paper)

LC 2013-002195

SUMMARY: This children's book, written by Jennifer Elvgren and illustrated by Fabio Santomauro, tells "the dramatic story of neighbors in a small Danish fishing village who, during the Holocaust, shelter a Jewish family waiting to be ferried to safety in Sweden. It is 1943 in Nazi-occupied Denmark. Anett and her parents are hiding a Jewish woman and her son, Carl, in their cellar until a fishing boat can take them across the sound to neutral Sweden." (Publisher's note)

REVIEW: *Booklist* v110 no17 p94 My 1 2014 Ilene Cooper

REVIEW: *Bull Cent Child Books* v67 no9 p452 My 2014 H. M.

"The Whispering Town". "[Jennifer] Elvgren's focused, unsentimentalized narrative is an ideal selection for introducing younger children to the many who stood up to do what was right during the Nazi regime. The spare storytelling style is perfectly matched with the sophisticated yet accessible illustrations, composed of black lines, fields of digital color, and scratchy pen details. A limited palette wherein grays and blues dominate plays to the mystery of the story while the contrasting splashes of dark red add interest. An author's note provides background information and links the events of the story to an actual occurrence in the fishing village of Gilleleje. This is a notable early introduction to the Danish resistance that deserves wide readership."

REVIEW: *Kirkus Rev* v82 no4 p246 F 15 2014

REVIEW: *N Y Times Book Rev* p22 Ap 6 2014 ELIZABETH WEIN

ELYA, SUSAN MIDDLETON, 1955-. Fire! Fuego! Brave bomberos; [by] Susan Middleton Elya 40 p. 2012 Bloomsbury Children's Books

1. Children's literature 2. Fire fighters—Fiction 3. Picture books for children 4. Spanish language—Vocabulary—Juvenile literature 5. Stories in rhyme

ISBN 1599907593; 9781599904610 (hardcover : alk. paper); 9781599907598 (reinforced : alk. paper)
LC 2011-004934

SUMMARY: This picture book depicts the story of a group of firefighters, "four bomberos and el capitán," as they "race to gear up and get to the fire after the alarm sounds." The book describes various firefighting themes such as the fire station Dalmatian, the fire pole, and rescuing a cat. Author Susan Middleton Elya incorporates Spanish vocabulary words into the text, and adds "context clues as well as words that are close to English [to] make most of the Spanish vocabulary easy to decode." (Kirkus Reviews)

REVIEW: *Booklist* v108 no16 p69 Ap 15 2012 Angie Zapata

REVIEW: *Kirkus Rev* v80 no4 p394 F 15 2012

"Fire! Fuego! Brave Bomberos." " [Susan Middleton] Elya has proven herself a master at painlessly weaving Spanish vocabulary into her stories, and this latest is no exception. Four bomberos and el capitán race to gear up and get to the fire after the alarm sounds. . . . Firefighting is a perennially popular topic, and while the actual story here is rather unexceptional, Elya makes this book stand out in other ways. . . . Context clues as well as words that are close to English make most of the Spanish vocabulary easy to decode. . . . [Dan] Santat's illustrations also help to set this firefighter book apart."

REVIEW: *Publ Wkly* v259 no11 p56 Mr 12 2012

EMERY, ELIZABETH. Photojournalism and the origins of the French writer house museum (1881-1914); privacy, publicity, and personality; [by] Elizabeth Emery xii, 262 p. 2012 Ashgate

1. Authors, French—Homes and haunts—France 2. Historic house museums—France 3. Historical literature 4. Literary landmarks—France 5. Photojournalism—France
ISBN 9781409408772 (hardcover : alk. paper)
LC 2011-038474

SUMMARY: In this book, author Elizabeth Emery "asks fundamental questions about the French heritage industry, and its particular penchant for the transformation of writers' houses into museums. Why, she asks, did these homes become so linked to their owners' work at the end of the nineteenth century that they started being preserved as museums, and how did this process become institutionalized in the twentieth century?" (Times Literary Supplement)

REVIEW: *TLS* no5755 p27 Jl 19 2013 NICHOLAS WHITE

"Photojournalism and the Origins of the French Writer House Museum (1881-1914): Privacy, Publicity, and Personality." "Pierre Loti's house in Rochefort is a conspicuous example of that modem phenomenon to which Elizabeth Emery's fine book bears eloquent testimony--the emergence during the belle époque of the French writer house museum. Emery asks fundamental questions about the French heritage industry, and its particular penchant for the transformation of writers' houses into museums. . . . Emery wears her remarkable erudition lightly."

EMKE, GERALD MICHAEL. Cyber Assassin; Cyber Crime Adventures of Mick Kelly; [by] Gerald Michael Emke 292 p. 2013 CreateSpace Independent Publishing Platform

1. Computer crimes 2. Computer hackers 3. Crime—Fiction 4. Intelligence service—Fiction 5. Suspense fiction
ISBN 1492942146; 9781492942146

SUMMARY: "In this thriller, a freelance hacker uses his expertise at a covert U.S. intelligence unit trying to keep America's computer networks secure. After leaving government work and retiring to his cabin in Bliss, Mich., superhacker Mick Kelly remains in touch with his former superior, Air Force Col. Tammi Chan, who hires him for some 'off the books' jobs that require a little wetwork. . . . Unfortunately, Mick becomes vulnerable when his past comes back to betray him." (Kirkus Reviews)

REVIEW: *Kirkus Rev* v81 no24 p387 D 15 2013

"Cyber Assassin: Cyber Crime Adventures of Mick Kelly". "Both these characters lend an emotional note to what is otherwise a coldblooded exercise in cyberwarfare and violence. Part of the novel's problem is the fact that it struggles to build suspense over the course of Mick's four assignments. The outcomes of the individual episodes never seem in doubt. Author [Gerald Michael] Emke appears to be on firmer footing when describing how to break into a secure computer system than when dramatizing human relationships. In particular, Mick's hero status is a little too good to be true; he comes across as more of a comic book superhero or perhaps the extreme wish fulfillment of a computer nerd. Sharp writing about computers and weapons systems, but the human element doesn't quite boot up."

EMMETT, CHAD F. Sex and world peace. See Hudson, V. M.

EMSLEY, CLIVE. Soldier, Sailor, Beggarman, Thief; Crime and the British Armed Services since 1914; [by] Clive Emsley 256 p. 2013 Oxford University Press

1. Historical literature 2. Military offenses—Great Britain—History—20th century 3. Soldiers—Conduct of life 4. War and crime—Great Britain—History—20th century 5. War crimes—Great Britain—History—20th century
ISBN 0199653712; 9780199653713
LC 2012-537395

SUMMARY: This book, by Clive Emsley, presents a "serious investigation of criminal offending by members of the British armed forces both during and immediately after these wars. Its particular focus is the two world wars but, recognising the concerns and the problems voiced in recent years about veterans of the Falklands, the Gulf wars, and the campaign in Afghanistan, Clive Emsley concludes his narrative in the present." (Publisher's note)

REVIEW: *Am Hist Rev* v119 no1 p255 F 2014 Jessica Meyer

REVIEW: *Choice* v51 no1 p152 S 2013 P. T. Smith

"Soldier, Sailor, Beggerman, Thief: Crime and the British Armed Services Since 1914." "The last few years have seen an impressive output of books about police and crime, much of it generated by former students or colleagues of [author] Clive Emsley. . . . Little has been done on the military side of criminal justice, here associated with the world wars. Much crime was carried out by young males and was opportunistic and impulsive, not simply the deeds of a separate criminal class. . . . Emsley goes through the various types of crimes servicemen committed, from drunken violence to murder and, more commonly, pilferage and desertion. . . . This is a scholarly, well-documented account, and much of the book is given over to colorful specific accounts."

REVIEW: *Hist Today* v63 no10 p60 O 2013 GARY SHEFFIELD

ENCYCLOPEDIA OF ALZHEIMER'S DISEASE; with directories of research, treatment and care facilities; viii, 447 p. 2012 McFarland

1. Alzheimer's disease—Diagnosis—Methodology 2. Alzheimer's disease—Prevention 3. Medical literature
ISBN 9780786464586 (softcover: alk. paper); 0786464585
LC 2011-046545

SUMMARY: This reference volume discusses Alzheimer's disease. "For this second edition . . . medical writer [Elaine A.] Moore has updated her alphabetical entries. This volume notes discontinued trials and reflects the current emphasis on lifestyle changes to reduce the risk of Alzheimer's disease, relevant environmental factors, and the search for better diagnostic techniques. Black-and-white diagrams aid the entries' explanations. Three revised sections are featured." (Choice)

REVIEW: *Choice* v49 no11 p2028 Jl 2012 T. M. Racz

"Encyclopedia of Alzheimer's Disease: With Directories of Research, Treatment, and Care Facilities". "For this second edition . . . medical writer [Elaine A.] Moore has updated her alphabetical entries. This volume notes discontinued trials and reflects the current emphasis on lifestyle changes to reduce the risk of Alzheimer's disease, relevant environmental factors, and the search for better diagnostic techniques. Black-and-white diagrams aid the entries' explanations. Three revised sections are featured. . . . This volume will be useful in college, university, and public libraries."

REVIEW: *Libr J* v137 no14 p130 S 1 2012 Laurie Selwyn

ENCYCLOPEDIA OF AMERICAN INDIAN ISSUES TODAY; 868 p. 2013 Greenwood

1. Encyclopedias & dictionaries 2. Indians of North America—Education 3. Indians of North America—Encyclopedias 4. Indians of North America—Government relations 5. Indians of North America—Social conditions 6. Indians of North America—Sovereignty
ISBN 0313381445; 9780313381447 (cloth : alk. paper); 9780313381454 (ebook)
LC 2012-031756

SUMMARY: Editor Russell M. Lawson's book "features subjects commonly discussed, including reservations, poverty, sovereignty, the problem of solid waste on reservations, and the lives of urban Indians, among other contemporary issues. Organized into ten sections, the book also provides helpful sidebars and informative essays to address topics on casinos and gaming, sexual identity, education, and poverty." (Publisher's note)

REVIEW: *Booklist* v109 no22 p55 Ag 1 2013 Mary Ellen Snodgrass

REVIEW: *Choice* v51 no1 p53 S 2013 M. Cedar Face

"Encyclopedia of American Indian Issues Today." "This two-volume set explores, within historical, social, and cultural contexts, contemporary issues facing Native peoples. Lengthy, signed entries are organized into ten topical sections that cover demographics, economy and work, education, health, identity and spirituality, sovereignty and the federal relationship, law and politics, expression and the arts, the environment, and Canadian and other indigenous issues . . . ranging from casinos to poverty, activism, domestic violence, mascots, repatriation, and tribal courts. . . . Editor [Russell M.] Lawson (Bacone College) has written and edited other reference works in the field of history. A good starting point for undergraduate research, this set is distinctive."

REVIEW: *Libr J* v138 no12 p103 Jl 1 2013 Patricia Ann Owens

THE ENCYCLOPEDIA OF CARIBBEAN RELIGIONS; Volume 1: a - L; Volume 2: M - Z; 640 p. 2013 Univ of Illinois Pr

1. Caribbean Area—Religion 2. Encyclopedias & dictionaries 3. Imperialism—Religious aspects 4. Rastafari movement 5. Vodou
ISBN 0252037235; 9780252037238

SUMMARY: This book covers "Caribbean religious phenomena from a Caribbean perspective. . . . Organized alphabetically, entries examine how Caribbean religious experiences have been shaped by and have responded to the processes of colonialism and the challenges of the postcolonial world.." Topics discussed include "Vodou, Rastafari, Sunni Islam, Sanatan Dharma, Judaism, and the Roman Catholic and Seventh-day Adventist churches." (Publisher's note)

REVIEW: *Booklist* v109 no12 p44 F 15 2013 Christopher McConnell

REVIEW: *Choice* v51 no7 p1180-1 Mr 2014 K. M. Simmons

"The Encyclopedia of Caribbean Religions." "This encyclopedia covers an impressive scope of material--over 100 entries, many with multiple subsections--in its two volumes. The editors do a fine job of including a vast array of information while creating a sense of relative cohesion. As with any encyclopedia with entries from different contributors, some inconsistencies in levels of substance and argumentation are evident. . . . A careful teacher or scholar surely would be wary of making such quick categorical claims about a cohesive 'African traditional religion' and 'its' origins or performances before a classroom or in print. Yet, such moments are easy to locate throughout the encyclopedia."

REVIEW: *Libr J* v138 no4 p90 Mr 1 2013 Annette Haldeman

ENCYCLOPEDIA OF GLOBAL BRANDS; 1183 p. 2013 St. James Press, A part of Gale, Cengage Learning

1. Brand name products—Encyclopedias 2. Branding (Marketing) 3. Corporations—Encyclopedias 4. Emerging markets 5. Encyclopedias & dictionaries
ISBN 1558622276; 9781558622272 (set); 9781558622289 (vol. 1); 9781558622296 (vol. 2)
LC 2013-012023

SUMMARY: This encyclopedia of global brands "centers on brands that have strong public awareness, dominance in the product's category, financial status, and potential for future success. . . . The A-Z entries are written in a case-study style, focusing on a company's background and branding practices. Entries begin with . . . [an] 'At a Glance' overview. The information following includes brand origins, elements, identity, strategy, equity, awareness, and outlook." (Booklist)

REVIEW: *Booklist* v110 no4 p34-6 O 15 2013 Jennifer Adams

"Encyclopedia of Global Brands." "Because of the vast number, not every global brand one would expect is included; however, the 269 represented will delight those looking for a brand-specific overview of new and established products flourishing in the global marketplace. . . . Since brand information is often held tightly to the chest, this two-volume set is a researcher's delight. Information was culled from marketing textbooks, domestic and international business journals, and trade publication brand rankings. This reference set is useful for those who are looking for information on the world's most influential brands, and it is recommended for most academic and large public libraries."

REVIEW: *Choice* v51 no5 p810 Ja 2014 L. Kong

THE ENCYCLOPEDIA OF GREEK TRAGEDY; 1808 p. 2014 Wiley-Blackwell

1. Encyclopedias & dictionaries 2. Greek drama (Tragedy)—Encyclopedias 3. Mythology in literature 4. Theater—Greece—History—To 500—Encyclopedias 5. Tragedy

ISBN 9781444335927 (set)

LC 2012-031788

SUMMARY: This encyclopedia of Greek tragedies "was created for readers who want context while attempting to truly understand these ancient works. . . . The three-volume set features 819 signed entries, including one for each of the 32 extant tragedies as well as the one surviving satyr play, 'Cyclops'. Outside of the plays themselves, topics range from the general, like Myth and Rhetoric, to the specific, such as Reception of Greek tragedy in Japanese literature and Performance." (Booklist)

REVIEW: *Booklist* v110 no6 p29-30 N 15 2013 Emily Compton-Dzak

"The Encyclopedia of Greek Tragedy." "'The Encyclopedia of Greek Tragedy' was created for readers who want context while attempting to truly understand these ancient works. Contextual information on topics such as political environment, the type of theaters used, and culture, according to the editor, gives readers the ability to comprehend Greek tragedies 'on their own terms, and not from a modern perspective alone.' . . . This encyclopedia is painstakingly thorough in its treatment of Greek tragedy. . . . Although the intended audience includes students and researchers, the content is accessible to anyone with an interest in Greek tragedy. This comprehensive set is recommended for academic, large public, and, when appropriate, high-school libraries."

REVIEW: *Choice* v51 no6 p976 F 2014 F. W. Jenkins

ENCYCLOPEDIA OF HUMAN MEMORY; 1262 p. 2013 Greenwood

1. Encyclopedias & dictionaries 2. Memory—physiology—Encyclopedias—English 3. Memory Disorders—Encyclopedias—English 4. Models, Neurological—Encyclopedias—English 5. Neuropsychological Tests—Encyclopedias—English

ISBN 9781440800252 (v. 1 : hbk. : acid-free paper); 9781440800269 (v. 1 : ebook)

LC 2013-010932

SUMMARY: This encyclopedia covers "various psychological and physiological systems of memory, such as short-term or procedural memory . . . the principles that underlie effective encoding, storage, and construction of memories; and . . . often misconceptualized conditions like 'amnesia' or how our memories are stored in bits and pieces rather than linearly like a recorded tape or video." (Publisher's note)

REVIEW: *Booklist* v110 no12 p40 F 15 2014 Janet Pinkley

"Encyclopedia of Human Memory." "Despite the complexity of the human memory, 'Encyclopedia of Human Memory' does a brilliant job of approaching this abstract topic and making it accessible to the layperson. . . . The encyclopedia is easy to navigate, with the alphabetical list of entries and the topical arrangement of entries at the beginning of each volume. Additionally, there is a highly detailed index at the back of volume 3 and helpful cross-referencing within entries to direct readers to other relevant entries. . . . This set would be a good addition for public libraries, high-school libraries, and undergraduate libraries; the entries are written in such a way that readers do not need to have previous knowledge of the topic."

REVIEW: *Choice* v51 no10 p1778 Je 2014 A. J. Trussell

ENCYCLOPEDIA OF JAPANESE AMERICAN INTERNMENT; 342 p. 2013 Greenwood, An Imprint of ABC-CLIO, LLC

1. Encyclopedias & dictionaries 2. Japanese Americans—Biography—Encyclopedias 3. Japanese Americans—Evacuation and relocation, 1942-1945—Encyclopedias 4. United States—History—World War, 1939-1945 5. World War, 1939-1945—Japanese Americans—Encyclopedias

ISBN 9780313399152 (hardcopy : alk. paper)

LC 2013-000311

SUMMARY: "This volume covers one of the most notorious chapters in American history: the internment of 120,000 Japanese Americans, many of them for close to four years, as sanctioned by the U.S. government. Known by euphemisms like 'citizen isolation camps' or 'assembly centers,' the last of the camps did not close until six months after the end of WWII." This reference book includes a chronology, a bibliography, a list of camp locations, and primary documents as well as topical entries. (Booklist)

REVIEW: *Booklist* v110 no2 p50 S 15 2013 Michael Tosko

"Encyclopedia of Japanese American Internment." "The volume begins with an in-depth introduction of more than 20 pages. . . . A detailed 15-page chronology helps set up the main entries, which make up the bulk of the volume. . . . The volume concludes with 15 primary resources. . . . Even the text of signs titled 'Instructions to All Persons of Japanese Ancestry' is included, telling citizens what they can and cannot bring with them to the camps ('no personal items'). Many of the primary sources here are personal letters to and from internees. In sum, this is an excellent, handy reference source on one of the less heroic but still vitally important aspects of American history. Recommended for all types of libraries."

REVIEW: *Choice* v51 no4 p612 D 2013 T. S. H. Chan

REVIEW: *Libr J* v138 no20 p1 N 15 2013

ENCYCLOPEDIA OF MAJOR MARKETING STRATEGIES; xiii, 431 p. 2013 Gale/Cengage Learning

1. Advertising 2. Advertising campaigns—History—21st century 3. Advertising campaigns—United States—History—21st century 4. Encyclopedias & dic-

tionaries 5. Marketing—History—21st century—Encyclodpedias
ISBN 1414499213 (hardback); 9781414499215 (hardback)
LC 2013-011846

SUMMARY: This reference work "provides information on 100 of the most innovative and memorable advertising campaigns between 2010 and 2013. . . . Each campaign receives a situational analysis of why the campaign was needed, the target market that the campaign was intended to address, how the company introduced and promoted the campaign, and the campaign's outcome." (Booklist)

REVIEW: *Booklist* v110 no5 p41-2 N 1 2013 David Tyckoson

"Encyclopedia of Major Marketing Strategies." "This new update to Gale's 'Encyclopedia of Major Marketing Campaigns' set provides information on 100 of the most innovative and memorable advertising campaigns between 2010 and 2013. From 'The Priceline Negotiator Lives' to the 'Most Interesting Man in the World,' this work documents the motivation and logic behind some of the most recent successful advertising campaigns--and it explains why the campaigns were so successful. . . . This work is a useful addition for any business library--and fun reading for those who want to know why their favorite advertising campaign was so effective. Recommended for large academic and public libraries."

REVIEW: *Choice* v51 no4 p612-3 D 2013 E. J. Wood

"Encyclopedia of Major Marketing Strategies." "Like volumes 1 . . . and 2 . . . of the 'Encyclopedia of Major Marketing Campaigns,' edited by Thomas Riggs, this third volume . . . documents the coordination of marketing elements that work together to increase sales and/or market share of a product or brand. . . . Besides directory information, the encyclopedia's entry head now lists campaign theme, country context, primary media used, market sector, and date of implementation. Although occasionally misleading . . . capsule summaries generally are good. . . . Articles are descriptive yet succinct and to the point, with bulleted take-aways beginning each section. . . . Outcomes clearly benchmark a campaign's impact in terms of sales increases, market share, or awards and public recognition."

ENCYCLOPEDIA OF NATIONAL DRESS; traditional clothing around the world; 2 v. (xv, 813 p.) 2013 ABC-CLIO

1. Clothing & dress—Religious aspects 2. Clothing & dress—Social aspects 3. Clothing and dress—Encyclopedias 4. National characteristics 5. Social science literature
ISBN 0313376360; 9780313376368 (set); 9780313376375 (ebook); 9780313376382 (v. 1); 9780313376405 (v. 2)
LC 2012-040568

SUMMARY: In this book, edited by Jill Condra, "contributors examine clothing that is symbolic of the people who live in regions all over the world, providing a historical and geographic perspective that illustrates how people dress and explains the reasons behind the material, design, and style. Each entry in the encyclopedia includes a short historical and geographical background for the topic before discussing the clothing of people in that country or region of the world." (Publisher's note)

REVIEW: *Booklist* v110 no2 p50 S 15 2013 Lindsay Harmon

REVIEW: *Choice* v51 no5 p810 Ja 2014 R. Tolley-Stokes

"Encyclopedia of National Dress: Traditional Clothing Around the World." "This two-volume set examines over 130 nations and autonomous regions' national dress, folk costumes, and ethnic dress worn on special occasions or for festivals. The focus is on dress that is distinctive to wearers' lifestyles and reflective of their history. Readers glimpse the uniqueness of dress existing in various countries worldwide, as the editor presents historic context for each chapter. By staying away from 'judging the ways in which ethnic expression changed and mutated with events such as colonialism,' the editor allows individual interpretation of meaning."

REVIEW: *Libr J* v138 no12 p105 Jl 1 2013 Michael Bemis

REVIEW: *SLJ* v59 no10 p1 O 2013 Ann West LaPrise

ENCYCLOPEDIA OF PHILOSOPHY AND THE SOCIAL SCIENCES; 1145 p. 2013 SAGE Publications, Inc.

1. Academic discourse 2. Encyclopedias & dictionaries 3. Philosophy & social sciences 4. Philosophy and social sciences—Encyclopedias 5. Social theory
ISBN 9781412986892
LC 2013-003423

SUMMARY: Edited by Byron Kaldis, "this encyclopedia is purposefully multi- and inter-disciplinary. Knowledge boundaries are both delineated and crossed over. The goal is to convey a clear sense of how philosophy looks at the social sciences and to mark out a detailed picture of how the two are interrelated: interwoven at certain times but also differentiated and contrasted at others." (Publisher's note)

REVIEW: *Booklist* v109 no22 p55 Ag 1 2013 Brian Odom

REVIEW: *Choice* v51 no2 p226-7 O 2013 M. Meola

"Encyclopedia of Philosophy and the Social Sciences." "This two-volume A to Z encyclopedia comprises 402 entries written by 396 contributors on ideas and concepts relating to philosophy and the social sciences. . . . The entries are clearly written, informative, and instructive. In most cases they explain the significance of a particular philosophy term to the social sciences, a feature that distinguishes this work from a general encyclopedia of philosophy. [Editor Bryon] Kaldis . . . is the lead editor of an eight-person editorial board that has assembled an impressive international list of contributors, some of whom are leaders in their fields."

REVIEW: *Libr J* v138 no18 p118 N 1 2013 Julie Seifert

ENCYCLOPEDIA OF SCHOOL HEALTH; 744 p. 2013 SAGE Publications

1. Adolescent—United States 2. Child—United States 3. Health Promotion—methods—United States 4. Medical literature 5. School Health Services—organization & administration—United States
ISBN 9781412996006 (hardcover)
LC 2013-012971

SUMMARY: This encyclopedia covers "health topics and issues related to the eight components of the coordinated school program: 'Health Education/Instruction'; 'Health Services'; 'School Environment'; 'Physical Education'; 'Nutrition Services'; 'Counseling, Psychological, and Social Services'; 'Health Promotion for School Staff'; and 'Family and Community Involvement.' A reader's guide is located at the beginning,b and an alphabetized index at the end."

(Choice: Current Reviews for Academic Libraries)

REVIEW: *Choice* v51 no7 p1186-7 Mr 2014 L. Synovitz

"Encyclopedia of School Health." "This comprehensive encyclopedia, with entries by 200-plus professional contributors, is well organized according to health topics and issues related to the eight components of the coordinated school program. . . . A few tables are included, but if the cost is not prohibitive, the editors of this encyclopedia should consider adding some photographs or other color graphics to a second edition. This work is extraordinary in its depth and breadth. It will be useful for undergraduate and graduate students who are obtaining degrees in health education, nursing, counseling, psychology, or nutrition. Those employed in related areas also will find it extremely useful. This is the first encyclopedia on school health to be published; no comparable work exists."

THE ENCYCLOPEDIA OF THE DEAD; 199 1989 Farrar, Straus & Giroux

1. Death—Fiction 2. Fables 3. Prostitutes—Fiction 4. Serbo-Croatian fiction—Translations into English 5. Short stories—By individual authors

ISBN 0-374-14826-0

LC 88-3-1877

SUMMARY: This is a collection of short stories by the Yugoslav author. The title piece is about a biographical dictionary devoted to the lives of unknown people. In the "Book of Kings and Fools," the author recounts the genesis of the anti-Semitic forgery—the Protocols of the Elders of Sion. "Simon Magus" and "The Legend of the Sleepers" are variations on ancient legends. "Last Respects" commemorates a Hamburg prostitute. "'The Story of the Master and the Disciple,' about an intellectual engagement between a reputable scholar and his inquisitive student, and 'The Mirror of the Unknown,' about a young girl's crime-solving clairvoyance . . . {are both set in the} world of Eastern European Jews." (Nation)

REVIEW: *TLS* no5767 p16 O 11 2013

"The Encyclopedia of the Dead." "Danilo Kiš . . . has been authoritatively admired across the Channel and the Atlantic . . . but I found his effect cumulatively unimpressive. He strikes me as a highly deliberate and self-conscious author of vaguely Pyrrhic books: great quantities of description, or, later, event, that leave one with the feeling of having read nothing at all. . . . The prevailing tone is one of dutiful, dependable academic narration, and even when the stories are told by a persona, there is a whiff of : erudition and privileged access to them. . . . These stories are not so much chronicles of deaths foretold, as deaths twice-told."

THE ENCYCLOPEDIA OF THE GOTHIC; 2 volumes (xxxi, 838 p.) 2013 Wiley-Blackwell

1. Encyclopedias & dictionaries 2. Gothic fiction (Literary genre)—Encyclopedias 3. Gothic revival (Art)—Encyclopedias 4. Gothic revival (Literature)—Encyclopedias 5. Horror in mass media—Encyclopedias

ISBN 9781405182904 (set)

LC 2012-031784

SUMMARY: This encyclopedia on the subject of the Gothic, edited by William Hughes, David Punter, and Andrew Smith, "cover[s] all aspects of the Gothic as it is currently taught and researched, along with the development of the genre and its impact on contemporary culture." It "extends beyond a purely literary analysis to explore Gothic elements of film, music, drama, art, and architecture." (Publisher's note)

REVIEW: *Choice* v50 no12 p2197 Ag 2013 R. B. Meeker

REVIEW: *TLS* no5770 p12 N 1 2013 PHIL BAKER

"The Encyclopedia of the Gothic." "The present publication is another landmark, with around 250 entries by over 130 writers. It is bedevilled by the knowledge that an encyclopedia--that very Enlightenment form--of such an anti-Enlightenment business as the gothic is something of a contradiction in terms. The editors discuss this in their introduction rather than attempt any definition or parameters, and this lack of definition haunts the whole project, until the subject seems sublimely vast. . . . All entries are alphabetical, without any further attempt to arrange or subordinate them, but some are more major than others, and it is possible for the wandering reader to piece together an overview of the subject."

ENCYCLOPEDIA OF THE U.S. PRESIDENCY; a historical reference; 6 v., 2500 p. 2013 Facts On File

1. Encyclopedias & dictionaries 2. Presidents—United States—Encyclopedias, Juvenile 3. Presidents—United States—History—Encyclopedias, Juvenile 4. United States—History—Dictionaries 5. United States—Politics & government—Dictionaries

ISBN 0816067449 (hardcover); 9780816067442 (hardcover)

LC 2010-020746

SUMMARY: This six-volume set looks at the American presidency. The "opening volume includes 19 thematic essays dealing with various topics surrounding the history of the presidency including 'Origins of the Presidency,' 'Presidency and the Politics of Race,' and 'The Presidency and Popular Culture.' The ensuing volumes follow a chronological arrangement of individually signed entries covering from Washington to Obama." (Library Journal)

REVIEW: *Booklist* v109 no18 p34 My 15 2013 Ken Black

REVIEW: *Choice* v51 no1 p54 S 2013 W. Jakub

"Encyclopedia of the U.S. Presidency." "This encyclopedia is one of many comprehensive works currently in print on the topic of the US presidency. This six-volume set provides complete coverage of every president and administration, with a chapter devoted to each. . . . Following the comprehensive articles in this set are short A-to-Z entries encompassing significant events, significant pieces of legislation, notable presidential actions, and major accomplishments of the presidencies. . . . Overall this work is well researched, well written, and easily understood."

REVIEW: *Libr J* v138 no7 p110 Ap 15 2013 Brian Odom

REVIEW: *SLJ* v59 no8 p63 Ag 2013 Mary Mueller

ENCYCLOPEDIA OF U.S. MILITARY INTERVENTIONS IN LATIN AMERICA; 2 v. (xxiv, 804 p.) 2013 ABC-CLIO

1. Encyclopedias & dictionaries

ISBN 9781598842593 (hbk. : alk. paper); 9781598842609 (ebook)

LC 2012-043074

SUMMARY: "This two-volume encyclopedia defines military interventions and their scope to include indirect interventions, as in proxy wars and support for dictatorships.

Included are entries on obvious topics, such as the invasion of Grenada and the occupations of Cuba and Nicaragua, as well as lesser-known episodes (the Baltimore affair) and broader concepts related to the central theme (e.g., articles on women and race)." (Choice: Current Reviews for Academic Libraries)

REVIEW: *Booklist* v110 no4 p36 O 15 2013 Mary Ellen Snodgrass

REVIEW: *Choice* v51 no5 p811 Ja 2014 L. Gardinier

"Encyclopedia of U.S. Military Interventions in Latin America." "Editor [Alan] McPherson . . . smartly instructed contributors to summarize the connections to military intervention in the first paragraph of each entry, maintaining the focus throughout. The scope, however, naturally emphasizes actors at the state and international levels: politicians, militaries, and governments. This approach means that the power of the general populace and its roles in these historical episodes--whether through protests, movements, or membership in civic organizations--sometimes is neglected. The index is inconsistent, making the electronic edition with full-text searching a more attractive option."

ENCYCLOPEDIA OF UTILITARIANISM; 608 p. 2013 Bloomsbury

1. Encyclopedias & dictionaries 2. Historical literature 3. Philosophy—History 4. Utilitarianism 5. Utilitarianism—Encyclopedias
ISBN 9780826429896 (hardcover : alk. paper)
LC 2012-039263

SUMMARY: Edited by James E. Crimmins, this book "captures the complex developmental history and the multi-faceted character of utilitarianism. . . . Studies of utilitarianism hitherto have been notably compartmentalised, focusing on utilitarian ethics, or the socio-political utilitarianism epitomized in Benthamism, or the genesis of Austrian jurisprudence, but never making these various aspects available for comparative study within a single work." (Publisher's note)

REVIEW: *Choice* v51 no4 p602-4 D 2013 R. K. Rowe

"The Bloomsbury Encyclopedia of Utilitarianism." "This volume is far more than a reference work on utilitarian ethical thought--it is a compendium of the idea of utility as a value, goal, or principle in all aspects of human life, spanning a time from antiquity to the Internet. . . . Editor [James E.] Crimmins aptly compares the utilitarian tradition to a living tree with roots in antiquity and branches that cross many fields and traditions throughout history. This work . . . illustrates this metaphor . . . relevant entries. They include historical figures, classical utilitarian philosophers, more-recent figures and schools, . . . related schools of thought, the many forms of utilitarianism, key concepts and issues, and emerging issues and ideas for the contemporary world."

ENDE, MICHAEL. Momo; 240 p. 2013 Pgw

1. Fantasy fiction 2. Social criticism 3. Technology—Social aspects 4. Urban life 5. Young adult fiction
ISBN 1938073142; 9781938073144

SUMMARY: In this book by Michael Ende, "After the sweet-talking gray men come to town, life becomes terminally efficient. Can Momo, a young orphan girl blessed with the gift of listening, vanquish the ashen-faced time thieves before joy vanishes forever? With . . . new drawings by Marcel Dzama and a new translation from the German by Lucas Zwirner, this all-new 40th anniversary edition celebrates the book's first U.S. publication in over 25 years." (Publisher's note)

REVIEW: *Kirkus Rev* v81 no12 p88 Je 15 2013

REVIEW: *Voice of Youth Advocates* v36 no4 p79-80 O 2013 Jennifer Miskec

"Momo." "Though [author Michael] Ende is more well known for his novel (and its filmic adaptation) 'The Neverending Story,' 'Momo' is the novel that first earned him literary acclaim. This edition celebrates Momo's fortieth anniversary with a new translation and new illustrations. Despite being forty years old, Ende's critique of contemporary culture--efficiency over quality, arbitrary deadlines instead of organic intervals, and even technology (like radios and books on tape) over human interaction--still rings true. Ende's story is heavy handed and will probably be more attractive to luddite adults than teen readers, though light fantasy and Ende fans might be intrigued by Ende's fairy-tale worlds."

ENDY, DREW. Synthetic aesthetics. See Schyfter, P.

ENERGY INDUSTRIES AND SUSTAINABILITY; 171 p. 2013 Berkshire Publishing

1. Emissions trading 2. Energy industries—Environmental aspects 3. Environmental literature 4. Renewable energy sources 5. Sustainability
ISBN 9781614729907 (pbk.: alk. paper)
LC 2013-032126

SUMMARY: This book "covers the exploitation of energy resources—such as coal, petroleum, and wood—and the innovations that can provide the energy we need for a cleaner, safer, and more sustainable future. Forty expert authors explain concepts such as 'materials substitution' and the 'polluter pays principle' and examine the industries and practices that bring us energy from the sun, water, and wind." (Publisher's note)

REVIEW: *Choice* v51 no9 p1646 My 2014 T. M. Marini

"Energy Industries and Sustainability". "This accessible book focuses on 'the exploitation of energy resources . . . and the innovations that may provide the energy we need for a cleaner, safer, and more sustainable future.' . . . Contributors provide compelling reasons to reduce dependence on traditional energy resources and shift to alternative energy (e.g., solar, wind, water), but they also address the barriers these new technologies face. . . . However, readers will find few if any opposing viewpoints from industries such as coal, gas, nuclear, or petroleum. This is especially relevant when emphasizing new technologies, which often look promising until the realities of cost and regulations are considered."

REVIEW: *Libr J* v139 no2 p96 F 1 2014 Judy Quinn

ENGINEERING THE HUMAN; 180 p. 2012 Springer

1. Biotechnology 2. Genetic engineering 3. Human genetics 4. Science fiction 5. Scientific literature
ISBN 9783642350955
LC 2012-955747

SUMMARY: "The volume is collection of articles treating the topic of human improvement/enhancement from a variety of perspectives--philosophical, literary, medical, genetic, sociological, legal etc" Topics include "genetic engineering, cloning, artificial implants and artificial intelligence etc. . . . The book . . . targets a non-specialist audience with an interest in philosophical, sociological, scientific and legal issues." (Publisher's note)

REVIEW: *Choice* v51 no7 p1242 Mr 2014 R. A. Hoots

"Engineering the Human: Human Enhancement Between Fiction and Fascination." "This provocative series of articles, fluidly translated from the Dutch, reads like a contemporary version of 'Brave New World'. . . . Drawing from today's common culture, the articles consider sociological, ethical, scientific, historical, and legal aspects to the human fantasy of extending life by delaying senescence. Many of the scenarios presented are compelling, and the potential outcomes will excite the imagination of a wide audience. . . . Highly recommended."

ENGLE, MARGARITA. Silver people; voices from the Panama Canal; [by] Margarita Engle 272 p. 2014 Houghton Mifflin Harcourt

1. Children's stories 2. Novels in verse 3. Racism—Fiction 4. Rain forests—Fiction 5. Segregation—Fiction
ISBN 0544109414; 9780544109414 (hardback)
LC 2013-037485

SUMMARY: This children's book, by Margarita Engle, is an "exploration of the construction of the Panama Canal. . . . Mateo, a 14-year-old Cuban lured by promises of wealth, journeys to Panama only to discover the recruiters' lies and a life of harsh labor. However, through his relationships with Anita, an 'herb girl,' Henry, a black Jamaican worker, and Augusto, a Puerto Rican geologist, Mateo is able to find a place in his new land." (Kirkus Reviews)

REVIEW: *Booklist* v110 no14 p73 Mr 15 2014 Michael Cart

REVIEW: *Bull Cent Child Books* v67 no6 p308 F 2014 Karen Coats

"Silver People: Voices From the Panama Canal." "As always, [Margarita]Engle's poetry captures with sympathetic wonder and delicate beauty the plight of these disenfranchised voices; here in particular she highlights the natural beauty and love that Mateo, Anita, and Henry find and cling to in the midst of their back- and heart-breaking labor. A prose epilogue in character from Augusto and a historical note from the author provide context for the Engle's project of giving voice to the 'silver people.'"

REVIEW: *Horn Book Magazine* v90 no2 p116-7 Mr/Ap 2014 KATHLEEN T. HORNING

"Silver People: Voices From the Panama Canal." "In melodic verses, [Margarita] Engle offers the voices of three . . . workers. . . . We also hear from Anita, a local girl who provides an account of how the canal work is changing the landscape. . . . Taken together, they provide an illuminating picture of the ecological sacrifices and human costs behind a historical feat generally depicted as a triumph. If there's any triumph at all here, it's in the relationships among the four principal players who survive and ultimately thrive on a newly formed island in the middle of the canal, an island that was once a mountaintop."

REVIEW: *Kirkus Rev* v82 no2 p153 Ja 15 2014

REVIEW: *SLJ* v60 no3 p138 Mr 2014 Ellen Norton

REVIEW: *Voice of Youth Advocates* v36 no5 p56-7 D 2013 Lucy Schall

ENGLISH HISTORICAL DOCUMENTS; 1392 p. 2011 Routledge

1. Great Britain—Church history—16th century 2. Great Britain—History—Elizabeth, 1558-1603—Sources 3. Great Britain—Social conditions—History 4. History—Sources
ISBN 0415199093 (v. V; 0415350972 (v. V; 9780415199094 (v. V; 9780415350976 (v. V
LC 2010-015451

SUMMARY: Edited by Ian W. Archer and F. Douglas Price, "This long awaited volume covers 1558-1603, the reign of Elizabeth I, when government, culture, religion and foreign policy all underwent profound change. This volume includes informative introductory pieces for the parts and sections and editorial comment is directed towards making sources intelligible rather than drawing conclusions from them." (Publisher's note)

REVIEW: *Engl Hist Rev* v128 no534 p1222-4 O 2013 Stephen Alford

"English Historical Documents: 1558-1603." "Sixty years is rather a long time to wait for any book, more so one in a distinguished series such as English Historical Documents. Douglas Price was commissioned to edit the volume covering the years between 1558 and 1603 by Eyre & Spottiswoode in 1950. . . . This typescript was discovered by Ian Archer, Price's successor as tutor and fellow in History at Keble College, Oxford; and it is Archer who, in an act of homage and heroism, has at last brought the project to an end. . . . Very little is missing from this volume. . . . . In fact, if one were to sit down with the book and read every document through to the very end, one would have a rich sense of the later Tudor world."

ENGMAN, CAMILLA.il. The voyage. See Salinas, V.

ENIA, DAVIDE. On earth as it is in heaven; [by] Davide Enia 320 p. 2014 Farrar, Straus and Giroux

1. Bildungsromans 2. Boxing stories 3. FICTION—Family Life 4. FICTION—Historical 5. FICTION—Literary 6. Mafia—Fiction 7. Masculinity
ISBN 9780374130046 (hardback)
LC 2013-034091

SUMMARY: "This Sicilian novel encompasses a multigenerational family—against a backdrop of war and the Mafia—as it tells the story of how a boy becomes a boxer and a man. This debut by an Italian novelist with previous playwriting experience shows the maturation of a 9-year-old boy into a champion-caliber boxer, following in the footsteps of the father he never knew and the uncle who has trained him." (Kirkus Reviews)

REVIEW: *Booklist* v110 no12 p23-4 F 15 2014 Bill Ott

REVIEW: *Kirkus Rev* v82 no3 p182 F 1 2014

"On Earth As It Is In Heaven". " This Sicilian novel encompasses a multigenerational family—against a backdrop of war and the Mafia—as it tells the story of how a boy becomes a boxer and a man. . . . The first-person narrative leaps around chronologically while rarely straying far from Palermo, where Enia was raised. . . . Though it can be a struggle to keep the narrative strands straight and see how they connect, a virtuoso climax ties everything together. The over-the-top clichés seem to come with the fictional territory as the novel explores just what it means to be a man."

REVIEW: *N Y Times Book Rev* p26 My 4 2014 Carmela Ciuraru

ENJOY THE EXPERIENCE; Homemade Records 1958-1992; 512 p. 2013 Sinecure Books

1. Album cover art 2. Music industry—History 3. Music literature 4. Sound recording industry 5. Sound recordings—Album covers

ISBN 1938265041; 9781938265044

SUMMARY: This book presents "the largest collection of American private-press vinyl ever amassed and presented, featuring more than 1,000 cover reproductions from 1958-1992. The musicians here range from awkward teen pop combos to pizza-parlor organists; religious cult leaders to Sinatra imitators. But this is not a novelty show: also profiled and discussed are some of the most highly regarded rock, soul, jazz, funk and singer/songwriter albums from the latter half of the twentieth century." (Publisher's note)

REVIEW: *Bookforum* v20 no4 p50 D 2013/Ja 2014 DAMON KRUKOWSKI

"Enjoy the Experience: Homemade Records 1958-1992." "The private-press LPs documented in this spectacularly fun coffee-table book routinely cross those boundaries--sometimes with an eye toward the slick, other times toward the sick, but rarely with hopes for anything like popular approval. . . . It's unmistakable that many of the album covers in 'Enjoy the Experience' have the novelty, mystery, and visual appeal that translate into consumer desirability. Indeed, that desirability underlies much of the book's raison d'être. Like gallerists or fine-art collectors, the editors of 'Enjoy the Experience' have, in cataloguing their passion, marketed it as well, and the texts in the book underscore this transformation of dross into gold."

ENMARCH, ROLAND.ed. Ancient Egyptian literature. See Ancient Egyptian literature

ENNIS, HELEN. Margaret Michaelis; love, loss and photography; [by] Helen Ennis

1. Biography (Literary form) 2. Michaelis, Margaret 3. Photography—Australia 4. Spain—History—Civil War, 1936-1939 5. Women photographers

ISBN 0-642-54120-5

SUMMARY: This book presents a biography of photographer Margaret Michaelis, whose "life in Europe was dislocated by the rise of fascism and the outbreak of World War II, following which she suffered acute personal losses and challenges in finding a new path for her art and life in Australia. . . . Crucial to the story are the dozens of love letters exchanged between Michaelis and her first husband, a prominent German anarchist imprisoned during the Spanish Civil War." (Publisher's note)

REVIEW: *Choice* v51 no10 p1740-1 Je 2014 C. Chiarenza

"Margaret Michaelis: Love, Loss, and Photography". "A natural storyteller, [Helen] Ennis prepared a brilliant biography by extrapolating from some fragments of known and discovered information about Michaelis, a simple, ordinary, yet mysterious, complex, troubled, and unusual woman who, for less than half her adult life, made photographs for a living. Ennis's insight, knowledge, and dedicated research provide not just a biography but a moving distillation of 20th-century history via a taste f some lives involved physically, intellectually, and emotionally in such pivotal events as the Holocaust and the Spanish Civil War."

ENRICO, JEANETTE.ed. Out-of-style. See Out-of-style

ENRIGUE, ALVARO. Hypothermia; [by] Alvaro Enrigue 183 p. 2013 Dalkey Archive Press

1. Alienation (Social psychology)—Fiction 2. Endangered languages 3. Fathers 4. Mental illness—Fiction 5. Short story (Literary form)

ISBN 9781564788733 (pbk. : alk. paper)

LC 2013-001673

SUMMARY: This book presents short stories by Álvaro Enrigue. " In 'Gula, or: The Invocation,' a doubtful father reluctantly writes a story which sacrifices his pet cat in order to save his family; in 'Outrage' a mentally unhinged garbage collector goes on a crime spree; and in 'The Extinction of Dalmation,' we find Tuone Udina, the intellectually-and hearing-challenged last living speaker of the Dalmatian language in a remote corner of Croatia." (Publishers Weekly)

REVIEW: *World Lit Today* v87 no6 p62-4 N/D 2013 Catharine E. Wall

"Hypothermia." "'Hypothermia' comprises twenty carefully sequenced stories. . . . The stories, too, are intricately structured and feature an eclectic selection of epigraphs, narrative voices, and modes, characters, and concerns while set mainly during recent years in Washington, DC, or Mexico, DF. . . . This neatly woven hook gathers force from each text and section to the next. . . . Brendan Riley's graceful translation and the inclusion of 'Hypothermia' alongside other distinguished works of Latin American literature in the press's list of publications bode well for future translations into English of [Álvaro] Enrigue's fiction."

ENSURING A SUSTAINABLE FUTURE; making progress on environment and equity; 384 p. 2014 Oxford University Press

1. Conservation of Natural Resources 2. Environmental Health 3. Environmental literature 4. Health Policy 5. Socioeconomic Factors

ISBN 9780199974702 (alk. paper)

LC 2013-023768

SUMMARY: This book "focuses on organizing poor and marginalized communities, improving their health, and providing (preferably green) jobs. Many of the 13 chapters present wide-ranging case studies—for example, urban transport in India, nutrition in Montreal, agriculture in the Andes, recycling by the poor in Vancouver, and clean energy development in remote northern Canada, among others." (Choice: Current Reviews for Academic Libraries)

REVIEW: *Choice* v51 no9 p1613-4 My 2014 B. C. Wyman

"Ensuring a Sustainable Future: Making Progress on Environment and Equity". "Edited by public health academics/researchers [Jody] Heymann . . . and [Magda] Barrera . . . the work focuses on organizing poor and marginalized communities, improving their health, and providing (preferably green) jobs. . . .There is ample documentation, but the strung-together summaries of research findings are often tedious. Many figures are poorly printed. The book is not a strong choice for undergraduates, but it can possibly serve as a supplemental graduate text in environmental-related disciplines. Practitioners could find some of the case studies useful."

EP VOLUME 1; The Italian Avant-Garde 1968-1976; 224

p. 2013 Sternberg Press
1. Architecture—Italy 2. Art literature 3. Avant-garde (Arts) 4. Design—Italy—History—20th century 5. Italian arts—20th century
ISBN 3943365492; 9783943365498

SUMMARY: This book on the Italian Avant-Garde during the 1960s and 1970s "emphasizes the multiple correspondences between well-known radical design groups like Arte Povera, Archizoom, and Superstudio . . . and previously overlooked spaces, works, and performances generated by Zoo, Gruppo 9999, and Cavart. Newly commissioned interviews and essays by historians, curators and critics shed new light on the era under scrutiny, while contemporary practitioners, discuss its complex legacy." (Publisher's note)

REVIEW: *TLS* no5751 p27 Je 21 2013 JOHN FOOT

"EP: The Italian Avant-Garde, 1968-76." "This volume, lovingly edited by Catharine Rossi and Alex Coles, brings together some of the main actors from that season of innovation (and, at times, excess). Through a combination of different media (interviews, notes, articles, photographs, designs, maps, political posters) their book captures some of the spirit of the period - both in terms of its form and its content. . . . Sometimes, the language in EP here appears arcane and confused, but the images and the range of the work presented are fascinating and stimulating, and provide a strong basis for future editions of this enterprising journal-book series."

EPHRON, NORA, 1941-2012. The Most of Nora Ephron; [by] Nora Ephron 576 p. 2013 Alfred A. Knopf
1. Aging 2. Anthologies 3. Essays 4. Love stories 5. Women
ISBN 038535083X; 9780385350839 (hardcover)
LC 2013-016426

SUMMARY: This posthumously-published book collects writings by Nora Ephron. Ephron and her editor "decided to structure it around the subject matters she explored and the genres she used to explore them. As a result, the text of her novel Heartburn (1983) is included, as is the screenplay for Ephron's most beloved movie, When Harry Met Sally, and her late-in-life play, Lucky Guy. The remainder of the anthology consists of much briefer entries across a . . . diverse set of topics." (Kirkus Reviews)

REVIEW: *Booklist* v110 no1 p26-7 S 1 2013 Donna Seaman

"The MOST of Nora Ephron". "No matter how versed in Ephron's cherished work a reader may be, she or he will be dazzled and touched anew by this life-spanning, life-embracing collection that so richly showcases her clarity, brio, and candor. . . . A canny interpreter of the Zeitgeist, Ephron threshed topics social, cultural, and political, and shared her passion for food. Nearly 80 stellar essays are accompanied by Ephron's novel, 'Heartburn,' her play, 'Lucky Guy,' and her acclaimed, oft-quoted screenplay for When Harry Met Sally. A tonic and essential celebration of a scintillating and mighty writer."

REVIEW: *Commentary* v136 no5 p48-50 D 2013 TERRY TEACHOUT

REVIEW: *Kirkus Rev* v81 no20 p215 O 15 2013

REVIEW: *Libr J* v138 no10 p80 Je 1 2013

REVIEW: *Libr J* v138 no16 p75 O 1 2013 Meagan Lacy

REVIEW: *N Y Rev Books* v60 no18 p18-21 N 21 2013 Francine Prose

REVIEW: *N Y Times Book Rev* p36 D 8 2013 GAIL COLLINS

REVIEW: *Publ Wkly* v260 no36 p51 S 9 2013

REVIEW: *TLS* no5790 p5 Mr 21 2014 LIDIJA HAAS

THE EPIC OF GESAR OF LING; Gesar's magical birth, early years, and coronation as king; lxi, 618 p. 2012 Shambhala
1. Buddhist literature, Tibetan 2. Epic literature 3. Epic literature, Tibetan—Translations into English 4. Gesar (Legendary character) 5. Kings & rulers—Fiction
ISBN 9781590308424 (hardcover: alk. paper)
LC 2011-014496

SUMMARY: Translated by Robin Kornman, Lama Chönam, and Sangye Khandro, "The Gesar epic tells how the king, an enlightened warrior, in order to defend Tibet and the Buddhist religion from the attacks of surrounding demon kings, conquers his enemies one by one in a series of adventures and campaigns that take him all over the Eastern world." (Publisher's note)

REVIEW: *TLS* no5790 p28 Mr 21 2014 MATTHEW T. KAPSTEIN

"The Epic of Gesar of Ling: Gesar's Magical Birth, Early Years, and Coronation As King" and "The Song of King Gesar." "The initiative for the present, outstanding translation of the first three episodes—the prologue in the heavens where the hero's incarnation is planned, the trickster-like birth and youth of Gesar, and his rise to kingship through victory in the horse race—came from the late Robin Kornman. . . . Those inspired by the magical world of the Tibetan epic, in which nothing happens quite by chance, will regard it as no accident that publication of the first English translation of the Gesar epic has coincided with a contemporary Tibetan novelist's retelling of the saga, Alai's 'Song of King Gesar.' . . . Alai's novel offers an accessible introduction to the Gesar story and its place in Tibetan culture."

EPPERSON, MICHAEL. Foundations of relational realism; a topological approach to quantum mechanics and the philosophy of nature; [by] Michael Epperson xx, 419 p. 2013 Lexington Books
1. Philosophy of nature 2. Physics literature 3. Quantum logic 4. Quantum theory—Philosophy 5. Topology
ISBN 9780739180327 (cloth : alkaline paper)
LC 2013-010287

SUMMARY: In this book, authors Michael Epperson and Elias Zafiris "return to ordinary quantum mechanics and propose sheaf theory, a theory that grew out of the abstract algebra of topology and set theory, as a solution to the stubborn paradoxes found in quantization attempts. They then compare the theory's interpretive value to the category scheme found in [Alfred North] Whitehead's 'Process and Reality' (1929)." (Choice: Current Reviews for Academic Libraries)

REVIEW: *Choice* v51 no7 p1258 Mr 2014 C. Lee

"Foundations of Relational Realism: A Topological Approach to Quantum Mechanics and the Philosophy of Nature." "The authors begin with the famous 1935 paper on quantum theory and reality by Einstein, Podolsky, and Rosen, but skip the more contemporary interventions by going straight to their own theories. The reader is well advised to come with advanced knowledge of quantum mechanics, logic, and Whiteheadian philosophy. Part of the 'Contemporary Whitehead Studies' series. . . . Recommended."

EPSTEIN, DAVID. The sports gene; inside the science of extraordinary athletic performance; [by] David Epstein 352 p. 2013 Current

1. Athletes 2. Athletic ability—Physiological aspects 3. Human genetics 4. Sports—Physiological aspects 5. Sports literature

ISBN 1591845114; 9781591845119

LC 2013-013443

SUMMARY: In this book, David Epstein investigates the connection between genetics and athletic ability. "Drawing on interviews with athletes and scientists, he points out that 'a nation succeeds in a sport not only by having many people who practice prodigiously at sport-specific skills, but also by getting the best all-around athletes into the right sports in the first place.'" (Publishers Weekly)

REVIEW: *Kirkus Rev* v81 no13 p270 Jl 1 2013

REVIEW: *New Statesman* v142 no5172 p46-7 Ag 30 2013 Ed Smith

REVIEW: *New York Times* v162 no56227 pD3 Ag 13 2013 CHRISTINE ASCHWANDEN

REVIEW: *New Yorker* v89 no27 p76-80 S 9 2013 Malcolm Gladwell

"The Sports Gene: Inside the Science of Extraordinary Athletic Performance" and "The Secret Race: Inside the Hidden World of the Tour de France: Doping, Cover-Ups and Winning at All Costs." "In 'The Sports Gene,' there are countless . . . examples of all the ways that the greatest athletes are different from the rest of us. . . . They carry genes that put them far ahead of ordinary athletes. . . . 'The Secret Race' deserves to be read alongside 'The Sports Gene,' because it describes the flip side of the question that Epstein explores. . . . [Tyler] Hamilton was a skier who came late to cycling, and he paints himself as an underdog. . . . His book is supposed to serve as his apology. At that task, it fails."

REVIEW: *Publ Wkly* v260 no28 p162 Jl 15 2013

REVIEW: *Sci Am* v309 no2 p96 Ag 2013

REVIEW: *Science* v342 no6158 p560-1 N 1 2013 Dov Greenbaum Jieming Chen Mark Gerstein

REVIEW: *TLS* no5777/8 p38 D 20 2013 MICHAEL BELOFF

"The Sports Gene." "David Epstein, an avid athlete and award-winning sports journalist, has entered the arena with zest. He takes deliberate aim at the thesis associated with Malcolm Gladwell in his influential book 'Outliers' (and more recently with the 'Times' columnist and former international table tennis player Matthew Syed in Bounce) that it is, in the hallowed saw, the 99 per cent perspiration and not the 1 per cent inspiration which is the recipe for genius. . . . 'The Sports Gene' is an enjoyable mixture of easily digestible science, anecdote and argument; but David Epstein has not so much closed off a debate as reignited it."

EPSTEIN, EDWARD. Three Days in May; Sex, Surveillance, and DSK; [by] Edward Epstein 2012 Melville House Pub.

1. France—Politics & government—1958- 2. Intelligence service 3. Political science literature 4. Sex scandals 5. Strauss-Kahn, Dominique, 1949-

ISBN 9781612191966 1612191967

SUMMARY: In this book about the 2011 sex scandal surrounding French politician Dominique Strauss-Kahn, "the story . . . turns into a speculative one about Mr. Strauss-Kahn being set up, probably by French intelligence services." Evidence presented includes "strange calls between the French-owned hotel and Parish, the disappearance of Mr. Strauss-Kahn's BlackBerry, a man repeatedly lurking behind him, the curious dance of two security men after Ms. [Nafi] Diallo was persuaded to call the police." (Economist)

REVIEW: *Economist* v403 no8784 p88 My 12 2012

"Three Days in May: Sex, Surveillance and DSK" and "DSK: The Scandal That Brought Down Dominique Strauss-Kahn." "Two new books tell the story from very different angles. Their one point in common is what happened in suite 2806 of the Sofitel . . . For Edward Epstein the story then turns into a speculative one about Mr. Strauss-Kahn being set up, probably by French intelligence services. . . . Yet ultimately Mr. Epstein's case ins unconvincing . . . John Solomon's book makes much more sense."

EPSTEIN, JAMES. Scandal of colonial rule; power and subversion in the British Atlantic during the age of revolution; [by] James Epstein xxiii, 289 p. 2012 Cambridge University Press

1. Criminal justice, Administration of—Trinidad—History—19th century 2. HISTORY—Europe—Great Britain 3. Historical literature 4. Slavery—Trinidad—History—19th century

ISBN 9780521176774 (paperback); 9781107003309 (hardback)

LC 2011-033926

SUMMARY: This book by James Epstein "is centred on Trinidad at the turn of the nineteenth century." It looks at "the trial in Britain of Thomas Picton, Trinidad's first British governor (1797–1803). . . . The colonial violence in Trinidad that initially so shocked the British public, Epstein argues . . . was not 'an aberration in evolving modes of liberal rule,' but rather reveals the 'deeper domestic and colonial shift to an officially sanctioned authoritarianism'". (Social History)

REVIEW: *Engl Hist Rev* v129 no536 p228-9 F 2014 Christer Petley

"Scandal of Colonial Rule: Power and Subversion in the British Atlantic During the Age of Revolution". "Absorbing. . . . [James] Epstein skilfully examines these questions in a book that sheds important new light on imperial history through the lens of debates and events surrounding Trinidad at the turn of the nineteenth century. . . . The result is an imaginative and engrossing study, a model of painstaking scholarship, which is marked by its compelling arguments and incisive writing. . . . Epstein therefore provides us with vividly fresh perspectives and inspiration for new work on Caribbean, Atlantic, British, and imperial history, helping us to imagine exciting scholarly futures for these intersecting fields."

EPSTEIN, LAWRENCE J. The basic beliefs of Judaism; a twenty-first-century guide to a timeless tradition; [by] Lawrence J. Epstein 203 p. 2013 Jason Aronson

1. God (Judaism) 2. Jewish ethics 3. Jewish way of life 4. Judaism 5. Religious literature

ISBN 9780765709691 (cloth : alk. paper); 9780765709707 (electronic)

LC 2013-015985

SUMMARY: In this book, Lawrence J. Epstein "culls from nearly 3,000 years of Jewish moral, ethical, and philosophical thought to present an overview of fundamentals for an educated, 21st-century audience. In ten chapters, he discusses themes such as the mystery of God, the suffering of the innocent, and ethical foundations for a good life, from a broad array of Jewish perspectives." (Choice: Current Reviews for Academic Libraries)

REVIEW: *Choice* v51 no7 p1231-2 Mr 2014 D. Mizrachi

"The Basic Beliefs of Judaism: A Twenty-First-Century Guide to a Timeless Tradition." "This is not a reference book; the author recommends reading the chapters in order 'because the material . . . is presented in an intellectually hierarchical fashion, with one section leading to the next.' Because of the vastness of the sources from which he draws, only a select essence can be conveyed. Biblical, Talmudic, and medieval sources are cited, as are Enlightenment, Reform, Conservative, and contemporary Jewish thinkers. The discussions are thoughtful and balanced. Readers from all backgrounds are challenged to engage with the issues further by using chapter exercises and the extensive bibliography."

EPSTEIN, RICHARD A. The classical liberal constitution; [by] Richard A. Epstein 2013 Harvard University Press

1. Constitutional law—United States 2. Liberalism 3. Political philosophy 4. Property rights 5. Separation of powers

ISBN 9780674724891 hardcover

SUMMARY: "Grounded in the thought of Locke, Hume, Madison, and other Enlightenment figures, the classical liberal tradition emphasized federalism, restricted government, separation of powers, property rights, and economic liberties. The most serious challenge to this tradition, [author Richard A.] Epstein contends, has come from New Deal progressives and their intellectual defenders." (Publisher's note)

REVIEW: *Choice* v52 no1 p160 St 2014 D. P. Ramsey

REVIEW: *Commentary* v137 no6 p59-61 Je 2014 TARA HELFMAN

REVIEW: *Ethics* v125 no1 p254-8 O 2014 KEITH E. WHITTINGTON

REVIEW: *Natl Rev* v66 no4 p43-4 Mr 10 2014 ROBERT F. NAGEL

"The Classical Liberal Constitution: The Uncertain Quest for Limited Government". "In this comprehensive, nuanced, and sophisticated volume, [Richard A.] Epstein proposes that courts enforce a constitution that gets its meaning from the principles of classical liberalism. Although he asserts that classical liberalism was the political philosophy of all the Framers, today his is a lonely voice that, if heeded, would significantly reshape constitutional jurisprudence and radically alter American politics. . . . In short, the classical-liberal constitution would effectively disenfranchise most of the modern progressive movement. As attractive as this idea may seem at first, like many pleasant dreams, it appears less desirable in the light of day."

REVIEW: *New Repub* v244 no28 p31-5 My 26 2014 Cass R. Sunstein

"The Classical Liberal Constitution: The Uncertain Quest for Limited Government." "Most constitutional scholars continue to think that [author Richard A.] Epstein's views are eccentric, but his views have had a large influence. Epstein is far too independent-minded to lead or follow any ideological movement, but it Tea Party constitutionalism has academic roots, or a canonical set of texts, they consist of Epstein's writings. . . . Epstein has now produced a full-scale and full-throated defense of his unusual vision of the Constitution. This book is his magnum opus. . . . When Epstein comes to constitutional law, he is, in a sense, a stranger in a strange land."

ERDRICH, LOUISE, 1954-. The round house; [by] Louise Erdrich 321 p. 2012 Harper

1. FICTION—General 2. Indian families—Fiction 3. Indian reservations—Fiction 4. Indian women—Crimes against—Fiction 5. Life change events—Fiction 6. Ojibwa Indians—North Dakota—Fiction

ISBN 9780062065261 (ebook); 9780062065254 (paperback); 9780062065247 (hardcover); 0062065246 (hardcover)

LC 2012-005381

SUMMARY: This book by Louise Erdrich, "[s]et on an Ojibwe reservation in North Dakota . . . focuses on 13-year-old Joseph. After his mother is brutally raped yet refuses to speak about the experience, Joe must not only cope with her slow physical and mental recovery but also confront his own feelings of anger and helplessness. Questions of jurisdiction and treaty law complicate matters. Doubting that justice will be served, Joe enlists his friends to help investigate the crime." (Library Journal)

REVIEW: *Commonweal* v140 no19 p30-2 D 6 2013 Alyssa Rosenberg

REVIEW: *TLS* no5751 p20 Je 21 2013 ALISON KELLY

"The Round House." "While Joe the narrator is an adult, Joe the amateur sleuth is thirteen, and this creates occasional problems of plausibility: one minute he is watching television, filching cigarettes or riding around on his bike with his friends; the next staking out the house of a foul-mouthed, pugilistic ex-army priest who is on his list of suspects. . . . These shifts mirror an uneasiness--or, more positively, a fluidity--of genre. . . . Perhaps what the book calls for is openness to a new departure on [Louise] Erdrich's part. It is as political as her previous novels. Its villain is an embodiment of a legendary evil spirit. But its hero represents a younger generation of Native Americans who are partly shaped by the myths of the television age."

REVIEW: *Women's Review of Books* v30 no3 p26-7 My/Je 2013 A. J. Verdelle

ERNE, LUKAS. Shakespeare and the Book Trade; [by] Lukas Erne xvi, 302 p. 2013 CAMBRIDGE UNIVERSITY PRESS

1. Book industries and trade—England—History—16th century 2. Book industries and trade—England—History—17th century 3. Historical literature 4. Literature publishing—England—History—16th century 5. Literature publishing—England—History—17th century

ISBN 9780521765664

LC 2012-039597

SUMMARY: This book "examine[s] the publication, constitution, dissemination and reception of [William] Shakespeare's printed plays and poems in his own time and to argue that their popularity in the book trade has been greatly underestimated. [Lukas] Erne uses evidence from Shakespeare's publishers and the printed works to show that . . . 'Shakespeare' became a name from which money could be made, a book-trade commodity in which publishers had significant investments." (Publisher's note)

REVIEW: *Choice* v51 no9 p1591 My 2014 E. D. Hill

REVIEW: *TLS* no5767 p23-4 O 11 2013 H. R. WOUDHUYSEN

"Shakespeare and the Book Trade" and "Shakespeare's Stationers: Studies in Cultural Bibliography." "The two books under review are part of a further line of investigation which seeks to see the poet and playwright in relation to the book trade and the stationers with whom he or his theatrical colleagues dealt. Lukas Erne and the contributors to the volume that Marta Straznicky has edited share an interest in many of the same sorts of questions. . . . [Erne's] argument . . . is essentially straightforward, clearly argued, with plenty of supporting evidence, and written in an elegant and eminently reasonable style. . . . These appendices are useful and fuller than the account of '[William] Shakespeare's publishers, 1593-1622' that Erne offers, but could still be improved. There is almost no mention of modem editions of Shakespeare's plays and poems in either Erne's book or Straznicky's collection."

ERRINGTON, FREDERICK. The noodle narratives. See Gewertz, D.

ESBAUM, JILL. I hatched!; 40 p. 2014 Dial Books for Young Readers

1. Animals—Infancy—Fiction 2. Birds—Fiction 3. Children's stories 4. Killdeer 5. Stories in rhyme

ISBN 0803736886; 9780803736887 (hardcover)

LC 2012-006100

SUMMARY: In this book, by Jill Esbaum, "a baby chick bursts from his egg and into the world with . . . enthusiasm, awe, and I-can't-help-myself energy. . . . Jen Corace's . . . artwork is alive with critters and curiosities and surprises--the biggest of which? The hatching of a new baby sister, to the absolute delight of her now 'expert' big brother!" (Publisher's note)

REVIEW: *Booklist* v110 no9/10 p116 Ja 1 2014 Ann Kelley

REVIEW: *Bull Cent Child Books* v67 no7 p355 Mr 2014 J. H.

"I Hatched!." "[Jill] Esbaum's text is as quick-paced and lively as the killdeer chick himself, and the well-crafted rhymes are amusing as well as informative. Unfortunately, [Jen] Corace's ink, watercolor, and pencil images are sometimes too busy and the chick's figure too undefined for a text that focuses on the specific details of a real bird's appearance and actions. . . . The chick himself is cute and personable, but it is sometimes tricky to pick him out against his similarly colored backgrounds, making this challenging for large-group viewing. Still, resourceful adults with access to bird guides and photos of actual killdeer can supplement the art after sharing the entertaining and instructive text."

REVIEW: *Kirkus Rev* v81 no22 p104 N 15 2013

REVIEW: *N Y Times Book Rev* p18 F 16 2014 SARAH HARRISON SMITH

REVIEW: *Publ Wkly* v260 no42 p50 O 21 2013

REVIEW: *SLJ* v60 no1 p68 Ja 2014 Brooke Rasche

ESCOFFIER, MICHAEL. The day I lost my superpowers; 32 p. 2014 Enchanted Lion Books

1. Children's stories 2. Imagination—Fiction 3. Parent & child—Fiction 4. Play—Fiction 5. Superheroes—Fiction

ISBN 9781592701445 (hardback)

LC 2014-000088

SUMMARY: "When the narrator of this tale . . . is first launched into the air by an obliging adult, she discovers that she can 'fly.' What follows is a chain of supcrpowers that she discovers, from walking on the ceiling (doing a headstand) to making things disappear (eating the cupcake on the table). A dog-assisted flight through the backyard (via a pulley in the tree) causes a crash, though, and she's convinced that she's lost all of her superpowers." (Bulletin of the Center for Children's Books)

REVIEW: *Booklist* v110 no16 p53 Ap 15 2014 Daniel Kraus

REVIEW: *Bull Cent Child Books* v67 no10 p514 Je 2014 T. A.

"The Day I Lost My Superpowers". "Whilc its brevity and relatively simple vocabulary would suggest a younger audience, the joy here is in recognizing the understated mismatch between the girl's narration and the accompanying illustrations, a process that requires a bit more sophistication. The scrawled earthtoned illustrations, with a crayony graininess that ranges from saturated planes of color to scribbly linework, effectively carry the spunk of the tale. . . . Though a superhero themed storytime would be an obvious use, this might also be an interesting way to introduce kids in the classroom to the concept of the unreliable narrator."

REVIEW: *Horn Book Magazine* v90 no4 p77 Jl/Ag 2014 KITTY FLYNN

REVIEW: *Kirkus Rev* v82 no6 p268 Mr 15 2014

REVIEW: *SLJ* v60 no10 p81 O 2014 Joy Fleishhacker

ESCUDIER, MARCEL. A dictionary of mechanical engineering. See Atkins, T.

ESKIN, MICHAEL.ed. Durs Grünbein. See Durs Grünbein

ESNOUF, CATHERINE.ed. Food system sustainability. See Food system sustainability

ESPOSITO, DOMENICO. Herculaneum. See Guidobaldi, M.P.

ESSIF, LES. American "unculture" in French drama; Homo Americanus and the post-1960 French resistance; [by] Les Essif xiii, 341 p. 2013 Palgrave Macmillan

1. Americans in literature 2. Culture in literature 3. French drama—20th century—History and criticism 4. Historical literature 5. National characteristics, American, in literature

ISBN 9781137299024

LC 2013-010734

SUMMARY: This book by Les Essif examines "the vision of the US as presented in French plays. . . . The author examines 23 plays dating between 1965 and 2003, analyzing them for what they show about the 'uncultured' (Jean Baudrillard's term) homo Americanus as opposed to homo Gallicanus. The plays represent the work of leading dramatists, including René de Obaldia, Fernando Arrabal, [and] Armand Catti." Topics include "the Western frontier . . . the capitalist system, and civic disintegration." (Choice)

REVIEW: *Choice* v51 no4 p642-3 D 2013 H. Londré

"American 'Unculture' in French Drama: Homo Americanus and the Post-1960 French Resistance." "Embracing a huge issue in cultural studies--European and even non-Western concern about globalization as the inevitable spread of US cultural norms with all their flaws--[Les] Essif . . . looks at the specifics in considering the vision of the US as presented in French plays. . . . the plays offer Americans an intriguing opportunity to see themselves as others see them. However, consistent with the concept of American hyper-reality, Essif himself often blurs the distinction between the theatricalized conceit and the presumably more nuanced reality of American culture."

ETKIND, ALEXANDER. Warped mourning; stories of the undead in the land of the unburied; [by] Alexander Etkind 328 p. 2013 Stanford University Press

1. Collective memory and literature—Russia (Federation) 2. Collective memory and literature—Soviet Union 3. Grief in literature 4. Literature—History & criticism 5. Russian literature—20th century—History and criticism 6. Socialism and literature—Soviet Union 7. Victims of state-sponsored terrorism—Soviet Union
ISBN 9780804773928 (cloth : alk. paper); 9780804773935 (pbk. : alk. paper)
LC 2012-028868

SUMMARY: "This book's premise is that late Soviet and post-Soviet culture, haunted by its past, has produced a unique set of memorial practices. More than twenty years after the collapse of the Soviet Union, . . . the events of the mid-twentieth century are still very much alive, and still contentious. [Author] Alexander Etkind shows how post-Soviet Russia has turned the painful process of mastering the past into an important part of its political present." (Publisher's note)

REVIEW: *Choice* v51 no3 p463-4 N 2013 C. A. Rydel

REVIEW: *Economist* v406 no8827 p83-4 Mr 16 2013

REVIEW: *TLS* no5786 p11 F 21 2014 POLLY JONES

"Warped Mourning: Stories of the Undead in the Land of the Unburied." "[Author Alexander] Etkind's achievement lies in revealing the unusual ways in which the Stalinist past kept bubbling to the surface, in fiction and film, even when state commitment to confronting it was consistently weak. . . . Etkind's account gives very little sense of the rich engagement with Stalinism in realist and documentary literature of the Khrushchev 'thaw' and especially of the glasnost era. . . . A work of great ambition that engages a century of thinking about trauma, 'Warped Mourning' does not always clarify the contradictions between its many theoretical models. The book's value lies in its invigoratingly close readings and polemical ideas."

EUGENIA, MARIA. Ink-blot; [by] Maria Eugenia 28 p. 2014 Orca Book Pub

1. Body image 2. Children's stories 3. Girls—Fiction 4. Personal beauty 5. Self-perception
ISBN 1927583225; 9781927583227

SUMMARY: This children's book "portray[s] girls of all different shapes and sizes and the self-doubt they experience. But not Ink-blot. She may be the 'messiest,' loosest-drawn girl in the story, but she has no doubts about herself. We see her glee as she rides her bike across the pages, plays with her dog and reads a book. She is not spending her time picking apart her appearance—she is too busy doing the things she enjoys." (Publisher's note)

REVIEW: *Kirkus Rev* v82 no1 p18 Ja 1 2014

"Ink-Blot". "This quirky—odd, even—paean to female self-respect preaches too baldly and too briefly. . . . Page after page, girls with exaggerated features rendered in bold, expressive colors catalog their supposed failings, until readers return to Ink-blot, who may 'really [be] BADLY DRAWN' but who 'COULDN'T CARE LESS! She's too busy having fun.' It is as unvarnished a piece as can be imagined, and to what end? . . . The pictures are very ugly indeed, and while this may be a transgressive and rebellious artistic act, it comes off the page as off-putting in the extreme. Moreover, as the message is aimed at preteen girls, the picture-book format seems an ineffective way to reach them. This didactic little piece will likely leave readers puzzled rather than liberated."

EULBERG, ELIZABETH. Better off friends; [by] Elizabeth Eulberg 288 p. 2014 Point

1. Best friends—Fiction 2. Best friends—Juvenile fiction 3. Dating (Social customs)—Fiction 4. Dating (Social customs)—Juvenile fiction 5. Friendship—Fiction 6. Friendship—Juvenile fiction 7. Interpersonal relations—Fiction 8. Interpersonal relations—Juvenile fiction 9. Love stories 10. Teenagers—Juvenile fiction
ISBN 0545551455; 9780545551458 (jacketed hardcover)
LC 2013-019024

SUMMARY: In this book by Elizabeth Eulberg, "for Macallan and Levi, it was friends at first sight. veryone says guys and girls can't be just friends, but these two are. Guys won't ask Macallan out because they think she's with Levi, and Levi spends too much time joking around with Macallan, and maybe not enough time with his date. They can't help but wonder . . . are they more than friends or are they better off without making it even more complicated?" (Publisher's note)

REVIEW: *Booklist* v110 no11 p63 F 1 2014 Sarah Bean Thompson

REVIEW: *Bull Cent Child Books* v67 no6 p308-9 F 2014 Karen Coats

"Better Off Friends." "[Elizabeth] Eulberg openly acknowledges her debt to . . . screenwriter Nora Ephron, as she should: age and material considerations aside, Levi's and Macallan's characters are similar to Harry's and Sally's as well. . . . Heck, even the boyfriends and girlfriends they leave along the way are supportive of their eventual, inevitable coupling. The fits and starts of their relationship provide that delicate sense of frustration and suspense that readers are looking for, and teens seeking light romance laced with just enough melancholy, setbacks, and relatable insecurities to make them want nothing but happiness for the characters will enjoy this."

REVIEW: *Kirkus Rev* v81 no23 p190 D 1 2013

REVIEW: *Publ Wkly* v260 no51 p61 D 16 2013

REVIEW: *SLJ* v60 no5 p107 My 2014 Martha Baden

REVIEW: *Voice of Youth Advocates* v37 no1 p64 Ap 2014 Kimberly Bower

EUROPEAN COSMOPOLITANISM IN QUESTION; xi, 204 p. 2012 Palgrave Macmillan

1. Cosmopolitanism—Social aspects—Europe 2. Eurocentrism 3. Globalization—Social aspects—Europe 4. Sociology—Philosophy 5. Sociology literature

ISBN 0230302629; 0230302637 (pbk.); 9780230302624; 9780230302631 (pbk.)

LC 2011-279185

SUMMARY: In this book, the authors "collectively explore solutions to two major problems in the sociology of cosmopolitanism proposed by Ulrich Beck. . . . The first major problem in the sociology of cosmopolitanism is its Eurocentric bias. . . . the second major problem in the sociology of cosmopolitanism . . . [is] a failure to articulate cosmopolitanism as an object of sociological study." (Contemporary Sociology)

REVIEW: *Contemp Sociol* v43 no1 p110-2 Ja 2014 Hiro Saito

"European Cosmopolitanism in Question". "A critical and timely intervention in the emerging research on cosmopolitanism. . . . the book's aim to deconstruct Eurocentrism may not resonate with non-European sociologists as much as with their European colleagues. Instead, the real value of the book lies in its attempt to resolve the second major problem in the sociology of cosmopolitanism: a failure to articulate cosmopolitanism as an object of sociological study. . . . But chapters in the book do not fully follow through in their attempt to inject conceptual and empirical rigor into the sociology of cosmopolitanism. . . . Despite its limitations, this book is a must-read for sociologists interested in cosmopolitanism."

EVANS, C. STEPHEN. God and moral obligation; [by] C. Stephen Evans vii, 199 p. 2013 Oxford University Press

1. Conscience 2. Divine commands (Ethics) 3. Duty 4. Philosophical literature 5. Religion and ethics

ISBN 0199696683 (hbk.); 9780199696680 (hbk.)

LC 2013-409928

SUMMARY: In this book on religion and morality, C. Stephen Evans argues that "it is not quite right to say that there would be nothing left of morality if God did not exist, but moral obligations do depend on God ontologically. Such obligations are best understood as God's commands or requirements, communicated to humans in a variety of ways, including conscience." (Publisher's note)

REVIEW: *Choice* v51 no3 p474 N 2013 F. G. Kirkpatrick

REVIEW: *TLS* no5759 p28 Ag 16 2013 JOHN COTTINGHAM

"From Morality to Metaphysics: The Theistic Implications of Our Ethical Commitments," "God and Moral Obligation," and "Good God: The Theistic Foundations of Morality." "In . . . a powerful and carefully organized study, Angus Ritchie goes systematically through the main options available to the secularist, and finds them all wanting. . . . Stephen Evans's superbly lucid book . . . provides one of the best overviews of the current debate on this matter that one could hope for. . . . David Baggett and Jerry Walls . . . work carefully and conscientiously through some of the manoeuvres in the recent literature on the Euthyphro debate. . . . The overall impression left by all four books is of a rich and fertile area of research."

EVANS, JOHN W. Young widower; a memoir; [by] John W. Evans 200 p. 2014 University of Nebraska Press

1. Loss (Psychology)—Case studies 2. Memoirs 3. Widowers—United States—Biography 4. Widowers—United States—Psychology 5. Widowhood—United States—Case studies 6. Wives—Death—Psychological aspects—Case studies 7. Young men—United States—Biography

ISBN 0803249527; 9780803249523 (paperback); 9780803254015 (pdf)

LC 2013-032472

SUMMARY: In this memoir, author John W. Evans "was twenty-nine years old and his wife, Katie, was thirty. They had met in the Peace Corps in Bangladesh, taught in Chicago, studied in Miami, and were working for a year in Romania when they set off with friends to hike into the Carpathian Mountains. In an instant their life together was shattered. Katie became separated from the group. When Evans finally found her, he could only watch helplessly as she was mauled to death by a brown bear." (Publisher's note)

REVIEW: *Kirkus Rev* v82 no3 p176 F 1 2014

"Young Widower: A Memoir". "[John W.] Evans recalls their brief life as a couple in flashbacks, eschewing chronology. Though he vividly recounts the circumstances of Katie's exceptional death, this is the author's story, a memoir of grieving and consolation, of trying to define a young widower's public face and private essence. . . . The emotional narrative is a study in loss, a confession and a search for meaning. . . . An urgent, palpably emotional account of coping with extreme grief."

EVANS, JULIAN.tr. The Foundling Boy. See Déon, M.

EVANS, PETER, 1933-. Ava Gardner; the secret conversations; [by] Peter Evans 293 pages, [8] pages of plates 2013 Simon & Schuster

1. Biographies 2. Man-woman relationships 3. Motion picture actors and actresses—United States—Biography 4. Motion picture industry—United States 5. Women in the motion picture industry

ISBN 1451627696 (hardcover); 9781451627695 (hardcover)

LC 2012-048411

SUMMARY: This book on the life and career of Ava Gardner, "based on the movie star's late-night ramblings" presents "an unvarnished account of her marriages and affairs in golden-age Hollywood. . . . British journalist [Peter] Evans . . . encouraged her to focus on her personal life, and she let loose with plenty of frank, bawdy material about husbands Mickey Rooney, Artie Shaw and Frank Sinatra, plus a long list of lovers topped by Howard Hughes and George C. Scott." (Kirkus Reviews)

REVIEW: *New Yorker* v89 no25 p64-9 Ag 26 2013 David Denby

"Ava Gardner: The Secret Conversations." "Gardner died in 1990, at the age of sixty-seven, ut her voice comes alive in a new book. . . . Running out of money, she approached Peter Evans, an English journalist . . . and asked his help with a memoir. . . . She would drink late, and then call him. . . . Evans took notes and, in the morning, turned them into orderly speech. . . . Eventually, they settled into long conversations, but there was a problem: Gardner's natural candor struggled against her fear of violating confidences. . . . The manuscript, twice abandoned, turns out to be a bristling look at Hollywood attitudes and sexual manners in the pre-feminist period, when a woman could hold her own only by giving up as much as she took."

EVANS, ROB. Undercover; The True Story of Britain's Secret Police; [by] Rob Evans 352 p. 2013 Faber and Faber
1. Investigative reporting 2. Police—Political activity 3. Police—Sexual behavior 4. Police corruption—Great Britain 5. Undercover operations
ISBN 0571302173; 9780571302178

SUMMARY: Written by Rob Evans and Paul Lewis, this book describes how, in order to spy on political activists, "Police stole the identities of dead people to create fake passports, driving licences and bank accounts. They then went deep undercover for years, inventing whole new lives so that they could live incognito among the people they were spying on. They used sex, intimate relationships and drugs to build their credibility." (Publisher's note)

REVIEW: *London Rev Books* v35 no21 p8-10 N 7 2013 Katrina Forrester
"Undercover: The True Story of Britain's Secret Police." "In 'Undercover,' Rob Evans and Paul Lewis draw on the testimonies of activists and whistleblowers to chart the history of secret policing. Their prize source is the former undercover officer Peter Francis, who spied on minor anti-fascist and antiracist groups in North London in the early 1990s before infiltrating his target group, Anti-Fascist Action. . . . It is thanks to Francis--who initially gave interviews to Evans and Lewis as an anonymous whistleblower, but has since revealed his identity--that the way the SDS operated is now known in some detail."

REVIEW: *New Statesman* v142 no5166 p51 Jl 12 2013 Alan White

EVANS, SHANE.il. Art from her heart: folk artist Clementine Hunter. See Whitehead, K.

EVE, HELEN. Stella; a novel; [by] Helen Eve 336 p. 2014 St. Martin's Griffin
1. Americans—England—Fiction 2. Boarding schools—Fiction 3. Cliques (Sociology)—Fiction 4. JUVENILE FICTION—Girls & Women 5. JUVENILE FICTION—School & Education 6. Popularity—Fiction 7. School stories 8. Schools—Fiction
ISBN 9781250043061 (trade paperback); 9781250048172 (hardback)
LC 2013-046168

SUMMARY: In this book, "Caitlin's world is shattered when her parents decide to get a divorce and ship her to a boarding school in England. While at Temperley, Caitlin comes in contact with Stella and her elite crew and quickly gets caught up in the unwritten social hierarchy. . . . Stella uses Caitlin to be her greatest ally among their peers; however, as Caitlin begins to shed her wallflower status, she slowly becomes a threat to Stella's carefully created empire." (VOYA Reviews)

REVIEW: *Kirkus Rev* v81 no24 p292 D 15 2013
"Stella". "A clash between boarding school rivals becomes a platform for a thought-provoking, in-depth dual character study. Caitlin finds herself suddenly moved from Manhattan to a posh boarding school in England when her parents divorce. There, shy Caitlin admires the beautiful, brilliant Stella, who rules the school with her posse of five friends, the Stars. . . . The author makes deliberate reference to Great Expectations, writing Stella as a modern-day Estella, taught to break hearts. This time, however, the focus falls on the effect of that upbringing on Stella instead of on the boys she targets. A fizzy, fashionable, schoolgirl rivalry with depth."

REVIEW: *Publ Wkly* v260 no52 p52 D 23 2013

REVIEW: *Voice of Youth Advocates* v37 no1 p64 Ap 2014 Courtney M. Krieger

EVOLUTION, GAMES, AND GOD; the principle of cooperation; xii, 400 p. 2013 Harvard University Press
1. Altruism 2. Cooperation 3. Evolution (Biology)—Philosophy 4. Evolution (Biology)—Social aspects 5. Religious literature 6. Scientific literature 7. Self-sacrifice
ISBN 9780674047976 (hardcover: alk. paper)
LC 2012-041386

SUMMARY: This book explores "how cooperation, working alongside mutation and natural selection, plays a critical role in populations from microbes to human societies. . . . Assembling experts in mathematical biology, history of science, psychology, philosophy, and theology, [editors] Martin Nowak and Sarah Coakley take an interdisciplinary approach to the terms 'cooperation' and 'altruism.'" (Publisher's note)

REVIEW: *Choice* v51 no3 p486 N 2013 A. C. Love

REVIEW: *TLS* no5792 p29 Ap 4 2014 DENIS ALEXANDER
"Evolution, Games, and God: The Principle of Cooperation." "'Evolution, Games, and God' is a fine collection of twenty essays bringing this discussion right up to the present day. . . . This is an important volume because it completely subverts the idea that the evolutionary narrative is in some profound sense antithetical to theology. Not so. The 'selfish gene' as a metaphor makes no sense of biological realities. Co-operation is here to stay, as important at the level of interacting genes in genomics as it is at the level of interaction between organisms."

EXPLAINING COMPLIANCE; business responses to regulation; xiv, 386 p. 2011 Edward Elgar
1. Compliance 2. Corporate governance 3. Social science literature 4. Trade regulation—Economic aspects 5. Trade regulation—Social aspects
ISBN 1848448856 (hbk.); 9781848448858 (hbk.)
LC 2011-931002

SUMMARY: "This collection of sixteen . . . empirically based articles . . . illustrates how central sociology and sociological thinking are in developing understandings of how business corporations behave in response to regulation." The book's four themes are "(1) motives for compliance, (2) organizational capacities and characteristics, (3) regulation and enforcement of compliance and (4) social and economic environments for regulation and compliance." (British Journal of Sociology)

REVIEW: *Br J Sociol* v65 no1 p196-7 Mr 2014 Siân Lewin
"Explaining Compliance: Business Responses to Regulation". "This innovative book dispels the notion that there can be a single coherent theory of regulatory compliance based on a simple model of deterrence and rational choice, and shows how more social constructionist approaches can

enrich our understandings of what it means for a business to respond to regulation. Suitable for graduate students and academics working in the field of regulation across a number of disciplines . . . 'Explaining Compliance' opens up the field for further research in this significant area of social and political life and will help to ensure this more nuanced, dynamic, complex and pluralistic view of regulatory compliance is incorporated into regulatory policy."

EXPLORER; the lost islands; 128 p. 2013 Abrams Books

1. Explorers—Fiction 2. Graphic novels 3. Islands—Fiction 4. Loneliness—Fiction 5. Radio broadcasters—Fiction

ISBN 1419708813 (hardcover); 141970883X (pbk.); 9781419708817 (hardcover); 9781419708831 (pbk.)

LC 2013-935794

SUMMARY: In this follow-up to "Explorer: The Mystery Boxes," Kazu Kibuishi and a crew of cartoonists again take turns weaving seven tales based around a loose theme. This time the motif is islands, and the contributors are left to interpret it in illustrated shorts. Some, by using their strange and remote settings as microcosms, underscore the value of hard work . . . or finding one's niche . . . , while others examine more abstract concepts such as exploration and isolation." (Publishers Weekly)

REVIEW: *Booklist* v110 no6 p32-3 N 15 2013 Candice Mack

"Explorer: The Lost Islands." "Best known for his celebrated series 'Flight and Amulet,' award-winning comics creator and editor [Kazu] Kibuishi presents the second volume of his comics anthology geared toward middle-school readers. . . . Each fun and fantastical story centers on the theme of islands, both in a physical and philosophical sense. . . . Though not as inventive as its debut volume, this sophomore effort's solid artwork, dialogue, and stories will still be a great introductory title for young or struggling middle-school readers starting to explore the world of graphic novels."

REVIEW: *Bull Cent Child Books* v67 no4 p221 D 2013 E. B.

REVIEW: *Horn Book Magazine* v90 no1 p94 Ja/F 2014 JENNIFER M. BRABANDER

REVIEW: *Kirkus Rev* v81 no18 p311 S 15 2013

REVIEW: *Publ Wkly* v260 no36 p59 S 9 2013

REVIEW: *Publ Wkly* p95-6 Children's starred review annual 2013

EXPLORER; the mystery boxes; 126 p. 2012 Abrams Books

1. Boxes—Fiction 2. Boxes—Juvenile fiction 3. Fantasy in literature 4. Graphic novels 5. Short stories

ISBN 1419700103 (hardcover with jacket); 9781419700095 (pbk.); 9781419700101 (hardcover with jacket)

LC 2011-025343

SUMMARY: This collection of short stories offers "[s]even . . . stories [which] answer one simple question: what's in the box? . . . [E]ach of these . . . illustrated short graphic works revolves around a central theme: a mysterious box and the marvels--or mayhem--inside. Artists include . . . Kazu Kibuishi, Raina Telgemeier ('Smile'), and Dave Roman ('Astronaut Academy'), as well as Jason Caffoe, Stuart Livingston, Johane Matte, Rad Sechrist (all contributors to the . . . comics anthology series 'Flight'), and . . . artist Emily Carroll." (Publisher's note)

REVIEW: *Booklist* v108 no12 p37 F 15 2012 Candice Mack

REVIEW: *Bull Cent Child Books* v65 no10 p515-6 Je 2012 K. C.

REVIEW: *Horn Book Magazine* v88 no3 p88 My/Je 2012 Robin Brenner

"Explorer: The Mystery Boxes." "[Kazu] Kibuishi is known for Amulet, his epic fantasy comic series. . . . More cohesive in theme and targeted toward younger readers, this new installment in the Explorer comics series shares the artistry, vivid atmosphere, and accomplishment in the telling short-form stories that make the Flight series so successful. . . . Spooky cautionary stories, slapstick humor, and enticing tales of enchantment fill these pages. All of the contributors have honed their artistic and narrative craft in both print and animation. . . . [T]his standout anthology will leave its audience with a fresh appetite for more from both the series and the individual contributors."

REVIEW: *Kirkus Rev* v80 no2 p188 Ja 15 2012

REVIEW: *Publ Wkly* v259 no7 p59 F 13 2012

REVIEW: *SLJ* v58 no3 p188-9 Mr 2012 Benjamin Russell

REVIEW: *Voice of Youth Advocates* v35 no1 p58 Ap 2012 Laurie Cavanaugh

EXTENCE, GAVIN. The Universe Versus Alex Woods; [by] Gavin Extence 320 p. 2014 Little Brown & Co.

1. Bullying—Juvenile fiction 2. Epileptics 3. Friendship—Fiction 4. Paranormal fiction 5. Young adult fiction

ISBN 031624659X; 9780316246590

SUMMARY: In this book, by Gavin Extence, "a rare meteorite struck Alex Woods when he was ten years old, leaving scars and marking him for an extraordinary future. The son of a fortune teller, bookish, and an easy target for bullies, Alex hasn't had the easiest childhood. But when he meets curmudgeonly widower Mr. Peterson, he finds an unlikely friend. Someone who teaches him that that you only get one shot at life. That you have to make it count." (Publisher's note)

REVIEW: *Booklist* v110 no14 p8 Mr 15 2014

"The Death of Bees," "Help for the Haunted," and "The Universe Versus Alex Woods". "With their parents dead and buried in the backyard, Scottish teens Marnie and Nelly are finally free from a childhood wracked with abuse. If only the neighbors dog would quit digging in the garden. . . . Sylvie is dealing with taunting classmates, her erratic older sister, and the unsolved murder of her ghost-hunting parents. But perhaps more problematic are the cursed remnants of her parents' work still lingering in the basement. . . . It all begins when Alex is hit on the head by a meteorite, and it all ends when he is arrested trying to reenter England with several grams of marijuana, lots of cash, and the ashes of Mr. Peterson."

REVIEW: *Libr J* v138 no9 p69 My 15 2013 Jan Blodgett

REVIEW: *Publ Wkly* v260 no16 p28 Ap 22 2013

EYMAN, SCOTT. You must remember this. See Wagner, R.

EZNACK, LUCILE. Crises in the Atlantic alliance; affect and relations among NATO members; [by] Lucile Eznack xi, 193 p. 2012 Palgrave Macmillan

1. Alliances (International relations) 2. Historical literature 3. International relations—Psychological aspects 4. International relations literature 5. Security, International
ISBN 9781137289315 (alk. paper)
LC 2012-024714

SUMMARY: This book by Lucile Eznack "examines the role played by affect and emotions to provide a new perspective on alliances and friendly relations among states. . . . Using empirical data and close examinations of the decision-makers in Atlantic alliance countries during the 1956 Suez Crisis, the 1966 NATO crisis, and the 2003 Iraq crisis, Eznack constructs a new history and theory of the workings of alliances." (Publisher's note)

REVIEW: *Choice* v51 no1 p159 S 2013 R. C. Hendrickson

"Crises in the Atlantic Alliance: Affect and Relations Among NATO Members." "[Author Lucile] Eznack . . . provides a novel contribution to the literature on the North Atlantic Treaty Organization (NATO). She maintains that 'affect,' which can loosely be viewed as member states' emotional ties to one another, must be a variable for consideration when seeking to understand the reasons for crises within NATO, the manner in which such events proceed, and how these troubles are rather quickly overcome. . . . The book is exceptionally well organized. She uses three cases: the Suez Canal Crisis in 1956, France's withdrawal from NATO's military command in 1966, and the intra-alliance dispute over US foreign policy toward Iraq in 2002-03."

F

THE FABLIAUX; a new verse translation; 982 p. 2013 Liveright Publishing Corporation, a Division of W. W. Norton & Company

1. Fabliaux 2. Fabliaux—Translations into English 3. French poetry—To 1500 4. French poetry—To 1500—Translations into English 5. Human sexuality in literature 6. Humorous poetry
ISBN 9780871403575 (hardcover)
LC 2013-002314

SUMMARY: This collection presents an English translation of the medieval French tales known as the Fabliaux. "Composed between the twelfth and fourteenth centuries, these virtually unknown erotic and satiric poems lie at the root of the Western comic tradition. Passed down by the anticlerical middle classes of medieval France, 'The Fabliaux' depicts priapic priests, randy wives, and their cuckolded husbands in tales that are shocking even by today's standards." (Publisher's note)

REVIEW: *Booklist* v109 no19/20 p15 Je 1 2013 Donna Seaman

REVIEW: *N Y Rev Books* v60 no19 p44-6 D 5 2013 Christopher Ricks

"The Fabliaux." "The fabliau, then, is a short story that is a tall story. It combines a burly blurting of dirty words with a reveling in humiliations that are good unclean fun. . . . Yet the obvious snag rises at once: Is it any longer possible, these days, to thrill to indecorum, given the fact that decorum has long since vacated the field? . . . Although it is not the same as altogether recognizing the problem, 'The Fabliaux' does nod toward the difficulty, here in our un-outrageable world. when it comes to these 'outrageously obscene, anticlerical, misogynistic fabliaux, which wildly violate any notion of bourgeois respectability.' . . . A bland editorial hand is therefore called for and called upon."

FABRE, CECILE. Cosmopolitan war; [by] Cecile Fabre xiii, 309 p. 2012 Oxford University Press

1. Cosmopolitanism 2. Just war doctrine 3. Philosophical literature 4. War & ethics 5. War (Philosophy)
ISBN 0199567166; 9780199567164
LC 2012-454676

SUMMARY: In this book, "Cécile Fabre articulates and defends an ethical account of war in which the individual, as a moral and rational agent, is the fundamental focus for concern and respect—both as a combatant whose acts of killing need justifying and as a non-combatant whose suffering also needs justifying. She takes as her starting point a political morality to which the individual, rather than the nation-state, is central, namely cosmopolitanism." (Publisher's note)

REVIEW: *Ethics* v124 no2 p406-12 Ja 2014 SETH LAZAR

"Cosmopolitan War". "a trenchant attempt to develop a plausible theory of the morality of war from cosmopolitan foundations. In it, [Cécile] Fabre secures her position as one of the leading revisionist just war theorists . . . but she adds something distinctive and compelling to the debate: a thoroughgoing integration of the morality of war into broader questions of global justice, deploying the tools of political as well as moral philosophy. . . . The book is a tightly integrated whole. . . . field. That said, there are of course weaknesses in the argument."

FABRICANT, MICHAEL. Charter schools and the corporate makeover of public education; what's at stake?; [by] Michael Fabricant xiii, 151 p. 2012 Teachers College

1. Business and education—United States 2. Charter schools—United States 3. Education—Aims and objectives—United States 4. Education—Economic aspects—United States 5. Educational literature
ISBN 9780807752852 (pbk. : alk. paper)
LC 2011-031855

SUMMARY: This book examines "development of charter schools within the broader social trend toward privatizing public institutions. . . . According to [Michael] Fabricant and [Michelle] Fine, the movement toward a market-driven public sphere reflects the nation's weakening 'commitments to shared fates, democratic participation, concerns for equity, and deep accountability'." (Harvard Educational Review)

REVIEW: *Choice* v50 no12 p2287 Ag 2013 R. Roth

REVIEW: *Harv Educ Rev* v84 no1 p125-33 Spr 2014 E.L.E. Y.Y. A.M.N.

"Schooling Hip-Hop: Expanding Hip-Hop Based Education Across the Curriculum," "Charter Schools and the Corporate Makeover of Public Education: What's At Stake?" and "Global Education Policy and International Development: New Agendas, Issues and Policies." "The authors face a difficult challenge as they attempt to move hip-hop pedagogical scholarship beyond a conversation about lyrics and instructional content. . . . For the most part, the authors in Schooling Hip-Hop achieve this feat. . . . Michael Fabricant and Michelle Fine write with a sense of urgency. . . Their imaginative investigation reveals the intricate network of decisions . . . that have created the current charter school landscape. . . . A timely compendium of studies aimed at elucidating the specific social, historical, political, and economic conditions that have shaped global education policies (GEPs) in diverse contexts."

FACTOR, ELIZABETH.ed. Big Tent. See Big Tent

FACTOR, MALLORY.ed. Big Tent. See Big Tent

FADER, JAMIE J. Falling back; incarceration and transitions to adulthood among urban youth; [by] Jamie J. Fader 256 p. 2013 Rutgers University Press

1. African American youth 2. Coming of age 3. Juvenile corrections—Pennsylvania—Philadelphia 4. Juvenile delinquents—Pennsylvania—Philadelphia 5. Juvenile delinquents—Rehabilitation—Pennsylvania—Philadelphia 6. Juvenile justice, Administration of—Pennsylvania—Philadelphia 7. Mountain Ridge Academy 8. Social science literature 9. Urban youth

ISBN 0813560748; 9780813560731 (pbk. : alk. paper); 9780813560748 (hardcover : alk. paper); 9780813560755 (e-book)

LC 2012-033333

SUMMARY: Author Jamie J. Fader's book is "based on over three years of ethnographic research with black and Latino males on the cusp of adulthood and incarcerated at a rural reform school designed to address 'criminal thinking errors' among juvenile drug offenders. Fader observed these young men as they transitioned back to their urban Philadelphia neighborhoods, resuming their daily lives and struggling to adopt adult masculine roles." (Publisher's note)

REVIEW: *Choice* v51 no1 p172 S 2013 J. H. Larson

"Falling Back: Incarceration and Transitions to Adulthood Among Urban Youth." "This exemplary book addresses the 'complex and manifold character' of urban delinquent behavior. The author is guided by pioneering sociologists who crafted approaches to unraveling and understanding the everyday lives of urban African American youth. . . . [Author Jamie J.] Fader . . . draws upon her academic training and professional experience to clearly articulate her methodological approach, enriched by informative case studies of the youth. . . . Readers move inside youthful experiences encountered in incarceration. . . . Subsequent chapters vividly portray personal and social identity struggles and expose the myths associated with the lives of urban youth."

FAGEN, DONALD, 1948-. Eminent hipsters; [by] Donald Fagen 176 p. 2013 Viking

1. Concert tours 2. Memoirs 3. Rock musicians—United States—Biography 4. Steely Dan (Musical group)

ISBN 0670025518; 9780670025510

LC 2013-017054

SUMMARY: This book, by Donald Fagen, is a "work of memoir and criticism by the cofounder of Steely Dan . . . . Fagen begins by introducing the 'eminent hipsters' that spoke to him as he was growing up . . . [and] how, coming of age during the paranoid Cold War era, one of his primary doors of escape became reading science fiction, and of his invigorating trips into New York City to hear jazz." He describes his "mind-expanding years at Bard College, . . . where he first met his future musical partner Walter Becker." (Publisher's note)

REVIEW: *Booklist* v110 no3 p12 O 1 2013 Carl Hays

REVIEW: *Kirkus Rev* v81 no17 p53 S 1 2013

REVIEW: *Libr J* v139 no2 p46 F 1 2014 Douglas King

REVIEW: *New York Times* v163 no56339 pC1-4 D 3 2013 JANET MASLIN

"Eminent Hipsters." "If you like Steely Dan's greatest hits too much, Donald Fagen of that band probably hates you already. . . . But the TV babies in his concert audiences probably won't be the readers of his book, 'Eminent Hipsters.' It's too sly and idiosyncratic and unpredictable for them. . . . The whole second half of 'Eminent Hipsters' is devoted to describing Mr. Fagen's complaints about being on a bus tour. . . . 'Eminent Hipsters' is as bleakly funny about the aging rocker's plight . . . as Steely Dan always has been about its perversely chosen subjects. . . . Mr. Fagen's cranky new incarnation is just as thornily entertaining as his cranky old one."

REVIEW: *Publ Wkly* v260 no30 p58 Jl 29 2013

REVIEW: *TLS* no5771 p27 N 8 2013 LOU GLANDFIELD

FAHEY, DAVID M.ed. Alcohol and drugs in North America. See Alcohol and drugs in North America

FAILURE AND NERVE IN THE ACADEMIC STUDY OF RELIGION; essays in honor of Donald Wiebe; ix, 243 p. 2012 Equinox

1. Religion—Hermeneutics 2. Religion—Study & teaching—History 3. Religion—Study and teaching 4. Religious literature

ISBN 9781845538989 (hardcover)

LC 2012-021686

SUMMARY: This book "presents a . . . critique of the unwillingness of modern scholars to publicly distinguish research into comparative religion from confessional studies written within denominationally-affiliated institutions. The book offers the nineteenth-century founders of the study of religion as a . . . corrective. . . . The book argues that conceptualizing religion as part of the world of human action and experience is the first requirement for the study of religion." (Publisher's note)

REVIEW: *J Am Acad Relig* v82 no1 p264-70 Mr 2014 Tim Jensen

"Failure and Nerve in the Academic Study of Religion: Essays in Honor of Donald Wiebe". "Wiebe's 1984 programmatic article is programmatic also for the essays following it. Whether editors and contributors have been trained by Wiebe, by students of Wiebe, or not: they all 'feel at home' with and are capable of that kind of critical thinking about religion, or, maybe more important, about the study of religion, that characterizes the oeuvre of Wiebe. . . . What is more, the book actually does what the editors say that it does, namely 'documents, refines, and examines' . . . the study of religion in ways variously framed by Wiebe's article. . . . The essays are all well written, all worthwhile reading."

FAIRBAIRN, DAPHNE J. Odd couples; extraordinary differences between the sexes in the animal kingdom; [by] Daphne J. Fairbairn 312 p. 2013 Princeton University Press

1. Animal reproduction 2. Scientific literature 3. Sex differences 4. Sexual behavior in animals 5. Sexual dimorphism (Animals)
ISBN 9780691141961 (hardcover: alk. paper)
LC 2012-046578

SUMMARY: This book by Daphne J. Fairbairn "explores the great size differences between the sexes that exist among many species in the animal world. The book opens with a discussion of why male and female animals differ, and ends with an overview of the diversity of sexual differences. The chapters between covers eight species exhibiting widely disparate sexual differences." (SB&F: Your Guide to Science Resources For All Ages)

REVIEW: *Choice* v51 no3 p491 N 2013 L. T. Spencer

REVIEW: *Libr J* v138 no10 p130 Je 1 2013 Marianne Stowell Bracke

REVIEW: *Nat Hist* v121 no4 p40-1 My 2013 LAURENCE A. MARSCHALL

REVIEW: *New Sci* v218 no2915 p52 My 4 2013

REVIEW: *Publ Wkly* v260 no12 p57-8 Mr 25 2013

REVIEW: *Sci Am* v308 no5 p82 My 2013 Anna Kuchment

FAIRMAN, JULIE A.ed. Routledge handbook on the global history of nursing. See Routledge handbook on the global history of nursing

FAIRY TALE COMICS; Classic Tales Told by Extraordinary Cartoonists; 128 p. 2013 First Second
1. Comic books, strips, etc. 2. Dogs—Fiction 3. Fairy tales 4. Princesses—Fiction 5. Rapunzel (Tale)
ISBN 1596438231 (hardcover); 9781596438231 (hardcover)

SUMMARY: In this book, editor Chris Duffy "has assembled a . . . lineup of comics versions of more than a dozen fairy tales in this . . . follow-up to 'Nursery Rhyme Comics.' Favorites like 'The Twelve Dancing Princesses' and 'Rapunzel' (whose heroines gain significant agency) join rarities like 'The Small Tooth Dog' and 'The Boy Who Drew Cats.'" (Publishers Weekly)

REVIEW: *Booklist* v109 no19/20 p59 Je 1 2013 Jesse Karp

REVIEW: *Bull Cent Child Books* v67 no3 p149 N 2013 K. C.

REVIEW: *Kirkus Rev* v81 no16 p76 Ag 15 2013

REVIEW: *N Y Times Book Rev* p24 N 10 2013 MARIA TATAR

"Tales From the Brothers Grimm," "Michael Hague's Read-To-Me Book of Fairy Tales," and "Fairy TAle Comics." "Lisbeth Zwerger's 'Tales From the Brothers Grimm' and Michael Hague's 'Read-to-me Book of Fairy Tales' draw children into nostalgic fairy-tale worlds with the seductive beauty of their illustrations. 'Fairy Tale Comics,' edited by Chris Duffy and animated by 17 cartoonists and illustrators, by contrast, refashions classic tales with bold creativity. . . . Though Zwerger's watercolors are sometimes disturbing, the decorative beauty of her work also functions as an antidote to the violent content of the tales. This dynamic is reversed in Hague's 'Read-to-Me Book of Fairy Tales'."

REVIEW: *Publ Wkly* p96 Children's starred review annual 2013

REVIEW: *Publ Wkly* v260 no25 p175 Je 24 2013

REVIEW: *SLJ* v59 no9 p168 S 2013 Barbara M. Moon

FALCONER, J. R. D. Crime and community in Reformation Scotland; negotiating power in a burgh society; [by] J. R. D. Falconer xiii, 214 p. 2013 Pickering & Chatto
1. Crime—Scotland—Aberdeen—History—16th century—Sources 2. Crime—Scotland—History—16th century 3. Criminal behavior—Scotland—Aberdeen—History—16th century—Sources 4. Criminal behavior—Scotland—History—16th century 5. Historical literature
ISBN 1848933274 (hbk.); 9781848933279 (hbk.)
LC 2012-537334

SUMMARY: This book by J. R. D. Falconer "focuses on crime in Aberdeen in the second half of the sixteenth century, primarily using burgh council and court records. However, it seeks to do more than simply outline patterns of offending, cases, procedures and punishments. At its heart is the argument that crimes which might be regarded as 'petty' carried a deeper social meaning, and formed attempts to negotiate power structures and relationships within the burgh." (English Historical Review)

REVIEW: *Engl Hist Rev* v129 no536 p196-8 F 2014 John McCallum

"Crime and Community in Reformation Scotland: Negotiating Power in a Burgh Society". "The social history of early modern Scotland's burghs remains relatively patchy in coverage, both geographically and thematically. It is therefore welcome that J.R.D. Falconer's revised doctoral dissertation undertakes extended study of a theme within a single burgh, taking us beyond the overviews and shorter studies which have been the dominant mode of publication to date. . . . The book is not always the easiest of reads, and there is a slight tendency to repeat the central claims rather too frequently. But through its close examination of the archival records . . . it should make it harder for Scottish historians to forget that there is no such thing as a meaningless crime."

FALKENSTERN, LISA.il. Professor Whiskerton presents Steampunk ABC. See Falkenstern, L.

FALKENSTERN, LISA. Professor Whiskerton presents Steampunk ABC; [by] Lisa Falkenstern 32 p. 2014 Two Lions
1. Airships 2. Alphabet books 3. Inventions—Juvenile literature 4. Mice—Juvenile fiction 5. Steampunk culture
ISBN 9781477847220 (trade pbk: alk. paper)
LC 2013-958175

SUMMARY: This alphabet book by Lisa Falkenstern has a steampunk theme and stars "two adorable mice, dressed in Victorian clothing, who use gadgets and found objects to invent machines, mostly using everyday tools. A is for Anvil; M is for Monkey wrench; P is for Periscope; Q is for Quartz; W is for Windsock; X Marks the spot; Z is for Zeppelin." On "the last page . . . the mice float off on the zeppelin that they have contrived to build." (Kirkus Reviews)

REVIEW: *Kirkus Rev* v82 no3 p214 F 1 2014

"Professor Whiskerton Presents Steampunk ABC". "Here's another ABC book that takes an unusual theme and manipulates the device for a very sophisticated audience.

Picture-book-age children will not be familiar with the term 'steampunk,' which is best known as a subgenre of fantasy and science fiction. . . . Though there is no narrative as such, savvy readers will wonder what the various contrivances are leading to, if anything. The last page reveals the answer, as the mice float off on the zeppelin that they have contrived to build. The intricately detailed illustrations are quite fascinating and eye-catching. . . . Though just a context-void bagatelle for actual children, perhaps teen and adult steampunk enthusiasts will take a look."

REVIEW: *Publ Wkly* v261 no7 p95 F 17 2014

REVIEW: *SLJ* v60 no5 p80 My 2014 Diane McCabe

FALLAW, BEN. Religion and state formation in postrevolutionary Mexico; [by] Ben Fallaw xx, 329 p. 2013 Duke University Press

1. Church and state—Mexico—History—20th century 2. Historical literature
ISBN 0822353229; 9780822353225 (cloth : alk. paper); 9780822353379 (pbk. : alk. paper)
LC 2012-011623

SUMMARY: In this book, author Ben Fallaw "argues that previous scholarship has not appreciated the pervasive influence of Catholics and Catholicism on postrevolutionary state formation. By delving into the history of four understudied Mexican states, he is able to show that religion swayed regional politics." (Publisher's note)

REVIEW: *Am Hist Rev* v119 no1 p222-3 F 2014 Edward Wright-Ríos

REVIEW: *Choice* v51 no1 p144 S 2013 J. B. Kirkwood

"Religion and State Formation in Postrevolutionary Mexico." "In this impressively researched, organized, and written work, [Ben] Fallaw examines one of the major themes facing Mexico in the 1930s--the conflict between the Catholic Church and the state. As a result of his carefully crafted investigation, Fallaw concludes that during the postrevolutionary years, Mexico's Catholic Church simultaneously fought the proposed changes of the state while . . . shaping the relations between the postrevolutionary state and the Church. . . . Fallaw's research convincingly argues that the actions of diverse characters . . . contributed to the national state's 'tacit recognition of defeat on the religious question.'"

FALTIS, CHRISTIAN J. The arts and emergent bilingual youth; building culturally responsive, critical and creative education in school and community contexts; [by] Christian J. Faltis xix, 220 p. 2013 Routledge

1. Arts—Study and teaching—United States 2. Bilingual students 3. Education, Bilingual—United States 4. Educational literature 5. Multicultural education—United States
ISBN 9780203124680 (alk. paper); 9780415509732 (alk. paper); 9780415509749 (alk. paper)
LC 2012-040373

SUMMARY: In this book, "arguing for the vital role of the arts in the academic development of bilingual youth, [Sharon Verner] Chappell . . . and [Christian J.] Faltis . . . make the link between second language acquisition theory and arts education. . . . The heart of the book is the suggestion that bilingual children be provided with the opportunity to tell their own stories through traditional and technological media." (Choice: Current Reviews for Academic Libraries)

REVIEW: *Choice* v51 no7 p1274 Mr 2014 A. Anderberg

"The Arts and Emergent Bilingual Youth: Building Culturally Responsive, Critical, and Creative Education in School and Community Contexts." "The heart of the book is the suggestion that bilingual children be provided with the opportunity to tell their own stories through traditional and technological media. Artists' projects and statements are thoughtfully described and supported by useful photographs. . . . Readers seeking to understand the academic achievement gap will appreciate the original perspective presented but may find some of the language tedious. . . . This book represents an important perspective and provides strategies for engaging bilingual youth in rigorous and evidence-based reflection centered on the arts."

FAMILY TROUBLE; memoirists on the hazards and rewards of revealing family; 232 p. 2013 University of Nebraska Press

1. Authorship—Moral & ethical aspects 2. Autobiography—Authorship—Anecdotes 3. Biographers—United States—Anecdotes 4. Essay (Literary form) 5. Family secrets—Anecdotes 6. Memoirs
ISBN 9780803246928 (pbk. : alk. paper)
LC 2012-048021

SUMMARY: This book, edited by Joy Castro, "navigates the emotional and literary minefields that any writer of family stories or secrets must travel when depicting private lives for public consumption. Essays by twenty-five memoirists . . . explore the fraught territory of family history told from one perspective, which, from another angle in the family drama, might appear quite different indeed." (Publisher's note)

REVIEW: *Kirkus Rev* v81 no16 p179 Ag 15 2013

"Family Trouble: Memoirists on the Hazards and Rewards of Revealing Family." "A chorus of noteworthy memoirists reflects on the ethical consequences of airing dirty laundry. 'With family stories, the stakes are always high,' writes [editor Joy] Castro . . . , who published her harrowing experiences as the abused child of fundamentalist parents. . . . This conundrum of writing within the 'self-disclosing genre of our reality-hungry era' is pondered throughout 25 reflective essays from a wide-ranging group of writers."

REVIEW: *Publ Wkly* v260 no33 p59 Ag 19 2013

FAN, TERRY.il. Rooftoppers. See Rundell, K.

FANNING, DIANE. Chain reaction; [by] Diane Fanning 233 p. 2014 Severn House Pub Ltd

1. Bombings—Fiction 2. Detective & mystery stories 3. High schools 4. Terrorism investigation 5. Women detectives—Fiction
ISBN 0727883410; 9780727883414

SUMMARY: Author Diane Fanning's "seventh Lucinda Pierce mystery . . . finds the Virginia homicide investigator as touchy and driven as ever. When a bomb explodes at Woodrow Wilson High School, killing a janitor and a student, competing agencies investigate--the FBI, in the person of Pierce's boyfriend, Jake Lovett, plus ATF and Homeland Security. Pierce doubts the bombing is terrorism related, but hers is not a popular opinion." (Publishers Weekly)

REVIEW: *Booklist* v110 no13 p20-1 Mr 1 2014 Barbara Bibel

"Chain Reaction." "A bomb blast rocks a high school on a Sunday afternoon, killing a janitor and an unidentified student. Homicide detective Lucinda Pierce arrives at the scene to find herself removed from the case. The FBI and Homeland Security, convinced that the bomb is the work of a terrorist group, do not think the locals can handle it. Lucinda is annoyed and convinced that there are other motives. . . . Meanwhile, she is also dealing with a young girl who has been abused by her mother's boyfriend. . . .The two cases and the subplot involving feuding federal agencies combine to provide a timely and involving case."

FANTASKEY, BETH. Buzz kill; [by] Beth Fantaskey 368 p. 2014 Houghton Mifflin Harcourt

1. Coaches (Athletics)—Fiction 2. Dating (Social customs)—Fiction 3. High schools—Fiction 4. Murder—Fiction 5. Mystery and detective stories 6. Schools—Fiction

ISBN 0547393105; 9780547393100

LC 2013-011423

SUMMARY: In this book, by Beth Fantaskey, "when the widely disliked Honeywell Stingers football coach is found murdered, 17-year-old Millie is determined to investigate. She is chasing a lead for the school newspaper—and looking to clear her father, the assistant coach, and prime suspect. . . . Millie joins forces with her mysterious classmate Chase who seems to want to help her even while covering up secrets of his own." (Publisher's note)

REVIEW: *Booklist* v110 no17 p52 My 1 2014 Krista Hutley

REVIEW: *Bull Cent Child Books* v67 no10 p515 Je 2014 K. Q. G.

"Buzz Kill". "Although at times Millie seems almost precious with adorkability, her narration reveals some of the neuroses behind the quirky façade, and she's utterly believable as a weird kid who'd like to be less weird if she could only figure out how. Chase makes a swoonworthy romantic counterpart, and the revelation of his past mistakes give him a depth not often seen in the genre—readers will argue whether that past makes him more sympathetic or completely undateable. Fans looking for a less prim and proper Nancy Drew (and a few more lustful kisses) will find her here."

REVIEW: *Kirkus Rev* v82 no7 p100 Ap 1 2014

REVIEW: *Publ Wkly* v261 no13 p66-7 Mr 31 2014

REVIEW: *SLJ* v60 no4 p162 Ap 2014 Diana Pierce

REVIEW: *Voice of Youth Advocates* v36 no6 p58 F 2014 Marissa Wolf

FARAONE, CHRISTOPHER A.ed. Greek and Roman animal sacrifice. See Greek and Roman animal sacrifice

FARIS, DAVID M. Dissent and revolution in a digital age; social media, blogging and activism in Egypt; [by] David M. Faris xi, 267 p. 2013 I.B. Tauris

1. Dissenters—Egypt—History—21st century 2. Internet—Political aspects—Egypt 3. Political activists—Egypt 4. Political science literature 5. Social media—Political aspects—Egypt

ISBN 1780761503 (hbk.); 9781780761503 (hbk.)

LC 2012-533383

SUMMARY: "In this book, [David M.] Faris . . . analyzes how social media networks (SMNs) have affected Egyptian politics over the past decade. . . .The book concentrates on developing a theoretical understanding of the centrality of SMNs to political change. . . . Faris's conclusion is that social media contribute to the speed and efficacy of revolutionary movements . . . but that social media networks are not sufficient in themselves to effect regime collapse or change." (Choice: Current Reviews for Academic Libraries)

REVIEW: *Choice* v51 no6 p1085-6 F 2014 P. Rowe

"Dissent and Revolution in a Digital Age: Social Media, Blogging and Activism in Egypt." "In this book, [David M.] Faris . . . analyzes how social media networks (SMNs) have affected Egyptian politics over the past decade. . . . Aside from some lengthy discussion of social media theory, the book is an excellent resource for those interested in online activism and the politics of the Arab Spring. Lay readers will be interested in its reliable and readable recounting of Egyptian politics at a key moment in history. . . . Recommended."

FARISH, MURRAY. Inappropriate behavior; stories; [by] Murray Farish 224 p. 2014 Milkweed Editions

ISBN 9781571311078 (paperback: acid-free paper); 1571311076 (paperback: acid-free paper)

LC 2013-037871

SUMMARY: The stories in this collection, by Murray Farish, "are stories of people seeking desperately for a way to connect, to be understood, and, more often than not, failing horribly in the attempt. From the personal account of someone easily recognized as a young John Hinckley Jr., to the . . . title story, in which a couple stretched to their limit after a layoff struggles to care for their emotionally unbalanced young son, this collection draws a bead on our national identity." (Publisher's note)

REVIEW: *Kirkus Rev* v82 no3 p184 F 1 2014

"Inappropriate Behavior: Stories". "Edgy writing in an unnerving collection of short fiction. . . . Though well-done, the best of the lot are those created from pure imagination. [Murray] Farish works best when he is left to his own devices. . . . The titular story is almost a tour de force. . . . Almost. Its penultimate section is a steady barrage of questions about life and substance in America that generates frightening momentum as it moves over several pages. Stop there. It loses its punch with the actual ending. This collection of stories is intriguing but misses as standout fiction through uneven writing and trying too hard to be oddly curious."

REVIEW: *Publ Wkly* v260 no51 p34-5 D 16 2013

FARIZAN, SARA. If you could be mine; a novel; [by] Sara Farizan 256 p. 2013 Algonquin

1. Best friends—Fiction 2. Friendship—Fiction 3. Lesbians—Fiction 4. Love—Fiction 5. Young adult fiction

ISBN 1616202513 (hardcover); 9781616202514 (hardcover)

LC 2013-008931

SUMMARY: This novel, set in Iran, 17-year-old Sahar, who has wanted to marry her best friend Nasrin since they were six years old, dreams of living openly with her lover. Nasrin prefers to accept an arranged marriage, while intending to continue their illicit affair. Exposed to a world of sexual diversity by her gay cousin and made desperate by Nasrin's impending marriage, Sahar explores the one legal option for the two of them to be together: her own sex reassignment surgery." (Publishers Weekly)

REVIEW: *Booklist* v110 no4 p60 O 15 2013 Ilene Cooper

REVIEW: *Booklist* v110 no14 p24 Mr 15 2014

REVIEW: *Booklist* v109 no21 p65 Jl 1 2013 Michael Cart

REVIEW: *Booklist* v110 no9/10 p83 Ja 1 2014 MICHAEL CART

"Ghost Hawk," "Looks Like Daylight," and "If You Could Be Mine". "[Susan] Cooper's heartfelt historical fantasy about the magical relationship between two boys, Native American Little Hawk and trader's son John, is richly plotted, beautiful in tone, and serious in theme as it examines the injustices of early colonial life. . . . Canadian author [Deborah] Ellis has interviewed 45 young Native people from Canada and the U.S. The 9- to 18-year-olds tell her about the often appalling conditions of their lives, which are blighted by alcohol and drug abuse, poverty, suicide, broken families, and more. 'That they are here at all,' Ellis movingly writes, 'is a miracle.' . . . [Sara] Farizan's unusual first novel tells an important story about the stubbornness of love and offers an inside look at secret gay life in Iran."

REVIEW: *Booklist* v110 no14 p87 Mr 15 2014 Heather Booth

REVIEW: *Bull Cent Child Books* v67 no2 p86-7 O 2013 K. C.

"If You Could Be Mine." "While the Koran explicitly forbids homosexuality, it is mute on the subject of surgically changing one's gender, according to the Islamic Republic of Iran. Sahar therefore decides that gender reassignment is the only way for her to prevent the loss of Nasrin, whom Sahar has loved since they were children together, when Nasrin is betrothed to a doctor. . . . [Author Sara] Farizan frankly tackles many timely issues in this book, and many Western readers will be shocked by the dangers Sahar Faces. Unfortunately, the author ends up telling more than showing her story, as Sahar reflects on her situation and engages in purposive conversations about social issues, surgical procedures, and her options."

REVIEW: *Horn Book Magazine* v89 no6 p91 N/D 2013 CLAIRE E. GROSS

REVIEW: *Kirkus Rev* v81 no13 p91 Jl 1 2013

REVIEW: *Kirkus Rev* p64 2013 Guide to BookExpo America

REVIEW: *N Y Times Book Rev* p34 S 22 2013 Jessica Bruder

REVIEW: *Publ Wkly* v260 no43 p57 O 28 2013

REVIEW: *Publ Wkly* v260 no23 p79 Je 10 2013

REVIEW: *SLJ* v59 no7 p92 Jl 2013 Kathleen E. Gruver

FARJEON, ELEANOR, 1881-1965. Like Sorrow or a Tune; A New Selection of Poems; [by] Eleanor Farjeon 160 p. 2013 Laurel Books

1. Bereavement 2. Children's poetry 3. English poetry 4. Poems—Collections 5. Sonnets
ISBN 1873390149; 9781873390146

SUMMARY: This book of poetry by Eleanor Farjeon presents a "thematically arranged collection of her work for children and adults," edited by Anne Harvey. (Times Literary Supplement) It includes "sonnets touching on her grief" for poet Edward Thomas following his death in the First World War. The book also includes a preface by Piers Plowright. (Publisher's note)

REVIEW: *TLS* no5769 p23 O 25 2013 JOHN GREENING

"Like Sorrow or a Tune: A New Selection of Poems" and "Selected Poems and Prose." "[Eleanor Farjeon's] own poems about [Edward Thomas] are the serious heart of 'Like Sorrow or a Tune,' and may be considered very successful sonnets, but the bulk of her work is for children. . . . For all [Anne] Harvey's advocacy . . . this verse does require modem adult readers to make allowances. Where she reaches for greater depths, she is too often remarking on a mystery, rather than recreating it. In the end, it is Harvey ' s own commentary and the relationship with Thomas that give this book its interest. . . . Although there has been no lack of recent editions, [David] Wright's judicious selection . . . is certainly worth reviving. . . . With Wright's succinct notes, this might be considered the most fully representative edition of Thomas's work."

FARKAS, ENDRE.ed. Language matters. See Language matters

FARLEY, BRIANNE.il. Ike's incredible ink. See Farley, B.

FARLEY, BRIANNE. Ike's incredible ink; [by] Brianne Farley 32 p. 2013 Candlewick Press

1. Adventure stories for children 2. Authorship—Juvenile literature 3. Ink 4. Picture books for children 5. Writer's block
ISBN 0763662968; 9780763662967
LC 2012-947261

SUMMARY: In this children's picture book by Brianne Farley, "Ike--an inkblot . . . is also a blocked writer. Like many before him, he procrastinates . . . and then he decides that his story demands ink made from exceptional ingredients: shadows, the feathers of a booga-bird, and the essence of the dark side of the moon. . . . After some chaotic concocting . . . Ike sits down to write and, sure enough, a story inspired by his ink quest materializes." (Publishers Weekly)

REVIEW: *Bull Cent Child Books* v67 no2 p87 O 2013 J. H.

REVIEW: *Kirkus Rev* v81 no12 p89 Je 15 2013

REVIEW: *N Y Times Book Rev* p16 Ag 25 2013 DAN YACCARINO

"Brush of the Gods," "Ike's Incredible Ink," and "The Day the Crayons Quit." "Four new books on art and white inspires it are just right for children who dream of being artists. . . . 'Brush of the Gods' [is] written by the veteran author Lenore Look, with illustrations by Meilo So evoking sumi ink paintings. . . . A blot of ink creating its own ink to write a story? Although I found the illustrations endearing, the narrative's lack of internal logic was a stumbling block I had a hard time getting over. . . . Although the crayons' wacky voices are believably the kind of thing creative kids come up with when they're daydreaming, [Drew] Daywalt's clever conceit seems stretched to its limit."

REVIEW: *Publ Wkly* v260 no21 p58 My 27 2013

REVIEW: *SLJ* v59 no7 p61 Jl 2013 Joan Kindig

FARMELO, GRAHAM. Churchill's bomb; how the United States overtook Britain in the first nuclear arms race; [by] Graham Farmelo 576 p. 2013 Basic Books

1. Atomic bomb—Great Britain—History 2. Historical literature 3. Nuclear weapons—Government policy—

Great Britain—History 4. Nuclear weapons—Government policy—United States—History 5. World War, 1939-1945—Science—Great Britain

ISBN 0465021956; 9780465021956 (hardcover: alk. paper)

LC 2013-940827

SUMMARY: Author Graham Farmelo describes how "the British set out to investigate the possibility of building nuclear weapons before their American colleagues [and how] Prime Minister Winston Churchill did not make the most of his country's lead and was slow to realize the Bomb's strategic implications. Contrasting Churchill's often inattentive leadership with Franklin Roosevelt's decisiveness, [Farmelo] reveals the secret history of the weapon that transformed modern geopolitics." (Publisher's note)

REVIEW: *Choice* v51 no8 p1423 Ap 2014 M. Schiff

"Churchill's Bomb: How the United States Overtook Britain in the First Nuclear Arms Race". "Its conceit is that although Winston Churchill strongly promoted nuclear energy for both industrial and military purposes before WWII, with Britain being the world leader in nuclear science, his push for a British bomb during the war proved both awkwardly handled and shortsighted to boot. . . .This is not the whole story, however, since, ironically, Churchill, an original Cold Warrior, became so horrified at the prospect of a nuclear holocaust that he subsequently pursued a policy of détente with Russia. Was Churchill right or wrong? The reader can decide. Meanwhile, [Graham] Farmelo . . . tells the story with verve and in fascinating, illuminating detail."

REVIEW: *Economist* v409 no8856 p88-9 O 5 2013

REVIEW: *Kirkus Rev* v81 no14 p128 Jl 15 2013

REVIEW: *Libr J* v138 no14 p124 S 1 2013 Ed Goedeken

REVIEW: *N Y Rev Books* v51 no7 p44-6 Ap 24 2014 Freeman Dyson

"Churchill's Bomb: How the United States Overtook Britain in the First Nuclear Arms Race." "The title, 'Churchill's Bomb,' is misleading. The title was probably chosen by the publisher to attract readers rather than to describe the book. Graham Farmelo's main subject is the personal rivalry surrounding the British nuclear weapons project, in which Winston Churchill played a leading part. But the book is not a history of the bomb. It does not answer some of the obvious questions that a reader might ask."

REVIEW: *N Y Times Book Rev* p12-3 D 1 2013 BENJAMIN SCHWARZ

FARMER, NANCY. The lord of Opium; [by] Nancy Farmer 432 p. 2013 Atheneum Books for Young Readers

1. Cloning—Fiction 2. Drug traffic—Fiction 3. Environmental degradation—Fiction 4. Science fiction 5. Speculative fiction

ISBN 1442482540 (hardcover); 9781442482548 (hardcover)

LC 2012-030418

SUMMARY: This book is the sequel to Nancy Farmer's "The House of the Scorpion." Here, "Matt was a clone of El Patrón, drug lord of Opium, but with El Patrón dead, Matt is now considered by international law to be fully human and El Patrón's rightful heir. But it's a corrupt land . . . ruled over by drug lords and worked by armies of Illegals turned into 'eejits,' or zombies. Matt wants to bring reform." (Kirkus Reviews)

REVIEW: *Booklist* v109 no19/20 p75 Je 1 2013 Suanne Roush

REVIEW: *Booklist* v110 no8 p55-8 D 15 2013 Lynn Rutan

"The Lord of Opium." "[Nancy] Farmer's long-awaited sequel to the award-winning 'The House of the Scorpion' . . . examines fascinating issues, introduces colorful new characters, and extends readers' understanding of this vividly realized world. [Raul] Esparza reads with a smooth fluidity and brings a wonderful authenticity to the many Spanish words and names. He distinguishes the major voices (from a large cast of characters) with changes in pitch and volume. The evil One Eye almost bellows, the eejit Waitress speaks in a low monotone, and Matt is given a slightly higher, youthful sound. This excellent production will be embraced by fans of the previous book."

REVIEW: *Bull Cent Child Books* v67 no5 p265 Ja 2014 A. M.

"The Lord of Opium." "Picking up only moments after its predecessor, this narrative offers an intriguing sequel that unfortunately doesn't reach the level of the previous title. [Nancy] Farmer succeeds in providing just enough detail to allow unfamiliar readers to follow the plot, but any emotional connection to Matt as a character remains grounded in the initial story. While Matt continues the worthy thematic struggle of figuring out who he is under the shadow of what others want him to be, he eventually becomes little more than a vessel by which to explore El Patrón's vicious legacy, a focus that diffuses energy and slows pacing. New characters are compelling, though."

REVIEW: *Horn Book Magazine* v89 no5 p94 S/O 2013 JONATHAN HUNT

"The Lord of Opium." "[Nancy] Farmer introduces some vivid new characters to her already colorful cast, enlarges the scope of her world-building, and eschews the quest plot that characterizes most of her work for a more nuanced one of mystery and intrigue. Yet ethical dilemmas remain at the heart of this novel, and, if anything, become elevated because of Matt's newfound power and responsibility. 'Where did it all end? How much wickedness could you do in the service of good before it turned into pure evil?' The landscape of dystopian literature has changed significantly since the first book, but this sequel is still a cut above the rest."

REVIEW: *Kirkus Rev* p65 2013 Guide 20to BookExpo America

REVIEW: *Kirkus Rev* p52-3 Ag 15 2013 Fall Preview

REVIEW: *Kirkus Rev* v81 no14 p33 Jl 15 2013

REVIEW: *Publ Wkly* p113 Children's starred review annual 2013

REVIEW: *Publ Wkly* v260 no25 p174 Je 24 2013

REVIEW: *SLJ* v59 no9 p156 S 2013 Janice M. Del Negro

REVIEW: *SLJ* v60 no2 p56 F 2014 Sarah Flood

REVIEW: *Voice of Youth Advocates* v36 no3 p74 Ag 2013 Kathleen Beck

FARR, DONALD. Mustang, fifty years; celebrating America's only true pony car; [by] Donald Farr 256 p. 2013 Motorbooks

1. Automobile racing 2. Historical literature 3. Mustang automobile—History 4. TRANSPORTATION—Automotive—History 5. TRANSPORTATION—Automotive—Pictorial

ISBN 9780760343968 (hardback)

LC 2013-011840

SUMMARY: This book on Mustang automobiles by Donald Farr "provides a comprehensive recounting of the car's gestation as a design study in the early 1960s, its splashy debut at the 1964 New York World's Fair and its tumultuous life up through the fifth-generation model that is entering its final model year. The book concludes with sections ofn Mustangs for racing, in pop culture and for hobbyists and collectors." (New York Times, Late New York Edition)

REVIEW: *New York Times* v163 no56344 p11 D 8 2013 CHARLES McEWEN JOSEPH SIANO JERRY GARRETT JULIA S. MAYERSOHN RICHARD S. CHANG

"Hunt vs. Lauda: The Epic 1976 Formula 1 Season," "Mustang Fifty Years: Celebrating America's Only True Pony Car," and "The Real Way Round". "This book appears to have been published to coincide with Ron Howard's movie 'Rush,' which dramatizes the battle for the 1976 Formula One drivers championship. . . . and 'rush' is what comes to mind when I think about the effort behind this book. . . . 'Mustang Fifty Years' is a voluminous book that tracks the life of a Ford that's as famous as the Model T. . . . While not exactly a beach read, the book is more digestible, even for general audiences, than its dauntingly encyclopedic appearance might suggest. . . . Libraries are full of reflective, overthought travelogues. If you prefer yours presented with all the cheer of a tale tale told in a pub and put together with the artistic élan of a family Christmas newsletter, you will strike gold with 'The Real Way Round'."

FARRANT, NATASHA. After Iris; [by] Natasha Farrant 272 p. 2013 Dial Books for Young Readers

1. Au pairs—Fiction 2. Brothers and sisters—Fiction 3. Children's literature 4. Diaries—Fiction 5. Family life—England—London—Fiction 6. Grief—Fiction 7. Twins—Fiction 8. Video recordings—Production and direction—Fiction

ISBN 0803739826 (hardcover); 9780803739826 (hardcover)

LC 2012-039136

SUMMARY: In this book, 12-year-old "Bluebell Gadsby's family has been collapsing ever since Blue's twin sister. Iris, died three years ago. Blue's father is working on the other side of the country, and their mother is traveling overseas, which leaves new au pair Zoran in charge. Between Blue's older sister Flora's rebelliousness, her two younger siblings' antics, and the family's pet rats, which live in the garden of their London home, Zoran has his hands full." (Publishers Weekly)

REVIEW: *Bull Cent Child Books* v67 no1 p17 S 2013 D. S.

"After Iris." "Three years ago, Bluebell Gadsby's twin sister, Iris, died, and it seems to twelve-year-old Bluebell like she's the only one in their noisy English family who still misses her. . . . [Author Natasha] Farrant writes with the effervescent, engaging style of her countrywomen Sue Limb or Hilary McKay. . . . The book isn't as successful as McKay's work, though, in balancing the loss with the cheerful chaos; the parents' abdication is too complete for a satisfactory resolution, so the happy ending is not only overcontrived (Dad returns home in a helicopter, bringing the two lost youngest children and a Hollywood producer) but also superficial and dishonest in so easily redeeming irredeemable parental failure."

REVIEW: *Horn Book Magazine* v89 no5 p94-5 S/O 2013 SARAH ELLIS

REVIEW: *Kirkus Rev* p74 N 15 2013 Best Books

REVIEW: *Kirkus Rev* v81 no10 p91 My 15 2013

REVIEW: *N Y Times Book Rev* p16 Jl 14 2013 EMMA BROCKES

REVIEW: *Publ Wkly* v260 no23 p78 Je 10 2013

REVIEW: *SLJ* v59 no7 p79 Jl 2013 Carol A. Edwards

REVIEW: *Voice of Youth Advocates* v36 no3 p60 Ag 2013 Sherri Rampey

FARRAR, CHRISTI SHOWMAN.ed. Magill's Literary Annual 2013. See Magill's Literary Annual 2013

FARRELL, JOSEPH. Sicily; A Cultural History; [by] Joseph Farrell 256 p. 2013 Interlink Pub Group Inc

1. Historical literature 2. Mafia—Italy—Sicily 3. Sicily (Italy)—Civilization—Arab influences 4. Sicily (Italy)—Description & travel 5. Sicily (Italy)—History

ISBN 1566569524; 9781566569521

SUMMARY: This book by Joseph Farrell presents a cultural history of Sicily, Italy. Arguing that "there is more to Sicily than the Godfather and the mafia," the author emphasizes that "Sicily was the land in the center of the Mediterranean where the great civilizations of Europe and Northern Africa met. . . . . Visitors will find in an out-of-the-way town an Aragonese castle . . . [and] see red Muslim-styles domes over a Christian shrine." (Publisher's note)

REVIEW: *TLS* no5754 p29 Jl 12 2013 IAN THOMSON

"Sicily: A Cultural History." "In his absorbing cultural history of the island, [Joseph] Farrell dilates knowledgeably on the Mafia and its crimes. . . . Farrell is rightly impatient of romantic, Hollywood representations of the Mafia as a sort of benevolent freemasonry. . . . Though he casts an appalled eye on organized crime, 'Sicily' is far from a sombre book. Descriptions of Sicilian marzipan sweets . . . jostle alluringly with reflections on wine and pasta dishes. . . . Joseph Farrell has written a marvellous guide to an island of bewildering mixed bloods and ethnicities."

FARRELL, MARY CRONK. Pure grit; how American World War II nurses survived battle and prison camp in the Pacific; [by] Mary Cronk Farrell 160 p. 2014 Abrams Books for Young Readers

1. Historical literature 2. Military nursing—United States—History—Juvenile literature 3. Nurses—United States—History—20th century 4. Prisoners of war—Philippines—Juvenile literature 5. Prisoners of war—United States—Juvenile literature 6. World War, 1939-1945—Campaigns—Philippines—Juvenile literature 7. World War, 1939-1945—Medical care—United States 8. World War, 1939-1945—Prisoners and prisons, Japanese—Juvenile literature

ISBN 1419710281; 9781419710285 (hardcover : alk. paper)

LC 2013-017134

SUMMARY: This book, by Mary Cronk Farrell, focuses on American World War II Navy and Army nurses who were stationed in the Pacific. "Nurses, deeply engaged in caring for desperately wounded soldiers, were sent to Bataan. After living on near-starvation rations, the nurses on Bataan were evacuated to Corregidor. . . . A few were rescued from Corregidor before it too fell to enemy forces. . . . The remaining nurses were then imprisoned . . . and not released until late winter of 1945." (Kirkus Reviews)

REVIEW: *Booklist* v110 no12 p74-5 F 15 2014 Carolyn Phelan

REVIEW: *Bull Cent Child Books* v67 no8 p404 Ap 2014 E. B.

"Pure Grit: How American World War II Nurses Survived Battle and Prison Camp in the Pacific". "[Mary Cronk] Farrell tells the gripping story of the nurses' three year ordeal on the college grounds of Santo Tomas in Manila and at the inland encampment of Los Baños at Laguna de Bay. . . Although the discussion of the Japanese military advance is flag-wavingly pro-American, Farrell tempers the narration with a discussion of how the popular press demonized the captors beyond their actual transgressions. This valuable account shifts the focus from World War II nurses as 'angels of mercy' to POWs, and replays the rout at Bataan with women rather than men in the starring roles."

REVIEW: *Horn Book Magazine* v90 no2 p138-40 Mr/Ap 2014 BETTY CARTER

"Pure Grit: How American World War II Nurses Survived Battle and Prison Camp in the Pacific." "Using information taken mainly from historical interviews and modern correspondence with the subjects' relatives, [Mary Cronk] Farrell directly confronts the horrors of war and the years of inhumane treatment in the POW camps. These women--malnourished, ill with diseases such as malaria, dysentery, and beriberi--established multiple hospital sites and often shouldered doctors' medical duties. Many returned home with disabilities and lifelong medical problems; though many suffered from PTSD, no mental health services were available to them."

REVIEW: *Kirkus Rev* v82 no2 p227 Ja 15 2014

REVIEW: *SLJ* v60 no4 p187 Ap 2014 Jackie Partch

REVIEW: *Voice of Youth Advocates* v37 no1 p92 Ap 2014 Rebecca Denham

FARREY, BRIAN. The Shadowhand Covenant; [by] Brian Farrey 384 p. 2013 HarperCollins

1. Conspiracies—Fiction 2. Fantasy 3. Fantasy fiction 4. Magic—Fiction 5. Nomads 6. Racism—Fiction
ISBN 0062049313; 9780062049315 (hardback)
LC 2013-021825

SUMMARY: In this book by Brian Farrey, "trouble is brewing in the Five Provinces. Mysterious magical artifacts have gone missing from the royal vaults. Master thieves from a secret society known as the Shadowhands are disappearing. And without explanation, the High Laird has begun imprisoning the peaceful Sarosan people. Jaxter Grimjinx and his parents receive a summons from the Shadowhands—a summons that they would be foolish to ignore—and Jaxter is thrust into the heart of the conspiracy." (Publisher's note)

REVIEW: *Booklist* v110 no4 p53 O 15 2013 Francisca Goldsmith

REVIEW: *Kirkus Rev* v81 no16 p135 Ag 15 2013

"The Shadowhand Covenant." "Making enemies-but-friends with two Sarosan kids, Jaxter and Maloch tumble their way through escapes, traps and fights with creepy monsters, while trying to untangle which adults committed which bad deed. Always 'flippant when faced with danger,' Jaxter narrates in humorous first-person. . . . Well-meaning but worrisome romanticization of simple, dark-skinned nomads somewhat undermines [author Brian] Farrey's explicit anti-racism. High-spirited fun, with complexity and surprises."

REVIEW: *SLJ* v60 no1 p80 Ja 2014 Stacy Dillon

FASCHING-VARNER, KENNETH JAMES. Working through whiteness; examining white racial identity and profession with pre-service teachers; [by] Kenneth James Fasching-Varner xii, 147 p. 2012 Lexington Books

1. Critical race theory 2. Social science literature 3. Student teachers—United States—Case studies 4. Teacher education—Social aspects 5. Teachers, White—Training of—United States—Case studies 6. Whites—Race identity—United States—Case studies
ISBN 9780739176863 (cloth : alk. paper)
LC 2012-044030

SUMMARY: This book, written by Kenneth Fasching-Varner, "examines the nature of white racial identity as seen through the narratives of nine pre-service teachers as well as his own struggles with racial identity. This text draws on racial identity, Critical Race theory, and discourse and narrative analysis to reveal how participants in the study used discourse structures to present beliefs about race and their own understandings." (Publisher's note)

REVIEW: *Choice* v51 no2 p320-1 O 2013 P. M. Del Prado Hill

"Working Through Whiteness: Examining White Racial Identity and Profession With Pre-Service Teachers." "[Author Kenneth James] Fasching-Varner . . . examines the preparation of white teachers, a complex, challenging topic given that the majority of the teaching force is white while the school-age population is increasingly nonwhite. The author positions his work within critical race theory and white racial identity theory and provides an extensive review of the literature to establish a helpful frame of reference. . . . This book should generate important conversations about race in order to improve schooling for all children."

THE FAST-CHANGING ARCTIC; rethinking Arctic security for a warmer world; xi, 395 p. 2013 University of Calgary Press

1. Global warming—Arctic regions 2. Political science literature 3. Security, International—Arctic regions
ISBN 9781552386460 (pbk.)
LC 2013-412072

SUMMARY: This book on political and environmental issues facing the Arctic regions was edited by Barry Scott Zellen. It covers topics such as "sovereignty, strategic defense, national and environmental security, and global economics. Some of these essays consider the probable rush to grab territories, and to exploit new transportation routes and newly accessible natural resources." (Choice: Current Reviews for Academic Libraries)

REVIEW: *Choice* v51 no7 p1304 Mr 2014 B. Galbraith

"The Fast-Changing Arctic: Rethinking Arctic Security for a Warmer World." "How can the Arctic nations peacefully manage these conflicting demands? What about the demands of non-Arctic nations that want a part of the spoils? Who will have the right to create and enforce environmental standards and rules? How will indigenous peoples fare? This is an excellent collection of essays from knowledgeable people. It is a must for anyone interested in geopolitics, international relations, and northern studies. . . . Highly recommended."

FATTAL, JOSH. A sliver of light. See Bauer, S.

FAULKNER, MATT. Gaijin; American prisoner of war; [by] Matt Faulkner 144 p. 2014 Disney-Hyperion Books
1. Graphic novels 2. Japanese Americans—Evacuation and relocation, 1942-1945—Fiction 3. Japanese Americans—Evacuation and relocation, 1942-1945—Juvenile fiction 4. Racially mixed people—Fiction
ISBN 1423137353; 9781423137351
LC 2013-029795

SUMMARY: In this graphic novel by Matt Faulkner, "with a white mother and a Japanese father, Koji Miyamoto quickly realizes that his home in San Francisco is no longer a welcoming one after Pearl Harbor is attacked. And once he's sent to an internment camp, he learns that being half white at the camp is just as difficult as being half Japanese on the streets of an American city during WWII." (Publisher's note)

REVIEW: *Booklist* v110 no16 p41 Ap 15 2014 Sarah Hunter

REVIEW: *Bull Cent Child Books* v67 no10 p516 Je 2014 E. B.

"Gaijin: American Prisoner of War". "In this graphic work of historical fiction, Koji Miyamoto turns thirteen the day the Japanese attack Pearl Harbor, and the San Francisco teen finds his life spinning out of control. . . . Frames are laid out with all the orderly crispness of a cleanly deployed executive order but are densely filled with figures that roil with emotion and colors that change to lurid red-streaked hues when Koji's nightmares and fears hold sway. The particular trials of a biracial internee add a fresh dimension to the canon of relocation-camp fiction, and an endnote offers background on the Faulkner family history that inspired this title."

REVIEW: *Horn Book Magazine* v90 no4 p91-2 Jl/Ag 2014 JONATHAN HUNT

REVIEW: *Kirkus Rev* v82 no8 p234 Ap 15 2014

REVIEW: *SLJ* v60 no5 p120 My 2014 Benjamin Russell

REVIEW: *Voice of Youth Advocates* v37 no2 p57 Je 2014 Marissa Wolf

REVIEW: *Voice of Youth Advocates* v37 no3 p54-5 Ag 2014 KAT KAN

FAULKS, SEBASTIAN, 1953-. Jeeves and the Wedding Bells; [by] Sebastian Faulks 336 p. 2013 St. Martin's Press
1. FICTION—Historical 2. FICTION—Humorous 3. Jeeves (Fictitious character)—Fiction 4. Single men—Fiction 5. Valets—Fiction 6. Weddings—Fiction 7. Wooster, Bertie (Fictitious character)—Fiction
ISBN 1250047595; 9781250047595
LC 2013-027676

SUMMARY: In this book by Sebastian Faulks, "P.G. Wodehouse's debonair Bertie Wooster and redoubtable butler Jeeves are back, with Bertie downcast because Georgina Meadowes is marrying someone else. His promise to help friend Peregrine 'Woody' Beeching with his own star-crossed romance leads to Jeeves's impersonating a lord and Bertie acting as manservant, all in the vicinity of the doubtless puzzled Georgina." (Library Journal)

REVIEW: *Booklist* v110 no9/10 p66 Ja 1 2014 Neal Wyatt

REVIEW: *Booklist* v110 no3 p32 O 1 2013 Bill Ott

"Jeeves and the Wedding Bells." "Young Faulksie just may have the gray matter to make a go of it. The first order of business when attempting to offer homage to Sir Pelham Grenville is to construct a plot as screwball crazy as anything [William] Shakespeare ever concocted in the Forest of Arden. . . . The plan, for reasons only a savvy Hegelian could fathom, involves Bertie posing as a manservant and Jeeves as his master. Brilliant stroke, that, allowing Jeeves to show his stuff at dinner-table chitchat and Bertie to, well, spill the gravy. . . . OK, fine, this P G. poseur gets the plot right, but what about the all-important patter? . . . But Faulksie nails it again, evoking rather than imitating, but doing so in perfect pitch."

REVIEW: *Kirkus Rev* p15 N 15 2013 Best Books

REVIEW: *Kirkus Rev* v81 no18 p321 S 15 2013

REVIEW: *Libr J* v138 no10 p78 Je 1 2013

REVIEW: *N Y Times Book Rev* p10 D 1 2013 CHRISTOPHER BUCKLEY

REVIEW: *TLS* no5777/8 p24 D 20 2013 JONATHAN BARNES

FAYE, LYNDSAY. Seven for a secret; [by] Lyndsay Faye 464 p. 2013 Amy Einhorn Books
1. Free African Americans—New York (State)—New York—Fiction 2. Historical fiction 3. Police—New York (State)—New York—Fiction 4. Slave trade—United States—History 19th century—Fiction 5. Underground Railroad—Fiction
ISBN 0399158383; 9780399158384
LC 2013-008127

SUMMARY: In this book, by Lyndsay Faye, "six months after the formation of the NYPD . . . Timothy Wilde, thinks himself well versed in his city's dark practices--until he learns of . . . 'blackbirders,' who snatch free Northerners of color . . . and sell them South . . . . as plantation property. Lucy Adams staggers into Timothy's office to report a robbery and is asked what was stolen, her reply is, 'My family.'" (Publisher's note)

REVIEW: *Booklist* v110 no13 p31 Mr 1 2014 Pam Spencer Holley

"Seven for a Secret." "Following the dramatic musical beginning, narrator [Steven] Boyer's nimble vocals whirl the reader through the effortless use of period slang; the varied accents of Irish, German, British, and Dutch immigrants; and the rich, lazy speech of the Southern blackbirders. Boyer distinguishes between the brothers; the confident resonance of Valentine and the soft introspection of Timothy that counters his determined speech, with its false sense of bravado, when faced with danger. . . .No matter how much Timothy's life is in perilous straits, when he talks to other victims, his softer, warmer tones are evident, as is his heartfelt grief when a friend is killed."

REVIEW: *Booklist* v110 no1 p48 S 1 2013 Michele Leber

REVIEW: *Libr J* v138 no14 p94 S 1 2013 Catherine Lantz

REVIEW: *Libr J* v138 no7 p53 Ap 15 2013 Barbara Hoffert

REVIEW: *N Y Times Book Rev* p17 S 22 2013 MARILYN STASIO

"W is for Wasted," "Then We Take Berlin," and "Seven For a Secret." "A painstaking plot wrangler, [Sue] Grafton carefully merges both narratives in a sad but satisfying conclusion. The problems arise from her efforts to work Kinsey's personal history into the story. . . . John Lawton's stylish spy thriller . . . is a splendid introduction to John Wilfrid (Wilderness) Holderness. . . . Timothy Wilde, who rescued child prostitutes in Lyndsay Faye's rip-roaring novel 'The Gods of Gothan' returns in 'Seven for a Secret' as the protector of lovely Lucy Adams, who lost her family to slave catchers."

REVIEW: *Publ Wkly* v260 no30 p46 Jl 29 2013

FEARNLEY, PAUL. Hunt vs. Lauda; the epic 1976 season in Formula One; [by] Paul Fearnley 160 p. 2013 David Bull Pub.

1. Automobile racing 2. Formula One automobiles 3. Hunt, James, 1947-1993 4. Lauda, Niki, 1949- 5. Sports literature

ISBN 9781935007197

LC 2013-939866

SUMMARY: This book on Formula 1 racing recounts "the dramatic battle for the 1976 World Championship between two very different drivers: the freewheeling Englishman James Hunt and his canny Austrian rival Niki Lauda. . . . Ferrari's defending World Champion Niki Lauda led early on before suffering serious burns in a near-fatal accident at the Nurburgring. Just five weeks later he was back, hoping to fend off McLaren's unpredictable upstart James Hunt." (Publisher's note)

REVIEW: *New York Times* v163 no56344 p11 D 8 2013 CHARLES McEWEN JOSEPH SIANO JERRY GARRETT JULIA S. MAYERSOHN RICHARD S. CHANG

"Hunt vs. Lauda: The Epic 1976 Formula 1 Season," "Mustang Fifty Years: Celebrating America's Only True Pony Car," and "The Real Way Round". "This book appears to have been published to coincide with Ron Howard's movie 'Rush,' which dramatizes the battle for the 1976 Formula One drivers championship. . . . and 'rush' is what comes to mind when I think about the effort behind this book. . . . 'Mustang Fifty Years' is a voluminous book that tracks the life of a Ford that's as famous as the Model T. . . . While not exactly a beach read, the book is more digestible, even for general audiences, than its dauntingly encyclopedic appearance might suggest. . . . Libraries are full of reflective, overthought travelogues. If you prefer yours presented with all the cheer of a tale tale told in a pub and put together with the artistic élan of a family Christmas newsletter, you will strike gold with 'The Real Way Round'."

FEARON, PETER.ed. The Great Depression of 1930s. See The Great Depression of 1930s

FEDER, JANE. Spooky friends; starring Scarlet and Igor; 40 p. 2013 Scholastic Press

1. Best friends—Fiction 2. Best friends—Juvenile fiction 3. Children's stories 4. Friendship—Fiction 5. Friendship—Juvenile fiction 6. Mummies—Fiction 7. Mummies—Juvenile fiction 8. Vampires—Fiction 9. Vampires—Juvenile fiction

ISBN 0545478154; 9780545478151 (hardcover : alk. paper); 9780545478168 (pbk. : alk. paper)

LC 2012-014786

SUMMARY: In this book by Jane Feder and illustrated by Julie Downing "Scarlet is a feisty little Vampire, and her best friend, Igor, is a roly-poly little Mummy. Together, they star in three humorous, heartwarming stories about two friends who never agree on anything. That is--until they discover different ideas can become even better ideas when they cooperate." (Publisher's note)

REVIEW: *Bull Cent Child Books* v67 no2 p87-8 O 2013 H. M.

"Spooky Friends," "This easy reader recounts the adventures of Scarlet, a vampire, and Igor, a mummy, best Friends who can't agree on anything. . . . Underlying the disagreements is a real strength: while Scarlet and Igor are not good at agreeing, they are really good at resolving disagreements, and that is what carries their friendship. The illustrations are pen and watercolor, enhanced digitally, and the focus in each composition rests squarely on the twosome. . . . Plenty of repetition, picture clues, and extensive spacing between lines make this an ideal choice for beginning readers, and with only two or three sentences per page, the narrative itself is very accessible--even Scarlet and Igor can agree on that."

REVIEW: *Horn Book Magazine* v89 no5 p65 S/O 2013 CYNTHIA K. RITTER

"Spooky Friends." "In three brief stories, vampire Scarlet and mummy Igor argue over what to do and eat, what to name a kitten, and whether to draw or paint. Eventually this odd-couple learns how to compromise and work together. [Jane] Feder's early-reader text addresses experiences that are relatable to children, and it includes useful repetition and age-appropriate vocabulary. [Julie] Downing gives the 'spooky friends' distinct and humorous personalities, while the generous white space in her spare pen and watercolor illustrations allows new readers to easily digest the entertaining action."

REVIEW: *Kirkus Rev* v81 no15 p8 Ag 1 2013

REVIEW: *SLJ* v59 no7 p62 Jl 2013 Scarlet

FEIFER, GREGORY. Russians; the people behind the power; [by] Gregory Feifer 384 p. 2013 Twelve

1. Journalism 2. National characteristics, Russian 3. Political culture—Russia (Federation) 4. Social values—Russia (Federation)

ISBN 1455509647; 9781455509645 (hardcover)

LC 2013-021656

SUMMARY: This book by Gregory Feifer "explores the seeming paradoxes of life in Russia by unraveling the nature of its people: what is it in their history, their desires, and their conception of themselves that makes them baffling to the West? Using the insights of his decade as a journalist in Russia, Feifer corrects pervasive misconceptions by showing that much of what appears inexplicable about the country is logical when seen from the inside." (Publisher's note)

REVIEW: *Kirkus Rev* v82 no1 p163 Ja 1 2014

REVIEW: *N Y Times Book Rev* p13 F 23 2014 JOSHUA RUBENSTEIN

"Russians: The People Behind the Power" and "Words Will Break Cement: The Passion of Pussy Riot." "Gregory Feifer's 'Russians: The People Behind the Power' joins a list of classic books by Western correspondents who have covered the politics and culture of what was once the Soviet Union. . . . The particular strength of his account is how he places his reporting of the country's myriad and devastating problems within a broad understanding of Russian . . . history. . . . 'Words Will Break Cement' makes clear that Pussy Riot is more than just a small group of disorderly anarchists."

REVIEW: *New York Times* v163 no56416 pC1-4 F 18 2014

MICHIKO KAKUTANI
"Russians: The People Behind the Power." "With 'Russians,' [author Gregory] Feifer gives us a revealing, opinionated primer on the country. . . . It is a collagelike book, consisting of historical asides, family reminiscences, interviews with public figures and ordinary people, political assessments and sharp snapshots of the country across its nine time zones, from the gaudy Moscow restaurants and clubs that cater to the showboating new rich to the distant wastelands of Siberia, where cold and poverty still define daily life. . . . What Mr. Feifer does very well is give the lay reader a spirited introduction to this complex country and its torturous past."

FEINBERG, RICHARD.ed. Polynesian outliers. See Polynesian outliers

FEINGOLD, MORDECHAI. Newton and the origin of civilization; [by] Mordechai Feingold ix, 528 p. 2013 Princeton University Press

1. Bible—Chronology 2. Chronology, Historical—History—17th century 3. Civilization, Ancient—Philosophy 4. Historical literature 5. Philosophers—England—Biography 6. Public opinion—Europe—History—17th century 7. Scientists—England—Biography 8. Scientists—Great Britain—Biography

ISBN 9780691154787 (hardcover : acid-free paper)
LC 2012-024733

SUMMARY: This book examines the reception of "Isaac Newton's 'Chronology of Ancient Kingdoms Amended,' published in 1728. . . . This book tells the story of how one of the most celebrated figures in the history of mathematics, optics, and mechanics came to apply his unique ways of thinking to problems of history, theology, and mythology, and of how his radical ideas produced an uproar that reverberated in Europe's learned circles throughout the eighteenth century and beyond." (Publisher's note)

REVIEW: *London Rev Books* v35 no19 p16-8 O 10 2013 Jonathan Rée

"Newton and the Origin of Civilisation." "The exuberant new book by Jed Buchwald and Mordechai Feingold raises the stakes by arguing that Newton's biblical lucubrations are just as scientific as his theory of gravitation, and scientific in much the same way. . . . Their main concern is to demonstrate parallels between the intellectual methods of the 'Chronology' and those of Newton's contributions to natural science. Newton questioned the evidence of his historical sources, they say, just as he questioned the evidence of the senses, subjecting it to a characteristic blend of experimental manipulation and mathematical synthesis."

FEINSTEIN, JOHN. Foul trouble; [by] John Feinstein 400 p. 2013 Alfred A. Knopf

1. African Americans—Fiction 2. Basketball—Fiction 3. Basketball—Juvenile literature 4. College athlete recruitment 5. School sports 6. Young adult fiction

ISBN 0375869646; 9780375869648 (trade); 9780375871696 (pbk.); 9780375982460 (lib. bdg.)
LC 2012-042982

SUMMARY: In this basketball novel by John Feinstein, "Danny Wilcox is Terrell's best friend and teammate, and a top prospect himself, but these days it seems like everyone wants to get close to Terrell: the sneaker guys, the money managers, the college boosters. They show up offering fast cars, hot girls, and cold, hard cash. They say they just want to help, but their kind of help could get Terrell disqualified." (Publisher's note)

REVIEW: *Booklist* v110 no1 p109 S 1 2013 John Peters

REVIEW: *Bull Cent Child Books* v67 no3 p152 N 2013 E. B.

"Foul Trouble." "[Author John] Feinstein puts his Sports Beat series on hold to offer a slightly older audience a page-turner on the underbelly of college basketball recruitment. . . . There's really nothing here that thoughtful readers of sports scandals haven't heard before, but laying it all out in a work of fiction offers a visceral evocation of just how difficult it is for a highly recruited player to keep his grades up, his ego in check, and his moral compass steady. As always, Feinstein does a lot of real world name-dropping, but he assigns the most dastardly ploys to a fictitious basketball program."

REVIEW: *Kirkus Rev* v81 no20 p65 O 15 2013

REVIEW: *Voice of Youth Advocates* v36 no5 p57 D 2013 KaaVonia Hinton

FELDSTEIN, RUTH. How it feels to be free; black women entertainers and the civil rights movement; [by] Ruth Feldstein 304 p. 2013 Oxford University Press

1. African American women entertainers—Political activity—History—20th century 2. African American women political activists—History—20th century 3. African Americans—Civil rights—History—20th century 4. African Americans—Music—Political aspects—History—20th century 5. Historical literature 6. Performing arts—Political aspects—United States—20th century

ISBN 0195314034; 9780195314038 (alk. paper)
LC 2013-019878

SUMMARY: In this book on the U.S. Civil Rights movement of the 20th century, "Ruth Feldstein examines celebrated black women performers, illuminating the risks they took, their roles at home and abroad, and the ways that they raised the issue of gender amid their demands for black liberation. Feldstein focuses on six women who made names for themselves in the music, film, and television industries: Simone, Lena Horne, Miriam Makeba, Abbey Lincoln, Diahann Carroll, and Cicely Tyson." (Publisher's note)

REVIEW: *Choice* v52 no1 p80 St 2014 T. F. DeFrantz

REVIEW: *New York Times* v163 no56383 pC4 Ja 16 2014 FARAH JASMINE GRIFFIN

"How It Feels To Be Free: Black Women Entertainers and the Civil Rights Movement". "Ruth Feldstein's important new book . . . is an original exploration of the little-known but central role that black entertainers, especially black women, played in helping communicate and forward the movement's goals. . . . Ms. Feldstein convincingly argues that 'culture was a key battleground in the civil rights movement' and that the women in this book anticipated much of what would later emerge in the more militant black power movement and in second-wave feminism. Though a scholarly book, it should be of interest to an intelligent, general readership."

FEMINIST AND CRITICAL PERSPECTIVES ON CARIBBEAN MOTHERING; 282 p. 2013 Africa World Press

1. Motherhood—Caribbean Area 2. Motherhood in literature 3. Mothers—Caribbean Area 4. Social science literature 5. Women—Caribbean Area
ISBN 9781592219223 (hard cover); 9781592219230 (pbk.)
LC 2012-049885

SUMMARY: This book presents "a collection of essays, which examine the multiple definitions and images of mothering and motherhood from childbirth as the initial site to surrogate, communal, and extended parenthood in the stories of generations of women that include grandmothers, godmothers, sisters and aunts." Topics discussed include "social class, language, cultural chauvinism, physical and psychological exile, racial politics, and colonial sovereignty barriers." (Publisher's note)

REVIEW: *Choice* v51 no7 p1314 Mr 2014 J. C. Richards

"Feminist and Critical Perspectives on Caribbean Mothering." "[Dorsía Smith] Silva . . . and Alexander . . . have gathered a talented group of Caribbean feminist writers interested in historical and contemporary mothering practices. Historically, motherhood is a highly esteemed occupation in the islands, affording prestige and power in recognition of women's skillful management of families' needs, often including adopted children and childless women. A variety of texts weave poetry and narrative together, reflecting traditional elements of storytelling. . . . Recommended."

FEMINIST WRITINGS FROM ANCIENT TIMES TO THE MODERN WORLD; a global sourcebook and history; 2 v. (xlvi, 718 p.) 2011 Greenwood

1. Anthologies 2. Clinton, Hillary Rodham, 1947- 3. Enheduanna 4. Feminism—History 5. Feminism and literature—History 6. Feminist criticism 7. Feminist literature—History 8. Feminists 9. Truth, Sojourner, d. 1883
ISBN 9780313345807 (hardback : set : acid-free paper); 9780313345814 (ebk); 9780313345821 (hardback : v. 1 : acid-free paper); 9780313345838 (ebk : v. 1); 9780313345845 (hardback : v. 2 : acid-free paper); 9780313345852 (ebk : v. 2)
LC 2011-009468

SUMMARY: "This two-volume anthology features feminist writings that focus on women's resistance to male privilege and power in cultures and religions around the world and in all time periods. The 230 entries include poems, letters, essays, speeches, court decisions, and other documents that address feminist thought. . . . This . . . set . . . includes well-known feminist writers such as Sappho, Mary Wollstonecraft, Margaret Fuller, Sojourner Truth, and Hillary Rodham Clinton as well as lesser-known feminists such as Enheduanna, of Sumer; Yeshe Tsogyal, of Tibet; and Nawal El Saadawi, of Egypt." (Booklist)

REVIEW: *Booklist* v108 no13 p60 Mr 1 2012 Merle Jacob

Feminist writings from ancient times to the modern world: A global sourcebook and history. "This two-volume anthology features feminist writings that focus on women's resistance to male privilege and power in cultures and religions around the world and in all time periods. The 230 entries include poems, letters, essays, speeches, court decisions, and other documents that address feminist thought. . . . This valuable set . . . includes well-known feminist writers such as Sappho, Mary Wollstonecraft, Margaret Fuller, Sojourner Truth, and Hillary Rodham Clinton . . . For writers who are not well known, the discussion of their impact during their lifetime and later will help students understand their place in the history of feminist thought."

REVIEW: *Choice* v49 no7 p1226 Mr 2012 K. Rosneck

FENDELMAN, HELAINE W.ed. Appraising art. See Appraising art

FENN, ELIZABETH A. Encounters at the heart of the world; a history of the Mandan people; [by] Elizabeth A. Fenn 480 p. 2014 Hill and Wang, a division of Farrar, Straus and Giroux

1. Historical literature 2. Lewis & Clark Expedition (1804-1806) 3. Mandan (North American people) 4. Native Americans—History 5. Native Americans—North Dakota—History
ISBN 0809042398; 9780809042395 (hardback)
LC 2013-032994

SUMMARY: This book, by Elizabeth A. Fenn, tells the "history of the tribe that once thrived on the upper Missouri River in present-day North Dakota. . . . Peaking at a population of 12,000 by 1500, and still a vital presence when Lewis and Clark visited in 1804, the Mandans were besieged by a 'daunting succession of challenges,' including Norway rats that decimated their corn stores, two waves of smallpox, whooping cough, and cholera, reducing their numbers to 300 by 1838." (Booklist)

REVIEW: *Booklist* v110 no9/10 p24 Ja 1 2014 Deborah Donovan

REVIEW: *Kirkus Rev* v82 no2 p22 Ja 15 2014

"Encounters at the Heart of the World: A History of the Mandan People". "A nonpolemical, engaging study of a once-thriving Indian nation of the American heartland whose origins and demise tell us much about ourselves. . . . [A] thorough mosaic of Mandan history and culture. . . . In addition to her comprehensive narrative, [Elizabeth A.] Fenn intersperses throughout the narrative many helpful maps and poignant drawings by George Catlin and others. An excellent contribution to the truth telling of the American Indian story."

REVIEW: *Libr J* v139 no4 p98 Mr 1 2014 John R. Burch

REVIEW: *Nation* v298 no12 p40-3 Mr 24 2014 RICHARD WHITE

"Encounter at the Heart of the World: A History of the Mandan People." "Elizabeth Fenn's 'Encounters at the Heart of the World' is part of a small renascence in historical writing. . . . She has written a profoundly spatial history rooted in a place made by the Mandans and their neighbors, the Hidatsas and Arikaras. . . . There are moments when Fenn strains too hard to narrate the periods during which much about the Mandans is unknown. . . . On the whole, however, Fenn is careful with her evidence."

REVIEW: *Publ Wkly* v260 no47 p40-1 N 18 2013

FENNELL, JACK, 1983-.tr. The Short Fiction of Flann O'Brien. See The Short Fiction of Flann O'Brien

FENSTER, J. M. (JULIE M.) For the Next Generation; A Wake-up Call to Solve Our Nation's Problems; [by] J. M. (Julie M.) Fenster 288 p. 2013 St Martins Pr

1. Parents—Political activity 2. Partisanship 3. Politi-

cal science literature 4. United States—Politics & government 5. Women legislators
ISBN 1250000998; 9781250000996

SUMMARY: In this book, U.S. legislator Debbie Wasserman Schultz "recalls her experiences with the legislative process of partisanship and gridlock that threatens any efforts at constructive legislation, ultimately at the cost of American children. Noting how few women with young children are members of Congress, Schultz appeals for resolution of political discord and issues a challenge to adopt a parent's perspective on how lawmaking or the lack of it will affect future generations." (Booklist)

REVIEW: *Booklist* v110 no1 p7-18 S 1 2013 Vanessa Bush

"For the Next Generation: A Wake Up Call to Solving Our Nation's Problems." "Noting how few women with young children are members of Congress, [Debbie Wasserman] Schultz appeals for resolution of political discord and issues a\ challenge to adopt a parent's perspective on how lawmaking or the lack of it will affect future generations. Throughout, she offers remembrances of her three children growing up--constant reminders of the significance of her job to the future of her children and other children. An interesting perspective on parenting and lawmaking."

REVIEW: *Kirkus Rev* v81 no19 p20 O 1 2013

REVIEW: *Libr J* v137 no18 p55 N 1 2012 Barbara Hoffert

REVIEW: *Publ Wkly* v260 no32 p51 Ag 12 2013

FENTON, LAURENCE. Palmerston and The Times; foreign policy, the press and public opinion in mid-Victorian Britain; [by] Laurence Fenton 213 p. 2013 I.B. Tauris
1. Historical literature 2. Press and politics—Great Britain—History—19th century
ISBN 1780760744 (hbk.); 9781780760742 (hbk.)
LC 2012-277283

SUMMARY: In this book, author Laurence Fenton "explores the highly-charged rivalry between . . . [Lord Palmerston—the dominant figure in foreign affairs in the mid-nineteenth century—and 'The Times,' the first global newspaper] revealing the personal and political differences at the heart of an antagonism that stretched over the course of three decades." (Publisher's note)

REVIEW: *Am Hist Rev* v119 no1 p253-4 F 2014 Michelle Tusan

"Palmerston and The Times: Foreign Policy, the Press and Public Opinion in Mid-Victorian Britain". "Importantly, this work provides a snapshot of the world before and after the repeal of the so-called taxes on knowledge. Historians understand the end of the stamp tax and other taxes in the mid-1850s as a turning point in the transformation of the press into a fair and balanced voice in politics. The democratization of the press into the Fourth Estate is often cast as a direct challenge to the political elite's dominance of the news media. [Laurence] Fenton's story reveals that this process was not so straightforward."

REVIEW: *Choice* v51 no1 p152 S 2013 P. T. Smith

FERGUSON, ALEX, 1941-. Alex Ferguson; My Autobiography; [by] Alex Ferguson 416 p. 2013 Trafalgar Square
1. Autobiography 2. Manchester United (Soccer team) 3. Soccer—Great Britain 4. Soccer managers 5. Sports business
ISBN 0340919396; 9780340919392

SUMMARY: This presents an autobiography of British soccer team manager Alex Ferguson, "from his very early days in the tough shipyard areas of Govan. Sir Alex announced his retirement as manager of Manchester United after 27 years in the role. He has gone out in a blaze of glory, with United winning the Premier League for the 13th time, and he is widely considered to be the greatest manager in the history of British soccer." (Publisher's note)

REVIEW: *London Rev Books* v36 no1 p31-3 Ja 9 2014 David Runciman

"My Autobiography". "Alex Ferguson is a conspiricist. . . . Ferguson may be a conspiracy theorist as well, but if so he isn't letting on. . . . When it comes to the football business itself Ferguson is much less reticent. He lets us in on the full range of his suspicions. . . . 'My Autobiography' is not an easy read. It is a hectoring, petty, repetitive book. . . . It's like being stuck in a room with the man himself as his mind whirrs away through its grudges and grievances and no one else gets a chance to put a word in. . . . It's ugly, it's grinding, but it gives you the flavour of the man."

FERGUSON, FRANK.ed. A north light. See Hewitt, J.

FERGUSON, WILL, 1964-. 419; [by] Will Ferguson 411 p. 2013 Penguin Group USA
1. Criminal investigation 2. Detective & mystery stories 3. Fiction 4. Internet fraud 5. Swindlers & swindling—Nigeria 6. Theft
ISBN 0143188720; 9780143188728

SUMMARY: This book, by Will Ferguson, "details the linked lives of four individuals, three African and one Canadian, drawn together by Nigeria's bloody, exploited history. Laura seeks justice for her murdered father; amoral Winston chases wealth at any cost; Nnamdi and Amina seek only honest employment and a chance to raise Amina's child. Greed contends with generosity and vengeance with forgiveness in a world where the bad prosper and acts of charity are harshly punished." (Publishers Weekly)

REVIEW: *Booklist* v109 no22 p33 Ag 1 2013 Christine Tron

REVIEW: *Quill Quire* v78 no3 p28 Ap 2012 James Grainger

"419." "[Will] Ferguson has entered the ranks of literary novelists with 419, a story that follows a Canadian editor from her comfortable life in Calgary to neo-liberalism's lawless frontiers in the oil- and blood-drenched streets and backwaters of Nigeria. . . . The novel comes to life when Ferguson dispenses with jarring short scenes and fully immerses readers in the intersecting stories that propel the narrative toward a series of dramatic collisions and reconciliations. Ferguson's eye for local detail and power dynamics animates [the plot]. . . . Even better are the scenes that take readers into the surreal criminal underworld of Nigeria's 419 Internet scams. . . . The novel is further enlivened by sharp dialogue and imagery."

REVIEW: *TLS* no5775 p22 D 6 2013 JAMIE JOSEPH

FERMOR, PATRICK LEIGH. The Broken Road; From the Iron Gates to Mount Athos; 384 p. 2014 Random House Inc New York Review Books
1. Athos (Greece) 2. Europe, Eastern—Description & travel 3. Istanbul (Turkey)—Description & travel 4.

Mediterranean Region—Description & travel 5. Travelers' writings
ISBN 1590177541; 9781590177549
LC 2013-043609

SUMMARY: This book is Sir Patrick Leigh Fermor's "final posthumous volume. . . . It takes the author from the Danube's Iron Gates to Mount Athos and Constantinople. . . . The book brings two texts: a detailed diary of his time on Mount Athos and a descriptio of the journey there. This last was written up from memory in the 1960s as some of Sir Patrick's contemporary notes had been stolen in Munich." (Economist)

REVIEW: *Booklist* v110 no11 p12 F 1 2014 Brad Hooper

REVIEW: *Economist* v408 no8853 p90 S 14 2013

"The Broken Road: From the Iron Gates to Mount Athos." "The pages are filled with brilliant evocations of his life on the road, none richer than the time he spent in a Romanian brothel. A flavour of the 'Pure Paddy' style is his description of the high-pitched Russians who drive carriages around Bucharest. . . . The only part republished here is the full contemporary account of his time at Mount Athos. The book is occasionally interrupted with later asides by the author on the fate of particular places or people, which drain a portion of the magic out of the account. . . . It is a fitting epilogue to 20th-century travel writing and essential reading for devotees of Sir Patrick [Leigh Fermor's] other works--though eclipsed by his earlier books and the world they conjured."

REVIEW: *Kirkus Rev* v82 no2 p169 Ja 15 2014

REVIEW: *London Rev Books* v35 no21 p15-6 N 7 2013 Neal Ascherson

REVIEW: *N Y Times Book Rev* p12 Mr 9 2014 ROBERT F. WORTH

REVIEW: *New Statesman* v142 no5175 p58-9 S 13 2013 Jeremy Seal

REVIEW: *N Y Rev Books* v61 no11 p63-5 Je 19 2014 Daniel Mendelsohn

"The Broken Road: From the Iron Gates to Mount Athos." "The author's chattiness, his inexhaustible willingness to be distracted, his susceptibility to detours geographical, intellectual, aesthetic, and occasionally amorous constitute, if anything, an essential and self-conscious component of the style that has won him such an avid following. . . . The irony of the publication of his final, posthumous work is that it creates, retrospectively and almost accidentally, something of [a] meaningful arc for the entire trilogy. By the end, the lacquered manner has dissolved, and a different, far more touching and sympathetic hero emerges."

REVIEW: *TLS* no5765 p21 S 27 2013 BEN DOWNING

REVIEW: *Va Q Rev* v90 no3 p195-8 Summ 2014 John Lingan

FERN, TRACEY. Dare the wind; [by] Tracey Fern 40 p. 2014 Farrar, Straus and Giroux

1. Biography (Literary form) 2. Children's nonfiction 3. Women sailors—Biography—Juvenile literature
ISBN 0374316996; 9780374316990 (hard)
LC 2013-007868

SUMMARY: Author Tracey Fern presents a biography of Ellen Prentiss. "As soon as she met a man who loved sailing like she did, she married him. When her husband was given command of a clipper ship custom-made to travel quickly, she knew that they would need every bit of its speed for their maiden voyage: out of New York City, down around the tip of Cape Horn, and into San Francisco, where the Gold Rush was well under way." (Publisher's note)

REVIEW: *Booklist* v110 no8 p37 D 15 2013 Carolyn Phelan

REVIEW: *Bull Cent Child Books* v67 no6 p310 F 2014 Elizabeth Bush

"Dare the Wind: The Record-Breaking Voyage of Eleanor Prentiss and the Flying Cloud." "While children have access to many picture-book biographies of women ahead of their time, [Tracey] Fern offers the story of a woman who could be considered relatively rare even in our own era, as a skillful and, as the concluding notes point out, daringly progressive navigator. [Emily Arnold] McCully's watercolors capture the sea in many moods, from eerily glassy doldrums that left the Flying Cloud with sails drooping, to the wind-whipped waves that pressed the ship sideways as it neared Cape Horn. A map, a brief glossary of nautical terms, and resources and notes on the Flying Cloud are included."

REVIEW: *Horn Book Magazine* v90 no2 p140 Mr/Ap 2014 PAMELA YOSCA

REVIEW: *Kirkus Rev* v81 no24 p93 D 15 2013

"Dare the Wind: The Record-Breaking Voyage of Eleanor Prentiss and the Flying Cloud". "A lively, true story about a 19th-century woman and the 15,000-mile sailing journey she navigated. With animated language full of the vigor of the sea itself, [Tracey] Fern relates the story of Ellen Prentiss Creesy, who, while growing up in Marblehead, Mass., was taught to both sail and navigate by her sea-captain father. . . . [Emily Arnold] McCully's expertly rendered watercolor illustrations evoke, in double-page spreads, the rich atmosphere of the sea in all its moods."

REVIEW: *Publ Wkly* v260 no48 p59 N 25 2013

REVIEW: *SLJ* v60 no4 p179 Ap 2014 Misti Tidman

FERNANDES, BONNIE JUETTNER. The Large Hadron Collider; [by] Bonnie Juettner Fernandes 48 p. 2013 Norwood House Press

1. Children's nonfiction 2. Laboratories 3. Large Hadron Collider (France and Switzerland)—Juvenile literature 4. Particle physics 5. Scientific literature
ISBN 9781599536002 (library edition : alk. paper); 9781603575805 (pbk. edition : alk. paper)
LC 2013-012254

SUMMARY: "This short, illustrated book in the A Great Idea series introduces the Large Hadron Collider (LHC), designed to test certain theories in particle physics. Supported by many nations and built near Geneva, Switzerland, the LHC is a 16.8-mile circular tunnel. [Bonnie Juettner] Fernandes discusses the challenging construction of the facility as well as a few of its purposes and achievements." (Booklist)

REVIEW: *Booklist* v110 no3 p78-80 O 1 2013 Carolyn Phelan

"The Large Hadron Collider." "This short, illustrated book in the 'A Great Idea' series introduces the Large Hadron Collider (LHC), designed to test certain theories in particle physics. . . . The author writes in clear language, explaining most terms and concepts introduced along the way. Students who have studied some physics will especially appreciate the detailed explanations of what happens within the collider. This is one of the few books on the subject published for young people, and readers need not comprehend everything about the LHC to gain an appreciation for the accomplishment it represents." (Publisher's note)

FERNANDEZ, LUIS. Shutting down the streets; political violence and social control in the global era; [by] Luis Fernandez 207 p. 2011 New York University Press

1. Anti-globalization movement 2. Globalization—Political aspects 3. Political violence 4. Social control 5. Social science literature

ISBN 0814708730 (ebook); 0814740995 (cl: alk. paper); 0814741002 (pb: alk. paper); 9780814708736 (ebook); 9780814740996 (cl: alk. paper); 9780814741009 (pb: alk. paper)

LC 2011-017987

SUMMARY: This book, "based on direct observation of more than 20 global summits, . . . demonstrates that social control is not only global, but also preemptive, and that it relegates dissent to the realm of criminality. The charge is insurrection, but the accused have no weapons. The authors document in detail how social control forecloses the spaces through which social movements nurture the development of dissent and effect disruptive challenges." (Publisher's note)

REVIEW: *Am J Sociol* v118 no5 p1454-6 Mr 2013 Patrick Gillham

REVIEW: *Contemp Sociol* v43 no2 p267-9 Mr 2014 Kevin B. Anderson

"Shutting Down the Streets: Political Violence and Social Control in the Global Era". "The discussion of state repression and social control at the various global summits . . . is a particularly cogent part of this book. . . . The biggest problem I had with this book's uncritical recourse to [Michel] Foucault, and in particular to his concept of resistance, is that Foucault's writings on resistance explicitly reject utopian or Marxian forms of thinking that would conceptualize real alternatives to the given social arrangements. . . .Despite such shortcomings, 'Shutting Down the Streets' remains an original work, fired by a commitment to social justice."

FERNANDEZ, OSCAR E. Everyday calculus; discovering the hidden math all around us; [by] Oscar E. Fernandez 168 p. 2014 Princeton University Press

1. Calculus—Popular works 2. Equations 3. Mathematical literature 4. Mathematical models 5. Stock exchanges

ISBN 0691157553; 9780691157559 (hardcover: acid-free paper)

LC 2013-033097

SUMMARY: In this book on calculus, author Oscar E. Fernandez "suggests we should be 'listening to the message' in the mathematics to learn about the world around us, arguing that mathematical equations 'can be seen, heard, and felt all around us every day'. . . . To illustrate the universal application of mathematics he shows that the essentially identical equations describe the spread of an infectious disease and the sustainability of fish populations." (SB&F: Your Guide to Science Resources for All Ages)

REVIEW: *Choice* v52 no2 p299 O 2014 N. W. Schillow

REVIEW: *Publ Wkly* v261 no9 p55-6 Mr 3 2014

FERNÁNDEZ-ARMESTO, FELIPE. Our America; a Hispanic history of the United States; [by] Felipe Fernández-Armesto 416 p. 2014 W.W. Norton & Co. Inc.

1. Hispanic Americans—History 2. Historical literature

ISBN 0393239535; 9780393239539 (hardcover)

LC 2013-037336

SUMMARY: Written by Felipe Fernández-Armesto, "this . . . narrative begins with the explorers and conquistadores who planted Spain's first colonies in Puerto Rico, Florida, and the Southwest. Missionaries and rancheros carry Spain's expansive impulse into the late eighteenth century. . . . In the Hispanic resurgence that follows, it is the peoples of Latin America who overspread" the U.S., "from the Hispanic heartland in the West to major cities." (Publisher's note)

REVIEW: *Booklist* v110 no7 p11 D 1 2013 Jay Freeman

REVIEW: *Economist* v410 no8871 p69-70 Ja 25 2014

REVIEW: *Kirkus Rev* v81 no24 p27 D 15 2013

"Our America: A Hispanic History of the United States". "A welcome corrective to Anglocentric versions of American history, which continue to dominate the textbook market. . . . [Felipe] Fernández-Armesto makes numerous important observations, noting that Spain's New World empire grew so large in part due to competition with those other European powers, and he takes in episodes of history that are largely overlooked—e.g., the El Paso 'salt war,' in which Anglos and Hispanics fought for control of that critically important resource. The correctives are useful and necessary, and it is easy to imagine that this book will become required reading in ethnic-studies courses—and, with luck, in American history survey courses as well."

REVIEW: *Libr J* v138 no13 p57 Ag 1 2013 Barbara Hoffert

REVIEW: *N Y Times Book Rev* p8-9 Ja 19 2014 JULIO ORTEGA

"Our America: A Hispanic History of the United States." "In 'Our America,' Felipe Fernández-Armesto . . . recasts the pilgrimage of Hispanics in the United States as a rich and moving chronicle for our very present. His book navigates five centuries of painful documents, atrocious statements and dubious literature to argue that the United States was, from its beginning, as much a Spanish colonial southern enterprise as an unending march westward. . . . The book is especially adept at following the construction of the United States territory as it defined its borders beginning in the early 1800s."

REVIEW: *Publ Wkly* v260 no40 p40 O 7 2013

REVIEW: *TLS* no5795 p5 Ap 25 2014 HENRY KAMEN

"Our America: A Hispanic History of the United States." "'Our America' is a brilliant, difficult book which seeks 'to show that there are other US histories than the standard Anglo narrative' by focusing on 'Hispanic influence in the country's past and future.' . . . To round off his discussion, Fernández-Armesto touches on fundamental questions that add a good measure of perspective to his primarily historical essay, but also court controversy. . . . This discussion is admirably balanced and perceptive. . . . There is much to learn, however, and much also to ponder, in this fluent and vigorous plea for a more positive approach to the present and future role of a major group of US citizens."

FERNÁNDEZ BRAVO, ÁLVARO.ed. New Argentine and Brazilian cinema. See New Argentine and Brazilian cinema

FERRANTE, ELENA. The Story of a New Name; [by]

Elena Ferrante 480 p. 2013 Penguin Group USA

1. Female friendship—Fiction 2. Historical fiction 3. Italy—Fiction 4. Marriage—Fiction 5. Women—Italy—Social conditions

ISBN 1609451341; 9781609451349

SUMMARY: This book, by Elena Ferrante, is "the second in a trilogy. . . . [It] rejoins narrator Elena Greco and her 'brilliant friend' Lina Cerullo as they leave behind their claustrophobic Italian girlhood and enter the tumultuous world of young womanhood. . . . Against the backdrop of 1960s/70s Naples, the previously inseparable girls embark on diverse paths. At 16, Lila has married the prosperous local grocer. . . . Conversely Elena has chosen education." (Publishers Weekly)

REVIEW: *Bookforum* v20 no5 p30 F/Mr 2014 MINNA PROCTOR

REVIEW: *Booklist* v110 no2 p31 S 15 2013 Cortney Ophoff

REVIEW: *Economist* v409 no8856 p89 O 5 2013

"The Story of a New Name." "Elena Ferrante may be the best contemporary novelist you have never heard of. The Italian author has written six lavishly praised novels. But she writes under a pseudonym and will not offer herself for public consumption. Her characters likewise defy convention. . . . 'The Story of a New Name,' the second volume in a magisterial Neapolitan trilogy, is an intense portrait of one woman's struggle against the misogyny of 1960s Naples. . . . Ms. Ferrante's voice is startlingly honest and modern in her descriptions of the psychic toll this world takes on two young women. . . . If the best prose is like glass-communicating without calling attention to itself--Ms. Ferrante's is crystal, and her storytelling both visceral and compelling."

REVIEW: *Kirkus Rev* v81 no15 p329 Ag 1 2013

REVIEW: *N Y Times Book Rev* p19 S 29 2013 Elena Ferrante

"The Story of a New Name." "Every so often you encounter an author so unusual it takes a while to make sense of her voice. The challenge is greater still when this writer's freshness has nothing to do with fashion, when it's imbued with the most haunting music at all, the echoes of literary history. Elena Ferrante is this rare bird: so deliberate in building up her story that you almost give up on it, so gifted that by the end she has you in tears. 'The Story of a New Name' is the second part of a trilogy that began with 'My Brilliant Friend'. . . . Despite its gender and class insights, Ferrante's novel wears its analysis lightly. . . . As a translator, Ann Goldstein does Ferrante a great service. Like the original Italian, the English here is disciplined, precise."

REVIEW: *New Yorker* v89 no37 p83-1 N 18 2013

REVIEW: *TLS* no5773 p19 N 22 2013 CATHARINE MORRIS

"The Story of a New Name." "[Elena] Ferrante' s imprint is firmly there in its forensic attention to psychological states; and its scale has perhaps made it more personal, not less. . . . Scenes of high emotion . . . are all the more powerful for being simply rendered. . . . One of Ferrante's greatest virtues is her doggedness in unearthing--and fearlessness in articulating--thoughts that usually remain unspoken. . . . Ferrante is also a master of the conflicted state, and of moments of self-analysis and correction. . . . Her translator Ann Goldstein has served it beautifully."

FERREIRA, PEDRO G. The perfect theory; a century of geniuses and the battle over general relativity; [by] Pedro G. Ferreira 304 p. 2014 Houghton Mifflin Harcourt

1. General relativity (Physics)—History—20th century 2. Physicists—Biography 3. Physics—History—20th century 4. Science and civilization—History—20th century 5. Scientific literature

ISBN 0547554893; 9780547554891 (hardback)

LC 2013-021741

SUMMARY: In this book on Albert Einstein's theory of relativity, author Pedro G. Ferreira "shares the story of general relativity's revival and application to previously unobservable objects like quasars and black holes. Ferreira's book is also about the people who find joy and excitement in discovering the secrets of the universe. . . . International collaboration made confirmation of [Einstein's] theory possible, while overturning some initial conclusions." (Publishers Weekly)

REVIEW: *Booklist* v110 no7 p19 D 1 2013 Bryce Christensen

REVIEW: *Choice* v51 no12 p2225 Ag 2014 M. Mounts

REVIEW: *Kirkus Rev* v81 no24 p123 D 15 2013

"The Perfect Theory: A Century of Geniuses and the Battle Over General Relativity". "An enthusiastic and comprehensible popular account of how Albert Einstein's Theory of Relativity continues to generate new knowledge as well as hints of more secrets to be revealed. . . . [Pedro G.] Ferreira does not downplay relativity's complexity and avoids the easy route of oversimplifying it into a cosmic magic show. The result is one of the best popular accounts of how Einstein and his followers have been trying to explain the universe for decades."

REVIEW: *Libr J* v138 no15 p47 S 15 2013

REVIEW: *Publ Wkly* v260 no51 p51 D 16 2013

REVIEW: *Sci Am* v310 no2 p76 F 2014 Lee Billings

FERRENDELLI, BETTA. The Friday Edition; [by] Betta Ferrendelli 308 p. 2012 CreateSpace Independent Publishing Platform

1. Alcoholics—Fiction 2. Detective & mystery stories 3. Murder—Fiction 4. Reporters & reporting—Fiction 5. Sisters—Fiction

ISBN 1480263184; 9781480263185

SUMMARY: In this book, "Sam won't admit that her [alcohol] problem has caused her to lose custody of her daughter and also to miss her sister's important phone call—her last communication before falling to her death from an apartment balcony. Convinced her sister would never commit suicide, Sam searches for her killer, following a trail of corruption involving drug cartels and some of the highest ranking members of a police department outside Denver." (Kirkus Reviews)

REVIEW: *Kirkus Rev* p17 D 15 2013 supplemet best books 2013

"The Friday Edition". "Struggling with personal demons, weight problems and alcoholism, Sam is a carefully crafted, realistically flawed character. Her mistakes and missteps have a humanizing effect, and though she may be exasperating at times, most readers will find themselves steadfastly in her corner. Secondary characters are similarly complex. . . . [Betta] Ferrendelli deftly avoids formulaic resolutions with outcomes that are nuanced and often unexpected. . . . Minor issues aside, Ferrendelli's debut will leave many readers hoping for more from this vulnerable, highly sympathetic heroine. A smart, nimble treat of a mystery that provides ample foundation for growth."

REVIEW: *Kirkus Rev* v81 no18 p57 S 15 2013

FERRI, GIULIANO.il. A taste of freedom. See Kimmel, E. C.

FERRIS, MONICA. The drowning spool; [by] Monica Ferris 304 p. 2014 Berkley Hardcover

1. Devonshire, Betsy (Fictitious character)—Fiction 2. Drowning—Fiction 3. FICTION—Mystery & Detective—General 4. FICTION—Mystery & Detective—Women Sleuths 5. Needlework—Fiction 6. Needleworkers—Crimes against—Fiction 7. Needleworkers—Fiction 8. Women detectives—Fiction

ISBN 9780425270080 (hardback)

LC 2013-039583

SUMMARY: "This seventeenth in the popular series starring Betsy Devonshire, owner of a needlecraft shop in rural Minnesota, finds Betsy taking a swim class in a senior complex called Watered Silk. The body of a young woman is found a few days later floating in the pool, and a young man working the front desk is fired. Betsy, a friend of the fired boy's aunt, is asked by the aunt to investigate. Then a resident of Watered Silk is also murdered." (Booklist)

REVIEW: *Booklist* v110 no12 p31-2 F 15 2014 Amy Alessio

"The Drowning Spool." "This seventeenth in the popular series starring Betsy Devonshire, owner of a needlecraft shop in rural Minnesota, finds Betsy taking a swim class in a senior complex called Watered Silk. . . . [Monica] Ferris skillfully sews in details about punch needlepoint among scenes discussing the emotionally moving circumstances of the victims. Unlike many overly amiable amateur-sleuth tales, Betsy's suspects lie to her and sometimes turn belligerent, offering a refreshingly realistic break from typical cozy fare. Fans of Livia Washburn's Phyllis Newsom stories, boasting a similar style, may also enjoy Ferris' series."

REVIEW: *Kirkus Rev* v82 no2 p273 Ja 15 2014

REVIEW: *Publ Wkly* v260 no52 p36 D 23 2013

FEST, JOACHIM. Not I; memoirs of a German childhood; 464 p. 2013 Other Press

1. Anti-Nazi movement—Germany—World War II—Biography 2. Historians—Germany—Biography 3. Memoirs 4. National socialism

ISBN 1590516109; 9781590516102 (hardcover)

LC 2013-018230

SUMMARY: This memoir, by Joachim Fest, presents a "portrait of a . . . anti-Nazi family in Berlin who managed to hang on to their moral convictions during the brutalizing Hitler years. . . . One of five children born to a politically committed teacher, Johannes Fest, who was alarmed by the ascent of the Nazi Party at the expense of the Weimar Republic, the author and his siblings grew up in a middle-class Berlin suburb and were duly inculcated . . . about the perils of surrendering to Nazi lawlessness." (Kirkus Reviews)

REVIEW: *America* v211 no2 p42-3 Jl 21 2014 Brenna Moore

REVIEW: *Commonweal* v141 no11 p26-9 Je 13 2014 John Connelly

REVIEW: *Kirkus Rev* v81 no23 p102 D 1 2013

REVIEW: *N Y Times Book Rev* p17 Mr 2 2014 BARRY GEWEN

REVIEW: *New York Times* v163 no56417 pC4 F 19 2014 WILLIAM GRIMES

"Not I: Memoirs of a German Childhood". "[A] quietly compelling, elegantly expressed memoir. . . . The book . . . describes in rich detail the moral education and day-to-day experiences of a sensitive, if smart-alecky member of . . . the high-minded, educated middle stratum, a cultural elite whose members, typically, refused to believe that the country of Schiller and Goethe could entrust their fate to a barbarian. . . . 'Not I' shrinks the Wagnerian scale of German history in the 1930s and 1940s to chamber music dimensions. It is intensely personal, cleareyed and absolutely riveting, partly because the author, thrust into an outsider's position, developed a keen appreciation of Germany's contradictions and paradoxes."

REVIEW: *New Yorker* v90 no7 p73-1 Ap 7 2014

"Not I: Memoirs of a German Childhood." "This remarkable memoir by the late German historian and biographer of Hitler opens in the nineteen-twenties in a Berlin suburb, where the Fest family enjoys a relatively peaceful existence. The story proceeds through the grand historical events of the next twenty years, as [author Joachim] Fest's father, an active supporter of the Weimar Republic, is fired from his job as a headmaster, and one after another of his children is pulled into the service of the Nazis."

FFORDE, JASPER. The song of the Quarkbeast; [by] Jasper Fforde 304 p. 2013 Houghton Mifflin Harcourt

1. Corporations—Corrupt practices—Fiction 2. Fantasy 3. Kings & rulers—Fiction 4. Magic—Fiction 5. Wizards—Fiction

ISBN 054773848X; 9780547738482

LC 2012-047318

SUMMARY: This is the second book in Jasper Fforde's Chronicles of Kazam series. Here, now "that magical power is on the rise again, the despotic King Snodd IV hopes to cash in, specifically by putting the wizards who work at Kazam Mystical Arts Management under his control by proposing they merge with iMagic, the rival house led by the Amazing Blix, a questionable character with a new royal appointment: Court Mystician." (Publishers Weekly)

REVIEW: *Horn Book Magazine* v89 no5 p95 S/O 2013 DEIRDRE F. BAKER

"The Song of the Quarkbeast." "[Jasper] Fforde creates a clever, comical world in which flying carpets go supersonic, the Quarkbeast . . . defies the laws of physics, public events are accompanied by 'tents with traveling knee replacement surgeons,' and human nature is much as we know it. Fforde's prose perfectly suits Jennifer's character: a brisk pace, no dawdling, and every sentence with a precise destination. Imaginatively energetic and made more so by a gloriously formidable female protagonist."

REVIEW: *Kirkus Rev* v81 no13 p235 Jl 1 2013

REVIEW: *Publ Wkly* p84-5 Children's starred review annual 2013

REVIEW: *Publ Wkly* v260 no28 p173 Jl 15 2013

FIELD, P. J. C.ed. Le morte Darthur. See Le morte Darthur

FIELDS, TRICIA. Wrecked; a mystery; [by] Tricia Fields 320 p. 2014 Minotaur Books

1. Detective & mystery stories 2. Missing persons—Fiction 3. Murder—Investigation—Fiction 4. Women police chiefs—Fiction

ISBN 1250021375; 9781250021373 (hardback)

LC 2013-033451

SUMMARY: In this book, by Tricia Fields, "Police Chief Josie Gray is living every cop's worst nightmare: a murder suspect who she knows personally. Even worse, it's her longtime boyfriend, Dillon Reese. . . . As suspicions split the department, Josie struggles with her choices on the night she last saw Dillon. If she had acted on her instincts, would the innocent woman still be alive? Unable to stay on the sidelines, Josie investigates on her own terms." (Publisher's note)

REVIEW: *Booklist* v111 no2 p67 S 15 2014 Lizzie Matkowski

REVIEW: *Booklist* v110 no12 p36 F 15 2014 Michele Leber

REVIEW: *Kirkus Rev* v82 no4 p313 F 15 2014

"Wrecked". "In [Tricia] Fields' . . . third novel featuring Josie Gray, the Texas police chief's latest case hits far too close to home. Josie's desperate race to save Dillon is all too plausible, though it would have been even more effective without a catalog of even minor characters' wardrobes, hairstyles and home furnishings. The prize-winning Fields compellingly evokes the remote Texas border town but compromises the suspense with Josie's self-obsessed guilt and anxiety and the book's inconsistent pacing."

REVIEW: *Libr J* v139 no4 p73 Mr 1 2014 Teresa L. Jacobsen

REVIEW: *Publ Wkly* v261 no2 p51 Ja 13 2014

FIGART, DEBORAH M.ed. Handbook of research on gender and economic life. See Handbook of research on gender and economic life

FIGLER, JEFF. Collectible Wisdom; FAVORITE COLUMNS FROM THE COLLECTIBLES GURU; [by] Jeff Figler 364 p. 2013 CreateSpace Independent Publishing Platform

1. Collectibles 2. Collectibles—Provenance 3. Collectibles—Sales & prices 4. Collectors & collecting 5. Do-it-yourself literature

ISBN 1482669358; 9781482669350

SUMMARY: "In a book of his newspaper columns, [Jeff] Figler . . . offers practical help to amateurs and explores the wide and peculiar world of collectibles. . . . Figler considers many different genres of collectibles, focusing especially on comic books, sports and other pop-culture memorabilia, but also highlighting more unusual items. . . . He discusses in-person and online auctions and how to evaluate items according to provenance, quality and rarity." (Kirkus Reviews)

REVIEW: *Kirkus Rev* v81 no24 p347 D 15 2013

"Collectible Wisdom: Favorite Columns From the Collectibles Guru". "[Jeff Figler's] latest book is full of useful advice for beginners, and its conversational tone and bite-size articles make it an easy, pleasant read. . . . Fascinating trivia abounds. . . . Only very occasionally is the author's approach too simplistic; most readers will already know about reserve prices, for example. The book's format as a collection of columns means that information is often repeated, and many lists of rare items and their selling prices seem like filler. If the material had been arranged into longer, thematic chapters, it might have reduced such duplicate material and rendered it more readable to moderately interested nonprofessionals. Nevertheless, Figler's enthusiasm is infectious."

FIJAŁKOWSKI, KRZYSZTOF.tr. A World Without Wall Street? See Morin, F.

FILER, NATHAN. The Shock of the Fall; [by] Nathan Filer 320 p. 2014 The Borough Press

1. Brothers—Fiction 2. Mental illness—Fiction 3. Psychiatric hospitals 4. Psychological fiction 5. Schizophrenia

ISBN 000749145X; 9780007491452

SUMMARY: This book by Nathan Filer, which won the Costa Book Award, follows the "journey of a teenager living and coming to terms with schizophrenia. Nineteen-year-old Matthew Homes tells the story of his life, thoughts and experiences stemming from the death of his elder brother as a child. Matthew's account is made up of diary-like entries and is fragmented, hopping in and out of different stories from separate times." (Psychologist)

REVIEW: *London Rev Books* v36 no4 p33 F 20 2014 Thomas Jones

"The Shock of the Fall". "The Costa [Book Award] judges said that 'The Shock of the Fall' is 'so good it will make you feel a better person', though that may be the last thing anyone should ask of a novel. . . . 'The Shock of the Fall' is an impressive feat of storytelling: it's never confusing and has plenty of narrative momentum. . . . As a story of a boy and his family struggling through grief, the book is often very affecting. [Nathan] Filer displays control of the narrative voice, too. . . . The techniques of suspense—the deliberate withholding of information till the moment of maximum impact, while keeping readers turning the pages in the meantime—work against the story here. . . . Throughout the novel, we hear Matt's voice, but we don't get inside his head."

FINCH, ANNIE. Spells; new & selected poems; [by] Annie Finch xii, 215 p. 2013 Wesleyan University Press

1. American poetry 2. Feminist poetry 3. Magic 4. Neopaganism 5. Versification

ISBN 9780819572691 (cloth)

LC 2012-044385

SUMMARY: "Annie Finch's 'Spells' brings together her most memorable and striking poems written over forty years. Finch's uniquely mysterious voice moves through the book, revealing insights on the classic themes of love, spirituality, death, nature, and the patterns of time. A feminist and pagan, Finch writes poems as 'spells' that bring readers to experience words not just in the mind, but in the body." (Publisher's note)

REVIEW: *World Lit Today* v88 no1 p69-70 Ja/F 2014 Jeanetta Calhoun Mish

"Spells: New and Selected Poems." "When opening a book of poetry by Annie Finch, the first thing a reader will notice is that the poems are dense--dense in language, dense in emotion. The complex density of Finch's work arises not from a desire to write obtuse or esoteric poetry but from the poet's deep knowledge of received poetic forms and modes as well as her woman and nature-centered philosophy. . . . Everyone should have a copy of Annie Finch's 'Spells' on their shelf, for those hours when patterned rhythm and sound seem the best approximation of the soul's speaking."

FINCH, TIM. The house of journalists; [by] Tim Finch 304 p. 2013 Farrar, Straus and Giroux

1. Authors, Exiled—Fiction 2. Journalists—Fiction 3. Refugees—Fiction 4. Satire
ISBN 0374173184; 9780374173180 (hardcover)
LC 2013-006520

SUMMARY: This book, by Tim Finch, centers around a "refuge for writers in exile. . . . Home to a select group of fellows, the House is located in . . . London. . . . As the fellows strive to remake their lives, they are urged to share their tales. . . Only one man manages to guard his past: the mysterious new fellow AA." (Publisher's note)

REVIEW: *Booklist* v110 no1 p38 S 1 2013 Carl Hays

REVIEW: *Columbia J Rev* v52 no3 p60-1 S/O 2013 TREVOR QUIRK

REVIEW: *Kirkus Rev* v81 no15 p312 Ag 1 2013

REVIEW: *Kirkus Rev* p18 Ag 15 2013 Fall Preview

REVIEW: *N Y Times Book Rev* p25 S 29 2013 Tim Finch

"The House of Journalists." "Former BBC reporter Tim Finch's clever novel . . . descends into antic black comedy, saturated as it is with characters . . . who lend themselves to caricature. . . . As a novelist, he is less preoccupied with individual stories of exile than with the subject of storytelling itself. Although the personal histories of the refugees are evocatively told, a generic quality haunts them, as if each had mostly allegorical purpose. . . . The novel, aware of its own status as story, is dryly self-referential. It presents itself as a thriller, but the understated plot undermines that visit."

REVIEW: *New Statesman* v142 no5171 p45 Ag 23 2013 Olivia Laing

REVIEW: *Publ Wkly* v260 no24 p36 Je 17 2013

FINCHAM, ANDREW.ed. Ljubljana Tales. See Ljubljana Tales

FINE, MICHELLE. Charter schools and the corporate makeover of public education. See Fabricant, M.

FINE, SARAH. Scan; [by] Sarah Fine 336 p. 2014 G. P. Putnam's Sons, an imprint of Penguin Group (USA) Inc.

1. Adventure and adventurers—Fiction 2. Extraterrestrial beings—Fiction 3. Fathers and sons—Fiction 4. Inventors and inventions—Fiction 5. Science fiction
ISBN 9780399160653 (hardcover)
LC 2013-023623

SUMMARY: In this book by Walter Jury and S. E. Fine, Tate discovers that "very little of the human population is actually human anymore (a small alien invasion, the H2s, has grown exponentially in the past 400 years), and the physical and mental training his father put Tate through was to help him defend the human survivors. Complicating things is his realization that his beloved girlfriend is an alien." (Bulletin of the Center for Children's Books)

REVIEW: *Booklist* v110 no18 p65 My 15 2014 Summer Hays

REVIEW: *Bull Cent Child Books* v67 no10 p525 Je 2014 A. S.

"Scan". "Both readers and Täte are playing catch-up from the start, with Täte learning most of the story in one urgent telling from his dying father and then having no one that he is certain he can trust; readers will also spot inconsistencies and careful not-quite-truths in those he meets.This is one of those enormously satisfying books where everyone has such complex, layered motivations that few emerge as truly admirable or evil. Add in the fact that there is perhaps a third group, a terrifying reason why the H2s came to Earth in the first place, that may play some role in a sequel, and the resulting thoughtful yet exciting adventure will satisfy both action and science fiction fans."

REVIEW: *Kirkus Rev* v82 no7 p105 Ap 1 2014

REVIEW: *Publ Wkly* v261 no10 p66 Mr 10 2014

REVIEW: *SLJ* v60 no5 p132 My 2014 Saleena L. Davidson

REVIEW: *SLJ* v60 no9 p68 S 2014 Suzanne Dix

REVIEW: *Voice of Youth Advocates* v37 no1 p83 Ap 2014 Lynne Farrell Stover

FINK, BEN.il. Farmstead egg guide and cookbook. See Golson, T.

FINK, SHERI. Five days at memorial; life and death in a storm-ravaged hospital; [by] Sheri Fink 432 p. 2013 Crown Publishers

1. Disaster hospitals—Louisiana—New Orleans—Case studies 2. Disaster medicine—Louisiana—New Orleans—Case studies 3. Forensic pathology—Louisiana—New Orleans—Case studies 4. Health facilities—Louisiana—Administration—Case studies 5. Hurricane Katrina, 2005 6. Journalism
ISBN 0307718964; 9780307718969
LC 2013-019693

SUMMARY: Author Sheri Fink's book "unspools the mystery of what happened in" the days after Hurricane Katrina, "bringing the reader into a hospital fighting for its life and into a conversation about the most terrifying form of health care rationing. . . . Fink exposes the hidden dilemmas of end-of-life care and reveals just how ill-prepared we are in America for the impact of large-scale disasters--and how we can do better." (Publisher's note)

REVIEW: *Bookforum* v20 no3 p14 S-N 2013 JEFF SHARLET

REVIEW: *Booklist* v110 no7 p37 D 1 2013 Sue-Ellen Beauregard

REVIEW: *Booklist* v109 no22 p11 Ag 1 2013 Keii Graff

REVIEW: *Christ Century* v131 no3 p32-3 F 5 2014 William Willimon

REVIEW: *Kirkus Rev* p23 Ag 15 2013 Fall Preview

REVIEW: *Kirkus Rev* v81 no14 p19 Jl 15 2013

REVIEW: *Libr J* v138 no21 p26 D 1 2013 Mahnaz Dar Bette-Lee Fox Liz French Margaret Heilbrun Barbara Hoffert Stephanie Klose Annalisa Pesek Henrietta Thornton-Verma Wilda Williams

REVIEW: *Libr J* v138 no21 p58 D 1 2013 Mary Knapp

REVIEW: *Libr J* v138 no14 p132 S 1 2013 Kathleen Arsenault

REVIEW: *N Y Times Book Rev* p20 S 8 2013 SHERWIN B. NULAND

REVIEW: *N Y Times Book Rev* p24 N 3 2013

REVIEW: *New Statesman* v143 no8 p50 F 28 2014

REVIEW: *New York Times* v162 no56249 pC6 S 4 2013 JASON BERRY

"Five Days at Memorial: Life and Death in a Storm-Ravaged Hospital." "In her book . . . Dr. Sheri Fink explores the excruciating struggle of medical professionals deciding to give fatal injections to those at the brink of death. Dr. Fink, a physician turned journalist, won a Pulitzer Prize for her investigation of these events in a 2009 joint assignment for ProPublica and the New York Times Magazine. This book is much more than an extension of that report. Although she had the material for a gripping disaster story, Dr. Fink has slowed down the narrative pulse to investigate situational ethics. . . . This approach is a literary gamble. . . . But Dr. Fink . . . more than delivers."

REVIEW: *Publ Wkly* v260 no27 p78 Jl 8 2013

REVIEW: *Time* v182 no13 p68 S 23 2013 Radhika Jones

"Five Days at Memorial: Life and Death in a Storm-Ravaged Hospital." "The story of what happened at Memorial unfolds with creeping doom. [Sheri] Fink interviewed hundreds of sources, creating detailed portraits of the staff and patients and a terrifying sense of atmosphere. . . . Fink . . . writes powerfully of the investigation into the Memorial deaths and, in her epilogue, of subsequent disasters. . . . Her findings are troublingly murky. . . . But in chronicling the devastating events at Memorial, Fink shows how important these discussions are, in a time of crisis or not. For the need to draw a line between life and death doesn't always announce itself with storms and floods."

FINKEL, DAVID. Thank You for Your Service; [by] David Finkel 272 p. 2013 Farrar, Straus and Giroux

1. HISTORY—Military—United States 2. HISTORY—Military—Veterans 3. Iraq War, 2003-2011—Psychological aspects 4. Iraq War, 2003-2011—Veterans—United States 5. Journalism 6. Post-traumatic stress disorder—United States

ISBN 0374180660; 9780374180669

LC 2013-021990

SUMMARY: In this book, author David Finkel "has embedded with some of the men of the 2-16 [Infantry Battalion]--but this time he has done it . . . after their deployments have ended. He is with them in their most intimate, painful, and hopeful moments as they try to recover, and in doing so, he creates a . . . portrait of what life after war is like." (Publisher's note)

REVIEW: *Am Sch* v83 no1 p123-5 Wint 2014 NEIL SHEA

REVIEW: *Bookforum* v20 no3 p7 S-N 2013 JEFF STEIN

"Breach of Trust: How Americans Failed Their Soldiers and Their Country: and "Thank You for Your Service." "[Andrew] Bacevich, a West Point graduate . . . now writes perceptive, bristling essays and books from his perch at Boston University. . . . If [David] Finkel weren't such a vivid, compelling, heartrending writer, you'd never get through his agonizing weave of battles, from the bomb-strewn highways of Iraq to the psycho clinics of VA hospitals and many ruined homes in between. . . . ['Breach of Trust' is a] gripping, appropriately lacerating book."

REVIEW: *Booklist* v110 no15 p37 Ap 1 2014 Joyce Saricks

REVIEW: *Booklist* v110 no1 p28 S 1 2013 Carol Haggas

"Thank You for Your Service." "[David] Finkel stays with the men of the 2-16 Infantry Battalion, whom he shadowed in 'The Good Soldiers' (2009), who return home to Ft. Riley, Kansas. . . . . It is impossible not to be moved, outraged, and saddened by these stories, and Finkel's deeply personal brand of narrative journalism is both heartbreaking and gut-wrenching in its unflinching honesty. When it comes to caring for the nearly 500,000 mentally wounded veterans of the long wars in Iraq and Afghanistan, it is a case of a mission most definitely not accomplished."

REVIEW: *Economist* v409 no8865 p85-8 D 7 2013

REVIEW: *Kirkus Rev* p23 Ag 15 2013 Fall Preview

REVIEW: *Kirkus Rev* v81 no14 p304 Jl 15 2013

REVIEW: *Libr J* v138 no8 p61 My 1 2013

REVIEW: *Libr J* v139 no3 p61 F 15 2014 Kelly Sinclair

REVIEW: *N Y Times Book Rev* p26 O 6 2013

REVIEW: *N Y Times Book Rev* p12 S 29 2013 David Finkel

REVIEW: *New York Times* v162 no56276 pC1-7 O 1 2013 MICHIKO KAKUTANI

REVIEW: *Publ Wkly* v260 no28 p160 Jl 15 2013

FINKEL, ELIZABETH. The Genome Generation; [by] Elizabeth Finkel 256 p. 2012 Melbourne University Publishing

1. DNA—Research 2. Genetic research 3. Genomics 4. RNA—Research 5. Science—Popular works

ISBN 0522856470; 9780522856477

SUMMARY: This book, by Elizabeth Finkel, covers revolutionary genetic developments in areas as diverse as medicine, agriculture, and evolution. From Botswana to Boston and from Australia to Mexico, the contributors to this work reveal what it means to be part of the genome generation. [It answers questions] such as What have we learned about evolution? How has it changed the way we practice medicine, grow crops, and breed livestock? and Is the genomic revolution an overhyped flop?" (Publisher's note)

REVIEW: *Choice* v51 no1 p104 S 2013 R. A. Hoots

"The Genome Generation." "With consummate skill and a flair for storytelling, [author Elizabeth] Finkel, an award-winning journalist and molecular biologist, uncoils the mystery of the genome and its ramifications. Beginning with a recapitulation of the conceptual development of the gene from its abstract perception by Mendel and Darwin to its dramatic emergence as part of the macromolecular DNA, the chapters continue with the paradigm shifts that the new knowledge engenders. . . . The text interweaves anecdotes, metaphors, and concrete comparisons to translate the genomic vernacular for laypersons."

FINKELSTEIN, JEFF.il. Seder in the desert. See Korngold, J.

FINKELSTEIN, NORMAN H. Schools of hope; the Rosenwald Schools of the American South; [by] Norman H. Finkelstein 80 p. 2014 Calkins Creek

1. African American schools 2. African Americans—Education—History 3. Historical literature 4. Philanthropists—History 5. Rosenwald, Julius, 1862-1932

ISBN 1590788419; 9781590788417
LC 2013-951346

SUMMARY: "When Booker T. Washington, the famed African American educator, asked Julius Rosenwald, the wealthy president of Sears, Roebuck and Company and noted philanthropist, to help him build well-designed and fully equipped schools for black children, the face of education in the South changed for the better. . . . In this inspiring story, noted nonfiction writer Norman H. Finkelstein spotlights one man's legacy and the power of community action." (Publisher's note)

REVIEW: *Booklist* v110 no11 p60-1 F 1 2014 Ilene Cooper

"Schools of Hope: How Julius Rosenwald Helped Change African American Education". "[Norman H.] Finkelstein does a solid job of introducing both a person and a history most readers will know nothing about. . . . The text is a bit repetitive in places, but it clearly explains how the schools were built, the enthusiasm for them, their successes, and how the legacy of the Rosenwald schools lives on. The archival photographs are particularly well chosen and often moving. An introduction by Rosenwald's grandson adds further insight."

REVIEW: *Bull Cent Child Books* v67 no10 p517 Je 2014 E. B.

"Schools of Hope: How Julius Rosenwald Helped Change African American Education". "This work delves more deeply into Rosenwald's other charitable work and ably contextualizes the school-building program within the 'separate but equal' social mandate that was then the law of the land. Plenty of black and white photos and architectural plans provide a vivid picture of the before-and-after state of post-Civil War black schools, and they also bring readers up to date on current preservation efforts. Index, citations, and print and online sources are included."

REVIEW: *Horn Book Magazine* v90 no3 p109 My/Je 2014 DEAN SCHNEIDER

REVIEW: *Kirkus Rev* v82 no6 p84 Mr 15 2014

REVIEW: *SLJ* v60 no3 p180 Mr 2014 Lisa Crandall

FINOCCHIARO, MAURICE A. The Routledge guidebook to Galileo's Dialogue; [by] Maurice A. Finocchiaro xviii, 357 p. 2014 Routledge-Taylor and Francis

1. Astronomy 2. Historical literature 3. Religion & science—History

ISBN 9780415503679 (alk. paper); 9780415503686 (pbk.: alk. paper)
LC 2013-005749

SUMMARY: This book looks at Gallileo's text "Dialogue". "The core of the book is an exposition of the critical reasoning used by Galileo in his text, breaking open the most important ideas through methodological steps. . . . Due to his problem with the church, Galileo claimed that he was treating both philosophies equally; [Maurice A.] Finocchiaro reveals how well Galileo succeeded at this attempt. The book concludes with remarks on Galileo's legacy." (Choice: Current Reviews for Academic Libraries)

REVIEW: *Choice* v51 no8 p1424 Ap 2014 M.-K. Hemenway

"The Routledge Guidebook to Gallileo's Dialogue". "Well-known Galileo expert [Maurice A.] Finocchiaro . . . provides the necessary guidance to understand the historical context, the intellectual background, and the key arguments that Galileo presented on both sides. . . . Useful diagrams illustrate important points in the arguments. . . . The author provide the presuppositions for many points, revealing a more complete understanding of them. . . . Part of 'The Routledge Guides to the Great Books' series, it will be a good resource for faculty using a great books curriculum."

FIORELLA, SAM. Influence marketing. See Brown, D.

THE FIRST DRAWING; 40 p. 2013 Little Brown & Co

1. Cave dwellers—Fiction 2. Cave paintings—Fiction 3. Children's stories 4. Drawing—Fiction 5. Imagination—Fiction 6. Prehistoric peoples—Fiction

ISBN 0316204781; 9780316204781
LC 2013-001269

SUMMARY: In this picture book, Caldecott Medalist Mordicai Gerstein tells the tale "of a boy living 30,000 years ago with his pet wolf and his very extended family. Using narrative direct address . . . to effectively bridge the gap between prehistoric times and the present, the story follows the boy on his fanciful discoveries of wooly mammoths in clouds, bears in stones and horses galloping on cave walls." (Kirkus Reviews)

REVIEW: *Booklist* v109 no22 p87 Ag 1 2013 Ilene Cooper

REVIEW: *Bull Cent Child Books* v67 no3 p153 N 2013 D. S.

"The First Drawing." "[Author Mordicai] Gerstein's second-person narration follows an imaginative stone-age child, who keeps seeing images of the local animals in firelight flickers on cave walls. . . . Though this is, according to a note, inspired by the Paleolithic era art in the Ghauvet-Pont d'Arc cave in Southern France, it's less about the stone age than it is about art, and the story offers a creative approach to get kids thinking about that paradigm shift into artistic representation. The illustrations enhance the connection between the young Paleolithic artist and young current artists by framing the stone-age visuals with a contemporary echo, a kid in modern blue jeans drawing away and producing a picture of the contemporary equivalents of the mastodons and wolves."

REVIEW: *Horn Book Magazine* v89 no5 p73-4 S/O 2013 JOANNA RUDGE LONG

REVIEW: *Kirkus Rev* v81 no15 p139 Ag 1 2013

REVIEW: *Nat Hist* v121 no9 p44 N 2013 Dolly Setton

REVIEW: *Publ Wkly* p28-9 Children's starred review annual 2013

REVIEW: *Publ Wkly* v260 no25 p171 Je 24 2013

REVIEW: *SLJ* v59 no8 p74 Ag 2013 Sara-Jo Lupo Sites

FISCHER, JAMES. Game math; [by] James Fischer 48 p. 2014 Mason Crest

1. Estimates 2. Games 3. Logic 4. Mathematical literature 5. Mathematical recreations—Juvenile literature

ISBN 9781422229019 (series); 9781422229071 (hardcover)
LC 2013-015666

SUMMARY: This book by Rae Simons is part of the Math 24/7 series, which "emphasizes how math skills come into play at all times and in all places, from the kitchen to the soccer field. . . . Guided questions walk readers through the process and provide practice problems. . . . In 'Game Math,'

Mason is surprised to discover that many of his favorite games incorporate such concepts as probability, coordinates, estimation, and logic." (Booklist)

REVIEW: *Booklist* v110 no5 p56 N 1 2013 Angela Leeper

"Culinary Math," "Fashion Math," and "Game Math." "The Math 24/7 series emphasizes how math skills come into play at all times and in all places, from the kitchen to the soccer field. Each book centers on a young person who is involved in a series of scenarios that requires real-world math to solve a problem. . . . In 'Culinary Math,' a culinary student uses estimating to budget his grocery shopping, multiplication to determine a food's calorie content, and fractions to measure ingredients. In 'Fashion Math,' a budding fashion designer uses math to convert sizes, choose enough fabric for a pattern, and determine prices to make a profit. In Game Math, Mason is surprised to discover that many of his favorite games incorporate such concepts as probability, coordinates, estimation, and logic."

FISCHER, PETER S. Me and Murder, She Wrote; [by] Peter S. Fischer 264 p. 2013 The Grove Point Press

1. Marcus Welby, MD (TV program) 2. Memoirs 3. Murder, She Wrote (TV program) 4. Television producers & directors 5. Television writers

ISBN 0988657139; 9780988657137

SUMMARY: In this book, Peter S. Fischer "focuses primarily on his career in Hollywood, starting with his early success as the writer of a 1971 TV movie of the week called The Last Child and ending with his retirement shortly after a long tenure as a TV writer and producer. . . . Fischer tells of writing episodes of famous programs . . . and winning an Edgar Award and two Golden Globes for Murder, She Wrote. The author also discusses his work on other promising but less-successful shows." (Kirkus Reviews)

REVIEW: *Kirkus Rev* v81 no21 p64 N 1 2013

REVIEW: *Kirkus Rev* p19 D 15 2013 supplemet best books 2013

"Me and Murder, She Wrote". "The narrative flows briskly as [Peter S.] Fischer tells of writing episodes of famous programs such as Marcus Welby, M.D. and winning an Edgar Award and two Golden Globes for Murder, She Wrote. . . . Overall, Fischer provides an engaging glimpse into the interpersonal relationships that enriched his life and career; for example, the camaraderie Fischer shared with TV stars Angela Lansbury and Peter Falk developed into long-standing friendships. Fischer further pays homage to his love of film and television by including a trivia question at the end of each chapter. A warm, affectionate autobiography that will likely appeal to TV history buffs."

REVIEW: *Publ Wkly* v260 no41 p25-6 O 14 2013

FISCHLIN, DANIEL. The fierce urgency of now. See Lipsitz, G.

FISCHLIN, DANIEL.ed. The Tempest. See The Tempest

FISHER, MELISSA S. Wall street women; [by] Melissa S. Fisher xii, 227 p. 2012 Duke University Press

1. Financial crises—United States—History—21st century 2. Financial services industry—United States 3. Global Financial Crisis, 2008-2009 4. Sex role in the work environment—New York (State)—New York 5. Social science literature 6. Women employees 7. Women in the professions 8. Women stockbrokers—New York (State)—New York

ISBN 9780822353300 (cloth ; alk. paper); 9780822353454 (pbk. : alk. paper)

LC 2012-011599

SUMMARY: In this book of historical ethnography, author Melissa S. Fisher "tells the story of the first generation of women to establish themselves as professionals on Wall Street. Since these women, who began their careers in the 1960s, faced blatant discrimination and barriers to advancement, they created formal and informal associations to bolster one another's careers." (Publisher's note)

REVIEW: *Am J Sociol* v119 no2 p575-7 S 2013 Louise Marie Roth

REVIEW: *Bus Hist Rev* v87 no3 p591-4 Aut 2013 Janette Rutterford

"Wall Street Women." "Melissa Fisher, who teaches anthropology at Georgetown University, applies her focus to a cohort of women who worked in Wall Street from the 1960s to the twenty-first century, the pioneers in the feminization of finance. . . . The author bases her story on detailed case studies of the first generation of women who entered Wall Street in the 1960s. . . . As an anthropologist. Fisher is not just interested in what these pioneering women have to say, but also in what they wore, how they related to each other, and even the décor of the rooms where they met."

REVIEW: *Libr J* v137 no10 p110 Je 1 2012 Rebekah Wallin

REVIEW: *Publ Wkly* v259 no19 p42 My 7 2012

FISHMAN, SETH. The well's end; [by] Seth Fishman 352 p. 2014 G.P. Putnam's Sons, an imprint of Penguin Group (USA) Inc.

1. Adventure and adventurers—Fiction 2. Boarding schools—Fiction 3. Fathers and daughters—Fiction 4. Schools—Fiction 5. Science fiction 6. Single-parent families—Fiction 7. Survival—Fiction 8. Virus diseases—Fiction

ISBN 0399159908; 9780399159909 (hardback)

LC 2013-022716

SUMMARY: In this book, by Seth Fishman, "a deadly virus and an impossible discovery unite. . . . Sixteen-year-old Mia Kish's small town of Fenton, Colorado is known for . . . one of the ritziest boarding schools in the country, Westbrook Academy. But when emergency sirens start blaring and Westbrook is put on lockdown, quarantined and surrounded by soldiers who shoot first and ask questions later, Mia realizes she's only just beginning to discover what makes Fenton special." (Publisher's note)

REVIEW: *Bull Cent Child Books* v67 no8 p405 Ap 2014 A. S.

"The Well's End". "There's a cool core to the novel, magical water that only appears in a seventeen-year-cycle and that can be used as both a devastating weapon and a healing element. However, its impact is diminished by the book's uninspiring bad guy . . . by the the too-frequent references to Mia's childhood fall down a well, and by awkward exposition scenes that get the teens up to date on how the grownups have been mishandling the situation. Even with the flaws, there are strengths: Mia's (ill-advised) steamy romance with a new student develops at an authentically frantic pace that matches the adrenaline rush of the rest of the novel, and a cliffhanger end opens up a new plot thread that may be worth pursuing."

FITZGERALD, LAURA MARX. Under the egg; [by] Laura Marx Fitzgerald 256 p. 2014 Dial Books for Young Readers, an imprint of Penguin Group (USA) Inc.

1. Art—Fiction 2. Friendship—Fiction 3. Holocaust, Jewish (1939-1945)—Fiction 4. Mystery and detective stories 5. Neighborhoods—Fiction 6. Recluses—Fiction

ISBN 0803740018; 9780803740013 (hardcover)
LC 2013-017790

SUMMARY: In this book, by Laura Marx Fitzgerald, "Theodora Tenpenny spills a bottle of rubbing alcohol on her late grandfather's painting [and] discovers . . . an old Renaissance masterpiece underneath. That's great news for Theo, who's struggling to hang onto her family's . . . townhouse and support her unstable mother. . . . There's just one problem: Theo's grandfather was a security guard at the Metropolitan Museum of Art, and she worries the painting may be stolen." (Publisher's note)

REVIEW: *Booklist* v110 no11 p57 F 1 2014 Carolyn Phelan

REVIEW: *Bull Cent Child Books* v67 no7 p355 Mr 2014 A. A.

REVIEW: *Horn Book Magazine* v90 no2 p118 Mr/Ap 2014 SHARA L. HARDESON

"Under the Egg". "After delving into her grandfather's military past—he was one of the famous Monuments Men—[Theodora] realizes the mystery stretches all the way back to Nazi Germany and Hitler's fine-art plundering. [Laura Marx] Fitzgerald moves beyond the all-too-familiar conventions of the 'X marks the spot' story line to offer a gripping mystery with high stakes and moving historical context (and in fact the WWII flashbacks are more vivid than her modern settings and characters); her focus on restitution and the personal value of art adds considerable depth to the narrative. Fans of Blue Balliett's art mysteries . . . will likely appreciate this similar fare."

REVIEW: *Kirkus Rev* v81 no24 p296 D 15 2013

"Under the Egg". "This debut novel weaves art appreciation, restoration and dating techniques, and bits of history from the Renaissance and World War II into a fast-paced mystery. . . . All the characters are relatively flat, including first-person protagonist Theodora, but an original plot with humorous swipes at rich-and-famous lifestyles and authentic references to New York City will keep readers interested. Occasionally, there are awkward or dense passages, but they are balanced by quirky encounters, as with Eddie, a tattooed librarian. If Dan Brown of The Da Vinci Code wrote middle-grade novels, this would be the one."

REVIEW: *Publ Wkly* v260 no51 p59-61 D 16 2013

REVIEW: *SLJ* v60 no2 p84 F 2014 Kiera Parrott

FITZGERALD, SARAH MOORE. Back to Blackbrick; [by] Sarah Moore Fitzgerald 208 p. 2013 Simon & Schuster

1. Alzheimer's patients 2. Fantasy fiction 3. Grandfathers—Fiction 4. Stablehands 5. Time travel—Juvenile fiction

ISBN 1442481552; 9781442481558

SUMMARY: In this book by Sarah Moore Fitzgerald about Alzheimer's disease and time travel, "Cosmo knows his Granddad is losing his mind. So on one of the rare occasions when Granddad seems to recognise him, Cosmo is bemused that he gives him a key to Blackbrick Abbey and urges him to go there. Cosmo shrugs it off, but gradually Blackbrick draws him in. Cosmo arrives there, scared and lonely, and is dropped off at the crumbling gates of a huge house." (Publisher's note)

REVIEW: *Bull Cent Child Books* v67 no2 p88-9 O 2013 J. H.

"Back to Blackbrick." "Young Cosmo is unwilling to accept that there is no cure for his grandfather's Alzheimer's, and he tries to prime Granddad's memory so that the man can at least stay in his own home. . . . Entering the gates of Blackbrick, Cosmo is transported back in time and meets Kevin--Granddad as a sixteen-year-old stable boy. . . . The book is a thoughtful blend of time travel adventure and family drama, and Cosmo's voice balances wry humor with deeply felt angst over his grandfather's illness. . . . Fans of gentle fantasies and readers with relatives suffering similar physical challenges will find Cosmo a worthwhile companion."

FITZGERALD, WILLIAM. How to read a Latin poem; if you can't read Latin yet; [by] William Fitzgerald ix, 278 p. 2013 Oxford University Press

1. Latin poetry—Appreciation 2. Latin poetry—History and criticism 3. Latin poetry—Translations into English 4. Literary critiques 5. Poetry (Literary form)—Translating

ISBN 0199657866; 9780199657865
LC 2012-532357

SUMMARY: It was the author's intent "to give the reader with little or no knowledge of Latin or the classical world a feel for the character of Roman poetry in the original language. We are offered word-by-word analysis and translation of classic texts, with . . . explanation of how meaning gradually emerges from a language which (unlike English) does not depend on word order to make sense." (Times Literary Supplement)

REVIEW: *Choice* v51 no7 p1210 Mr 2014 M. L. Goldman

REVIEW: *Classical Rev* v64 no1 p312 Ap 2014 Alan Beale

REVIEW: *TLS* no5751 p25 Je 21 2013 ROY GIBSON

"How to Read a Latin Poem: If You Can't Read Latin Yet." "Despite the schoolmasterly 'yet' of the title . . . this short book is no cautiously chaperoned tour of the territory. . . . We are offered word-by-word analysis and translation of classic texts, with deft explanation of how meaning gradually emerges from a language which (unlike English) does not depend on word order to make sense. . . . [William] Fitzgerald proves an inspiring guide to the richness and (rarely emphasized) strangeness of Virgil's Latin. He also offers stimulating asides on the stark juxtapositions of vocabulary that are inevitable in a language which dispenses with definite and indefinite articles and has no need of many of the prepositions which litter English."

FITZPATRICK, HUNTLEY. What I thought was true; [by] Huntley Fitzpatrick 416 p. 2014 Dial

1. Dating (Social customs)—Fiction 2. Family life—Connecticut—Fiction 3. Islands—Fiction 4. Love stories 5. Old age—Fiction 6. People with disabilities—

Fiction 7. Social classes—Fiction
ISBN 0803739095; 9780803739093 (hardback)
LC 2013-027029

SUMMARY: This book, by Huntley Fitzpatrick, is a "love story [that] shows the clash between classes in a New England beach community. . . Gwen, whose mother is a house cleaner, has . . . [a poor] reputation among the members of the boys' swim team, including rich Cass. . . . After a humiliating run-in with him at a party, it's hard for Gwen to believe that he wants more from her than a quick fling, but over the course of the summer, he gradually wins her trust and her heart." (Publishers Weekly)

REVIEW: *Booklist* v110 no15 p87-8 Ap 1 2014 Lexi Walters Wright

REVIEW: *Kirkus Rev* v82 no5 p109 Mr 1 2014

"What I Thought Was True". "A teenage girl struggles with class divisions, sex and the tricky art of communication. . . . What starts out as snappy chick-lit writing quickly becomes deeper and more complex, as [Huntley] Fitzpatrick beautifully portrays a teenager's wobbly foray into sex as well as her dawning awareness of the power that actions and incautiously chosen words have to hurt others. A late revelation will surprise readers as much as it does Gwen; natural dialogue and authentic characters abound. Much deeper than the pretty cover lets on."

REVIEW: *Publ Wkly* v261 no3 p58-9 Ja 20 2014

REVIEW: *SLJ* v60 no3 p157 Mr 2014 Candyce Pruitt-Goddard

REVIEW: *Voice of Youth Advocates* v37 no1 p65 Ap 2014 Jim Nicosia

FIZZY'S LUNCH LAB; super supper throwdown; 64 p. 2014 Candlewick Press

1. Children's recipes & cookbooks 2. Children's stories 3. Cooking competitions 4. Dinners & dining 5. Nutrition—Juvenile literature
ISBN 9780763668839 (pbk.); 9780763672799 (hardcover)
LC 2013-944010

SUMMARY: In this book, "the characters from the PBS Kids' show Fizzy's Lunch Lab teach kids about the importance of good nutrition. Professor Fizzy, the master of healthy eating, takes on Fast Food Freddy, greasy food expert. The challenge? The titular cook-off: Each chef will design a meal that three kids will then taste test. . . . Throughout, Sully the Cell interjects to explain how the right foods are used to fuel the body, and Cpl. Cup provides the recipes that help Fizzy win the cook-off." (Kirkus Reviews)

REVIEW: *Kirkus Rev* v82 no5 p81 Mr 1 2014

"Super Supper Throwdown". "The characters from the PBS Kids' show Fizzy's Lunch Lab teach kids about the importance of good nutrition. Professor Fizzy, the master of healthy eating, takes on Fast Food Freddy, greasy food expert. The challenge? The titular cook-off: Each chef will design a meal that three kids will then taste test. . . . The brightly colored digital illustrations match the TV show to a T, inelegantly making the leap to the page. Better than many at explaining the hows and whys of healthy eating but still a TV show on paper."

FLAGG, FANNIE, 1944-. The All-Girl Filling Station's Last Reunion; a novel; [by] Fannie Flagg 352 p. 2013 Random House Inc

1. FICTION—Contemporary Women 2. FICTION—Historical 3. FICTION—Humorous 4. Family secrets—Fiction 5. Female friendship—Fiction 6. Service stations—Fiction 7. Women—Fiction
ISBN 1400065941; 9781400065943
LC 2013-030030

SUMMARY: This book, by Fannie Flagg, is a "comic mystery novel about two women who are forced to reimagine who they are. Mrs. Sookie Poole of Point Clear, Alabama, has just married off the last of her daughters. . . . The only thing left to contend with is her mother, . . . Lenore Simmons Krackenberry. . . . One day, . . . Sookie discovers a secret about her mother's past that . . . calls into question everything she ever thought she knew about herself, her family, and her future." (Publisher's note)

REVIEW: *Booklist* v110 no4 p15 O 15 2013 Rebecca Vnuk

REVIEW: *Booklist* v109 no19/20 p125-7 Je 1 2013 Sue-Ellen Beauregard

REVIEW: *Kirkus Rev* v81 no19 p304 O 1 2013

REVIEW: *Libr J* v138 no18 p77 N 1 2013 Shannon Marie Robinson

REVIEW: *Libr J* v139 no6 p56 Ap 1 2014 Donna Bachowski

REVIEW: *Libr J* v138 no10 p78 Je 1 2013

REVIEW: *N Y Times Book Rev* p23 N 17 2013 MARILYN STASIO

"Critical Mass," "The All-Girl Filling Station's Last Reunion," and "Country Hardball." "The drug subplot is an unnecessary complication in an already busy story told in two parallel narratives set in different countries, running on separate timelines and involving four generations of characters. But if the plot mechanics are unwieldy, the character of Martina is the serene center of this fractured universe. . . . Steve Weddle's writing is downright dazzling in 'Country Hardball'. . . . Sookie's detective work, tracing her new identity, takes her all the way to Pulaski, Wis., and into the lives of four ebullient sisters who ran their father's gas station during World War II. Honestly, who wouldn't want to be part of that family?"

REVIEW: *Publ Wkly* v260 no27 p16-22 Jl 8 2013 SHANNON MAUGHAN

FLATT, LIZANN. Shaping Up Summer; 32 p. 2014 Pgw

1. Children's nonfiction 2. Geometry in nature 3. Mathematics—Juvenile literature 4. Shapes—Juvenile literature 5. Summer—Juvenile literature
ISBN 1926973879; 9781926973876

SUMMARY: This book, focused on shapes and the summer season, is part of Lizann Flatt and Ashley Barron's "Math in Nature" series. "Moles dig out tunnels in the shapes of rectangles, triangles and squares, while ghost crabs use the sand excavated from their holes to build spheres, prisms and cylinders. . . . From shapes, Flatt moves on to explore such relational concepts as above, below, under, over, beside, etc." (Kirkus Reviews)

REVIEW: *Kirkus Rev* v82 no2 p170 Ja 15 2014

"Shaping Up Summer". "[Lizann] Flatt and [Ashley] Barron's fourth and final entry in the Math in Nature series rounds out the seasons with a look at shapes in the summer. From 2-D to 3-D, Flatt explores all sorts of shapes, though only rarely do either the text or the gorgeous cut-paper collages reflect shapes actually found in nature. . . . . Barron's artwork continues to be the major draw, as this latest shares the flaws of the other books in the series. The rhythm and rhyme are inconsistent, sometimes dropping altogether, and the book lacks an answer key. . . . The audience isn't clear—those who are drawn to picture books may find themselves in over their heads, as the concepts and vocabulary are not explained."

REVIEW: *SLJ* v60 no4 p180 Ap 2014 Jasmine L. Precopio

FLEEGLER, ROBERT L. Ellis Island nation; immigration policy and American identity in the twentieth century; [by] Robert L. Fleegler 270 p. 2013 University of Pennsylvania Press

1. Acculturation—United States—HIstory—20th century 2. Historical literature 3. Immigrants—United States—HIstory—20th century 4. Multiculturalism—United States—HIstory—20th century

ISBN 9780812245097 (hardcover : alk. paper)

LC 2012-031343

SUMMARY: This book on 20th-century immigration to the U.S. by Robert L. Fleegler "describes how contributionism eventually shifted the focus of the immigration debate from assimilation to a Cold War celebration of ethnic diversity and its benefits--helping to ease the passage of 1960s immigration laws that expanded the pool of legal immigrants and setting the stage for the identity politics of the 1970s and 1980s." (Publisher's note)

REVIEW: *Choice* v51 no4 p709 D 2013 C. K. Piehl

"Ellis Island Nation: Immigration Policy and American Identity in the Twentieth Century." "In this thoughtful, timely volume, [Robert L.] Fleegler . . . focuses on the crucial era between the Johnson-Reed Act (1924), which hardened restrictionism that governed US policy, and the 1965 Hart-Celler Act. . . . In a helpful epilogue, Fleegler outlines how Hart-Celler has influenced immigration policy since. An outstanding, extremely useful book for a wide range of students, scholars, and professionals seeking perspectives on the current immigration debates."

FLEMING, JOHN, 1919-2001. A world history of art. See Honour, H.

FLEMING, MICHAEL.il. Ten eggs in a nest. See Sadler, M.

FLEMING, THEODORE H. The ornaments of life. See Kress, W. J.

FLETCHER, MARTIN. Jacob's oath; a novel; [by] Martin Fletcher 336 p. 2013 Thomas Dunne Books

1. Brothers and sisters—Fiction 2. FICTION—Jewish 3. Historical literature 4. Holocaust survivors—Fiction 5. Jewish families—Fiction 6. Revenge—Fiction

ISBN 9781250027610 (hardback)

LC 2013-020532

SUMMARY: In this historical novel by Martin Fletcher "As World War II winds to a close, Europe's roads are clogged with twenty million exhausted refugees walking home. Among them are Jacob and Sarah, lonely Holocaust survivors who meet in Heidelberg. But Jacob is consumed with hatred and cannot rest until he has killed his brother's murderer, a concentration camp guard nicknamed 'The Rat.' Now he must choose between revenge and love, between avenging the past and building a future." (Publisher's note)

REVIEW: *Booklist* v110 no1 p46 S 1 2013 Thomas Gaughan

REVIEW: *Kirkus Rev* v81 no16 p284 Ag 15 2013

"Jacob's Oath." "A Holocaust survivor must choose between keeping the woman he loves and seeking revenge against the camp guard who beat his younger brother to death. . . . With an emotionally agile tone, [author Martin] Fletcher . . . captures the chaos and desperation that followed the end of World War II in Europe. While some of the characters feel hollow, Fletcher does a particularly good job of bringing the titular character to life, imbuing him with a dark side brought to the fore by the horrors he's experienced. An expressive and generally well-told story of love and hatred, revenge and recovery."

REVIEW: *Publ Wkly* v260 no32 p37 Ag 12 2013

FLIOTSOS, ANNE.ed. International women stage directors. See International women stage directors

FLIP FLAP FARM; 26 p. 2014 Candlewick Press

1. Animals—Juvenile fiction 2. Domestic animals 3. Farms—Juvenile literature 4. Picture books for children 5. Toy & movable books

ISBN 0763670677; 9780763670672

LC 2013-943076

SUMMARY: In this flip book, by Axel Scheffler, readers can mix and match pages to create different animals. "What do you get when you cross a goat with a turkey? Why, a gurkey, of course! What about a pig with a sheep? Well, that would be a peep, naturally!" The book features "split pages and spiral binding . . . [and] 121 possible combinations." (Publisher's note)

REVIEW: *Bull Cent Child Books* v67 no7 p376 Mr 2014 D. S.

"Flip Flap Farm." "Eleven common animals are introduced here with a jaunty two-stanza verse . . . and a simple, hearty full-page illustration. The trick here, however, is that the spiral-bound pages are horizontally bisected at a neatly hybrid point in both text and art, so that viewers can turn the above sheep into a 'shabbit,' a 'shicken,' or a 'shig.' The verse here is cheerful, but it's mostly greeting-card-style filler, failing to add anything to the concept or to maximize the humor potential of the mismatched couplings the way text in other such split-page books . . . does."

REVIEW: *Kirkus Rev* v82 no2 p228 Ja 15 2014

REVIEW: *Publ Wkly* v260 no51 p60 D 16 2013

FLISAR, EVALD.tr. The master of insomnia. See The master of insomnia

FLOCA, BRIAN.il. Marty McGuire has too many pets! See Messner, K.

FLOHR, MIKO. The world of the Fullo; work, economy, and society in Roman Italy; [by] Miko Flohr xvi, 401 p. 2013 Oxford University Press CPI Group (UK) Ltd.

1. Artisans—History 2. Historical literature 3. Textile industry—History
ISBN 0199659354 (hbk.); 9780199659357 (hbk.)
LC 2013-937237

SUMMARY: Written by Miko Flohr, "'The World of the Fullo' takes a detailed look at the fullers, craftsmen who dealt with high-quality garments, of Roman Italy. Analyzing the social and economic worlds in which the fullers lived and worked, it tells the story of their economic circumstances, the way they organized their workshops, the places where they worked in the city, and their everyday lives on the shop floor and beyond." (Publisher's note)

REVIEW: *TLS* no5790 p13 Mr 21 2014 GREG WOOLF

"The World of the Fullo: Work, Economy, and Society in Roman Italy." "The evidence for fulling is of the worst kind, plentiful but ambiguous, and has been the support for all sorts of anachronistic and frankly fanciful reconstructions. But in 'The World of the Fullo' [author Miko] Flohr has been prepared to scrub this data clean with as much effort as the poor workers who trod for hours in stalls in the semi-darkness at the back of pokey shops, and the author has wielded his shears without mercy on the work of his predecessors. . . . Miko Flohr's reconstruction of Roman fulling sets out to offer a contribution to the long-stalled debates over the ancient economy, but what is most fascinating in his account are these glimpses of life and work—grubby and proud—in the Roman rag trade."

FLOOD, CYNTHIA. Red Girl Rat Boy; [by] Cynthia Flood 192 p. 2013 Biblioasis

1. Activists 2. British Columbia—Fiction 3. Canadian fiction 4. Human sexuality—Fiction 5. Short stories
ISBN 1927428416; 9781927428412 (pbk.)
LC 2013-464499

SUMMARY: This book, by Cynthia Flood, presents short stories featuring "women. Young women, old women. The hair-obsessed, the politically driven, . . . the awkward and compulsive and alone. Sleep-deprived and testy. Exhausted and accepting. Among the innumerable wives, husbands, sisters, and in-laws vexed by short temper and insecurity throughout the collection, Cynthia Flood's protagonists stand out as masters of a reality that the rest of the world will only partially understand." (Publisher's note)

REVIEW: *Quill Quire* v79 no8 p29-30 O 2013 Michael Bryson

"Red Girl Rat Boy." "This relatively slim collection of 11 stories features a large wildcat, domestic troubles, and memories of the West Coast's extreme left in the 1960s and '70s. 'Blue Clouds' and 'Dirty Work,' for example, recount class struggle and the sex lives of 'contacts' and 'comrades,' but they are more anthropologically interesting than examples of stunning short-story technique. . . . As we have come to expect, [author Cynthia] Flood's stories reward attentive reading. Realism is the dominant technique, but there are also quirks that bend the reader's ear and excite."

FLORENCE, CURTIS S.ed. Economics and youth violence. See Economics and youth violence

FLORIAN, DOUGLAS, 1950-. Poem Depot; Aisles of Smiles; [by] Douglas Florian 160 p. 2014 Dial Books for Young Readers

1. Animals—Juvenile poetry 2. Children's poetry 3. Families—Juvenile poetry 4. Poems—Collections 5. Schools
ISBN 9780803740426 (hardcover)
LC 2013-017299

SUMMARY: This book by Douglas Florian presents a "ollection of drawings and brief poems on a host of silly subjects." It is "posited as a superstore of verse on assorted topics children care about—school, family, animals, food and the like." Several poems "employ wordplay to elicit a chuckle or illustrate . . . nonsensical truisms about language." (Kirkus Reviews)

REVIEW: *Booklist* v110 no14 p67 Mr 15 2014 Carolyn Phelan

REVIEW: *Bull Cent Child Books* v67 no10 p517 Je 2014 D. S.

REVIEW: *Horn Book Magazine* v90 no4 p112 Jl/Ag 2014 SUSAN DOVE LEMPKE

REVIEW: *Kirkus Rev* v81 no24 p139 D 15 2013

"Poem Depot: Aisles of Smiles". "Gifted poet and illustrator Florian (Poem Runs: Baseball Poems, 2012, etc.) here presents a chunky collection of drawings and brief poems on a host of silly subjects. Posited as a superstore of verse on assorted topics children care about—school, family, animals, food and the like—one also can't help thinking this "depot" represents a midway point for a number of poems that haven't quite reached their creative destinations. To be truly effective, light or nonsensical verse should be as tight in its poetic construction as it is loosely suggestive in metaphorical associations, and a number of the works assembled here simply read as not fully cooked."

REVIEW: *Publ Wkly* v260 no45 p73 N 11 2013

REVIEW: *SLJ* v60 no2 p119 F 2014 Magdaline Henderson-Diman

FLORIDA, RICHARD L., 1957-.ed. The creative class goes global. See The creative class goes global

FLORIO, GWEN. Montana; [by] Gwen Florio 208 p. 2013 The Permanent Press

1. Detective & mystery stories 2. Drug traffic—Fiction 3. Murder—Investigation—Fiction 4. Whites—Relations with Indians—Fiction 5. Women journalists—Fiction
ISBN 1579623360; 9781579623364
LC 2013-021081

SUMMARY: In this book, by Gwen Florio, "foreign correspondent Lola Wicks is looking forward to a restful reentry at a friend's Montana cabin. Instead, she's greeted by her former colleague's corpse. . . . Lola doesn't trust that the local sheriff has the skills to find Mary Alice's killer, so she extends her stay and uses her investigative expertise to reconstruct Mary Alice's last days. She learns that there's a lot more than meets the eye going on in Magpie, Montana." (Booklist)

REVIEW: *Booklist* v110 no3 p38-9 O 1 2013 Karen Keefe

"Montana." "Returning from assignment in Afghanistan, foreign correspondent Lola Wicks is looking forward to a restful reentry at a friend's Montana cabin. Instead, she's greeted by her former colleague's corpse. Lola learns that Mary Alice had been writing for the local paper, digging into the past of Native American gubernatorial candidate Johnny

Running Wolf Lola doesn't trust that the local sheriff has the skills to find Mary Alice's killer, so she extends her stay and uses her investigative expertise to reconstruct Mary Alice's last days. . . . The sparsely populated Big Sky setting will be one of the major sources of appeal for readers of this gripping debut mystery."

REVIEW: *Kirkus Rev* v81 no15 p319 Ag 1 2013

REVIEW: *Kirkus Rev* p7-8 Ag 15 2013 Fall Preview

REVIEW: *Publ Wkly* v260 no31 p49 Ag 5 2013

FLOWERS, PAM. Ordinary dogs, extraordinary friendships; stories of loyalty, courage, and compassion; [by] Pam Flowers 144 p. 2013 Alaska Northwest Books

1. Dogs—Juvenile literature 2. Dogsledding 3. Human-animal relationships—Anecdotes 4. Loyalty 5. Sled dogs

ISBN 0882409166; 9780882409160 (pbk. : alk. paper)

LC 2013-017986

SUMMARY: Author Pam Flowers "shares positive character traits [she] has observed in her thirty-two years of working with dogs [as an explorer.] Eleven spellbinding and valuable stories of wisdom, loyalty, courage, and even good judgment fill the pages of this book for dog lovers of all ages." (Publisher's note)

REVIEW: *Kirkus Rev* v81 no16 p304 Ag 15 2013

"Ordinary Dogs, Extraordinary Friendships: Stories of Loyalty, Courage, and Compassion." "[Author Pam] Flowers . . . is a sled-dog musher in Alaska. Her attachment to her loyal and hardworking dogs is unmistakable. She introduces readers to some of her favorite canine friends, each chapter offering in clear, engaging prose another portrait of a treasured dog. . . . Baskin's pen-and-ink illustrations nicely capture the flavor of the text, with the canines' facial expressions reflecting the appropriate and touching anthropomorphizing nature of the tales. These dog stories are so clearly based on love and respect and include many details about long, arduous and thrilling journeys across the Arctic landscape, that they are sure to entertain and perhaps even inspire readers."

FLUEHR-LOBBAN, CAROLYN. Historical dictionary of the Sudan; [by] Carolyn Fluehr-Lobban lxxiii, 546 p. 2013 Scarecrow Press

1. Africa—Maps 2. Encyclopedias & dictionaries 3. Sudan—History

ISBN 0810861801; 9780810861800 (cloth : alk. paper); 9780810879409 (ebook)

LC 2012-043839

SUMMARY: Author Robert S. Kramer's fourth edition of the book features a historical dictionary of the Republic of Sudan, a large country in Africa. The 700 entries "deal with important personalities, politics, the economy, society, culture, religion and inevitably the civil war. There are also appendixes and an extensive bibliography." The book also includes "a detailed chronology tracing its relatively few successes and numerous failures." (Publisher's note)

REVIEW: *Choice* v51 no1 p56 S 2013 D. Altschiller

"Historical Dictionary of the Sudan." "Since the third edition . . . the Republic of Sudan has been partitioned, leading to the independence of the Republic of South Sudan in July 2011. As a result of this major development, this dictionary has been greatly expanded to include much new information. . . . In addition, new maps, charts, illustrations, and tables have been added. Authors [Robert S.] Kramer . . . , [Richard A.] Lobban . . . , and [Carolyn] Fluehr-Lobban . . . are experts active in the Sudan Studies Association. . . . A recurring problem with Scarecrow's historical dictionaries is that the entries do not cite any sources. . . . Nevertheless, this is an outstanding ready-reference source providing hard-to-find information."

FLUKE, JOANNE. Blackberry pie murder; [by] Joanne Fluke 368 p. 2014 Kensington Pub Corp

1. Bakers—Fiction 2. Detective & mystery stories 3. Food habits—Fiction 4. Murder investigation—Fiction 5. Traffic accidents—Fiction

ISBN 0758280378; 9780758280374

SUMMARY: In this book, by Joanne Fluke, "Hannah finds yet another dead body—that of the unidentified man she hit and apparently killed while driving on a highway during a summer rainstorm. Of course, it was an accident, but Hannah winds up arrested and arraigned. . . . Hannah learns that the stains on the victim's shirt are not blood but blackberry pie—and an autopsy reveals that he was dead before her car hit him. Hannah is now free to look for a killer." (Publishers Weekly)

REVIEW: *Booklist* v110 no12 p30 F 15 2014 Amy Alessio

REVIEW: *Kirkus Rev* v82 no4 p317 F 15 2014

"Blackberry Pie Murder". "Lake Eden's favorite baker, Hannah Swensen (Red Velvet Cupcake Murder, 2013, etc.), finds herself on the wrong end of a police investigation. Dodging lightning on an icy road, Hannah finds herself facing a driver's worst nightmare: Her car hits something, and all of a sudden, there's a body lying on the pavement. Hours later, her mother's fiance, Doc Knight, delivers his terrible findings. The man she hit was alive when Hannah struck him, and he died on impact. . . . Once sprung, amateur sleuth Hannah is faced with an unusual case. She knows who the killer is, but who's the victim? . . . . It's amazing how little a vehicular homicide charge changes Hannah's life in Fluke's good-natured 19th."

REVIEW: *Publ Wkly* v261 no1 p35-6 Ja 6 2014

REVIEW: *Publ Wkly* v261 no21 p54-5 My 26 2014

FLYNN, DENNIS O. China and the birth of globalization in the 16th century. See Giráldez, A.

FLYNN, FRANCIS J. The exorcism of little Billy Wagner; [by] Francis J. Flynn 2013 Janus Publishing

1. Catholic Church—United States 2. Church & politics—Catholic Church 3. Demoniac possession 4. Exorcism 5. Religious satire

SUMMARY: In this novel by Francis J. Flynn, "Twelve-year-old Little Billy Wagner is possessed; the question is by what? When the medical community throws up their arms about what to do about Billy, his parents turn to their own Catholic Church to investigate whether their son is demonically possessed." The book is a "satire about what happens when everything becomes politicized and the resulting collateral damage that leaves no one unharmed, especially one Little Billy Wagner." (Publisher's note)

REVIEW: *Kirkus Rev* v81 no16 p23 Ag 15 2013

"The Exorcism of Little Billy Wagner." "In [Francis] Flynn's novel, the strange behavior of a 12-year-old boy mobilizes his whole town. The short novel opens with a crisis in faith. In Saint Anthony's parish in Gateway City, Mo., surly, big-for-his-age Billy Wagner has begun acting very strangely--barricading himself in his room, playing with knives, etc. His frantic parents have had no success talking to him, so they write a letter to the bishop of their diocese, wondering if an exorcism might be in order. . . . The one-liners are good for serious laughs, but the occasional swerves into emotion are just as affecting, and the revelations of church corruption in the climactic courtroom trial are expertly handled. A fun, fascinating send-up of the modern Catholic Church."

REVIEW: *Kirkus Rev* v81 no14 p398 Jl 15 2013

FOKKENS, HARRY.ed. The Oxford handbook of the European Bronze Age. See The Oxford handbook of the European Bronze Age

FOLEY, LIZZIE K. Remarkable; a novel; [by] Lizzie K. Foley 325 p. 2012 Dial Books for Young Readers

1. Ability—Fiction 2. Children—Fiction 3. Community life—Fiction 4. Eccentrics and eccentricities—Fiction 5. Fantasy fiction 6. Humorous stories 7. Pirates—Fiction 8. Secrets—Fiction 9. Young adult fiction
ISBN 9780803737068 (hardcover)
LC 2011-021641

SUMMARY: This book presents the story of an average girl named Jane Doe who lives in "the town of Remarkable, so named for its abundance of talented citizens, everyone lives up to its reputation. . . . Jane should be just as remarkable. Instead, this average 10-year-old girl is usually overlooked. . . . Mix in a rival town's dispute over jelly, hints of a Loch Ness Monster-like creature and a psychic pizzeria owner who sees the future in her reflective pizza pans. . . . With the help of her quiet Grandpa John, who's also forgotten most of the time, Jane learns to be true to herself and celebrate the ordinary in life." (Kirkus)

REVIEW: *Booklist* v108 no14 p57 Mr 15 2012 Ann Kelley

REVIEW: *Horn Book Magazine* v88 no2 p103-4 Mr/Ap 2012 Susan Dove Lempke

REVIEW: *Kirkus Rev* v80 no4 p395 F 15 2012

"Remarkable." "The title of this debut says it all. In the town of Remarkable, so named for its abundance of talented citizens, everyone lives up to its reputation. . . . Jane should be just as remarkable. Instead, this average 10-year-old girl is usually overlooked. . . . Mix in a rival town's dispute over jelly, hints of a Loch Ness Monster-like creature and a psychic pizzeria owner who sees the future in her reflective pizza pans, and this uproarious mystery becomes--if even possible--a whole lot funnier. With the help of her quiet Grandpa John, who's also forgotten most of the time, Jane learns to be true to herself and celebrate the ordinary in life. Foley tightly weaves the outlandish threads into a rich, unforgettable story that's quite simply--amazing."

REVIEW: *Publ Wkly* v259 no11 p61 Mr 12 2012

REVIEW: *SLJ* v58 no4 p162 Ap 2012 Clare A. Dombrowski

REVIEW: *Voice of Youth Advocates* v35 no3 p277-8 Ag 2012 Paisley Adams

REVIEW: *Voice of Youth Advocates* v35 no3 p277 Ag 2012 Ursula Adams

FOLEY, MICHAEL STEWART. Front porch politics; the forgotten heyday of American activism in the 1970s and 1980s; [by] Michael Stewart Foley 432 p. 2013 Hill and Wang

1. HISTORY—United States—20th Century 2. Historical literature 3. Political activists—United States—History—20th century 4. Political participation—United States—History—20th century 5. Protest movements—United States—History—20th century
ISBN 9780809054824 (hardback)
LC 2013-014769

SUMMARY: This book by Michael Stewart Foley examines "the lesser-known community-organizing endeavors that surged in the '70s and '80s, taking shape around bread-and-butter issues like jobs and housing. By chiefly examining small-scale, local efforts, Foley builds a case that the '60s movements influenced civic action across the political spectrum, changing the look of democracy in the United States." (Bookforum)

REVIEW: *Bookforum* v20 no3 p52 S-N 2013 SARA MARCUS

"Front Porch Politics: The Forgotten Heydey of American Activism in the 1970s and 1980s." "[Michael Stewart] Foley has done important work by assembling these disparate histories into a single, readable volume. . . . His focus on accidental activists is helpful, too, in challenging the easy opposition of extreme politicos and complacent Middle Americans. . . . Yet this model risks oversimplifying the issues. .. . . Foley consistently plays up the central importance of citizen action, even when it fails, as many of the campaigns in the book ultimately did. And this bias distorts the thrust of his argument: He laments the passing of front-porch politics (and exaggerates the death of community organizing in the process), but he doesn't fully address the paradoxes in his own stories."

REVIEW: *Booklist* v109 no22 p11 Ag 1 2013 Mary Carroll

REVIEW: *Kirkus Rev* v81 no12 p47-8 Je 15 2013

FOLKLORE & FAIRY TALE FUNNIES; 64 2000 HarperCollins Pubs.

1. Children's literature—Works—Grades two through six 2. Children's literature—Works—Preschool through grade two 3. Comic books, strips, etc. 4. Comic books, strips, etc.—Juvenile literature 5. Fairy tales 6. Folklore 7. Folklore—Juvenile literature 8. Young adult literature—Works
ISBN 0-06-028624-5
LC 99-5-1484

SUMMARY: In this anthology of comics based on folklore and fairy tales, edited by Art Spiegelman, "17 contributors" present "a dozen cartoon folktales or folktale spin-offs, five single-page or spread-sized visual puzzles and two role-playing board games." Tales include "Jack and the Beanstalk" and "Humpty Dumpty." (Kirkus Reviews)This is a "collection of 16 contemporary artists' comics-style interpretations of folklore and fairy-tale plots and themes. . . . All ages." (N Y Times Book Rev)

REVIEW: *Booklist* v110 no13 p46 Mr 1 2014 SARAH HUNTER

"Hello Kitty: Here We Go!," "Little Lit: Folklore & Fairy Tale Funnies," and "Nursery Rhyme Comics: 50 Timeless Rhymes From 50 Celebrated Cartoonists." "Hello Kitty is cute, cute, cute! And in this collection of short, wordless comics, she spoofs everything from James Bond flicks to Chandleresque noir. Kids won't be able to resist the cheerful, bubbly art, and parents will chuckle over the artists' clever visual jokes. . . . [Art] Spiegelman and his wife, Françoise Mouly . . . invited 15 stellar talents to create original graphic stories that poke often ironic fun at tales. . . . It's an extravagant treat for readers of all ages. . . . Having 50 of the finest cartoonists draw simple nursery rhymes, each no more than two or three pages long, is such a crazy move that it's borderline genius."

FONG, KEVIN. Extreme medicine; how exploration transformed medicine in the twentieth century; [by] Kevin Fong 304 p. 2014 The Penguin Press

1. Adventure travel—Health aspects 2. Extreme environments—Health aspects 3. First aid in illness and injury 4. Historical literature 5. Space flight—Health aspects

ISBN 1594204705; 9781594204708

LC 2013-028124

SUMMARY: This book, by Kevin Fong, "explores different limits of endurance. . . . The challenges of Arctic exploration created opportunities for breakthroughs in open heart surgery; battlefield doctors pioneered techniques for skin grafts, heart surgery, and trauma car; underwater and outer space exploration have revolutionized our understanding . . . fundamentally changing our ideas about the nature of life and death." (Publisher's note)

REVIEW: *Booklist* v110 no8 p6 D 15 2013 Tony Miksanek

REVIEW: *Choice* v51 no11 p2018 Jl 2014 I. Richman

REVIEW: *Kirkus Rev* v81 no24 p137 D 15 2013

"Extreme Medicine: How Exploration Transformed Medicine in the Twentieth Century". "[Kevin] Fong shares a unique point of view on the development of intensive care as a medical discipline. . . . Fong believes that the demands of manned space flights to Mars will drive new frontiers of medicine. Today, we are only beginning to deal with medical problems (e.g., loss of calcium in bones, inner-ear problems with balance) faced by astronauts who spend time in zero-gravity environments and then return to Earth. A medical thriller of the first order."

REVIEW: *Libr J* v139 no3 p123 F 15 2014 Susanne Caro

REVIEW: *N Y Times Book Rev* p18 Mr 23 2014 VICTORIA SWEET

REVIEW: *Publ Wkly* v260 no49 p73 D 2 2013

REVIEW: *Sci Am* v310 no2 p76 F 2014 Lee Billings Rachel Feltman

"Extreme Medicine: How Exploration Transformed Medicine in the Twentieth Century." "In 'Extreme Medicine,' [author Kevin Fong] writes of . . . medical advancements that have pushed the boundaries of possibility. . . . Fong interweaves historical accounts with engrossing stories of clinical doctors charting new territories to save their patients. In each case, their encounter with physical extremes powered rapid medical advances. . . . The book shows how, 'by probing the very limits of our biology, we may ultimately return with a better appreciation of precisely how our bodies work, what life is, and what it means to be human.'"

FOOD AND DRINK IN AMERICAN HISTORY; a "full course" encyclopedia; 3 v. (xlix, 1473, I-40 p.) 2013 ABC-CLIO

1. Cooking, American—Encyclopedias 2. Encyclopedias & dictionaries 3. Food—Encyclopedias 4. Food—History 5. Food habits—United States—Encyclopedias

ISBN 9781610692328 (hardback)

LC 2013-007323

SUMMARY: This encyclopedia on food and drink in American history "comprises two volumes containing more than 600 alphabetically arranged historical entries on American foods and beverages, as well as dozens of historical recipes for traditional American foods; and a third volume of more than 120 primary source documents." Topics include "tuna fish . . . the canning industry" and the role of "taxation on beverages like tea, rum and whisky" in American political history. (Publisher's note)

REVIEW: *Booklist* v110 no13 p32 Mr 1 2014 Christine Bulson

"Food and Drink in American History: A 'Full Course' Encyclopedia." "[Andrew F.] Smith is a prolific author on food and drink in the U.S., including editing the second edition of 'The Oxford Encyclopedia of Food and Drink in America' (2013). When a reviewer sees a new source with the same author-editor and a similar title, entries, bibliographies, and appendixes, a red flag appears. There is no question that these titles are similar. However, the historical recipes and primary sources of the ABC-CLIO title are unique and useful for research projects. Libraries that own the Oxford encyclopedia will need to decide if both sources are necessary and affordable. 'Food and Drink in American History' is recommended for culinary, sociology, U.S. history, and nutrition collections."

REVIEW: *Choice* v51 no8 p1378 Ap 2014 S. A. Marien

REVIEW: *Libr J* v139 no1 p1 Ja 2014

REVIEW: *SLJ* v60 no4 p66 Ap 2014 Ann West LaPrise

FOOD SYSTEM SUSTAINABILITY; insights from duALIne; 2013 Cambridge University Press

1. Ecological impact 2. Food industry 3. Food security 4. Food waste 5. Sustainable development

ISBN 9781107036468

LC 2012-037614

SUMMARY: This book, edited by Catherine Esnouf and Marie Russel, explores how "as western-style food systems extend further around the world, food sustainability is becoming an increasingly important issue. . . . From 2009 to 2011, the duALIne project, led by INRA and CIRAD, assembled a team of experts to investigate food systems downstream of the farm, from the farm gate, to consumption and the disposal of waste." (Publisher's note)

REVIEW: *Choice* v51 no5 p857 Ja 2014 E. G. Harrington

"Food System Sustainability: Insights From duALIne." "A few chapters have a noticeable French slant, since INRA and GIRAD, two French agricultural research organizations, led the project, but overall, the authors stress the need to take a global and multidisciplinary approach to meeting the food security challenges of the future in a sustainable way. This volume is full of food for thought for advanced students, researchers, and policy makers in agricultural economics, public health, and sociology."

FOOTE, JEFFREY. Beyond addiction; how science and kindness help people change; [by] Jeffrey Foote 336 p. 2014 Scribner

1. Addicts—Behavior modification 2. Addicts—Rehabilitation 3. Compulsive behavior—Patients—Rehabilitation 4. Self-help materials 5. Substance abuse—Patients—Rehabilitation
ISBN 1476709475; 9781476709475 (hardback); 9781476709482 (trade paperback)
LC 2013-032603

SUMMARY: In this book, "addressing family members who feel helpless when faced with addiction," the authors "draw on 40 years of substantiated analysis and clinical research from their Manhattan-based Center for Motivation and Change, a collective recovery treatment program. . . . All three are aggressive proponents of the Community Reinforcement Approach and Family Training rehabilitation strategy, which introduces a real-world, motivational, coordinated approach to a loved one's substance abuse." (Kirkus Reviews)

REVIEW: *Kirkus Rev* v81 no24 p205 D 15 2013

"Beyond Addiction: How Science and Kindness Help People Change". "A sensible, family-focused guide to substance abuse. . . . Bulleted lists and helpful exercises further assist families with identifying the stages of drug abuse, coping mechanisms, modes of self-care, limitations and the importance of positive communication. . . . The authors also include a lengthy, significant chapter on treatment options and available levels of care, all stated, as is most of the book's text, in accessible, everyday language. Objectively written and conveyed with congenial authority, the book offers collective hope to families of substance abusers. Essential outreach on embracing and effectively managing a loved one's addiction."

REVIEW: *Publ Wkly* v260 no50 p60 D 9 2013

FORAY, JENNIFER L. Visions of empire in the Nazi-occupied Netherlands; [by] Jennifer L. Foray xiv, 337 p. 2012 Cambridge University Press

1. Anti-Nazi movement 2. Decolonization—Indonesia—History 3. Decolonization—Netherlands—History 4. Dutch—Indonesia—History—20th century 5. Ethical Policy (Dutch East Indies, 1901-1942) 6. HISTORY—Europe—General 7. Historical literature 8. Imperialism—History—20th century 9. World War, 1939-1945—Netherlands 10. World War, 1939-1945—Underground movements—Netherlands
ISBN 9781107015807 (hardback)
LC 2011-022034

SUMMARY: "This book explores how the experiences of World War II shaped and transformed Dutch perceptions of their centuries-old empire. Focusing on the work of leading anti-Nazi resisters, Jennifer L. Foray examines how the war forced a rethinking of colonial practices and relationships. As Dutch resisters planned for a postwar world bearing little resemblance to that of 1940, they envisioned a wide range of possibilities for their empire . . . and its most prized colony in the East Indies." (Publisher's note)

REVIEW: *Am Hist Rev* v118 no4 p1265-6 O 2013 L. J. Butler

"Visions of Empire in the Nazi-Occupied Netherlands." "The last phase of Dutch colonialism has suffered undue historiographical neglect. This very welcome book represents a major step towards rectifying this anomaly. Jennifer L. Foray has produced an engaging, stimulating, and ultimately convincing study, based on careful and exhaustive research, which amply reinforces and develops existing interpretations of the corrosive influence of war on European colonialism, while clarifying the metropolitan underpinnings of late colonial rule. This scholarly yet highly readable book examines how World War II, particularly almost five years of German occupation, fundamentally altered Dutch people's views of their overseas empire."

FORBES, JAMES R. Spacecraft dynamics and control. See De Ruiter, A. H. J.

FORBES, NANCY. Faraday, Maxwell, and the electromagnetic field. See Mahon, B.

FORD, A. G.il. Under the Same Sun. See Under the Same Sun

FORD, GABRIELLE. Gabe & Izzy; Standing up for America's bullied; [by] Gabrielle Ford 192 p. 2014 Penguin Group USA

1. Bullying 2. Dogs 3. Human-animal relationships 4. Memoirs 5. People with mental disabilities, Writings of
ISBN 080374062X; 9780803740624

SUMMARY: This book, by Gabrielle Ford, "true story of the young woman dubbed 'The Voice of America's Bullied'. . . . Ford developed a degenerative muscle disease, and was harassed by bullies as a result. . . .Then Gabe got a dog, Izzy, who developed an uncannily similar disorder. They were invited to appear on Animal Planet to talk about their bond, . . . and so began Gabe's career as an anti-bullying advocate." (Publisher's note)

REVIEW: *Booklist* v110 no13 p56-8 Mr 1 2014 John Peters

REVIEW: *Kirkus Rev* v82 no2 p140 Ja 15 2014

"Gabe & Izzy: Speaking Up for America's Bullied". "[Gabrielle] Ford's motivational story of overcoming bullying and disability will appeal to dog lovers as well as kids coping with bullying. . . . Their intriguing story is more told than shown; many major events read like summaries. The author's conversational tone softens the issues of disability and bullying for young readers, but it also glosses over incidents that invite deeper reflection. . . . This canine tale is a fine beginning resource for bullied kids and the adults who care about them."

REVIEW: *Voice of Youth Advocates* v36 no6 p80 F 2014 Barbara Fecteau

FORMENTO, ALISON. These rocks count!; [by] Alison Formento 32 p. 2014 Albert Whitman & Company

1. Counting 2. Geology—Juvenile literature 3. Picture books for children 4. Rocks—Fiction 5. School field trips—Fiction
ISBN 9780807578704 (hardback)
LC 2013-031235

SUMMARY: This counting book presents "a look at the ways people use rocks. Ranger Pedra meets the students and introduces them to the notion that rocks have stories to tell. The class counts what they 'hear' from a boulder: one sculptor, two cement trucks, three beetles, four oceanside mounds of drying salt, five baby turtles in the sand, six stalactites dripping water, seven gems, a sidewalk comprising eight pieces of slate, nine bricks and 10 panes of glass." (Kirkus

Reviews)

REVIEW: *Kirkus Rev* v82 no1 p232 Ja 1 2014

"These Rocks Count!". " Mr. Tate's class disappoints their fans with this outing to Rocky Ridge Mountain and a look at the ways people use rocks. . . . [Sarah] Snow's digital collages are well-suited to the subject matter, though the people seem more wooden and obviously digital than in previous entries. Overall, the team of Formento and Snow has not been able to capture the same winning combination of education and story as they did with their first, 'This Tree Counts!' (2010). This latest has the same ambiguous-audience problem that plagued 'These Seas Count!' (2013). . . . An uneven flow may also cause readers to lose interest midway."

REVIEW: *Publ Wkly* v261 no5 p54-5 F 3 2014

REVIEW: *SLJ* v60 no3 p111 Mr 2014 Kathleen Kelly MacMillan

FORRESTER, SIBELAN.ed. Baba Yaga. See Baba Yaga

FORSYTH, JANICE.ed. Aboriginal peoples and sport in Canada. See Aboriginal peoples and sport in Canada

FORSYTH, MARK. Horologicon; [by] Mark Forsyth 286 p. 2013 Penguin Group USA

1. Curiosities & wonders 2. Encyclopedias & dictionaries 3. English language—Archaisms 4. English language—Etymology 5. English language—Obsolete words 6. Everyday life 7. Vocabulary

ISBN 0425264378; 9780425264379

LC 2013-021235

SUMMARY: "The 'Horologicon' (or book of hours) contains the most extraordinary words in the English language, arranged according to what hour of the day you might need them. From Mark Forsyth, the author of . . . 'The Etymologicon,' comes a book of weird words for familiar situations. From ante-jentacular to snudge by way of quafftide and wamblecropt, at last you can say, with utter accuracy, exactly what you mean." (Publisher's note)

REVIEW: *N Y Times Book Rev* p19 D 22 2013 MOIGNON FOGARTY

"The Book of Jezebel: An Illustrated Encyclopedia of Lady Things," "The Horologicon: A Day's Jaunt Through the Lost Words of the English Language," "Wordbirds: An Irreverent Lexicon for the 21st Century." "'The Book of Jezebel' is drawn from the energetic contributors to the Jezebel.com blog, and its editor, Anna Holmes . . . takes care to note that what appears to be a colorful encyclopedia is actually a work fo both fact and opinion. . . . Once you pick up 'The Horologicon' it's hard to put down. As a devotee of useful tips, I approached Mark Forsyth's book with skepticism. . . . Liesl Schillinger's 'Wordbirds' embraces the theme of birds. . . . While 'The Horologicon' shines a light on the past, 'Wordbirds' does the same for our times."

FORSYTHE, CLARKE D. Abuse of discretion; the inside story of Roe v. Wade; [by] Clarke D. Forsythe 496 p. 2012 Encounter Books

1. Abortion—Government policy—United States 2. Abortion—Law and legislation—United States 3. Historical literature 4. Political questions and judicial power—United States 5. Trials (Abortion)—United States

ISBN 9781594036927 (hardcover : alk. paper); 9781594036934 (ebook)

LC 2013-003349

SUMMARY: This book, by Clarke D. Forsythe, "is a critical review of the behind-the-scenes deliberations that went into the Supreme Court's abortion decisions . . . . The first half of the book looks at the mistakes made by the Justices, based on the case files, the oral arguments, and the Justices' papers. The second half of the book critically examines the unintended consequences of the abortion decisions in law, politics, and women's health." (Publisher's note)

REVIEW: *Natl Rev* v65 no22 p48-9 N 25 2013 RAMESH PONNURU

"Abuse of Discretion: The Inside Story of Roe v. Wade." "A longtime legal strategist for the pro-life movement, [Clarke D.] Forsythe has gone deep into the archives to shed new light on Roe and its companion case, Doe v. Bolton. Even people who have studied the issue will learn something new. . . . Forsythe does not render harsh judgments on any of the justices he discusses, but the reader has sufficient evidence to conclude that some of the justices were politicians in robes, and shifty politicians at that."

FORT, RODNEY. 15 sports myths and why they're wrong; [by] Rodney Fort viii, 299 p. 2013 Stanford Economics & Finance, an imprint of Stanford University Press

1. College sports—Economic aspects—United States 2. Economics literature 3. Professional sports—Economic aspects—United States 4. Sports—Economic aspects—United States 5. Sports literature

ISBN 0804774366; 9780804774369 (cloth : acid-free paper)

LC 2013-014691

SUMMARY: In this book, authors Rodney Fort and Jason Winfree "bust some of the most widespread urban legends about college and professional athletics. Each chapter takes apart a common misconception, showing how the assumptions behind it fail to add up. . . . [They] reveal how these myths perpetuate themselves and, ultimately, how they serve a handful of powerful parties--such as franchise owners, reporters, and players--at the expense of the larger community of sports fans." (Publisher's note)

REVIEW: *Choice* v51 no7 p1270-1 Mr 2014 D. A. Coffin

"15 Sports Myths and Why They're Wrong." "The authors approach the issues by using a variant of the 'principal-agent' model, in which university administrators are the principals and athletic directors are their agents. This is a useful approach, and the authors generally use it well. . . . There is little to disagree with in the authors' analysis, given their starting point. What is less clear is to whom this work is directed. Two potential audiences are general readers interested in the role of sports in society and students enrolled in sports economics courses (and their instructors). This reviewer's somewhat reluctant conclusion is that the results fall awkwardly between these two audiences."

FORTENBERRY, JULIE.il. Sadie's Lag Ba'omer mystery. See Korngold, J.

FORTENBERRY, JULIE.il. Sadie's almost marvelous menorah. See Korngold, J.

FORTES, DOMINIC. Planetary geology. See Vita-Finzi, C.

FORTIN, JEFFREY A.ed. Atlantic biographies. See Atlantic biographies

FORTUNATI, LEOPOLDINA.ed. Migration, diaspora, and information technology in global societies. See Migration, diaspora, and information technology in global societies

FORWARD, TOBY. Fireborn; [by] Toby Forward 432 p. 2013 Bloomsbury

1. Apprentices—Fiction 2. Fantasy 3. Fire—Fiction 4. JUVENILE FICTION—Action & Adventure—General 5. JUVENILE FICTION—Fantasy & Magic 6. JUVENILE FICTION—General 7. Wizards—Fiction

ISBN 1599908891; 9781599908892 (hardback)

LC 2013-012055

SUMMARY: In this book, the prequel to Toby Forward's book "Dragonborn," "when greedy wizard Slowin steals both name and power from his apprentice, Bee, the conflagration affects magic everywhere. Meanwhile, twelve-year-old Cabbage's own master, Flaxfield, suddenly loses all his magic, and Cabbage finds that he and a newm friend, Perry the (Hobbit-like) roffle, are the only ones with the ability to amend the situation." (Horn Book Magazine)

REVIEW: *Horn Book Magazine* v89 no6 p91-2 N/D 2013 DEIRDRE F. BAKER

"Fireborn." "[Toby] Forward's sturdy, precise manner of expression has deepened as he has moved backwards from 'Dragonborn' . . . to its prequel, 'Fireborn'; indeed, here his prose often takes on a luminous quality that suits the story's fire imagery. . . . Memorable, convincing adult figures mingle with the young protagonists in this story, but the curiosity, courage, and talents of Bee, Cabbage, and Perry, growing into adolescence, are at its heart. An intelligent, down-to-earth wisdom runs throughout, as enriching as any magic."

REVIEW: *Kirkus Rev* v81 no21 p35 N 1 2013

REVIEW: *SLJ* v60 no2 p86 F 2014 Eva Mitnick

REVIEW: *Voice of Youth Advocates* v36 no6 p70 F 2014 Maia Raynor

REVIEW: *Voice of Youth Advocates* v36 no6 p69-70 F 2014 Deena Viviani

FORWOOD, GILLIAN. Lina Bryans; rare modern, 1909-2000; [by] Gillian Forwood 214 2003 Miegunyah Press

1. Artists 2. Australian painting—20th century 3. Biography (Literary form) 4. Painters

ISBN 0-522-85037-5

LC 2003—447443

SUMMARY: This book by Gillian Forwood presents a biography of painter Lina Bryans. "A rare feminist raised within the confines of one of Melbourne's elite Jewish families and apolitical in public, Bryans was an unwitting early role model for liberated women artists in Australia. She braved divorce to live a bohemian life as a painter at a time when unmarried women with children were scorned." (Choice: Current Reviews for Academic Libraries)

REVIEW: *Choice* v51 no10 p1741 Je 2014 M. R. Vendryes

"Lina Bryans: Rare Modern, 1909-2000". "Bryans, a talented self-taught painter, is finally given due credit for her contributions to Australian art, particularly mid 20th-century painting in Melbourne. . . . [Gillian] Forwood's admirable tribute to Bryans charts her development with biographical details punctuated by mostly color reproductions of Bryans' best work. . . . This biography of Bryans is organized chronologically to highlight her involvement in the arts at crucial moments in Melbourne's history."

FOSCARI, ANTONIO. Tumult and Order. See Tumult and Order

FOSTER, CECIL. Independence; [by] Cecil Foster 328 p. 2014 Harper Collins Canada

1. Barbados—History 2. Coming of age 3. Friendship—Fiction 4. Grandparent & child—Fiction 5. Historical fiction

ISBN 1443415057; 9781443415057

SUMMARY: This book, by Cecil Foster, looks at newly independent Barbados in the 1960s, "as seen through the eyes of 13-year-old Christopher Lucas. Like his childhood friend and neighbour Stephie, Christopher is a 'grandmother chile,' raised under old-fashioned customs. . . . Christopher and Stephie's mothers live and work 'over-'n'-away' in Canada. . . . Christopher must reconcile all the changes taking place around him and inside him without the help of a father or mother." (Quill & Quire)

REVIEW: *Quill Quire* v80 no2 p24-5 Mr 2014 Safa Jinje

"Independence". "Cecil Foster was 12 years old in 1966 when Barbados gained independence from Britain. Foster's first novel in almost a dozen years delves into the formative period of the newly liberated nation, as seen through the eyes of 13-year-old Christopher Lucas. . . 'Independence' is a richly detailed novel, offering a vivid portrait of a Bajan society in flux. The land, the flavourful food (and its strenuous preparation), the packed dance halls, and the sweltering heat all feel so present and real that readers may find themselves tasting the salt of an imagined sea breeze."

FOSTER, LORI. Turn Up the Heat; Love Won't Wait / Beach House Beginnings / Strong Enough to Love; [by] Lori Foster 336 p. 2013 Harlequin Books

1. Human sexuality—Fiction 2. Love stories 3. Man-woman relationships—Fiction 4. Premarital sex 5. Single women—Fiction

ISBN 0373778384; 9780373778386

SUMMARY: This collection of romance novellas, by Lori Foster, Christie Ridgway, and Victoria Dahl, "explore[s] a 'sex-only lovers' theme as a first step on the risky road to love. Three once-burned-in-love, twice-shy characters decide to explore passion rather than love by picking a sexual partner they decide won't have access to their vulnerable emotional selves." (Kirkus Reviews)

REVIEW: *Kirkus Rev* v81 no24 p252 D 15 2013

"Turn Up the Heat". " Three sizzling tales explore a "sex-only lovers" theme as a first step on the risky road to love. Three once-burned-in-love, twice-shy characters decide to explore passion rather than love by picking a sexual partner they decide won't have access to their vulnerable emotional selves. In [Lori] Foster's 'Love Won't Wait,' waitress Merrily is too old to be a virgin, and most men consider her virginity a challenge to conquer. She decides to proposition her customer/crush, Brick. . . . Three romance novelists known for sizzling, emotional stories deliver an entertaining, diverting set of novellas hot enough to warm a cold winter night."

FOSTER, PAUL.ed. William Hayley (1745-1820), Selected Poetry. See William Hayley (1745-1820), Selected Poetry

FOSTER, PAUL.ed. William Hayley (1745-1820), Poet, Biographer and Libertarian. See Barsham, D.

FOTHERINGHAM, EDWIN.il. A Home for Mr. Emerson. See Kerley, B.A.

FOTHERINGHAM, EDWIN.il. Tony Baloney. See Ryan, P. M.

FOTIADE, RAMONA. À bout de souffle; [by] Ramona Fotiade 142 p. 2013 I.B. Tauris

1. Film criticism 2. French films 3. Godard, Jean Luc, 1930- 4. Motion pictures—History—20th century 5. À bout de souffle (Film)

ISBN 9781780765082 (hardcover); 9781780765099 (softcover)

LC 2012-277892

SUMMARY: "In this original guide to the film, Ramona Fotiade analyses in depth its production and reception, as well as its mise-en-scène and editing. She situates À Bout de souffle in relation to Godard's filmography and critical writings up to 1960, focusing on a narrative and visual discourse that is now identified with a distinctive strand in postmodern French cinema." (Publisher's note)

REVIEW: *TLS* no5781 p27 Ja 17 2014 JEROME DE GROOT

"À Bout De Souffle." "[Author Ramona] Fotiade grounds [filmmaker Jean-Luc] Godard's work in several contexts. She considers his film criticism in some detail to emphasize the development of a serious and engaged manifesto for the film, accounting for a desire for conscious innovation rather than accidental amateurish effect. The work on Godard's theories of montage is excellent. Fotiade outlines the production process and explains how some decisions that seem important were simply down to budget. . . . Her work on Godard's early short movies is important, and locates his later approaches in some of these short and rare pieces. . . . Fotiade's account gives Godard intellectual and aesthetic control over what he was doing."

FOUR DAYS; the historical record of the death of President Kennedy; 143 p. 1964 American Heritage Pub. Co.

1. Historical literature 2. Presidents—Assassination—United States—History 3. United States—History—1961-1969

LC 6401-5726

SUMMARY: "This . . . coffee-table book . . . covers the days of national shock, from [John F.] Kennedy's assassination in Dallas to his funeral cortege in Washington. . . . It includes . . . [an] eyewitness piece by U.P.I's Merriman Smith, dean of the White House correspondents, who spread the news of the shooting around the world." (New York Times Book Review)

REVIEW: *N Y Times Book Rev* p24 O 27 2013 JILL ABRAMSON

"The Making of a President 1960," "Four Days: The Historical Record of the Death of President Kennedy," and "The Kennedy Tapes: Inside the White House During the Cuban Missile Crisis." "The classic that gave birth to the campaign book genre provides fly-on-the-wall detail about every aspect of [John F.] Kennedy's climb to the White House. Although everyone knows how the story ends, [Theodore H.] White builds considerable narrative tension. . . . This slim coffee-table book, full of arresting photographs, covers the days of national shock, from Kennedy's assassination in Dallas to his funeral cortege in Washington, with raw intensity. . . . This book of transcriptions gives readers the opportunity to sit in as history is being made by a small group of advisers, led by a stoical president."

FOURARI, CLARICE MARIE. Faith in Family; One Women's Journey Through Trauma Leads Her to Embrace Family; [by] Clarice Marie Fourari 226 p. 2013 Createspace Independent Pub

1. Breast cancer 2. Emotional trauma 3. Faith 4. Families 5. Memoirs 6. Self-help materials

ISBN 1491046678; 9781491046678

SUMMARY: This book by Clarice Marie Fourari presents an "in-depth examination of her life, including her parents' marriage and subsequent divorce, her birth father's suicide and several other family tragedies." Particular focus is given to her struggle with breast cancer. "As she makes her way through biopsies, chemotherapy and reconstructive surgery, Fourari decides to slow down her life and savor the things that matter—namely, her family and her faith." (Kirkus Reviews)

REVIEW: *Kirkus Rev* v82 no2 p332 Ja 15 2014

"Faith in Family: One Woman's Journey Through Trauma Leads Her to Embrace Family". " While her story is certainly relatable and engaging, readers are likely to have heard the lessons before. Overall, the book walks the line between being a memoir and a self-help guide without ever clearly settling on one side or the other. . . . The book stays true to its intention to explore the importance of family by including a large cast of characters, which can make the story drag at times, especially when those characters rarely play a large role in the narrative. Nevertheless, [Clarice Marie] Fourari's approachability and humor are inspiring and engaging, and readers struggling with illness are sure to find comfort in these pages. Standard self-help fare, but humorous and thorough."

FOURNIER, MARCEL. Emile Durkheim; [by] Marcel Fournier 700 p. 2012 John Wiley & Sons Inc

1. Biography (Literary form) 2. Durkheim, Émile, 1858-1917 3. Sociologists—Biography 4. Sociology—History 5. Sociology—Methodology

ISBN 074564645X; 9780745646459

SUMMARY: This book examines the"life and thought of Émile Durkheim, one of the great founding fathers of sociology. . . . He brought about a revolution in the social sciences: the defence of the autonomy of sociology as a science, the systematic elaboration of rules and methods for studying the social, the condemnation of racial theories, the critique of

Eurocentrism and the rehabilitation of the humanity of 'the primitive'." (Publisher's note)

REVIEW: *Br J Sociol* v64 no3 p551-2 S 2013 Mark Erickson

REVIEW: *Choice* v51 no3 p556 N 2013 P. Kivisto

REVIEW: *Contemp Sociol* v43 no2 p165-71 Mr 2014 David N. Smith

"Émile Durkheim: 1858-1917" and "Émile Durkheim: A Biography". "[Marcel] Fournier offers rich new evidence concerning Durkheim's ill-starred encounter with his critics, much of which should cast doubt, at the very least, on the still-current stereotype. But Fournier also shows that, from the very start, many of Durkheim's critics seemed almost immune to his actual words; indeed, some seemed positively enamored of the image of Durkheim the Metaphysician, elevating Society over the Individual. Fournier's chronicle allows us to see how this happened, year by year, as if we were watching time-lapse photography. . . . What Fournier offers, above all, is material drawn from Durkheim's correspondence. . . . Only dedicated specialists will have the patience to wade through the endless detail, and few will regard Fournier's attempt to turn this detail into a rounded biography as a literary success. . . . But Fournier offers many invaluable nuggets."

REVIEW: *Contemp Sociol* v43 no2 p161-5 Mr 2014 Massimo Borlandi

REVIEW: *TLS* no5735 p5-7 Mr 1 2013 BERNICE MARTIN

FOWLER, CHRISTOPHER. The Invisible Code; a Peculiar Crimes Unit mystery; [by] Christopher Fowler 368 p. 2013 Bantam Books

1. Bryant, Arthur (Fictitious character)—Fiction 2. Crime—Fiction 3. Detective & mystery stories 4. May, John (Fictitious character)—Fiction 5. Murder—Investigation—Fiction 6. Police—England—London—Fiction

ISBN 0345528654; 9780345528650 (acid-free paper)
LC 2012-048699

SUMMARY: This book, by Christopher Fowler, is part of the Peculiar Crimes Unit Mystery series. "London's craftiest and boldest detectives, Arthur Bryant and John May, are back in this deviously twisting mystery of black magic, madness, and secrets hidden in plain sight. . . . Called into headquarters by Oskar Kasavian, the head of Home Office security, Bryant and May are shocked to hear that their longtime adversary now desperately needs their help." (Publisher's note)

REVIEW: *Kirkus Rev* v81 no24 p34 D 15 2013

REVIEW: *N Y Times Book Rev* p19 Ja 5 2014 MARLIYN STASIO

"Dark Times in the City," "The Invisible Code," and "The Midas Murders." "In Gene Kerrigan's novel 'Dark Times in the City' . . . Kerrigan writes with a grim elegance that takes the edge off the blunt language and brutal deeds of his underworld villains and spares some grace for their hapless victims. . . . There are witches on Fleet Street in 'The Invisible Code.' . . . There are also devils and demons and ladies who lunch in Christopher Fowler's latest madcap mystery about the strange police detectives in London's Peculiar Crimes Unit. . . . In 'The Midas Murders' . . . , a new police procedural (its rhetorical excesses intact in Brian Doyle's translation) from Pieter Aspe. . . . It's all intricately plotted by Aspe."

REVIEW: *New York Times* v163 no56355 pC7 D 19 2013 JANET MASLIN

"The Invisible Code: A Peculiar Crimes Unit Mystery". "[Christopher Fowler's] strengths are humor and Holmesian cogitation. . . . Mr. Fowler's small but ardent American following deserves to get much larger. and 'The Invisible Code' is a delightful introduction to his work. . . . 'The Invisible Code' has immense charm, but its plotting will satisfy serious mystery fans, too. . . . Mr. Fowler creates a fine blend of vivid descriptions . . . quick thinking and artful understatement. . . . Mr. Fowler's many other works would also be welcome here, since he has written much more than this detective series."

REVIEW: *Publ Wkly* v260 no40 p30 O 7 2013

FOWLER, CHRISTOPHER. The memory of blood; a Peculiar Crimes Unit mystery; [by] Christopher Fowler 333 p. 2012 Bantam Books

1. Bryant, Arthur (Fictitious character)—Fiction 2. Detective & mystery stories 3. Infanticide—Fiction 4. May, John (Fictitious character)—Fiction 5. Murder—Investigation—Fiction 6. Police—England—London—Fiction

ISBN 9780345528636 (acid-free paper); 9780345532138 (ebook)
LC 2011-017511

SUMMARY: In this book, "the Peculiar Crimes Unit . . . celebrates its new digs in Caledonian Road by investigating a murder whose leading suspect is Mr. Punch, of Punch and Judy fame. The party to celebrate the opening of Ray Pryce's The Two Murderers . . . comes to a crashing end with the news that theater owner Robert Kramer's 1-year-old son Noah has been hurled from his nursery window. Marks from the hands of a life-size puppet of Punch lying nearby are around the infant's neck; the nursery door is locked from the inside; and the window is utterly inaccessible from the outside. . . . Called to the scene by the bizarre nature of the crime, Arthur Bryant and John May find many outsized egos . . . but no answers to the obvious questions." (Kirkus)

REVIEW: *Booklist* v108 no13 p49 Mr 1 2012 Allison Block

REVIEW: *Kirkus Rev* v80 no4 p348 F 15 2012

"The Memory of Blood." "The Peculiar Crimes Unit (Bryant & May Off the Rails, 2010, etc.) celebrates its new digs in Caledonian Road by investigating a murder whose leading suspect is Mr. Punch, of Punch and Judy fame. . . . Though no single element stands out, Fowler achieves a fine balance between the impossible crime, the juggling of suspects and motives, Mr. Bryant's flights of recondite erudition, the planting and decoding of clues and the obligatory plots to discredit and disband the PCU."

REVIEW: *Libr J* v137 no1 p77 Ja 1 2012 Wilda Williams

REVIEW: *Publ Wkly* v259 no8 p149 F 20 2012

FOWLER, THERESE ANNE. Z; A Novel of Zelda Fitzgerald; [by] Therese Anne Fowler 375 p. 2013 St. Martin's Press

1. Authors—Fiction 2. Authors' spouses—Fiction 3. Historical fiction 4. Nineteen twenties—Fiction

ISBN 1250028655 (hardcover); 9781250028655 (hardcover)

LC 2013-003452

SUMMARY: This novel by Therese Anne Fowler follows "Jazz Age legends F. Scott and Zelda Fitzgerald. . . . The famous couple have a whirlwind courtship in Montgomery, Ala., where Scott was briefly stationed at the end of WWI, and Zelda was the talk of the town. Then Fowler unfolds the next 20 years: the couple's New York celebrity after 'This Side of Paradise'; the years in Paris with the other 'Lost Generation' expats; and their return to the U.S. to treat Zelda's schizophrenia." (Publishers Weekly)

REVIEW: *Booklist* v109 no12 p37 F 15 2013 Allison Block

REVIEW: *Kirkus Rev* v81 no1 p9 Ja 1 2013

REVIEW: *Libr J* v137 no16 p54 O 1 2012 Barbara Hoffert

REVIEW: *Libr J* v138 no1 p84 Ja 1 2013 Shannon Marie Robinson Andrea Brooks Sally Bissell

REVIEW: *N Y Times Book Rev* p16 Ap 21 2013 PENELOPE GREEN

REVIEW: *New Statesman* v142 no5157 p42-3 My 10 2013 Sarah Churchwell

REVIEW: *Publ Wkly* v260 no7 p37-8 F 18 2013

REVIEW: *Publ Wkly* v260 no14 p13 Ap 8 2013 Seth Satterlee

REVIEW: *TLS* no5749 p17-8 Je 7 2013 PAULA BYRNE

"Melting the Snow on Hester Street," "Z: A Novel of Zelda Fitzgerald," and "Beautiful Fools: The Last Affair of Zelda and Scott Fitzgerald." "[Daisy] Waugh creates the early Hollywood world with verve and conviction in this taut, clever and moving novel. . . . Capturing that voice is no easy feat and [Therese Anne] Fowler does not succeed. Nor does she believe that Zelda was insane, although a cursory glance at the family lineage reveals a long history of mental illness and suicide on both sides. . . . To underplay this, as Fowler's novel does, is to deny her painful and courageous struggle to come to terms with her pitiful condition. . . . R. Clifton Spargo's 'Beautiful Fools' . . . is historical fiction at its best, imaginatively filling the gaps and bringing us intimately into a portrait of a marriage."

FOX, AARON S. Shoe Shine Lady; [by] Aaron S. Fox 238 p. 2013 CreateSpace Independent Publishing Platform

1. Businesspeople—Fiction 2. Cities & towns—Fiction 3. Marriage—Fiction 4. Psychological fiction 5. Steel mills

ISBN 1484089804; 9781484089804

SUMMARY: In this book, "Belle Reinker's life is defined by the West-Penn steel mill. . . Belle's father and her husband, Mike, both work at the mill, and Belle is the secretary of the union. But when the mill refuses to renew its contract with the union and the workers go on strike, Belle knows it signals the beginning of the end. . . . Without telling her family, Belle takes out a second mortgage and sets up a shoeshine stand in a nearby hotel. Her business thrives, but her marriage is strained." (Kirkus Reviews)

REVIEW: *Kirkus Rev* v82 no1 p310 Ja 1 2014

"Shoe Shine Lady". "[Aaron S.] Fox succeeds in bringing the town to life and deftly establishes the conflict between the forces that divide it. Unfortunately, the multifaceted premise is sometimes undermined by awkward writing. Even though Fox emphasizes that his characters are direct straight shooters, he sprinkles pretentious vocabulary throughout the story. Mill workers nurse their beers in "tenebrous saloons," a planned lodge is hailed as "cynosure of the entire valley," and the old steel mill is "fuliginous." In most cases, simpler language would have enhanced the story. A worthwhile, though a bit overwritten, American story about family, friendship and hard work."

FOX, ADRIAN.ed. Antarctic Peninsula. See Antarctic Peninsula

FOXHALL, KATHERINE. Health, medicine, and the sea; Australian voyages, c.1815-1860; [by] Katherine Foxhall xi, 250 p. 2012 Manchester University Press Distributed in the U.S. by Palgrave Macmillan

1. Convict ships—Health aspects 2. Historical literature 3. History, 19th Century—Australia 4. History, 19th Century—Great Britain 5. Naval Medicine—history—Australia 6. Naval Medicine—history—Great Britain 7. Oceans and Seas—Australia 8. Oceans and Seas—Great Britain 9. Penal transportation—Australia—History—19th century 10. Prisoners—Australia—History—19th century 11. Prisoners—Health and hygiene 12. Prisoners—Transportation—Medical care—History—19th century 13. Prisoners—history—Australia 14. Prisoners—history—Great Britain 15. Transients and Migrants—history—Australia 16. Transients and Migrants—history—Great Britain 17. Travel Medicine—history—Australia 18. Travel Medicine—history—Great Britain

ISBN 0719085713; 9780719085710 (pbk.)

LC 2012-406882

SUMMARY: This "book about health, medicine, and sea voyages to Australia . . . focus[es] on voyaging emigrants and convicts—and their transformation into 'colonists' at the end of their journeys." Author Katherine Foxhall shows "how colonialism and its dynamics can shed light on the worlds of emigrants and their experiences of health and illness." (American Historical Review)

REVIEW: *Am Hist Rev* v119 no2 p505-6 Ap 2014 Catharine Coleborne

REVIEW: *Engl Hist Rev* v129 no536 p230-1 F 2014 Zoë Laidlaw

"Health, Medicine and the Sea: Australian Voyages c.1815-1860". "Structured to resemble a voyage from the British Isles to Australia, Katherine Foxhall's book opens the reader's eyes to an often overlooked component of convict and emigrant experience. . . . This is an excellent and persuasive work, marrying the histories of medicine, penal transportation, and colonialism with maritime geography. . . . This is a work which will challenge historians of empire and migration to give more thought to those (often) apparently static chapters in travelogues and diaries in which passengers simply glided across the sea, eventually to emerge onto dry land and back into 'history'. Foxhall shows that we should not ignore the journey itself, whether for free or enchained."

REVIEW: *History* v99 no334 p186-7 Ja 2014 Jonathan Lamb

FOXLEE, KAREN. The midnight dress; [by] Karen Foxlee 288 p. 2013 Alfred A. Knopf

1. Alcoholism—Fiction 2. Eccentrics and eccentricities—Fiction 3. Friendship—Fiction 4. Mystery and detective stories 5. Schools—Fiction 6. Sewing—Fiction

7. Single-parent families—Fiction
ISBN 0375856455; 9780375856457; 9780375956454 (library binding); 9780449818213 (ebook)
LC 2012-029108

SUMMARY: In this book by Karen Foxlee, "Rose doesn't expect to fall in love with the . . . town of Leonora. Nor does she expect to become fast friends with . . . Pearl Kelly, organizer of the high school float at the annual Harvest Festival parade. Pearl convinces Rose to visit Edie Baker, once a renowned dressmaker, now a rumored witch. Together Rose and Edie hand-stitch [a dress] for Rose to wear at the Harvest Festival--a dress that will have long-lasting consequences." (Publisher's note)

REVIEW: *Booklist* v110 no4 p48 O 15 2013 Lexi Walters Wright

REVIEW: *Bull Cent Child Books* v67 no5 p266 Ja 2014 K. C.

"The Midnight Dress." "Each chapter starts with either an unfolding description of what happened or an update on the investigation, then shifts to flashbacks of the events that lead up to the night of the festival, keeping the mystery taut but also reminding readers that Rose's year of hope and transformation did not end well. Rose spends much of her time in the green world of the rain forest and beach that make up the edges of the town; her mental and emotional awakening is conveyed by her growing physical ability to navigate the terrain, which is described with alluring and loving detail. Readers who appreciate layered coming-of-age stories cut short by tragedy and tinged with mystery will enjoy this, especially if they have an affinity for wild spaces."

REVIEW: *Horn Book Magazine* v90 no1 p90 Ja/F 2014 KATRINA HEDEEN

"The Midnight Dress." "Though ostensibly the tale of a magical midnight-blue dress, there are many story lines within [Karen] Foxlee's complex novel: Pearl and Rose's close but strained friendship; the girls' tip-toeing into their own sexual relationships; Edie Baker's sad history; the powerful lure of the neighboring mountain, described vividly and mystically; Rose's relationship with her impenetrable father and Pearl's tireless search for her own one-night-stand dad; and also, importantly, the narration (in italics opening each chapter) of the investigation into the tragedy that befalls one of the girls. Though the layers are many, they coalesce into a dreamlike, eerie whole told in mesmerizing, sensuous prose."

REVIEW: *Kirkus Rev* v81 no17 p90 S 1 2013

REVIEW: *Publ Wkly* v261 no1 p53-4 Ja 6 2014

REVIEW: *Publ Wkly* p130-2 Children's starred review annual 2013

REVIEW: *Publ Wkly* v260 no36 p59 S 9 2013

REVIEW: *SLJ* v59 no10 p1 O 2013 Georgia Christgau

REVIEW: *SLJ* v60 no1 p58 Ja 2014 Amanda Raklovits

REVIEW: *Voice of Youth Advocates* v36 no6 p58 F 2014 Meghann Meeusen

FRAILE, MEDARDO. Things look different in the light and other stories. See Things look different in the light and other stories

FRAME, JANET, 1924-2004. In the memorial room; a novel; [by] Janet Frame 208 p. 2013 Counterpoint

1. Authors 2. Authorship—Fiction 3. FICTION—Literary 4. Literature—Scholarships, fellowships, etc. 5. Memorials 6. Memory—Fiction
ISBN 1619021757; 9781619021754 (hardback)
LC 2013-018057

SUMMARY: In this book, author Janet Frame "portray[s] historical fiction writer Harry Gill's travails after being awarded the annual Watercress-Armstrong Fellowship. The award, given in honor of the (fictional) poet Margaret Rose Hurndell, requires him to travel to Menton, [France] where Hurndell once lived. Harry finds himself struggling to turn his good fortune into productivity." (Publishers Weekly)

REVIEW: *Kirkus Rev* v81 no21 p38 N 1 2013

REVIEW: *Libr J* v138 no18 p78 N 1 2013 Faye Chadwell

REVIEW: *N Y Times Book Rev* p24 N 24 2013 SCOTT BRADFIELD

"In the Memorial Room." "This short, funny and often beautifully written novel . . . provides an excellent occasion for remembering the weird wisdom and genuine talent of Janet Frame. . . . 'In the Memorial Room' is filled with terrifyingly beautiful reflections on how reading books (and even reading them) can feel like digging your own grave. It also serves as a sly warning to those of us who obsessively cherish the works of writers--even writers as good as Janet Frame. Watch out! The death you memorialize may well be your own."

REVIEW: *Publ Wkly* v260 no31 p43 Ag 5 2013

FRAME, RONALD. Havisham; [by] Ronald Frame 357 p. 2013 Faber & Faber

1. Dickens, Charles, 1812-1870 2. Emotional trauma 3. Fan fiction 4. Heiresses 5. Rich people—Fiction
ISBN 0571288286; 1250037271; 9780571288281; 9781250037275

SUMMARY: Written by Ronald Frame, this novel describes how "Before she became the immortal and haunting Miss Havisham of [Charles Dickens's novel] 'Great Expectations,' she was Catherine, a young woman with all of her dreams ahead of her." This book "unfurls the psychological trauma that made young Catherine into Miss Havisham and cursed her to a life alone, roaming the halls of the mansion in the tatters of the dress she wore for the wedding she was never to have." (Publisher's note)

REVIEW: *Kirkus Rev* p15 N 15 2013 Best Books

REVIEW: *Kirkus Rev* v81 no18 p5 S 15 2013

REVIEW: *N Y Times Book Rev* p15 D 1 2013 JANE SMILEY

REVIEW: *N Y Times Book Rev* p80 D 8 2013

REVIEW: *New Yorker* v89 no43 p67-1 Ja 6 2014

"Havisham." "This literary prequel imagines the life of Catherine Havisham, from privileged childhood to the macabre death scene of Dickens's 'Great Expectations.' Adopting a character whose fate is sealed reduces the potential for surprise, but Frame's book is a pleasurable read. He wisely refrains from mimicking Dickens's style, writing in Catherine's voice (which reaches us, strangely, from beyond the grave). . . . The novel runs into trouble, though, as its time line catches up to the story we know."

REVIEW: *New Yorker* v89 no43 p67-1 Ja 6 2014

REVIEW: *Publ Wkly* v260 no31 p44 Ag 5 2013

REVIEW: *TLS* no5718 p20 N 2 2012 TREV BROUGH-

TON

FRANCIS, GAVIN. Empire Antarctica; ice, silence, and emperor penguins; [by] Gavin Francis 304 p. 2013 Counterpoint

1. Antarctica –Discovery & exploration 2. Emperor penguin 3. Memoirs 4. Natural history—Antarctica
ISBN 1619021846; 9781619021846
LC 2013-018055

SUMMARY: This book presents an "account of [author Gavin Francis'] 14 months at Halley, a British research station on the coast of Antarctica. . . . While providing thoughtful observations on the life cycle and mating habits of . . . [Emperor] penguins, [Gavin] Francis also offers a history lesson about past Antarctic pioneers--Ernest Shackleton, Apsley Cherry-Garrard, William Spears Bruce--regaling the reader with the triumphs and failures of his predecessors." (Publishers Weekly)

REVIEW: *Booklist* v110 no2 p22 S 15 2013 Nancy Bent

"Empire Antarctica: Ice, Silence, and Emperor Penguins." "In this lyrical book, [Gavin]n Francis plumbs his fascination with the barren continent, the very blankness of which intrigued him, empty as it is of human history or cultural memory. . . . Woven into the narrative are stories from past Antarctic explorers, most notably the disaster and miraculous escape of the [Ernest] Shackleton expedition, as well as lesser-known biologists and their early notes on emperor penguins and the embryology of their eggs. Francis is an' evocative writer; we feel the cold and the dark, revel in the silence, and find kinship with the penguins."

REVIEW: *Economist* v409 no8858 p89 O 19 2013

REVIEW: *Kirkus Rev* v81 no17 p54 S 1 2013

REVIEW: *Libr J* v138 no12 p100 Jl 1 2013 Sue O'Brien

REVIEW: *Publ Wkly* v260 no26 p76 Jl 1 2013

REVIEW: *TLS* no5743 p8-9 Ap 26 2013 RICHARD HAMBLYN

FRANCIS, MATTHEW. Muscovy; [by] Matthew Francis 80 p. 2013 Faber & Faber

1. Boyle, Robert, 1627-1691 2. English poetry 3. Historical poetry 4. Poems—Collections 5. Russia—In literature
ISBN 0571297358 (hbk.); 9780571297351 (hbk.)

SUMMARY: This book of poetry "explores a world of marvels, real and fantastic. A man takes off for the moon in an engine drawn by geese, a poltergeist moves into a remote Welsh village, and a party of seventeenth-century Englishmen encounter the wonders of Russia--sledges, vodka, skating and Easter eggs. The scientist Robert Boyle basks in the newly discovered radiance of phosphorus . . . and the theme of light in darkness is taken up by the more personal poems in the book." (Publisher's note)

REVIEW: *TLS* no5770 p28 N 1 2013 WILLIAM WOOTTEN

"Muscovy." "[Matthew] Francis's last collection, 'Muscovy' not only finds the past a foreign country, it also visits other countries there. In so doing it tells of things done differently, it brings home the strange and wonderful. . . . Matthew Francis is most himself when done up in period costume or moving through a labyrinth. In his meticulous arrangements of stress and syllable and stanza, in his Oulipian schemes, he is a poet of conspicuous and inventive formal accomplishment. But, as with his adaptation and inhabiting of his source material, the artifice is worked on by a strong, sensuous imagination. 'Muscovy' is not only an impressive collection but one which offers rich pleasures."

FRANK, JEFFREY. Ike and dick; portrait of a strange political marriage; [by] Jeffrey Frank 448 p. 2013 Simon & Schuster

1. Historical literature 2. Presidents—United States—Biography
ISBN 1416587012; 9781416587019 (hardcover); 9781416588207 (ebook)
LC 2012-015138

SUMMARY: Author Jeffrey Frank's book on the "1952 presidential election focuses on Republican vice presidential candidate" Richard Nixon. "Easily winning the Republican presidential nomination, Eisenhower left the choice of a running mate to advisers, who picked Nixon: a first-term senator, he was much younger, politically astute, and possessing suitably fierce anticommunist credentials." (Publishers Weekly)

REVIEW: *Booklist* v109 no7 p11 D 1 2012 Gilbert Taylor

REVIEW: *Economist* v406 no8821 p73 F 2 2013

REVIEW: *Kirkus Rev* v80 no22 p11 N 15 2012

REVIEW: *Libr J* v137 no20 p90 D 1 2012 Karl Helicher

REVIEW: *N Y Rev Books* v60 no6 p6-10 Ap 4 2013 Russell Baker

REVIEW: *N Y Times Book Rev* p30 N 17 2013

"Blasephemy," "The Story of Ain't: America, Its Language and the Most Controversial Dictionary Ever Published," and "Ike and Dick: Portrait of a Strange Political Marriage." "[Sherman] Alexie has carved out a space in American literature as an audacious observer of the Native American experience in the Pacific Northwest. . . . [David] Skinner's spry cultural history revisits the brouhaha that greeted Webster's Third and describes the societal metamorphoses that have shaped our language. . . . [Jeffrey] Frank skillfully examines the embittering relationship that shaped the American agenda for decades: President Dwight Eisenhower . . . and his two-term vice president, Richard Nixon."

REVIEW: *N Y Times Book Rev* p1-18 F 17 2013 Joe Scarborough

REVIEW: *Natl Rev* v65 no6 p42-3 Ap 8 2013 VINCENT J. CANNATO

REVIEW: *Publ Wkly* v259 no37 p42 S 10 2012

FRANK, JOAN. Make it stay; [by] Joan Frank 160 p. 2012 The Permanent Press

1. Couples—Fiction 2. Fiction 3. Interpersonal relations—Fiction 4. Male friendship—Fiction 5. Married people—Fiction
ISBN 9781579622275
LC 2011-048286

SUMMARY: This book is a "novel that peers into relationships in the small town of Mira Flores in northern California. Rachel, the narrator, writes books and deeply loves her husband Neil, a lawyer who has occasional doubts about their marriage. His best friend is Mike, the man who saved him from drowning in the South Pacific. Mike sells exotic fish and is married to Tilda, the only character who has an underlying streak of meanness and deceit. . . . When disaster strikes one of them, the rest are devastated." (Kirkus)

REVIEW: *Booklist* v108 no14 p20 Mr 15 2012 Cortney Ophoff

REVIEW: *Kirkus Rev* v80 no4 p335 F 15 2012

"Make It Stay." " A novel that peers into relationships in the small town of Mira Flores in northern California, . . . The mix of personalities is perfect: a woman who loves unconditionally; her loyal but sometimes shaky spouse; his do-anything-for-you and screw-anything-that-moves friend; and a woman who serves expensive steaks she obtains with 'five-finger discounts.' . . . There comes a moment when everything seems perfect with the foursome, when one of the characters wants that situation to last forever, to 'make it stay.' But happily-ever-afters are for fairy tales, and nothing good lasts forever. First-class fiction."

REVIEW: *Publ Wkly* v259 no5 p33 Ja 30 2012

FRANKLIN, JANET.ed. Vegetation ecology. See Vegetation ecology

FRANKLIN, SARAH, 1960-. Biological relatives; IVF, stem cells, and the future of kinship; [by] Sarah Franklin 376 p. 2013 Duke University Press

1. Biology—Social aspects 2. Feminist anthropology 3. Fertilization in vitro, Human—Social aspects 4. Historical literature 5. Kinship—Philosophy

ISBN 9780822354857 (cloth: alk. paper); 9780822354994 (pbk.: alk. paper)

LC 2013-018962

SUMMARY: "In 'Biological Relatives,' Sarah Franklin explores how the normalization of IVF has changed how both technology and biology are understood. Drawing on anthropology, feminist theory, and science studies, Franklin charts the evolution of IVF from an experimental research technique into a global technological platform used for a wide variety of applications, including genetic diagnosis, livestock breeding, cloning, and stem cell research." (Publisher's note)

REVIEW: *Choice* v51 no11 p2019 Jl 2014 S. M. Weiss

REVIEW: *Science* v344 no6182 p361-2 Ap 25 2014 Charis Thompson

"Biological Relatives: IVF, Stem Cells, and the Future of Kinship." "The book's title is a pun on our ability to use new reproductive biology techniques to make new kinds of relatives and families and on the ways in which reproduction has changed relative to those techniques. . . . Reading the book illuminates ways to see across divides, and there are some striking images along the way. . . The scholars [author Sarah] Franklin taps are not usually read together, and without her own body of work over the years, there would not be a field for the book to serve as an archive. It would also be easy to miss how generous this aspect of the book is. Franklin need not have, and yet does, distribute credit widely."

FRANZEN, JONATHAN, 1959-.tr. The Kraus Project. See The Kraus Project

FRASER, ANTONIA, 1932-. Perilous question; reform or revolution? Britain on the brink, 1832; [by] Antonia Fraser 320 p. 2013 PublicAffairs

1. Great Britain—Politics & government—1830-1837 2. Historical literature 3. Political reform 4. Representation of the People Act, 1832 (Great Britain) 5. Representative government

ISBN 1610393317; 9781610393317 (hardcover); 9781610393324 (electronic)

LC 2013-933913

SUMMARY: This book by Antonia Fraser examines "the tempestuous two-year period in Britain's history leading up to the passing of the Great Reform Bill in 1832. . . . The underlying grievance was the fate of the many disfranchised people. They were ignored by a medieval system of electoral representation that gave, for example, no votes to those who lived in the new industrial cities . . . while allocating two parliamentary representatives to a village long since fallen into the sea." (Publisher's note)

REVIEW: *Choice* v51 no1 p152-3 S 2013 P. Stansky

"Perilous Question: Reform or Revolution? Britain on the Brink, 1832." "This is a wonderful account of the passing of the Reform Act of 1832, which marginally increased the electorate to include middle-class male property owners and reluctantly introduced the idea that the number of voters might be further expanded. [Author Antonia] Fraser has previously mostly written about Britain in the 17th century, but here she expands her range with great deftness and a fine sense of the mostly aristocratic players in the story. It was not as if the unenfranchised lacked power, as amply demonstrated in riots and considerable property damage."

REVIEW: *Hist Today* v63 no7 p62-3 Jl 2013 STEPHEN FARRELL

REVIEW: *Kirkus Rev* v81 no7 p321 Ap 1 2013

REVIEW: *Libr J* v139 no6 p59 Ap 1 2014 Forrest E. Link

REVIEW: *Libr J* v138 no10 p121 Je 1 2013 Megan H. Fraser

REVIEW: *N Y Rev Books* v61 no1 p45-7 Ja 9 2014 Alan Ryan

"Perilous Question: Reform or Revolution? Britain on the Brink, 1832." "It is more than forty years since Antonia Fraser revealed a formidable talent for writing serious and well-researched books on history for a wide audience. . . . All her familiar virtues are on display, and if readers know the dénouement before they open the book--Britain did not experience a revolution in 1832--the story contains enough plot twists to satisfy the most avid mystery reader. . . . The one complaint one might level at 'Perilous Question' is that it barely glances, not so much at the slow advance of democracy in Britain, as at the wider changes of which the Reform Act was a part. . . . Whatever 'Perilous Question' lacks by way of analysis it more than makes up in high spirits and literary verve."

REVIEW: *Natl Rev* v65 no18 p53-4 S 30 2013 KELLY JANE TORRANCE

REVIEW: *New Yorker* v89 no22 p67 Jl 29 2013

REVIEW: *TLS* no5747 p34 My 24 2013 ROBERT SAUNDERS

"The Perilous Question: The Drama of the Great Reform Bill 1832." "Antonia Fraser's splendid book . . . captures superbly the sense of a nation in storm, as well as the intolerable pressures on those at the heart of government. . . . it is a particular strength of Fraser's account that she restores the monarchy to centre stage. . . . The nineteenth century marks new territory for Fraser, and there are inevitably some fumbles. . . . Judged on its own terms, however, this is popular history of a very high order. Elegantly written, lavishly illustrated and deftly argued, it is a brilliant and entertaining evocation of a turning point in British history."

FRAWLEY, KEITH.il. Teeny Tiny Trucks. See McCanna, T.

FRÉCHET, ROBYN.tr. Philo of Alexandria. See Philo of Alexandria

FREEDMAN, CARL. Versions of Hollywood Crime Cinema; Studies in Ford, Wilder, Coppola, Scorsese and Others; [by] Carl Freedman 184 p. 2013 University of Chicago Press

1. Crime films 2. Crime in motion pictures 3. Crime on television 4. Film criticism 5. Television crime shows
ISBN 1841507245; 9781841507248

SUMMARY: This book on crime film and television "offers a series of critical readings spanning several genres. From among the mob movies, [Carl] Freedman focuses on Francis Ford Coppola's Godfather trilogy. . . . Turning his attention to other genres, Freedman also looks at film noir and Westerns, in addition to films for which crime is significant but not central, from horror movies like Stanley Kubrick's The Shining to science fiction and social realist films like The Grapes of Wrath." (Publisher's note)

REVIEW: *Choice* v51 no5 p841-2 Ja 2014 S. C. Dillon

"Versions of Hollywood Crime Cinema: Studies in Ford, Wilder, Coppola, Scorsese, and Others." "The writing is always intellectual and precise, even if this sequence seems flat compared to the author's earlier work and to numerous lively discussions elsewhere. . . . Two sections consider film noir and the John Wayne western, each with paired essays. The second of each pair . . . are both stimulating. Something of an incomplete project in itself, this heterogeneous volume is at times terrific, at other times merely smart and competent."

FREEDMAN, ERIC. Presidents and Black America; a documentary history; [by] Eric Freedman xxxiv, 546 p. 2011 CQ Press

1. African Americans—Attitudes—History—Sources 2. Presidents—Relations with African Americans—History—Sources 3. Presidents—United States—Racial attitudes—Sources 4. Reference books 5. United States
ISBN 1608710084; 9781608710089 (cloth : alk. paper)
LC 2011-032618

SUMMARY: This reference book "features a mixture of primary source material with introductory essays outlining each president's views on blacks in America. . . . The work is arranged in chronological order, with each chapter covering a president. . . . Chapters open with an introductory essay. . . . One can clearly see how the successive Republican presidencies of Harding, Coolidge, and Hoover turned American blacks . . . to the Democratic party of Franklin Roosevelt." (Booklist)

REVIEW: *Booklist* v108 no15 p36 Ap 1 2012 Ken Black

"Presidents and Black America: A Documentary History." "This outstanding work features a mixture of primary source material with introductory essays outlining each president's views on blacks in America. . . . Chapters open with an introductory essay referring to each document within the chapter. These essays—replete with footnotes—serve as excellent resources for further research. . . . With the prevalence of primary source material on the Internet, any collection of such documents in book form is ultimately dependent upon its editorial content, and this volume rises to the occasion. This well-edited, well-written work belongs on the shelves of all libraries."

REVIEW: *Choice* v49 no10 p1851 Je 2012 T. M. Hughes

"Presidents and Black America: A Documentary History." "This book uses information from letters, diary entries, addresses, and other primary documents to examine how each president responded to political and social issues related to black Americans. . . . This volume succeeds in using leaders' own words to illustrate their perceptions, actions, and, in some cases, contradictions regarding slavery, racial and social injustices, segregation, and related issues. This work is a timely resource for those researching various presidents' navigation of the waters of race in the US, particularly in relation to black Americans."

REVIEW: *Libr J* v137 no10 p124 Je 1 2012 Donald Altschiller

FREEDMAN, ESTELLE B. Redefining rape; sexual violence in the era of suffrage and segregation; [by] Estelle B. Freedman 387 p. 2013 Harvard University Press

1. Citizenship—United States—History 2. Civil rights—United States—History 3. Historical literature 4. Rape—United States—History 5. Women's rights—United States—History
ISBN 9780674724846 (alk. paper)
LC 2013-002883

SUMMARY: This book "demonstrates that power and privilege fundamentally shape the meanings of rape--its legal definitions, cultural representations, and human impact. Focusing especially on 1850-1950, [Estelle B.] Freedman . . . argues that rape and citizenship are inextricably bound. Contests over who may--and may not--claim protection from sexual violence and accusations of rape illustrate this." (Choice: Current Reviews for Academic Libraries)

REVIEW: *Choice* v51 no5 p903-4 Ja 2014 S. Burch

"Redefining Rape: Sexual Violence in the Era of Suffrage and Segregation." "This stunning US history demonstrates that power and privilege fundamentally shape the meanings of rape--its legal definitions, cultural representations, and human impact. . . . Connections to broader histories of racial, class, and gender injustice drew attention to activists' work, and [Estelle B.] Freedman deserves praise for critically examining their different attitudes and aspirations. She also astutely acknowledges regional differences in legal constructions, representations, and experiences of rape and sexual violence. Insightful critiques of sodomy laws, male youth, and men of color distinguish this book. . . . Closer study of disability and ableism might have enhanced the work."

FREEDMAN, LAWRENCE. Strategy; a history; [by] Lawrence Freedman 768 p. 2013 Oxford University Press, USA

1. Historical literature 2. Military history 3. POLITICAL SCIENCE—History & Theory 4. Strategic culture 5. Strategic planning 6. Strategy—History
ISBN 9780199325153 (hardback)
LC 2013-011944

SUMMARY: In this book, author Lawrence Freedman "outlines past and present strategies of force and mind. His encyclopedic review begins with [Carl] von Clausewitz's ideas on military power, and moves into futurist [Herman] Kahn's contributions on deterrence in thermonuclear warfare. . . . Bottom-up strategies he includes thinkers such as [Karl] Marx, [Vladimir] Lenin, Mao Zedong, and Martin Luther King, Jr." (Publishers Weekly)

REVIEW: *Choice* v51 no11 p2064 Jl 2014 C. Potholm II

REVIEW: *Economist* v409 no8860 p88-9 N 2 2013

REVIEW: *Hist Today* v64 no6 p64 Je 2014 Jeremy Black

REVIEW: *Kirkus Rev* v81 no17 p55 S 1 2013

REVIEW: *Natl Rev* v66 no1 p38-40 Ja 27 2014 VICTOR DAVIS HANSON

"Strategy: A History". "In the world of [Lawrence] Freedman, almost everything becomes strategic and everyone a strategist of some sort, from a comic dramatist to a CEO to a community organizer. But to paraphrase Frederick the Great, does he who defines strategy as everything risk reducing it to nothing? In some sense, he does. . . . The text is vast and displays an enormous amount of knowledge, but it can also make for slow reading. . . . He has written a vast exploration of strategy that is difficult to read, full of surprises, and marked by unsurpassed erudition. It also is witty and reminds us that he in the world who knows most about strategy may be the one who is the most unimpressed with it."

REVIEW: *Parameters: U.S. Army War College* v44 no2 p103-7 Summ 2014 Lawrence Freedman

FREEDMAN, RUSSELL, 1929-. Angel Island; gateway to Gold Mountain; 96 p. 2013 Clarion Books

1. Historical literature

ISBN 0547903782; 9780547903781 (hardcover)

LC 2012-036532

SUMMARY: This book is a "history of Angel Island and its legacy in the American immigration narrative. Detailed descriptions of the island, the actual building, the events that took place there, and the people who passed through its doors are sprinkled with the emotional poems, quotes, and other writings that were discovered covering the walls of the areas where the detainees were housed." (School Library Journal)

REVIEW: *Booklist* v110 no5 p58 N 1 2013 Michael Cart

"Angel Island: Gateway to Gold Mountain." "Called the 'Ellis Island of the West,' Angel Island, located in San Francisco Bay, was once the busiest immigration station on the West Coast. For generations of Asian immigrants, it was the first stop upon landing in America. . . . [Russell] Freedman chronicles all of this in his carefully researched and clearly written history, which is lavishly illustrated with black-and-white photographs and drawings. Appended are a selected bibliography and notes identifying the sources of all quoted material. Now a National Historic Landmark, Angel Island is a place where we can learn from the past, as is Freedman's important book."

REVIEW: *Bull Cent Child Books* v67 no6 p311 F 2014 Elizabeth Bush

REVIEW: *Horn Book Magazine* v89 no6 p114-5 N/D 2013 DEAN SCHNEIDER

"Angel Island: Gateway to Gold Mountain." "Chinese immigrants on the West Coast faced great discrimination, and Angel Island became a detention center and barrier for many. [Russell] Freedman weaves a clear and straightforward narrative history with abundant quotations, excerpts from diaries and wall poems, and archival photographs. This is a clearly written account of a lesser-known side of American immigration history that may add to readers' understanding of current political debate. Thorough source notes and a selected bibliography round out the engaging volume."

REVIEW: *Kirkus Rev* v81 no21 p180 N 1 2013

REVIEW: *Publ Wkly* v260 no42 p54 O 21 2013

REVIEW: *SLJ* v59 no9 p182 S 2013 Jody Kopple

REVIEW: *Voice of Youth Advocates* v36 no6 p80 F 2014 Kristi Sadowski

FREEDMAN, SAMUEL G. Breaking the line; the season in Black college football that transformed the sport and changed the course of civil rights; [by] Samuel G. Freedman 336 p. 2013 Simon & Schuster

1. African American football players—Biography 2. College sports—United States—History 3. Discrimination in sports—United States—History 4. Football—United States—History 5. Sports literature

ISBN 1439189773; 9781439189771 (hardcover); 9781439189788 (trade pbk.)

LC 2012-042465

SUMMARY: Author Samuel G. Freedman's book "brings to life the historic saga of the battle for the 1967 black college championship, culminating in a riveting, excruciatingly close contest." He "traces the rise of these four leaders and their teammates as they storm through the season. Together they helped compel the segregated colleges of the South to integrate their teams and redefined who could play quarterback in the NFL, who could be a head coach, and who could run a franchise as general manager." (Publisher's note)

REVIEW: *Booklist* v109 no19/20 p14 Je 1 2013 Mark Levine

REVIEW: *Kirkus Rev* v81 no13 p77 Jl 1 2013

REVIEW: *Libr J* v138 no11 p97 Je 15 2013 John Maxymuk

REVIEW: *N Y Times Book Rev* p38 O 13 2013 Jay Jennings

"American Pastimes: The Very Best of Red Smith," "Breaking the Line: The Season in Black College Football that Transformed the Sport and Changed the Course of Civil Rights," and "A Chance to Win: Boyhood, Baseball, and the Struggle for Redemption in the Inner City." "Smith rarely sounds dated or overwrought. Whatever the subject, the authority of his prose never flags. . . . It's probably not fair to blame the author for overstatement in a subtitle. . . . [Samuel G.] Freedman never makes the case for the latter in what is a dutiful, near-hagiographic dual biography of Eddie Robinson and Jake Gaither. . . . The sport is merely the occasion for [Jonathan] Schuppe's deep excavation into four hard-knock lives in Newark. . . The 'cycle' in the rough neighborhoods Schuppe vividly captures is not something you hit for but something that hits you, repeatedly."

FREELY, MAUREEN.tr. The Time Regulation Institute. See Tanpınar, A. H.

FREEMAN, CAITLIN. Modern art desserts. See Duggan, T.

FREEMAN, MARTHA, Who stole New Year's Eve?; 224 p. 2013 Holiday House

1. Carnivals—Fiction 2. Friendship—Juvenile fiction 3. Ice carving—Fiction
ISBN 0823427501; 9780823427505 (hardcover)
LC 2012-019674

SUMMARY: In this book by Martha Freeman, part of the "Chickadee Court Mystery" series, "twelve-year-old sleuths, Yasmeen and Alex, are having friendship issues. Yasmeen thinks that she's being replaced by a new girl who has come to Chickadee Court. Then, the whole gang comes together to solve the frosty mystery [of stolen ice sculptures]. The clues lead to a fracking operation and the laboratory of a professor who is racing to invent a new alternative fuel before his competitors do." (Publisher's note)

REVIEW: *Horn Book Magazine* v89 no6 p63 N/D 2013 MARTHA V. PARRAVANO

"Who Stole New Year's Eve?" "When all the ice sculptures intended for the town's annual Ice Carnival are stolen, eleven-year-old Alex Parakeet and the rest of the kid sleuths on Chickadee Court follow clues . . . to solve the case. Adding even more interest is Alex's newly complicated personal life, as best friend Yasmeen is threatened by Alex's friendship with newcomer Eve. . . . This fifth mystery in the [Chickadee Court Mystery] series is solid and satisfying, set against a background of holiday celebrations and enhanced with much humor and intrigue."

REVIEW: *SLJ* v60 no1 p81 Ja 2014 Kira Moody

FREITAS, DONNA. Gold medal winter; [by] Donna Freitas 320 p. 2014 Arthur A. Levine Books

1. Competition (Psychology)—Fiction 2. Competition (Psychology)—Juvenile fiction 3. Dominican Americans—Fiction 4. Figure skating stories 5. Ice skating—Fiction 6. Winter Olympics—Fiction 7. Winter Olympics—Juvenile fiction 8. Women figure skaters—Juvenile fiction
ISBN 0545643775 (hardcover : alk. paper); 0545643783 (pbk. : alk. paper); 9780545643771 (hardcover : alk. paper); 9780545643788 (pbk. : alk. paper)
LC 2013-029144

SUMMARY: In this book, "fifteen-year-old Esperanza Flores . . . wins a place on the Olympic figure-skating team after a leading competitor injures herself too badly to go. . . . She's daunted, however, by the bullying of the other members of the team, who resent Espi's displacement of their former teammate; she's also . . . intrigued by the attentions of two young male Olympians, one a famous figure skater and the other a quiet hockey player." (Bulletin of the Center for Children's Books)

REVIEW: *Booklist* v110 no9/10 p104 Ja 1 2014 Kay Weisman

REVIEW: *Bull Cent Child Books* v67 no6 p311-2 F 2014 Deborah Stevenson

"Gold Medal Winter." "There's a generic flavor throughout as Espi triumphs against all obstacles--so generic, in fact, that the location of the actual Olympics is never actually given. The story is, however, sweet and innocent, with Espi reading much younger than fifteen (and the portrait of the Olympic Village thoroughly sanitized), and the details of skating practice, morning television appearances, and Vera Wang costumes are fresh and specific enough to advance the wish-fulfillment. Armchair ice princesses looking for a sports fairy tale will likely overlook the book's weaknesses and find it a cozy accompaniment to the Winter Olympics."

REVIEW: *Kirkus Rev* v81 no23 p219 D 1 2013

REVIEW: *SLJ* v60 no2 p86 F 2014 Jennifer Schultz

REVIEW: *Voice of Youth Advocates* v36 no6 p58-9 F 2014 Julie Hanson

FRENCH DECADENT TALES; l, 231 p. 2013 Oxford University Press

1. Anthologies 2. Decadence (Literary movement)—France 3. French fiction—19th century 4. Short stories, French—Translations into English
ISBN 0199569274; 9780199569274
LC 2013-431424

SUMMARY: This book "brings together 36 of the best decadent tales from the French fin-de-siècle, including work by well-known writers such as [Guy de] Maupassant . . . [and Octave] Mirbeau. . . . Stephen Romer's . . . introduction provides . . . context for the stories, underscoring the principal literary, philosophical, scientific, and political trends of the time, which fed into their authors' loathing of the modern world, and the discovery of the Unconscious." (Publisher's note)

REVIEW: *TLS* no5761 p19 Ag 30 2013 GRAHAM ROBB

"French Decadent Tales." "Stephen Romer's beautifully translated anthology . . . is not, he admits, wholly representative of the French fin-de-siècle 'Decadent' coteries and their 'feckless retinue of disabused young men'. He has chosen thirty-six unusually well-crafted tales of modem urban life by fourteen authors, from Barbey d'Aurevilly to Pierre Louys, favouring the blackly humorous and the uncanny, and avoiding Decadent kitsch. . . . Almost all these writers, as Romer ruefully remarks, are misogynistic. . . . Stephen Romer's diligent inspection of the 'writhing snake-pit' of Decadents has also turned up some minor, forgotten masterpieces by Gustave Geoffroy, Jean Lorrain and Georges Rodenbach."

FRENCH, HENRY. Man's estate; landed gentry masculinities, c.1660-c.1900; [by] Henry French viii, 281 p. 2012 Oxford University Press

1. Gentry—England—History—18th century 2. Gentry—England—History—19th century 3. Gentry—Great Britain 4. Historical literature 5. Human life cycle 6. Masculinity—England—History—18th century 7. Masculinity—England—History—19th century 8. Masculinity—History 9. Men—Great Britain
ISBN 0199576696 (hbk.); 9780199576692 (hbk.)
LC 2012-931196

SUMMARY: This book by Henry French and Mark Rothery focuses "on a particular social group, the English landed gentry" over "a time span of several hundred years. The authors move beyond the study of printed conduct literature . . . by examining the values expressed in family correspondence in order to get closer to social practices." The book "concentrates on four important periods in the life-course . . . : schooling, university, foreign travel, and marriage and family life." (Publisher's note)

REVIEW: *Am Hist Rev* v118 no4 p1247-9 O 2013 James Rosenheim

"Man's Estate: Landed Gentry Masculinities, c. 1660-c. 1900" and "The Little Republic: Masculinity and Domestic

Authority in Eighteenth-Century Britain." "These two volumes add significantly to a growing literature on the place of men and the nature of masculinity in the context of the seventeenth-, eighteenth-, and nineteenth-century English family and home. Drawing on both the strengths and the gaps left by recent studies of masculinity, gender relations, the household, and the world beyond the home (a literature that each book in its way parses, praises, and provides with critique), Karen Harvey and the team of Henry French and Mark Rothery ambitiously undertake to bring clarity to what is a still rather muddled history of men and manhood. They succeed admirably."

REVIEW: *Choice* v50 no5 p951-2 Ja 2013 J. Sainsbury

REVIEW: *Engl Hist Rev* v128 no535 p1591-3 D 2013 Ben Griffin

REVIEW: *History* v98 no330 p286-90 Ap 2013 Anthony Fletcher

FRENCH, HOWARD W. China's second continent; how a million migrants are building a new empire in Africa; [by] Howard W. French 304 p. 2014 Alfred A. Knopf

1. Africa—Foreign relations—China 2. Chinese—Africa, Sub-Saharan 3. Immigrants—Africa, Sub-Saharan 4. Political science literature

ISBN 0307956989; 9780307946652 (pbk.); 9780307956989 (hardcover)

LC 2013-026930

SUMMARY: In this book, Howard W, French "sought to understand China's ties to Africa through the experiences of Chinese migrants and long-term residents. French interviewed friends, other contacts, officials, and perfect strangers on such subjects as resource depletion, infrastructure building, rapid growth, cultural dependency, and rampant colonialism. He learned that in the spirit of noninterference, China pays little attention to things like local laws, democracy, and human rights." (Library Journal)

REVIEW: *Booklist* v110 no13 p6 Mr 1 2014 Brendan Driscoll

"China's Second Continent: How a Million Migrants Are Building a New Empire in Africa". "[Howard W.] French . . . has the advantage of significant personal experience in both Africa and China. He also speaks Mandarin, so he can converse directly with some of the million or so members of the Chinese diaspora in Africa. . . . Interacting with Chinese and Africans in Mozambique, Sierra Leone, Namibia, and elsewhere, French capably illustrates that although the Chinese omnipresence in Africa may be a form of soft imperialism, it is also a result of the crushing pressures . . of modern Chinese society. . . . If French is sympathetic to the plight of many Chinese immigrants, however, he remains critical of their casual racism and general callousness about their African hosts."

REVIEW: *Economist* v412 no8901 p76-7 Ag 23 2014

REVIEW: *Kirkus Rev* v82 no8 p3 Ap 15 2014

REVIEW: *Libr J* v139 no4 p98 Mr 1 2014 Bonnie Tollefson

REVIEW: *N Y Times Book Rev* p13 Jl 13 2014 ALEXIS OKEOWO

REVIEW: *Nation* v299 no16 p30-3 O 20 2014 AUDREA LIM

REVIEW: *New York Times* v163 no56560 p13 Jl 12 2014 ALEXIS OKEOWO

REVIEW: *Publ Wkly* v261 no5 p45 F 3 2014

FRENCH, NICCI. Waiting for Wednesday; a Frieda Klein Mystery; [by] Nicci French 384 p. 2013 Pamela Dorman Books/Viking

1. Detective & mystery stories 2. Murder—Investigation—Fiction 3. Secrecy—Fiction 4. Serial murders—Fiction 5. Women psychotherapists—Fiction

ISBN 0670015776; 9780670015771

LC 2013-016793

SUMMARY: "In [Nicci] French's third novel . . . featuring London psychotherapist Frieda Klein, seemingly average mother Ruth Lennox is found murdered without apparent reason. As details of her secret life emerge, the cast of characters expose a web of tangled lives. Frieda gets involved when her teenage niece befriends the dead woman's son. The pace picks up after one of Frieda's patients, during therapy, makes an offhand remark that leads Frieda to believe a serial killer is at work." (Library Journal)

REVIEW: *Booklist* v110 no12 p34 F 15 2014 Michele Leber

"Waiting for Wednesday". "By all accounts Ruth Lennox—a wife and mother of three teenagers who was universally liked—led a perfect life until she was murdered in her London home, likely in a burglary gone wrong. But when the prime suspect is ruled out, DCI Malcolm Karlsson approaches psychotherapist Frieda Klein for help. The big question, to Klein, is what the victim's secrets were, and a shocking one sets the case on end. . . . There's enough backstory for this third Frieda Klein mystery to stand alone, but the greatest pleasure is in following the series from the beginning to see the evolution of Klein, a detective of the mind, who endures a rough patch here but makes it through the darkness. Another compelling entry In this complex, suspenseful series."

REVIEW: *Kirkus Rev* v82 no7 p40 Ap 1 2014

REVIEW: *Libr J* v139 no2 p67 F 1 2014 Susan Carr

REVIEW: *Publ Wkly* v261 no1 p34 Ja 6 2014

FRENETTE, BETHANY. Burn bright; a Dark star novel; [by] Bethany Frenette 352 p. 2013 Hyperion

1. Demonology—Fiction 2. Mothers and daughters—Fiction 3. Psychic ability—Fiction 4. Superheroes—Fiction 5. Supernatural—Fiction

ISBN 9781423146667

LC 2013-001576

SUMMARY: In this sequel to Bethany Frenette's "Dark Star," a new demon in town named Susannah is looking for the girl with the power to open pathways to the Beneath. . . . Audrey's boyfriend, Leon, is her Guardian, meaning he is mystically bound to protect her and has been granted magic abilities to do so—chiefly, he can sense when she is in danger and teleport to save her. That's why it's concerning when Audrey has an encounter with a group of Harrowers led by Susannah and Leon doesn't show." (Kirkus Reviews)

REVIEW: *Kirkus Rev* v82 no1 p130 Ja 1 2014

"Burn Bright". "Against this relationship drama, Audrey's two best friends pursue interesting subplots, Susannah launches a series of testing attacks against the Guardians, and Audrey's mother, more like Cassandra Clare's Shadowhunters than the superhero Audrey's narration promises, fights no crime. The plot's uneven, but dialogue and characters are strong. In the last 50 pages or so, the story really comes to life for those readers patient enough to have made it through the first 290. A demon-hunting fix for readers who can forgive page-padding."

FRENKEL, EDWARD. Love and math; the heart of hidden reality; [by] Edward Frenkel 304 p. 2013 Basic Books

1. Antisemitism 2. Mathematical literature 3. Mathematicians—United States—Biography 4. Mathematics—Miscellanea
ISBN 0465050743; 9780465050741 (hardback)
LC 2013-017372

SUMMARY: This book by Edward Frenkel "tells two intertwined stories: of amazing mathematics and of the journey of one young man learning and living it. Growing up in Russia, Frenkel was denied entrance to university to study mathematics because he was Jewish. Yet with the help of his mentors he circumvented the system to become one of the twenty-first century's leading mathematicians. He now works on one of the biggest ideas to come out of mathematics in the last 50 years." (Publisher's note)

REVIEW: *Booklist* v110 no4 p6-7 O 15 2013 Bryce Christensen

REVIEW: *Choice* v51 no7 p1257 Mr 2014 J. Johnson

"Love and Math: The Heart of Hidden Reality." "Throughout the book, [Edward] Frenkel documents his growing love affair with the subject, sharing interesting mathematical insights with readers and trying to kindle their love affair as well. Frenkel discusses his current mathematics efforts in the Langlands Program, a quest toward a grand unified theory in mathematics that allows the solution of an array of problems via translations of research ideas between diverse fields. The book is best read along with a viewing of Frenkel's film Rites of Love and Math. Together, the two are a significant step forward in helping all learners understand how love and math fit together."

REVIEW: *Kirkus Rev* v81 no18 p101 S 15 2013

REVIEW: *N Y Rev Books* v60 no19 p27-9 D 5 2013 Jim Holt

"Love and Math: The Heart of Hidden Reality." "Winsome. . . . As far as I know, [Edward] Frenkel is the first to try to explain the Langlands Program--for him, 'the source code of all mathematics'-- to readers without any mathematical background. His book, then, is three things: a Platonic love letter to mathematics; an attempt to give the layman some idea of its most magnificent drama-in-progress; and an autobiographical account, by turns inspiring and droll, of how the author himself came to be a leading player in that drama."

REVIEW: *N Y Times Book Rev* p15 O 27 2013 LEONARD MLODINOW

"Love and Math: The Heart of Hidden Reality." "After describing how he got into the field, 'Love and Math' is mostly devoted to the math. . . . [Edward] Frenkel aims to make it understandable, even beautiful. . . . Frenkel concedes that 'one can get a headache' trying to keep track of this 'stuff,' and if there's a drawback to this book, that's it. Those not familiar with higher math might feel overwhelmed instead of moved--as one would hope--by Frenkel's passion of the 'exquisite harmony' of mathematics and how it 'unites us across culture, continents, and centuries.'"

REVIEW: *New York Times* v163 no56325 pD5 N 19 2013 AMIR ALEXANDER

"Love & Math: The Heart of Hidden Reality." "The story of [Edward Frenkel's] professional triumph against heavy odds is deeply satisfying. . . . But his true answer to the bigotry he encountered in his youth lies in his passion for mathematics--the 'love' of the book's title. . . . He does his best to explain the substance of his work to the lay reader, but this, he admits, is no easy task. . . . Impressively, he does not give up. Believing that mathematics is a common human possession, he explains each concept in nontechnical terms, relying heavily on analogies from daily life. In the end, lay readers will probably acquire no more than a superficial sense of all this technical work. But far more important, they will gain an understanding of what modern mathematics is all about."

REVIEW: *Publ Wkly* v260 no32 p49 Ag 12 2013

REVIEW: *Sci Am* v309 no4 p94 O 2013 John Matson

FREUDENBERGER, NELL. The newlyweds; a novel; [by] Nell Freudenberger 337 p. 2012 Knopf

1. FICTION—Contemporary Women 2. FICTION—Family Life 3. FICTION—Literary 4. Marriage in literature 5. Newlyweds—Fiction
ISBN 0307268845; 9780307268846
LC 2011-044116

SUMMARY: This book by Nell Freudenberger "examines a marriage arranged via the Internet. . . . Amina wanted to escape from her family's straitened circumstances in Bangladesh; George wanted someone who "did not play games." . . . So here she is, in the fall of 2005 in . . . Rochester, N.Y., recently married, working in retail while she studies for a teaching certificate. . . . [S]he's uncertain how to bridge the gulf between [her] two selves. She makes a much-needed friend in George's cousin Kim . . . so when it turns out that she and George have been hiding something important from Amina, it's . . . shattering. However, it does prompt George to agree to bring Amina's parents to America, and she goes to collect them in Bangladesh, where several old family conflicts flare anew." (Kirkus Reviews)

REVIEW: *Bookforum* v19 no1 p25 Ap/My 2012 Jessica Joffe

"The Newlyweds." "The novel grew out of [Nell Freudenherger's] . . . experience she had sitting next to a young Bangladeshi woman on a plane. The woman, Farah, had moved to Rochester from Dhaka to marry a man she had met on the Internet. . . . And that is exactly how it reads: less like a novel than an exhaustively detailed 352-page reportage of Farah's journey. We meet her fictional alter ego, Amina, the beautiful young Desi, as she is learning to adjust to suburban American life and a new marriage to a man she barely knows. . . . Freudenberger goes into minute detail, jotting down not only the contents of Amina's head, which is filled with some of the twee-est thoughts in literary history, . . . but also everything else she notices."

REVIEW: *Booklist* v108 no17 p81 My 1 2012 Donna Seaman

"The Newlyweds." "Amina is a marvelously wily narrator, and [Nell] Freudenberger . . . greatly advances her standing as a writer skilled in understatement and deadpan wit as she continues her signature exploration of the dynamics between Americans and Southeast Asians in this exceptionally intimate, vivid, and suspenseful novel. . . . This classic tale of missed chances, crushing errors of judgment, and scarring sacrifices, all compounded by cultural differences, is perfectly pitched, piercingly funny, and exquisitely heartbreaking."

REVIEW: *Economist* v404 no8798 p74-5 Ag 18 2012

REVIEW: *Kirkus Rev* v80 no8 p123 Ap 15 2012

"The Newlyweds." "[Nell] Freudenberger does well in capturing the off kilter feelings of a young woman in a country so unlike her birthplace, and the cultural differences prompt some enjoyably wry humor. The characters are all well drawn, if a trifle pallid, which points to a larger problem. Freudenberger's tone is detached and cool throughout, even when violent incidents are described, which makes it difficult to emotionally engage with the story. The novel is carefully researched rather than emotionally persuasive. Well executed but a bit too obviously studied--more willed than felt."

REVIEW: *Libr J* v137 no7 p76-7 Ap 15 2012 Christine DeZelar-Tiedman

REVIEW: *N Y Times Book Rev* p1 Ap 29 2012 MOHSIN HAMID

REVIEW: *N Y Times Book Rev* p26 My 6 2012

REVIEW: *Publ Wkly* v259 no10 p44-5 Mr 5 2012

REVIEW: *TLS* no5707/5708 p22 Ag 17 2012 Fran Bigman

FREYTAG, LORNA.il. My humongous hamster. See Freytag, L.

FREYTAG, LORNA. My humongous hamster; [by] Lorna Freytag 32 p. 2014 Henry Holt and Co

1. Children's stories 2. Hamsters—Fiction 3. Imagination 4. Pets—Juvenile literature 5. Size—Fiction
ISBN 0805099182; 9780805099188 (hardback)
LC 2013-036531

SUMMARY: Written and illustrated by Lorna Freytag, this book describes how "whether taking a spin on the Ferris wheel, stopping a burglary in progress, napping at the foot of a mountain, or gazing longingly off into a sunset, Humongous Hamster is a hero every kid will adore. He eats trees like broccoli, gives kids a ride to the park, and scares the neighbor's cat." (Publisher's note)

REVIEW: *Bull Cent Child Books* v67 no7 p356 Mr 2014 J. H.

"My Humongous Hamster." "There isn't much substance to the story, but it is a kid-pleasing concept, and the images of the giant hamster, his beady black eyes shining against his reddish-brown fur, looming large against a city skyline like a benevolent Godzilla, will likely incite plenty of giggles. The digital alterations to the photographs are somewhat crude, though, with shadows sometimes missing or misplaced and a lack of depth in some images. This might still work in a fanciful storytime about oversized pets. . . . A creative and tech-savvy teacher or parent could also use this as a springboard for a similar imaginative photo/story project."

REVIEW: *Kirkus Rev* v82 no2 p189 Ja 15 2014

REVIEW: *Publ Wkly* v260 no50 p69 D 9 2013

FRIED, MICHAEL, 1939-. Flaubert's gueuloir; on Madame Bovary and Salambo; [by] Michael Fried ix, 184 p. 2012 Yale University Press

1. Literary critiques 2. Oral reading
ISBN 030018705X (hardcover); 9780300187052 (hardcover)
LC 2012-007287

SUMMARY: This book on Gustav Flaubert examines the "approach to Flaubert's well-known practice of the 'gueuloir' (i.e., loud recitation)." It "argues that the defining stylistic feature of 'Madame Bovary' is the coexistence of two antithetical or seemingly antithetical characteristics: intention and automaticity, each inextricably implicated in the other. In 'Salammbô,' on the other hand, Fried sees an exemplary work of modern literature that is exclusively the product of conscious intention." (Choice: Current Reviews for Academic Libraries)

REVIEW: *Choice* v50 no7 p1250-1 Mr 2013 C. B. Kerr

"Flaubert's 'gueueloir': On 'Madame Bovary' and 'Salammbô." "One hundred years ago, French critic Albert Thibaudet observed that Flaubert was not a 'naturally' gifted writer, that he needed to read his sentences out loud in order to hear and correct the defects in his prose. What makes [Michael] Fried's approach to Flaubert's well-known practice of the 'gueuloir' (i.e., loud recitation) original and thought provoking is that he shows how Flaubert's drive for perfection did not, in fact, lead to elimination of repetitions. Fried . . . examines authorial will and habit. . . . A fascinating study of 19th-century literature, painting, and criticism. Summing Up: Recommended."

REVIEW: *Libr J* v137 no19 p82 N 15 2012 Erica Swenson Danowitz

REVIEW: *London Rev Books* v36 no2 p30 Ja 23 2014 Paul Grimstad

FRIED WALLEYE AND CHERRY PIE; midwestern writers on food; 280 p. 2013 University of Nebraska Press

1. Authors, American—Middle West—Miscellanea 2. COOKING—Essays 3. Cookbooks 4. Cooking—Middle West 5. Cooking, American—Midwestern style 6. Food habits—Middle West—Anecdotes 7. International cooking—Anecdotes
ISBN 080323645X; 9780803236455 (pbk.)
LC 2013-022747

SUMMARY: Editor Peggy Wolff's book features a collection of recipes from "thirty midwestern writers. . . . In a meditation on comfort food, Elizabeth Berg recalls her aunt's meatloaf. Stuart Dybek takes us on a school field trip to a slaughtering house, while Peter Sagal grapples with the ethics of paté. Parsing Cincinnati five-way chili, Robert Olmstead digresses into questions of Aztec culture. Harry Mark Petrakis reflects on owning a South Side Chicago lunchroom, while Bonnie Jo Campbell nurses a sweet tooth through a fudge recipe." (Publisher's note)

REVIEW: *Booklist* v110 no3 p26 O 1 2013 Mark Knoblauch

REVIEW: *N Y Times Book Rev* p25 D 15 2013 JENNY ROSENSTRACH

"Biting Through the Skin: An Indian Kitchen in America's Heartland," "Three Squares: The Invention of the American Meal," and "Fried Walleye and Cherry Pie: Midwestern Writers on Food." "In Nine Mukerjee Furstenau's memoir, 'Biting Through the Skin: An Indian Kitchen in America's Heartland' . . . , the author uses family recipes to bridge two worlds. . . . In the engrossing 'Three Squares: The Invention of the American Meal' . . . , Abigail Carroll lays down some historical context, reminding us dinner became a signifier of class. . . . In Peggy Wolff's 'Fried Walleye and Cherry Pie' . . . the quality of the writing is uneven, but Heartland natives will embrace the recipes."

REVIEW: *Publ Wkly* v260 no33 p54 Ag 19 2013

REVIEW: *TLS* no5793 p26 Ap 11 2014 CLAIRE HAZELTON

"Fried Walleye and Cherry Pie: Midwestern Writers on Food." "[Editor] Peggy Wolff begins this anthology of food writing with a childhood memory—a mined batch of chocolate chip biscuits. In spite of the biscuits' shortcomings, the memory carries with it the scent of home. Like many of the pieces compiled here, Wolff describes how food and place first became intertwined in childhood. . . . 'Fried Walleye and Cherry Pie' reads like a feast and road trip combined, taking in Iowa, the so-called 'pork tenderloin corridor' (where pork sandwiches are so popular they are served in gas stations and fine restaurants alike), and skirting the 'tan' landscape of the 'Corn Belt.' The book ends with a selection of desserts, allowing Peggy Woolf to reminisce about pie."

FRIEDBERG, AARON L. A contest for supremacy; [by] Aaron L. Friedberg p. cm. 2011 W. W. Norton & Co.

1. China—Economic conditions 2. China—Relations—United States 3. Nonfiction 4. World politics
ISBN 9780393068283
LC 2011-017661

SUMMARY: It was the author's intent to demonstrate "that a growing Sino-American rivalry is forthcoming and inevitable.. . . The U.S. policy over the past 60 years has passed through phases of containment, alignment and the current uneasy mix of the two, 'congagement,' which has been severely challenged since Tiananmen Square . . . With its newfound economic muscle, China will most likely follow the historic precedent of previous hegemons in the throes of intense expansion . . . and seek to dominate 'its neighbors, its regions, and, if it can, the world.' . . . Friedberg lays out the various ongoing arguments for containment or alignment, as well as what he extrapolates Chinese intentions to be-avoid confrontation, build comprehensive national power and advance incrementally." (Kirkus)

REVIEW: *Choice* v49 no7 p1349 Mr 2012 M. G. Roskin

REVIEW: *N Y Rev Books* v59 no3 p47-9 F 23 2012 Richard Bernstein

"A Contest for Supremacy: China, America, and the Struggle for Mastery in Asia." "In 'A Contest for Supremacy: China, America, and the Struggle for Mastery in Asia,' Aaron L. Friedberg provides the most informed, cogent, and well-developed warning of the Chinese threat that I have seen. . . . In the end, Friedberg's book is not entirely persuasive on his essential points: that China's goal is to supplant the United States in Asia, that it is winning the contest for power and influence there, and that it is the very nature of the United States as a champion of antiauthoritarian ways that is at the crux of the conflict."

FRIEDLANDER, CYNTHIA LEEDS. Breastless Intimacy; A Celebration of Love, Loss and Learning; [by] Cynthia Leeds Friedlander 200 p. 2013 Word Craft Press

1. Body image 2. Breast cancer patients' writings 3. Intimacy (Psychology) 4. Mastectomy 5. Memoirs
ISBN 0989953629; 9780989953627

SUMMARY: This "memoir recounts . . . the author's life after a bilateral mastectomy. Three months after her sister lost a two-year battle with breast cancer, [Cynthia Leeds] Friedlander . . . received a diagnosis of stage 0 breast cancer. Although the condition was noncancerous, she made the decision to remove both breasts." She discusses "her life as a divorced woman in her late 40s, experiencing intimacy after her surgery and all the bouts of self-consciousness and inadequacy that came with it." (Kirkus Reviews)

REVIEW: *Kirkus Rev* v82 no2 p388 Ja 15 2014

"Breastless Intimacy". "Written in a clear, determined voice, each piece stands alone, though there's a sense of continuity as well as some repetition. Ranging from poetic prose to reflective musings, the writing is open and honest. . . . While this book isn't directed at those with advanced breast cancer, [Cynthia Leeds] Friedlander's experiences may help other women dealing with a similar precancerous condition by providing them with a better understanding of the consequences of taking aggressive action. . . . All of her heartbreak, tears and success led her to one conclusion: 'Well-being always comes from within.' An illuminating collection of writing that's full of introspection and emotional transcendence."

FRIEDLÄNDER, SAUL, 1932-. Franz Kafka; the poet of shame and guilt; [by] Saul Friedländer 183 p. 2013 Yale University Press

1. Authors—Family relationships 2. Authors—Sexual behavior 3. Authors, Austrian—20th century—Biography 4. Biographies 5. Jewish authors—Austria—Biography
ISBN 9780300136616 (cloth : alk. paper)
LC 2012-034381

SUMMARY: This book "investigates some of the sources of [Franz] Kafka's personal anguish and its complex reflections in his imaginary world. Saul Friedländer probes major aspects of Kafka's life (family, Judaism, love and sex, writing, illness, and despair) that until now have been skewed by posthumous censorship." (Publisher's note)

REVIEW: *Choice* v51 no1 p81 S 2013 S. Gittleman

REVIEW: *N Y Rev Books* v60 no16 p17-9 O 24 2013 John Banville

"Kafka: The Decisive Years," "Kafka: The Years of Insight," and "Franz Kafka: The Poet of Shame and Guilt." "It is to [Saul] Friedländer's credit that he notes 'the ongoing influence of Expressionism' and contemporary works of fantastic literature . . . on Kafka's literary sensibility.. . . . Reiner Stach, in his ongoing biography of Kafka, strives for a similarly intimate knowledge of his subject, and of the time and place in which he lived and worked. Stach is at once highly ambitious and admirably unassuming. . . . On the evidence of the two volumes that we already have, this is one of the great literary biographies."

FRIEDMAN, CEIL.tr. Herculaneum. See Guidobaldi, M.P.

FRIEDMAN, LAURIE B. Too good to be true; [by] Laurie B. Friedman 158 p. 2014 Darby Creek

1. Dating (Social customs)—Fiction 2. Diaries—Fiction 3. Friendship—Fiction 4. Interpersonal relations—Fiction 5. Psychological fiction
ISBN 1467709263; 9781467709262 (trade hard cover: alk. paper)
LC 2013-026434

SUMMARY: In this book, by Laurie Friedman, "eighth grade is off to a surprisingly promising start for April Sinclair. . . Making the dance team is the icing on the cake.

But with one unexpected move from her hot neighbor, Matt Parker, April's life starts to spin out of control. In the blink of an eye, her best friend is furious, her boyfriend dumps her, and the girls on the dance team don't want anything to do with her. How could things go so wrong so fast?" (Publisher's note)

REVIEW: *Kirkus Rev* v82 no4 p179 F 15 2014

"Too Good To Be True". "[Laurie] Friedman sensitively explores the emotional upheavals that sometimes accompany the middle school years. The revelation of April's clandestine kiss with Matt wreaks havoc in her life. April's lament, 'Can a girl make a mistake without her life falling apart?' highlights the intense pressures of middle school social life. Relying on the sage counsel of both her grandmother and father, April navigates her way. Readers will empathize as April displays spunk and resilience in addressing her mistakes and remaining true to herself."

REVIEW: *SLJ* v60 no4 p145 Ap 2014 Amy Commers

REVIEW: *Voice of Youth Advocates* v37 no1 p65 Ap 2014 Heather Christensen

FRIEDMAN, LAWRENCE J. The lives of Erich Fromm; love's prophet; [by] Lawrence J. Friedman 456 p. 2013 Columbia University Press

1. Biography (Literary form) 2. Love 3. Psychoanalysts—Germany—Biography 4. Psychoanalysts—United States—Biography

ISBN 0231162588; 9780231162586 (cloth : alk. paper); 9780231531061 (e-book)

LC 2012-024631

SUMMARY: This book, by Lawrence J. Friedman, offers an overview of the works and thought of Erich Fromm, "political activist, psychologist, psychoanalyst, philosopher, and one of the most important intellectuals of the twentieth century. Known for his theories of personality and political insight, Fromm dissected the sadomasochistic appeal of brutal dictators while also eloquently championing love. . . . this biography revisits the thinker's most important works." (Publisher's note)

REVIEW: *America* v209 no2 p33-4 Jl 15 2013 MICHAEL M. CANARIS

REVIEW: *Choice* v51 no2 p357 O 2013 C. J. Churchill

"The Lives of Erich Fromm: Love's Prophet." "[Author Lawrence J.] Friedman . . . provides a deep, insightful, and very human portrait of one of the great public intellectuals of the 20th century. Readers will perhaps be surprised to learn of Fromm's significant influence on political figures like Adlai Stevenson and J. William Fulbright; or of his important role in the founding of groups like SANE and Amnesty International; or that while he earned significant wealth through the sales of his books, he gave a very large amount of it away to progressive causes--this in keeping with his commitment to Jewish ethics and principle of social democracy. . . . Friedman treats Fromm with a humanism and depth of curiosity that Fromm would have appreciated."

REVIEW: *Kirkus Rev* v80 no23 p118 D 1 2012

REVIEW: *Libr J* v138 no1 p99 Ja 1 2013 E. James Lieberman

REVIEW: *N Y Rev Books* v60 no13 p61-3 Ag 15 2013 Alan Ryan

"The Lives of Erich Fromm: Love's Prophet." "Lawrence Friedman's biography has many virtues; it is meticulous, detailed, friendly to its subject but not uncritical, the result of many years of archival investigation and interviews with people who knew Fromm well. . . . Erich Fromm himself was a far from careful scholar, but The Lives of Erich Fromm is a reassuringly solid piece of work. What makes it a model of intellectual biography, however, is the way it illuminates the Erich Fromm who became famous in America in the 1950s, by seeing him in his many different settings--geographical, social, intellectual, and emotional."

REVIEW: *Publ Wkly* v259 no50 p51 D 10 2012

REVIEW: *Rev Am Hist* v42 no1 p140-5 Mr 2014 Robert Genter

"The Lives of Erich Fromm: Love's Prophet." "In this well-researched and splendidly written biography, Lawrence Friedman reveals the many 'lives' of this influential European intellectual--psychoanalyst, social psychologist, peace activist, self-help guru, German elitist, democratic socialist, radical humanist, and religious thinker. . . . If anything, Friedman should have done a bit more to explain Fromm's readership, describing the general reception of his books outside of academic reviews to explain why, for example, millions of copies of 'The Art of Loving' have been sold over the decades."

REVIEW: *TLS* no5771 p12 N 8 2013 PAUL REITTER

"The Lives of Erich Fromm: Love's Prophet." "Lawrence J. Friedman's biography tracks Fromm through the various phases of his life in detail, providing a thickness of description that hasn't been available before. . . . What occasionally feels unsatisfying is Friedman's mode of contextualization. . . . The greater disappointment, however, is that Friedman doesn't consistently shine where he promises real illumination. He maintains that his book will bring to light the connections between Fromm's personal circumstances and his major works, but while he ably reconstructs those circumstances and judiciously assesses Fromm's writings, his linking of the latter with the former often fails to deliver subtle or penetrating insights. . . . But these are minor disappointments."

FRIEL, HOWARD. Chomsky and Dershowitz; on endless war and the end of civil liberties; [by] Howard Friel 376 p. 2014 State University of New York Press

1. Civil rights—United States 2. Political science literature 3. War

ISBN 1566569427; 9781438449753 (hardcover: alk. paper); 9781566569422

LC 2013-023663

SUMMARY: This book, by Howard Friel, "using the works of intellectuals Alan Dershowitz of Harvard and Noam Chomsky of MIT as metaphors, . . . considers how attitudes and public policy on international law have changed since the terrorist attacks of 9/11. . . . [It] argues that Dershowitz has not honored his commitment to international law and human rights, while Chomsky has remained steadfast in his challenge to any nation . . . to threaten or use force in intervening in the affairs of other nations." (Booklist)

REVIEW: *Booklist* v110 no6 p10-1 N 15 2013 Vanessa Bush

"Chomsky and Dershowtiz: On Endless War and the End of Civil Liberties". "Declining civil liberties in the U.S. is a direct result of long U.S. support for violations of international law and human rights, including the Israeli-Palestinian conflict, argues Yale scholar [Howard] Friel. Using the works of intellectuals Alan Dershowitz of Harvard and Noam Chomsky of MIT as metaphors, Friel considers how attitudes and public policy on international law have changed since the terrorist attacks of 9/11."

REVIEW: *Libr J* v139 no2 p86 F 1 2014 Stephen Kent Shaw

FRIERSON, PATRICK R. What is the human being?; [by] Patrick R. Frierson ix, 322 p. 2013 Routledge

1. Existentialism 2. Human beings 3. Philosophical anthropology 4. Philosophical literature
ISBN 9780203070314 (e-book); 9780415558440 (hardback : alk. paper); 9780415558457 (pbk. : alk. paper)
LC 2012-029613

SUMMARY: This book by Patrick R. Frierson is part of the "Kant's Questions" series. "Framed in terms of [Immanuel] Kant's quest for an account of human nature, the book presents the whole of Kantian philosophy as a single anthropological project. The first section lays out Kant's view of human nature. . . . The final section defends Kant's view of human nature in light of more contemporary scientific naturalism, historicism, and existentialism." (Choice)

REVIEW: *Choice* v51 no4 p649-50 D 2013 L. A. Wilkinson

"What is the Human Being?" "In this excellent introduction to [Immanuel] Kant, [Patrick R.] Frierson . . . distills the profound complexity of Kantian philosophy into a remarkably accessible, concise, and well-argued contribution to the Routledge 'Kant's Questions' series. Framed in terms of Kant's quest for an account of human nature, the book presents the whole of Kantian philosophy as a single anthropological project. . . . Overall, Frierson's ability to simplify Kantian philosophy, without sacrificing philosophical rigor, makes for one of the best available contemporary introductions to Kant."

FRIESEN, JONATHAN. Mayday; a novel; [by] Jonathan Friesen 320 p. 2013 Puffin Books, an imprint of Penguin Group (USA) Inc.

1. Coma—Fiction 2. Self-sacrifice 3. Sisters—Fiction 4. Soul—Fiction 5. Speculative fiction
ISBN 9780142412299 (pbk.: alk. paper)
LC 2013-017913

SUMMARY: In this book by Jonathan Friesen, "even as her own soul hovers in the 'middle' space, her body barely clinging to life in a hospital room, 18-year-old Crow's thoughts are consumed with protecting her sister. When given the chance to go on a 'walkabout'—an opportunity to revisit her life and make things right—Crow learns that there may have been another side to the people and events that defined her. The only catch is that she must return as someone other than herself." (Kirkus Reviews)

REVIEW: *Bull Cent Child Books* v67 no9 p453 My 2014 K. C.

"Mayday". "While the premise is promising, the plotting is leggy and disjointed. . . . The other characters all too readily accept the sudden appearance, disappearance, and shape-shifting of these newcomer Shanes who are weirdly knowledgeable about everyone's lives. Addy herself is unconvincingly naive and untroubled, especially after she is assaulted by her stepfather. Crow, however, has a believably cynical disposition that is most evident in the harsh, angry tenor of her narration of past events. As she sees herself through the eyes of the Shanes, she confronts her damage with a gentleness she had previously reserved only for others; readers who are overly critical of themselves may find here a model for widening perspective."

REVIEW: *Kirkus Rev* v82 no4 p148 F 15 2014

REVIEW: *Voice of Youth Advocates* v37 no2 p74 Je 2014 Richard Vigdor

FRIESEN, T. MAX. When worlds collide; hunter-gatherer world-system change in the nineteenth-century Canadian Arctic; [by] T. Max Friesen xv, 260 p. 2013 University of Arizona Press

1. Acculturation—Yukon—Herschel Island 2. Anthropology literature 3. Ethnohistory—Yukon—Herschel Island 4. Hunting and gathering societies—Yukon—Herschel Island 5. Inuvialuit Eskimos—Colonization 6. Inuvialuit Eskimos—History—19th century 7. Inuvialuit Eskimos—Hunting
ISBN 9780816502448 (cloth : acid-free paper)
LC 2012-034299

SUMMARY: For this book, "Max Friesen has adapted and expanded world-system theory in order to develop a model that explains how hunter-gatherer interaction networks, or world-systems, are structured--and why they change. He has utilized this model to better understand the development of Inuvialuit society in the western Canadian Arctic over a 500-year span, from the pre-contact period to the early twentieth century." (Publisher's note)

REVIEW: *Choice* v51 no6 p1055 F 2014 J. S. Krysiek

"When Worlds Collide: Hunter-Gatherer World-System Change in the Nineteenth-Century Canadian Arctic." "Those familiar with Immanuel Wallerstein's world-system theory will appreciate . . . [T. Max] Friesen's examination of some of Canada's Inuit in centuries prior to the 20th century. . . . Friesen makes an important contribution to world-system literature; he also underscores the value of archaeological excavations, upon which he bases his analysis. Scholars who employ a Wallerstein-inspired approach in their own research, as well as archaeologists, particularly those involved in Arctic research, will read this work with interest. However, readers who could care less about excavated artifacts, trade items, and preciosities may find this book dull and uninspiring."

FRIEZE, DONNA-LEE.ed. Totally unofficial. See Totally unofficial

FRITSCH, RON. Promised Valley Peace; [by] Ron Fritsch 274 p. 2013 Createspace Independent Pub

1. Horses—Fiction 2. Imaginary wars & battles—Fiction 3. Land tenure—Fiction 4. Prehistoric peoples—Fiction 5. War stories
ISBN 1493672339; 9781493672332

SUMMARY: This book "is the fourth and last novel in Ron Fritsch's allegorical Promised Valley series. The conspirators and their allies from the first three novels give up on the gods, whose existence many of them doubt, and discover how to use horses in warfare. They prepare to employ them in a last battle to bring the prehistoric enemy hunters and farmers together as one people in a 'new kingdom' and end warfare between them forever." (Publisher's note)

REVIEW: *Kirkus Rev* v82 no2 p372 Ja 15 2014

"Promised Valley Peace". "The novel convincingly depicts a society in which homosexual relationships are conducted openly with no lessening of public esteem, and [Ron] Fritsch handles the theme with a no-fuss skill reminiscent of Mary Renault's. . . . Fritsch tells a very detailed, very human story, although the opening 10 pages, a stultifying, bullet-point plot summary of the previous books in the series, may alienate new readers. . . . The interminable threat of war allows Fritsch to make the conflict an allegory for every human conflict to come. There's a sad moment of irony when a character late in the book hopes that their peoples will 'never go to war again.' A wise, bittersweet conclusion to a sprawling tale of prehistoric war and peace."

FROM BEASTS TO SOULS; gender and embodiment in Medieval Europe; ix, 269 p. 2013 University of Notre Dame Press

1. Animals in literature 2. Historical literature 3. Literature, Medieval—History and criticism 4. Sex role in literature 5. Soul in literature

ISBN 0268022321 (pbk. : alk. paper); 9780268022327 (pbk. : alk. paper)

LC 2013-000463

SUMMARY: This book "raises the issues of species and gender in tandem, asking readers to consider more fully what happens to gender in medieval representations of nonhuman embodiment. The contributors reflect on the gender of stones and the soul, of worms and dragons, showing that medieval cultural artifacts, whether literary, historical, or visual, do not limit questions of gender to predictable forms of human or semi-human embodiment." (Publisher's note)

REVIEW: *Choice* v51 no6 p986-7 F 2014 A. P. Church

"From Beasts to Souls: Gender and Embodiment in Medieval Europe." "Readers who share the presuppositions of post-humanism and gender studies will find this book appealing, but others may be more skeptical. In essay after essay, contributors posit more speculative questions than they clearly prove through propositions and conclusions. . . . The anthology's contributors are an elite group of illuminati, educated and employed at the best schools. . . . Nevertheless, this book raises more questions than may be satisfactorily answered, especially for those who find it impossible, impractical, and maybe even undesirable to discard or deconstruct what humanistic culture accepts as constructed."

FROM PLUNDER TO PRESERVATION; Britain and the heritage of empire, c.1800-1940; xii, 304 p. 2013 Published for the British Academy by Oxford University Press

1. Antiquities—Collection and preservation—Corrupt practices—Congresses 2. Antiquities—Collection and preservation—Moral and ethical aspects—Congresses 3. Archaeology—Moral and ethical aspects—Congresses 4. Cultural property—Protection—Moral and ethical aspects—Congresses 5. Historic preservation—Great Britain—History—Congresses 6. Historical literature 7. Imperialism—Congresses 8. Pillage—Congresses

ISBN 0197265413 (hbk.); 9780197265413 (hbk.)

LC 2012-277798

SUMMARY: "What was the effect of the British Empire on the cultures and civilisations of the peoples over whom it ruled? This book takes a novel approach to this important and controversial subject by considering the impact of empire on the idea of 'heritage'." . . . It offers "a vivid story of how our current understanding of the diverse heritages of world history was forged in the crucible of the British Empire." (Publisher's note)

REVIEW: *TLS* no5783 p29 Ja 31 2014 KRISHAN KUMAR

"From Plunder to Preservation: Britain and the Heritage of Empire, c. 1800-1940." "Is the obsession with origins part of the reason for the European passion for preserving ancient monuments? And is that passion greater in Europe than elsewhere? . . . In that sense the European empires might count among their legacies an attitude towards the past that, contrary to many traditions, puts objects on a par with ideas and beliefs. It is one of the many strengths of this lively handsomely produced and beautifully illustrated collection of essays that it provides ample material for reflecting on this."

FROM POSTWAR TO POSTMODERN; art in Japan, 1945-1989; 464 p. 2013 Museum of Modern Art

1. Art literature 2. Japan—History—1945-1989 3. Japanese art—20th century 4. Photography—Japan 5. Video art

ISBN 9780822353683

LC 2012-952761

SUMMARY: In this book on Japanese art in the mid-to-late 20th century, "an array of key documents, artist manifestos, critical essays, and roundtable discussions are translated into English for the first time. The pieces cover a broad range of artistic mediums--including photography, film, performance, architecture, and design--and illuminate their various points of convergence in the Japanese context." (Publisher's note)

REVIEW: *Art Am* v101 no10 p75 N 2013

"Hybrid Culture: Japanese Media Arts in Dialogue With the West," "Japan's Modern Divide: The Photographs of Hiroshi Hamaya and Kansuke Yamamoto," and "From Postwar to Postmodern: Art in Japan 1945-1989: Primary Documents." "Sharing a high regard for precision, Japanese artists and engineers collaborate in ways that subtly meld Eastern and Western concepts, pure art and technical prowess, futurity and tradition. . . . Japanese photography bifurcated in the 1930s into a documentary stream, represented by Hiroshi Hamaya, and an experimental stream, exemplified by Kansuke Yamamoto. Five essayists discuss the artists' careers, illustrated by some 100 contrasting images. . . . Manifestos, essays and debates from Japan's fervent postwar era appear in English for the first time, accompanied by more than 20 new scholarly articles."

REVIEW: *Choice* v50 no12 p2198 Ag 2013 J. B. Gregory

FROST, MARK. Alliance; [by] Mark Frost 352 p. 2014 Random House Inc

1. Adventure stories 2. Good and evil—Fiction 3. Paranormal fiction 4. Secret societies—Fiction 5. Superheroes—Fiction

ISBN 0375870466; 9780375870460 (hardback)

LC 2013-041891

SUMMARY: This book is part of Mark Frost's "Paladin Prophecy" series. "Several months have passed since Will and his roommates defeated the Knights of Charlemagne, but many questions remain about the Knights, their ties to the monsters of the Never-Was and the disappearance of Will's parents. A wealthy school donor emerges as a major player in the conspiracy, so Will and his friends develop a risky plan to use their extraordinary abilities . . . to infiltrate and search his island home." (Kirkus Reviews)

REVIEW: *Kirkus Rev* v81 no24 p211 D 15 2013

"Alliance". "Will West faces old and new adversaries during summer vacation in this sloppy sequel to 'The Paladin Prophecy'. . . . Unfortunately, Frost's everything-plus-the-kitchen-sink approach to worldbuilding doesn't make more sense the second time around; even with a clumsy extended recap in the first chapter, the mix of secret societies, genetic manipulation, guardian angels and monsters from another dimension is hard to keep straight. The busy plot leaves little space for characterization . . . making the love triangle feel perfunctory, and Will's cross-country coach, Jericho, only appears when Will needs a convenient source of generic Native American mysticism and lore. When the obligatory cliffhanger ending comes, it's hard to care what happens next."

REVIEW: *SLJ* v60 no2 p104 F 2014 Saleena L. Davidson

REVIEW: *SLJ* v60 no4 p63 Ap 2014 Sarah Flood

REVIEW: *Voice of Youth Advocates* v37 no1 p81 Ap 2014 Bonnie Kunzel

FROST, NATASHA A. The punishment imperative. See Clear, T. R.

FRY, ERIN. Secrets of the Book; [by] Erin Fry 272 p. 2014 Amazon Childrens Pub

1. Books & reading—Fiction 2. Fantasy fiction 3. Magic—Fiction 4. Pandora (Greek mythology) 5. People with disabilities—Fiction

ISBN 1477847162; 9781477847169

SUMMARY: This book by Erin Fry follows "Spencer, a sixth-grader" and "his best friend, Gregor. . . . The boys get mixed up in mysterious goings-on when Ed, an elderly man that Spencer visits at a local nursing home, entrusts Spencer with a book and then promptly disappears. The story rushes on from there as Spencer brings to life (then loses) Socrates and finds himself pursued by a shadowy bad guy with a German accent. " (Kirkus Reviews)

REVIEW: *Booklist* v110 no11 p66 F 1 2014 Kathleen Isaacs

REVIEW: *Bull Cent Child Books* v67 no7 p356 Mr 2014 A. M.

REVIEW: *Kirkus Rev* v82 no1 p144 Ja 1 2014

"Secrets of the Book". "This mildly engaging fantasy features a magical book, famous figures from the past and a decidedly unheroic narrator who nevertheless manages (with some help) to save the world. . . . [Erin] Fry offers plenty of action to move the plot along, not giving readers too much time to puzzle over the mechanics of her magic. The casual, colloquial tone, sprinkled with humorous observations and asides, manages to sound enough like that of a sixth-grader to aid in the suspension of disbelief, though Spencer's reactions to Ed's granddaughter Mel seem a bit flowery for the average middle school boy. Fry breaks no new ground, but she does provide undemanding entertainment for fantasy fans and history buffs."

REVIEW: *Publ Wkly* v260 no48 p57-8 N 25 2013

REVIEW: *SLJ* v60 no4 p146 Ap 2014 Beth L. Meister

FU, KIM. For today I am a boy; [by] Kim Fu 256 p. 2014 Houghton Mifflin Harcourt

1. Bildungsromans 2. Brothers and sisters—Fiction 3. Chinese—Canada—Fiction 4. FICTION—Coming of Age 5. FICTION—Cultural Heritage 6. FICTION—Literary 7. Fathers and sons—Fiction 8. Gender identity—Fiction

ISBN 0544034724; 9780544034723 (hardback)

LC 2013-027720

SUMMARY: In this book, by Kim Fu, "a young man wrestles with gender expectations and his own gender identity. . . . Growing up in exurban Ontario, Peter was always the outlier, preferring his three sisters' girlish behavior over that of his rough-and-tumble male classmates. But his attempts to push his boyishness aside--cooking while wearing a much-loved apron, for instance--incur the wrath of his father, a conservative Chinese immigrant." (Kirkus Reviews)

REVIEW: *Booklist* v110 no5 p24-5 N 1 2013 Michael Cart

"For Today I Am A Boy." "Peter's Chinese name may be Juan Chaun ('Powerful King'), but when he is in the first grade, he declares, 'I want to be a mommy.' . . . In her episodic first novel, Canadian author [Kim] Fu does an excellent job of conveying the desperation of one trapped in the wrong body as well as the confusion and frustration of that condition. In a larger sense, she examines what it means to be a woman when, like Peter, you're born a man. An interesting, thought-provoking novel."

REVIEW: *Kirkus Rev* v81 no20 p86 O 15 2013

REVIEW: *N Y Times Book Rev* p18 F 2 2014 JIAYANG FAN

"For Today I Am a Boy." "In her sensitively wrought debut novel, 'For Today I Am a Boy,' set in a sleepy and predominantly white town in Ontario, Kim Fu invites us inside the Huang household, where patriarchy rules [and] the mother tongue is forbidden. . . . Fu, a 26-year-old Chinese-Canadian . . . is intimately attuned to the anxieties of first-generation go-getters. . . . The story of dictatorial parents and subjugated children is not a new one, but Fu cleverly juxtaposes the narrative of the father's attempt at cultural acclimation with the son's search for a female form."

REVIEW: *Publ Wkly* v260 no37 p24 S 16 2013

REVIEW: *Quill Quire* v80 no4 p27 My 2014 Emma Renda

FUCHS, BARBARA. The poetics of piracy; emulating Spain in English literature; [by] Barbara Fuchs 186 p. 2013 PENN/University of Pennsylvania Press

1. English literature—Early modern, 1500-1700—History and criticism 2. English literature—Spanish influences 3. Imitation in literature 4. Literature—History & criticism 5. Piracy (Copyright)

ISBN 9780812244755 (hardcover : acid-free paper)

LC 2012-031344

SUMMARY: In this book on early modern English literature, "Barbara Fuchs traces how Spanish material was transmitted into English writing, entangling English literature in questions of national and religious identity, and how piracy came to be a central textual metaphor, with appropriations from Spain triumphantly reimagined as heroic looting." (Publisher's note)

REVIEW: *Choice* v51 no5 p832 Ja 2014 K. M. Sibbald

"The Poetics of Piracy: Emulating Spain in English Literature." "A highly intelligent romp through 'theatrical mobility,' this is a good read stressing that transnational exchange is not merely stereotyping but instead engaged, self-aware dialogue between practitioners and their historical traditions. A powerful argument for reinscribing the Spanish legacy that cultural legatees--English and American--have so often tried to erase, this book should appeal to a wide readership irrespective of national interests and linguistic frames. . . . Highly recommended."

REVIEW: *TLS* no5768 p27 O 18 2013 HANNAH LEAH CRUMMÉ

FUCILE, TONY.il. Mitchell goes bowling. See Durand, H.

FUDGE, THOMAS A. The trial of Jan Hus; medieval heresy and criminal procedure; [by] Thomas A. Fudge xxiii, 392 p. 2013 Oxford University Press

1. Church history—Middle Ages, 600-1500 2. Criminal procedure (Canon law)—History—To 1500 3. Heresy (Canon law)—History—To 1500 4. Historical literature 5. Trials (Heresy)—Germany—Konstanz

ISBN 9780199988082 (hardcover : alk. paper)

LC 2012-040610

SUMMARY: This book, written by Thomas A. Fudge, "offers the first English-language examination of the indictment, relevant canon law, and questions of procedural legality." It "shows how this popular and successful priest became a criminal suspect and a convicted felon, and why he was publicly executed, providing critical insight into what may have been the most significant heresy trial of the Middle Ages." (Publisher's note)

REVIEW: *Choice* v51 no2 p329 O 2013 L. W. Marvin

"The Trial of Jan Hus: Medieval Heresy and Criminal Procedure." "This 'legal exegesis' meticulously analyzes the infamous trial, conviction, and execution of the Czech priest Jan Hus before and at the Council of Constance (1414-18). Hus appealed to the papacy when lower court rulings went against him, but eventually decided the pope could not be fair, so he appealed to Christ as supreme court justice. No earthly court then or now would accept that. Hus could have spared himself execution by recanting, but he refused. [Author Thomas A.] Fudge . . . painstakingly examines the case for and against Hus. . . . Fudge concludes that based on medieval ecclesiastical and legal procedure rather than modern notions of justice, Hus received due process."

FUECHTNER, VERONIKA.ed. Imagining Germany Imagining Asia. See Imagining Germany Imagining Asia

FUGA, NINA.il. Chasing the rose. See Di Robilant, A.

FUHRMANN, MATTHEW.ed. The nuclear renaissance and international security. See The nuclear renaissance and international security

FÜHMANN, FRANZ, 1922-1984. The Jew Car; Fourteen Days from Two Decades; 256 p. 2013 University of Chicago Press

1. Autobiographical fiction 2. Germany—Politics & government—1933-1945 3. National socialism 4. Nazis 5. Prisoners of war—Fiction

ISBN 0857420860; 9780857420862

SUMMARY: This book presents "a cycle of autobiographical stories which chronicles the author's relationship with Nazi ideology, from his embrace of it during the Depression to his ultimate disenchantment, which began while he was a Soviet prisoner of war. [Franz] Fühmann pairs phases of his youth with key moments in the Third Reich's rise and fall." (Times Literary Supplement)

REVIEW: *London Rev Books* v36 no1 p23-4 Ja 9 2014 Neal Ascherson

"Red Love: The Story of an East German Family" and "The Jew Car". "These two excellent hooks show that passion and commitment were often present too: not just fanatical excitement, but the genuine subjective passion to contribute to the systems' goals, beneath the outer show of marching, chanting and resolution-signing demanded by the dictatorships. . . . 'To read The Jew Car' is to be reminded that the precondition for mass belief in Hitlerism was a degree of ignorance and credulity perhaps impossible today. . . . It's unlikely that everything happened just as he describes it, and there are some very large omissions. . . . But this is, even so, one of the most honest and revealing accounts of the long rearguard action conducted by blind faith in Fatherland and Führer against disenchantment. . . . 'Red Love' is a silly title for a serious, very moving book."

REVIEW: *TLS* no5765 p20 S 27 2013 DANIEL MEDIN

"The Jew Car" and "The Devil's Workshop." "[Franz] Fühmann pairs phases of his youth with key moments in the Third Reich's rise and fall--a set of parallel narratives that justify calling the book a novel and allow the story of a life to stand in for the story of a nation. . . . Driven by [Jáchuym] Topol's ingenuity and mischief, these commercial passages are easily the funniest of the novel. . . . In the novel's second part, the humour grows corrosive. . . . 'The Devil's Workshop' is a miracle of compression, its scope greater than ought to be possible for a book of its length. It should help to cement Jáchym Topol's reputation as one of the most original and compelling European voices at work today."

FULDA, BERNHARD. Max Pechstein: The Rise and Fall of Expressionism; [by] Bernhard Fulda xvi, 432 p. 2012 De Gruyter

1. Art and society—Germany—History—20th century 2. Art literature 3. Artists—Germany—Biography 4. Expressionism (Art)

ISBN 9783110296624 (alk. paper)

LC 2012-035962

SUMMARY: This book on artist Max Pechstein "employs the genre of biography to investigate how Pechstein achieved his status during his lifetime, as well as what contributed to its decline after his death. . . . The book's chapters divide his career into six periods, providing a . . . view of how that career was constructed within the German art world." (Burlington Magazine)

REVIEW: *Burlington Mag* v156 no1330 p37-8 Ja 2014 WILLIAM S. SIMMONS

"Max Pechstein: The Rise and Fall of Expressionism". "Making use of a wealth of existing scholarship, as well as many new sources, the book's chapters divide his career into six periods, providing a thorough view of how that career was constructed within the German art world. . . . Pechstein's career seems to have come full circle in this late return to a conservative stress on the craft of painting and to the radical escape from modernity into South Seas primitivism. A series of nine paintings of sunflowers in 1948 also suggests a reconnection with [Vincent] Van Gogh. Such recognitions are possible because of what the reader has learned from the thorough documentation and insightful analysis of

Pechstein's career provided by this critical biography."

FULLERTON, SUSANNAH. Happily Ever After; Celebrating Jane Austen's Pride and Prejudice; [by] Susannah Fullerton 240 p. 2013 Frances Lincoln Publishers Ltd

1. Austen, Jane, 1775-1817 2. Austen, Jane, 1775-1817—Characters 3. Free indirect speech 4. Irony in literature 5. Literary critiques

ISBN 0711233748; 9780711233744

SUMMARY: This book tells "the tale of how 'Pride and Prejudice' came to be written, its first reception in a world that didn't take much notice of it and then its growing popularity. As well as discussing the famous characters . . . Susannah Fullerton looks at the style of the novel - its wicked irony, its brilliant structuring, its revolutionary use of the technique known as 'free indirect speech'." (Publisher's note)

REVIEW: *TLS* no5761 p11 Ag 30 2013 ALICIA RIX

"Happily Ever After: Celebrating Jane Austen's 'Pride and Prejudice,'" and "The Cambridge Companion to 'Pride and Prejudice'." "An enjoyable and loyally enthusiastic tribute to 'Pride and Prejudice,' written largely for, and often about, die-hard Janeites. . . . The book contains thoughtful plot and character summaries useful for orienting the school student, and is full of trivia for Austen enthusiasts. . . . It is also delightfully illustrated. . . . The last four essays of the intelligent and accessible 'Cambridge Companion to "Pride and Prejudice"' consider the novel's afterlife as a cultural industry. . . . The Companion's heady journey through the novel's 'proliferation' and expansion . . . is balanced; however, by essays addressing the novel's style, topography, and literary and historical contexts."

FUMIHIKO SUMITOMO.ed. From postwar to postmodern. See From postwar to postmodern

FUNK, MCKENZIE. Windfall; the booming business of global warming; [by] McKenzie Funk 320 p. 2014 Penguin Press

1. Business literature 2. Clean energy investment 3. Energy industries 4. Entrepreneurship 5. Global warming—Economic aspects

ISBN 1594204012; 9781594204012 (hardback)

LC 2013-028118

SUMMARY: This book, by McKenzie Funk, is an "investigation into how people around the globe are cashing in on [global] warming. . . . Global warming's physical impacts can be separated into three broad categories: melt, drought, and deluge. Funk travels to two dozen countries to profile entrepreneurial people who see in each of these forces a potential windfall." (Publisher's note)

REVIEW: *Bookforum* v20 no5 p15-6 F/Mr 2014 JULIET EILPERIN

"Windfall: The Booming Business of Global Warming." "[McKenzie] Funk's business survey-cum-travelogue exposes in vivid detail exactly how certain individuals, companies, and nations are taking advantage of a changing climate, while others are losing out. . . . Funk's unsparing focus on the mechanics of planning ahead for the many contingencies and emergencies of a warming world makes for an arresting book. Watching the various players in the emerging new climate economy deal with the inevitability of global warming in real time is fascinating, if also fairly depressing, reading. . . . The book's main strength lies in Funk's ability to bring to the fore many of the people long dug into the trenches of the climate-adaptation battle."

REVIEW: *Kirkus Rev* v81 no24 p70 D 15 2013

REVIEW: *New Sci* v221 no2962 p52-3 Mr 29 2014 Fred Pearce

REVIEW: *Orion Magazine* v33 no3 p98-9 My/Ag 2014 Kathryn Flagg

REVIEW: *Publ Wkly* v260 no45 p60-1 N 11 2013

REVIEW: *Sci Am* v310 no1 p78 Ja 2014 Lee Billings

FURSTENAU, NINA MUKERJEE. Biting through the skin; an Indian kitchen in America's heartland; [by] Nina Mukerjee Furstenau 168 p. 2013 University of Iowa Press

1. Bengali Americans—Biography 2. Bengali Americans—Food 3. Bengali Americans—Social life and customs 4. Cookbooks 5. Cooking, Indic 6. Food habits—India—Bengal 7. Food habits—Kansas 8. Memoirs

ISBN 1609381858 (pbk. : alk. paper); 9781609381851 (pbk. : alk. paper)

LC 2013-005215

SUMMARY: "At once a traveler's tale, a memoir, and a mouthwatering cookbook, 'Biting through the Skin' offers a first-generation immigrant's perspective on growing up in America's heartland. Author Nina Mukerjee Furstenau's parents brought her from Bengal in northern India to the small town of Pittsburg, Kansas, in 1964 . . . Her parents transferred the cultural, spiritual, and family values they had brought . . . through the rituals of cooking, serving, and eating Bengali food." (Publisher's note)

REVIEW: *N Y Times Book Rev* p25 D 15 2013 JENNY ROSENSTRACH

"Biting Through the Skin: An Indian Kitchen in America's Heartland," "Three Squares: The Invention of the American Meal," and "Fried Walleye and Cherry Pie: Midwestern Writers on Food." "In Nine Mukerjee Furstenau's memoir, 'Biting Through the Skin: An Indian Kitchen in America's Heartland' . . . , the author uses family recipes to bridge two worlds. . . . In the engrossing 'Three Squares: The Invention of the American Meal' . . . , Abigail Carroll lays down some historical context, reminding us dinner became a signifier of class. . . . In Peggy Wolff's 'Fried Walleye and Cherry Pie' . . . the quality of the writing is uneven, but Heartland natives will embrace the recipes."

FURUHATA, YURIKO, 1973-. Cinema of actuality; Japanese avant-garde filmmaking in the season of image politics; [by] Yuriko Furuhata 280 p. 2013 Duke University Press

1. Avant-garde (Arts) 2. Film criticism 3. Film theory 4. Motion picture literature 5. Motion pictures—Japan—History—20th century 6. Motion pictures—Political aspects—Japan—History—20th century

ISBN 9780822354901 (cloth : alk. paper); 9780822355045 (pbk. : alk. paper)

LC 2013-011687

SUMMARY: In this book, "Yuriko Furuhata explores how avant-garde Japanese films of the 1960s and early 1970s integrated themselves into other media forms, including the manga cartoon, the still photograph, television and, most importantly, journalism in print and on screen. In so doing, she explores the political function of the image in a turbulent age." (Times Literary Supplement)

REVIEW: *TLS* no5772 p31 N 15 2013 ALEXANDER JACOBY

"Cinema of Actuality: Japanese Avant-Garde Filmmaking in the Season of Image Politics." "[Yuriko] Furuhata usefully sets key films . . . in the context of the influential landscape theory. . . . She convincingly shows how awareness of it is a prerequisite for understanding some of the era's key films, writing suggestively on how they expose the use of urban planning as a force for social control. Some of the book's theoretical underpinnings feel more awkward. . . .It might also be said that the book is sometimes repetitious, and the writing somewhat ponderous. Nevertheless, at her best Furuhata convincingly sketches the intellectual and social environment that gave birth to some of Japan's most distinctive films."

FURUTO, SHARLENE B. C. L.ed. Social welfare in East Asia and the Pacific. See Social welfare in East Asia and the Pacific

G

GABORIK, PATRICIA.tr. In broad daylight. See In broad daylight. See Pedulla, G.

GABRIEL, RICHARD A. Between flesh and steel; a history of military medicine from the Middle Ages to the war in Afghanistan; [by] Richard A. Gabriel 312 p. 2013 Potomac Books

1. Historical literature 2. History, Early Modern 1451-1600 3. History, Modern 1601- 4. Military Medicine—history 5. War 6. Weapons—history 7. Wounds and Injuries—surgery

ISBN 1612344208; 9781612344201 (cloth : alk. paper); 9781612344218 (e-book)

LC 2012-039781

SUMMARY: Author Richard A. Gabriel's book "traces the historical development of military medicine from the Middle Ages to modern times. . . . Gabriel focuses on three key elements: the modifications in warfare and weapons whose increased killing power radically changed the medical challenges that battle surgeons faced in dealing with casualties, advancements in medical techniques that increased the effectiveness of military medical care, and changes that finally brought about the establishment of military medical care system in modern times." (Publisher's note)

REVIEW: *Choice* v51 no1 p114 S 2013 M. W. Carr

"Between Flesh and Steel: A History of Military Medicine From the Middle Ages to the War in Afghanistan." "Examining military medicine from the 1400s to today's wars in Iraq and Afghanistan, [author Richard A.] Gabriel . . . succinctly documents and describes military medical care along with the cultural, political, and engineering influences on military medicine in various time periods. . . . The ability of medical care givers to evacuate, treat, and save wounded soldiers is impressive, but as Gabriel explains, the lethality of modern weapons . . . make doing so increasingly difficult. . . . 'Between Flesh and Steel' provides an excellent examination of medicine and war."

GADDIS, WILLIAM, 1922-1998. JR; [by] William Gaddis 726 1975 Knopf

1. Capitalists & financiers—Fiction 2. Collectors & collecting 3. Corporations 4. Humorous stories 5. Teenagers—Fiction

ISBN 0-394-49550-0; 0-394-73142-5 (paperback)

LC 75-8-230

SUMMARY: In this book, "JR, ambitious sixth-grader in torn sneakers, bred on the challenge of 'free enterprise' and fired by heady mail-order promises of 'success' . . . parlays a deal for thousands of surplus Navy picnic forks . . . into a nationwide, hydra-headed 'family of companies.' The JR Corp and its Boss engulf brokers, lawyers, Congressmen, disaffected school teachers . . . and a fledgling composer." (Publisher's note)

"JR, ambitious sixth-grader in torn sneakers, bred on the challenge of 'free enterprise' and fired by heady mail-order promises of 'success' . . . parlays a deal for thousands of surplus Navy picnic forks . . . into a nationwide, hydra-headed 'family of companies.' The JR Corp and its Boss engulf brokers, lawyers, Congressmen, disaffected school teachers and disen-franchised Indians, drunks, divorcees, secondhand generals, and a fledgling composer. . . . [Most of the book consists of the conversation of the characters] talking to each other, at each other, into phones, on intercoms, [and] from TV screens and radios." (Publisher's note)

REVIEW: *TLS* no5750 p16 Je 14 2013

"JR." "The novel is brutally hard to read, the reader's well-being treated with indifference or sadism. Seven hundred densely packed pages without chapter division or other landmarks . . . written almost exclusively in torrents of halting, gabbling dialogue, mostly un-attributed . . . by speakers often inarticulate, drunk or mad, often changing character while I stopped to bat an eyelid. It gets easier as the voices become familiar and the jokes more frequent; Mr [William] Gaddis has a remarkable ear for the innumerable varieties of pathetic or pompous or passionate incoherence. If the texture of the writing were all, this would be fine, but there is a plot of exceptional complexity . . . the narrative thread desperately easy to lose."

GAGNE, TAMMY. Buster Posey; [by] Tammy Gagne 32 p. 2014 Mitchell Lane Publishers

1. Baseball players—United States—Biography—Juvenile literature 2. Children's nonfiction 3. Football—Awards—United States 4. Sports injuries

ISBN 9781612284583 (library bound)

LC 2013-023055

SUMMARY: This book on football player Buster Posey is part of the "Robbie Reader: Contemporary Biography" series, which presents "a brief look at each player's childhood and high-school

play before launching into their award-winning sports careers. . . . 'Buster Posey' shows how this catcher and first baseman overcame injury to earn the National League MVP Award." (Booklist)

REVIEW: *Booklist* v110 no13 p66 Mr 1 2014 Angela Leeper

"Andrew Luck," "Buster Posey," and "Joe Flacco." "Good sports biographies are a must for any school or public library, and these titles in the Robbie Reader: Contemporary Biography series satisfy this need. Each book begins with a dramatic scene from the athlete's pro career, which ensures further reading. The large, accessible text continues with a brief look at each player's childhood and high-school play before launching into their award-winning sports careers. . . . A chronology, glossary, career statistics, and other back matter will further gratify sports enthusiasts."

GAIDUK, ILYA V. Divided together; the United States and the Soviet Union in the United Nations, 1945-1965; [by] Ilya V. Gaiduk xx, 328 p. 2012 Woodrow Wilson Center Press Stanford University Press

1. Cold War 2. Historical literature 3. United Nations—History

ISBN 9780804782920 (cloth)

LC 2011-053432

SUMMARY: This book by Ilya V. Gaiduk "studies US and Soviet policy toward the United Nations during the first two decades of the Cold War. It sheds new light on a series of key episodes, beginning with the prehistory of the UN, an institution that aimed to keep the Cold War cold. Gaiduk employs previously secret Soviet files on UN policy, greatly expanding the evidentiary basis for studying the world organization." (Publisher's note)

REVIEW: *Am Hist Rev* v119 no2 p482 Ap 2014 Jussi M. Hanhimäki

REVIEW: *Choice* v51 no1 p159 S 2013 D. J. Dunn

"Divided Together: The United States and the Soviet Union in the United Nations, 1945-1965." "[Ilya V.] Gaiduk, former research fellow at the Institute of World History in Moscow who died unexpectedly in 2011, wrote an interesting history of US-Soviet relations in the UN from 1945 to 1965. Although not a detailed history of US-Soviet interaction at the UN for that period, it does cover . . . the strained relationship during the Stalin and Khrushchev eras of the Cold War. Based upon research in the archives of Russia and the US, the book reveals new details about such events as the Berlin Crisis and the Korean War and makes clear that the Soviets considered the UN to be a pliant tool of the US and, therefore, tried to frustrate its work and refused to pay its share of UN costs."

GAILEY, SAMUEL W. Deep Winter; a novel; [by] Samuel W. Gailey 304 p. 2014 Blue Rider Press

1. FICTION—Thrillers 2. Friendship—Fiction 3. Murder—Investigation—Pennsylvania—Fiction 4. People with mental disabilities—Fiction 5. Police—Fiction

ISBN 9780399165962 (hardback)

LC 2013-036456

SUMMARY: In this book, "Danny Bedford—fat, mentally slow, and considered harmless by most folks in the small town of Wyalusing, Pa.—discovers Mindy Knolls's battered body in her trailer on her birthday in 1984. . . . A dispirited and confused Danny, suspected of Mindy's murder, wanders the woods while some hunt to capture and others to kill him. Some townspeople doubt his guilt, but few are willing to stand up for him." (Publishers Weekly)

REVIEW: *Booklist* v110 no9/10 p48-9 Ja 1 2014 Don Crinklaw

REVIEW: *Kirkus Rev* v82 no2 p222 Ja 15 2014

"Deep Winter". "Screenwriter [Samuel W.] Gailey's first novel owes a tip of the hat to John Steinbeck's Of Mice and Men. . . . What follows is a race to pin the crime on the innocent man by some of the most odious characters this side of the Evil Empire, including an extraneous drunken state police officer. Gailey writes visually, rendering the characters and action both vivid and alive. But his townsfolk behave so shamefully toward Danny, and the villain is so despicable, that the book often reads more like a fairy tale than a novel. Gailey's writing is the saving grace in this tale of good versus evil."

REVIEW: *N Y Times Book Rev* p15 F 16 2014 MARILYN STASIO

REVIEW: *Publ Wkly* v260 no50 p48-9 D 9 2013

GAIMAN, NEIL, 1960-. Fortunately, the milk; [by] Neil Gaiman 128 p. 2013 Harper, an imprint of HarperCollinsPublishers

1. Adventure and adventurers—Fiction 2. Family storytelling 3. Fathers—Fiction 4. Humorous stories 5. Space and time—Fiction

ISBN 0062224077; 9780062224071 (hardcover bdgs)

LC 2012-050670

SUMMARY: This children's picture book by Neil Gaiman is "about a father who has taken an excessively long time to return from the corner store with milk for his children's breakfast." He "is abducted by aliens, made to walk the plank by pirates, and rescued by a stegosaurus in a balloon, among other outrageous escapades." (Publishers Weekly)

REVIEW: *Booklist* v110 no18 p72 My 15 2014

REVIEW: *Booklist* v110 no16 p62 Ap 15 2014 Brian Wilson

REVIEW: *Booklist* v109 no17 p74 My 1 2013 Gillian Engberg

REVIEW: *Booklist* v109 no21 p74 Jl 1 2013 Thom Barthelmess

REVIEW: *Bull Cent Child Books* v67 no2 p89-90 O 2013 K. Q. G.

"Fortunately, the Milk." "The cheerful pell-mell absurdity of this brief but delightful bit of whimsy is contagious, and readers will be swept along with the action just as the dad is swept up into Steg's balloon. [Illustrator Skottie] Young's pen and ink illustrations have an energetic flair, with scritch-scratchy linework and a fatherly hero who bears quite the resemblance to Gaiman himself; the goofiness is mostly all in fun, but one illustration of prehistoric tribesmen unfortunately teeters toward stereotyping. Offspring of parents with a penchant for hyperbole will sympathetically roll their eyes even as they delight in the dad's constant reassurance that the milk is just fine while he describes battling off buccaneers and an angry god."

REVIEW: *Horn Book Magazine* v89 no6 p92-3 N/D 2013 SARAH ELLIS

REVIEW: *Kirkus Rev* v81 no13 p285 Jl 1 2013

REVIEW: *Publ Wkly* v260 no28 p171-2 Jl 15 2013

REVIEW: *SLJ* v60 no3 p70 Mr 2014 Jennifer Verbrugge

REVIEW: *SLJ* v59 no10 p1 O 2013 Amy Shepherd

GAL, OFER. Baroque science. See Chen-Morris, R.

GALATEO, OR, THE RULES OF POLITE BEHAVIOR; 144 p. 2013 The University of Chicago Press

1. Conversation—Early works to 1800 2. Etiquette—Handbooks, manuals, etc. 3. Etiquette, Medieval—

Early works to 1800 4. Flattery 5. Handbooks, vademecums, etc.
ISBN 9780226010977 (cloth : alk. paper)
LC 2013-005588

SUMMARY: This etiquette guide, "first published in 1558 . . . was reading matter for noblemen, hauts bourgeois, and men in high places. . . . Many of the key entries . . . pertain to the different forms of address, flattery, and designations for rank or social status. [Giovanni] della Casa assails the rising tides of flattery, intended to gain status or security from the powerful. M. F. Rusnak's edition seeks to put 'Galateo' into a rhetorical tradition with roots in the ancient world." (Times Literary Supplement)

REVIEW: *Choice* v51 no4 p649 D 2013 D. Stewart

REVIEW: *N Y Times Book Rev* p12 Je 2 2013 JUDITH MARTIN

REVIEW: *Publ Wkly* v260 no14 p53-4 Ap 8 2013

REVIEW: *TLS* no5759 p35 Ag 16 2013 LAURO MARTINES

"Galateo: Or, the Rules of Polite Behavior." "Composed by a worldly archbishop, 'Galateo' was reading matter for noblemen,m hauts bourgeois, and men in high places. It has all the well-known admonitions. . . . Many of the key entries, however, pertain to the different forms of address, flattery, and designations for rank or social status. . . . M. F. Rusnak's edition seeks to put 'Galateo' into a rhetorical tradition with roots in the ancient world. This approach is certainly defensible, but it floats the work in a political and social vacuum."

GALBRAITH, BREE. Once upon a balloon; [by] Bree Galbraith 32 p. 2013 Orca Book Publishers
1. Balloons 2. Brothers—Juvenile fiction 3. Children's stories 4. Imagination 5. Picture books for children
ISBN 9781459803244 (hardcover); 9781459803251 (electronic edition; 9781459803268 (electronic edition
LC 2013-935385

SUMMARY: Written by Bree Galbraith and illustrated by Isabelle Malenfant, this picture book describes how "Theo is brokenhearted when he accidentally lets go of the string of his party balloon. As he watches it float out of sight, Theo wonders where his balloon might have gone. Luckily, his older brother Zeke knows everything about everything. Zeke explains that it is a little-known fact that all lost balloons end up in Chicago, the Windy City." (Publisher's note)

REVIEW: *Kirkus Rev* v81 no18 p83 S 15 2013

REVIEW: *Quill Quire* v79 no7 p34 S 2013 Sarah Sawler

"Once Upon a Balloon." "In Vancouver graphic designer Bree Galbraith's debut picture book, young Theo's tale begins with a common childhood heartbreak: a balloon slipping from his grasp and floating away. . . . Galbraith demonstrates an intimate understanding of a child's inquisitive, innocent nature. . . . The fantastical storyline is enhanced by Isabelle Malenfant's whimsical illustrations. . . . Children will be delighted as Theo persists (and succeeds) in trying to help Frank, and adult readers may be reminded of something too easily forgotten: that a childlike sense of wonder is something to be treasured."

GALBRAITH, KATE. The great Texas wind rush; how George Bush, Ann Richards, and a bunch of tinkerers helped the oil and gas state win the race to wind power; [by] Kate Galbraith viii, 199 p. 2013 University of Texas Press
1. Historical literature 2. Renewable energy sources—Texas 3. Richards, Ann, 1933-2006 4. Texas—Politics & government 5. Wind power—Government policy—Texas
ISBN 9780292735835 (cloth: alk. paper)
LC 2012-044363

SUMMARY: In this book on the development of wind power in Texas, authors Kate Galbraith and Asher Price "explain the policies and science that propelled the 'windcatters' to reap the great harvest of Texas wind. They also explore what the future holds for this relentless resource that is changing the face of Texas energy." (Publisher's note)

REVIEW: *Choice* v51 no9 p1682 My 2014 D. L. Feldman

"The Great Texas Wind Rush: How George Bush, Ann Richards, and a Bunch of Tinkerers Helped the Oil and Gas State Win the Race to Wind Power". "An entertaining, fast-paced, insightful snapshot as to how Texas catapulted itself into the top spot for US wind-energy production. . . . Students will enjoy the colorful anecdotes and political insights into debates over wind-power development, while scholars will benefit from the authors' efforts to frame these developments within larger national and regional trends. . . . Efforts to distill lessons generalizable to other states are less successful, however, if only because oversimplification of other states' efforts—and brevity of discussion—diminish the impact of their arguments."

GALBRAITH, KATHRYN. Two bunny buddies; 32 p. 2014 Harcourt Children's Books, Houghton Mifflin Harcourt
1. Children's stories 2. Emotions (Psychology)—Juvenile literature 3. Friendship—Fiction 4. Rabbits—Fiction 5. Sharing
ISBN 9780544176522
LC 2013-020192

SUMMARY: In this children's book, "two bunnies . . . set off together . . . down a long path under the hot sun. When the path divides, the bunnies disagree on which way to travel, and an argument ensues. Names are flung . . . and the rabbits part company, each continuing to hike alone. After finding berries and clover, both bunnies are sad without a companion to share their discoveries. The rabbits gather food to take back and then reverse directions to meet in the middle, friends once again." (Kirkus Reviews)

REVIEW: *Booklist* v110 no13 p79 Mr 1 2014 Kara Dean

REVIEW: *Bull Cent Child Books* v67 no9 p453 My 2014 T. A.

REVIEW: *Kirkus Rev* v82 no5 p89 Mr 1 2014

"Two Bunny Buddies". "In this simple but insightful story, two rabbits discover that lunch with a pal is more fun than eating alone. . . . The minimal text conveys an entire plot full of humor and emotion in just a few words, effectively using action verbs, repetition and occasional rhyming word pairs ('One bunny sighs. / One bunny cries'). Deftly designed cartoon-style illustrations use simple shapes outlined in thick, black strokes set against pastel backgrounds, which will show up well in group readings. . . . Learning how to navigate the path of friendship is an important part of life, and these bunny buddies learn a lesson that is gently, beautifully shown rather than told."

REVIEW: *Publ Wkly* v260 no50 p69 D 9 2013

REVIEW: *SLJ* v60 no2 p72 F 2014 Linda Ludke

GALBRAITH, KATHRYN O. Where is baby?; 32 p. 2013 Peachtree Publishers

1. Animal defenses—Juvenile literature 2. Animals—Infancy—Juvenile literature 3. Children's nonfiction 4. Infants—Juvenile literature 5. Pregnancy
ISBN 1561457078; 9781561457076
LC 2012-033522

SUMMARY: This book, by Kathryn O. Galbraith and illustrated by John Butler, presents an "introduction to animal babies [that] focuses on how they keep themselves safe by hiding. Each page spread that follows features a baby animal and explains where and how it hides. The acrylic-and-colored-pencil illustrations depict cuddly baby animals up close, allowing readers to see their faces as well as their textures and colorations in great detail." (Kirkus Reviews)

REVIEW: *Kirkus Rev* v81 no16 p167 Ag 15 2013

"Where Is Baby?" "This sweet, simple introduction to animal babies focuses on how they keep themselves safe by hiding. . . . Though limited to only a short sentence on most pages, the language is quietly poetic, with audience-appropriate descriptive vocabulary. The acrylic-and-colored-pencil illustrations depict cuddly baby animals up close, allowing readers to see their faces as well as their textures and colorations in great detail. While the illustrations are lovely, a few will likely provoke some consternation, as children will wonder why the animals are so easy to spot when they are supposed to be hiding by blending into the background."

THE GALE ENCYCLOPEDIA OF NURSING AND ALLIED HEALTH; 6 v. (xxvi, 3784 p.) 2013 Gale Cengage Learning

1. Allied Health Personnel—Encyclopedias—English 2. Medical literature 3. Medicine—Encyclopedias 4. Nursing—Encyclopedias 5. Nursing—Encyclopedias—English 6. Nursing Care—Encyclopedias—English
ISBN 9781414498881 (set : alk. paper)
LC 2012-034778

SUMMARY: This book is the third edition of an encyclopedia of nursing and allied health fields. Its "more than 1,000 alphabetically arranged entries, of which about 100 are new, cover topics in body systems and functions, conditions and common diseases, contemporary health care issues and theories, techniques and practices, and devices and equipment. The Encyclopedia covers all major health professions, including nursing, physical therapy, occupational therapy, respiratory therapy and more." (Publisher's note)

REVIEW: *Choice* v51 no5 p806 Ja 2014 L. M. McMain

"The Gale Encyclopedia of Nursing and Allied Health." "Expanded to six volumes, with over 150 new entries, this third edition is destined to outshine the previous ones. . . . Written to be understandable to educated laypeople, the six volumes feature excellent photos, illustrations, charts, and graphs. . . . Entries are consistently arranged to include a definition; description; information on prevention and function, as appropriate; key terms; and a list of resources. This will be a valuable resource for all public and academic libraries, especially those serving nursing and allied health science students."

GALEN, SHANA. Sapphires Are an Earl's Best Friend; [by] Shana Galen 352 p. 2014 Sourcebooks Inc

1. Courtesans 2. Fathers & sons—Fiction 3. Love stories 4. Nobility (Social class)—Great Britain—Fiction 5. Spy stories
ISBN 140226979X; 9781402269790

SUMMARY: In this book, by Shana Galen, "Lily Dawson . . . plays the role of the courtesan flawlessly while her real purpose is spying in the service of the Crown. Her mission now is to seduce a duke to test his true loyalties. She'll do it, even though the man she really wants is Andrew Booth-Payne, Earl of Darlington—the duke's son. Andrew is furious when he finds himself rivaling his father for Lily's attention. When he uncovers Lily's mission, Andrew is faced with impossible choices." (Publisher's note)

REVIEW: *Kirkus Rev* v82 no4 p219 F 15 2014

"Sapphires Are An Earl's Best Friend". " Lily Dawson's reputation as the Countess of Charm, a renowned courtesan, is secretly a cover for her intelligence gathering, and her current mission is compromised when the only man she's ever loved finally notices her—just as she is trying to seduce his father. . . . The third installment in the Jewels of the Ton trilogy, the novel finishes off a series that nods to the demimonde, international intrigue, and various secrets and lies, which keeps the plots afloat and the relationships steamy and emotionally satisfying. The courtesans are never as wicked as they pretend, but the road to happily-ever-after is intense, conflicted, suspenseful and fun."

REVIEW: *Publ Wkly* v261 no3 p37 Ja 20 2014

GALITSKI, VICTOR, JR. Exploring quantum mechanics. See Kogan, V.

GALLAGER, DAVID A.ed. Appraising art. See Appraising art

GALLAND, NICOLE. Godiva; [by] Nicole Galland 336 p. 2013 HarperCollins

1. Godiva, fl. 1040-1080 2. Great Britain—Kings & rulers—Fiction 3. Historical fiction 4. Human sexuality—Fiction 5. Nobility (Social class)—Great Britain—Fiction
ISBN 0062026887; 9780062026880

SUMMARY: In this book, Nicole Galland explores the story of the historical figure Lady Godiva. "Her Countess Godiva cheerfully flirts her way to whatever she wants until she finds herself in conflict with an unjust king, who demands that Godiva either surrender Coventry to him or ride naked through town as punishment. Further complicating matters are the problems of Godiva's best friend, an abbess facing the consequences of having succumbed to sexual temptation." (Library Journal)

REVIEW: *Booklist* v109 no21 p43-4 Jl 1 2013 Julie Trevelyan

REVIEW: *N Y Times Book Rev* p34 S 8 2013 Alex Kuczynski

"Godiva." "You'll need lots of sugary cocktails to soldier your way through [Nicole] Galland's retelling of the events leading up to Lady Godiva's mythic ride through the streets of Coventry. . . . The actual Lady Godiva . . . is an intriguing historical figure. But in this mawkish telling she comes off like a scheming, chortling Samantha from 'Sex and the City. . . . Galland's description of the ride is convincing. . . . But these passages . . . aren't enough to rescue 'Godiva' from self-satire. After reading the novel you may well feel you've witnessed a piece of medieval high camp or spent the weekend at a Renaissance Faire trying to escape the pawing hands of a sweaty, sexually voracious jouster."

GALLATI, BARBARA DAYER. Beauty's Legacy; Gilded Age Portraits in America; [by] Barbara Dayer Gallati 184 p. 2013 Giles

1. American portrait painting—History—19th century 2. Art catalogs 3. Art literature 4. Clothing & dress in art 5. Portrait miniatures

ISBN 1907804188; 9781907804182

SUMMARY: This book "examines the remarkable resurgence of portraiture in the United States at the end of the nineteenth century. It features over fifty paintings, including works by John Singer Sargent, William Bouguereau, and James Montgomery Flagg, and twenty-five miniature portraits of reigning social celebrities from Peter Marié's famous collection Gallery of Beauty. A chapter by leading fashion historian Valerie Steele reveals how important beauty and fashion were in Gilded Age America." (Publisher's note)

REVIEW: *Choice* v51 no7 p1201 Mr 2014 J. K. Dabbs

"Beauty's Legacy: Gilded Age Portraits in America." "The varying styles of [John Singer] Sargent, [Daniel] Huntington, and [Alexandre] Cabanel are complemented by works by lesser-known artists (including women). The book gives equal attention to miniatures, which were popular emblems of beauty in the period. In addition to entries on the portraits and their creators, readers will find a substantive essay by [Barbara Dayer] Gallati . . . on the renewed importance of portraiture in America's Gilded Age. The two other essays . . . are fascinating but less developed. This well-produced volume is a useful contribution to American art/ cultural history."

GALLO, CARMINE. Talk like TED; the 9 public speaking secrets of the world's top minds; [by] Carmine Gallo 288 p. 2014 St. Martin's Press

1. Advice literature 2. Business presentations 3. Public speaking 4. TED Conference 5. Teaching—Methodology

ISBN 1250041120; 9781250041128 (hardcover: alk. paper)

LC 2013-031049

SUMMARY: In this book about public speaking, author Carmine Gallo "identifies the common elements that make TED Talks so successful. He offers nine secrets, including mastering the art of storytelling, being passionate about the subject matter, speaking conversationally, using humor, . . . and keeping presentations to 18 minutes. Gallo divides the lessons into three parts, focusing on the emotional, novel, and memorable." (Booklist)

REVIEW: *Booklist* v110 no21 p55 Jl 1 2014 Joyce Saricks

REVIEW: *Booklist* v110 no9/10 p28 Ja 1 2014 Vanessa Bush

REVIEW: *Booklist* v110 no21 p55 Jl 14 2014 Joyce Saricks

REVIEW: *Kirkus Rev* v82 no4 p24 F 15 2014

"Talk Like TED: The 9 Public-Speaking Secrets of the World's Top Minds". "[Carmine] Gallo's practical orientation assists his selection of the methods and tactics the speakers employ, and the author holds himself to the same standards he recommends for others. Gallo brings the narrative to life with plenty of examples-e.g., a speech by Harvard neuroanatomist Dr. Jill Bolte Taylor about growing up or Bill Gates' effective presentation of the reality of mosquito-borne disease. The author also includes successful outlines and guides to using both audio-visual aides and effective body language. Dramatic composition and vigorous presentation make this a powerful tool to improve mastery of speaking skills."

REVIEW: *Libr J* v139 no13 p49 Ag 1 2014 Cheryl Youse

REVIEW: *Libr J* v139 no7 p93 Ap 15 2014 Elizabeth Nelson

REVIEW: *Publ Wkly* v260 no52 p1 D 23 2013

GALLOWAY, ANDREW.ed. Answerable style. See Answerable style

GALVESTON, LOUISE. By the grace of Todd; [by] Louise Galveston 240 p. 2014 Razorbill

1. Bullying—Fiction 2. Cleanliness—Fiction 3. Humorous stories 4. Popularity 5. Size—Fiction

ISBN 9781595146779 (hardback)

LC 2013-029787

SUMMARY: In this book, "Todd's reluctance to pick up his dirty laundry has led to the spontaneous generation of a civilization of ant-sized people . . . who call themselves Toddlians. . . . After Max, the most popular and powerful kid at school, chooses Todd to be his science-project partner, Todd accidentally reveals the Toddlians' existence to him; Max then decides their science project should be to train the Toddlians to perform in a circus." (Bulletin of the Center for Children's Books)

REVIEW: *Booklist* v110 no11 p67 F 1 2014 Peggy Hailey

REVIEW: *Bull Cent Child Books* v67 no6 p312 F 2014 Thaddeus Andracki

"By the Grace of Todd." "Todd's troubles with family, school, and friends are pretty standard middle-school fare, but the generosity toward Todd as a character through his sloppiness and self-absorption is refreshing, and the zany science fiction/fantasy premise is skillfully executed. The Toddlians, too, are entertaining. . . . The gratifying conclusion sees the Toddlians to safety, and an epilogue that reveals that the whole story has been recounted by an elder of Toddlandia suggests that the Toddlians might return for future adventures, sure to be welcome news to the fans of both the smart and the gross that will take to this one."

REVIEW: *Kirkus Rev* v81 no23 p156 D 1 2013

REVIEW: *Publ Wkly* v260 no49 p83 D 2 2013

GAMBATESA, FRANCESCA.il. Naples! See De Laurentiis, G.

GAMING; from Atari to Xbox; xviii, 158 p. 2012 Rosen Pub. Group

1. Computer games 2. Electronic games 3. Popular culture studies 4. Video games 5. Video games—History

ISBN 1615307044; 9781615307043 (library binding)

LC 2011-035886

SUMMARY: Editor Michael Ray discusses video games. "[E]lectronic games have evolved both visually and substantially since the early days of Spacewar! and Pong . . . [The book discusses] the development of electronic gaming including arcade and early home video consoles through massive multiplayer online games, and examines some of the most popular games of all time." (Publisher's note)

REVIEW: *Voice of Youth Advocates* v35 no3 p292 Ag 2012 Meghann Meeusen

REVIEW: *Voice of Youth Advocates* v36 no4 p94-5 O 2013 Heather Christensen

"Architects of the Information Age," "Gaming: From Atari to Xbox 3," "Breakthroughs in Telephone Technology." "Britannica gives readers a chronological perspective of computer and information technology in this five book series. Each book introduces a particular topic and then more fully explores it from its historic roots to the most recent innovations and developments. . . . 'Architects of the Information Age' provides biographical information on over fifty movers and shakers in the history of computers. Although illustrated with both black-and-white and color photographs, readers may be disappointed to discover that few of the entries include portraits of the subjects. . . . Overall, this is a well-developed series on an ever-changing topic."

GANDA, KANCHAN M. Dentist's guide to medical conditions, medications, and complications; [by] Kanchan M. Ganda xv, 774 p. 2013 Wiley-Blackwell

1. Dental Care for Chronically Ill 2. Medical History Taking 3. Medical literature 4. Pharmaceutical Preparations, Dental—administration & dosage 5. Pharmaceutical Preparations, Dental—contraindications 6. Stomatognathic Diseases—complications 7. Stomatognathic Diseases—drug therapy

ISBN 1118313895 (softback: alk. paper); 9781118313893 (softback: alk. paper)

LC 2013-003815

SUMMARY: "This textbook by [Kanchan M.] Ganda . . . provides dental students and practitioners with a comprehensive overview of medicine and its role within dentistry. The book is divided into 21 macro sections, each of which covers a specific bodily system . . . disease category . . . or other broad topic. . . . Within each section are subsections that include descriptions of diseases, diagnostics, pharmacologic and other treatment options, [and] management guidelines." (Choice: Current Reviews for Academic Libraries)

REVIEW: *Choice* v51 no8 p1373 Ap 2014 M. P. MacEachern

"Dentist's Guide to Medical Conditions, Medications, and Complications". "This reviewer did not find the book to be logically organized. The introduction did not adequately describe what was to follow. The index, though, serves its purpose and makes navigating the book possible. The book's biggest limitation is its lack of references. An exhaustive list of suggested readings appears in the 42-page appendix, but these readings are not directly associated with any of the preceding text. In other words, all content in this substantial book, including the management recommendations, is unreferenced. Though this book will be useful to those in the dental professions, readers should go further and seek out the actual evidence when making their clinical decisions."

GANDERT, MIGUEL A.il. Hotel Mariachi. See Hotel Mariachi

GANDHI, ARUN. Grandfather Gandhi; [by] Arun Gandhi 48 p. 2012 Atheneum Books for Young Readers

1. Children's nonfiction 2. Pacifists—India—Biography—Juvenile literature 3. Statesmen—India—Biography—Juvenile literature

ISBN 144242365X; 9781442423657 (hardcover)

LC 2011-033058

SUMMARY: In this book, by Arun Gandhi and Bethany Hegedus, illustrated by Evan Turk, "Mahatma Gandhi's grandson tells the story of how his grandfather taught him to turn darkness into light. . . . When an older boy pushes him on the soccer field, his anger fills him in a way that surely a true Gandhi could never imagine. Can Arun ever live up to the Mahatma? Will he ever make his grandfather proud?" (Publisher's note)

REVIEW: *Booklist* v110 no8 p35-7 D 15 2013 Thom Barthelmess

REVIEW: *Horn Book Magazine* v90 no2 p140-1 Mr/Ap 2014 KATHLEEN T. HORNING

"Grandfather Gandhi." "Unusual for its child-centered and intimate portrait of Gandhi (we learn, for example, that he smelled like peanut oil), the graceful narrative is nearly outdone by the vivid mixed-media illustrations, rendered in watercolor, paper collage, cotton fabric, cotton, yarn, gouache, pencil, tea, and tinfoil. The cotton yarn, handspun on an Indian book charkha, gives the pictures such a three-dimensional look that one feels as though it could be plucked right off Gandhi's spinning wheel. But it's more than just an attractive effect--the yarn becomes a visual metaphor for anger channeled into light."

REVIEW: *Kirkus Rev* v82 no2 p121 Ja 15 2014

REVIEW: *Publ Wkly* v260 no51 p63 D 16 2013

REVIEW: *SLJ* v60 no2 p119 F 2014 Jody Kopple

GANDOLFO, JEAN-PAUL. The Lumière autochrome. See Lavedrine, B.

GANDULLA, STEPHANIE.ed. The archaeology of French and Indian War frontier forts. See The archaeology of French and Indian War frontier forts

GANN, ALEXANDER.ed. The annotated and illustrated double helix. See Watson, J.

GANSWORTH, ERIC. If I ever get out of here; [by] Eric Gansworth 368 p. 2013 Arthur A. Levine Books

1. Families of military personnel—Fiction 2. Families of military personnel—Juvenile fiction 3. Friendship—Fiction 4. Friendship—Juvenile fiction 5. Historical fiction 6. Identity (Psychology)—Juvenile fiction 7. Identity—Fiction 8. Indians of North America—New York (State)—Fiction 9. Race relations—Fiction 10. Tuscarora Indians—Fiction 11. Tuscarora Indians—Juvenile fiction 12. Tuscarora Nation Reservation (N.Y.)—Fiction

ISBN 0545417309; 9780545417303 (hardcover : alk. paper); 9780545417310 (paperback)

LC 2012-030553

SUMMARY: In this book "Lewis lives in abject poverty on the reservation. . . . He's the only Indian in the class for smart kids. And he's in middle school. Times are tough. When

George, a military kid, arrives, the two bond over their mutual appreciation of music. Lewis shares select pieces of his life with George. . . . Forces of nature eventually compel Lewis to face everything: the bully, what he is hiding and his own shame." (Kirkus Reviews)

REVIEW: *Booklist* v110 no1 p103 S 1 2013 Thom Barthelmess

REVIEW: *Horn Book Magazine* v89 no5 p97 S/O 2013 DEAN SCHNEIDER

"If I Ever Get Out of Here." "Beatles music provides common ground for the two boys, and titles for the novel's three sections (and the author's original paintings) are riffs on Beatles songs, while chapter titles alternate between Beatles and Paul McCartney post-Beatles tunes. . . . [Eric] Gansworth's YA debut is a fine story with depth and heart; like Sherman Alexie's 'The Absolutely True Story of a Part-Time Indian' . . . it is engaging and authentic. Readers will welcome the inclusion of a playlist and discography."

REVIEW: *Kirkus Rev* v81 no12 p90-1 Je 15 2013

REVIEW: *Publ Wkly* v260 no26 p90 Jl 1 2013

REVIEW: *SLJ* v59 no9 p142 S 2013 Evelyn Khoo Schwartz

REVIEW: *Voice of Youth Advocates* v36 no4 p62 O 2013 Vikki Terrile

GANTOS, JACK. Rotten Ralph's rotten family; [by] Jack Gantos 48 p. 2014 Farrar Straus & Giroux

1. Behavior—Fiction 2. Cats—Fiction 3. Children's stories 4. Families—Fiction 5. Farms—Juvenile literature

ISBN 0374363536; 9780374363536 (hardback)

LC 2013-022076

SUMMARY: In this children's book, by Jack Gantos, "Rotten Ralph's owner, Sarah, is fed up with her red rascal's behavior. Ralph is tired of Sarah trying to change him. He misses his cat family, which never made him alter a thing about himself. But in this . . . adventure for newly independent readers, the world's favorite rotten red cat gets tripped up when he runs away for a journey down memory lane." (Publisher's note)

REVIEW: *Booklist* v110 no9/10 p104 Ja 1 2014 Carolyn Phelan

REVIEW: *Horn Book Magazine* v90 no5 p108 S/O 2014 ROBIN L. SMITH

REVIEW: *Kirkus Rev* v82 no2 p160 Ja 15 2014

"Rotten Ralph's Rotten Family". "Just how did Rotten Ralph get so rotten? Poor, beleaguered Sarah is at her wits' end with her beloved Rotten Ralph when she cannot find a catsitter willing to care for him. . . . Poor Ralph returns to Sarah a reformed cat and proceeds to clean his room, tidy the house and prepare her a fancy breakfast in bed. However, fans of Ralph's rotten ways needn't be concerned about this apparent transformation, as a closing line asserts that he's grateful not for some internal change, but for the knowledge that Sarah loves him enough that he can do whatever he wants. Rot on, Ralph!"

REVIEW: *SLJ* v60 no4 p120 Ap 2014 Gloria Koster

GAQUIN, DEIRDRE A.ed. State and Metropolitan Area Data Book 2013. See State and Metropolitan Area Data Book 2013

GARCIA, JUSTIN R. Evolution and human sexual behavior; [by] Justin R. Garcia xix, 357 p. 2013 Harvard University Press

1. Human evolution 2. Scientific literature 3. Sex 4. Sex (Biology) 5. Sex (Psychology)

ISBN 9780674072732 (hbk. : alk. paper)

LC 2012-037630

SUMMARY: In this book, "through a synthesis of theory and a review of studies, [Peter B.] Gray and [Justin R.] Garcia tackle human sexual behavior from an evolutionary perspective. Across the book's 12 chapters they answer questions about the evolution of sexual reproduction, love, monogamy, and sex differences in reproductive behavior. The authors use a cross cultural and contextually-dependent approach and take readers far from their own bedrooms." (American Journal of Human Biology)

REVIEW: *Choice* v51 no4 p731 D 2013 S. M. Valente

"Evolution and Human Sexual Behavior." "This book explores, from an evolutionary perspective, the patterns and variations in human sexual behavior across cultures and disciplines. [Peter B.] Gray . . . and [Justin R.] Garcia . . . . examine why sex has fascinated society across time and ask about love, marriage, bonding, adolescent sex, reproductive anatomy and physiology, sexual responses, babies, and fertilization. Sexual learning and play among primates contrasts with human hunter-gatherer societies and current society, and the authors weave together the research from animals and humans about peripartum shifts in sexual behavior. . . . An intriguing treatment of an intriguing subject."

GARDINER, JOHN ELIOT. Music in the Castle of Heaven; A Portrait of Johann Sebastian Bach; [by] John Eliot Gardiner 608 p. 2013 Random House Inc

1. Bach, Johann Sebastian, 1685-1750 2. Biography (Literary form) 3. Composers—Germany—Biography 4. Music—18th century 5. Music literature

ISBN 0375415297; 9780375415296

LC 2013-030398

SUMMARY: "[Author John Eliot] Gardiner's background as a historian has encouraged him to search for ways in which scholarship and performance can cooperate and fruitfully coalesce. This has entailed piecing together the few biographical shards, scrutinizing the music, and watching for those instances when [composer Johann Sebastian] Bach's personality seems to penetrate the fabric of his notation." (Publisher's note)

REVIEW: *Libr J* v138 no11 p62 Je 15 2013 Barbara Hoffert

REVIEW: *New Statesman* v142 no5182 p47-50 N 1 2013 James Naughtie

REVIEW: *TLS* no5777/8 p31 D 20 2013 NICHOLAS KENYON

"Music in the Castle of Heaven: A Portrait of Johann Sebastian Bach." "For [author John Eliot] Gardiner, Bach needs to escape from the confining and limited image of his personality as expressed by both scholars and performers across the years, so that he can live again in the 'rich, sonorous world' of his music. . . . This is scarcely a new or radical thought, but it animates this book with a rare fervour and excitement. . . . it is a significant contribution to English-language Bach studies, exhaustively researched and up to date in its scholarship. . . . John Eliot Gardiner writes magnificently throughout, with dramatic flourishes worthy of Bach himself."

REVIEW: *Choice* v51 no10 p1811 Je 2014 J. P. Ambrose

REVIEW: *Economist* v409 no8857 p96 O 12 2013

"Bach: Music in the Castle of Heaven". "Billed as a portrait of Johann Sebastian Bach, it is inevitably also a portrait of John Eliot Gardiner. . . . Sir John is better placed than most to convey what it would have been like for Bach himself to stand in front of his musicians, and what went on in the composer's mind when he wrote the music. . . . This book is not a biography int he conventional sense . . . but an attempt to uncover the man through his music. . . . Sir John analyses many of these cantatas in scholarly detail. . . . You either have to know the music very well or listen to it as you go through the text to make sense of it. Sir John's book is not Bach for beginners, but it is very rewarding."

REVIEW: *Kirkus Rev* v81 no20 p216 O 15 2013

REVIEW: *N Y Rev Books* v61 no3 p23-5 F 20 2014 George B. Stauffer

"Bach: Music in the Castle of Heaven". "A lively new book by the distinguished British conductor John Eliot Gardiner. . . . Gardiner has devoted his life to the performance of [Johann Sebastian] Bach's vocal works . . . and the biographical gaps he seeks to close in his lengthy study have perplexed Bach scholars for more than two hundred years. . . . He believes the key to unlocking Bach's concealed character lies in the music itself. . . . Gardiner limits himself to Bach's vocal works—a restriction that raises problems. . . . By excluding Bach's keyboard and instrumental pieces from discussion. . . Gardiner disregards telling evidence that he himself deems critical for understanding Bach's character."

REVIEW: *N Y Times Book Rev* p73 D 8 2013 ZACHARY WOOLFE

REVIEW: *New York Times* v163 no56340 pC7 D 4 2013 JAMES R. OESTREICH

"Bach: Music in the Castle of Heaven". "Not to proclaim that an author's first book will necessarily stand as his magnum opus, but it is hard to imagine what the English maestro John Eliiot Gardiner, 70, might do to surpass 'Bach: Music in the Castle of Heaven' in commitment, scope, and comprehensiveness. . . His stated goals are to provide a 'corrective to the old hagiolatry' to get at the 'Bach as mensch' who always eludes us, to find the man in his creation. He is in an excellent position to do this since Bach was as much performer as composer. . . . His book is dense with fact and full of diversions, with copious footnotes leading every which way. . . . But the book is also rich in informed conjecture."

REVIEW: *New Yorker* v89 no47 p79-1 F 3 2014

GARDNER, MARK LEE. Shot All to Hell; Jesse James, the Northfield Raid, and the Wild West's Greatest Escape; [by] Mark Lee Gardner 320 p. 2013 HarperCollins

1. Historical literature 2. James, Frank, 1844-1915 3. James, Jesse, 1847-1882 4. Outlaws—West (U.S.)—Biography 5. United States—History—Civil War, 1861-1865

ISBN 0061989479; 9780061989476

SUMMARY: This book looks at "Jesse James (1847–1882), Frank James (1843–1915) and the Younger brothers . . . Confederate sympathizers, most participated as 'bushwackers' in the nasty partisan insurgency that wracked Missouri during the Civil War. . . . They later coalesced into a criminal band that traveled widely and became national news. [Mark Lee] Gardner summarizes their lives . . . before settling in to describe their last, spectacularly bungled 1876 robbery of a Northfield, Minn., bank." (Kirkus Reviews)

REVIEW: *Booklist* v109 no21 p8 Jl 1 2013 Jay Freeman

REVIEW: *Kirkus Rev* v81 no13 p159 Jl 1 2013

REVIEW: *N Y Times Book Rev* p22 S 22 2013 GREG TOBIN

"The Lost Cause: The Trials of Frank and Jesse James" and "Shot All to Hell: Jesse James, the Northfield Raid, and the Wild West's Greatest Escape." "Two narratives of parallel interest and construction . . . recount the oft-told tale of the brothers and their gang. . . . Both books read like extended episodes of 'Law & Order,' set in the midwest, in the years immediately after the Civil War. Both provide detailed accountings of Jesse's and his fellows' movements. And both are equal parts violent melodrama and meticulous procedural, wrapped in vivid packages with enough bloody action to engage readers enthralled by tales of good versus evil."

REVIEW: *Publ Wkly* v260 no21 p46-7 My 27 2013

GARDNER, MARTIN, 1914-2010. Undiluted hocus-pocus; the autobiography of Martin Gardner; [by] Martin Gardner 288 p. 2013 Princeton University Press

1. Journalists—United States—Biography 2. Magicians—United States—Biography 3. Mathematical recreations—United States—History—20th century 4. Mathematics—Social aspects—United States—History—20th century 5. Memoirs 6. Science—Social aspects—United States—History—20th century 7. Science writers—United States—Biography

ISBN 0691159912; 9780691159911 (hardcover: acid-free paper)

LC 2013-016324

SUMMARY: In this autobiography, author Martin Gardner "gives [a] look into his diverse life and interests outside the cultural mainstream, from religion, science fiction, and poetry to magic, chess, and learning to play the saw. After leading a double life as an amateur magician and philosophy major . . . Gardner was determined to make a living as a writer. He . . . eventually landed in New York City, where his Mathematical Games column in Scientific American ran for more than 25 years." (Publishers Weekly)

REVIEW: *Choice* v51 no8 p1441 Ap 2014 J. T. Noonan

REVIEW: *Libr J* v138 no18 p114 N 1 2013 William Baer

REVIEW: *N Y Times Book Rev* p22 Ja 12 2014

REVIEW: *N Y Times Book Rev* p12-3 Ja 5 2014 TELLER

"Undiluted Hocus-Pocus: The Autobiography of Martin Gardner." "'Undiluted Hocus-Pocus: The Autobiography of Martin Gardner' is the 'disheveled memoir' of the beloved 'Scientific American' columnist, journalist and author or editor of more than 100 books of philosophy, humor, mathematics, poetry, puzzles, fiction, science, anthologies and annotations. . . . Gardner . . . wrote 'Undiluted Hocus-Pocus' at the age of 95 in a one-room assisted-living apartment in Norman, Okla. . . . Gardner was a child of faith and skepticism. . . Gardner writes with such frank pleasure, you find yourself surveying your own life for piquant and vivid memories."

REVIEW: *Publ Wkly* v260 no33 p58 Ag 19 2013

REVIEW: *TLS* no5784 p25 F 7 2014 MICHAEL SALER

"Undiluted Hocus-Pocus: The Autobiography of Martin Gardner." "[Author Martin] Gardner published over seventy books in his lifetime and completed this autobiography shortly before his death at the age of ninety-five in 2010. . . . While Gardner was self-deprecating, he was not being falsely modest in calling 'Undiluted Hocus Pocus' ' these disheveled memoirs.' Fans will be grateful for a new opportunity to spend time in his company, but much of the book repeats material from his other works and reads like an early draft."

GARDNER, SALLY. Operation Bunny; The Fairy Detective Agency's First Case; [by] Sally Gardner 192 p. 2014 Henry Holt and Co

1. Adoption—Fiction 2. Cats—Fiction 3. Fairies—Fiction 4. Foundlings—Fiction 5. Magic—Fiction 6. Mystery and detective stories 7. Witches—Fiction
ISBN 0805098925; 9780805098921 (hardback); 9781250050533 (paperback)
LC 2013-037809

SUMMARY: Written by Sally Gardner and illustrated by David Roberts, this book is part of the Wings & Co. series. "When Emily Vole inherits an abandoned shop, she discovers a magical world she never knew existed. . . . With the help of a talking cat called Fidget and a grumpy fairy detective called Buster, it is up to Emily to save the fairies and get to the bottom of Operation Bunny." (Publisher's note)

REVIEW: *Booklist* v110 no9/10 p113-4 Ja 1 2014 Sarah Hunter

"Operation Bunny." "Discovering fairies, witches, and a secret magical shop along the way, Emily becomes an ace detective specializing in magical crimes. [David] Roberts' stylized cartoony illustrations--mostly of cute bunnies--scatter over almost every page, adding a delightful touch to the madcap caper. Emily is a no-nonsense, brave girl detective, and young readers looking for silly magical adventures will find much to love. Want more? You're in luck: this is the first title in the Wings & Co. series."

REVIEW: *Bull Cent Child Books* v67 no7 p357 Mr 2014 J. H.

"Operation Bunny: Wings & Co.: The Fairy Detective Agency's First Case." "The writing in this British import is so focused on being arch that it's tough for the story to get any real momentum, and the lack of tonal differentiation means it's a challenge to keep everything straight (explanations of the parameters and roles of the fairies are particularly incomplete). Nonetheless, the characterizations are entertaining (especially Fidget), the satirical edge of the writing can be amusing, and the Cinderella/Harry Potter rags-to-witches plot has appeal. . . . Though billed as both fantasy and mystery, this title (the first in a series) is heavier on the fantasy than the mystery, and fans of Roald Dahl or the Clover Twig series may find some new favorite characters here."

REVIEW: *Horn Book Magazine* v90 no2 p118-9 Mr/Ap 2014 MONICA EDINGER

REVIEW: *Kirkus Rev* v81 no24 p169 D 15 2013

REVIEW: *N Y Times Book Rev* p21 Mr 16 2014 KATHERINE RUNDELL

REVIEW: *Publ Wkly* v260 no48 p57 N 25 2013

REVIEW: *SLJ* v60 no3 p111 Mr 2014 Amy Holland

GARFIELD, LEON. Smith; the story of a pickpocket; [by] Leon Garfield 195 p. 2013 New York Review of Books

1. Adventure stories 2. JUVENILE FICTION—Action & Adventure—General 3. JUVENILE FICTION—Classics 4. JUVENILE FICTION—Law & Crime 5. Robbers and outlaws—Fiction
ISBN 9781590176757 (hardback)
LC 2013-018766

SUMMARY: In this book, "seconds after twelve-year-old Smith picks the bulging pocket of an old gentleman . . . two men in brown appear, and from the doorway where he is hiding, Smith witnesses the murder and violent search of his victim. Terrified, he flees the scene of the crime. A quarter of a mile off Smith stops. What has he stolen that is worth the life of a man? He stares at his loot bitterly. It is a document—and Smith cannot read." (Publisher's note)

REVIEW: *Kirkus Rev* v82 no1 p362 Ja 1 2014

"Smith: The Story of a Pickpocket". "The succeeding entanglement takes Smith from genteel comfort to the horrors of Newgate in the company of pharisees and publicans, honest rogues and the devil's cajoling disciple. A disquieting story, told with Mr. [Leon] Garfield's customary elan; a story that is both somber and sardonic, leavened with raucous good spirits and simple compassion. More Hogarth than Cruikshank, this lacks the gusto of 'Devil in the Fog' (1966) but readers who respond to the author will follow him here."

GARLAND IN HIS OWN TIME; a biographical chronicle of his life, drawn from recollections, interviews, and memoirs by family, friends, and associates; xxxviii, 250 p. 2013 University of Iowa Press

1. Authors, American—19th century—Biography 2. Authors, American—20th century—Biography
ISBN 1609381629 (softcover : acid-free paper); 9781609381622 (softcover : acid-free paper)
LC 2012-915018

SUMMARY: This book, edited by Keith Newlin, is a biography of writer Hamlin Garland. "Garland had a considerable reputation as a radical writer whose realistic stories and polemical essays agitating for a literature that accurately represented American life riled the nation's press. . . . The sixty-six reminiscences in 'Garland in His Own Time' offer . . . [a] complement to his self-portrait by giving the perspectives of family, friends, fellow writers." (Publisher's note)

REVIEW: *Choice* v51 no2 p258 O 2013 R. Mulligan

"Garland in His Own Time: A Biographical Chronicle of His Life, Drawn From Recollections, Interviews and Memoirs by Family Friends, and Associates." "Drawn from more than 60 recollections by luminaries such as Walt Whitman, William Dean Howells, and Theodore Roosevelt, but also from ordinary Midwest citizens . . . , 'Garland in His Own Time' connects disparate voices to create a fine critical biography. Described as . . . a populist who became an elitist, a Midwestern farmer who settled in Hollywood, Garland emerges as a complex figure. . . . In thoughtfully selecting, arranging, and contextualizing the voices of those who knew Garland best, [editor Keith] Newlin creates an honest portrait that identifies Garland as an influential writer."

GARMEY, JANE. Private gardens of the Hudson Valley; [by] Jane Garmey 240 p. 2013 Monacelli Press

1. Horticultural literature 2. Hudson River Valley (N.Y. & N.J.) 3. Landscape architecture—United States 4. Photography of gardens 5. Views
ISBN 9781580933483
LC 2013-935923

SUMMARY: Written by Jane Garmey, with photography by

John M. Hall, this book "surveys the majestic landscape that borders the Hudson River, an area rich in history and unique garden designs. The scenery, which encompasses riverfront meadows, craggy hills, and long open valleys, is inherently dramatic. Twenty-six private gardens are presented here, chosen to establish a sense of place and to convey the romance of the landscape." (Publisher's note)

REVIEW: *N Y Times Book Rev* p53 D 8 2013 ALIDA BECKER

"City Parks: Public Places, Private Thoughts," "Private Gardens of the Hudson Valley," and "Quiet Beauty: The Japanese Gardens of North America." "The 18 contributors to Catie Marron's 'City Parks: Public Places, Private Thoughts' have . . . [created] an eloquent reminder of the way shard landscapes can provide intimate inspiration. . . . In 'Private Gardens of the Hudson Valley,' Jane Garmey and John M. Hall's follow-up . . . There's also some interesting whimsy. . . . Just flipping through the pages of 'Quiet Beauty: The Japanese Gardens of North America' will instantly lower your blood pressure."

GARNETT, JANE. Spectacular Miracles. See Rosser, G.

GAROOGIAN, DAVID.ed. Profiles of California, 2013. See Profiles of California, 2013

GARRETT, CRAIG.ed. Vitamin D2. See Vitamin D2

GARRETT, PAUL RUSSELL.tr. The Contract Killer. See Andersen, B.

GARRETT, WENDELL.ed. Appraising art. See Appraising art

GARRINGTON, ABBIE. Haptic modernism; touch and the tactile in modernist writing; [by] Abbie Garrington viii, 208 p. 2013 Edinburgh University Press

1. Human body in literature 2. Joyce, James, 1882-1941 3. Literary critiques 4. Modernism (Literature) 5. Touch in literature 6. Woolf, Virginia, 1882-1941
ISBN 9780748641741 (hbk.); 9780748682539 (webready PDF); 9780748682546 (epub.)
LC 2013-363592

SUMMARY: "This book contends that the haptic sense--combining touch, kinaesthesis and proprioception--was first fully conceptualised and explored in the modernist period, in response to radical new bodily experiences brought about by scientific, technological and psychological change." It explores the role of the haptic in "the work of four major writers of the modernist canon--James Joyce, Virginia Woolf, D. H. Lawrence and Dorothy Richardson." (Publisher's note)

REVIEW: *Choice* v51 no4 p629 D 2013 A. J. Barlow

"Haptic Modernism: Touch and the Tactile in Modernist Writing" and "Sonic Modernity: Representing Sound in Literature, Culture and the Arts." "These two volumes add to knowledge of the modernist period within a modernist frame: the scholarship reflects a modernist eye for derail and respect for nuance. By focusing on sound and touch, respectively, [Sam] Halliday . . . and [Abbie] Garrington . . . bring to light less explored areas of care and craft and in so doing demonstrate the knowledge base and intellectual confidence that made modernism possible. The range of writers considered in each volume is impressive."

GARTH EVANS SCULPTURE; Beneath the Skin; 224 p. 2013 Palgrave Macmillan

1. American sculpture 2. Art literature 3. British sculpture 4. Evans, Garth 5. Sculptors
ISBN 1781300046; 9781781300046

SUMMARY: In this book, "editor [Ann] Compton . . . and others examine [Garth] Evans's emergence as a figure who straddles Britain's large-scale constructivist mode and . . . more intimately scaled works made from plywood, cardboard, and ceramic. . . . The catalogue begins with an interview with the artist and Jon Wood . . . and ends with written fragments by Evans. In between, essays focus on different moments in Evans's career." (Choice: Current Reviews for Academic Libraries)

REVIEW: *Choice* v51 no8 p1388-9 Ap 2014 J. Simon

"Garth Evans Sculpture: Beneath the Skin". "This profusely illustrated exhibition catalogue for the British Arts Council handsomely presents this distinctive sculptor. . . essays focus on different moments in Evans's career, with varying success and differences in tone; they range from personal recollection to scholarly investigation. Anna Lovatt . . .offers thoughtful and illuminating readings of Evans's 1980s wall-mounted structures, with their lively painted, multiple geometric surfaces. Leila Philip's recounting of a studio visit provides not only a needed awareness of sculptural scale (including photographs of the works in situ), but also a sophisticated understanding of the bodily import of the works and their self-conscious art historical references."

GARZA, DAVID L. Disrupting HR; An Introduction to a New HR Doctrine; [by] David L. Garza 220 p. 2013 CreateSpace Independent Publishing Platform

1. Business literature 2. Business models 3. Personnel departments 4. Personnel departments—Employees 5. Resource allocation
ISBN 1481175718; 9781481175715

SUMMARY: This book "lays out a new doctrine that innovative HR leaders may use to rebuild their departments to fit new business realities. [David L.] Garza divides his plan into 'ethos' (theory) and 'praxis' (practice). . . . HR departments, he writes, need to change from a 'push' system, in which they come up with products and push them into practice, to a 'pull' system, in which the company states its needs and HR designs products to meet them." (Kirkus Reviews)

REVIEW: *Kirkus Rev* v81 no24 p385 D 15 2013

"Disrupting HR: An Introduction to a New HR Doctrine". "[David L.] Garza's debut work presents a new doctrine to help bring human resources departments into the modern era. . . . Garza's prose style is dense and occasionally technical, but he leavens it with lighter vignettes at the beginning of each chapter. Persistent readers will be rewarded with a detailed road map for redesigning HR policies to suit any company's specific circumstances. An intriguing, if rather dry, book about possibilities for the future of HR."

GARZA, XAVIER. Maximilian and the bingo rematch; a Lucha libre sequel; [by] Xavier Garza 208 p. 2013 Cinco Puntos Press

1. Aunts—Fiction 2. Dating (Social customs)—Fiction 3. Graphic novels 4. Mexican Americans—Fiction 5. Wrestling—Fiction
ISBN 9781935955467 (paperback); 9781935955597 (hardcover)
LC 2012-043173

SUMMARY: This is the second in Xavier Garza's Max's Lucha Libre Adventures series. Here, "suddenly everybody seems to be fighting: a couple of cranky tías who, like lucha libre rudos, will stop at nothing to triumph in the church's lotería game; his masked uncles going for the tag-team title of the world; and a green-eyed vixen named Paloma who challenges his love for Cecilia. Will good triumph over evil?" (Publisher's note)

REVIEW: *Bull Cent Child Books* v67 no6 p312-3 F 2014 Elizabeth Bush
"Maximilian and the Bingo Rematch." "The juxtaposition of wryly narrated middle-school woes against the background of professional lucha libre wrestling continues to be a winner, and the bilingual text, heavy on conversation and idiom, can be engaged with, toyed with, or ignored, as the English or Spanish language reader prefers. This series should definitely be on the radar of bilingual classroom teachers, though, whose students can meet on common literary ground, while stretching across the gutter to appropriate the chatter of their classmates."

REVIEW: *Kirkus Rev* v81 no13 p93 Jl 1 2013

REVIEW: *Kirkus Rev* p46 2013 Guide 20to BookExpo America

REVIEW: *SLJ* v59 no7 p80 Jl 2013 Ted McCoy

GASIOROWSKI, MARK.ed. The government and politics of the Middle East and North Africa. See The government and politics of the Middle East and North Africa

GASTON, THEODORA GETTY. Alone Together; My Life With J. Paul Getty; [by] Digby Diehl 416 p. 2013 HarperCollins
1. Businesspeople 2. Getty, J. Paul (Jean Paul), 1892-1976 3. Marriage 4. Memoirs 5. Millionaires
ISBN 0062219715; 9780062219718

SUMMARY: This book is a memoir of the author's marriage to J. Paul Getty. "Getty married [Theodora Getty] Gaston in Rome on the eve of World War II and demanded she break off her studies to return home with him. Gaston remained in Italy to finish her studies, only to become a prisoner of war. . . . When Gaston returned to the States in 1942, it was to an increasingly stingy husband who now spent most of his time working, traveling and having affairs that he denied." (Kirkus Reviews)

REVIEW: *Booklist* v110 no2 p16 S 15 2013 Carol Haggas

REVIEW: *Kirkus Rev* v81 no16 p269 Ag 15 2013

REVIEW: *N Y Times Book Rev* p10 S 1 2013 JUDITH NEWMAN
"Alone Together: My Life With J. Paul Getty." "It's a blueprint for living peacefully with a brilliant and monstrously selfish man. . . . This book . . . is the kindest, most understanding memoir of a narcissist you'll ever read. And it's still appalling. . . . 'Alone Together' is a private memoir of a public man, and a very whitewashed one. We hear about the little Donald Duck stuffed toys the exchanged, but nothing substantive about his business, his relationships with world leaders, his other wives and children, or the famous kidnapping and mutilation of his grandson. . . . Much here reflects the fond, and I suspect unreliable, memories of a lovely and loving, now 99-year-old woman."

GATES, ROBERT MICHAEL, 1943-. Duty; memoirs of a Secretary at war; [by] Robert Michael Gates 640 p. 2014 Alfred A. Knopf
1. Afghan War, 2001-—Personal narratives, American 2. Cabinet officers—United States—Biography 3. Civil-military relations—United States—History—21st century 4. Iraq War, 2003-2011—Personal narratives 5. Memoirs 6. War on Terrorism, 2001-2009—Personal narratives, American
ISBN 0307959473; 9780307959478 (hardcover)
LC 2013-026348

SUMMARY: In this book, author Robert M. Gates "takes us behind the scenes of his nearly five years as a secretary at war: the battles with Congress, the two presidents he served, the military itself, and the vast Pentagon bureaucracy; his efforts to help Bush turn the tide in Iraq; his role as a guiding, and often dissenting, voice for [Barack] Obama; the ardent devotion to and love for American soldiers—his 'heroes'—he developed on the job." (Publisher's note)

REVIEW: *Booklist* v110 no9/10 p25 Ja 1 2014 Jay Freeman

REVIEW: *Booklist* v110 no19/20 p121-2 Je 1 2014 Alan Moores

REVIEW: *Choice* v52 no2 p346 O 2014 M. A. Genovese

REVIEW: *Commentary* v137 no4 p52-4 Ap 2014 ARTHUR HERMAN

REVIEW: *Commonweal* v141 no10 p20-2 Je 1 2014 Alan Wolfe

REVIEW: *Libr J* v139 no7 p48 Ap 15 2014 Kelly Sinclair

REVIEW: *N Y Times Book Rev* p22 F 2 2014 GREGORY COWLES

REVIEW: *N Y Times Book Rev* p1-18 Ja 19 2014 Thomas E. Ricks

REVIEW: *Natl Rev* v66 no3 p42-4 F 24 2014 BING WEST
"Duty: Memoirs of a Secretary at War". "[Robert Gates'] powerful memoir is insightful, tendentious, angry, elucidating, contradictory, and honest. . . . While he packed too much into one book, students of political power will study, not just skim, this book. . . . Yet in all three of these key and disastrous decisions, Gates is silent about his participation in any argument or action. Did he agree or disagree? What was his role? His memoir does not tell us. This omission by silence is the central flaw in the book."

REVIEW: *New Repub* v244 no23 p48-53 Mr 3 2014 Max Boot

REVIEW: *New Statesman* v143 no5194 p48-9 Ja 24 2014 John Bew

REVIEW: *New York Times* v163 no56376 pC1-7 Ja 9 2014 MICHIKO KAKUTANI

REVIEW: *Parameters: U.S. Army War College* v44 no2 p110-1 Summ 2014 Robert M. Gates

REVIEW: *Time* v183 no2 p11 Ja 20 2014 Michael Crowley

GATRELL, VIC. The First Bohemians; Life and Art in London's Golden Age; [by] Vic Gatrell 512 p. 2014 Penguin Global

1. British art—18th century 2. Historical literature 3. London (England)—History—18th century 4. London (England)—Intellectual life—18th century 5. London (England)—Social life & customs

ISBN 1846146771; 9781846146770

SUMMARY: This book by Vic Gatrell presents a "look at the artists and writers who lived in and around Covent Garden and Soho during the 18th century." The author explores "how the scurrilous behaviour of London's residents often inspired some of the finest works of art and literature. . . . Mr. Gatrell uses these figures to evoke the excesses and eccentricities of British life in the 18th century." (Economist)

REVIEW: *Economist* v405 no8855 p79-80 S 28 2013

"The First Bohemians: Life and Art in London's Golden Age." "Vic Gatrell . . . has written an entertaining look at the artists and writers who lived in and around Covent Garden and Soho during the 18th century. . . . Mr. Gatrell does a fine job of tracing how the scurrilous behaviour of London's residents often inspired some of the finest works of art and literature. . . . This richness of detail makes 'The First Bohemians' a pleasure to read. Occasionally Mr. Gatrell gets carried away, particularly when describing the bohemian excess of London's inhabitants. . . . But with over 200 images reproduced in his book, many of which have rarely been seen before, his enthusiasm feels infectious."

REVIEW: *New Statesman* v142 no5179 p43-4 O 11 2013 Frances Wilson

GAUTIER, MARY L. American Catholics in transition. See Dillon, M.

GAVIN, RICK. Nowhere Nice; [by] Rick Gavin 288 p. 2013 Minotaur Books

1. Adventure stories 2. Crime—Fiction 3. Drug dealers—Fiction 4. Revenge—Fiction 5. Theft—Fiction

ISBN 0312583192; 9780312583194 (hardcover)

LC 2013-024713

SUMMARY: In this noir novel by Rick Gavin, "The last time Nick Reid and his pal Desmond tangled with that crazy meth-dealer Boudrot, Boudrot landed in jail and Nick and Desmond helped themselves to the several hundred grand in cash hidden in his trailer. . . . But that Boudrot is even meaner and crazier than they've bargained for, and Nick and Desmond will be lucky to make it through alive on this wild, wacky chase through the Mississippi Delta." (Publisher's note)

REVIEW: *Booklist* v110 no3 p39 O 1 2013 Thomas Gaughan

REVIEW: *Kirkus Rev* v81 no22 p11 N 15 2013

REVIEW: *Libr J* v138 no18 p72 N 1 2013 Teresa L. Jacobsen

REVIEW: *N Y Times Book Rev* p27 D 15 2013 MARILYN STASIO

"Dust," Nowhere Nice," and "City of Lies." "[Author] Patricia Cornwell's imperious forensic scientist, Kay Scarpetta, shows uncharacteristic signs of vulnerability at the beginning of 'Dust.' . . . There's plenty going on at Scarpetta's bustling lab. . . . Buckle up for a rowdy ride with [author] Rick Gavin in 'Nowhere Nice' . . . , the latest in a riotous series set in the Mississippi Delta. . . . Calling these characters colorful doesn't begin to get at the rich regional nuances that Gavin mines at every pit stop from Arkansas to Alabama. . . . A sensitive hero is a good thing to have in a tough crime novel--up to a point. That point is passed in R. J. Ellory's 'City of Lies' . . . , when the doting author allows these tender feelings to soften his protagonists's brain."

REVIEW: *Publ Wkly* v260 no31 p47 Ag 5 2013

GAVIN, ROHAN. Knightley and son; [by] Rohan Gavin 320 p. 2014 Bloomsbury

1. Coma—Patients—Fiction 2. Conspiracies—Fiction 3. Fathers and sons—Fiction 4. Memory—Fiction 5. Mystery and detective stories

ISBN 9781619631533 (hardback)

LC 2013-034316

SUMMARY: In this book, "since 13-year-old Darkus Knightley's parents split, he sees his father, Alan—a detective of obsessive professional dedication—once a week. Darkus' sponge of a brain has absorbed the details of every former case of his father's, which fuel conversation during their visits. The conversations tend to be one-sided, though, as Alan has been comatose for four years. One evening, Alan miraculously wakes from his coma, ready to investigate a series of bizarre crimes." (Kirkus Reviews)

REVIEW: *Booklist* v110 no17 p58 My 1 2014 Carolyn Phelan

REVIEW: *Bull Cent Child Books* v67 no9 p454 My 2014 K. Q. G.

"Knightley & Son: Cracking the Code". "The father-son relationship adds a bit of pathos to all the logic, with Darkus wondering if his father sees him as anything other than a useful detecting tool. The mystery is genuinely compelling, with the appropriate MacGuffins and red herrings, and the bad guys get their comeuppance (two of them quite gruesomely). A few hints at the conclusion, however, point toward a sequel, and readers can hope that Darkus' snarky stepsister and gadget-loving teacher will play bigger parts in upcoming installments."

REVIEW: *Kirkus Rev* v82 no4 p149 F 15 2014

"Knightley and Son". " Heaps of mystery, dry humor and tweed abound in this exemplar of crime fiction à la Doyle. . . . Even if Gavin didn't disclaim his affinity for Sherlock Holmes, it would be abundantly evident; Darkus' skill at deduction, perpetual observation and sang-froid are spot-on Holmes-ian. Don't expect a puttering Watson, though. Darkus' sidekick and stepsister, Tilly, is wrought with sass, intelligence and a never-ending supply of hair dye. Heroes, villains and settings are all fully realized through proficient description, and contemporary technology gives way to sheer brainpower. A rousing page-turner with one fault: It ends."

REVIEW: *Publ Wkly* v261 no3 p56 Ja 20 2014

REVIEW: *SLJ* v60 no4 p146 Ap 2014 Saleena L. Davidson

REVIEW: *Voice of Youth Advocates* v37 no2 p74-5 Je 2014 Erin Wyatt

GAWRYCH, GEORGE W. The young Atatürk; from Ottoman soldier to statesman of Turkey; [by] George W. Gawrych xiv, 267 p. 2013 I.B. Tauris Distributed in the U.S. & Canada Exclusively by Palgrave Macmillan

1. Historical literature 2. Presidents—Turkey—Biography

ISBN 1780763220; 9781780763224

LC 2013-431539

SUMMARY: This book is the "winner of a 2014 Distinguished Book Award from The Society of Military History" and was s"hortlisted for the 2014 Longman-History Today Book Prize." It looks at the early career of Turkish staesman Mustafa Kemal, "from the War of Independence to the founding of the Republic --and shows that it is only by understanding Kemal's military career that one can fully comprehend how he evolved as one of the twentieth century's most extraordinary statesmen." (Publisher's note)

REVIEW: *Choice* v51 no4 p707 D 2013 R. W. Zens

REVIEW: *TLS* no5772 p22 N 15 2013 WILLIAM ARMSTRONG

"The Young Atatürk: From Ottoman Soldier to Statesman of Turkey." "George W. Gawrych focuses primarily on the military aspect of the 'young Atatürk' and states clearly that he does not aim to provide a comprehensive assessment of the broader legacy of his subject. That being said, he does leave the reader wishing for a rather more comprehensive appraisal; the 'young Atatürk', may be inextricable from the 'military Atatürk,' but considering either with only minimal reference to the broader sweep of Ottoman decline and republican renaissance makes for pretty dry reading."

GAY, MARIE-LOUISE. Read Me a Story, Stella; [by] Marie-Louise Gay 32 p. 2013 Pgw

1. Books & reading—Juvenile fiction 2. Brothers & sisters—Juvenile fiction 3. Children's literature 4. Everyday life 5. Nature—Juvenile literature

ISBN 1554982162; 9781554982165

SUMMARY: "In this lovely addition to Marie-Louise Gay's renowned Stella series, Stella introduces little brother Sam to the pleasures of reading. Sam is as busy and worried as ever, and Stella almost always has her nose in a book these days, but she finds time to help him out, while sharing her new pastime with contagious enthusiasm." (Publisher's note)

REVIEW: *Bull Cent Child Books* v67 no1 p19-20 S 2013 H. M.

"Read Me a Story, Stella." "Stella spends most of the story with her nose in one of her books, and throughout the day she shares tidbits of stories and facts with her brother, from folklore references to information about caterpillars to poetry about bunnies for the benefit of Sam's carrot garden. The literary references are perfectly organic to the storyline--neither pedantic nor obvious. . . . [Author and illustrator Marie-Louise] Gay's watercolor compositions dominate each spread, with text only filling the minimal white strip at the bottom. . . . This is an excellent model both of positive sibling relations and of the way books and stories can naturally play into everyday life."

REVIEW: *Kirkus Rev* v81 no15 p343 Ag 1 2013

REVIEW: *Publ Wkly* v260 no28 p168 Jl 15 2013

REVIEW: *SLJ* v59 no9 p120 S 2013 Catherine Callegari

GAYDOS, MICHAEL. Heaven's War. See Harris, M.

GAYFORD, MARTIN. Michelangelo; His Epic Life; [by] Martin Gayford 688 p. 2013 Fig Tree

1. Artists—Italy—Biography 2. Biography (Literary form) 3. Michelangelo Buonarroti, 1475-1564 4. Renaissance art—Italy 5. Sculptors—Italy—Biography

ISBN 1905490542; 9781905490547

SUMMARY: This book by Martin Gayford presents a biography of the artist Michelangelo Buonarroti. "At 31 he was considered the finest artist in Italy, perhaps the world; long before he died at almost 90 he was widely believed to be the greatest sculptor or painter who had ever lived. . . . For decade after decade, he worked near the dynamic centre of events: the vortex at which European history was changing from Renaissance to Counter Reformation." (Publisher's note)

REVIEW: *Apollo: The International Magazine for Collectors* v178 no615 p103 D 2013

REVIEW: *Apollo: The International Magazine for Collectors* v179 no618 p192-3 Mr 2014 Paul Joannides

"Michelangelo: His Epic Life". "[Martin] Gayford has no track record as a scholar of the Renaissance . . . and he does not tell us why he decided to write this one:presumably it was a labour of love. But he has mastered the sources and, without entrenched positions—or ego—to defend, has produced an account that is measured, detached but sympathetic, and guided by a profound awareness of the magnitude of Michelangelo's achievement: hence the subtitle. The book is consistently readable; particularly admirable—perhaps a consequence of Gayford's practice as a journalist and reviewer—is the ease and flexibility with which he moves. . . . This results in a densely textured and convincing account."

REVIEW: *Economist* v409 no8866 p91 D 14 2013

REVIEW: *TLS* no5802 p24 Je 13 2014 BRUCE BOUCHER

GAYFORD, MARTIN. Man with a blue scarf; [by] Martin Gayford 248 2010 Thames & Hudson

1. Art critics 2. Art literature 3. Artists 4. Painters 5. Portrait painting

ISBN 9780500238752; 0-500-23875-8

SUMMARY: English artist Lucian Freud "spent seven months painting a portrait of the art critic Martin Gayford. Gayford describes the process chronologically, from the day he arrived for the first sitting through to his meeting with the couple who bought the finished painting. . . . The book is illustrated throughout with photographs by David Dawson of Freud at work, with paintings by Freud from the 1940s to the present, and images by other artists discussed by Freud with Gayford." (Publisher's note)

REVIEW: *London Rev Books* v35 no23 p3-8 D 5 2013 Julian Barnes

"Man With a Blue Scarf: On Sitting for a Portrait By Lucian Freud" and "Breakfast With Lucian: A Portrait of the Artist". "[Martin] Gayford's 'Man With a Blue Scarf' . . . is one of the best books about art, and the making of art, that I have ever read. . . . Gayford is also funny and honest about what a sitter goes through. . . . [Geordie] Greig's book is more substantial than it first appears. . . . Whether Freud himself would have felt his 'confidence and trust' had been misplaced is another matter. Greig's book will certainly do Freud's personal reputation harm. But it will also, I think, harm the way we look at some of his paintings, and perhaps harm the paintings themselves—at least until a different generation of viewers comes along."

GEARTY, CONOR.ed. The Cambridge companion to human rights law. See The Cambridge companion to human rights law

GEBHART, RYAN. There will be bears; [by] Ryan Gebhart 224 p. 2014 Candlewick Press

1. Adventure stories 2. Bears—Juvenile fiction 3. Grandparent & child 4. Grandparent & child—Fiction 5. Hunting stories 6. Wilderness survival—Fiction

ISBN 0763665215; 9780763665210

LC 2013-946620

SUMMARY: In this book, by Ryan Gebhart, "thirteen-year-old Tyson loves hanging out with his . . . Grandpa Gene. . . . So when Grandpa Gene has to move to a nursing home that can manage his kidney disease, Tyson feels like he's losing his only friend. Not only that, but Tyson was counting on Grandpa Gene to take him on his first big hunt. So in defiance of Mom and Dad's strict orders, and despite reports of a . . . man-eating grizzly named Sandy, the two sneak off to the Grand Tetons." (Publisher's note)

REVIEW: *Booklist* v110 no16 p52 Ap 15 2014 Julia Smith

REVIEW: *Bull Cent Child Books* v67 no10 p518 Je 2014 E. B.

"There Will Be Bears". "It's a pretty insane idea, fraught not only with danger to Gramps' fragile health but also with the very real threat from a rogue grizzly that has mauled tourists and hunters over the past few weeks. The book is strongly written, and Tyson's emotional turmoil, which he glibly covers with barbed observations and self-deprecating humor, is painfully real. The gorily precise details of the elk kill and butchering also add compelling dimension to a familiar story of coming to terms with the debility of a beloved grandparent. Family stories and adventure tales are often relegated to separate pigeonholes, and this title offers fresh crossover appeal."

REVIEW: *Horn Book Magazine* v90 no2 p119 Mr/Ap 2014 DEAN SCHNEIDER

"There Will Be Bears". "The combination of an inexperienced boy, a sickly seventy seven-year-old man, and a killer grizzly bear reported in the park is a dangerous one. How much is it worth to prove yourself, or to have one last adventure? [Ryan] Gebhart crafts a satisfyingly complicated realistic drama that deals with big issues. When Tyson disembowels an elk and is confronted by the blood and guts, he wonders, 'Is this what I am? Just a pile of veins and tendons and muscle?' Tyson is a likable protagonist in a well-paced tale that will hold young readers in its grip."

REVIEW: *Kirkus Rev* v82 no4 p153 F 15 2014

"There Will Be Bears". "Tyson is quirky, awkward and lovable; a perfect middle school boy. He is also, at times, laugh-out-loud funny, but his best qualities are his fierce love for his family and his unwavering desire to be true to himself. It is this inner strength that carries the story through some eyebrow-raising moments. While honesty is emphasized, the lies surrounding the secret hunting trip are brushed aside as necessary for the greater good. Occasionally salty vocabulary and adolescent innuendo are developmentally spot-on. A quirky, sweet adventure for middle school boys."

REVIEW: *Publ Wkly* v261 no7 p100 F 17 2014

REVIEW: *SLJ* v60 no6 p101 Je 2014 Bob Hassett

REVIEW: *Voice of Youth Advocates* v37 no2 p58 Je 2014 Joanna Lima

GEDDES, LINDA. Bumpology; the myth-busting pregnancy book for curious parents-to-be; [by] Linda Geddes 309 p. 2013 Simon & Schuster Paperbacks

1. Advice literature 2. Childbirth—Popular works 3. Infants—Care—Popular works 4. Pregnancy—Popular works 5. Prenatal care 6. Prenatal influences

ISBN 1451684991; 9781451684995; 9781451685763 (trade pbk.)

LC 2013-026987

SUMMARY: "The moment she discovers she's pregnant, every woman suddenly has a million questions about the life that's developing inside her. . . . In 'Bumpology,' [author Linda] Geddes discusses the latest research on every topic that expectant parents encounter, from first pregnancy symptoms to pregnancy diet, the right birth plan, and a baby's first year." (Publisher's note)

REVIEW: *Kirkus Rev* v82 no3 p130 F 1 2014

"Bumpology: The Myth-Busting Pregnancy Book for Curious Parents-to-Be". "[Linda] Geddes addresses the multitude of concerns any woman experiencing pregnancy for the first time may have and offers solid, no-nonsense answers, effectively alleviating much of the guilt, anxiety and doubt any new parent may face. She also includes a helpful glossary for readers unfamiliar with the many new terms they will encounter, including, among dozens of others, bilirubin, hindmilk, syntocinon and ventouse. Straightforward, stress-reducing answers to the most common pregnancy and post-pregnancy questions."

REVIEW: *Publ Wkly* v261 no3 p47-8 Ja 20 2014

GEFTER, AMANDA. Trespassing on Einstein's lawn; a father, a daughter, the meaning of nothing, and the beginning of everything; [by] Amanda Gefter 418 p. 2014 Bantam Books

1. Beginning 2. Fathers & daughters 3. Memoirs 4. Physics—Philosophy 5. Quantum theory 6. Science journalism

ISBN 034553963X; 9780345531438 (hardback : acid-free paper)

LC 2013-013874

SUMMARY: "Part science writing and part memoir, this adventurous fact-finding romp takes readers across the landscape of ideas about the universe, calling on the expertise of the biggest names in science--and also the author's lifelong partner in her pursuit of the meaning of everything: her father." Author Amanda Gefter "describes how she jump-started her career by crashing physics conferences and faking her way into interviews with world-famous physicists." (Kirkus Reviews)

REVIEW: *Kirkus Rev* v82 no2 p239 Ja 15 2014

REVIEW: *N Y Times Book Rev* p20 Mr 2 2014 ROBIN MARANTZ HENIG

"Trespassing on Einstein's Lawn: A Father, a Daughter, the Meaning of Nothing, and the Beginning of Everything." "Father-daughter memoirs have an inherent appeal, especially when the father and daughter are on an almost preposterous quest. There's such a quest in 'Trespassing on Einstein's Lawn': to uncover the nature of reality. . . . What we're left with, finally, is being inside Gefter's head as she falls deeper into the thickets of cosmology and quantum theory--and, later, as she hangs out with famous physicists. . . . Rather than applying her smarts to filter out complexities and distill a digestible story, she opted to make this more of a narrative, by explicating her every thought, no matter how convoluted, and leading us down whatever trail she imagined or explored."

GEIMER, SAMANTHA. The girl; a life in the shadow of Roman Polanski; [by] Samantha Geimer 272 p. 2013 Atria Books

1. Memoirs 2. Rape victims—United States—Biography 3. Sexually abused teenagers—United States—Biography

ISBN 9781476716831 (hardcover : alk. paper); 9781476716848 (pbk. : alk. paper)

LC 2013-027264

SUMMARY: It was the author's intent "to reclaim her identity as "more than Sex Victim Girl" and redress long-forgotten misconceptions" surrounding her rape at age 13 by director Roman Polanski. "She knows now she was raped, but observes the '70s shifting sexual climate blurred lines. Sex occurred between people of different ages without "calculation or malice," she writes. . . . Now Geimer saves her vitriol for the 'victim industry,' represented by Dr. Phil and Nancy Grace." (Maclean's)

REVIEW: *N Y Times Book Rev* p19 S 22 2013 LISA SCHWARZBAUM

"The Girl: A Life in the Shadow of Roman Polanski." "Written with the journalist Judith Newman and with input from [Samantha] Geimer's lawyer, Lawrence Silver, 'The Girl' is a feisty, almost jaunty you're-not-the-boss-of-me account of a really awful thing and its long aftermath. It's also an exercise that uses autobiography as a feminist tactic for Geimer to own her sexuality, acknowledge her crummy but eventually better lifestyle choices in the years after the rape, and cash in on her right to tell the story her way."

REVIEW: *New York Times* v162 no56247 pC3 S 2 2013 JANET MASLIN

GELB, ALAN. Conquering the college admissions essay in 10 steps; crafting a winning personal statement; [by] Alan Gelb xii, 210 p. 2013 Ten Speed Press

1. College applications—United States 2. EDUCATION—Higher 3. Essay—Authorship 4. Exposition (Rhetoric) 5. LANGUAGE ARTS & DISCIPLINES—Composition & Creative Writing 6. STUDY AIDS—College Entrance 7. Universities and colleges—United States—Admission

ISBN 9781607743668 (pbk.)

LC 2013-011730

SUMMARY: Written by Alan Gelb, this book is "A guide to crafting a meaningful and polished college admissions essay that gets students into the school of their dreams by expressing their unique personality, strengths, and goals." It aims to help applicants to "Stand out from the crowd with a memorable, meaningful personal statement that will capture the attention of college admissions officers." (Publisher's note)

REVIEW: *Voice of Youth Advocates* v36 no4 p97-8 O 2013 Lindsay Grattan

"Conquering the College Admissions Essay in 10 Steps." "In the second edition of 'Conquering the College Admissions Essay in 10 Steps,' [Alan] Gelb focuses on one major aspect of the college admissions process: the personal essay. . . . Gelb outlines the road to a successful essay in ten steps. . . . He explains everything from choosing a compelling topic that captures the interest and attention of the admissions staff to point of view, structure, tone, and conflict. His tips on self-editing and proofreading are vital to a well-written narrative. Perhaps the biggest bonus of the book is the inclusion of several personal essays written by students who were accepted into their college of choice."

GELLATELY, ROBERT. Stalin's curse; battling for communism in war and Cold War; [by] Robert Gellately 496 p. 2013 Knopf

1. Communism—Europe—History—20th century 2. Historical literature 3. Soviet Union—Relations—United States

ISBN 0307269159; 9780307269157

LC 2012-028768

SUMMARY: Author Robert Gellately presents an "account based on newly released Russian documentation that reveals Joseph Stalin's true motives--and the extent of his enduring commitment to expanding the Soviet empire--during the years in which he seemingly collaborated with Franklin D. Roosevelt, Winston Churchill, and the capitalist West." (Publisher's note)

REVIEW: *Booklist* v109 no11 p13 F 1 2013 Gilbert Taylor

REVIEW: *Choice* v51 no1 p142 S 2013 D. J. Dunn

REVIEW: *Economist* v406 no8829 p82 Mr 30 2013

REVIEW: *Kirkus Rev* v80 no24 p236 D 15 2012

REVIEW: *Libr J* v138 no4 p81 Mr 1 2013 Jacob Sherman

REVIEW: *New Statesman* v142 no5153/5154 p135 Ap 12 3013 Robert Service

REVIEW: *Publ Wkly* v259 no52 p45 D 24 2012

REVIEW: *TLS* no5769 p26 O 25 2013 GEOFFREY SWAIN

"Stalin's Curse: Battling For Communism in War and Cold War." "[Robert] Gellately is right that [Joseph] Stalin wanted to export revolution, but the way he sets about explaining this is not entirely successful. Gellately states that he is not writing a biography of Stalin, but he does nevertheless feel the need to catalogue every one of Stalin's crimes. . . . This means that although Gellately's sources are up to date, inevitably his broad-brush approach leads to rather superficial summaries and the occasional error of detail. The second consequence is more serious. The decision to list Stalin's crimes detracts from the central purpose of the book."

GELLMAN, ERIK S. Death blow to Jim Crow; the National Negro Congress and the rise of militant civil rights; [by] Erik S. Gellman xiii, 354 p. 2012 University of North Carolina Press

1. African Americans—Civil rights—History—20th century 2. African Americans—History—1877-1964 3. African Americans—Segregation—History—20th century 4. Civil rights movements—United States—History—20th century 5. Historical literature 6. Race discrimination—United States—History—20th century

ISBN 9780807835319 (cloth : alk. paper)

LC 2011-022145

SUMMARY: This book on civil rights activism by Erik S. Gellman "focuses on the National Negro Congress (NNC) and its independent youth affiliate, the Southern Negro Youth Congress (SNYC). To evidence the NNC's and SNYC's careers, Gellman fixes on operations in five locations--Chicago; Columbia, South Carolina; New York

City; Richmond, Virginia; and Washington, D.C. The black intellectual activist attorney John Preston Davis (1905–73) serves as Gellman's main character." (Reviews in American History)

REVIEW: *Am Hist Rev* v118 no4 p1196 O 2013 Cornelius L. Bynum

"Death Blow to Jim Crow: The National Negro Congress and the Rise of Militant Civil Rights." "In examining how the National Negro Congress (NNC) became the "black vanguard" of a coalitional effort to extend New Deal progressivism and defeat fascism at home and abroad through 'interracial, labor-based alliances of radicals and liberals,' Erik S. Gellman's 'Death Blow to Jim Crow' fills a considerable gap in the literature on radicalism and civil rights in the United States during the interwar years. . . . 'Death Blow to Jim Crow' is a good example of how competent research and nuanced argumentation can yield scholarly discoveries even in exhaustively studied areas of American history."

REVIEW: *J Am Hist* v99 no3 p962 D 2012 Cynthia Taylor

REVIEW: *Rev Am Hist* v41 no3 p507-12 S 2013 Thomas J. Davis

"Death Blow to Jim Crow: The National Negro Congress and the Rise of Militant Civil Rights." "[Erik S.] Gellman's assessments too often confuse the sweeping movements of an era with the acts of his selected organizations and individuals. . . .Moreover, while Gellman casts the NNC as one among many actors, he persistently positions the NNC not even as primus inter pares but as indispensable. He casts the NNC as the but-for-cause for far too much. . . . Positioning the NNC as the sine qua non of black radicalism from 1938 to 1947 mistakes not only the era but the efforts of many of the people Gellman parades through his essays."

GENDERED LIVES; Gender Inequalities in Production and Reproduction; 256 p. 2013 Edward Elgar Pub.

1. Gender inequality 2. Gender mainstreaming 3. Sex discrimination 4. Sexual division of labor 5. Social science literature

ISBN 1781004080; 9781781004081

SUMMARY: This book "examines how gender inequalities in contemporary societies are changing and how further changes towards greater gender equality might be achieved. The focus of the book is on inequalities in production and reproductive activities, as played out over time and in specific contexts. It examines the different forms that gendered lives take in the household and the workplace, and explores how gender equalities may be promoted in a changing world." (Publisher's note)

REVIEW: *Contemp Sociol* v43 no2 p287-8 Mr 2014

"Gendered Lives: Gender Inequalities in Production and Reproduction". "A collection of chapters written by various authors. Editors Jacqueline Scott, Shirley Dex, and Anke Plagnol seek to examine how gender inequality in the contemporary United Kingdom is changing and how continued steps toward greater gender equality can be achieved. Inequalities in work and family both now, over time, and in specific contexts are examined. The authors also focus on how lives and structure are changing, and how policy can promote these changes."

GENDERING THE FAIR; histories of women and gender at world's fairs; viii, 243 2010 University of Illinois Press

1. Exhibitions—History—19th century 2. Women—History—19th century

ISBN 9780252035586; 0252035585; 9780252077494; 0252077490

LC 2010-016580

SUMMARY: The book offers an "array of essays exploring world's fairs from a feminist perspective. Rather than presenting the essays chronologically, [the editors] have arranged them around three central themes: gender and the project of nation building, women's activism, and space and culture." Topics discussed include "the Board of Lady Managers and the Woman's Building at the Chicago Worlds's Fair of 1893 . . . the construction of an imperial American masculinity at the 1915 Panama-Pacific International Exposition . . . [and] the focus on women's work rather than domestic achievement at a series of Chicago expositions during the 1920s." (Journal of American History)

REVIEW: *J Am Hist* v98 no3 p862-3 D 2011 Melissa R. Klapper

"Gendering the Fair: Histories of Women and Gender at World's Fairs." "In 'Gendering the Fair' T. J. Boisseau and Abigail M. Markwyn have assembled a nice array of essays exploring world's fairs from a feminist perspective. Rather than presenting the essays chronologically, they have arranged them around three central themes: gender and the project of nation building, women's activism, and space and culture. . . . Sarah J. Moore analyzes the construction of an imperial American masculinity at the 1915 Panama-Pacific International Exposition; Markwyn examines the physical and cultural spaces allotted to women at the same exposition; Anne Clendinning traces the ironies of peace activism at the 1924 British Empire Exhibition glorifying colonial conquest; Boisseau reveals the focus on women's work rather than domestic achievement at a series of Chicago expositions during the 1920s; and Mary Pepchinski studies the architectural features of woman's buildings at several American and European fairs from 1893 to 1939. . . . World's fairs and expositions . . . [a]s the essays in 'Gendering the Fair' amply demonstrate, . . . deserve continued attention by historians."

GENDRON, ROBIN S.ed. Aluminum Ore. See Aluminum Ore

GENSLER, SONIA. The dark between; [by] Sonia Gensler 352 p. 2013 Alfred A. Knopf

1. Dead—Fiction 2. Experiments—Fiction 3. Historical fiction 4. Spiritualism—History 5. Young adult fiction

ISBN 9780375867026; 9780375967023 (lib. bdg.)

LC 2012-036208

SUMMARY: This young adult novel, by Sonia Gensler, describes how "At the turn of the twentieth century, Spiritualism and séances are all the rage--even in the scholarly town of Cambridge, England. While mediums dupe the grief-stricken, a group of local fringe scientists seeks to bridge the gap to the spirit world by investigating the dark corners of the human mind. Each running from a shadowed past, Kate, Asher, and Elsie take refuge within the walls of Summerfield College." (Publisher's note)

REVIEW: *Booklist* v109 no22 p77 Ag 1 2013 Sarah Hunter

REVIEW: *Bull Cent Child Books* v67 no2 p90-1 O 2013 E. B.

"The Dark Between." "Three teens converge at Summerfield College in Cambridge in 1901: Kate, who has just lost her job playing a spirit at Mrs. Martineau's sham seances; Elsie, the ailing niece of Mrs. Thompson, the college president; and Asher, an American paying a courtesy call on behalf of his parents. What appears at first to be coincidence begins to seem inevitable once the trio discover that their respective parents and the Thompsons have long shared an interest in spiritualism and its possible relation to the fascinating new field of psychology. . . . The melodrama here somewhat overshadows what could have been a fascinating examination of the overlapping study of mind and soul, body and disembodiment, at the close of the Victorian period."

REVIEW: *Kirkus Rev* v81 no2 p85-8 Je 1 2013

REVIEW: *SLJ* v59 no10 p1 O 2013 Jessica Miller

GENTILI, GRAZIANO. Regular functions of a quaternionic variable; [by] Graziano Gentili xix, 185 p. 2013 Springer

1. Complex analysis (Mathematics) 2. Functions of several complex variables 3. Functions, Quaternion 4. Mathematical literature 5. Quaternion functions 6. Regular functions (Mathematics)
ISBN 3642338704 (alk. paper); 9783642338700 (alk. paper)
LC 2012-954238

SUMMARY: Authors Graziano Gentili, Caterina Stoppato, and Daniele C. Struppa "document their own very recent theory of quaternionic regular functions, a development that parallels familiar complex function theory spectacularly well. This user-friendly primary source confirms that quaternionic calculus is not a dead end, and clearly answers a popular question regarding the analogy of complex function theory (complex analysis) with quarternionic variables." (Choice)

REVIEW: *Choice* v51 no1 p119 S 2013 D. V. Feldman

"Regular Functions of a Quaternionic Variable." "Here, [authors Graziano] Gentili . . . , [Caterina] Stoppato . . . , and [Daniele C.] Struppa . . . document their own very recent theory of quaternionic regular functions, a development that parallels familiar complex function theory spectacularly well. This user-friendly primary source confirms that quaternionic calculus is not a dead end, and clearly answers a popular question regarding the analogy of complex function theory (complex analysis) with quarternionic variables, making it an excellent basis for a capstone course."

GEORGE-WARREN, HOLLY. A man called destruction; the life and music of Alex Chilton, from Box Tops to Big Star to backdoor man; [by] Holly George-Warren 384 p. 2014 Viking

1. Big Star (Musical group) 2. Biography (Literary form) 3. Box Tops (Musical group) 4. Rock musicians—United States—Biography
ISBN 0670025631; 9780670025633
LC 2013-041158

SUMMARY: This biography, by Holly George-Warren, tells the story of musician Alex Chilton, "beginning with teenage rock stardom and heading downward. Following stints leading 60s sensation the Box Tops and pioneering 70s popsters Big Star, Chilton became a dishwasher. Yet he rose again in the 80s as a solo artist, producer, and trendsetter, coinventing the indie-rock genre. . . . The 90s. . . [ushered] him back to the spotlight before his untimely death in 2010." (Publisher's note)

REVIEW: *Bookforum* v20 no5 p45 F/Mr 2014 CARL WILSON

"A Man Called Destruction: The Life and Music of Alex Chilton, From Box Tops to Big Star to Backdoor Man." "[A] thorough but slow-paced account of Chilton's life. . . . Chilton's story doesn't read mainly as one of missed opportunity. Yes, he could have dedicated himself to producing pop masterpieces, but he probably changed music and culture just as effectively with his elusiveness. . . . As I worked my way through the book's steady procession of neutrally narrated anecdotes of recording-session anarchy, lazy days and debauched nights, broken friendships and bruising romances, off-the-cuff performances and hastily assembled bands, I kept being startled to realize how young Chilton still was, chapter by chapter and event by event."

REVIEW: *Booklist* v110 no14 p40-1 Mr 15 2014 Ben Segedin

REVIEW: *Kirkus Rev* v82 no3 p170 F 1 2014

"A Man Called Destruction: The Life and Music of Alex Chilton, From Box Tops to Big Star to Backdoor Man". "A thoroughly reported biography illuminating the life and work of one of the more mystifying and influential cult figures in rock. . . . It may be hard to find the common denominator, but veteran rock journalist [Holly] George-Warren . . . connects the dots, showing how it all fit together. . . . As an artist who 'left behind . . . many lifetimes of brilliant music, a legacy that will inspire generations to come,' Chilton receives the biography he deserves."

REVIEW: *Libr J* v139 no3 p107 F 15 2014 Dave Valencia

REVIEW: *New York Times* v163 no56450 pC1-4 Mr 24 2014 JANET MASLIN

REVIEW: *N Y Times Book Rev* p38-9 Je 1 2014 HOWARD HAMPTON

GEORGE, BOBBY. Montessori shape work; [by] Bobby George 18 p. 2013 Abrams Appleseed

1. Board books 2. Children's nonfiction 3. Montessori method of education 4. Shapes—Juvenile literature 5. Triangles
ISBN 9781419709357
LC 2012-049489

SUMMARY: In this children's picture book, "shapes are presented from the concrete to the abstract. Three varieties of triangles, all with a tactile feature created by cutting away the top layer of the board page, are presented, allowing readers to feel and understand the geometric concept. On the following pages, these triangles are more specifically named . . . and shown in their real-world contexts. . . . Rounds (circle, ellipse, and oval) come next." (Kirkus Reviews)

REVIEW: *Kirkus Rev* v82 no1 p22 Ja 1 2014

"Shape Work". "Montessori experts offer a handsome, in-depth exploration of shapes. . . . [Alyssa] Nassner's crystal-clear graphics in natural colors against faux wood grain, give the book much-needed warmth. This is an advanced take on shapes, with mathematically accurate vocabulary ('rhombus' is used rather than the more colloquial 'diamond,' for example), and shapes are flipped and turned when presented as real-world objects (the egg-shaped 'oval' is shown narrow end up in its abstract form and with narrow side down as a balloon). There are some clever and surprising things used to illustrate where shapes can be found, such as the black pentagons found on the typical soccer ball."

GEORGE, ELIZABETH, 1949-. The edge of the water; [by] Elizabeth George 448 p. 2014 Viking, published by Penguin Group

1. Abandoned children—Fiction 2. Interpersonal relations—Fiction 3. Psychic ability—Fiction 4. Seals (Animals)—Fiction 5. Secrets—Fiction 6. Selkies—Fiction 7. Sexual orientation—Fiction 8. Speculative fiction
ISBN 0670012971; 9780670012978 (hardcover)
LC 2013-014160

SUMMARY: In this book, by Elizabeth George, "strange things are happening on Whidbey Island, and Becca King, is drawn into the maelstrom of events. . . . Still on the run from her criminal stepfather, Becca is living in a secret location. Even Derric, the Ugandan orphan with whom Becca shares a close, romantic relationship, can't be allowed to know her whereabouts. As secrets of the past and present are revealed, Becca becomes aware of her growing paranormal powers." (Publisher's note)

REVIEW: *Booklist* v110 no8 p45 D 15 2013 Debbie Carron

REVIEW: *Booklist* v110 no1 p65 S 1 2013 Gillian Engberg

"Dangerous," "Desert Tales," and "The Edge of the Water." "The acclaimed, best-selling author [Shannon Hale] takes a new direction in this fantasy adventure, in which an unsuspecting heroine discovers a terrifying plot against society-and falls in love along the way. . . . In this new companion to the blockbuster Wicked Lovely series, [Melissa] Marr focuses on faery Rika, whose free, isolated existence in the Mojave Desert is transformed by both a king's power and a new romance. . . . The second YA title from best-selling adult crime novelist [Elizabeth] George is the first entry in a new paranormal mystery series set on Washington state's Whidbey Island."

REVIEW: *Kirkus Rev* v82 no3 p77 F 1 2014

REVIEW: *SLJ* v60 no5 p130 My 2014 Elisabeth Gattullo Marrocolla

REVIEW: *Voice of Youth Advocates* v36 no6 p71 F 2014 Madeline Miles

REVIEW: *Voice of Youth Advocates* v36 no6 p70 F 2014 Debbie Wenk

GEORGE, JEAN CRAIGHEAD, 1919-2012. Galapagos George; [by] Jean Craighead George 40 p. 2014 HarperCollins Publishers

1. Darwin, Charles, 1809-1882 2. Evolution (Biology)—Juvenile literature 3. Galapagos tortoise—Evolution—Juvenile literature 4. Galapagos tortoise—Juvenile literature 5. Galapagos tortoise—Migration—Juvenile literature
ISBN 0060287934; 9780060287931 (trd. bdg.); 9780060287948 (lib. bdg.)
LC 2011-030446

SUMMARY: This book, by Jean Craighead George, "is the story of the famous Lonesome George, a giant tortoise who was the last of his species, lived to be one hundred years old, and became known as the rarest creature in the world. His story gives us a glimpse of the amazing creatures inhabiting the ever-fascinating Galápagos Islands." (Publisher's note)

REVIEW: *Booklist* v110 no9/10 p92 Ja 1 2014 Randall Enos

REVIEW: *Horn Book Magazine* v90 no2 p141-2 Mr/Ap 2014 BETTY CARTER

REVIEW: *Kirkus Rev* v82 no4 p113 F 15 2014

"Galápagos George". "[Wendell] Minor's paintings are gorgeous, befitting the awesome Galápagos scenery and including representative plants and animals. But the posthumously published text oversimplifies. It describes [Charles] Darwin speculating about the giant tortoises' common ancestor, but at the time, he didn't realize they were different species. It condenses the adaptation process. Even the backmatter doesn't use the phrase 'natural selection,' and the very important term 'evolution' is defined incorrectly. A heartfelt if imperfect tribute to one George by another who will also be missed."

REVIEW: *Publ Wkly* v261 no5 p56 F 3 2014

REVIEW: *SLJ* v60 no3 p172 Mr 2014 Frances E. Millhouser

GEORGE, JENNIFER.ed. The art of Rube Goldberg. See The art of Rube Goldberg

GEORGE, JUNE. Montessori shape work. See George, B.

GEORGE, ROSE. Ninety percent of everything; inside shipping, the invisible industry that puts clothes on your back, gas in your car, and food on your plate; [by] Rose George 304 p. 2013 Metropolitan Books

1. Container ships 2. Freight and freightage—History 3. Journalism 4. Shipping (Water transportation) 5. Shipping—History
ISBN 9780805092639
LC 2013-000293

SUMMARY: In this book, author "Rose George . . . sails from Rotterdam to Suez to Singapore on ships the length of football fields . . . she patrols the Indian Ocean with an anti-piracy task force; she joins seafaring chaplains, and investigates the harm that ships inflict on endangered whales. Sharply informative and entertaining, 'Ninety Percent of Everything' reveals . . . an unseen world that holds the key to our economy, our environment, and our very civilization." (Publisher's note)

REVIEW: *Booklist* v109 no21 p7 Jl 1 2013 Carl Hays

REVIEW: *Kirkus Rev* v81 no9 p48 My 1 2013

REVIEW: *Kirkus Rev* p26 2013 Guide to BookExpo America

REVIEW: *N Y Rev Books* v61 no6 p28-32 Ap 3 2014 Maya Jasanoff

"Ninety Percent of Everything: Inside Shipping, the Invisible Industry That Puts Clothes on Your Back, Gas in Your Car, and Food on Your Plate." "[Author Rose] George organizes the book loosely around her voyage, using each stage to delve into associated aspects of merchant shipping. Her choppy, hard-edged prose rebuffs hopeful illusions about the sea. . . . George dedicates two excellent chapters to the best-known form of lawlessness, the Somali pirates who have been the scourge of merchant shipping since the early 2000s."

REVIEW: *New York Times* v162 no56292 pC1-7 O 17 2013 DWIGHT GARNER

REVIEW: *Orion Magazine* v33 no3 p101-2 My-Ag 2014 Elizabeth Kennedy

GERHARDT, ROBERT E. Michiel van Musscher (1645-

1705); [by] Robert E. Gerhardt 2012 WBOOKS
1. Art literature 2. Biographies 3. Dutch art—History 4. Dutch painters 5. Van Musscher, Michiel
ISBN 9789040007132; 9789040007217

SUMMARY: This book by Robert E. Gerhardt and Francis Griep-Quint accompanied a 2012 exhibition at the Museum van Loon. "The exhibition on Michiel van Musscher does not only display his more famous paintings from Dutch collections and the museum itself, but also a significant number of paintings from foreign museums and national and international private collections, which are normally not accessible to the public." (Publisher's note)

REVIEW: *Burlington Mag* v155 no1327 p719-20 O 2013 EDDY SCHAVEMAKER

"Michiel van Musscher (1645-1705). The Wealth of the Golden Age." "Michiel van Musscher (1645-1705) painted highly finished, cabinet-size portraits and scenes of everyday life for the Amsterdam elite. Like many successful Dutch artists of his generation, he fell from favour in the nineteenth century. . . . This publication accompanied a recent exhibition held at the Museum van Loon, Amsterdam, that presented an opportunity for scholars and the general public to acquaint themselves with Van Musscher's work. . . . In the present publication the chapters about the artist's life, training, stylistic development, patrons and critical fortunes contain a wealth of information, but the authors have struggled to present it in a lucid fashion."

GERHARDT, UTA. The social thought of Talcott Parsons; methodology and American ethos; [by] Uta Gerhardt xii, 444 p. 2011 Ashgate
1. Social theory 2. Sociology—United States—History 3. Sociology—United States—Methodology 4. Sociology literature
ISBN 9781409427674 (hbk.; alk. paper); 9781409427681 (ebook)
LC 2011-017895

SUMMARY: This book on sociologist Talcott Parsons "explores the debates in which Parsons was engaged throughout his life, with the Frankfurt School, C. Wright Mills and the young radicals among the 'disobedient' student generation, as well as economism and utilitarianism in social theory." Author Uta Gerhardt takes up themes in current research and theory—including social inequality, civic culture, and globalization." (Publisher's note)

REVIEW: *Contemp Sociol* v43 no1 p90-2 Ja 2014 Isaac Ariail Reed

"The Social Thought of Talcott Parsons: Methodology and American Ethos". "This book is a sprawling labor of love, flawed but useful, and intensely focused on certain debates between theorists as a route into the larger problems of the discipline. Uta Gerhardt has as her goal nothing less than the revival of the discipline's most typified, stereotyped, and negatively cathected theorist. The means she chooses for pursuing this end are intellectual history, conceptual exegesis, and polemic against other Parsons interpreters. She is well-armed for the third task, well-practiced at the second, but ultimately most successful, in this text, at the first."

GERMAN TEXT CRIMES; writers accused, from the 1950s to the 2000s; 242 p. 2013 Rodopi
1. Censorship 2. German literature—20th century—History and criticism 3. Historical literature 4. Law and literature—Germany 5. Scandals
ISBN 9042036907 (hd.bd.); 9789042036901 (hd.bd.)
LC 2013-380296

SUMMARY: This book, edited by Tom Cheesman, looks at 'scandals and legal actions implicating writers of German literature since the 1950s. Topics range from literary echoes of the 'Heidegger Affair' to recent incitements to murder businessmen (agents of American neo-liberal power) in works by Rolf Hochhuth and others; GDR songwriters' cat-and-mouse games with the Stasi; [and] feminist debates on pornography." (Publisher's note)

REVIEW: *TLS* no5771 p27 N 8 2013 HOUMAN BAREKAT

"German Text Crimes: Writers Accused, From the 1950s to the 2000s." "The cultural politics of the Cold War feature prominently, as in David Robb's chapter on 'Text Crimes against the GDR's Revolutionary Heritage'. . . . Notwithstanding its rather clunky frame of reference--and the somewhat inappropriate punning of the title--German Text Crimes is a thought-provoking study of the relationship between politics and the arts, as well as an valuable contribution to the ever-growing scholarship on historical memory."

GERRITSEN, TESS. Keeper of the bride; [by] Tess Gerritsen 250 p. 2013 Severn House
1. Bombings—Fiction 2. Crime—Fiction 3. Love stories 4. Police—Fiction 5. Weddings—Fiction
ISBN 0727881221; 9780727881229

SUMMARY: In this book, by Tess Gerritsen, "Nina Cormier was jilted at the altar, but what a break that turns out to be: the church blows up just as she is leaving. . . . The bomb squad investigates, headed by Detective Sam Navarro, and all leads point to Nina's ex-husband as the prime suspect. Nina is heartbroken and scared; Sam is brave and strong; and both are determined to keep it all professional. But when someone tries to run Nina off the road, Sam steps in to make sure she's safe." (Booklist)

REVIEW: *Booklist* v110 no2 p42-4 S 15 2013 Stacy Alesi

"Keeper of the Bride." "Nina Cormier was jilted at the altar, but what a break that turns out to be: the church blows up just as she is leaving (and when she would have been saying vows had the marriage happened). . . .This fast-paced story, reissued here in hardcover following its original publication in 1996 as a Harlequin paperback, boasts some nice plot twists and two likable protagonists. Rizzoli & Isles fans may think of this as Gerritsen-lite, but Sandra Brown readers will love it."

GERSHATOR, PHILLIS, 1942-. Time for a hug; [by] Phillis Gershator p. cm. 2012 Sterling Pub. Co.
1. Activities of daily living 2. Children's stories 3. Hugging—Fiction 4. Rabbits—Fiction 5. Stories in rhyme 6. Time—Juvenile literature
ISBN 9781402778629
LC 2011-021209

SUMMARY: In this children's book, by Phillis Gershator & Mim Green, "two bunnies, one small and orange and the other bigger and gray, wake up at 8:00 to begin a day chock-full of activities that preschoolers will recognize. Washing faces, getting dressed, baking a pie, playing with puppets, reading a book, bathing, brushing teeth and hopping off to bed are all portrayed in [David] Walker's softly colored full-page and double-page spreads or vignettes." (Kirkus Reviews)

REVIEW: *Kirkus Rev* v82 no1 p2 Ja 1 2014

"Time for a Hug". "[A] sweet, brief rhyming tale celebrating hugs at any hour of the day. . . . As times passes, young readers will enjoy looking for the clock ticking off each hour until bedtime. Most hours prove to be a perfect moment to embrace. 'Two o'clock, three o'clock. What shall we do? / Bounce a ball, ride a bike, climb a tree, / go on a hike. Smell a flower, chase a bug—What time is it? / Time for a hug!' The pleasingly predictable rhyme will have preschoolers chiming in all the way to the page where the covers are pulled up. Worth a pause and may well inspire a hug or two."

GERSTEIN, DAVID.ed. Walt Disney's Mickey Mouse color Sundays. See Walt Disney's Mickey Mouse color Sundays

GERSTEIN, MORDICAI, 1935-.il. The first drawing. See The first drawing

GERSTEIN, MORDICAI, 1935-. You can't have too many friends!; [by] Mordicai Gerstein 32 p. 2014 Holiday House

1. Children's stories 2. Ducks—Fiction 3. Friendship—Fiction 4. Humorous stories 5. Jellybeans 6. Kings, queens, rulers, etc.—Fiction

ISBN 082342393X; 9780823423934 (hardcover)

LC 2013-020997

SUMMARY: This children's book, by Mordicai Gerstein, is an "adaptation of 'Drakestail,' a classic French fairytale[.] Duck goes on an epic quest to retrieve jellybeans from the king with lots of help from his unusual friends." (Publisher's note) "These new friends all come in handy when the king declines to give back the candy." (Horn Book Magazine)

REVIEW: *Booklist* v110 no15 p95 Ap 1 2014 Kay Weisman

REVIEW: *Horn Book Magazine* v90 no2 p102 Mr/Ap 2014 DOVE LEMPKE

"You Can't Have Too Many Friends!" "Listening children will anticipate the role of each of Duck's pals and will enjoy seeing the king's nasty acts rightfully rewarded, especially when he's chased naked out of his bathtub by the wasps. This is anything but a heavy handed moral treatment, though--[Mordicai] Gerstein's pen-and-ink, acrylic, and colored-pencil illustrations employ a cheerful palette, with scribbly lines and dialogue bubbles. Each picture includes humorous details such as the web-footed claw bathtub and the queen's fuzzy slippers. And in the end, the king makes reparations, sitting down to a jelly-bean feast with Duck and his odd group of friends."

REVIEW: *Kirkus Rev* v82 no3 p207 F 1 2014

REVIEW: *SLJ* v60 no4 p120 Ap 2014 Marilyn Taniguchi

GERT, JOSHUA. Normative bedrock; response-dependence, rationality, and reasons; [by] Joshua Gert x, 218 p. 2012 Oxford University Press

1. Color (Philosophy) 2. Naturalism 3. Normativity (Ethics) 4. Philosophical literature 5. Reason

ISBN 9780199657544

LC 2012-532286

SUMMARY: "This book argues that we can 'demystify' the normative by applying the philosophical method 'linguistic naturalism' to 'basic' normative concepts: those 'not defined in terms of other concepts, and that one learns to apply non-inferentially'. . . . This method treats those concepts as response-dependent, and as in this way similar to colour concepts." (Analysis)

REVIEW: *Ethics* v124 no3 p608-12 Ap 2014 BART STREUMER

REVIEW: *TLS* no5768 p7-8 O 18 2013 ALLAN GIBBARD

"Shaping the Normative Landscape" and "Normative Bedrock" Response-Dependence, Rationality, and Reasons." "[David] Owens's many examples convince me that this really is how we understand promises. . . . Central to Owens's book is the claim that a nonnative status can matter even apart from the good its recognition fosters. Not all acts are for goods, and some of our interests are purely normative. . . . Response-dependence has been at the centre of much discussion of normative concepts in recent decades, but understanding the response in terms of goal puzzlement is [Joshua] Gert's distinctive contribution, as far as I know. . . . Both books are models of philosophy as a cumulative enterprise that builds originally on what has been done before. Each changes one's view of an important subject."

GERTLER, MERIC.ed. The creative class goes global. See The creative class goes global

GERTZ, SEBASTIAN RAMON PHILIPP.tr. Aeneas of Gaza. See Aeneas of Gaza

GERVAIS, BERNADETTE. Birds of a feather. See Pittau, F.

GESSEN, MASHA. Words will break cement; the passion of Pussy Riot; [by] Masha Gessen 320 p. 2014 Riverhead Books

1. Punk rock music—Political aspects—Russia (Federation) 2. Resistance to government 3. Revolutionary literature 4. Russia (Federation)—Politics & government

ISBN 1594632197; 9781594632198

LC 2013-046520

SUMMARY: "Drawing on her exclusive, extensive access to the members of Pussy Riot and their families and associates, [author Masha Gessen] reconstructs the fascinating personal journeys that transformed a group of young women into artists with a shared vision, gave them the courage and imagination to express it unforgettably, and endowed them with the strength to endure the devastating loneliness and isolation that have been the price of their triumph." (Publisher's note)

REVIEW: *America* v210 no20 p34-5 Je 23 2014 LISA A. BAGLIONE

REVIEW: *Kirkus Rev* v82 no2 p210 Ja 15 2014

"Words Will Break Cement: The Passion of Pussy Riot". "The problem with this illuminating book is that [Masha] Gessen . . . is both too close and not close enough. While she lacked access to the incarcerated members once worldwide attention justified a book such as this (likely to capitalize on the profile it helps raise, just as it analyzes how some involved have hopes of capitalizing), she does not provide the detail required by those readers who may not understand the intricacies and absurdities of the Russian legal system. The reporting of the trial is the most vivid. . . . An uneven but revelatory introduction to the story, though certainly not the last word."

REVIEW: *New York Times* v163 no56377 pC5 Ja 10 2014 ALEXANDRA NAZARYAN

"Words Will Break Cement: The Passion of Pussy Riot". "Urgent. . . . Damning. . . . [Masha Gessen's] subject is the punk band Pussy Riot, three of whose members were given two-year prison sentences for their minute-long 'punk prayer' performed in a cathedral in 2012. . . . Ms. Gessen is a largely dispassionate observer. . . . She is not the first to tell Pussy Riot's story . . . . But she tells it more thoroughly, her anger at Russia's 'overwhelming mediocrity' scorching every page. . . . Much here will be new to the American reader. All of it is infuriating."

REVIEW: *TLS* no5807 p7 Jl 18 2014 FERNANDA EBERSTADT

GEWERTZ, DEBORAH. The noodle narratives; the global rise of an industrial food into the twenty-first century; [by] Deborah Gewertz 216 p. 2013 University of California Press

1. Historical literature 2. Noodles—Social aspects—Japan 3. Noodles—Social aspects—Papua New Guinea 4. Noodles—Social aspects—United States 5. Noodles industry—Social aspects—Japan 6. Noodles industry—Social aspects—Papua New Guinea 7. Noodles industry—Social aspects—United States

ISBN 9780520276338 (cloth: alk. paper); 9780520276345 (pbk.: alk. paper)
LC 2012-046523

SUMMARY: In this book, authors Frederick Errington, Tatsuro Fujikura and Deborah Gewertz "examine the history, manufacturing, marketing, and consumption of instant noodles. By focusing on three specific markets, they reveal various ways in which these noodles enable diverse populations to manage their lives. The first market is in Japan. . . . The second is in the United States. . . . The third is in Papua New Guinea, where instant noodles arrived only recently." (Publisher's note)

REVIEW: *Choice* v51 no8 p1446 Ap 2014 J. M. Deutsch

"The Noodle Narratives: The Global Rise of an Industrial Food Into the Twenty-First Century". "Introductory chapters detail the history, industrialization, and rapid rise of instant noodles and analyze the components from commodities, chemical, and physiological perspectives. Central chapters make a clear case in each culture for instant noodles as technological and marketing phenomenon (Japan); desperation and transition food (US); and status industrial food (Papua New Guinea). The engaging, accessible writing style is supported with extensive notes and references."

REVIEW: *TLS* no5780 p26-7 Ja 10 2014 MARION RANKINE

"The Noodle Narratives: The Global Rise of an Industrial Food Into the Twenty-First Century." "Such is the dubious triumph of capitalism and globalization that it is now possible to learn a great deal about history, economics and culture through the lens of a single food product. . . . 'The Noodle Narratives' focuses on 'a uniquely universal, inexpensive, relatively low-profile belly filler'--instant noodles. They are, according to the book's authors, 'one of the most remarkable foods ever,' a statement which seems far-fetched considering their otherwise impartial approach. . . . The book plunges into a noodle-centric investigation of three very different markets: Japan, the United States and Papua New Guinea."

GEZARI, VANESSA M. The tender soldier; a true story of war and sacrifice; [by] Vanessa M. Gezari 336 p. 2013 Simon & Schuster

1. Afghan War, 2001—Campaigns—Afghanistan—De Maywand Kārīz 2. Anthropologists—United States—Biography 3. Applied anthropology—Afghanistan 4. Applied anthropology—United States—Moral and ethical aspects 5. Counterinsurgency—Afghanistan—De Maywand Kārīz 6. Journalism 7. Social sciences—Research—United States—Moral and ethical aspects

ISBN 1439177392; 9781439177396
LC 2013-001090

SUMMARY: This book, by Vanessa M. Gezari, looks at the U.S. "Pentagon's controversial attempt to bring social science to the battlefield, a program, called the Human Terrain System. . . . Gezari follows . . . three idealists from the hope that brought them to Afghanistan through the events of the fateful day when one is gravely wounded, an Afghan is dead, and a proponent of cross-cultural engagement is charged with his murder." (Publisher's note)

REVIEW: *Kirkus Rev* v81 no2 p53 Je 1 2013

REVIEW: *New York Times* v162 no56242 pC2 Ag 28 2013 JAMES DAO

"The Tender Soldier: A True Story of War and Sacrifice." "As Neil Sheehan's 'Bright Shining Lie' did with Vietnam, Ms. [Vanessa] Gezari's deft if less sweeping narrative dissects the hopes, hubris and shortcomings of America's efforts to nation-build in Afghanistan while fighting a war there. . . . Ms. Gezari brings to life other important figures in the program. . . . More important, she investigates the Afghan who doused Ms. [Paula] Lloyd with gasoline and set her on fire. . . . It is a testament to the book's strengths that it left me wanting more. . . . Ms. Gezari's book powerfully humanizes the ways the counterinsurgency effort played out in Afghanistan."

REVIEW: *Publ Wkly* v260 no16 p40 Ap 22 2013

G.H. MEAD; a reader; xxiv, 342 p. 2011 Routledge

1. Democracy 2. Social psychology 3. Social sciences—Philosophy 4. Sociology literature

ISBN 9780203869550 (ebook); 9780415556255 (cloth: alk. paper); 9780415556262 (limp: alk. paper)
LC 2010-040395

SUMMARY: This book, part of the Routledge Classics in Sociology series, "introduces social scientists to the ideas of George Herbert Mead (1863-1931). . . . It is the first to critically assess all of Mead's writings and draw out the aspects that are central to his system of thought. The book is divided into three parts (social psychology, science and epistemology, and democratic politics), comprising a total of 30 chapters - a third of which are published here for the first time." (Publisher's note)

REVIEW: *Contemp Sociol* v43 no2 p237-9 Mr 2014 Priscilla Dunk-West

"G. H. Mead: A Reader". "The publication of 'G.H. Mead: A Reader' has the welcome potential to incite a Meadian renaissance. This is because although George Herbert Mead is a prominent theorist, his publications can be difficult to access. Early writing about Mead is obfuscated by questions around authenticity and authorship of the source material cited and this volume is a welcome antidote to this problem. . . . The editor, Filipe Carriera da Silva, notes that his selection of Mead's work has been carefully considered in relation to what already exists in the literature. In what must have been a difficult task, he has skillfully selected 'the most relevant of Mead's contributions to contemporary social sciences'."

GHANNAM, FARHA. Live and die like a man; gender dynamics in urban Egypt; [by] Farha Ghannam xii, 222 p. 2013 Stanford University Press

1. Anthropology literature 2. Masculinity—Egypt 3. Men—Socialization—Egypt 4. Sex role—Egypt 5. Social norms—Egypt

ISBN 9780804783286 (cloth : alk. paper); 9780804783293 (pbk. : alk. paper)

LC 2013-021485

SUMMARY: In this book, "anthropologist Farha Ghannam utilizes 20 years of field research in the working-class neighborhood of al-Zawiya al-Hamra' to deconstruct the notion of masculinity. . . . Ghannam examines the meaning of masculinity through several processes: growing up, marriage, find a career, aging, and death." (Middle East Journal)

REVIEW: *Middle East J* v68 no1 p161-2 Wint 2014 Mona L. Russell

"To Live and Die Like a Man: Gender Dynamics in Urban Egypt." "In this groundbreaking work, anthropologist Farha Ghannam utilizes 20 years of field research in the working-class neighborhood of al-Zawiya al-Hamra' to deconstruct the notion of masculinity. . . . Ghannam excels at thick description. . . . Particularly poignant is her chapter on death. . . . There is little to criticize in this seminal work. . . . This work is a huge step forward in the field of Middle Eastern Studies. Little work has been done on masculinity in general, and even less on what it means for the ordinary man."

GHARIPOUR, MOHAMMAD. Persian gardens and pavilions; reflections in history, poetry and the arts; [by] Mohammad Gharipour xx, 233 p. 2013 I.B. Tauris

1. Architecture in art 2. Gardens in art 3. Gardens, Persian—History 4. Historical literature 5. Pavilions—Iran—History

ISBN 178076121X; 9781780761213

LC 2013-370216

SUMMARY: In this book, "Mohammad Gharipour places both the garden and the pavilion within their historical, literary and artistic contexts, emphasizing the importance of the pavilion. . . . He does so by examining the representations of gardens and pavilions in religious texts . . . the poetry of major Persian poets . . . miniature painting, sculpture and carpets, as well as accounts of travelers to Persia." (Publisher's note)

REVIEW: *Choice* v51 no6 p988-9 F 2014 L. Nees

"Persian Gardens and Pavilions: Reflections in History, Poetry and the Arts." "This fine book by [Mohammad] Gharipour . . . focuses on Persian gardens and the permanent or temporary structures within them, from the 15th through the 18th centuries. It also includes a useful, concise survey of references to gardens in earlier literature. . . . A scholarly book with a wide scope, it includes an extensive apparatus of glossary, notes and sources, and 100 illustrations. . . . The author systematically investigates many questions, especially with regard to structures, such as tents, or thrones in gardens, along with what can be said about the types and arrangements of plants."

GHATTAS, KIM. The secretary; a journey with Hillary Clinton from Beirut to the heart of American power; [by] Kim Ghattas 368 p.

1. Cabinet officers—United States—Biography 2. Journalism 3. Women cabinet officers—United States—Biography

ISBN 9780805095111

LC 2012-043835

SUMMARY: This book "tells the story of Hillary Clinton's tenure as Secretary of State, from the first days of the [Barack] Obama administration, to the drama of Wikileaks, to the 'Arab Spring' uprisings, and the standoff with Iran. Through [Kim] Ghattas' eyes, we see Clinton under the intense professional spotlight commanded by the world's chief diplomat, but also in the softer lighting of the more personal nuances of foreign relations." (Publisher's note)

REVIEW: *Booklist* v109 no12 p10 F 15 2013 Vanessa Bush

REVIEW: *Choice* v51 no6 p1094-5 F 2014 J. P. Dunn

"The Secretary: A Journey With Hillary Clinton from Beirut to the Heart of American Power." "[Kim] Ghattas, a Lebanese-born BBC correspondent, traveled with Secretary of State Hillary Clinton for four years and for much of Hillary's recordbreaking one million miles. Her portrait of Clinton as individual, diplomat, [and][personality . . . is a unique kind of study. . . . Critics will consider the volume an Obama/Clinton apologia, and such early journalist accounts seldom stand the test of time against later in-depth scholarship. But the book is a good first-blush introduction to the role of Hillary Clinton in the diplomacy of the first Obama administration. Whatever readers' politics, the volume is an engaging and enjoyable read."

REVIEW: *Kirkus Rev* v80 no24 p286 D 15 2012

REVIEW: *Libr J* v138 no4 p82 Mr 1 2013 Zachary Irwin

REVIEW: *Publ Wkly* v259 no52 p44 D 24 2012

GHORBANI, REZA. Secrets to a Pain Free Life; [by] Reza Ghorbani 232 p. 2013 Truceuticals Incorporated

1. Analgesia 2. Chronic pain—Treatment 3. Holistic medicine 4. Medical literature 5. Pain management

ISBN 0989823016; 9780989823012

SUMMARY: In this book, Reza Ghorbani, "a medical doctor and pain-management specialist, provides . . . facts . . . about the history of pain treatment, current attitudes toward pain management, the uses of prescription medications and natural remedies, and his own all-natural pain relief medication. The book categorizes pain into various types—acute, chronic, referred and phantom—and describes each in physiological detail." (Kirkus Reviews)

REVIEW: *Kirkus Rev* v81 no24 p395 D 15 2013

"Secrets to a Pain Free Life". "[Reza] Ghorbani, a medical doctor and pain-management specialist, provides intriguing facts here about the history of pain treatment, current attitudes toward pain management, the uses of prescription medications and natural remedies, and his own all-natural pain relief medication. . . . The book includes an illuminating description of the process of getting a new drug to the marketplace. . . . The author does discuss the merits of his own product, but he's never heavy-handed, and the book doesn't come off as an advertisement. Although it's a bit repetitive at times, it remains highly readable throughout. A hopeful, helpful resource for readers who might want to reach for something other than aspirin."

GIAMMETTI, GIANCARLO. Private; [by] Giancarlo Giammetti 380 p. 2013 Assouline

1. Celebrities 2. Fashion—History—20th century 3. Fashion designers 4. Memoirs 5. Valentino, 1932-
ISBN 1614281416; 9781614281412

SUMMARY: This book by Giancarlo Giammettti is "filled with images of those who were once known as the 'beautiful people'." It "is an exploration of the life of Mr. Giammetti and his partner, Valentino, couturier to royalty and stars. It moves backward and forward in time, from an Italian childhood through 50 years of fashion, with a certain focus on the carefree 1970s." (New York Times)

REVIEW: *New York Times* v163 no56362 pE5 D 26 2013 SUZY MENKES

"Private: Giancarlo Giammetti". "The appeal of 'Private' is not that Mr. Giammetti has made his life public by writing it, but that the book is a visual link to a world that has a blue-sky happiness. . . . He explains in the frank text that at one point their personal relationship broke up, yet the couple's two mothers remained inseparable friends. . . . The book is also a peek at an era, before the wide use of digital cameras, when the paparazzi . . . could be kept at bay. . . . For most of the images, though, there is a rollicking freedom, since people knew that their personal sunshine and shadows would remain inside the closed world of a photo album."

GIBB, SARAH.il. Beauty and the beast. See Beauty and the beast

GIBERSON, KARL W. The anointed; evangelical truth in a secular age; [by] Karl W. Giberson 384 2011 Belknap Press of Harvard University Press

1. Anti-intellectualism 2. Church & politics—Evangelical churches 3. Creationism 4. Evangelical churches—United States 5. Protestant fundamentalism 6. Social science literature
ISBN 9780674048188
LC 2011-019826

SUMMARY: "Exploring intellectual authority within evangelicalism, [authors Randall J. Stephens and Karl W. Giberson] reveal how America's populist ideals, anti-intellectualism, and religious free market, along with the concept of anointing--being chosen by God to speak for him like the biblical prophets--established a conservative evangelical leadership isolated from the world of secular arts and sciences." (Publisher's note)

REVIEW: *Choice* v49 no7 p1280 Mr 2012 A. W. Klink

REVIEW: *Christ Century* v128 no23 p38-9 N 15 2011 Matthew Avery Sutton

REVIEW: *J Relig* v93 no4 p531-2 O 2013 ROGER G. ROBINS

REVIEW: *Rev Am Hist* v42 no1 p174-80 Mr 2014 Mark A. Lempke

"The Anointed: Evangelical Truth in a Secular Age" and "Moral Minority: The Evangelical Left in an Age of Conservatism." "Collectively, these two books do their readers a great service, challenging the stereotypical perception of evangelicals in ways that may surprise even the evangelical community itself. . . . 'Moral Minority' turns its gaze to the Evangelical Left that formed in conversation with, rather than opposition to, the social movements of the late 1960s and early 1970s. 'The Anointed,' meanwhile, is decidedly presentist, exploring how some contemporary evangelicals acquire their understanding of science, American history, child rearing, and other topics through a litany of dubious authorities."

GIBSEN, COLE. Shinobi; [by] Cole Gibsen 288 p. 2014 Flux

1. High schools—Fiction 2. Love—Fiction 3. Martial arts—Fiction 4. Paranormal romance stories 5. Reincarnation—Fiction 6. Samurai—Fiction 7. Schools—Fiction 8. Supernatural—Fiction
ISBN 9780738739113
LC 2013-038149

SUMMARY: In this book, "Rileigh, a beautiful reincarnated samurai, is starting a new life in the finale to the Katana trilogy. . . . However, before she and Kim can begin a normal life as contemporary older teens, their powerful nemesis, the murderer Sumi, is back to get what she's always wanted: Kim. Sumi performs a ritual that enables her to switch bodies with Rileigh. Rileigh is horrified . . . if she can't find a way back into her own body quickly, she will be stuck forever." (Kirkus Reviews)

REVIEW: *Kirkus Rev* v82 no3 p72 F 1 2014

"Shinobi". "Rileigh is horrified to find her psyche and soul trapped within the body of the woman she's loathed for centuries, and her ki is weakening by the moment. If she can't find a way back into her own body quickly, she will be stuck forever. With Kim by her side, she begins a fraught journey to regain her identity and convince her fellow samurai that she is Rileigh, though in the wrong body. Adding dimension to the tale, the engrossing flashback chapters to 1400s Japan detail Sumi's heart-poisoning history in the hands of a cruel kidnapper. A swift tale of romance for the young teen with a warrior heart."

REVIEW: *Voice of Youth Advocates* v37 no1 p81 Ap 2014 Valerie Burleigh

GIBSON, KAREN BUSH. Women in space; 23 stories of first flights, scientific missions, and gravity-breaking adventures; [by] Karen Bush Gibson 240 p. 2014 Chicago Review Press

1. Children's nonfiction 2. Outer space—Exploration—History 3. United States. National Aeronautics & Space Administration 4. Women astronauts—Biography—Juvenile literature 5. Women in astronautics—Juvenile literature
ISBN 9781613748442 (cloth); 1613748442
LC 2013-024950

SUMMARY: This book, by Karen Bush Gibson, "profiles 23 pioneers, including Eileen Collins, the first woman to command the space shuttle; Peggy Whitson, who logged more than a year in orbit aboard the International Space Station; and Mae Jemison, the first African American woman in space; as well as astronauts from Japan, Canada, Italy, South Korea, France, and more." (Publisher's note)

REVIEW: *Booklist* v110 no13 p58 Mr 1 2014 John Peters

REVIEW: *Kirkus Rev* v82 no1 p202 Ja 1 2014

"Women in Space: 23 Stories of First Flights, Scientific

Missions, and Gravity-Breaking Adventures". "Sidebars supply factual information on such topics as training, experiments, sleeping and eating in space, and the physical and psychological effects of space travel. This workmanlike book is most valuable for the profiles on cosmonauts and international women astronauts, subjects that have received scant attention. An informative introductory overview of the many important contributions women have made to space exploration."

REVIEW: *Publ Wkly* v260 no47 p55 N 18 2013

REVIEW: *SLJ* v60 no3 p180 Mr 2014 Patricia Ann Owens

REVIEW: *Voice of Youth Advocates* v37 no1 p92 Ap 2014 Charla Hollingsworth

GIBSON, REX.ed. The Tempest. See The Tempest

GIBSON, ROY K. Reading the Letters of Pliny the Younger; an introduction; [by] Roy K. Gibson xi, 350 p. 2012 Cambridge University Press

1. Latin authors 2. Latin letters 3. Letter writing, Latin—History—To 1500 4. Pliny, the Younger, ca. 61-ca. 112 5. Villa of Pliny the Younger (San Giustino, Italy)
ISBN 9780521842921 (hardback)
LC 2011-042605

SUMMARY: Written by Roy K. Gibson and Ruth Morello, "This is the first general introduction to Pliny's 'Letters' published in any language, combining close readings with broader context and adopting a fresh and innovative approach to reading the letters as an artistically structured collection. . . . Four detailed appendices give . . . historical and scholarly context, including a . . . timeline . . . , detailed bibliographical help . . . and a summary of the main characters." (Publisher's note)

REVIEW: *Classical Rev* v63 no2 p453-5 O 2013 Kathryn Williams

"Reading the 'Letters' of Pliny the Younger: An Introduction." "Pliny's ten books of letters cover a vast array of addressees, topics and themes. . . . Yet [authors Roy K. Gibson and Ruth Morello] also demonstrate how fruitful the focus on letter cycles of individuals or themes can be. . . . The aim of the volume is to provide a 'general literary-historical introduction' . . . to Pliny's collection. . . . Reconsideration of the role of Book 10 is a fitting way to conclude the volume. It caps a series of insightful chapters which introduce Pliny's letters to new readers, stimulate those who know the letters through anthologies to read the entire collection, and entice those already familiar with the collection to reread and reevaluate this kaleidoscopic mosaic."

GIDWITZ, ADAM. The Grimm conclusion. See The Grimm conclusion

GIEMZA, BRYAN. Irish Catholic writers and the invention of the American South; [by] Bryan Giemza xi, 361 p. 2013 Louisiana State University Press

1. American literature—Southern States—History and criticism 2. Authors, American—Southern States—History and criticism 3. Irish American Catholics—Southern States 4. Literature—History & criticism
ISBN 9780807150900 (cloth : alk. paper)
LC 2012-048402

SUMMARY: In this book, "Bryan Giemza retrieves a missing chapter of Irish Catholic heritage by canvassing the literature of American Irish writers from the U.S. South. . . . Some familiar names arise in an Irish context, including Joel Chandler Harris and Kate (O'Flaherty) Chopin. Giemza also examines the works of twentieth-century writers, such as Margaret Mitchell, John Kennedy Toole, and Pat Conroy. For each author, Giemza traces how Catholicism influenced faith and ethnic identity." (Publisher's note)

REVIEW: *Choice* v51 no6 p1002-3 F 2014 R. R. Joly

"Irish Catholic Writers and the Invention of the American South." "[Bryan] Giemza . . . probes the Irish Catholic literary sensibility in the South from its genesis to the present. . . .Giemza's wide sweep includes the stalwart Cormac McCarthy, Anne Rice, Valerie Sayers, and Lafcadio Hearn; in one astute chapter he considers getting past the enigma of Irish identity in a region widely settled by Irish Scot Protestants. This volume supplements Gimaza's edited collection, 'Rethinking the Irish in the American South'. . . . Recommended."

GIERACH, JOHN. All Fishermen Are Liars; [by] John Gierach 224 p. 2014 Simon & Schuster

1. Fishes 2. Fly fishing—Anecdotes 3. Hydrology 4. Sports literature 5. Travelers' writings
ISBN 145161831X; 9781451618310
LC 2013-012784

SUMMARY: In this book, author John Gierach "travels across North America from the Pacific Northwest to the Canadian Maritimes to seek out quintessential fishing experiences. Whether he's fishing a busy stream or a secluded lake amid snow-capped mountains, Gierach insists that fishing is always the answer—even when it's not clear what the question is." (Publisher's note)

REVIEW: *Booklist* v110 no15 p12 Ap 1 2014 John Rowen

REVIEW: *Kirkus Rev* v82 no5 p19 Mr 1 2014

"All Fisherman Are Liars". "The writer's single-minded devotion to his fisherman's M.O. in those pretty mountain streams naturally won't mean much to piscatorial agnostics who never had the pleasure of outsmarting a trout in its home environs. . . . Certainly, there are many sweet, folksy passages on ichthyology and the cultural anthropology of those folks who take so happily to the outdoor life, yet the book remains primarily a fisherman's testimony to the faithful. . . . Elegiac tribute to the elusive art and ineffable pleasure of fly-fishing, with plenty of information about how it's done by true practitioners."

REVIEW: *Publ Wkly* v261 no4 p183 Ja 27 2014

GIFF, PATRICIA REILLY, 1935-. Winter sky; [by] Patricia Reilly Giff 160 p. 2014 Wendy Lamb Books, an imprint of Random House Children's Books

1. Courage—Fiction 2. Detective & mystery stories 3. Family life—Fiction 4. Fire fighters—Fiction 5. Friendship—Fiction
ISBN 0375838929; 9780375838927 (hardback); 9780385371926 (lib. bdg.)
LC 2013-022399

SUMMARY: In this book, by Patricia Reilly Giff, "Siria's dad is a firefighter who doesn't know that someone special watches out for him; each time his daughter hears a siren, she sneaks out of her apartment building to chase his fire truck and make sure he is safe. During one such nightly pursuit, Siria discovers evidence of what she believes to be arson. Who could be purposely setting fires? When clues point to someone close to home, Siria must find the strength to unravel the mystery." (School Library Journal)

REVIEW: *Booklist* v110 no12 p83 F 15 2014 Gail Bush

REVIEW: *Booklist* v110 no18 p72 My 15 2014 Heather Booth

REVIEW: *Bull Cent Child Books* v67 no5 p267 Ja 2014 A. A.

"Winter Sky." "With simple prose and an appreciation for the growing sense of freedom and responsibility of late childhood, [Patricia Reilly] Giff creates a gentle and enjoyable read with a light touch of suspense. While Siria's insistence on these dangerous late-night excursions and her reluctance to confide in an adult go on a bit longer than believable, the book effectively captures the mind of a preteen who feels deeply responsible for those around her. The mystery element will keep young readers guessing, while the themes of loneliness, friendship, and family will resonate strongly. Siria's late-night sleuthing and realistic friendships--along with a well-worn dog-adoption subplot--also make this a potential readaloud for an upper elementary classroom."

REVIEW: *Kirkus Rev* v81 no23 p106 D 1 2013

REVIEW: *Publ Wkly* v261 no13 p62 Mr 31 2014

REVIEW: *Publ Wkly* v260 no43 p60-1 O 28 2013

REVIEW: *SLJ* v60 no1 p81 Ja 2014 Kerry Roeder

REVIEW: *SLJ* v60 no3 p72 Mr 2014 Kira Moody

GIFFELS, DAVID. The hard way on purpose; essays and dispatches from the rust belt; [by] David Giffels 272 p. 2014 Scribner

1. BIOGRAPHY & AUTOBIOGRAPHY—Personal Memoirs 2. Essay (Literary form) 3. HISTORY—United States—State & Local—Midwest (IA, IL, IN, KS, MI, MN, MO, ND, NE, OH, SD, WI) 4. SOCIAL SCIENCE—Regional Studies

ISBN 1451692749; 9781451692747 (pbk.)

LC 2013-032606

SUMMARY: "In 'The Hard Way on Purpose,' David Giffels takes us on an insider's journey through the wreckage and resurgence of America's Rust Belt. A native who never knew the good times, yet never abandoned his hometown of Akron, Giffels plumbs the touchstones and idiosyncrasies of a region where industry has fallen. . . . Giffels's linked essays are about coming of age in the Midwest and about the stubborn, optimistic, and resourceful people who prevail there." (Publisher's note)

REVIEW: *Kirkus Rev* v82 no4 p38 F 15 2014

"The Hard Way on Purpose: Essays and Dispatches From the Rust Belt". "Appealing, original fusion of personal essay collection and Rust Belt post-mortem. [David] Giffels . . . takes an audacious approach to considering his 1970s adolescence in Akron, Ohio, and his life there ever since. . . . While his essays are funny and crisply rendered, there's an undertone of wonderment at the sheer loss of functionality and productive might in such places. . . . The author's tone is relaxed and approachable, yet he never loses sight of the social costs incurred by the alleged obsolescence of the blue-collar Midwest. These seasoned dispatches convey an important narrative of regional marginalization; Giffels' work deserves to avoid that fate."

REVIEW: *N Y Times Book Rev* p11 My 4 2014 BETH MACY

REVIEW: *Publ Wkly* v261 no3 p43 Ja 20 2014

GIFFORD, JOHN. Dundee and Angus; [by] John Gifford 754 p. 2012 Yale University Press

1. Angus (Scotland) 2. Architectural literature 3. Architecture—Scotland 4. Buildings—History 5. Dundee (Scotland)

ISBN 0300141718; 9780300141719

SUMMARY: Written by John Gifford, "This volume in the Buildings of Scotland series explores the rich architectural diversity of Dundee and Angus. Dundee, the fourth-largest city in Scotland, boasts some of the country's finest ecclesiastical, public, industrial, and commercial buildings. . . . Beyond Dundee lies the predominantly rural county of Angus, where visitors can see stunning Pictish and early Christian monuments, castles, country houses, and the famed Bell Rock Lighthouse." (Publisher's note)

REVIEW: *Burlington Mag* v155 no1327 p706 O 2013 LIZZIE SWARBRICK

"The Buildings of Scotland: Dundee and Angus." "The late John Gifford's volume 'Dundee and Angus' represents a significant step towards the completion of the Pevsner Architectural Guides project. The Buildings of Scotland series, begun in the 1970s, is making substantial progress with the publication of this book, leaving just four volumes before Scotland is comprehensively covered. . . . The scope of the book, its useful format, and the quality of its reproductions makes 'Dundee and Angus' a learned and sturdy companion for all those interested in the region, which it is a pleasure to see brought to the public's attention."

GIFFORD, PEGGY. The great big green; 32 p. 2014 Boyds Mills Press

1. Children's poetry 2. Color—Juvenile literature 3. Earth (Planet)—Juvenile literature 4. Green 5. Picture books for children

ISBN 1620916290; 9781620916292

LC 2013-947714

SUMMARY: This children's book, written by Peggy Gifford and illustrated by Lisa Desimini, is "both a riddle and an ode to the earth. . . . Perfect for budding environmentalists and lovers of poetry alike, . . . [it] is illustrated with . . . [a] mix of collage and painting." (Publisher's note) The text and illustrations highlight the green plants, animals, and objects which populate the earth. "There are green socks, a green light for 'go' and an old green door." (Kirkus Reviews)

REVIEW: *Kirkus Rev* v82 no4 p209 F 15 2014

"The Great Big Green". " An abundantly illustrated puzzle poem provides a spectacular celebration of green in the world. . . . The text reads aloud beautifully, building to the question, 'Have you guessed yet?' and the final answer, revealed not in words but in a familiar image of Earth from space, with previous elements cleverly placed. [Lisa] Desimini's imaginative illustrations complement and extend the graphically flexible text. Done with scanned textures and images combined into mixed-media collages, these are both realistic and imaginative, full of whimsy. . . . Two fertile imaginations grow a grand salute."

REVIEW: *Publ Wkly* v261 no5 p54 F 3 2014

REVIEW: *SLJ* v60 no5 p80 My 2014 Nancy Jo Lambert

GIGANTE, DENISE. The Keats brothers; [by] Denise Gigante ix, 499p. 2011 Belknap Press of Harvard University Press

1. Biographies 2. British Americans 3. Keats, George 4. Keats, John, 1795-1821 5. Poets—Family relationships
ISBN 9780674048560
LC 2011-014487

SUMMARY: This book examines the impact of "George [Keats]'s 1818 move to the western frontier of the United States," which "created in John [Keats] an abysm of alienation and loneliness that would inspire the poet's most plangent and sublime poetry. [Author] Denise Gigante's account of this emigration places John's life and work in a transatlantic context . . . while revealing the emotional turmoil at the heart of some of the most lasting verse in English." (Publisher's note)

REVIEW: *Choice* v49 no7 p1258 Mr 2012 R. K. Mookerjee

REVIEW: *Kenyon Review* v36 no1 p242-50 Wint 2014 STANLEY PLUMLY

REVIEW: *N Y Rev Books* v60 no17 p96-9 N 7 2013 Richard Holmes

"The Keats Brothers: The Life of John and George" and "John Keats: A New Life." "[Denise] Gigante's style as biographer is bustling and informative, if sometimes rather impressionistic. She loves lists and inventories. . . . The familiarity of [John] Keats's story is precisely the thing that makes it such a challenge for any new biographer. Nicholas Roe confronts this . . . with an unusual combination of scholarship, speculation, and deep background research. Though traditional in form, the whole biography is astonishingly fresh and observant, with a magical sense of Keats's shifting moods and workplaces. Meticulously researched and precisely visualized, it produces a hypnotic portrait of Keats."

REVIEW: *N Y Times Book Rev* p28 N 3 2013 IHSAN TAYLOR

"The Keats Brothers: The Life of John and George," "Far From the Tree: Parents, Children, and the Search for Identity," and "The City of Devi." "[A] savvy pairing of the lives of John Keats (1795-1821) and George Keats, whose emigration to America and fluctuating fortunes on the Western frontier inspired his brother's most sublime poetry. . . . One of the Book Review's 10 Best books of 2012, this passionate and affecting work complicates everything we thought we knew about love, sacrifice and success. . . . India and Pakistan are on the brink of nuclear war in [Manil] Suri's third novel, which completes a loose trilogy."

REVIEW: *TLS* no5723 p3-4 D 7 2012 JONATHAN BATE

GILBERT, ELIZABETH, 1969-. The Signature of All Things; a novel; [by] Elizabeth Gilbert 512 p. 2013 Penguin Group USA

1. Enlightenment—Fiction 2. FICTION—Historical 3. FICTION—Literary 4. Industrial revolution—Fiction 5. Painters—Fiction 6. Women botanists—Fiction
ISBN 0670024856; 9780670024858
LC 2013-017045

SUMMARY: This book follows Alma Whittaker. "Born in 1800, Alma learns Latin and Greek, understands the natural world, and reads everything in sight. Despite her wealth and education, Alma is a woman, and a plain one at that, two facts that circumscribe her opportunities. Resigned to spinsterhood, ashamed and tormented by her erotic desires, Alma finds a late-in-life soul mate in Ambrose Pike, a talented botanical illustrator and spiritualist." (Publishers Weekly)

REVIEW: *Booklist* v109 no22 p45 Ag 1 2013 Joanne Wilkinson

REVIEW: *Booklist* v110 no15 p36 Ap 1 2014 Joy Matteson

REVIEW: *Kirkus Rev* p6 2013 Guide 20to BookExpo America

REVIEW: *Kirkus Rev* p6 2013 Guide 20to BookExpo America Megan Labrise

REVIEW: *Kirkus Rev* v81 no2 p12-3 Je 1 2013

REVIEW: *Libr J* v138 no8 p59 My 1 2013

REVIEW: *Libr J* v139 no2 p43 F 1 2014 Wendy Galgan

REVIEW: *N Y Rev Books* v60 no18 p54-6 N 21 2013 April Bernard

"The Signature of All Things" and "Archangel." "Andrea Barrett is a splendid writer of what, for lack of any better term, we call literary fiction; Elizabeth Gilbert . . . is an energetic scribbler. Barrett writes of science and scientists from profound understanding and passion, exploring how scientific reason and human feeling collide and illuminate one another. Gilbert's novel is another matter. . . .Inside this big sloppy novel, there is a good short story longing to get out. . . . Like [Charles] Darwin, and [Albert] Einstein, and all her other heroes, Barrett the storyteller pulls us relentlessly away from false comforts, into the dazzling, often chaotic, world as it really is."

REVIEW: *N Y Times Book Rev* p26 O 6 2013

REVIEW: *N Y Times Book Rev* p1-33 S 29 2013 Barbara Kingsolver

"The Signature of All Things." "Expansive. . . . A scientifically minded reader might want a few more details about what Alma sees through her microscope as she classifies her discoveries. . . . Real events provide ample substrate for a novel that entwines the historic and the imagined so subtly as to read like good nonfiction for most of its first half. It crosses over to page turner after the introduction of the author's most beguiling invention, the deliciously named Ambrose Pike. . . . Their mutual captivation proceeds too quickly into what may be the most thrillingly bizarre marriage proposal in literature. . . . The book's locales are captured in glittering portraits. . . . The narrative stretches but its center holds."

REVIEW: *New York Times* v163 no56275 pC1-4 S 30 2013 JANET MASLIN

REVIEW: *New Yorker* v89 no31 p1 O 7 2013

REVIEW: *Orion Magazine* v33 no2 p69-70 Mr/Ap 2014 Bill Roorbach

REVIEW: *Publ Wkly* v261 no1 p52 Ja 6 2014

REVIEW: *Publ Wkly* v260 no26 p62 Jl 1 2013

REVIEW: *Quill Quire* v79 no6 p29-31 Jl/Ag 2013

GILCHRIST, ELLEN, 1935-. Acts of God; stories; [by] Ellen Gilchrist 256 p. 2014 Algonquin Books of Chapel Hill

1. American short stories 2. Determination (Personality trait) 3. Life change events—Fiction 4. Older people—Fiction 5. Terrorism—Fiction
ISBN 161620110X; 9781616201104 (alk. paper)
LC 2013-043330

SUMMARY: The short stories in this collection by Ellen

Gilchrist "reflect recent national events and current social and political conditions that put individuals' moxie to the test. . . . 'Toccata and Fugue in D Minor' . . . sees three middle-aged women . . . off to a vacation in Italy, but they are sidelined along the way by terrorist activity; in post-Katrina New Orleans in the title story, an elderly couple's last effort at independence from caretakers and infirmities has fatal results." (Booklist)

REVIEW: *Booklist* v110 no11 p19 F 1 2014 Brad Hooper

"Acts of God." "[Ellen] Gilchrist's deliciously wise and humorous voice abides best in the short story form, and her new collection of 10 stories will say to her fans that their reconnection to this openhearted writer from the South is a pure old-home-week experience (especially given that recurring Gilchrist characters make welcome appearances). A thematic connection unifies the stories, which generally reflect recent national events and current social and political conditions that put individuals' moxie to the test."

REVIEW: *Kirkus Rev* v82 no3 p305 F 1 2014

"Acts of God". " Disaster becomes the impetus for renewed faith in goodness, love and spiritual uplift in these 10 stories about kindhearted Southerners from [Ellen] Gilchrist. . . . In 'Toccata and Fugue in D Minor,' three Southern ladies (former sorority sisters) on their way to a vacation in Italy are delayed at Heathrow Airport during a bomb scare and share life stories with others stuck over free drinks and hors d'oeuvres in the first-class lounge—the sense of privilege, taken for granted by the author, may grate on readers. . . . The volume's first hint of diversity appears in the final story, about a black child saved by kindly white plantation owners in 1901. Overly sentimental."

REVIEW: *N Y Times Book Rev* p9 My 4 2014 DANIEL HANDLER

REVIEW: *Publ Wkly* v260 no51 p34 D 16 2013

GILDER, GEORGE F., 1939-. Knowledge and power; the information theory of capitalism and how it is revolutionizing our world; [by] George F. Gilder 348 p. 2013 Regnery

1. Capitalism 2. Economic policy 3. Economics literature 4. Entrepreneurship 5. Information theory in economics

ISBN 1621570274; 9781621570271

SUMMARY: In this book, George Gilder "breaks away from the supply-side model of economics to present a new economic paradigm: the epic conflict between the knowledge of entrepreneurs on one side, and the blunt power of government on the other. The knowledge of entrepreneurs, and their freedom to share and use that knowledge, are the sparks that light up the economy and set its gears in motion." (Publisher's note)

REVIEW: *Natl Rev* v65 no15 p42-4 Ag 19 2013 JAMES V. DELONG

"Knowledge and Power: The Information Theory of Capitalism and How It Is Revolutionizing Our World." "Don't sit down with George Gilder's 'Knowledge and Power' with the idea that you are about to read a book. You are entering into an evening of rambling discussion with a thinker who is revisiting ideas that have animated him for almost half a century, as he delves more deeply into what he was trying to say all those years ago in 'Microcosm' . . . or finally understands what Andy Viterbi of Qualcomm was telling him about information theory in 1993. The work has the texture of a conversation, as threads are plucked, dropped, and found again a few chapters later."

GILES, AUDREY R.ed. Aboriginal peoples and sport in Canada. See Aboriginal peoples and sport in Canada

GILES, GAIL. No Returns; [by] Gail Giles 246 p. 2014 Running Fox Books

1. Bands (Musical groups)—Fiction 2. Devil—Fiction 3. Missing persons—Fiction 4. Paranormal fiction 5. Teenage musicians

ISBN 1940320046; 9781940320045

SUMMARY: This book is "the first in a series featuring three teenage musicians in an unwitting Faustian bargain, a mysterious librarian and a supernatural James Cagney wannabe. Pod, Manny and Flaco are practicing in Pod's family barn, preparing for an upcoming battle-of-the-bands competition, when a combination of a dead rat and inspired lyrics somehow results in the boys' accidentally selling their souls for superstardom." (Kirkus Reviews)

REVIEW: *Kirkus Rev* v82 no2 p360 Ja 15 2014

"No Returns: Book One of the Battleband Saga". "The three main characters are the strongest part of the story, and Pod, in particular, is appealingly quirky and believable. The primary demonic force (whose name is Fred) is effectively menacing as he puts on gangster mannerisms. . . . The colorful cast often makes up for a plot that sometimes relies on predictable twists, although many of the antagonists, including Noah, tend to be overly simplistic stock character types. The novel's numerous songs link the story to Goethe's Faust and provide a welcome additional dimension to the story, but the plot thread sometimes gets lost amid the sprawl of song lyrics, making it difficult for readers to always grasp precisely what's going on."

GILES, LAMAR. Fake ID; [by] Lamar Giles 320 p. 2014 Amistad

1. African Americans—Fiction 2. Conspiracies—Fiction 3. Mystery and detective stories 4. Witness protection programs—Fiction 5. Young adult fiction

ISBN 0062121847; 9780062121844 (hardback)

LC 2013-032149

SUMMARY: In this novel by Lamar Giles, "Nick Pearson is hiding in plain sight. In fact, his name isn't really Nick Pearson. He shouldn't tell you his real name, his real hometown, or why his family just moved to Stepton, Virginia. And he definitely shouldn't tell you about his friend Eli Cruz and the major conspiracy Eli was uncovering when he died. About how Nick had to choose between solving Eli's murder with his . . . sister, Reya, and 'staying low-key' like the Program said to do." (Publisher's note)

REVIEW: *Booklist* v110 no9/10 p106 Ja 1 2014 Kara Dean

REVIEW: *Bull Cent Child Books* v67 no7 p358 Mr 2014 E. B.

"Fake ID." "[L. R.] Giles ups the ante of YA witness-protection tales with a chilling foray into a much broader conspiracy, teasing readers with plausible suspects and clever misdirections that play off the tropes of running-from-the-mob stories. Dialogue is razor sharp, and family dynamics within Nick's stressed-out household are poignant and unsettling. Nick gets to the sorry bottom of the mystery, but the resolution hints at a troubling near future for both the emotionally exhausted young man and his latest hometown. Of course, some grace-saving sequel might come along to smooth away ambiguities, but teens who are willing to trade off a happy ending for a truthful one will be just as content to leave Nick right where Giles has steered him."

REVIEW: *Kirkus Rev* v81 no21 p207 N 1 2013

REVIEW: *SLJ* v60 no3 p158 Mr 2014 Ryan P. Donovan

GILI, OBERTO.il. City Parks. See City Parks

GILL, A. A. To America with love; [by] A. A. Gill 256 p. 2013 Simon & Schuster

1. HISTORY—United States—General 2. SOCIAL SCIENCE—Customs & Traditions 3. TRAVEL—Special Interest—General 4. Travelers' writings

ISBN 1416596216; 9781416596219 (hardback); 9781439100448 (trade paperback)

LC 2013-019543

SUMMARY: This book is Scottish-born A.A. Gill's tribute to America. He "devotes his . . . to defending the country's earnest belief in government by the people, as well as its brashness of character, frank celebration of success, sublime sense of nature, and childish delight in speechifying and hucksterism, among other things." (Publishers Weekly)

REVIEW: *Booklist* v109 no19/20 p15 Je 1 2013 Mary Carroll

REVIEW: *Kirkus Rev* v81 no2 p53-4 Je 1 2013

REVIEW: *New York Times* v162 no56236 pC6 Ag 22 2013 MICHIKO KAKUTANI

"To America With Love." "In his new book . . . A. A. Gill attempts to make up for his fellow Britons' grouchiness, sending the United States a frilly, funny valentine. . . . Mr. Gill . . . is a writer with several octaves to his voice, capable of being outrageous and lyrical, comic and profane, crotchety and meditative. At his best, he writes with enormous energy and verve, channeling Evelyn Waugh and Clive James, and this volume certainly has its share of entertaining anecdotes and sparkling asides. But this book can also feel lazy and outdated. Many of Mr. Gill's observations, perhaps unavoidably, retrace ground covered more than a century and a half ago by Alexis de Tocqueville, not to mention aperçus served up by the seemingly endless stream of foreign writers since."

REVIEW: *Publ Wkly* v260 no21 p50 My 27 2013

GILL, J. DUDDY. The secret of Ferrell Savage; [by] J. Duddy Gill 176 p. 2014 Atheneum Books for Young Readers

1. Best friends—Fiction 2. Family life—Colorado—Fiction 3. Friendship—Fiction 4. Racing—Fiction 5. Secrets—Fiction 6. Sledding—Fiction 7. Young adult fiction

ISBN 1442460172; 9781442460171 (hardcover)

LC 2012-051500

SUMMARY: In this book, by Jennifer Duddy Gill, "Ferrell Savage is finally twelve, and finally eligible to compete in The Big Sled Race on Golden Hill—the perfect chance to impress Mary Vittles. . . . [But], it turns out that his great, great, great uncle had an encounter with Mary's great, great grandfather. And the encounter was, well, let's just say—edible. Sure, the circumstances were extreme, but some facts might just be romantically indigestible." (Publisher's note)

REVIEW: *Booklist* v110 no11 p68 F 1 2014 Martha Edmundson

REVIEW: *Bull Cent Child Books* v67 no7 p358-9 Mr 2014 T. A.

REVIEW: *Kirkus Rev* v81 no24 p115 D 15 2013

"The Secret of Ferrell Savage". "A debut that reads like an early draft of a successful story of mild middle school drama. . . . That would be a perfectly fine premise for a book, but unfortunately, it's not the premise for this book. No, this book's premise is that Ferrell's great-great-uncle was an infamous (real-life) cannibal and Mary's ancestor his victim. . . . That's his secret, but he doesn't know it yet. (Readers do, thanks to the cover, and they have to endure a lot of obvious misdirection before Ferrell learns.) . . . Tendentiously cute names . . . distract more than they amuse. Strip the cannibalism, the clumsy, plot-driven characterization and the dopey names, and this could be quite a sweet story."

REVIEW: *SLJ* v60 no3 p139 Mr 2014 Amy Seto Musser

GILLAIN, ANNE. Francois Truffaut; The Lost Secret; 376 p. 2013 Indiana Univ Pr

1. Emotional trauma 2. Film criticism 3. Memory in motion pictures 4. Motion picture producers & directors 5. Truffaut, François, 1932-1984

ISBN 0253008344; 9780253008343

SUMMARY: In this book, "taking a psycho-biographical approach, [Anne] Gillain shows how [François] Truffaut's creative impulse was anchored in his personal experience of a traumatic childhood that left him lonely and emotionally deprived. . . . She demonstrates how involuntary memories arising from Truffaut's childhood not only furnish a succession of motifs that are repeated from film to film, but also govern every aspect of his mise en scène and cinematic technique." (Publisher's note)

REVIEW: *Choice* v51 no3 p466 N 2013 M. Yacowar

REVIEW: *Film Q* v67 no1 p79-80 Fall 2013 DAVID STERRITT

REVIEW: *N Y Rev Books* v60 no8 p35-6 My 9 2013

"Seeing Red—Hollywood's Pixeled Skins: American Indians and Film," "François Truffaut: The Lost Secret," and "The B Word: Bisexuality in Contemporary Film and Television". "A dazzling anthology of film reviews . . . highlights past American Indian stereotypes to suggest ways of seeing aboriginal peoples more clearly today. . . . Considered by many to be the best book on the interpretation of [François] Truffaut's films, this French translation shows how Truffaut's creative impulse was anchored in his personal experience of a traumatic childhood. . . . Viewing films as diverse as 'Brokeback Mountain' . . and 'Mulholland Drive' through a bisexual lens, 'The B Word' transforms films commonly read as homosexual or heterosexual."

GILLESPIE, MICHELE. Katharine and R.J. Reynolds; partners of fortune in the making of the new south; [by] Michele Gillespie p. cm. 2012 The University of Georgia Press

1. Biography (Literary form) 2. Businessmen—United States—Biography 3. Businesswomen—United States—Biography

ISBN 0820332267 (hardcover: alk. paper); 9780820332260 (hardcover: alk. paper)

LC 2012-010004

SUMMARY: This book presents a dual biography of Katharine and R.J. Reynolds. "Katharine gave R.J. advice about trends and consumer tastes. He gave her freedom to build Reynolds Estate, which was to include a house . . . schools, and churches. Never challenging the current political or social status quo, they worked to improve the town of Winston-Salem, NC, including their factories there, knowing that better conditions for the African American community would lead to a better workforce." (Library Journal)

REVIEW: *Am Hist Rev* v119 no1 p190-1 F 2014 Mary E. Frederickson

"Katharine and R. J. Reynolds: Partners of Fortune in the Making of the New South". "Carefully researched and elegantly written, this thoughtful and engaging dual biography of Katharine and R. J. Reynolds is a story that needed to be told. Michele Gillespie gives us two larger than life characters whose narratives unfold on a 'big southern stage' that stretched from North Carolina to New York and encompassed a broad swath of American life. . . . A sophisticated study that will appeal to a broad range of readers within and beyond the academy, Gillespie's work pivots on her keen insights about the dynamics of power in a political culture built on intricate hierarchies of race, class, and gender."

REVIEW: *Choice* v50 no7 p1316 Mr 2013 B. M. Banta

REVIEW: *J Am Hist* v100 no2 p552 S 2013 Bruce W. Eelman

REVIEW: *Libr J* v137 no15 p76 S 15 2012 June Parker

GILLESPIE, SUSAN H.tr. Philosophy of dreams. See Philosophy of dreams

GILLIOM, JOHN. SuperVision; an introduction to the surveillance society; [by] John Gilliom viii, 188 p. 2013 University of Chicago Press

1. Electronic surveillance—Social aspects 2. Information technology—Social aspects 3. Mass surveillance 4. Privacy, Right of 5. Social science literature

ISBN 0226924432 (cloth : alkaline paper); 0226924440 (paperback : alkaline paper); 9780226924434 (cloth : alkaline paper); 9780226924441 (paperback : alkaline paper)

LC 2012-014021

SUMMARY: This book, by John Gilliom and Torin Monahan, "uses examples drawn from everyday technologies to show how surveillance is used, who is using it, and how it affects our world. Beginning with a look at the activities and technologies that connect most people to the surveillance matrix, from identification cards to GPS devices in our cars to Facebook, John Gilliom and Torin Monahan invite readers to critically explore surveillance as it relates to issues of law, power, freedom, and inequality." (Publisher's note)

REVIEW: *Choice* v51 no1 p164 S 2013 J. A. Stever

"SuperVision: An Introduction to the Surveillance Society." "[Authors John] Gilliom . . . and [Torin] Monahan . . . argue that contemporary society has become a de facto panopticon. Their thesis is that digital technology and the Internet allow a few centrally located institutions to monitor and manipulate the behavior of modern citizens. Unsuspecting citizens who enjoy the convenience of cell phones, credit cards, and Internet searches do not understand that they use these technological marvels at a price. . . . The authors correctly point out that pervasive surveillance is not a good thing."

GILMAN, RICHARD. Angels Ten!; [by] Richard Gilman 136 p. 2012 FriesenPress

1. Fighter pilots—Great Britain—Biography 2. Great Britain. Royal Air Force 3. Memoirs 4. World War, 1939-1945—British aerial operations 5. World War, 1939-1945—British personal narratives

ISBN 1770972765; 9781770972766

SUMMARY: Written by World War II Royal Air Force pilot Richard Gilman, this "collection of personal memoirs" describes his time as a Spitfire pilot. "It was a time of undeniable excitement and indelible pain. These stories are important because they help us understand a little of what war was like, how it felt." (Publisher's note)

REVIEW: *Kirkus Rev* v81 no16 p15 Ag 15 2013

"Angels Ten! Memoirs of a WWII Spitfire Pilot." "An airman recalls his brushes with death--including four crashes while serving as a fighter pilot--in this sharply pitched World War II memoir. Born in Vancouver but raised in England, [author Richard] Gilman enlisted in the Royal Air Force at the tender age of 18. . . . Crisp prose and laconic humor bring the book's collection of hair-raising stories to life, as do his well-chosen black-and-white photographs. Gilman rarely gets caught up in the jargon of the cockpit, and in pursuing his personal story, he avoids the lethargy of potted history. . . . A highly engaging memoir of flying the not-so-friendly skies."

REVIEW: *Kirkus Rev* v81 no14 p382 Jl 15 2013

GING, DEBBIE. Men and masculinities in Irish cinema; [by] Debbie Ging ix, 252 p. 2013 Palgrave Macmillan

1. Film criticism 2. Irish films 3. Masculinity in motion pictures 4. Men in motion pictures 5. Motion pictures—Ireland

ISBN 0230232000; 9780230232006 (hbk.)

LC 2012-034821

SUMMARY: This book is a "study of men and masculinities in Irish cinema that informs a host of topics, including gender theory, studies of national cinema, and masculinity in cinema and film culture." Author Debbie Ging "has produced an integral list of films on Irish masculinity and discusses them in the context of when they were produced and in their relationship to other films, including those of Great Britain and the US." (Choice)

REVIEW: *Choice* v51 no1 p83-4 S 2013 G. R. Butters Jr.

"Men and Masculinities in Irish Cinema." "[author Debbie] Ging . . . has delivered an ingenious new study of men and masculinities in Irish cinema that informs a host of topics, including gender theory, studies of national cinema, and masculinity in cinema and film culture. Not only has Ging produced a work that adds greatly to a discussion of these topics but she has created a book that should serve as a model for how to do true interdisciplinary work in cinema studies. A great deal of the strength in this volume is the author's knowledge base; she has produced an integral list of films on Irish masculinity and discusses them in the context of when they were produced and in their relationship to other films, including those of Great Britain and the US."

GINSBERG, ALEXANDRA DAISY. Synthetic aesthetics.

See Schyfter, P.

GIRARD, GEOFFREY. Cain's blood; a novel; [by] Geoffrey Girard 352 p. 2013 Simon & Schuster

1. Biological weapons—Fiction 2. Cloning—Fiction 3. FICTION—Horror 4. FICTION—Science Fiction—Military 5. FICTION—Thrillers 6. Horror tales, American 7. Murder—Fiction 8. Science fiction 9. Serial murderers—Fiction 10. Spy stories 11. Young men—Fiction

ISBN 9781476704043 (hardback)

LC 2013-001819

SUMMARY: "The DNA of the world's most notorious serial killers has been cloned by the U.S. Department of Defense to develop a new breed of bioweapon. Now in Phase Three, the program includes dozens of young men who have no clue as to their evil heritage.... A man with demons of his own, former black ops soldier Shawn Castillo is hot on their trail." (Publisher's note)

REVIEW: *Booklist* v109 no22 p50 Ag 1 2013 Daniel Kraus

REVIEW: *Kirkus Rev* v81 no16 p252 Ag 15 2013

"Cain's Blood." A former Black Ops soldier with a troubled history is called in after a deranged geneticist creates multiple clones of famous serial killers and then releases them into the world. When a group of six teens commit several ghastly murders while escaping from a facility for troubled boys attached to DSTI, a biotech company with ties to the military, Shawn Castillo is called in. . . The prose is clean and competent, but the dialogue is awkward. The characters, especially Castillo, are paper thin, but readers looking for a sadistic thrill will hardly notice. Mostly suited for horror fans with an interest in real-life serial killers and with exceptionally strong stomachs."

REVIEW: *Publ Wkly* v260 no30 p44 Jl 29 2013

GIRLING, RICHARD. The Hunt for the Golden Mole; All Creatures Great & Small and Why They Matter; [by] Richard Girling 312 p. 2014 Pgw

1. Animals—Classification 2. Identification of animals 3. Journalism 4. Moles (Animals) 5. Rare animals

ISBN 1619024500; 9781619024502

SUMMARY: "Taking as its narrative engine the hunt for an animal that is legendarily rare, Richard Girling writes [a]. . . history of humankind's interest in hunting and collecting—what prompts us to do this? What good might come of our need to catalog all the living things of the natural world? . . . The Somali mole of the title, first described in print in a text book published in 1964, had as sole evidence of its existence only the fragment of a jaw bone found in an owl pellet." (Publisher's note)

REVIEW: *Booklist* v111 no3 p14 O 1 2014 Carol Haggas

REVIEW: *Kirkus Rev* v82 no19 p10 O 1 2014

REVIEW: *Nat Hist* v122 no8 p46 O 2014 LAURENCE A. MARSCHALL

REVIEW: *New Sci* v222 no2974 p47 Je 21 2014 Adrian Barnett

"The Hunt for the Golden Mole: All Creatures Great and Small and Why They Matter" and "Cold Blood: Adventures With Reptiles and Amphibians." "[Author Richard] Girling deftly combines broad themes with detailed content, exploring humanity's relationship with the natural world by taking wide narrative strides, and then pausing for close analysis. . . . [Author Richard] Kerridge writes no less eloquently, but the style and the focus are different. . . . Kerridge reserves some of his finest writing to describe the animals themselves."

REVIEW: *Publ Wkly* v261 no34 p90 Ag 25 2014

REVIEW: *TLS* no5809 p30 Ag 1 2014 JENNIE ERIN SMITH

GIRÁLDEZ, ARTURO. China and the birth of globalization in the 16th century; [by] Arturo Giráldez 284 2010 Ashgate Variorum

1. China—Foreign economic relations—History 2. Globalization—History 3. Historical literature 4. Interdisciplinary approach to knowledge 5. World history

ISBN 9780754668589; 0754668584

SUMMARY: "Including 11 essays published over the last 15 years, this volume by Dennis O. Flynn and Arturo Giraldez concerns the origins and early development of globalization. It opens with their 1995 'Silver Spoon' essay and a theoretical essay published in 2002. Subsequent sections deal with Pacific Ocean exchanges, interconnections between the Spanish, Ottoman, Japanese and Chinese empires, and the necessity of multidisciplinary approaches to global history." (Publisher's note)

REVIEW: *Engl Hist Rev* v128 no534 p1220-2 O 2013 Anne Gerritsen

"China and the Birth of Globalization in the 16th Century." "Dennis O. Flynn and Arturo Giráldez take issue with the conventional argument that the European demand for Asian silks, spices and porcelain, combined with the lack of desire for European goods in Asia, led to an inevitable trade deficit and a flow of precious metals to Asia. Instead of this trade deficit argument (which merely highlights European dynamics while casting China in a passive and static role), Flynn and Giráldez propose a more nuanced narrative. . . . More significant, however, is the absence in these articles of a critical engagement with the field of global history."

GITLIN, DANIELLA.tr. Operation massacre. See Operation massacre

GITLIN, MARTY. Joe Flacco; Super Bowl mvp; [by] Marty Gitlin 32 p. 2013 ABDO Pub. Co.

1. Baltimore Ravens (Football team) 2. Children's nonfiction 3. Flacco, Joe, 1985- 4. Super Bowl (Football game) 5. Super Bowl Most Valuable Player Award

ISBN 9781617836992

LC 2013-934739

SUMMARY: This book on football player Joe Flacco is part of the "Playmakers" series. Each book in the series has "an opening chapter highlighting one of the football player's greatest accomplishments" followed by "a look at each athlete's childhood and his path from high school to college to professional football. . . . 'Joe Flacco' explains how after many near-misses over several years, the Baltimore Raven helped his team win the Super Bowl and earned the status of Super Bowl MVP." (Booklist)

REVIEW: *Booklist* v110 no11 p55 F 1 2014 Angela Leeper

"Colin Kaepernick: NFL Phenom," "Joe Flaco: Super Bowl MVP," and "Robert Griffin III: RGIII--NFL Sensation." "Each book immediately hooks young sports enthusiasts with an opening chapter highlighting one of the football player's greatest accomplishments. The concise text continues with a look at each athlete's childhood and his path from high school to college to professional football. . . . Numerous color photos of the quarterbacks in action both on and off the field and interesting sidebars . . . keep the text exciting, especially for reluctant readers. Additional fun facts and quotes make these books good choices for recreational reading or biography studies."

GLADSTONE, WAYNE. Notes from the Internet Apocalypse; [by] Wayne Gladstone 224 p. 2014 Thomas Dunne Books

1. Computer system failures 2. FICTION—General 3. Humorous stories 4. Internet—Fiction 5. Satire
ISBN 9781250045027 (hardback)
LC 2013-030996

SUMMARY: In this book by Wayne Gladstone, "when the Internet suddenly stops working, society reels from the loss of flowing data and streaming entertainment. Addicts wander the streets talking to themselves in 140 characters or forcing cats to perform tricks for their amusement, while the truly desperate pin their requests for casual encounters on public bulletin boards. The economy tumbles and the government passes the draconian NET Recovery Act." (Publisher's note)

REVIEW: *Booklist* v110 no13 p19 Mr 1 2014 Cortney Ophoff

REVIEW: *Kirkus Rev* v82 no1 p282 Ja 1 2014

"Notes From the Internet Apocalypse". "An outlandishly specific takedown of online culture via the popular apocalypse comedy genre. Readers who don't dabble regularly on the Web won't get it, but fans of sites like Reddit, Instagram or Facebook (or streaming pornography, come to think of it) should find themselves howling at this profane, very funny comedy about our worldwide addiction to the Internet. . . . Strikingly similar to fellow Cracked.com contributor David Wong's (Jason Pargin's) John Dies at the End, there's a surprising amount of pathological drama at the book's denouement that shows there's a lot of brains behind all those dirty jokes. An acid cultural satire that skewers what we would miss most about the online world."

REVIEW: *Publ Wkly* v260 no50 p52 D 9 2013

GLADWELL, MALCOLM, 1963-. David and Goliath; underdogs, misfits, and the art of battling giants; [by] Malcolm Gladwell 304 p. 2013 Little, Brown & Co.

1. Achievement 2. Business literature 3. Disabilities 4. Dyslexia 5. Motivation (Psychology) 6. Opportunity 7. Struggle—Psychological aspects 8. Success
ISBN 9780316204361 (hardcover); 0316204366; 9780316239851 (large print)
LC 2013-941807

SUMMARY: In this book, author Malcolm Gladwell "examines and challenges our concepts of 'advantage' and 'disadvantage' in a way that may seem intuitive to some and surprising to others. Beginning with the classic tale of David and Goliath and moving through history with figures such as Lawrence of Arabia and Martin Luther King Jr., Gladwell shows how, time and again, players labeled 'underdog' use that status to their advantage and prevail through the elements of cunning and surprise." (Booklist)

REVIEW: *Atlantic* v312 no3 p36-8 O 2013 TINA ROSENBERG

"David and Goliath: Underdogs, Misfits, and the Art of Battling Giants." "Gladwell, who half a decade ago brought us tales of top dogs in 'Outliers: The Story of Success', is still worrying the same bone: Who gets ahead, and how? . . . In his pages, the underdogs win, mostly by dint of the sort of upstart individual agency he downplayed in 'Outliers'. . . . Yet you'll look in vain for reasons to believe that these exceptions prove any real-world rules about underdogs. In life, it's hard to turn obstacles into blessings, and giants are by now adept at the art of battling insurgents."

REVIEW: *Bookforum* v20 no4 p18-51 D 2013/Ja 2014 JIM NEWELL

REVIEW: *Booklist* v110 no3 p8 O 1 2013 David Siegfried

"David and Goliath: Underdogs, Misfits and the Art of Battling Giants". "Here he examines and challenges our concepts of 'advantage' and 'disadvantage' in a way that may seem intuitive to some and surprising to others. . . . Beginning with the classic tale of David and Goliath and moving through history with figures such as Lawrence of Arabia and Martin Luther King Jr., [Malcolm] Gladwell shows how, time and again, players labeled 'underdog' use that status to their advantage and prevail through the elements of cunning and surprise. . . . As usual, Gladwell presents his research in a fresh and easy-to-understand context, and he may have coined the catchphrase of the decade, 'Use what you got.'"

REVIEW: *Christ Century* v131 no1 p38-40 Ja 8 2014 Bromleigh McCleneghan

REVIEW: *Economist* v409 no8858 p89 O 19 2013

"David and Goliath: Underdogs, Misfits and the Art of Battling Giants". "A superbly fluid writer, Mr. [Malcolm] Gladwell once again traffics in anecdotes and covers a lot of ground. . . . These . . . stories are entertainingly told. But with each passing chapter the book grows less organised, and Mr. Gladwell's lessons increasingly vague or thuddingly obvious. . . . Mr. Gladwell's earlier books, particularly 'The Tipping Point,' his first, were genuinely thought-provoking. This one is about as insightful as a fortune cookie. Read something else."

REVIEW: *Kirkus Rev* v81 no17 p55 S 1 2013

REVIEW: *Kirkus Rev* p20 Ag 15 2013 Fall Preview

REVIEW: *Libr J* v138 no18 p58 N 1 2013 Heather Malcolm

REVIEW: *Libr J* v138 no9 p54 My 15 2013 Barbara Hoffert

REVIEW: *N Y Rev Books* v60 no18 p26-9 N 21 2013 Freeman Dyson

REVIEW: *N Y Times Book Rev* p14 O 13 2013 JOE NOCERA

REVIEW: *Natl Rev* v65 no24 p48-9 D 31 2013 SARAH RUDEN

REVIEW: *New Repub* v244 no19 p39-43 N 25 2013 John Gray

REVIEW: *New York Times* v163 no56278 pC4 O 3 2013 JANET MASLIN

"David and Goliath: Underdogs, Misfits, and the Art of Battling Giants". "The world becomes less complicated with a Malcolm Gladwell book in hand. Mr. Gladwell raises questions—should David have won his fight with Goliath?—that are reassuringly clear even before they are answered. His answers are just tricky enough to suggest that the reader has learned something, regardless of whether that's true. . . . The book's middle section is the messiest . . . but it is Mr. Gladwell's gift to paste together the incongruous."

REVIEW: *Quill Quire* v79 no10 p29 D 2013 Shaun Smith

GLASER, GABRIELLE. Her best-kept secret; why women drink—and how they can regain control; [by] Gabrielle Glaser 256 p. 2013 Simon & Schuster

1. Alcoholics Anonymous 2. Alcoholism 3. Social science literature 4. Women—Alcohol use—United States 5. Women alcoholics—Rehabilitation—United States
ISBN 1439184380; 9781439184387
LC 2013-001088

SUMMARY: This book by Gabrielle Glaser looks at U.S. women's alcohol consumption. She "traces the increasingly besotted history of women's relationship with alcohol (focusing mostly on middle-class women), but . . . argues against the efficacy of Alcoholics Anonymous (AA) for women. Rather than guiding women down a healing path of humility and acceptance, AA and its Twelve Steps, Glaser argues, have failed to protect women from predatory men, thereby consigning many" women to failure. (Publishers Weekly)

REVIEW: *Kirkus Rev* v81 no10 p59 My 15 2013

REVIEW: *N Y Times Book Rev* p18 N 17 2013 IRIN CARMON

"Drink: The Intimate Relationship Between Women and Alcohol" and "Her Best-Kept Secret: Why Women Drink--and How They Can Regain Control." "A temptation for many trend journalists and headline writers (a temptation to which Johnston sometimes succumbs) is to see women's higher rates of alcohol abuse and dependency as the uneasy consequence of female liberation. . . . [Ann Dowsett] Johnson's choice to blend memoir and reporting makes her book feel unfinished, too entangled in raw heartbreak to arrive at clarity. . . . Despite its pulpy title, 'Her Best-Kept Secret' is the more substantial book, interested in hard facts and nuance rather than hand-wringing. It is strongest when detailing how the American story of addiction and recovery was shaped for and by men."

REVIEW: *Publ Wkly* v260 no18 p50 My 6 2013

GLASS, JULIA. And the Dark Sacred Night; A Novel; [by] Julia Glass 400 p. 2014 Pantheon Books

1. Birthfathers—Fiction 2. FICTION—Family Life 3. FICTION—Literary 4. FICTION—Sagas 5. Family secrets—Fiction 6. Unemployed—Fiction
ISBN 0307377938; 9780307377937 (hardcover)
LC 2013-024331

SUMMARY: This book, by Julia Glass, is "the story of a middle-aged man who searches for his father. . . . Kit Noonan's life is stalled: unemployed, twins to help support, a mortgage to pay—and a frustrated wife, who is certain that more than anything else, Kit needs to solve the mystery of his father's identity. He begins with a visit to his former stepfather, Jasper, a take-no-prisoners Vermont outdoorsman. But it is another person who has kept the secret: Lucinda Burns." (Publisher's note)

REVIEW: *Booklist* v110 no11 p20 F 1 2014 Kerri Price

"And the Dark Sacred Night." "Convinced that deep-seated identity issues are fueling Kit's inertia-inducing depression, his wife urges him to find the identity of his biological father, a fact his otherwise loving mother refuses to divulge. . . . Woven throughout the narrative are flashbacks to key events in Kit's history, including the tender and beautifully told story of the relationship between Kit's mother and father. Divided into sections written from the perspective of key characters. Glass explores the pain of family secrets, the importance of identity, and the ultimate meaning of family."

REVIEW: *Booklist* v110 no9/10 p20 Ja 1 2014 Brad Hooper

"All the Light We Cannot See," "And the Dark Sacred Night," and "Lovers at the Chameleon Club, Paris 1932." "[Anthony] Doerr's brilliance as a short story writer was established by the popular 'Shell Collector' (2001), but his work in the novel form has also been exceptional; his latest one, about a young couple in Europe, will attest to that. . . . [Julia] Glass won the National Book Award for 'Three Junes' (2002), and she has been on serious fiction readers' radar ever since; they will not be disappointed in her latest novel, about family secrets. . . . One of the finest current literary-fiction writers, [Francine] Prose presents a novel focused on a Paris jazz club and its fascinating clientele in the 1920s and 1930s."

REVIEW: *Kirkus Rev* v82 no4 p103 F 15 2014

"And the Dark Sacred Night". " Jasper is a lovable creation, tough but gentle, worried that he was not much of a father to his own sons, let alone Kit. . . . While all of the characters Kit encounters have idiosyncratic charm, Kit himself is an overly sensitive, navel-gazing bore. Nevertheless, a new extended family develops, though not without trials and tears. Why Daphne keeps her secret in the 21st century is hard to fathom, and it's just one of the creaking contrivances that fans of [Julia] Glass' empowering tear-jerkers will have to overlook."

REVIEW: *Libr J* v139 no2 p65 F 1 2014 Leslie Patterson

REVIEW: *N Y Times Book Rev* p12 My 4 2014 CAROL ANSHAW

REVIEW: *New Yorker* v90 no11 p75-1 My 5 2014

GLASSON, TRAVIS. Mastering Christianity; missionary Anglicanism and slavery in the Atlantic world; [by] Travis Glasson x, 318 p. 2012 Oxford University Press

1. Historical literature 2. Missions, British 3. Racism—Great Britain—History 4. Slavery and the church—Church of England—History
ISBN 0199773963 (alk. paper); 9780199773961 (alk. paper)
LC 2011-008489

SUMMARY: This book by Travis Glasson recounts how "Beginning in 1701, missionary-minded Anglicans launched . . . efforts to Christianize the enslaved people of Britain's colonies. Hundreds of clergy traveled to widely-dispersed posts in North America, the Caribbean, and West Africa under . . . the Society for the Propagation of the Gospel in Foreign Parts (SPG). . . . Yet, only a minority of enslaved people embraced Anglicanism, while a majority rejected it." (Publisher's note)

REVIEW: *Am Hist Rev* v118 no1 p154-5 F 2013 ROBERT OLWELL

REVIEW: *Engl Hist Rev* v128 no534 p1248-9 O 2013 Sylvia R. Frey

"Mastering Christianity: Missionary Anglicanism and Slavery in the Atlantic World." "Over the course of the last decade there have been a number of studies of Protestant missionary activities among Atlantic black populations, but, for the most part, missionary Anglicanism has played only a peripheral role. Yet, as Travis Glasson demonstrates here, Anglicanism was far from a marginal institution. . . .

The book succeeds on several levels--in its thorough-going revision of Anglican humanitarianism, in its exhaustive examination of the role played by the SPG's identification with slave-holding society as a dynamic factor in its failure to realise the missionary goal of Christianising black Atlantic populations."

REVIEW: *J Am Hist* v100 no2 p503 S 2013 Dee E. Andrews

REVIEW: *J Relig* v94 no1 p114-6 Ja 2014 REBECCA ANNE GOETZ

GLEASON, COLLEEN. The clockwork scarab; [by] Colleen Gleason 356 p. 2013 Chronicle Books

1. Detective and mystery stories 2. Mystery and detective stories 3. Scarabs—Fiction 4. Scarabs—Juvenile fiction 5. Secret societies—Fiction 6. Secret societies—Juvenile fiction 7. Time travel—Fiction 8. Time travel—Juvenile fiction

ISBN 1452110700; 9781452110707 (alk. paper)

LC 2012-036578

SUMMARY: This is the first book in Colleen Gleason's Stoker and Holmes series. The "narrative switches between two young women living in 1889 London: observant and cerebral Alvermina Holmes (she goes by Mina . . .), the niece of Sherlock Holmes; and Evaline Stoker, the headstrong (and physically strong) younger sister to Bram, and member of a proud line of vampire hunters." They "investigate the connection between the disappearance of a young woman and several recent murders." (Publishers Weekly)

REVIEW: *Booklist* v110 no1 p113 S 1 2013 Ilene Cooper

REVIEW: *Horn Book Magazine* v89 no5 p98-9 S/O 2013 ELISSA GERSHOWITZ

"The Clockwork Scarab." "In this first series entry, [Colleen] Gleason lays the foundation for future volumes, but there's still a lot of ground to cover: for example, even though Evaline's vampire-hunting legacy is alluded to, there's not a fanged creature in sight; also, we don't know much about Dylan's backstory. The mystery itself is not [Arthur] Conan Doyle-caliber: as is often the case with latter-day Holmes adventures, there's a supernatural component, and the details are murky. But the fun comes from the voices of the two main characters whose alternating narration includes quick-witted sparring, slowly developing friendship, and grudging admiration for each other's very different strengths, along with cameo appearances by their famous relatives."

REVIEW: *Kirkus Rev* v81 no14 p208 Jl 15 2013

REVIEW: *N Y Times Book Rev* p23 O 13 2013 ALEXANDRA MULLEN

REVIEW: *Publ Wkly* v260 no30 p69 Jl 29 2013

REVIEW: *SLJ* v59 no9 p157 S 2013 Jennifer Prince

REVIEW: *Voice of Youth Advocates* v36 no4 p81 O 2013 Katie Mitchell

GLEIS, JOSHUA L. Hezbollah and Hamas; a comparative study; [by] Joshua L. Gleis x, 249 p. 2012 Johns Hopkins University Press

1. Arab-Israeli conflict 2. Islam and politics 3. Islamic fundamentalism 4. Political science literature

ISBN 1421406144 (hdbk.: alk. paper); 1421406152 (pbk.: alk. paper); 1421406713 (electronic); 9781421406145 (hdbk.: alk. paper); 9781421406152 (pbk.: alk. paper); 9781421406718 (electronic)

LC 2011-048392

SUMMARY: "'Hezbollah and Hamas' draws from primary interviews and documents coupled with a thorough review of current scholarship. This is a portrait of the organizations' roots, histories, ideologies, relationships, tactics, political outlooks, and futures. [Editors] Joshua L. Gleis and Benedetta Berti present organization charts, maps, and a case study of the TriBorder Area in South America, which frequently serves as an operational center for terrorist groups." (Publisher's note)

REVIEW: *Choice* v50 no6 p1130 F 2013 G. E. Perry

REVIEW: *TLS* no5791 p28 Mr 28 2014 GERARD RUSSELL

"Hezbollah: The Global Footprint of Lebanon's Party of God" and "Hezbollah and Hamas: A Comparative Study." "[Author Matthew] Levitt's book is comprehensive, and attempts to leaven its forensic detail by having each chapter (all of them dealing with a separate part of the world) plunge us straight into the middle of events, in the style of a thriller. So the book jumps confusingly about in time: a chronology would have been helpful. More significantly, this hampers a proper discussion of causality and development over time. . . . [Editors] Joshua L. Gleis and Benedetta Berti provide some context and a clearer narrative in their short book comparing Hamas and Hezbollah."

GLEIZER, DANIELA. Unwelcome exiles; Mexico and the Jewish refugees from Nazism, 1933-1945; [by] Daniela Gleizer xx, 334 p. 2014 Brill

1. Historical literature 2. Immigrants—Mexico—History—20th century 3. Jews—Mexico—History—20th century 4. World War, 1939-1945—Refugees—Mexico

ISBN 9789004259935 (hardback: acid-free paper)

LC 2013-031672

SUMMARY: "This book examines Mexico's reactions to Jews seeking refuge from Nazi Germany. . . . Although Mexican and international Jewish organizations petitioned for refuge, inopportune circumstances ranging from right-wing activism to the contradictory goals of government ministries and the disparate agendas of successive political leaders precluded a more humane outcome." (Choice: Current Reviews for Academic Libraries)

REVIEW: *Choice* v51 no9 p1658 My 2014 S. J. Gold

"Unwelcome Exiles: Mexico and the Jewish Refugees From Nazism, 1933-1945". "Using meticulous documentation, [Daniela] Gleizer . . . reveals the convoluted process by which only about 2,000 of approximately 500,000 haven-seekers found shelter in Mexico from the early 1930s to the end of WW II. . . . The book is packed with detailed information, not just concerning wartime Jewish resettlement, but also about Mexico's political history and understanding of national membership. Especially for readers interested in the Holocaust, Jewish studies, and Mexican history."

GLENNIE, SCOTT C. Kicking the Can; [by] Scott C. Glennie 438 p. 2013 Createspace Independent Pub

1. Health care reform—Political aspects 2. Health care reform—United States 3. Lung transplants 4. Medical policy 5. Political fiction

ISBN 1492815071; 9781492815075

SUMMARY: This novel by Scott C. Glennie "hinges on solving the U.S. health care crisis. Chris Drummond, due to his qualifications in 'acquisition and integration of physician practices,' is chosen to lead a team to find an inspired solution for the country's massive health care debt. The president, frustrated by the deadlocked government, puts together five groups to compete in a 'contest devised to bypass Congress and take the problem directly to the people.'" (Kirkus Reviews)

REVIEW: *Kirkus Rev* v82 no2 p358 Ja 15 2014

"Kicking the Can". "The primary plot . . . relies heavily on the author's extensive health care research, and, to his credit, he integrates it well; for the most part, it's never long-winded or extraneous. However, readers will have to arrive with an interest in complex governmental policy. There's some occasional clunky dialogue, particularly from Sarah . . . and there's a huge cast of characters for readers to follow. That said, [Scott C.] Glennie seems to know his audience, and he has a consistently good feel for the elements of a mainstream thriller. An ambitious novel but one that may lack universal appeal."

GLOAG, KENNETH.ed. The Cambridge companion to Michael Tippett. See The Cambridge companion to Michael Tippett

GLOBAL EDUCATION POLICY AND INTERNATIONAL DEVELOPMENT; new agendas, issues, and policies; 240 p. 2012 Bloomsbury Academic

1. Economic development—Developing countries 2. Education—Economic aspects—Developing countries 3. Education and globalization—Developing countries 4. Education and state—Developing countries 5. Educational literature

ISBN 9781441130358; 9781441143907; 9781441169839; 9781441170903

LC 2012-005874

SUMMARY: "This edited volume, which comprises 3 sections and 14 chapters, seeks to familiarize the nascent reader to the dialectics, tensions, and prospects of the emerging area of global educational policy (GEP) studies. . . . This volume deals with the long-standing topic of the movement of policy ideas across national borders." (Comparative Education Review)

REVIEW: *Harv Educ Rev* v84 no1 p125-33 Spr 2014 E.L.E. Y.Y. A.M.N.

"Schooling Hip-Hop: Expanding Hip-Hop Based Education Across the Curriculum," "Charter Schools and the Corporate Makeover of Public Education: What's At Stake?" and "Global Education Policy and International Development: New Agendas, Issues and Policies." "The authors face a difficult challenge as they attempt to move hip-hop pedagogical scholarship beyond a conversation about lyrics and instructional content. . . . For the most part, the authors in Schooling Hip-Hop achieve this feat. . . . Michael Fabricant and Michelle Fine write with a sense of urgency. . . Their imaginative investigation reveals the intricate network of decisions . . . that have created the current charter school landscape. . . . A timely compendium of studies aimed at elucidating the specific social, historical, political, and economic conditions that have shaped global education policies (GEPs) in diverse contexts."

GLOBAL MOBILE; applications and innovations for the worldwide mobile ecosystem; xi, 620 p. 2013 Information Today, Inc.

1. Information technology—Economic aspects 2. Mobile communication systems 3. Mobile computing 4. Social science literature 5. Technology & civilization

ISBN 1573874620 (paperback); 9781573874625 (paperback)

LC 2013-009194

SUMMARY: This book examines "mobile technology and its impacts on human life, work, and society. Thirty-one chapters examine the foundations of the worldwide mobile ecosystem and present an array of case studies and perspectives on how mobile is transforming human enterprise from business and healthcare to education, employment, entertainment, government, and the media." (Publisher's note)

REVIEW: *Choice* v51 no6 p1046 F 2014 C. Tappert

"Global Mobile: Applications and Innovations for the Worldwide Mobile System." "'Global Mobile,' edited by information technology researcher/educator [Peter A.] Bruck . . . and author/consultant [Madanmohan] Rao . . . describes the extensive impact of and developments in mobile technology throughout the world, facilitated by increases in computing power (at decreasing costs) and advances in 'optical transmission, data storage, screen resolution, and network switching.' . . . Overall, a useful overview of the wide-ranging influence of mobile technology."

GLOBAL PROJECTS; institutional and political challenges; xix, 452 p. 2011 Cambridge University Press

1. Economic development projects—Developing countries 2. Infrastructure (Economics)—Developing countries 3. International cooperation 4. Public-private sector cooperation—Developing countries 5. Social science literature

ISBN 0521181909 (paperback); 1107004926 (hardback); 9780521181907 (paperback); 9781107004924 (hardback)

LC 2010-050613

SUMMARY: "This book presents a new theoretical framework that allows us to analyze the institutional and social movement processes, both negative and positive, that surround global infrastructure projects as they confront cross-national and cross-sectoral . . . institutional differences. The value of this framework is illustrated through a series of studies on a wide range of infrastructure projects, including roads . . . airports, water supply and energy pipelines." (Publisher's note)

REVIEW: *Contemp Sociol* v43 no1 p115-7 Ja 2014 Göran Ahrne

"Global Projects: Institutional and Political Challenges". "It does not become very clear what really is gained by collapsing all kinds of different forms of knowledge or ignorance into the term institutional. Lumping all sorts of knowledge regarding legislation, technical solutions, or work practices together as institutional may instead hamper important insights. . . . One of the most interesting chapters of the book is the one that applies social movement theory. . . . The volume as a whole is rich in terms of empirical material, and most of the chapters apply sophisticated methods for the analysis of qualitative case studies. But its contribution to a theoretical understanding of processes of globalization is limited."

GLOCK-COOPER, ALLISON. Changers book one. See

Cooper, T.

A GLORIOUS ENTERPRISE; the Academy of Natural Sciences of Philadelphia and the making of American science; xvii, 437 p. 2012 University of Pennsylvania Press
1. Historical literature 2. Natural history—Research—Pennsylvania—Philadelphia 3. Science—History 4. Scientists—United States
ISBN 0812243803; 9780812243802 (alk. paper)
LC 2011-034991

SUMMARY: This book by Robert McCracken Peck and Patricia Tyson Stroud focuses on the history of the Academy of Natural Sciences of Philadelphia, which "stands today as the oldest natural history museum in the Western hemisphere. . . . What began as a small gathering of devoted amateurs has grown into a vibrant international center for scientific education and research." (Publisher's note)

REVIEW: *Audubon* v114 no4 p60 Jl/Ag 2012 Julie Leibach

REVIEW: *Choice* v50 no3 p503 N 2012 J. S. Schwartz

"A Glorious Enterprise: The Academy of Natural Sciences of Philadelphia and the Mythmaking of American Science." "This massive compendium . . . deal[s] with different aspects of the Academy of Natural Sciences of Philadelphia. . . . [Robert McCracken] Peck . . . and [Patricia Tyson] Stroud . . . describe how a group of amateur naturalists got together in 1812 for 'the purposes of rational, free, literary, and scientific conversation.' . . . This magnificent volume is beautifully illustrated, including excellent woodcuts, reproductions of Audubon's drawings, and oil paintings and stereographs. It should interest students of American history, American studies, art, as well as natural history and the voyages of exploration."

REVIEW: *Nat Hist* v120 no9 p37-8 N 2012 LAURENCE A. MARSCHALL

GODWIN, GAIL, 1937-. Flora; a novel; [by] Gail Godwin 288 p. 2013 Bloomsbury
1. Cousins—Fiction 2. Girls—Fiction 3. Guardian and ward—Fiction 4. Historical fiction 5. Orphans—Fiction 6. Sanatoriums
ISBN 1620401207; 9781620401200
LC 2012-036741

SUMMARY: In this book, "Helen, a writer, looks back to the fateful summer of 1945, when she was a precocious, motherless 10-year-old trying to make sense of a complicated and unjust world. Young Helen lives on a hill in North Carolina in an old . . . house that was once a sanatorium for folks she calls the Recoverers. Raised by her . . . grandmother, whom she worships, Helen is bereft after Nonie's sudden death" and she must live with her guileless cousin Flora. (Booklist)

REVIEW: *Booklist* v109 no12 p25 F 15 2013 Donna Seaman

REVIEW: *Kirkus Rev* v81 no4 p152 F 15 2013

REVIEW: *N Y Times Book Rev* p11 My 27 2013 LEAH HAGER COHEN

"Flora." "As the story unfolds, we realize it's populated almost exclusively by orphans of different stripes. It's a mark of [Gail] Godwin's light, sure touch that this doesn't feel contrived. On the contrary, it begins to feel natural, inevitable that beneath the surface of any individual we'll find a lonesome soul, cut adrift. . . . For most of the book, not much happens in the house on the mountaintop. . . . In old age, she'll recall it as having been 'for the most part a boring, exasperating summer'--by any reckoning a risky proposition for a novel. But Godwin makes use of the older Helen's voice to dispense snatches of foreboding. We understand that we're creeping toward some calamity whose unpredictable nature is precisely what keeps us reading."

REVIEW: *Publ Wkly* v260 no6 p37 F 11 2013

GOH SHUFEN. China Cmo. See Paull, G.

GOKHALE, SHANTA. Crowfall; [by] Shanta Gokhale 280 p. 2013 Penguin Viking
1. Friendship—Fiction 2. Indic literature—Translations into English 3. Marathi fiction 4. Urban life—Fiction
ISBN 0670086940; 9780670086948
LC 2013-413062

SUMMARY: Written by Shanta Gokhale, "'Crowfall' unobtrusively follows an eventful year in the lives of a group of friends--a journalist, a teacher, a musician and three painters--in Mumbai. Like the cycle of seasons, love and violence and heartbreak and joy pursue each other. . . . 'Crowfall' takes in art and identity, music and communal madness, and the clash of the old and the new to etch a finely nuanced portrait of contemporary Mumbai." (Publisher's note)

REVIEW: *World Lit Today* v88 no2 p58-9 Mr/Ap 2014 Saleem Peeradina

"Crowfall." "Shanta Gokhale's 'Crowfall' (originally in Marathi) starts with a paradox. Before she can begin telling her story, Anima, the central character, destroys the twelve volumes of her twelve-year-long chronicle of grief and nightmares that started with the mindless murder of her husband in the 1993 Bombay riots. . . . As a columnist and performing-arts critic, Gokhale speaks with authority on the city and its evolving culture. She speaks with no less empathy of the unique sensibilities of her characters. The nexus between artists, galleries, and art critics, a lucrative formula in the art world everywhere, is shown as a ringside spectator would see it."

GOLAN, AVIRAMA. Little Naomi, Little Chick; 34 p. 2013 Eerdmans Books for Young Readers
1. Animals—Infancy—Fiction 2. Chickens—Fiction 3. Children's stories 4. Farm life—Fiction 5. Nursery schools—Fiction 6. Schools—Fiction
ISBN 0802854273 (hbk.); 9780802854278 (hbk.)
LC 2013-000492

SUMMARY: In this book, by Avirama Golan, "Little Naomi has a busy day! She gets ready for school, plays with all her friends, builds with blocks, bakes mud pies, colors pictures, eats lunch, and helps mom with the shopping. Little Chick has to stay at home with the other barnyard animals, but that doesn't stop him from having adventures of his own." (Publisher's note)

REVIEW: *Booklist* v110 no4 p56 O 15 2013 Lolly Gepson

REVIEW: *Horn Book Magazine* v90 no1 p71 Ja/F 2014 ELISSA GERSHOWITZ

"Little Naomi, Little Chick." "This clever book tells two stories, one about a preschooler named Naomi, the other about a little chick. . . . . The chick and its friends--a duck, a mole, and a sheep--have small adventures that loosely parallel Naomi's experiences. . . . Although the farm story is wordless, the illustrations say it all, capturing, through cartoony creatures and slapstick reaction shots, the tale's humor and also its warmth. . . . Several visual elements . . . gracefully unite these two worlds of play."

REVIEW: *Kirkus Rev* v81 no17 p94 S 1 2013

REVIEW: *Kirkus Rev* p54 N 15 2013 Best Books

REVIEW: *Publ Wkly* v260 no28 p167 Jl 15 2013

REVIEW: *SLJ* v59 no10 p1 O 2013 Carol Connor

GOLDEMBERG, SILVANA. Victoria; [by] Silvana Goldemberg 136 p. 2014 Orca Book Pub

1. Families—Fiction 2. Paraná (Argentina) 3. Runaway teenagers—Fiction 4. Street children 5. Young adult fiction

ISBN 1896580955; 9781896580951

SUMMARY: In this book, "Victoria Díaz has already lost both parents. . . She and her younger, twin brothers live with an aunt and her boyfriend in Doña Norma's house until the boyfriend's sexual advances cause Victoria to run away. While she meets some well-meaning strangers, the streets of the city are rough, teeming with gang members, drug dealers and other unsavory characters. Victoria must navigate this chaotic world while trying to get back into school and reunite with her brothers." (Kirkus Reviews)

REVIEW: *Kirkus Rev* v82 no2 p100 Ja 15 2014

"Victoria". ". Native Argentine [Silvana] Goldemberg has an unending supply of obstacles to put in Victoria's path. The author dedicates the novel to 'the children who suffer from violence and poverty,' but she almost makes a mockery of their suffering through a combination of two-dimensional characters, hackneyed dialogue, unbelievable coincidences, poor transitions and a very tidy ending. Spanish and Italian words and South American slang provide some initial interest in the otherwise lackluster conversations, but they soon wear, especially when combined with the snippets of song lyrics scattered throughout the novel. Teen readers need realistic novels set in contemporary Latin America that capture culture while avoiding stereotypes, but Goldemberg's effort fails to engage."

THE GOLDEN FLEECE; manipulation and independence in humanitarian action; xviii, 318 p. 2012 Kumarian Press

1. Humanitarian assistance—Political aspects 2. Humanitarian intervention—Political aspects 3. International agencies 4. International relief—Political aspects 5. Nongovernmental organizations 6. Social science literature

ISBN 9781565494879 (cloth : alk. paper); 9781565494886 (pbk. : alk. paper); 9781565494893 (library networkable e-edition); 9781565494909 (consumer e-edition)

LC 2012-016566

SUMMARY: This book "examines the impact of manipulation on the effectiveness of humanitarian action . . . starting with the origins of organized humanitarianism in the mid-19th century and zeroes in on the twenty-plus years since the end of the Cold War. It examines whether instrumentalization has achieved its desired objectives . . . and whether the recent dramatic growth of relief work has opened up humanitarian action to greater manipulation." (Publisher's note)

REVIEW: *TLS* no5744 p27 My 3 2013 JONATHAN BENTHALL

"The Golden Fleece: Manipulation and Independence in Humanitarian Action." "The originality of . . . [the book] rests on its demonstration that there was never a golden age. . . . The editor, Antonio Donini, of Tufts University and formerly of the UN, is one of the most thoughtful humanitarians in the world today and a staunch advocate for independence. He has assembled a team of authors who all draw on practical experience of providing institutional relief to victims of conflicts and 'natural' disasters. . . . There are weaknesses. . . . Little on faith-based aid agencies, and little on how funds for humanitarian action are mobilized. . . . But 'The Golden Fleece' is an indispensable collection. If read and absorbed by decision-makers, it might help to pre-empt future mistakes."

GOLDEN, JESS.il. Snow dog, sand dog. See Singleton, L. J.

GOLDHAGEN, DANIEL JONAH. The Devil That Never Dies; The Rise and Threat of Global Antisemitism; [by] Daniel Jonah Goldhagen 432 p. 2013 Little, Brown and Co.

1. Antisemitism—History—20th century 2. Antisemitism—History—21st century 3. Arab-Israeli conflict 4. Globalization—Social aspects 5. Social science literature

ISBN 031609787X; 9780316097871

LC 2013-941806

SUMMARY: In this book, by Daniel Jonah Goldhagen, "reveals the unprecedented, global form of [antisemitism]; its strategic use by states; its powerful appeal to individuals and groups; and how technology has fueled the flames that had been smoldering prior to the millennium." (Publisher's note)

REVIEW: *Booklist* v110 no2 p8 S 15 2013 Jay Freeman

REVIEW: *Kirkus Rev* v81 no15 p268 Ag 1 2013

REVIEW: *Libr J* v138 no7 p58 Ap 15 2013 Barbara Hoffert

REVIEW: *Libr J* v138 no14 p124 S 1 2013 Joel Neuberg

REVIEW: *N Y Times Book Rev* p28 O 13 2013 JEFFREY GOLDBERG

"The Devil That Never Dies: The Rise and Threat of Global Antisemitism." "The most effective and disturbing argument [Daniel Jonah] Goldhagen musters in this new book is that the resurgence of rhetorically and sometimes physically violent anti-Semitism over the past dozen years or so is shocking in part because it does not seem to shock. . . . This is a fine point to make. Unfortunately, Goldhagen undermines himself by, among other things, allowing his anger to get the best of him. 'The Devil That Never Dies' is written in a hyperventilating style, starting with its title. . . . Most of these statements are easily found on the Internet, where Goldhagen appears to have done much of his research, but there is real utility to his efforts."

GOLDHAMMER, ARTHUR.tr. Algerian chronicles. See Camus, A.

GOLDHAMMER, ARTHUR.tr. Capital in the twenty-first century. See Piketty, T.

GOLDHAMMER, ARTHUR.tr. The society of equals. See

Rosanvallon, P.

GOLDHAMMER, ARTHUR.tr. Tocqueville. See Tocqueville

GOLDIE, SONIA. Ghosts; 40 p. 2013 Enchanted Lion Books

1. Balls (Parties) 2. Children's stories 3. Dwellings—Juvenile literature 4. Ghost stories 5. Ghosts—Fiction
ISBN 9781592701421 (alk. paper)
LC 2013-030049

SUMMARY: In this book, Sonia Goldie and Marc Boutavant "put to rest the old stereotype of sheet-wearing, ball-dragging, 'Boo'-shrieking ghosts and present an array of imaginative household haunters, each with its own unique traits and looks. For example, a gluttonous kitchen ghost gobbles up food from the fridge; the ghost of the attic 'likes to spend his time remembering the good old days.' Most of the specters are more peculiar than scary." (School Library Journal)

REVIEW: *Booklist* v110 no9/10 p96 Ja 1 2014 Sarah Hunter

"Ghosts." "In short, there's a ghost for pretty much everything, but [Marc] Boutavant's bright, colorful, and playful illustrations of the friendly animal-shaped ghosts in their favorite haunts keep these spooks from ever being scary. In fact, it seems like there's a playful apparition behind every creak and shifting window shade--nothing to be scared of after all. [Sonia] Goldie's charmingly off-kilter descriptions of everyday ghosts paired together with the cheery childlike illustrations make for a delightful oddball treat."

REVIEW: *Kirkus Rev* v81 no20 p251 O 15 2013

REVIEW: *Publ Wkly* v260 no41 p59 O 14 2013

REVIEW: *SLJ* v60 no2 p72 F 2014 Yelena Alekseyeva-Popova

GOLDIN, IAN. Divided Nations; Why Global Governance Is Failing, and What We Can Do About It; [by] Ian Goldin 200 p. 2013 Oxford University Press

1. Climatic changes—International cooperation 2. Emigration & immigration—International cooperation 3. International cooperation 4. International organization 5. Political science literature
ISBN 0199693900; 9780199693900

SUMMARY: In this book, Ian Goldin "argues that the global community is at a crossroads. Hyperconnectivity means that local hazards . . . have the potential to blossom into global catastrophes . . . hence the clear need for greater international cooperation. Focusing on the areas of climate change, cybersecurity, pandemics, migration, and finance, Goldin finds the current global architecture, largely designed in the wake of WW II, woefully inadequate to the task." (Choice: Current Reviews for Academic Libraries)

REVIEW: *Choice* v51 no8 p1486-7 Ap 2014 M. F. Farrell

"Divided Nations: Why Global Governance Is Failing, and What We Can Do About It". "[Ian] Goldin . . . brings a wealth of experience as a practitioner with a variety of international organizations along with solid academic credentials to this thoughtful and clearly written study of global governance. . . . Emphasizing the need to balance legitimacy and effectiveness, Goldin recommends specific reforms for existing institutions. . . . While the recommendations are left at a fairly general level, this thoughtful, well-informed work provides very helpful guidance through the crowded terrain of global governance issues today."

REVIEW: *Libr J* v138 no8 p92 My 1 2013 Veronic Arellano

REVIEW: *Publ Wkly* v260 no13 p54-5 Ap 1 2013

GOLDMAN, ADAM. Enemies Within; Inside the Nypd's Secret Spying Unit and the Most Dangerous Terror Plot Since 9/11; [by] Adam Goldman 352 p. 2013 Simon & Schuster

1. Intelligence service—United States 2. Journalism 3. New York (N.Y.). Police Dept. 4. Terrorism—New York (State) 5. Terrorism—United States—Prevention
ISBN 1476727937; 9781476727936

SUMMARY: This book examines " the NYPD's post-9/11 counterterrorism intelligence unit amid the almost-undetected 2009 plot to bomb the subway system." Following the September 11, 2001 terrorist attacks, "the NYPD began an unprecedented intelligence-gathering campaign to bolster anti-terrorism security. . . . Headed by former CIA analyst David Cohen . . . the I.D. began operating like an international spy unit rather than a division of the police department." (Kirkus Reviews)

REVIEW: *Commentary* v136 no4 p42-4 N 2013 ROBERT McMANUS

REVIEW: *Kirkus Rev* v81 no19 p49 O 1 2013

REVIEW: *Libr J* v138 no6 p58 Ap 1 2013 Barbara Hoffert

REVIEW: *N Y Times Book Rev* p26 O 13 2013 TARA McKELVEY

"Enemies Within: Inside the NYPD's Secret Spying Unit and Bin Laden's Final Plot Against America." "Unlike other accounts of New York's counterterrorism efforts . . . 'Enemies Within' does not glorify the work of the cops. Instead, it attempts to portray [David] Cohen as a sinister force, a man who oversees a network of surveillance operations that tramples on civil liberties. . . . Despite the authors' efforts to blacken Cohen and his unit, the squad does not come off all that badly. In this account, at least, they seem clownish but relatively harmless. . . . As for [Matt] Apuzzo and [Adam] Godlman's actual argument, it seems confused. . . . Apuzzo and Goldman fail to present sufficient evidence for either case."

GOLDMAN, LAWRENCE. The Life of R. H. Tawney; Socialism and History; [by] Lawrence Goldman 432 p. 2013 Bloomsbury USA Academic

1. Biography (Literary form) 2. Historians—Great Britain—Biography 3. Historical literature 4. Socialists—Great Britain—Biography 5. Tawney, R. H. (Richard Henry), 1880-1962
ISBN 1780937040; 9781780937045

SUMMARY: "R. H. Tawney was the most influential theorist and exponent of socialism in Britain in the 20th century and also a leading historian. Based on papers deposited at the London School of Economics including a collection of personal material previously held by his family, this book provides the first detailed biography. [Author] Lawrence Goldman shows that to understand Tawney's work it is necessary to understand his life." (Publisher's note)

REVIEW: *TLS* no5781 p3 Ja 17 2014

REVIEW: *TLS* no5781 p3-5 Ja 17 2014 STEFAN COLLINI

"The Life of R. H. Tawney: Socialism and History" and "Richard Hoggart: Virtue and Reward." "The appearance of these two sharply contrasting biographies ought to go some way towards disturbing . . . complacent preconceptions. . . . To say that Fred Inglis wears his heart on his sleeve would be to understate his forthrightness. His prose is characterized by what might be called exuberant lyricism. . . . In the cases of both R. H. Tawney and Richard Hoggart, the exemplary quality of their own characters stands high in all recollections and celebrations of them. Even in the face of the complacent disdain that I mentioned at the outset, it is difficult to come away from these two biographies without feeling renewed admiration for their subjects."

GOLDSCHMIDT, TYRON.ed. The puzzle of existence. See The puzzle of existence

GOLDSMITH, CONNIE. Traumatic brain injury; from concussion to coma; [by] Connie Goldsmith 88 p. 2014 Twenty-First Century Books

1. Brain—Diseases—Juvenile literature 2. Brain—Wounds and injuries—Juvenile literature 3. Children's nonfiction 4. Neurology—Juvenile literature 5. Traumatology

ISBN 1467713481; 9781467713481 (lib. bdg.: alk. paper)

LC 2013-001346

SUMMARY: This juvenile nonfiction book, by Connie Goldsmith, explores traumatic brain injury, including "the different types of TBIs, what causes them, and how they are diagnosed and treated. . . . [It also profiles] National Hockey League player Derek Boogaard and U.S. Representative Gabby Giffords, both of whom sustained TBIs, with dramatically different outcomes. . . . [Finally, it previews] medical technologies that help victims recover and promise hope for the future." (Publisher's note)

REVIEW: *Booklist* v110 no7 p53 D 1 2013 Martha Edmundson

REVIEW: *Kirkus Rev* v81 no24 p167 D 15 2013

"Traumatic Brain Injury: From Concussion to Coma". "[Connie] Goldsmith provides basic information about the brain and the definition of TBI as well as explaining the different types of concussions. Individual chapters explore currently prominent themes, especially sports-related injuries, war wounds and damage caused by motor vehicle accidents. Even an event as common as falling down is examined. . . . A lot of ground is covered in this slim volume, but it is a solid introduction to the topic. It makes good use of graphics, photographs and sidebars to deliver complicated information."

REVIEW: *SLJ* v60 no2 p124 F 2014 Tammy Turner

REVIEW: *Voice of Youth Advocates* v37 no1 p92 Ap 2014 Morgan Brickey

GOLDSTEIN, ALYOSHA. Poverty in common; the politics of community action during the American century; [by] Alyosha Goldstein xii, 379 p. 2012 Duke University Press

1. Community development—United States—History—20th century 2. Economic assistance, Domestic—United States—History—20th century 3. Historical literature 4. Poverty—Government policy—United States—History—20th century 5. Public welfare—United States—History—20th century 6. Social service—United States—History—20th century

ISBN 9780822351672 (cloth : alk. paper); 9780822351818 (pbk. : alk. paper)

LC 2011-041901

SUMMARY: This book on the history of community-based antipoverty programs "attempts to tease out the evolving interactions of government rhetoric, poverty programs, and bottom-up organizing for social services and material resources. . . . The book is a chronologically organized series of brief case studies of community organizing . . . unified by a larger history of the idea that programs to strengthen community action and increase activism by the poor are a key to fighting poverty." (Reviews in American History)

REVIEW: *Am Hist Rev* v118 no2 p547-8 Ap 2013 MARK EDWARD BRAUN

REVIEW: *J Am Hist* v99 no4 p1280-1 Mr 2013 Jennifer Frost

REVIEW: *Polit Sci Q (Wiley-Blackwell)* v128 no1 p190-1 Spr 2013 ROSE ERNST

REVIEW: *Rev Am Hist* v41 no3 p513-8 S 2013 Annelise Orleck

"Poverty in Common: The Politics of Community Action During the American Century." "Rich in detail and analytically complex, the book attempts to tease out the evolving interactions of government rhetoric, poverty programs, and bottom-up organizing for social services and material resources. . . . I don't really disagree with any of the fundamentals of [Alyosha] Goldstein's argument in this complex and fascinating study. . . . Still, I think that this book somewhat underplays the impact and extent of the 'unruly surplus' that spilled out of the call for democratic participation."

GOLDSTEIN, REBECCA, 1950-. Plato at the Googleplex; why philosophy won't go away; [by] Rebecca Goldstein 480 p. 2014 Pantheon

1. Ethics 2. Imaginary conversations 3. Philosophical literature 4. Philosophy—History—21st century

ISBN 0307908879; 9780307378194 (hardback)

LC 2013-029660

SUMMARY: In this book, Rebecca Newberger Goldstein "provides a . . . plunge into the drama of philosophy, revealing its hidden role in today's debates on religion, morality, politics, and science. At the origin of Western philosophy stands Plato. . . . On her way to considering the place of philosophy in our ongoing intellectual life, Goldstein tells a new story of its origin, re-envisioning the extraordinary culture that produced the man who produced philosophy." (Publisher's note)

REVIEW: *America* v211 no10 p42-4 O 13 2014 M. ROSS ROMERO

REVIEW: *Atlantic* v313 no3 p36-8 Ap 2014 CLANCY MARTIN

"Plato at the Googleplex: Why Philosophy Won't Go Away". "[An] ingenious, entertaining, and challenging new book. . . . Every generation could use a Plato to tackle those genuinely human lessons. That is the creative, verging on wacky, premise that has inspired [Rebecca Newberger] Goldstein's approach to demonstrating why philosophy won't (and had better not) go away. She transports Plato into the 21st century and, adopting his own preferred literary form, puts him into fictional dialogue with a variety of contemporary characters. . . . She ratchets up the entertainment value . . . eager for drama and topical issues. . . . This sounds dangerously facile and cute, but Goldstein mostly pulls it off, cleverly weaving passages directly from Plato's dialogues into her own."

REVIEW: *Booklist* v110 no12 p3 F 15 2014 Bryce Christensen

REVIEW: *Kirkus Rev* v81 no24 p307 D 15 2013

REVIEW: *Libr J* v139 no2 p78 F 1 2014 Robert C. Robinson

REVIEW: *N Y Times Book Rev* p16 Ap 20 2014 ANTHONY GOTTLIEB

REVIEW: *Publ Wkly* v261 no1 p45 Ja 6 2014

GOLEMBIEWSKI, CAROL. The Projection Room; Two from the Cubist Mist; [by] Carol Golembiewski 248 p. 2013 Author Solutions

1. Art museums 2. Horror tales 3. Milwaukee Art Museum 4. Museums—Fiction 5. Paranormal fiction
ISBN 1458207420; 9781458207425

SUMMARY: In this supernatural novel by Carol Golembiewski, "Years after an artist captures a macabre vision during World War I, his paintings unleash their remarkable powers onto a museum and all who dare to enter the Projection Room. . . . His widow sells both paintings to a Milwaukee museum that is testing a new technology that projects images and allows patrons to experience art three dimensionally." (Publisher's note)

REVIEW: *Kirkus Rev* p20 D 15 2013 supplemet best books 2013

REVIEW: *Kirkus Rev* v81 no16 p7 Ag 15 2013

"The Projection Room." "Cubist art runs amok and slaughters museum staff in this arty, high-concept supernatural thriller debut. . . . Art teacher [and author Carol] Golembiewski creates an intriguing new menace which works its mayhem as artists do, by creatively reimagining space and structure—but with grisly real-world effects. Although the overall conceit is a bit cartoonish, she grounds it in subtle, psychologically realistic prose and a gallery full of sharply etched characters. . . . Although the subject matter may be lurid at times, the author's fine brushwork keeps the picture sharp. An original, entertaining horror fantasy."

GOLENBOCK, PETER. They called me god. See Harvey, D.

GOLSON, TERRY. Farmstead egg guide and cookbook; 192 p. 2013 Houghton Mifflin Harcourt

1. Chickens 2. Cookbooks 3. Cooking (Eggs) 4. Egg gathering 5. Poultry farms
ISBN 1118627954; 9781118627952
LC 2013-027719

SUMMARY: This book, by Terry Golson, discusses keeping chickens and presents a variety of egg recipes. "In the first part of the book, Golson . . . presents a brief overview of keeping chickens, discussing raising layers and how to handle fresh eggs. The majority of the work is devoted to a bounty of recipes featuring eggs as the main ingredient, ranging from the simplest forms of fried, poached, and shirred eggs to quiches, custards, sauces, and soufflés." (Library Journal)

REVIEW: *Booklist* v110 no12 p12-3 F 15 2014 Mark Knoblauch

"The Farmstead Egg Guide & Cookbook". "[Terry] Golson has taken to raising her own eggs from a backyard chicken flock. For those similarly inclined, she offers plenty of practical advice, beginning with the necessity to check local regulations to be sure the community has no bans against poultry, which can be noisy enough to offend neighbors. Golson also cautions that no matter how tasty one's own hand-raised eggs can be, their costs can never hope to compete with eggs raised with the economies of scale that modern industrial egg production achieves. For those who don't have room for a backyard coop, Golson provides a number of egg recipes, ranging from the simplest boiled egg through complex quiches and silky baked custards."

REVIEW: *Libr J* v139 no1 p1 Ja 2014

REVIEW: *Publ Wkly* v261 no1 p46-7 Ja 6 2014

GOMAN, CAROL KINSEY. Every body's talking. See Jackson, D. M.

GÓMEZ-GALVARRIATO, AURORA. Industry and revolution; social and economic change in the Orizaba Valley, Mexico; [by] Aurora Gómez-Galvarriato 351 p. 2013 Harvard University Press

1. Historical literature 2. Textile industry—Mexico—Orizaba (Veracruz-Llave)—History—19th century 3. Textile industry—Mexico—Orizaba (Veracruz-Llave)—History—20th century 4. Textile workers—Mexico—Orizaba (Veracruz-Llave)—History—19th century 5. Textile workers—Mexico—Orizaba (Veracruz-Llave)—History—20th century
ISBN 9780674072725 (alk. paper)
LC 2012-038237

SUMMARY: In this book on the Mexican Revolution, "by tracing the introduction of mechanized industry into the [Orizaba] valley, [Aurora Gomez-Galvarriato] connects the social and economic upheaval unleashed by new communication, transportation, and production technologies to the political unrest of the revolutionary decade. Industry and Revolution makes an . . . argument that the Mexican Revolution cannot be understood apart from the changes wrought by the Industrial Revolution." (Publisher's note)

REVIEW: *Choice* v51 no5 p898 Ja 2014 J. B. Kirkwood

"Industry and Revolution: Social and Economic Change in the Orizaba Valley, Mexico." "Mexican economic historian [Aurora] Gómez-Galvarriato's sophisticated analysis of economic and labor history investigates the intersections of the Industrial Revolution in the textile industry with the revolutionary changes taking place in the Mexican political and social arena in 1910. . . . She convincingly argues that these workplace changes found a receptive audience with the broader demands being made across the nation with the outbreak of the revolution. . . . Through careful research in government and textile company archives, oral history, and local and national newspapers, the author demonstrates that industrial labor won important postrevolutionary gains in how laborers worked and lived."

GOMI, TARO, 1945-. Wiggle!; [by] Taro Gomi 16 p. 2013 Chronicle Books LLC

1. Animals—Fiction 2. Animals—Juvenile fiction 3. Board books 4. Elephants—Juvenile fiction 5. Fingers 6. Toy and movable books 7. Toy and movable books—Specimens
ISBN 9781452108360 (alk. paper)
LC 2012-039631

SUMMARY: In this children's book by Taro Gomi, "every spread is missing a key element of a featured animal—from an elephant's trunk to a penguin's beak, these creatures are incomplete. And it's up to young readers to help them out! Kids can finish the illustration by wiggling their fingers through suitably placed die-cuts." (Publisher's note)

REVIEW: *Kirkus Rev* v82 no1 p10 Ja 1 2014

"Wiggle!" "Readers' digits become a cat's tail, a rattlesnake's rattle, a chameleon's tongue and more in the Japanese illustrator's recognizably whimsical watercolor cartoons, done in colors both bright and muted. Some of the finger animations work well, like the sea gull wing and the elephant trunk, but others look odd or incomplete, such as the penguin beak and the deer antlers. . . . The die-cut holes appear on both the left and right sides of the double-page spread, but only one hole is needed to create the animation effect, making the page layout look unfinished."

GONEAU, MARTIN.il. Pre- and re-, mis- and dis. See Cleary, B. P.

GONZALEZ, THOMAS.il. The house on Dirty-Third Street. See Kittinger, J. S.

GONZÁLEZ, ALESSANDRA L. Islamic feminism in Kuwait; the politics and paradoxes; [by] Alessandra L. González 254 p. 2013 Palgrave Macmillan

1. Feminism & Islam 2. Feminism—Kuwait—Case studies 3. Feminism—Religious aspects—Islam 4. Muslim women—Kuwait—Case studies 5. Social science literature 6. Women—Kuwait 7. Women in Islam—Kuwait—Case studies
ISBN 1137304731; 9781137304735 (hardback)
LC 2012-034804

SUMMARY: Author Alessandra L. González's book focuses on women's rights concerning Islamic Feminism in Kuwait. "This book highlights the voices of cultural elites in the oil-rich State of Kuwait, where we have been witness to a modern suffrage movement since when women were given their political rights in 2005. The result is a new brand of feminism, one born out of a traditional and culturally conservative climate, which gives Islamic Feminists in Kuwait the edge they need to soar to new heights." (Publisher's note)

REVIEW: *Choice* v51 no1 p172 S 2013 A. Rassam

"Islamic Feminism in Kuwait: The Politics and Paradoxes." "Who are the advocates of Islamic feminism? What are their goals? What tactics do Islamic feminists employ to achieve these goals? These are some of the questions that [author Alessandra] González sets out to answer in her study of Islamic feminism in Kuwait. Basing her book on interviews and a survey of over one thousand Kuwaiti college students conducted in 2008, the author reveals the complexities and paradoxes inherent in the relationship between gender, religion, and social traditions in a Muslim society. . . . From this perspective, Islamic feminism can be seen as an effective negotiating strategy that takes into account religious authority and familial and communal responsibilities."

GOOCH, BRAD. Flannery; a life of Flannery O'Connor; [by] Brad Gooch 448 2009 Little, Brown and Co.

1. Authors 2. Authors, American 3. Biography, Individual 4. Novelists 5. Short story writers 6. Women authors
ISBN 978-0-316-00066-6; 0-316-00066-3
LC 2008—28504

SUMMARY: This biography of writer Flannery O'Connor, by Brad Gooch, focuses on "O'Connor's significant friendships—with Robert Lowell, Elizabeth Hardwick, Walker Percy, and James Dickey among others—and her deeply felt convictions, as expressed in her communications with Thomas Merton, Elizabeth Bishop, and Betty Hester. . . . O'Connor's capacity to live fully—despite the chronic disease that eventually confined her to her mother's farm in Georgia" is also discussed. (Publisher's note)

REVIEW: *Choice* v51 no10 p1741-2 Je 2014 J. W. Hall

"Flannery: A Life of Flannery O'Connor". "[Brad] Gooch . . . develops a fascinating narrative of O'Connor (1925-64), who was intensely serious about her Catholicism and her writing but who could speak wryly of nuns and novelists. Gooch's reference to his subject as 'Flannery' from chapter 4 onward is misleading (not to mention distracting), because his research is not casual, as 60 pages of acknowledgments and notes attest. He describes O'Connor's relationships with Erik Langkjaer, Betty Hester, and others in unprecedented detail. . . . [A] moving, readable study."

GOOD, PHYLLIS. Fix-it and forget-it new cookbook; 250 new delicious slow cooker recipes; [by] Phyllis Good 384 p. 2013 Good Books

1. Cookbooks 2. Cooking (Chicken) 3. Desserts 4. Slow cooking 5. Soups
ISBN 1561488003; 9781561488001 (pbk.)
LC 2013-943873

SUMMARY: In this slow-cooker cookbook, "[Phyllis] Good provides plenty of practical tips about what she calls a near miracle appliance. . . . Many of the 250 recipes are for main dishes made with chicken, turkey, pork, or beef. But she gives even more space to pasta, soups, quiches, appetizers, breakfasts, breads, and desserts." (Booklist)

REVIEW: *Booklist* v110 no3 p29 O 1 2013 Karen Springen

"Fix-it and Forget-It New Cookbook: 250 New Delicious Slow Cooker Recipes." "Fans of [Phyllis] Good's best-selling slow-cooker recipe books won't be disappointed with her latest installment. Good provides plenty of practical tips about what she calls a near miracle appliance. . . . Each recipe comes with a photo, some (such as mashed potatoes) get a 'quick and easy' label, and several get a bonus tip from Good (such as 'cooking wine is wine with salt added'). With good recipes and good vibes, the latest Fix-It and Forget-It cookbook is bound to be a best-seller."

GOODBY, JOHN. The Poetry of Dylan Thomas; Under the Spelling Wall; [by] John Goodby 512 p. 2013 Oxford Univ Pr

1. English poetry—History & criticism 2. Gender in literature 3. Literature—History & criticism 4. Modernism (Literature) 5. Thomas, Dylan, 1914-1953
ISBN 1846318769; 9781846318764

SUMMARY: This book on poet Dylan Thomas, by John Goodby, "is the first study of poet to show how his work may be read in terms of contemporary critical concerns, using theories of modernism, the body, gender, the carnivalesque, language, hybridity and the pastoral in order to view it in an original light." (Publisher's note)

REVIEW: *Choice* v51 no8 p1399 Ap 2014 R. K. Mookerjee

"The Poetry of Dylan Thomas: Under the Spelling Wall". "The analysis is particularly impressive when focused on formal issues: the emphasis on process in Thomas's 'mannerist' modernism; the subtle manipulation of sounds that characterizes his poetic speech (with its echoes of dialect); the coexistence of Romantic and avant-garde poetics in his work. Somewhat fraught questions such as Thomas's relationship to 'colonialist' ideas and his struggle with sexual compulsions are explored in a lucid, evidence-based manner with the dual purpose of redeeming a great poet and improving understanding of his poetry. Aimed equally at the scholarly community and the poet's devoted readers, this study is authoritative, detailed, and insightful."

GOODE, DIANE.il. Outside the box. See Wilson, K.

GOODE, J. J. Pok Pok. See Pok Pok

GOODHART, DAVID. The British Dream; Successes and Failures of Post-war Immigration; [by] David Goodhart 416 p. 2013 Atlantic Books

1. Great Britain—Politics & government 2. Great Britain—Race relations 3. Immigrants—Great Britain 4. Political science literature 5. Social integration
ISBN 1843548054; 9781843548058

SUMMARY: It was the author's intent to demonstrate "that if Britain is to avoid a narrowing of the public realm and sharply segregated cities, as in many parts of the US, its politicians and opinion leaders must do two things. Firstly, as advocated by the center right, they need to bring immigration down to more moderate and sustainable levels. Secondly, as advocated by the center left, they need to shape a progressive national story about openness and opportunity." (Publisher's note)

REVIEW: *Economist* v407 no8832 p90 Ap 20 2013

REVIEW: *London Rev Books* v35 no12 p7-9 Je 20 2013 Jonathan Portes

REVIEW: *New Statesman* v142 no5153/5154 p142-3 Ap 12 3013 Jon Cruddas

REVIEW: *TLS* no5759 p33 Ag 16 2013 K. BISWAS

"The British Dream: Successes and Failures of Post-War Immigration." "Overlapping statistics and projections place foreign-born and ethnic minority data incongruously side by side, blurring the boundaries between concerns with immigration and with race. . . . [David Goodhart] rarely points towards anything conclusive. . . . He . . . bafflingly posits that it is not racist 'to assume that one member of a group is likely to share the common characteristics of the group'. . . . 'The British Dream' does little to acknowledge the wealth of human experience within waves of migration, instead choosing to see monolithic ethnic blocks, only to dismiss them. . . . Indeed, given that Goodhart is a prominent public thinker, his policy proposals are surprisingly non-intellectual."

GOODMAN, GABRIEL. The alliance; [by] Gabriel Goodman 103 p. 2013 Darby Creek

1. Friendship—Fiction 2. Gay-straight alliances in schools—Fiction 3. High schools—Fiction 4. School stories 5. Schools—Fiction
ISBN 1467705950 (library); 9781467705950 (library)
LC 2012-032139

SUMMARY: This teen novel, by Gabriel Goodman, is part of the "Surviving Southside" series. "'One Down . . . You're Next.' Or so said the note Carmen Mendoza found in her locker. Carmen is out, loud, and proud, so the threat doesn't faze her . . . much. . . . Jamie Ballard is the 'one down.' Jamie was Scott King's best friend. . . . Now Scott has to do something, even if it costs him his reputation. If Carmen and Scott can figure out how to get along, they'll be an unstoppable alliance." (Publisher's note)

REVIEW: *Horn Book Magazine* v89 no6 p125-6 N/D 2013 Katrina Hedeen

"Revenge of a Not-So-Pretty Girl," "Me, Him, Them and It," and "The Alliance". [In 'Revenge of a Not-So-Pretty Girl,] abused fourteen-year-old Faye hates her Brooklyn Catholic school. . . . Characters and place ring true in a story about learning what (and who) is really important in life. . . . The difficult decision [in 'Me, Him, Them, and It] becomes whether to keep the baby or give it up, and the narrative's ongoing debate will keep readers guessing. This is a compelling pregnant-teen story, and the topic is given sensitive treatment by [Caela] Carter. . . . [In 'The Alliance', part of the Surviving Southside series,] out-and proud Carmen teams up with oblivious jock Scott to start a gay-straight alliance group after his best friend Jamie is bullied into suicide. The issue is given formulaic packaging, but this hi-lo problem novel is a gap-filler."

GOODMAN, PAUL, 1911-1972. Growing up absurd; Problems of youth in the organized society; [by] Paul Goodman 2012 New York Review Books

1. Capitalism—United States—Social aspects 2. Industries—Social aspects 3. Social criticism 4. United States—Social life & customs—20th century 5. Youth culture—United States
ISBN 9781590175811 paperback

SUMMARY: "Paul Goodman's 'Growing Up Absurd' was a runaway best seller when it was first published in 1960, and it became one of the defining texts of the New Left. . . . For Goodman, the unhappiness of young people was a concentrated form of the unhappiness of American society as a whole, run by corporations that provide employment (if and when they do) but not the kind of meaningful work that engages body and soul." (Publisher's note)

REVIEW: *Commonweal* v140 no18 p33-4 N 15 2013 Nathan Schneider

"Growing Up Absurd." "Nearly everything that Paul Goodman complained about in 'Growing Up Absurd'--his influential critique of 1950s America, originally published in 1960 and recently reissued by New York Review Books--is now worse. . . . This book is above all a thing of its time and place (and gender and race). Goodman did sometimes recognize that the average white man's plight under capitalism was related to his relationship to a social order that excluded too many people, but for the most part 'Growing Up Absurd' keeps the marginalized on the margins."

REVIEW: *New Statesman* v141 no5132 p42-3 N 16 2012 Adam Kirsch

GOODMAN, SUSAN E. How do you burp in space?; and other tips every space tourist needs to know; [by] Susan E. Goodman 80 p. 2013 Bloomsbury Pub. Distributed by Macmillan Publishers

1. Children's literature 2. Interplanetary voyages—Juvenile literature 3. Manned space flight—Juvenile literature 4. Outer space—Juvenile literature 5. Space tourism—Juvenile literature

ISBN 1599900688; 9781599900681 (hardback); 9781599909349 (reinforced)

LC 2011-035303

SUMMARY: In this children's book, author Susan E. Goodman "gives readers who will be the first generation of true space tourists general advice about how to prepare for the trip, what to pack, what food and accommodations will be like, and recreational opportunities both in Earth's orbit and on the moon. She also highlights some hazards, such as drinking carbonated drinks: Burping in microgravity brings up more than just CO2." (Kirkus Reviews)

REVIEW: *Bull Cent Child Books* v67 no1 p20-1 S 2013 E. B.

"How Do You Burp in Space?: And Other Tips Every Space Tourist Needs to Know." "Children's departments are, in general, amply supplied with books on how to become an astronaut NASA-style, and [author Susan E.] Goodman herself has contributed a tide of this variety, 'Ultimate Field Trip 5: Blasting Off to Space Academy'. With the possibility of space tourism on the horizon, it's possible that kids will find extraterrestrial opportunities through pleasure-seeking vacations, not just scientific research. . . . Illustrations (full color to come) are an entertaining blend of astronaut and space photographs, many embellished with cartoon figures that reinterpret them as a tourist experience, such as the space-walking astronaut signaling a cartoon taxi."

REVIEW: *Kirkus Rev* v81 no12 p92 Je 15 2013

REVIEW: *SLJ* v59 no4 p178 Ap 2013 John Peters

GOODWIN, DORIS KEARNS, 1943-. The Bully Pulpit; Theodore Roosevelt, William Howard Taft, and the Golden Age of Journalism; [by] Doris Kearns Goodwin 848 p. 2013 Simon & Schuster

1. Historical literature 2. Journalism—History 3. Press and politics—United States—History—20th century 4. Progressivism (United States politics)—History—20th century 5. Roosevelt, Theodore, 1858-1919 6. Taft, William H. (William Howard), 1857-1930 7. United States—Politics & government—20th century

ISBN 141654786X; 9781416547860

LC 2013-032709

SUMMARY: This book, by Doris Kearns Goodwin, examines "the friendship of two very different Presidents, [Theodore] Roosevelt and William Howard Taft. . . . Though the book is primarily concerned with the intervening private lives of two politicians, a prominent second narrative emerges as Goodwin links both presidents' fortunes to the rise of 'muckraking' journalism, specifically the magazine 'McClure's' and its influence over political and social discussion." (Publishers Weekly)

REVIEW: *Booklist* v110 no6 p10 N 15 2013 Jay Freeman

REVIEW: *Booklist* v110 no9/10 p68 Ja 1 2014 Allan Moores

REVIEW: *Choice* v51 no10 p1873 Je 2014 M. J. Birkner

REVIEW: *Christ Century* v131 no9 p3 Ap 30 2014 John M. Buchanan

REVIEW: *Christ Century* v130 no25 p22 D 11 2013

REVIEW: *Columbia J Rev* v52 no5 p60-1 Ja 2014 JULIA M. KLEIN

"The Bully Pulpit: Theodore Roosevelt, William Howard Taft, and the Golden Age of Journalism". "[Doris Kearns Goodwin] is an assiduous researcher and a lucid writer who dares to tackle seemingly well-worn, subjects like the big game of presidential history. . . . Goodwin's signature talent is to reconfigure the contours of the genre by exploring historically significant relationships. . . . Goodwin's strength is her deep empathy for her subjects. Its fipside is a tendency to sand away hard edges, to endow the past with a gauzily nostalgic glow. The sometimes inept Taft, scorned by history, has never seemed as heroic as he does here. . . . Goodwin has produced a readable testament to the Progressive Era."

REVIEW: *Economist* v409 no8862 p85-6 N 16 2013

"The Bully Pulpit: Theodore Roosevelt and the Golden Age of Journalism". "This sophisticated, character-driven book tells two big stories. . . . The book is a striking reminder that the Republican Party was once the more progressive of America's two political parties. . . . Despite its great length—and the occasional sense that this in fact might be two books, rather than one—this is a fascinating work, even a timely one. . . . It captures the way a political party can be destroyed by factionalism, and it shows the important role investigative journalists play in political life."

REVIEW: *Kirkus Rev* v81 no21 p237 N 1 2013

REVIEW: *Libr J* v138 no9 p54 My 15 2013 Barbara Hoffert

REVIEW: *Libr J* v139 no2 p46 F 1 2014 Forrest E. Link

REVIEW: *Libr J* v138 no21 p110 D 1 2013 William D. Pederson

REVIEW: *N Y Rev Books* v61 no3 p28-30 F 20 2014 Susan Dunn

"The Bully Pulpit: Theodore Roosevelt, William Howard Taft, and the Golden Age of Journalism". "Doris Kearns Goodwin's exuberant new book . . . offers a sprawling panorama centered for the most part on TR, the reformer in the White House, whom she portrays . . . as an inspired crusader. . . . Goodwin is a superb storyteller, an author of fascinating narratives that are rich in hard-won detail, though 'The Bully Pulpit' offers no distinctive interpretation of Roosevelt and his era. . . . Ultimately more transformative than Theodore Roosevelt's reforms were his personality, his energy, and, as Goodwin shows, his seizing of the bully pulpit that prepared the political landscape for expansive new concepts of government, rights, and community."

REVIEW: *N Y Times Book Rev* p34 N 24 2013

REVIEW: *N Y Times Book Rev* p28 O 5 2014 IHSAN TAYLOR

REVIEW: *N Y Times Book Rev* p1-21 N 17 2013 Bill Keller

REVIEW: *New Repub* v244 no24 p39-45 Mr 24 2014 Jackson Lears

"The Bully Pulpit: Theodore Roosevelt, William Howard Taft, and the Golden Age of Journalism." "The most popular . . . version of progressive reform . . . puts Theodore Roosevelt at the center of events. . . . This is the story retold by Doris Kearns Goodwin in her thoroughly mediocre book. . . . On this view, progressive reform was commanded by metropolitan elites with a sense of noblesse oblige. . . . This sprawling book is very much a Washington insider's view of the Progressive Era. Progressivism, in Goodwin's account, is a movement made by Big Men—Presidents Roosevelt and Taft, accompanied by a retinue of senators, congressmen, and judges. . . . Despite its bulk, Goodwin's book tells us next to nothing about the cultural and social setting of progressive political struggles."

REVIEW: *New York Times* v163 no56318 pC1-2 N 12 2013 MICHIKO KAKUTANI

REVIEW: *New Yorker* v89 no37 p78-1 N 18 2013

GOODYEAR, DANA. Anything that moves; renegade chefs, fearless eaters, and the making of a new American food culture; [by] Dana Goodyear 272 p. 2013 Riverhead Books, a member of Penguin Group (USA) Inc.

1. COOKING—Essays 2. Cooking—Social aspects—United States 3. Cooks—United States 4. Extremists—United States 5. Food—Social aspects—United States 6. Food habits—United States 7. Gourmets—United States 8. SOCIAL SCIENCE—Popular Culture 9. Social science literature

ISBN 1594488371; 9781594488375 (hardback)

LC 2013-025054

SUMMARY: Author Dana Goodyear's book is "an attempt to understand the implications of the way we eat. This is a universe populated by insect-eaters and blood drinkers, avant-garde chefs who make food out of roadside leaves and wood, and others who serve endangered species and Schedule I drugs--a cast of characters, in other words, who flirt with danger, taboo, and disgust in pursuit of the sublime." The book is a "look into the raucous, strange, fascinatingly complex world of contemporary American food culture, and the places where the extreme is bleeding into the mainstream." (Publisher's note)

REVIEW: *Atlantic* v312 no4 p40-4 N 2013 LAURA SHAPIRO DANA GOODYEAR

"Anything That Moves: Renegade Chefs, Fearless Eaters, and the Making of a New American Food Culture." "[Dana Goodyear]'s a wonderfully engaging writer and a first-rate reporter. . . . 'Anything That Moves' is a chronicle of what she calls 'extreme foodie-ism"--today's culinary quest for the forbidden, the unexplored, the offmenu, and the occasionally toxic. . . . If Goodyear was ever tempted to step back and dismiss any of this activity as the culinary equivalent of gathering at Stonehenge to look for druids, there's no sign of such doubts. She takes these cooks and eaters at their word; they represent 'a new American food culture' forging its way toward the mainstream. . . . The mainstream, however, seems awfully removed from a lot of what's going on in this movement."

REVIEW: *Booklist* v110 no4 p8 O 15 2013 Mark Knoblauch

REVIEW: *Kirkus Rev* v81 no15 p193 Ag 1 2013

REVIEW: *Kirkus Rev* p24 Ag 15 2013 Fall Preview

REVIEW: *N Y Rev Books* v60 no20 p65-6 D 19 2013 Jason Epstein

REVIEW: *N Y Times Book Rev* p26 D 15 2013 THOMAS McNAMEE

REVIEW: *New York Times* v163 no56314 pC23-6 N 8 2013 DWIGHT GARNER

GOODYEAR, FRANK H. A president in Yellowstone; the Frank Jay Haynes photographic album of Chester Arthur's 1883 expedition; [by] Frank H. Goodyear 147 p. 2013 University of Oklahoma Press

1. Historical literature 2. Photographs 3. Presidents—Travel—Yellowstone National Park—History—19th century—Pictorial works 4. Presidents—United States—Biography—Pictorial works

ISBN 9780806143552 (hardcover : alk. paper)

LC 2012-036675

SUMMARY: This book, written by Frank H. Goodyear III, recounts how "On the morning of July 30, 1883, President Chester A. Arthur embarked on a trip of historic proportions. His destination was Yellowstone National Park. . . . Also slated to join the expedition was a young photographer, Frank Jay Haynes. This elegant--and fascinating--book showcases Haynes's remarkable photographic album from their six-week journey." (Publisher's note)

REVIEW: *Choice* v51 no4 p624-5 D 2013 P. D. Thomas

"A President in Yellowstone: The F. Jay Haynes Photographic Album of Chester Arthur's 1883 Expedition." "This handsomely published, attractively illustrated, and engaging volume ostensibly presents a photographic record of President Chester Arthur's 1883 odyssey in Yellowstone, but it presents as well an incisive review of the politics and competing economic interests that sought to essentially privatize Yellowstone. . . . It also provides insight into Arthur's aversion to reporters, which led General Philip Sheridan to suggest that Frank Jay Haynes accompany the party as a photographer. Haynes took the 104 photographs that appear in this album, using a large-format camera that produced 8 x 10 inch negatives and a smaller stereograph camera."

GORDIS, DANIEL. Menachem Begin: the battle for Israel's soul; [by] Daniel Gordis 320 p. 2014 Nextbook; Schocken

1. Biography (Literary form) 2. Prime ministers—Israel—Biography 3. Revisionist Zionists—Israel—Biography

ISBN 9780805243123

LC 2013-023333

SUMMARY: In this biography of Menachem Begin, Daniel Gordis "re-examines the controversial Israeli leader in order 'to look at his life through the lens of the passion he still evokes'. . . . Begin . . . committed himself to two basic ideas: the Jews must have their own state; independence required military strength. . . . Gordis delineates the fierce controversies within the Zionist communities and focuses especially on the rivalry between Begin and David Ben-Gurion." (Kirkus Reviews)

REVIEW: *Commentary* v137 no4 p54-6 Ap 2014 STEPHEN DAISLEY

REVIEW: *Kirkus Rev* v81 no24 p73 D 15 2013

"Menachem Begin: The Battle for Israel's Soul". "[Daniel] Gordis delineates the fierce controversies within the Zionist communities and focuses especially on the rivalry between Begin and David Ben-Gurion, a battle between Begin's 'romantic preoccupation' with Jewish victimization and Ben-Gurion's pragmatic belief that Israel needed to move beyond the past. . . . For Gordis, Begin stands as an exemplary leader whose selflessness and deep loyalty to the Jewish people and to Israel should inspire any who may question "the legitimacy of love for a specific people or devotion to its ancestral homeland."

REVIEW: *Libr J* v138 no16 p58 O 1 2013 Barbara Hoffert

REVIEW: *Natl Rev* v66 no5 p40-1 Mr 24 2014 DAVID G. DALIN

"Menachem Begin: The Battle for Israel's Soul." "In this immensely thoughtful and nuanced new biography, Daniel Gordis . . . reflects on Begin's enduring contribution to the State of Israel. . . . In his very balanced discussion of Begin's involvement in . . . controversial military actions against the British, Gordis analyzes the emerging political rivalry between Begin and David Ben-Gurion. . . . This book is beautifully written and insightful, and demonstrates conclusively that Menachem Begin was, together with Ben-Gurion, one of the two most important and influential of Israel's founders. . . . It is an important contribution to contemporary scholarship about the political history of the modern Jewish state."

REVIEW: *Publ Wkly* v260 no48 p40-1 N 25 2013

GORDON, AMY. Painting the rainbow; [by] Amy Gordon 169 p. 2014 Holiday House

1. Cousins—Fiction 2. Family life—New Hampshire—Fiction 3. Family problems—Fiction 4. Friendship—Fiction 5. Historical fiction 6. Japanese Americans—Evacuation and relocation, 1942-1945—Fiction 7. Secrets—Fiction

ISBN 9780823425259 (hardcover)

LC 2013-020999

SUMMARY: This book follows "two young cousins . . . during a fraught vacation at their family's lake house . . . overshadowed by the mystery of their uncle's long-ago death. Cousins Holly Swanson and Ivy Greenwood have very different personalities, but that has never mattered before. During the summers, they've always been inseparable. But this summer of 1965, with Ivy's parents fighting more than ever and Holly showing interest in local boys, they can't seem to find any common ground." (Kirkus Reviews)

REVIEW: *Booklist* v110 no16 p61 Ap 15 2014 Courtney Jones

REVIEW: *Bull Cent Child Books* v67 no11 p574-5 Jl/Ag 2014 A. A.

REVIEW: *Kirkus Rev* v82 no5 p141 Mr 1 2014

"Painting the Rainbow". "Mixing diary entries and letters into the narrative, [Amy] Gordon delivers a sweet albeit convenient story about familial rupture and healing. The cast of characters is well-imagined, and the plot is infused with the inevitable repercussions of history, both immediate and those of a more global nature. However, events are repeatedly too advantageous to be ultimately satisfying. Hidden diaries, letters and pictures are discovered with alarming regularity. Perhaps acknowledging this narrative ease, the publisher recommends this book for ages 8-12, but the girls' dawning understanding of the complex world of adulthood pushes it a little older. A story about a tumultuous family that lacks a certain element of hardship needed to make a book truly gripping."

REVIEW: *SLJ* v60 no3 p139 Mr 2014 Marie Orlando

GORDON, DAVID.il. Motor dog. See Cyrus, K.

GORDON, EDWARD E. Future jobs; solving the employment and skills crisis; [by] Edward E. Gordon 203 p. 2013 Praeger

1. Economics literature 2. Education—United States 3. Labor market—United States 4. Manpower policy—United States 5. Occupations—United States—Forecasting 6. Skilled labor—United States

ISBN 9781440829338 (hardcopy : alk. paper)

LC 2013-027612

SUMMARY: This book by Edward E. Gordon "offers an economic and historical perspective on the evolution of jobs and careers, explains how technology has permanently altered the U.S. job/labor market, and provides practical information for businesses seeking qualified workers, educators preparing students for careers, unemployed or underemployed individuals, and those interested in changing careers." (Publisher's note)

REVIEW: *Choice* v51 no6 p1057 F 2014 G. E. Kaupins

"Future Jobs: Solving the Employment and Skills Crisis." "[Edward E.] Gordon, a business consultant, examines how the US can reduce workforce skills shortages by offering comprehensive regional solutions. In the book's first part, he discusses jobs that will be in high demand in the digital age, including science, technology, engineering, and math (STEM) occupations along with research and development, information technology, operations, management, and sales. Gordon also addresses issues contributing to labor shortages, such as baby boomer retirements, fixation on short-term profits, educational mediocrity, the high school dropout rate, and an increasing gap between worker skills and job requirements. . . . Recommended."

GORDON, GUS.il. Herman and Rosie. See Gordon, G.

GORDON, GUS. Herman and Rosie; 32 p. 2013 Roaring Brook Press

1. Crocodiles—Fiction 2. Deer—Fiction 3. Friendship—Fiction 4. Jazz—Fiction 5. Loneliness—Fiction 6. Picture books for children

ISBN 1596438568; 9781596438569 (hardcover: alk. paper)

LC 2012-037557

SUMMARY: In author Gus Gordon's book, "once upon a time in a very busy city, on a very busy street, in two very small apartments, lived...Herman and Rosie. Herman liked playing the oboe, the smell of hot dogs in the winter, and watching films about the ocean. Rosie liked pancakes, listening to old jazz records, and watching films about the ocean. They both loved the groovy rhythm of the city, but sometimes the bustling crowds and constant motion left them lonely, until one night" something happens. (Publisher's note)

REVIEW: *Booklist* v110 no3 p53 O 1 2013 Ann Kelley

"Herman and Rosie". "There are so many great New York love stories, and here's another. . . . This Australian picture book doesn't skimp on fantastic details. . . . [Gus] Gordon's heavily lined characters and collage backgrounds give rise to the vibrant Big Apple, populated by all species and anchored by two endearing artistic types. The illustrations include scenes depicted on postcards as the duo moves around the city, maps of their wanderings, and even a page comprised entirely of neon signs . , , that light up the night sky. Not since Petra Mathers' 'Sophie and Lou' (1991) has a picture book, the arts, and romance converged so charmingly."

REVIEW: *Bull Cent Child Books* v67 no4 p211-2 D 2013

J. H.

REVIEW: *Kirkus Rev* v81 no16 p166 Ag 15 2013

REVIEW: *N Y Times Book Rev* p15 D 22 2013 SARAH HARRISON SMITH

"Herman and Rosie," "Frog Trouble: Deluxe Songbook," "Never Play Music Right Next to the Zoo." "Music is the food of love for Herman, a crocodile who plays oboe, and his neighbor Rosie, a doe who sings jazz at the Mangy Hound. . . . You might have been so distracted by [author Sandra] Boynton's prolific literary production that you missed her musical endeavors . . . In 'Frog Trouble,' she illustrates 12 witty children's country songs with pictures of the adorably smiley animals who ostensibly sing them. . . . In [author John] Lithgow's zany and toe-tapping song, illustrated with comic abandon by [illustrated by Leeza] Hernandez, all sorts of unexpected things happen when a boy and his family attend an outdoor concert at a city zoo."

REVIEW: *Publ Wkly* p52 Children's starred review annual 2013

REVIEW: *Publ Wkly* v260 no31 p69 Ag 5 2013

REVIEW: *SLJ* v59 no10 p1 O 2013 Miriam Lang Budin

GORDON, PETER E.ed. Weimar thought. See Weimar thought

GORDON, ROBERT. Respect yourself; Stax Records and the soul explosion; [by] Robert Gordon 480 p. 2013 Bloomsbury

1. Historical literature 2. Music & race 3. Music industry—History

ISBN 1596915773; 9781596915770 (alk. paper)

LC 2013-014533

SUMMARY: This book by Robert Gordon on the history of Stax Records "situat[es] the story of Stax within the cultural history of the 1960s in the South. . . . Gordon . . . narrates the stories of the many musicians who called Stax home, from . . . Otis Redding to Isaac Hayes, Sam and Dave, and the Staples Singers, as well as the creative marketing and promotional strategies. . . . By the early 1970s, bad business decisions and mangled personal relationships shuttered the doors of Stax." (Publishers Weekly)

REVIEW: *Bookforum* v20 no3 p57 S-N 2013 DOUGLAS WOLK

"Respect Yourself: Stax Records and the Soul Explosion." "That's a compelling story, and Robert Gordon's well placed to tell it. . . . Despite 'Respect Yourself's subtitle, there's not much here about Stax's sound in the context of the '60s and '70s 'soul explosion'. . . . Where Gordon digs deeper, though, is the story of the people behind Stax. . . . There's a natural temptation, when an institution that used to be good heads downhill, to find some outside force to blame. It's reasonable to argue that the disastrous disorganization of Union Planters or the devouring capitalism of CBS or the pervasive racism of Memphis had a little, or a lot, to do with why Stax failed, and Gordon gives space to all of those arguments, as well as taking some carefully honed jabs at Johnny Baylor."

REVIEW: *Booklist* v110 no5 p21 N 1 2013 June Sawyers

REVIEW: *Kirkus Rev* v81 no19 p95 O 1 2013

REVIEW: *Libr J* v139 no2 p77 F 1 2014 Barry Zaslow

REVIEW: *N Y Times Book Rev* p62-3 D 8 2013 ELSA DIXLER

"Respect Yourself: Stax Records and the Soul Explosion." "[Robert] Gordon . . . profiles singers, songwriters and producers. But he has also written a social history, viewing the company that for more than 15 years produced some of the most popular and important music in American as part of the history of Memphis and of the civil rights movement. . . . Gordon presents this complicated story clearly, teasing out the various details of the business and of personal relationships. . . . The voices of the members of the Stax family, and Gordon's deep knowledge of Memphis, give this book a significance that extends beyond a single recording studio."

REVIEW: *Publ Wkly* v260 no36 p49-50 S 9 2013

REVIEW: *Va Q Rev* v90 no2 p207-11 Spr 2014 Preston Lauterbach

GORDON, STEPHEN G. Expressing the inner wild; tattoos, piercings, jewelry, and other body art; [by] Stephen G. Gordon 56 p. 2014 Twenty-First Century Books

1. Beauty, Personal—Juvenile literature 2. Body marking—Juvenile literature 3. Fashion—Juvenile literature 4. Jewelry—Juvenile literature 5. Social science literature 6. Tattooing—Juvenile literature

ISBN 1467714674; 9781467714679 (lib. bdg. : alk. paper)

LC 2013-011192

SUMMARY: Author Stephen G. Gordon presents information "about all the amazing ways people around the globe and across the centuries have been creatively transforming their hair, lips, fingers, toes, eyelashes, ears . . . with jewelry, makeup, inks, piercings, and other decorations. From African tribal body paint to ear plugs, tattoo pantyhose, and nail art for guys." (Publisher's note)

REVIEW: *Booklist* v110 no9/10 p82 Ja 1 2014 J. B. Petty

REVIEW: *Bull Cent Child Books* v67 no7 p359 Mr 2014 E. B.

"Expressing the Inner Wild: Tattoos, Piercings, Jewelry, and Other Body Art." "Discussion is neatly organized, but coverage never expands beyond brief observations into substantive explorations. Topics appear to be limited to body art that spans a significant time range, and thus scarification makes the cut (so to say), while other permanent modifications such as foot-binding and skullshaping, which have passed into history, do not. Readers who get beyond browsing the striking color photographs will probably recognize that this slim volume isn't going to delve into the embellishment of human civilization, but it might lead to further reading on a newly whetted interest."

REVIEW: *SLJ* v60 no2 p124 F 2014 Lindsay Klemas

GORDY, ERIC. Guilt, responsibility, and denial; the past at stake in post-Milošević Serbia; [by] Eric Gordy xv, 256 p. 2013 University of Pennsylvania Press

1. Social science literature 2. Yugoslav War, 1991-1995—Serbia—Influence

ISBN 0812245350 (hardcover: alk. paper); 9780812245356 (hardcover: alk. paper)

LC 2013-011474

SUMMARY: This book "sets out to trace the political, social, and moral challenges that Serbia faced from 2000 onward, offering an . . . account of what was demanded of the country's citizens as well its political leadership—and how these challenges were alternately confronted and ignored.

Eric Gordy makes extensive use of Serbian media to capture the internal debate surrounding the legacy of the country's war crimes." (Publisher's note)

REVIEW: *Choice* v51 no9 p1676-7 My 2014 W. R. Pruitt

"Guilt, Responsibility, and Denial: The Past at Stake in Post-Milošević Serbia". "[Eric] Gordy . . . has compiled an uneven assessment of post-Milosevic Serbia. . . . Unfortunately, the work never seems to find its voice or its purpose. The book is said to be organized by 'moments' and 'non-moments,' though distinguishing what these terms mean or why one event is a moment and another a non-moment is nigh impossible. While using social media and online discussion boards as evidence may appeal to the lay reader, it does little to engage in a theoretical explanation of post-Milosevic Serbia. . . . However, this book may still appeal to those with a specific interest in Serbia or its rebuilding after Milosevic's regime finally was stopped."

GORMAN, HUGH S. The story of N; a social history of the nitrogen cycle and the challenge of sustainability; [by] Hugh S. Gorman xiii, 241 p. 2012 Rutgers University Press

1. Environmental literature 2. Historical literature 3. Nature—Effect of human beings on 4. Nitrogen—Environmental aspects 5. Nitrogen cycle 6. Nitrogen fertilizers 7. Nitrogen in agriculture 8. Sustainable development

ISBN 0813554381; 9780813554389 (hardcover : alk. paper); 9780813554396 (e-book)

LC 2012-009901

SUMMARY: In this book, author Hugh S. "Gorman analyzes the notion of sustainability from a fresh perspective--the integration of human activities with the biogeochemical cycling of nitrogen--and provides a supportive alternative to studying sustainability through the lens of climate change and the cycling of carbon." (Publisher's note)

REVIEW: *Choice* v51 no1 p98 S 2013 T. R. Blackburn

"The Story of N: A Social History of the Nitrogen Cycle and the Challenge of Sustainability." "This piquantly titled monograph, part of the 'Studies in Modern Science, Technology, and the Environment' series, views human history as a function of the growing ability of agriculture to sustain large populations. [Author Hugh S.] Gorman . . . traces the evolution of the decreasing ratio of farmers to urbanites as farmers learned to supply crops with 'fixed' (in forms other than the unreactive gaseous element) nitrogen, thus greatly increasing the food-producing efficiency of farming. . . . A well-written, well-documented, and fascinating work, accessible to laypersons and useful to students and professionals."

GOSCILO, HELENA.ed. Baba Yaga. See Baba Yaga

GOTT, TED. Gorilla; [by] Ted Gott 232 p. 2013 University of Chicago Press

1. Apes in art 2. Apes in literature 3. Gorilla 4. Human-animal relationships 5. Natural history literature

ISBN 178023029X; 9781780230290

SUMMARY: In this book, Ted Gott and Kathryn Weir "describe how early European observations of gorillas in their native Africa were the genesis of literary and artistic representations such as King Kong. At the same time, gorillas became symbolic of sexuality and subconscious, uncontrolled urges, and influenced theories of criminality. It was not until Dian Fossey's research in the 1960s and 1970s that many misconceptions about the gorilla--specially their violence--were dispelled." (Publisher's note)

REVIEW: *TLS* no5772 p26 N 15 2013 BARBARA J. KING

"Gorilla" and "Monkey." "Primates feature in two new volumes from Reaktion Books' Animal series. . . . Gorgeously illustrated, both books convey fascinating information about some of our closest relatives, but 'Gorilla' is by far the more successful endeavour. . . . The selection of two art experts . . . to write a book about apes does have its drawbacks. Short shrift is given to fieldwork on gorillas . . . By contrast, chapters that focus on the use of the gorilla in visual media convey stunningly how these apes have been persistently co-opted by those in power to vilify persons or social groups considered marginal or inferior. . . . The same is true for many monkeys, and a strength of Desmond Morris's 'Monkey' is his unsettling portrayal of how thoroughly our own primate species is willing to exploit its near relatives."

GOTTFREDSON, FLOYD. Walt Disney's Mickey Mouse color Sundays. See Walt Disney's Mickey Mouse color Sundays

GOTTLIEB, RICHARD.ed. The Complete Directory for People With Chronic Illness 2013/14. See The Complete Directory for People With Chronic Illness 2013/14

GOULET, MARY ELLEN. Reveille in Hot Springs; The Battle to Save Our VA; [by] Mary Ellen Goulet 236 p. 2013 CreateSpace Independent Publishing Platform

1. Hot Springs (S.D.) 2. Medical care of veterans—United States 3. United States. Dept. of Veterans Affairs 4. Veterans—Mental health services 5. Veterans' hospitals—United States

ISBN 1484053982; 9781484053980

SUMMARY: This book presents "a series of short testimonies by U.S. military veterans about their treatment at a Hot Springs, S.D., veterans facility. Freelance writer [Mary Ellen] Goulet gathered this collection primarily as a reaction to the U.S. government's announced decision in December 2011 to close the veterans hospital in Hot Springs and pull the plug on its good works. The shutdown would require veterans to seek help hours away without reimbursement of travel expenses." (Kirkus Reviews)

REVIEW: *Kirkus Rev* v81 no24 p242 D 15 2013

"Reveille in Hot Springs: The Battle to Save Our VA". "A series of short testimonies by U.S. military veterans about their treatment at a Hot Springs, S.D., veterans facility. Freelance writer [Mary Ellen] Goulet gathered this collection primarily as a reaction to the U.S. government's announced decision in December 2011 to close the veterans hospital in Hot Springs and pull the plug on its good works. . . . Each of the vignettes is brief—typically five pages or so—but harrowing. Goulet often lets the veterans speak for themselves about their war experiences and their profound aftereffects. . . . The author fashions the veterans' words into engaging narratives without overpolishing them, giving a rattling, unvarnished rawness to the material."

GOVENAR, ALAN. Deep Ellum; the other side of Dallas;

[by] Alan Govenar x, 307 p. 2013 Texas A&M University Press

1. African Americans—Texas—Dallas—Music—History and criticism 2. Historical literature 3. Popular music—Texas—Dallas—History and criticism

ISBN 1603449582 (pbk. : alk. paper); 9781603449588 (pbk. : alk. paper)

LC 2012-041446

SUMMARY: This book on the Deep Ellum district of Dallas, Texas "strips away layers of myth to illuminate the cultural milieu that spawned such seminal blues and jazz musicians as Blind Lemon Jefferson, Buster Smith, and T-Bone Walker and that was also an incubator for the growth of western swing. Expanding upon the original 1998 publication," this "edition offers new research on Deep Ellum's vital cross-fertilization of white and black musical styles." (Publisher's note)

REVIEW: *Choice* v51 no6 p1013-4 F 2014 D.-R. de Lerma

"Deep Ellum: The Other Side of Dallas." "The book is lavishly illustrated . . . with photographs, record labels, and newspaper advertisements, all of which support an engaging text. What particularly justifies this second edition are the 50 pages of disciplined discography with labels, dates, and personnel of those 78 rpm discs from Brunswick, Columbia, Victor, and Vocalion that gave sonoric documentation to the work of so many individuals from earlier days who had connections with Dallas history. . . . Recommended"

THE GOVERNMENT AND POLITICS OF THE MIDDLE EAST AND NORTH AFRICA; 2014 Westview Press

1. Africa, North—Foreign relations 2. Africa, North—Politics & government 3. Middle East—Foreign relations 4. Middle East—Politics & government 5. Political science literature

ISBN 9780813348650 (pbk.); 9780813348667 (e-book)

LC 2013-012742

SUMMARY: This book, edited by Mark Gasiorowski, David E. Long and Bernard Reich, "provide[s] . . . coverage of the domestic politics and foreign policies of all countries in [the Middle East and North Africa.] . . . Specialists contribute authoritative overviews of the government and politics of each country using a common framework to create consistency throughout the book, examining each country's historical background, political environment, political structure and dynamics, and foreign policy." (Publisher's note)

REVIEW: *Choice* v51 no6 p982-3 F 2014 D. Altschiller

"The Government and Politics of the Middle East and North Africa." "First published in 1980, this title, now in its seventh edition . . . contains updated and revised information and includes a few new contributors. . . .Written by academic specialists, the lucidly written chapters include helpful bibliographies (some are annotated). The index is well organized. Since many parts of the Middle East are undergoing major upheavals, the narrative sections on recent trends are already dated in some cases (Syria, Libya, Egypt, Tunisia). Nevertheless, this anthology provides useful background and ready-reference information."

GOWNLEY, JIMMY. The dumbest idea ever!; [by] Jimmy Gownley 240 p. 2014 Graphix / Scholastic

1. Cartoonists 2. Catholic schools 3. Chickenpox 4. Graphic nonfiction 5. High school students

ISBN 0545453461; 9780545453462; 9780545453479

LC 2013-939128

SUMMARY: In this juvenile graphic novel memoir, by Jimmy Gownley, "at thirteen, Jimmy was popular, at the top of his class, and the leading scorer on his basketball team. But . . . when chicken pox forced him to miss the championship game . . . , he got pneumonia and missed . . . school. Before Jimmy knew it, his grades were sinking and nothing seemed to be going right. How would Jimmy turn things around, get back on top at school, and maybe even get a date with the cutest girl in school?" (Publisher's note)

REVIEW: *Booklist* v110 no8 p34 D 15 2013 Francisa Goldsmith

REVIEW: *Horn Book Magazine* v90 no2 p142 Mr/Ap 2014 SAM BLOOM

"The Dumbest Idea Ever!." "Eventually--with a great deal of support from his parents, Catholic school friends, and girlfriend Ellen--Jimmy published his first graphic novel when he was fifteen, and the rest is history. The cherub-faced, clean-living teens aren't the most scintillating characters; however, Jimmy is a likable (if 'big-headed') kid, and the visuals are strong. [Jimmy] Gownley's art is clean and simple. The overall feel is similar to that of old Archie comics: entertaining, but not much going on under the surface. That likely won't deter tween readers, who will fall for--and possibly try to emulate--Gownley's story."

REVIEW: *Kirkus Rev* v81 no23 p187 D 1 2013

REVIEW: *Publ Wkly* v260 no49 p87 D 2 2013

REVIEW: *SLJ* v60 no5 p122 My 2014 Kiera Parrott

GRABENSTEIN, CHRIS. Treasure hunters. See Treasure hunters

GRABNER, SABINE.ed. Orient & Occident. See Orient & Occident

GRABOWSKI, JAN. Hunt for the Jews; betrayal and murder in German-occupied Poland; [by] Jan Grabowski 320 p. 2013 Indiana University Press

1. Historical literature 2. Holocaust, Jewish (1939-1945)—Poland—Dąbrowa Tarnowska (Powiat) 3. Jews—Poland—Dąbrowa Tarnowska (Powiat)—History—20th century 4. World War, 1939-1945—Collaborationists

ISBN 9780253010742 (cl : alk. paper); 9780253010872 (eb)

LC 2013-012259

SUMMARY: This book by Jan Grabowski looks at "the Nazi hunt for Jews (Judenjagd) in Dabrowa Tarnowska, a rural county in southeastern Poland, where a majority of the Jews, both neighbors and refugees fleeing the ghettos of Poland, went into hiding, and where many of them perished as a consequence of betrayal by their Polish neighbors." (Choice: Current Reviews for Academic Libraries)

REVIEW: *Choice* v51 no7 p1284-5 Mr 2014 J. Fischel

"Hunt for the Jews: Betrayal and Murder in German-Occupied Poland." "[Jan] Grabowski is unrelenting in describing how, between 1942 and 1945, Jews were hunted down by the Polish 'blue' police, whose treatment of Jews matched that of their German counterparts. . . . One concludes from Grabowski's important study that without the often unforced, and sometimes enthusiastic, support of non-German volunteers and helpers, the Germans would not have succeeded as completely as they did during the Holocaust. . . . Recomended."

REVIEW: *Kirkus Rev* v81 no16 p138 Ag 15 2013

GRADY, FRANK.ed. Answerable style. See Answerable style

GRAEDON, ALENA. The word exchange; a novel; [by] Alena Graedon 384 p. 2014 Doubleday

1. Missing persons—Fiction 2. Speculative fiction 3. Technology—Fiction 4. Transmission of texts—Fiction 5. Young women—Fiction

ISBN 0385537654; 9780385537650 (hardback)

LC 2013-033165

SUMMARY: This book "explores a near-future America that's shifted almost exclusively to smart technologies, where print is only a nostalgia. . . . Anana Johnson works closely with her . . . father Doug, a famous lexicographer, at the North American Dictionary of the English Language. But when Doug goes missing, what once seemed like a luddite's quaint conspiracy theory takes on new plausibility . . . as the city quickly falls victim to a fast-spreading 'word flu' virus." (Publishers Weekly)

REVIEW: *Booklist* v110 no13 p23 Mr 1 2014 Keir Graff

"The Word Exchange". "What if we became so dependent on our gadgets that we lost our ability to speak? That's the big idea in [Alena] Graedon's entertainingly scary debut, a bibliothriller of epidemic proportions. . . . Graedon's fears about technology are clearly evident. There are a few stutters in the structure and pacing, but this is a remarkable first novel, combining a vividly imagined future with the fondly remembered past to offer a chilling prediction of where our unthinking reliance on technology is leading us. And, as you'd expect, Graedon's word choice is exquisite."

REVIEW: *Kirkus Rev* v82 no5 p293 Mr 1 2014

REVIEW: *N Y Times Book Rev* p19 My 4 2014 LIESL SCHILLINGER

GRAEGIN, STEPHANIE.il. You were the first. See You were the first

GRAFTON, SUE, 1940-. W is for wasted; [by] Sue Grafton 496 p. 2013 A Marian Wood Book/Putnam

1. FICTION—Mystery & Detective—General 2. FICTION—Mystery & Detective—Women Sleuths 3. Homeless persons—Fiction 4. Millhone, Kinsey (Fictitious character)—Fiction 5. Women private investigators—Fiction

ISBN 0399158987; 9780399158988 (hardback)

LC 2013-019292

SUMMARY: In this book, by Sue Grafton, two dead bodies are found. "The first was a local PI of suspect reputation. The other was on the beach six weeks later. A slip of paper with [detective Kinsey] Millhone's name and number was in his pants pocket. As Kinsey digs deeper into the mystery of the John Doe, some very strange linkages begin to emerge. And before long at least one aspect is solved as Kinsey literally finds the key to his identity." (Publisher's note)

REVIEW: *Booklist* v109 no22 p43-4 Ag 1 2013 Stephanie Zvirin

REVIEW: *Kirkus Rev* v81 no15 p190 Ag 1 2013

REVIEW: *Libr J* v138 no14 p94 S 1 2013 Linda Oliver

REVIEW: *Libr J* v138 no21 p54 D 1 2013 Joyce Kessel

REVIEW: *N Y Times Book Rev* p17 S 22 2013 MARILYN STASIO

"W is for Wasted," "Then We Take Berlin," and "Seven For a Secret." "A painstaking plot wrangler, [Sue] Grafton carefully merges both narratives in a sad but satisfying conclusion. The problems arise from her efforts to work Kinsey's personal history into the story. . . . John Lawton's stylish spy thriller . . . is a splendid introduction to John Wilfrid (Wilderness) Holderness. . . . Timothy Wilde, who rescued child prostitutes in Lyndsay Faye's rip-roaring novel 'The Gods of Gothan' returns in 'Seven for a Secret' as the protector of lovely Lucy Adams, who lost her family to slave catchers."

REVIEW: *Publ Wkly* v260 no48 p49 N 25 2013

REVIEW: *Publ Wkly* v260 no27 p65 Jl 8 2013

GRAHAM, BOB.il. The silver button. See Graham, B.

GRAHAM, BOB. The silver button; [by] Bob Graham 32 p. 2013 Candlewick Press

1. Children's stories 2. Cities & towns—Juvenile literature 3. Everyday life 4. Time—Juvenile literature 5. Urban life—Juvenile fiction

ISBN 0763664375; 9780763664374

LC 2012-947825

SUMMARY: In this book, by Bob Graham, "at the same moment that Jodie's baby brother takes his first step, a city's worth of moments unfold. From an ordinary scene of an apartment strewn with child's artwork and toys to a bird's-eye view of a city morning pulsing with life, Bob Graham celebrates a whole world-vision in a single moment, encouraging readers to stop, observe, and savor the world around them." (Publisher's note)

REVIEW: *Booklist* v110 no2 p73 S 15 2013 Ilene Cooper

REVIEW: *Bull Cent Child Books* v67 no3 p154 N 2013 T. A.

"The Silver Button." "[Author and illustrator Bob] Graham, always a gentle observer of the quotidian, regales audiences with a steadily zooming-out cross-section of city life to illustrate the millions of events packed into a minute. Graham's prose is both simple and quietly lyrical . . . , with a focused present tense that enhances the book's encapsulation of a moment, while his signature line and watercolor illustrations with their gentle hues and rounded features enhance the tenderness of this tale. The richly packed cityscapes and scenes of Jodie's apartment . . . alternate with panels that focus on the connections that are continually occurring between people at any given time."

REVIEW: *Kirkus Rev* v81 no15 p303 Ag 1 2013

REVIEW: *Publ Wkly* v260 no35 p59 S 2 2013

REVIEW: *Publ Wkly* p54 Children's starred review annual 2013

REVIEW: *SLJ* v59 no9 p120 S 2013 Amy Lilien-Harper

REVIEW: *SLJ* v60 no2 p30 F 2014 Brenda Dales

GRAHAM, JORIE, 1950-. Place; new poems; [by] Jorie Graham 79 p. 2012 Ecco

1. American poetry 2. Environmental protection 3. Nature—Poetry 4. Parenthood 5. Poems—Collections
ISBN 0062190644; 9780062190642

SUMMARY: This is "[Jorie] Graham's 12th book" and "continues in the . . . vein of her recent politically and environmentally concerned collections . . . , but adds a powerful thread about a parent's apprehension that her child has grown and is inheriting the (broken) world. . . . For Graham, life's most powerful experience may be ambivalence, as in competing passions, which becomes a startling kind of abundance." (Publishers Weekly)

REVIEW: *Economist* v405 no8814 p86 D 8 2012

REVIEW: *N Y Rev Books* v59 no14 p64-5 S 27 2012 Dan Chiasson

REVIEW: *Publ Wkly* p34 My 21 2012

REVIEW: *TLS* no5763 p22 S 13 2013 OLI HAZZARD

"The Taken-Down God" and "P L A C E." "'The Taken Down God' is Jorie Graham's second volume of selected poems . . . and includes work from five collections. . . . Its judicious selection from these books provides a comprehensive introduction to Graham's development over the past fifteen years, and in some ways represents a useful way in which to encounter a poet whose work can be uneven--a characteristic that is perhaps inseparable from her salutary desire for continual change. . . .'I was a hard thing to undo', she writes . . . and it is with this declaration in mind that Jorie Graham's ambitious, densely tangled work should be approached. It rewards the effort."

GRAHAM, JORIE, 1950-. The Taken-Down God; Selected Poems 1997-2008; [by] Jorie Graham 144 p. 2013 Carcanet Press Ltd

1. American poetry 2. Language & languages 3. Nature—Poetry 4. Poems—Collections 5. Political poetry
ISBN 1847771947; 9781847771940

SUMMARY: In this poetry collection, Jorie Graham "selects from the full range of her five most recent books. . . . Here we follow her through the later environmental and political poems of 'Overlord,' 'Sea Change' and other collections. . . . Jorie Graham's poems address a planet spinning towards an unknowable future." (Publisher's note)

REVIEW: *TLS* no5763 p22 S 13 2013 OLI HAZZARD

"The Taken-Down God" and "P L A C E." "'The Taken Down God' is Jorie Graham's second volume of selected poems . . . and includes work from five collections. . . . Its judicious selection from these books provides a comprehensive introduction to Graham's development over the past fifteen years, and in some ways represents a useful way in which to encounter a poet whose work can be uneven--a characteristic that is perhaps inseparable from her salutary desire for continual change. . . .'I was a hard thing to undo', she writes . . . and it is with this declaration in mind that Jorie Graham's ambitious, densely tangled work should be approached. It rewards the effort."

GRAINGER, JOHN D. The Battle for Syria, 1918-1920; [by] John D. Grainger viii, 261 p. 2013 Boydell Press

1. Great Britain—Military history 2. Historical literature 3. Megiddo, Battle of, Israel, 1918
ISBN 1843838036; 9781843838036
LC 2012-462779

SUMMARY: "This book charts the continuing war between Britain and France on the one side and the Turkish Empire on the other following the British capture of Jerusalem in 1917. It outlines how the British prepared for their advance, bringing in Indian and Australian troops; how the Turks were defeated at the great Battle of Megiddo in September 1918; and how Damascus fell." (Publisher's note)

REVIEW: *Middle East J* v67 no3 p497 Summ 2013 A. B. G.

REVIEW: *TLS* no5751 p11 Je 21 2013 JAMES BARR

"The Battle for Syria, 1918-1920." "[John D.] Grainger, who has written widely about ancient and modem military campaigns, mixes personal memoirs, regimental histories and the war diaries of the fighting units to retell this story. He is a military historian of the old school, and he might have got away with the details of precisely which units were involved at every step if he had also provided the reader with compelling pen portraits of the leading generals, and a mastery of their tactics and of the politics they had to grapple with. Alas, the characters are flat and the narrative lacks clarity. Occasionally the trundling cogs inside the author's brain are audible. . . . The book's most fundamental flaw is its failure to set out the political background clearly at the outset."

GRAND, STEPHEN R. The Arab awakening. See Pollack, K. M.

GRANDE, JAMES.ed. The opinions of William Cobbett. See The opinions of William Cobbett

GRANDIN, GREG. The empire of necessity; freedom, slavery, and deception in the New World; [by] Greg Grandin 320 p. 2013 Metropolitan Books/Henry Holt and Company

1. Historical literature 2. Slave insurrections—South America—History—19th century 3. Slave trade—South America—History—19th century 4. Slavery—South America—History—19th century
ISBN 0805094539; 9780805094534 (hardcover)
LC 2013-014309

SUMMARY: "Drawing on research on four continents, 'The Empire of Necessity' explores the multiple forces that culminated in [an] extraordinary event--an event that already inspired Herman Melville's masterpiece Benito Cereno. Now historian Greg Grandin . . . uses the dramatic happenings of that day to map a new transnational history of slavery in the Americas, capturing the clash of peoples, economies, and faiths that was the New World in the early 1800s." (Publisher's note)

REVIEW: *Am Sch* v83 no1 p119-21 Wint 2014 FERGUS M. BORDEWICH

REVIEW: *Bookforum* v20 no5 p37 F/Mr 2014 VICTOR LAVALLE

REVIEW: *Booklist* v110 no7 p6 D 1 2013 Jay Freeman

REVIEW: *Economist* v410 no8870 p83 Ja 18 2014

REVIEW: *Kirkus Rev* v81 no23 p30 D 1 2013

REVIEW: *Libr J* v139 no5 p128 Mr 15 2014 Robert B. Slater

REVIEW: *Libr J* v138 no9 p56 My 15 2013 Barbara Hoffert

REVIEW: *N Y Times Book Rev* p18 Ja 12 2014 ANDREW DELBANCO

"The Empire of Necessity: Slavery, Freedom, and Deception in the New World." "For nearly four centuries, as Greg Grandin writes in his powerful new book, slavery was the 'flywheel' that drove the global development of everything from trade and insurance to technology, religion and medicine. . . . Beginning in 1804 with their embarkation from West Africa, he follows a particular group of slaves to a British slave ship until it is seized . . . by a French pirate. . . . 'The Empire of Necessity' is also a significant contribution to the largely impossible yet imperative effort to retrieve some trace of the countless lives that slavery consumed."

REVIEW: *New Yorker* v90 no4 p73-1 Mr 17 2014

GRANT, SARA. Half lives; [by] Sara Grant 400 p. 2013 Little, Brown and Co.

1. Cults—Fiction 2. Dystopias 3. Nevada—Fiction 4. Radioactive waste disposal—Fiction 5. Science fiction 6. Survival—Fiction

ISBN 031619493X; 9780316194938

LC 2012-031405

SUMMARY: In this book, "17-year-old Icie's normal life is disrupted when her government advisor parents alert her to a biological threat and tell her to get to a shelter outside Las Vegas. . . . Alternating with Icie's tale is the story of a mountain cult in the future, in which teenagers like Beckett and Harper face the mysteries of the same base Icie and her friends are running toward, as well as their own connections to her world." (Publishers Weekly)

REVIEW: *Bull Cent Child Books* v67 no2 p91-2 O 2013 A. M.

"Half Lives." "Told in chapters alternating between Icie's present and Beckett's future, this novel offers a harrowing survival story that raises powerful questions about what it takes physically and spiritually to survive a global catastrophe. Icie's narrative packs a particularly powerful emotional punch, with its cast of compelling characters who struggle with their best and worst impulses in the face of dire circumstances. The other half of the novel is less emotional than intellectual, exploring the evolution of language and culture in the absence of its original context, offering an interesting contrast to Icie's intensely personal journey. On the whole, this highly original read gives science fiction fans a thoughtful apocalyptic tale for both the heart and the head."

REVIEW: *Kirkus Rev* v81 no10 p93 My 15 2013

REVIEW: *Publ Wkly* v260 no23 p79 Je 10 2013

REVIEW: *Voice of Youth Advocates* v36 no2 p77 Je 2013 Morgan Brickey

GRASSO, JOHN. Historical dictionary of football; [by] John Grasso 559 p. 2013 Scarecrow Press, Inc., a wholly owned subsidiary of The Rowman & Littlefield Pub. Group, Inc.

1. Encyclopedias & dictionaries 2. Football—History 3. Football—United States—Dictionaries 4. Football players 5. Football teams 6. Sports—Dictionaries

ISBN 9780810878563 (cloth : alk. paper)

LC 2013-001762

SUMMARY: This book, written by John Grasso, "covers the history of American football through a chronology, an introductory essay, appendixes, and an extensive bibliography. The dictionary section has over 600 cross-referenced entries on both amateur (collegiate) and professional players, coaches, teams and executives from all eras." (Publisher's note)

REVIEW: *Choice* v51 no4 p601-2 D 2013 J. R. Bailey

"Historical Dictionary of Football." "In over 600 entries on collegiate and professional American football players, coaches, teams, leagues, and executives, [author John] Grasso . . . addresses the history of the sport. Individual entries are up to two pages long and have boldface cross-references to other articles. The book begins with a historical chronology of football and a good introductory essay that should provide novices with a basic understanding of this predominantly North American sport. Biographical entries include date and place of birth and death (if deceased). . . . Entries for leagues, teams, and universities are particularly well-written and interconnect with the biographies to place individuals in the broader context of the history of the sport."

GRATTON, TESSA. The Curiosities. See Stiefvater, M.

GRAVEL, ÉLISE, 1977-. The fly; [by] Élise Gravel 32 p. 2014 Tundra Books of Northern New York

1. Children's nonfiction 2. Flies 3. Flies—Behavior 4. Housefly 5. Natural history—Juvenile literature

ISBN 177049636X; 9781770496361 (hardcover); 9781770496385 (ebk.)

LC 2013-940756

SUMMARY: This children's book, part of Elise Gravel's "Disgusting Critters" series, is an "illustrated non-fiction book about the house fly. . . . It covers such topics as the hair on the fly's body (requires a lot of shaving), its ability to walk on the ceiling (it's pretty cool, but it's hard to play soccer up there), and its really disgusting food tastes (garbage juice soup followed by dirty diaper with rotten tomato sauce, for example)." (Publisher's note)

REVIEW: *Bull Cent Child Books* v67 no9 p455 My 2014 J. H.

"The Fly" and "The Worm". "Perhaps you've said to yourself, 'why aren't there more easy reader titles about vermin?' Well, worry no more. [Elise] Gravel's new series nicely fills that particular niche, serving up nuggets of introductory information about 'Disgusting Critters' with a heaping helping of humor. . . . The amusing digital artwork, rendered appropriately in earth tones with pops of brighter reds or pink on matte pages, is modern, fresh, and funny. . . . While some readers may need help to decode words like 'muscidae' or 'hermaphrodites' (defined within the text), the writing is generally quite accessible to older primary graders; reluctant older readers may find these titles appealing as well."

REVIEW: *Kirkus Rev* v82 no2 p312 Ja 15 2014

"The Fly". "The author of the rousingly revolting 'Day in the Office of Doctor Bugspit' . . . dishes out more dirt with this appetite-spoiling introduction to the ubiquitous fly clan. Focusing particularly on houseflies (Muscidae), [Elise] Gravel ties snippets of natural science . . . to humorous scenarios. . . . The black, blue, puce and red illustrations feature bulbous, anthropomorphic figures with limp wings and tubular noses, along with the occasional accessory. . . . . Young readers will at least come away with a thorough understanding of how unsanitary these insects are and also, perhaps, clearer pictures of their physical makeup, life cycle and even some of the differences among fly species."

REVIEW: *Quill Quire* v80 no1 p46-7 Ja/F 2014 Sarah Sorensen

"The Worm" and "The Fly". "The Disgusting Critters series [is] an amusing group of books for beginning readers that successfully mixes fact and humour to introduce youngsters to creatures gros and small. The first two books in the series focus on worms and flies, and while they are chock full of great information, Gravel also packs each book with enough laugh-out-loud jokes and vibrant illustrations to keep the tone light and entertaining. . . . Gravel's books, with their bouncing humour, fast pace, and visual treats, would not feel out of place alongside Tedd Arnold's popular Fly Guy fiction series. The interplay of text and illustration should strike all the right notes for gross-out loving young readers."

REVIEW: *SLJ* v60 no6 p137 Je 2014 Patricia Manning

GRAVEL, ÉLISE, 1977-. The worm; [by] Élise Gravel 32 p. 2014 Tundra Books of Northern New York

1. Children's nonfiction 2. Habitat (Ecology) 3. Natural history—Juvenile literature 4. Worms 5. Worms—Behavior

ISBN 1770496335; 9781770496330 (hardcover); 9781770496354 (ebk.)

LC 2013-940757

SUMMARY: This children's book, part of Elise Gravel's "Disgusting Critters" series, is an "illustrated non-fiction book about the worm. . . . It covers such topics as the worm's habitats (sometimes they live inside other animals), its anatomy (its muscle tube is slimy and gross), and its illustrious history (worms have been on earth for 120 million years). Although silly . . . [it] contains real information that will tie in with curriculum." (Publisher's note)

REVIEW: *Bull Cent Child Books* v67 no9 p455 My 2014 J. H.

"The Fly" and "The Worm". "Perhaps you've said to yourself, 'why aren't there more easy reader titles about vermin?' Well, worry no more. [Elise] Gravel's new series nicely fills that particular niche, serving up nuggets of introductory information about 'Disgusting Critters' with a heaping helping of humor. . . . The amusing digital artwork, rendered appropriately in earth tones with pops of brighter reds or pink on matte pages, is modern, fresh, and funny. . . . While some readers may need help to decode words like 'muscidae' or 'hermaphrodites' (defined within the text), the writing is generally quite accessible to older primary graders; reluctant older readers may find these titles appealing as well."

REVIEW: *Quill Quire* v80 no1 p46-7 Ja/F 2014 Sarah Sorensen

"The Worm" and "The Fly". "The Disgusting Critters series [is] an amusing group of books for beginning readers that successfully mixes fact and humour to introduce youngsters to creatures gros and small. The first two books in the series focus on worms and flies, and while they are chock full of great information, Gravel also packs each book with enough laugh-out-loud jokes and vibrant illustrations to keep the tone light and entertaining. . . . Gravel's books, with their bouncing humour, fast pace, and visual treats, would not feel out of place alongside Tedd Arnold's popular Fly Guy fiction series. The interplay of text and illustration should strike all the right notes for gross-out loving young readers."

REVIEW: *SLJ* v60 no6 p137 Je 2014 Patricia Manning

GRAVES, JANE. Cowboy Take Me Away; [by] Jane Graves 464 p. 2013 Grand Central Pub.

1. Animal shelters 2. Bullfighters 3. Human-animal relationships—Fiction 4. Love stories 5. Man-woman relationships—Fiction

ISBN 1455515191 (paperback); 9781455515196 (paperback)

SUMMARY: This is the first in Jane Graves's Rainbow Valley series. "Luke Dawson was the town's teenage bad boy, now made good as a bull rider but forced to convalesce in his hated hometown after a knee injury. Shannon North, his estranged high school love, runs the local animal shelter with overachiever's passion." (Publishers Weekly)

REVIEW: *Booklist* v109 no16 p24 Ap 15 2013 Shelley Mosley

REVIEW: *Booklist* v110 no2 p49 S 15 2013 Donna Seaman

"The Accidental Bride," "Any Duchess Will Do," and "Cowboy Take Me Away." "Jilly loves being a chef, but the stress is killing her. Off she goes to the Lost Creek Resort in Wyoming for a calming knitting retreat, but instead, she meets Walker Hale. . . . With just one day to select a bride, the future Duchess of Halford, Griffin chooses serving girl Pauline, as RITA Award-winning [Tessa] Dare continues her sparkling and sexy Spindle Cove series. . . . Graves launches a new series with this charming, emotionally rich novel about the return to Rainbow Valley, Texas, of champion bull rider Luke Dawson and Shannon North, who left her big-city career to run a no-kill animal shelter."

REVIEW: *Publ Wkly* v260 no12 p49 Mr 25 2013 Stephanie Kip Rostan

GRAVES, JENNIFER. Framing fat; competing constructions in contemporary culture; [by] Jennifer Graves 192 p. 2013 Rutgers University Press

1. Body image—United States 2. Food habits—United States—History 3. Obesity—Social aspects—United States—History 4. Overweight persons—Psychology 5. Overweight persons—Social conditions 6. Social science literature

ISBN 0813560918; 0813560926; 9780813560915 (pbk. : alk. paper); 9780813560922 (hardcover : alk. paper)

LC 2012-033362

SUMMARY: Author Samantha Kwan's book focuses on obesity in the U.S, "specifically where issues of beauty, health, choice and responsibility, and social justice are concerned." The author examines "how laypersons respond to these conflicting messages and illustrate the gendered, raced, and classed implications within them. In doing so, they shed light on how dominant ideas about body fat have led to the moral indictment of body nonconformists, essentially 'framing' them for their fat bodies." (Publisher's note)

REVIEW: *Choice* v51 no1 p173 S 2013 J. L. Croissant

"Framing Fat: Competing Constructions in Contemporary Culture." "[Samantha] Kwan . . . and [Jennifer] Graves . . . provide a sociological analysis of discourses surrounding obesity in US popular and medical cultures. Taking a social problems approach, they examine how the fashion/beauty industry provides a general backdrop for medical, neoliberal, and size-acceptance movements in constructing or resisting obesity as a problem. . . . While highly descriptive and empirically rich and exemplary in its exposition of framing theory and its core concepts, the book nonetheless lacks some explanatory weight."

REVIEW: *Contemp Sociol* v42 no6 p887-8 N 2013

GRAVES, ROBERT, 1895-1985. Selected poems; [by] Robert Graves 2012 Faber and Faber

1. Anthologies 2. English love poetry 3. English poetry—20th century 4. Poems—Collections 5. War poetry, English

ISBN 9780571283835 paperback

SUMMARY: "This is a new and essential selection from the range and bulk of Robert Graves' poetry, edited by Ulster poet Michael Longley. This edition will restore Graves to view as a major twentieth century poet, and demonstrate his manifold achievement as war poet, as love poet, and as--in the round--a secular visionary." (Publisher's note)

REVIEW: *Economist* v408 no8849 p70-1 Ag 17 2013

REVIEW: *London Rev Books* v35 no6 p31-4 Mr 21 2013 Peter Howarth

REVIEW: *N Y Rev Books* v60 no11 p60-2 Je 20 2013 Edward Mendelson

"Selected Poems" and "The Selected Letters of Anthony Hecht." "Anthony Hecht, more than any other American poet of the past half-century, wrote as a champion of traditional forms and elevated syntax. . . . More than any other critic, [J. D.] McClatchy--Hecht's literary executor and editor of a well-judged and deftly annotated Selected Poems--is alert to Hecht's double edge, his oscillation between formal, aristocratic disdain and abased, formless despair. . . . Except for the dreary sans-serif typeface used for the letters (the introduction and headnotes are more legible), this is a model edition. The letters themselves are vastly interesting for what Hecht says about himself and his poems, less so about everything else."

REVIEW: *New Statesman* v142 no5169 p43 Ag 9 2013

REVIEW: *Sewanee Rev* v122 no1 pxi-xiv Wint 2014 David Middleton

REVIEW: *TLS* no5723 p23 D 7 2012

REVIEW: *TLS* no5709 p22-3 Ag 31 2012 Andrew Mcculloch

REVIEW: *TLS* no5759 p34 Ag 16 2013 ELIZABETH SCOTT-BAUMANN

"Selected Poems: Secular and Sacred." "[Robin] Holloway . . . is frank about the unscholarly nature of his editorial procedure: 'this is absolutely a personal selection, relying upon taste, ear, pleasure, feeling, as criteria and guides'. Though the editor has an evident and appealing enthusiasm for [Richard] Crashaw, he also dismisses much of the poetry. . . .This results in a curious combination of insisting on an aesthetic rather than a historical reading of Crashaw, while also acknowledging that much of it falls short of such an approach. . . . Holloway's friendly and witty approach may find Crashaw a new audience as much by acknowledging his weaknesses for the modem reader as by championing his strengths."

GRAVES, SUE. I didn't do it; [by] Sue Graves 28 p. 2013 Free Spirit Publishing

1. Blame 2. Emotions (Psychology)—Juvenile literature 3. Emotions (Psychology) in children 4. Picture books for children 5. Truthfulness and falsehood in children—Juvenile literature

ISBN 1575424452; 9781575424453

LC 2013-012340

SUMMARY: This book by Sue Graves is part of the Our Emotions and Behavior series, which offers "young children and their caregivers help with hard-to-manage feelings and inappropriate actions. . . . A fictional story portrays a child struggling with a particular emotion. Each story takes the main character through several misdeeds or scenarios, looking at the same theme in slightly different ways." This entry looks at lying. (Booklist)

REVIEW: *Booklist* v110 no2 p64 S 15 2013 Carolyn Phelan

"I Didn't Do It!," "I Hate Everything!," and ""Take a Deep Breath." "Books in the Our Emotions and Behavior series offer young children and their caregivers help with hard-to-manage feelings and inappropriate actions. . . . Each story takes the main character through several misdeeds or scenarios, looking at the same theme in slightly different ways. The simple texts are direct, and the endings are consistently upbeat. . . . Bright but sometimes too intensely colored, the cartoon-style digital illustrations are generally easy to interpret. Advising adults on using the book with children, the final two-page section suggests related activities. These purposeful books will be useful in many libraries."

GRAVES, SUE. I hate everything!; [by] Sue Graves 28 p. 2013 Free Spirit Publishing

1. Anger—Juvenile literature 2. Anger in children—Juvenile literature 3. Emotions (Psychology) in children 4. Picture books for children

ISBN 1575424436; 9781575424439

LC 2013-012336

SUMMARY: This book by Sue Graves is part of the Our Emotions and Behavior series, which offers "young children and their caregivers help with hard-to-manage feelings and inappropriate actions. . . . A fictional story portrays a child struggling with a particular emotion. Each story takes the main character through several misdeeds or scenarios, looking at the same theme in slightly different ways." Here, "Sam has difficulty controlling his anger . . . but Aunt Meg's suggestions give him some tools to try." (Booklist)

REVIEW: *Booklist* v110 no2 p64 S 15 2013 Carolyn Phelan

"I Didn't Do It!," "I Hate Everything!," and ""Take a Deep Breath." "Books in the Our Emotions and Behavior series offer young children and their caregivers help with hard-to-manage feelings and inappropriate actions. . . . Each story takes the main character through several misdeeds or scenarios, looking at the same theme in slightly different ways. The simple texts are direct, and the endings are consistently upbeat. . . . Bright but sometimes too intensely colored, the cartoon-style digital illustrations are generally easy to interpret. Advising adults on using the book with children, the final two-page section suggests related activities. These purposeful books will be useful in many libraries."

REVIEW: *Kirkus Rev* v81 no17 p94 S 1 2013

GRAVES, SUE. Take a deep breath; [by] Sue Graves 28 p. 2013 Free Spirit Publishing

1. Breathing exercises 2. Emotions (Psychology) in children 3. Fear in children—Juvenile literature 4. Picture books for children 5. Stage fright

ISBN 1575424460; 9781575424460

LC 2013-012339

SUMMARY: In this book by Sue Graves, "Lucy is afraid of

dogs, Josh doesn't like to go in the pool, Dan doesn't want the nurse to touch his bruised knee, and Ben is afraid to go on stage in front of people. Follow along as these friends learn that when something scares them, they can take a deep breath and feel brave enough to get through their ordeals." (Publisher's note)

REVIEW: *Booklist* v110 no2 p64 S 15 2013 Carolyn Phelan

"I Didn't Do It!," "I Hate Everything!," and ""Take a Deep Breath." "Books in the Our Emotions and Behavior series offer young children and their caregivers help with hard-to-manage feelings and inappropriate actions. . . . Each story takes the main character through several misdeeds or scenarios, looking at the same theme in slightly different ways. The simple texts are direct, and the endings are consistently upbeat. . . . Bright but sometimes too intensely colored, the cartoon-style digital illustrations are generally easy to interpret. Advising adults on using the book with children, the final two-page section suggests related activities. These purposeful books will be useful in many libraries."

GRAVES, WILL. Robert Griffin lll; RGlll - NFL sensation; [by] Will Graves 32 p. 2013 ABDO Pub. Co.

1. Children's nonfiction 2. Football players 3. Griffin, Robert, 1990- 4. Track & field athletes 5. Washington Redskins (Football team)
ISBN 9781617837005
LC 2013-934740

SUMMARY: This book on football player Robert Griffin III is part of the "Playmakers" series. Each book in the series has "an opening chapter highlighting one of the football player's greatest accomplishments" followed by "a look at each athlete's childhood and his path from high school to college to professional football. . . . 'Robert Griffin III' tells how, instead of adapting to the Redskins' style of play, the Heisman Trophy winner brought needed change to his team." (Booklist)

REVIEW: *Booklist* v110 no11 p55 F 1 2014 Angela Leeper

"Colin Kaepernick: NFL Phenom," "Joe Flaco: Super Bowl MVP," and "Robert Griffin III: RGIII--NFL Sensation." "Each book immediately hooks young sports enthusiasts with an opening chapter highlighting one of the football player's greatest accomplishments. The concise text continues with a look at each athlete's childhood and his path from high school to college to professional football. . . . Numerous color photos of the quarterbacks in action both on and off the field and interesting sidebars . . . keep the text exciting, especially for reluctant readers. Additional fun facts and quotes make these books good choices for recreational reading or biography studies."

GRAVETT, EMILY.il. Matilda's cat. See Gravett, E.

GRAVETT, EMILY. Matilda's cat; 32 p. 2013 Simon & Schuster Books for Young Readers

1. Cats—Fiction 2. Children's stories 3. Human-animal relationships—Fiction 4. Pets—Juvenile literature 5. Play
ISBN 1442475277; 9781442475274 (hardcover)
LC 2012-049731

SUMMARY: In this book, by Emily Gravett, "Matilda is desperate to figure out what her cat will enjoy. She tries everything she can think of: climbing trees, playing with wool, even tea parties and dress-up games, but as Matilda gets more and more creative in her entertainment attempts, her cat moves from unimpressed to terrified. Will Matilda ever figure out what her cat likes?" (Publisher's note)

REVIEW: *Booklist* v110 no13 p77 Mr 1 2014 Sarah Hunter

REVIEW: *Bull Cent Child Books* v67 no7 p359-60 Mr 2014 J. H.

REVIEW: *Kirkus Rev* v82 no2 p120 Ja 15 2014

"Matilda's Cat". "A master of animal countenance, [Emily] Gravett pairs an expressive cat with a busy kid and winks at the difference between textual and visual message. . . . Each spread shows Matilda playing at one thing while the text claims that her orange tabby enjoys it. . . . Matilda sports a head-to-toe tabby suit, linking cat and girl all along; the shrewd and skillful art implies sly underlying affection even when the cat's nonplussed, worried or asleep. Even Matilda's cat would like this."

REVIEW: *N Y Times Book Rev* p22 Mr 16 2014 SARAH HARRISON SMITH

REVIEW: *Publ Wkly* v261 no1 p57 Ja 6 2014

REVIEW: *SLJ* v60 no4 p121 Ap 2014 Luann Toth

GRAY, JASON. Glimpses through the forest; memories of gabon; [by] Jason Gray 288 p. 2013 Peace Corps Writers

1. Americans—Africa 2. Gabon 3. Memoirs 4. Peace Corps (U.S.) 5. World Wide Fund for Nature (1998-)
ISBN 9781935925309 (pbk.)
LC 2013-934691

SUMMARY: "An . . . account of life in Gabon, particularly around the Ndougou Lagoon, this new book by Jason Gray leaves us . . . having shared in his experiences. Gray's underlying reverence for Gabon and its people comes out strongly in this recounting of his three years . . . with the Peace Corps and the World Wide Fund for Nature." (Publisher's note)

REVIEW: *Kirkus Rev* v81 no16 p27 Ag 15 2013

"Glimpses Through the Forest: Memories of Gabon Peace Corps Writers." "A former Peace Corps volunteer reminisces about . . . his three years in Gabon, where the people, the countryside and nature captured his heart. For debut travel writer [Jason] Gray, the coastal West African country of Gabon . . . was about the most extreme contrast to his native Montana he could have wished for. . . . At the center of the country is oil revenue, but, with only passing references made to the presence of international companies, Gray's efforts to avoid political controversy lead him to give no opinion on the matter--a shortcoming of this otherwise engaging portrait of a society caught between ancient and modern ways. A personal, somewhat overly romantic account of life far away from home."

GRAY, MEL.ed. Decolonizing social work. See Decolonizing social work

GRAY, PAUL BRYAN. A clamor for equality; emergence and exile of Californio activist Francisco P. Ramírez; [by] Paul Bryan Gray xviii, 390 p. 2012 Texas Tech University Press

1. Exiles—Mexico—Ensenada (Baja California)—Biography 2. Historical literature 3. Lawyers—California—Los Angeles—Biography 4. Mexican American

journalists—California—Biography 5. Mexican Americans—California—Biography 6. Mexican Americans—Civil rights—California—History 7. Political activists—California—Biography
ISBN 9780896727632 (alk. paper)
LC 2012-020658

SUMMARY: This book "details the remarkable life of Francisco P. Ramirez, who, at eighteen years old, launched El Clamor Publico (The Public Outcry), a Spanish-language weekly in 1850s Los Angeles. . . . As a lawyer, publisher, and Republican political activist, Ramírez witnessed and participated in Los Angeles's transition from Mexican pueblo to American city." (American Historical Review)

REVIEW: *Am Hist Rev* v119 no1 p181-2 F 2014 Thomas R. Clark

"A Clamor for Equality: Emergence and Exile of California Activist Francisco P. Ramírez". "While [Paul Bryan] Gray provides colorful vignettes and intriguing detail, readers of this journal may find his reluctance to engage more recent historiography frustrating. The book is, in short, an old-fashioned biography: heavy on chronological detail and short on interpretation. . . . It is unfair, however, to criticize Gray for the book that he did not write. Gray set out to write a biography of an inspiring but neglected activist for racial equality, and he succeeded. Gray did not set out to write an academic work of transnational or borderlands history. But he has provided a provocative starting point for those who might."

REVIEW: *J Am Hist* v100 no2 p527-8 S 2013 Harold Brackman

REVIEW: *N Y Rev Books* v60 no8 p27 My 9 2013

GRAY, PETER B. Evolution and human sexual behavior. See Garcia, J. R.

GRAY, RICHARD. After the fall; American literature since 9/11; [by] Richard Gray 2011 John Wiley & Sons

1. Literary critiques 2. September 11 Terrorist Attacks, 2001—Influence 3. September 11 Terrorist Attacks, 2001, in literature 4. Terrorism & literature 5. War on Terrorism, 2001-2009, in literature
ISBN 9780470657928

SUMMARY: This book, by Richard Gray, analyzes American literature since September 11, 2001. "Several of the novels he analyzes, such as those by Mohsin Hamid and Joseph O'Neill, are not by Americans, and many of the works he indexes are not about 9/11 at all, but rather reflect an awareness of transnational divisions Gray sees as now inextricably linked to discourse sparked by the event." (American Literature)

REVIEW: *Am Lit* v85 no3 p604-6 S 2013 Hillary Chute

"9/11 and the Literature of Terror" and "After the Fall: American Literature Since 9/11." "Randall's introduction lays out compelling questions about how the event of 9/11 might be understood to place pressure on the endeavor of fiction. . . . Randall's account of the word-and-image problem plaguing novelists is fascinating, as is his assessment of the amplification of documentary after 9/11. . . . But if these authors lament what [Richard] Gray calls 'the seductive pieties' that structure much of American fiction, they also reveal what feels like their own pieties here (realism/domestic= bad; hybrid/global= good)."

REVIEW: *Choice* v49 no5 p878-9 Ja 2012 A.-P. Durand

GRAY, RITA. Have you heard the nesting bird?; [by] Rita Gray 32 p. 2014 Houghton Mifflin Books for Children/Houghton Mifflin Harcourt

1. Birds—Behavior—Juvenile literature 2. Birds—Nests—Juvenile literature 3. Birdsongs—Juvenile literature 4. Picture books for children 5. Robins
ISBN 054410580X; 9780544105805
LC 2013-017621

SUMMARY: This children's book, written by poet Rita Dove and illustrated by Kenard Pak, features "all the different bird calls in counterpoint to the pervasive quiet of a mama bird waiting for her eggs to hatch. Fun and informative back matter takes the shape of an interview so that readers learn more right from the bird's bill." (Publisher's note)

REVIEW: *Booklist* v110 no11 p56 F 1 2014 Carolyn Phelan

"Have You Heard the Nesting Bird?." "The appended 'A Word with the Bird' section, cleverly written as a Q&A with the robin, offers a short, highly readable account of life in the nest before and after the eggs hatch. . . . The pleasing text is well constructed, with rhythm and rhyme altered in different types of stanzas, and distinctive birdsongs included in the verse. In his picture-book debut, [Kenard] Pak's collage-style artwork is distinctive, dynamic, and rewarding to look at again and again. Retro in style, the watercolor-and-digital-media illustrations make good use of varied perspectives, layouts, and lighting effects A beautifully crafted, informative picture book."

REVIEW: *Bull Cent Child Books* v67 no8 p405 Ap 2014 E. B.

REVIEW: *Kirkus Rev* v82 no3 p62 F 1 2014

"Have You Heard the Nesting Bird?" "This charming and unusual nature story contributes something new to the overstuffed field of bird-related picture books. [Rita] Gray's simple rhymes and accurate bird calls are attractively complemented by [Kenard] Pak's textured watercolor-resist illustrations in soft greens, browns and grays. Each bird is humorously but accurately depicted. A final 'Word with the Bird' in Q-and-A format explains in detail why the robin is silent while hatching her eggs and answers many other useful questions, including the role of the father bird and what happens to the babies after they leave the nest. As welcome as the robin in springtime."

REVIEW: *Publ Wkly* v260 no51 p63 D 16 2013

REVIEW: *SLJ* v60 no2 p119 F 2014 Frances E. Millhouser

GRAY, TRUDY. Manette's Cafe; [by] Trudy Gray 2013 Trudy Gray

1. Chicago (Ill.)—Fiction 2. Historical fiction 3. Man-woman relationships—Fiction 4. Self-realization—Fiction 5. Women immigrants—Fiction
ISBN 0615857825; 9780615857824

SUMMARY: This book by Trudy Gray "is set in a small town outside of Chicago, before and during Prohibition. Manette, a young immigrant from Belgium, runs away from home to follow her fiance to the New World. The year is 1914. The marriage does not last. Manette struggles with poverty, raising five children, and brewing illegal beer. She meets people who become close friends, others who turn out to be unreliable. In the end she gains insight and makes a decision that startles her family." (Publisher's note)

REVIEW: *Kirkus Rev* v82 no2 p348 Ja 15 2014

"Manette's Cafe". "An inspiring . . . historical novel about a woman determined to survive life's challenges at any cost. . . . [Trudy] Gray effectively portrays Manette's impressive strength and courage as she moves past obstacles and matures beyond her years. Through the lens of Manette's own war for independence, the author treats the reader to a rich account of Prohibition and World War I-era America. Readers may find that this plucky heroine and her well-told story will stay with them long after her story ends. An engaging historical tale of self-discovery in the early 20th century."

GRAY, VIRGINIA. Interest groups and health care reform across the United States. See Lowery, D.

GRAYBILL, ANDREW R. The red and the white; a family saga of the American West; [by] Andrew R. Graybill 368 p. 2013 Liveright

1. Historical literature 2. Interracial marriage—West (U.S.)—History—19th century 3. Marias Massacre, Mont., 1870 4. Piegan Indians 5. Whites—West (U.S.)—Relations with Indians

ISBN 0871404451; 9780871404459 (hardcover)

LC 2013-011167

SUMMARY: Author Andrew R. Graybill "sheds light on the overlooked interracial Native-white relationships critical in the development of the trans-Mississippi West in this multi-generational saga. Beginning in 1844 with the marriage of Montana fur trader Malcolm Clarke and his Piegan Blackfeet bride, Coth-co-co-na, Graybill traces the family from the mid-nineteenth century, when such mixed marriages proliferated, to the first half of the twentieth." (Publisher's note)

REVIEW: *J Am Hist* v101 no2 p591 S 2014

REVIEW: *Kirkus Rev* v81 no16 p81 Ag 15 2013

REVIEW: *Libr J* v138 no13 p107 Ag 1 2013 John R. Burch

REVIEW: *TLS* no5791 p25 Mr 28 2014 MICK GIDLEY

"The Red and the White: A Family Saga of the American West." "Malcolm Clarke was a white Montanan who had ventured westwards in 1841. . . . In 'The Red and the White,' relying on a very impressive range of written and, where available, oral sources, Andrew R. Graybill recounts the fortunes of key members of Clarke's family, each of whom achieved distinction in Montana. . . . In a series of mini-essays woven into the narrative, Graybill also relates these personal stories to larger movements of which they were a part, including the high rate of interracial marriage during the fur trade, military excursions against the Plains tribes after the Civil War . . . , and the vogue for Indianesque crafts early in the twentieth century."

GRAZIOSI, BARBARA. The Gods of Olympus; A History; [by] Barbara Graziosi 304 p. 2014 Henry Holt & Co

1. Greek goddesses 2. Greek gods 3. Greek mythology 4. Historical literature 5. Religion & sociology

ISBN 0805091572; 9780805091571

SUMMARY: "This is a study of how the cult of Olympus flourished in ancient Greece and spread through conquest. Alexander was the prime catalyst as he conquered lands from India to Africa and brought his gods along to marginalize the local gods. . . . When the Romans took Greece, they translated the entire pantheon to Rome. They adopted the Greek culture for the simple reason that it was predominant in the regions they conquered, and they tended to maintain local rule." (Kirkus Reviews)

REVIEW: *Booklist* v110 no11 p3 F 1 2014 Lynn Weber

REVIEW: *Kirkus Rev* v82 no1 p74 Ja 1 2014

"The Gods of Olympus: A History". "The author leaves aside the secondary gods, demigods and Roman household gods but not the soi-disant gods such as Alexander the Great and Julius Caesar, who spread the word. This is a study of how the cult of Olympus flourished in ancient Greece and spread through conquest. . . . Ultimately, the gods were turned away but not forgotten. . . . [Barbara] Graziosi's easy style and focus on the history of the world as told by the gods of Olympus make this a book to savor."

REVIEW: *Libr J* v138 no21 p110 D 1 2013 Margaret Heller

REVIEW: *Publ Wkly* v260 no44 p55 N 4 2013

REVIEW: *TLS* no5814 p22 S 5 2014 HELEN MORALES

GREAT DEEDS IN IRELAND; Richard Stanihurst's De Rebus in Hibernia Gestis; 544 p. 2013 Stylus Pub Llc

1. Great Britain—History—William I, 1066-1087 2. Historical literature 3. Ireland—History—To 1603 4. Ireland—Social life & customs 5. Latin literature—Translations into English

ISBN 190900572X; 9781909005723

SUMMARY: This book, edited by John Barry and Hiram Morgan, offers "the first full translation of the controversial Latin history of Ireland by the [16th-century] . . . Dublin intellectual, Richard Stanihurst. . . . [It] provides a contemporary account of Ireland's geography and people and what the author considered to be the greatest event in Irish history--the Anglo-Norman conquest." (Publisher's note)

REVIEW: *TLS* no5749 p13 Je 7 2013 ANDREW HADFIELD

"Great Deeds in Ireland: Richard Stanihurst's 'De Rebus in Hibernia Gestis'." "John Barry and Hiram Morgan should be congratulated for this splendid edition. . . . 'De Rebus in Hibernia Gestis'--a humanist text written for a European audience that makes a special case for the importance of the Old English in Ireland--allows us to see how complicated national representations were transformed when they were transported and translated into new places for new readers. The introduction is substantial and informative, and is especially good on the style and sources of De Rebus, as well as the ways in which it was subsequently read. The text has been translated with admirable vigour and panache, a modem rendition of a work that was the state of the art when it first appeared."

THE GREAT DEPRESSION OF 1930S; lessons for today ; 2013 Oxford University Press

1. Depressions—1929 2. Financial crises 3. Great Britain—Economic conditions—1918-1945 4. Historical literature 5. United States—Economic conditions—1918-1945

ISBN 9780199663187

SUMMARY: This book, edited by Nicholas Crafts and Peter Fearon, presents an "introduction to the Great Depression as it affected the advanced countries in the 1930s.The contributions . . . cover in detail the experiences of Britain, Germany, and, the United States. . . . The crisis entailed the collapse of the international monetary system, sovereign default, and banking crises in many countries. . . . The responses included protectionism, regulation, fiscal and monetary stimulus, and the New Deal." (Publisher's note)

REVIEW: *Choice* v51 no5 p888-9 Ja 2014 R. E. Schenk

"The Great Depression of the 1930s: Lessons for Today." " None of the 14 papers of this volume, written by 18 economists and historians engaged in research about the Great Depression, contests this thesis, though all reject the monetarist framework of Friedman-Schwartz. The papers extend and modify Friedman-Schwartz in several ways. There is more emphasis on events in and circumstances of Britain, France, and Germany. . . . No paper disputes that central banks learned from the 1930s, and their response to the recent financial crisis reflected lessons learned. . . . Highly recommended."

GREAT DISCOVERIES IN MEDICINE; 304 2011 Thames & Hudson

1. Historical literature 2. Medical equipment—History 3. Medical innovations 4. Medical sciences—History 5. Medicine—History

ISBN 9780500251805; 0500251800
LC 2011-922602

SUMMARY: This book provides an "account of the evolution of medical knowledge and practice from ancient Egypt, India, and China to the latest technology. . . . Topics include humors & pneumas, Islamic medicine, pathological anatomy, neuron theory, bedlam & beyond, parasites & vectors, hormones, the genetic revolution, defibrillators, the endoscope, medical robots, typhus, tuberculosis, smallpox, HIV, and more." (Publisher's note) "The volume is divided into sections that address different areas of medicine and studies of the body from the ancient world to modern times: tools, contagious diseases, remedies, surgery, and various technological innovations." (Publishers Weekly)

REVIEW: *Choice* v49 no7 p1299 Mr 2012 R. D. Arcari

REVIEW: *Libr J* v136 no20 p139-40 D 1 2011 Kathy Arsenault

REVIEW: *TLS* no5691 p26 Ap 27 2012 Christopher Lawrence

"The Oxford Handbook of the History of Medicine" and "Great Discoveries in Medicine." "The contributors assembled by Mark Jackson for 'The Oxford Handbook of the History of Medicine' have produced essays of almost uniformly high quality. . . . The usual modern suspects are here: sexuality, old age, the mad, death, chronic illness, oral history, film, environment, but also an eloquent, elegantly argued plea for the incorporation of animals into a history largely concerned with humans. Apart from reflecting and embodying broader modem concerns, these historical essays all make a case . . . for according the history of medicine a place in medical policymaking. . . . ['Great Discoveries in Medicine'] does start with the ancient Egyptians, and takes in all the familiar highlights: the circulation of the blood, insulin, the Pill - but no abortion or euthanasia. . . . Anyone loosely connected with the subject will spot the impeccable historical credentials of many of the authors enrolled here: Andrew Scull on Bedlam, Vivian Nutton on humours, Michael Worboys on germs, Mark Harrison on typhus. Yet, however hard most of these writers try to escape the shackles of teleology, the predetermined meanings of everyday language carry the message of their narratives."

THE GREAT EUROZONE DISASTER; from crisis to global New Deal; ix, 274 p. 2012 Zed Books

1. Economics literature 2. Eurozone 3. Financial crises—European Union countries 4. Monetary policy—European Union countries

ISBN 9781780324791 (hb)
LC 2012-474472

SUMMARY: This book by Heikki Patomäki presents an "analysis of the financial crisis in Europe. He examines its causes and explores . . . solutions. . . . One of Patomäki's major critiques is that there has been a misguided reliance on neoclassical theory in the formulation of monetary policy. . . . He advocates instead a 'global Keynesian' approach, which would make it easier to achieve international policy solutions and economic as well as financial stability." (Choice)

REVIEW: *Choice* v51 no4 p693-4 D 2013 H. D. Renning

"The Great Eurozone Disaster: From Crisis to Global New Deal." "[Heikki] Patomäki . . . has produced an ambitious and remarkably persuasive analysis of the financial crisis in Europe. He examines its causes and explores desirable, though not easily realizable, solutions to it. . . . The book has been very well translated from the Finnish. This is a valuable resource for both economists and political scientists concerned with modern Europe and worldwide economic and political integration. Elaborate endnotes (almost 50 pages) and a lengthy bibliography. . . . Highly recommended."

THE GREAT WARDROBE ACCOUNTS OF HENRY VII AND HENRY VIII; liv, 335 p. 2012 London Record Society Boydell Press Boydell & Brewer, Inc.

1. Accounts 2. Clothing and dress—England—History—15th century 3. Great Britain—History—Henry VII, 1485-1509 4. Great Britain—History—Henry VIII, 1509-1547 5. Henry VII, King of England, 1457-1509 6. Henry VIII, King of England, 1491-1547

ISBN 0900952520 (hardcover); 9780900952524 (hardcover)
LC 2012-494413

SUMMARY: "By the late fifteenth century the Great Wardrobe, the section of the royal household that supplied the king and his household with clothing and furnishings, was well established in the London parish of St Andrew by the Wardrobe." Edited by Maria Hayward, "This volume provides an edition and calendar of the accounts for 1498-99 and 1510-11, as well as the section of the 1544 account relating to Henry VIII's campaign in France." (Publisher's note)

REVIEW: *Engl Hist Rev* v128 no534 p1207-8 O 2013 Steven Gunn

"The Great Wardrobe Accounts of Henry VII and Henry VIII." "The records of the early Tudor Great Wardrobe . . . show how kings and their courtiers dressed, at a time when social rank, political power and familiarity with foreign fashion were readily displayed in clothing. . . . In the present volume [editor Maria Hayward] provides an edition of accounts for the years 1498-9, 1510-11 and 1543-4. These illustrate different parts of the period, under Henry VII, the young Henry VIII and his older self. . . . The combination of . . . telling detail with wider analysis will make this a useful volume."

GREBE, ANJA. The Vatican; All the Paintings : The Complete Collection of Old Masters, Plus More Than 300 Sculptures, Maps, Tapestries, and Other Artifacts; [by]

Anja Grebe 525 p. 2013 Black Dog & Leventhal Pub
1. Art catalogs 2. Art literature 3. Christianity & art—Catholic Church 4. Painting—Italy—History 5. Vatican City
ISBN 1579129439; 9781579129439

SUMMARY: This book "illustrates all the works of art on display in the Vatican and underscores the variety of its art, including works that popes commissioned from painters as well as works that were accumulated for art appreciation and prestige beginning in the 17th century. The book is divided into 22 sections representing the museums and areas of the Vatican. This includes the Pinacoteca (painting gallery), with paintings given to or purchased by the popes." (Library Journal)

REVIEW: *Booklist* v110 no6 p18-9 N 15 2013 Donna Seaman

"The Vatican: All the Paintings; The Complete Collection of Old Masters Plus More than 300 Sculptures, Maps,Tapestries, and Other Artifacts." "Ross King, author of many works of vivid art history . . . introduces this sumptuous showcase of 976 of the Vatican's art treasures. . . . Now everyone everywhere can experience the Vatican's magnificent collections in this veritable pageant of art history. Art historian [Anja] Grebe provides to-the-point commentary, covering various popes' commissioning of specific works and, beginning in the seventeenth century, avid acquisition of masterpieces."

GRECO, ALBERT N. The book publishing industry. See Milliot, J.

GREEK AND ROMAN ANIMAL SACRIFICE; ancient victims, modern observers; xiv, 209 p. 2012 Cambridge UP
1. Animal sacrifice—Greece—History—To 1500—Congresses 2. Animal sacrifice—Rome—History—To 1500—Congresses 3. Divination—Greece—History—To 1500—Congresses 4. Divination—Rome—History—To 1500—Congresses 5. Historical literature
ISBN 1107011124; 9781107011120
LC 2011-279382

SUMMARY: In this collection of essays on Greek and Roman animal sacrifice, edited by Christopher A. Faraone and F. S. Naiden, the contributors evaluate "the views of Walter Burkert, the late J.-P. Vernant, and Marcel Detienne" (Publisher's note), whose views on the subject are here critiqued for their adherence to Marxist and Durkheimian ideas concerning religion. (Times Literary Supplement)

REVIEW: *TLS* no5748 p9-10 My 31 2013 PETER THONEMANN

"Greek and Roman Animal Sacrifice: Ancient Victims, Modern Observers" and "Smoke Signals for the Gods: Ancient Greek Sacrifice From the Archaic Through Roman Periods." "The essays in 'Greek and Roman Animal Sacrifice struggle to come up with any real alternative. . . . No such infirmity of purpose impedes [F. S.] Naiden's Smoke Signals for the Gods, which offers a massive and sustained challenge to the Durkheimian vision of ancient sacrifice. . . . Naiden's attempt to return to a pre-Durkheimian theory of religious action, based around meaningful personal encounters and communications with the divine, fails to persuade."

GREEN, FELICITY. Montaigne and the life of freedom; [by] Felicity Green a xiii, 246 p. 2012 Cambridge University Press
1. Historical literature 2. Liberty in literature 3. Philosophical literature 4. Self in literature
ISBN 9781107024397 (hardback)
LC 2012-002691

SUMMARY: This book by Felicity Green presents a "revisionist reading of [Michel de] Montaigne's . . . ['Essais'] centred on one of his deepest but hitherto most neglected preoccupations: the need to secure for himself a sphere of liberty and independence that he can properly call his own, or himself. 'Montaigne and the Life of Freedom' restores the Essais to its historical context by examining the sources, character and significance of Montaigne's project of self-study." (Publisher's note)

REVIEW: *TLS* no5746 p25 My 17 2013 JOHN O'BRIEN

"Montaigne and the Life of Freedom." "Her opening chapter makes a number of important methodological distinctions. . . . Such a refocusing of these issues is very welcome. [Felicity] Green's intellectual acumen, clarity of argument, coherent presentation and incisive style will ensure that her case will receive due hearing. . . . Felicity Green offers a stimulating and challenging account of her topic, one that calls us back to a very specific historical approach. She herself admits that her angle of attack is, and wishes to be, particular and even polemical. Her Montaigne would have been recognizable to Montaigne's disciple Pierre Charron, but it only exhibits one aspect of the many-sided writer and thinker we find in the 'Essais'."

GREEN, JOEL B. ed. The world of the New Testament. See The world of the New Testament

GREEN, KRISTIN. Plantiful; start small, grow big with 150 plants that spread, self-sow, and overwinter; [by] Kristin Green 224 p. 2014 Timber Press
1. Annuals (Plants) 2. Gardening 3. Horticultural literature 4. Plant propagation 5. Planting (Plant culture)
ISBN 1604693878; 9781604693874
LC 2013-019896

SUMMARY: In this book, "Kristen Green highlights plants that help a garden quickly grow by self-sowing and spreading and teaches you how to expand the garden and extend the life of a plant by overwintering. The book features plant profiles for 50 self-sowers . . . 50 spreaders . . . and 50 plants that overwinter. . . . Additional gardening tips, design ideas, and inspirational photos will motivate and inspire gardeners of all levels." (Publisher's note)

REVIEW: *Booklist* v110 no8 p16 D 15 2013 Carol Haggas

"Plantiful: Start Small, Grow Big With 150 Plants That Spread, Self-Sow, and Overwinter". "Lest one think this willy-nilly approach is a 'love 'em and leave 'em' proposition, [Kristin] Green cautions that there is a fine line between exuberance and invasiveness and encourages a judicious application of editorial control in weeding out any interlopers. Gorgeous photographs illustrate cunning design suggestions, while concise plant profiles give snapshots of VIP volunteers. Basic cultural techniques, handy references, and helpful resources augment this guide to enthusiastic gardening."

REVIEW: *Libr J* v139 no3 p122 F 15 2014 Bonnie Poquette

REVIEW: *Publ Wkly* v260 no49 p80 D 2 2013

GREEN, MIM. Time for a hug. See Gershator, P.

GREEN, SIMON. Dumfries House; An Architectural Story; [by] Simon Green 280 p. 2014 Royal Commission on the Ancient & Historical Monuments of Scotland

1. Architectural literature 2. Architecture—Scotland 3. Country homes 4. Historic buildings 5. Historic preservation
ISBN 1902419855; 9781902419855

SUMMARY: This book on the estate known as Dumfries House in Scotland "draws on previously unpublished documents from the extensive archives of the Bute family, who lived in the house from the early nineteenth century until the death of Lady Bute in 1993, along with a wealth of photographs, plans and drawings from the National Trust for Scotland and the Royal Commission on the Ancient and Historical Monuments of Scotland." (Publisher's note)

REVIEW: *Apollo: The International Magazine for Collectors* v179 no617 p85 F 2014

"Dumfries House: An Architectural Story," "Piero della Francesca: Artist and Man," and "Whistler: A Life for Art's Sake". "This study, which draws on previously unpublished archival material, opens up the house and its history as never before—apt for a building and collection that has recently been saved for the public. . . . James Banker couches the Tuscan painter's achievements carefully within the social and artistic contexts of his time, making compelling claims about the dating of certain works, and offering a new interpretation of the enigmatic Flagellation of Christ. . . . This is the first full biography of [James] Whistler for more than 20 years. Making use of the painter's private correspondence, historian Daniel Sutherland presents a more introspective figure than the truculent eccentric who has entered the public consciousness."

GREEN, TIM, 1963-. New kid; [by] Tim Green 320 p. 2014 HarperCollins

1. Baseball—Fiction 2. Baseball stories 3. Fathers and sons—Fiction 4. Interpersonal relations—Fiction 5. Moving, Household—Fiction 6. Schools—Fiction
ISBN 0062208721; 9780062208729 (hardback)
LC 2013-032816

SUMMARY: In this "baseball novel," by Tim Green, "Tommy's the new kid in town--who now goes by the name Brock--and he's having a hard time fitting in. Thanks to a prank gone wrong, he may be able to settle in on the baseball team. But can he prove himself before he becomes a new kid . . . again?" (Publisher's note)

REVIEW: *Bull Cent Child Books* v67 no7 p360 Mr 2014 E. B.

"New Kid." "Make no mistake, though, this is still solidly within [Tim] Green's familiar sports territory, and Brock grows into a promising pitcher even as he struggles to get his father to explain their bizarre situation. Witness in protection? Good guy secret agent? Bad guy thug? Readers are as confounded as Brock about his father's situation and his real status, and it is this ambiguity that elevates the title from the mundane to the engrossing. A bittersweet ending that diverges from the pattern of middle-grade sports plots will shake series fiction readers out of their comfort zone and ready them for the challenging work of YA sports writers awaiting them down the line."

REVIEW: *Kirkus Rev* v82 no2 p114 Ja 15 2014

"New Kid". "Best-selling author and former NFL defensive end [Tim] Green delivers a riveting book about the complexities of being a teenager caught in unusual circumstances beyond his control. His writing is both compelling and intelligent, and even thc implausible scenes—like a visit from a baseball great—still maintain a feel of authenticity. Even readers who aren't sports fans will find plenty of familiar drama and entertainment in this book. Exciting, romantic and thought-provoking, this book scores a home run."

REVIEW: *SLJ* v60 no2 p86 F 2014 Brenda Kahn

GREEN, TOBY. The rise of the trans-Atlantic slave trade in western Africa, 1300-1589; [by] Toby Green xxvi, 333 p. 2012 Cambridge University Press

1. Creoles—Africa, West—History 2. Historical literature 3. Slave trade—Africa, West—History 4. Slave trade—America—History 5. Slavery—History
ISBN 1107014360 (hbk.); 9781107014367 (hbk.)
LC 2011-015312

SUMMARY: "Drawing on many new sources, [author] Toby Green challenges current quantitative approaches to the history of the slave trade. New data on slave origins can show how and why Western African societies responded to Atlantic pressures. Green . . . uses the idea of creolization--the formation of mixed cultural communities in the era of plantation societies--to argue that preceding social patterns in both Africa and Europe were crucial." (Publisher's note)

REVIEW: *Engl Hist Rev* v128 no534 p1205-7 O 2013 Akin Ogundiran

"The Rise of the Trans-Atlantic Slave Trade in Western Africa, 1300-1589." "This is a story of the roles that the Cabo Verde and the Upper Guinea areas of Western Africa played in the rise of the Atlantic World. Toby Green presents his case for West Africa being the first theatre of the economic, political, and cultural developments that we have come to associate with the Atlantic world with a decade-by-decade analysis of archival records from about half a dozen countries. . . . The author has made a string of overlapping and well-structured arguments in this book. . . . Overall, this book is a transnational history par excellence, with multiple places, communities, regions, peoples, cultures, identities, and overlapping agendas in simultaneous dialogues."

GREENAWAY, P. CHRISTINA. Written in Ruberah; Age of Jeweled Intelligence; [by] P. Christina Greenaway 420 p. 2013 girl by the sea

1. Cornwall (England: County)—Fiction 2. Fantasy fiction 3. Good & evil—Fiction 4. Love stories 5. Magic—Fiction
ISBN 0615949878; 9780615949871

SUMMARY: In this book, "New York real estate broker Miriam Lewis takes off for a brief getaway to a remote inn on the rugged cliffs of Cornwall. . . . Entering Cornwall, Miriam crosses the River Tamar and glimpses a luminous girl floating in the river. A memory from long, long ago begins to unfold in Miriam's thoughts—something about a promise she made to perform a selfless act of courage. Could it be true? Could she ever rise to such heroism or is it just a hallucination?" (Publisher's note)

REVIEW: *Kirkus Rev* v82 no3 p123 F 1 2014

REVIEW: *Kirkus Rev* v82 no2 p380 Ja 15 2014

"Written in Ruberah: Age of Jeweled Intelligence". "Although they are deeply entangled in these ancient dramas, Miriam and Mitch (who's carrying the spirit of Da'krah, though he doesn't know it) are also the focus of a sorcery-fueled romantic-triangle plot of their own, which is energetically handled. [Christina] Greenaway juggles the many strands of her lushly descriptive book with ease, managing to bring all of these characters, from all their separate time periods, together in a rousing climax that invests just as much energy in high fantasy as modern romance, with winning results. The richly imagined story of a modern woman bearing ancient responsibilities."

GREENBERG, JAN. The mad potter; George E. Ohr, eccentric genius; [by] Jan Greenberg 56 p. 2013 Roaring Brook Press

1. Art—Biography 2. Art pottery, American—Mississippi—Biloxi—Juvenile literature 3. Biographies 4. Potters—United States—Biography—Juvenile literature
ISBN 159643810X; 9781596438101 (hardcover : alk. paper)
LC 2012-047601

SUMMARY: This children's book is a biography of American potter George E. Ohr. "Ohr's eccentricities and his penchant for self-promotion are clearly presented. . . . What makes a George E. Ohr vase sell at auction nowadays for $84,000, and is he really America's greatest art potter? Certainly his work is whimsical . . . vases tilting like leaning towers, a teapot with a spout like an open-mouthed serpent, and all manner of wrinkled, twisted and squashed vessels." (Kirkus Reviews)

REVIEW: *Booklist* v110 no9/10 p13-6 Ja 1 2014

"Becoming Ben Franklin: How a Candle-Maker's Son Helped Light the Flame of Liberty," "The Mad Potter: George E. Ohr, Eccentric Genius," and "The Boy Who Loved Math: The Improbable Life of Paul Erdos." "In this handsomely designed, solidly researched, and beautifully written biography, [Russell] Freedman uses well-chosen quotes, anecdotes, and illustrations as he traces Ben Franklin's improbable journey. . . . Intelligently written and beautifully illustrated, this engaging book describes the life and flamboyant personality of Mississippi potter George Ohr. . . . This unusual picture book introduces eccentric mathematician Paul Erdos and his unconventional life. Lively writing and vivid artwork combine to make this a memorable biography."

REVIEW: *Booklist* v110 no5 p66 N 1 2013 Carolyn Phelan

"The Mad Potter: George E. Ohr, Eccentric Genius." "The artist comes to life in this clearly written narrative, full of well-chosen details and anecdotes. Fine vintage photos show Ohr at work and with his family. Viewers accustomed to the usually staid photographs from the period will be amused by pictures in which Ohr's tomfoolery and bravado are as evident as his wild mustache. Throughout the book, color photos of his art pottery remind readers that Ohr's story is worth telling not just because it's entertaining, but because his pots are unique and beautiful. This informative introduction to the artist who made them closes with exemplary back matter that will help readers of all ages approach art with enthusiasm and confidence."

REVIEW: *Bull Cent Child Books* v67 no4 p212 D 2013 D. S.

REVIEW: *Horn Book Magazine* v90 no1 p109 Ja/F 2014 JOANNA RUDGE LONG

REVIEW: *Kirkus Rev* v81 no19 p205 O 1 2013

REVIEW: *Publ Wkly* v260 no33 p70 Ag 19 2013

REVIEW: *SLJ* v59 no9 p184 S 2013 Daryl Grabarek

GREENBERG, JOEL. A feathered river across the sky; the passenger pigeon's flight to extinction; [by] Joel Greenberg 304 p. 2014 Bloomsbury

1. Bird extinctions—History 2. Environmental literature 3. Extinct birds 4. Historical literature 5. Passenger pigeon
ISBN 9781620405345 (alk. paper)
LC 2013-016927

SUMMARY: "Passenger pigeons inspired awe in the likes of Audubon, Henry David Thoreau, James Fenimore Cooper, and others, but no serious effort was made to protect the species until it was way too late. [Joel] Greenberg's . . . story of the passenger pigeon provides a cautionary tale of what happens when species and natural resources are not harvested sustainably." (Publisher's note)

REVIEW: *Booklist* v110 no5 p8 N 1 2013 Dane Carr

REVIEW: *Kirkus Rev* v81 no22 p48 N 15 2013

REVIEW: *N Y Rev Books* v61 no1 p35-7 Ja 9 2014 Elizabeth Kolbert

REVIEW: *New Yorker* v89 no43 p62-1 Ja 6 2014

"A Feathered River Across the Sky: The Passenger Pigeon's Flight to Extinction." "'A Feathered River Across the Sky: The Passenger Pigeon's Flight to Extinction' . . . [is] Joel Greenberg's study of a bird that really did vanish after near-ubiquity, and that really is the subject of Frankenpigeon dreams of resurrection. . . . A painstaking researcher, Greenberg writes with a naturalist's curiosity about the birds. . . . Greenberg's book is rich in natural history, but when it comes to human history he is more of an environmentalist looking back in anger."

REVIEW: *New Yorker* v89 no43 p62-1 Ja 6 2014

GREENE, DANA. Denise Levertov; a poet's life; [by] Dana Greene p. cm. 2012 University of Illinois Press

1. Biographies 2. Jewish Christians—Biography 3. Poets, American—20th century—Biography
ISBN 9780252037108 (cloth : alk. paper); 9780252094217 (electronic)
LC 2012-023708

SUMMARY: In this biography of poet Denise Levertov, author "Dana Greene examines Levertov's interviews, essays, and self-revelatory poetry to discern the conflict and torment she both endured and created in her attempts to deal with her own psyche, her relationships with family, friends, lovers, colleagues, and the times in which she lived." (Publisher's note)

REVIEW: *America* v209 no2 p30-3 Jl 15 2013 DAVID LEIGH

REVIEW: *Choice* v51 no10 p1742 Je 2014 D. D. Kummings

REVIEW: *Choice* v50 no7 p1244 Mr 2013 D. D. Kummings

REVIEW: *Kirkus Rev* v80 no20 p90 O 15 2012

REVIEW: *Libr J* v137 no14 p100 S 1 2012 Denise J. Stankovics

REVIEW: *TLS* no5747 p22 My 24 2013 ERIC ORMSBY

"Denise Levertov: A Poet's Life" and "A Poet's Revolution: The Life of Denise Levertov." "Both Dana Greene and Donna Krolik Hollenberg document Levertov's career in considerable detail but without ever coming to grips with the genuine puzzle that her work presents. . . . Levertov's life is intrinsically interesting. . . .Of the two accounts, Hollenberg's is the fuller and more illuminating. She has delved deeper into the sources; she offers more specific detail. . . . Hollenberg is also good at evoking the places that were significant for Levertov."

REVIEW: *Women's Review of Books* v31 no1 p18-20 Ja/F 2014 Kate Daniels

GREENE, HARRY W. Tracks and shadows; field biology as art; [by] Harry W. Greene 296 p. 2013 University of California Press

1. Biologists—United States—Biography 2. NATURE—Animals—General 3. NATURE—Environmental Conservation & Protection 4. Nature 5. SCIENCE—Life Sciences—Biology—General 6. Science—Popular works

ISBN 0520232755; 9780520232754 (hardback)

LC 2013-020395

SUMMARY: This book is a memoir by "herpatologist and Cornell University professor [Harry W.] Greene. . . . Evocations of his Texas and Oklahoma childhood reveal a lifelong fascination with reptiles, specifically snakes, which launched a career in academia and research circling the globe." He reflects "on humanity's interconnectedness with the Earth and all its inhabitants." (Publisher's Weekly)

REVIEW: *Booklist* v110 no5 p8 N 1 2013 Colleen Mondor

REVIEW: *Nat Hist* v122 no2 p44 Mr 2014 LAURENCE A. MARSCHALL

REVIEW: *Publ Wkly* v260 no33 p59 Ag 19 2013

REVIEW: *Science* v342 no6164 p1320 D 13 2013 Frances Bonier

"Tracks and Shadows: Field Biology As Art." "[Author Harry W.] Greene's book reads as an ode to organismal biology; a defense of the value of basic natural history research; and a love story about snakes, wild places, and learning through the art of observation and inquiry. The book is far more than a memoir--as eclectic as its author . . . , it encompasses biographical essays on friends and mentors, popular science writing about his beloved snakes, and philosophical ponderings of existential quandaries. . . . From vivid and touching stories about his experiences as an ambulance driver, to detailed descriptions of the biology and evolution of snakes, to appreciations on deserts and tropical forests, Greene engages readers from beginning to end."

GREENE, JACK P. Evaluating empire and confronting colonialism in eighteenth-century Britain; [by] Jack P. Greene xx, 385 p. 2013 Cambridge University Press

1. Discourse analysis—History—18th century 2. HISTORY—Europe—Great Britain 3. Historical literature 4. Imperialism—Public opinion—History—18th century

ISBN 1107030552 (hardback); 1107682983 (paperback); 9781107030558 (hardback); 9781107682986 (paperback)

LC 2012-021362

SUMMARY: Written by Jack P. Greene, "This volume comprehensively examines the ways metropolitan Britons spoke and wrote about the British Empire during the short eighteenth century, from about 1730 to 1790. The work argues that . . . a growing familiarity with the character of overseas territories and their inhabitants during and after the Seven Years' War produced a substantial critique of empire." (Publisher's note)

REVIEW: *Choice* v51 no2 p339-40 O 2013 E. J. Jenkins

"Evaluating Empire and Confronting Colonialism in Eighteenth-Century Britain." "Britons' discourse about their empire underwent a major shift from the 1760s, according to [author Jack P.] Greene. . . . After the Seven Years' War ended in 1763, . . . the language appearing in contemporary primary sources became increasingly critical, demonstrating that as Britons gained access to more information from abroad, they became disenchanted by evidence of oppression in their current and former colonial possessions. Greene argues that the language of justice, liberty, and humanity gave way to protests about slavery . . . and the oppression of indigenous peoples. . . . Greene's expertise and research from a wide array of primary sources has produced an excellent book."

REVIEW: *Hist Today* v64 no1 p58-9 Ja 2014 Frank O'Gorman

" Evaluating Empire and Confronting Colonialism in Eighteenth-Century Britain." "The purposes of this book are singular and, to an extent, groundbreaking. . . . [Jack P.] Greene's method is to establish a clear theme at the start of each chapter and then to furnish detailed illustrations and examples. He deploys succinct summaries of his sources while enabling his authors to speak for themselves. . . . What we have, then, is an enormously learned, clearly organised and chronologically-based outline of a vast mass of literature on the 18th-century British Empire and its critics. . . . Such a work has its limitations. . . . Nevertheless one cannot imagine anyone failing to profit by immersing themselves in Jack Greene's elegantly written pages."

GREENE, JOSHUA. Moral tribes; emotion, reason, and the gap between us and them; [by] Joshua Greene 432 p. 2013 Penguin Press

1. Civilization 2. Emotions 3. Ethics 4. Evolutionary psychology 5. Neurosciences & the humanities 6. Psychological literature 7. Psychology & ethics

ISBN 1594202605; 9781594202605

LC 2013-007775

SUMMARY: In this book, "[Joshua] Greene, a philosopher and scientist, draws on research in psychology and neuroscience to explore the roots of morality, particularly the tragedy of commonsense morality, when people of different races, religions, ethnic groups, and nationalities share the same sense of morality but apply it from different perspectives in whose differences lie the roots of conflict. Us-versus-them conflicts date back to tribal life." (Booklist)

REVIEW: *Atlantic* v312 no4 p102-18 N 2013 ROBERT WRIGHT

"Moral Tribes: Emotion, Reason, and the Gap Between Us and Them" and "Just Babies: The Origins of Good and Evil." "[Joshua] Greene writes that his book is about 'the central tragedy of modern life.' He's not alone in thinking this is high-gravitas stuff. The Yale psychologist Paul Bloom, who also studies the biological basis of morality, has a new book called 'Just Babies', about the emergence of moral inclinations in infants and toddlers. . . . Anyone who doubts that basic moral impulses are innate will have Paul Bloom's book to contend with. . . . If Greene thinks that getting people to couch their moral arguments in a highly reasonable language will make them highly reasonable, I think he's underestimating the cleverness and ruthlessness with which our inner animals pursue natural selection's agenda."

REVIEW: *Choice* v51 no9 p1606 My 2014 S. A. Mason

REVIEW: *Kirkus Rev* v81 no18 p45 S 15 2013

REVIEW: *New Repub* v244 no18 p48-51 N 11 2013 Thomas Nagel

REVIEW: *Publ Wkly* v260 no34 p59 Ag 26 2013

GREENE, M. J. A Conflict of Interest; [by] M. J. Greene 270 p. 2013 Author Solutions

1. Afghanistan—Social conditions 2. Bootlegging 3. Corporations—Corrupt practices 4. Memoirs 5. Whistleblowers

ISBN 1491709308; 9781491709306

SUMMARY: This book by M. J. Greene is a "memoir about her three-year sojourn in the war-ravaged nation. When the Australian native landed in Kabul in 2007 at age 37, she yearned for adventure, so she took a job as a general manager for a company providing supplies to defense organizations. . . . Shortly after starting her job, Greene suspected that someone within the company was selling alcohol illegally on the black market; worse still, she found out that she had been set up as the scapegoat." (Kirkus Reviews)

REVIEW: *Kirkus Rev* v82 no3 p381 F 1 2014

"A Conflict of Interest". " The frightening odyssey of a business executive who went to work in Afghanistan and ended up fighting a personal war against corruption. . . . This tautly written book is filled with mind-twisting intrigue as [M. J.] Greene recounts how she secretly gathered evidence to expose the conspiracy. Her story contains all the suspense of a mystery novel, but readers may find it all the more unnerving because it happened to a real-life, honest person. . . . Greene, in this fine memoir, shows that her keen sense of intuition and unwavering belief in what she thought was right proved to be her greatest survival tools. A harrowing, inspiring true story of a woman caught in a cesspool of corruption who refused to become dirty herself."

REVIEW: *Kirkus Rev* v82 no4 p86 F 15 2014

"A Conflict of Interest". "The frightening odyssey of a business executive who went to work in Afghanistan and ended up fighting a personal war against corruption. . . . This tautly written book is filled with mind-twisting intrigue as [M. J.] Greene recounts how she secretly gathered evidence to expose the conspiracy. Her story contains all the suspense of a mystery novel, but readers may find it all the more unnerving because it happened to a real-life, honest person. . . . Greene, in this fine memoir, shows that her keen sense of intuition and unwavering belief in what she thought was right proved to be her greatest survival tools. A harrowing, inspiring true story of a woman caught in a cesspool of corruption who refused to become dirty herself."

GREENE, MEG. Elena Kagan; a biography; [by] Meg Greene xiv, 172 p. 2014 Greenwood

1. Biography (Literary form) 2. Government attorneys—United States—Biography 3. Judges—United States—Biography 4. Law teachers—United States—Biography 5. Lawyers—United States—Biography

ISBN 1440828970; 9781440828973 (hardback)

LC 2013-031449

SUMMARY: This biography of Elena Kagan, by Meg Greene, part of the Greenwood Biographies series, "focuses on the Supreme Court Justice's impressive law career, including serving as a law clerk to Thurgood Marshall, becoming the first female dean of Harvard Law School, and being appointed the first female solicitor general. The book also devotes considerable attention to Kagan's legal arguments and even explains how she did not always agree with her esteemed boss." (Booklist)

REVIEW: *Booklist* v110 no14 p71 Mr 15 2014 Angela Leeper

"Elena Kagan: A Biography" and "Malcolm X: A Biography". "Biographies are a staple of any school library, and, luckily, these titles in the Greenwood Biographies series make it easier for teens to discover noteworthy Americans, whether for academic or personal research. The thorough coverage begins with a look at each individual's formative years . . . and shows how these events shaped personal and career paths. . . . Black-and-white photos, time lines, and extensive bibliographies round out these solid bios."

GREENE, STEPHANIE. Princess Posey and the Christmas magic; [by] Stephanie Greene 96 p. 2013 G.P. Putnam's Sons

1. Christmas—Fiction 2. Guilt—Fiction 3. Magic—Fiction 4. Santa Claus—Juvenile fiction 5. Truthfulness & falsehood

ISBN 0399163638; 9780399163630 (hardcover)

LC 2012-046089

SUMMARY: In this book, by Stephanie Greene, "Posey is sure Santa will bring her a real magic wand for Christmas--it will help her do so many wonderful things! But when an accident leads to a little white lie, she worries Santa won't come at all. Will Princess Posey's sparkly tutu help her find the courage to fix things?" (Publisher's note)

REVIEW: *Horn Book Magazine* v89 no6 p64 N/D 2013 MARTHA V. PARRAVANO

"Princess Posey and the Christmas Magic." "In her latest easy-to-read adventure, first grader Posey worries that Santa won't come to her house this year: she has failed to tell her mom the whole truth about an incident involving her baby brother and the Christmas tree. A full confession (as always, made easier by donning her empowering pink tutu) eases her guilt. Meanwhile, she helps Gramps become a more confident dancer. . . . A warm family story told in ten brief, generously leaded chapters, with a likable, kindhearted protagonist."

REVIEW: *Kirkus Rev* v81 no15 p179 Ag 1 2013

REVIEW: *SLJ* v59 no10 p1 O 2013 Virginia Walter

GREENE, THOMAS CHRISTOPHER. The headmaster's wife; [by] Thomas Christopher Greene 288 p. 2014 Thomas Dunne Books

1. Boarding schools—Fiction 2. Grief—Fiction 3. Marriage—Fiction 4. Psychic trauma—Fiction 5. Psychological fiction 6. School principals—Fiction

ISBN 1250038944; 9781250038944 (hardcover: alk. paper)

LC 2013-031656

SUMMARY: "Arthur Winthrop is the Headmaster of Vermont's elite Lancaster School. It is the place he feels has given him his life, but is also the site of his undoing. . . . Found wandering naked in Central Park, he begins to tell his story to the police, but his memories collide into one another, and the true nature of things, a narrative of love, of marriage, of family and of a tragedy Arthur does not know how to address emerges." (Publisher's note)

REVIEW: *Booklist* v110 no11 p23 F 1 2014 Carol Haggas

REVIEW: *Kirkus Rev* v82 no1 p274 Ja 1 2014

"The Headmaster's Wife". "A headmaster and his wife suffer intimations of mortality on a bucolic Vermont campus. The first half of Greene's fourth novel (Envious Moon, 2007, etc.) unfolds like a conventional academic tale. . . . Just as we begin to understand that this is no ordinary interrogation, the novel takes a wholly unexpected twist, which is then compounded by another, even more surprising one. Up to this point, readers will suspect only that the story could be taking place anytime in the last 40 years or so. Although the puzzle element threatens to overwhelm the narrative, this is a moving testament to the vicissitudes of love and loss, regret and hope."

REVIEW: *Publ Wkly* v260 no45 p46 N 11 2013

GREENFIELD, JEFF. If Kennedy Lived; The First and Second Terms of President John F. Kennedy: an Alternate History; [by] Jeff Greenfield 256 p. 2013 Penguin Group USA

1. American alternate histories (Fiction) 2. Civil rights movements 3. Cold War, 1945-1989 4. Kennedy, John F. (John Fitzgerald), 1917-1963 5. United States—Politics & government

ISBN 0399166963; 9780399166969

SUMMARY: In this alternate history, author Jeff Greenfield "speculates how much different the nation and the world would have been if [John F.] Kennedy had been only wounded by [Lee Harvey] Oswald and gone on to serve two full terms. Here, Kennedy . . . ushers in a relatively peaceful era--compared to the real 1960s--in which the Cold War ends, the United States avoids entrapment in Vietnam, and student protests call for more progressive politics than JFK is already advocating." (Library Journal)

REVIEW: *Kirkus Rev* v81 no22 p248 N 15 2013

REVIEW: *Libr J* v138 no8 p60 My 1 2013

REVIEW: *N Y Times Book Rev* p34 O 27 2013 Jacob Heilbrunn

"The Interloper: Lee Harvey Oswald Inside the Soviet Union," "JFK, Conservative," and "If Kennedy Lived: The First and Second Terms of President John F. Kennedy: An Alternate History." "In this penetrating study of Oswald's pivotal sojourn in the Soviet Union, [Peter] Savodnik outlines the pitiable delusions and hopes Oswald harbored both in America and abroad. Savodnik, a gifted writer, draws on archival documents and interviews . . . to explain the murderous rage that prompted him to assassinate John F. Kennedy. . . . [Ira] Stoll . . . provides a wonderfully mischievous analysis. . . . In his diverting 'If Kennedy Lived,' [Jeff] Greenfield . . . asks how things might have played out had John F. Kennedy survived."

REVIEW: *N Y Times Book Rev* p1-24 O 27 2013 Jill Abramson

"If Kennedy Lived: The First and Second Terms of President John F. Kennedy: An Alternate History," "The Dark Side of Camelot," and "President Kennedy: Profile of Power." "The loathsomely titled 'If Kennedy Lived' . . . imagines a completed first Kennedy term and then a second. . . . 'President Kennedy: Profile of Power' is a minutely detailed chronicle of the Kennedy White House. As a primer on Kennedy's decision-making . . . the book is fascinating. What's missing is a picture of Kennedy's personal life. . . . In 'The Dark Side of Camelot,' [Seymour M.] Hersh wildly posits connections between the Kennedys and the mob."

GREENING INDIA'S GROWTH; costs, valuations and trade-offs; 208 p. 2014 Routledge

1. Economic development—Environmental aspects—India 2. Environmental economics 3. India—Environmental conditions 4. Political science literature 5. Sustainable development—India

ISBN 9780415719353 (hbk: alk. paper)

LC 2013-025148

SUMMARY: This book by Muthukumara Mani "analyses India's growth from an economic perspective and assesses whether India can grow in a 'green' and sustainable manner." Topics include "the physical and monetary costs and losses of environmental health and natural resources driven by economic growth . . . the value of ecosystem services from the major biomes in India . . . [and] trade-offs between economic growth and environmental sustainability." (Publisher's note)

REVIEW: *Choice* v51 no9 p1647 My 2014 J. Bhattacharya

"Greening India's Growth: Costs, Valuations, and Trade-Offs". "These questions are easy to pose but tough to answer dispassionately with cold, hard numbers. This volume, based on research conducted under the auspices of the World Bank and edited by stalwart environmental economist [Muthukumara S.] Mani, attempts to do exactly that. . . . The volume is exceptionally well written, especially considering the technical nature of the subject matter. The conclusion leaves the reader with hope that policy action today could make matters better for millions to come."

GREENLY, LARRY. Eugene Bullard; world's first Black fighter pilot; [by] Larry Greenly 160 p. 2012 Junebug Books

1. African American fighter pilots—Biography 2. African American fighter pilots—France—Biography 3. Biography (Literary form) 4. Fighter pilots—France—Biography 5. Race discrimination—United States—History—20th century 6. World War, 1914-1918—Aerial operations, French 7. World War, 1939-1945—Aerial operations, French

ISBN 158838280X; 9781588382801

LC 2012-036425

SUMMARY: This book, by Larry Greenly, "tells the story of pioneering black aviator Eugene Bullard from his birth in 1895 to his combat experiences in both World War I and II and, finally, his return to America. . . . He ran away from home at twelve and eventually made his way to France, where he joined the French Foreign Legion and later the Lafayette Flying Corps, to become the world's first black fighter pilot." (Publisher's note)

REVIEW: *Booklist* v110 no11 p58 F 1 2014 J. B. Petty

"Eugene Bullard: World's First Black Fighter Pilot." "Though his heroic deeds brought recognition from the French, a white American doctor in Paris became a constant stumbling block for further progress in Eugene's life and career. When Bullard returned to the U.S., he faced racial bias until his death in 1961. Using Bullard's memoirs and other sparse information about him, [Larry] Greenly crafts a moving, novelistic biography that portrays Bullard's courage throughout his life. Meanwhile, the black-and white photos, of everything from a teenage Bullard boxing to wartime aircrafts, add plenty of historical flavor."

REVIEW: *Kirkus Rev* v81 no22 p185 N 15 2013

REVIEW: *Voice of Youth Advocates* v36 no6 p80 F 2014 Stacy Holbrook

GREENSPAN, ALAN, 1926-. The Map and the Territory; Risk, Human Nature, and the Future of Forecasting; [by] Alan Greenspan 496 p. 2013 Penguin Group USA

1. Economic forecasting 2. Economics literature 3. Financial crises 4. Financial risk 5. United States—Economic policy

ISBN 1594204810; 9781594204814

SUMMARY: This book by Alan Greenspan is "integrates the history of economic prediction, the new work of behavioral economists, and the fruits of the author's own . . . career to offer a . . .grounding in what we can know about economic forecasting and what we can't.The book explores how culture is and isn't destiny and probes what we can predict about the world's biggest looming challenges, from debt and the reform of the welfare state to natural disasters in an age of global warming." (Publisher's note)

REVIEW: *Bookforum* v20 no4 p12-51 D 2013/Ja 2014 HELAINE OLEN

REVIEW: *Booklist* v110 no5 p6 N 1 2013 Mary Whaley

REVIEW: *Choice* v51 no6 p1060 F 2014 J. Prager

REVIEW: *Economist* v409 no8861 p87-8 N 9 2013

"The Map and the Territory: Risk, Human Nature and the Future of Forecasting." "'The Map and the Territory' could have been fascinating. The book aims to explain the economy's recent troubles by offering a 'macro view' of how everything works. A new, lucid set of macroeconomic principles would have been something new for Mr. [Alan] Greenspan. . . . But hopes for clarity prove as unjustified as 1990s share prices. The book is a difficult read, jumbled and confused. . . . Though occasionally arresting, these globs of discussion never coalesce into a sustained argument."

REVIEW: *Kirkus Rev* v81 no19 p215 O 1 2013

REVIEW: *Libr J* v138 no9 p56 My 15 2013 Barbara Hoffert

REVIEW: *N Y Times Book Rev* p24 N 17 2013 N. GREGORY MANKIW

REVIEW: *New Repub* p35-9 D 2013/Ja 2014 Robert M. Solow

REVIEW: *New York Times* v163 no56296 pC4 O 21 2013 BINYAMIN APPELBAUM

GREENWALD, ALICE M.ed. The stories they tell. See The stories they tell

GREENWALD, GLENN, 1967-. No place to hide; Edward Snowden, the NSA, and the U.S. surveillance state; [by] Glenn Greenwald 320 p. 2014 Henry Holt & Co.

1. Intelligence service—United States 2. Mass surveillance 3. Memoirs 4. Snowden, Edward Joseph, 1983- 5. United States. National Security Agency

ISBN 162779073X; 9781627790734 (hardcover); 9781627790741 (electronic bk.)

LC 2014-932888

SUMMARY: This book tells how "In May 2013, [author] Glenn Greenwald set out for Hong Kong to meet an anonymous source who claimed to have astonishing evidence of pervasive government spying. . . . That source turned out to be the 29-year-old NSA contractor Edward Snowden, and his revelations about the agency's widespread, systemic overreach proved to be some of the most explosive and consequential news in recent history." (Publisher's note)

REVIEW: *Columbia J Rev* v53 no2 p52-7 Jl/Ag 2014 MALCOLM FORBES

REVIEW: *Economist* v411 no8887 p79 My 17 2014

REVIEW: *Harper's Magazine* v328 no1969 p83-5 Je 2014 Joshua Cohen

REVIEW: *Kirkus Rev* v82 no12 p292 Je 15 2014

REVIEW: *Libr J* v139 no11 p109 Je 15 2014 Amanda Mastrull

REVIEW: *London Rev Books* v36 no18 p11-2 S 25 2014 Andrew O'Hagan

REVIEW: *N Y Rev Books* v61 no12 p16-20 Jl 10 2014 Sue Halpern

REVIEW: *N Y Times Book Rev* p14-5 Je 8 2014 MICHAEL KINSLEY

REVIEW: *New Statesman* v143 no5211 p46-7 My 23 2014 David Aaronovitch

REVIEW: *New York Times* v163 no56500 pC1-4 My 13 2014 MICHIKO KAKUTANI

REVIEW: *New Yorker* v90 no14 p72-1 My 26 2014

"No Place to Hide: Edward Snowden, the NSA, and the US Surveillance State." "Early in this effective memoir of Edward Snowden's revelations about National Security Agency spying, Greenwald recalls meeting Snowden in a Hong Kong hotel conference room next to 'a huge, green, plastic alligator.' Greenwald found his youth 'disorienting,' having assumed that someone willing to risk his future must be near retirement. He veers between frustration with the deliberations at the 'Guardian,' his journalistic home at the time, and acknowledgment of the 'remarkable speed and boldness' with which it published, despite pressure from two governments."

REVIEW: *Publ Wkly* v261 no21 p12 My 26 2014 ALEX CROWLEY

REVIEW: *Publ Wkly* v261 no4 p108-12 Ja 27 2014

REVIEW: *TLS* no5807 p27 Jl 18 2014 CHRISTOPHER COKER

GREENWAY, ALICE. The Bird Skinner; [by] Alice Greenway 320 p. 2014 Pgw

1. Love stories 2. Maine—Fiction 3. Older men—Fiction 4. Ornithologists 5. Recluses—Fiction

ISBN 0802121047; 9780802121042

SUMMARY: The protagonist of this novel by Alice Greenway, "Jim Kennoway was once an esteemed member of the ornithology department at the Museum of Natural History in New York, collecting and skinning birds as specimens. Slowing down from a hard-lived life and a recent leg amputation, Jim retreats to an island in Maine: to drink, smoke, and to be left alone." (Publisher's note)

REVIEW: *Booklist* v110 no6 p20 N 15 2013 Joanne Wilkinson

REVIEW: *Kirkus Rev* v81 no20 p211 O 15 2013

REVIEW: *Libr J* v139 no4 p82 Mr 1 2014 Leslie Patterson

REVIEW: *N Y Times Book Rev* p13 Ja 12 2014 JOANNA HERSHON

"The Bird Skinner." "If there were a prize for ornery old men, the ornithologist Jim Kennoway in Alice Greenway's novel 'The Bird Skinner,' would trounce every recluse in New England. Refusing help . . . , he's drinking and smoking himself to death on an island in Maine. . . . If this premise sounds familiar--striking young woman brings hope to forsaken old man--the style with which Greenway weaves her tale of memory and loss is bracing in its restraint. . . . Jim's memories of his wife give the novel its erratic heartbeat. . . . With an attention to detail that's both poetic and precise . . . Greenway evokes so much more than the weather and mood of her locales."

GREER, GERMAINE, 1939-. White Beech; The Rainforest Years; [by] Germaine Greer 384 p. 2014 St. Martin's Press

1. Forest conservation—Australia 2. Forest reserves—Australia 3. Historical literature 4. Memoirs 5. Reforestation

ISBN 162040611X; 9781620406113

SUMMARY: This book, by Germaine Greer, describes how on "one bright day in December 2001, sixty-two-year-old Germaine Greer found herself confronted by an irresistible challenge in the shape of sixty hectares of dairy farm, one of many in southeast Queensland, Australia, which, after a century of logging, clearing, and downright devastation, had been abandoned to their fate." Greer then describes how she rebuilt and restored the farm's ecosystem. (Publisher's note)

REVIEW: *Booklist* v110 no19/20 p9 Je 1 2014 Donna Seaman

REVIEW: *Kirkus Rev* v82 no12 p3 Je 15 2014

REVIEW: *Libr J* v139 no3 p74 F 15 2014 Barbara Hoffert

REVIEW: *Libr J* v139 no6 p109 Ap 1 2014 Diana Hartle

REVIEW: *New Statesman* v143 no5195 p48-9 Ja 31 2014 Richard Mabey

REVIEW: *New York Times* v163 no56564 pC1-6 Jl 16 2014 DWIGHT GARNER

REVIEW: *Publ Wkly* v261 no13 p52 Mr 31 2014

REVIEW: *TLS* no5795 p30 Ap 25 2014 GHILLEAN PRANCE

"White Beech: The Rainforest Years." "'White Beech' is something of a departure for Germaine Greer. . . . She bought a dilapidated property in the subtropical rainforest zone of Southern Queensland and went about rehabilitating it. The story takes us from the initial search for a suitable site to the handing over to a charity of a regenerating and functional forest. This is much more than a simple account of the forest restoration because . . . Greer has had to do extensive research in many areas. There is an impressive amount here about Australian history, its native peoples, . . . and its plants and animals. . . . Greer states that 'If I have written this book properly, it will convey the deep joy that rebuilding wild nature can bring.' She has certainly achieved her goal."

GREGORY, PETER J.ed. Soil conditions and plant growth. See Soil conditions and plant growth

GREGSON, J. M. Cry of the Children; [by] J. M. Gregson 224 p. 2014 Severn House Pub Ltd

1. Detective & mystery stories 2. Missing children—Fiction 3. Murder—Fiction 4. Murder investigation—Fiction 5. Police—Fiction

ISBN 0727882864; 9780727882868

SUMMARY: In this book, by J.M. Gregson, "when seven-year-old Lucy Gibson disappears into thin air at the local funfair, Chief Superintendent Lambert, along with DS Bert Hook and DS Ruth David have a race against time to discover who took the young girl—and to prevent more children from going missing before it's too late." (Publisher's note)

REVIEW: *Booklist* v110 no6 p23 N 15 2013 Emily Melton

REVIEW: *Kirkus Rev* v81 no24 p187 D 15 2013

"Cry of the Children". "Chief Supt. John Lambert and DS Bert Hook . . . face what every policeman dreads: a child-killer. When 24 hours pass with no result after Anthea Gibson first reports the disappearance of her 7-year-old daughter, Lucy, from the village fair, Lambert and Hook know that the outcome won't be good. . . . And once it's a case of murder, they bear down even harder, trying to stop the killer before more children come to harm. [J. M.] Gregson knows when to up the ante and when to bring his case to a close in this tense procedural."

REVIEW: *Publ Wkly* v260 no44 p51 N 4 2013

GREIG, GEORDIE. Breakfast with Lucian; the astounding life and outrageous times of Britain's great modern painter; [by] Geordie Greig 272 p. 2013 Farrar Straus & Giroux

1. BIOGRAPHY & AUTOBIOGRAPHY—Artists, Architects, Photographers 2. BIOGRAPHY & AUTOBIOGRAPHY—Personal Memoirs 3. Biographies 4. Painters—Great Britain—Biography

ISBN 0374116482; 9780374116484 (hardback)

LC 2013-022509

SUMMARY: This book traces the life of artist Lucian Freud, "from his Jewish German family's escape from the Nazis to his starving-artist years. Impudent, ambitious, and voracious, Freud did have a lot to hide. His prodigious sex life, a dizzying carousel of simultaneous partners, resulted in at least 14 children. Because he often paid his enormous gambling debts with paintings, a bookie owns the world's largest private Lucian Freud collection." (Booklist)

REVIEW: *Apollo: The International Magazine for Collectors* v178 no614 p23 N 2013 Thomas Marks

REVIEW: *Apollo: The International Magazine for Collectors* v178 no612 p119 S 2013

REVIEW: *Booklist* v110 no5 p20 N 1 2013 Donna Seaman

"Breakfast With Lucian: The Astounding Life and Outrageous Times of Britain's Great Modern Painter." "[Geordie] Greig, a prominent newspaper editor, managed to get close to [Lucian] Freud during the painter's last decade, meeting him regularly for breakfast near his London home and studio.. . . Greig's vivid, swiftly flowing, bracingly candid, alluringly illustrated chronicle of the exploits and accomplishments of this renowned renegade artist is as arresting, discomfiting, and unforgettable as a Freud portrait."

REVIEW: *Economist* v409 no8859 p94 O 26 2013

"Breakfast With Lucian: The Astounding Life and Outrageous Times of Britain's Great Modern Painter." "Spirited. . . . A dedicated networker and an inspired gossip, Mr. [Geordie] Greig has produced a small, highly readable life of the artist. . . . The book focuses not on his painting but on his celebrity. . . . Mr. Greig is [Lucian] Freud's [James] Boswell. . . . Mr. Grieg writes of Freud's art and his life being seamlessly joined. . . . Mr. Greig's is a compelling portrait of a complete amoralist who became a monstre sacré."

REVIEW: *Kirkus Rev* v81 no18 p81 S 15 2013

REVIEW: *Libr J* v138 no18 p85 N 1 2013 Julia A. Watson

REVIEW: *London Rev Books* v35 no23 p3-8 D 5 2013 Julian Barnes

REVIEW: *N Y Times Book Rev* p11 D 1 2013 FRANCINE PROSE

REVIEW: *New York Times* v163 no56328 pC21-5 N 22 2013 DWIGHT GARNER

"Breakfast With Lucian: The Astounding Life and Outrageous Times of Britain's Great Modern Painter." "I don't mean to make [Lucian] Freud sound insecure and vile. Geordie Greig does a handy enough job of that in his new book . . . a volume of prying and sabotage dressed up to resemble a book of love. . . . It displays little feeling for Freud's work. Its history is patchy. Its tone is frequently what you'd get if you set Robin Leach loose at the Tate Modern. . . . 'Breakfast With Freud' is seldom boring, though, which is something. It is so force-fed with gossip and incident . . . that Freud comes of as equal parts Cecil Beaton . . . and Charles Bukowski. . . . You turn each page the way a rat hits the little lever for another pellet of crack."

REVIEW: *New York Times* v163 no56328 pC21-5 N 22 2013 DWIGHT GARNER

REVIEW: *New Yorker* v89 no34 p79-1 O 28 2013

"Breakfast With Lucian." "[An] admiring but acerbic biography of the painter. The book focusses on personal matters: [Lucian] Freud, who had hundreds of lovers and fathered at least a dozen children, had ample fuel for his emotionally charged paintings, which, by the time of his death, in 2011, were selling for up to eight figures. [Geordie] Greig weaves in the story of his obsession with the painter, which eventually became a friendship, and led to a series of interviews over breakfast in a London restaurant. The Freud who emerges in this account is a slippery figure, not only for journalists who tried to explain him but also for his intimates."

REVIEW: *Publ Wkly* v260 no25 p21-6 Je 24 2013 JAMES H. MILLER

REVIEW: *TLS* no5776 p11 D 13 2013 KEITH MILLER

GREIG, HANNAH. The beau monde; fashionable society in Georgian London; [by] Hannah Greig 352 p. 2013 Oxford University Press

1. Fashion—England 2. Fashion—History—18th century 3. Historical literature 4. London (England)—History—18th century 5. London (England)—Social life & customs—18th century

ISBN 9780199659005 (hardback)

LC 2013-936233

SUMMARY: This book by Hannah Greig describes how, "Caricatured for extravagance, vanity, glamorous celebrity and, all too often, embroiled in scandal and gossip, 18th-century London's fashionable society had a well-deserved reputation for frivolity. . . . 'The Beau Monde' leads us on a tour of this exciting new world, from court and parliament to London's parks, pleasure grounds, and private homes." (Publisher's note)

REVIEW: *Choice* v51 no8 p1478 Ap 2014 M. H. Markus

REVIEW: *Economist* v409 no8858 p87-8 O 19 2013

REVIEW: *TLS* no5791 p27 Mr 28 2014 ANTHONY FLETCHER

"The Beau Monde: Fashionable Society in Georgian London." "[Author Hannah Greig] tackles the challenge posed by her title, 'The Beau Monde,' head on, wrestling with it, taking it apart, even adding a dense but deeply researched 'supplementary essay' on the uses and meanings of the term. All this pays off, for her vivid and playful book tantalizes us, just as the leaders of fashionable London society between the 1690s and the early 1800s did the general public, which could not quite come to terms with their mercurial power. As Greig shows cleverly, the 'Beau Monde' was constantly in flux: it spent a great deal of time itself discussing who was in and who was out. . . . Hannah Greig moves with faultless poise through the London scenes that she has so carefully and memorably anatomized."

GRENIER, ROGER. A box of photographs; [by] Roger Grenier 109 p. 2013 University of Chicago Press

1. Authors, French—20th century—Biography 2. Essays 3. Paris (France)—History 4. Photography—History—20th century

ISBN 0226308316 (cloth : alkaline paper); 9780226308319 (cloth : alkaline paper)

LC 2012-037369

SUMMARY: In this book Roger Grenier's "short personal essays revisit his childhood and young-adult life in Paris while explaining his enduring connection with photography. Through . . . anecdotes, Grenier blends his own history with that of photography, and explains how the medium has influenced his entire life. He begins with early photographic history and its practitioners . . . and . . . weaves these histories into his own memories." (Library Journal)

REVIEW: *Libr J* v138 no8 p77 My 1 2013 Shauna Frischkorn

REVIEW: *TLS* no5763 p30 S 13 2013 PETER READ

"A Box of Photographs." "Divided into short chapters, like selections from a newspaper column or pages from a photo album, 'A Box of Photographs' tells in words and images the story of a life spent with cameras and typewriters, while also tracing a path through the social and cultural history of twentieth-century France. . . . We get the message that Roger Grenier cares as much about language as he does about photography. . . . [Albert] Camus promoted a brand of 'joumalisme critique' which combined accurate reporting with explicit awareness of the moral or philosophical consequences of situations and events, an ideal that clearly underpins Grenier's own empathetic values, concise narrative style and understated ability to draw conclusions from anecdotes and experiences."

GRESH, KRISTEN. She who tells a story; women photographers from Iran and the Arab world; [by] Kristen Gresh 164 p. 2013 MFA publications, Museum of Fine Arts, Boston

1. Art literature 2. Photography—Arab countries—Exhibitions 3. Photography—Iran—Exhibitions 4. Women photographers—Arab countries—Exhibitions 5.

Women photographers—Iran—Exhibitions
ISBN 0878468048; 9780878468041
LC 2013-938797

SUMMARY: This book, by Kristen Gresh, "introduces the pioneering work of 12 leading women photographers from Iran and the Arab world: Jananne Al-Ani, Boushra Almutawakel, Gohar Dashti, Rana El Nemr, Lalla Essaydi, Shadi Ghadirian, Tanya Habjouqa, Rula Halawani, Nermine Hammam, Rania Matar, Shirin Neshat and Newsha Tavakolian." (Publisher's note)

REVIEW: *Bookforum* v20 no5 p24-5 F/Mr 2014 Christopher Lyon

"Co-Mix: A Retrospective of Comics, Graphics and Scraps," "She Who Tells a Story: Women Photographers From Iran and the Arab World," and "Lumiere Autochrome: History, Technology, and Preservation." "'Co-Mix' . . . perform[s] the jujitsu flip of mimicking a high-art exhibition catalogue in the quintessential low-art medium of comics. . . . Though Shirin Nesbat is well represented and an obvious inspiration for the other eleven younger artists featured, much of this work could be called post-Neshat, because it favors a less fussy approach, and is more narrative driven. . . . A kind of Swiss Army knife of a book, covering not only the Lumière family's pioneering photographic inventions, dating to the mid-1880s, but also the history of color photography and technical details of processes\ and preservation. . . . An essential resource for students and collectors of photography."

REVIEW: *Choice* v51 no4 p625 D 2013 J. Natal

GRIEP-QUINT, FRANCIS. Michiel van Musscher (1645-1705). See Gerhardt, R. E.

GRIFFEL, MARGARET ROSS. Operas in English; a dictionary; [by] Margaret Ross Griffel 2 v. (xxvi, 984 p.) 2013 Scarecrow Press

1. Encyclopedias & dictionaries 2. Music—Dictionaries 3. Opera—Dictionaries 4. Operas 5. Operas—Discography
ISBN 0810882728 (hardcover); 9780810882720 (hardcover)
LC 2012-031874

SUMMARY: This "is a companion volume to [Margaret Ross] Griffel's 'Operas in German.' The major portion of the book is an alphabetical listing of 3,500 operas. Generally, each entry provides the number of acts; composer; librettist; original language and source of the libretto; date, place, and cast of first performance; a . . . summary of the plot, with names and vocal ranges of the main characters; critical editions of the score; bibliography; and discography." (Booklist)"This is a companion volume to Griffel's Operas in German. The major portion of the book is an alphabetical listing of 3,500 operas. Generally, each entry provides the number of acts; composer; librettist; original language and source of the libretto; date, place, and cast of first performance; a . . . summary of the plot, with names and vocal ranges of the main characters; critical editions of the score; bibliography; and discography. . . . A selective bibliography and an index of characters and names conclude the volume." (Booklist)

REVIEW: *Booklist* v109 no17 p72 My 1 2013 Steven York

REVIEW: *Choice* v50 no11 p1982-3 Jl 2013 C. A. Kolczynski

"Operas in English: A Dictionary." "A greatly expanded and revised edition of [author Margaret Ross] Griffel's 1999 publication . . . featuring some 900 new terms, this dictionary has its main listings in the first volume and the appendixes and index in the second. . . . Entries have librettist, composer, voice types, plot précis, and more. Information about the location and availability of scores and librettos is especially valuable. The addition of some performance reviews and notable videographies and discographies is extremely useful."

REVIEW: *Libr J* v138 no7 p108 Ap 15 2013 Jennifer Stith

GRIFFIN, ADELE. Loud awake and lost; [by] Adele Griffin 304 p. 2013 Alfred A. Knopf

1. Amnesia—Fiction 2. Love—Fiction 3. Memory—Fiction 4. Traffic accidents—Fiction 5. Young adult fiction
ISBN 0385752733; 9780385752725 (hardcover); 9780385752732 (hardcover library binding); 9780385752756 (trade pbk.)
LC 2012-049042

SUMMARY: In this book, "Ember was seriously injured in a car crash, but worse, she killed her passenger, a young man named Anthony. Along with brain trauma and back injuries, she has no memory of the six weeks prior to the accident. Eight months later, she returns from the rehab facility to her home in New York City. Friends and family are on eggshells. . . . Then she meets Kai, so free and different from her old friends, and he makes her want to wake up again. But what will she find when she does?" (Booklist)

REVIEW: *Booklist* v110 no12 p95-6 F 15 2014 Edie Ching

"Loud Awake and Lost." "This passionate story of love and loss is narrated with intensity by [Abby] Craden. She brings forth Em's confusion and hesitancy with a soft voice that often moves from uncertainty to panic. Voices of secondary characters, especially best friend Rachel, go from patient and supportive to irritated and pained when Ember seems to shut them out. Craden captures the intensity of Em's emotions as she struggles to regain her memory and explores her passionate feelings for the mysterious and elusive Kai. The feelings are all there in Craden's reading, and Em's emotions fluctuate with her increasing awareness of her past. This mystery about identity and love will leave listeners holding their breath at times."

REVIEW: *Booklist* v110 no5 p60 N 1 2013 Ilene Cooper

"Loud Awake and Lost." "Two-time National Book Award finalist [Adele] Griffin continues her exploration of the inner workings of the mind in this moving and surprising story. . . . Griffin's writing is exquisite, teasing meaning and memory from her sentences. Even in the smallest moments, she captures the incredible stamina it takes to rebound from a devastating accident, while at the same time showing how the injured can spin a protective cocoon. Ember and all the characters--parents, pals, an old boyfriend--seem walk-through- the-door real. When the final twist arrives, readers may skip back through the pages to figure out why they didn't see it coming, but it doesn't negate the underpinnings of this emotional journey."

REVIEW: *Bull Cent Child Books* v67 no4 p213 D 2013 D. S.

REVIEW: *Kirkus Rev* p53 Ag 15 2013 Fall Preview

REVIEW: *Kirkus Rev* v81 no18 p115 S 15 2013

REVIEW: *Kirkus Rev* v81 no16 p365 Ag 15 2013

REVIEW: *Publ Wkly* v261 no1 p53 Ja 6 2014

REVIEW: *Voice of Youth Advocates* v36 no5 p59-60 D 2013 Allison Hunter Hill

GRIFFIN, MICHAEL. Enlightenment in ruins; the geographies of Oliver Goldsmith; [by] Michael Griffin 209 p. 2013 Bucknell University Press The Rowman & Littlefield Pub. Group, Inc.

1. Authors, Irish—18th century—Biography 2. Biography (Literary form) 3. Irish literature—18th century—History and criticism 4. Irish poets 5. Political poetry
ISBN 9781611485059 (cloth : alk. paper)
LC 2013-015895

SUMMARY: This book by Michael Griffin describes how Irish poet "Oliver Goldsmith (1728-1774) moved between the genres and geographies of enlightenment writing with considerable dexterity. . . . Griffin places Goldsmith in two contexts: one is the intellectual and political culture in which he worked as a professional author living in London; the other is that of his nationality and his as yet unstudied Jacobite politics." (Publisher's note)

REVIEW: *Choice* v51 no6 p1003 F 2014 M. H. Kealy

REVIEW: *TLS* no5784 p21 F 7 2014 NORMA CLARKE

"Enlightenment in Ruins: The Geographies of Oliver Goldsmith." "As the social contract of the post-war era in the twentieth century begins to acquire a copper tinge--our very own golden age--Goldsmith might have something to tell us about what Michael Griffin in this very welcome book calls 'the destructive negligence of the rich.' . . . Griffin's aim is to restore the full Irish context. . . . The Goldsmith who emerges here is a complex, dissident thinker writing for a popular readership unlikely to share his views. . . . This book is a model of historically informed literary analysis, beautifully written and assiduously researched. It is a relief to encounter Goldsmith free of Boswell's anecdotage."

GRIFFITH, NICOLA. Hild; a novel; [by] Nicola Griffith 560 p. 2013 Farrar Straus & Giroux

1. Christian saints—England—Northumbria (Region)—Fiction 2. Christian women saints—England—Whitby—Fiction 3. FICTION—Historical 4. FICTION—Literary 5. Women—History—Middle Ages, 500-1500—Fiction
ISBN 0374280878; 9780374280871
LC 2013-022510

SUMMARY: This book by Nicola Griffith presents a "fictional coming-of-age story about real-life Saint Hilda of Whitby, who grew up pagan in seventh-century Britain. Daughter of a poisoned prince and a crafty noblewoman, quiet, bright-minded Hild arrives at the court of King Edwin of Northumbria, where the six-year-old takes on the role of seer/consiglieri for a monarch troubled by shifting allegiances and Roman emissaries attempting to spread their new religion." (Publishers Weekly)

REVIEW: *Bookforum* v20 no4 p28 D 2013/Ja 2014 JENNY DAVIDSON

"Hild." "[Nicola] Griffith realistically represents the brutality of everyday life in this milieu. . . . In its ambition and intelligence, 'Hild' might best be compared to Hilary Mantel's novels about Thomas Cromwell. Griffith does not have the extraordinary ability displayed in Mantel's 'Wolf Hall' to render densely populated political negotiations as vividly and concretely as one might describe the relationships between three or four members of a family . . . but she has other gifts Mantel doesn't, especially that sharp eye for what happens to plants and animals . . . over the course of the seasons, as well as an understated and just-lyrical-enough prose style that delights the reader locally without ever distracting from the forward movements of character and plot."

REVIEW: *Booklist* v110 no3 p41 O 1 2013 Kerri Price

REVIEW: *Kirkus Rev* v81 no17 p9 S 1 2013

REVIEW: *Libr J* v139 no9 p70 My 15 2014 ALA Rusa-Codes

REVIEW: *Libr J* v138 no11 p60 Je 15 2013 Barbara Hoffert

REVIEW: *Publ Wkly* v260 no25 p140 Je 24 2013

GRIFFITHS, DEAN.il. The stowaways. See Marentette, M.

GRIFFITHS, KATE. Adapting Nineteenth-Century France. See Watts, A.

GRIFFITHS, PAUL. Genetics and philosophy; an introduction; [by] Paul Griffiths viii, 270 p. 2013 Cambridge University Press

1. Developmental genetics 2. Genes 3. Genetics—Philosophy 4. Genomics 5. Scientific literature
ISBN 0521173906 (paperback); 1107002125 (hardback); 9780521173902 (paperback); 9781107002128 (hardback)
LC 2012-042715

SUMMARY: In this book, "Paul Griffiths and Karola Stotz show how the concept of the gene has evolved and diversified across the many fields that make up modern biology. By examining the molecular biology of the 'environment,' they situate genetics in the developmental biology of whole organisms, and reveal how the molecular biosciences have undermined the nature/nurture distinction." (Publisher's note)

REVIEW: *Choice* v51 no7 p1242-3 Mr 2014 D. L. Beach

"Genetics and Philosophy: An Introduction." "[Paul] Griffiths and [Karola] Stotz . . . explore the development of genetic ideals and scientific thought from the early exploration of heredity through modern genomic analysis. The history of the field is particularly well developed in early chapters. . . . The 'Further Reading' sections of each chapter complement the work, providing expanded background information and context. A valuable resource for students and other readers interested in science and philosophy and the history of these fields, along with modern applications of genetic information, including the bioethics of genomic analysis. . . . Highly recommended."

GRIG, LUCY.ed. Two Romes: Rome and Constantinople in Late Antiquity. See Two Romes: Rome and Constantinople in Late Antiquity

GRIGSBY, MARY. Noodlers in Missouri; fishing for identity in a rural subculture; [by] Mary Grigsby 164 p. 2012 Truman State University Press

1. Catfishing—Missouri 2. Fishers—Missouri—Interviews 3. Fishing—Missouri—Psychological aspects 4. Fishing—Social aspects—Missouri 5. Identity (Psy-

chology)—Missouri 6. Sociology literature 7. Subculture—Missouri
ISBN 9781612480619 (pbk. : alk. paper); 9781612480626 (ebk.)
LC 2012-002457

SUMMARY: "In this inside look at the folk tradition of hand-fishing, Mary Grigsby interviews thirty Missouri noodlers to examine this sport's appeal. The skill of catching spawning catfish with the bare hands is passed down through generations and builds a sense of community among participants despite or perhaps because of its illegality." (Publisher's note)

REVIEW: *Contemp Sociol* v42 no5 p762-3 S 2013

"Noodlers in Missouri: Fishing for Identity in a Rural Subculture." "Mary Grigsby's 'Noodlers in Missouri' offers a fascinating ethnography of the southern rural subculture of handfishing, also known as noodling, in Missouri. The details of this folk tradition and the stories of those with whom Grigsby worked in creating the book are readily engaging, providing a compelling read for those unfamiliar with the practice of handfishing. In each chapter, Grigsby elaborates on a different facet of noodling, ultimately building a contemporary portrait of this practice in Missouri, where handfishing is currently illegal."

GRIMES, JILL.ed. Sexually transmitted disease. See Sexually transmitted disease

GRIMES, MARTHA, 1931-. The way of all fish; novel; [by] Martha Grimes 352 p. 2014 Scribner
1. Assassins—Fiction 2. Authorship—Fiction 3. Humorous stories 4. Literary agents 5. Publishers & publishing—Fiction
ISBN 1476723958; 9781476723952 (hc); 9781476723976 (tp)
LC 2013-016760

SUMMARY: In this novel, by Martha Grimes, "Candy and Karl, hitmen with a difference—they have scruples—once again venture into the murky Manhattan publishing scene. This time they come to the aid of a writer who is being sued by her unscrupulous literary agent, L. Bass Hess, a man determined to get a 15 percent commission for a book he didn't sell." (Publisher's note)

REVIEW: *Booklist* v110 no9/10 p53 Ja 1 2014 Michele Leber

REVIEW: *Kirkus Rev* v82 no1 p176 Ja 1 2014

"The Way of All Fish". "Unlikely alliances form in a plot to neutralize an author's greedy former agent. . . . As one caper follows another, from Manhattan to Sewickley, Pa., to the Everglades, Cindy loses her importance to the conspirators. [Martha] Grimes . . . brings a crazy-quilt sensibility to a romp that ultimately sags a bit under the weight of its own cleverness. Despite its pallid heroine, however, this sendup of the book world, in which hit men apparently have more integrity than publishers, is great fun."

REVIEW: *Libr J* v138 no13 p54 Ag 1 2013 Barbara Hoffert

REVIEW: *Publ Wkly* v260 no47 p32-3 N 18 2013

GRIMES, NIKKI. Words With Wings; [by] Nikki Grimes 96 p. 2013 Boyds Mills Press
1. Authorship 2. Child authors 3. Divorce—Fiction 4. Imagination 5. Novels in verse
ISBN 1590789857; 9781590789858

SUMMARY: In this book, by Nikki Grimes, "Gabby . . . is a daydreamer, and words fire her imagination, creating new worlds for her to inhabit. After her parents separate and Gabby must go to a different school, her daydreams become increasingly vivid, intruding on the realities of the classroom and schoolwork. To Gabby's occasional puzzlement, her mother worries . . . but her wonderful new teacher is more patient, wisely helping her capture her daydreams on paper and inspiring a new dream to become an author." (Booklist)

REVIEW: *Booklist* v110 no2 p67 S 15 2013 Michael Cart

"Words With Wings." "[Nikki] Grimes, recipient of the 2006 NCTE Award for Excellence in Poetry for Children, has written a novel in verse that is an enthusiastic celebration of the power of words and imagination and a dramatic demonstration that daydreamers are, as Gabby hopes, 'cool.' Always accessible. Grimes' language is vivid, rhythmic, and figurative: Gabby says her dreams are 'fancy dancing in my mind,' for example, and thoughts of a circus are a 'trampoline to the big top.' Plain or fancy, Grimes' words speak to the daydreamer in every reader."

REVIEW: *Bull Cent Child Books* v67 no4 p213-4 D 2013 K. C.

REVIEW: *Kirkus Rev* p75 N 15 2013 Best Books

REVIEW: *Kirkus Rev* p39-40 Ag 15 2013 Fall Preview

REVIEW: *Kirkus Rev* v81 no15 p106 Ag 1 2013

REVIEW: *Publ Wkly* v260 no31 p73 Ag 5 2013

REVIEW: *SLJ* v60 no4 p53 Ap 2014 Sharon Grover Liz Hannegan

GRIMLY, GRIS.il. Gris Grimly's Frankenstein, or, The modern Prometheus. See Gris Grimly's Frankenstein, or, The modern Prometheus

GRIMLY, GRIS.il. The Annotated Frankenstein; 387 p. 2012 The Belknap Press of Harvard University Press
1. Frankenstein's monster (Fictitious character)—Fiction 2. Frankenstein, Victor (Fictitious character)—Fiction 3. Horror tales 4. Modernity 5. Scientists—Fiction
ISBN 9780674055520 (alk. paper)
LC 2012-024171

SUMMARY: This annotated edition of the novel "Frankenstein" by Mary Shelley "situate[s] the novel in its philosophical, literary, biographical and historical contexts, and provides . . . illustrations and . . . appendices (including examinations of the revised edition of 1831 and a timeline which juxtaposes the novel's episodes with concurrent historical events)." (Times Literary Supplement)

REVIEW: *Choice* v50 no6 p1053 F 2013 J. T. Lynch

REVIEW: *Libr J* v137 no20 p85-7 D 1 2012 Morris Hounion

REVIEW: *TLS* no5745 p12-3 My 10 2013 MICHAEL SALER

"The Lady and Her Monsters: A Tale of Dissections, Real-Life Dr. Frankensteins, and the Creation of Mary Shelley's Masterpiece" and "The Annotated Frankenstein." "[Roseanne Montillo's] book is gripping, as she is drawn to the many sensationalistic aspects surrounding Frankenstein's gestation and Shelley's tempestuous, often tragic, life. . . .

Her book is no more sophisticated as literary criticism. . . . 'The Annotated Frankenstein' is an ideal vehicle for . . . a more sustained engagement with the novel's complexities. . . . It should appeal to scholars familiar with the novel as well as those exploring it for the first time."

THE GRIMM CONCLUSION; 368 p. 2013 Dutton Children's Books

1. Adventure and adventurers—Fiction 2. Brothers and sisters—Fiction 3. Characters in literature—Fiction 4. Fairy tales 5. Humorous stories

ISBN 0525426159; 9780525426158 (hardcover)

LC 2013-021686

SUMMARY: In this book by Adam Gidwitz and illustrated by Hugh D'Andrade, "two children venture through forests, flee kingdoms, face ogres and demons and monsters, and, ultimately, find their way home. Oh yes, and they may die. Just once or twice." (Publisher's note) "An omniscient narrator comments throughout, offering warnings, consolation, and explanations." (Horn Book Magazine)

REVIEW: *Booklist* v110 no6 p48-9 N 15 2013 Sarah Hunter

REVIEW: *Horn Book Magazine* v90 no1 p91 Ja/F 2014 SUSAN DOVE LEMPKE

"The Grimm Conclusion." "Readers of [Adam] Gidwitz's previous two books . . . will not be surprised that the sister and brother in this story both endure terrible adventures, including death. . . . This is gruesome, grisly, grim fun. . . . This volume is filled with metafictive references to the previous books and their characters; it also introduces some entertaining new characters, from a terrifying ogre named Malchizedek and a dimwitted prince to three ravens who offer their own arch commentary on events. Despite the gleeful horror, this is ultimately a warm and empathetic novel about devotion, and it will make a great read-aloud to groups that can handle the gore."

REVIEW: *Kirkus Rev* v81 no18 p291 S 15 2013

REVIEW: *Publ Wkly* p77 Children's starred review annual 2013

GRIMM, DAVID. Citizen canine; our evolving relationship with cats and dogs; [by] David Grimm 352 p. 2014 PublicAffairs

1. Animal rights 2. Human-animal relationships—History 3. Journalism 4. Pets—History 5. Pets—Social aspects—History

ISBN 1610391330; 9781610391337 (hardcover)

LC 2013-043916

SUMMARY: Author David Grimm "investigates the ever-changing roles played by cats and dogs throughout history and travels the U.S. speaking to those on the cutting edge of animal science and welfare. He visits the Washington National Cathedral for the Blessing of the Animals and rides along with a detective in the LAPD's Animal Cruelty Task Force. . . . He also attends a Military Working Dog program . . . and argues against harmful pit bull stereotype." (Publishers Weekly)

REVIEW: *Booklist* v110 no14 p37 Mr 15 2014 Nancy Bent

REVIEW: *Kirkus Rev* v82 no5 p49 Mr 1 2014

"Citizen Canine: Our Evolving Relationship With Cats and Dogs". "Science deputy news editor [David] Grimm . . . looks at the pros and cons of granting citizenship to our pets-a far-out idea, to be sure, but one gaining traction with some on the fringe of the animal rights movement. . . . He does not subscribe to giving animals citizenship, but he does believe 'that the quest for inclusion defines us all, animal and man.' A challenging notion that fails to adequately address the implicit downgrading of our broader responsibilities as citizens."

REVIEW: *Libr J* v139 no6 p106 Ap 1 2014 Eva Lautemann

REVIEW: *New York Times* v163 no56475 pC25-8 Ap 18 2014 MICHIKO KAKUTANI

REVIEW: *Publ Wkly* v261 no2 p59 Ja 13 2014

GRIS GRIMLY'S FRANKENSTEIN, OR, THE MODERN PROMETHEUS; 208 p. 2013 Balzer + Bray

1. Canon (Literature) 2. Graphic novels 3. Horror stories 4. Monsters—Fiction 5. Scientists—Fiction

ISBN 0061862975; 9780061862977 (trade bdg.)

LC 2010-046237

SUMMARY: This is a graphic novel version of Mary Shelley's "Frankenstein" by Gris Grimly. "Spidery ink lines and a palette of jaundiced yellows and faded sepias plumb the darkness of the writer's imaginings. Frankenstein's bone-embellished military jacket and pop-star shock of hair turn him into a sort of anachronistic punk scientist." Focus is given to "the monster's self-loathing and Frankenstein's ruin." (Publishers Weekly)

REVIEW: *Bull Cent Child Books* v67 no2 p113-4 O 2013 K. C.

"Gris Grimly's Frankenstein." "While most everyone knows the story of Frankenstein and his monstrous creation, approaching the original text can be a daunting prospect. [Adaptor and illustrator Gris] Grimly succeeds admirably, following the novel by first setting the scene through letters from Captain Walton (the eventual finder of the monster) reproduced in a sepia font resembling handwriting on parchment, before moving into a more recognizable graphic narrative format. . . . Grimly proves himself a more adept assembler of parts than his subject proved to be; his product is no monster, but a pastiche of style and substance that will reanimate the original for yet another generation of readers."

REVIEW: *Horn Book Magazine* v89 no5 p68 S/O 2013 KATIE BIRCHER

"Gris Grimly's 'Frankenstein, or, the Modern Prometheus'." "Adeptly 'assembled from the original text,' this graphic novel adaptation abridges [Mary] Shelley's tale while staying true to its spirit. The inventive illustrations relocate Frankenstein and his creation to a goth-y, Tim Burton-esque time-out-of-time with a mix of modern, nineteenth-century, and steampunk sensibilities. A muted palette of sepia, gray, and olive tones is effectively punctuated by black, pinks, and purples, and, in more gruesome moments, bilious green. Grimly makes excellent use of his format with dynamic shapes, sizes, and pacing of panels."

REVIEW: *Kirkus Rev* v81 no14 p341 Jl 15 2013

REVIEW: *Publ Wkly* v260 no22 p63 Je 3 2013

REVIEW: *Publ Wkly* p134-6 Children's starred review annual 2013

REVIEW: *SLJ* v59 no7 p105 Jl 2013 Peter Blenski

REVIEW: *Voice of Youth Advocates* v36 no4 p86 O 2013 Stacy Holbrook

"Gris Grimly's Frankenstein." "'Gris Grimiy's Frankenstein' is an illustrated version of the original 1818 work by

Mary Shelley. . . . Using most of Shelley's original text. Grimly breathes life into this classic by telling the tale simultaneously through his gothic illustrations. Any text omitted from the original work is instead told through comic-style panels; though no text appears in these panels, the artwork stands on its own to represent the story. . . . Grimly's version has a whimsical quality that will draw teens in and allow them to better access this classic novel."

GRISHAM, JOHN, 1955-. Sycamore Row; [by] John Grisham 464 p. 2013 Random House Inc Doubleday

1. Criminal defense lawyers—Fiction 2. Inheritance and succession—Fiction 3. Legal stories 4. Race relations—Fiction

ISBN 0385537131; 9780385537131

LC 2013-362251

SUMMARY: In this novel, by John Grisham, attorney "Jake Brigance once again finds himself embroiled in a fiercely controversial trial . . . that will expose old racial tensions and force Ford County, [Mississippi] to confront its tortured history. Seth Hubbard is a wealthy man dying of lung cancer. . . . Before he hangs himself from a sycamore tree, Hubbard leaves a new, handwritten, will. It is an act that drags his adult children, his black maid, and Jake into . . . conflict." (Publisher's note)

REVIEW: *Booklist* v110 no17 p64 My 1 2014 Mary McCay

REVIEW: *Kirkus Rev* v81 no22 p222 N 15 2013

REVIEW: *Libr J* v139 no2 p43 F 1 2014 Suanne Roush

REVIEW: *N Y Times Book Rev* p14 N 10 2013 CHARLIE RUBIN

"Sycamore Row." "[John] Grisham's 26th adult novel and one of his finest. . . . 'Sycamore Row' is a true literary event--the sequel, nearly a quarter-century later, to 'A Time to Kill,' Grisham's first and perhaps best-regarded novel. . . . This grand, refreshing book . . . reminds us that the best legal fiction is written by lawyers . . . but this novel is unavoidably, and thankfully, about far more than just probating a will. Law is indistinguishable from the history of race in the South. . . . I believe these two books about Clanton will now be read back to back--and, standing together, at least dispel the long shadow of Harper Lee (not a lawyer)."

REVIEW: *New York Times* v162 no56306 pC1-2 O 31 2013 JANET MASLIN

REVIEW: *Publ Wkly* v261 no4 p186 Ja 27 2014

GROOT, TRACY. The sentinels of Andersonville; [by] Tracy Groot 368 p. 2014 Tyndale House Publishers, Inc.

1. Historical fiction 2. Prisoner-of-war escapes—Fiction 3. Prisoners of war—Georgia—Fiction 4. United States—History—Civil War, 1861-1865—Prisoners and prisons—Fiction

ISBN 1414359489; 9781414359489 (hc)

LC 2013-031516

SUMMARY: In this book, Tracy Groot "uses the Civil War atrocity at Andersonville Prison, where 13,000 Union prisoners died in a single year, as the background for a . . . retelling of the story of the Good Samaritan. Three young Southerners—two Confederate soldiers and a young woman who lives in the town nearest Andersonville—come to understand the true conditions in the prisoner-of-war camp, and must decide what they can do." (Publishers Weekly)

REVIEW: *Kirkus Rev* v82 no2 p254 Ja 15 2014

"The Sentinels of Andersonville". "Violet realizes that the Union soldiers are not the vermin she's been led to believe they are. Distraught over the conditions at Andersonville, as well as the complacency in Americus, Violet, Dance, Emery and Dr. Stiles found the Friends of Andersonville. Intended to open the eyes of Southern citizens to the truth and to improve conditions for the soldiers held at Andersonville, the group instead challenges everyone's moral fortitude. When mercy is seen as treason, even the heroes are endangered. Christy-award winning novelist [Tracy] Groot . . . unflinchingly examines the consequences of becoming a good Samaritan in this richly detailed, engrossing historical fiction."

GROSS, NEIL. Why are professors liberal and why do conservatives care?; [by] Neil Gross 400 p. 2013 Harvard University Press

1. College teachers—Attitudes 2. College teachers—United States—Political activity 3. Conservatism—United States 4. Liberalism—United States 5. Political science literature

ISBN 0674059093; 9780674059092 (hardcover : alk. paper)

LC 2012-031469

SUMMARY: In this book, author Neil Gross "explains how academic liberalism became a self-reproducing phenomenon, and why Americans on both the left and right should take notice. . . . Gross argues that 'political typing' plays an overlooked role. . . . The professoriate developed a reputation for liberal politics early in the twentieth century. As this perception spread, it exerted a self-selecting influence on bright young liberals, while deterring equally promising conservatives." (Publisher's note)

REVIEW: *Choice* v51 no1 p122 S 2013 M. Oromaner

REVIEW: *Kirkus Rev* v81 no2 p259 Ja 15 2013

REVIEW: *Libr J* v138 no5 p115 Mr 15 2013 Elizabeth Hayford

REVIEW: *Natl Rev* v65 no8 p59-61 My 6 2013 ROBERT VERBRUGGEN

"Why Are Professors Liberal and Why Do Conservatives Care?" "His results are worth considering, even if the book in which he presents them will grate on right-leaning readers from time to time. . . . Unfortunately, as empirically oriented as [Neil] Gross is, he often cannot resist the subtle jab at conservatives . . . Gross is at his best when he's explaining his surveys and experiments and using them to evaluate competing theories of professors' liberalism--and fortunately, he spends a lot of time doing that. Readers will gain a nuanced understanding of the subject, and conservative readers in particular will find many interesting nuggets here. The condescension is unfortunate, but a price worth paying."

REVIEW: *Publ Wkly* v260 no8 p157 F 25 2013

GROSSMAN, DAVID. Falling out of time; 208 p. 2014 Alfred A. Knopf

1. Bereavement—Fiction 2. Death—Fiction 3. Experimental fiction 4. Fathers 5. Grief—Fiction

ISBN 0385350139; 9780345805850 (trade pbk.); 9780385350136 (hardcover); 9780385350143 (ebook)

LC 2013-017532

SUMMARY: In this book by Daniel Grossman, "a bereaved father, who, after five years, still cannot come to terms with his son's death, leaves his wife and home to try to find the 'there,' where the boy's soul resides. As he relentlessly walks through and around his village, the Walking Man is joined by others who have lost their children." (Publishers Weekly)

REVIEW: *Booklist* v110 no11 p24 F 1 2014 Bryce Christensen

REVIEW: *Kirkus Rev* v82 no3 p114 F 1 2014

"Falling Out of Time". "A genre-crossing, pensive, peripatetic novel by Israeli author [Daniel] Grossman. . . . A blend of verse, drama and prose that recalls Karl Kraus' blistering 'Last Days of Mankind' (1919) in both subject and form. Where Kraus described the self-immolation of Europe in World War I, Grossman ponders a world in which '[c]old flames lapped around us,' a world caught up in formless, chaotic conflict about which we know only a few things—especially that people, young people, have died. . . . Though death is final, the fact of death continues to reverberate among the living, awed and heartbroken. Rich, lyrical, philosophically dense—not an easy work to take in but one that repays every effort."

REVIEW: *Libr J* v138 no16 p59 O 1 2013 Barbara Hoffert

REVIEW: *N Y Rev Books* v61 no10 p56-7 Je 5 2014 Adam Kirsch

"Falling Out of Time." "[Author David] Grossman's two masterpieces [are] 'See Under: Love' and 'To the End of the Land.' . . . 'Falling Out of Time,' Grossman's spare and poetic new book, forms a conclusion to this sequence so natural, so seemingly inevitable, that it is uncanny. . . . In August 2006, his younger son, Uri, was killed in combat. . . . It is impossible to read 'Falling Out of Time' otherwise than as Grossman's response to Uri's death. . . . 'Falling Out of Time' is not really fiction. It is, rather, a poetic drama, proceeding almost entirely in alternating monologues, which could easily be imagined on stage."

REVIEW: *N Y Times Book Rev* p26 Jl 27 2014

REVIEW: *N Y Times Book Rev* p12 Jl 20 2014 EDWARD HIRSCH

REVIEW: *Publ Wkly* v261 no4 p166-7 Ja 27 2014

REVIEW: *TLS* no5797 p19-20 My 9 2014 CLIVE SINCLAIR

GROSSMAN, EDITH.tr. In the Night of Time. See In the Night of Time

GROSSMAN, PAUL. Brotherhood of fear; a Willi Kraus novel; [by] Paul Grossman 320 p. 2014 St. Martin's Press

1. Antisemitism—Fiction 2. Detective & mystery stories 3. Detectives—France—Paris—Fiction 4. Jews—Fiction 5. Murder—Investigation—Fiction
ISBN 1250011590; 9781250011596 (hardcover)
LC 2013-031354

SUMMARY: This book, by Paul Grossman, is set in "Paris, 1933. A refugee with no papers, no legal status, and few resources, Willi Kraus lives in fear of deportation back to Nazi Germany. His reputation as a top sleuth however precedes him, and he's soon enlisted to work as a private eye. . . . Seduced by a sultry but troubled young French girl and befriended by France's most flamboyant financier, Willi finds himself unwittingly drawn into a murder mystery." (Publisher's note)

REVIEW: *Booklist* v110 no12 p30-1 F 15 2014 Bill Ott

"Brotherhood of Fear." "The prewar tension is palpable here, as the French simultaneously worry about the Fascist threat and attempt to distance themselves from it. Willi, as a Jewish refugee, is an unwelcome reminder of the gathering storm. [Paul] Grossman nails the casual anti-Semitism of the French toward Willi and the world situation, and if the plot gets a little hinky toward the end, the novel still works well as an atmospheric look at a setting thriller readers familiar with the works of Alan Furst know and love: Paris on the eve of war."

REVIEW: *Kirkus Rev* v82 no2 p243 Ja 15 2014

REVIEW: *Publ Wkly* v260 no51 p38 D 16 2013

GROSSMAN, RICHARD S. Wrong; nine economic policy disasters and what we can learn from them; [by] Richard S. Grossman 266 p. 2013 Oxford University Press

1. Economic policy—Case studies 2. Economics literature 3. Financial crises—Case studies 4. Free enterprise 5. Gold standard 6. Monetary policy
ISBN 9780199322190 (alk. paper)
LC 2013-007697

SUMMARY: This book by Richard S. Grossman examines "the poor thinking behind nine of the worst economic policy mistakes of the past 200 years, missteps whose outcomes ranged from appalling to tragic. Grossman tells the story behind each misconceived economic move, explaining why the policy was adopted, how it was implemented, and its short- and long-term consequences. In each case, he shows that the main culprits were policy makers who were guided by ideology rather than economics." (Publisher's note)

REVIEW: *Choice* v51 no7 p1271 Mr 2014 R. E. Schenk

"Wrong: Nine Economic Policy Disasters and What We Can Learn From Them." "[Richard S.] Grossman gives enough background for nonacademic readers to understand the situation, and he clearly explains the policy mistakes. The weakest aspect of the book is his attempt to link policy mistakes by arguing that ideology was their source. Most economists could construct equally plausible cases that the influence of special interests caused these mistakes. This weakness is most evident when, after explaining for several pages why special interests have undue influence on trade policy, Grossman declares that the Smoot-Hawley Tariff resulted from ideology because 'high tariffs were a central part of the Republican Party's political creed.'"

GROSSO, CHRIS. Indie spiritualist; a no bullshit exploration of spirituality; [by] Chris Grosso 272 p. 2014 Atria Books/Beyond Words

1. Self-acceptance 2. Self-help materials 3. Self-realization 4. Spiritual life 5. Spirituality
ISBN 1582704627; 9781476747088 (ebook); 9781582704623 (paperback)
LC 2013-041880

SUMMARY: In this book, author Chris Grosso presents a "collection of stories and musings about his meandering journey of self-inquiry, recovery, and acceptance shows what it means to live a truly authentic spiritual life. . . . [It] encourages you to accept yourself just as you are, in all your humanity and imperfect perfection." (Publisher's note)

REVIEW: *Booklist* v110 no11 p3 F 1 2014 Francisca Goldsmith

REVIEW: *Kirkus Rev* v82 no2 p76 Ja 15 2014

"Indie Spiritualist: A No Bullshit Exploration of Spirituality". "In a mixed bag of introspective insights and navel-gazing, Grosso tells the story of how he finally entered recovery after years of drug and alcohol abuse, which set him on the path of investigating his spiritual side far outside of organized religion. It's a bit like mid-1990s MTV meets New-Age mysticism, and they have a tattooed hipster baby. To give the author credit, it sounds like he was truly messed up before he got his act together, and his explorations may appeal to Daily Show viewers who feel like they need a shot of new-time religion. The book is composed of short, easily consumed chapters kicked off with quotes from usual suspects."

REVIEW: *Libr J* v139 no3 p86 F 15 2014 Graham Christian

REVIEW: *Publ Wkly* v261 no3 p49 Ja 20 2014

GROTH, GARY.ed. Walt Disney's Mickey Mouse color Sundays. See Walt Disney's Mickey Mouse color Sundays

GROTH, GARY.ed. Walt Disney's Donald Duck. See Barks, C.

GROVER, LORIE ANN. Big Hug for Little Cub; [by] Lorie Ann Grover 18 p. 2014 Scholastic

1. Animal stories 2. Animal young—Juvenile fiction 3. Lions—Juvenile literature 4. Meerkat 5. Mother & child—Fiction
ISBN 0545530911; 9780545530910

SUMMARY: This children's book presents a "day-in-the-life tale of a lion cub and his mother. From morning until night, the little wild cat enjoys pouncing, playing, exploring and preening while his momma looks on and offers a helping paw when needed. The youngster encounters a fellow cub and a couple of meerkats before hunkering down with momma for the night." (Kirkus Reviews)

REVIEW: *Kirkus Rev* v82 no2 p322 Ja 15 2014

"Big Hug For Little Cub". "Each double-page spread (on thinner-than-normal board-book stock) provides a different view of the grassland setting in both bright and muted earth tones. [Rosalinda] Kightley's paintings, which have the look of acrylic on canvas, are deft at capturing the sunny yellow cub and his playmate in motion. This is a kinder and gentler savanna. . . . In gentle rhyming couplets meted out in one or two couplets per page, the first-person-narrator cub describes the action. . . . As realism is not the object here, these lions are cute, cuddly and toothless, safe for sharing a crib with baby."

REVIEW: *Kirkus Rev* v82 no13 p3 Jl 1 2014

REVIEW: *Publ Wkly* v260 no48 p55 N 25 2013

GROVIER, KELLY. 100 works of art that will define our age; [by] Kelly Grovier 320 p. 2013 Thames & Hudson

1. Art criticism 2. Art literature 3. Artists 4. Modern art—20th century 5. Modern art—21st century
ISBN 9780500239070 (hardcover)
LC 2013-934846

SUMMARY: In this book, "Kelly Grovier curates a . . . list of one hundred paintings, sculptures, drawings, installations, performances, and video pieces that have made the greatest impact from 1989 to the present. . . . Many of the pieces reflect the cultural upheavals of recent times, from the collapse of the Berlin Wall to the blossoming of the Arab Spring." (Publisher's note)

REVIEW: *Publ Wkly* v260 no40 p44 O 7 2013

REVIEW: *TLS* no5792 p3-4 Ap 4 2014 KEITH MILLER

"100 Works of Art That Will Define Our Age." "Kelly Grovier's hecatomb to posterity is prefaced with a brisk and cogent essay proclaiming the capacity of some artworks to make themselves heard, or felt, across time—a necessary precondition for any sort of immortality. . . . In practice, Grovier's canon is fairly, but by no means exclusively, Western, and restricts itself to works from 1989 onwards. . . . The book is set out as a series of large and generally good reproductions of works, ordered alphabetically by artist, each garnished with a half-page or so's worth of citation, prefaced by a short apophthegm or rhetorical question in bold type."

GRUMDAHL, DARA MOSKOWITZ. Drink this; [by] Dara Moskowitz Grumdahl 348 2009 Ballantine Books

1. Food & wine pairing 2. Food writing 3. Wine & wine making 4. Wine industry 5. Wine lists
ISBN 0345511654; 9780345511652
LC 2009-036047

SUMMARY: This book by Dara Moskowitz Grumdahl "explains how to negotiate wine lists in restaurants, how to build your own wine collections, how and with what to serve wines, and how to comprehend the layouts of wine shops, all underscored by her fundamental principle that wine is about how and where grapes are grown." (Booklist)

REVIEW: *Booklist* v110 no3 p27 O 1 2013 Brad Hooper

"Drink This: Wine Made Simple," "Inventing Wine: A New History of One of the World's Most Ancient Pleasures," and "Unquenchable: A Tipsy Quest for the World's Best Bargain Wines." "[Dara Moskowitz Grumdahl] carefully explains how to negotiate wine lists in restaurants, how to build your own wine collections, how and with what to serve wines, and how to comprehend the layouts of wine shops. . . . The book's format is both attractive and comfortable. . . . In highly readable prose, [Paul] Lukacs tells the story of winemaking's worldwide history, recounting such ever-fascinating stories as the discovery of champagne. . . . This is a lively, entertaining tour of wines and a personal look at some of [Natalie] MacLean's favorite wines."

GSCHWANDTNER, CHRISTINA M. Postmodern apologetics?; arguments for God in contemporary philosophy; [by] Christina M. Gschwandtner xxvi, 352 p. 2012 Fordham University Press

1. Apologetics 2. Continental philosophy 3. God (Christianity) 4. Phenomenological theology 5. Phenomenology & religion 6. Philosophical literature 7. Philosophical theology 8. Philosophy, French
ISBN 0823242749; 9780823242740 (cloth : alk. paper); 9780823242757 (pbk. : alk. paper)
LC 2012-031535

SUMMARY: This book, by Christina M. Gschwandtner, "provides an introduction to the emerging field of continental philosophy of religion by treating the thought of its most important representatives, including its appropriations by several thinkers in the United States. The book thus both provides an introduction to important contemporary thinkers, many of whom have not yet received much treatment in

English, and also argues that their philosophies can be read as providing an argument for Christian faith." (Publisher's note)

REVIEW: *Choice* v51 no1 p96 S 2013 S. Young

"Postmodern Apologetics?: Arguments for God in Contemporary Philosophy." "[Author Christina M.] Gschwandtner . . . surveys writings on religion from a dozen key phenomenological figures, asking whether this bourgeoning interest in religious phenomenology might signal a new kind of defense of the (Christian) faith. . . . The author's own critique and evaluation is light, and broader issues of philosophical and theological context receive scant attention. A comparative chapter on Anselm, and her concluding discussion of religion as experience of excess, will leave readers wishing the author had shared more of her own evaluation of the subjects of her investigation."

GUARNACCIA, STEVE.il. Cinderella. See Guarnaccia, S.

GUARNACCIA, STEVE. Cinderella; a fashionable tale; [by] Steve Guarnaccia 32 p. 2013 Abrams Books for Young Readers

1. Cinderella (Legendary character) 2. Cinderella (Tale) 3. Fairy tales 4. Fashion 5. Folklore
ISBN 9781419709869
LC 2013-006459

SUMMARY: In this fashion-focused retelling of the Cinderella story, "a Twiggylike heroine is attended by a miniature fairy godfather—Karl Lagerfeld's doppelgänger. The drama reaches its zenith when Cinderella tries on different options for the ball. She chooses a Vivienne Westwood: the 'Statue of Liberty Dress'." (School Library Journal)

REVIEW: *Kirkus Rev* v82 no2 p46 Ja 15 2014

"Cinderella: A Fashionable Tale". "A crisp, modern take on the oft-told tale: deliciously subversive and visually captivating. Electrolux vacuum in hand, this Twiggy-esque Cinderella is fresh, bright and absolutely unexpected in her patchwork shift (of designer patterns). Here, the confines of fairy-tale dress are shed, and the Perrault story becomes the perfect vehicle to celebrate fashion—and the real-life mavericks who redefined beauty in the 20th and 21st centuries. . . . [Steven] Guarnaccia's simple, sophisticated drawings imply a luxuriousness brought to life. "

REVIEW: *SLJ* v60 no1 p66 Ja 2014 Wendy Lukehart

GUDE, PAUL. When Elephant met Giraffe; [by] Paul Gude 56 p. 2013 Disney-Hyperion Books

1. Animal stories 2. Bashfulness 3. Elephants—Fiction 4. Friendship—Fiction 5. Giraffe—Fiction
ISBN 9781423163039
LC 2012-015041

SUMMARY: In this book, "three short stories depict the budding friendship between a lively elephant and a silent giraffe, beginning with their initial meeting in 'The Water Hole.' . . . In 'Pretzels,' Giraffe decides to whip up some pretzels. . . . 'The Bossy Pirate' finds Elephant so narrowly dictating the pair's pretend play that Giraffe gives up and reads a book instead, until Elephant acquiesces that each friend can choose a pretend identity." (Bulletin of the Center for Children's Books)

REVIEW: *Kirkus Rev* v81 no24 p129 D 15 2013

"When Elephant Met Giraffe". "[Paul] Gude's flat, cartoonish digital art depicts Elephant heading off for a swim in the first story. . . . Sly humor punctuates the stories, which inevitably center on conflict arising from the friends' very different personalities. At first blush, the picture book reads like an early reader in some ways, with its discrete, tightly paced stories and odd-couple characters, but the vocabulary isn't quite controlled enough to be accessible to independent emergent readers. A humorous picture book about two new, unlikely pals."

GUDE, PAUL.il. When Elephant met Giraffe. See Gude, P.

GUENOUN, DENIS. About Europe; philosophical hypotheses; [by] Denis Guenoun xiii, 324 p. 2013 Stanford University Press

1. Europe—History 2. European studies 3. History—Philosophy 4. Philosophical literature 5. Philosophy & history
ISBN 9780804773850 (cloth : alk. paper); 9780804773867 (pbk. : alk. paper)
LC 2012-045372

SUMMARY: Written by Denis Guénoun and translated by Christine Irizarry, "This book reflects on Europe and its changing boundaries over the span of twenty centuries. A work of philosophy, it consistently draws on concrete events. . . . Empire, Church, and EU: all have been constructed in contrast to an Oriental 'other.' The stakes of Europe, then, are as much metaphysical as political." (Publisher's note)

REVIEW: *TLS* no5787 p7-8 F 28 2014 SIMON GLENDINNING

"About Europe: Philosophical Hypotheses." "The idea of the global spreading of the Greek-then-Roman-then-Germanic world has been the mainstay of the philosophy of world history, and provides a point of departure for [author Denis] Guénoun's philosophy of Europe. . . . Guénoun's reflections on Europe's emerging cultural identity are rich and fascinating, and English-speaking readers can be extremely grateful to Christine Irizarry for her fluent and elegant translation. However, while it may be a general fault of the book that it is quite so Franco-German-centred, it seems extraordinary to omit Britain ('England') from the story altogether."

GUHA, RAMACHANDRA, 1958-. Gandhi before India; [by] Ramachandra Guha 672 p. 2014 Alfred A. Knopf

1. Biographies 2. East Indians—South Africa—Politics and government 3. Statesmen—India—Biography
ISBN 0385532296; 9780385532297
LC 2013-025014

SUMMARY: This biography "takes us from Mohandas Gandhi's birth in 1869 through his upbringing in Gujarat, his two years as a student in London, and his two decades as a lawyer and community organizer in South Africa." Author Ramachandra Guha "makes clear that Gandhi's work in South Africa—far from being a mere prelude to his accomplishments in India—was profoundly influential on his evolution as a political thinker, social reformer, and beloved leader." (Publisher's note)

REVIEW: *Booklist* v110 no13 p15 Mr 1 2014 Jay Freeman

REVIEW: *Booklist* v110 no19/20 p25 Je 1 2014 Donna Seaman

REVIEW: *Choice* v51 no12 p2241 Ag 2014 J. O. Gump

REVIEW: *Economist* v409 no8857 p97-8 O 12 2013

"Gandhi Before India". "[This book] by Ramachandra Guha, India's leading historian, offers plenty. The first of two volumes, it deals with [Mohandas] Gandhi's life up to 1914. . . . A fluent writer, Mr. Guha is alert to Gandhi's many apparent inconsistencies. . . . Rather than lingering on Gandhi's own well-studied words, Mr. Guha has unearthed a wealth of previously overlooked school reports, diaries, letters and articles by collaborators and opponents of Gandhi. The result is a striking depiction of his transformation into mid-adulthood."

REVIEW: *Hist Today* v64 no2 p65 F 2014 Mihir Bose

"Gandhi Before India". "[Ramachandra] Guha approaches his subject as an admirer, although yet another book on Gandhi seems an overkill. Guha argues that, while we know much of what Gandhi thought, we do not know enough of what the world around him thought. . . . Guha's research cannot be doubted and he does not gloss over uncomfortable facts. . . . However Guha does not sustain his thesis that Gandhi's Satyagraha is a ready answer to all oppressive regimes, from racism in the US Deep South to those seeking to bring down the Berlin Wall and the battles for democracy in the Arab Spring."

REVIEW: *Kirkus Rev* v82 no5 p34 Mr 1 2014

REVIEW: *Libr J* v139 no4 p97 Mr 1 2014 Zachary Irwin

REVIEW: *N Y Times Book Rev* p14 My 11 2014 JYOTI THOTTAM

REVIEW: *N Y Times Book Rev* p30 My 18 2014

REVIEW: *New Repub* v244 no29 p53-7 Je 9 2014 Maya Jasanoff

"Gandhi Before India." "'Gandhi Before India,' the first volume of Ramachandra Guha's projected two-part biography, traces Gandhi's activities up to 1914, when he returned permanently to India. The central achievement of this book is to establish the South African period . . . as foundational to Gandhi's later career, and worth sustained attention in its own right. . . . Guha has turned up troves of hitherto unused private papers belonging to Gandhi's many close friends and colleagues, to develop a far more rounded portrait. Deeply contextualized, dextrously research, and judiciously written, this deserves to become the landmark biography of the early Gandhi."

REVIEW: *New York Times* v163 no56501 pC4 My 14 2014 MARTIN MEREDITH

REVIEW: *New Yorker* v90 no14 p72-1 My 26 2014

"Gandhi Before India." "Covering Gandhi's life from his birth, in 1869, to his mid-forties—with a focus on his time in South Africa—this study makes clear that sangfroid and uncanny self-assurance in the face of ugly opposition were evident from the beginning. Yet this is no hagiography: [author Ramachandra] Guha notes Gandhi's early obliviousness toward South Africa's native population, and his thoughtless treatment of his wife. He never writes as though Gandhi's destiny were a foregone conclusion."

REVIEW: *Publ Wkly* v261 no3 p42 Ja 20 2014

REVIEW: *TLS* no5777/8 p8-9 D 20 2013 R. W. JOHNSON

"Gandhi Before India." "What is at work here is what one may term iconic moral inflation. . . . What Guha does show is that Gandhi's career in South Africa was no mere sideshow, the prelude to the main act in India, but that it was where Gandhi learnt how to be a mystic and a politician, and also where he learnt and perfected satyagraha. . . . Guha has done his work well, even tracing a letter from Muhammad Ali Jinnah supporting Gandhi's early work in Natal. . . . Ramachandra Guha's book is suffused with a sort of euphoric glow from the Gandhi-yet-to-come era in India, but it would be fairer to judge his actions against what happened in South Africa."

GUHRKE, LAURA LEE. When the Marquess Met His Match; An American Heiress in London; [by] Laura Lee Guhrke 384 p. 2013 HarperCollins

1. Americans—Great Britain—Fiction 2. Heiresses 3. Love stories 4. Man-woman relationships—Fiction 5. Marriage brokerage

ISBN 006211817X; 9780062118172

SUMMARY: In this book, by Laura Lee Guhrke, "Lady Belinda Featherstone, a former American heiress and now the quite happy widow of the Earl of Featherstone, has become the matchmaker of choice for aspiring American debutantes in London—and keeping them safe from philandering fortune hunters is one of her goals. So when the infamous . . . Marquess of Trubridge asks for her help, naturally she refuses." (Library Journal)

REVIEW: *Booklist* v110 no6 p27 N 15 2013 John Charles

"When the Marquess Met His Match." "Lady Belinda Featherstone might be the best matchmaker in England, but even she has her limits. . . . In her latest flawlessly written romance, [Laura Lee] Guhrke launches a new series by elegantly scrutinizing the trade in American wealth for British titles with skillfulness reminiscent of that of Edith Wharton and a sophisticated sense of wit in the vein of Oscar Wilde. Graced with an abundance of memorable characters and rich in lush sensuality, 'When the Marquess Met His Match' is pure reading bliss."

GUIBERSON, BRENDA Z., 1946-. The greatest dinosaur ever; [by] Brenda Z. Guiberson 32 p. 2013 Henry Holt and Company

1. Children's nonfiction 2. Competition (Psychology) 3. Dinosaurs 4. Dinosaurs—Juvenile literature 5. Dinosaurs—Pictorial works 6. Paleontology—Juvenile literature

ISBN 0805096256; 9780805096255 (hardcover)

LC 2013-001725

SUMMARY: This book, by Brenda Z. Guiberson and illustrated by Gennady Spirin, features "facts and . . . illustrations [designed to] inspire young readers to choose their own favorite dinosaurs! Which dinosaur was the greatest? Was it the tallest, the biggest, the strongest, the smartest, the weirdest, the fastest, or the smallest? Or was it the oldest bird, the best parent, the one with the best night vision, the best armor, or the longest tail spikes?" (Publisher's note)

REVIEW: *Booklist* v110 no5 p53 N 1 2013 Carolyn Phelan

REVIEW: *Bull Cent Child Books* v67 no3 p155 N 2013 E. B.

"The Greatest Dinosaur Ever." "A dozen dino contenders vie for the honor of 'the greatest dinosaur that ever lived,' and each is allowed only a few lines in which to make his or her case. . . . While status wrangling is the ostensible focus here, the real pleasure is in perusing [illustrator Gennady] Spirin's full-bleed full-spread oil paintings, which bring an unusual beauty to a genre more notable for gory scenes of predation. Spirin's pictures are intricately detailed, subtle in hue, and textured to resemble the finely crackled varnish of the Old Masters. A closing spread offers thumbnail portraits of the featured dinosaurs along with fast facts of name meaning, size, period, and location not explicitly covered in the main text."

REVIEW: *Kirkus Rev* v81 no16 p124 Ag 15 2013

REVIEW: *SLJ* v59 no9 p176 S 2013 Leila Sterman

GUICCIARDINI, DESIDERIA.il. I didn't do it. See Graves, S.

GUICCIARDINI, DESIDERIA.il. I hate everything! See Graves, S.

GUICCIARDINI, DESIDERIA.il. Take a deep breath. See Graves, S.

GUIDOBALDI, MARIA PAOLA. Herculaneum; art of a buried city; 352 p. 2013 Abbeville Press

1. Archaeological literature 2. Architecture, Domestic—Italy—Herculaneum (Extinct city) 3. Excavations (Archaeology)—Italy—Herculaneum (Extinct city) 4. Mural painting and decoration, Roman—Italy—Herculaneum (Extinct city)
ISBN 9780789211460 (hardback)
LC 2013-031198

SUMMARY: This book looks at "Herculaneum, the ancient Roman town on the west slope of Mt. Vesuvius that was buried in the eruption of 79 CE." It was "written by [Maria Paola] Guidobaldi, the director of excavations, and [Domenico] Esposito, a classical archaeologist who was also an excavator at the site. . . . The majority of the text describes the layout and decoration of 17 houses and 2 villas. Special emphasis is given to wall paintings." (Choice: Current Reviews for Academic Libraries)

REVIEW: *Choice* v51 no8 p1390-1 Ap 2014 F. Van Keuren
"Herculaneum: Art of a Buried City". "This lavishly illustrated volume forms a valuable, up-to-date introduction to Herculaneum, the ancient Roman town on the west slope of Mt. Vesuvius that was buried in the eruption of 79 CE. Written by [Maria Paola] Guidobaldi, the director of excavations, and [Domenico] Esposito, a classical archaeologist who was also an excavator at the site, this volume is an English translation from the Italian edition, 'Ercolano' (2008). The two editions are identical, except for the omission in this English translation of the glossary; this omission leaves much terminology unexplained, especially relating to house plans."

REVIEW: *N Y Rev Books* v61 no5 p23-5 Mr 20 2014 Ingrid D. Rowland

REVIEW: *Publ Wkly* v260 no48 p48 N 25 2013

GUINN, JEFF. Manson; the life and times of Charles Manson; [by] Jeff Guinn 512 p. 2013 Simon & Schuster

1. Biographies 2. Criminals—United States—Biography 3. Cults 4. Murderers—United States—Biography
ISBN 1451645163; 9781451645163
LC 2012-050176

SUMMARY: This book by Jeff Guinn "reexamines the life of Charles Manson, interviewing Manson's sister and cousin, who have not previously spoken out, and gleaning new information from childhood friends, cellmates, and Manson Family members. Guinn argues that while Manson spouted incoherent race-war rhetoric, the killings were in fact related to his failed ambitions to be a rock star." (Library Journal)

REVIEW: *Booklist* v109 no19/20 p23 Je 1 2013 Ray Olson

REVIEW: *Kirkus Rev* v81 no12 p50 Je 15 2013

REVIEW: *Libr J* v138 no5 p93 Mr 15 2013 Barbara Hoffert

REVIEW: *Libr J* v139 no4 p56 Mr 1 2014 Victoria A. Caplinger

REVIEW: *London Rev Books* v35 no21 p20-2 N 7 2013 Christian Lorentzen
"Manson: The Life and Times of Charles Manson." "'Manson: The Life and Times of Charles Manson' is a cradle-to-grave treatment, though the graves belong to other people. The subject remains in California, an inmate at Corcoran State Prison, where he issues statements his followers disseminate via the website of his Air Trees Water Animals organisation. . . . [Author Jeff] Guinn explains a lot in his usefully linear book. . . . The story lingers and books like Guinn's are written to remind the Baby Boomers why they cut their hair and switched from hallucinogens to antidepressants."

REVIEW: *N Y Times Book Rev* p14 Ag 18 2013 ANN RULE
"Manson; The Life and Times of Charles Manson." "A great deal of the story of Manson's roots has been apocryphal. [Jeff] Guinn's research, which turned up family members never before interviewed, along with individuals Manson related to intensely or only peripherally, attempts to set the record straight. . . . Though most of the literate world knows what's to come, Guinn ably maintains suspense. Even if 'Manson' is occasionally tedious, recounting over and over the Family's peripatetic adventures . . . it stands as a definitive work: important for students of criminology, human behavior, popular culture, music, psychopathology and sociopathology, and compulsively readable for anyone who relishes nonfiction."

REVIEW: *N Y Times Book Rev* p34 Ag 25 2013

REVIEW: *Natl Rev* v65 no17 p39-40 S 16 2013 FLORENCE KING
"Manson: The Life and Times of Charles Manson." "Sometimes a book is so good that the reviewer does not know where to begin. It doesn't happen often, but this is one of those times. I have tried out a dozen different ledes but they all seemed inadequate to the task. I can't sit here any longer staring at a blank screen or I'll miss my deadline, so I'll get right to it: Jeff Guinn, a former investigative reporter with books on Wyatt Earp and Bonnie and Clyde to his credit, has produced not only the best biography of Charles Manson, but the best study of American true crime since Victoria Lincoln's 'A Private Disgrace: Lizzie Borden by Daylight'."

REVIEW: *New York Times* v162 no56221 pC1-4 Ag 7 2013 JANET MASLIN

REVIEW: *Publ Wkly* v260 no19 p57 My 13 2013

GUNNISON, ELAINE. Offender reentry. See Helfgott, J. B.

GUNTER, MICHAEL M., 1943-.ed. The Kurdish spring. See The Kurdish spring

GUO JIAN.ed. Tombstone. See Tombstone

GURGANUS, ALLAN, 1947-. Local souls; novellas; [by] Allan Gurganus 352 p. 2013 Liveright Publishing Corporation

1. Friendship—Fiction 2. Missing persons—Fiction 3. Mothers & daughters—Fiction 4. North Carolina—Fiction 5. Novellas (Literary form)
ISBN 087140379X; 9780871403797 (hardcover)
LC 2013-016662

SUMMARY: This book by Allan Gurganus presents "three novellas set in Falls, NC, the mythic town in his . . . first novel, 'Oldest Living Confederate Widow Tells All'. In 'Fear Not,' a banker's daughter hunts for the child she was forced to give up at birth. In 'Saints Have Mothers,' a cult grows up around a vanished high school valedictorian. In 'Decoy,' the eroticized bond between two married men is tested by an epic flood." (Library Journal)

REVIEW: *Booklist* v109 no21 p28 Jl 1 2013 Brad Hooper

REVIEW: *Kirkus Rev* v81 no21 p252 N 1 2013

REVIEW: *Libr J* v138 no7 p54 Ap 15 2013 Barbara Hoffert

REVIEW: *N Y Rev Books* v61 no8 p38-9 My 8 2014 Darryl Pinckney

REVIEW: *N Y Times Book Rev* p17 O 13 2013 JAMIE QUATRO

"Local Souls: Novellas." "If there remains any doubt of [Alan Gurganus's] literary greatness, his fifth book, 'Local Souls,' should put it to rest forever. . . . 'Local Souls' ios a tour de force in the tradition of [Nathaniel] Hawthorne. It shows that Gurganus's vast creative an imaginative powers, still rooted in the local, are increasingly universal in scope and effect. The book is an expansive work of love. . . . The prose is taut with the electric charge of internal rhyme, assonance and alliteration. . . . But such sentences are only half the wonder. Each novella concerns an isolated character desperate to know and connect with another."

REVIEW: *N Y Times Book Rev* p26 O 20 2013

REVIEW: *New York Times* v163 no56270 pC1-6 S 25 2013 DWIGHT GARNER

REVIEW: *New Yorker* v89 no31 p1 O 7 2013 Thomas Mallon

"Local Souls." "Despite his Iowa M.F.A., [Alan] Gurganus writes novels and short stories that don't follow the usual workshop rule to show instead of tell. Nor do they break it in any simple way. Rather, they show you and tell you and then show you some more and tell you again. Along the way, adjectives compound themselves into Lego towers, and syntax performs triple Salchows that can land in a perfect-ten fragment instead of a sentence. . . . With three first-person narrators, 'Local Souls' stays true to its author's vocal aesthetic. . . . Gurganus splendidly allows the flood to be a deus ex machina that resolves nothing; it merely brings existing perplexities into higher relief."

REVIEW: *Publ Wkly* v260 no30 p1 Jl 29 2013

GUSTAFSON, THANE. Wheel of fortune; the battle for oil and power in Russia; [by] Thane Gustafson 662 p. 2012 Harvard University Press

1. Historical literature 2. Petroleum industry and trade—Government policy—Russia (Federation) 3. Petroleum industry and trade—Political aspects—Russia (Federation) 4. Petroleum industry and trade—Russia (Federation) 5. Russia (Federation)—Politics & government
ISBN 0674066472 (hardcover); 9780674066472 (hardcover)
LC 2012-007731

SUMMARY: This book, by Thane Gustafson, profiles how "the Russian oil industry--which vies with Saudi Arabia as the world's largest producer and exporter of oil, providing nearly 12 percent of the global supply--is facing mounting problems that could send shock waves through the Russian economy and worldwide. . . . [This book] provides an authoritative account of this vital industry from the last years of communism to its uncertain future." (Publisher's note)

REVIEW: *Choice* v50 no8 p1513 Ap 2013 Y. Polsky

REVIEW: *Kirkus Rev* v80 no21 p45 N 1 2012

REVIEW: *London Rev Books* v35 no11 p30-2 Je 6 2013 Tony Wood

REVIEW: *Publ Wkly* v259 no41 p53 O 8 2012

REVIEW: *TLS* no5750 p10 Je 14 2013 PETER RUTLAND

"Wheel of Fortune: The Battle for Oil and Power in Russia" and "The Oil Road: Journeys From the Caspian Sea to the City of London." "Thane Gustafson has produced what will surely be the definitive work on this subject. . . . Having been present at the creation, he is uniquely placed to combine an insider's knowledge of how the industry works with academic analytical skills and a sophisticated understanding of Russian culture and politics. . , . In contrast to Gustafson's highly sympathetic account, James Marriott and Mika Minio-Paluello's book seeks to expose a sinister 'carbon web' of oilmen and their political cronies. . . . The authors try to evoke the richness of the places en route and the people whose lives are affected. Unfortunately, they have neither the local knowledge nor vivid enough personal encounters to pull this off."

GUSTAVSON, ADAM.il. Charlie Bumpers vs. the Teacher of the Year. See Harley, Bi.

GUTERL, MATTHEW PRATT. Josephine Baker and the Rainbow Tribe; [by] Matthew Pratt Guterl 288 p. 2014 The Belknap Press of Harvard University Press

1. African American entertainers—France—Biography 2. Americans—France—History—20th century 3. Biography (Literary form) 4. Dancers—France—Biography
ISBN 9780674047556 (alk. paper)
LC 2013-037831

SUMMARY: This book by Matthew Pratt Guterl describes how, "Her performing days numbered, Baker settled down in a sixteenth-century chateau she named Les Milandes, in the south of France. Then, in 1953, she did something completely unexpected and, in the context of racially sensitive times, outrageous. Adopting twelve children from around the globe, she transformed her estate into a theme park, complete with rides, hotels, a collective farm, and singing and dancing." (Publisher's note)

REVIEW: *Booklist* v110 no15 p9-10 Ap 1 2014 Eloise Kinney

REVIEW: *Choice* v52 no1 p80-1 St 2014 M. D. Whitlatch

REVIEW: *New Yorker* v90 no13 p91-1 My 19 2014

"Josephine Baker and the Rainbow Tribe." "The familiar image of Josephine Baker—sensational dancer of Jazz Age Paris, pioneering black superstar—is important to this account of her later life. Unable to have children, she adopted twelve children from various racial and religious backgrounds and reared them in a castle in France. She saw this Rainbow Tribe as proof of the possibilities of racial harmony. . . . [author Matthew Pratt] Guterl is astute about the contradictions in Baker's experiment and her celebrity, both of which rested on her capacity for reinvention.

GUTFELD, GREG. Not cool; the hipster elite and their war on you; [by] Greg Gutfeld 272 p. 2014 Crown Forum

1. Conduct of life—Humor 2. Cool (The concept) 3. Elite (Social sciences)—Humor 4. Personality & politics 5. Social commentary 6. United States—Politics & government 7. United States—Social life & customs

ISBN 9780804138536 (hardback); 9780804138550 (paperback)

LC 2013-050828

SUMMARY: "In 'Not Cool,' Greg Gutfeld . . . lays out the battle plan for reclaiming the real American ideal of cool—building businesses, protecting freedom at home and abroad, taking responsibility for your actions, and leaving other people alone to live as they damn well please. 'Not Cool' fights back against the culture of phonies, elitists, and creeps who want your soul." (Publisher's note)

REVIEW: *Natl Rev* v65 no6 p38-9 Ap 7 2014 FLORENCE KING

"Not Cool: The Hipster Elite and Their War on You." "[Greg] Gutfield's many no-holds-barred remarks are saved from obscenity by being funny, but I never expected him to turn into my grandmother. . . . Gutfield has a real fear that the uncool majority is letting the cool win without putting up a fight. . . . Obviously 'Not Cool' is a wonderful book, but it is also something more. . . . A longstanding problem of American writing has sorted itself out. . . . Our only bona fide misanthrope was Ambrose Bierce, and Greg Gutfield is his heir."

GUTIERREZ, ELISA.il. Letter lunch. See Gutierrez, E.

GUTIERREZ, ELISA. Letter lunch; 32 p. 2014 Owlkids Books, Inc.

1. Alphabet—Juvenile literature 2. Cooking 3. Luncheons 4. Picture books for children 5. Stories without words

ISBN 1771470003; 9781771470001

LC 2013-948985

SUMMARY: In this book, by Elisa Gutierrez, "the cupboards are empty, as is the fridge. Thus begins the adventure of a hungry brother and sister as they try to figure out what's for lunch. But there's nothing ordinary about the feast the siblings . . . are cooking up. From letter-picking in their backyard to browsing through the alphabet at the local market, . . . the two chefs and letter foragers set out to create a feast of consonants that's seasoned with . . . vowels." (Publisher's note)

REVIEW: *Booklist* v110 no13 p63 Mr 1 2014 Ilene Cooper

REVIEW: *Kirkus Rev* v82 no2 p214 Ja 15 2014

"Letter Lunch". " Hold onto your vowels and get ready for an alphabetic romp—graphic style. . . . Cut-paper collage and mixed media carry out this visual venture with basic shapes and dots and lines for eyes and mouths. Some background scenes and people are drawn with just white outlines, and each letter is blocked in different colors. Sharp eyes will notice a clue to the story in the list of letter ingredients the boy and girl make as they leave the kitchen: It contains no vowels. . . . [Eliza] Gutiérrez's comic-strip story feels pleasingly fresh. Obviously, this wordless, multipaneled narrative is not for beginners learning the alphabet, but it is an inventive boon for language teachers and others. This recipe spells out delicious wordplay and appreciation."

REVIEW: *Publ Wkly* v261 no1 p55-7 Ja 6 2014

REVIEW: *Quill Quire* v80 no2 p34-5 Mr 2014 Emily Donaldson

REVIEW: *SLJ* v60 no2 p119 F 2014 April Sanders

GUTIERREZ, LALEI E. Eight Pathways of Healing Love. See Belzunce, P. R.

GUTSCHOW, NIELS.ed. A Blessing in Disguise. See A Blessing in Disguise

GUY, JOHN. The Children of Henry VIII; [by] John Guy 272 p. 2013 Oxford University Press

1. Elizabeth I, Queen of England, 1533-1603 2. Great Britain—History—Tudors, 1485-1603 3. Henry VIII, King of England, 1491-1547 4. Historical literature 5. Tudor, House of

ISBN 0192840908 (hardcover); 9780192840905 (hardcover)

SUMMARY: This book by John Guy looks at "the heirs of Henry VIII. . . . Rather than attempt the massive undertaking of covering in depth the histories of Edward, Mary, and Elizabeth, Guy has chosen to give the most salient details regarding the monarchs . . . present[ing] an overall picture of their lives and upbringings under Henry's rule and during their later reigns. His particular focus is on how their relationships with each other--and . . . their father--affected them." (Library Journal)

REVIEW: *Booklist* v109 no21 p14 Jl 1 2013 Gilbert Taylor

REVIEW: *Choice* v51 no4 p714 D 2013 D. R. Bisson

REVIEW: *Kirkus Rev* v81 no6 p91 Mr 15 2013

REVIEW: *Libr J* v138 no7 p91 Ap 15 2013 Kathleen McCallister

REVIEW: *TLS* no5766 p24 O 4 2013 CHRIS SKIDMORE

"The Children of Henry VIII." "[John] Guy wears his learning lightly here, perhaps understandably so, since this book is so short. It seems remarkable even to attempt to cover an eighty-year chronology that stretches from the death of Henry VII's eldest son, Arthur, to the Spanish Armada, in under 200 pages. Nevertheless, with the panache for which Guy's work has become known, 'The Children of Henry VIII' portrays the childhood nightmares of Britain's most celebrated dysfunctional family. . . . Guy succeeds in not simply retelling a well-worn narrative by giving a detailed re-examination of original letters and sources. . . . A portrait miniature of a book, skilfully portraying the character of an age, yet managing to do so with enough detail and care to bring its subjects to life."

GUYNUP, SHARON. Tigers Forever. See Winter, S.

GUZMAN, ANDREW T. Overheated; The Human Cost of Climate Change; [by] Andrew T. Guzman 280 p. 2013 Oxford University Press

1. Climatic changes—Economic aspects 2. Climatic changes—Effect of human beings on 3. Climatic changes—Social aspects 4. Human ecology 5. Political science literature

ISBN 0199933871 (hardcover); 9780199933877 (hardcover)

LC 2012-047000

SUMMARY: This book, by Andrew T. Guzman, discusses the political aspects surrounding climate change. "Guzman takes climate change out of the realm of scientific abstraction to explore its real-world consequences. . . . He takes as his starting point a fairly optimistic outcome in the range predicted by scientists. . . Even this modest rise would lead to catastrophic . . . problems. . . . He shows in vivid detail how climate change is already playing out in the real world." (Publisher's note)

REVIEW: *Choice* v51 no1 p110-1 S 2013 E. J. Kormondy

"Overheated: The Human Cost of Climate Change." "Law professor [Andrew T.] Guzman . . . states that 'this is not a feel-good book.' Instead, it is a hard-hitting, well-documented overview of the problems an increasingly heated world is currently facing, coupled with what lies ahead--'unprecedented migrations, famine, war, and disease.' The author focuses on the possible devastating effects of a potential two-degree Celsius temperature increase by the end of the 21st century. . . . Writing in the first person, the author adroitly employs analogues (e.g., 'hiding under the covers') that facilitate comprehension of the untoward outcomes of an overheated world."

H

HAAS, EVE. The secrets of the notebook; a woman's quest to uncover her royal family secret; [by] Eve Haas 280 p. 2013 Arcade Publishing

1. Family histories 2. Family secrets 3. Jews, German—History 4. Memoirs 5. Princes—Germany

ISBN 1611459060; 9781611459067 (alk. paper)

LC 2013-022497

SUMMARY: Author "Eve Haas is the daughter of a German Jewish family that took refuge in London after Hitler came to power. Following a terrifying air raid in the blitz, her father revealed the family secret, that her great-great grandmother Emilie was married to a Prussian prince. He then showed her the treasured leather-bound notebook inscribed to Emilie by the prince." (Publisher's note)

REVIEW: *Booklist* v110 no4 p14 O 15 2013 Hazel Rochman

REVIEW: *Kirkus Rev* v81 no16 p219 Ag 15 2013

"The Secrets of the Notebook: A Woman's Quest to Uncover Her Royal Family Secret Arcade." "World War II had just begun when Haas' father decided to show her a notebook he told her had belonged to his great-grandfather Prince Augustus of Prussia but had been written by Augustus' daughter, Charlotte. . . . Haas began an odyssey that would take her from her home in London to archives in East Germany that no one from the West had entered in more than 40 years. The information she found not only offered exciting glimpses into a bygone world, but also revealed that Augustus was a social progressive who supported Jews during a time of fierce anti-Semitism. . . . A mostly pedestrian treatment of an intriguing topic."

HAAS, JESSIE. Bramble and Maggie give and take; 56 p. 2013 Candlewick Press

1. Children's literature 2. Horsemanship—Fiction 3. Horses—Juvenile fiction 4. Pets

ISBN 9780763650216

LC 2012-942618

SUMMARY: In this book, by Jessie Haas, "Bramble, an opinionated mare, isn't about to be taken advantage of. For instance, she knows all about rides: 'The rider sat in the saddle. The horse did all the hard work.' Young Maggie, as always, has Bramble's number, and with a little judicious bribery (give-and-take, thinks Bramble), they are soon having adventures together, Maggie in the saddle, Bramble content." (Kirkus Reviews)

REVIEW: *Booklist* v109 no15 p76 Ap 1 2013 Carolyn Phelon

REVIEW: *Bull Cent Child Books* v66 no9 p419 My 2013 D. S.

REVIEW: *Horn Book Magazine* v89 no2 p102 Mr/Ap 2013 JULIE ROACH

"Bramble and Maggie: Give and Take." "In four chapters, beginning readers will get to know [Maggie and her horse Bramble] better, along with their neighbors and a broader meaning of the phrase 'give and take.' Readers learn from the very first page, when Maggie suggests going for a ride, that Bramble in particular has strong opinions and dry wit . . . . For new readers gaining confidence, the simple sentences are peppered with more challenging vocabulary, and they building complexity over the course of the book. The soft gouache illustrations delicately draw out and supplement the text's humor in both spot art and full spreads."

REVIEW: *Kirkus Rev* v81 no3 p233 F 1 2013

REVIEW: *SLJ* v59 no6 p86 Je 2013 Melissa Smith

HAAS, MARK L.ed. The Arab Spring. See The Arab Spring

HABER, STEPHEN H. Fragile by design. See Calomiris, C. W.

HABERMAN, DAVID L. People trees; worship of trees in Northern India; [by] David L. Haberman xiii, 239 p. 2013 Oxford University Press

1. Animism 2. Hinduism—Sacred books 3. Historical literature 4. India, North—Religion 5. Social science literature 6. Tree worship—India, North 7. Trees—Religious aspects

ISBN 9780199929160; 9780199929177

LC 2012-038598

SUMMARY: This book by David Haberman "is about religious conceptions of trees within the cultural world of tree worship at the tree shrines of northern India. Sacred trees have been worshiped for millennia in India, and today tree worship continues there in abundance among all segments of society." The book "reevaluates concepts such as animism, anthropomorphism, and personhood." (Publisher's note)

REVIEW: *Choice* v51 no2 p280 O 2013 R. C. Rinehart

"People Trees: Worship of Trees in Northern India." "In this engaging and accessible book, [author David L.] Haberman . . . explores the widespread worship of trees by Hindus throughout northern India. . . . Haberman argues that, while scholars of religion have moved past such theories, much may be learned from a close analysis of the practices of those who consider trees conscious beings worthy of worship. . . . Significantly, evidence for tree worship is widely attested throughout the history of India, from the Indus Valley civilization to numerous tales in the Vedas, Upanishads, Puranas, and vernacular traditions. Haberman's book brings attention to an important yet understudied aspect of Hindu religious experience."

HABERMAS, JÜRGEN, 1929-. The future of human nature; [by] Jürgen Habermas 127 2003 Polity

1. Bioethics 2. Biotechnology 3. Eugenics—Moral and ethical aspects 4. Human beings 5. Philosophical literature
ISBN 0-7456-2986-5
LC 2002—192476

SUMMARY: In this book, Jürgen Habermas considers "that the question of what constitutes authentic human esistence is central to thinking about the new biotechnologies. . . . If new biotechnologies make it possible to create new human beings, they also make it impossible to to avoid questions about what it means to be human—questions that cannot be answered by science." (Times Literary Supplement)

REVIEW: *Contemp Sociol* v43 no2 p155-60 Mr 2014 Graham Scambler

"The Future of Human Nature," "The Politics of Life Itself: Biomedicine, Power, and Subjectivity in the Twenty-First Century," and "The New Medical Sociology: Social Forms of Health and Illness". "[Jürgen Habermas's] short volume comprises three pieces of direct relevance to medical sociology dating back to 2001: the first two are expanded versions of lectures delivered at the Universities of Zurich and Marburg and the third is based on a speech he gave on receiving the Peace Prize of the German Book Trade. . . . [Nikolas] Rose traverses similar territory but takes a very different route. Drawing on explicitly Foucauldian theoretical foundations as well as his previous work, he takes off from the current and growing ambiguity around notions of the normal. . . . Bryan Turner has decisively intervened in medical sociology's development more than once. His 'The New Medical Sociology' consolidates his reputation."

HABITABILITY OF OTHER PLANETS AND SATELLITES; xxix, 419 p. 2013 Springer

1. Exobiology 2. Habitable planets 3. Life on other planets 4. Outer space—Exploration 5. Scientific literature
ISBN 9400765452 (hdbk. : acid-free paper); 9789400765450 (hdbk. : acid-free paper)
LC 2013-943260

SUMMARY: "This edited collection of short papers covers a range of topics relevant to questions of habitability on planetary bodies other than Earth. It is divided into eight parts: habitability parameters, impact craters, field studies, the search for habitable worlds, alternatives to terrestrial life, technical applications, future space missions, and conclusions." (Choice: Current Reivews for Academic Libraries)

REVIEW: *Choice* v51 no7 p1240 Mr 2014 P. K. Strother

"Habitability of Other Planets and Satellites." "Chapter authors cover quite a bit of ground; the book is perhaps suitable as a primer in aspects of astrobiology associated with questions of habitability of other planets and moons. Some chapters are quite technical, while others can be easily understood by readers without a science background. Most of the authors are European, so the book also serves to emphasize a European perspective on these research topics. There are some fundamental differences in how researchers approach the possibility of life on other planets, and editors [Jean-Pierre] de Vera . . . and [Joseph] Seckbach . . . have allowed these different approaches to be expressed without imposing a singular philosophy."

HACK, HENRY. Mommy, Mommy; A Danny Boyland Novel; [by] Henry Hack 296 p. 2013 Createspace Independent Pub

1. Child abuse—Fiction 2. Detective & mystery stories 3. Missing persons—Fiction 4. Mothers & sons—Fiction 5. Serial murderers—Fiction
ISBN 1491239492; 9781491239490

SUMMARY: In this book, "a detective faces off against a dangerous killer. . . . Frankie Chandler has bounced around foster homes ever since his father died and his mother, Angela, left him. What upsets Frankie is not that Angela fled the police, who suspected her husband's stumble down the stairs was no accident, but that she deserted her own son. Years later . . . a series of murders of women the same age and appearance catches the attention of homicide investigator Danny Boyland." (Kirkus Reviews)

REVIEW: *Kirkus Rev* v82 no2 p334 Ja 15 2014

"Mommy, Mommy: A Danny Boyland Novel". "The incisive study of a murderer. . . . [Frankie Chandler's] account is so impassioned . . . that Danny winds up playing second fiddle in his third literary turnout. As such, his much-praised investigatory skills—the director of the FBI even vouches for him—aren't really on display this book, since he tends to have revelations only after another person is found dead. . . . Pitied or not, Frankie is a terrifying killer as he goes through a list of 32 females who resemble his mother; though he's well into his 20s, he still refers to Angela as 'Mommy.' May not stir much interest in the Danny Boyland series, but a mesmerizing killer makes this story a triumph."

HACKEL, STEVEN W. Junípero Serra; California's founding father; [by] Steven W. Hackel 352 p. 2013 Hill and Wang, A division of Farrar, Straus and Giroux

1. Biography (Literary form) 2. Missionaries—California—Biography 3. Missions, Spanish—California—History
ISBN 9780809095315 (hardcover)
LC 2013-015253

SUMMARY: This book presents a biographyof missionary Junípero Serra. "Hcould imagine no greater service to God than converting Indians, and in 1749 he set off for the new world. In Mexico, Serra first worked as a missionary to Indians and as an uncompromising agent of the Inquisition. . . . With a potent blend of Franciscan piety and worldly cunning, he outmaneuvered Spanish royal officials, rival religious orders, and avaricious settlers to establish himself as a peerless frontier administrator." (Publisher's note)

REVIEW: *America* v210 no9 p33-5 Mr 17 2014 THOMAS RZEZNIK

"Junípero Serra: Californias Founding Father" and "Journey to the Sun: Junípero Serra's Dream and the Founding of California". "Both authors reveal an appreciation for Serra's life and legacy, but they employ different narrative styles and differ in their characterization of their shared subject. [Steven W.] Hackel, a historian who has written about Indian-Spanish relations in the colonial missions, provides the crisper biography. Though still lively and engaging, his is the more academic study, exhibiting his broad command not just of Serra's own writings, but of the social, political and religious context of his times. [Gregory] Orfalea, in contrast, employs a more literary approach to his tale. His account can be imaginative or impressionistic at times, but he wants readers to experience the sights, sounds and spectacle of Serra's travels and ministry."

REVIEW: *Choice* v51 no5 p904-5 Ja 2014 S. Pitti

REVIEW: *Commonweal* v141 no11 p35-8 Je 13 2014 Patrick Jordan

REVIEW: *Kirkus Rev* v81 no16 p118 Ag 15 2013

REVIEW: *Libr J* v138 no13 p104 Ag 1 2013 Crystal Goldman

REVIEW: *Publ Wkly* v260 no27 p79 Jl 8 2013

HADADI, HODA. il. Deep in the Sahara. See Cunnane, K.

HADAS-LEBEL, MIREILLE. Philo of Alexandria; a thinker in the Jewish diaspora; xvi, 241 p. 2012 Brill

1. Alexandria (Egypt)—History 2. Hellenism 3. Historical literature 4. Jewish philosophers 5. Jewish philosophy 6. Judaism and philosophy 7. Philo, of Alexandria 8. Philosophers, Ancient

ISBN 9789004209480 (hardback : alk. paper)

LC 2012-017637

SUMMARY: This book by Mireille Hadas-Lebel discusses how "Philo (20BCE?-45CE?) is the most illustrious son of Alexandrian Jewry and the first major scholar to combine a deep Jewish learning with Greek philosophy. . . . This monograph provides a guide to Philo's life, his thought and his action, as well as his continuing influence on theological and philosophical thought." (Publisher's note)

REVIEW: *Classical Rev* v63 no2 p390-2 O 2013 Jutta Leonhardt-Balzer

"Philo of Alexandria: A Thinker in the Jewish Diaspora." "Nine years after the publication of the French original [author Mireille Hadas-Lebel's] book has been translated into English. . . . The book has nine main chapters, outlining Philo's life, thought and impact, mainly based on the evidence of the ancient sources. . . . The book is an introduction to Philo for the general reader rather than someone with a more specialised interest, although its broad use of the ancient sources also makes it a good read for the experts. Each chapter can be read by itself and there is little overlap. The English edition has been well prepared, although there are some slight oversights."

HADDAD, JOHN R. America's first adventure in China; trade, treaties, opium, and salvation; [by] John R. Haddad 294 p. 2013 Temple University Press

1. Historical literature 2. Missions, American—China—History—19th century 3. Opium trade—China—History—19th century

ISBN 1439906890; 9781439906897 (cloth : alk. paper)

LC 2012-040901

SUMMARY: In the book, author "John Haddad provides a colorful history of the evolving cultural exchange and interactions between these countries. He recounts how American expatriates adopted a pragmatic attitude--as well as an entrepreneurial spirit and improvisational approach--to their dealings with the Chinese. Haddad shows how opium played a potent role in the dreams of Americans who either smuggled it or opposed its importation, and he considers the missionary movement." (Publisher's note)

REVIEW: *Choice* v51 no1 p147 S 2013 D. L. Wilson

"America's First Adventure in China: Trade, Treaties, Opium, and Salvation." "[Author John R.] Haddad . . . tells a powerful story of the first epoch of Sino-American relations. . . . The US citizens who made these early travels did so without any protection from their government, because they represented a small, weak nation. . . . The book's organization provides a clear picture of the progression of Sino-American relations in the early years. . . . Haddad bases his important synthesis on a wide range of English-language materials, journals, memoirs, and scholarly accounts that focus on more specific details, and does not utilize any significant Chinese source materials."

REVIEW: *Libr J* v138 no8 p91 My 1 2013 Susan G. Baird

HADDIX, CHUCK. Bird; the life and music of Charlie Parker; [by] Chuck Haddix 190 p. 2013 University of Illinois Press

1. Jazz musicians—United States—Biography

ISBN 9780252037917 (hardcover : alk. paper); 9780252095177 (e-book)

LC 2013-003509

SUMMARY: Written by Chuck Haddix, "'Bird: The Life and Music of Charlie Parker' tells the story of his life, music, and career. This new biography . . . weaves together firsthand accounts from those who knew him with new information about his life and career to create a . . . narrative portrait of a tragic genius." (Publisher's note)

REVIEW: *Booklist* v110 no1 p23 S 1 2013 Mark Levine

REVIEW: *Commentary* v136 no2 p58-61 S 2013 TERRY TEACHOUT

REVIEW: *London Rev Books* v36 no2 p26-9 Ja 23 2014 Ian Penman

REVIEW: *N Y Times Book Rev* p51 D 8 2013 DAVID HAJDU

"Kansas City Lightning: The Rise and Times of Charlie Parker" and "Bird: The Life and Music of Charlie Parker." "'Lightning: The Rise and Times of Charlie Parker' is . . . a virtuoso performance of musical-literary mimesis. . . . In jazz scholarship, few writers have been as devoted to their subjects as Crouch has been to Parker. . . . 'Bird,' by Chuck Haddix . . . has also recently been published, and its benign but bloodless presentation of the facts about Parker's life reminds one of the value of critical analysis and interpretation. . . . The information in Haddix's book is not always accurate, either."

HADLEY, TESSA. Clever Girl; A Novel; [by] Tessa Hadley 256 p. 2013 Jonathan Cape

1. Historical fiction 2. Life change events—Fiction 3. Single mothers—Fiction 4. Teenage pregnancy—Fiction 5. Women—Great Britain
ISBN 0062270397; 0224096524; 9780062270399; 9780224096522

SUMMARY: In this book, by Tessa Hadley, "one relatively ordinary life, chronicled from the 1950s to the 1990s in England, mirrors enormous shifts in style, attitude and choice, especially for women. . . . Growing up in the postwar decade without a father . . . [Stella] experiences a childhood bound by convention and a shortage of cash. . . . Stella falls pregnant and becomes a single mother herself, a choice which derails her hopes for college." (Kirkus Reviews)

REVIEW: *Booklist* v110 no7 p20 D 1 2013 Michele Leber

REVIEW: *Kirkus Rev* v81 no21 p133 N 1 2013

REVIEW: *Libr J* v138 no21 p90 D 1 2013 Joyce Townsend

REVIEW: *N Y Times Book Rev* p17 Mr 16 2014 MEG WOLITZER

REVIEW: *N Y Times Book Rev* p25 Mr 23 2014

REVIEW: *New Statesman* v142 no5155 p47-8 Ap 26 2013 Claire Lowdon

REVIEW: *New York Times* v163 no56453 pC4 Mr 27 2014 John Williams

REVIEW: *Publ Wkly* v260 no44 p42 N 4 2013

REVIEW: *TLS* no5749 p20 Je 7 2013 ALEX CLARK

"Clever Girl." "[Tessa] Hadley's achievement in her fifth novel is to express a life significantly shaped and often constrained by discomfort --physical, mental, emotional--but a life that nonetheless progresses, mutating from circumstance to circumstance, decade to decade. . . . The details of the past--minute, sensory, utterly present in recollection--are at once revelatory and esoteric; they confront us with a quick apprehension of the truth but leave us none the wiser as to its overall design. . . . The precision with which Hadley allows Stella to retell her life . . . is unsurprising; this is what she does, this beautiful brand of observation, both scrupulous and ambiguous. But her foray into the first person . . . makes her observations paradoxically more strange."

HAEFELI, EVAN. New Netherland and the Dutch origins of American religious liberty; [by] Evan Haefeli xiv, 355 p. 2012 University of Pennsylvania Press

1. Dutch—United States—History—17th century 2. Historical literature 3. Religious tolerance—United States—History—17th century
ISBN 9780812244083 (hardcover: alk. paper)
LC 2011-046060

SUMMARY: This book by Evan Haefeli "offers a new reading of the way tolerance operated in colonial America. Using sources in several languages and looking at laws and ideas as well as their enforcement and resistance, Evan Haefeli shows that, although tolerance as a general principle was respected in the colony, there was a pronounced struggle against it in practice. Crucial to the fate of New Netherland were the changing religious and political dynamics within the English empire." (Publisher's note)

REVIEW: *Am Hist Rev* v118 no5 p1510-1 D 2013 Charles H. Parker

REVIEW: *Choice* v50 no3 p553 N 2012 D. R. Mandell

REVIEW: *J Am Hist* v101 no2 p555-7 S 2014

REVIEW: *Rev Am Hist* v42 no1 p7-12 Mr 2014 John D. Krugler

"New Netherland and the Dutch Origins of American Religious History." "Evan Haefeli has done an excellent job of positioning New Netherland in the context of the Dutch nation and its expansive worldwide empire that stretched from the Far East to South America and to the West Indies. In focusing on the Dutch colony that eventually became New York, he argues that the colony deserves greater recognition for its contribution to American religious liberty. This is a book that historians of religion and politics in the seventeenth-century will want to read. . . . New Netherland is more provocative than convincing. Haefeli has done a masterful job of presenting and analyzing an array of terms that are vital for understanding religion in New Netherland."

HAGAN, JOHN. Who are the criminals?; the politics of crime policy from the age of Roosevelt to the age of Reagan; [by] John Hagan 301 2010 Princeton University Press

1. Crime—Government policy—United States—History—20th century 2. Criminal justice, Administration of—United States—History—20th century 3. Mandatory minimum sentences 4. Social science literature 5. Subprime mortgages—Law & legislation 6. United States—Politics & government—1981-1989
ISBN 0-691-14838-4; 978-0-691-14838-0
LC 2010--18663

SUMMARY: "Hagan argues that the recent history of American criminal justice can be divided into two eras—the age of Roosevelt (roughly 1933 to 1973) and the age of Reagan (1974-2008). A focus on rehabilitation, corporate regulation, and the social roots of crime in the earlier period was dramatically reversed in the later era." (Publisher's note) Index."Hagan argues that the recent history of American criminal justice can be divided into two eras—the age of Roosevelt (roughly 1933 to 1973) and the age of Reagan (1974-2008). A focus on rehabilitation, corporate regulation, and the social roots of crime in the earlier period was dramatically reversed in the later era." (Publisher's note) Index.

REVIEW: *Contemp Sociol* v42 no5 p683-6 S 2013 Michael Levi

"Who Are the Criminals? The Politics of Crime Policy From the Age of Roosevelt to the Age of Reagan." "[Author John] Hagan notes the importance to Reagan crime policies not just of sloganistic thinking about outgroups but also of '(1) data revealing that the majority of crimes were committed by a small minority of highly active offenders, and (2) studies challenging the value of indeterminate sentences in reducing criminal behavior.' . . . Importantly, he connects the sub-prime issues to both crime reduction (homeowners are less criminal, at least when able to prepay loans), and to white-collar (and, understressed in the book, lower level white/blue collar) victimization of poor and blacks."

REVIEW: *Contemp Sociol* v42 no5 p679-83 S 2013 William S. Laufer

HAGEN, BETHANY. Landry Park; [by] Bethany Hagen 384 p. 2013 Dial Books for Young Readers

1. Elite (Social sciences) 2. Justice—Fiction 3. Nuclear energy—Fiction 4. Science fiction 5. Social classes—Fiction
ISBN 9780803739482 (hardcover)
LC 2012-045144

SUMMARY: In this book, "sixteen-year-old Madeline

Landry is practically Gentry royalty. Her ancestor developed the nuclear energy that has replaced electricity. . . . But when she learns about the devastating impact the Gentry lifestyle . . . is having on those less fortunate, her whole world is turned upside down. As Madeline begins to question everything she has been told, she finds herself increasingly drawn to handsome, beguiling David Dana, who seems to be hiding secrets of his own." (Publisher's note)

REVIEW: *Bull Cent Child Books* v67 no6 p314 F 2014 Kate Quealy-Gainer

Title:"Landry Park." "The dystopian world here, containing an ironfisted upper class lording over a weaker population, is by now a familiar one in YA lit, but it's the upper-class perspective of Madeline's narration that makes this a compelling, thoughtful look at the structuring of power and what it takes to dismantle it. [Bethany] Hagen manages to humanize the elite without absolving them, focusing on Madeline and David as they struggle to make the choice between a comfortable life and a comfortable conscience; especially moving is their ultimate realization that merely providing resources to the Rootless while enjoying the fruits of their diseased labor is the worst kind of charity."

REVIEW: *Kirkus Rev* v81 no24 p163 D 15 2013

"Landry Park". "Regency romance sits uneasily in a dystopian throwback future. . . . From within the cozy confines of her silken prison, Madeline realizes that forcing children to dispose of spent uranium while providing only enough medical care for them to stay fertile is a little gauche. Along with a few interestingly complex secondary characters, Madeline learns about the caricatured evil underlying her luxuries. Will she be able to assuage her conscience by merely scattering largesse to the populace out of a sense of noblesse oblige, or will she be forced to make any actual sacrifices? Regency romances can combine well with science fiction . . . but this awkward merger of the two will convince few."

REVIEW: *Publ Wkly* v260 no47 p53 N 18 2013

REVIEW: *SLJ* v60 no3 p158 Mr 2014 Shelley Diaz

REVIEW: *Voice of Youth Advocates* v36 no6 p71 F 2014 Walter Hogan

HAGENA, KATHARINA. The taste of apple seeds; 241 p. 2013 Atlantic

1. Families—Fiction 2. Grandmothers—Fiction 3. Grandparent and child—Fiction 4. Inheritance and succession—Fiction 5. Loss (Psychology)—Fiction 6. Psychological fiction

ISBN 0857890980 (hbk.); 0857890999; 9780857890986 (hbk.); 9780857890993

LC 2013-376392

SUMMARY: In this internationally bestselling book, by Katharina Hagena, "when Iris unexpectedly inherits her grandmother's house in the country, she also inherits the painful memories that live there. Iris gives herself a one-week stay at the old house, after which she'll make a decision: keep it or sell it. The choice is not so simple, though, for her grandmother's cottage is an enchanting place, where . . . the darkest family secrets never stay buried." (Publisher's note)

REVIEW: *Booklist* v110 no11 p25 F 1 2014 Deborah Donovan

REVIEW: *Kirkus Rev* v82 no1 p248 Ja 1 2014

"The Taste of Apple Seeds". "This book was an international best-seller. In [Jamie] Bulloch's translation from the German, nature imagery is colorfully transcribed, which is fortunate, since [Katharina] Hagena's descriptions of the lake, forest and gardens surrounding the ancestral apple farm of the Deelwater family are among this novel's principal charms. . . . Whimsy abounds, striking a discordant note with the overall meditative tone of the book. . . . Since much of the nuanced wit is perhaps lost in translation, what remains is a decorative but aimless family chronicle. Matriarch Bertha's decline is, however, viscerally felt and vividly detailed."

HAGHER, IYORWUESE. A Day in Mexico City; And Other Poems; [by] Iyorwuese Hagher 204 p. 2009 Author Solutions

1. Africa—Social conditions 2. Mexico City (Mexico)—Social conditions 3. Nigeria—Social conditions 4. Poems—Collections 5. Poverty

ISBN 1438946929; 9781438946924

SUMMARY: "In this collection, Nigeria's former envoy to Mexico reflects on life in Mexico but also makes strong statements about life in the developing world. He takes issues with poverty and its causes: bad leadership, lack of democracy, injustice, corruption and greed. The poems offer hope in the human condition, and empathize with the suffering of the downtrodden, the poor and the weak." (Publisher's note)

REVIEW: *Kirkus Rev* v81 no24 p77 D 15 2013

"A Day In Mexico City". "Outraged, sorrowful and occasionally hopeful post-colonial free verse that gives voice to the oppressed. In his unflinching debut, [Iyorwuese] Hagher seeks to redeem the struggling African continent through the power of myth, song and poetry, but he finds it a rough go, even from the outset. . . . The epic of celebration and heroism is not fulfilled here, but the seeds of resurrection are sown in some of Hagher's longer, more explicitly African pieces . . . in which the long arcs of African histories are revealed and celebrated. Ambitious yet aware of its own futility, Hagher's project necessarily means poetry that is, by turns, bombastic, messy and opaque, but it can be remarkably powerful, too. Meaningful, edifying verse that tells of a beleaguered people."

HAGLER, GINA. Modeling ships and space craft; the science and art of mastering the oceans and sky; [by] Gina Hagler xiv, 249 p. 2013 Springer

1. Aerodynamics—Simulation methods 2. Hydrodynamics—Simulation methods 3. Scientific literature 4. Ship models 5. Space vehicles—Models

ISBN 1461445957 (pbk. : alk. paper); 9781461445951 (pbk. : alk. paper)

LC 2012-945938

SUMMARY: This book "begins with the theories of Aristotle and Archimedes, moving on to examine the work of Froude and Taylor, the early aviators and the Wright Brothers, Goddard and the other rocket men, and the computational fluid dynamic models of our time. It examines the ways each used fluid dynamic principles in the design of their vessels. In the process, this book covers the history of hydrodynamic (aero and fluid) theory and its progression." (Publisher's note)

REVIEW: *Choice* v51 no5 p859 Ja 2014 A. M. Strauss

"Modeling Ships and Space Craft: The Science and Art of Mastering the Oceans and Sky." "This book has a misleading title. Only about one quarter of the book is about modeling, and the modeling is mostly about ships, with only a little bit devoted to spacecraft. . . . the text lacks equations and does not cover dimensional analysis and its central role in modeling. . . . The graphics are poor; some figures are mysterious since they do not seem to convey any information. . . . Nonetheless, the book does contain some good writing and interesting information on the history of technology."

HAGUE, MICHAEL.il. The hobbit. See The hobbit

HAGUE, MICHAEL.il. Michael Hague's read-to-me book of fairy tales. See Michael Hague's read-to-me book of fairy tales

HAGY, ALYSON. Boleto; a novel; [by] Alyson Hagy 251 p. 2012 Graywolf Press

1. Fiction 2. Horse trainers—Fiction 3. Horses—Fiction 4. Horses—Training—Fiction 5. Horses in literature 6. Human-animal relationships—Fiction 7. Human-animal relationships in literature 8. Polo—Fiction 9. Polo in literature 10. Sports business

ISBN 1555976123; 9781555976125 (alk. paper)

LC 2012-931912

SUMMARY: This book "opens with Will [Testerman] buying a beautiful 2-year-old filly for a bargain price. She will be a 'development project' for the patient Will. He talks to her a lot, building trust. He won't ride her yet . . . but they'll be going to California together to meet Don Enrique. . . . It turns out Don Enrique is an Argentine businessman who hosts polo games. His manager is a swine. Five frightened, underfed Argentine teenagers do the barn work. Will's fantasy of learning the polo business, unwisely based on a single conversation with the Don, begins to crumble. Will his innate decency hobble him with this tough, mercenary crowd? And can he protect his beloved filly from these rapacious rich folks?" (Kirkus Reviews)

REVIEW: *Booklist* v108 no14 p17 Mr 15 2012 Joanne Wilkinson

REVIEW: *Kirkus Rev* v80 no8 p39 Ap 15 2012

"Boleto." "He's come of age, but the appealing young cowboy still has life lessons to learn in this beautifully observed third novel from [Alyson] Hagy. . . . he novel opens with Will buying a beautiful 2-year-old filly for a bargain price. She will be a 'development project' for the patient Will. He talks to her a lot, building trust. He won't ride her yet . . . but they'll be going to California together to meet Don Enrique. . . . Hagy demonstrates an easy mastery of her material; whether it's horsey stuff, a sex scene or an ugly poker game, she nails it. . . . Plot lags behind character, but Hagy reads horses and people so well you won't mind. . . so much."

REVIEW: *Libr J* v137 no6 p71 Ap 1 2012 John R. Cecil

REVIEW: *N Y Times Book Rev* p56 N 10 2013 IHSAN TAYLOR

REVIEW: *New Yorker* v88 no16 p125 Je 4 2012

REVIEW: *Orion Magazine* p74-5 S/O 2012 Joe Wilkins

REVIEW: *Publ Wkly* v259 no8 p139 F 20 2012

HAHN, BARBARA. Making tobacco bright; creating an American commodity, 1617-1937; [by] Barbara Hahn x, 236 p. 2011 Johns Hopkins University Press

1. Agricultural literature 2. Historical literature 3. Tobacco—United States—History 4. Tobacco—Virginia—History 5. Tobacco industry—United States—History 6. Tobacco industry—Virginia—History

ISBN 1421402866 (hardcover : acid-free paper); 9781421402864 (hardcover : acid-free paper)

LC 2011-013289

SUMMARY: "In her sweeping history of the American tobacco industry, Barbara Hahn traces the emergence of the tobacco plant's many varietal types, arguing that they are products not of nature but of economic relations and continued and intense market regulation. Hahn focuses her study on the most popular of these varieties, Bright Flue-Cured Tobacco. . . . Combining economic theory with the history of technology, 'Making Tobacco Bright' revises several narratives in American history." (Publisher's note)

REVIEW: *Am Hist Rev* v117 no5 p1611 D 2012 Jeannie Whayne

REVIEW: *Choice* v49 no8 p1498 Ap 2012 T. E. Sullivan

REVIEW: *J Am Hist* v99 no3 p963-4 D 2012 Russell R. Menard

REVIEW: *Rev Am Hist* v42 no1 p20-2 Mr 2014 Eldred E. "Wink" Prince Jr.

"Making Tobacco Bright: Creating an American Commodity, 1617-1937." "Agriculture is a place where history and science meet, and Barbara Hahn displays a command of both disciplines in this challenging book. Hahn rolls out her thesis early: the so-called varieties of tobacco such as Burley and Bright have little to do with genetics. Rather, they resulted from different methods of cultivation, harvesting, curing, and readying for market. Further, these husbandry variations were themselves responses to markets, government policies, and technology. . . . 'Making Tobacco Bright' is more than simply another history of tobacco culture. Rather, the book makes a unique and valuable contribution by weaving familiar historical threads into a new pattern."

HAHN, REBECCA. A creature of moonlight; [by] Rebecca Hahn 224 p. 2014 Houghton Mifflin Harcourt

1. Dragons—Fiction 2. Fantasy 3. Flowers—Fiction 4. Forests and forestry—Fiction 5. Identity—Fiction 6. Magic—Fiction 7. Princesses—Fiction

ISBN 054410935X; 9780544109353

LC 2013-020188

SUMMARY: In this novel, by Rebecca Hahn, "as the only heir to the throne, Marni should have been surrounded by wealth and privilege, not living in exile—but now the time has come when she must choose between claiming her birthright as princess of a realm whose king wants her dead, and life with the father she has never known: a wild dragon who is sending his magical woods to capture her." (Publisher's note)

REVIEW: *Bull Cent Child Books* v67 no9 p456 My 2014 K. Q. G.

"A Creature of Moonlight". "This is fairy-tale fantasy at its best, with evocative prose and simple storytelling deftly conveying a powerful emotional core that will haunt readers long after the pages end. The fairy forest has an appropriately ethereal feel while the royal court is full of sharp edges and shady people, but both places are dangerous for Marni, whose presence means an opportunity to grab power more than a chance to welcome kin home. Though mainly a character study of a girl divided by her heritage, it's also a strong indictment of the idea that love is the same thing as possession and an exploration of the way that such interpretations of love lead to destruction."

REVIEW: *Horn Book Magazine* v90 no4 p92-3 Jl/Ag 2014 CYNTHIA K. RITTER

REVIEW: *N Y Times Book Rev* p19 Je 15 2014 JENNIFER A. NIELSEN

HAIKU IN ENGLISH; the first hundred years; 464 p. 2013 W. W. Norton & Company

1. English haiku 2. English poetry—History & criticism 3. Haiku 4. Haiku—Explication 5. Haiku—History & criticism 6. Poems—Collections
ISBN 0393239470; 9780393239478 (hardcover)
LC 2013-014060

SUMMARY: This book is an "anthology of more than 800 . . . chosen poems that were originally written in English by over 200 poets from around the world. Although haiku originated as a Japanese art form, it has found a . . . home in the English-speaking world. This collection tells the story for the first time of Anglophone haiku, charting its evolution over the last one hundred years and placing it within its historical and literary context." (Publisher's note)

REVIEW: *Booklist* v109 no22 p21 Ag 1 2013 Donna Seaman

REVIEW: *Choice* v51 no6 p1003-4 F 2014 R. T. Prus

"Haiku in English: The First Hundred Years." "A splendid collection. It operates on several levels. In its purest form, haiku startles readers into an awareness of their presence in a world of flux. The poems collected here achieve this level of satisfaction and more. . . . The arrangement of the poems in this gathering provides a history of the form in English, demonstrating how the language bent the form without breaking it. Billy Collins provides an insightful introduction, and [Jim] Kacian gives a lucid analysis of the transformation of the genre as it entered English language literature with Ezra Pound and the modernists and continues to the present. Collins's opening and Kacian's closing provide fitting bookends to the collection and become apt metaphors for the genre."

HAIRSTON, ERIC ASHLEY. The ebony column; classics, civilization, and the African American reclamation of the West; [by] Eric Ashley Hairston xvi, 262 p. 2013 University of Tennessee Press

1. American literature—African American authors—History and criticism 2. American literature—Classical influences 3. Classicism in literature 4. Historical literature 5. Race relations in literature
ISBN 157233942X (hardcover); 9781572339422 (hardcover)
LC 2013-001464

SUMMARY: This book "probes classicism's impact on Phillis Wheatley, Frederick Douglass, Anna Julia Cooper, and W. E. B. Du Bois. . . . The author contends that overlooking these individuals' forays in antiquity's archives limits one's understanding of America. . . . His research suggests that black writers used epics, oratorical treatises, and curricular philosophies both to critique racial injustice and to claim a stake in national identity." (Choice: Current Reviews for Academic Libraries)

REVIEW: *Choice* v51 no6 p1004 F 2014 M. D. Hill

"The Ebony Column: Classics, Civilization, and the African American Reclamation of the West." "[Eric Ashley] Hairston . . . zestfully probes classicism's impact on Phillis Wheadey, Frederick Douglass, Anna Julia Cooper, and W. E. B. Du Bois. . . . When he analyzes piety, virtue, femininity, and culture, Hairston not only reshapes debates about these authors, but he also attacks theories that link classical education to white elitism. . . . This study complicates the reader's grasp of American cultural syncretism. Although Hairston occasionally romanticizes antiquity's prejudices and oversimplifies oppositional reasoning, his apologetics benefit from copious support and cogent thinking. His insistence that black voice absorbs classical tones must be heeded."

HAITI AND THE AMERICAS; 256 p. 2013 Jackson

1. Haiti—Foreign relations 2. Haiti—History 3. Historical literature 4. Pan-Africanism
ISBN 9781617037573 (cloth : alk. paper); 9781617037580 (ebook)
LC 2012-038298

SUMMARY: This book "brings together an interdisciplinary group of essays to examine the influence of Haiti throughout the hemisphere, to contextualize the ways that Haiti has been represented over time, and to look at Haiti's own cultural expressions in order to think about alternative ways of imagining its culture and history." (Publisher's note)

REVIEW: *Choice* v51 no4 p682-3 D 2013 I. M. de Assis-Wilson

"Haiti and the Americas." "Contesting, revising, and reclaiming Haiti's representations in the imaginary of the 'New World,' this thought-provoking collection looks at Haiti as a vital crossroads in the Americas. Written by established and rising scholars (inside and outside the US), the essays coalesce into a provocative argument for advancing scholarship in Haitian studies. . . . In sum, the volume stands as a multidisciplinary approach to the historical/cultural positioning of Haiti in the Americas--a vital resource encapsulating Latin American history, cultural studies, art history, film/literary studies, and political theory. . . . Highly recommended."

HALE, CHRISTOPHER. Massacre in Malaya; Exposing Britain's My Lai; [by] Christopher Hale 432 p. 2013 Trafalgar Square

1. Batang Kali (Selangor) 2. Great Britain. Army 3. Historical literature 4. Malaya—History—Malayan Emergency, 1948-1960 5. Massacres
ISBN 0752487019; 9780752487014

SUMMARY: It was the author's intent to demonstrate "that British tactics in Malaya were more ruthless than historians have so far conceded. Like the conflict in colonial Kenya against the Mau-Mau, British tactics in Malaya involved massive resettlement programs, ethnic cleansing, indiscriminate aerial bombing, and the brutal exploitation of aboriginal forces." (Publisher's note)

REVIEW: *London Rev Books* v36 no4 p19-20 F 20 2014 Neal Ascherson

"Massacre in Malaya: Exposing Britain's My Lai". "The first thing to know about this big book is that it's not really about the 'massacre in Malaya', the crime the media sometimes call 'Britain's My Lai'. Only a few pages deal in detail with the Batang Kali killings in December 1948. . . . Instead,

Christopher Hale . . . has put together a massive history of the British presence on the Malay peninsula. . . . That's not to say that Hale has simply pasted 'Massacre' on the cover to help the book sell. This is a pungently hostile history of British colonial strategy and tactics in the region, and he obviously feels that Batang Kali is somehow representative of that history. . . . Hale isn't wrong to see in Batang Kali some obscene reflections of older failures."

HALE, NATHAN. Donner dinner party; [by] Nathan Hale 123 p. 2013 Harry N Abrams Inc

1. Cannibalism 2. Donner Party 3. Graphic nonfiction 4. Overland journeys to the Pacific 5. Pioneers
ISBN 1419708562; 9781419708565

SUMMARY: In this graphic novel, author Nathan Hale "tells the harrowing story of the ill-fated Donner party. Beginning with their departure from Springfield, Illinois, in 1846, Hale depicts the party's progress . . . and includes lots of factual details, such as a roster of everyone in the party, how they died, and a helpful map showing just how . . . close they came to California before meeting their grisly end." (Booklist)

REVIEW: *Booklist* v110 no4 p39 O 15 2013 Sarah Hunter

"Nathan Hale's Hazardous Tales: Donner Dinner Party." "Hale, still narrating juicy history tales . . . with the help of a British soldier and an effusive, bumbling executioner, tells the harrowing story of the ill-fated Donner party. . . . Hale depicts the party's progress in small but clear panels and includes lots of factual details, such as a roster of everyone in the party, how they died, and a helpful map. . . despite the gruesome facts. Hale keeps it relatively light and lifts the mood with some much-needed humor. . . . This informative graphic novel capitalizes on enticingly gross history to great effect, balancing raw facts with strong storytelling."

REVIEW: *N Y Times Book Rev* p38 N 10 2013 BETSY BIRD

"The Great American Dust Bowl" and "Donner Dinner Party." "Don Brown and Nathan Hale use impressive artistry to recount two of the American West's most infamous tragedies in graphic-novel form. . . . Yet while Brown's narrative focuses on extreme woe's, there's something curiously undramatic about his illustrations. It's as if he wants to rein in the atrocious elements of his story even as he bring them to light. You come to wonder if his reluctance to heighten the action with more exciting pictures is part of a refusal to sensationalize. . . .'Donner Dinner Party' is, as it boats, 'dire and disgusting, but a testament to the human will to survive. . . . Most children will probably prefer Hale's blood-soaked adventures over Brown's careful and grim account of an environmental catastrophe."

HALE, SHANNON. Dangerous; [by] Shannon Hale 400 p. 2014 Bloomsbury/Walker

1. Adventure and adventurers—Fiction 2. Astronautics—Fiction 3. Love—Fiction 4. People with disabilities—Fiction 5. Science fiction
ISBN 1599901684; 9781599901688 (hardback)
LC 2013-034322

SUMMARY: In this book, "Maisie Danger Brown just wanted to get away from home for a bit and see something new. She never intended to fall in love with a boy at space camp. And she certainly never intended to stumble into a frightening plot that just might destroy everything and everyone she cares about. But now there's no going back--Maisie's the only thing standing between danger and annihilation. She must become the hero the world needs, before she loses her heart . . . and her life." (Publisher's note)

REVIEW: *Booklist* v110 no1 p65 S 1 2013 Gillian Engberg

"Dangerous," "Desert Tales," and "The Edge of the Water." "The acclaimed, best-selling author [Shannon Hale] takes a new direction in this fantasy adventure, in which an unsuspecting heroine discovers a terrifying plot against society-and falls in love along the way. . . . In this new companion to the blockbuster Wicked Lovely series, [Melissa] Marr focuses on faery Rika, whose free, isolated existence in the Mojave Desert is transformed by both a king's power and a new romance. . . . The second YA title from best-selling adult crime novelist [Elizabeth] George is the first entry in a new paranormal mystery series set on Washington state's Whidbey Island."

REVIEW: *Booklist* v110 no15 p83 Ap 1 2014 Krista Hutley

REVIEW: *Bull Cent Child Books* v67 no8 p406 Ap 2014 A. S.

"Dangerous". "There are few truly good or evil folks in this novel, as everyone seems driven by multiple, intricately layered motives. Not much is made of the fact that Maisie only has one arm, other than through descriptions of the alien supercharged robotic arm she makes for herself, and the absence of earnest efforts at proving Maisie is like the others is refreshing. [Shannon] Hale fans will easily find much to appreciate in the well-developed setting and sturdy girl characters in this new genre for the author."

REVIEW: *Kirkus Rev* v82 no3 p243 F 1 2014

REVIEW: *Publ Wkly* v261 no2 p70 Ja 13 2014

REVIEW: *SLJ* v60 no3 p159 Mr 2014 Kathleen E. Gruver

REVIEW: *Voice of Youth Advocates* v37 no2 p75 Je 2014 Jessica Miller

HALES, ROBERT. Islamic and Oriental Arms and Armour; A Lifetime's Passion; [by] Robert Hales 400 p. 2013 Robert Hales C.I. Ltd

1. Art literature 2. Collections 3. Historical literature 4, Islamic armor 5. Islamic weapons
ISBN 0992631505; 9780992631505

SUMMARY: Written by Robert Hales, this book "illustrates over 1,000 items of Islamic and Oriental arms and armour which represent the finest and most interesting examples originating from Islamic and Hindu cultures and beyond, including Russia, China, Tibet, Mongolia, Korea and South East Asia. . . . Divided into four sections: daggers, swords, firearms, and armour, with the occasional transgression, the publication also includes a useful glossary of terms." (Publisher's note)

REVIEW: *Apollo: The International Magazine for Collectors* v179 no617 p92-3 F 2014 Lucien de Guise

REVIEW: *Apollo: The International Magazine for Collectors* v178 no614 p121 N 2013

"Anti-Ugly: Excursions in English Architecture and Design," "Islamic and Oriental Arms and Armour: A Lifetime's Passion," and "The Image of Venice: Fialetti's View and Sir Henry Wotton." "Some 50 . . . pieces are collected in ['Anti-Ugly'], which focuses on English architecture. A reminder, if one were needed, of [author Gavin] Stamp's . . . wit. . . . After discovering antique weaponry in the mid 1960s, [author] Robert Hales went on to spend almost 30 years as a highly respected dealer. . . . ['Islamic and Oriental Arms and Armour'] reproduces many of the daggers, swords, firearms and armour that passed through his hands. . . . Odoardo Fiaietti's early 17th-century view of Venice has spent 400 years in relative obscurity. . . . Its recent restoration and public exhibition have inspired ['The Image of Venice']."

HALEVI, YOSSI KLEIN. Like dreamers; the story of the Israeli paratroopers who reunited Jerusalem and divided a nation; [by] Yossi Klein Halevi 608 p. 2013 HarperCollins Publishers

1. Arab-Israeli conflict—1967-1973 2. Arab-Israeli conflict—1973-1993 3. Journalism

ISBN 0060545763; 9780060545765 (hardcover : alk. paper); 9780060545772 (pbk. : alk. paper); 9780062274823 (epub)

LC 2013-018850

SUMMARY: In this book, author Yossi Klein Halevi, "interweaves the stories of a group of 1967 paratroopers who reunited Jerusalem, tracing the history of Israel and the divergent ideologies shaping it from the Six-Day War to the present. Following the lives of seven young members from the 55th Paratroopers Reserve Brigade . . . Halevi reveals how this band of brothers played pivotal roles in shaping Israel's destiny long after their historic victory." (Publisher's note)

REVIEW: *Booklist* v110 no2 p7 S 15 2013 Jay Freeman

REVIEW: *Commentary* v136 no5 p39-41 D 2013 STEPHEN DAISLEY

REVIEW: *Kirkus Rev* v81 no16 p279 Ag 15 2013

REVIEW: *Libr J* v139 no6 p56 Ap 1 2014 Ilka Gordon

REVIEW: *N Y Times Book Rev* p20 O 20 2013 JODI RUDOREN

"Like Dreamers: The Story of the Israeli Paratroopers Who Reunited Jerusalem and Divided a Nation." "[Yossi Klein] Halevi expertly employs a traditional journalistic form: he isolates seven paratroopers from that 'mythic moment' and reconstructs their lives, before and since, to render a complicated history intimate, human, relatable. His meticulous, sensitive, detailed reporting--the book is the work of more than a decade--is incredibly effective at making the small big. Over and over again, anecdotes about one religious settler or one secular kibbutznik resonate as powerful metaphors for the state's challenges. . . . It is refreshingly free of prescriptive language and judgment about a subject too often overwhelmed by people screaming past one another."

REVIEW: *New York Times* v163 no56271 pC2 S 26 2013 ETHAN BRONNER

HALEY, DAVID W.ed. The infant mind. See The infant mind

HALFMANN, DREW. Doctors and demonstrators; how political institutions shape abortion law in the United States, Britain, and Canada; [by] Drew Halfmann xi, 354 p. 2011 University of Chicago Press

1. Abortion—Law and legislation—Canada 2. Abortion—Law and legislation—Great Britain 3. Abortion—Law and legislation—United States 4. Abortion—Political aspects—Canada 5. Abortion—Political aspects—Great Britain 6. Abortion—Political aspects—United States 7. Political science literature

ISBN 0226313425 (cloth: alk. paper); 0226313433 (pbk.: alk. paper); 9780226313429 (cloth: alk. paper); 9780226313436 (pbk.: alk. paper)

LC 2011-003353

SUMMARY: The article discusses political aspects of abortion in the United States, Britain, and Canada. "In the United States, federalism, judicial review, and a private health care system contributed to the public definition of abortion as an individual right rather than a medical necessity. Meanwhile . . . the porous structure of American political parties gave pro-choice and pro-life groups the opportunity to move the issue onto the political agenda." (Publisher's note)

REVIEW: *Am J Sociol* v118 no4 p1112-4 Ja 2013 Myra Marx Ferree

REVIEW: *Contemp Sociol* v43 no1 p16-29 Ja 2014 Edwin Amenta

"The Fifth Freedom:Jobs, Politics, and Civil Rights in the United States, 1941-1972," "Doctors and Demonstrators: How Political Institutions Shape Abortion Law in the United States, Britain, and Canada," and "The Civil Rights Movement and the Logic of Social Change". "[Joseph E.] Luders analyzes a series of civil rights campaigns and policy debates, with business as well as government targets. His cost perspective yields insights about the influence of protest generally. . . With its combination of historical sophistication, astute political analysis, and quantitative examinations of lower-level political battles, this study's venal sins are mainly of omission. . . . [Drew] Halfmann demonstrates his arguments by comparative analyses, process tracing, and within-case analyses across three countries and several decades with meticulous and impressive archival research. His comparative approach cries out for imitation."

REVIEW: *Contemp Sociol* v42 no6 p843-4 N 2013 HAHRIE HAN

REVIEW: *Women's Review of Books* v29 no4 p9-11 Jl/Ag 2012 Miriam Smith

HALL, CARLA. Cooking with Carla; new comfort foods from around the world; [by] Carla Hall 240 p. 2014 Atria Books

1. Comfort food 2. Cookbooks 3. International cooking

ISBN 145166222X (hardback); 9781451662221 (hardback)

LC 2013-035094

SUMMARY: This cookbook by Carla Hall "centers on the philosophy that food and dishes are pretty much the same the world 'round; you change them by changing their spices. She starts with an easy foundational dish (with a heavy emphasis on vegetables), say, roasted fingerling potatoes, followed by at least two variations." Recipes include "baked corn pudding, hot fried chicken, and rustic bacon-apple pie." (Booklist)

REVIEW: *Booklist* v110 no13 p11 Mr 1 2014 Barbara Jacobs

"Carla's Comfort Foods: Favorite Dishes From Around the World". "What's even better in [Carla Hall's] second recipe collection . . . is her enthusiastic and knowledgeable embrace of all things spice, whether it be a mild lemongrass or a heated habanero chili. . . . Hall won't let any home chef flounder. Each dish includes a snappy personal introduction, directions (naturally), and Carla's tips, ranging from ideas for swap-outs (substitute curry powder for vadouvan) to specific explanations about certain ingredients. Sidebars also show off her chatty style, such as her first experience cooking red lentils. Get ready for 111 different goodnesses, including baked corn pudding, hot fried chicken, and rustic bacon-apple pie. Nothing says lovin' better."

REVIEW: *Libr J* v139 no3 p124 F 15 2014 Lisa Campbell

REVIEW: *Publ Wkly* v261 no3 p45-6 Ja 20 2014

HALL, CAROL M.ed. Novel ecosystems. See Novel ecosystems

HALL, DAVID D. A reforming people; Puritanism and the transformation of public life in New England; [by] David D. Hall xvii, 255 p. 2011 Alfred A. Knopf

1. Historical literature 2. Local government—New England—History—17th century 3. Puritans—New England—History—17th century 4. Religion and politics—New England—History—17th century
ISBN 0679441174; 9780679441175
LC 2010-051851

SUMMARY: The book "explor[es] how first-generation New Englanders structured institutions to achieve their social vision. [David D.] Hall argues that the mainstream migrants to the four orthodox New England colonies . . . aimed to create not only a godly society but one that promoted harmony and equity." Topics include the creation of central governments . . . the practices of church governance and membership, and the reformation of English legal codes." (Journal of American History)

REVIEW: *Am Hist Rev* v117 no2 p517-8 Ap 2012 John McWilliams

REVIEW: *Choice* v49 no4 p752 D 2011 R. P. Gildrie

REVIEW: *J Am Hist* v98 no3 p814-5 D 2011 Carla Gardina Pestana

A Reforming People: Puritanism and the Transformation of Public Life in New England "In A Reforming People David D. Hall returns to the Puritans, exploring how first-generation New Englanders structured institutions to achieve their social vision. Hall argues that the mainstream migrants to the four orthodox New England colonies (Plymouth, Massachusetts, New Haven, and Connecticut) aimed to create not only a godly society but one that promoted harmony and equity. In clear, elegant prose Hall reviews the creation of central governments, the business of land distribution and taxation that occupied towns, the practices of church governance and membership, and the reformation of English legal codes. A chapter on each of those topics is followed by a case study focused on Cambridge, Massachusetts, under the ministry of Thomas Shepard."

REVIEW: *N Engl Q* v85 no2 p365-8 Je 2012 Stephen Foster

REVIEW: *Rev Am Hist* v41 no3 p389-93 S 2013 Nicholas Tyacke

"A Reforming People: Puritanism and the Transformation of Public Life in New England." "Especially to be welcomed, not least because of the comparative dimension provided by the author as regards developments in America and England. [David D.] Hall is also unusual in being concerned with the civil as well as the religious aspects of New England Puritanism. . . . One would have liked more discussion of those many colonists who were excluded from church membership under the 'gathered' congregational system and, as a consequence, unable to become freemen."

HALL, EDITH. Adventures with Iphigenia in Tauris, a cultural history of Euripides' Black Sea tragedy; [by] Edith Hall 378 p. 2012 Oxford University Press

1. Historical literature 2. Influence (Literary, artistic, etc.) 3. Iphigenia (Greek mythology) 4. Mythology in literature 5. Setting (Literature)
ISBN 9780195392890
LC 2012-008796

SUMMARY: This book on Euripides's play "Iphigenia in Tauris" explores "cultural history of this play, giving as much weight to the impact of the play on subsequent Greek and Roman art and literature as on its manifestations since the discovery of the sole surviving medieval manuscript in the 1500s. The book argues that the reception of the play is bound up with its spectacular setting on the southern coast of the Crimean peninsula in what is now the Ukraine." (Publisher's note)

REVIEW: *Choice* v50 no11 p2010 Jl 2013 S. E. Goins

REVIEW: *Classical Rev* v64 no1 p33-4 Ap 2014 Michael Lloyd

REVIEW: *TLS* no5762 p11-2 S 6 2013 MARINA WARNER

"Adventures With Iphigenia in Tauris: A Cultural History of Euripides' Black Sea Tragedy." "In this superb and richly detailed study . . . Edith Hall has orchestrated, with impassioned and assiduous attention, this remarkable afterlife of Iphigenia. . . . She has compiled an exhaustive history of the play as manifest in different performed variations, and dug as deep as she can--even through the ephemeral records of student productions--and has discovered some tremendous visual evidence, ranging from images on pots to theatrical posters and such like."

HALL, JOHN M.il. Private gardens of the Hudson Valley. See Garmey, J.

HALL, KATHARINE. Polar bears and penguins; a compare and contrast book; [by] Katharine Hall 32 p. 2014 Sylvan Dell Publishing

1. Adaptation (Biology)—Juvenile literature 2. Animals—Polar regions—Juvenile literature 3. Penguins—Juvenile literature 4. Polar bear—Juvenile literature
ISBN 9781628552096 (English hardcover); 9781628552188 (English pbk.)
LC 2013-044813

SUMMARY: In this book, by Katharine Hall, "a set of comparisons presents new and pre-readers with elementary pointers on both the poles and differences between animals. Photos of polar bears and of penguins on alternating spreads or pages with a few accompanying lines of simply phrased observations highlight differences between the two creatures . . . as well as their respective Arctic and Antarctic habitats." (Kirkus Reviews)

REVIEW: *Kirkus Rev* v82 no4 p249 F 15 2014

"Polar Bears and Penguins". "A set of comparisons presents new and pre-readers with elementary pointers on both the poles and differences between animals. . . . Though the . . . quiz rather unfairly covers material not previously presented, and one 'photo' is actually a collage with northern lights clumsily Photoshopped in behind a polar bear, the overall approach will at least lay some groundwork for later geographical and animal study. A utilitarian, if not quite seamless, introduction to several natural history subjects, it will do till something more artful comes along."

REVIEW: *SLJ* v60 no6 p137 Je 2014 Denise Schmidt

HALL, MARK DAVID. Roger Sherman and the creation of the American republic; [by] Mark David Hall xi, 224 p. 2013 Oxford University Press

1. Calvinism—United States 2. Church & state—United States 3. Founding Fathers of the United States 4. Historical literature 5. Sherman, Roger, 1721-1793 6. Statesmen—United States—Biography
ISBN 9780199929849
LC 2012-018343

SUMMARY: In this book, author "Mark David Hall explores [Roger] Sherman's political theory and shows how it informed his many contributions to America's founding. A close examination of Sherman's religious beliefs provides insight into how those beliefs informed his political actions. Hall shows that Sherman, like many founders, was influenced by Calvinist political thought." (Publisher's note)

REVIEW: *Am Hist Rev* v118 no4 p1177-8 O 2013 Nicholas P. Miller

"Roger Sherman and the Creation of the American Republic." "This concise and readable political and intellectual biography argues that Roger Sherman--tradesman, politician, and Reformed thinker from Connecticut--should rank among the first tier of American constitutional founders. It is a compelling case, I believe, though not for all the reasons that Mark David Hall proposes. . . . It is on the question of religion and religious liberty that Hall's argument is at its weakest. . . . It is simply a false choice to say that we must decide between the skeptical Enlightenment views of Jefferson and Madison and the Reformed establishment views of Sherman and his New England allies."

REVIEW: *J Am Hist* v100 no3 p817-8 D 2013 Jane E. Calvert

HALL, PAMELA. Miss you like crazy; 32 p. 2014 Tanglewood

1. Children's stories 2. Mother and child—Fiction 3. Separation anxiety 4. Squirrels—Fiction 5. Working mothers
ISBN 1933718919; 9781933718910 (hardback)
LC 2013-038081

SUMMARY: In this book, written by Pamela Hall and illustrated by Jennifer A. Bell, "Walnut and his mom agree that it would be fun if he could go to work with her, and they fantasize about the adventures they could share. Though it can't always happen, Walnut's mother assures him that he is always on her mind, and together they find ways to have a physical presence for each other when at work or school." (Publisher's note)

REVIEW: *Booklist* v110 no15 p93-4 Ap 1 2014 Connie Fletcher

REVIEW: *Kirkus Rev* v82 no4 p125 F 15 2014

"Miss You Like Crazy". "Most of the tale is imaginative banter, but [Pamela] Hall adroitly touches on the question kids are really asking: Why is work so important it takes a parent away? Bell's fuzzy-tailed critters and soft, warm hues create a cozy environment for comforting a little one's fears. The end feels a bit like a tacked-on separation-anxiety solution (Mom sends a note and a photo to school with Walnut), but that doesn't undercut the sensitivity of the whole story. Hassled parents will appreciate having yet another resource to combat this common childhood worry."

REVIEW: *Publ Wkly* v261 no6 p87-8 F 10 2014

REVIEW: *SLJ* v60 no4 p122 Ap 2014 Michelle Anderson

HALL, TARQUIN. The case of the love commandos; from the files of Vish Puri, India's most private investigator; [by] Tarquin Hall 320 p. 2013 Simon & Schuster

1. Caste—India 2. Detective & mystery stories 3. Murder—Investigation—Fiction 4. Private investigators—India—Fiction
ISBN 1451613261; 9781451613261 (hardcover); 9781451613285 (pbk.)
LC 2013-009100

SUMMARY: In this book by Tarquin Hall, "when Ram and Tulsi fall in love, [her] parents are dead set against the union. She's from a high-caste family; he's an Untouchable. Tulsi's father locks her up and promises to hunt down [Ram]. Volunteers dedicated to helping mixed-caste couples, come to the rescue. After they liberate Tulsi, Ram is mysteriously snatched from . . . hiding. It falls to Vish Puri to track down Ram and reunite the star-crossed lovers." (Publisher's note)

REVIEW: *Booklist* v110 no1 p44 S 1 2013 Connie Fletcher

"The Case of the Love Commandos." "Vish Puri of Delhi, head of Most Private Investigators, Ltd., is regarded by many (and himself) as the best private eye in India. . . . Puri's love of food--and Hall's descriptions of the dishes he enjoys--is one of the delights of this series. . . . As in any Puri novel, a great deal of humor about Puri's family life is mixed with skillful plotting and realistic descriptions of contemporary India's overflowing street life. [Tarquin] Hall, a British journalist . . . has lived in South Asia for more than a decade."

REVIEW: *Kirkus Rev* v81 no19 p62 O 1 2013

REVIEW: *Publ Wkly* v260 no31 p48 Ag 5 2013

HALLETT, BRIEN. Declaring war; Congress, the president, and what the constitution does not say; [by] Brien Hallett xvii, 273 p. 2012 Cambridge University Press

1. LAW—Constitutional 2. Political science literature 3. Separation of powers 4. War and emergency powers—United States 5. War, Declaration of—United States
ISBN 9781107026926 (hardback); 9781107608573 (paperback)
LC 2012-012603

SUMMARY: In this book, Brien Hallett "directly challenges the 200-year-old belief that the Congress can and should declare war. By offering a detailed analysis of the declarations of 1812, 1898, and the War Powers Resolution of 1973, the book demonstrates the extent of the organizational and moral incapacity of the Congress to declare war." (Publisher's note)

REVIEW: *Choice* v51 no1 p165 S 2013 M. A. Sollenberger

"Declaring War: Congress, the President, and What the Constitution Does Not Say." "In an ambitious book on the act of declaring war, [Brien] Hallett . . . sets out to show that presidential tyranny is real and that Congress is largely to blame. While the topic of war is an important one, Hallett provides a strained and at times confusing analysis. He focuses on the War of 1812 as the precedent that has given all future presidents the freedom to commit the country to war without a formal declaration from Congress. . . .By providing such a narrow definition, Hallett declares that the Constitution has been repeatedly violated. With that said, the book offers a unique perspective on the war power that some readers might find interesting."

HALLETT, MARK.il. Scaly spotted feathered frilled. See Thimmesh, C.

HALLIDAY, SAM. Sonic Modernity; Representing Sound in Literature, Culture, and the Arts; [by] Sam Halliday 224 p. 2013 Oxford University Press

1. Modernism (Aesthetics) 2. Philosophical literature 3. Sound in art 4. Sound in literature 5. Sound in mass media 6. Sound in motion pictures

ISBN 0748627618; 9780748627615

SUMMARY: This book, edited by Sam Halliday, "reveals the many roles and forms of sound in modernism. Drawing on a wealth of texts and thinkers, the book shows the distinctive nature of sonic cultures in modernity. Arguing that these cultures are not reducible to sound alone, the book further shows that these encompass representations of sound in 'other' media: especially literature; but also, cinema and painting." (Publisher's note)

REVIEW: *Choice* v51 no4 p629 D 2013 A. J. Barlow

"Haptic Modernism: Touch and the Tactile in Modernist Writing" and "Sonic Modernity: Representing Sound in Literature, Culture and the Arts." "These two volumes add to knowledge of the modernist period within a modernist frame: the scholarship reflects a modernist eye for derail and respect for nuance. By focusing on sound and touch, respectively, [Sam] Halliday . . . and [Abbie] Garrington . . . bring to light less explored areas of care and craft and in so doing demonstrate the knowledge base and intellectual confidence that made modernism possible. The range of writers considered in each volume is impressive."

REVIEW: *TLS* no5769 p31 O 25 2013 SERENA GOSDEN

"Sonic Modernity: Representing Sound in Literature, Culture and the Arts." "Conceptually expansive and revealingly oxymoronic, Sam Halliday's exploration of the effect of technological development on modernism's relationship with sound is thorough and illuminating. . . . The notion that it is not silence so much as the 'wrong sound' that disintegrates humanity is a point that resonates most in its twentieth-century context. To mix, perhaps appropriately, a sensory metaphor, 'Sonic Modernity' is a book that gives voice to much of what has been hiding in plain sight."

HALLIWELL, MARTIN. Therapeutic revolutions; medicine, psychiatry, and American culture, 1945-1970; [by] Martin Halliwell 400 p. 2013 Rutgers University Press

1. Historical literature 2. History, 20th Century—United States 3. Mental Disorders—history—United States 4. Mental Disorders—therapy—United States 5. Psychiatry—history—United States 6. Social Conditions—United States 7. Therapeutics—history—United States

ISBN 9780813560649 (hardcover : alk. paper); 9780813560656 (pbk. : alk. paper); 9780813560663 (e-book)

LC 2012-023503

SUMMARY: This book "examines the evolving relationship between American medicine, psychiatry, and culture from World War II to the dawn of the 1970s. In this richly layered intellectual history, Martin Halliwell ranges from national politics, public reports, and healthcare debates to the ways in which film, literature, and the mass media provided cultural channels for shaping and challenging preconceptions about health and illness." (Publisher's note)

REVIEW: *Choice* v51 no1 p168 S 2013 B. C. Beins

"Therapeutic Revolutions: Medicine, Psychiatry, and American Culture, 1945-1970." "People's lives are complicated in the best of circumstances, but societal change can amplify the complexities. This theme pervades [author Martin] Halliwell's 'Therapeutic Revolutions: Medicine, Psychiatry, and American Culture, 1945-1970.' A blend of complex factors affected society in this quarter century. Veterans returned from the war, requiring medical and psychiatric care; the government began to institutionalize the health care system and medical research; and modernization of social roles began. This book outlines these changes from a cultural perspective. Halliwell . . . uses the lens of Freudian theory."

HALLWARD-DRIEMEIER, MARY. Enterprising women; expanding economic opportunities in africa; [by] Mary Hallward-Driemeier xxix, 274 p. 2013 World Bank

1. Businesswomen—Africa, Sub-Saharan 2. Economics literature 3. Women—Africa, Sub-Saharan—Economic conditions 4. Women—Africa, Sub-Saharan—Social conditions 5. Women—Employment—Africa, Sub-Saharan

ISBN 9780821397039; 9780821398098 (electronic)

LC 2012-049861

SUMMARY: This book, part of the African Development Forum series, "brings together new household and enterprise data from 41 countries in Sub-Saharan Africa . . . . Four key areas of the agenda for expanding women's economic opportunities in Africa are analyzed: strengthening women's property rights. . .improving women's access to finance; building human capital . . . and strengthening women's voices in business environment reform." (Publisher's note)

REVIEW: *Choice* v51 no6 p1060 F 2014 J. E. Weaver

"Enterprising Women: Expanding Economic Opportunities in Africa." "Part of the 'African Development Forum' series, this volume, sponsored by the Agence Française de Development and the World Bank, focuses on improving the work environment for women in Africa, especially entrepreneurs. In sub-Saharan Africa, women are economically active but often in low-productivity endeavors. This work asserts that both individuals and society would benefit if women were engaged in more highly productive work.. . . . This is a repetitive, data-filled work, with numerous references to relevant literature. Data are clearly explained and carefully analyzed. . . .Recommended."

HALPERIN, MARK. Double Down; Game Change 2012; [by] Mark Halperin 499 p. 2013 Penguin Group USA

1. Obama, Barack, 1961- 2. Political campaigns—United States—History—21st century 3. Political science literature 4. Presidential candidates—United States 5. Presidents—United States—Election—2012 6. Romney, Mitt, 1947- 7. United States—Politics & government

ISBN 1594204403; 9781594204401 (hardback)
LC 2013-431166

SUMMARY: This book by Mark Halperin and John Heileman chronicles the 2012 U.S. Presidential election. "Their focus is always on the candidates with the most buzz among not just voters, but the Washington, D.C., cognoscenti." Candidates profiled include Barack Obama, Mitt Romney, Jon Huntsman, Newt Gingrich, and Chris Christie. (Kirkus Reviews)

REVIEW: *Choice* v52 no1 p163 St 2014 R. E. O'Connor

REVIEW: *Economist* v409 no8861 p88-9 N 9 2013

"Double Down: Game Change 2012". "Sharp insights buttressed by startling indiscretions fill 'Double Down,' a new account of Barack Obama's win over his 2012 Republican rival, Mitt Romney. This gripping book—a sequel to 'Game Change,' a bestseller about Mr. Obama's 2008 path to the White House—cements the status of the authors as unrivalled chroniclers of campaign politics. . . . The most interesting revelations involve Mr. Obama. . . . In short, presidential elections repel the well-adjusted and attract the distinctly odd. Then they strip those oddballs of what is left of their self-respect. A great but depressing read."

REVIEW: *Economist* v409 no8865 p85-8 D 7 2013

REVIEW: *Kirkus Rev* v81 no24 p316 D 15 2013

"Double Down". "Gossipy insider's account of the presidential election of 2012. . . . Not surprisingly, their views are conventional and close to the center, their attention trained on politics as sport (or, as the title suggests, as a high-stakes poker game) and politicians as personalities. . . . Still, [Mark] Halperin and [John] Heilemann offer a highly entertaining, dishy read, full of astonishing revelations about the strengths and, most intriguingly, the foibles of the nation's political stars and egos, including unforgettable portraits of former House Speaker Newt Gingrich and New Jersey Gov. Chris Christie in particular."

REVIEW: *Libr J* v139 no3 p61 F 15 2014 Sean Kennedy

REVIEW: *Libr J* v138 no11 p62 Je 15 2013 Barbara Hoffert

REVIEW: *N Y Rev Books* v61 no1 p32-4 Ja 9 2014 Andrew Hacker

"Double Down: Game Change 2012," "The Gamble: Choice and Chance in the 2012 Presidential Election," and "The Fracturing of the American Corporate Elite". " While 'Double Down' makes for intriguing reading, it tells us little about the election. . . . 'The Gamble'—a title never fully explained—argues that a complex of 'structural conditions' meant that Mitt Romney never had a chance. . . . Mark Mizruchi, in 'The Fracturing of the American Corporate Elite,' explains why corporations have become less openly political. . . . Mizruchi makes a convincing case."

REVIEW: *N Y Times Book Rev* p1-47 N 10 2013 Michael Kinsley

REVIEW: *Nation* v297 no22 p6-8 D 2 2013 Eric Alterman

REVIEW: *New Statesman* v142 no5187 p43 D 6 2013 Nicky Woolf

REVIEW: *New Statesman* v142 no5188 p43 12/092013 Nicky Woolf

REVIEW: *New York Times* v163 no56311 pC1-4 N 5 2013 MICHIKO KAKUTANI

REVIEW: *New Yorker* v89 no37 p83-1 N 18 2013

HALPERN, NIKKI.tr. The faith of remembrance. See Wachtel, N.

HALPIN, ABIGAIL.il. The problem with being slightly heroic. See The problem with being slightly heroic

HALPIN, BRENDAN. A really awesome mess; [by] Brendan Halpin 288 p. 2013 Egmont USA

1. Boarding schools—Fiction 2. Chinese Americans—Fiction 3. Emotional problems—Fiction 4. Psychotherapy—Fiction 5. Schools—Fiction 6. Young adult fiction
ISBN 160684363X; 9781606843635 (hardcover)
LC 2012-045978

SUMMARY: In this book, "a group of teens at a live-in institution for troubled young people bond, pull off a caper and overcome their issues. . . . Emmy, adopted from China by white parents, feels out of place and unwanted in her family. She is sent to Heartland Academy after retaliating against a tormentor at school. . . . Justin, who resents his father's absence, comes to Heartland following a suicide attempt and after being caught receiving oral sex from a girl he met earlier that day." (Kirkus Reviews)

REVIEW: *Booklist* v109 no21 p70 Jl 1 2013 Courtney Jones

REVIEW: *Bull Cent Child Books* v67 no2 p80-1 O 2013 K. C.

"A Really Awesome Mess." "Adopted from China just when her parents found out they were pregnant, Emily has always felt unsure of her place in her family and the world. She responds to a cruel sexting episode by becoming anorexic and launching an online bullying campaign against the offending boy and winds up at Heartland Academy, where she meets Justin. . . . Justin and Emily alternate as narrators of this ultimately feel-good story of kids whose identity issues and behavioral responses are just a tad more intense than the norm. . . . There are messages conveyed, sure, but they're reassuring ones: that broken can be funny as well as tragic, resilience is possible, and support is where you find it, as long as the grownups don't find out."

REVIEW: *Kirkus Rev* v81 no2 p79 Je 1 2013

REVIEW: *SLJ* v59 no8 p110 Ag 2013 Jennifer Rothschild

REVIEW: *Voice of Youth Advocates* v36 no3 p58-60 Ag 2013 Mark Letcher

HAMBLY, BARBARA. Kindred of Darkness; A vampire kidnapping; [by] Barbara Hambly 256 p. 2014 Severn House Pub Ltd

1. Books & reading—Fiction 2. Businesspeople—Fiction 3. Fantasy fiction 4. Kidnapping—Fiction 5. Vampires—Fiction
ISBN 0727883429; 9780727883421

SUMMARY: In this book, by Barbara Hambly, "James Asher and his wife Lydia's baby daughter Miranda is kidnapped by the Master Vampire of London. . . . The Master Vampire's instructions [are to] keep out of the way of the human networks that serves the vampires, destroy the interloper who seeks to seize control of the London Nest, and find the key to the Nest's tortuous inner workings: The Book of the Kindred of Darkness." (Publisher's note)

REVIEW: *Booklist* v110 no12 p38 F 15 2014 David Pitt

REVIEW: *Kirkus Rev* v82 no3 p272 F 1 2014

"The Kindred of Darkness". "On the eve of World War I, a couple fights to rescue their daughter from a vampire's clutches. . . . Avowed series hero James . . . is more pallid a character than his centuries-old quarry, and his Oxford-educated, scientifically minded wife is too vain to wear her glasses even when she's hunting vampires in the dark. Although [Barbara] Hambly's fans may enjoy returning to her carefully constructed and lavishly detailed world, the uninitiated may be less enthralled."

REVIEW: *Libr J* v139 no3 p76 F 15 2014 Megan M. McArdle

REVIEW: *Publ Wkly* v261 no4 p174 Ja 27 2014

HAMBURGER, MICHAEL, 1924-2007.tr. Glowing enigmas. See Glowing enigmas

HAMERSTONE, JAMES. A woman's framework for a successful career and life; [by] James Hamerstone xii, 205 p. 2013 Palgrave Macmillan

1. Advice literature 2. Career development 3. Women—Employment 4. Women professional employees 5. Work-life balance

ISBN 9781137293183 (hc : alk. paper); 9781137293190 (pbk : alk. paper)

LC 2013-000422

SUMMARY: "This book presents strategies for building a successful career. . . . Factual content, including research findings, is interspersed with scenarios addressing comraon workplace concerns. The authors advise women that success requires balancing a career and personal life. They stress the need for personal and professional support and knowledge of technical and communications skills." (Choice: Current Reviews for Academic Libraries)

REVIEW: *Choice* v51 no6 p1058 F 2014 E. G. Ferris

"A Woman's Framework for a Successful Career and Life." "Although the work is targeted toward college women, others in this age group and beyond can benefit from its guidelines. [James] Hamerstone (an academic) and [Lindsay Musser] Hough (a consultant) design the work so that it is structured enough to use in a career development class yet practical enough for personal use. The content is timely. . . . Some readers may question that one of the authors is male, but the tone and presentation of material should allay these concerns. The book's strength is in its breadth and practicality. It offers useful career information and insights for general audiences, students, and teachers."

HAMETZ, MAURA E. In the name of Italy; nation, family, and patriotism in a fascist court; [by] Maura E. Hametz x, 278 p. 2012 Fordham University Press

1. Administrative courts—Italy 2. Fascism—Italy 3. Historical literature 4. Italianization 5. Law—Political aspects—Italy 6. National characteristics, Italian 7. Trials—Italy—Trieste

ISBN 9780823243396 (hbk.)

LC 2012-002895

SUMMARY: This book by Maura E. Hametz chronicles "Luigia Barbarovich Paulovich's successful struggle to keep the Fascist regime from 'restoring' her name to its supposedly Italian version of Paoli as it attempted to Italianise its recently acquired eastern border territories. . . . This episode, which unfolds between 1930 and 1932, to investigate a variety of themes in Fascist Italy that allowed Paulovich to succeed in her struggle." (Modern Italy)

REVIEW: *Am Hist Rev* v119 no1 p271 F 2014 David I. Kertzer

"In the Name of Italy: Nation, Family and Patriotism in a Fascist Court". "[Maura E.] Hametz presents her book as a micro-history, and in many ways it follows the example of other such works that have used archival court documents to shed light on formerly obscure individuals in order to illuminate larger historical dynamics. She is constrained, however, by the relatively modest materials she has unearthed on the family that is the focus of her work. . . . 'In the Name of Italy' offers a useful case study of the continuities found in the administrative machinery of the Italian fascist regime and a provocative example of the politics of naming. It also contributes to our understanding of that fascinating multicultural mix that was Trieste."

REVIEW: *Choice* v50 no8 p1510 Ap 2013 P. Lorenzini

HAMID, MOHSIN, 1971-. How to Get Filthy Rich in Rising Asia; [by] Mohsin Hamid 240 p. 2013 Riverhead Books Inc.

1. Economic change 2. Man-woman relationships 3. Rich people—Fiction 4. Satire 5. Self-realization—Fiction

ISBN 1594487294; 9781594487293

LC 2012-039847

SUMMARY: This book, by Mohsin Hamid, presents the "tale of a man's journey from impoverished rural boy to corporate tycoon [and] steals its shape from the business self-help books devoured by ambitious youths all over 'rising Asia.' It follows its nameless hero to the sprawling metropolis where he begins to amass an empire built on that most fluid, and increasingly scarce, of goods: water. Yet his heart remains set on something else, on the pretty girl whose star rises along with his." (Publisher's note)

REVIEW: *Bookforum* v19 no5 p26 F/Mr 2013 SIDDHARTHA DEB

REVIEW: *Economist* v407 no8830 p98 Ap 6 2013

REVIEW: *Kirkus Rev* p18 N 15 2013 Best Books

REVIEW: *Kirkus Rev* v81 no9 p13 My 1 2013

REVIEW: *Libr J* v137 no16 p56 O 1 2012 Barbara Hoffert

REVIEW: *London Rev Books* v35 no12 p29-30 Je 20 2013 Nick Richardson

REVIEW: *N Y Rev Books* v60 no7 p33-5 Ap 25 2013 Pankaj Mishra

REVIEW: *N Y Times Book Rev* p28 Ap 20 2014 IHSAN TAYLOR

REVIEW: *New Statesman* v142 no5151/5152 p83-4 Mr 29 2013 Hannah Rosefield

REVIEW: *New York Times* v162 no56055 pC19-22 F 22 2013 MICHIKO KAKUTANI

"How to Get Filthy Rich in Rising Asia." "Mr. [Mohsin] Hamid's new novel . . . tells a compelling story that works on two levels . . . as a deeply moving and highly specific tale of love and ambition, and as a larger, metaphorical look at the mind-boggling social and economic changes sweeping 'rising Asia'. . . . The story is couched as a kind of self-help book and told in the second person. . . . What might initially seem like a clumsy narrative technique is actually a device that allows Mr. Hamid to zoom in and out from his hero's life. . . . With 'How to Get Filthy Rich in Rising Asia' Mr. Hamid reaffirms his place as one of his generation's most inventive and gifted writers."

REVIEW: *New York Times* v162 no56092 p9 Mr 31 2013 PARUL SEHGAL

"How to Get Filthy Rich in Rising Asia." "The marriage of these two curiously compatible genres--self-help and the old-fashioned bildungsroman--is just one of the pleasures of Mohsin Hamid's shrewd and slippery new novel, a rags-to-riches that works on a head-splitting number of levels. It's a love story and a study of seismic social change. It parodies a get-rich-quick book and gestures to a new direction for the novel, all in prose so pure and purposeful it passes straight into the bloodstream. It intoxicates."

REVIEW: *New York Times* v162 no56055 pC19-22 F 22 2013 MICHIKO KAKUTANI

REVIEW: *Orion Magazine* v32 no4 p68 Jl/Ag 2013 Christopher Merrill

REVIEW: *Publ Wkly* v259 no49 p51 D 3 2012

REVIEW: *Publ Wkly* v260 no17 p127 Ap 29 2013

REVIEW: *Time* v181 no9 p53 Mr 11 2013 Rob Spillman

"How to Get Filthy Rich in Rising Asia." "Mohsin Hamid's new novel is a love story and bildungsroman disguised as a self-help book, and the result has all the inventiveness, exuberance and pathos that the writer's fans have come to expect. . . . The great trick of 'How to Get Filthy Rich in Rising Asia' is in how it creates so much empathy for its narrator, who hacks through thickets of bureaucracy, tribalism and religious violence on his resolute quest for lucre. . . . Hamid keeps the direct second-person address throughout . . . . and while it's nimbly applied, it has its limits"

REVIEW: *TLS* no5741 p26 Ap 12 2013 PETER C. BAKER

REVIEW: *World Lit Today* v87 no4 p58-9 Jl/Ag 2013 Jim Hannan

HAMILTON-PATERSON, JAMES. Under the Radar; A Novel; [by] James Hamilton-Paterson 320 p. 2013 Faber and Faber

1. Air pilots 2. Bombers (Airplanes) 3. Cold War, 1945-1989—Fiction 4. Gays—Fiction 5. War stories

ISBN 057127398X; 9780571273980

SUMMARY: This book by James Hamilton-Paterson tells "the story of Squadron-Leader Amos McKenna, a Vulcan pilot who is suffering from desires and frustrations that are tearing his marriage apart and making him question his ultimate loyalties. Relations with the American cousins are tense; the future of the RAF bomber fleet is in doubt. And there is a spy at RAF Wearsby, who is selling secrets to his Russian handlers in seedy East Anglian cafes." (Publisher's note)

REVIEW: *TLS* no5746 p20 My 17 2013 JEROME BOYD MAUNSELL

"Under the Radar." "The real meat of the story--and its main strength--is in its delineation of daily life as a nuclear bomber. . . . The rhythms of work, of a job that is also an all-encompassing way of life, dominate; the minutiae of the physical and mental exertions of pilots' lives are expertly recreated. . . . Very few bombs are actually dropped, which makes the ethical freight of the novel lighter than it might have been. . . . 'Under the Radar' is very precisely researched, almost to a fault, overflowing into appendices on facts and technicalities. . . . Yet this is a sombre, muted book, falling somewhere between a thriller and something more reflective."

HAMILTON, PATRICK L. Of space and mind; cognitive mappings of contemporary Chicano/a fiction; [by] Patrick L. Hamilton x, 214 p. 2011 University of Texas Press

1. American fiction—20th century—History and criticism 2. American fiction—Mexican American authors—History and criticism—Theory, etc 3. Cognitive maps (Psychology) 4. Literary critiques 5. Mexican Americans in literature

ISBN 0292723636 (cloth : alk. paper); 9780292723634 (cloth : alk. paper)

LC 2010-026137

SUMMARY: It was the author's intent "to expand our understandings of the cultural interactions within the United States that are communicated by Chicano/a fiction. He argues that the narrative ethics of 'resistance' within the Chicano/a canon is actually complemented by ethics of 'persistence' and 'transformation' that imagine cultural differences within the United States as participatory and irreducible to simple oppositions." (Publisher's note)

REVIEW: *Am Lit* v85 no3 p598-600 S 2013 José E. Limón

"Mythohistorical Interventions: The Chicano Movement and Its Legacies" and "Of Space and Mind: Cognitive Mappings of a Contemporary Chicano/a Fiction." "These books offer competent close readings of their chosen texts in the service of their respective arguments. However, each argument is questionable on a sociological scale but in a way not necessarily of the author's own making. . . . Rather than reflective, this cultural production is better seen as refractive; rather than producing a collective counter-consensus among US Mexicans, it should be viewed, at best, as vanguardist."

HAMILTON, TYLER. The Secret Race; Inside the Hidden World of the Tour de France: Doping, Cover-ups, and Winning at All Costs; [by] Tyler Hamilton 290 p. 2012 Bantam Books

1. Armstrong, Lance, 1971- 2. Doping in sports 3. Sports—Corrupt practices 4. Sports literature 5. Tour de France (Bicycle race)

ISBN 0345530411; 9780345530417

SUMMARY: This book, by Tyler Hamilton and Daniel Coyle, winner of the 2012 William Hill Sports Book of the Year Award, offers a "look at the world of professional cycling--and the doping issue surrounding this sport and its most iconic rider, Lance Armstrong. . . . [The book] . . . takes us . . . inside a shadowy . . . world of unscrupulous doctors, . . . team directors, and athletes so relentlessly driven to succeed that they would do anything . . . to gain the edge they need to win." (Publisher's note)

REVIEW: *Economist* v405 no8814 p85 D 8 2012

REVIEW: *Kirkus Rev* v80 no22 p219 N 15 2012

REVIEW: *London Rev Books* v34 no22 p5-9 N 22 2012 David Runciman

REVIEW: *N Y Times Book Rev* p45 N 11 2012 GEOFFREY WHEATCROFT

REVIEW: *New Statesman* v141 no5124 p64-54 S 21 2012 Gary Imlach

REVIEW: *New Yorker* v89 no27 p76-80 S 9 2013 Malcolm

Gladwell "The Sports Gene: Inside the Science of Extraordinary Athletic Performance" and "The Secret Race: Inside the Hidden World of the Tour de France: Doping, Cover-Ups and Winning at All Costs." "In 'The Sports Gene,' there are countless . . . examples of all the ways that the greatest athletes are different from the rest of us. . . . They carry genes that put them far ahead of ordinary athletes. . . . 'The Secret Race' deserves to be read alongside 'The Sports Gene,' because it describes the flip side of the question that Epstein explores. . . . [Tyler] Hamilton was a skier who came late to cycling, and he paints himself as an underdog. . . . His book is supposed to serve as his apology. At that task, it fails."

HAMMEL, ALICE M. Teaching music to students with autism; [by] Alice M. Hammel xvii, 164 p. 2013 Oxford University Press

1. Autistic children—Education 2. Children with autism spectrum disorders—Education 3. Educational literature 4. Music—Instruction and study 5. Special education
ISBN 9780199856763 (pbk.: alk. paper); 9780199856770 (hardcover: alk. paper)
LC 2012-051118

SUMMARY: In this book on music education for students with autism, "the authors focus on understanding autism, advocating for students and music programs, and creating and maintaining a team approach by working together with colleagues effectively. A significant portion of the book is focused on understanding and overcoming the communication, cognition, behavior, sensory, and socialization challenges inherent in working with students with autism." (Publisher's note)

REVIEW: *Choice* v51 no8 p1410 Ap 2014 A. C. Shahriari
"Teaching Music to Students With Autism". "The book is a helpful support for those needing encouragement and a general resource for those wishing to communicate more effectively with parents, colleagues, and administration in order to help students attain an optimal learning environment. . . . What is lacking is a thorough presentation of effective pedagogies for 'teaching music to students with autism.' . . . This preoccupation with addressing behavioral issues—rather than offering strategies for teaching music—serves as a sort of bias. Nevertheless, because there is a dearth of literature on effective strategies for teaching music to children with autism, this book is a worthwhile contribution to the literature."

HAMMERICH, KAI. Fish can't see water. See Lewis, R. D.

HAMMETT, CHAD.ed. Two Prospectors. See Two Prospectors

HAMMETT, JERILOU.ed. The architecture of change. See The architecture of change

HAMMOND, PAUL.tr. Our lady of the assassins. See Our lady of the assassins

HAMPSON, ROBERT. Conrad's Secrets; [by] Robert Hampson 312 p. 2012 Palgrave Macmillan

1. Conrad, Joseph, 1857-1924 2. Historical criticism (Literature) 3. Illegal arms transfers 4. Secrecy in literature 5. Slave trade in literature
ISBN 0230507832; 9780230507838

SUMMARY: In this book, Robert Hampson "considers 'secrets,' areas of knowledge that would have been familiar to [Joseph] Conrad but are unfamiliar to modern readers. For example, Hampson looks at gunrunning and slave trading in the Malay Archipelago in relationship to 'Almayer's Folly,' 'An Outcast of the Islands,' and 'The Rescue,' arguing that Conrad was familiar with these practices and that understanding such practices aids in understanding the novels." (Choice: Current Reviews for Academic Libraries)

REVIEW: *Choice* v50 no7 p1244-5 Mr 2013 J. G. Peters
"Conrad's Secrets." "[Robert] Hampson is one the most prominent Conrad scholars in the world. This is his third book on Conrad, and all are valuable contributions to Conrad studies. Here Hampson considers 'secrets,' areas of knowledge that would have been familiar to Conrad but are unfamiliar to modern readers. For example, Hampson looks at gunrunning and slave trading in the Malay Archipelago in relationship to 'Almayer's Folly,' 'An Outcast of the Islands,' and 'The Rescue,' arguing that Conrad was familiar with these practices and that understanding such practices aids in understanding the novels. . . . Hampson's point of entry is original, and he presents good evidence in support of reading Conrad armed with a knowledge of his 'secrets.' Summing Up: Recommended."

REVIEW: *TLS* no5719 p26 N 9 2012 ALEXANDRA LAWRIE

HAMSCHA, SUSANNE. The Fiction of America; Performance and Cultural Imaginary in Literature and Film; [by] Susanne Hamscha 350 p. 2013 University of Chicago Press

1. American films 2. Literature—History & criticism 3. National characteristics, American 4. Popular culture—United States 5. United States—Civilization
ISBN 3593398729; 9783593398723

SUMMARY: This book by Susanne Hamscha "juxtaposes classic literature of the American Renaissance with twentieth-century popular culture . . . to investigate how the 'Americanness' of American culture constitutes itself in the interplay of the cultural imaginary and performance. Conceptualizing 'America' as a transhistorical practice, Susanne Hamscha reveals disruptive, spectral moments in the narrative of 'America,' which confront American culture with its inherent inconsistencies." (Publisher's note)

REVIEW: *Choice* v51 no7 p1196-7 Mr 2014 D. E. Magill
"The Fiction of America: Performance and the Cultural Imaginary in Literature and Film." "[Susanne] Hamscha demonstrates her theories through readings that juxtapose classic American literary texts with contemporary pop culture texts. Placing Walt Whitman alongside Spiderman or [Ralph Waldo] Emerson against Finding Nemo allows her to both reveal the performance's ideal America and locate the instabilities at work in their structures. Hamscha's work engages productively with theories of nation, identity, and form to disrupt easy understanding of America and its many productions. . . . Recommended."

HAN HAN. This Generation; Dispatches from China's

Most Popular Literary Star (And Race Car Driver); [by] Han Han 288 p. 2012 Simon & Schuster

1. China—Civilization 2. China—Politics & government 3. China—Social conditions 4. Essays 5. Popular culture—China

ISBN 1451660006; 9781451660005

SUMMARY: In this book, race car driver Han Han offers "blog posts in his first-ever volume . . . [that] introduce us to pedestrian observations on any number of subjects. Han reflects on the value of requiring the writing of essays in an academic setting." Other topics include "the faltering management of the Chinese government by its officials," "political reform," and "prostitutes." (Kirkus Reviews)

REVIEW: *Kirkus Rev* v80 no17 p137 S 1 2012

REVIEW: *N Y Rev Books* v60 no16 p49-51 O 24 2013 Perry Link

"For a Song and a Hundred Songs: A Poet's Journey Through a Chinese Prison," "This Generation: Dispatches From China's Most Popular Literary Star (and Race Car Driver)," and "Ai Weiwei's Blog: Writings, Interviews, and Digital Rants, 2006-2009." "A great virtue of Liao Yiwu's new book . . . is that it suggests what we have to look at before crediting the regime with efficiency. It shows that not only cleverness but a beastly ruthlessness undergirds the resilience. . . . Many of Han Han's views, although artfully put, are unsurprising versions of what other critics of the regime have been saying for years. . . . But Han Han does more than just put well-known complaints into clever form. On some topics he is uniquely astute. . . . Ai [Weiwei's] creativity seems to come in bursts. He lacks the reflective mood that allows Han Han to achieve analytic depth, and his essays are not as carefully written as Han Han's. But his intuitive eruptions sometimes yield stark, profound perceptions."

REVIEW: *Publ Wkly* v259 no31 p47 Jl 30 2012

REVIEW: *TLS* no5727 p30 Ja 4 2013 KATE MERKEL-HESS

HAN, JENNY. Fire with fire; [by] Jenny Han 528 p. 2013 Simon & Schuster Books for Young Readers

1. Friendship—Fiction 2. High schools—Fiction 3. Islands—Fiction 4. Revenge—Fiction 5. Schools—Fiction

ISBN 9781442440784 (hardcover)

LC 2013-000541

SUMMARY: This young adult novel is "Book two of a trilogy from 'New York Times' bestselling author Jenny Han and Siobhan Vivian. Lillia, Kat, and Mary had the perfect plan. Work together in secret to take down the people who wronged them. But things didn't exactly go the way they'd hoped at the Homecoming Dance." (Publisher's note)

REVIEW: *Booklist* v110 no1 p114 S 1 2013 Ann Kelley

REVIEW: *Kirkus Rev* v81 no16 p99 Ag 15 2013

"Fire With Fire." "Revenge might be a dish best served cold but not when it's as unappetizing and bloated as this sequel to 'Burn for Burn.' At first, in the aftermath of the homecoming debacle, Kat, Lillia and Mary think they're done with revenge. But then they regroup and focus their efforts on one person: star quarterback Reeve. . . . The movement of Lillia to the forefront of the novel and the slow growth of her feelings for Reeve are compelling, but Kat's relegation to the sidelines and the strange supernatural powers that Mary discovers make the book feel uneven. When the truth about Mary is finally revealed, it's just a distraction from the more interesting plot points--and feels totally unnecessary."

REVIEW: *SLJ* v59 no10 p1 O 2013 Brandy Danner

HAN, JENNY. To all the boys I've loved before; [by] Jenny Han 368 p. 2014 SSBFYR

1. Dating (Social customs)—Fiction 2. Love—Fiction 3. Love letters 4. Love stories 5. Sisters—Fiction 6. Young adult fiction

ISBN 1442426705; 9781442426702 (hardback); 9781442426719 (paperback)

LC 2013-022311

SUMMARY: In this book, by Jenny Han, "Lara Jean Song keeps her love letters in a hatbox. . . . They aren't love letters that anyone else wrote for her; these are ones she's written. One for every boy she's ever loved—five in all. When she writes, she pours out her heart and soul and says all the things she would never say in real life, because her letters are for her eyes only. Until the day her secret letters are mailed, and suddenly, Lara Jean's love life goes from imaginary to out of control." (Publisher's note)

REVIEW: *Booklist* v110 no14 p78 Mr 15 2014 Sarah Bean Thompson

REVIEW: *Kirkus Rev* v82 no4 p145 F 15 2014

"To All the Boys I've Loved Before". " An ultimately compelling exploration of teenage growth and young love. . . . . It's difficult to see this book as a love triangle—Josh is bland as oatmeal, and Peter is utterly charismatic. Meanwhile, readers may find that Lara Jean sometimes seems too naïve and rather young for 16—though in many ways, this makes her feel more realistic than many of the world-weary teens that populate the shelves. Regardless, readers will likely be so swept up in the romance they can read past any flaws."

REVIEW: *Publ Wkly* v261 no5 p58 F 3 2014

REVIEW: *SLJ* v60 no4 p164 Ap 2014 Miranda Doyle

REVIEW: *Voice of Youth Advocates* v37 no1 p66 Ap 2014 Sarah Flowers

HAN, SALLIE. Pregnancy in practice; expectation and experience in the contemporary US; [by] Sallie Han ix, 195 p. 2013 Berghahn Books

1. Anthropology, Cultural—United States 2. Pregnancy—Social aspects 3. Pregnancy—ethnology—United States 4. Pregnant women 5. Showers (Parties) 6. Social science literature

ISBN 9780857459879 (hardback : alk. paper); 9780857459886 (institutional ebook)

LC 2013-005549

SUMMARY: This book by Sallie Han presents "an ethnographic account of 'ordinary' pregnancy. The author considers the importance and meaning of 'everyday experiences' through six thematic chapters organized chronologically throughout the pregnancy and birth experience. Topics include reading books on pregnancy, viewing and sharing ultrasound images of the fetus, planning the baby's nursery, baby showers, and more." (Choice: Current Reviews for Academic Libraries)

REVIEW: *Choice* v51 no7 p1253 Mr 2014 M. L. Charleroy

"Pregnancy in Practice: Expectation and Experience in the Contemporary US." "[Sallie] Han constructs her argument by drawing on interviews with pregnant women and their friends, family, and partners, and birth professionals in Ann Arbor, Michigan. In addition to conducting personal interviews, Han observed office visits and childbirth education classes, and she even completed a doula training course. Based on this ethnographic research, Han describes routine pregnancies of American middle-class women, essentially reorienting anthropological study of birth and reproduction, which previously focused on the medical and technical aspects of giving birth. . . . Recommended."

HANABUSA, CHIAKI.ed. Two lamentable tragedies. See Two lamentable tragedies

HANBURY-TENISON, WILLIAM.tr. The Memoirs of Jin Luxian. See Jin Luxian

HANCOCK, JAMES GULLIVER.il. Underworld. See Price, J.

HANCOCK, NUALA. Charleston and Monk's House; the intimate house museums of Virginia Woolf and Vanessa Bell; [by] Nuala Hancock x, 226 p. 2012 Edinburgh University Press

1. Historic house museums—England 2. Historical literature

ISBN 0748646736; 9780748646739

LC 2012-551999

SUMMARY: This book by Nuala Hancock looks at two historic house museums commemorating the lives of Virginia Woolf and Vanessa Bell. The "book emerges from her research residency at Charleston, interspersed with regular visits to Monk's House as a volunteer steward." She explores "how these houses work as memorial sites and businesses, how each constitutes a situated, material biography of its former inhabitants, to be packaged and sold to a thriving tourist industry." (Times Literary Supplement)

REVIEW: *TLS* no5769 p14-5 O 25 2013 AMBER K. REGIS

"Charleston and Monk's House: The Intimate House Museums of Virginia Woolf and Vanessa Bell," "In the Hollow of the Wave: Virginia Woolf and Modernist Uses of Nature," and "Virginia Woolf and the Theater." "[Nuala] Hancock understands better than most the performances required by a house museum. . . . The result is a strikingly personal, reflective account of how these houses work as memorial sites and businesses. . . . Over six chapters, [Bonnie Kime] Scott demonstrates the revisionary potential of posthuman and ecocritical approaches to literary study. . . . [Steven D.] Putzel identifies the essence of Woolf s fully developed sense of the theatre."

HANCOX, DAN. The village against the world; [by] Dan Hancox 240 p. 2013 Verso

1. Journalism 2. Political leadership—Spain—Marinaleda 3. Utopian socialism—Spain—Marinaleda—History 4. Utopias—History—20th century

ISBN 1781681309 (hc); 9781781681305 (hc)

LC 2012-474499

SUMMARY: This book describes how "For the last thirty-five years the small Andalusian village of Marinaleda has been the centre of a tireless struggle to create a living utopia. [Author] Dan Hancox reveals the fascinating history of a community that seized the land owned by wealthy aristocrats in order to work it themselves. Since the 1980s, led by the charismatic mayor, Juan Manuel Sánchez Gordillo, the villagers have been fighting for a better life." (Publisher's note)

REVIEW: *New Statesman* v142 no5183 p44-5 N 8 2013 Fiona Sampson

REVIEW: *TLS* no5776 p31 D 13 2013 JULIUS PURCELL

"The Village Against the World." "[Author Dan] Hancox is an insightful chronicler of a globalized generation carving what he terms 'a new sincerity' out of the ruins of recession. . . . Hancox is delighted by Marinaleda life. . . . Few readers will be left unmoved by Hancox's historic portrait of Andalusia, with its nobles who sat on uncultivated estates as the people starved, yet even left-leaning readers will baulk at the mayor's tub-thumping style. . . . Hancox tries, but never quite manages, to dispel doubts about this supposed Utopia."

HAND, D. J. (DAVID J.), 1950-. The improbability principle; why coincidences, miracles, and rare events happen every day; [by] D. J. (David J.) Hand 288 p. 2014 Scientific American/Farrar, Straus and Giroux

1. BUSINESS & ECONOMICS—Statistics 2. BUSINESS & ECONOMICS—Strategic Planning 3. MATHEMATICS—Probability & Statistics—General 4. Mathematical literature 5. Probabilities

ISBN 9780374175344 (hardback)

LC 2013-034007

SUMMARY: This book presents an "introduction to probability that mixes counterintuitive anecdotes with . . . doses of statistics. Thus, through the 'law of truly large numbers,' [David J. Hand] reveals that, among the billions of events we experience throughout our lives, outrageous ones are bound to occur. Meanwhile, the "'aw of selection' reveals how probabilities can be made to appear artificially high due to selecting criteria after an event." (Publishers Weekly)

REVIEW: *Booklist* v110 no9/10 p29 Ja 1 2014 Bridget Thoreson

REVIEW: *Choice* v52 no1 p116 St 2014 J. T. Noonan

REVIEW: *Kirkus Rev* v82 no3 p20 F 1 2014

"The Improbability Principle: Why Coincidences, Miracles, and Rare Events Happen Every Day". "Enlightening and entertaining explanation of why extraordinary events are to be expected. Former Royal Statistical Society president [David J.] Hand . . . is an erudite but utterly unpretentious guide to the often confusing and counterintuitive subject of probability and its underappreciated complement, improbability. . . . Without taxing casual readers with strenuous math, the author coolly examines many fascinating examples of the unlikely. . . . Ably and assuredly demystifies an ordinarily intimidating subject."

REVIEW: *Libr J* v139 no4 p109 Mr 1 2014 Harold D. Shane

REVIEW: *New Sci* v221 no2960 p51 Mr 15 2014 Jonathon Keats

"The Improbability Principle: Why Coincidences, Miracles, and Rare Events Happen Every Day". "[A] lucid overview of the mathematics of chance and the psychological phenomena that can make probability seem counter-intuitive to so many. . . . The concepts underlying [David J.] Hand's laws will be familiar to all who have studied probability. His improbability principle is simply a conceit for assembling them in a book. But as an organisational scheme, it serves the purpose exceptionally well. Hand has written a superlative introduction to critical thinking, accessible to everybody, regardless of mathematical ability—and essential if your probability of taking a university-level maths class is less than zero."

REVIEW: *Publ Wkly* v260 no49 p73 D 2 2013

REVIEW: *Sci Am* v310 no5 p80 My 2014 Steve Mirsky

"The Improbability Principle: Why Coincidences, Miracles, and Rare Events Happen Every Day." "[E. G.] Bulwer-Lytton is the guy who . . . has a contest named for him that rewards the worst fictional sentence. 'The Improbability Principle' is not eligible, because it is a work of nonfiction, and it is good. 'The law,' writes the learned [D. J.] Hand, 'of truly large numbers . . . says that, with a large enough number of opportunities, any outrageous thing is likely to happen.' Lotteries are wonderful examples of how events that appear virtually impossible actually become inevitable given enough time and trials."

REVIEW: *Science* v345 no6202 p1253 S 12 2014 Eve Limbrick-Oldfield

HANDBOOK OF ENERGY, VOLUME I; Diagrams, Charts, and Tables; 1034 p. 2013 Elsevier Science

1. Energy consumption 2. Industries—Power supply 3. Power resources 4. Renewable energy sources 5. Scientific literature

ISBN 030648191X; 9780306481918

SUMMARY: This book, edited by Cutler J. Cleveland and Christopher Morris, examines "all phases of energy and its role in society, including its social, economic, political, historical, and environmental aspects. . . . . It focuses on visual, graphic, and tabular information in a schematic format." (Publisher's note)

REVIEW: *Choice* v51 no7 p1250 Mr 2014 F. Potter

"Handbook of Energy: Diagrams, Charts, and Tables." "This handbook, edited by [Cutler J.] Cleveland . . . and [Christopher] Morris . . . is a comprehensive resource on all aspects of energy. . . .There is no text beyond the figure captions and the contents of the color charts, diagrams, and tables themselves. The book also lacks an index to supplement the brief table of contents. However, there is a plethora of online sources along with numerous book and journal references for further research. This authoritative resource will be valuable for audiences in disparate fields of interest. . . . Highly recommended."

HANDBOOK OF RESEARCH ON GENDER AND ECONOMIC LIFE; 612 p. 2013 Edward Elgar Pub.

1. Economics literature 2. Feminist economics 3. Gender—Economic aspects 4. Gender role—Economic aspects 5. Women—Economic conditions

ISBN 9780857930941 (hardback)

LC 2013-932067

SUMMARY: Edited by Deborah M. Figart and Tonia L. Warnecke, "this volume brings together various theoretical and empirical contributions of well-known feminist economists covering a wide range of time-appropriate topics across countries. They include formal and informal labor market participation, the care economy, employment policies that affect women, and education, health, and welfare." (Choice: Current Reviews for Academic Libraries)

REVIEW: *Choice* v51 no8 p1456 Ap 2014 S. Chaudhuri

"Handbook of Research on Gender and Economic Life". "This volume brings together various theoretical and empirical contributions of well-known feminist economists covering a wide range of time appropriate topics across countries. They include formal and informal labor market participation, the care economy, employment policies that affect women, and education, health, and welfare. A must read for faculty, students, and practitioners of economics, feminist economics, sociology, and public and health policy."

HANDBOOK OF U.S. LABOR STATISTICS, 2013; Employment, Earnings, Prices, Productivity, and Other Labor Data; 536 p. 2013 Rowman & Littlefield Pub Inc

1. Economic sectors 2. Production (Economic theory) 3. Reference books 4. United States—Economic conditions—Statistics 5. United States. Bureau of Labor Statistics 6. United States. Bureau of the Census

ISBN 159888610X; 9781598886108

SUMMARY: Edited by Mary Meghan Ryan, "This volume presents data from the U.S. Bureau of Labor Statistics in approximately 225 tables. Topics addressed include unemployment, wages and productivity, price indexes, consumer income and expenditures, occupational safety and health, 'green' jobs, and more. Tables and figures are displayed in user-friendly formats, with supporting text and bulleted lists of highlights for each general heading." (Booklist)

REVIEW: *Booklist* v110 no1 p62 S 1 2013 Jennifer Michaelson

REVIEW: *Choice* v51 no2 p236-8 O 2013 S. Freedman

"Handbook of U.S. Labor Statistics: Employment, Earnings, Prices, Productivity, and Other Labor Data." "This 16th edition . . . is timely and useful, with updated chapter topics (e.g., in chapter 12, material on the American Time Use Survey) and new material on topics such as elder care and green jobs, technologies, and practices. Employment and labor statistics derive from both the government and the private sector. The historical publication data and some tables on unemployment go back to the 1940s, highlighting data culled from the Bureau of Labor Statistics . . . and the Census Bureau . . . websites. This ready-reference volume includes over 225 tables and figures with trend analysis, organized by subject in 15 chapters."

HANDBOOK OF WATER ANALYSIS; xvi, 979 p. 2013 CRC Press, Taylor & Francis Group

1. Chemical literature 2. Chromatographic analysis 3. Endocrine disruptors 4. Water—Analysis—Handbooks, manuals, etc 5. Water sampling

ISBN 9781439889640 (hardcover: alk. paper)

LC 2013-020078

SUMMARY: This third edition of editors Leo M. L. Nollet's and Leen S.P. De Gelder's book on water analysis "addresses the importance of sampling methods and discusses and compares various storage containers; an extensive table presents recommendations for storage containers. Up-to-date instrumental methods of analysis, including current electrode sensors, the full spectrum of chromatography methods, atomic absorption techniques, etc., are presented." (Choice: Current Reviews for Academic Libraries)

REVIEW: *Choice* v51 no8 p1430-1 Ap 2014 A. S. Casparian

"Handbook of Water Analysis". "This third edition . . . has

been expanded from 26 to 32 chapters, which are grouped into 12 sections to enhance information access. . . . Up-to-date instrumental methods of analysis, including current electrode sensors, the full spectrum of chromatography methods, atomic absorption techniques, etc., are presented. . . . Data tables throughout appear up-to-date, exceptionally well organized, and easy to understand. Though some details of instrumental methods have been omitted, end-of-chapter references are provided for interested readers to obtain more information. This book is valuable as a working reference manual, and is most suitable for graduate students, researchers, and practitioners in the field of water analysis."

HANDLER, CHELSEA, 1975-. Uganda Be Kidding Me; [by] Chelsea Handler 272 p. 2014 Grand Central Publishing

1. Africa—Description & travel 2. American wit & humor 3. Germany—Description & travel 4. Safaris 5. Travel—Humor 6. Travelers' writings
ISBN 1455599735; 9781455599738
LC 2013-043016

SUMMARY: This book presents a collection of travel essays by comedian Chelsea Handler. "On safari in Africa, it's anyone's guess as to what's more dangerous: the wildlife or Chelsea. But whether she's fumbling the seduction of a guide by not knowing where tigers live (Asia, duh) or wearing a bathrobe into the bush because her clothes stopped fitting seven margaritas ago, she's always game for the next misadventure." (Publisher's note)

REVIEW: *Booklist* v110 no13 p14 Mr 1 2014 Ann Kelley

REVIEW: *Booklist* v110 no5 p4 N 1 2013 Brad Hooper

"Like A Mighty Army," "A Nice Little Place on the North Side: Wrigley Field at One Hundred," and "Uganda Be Kidding Me." "The seventh volume in the best selling Safehold series of sf novels sees the heretofore unchallenged and repressive rule of the Church of God Awaiting being threatened. . . . Conservative commentator [George] Will has always held baseball in a special place in his heart, and in his new book, he gives free rein to his passion, imparting the history of Wrigley Field, home of the Chicago Cubs. . . . In comedian and best-selling author [Chelsea] Handler's new hook, she talks about her travels."

REVIEW: *Kirkus Rev* v82 no3 p194 F 1 2014

"Uganda Be Kidding Me". "Her shtick remains intact: an unapologetic stream of calculated outrageousness, including casual near-racism, abuse heaped on friends and family, overindulgence in various intoxicating substances, sexual frankness and scatological misadventure. . . . The results are fitfully funny, though the author's grotesque sense of privilege and entitlement begins to grate; though this tone is certainly also part of [Chelsea] Handler's highly polished comic persona, readers not blessed with the TV star's wealth and coterie of pampering enablers may begin to resent her petty complaints and blithe disregard for consequences. . . . Fans of Handler's outrageous persona will find much to enjoy; the unconverted will remain so."

REVIEW: *N Y Times Book Rev* p26 Mr 23 2014 GREGORY COWLES

HANFLING, EDWARD. Two Hundred and Forty Years of New Zealand Painting. See Dunn, M.

HANLEY, MARY STONE.ed. Culturally relevant arts education for social justice. See Culturally relevant arts education for social justice

HANLON, DAVID R. Illuminated shadows; the Calotype in Nineteenth Century America; 246 p. 2013 Carl Mautz Pub.

1. Calotype—History 2. Photography—Negatives 3. Photography—United States—History 4. Photography literature 5. Talbot, William Henry Fox, 1800-1877
ISBN 9781887694315 (hardcover); 9781887694322 (collector's edition)
LC 2013-939320

SUMMARY: This book looks at "the photographic process of calotype" as used in the United States. Author David R. Hanlon "opens with the earliest experiments beginning in the 1820s. In ten chapters he charts the multiple uses, commercial context, and aesthetics of the process until about 1870, when the paper negative was discontinued in favor of glass." (Choice: Current Reviews for Academic Libraries)

REVIEW: *Choice* v51 no9 p1577-8 My 2014 P. C. Bunnell

"Illuminating Shadows: The Calotype in 19th-Century America". "Previous publications have addressed the calotype in various countries, but this is the first in-depth study of its use in the US. Well researched and modestly illustrated, it documents an overlooked aspect of American history. [David R.] Hanlon . . . a professor of photographic history, opens with the earliest experiments beginning in the 1820s. In ten chapters he charts the multiple uses, commercial context, and aesthetics of the process until about 1870, when the paper negative was discontinued in favor of glass. Excellent notes, appendixes, and bibliography."

HANN, ANDREW.ed. Slavery and the British Country House. See Slavery and the British Country House

HANNA, ERIKA. Modern Dublin; urban change and the Irish past, 1957-1973; [by] Erika Hanna vi, 230 p. 2013 Oxford University Press

1. City planning—Ireland—Dublin—History—20th century 2. Historical literature 3. Urban policy—Ireland—Dublin—History—20th century
ISBN 0199680450 (hbk.); 9780199680450 (hbk.)
LC 2013-474169

SUMMARY: This book by Erika Hanna explores "social and cultural change in 1960s Ireland. . . . Using approaches from urban studies and cultural geography, the author reveals Dublin as a place of complex exchange between a variety of interest groups with different visions for the built environment, and thus for society and the independent nation." (Publisher's note)

REVIEW: *Choice* v51 no9 p1670-1 My 2014 A. H. Plunkett

"Modern Dublin: Urban Change and the Irish Past, 1957-1973". "[Erika] Hanna . . . skillfully explores five preservationist battles in Dublin between 1957 and 1973, as the city became a highly contested site where urban planners, architects, politicians, developers, preservationists, students, and poor residents pursued different visions of its future. . . . Hanna concludes that by the late 1970s, many Georgian buildings and traditional communities had been obliterated, but a new awareness of the importance of preserving what remained, and of the meaning and costs of modernization in the urban environment, had emerged. This insightful study will be of interest to students of Ireland, architectural history, and urban studies."

HANNAH, SOPHIE. Kind of cruel; [by] Sophie Hannah 448 p. 2013 Penguin Books

1. Insomnia—Fiction 2. Murder—Investigation—Fiction 3. Recovered memory—Fiction 4. Secrets—Fiction 5. Suspense fiction
ISBN 9780670785858
LC 2012-046995

SUMMARY: This book "explores the differences between feelings and memories. Insomniac Amber Hewerdine's visit to a hypnotherapist in Silsford, England, leads to her involvement in the investigation of the murder of Katharine Allen, a primary school teacher. At the crime scene is a piece of paper with the enigmatic words of the title. . . . An earlier murder, by arson, of Amber's best friend, raises the tension." (Publishers Weekly)

REVIEW: *Booklist* v109 no17 p30 My 1 2013 Michele Leber

REVIEW: *Booklist* v110 no9/10 p63-6 Ja 1 2014 Karen Harris

"Kind of Cruel." "In [Sophie] Hannah's seventh thriller featuring British detectives Waterhouse and Zailer, a woman finds herself in the middle of a murder investigation. . . . A host of secrets are uncovered, raising issues connected to previous events in Amber's past that have never been explained. . . . [Elizabeth] Sastre, reading in a mildly accented, nuanced British voice, displays considerable versatility. She is adept at evoking male and female characters of various ages, classes, and, most important, emotional states, which are crucial to the effectiveness of this unusual and compelling psychological thriller."

REVIEW: *Kirkus Rev* v81 no12 p19 Je 15 2013

REVIEW: *Libr J* v138 no10 p98 Je 1 2013 Linda Oliver

REVIEW: *Libr J* v138 no3 p72 F 15 2013 Barbara Hoffert

REVIEW: *Publ Wkly* v260 no24 p43 Je 17 2013

HANNAH, SOPHIE. The Orphan Choir; A Novel; [by] Sophie Hannah 304 p. 2013 Hammer

1. Children's choirs 2. Dwellings—Fiction 3. Mothers—Fiction 4. Paranormal fiction 5. Psychological fiction
ISBN 0099579995; 1250041023; 9780099579991; 9781250041029

SUMMARY: This novel, by Sophie Hannah, "explores the psyche of a woman whose life is troubled by a noisy neighbor and the enforced absence of her own small child. . . . Joseph attends an exclusive private school in Cambridge, and . . . is required to board at the school. That means Louise and her husband, Stuart, only see Joseph . . .during breaks. . . . She keeps hearing the voices of singing children, a choir like Joseph's, wherever she is. And it appears no one else can hear the choir but her." (Kirkus Reviews)

REVIEW: *Booklist* v111 no2 p66-7 S 15 2014 Renee Young

REVIEW: *Booklist* v110 no5 p31 N 1 2013 Michele Leber

"The Orphan Choir." "Louise Beeston is teetering on the edge of sanity. She has virtually lost her only child, seven-year-old Joseph, who is required to be a boarder at Savior College School as a member of its 16-boy choir. Then her sleep is badly disrupted by loud music played late at night by next-door neighbor Justin Clay, until she retaliates in kind, with advice from a city-council environmental-health officer. . . . This stand-alone novel, a break from [Sophie] Hannah's series of psychological police procedurals . . . is a riveting story in which suspense snowballs to a climax that is all the more dire for its everyday contemporary English setting. Absolutely haunting, in every sense of the word."

REVIEW: *Kirkus Rev* v81 no21 p132 N 1 2013

REVIEW: *Libr J* v138 no15 p46 S 15 2013

REVIEW: *Libr J* v138 no18 p78 N 1 2013 Jane Jorgenson

REVIEW: *N Y Times Book Rev* p30-1 Je 1 2014 TERRENCE RAFFERTY

REVIEW: *New York Times* v163 no56397 pC7 Ja 30 2014 - John Williams

REVIEW: *TLS* no5749 p21 Je 7 2013 SARAH CURTIS

HANNAHAM, JAMES. Kara Walker. See Als, H.

HANNIBAL, MARY ELLEN. The Spine of the Continent; The Most Ambitious Wildlife Conservation Project Ever Undertaken; [by] Mary Ellen Hannibal xv, 272 p. 2012 Globe Pequot Pr

1. Canadian Rockies (B.C. & Alta.) 2. Ecosystem management 3. Environmental literature 4. Rocky Mountains—Environmental conditions 5. Wilderness areas—North America 6. Wilderness areas—Rocky Mountains Region 7. Wildlife conservation—North America 8. Wildlife conservation—Rocky Mountains Region
ISBN 076277214X; 9780762772148
LC 2012-020223

SUMMARY: This book, by Mary Ellen Hannibal, describes the author's "travels [throughout] the length of North America and reports on efforts to create a wildlife corridor through Canada, the United States, and Mexico, begun with the purpose of protecting landscapes so that animals and plants have room to roam." (Publisher's note)

REVIEW: *Booklist* v109 no1 p20-2 S 1 2012 Carl Hays

"The Spine of the Continent: The Most Ambitious Wildlife Conservation Project Ever Undertaken." "A large-scale environmental project spearheaded by conservation biologist Michael Soulé and appropriately named the Spine of the Continent (SOC) Initiative, was recently launched to make sure the Rockies are knit together as an interconnected ecosystem. . . . Many protected wildlife zones along this corridor . . . have become isolated from each other due to highways and urban development. . . . [Mary Ellen] Hannibal's captivating true-life narrative tells the stories of those devoted to Soulé's vision and provides an inspiring example to follow for environmentalists on every continent."

REVIEW: *Choice* v51 no2 p290-1 O 2013 K. K. Goldbeck-DeBose

REVIEW: *Kirkus Rev* v80 no14 p1472 Jl 15 2012

REVIEW: *Publ Wkly* v259 no28 p53 Jl 9 2012

HANS BLUMENBERG, JACOB TAUBES; Briefwechsel; 2013 Suhrkamp

1. Blumenberg, Hans 2. Germany (West)—Intellectual

life 3. Letters 4. Philosophers—Germany—Correspondence 5. Taubes, Jacob

SUMMARY: Edited by Herbert Kopp-Oberstebrink and Martin Treml, "The correspondence between Hans Blumenberg and Jacob Taubes is a document of a rich though not entirely smooth relationship between two intellectuals who could not have been more different: On the one hand, Hand Blumenberg, whose works constitute one of the most impressive contributions to 20th century German philosophy; on the other hand, the philosopher of religion Jacob Taubes." (Publisher's note)

REVIEW: *TLS* no5796 p26 My 2 2014 JOE PAUL KROLL

"Hans Blumenberg and Jacob Taubes: Briefwechsel 1961-1981." "An interdisciplinary study group in the humanities, 'Poetik und Hermeneutik' rivalled the Frankfurt School not in political resonance, but in long-term influence as a force for the renewal of (West) German intellectual life in the post-war era. Founded in 1963, its early and defining members included Hans Blumenberg and Jacob Taubes, whose uneasy encounter of minds and temperaments is documented in this thoroughly edited and extensively annotated volume of correspondence. . . . Although this volume documents a failed attempt at mutual understanding, the testimony it gives to the divisive power of arcane problems is impressive in itself."

HANSEN, PETER H. The summits of modern man; mountaineering after the enlightenment; [by] Peter H. Hansen x, 380 p. 2013 Harvard University Press

1. Historical literature 2. Modernity 3. Mountaineering—History 4. Mountaineering—Philosophy 5. Mountaineers
ISBN 9780674047990 (alk. paper)
LC 2012-040365

SUMMARY: In this book, "historian Peter Hansen traces our complicated relationship with mountains, from the Himalaya to the European Alps. By exploring themes such as why we feel the need to dominate nature and what do these first ascents truly accomplish, he explores how the birth of mountaineering has shaped modern society." (Australian Geographic)

REVIEW: *Choice* v51 no3 p504 N 2013 R. W. Roberts

REVIEW: *Hist Today* v63 no10 p64 O 2013 CLARE ROCHE

REVIEW: *TLS* no5756 p3-4 Jl 26 2013 ADAM THORPE

"The Summits of Modern Man: Mountaineering After the Enlightenment." "[A] learned and complex analysis of 'multiple modernities' as seen through the prism of mountaineering. . . . While the book's passages on Savoy politics make for a stiff climb, not helped by the author's rigorous denial of picturesque digression, they are necessary to the whole. . . . The complex time knot thus created makes this one of the most revealing accounts of the Everest expedition that I have read. But [Peter H.] Hansen provokingly leaves us, after a commentary on the way climate change has taken the zip out of our species' sovereignty, with the Rückenfigur of Ötzi, the Neolithic individual revealed by melting ice on the Austrian-Italian frontier.:

HANSEN, VALERIE. The Silk Road; a new history; [by] Valerie Hansen xi, 304 p., [16] p. of plates 2012 Oxford University Press

1. Historic sites—Silk Road 2. Historical literature 3. Trade routes—Asia—History
ISBN 0195159314 (hardcover : acid-free paper); 9780195159318 (hardcover : acid-free paper); 9780199978601 (ebook); 0199978603 (ebook)
LC 2011-041804

SUMMARY: This book by Valerie Hansen "examines the Silk Road. . . . Organizing the text around the seven Silk Road cities of Niya, Kucha, Turfan, Samarkand, Chang'an, Dunhuang, and Khotan, the author takes the position that the Silk Road was made up of local and small-scale trade, not the large commercial routes that we have come to associate with it. More significant, she writes, its true importance lies in the movement of ideas." (Library Journal)

REVIEW: *Choice* v50 no7 p1310 Mr 2013 J. K. Skaffi

REVIEW: *Libr J* v137 no11 p87 Je 15 2012 Melissa Aho

REVIEW: *Publ Wkly* p49 My 21 2012

REVIEW: *TLS* no5777/8 p33 D 20 2013 DAVID MORGAN

"The Silk Road: A New History." "Valerie Hansen, by contrast, focuses her attention on seven places along the supposed road: Niya, Kucha, Turfan, Samarkand, Chang'an (Xi'an), Dunhuang and Khotan. . . . Whereas many studies of the Silk Road concentrate on the remarkable art which has been unearthed along it, Valerie Hansen deals with what may be learnt from documentary evidence. . . . Even more striking, perhaps, is Hansen's entirely persuasive argument that, considered as a route which ran all the way from China, across Central Asia and to Persia, the Silk Road did not really exist at all."

HANSON, WARREN. It's Monday, Mrs. Jolly Bones; [by] Warren Hanson 32 p. 2013 Beach Lane Books

1. Chores 2. Housekeeping—Fiction 3. Humorous stories 4. Stories in rhyme 5. Week—Fiction
ISBN 1442412291; 9781442412293 (hardcover)
LC 2010-004309

SUMMARY: This book-length ballad focuses on "Mrs. Jolly Bones [who] is a woman who keeps a serious housekeeping schedule--in her own peculiar way. Monday is for doing laundry, which concludes with throwing all the clothes out the window; Tuesday's gardening ends with a garden-wrecking dance . . . ; Wednesday's housecleaning culminates in a toilet-bowl bath, etc. Finally Sunday comes, and a blissful day of rest comes to a celebratory finale." (Bulletin of the Center for Children's Books)

REVIEW: *Booklist* v109 no13 p70-1 Mr 1 2013 Ann Kelley

REVIEW: *Bull Cent Child Books* v66 no8 p377-8 Ap 2013 Deborah Stevenson

"It's Monday, Mrs. Jolly Bones!" "In this rollicking ballad, Mrs. Jolly Bones is a woman who keeps a serious housekeeping schedule--in her own peculiar way. Monday is for doing laundry, which concludes with throwing all the clothes out the window; Tuesday's gardening ends with a garden-wrecking dance. . . . [Warren] Hanson writes with an appealingly larky joie de vivre; the combination of drudgery and absurdity is amusing, and the crisp scansion makes the verse dance. Though the abundance of dark-lined elements (offset only by delicate, pale touches of watercolor) overbusies some scenes, [Tricia] Tusa's scrabbly outlining and rich detailing expand on the text's chaotic humor."

REVIEW: *Horn Book Magazine* v89 no2 p86 Mr/Ap 2013 KITTY FLYNN

REVIEW: *Kirkus Rev* v81 no3 p117 F 1 2013

REVIEW: *Publ Wkly* v260 no3 p64 Ja 21 2013

REVIEW: *SLJ* v59 no2 p74-6 F 2013 Mary Hazelton

HAQQANI, HUSAIN. Magnificent delusions; Pakistan, the United States, and an epic history of misunderstanding; [by] Husain Haqqani 432 p. 2013 PublicAffairs

1. National security 2. Political science literature 3. Terrorism
ISBN 1610393171; 9781610393171 (us hardcover); 9781610393188 (e-bk.); 9781610394093 (international hc); 9781610394109 (international pb)
LC 2013-948306

SUMMARY: This book by Husain Haqqani describes how "the relationship between America and Pakistan is based on mutual incomprehension and always has been. Pakistan—to American eyes—has gone from being a quirky irrelevance, to a stabilizing friend, to an essential military ally, to a seedbed of terror. America—to Pakistani eyes—has been a guarantee of security, a coldly distant scold, an enthusiastic military enabler, and is now a threat to national security and a . . . humiliation." (Publisher's note)

REVIEW: *Kirkus Rev* v81 no20 p119 O 15 2013

REVIEW: *N Y Rev Books* v61 no5 p26-8 Mr 20 2014 Anatol Lieven

"No Exit From Pakistan: America's Tortured Relationship With Islamabad," "The Way of the Knife: The CIA, a Secret Army, and a War at the Ends of the Earth," and "Magnificent Delusion: Pakistan, the United States, and an Epic History of Misunderstanding". "'The Way of the Knife' . . . [is a] powerful exposé. . . . It would . . . be a pity if Pakistanis simply dismiss [Husain] Haqqani's book, because if it does not contain nearly enough that Americans need to hear, it contains a great deal that Pakistanis badly need to hear, and that they very rarely do hear from their own media. . . . [Daniel] Markey has little to suggest beyond the development of new drone technology, and the possible extension of missile attacks to new parts of Pakistan."

REVIEW: *New York Times* v163 no56391 pC30 Ja 24 2014 DECLAN WALSH

"Magnificent Delusions: Pakistan, the United States, and an Epic History of Misunderstanding" and "Getting Away With Murder: Benazir Bhutto's Assassination and the Politics of Pakistan". "Mr. [Husain] Haqqani is eminently qualified to tell this story. . . . His history relies heavily on American cables and memoirs, which serves well to illuminate some episodes. . . . But at other times, the lack of Pakistani voices feels one-sided. . . . And there is a disappointing lack of detail from the recent period when Mr. Haqqani himself was a central participant in the action. . . . As a diplo-sleuth, Mr. Heraldo [Muñoz] provides some revealing detail on this important story. But, alas, he is no Agatha Christie. A dutiful rehashing of Pakistani history is insightful but sprinkled with careless errors. And, ultimately, he fails to go much further into [Benazir] Bhutto's death than his well-regarded United Nations report."

REVIEW: *Publ Wkly* v260 no36 p47-8 S 9 2013

HARADA, VIOLET H.ed. Growing schools. See Growing schools

HARASIMOWICZ, ELLEN.il. Handle with care. See Burns, L. G.

HARBACH, CHAD.ed. MFA vs NYC. See MFA vs NYC

HARDER, ANNETTE.ed. Aetia. See Aetia

HARDING, ANTHONY.ed. The Oxford handbook of the European Bronze Age. See The Oxford handbook of the European Bronze Age

HARDING, JAMES M. The ghosts of the avant-garde(s); exorcising experimental theater and performance; [by] James M. Harding ix, 234 p. 2013 University of Michigan Press

1. Arts & society 2. Avant-garde (Arts) 3. Experimental drama—History and criticism 4. Experimental theater—History and criticism 5. Sociology literature
ISBN 9780472118748 (hardback : acid-free paper)
LC 2012-042609

SUMMARY: "'The Ghosts of the Avant-Garde(s)' offers a strikingly new perspective on key controversies and debates within avant-garde studies and on contemporary forms of avant-garde expression within a global political economy. . . . James M. Harding revisits iconic sites of early twentieth-century avant-garde performance to examine how European avant-gardists attempted . . . to employ that discourse as a strategy for enforcing uniformity among a . . . diverse group of artists." (Publisher's note)

REVIEW: *Choice* v51 no5 p839-40 Ja 2014 M. S. LoMonaco

REVIEW: *TLS* no5784 p27 F 7 2014 NICHOLAS RIDOUT

"The Ghosts of the Avant-Garde(s): Exorcising Experimental Theatre and Performance." "Here James M. Harding takes Peter Bürger's influential 'Theory of the Avant-Garde' to task for establishing a critical orthodoxy that fails to consider the multiplicity of avant-gardes. . . . In Harding's examination of the critical discourses of and about the various avant-gardes, however, it is precisely such 'hybrid vanguardism' that offers an open and dynamic alternative to a coherent of 'monolithic' avant-garde project . . . The repeated appearance of avant-gardes, Harding also suggests, is due to their failure: a successful avant-garde would render all future ones obsolete in advance."

HARDING, LUKE. The Snowden Files; The True Inside Story on the World's Most Wanted Man; [by] Luke Harding 352 p. 2014 Guardian Faber Publishing

1. Journalism 2. Leaks (Disclosure of information) 3. Snowden, Edward Joseph, 1983- 4. United States. National Security Agency 5. Whistleblowing
ISBN 0804173524; 1783350350; 9780804173520; 9781783350353

SUMMARY: This book looks at "Edward Snowden . . . a 29-year-old computer genius working for the National Security Agency when he shocked the world by exposing the near-universal mass surveillance programs of the United States government. His whistleblowing has shaken the leaders of nations worldwide, and generated a passionate public debate on the dangers of global monitoring and the threat to individual privacy." (Publisher's note)

REVIEW: *Kirkus Rev* v82 no5 p310 Mr 1 2014

REVIEW: *London Rev Books* v36 no4 p9-10 F 20 2014 Daniel Soar

"The Snowden Files: The Inside Story of the World's Most Wanted Man". "A super-readable, thrillerish account of the events surrounding the reporting of the documents, with a few interludes sketching out what some of the stories have revealed. If you're only going to read one of all the books coming out around [Edward] Snowden—Harding's is the first of several—then [Glenn] Greenwald's, due soon, will almost certainly be the one to choose: it's the most likely to have new information, and a swinging style. But Harding's is a handy guide to much of what happened. . . . Despite not having seen much at first hand, Harding has done an amazing—and speedy— job of assembling material from a wide variety of sources and turning it into an exciting account."

REVIEW: *N Y Rev Books* v61 no12 p16-20 Jl 10 2014 Sue Halpern

REVIEW: *New Statesman* v143 no5192 p52-3 Ja 10 2014 Tom Gatti

REVIEW: *New Statesman* v143 no5211 p46-7 My 23 2014 David Aaronovitch

REVIEW: *New York Times* v163 no56403 pC1-4 F 5 2014 MICHIKO KAKUTANI

REVIEW: *TLS* no5793 p3-5 Ap 11 2014 EDWARD N. LUTTWAK

HARDING, PAUL. Enon; [by] Paul Harding 256 p. 2013 Random House Inc

1. Bereavement—Fiction 2. Families—Fiction 3. Grandsons—Fiction 4. Loss (Psychology)—Fiction 5. Psychological fiction
ISBN 1400069432; 9781400069439
LC 2013-007985

SUMMARY: This book by Paul Harding "covers a year in the life of Charlie Crosby . . . as he mourns the death of his 13-year-old daughter in an accident. After smashing his hand against a wall in a rage, he loses his wife and develops a slow-growing addiction to painkillers and alcohol that leads him to break-ins and other foolhardy decisions. But Harding is less concerned with plot as with what's swimming in Charlie's head, and themes of nature and time abound." (Kirkus Reviews)

REVIEW: *Booklist* v109 no22 p29 Ag 1 2013 Donna Seaman

REVIEW: *Economist* v408 no8854 p92 S 21 2013

"Enon." "A beautifully melancholic new novel by Paul Harding. . . . All this sounds heavy going. Yet Mr. Harding ensures that Charlie, despite his sorrow, is still good company. Even as he slides further into despair, his perception warped by grief and drug addiction, Charlie wryly observes his own wretchedness. . . . And there is lightness int he narrative, largely in memories of Kate and recollections of Charlie's own childhood. . . . As with 'Tinkers,' the language of 'Enon' glimmers without feeling precious. . . . With Charlie, Mr. Harding captures the poignant aches of parenthood. . . . And he turns the fictional town of Enon into a vital, storied, memorable place, well worth visiting."

REVIEW: *Kirkus Rev* p9 Ag 15 2013 Fall Preview

REVIEW: *Kirkus Rev* p19 N 15 2013 Best Books

REVIEW: *Kirkus Rev* v81 no15 p144 Ag 1 2013

REVIEW: *Libr J* v138 no7 p54 Ap 15 2013 Barbara Hoffert

REVIEW: *N Y Times Book Rev* p18 S 22 2013 MARK SLOUKA

REVIEW: *New York Times* v163 no56271 pC2 S 26 2013 Susannah Meadows

REVIEW: *New Yorker* v89 no28 p1 S 16 2013

REVIEW: *Publ Wkly* v260 no27 p64 Jl 8 2013

HARDING, THOMAS. Hanns and Rudolf; The True Story of the German Jew Who Tracked Down and Caught the Kommandant of Auschwitz; [by] Thomas Harding 352 p. 2013 Simon & Schuster

1. Alexander, Hanns 2. Auschwitz (Poland : Concentration camp) 3. Historical literature 4. Hoess, Rudolf, 1900-1947 5. Nazi hunters
ISBN 1476711844; 9781476711843

SUMMARY: In this book, Thomas Harding profiles "Rudolf Höss (1900–1947), the coldly efficient lapsed-Catholic commandant of Auschwitz . . . [and] Hanns Alexander (1917–2006) . . . a German Jewish émigré in the service of the British Army dead-set on hunting down Rudolf . . . and bringing him to justice." The book concludes "when Hanns and Rudolf finally come face to face on a farm where the war criminal had been desperately trying to elude his pursuers." (Publishers Weekly)

REVIEW: *Economist* v408 no8851 p73-4 Ag 31 2013

"Hanns and Rudolf: The True Story of the German Jew Who Tracked Down and Caught the Kommandant of Auschwitz." "A gripping new book. . . . Mr. [Thomas] Harding does not change existing views of Rudolf [Höss] . . . . Yet he has unearthed chilling details of Rudolf's family life at his Auschwitz villa. . . . Mr. Harding also impressively recovers Hanns [Alexander's] story. . . . Mr. Harding begins his book with a promise to challenge 'the traditional portrayal of the hero and the villain'. Fortunately his narrative is not so morally muddy. Rudolf is shown as a man who, owing to circumstance and character, embraced evil. Hanns did the opposite."

REVIEW: *Kirkus Rev* v81 no14 p272 Jl 15 2013

REVIEW: *Libr J* v138 no7 p58 Ap 15 2013 Barbara Hoffert

REVIEW: *Publ Wkly* v260 no26 p82 Jl 1 2013

HARDY, NICOLE. Confessions of a latter day virgin; a memoir; [by] Nicole Hardy 304 p. 2013 Hyperion

1. Chastity 2. Ex-church members—Church of Jesus Christ of Latter-day Saints—Biography 3. Memoirs 4. Mormon women 5. Spiritual biography
ISBN 9781401341862
LC 2012-045975

SUMMARY: This memoir by Nicole Hardy tells the story "of a headstrong, dramatic dreamer who grew up wanting much more for herself than the marriage and children her church [the Church of Jesus Christ of Latter-Day Saints] deemed necessary for eternal life, and yet remained wary of defying her faith's conception of spiritual fulfillment. She aspires to write . . . and in the meantime her heart is broken by the fact that non-Mormon men who might fulfill her are off limits." (New York Times Book Review)

REVIEW: *Booklist* v109 no19/20 p19 Je 1 2013 Allison Block

REVIEW: *Kirkus Rev* v81 no13 p69 Jl 1 2013

REVIEW: *N Y Times Book Rev* p20 S 22 2013 CARLENE BAUER

"Confessions of a Latter-Day Virgin: A Memoir." "There are wisecracks to spare and no shortage of wry asides. But laced as it is with a tortured strain of self-denial . . . [Nicole] Hardy's story may seem appealing--and comprehensible--only to those who have been raised in conservative Christian churches. Through quite a bit of the book she defensively chafes against the numerous platitudes issued by her fellow faithful. Yet while she has good reason to erupt at the bad theology . . . the memoir can read uncomfortably like a string of tantrums. . . . We don't see enough of [God] in her book. A fuller glimpse would have made this a consistently, rather than fitfully, powerful document of what a liberated woman's faith looks and sounds like."

REVIEW: *Publ Wkly* v260 no21 p45-6 My 27 2013

HARLEY, BILL. Charlie Bumpers vs. the Teacher of the Year; 160 p. 2013 Peachtree Publishers

1. Behavior—Fiction 2. Family life—Fiction 3. Humorous stories 4. Orderliness—Fiction 5. School stories 6. Schools—Fiction 7. Teachers—Fiction
ISBN 1561457329; 9781561457328
LC 2013-004850

SUMMARY: In this book written by Bill Harley and illustrated by Adam Gustavson, "Shortly before school starts, Charlie Bumpers learns that he will have the strictest teacher in the whole school for fourth grade. It doesn't matter that she's been named Teacher of the Year. He's still afraid of her. . . . How will he survive a year under a teacher who is just waiting for him to make another stupid mistake?" (Publisher's note)

REVIEW: *Bull Cent Child Books* v67 no2 p92-3 O 2013 T. A.

"Charlie Bumpers vs. The Teacher of the Year." "Ever since an incident last year in which he discovered Mrs. Burke's intimidating disciplinary demeanor, Charlie's tried to avoid the teacher, but now that he's assigned to her classroom for fourth grade it looks like there's no escape. . . . Narrator Charlie is personable and well-rounded as a Ramona Quimby-esque protagonist who faces a series of kid-familiar challenges in trying his best to do the right thing. . . . Black and white spot art in India ink and watercolor effectively adds a bit of silly realism. . . . Charlie Bumpers' first adventures are the start of a proposed series, and readers will welcome him as a bumbling but generous addition to the ranks of novels for novices."

REVIEW: *Kirkus Rev* v81 no17 p95 S 1 2013

REVIEW: *Publ Wkly* v260 no30 p68 Jl 29 2013

REVIEW: *SLJ* v59 no9 p122 S 2013 Laura Stanfield

HARMON, LIN.ed. Dictionary of environmental and climate change law. See Dictionary of environmental and climate change law

HARPER, CHARISE MERICLE.il. Alien encounter. See Harper, C. M.

HARPER, CHARISE MERICLE. Alien encounter; [by] Charise Mericle Harper 208 p. 2014 Christy Ottaviano Books, Henry Holt & Company

1. Extraterrestrial beings—Fiction 2. Family life—Northwest, Pacific—Fiction 3. Friendship—Fiction 4. Humorous stories 5. Yeti—Fiction
ISBN 0805096213; 9780805096217 (hardback)
LC 2013-039906

SUMMARY: This book, the first in Charise Mericle Harper's "Sasquatch and Aliens" series, "introduces a pair of nine-year-old boys who are propelled into an adventure that may or may not involve otherworldly creatures. Anxiety-prone Morgan first meets new kid Lewis as Lewis is hanging from a tree by his underwear. After Morgan reluctantly rescues Lewis (whose family just bought a creepy motel), a tentative friendship is born." (Publishers Weekly)

REVIEW: *Booklist* v110 no15 p88 Ap 1 2014 J. B. Petty

REVIEW: *Bull Cent Child Books* v67 no9 p457 My 2014 T. A.

REVIEW: *Horn Book Magazine* v90 no2 p119-20 Mr/Ap 2014 SARAH ELLIS

REVIEW: *Kirkus Rev* v82 no3 p234 F 1 2014

"Alien Encounter". "In this stretched-out series opener, two lads do little more than hang out for chapter after chapter between encounters with (putatively) an almond-eyed alien and a sasquatch while the author hints at hidden doings. . . . The 9-year-old narrator continues in a mix of chatty prose, comical line drawings, lists and acrostics to introduce his (seemingly) typical family and small town. . . . Lots of tantalizing setup plus not quite enough plot fails to equal a story that stands on its own."

REVIEW: *SLJ* v60 no3 p112 Mr 2014 Gerry Larson

HARPER, CHARISE MERICLE. Dreamer, wisher, liar; [by] Charise Mericle Harper 352 p. 2014 Balzer + Bray, an imprint of HarperCollinsPublishers

1. Babysitter—Fiction 2. Fantasy fiction 3. Magic—Fiction 4. Mothers and daughters—Fiction 5. Wishes—Fiction
ISBN 0062026755; 9780062026750 (hardcover bdg.)
LC 2013-008222

SUMMARY: This book is a "story about one girl's transformative summer full of friendship, secret magic, and family. . . . When her best friend is moving away and her mom has arranged for some strange little girl to come and stay with them, Ash . . . is expecting the worst summer of her life. Then seven-year-old Claire shows up. Armed with a love of thrift-store clothes and an altogether too-sunny disposition, Claire proceeds to turn Ash's carefully constructed life upside down." (Publisher's note)

REVIEW: *Booklist* v110 no13 p73 Mr 1 2014 Erin Downey Howerton

REVIEW: *Bull Cent Child Books* v67 no9 p456-7 My 2014 K. Q. G.

REVIEW: *Kirkus Rev* v82 no5 p117 Mr 1 2014

"Dreamer, Wisher, Liar". "Bracing for a lonely summer, Ash is surprised when the little girl she babysits and some unexpected time travel open new horizons. . . . Though she's busy with Claire, Ash becomes distracted after finding a jar labeled 'wishes' in the basement that transports her into the lives of two girls living when her parents were young. . . . Ash tells her summer saga in a humorous, chatty, somewhat-vulnerable voice, and although the time-travel thread initially feels disconnected from the plotline, the past and present eventually sync. Spot art line drawings feature chapter elements. Amusing, heartfelt time travel about friends and wishes-old and new."

REVIEW: *Publ Wkly* v261 no6 p89 F 10 2014

REVIEW: *SLJ* v60 no4 p146 Ap 2014 Annette Herbert

REVIEW: *Voice of Youth Advocates* v36 no6 p71 F 2014 Juidth Hayn

HARRINGTON, JOEL F. The faithful executioner; life and death, honor and shame in the turbulent sixteenth century; [by] Joel F. Harrington 320 p. 2013 Farrar Straus & Giroux

1. Crime—Germany—Nuremberg History 2. Criminal procedure—Germany—Nuremberg—History 3. Executions and executioners—Germany—Nuremberg—Biography 4. HISTORY—Europe—Germany 5. HISTORY—Modern—16th Century 6. Historical literature

ISBN 0809049929 (hardcover); 9780809049929 (hardcover)

LC 2012-029017

SUMMARY: This book, by Joel F. Harrington, "takes us deep inside the alien world and thinking of Meister Frantz Schmidt of Nuremberg, who, during forty-five years as a professional executioner, personally put to death 394 individuals and tortured, flogged, or disfigured many hundreds more. But the picture that emerges of Schmidt from his personal papers is not that of a monster. Could a man who routinely practiced such cruelty also be insightful, compassionate--even progressive?" (Publisher's note)

REVIEW: *Choice* v51 no3 p537-8 N 2013 P. G. Wallace

REVIEW: *Hist Today* v63 no6 p55-6 Je 2013 KAT HILL

"The Faithful Executioner: Life and Death, Honour and Shame in the Turbulent Sixteenth Century." "In this vividly drawn portrait of the life of an early modern executioner, Meister Franz Schmidt, Joel Harrington immerses us in the world of crime, violence and honour of 16th-and 17th-century Germany. . . . Finely researched and crafted, this tale of a man at the margins of respectability demands that we do not see the executioner in comic book terms as a symbol of a violent, alien age and so opens a window onto the norms, codes of honour and social structures of early modern Germany."

REVIEW: *Kirkus Rev* v81 no1 p48 Ja 1 2013

REVIEW: *Publ Wkly* v259 no51 p50 D 17 2012

REVIEW: *TLS* no5762 p3-4 S 6 2013 RICHARD J. EVANS

"The Faithful Executioner: Life and Death, Honour and Shame in the Turbulent Sixteenth Century." "Master Frantz [Schmidt] was not an introspective diarist, but [Joel F.] Harrington brings out with great interpretative acuity his vision of the moral values with whose enforcement he was charged. He provides a richly detailed and utterly absorbing account of a world of violence, pain and suffering into which it would be difficult for the modern reader to enter through less sympathetic accounts. . . . Harrington describes this world of fixed hierarchies and rigid demarcations of status very well, but he could perhaps have brought out more clearly the symbolic nature of its constituent elements."

HARRINGTON, KAREN. Sure signs of crazy; [by] Karen Harrington 288 p. 2013 Little Brown & Co

1. Coming of age—Fiction 2. Family problems—Fiction 3. Mental illness—Fiction 4. Young adult fiction

ISBN 0316210587 (hardcover); 9780316210584 (hardcover)

LC 2012-030683

SUMMARY: In this book, "worried that she will grow up to be crazy like her mother or alcoholic like her father, rising seventh-grader Sarah Nelson takes courage from Harper Lee's 'To Kill a Mockingbird,' writing letters to Atticus Finch and discovering her own strengths. . . . She describes the events of the summer she turns 12, gets her period, develops a crush on a neighbor and fellow word lover, and comes to terms with her parents' failings." (Kirkus Reviews)

REVIEW: *Booklist* v109 no22 p74 Ag 1 2013 Abby Nolan

REVIEW: *Bull Cent Child Books* v67 no2 p93 O 2013 J. H.

REVIEW: *Horn Book Magazine* v89 no6 p94 N/D 2013 ELISSA GERSHOWITZ

"Sure Signs of Crazy." "'You've never met anyone like me,' begins this affecting book, 'Unless, of course, you've met someone who survived her mother trying to drown her and now lives with an alcoholic father.' . . . Te book is never maudlin, even at the breath-catching climax when Sarah goes to see her mother. And if there are a few too many plot points and the protagonist's voice sounds less like a just-turned-twelve-year-old's and more like a highly self-aware (and impossibly resilient) grownup, it's well worth looking past in order to appreciate the extraordinary heart of the story."

REVIEW: *Kirkus Rev* p76 N 15 2013 Best Books

REVIEW: *Kirkus Rev* v81 no10 p94 My 15 2013

REVIEW: *Publ Wkly* v260 no21 p59 My 27 2013

REVIEW: *SLJ* v59 no8 p100 Ag 2013 Marie Orlando

REVIEW: *Voice of Youth Advocates* v36 no5 p61 D 2013 Riley Carter

REVIEW: *Voice of Youth Advocates* v36 no5 p60-1 D 2013 Kim Carter

HARRIS-GERSHON, DAVID. What do you buy the children of the terrorist who tried to kill your wife?; a memoir; [by] David Harris-Gershon 332 p. 2013 Pgw

1. Arab-Israeli conflict—1993—Peace 2. Dialogue 3. Historical literature 4. Memoirs 5. Terrorism victims' families

ISBN 1851689966; 9781851689965

SUMMARY: Author David Harris-Gershon presents a memoir "about the roots of terrorism and the nature of victimhood. After the author struggled for years with the emotional aftermath of his wife's traumatic injuries from the 2002 terrorist bombing of Hebrew University, this book is as much about trying to write about what happened as it is an attempt to understand the Israeli-Palestinian conflict. Harris-Gershon details the couple's personal story while juxtaposing it with his ongoing historical research." (Booklist)

REVIEW: *TLS* no5783 p24 Ja 31 2014 NICHOLAS BLINCOE

"What Do You Buy the Children of the Terrorist Who Tried to Kill Your Wife?" "In July 2002, Mohammad Odeh . . . planted a rucksack bomb in the cafeteria of the Hebrew University. The explosion . . . injured . . . the wife of [author] David Harris-Gershon. These memoirs start with Harris-

Gerson's struggle to accept that he has post-traumatic stress, though he was not the one blown up. The story ends in Silwan with his meeting Odeh's family. . . . It would be easy to ridicule him, as he spins a work of therapy into a quixotic peace mission, yet Harris-Gershon's instincts are sound. . . . Harris-Gershon's book succeeds, at last, because he shows how easy it is to talk."

HARRIS, BERT. Banking Lite; [by] Bert Harris 440 p. 2013 Createspace Independent Pub

1. Bank of America Corp. 2. Bankers 3. Banking industry 4. Community banks 5. Memoirs

ISBN 1492711853; 9781492711858

SUMMARY: In this book, author Bert Harris "offers an insider's look at the long-gone era of small-town banking while chronicling the shift to a less personal, more complex way of doing business. After launching his career with an entry-level position in a Colorado bank in the early 1960s, Harris soon moved on to become a National Bank Examiner. By his mid-20s, he was running his own bank in Greybull, Wyo. But the good times didn't last." (Kirkus Reviews)

REVIEW: *Kirkus Rev* v82 no3 p366 F 1 2014

REVIEW: *Kirkus Rev* v82 no5 p23 Mr 1 2014

"Banking Lite". "Anyone with an interest in banking will appreciate his observations on the minutiae of lending and borrowing, and many of his stories earn a chuckle, such as a practical joke involving two friends and a fake marriage. In fact, he manages to recall the names and key characteristics of seemingly everyone he's done business with over the years; either he has a remarkable memory or he kept voluminous diaries. Yet there's not a lot of personality on display. . . . Still, [Bert] Harris is a keen observer of human nature, and as a chronicle of small-town life and business, the book can be charming. . . . A thoughtful look at a vanishing corner of the banking industry."

HARRIS, ELIZABETH.tr. This is the garden. See Mozzi, G.

HARRIS, EVE. The Marrying of Chani Kaufman; [by] Eve Harris 384 p. 2014 Grove Press, Black Cat

1. Arranged marriage—Fiction 2. Love stories 3. Marriage—Fiction 4. Orthodox Jews 5. Rabbis—Fiction

ISBN 0802122736; 9780802122735

SUMMARY: This book by Eve Harris was longlisted for the Man Booker Prize. It is set in 2008 in London's Orthodox Jewish community, where "Chani Kaufman and Baruch Levy are getting married after a mere three dates. Opening with their wedding ceremony, the story loops back to the couple's first encounter, the matchmaker's involvement, the courtship, the parents' reactions (his mother doesn't approve) and the proposal." (Kirkus Reviews)

REVIEW: *Booklist* v110 no14 p48-9 Mr 15 2014 Barbara Bibel

"The Marrying of Chani Kaufman." "[Eve] Harris takes readers into the insular ultra- Orthodox Jewish community in London. It is 2008, and 19-year-old Chani Kaufman is about to marry Baruch, a young man whom she has seen only four times. . . . The book introduces readers to a little-known way of life and asks us to consider the role of faith and family in today's world. Anyone interested in relationships will enjoy this fascinating take on the subject; in fact, Jane Austen fans will find much that is familiar in the well-developed characters and the social conventions they must navigate."

REVIEW: *Kirkus Rev* v82 no6 p127 Mr 15 2014

REVIEW: *Libr J* v139 no7 p77 Ap 15 2014 Barbara Love

REVIEW: *TLS* no5766 p21 O 4 2013 CLIVE SINCLAIR

HARRIS, JOHANNA. Use Protection; An Employee's Guide to Advancement in the Workplace; [by] Johanna Harris 162 p. 2013 CreateSpace Independent Publishing Platform

1. Career development 2. Employment interviewing 3. Labor laws & legislation 4. Self-help materials 5. Success in business

ISBN 1492961841; 9781492961840

SUMMARY: In this book, "an attorney draws on her experience in labor law to guide employees through some of the working world's legal minefields." Topics include "how to read an offer letter, what is and is not covered by the Family Medical Leave Act, and how to file or respond to a harassment claim. [Johanna] Harris encourages employees to fully understand their rights and responsibilities under federal and state laws, as well as under their companies' policies." (Kirkus Reviews)

REVIEW: *Kirkus Rev* v82 no1 p330 Ja 1 2014

"Use Protection: An Employee's Guide to Advancement in the Workplace". "[Johanna] Harris takes a cleareyed but optimistic view of the corporate world while warning workers that a human resources department exists for the benefit of the company, not the employee. . . . . Although the book opens with a rather off-putting disclaimer . . . the tone for the rest of the book is far more matter-of-fact. The well-written narrative avoids most legal jargon and leaves readers feeling hopeful about the possibility of a corporate world staffed by well-informed, reasonable people who appropriately deal with consequences. A readable, highly informative guide to employment law and policy."

HARRIS, KAPLAN.ed. The selected letters of Robert Creeley. See The selected letters of Robert Creeley

HARRIS, MARK. Five Came Back; A Story of Hollywood and the Second World War; [by] Mark Harris 480 p. 2014 Penguin Group USA

1. Historical literature 2. Motion picture industry—California—Los Angeles—History 3. Motion picture producers & directors 4. Motion pictures—United States—History 5. World War, 1939-1945—Motion pictures and the war

ISBN 1594204306; 9781594204302

LC 2013-039983

SUMMARY: This book tells "the untold story of how Hollywood changed World War II, and how World War II changed Hollywood, through the prism of five film directors caught up in the war: John Ford, William Wyler, John Huston, Frank Capra, and George Stevens." (Publisher's note)

REVIEW: *Booklist* v110 no12 p10 F 15 2014 Bill Ott

REVIEW: *Commentary* v137 no5 p78-81 My 2014 TERRY TEACHOUT

REVIEW: *Film Q* v67 no3 p80-2 Spr 2014 DAVID STERRITT

REVIEW: *Kirkus Rev* v82 no1 p192 Ja 1 2014

"Five Came Back: A Story of Hollywood and the Second World War". "A comprehensive, cleareyed look at the careers of five legendary directors who put their Hollywood lives on freeze-frame while they went off to fight in the only ways they knew how. . . . Arranged chronologically (beginning in 1938), the text generally includes the doings of each of the five (John Ford, George Stevens, John Huston, William Wyler and Frank Capra) in each of the chapters, with [Mark] Harris artfully intercutting events from his principals' private as well as professional lives. Harris segues seamlessly to scenes all over the world. . . . As riveting and revealing as a film by an Oscar winner."

REVIEW: *Libr J* v138 no14 p87 S 1 2013

REVIEW: *Libr J* v139 no4 p92 Mr 1 2014 Richard Dickey

REVIEW: *N Y Times Book Rev* p30 Je 29 2014 Andrew O'Hehir

REVIEW: *Nation* v298 no26 p35-7 Je 23 2014 NOAH ISENBERG

REVIEW: *New Repub* v244 no26 p56-8 Ap 21 2014 David Thomson

"Five Came Back: A Story of Hollywood and the Second World War." "An exceptional movie book has just been published. It is called 'Five Came Back: A Story of Hollywood and the Second World War,'' by Mark Harris. It is a history of American documentary films made during World War II as told through five feature-film directors who felt compelled to serve a just war. . . . The five are John Ford, George Stevens, John Huston, William Wyler, and Frank Capra. I recommend the book for its narrative sweep, its revelation of character, and for the many ironies that attend the idea of 'documentary.'"

REVIEW: *New York Times* v163 no56429 pC4 Mr 3 2014 THOMAS DOHERTY

REVIEW: *New Yorker* v90 no4 p69-1 Mr 17 2014

REVIEW: *Publ Wkly* v261 no2 p64 Ja 13 2014

REVIEW: *Sight Sound* v24 no6 p104-5 Je 2014 David Thomson

HARRIS, MARK.ed. Running the Whale's Back. See Running the Whale's Back

HARRIS, MICAH. Heaven's War; [by] Micah Harris 118 2003 Image Comics

1. Adventure graphic novels 2. Crowley, Aleister, 1875-1947 3. Fantasy graphic novels 4. Graphic novels 5. Lewis, C. S. (Clive Staples), 1898-1963 6. Tolkien, J. R. R. (John Ronald Reuel), 1892-1973

ISBN 1-58240-330-9

SUMMARY: In this graphic novel, "J.R.R. Tolkien and C.S. Lewis are called upon by eccentric fellow fantasist Charles Williams to join him against occultist Aleister Crowley. Crowley seeks an entrance into the Heavenly realms with the intent of manipulating the angelic battles that shape human history and thus mold the world according to his will. Their conflict with Crowley will take this trio of authors . . . to the very edge of Heaven." (Publisher's note)In 1938, as the world moves toward global war, a secret angelic battle is waged in the heavenly realms to determine mankind's fate. The infamous Aleister Crowley plans to manipulate those angelic struggles and thus shape the world according to his will. Only The Inklings" - fantasy authors J.R.R. Tolkien, C.S. Lewis, and Charles Williams - oppose him. They must decipher a landscape of sacred geometry to intercept Crowley at the threshold of heaven. And, for one of the Inklings, the pursuit will reach outside time itself. The book includes annotations after the story, to explain historical and literary references.

REVIEW: *Booklist* v110 no13 p35-6 Mr 1 2014 Ray Olson

"Heaven's War." "Both [Charles] Williams and [Aleister] Crowley move mystically through time as they converge on a gateway to heaven that the Knights Templar spirited from the Holy Land to Rennes-le- Château, France. Readers of 'The Da Vinci Code' . . . and Crowley devotees will recognize that French village, and they, along with those who have never heard of it before, including the huge fandoms of Lewis and Tolkien, will probably greatly enjoy [Micah] Harris' outré concoction, which he helpfully annotates in a 14-page appendix. [Michael] Gaydos' black-and-white artwork, while crying out for color when its smaller details look like clumps of straw, is handsome and appropriate."

REVIEW: *Kirkus Rev* v80 no13 p1330 Jl 1 2012

REVIEW: *Libr J* v137 no20 p46-8 D 1 2012 Jessi Brown

HARRIS, ROBERT. An Officer and a Spy; [by] Robert Harris 448 p. 2014 Random House

1. FICTION—Espionage 2. FICTION—Historical 3. FICTION—Thrillers 4. Historical fiction 5. Intelligence officers—France—Fiction 6. Picquart, Georges

ISBN 0385349580; 9780385349581

LC 2013-044985

SUMMARY: This book, by Robert Harris, is set in "Paris in 1895. Alfred Dreyfus, a young Jewish officer, has just been convicted of treason, sentenced to life imprisonment at Devil's Island, and stripped of his rank. Among the witnesses to his humiliation is Georges Picquart, the . . . head of the counterespionage agency that 'proved' Dreyfus had passed secrets to the Germans. Picquart [soon] stumbles on information that leads him to suspect that there is still a spy at large in the French military." (Publisher's note)

REVIEW: *Booklist* v110 no7 p28 D 1 2013 Christine Tran

REVIEW: *Kirkus Rev* v81 no22 p198 N 15 2013

REVIEW: *Libr J* v139 no8 p42 My 1 2014 Sean Kennedy

REVIEW: *N Y Times Book Rev* p26 F 16 2014 GREGORY COWLES

REVIEW: *N Y Times Book Rev* p12 F 2 2014 LOUIS BEGLEY

"An Officer and a Spy." "The Dreyfus Affair . . . began on the morning of Oct. 15, 1894, with the arrest for high treason of Capt. Alfred Dreyfus. . . . Robert Harris, in his fine novel 'An Officer and a Spy,' lucidly retells the famous, bizarrely complicated and chilling story. . . . Drawing on the vast trove of books about the affair and some newly available materials, Harris tells a gripping tale. . . . Yet if the novel has a fault, it is precisely the decision to view the affair through [Col. Georges] Picquart's eyes. The focus is necessarily too narrow, failing to take in the historical background, without which some of what happened may seem more puzzling than it was."

REVIEW: *New Statesman* v142 no5183 p43 N 8 2013 Douglas Hurd

REVIEW: *New York Times* v163 no56402 pC1-4 F 4 2014 JANET MASLIN

"An Officer and a Spy." "Robert Harris's novel 'An Officer and a Spy' has a point of high drama when the main character, Col. Georges Picquart, is ushered into a room full of atypical characters: people who will actually listen to him. For the first three-quarters of this book Picquart has operated quietly, trying to piece together the facts of the infamous Dreyfus affair, which culminated in the conviction, humiliation and banishment of Alfred Dreyfus, a French officer convicted on impossibly scanty evidence of being a German spy. . . . Try as he might, Mr. Harris does not inject much verve into this string of discoveries. If anything, he invents seemingly endless ways of describing office meetings."

REVIEW: *Publ Wkly* v260 no47 p35 N 18 2013

REVIEW: *TLS* no5771 p21 N 8 2013 LESLEY CHAMBERLAIN

HARRIS, ROBIE H., 1940-. When lions roar; [by] Robie H. Harris 32 p. 2013 Orchard Books

1. Emotions—Fiction 2. Emotions—Juvenile fiction 3. Fear—Fiction 4. Fear—Juvenile fiction 5. Noise—Fiction 6. Noise—Juvenile fiction 7. Picture books for children

ISBN 0545112834; 9780545112833

LC 2012-005622

SUMMARY: In this children's picture book, by Robie H. Harris, illustrated by Chris Raschka, "a young child is frightened when lions roar, monkeys screech, and lightning cracks; but these are just a few of the scary things. This large storybook shows the many circumstances that are scary for him, one on each page, until he sits down, shuts his eyes, and tells the scary to go away. Then the quiet comes back so he opens his eyes, stands up, and finds that his world is much better." (Children's Literature)

REVIEW: *Booklist* v109 no22 p75 Ag 1 2013 Ann Kelley

REVIEW: *Horn Book Magazine* v89 no5 p74 S/O 2013 KATHLEEN T. HORNING

"When Lions Roar." "[Chris] Raschka's crayon and watercolor illustrations, using flat colors in orange, blue, green, and yellow, take the child through 'the scary' until he/she is able to find calming spaces. Raschka once again shows his remarkable skill at using line and color to illustrate abstract concepts for young children. At the same time, his pictures provide a narrative context that's not obvious in the text itself: when a mom and a dad take their timid child to the zoo, they are hit by a sudden thunderstorm."

REVIEW: *Kirkus Rev* v81 no15 p201 Ag 1 2013

REVIEW: *Publ Wkly* p39 Children's starred review annual 2013

REVIEW: *Publ Wkly* v260 no33 p64 Ag 19 2013

REVIEW: *SLJ* v59 no9 p122 S 2013 Maryann H. Owen

HARRIS, ROBIN. Not for turning; the life of Margaret Thatcher; [by] Robin Harris 512 p. 2013 Thomas Dunne Books/St. Martin's Press

1. BIOGRAPHY & AUTOBIOGRAPHY—Political 2. BIOGRAPHY & AUTOBIOGRAPHY—Presidents & Heads of State 3. Biographies 4. HISTORY—Europe—Great Britain 5. Prime ministers—Great Britain—Biography 6. Women prime ministers—Great Britain—Biography

ISBN 9781250047151 (hardback)

LC 2013-023171

SUMMARY: In this book, " Margaret Thatcher's "speechwriter, close adviser and the draftsman of both volumes of her autobiography . . . tells the . . . story of her life, from humble beginnings above her father's grocery store in Grantham, her early days as one of the first women in Westminster . . . and then on to her groundbreaking career as Prime Minister." (Publisher's note)

REVIEW: *Kirkus Rev* v81 no19 p14 O 1 2013

REVIEW: *New Yorker* v89 no23 p68-72 Ag 5 2013 John Lanchester

REVIEW: *TLS* no5749 p3-7 Je 7 2013 FERDINAND MOUNT"Not for Turning: The Life of Margaret Thatcher," "A Journey With Margaret Thatcher: Foreign Policy Under the Iron Lady" and "The Real Iron Lady: Working With Margaret Thatcher." "Even her most loyal of ghosts, Robin Harris, . . . accuses her of being a naive and hopeless picker of ministers. This is surely an unrealistic criticism. . . . In his absorbing accounts of the negotiations he himself was involved in . . . [Robin Renwick] he depicts a demanding but entirely rational boss. . . .The freshest part of his account is of the encouragement she gave F. W. de Klerk and the steady pressure she exerted for the release of Nelson Mandela. . . . [Gillian] Shephard's accounts of Mrs Thatcher's encounters with unfamous cogs in the political world supplement this picture on the domestic front."

HARRIS, ROSIE. Stolen Moments; [by] Rosie Harris 384 p. 2013 Severn House Pub Ltd

1. Chartism 2. Love stories 3. Mines & mineral resources—Fiction 4. Social classes—Fiction 5. Wales—Fiction

ISBN 0727883267; 9780727883261

SUMMARY: In this book, "when nanny Kate Stacey meets David, her employer Lady Helen Sherwood's brother, the couple falls instantly in love. But David's father wants him to marry a woman who will enhance his Welsh mining empire and . . . persuades Helen's husband to fire Kate. . . . But Kate is made of sterner stuff and travels to Wales, where she's heard that David has been called to quell a miners' uprising." (Booklist)

REVIEW: *Booklist* v110 no5 p36-7 N 1 2013 Pat Henshaw

"Stolen Moments." "Set in the early days of Wales' Chartist Movement, [Rosie] Harris' . . . latest finds that the path toward love between someone of the upper class and a servant isn't straightforward or smooth. When nanny Kate Stacey meets David, her employer Lady Helen Sherwood's brother, the couple falls instantly in love. But David's father wants him to marry a woman who will enhance his Welsh mining empire and already has a girl picked out for him. Harris adeptly mixes Welsh history with gentle romance while giving readers a graphic depiction of the disgraceful conditions of the time."

HARRIS, SAM, 1967-. Lying; [by] Sam Harris 105 p. 2013 Four Elephants Press

1. Deception 2. Ethics 3. Honesty 4. Philosophical literature 5. Truthfulness & falsehood

ISBN 9781940051000

LC 2013-947127

SUMMARY: In this book, "neuroscientist Sam Harris argues that we can radically simplify our lives and improve society by merely telling the truth in situations where others often lie. He focuses on 'white' lies--those lies we tell for the purpose of sparing people discomfort--for these are the lies that most often tempt us. And they tend to be the only lies that good people tell while imagining that they are being good in the process." (Publisher's note)

REVIEW: *Bookforum* v20 no5 p52 F/Mr 2014 CLANCY MARTIN

"Lying." "Sam Harris . . . argues the difficult case that it is always wrong to lie--whether you're deceiving others or yourself. Of course Harris is right some of the time. . . .But Harris oversimplifies both the act and the morality of lying. . . . Real life requires more nuance about truthfulness and lying than you find in Harris's all-or-nothing approach. . . . One thing I like about Harris's book is his observation that there's something degrading about lying, both for the liar and his intended dupe."

HARRIS, TODD.il. The Hero's Guide to Being an Outlaw. See Healy, C.

HARRIS, WILLIAM. Lebanon; a history, 600-2011; [by] William Harris xxv, 360 p. 2012 Oxford University Press

1. Christians—Lebanon 2. Historical literature 3. Islam & politics—Lebanon 4. Lebanon—Politics & government 5. Sectarian conflict—History

ISBN 9780195181111 (hardcover : alk. paper); 9780195181128 (pbk. : alk. paper)
LC 2011-042934

SUMMARY: In this book, author "William Harris narrates the history of the sectarian communities of Mount Lebanon and its vicinity. . . . Harris contends that Lebanon has not found a new equilibrium and has not transcended its sects. In the early twenty-first century there is an uneasy duality: Shia have largely recovered the weight they possessed in the sixteenth century, but Christians, Sunnis, and Druze are two-thirds of the country." (Publisher's note)

REVIEW: *Choice* v50 no8 p1502 Ap 2013 N. E. Bou-Nacklie

REVIEW: *Middle East J* v67 no4 p648-9 Aut 2013 Peter Sluglett

"Lebanon: A History, 600-2011." "This book is a welcome edition to the historiography of the modern Middle East. It is based mostly on secondary sources, although the author has made intelligent use of 20th century editions of Arabic chronicles for all periods in Lebanese history. . . . The story is compelling, and for the most part he tells it well. It is an impressive achievement in a number of ways. . . . Almost inevitably, the book has defects, but they are not such as to detract from the book's overall standing."

REVIEW: *TLS* no5763 p24 S 13 2013 T. J. GORTON

"Lebanon: A History, 600-2011" and "Lebanon: After the Cedar Revolution." "Two new books provide timely historical context and up-to-date analysis of the endemic and external troubles afflicting the tiny state. . . . [William] Harris's book shows no signs of bias and is certainly not superficial. Harris displays an intimate knowledge of Arabic. . . . This book will provide scholars with a useful and overdue reference: but it is a pity that, like too many books of academic history, it is written in a pedestrian prose that does not do justice to Lebanon's colourful drama. . . . 'Lebanon: After the Cedar Revolution' is a collection of essays focusing on the country before and since the assassination in 2005 of the former Prime Minister, Rafiq Hariri, and several dozen others. . . . Overall, there is a deft balance between scholarly discourse and the personal observation of an insider."

HARRISON, CAROL. The art of listening in the early church; [by] Carol Harrison x, 302 p. 2013 Oxford University Press

1. Christian education—History—Early church, ca. 30-600 2. Church history—Primitive and early church, ca. 30-600 3. Historical literature 4. Listening—Religious aspects—Christianity 5. Oral communication—Religious aspects—Christianity 6. Prayer—Christianity—History—Early church, ca. 30-600 7. Preaching—History—Early church, ca. 30-600

ISBN 0199641439 (hardcover); 9780199641437 (hardcover)
LC 2012-277847

SUMMARY: In this book, Carol Harrison argues "that what illiterate early Christians heard both formed their minds and souls and, above all, enabled them to become 'literate' listeners; able not only to grasp the rule of faith but also tacitly to follow the infinite variations on it which were played out in early Christian teaching, exegesis and worship." (Publisher's note)

REVIEW: *Choice* v51 no9 p1610-1 My 2014 A. W. Klink

"The Art of Listening in the Early Church". "In this important contribution to patristics, [Carol] Harrison . . . explores how practices of listening and speaking shaped Christianity's transmission to largely illiterate audiences in the fourth and fifth centuries. It employs a sophisticated interdisciplinary framework to understand how preachers and hearers understood the importance of listening for Christian formation in both cultural and theological contexts. . . . Students of early Christian history and theology will find this book worthwhile."

HARRISON, GUY P. Think; why you should question everything; [by] Guy P. Harrison 300 p. 2013 Prometheus Books

1. Critical thinking—Miscellanea 2. PHILOSOPHY—Logic 3. Reasoning—Miscellanea 4. SCIENCE—Philosophy & Social Aspects 5. Science—Methodology 6. Skepticism—Miscellanea

ISBN 1616148071; 9781616148072 (pbk.)
LC 2013-024867

SUMMARY: Author Guy P. Harrison presents an "approach to science, skepticism, and critical thinking [designed to] enlighten and inspire readers of all ages. [He] shows you how to better navigate through the maze of biases and traps that are standard features of every human brain. Harrison shows how it's in everyone's best interest to question everything. He brands skepticism as a constructive and optimistic attitude." (Publisher's note)

REVIEW: *Horn Book Magazine* v90 no1 p111-2 Ja/F 2014 BART HELMESS

"Thomas Jefferson: Life, Liberty and the Pursuit of Everything." "On the cover of this striking picture book biography, Jefferson poses proudly in the foreground with his celebrated home standing on a hill in the distance. . . . A series of spreads, with [Maira] Kalman's familiar primitivist rendering and chromatic brilliance, details Jefferson's work as collector, architect, horticulturalist, and musician. . . . Kalman . . . addresses all of this with a colloquial, occasionally arch, and whimsical narrative, heavy with historical import and dotted with trivia. . . . The vibrant imagery, frank content, and disarming language combine in a nuanced portrait that respects its subject and its audience in equal measure."

REVIEW: *Kirkus Rev* v81 no22 p105 N 15 2013

REVIEW: *Libr J* v138 no18 p107 N 1 2013 Dale Farris

REVIEW: *N Y Times Book Rev* p14 Ja 12 2014 HAROLD HOLZER

REVIEW: *Publ Wkly* v260 no33 p54 Ag 19 2013

REVIEW: *Publ Wkly* v260 no43 p63 O 28 2013

REVIEW: *SLJ* v60 no1 p114 Ja 2014 Jody Kopple

HARRISON, KIM. The Undead Pool; [by] Kim Harrison 432 p. 2014 HarperCollins

1. Bounty hunters—Fiction 2. Demonology 3. Fantasy fiction 4. Magic—Fiction 5. Vampires—Fiction

ISBN 0061957933; 9780061957932

SUMMARY: In this book, "witch and day-walking demon Rachel Morgan has managed to save the demonic ever-after from shrinking, but at a high cost. Now, strange magic is attacking Cincinnati and the Hollows, causing spells to backfire or go horribly wrong, and the truce between the Inderlander and human races is shattering. Rachel must stop this dark necromancy before an all-out supernatural war breaks out." (Publisher's note)

REVIEW: *Kirkus Rev* v81 no24 p302 D 15 2013

"The Undead Pool". "After so many series installments infused with daywalking demon Rachel Morgan's self-doubt, neuroses and rash behavior, it's nice to see her finally achieve some emotional maturity, expand her circle of trust and seize some happiness for a change. . . . . Fans will relish the moment and will also dig into the rest of the plot, which features Harrison's usual (and usually enjoyable) Evil Conspiracy and labyrinthine plot twists, Rachel rushing to save the day. . . . A great ride in and of itself, rather than simply a buildup to the finale, which is sure to be whiz-bang."

REVIEW: *Libr J* v138 no16 p56 O 1 2013 Barbara Hoffert

REVIEW: *Libr J* v139 no3 p76 F 15 2014 Megan M. McArdle

REVIEW: *Publ Wkly* v261 no1 p38 Ja 6 2014

HARRISON, NANCY. Appraising art. See Appraising art

HARRISON, S. J.ed. Louis MacNeice. See Louis MacNeice

HARRISON, THEA. Falling Light; [by] Thea Harrison 304 p. 2014 Berkley Pub Group

1. Devil—Fiction 2. Fantasy fiction 3. Good & evil—Fiction 4. Love stories 5. Soul mates

ISBN 0425255107; 9780425255100

SUMMARY: In this book, "Michael, a warrior who has fought the renegade Deceiver over time and space, and Mary, a healer who has suffered much from the Deceiver's onslaughts, were once "creatures of power and fire." Now the reincarnated soulmates continue the Good vs. Evil battle [author Thea] Harrison launched in 'Rising Darkness'." (Publishers Weekly)

REVIEW: *Kirkus Rev* v82 no2 p92 Ja 15 2014

"Falling Light". "[Thea] Harrison builds a creative, fascinating urban fantasy world that looks a lot like ours but with one troubling supervillain who has slashed and burned his way through human history. In this second of two installments, Michael and Mary just might be able to stop the demonic Deceiver once and for all, with help from the enigmatic Astra, some Native American wisdom and heroes, and some ancient and powerful allies. Beautifully written, boldly imaginative, action-packed and captivating."

REVIEW: *Publ Wkly* v260 no52 p38-9 D 23 2013

HART, CARL. High Price; A Neuroscientist's Journey of Self-discovery That Challenges Everything You Know About Drugs and Society; [by] Carl Hart 352 p. 2013 HarperCollins

ISBN 0062015885; 9780062015884

SUMMARY: In this book, "combining memoir, popular science, and public policy" author Carl Hart "lambasts current drug laws as draconian and repressive, arguing that they're based more on assumptions about race and class than on a real understanding of the physiological and societal effects of drugs. . . . Central to his work is the idea that addiction is actually a combination of physiological and social factors, and the use of drugs does not itself lead to violence and crime." (Publishers Weekly)

REVIEW: *Kirkus Rev* v81 no9 p50 My 1 2013

REVIEW: *Libr J* v138 no9 p93 My 15 2013 Dale Farris

REVIEW: *Publ Wkly* v260 no16 p48-9 Ap 22 2013

REVIEW: *Sci Am* v308 no6 p88 Je 2013 Anna Kuchment

"High Price: A Neuroscientist's Journey of Self-Discovery That Challenges Everything You Know About Drugs and Society." "[Carl] Hart . . . uses a mix of personal narrative and scientific research to argue for the decriminalization of drugs. When crack cocaine spread through his predominately poor, black Miami neighborhood in the 1980s, Hart blamed the drug for increases in crime and gun violence. But later research by Hart and others showed that crack was not particularly addictive, nor did it make users more impulsive or violent, leading him to a revelation: although drugs can exacerbate social problems, they are rarely the cause. Hart's account of rising from the projects to the ivory tower is as poignant as his call to change the way society thinks about race, drugs and poverty."

HART, D. G. Calvinism; a history; [by] D. G. Hart 376 p. 2013 Yale University Press

1. Calvinism—History 2. Church history 3. HISTORY—World 4. Historical literature 5. RELIGION—Christianity—Calvinist 6. RELIGION—History

ISBN 9780300148794 (hardback)

LC 2013-003010

SUMMARY: Written by D. G. Hart, "This briskly told history of Reformed Protestantism takes these churches through their entire 500-year history--from sixteenth-century Zurich and Geneva to modern locations as far flung as Seoul and São Paulo. D. G. Hart explores specifically the social and political developments that enabled Calvinism to establish a global presence." (Publisher's note)

REVIEW: *Choice* v51 no4 p655 D 2013 J. W. McCormack

REVIEW: *Christ Century* v131 no8 p36-7 Ap 16 2014 James Bratt

REVIEW: *Christ Today* v57 no5 p74 Je 2013

REVIEW: *TLS* no5776 p10 D 13 2013 PETER MAR-

SHALL
"Calvinism: A History." "Calvin himself is a relatively minor player in Darryl Hart's 'Calvinism: A history,' which crosses five centuries and as many continents. . . . Much of the interest of this expansive and informative account comes from observing how a religious ethos originating in the city-states of Switzerland has both nurtured and transcended an intense denominationalism in settings across the globe. . . . For anyone fascinated by the institutional history of Calvinist churches. Hart is a mine of information and analysis. . . . His concern with disentangling the knots of modem American Calvinism, meanwhile, causes him to leave some European--and particularly British--threads hanging."

HART, DAVID BENTLEY. The experience of God; being, consciousness, bliss; [by] David Bentley Hart 376 p. 2013 Yale University Press
1. Experience (Religion) 2. God 3. God (Christianity) 4. God (Islam) 5. God (Judaism) 6. Religious literature
ISBN 9780300166842 (cloth : alk. paper)
LC 2013-007118

SUMMARY: In this book, "David Bentley Hart pursues a clarification of how the word 'God' functions in the world's great theistic faiths. . . . Hart explores how these . . . traditions treat humanity's knowledge of the divine mysteries. Constructing his argument around three principal metaphysical 'moments' . . . the author demonstrates an essential continuity between our fundamental experience of reality and the ultimate reality to which that experience inevitably points." (Publisher's note)

REVIEW: *Choice* v51 no7 p1232 Mr 2014 J. P. Blosser

REVIEW: *Commonweal* v141 no3 p23-5 F 7 2014 Michael Robbins

"The Experience of God: Being, Consciousness, Bliss". "David Bentley Hart's brilliant, frustrating new book . . . is . . . wonderfully ecumenical: he draws with ease on the Upanishads, Sufi poetry, Islamic philosophy, and the Church Fathers. . . . Hart, often a subtle and eloquent writer, has come down with Harold Bloom Syndrome, whose sufferers reiterate perfectly good themes until they lose their rhetorical force. . . . These faults, however, do not sink 'The Experience of God.' Hart is a phenomenally gifted thinker who recalls believers of all faiths to the best of their traditions, challenges unbelievers to examine their own metaphysical presuppositions, and does these with tremendous gusto."

REVIEW: *Harper's Magazine* v327 no1960 p81-3 S 2013 Jane Smiley

REVIEW: *Natl Rev* v65 no20 p60-1 O 28 2013 SARAH RUDEN

"The Experience of God: Being, Consciousness, Bliss." "David Bentley Hart is probably the greatest living scholarly defender of religious thought. in three magisterial sections--on being, consciousness, and bliss--Hart insists on the weaknesses of claims that these phenomena can be fully accounted for through materialistic or deistic theories, a fundamental conclusion of the latter being that God, though the creator and also the source of human reason, does not either inhere or intervene in what he created. the book makes, in general, a very solid case against both prominent atheists' logical stumbling and others' sloppy attempts to split the difference between religion and no-religion. But it is disappointing that, even for me . . . this new book is hard going."

REVIEW: *New Yorker* v90 no1 p107-1 F 17 2014

REVIEW: *TLS* no5816 p26 S 19 2014 ANDREW DAVISON

HART, KIMBERLY. And then we work for God; rural Sunni Islam in western Turkey; [by] Kimberly Hart 304 p. 2013 Stanford University Press
1. Islam—Turkey—Customs and practices 2. Islam and culture—Turkey 3. Rural population—Turkey 4. Social science literature
ISBN 9780804783309 (cloth: alk. paper);
9780804786607 (pbk.: alk. paper)
LC 2013-013864

SUMMARY: "Turkey's contemporary struggles with Islam are often interpreted as a conflict between religion and secularism played out most obviously in the split between rural and urban populations." Written by Kimberly Hart, "Exploring religious expression in two villages, this book considers rural spiritual practices and describes a living, evolving Sunni Islam, influenced and transformed by local and national sources of religious orthodoxy." (Publisher's note)

REVIEW: *Choice* v51 no4 p686 D 2013 A. Rassam

REVIEW: *Middle East J* v68 no3 p481-3 Summ 2014 Banu Eligür

"And Then We Work for God: Rural Sunni Islam in Western Turkey." "In 'And Then We Work for God,' Kimberly Hart examines how Turkish villagers interpret and practice Sunni Islam in their daily lives. . . . One of the major problems of the book is its descriptive nature. The book does not analyze the reasons Yeniyurt and Kayalarca villagers interpret Sunni Islam in different ways and when this divergence started. . . . Yet, most problematic are crucial mistakes regarding basic facts of Turkish history and politics. . . . Hart also makes ahistorical and sweeping generalizations about Turkish history without providing any evidence or a reference. . . . Regrettably, significant deficiencies in the book's analysis and research impede it from making a valuable contribution."

HART, RODERICK P. Political tone; how leaders talk and why; [by] Roderick P. Hart 293 p. 2013 University of Chicago Press
1. Bush, George W. (George Walker), 1946- 2. Clinton, Bill, 1946- 3. Obama, Barack, 1961- 4. Palin, Sarah, 1964- 5. Political oratory 6. Political oratory—United States 7. Political science literature 8. Politicians—Language 9. Rhetoric—Political aspects 10. United States—Politics & government
ISBN 9780226023014 (cloth : alkaline paper);
9780226023151 (paperback : alkaline paper)
LC 2012-048344

SUMMARY: In this book, "Roderick P. Hart, Jay P. Childers, and Colene J. Lind analyze a range of texts--from speeches and debates to advertising and print and broadcast campaign coverage--using a sophisticated computer program . . . Beginning with a look at how societal forces like diversity and modernity manifest themselves as political tones . . . , the authors proceed to consider how individual leaders have used tone to convey their messages." (Publisher's note)

REVIEW: *Choice* v51 no4 p626 D 2013 P. J. Gehrke

"Political Tone: How Leaders Talk and Why." "[Authors Roderick P.] Hart . . . , [Jay P.] Childers . . . , and [Colene J.] Lind . . . analyzed approximately 30,000 texts (1948-2008) from politicians, journalists, and citizens, focusing on discourse about presidents and presidential elections. . . . In four chapters, the authors provide both diachronic analysis of changes in certain political tones. . . . In the subsequent four chapters, they study specific politicians: Bill Clinton, George W. Bush, Barack Obama, and Sarah Palin. The analysis of word choice (without paralanguage or kinesics) limits the dimensions of tone the book addresses. . . . Hand-wringing about methodology . . . is . . . excessive. . . . But when the authors move . . . to . . . specific texts, their analysis shines."

HARTMAN, BRUCE. The Rules of Dreaming; [by] Bruce Hartman 298 p. 2013 Swallow Tail Press

1. Detective & mystery stories 2. Literature—Philosophy 3. Medical fiction 4. Mentally ill—Fiction 5. Psychiatrists—Fiction

ISBN 0988918102; 9780988918108

SUMMARY: This book follows "Dr. Ned Hoffmann, a new psychiatrist at a mental institution in a small town . . . [who] struggles with demanding bosses and baffling patients, including the schizophrenic grown children of an opera singer who died under suspicious circumstances. When one of Dr. Hoffmann's recent patients, Nicole, an anxious literature grad student, finally finds a topic for her dissertation, she discovers that life in her town is beginning to mirror art—in some disconcerting ways." (Kirkus Reviews)

REVIEW: *Kirkus Rev* v81 no13 p119 Jl 1 2013

REVIEW: *Kirkus Rev* p22-4 D 15 2013 supplemet best books 2013

"The Rules of Dreaming". "In this intricately plotted novel, [Bruce] Hartman . . . spins the familiar trappings of gothic mystery together with a fresh postmodern sensibility, producing a story that's as rich and satisfying as it is difficult to categorize. . . . Hartman impressively turns literary theory into something sexy and menacing, weaving the real-life works of writer E.T.A. Hoffmann and composers Robert Schumann and Jacques Offenbach, among others, into his characters' increasingly muddled lives. . . . For the most part, Hartman brings a light touch to potentially weighty material. Though the novel's philosophical twists and turns are fascinating, the story also succeeds as an old-fashioned whodunit, and the writing is full of descriptive gems."

HARTMAN, STEVEN.tr. Sleet. See Dagerman, S.

HARTNETT, SONYA, 1968-. The children of the King; [by] Sonya Hartnett 265 p. 2012 Penguin Books (Australia)

1. Friendship—Fiction 2. Great Britain—History—Richard III, 1483-1485 3. Historical fiction 4. World War, 1939-1945—Evacuation of civilians—Great Britain 5. World War, 1939-1945—Great Britain—Fiction

ISBN 0763667358; 9780670076130; 9780763667351

LC 2013-414845

SUMMARY: This book, by Sonya Hartnett, "takes place in England during World War II. . . . Siblings Cecily and Jeremy, along with their mother Heloise, are sent to the northern countryside to live with Heloise's brother, Peregrine Lockwood, in mysterious Heron Hall. . . . The family winds up taking in May Bright, a 10-year-old refugee from London. The two girls become fast friends and . . . come across two boys in the ruins of a nearby castle." (School Library Journal)

REVIEW: *Booklist* v110 no9/10 p96 Ja 1 2014 Carolyn Phelan

REVIEW: *Bull Cent Child Books* v67 no7 p347-8 Mr 2014 Deborah Stevenson

"With skilled layering . . . . [Sonya] Hartnett embraces this scenario in a way that its fans will appreciate but also subtly tweaks it, making classic pleasures and contemporary judgment strangely comfortable partners. Her writing is superb, carrying echoes of [Jane] Austen but also touched with a perceptive yet incisive wit that recalls Muriel Spark, and the book stealthily alludes to the Lockwoods' considerable privilege and shades its dismantling. . . . Together, it's an atmospheric concoction, haunted in the nicest possible ways, and readable at various levels of sophistication. . . . Fans of classic children's literature will delight in seeing a familiar plot so richly interpreted, and sharp readers will appreciate the provocative new resonance under the old story."

REVIEW: *Horn Book Magazine* v90 no2 p120 Mr/Ap 2014 RUSSELL PERRY

"The Children of the King." "As always, [Sonya] Hartnett's gift for language deftly conveys both the sublime and the mundane in life. . . . Hartnett grounds the relatively minor fantasy presence in the book with a heartfelt examination of the pain and hardships, endured by civilians in wartime. Cecily is a naive, spoiled, but well-intentioned heroine, effectively contrasted by the quietly independent and mature May and impetuous, brave Jeremy. Over the course of the story, Hartnett's characters waver between feelings of helplessness, anger, and fear; ultimately, they find the necessary resolve to carry on."

REVIEW: *Kirkus Rev* v82 no2 p126 Ja 15 2014

"The Children of the King". "Through her likable, vividly wrought characters, [Sonya] Hartnett respectfully captures the depth and ferocity of childhood. The poetic descriptions of the girls' rural wanderings are to be savored like the best tea and biscuits, but the masterful lyricism never slows the suspenseful story of Cecily and May's discovery of two 'horrid boys' in velvet jackets, hiding among nearby castle ruins…or the rising tension between Jeremy and his mother as he battles his sense of helplessness as others fight the war. Uncle Peregrine tells a 450-year-old story whose themes are curiously relevant to World War II England…perhaps even to the be-velveted boys-in-hiding. Mystery and history dance a mesmerizing waltz in this poignant, thoroughly entertaining novel."

REVIEW: *SLJ* v60 no3 p140 Mr 2014 Jesten Ray

REVIEW: *Voice of Youth Advocates* v37 no1 p66 Ap 2014 Jen McIntosh

HARUN, ADRIANNE. A man came out of a door in the mountain; [by] Adrianne Harun 272 p. 2014 Penguin Books

1. FICTION—Fairy Tales, Folk Tales, Legends & Mythology 2. FICTION—Literary 3. Missing persons—Fiction 4. Revenge—Fiction 5. Teenagers—Fiction

ISBN 0670786101; 9780670786107 (pbk.)

LC 2013-035043

SUMMARY: In this book, by Adrianne Harun, "girls, mostly Native, are vanishing from the sides of a notorious highway in the isolated Pacific Northwest. Leo Kreutzer and his friends are barely touched by these disappearances—until a series of enigmatic strangers arrive in their remote mountain town, beguiling and bewitching them." (Publisher's note)

REVIEW: *Booklist* v110 no11 p35 F 1 2014 Sarah Hunter

REVIEW: *Kirkus Rev* v82 no2 p234 Ja 15 2014

"A Man Came Out of a Door in the Mountain". "All of the friends are in late adolescence and trying to make sense of life in their remote logging town. And then a number of strangers appear, bringing mystery and allure to their lives: Kevin Seven does dazzling card tricks and starts to mentor Ursie, who'd never before even shuffled a deck, while fragile and self-possessed Hana Swann, with preternaturally white skin, calmly tries to convince Bryan of the rationality of getting revenge on Gerald Flacker, a local drug dealer seemingly in league with the devil. Through a complex narrative structure, [Adrianne] Harun manages to invest all of her action—slow as it sometimes is—with an aura of myth and folk legend that raises it above the lurid and sensational."

REVIEW: *Libr J* v139 no9 p38 My 15 2014 Deb West

REVIEW: *N Y Times Book Rev* p29 Ap 6 2014 CLAIRE VAYE WATKINS

REVIEW: *Publ Wkly* v260 no48 p28 N 25 2013

HARVEY, ANNE.ed. Like Sorrow or a Tune. See Farjeon, E.

HARVEY, CHESTER.il. Mastering iron. See Knowles, A. K.

HARVEY, DOUG. They called me god; the best umpire who ever lived; [by] Doug Harvey 288 p. 2014 Gallery Books

1. Baseball players—Family relationships 2. Baseball teams 3. Baseball umpires—United States—Biography 4. Major League Baseball (Organization) 5. Memoirs
ISBN 1476748780 (); 9781476748788 (hardback)
LC 2013-048063

SUMMARY: This memoir, by baseball umpire Doug Harvey, "takes the reader behind the plate for some of baseball's most memorable moments, including Roberto Clemente's three thousandth and final hit, the . . . three-and-two pinch-hit home run by Kirk Gibson in the '88 World Series, . . . [and] the close-fought '68 World Series, when Doug called St. Louis Cardinal Lou Brock out at home plate." (Publisher's note)

REVIEW: *Kirkus Rev* v82 no4 p28 F 15 2014

"They Called Me God: The Best Umpire Who Ever Lived". "A breezy and sometimes-grumpy memoir about his years in major league baseball. There is no shortage of self-regard (see the subtitle), and the author repeatedly reminds readers that he was the best. Later in his text, he even repeats, virtually verbatim, a story he'd told earlier about being named the second-greatest umpire of all time. In most other ways, the text is yawningly conventional. . . . A soufflé of anecdote, revenge served cold and self-promotion."

HARVEY, KAREN. The little republic; masculinity and domestic authority in eighteenth-century Britain; [by] Karen Harvey xii, 218 p. 2012 Oxford University Press

1. Families 2. Great Britain—Social life & customs—18th century 3. Historical literature 4. Households—Great Britain—History—18th century 5. Masculinity—History 6. Men—Conduct of life—History—18th century 7. Men—Great Britain 8. Men—Great Britain—Identity—History—18th century 9. Men—Great Britain—Social life and customs—18th century
ISBN 0199533849 (hbk.); 9780199533848 (hbk.)
LC 2012-406313

SUMMARY: In this book, "Karen Harvey explores how [18th century British] men represented and legitimized their domestic activities. She considers the relationship between discourses of masculinity and domesticity, and whether there was a particularly manly attitude to the domestic. In doing so, Harvey suggests that . . . the 'house' foregrounds a different domestic culture, one in which men and masculinity were central." (Publisher's note)

REVIEW: *Am Hist Rev* v118 no4 p1247-9 O 2013 James Rosenheim

"Man's Estate: Landed Gentry Masculinities, c. 1660-c. 1900" and "The Little Republic: Masculinity and Domestic Authority in Eighteenth-Century Britain." "These two volumes add significantly to a growing literature on the place of men and the nature of masculinity in the context of the seventeenth-, eighteenth-, and nineteenth-century English family and home. Drawing on both the strengths and the gaps left by recent studies of masculinity, gender relations, the household, and the world beyond the home (a literature that each book in its way parses, praises, and provides with critique), Karen Harvey and the team of Henry French and Mark Rothery ambitiously undertake to bring clarity to what is a still rather muddled history of men and manhood. They succeed admirably."

REVIEW: *Choice* v50 no6 p1146 F 2013 J. Sainsbury

REVIEW: *Engl Hist Rev* v128 no535 p1590-1 D 2013 Faramerz Dabhoiwala

REVIEW: *History* v98 no330 p286-90 Ap 2013 Anthony Fletcher

HARVEY, ROSALIND.tr. Quesadillas. See Quesadillas

HARWARD, BRIAN M. Presidential campaigns. See Shea, D. M.

HARWOOD, RUSSELL. China's new socialist countryside; modernity arrives in the Nu River Valley; [by] Russell Harwood 230 p. 2013 University of Washington Press

1. Rural development—China—Nujiang Lisuzu Zizhizhou 2. Rural population—China—Nujiang Lisuzu Zizhizhou 3. Social science literature
ISBN 9780295993256 (hb: alk. paper); 9780295993386 (pb: alk. paper)
LC 2013-027329

SUMMARY: "This case study examines the impact of economic development on ethnic minority people living along the upper-middle reaches of the Nu (Salween) River in Yunnan." It "explores how compulsory education, conservation programs, migration for work, and the expansion of social and economic infrastructure are not only transforming livelihoods, but also intensifying the Chinese Party-state's capacity to integrate ethnic minorities into its political fabric and the national industrial economy." (Publisher's note)

REVIEW: *Choice* v51 no8 p1466-7 Ap 2014 A. Y. Lee

"China's New Socialist Countryside: Modernity Arrives in the Nu River Valley". "This book is an ethnographic study of ethnic minorities in Gongshan County along the Nu River Valley in Yunnan Province, China, including the Lisu, Nu, Dulong, and Tibetan peoples. The study focuses on the consequences of economic and educational intervention programs imposed on local communities by the party-state government. . . . More importantly, [Russell] Harwood brings up questions that are applicable to situations beyond the communities in Gongshan, such as conservation of minority cultures and livelihoods against the background of globalization, as well as structured inequalities in the process of urbanization and market-oriented economic development."

HASKELL, FRANCIS, 1928-2000. The king's pictures; the formation and dispersal of the collections of King Charles I and his Courtiers; [by] Francis Haskell 260 p. 2013 Yale University Press

1. Art history 2. Art literature 3. Charles I, King of England, 1600-1649 4. Historical literature 5. Private art collections

ISBN 9780300190120 (cl : alk. paper)

LC 2013-944778

SUMMARY: In this book, author Francis Haskell notes that "in the first half of the 17th century, masterpieces by Titian, Raphael, and Leonardo, among others, were the objects of fervent pursuit by art connoisseurs. . . . Haskell traces the fate of collections extracted from Italy, Spain, and France by King Charles I and his circle, which, after a brief stay in Britain, were largely dispersed after the Civil War to princely galleries across the Continent." (Publisher's note)

REVIEW: *Apollo: The International Magazine for Collectors* v179 no616 p90-1 Ja 2014 Robert O'Byrne

"The King's Pictures: The Formation and Dispersal of the Collections of Charles I and His Courtiers". "One of the pleasures of 'The King's Pictures' is precisely the impression it conveys of listening to someone talk with articulate enthusiasm (which is certainly not always the case in the lecture hall). A great deal of information and opinion is conveyed with seeming effortlessness, and one's attention is held from start to finish. [Karen] Serres' own interventions, primarily in the form of footnotes on the latest research, are equally deft. In addition, the book is fulsomely illustrated, making it a pleasure to view as well as read."

REVIEW: *Burlington Mag* v156 no1334 p319 My 2014 DESMOND SHAWE-TAYLOR

REVIEW: *Choice* v51 no7 p1202 Mr 2014 C. A. Hanson

REVIEW: *N Y Rev Books* v61 no2 p12-3 F 6 2014 Charles Hope

"The King's Pictures: The Formation and Dispersal of the Collections of Charles I and His Courtiers." "Although [Francis] Haskell apparently continued to assemble material about the subject after 1995, it seems evident that be would not have published his lectures without additional research, which would have extended the scope of the book. . . . But even though a great deal of new material has come to light since Haskell's death, to which reference has been added in the notes, the book was certainly worth publishing, since it is such a lively and intelligent survey of the subject."

HASKELL, MOLLY. My brother my sister; story of a transformation; [by] Molly Haskell 224 p. 2013 Viking

1. Families of transgender people 2. Male-to-female transsexuals 3. Memoirs 4. Older transsexuals 5. Sex change—United States—Case studies 6. Transsexuals—Family relationships 7. Transsexuals—United States—Biography

ISBN 9780670025527

LC 2013-016961

SUMMARY: Author Molly "Haskell's 'My Brother My Sister' gracefully explores a delicate subject, this time from the perspective of a family member. Haskell chronicles her brother Chevey's transformation through a series of psychological evaluations, grueling surgeries, drug regimens, and comportment and fashion lessons as he becomes Ellen. Despite Haskell's liberal views on gender roles, she was dumbfounded by her brother's decision." (Publisher's note)

REVIEW: *Booklist* v109 no22 p12-3 Ag 1 2013 Donna Chavez

REVIEW: *Kirkus Rev* v81 no16 p51 Ag 15 2013

"My Brother My Sister: Story of a Transformation." "Feminist film critic [Molly] Haskell . . . delves into the dramatic, deeply personal tale of her brother's transformation, in his early 60s, from a man into a woman. . . . With candor and sly humor, the author questions her ideas about womanhood and considers the relationship between gender and identity as they relate to Ellen, herself, and myriad films and other aspects of popular culture. At the heart of this intelligent memoir lies the process through which Ellen's transsexualism became, then faded from being, the primary fact of the siblings' respective lives. A discerning, vital memoir."

REVIEW: *Publ Wkly* v260 no26 p79 Jl 1 2013

HASSAN, ROBERT. The age of distraction; reading, writing, and politics in a high-speed networked economy; [by] Robert Hassan xv, 221 p. 2012 Transaction Publishers

1. Distraction (Psychology)—Social aspects 2. Information technology—Social aspects 3. Social science literature 4. Technology & civilization 5. Time—Sociological aspects

ISBN 9781412843065 (hardcover)

LC 2011-012445

SUMMARY: This book, by Robert Hassan, examines "the trajectory of modernity into late-modernity, and illustrate how the arc of progress has transformed. New modes of time, technology, and reading and writing are helping create a faster world where we know less about more—and forget what we know evermore quickly." (Publisher's note)

REVIEW: *Contemp Sociol* v43 no1 p133-4 Ja 2014

"The Age of Distraction: Reading, Writing, and Politics in a High-Speed Networked Economy". "Many interesting books are created these days in Australia, and this is another one. . . . [Robert] Hassan is sounding as much a eulogy for a receding past as he is aiming toward an improved future. . . . The book is chock full of literary, philosophical, and historical references, almost becoming too much of a very good thing, yet the point is well made. . . . a valuable book if one frets about the future of political and literate culture."

HASSETT, ANN. Come back, Ben; 32 p. 2013 Holiday House

1. Balloons 2. Boys—Fiction 3. Imaginary voyages 4. Moon—Juvenile literature 5. Space travelers

ISBN 0823425991; 9780823425990 (hardcover)

LC 2011-049310

SUMMARY: In this children's picture book, "happy-go-lucky Ben has a balloon that lifts him up and off the page. With a smile on her face, Ben's sister says, 'Bye, Ben'. . . . As Ben begins his ascent, the window bids him "Come back, Ben," as do the bees, the trees . . . and many more 'friends.' . . . When the child reaches the Moon, he cleverly arranges his descent and down he comes, past all of the friends who await his return." (School Library Journal)

REVIEW: *Bull Cent Child Books* v67 no2 p93-4 O 2013 H. M.

"Come Back, Ben" and "Pete Won't Eat." "These two offerings from the Holiday House 'I Like to Read' series offer simple storylines, lots of vowel sound repetition, and an extra-large font size to make reading more approachable for new readers. In [author Ann] Hassett's 'Come Back, Ben', a boy flies off on a balloon past a series of passers-by until eventually landing on the moon, where he fills his pocket with moon rocks and sends himself floating back to earth. . . . In [author and illustrator Emily Arnold] McGully's 'Pete Won't Eat', a pig named Pete refuses to eat his bowl of green slop. . . . McGully's line and watercolor illustrations feature . . . plenty of text-to-image pairing within the story to guide young readers."

REVIEW: *Horn Book Magazine* v90 no1 p73 Ja/F 2014 JULIE ROACH

REVIEW: *Kirkus Rev* v81 no14 p213 Jl 15 2013

REVIEW: *Kirkus Rev* p55 N 15 2013 Best Books

REVIEW: *SLJ* v59 no8 p74 Ag 2013 Joan Kindig

HASSETT, JOHN.il. Come back, Ben. See Hassett, A.

HASTINGS, MAX. Catastrophe 1914; Europe goes to war; [by] Max Hastings 672 p. 2013 Alfred A. Knopf

1. HISTORY—Europe—General 2. HISTORY—Military—World War I 3. HISTORY—Modern—20th Century 4. Historical literature 5. World War, 1914-1918—Causes

ISBN 0307597059; 9780307597052 (hardback); 9780307743831 (paperback)

LC 2013-027865

SUMMARY: Author Max Hastings "traces the path to [World War I] making clear why Germany and Austria-Hungary were primarily to blame, and describes the gripping first clashes in the West, where the French army marched into action. Hastings gives us frank assessments of generals and political leaders. He argues passionately against the contention that the war was not worth the cost, maintaining that Germany's defeat was vital to the freedom of Europe." (Publisher's note)

REVIEW: *Booklist* v110 no2 p16 S 15 2013 Margaret Flanagan

REVIEW: *Choice* v51 no6 p1083 F 2014 A. M. Mayer

REVIEW: *Commonweal* v141 no8 p20-2 My 2 2014 James J. Sheehan

REVIEW: *Kirkus Rev* v81 no16 p268 Ag 15 2013

"Catastrophe 1914: Europe Goes to War." "Does the world need another book on that dismal year? Absolutely, if it's by [author Max] Hastings. . . . After many accounts of World War II, the veteran military historian tries his hand, with splendid results. . . . Readers accustomed to Hastings' vivid battle descriptions, incisive anecdotes from all participants, and shrewd, often unsettling opinions will not be disappointed. Among the plethora of brilliant accounts of this period, this is one of the best."

REVIEW: *Libr J* v138 no7 p54 Ap 15 2013 Barbara Hoffert

REVIEW: *Libr J* v138 no18 p53 N 1 2013 Edwin B. Burgess Margaret Heilbrun

REVIEW: *N Y Times Book Rev* p16-7 My 18 2014 ADAM HOCHSCHILD

REVIEW: *N Y Times Book Rev* p17 O 27 2013 MAX BOOT

"Catastrophe 1914: Europe Goes to War." "Max Hastings does an excellent job of assembling a chronicle of the war's first few months. . . . that puts paid to . . . [erroneus] perceptions [of World War I]. . . . He does not break new historiographical ground, but rather skillfully marshals evidence assembled by several generations of scholars into a highly readable narrative that should--but won't--be the last word on the subject. . . . 'Catastrophe 1914' brilliantly shows how, within its first few months, World War I came to assume the dispiriting and bloody form it would hold for the next four years."

REVIEW: *New Statesman* v142 no5177 p58-63 S 27 2013 Richard Overy

REVIEW: *New York Times* v163 no56293 pC27 O 18 2013 HEW STRACHAN

REVIEW: *TLS* no5772 p3-4 N 15 2013 WILLIAM PHILPOTT

"The War That Ended Peace: How Europe Abandoned Peace for the First World War," "Catastrophe: Europe Goes to War 1914," and "1914: Fight the Good Fight: Britain, the Army and the Coming of the First World War." "In Britain, the centenary wars are already raging between government and historians, largely over whether we should still be wearing the patriotic cloak that nations donned in the face of aggression by traditional enemies. Max Hastings and Allan Mallinson still wear it. For Hastings the guilt of Germany is firmly established. . . . Margaret Macmillan's judgement in 'The War that Ended Peace' is more balanced, although German intentions and action remain central to the war's origins. . . . Mallinson dissects military affairs (and political deficiencies) with a trained soldierly eye."

HATCH, MARK. The maker movement manifesto; rules for innovation in the new world of crafters, hackers, and tinkerers; [by] Mark Hatch viii, 213 p. 2014 McGraw-Hill Education

1. Business literature 2. Diffusion of innovations—Economic aspects 3. Industrial arts 4. Manufactures 5. Technological innovations—Economic aspects

ISBN 0071821120 (alk. paper); 9780071821124 (alk. paper)

LC 2013-017764

SUMMARY: In this book, TechShop CEO Mark Hatch "describes the remarkable technologies and tools now accessible to you and shares stories of how ordinary people have devised extraordinary products, giving rise to successful new business ventures. He explains how economic upheavals are paving the way for individuals to create, innovate, make a fortune--and even drive positive societal change--with nothing more than their own creativity and some hard work." (Publisher's note)

REVIEW: *Choice* v51 no7 p1235-6 Mr 2014 M. S. McCullough

"The Maker Movement Manifesto: Rules for Innovation in the New World of Crafters, Hackers, and Tinkerers." "[Mark] Hatch presents dozens of real-life examples, giving the impression that everyone can become successful, though it may take many failed attempts. . . . This is not a how-to book . . .but a why-do-it, positive, upbeat book, written in an easy-to-read, conversational style. Any negative reactions or experiences people or corporations may have to makerspaces are not discussed. Hatch makes his audience want to begin experimenting and to have maker facilities in every city. Much of the book makes references to Hatch's TechShop. Overall, a good overview of an important trend."

HATKE, BEN. The Return of Zita the Spacegirl; [by] Ben Hatke 240 p. 2014 First Second

1. Good & evil—Fiction 2. Graphic novels 3. Prisoners—Fiction 4. Science fiction 5. Space flight—Fiction
ISBN 1626720584; 9781626720589

SUMMARY: In this graphic novel, by Ben Hatke, "Zita the Spacegirl has saved planets, battled monsters, and wrestled with interplanetary fame. But she faces her biggest challenge yet in the third and final installment of the Zita adventures. Wrongfully imprisoned on a penitentiary planet, Zita has to plot the galaxy's greatest jailbreak before the evil prison warden can execute his plan of interstellar domination!" (Publisher's note)

REVIEW: *Booklist* v110 no13 p51 Mr 1 2014 Ian Chipman

"The Return of Zita the Spacegirl." "Although Zita is a great, cheerworthy lead, [Ben] Hatke has always had a particular knack for surrounding her with crazy-inventive oddballs, from cuddly rocks and wisecracking rag piles to broken-down battle orbs and lime-Jell-O-blob leviathans. And the villains! There's no mistaking the pure-evil tentacle bots or the pistol-faced hulks for what they are, and they're just vanquishable enough to make the action really zing.As this fine adventure comes to its final pages, Hatke leaves the door just a bit ajar for more interstellar exploits. An afterword supplies fans with the history of Zita's character, from doodle to webcomic to the heroine fans know and love."

REVIEW: *Kirkus Rev* v82 no8 p72 Ap 15 2014

REVIEW: *SLJ* v60 no5 p122 My 2014 Barbara M. Moon

HATSUE NAKAWAKI. Wait! wait!; [by] Hatsue Nakawaki 24 p. 2013 Enchanted Lion Books

1. Animals—Fiction 2. JUVENILE FICTION—Concepts—General 3. JUVENILE FICTION—Family—Parents 4. JUVENILE FICTION—Imagination & Play 5. JUVENILE FICTION—Nature & the Natural World—General (see also headings under Animals) 6. Parent and child—Fiction 7. Picture books for children
ISBN 1592701388 (hardcover); 9781592701384 (hardcover)
LC 2013-011003

SUMMARY: This book by Hatsue Nawaki "follows a young child's discovery of other creatures. This discovery comes with the recognition that while other creatures can suddenly appear they can also go away and disappear just as quickly. But the delightful appearance of a dad and his playful swoop of his toddler up onto his shoulders will remind little ones that the people who love them will always be there and will never, ever not come back." (Publisher's note)

REVIEW: *Horn Book Magazine* v89 no5 p77 S/O 2013 MARTHA V. PARRAVANO

"Wait! Wait!" "Illustrator [Komako] Sakai . . . once again captures, in minimalist double-page spreads, the body language and characteristics of a curious young child interacting with her world. Acrylic and oil-pencil illustrations in the softest of palettes reveal her determination in pursuing her hoped-for new friends and her bafflement when they run away--as well as her ability to switch gears when a new experience is offered. The pacing, amount of text, and judicious use of repetition suit the book perfectly for preschoolers; the page turns are particularly effective. A welcome picture book from an author and illustrator who clearly understand young children and convey that understanding with gentle eloquence."

REVIEW: *Kirkus Rev* p60-1 N 15 2013 Best Books

REVIEW: *Kirkus Rev* v81 no12 p107 Je 15 2013

REVIEW: *Publ Wkly* v260 no19 p66 My 13 2013

REVIEW: *Publ Wkly* p55-6 Children's starred review annual 2013

REVIEW: *SLJ* v59 no9 p128 S 2013 Amy Lilien-Harper

HATVANY, AMY. Safe with me; a novel; [by] Amy Hatvany 352 p. 2013 Atria Books

1. Bereavement—Psychological aspects 2. Children—Death—Psychological aspects—Fiction 3. Friendship—Fiction 4. Liver—Transplantation—Patients—Fiction 5. Psychological fiction 6. Transplantation of organs, tissues, etc. in children 7. Transplantation of organs, tissues, etc. in children—Fiction
ISBN 9781476704418
LC 2013-017478

SUMMARY: In this book by Amy Hatvany,"Hannah is still reeling with grief" after the accidental death of her daughter "when she unexpectedly stumbles into the life of the Bell family, whose fifteen-year-old daughter, Maddie, survived only because Hannah's daughter had died. Mesmerized by this fragile connection to her own daughter and afraid to reveal who she actually is, Hannah develops a surprising friendship with Maddie's mother, Olivia." (Publisher's note)

REVIEW: *Booklist* v110 no9/10 p44-6 Ja 1 2014 Rebecca Vnuk

"Safe With Me." "Hannah and Olivia become friends by chance--the two women hit it off when Olivia brings her teenage daughter, Maddie, into Hannah's salon for a makeover on a whim. Each woman could really use a friend, as Hannah's still mourning the accidental death of her daughter, while Olivia struggles to hide the fact that her high-powered husband abuses her. . . . [Amy] Hatvany does a marvelous job of not letting the plot get too maudlin or 'ripped from the headlines,' and her characters have warmth and depth. Readers will find themselves cheering for these women. A good pick for women's-fiction fans."

REVIEW: *Kirkus Rev* v82 no1 p275 Ja 1 2014

HAUBER, MARK E. The book of eggs; a life-size guide to the eggs of six hundred of the world's bird species; [by] Mark E. Hauber 655 p. 2014 University of Chicago Press

1. Bird eggs 2. Bird watching—Guidebooks 3. Birds—Breeding 4. Birds—Eggs 5. Birds—Eggs—Classification 6. Birds—Eggs—North America—Pictorial works 7. Birds—Nests 8. Identification of birds 9. Nature

photography 10. Nature study
ISBN 9780226057781 (cloth: alk. paper)
LC 2013-042253

SUMMARY: Written by Mark E. Hauber, "'The Book of Eggs' introduces readers to eggs from six hundred species—some endangered or extinct—from around the world and housed mostly at Chicago's Field Museum of Natural History. Organized by habitat and taxonomy, the entries include newly commissioned photographs that reproduce each egg in full color and at actual size, as well as distribution maps and drawings and descriptions of the birds and their nests where the eggs are kept warm." (Publisher's note)

REVIEW: *New Sci* v222 no2968 p47 My 10 2014 Adrian Barnett

"The Book of Eggs: A Life-Size Guide to the Eggs of Six Hundred of the World's Bird Species." "Beyond the brown and white eggs we are used to, there is a dazzling array of colours and patterns. . . . Each of the book's 600 eggs is photographed life size, with magnified views of the smaller ones to allow us to appreciate the detail. For each, a summary of breeding biology links form to function. . . . Altogether, this book achieves a fine synergy between informative text and beautiful photographs."

HAUERWAS, STANLEY, 1940-. Approaching the end; eschatological reflections on church, politics, and life; [by] Stanley Hauerwas a xvii, 251 p. 2013 William B. Eerdmans Publishing Company

1. Christian life 2. Christianity and politics 3. Eschatology 4. Religious literature
ISBN 0802869599 (pbk.: alk. paper); 9780802869593 (pbk.: alk. paper)
LC 2013-031430

SUMMARY: "In this book Stanley Hauerwas explores the significance of eschatological reflection for helping the church negotiate the contemporary world . . . addressing such issues as the divided character of the church, the imperative of Christian unity, and the necessary practice of sacrifice. In Part Three . . . Hauerwas moves from theology and the church as a whole to focusing on how individual Christians should live in light of eschatology." (Publisher's note)

REVIEW: *Choice* v51 no10 p1820 Je 2014 E. B. Scott

REVIEW: *Christ Century* v131 no6 p37-9 Mr 19 2014 Clay Thomas

REVIEW: *Commonweal* v141 no4 p32-4 F 21 2014 William L. Portier

"Approaching the End: Eschataological Reflections on Church, Politics, and Life". "Any new book bearing [Stanley] Hauerwas's name is noteworthy, and the latest one doesn't disappoint. . . . A review cannot do justice to this extraordinarily honest account of Christian unity from the perspective of a self-described 'high church Mennonite' and 'congregationalist with Catholic sensibilities.' . . . Such an engaging intellectual retrospective by a world-class theologian deserves wide readership, both among those committed to the Lordship of Christ and the continuing life of the church, and among those simply interested in what it means to be human."

HAUGELAND, JOHN. Dasein disclosed; John Haugeland's Heidegger; [by] John Haugeland 2013 Harvard University Press

1. Being & Time (Book : Heidegger) 2. Continental philosophy 3. Heidegger, Martin, 1889-1976 4. Ontology 5. Philosophical literature
ISBN 9780674072114 (alk. paper)
LC 2012-028995

SUMMARY: This book, edited by Joseph Rouse, presents the writings of John Haugeland, "a man widely acknowledged as one of [Martin] Heidegger's preeminent and most provocative interpreters. . . . 'Being and Time' has inspired copious commentary. . . . Haugeland aspired to a sweeping reevaluation of Heidegger's magnum opus and its conception of human life as Dasein--a reevaluation focused on Heidegger's effort to reawaken philosophically dormant questions of what it means 'to be.'" (Publisher's note)

REVIEW: *TLS* no5775 p29 D 6 2013 TAYLOR CARMAN

"Dasein Disclosed: John Haugeland's Heidegger." "The late John Haugeland was well known among philosophers as an ingenious interpreter of Martin Heidegger's 'Being and Time.' Central to his reading of that difficult text was his denial of what had seemed obvious to most other readers: that Heidegger's word Dasein (which in ordinary German just means existence) refers to the individual human being. . . . The envisioned opus was to be called 'Dasein Disclosed,' and the unfinished manuscript forms the central hundred pages or so of the present volume, which now bears that title. It has been edited with great intelligence and care by Joseph Rouse, who has included ten additional essays (two previously unpublished)."

HAUSER, THOMAS. Straight writes and jabs; an inside look at another year in boxing; [by] Thomas Hauser 250 p. 2013 University of Arkansas Press

1. Boxing 2. Doping in sports 3. Moore, Archie 4. Sports literature 5. Steward, Emanuel, 1944-2012
ISBN 9781557286444 (pbk. : alk. paper)
LC 2013-942079

SUMMARY: This book on boxing by Thomas Hauser presents an "overview" of the sport in 2012. Topics include "the presence of performance-enhancing drugs in boxing . . . late champion Archie Moore . . . the September 15 fight between Sergio Martinez and Julio Cesar Chavez Jr. . . . [and] a . . . tribute to Emanuel Steward, the longtime trainer of champions, who passed in 2012." (Booklist)

REVIEW: *Booklist* v110 no4 p9 O 15 2013 Wes Lukowsky

"Straight Writes and Jabs: An Inside Look at Another Year in Boxing." "For the last few years 'Booklist' has heaped praise on [Thomas] Hauser's annual look back at the previous year in boxing. This year is no different. Why is Hauser one of the best sports journalists working today? He is an unashamed lover of boxing but never hesitates in exposing its flaws. In this overview of 2012, he does some of his best work, especially an extended piece on the presence of performance-enhancing drugs in boxing. . . . Wonderful writing from a world-class journalist."

HAUTALA, RICK, 1940-2013. The dead lands; [by] Rick Hautala 232 p. 2014 JournalStone

1. Detective & mystery stories 2. Ghost stories 3. Good & evil—Fiction 4. Murder investigation—Fiction 5. Supernatural
ISBN 9781940161303 (pbk.: alk. paper); 9781940161310 (e-bk.: alk. paper); 9781940161327 (hardcover: alk. paper)
LC 2013-952623

SUMMARY: In this book, "when modern 16-year-old Megan McGowan falls to her death from the cliffs at Fort Williams, the spirit of Abby Cummings, who died in a shipwreck off the Maine coast in 1883, awakens to help her. Abby has risen several times over the years to help the spirits of the conflicted departed move on by resolving the issues they left unfinished in life. Now the girls must discover what is holding Megan back, and that means finding out if her fall was an accident, suicide or murder." (Kirkus Reviews)

REVIEW: *Kirkus Rev* v82 no2 p220 Ja 15 2014

"The Dead Lands". "[Rick] Hautala died in early 2013, and this, his last novel, shows signs of premature separation. Obviously planned as the start of a series, this stiff, melodramatic offering would have improved over subsequent drafts had its author lived. Clichéd characters, an obvious mystery, a fuzziness to the supernatural logic, and a rushed, unsatisfying climax belie Hautala's Bram Stoker Lifetime Achievement Award. An unease in balancing child and (frequently foulmouthed) adult characters further marks the story as still in development. Nevertheless, kids who find their curiosity piqued by unresolved questions about Abby's world may hope for the stories to continue, as a tantalizing ending suggests. Not, alas, quite ready for prime time."

HAUTMAN, PETE, 1952-. The Cydonian pyramid; [by] Pete Hautman 368 p. 2013 Candlewick Press

1. Fantasy fiction 2. Religion & science 3. Religions 4. Science fiction 5. Time travel

ISBN 0763654043 (reinforced); 9780763654047 (reinforced)

LC 2012-942673

SUMMARY: This novel, by Pete Hautman, is part of the "Klaatu Diskos" series. "More than half a millennium in the future, in the shadow of the looming Cydonian Pyramid, a pampered girl named Lah Lia has been raised for one purpose: to be sacrificed. . . . But just as she is about to be killed, a strange boy appears from the diskos, providing a cover of chaos that allows her to escape and launching her on a time-spinning journey in which her fate is irreversibly linked to his." (Publisher's note)

REVIEW: *Booklist* v110 no12 p95 F 15 2014 Rachel Reinwald

REVIEW: *Bull Cent Child Books* v67 no1 p22-3 S 2013 K. C.

"The Cydonian Pyramid." "In the first volume of the Klaatu Diskos trilogy . . . Tucker Feye met Lah Lia . . . and their faces became intertwined. This second volume reveals Lah Lia's origins as a Pure Girl, one of the few selected by the priests in her time to be sacrificed and thrown into the diskos as a spectacle to keep the people in line. . . . As in the first volume, interstitial passages provide history and context for the peoples that Lah Lia encounters and intrigue readers with thought-provoking glimpses of the changes that technology can bring about (and may yet in the human world as well). Lah Lia is a compelling character that readers will be glad to see developed and given equal time with Tucker Feye. . . ."

HAUTMAN, PETE, 1952-. The Klaatu terminus; [by] Pete Hautman 368 p. 2014 Candlewick Press

1. Families—Fiction 2. Science fiction 3. Space & time—Fiction 4. Time travel—Fiction 5. Wisconsin—Fiction

ISBN 0763654051; 9780763654054

LC 2013-944132

SUMMARY: In this series finale, Pete Hautman "weaves several diverging time streams into one . . . masterwork. . . . In a far distant future, Tucker Feye and . . . Lia find themselves atop a crumbling pyramid in an abandoned city. In present-day Hopewell, Tucker's uncle Kosh faces armed resistance . . . as he attempts to help a terrorized woman named Emma. . . . And on a train platform in 1997, a seventeen-year-old Kosh is given an instruction that will change his life." (Publisher's note)

REVIEW: *Booklist* v110 no15 p82 Ap 1 2014 Daniel Kraus

REVIEW: *Bull Cent Child Books* v67 no9 p458 My 2014 K. C.

"The Klaatu Terminus." "Characters who have been important in the first two books are brought into the mix, and [Pete] Hautman deftly manages to bring their stories together amidst more harrowing danger and intricately timed escapes. Readers will need to pay close attention to understand just when the individual scenes are taking place as the characters enter and exit portals and move between by-now-familiar parts of Wisconsin's present, past, and future. Hautman closes the series the way a middle-grade sci-fi series should be closed: all questions are answered, and the good guys survive, prosper, and eventually get married to the right people, while the bad guys get their throats ripped out by jaguars or suffocate in the unbreathable air on Mars."

REVIEW: *Horn Book Magazine* v90 no3 p87-8 My/Je 2014 LAUREN ADAMS

REVIEW: *Kirkus Rev* v82 no4 p178 F 15 2014

REVIEW: *SLJ* v60 no7 p53 Jl 2014 Elizabeth L. Kenyon

REVIEW: *SLJ* v60 no4 p166 Ap 2014 Sabrina Carnesi

REVIEW: *Voice of Youth Advocates* v37 no1 p82 Ap 2014 Tanya Paglia

HAWKES, KEVIN.il. Meanwhile back at the ranch. See Meanwhile back at the ranch

HAWKING, S. W. (STEPHEN W.), 1942-. My brief history; [by] S. W. (Stephen W.) Hawking 144 p. 2013 Bantam Books

1. Autobiographies 2. Black holes (Astronomy) 3. Cosmology 4. Physicists—Great Britain—Biography

ISBN 9780345535283

LC 2013-027938

SUMMARY: In this autobiography, Stephen Hawking "opens up about the challenges that confronted him following his diagnosis of ALS at age twenty-one. Tracing his development as a thinker, he explains how the prospect of an early death urged him onward through numerous intellectual breakthroughs, and talks about the genesis of his masterpiece 'A Brief History of Time'." (Publisher's note)

REVIEW: *Libr J* v138 no21 p58 D 1 2013 Judith Robinson

REVIEW: *New Sci* v219 no2936 p50 S 28 2013 Sumit Paul-Choudhury

"My Brief History." "[Stephen Hawking's] appeal rests on intertwined elements. He is the stricken genius whose intellect transcends his physicality. He is a bestselling author though he can barely talk, a frequent TV guest star though he can barely move. He is a cyborg whose humanity is inseparable from his machines, with a voice both utterly synthetic and brimming with personality. He is the cosmologist who would know the mind of God—and help the rest of us know it, too. . . . The book tells Hawking's story in his own words, including details of his upbringing and formative years. His clarity, wit and determination are evident, his understatement and good humour occasionally moving. But it's a terse, somewhat sparse read, lacking the elaboration that might offer real insight."

REVIEW: *New Statesman* v142 no5179 p44-6 O 11 2013 Ian Stewart

HAWKINS, DONALD T.ed. Personal archiving. See Personal archiving

HAWKINS, KATE.ed. Women, sexuality and the political power of pleasure. See Women, sexuality and the political power of pleasure

HAWKINS, RACHEL. Rebel belle; [by] Rachel Hawkins 352 p. 2014 G. P. Putnam's Sons, an imprint of Penguin Group (USA) Inc.

1. Debutantes—Fiction 2. High schools—Fiction 3. Magic—Fiction 4. Oracles—Fiction 5. Schools—Fiction 6. Supernatural—Fiction 7. Young adult fiction
ISBN 0399256938; 9780399256936 (hardback)
LC 2013-027102

SUMMARY: In this young adult novel by Rachel Hawkins, the first in a projected series, "Harper Price, peerless Southern belle, was born ready for a Homecoming tiara. But after a strange run-in at the dance imbues her with incredible abilities, Harper's destiny takes a turn for the seriously weird. She becomes a Paladin, one of an ancient line of guardians with agility, super strength and lethal fighting instincts." (Publisher's note)

REVIEW: *Booklist* v110 no15 p87 Ap 1 2014 Anne O'Malley

REVIEW: *Bull Cent Child Books* v67 no8 p406-7 Ap 2014 K. C.

"Rebel Belle". "Harper is as quippy as you please, with a sass born of a sharp intellect and an easy assurance that if one just follows the time-tested rules of Southern tradition and decorum, all will be well; after all, she herself bears witness to the effectiveness of proper footwear. The twist at the end is as surprising as it is delicious, hinting at further tests of aggressive politeness as she, David, and her set of belles and beaux set out to save—or perhaps doom—the world. Fans of Michèle Jaffe will not want to miss this."

REVIEW: *Kirkus Rev* v82 no3 p251 F 1 2014

REVIEW: *SLJ* v60 no4 p147 Ap 2014 Colleen S. Banick

REVIEW: *Voice of Youth Advocates* v37 no1 p82 Ap 2014 Elizabeth Norton

HAXELL, KATE. The knitted alphabet; [by] Kate Haxell 256 p. 2013 Barrons Educational Series, Inc.

1. Alphabets 2. Do-it-yourself literature 3. Handicraft 4. Knitting 5. Knitting—Patterns
ISBN 9781438002958
LC 2013-941173

SUMMARY: "This book shows readers how to hand knit every letter of the alphabet, plus numbers and punctuation marks, in 26 different fonts--from simple classic lettering to more ornate calligraphy and contemporary handwritten styles." It includes "patterns for 26 different alphabets, including numbers, punctuation, emoticons and dingbats" and patterns for ten projects. (Publisher's note)

REVIEW: *Booklist* v110 no8 p16 D 15 2013 Barbara Jacobs

"The Knitted Alphabet: How to Knit Letters From A to Z." "Pure graphic designers might quarrel with [Kate] Haxell and [Sarah] Hazell's descriptions-classification of alphabets. But knitters and sewers will welcome this extremely detailed, comprehensive, and creative look at personalizing thread-based projects. . . . Though the actual alphabet patterns are more than a bit quirky--after all, how can you label five different decades as retro?--the swatches and 10 projects will boost use. . . . This inspired book is a first class."

HAYASAKI, ERIKA. The death class; a true story about life; [by] Erika Hayasaki 288 p. 2014 Simon & Schuster

1. College students—United States 2. Death—Social aspects 3. Memoirs 4. Thanatology 5. Thanatology—United States
ISBN 1451642857; 9781451642858
LC 2013-002025

SUMMARY: In this book, journalist Erika Hayasaki "chronicles her years shadowing Dr. Norma Bowe, the 'professor of death' at Kean University in Union, N.J. Bowe's class, Death in Perspective, had a three-year waiting list. . . . In the course of dogging the professor over the semester, involving visits to cemeteries, a hospice, death row at a state prison, mortuary, and psych hospital, . . . Hayasaki unearths the wrenching personal stories of these traumatized students--and that of Bowe herself." (Publishers Weekly)

REVIEW: *Booklist* v110 no5 p6 N 1 2013 Vanessa Bush

REVIEW: *Kirkus Rev* v81 no22 p73 N 15 2013

REVIEW: *N Y Times Book Rev* p21 Ja 26 2014 PAIGE WILLIAMS

"Things I've Learned From Dying: A Book About Life" and "The Death Class: A True Story About Life." "In the latest memoir by David R. Dow . . . three important figures in his life are in danger. . . . Dow tells the story of trying to save all three. Each narrative is in its own way gutting. . . . A warm and fluid writer, he is also often funny, and angry, and embraces his own imagination. . . . The extended deliberations . . . can feel a bit repetitive. . . . Erika Hayasaki . . . began following a course called Death in Perspective . . . , which was taught by Norma Bowe, a registered nurse. . . . The book's strength lies in the well-observed details of the lives portrayed, and in the recognition that the work Bowe and her students are doing is messy, necessary stuff."

REVIEW: *Publ Wkly* v260 no42 p41 O 21 2013

HAYDER, MO. Skin; [by] Mo Hayder 384 p. 2009 Bantam Press

ISBN 9780802198013 (ebook); 9780802145178 (paperback); 9780802119308 (hardcover)
LC 2009-437589

SUMMARY: In this novel, by Mo Hayder, "when the decomposed body of a young woman is found near some railway tracks just outside Bristol one hot May morning, all indications are that she committed suicide. . . . But DI Jack Caffery is not so sure. . . . Police diver Flea Marley is working alongside Caffery. . . . And then she makes a discovery that changes everything." (Publisher's note)

REVIEW: *Horn Book Magazine* v89 no5 p107 S/O 2013 KATRINA HEDEEN

"Skin." "Sep's agony over hiding her changing skin (especially from Joshua, who readers will suspect would love her regardless) is heartbreaking. Then comes an epiphany-like shift, after which she's at peace; though it's abrupt, this change feels credible due to the ongoing themes of Sep's passion for studying unique physical attributes of rare animal species as well as her growing awareness of and appreciation for her body, evidenced by her dutiful practice of jazz dance, yoga, and mindfulness. The teen's turmoil over a disease that is literally only skin-deep is poignant, and given respectful treatment by Napoli; readers will empathize with Sep's feelings, fears, and actions."

HAYES-MARTIN, MARYLIN. Common Thread-Uncommon Women; [by] Marylin Hayes-Martin 278 p. 2013 Author Solutions

1. Assimilation (Sociology) 2. Families—Fiction 3. Families of military personnel 4. Historical fiction 5. Native American women—Fiction

ISBN 1481705601; 9781481705608

SUMMARY: In this book, "four generations of Native American women navigate life in a patriarchal American society in this debut historical novel." Author Marylin Hayes-Martin "tells the story of the female lineage of her real-life family from the Civil War era to World War II. The story begins with Martin's great-grandmother Minerva, a Native American woman married to a white Confederate soldier." (Kirkus Reviews)

REVIEW: *Kirkus Rev* v82 no1 p342 Ja 1 2014

"Common Thread-Uncommon Women". " The novel's dialogue and internal monologues can sometimes feel a bit clichéd, but overall, [Marylin] Martin's prose is consistently clear and polished. The storyline is easy to follow, and provides a fast, engaging read. At times, it seems overly idealistic in its portrayal of the women's unwavering strength, and the characters might have felt more fully realized if Martin had addressed their internal struggles more often. However, the author conveys their actions in a manner that feels historically accurate for their time periods. . . . An absorbing, warmly written historical tale."

HAYES, ALFRED. In love; [by] Alfred Hayes xiii, 130 p. 2013 New York Review Books

1. Bars (Drinking establishments)—Fiction 2. Loss (Psychology) 3. Love stories 4. Man-woman relationships—Fiction

ISBN 9781590176665 (pbk. : alk. paper)

LC 2013-008974

SUMMARY: This book is set in "New York in the 1950s. A man on a barstool is telling a story about a woman he met in a bar. . . . They'd gone out, they'd grown close, but as far as he was concerned it didn't add up to much. He was a busy man. Then one day, out dancing, she runs into a rich awkward lovelorn businessman. He'll pay for her to be his, pay her a lot. And now the narrator discovers that he is as much in love with her as she is with him." (Publisher's note)

REVIEW: *TLS* no5766 p20 O 4 2013 MARTIN SCHIFINO

"In Love" and "My Face for the World To See." "Alfred Hayes once seemed poised to become an American classic, before nearly everyone forgot he existed. . . . Most of his fiction, much of it first-rate, is out of print. . . . As a novelist, he has just about held on to posterity on the strength of one book, 'In Love' (1953), which revives interest every time it is reissued, though somehow never secures a firmer status than that of a 'lost classic' or 'minor masterpiece'. . . . The simultaneous publication of two of his best novels by NYRB Classics is a step in the right direction. Both volumes are elegantly produced and feature insightful introductions that put the writing in context, identify elective affinities, and even venture to explain the author's eclipse."

HAYES, ALFRED. My face for the world to see; [by] Alfred Hayes xii, 131 p. 2013 New York Review Books/ NYRB

1. Actresses—Fiction 2. Hollywood (Los Angeles, Calif.)—Fiction 3. Love stories 4. Motion picture industry—Fiction 5. Screenwriters

ISBN 9781590176672 (pbk. : alk. paper)

LC 2013-008975

SUMMARY: This book "is set in Hollywood. . . . At a party, the narrator, a screenwriter, rescues a young woman who staggers with drunken determination into the Pacific. He is living far from his wife in New York and long ago shed any illusions about the value of his work. He just wants to be left alone. And yet without really meaning to, he gets involved with the young woman, who has, it seems, no illusions about love, especially with married men." (Publisher's note)

REVIEW: *New Statesman* v142 no5172 p51-3 Ag 30 2013 Leo Robson

REVIEW: *TLS* no5766 p20 O 4 2013 MARTIN SCHIFINO

"In Love" and "My Face for the World To See." "Alfred Hayes once seemed poised to become an American classic, before nearly everyone forgot he existed. . . . Most of his fiction, much of it first-rate, is out of print. . . . As a novelist, he has just about held on to posterity on the strength of one book, 'In Love' (1953), which revives interest every time it is reissued, though somehow never secures a firmer status than that of a 'lost classic' or 'minor masterpiece'. . . . The simultaneous publication of two of his best novels by NYRB Classics is a step in the right direction. Both volumes are elegantly produced and feature insightful introductions that put the writing in context, identify elective affinities, and even venture to explain the author's eclipse."

HAYES, NED. Sinful Folk; A Novel of the Middle Ages; [by] Ned Hayes 362 p. 2014 Itasca Books

1. Antisemitism—Fiction 2. Ex-nuns 3. Great Britain—History—14th century 4. Historical fiction 5. Mothers—Fiction

ISBN 0985239301; 9780985239305

SUMMARY: In this book, set in 1377," four children were burned to death in a suspicious house fire. Villagers traveled hundreds of miles across England to demand justice." Author Ned Hayes follows "Mear, a former nun who has lived for a decade disguised as a mute man, raising her son quietly in this isolated village. For years, she has concealed herself and all her history. But on this journey, she will find the strength to claim the promise of her past and create a new legacy." (Publisher's note)

REVIEW: *Booklist* v110 no12 p36 F 15 2014 Joanne Wilkinson

"Sinful Folk." "In December of 1377, five children are burned in a suspicious house fire. Awash in paranoia and prejudice, the fathers suspect it is the work of Jews and set out to seek justice from the king, loading the charred bodies of their boys onto a cart. . . . Brilliantly conceived and beautifully executed, [Ned] Hayes' novel is woven through with a deep knowledge of medieval history, all conveyed in mesmerizing prose. At the center of the novel is Mear, a brave and heartbreaking character whose story of triumph over adversity is a joy to read."

HAYES, PATRICK J. A Catholic brain trust; the history of the Catholic Commission on Intellectual and Cultural Affairs, 1945-1965; [by] Patrick J. Hayes vii, 431 p. 2011 University of Notre Dame Press

1. Catholic intellectuals 2. Catholics—United States—Iintellectual life—20th century 3. Historical literature 4. Murray, John Courtney, 1904-1967 5. Religious history
ISBN 0268031096 (cloth : alk. paper); 9780268031091 (cloth : alk. paper)
LC 2010-052720

SUMMARY: In this book, "Patrick J. Hayes chronicles the history and assesses the achievement of the organization . . . [U.S. Catholic] scholars created, the Catholic Commission on Intellectual and Cultural Affairs (CCICA). Hayes's . . . account reveals a postwar moment ripe for just such an undertaking. It was a period of religious enthusiasm throughout the country and Catholics' place in national life had improved notably since the dark days of Al Smith's presidential bid. . . . As polymaths and intellectual leaders, . . . CCICA members abandoned the defensive crouch long associated with Catholic engagement in the public square. . . . The group's debate on Catholic conceptions of religious liberty . . . saw John Courtney Murray defending American notions of religious pluralism." (Commonweal)

REVIEW: *Am Hist Rev* v117 no5 p1622-3 D 2012 David S. Bovée

REVIEW: *Commonweal* v139 no7 p23-4 Ap 6 2012 James P. McCartin

"A Catholic Brain Trust: The History of the Catholic Commission on Intellectual and Cultural Affairs." "In 'A Catholic Brain Trust,' Patrick J. Hayes chronicles the history and assesses the achievement of the organization . . . [U.S. Catholic] scholars created, the Catholic Commission on Intellectual and Cultural Affairs (CCICA). Hayes's thorough and well-documented account reveals a postwar moment ripe for just such an undertaking. It was a period of religious enthusiasm throughout the country and Catholics' place in national life had improved notably since the dark days of Al Smith's presidential bid. . . . As polymaths and intellectual leaders, . . . CCICA members abandoned the defensive crouch long associated with Catholic engagement in the public square."

REVIEW: *J Am Hist* v99 no3 p982-3 D 2012 Kathleen Sprows Cummings

HAYHURST, DIRK. Bigger Than the Game; Restitching a Major League Life; [by] Dirk Hayhurst 320 p. 2014 Kensington Pub Corp

1. Baseball injuries 2. Baseball players—Health 3. Memoirs 4. Pitchers (Baseball) 5. Toronto Blue Jays (Baseball team)
ISBN 0806534877; 9780806534879

SUMMARY: This book, by Dirk Hayhurst, "tells a story about what lies beneath the often gilded uniform of the professional player. . . . Hayhurst . . . [explores] often shunned topics like the rampancy of prescription drug abuse among major league athletes, the stigma of depression among athletes, and the damning consequences of violating the codes of the locker room." (Publisher's note)

REVIEW: *Kirkus Rev* v82 no3 p212 F 1 2014

"Bigger Than the Game". "A revealing yet occasionally tedious, seasonlong account of a major league pitcher on the outs. . . . Rarely does an athlete admit publicly to feeling anxious, afraid or depressed, but [Dirk] Hayhurst candidly shows readers that he was fraying both emotionally and physically. (One line sums it up nicely: 'Arm pain can make your whole life hurt.') However, the author draws out his emotionally honest story with unnecessary, lengthy accounts of interactions with coaches and trainers, as well as intimate conversations with his wife. Several chapters devoted to his rehabilitation program lend no insight or deeper understanding of his pain. A flawed yet unique, personal story of an athlete's anguish at the end of his career."

REVIEW: *Libr J* v139 no3 p109 F 15 2014 Jim Burns

HAYLEY, WILLIAM, 1745-1820. William Hayley (1745-1820), Selected Poetry. See William Hayley (1745-1820), Selected Poetry

HAYNES, STEPHEN R. The last segregated hour; the Memphis kneel-ins and the campaign for Southern church desegregation; [by] Stephen R. Haynes xi, 314 p. 2013 Oxford University Press

1. Blacks—Segregation—United States 2. Historical literature 3. Segregation—Religious aspects—Christianity—History—20th century
ISBN 9780195395051
LC 2012-003851

SUMMARY: This book presents an account "of a church desegregation campaign in Memphis. . . . These kneel-ins carried a different weight than other protest activities, as activists sought to expose moral hypocrisy and reconcile the church to Christ's teachings of brotherhood and love. . . . [Stephen R.] Haynes focuses on kneel-ins at the 3,500-member Second Presbyterian Church (SPC), where lay leaders routinely blocked integrated groups over a ten-month period beginning in early 1964." (Journal of American History)

REVIEW: *Choice* v50 no9 p1642 My 2013 S. A. Johnson

REVIEW: *J Am Hist* v100 no3 p911-2 D 2013 Carter Dalton Lyon

REVIEW: *Rev Am Hist* v41 no3 p540-4 S 2013 Paul Harvey

"The Last Segregated Hour: The Memphis Kneel-Ins and the Campaign for Southern Church Desegregation." "To my knowledge, this is the first full-length work investigating the history of kneel-ins in one city. . . . [Stephen R.] Haynes comes at this book with a unique set of qualifications. And he delivers on the promise, making this the finest study of the church kneel-ins that I have read, and more generally a signal contribution to Civil Rights Movement historiography. . . . Beyond being a local study of the kneel-ins in Memphis, this book is also a broad-based theological and cultural exploration of the requirements of reconciliation."

HAYS, BETSY A. Land your dream career; eleven steps to

take in college; [by] Betsy A. Hays 226 p. 2013 Rowman & Littlefield Publishers, Inc.

1. Advice literature 2. College graduates—Employment 3. College students 4. Job skills 5. Social networks
ISBN 1442219467; 9781442219465 (cloth : alk. paper); 9781442219489 (electronic)
LC 2012-045227

SUMMARY: In this book, authors Tori Randolph Terhune and Betsy A. Hays "show readers what they can do in college to successfully pave the way for future employment. . . The authors provide eleven easy-to-follow strategies for effectively using time on campus to start building a career. Terhune and Hays lead students through content designed to help [them] set themselves up for success, without focusing on grades or papers." (Publisher's note)

REVIEW: *Booklist* v109 no14 p35 Mr 15 2013 Barbara Jacobs

REVIEW: *Choice* v51 no2 p314-5 O 2013 C. J. Kohen

"Land Your Dream Career: Eleven Steps to Take in College." "This book provides useful career strategies and advice to current college students. [Authors Tori Randolph] Terhune and [Betsy A.] Hays . . . have created a very readable work providing straightforward advice; useful anecdotes modeling successful behaviors; helpful tips throughout each section; and a cheat sheet to summarize key points. They discuss the importance of students' cultivating behaviors such as strong communication skills, politeness, honesty, time management, prioritization, integrity, professionalism, goal setting, clarity, and organizational skills. Separate chapters are devoted to networking and using social media. Stories of individuals throughout the chapters illustrate the behaviors and skills discussed."

REVIEW: *Libr J* v138 no6 p88 Ap 1 2013 Sara Holder

HAYS, TOMMY. What I came to tell you; [by] Tommy Hays 304 p. 2013 Egmont USA

1. Artists—Fiction 2. Death—Fiction 3. Friendship—Fiction 4. Grief—Fiction 5. Young adult literature
ISBN 9781606844335 (hardcover)
LC 2012-046189

SUMMARY: In this book, "when Grover's mom died in a terrible accident, it shattered his family. His sister, Sudie, cries all the time; his dad puts all his energy into his job as the director of the Thomas Wolfe house; and the only thing Grover wants to do is make beautiful weavings out of leaves, branches, and bamboo in the canebrake. . . . Luckily, when a new family--also missing a parent--moves in across the street, Grover and his father learn how to share their grief and help each other move forward." (Booklist)

REVIEW: *Booklist* v110 no1 p121-2 S 1 2013 Sarah Hunter

"What I Came to Tell You." "When Grover's mom died in a terrible accident, it shattered his family. . . . Luckily, when a new family--also missing a parent--moves in across the street, Grover and his father learn how to share their grief and help each other move forward. Hays' story is filled with touching honesty and youthful wisdom, all of which help undergird Grover's own discovery of the healing power of family, love, and art. Although the Thomas Wolfe references will likely be lost on its intended audience, the book's quiet story of a young boy experiencing a tragic loss and learning how to live life in spite of it is nonetheless moving."

REVIEW: *Bull Cent Child Books* v67 no2 p94 O 2013 K. C.

REVIEW: *Kirkus Rev* v81 no14 p141 Jl 15 2013

REVIEW: *Publ Wkly* v260 no31 p72 Ag 5 2013

REVIEW: *Publ Wkly* p82 Children's starred review annual 2013

HAYTON, DAVID, 1949-. The Anglo-Irish experience, 1680-1730; religion, identity and patriotism; [by] David Hayton xvii, 225 p. 2012 Boydell Press

1. British—Ireland—History—17th century 2. British—Ireland—History—18th century 3. Historical literature 4. Nationalism—Ireland—History—17th century 5. Nationalism—Ireland—History—18th century
ISBN 1843837463 (hbk.); 9781843837466 (hbk.)
LC 2012-450875

SUMMARY: This book presents previously uncollected historical essays by D. W. Hayton. "The wars and revolutions of seventeenth-century Ireland established in power a ruling class of Protestant landowners whose culture and connexions were traditionally English, but whose interests and political loyalties were increasingly Irish. . . . 'The Anglo-Irish Experience' explores the religious, intellectual and political culture of this new elite during a period of change and adjustment." (Publisher's note)

REVIEW: *Engl Hist Rev* v129 no536 p216-7 F 2014 T.C. Barnard

"The Anglo-Irish Experience, 1680-1730: Religion, Identity and Patriotism". "David Hayton confirmed his reputation as the most penetrating analyst of public politics in later Stuart and early Hanoverian Ireland. In drawing together a second collection of hitherto scattered essays, he consolidates and extends that deservedly high regard. He brings to his analysis of individuals, groups, institutions, attitudes and episodes an unrivalled familiarity with the unpublished sources. . . . To read any of these essays is to be reminded of the more durable attractions of secure evidence, precise analysis and careful comparison. . . . With subtlety and sensitivity, he traces how outsiders' (especially English) perceptions of the Irish shifted from attributions of barbarism to comedy."

HAYWARD, MARIA.ed. The Great wardrobe accounts of Henry VII and Henry VIII. See The Great wardrobe accounts of Henry VII and Henry VIII

HAYWOOD, IAN. Romanticism and caricature; [by] Ian Haywood 237 p. 2013 Cambridge University Press

1. Caricature in literature 2. English literature—18th century—History and criticism 3. English literature—19th century—History and criticism 4. Literature—History & criticism 5. Romanticism
ISBN 9781107044210 (hardback: alk. paper)
LC 2013-013493

SUMMARY: In this book, "Ian Haywood explores the 'Golden Age' of caricature through the close reading of key, iconic prints by artists including James Gillray, George and Robert Cruikshank, and Thomas Rowlandson. This approach both illuminates the visual and ideological complexity of graphic satire and demonstrates how this art form transformed Romantic-era politics into a unique and compelling spectacle of corruption, monstrosity and resistance." (Publisher's note)

REVIEW: *TLS* no5795 p26 Ap 25 2014 GREGORY DART

"Romanticism and Caricature." "Ian Haywood's book offers a compelling account of political caricature in the Romantic period, while also placing it in the broader context of British visual culture, from Restoration to Reform. . . . Always attentive to the peculiar mixture of intertextuality and topicality inherent in the genre, Haywood also offers fascinating speculations on its innate tendency towards self-reflexiveness. . . . Aware of caricature's rich, even paradoxical status as a kind of forgery to expose forgeries, Ian Haywood's book offers an inventive and highly informative tour of the genre, making a welcome contribution to a growing field."

HAZARD, ANTHONY Q. Postwar anti-racism; the United States, UNESCO, and "race", 1945-1968; [by] Anthony Q. Hazard xii, 252 p. 2012 Palgrave Macmillan

1. Anti-racism—United States—History—20th century 2. Historical literature
ISBN 9781137003836 (hbk.: alk. paper)
LC 2012-035087

SUMMARY: In this book, "Anthony Q. Hazard, Jr., examines the postwar anti-racist activities of the United Nations Educational, Scientific and Cultural Organization (UNESCO) and the role of the United States in shaping those efforts at home and abroad. . . . Hazard argues that American officials dominated UNESCO's budget planning and its agenda in the 1950s, fostering a type of anti-racism that supported American Cold War diplomatic goals and deflected international criticism." (American Historical Review)

REVIEW: *Am Hist Rev* v119 no1 p159-60 F 2014 Michelle Brattain

"Postwar Anti-racism: The United States, UNESCO, and 'Race,' 1945-1968". "[Anthony Q. Hazard] stakes out ambitious arguments that are often plausible, but are unfortunately not always well supported. While Hazard can show how UNESCO's early actions frequently served American interests at home and abroad, his book reveals little about how the United States actually produced these actions. . . . Throughout the book Hazard relies heavily on published reports, public statements, conferences, and newspapers. . . . Hazard has done scholars a service by shining light on UNESCO's public presence in the United States, particularly its conferences on Asia and Africa. But what is often lacking is a richer context for evaluating these UNESCO products, whether in the United States or abroad."

REVIEW: *Choice* v50 no12 p2298 Ag 2013 K. K. Hill

REVIEW: *Engl Hist Rev* v129 no539 p1017-8 Ag 2014 Ryan Shaffer

HAZELL, SARAH. The knitted alphabet. See Haxell, K.

HEAD, RANDOLPH C. A concise history of Switzerland. See Church, C. H.

HEAD, SIMON. Mindless; why smarter machines are making dumber humans; [by] Simon Head 240 p. 2013 Basic Books

1. Business—Data processing—Psychological aspects 2. Business literature 3. Industries—Technological innovations—Psychological aspects 4. Knowledge management 5. Mental efficiency 6. Technology—Social aspects
ISBN 0465018440; 9780465018444 (hardback)
LC 2013-041878

SUMMARY: In this book, "Simon Head argues that Computer Business Systems (CBSs) . . . have come to trump human expertise, dictating the goals and strategies of a wide array of businesses, and de-skilling the jobs of middle class workers in the process. CBSs are especially dysfunctional, Head argues, when they apply their disembodied expertise to transactions between humans, as in health care, education, customer relations, and human resources management." (Publisher's note)

REVIEW: *Kirkus Rev* v82 no2 p199 Ja 15 2014

REVIEW: *N Y Rev Books* v61 no6 p35-7 Ap 3 2014 Robert Skidelsky

HEADLEY, CLEVIS.ed. Haiti and the Americas. See Haiti and the Americas

HEALEY, NICOLA. Dorothy Wordsworth and Hartley Coleridge; the poetics of relationship; [by] Nicola Healey xiv, 272 p. 2012 Palgrave Macmillan

1. Identity (Philosophical concept) in literature 2. LITERARY CRITICISM—European—English, Irish, Scottish, Welsh 3. LITERARY CRITICISM—Poetry 4. LITERARY CRITICISM—Women Authors 5. Poets, English—19th century—Family relationships 6. Romanticism—England
ISBN 9780230277724 (hardback)
LC 2012-006104

SUMMARY: This book by Nicola Healey "a reassessment of the writings of Hartley Coleridge and Dorothy Wordsworth and presents them in a new poetics of relationship, re-evaluating their relationships with William Wordsworth and Samuel Taylor Coleridge to restore a more accurate understanding of Hartley and Dorothy as independent and original writers." (Publisher's note)

REVIEW: *TLS* no5771 p10-1 N 8 2013 TOM DURNO

"Dorothy Wordsworth: Wonders of the Everyday," "Dorothy Wordsworth and Hartley Coleridge: The Poetics of Relationship," and "Wordsworth and Coleridge: Promising Losses." "Both book and exhibition testify to [Pamela] Woof's own efforts over many years to sustain and develop work on Dorothy Wordsworth. . . . Because of such admissions that she was no full poet, [Nicola] Healey's account of Hartley's verse seems more novel than her reading of Dorothy's works. Where Woof gives space to Dorothy's non-literary life alongside her texts, Healey's framing of Dorothy's writing in primarily literary terms is undermined by Dorothy's own discomfort with her poetic identity. . . . [Peter] Larkin's essays span thirty years, reflecting a careful tuning-in to the grain of these poets' respective voices, and are divided into discrete sections on them."

THE HEALTH CARE CASE; the Supreme Court's decision and its implications; xiv, 386 p. 2013 Oxford University Press

1. Health care reform—Economic aspects—United States 2. Health care reform—United States 3. Health insurance—Law and legislation—United States 4.

Medical care—Finance—Law and legislation—United States 5. Political science literature
ISBN 0199301050 (hbk.); 0199301069 (pbk.); 9780199301058 (hbk.); 9780199301065 (pbk.)
LC 2012-051327

SUMMARY: "This work offers an array of legal perspectives on NFIB v. Sebelius (2012), the case where Chief Justice Roberts surprised many by writing a majority opinion upholding the individual mandate based on Congress's taxing power. The decision. . . , has unleashed discussions relating to the chief justice's motives, the significance of the decision for the law, and its importance to Constitutional law and the role of the federal government." (Choice: Current Reviews for Academic Libraries)

REVIEW: *Choice* v51 no7 p1308-9 Mr 2014 J. F. Kraus

"The Health Care Case: The Supreme Court's Decision and Its Implications." "If readers are looking for definitive answers, they should look elsewhere. . . . Depending on the chapter, the chief [justice] is a statesman, a cynic, or someone who clearly misinterpreted the commerce and the necessary and proper clauses. This is the book's strength. The diversity of ideological and legal perspectives, and the different interpretations of the case's significance, makes this a good read for anyone interested in NFIB v. Sebelius and the Patient Protection and Affordable Care Act."

HEALY, CHRISTOPHER. The Hero's Guide to Being an Outlaw; 528 p. 2014 Harpercollins Childrens Books
1. Adventure stories 2. Bounty hunters—Fiction 3. Humorous stories 4. Princes—Fiction 5. Princesses—Fiction
ISBN 006211848X; 9780062118486

SUMMARY: "The League of Princes returns in the hilariously epic conclusion to the hit series that began with Christopher Healy's 'The Hero's Guide to Saving Your Kingdom.' . . . Posters plastered across the thirteen kingdoms are saying that Briar Rose has been murdered—and the four Princes Charming are the prime suspects. Now they're on the run in a desperate attempt to clear their names." (Publisher's note)

REVIEW: *Kirkus Rev* v82 no5 p103 Mr 1 2014

"The Hero's Guide to Being an Outlaw". "While initially portrayed as more competent than their princes, the princesses soon reveal themselves as just as hilariously dysfunctional. Throughout the heroes' and heroines' travels, the anti-prince conspiracy is revealed in each kingdom—it's directly related to loose ends from 'The Hero's Guide to Storming the Castle' (2013). Side characters make comedic final appearances, and a surprise villain team-up provides closure to the trilogy. Part screwball comedy, part sly wit and all fun."

REVIEW: *SLJ* v60 no4 p147 Ap 2014 Mary Beth Rassulo

HEARN, CHESTER G. Lincoln and McClellan at war; [by] Chester G. Hearn 257 p. 2012 Louisiana State University Press
1. Command of troops—History—19th century 2. Historical literature
ISBN 9780807145524 (cloth : alk. paper); 9780807145531 (pdf)
LC 2012-004477

SUMMARY: "At the beginning of the Civil War, President Abraham Lincoln and his highest-ranking general, George B. McClellan, agreed that the United States must preserve the Union. Their differing strategies for accomplishing that goal, however, created constant conflict. In 'Lincoln and McClellan at War,' Chester G. Hearn explores this troubled relationship, revealing its complexity and showing clearly why the two men--both inexperienced with war--eventually parted ways." (Publisher's note)

REVIEW: *Choice* v50 no9 p1698-9 My 2013 D. L. Wilson

REVIEW: *Rev Am Hist* v42 no1 p78-83 Mr 2014 Kathryn Shively Meier

"Lincoln and McClellan at War." "Chester Hearn's new analysis of McClellan does not meaningfully diverge from its predecessors, but rather it filters McClellan's politics and generalship through the prism of his relationship to Lincoln as the two attempted to craft early Union military strategy. . . . Throughout the narrative, Hearn pays careful attention to the details of McClellan's strategic thinking, but disappointingly, he does not always follow through at the tactical level. . . . Hearn's greatest strength is his ability to convey the contingency of events that affected McClellan's and, secondarily, Lincoln's abilities to make strategic decisions."

HEARSON, RUTH.il. Leo loves baby time. See McQuinn, A.

HEASLEY, GWENDOLYN. Don't call me baby; 304 p. 2014 HarperTeen
1. Blogs 2. Internet & teenagers 3. Mothers & daughters—Fiction 4. Young adult fiction
ISBN 0062208527; 9780062208521 (pbk.)
LC 2013-956490

SUMMARY: In this book, by Gwendolyn Heasley, "Imogene's mother has been writing [a] . . . blog about her since before she was born. The thing is, Imogene is fifteen now, and her mother is still blogging about her. . . . When a mandatory school project compels Imogene to start her own blog, Imogene is reluctant to expose even more of her life online . . . until she realizes that the project is the opportunity she's been waiting for to define herself for the first time." (Publisher's note)

REVIEW: *Bull Cent Child Books* v67 no11 p577 Jl/Ag 2014 K. C.

REVIEW: *Kirkus Rev* v82 no5 p93 Mr 1 2014

"Don't Call Me Baby". " Imogene's mother is a prolific professional blogger, continually blogging about her unfortunate daughter's every cute smile and dirty diaper to her large online audience since she was a baby. Now that she is 15, however, 'Babylicious' is beginning to resent the fact that every intimate detail of her daily life is subject to public scrutiny. . . . As the witty story unfolds, mommies and daughters learn to give each other some space and that the Internet is no substitute for real-life experience. [Gwendolyn] Heasley delivers her message without compromising frothy fun. This surprisingly poignant comedy about teen-parent communication has enough bite to pique the interest of any teenager having trouble interacting meaningfully with her parents."

REVIEW: *SLJ* v60 no5 p131 My 2014 Amanda Raklovits

HEAVEN, HELL, AND THE AFTERLIFE; eternity in Judaism, Christianity, and Islam; xxii, 223 p. 2013 Praeger
1. Eternity 2. Future life 3. Jewish theology 4. Judaism—Customs & practices 5. Religious literature
ISBN 9781440801839 (alk. paper)

LC 2012-048027

SUMMARY: This book "primarily deals with the afterlife as gleaned from Jewish scriptures, Philo, Josephus, and the Dead Sea Scrolls. The contributors provide a thorough treatment of the varieties of views in Judaism. The writers demonstrate . . . that Sheol, the Hebrew word variously translated as the 'grave' and "the abode of the dead," is free from any ideas of rewards and punishments, and that no developed concept of the afterlife exists in the Hebrew Bible." (Choice: Current Reviews for Academic Libraries)

REVIEW: *Choice* v51 no7 p1182 Mr 2014 W. J. Pankey

"Heaven, Hell and the Afterlife: Eternity in Judaism, Christianity, and Islam." "[J. Harold] Ellens's edited three-volume set . . . is an ambitious attempt to make meaning of these three concepts as found in Judaism, Christianity, and Islam. . . . In this reviewer's opinion, the contributors fail to see that the sayings of Jesus do carry the idea of retribution and final judgment. They are correct, however, in demonstrating that the church has embellished the afterlife far beyond what scant New Testament evidence exists. . . . This set provides readers with a wealth of material on various views of the afterlife. While not all readers will come to the same conclusions as the contributors, these writers have provided stimulating material that is sure to spark further discussion."

HEBLE, AJAY. The fierce urgency of now. See Lipsitz, G.

HECHT, JENNIFER MICHAEL. Stay; a history of suicide and the philosophies against it; [by] Jennifer Michael Hecht 264 p. 2013 Yale University Press

1. Communities 2. Historical literature 3. Philosophical literature 4. Philosophy—History 5. Suicide 6. Suicide—Moral & ethical aspects 7. Suicide—Prevention
ISBN 9780300186086 (cloth : alk. paper)
LC 2013-016107

SUMMARY: "In this sweeping intellectual and cultural history, poet and historian Jennifer Michael Hecht channels her grief for two friends lost to suicide into a search for history's most persuasive arguments against the irretrievable act, arguments she hopes to bring back into public consciousness. . . . By examining how people in other times have found . . . reasons to stay alive when suicide seems a tempting choice, she makes a . . . intellectual and moral case against suicide." (Publisher's note)

REVIEW: *New Yorker* v89 no40 p89-1 D 9 2013

"Stay." "[Author Jennifer Michael Hecht] offers a history of suicide and of arguments against it. She recounts episodes from the canon of voluntary self-murder, including the deaths of Socrates, Cato, Samson, Sylvia Plath, and even Jesus--whose end, according to some scholars, was tantamount to suicide. After studies showed that sensationalized accounts of suicide inspired imitators, journalists began to tread lightly. Hecht puzzles through the anti-suicide insights of Western thinkers such as the neoclassical Aquinas, the 'Zen-like' Arthur Schopenhauer, and the rational Kant."

HECHT, MARY A. 250 Tips for Staying Young; A Guide to Aging Well; [by] Mary A. Hecht 104 p. 2013 CreateSpace Independent Publishing Platform

1. Aging 2. Older people—Sexual behavior 3. Personal finance 4. Retirement 5. Self-help materials
ISBN 1490565108 (pbk.); 9781490565101 (pbk.)

SUMMARY: In this book on aging, "the author talks openly about the aging body, eyes, ears, nose, throat, teeth, face, hair, skin and mind. . . . She also appends several short anecdotes and vignettes at the end of each chapter in which real people relate their own relevant experiences." Topics include "finances in retirement, protection from identity theft and mugging, leaving a legacy, and the often taboo topic of aging and sex." (Kirkus Reviews)

REVIEW: *Kirkus Rev* v82 no1 p102 Ja 1 2014

"250 Tips For Staying Young: A Guide to Aging Well". "An engaging, frank handbook that focuses on how to avoid looking and feeling old. [Mary A.] Hecht . . . has written a guide that approaches aging with honesty, humor and insight. She takes somewhat of a risk of alienating her intended audience by addressing the unpleasant aspects of aging in Part 1. . . . But Hecht tempers what could be unsettling for the reader by including specific, easy solutions in each chapter. . . . Hecht approaches each of these subjects without being judgmental as she explains her point of view in language that is simple yet not condescending. Chapters are brief and to the point; some readers may in fact find the content a bit too cursory rather than comprehensive."

HEFFER, SIMON. High Minds; The Victorians and the Birth of Modern Britain; [by] Simon Heffer 896 p. 2013 Random House Books

1. Democracy—Great Britain 2. Great Britain—Intellectual life—19th century 3. Great Britain—Politics & government—1837-1901 4. Historical literature 5. Social reformers—Great Britain—Biography
ISBN 1847946771; 9781847946775

SUMMARY: "Simon Heffer's new book forms an ambitious exploration of the making of the Victorian age and the Victorian mind. . . . It traces the evolution of British democracy and shows how early laissez-faire attitudes to the lot of the less fortunate turned into campaigns to improve their lives and prospects. It analyses the birth of new attitudes to education, religion and science." (Publisher's note)

REVIEW: *Hist Today* v63 no11 p65 N 2013 GEOFFREY BEST

REVIEW: *New Statesman* v142 no5178 p45-6 O 4 2013 Tristram Hunt

REVIEW: *TLS* no5785 p22-3 F 14 2014 CLARE PETTITT

"High Minds: The Victorians and the Birth of Modern Britain" and "Victoria's Madmen: Revolution and Alienation." "Both [Simon] Heffer's and [Clive] Bloom's histories . . . get the dragnets out, gathering great tankloads of Victorian specimens. . . . Rather than setting up a question that needs an answer, both these authors start their books by telling us off. . . . Heffer makes use of archives that are familiar to nineteenth-century historians, but what he does with them is disappointing. . . . Bloom undoubtedly has an instinct for juicy quotations, and 'Victoria's Madmen' is perhaps best approached as a sort of common-place book, but . . . there are no footnotes. . . . Many of Bloom's sentences are improbably long, grammatically challenged and disorientating to read."

HEFFER, SIMON. Simply English; An A-Z of Avoidable Errors; [by] Simon Heffer 400 p. 2014 Random House Books

1. Authorship—Style manuals 2. Comparative gram-

mar—Handbooks, manuals, etc. 3. English language—Errors of usage 4. English language—Usage 5. Linguistic usage
ISBN 1847946763; 9781847946768

SUMMARY: "In 'Simply English' he offers [a] useful A-Z guide to frequent errors, common misunderstandings and stylistic howlers. . . . With articles on everything from punctuation to tabloid English to adverbs and adjectives, 'Simply English' is [a] companion for anyone who cares about the language and wants to use it correctly." (Publisher's note)

REVIEW: *New Statesman* v143 no5211 p48 My 23 2014

REVIEW: *TLS* no5794 p27 Ap 18 2014 MICHAEL CAINES

"Simply English: An A to Z of Avoidable Errors." "Simon Heffer intends 'Simply English' to complement 'Strictly English' (2010), a guide to writing proper, avoiding vulgarities and the like. In this A to Z of grammatical terms, howlers and catachreses, the uncertain language-user may learn that a muscle is part of the body but a mussel is a bivalve—and that immolation is not death by fire but the sacrifice of a life. . . . There are also longer entries in which Heffer offers some more general guidelines; many would-be professional writers would do well to read and heed them, even (perhaps particularly) if they disagree. . . . Yet this book's usefulness is not without limits."

HEFFRON, MARGERY M. Louisa Catherine; the other Mrs. Adams; [by] Margery M. Heffron 416 p. 2014 Yale University Press

1. Biography (Literary form) 2. Politicians' spouses 3. Presidents' spouses—United States—Biography
ISBN 9780300197969 (cloth: alk. paper)
LC 2013-042868

SUMMARY: "Louisa Catherine Johnson Adams, wife and political partner of John Quincy Adams, became one of the most widely known women in America when her husband assumed office as sixth president in 1825. . . . Louisa left behind a trove of journals, essays, letters, and other writings, yet no biographer has mined these riches until now. [Author] Margery Heffron brings Louisa out of the shadows at last to offer the first full and nuanced portrait of an extraordinary first lady." (Publisher's note)

REVIEW: *Choice* v52 no2 p328 O 2014 H. Aquino

REVIEW: *N Y Rev Books* v61 no10 p45-7 Je 5 2014 Susan Dunn

"John Quincy Adams: American Visionary," "Louisa Catherine: The Other Mrs. Adams," and "A Traveled First Lady: Writings of Louisa Catherine Adams." "As Fred Kaplan demonstrates in his engaging, well-crafted, and deeply researched biography . . . this supremely successful diplomat and shrewd practitioner of realpolitik had a personality quite unsuited for a life in politics. . . . In 'Louisa Catherine: The Other Mrs. Adams,' Margery Heffron's insightful and entertaining though unfinished book . . . we enter deeply into the damaged family life of John Quincy and Louisa. . . . A fine new sampling of Louisa's writings, 'A Traveled First Lady: Writings of Louisa Catherine Adams' [is] edited by Margaret A. Hogan and C. James Taylor."

REVIEW: *N Y Times Book Rev* p34 My 11 2014

REVIEW: *N Y Times Book Rev* p1-17 My 4 2014 Virginia DeJohn Anderson

REVIEW: *New Yorker* v90 no11 p71-1 My 5 2014

"John Quincy Adams: American Visionary" and "Louisa Catherine: The Other Mrs. Adams." "[John Quincy Adams's] latest biographer, Fred Kaplan . . . argues that Adams doesn't fully deserve his reputation for coldness, but, for all its diligence, 'John Quincy Adams: American Visionary' . . . never really succeeds in raising the sixth President's temperature. . . . [Author Margery M.] Heffron's agreeably written biography—cut short by the death of the author, in December, 2011—leaves Louisa [Catherine Adams] on the threshold of the Adamses' unhappy years in the White House. Another writer will have to finish her story."

HEGARTY, PATRICIA. Five black cats; [by] Patricia Hegarty 22 p. 2013 Tiger Tales

1. Board books 2. Cats—Fiction 3. Ghosts—Juvenile literature 4. Halloween—Fiction 5. Stories in rhyme
ISBN 1589256115 (board book); 9781589256118 (board book)
LC 2013-009974

SUMMARY: In this children's book by Patricia Hegarty, "a troop of cats traverse a spooky landscape as they make their way to a party hosted by ghosts. Each double-page spread shows the felines' encounters with the likes of an owl, jack-o'-lanterns or a bat. . . . The sleek, slightly retro art, likely created using a computer, depicts the cats cavorting at night through a shadowy cityscape, the countryside and a haunted house." (Kirkus Reviews)

REVIEW: *Kirkus Rev* v81 no19 p358 O 1 2013

REVIEW: *Kirkus Rev* v82 no1 p34 Ja 1 2014

"Five Black Cats". "One or two of these creepy meetings may be too abstract for the youngest readers, as the cats hear eerie noises with no discernible source on the page. The text, which consists of one rhyming couplet per scene, mostly scans despite a couple of wobbles. . . . A brighter color palette would have given the project a friendlier, more universal appeal. Luckily, the well-lit, final party scene provides a playful conclusion. For toddlers unafraid of typical Halloween imagery. "

HEGEDUS, BETHANY. Grandfather Gandhi. See Gandhi, A.

HEGLAND, MARY ELAINE. Days of revolution; political unrest in an Iranian village; [by] Mary Elaine Hegland 352 p. 2014 Stanford University Press

1. Historical literature 2. Political culture—Iran 3. Villages—Iran—Case studies
ISBN 9780804775670 (cloth: alk. paper); 9780804775687 (pbk.: alk. paper)
LC 2013-026629

SUMMARY: Written by Mary Elaine Hegland, "'Days of Revolution' offers an insider's view of how regular people were drawn into, experienced, and influenced the 1979 Revolution and its aftermath. Conventional wisdom assumes Shi'a religious ideology fueled the revolutionary movement. But Hegland counters that the Revolution spread through much more pragmatic concerns: growing inequality, lack of development and employment opportunities, government corruption." (Publisher's note)

REVIEW: *Choice* v51 no8 p1470 Ap 2014 G. M. Farr

REVIEW: *Middle East J* v68 no3 p474-5 Summ 2014 Jonathan G. Katz

"Days of Revolution: Political Unrest in an Iranian Village." "In this fascinating study, written with the hindsight of 34 years, [author Mary Elaine] Hegland shows that in Iran, no less than in America, the . . . adage that 'all politics is local' applies. . . . Hegland analyzes the course of the village revolution through the lens of tayefehkashi, the competition for local dominance between extended kinship groups. . . . Hegland's final chapter, written following visits to Iran in 2003 and 2008, recounts the changes that 'Aliabad has undergone in her absence."

HEIKKINEN, KAY.tr. Ben Barka Lane. See Saeed, M.

HEILEMANN, JOHN. Double Down. See Halperin, M.

HEILIGMAN, DEBORAH. The boy who loved math; the improbable life of Paul Erdos; [by] Deborah Heiligman 48 p. 2013 Roaring Brook Press

1. Biographies 2. Gifted children 3. Mathematicians—Hungary—Biography—Juvenile literature 4. Picture books for children

ISBN 1596433078; 9781596433076 (hardcover)

LC 2012-029744

SUMMARY: This book is a biography of mathematician Paul Erdös. He was a child prodigy who had to be homeschooled due to his inability to sit still and follow rules. "High school was a better fit, and he made friends with students who shared his love of math. His skills became famous, but Erdös didn't know how to do laundry, cook, or even butter his own bread. He 'didn't fit into the world in a regular way.' So, he created a life that fit him instead." (School Library Journal)

REVIEW: *Booklist* v109 no19/20 p82 Je 1 2013 Carolyn Phelan

REVIEW: *Booklist* p4-10 Ja 1 2014 Supplement Gillian Engberg

"The Boy Who Loved Math: The Improbable Life of Paul Erdos," "Little Red Writing," and "Flight of the Honey Bee." "Mathematician Paul Erdos is the subject of this inventive, entertaining picture-book biography. . . . The colorful, energetic artwork, organized in a well-designed mix of spot scenes with full-page spreads, further expands the concepts with decorative elements. . . . [An] uproarious retelling of 'Little Red Riding Hood' . . . [Melissa] Sweet's exuberant illustrations reinforce the concepts with wit and energy. A perfect prompt for beginning writers to borrow from Little Red's basket of words and try their own stories. . . . [Raymond] Huber . . . shows an obvious understanding of both honeybees and of what will interest young children in this attractive offering. . . . One of the most informative--and beautiful--picture books about honeybees."

REVIEW: *Booklist* v110 no9/10 p13-6 Ja 1 2014

"Becoming Ben Franklin: How a Candle-Maker's Son Helped Light the Flame of Liberty," "The Mad Potter: George E. Ohr, Eccentric Genius," and "The Boy Who Loved Math: The Improbable Life of Paul Erdos." "In this handsomely designed, solidly researched, and beautifully written biography, [Russell] Freedman uses well-chosen quotes, anecdotes, and illustrations as he traces Ben Franklin's improbable journey. . . . Intelligently written and beautifully illustrated, this engaging book describes the life and flamboyant personality of Mississippi potter George Ohr. . . . This unusual picture book introduces eccentric mathematician Paul Erdos and his unconventional life. Lively writing and vivid artwork combine to make this a memorable biography."

REVIEW: *Bull Cent Child Books* v66 no11 p511 Jl/Ag 2013 F. B.

REVIEW: *Horn Book Magazine* v89 no3 p106 7 My/Je 2013 SAM BLOOM

REVIEW: *Kirkus Rev* p56 N 15 2013 Best Books

REVIEW: *Kirkus Rev* v81 no8 p87-8 Ap 15 2013

REVIEW: *N Y Times Book Rev* p14 Jl 14 2013 NATE SILVER

"The Boy Who Loved Math: The Improbable Life of Paul Erdos" and "On a Beam of Light: A Story of Albert Einstein." "Erdos is the hero of Deborah Heiligman's energetic new children's book, 'The Boy Who Loved Math.' It should make excellent reading for nerds of all ages. The book is not a mathematics primer. Heiligman incudes a straightforward discussion about how prime numbers work, and there are LeUyen Pham's precise and playful illustrations, which are full of hidden mathematical allusions and puzzles. But Heiligman focuses on Erdos's personal story. . . . Perhaps appropriately, 'On a Beam of Light' has a daydreamy feel. The prose isn't as wry as Heiligman's and the illustrations (beautifully done by Vladimir Radunsky) are more whimsical."

REVIEW: *Publ Wkly* v260 no22 p59 Je 3 2013

REVIEW: *Publ Wkly* p56 Children's starred review annual 2013

REVIEW: *SLJ* v59 no5 p92 My 2013 Sara-Jo Lupo Sites

HEILIGMAN, DEBORAH. Snow Dog, Go Dog; 32 p. 2013 Amazon Children's Pub.

1. Dogs—Juvenile fiction 2. Human-animal relationships 3. Picture books for children 4. Sledding 5. Snow—Juvenile literature

ISBN 1477817247; 9781477817247

SUMMARY: In this children's picture book, "Tinka, an exuberant Labrador retriever is excited about winter as she begins her rambunctious romp through the falling snow. She runs to and fro, hides behind a snow polar bear and joins her human friend for a harrowing sled ride. She has a romping good time with another dog and wanders far away as they play chase and race. . . . Then a car appears. Her human friend has found her. He has brought her favorite toy and a dog treat." (Children's Literature)

REVIEW: *Booklist* v110 no3 p102-3 O 1 2013 Connie Fletcher

"Snow Dog, Go Dog." "This takes readers through a snowy outing, from the first flurries to the great heaps of snow in which Tinka and his boy revel. There is a nice narrative arc here, complete with suspense as Tinka dashes off and is temporarily lost. As before, the bouncy rhymes mimic Tinka's playful nature. . . . The bright, textured acrylics form a nice contrast between Tinka's gold coloring and the icy-blue snowscape, while Tinka's comically elongated snout points out the highlight of each scene. A cozy ending rounds off this satisfying adventure."

REVIEW: *SLJ* v60 no3 p112 Mr 2014 Sharon Grover

HEIM, MICHAEL HENRY, 1943-2012.tr. The encyclopedia of the dead. See The encyclopedia of the dead

HEIMLICH, HENRY J. Heimlich's maneuvers; my seventy years of lifesaving innovation; [by] Henry J. Heimlich 230 p. 2014 Prometheus Books

1. Heimlich Maneuver—history 2. Medical innovations 3. Memoirs 4. Physicians—Autobiography 5. Physicians—Biography
ISBN 9781616148492 (pbk.)
LC 2013-036223

SUMMARY: Author Henry J. Heimlich's "memoir looks beyond the invention of the author's eponymous technique, which has saved countless choking victims since 1974. The book begins with Heimlich's comfortable childhood in New Rochelle, N.Y.--filled with daydreams of 'medical discovery'--and follows him through his training at Cornell Medical College, his service in the Navy during WWII at a Gobi Desert hospital, his marriage, and his establishment of a remarkable surgical practice." (Publishers Weekly)

REVIEW: *Booklist* v110 no9/10 p29-30 Ja 1 2014 Tony Miksanek

"Heimlich's Maneuvers: My Seventy Years of Lifesaving Innovation." "[Henry J.] Heimlich is a real-life medical version of TV's MacGyver. While stationed in the Gobi Desert during WWII, he devised a simple cure for trachoma (a leading cause of blindness) by mixing pulverized sulfa antibiotic tablets with shaving cream.. . . . In his uplifting memoir, the retired thoracic surgeon and medical innovator comes across as a man with big ideas and lofty ideals, a caring physician who combines common sense and knowledge to make the world a safer place."

REVIEW: *Kirkus Rev* v81 no24 p122 D 15 2013

REVIEW: *Publ Wkly* v260 no48 p42-3 N 25 2013

A HEINRICH SCHÜTZ READER; letters and documents in translation; xxviii, 283 p. 2013 Oxford University Press

1. Anthologies 2. Composers—Germany—Biography 3. Gabrieli, Giovanni, 1557-1612 4. History—Sources
ISBN 9780199812202 (alk. paper)
LC 2012-011188

SUMMARY: This collection, edited by Gregory S. Johnston, presents "more than 150 documents by or about Heinrich Schütz, from his earliest studies under Giovanni Gabrieli to accounts of his final hours. . . . Dedications and prefaces of his printed music, letters and memoranda, poetry and petitions, travel passes and contracts, all offer immediate and unabridged access to the composer's life." (Publisher's note)

REVIEW: *Choice* v51 no8 p1411 Ap 2014 J. M. Edwards

"A Heinrich Schütz Reader: Letters and Documents in Translation". "Working with original manuscripts and early prints, [Gregory S.] Johnston offers the most comprehensive collection of Schütz documents (correspondence, prefaces, memoranda, contracts, and so on) to date—including material previously unavailable in English translation or even difficult to find in its original languages. . . . The explanatory footnotes (thankfully, not endnotes) provide historical and geographical context, background information about people referenced, and illumination of literary references. However, explanations appear only on the first occurrence of a word or phrase, which will be somewhat problematic for a reader who is sampling."

HEINRICHS, ANN. Brazil; [by] Ann Heinrichs 144 p. 2013 Children's Press, an imprint of Scholastic Inc.

1. Brazil—History 2. Brazil—Politics & government 3. Brazil—Social conditions 4. Brazil—Social life & customs 5. Children's nonfiction
ISBN 0531236757; 9780531236758 (library binding)
LC 2013-000089

SUMMARY: This book, by Ann Heinrichs, focuses on Brazil. The "country's culture, history, and geography are explored in detail, allowing readers a chance to see how people live. . . . Sidebars highlight especially interesting people, places, and events . . . [and] recipes give readers the opportunity to experience foreign cuisine first-hand." (Publisher's note)

REVIEW: *Booklist* v110 no9/10 p94 Ja 1 2014 Susan Dove Lempke

"Brazil," "Ireland," "North Korea." "For reliably accurate, attractively presented and well-calibrated information, the longstanding 'Enchantment of the World' series remains a superior choice. . . . Although the basic structure holds true to past versions, the updated photographs are truly eye-popping and take care to portray the countries as modern. . . . 'Brazil' . . . conveys an excitement about the country and its people as well as its plentiful animals and plants. It might not be necessary for libraries to replace 'Ireland,' since it hasn't changed radically, but this is a solid offering with updated statistics. 'North Korea' has a new author and a strong political focus, discussing life under the new leader, Kim Jong-un."

HEINRICHS, ANN. The Shipbuilder; [by] Ann Heinrichs 48 p. 2013 Marshall Cavendish

1. Children's nonfiction 2. Historical literature 3. Shipbuilding—United States—History—Juvenile literature 4. Shipwrights—United States—Juvenile literature
ISBN 0761400052; 9780761400059 (print); 9781608709878 (ebook)
LC 2011-028344

SUMMARY: This book on shipbuilders and shipbuilding in colonial America, by Christine Petersen, is part of the Colonial People series. It "introduces the master shipbuilder as well as the many skilled tradespeople needed to make a sailing ship." It includes "a description of the craftsman's process" and is "illustrated with tinted engravings and paintings from earlier eras as well as . . . color photos of artifacts and replicas." (Booklist)

REVIEW: *Booklist* v110 no4 p45 O 15 2013 Carolyn Phelan

"The Gunsmith," "The Merchant," and "The Shipbuilder." "Attractively designed, the books in the Colonial People series present and discuss the roles of individual trades from colonial America. . . . The publisher indicates the reading level as four, and while the books' relatively large type and square format are consistent with a fourth-grade audience, the readability level appears to be several grades higher. . . . In each book, the informative text is illustrated with tinted engravings and paintings from earlier eras as well as excellent color photos of artifacts and replicas and reenactments of historical trades in Colonial Williamsburg."

REVIEW: *SLJ* v60 no2 p117 F 2014 Lucinda Snyder Whitehurst

HEIVOLL, GAUTE. Before I burn; 336 p. 2014 Graywolf Press

1. Arson 2. Motivation (Psychology) 3. Norway—Fiction 4. Pyromania 5. True crime stories

ISBN 1555976611; 9781555976613 (alk. paper)
LC 2013-946919

SUMMARY: This book, by Gaute Heivoll, is "based on the true account of Norway's most dramatic arson case . . . An arsonist targets a small town for one long, terrifying month. . . . Amid the chaos, only a day before the last house is set afire, the community comes together for the christening of a young boy. . . . As he grows up, stories about the time of fear and fire become deeply engrained in his young mind until, as an adult, he begins to retell the story." (Publisher's note)

REVIEW: *Booklist* v110 no5 p28 N 1 2013 Stephanie Turza

"Before I Burn." "[Gaute] Heivoll, a Finsland native born in the midst of the arsonist's spree, grows up determined to uncover the true motives behind the arsonist's crimes. Heivoll pours his own experiences into 'Before I Burn,' blending autobiographical details with a true story to create a thrilling and poetic novel. In this dark and powerful examination of two men's obsessions, Heivoll's introspection and attention to detail are unparalleled. Fans of 'In Cold Blood' (1965) and 'The Devil in the White City' (2003) will appreciate the chilling true-crime angle, while Heivoll's dazzling prose will quickly enchant those unfamiliar with this Scandinavian writer. An absorbing story of compulsion, obsession, and the power of desire."

REVIEW: *Kirkus Rev* v81 no21 p156 N 1 2013

REVIEW: *New York Times* v163 no56397 pC7 Ja 30 2014 John Williams

REVIEW: *World Lit Today* v88 no1 p65 Ja/F 2014

HELD, SHAI, 1971-. Abraham Joshua Heschel; The call of transcendence; [by] Shai Held 2013 Indiana University Press

1. God (Judaism) 2. Heschel, Abraham Joshua, 1907-1972 3. Jewish theology 4. Religious literature 5. Transcendence of God

ISBN 9780253011268 hardcover

SUMMARY: "In this sympathetic, yet critical, examination, Shai Held elicits the overarching themes and unity of Heschel's incisive and insightful thought. Focusing on the idea of transcendence--or the movement from self-centeredness to God-centeredness--Held puts Heschel into dialogue with contemporary Jewish thinkers, Christian theologians, devotional writers, and philosophers of religion." (Publisher's note)

REVIEW: *N Y Times Book Rev* p23 F 16 2014 MARC TRACY

"Abraham Joshua Heschel: The Call of Transcendence." "Situating Heschel in his time and place is not a purpose of 'Abraham Joshua Heschel: The Call of Transcendence,' a short, overly dense and academic examination of Heschel's theology. I would not be surprised to learn that it is adapted only slightly from [author Shai] Held's dissertation. . . . If you hack through the opaque theological thicket, Held's purpose begins to emerge. It helps to know that Held is a co-founder of Machon Hadar, a Manhattan-based institute of Jewish learning committed to egalitarianism. . . . Held retroactively enrolls Heschel in the school."

HELFGOTT, JACQUELINE B.ed. Criminal psychology. See Criminal psychology

HELFGOTT, JACQUELINE B. Offender reentry; beyond crime and punishment; [by] Jacqueline B. Helfgott x, 241 p. 2013 Lynne Rienner Publishers

1. Criminal Justice, Administration of—United States 2. Criminals—Rehabilitation—United States 3. Ex-convicts—Services for—United States 4. Prisoners—Deinstitutionalization—United States 5. Social science literature

ISBN 9781588269126 (hc : alk. paper)
LC 2013-012998

SUMMARY: In this "exploration of the core issues surrounding offender reentry, Elaine Gunnison and Jacqueline Helfgott highlight the constant tension between policies meant to ensure smooth reintegration and the social forces especially the stigma of a criminal record that can prevent it from happening. Gunnison and Helfgott focus on the factors that enhance reentry success as they address challenges related to race, class, and gender." (Publisher's note)

REVIEW: *Choice* v51 no6 p1101-2 F 2014 C. Powell

"Offender Reentry: Beyond Crime & Punishment." "This book should he required reading for all advocates for the 'culture of control,' as it offers considerable support for recent moves within the community corrections systems toward giving offenders the benefit of the doubt. The authors . . . should be congratulated for bringing together and making clear the rich range of statistical data that clearly establishes the perennial difficulties involved in achieving 'successful reintegration.' . . . Arguably, however, the authors fail to acknowledge that an alternative way of understanding criminal justice is to focus on the ideological implications of the outcomes they describe so powerfully, outcomes that reproduce the exclusion of already marginalized groups."

HELLARD, SUE.il. Princesses are not just pretty. See Lum, K.

HELQUIST, BRETT.il. The fort that Jack built. See Ashburn, B.

HELQUIST, BRETT.il. The Shadowhand Covenant. See Farrey, B.

HELVIG, KRISTI. Burn out; [by] Kristi Helvig 272 p. 2014 EgmontUSA

1. Government, Resistance to—Fiction 2. JUVENILE FICTION—Action & Adventure—Survival Stories 3. JUVENILE FICTION—Fantasy & Magic 4. JUVENILE FICTION—Science Fiction 5. Mercenary troops—Fiction 6. Orphans—Fiction 7. Science fiction 8. Survival—Fiction 9. Weapons—Fiction

ISBN 9781606844793 (hardback)
LC 2013-018280

SUMMARY: In this book, "Tora Reynolds, the daughter of a famous weapons developer, spends her days isolated in an underground bunker. . ., The Earth has become a monstrously inhospitable place, with an angry sun that has shriveled the land to dust. . . . When Tora is unexpectedly approached by Markus, a friend of her father's with a disreputable past, she is cast into a dangerous game in which Markus' group and the oppressive Consulate vie for access to her deadly arsenal." (Kirkus Reviews)

REVIEW: *Booklist* v110 no15 p80 Ap 1 2014 Daniel Kraus

REVIEW: *Bull Cent Child Books* v67 no8 p407 Ap 2014 A. S.

REVIEW: *Kirkus Rev* v82 no5 p105 Mr 1 2014

"Burn Out". "In an unrecognizable future, the sun has ballooned to epic proportions, leaving the Earth charred, desiccated and nearly vacant, as a teenage girl tries to hold on to her sanity and secrets. . . . Tora is whip-smart and sharp-tongued, and though she possesses enough munitions to blow up a spaceship, her sarcasm is by far her most useful tool. Helvig builds a rock-solid future world and provides enough staggering plot twists and turns to keep pages flying to the gut-wrenching cliffhanger. A scorching series opener not to be missed."

REVIEW: *Publ Wkly* v261 no4 p194 Ja 27 2014

REVIEW: *SLJ* v60 no7 p103 Jl 2014 Gretchen Kolderup

HELWIG, DAVID, 1938-. Clyde; [by] David Helwig 246 p. 2013 Bunim and Bannigan

1. Canada—Fiction 2. Friendship—Fiction 3. Marriage—Fiction 4. Memory—Fiction 5. Psychological fiction

ISBN 9781933480367 (alk. paper)

LC 2013-940038

SUMMARY: In this book by David Helwig, "betrayed by his oldest friend, a boyhood companion, his gingerly constructed career at stake, Clyde Bryanton, property developer and Ottawa political consultant, unpeels layers and layers of memory, a half century of getting along by going along. . . . Clyde is as baffled by the emotions that occasionally sound from his depths as he is by his mentors, the banker and the senator who manipulate money and power in a small Canadian city." (Publisher's note)

REVIEW: *Quill Quire* v80 no2 p26 Mr 2014 Kamal Al-Solaylee

"Clyde". "If all this tells you more about his friends and family than the man himself it's because—and herein lies both the strength and weakness of 'Clyde'—[David] Helwig structures the novel around his main character's recollections of the people who shaped his life from the 1940s to the 1990s. . . . Helwig confuses detail and narrative abundance with insight and meaning. At the end of this ultimately entertaining and fast read, you may well wonder what the author is trying to convey. 'Clyde' is a character study, a rake's progress of sorts, and on those terms, it succeeds. However, that success comes at a hefty expense, including underdeveloped supporting characters—and a hackneyed plot device by which the death of a childhood friend triggers Clyde's memories."

HEMINGWAY, ANDREW. The mysticism of money; precisionist painting and machine age America; George Ault, Stefan Hirsch, Louis Lozowick; [by] Andrew Hemingway 260 p. 2012 Periscope Pub., Ltd.

1. Art & economics 2. Art & society 3. Art—Political aspects 4. Art—United States—History 5. Art literature 6. Historical literature 7. Precisionism (Art movement)

ISBN 9781934772805

LC 2011-944523

SUMMARY: This book by Andrew Hemingway "overturns orthodox views of Precisionist art and, more generally, of American Modernism. A trio of neglected artists--Stefan Hirsch, Louis Lozowick, and George C. Ault--are finally accorded in-depth analysis; and, drawing on an unrivaled knowledge of left-leaning politics, Hemingway connects Precisionism to a milieu in which experimental theater, a wave of 'little magazines,' and engagement with communist politics stirred debate and conflict." (Publisher's note)

REVIEW: *Choice* v51 no2 p247-8 O 2013 R. L. McGrath

"The Mysticism of Money: Precisionist Painting and Machine Age America." "This book by [author Andrew] Hemingway . . . is as perplexing as its title. It is the product of the most far-ranging erudition and thoughtful research ever expended on an American art movement. It is also the result of a tired, tiresome, neo-Marxist analysis of artworks that is, in this reviewer's judgment, wide of the mark. . . . This is no small contribution to the history of art. Yet, despite all, the exegetical key to the meanings of these canvases remains elusive. Somehow, this art manages to evade even the most penetrating analysis. One thing, however, is clear; anyone wishing to deal with American art of the 1920s and 1930s will need to consult this remarkable book."

HEMINGWAY, ERNEST, 1899-1961. The Letters of Ernest Hemingway; 1923-1925; 515 p. 2013 Cambridge University Press

1. Americans—France 2. Authors—Correspondence 3. Dos Passos, John, 1896-1970 4 Novelists, American—20th century—Correspondence

ISBN 0521897343; 9780521897341

LC 2012-429205

SUMMARY: This book, the second in a collection of writer Ernest Hemingway's letters, "illuminates Hemingway's literary apprenticeship in the legendary milieu of expatriate Paris in the 1920s. We witness the development of his friendships with the likes of Sylvia Beach, F. Scott Fitzgerald and John Dos Passos. . . . In this period, Hemingway publishes his first three books, including 'In Our Time' . . . and discovers a lifelong passion for Spain and the bullfight." (Publisher's note)

REVIEW: *America* v210 no6 p33-5 F 24 2014 JON M. SWEENEY

REVIEW: *Booklist* v110 no3 p14-5 O 1 2013 Steve Paul

REVIEW: *Choice* v51 no10 p1802 Je 2014 S. Miller

REVIEW: *Libr J* v138 no14 p107 S 1 2013 William Gargan

REVIEW: *N Y Times Book Rev* p27 N 24 2013 MICHAEL GORR

"The Letters of Ernest Hemingway: 1924-1925". "The second volume of 'The Letters of Ernest Hemingway' documents the years in which he became himself. . . . I suspect, however, that those who love his posthumous memoir, 'A Moveable Feast,' will be surprised by how little of letters these letters contain. . . . There's no account of the city itself, not even in the letters to his parents back home in Illinois. . . . [F. Scott] Fitzgerald himself is, however, present as the recipient of some of this book's richest letters. . . . His style here is at once close to and yet unutterably distant from that of his fiction. The language is often bone-simple, and yet its minimalism rarely seems the product of deliberate choice."

REVIEW: *Publ Wkly* v260 no34 p63 Ag 26 2013

REVIEW: *TLS* no5792 p23 Ap 4 2014 SARAH GRAHAM

"The Letters of Ernest Hemingway: Volume II, 1923-1925." "Hemingway emerges as more vulnerable than his public persona usually allows, and more entertaining, too.

The letters confirm his reputation for machismo. There is evidence that his boundless energy could seem bullying . . . and his obsession with vigorous outdoor sports, especially bullfighting, is clear. . . . Despite the less appealing aspects of his character, Hemingway is passionate about literature, an astute critic and a generous, supportive friend, comfortable with expressing his love for others. . . . This essential volume, beautifully presented and annotated with tremendous care and extraordinary attention to detail, offers readers a Hemingway who is both familiar and new."

HEMPHILL, STEPHANIE. Hideous love; the story of the girl who wrote Frankenstein; [by] Stephanie Hemphill 320 p. 2013 Balzer + Bray, an imprint of HarperCollinsPublishers

1. Authorship—Fiction 2. Love—Fiction 3. Novels in verse

ISBN 0061853313; 9780061853319 (hardcover bdg.)

LC 2013-000237

SUMMARY: This book is a "fictionalized verse biography of" author Mary Shelley. Stephanie Hemphill "explores the particular challenges facing a gifted female artist who allies herself with a renowned male poet. Central to the plot is the parentage of Mary Wollstonecraft Godwin Shelley, daughter of Mary Wollstonecraft, the pioneering feminist philosopher who died days after Mary was born, and William Godwin, a radical political philosopher who espoused free love for all but his daughters." (Kirkus Reviews)

REVIEW: *Booklist* v110 no3 p90-1 O 1 2013 Daniel Kraus

REVIEW: *Bull Cent Child Books* v67 no3 p156-7 N 2013 K. C.

REVIEW: *Horn Book Magazine* v89 no5 p100 S/O 2013 DEIRDRE F. BAKER

"Hideous Love: The Story of the Girl Who Wrote Frankenstein." "Although she tries to affect Mary's voice, [Stephanie] Hemphill meets the reader closer to the twenty-first century than the early nineteenth, with verse that reads like short journal entries and incorporates modern-day turns of phrase ('staying on task,' '[this] might not be the greatest plan,' and the like). Hemphill's own style doesn't have notable poetic verve, but even so she succeeds in producing an informative, mildly impressionistic introduction to Mary's life. This is richer as history than character study, but it's a good beginning for readers curious about the author of Frankenstein."

REVIEW: *Kirkus Rev* v81 no17 p96 S 1 2013

REVIEW: *Publ Wkly* v260 no36 p58 S 9 2013

REVIEW: *SLJ* v59 no9 p158 S 2013 Barbara M. Moon

HENDERSON, BILL.ed. The Pushcart Prize Xxxviii. See The Pushcart Prize Xxxviii

HENDERSON, BONNIE. The next tsunami; living on a restless coast; [by] Bonnie Henderson 320 p. 2014 Oregon State University Press

1. Geology—Northwest, Pacific 2. Horning, Tom 3. Natural history literature 4. Tsunami hazard zones—Pacific Coast (America) 5. Tsunamis—Pacific Coast (America)

ISBN 9780870717321 (alk. paper)

LC 2013-040039

SUMMARY: This book on tsunamis in the U.S. Northwest, by Bonnie Henderson, "begins with a tsunami that hit Seaside, Ore., in 1964, and follows the career of Tom Horning, then a boy in Seaside, whose life is interwoven with the story of the scientific realization that the Earth's crust is made up of moving plates, something still hotly debated 50 years ago." (Publishers Weekly)

REVIEW: *Kirkus Rev* v82 no4 p143 F 15 2014

"The Next Tsunami". "The author does service in pointing to possible events that have long been overshadowed by projections of the next major earthquake in the vastly more populated areas to the south. Although her prose is more scattershot than the densely layered encyclopedism of John McPhee's geological writings, she covers a great deal of scientific ground while never losing sight of the human interest side of the story. As with McPhee, there's poetry to her ground truthing, too. . . . Of more than local interest, though Northwesterners should pay particularly close attention to the news [Bonnie] Henderson brings."

REVIEW: *Publ Wkly* v261 no5 p48 F 3 2014

HENDERSON, JASON. Street fight; the politics of mobility in San Francisco; [by] Jason Henderson 256 p. 2013 University of Massachusetts Press

1. City planning—California—San Francisco 2. Political science literature 3. San Francisco (Calif.)—Politics & government 4. Transportation planning—California—San Francisco 5. Urban transportation—Political aspects—California—San Francisco

ISBN 9781558499980 (hardcover : alk. paper); 9781558499997 (pbk. : alk. paper)

LC 2012-050132

SUMMARY: In this book, "Through a detailed case study of San Francisco, Jason Henderson examines how this is not just a struggle over what type of transportation is best for the city, but a series of ideologically charged political fights over issues of street space, public policy, and social justice." (Publisher's note)

REVIEW: *Choice* v51 no2 p355 O 2013 R. A. Beauregard

"Street Fight: The Politics of Mobility in San Francisco." "In his study of the 'politics of mobility,' [author Jason] Henderson . . . describes 50 years of controversy in San Francisco over the building and demolition of freeways, the construction of bike lanes, the financing of city transit, and the elimination of parking requirements. The author focuses on the political activities of three ideological groups: progressives who want to limit automobility and instead champion alternative modes of mobility; neoliberals who want to manage mobility through market pricing; and conservatives calling for more highways, fewer restrictions, and lower costs for car users. Henderson, in line with other progressives, argues that improved livability in cities means less automobility."

HENDERSON, MERYL.il. Scorpions! See Pringle, L.

HENDRICK, JOSHUA D. Gülen; the ambiguous politics of market Islam in Turkey and the world; [by] Joshua D. Hendrick xvi, 276 p. 2013 NYU Press

1. Gülen movement 2. Gülen, Fethullah, 1941- 3. Islam—Economic aspects—Turkey 4. Political science literature

ISBN 9780814770986 (hardback); 9781479800469 (paper)
LC 2013-006919

SUMMARY: "In Gülen, [author] Joshua D. Hendrick suggests that . . . the Gülen Movement, despite both praise and criticism, should be given credit for playing a significant role in Turkey's rise to global prominence. Drawing on 14 months of ethnographic fieldwork in Turkey and the U.S., Hendrick examines the Gülen Movement's role in Turkey's recent rise, as well as its strategic relationship with Turkey's Justice and Development Party-led government." (Publisher's note)

REVIEW: *Middle East J* v68 no1 p178-9 Wint 2014 Ahmet T. Kuru

REVIEW: *N Y Rev Books* v61 no6 p18-22 Ap 3 2014 Christopher de Bellaigue

"The Rise of Turkey: The Twenty-First Century's First Muslim Power," "Gülen: The Ambiguous Politics of Market Islam in Turkey and the World," and "İmamin Ordusu." "'The Rise of Turkey: The Twenty-First Century's First Muslim Power' . . . might have struck one as triumphal. . . . 'Gülen: The Ambiguous Politics of Market Islam in Turkey and the World' is . . . a helpful and detailed account of a movement that is defined . . . by obfuscation. . . . In 2011, a journalist called Ahmet Şik brought out a book . . . that shows how the Gülenists took control of the police force over a period of two decades. 'The Imam's Army' is full of fascinating details."

HENDRIX, JOHN.il. Rutherford B., who was he? See Singer, M.

HENICAN, ELLIS. The party's over. See Crist, C.

HENKES, KEVIN, 1960-. The year of Billy Miller; [by] Kevin Henkes 240 p. 2013 Harpercollins Childrens Books

1. Family life—Wisconsin—Fiction 2. Humorous stories 3. Interpersonal relations—Juvenile fiction 4. School stories 5. Schools—Fiction
ISBN 0062268120 (hardcover); 9780062268129 (hardcover); 9780062268136 (library)
LC 2012-050373

SUMMARY: This book follows second-grader Billy Miller. It's the "year of several dilemmas for the boy, including the fear he might 'start forgetting things' due to bumping his head while on vacation over the summer. Then there's the habitat diorama that Billy is assigned--the bat cave he creates doesn't turn out quite like he'd hoped." His relationships with his teacher, father, mother, and sister are examined. (Publishers Weekly)

REVIEW: *Booklist* v109 no21 p75-6 Jl 1 2013 Ilene Cooper

REVIEW: *Bull Cent Child Books* v67 no3 p157 N 2013 J. H.

"The Year of Billy Miller." "A school year in the life of second-grader Billy Miller is presented here in four complete episodes, with each set during a different time of year and focusing on a different relationship in Billy's life. . . . The action is fairly mild, but Billy's second-grade thoughts and actions are solid and believable, and the relationships between Billy and the other characters (Billy's father and sister are particularly dimensional) are warmly and credibly rendered. The large print, occasional black and white spot art, and strong story structure will bolster young chapter-book readers as well."

REVIEW: *Horn Book Magazine* v89 no5 p101 S/O 2013 THOM BARTHELMESS

REVIEW: *Kirkus Rev* v81 no14 p32 Jl 15 2013

REVIEW: *Kirkus Rev* p40 Ag 15 2013 Fall Preview

REVIEW: *Kirkus Rev* p76 N 15 2013 Best Books

REVIEW: *Kirkus Rev* p47 2013 Guide 20to BookExpo America

REVIEW: *Publ Wkly* v260 no27 p88 Jl 8 2013

REVIEW: *SLJ* v59 no7 p63 Jl 2013 Cheryl Ashton

HENKES, KEVIN, 1960-.il. The year of Billy Miller. See Henkes, K.

HENNEBERG, SUSAN. Twitter safety and privacy; a guide to microblogging; [by] Susan Henneberg 64 p. 2014 Rosen Central

1. Children's nonfiction 2. Cyberbullying 3. Identity theft 4. Online social networks—Security measures 5. Twitter (Web resource)
ISBN 1448895723 (library binding); 144889588X (pbk.); 9781448895724 (library binding); 9781448895885 (pbk.)
LC 2012-277793

SUMMARY: This book on the social media website Twitter is part of the "21st Century Safety and Privacy" series, which "focuses on safe use of the Internet and social media, explaining each activity, noting pleasures as well as perils, and offering suggestions for minimizing risk. The information is organized into short chapters." The book also discusses cyberbullying and identity theft. (Booklist)

REVIEW: *Booklist* v110 no12 p71 F 15 2014 Kathleen Isaacs

"Downloading and Online Shopping Safety and Privacy," "Facebook Safety and Privacy," and "Twitter Safety and Privacy: A Guide to Microblogging." "This timely series focuses on safe use of the Internet and social media, explaining each activity, noting pleasures as well as perils, and offering suggestions for minimizing risk. The information is organized into short chapters liberally laced with appropriate subheadings, photographs of young users, and boxes to break up the text and presented in an oversize, easy-to-read font. . . . In spite of similarities across the titles, there is enough specific information in each to justify purchasing the full series. There are older teen faces on the covers, but this would be most useful for middle-schoolers just entering the social media world."

HENRY ANTHONY, RONDA C. Searching for the new Black man; Black masculinity and women's bodies; [by] Ronda C. Henry Anthony xi, 192 p. 2013 University Press of Mississippi

1. American literature—African American authors—History and criticism 2. Femininity in literature 3. Human body in literature 4. Masculinity in literature 5. Social science literature
ISBN 9781617037344 (cloth : alk. paper)
LC 2012-044792

SUMMARY: In this book, "using Frederick Douglass's slave narratives, the political and literary texts of W. E. B. Du Bois, the novels of James Baldwin and Walter Mosley, and the autobiographical writings of Barack Obama, the author demonstrates how black masculinity is often created through claims to the patriarchal power of white masculinity, a move that comes at the expense of black women and their bodies." (Choice: Current Reviews for Academic Libraries)

REVIEW: *Choice* v51 no5 p833 Ja 2014 D. E. Magill

"Searching for the New Black Man: Black Masculinity and Women's Bodies." "[Ronda C.] Henry Anthony is indebted to Maurice Wallace, Mark Anthony Neal, David Ikard, and Jeffrey Leak among others (though not explicitly bell hooks); she extends their work fruitfully with her focus on black women's bodies and power, which allows her to articulate a stronger black feminist position for men and women to inhabit. This study is a strong contribution to gender studies, feminist studies, body studies, and African American studies. It usefully complicates ideals of black masculinities and pushes readers to reconsider gender relations and the powerful implications of race."

HENRY, APRIL. The girl who was supposed to die; [by] April Henry 224 p. 2013 Christy Ottaviano Books, Henry Holt and Company

1. Adventure and adventurers—Fiction 2. Amnesia—Fiction 3. Biological warfare—Fiction 4. Identity theft—Fiction 5. JUVENILE FICTION—Action & Adventure—General 6. JUVENILE FICTION—Family—General (see also headings under Social Issues) 7. JUVENILE FICTION—Mysteries & Detective Stories 8. JUVENILE FICTION—Social Issues—Friendship 9. Mystery and detective stories 10. Survival—Fiction

ISBN 0805095411 (hardcover); 9780805095418 (hardcover)

LC 2013-001698

SUMMARY: This book by April Henry presents a "tale of abduction, escape, and paranoia. Cady, 16, wakes up on the floor of a cabin. Two of her fingernails have been yanked out. A man says, 'Take her out back and finish her off.' Worst of all, she has total amnesia. To her shock, she discovers that she knows how to fight--she beats up her captor and flees, and what follows is 28 hours of outfoxing an unknown enemy who wants her, and apparently her family, dead." (Booklist)

REVIEW: *Booklist* v110 no6 p55-6 N 15 2013 Pam Spencer Holley

"The Girl Who Was Supposed to Die." "Gaining consciousness, a young girl awakens in a deserted cabin and doesn't remember who she is or what has happened. As she is being dragged outside by a man, she grabs a stone, decks him, and escapes in his car. . . . Narrator [Cristina] Panfilio initially relates Cady's situation in very practical, measured tones as she analyzes where she is and what she can do, but as the danger heightens, the tempo increases, and Cady's voice becomes higher pitched with worry. Panfilio gives nice-guy Ty a low, silky,\ and calming voice, while the man who terrorizes Cady gets a nasal, high-pitched voice. East-paced, suspenseful incidental music adds to this action-filled tale."

HENRY, CLARENCE BERNARD. Quincy Jones; his life in music; [by] Clarence Bernard Henry 192 p. 2013 University Press of Mississippi

1. Biographies 2. Composers—Biography 3. Jazz musicians—United States—Biography 4. Music industry—History

ISBN 9781617038617 (cloth : alk. paper); 9781617038624 (ebook)

LC 2013-009232

SUMMARY: In this book on musician Quincy Jones, author "[Clarence BernardHenry chronicles Jones' career, from young trumpeter with the bands of Lionel Hampton and Dizzy Gillespie to groundbreaking career as a recording industry executive to composer for Hollywood films. Jones, a multiple Grammy Award winner, has worked with iconic musicians, including Louis Armstrong, Miles Davis, Ella Fitzgerald, Frank Sinatra, and Ray Charles, and contributed his work to humanitarian causes." (Booklist)

REVIEW: *Booklist* v110 no1 p25 S 1 2013 Vanessa Bush

"Quincy Jones: His Life in Music." "Though probably best known for producing Michael Jackson's 'Thriller,' Jones has seen major success and influence as a composer and an arranger of jazz, blues, gospel, soul, and classical music for more than 60 years. . . . [Clarence Bernard] Henry regards Jones as part of the canon of master musicians, including [Johann Sebastian] Bach, [Ludwig van] Beethoven, [Aaron] Copland, and [Leonard] Bernstein. Fans of Jones will appreciate this biography of the musical experience of an iconic musician."

HENRY, CLEMENT.ed. The Arab Spring. See The Arab Spring

HENRY, DAVID. Furious cool; Richard Pryor and the world that made him; [by] David Henry 400 p. 2013 Algonquin Books

1. Biographies 2. Comedians—United States—Biography 3. Drug abuse 4. Motion picture actors and actresses—United States—Biography

ISBN 1616200782; 9781616200787

LC 2013-019665

SUMMARY: In this biography of Richard Pryor, authors David Henry and Joe Henry "bring him to life both as a man and as an artist, providing an in-depth appreciation of his talent and his lasting influence, as well as an . . . examination of the world he lived in and the influences that shaped both his persona and his art." (Publisher's note)

REVIEW: *Booklist* v110 no11 p38 F 1 2014 Sue-Ellen Beauregard

"Furious Cool: Richard Pryor and the World That Made Him." "[Dion] Graham absolutely shines in his reading of this revealing portrait of comedic genius Richard Pryor. . . . Graham smoothly morphs into Pryor's voice when reciting his many stand-up routines, album cuts, or television appearances, and at times it almost seems like Pryor himself is speaking. . . . But more than merely impersonating Pryor, Graham puts heart and soul into his reading so we feel that Graham is touched by the 'groundbreaking genius' of Pryor. . . . Filled with profanity and strong language, this is not for the faint of heart, but a watered-down portrait would be inauthentic. The writing is fantastic and the reading even better."

REVIEW: *Booklist* v110 no2 p13 S 15 2013 Vanessa Bush

"Furious Cool: Richard Pryor and the World That Made Him." "The Henrys [David Henry and Joe Henry] detail Pryor's early struggle with double-consciousness: cleaning up his act to get ahead (à la Bill Cosby) while wanting a release from containment. When he found his own voice, Pryor got mixed reactions, both horror at his rawness and liberal use of the n-word and elation at his liberating frankness. Drawing on interviews with Pryor's friends, family, and colleagues as well as his personal writings, the Henrys portray a man of enormous talent, a one-man theater of raw emotions as he torqued through success and a spectacular crash through drugs, violence, forgettable movie roles, and self-immolation. A beautifully written account of the troubled life of a manic genius."

REVIEW: *Booklist* v110 no11 p37 F 1 2014 Joyce Saricks

REVIEW: *Booklist* v110 no5 p18 N 1 2013 Donna Seaman

"Anything Goes: A History of American Musical Theatre," "Furious Cool: Richard Pryor and the World That Made Him," and "Kansas City Lightning: The Rise and Times of Charlie Parker." "[Ethan] Mordden traces the evolution of the musical, a quintessential American art form, and analyzes dozens of standout examples in this comprehensive, witty, and sassy history. . . . Richard Pryor drew on his difficult life and ferocious energy to create his blazing comedy, and the brothers [David Henry and Joe] Henry detail every facet of his troubled life in this superbly written account of a manic genius. . . . [Stanley] Crouch captures with novelistic verve the early years of jazz master Charlie Parker's short life in Kansas City, capturing the excitement of his artistic daring."

REVIEW: *Choice* v51 no10 p1807 Je 2014 T. F. DeFrantz

REVIEW: *Kirkus Rev* v81 no16 p48 Ag 15 2013

REVIEW: *Kirkus Rev* p24-5 Ag 15 2013 Fall Preview

REVIEW: *Libr J* v138 no14 p112 S 1 2013 Terry Hong

REVIEW: *Libr J* v138 no18 p104 N 1 2013 Molly McArdle

REVIEW: *Libr J* v139 no2 p46 F 1 2014 Mark John Swails

REVIEW: *N Y Times Book Rev* p8 Ja 5 2014 MEL WATKINS

REVIEW: *Publ Wkly* v260 no45 p8 N 11 2013

REVIEW: *Publ Wkly* v261 no13 p62 Mr 31 2014

REVIEW: *Sight Sound* v23 no12 p104-5 D 2013 Nick Pinkerton

HENRY, EDWARD R.ed. Early and middle woodland landscapes of the Southeast. See Early and middle woodland landscapes of the Southeast

HENRY, JED.il. My dream playground. See Becker, K. M.

HENRY, JOE. Furious cool. See Henry, D.

HENSHALL, KENNETH. Historical dictionary of Japan to 1945; [by] Kenneth Henshall xxxi, 596 p. 2014 The Scarecrow Press, Inc.

1. Encyclopedias & dictionaries 2. History—Dictionaries 3. Japan—History 4. Japan—Military history
ISBN 9780810878716 (cloth: alk. paper)
LC 2013-022050

SUMMARY: This historical dictionary of Japan, by Kenneth Henshall, "starts with a summary chronology from prehistory to 1945. . . . Fully half the chronology is devoted to the last 150 years. A brief narrative history follows, divided into several well-established eras. The dictionary entries comprise the bulk of the volume, along with 13 appendixes consisting mostly of historical documents." (Choice: Current Reviews for Academic Libraries)

REVIEW: *Choice* v51 no8 p1378 Ap 2014 M. M. Bohn

"Historical Dictionary of Japan to 1945". "This one disappoints, mainly because the author is given to editorializing rather than presenting facts in an objective and dispassionate manner. . . . Although Japan has a long and eventful history, fully half the chronology is devoted to the last 150 years. . . . An index would have been useful. . . . [Kenneth] Henshall frequently equivocates, stating x or y as fact, then declaring that 'some scholars argue . . .' the opposite. . . . He editorializes more often than seems appropriate. This is particularly apparent when he addresses Japanese nationalism in an extended dictionary entry and when he comments on Japanese 'brutality.' The organization of the entries also leaves something to be desired."

REVIEW: *Libr J* v139 no6 p112 Ap 1 2014 Judy Quinn

HENTITIUK, VALERIE.ed. A literature of restitution. See A literature of restitution

HEPINSTALL, KATHY. Blue asylum; a novel; [by] Kathy Hepinstall 270 p. 2012 Houghton Mifflin Harcourt

1. Asylums—Fiction 2. FICTION—Historical 3. FICTION—Literary 4. Plantation owners' spouses—Virginia—Fiction 5. Psychiatric hospital patients—Fiction
ISBN 9780547712079 (hardback)
LC 2011-029653

SUMMARY: In this book, "Iris Dunleavy must be mad. Why else would she have accompanied slaves trying to escape from her husband's Virginia plantation? When she arrives at the asylum on Florida's Sanibel Island in 1864 after being declared insane by a doctor and a judge, she tries to convince her captors of her sanity. Although the patients generally receive humane treatment, Dr. Cowell, the superintendent, applies the "water treatment" to those like Iris who remain defiant. As Iris's friendship with Ambrose Weller, a Confederate soldier who cannot cope with battlefield memories, deepens, Dr. Cowell's own attraction to the rebellious Iris grows. Determined to escape with Ambrose, Iris enlists the help of Dr. Cowell's 12-year-old son." (Libr J)

REVIEW: *Booklist* v108 no11 p38 F 1 2012 Mary Ellen Quinn

REVIEW: *Kirkus Rev* v80 no8 p13 Ap 15 2012

"Blue Asylum." "[Kathy] Hepinstall's latest novel . . . refracts the Civil War through the lenses of parallel conflicts: husbands and wives, fathers and sons, doctors and patients. Given rich psychological dimensions, each character strives to negotiate the lines balancing desire and control, power and compassion. The lines converge within the character of Iris, who longs for adventure. . . . When Robert Dunleavy, plantation owner and slaveholder, comes to town, Iris is enthralled. . . until she discovers the ugly underbelly of slavery. After embarrassing Robert, Iris is committed to Sanibel Asylum. . . . A fine novel embroidered with rich imagery."

REVIEW: *Libr J* v137 no2 p56-7 F 1 2012 Kathy Piehl

REVIEW: *Publ Wkly* v259 no4 p141 Ja 23 2012

HERALD, DIANA TIXIER. Genreflecting; a guide to popular reading interests; [by] Diana Tixier Herald 622 p. 2013 Libraries Unlimited

1. American fiction—Stories, plots, etc 2. English fiction—Stories, plots, etc 3. Fiction—Bibliography 4. Fiction genres—Bibliography 5. Popular literature—Stories, plots, etc 6. Reading interests 7. Reference books

ISBN 9781598848403 (Hardcopy: acid-free paper); 1598848402

LC 2012-051480

SUMMARY: This book for librarians on popular reading interests features "chapters devoted to each major genre with an overview of the genre's characteristics and appeal elements followed by definitions of popular subgenres, lists of benchmark titles, reader favorites, book-group selections, and resources for further investigation. Parts I and 2 focus on readers'-advisory services in the public library for the novice. . . . The chapters on the genres, found in part 3, are the series' stock-in-trade." (Booklist)

REVIEW: *Booklist* v110 no2 p4 S 15 2013 Kaite Mediatore Stover

"Genreflecting: A Guide to Popular Reading Interests". "Parts I and 2 focus on readers'-advisory services in the public library for the novice. Much of this material can be found in other readers'-advisory tools. The chapters on the genres, found in part 3, are the series' stock-in-trade. For this latest edition, the old standby chapter on westerns has been reduced in order to devote more pages to new chapters, such as 'Other Popular Reading Interests,' which serves as an excellent introduction to three areas of fiction that can present the greatest challenges to readers' advisors. . . . Libraries looking to add a compact readers'-advisory training resource for staff that can do double-duty at the public-service desk for patrons have a solid choice in this volume."

REVIEW: *Libr J* v138 no15 p80 S 15 2013 Kendra Auberry

REVIEW: *Voice of Youth Advocates* v36 no3 p94 Ag 2013 Geri Diorio

HERBACH, GEOFF. I'm with stupid; [by] Geoff Herbach 320 p. 2013 Sourcebooks Fire

1. Anxiety—Fiction 2. Athletes—Fiction 3. High schools—Fiction 4. Identity—Fiction 5. Schools—Fiction 6. Sports stories

ISBN 1402277911; 9781402277917 (tp : alk. paper)

LC 2012-042814

SUMMARY: This book explores a "Wisconsin football phenom's high-school years. The pressure is truly on as Felton, a senior, has to cope with the stresses of college recruitment. When his girlfriend, Aleah, breaks off their long-distance romance, and the brother of the bullied freshman he mentors kills himself, Felton violently unravels. Identifying with Shakespeare's Hamlet, Felton struggles with his own royal role as sports hero and his father's legacy as angry suicide." (Booklist)

REVIEW: *Booklist* v110 no6 p55 N 15 2013 Karen Cruze

REVIEW: *Booklist* v109 no19/20 p91 Je 1 2013 Karen Cruze

REVIEW: *Booklist* v110 no1 p107 S 1 2013

"Becoming Babe Ruth," "I'm With Stupid," and "Tap Out." "This engaging rags-to-riches chronicle puts an emphasis on Ruth's early school years before vividly capturing his larger-than-life career, accomplishments, and charm. The art, like the Babe, is irrepressible. . . . The second sequel to 'Stupid Fast' (2011) loses no steam, as football phenom Felton suffers the pressures of college recruitment while dealing with long-distance romance, suicide, and alcoholism. . . . Gritty, bloody, and chilling, this is an unblinking look at 17-year-old Tony, who uses a local mixed-martial-arts gym as inspiration to disengage from the drug dealers running his trailer park."

REVIEW: *Kirkus Rev* v81 no7 p235 Ap 1 2013

REVIEW: *SLJ* v59 no10 p1 O 2013 Heather Webb

REVIEW: *Voice of Youth Advocates* v36 no2 p58 Je 2013 Judith A. Hayn

HERBAL MEDICINES; 928 p. 2013 Pharmaceutical Pr

1. Herbal medicine 2. Medical literature 3. Pharmaceutical chemistry 4. Pharmacopoeias 5. Photochemistry

ISBN 0857110357; 9780857110350

SUMMARY: This book "provides a comprehensive single source of scientifically rigorous, impartial information on 180 of the most commonly used herbal medicinal products. The monographs are extensively referenced, detailing photochemical, pharmacological and clinical aspects of each herb (use, dose, adverse effects, interactions, etc)." (Publisher's note)

REVIEW: *Choice* v50 no11 p1985 Jl 2013 J. S. Whelan

"Herbal Medicines." "'Herbal Medicines' is one of the most authoritative print references on medicinal herbs available. . . . The entries are meant as a reference and guide for health professionals as they review patient medications. Monographs provide information on chemical constituents and their structures, dosage, quality of products, pharmacological action, contraindications, and side effects. . . . This fourth edition . . . adds 30 new monographs and 60 color photos of herb plants and crude drugs, along with updated, expanded references."

HERMAN, ARTHUR. The cave and the light; Plato versus Aristotle and the struggle for the soul of Western civilization; [by] Arthur Herman 720 p. 2010 Random House

1. Civilization, Western—Greek influences 2. Philosophical literature 3. Philosophy, Ancient

ISBN 0553807307; 9780553807301 (acid-free paper)

LC 2010-008230

SUMMARY: This book, by Arthur Herman, is an "account of how the two greatest thinkers of the ancient world, Plato and Aristotle, laid the foundations of Western culture—and how their rivalry shaped the essential features of our culture down to the present day. . . . From Martin Luther . . . to Karl Marx . . . heroes and villains of history have been inspired . . . by these two master philosophers." (Publisher's note)

REVIEW: *Choice* v51 no6 p1066 F 2014 R. T. Ingoglia

REVIEW: *Commentary* v136 no4 p48-9 N 2013 PASCAL-EMMANUEL GOBRY

REVIEW: *Kirkus Rev* v81 no14 p291 Jl 15 2013

REVIEW: *Libr J* v138 no16 p89 O 1 2013 Margaret Heller

REVIEW: *Natl Rev* v65 no23 p54-5 D 16 2013 BRIAN C. ANDERSON

"The Cave and the Light: Plato Versus Aristotle, and the Struggle for the Soul of Western Civilization". "This book is unfashionably ambitious history, with a sweep and drama worthy of Arnold Toynbee. . . . [Arthur] Herman's pursuit of his thesis at times leads him to ignore or downplay significant distinctions. . . . The author's judgment about particular thinkers is usually sound, but it isn't infallible. . . . But any book as bold as 'The Cave and the Light' is bound to provoke disagreements and contrary assessments of particular individuals and eras. Herman has given us a wonderful introduction to the intellectual history of the West. In a saner era, it would be on every college freshman's reading list."

REVIEW: *Publ Wkly* v260 no29 p58 Jl 22 2013

HERNANDEZ, ANABEL. Narcoland; the Mexican drug lords and their godfathers; 304 p. 2013 Verso

1. Corruption—Mexico 2. Drug control—Mexico 3. Drug traffic—Mexico 4. Historical literature 5. Organized crime—Mexico
ISBN 9781781680735 (alk. paper)
LC 2013-011559

SUMMARY: "The definitive history of the drug cartels, 'Narcoland' takes readers to the front lines of the 'war on drugs,' which has so far cost more than 60,000 lives in just six years. [Author Anabel] Hernández explains in riveting detail how Mexico became a base for the mega-cartels of Latin America and one of the most violent places on the planet." (Publisher's note)

REVIEW: *Booklist* v109 no22 p13 Ag 1 2013 Jay Freeman

REVIEW: *Columbia J Rev* v52 no4 p55-7 N/D 2013 MARCELA VALDES

"Narcoland: The Mexican Drug lords and Their Godfathers" and "The Beast: Riding the Rails and Dodging Narcos on the Migrant Trail." "How did the Mexican government lose control of its traffickers? An answer can be found in two new books: [Anabel] Hernández' 'Narcoland: The Mexican Drug Lords and Their Godfathers' and Óscar Martínez' 'The Beast: Riding the Rails and Dodging Narcos on the Migrant Trail.' Together they provide a top-down, bottom-up view of how Mexican cartels have consolidated and corporatized in the past two decades."

REVIEW: *Kirkus Rev* v81 no14 p79 Jl 15 2013

REVIEW: *London Rev Books* v36 no9 p21-3 My 8 2014 Álvaro Enrigue

REVIEW: *Publ Wkly* v260 no24 p50 Je 17 2013

HERNANDEZ, LEEZA.il. Never play music right next to the zoo. See Lithgow, J.

HERODOTUS, CA. 484 B.C.-425 B.C. The Histories; [by] ca. 484 B.C.-425 B.C. Herodotus 880 p. 2014 Viking Adult

1. Greece—History—To 146 B.C 2. History, Ancient
ISBN 0670024899 (hbk.); 9780670024896 (hbk.)
LC 2012-474647

SUMMARY: This book by Herodotus, translated by Tom Holland, "is the earliest surviving work of nonfiction and a thrilling narrative account of (among other things) the war between the Persian Empire and the Greek city-states in the fifth century BC." This edition includes "an introduction and notes by Professor Paul Cartledge, a translator's preface, an index of significant persons and places, maps, and a supplementary index." (Publisher's note)

REVIEW: *Economist* v408 no8854 p92-3 S 21 2013

REVIEW: *Hist Today* v63 no10 p58-9 O 2013 PAUL CARTLEDGE

REVIEW: *Kirkus Rev* v82 no9 p55 My 1 2014

REVIEW: *London Rev Books* v36 no7 p29-31 Ap 3 2014 Peter Green

REVIEW: *New Statesman* v142 no5180 p42 O 18 2013 Peter Jones

REVIEW: *TLS* no5772 p8-9 N 15 2013 EDITH HALL

"The Histories". "Herodotus . . . needs a versatile translator who appreciates his hybridity. Enter Tom Holland, a distinguished and highly readable author of both historical nonfiction dealing with ancient empires . . . and popular fantasy novels. He knows more than most of us about how to evoke both real and imagined scenarios with economy, elegance and gusto. Although there is no shortage of rival translations on the market, the Herodotus of Holland has therefore been eagerly awaited. . . . This is a twenty-first-century Herodotus. It is a Herodotus whose tongue is often in his cheek. . . But this is also the Herodotus of a translator who respects the old-fashioned niceties of rhetoric and prose style."

HERRERA, ROBIN. Hope is a ferris wheel; [by] Robin Herrera 272 p. 2014 Amulet Books

1. Clubs—Fiction 2. Friendship—Fiction 3. Poetry—Fiction 4. Trailer camps—Fiction 5. Young adult fiction
ISBN 1419710397; 9781419710391 (alk. paper)
LC 2013-026392

SUMMARY: In this book, by Robin Herrera, "ten-year-old Star Mackie lives in a trailer park with her flaky mom and her melancholy older sister. . . . Moving to a new town has made it difficult for Star to make friends, when her classmates tease her because of where she lives and because of her layered blue hair. But when Star starts a poetry club, she develops a love of Emily Dickinson and . . . learns some important lessons about herself and comes to terms with her hopes for the future." (Publisher's note)

REVIEW: *Booklist* v110 no13 p73 Mr 1 2014 Jeanne Fredriksen

REVIEW: *Bull Cent Child Books* v67 no9 p458-9 My 2014 K. C.

REVIEW: *Horn Book Magazine* v90 no3 p88 My/Je 2014 ROBIN L. SMITH

REVIEW: *Kirkus Rev* v82 no4 p331 F 15 2014

"Hope is a Ferris Wheel". "Debut author [Robin] Herrera deftly combines family drama with a school and friendship story. . . . The author handles the Mackie family's financial and domestic situation with delicacy and respect, allowing readers to gradually get to know the difficulties her characters face. . . . Some readers may find the overall story arc predictable, and unfortunately, charismatic secondary characters occasionally outshine Star. . . . Well-constructed, thought-provoking and appealing, this first effort bodes well for the author's future despite some minor missteps."

REVIEW: *SLJ* v60 no4 p148 Ap 2014 B. Allison Gray

HERRIN, JUDITH. Margins and metropolis; authority across the Byzantine Empire; [by] Judith Herrin xxiv, 365 p. 2013 Princeton University Press

1. Authority—Social aspects—Byzantine Empire—History 2. Borderlands—Byzantine Empire—History 3. Christianity and politics—Byzantine Empire—History

4. City and town life—Byzantine Empire—History 5. Historical literature
ISBN 9780691153018 (acid-free paper)
LC 2012-038201

SUMMARY: "This volume explores the political, cultural, and ecclesiastical forces that linked the metropolis of Byzantium to the margins of its far-flung empire. Focusing on the provincial region of Hellas and Peloponnesos in central and southern Greece, Judith Herrin shows how the prestige of Constantinople was reflected in the military, civilian, and ecclesiastical officials sent out to govern the provinces." (Publisher's note)

REVIEW: *N Y Rev Books* v60 no18 p68-70 N 21 2013 G. W. Bowersock

"Margins and Metropolis: Authority Across the Byzantine Empire" and "'Unrivalled Influence: Women and Empire in Byzantium." "For [Judith Herrin] there would have been no Europe without Byzantium. She returns to this view once again in introducing the first of her two new volumes of collected essays on Byzantine history. She is a forceful advocate of this hypothesis. . . . Herrin's comparative perspective on Byzantium, European Christendom, and Islam reflects a lifetime of distinguished work on the Byzantine Empire. With these two new volumes, comprising comprising papers written over many years between the late 1960s and the present, we can watch her interests develop across a long period in which Byzantine studies grew dramatically from academic obscurity into an industry."

HERRIN, JUDITH. Unrivalled influence; women and empire in Byzantium; [by] Judith Herrin 328 p. 2013 Princeton University Press

1. Historical literature 2. Upper class women—Byzantine Empire 3. Women—Byzantine Empire—History—Middle Ages, 500-1500 4. Women—Byzantine Empire—Social conditions 5. Women and religion—Byzantine Empire
ISBN 9780691153216 (alk. paper)
LC 2012-038153

SUMMARY: This book "explores the exceptional roles that women played in the vibrant cultural and political life of medieval Byzantium. . . . Judith Herrin sheds light on the importance of marriage in imperial statecraft, the tense coexistence of empresses in the imperial court, and the critical relationships of mothers and daughters. She looks at women's interactions with eunuchs, the in-between gender in Byzantine society, and shows how women defended their rights to hold land." (Publisher's note)

REVIEW: *N Y Rev Books* v60 no18 p68-70 N 21 2013 G. W. Bowersock

"Margins and Metropolis: Authority Across the Byzantine Empire" and "'Unrivalled Influence: Women and Empire in Byzantium." "For [Judith Herrin] there would have been no Europe without Byzantium. She returns to this view once again in introducing the first of her two new volumes of collected essays on Byzantine history. She is a forceful advocate of this hypothesis. . . . Herrin's comparative perspective on Byzantium, European Christendom, and Islam reflects a lifetime of distinguished work on the Byzantine Empire. With these two new volumes, comprising comprising papers written over many years between the late 1960s and the present, we can watch her interests develop across a long period in which Byzantine studies grew dramatically from academic obscurity into an industry."

HERRING, M.L.il. Ellie's log. See Li, J.

HERRNDORF, WOLFGANG. Why we took the car; [by] Wolfgang Herrndorf 256 p. 2014 Arthur A. Levine Books

1. Automobile theft—Fiction 2. Automobile theft—Juvenile fiction 3. Friendship—Fiction 4. Friendship—Juvenile fiction 5. Immigrants—Fiction 6. Immigrants—Germany—Berlin—Juvenile fiction 7. Juvenile delinquency—Fiction 8. Juvenile delinquents—Germany—Juvenile fiction 9. Road fiction 10. Russians—Germany—Berlin—Fiction 11. Russians—Germany—Berlin—Juvenile fiction 12. Self-esteem—Fiction 13. Self-esteem—Juvenile fiction
ISBN 0545481805; 9780545481809 (hardcover : alk. paper); 9780545481816 (pbk. : alk. paper)
LC 2012-044118

SUMMARY: In this book by Wolfgang Herrndorf "Tschick shows up at Mike's house out of the blue. Turns out he wasn't invited to Tatiana's party either, and he's ready to do something about it. Forget the popular kids: Together, Mike and Tschick are heading out on a road trip. No parents, no map, no destination. Will they get hopelessly lost in the middle of nowhere? Probably. Will they meet crazy people and get into serious trouble? Definitely. But will they ever be called boring again?" (Publisher's note)

REVIEW: *Booklist* v110 no8 p48 D 15 2013 Sarah Bean Thompson

REVIEW: *Bull Cent Child Books* v67 no6 p315 F 2014 Karen Coats

"Why We Took the Car." "The narrative style in this translated text is completely without imagery or metaphor, save the overarching metaphor of the road trip itself; Mike merely describes everything that happens as it happens while filling in some gaps about his home life. Only towards the end does anything like a theme emerge, as Mike reflects on how unfairness of the class difference between him and Tschick results in their differential treatment under the law, how getting in legal trouble elevates your social status in high school, and how there are worse things than having an alcoholic mother."

REVIEW: *Horn Book Magazine* v90 no1 p91-2 Ja/F 2014 JESSICA TACKETT MACDONALD

REVIEW: *Kirkus Rev* v81 no22 p116 N 15 2013

REVIEW: *N Y Times Book Rev* p15 Ja 12 2014 PETER BEHRENS

"The Scar Boys" and "Why We Took the Car." "In Len Vlahos's debut novel, the Scar Boys are a punk band from Yonkers that hits the road riding a rusty van and working out personal problems while playing gigs in college towns. . . . Playing and touring demand creativity and commitment, forcing the Scar Boys--actually three guys and a girl--to come of age in this wry, stylish tale. . . . In Wolfgang Herrndorf's 'Why We Took the Car,' originally published in German and ably translated by Tim Mohr, the title question never really gets answered. . . . By no means a wholesome story, 'Why We Took the Car' is exuberant and without a mean bone in its narrative. American teenagers shouldn't have trouble relating to Mike and Tschick."

REVIEW: *Publ Wkly* v260 no43 p63 O 28 2013

REVIEW: *Voice of Youth Advocates* v36 no5 p61 D 2013 Cathy Fiebelkorn

HERRNSTEIN, RICHARD J. The bell curve. See Murray, C.

HERSCH, MATTHEW H. Inventing the American Astronaut; [by] Matthew H. Hersch 2012 Palgrave Macmillan

1. Astronauts—United States 2. Historical literature 3. Manned space flight—History 4. Project Apollo (U.S.) 5. United States. National Aeronautics & Space Administration

ISBN 1137025271; 9781137025272

SUMMARY: This book presents "an astronaut-focused history of NASA's first 30 years." Author Matthew Hersch "debuts with an analysis of the astronauts as a special subset of professional skilled laborers, along with an examination of their part in the evolution of the technological systems developed for the Apollo program and beyond." (Kirkus Reviews)

REVIEW: *Am Hist Rev* v119 no1 p201-2 F 2014 Amy E. Foster

"Inventing the American Astronaut"."What [Matthew H.] Hersch does best is uncover the real story behind 'The Right Stuff' by offering insight into the world of the astronaut office. . . . Hersch's research and argument leave no doubt that NASA has struggled to define its scientific purpose and that many of the pilot-astronauts showed ambivalence, even hostility, to their scientist colleagues, but what gets lost is the deeper sense of pride that the astronauts felt about the work they did, particularly during the Apollo program. . . . Useful for college-level history, political science, and space policy courses and accessible to a broader audience with an interest in the human spaceflight program, Hersch's work is commendable for its demystification of this profession."

REVIEW: *Choice* v50 no10 p1858 Je 2013 J. Z. Kiss

REVIEW: *J Am Hist* v100 no3 p915 D 2013 James Spiller

REVIEW: *Kirkus Rev* v80 no18 p364 S 15 2012

HERSCHDORFER, NATHALIE.ed. Le corbusier and the power of photography. See Le corbusier and the power of photography

HERSH, SEYMOUR, 1937-. The dark side of Camelot; [by] Seymour Hersh 498 1997 Little, Brown

1. Attorneys general 2. Biography, Individual 3. Historical literature 4. Members of Congress 5. Political leaders 6. Presidential candidates 7. Presidents 8. Senators 9. Siblings of presidents 10. United States—Politics and government—1961-1963

ISBN 0-316-35955-6

LC 97-7-5404

SUMMARY: This book argues that President John F. "Kennedy's private life and personal obsessions--his character--affected the affairs of the [United States] and its foreign policy far more than has ever been known." (Publisher's note) The author "posits connectionos between the Kennedys and the mob." (New York Times Book Review)This book argues that President "Kennedy's private life and personal obsessions—his character—affected the affairs of the {United States} and its foreign policy far more than has ever been known." (Author's note) Index.

REVIEW: *N Y Times Book Rev* p1-24 O 27 2013 Jill Abramson

"If Kennedy Lived: The First and Second Terms of President John F. Kennedy: An Alternate History," "The Dark Side of Camelot," and "President Kennedy: Profile of Power." "The loathsomely titled 'If Kennedy Lived' . . . imagines a completed first Kennedy term and then a second. . . . 'President Kennedy: Profile of Power' is a minutely detailed chronicle of the Kennedy White House. As a primer on Kennedy's decision-making . . . the book is fascinating. What's missing is a picture of Kennedy's personal life. . . . In 'The Dark Side of Camelot,' [Seymour M.] Hersh wildly posits connections between the Kennedys and the mob."

HERTZ, NEIL. Pastoral in Palestine; [by] Neil Hertz 122 p. 2013 Prickly Paradigm Press

1. Abu Dis (West Bank) 2. Americans—West Bank 3. Arab-Israeli conflict—1993- 4. Memoirs 5. Palestinian Arabs—Social conditions 6. Social criticism

ISBN 9780984201037 (alk. paper)

LC 2012-948395

SUMMARY: "In 2011, Neil Hertz lived in Ramallah in Palestine's occupied West Bank and taught in Abu Dis, just outside Jerusalem. With 'Pastoral in Palestine,' he offers a personal take on the conflict. . . . Illustrated throughout with full-color photographs taken by the author, 'Pastoral in Palestine' puts a human face to politics in the Middle East." (Publisher's note)

REVIEW: *World Lit Today* v88 no2 p72 Mr/Ap 2014 Adele Newson-Horst

"Pastoral in Palestine." "In the late winter and spring of 2011, Neil Hertz . . . lived in Ramallah and taught just outside of East Jerusalem at the Abu Dis campus of Al-Quds University in a collaborative program developed by the university and Bard College. 'Pastoral in Palestine' was written during and in response to that experience. It is travel literature, social commentary, and political commentary all in one. Alternately tragic, humorous, and discerning, it reveals as much about life in the Occupied Territories of the West Bank as it does the author. . . . Though a slender volume (122 pages), with photographs he himself took and a few from the Internet, it is weighty in its effect."

HERZOG, JONATHAN P. The spiritual-industrial complex; America's religious battle against communism in the early Cold War; [by] Jonathan P. Herzog 273 2011 Oxford University Press

1. Civil religion—United States 2. Cold War, 1945-1989—Religious aspects 3. Historical literature 4. Religion & politics—United States—History 5. United States—Church history—20th century 6. United States—Religion—1945-

ISBN 0195393465; 9780195393460

LC 2010-053172

SUMMARY: This book by Jonathan P. Herzog "shows that American leaders in the early Cold War years considered the conflict to be profoundly religious; they saw Communism not only as godless but also as a sinister form of religion. Fighting faith with faith, they deliberately used religious beliefs and institutions as part of the plan to defeat the Soviet enemy." (Publisher's note)

REVIEW: *J Am Hist* v99 no1 p352-3 Je 2012 Jason W. Stevens

REVIEW: *Rev Am Hist* v42 no2 p351-9 Je 2014 Mark Hulsether

"The Spiritual-Industrial Complex: America's Religious Battle Against Communism in the Early Cold War" and "Embattled Ecumenism: The National Council of Churches, the Vietnam War, and the Trials of the Protestant Left." "[Author Jonathan P.] Herzog clearly demonstrates that religious anticommunism was pervasive and highly orchestrated during the 1940s and 1950s. . . . Nevertheless, much hinges on his premises about communism, secularism, and sacralization. . . . 'Embattled Ecumenism' is impressive in depth of research. . . . 'Embattled Ecumenism' is a substantive monograph, based on deep and original research, and deserves a reading from cultural historians as well as scholars in religious studies, American Studies, and Protestant ecumenism. But like all projects, it has both strengths and weaknesses."

HETHERINGTON, TIANI.ed. Decolonizing social work. See Decolonizing social work

HEWITT, DAVID.ed. The Edinburgh edition of the Waverley novels. See The Edinburgh edition of the Waverley novels

HEYMANN, JODY. Children's chances; how countries can move from surviving to thriving; [by] Jody Heymann xi, 394 p. 2013 Harvard University Press

1. Child welfare 2. Children—Government policy 3. Children—Services for 4. Children—Social conditions 5. Public administration literature

ISBN 0674066812; 9780674066816 (alk. paper)

LC 2012-030829

SUMMARY: Author Judy Heymann's book focuses on "a transformational shift from focusing solely on survival to targeting children's full and healthy development." The book tells "the story of what works and what countries around the world are doing to ensure equal opportunities for all children. Covering poverty, discrimination, education, health, child labor, child marriage, and parental care," it "identifies the leaders and the laggards, highlights successes and setbacks, and provides a guide for what needs to be done to make equal chances for all children a reality." (Publisher's note)

REVIEW: *Choice* v51 no1 p115 S 2013 K. H. Jacobsen

"Children's Chances: How Countries Can Move From Surviving to Thriving." "'Children's Chances' is a report from the World Policy Analysis Center, formerly located at McGill University and now housed at the UCLA School of Public Health; [author Jody] Heymann is director of the center. The work compares data on child-related social policies from all the member states of the United Nations. The nine chapters examine how policies on education, child labor, child marriage, health care access, discrimination, and other issues influence child health and development. . . . No previous analysis has so conveniently compiled comprehensive global information about such a wide range of public policies related to child development."

HEYMANN, JODY.ed. Ensuring a sustainable future. See Ensuring a sustainable future

HICKMAN, TRACY. Wayne of Gotham; [by] Tracy Hickman 296 p. 2012 It Books

1. Batman (Fictitious character) 2. Family secrets—Fiction 3. Fathers & sons—Fiction 4. Graphic novels 5. Murder—Fiction

ISBN 0062074202 (hardcover); 9780062074201 (hardcover)

LC 2012-288081

SUMMARY: In this book by Tracy Hickman, "Bruce Wayne, Gotham City's dark knight, discovers that the primeval event of his life--the murder of his parents . . . may hold clues to the nature of his worst enemies. . . . Bruce's father, Thomas . . . [used] the Wayne fortune to finance research into eugenics. . . . Back in the present, Bruce/Batman . . . uncovers his father's part in the creation of the '50s-era gang of vigilantes called The Apocalypse." (Kirkus Reviews)

REVIEW: *Booklist* v110 no13 p30 Mr 1 2014 Joyce Saricks

"Wayne of Gotham." "Driven by compelling sound effects and a full score, [Tracy] Hickman's darkly disturbing exploration of the origins of Batman makes compulsive listening. The story lines alternate between Thomas and Bruce Wayne, father and son, in the 1950s and the present day. . . . [Richard] Rohan reads at a brisk pace, underlining the urgency of both plots. The large cast, identified at the end of the recording, provides distinctive voices for the richly drawn characters. But the sound effects and score set this recording apart from other full-cast readings, creating aural images that propel the story and reinforce the nightmare tone that reflects Batman's physical and emotional peril as he discovers the secrets of his family's past."

REVIEW: *Booklist* v108 no21 p40 Jl 1 2012 David Pitt

REVIEW: *Kirkus Rev* v80 no14 p1428 Jl 15 2012

HICKS, FAITH ERIN.il. The Adventures of Superhero Girl. See Hicks, F. E.

HICKS, FAITH ERIN. The Adventures of Superhero Girl; 112 p. 2013 Dark Horse Comics

1. Crime—Fiction 2. Criminals 3. Graphic novels 4. Superhero comic books, strips, etc. 5. Women superheroes

ISBN 1616550848; 9781616550844 (hardcover)

SUMMARY: This graphic novel features "Superhero Girl [who] has some Superman-like powers, although she can't fly, just leap over tall buildings, and she works to protect the small town where she went to get away from her charismatic superhero brother, Kevin. She fights bad-guy ninjas, bank robbers, even a tentacled space monster, but she also struggles to pay rent . . . and she has to deal with her future supervillain self." (Voice of Youth Advocates)

REVIEW: *Publ Wkly* v260 no4 p159 Ja 28 2013

REVIEW: *Voice of Youth Advocates* v37 no1 p28-9 Ap 2014 AMANDA FOUST JACK BAUR

REVIEW: *Voice of Youth Advocates* v36 no2 p52-3 Je 2013 KAT KAN

"Reed Gunther Vol. 2: Monsters and Mustaches!," "The Adventures of Superhero Girl," and "Nothing Can Possibly Go Wrong." "'Reed Gunther Vol. 2: Monsters and Mustaches!' recounts more weird Western adventures of Reed Gunther. . . . This volume includes a flashback story in which Reed tells how he and Sterling met. Every story involves some kind of monster. . . . The monsters aren't horribly scary; there's lots of action but not much actual violence; and Reed's 'cussin' runs to such phrases as 'bourbon and raw eggs!' and 'sweet sarsaparilla!,' making this book suitable for anyone in upper elementary through high school. . . . 'Superhero Girl' has some Superman-like powers, although she can't fly, just leap over tall buildings, and she works to protect the small town where she went to get away from her charismatic superhero brother, Kevin. . . . [Faith Erin] Hicks covers a lot of the questions some people might ask about superheroes, such as how can they pay for things if they're not superrich like Bruce Wayne, and how can they truly separate their lives as superheroes from their 'regular' lives, and she does it with lots of humor, fun, and just a touch of snark. . . . Hicks adapted and illustrated 'Nothing Can Possibly Go Wrong' from a prose novel written by Prudence Shen. . . . This is a fantastic distillation of all the high school and coming-of-age tropes found in YA fiction, illustrated in energetic black and white by Hicks. School election shenanigans, nerds vs. popular kids, family dynamics, friends becoming rivals, underdogs entering a major competition, sneaking out for a road trip—it's all here."

HICKS, KELLI L. Winning by teamwork; [by] Kelli L. Hicks 24 p. 2013 Rourke Educational Media

1. Children—Conduct of life—Juvenile literature 2. Children's nonfiction 3. Cooperation 4. Sportsmanship 5. Teamwork (Sports)

ISBN 9781621699033

LC 2013-937298

SUMMARY: This book on teamwork by Kelli L. Hicks is part of the Social Skills series, which "takes one aspect of a winning attitude and explains why it might be a worthy goal. . . . 'Winning by Teamwork' . . . alternat[es] modern examples of good sportsmanship with photos of a U.S. Olympics team. Babe Ruth, and a famous college basketball handshake between a white and black player." (Booklist)

REVIEW: *Booklist* v110 no5 p56 N 1 2013 Daniel Kraus

"Winning By Giving," "Winning By Teamwork," and "Winning By Waiting." "Each cheerful title in the Social Skills series takes one aspect of a winning attitude and explains why it might be a worthy goal. 'Winning by Giving' defines philanthropy and then suggests that readers give their kindness, talents, and time to family, friends, and the community. 'Winning by Teamwork' is the series standout, alternating modern examples of good sportsmanship with photos of a U.S. Olympics team, Babe Ruth, and a famous college basketball handshake between a white and black player. 'Winning by Waiting' teaches a lesson well suited to impatient children to appreciate the strategy of the tortoise. . . . Though the text can be a bit cornball, the clean design and bright full-bleed photos of giddy kids make these books suitable and approachable tools in addressing those, shall we say, character quirks out there."

HICKS, PATRICK. The Commandant of Lubizec; A Novel of the Holocaust and Operation Reinhard; [by] Patrick Hicks 256 p. 2014 Random House

1. Concentration camps—Fiction 2. Historical fiction 3. Holocaust, Jewish (1939-1945)—Fiction 4. Military personnel—Fiction 5. World War, 1939-1945—Concentration camps—Poland

ISBN 1586422200; 9781586422202

SUMMARY: This book follows "Hans-Peter Guth . . . a devoted family man, the type who takes his kids camping. . . . He's also a mass murderer, responsible for the deaths of—by his own estimation—a million Jews. Guth is commandant of the Lubizec death camp in Poland, where trainloads of Jews are unloaded, stripped naked, shaved, then crammed into gas chambers. Of course, Guth himself never lays a finger on anyone—he leaves that to his sadistic guards—but he certainly runs the show." (Kirkus Reviews)

REVIEW: *Kirkus Rev* v82 no3 p6 F 1 2014

"The Commandant of Lubizec". "A heart-rending novel about a Nazi death camp that didn't exist—but could have. . . . [Patrick] Hicks . . . tells the story of the fictional Lubizec as if it were a historical account, complete with footnotes and quotes from future fictional documentaries, to devastating effect. Of course, most of the things that happened in Hicks' fictional camp happened in the real death camps, but Hicks' documentary style not only adds a layer of realism to the story, but also allows him to comment on certain inherent problems with books on the subject. . . . Hicks' prose is clear and unflinching, and while, as a result, there are many difficult-to-read scenes, this is as it should be. Thought-provoking and gut-wrenchingly powerful."

REVIEW: *Publ Wkly* v260 no44 p42 N 4 2013

HIGASHIDA, NAOKI. The reason I jump; 176 p. 2013 Random House

1. Autism 2. Autistic people—Japan—Biography 3. Autistic people—Psychology 4. Autistic people's writings 5. Memoirs

ISBN 0812994868; 9780812994865 (acid-free paper)

LC 2012-045703

SUMMARY: In this book, "a 13-year-old Japanese author illuminates his autism from within. . . . The book takes the form of a series of straightforward questions followed by answers. . . . He describes the difficulty of expressing through words what the brain wants to say, the challenge of focusing and ordering experience, the obsessiveness of repetition, the comfort found in actions that others might find odd, and the frustration of being the source of others' frustration." (Kirkus Reviews)

REVIEW: *Kirkus Rev* v81 no13 p299 Jl 1 2013

REVIEW: *Libr J* v139 no7 p48 Ap 15 2014 Douglas C. Lord

REVIEW: *N Y Times Book Rev* p27 Ag 25 2013 SALLIE TISDALE

"The Reason I Jump: The Inner Voice of a Thirteen-Year-Old Boy With Autism." "The author, Naoki Higashida, was 13 years old at the time he wrote the memoir, and nonverbal. He wrote by spelling out words on a Japanese alphabet letter board. . . . Higashida is bright and thoughtful. . . . The book comes to English readers through the passionate efforts of David Mitchell . . . and his wife, KA Yoshida, [who] provided the translation. . . . 'The Reason I Jump' makes for odd reading. . . . The constant presumption that he speaks for 'people with autism' and 'us kids with autism' is jarring. . . . Unfortunately, it's impossible to sort out what is Higashida here and what is Mitchell. . . . The parents of an autistic child may not be the best translators for a book by an autistic child."

REVIEW: *New Statesman* v142 no5167 p46-7 Jl 19 2013 Caroline Crampton

REVIEW: *Publ Wkly* v260 no36 p15 S 9 2013 Jessamine Chan

REVIEW: *TLS* no5766 p26-7 O 4 2013 ADAM WISHART

HIGDON, DAVID LEON. Wandering into Brave New World; [by] David Leon Higdon 255 p. 2013 Rodopi
1. Caste—India 2. Influence (Literary, artistic, etc.) 3. Literature—History & criticism
ISBN 9042037164 (pbk.); 9789042037168 (pbk.)
LC 2013-362109

SUMMARY: This book by David Leon Higdon "explores the historical contexts and contemporary sources of Aldous Huxley's 1932 novel [Brave New World]. . . . This new study addresses a number of questions which still remain open. Did his round-the-world trip in 1925-1926 provide material for the novel? Did India's caste system contribute to the novel's human levels? Is there an overarching pattern to the names of the novel/s characters?" (Publisher's note)

REVIEW: *TLS* no5770 p30-1 N 1 2013 JONATHAN TAYLOR
"Wandering Into 'Brave New World'." "It is in this sense--of 'Brave New World' as contemporary satire, as opposed to futuristic prophecy--that [David Leon] Higdon's book is justified in its exhaustive tracing of connections between, on the one hand, [Aldous] Huxley's novel and, on the other, contexts such as Henry Ford's assembly line, Freudian psychoanalysis, the Indian caste system, the failure of imperialism in India and Indonesia, Hollywood high society, and the 'Indian' Reservations in New Mexico. . . . In this context, it is not right to claim that speculative fiction is really just about the present: rather, in Huxley's vision, it would seem that past, present and future overlap."

HIGGINBOTHAM, SUSAN. The Woodvilles; The Wars of the Roses and England's Most Infamous Family; [by] Susan Higginbotham 232 p. 2014 Trafalgar Square
1. Great Britain—History—Edward IV, 1461-1483 2. Great Britain—History—Wars of the Roses, 1455-1485 3. Historical literature 4. Plantagenêt, House of 5. Tudor, House of
ISBN 0752488120; 9780752488127

SUMMARY: This is the story of the family whose fates would be inextricably intertwined with the fall of the Plantagenets and the rise of the Tudors: Richard, the squire whose marriage to a duchess would one day cost him his head . . . Elizabeth, the commoner whose royal destiny would cost her three of her sons . . . and Edward, whose military exploits would win him the admiration of Ferdinand and Isabella. This history includes little-known material such as private letters and wills." (Publisher's note)

REVIEW: *TLS* no5776 p31 D 13 2013 AMY LICENCE
"The Woodvilles: The Wars of the Roses and England's Most Infamous Family." "Here, at last, is a long overdue reassessment of one of the most controversial families of fifteenth-century England. . . . In [author] Susan Higginbotham's account, the family emerges as made up of cultured, intelligent and significant individuals. . . . With meticulous research, Higginbotham fleshes out the key figures. . . . 'The Woodvilles' is a welcome addition to fifteenth-century social and political history, highlighting those close to the throne. Higginbotham has much to say about the way in which her subjects' reputations were formed and recorded and, with her extensive use of primary sources, offers conclusive answers to their critics."

HIGGINS, ANNE KEENAN.il. Starring Jules (super-secret spy girl). See Ain, B.

HIGGINS, JACK. The death trade; [by] Jack Higgins 336 p. 2013 G.P. Putnam's Sons
1. Intelligence officers—Fiction 2. Iran—Fiction 3. Nuclear weapons 4. Scientists—Fiction 5. Spy stories
ISBN 0399165894; 9780399165894
LC 2013-015509

SUMMARY: This book, by Jack Higgins, "pits . . . Sean Dillon and Sara Gideon against the nuclear ambitions of Iran. An . . . Iranian scientist has made a . . . breakthrough in nuclear weapons research, but he can't stand the thought of his regime owning the bomb. He would run if he could, but if he does, his family dies. . . . It is up to Sean Dillon and the rest of the small band known as the Prime Minister's private army to think of a plan." (Publisher's note)

REVIEW: *Booklist* v110 no8 p21-2 D 15 2013 David Pitt
"The Death Trade." "An Iranian medical researcher, forced into applying his work on medical isotopes to nuclear weapons research, is dangerously close to perfecting a more powerful, cheaper nuclear bomb. The man's family is being held captive by the Iranian government so there's little chance he would ever defect, but the British . . . see a window of opportunity. . . . This is another sturdy action thriller with political overtones from one of the masters of the genre. Fans of the long-running Dillon series will flock to this latest entry, and the reappearance of Sara Gideon . . . injects the book with some serious new energy. Good stuff."

REVIEW: *Kirkus Rev* v81 no24 p184 D 15 2013
REVIEW: *Publ Wkly* v260 no41 p38 O 14 2013

HIGGINS, JOANNA. Waiting for the queen; [by] Joanna Higgins 256 p. 2013 Milkweed Editions
1. Friendship—Fiction 2. Frontier and pioneer life—Pennsylvania—Fiction 3. Historical fiction 4. Shakers—Fiction 5. Slavery—Fiction 6. Social classes—Fiction
ISBN 1571317007; 9781571317001 (alk. paper)
LC 2012-042167

SUMMARY: In this book, "Eugenie, 15 and haunted by the horrors [of the French Revolution] they've escaped, arrives unprepared for the harshly primitive conditions they find [in America], and she's annoyed by her unrealistic mother's matchmaking with an unpleasant young noble. In alternating chapters, her story is contrasted with that of Quaker Hannah, who . . . has been hired to help the French out for a year but whose faith keeps her from the subservience the noblemen demand." (Kirkus Reviews)

REVIEW: *Booklist* v110 no5 p81-2 N 1 2013 Anne O'Malley
"Waiting for the Queen." "[Joanna] Higgins bases her story on an actual Pennsylvania settlement of French gentry who fled their homeland. Eugenie and Hannah narrate alternating chapters, offering sharply contrasting glimpses of what the French and Americans each held dear. The French naively await the arrival of Marie Antoinette, and their superior attitudes will incense readers who will figure that the royals are lucky to have gotten out with their heads. Eugenie's and Hannah's thought processes carry the story forward as they wrestle with notions of justice and gradually come together in friendship. Eugenie's transformation may seem a bit over the top as she embraces liberté, égalité, ana fraternité, but the

unique setting offers a fresh look at early America."

REVIEW: *Kirkus Rev* v81 no14 p160 Jl 15 2013

REVIEW: *Voice of Youth Advocates* v36 no3 p61 Ag 2013 Amanda MacGregor

HIGGINS, KRISTAN. The Perfect Match; [by] Kristan Higgins 448 p. 2013 Harlequin Books

1. College teachers—Fiction 2. Green cards 3. Love stories 4. Marriages of convenience 5. Stepsons

ISBN 0373778198; 9780373778195

SUMMARY: In this book by Kristan Higgins, "Honor Holland has just been . . . rejected by her lifelong crush. And now [he] is engaged to her best friend. British professor Tom Barlow just wants to do right by his unofficial stepson, Charlie, but his visa is about to expire. Honor agrees to help Tom with a marriage of convenience--and make her ex jealous. As sparks start to fly between Honor and Tom, they might discover that [the] relationship is far too perfect to be anything but true love." (Publisher's note)

REVIEW: *Booklist* v110 no4 p23 O 15 2013 Aleksandra Walker

REVIEW: *Kirkus Rev* v81 no21 p137 N 1 2013

REVIEW: *N Y Times Book Rev* p30 F 9 2014 Sarah MacLean

"The Luckiest Lady in London," "The Perfect Match," and "The Last Man on Earth." "[Author Sherry] Thomas is known for a lush style that demonstrates her love of her second language, and ['The Luckiest Lady in London'] edges into historical fiction with its transporting prose even as it delivers on heat and emotion and a well-earned happily ever after. . . . In 'The Perfect Match' . . . [author Kristan] Higgins offers readers a journey filled with tears and laughter and the best kind of sighs. . . . Few things are more fun than an enemies-to-lovers romance, and [author Tracy Anne] Warren delivers with 'The Last Man on Earth.'"

REVIEW: *Publ Wkly* v260 no38 p63 S 23 2013

HIGGINS, NADIA. Deadly adorable animals; [by] Nadia Higgins 32 p. 2013 Lerner Publications Co.

1. Animal attacks 2. Animal chemical defenses—Juvenile literature 3. Animal defenses—Juvenile literature 4. Children's nonfiction 5. Dangerous animals

ISBN 9781467705981 (lib. bdg. : alk. paper)

LC 2012-015331

SUMMARY: This book by Nadia Higgins encourages the reader to "Imagine a creature that would gnaw on the tail of a crocodile or crush a seal's skull with its razor-sharp teeth. Are you picturing a grizzly or other tough-looking critter? If so, you're wrong! The animals that do these things are none other than adorable otters and fluffy polar bears! Many adorable animals can actually be pretty vicious. Find out which cuties are killers and see how they take down their prey." (Publisher's note)

REVIEW: *Voice of Youth Advocates* v36 no4 p95-6 O 2013 Mary Ellen Snodgrass

"Deadly High-Risk Jobs" and "Deadly Adorable Animals." "A compilation of twelve risky careers, [author Elaine] Landau's text juxtaposes entertainers--stunt actors, rodeo riders, and car racers--with serious risk-takers in law enforcement, the military, and space exploration. . . . A zoological gallery balancing catchy close-ups with alerts to perils, [author Nadia] Higgins's sampling presents a realistic glimpse of the animal kingdom. . . . While the two titles reviewed here are excellent resources, another title in the series, 'Deadly Danger Zones,' suffers from poor editorial guidance and mixing of fact with fiction."

HIGGINS, NADIA. Natural disasters through infographics; [by] Nadia Higgins 32 p. 2014 Lerner Publications Company

1. Children's nonfiction 2. Earthquakes 3. Natural disasters—Juvenile literature 4. Tsunamis 5. Volcanoes

ISBN 9781467712873 (lib. bdg.: alk. paper)

LC 2013-006928

SUMMARY: In this book, part of Nadia Higgins' "Super-science Infographics" series, "children will learn how to track the course of a tsunami, classify an earthquake, and identify one of four different types of volcanoes. They will learn about some of the biggest and most destructive natural disasters. . . . After educating readers on the events and dangers, the author provides survival tips on what to do if one of these three natural disasters occurs." (Children's Literature)

REVIEW: *Booklist* v110 no3 p80 O 1 2013 John Peters

HIGGS, COLIN. Long-term athlete development. See Balyi, I.

HIGGS, ERIC S.ed. Novel ecosystems. See Novel ecosystems

HIGHAM, NICHOLAS J. The Anglo-Saxon world; [by] Nicholas J. Higham 496 p. 2013 Yale University Press

1. Anglo-Saxon art 2. Anglo-Saxons 3. Coins, Anglo-Saxon 4. Historical literature 5. Interdisciplinary approach to knowledge

ISBN 9780300125344 (cl : alk. paper)

LC 2013-005724

SUMMARY: In this book, "N. J. Higham and M. J. Ryan reexamine Anglo-Saxon England in the light of new research in disciplines as wide ranging as historical genetics, paleobotany, archaeology, literary studies, art history, and numismatics. The result is the definitive introduction to the Anglo-Saxon world, enhanced with a rich array of photographs, maps, genealogies, and other illustrations." (Publisher's note)

REVIEW: *Choice* v51 no4 p714-5 D 2013 E. J. Kealey

REVIEW: *Publ Wkly* v260 no27 p73 Jl 8 2013

REVIEW: *TLS* no5780 p25 Ja 10 2014 GEORGE MOLYNEAUX

"The Anglo-Saxon World." "For the upper echelons of English society, 1066 was disastrous, but there was much which the Conquest did not sweep away. . . . Such themes are prominent in Nicholas Higham and Martin Ryan's new survey of the pre-Conquest period. The Anglo-Saxon World. While being careful to avoid teleology and national triumphalism, they present a fairly conventional narrative, starting with Roman Britain, the fifth-century collapse of many of its political and economic structures, and the settlement in the south and east of non- Christian speakers of Germanic dialects, from which modem English has evolved."

HIGSON, CHARLIE. The sacrifice; [by] Charlie Higson

484 p. 2013 Hyperion
1. Dystopias 2. Horror stories 3. Horror tales 4. London (England)—Fiction 5. Survival—Fiction 6. Young adult fiction 7. Zombies 8. Zombies—Fiction
ISBN 9781423165651
LC 2012-036699

SUMMARY: Part of author Charlie Higson's Enemy series, this young adult zombie novel "picks up after Small Sam and The Kid arrive at the Tower of London at the end of 'The Dead.' Though Sam finds safety and friendship at the Tower with Jordan Hordern's crew, he can't settle down. The only thing he wants is to be reunited with his sister, Ella. Despite Ed's protests, Sam and the Kid strike out westward, through the no-go zone." (Publisher's note)

REVIEW: *Booklist* v109 no22 p90-2 Ag 1 2013 Daniel Kraus

REVIEW: *Voice of Youth Advocates* v36 no4 p81-2 O 2013 Ava Ehde

"The Sacrifice: An Enemy Novel." "This suspenseful, longed-for, fourth novel of the Enemy series takes the reader into the heart of London where the kids must now venture out to find family or replenish their food and water in order to survive. The disaster last year created a sickness which either wiped out everyone over the age of fourteen or turned them into diseased zombies with an insatiable hunger for children. . . . Death, religion, friendship, survival, power, politics, and fear are explored throughout this installment. . . . The solid writing is, at times, brilliant, such as the Kid's description of music. . . . This popular, dark dystopian tale with its combination of adventure, horror and suspense will appeal to many at both public and school libraries."

HILGERT, JEFFREY. Hazard or hardship; crafting global norms on the right to refuse unsafe work; [by] Jeffrey Hilgert x, 207 p. 2013 ILR Press, an imprint of Cornell University Press
1. Employee rights 2. Industrial safety—Law and legislation 3. Labor laws and legislation 4. Right to refuse hazardous work 5. Social science literature
ISBN 0801451892 (cloth); 9780801451898 (cloth)
LC 2013-004467

SUMMARY: This book by Jeffrey Hilgert "focuses on International Labor Organization Convention 155 (1981), which defined occupational safety and health as a human right, and on North American laws that protect employer prerogatives." According to the author, "international standards provide refusal rights that are too limited, allowing employers to discriminate against workers who band together to refuse to work in hazardous environments." (Choice: Current Reviews for Academic Libraries)

REVIEW: *Choice* v51 no9 p1677 My 2014 D. B. Robertson

"Hazard or Hardship: Crafting Global Norms on the Right to Refuse Unsafe Work". "[Jeffrey] Hilgert . . . a scholar/activist, earnestly details the shortcomings of current protections for such workers. . . . Current legal protections are inadequate because they are too narrow and disconnected from freedom of association, says Hilgert: 'what is needed is a radical reshaping of social consciousness on the advocacy of labor rights in the working environment.' This valuable book is useful for research libraries, graduate students, and upper-level undergraduate students interested in industrial relations, human rights, and the work environment."

HILL, LEA M. The Society of Sylphs; [by] Lea M. Hill 269 p. 2013 Best Bilingual Solutions
1. Autistic youth 2. Communication 3. Fantasy fiction 4. Friendship—Fiction 5. Spirits
ISBN 1619955555; 9781619955554

SUMMARY: In this book, "a boy with autism makes friends with a sylph, who helps him communicate. Luranna is a young sylph, an air elemental invisible to most humans. . .. Eddie is a bright 12-year-old boy with autism. . . . One stormy night, Pam goes out to meet some friends for a few beers by the ocean. . . . After they both witness a terrible accident, Eddie needs Luranna's assistance to communicate, and Luranna learns some lessons about trust, courage and friendship." (Kirkus Reviews)

REVIEW: *Kirkus Rev* v82 no3 p345 F 1 2014

"The Society of Sylphs: How an Autistic Boy and a Mystical Being Find Their Voices Through Human Tragedy". "In her debut novel, [Lea M.] Hill . . . does a fine job of describing Eddie's rapt obsessions and how others often fail to understand the autistic child's point of view. . . . The sylph's story, however, succeeds less well, as Luranna decides to keep a secret for flimsy reasons, seemingly only to postpone the story's ending. A sylph gathering in Iceland initially sounds exciting, but it turns out to be an annual meeting with an agenda and stuffy speeches. . . . A YA novel that's sympathetic to those with autism but ultimately unsatisfying."

HILL, MARC LAMONT.ed. Schooling hip-hop. See Schooling hip-hop

HILL, SUSAN, 1942-. The mist in the mirror; a ghost story; [by] Susan Hill 288 p. 2014 Vintage Books, A Division of Random House, LLC.
1. Adventure & adventurers 2. Detective & mystery stories 3. Explorers—Fiction 4. Ghost stories 5. Secrets—Fiction
ISBN 0345806670; 9780345806673
LC 2013-030742

SUMMARY: In this book, "Sir James Monmouth has made his life traveling . . . in the footsteps of his hero, the famous (or infamous) Conrad Vane. On his arrival in England, Monmouth plans to learn the history surrounding Vane, from his early life onward. Though all those he meets try to dissuade him from this quest, citing feelings of wariness and concern for Monmouth, he soldiers on, tracking down a surprising connection between Vane's life and his own." (Kirkus Reviews)

REVIEW: *Booklist* v110 no9/10 p62 Ja 1 2014 Carol Haggas

REVIEW: *Kirkus Rev* v82 no2 p94 Ja 15 2014

"The Mist in the Mirror". "The moody countryside wanderings of an adventurer [Susan] Hill . . . sends on a glacially paced adventure in search of the truth about his hero. . . Although Lady Quincebridge insists that Monmouth give up when the madness of researching Vane begins to infect him as an illness, Monmouth cannot rest until he understands how their lives are intertwined. His journey to Kittiscar Hall holds secrets that Monmouth had never guessed and yet always instinctively knew—and not only secrets, but danger too. The eponymous mist seems to cloud the writing, and the meandering tale ends quickly with a conclusion that still seems obscure. Even if Monmouth doesn't deserve the truth, doesn't the loyal reader?"

REVIEW: *Publ Wkly* v260 no49 p65-6 D 2 2013

REVIEW: *Publ Wkly* v260 no49 p59 D 2 2013

HILLABY, CAROLINE. The Palgrave dictionary of medieval Anglo-Jewish history. See Hillaby, J.

HILLABY, JOE. The Palgrave dictionary of medieval Anglo-Jewish history; [by] Joe Hillaby xix, 447 p. 2013 Palgrave Macmillan

1. Historical literature 2. Jews—England—History—To 1500—Dictionaries 3. Jews—England—Social conditions—To 1500—Dictionaries 4. Jews—Legal status, laws, etc.—England—History—To 1500—Dictionaries
ISBN 9780230278165
LC 2012-048103

SUMMARY: This historical dictionary looks at Jews and Jewish culture in medieval England. "The introduction by Joe Hillaby and Caroline Hillaby provides 'an over-view of the history of English medieval Jewry.' This is followed by 'Statutory and Other Key Documents'. . . . Topics include 'Women of the Medieval Anglo-Jewry,' 'Libraries and Books,' and 'Herb Gardens.'" (Choice: Current Reviews for Academic Libraries)

REVIEW: *Choice* v51 no9 p1572 My 2014 W. Baker

"The Palgrave Dictionary of Medieval Anglo-Jewish History". "This new dictionary complements and adds considerably to William Rubinstein's edited 'The Palgrave Dictionary of Anglo-Jewish History'. . . which covers a subsequent historical period. The main body of the Hillabys' text consists of 'Topographical, Biographical and General Entries,' beginning with 'Aaron' and concluding with 'York, Josce, d. 1190, and Benedict, d. 1189, of'. . . . Essentially the first book of its kind, this clearly written, well-printed, and sturdily bound and illustrated work is an indispensable reference tool."

HILLERMAN, ANNE. Spider Woman's Daughter; [by] Anne Hillerman 320 p. 2013 HarperCollins

1. Detective & mystery stories 2. Indian reservation police 3. Indians—Antiquities 4. Navajo Indians—Fiction 5. Police—Fiction
ISBN 0062270486; 9780062270481

SUMMARY: In this book, Anne Hillerman revives the characters Joe Leaphorn and Jim Chee from the stories of her late father, Tony Hillerman. Chee's wife Officer Bernadette Manuelito "sees a gunman shoot Leaphorn in a restaurant parking lot, but isn't close enough to stop the shooter from driving off. With Leaphorn comatose, Chee is named head investigator. . . . Leaphorn's current job evaluating a collection that the American Indian Resource Center is acquiring may provide a clue to his attacker." (Publishers Weekly)

REVIEW: *Booklist* v110 no2 p37-8 S 15 2013 Stephanie Zvirin

"Spider Woman's Daughter." "[Anne] Hillerman builds upon characters and themes from her father's 'Thief of Time' (1988), applying her own knowledge of contemporary Navajo culture. The spiritual elements prominent in previous Leaphorn-Chee books are downplayed, and the measured plot (with perhaps too much attention to the desert landscape) has few surprises. What intrigues is Bernie herself, a devoted young Native American balancing her heritage and family obligations with the demands of a difficult job."

REVIEW: *Kirkus Rev* v81 no13 p157 Jl 1 2013

REVIEW: *Publ Wkly* v260 no28 p147 Jl 15 2013

HILLIARD, CHRISTOPHER. English as a vocation; the Scrutiny movement; [by] Christopher Hilliard ix, 298 p. 2012 Oxford University Press

1. Criticism—England—Cambridge—History—20th century 2. Criticism—Study and teaching (Higher)—England—Cambridge—History—20th century 3. Historical literature
ISBN 0199695172; 9780199695171
LC 2012-454530

SUMMARY: This book by Christopher Hilliard "is a history of the most influential movement in modern British literary criticism. F. R. Leavis and his collaborators on the Cambridge journal 'Scrutiny' from the 1930s to the 1950s demonstrated compelling ways of reading modernist poetry, Shakespeare, and the 'texts' of advertising. Crucially, they offered a way of teaching critical reading. . . . This book shows how a small critical school turned into a movement with an international reach." (Publisher's note)

REVIEW: *London Rev Books* v35 no17 p10-2 S 12 2013 John Mullan

"Memoirs of a Leavisite: The Decline and Fall of Cambridge English," "English As a Vocation: The 'Scrutiny' Movement," and "The Two Cultures? The Significance of C. P. Snow." "[Author David] Ellis is well aware of Leavis's joyless reputation and tries to redeem it. . . . Christopher Hilliard's 'English as a Vocation' shows that applicants to Downing were expected already to have read large swathes of Shakespeare, 17th-century poetry, Romantic poetry and 19th-century fiction. . . . In the year of his retirement from his readership in the Cambridge English Faculty [author F. R. Leavis] achieved notoriety with his riposte to C.P. Snow's lecture 'The Two Cultures and the Scientific Revolution'. . . . The performance survives rather well."

REVIEW: *TLS* no5721 p3-5 N 23 2012 STEFAN COLLINI

HILLS, TAD.il. Duck & Goose go to the beach. See Hills, T.

HILLS, TAD. Duck & Goose go to the beach; 40 p. 2014 Schwartz & Wade

1. Adventure and adventurers—Fiction 2. Animal stories 3. Beaches—Fiction 4. Ducks—Fiction 5. Friendship—Fiction 6. Geese—Fiction
ISBN 0385372353; 9780385372350 (hardback); 9780385372374 (glb)
LC 2013-029728

SUMMARY: In this book, "a contented Goose comments on the loveliness of the here and now moment in the meadow just as good friend Duck conceives of the idea to set off on an adventure. Goose joins him despite being largely unimpressed with the plan, but upon arriving at the sandy shore, there is a sudden shift in opinions: Duck is put off by the noise, the water, and the sand, while Goose is positively thrilled by their new environs." (Bulletin of the Center for Children's Books)

REVIEW: *Booklist* v110 no15 p92 Ap 1 2014 Connie Fletcher

REVIEW: *Bull Cent Child Books* v67 no10 p521 Je 2014 H. M.

"Duck & Goose Go to the Beach". "The familiar dynamic of Duck and Goose . . . effectively drives this celebration of friendship and adventure. The playful language and birdy banter adds humor to the day-in-the-life plotline, while the switching perspectives contribute interest to what could otherwise present itself as a list of activities. Duck and Goose's faces are remarkably expressive, especially considering that they are all eyes and beak and the beaks don't change at all. The clean design keeps the two birds and the dynamic of the moment at the center of the action, and the peaceful palette of pale green field, turquoise water, and periwinkle sky provides a serene backdrop."

REVIEW: *Kirkus Rev* v82 no5 p76 Mr 1 2014

REVIEW: *Publ Wkly* v261 no11 p82-3 Mr 17 2014

REVIEW: *SLJ* v60 no4 p122 Ap 2014 Blair Christolon

HILLS, TAD.il. Rocket's mighty words. See Hills, T.

HILLS, TAD. Rocket's mighty words; 22 p. 2013 Schwartz & Wade Books

1. Birds—Fiction 2. Books & reading—Juvenile fiction 3. Dogs—Fiction 4. Learning 5. Vocabulary—Fiction
ISBN 0385372337; 9780385372336
LC 2012-049622

SUMMARY: In this children's book by Tad Hills, part of a series, "Rocket, the beloved dog from the 'New York Times' bestselling picture books 'How Rocket Learned to Read' and 'Rocket Writes a Story,' is back in a sturdy big board book for new readers. Preschoolers watch the little yellow bird teach Rocket simple words, like n-e-s-t and m-u-d." (Publisher's note)

REVIEW: *Kirkus Rev* v81 no16 p366 Ag 15 2013

REVIEW: *Kirkus Rev* v82 no1 p24 Ja 1 2014

"Rocket's Mighty Words". "[Tad] Hills' adorable black-and-white spotted dog named Rocket . . . returns in this oversized vocabulary primer. . . . Many of the charming images will be familiar to readers, as they have appeared before, in part or whole, in other Rocket adventures. Nothing really new here, but Rocket fans—at least those who don't consider themselves too old for board books—may enjoy using this as a tool for practicing word recognition with the sweet puppy they've come to love."

REVIEW: *Publ Wkly* v260 no31 p71 Ag 5 2013

REVIEW: *SLJ* v59 no10 p1 O 2013 Barbara Auerbach

HINCHMAN, KATHLEEN A.ed. Reconceptualizing the literacies in adolescent's lives. See Reconceptualizing the literacies in adolescent's lives

HINDLEY, KATE.il. How to wash a woolly mammoth. See Robinson, M.

HINDS, GARETH, 1971-.il. The most excellent and lamentable tragedy of Romeo & Juliet. See Hinds, G.

HINDS, GARETH, 1971-. The most excellent and lamentable tragedy of Romeo & Juliet; a play by William Shakespeare; 128 p. 2013 Candlewick Press

1. Graphic novels 2. Juliet (Fictitious character) 3. Love stories 4. Romeo (Fictitious character) 5. Shakespeare, William, 1564-1616—Adaptations
ISBN 0763659487 (hardcover); 0763668079 (pbk.); 9780763659486 (hardcover); 9780763668075 (pbk.)
LC 2012-950561

SUMMARY: This book by Gareth Hinds presents a graphic novel adaptation of William Shakespeare's play "Romeo and Juliet." "The most notable change between this story and Shakespeare's original is the creative license that Hinds takes with ethnicity--he makes the characters of African, Indian, and Caucasian descent in order to promote the universality of the story. The Shakespearean language is abridged but not adapted into contemporary English." (School Library Journal)

REVIEW: *Horn Book Magazine* v89 no6 p120-1 N/D 2013 JOANNA RUDGE LONG

"Romeo & Juliet." "Cleaving to [William] Shakespeare's words and his dramatic arc, [Gareth] Hinds . . . creates another splendid graphic novel, tracing each scene in taut, coherent, and expertly deployed dialogue. Hinds's characters. . . are poignantly specific yet as universal as this tragic tale of young love demands. . . . Expertly pacing the drama with varied frames, often with sharp, action-propelling angles, Hinds explicates and amplifies Shakespeare's story on every page. . . . From swirling action to subtly delineated emotion, he delivers the play's essence and beauty, its glorious language, furious conflict, yearning love, and wrenching tragedy."

HINKS, PETER P.ed. All men free and brethren. See All men free and brethren

HINTON, JAMES. The mass observers; a history, 1937-1949; [by] James Hinton xiv, 401 p. 2013 Oxford University Press

1. Historical literature 2. Popular culture—Great Britain—History—20th century 3. Public opinion—Great Britain—History—20th century 4. Social surveys—Great Britain—History—20th century 5. World War, 1939-1945—Social aspects—Great Britain
ISBN 0199671044 (hardcover); 9780199671045 (hardcover)
LC 2012-277332

SUMMARY: This book presents a "history of Mass-Observation, the independent social research organisation which, between 1937 and 1949, set out to document the attitudes, opinions, and every-day lives of the British people. Through a combination of anthropological fieldwork, opinion surveys, and written testimony solicited from hundreds of volunteers, Mass-Observation created a huge archive of popular life during a tumultuous decade which remains central to British national identity." (Publisher's note)

REVIEW: *TLS* no5767 p27 O 11 2013 JULIET GARDINER

"The Mass Observers: A History, 1937-1949." "[James] Hinton's subtitle misleads. The Mass Observers does not end in 1949 but usefully carries on until the 1970s, when the question of M-O's purpose became acute. By that time, it was unable to attract academic funding for its allegedly amateur, anecdotal research methods, so was obliged to compromise its principles and increasingly turn to undertaking market research projects . . . while valiantly trying to cling on to its raison d'être by publishing earlier material that had attempted to answer big questions."

HIRAIDE, TAKASHI, 1950-. The Guest Cat. See The Guest Cat

HIROSHI MASUDA. MacArthur in Asia; the general and his staff in the Philippines, Japan, and Korea; [by] Hiroshi Masuda xii, 320 p. 2013 Cornell University Press

1. Generals—United States—Biography 2. Historical literature 3. United States—Military history 4. World War, 1939-1945—Campaigns—Asia

ISBN 0801449391; 9780801449390 (cloth : alk. paper)

LC 2012-009130

SUMMARY: "General Douglas MacArthur's storied career is inextricably linked to Asia." In this book, Hiroshi Masuda "offers a new perspective on the American icon, focusing on his experiences in the Philippines, Japan, and Korea and highlighting the importance of the general's staff--the famous 'Bataan Boys' who served alongside MacArthur throughout the Asian arc of his career--to both MacArthur's and the region's history." (Publisher's note)

REVIEW: *Am Hist Rev* v119 no2 p492 Ap 2014 Marc Gallicchio

REVIEW: *Choice* v51 no2 p335-6 O 2013 J. Tucci

"MacArthur in Asia: The General and His Staff in the Philippines, Japan, and Korea." "General Douglas MacArthur has been the subject of numerous biographies and histories, but the vast majority available in English have been from the US perspective. [Author Hiroshi] Masuda . . . offers a fresh, scholarly, Japanese perspective on the full range of the general's career. In what is more a collective biography of MacArthur and the important staff officers around him . . . , Masuda succeeds in demonstrating how these 15 loyal subordinates were essential to MacArthur's command and eventual success, both in wartime and in the occupation of Japan. Although the author claims to cover MacArthur's entire career, . . . the New Guinea campaign and the Korean War . . . receive scant attention."

HIRSCH, JEFF. The darkest path; [by] Jeff Hirsch 336 p. 2013 Scholastic Press

1. Adventure stories 2. Brothers—Fiction 3. Brothers—Juvenile fiction 4. Cults—Fiction 5. Cults—Juvenile fiction 6. Dystopias—Juvenile fiction 7. Escapes—Fiction 8. Escapes—Juvenile fiction 9. Militia movements—Fiction 10. Militia movements—Juvenile fiction 11. Survival—Fiction 12. Survival—Juvenile fiction

ISBN 0545512239; 9780545512237 (hardcover); 9780545512244 (pbk.); 9780545512251 (e-book)

LC 2013-004367

SUMMARY: In this book, by Jeff Hirsch, protagonist Callum Roe is forced to "walk away from his younger brother when it becomes clear the boy has been swallowed up by the fanaticism of the Glorious Path, a military-religious cult that holds half of America under its sway. The brothers were kidnapped by the Path years before, and Cal never gave up on the idea of returning to their true home in Ithaca, New York. Forced to run, Cal treks . . . through the desert Southwest, seeking to cross into Federal territory." (Booklist)

REVIEW: *Booklist* v110 no3 p89-90 O 1 2013 Karen Cruze

"The Darkest Path." "Teen warriors populate a great deal of young-adult fiction. Coming up with a fresh take on these protagonists, especially in the dystopian genre, is not an easy feat, but in Callum Roe, Hirsch has created a hero who stands out. . . . Forced to run, Cal treks with his dog through the desert Southwest, seeking to cross into Federal territory. His encounters with those who help or hinder him always surprise. Only at the end of his journey, in a series of convenient plot twists, does the novel falter. Still, recommend this to thrill-seeking, adventure-loving readers."

REVIEW: *Kirkus Rev* v81 no17 p97 S 1 2013

REVIEW: *Voice of Youth Advocates* v36 no5 p74 D 2013 Jane Van Wiemokly

HIRTH, KENNETH G.ed. Merchants, markets, and exchange in the Pre-Columbian world. See Merchants, markets, and exchange in the Pre-Columbian world

A HISTORY OF JEWISH-MUSLIM RELATIONS; from the origins to the present day; 1145 p. 2013 Princeton University Press

1. Historical literature 2. Islam—Relations—Judaism—History 3. Jewish-Arab relations 4. Judaism—Relations—Islam—History

ISBN 069115127X; 9780691151274

LC 2013-937928

SUMMARY: This book, edited by Abdelwahab Meddeb and Benjamin Stora, is an "encyclopedic guide to the history of relations between Jews and Muslims around the world from the birth of Islam to today. . . . Part I covers the medieval period; Part II, the early modern period through the nineteenth century, in the Ottoman Empire, Africa, Asia, and Europe; Part III, the twentieth century, including the exile of Jews from the Muslim world, Jews and Muslims in Israel, and Jewish-Muslim politics." (Publisher's note)

REVIEW: *Booklist* v110 no9/10 p78 Ja 1 2014 Muhammed Hassanali

"A History of Jewish-Muslim Relations: From the Origins to the Present Day." "Although contemporary media may portray Muslim-Jewish relations from only the perspective of the Palestinian-Israeli lens . . . this book presents a far deeper and richer relationship between Muslims and Jews in areas that go beyond politics and religion. . . . There are two minor issues with this reference: a detailed table of contents is at the back of the volume (instead of the front), and a time line of events is conspicuously missing. . . . The essays presented here provide the general reader with a flavor of the rich Muslim-Jewish relationship since early Islam. An excellent reference for high-school students, general readers . . . and undergraduates looking for a starting point in their research."

HITCHINGS, HENRY. Sorry!; [by] Henry Hitchings 400 p. 2013 John Murray Publishers Ltd

1. Courtesy 2. Etiquette 3. Historical literature 4. Manners & customs 5. National characteristics, English

ISBN 1848546645; 9781848546646

SUMMARY: This book by Henry Hitchings examines the history "of English manners. From basic table manners to appropriate sexual conduct, via hospitality, chivalry, faux pas, and online etiquette, Hitchings traces the history of England's customs and courtesies." Writings on social mores by such authors as Jane Austen and Samuel Pepys are also discussed. (Publisher's note)

REVIEW: *Booklist* v110 no4 p5 O 15 2013 Bridget Thoreson

REVIEW: *Kirkus Rev* v81 no20 p2 O 15 2013

REVIEW: *New Statesman* v142 no5142 p42 Ja 25 2013 Simon Heffer

REVIEW: *Publ Wkly* v260 no25 p155 Je 24 2013

REVIEW: *TLS* no5770 p10 N 1 2013 NICOLA SCHULMAN

"Sorry! The English and Their Manners." "Sometimes the volume of material threatens to put Hitchings's nimbleness and his curiosity at odds with one another. Luckily, he is an elegant prose writer with a gift for category and conclusion, so, what might feel like an overwhelming slurry of observations and "did-you-knows" too good to be left out . . . always feels ventilated and discriminating. . . . On the whole, principles of conduct are what interest the author, more than the 'how-to' detail, and he has taken pains to avoid the obvious. . . . His chapter on euphemism is particularly good."

HITE, KATHERINE.ed. Sustaining human rights in the twenty-first century. See Sustaining human rights in the twenty-first century

HITI, SAMUEL.il. The endocrine and reproductive systems.. See Midthun, J.

HITI, SAMUEL.il. The skeletal and muscular systems. See Midthun, J.

HITTMAN, MICHAEL. Great Basin Indians; an encyclopedic history; [by] Michael Hittman 512 p. 2013 University of Nevada Press

1. Encyclopedias & dictionaries 2. Great Basin Indians 3. Indians of North America—Encyclopedias 4. Indians of North America—Great Basin—History—Encyclopedias 5. Indians of North America—Great Basin—Social life and customs—Encyclopedias 6. Indians of North America—History

ISBN 9780874179095 (cloth : alk. paper); 9780874179101 (ebook)

LC 2012-046512

SUMMARY: Written by Michael Hittman, this book "is organized in an encyclopedic format to allow full discussion of many diverse topics, including geography, religion, significant individuals, the impact of Euro-American settlement, wars, tribes and intertribal relations, reservations, federal policies regarding Native Americans, scholarly theories regarding their prehistory, and others." (Publisher's note)

REVIEW: *Choice* v51 no4 p614 D 2013 M. Cedar Face

"Great Basin Indians: An Encyclopedic History." "[Author Michael] Hittman . . . aims to provide an 'encyclopedic history' of Native peoples of the Great Basin, with entries that focus on individuals and tribes over time. . . . Entry chapters conclude with endnotes. Nearly half of the entries are biographies of prominent historic and contemporary individuals. . . . Given the dearth of encyclopedic works on Great Basin Indians, this book fills a gap. . . . Despite filling a need, Hittman's book does not totally hit the mark. Coverage is uneven, and entry selection is biased towards the author's research interests. The text is dense and the organization unwieldy, making the locating of information challenging at times."

REVIEW: *N Y Rev Books* v60 no8 p31 My 9 2013

HLASKO, MAREK. Beautiful Twentysomethings; [by] Marek Hlasko 232 p. 2013 NIU Press

1. Authors, Polish—20th century—Biography 2. Memoirs 3. Poland—Intellectual life—1945-1989 4. Polish authors—History

ISBN 9780875804774 (hardcover); 9780875806976 (softcover)

LC 2013-017701

SUMMARY: Translated by Ross Ufberg, "Marek Hłasko's literary autobiography is a vivid, first-hand account of the life of a young writer in 1950s Poland and a fascinating portrait of the ultimately short-lived rebel generation. Told in a voice suffused with grit and morbid humor, Hłasko's memoir was a classic of its time. In it he recounts his adventures and misadventures, moving swiftly from one tale to the next." (Publisher's note)

REVIEW: *TLS* no5792 p22 Ap 4 2014 PIOTR GWIAZDA

"Beautiful Twentysomethings." "First published in Paris in 1966, republished in Poland in 1988, and now for the first time available in English, 'Beautiful Twentysomethings' explains Hłasko's personal and political choices—which at least were choices. Readers interested in post-Second World War European history will find this memoir fascinating. . . . This is primarily a literary memoir. Hłasko adeptly recreates the world of his fellow writers, poets, critics, actors, film directors—the 'beautiful twentysomethings' of his title. . . . Ross Ufberg has successfully reproduced Hłasko's casual, fast-paced style in his translation."

HO, UFRIEDA. Paper sons and daughters; growing up Chinese in South Africa; [by] Ufrieda Ho viii, 229 p. 2012 Ohio University Press

1. Chinese—South Africa—Biography 2. Chinese—South Africa—Ethnic identity 3. Chinese—South Africa—History 4. Memoirs

ISBN 0821420208 (pbk. : acid-free paper); 0821444441 (electronic); 9780821420201 (pbk. : acid-free paper); 9780821444443 (electronic)

LC 2012-020804

SUMMARY: This "memoir describes with intimate detail what it was like to come of age in the marginalized Chinese community of Johannesburg during the apartheid era of the 1970s and 1980s. The Chinese were mostly ignored, as [Ufrieda] Ho describes it, relegated to certain neighborhoods and certain jobs, living in a kind of gray zone between the blacks and the whites. As long as they adhered to these rules, they were left alone." (Publisher's note)

REVIEW: *World Lit Today* v87 no6 p69-70 N/D 2013

"Paper Sons and Daughters." "Ufrieda Ho's memoir, subtitled 'Growing up Chinese in South Africa,' describes the lives of an illegal immigrant family who reside in the marginal space allotted to nonwhites in apartheid Johannesburg during the 1970s and '80s. Lacking a formal education and ineligible for most legitimate employment, father Ho Sing Kee becomes a shadowy gambling manager . . . in order to support his family."

HOAG, HEATHER J. Developing the Rivers of East and West Africa; An Environmental History; [by] Heather J. Hoag 304 p. 2013 Bloomsbury USA Academic

1. Historical literature 2. Human ecology—History 3. River ecology 4. Rivers—Africa 5. Water supply—Africa

ISBN 1441192379; 9781441192370

SUMMARY: This book by Heather J. Hoag "explores the role African waterways played in the continent's economic, social, and political development. . . . It analyzes key themes in Africa's modern history--European exploration, establishment of colonial rule, economic development, 'green' politics--and each case study provides a lens with which to view social, economic and ecological change in Africa." (Publisher's note)

REVIEW: *Choice* v51 no7 p1280 Mr 2014 J. R. Kenyon

"Developing the Rivers of East and West Africa: An Environmental History." "Serving as a useful introduction to hydrological themes in African environmental history, this book adds to the historical coverage of Africa's waterscapes. . . . One weakness of the book is its patchwork nature. Derived from a series of articles, the narrative jumps from one region and theme to the next, reducing the thrust of the argument. . . . Yet overall, [Heather J.] Hoag . . . presents a well-documented environmental history and delivers fascinating insights into how both East African and colonial populations have understood and misunderstood the rivers on which they depended."

HOAGLAND, EDWARD, 1932-. Children are diamonds; an African apocalypse; [by] Edward Hoagland 240 p. 2013 Arcade Publishing

1. Americans—Kenya—Fiction 2. Americans—South Sudan—Fiction 3. Child soldiers—Africa—Fiction 4. Humanitarian assistance—Africa—Fiction 5. War stories

ISBN 161145834X (hardcover); 9781611458343 (hardcover)

LC 2013-013603

SUMMARY: This novel, by Edward Hoagland, focuses on Hickey, "an American school teacher who . . . goes to Africa as an aid worker. Working for an agency in Nairobi, one of his jobs is to drive food and medical supplies to Southern Sudan to an aid station run by Ruth, a middle-aged woman, who acts as nurse, doctor, [and] feeder of starving children. When the violence . . . in the region increase . . . and aid workers are being slaughtered or evacuated, Hickey is asked to save Ruth." (Publisher's note)

REVIEW: *Booklist* v109 no19/20 p28 Je 1 2013 Donna Seaman

REVIEW: *Kirkus Rev* v81 no10 p13 My 15 2013

REVIEW: *N Y Times Book Rev* p26-8 D 8 2013

"The Accursed," "Children Are Diamonds: An African Apocalypse," "The American Way of Poverty: How the Other Half Still Lives." "['The Accursed' is Joyce Carol] Oates's extravagantly horrifying, funny prolix postmodern Gothic novel. . . . The adventure-seeking protagonist of [Edward] Hoagland's novel ['Children Are Diamonds: An African Apocalypse'] is swept up in the chaos of southern Sudan. . . . ['The American Way of Poverty'], based on [author Sasha] Abramsky's travels around the country meeting the poor, both describes and prescribes."

HOARE, PHILIP. The sea inside; [by] Philip Hoare 374 p. 2014 Melville House Publishing

1. Seas—Anecdotes 2. Seas—Popular works 3. Seas—Social aspects 4. Travelers' writings

ISBN 1612193595; 9781612193595 (pbk.)

LC 2013-047143

SUMMARY: In this book, author Philip Hoare, "sets out to rediscover the sea and its islands, birds, and beasts. Starting at his home on the shores of Britain's Southampton Water and moving in ever widening circles—like the migration patterns of whales—Hoare explores London, the Isle of Wight, the Azores, Sri Lanka, Tasmania, and New Zealand." (Publisher's note)

REVIEW: *Booklist* v110 no14 p37 Mr 15 2014 Nancy Bent

"The Sea Inside". "As [Phillip Hoare states in the opening pages of this lyrical book, the sea defines us, connects us, and separates us. When Hoare sets out on a journey to rediscover the sea, he also meditates on the past, on the whales, birds, and other animals he encounters and on the people who had been there before him. . . . Literary history and natural history entwine so seamlessly in Hoare's narrative that the barrier between readers and the sea within all of us blurs and disappears. . . . A good choice for teens interested in natural history and eco-adventures."

REVIEW: *Kirkus Rev* v82 no3 p317 F 1 2014

"The Sea Inside". "[An] absorbing book. . . . Anyone who has an affinity, indeed a need, for the water will understand the author's desire to swim every day near his home in Southampton, England. . . . His travels and his meandering, humorous writing take us from the Isle of Wight to the Azores, Sri Lanka, and the nearly primeval Tasmania and New Zealand, and Hoare delivers delightful descriptions of sea creatures and shore birds, bemoaning animals newly and nearly extinct. . . . While the author may digress occasionally, readers will relish his writing and devotion to nature and likely won't begrudge him a bit of family history here and there. A beautifully written memoir/travelogue with readable diversions into philosophy."

REVIEW: *London Rev Books* v35 no15 p40 Ag 8 2013 Kathleen Jamie

REVIEW: *N Y Times Book Rev* p26-7 Je 1 2014 LAWRENCE OSBORNE

REVIEW: *TLS* no5804 p28 Je 27 2014 IAIN BAMFORTH

HOBBIE, HOLLY. Gem; [by] Holly Hobbie 32 p. 2012 Little, Brown & Co.

1. Children's literature 2. Gardens—Fiction 3. Granddaughters 4. Picture books for children 5. Toads

ISBN 0316203343; 9780316203340

SUMMARY: This picture book "explores the wonders of spring through the eyes of a toad that survives the perils and pleasures of its trek to a country garden, where he encounters the author's granddaughter, Hope. Opening with a letter explaining how Hope's discovery of a toad named Gem inspired her to 'tell the story of Gem's spring journey,' [Holly] Hobbie wordlessly chronicles this odyssey in . . . watercolor, pen and ink illustrations. A palette of fresh greens and yellows heralds springtime, while varying frame sizes and perspectives allow readers to view the . . . toad's cross-country ramble from multiple angles." (Kirkus)

REVIEW: *Bull Cent Child Books* v65 no9 p460 My 2012 J. H.

REVIEW: *Kirkus Rev* v80 no4 p400 F 15 2012

"Gem." " Hobbie explores the wonders of spring through the eyes of a toad that survives the perils and pleasures of its trek to a country garden, where he encounters the author's granddaughter, Hope. Opening with a letter explaining how Hope's discovery of a toad named Gem inspired her to 'tell the story of Gem's spring journey,' Hobbie wordlessly chronicles this odyssey in luminous watercolor, pen and ink illustrations. A palette of fresh greens and yellows heralds springtime, while varying frame sizes and perspectives allow readers to view the realistically rendered toad's cross-country ramble from multiple angles. . . . A stunning gem indeed."

REVIEW: *Publ Wkly* v259 no6 p58 F 6 2012

REVIEW: *SLJ* v58 no3 p127 Mr 2012 Catherine Callegari

HOBBIE, HOLLY.il. The night before Christmas. See Moore, C. C.

HOBBS, RICHARD J.ed. Novel ecosystems. See Novel ecosystems

HOBERMAN, J. Film after film; or, what became of 21st-century cinema?; [by] J. Hoberman p. cm. 2012 Verso

1. Digital media—Philosophy 2. Motion picture literature 3. Motion pictures—History—21st century 4. Motion pictures—Reviews 5. September 11 Terrorist Attacks, 2001, in motion pictures
ISBN 9781844677511 (hardback : alk. paper)
LC 2012-015580

SUMMARY: In this book on 21st-century cinema, author J. Hoberman "contends that a distinct movement has emerged as a result of two factors. Firstly, the technological shift from the photographic to the digital--a process that had its origins in the 1980s, and began to gather pace in the mid-90s. Secondly, the events of September 11, 2001, watched live and on repeated loops all over the world--'a manmade cinematic event.'" (Times Literary Supplement)

REVIEW: *Film Q* v66 no2 p52-4 Wint 2012 Paul Thomas

REVIEW: *Libr J* v137 no12 p84 Jl 1 2012 Roy Liebman

REVIEW: *Sight Sound* v22 no11 p125 N 2012 Nick James

REVIEW: *TLS* no5749 p23-4 Je 7 2013 JOHN RIDPATH

"MP3: The Meaning of a Format," "In Broad Daylight: Movies and Spectators After the Cinema" and "Film After Film: Or, What Became of 21st Century Cinema." "it is clear that the story of recorded music (and audio, even) is necessarily a story of formats. Indeed, in 'MP3: The meaning of a format,' Jonathan Sterne argues that if there is such a thing as 'media theory', there should also be a 'format theory'. . . . Gabriele Pedullà's' In Broad Daylight' explores how the interconnected evolution of formats and devices has disrupted the relationship between cinema (as art form) and cinema (as place). . . . This new aesthetic of 'twenty-first century cinema' is explored more deeply in J. Hoberman's 'Film After Film'."

HOBGOOD, ALLISON P.ed. Recovering disability in early modern England. See Recovering disability in early modern England

HOBLIN, PAUL. Colin Kaepernick; NFL phenom; [by] Paul Hoblin 32 p. 2013 ABDO Pub. Co.

1. Children's nonfiction 2. Football players 3. Football players—Selection & appointment 4. Kaepernick, Colin 5. Quarterbacks (Football)
ISBN 9781617837012
LC 2013-934742

SUMMARY: This book on football player Colin Kaepernick is part of the "Playmakers" series. Each book in the series has "an opening chapter highlighting one of the football player's greatest accomplishments" followed by "a look at each athlete's childhood and his path from high school to college to professional football. 'Colin Kaepernick' describes how after being rejected from more than 100 colleges, he was recruited during a high-school basketball game to play quarterback for the University of Nevada." (Booklist)

REVIEW: *Booklist* v110 no11 p55 F 1 2014 Angela Leeper

"Colin Kaepernick: NFL Phenom," "Joe Flaco: Super Bowl MVP," and "Robert Griffin III: RGIII--NFL Sensation." "Each book immediately hooks young sports enthusiasts with an opening chapter highlighting one of the football player's greatest accomplishments. The concise text continues with a look at each athlete's childhood and his path from high school to college to professional football. . . . Numerous color photos of the quarterbacks in action both on and off the field and interesting sidebars . . . keep the text exciting, especially for reluctant readers. Additional fun facts and quotes make these books good choices for recreational reading or biography studies."

HOBSON, THEO. Reinventing liberal Christianity; [by] Theo Hobson 304 p. 2013 William B. Eerdmans Publishing Company

1. Church & state 2. Liberalism (Religion) 3. Liberty of conscience 4. Religious literature 5. Ritual
ISBN 0802868401; 9780802868404 (cloth : alk. paper)
LC 2013-014360

SUMMARY: In this book, author Theo Hobson argues that liberal Christianity "should and must be revived, because other strains of Christianity . . . uphold neither the separation of church and state nor the liberty of conscience that, he asserts, God wills. Perhaps the most important element in reviving liberal Christianity, Hobson says, is the revival of the cultic aspect of Christianity." (Booklist)

REVIEW: *Booklist* v110 no6 p16 N 15 2013 Ray Olson

"Reinventing Liberal Christianity." "Centuries in development, liberal Christianity crystallized in the tumultuous seventeenth century in England and reached an apotheosis when the U.S. emerged as the first explicitly liberal state. That culmination was and has continued to be hotly contested by preachers and theologians, poets and even politicians, whose ideas Hobson explains with brilliant clarity, always pointing out particular thinkers' weaknesses as well as strengths. The book is so engrossing and so illuminating that it is a must-read for everyone concerned with the future of Christianity and the liberal state."

REVIEW: *Choice* v51 no8 p1417 Ap 2014 C. H. Lippy

REVIEW: *Christ Century* v131 no5 p37-40 Mr 5 2014 Walter Brueggemann

REVIEW: *Commonweal* v140 no16 p23-7 O 11 2013 Gary Dorrien

REVIEW: *TLS* no5799 p24 My 23 2014 ANDREW DAVISON

HOCKETT, JEFFREY D. A storm over this court; law, politics, and Supreme Court decision making in Brown v. Board of Education; [by] Jeffrey D. Hockett x, 267 p. 2013 University of Virginia Press

1. African Americans—Civil rights 2. Discrimination in education—Law and legislation—United States 3. Political science literature 4. School integration—United States 5. Segregation in education—Law and legislation—United States

ISBN 9780813933740 (cloth : alk. paper); 9780813933757 (e-book)

LC 2012-035954

SUMMARY: In this book, "on the way to offering a new analysis of the basis of the Supreme Court's iconic decision in Brown v. Board of Education, Jeffrey Hockett critiques an array of theories that have arisen to explain it and Supreme Court decision making generally. Drawing upon justices' books, articles, correspondence, memoranda, and draft opinions, 'A Storm over This Court' demonstrates that the puzzle of Brown's basis cannot be explained by any one theory." (Publisher's note)

REVIEW: *Choice* v51 no6 p1095 F 2014 M. W. Bowers

"A Storm Over This Court: Law, Politics, and Supreme Court Decision Making in Brown v. Board of Education." "[Jeffrey D.] Hockett . . . notes that if scholars wish to 'explain the votes of nine justices in one Supreme Court ruling, then methodological diversity is a necessity.' In this work, he examines the landmark desegregation case of Brown v. Board of Education (1954) through a number of methodological lenses in order to increase the accuracy of the understanding of the factors behind the justices' votes in this unanimous decision. . . . This is a truly comprehensive work that is of interest not only to Brown scholars but also to those who seek to understand the process of judicial decision making. . . . Highly recommended."

HOCKING, AMANDA. Tidal; [by] Amanda Hocking 352 p. 2013 St. Martin's Griffin

1. Blessing and cursing—Fiction 2. JUVENILE FICTION—Fantasy & Magic 3. Love—Fiction 4. Seaside resorts—Fiction 5. Sirens (Mythology)—Fiction 6. Sisters—Fiction 7. Supernatural—Fiction

ISBN 1250008115; 9781250008114 (hardback)

LC 2013-009316

SUMMARY: In this book by Amanda Hocking, "now that Gemma has learned more about the bloodthirsty habits of her new clique, she and her sister, Harper, are doing their best to figure out a way to end the curse. Harper's friend Marcy introduces them to a bookseller who specializes in mythical creatures, and from her they learn that the specifics of the curse are written on a scroll carefully guarded by the chief siren, Penn. Destruction of that scroll will mean not only the end of the curse but also the end of the sirens." (Voice of Youth Advocates)

REVIEW: *Booklist* v109 no19/20 p95-6 Je 1 2013 Frances Bradburn

REVIEW: *Kirkus Rev* v81 no10 p95 My 15 2013

REVIEW: *Voice of Youth Advocates* v36 no2 p77-8 Je 2013 Heather Christensen

"Tidal: A Watersong." "Fans will be thrilled to get their hands on the latest in this [Watersong] series about mermaid mean girls (aka sirens). Now that Gemma has learned more about the bloodthirsty habits of her new clique, she and her sister, Harper, are doing their best to figure out a way to end the curse. . . . [Amanda] Hocking's use of alternating viewpoints . . . provides valuable clues about the history of the sirens and their place in Greek mythology. While there is plenty of intrigue, it often feels as if external forces move the plot forward rather than the internal drive or motivation of the characters. Nevertheless, teens looking for a quick, easy read will enjoy escaping into this steamy, suspenseful story."

HOCKING, JUSTIN. The great floodgates of the Wonderworld; A Memoir; [by] Justin Hocking 256 p. 2014 Graywolf Press

1. American love stories 2. Memoirs 3. Moby-Dick; or, The Whale (Book) 4. Rockaway Beach (New York, N.Y.) 5. Surfers

ISBN 1555976697; 9781555976699 (alk. paper)

LC 2013-946924

SUMMARY: In this memoir, author Justin Hocking "lands in New York hopeful but adrift—he's jobless, unexpectedly overwhelmed and disoriented by the city, struggling with anxiety and obsession, and attempting to maintain a faltering long-distance relationship. . . . Then he spies his first New York surfer hauling a board to the subway, and its not long before he's a member of the vibrant and passionate surfing community at Far Rockaway." (Publisher's note)

REVIEW: *Kirkus Rev* v82 no2 p23 Ja 15 2014

REVIEW: *N Y Times Book Rev* p16 Mr 9 2014 THAD ZIOLKOWSKI

REVIEW: *New Yorker* v90 no8 p83-1 Ap 14 2014

"The Great Floodgates of the Wonderworld: A Memoir." "In this appealing memoir, the young author finds salvation from a dead-end Manhattan office job in an activity not often associated with New York: surfing. As his excursions to Rockaway Beach become more and more frequent, he begins to draw parallels between himself and Melville's Ishmael, 'another disgruntled young New Yorker with a deep spiritual longing for the sea.' Hocking's 'obsession' with 'Moby-Dick' doesn't feel quite convincing, but the passages about surfing and the relationships it fosters are filled with excitement and tenderness."

HODGE, ROSAMUND. Cruel Beauty; [by] Rosamund Hodge 352 p. 2014 Balzer + Bray, an imprint of HarperCollinsPublishers

1. Blessing & cursing—Fiction 2. Demonology 3. Fantasy 4. Love stories 5. Marriage—Fiction

ISBN 0062224735; 9780062224736 (hardcover)

LC 2013-015418

SUMMARY: In this book, by Rosamund Hodge, "betrothed to the evil ruler of her kingdom, Nyx has always known her fate was to marry him, kill him, and free her people from his tyranny. On her seventeenth birthday, when she moves into his castle high on the kingdom's mountaintop, nothing is as she expected. Nyx knows she must save her homeland at all costs, yet she can't resist the pull of her sworn enemy--who's gotten in her way by stealing her heart." (Publisher's note)

REVIEW: *Bull Cent Child Books* v67 no6 p316 F 2014

Kate Quealy-Gainer

"Cruel Beauty." "While an obvious twist on "Beauty and the Beast," this also includes elements of 'Bluebeard,' 'East of Sun, West of Moon,' and Roman mythology, and the book totally immerses readers a world of dark magic and terrible bargains, where everything good comes at a cost. The push and pull romance between Nyx and Ignifex is pure fairy tale, but the characters themselves are complex and genuinely human as they struggle with their own culpability in a situation that forces them to choose between selfishness and selflessness. Additionally, Nyx's efforts to shed the assumptions of her father and shift the dynamics in her family while establishing her own identity will likely strike a deep chord with many adolescent readers."

REVIEW: *Kirkus Rev* v81 no22 p112 N 15 2013

REVIEW: *SLJ* v60 no2 p106 F 2014 Kristyn Dorfman

REVIEW: *Voice of Youth Advocates* v36 no6 p72 F 2014 Susan Redman-Parodi

HODGINS, PETER.ed. Settling and unsettling memories. See Settling and unsettling memories

HODGKINSON, JANE H. The earth as a cradle for life. See Stacey, F. D.

HODSON, SALLY. Granny's clan; a tale of wild orcas; [by] Sally Hodson 32 p. 2012 Dawn Publications

1. Killer whale—Behavior—Juvenile literature 2. Life sciences literature 3. Marine ecology 4. Whales—Behavior 5. Whales—Juvenile literature
ISBN 1584691719; 9781584691716 (hardback); 9781584691723 (pbk.)
LC 2011-049431

SUMMARY: In this book, Sally Hodson offers a "glimpse into the real world of a Pacific Northwest killer whale family or pod. Also known as an orca, 100-year-old granny and her family (the J-pod) interact with one another, just as humans do. Granny teaches her children, grandchildren and great-grandchildren, how and where to locate food, play nicely, avoid danger, sing orca songs, and coexist with people." (Children's Literature)

REVIEW: *Booklist* v109 no7 p58 D 1 2012 Francisca Goldsmith

REVIEW: *Kirkus Rev* v80 no17 p58 S 1 2012

REVIEW: *SLJ* v59 no3 p140 Mr 2013 Susan Scheps

HOEKSTRA, MISHA.tr. You disappear. See Jungersen,, C.

HOFF, DEREK S. The state and the stork; the population debate and policy making in US history; [by] Derek S. Hoff 378 p. 2012 The University of Chicago Press

1. Demography 2. Economic development 3. Historical literature 4. United States—Population
ISBN 0226347621 (cloth: alkaline paper); 9780226347622 (cloth: alkaline paper)
LC 2012-001903

SUMMARY: In this book, Derek S. Hoff "chronicles how economists, students of population, and political leaders have debated the effects of population growth on US economic development. He treats the colonial period through the late nineteenth century" in his first chapter. "The heart of Hoff's story, though, is the twentieth century, especially the period from the 1950s through the 1970s." (Population & Development Review)

REVIEW: *Am Hist Rev* v119 no1 p213-4 F 2014 Laura L. Lovett

"The State and the Stork: The Population Debate and Policy Making in US History". "'The State and the Stork' goes beyond a narrative survey of population issues in the United States to offer a focused history of the political economy of population. Hoff's careful analysis of the history of American economic thought and population policies from the colonial era to the present provides an important and welcome complement to histories of demographers, eugenicists, and politicians. . . . Hoff's thoughtful historical analysis of how the interplay between our dynamic economy and population has been imagined, debated, and enacted in policy provides a powerful model of how to understand the complex array of issues that will shape the political economy of population in the future."

REVIEW: *Choice* v50 no8 p1478-9 Ap 2013 R. M. Whaples

REVIEW: *J Am Hist* v100 no1 p276 Je 2013 Edward D. Berkowitz

REVIEW: *Rev Am Hist* v42 no1 p43-50 Mr 2014 Margo Anderson

HOFFER, PETER CHARLES. Prelude to revolution; the Salem gunpowder raid of 1775; [by] Peter Charles Hoffer 152 p. 2013 The Johns Hopkins University Press

1. Civil-military relations—Massachusetts—Salem—History—18th century 2. Collective memory—United States—Case studies 3. Colonists—Massachusetts—Salem—History—18th century 4. Gunpowder—Political aspects—Massachusetts—Salem—History—18th century 5. Historical literature 6. Raids (Military science)—History—18th century
ISBN 1421410052 (hardcover: acid-free paper); 1421410060 (paperback: acid-free paper); 9781421410050 (hardcover: acid-free paper); 9781421410067 (paperback: acid-free paper)
LC 2013-004818

SUMMARY: In this book, Peter Charles Hoffer "examines the British effort to confiscate colonists' weaponry in the Salem gunpowder raid of 1775. The author argues that the raid, in which the British commander and local Colonial officials negotiated a nonviolent and face-saving solution that averted armed conflict, was foremost in the minds of those who participated at Lexington and Concord, and served as an example of how cooler heads could prevent bloodshed that led to war." (Choice: Current Reviews for Academic Libraries)

REVIEW: *Choice* v51 no8 p1473-4 Ap 2014 J. C. Arndt

"Prelude to Revolution: The Salem Gunpowder Raid of 1775." "In this highly readable book, [Peter Charles] Hoffer not only offers a vivid portrayal of the characters and events associated with the raid, but provides readers with a compelling account of life on the eve of the Revolution. This superb little book will be of interest to anyone with an interest in the American Revolution or New England life in the 1770s, and would be excellent supplemental reading for all undergraduate students."

REVIEW: *N Engl Q* v87 no3 p546-8 S 2014 Daniel S. Soucier

HOFFMAN, ALICE, 1952-. The Museum of Extraordinary Things; a novel; [by] Alice Hoffman 384 p. 2014 Simon & Schuster Scribner

1. Fantasy fiction 2. Historical fiction 3. Immigrants—New York (State)—New York—Fiction 4. Russians—New York (State)—New York—Fiction 5. Young women—Fiction

ISBN 1451693567; 9781451693560

LC 2013-036572

SUMMARY: "Alice Hoffman's 'The Museum of Extraordinary Things' is the story of an electric and impassioned love between two vastly different souls in New York during the volatile first decades of the twentieth century. . . . With its colorful crowds of bootleggers, heiresses, thugs, and idealists, New York itself becomes a riveting character as Hoffman weaves her trademark magic, romance, and . . . storytelling." (Publisher's note)

REVIEW: *Booklist* v110 no8 p20 D 15 2013 Donna Seaman

REVIEW: *Booklist* v110 no3 p4 O 1 2013

REVIEW: *Kirkus Rev* v82 no3 p19 F 1 2014

REVIEW: *Libr J* v138 no14 p86 S 1 2013

REVIEW: *Libr J* v139 no6 p56 Ap 1 2014 Wendy Galgan

REVIEW: *Ms* v24 no1 p56-7 Wint/Spr 2014 Aryn Kyle

REVIEW: *N Y Times Book Rev* p18 Mr 2 2014 KATHARINE WEBER

"The Museum of Extraordinary Things." "'The Museum of Extraordinary Things' will not disappoint readers longing to be swept up by a lavish tale about strange yet sympathetic people, haunted by the past and living in bizarre circumstances. But those who have admired [author Alice] Hoffman's best and most gracefully literary novels . . . will be less enchanted, unable to ignore the hackneyed and thinly sketched writing that diminishes many scenes in these pages. 'The Museum of Extraordinary Things' is, in a way, a museum of Alice Hoffman's bag of plot tricks."

REVIEW: *Publ Wkly* v260 no47 p29 N 18 2013

REVIEW: *Publ Wkly* v261 no9 p10-1 Mr 3 2014

HOFFMAN, BEATRIX. Health care for some; rights and rationing in the United States since 1930; [by] Beatrix Hoffman xxxv, 319 p. 2012 University of Chicago Press

1. Health care rationing—United States—History 2. Health services accessibility—United States—History 3. Historical literature 4. Medical policy 5. Right to health—United States—History

ISBN 0226348032 (cloth: alkaline paper); 9780226348032 (cloth: alkaline paper)

LC 2012-000338

SUMMARY: Author Beatrix Rebecca Hoffman looks at "America's long tradition of unequal access to health care. . . . Hoffman argues that two main features have characterized the US health system: a refusal to adopt a right to care and a particularly American type of rationing." The book "shows that the haphazard way the US system allocates medical services—using income, race, region, insurance coverage, and many other factors—is a disorganized, illogical, and powerful form of rationing." (Publisher's note)

REVIEW: *Am Hist Rev* v119 no1 p214-5 F 2014 Beth Linker

"Health Care for Some: Rights and Rationing in the United States Since 1930". "In lesser hands, the history of U.S. health policy could be a dry and lifeless account that moves from one failed attempt at universal coverage to another over the last century. [Beatrix] Hoffman, by contrast, puts flesh on the story. . . . 'Health Care for Some' is a must-read not just for specialists in health care policy but for anyone who desires to be an informed citizen and user of the American health care system. . . . Hoffman has done . . . a great service in providing us with a smart, lively, and highly readable account of why we have inherited one of the most expensive and inefficient health care systems in the world."

REVIEW: *Choice* v50 no8 p1471 Ap 2013 T. P. Gariepy

REVIEW: *J Am Hist* v100 no1 p290-1 Je 2013 Jan Gregoire Coombs

REVIEW: *Libr J* v137 no14 p118 S 1 2012 Aaron Klink

REVIEW: *Publ Wkly* v259 no25 p45-6 Je 18 2012

HOFFMAN, CARA. Be safe I love you; A novel; [by] Cara Hoffman 304 p. 2014 Simon & Schuster

1. Brothers & sisters—Fiction 2. Depressed persons—Family relationships—Fiction 3. Post-traumatic stress disorder 4. Psychological fiction 5. Veteran reintegration—Fiction

ISBN 1451641311; 9781451641318 (hardcover); 9781451641325 (trade pbk.)

LC 2013-011118

SUMMARY: In this book, by Cara Hoffman, "Lauren Clay has returned from a tour of duty in Iraq just in time to spend the holidays with her family. Before she enlisted, Lauren, a classically trained singer, and her brother Danny, a bright young boy obsessed with Arctic exploration, made the most of their modest circumstances, escaping into their imaginations and forming an indestructible bond. Joining the army allowed Lauren to continue to provide for her family, but it came at a great cost." (Publisher's note)

REVIEW: *Booklist* v110 no11 p19 F 1 2014 Joanne Wilkinson

REVIEW: *Kirkus Rev* v82 no4 p223 F 15 2014

"Be Safe I Love You". ". For those who like their prose spare and unembellished, beware: [Cara] Hoffman has nothing in common with the Hemingway school of writing. But she does an admirable job of conveying the confusion and helplessness of a returning warrior with PTSD who is trying to reintegrate into society and finds it makes little sense. And Hoffman has a knack for bringing her characters to life while providing readers with a reason to care about them. . . . Hoffman weaves an intricate plot, but a tendency to overwrite shadows her story, leaving the reader to make a complicated literary journey that, for some, may not be worth the effort."

REVIEW: *Libr J* v139 no2 p65 F 1 2014 Lauren Gilbert

REVIEW: *N Y Times Book Rev* p20 My 25 2014 ALISSA J. RUBIN

REVIEW: *Publ Wkly* v261 no2 p46-7 Ja 13 2014

HOFFMAN, IAN. Jacob's new dress. See Hoffman, S.

HOFFMAN, SARAH. Jacob's new dress; 32 p. 2014 Al-

bert Whitman & Company
1. Children's stories 2. Clothing and dress—Fiction 3. Dresses—Fiction 4. Gender identity—Fiction 5. Sex role—Fiction
ISBN 0807563730; 9780807563731 (hardcover)
LC 2013-028443

SUMMARY: In this book, by Sarah Hoffman and Ian Hoffman, illustrated by Chris Case, "Jacob loves playing dress-up, when he can be anything he wants to be. Some kids at school say he can't wear 'girl' clothes, but Jacob wants to wear a dress to school. Can he convince his parents to let him wear what he wants?" The book addresses "challenges faced by boys who don't identify with traditional gender roles." (Publisher's note)

REVIEW: *Booklist* v110 no14 p82 Mr 15 2014 Michael Cart

REVIEW: *Bull Cent Child Books* v67 no8 p407-8 Ap 2014 T. A.

"Jacob's New Dress". "The thin plot and over-earnest take on its topic makes this story of gender nonconformity more therapeutic than entertaining, but Jacob's concrete emotional reactions to people's perceptions of his behavior ('Mom didn't answer. The longer she didn't answer, the less Jacob could breathe') might be helpful to youngsters in similar situations. . . . His characters' cartoonishness—big heads and dot eyes—also helps with their emotiveness. . . . This is still a welcome addition to the recent uptick in picture books about gender nonconforming kids."

REVIEW: *Kirkus Rev* v82 no2 p176 Ja 15 2014

"Jacob's New Dress". "A warmly illustrated picture book meant to comfort both boys who are gender-nonconforming and their parents. . . . The segments with Jacob's mom and dad seem aimed at parents as much as at children. Jacob's mom's look of concern when he first asks about the dress is poignant, and his dad's words of acceptance . . . could easily serve as a model for fathers in similar positions. What rings less true is the story's rosy end. Faced with Christopher's bullying comments and other kids' laughter, Jacob is so buoyed by his new dress that he stands up to Christopher himself, then sprints triumphantly across the playground. . . . Hopeful and affirming, but children familiar with bullying may find the conclusion too simple."

REVIEW: *Publ Wkly* v261 no3 p53 Ja 20 2014

REVIEW: *SLJ* v60 no2 p74 F 2014 Melissa Smith

HOFMANN, MICHAEL, 1957-.tr. Impromptus. See Benn, G.

HOFSTRA, WARREN R.ed. Sweet dreams. See Sweet dreams

HOGAN, DESMOND. A farewell to Prague; [by] Desmond Hogan 245 p. 2013 Dalkey Archive Press
1. AIDS patients—Fiction 2. Autobiographical fiction 3. Irish—Europe—Fiction 4. Irish—United States—Fiction
ISBN 9781564788542 (pbk. : acid-free paper)
LC 2013-003002

SUMMARY: In this "novel-cum-memoir" by Desmond Hogan, "Desmond, an Irish writer, drifts around Europe and the Southern states of America, mourning the death of his lover from AIDS: 'Marek's death was leading me from one path of search to another. The paths were cross-reaching, but where the new path was going I didn't know yet'." (Times Literary Supplement)

REVIEW: *TLS* no5756 p20 Jl 26 2013 KEITH HOPPER

"The Ikon Maker," "The House of Mourning and Other Stories," and "A Farewell to Prague." "'The Ikon Maker' acted as an iconoclastic outlier for a whole new wave of counterrealist writers, who took full advantage of the cultural dispensations of the post-censorship era. . . . 'The House of Mourning and Other Stories' . . . shows [Desmond] Hogan's aesthetic at its worst and best. The earliest of these stories are full of the bitterness of exile, and too often adopt a hectoring tone. As the collection progresses, though, Hogan's mode of poetical reportage reveals, with anthropological zeal, a dispossessed tribe of junkies, alcoholics and outcasts. In this lonely landscape there is grace and levity, too. . . . This edgeland existence finds full-length expression in Hogan's tender and lyrical novel-cum-memoir 'A Farewell to Prague'."

HOGAN, DESMOND. The house of mourning and other stories; [by] Desmond Hogan 240 p. 2013 Dalkey Archive Press
1. Drug addicts—Fiction 2. Ireland—Fiction 3. Irish Travellers (Nomadic people) 4. Loneliness—Fiction 5. Short stories
ISBN 1564788555; 9781564788559 (pbk. : acid-free paper)
LC 2013-005546

SUMMARY: This book, by Desmond Hogan, presents several short stories. "Focusing as always on the downtrodden and the eccentric, the misplaced and the dispossessed, Hogan's stories merge past with present, landscape with mindscape—distinctly Irish and burdened by history, while exhilaratingly and wholly universal and modern." (Publisher's note)

REVIEW: *TLS* no5756 p20 Jl 26 2013 KEITH HOPPER

"The Ikon Maker," "The House of Mourning and Other Stories," and "A Farewell to Prague." "'The Ikon Maker' acted as an iconoclastic outlier for a whole new wave of counterrealist writers, who took full advantage of the cultural dispensations of the post-censorship era. . . . 'The House of Mourning and Other Stories' . . . shows [Desmond] Hogan's aesthetic at its worst and best. The earliest of these stories are full of the bitterness of exile, and too often adopt a hectoring tone. As the collection progresses, though, Hogan's mode of poetical reportage reveals, with anthropological zeal, a dispossessed tribe of junkies, alcoholics and outcasts. In this lonely landscape there is grace and levity, too. . . . This edgeland existence finds full-length expression in Hogan's tender and lyrical novel-cum-memoir 'A Farewell to Prague'."

HOGAN, DESMOND. The ikon maker; [by] Desmond Hogan 144 p. 2013 Lilliput Press
1. Ireland—Fiction 2. Mothers & sons 3. Popular literature 4. Self-realization—Fiction 5. Suicide—Fiction
ISBN 1843513870 (pbk.); 9781843513872 (pbk.)
LC 2013-375826

SUMMARY: In this book, "Susan is forced to confront a ruptured relationship with her only son, and the ikons--feathers, beads, paper accumulated into shapes--marking the progress of his troubled childhood. As she pursues him across England, meeting friends and lovers left in his wake, she resigns herself to the man her son has become, and must face a new identity of her own." (Publisher's note)

REVIEW: *TLS* no5756 p20 Jl 26 2013 KEITH HOPPER

"The Ikon Maker," "The House of Mourning and Other Stories," and "A Farewell to Prague." "'The Ikon Maker' acted as an iconoclastic outlier for a whole new wave of counterrealist writers, who took full advantage of the cultural dispensations of the post-censorship era. . . . 'The House of Mourning and Other Stories' . . . shows [Desmond] Hogan's aesthetic at its worst and best. The earliest of these stories are full of the bitterness of exile, and too often adopt a hectoring tone. As the collection progresses, though, Hogan's mode of poetical reportage reveals, with anthropological zeal, a dispossessed tribe of junkies, alcoholics and outcasts. In this lonely landscape there is grace and levity, too. . . . This edgeland existence finds full-length expression in Hogan's tender and lyrical novel-cum-memoir 'A Farewell to Prague'."

HOGAN, MARGARET A.ed. A traveled first lady. See A traveled first lady

HOGSELIUS, PER. Red gas; Russia and the origins of European energy dependence; [by] Per Hogselius xii, 279 p. 2013 Palgrave Macmillan

1. Energy policy—European Union countries 2. Energy security—European Union countries 3. Gas industry—Europe 4. Historical literature
ISBN 1137286148; 1137293713; 9781137286147 (pbk.); 9781137293718
LC 2012-474297

SUMMARY: It was the author's intent to demonstrate "that the Russian 'energy weapon' is more perception than reality" through a "study of how Soviet exports of natural gas to Europe began." Author Per Högselius "shows how, time and again, economic and commercial rationales—fundamentally, Europe's demand for a popular new fuel and the Soviet ability to supply it—trumped Cold War rhetoric." (American Historical Review)

REVIEW: *Am Hist Rev* v119 no1 p280-1 F 2014 Simon Pirani

"Red Gas: Russia and the Origins of European Energy Dependence". "Per Högselius bases his trenchant argument that the Russian 'energy weapon' is more perception than reality on a wonderfully rounded study of how Soviet exports of natural gas to Europe began. . . . This is a pioneering work. . . . Russian gas exports to Europe have been the province not of historians but of energy specialists and political scientists trying to keep up with fast-moving events. The return to history is welcome. Högselius is admirably equipped for it, comfortable in several languages and as happy explaining what happened to the methane molecules and steel pipes as with events in boardrooms and embassies."

HOLDSWORTH, NADINE.ed. A concise companion to contemporary British and Irish drama. See A concise companion to contemporary British and Irish drama

HOLINATY, JOSH.il. No saints around here. See Toth, S. A.

HOLLAND, L. TAM. The counterfeit family tree of Vee Crawford-Wong; [by] L. Tam Holland 368 p. 2013 Simon & Schuster BFYR

1. Amerasians 2. Asian Americans—Fiction 3. Chinese Americans—Fiction 4. Families—Fiction 5. High schools—Fiction 6. School stories 7. Schools—Fiction
ISBN 144241264X (hardcover); 9781442412644 (hardcover); 9781442412651 (paperback); 9781442412668 (ebook)
LC 2012-014542

SUMMARY: In this book, Vee has to write an essay on family history, but all he "knows about his Texas grandparents is that their annual Christmas card always makes his mother cry; his father, meanwhile, left China for college and never looked back. Already in trouble for lackluster academics, Vee can't get his parents to talk about their pasts, so he completes the essay by inventing a backstory for his father's family in a fishing village along the Yangtze. After he gets away with that, he's on a roll." (Publishers Weekly)

REVIEW: *Bull Cent Child Books* v67 no2 p95-6 O 2013 K. C.

"The Counterfeit Family Tree of Vee Crawford-Wong." "Both Vee's Chinese father and his Texan mother are silent about their pasts, so when Vee faces a family history assignment, the sophomore cops one off the internet, inventing a grandfather who escaped the Nanking massacre. . . . Vee's narrative voice is lyrical, full of witty snark and credible sophomore angst, and [author L. Tam] Holland works in an effective metaphor of unearthing family histories that may never satisfy by giving Vee a fascination with Peking Man. Besides being a stylistically compelling coming-of-age narrative with a warm nuclear family dynamic, this will be a boon for collections in need of high-quality titles featuring contemporary Asian-American protagonists."

REVIEW: *Kirkus Rev* v81 no10 p95-6 My 15 2013

REVIEW: *Publ Wkly* v260 no20 p62 My 20 2013

REVIEW: *SLJ* v59 no10 p1 O 2013 Gerry Larson

HOLLAND, MARY. The beavers' busy year; [by] Mary Holland 32 p. 2014 Sylvan Dell Publishing

1. Beavers—Behavior 2. Beavers—Habitations—Juvenile literature 3. Beavers—Juvenile literature 4. Children's nonfiction 5. Picture books for children
ISBN 9781628552041 (English hardcover); 9781628552133 (English pbk.)
LC 2013-036382

SUMMARY: In this book by Mary Holland, "photographs document the beavers' activities through the course of a year. Do these beavers ever take a break? Follow along as they pop through the winter ice to begin the busy year of eating bark, building dams and gathering food just in time for winter to come again." (Publisher's note)

REVIEW: *Booklist* v110 no21 p61 Jl 1 2014 Erin Anderson

REVIEW: *Booklist* v110 no21 p61 Jl 14 2014 Erin Anderson

REVIEW: *SLJ* v60 no5 p147 My 2014 Susan E. Murray

HOLLAND, MAX. Blind over Cuba; [by] Max Holland x, 210 p. 2012 Texas A&M University Press

1. Aerial surveillance 2. Cuban Missile Crisis, 1962 3. Executive-legislative relations—United States 4. Historical literature 5. Intelligence service—Political

aspects—United States 6. Intelligence service—United States 7. Kennedy, John F. (John Fitzgerald), 1917-1963 8. National security—Political aspects—United States
ISBN 1603447687 (cloth : alk. paper); 1603447725 (e-book); 9781603447683 (cloth : alk. paper); 9781603447720 (e-book)
LC 2012-004754

SUMMARY: "In 'Blind over Cuba,' David M. Barrett and Max Holland challenge the popular perception of the Kennedy administration's handling of the Soviet Union's surreptitious deployment of missiles in the Western Hemisphere. Rather than epitomizing it as a masterpiece of crisis management . . . , Barrett and Holland make the case that the affair was . . . a close call stemming directly from . . . deep distrust between key administration officials and the intelligence community." (Publisher's note)

REVIEW: *Antioch Rev* v71 no4 p815-6 Fall 2013 Ken Bode

"Blind Over Cuba: The Photo Gap and the Missile Crisis." "With the passage of its fiftieth anniversary, the dominant historical interpretation of the Cuban Missile Crisis is that it revealed John F. Kennedy in his finest hour, courageous, cool, winner of a decisive victory over the Soviet Union. That take on history is not shared by [authors David M.] Barrett and [Max] Holland. [CIA director David] McCone is the central character in 'Blind Over Cuba,' a title referring to the several weeks when the CIA was prevented from flying U-2 surveillance missions over the island, exactly the time when the Soviets were secretly deploying missiles."

REVIEW: *Choice* v50 no9 p1710 My 2013 A. Klinghoffer

REVIEW: *J Am Hist* v100 no1 p262-4 Je 2013 Alice L. George

REVIEW: *Polit Sci Q (Wiley-Blackwell)* v128 no3 p587-8 Fall 2013 DAVID A. WELCH

HOLLAND, PETER, 1951-.ed. Medieval Shakespeare. See Medieval Shakespeare

HOLLAND, TOM.tr. The Histories. See Herodotus, c. 4. B. B. C.

HOLLENBERG, DONNA KROLIK. A poet's revolution; the life of Denise Levertov; [by] Donna Krolik Hollenberg 532 p. 2013 University of California Press

1. Biographies 2. Jewish Christians—Biography 3. Poets, American—20th century—Biography
ISBN 9780520272460 (cloth : alk. paper)
LC 2012-025828

SUMMARY: This biography of poet Denise Levertov "charts Levertov's early life in England as the daughter of a Russian Hasidic father and a Welsh mother, her experience as a nurse in London during WWII, her marriage to an American after the war, and her move to New York City where she became a major figure in the American poetry scene. The author chronicles Levertov's role as a passionate social activist in volatile times and her importance as a teacher of writing. " (Publisher's note)

REVIEW: *Choice* v51 no4 p637 D 2013 B. Wallenstein

REVIEW: *Libr J* v138 no6 p81 Ap 1 2013 Denise J. Stankovics

REVIEW: *Nation* v297 no19 p37 N 11 2013 ANGE MLINKO

REVIEW: *TLS* no5747 p22 My 24 2013 ERIC ORMSBY

"Denise Levertov: A Poet's Life" and "A Poet's Revolution: The Life of Denise Levertov." "Both Dana Greene and Donna Krolik Hollenberg document Levertov's career in considerable detail but without ever coming to grips with the genuine puzzle that her work presents. . . . Levertov's life is intrinsically interesting. . . .Of the two accounts, Hollenberg's is the fuller and more illuminating. She has delved deeper into the sources; she offers more specific detail. . . . Hollenberg is also good at evoking the places that were significant for Levertov."

REVIEW: *Women's Review of Books* v31 no1 p18-20 Ja/F 2014 Kate Daniels

HOLLINGWORTH, MILES. Saint Augustine of Hippo; An Intellectual Biography; [by] Miles Hollingworth 400 p. 2013 Oxford University Press

1. Augustine, Saint, Bishop of Hippo, 354-430 2. Biography (Literary form) 3. Conversion (Religion)—Christianity 4. Fathers of the church, Latin 5. Theologians
ISBN 0199861595; 9780199861590

SUMMARY: "Miles Hollingworth, though well versed in the latest scholarship, draws his inspiration largely from the actual narrative of Augustine's life. By this means he reintroduces a cardinal but long-neglected fact to the center of Augustinian studies: that there is a direct line from Augustine's own early experiences of life to his later commentaries on humanity." (Publisher's note)

REVIEW: *Libr J* v138 no4 p78 Mr 1 2013 Augustine J. Curley

REVIEW: *New Statesman* v142 no5163 p43 Je 21 2013 Philip Maughan

REVIEW: *TLS* no5776 p7-8 D 13 2013 LUCY BECKETT

"Saint Augustine of Hippo: An Intellectual Biography." "It soon becomes clear to the reader that Miles Hollingworth's book is not a biography. Still less is it an 'intellectual biography.' . . . Damagingly to the notion of an intellectual biography, Hollingworth quotes constantly from the whole extent of what Augustine wrote over more than four decades, but almost entirely ignores the particularity of his books except for the 'Confessions.' . . . This book's heart is in the right place. It demonstrates real and lively sympathy with Augustine and with the depth of his faith and of his intelligence. But it is inexcusably difficult to read."

HOLLIST, PEDE. So the Path Does Not Die; [by] Pede Hollist 296 p. 2008 African Books Collective

1. Africa—Fiction 2. Africans—United States 3. Bildungsromans 4. Female genital mutilation 5. Women—Africa
ISBN 9789956727377; 9956727377

SUMMARY: In this book by Pede Hollist, "protagonist Fina's search for happiness and belonging begins on the night of her aborted circumcision and continues through her teenage years in Freetown, Sierra Leone's capital; her twenties in the Washington Metropolitan Area; and ends with her return to Sierra Leone to work as an advocate for war-traumatized children." (Publisher's note)

REVIEW: *World Lit Today* v87 no5 p56-7 S/O 2013 Kathryn VanSpanckeren

"So the Path Does Not Die." "This absorbing novel vividly brings the African diaspora to life. . . . The story begins and ends in Africa and offers memorable characters from the US and Caribbean. From the young girl's perspective, we discover a world filled with wonder and also unpredictable violence. . . . At times . . . it almost becomes picaresque, and this is a strength--unexpected turns allow the writer to dwell on extremely different settings and give them close-grained treatment. [Pede] Hollist excels at social interaction, dialogue, clothing, economic detail, and depictions of social gatherings. . . . The characterizations and dialogue are strong and often funny."

HOLLY, MICHAEL ANN. The melancholy art; [by] Michael Ann Holly xxv, 194 p. 2013 Princeton University Press

1. Art & history 2. Art—Historiography 3. Art historians 4. Art literature 5. Melancholy

ISBN 0691139342 (cloth : alk. paper); 9780691139340 (cloth : alk. paper)

LC 2012-024515

SUMMARY: This book "looks at how melancholy suffuses the work of some of the twentieth century's most powerful and poetic writers on the history of art. . . . Though the objects art historians study are materially present . . . , the worlds from which they come are forever lost to time. . . . [Author] Michael Ann Holly traces how this disjunction courses through the history of art and shows how it can give rise to melancholic sentiments in historians who write about art." (Publisher's note)

REVIEW: *Apollo: The International Magazine for Collectors* v178 no615 p108-9 D 2013 Kathryn Murphy

REVIEW: *Burlington Mag* v156 no1330 p38-9 Ja 2014 DAVID CARRIER

REVIEW: *Choice* v51 no1 p62-3 S 2013 D. Pincus

"The Melancholy Art." "With the goal of bringing more passion into the writing of art history, [author Michael Ann] Holly . . . makes the argument for the recognition of melancholy--'the black bile of melancholy'--as a central fact of the discipline. . . . In this inquiry, 'The Melancholy Art' summons a cast of thousands, covering psychoanalysis, philosophy, and art history, and testifying to the authot's theoretical grounding. A select group of scholars, including Riegl, Heidegger, Warburg, Panofsky, Walter Benjamin, and Baxandall, are given extended treatment."

REVIEW: *Libr J* v138 no8 p77 My 1 2013 Ellen Bates

HOLMES, ANNA.ed. The book of Jezebel. See The book of Jezebel

HOLMES, MEGAN. The miraculous image in Renaissance Florence; [by] Megan Holmes 396 p. 2013 Yale University Press

1. Art literature 2. Christian art & symbolism 3. Christian art and symbolism—Italy—Florence 4. Devotional objects—Italy—Florence 5. Florentine art 6. Renaissance—Italy 7. Renaissance—Italy—Florence 8. Renaissance art

ISBN 9780300176605 (cl : alk. paper)

LC 2012-048819

SUMMARY: This book by Megan Holmes discusses how "In Renaissance Florence, certain paintings and sculptures of the Virgin Mary and Christ were believed to have extraordinary efficacy in activating potent sacred intercession. Cults sprung up around these 'miraculous images' in the city and surrounding countryside beginning in the late 13th century." (Publisher's note)

REVIEW: *Apollo: The International Magazine for Collectors* v178 no613 p120-1 O 2013 Richard Cork

"Spectacular Miracles: Transforming Images in Italy From the Renaissance to the Present" and "The Miraculous Image in Renaissance Florence." "These two defiant books, both focused on miraculous images in Italian art, are under no illusions about the hostility which their chosen subject can provoke. Jane Garnett and Gervase Rosser, co-authors of 'Spectacular Miracles,' . . . have written an impressively researched and perceptive study of miraculous images in Italy. . . . The simultaneous publication of another deeply considered book, 'The Miraculous Image in Renaissance Florence,' proves that this ambition is shared. Although the author, Megan Holmes, focuses on a far shorter period, her text is the fruit of long, sustained and carefully considered research."

REVIEW: *Choice* v51 no8 p1389 Ap 2014 J. B. Gregory

HOLMES, RICHARD, 1945-. Falling upwards; how we took to the air; [by] Richard Holmes 416 p. 2013 Pantheon Books

1. Ballooning—History 2. Balloonists—History 3. Flight—History 4. Historical literature 5. Hot air balloons

ISBN 0307379663; 9780307379665

LC 2013-011128

SUMMARY: This book by Richard Holmes looks at ballooning. He "mentions Daedalus and Icarus, some balloons in literature, films and popular culture, and then lifts off into another of his . . . histories. He notes that the French were the first to use balloons for military purposes (reconnaissance), then tells us about some of the most notable balloon pioneers, including André-Jacques Garnerin, who also pioneered parachutes." (Kirkus Reviews)

REVIEW: *Am Sch* v82 no4 p103-5 Aut 2013 Toby Lester

REVIEW: *Booklist* v110 no2 p8 S 15 2013 Rick Roche

REVIEW: *Economist* v407 no8835 p89 My 11 2013

REVIEW: *Kirkus Rev* p25 Ag 15 2013 Fall Preview

REVIEW: *Kirkus Rev* v81 no14 p112 Jl 15 2013

REVIEW: *Libr J* v138 no14 p137 S 1 2013 Lara Jacobs

REVIEW: *Libr J* v138 no9 p55 My 15 2013 Barbara Hoffert

REVIEW: *London Rev Books* v35 no15 p38-9 Ag 8 2013 Mike Jay

REVIEW: *N Y Rev Books* v60 no19 p4-8 D 5 2013 Graham Robb

"Falling Upwards: How We Took to the Air." "Far from being a straightforward history of the balloon, this is an uplifting celebration of its aesthetic appeal and its 'social and imaginative impact,' of the writing it inspired and of the 'strangely mesmerising' 'dash and eccentricity' of the balloonists themselves. . . . [Richard Holmes] has written a social history that, flighty but never flippant, touches down as though by accident in some remote and rarely visited corners of the mind. . . . There is, inevitably, a certain sameness in the ascending and descending, and it takes all of Holmes's skill as a biographer to keep the story bobbing merrily along. One starts to look forward to the deaths, as though they were the point of the whole adventure."

REVIEW: *N Y Times Book Rev* p19 N 17 2013 PAUL ELIE

REVIEW: *New Statesman* v142 no5156 p44-5 My 3 2013 Leo Robson

REVIEW: *New Yorker* v89 no33 p103-1 O 21 2013

REVIEW: *Smithsonian* v44 no6 p110 O 2013 Chloë Schama

REVIEW: *TLS* no5755 p30 Jl 19 2013 LILY FORD

HOLSINGER, BRUCE. A Burnable Book; a novel; [by] Bruce Holsinger 464 p. 2014 William Morrow

1. Betrayal—Fiction 2. Books and reading—Fiction 3. Courts and courtiers—Fiction 4. Historical fiction
ISBN 0062240323; 9780062240323 (hardcover); 9780062240330 (trade pbk.)
LC 2013-025522

SUMMARY: In this book, by Bruce Holsinger, "Geoffrey Chaucer asks fellow poet and dealer in information, John Gower, to find a cryptic manuscript that predicts specifically how the current monarch, Richard II, will be assassinated. Gower discovers that the book has been stolen from Westminster by an unidentified woman, later murdered; dying, she gave it to a common prostitute, who is now hiding it in London." (Publishers Weekly)

REVIEW: *Kirkus Rev* v82 no2 p242 Ja 15 2014

"A Burnable Book". "In 1385 London, the race is on to recover a missing book. . . . Possession of a 'burnable book,' one that embodies heresy and/or threats to the king's person, is high treason. [John] Gower and his friend Geoffrey Chaucer are hot on the tome's trail when Gower's sinister son, Simon, returns inopportunely from exile abroad. Although the burgeoning web of plots and plotlines is dauntingly complex, the determined reader will be rewarded with a fascinating overview of pre-Renaissance London at its best and worst. A highly literate thriller from medievalist [Bruce] Holsinger."

REVIEW: *Libr J* v138 no21 p92 D 1 2013 Catherine Lantz

REVIEW: *Libr J* v138 no16 p57 O 1 2013 Barbara Hoffert

REVIEW: *N Y Times Book Rev* p22 F 23 2014

REVIEW: *N Y Times Book Rev* p12 F 16 2014 SARAH DUNANT

"A Burnable Book." "Language, spoken and written, is at the center of [author Bruce Holsinger's] first novel, 'A Burnable Book.' The year is 1385. . . . Two men meet in a tavern. . . . Their names: John Gower and Geoffrey Chaucer. . . . We are in the genre of the historical thriller, where fact and fiction have a tendency to wantonly mingle. . . . Perhaps not surprisingly, Holsinger the scholar is more successful than Holsinger the thriller writer. His evocation of 14th-century London is the best thing in the book. . . . Adding more layers to keep readers guessing is an understandable temptation, but an author must gauge our credibility--and exhaustion--threshold. . . . Such plot contortion takes its toll on character."

REVIEW: *Publ Wkly* v261 no3 p32 Ja 20 2014

HOLT, KIMBERLY WILLIS. Dinner with the Highbrows; 40 p. 2014 Christy Ottaviano Books, Henry Holt & Company

1. Dinners and dining—Fiction 2. Etiquette—Fiction 3. Humorous stories 4. Restaurants—Fiction 5. Table etiquette
ISBN 9780805080889 (hardback)
LC 2013-021125

SUMMARY: In this book by Kimberly Willis Holt, Bernard's mother is "anxiously prepping her son with a heaping helping of dining etiquette for his upcoming dinner at the home of the Highbrows. He takes it all—the napkin placement, the compliments to the chef, and the offer to wash dishes—to heart, so imagine his surprise when the Highbrows take him to a fancy restaurant and he learns their table manners belie their last name." (Bulletin of the Center for Children's Books)

REVIEW: *Booklist* v110 no16 p54 Ap 15 2014 Maryann Owen

REVIEW: *Bull Cent Child Books* v67 no9 p459 My 2014 A. A.

"Dinner With the Highbrows". "While [Krysten] Brooker's expressive oil illustrations capture the Highbrows' high spirits (and Bernard's reserve) in depictions as generous and colorful as their manners, the frank but flat accompanying text is unfortunately unengaging. The book struggles to define its stance on etiquette, seeming to relish the Highbrows' antic misbehavior while listing the basics of table manners in the endpapers. Still, the underlying caution against assumptions and encouragement of zesty enjoyment of life provide solid messages. This appreciation for joie de vivre and occasional moments of real humor . . . Make this an enjoyable readaloud for kids learning about manners—and wishing they could behave like the Highbrows."

REVIEW: *Kirkus Rev* v82 no5 p72 Mr 1 2014

REVIEW: *Publ Wkly* v261 no1 p56 Ja 6 2014

REVIEW: *SLJ* v60 no4 p122 Ap 2014 Gay Lynn Van Vleck

HOLT, NATHALIA. Cured; how the Berlin patients defeated HIV and forever changed medical science; [by] Nathalia Holt 336 p. 2014 Dutton, published by the Penguin Group

1. Antiretroviral agents—History 2. Gene therapy—Germany—Berlin—History 3. HIV infections—Treatment—Germany—Berlin 4. Hydroxyurea (Drug) 5. Medical literature
ISBN 0525953922; 9780525953920
LC 2013-037181

SUMMARY: In this book, HIV researcher Nathalia Holt "offers increasing hope for a cure by spotlighting the two male 'Berlin Patients' . . . who chemically bombarded and expunged the HIV virus from their bodies. The author tracks the enduring histories of these men—German-born Christian Hahn and Timothy Brown, an American. . . . Holt also profiles HIV specialists Heiko Jessen, Bruce Walker and David Ho." (Kirkus Reviews)

REVIEW: *Kirkus Rev* v82 no2 p20 Ja 15 2014

"Cured: How the Berlin Patients Defeated HIV and Forever Changed Medical Science". "A fascinating discourse on how medical science is zeroing in on an HIV vaccine after several anomalous triumphs. . . . [Nathalia] Holt further supports her subject with graphic illustrations and a well-balanced assortment of interviews and opinions from doctors, genetic scientists and informed researchers, all unified in the global battle to find a cure. An astute AIDS retrospective blended with contemporary updates on aggressive medical strategies."

REVIEW: *Libr J* v138 no15 p47 S 15 2013

REVIEW: *N Y Times Book Rev* p30 My 11 2014 GEORGE JOHNSON

REVIEW: *Publ Wkly* v260 no44 p58 N 4 2013

HOLUB, JOAN. Little Red Writing; [by] Joan Holub 36 p. 2013 Chronicle Books

1. Authorship—Fiction 2. Authorship—Juvenile fiction 3. Creative writing—Fiction 4. Creative writing—Juvenile fiction 5. Humorous stories 6. Pencils—Fiction 7. Pencils—Juvenile fiction

ISBN 0811878694; 9780811878692 (alk. paper)

LC 2012-027737

SUMMARY: In this book author Joan Holub and illustrator Melissa Sweet present a "retelling of 'Little Red Riding Hood,' in which a brave, little red pencil finds her way through the many perils of writing a story, faces a ravenous pencil sharpener (the Wolf 3000) . . . and saves the day." (Publisher's note) "Little Red is eager to begin, and knowing that a good story often involves a journey, she sets off, armed with a basket of words for help along the way." (Booklist)

REVIEW: *Booklist* v110 no2 p72 S 15 2013 Thom Barthelmess

REVIEW: *Booklist* p4-10 Ja 1 2014 Supplement Gillian Engberg

"The Boy Who Loved Math: The Improbable Life of Paul Erdos," "Little Red Writing," and "Flight of the Honey Bee." "Mathematician Paul Erdos is the subject of this inventive, entertaining picture-book biography. . . . The colorful, energetic artwork, organized in a well-designed mix of spot scenes with full-page spreads, further expands the concepts with decorative elements. . . . [An] uproarious retelling of 'Little Red Riding Hood' . . . [Melissa] Sweet's exuberant illustrations reinforce the concepts with wit and energy. A perfect prompt for beginning writers to borrow from Little Red's basket of words and try their own stories. . . . [Raymond] Huber . . . shows an obvious understanding of both honeybees and of what will interest young children in this attractive offering. . . . One of the most informative--and beautiful--picture books about honeybees."

REVIEW: *Bull Cent Child Books* v67 no4 p217 D 2013 J. H.

REVIEW: *Horn Book Magazine* v90 no1 p73-4 Ja/F 2014 ROBIN L. SMITH

"Little Red Writing." "[Joan] Holub and [Melissa] Sweet, along with a cadre of pencils, pens, and erasers, team up to help young writers avoid pitfalls on their way to writing their own stories. Using every available inch of the book, including cover, endpapers, and title page, this energetic volume is full of fun and information. . . . With a plethora of punny speech bubbles, a variety of hand-lettering, and a joyful combination of watercolor, collage, and pencil lines, the book clearly reflects Sweet's delight in this project. Teachers and aspiring young writers will embrace this lively story."

REVIEW: *Kirkus Rev* p57 N 15 2013 Best Books

REVIEW: *Kirkus Rev* p40 Ag 15 2013 Fall Preview

REVIEW: *Kirkus Rev* v81 no16 p181 Ag 15 2013

REVIEW: *Publ Wkly* p46 Children's starred review annual 2013

REVIEW: *Publ Wkly* v260 no36 p56-7 S 9 2013

REVIEW: *SLJ* v59 no9 p122 S 2013 Teri Markson

HOLWAY, TATIANA. The flower of empire; the Amazon's largest water lily, the quest to make it bloom, and the world it helped create; [by] Tatiana Holway 328 p. 2013 Oxford University Press

1. Botanical gardens—England—History—19th century 2. British architecture—History 3. Greenhouses 4. Historical literature 5. Victoria amazonica

ISBN 0195373898; 9780195373899

LC 2012-034518

SUMMARY: The "central narrative of [Tatiana] Holway's book pivots around an 1837 British discovery in Guiana of an immense water lily, and the mission to make one bloom in England. Along with the story of a quest for germination is the author's . . . description of the botany-obsessed Victorian England where the building of glass greenhouses influenced the design of the Crystal Palace in Hyde Park for the Great Exposition of 1851." (Library Journal)

REVIEW: *Booklist* v109 no15 p10 Ap 1 2013 Carol Haggas

REVIEW: *Choice* v51 no5 p865 Ja 2014 D. H. Pfister

"The Flower of Empire: An Amazonian Water Lily, the Quest to Make It Bloom, and the World It Created." "Victorian sensibilities are very much a part of the account; few plants have been so written about and so lavishly illustrated. From the glasshouses of Chatsworth and Kew Gardens to the creation of the Crystal Palace, [Tatiana] Holway . . . takes many divergent paths, introducing the personalities involved and the botanical, architectural, and cultural themes centered on this fantastic water lily."

REVIEW: *Kirkus Rev* v81 no4 p234 F 15 2013

REVIEW: *Libr J* v138 no9 p86 My 15 2013 Kelsey Berry Philpot

REVIEW: *N Y Times Book Rev* p18-9 Je 2 2013 DOMINIQUE BROWNING

HOLY GHOST WRITER. The Sovereign Order of Monte Cristo; And the Newly Discovered Adventures of Sherlock Holmes; [by] Holy Ghost Writer 816 p. 2013 Createspace Independent Pub

1. Finn, Huckleberry (Fictitious character) 2. Historical fiction 3. Holmes, Sherlock (Fictitious character) 4. Slavery—Fiction 5. Southern States—Fiction

ISBN 1490406840; 9781490406848

SUMMARY: This book presents "a retelling of Alexandre Dumas' 1844 classic 'The Count of Monte Cristo' that continues the story of Edmond Dantès." It "offers 245 pages of new adventures for Dantès . . . narrated by Arthur Conan Doyle's equally classic detective Sherlock Holmes (with a guest appearance by Mark Twain's Huckleberry Finn). The new material, enough for a stand-alone novel by itself, is preceded by a 571-page recap of Dumas' original novel, also narrated by Holmes." (Kirkus Reviews)

REVIEW: *Kirkus Rev* v82 no3 p361 F 1 2014

"The Sovereign Order of Monte Cristo: Newly Discovered Adventures of Sherlock Holmes". "The new material, enough for a stand-alone novel by itself, is preceded by a 571-page recap of [Alexandre] Dumas' original novel, also narrated by Holmes. Given that the original is widely available in print and digital form, it's hard to imagine why one would want to read a version that eliminates Dumas' color and description. Holmes' voice often sounds more like a 21st-century man's . . . than [Arthur Conan] Doyle's meticulous, cerebral hero's. . . . The plot never quite gets going, as the novel turns out to be merely a setup for a yet-to-be-published volume. . . . It effectively turns Dantès from a flawed hero who realizes too late the price of revenge to a two-dimensional uber-mensch."

HOMANS, MARGARET. The imprint of another life; adoption narratives and human possibility; [by] Margaret Homans xi, 300 p. 2013 University of Michigan Press

1. Adoption in literature 2. American literature—History and criticism 3. Families in literature 4. Literature—History & criticism 5. Narration (Rhetoric)—Social aspects

ISBN 9780472118885 (cloth : acid-free paper)

LC 2013-006631

SUMMARY: This book "addresses a series of questions about common beliefs about adoption. Underlying these beliefs is the assumption that human qualities are innate and intrinsic, an assumption often held by adoptees and their families, sometimes at great emotional cost. This book explores representations of adoption--transracial, transnational, and domestic same-race adoption--that reimagine human possibility by questioning this assumption and conceiving of alternatives." (Publisher's note)

REVIEW: *Choice* v51 no6 p1004 F 2014 J. J. Benardete

"The Imprint of Another Life: Adoption Narratives and Human Possibility." "Well versed in the literature of adoption and with special sensitivity to the struggles of adoptees and their parents or guardians, [Margaret] Homans uses a rich variety of biographical and fictional accounts to illustrate the often harsh impact of contemporary, often transnational, adoption. . . . She finally and optimistically argues that although an adoptee's 'actual, much-desired origins cannot be recovered . . . origins can be satisfactorily invented'. . . . A fascinating study that offers rich literary insights. . . . Highly recommended."

HOMER (POET) The illiad; [by] Homer (Poet) 2011 Weidenfeld

1. Achilles (Greek mythology) 2. Epic poetry 3. Greek epic poetry 4. Translations 5. Trojan War

ISBN 1439163375; 9780297859734

LC 2010-051827

SUMMARY: This book offers a translation of the "Iliad," an ancient Greek epic by Homer. The story is as follows: "Man seduces another's wife then kidnaps her. The husband and his brother get a gang together to steal her back and take revenge. The woman regrets being seduced and wants to escape whilst the man's entourage resent the position they have been placed in. Yet the battle lines have been drawn and there is no going back. . . . [This translation is b]ased on the . . . M.L. West edition of the Greek." (Publisher's note) In addition, due to arguments for its spuriousness, the author "omits the entirety of Book 10." (TLS)

REVIEW: *Choice* v51 no8 p1397 Ap 2014 R. Cormier

REVIEW: *Classical Rev* v64 no1 p7-9 Ap 2014 Karin Johansson

REVIEW: *Classical Rev* v63 no2 p325-7 O 2013 Deborah Beck

"Homer: The Illiad." "[Author W. Allen] has written a lively, accessible and informative introduction to Homer's 'Iliad.' In 70 pages, the book discusses most of the questions that regularly arise when teaching the 'Iliad' to lower level students, supporting clear and engaging interpretative statements with relevant examples. The unpretentious and direct style makes the book welcoming to students, and even advanced readers will find insights that are new to them. The book includes a short preface, a map of Greece and Asia Minor, five chapters, an epilogue (consisting of a single brief paragraph) and suggestions for further reading."

REVIEW: *SLJ* v60 no3 p175 Mr 2014 Heather Talty

HOMER (POET) The Iliad; [by] Homer (Poet) 512 2011 Oxford University Press

1. Achilles (Greek mythology)—Poetry 2. Classical literature—Translations into English 3. Greek mythology—Poetry 4. Trojan War—Poetry

ISBN 0199235481; 9780199235483

SUMMARY: This book, a translation of Homer's "The Iliad" by Anthony Verity, recounts the Trojan War, "the story of Achilles' anger and Hector's death." (Publisher's note) "[Verity has] adopted something very like [Richmond] Lattimore's loose quasi-hexametrical line. . . . Verity also keeps carefully to Homeric line-numeration." (New Republic)

REVIEW: *Choice* v51 no8 p1397 Ap 2014 R. Cormier

REVIEW: *Classical Rev* v64 no1 p7-9 Ap 2014 Karin Johansson

REVIEW: *Classical Rev* v63 no2 p325-7 O 2013 Deborah Beck

"Homer: The Illiad." "[Author W. Allen] has written a lively, accessible and informative introduction to Homer's 'Iliad.' In 70 pages, the book discusses most of the questions that regularly arise when teaching the 'Iliad' to lower level students, supporting clear and engaging interpretative statements with relevant examples. The unpretentious and direct style makes the book welcoming to students, and even advanced readers will find insights that are new to them. The book includes a short preface, a map of Greece and Asia Minor, five chapters, an epilogue (consisting of a single brief paragraph) and suggestions for further reading."

REVIEW: *SLJ* v60 no3 p175 Mr 2014 Heather Talty

HONOUR, HUGH. A world history of art; [by] Hugh Honour 984 p. 2013 Laurence King Pub.

1. Art history 2. Art literature 3. Mosaics (Art) 4. Painting 5. Photography

ISBN 1780671172; 9781780671178

SUMMARY: This book on art history by Hugh Honour and John Fleming "is international in scope and comprehensive in its coverage of the visual arts, including painting, mosaic, drawing, printmaking, sculpture, architecture, and photography, as well as textiles, coins, pottery enamels, gold, and silver." (Publisher's note) It was the authors' intent that it should be "'exploratory rather than critical'." (Booklist)

REVIEW: *Booklist* v110 no9/10 p78 Ja 1 2014 Lindsay Harmon

"The Visual Arts: A History." "Originally published in 2009, this most recent edition of Honour and Fleming's classic art-history text is now being marketed to a general audience at a more affordable price. . . . This book aims to be comprehensive, as befitting its stated goal of being 'exploratory rather than critical.'. . . Unlike many art-history books, the focus here goes beyond Western art, and topics such as colonialism and indigenous art are addressed. . . . Classic art-history surveys are regularly updated but often at a significantly higher cost. At just $75, this book represents an affordable and comprehensive addition to academic, school, and public library collections."

HOOD, BRUCE. The Domesticated Brain; A Pelican Introduction; [by] Bruce Hood 352 p. 2014 Penguin Books Ltd
1. Comparative psychology 2. Evolutionary psychology 3. Neurosciences 4. Psychological literature 5. Social psychology
ISBN 0141974869; 9780141974866

SUMMARY: "In 'The Domesticated Brain,' renowned psychologist Bruce Hood explores the relationship between the brain and social behaviour, looking for clues as to origins and operations of the mechanisms that keep us bound together. How do our brains enable us to live together, to raise children, and to learn and pass on information and culture?" (Publisher's note)

REVIEW: *New Sci* v222 no2969 p47 My 17 2014 Jonathon Keats

"The Domesticated Brain." "Drawing on his research in developmental psychology, [author Bruce] Hood often enlists parallels between dogs and children to support the notion of human domestication. . . . Hood argues that our social adeptness is both a cause and an effect of our self-domestication, and suggests that our social behaviour is key to our species' success. . . . Hood is to be commended for writing 'The Domesticated Brain' at a level that anyone can understand. That said, in his effort to encompass all of psychology in just 300 pages . . . he often loses touch with his theme. The result is informative but, sadly, largely formless."

HOOD, SUSAN. Rooting for you; (a moving up story); 32 p. 2013 Disney-Hyperion
1. Children's stories 2. Courage 3. Daisies 4. Growth—Fiction 5. Seeds—Fiction
ISBN 9781423152309
LC 2012-006712

SUMMARY: This children's book presents "a story about a seed's journey from sprout to bloom. A nervous daisy seed, 'safe and sound,/down/down/down/here in the ground,' finally becomes bored and decides to begin his travels through soil, meeting a helpful worm and bravely passing a menacing spider." (School Library Journal)

REVIEW: *Kirkus Rev* v82 no3 p100 F 1 2014

"Rooting for You". "[Matthew] Cordell uses a flat, matte color palette of browns, greens, worm-pink and sky blue, with thick black line for details. He preserves the plant's personality throughout its growth spurt, successively using the same pale green hue and facial expressions for the seed, sprout and the flower's center. [Susan] Hood's rhyming text is charming, but the final gatefold, a full three pages tall, must be folded away and turned before its verse can be concluded on the final spread—a slight detraction from the flow. As sweet and benign as a summer daisy."

HOOPER, HADLEY.il. How I discovered poetry. See Nelson, M.

HOPE, ANNA. Wake; a novel; [by] Anna Hope 304 p. 2014 Random House Inc
1. FICTION—Historical 2. FICTION—Literary 3. FICTION—War & Military 4. Historical fiction 5. Veterans' families—Great Britain—History—20th century—Fiction 6. Women—Fiction 7. World War, 1914-1918—Repatriation of war dead—Great Britain—Fiction
ISBN 9780812995138 (hardback)
LC 2013-021327

SUMMARY: This novel by Anna Hope is set in "London, 1920. The city prepares to observe the two-year anniversary of Armistice Day with the burial of the unknown soldier. Many are still haunted by the war. . . . The lives of . . . three women are braided together, their stories gathering tremendous power as the ties that bind them become clear, and the body of the unknown soldier moves closer and closer to its final resting place." (Publisher's note)

REVIEW: *Booklist* v110 no5 p35 N 1 2013 Sarah Johnson

REVIEW: *Kirkus Rev* v81 no23 p201 D 1 2013

REVIEW: *Libr J* v138 no18 p82 N 1 2013 Mara Bandy

REVIEW: *N Y Times Book Rev* p30 Mr 23 2014 Abigail Meisel

REVIEW: *N Y Times Book Rev* p30 Mr 23 2014 Abigail Meisel

REVIEW: *Publ Wkly* v260 no44 p43 N 4 2013

REVIEW: *TLS* no5784 p20 F 7 2014 ALEX PEAKE-TOMKINSON

"The Lie" and "Wake." "The Orange Prize-winning author Helen Dunmore and the first-time novelist Anne Hope have both written novels that look back at the First World War from the vantage point of 1920. . . . Daniel Bramall, Dunmore's narrator in 'The Lie,' is a soldier who has returned to his native Cornwall from the trenches. . . . 'The Lie' is a substantial work, and Dunmore is able to crystallize tragedy in a simple sentence. . . . 'Wake' is unashamedly commercial fiction but not less affecting or skilful for that. Hope does make technical mistakes. . . . The novelist also occasionally resorts to banalities. . . . But given the breadth of Hope's ambition in this novel it seems churlish to dwell on them too long."

HOPF, TED. Reconstructing the Cold War; the early years, 1945 - 1958; [by] Ted Hopf ix, 305 pages 2012 Oxford University Press
1. China—Foreign relations—Soviet Union 2. Cold War 3. Cold War, 1945-1989 4. Group identity—Soviet Union 5. Historical literature 6. Social change—Soviet Union 7. Soviet Union—Civilization 8. Soviet Union—Foreign relations 9. Stalinism
ISBN 9780199858484 (hardback : alkaline paper)
LC 2011-047116

SUMMARY: This book by Ted Hopf describes how "During Stalin's rule, a discourse of danger prevailed in Soviet society. . . . Even under the rule of Stalin, Soviet society understood a socialist Soviet Union as a more secure, diverse, and socially democratic place. This discourse of difference . . . was empowered after Stalin's death, first by Beria, then by Malenkov, and then by Khrushchev, and rest of the post-Stalin Soviet leadership." (Publisher's note)

REVIEW: *Am Hist Rev* v118 no4 p1285-6 O 2013 Austin Jersild

"Reconstructing the Cold War: The Early Years, 1945-1958." "Ted Hopf, historian and international relations theorist, uses the methods of both fields to explain the evolution of Soviet foreign policy in the early stages of the Cold War. . . . Hopf brings a vast knowledge to this broad topic, with many unexpected and pleasing turns to sources and topics that do not usually surface in scholarship about foreign policy and the Cold War. . . . Hopf's rich and eclectic book will serve as an important guide to scholars eager to mine the many still untapped archival materials on international relations, foreign policy, and the Cold War."

REVIEW: *Choice* v50 no4 p753 D 2012 L. S. Hulett

HOPKINS, H. JOSEPH. The tree lady; [by] H. Joseph Hopkins 32 p. 2013 Beach Lane Books

1. Balboa Park (San Diego, Calif.) 2. Biographies 3. Horticulturists—California—San Diego—Biography—Juvenile literature 4. San Diego (Calif.)—History
ISBN 1442414022; 9781442414020 (hardcover)
LC 2012-032903

SUMMARY: This "picture book biography recalls the life and contributions of a horticulturist in the late 19th century. Kate Sessions populated San Diego's landscape with not lupines but trees. Her love for nature dated back to her childhood, where, in school, 'she liked studying wind and rain, muscles and bones, plants and trees. Especially trees.'" (Publishers Weekly)

REVIEW: *Booklist* v109 no19/20 p84 Je 1 2013 Ann Kelley

REVIEW: *Bull Cent Child Books* v67 no2 p96 O 2013 E. B.

REVIEW: *Horn Book Magazine* v89 no5 p122 S/O 2013 JONATHAN HUNT

"The Tree Lady: The True Story of How One Tree-Loving Woman Changed a City Forever." "[H. Joseph] Hopkins's text succinctly captures the highlights of his subject's life, punctuating each page with a variation of the refrain, 'But Kate did,' effectively underscoring Sessions's drive and determination. [Jill] McElmurry's gouache illustrations document the gradually changing landscape from barren desert to verdant garden. . . . This picture book biography captures the infectious passion Sessions had for her chosen vocation, but it's also a wonderful testament to urban planning and human ecology--and a great book for Arbor Day."

REVIEW: *Kirkus Rev* v81 no14 p135 Jl 15 2013

REVIEW: *Publ Wkly* v260 no27 p91 Jl 8 2013

REVIEW: *SLJ* v59 no10 p1 O 2013 Alyson Low

HOPKINSON, DEBORAH. The Great Trouble; a mystery of London, the blue death, and a boy called Eel; [by] Deborah Hopkinson 256 p. 2013 Alfred A. Knopf

1. Cholera—Fiction 2. Epidemics—Fiction 3. Historical fiction 4. Orphans—Fiction
ISBN 0375848185; 9780375848186 (hard cover); 9780375948183 (library binding)
LC 2012-032799

SUMMARY: Author Deborah Hopkinson's book, "equal parts medical mystery, historical novel, and survival story about the 1854 London cholera outbreak, . . . introduces Eel, a boy trying to make ends meet on Broad Street. When he visits one of his regular employers, he learns the man has fallen ill. Eel enlists the help of Dr. Snow, and together they work to solve the mystery of what exactly is causing the spread of cholera and how they can prevent it." (Booklist)

REVIEW: *Booklist* v110 no4 p51-2 O 15 2013 Sarah Bean Thompson

"The Great Trouble: A Mystery of London, The Blue Death, and a Boy Called Eel." "Steeped in rich fact and detailed explanations about laboratory research, [Deborah] Hopkinson's book uses a fictional story to teach readers about science, medicine, and history--and works in a few real-life characters, too. Eel serves as a peek into the lower class of London society and offers readers a way to observe--and hopefully, ask questions about--the scientific method. An author's note provides readers with a look at the real story behind the novel, making this a great choice for introducing readers to science and history."

REVIEW: *Booklist* v110 no9/10 p126 Ja 1 2014 Shari Fesko

REVIEW: *Bull Cent Child Books* v67 no3 p157-8 N 2013 E. B.

REVIEW: *Horn Book Magazine* v89 no6 p94-5 N/D 2013 DEAN SCHNEIDER

REVIEW: *Kirkus Rev* v81 no16 p109 Ag 15 2013

REVIEW: *Publ Wkly* p88 Children's starred review annual 2013

REVIEW: *Publ Wkly* v260 no35 p61 S 2 2013

REVIEW: *SLJ* v59 no10 p1 O 2013 Ragan O'Malley

HOPMAN, MARIANNE GOVERS. Scylla; myth, metaphor, paradox; [by] Marianne Govers Hopman xix, 300 p. 2012 Cambridge University Press

1. HISTORY—General 2. Historical literature 3. Monsters in art 4. Monsters in literature 5. Scylla and Charybdis (Greek mythology)
ISBN 9781107026766
LC 2012-017772

SUMMARY: This book "challenges the dominant view that a mythical symbol denotes a single, clear-cut 'figure' and proposes instead to conceptualize the name 'Scylla' as a combination of three concepts . . . whose articulation changes over time. While archaic and classical Greek versions usually emphasize the metaphorical coherence of Scylla's various components, the name is increasingly treated as a well-defined but also paradoxical construct from the late fourth century BCE onward." (Publisher's note)

REVIEW: *Classical Rev* v64 no1 p16-8 Ap 2014 Daniel W. Berman

REVIEW: *TLS* no5749 p10 Je 7 2013 HELEN MORALES

"Scylla: Myth, Metaphor, Paradox." "[Marianne Govers] Hopman does a real service through her meticulous collation of material. She is particularly good on how anxieties about female sexuality become more prominent in the Scyllas of classical Greece, and how descriptions of Scylla play a meta-poetic role in later Greek and Latin poetry. . . . It is an instructive book, if not a pleasurable one; the writing is as indigestible as Odysseus' swallowed crew. It also tends to misrepresent the position of mainstream scholarship. . . . Hopman has taken a large and unwieldy critical sledgehammer to crack a non-existent nut."

HOPPER, KEITH.ed. The Short Fiction of Flann O'Brien. See The Short Fiction of Flann O'Brien

HORN, CHRISTOPH.ed. Neoplatonism and the philosophy of nature. See Neoplatonism and the philosophy of nature

HORN, DARA. A guide for the perplexed; a novel; [by] Dara Horn 336 p. 2013 W W Norton & Co Inc

1. Cairo Genizah 2. Kidnapping—Egypt—Fiction 3. Schechter, S. (Solomon), 1847-1915 4. Sisters—Fiction 5. Speculative fiction

ISBN 0393064891; 9780393064896 (hardcover)

LC 2013-009456

SUMMARY: In this book by Dara Horn, "Josie's company produces Genizah, a Facebook-like digital archive that catalogs life in real time. . . . While working in Egypt . . . Josie is kidnapped. As the family deals with the aftermath. . . the narrative travels back in time to Solomon Schecter's expedition to Egypt to investigate the Cairo Genizah. . . . Both the real and fictional genizahs raise questions throughout the novel about how and why we choose what to remember or forget." (Library Journal)

REVIEW: *Booklist* v110 no2 p30 S 15 2013 Bill Ott

"A Guide for the Perplexed." "[A] richly textured blend of history, psychology, religion, and human emotion. . . . Yes, the novel is as intricately constructed as Joseph's coat of many colors, and, yes, it echoes the thematic density of the philosophical work after which it is named, but beneath all that beats the living heart of a very human drama, one that will have readers both caught up in the suspense and moved by the tragic dimensions of the unresolved dilemma at the core of the story."

REVIEW: *Kirkus Rev* v81 no15 p53 Ag 1 2013

REVIEW: *Libr J* v138 no7 p56 Ap 15 2013 Barbara Hoffert

REVIEW: *Libr J* v138 no12 p76 Jl 1 2013 Pamela Mann

REVIEW: *N Y Times Book Rev* p22 S 29 2013 Dara Horn

REVIEW: *Publ Wkly* v260 no24 p38 Je 17 2013

HORN, STACY. Imperfect harmony; finding happiness singing with others; [by] Stacy Horn 256 p. 2013 Algonquin Books of Chapel Hill

1. Choral singing—New York (State)—New York 2. Community choirs 3. Community music 4. Happiness 5. Music literature 6. Music psychology 7. Singing

ISBN 9781616200411

LC 2012-051349

SUMMARY: This book, by Stacy Horn, "unfolds the history of choral music, the neurological science underpinning what happens in listeners' and performers' brains, and the effort it takes to put on a performance. The choir community in this book is made up of both those at rehearsal and the composers and the singers of the past." (Booklist)

REVIEW: *Atlantic* v312 no3 p38 O 2013 STACY HORN Ann Hulbert

"Imperfect Happiness Singing With Others." "Horn evokes a devotional experience that has nothing to do with formal devoutness. Belonging to a chorus is a salve for the heart--a word that comes up often as she explores 'all the benefits that come from being in the middle of a song', blending in eclectic musical history and idiosyncratic memoir along the way. She duly invokes brain studies too. (Who doesn't these days?) But Horn's real feat is to soar beyond a purely, well, instrumental focus as she conveys the joys that await an amateur voice."

REVIEW: *Booklist* v109 no17 p58 My 1 2013 Bridget Thoreson

REVIEW: *Kirkus Rev* v81 no10 p63 My 15 2013

REVIEW: *Publ Wkly* v260 no15 p51 Ap 15 2013

HORN, STEVEN W. The pumpkin eater; a Sam Dawson mystery; [by] Steven W. Horn 370 p. 2013 Granite Peak Press

1. Cemeteries 2. Detective & mystery stories 3. Eugenics 4. Genetic engineering—Fiction 5. Photographers—Fiction

ISBN 9780983589402 (pbk.: alk. paper); 9780983589419 (hardback: alk. paper)

LC 2013-945056

SUMMARY: This mystery novel is part of Steven W. Horn's Sam Dawson series. "Sam uncovers eerie likenesses between the Iowa cemetery and one thousands of miles away in Cambridge, Colo. For example, Eugene Eris, a doctor, is buried in each, 18 months apart with the same birth dates and the same mysterious epitaph. . . . Ignoring threats . . . Sam digs through . . . layers of bureaucracy as he zeros in on Dr. Eris' place in the early 20th-century eugenics movement—and his hideous crimes." (Kirkus Reviews)

REVIEW: *Kirkus Rev* v81 no24 p13 D 15 2013

"The Pumpkin Eater: A Sam Dawson Mystery". "[Steven W.] Horn . . . has constructed a truly unsettling mystery backed by in-depth knowledge of science, Colorado bureaucracy and politics, and history. . . . The pieces fit together well. . . . Horn's characterization, dialogue and pacing are solid. . . . A few creaky tropes from mystery thrillers can be found here. . . . Horn plans further Sam Dawson mysteries, and criticisms aside, readers will look forward to the next outing. Dramatic and intelligent, this is a smart start to a new detective series."

REVIEW: *Kirkus Rev* v81 no20 p300 O 15 2013

HORNBAKER, TIM. Turning the Black Sox White; the misunderstood legacy of Charles A. Comiskey; [by] Tim Hornbaker 400 p. 2014 Sports Publishing

1. Baseball team owners—United States—Biography 2. Biography (Literary form) 3. Major League Baseball (Organization)—History—20th century

ISBN 1613216386; 9781613216385 (hardback)

LC 2013-041431

SUMMARY: In this book, "through . . . research from the National Archives, newspapers, and various other publications, [author] Tim Hornbaker not only tells the full story of [Charles Albert] Comiskey's incredible life and the sport at the time, but also debunks the 'Black Sox' controversy, showing that Comiskey was not the reason that the Sox threw the 1919 World Series." (Publisher's note)

REVIEW: *Kirkus Rev* v82 no2 p88 Ja 15 2014

"Turning the Black Sox White: The Misunderstood Legacy of Charles A. Comiskey." "Although the author is not a particularly elegant stylist, his depth of knowledge of this era of baseball history shines through. . . . [Tim] Hornbaker makes a sound case for why Comiskey has long been an inappropriate fall guy for the scandal. But this story only takes up a small part of Comiskey's life and this book. Why, then, give the book, which is not in fact about the Black Sox scandal on the whole, such a peculiar title, and why make it the foundation of the book's marketing campaign? In so doing, the author and the publisher do the larger story he tells a disservice. The history of baseball might be far different without Comiskey's role in it. This serviceable biography ensures that his role will not be forgotten."

REVIEW: *Libr J* v139 no3 p108 F 15 2014 Brett Rohlwing

HOROWITZ, BEN. The Hard Thing About Hard Things; Building a Business When There Are No Easy Answers; [by] Ben Horowitz 304 p. 2014 HarperCollins

1. Andreessen Horowitz (Company) 2. Business literature 3. Entrepreneurship 4. New business enterprises 5. Success in business

ISBN 0062273205; 9780062273208

SUMMARY: This book of business advice by Ben Horowitz, "a tech entreprneur turned venture capitalist" and the cofounder of Andreessen Horowitz, is "a compendium of . . . posts from his popular blog." Topics discussed include "minimizing office politics and how a startup executive might grow into managing a larger business." (Publishers Weekly)

REVIEW: *Booklist* v110 no14 p37 Mr 15 2014 Barbara Jacobs

"The Hard Thing About Hard Things: Building a Business When There Are No Easy Answers." "It's fairly evident that this is a collection of blogs, loosely strung together, united in their varied perspectives on startups, CEO-dom, and business in general. . . . [Ben Horowitz has] imparted some valuable insight on hard lessons learned that apply to any manager, whether In the executive suite or not. As with most experiential books, it is all about him--but it's written in such an engaging and universally acceptable manner that no one could object. . . . It's a refreshingly honest take, and his colorful (and, yes, profanity-laced) language breaks down any other misperceptions about the role and the person. Plus, his imagination is compelling."

REVIEW: *Economist* v410 no8878 p77-8 Mr 15 2014

"The Hard Thing About Hard Things: Building a Business When There Are No Easy Answers." "What makes this a compelling read is the first few chapters, where Mr. [Ben] Horowitz provides a blow-by-blow account of his own struggle as the boss of Loudcloud. . . Throughout all this, Mr. Horowitz learns plenty of lessons about managing a company, which he proceeds to recount in the rest of the book. . . . Not all his advice is compelling, but there is more than enough substance in Mr. Horowitz's impressive tome to turn it into a leadership classic."

REVIEW: *N Y Times Book Rev* p30 Ap 13 2014 Nancy Koehn

REVIEW: *Publ Wkly* v260 no52 p40 D 23 2013

HOROWITZ, DANIEL. Consuming pleasures; intellectuals and popular culture in the postwar world; [by] Daniel Horowitz xi, 491 p. 2012 University of Pennsylvania Press

1. Consumption (Economics)—Europe—Psychological aspects—20th century 2. Consumption (Economics)—United States—Psychological aspects—20th century 3. Historical literature 4. Intellectuals—Europe—Attitudes—History—20th century 5. Intellectuals—United States—Attitudes—History—20th century 6. Popular culture—Economic aspects—Europe—20th century 7. Popular culture—Economic aspects—United States—20th century

ISBN 9780812243956 (alk. paper)

LC 2011-034159

SUMMARY: This book on U.S. intellectual attitudes toward popular culture "reveals how a group of writers shifted attention from condemnation to critical appreciation, critiqued cultural hierarchies and moralistic approaches, and explored the symbolic processes by which individuals and groups communicate. Historian Daniel Horowitz traces the emergence of these new perspectives through a series of intellectual biographies." (Publisher's note)

REVIEW: *Choice* v50 no2 p345 O 2012 A. O. Edmonds

REVIEW: *Engl Hist Rev* v129 no536 p353-5 F 2014 Guy Ortolano

"Consuming Pleasures: Intellectuals and Popular Culture in the Postwar World". "[Daniel] Horowitz's preferred explanation would seem to acknowledge that the case is complicated, the reasons various, and the routes diverse, but that prudent demurral may leave the reader longing for . . . interpretative snap. . . . But [Daniel] Horowitz's ambition is less to offer an interpretation of post-war culture than to excavate a rich seam within it, and in this he succeeds magnificently. His book offers a fascinating study of more than a dozen major figures on both sides of the Atlantic, and it demonstrates beyond question that their work was part of a seminal shift in post-war—indeed, modern—intellectual history."

REVIEW: *J Am Hist* v99 no4 p1298-9 Mr 2013 Robert Vanderlan

REVIEW: *Rev Am Hist* v42 no1 p181-7 Mr 2014 Lawrence B. Glickman

HORVATH, POLLY. Lord and Lady Bunny—almost royalty!; 304 p. 2014 Schwartz & Wade books

1. Animal stories 2. Hippies—Fiction 3. Human-animal communication—Fiction 4. Kings, queens, rulers, etc.—Fiction 5. Rabbits—Fiction 6. Voyages and travels—Fiction

ISBN 0307980650; 9780307980656; 9780307980663 (glb); 9780307980670 (ebook)

LC 2012-027442

SUMMARY: Written by Polly Horvath and illustrated by Sophie Blackall, this book is a "sequel to 'Mr. and Mrs. Bunny--Detectives Extraordinaire!'--that even includes a guest appearance by J. K. Rowling a.k.a. 'Oldwhatshername'--Madeleine wants nothing more than to save money for college, but her impractical, ex-hippie parents are broke. When the family unexpectedly inherits a sweet shoppe in England that has the potential to earn serious profit, they see an answer to all their problems." (Publisher's note)

REVIEW: *Booklist* v110 no9/10 p113 Ja 1 2014 Thom Barthelmess

REVIEW: *Horn Book Magazine* v90 no1 p92 Ja/F 2014 JENNIFER M. BRABANDER

"Lord and Lady Bunny--Almost Royalty! By Mr. and Mrs. Bunny." "As in the first book, [Polly] Horvath includes plenty of satire (overly energetic scrapbooking moms; royals and their loyal followers; people who leave their money to cats); winks at children's literature (Horvath herself makes a bitingly funny appearance, at a book-signing seated next to Oldwhatshername, the elegant and svelte author of a ten-pound fantasy book); and, again, more lunacy than you can shake a carrot at. . . . One can only hope that Mr. and Mrs. B. have loads more madcap adventures to share with audiences--both bunny and human."

REVIEW: *Kirkus Rev* v81 no23 p163 D 1 2013

REVIEW: *SLJ* v60 no2 p88 F 2014 Rhona Campbell

HORWITZ, ALLAN V. Anxiety; a short history; [by] Allan V. Horwitz 208 p. 2013 Johns Hopkins University Press

1. Anxiety—history 2. Anxiety Disorders—history 3. Historical literature 4. Psychiatric drugs 5. Psychiatry
ISBN 142141080X (pbk.: alk. paper); 1421410818 (electronic); 9781421410807 (pbk.: alk. paper); 9781421410814 (electronic)
LC 2013-003541

SUMMARY: This book by Allan V. Horowitz examines "the sociocultural aspects of anxiety's past, present, and future. He begins in the classical period with Hippocrates and proceeds up to the present. Almost an entire chapter is devoted to the rise of Freud in the 20th century, when the modern definition of anxiety developed." (Publishers Weekly)

REVIEW: *Choice* v51 no9 p1629 My 2014 M. C. Matteis

REVIEW: *Libr J* v138 no15 p91 S 15 2013 E. James Lieberman

REVIEW: *New Sci* v221 no2955 p49-50 F 8 2014 Bob Holmes

"Anxiety: A Short History" and "My Age of Anxiety: Fear, Hope, Dread, and the Search for Peace of Mind". "[Allan V.] Horwitz, a sociologist of mental illness and mental health at Rutgers University in New Jersey, and [Scott] Stossel, editor of The Atlantic magazine, give remarkably similar historical overviews. They seem to have read the same sources, cite identical quotes from The Iliad, and come to the same conclusions. It's almost as if they had shared a desk at the library. Despite that, they have written very different books. Horwitz's book gives an objective, somewhat detached look at anxiety through the ages. . . . It's one thing to read a dispassionate discussion of whether social and economic pressures have medicalised anxiety, and quite another to read of Stossel's lifelong torture from overpowering anxiety, despite trying 20 different therapies and 28 different anti-anxiety drugs, none of which gave lasting relief."

REVIEW: *Publ Wkly* v260 no35 p50 S 2 2013

HORWITZ, DEBRA.ed. Decoding Your Dog. See Decoding Your Dog

HORÁČEK, PETR.il. Animal opposites. See Horacek, P.

HORÁČEK, PETR. Animal opposites; 20 p. 2013 Candlewick Press

1. Animals—Juvenile literature 2. Children's literature 3. Interactive books 4. Opposition (Linguistics) 5. Pop-up books
ISBN 0763667765; 9780763667764
LC 2012-950554

SUMMARY: In this book, illustrator Paetr Horacek contrasts 20 animals, using flaps, pop-ups, and . . . mixed-media paintings to highlight the differences between them." (Publishers Weekly)

REVIEW: *Bull Cent Child Books* v67 no2 p96-7 O 2013 J. H.

"Animal Opposites: A Pop-Up Book." "Pairs of oppositional adjectives are partnered with [author Petr] Horáček's vibrant mixed-media illustrations of animals in spreads enhanced by pop-up elements. . . . While kids may be disappointed by the one spread that features no interactive elements, many of the pop-ups are stunning in not only their construction and positioning but also in the motion of their revelation . . . The pages are thick and sturdy, and the pop-up construction, though less durable than the pages, is still solid enough to hold up to a fair amount of use; little ones may need a hand in reassembling the final, oversized fold-out of a large elephant to keep it in good shape. The large, high-contrast illustrations work effectively at a distance and up close."

REVIEW: *SLJ* v59 no9 p123 S 2013 Sandra Welzenbach

HOTES, JENNIFER L. Four rubbings; [by] Jennifer L. Hotes 372 p. 2013 Booktrope Editions

1. Cemeteries—Fiction 2. Ghost stories 3. Sepulchral monuments 4. Teenagers—Fiction 5. Young adult fiction
ISBN 9781620151631
LC 2013-947204

SUMMARY: In this book by Jennifer L. Hotes, "a group of teenage friends, led by young Josie, go out on Halloween night to visit a purportedly haunted cemetery and to take rubbings from the headstones there. While Josie hopes for some contact with the spirit of her dead mother, her friends Casey, Blaze and Seth are drawn to other graves. They find themselves called by the mysteries of the people laid to rest there and the loose ends of their lives." (Kirkus Reviews)

REVIEW: *Kirkus Rev* v82 no5 p63 Mr 1 2014

"Four Rubbings: The Stone Witch Series Volume 1". "The thoughtful, intelligent and altogether human narrative shows how lives can interweave even after death. [Jennifer L.] Hotes masterfully brings her characters to life, both the living and the dead, each of whom is vivid and involving. The supernatural is present but it's as subtle as a shadow on the moon. . . . On a technical level, the text is clean and professional, with welcome poise. . . . Although the book is the first in a series, the author makes sure that it's quite satisfying on its own. Quality YA suspense set in a world of full of fantastic possibilities."

REVIEW: *Kirkus Rev* v82 no4 p406 F 15 2014

"Four Rubbings: The Stone Witch Series Volume 1". "The thoughtful, intelligent and altogether human narrative shows how lives can interweave even after death. [Jennifer L.] Hotes masterfully brings her characters to life, both the living and the dead, each of whom is vivid and involving. The supernatural is present but it's as subtle as a shadow on the moon. . . . On a technical level, the text is clean and professional, with welcome poise. . . . Although the book is the first in a series, the author makes sure that it's quite satisfying on its own. Quality YA suspense set in a world of full of fantastic possibilities."

HOTZE, STEVEN F. Hypothyroidism, health & happiness; the riddle of illness revealed; [by] Steven F. Hotze 294 p. 2013 Advantage

1. Diagnosis 2. Hypothyroidism—Diagnosis—Popular works 3. Hypothyroidism—Popular works 4. Medical literature 5. Thyroid diseases
ISBN 1599323966 (hdbk.); 9781599323961 (hdbk.)
LC 2013-936084

SUMMARY: In this book, "the author argues that an overlooked epidemic of hypothyroidism is responsible for some of today's most commonly treated medical conditions. The reason for this medical mistake is twofold. First, the overly broad test used to diagnose thyroid conditions misses many abnormalities. Second, a heavy reliance on synthetic rather than naturally produced thyroid-replacement drugs actually prevents many patients from correcting their thyroid imbalances." (Kirkus Reviews)

REVIEW: *Kirkus Rev* v82 no1 p52 Ja 1 2014

"Hypothyroidism, Health and Happiness: The Riddle of Illness Revealed". "A physician argues that undiagnosed hypothyroidism is the cause of many common medical conditions. [Steven F.] Hotze . . . convincingly argues that the thyroid gland plays a vital role in overall well-being. After studying the issue for more than 20 years, he has condensed his findings into an accessible guide. . . . At times, the work reads like an extended advertisement for the author's clinic, but the evidence—written plainly for patients with wide-ranging medical issues—is convincing. The book is frustratingly free of dissenting opinions, but even those readers unconvinced that thyroid therapy is a cure-all may want to get their thyroids tested."

HOUGH, DOUGLAS E. Irrationality in health care; what behavioral economics reveals about what we do and why; [by] Douglas E. Hough xvii, 291 p. 2013 Stanford Economics and Finance, an imprint of Stanford University Press

1. Behavioral economics 2. Economics—Psychological aspects 3. Economics literature 4. Health behavior—United States 5. Medical care—United States 6. Medical economics—United States

ISBN 9780804777971 (cloth : alk. paper)

LC 2012-039953

SUMMARY: Written by Douglas Hough, "this book draws on behavioral economics as an alternative lens to provide more clarity in diagnosing the ills of health care today. A behavioral perspective makes sense of key contradictions--from the seemingly irrational choices that we sometimes make as consumers, to the incongruous behavior of providers, to the morass of the long-lived debate surrounding reform." (Publisher's note)

REVIEW: *Choice* v51 no2 p317 O 2013 J. P. Burkett

"Irrationality in Health Care: What Behavioral Economics Reveals About What We Do and Why." "All five titles listed on [author Douglas E.] Hough's website concern health care rather than behavioral economics (BE). Educated 'as a mainstream, neoclassical economist,' Hough . . . took to BE in the late 1980s. His book, written informally to popularize BE in the health care community, argues that BE helps explain 23 health care anomalies, each linked to a puzzle. . . . Unfortunately, the misuse of technical terms such as 'frame' defeats the book's purpose. . . . Confusion also mars Hough's treatment of commitment devices, endowment effects, hot states, hyperbolic discounting, loss aversion, overconfidence, projection bias, probability, and value and weighting functions."

REVIEW: *Science* v342 no6155 p196 O 11 2013 Richard S. Mathis

"Irrationality in Health Care: What Behavioral Economics Reveals About What We Do and Why." "An interesting perspective. . . . [Douglas E.] Hough carefully avoids using behavioral economics as an explanation of all things rational and irrational in U.S. health care. He is also realistic about the current status of behavioral economics as a 'young and imperfect science.' Recognizing the limitations of the advancing field, he does an excellent job of applying it to well-known conundrums. The book could have been improved had the author listed all of the factors that contribute to irrationality in one place. . . . My minor criticisms, however, should not dissuade either health care practitioners or members of the public from reading 'Irrationality in Health Care'."

HOUGH, LINDSAY MUSSER. A woman's framework for a successful career and life. See Hamerstone, J.

HOUGHTON MIFFLIN HARCOURT PUBLISHING CO.comp. The American Heritage dictionary of the English language. See The American Heritage dictionary of the English language

HOURAN, LORI HASKINS. Diary of a worm; teacher's pet; [by] Lori Haskins Houran 2013 HarperCollins

ISBN 9780062087041 ebook; 9780062087058 trade

SUMMARY: Written by Lori Haskins Houran and illustrated by John Nez, this "is a Level One I Can Read book. . . . Children already know and love Worm from the . . . picture book by Doreen Cronin and Harry Bills. Worm is all about having fun, respecting the earth, and never taking baths. Now he's the star of a series of I Can Read books with full-color illustrations." (Publisher's note)

REVIEW: *Bull Cent Child Books* v67 no1 p24-5 S 2013 H. M.

"Diary of a Worm: Teacher's Pet." "This easy reader based on Cronin and Bliss' Diary of a Worm . . . follows the premise of the original, sharing the entries Worm writes in his diary that address the trials and tribulations of being a worm. In this offering, Worm is trying to come up with the perfect gift for his teacher's birthday. . . . As is often the case when picture books are adapted into easy reader format, there isn't much new here; the dynamics among characters, the humor, and the diary format are more or less repackaged with somewhat simpler text and more visual clues. . . . Still, Worm was entertaining the first time around and proves entertaining once again in this format."

REVIEW: *Kirkus Rev* v81 no2 p108 Je 1 2013

REVIEW: *SLJ* v59 no6 p88 Je 2013 Melissa Smith

HOURIGAN, RYAN M. Teaching music to students with autism. See Hammel, A. M.

HOURIHAN, KELLY. 4 to 16 characters; [by] Kelly Hourihan 376 p. 2017 Lemon Sherbet Press

ISBN 9780989741101; 9780989741118; 9780989741125

LC 2013-946698

SUMMARY: In this book, "Jane Shilling is a sullen teenage girl with an alcoholic father and no friends; but on the Internet, nobody knows that. Told exclusively through online sources . . . this is the story of Jane's living more than one life. . . . The adults in her life would like to pull her back to reality. When Jane's online personas begin to fall apart, she'll need the help of Gary and Nora to speak her truth."

(Kirkus Reviews)

REVIEW: *Kirkus Rev* p24 D 15 2013 supplemet best books 2013

"4 to 16 Characters". "This Internet narrative is surprisingly compelling and effective. Readers gain a portrait of Jane's deceased mother in a short series of emails sent before her death. . . . The sci-fi fan fiction is a bit hard to contend with, but it also works as a means to show Jane's dissociation from the pain in her life. Readers should be prepared for total chat-speak immersion, from actions expressed between double colons to Gary's abbreviation-happy communiques. Throughout it all, though, Jane is a dynamic heroine, smart, angry and heartwarming in all the right ways."

REVIEW: *Kirkus Rev* v81 no21 p45 N 1 2013

HOUSE, KATHERINE L. The White House for kids; a history of a home, office, and national symbol: with 21 activities; [by] Katherine L. House 144 p. 2014 Chicago Review Press

1. Children's nonfiction 2. JUVENILE NONFICTION—History—United States—General 3. JUVENILE NONFICTION—Social Science—Politics & Government
ISBN 1613744617; 9781613744611 (pbk.)
LC 2013-038108

SUMMARY: This children's book, by Katherine L. House, offers an "educates young readers on the White House. Blending facts from numerous primary sources with engaging anecdotes . . . , this book provides the complete story of the presidents' home. Details on the many changes, updates, renovations, and redecorations that have occurred over the years are featured as well as a look at the daily lives of the White House's inhabitants." (Publisher's note)

REVIEW: *Booklist* v110 no12 p69-70 F 15 2014 Carolyn Phelan

REVIEW: *Kirkus Rev* v81 no24 p272 D 15 2013

"The White House For Kids: A History of a Home, Office, and National Symbol, With 21 Activities". "The latest installment in the For Kids series offers a biography of a house. . . . Young readers will certainly be drawn in by this kid-friendly approach to history. The series' signature activities include how to write a letter to the president, make stilts (since Theodore Roosevelt's children loved walking the house and gardens on stilts), bake Chelsea Clinton's chocolate-chip cookies and hold an egg race like the annual Easter Egg Roll at the White House. . . . An engaging history of a country through the biography of its most famous dwelling."

REVIEW: *SLJ* v60 no2 p125 F 2014 Lauren M. Sinacore

REVIEW: *Voice of Youth Advocates* v37 no3 p94 Ag 2014 Amy Cummins

HOUSE, RICHARD. The Kills; Sutler, The Massive, The Kill, and The Hit; [by] Richard House 1024 p. 2014 St. Martin's Press

1. Contractors 2. Embezzlement 3. Iraq War, 2003-2011 4. Murder—Fiction 5. Suspense fiction
ISBN 9781250052438; 1250052432

SUMMARY: This book made the longlist for the Man Booker Prize, and was originally published as four separate ebooks. "Book One, 'Sutler,' is the story of a contractor on the run from his post in Iraq, a patsy for an $53 million embezzlement scandal. . . . Along the way he meets . . . a student reading a novel entitled 'The Kill'. . . . The film of 'The Kill' is discussed in Book Two; Book Three consists of the novel in its entirety, before it is revisited in Book Four, 'The Hit'." (Times Literary Supplement)

REVIEW: *Kirkus Rev* v82 no11 p162 Je 1 2014

REVIEW: *Libr J* v139 no4 p64 Mr 1 2014 Barbara Hoffert

REVIEW: *Libr J* v139 no5 p64 Mr 15 2014 Barbara Hoffert

REVIEW: *TLS* no5763 p20 S 13 2013 LUKE BROWN

"The Kills". "'The Kills' consists of four 'thrillers' which were first published as separate ebooks. This is something of a red herring because none of the four is satisfying as a conventional thriller, and it is only together that they create the literary success that this year's judges of the Man Booker Prize rightly recognized by placing it on their longlist. The reader hoping for more than thematic coherence will frequently be disappointed: the novel's structure is more ambitious than this. Richard House has built the four parts to play off against each other, to explore how acts of greed and violence perpetuate themselves. This is where the novel's real originality lies, rather than in the accompanying video and audio clips that House has created and linked to in the ebook."

HOUSTON, KEITH. Shady characters; the secret life of punctuation, symbols, & other typographical marks; [by] Keith Houston 352 p. 2013 W W Norton & Co Inc

1. Historical literature 2. Punctuation—History 3. Signs and symbols—History 4. Type and type-founding—History 5. Writing—History
ISBN 0393064425; 9780393064421
LC 2013-017324

SUMMARY: This book is a "bestiary of lesser-known punctuation marks. . . . Nearly every punctuation symbol in this book gained its start from the annotation marks of monks, scribes, or scholars. (The chapter on daggers and asterisks, of course, uses those symbols to mark the asides.) Some game-changers, like the sudden confines of the typing press or the yet-more-restrictive typewriter, extend their influence across numerous chapters." (Publishers Weekly)

REVIEW: *Kirkus Rev* v81 no15 p63 Ag 1 2013

REVIEW: *Libr J* v138 no12 p102 Jl 1 2013 Robert Mixner

REVIEW: *Publ Wkly* v260 no27 p82 Jl 8 2013

REVIEW: *TLS* no5783 p21 Ja 31 2014 SEBASTIAN CARTER

"Shady Characters: Ampersands, Interrobangs, and Other Typographical Curiosities." "Even before the invention of minuscules, a detachment of symbols, abbreviate words and help the reader to perform this or that function. 'Shady Characters' is a collection of essays that describes many of them, and investigates their history. . . . 'Shady Characters' is produced to a high standard, and is printed in two colours throughout. . . . [Author Keith] Houston admits that his book will probably be dipped into in search of information on a particular punctuation sign, and provides cross-references accordingly; and that is probably the best way to use it."

HOWARD, A. G. Unhinged; a novel; [by] A. G. Howard 400 p. 2014 Amulet Books

1. Alice (Fictitious character : Carroll) 2. Characters in literature—Fiction 3. Fantasy fiction 4. Mental illness—Fiction 5. Mothers and daughters—Fiction 6.

Supernatural—Fiction
ISBN 1419709712; 9781419709715 (hardback)
LC 2013-026395

SUMMARY: In this young adult novel, by A. G. Howard, book two in the "Splintered" series, "Alyssa Gardner has been down the rabbit hole. . . . Now all she has to do is graduate high school. That would be easier without her mother, freshly released from an asylum, acting overly protective and suspicious. It would be much simpler if the mysterious Morpheus didn't show up for school one day to tempt her with another dangerous quest in the dark, challenging Wonderland." (Publisher's note)

REVIEW: *Booklist* v110 no8 p46 D 15 2013 Frances Bradburn

REVIEW: *Bull Cent Child Books* v67 no6 p316 F 2014 Alaine Martaus

"Unhinged." "As intense, dark, and weird as the first volume, this worthy sequel creates a parallel narrative that brings the action out of Wonderland and into Alyssa's hometown. Many of the story's initial strengths carry over, including the fantastical creatures, the exciting adventure, and Alyssa's struggle to understand and accept her dual nature as human and netherling. The narrative is slightly more effortful in its refashioning of [Lewis] Carroll's story, but fans of 'Splintered' will happily throw themselves back down the rabbit hole for this new exploit, and a final showdown that ends with three central characters in peril will have readers lining up for more."

REVIEW: *Kirkus Rev* v81 no23 p92 D 1 2013

REVIEW: *SLJ* v60 no2 p106 F 2014 Eliza Langhans

REVIEW: *Voice of Youth Advocates* v36 no6 p72 F 2014 Jessica Miller

HOWARD, DEBORAH. The Image of Venice; Fialetti's View and Sir Henry Wotton; [by] Deborah Howard 168 p. 2013 Paul Holberton Publishing

1. Art literature 2. Fialetti, Odoardo, 1573-1638 3. Italian art 4. Venice (Italy)—In art 5. Wotton, Henry, Sir, 1568-1639
ISBN 1907372628; 9781907372629

SUMMARY: Written by Henrietta Ryan and Deborah Howard, "This book explores the creation of one of [Venice's] largest surviving depictions, which has remained almost unknown to the wider public since its creation exactly four centuries ago. Signed and dated 1611, the painting is the work of the notable early seventeenth-century Bolognese artist Odoardo Fialetti." (Publisher's note)

REVIEW: *Apollo: The International Magazine for Collectors* v178 no614 p121 N 2013

"Anti-Ugly: Excursions in English Architecture and Design," "Islamic and Oriental Arms and Armour: A Lifetime's Passion," and "The Image of Venice: Fialetti's View and Sir Henry Wotton." "Some 50 . . . pieces are collected in ['Anti-Ugly'], which focuses on English architecture. A reminder, if one were needed, of [author Gavin] Stamp's . . . wit. . . . After discovering antique weaponry in the mid 1960s, [author] Robert Hales went on to spend almost 30 years as a highly respected dealer. . . . ['Islamic and Oriental Arms and Armour'] reproduces many of the daggers, swords, firearms and armour that passed through his hands. . . . Odoardo Fiaietti's early 17th-century view of Venice has spent 400 years in relative obscurity. . . . Its recent restoration and public exhibition have inspired ['The Image of Venice']."

HOWARD, ELIZABETH JANE, 1923-2014. All Change; [by] Elizabeth Jane Howard 592 p. 2014 Pan Books

1. Adultery—Fiction 2. English fiction 3. Great Britain—Social life & customs—20th century—Fiction 4. Social classes—Fiction 5. Social classes—Great Britain
ISBN 0330508989; 9780330508988

SUMMARY: In this novel by Elizabeth Jane Howard, part of The Cazalet Chronicles series, "It is the 1950s and as the Duchy, the Cazalets' beloved matriarch, dies, she takes with her the last remnants of a disappearing world--of houses with servants, of class and tradition--in which the Cazalets have thrived." (Publisher's note)

REVIEW: *London Rev Books* v36 no3 p31-2 F 6 2014 Tessa Hadley

"All Change". "The material of the chronicles seems like [Elizabeth Jane] Howard's natural and inevitable subject: the tangled but ordinary enough private lives of a fairly undistinguished upper-middle-class family, loosely based on her own, between the 1930s and 1950s. . . . She can give flat utterance to things which were more or less understood between her protagonists, but which they didn't have a language for. . . . Howard makes an effort to write the servants into the story; they're seen convincingly enough when they're functioning as part of the household, but she can't find the right tone to give them inner lives, and resorts to working-class voices out of central casting."

REVIEW: *TLS* no5775 p20 D 6 2013 FRANCES WILSON

"All Change." "Just shy of parody, [author Elizabeth Jane] Howard gives us the scourge of the middlebrow from the perspective of a man whose family consider themselves the backbone of England. . . . Howard's brilliance lies in her forensic depiction of sexual and emotional loneliness. . . . The problem with 'All Change' is that communications between the couples have improved. . . . The relationship between Edward and his second wife, Diana, is the only one to lift off the page. As his feisty mistress, Diana was an admirable figure, but as his spouse she is the enemy within. . . . Diana, Edward recognizes with horror, is the distinguished thing--a middlebrow."

HOWARD, PHILIP N. Democracy's fourth wave?; digital media and the Arab Spring; [by] Philip N. Howard xiv, 145 p. 2013 Oxford University Press

1. Arab Spring, 2010- 2. Information technology—Political aspects—Arab countries 3. Internet—Political aspects—Arab countries 4. Internet—Social aspects—Arab countries 5. Political science literature 6. Revolutions—Arab countries—History—21st century
ISBN 9780199936953 (hardcover : alk. paper); 9780199936977 (pbk. : alk. paper)
LC 2012-023604

SUMMARY: In this book, authors Philip N. Howard and Muzammil M. Hussain "study the role of digital media during the Arab Spring. They find that 'information infrastructure--especially mobile phone use--consistently appears as one of the key ingredients in parsimonious models for conjoined combinations of causes behind regime fragility and social movement success." (Choice: Current Reviews for Academic Libraries)

REVIEW: *Choice* v51 no4 p720 D 2013 A. R. Abootalebi

"Democracy's Fourth Wave?: Digital Media and the Arab Spring." "Digital media is undoubtedly changing the dynamics of state-society relations, but whether it is fundamentally changing the nature of governance itself remains a contentious issue. The authors' choice of title, intimately conjoining digital media with the 'fourth wave of democracy,' is misleading. Causes and consequences of social movements and collective action are complex and uncertain in many ways, including the degree of impact of digital media on the nature of governance."

HOWARD, RICHARD.tr. Alien hearts. See Maupassant, G. de

HOWARD, RYAN. Punch and Judy in 19th century America; a history and biographical dictionary; [by] Ryan Howard 275 p. 2013 McFarland

1. Actors—United States—Biography—Dictionaries 2. Historical literature 3. Puppet theater—United States—History—19th century 4. Theater—United States—History—19th century 5. Theatrical producers and directors—United States—Biography—Dictionaries
ISBN 0786472707; 9780786472703 (softcover : alk. paper)
LC 2013-004866

SUMMARY: This book, by Ryan Howard, covers the "hand-puppet play starring the characters Punch and Judy [that] was introduced from England and became extremely popular in the United States in the 1800s. This book details information on nearly 350 American Punch players. It explores the significance of the 19th-century American show as a reflection of the attitudes and conditions of its time and place." (Publisher's note)

REVIEW: *Choice* v51 no1 p43-4 S 2013 R. A. Naversen

"Punch and Judy in 19th Century America: A History and Biographical Dictionary." "[Author Ryan] Howard . . . draws on Paul McPharlin's 'The Puppet Theatre in America' (1949; with a 1969 supplement, 'Puppets in America Since 1948') and adds his own extensive research through newspapers, magazines, books, and public records to provide a chronicle of American Punch and Judy puppeteers and puppet makers during the 19th century. . . . Howard provides an extensive bibliographical dictionary on nearly 350 American Punch practitioners while also surveying the significance of these characters in light of the diverse racial, social, and cultural vicissitudes of the developing nation."

HOWE, ANTHONY.ed. The Oxford handbook of Percy Bysshe Shelley. See The Oxford handbook of Percy Bysshe Shelley

HOWE, R. BRIAN. Education in the best interests of the child; a children's rights perspective on closing the achievement gap; [by] R. Brian Howe 259 p. 2013 University of Toronto Press

1. Academic achievement 2. Children's rights 3. Démocratisation de l'enseignement 4. Educational change 5. Educational equalization 6. Educational literature 7. Enfants—Droits 8. Enseignement—Réforme 9. Succès scolaire
ISBN 144261451X (pbk.); 1442646586 (bound); 9781442614512 (pbk.); 9781442646582 (bound)
LC 2012-285744

SUMMARY: This book presents an "argument for addressing the achievement gap that exists among children by using a human rights perspective. . . . Specifically the authors cite international law and the Convention on the Rights of the Child as the catalyst for narrowing the achievement gap. Under this law, the 'best interest of the child' translates into addressing social issues . . . for the express benefit of those children experiencing poverty." (Choice: Current Reviews for Academic Libraries)

REVIEW: *Choice* v51 no5 p924-5 Ja 2014 L. T. Grover

"Education in the Best Interests of the child: A Children's Rights Perspective on Closing the Achievement Gap." "[R. Brian] Howe and [Katherine] Covell . . . offer up an excellent, compelling argument for addressing the achievement gap that exists among children by using a human rights perspective. The authors keep the generally accepted premise that education is the key to reducing disparity, and they make the case for three major policy recommendations that will reduce the achievement gap: implementing early childhood education, improving school practices, and transforming school cultures. . . . Though the concept of 'best interests' can be vague and complex, the authors successfully present the model in an understandable, applied, and research-based manner."

HOWELL, WILLIAM G. Thinking about the presidency; the primacy of power; [by] William G. Howell xiii, 185 p. 2013 Princeton University Press

1. Executive power—United States 2. Political science literature 3. Power (Social sciences) 4. Presidents—United States
ISBN 0691155348; 9780691155340 (hardcover: alk. paper)
LC 2012-042074

SUMMARY: In this book, the authors argue that U.S. presidents "'want a great deal more power than they can get' in order to tackle their many responsibilities, but their ambition is hemmed in by 'cultural ambivalence, political constraints, and an uncooperative world.' In challenging circumstances, failing to use the power available can be a catastrophe for the president, as the authors note in brief case studies of the Iran hostage crisis . . . and the debt ceiling debacle in 2011." (Choice)

REVIEW: *Choice* v51 no4 p728-9 D 2013 J. P. Crouch

"Thinking About the Presidency: The Primacy of Power". "[William G.] Howell . . . and [David Milton] Brent . . . have authored an insightful and thought-provoking book. In a brief but wide-ranging analysis, they develop their thesis: 'Power is the president's North Star.' The president lacks formal constitutional powers, but he is still expected to 'appear in command' by a public that requires him to be nothing less than 'everything.' . . . The book's combination of clear prose and scholarly heft makes it an attractive option for undergraduates and graduates interested in the presidency."

HOYT, ARD.il. Alice from Dallas. See Sadler, M.

HSIEH, ANDREW. The Lius of Shanghai. See Cochran, S.

HUA, JULIETTA. Trafficking women's human rights; [by] Julietta Hua xxix, 152 p. 2011 University of Minnesota Press

1. Feminism 2. Human rights 3. Human trafficking 4. Social science literature 5. Women—Legal status, laws,

etc 6. Women's rights
ISBN 0816675600 (alk. paper); 0816675619 (pb : alk. paper); 9780816675609 (alk. paper); 9780816675616 (pb : alk. paper)
LC 2011-016428

SUMMARY: "In 'Trafficking Women's Human Rights,' [author Julietta] Hua maps the ways in which government, media, and scholarship have described sex trafficking for U.S. consumption. As her investigation takes us from laws like the Victims of Trafficking and Violence Protection Act to political speeches and literary and media images, it uncovers dark assumptions about race, difference, and the United States' place in the world expressed--and often promoted--by such images." (Publisher's note)

REVIEW: *Choice* v49 no7 p1305 Mr 2012 B. Tavakolian

REVIEW: *Contemp Sociol* v42 no6 p848-50 N 2013 ANDREA D. MILLER

"Trafficking Women's Human Rights." "Julietta Hua's Trafficking Women's Human Rights' provides a critical lens to the human rights issue of human trafficking. Hua explores the framework of human trafficking itself, asking the reader to question the knowledge production that reproduces the ideologies of who counts as victim and oppressor. Her primary thesis considers the ways governmental and nongovernmental institutions, as well as news media, actually participate in defining the lens through which human trafficking is viewed and understood by the public at large."

REVIEW: *Ethn Racial Stud* v35 no9 p1703-4 S 2012 Bridget Anderson

HUBBARD, JENNIFER R. Until it hurts to stop; [by] Jennifer R. Hubbard 256 p. 2013 Viking, published by Penguin Group
1. Bullying—Fiction 2. High schools—Fiction 3. Hiking—Fiction 4. Interpersonal relations—Fiction 5. School stories 6. Schools—Fiction 7. Self-acceptance—Fiction 8. Young adult fiction
ISBN 9780670785209 (hardcover)
LC 2013-012795

SUMMARY: In this young adult novel, author Jennifer R. Hubbard describes how high school student "Maggie's self-esteem plummets . . . Hubbard demonstrates the intense fear, paranoia, and dread that can paralyze victims of bullying long past the days of actual incidents. . . . The stuttering, burgeoning romance between Maggie and Nick becomes the backdrop to a more important love story, that of Maggie and herself." (Booklist)

REVIEW: *Booklist* v110 no2 p77 S 15 2013 Courtney Jones

REVIEW: *Bull Cent Child Books* v67 no3 p158 N 2013 K. C.

"Until It Hurts to Stop." "[Author Jennifer R.] Hubbard effectively plays her metaphors close to the surface here: Maggie's painful past is the mountain she has to climb, and the rattlesnake she and Nick encounter is the anger and resentment that lie coiled inside her, waiting to strike. . . . If her self-involvement is a bit obvious, well, it might just need to be to make it clear to readers that being victimized can have damaging effects long after the abuse stops; Hubbard shows, with profound psychological insight, how Maggie's recognizing in Nick what she can't see in herself is a first step toward really putting her junior high past to rest. Readers will similarly see themselves in Maggie and, hopefully, stop punishing themselves with their own legacies of bullying."

REVIEW: *Kirkus Rev* v81 no16 p65 Ag 15 2013

REVIEW: *Publ Wkly* v260 no30 p69-70 Jl 29 2013

REVIEW: *Voice of Youth Advocates* v36 no4 p63-4 O 2013 Diane Colson

"Until It Hurts to Stop." "In junior high, Maggie was the target of fierce bullying by mean girls and their minions. Each day was a new ordeal filled with pranks and taunts. Now, two years later, Maggie has a different life. . . . Then, the worst of the mean girls, Raleigh, begins attending Maggie's high school, and Maggie's dread of public humiliation returns. . . . The book concludes realistically, with genuinely important insights into recovery from bullying. Recommend this title to readers affected by bullying from peers, as in Maggie's case, or from parents, as with Nick."

HUBBARD, JENNY. And we stay; [by] Jenny Hubbard 240 p. 2014 Delacorte Press
1. Boarding schools—Fiction 2. High schools—Fiction 3. Interpersonal relations—Fiction 4. Poetry—Fiction 5. School stories 6. Schools—Fiction 7. Suicide—Fiction
ISBN 0385740573; 9780375989551 (glb); 9780385740579 (hc)
LC 2013-002236

SUMMARY: In this book, by Jenny Hubbard "high school senior Paul Wagoner walks into his school library with a stolen gun, . . . threatens his girlfriend Emily Beam, then takes his own life. In the wake of the tragedy, an angry and guilt-ridden Emily is shipped off to boarding school in Amherst, Massachusetts, where she encounters a ghostly presence who shares her name. The spirit of Emily Dickinson and two quirky girls offer helping hands, but it is up to Emily to heal her own damaged self." (Publisher's note)

REVIEW: *Booklist* v110 no6 p39 N 15 2013 Ann Kelley

"And We Stay." "This novel is accomplished, polished, and mixes prose and poetry to stunning effect. . . . The third-person, present-tense voice is compelling. Sounding almost like stage directions ('Emily Beam is sighing all the time'), [Jenny] Hubbard's narrative tone will only make readers want to lean in closer. The poems themselves are insightful and poignant, illuminating the dark corners of Emily's psyche. And though Emily may be damaged and the winter of 1994 is long, happier times--and spring--seem on the horizon."

REVIEW: *Bull Cent Child Books* v67 no5 p268 Ja 2014 K. C.

"And We Stay." "[Jenny] Hubbard's language caresses the reader with both imagistic and sonic loveliness, incorporating lines from [Emily] Dickinson's poetry that propel Emily's insights at various moments and prompt poems of her own that catch at the throat as they chart her path through mourning. Clearly, she's grieving much more than the loss of Paul; her specific losses and their recompense become universally recognizable as the process of growing up itself, but as with so much of Dickinson's poetry, they inspire thoughtful reflection more than nostalgic or sentimental tears. Emily is a sharp-witted thinker's girl surprised by feeling, a character worthy of Dickinson's formidable legacy."

REVIEW: *Kirkus Rev* v81 no22 p115 N 15 2013

REVIEW: *Publ Wkly* v260 no42 p53 O 21 2013

REVIEW: *SLJ* v60 no1 p100 Ja 2014 Jill Heritage Maza

REVIEW: *Voice of Youth Advocates* v36 no5 p61-2 D 2013 Suzanne Osman

HUBER, PETER W. The cure in the code; how 20th century law is undermining 21st century medicine; [by] Peter W. Huber 304 p. 2013 Basic Books

1. Biomedical Research—legislation & jurisprudence—United States 2. Drug Industry—legislation & jurisprudence—United States 3. Legislation, Medical—United States 4. Political science literature 5. State Medicine—legislation & jurisprudence—United States

ISBN 9780465050680 (hardcover)

LC 2013-026302

SUMMARY: In this book, Peter Huber "contends that government intervention in the science and practice of medicine is impeding progress. The author claims that the advancement of molecular biology . . . allows for the practice of a new kind of individualized medicine . . . Huber makes the point that the kind of broad-based, double-blind experiments currently required before a drug can be marketed will become obsolete as . . . treatments can be individualized on the basis of genetic information." (Kirkus Reviews)

REVIEW: *Booklist* v110 no5 p9-10 N 1 2013 Tony Miksanek

"The Cure in the Code: How 20th Century Law is Undermining 21st Century Medicine." "Our ability to read the genetic code heralds a transformation of modern medicine. Yet many potential medical miracles remain throttled. Antiquated and stifling regulations and policies presently handcuff the evolution of molecular medicine. [Peter W.] Huber, a senior fellow at the Manhattan Institute for Policy Research, pleads for reforming the drug-licensing system and advocates 'a culture of discovery and creativity that is willing to take risks and invest patiently in the future, 'Although Huber's discussion of the topic is at times dense, his ardor for invigorating pharmaceutical progress is apparent on every page of this scholarly work."

REVIEW: *Kirkus Rev* v81 no19 p161 O 1 2013

REVIEW: *Natl Rev* v66 no1 p41-4 Ja 27 2014 KEVIN D. WILLIAMSON

REVIEW: *Publ Wkly* v260 no36 p47 S 9 2013

HUBER, RAYMOND. Flight of the honey bee; [by] Raymond Huber 32 p. 2013 Candlewick Press

1. Beehives 2. Female honeybees 3. Honeybee 4. Honeybees—Behavior 5. Honeybees—Juvenile literature 6. Picture books for children

ISBN 0763667609; 9780763667603

LC 2013-931462

SUMMARY: Author Raymond Huber presents an illustrated children's book. "A tiny honey bee emerges from the hive for the first time. Using sunlight, landmarks, and scents to remember the path, she goes in search of pollen and nectar to share with the thousands of other bees in her hive. She uses her powerful sense of smell to locate the flowers that sustain her, avoids birds that might eat her, and returns home to share her finds with her many sisters." (Publisher's note)

REVIEW: *Booklist* p4-10 Ja 1 2014 Supplement Gillian Engberg

"The Boy Who Loved Math: The Improbable Life of Paul Erdos," "Little Red Writing," and "Flight of the Honey Bee". "Mathematician Paul Erdos is the subject of this inventive, entertaining picture-book biography. . . . The colorful, energetic artwork, organized in a well-designed mix of spot scenes with full-page spreads, further expands the concepts with decorative elements. . . . [An] uproarious retelling of 'Little Red Riding Hood" . . . [Melissa] Sweet's exuberant illustrations reinforce the concepts with wit and energy. A perfect prompt for beginning writers to borrow from Little Red's basket of words and try their own stories. . . . [Raymond] Huber . . . shows an obvious understanding of both honeybees and of what will interest young children in this attractive offering. . . . One of the most informative—and beautiful—picture books about honeybees."

REVIEW: *Booklist* v110 no4 p46 O 15 2013 Carolyn Phelan

"Flight of the Honey Bee". "This brightly illustrated picture book achieves a good deal. The lively, realistic story is enhanced with apt imagery and vivid turns of phrase. Meanwhile, small-type sentences on each spread add intriguing related facts about honey bees. [Raymond] Huber . . . shows a good understanding of both honey bees and of what will interest young children. [Brian] Lovelock's illustrations, watercolor paintings with acrylic and colored-pencil elements, offer distinctive bee's-eye views of the world, whether showing landscapes from the air or close-ups of falling hail and bee-to-wasp combat. One of the most informative picture books about honey bees, this is surely among the most beautiful as well."

REVIEW: *Bull Cent Child Books* v67 no3 p158-9 N 2013 D. S.

REVIEW: *Horn Book Magazine* v89 no6 p115-6 N/D 2013 JENNIFER LU

REVIEW: *Kirkus Rev* v81 no16 p175 Ag 15 2013

"Flight of the Honey Bee." "A New Zealand import describes a worker honeybee's scouting mission. Naming his protagonist Scout for her current role in the hive, [author Raymond] Huber delivers a present-tense narrative of her odyssey. . . . [Illustrator Brian] Lovelock's full-bleed paintings, done in watercolor, acrylic ink and colored pencil, vary in perspective and scale, making the most of the autumn palette and refraining at all times from anthropomorphizing their subjects. While hardly the only bee book available, this handsome, respectful volume deserves a place on the shelf."

REVIEW: *SLJ* v59 no9 p176 S 2013 Margaret Bush

HUBKA, THOMAS C. Houses without names; architectural nomenclature and the classification of America's common houses; [by] Thomas C. Hubka x, 112 p. 2013 University of Tennessee Press

1. Architectural literature 2. Architecture—Terminology 3. Architecture and society—United States 4. Architecture, Domestic—United States—Classification 5. Vernacular architecture—United States—Classification

ISBN 1572339470 (paperback); 9781572339477 (pbk.)

LC 2013-001554

SUMMARY: This book by Thomas C. Hubka "aims to challenge 'the current way we see and interpret the common, everyday houses that surround us.' . . . First, by examining internal house features . . . he makes an argument for creating and using floor plans to define and classify these houses. . . . The book ends by using these techniques to create names for these house." (Choice: Current Reviews for Academic Libraries)

REVIEW: *Choice* v51 no6 p992-3 F 2014 L. B. Allsopp

"Houses Without Names: Architectural Nomenclature and the Classification of America's Common Houses." "Common houses in the US need 'meaningful names and classification . . . [in order] to recognize their role in the development of . . . domestic culture and its housing landscape,' notes [Thomas C.] Hubka. . . . In five chapters, the author clearly lays out problems, myths, and misconceptions, and then offers a solution. . . . Using clear, detailed graphics and black and-white photos, the author provides readers with a new tool for analyzing housing."

REVIEW: *Libr J* v139 no7 p92 Ap 15 2014 Valerie Nye

HUCKELBRIDGE, DANE. Bourbon; A History of the American Spirit; [by] Dane Huckelbridge 288 p. 2014 HarperCollins

1. Bourbon whiskey 2. Cooking (Bourbon whiskey) 3. Historical literature 4. Liquor industry—History 5. Prohibition

ISBN 0062241397; 9780062241399

SUMMARY: This book, by Dane Huckelbridge, is "the story of . . . bourbon whiskey. Its primary ingredient was discovered by Christopher Columbus. Its recipe was perfected on the Western frontier. In 1964, Congress passed a resolution declaring it to be a 'distinctive product of the United States.' First brewed by pioneers in in the backwoods of Appalachia, bourbon whiskey has become a modern multi-billion dollar international industry today." (Publisher's note)

REVIEW: *Kirkus Rev* v82 no4 p66 F 15 2014

"Bourbon: A History of the American Spirit". "A mirthful, erudite appreciation of bourbon and its striking history. . . . In this entertaining tour d'horizon of bourbon's birth and long, healthy life, the author dispels plenty of bogus history. . . . In one of the more sharp-eyed chapters, [Dane] Huckelbridge tells the tale of how class and ethnic bigotry played a leading role in the passage of Prohibition and how the need for tax revenues made Congress see the light through the amber liquid. A snappy history of the popular spirit's rise and continued ascent."

REVIEW: *Publ Wkly* v261 no2 p61-2 Ja 13 2014

HUDSON, KERRY. Tony Hogan bought me an ice-cream float before he stole my Ma; [by] Kerry Hudson 272 p. 2013 Penguin Books

1. Bildungsromans 2. Dysfunctional families—Scotland—Fiction 3. Mothers & daughters—Fiction 4. Working class families—Scotland—Fiction

ISBN 9780143124641

LC 2013-018974

SUMMARY: This book by Kerry Hudson "begins with our singular heroine's less than idyllic birth and quickly moves to a spectacular fight that lands Janie and her mother in a local women's shelter. From there it's on to a dodgy council flat and a succession of unsuitable men, including the hard-drinking, drug-dealing, ice-cream-buying Tony Hogan." (Publisher's note)

REVIEW: *Booklist* v110 no8 p20 D 15 2013 Ann Kelley

REVIEW: *Kirkus Rev* v81 no24 p135 D 15 2013

"Tony Hogan Bought Me an Ice-Cream Float Before He Stole My Ma". "The problems (in the novel and with it) begin with the protagonist's birth, because she is apparently the narrator as soon as she leaves the womb. And both her perceptive abilities and language (often foulmouthed) vary widely, as the reader must determine how much faith to put in a narrator who can neither walk nor talk. . . . Yet, it's a testament to the author's compelling voice that the reader feels he or she knows and cares about narrator Janie, her mother, Iris, and many of the ne'er-do-wells they encounter on life's crooked path. . . . A funny and dark sensibility can't quite overcome the flaws of this novel, which ends with plenty of unfinished business, suggesting a sequel or a series."

REVIEW: *Publ Wkly* v260 no51 p37 D 16 2013

HUDSON, VALERIE M. Sex and world peace; [by] Valerie M. Hudson xii, 289 p. 2012 Columbia University Press

1. International relations—Social aspects 2. Peace—Social aspects 3. Sex discrimination against women 4. Social science literature 5. War and society 6. Women and peace 7. Women and war

ISBN 9780231131827 (cloth: alk. paper); 9780231520096 (ebook)

LC 2011-048554

SUMMARY: This book "consolidates research across several disciplines to offer an explanation of how male-lead social structures came to dominate and how certain social structures and cultural shifts might remedy such gender inequities." Valerie M. Hudson "and co-authors' arguments draw on well-known concepts related to gender, culture and norms, social demography, political sociology, victimization, and crime/deviance, applied in an international context." (Contemporary Sociology)

REVIEW: *Choice* v50 no7 p1331 Mr 2013 K. Staudt

REVIEW: *Contemp Sociol* v43 no1 p93-5 Ja 2014 Jennifer Schwartz

"Sex and World Peace". "'Sex and World Peace' presents a convincing theoretical and empirical argument for considering women when studying problems of global inequality and violence. . . . A second important contribution of this book is an introduction to a wide audience of the impressive, publically-available WomanStats Database. . . . Finally, Valerie Hudson and co-authors compel readers to recognize the extent and nature of women's unequal treatment across the world and offer concrete, feasible actions for individuals and those in power, sidestepping the depression that readers sometimes feel accompanying sociological awakening to inequalities. . . . The book unfolds in a logical, interesting way."

HUDSPETH, ROBERT N.ed. The correspondence of Henry D. Thoreau. See The correspondence of Henry D. Thoreau

HUEMER, MICHAEL. The problem of political authority; an examination of the right to coerce and the duty to obey; [by] Michael Huemer xxviii, 365 p. 2013 Palgrave Macmillan

1. Authority 2. Obedience 3. Philosophical literature 4. Political science 5. Social contract

ISBN 9781137281647 (alk. paper); 9781137281654 (pbk.: alk. paper)

LC 2012-038844

SUMMARY: "This book examines theories of political authority, from the social contract theory, to theories of democratic authorization, to fairness- and consequence-based theories. Ultimately, no theory of authority succeeds, and thus no government has the kind of authority often ascribed to governments. The author goes on to discuss how voluntary and competitive institutions could provide the central goods for the sake of which the state is often deemed necessary." (Publisher's note)

REVIEW: *Ethics* v124 no2 p412-147 Ja 2014 GEORGE KLOSKO

"The Problem of Political Authority: An Examination of the Right to Coerce and the Duty to Obey". "Although Michael Huemer treads close to his zanier fellow travelers, he largely escapes their grasp because of greater philosophical sophistication. But he is not more moderate. . . . Although his conclusions are extreme, he attempts to establish them through clear, plausible arguments. Because his arguments are frequently of high quality, Huemer forces his readers to consider seriously views they would otherwise likely dismiss, while his assault on traditional opinions raises troubling questions for familiar positions. . . . As one may see, Huemer covers a great deal of ground and does so with a combination of ingenuity, philosophical sophistication, and the conviction of a zealot."

HUESTON, PENNY.tr. All the Way. See Darrieussecq, M.

HUEY, LOIS MINER. Ick! Yuck! Eew!; our gross American history; [by] Lois Miner Huey 48 p. 2014 Millbrook Press

1. Children's nonfiction 2. Hygiene—History 3. United States—History—18th century 4. United States—History—Juvenile literature
ISBN 9780761390916 (lib. bdg. : alk. paper)
LC 2013-004386

SUMMARY: "In this heavily illustrated book, [author Lois Miner] Huey seeks to help young readers experience history through the senses of smell, feel, and taste. . . . Those who like gross stuff will get a kick out of reading about the stinky living conditions, bug-infested and rotting food that people ate, the lack of dental and other personal hygiene, and other icky bits of eighteenth-century American history." (Booklist)

REVIEW: *Booklist* v110 no3 p50 O 1 2013 Kat Kan

REVIEW: *Bull Cent Child Books* v67 no3 p159 N 2013 E. B.

"Ick! Yuck! Eew!: Our Gross American History." "Eye-catching bookmaking is the draw in this quick overview of some of the nastier aspects of America before the arrival of hand sanitizer. . . . Text is broken into browsable chunks under subheadings; artifacts and period illustrations, along with splashes of indeterminate goo and crawling critters, march across every spread. There's not a lot of information here that isn't readily available in other sources on early America, and the rust-red interjections ('Cramps! Mess! Gross!'; "Pain! Scars! Eew!') get tiresome pretty fast."

REVIEW: *Kirkus Rev* v81 no15 p230 Ag 1 2013

REVIEW: *SLJ* v59 no9 p184 S 2013 Annette Herbert

HUGHES-HALLETT, LUCY. Gabriele d'Annunzio; poet, seducer and preacher of war; [by] Lucy Hughes-Hallett 608 p. 2013 Alfred A. Knopf

1. Biography (Literary form) 2. Fascism—Italy—History—20th century 3. Militarism—Italy—History—20th century 4. Nationalists—Italy—Biography 5. Poets, Italian—20th century—Biography 6. Politics and literature—Italy—History—20th century 7. World War, 1914-1918—Territorial questions—Croatia—Rijeka
ISBN 0307263932; 9780307263933
LC 2012-033943

SUMMARY: This book by Lucy Hughes Hallett presents a biography of "the Italian modernist writer and demagogue" Gabriele d'Annunzio. "He was a brilliant, scandalous literary celebrity . . . a ruthless seducer of women; an avowed Nietzschean superman and an effeminate voluptuary who loved fashion, furnishings, and flowers; and a blood-thirsty militarist who helped propel Italy into World War I with his pro-war oratory and reveled in the carnage he witnessed at the front." (Publishers Weekly)

REVIEW: *Booklist* v109 no21 p13 Jl 1 2013 Ray Olson

REVIEW: *Kirkus Rev* v81 no12 p51 Je 15 2013

REVIEW: *N Y Rev Books* v61 no4 p21-2 Mr 6 2014 David Gilmour

"Gabriele d'Annunzio: Poet, Seducer, and Preacher of War". "D'Annunzio's life outside literature suits his biographer, who is not a critic and whose primary intention is to depict the character and personality of her extraordinary subject. Her approach to her task is protean and impressionistic, sometimes pointillist, and generally impatient of conventional chronology. . . . All this is told with an empathy and craftsmanship that d'Annunzio would admire even if he might not appreciate every judgment. . . . The result is a magnificent and beautifully written book that makes readers feel they have really come to know d'Annunzio, his many faults, his fewer virtues, and his enormous talent for life."

REVIEW: *N Y Times Book Rev* p19 S 1 2013 SHERI BERMAN

"Gabriele D'Annunzio: Poet, Seducer, and Preacher of War". "[Lucy Hughes-Hallet's] book . . . is not a standard political biography, not even a standard biography. Consciously or unconsciously echoing the style of d'Annunzio's own autobiography . . . Hughes-Hallett makes 'use of techniques commoner in fiction-writing than in biography,' ignoring chronological order and alternating 'legato narrative with staccato glimpses of the man and fragments of his thought.' In practice, this often means lots of disconnected snippets of information thrown together with little apparent logic or context. . . . Hughes-Hallett spends little time discussing or analyzing actual political events or trends, focusing more on d'Annunzio's admittedly remarkable personal life."

REVIEW: *Natl Rev* v65 no20 p58-9 O 28 2013 DAVID PRYCE-JONES

REVIEW: *New Repub* v244 no22 p42-7 F 17 2014 Jonathan Galassi

"Gabriele D'Annunzio: Poet, Seducer, and Preacher of War". "As she creates her rich, effervescent, astute, involving portrait of the notorious 'poet, seducer, and preacher of war,' Hughes-Hallett spares us the whole ghastly blow-by-blow, focusing instead on representative vignettes while leaving us to understand that there were many more such in her subject's unflagging, jam-packed existence. It is a canny strategy that prevents her reader from sinking under the weight of D'Annunzio's overweening narcissism; it also underlines the unswervingly exterior character of her relentless subject."

REVIEW: *Publ Wkly* v260 no20 p44 My 20 2013

REVIEW: *World Lit Today* v88 no1 p67 Ja/F 2014

HUGHES, ALISON. On a scale of idiot to complete jerk; [by] Alison Hughes 144 p. 2014 Orca Book Publishers

1. Conduct of life—Fiction 2. Human behavior 3. Middle schools 4. School stories 5. Science projects
ISBN 9781459804845 (pbk.); 9781459804852 (electronic edition; 9781459804869 (electronic edition
LC 2013-954114

SUMMARY: In this book by Alison Hughes, "after establishing that jerks existed in prehistory using cave paintings and throughout history using folk tales and children's literature, eighth-grader J.J. Murphy explains the need for a scientific study of jerk-ishness and delineates the methods he'll use. . . . He . . . creates a scale he calls the Jerk-O-Meter, which runs from 'normal' through 'idiot' to 'complete jerk'." (Kirkus Reviews)

REVIEW: *Kirkus Rev* v82 no3 p256 F 1 2014

"On a Scale From Idiot to Complete Jerk". "Can a scientific study explain jerk-ish behavior, and will it earn J.J. a passing grade? . . . Canadian [Alison] Hughes' debut is constructed around the conceit that it is the actual science project that J.J. turns in. Though his voice rings true, the device wears thin quickly. With no through story to sustain it or continuing characters beyond the narrator, it's an occasionally amusing collection of anecdotes. Though it attempts Diary of a Wimpy Kid, it achieves lengthy science report. Skippable."

REVIEW: *Quill Quire* v80 no2 p35 Mr 2014 Cara Smusiak

"On a Scale From Idiot to Complete Jerk". "[A] quirky, funny glimpse into the life and mind of a 13-year-old boy. Structured as a science report written by J.J., 'On a Scale From Idiot to Complete Jerk' presents a narrative about human nature that middle-grade kids will find relatable, humorous, and genuine. . . . His case studies include not-quite-accurate line graphs, made-up pie charts, silly illustrations, unintentionally amusing interview and video transcripts, and recollections of events. . . . In addition to the unorthodox format, what makes this book work is its universal appeal. . . . Author Alison Hughes deserves an A+ for her smart, engaging middle-grade read."

HUGHES, GREGORY. Unhooking the moon; [by] Gregory Hughes 374 p. 2010 Quercus

1. Adventure stories 2. Brothers & sisters—Fiction 3. Father & child—Fiction 4. New York (N.Y.)—Fiction 5. Orphans—Fiction 6. Travelers—Fiction
ISBN 1623650208 (hardcover); 9781623650209 (hardcover)
LC 2010-478376

SUMMARY: In this book, orphans Bob and Marie Claire (aka Rat) travel from Winnipeg to New York City in search of their drug dealer uncle. "For lack of a better plan, they wander Manhattan and the Bronx asking passersby if they know him. This strategy leads to encounters with a host of colorful city types, notably a pair of softhearted con men and a lonely rising rap star." (Kirkus Reviews)

REVIEW: *Booklist* v110 no5 p62 N 1 2013 Michael Cart

REVIEW: *Bull Cent Child Books* v67 no3 p159-60 N 2013 D. S.

REVIEW: *Kirkus Rev* p76 N 15 2013 Best Books

REVIEW: *Kirkus Rev* p47 2013 Guide 20to BookExpo America

REVIEW: *Kirkus Rev* v81 no14 p24 Jl 15 2013

REVIEW: *N Y Times Book Rev* p39 N 10 2013 JOHN FREEMAN GILL

"Unhooking the Moon." "A dark undercurrent runs through this funny novel. . . . Once the pair reach New York, the book loses some of its magic. There are adventures with likable oddballs, but Gotham is not particularized as successfully as Winnipeg, and the result is something of a foreigner's fantasy of New York City. The problem is not just [Gregory] Hughes' occasional factual error . . . but also his reliance on stereotypes. . . . The occasional cartoonishness of the supporting characters is at odds with the very real perils the children confront. At times the novel feels inappropriately jocular for a story that takes on the deeply unamusing subjects of mental illness and child abuse. . . . The denouement is poignantly wrought, concluding on a note . . . of hope and fraternal love."

REVIEW: *Publ Wkly* v260 no35 p60-1 S 2 2013

REVIEW: *Voice of Youth Advocates* v36 no4 p64 O 2013 Nancy Wallace

REVIEW: *Voice of Youth Advocates* v36 no4 p64 O 2013 Mary Kusluch

HUGHES, MARK PETER. Lemonade Mouth puckers up; [by] Mark Peter Hughes 291 p. 2012 Delacorte Press

1. Bands (Music)—Juvenile fiction 2. Friendship—Fiction 3. High schools—Juvenile fiction 4. School stories 5. Young adult fiction
ISBN 0385737122; 9780385737128
LC 2012-289044

SUMMARY: In this young adult novel, by Mark Peter Hughes, "Olivia, Wen, Stella, Charlie, and Mo . . . [are] the members of the legendary band Lemonade Mouth. . . . But just how did this little group . . . end up rocketing from high school nobodies to household names? In their own words, the band tells the story of the momentous summer . . . [which] launched them on their roller-coaster ride to destiny." (Publisher's note)

REVIEW: *SLJ* v58 no12 p118-9 D 2012 Melissa Stock

REVIEW: *Voice of Youth Advocates* v35 no6 p564 F 2013 Lisa Martincik

"Lemonade Mouth Puckers Up." "After forming a surprisingly successful band and inspiring their fellow students at Opequonsett High School, the five quirky members of Lemonade Mouth are . . . scouted at a local concert by a major talent agent. . . . Different characters narrate each chapter, sometimes in a different font, and this continues to work well at providing different viewpoints and creating natural transitions in time. The band . . . has to remember what they value as, again and again, each chance at success comes with a concession to their message of being true to self over the images imposed by others."

HUGHES, SHIRLEY, 1927-. Hero on a bicycle; [by] Shirley Hughes 224 p. 2013 Candlewick Press

1. Families—Fiction 2. Florence (Italy)—History—Siege, 1944 3. Historical fiction 4. World War, 1939-1945—Italy—Fiction 5. World War, 1939-1945—Underground movements
ISBN 076366037X; 9780763660376
LC 2012-943650

SUMMARY: This book is set in Italy during World War II. "The narrative focuses on a city under German occupation, events being perceived principally through the eyes of three members of the Crivelli family: teenager Paolo, his older sister Constanza and Rosemary, their English-born mother. . . . When an opportunity arises for Paolo, Constanza and Rosemary to lend their practical support to the Partisan cause Paolo, in particular, seizes it enthusiastically." (School Librarian)

REVIEW: *Booklist* v109 no16 p67 Ap 15 2013 Kathleen Isaacs

REVIEW: *Booklist* v110 no14 p87 Mr 15 2014 Sharon Hrycewicz

REVIEW: *Bull Cent Child Books* v66 no9 p422 My 2013 E. B.

REVIEW: *Horn Book Magazine* v89 no2 p105-7 Mr/Ap 2013 ROGER SUTTON

REVIEW: *Kirkus Rev* p77 N 15 2013 Best Books

REVIEW: *Kirkus Rev* v81 no3 p232 F 1 2013

REVIEW: *N Y Times Book Rev* p25 My 12 2013 MONICA EDINGER

"Hero on a Bicycle." "Those . . . who find the excitement and anguish of World War II especially fascinating, along with others who enjoy a gripping wartime tale whatever the time period, are going to relish Shirley Hughes's realistic adventure. . . . Vividly evoking the closing-in conflict, with tanks rumbling along a nearby road, zooming fighter planes and relentless shellfire, Hughes ratchets up the tension. . . . Sensitively, she moves readers into the heads and hearts of the three family members. . . . Huge as the war is, this story is an intimate one."

REVIEW: *Publ Wkly* v260 no9 p70 Mr 4 2013

REVIEW: *Publ Wkly* p88-90 Children's starred review annual 2013

REVIEW: *SLJ* v59 no4 p164 Ap 2013 Renee Steinberg

REVIEW: *SLJ* v59 no9 p69 S 2013 Chani Craig

REVIEW: *Voice of Youth Advocates* v36 no2 p60 Je 2013 Nancy Pierce

HUGHES, WILLIAM.ed. The encyclopedia of the gothic. See The encyclopedia of the gothic

HUMAN WORK PRODUCTIVITY; a global perspective; xiv, 239 p. 2014 CRC Press

1. Business literature 2. Ergonomics 3. Human engineering 4. Industrial management 5. Labor productivity
ISBN 9781439874141 (hardback)
LC 2013-026058

SUMMARY: "This book examines how ergonomic improvements for the human operator and/or redesign and rearrangement of the workplace can boost individual productivity. It also covers the impact of the aging workforce, reports on an investigation of total productive maintenance, and considers the efficacy of workplace design from a maintenance perspective." Other topics include "work hours and their effect on productivity, the impact of technology, and productivity in a health care organization." (Publisher's note)

REVIEW: *Choice* v51 no8 p1452 Ap 2014 G. E. Kaupins

"Human Work Productivity: A Global Perspective". "A unique volume examining various aspects of industrial and manufacturing practices as they relate to human workplace productivity and international competitiveness. . . . Researchers from mostly Europe and North America contribute 10 academically oriented articles using considerable survey data. . . . These diverse articles also consider other factors that may affect work productivity, including education and population trends. . . . Recommended."

HUMANS AND THE ENVIRONMENT; new archaeological perspectives for the twenty-first century; 2013 Oxford University Press
ISBN 9780199590292

SUMMARY: This book, edited by Matthew I. J. Davies and Freda Nkirote M'Mbogori, "resituates the way in which archaeologists use and apply the concept of the environment. Each chapter critically explores the potential for archaeological data and practice to contribute to modern environmental issues, including problems of climate change and environmental degradation." (Publisher's note)

REVIEW: *Choice* v51 no8 p1449 Ap 2014 L. L. Johnson

"Humans and the Environment: New Archaeological Perspectives for the 21st Century". "The majority of the chapters that follow are aspirational: one can see through history and archaeology how past peoples succeeded in maintaining themselves sustainably; people today need to use this information to inform the future. . . . Much of the volume comes across as dated to an American anthropological archaeologist, because scholars trained only in archaeology find the idea of humans in nature rather than humans and nature new and somewhat difficult to encompass. The photos are not well reproduced, which is surprising in a volume at this price. Nevertheless, there is much of interest here for libraries."

HUNEVEN, MICHELLE. Off course; a novel; [by] Michelle Huneven 304 p. 2014 Sarah Crichton Books, Farrar, Straus and Giroux

1. American fiction 2. Doctoral students—Fiction 3. Man-woman relationships—Fiction 4. Mountain life—Fiction 5. Single women—Fiction
ISBN 0374224471; 9780374224479 (hardback)
LC 2013-036858

SUMMARY: In this novel, by Michelle Huneven, "Cressida Hartley, a gifted Ph.D. student in economics, moves into her parents' shabby A-frame cabin in the Sierras to write her dissertation. . . . Cress, increasingly resistant to her topic (art in the marketplace), allows herself to be drawn into the social life of the small mountain community. . . . As Cress tells her best friend back home in Pasadena, being a single woman on the mountain amounts to a form of public service." (Publisher's note)

REVIEW: *Booklist* v110 no13 p19 Mr 1 2014 Julie Trevelyan

REVIEW: *Kirkus Rev* v82 no3 p306 F 1 2014

REVIEW: *Libr J* v138 no18 p68 N 1 2013 Barbara Hoffert

REVIEW: *N Y Times Book Rev* p20 My 25 2014 NAOMI FRY

REVIEW: *New Yorker* v90 no9 p105-1 Ap 21 2014

"Off Course." "Any novel that has a bear and casual sex in the first chapter has to pay off somehow, and this one, [author Michelle] Huneven's fourth, is full of surprises. Cressida Hartley, with an economics dissertation to write, holes up in her parents' home high in California's Southern Sierra, and gets distracted by the locals. . . . Huneven's touch is sure, and her protagonist is simultaneously sympathetic and maddening. The landscape descriptions are erotic, and the erotic scenes have near-hallucinatory power."

REVIEW: *Publ Wkly* v260 no45 p45 N 11 2013

HUNSICKER, HARRY. The contractors; a thriller; [by] Harry Hunsicker 510 p. 2014 Thomas & Mercer

1. Detective & mystery stories 2. Drug traffic—Fiction 3. Government agencies—Contracting out 4. United States. Dept. of Homeland Security

ISBN 1477808728 (pbk.); 9781477808726 (pbk.)

LC 2013-906585

SUMMARY: In this thriller novel, by Harry Hunsicker, "Jon Cantrell, a disgraced ex-cop, works . . . [as] a DEA agent paid on a commission basis, patrolling . . . Dallas, Texas. . . . Cantrell and his partner . . . find themselves in possession of a star witness in an upcoming cartel trial that could destroy the largest criminal organization in the hemisphere. . . . All they have to do is safely deliver the witness to the US Attorney on the other side of the state." (Publisher's note)

REVIEW: *Booklist* v110 no9/10 p48 Ja 1 2014 Don Crinklaw

REVIEW: *Kirkus Rev* v82 no4 p287 F 15 2014

"The Contractors". "Veteran mystery writer [Harry] Hunsicker . . . turns in an ever-so-timely tale of mayhem and murder set on familiar Texas turf. . . . Hunsicker does good and useful work in sneaking a conversation about the international line into a whodunit. On the face of it, that story seems full of promise for disappointment: It's got dishy dames, rogue government types, crooked politicos and all the usual makings of the usual procedural. But Hunsicker adds contemporary twists that enrich the story, some of them subtle, others not so much."

REVIEW: *Publ Wkly* v260 no49 p64 D 2 2013

HUNT, BILL. Look Away, Look Away; Dixieland Short Stories of a Peculiar Nature; [by] Bill Hunt 196 p. 2013 CreateSpace Independent Publishing Platform

1. American short stories 2. Families—Fiction 3. Physician & patient 4. Recluses—Fiction 5. Southern States—Fiction

ISBN 1490423907; 9781490423906

SUMMARY: This book by Bill Hunt presents a "collection of short stories set in the American South. . . . The opening story, about an aging mixed-race hermit and her riches, as told to a rookie Latino reporter, sits alongside a doctor's account of an eerily intimate exchange with his new patient; the story of a family squatting and stealing to get by; and the tale of an uncultured Alabama father begrudgingly accompanying his wife and daughter on a trip to Europe." (Kirkus Reviews)

REVIEW: *Kirkus Rev* v82 no1 p306 Ja 1 2014

"Look Away, Look Away". "A playful collection of short stories set in the American South and featuring plenty of local color and family drama. . . . These stories range in tone from unsettling to nearly devastating, but they occasionally offer a glimmer of hope. With such ambitious scope, however, they sometimes fall short of their attempted depth, with subtleties often obscured by awkward prose and half-formed ideas. . . Readers may find some of the forced, stereotypical speech patterns uncomfortable at times. . . . However, the author's critique of social hierarchy is ultimately the book's engine, and although the collection may be a bit spotty, his picture of a complex society fully emerges by the end. A well-intentioned but inconsistent smorgasbord of Southern vignettes."

HUNT, JAMES PATRICK. The detective; [by] James Patrick Hunt 2014 Five star, A part of Gale, Cengage Learning

1. Detective and mystery stories 2. Holocaust survivors—Fiction 3. Jews—Crimes against 4. Murder—Investigation—Fiction 5. Police—Fiction

ISBN 1432828088 (hardcover); 9781432828080 (hardback)

LC 2013-040922

SUMMARY: In this book by James Patrick Hunt, "five dead bodies are sprawled on a subway platform.The two investigating detectives are introduced. They're not fond of each other. . . . One victim is Jewish, so the cops are off to interview a Nazi. . . . It's here that the story pauses for a discussion.Was Charles Manson like Hitler? Further on we get a biography of a Polish death-camp survivor." (Booklist)

REVIEW: *Booklist* v110 no9/10 p51 Ja 1 2014 Don Crinklaw

"The Detective." "This superb novel sets its stage expertly, in a couple of paragraphs. . . . It's okay to wonder, what the heck? but don't stop reading--this is scaffolding for the working out of a murder scheme as touching as it is sinister. The glitzy stuff is here: cocaine and gorgeous hookers, machine pistols and satchels of big bills. The detective work is a brilliant mix of plodding and intuition. One tiny out-of-place gesture, noticed and remembered, keeps the detectives asking questions after officialdom has decide-- wrongly--that the case is closed. That happens sometimes. Fine writing and storytelling."

REVIEW: *Kirkus Rev* v82 no6 p24 Mr 15 2014

HUNT, JONATHAN.tr. Time on my hands. See Vasta, G.

HUNT, LYNDA MULLALY. One for the Murphys; [by] Lynda Mullaly Hunt 224 p. 2012 Nancy Paulsen Books

1. Domestic fiction 2. Family life—Connecticut—Fiction 3. Family problems—Fiction 4. Foster home care—Fiction 5. JUVENILE FICTION—Family—Orphans & Foster Homes 6. JUVENILE FICTION—Family—Parents 7. JUVENILE FICTION—Social Issues—Self-Esteem & Self-Reliance 8. Mothers and daughters—Fiction 9. Stepfathers—Fiction

ISBN 0399256156; 9780399256158 (hardback)

LC 2011-046708

SUMMARY: This book by Lynda Mullaly Hunt follows "eighth-grader Carley Connors [as she] learns about a different kind of family life, first resisting and then resisting having to leave the loving, loyal Murphys. . . . She's torn between her love for her mother and her memory of the fight that sent her to the hospital, when her mother caught and held her for her stepfather. Slowly won over at home . . . Carley also finds a friend at school in the prickly, Wicked-obsessed Toni." (Kirkus Reviews)

REVIEW: *Booklist* v108 no18 p56 My 15 2012 Ann Kelley

REVIEW: *Horn Book Magazine* v88 no4 p117 Jl/Ag 2012 Rebecca Kirshenbaum

"One For the Murphys." "[Lynda Mullaly] Hunt successfully creates a portrait of a young girl's emerging understanding of the complexities of family and the awareness that loyalty is not the same as ignoring your own wants and needs. Carley's struggles with anger, regret, and self-worth both balance and deepen this coming-of-age tale. The novel speaks to the universal experience of growing up but will especially resonate with readers who have questioned the hands they have been dealt and wonder how to move forward nonetheless. Hunt's novel vacillates between uplifting and heartbreaking as Carley learns to love, be loved, and let go."

REVIEW: *Kirkus Rev* v80 no8 p100 Ap 15 2012

"One for the Murphys." " Sent to a foster home after a beating from her stepfather, eighth-grader Carley Connors learns about a different kind of family life, first resisting and then resisting having to leave the loving, loyal Murphys. Carley is a modern-day Gilly Hopkins, bright and strong, angry and deeply hurt. She's torn between her love for her mother and her memory of the fight that sent her to the hospital, when her mother caught and held her for her stepfather. . . . There's plenty of snappy dialogue as well. By the end of this poignant debut, readers will be applauding Carley's strength even if they're as unhappy as Carley is about the resolution. A worthy addition to the foster-family shelf."

REVIEW: *Publ Wkly* v259 no11 p61 Mr 12 2012

REVIEW: *SLJ* v58 no6 p124 Je 2012 Carol A. Edwards

REVIEW: *Voice of Youth Advocates* v35 no3 p262 Ag 2012 Maria K. Unruh

REVIEW: *Voice of Youth Advocates* v35 no3 p262 Ag 2012 Amber Brown

HUNTER, NICK. How carbon footprints work; [by] Nick Hunter 32 p. 2014 Gareth Stevens Publishing

1. Children's nonfiction 2. Ecological impact 3. Energy conservation—Juvenile literature 4. Environmental protection—Juvenile literature 5. Sustainable living—Juvenile literature

ISBN 1433995522 (library binding); 1433995530 (paperback); 9781433995521 (library binding); 9781433995538 (paperback)

LC 2012-277824

SUMMARY: This book, by Nick Hunter, explains "what exactly is a carbon footprint. . . . Content . . . takes on climate change, vehicle emissions, and wasting electricity. Practical solutions to reducing readers' carbon footprints compliment social studies and science information that augment what they encounter in the classroom." (Publisher's note)

REVIEW: *Booklist* v110 no12 p77-8 F 15 2014 Ilene Cooper

"How Carbon Footprints Work." "This title from the Eco Works series gives kids a good understanding of the term, but more importantly, it shows how each individual's carbon footprint affects the environment. . . . Controversial questions aren't avoided: 'What's the point of reducing your carbon footprint if more than 1 billion people in China are increasing their carbon dioxide emissions?' Illustrated with stock color photos, the text is occasionally broken up by 'Eco Facts' and other sidebars. A thought-provoking overview, and the good back matter will lead kids to more."

HUNTINGTON, SHEILA. Morning Glory Woman; [by] Sheila Huntington 284 p. 2013 CreateSpace Independent Publishing Platform

1. Classical antiquities thefts 2. Detective & mystery stories 3. Intelligence service—Fiction 4. Murder—Fiction 5. Organized crime—Fiction

ISBN 149225455X; 9781492254553

SUMMARY: In this book, "Professor Papandrou, a revered Greek archaeological professor, has been murdered, and a priceless 40,000-year-old Nemhi figurine has been stolen. The Athens Police ask the CIA for help and agents Matt Chaney and Leeza Findlay are assigned to the case. They uncover a worldwide crime organization named ARES, larger and more malevolent than the Mafia." (Publisher's note)

REVIEW: *Kirkus Rev* v81 no24 p397 D 15 2013

"Morning Glory Woman". "[Sheila] Huntington exuberantly fuses these elements into a subtle, shimmering mystery, often offering readers dazzling opulence. . . . The characters, meanwhile, are mostly well-drawn, red-blooded men and women who hold their torrid longings in check. . . . (However, one minor character refers to homosexuality as 'deviant,' which may offend some readers.) The villains are entertainingly bombastic, as well; in a flashback, Longhren says, 'No jail will hold me, and no matter how long it takes, I'll make you sorry you ever met me!' An often engaging romantic thriller."

HUNTLEY, HORACE.ed. Black workers' struggle for equality in Birmingham. See Black workers' struggle for equality in Birmingham

HURD, DOUGLAS, 1930-. Disraeli; Or, the Two Lives; [by] Douglas Hurd 320 p. 2013 Weidenfeld & Nicolson

1. Biography (Literary form) 2. Great Britain—History—Victoria, 1837-1901 3. Great Britain—Politics & government—1837-1901 4. Jewish politicians 5. Prime ministers—Great Britain—Biography

ISBN 0297860976; 9780297860976

SUMMARY: In this book, "Douglas Hurd and Edward Young explore the paradoxes at the centre of [Benjamin] Disraeli's 'two lives': a dandy and gambler on the one hand, a devoted servant and favourite Prime Minister of the Queen on the other. A passionately ambitious politician, he intrigued and manoeuvred with unmatched skill to get to--in his own words--'the top of the greasy pole,' but he also developed a set of ideas to which he was devoted." (Publisher's note)

REVIEW: *London Rev Books* v35 no23 p34-6 D 5 2013 John Pemble

"Disraeli: Or, the Two Lives," "The Great Rivalry: Gladstone and Disraeli," and "Disraeli; The Romance of Politics". "Douglas Hurd and Edward Young's 'Disraeli;or, the Two Lives,' and Robert O'Kell's 'Disraeli: The Romance of Politics' diverge when they come to [Benjamin] Disraeli's Byronism. Hurd and Young wave it aside. . . . O'Kell's interpretation is fundamentally different. . . . O'Kell pushes his argument too far by reading Byronic 'psychological romance' into virtually everything Disraeli wrote. . . . Dick Leonard's 'The Great Rivalry' . . . uses the old compare and contrast formula, hopping between the two protagonists, but updating the story with the recent work of Colin Matthew, Roy Jenkins, Richard Shannon, John Vincent, Sarah Bradford and Stanley Weintraub. Essentially it's drybones parliamentary history . . . and its verdict on the falling out hardly deepens our understanding."

REVIEW: *New Statesman* v142 no5167 p40 Jl 19 2013 Michael Prodger

REVIEW: *TLS* no5768 p10 O 18 2013 ROBERT SAUNDERS

"The Great Rivalry: Gladstone and Disraeli: A Dual Biography" and "Disraeli: Or the Two Lives." "[Dick] Leonard's dual biography is essentially a distillation of older, more authoritative studies, and offers very little that is new. There are so many quotations from previous writers that the early chapters, in particular, feel like the literary equivalent of a mix tape. . . . [Douglas] Hurd and [Edward] Young have a clearer sense of purpose and a stronger controlling argument. They present their biography of [Benjamin] Disraeli as a myth-busting exercise, intended to strip away the inflated claims made for Disraeli as a One Nation Conservative and a 'Tory Democrat'. . . . The result is a respectable and competent survey, but one that is unlikely to displace the competition."

HURLEY, DAN. Smarter; The New Science of Building Brain Power; [by] Dan Hurley 304 p. 2013 Penguin Group USA

1. Brain—Research 2. Fluid intelligence 3. Medical technology 4. Mental efficiency 5. Scientific literature
ISBN 1594631271; 9781594631276

SUMMARY: In this "account of the young science of brain training," author Dan Hurley "examines the research, describes heated debates at major science meetings, and chronicles his use of what he considers the most credible cognitive interventions to see whether he can improve his own intelligence. . . . After three and a half months of training, for two to three hours daily, tests show his fluid intelligence increased by 16 percent." (Kirkus Reviews)

REVIEW: *Kirkus Rev* v81 no24 p228 D 15 2013

"Smarter: The New Science of Building Brain Power". "In this conversational book, [Dan] Hurley examines the research, describes heated debates at major science meetings, and chronicles his use of what he considers the most credible cognitive interventions to see whether he can improve his own intelligence. . . . After three and a half months of training, for two to three hours daily, tests show his fluid intelligence increased by 16 percent. A highly accessible report on cutting-edge science with practical tips for readers bent on boosting their own intelligence."

REVIEW: *N Y Times Book Rev* p19 Mr 23 2014 ANNIE MURPHY PAUL

"Smarter: The New Science of Building Brain Power." "Like the early advocates of physical exercise, [author Dan] Hurley has a tough sell. The mental exercises recommended by the researchers he interviews are at once numbingly boring and exasperatingly difficult. . . . Hurley's book feels premature, like the crowning of a winner in a race that's only just begun. Its author may declare himself satisfied with the evidence generated so far, but the rest of us will need to see more proof that these exercises, unpleasant as they sound, have meaningful effects on the outcomes we care about: doing better at school and at work, remembering more accurately, solving problems more effectively."

REVIEW: *New Sci* v221 no2958 p52-3 Mr 1 2014 Kate Douglas

HURLEY, TONYA. Passionaries; [by] Tonya Hurley 368 p. 2014 Simon & Schuster Books for Young Readers

1. Conduct of life—Fiction 2. Good and evil—Fiction 3. Saints—Fiction 4. Speculative fiction
ISBN 9781442429543 (hardcover); 9781442429550 (pbk.)
LC 2013-019654

SUMMARY. "This second installment in [Tonya] Hurley's supernatural Catholic-themed trilogy finds three teens who have been reincarnated as saints grieving separately over the loss of their surprisingly shared beloved, Sebastian. There's Cecilia, the gritty musician; Lucy, the socialite; and Agnes, the good girl. The teens are dealing with the fame and notoriety of possibly being reincarnated martyred saints, when they learn that someone has stolen Sebastian's heart." (School Library Journal)

REVIEW: *Booklist* v110 no11 p64-5 F 1 2014 Ilene Cooper

"Passionaries." "Book two of the Blessed series follows the girls, now on their own, as they try to figure out their relevance, protect themselves, and keep their faith in Sebastian strong. This gory offering is no simple bridge book in a trilogy. There are professions of faith, horrifying murders, and the continuing mystery of their mission. [Tonya] Hurley, also author of the Ghostgirl series, has taken on a huge job, but for the most part, she handles her multinarrated saga well--though at times it seems as if no one will be left alive. The ending is particularly disturbing, but those who have made it this far through the grit, death, and incense will await the redemption of the final chapter."

REVIEW: *Kirkus Rev* v81 no23 p100 D 1 2013

REVIEW: *SLJ* v60 no2 p106 F 2014 Danielle Serra

HURTEAU, ROBERT. A worldwide heart; the life of Maryknoll Father John J. Considine; [by] Robert Hurteau xxxvi, 308 p. 2013 Orbis Books

1. Biography (Literary form) 2. Catholic press 3. Missiologists—United States—Biography
ISBN 9781626980211 (pbk.)
LC 2012-049629

SUMMARY: This book presents a biography of "John J. Considine, MM (1897-1982) . . . [who] was one of the leading figures in Catholic mission in the twentieth century this despite his never having served in an overseas mission assignment. From the time of his entry in 1915 into the Maryknoll Fathers and Brothers until his retirement in the mid-1970s, Considine was a tireless researcher, promoter, organizer of Catholic missions and their support institutions." (Publisher's note)

REVIEW: *America* v210 no3 p42-3 F 3 2014 THOMAS J. SHELLEY

"A Worldwide Heart: The Life of Maryknoll Father John J. Considine." "Although [Robert] Hurteau's sympathies are with Considine, he is scrupulously fair in judging the motives and assessing the achievements of both men. . . .. It is a welcome and much needed addition to the corpus of works on the American Catholic foreign missions. It must be admitted, however, that the wide range of Considine's interests and activities present a daunting challenge for even the most seasoned biographer to achieve a satisfying synthesis of his life and work."

HURWITZ, MICHELE WEBER. The summer I saved the world— in 65 days; [by] Michele Weber Hurwitz 272 p. 2014 Wendy Lamb Books, an imprint of Random House Children's Books

1. Conduct of life—Fiction 2. Family life—Illinois—Fiction 3. Friendship—Fiction 4. Helpfulness—Fiction 5. Neighbors—Fiction 6. Psychological fiction
ISBN 0385371063; 9780385371063 (trade); 9780385371070 (lib. bdg.); 9780385371094 (pbk.)
LC 2013-016843

SUMMARY: In this book, by Michele Weber Hurwitz, "thirteen-year-old Nina Ross is feeling kind of lost. . . . This summer, Nina decides to change things. She hatches a plan. There are sixty-five days of summer. Every day, she'll anonymously do one small but remarkable good thing for someone in her neighborhood, and find out: does doing good actually make a difference? Along the way, she discovers that her neighborhood, and her family, are full of surprises and secrets." (Publisher's note)

REVIEW: *Booklist* v110 no14 p80 Mr 15 2014 Magan Szwarek

REVIEW: *Bull Cent Child Books* v67 no9 p459-60 My 2014 D. S.

REVIEW: *Kirkus Rev* v82 no4 p163 F 15 2014

"The Summer I Saved the World...In 65 Days". "What happens when a teenage girl tries to change the world in 65 tiny ways? . . . Nina plans to perform 65 small, anonymous acts of kindness for her family and neighbors-one for each day of her summer. . . . Teens will easily ally with the kind-hearted, insecure Nina and be charmed by the humor and beautifully defined characters. The unpredictable domino effect of Nina's good deeds is a joy to behold. Joyful dividends are reaped from a teenager's secret acts of kindness in this appealingly, unabashedly feel-good story."

REVIEW: *Publ Wkly* v261 no4 p193-4 Ja 27 2014

REVIEW: *Voice of Youth Advocates* v37 no1 p67 Ap 2014 Barbara Johnston

HUSSAIN, MUZAMMIL M. Democracy's fourth wave? See Howard, P. N.

HUSSLEIN-ARCO, AGNES.ed. Orient & Occident. See Orient & Occident

HUSTAD, MEGAN. More than conquerors; a memoir of lost arguments; [by] Megan Hustad 240 p. 2014 Farrar, Straus and Giroux

1. BIOGRAPHY & AUTOBIOGRAPHY—Personal Memoirs 2. BIOGRAPHY & AUTOBIOGRAPHY—Religious 3. Children of missionaries—United States—Biography 4. Evangelicalism—Social aspects—United States 5. Evangelicalism—United States—Psychological aspects 6. Families—Religious life—United States—Case studies 7. Memoirs 8. Religion and social status—United States—Case studies 9. Social conflict—United States—Case studies
ISBN 9780374298838 (hardback)
LC 2013-038713

SUMMARY: In this book, "a daughter of evangelical missionaries reflects on the complexities of faith. [Megan] Hustad . . . was born in Minneapolis. . . . But her parents felt a religious calling, and soon, young Megan and her sister, Amy, were transported to the Caribbean island of Bonaire. . . . Escaping to New York City as soon as she could, Megan met people 'who associated religious belief with rank stupidity' . . . leading her to reconsider her own complicated connections to faith." (Kirkus Reviews)

REVIEW: *Bookforum* v20 no5 p42 F/Mr 2014 ANN NEUMANN

"More Than Conquerors:A Memoir of Lost Arguments." "[A] beautiful but ultimately unsatisfying new memoir: . . . In pieces, the book captures [Megan] Hustad's childhood and eventual falling away from her faith and her parents. . . . Along the way, 'More than Conquerors' attempts to make the case that the girls are disadvantaged by the legacy of their parents' faith. Thrift-store clothing, 'un-American teeth,' a 'peculiar accent,' and a Christian past are, we learn, their plight. . . . Hustad acknowledges that her actions and words are conflicting, but she never spells out just what that conflict means. The most important thing Hustad has going for her is that she can write. 'More Than Conquerors' is embroidered with gorgeous sentences."

REVIEW: *Booklist* v110 no11 p3-4 F 1 2014 Bridget Thoreson

REVIEW: *Kirkus Rev* v81 no23 p176 D 1 2013

REVIEW: *N Y Times Book Rev* p15 Mr 23 2014 JUSTIN ST. GERMAIN

"More Than Conquerors." "Early in 'More Than Conquerors,' a memoir of her family's life as Christian missionaries, Megan Hustad anticipates her readers' expectations. With a wry frankness typical of the book, she writes: 'This is not a story of judgmental zealots thumping pulpits. . . . This is not a story about pious blowhards whose unbending conviction alienated their children forever.' . . . At times, the book digresses and loses momentum. Letters and conversations appear in full; footnotes, lists, and quotations from Scripture and other sources abound. . . . But those are flaws of ambition, and 'More Than Conquerors' achieves far more than it fails to. Hustad has written a generous and arresting account of an upbringing that might have turned a lesser writer bitter."

REVIEW: *Publ Wkly* v260 no52 p48 D 23 2013

HUSTVEDT, SIRI. The blazing world; [by] Siri Hustvedt 368 p. 2014 Simon & Schuster

1. Death—Fiction 2. Psychological fiction 3. Sexism 4. Teachers—Fiction 5. Women artists—Fiction
ISBN 1476747237; 9781476747231 (hardback); 9781476747248 (paperback)
LC 2013-027172

SUMMARY: This novel by Siri Hustvedt presents a "purported collection of writings by and about an enigmatic artist, Harriet Burden, the tall, strong, erudite widow of a famous and secretive art dealer. Long enraged over the dismissive response to her work, Harriet launches a high-stakes gambit to expose the art world's persistent sexism. She convinces three male artists to pose as the creators of a sequence of her elaborate, allusive, and wildly provocative installations." (Booklist)

REVIEW: *Booklist* v110 no12 p23 F 15 2014 Donna Seaman

"The Blazing World". "[Siri] Hustvedt's . . . fascination with art and artists, a prime subject in her fiction and essays, propels her sixth novel through a labyrinth of masquerade and betrayal to profoundly unsettling truths. . . . Hustvedt subtly explores the intricate workings of the brain and the mysteries of the mind as she shrewdly investigates gender differences, parodies art criticism, and contrasts diabolical ambition and the soul-scouring inquiries of expressive art. A heady, suspenseful, funny, and wrenching novel of creativity, identity, and longing."

REVIEW: *Kirkus Rev* v81 no24 p234 D 15 2013

"The Blazing World". "As the story of Harry's life coheres—assembled from her notebooks, various pieces of journalism, and interviews with her children, the three male artists and other art-world denizens—it's the emotional content that seizes the reader. . . . [Siri] Hustvedt paints a scathing portrait of the art world, obsessed with money and the latest trend, but superb descriptions of Harry's work—installations expressing her turbulence and neediness—remind us that the beauty and power of art transcend such trivialities. . . . Blazing indeed: not just with Harry's fury, but with agonizing compassion for all of wounded humanity."

REVIEW: *N Y Times Book Rev* p1-20 Mr 30 2014 Fernanda Eberstadt

REVIEW: *N Y Times Book Rev* p32 Ap 6 2014

REVIEW: *New Yorker* v90 no17 p85-1 Je 23 2014

REVIEW: *Publ Wkly* v260 no51 p38 D 16 2013

REVIEW: *TLS* no5792 p19 Ap 4 2014 LIDIJA HAAS

"The Blazing World." "[Author Siri] Hustvedt frequently gives her interests and her reading on these subjects to characters in her fiction, but in her latest novel. 'The Blazing World,' they are more than themes—they structure the whole book, serving as plot and propulsive force. The novel is presented as an anthology, assembled by the fictional scholar I. V. Hess, of writing by and about an artist pointedly named Harriet Burden, who has achieved success only several years after her death, and whose work is still the subject of great dispute. . . . Still more obviously here than in her previous work, Hustvedt is a novelist of ideas, but one who routinely makes the case for not dividing them from feeling."

HUTCHINSON, BEN.ed. A literature of restitution . See A literature of restitution

HUTCHINSON, GEORGE.ed. American cocktail. See Miller, H.

HUTH, JOHN EDWARD. The lost art of finding our way; [by] John Edward Huth 544 p. 2013 The Belknap Press of Harvard University Press

1. Historical literature 2. Nautical astronomy 3. Naval art and science—History 4. Navigation—History 5. Wayfinding

ISBN 9780674072824 (alk. paper)

LC 2012-044083

SUMMARY: This book by John Edward Huth "offers a . . . short course in navigation that draws on Earth science, history, anthropology, neuroscience, archaeology, and linguistics. It provides both a primer on navigational techniques and a tour through 'the historical evolution of way finding.' Huth punctuates instruction on celestial navigation and reading wind, weather, and currents with . . . stories and images." (Science)

REVIEW: *Science* v341 no6146 p615 Ag 9 2013 Deirdre Lockwood

REVIEW: *TLS* no5768 p25 O 18 2013 CLAUDIO VITA-FINZI

"The Lost Art of Finding Our Way." "Much of 'The Lost Art of Finding Our Way' amounts to a manual of navigational aspects of astronomy, physical oceanography and climatology, and of the rudiments of boat design and handling, devised for an audience of ignorant but willing humans. . . . All of this is conveyed in fluent prose which wafts the reader painlessly over some nasty technical reefs. . . . How many readers of [John Edward] Huth's tract will respond to his message? Many will view traditional modes of navigation as they might to alternative medicine or manual typesetting. . . . Others will sympathize in recognition of the bond between the organic and inorganic worlds represented by intuitive voyaging."

HUTNER, GORDON.ed. Selected speeches and writings of Theodore Roosevelt. See Selected speeches and writings of Theodore Roosevelt

HYUN, JANE. Flex; the new playbook for managing across differences; [by] Jane Hyun 336 p. 2013 HarperBusiness

1. Business communication 2. Business literature 3. Diversity in the workplace—Management 4. Leadership 5. Management—Cross-cultural studies

ISBN 0062248529; 9780062248527 (hardback)

LC 2013-033052

SUMMARY: In this book, Jane Hyun and Audrey S. Lee "examine how 'infusing cultural proficiency initiatives into company-wide values, policies and programs achieves a demonstrable effect.' The authors report that the workforce is changing, growing more multicultural, younger and more female. These changes call for a much more nuanced response from corporate leaders to avoid pitfalls and achieve success." (Kirkus Reviews)

REVIEW: *Kirkus Rev* v82 no4 p96 F 15 2014

"Flex: The New Playbook for Managing Across Differences". "The authors seek to show readers how to reduce losses of time and resources incurred when the potential contributions of well-qualified recruits or hires are lost because management doesn't fully understand how to bring them on board. They discuss many ways of overcoming the business consequences of such failures to flex across the gap. '[O]ur experience has taught us that interpersonal dynamics can change when people with a drive for making a difference take the initiative and then influence others to multiply the effect,' they write. [Jane] Hyun and [Audrey S.] Lee offer convincing evidence to illustrate how to enhance communication skills across various workplace divides."

REVIEW: *Libr J* v139 no3 p116 F 15 2014 John Rodzvilla

REVIEW: *Publ Wkly* v261 no2 p63-4 Ja 13 2014

I

I LESSICI A PLATONE DI TIMEO SOFISTA E PSEUDO-DIDIMO; Introduzione ed edizione critica; 2012 DeGruyter

1. Ancient philosophy 2. Dialogues (Book : Plato) 3. Indexes 4. Philosophical literature 5. Timaeus (Book : Plato)

ISBN 9783110240801 hardcover

SUMMARY: "Two lexica to Plato have survived from Antiquity: the epitome of Timaeus and the so-called Pseudo-Didymus." Edited by Stefano Valente, "This is the first critical edition of these lexica relying on a complete survey of their textual traditions . . . , which are investigated in the Italian prefaces; it is also provided with an up-to-date picture of Timaeus, with an extensive inquiry into his sources and with an analysis of the mutual relationships between the two works." (Publisher's note)

REVIEW: *Classical Rev* v63 no2 p398-400 O 2013 A.R. Das

"I lessici a Platone di Timeo Sofista e Pseudo-Didimo." "This book provides a new edition of the Platonic lexica of 'Timaeus the Sophist' and 'pseudo-Didymus,' the only works of this kind extant from antiquity. . . . In spite of the uncertain relationship between the two texts, [editor Stefano Valente] identifies a number of important connections in his detailed introduction. Here, the lexica of 'Timaeus' and 'pseudo-Didymus' are presented together for the first time. . . . For those unfamiliar with ancient lexicography, [Valente's] volume may pose certain challenges, as he does not give information about the date and textual state of several of the sources he mentions."

IBATOULLINE, BAGRAM.il. The Snow Queen. See Andersen, H. C.

IBBOTSON, EVA. The abominables; [by] Eva Ibbotson 272 p. 2013 Harry N. Abrams

1. JUVENILE FICTION—Fantasy & Magic 2. JUVENILE FICTION—General 3. JUVENILE FICTION—Humorous Stories 4. Voyages and travels—Fiction 5. Yeti—Fiction
ISBN 1419707892; 9781419707896 (hardback)
LC 2013-005159

SUMMARY: This book, by Eva Ibbotson and illustrated by Fiona Robinson, "follows a family of yetis who are forced, by tourism, to leave their home in the Himalayas and make their way across Europe. Siblings Con and Ellen shepherd the yetis along their eventful journey, with the help of Perry, a good-natured truck driver. The yetis at last find their way to an ancestral estate in England--only to come upon . . . hunters who have set their sights on the most exotic prey of . . . Abominable Snowmen." (Publisher's note)

REVIEW: *Booklist* v110 no18 p60 My 15 2014

REVIEW: *Booklist* v110 no2 p65 S 15 2013 Carolyn Phelan

REVIEW: *Bull Cent Child Books* v67 no4 p217-8 D 2013 J. H.

REVIEW: *Horn Book Magazine* v89 no6 p95 N/D 2013 MONICA EDINGER

"The Abominables." "From Kenneth Grahame's reluctant dragon to Roald Dahl's BFG, endearing monsters are a staple of children's literature, now including Eva Ibbotson's yetis. . . . Wit, intelligence, a few royals, and a large assortment of schoolchildren manage to save the day. Completed after Ibbotson's death by her son and her editor, this is a romp that balances Ibbotson's trademark whimsical humor with understated opinions about outsider- and animal rights. Line illustrations, cozy but surreal, suit the tone admirably."

REVIEW: *Kirkus Rev* p41 Ag 15 2013 Fall Preview

REVIEW: *Kirkus Rev* v81 no15 p178 Ag 1 2013

REVIEW: *Publ Wkly* v260 no33 p67-8 Ag 19 2013

REVIEW: *Publ Wkly* p76 Children's starred review annual 2013

REVIEW: *SLJ* v59 no10 p1 O 2013 Elly Schook

IBBOTSON, EVA. One dog and his boy; [by] Eva Ibbotson 271 p. 2012 Scholastic Press

1. Children & animals—Psychological aspects 2. Children's literature 3. Dogs 4. Dogs—Fiction 5. Family life—England—London—Fiction 6. Human-animal relationships—Fiction 7. Pets 8. Voyages and travels—Fiction 9. Wealth—Fiction
ISBN 0545351960; 9780545351966
LC 2011-003773

SUMMARY: In this book, by Eva Ibbotson, "[all] Hal has ever wanted is a dog. His busy parents, hoping that he'll tire of the idea, rent a dog from Easy Pets, run by the heartless Mr. and Mrs. Carker. Hal and Fleck, the dog he chooses, bond immediately, and they are both heartbroken when Hal's mother, realizing that Hal's interest isn't waning, sneaks the dog back to Easy Pets. Hal decides to get Fleck back and run away to his grandparents." (Bulletin of the Center for Children's Books)

REVIEW: *Booklist* v108 no13 p89 Mr 1 2012 Kara Dean

REVIEW: *Bull Cent Child Books* v65 no8 p403-4 Ap 2012 J. H.

"One Dog and His Boy." "[Eva] Ibbotson thoughtfully picks apart the pet-rental business, characterizing dogs fittingly by breed. . . . While some of the adults are a bit exaggerated, the young characters are honest and real, and Hal's longing will resonate with many kids: 'Often and often when you wanted something and then got it, it was a disappointment. . . . But having a dog was completely different. He'd wanted it and wanted it and when it happened it was even better than he'd thought it would be.' Ibbotson's evocation of the emotional bond between humans and dogs and her descriptions of the dogs' personalities are especially strong. Animal lovers will lap this up, of course, but they also might walk away with a fresh perspective on pet ownership."

REVIEW: *Horn Book Magazine* v88 no3 p87 My/Je 2012 Roger Sutton

"One Dog and His Boy." "This (sadly) last of the late [Eva] Ibbotson's novels follows a classic formula. Boy gets dog, boy loses dog; that boy and dog will be reunited is never in doubt. . . . Hal's parents finally give in to his greatest wish and get him a dog for his birthday. What they don't tell him is that Fleck is only a rental. . . . Ibbotson leads a brisk chase across London and, eventually, cross country. . . . Their journey has welcome echoes of Dodie Smith. . . . If the world is not so neatly divided into selfish, superficial grownups and openhearted, brave kids (and dogs and grandparents), never mind: the appeal of Ibbotson's books has always been the author's firm loyalty to children."

REVIEW: *Kirkus Rev* v80 no1 p2440-1 Ja 1 2012

REVIEW: *Publ Wkly* v259 no3 p56 Ja 16 2012

REVIEW: *SLJ* v58 no3 p160 Mr 2012 Miriam Lang Budin

REVIEW: *SLJ* v59 no10 p1 O 2013 Jessica Gilcreast

IBRAHIM, SONALLAH. That smell, and; Notes from prison; 120 p. 2013 New Directions Pub.

1. Egypt—Fiction 2. Home detention 3. Political prisoners—Egypt—Fiction 4. Prison psychology 5. Psychological fiction
ISBN 9780811220361 (paperbook : alk. paper);

9780811220620 (ebook)
LC 2012-032484

SUMMARY: This book by Sonallah Ibrahim looks at "a man whose brutal incarceration has left him stripped of emotions and physical sensation. . . . Unable to write, the narrator cannot connect with anyone or anything: 'People walked and talked and acted as if I'd always been there with them and nothing had happened'. He is rendered impotent--sexually, politically, creatively." (Times Literary Supplement)

REVIEW: *London Rev Books* v35 no5 p15-6 Mr 7 2013 Adam Shatz

REVIEW: *TLS* no5771 p21 N 8 2013 LUCY POPESCU

"That Smell: And Notes From Prison." "With Egypt once more at a crossroads, Robyn Creswell's new translation of Sonallah Ibrahim's classic novella is timely. . . . Ibrahim paints a devastating portrait of a man whose brutal incarceration has left him stripped of emotions and physical sensation. . . . Ibrahim's stark, spare prose underlines the bleakness of his protagonist's life. . . . We now know the extent of [Gamal Abdel] Nasser's corruption, the sociological and political repression, the state-sanctioned torture and cult of personality, later mirrored by the regime of Hosni Mubarak. What is most remarkable is that Ibrahim managed to convey such a vivid sense of the country's stagnation while living through it."

ICONS OF THE AMERICAN COMIC BOOK; from Captain America to Wonder Woman; 2 v. (xv, 920 p.) 2013 Greenwood

1. Comic books, strips, etc.—History and criticism 2. Comic strip characters 3. Literature—History & criticism 4. Superhero comic books, strips, etc. 5. Superheroes
ISBN 0313399239 (hardcover); 9780313399237 (hardcover); 9780313399244 (ebook)
LC 2012-034779

SUMMARY: This reference book looks at American comic book icons. Editors Randy Duncan and Matthew J. Smith "explore the cultural influence of comics, moving beyond the striking art, fantastic colors, and word balloons to show 'far more meaning and significance within the identities of comic book heroes and characters than it would seem.' One hundred . . . profiles cover creators such Alan Moore, Frank Miller, Chris Ware, and the ubiquitous Stan Lee." (Library Journal)

REVIEW: *Booklist* v109 no16 p36-8 Ap 15 2013 Kathleen McBroom

REVIEW: *Choice* v50 no11 p1983 Jl 2013 W. L. Svitavsky

"Icons of the American Comic Book: From Captain America to Wonder Woman." "These volumes offer the useful approach of the publisher's 'Icons' series as a 'port of entry' for students and general readers. . . . The majority of the entries describe characters; others describe creators, publishers, titles, and phenomena of enduring significance. . . . While these volumes cover material that can be found elsewhere, they combine greater detail than can be found in many comics reference works with greater scope and rigor than can be found in most popular sources."

REVIEW: *Libr J* v138 no8 p100 My 1 2013 Laverne Mann

IDEA OF THE TEMPLE OF PAINTING; 2013 Pennsylvania State University Press

1. Art criticism 2. Art literature 3. Expression 4. Painting 5. Self-expression
ISBN 9780271059532 (cloth : alk. paper)
LC 2012-047291

SUMMARY: This book, by Giovanni Paolo Lomazzo, edited and translated by Jean Julia Chai, presents the writings of "perhaps the most imaginative writer on art in the sixteenth century, Giovan Paolo Lomazzo was also an ambitious painter, well-informed critic, and sarcastic wit. . . His greatest contribution to the history of art is his special treatment of expression and, in its more mature form, self-expression. . . [This book] embodies all his essential thoughts about art." (Publisher's note)

REVIEW: *Choice* v51 no6 p990-1 F 2014 P. Emison

"Idea of the Temple of Painting." "Though [Giovanni Paolo Lomazzo's] thought includes Neoplatonic intricacies, the translation is highly readable. [Jean Julia] Chai's nuanced introductory essay deftly places this late effort by the blind artist into both the context of Lomazzo's life and interests . . . and the complicated strands of 16th-century society and books. An abstruse author with a taste for allegory and the occult, Lomazzo, hitherto scarcely available in English, is presented with sympathy and clarity. His text highlights artists now obscure (e.g., Gaudenzio Ferrari), juxtaposing them with the highly famous: it is precious not least for this insight into how the world of art looked in the pivotal years around 1590."

AN IDEAL THEATER; founding visions for a new American art; 2013 Theatre Communications Group, Inc.

1. Regional theater 2. Theater—Political aspects 3. Theater—United States—History—20th century 4. Theater literature 5. Theatrical companies
ISBN 9781559364096

SUMMARY: This book, edited by Todd London, is a "documentary history of the American theatre movement as told by the visionaries who goaded it into being. This anthology collects over forty essays, manifestos, letters and speeches that are each introduced and placed in historical context by . . . London, who spent nearly a decade assembling this collection. This celebration of the artists who came before is an exhilarating look backward, as well as toward the future." (Publisher's note)

REVIEW: *Choice* v51 no7 p1225-6 Mr 2014 M. D. Whitlatch

"An Ideal Theater: Founding Visions for a New American Art." "The materials offer a panoramic view of American theater from the perspectives of many important theatrical visionaries of the past century. Essay subjects range from the development of modern American theater after WW I to the theatrical experimentation of the 1930s to the growth of regional theater after WW II to the political theater movement of the late 1950s and 1960s to the present. [Todd] London provides a brief introduction for each essay, and in these he places the piece in its historical context. 'Founding Visions' is an excellent addition to American theatrical scholarship."

IDEOLOGY AND FOREIGN POLICY IN EARLY MODERN EUROPE (1650-1750); xi, 320 p. 2011 Ashgate

1. Historical literature 2. Ideology—Europe—History—17th century 3. Ideology—Europe—History—18th century 4. Political culture—Europe—History—17th

century 5. Political culture—Europe—History—18th century
ISBN 1409419134 (hardcover : alk. paper); 9781409419136 (hardcover : alk. paper)
LC 2011-009339

SUMMARY: Edited by David Onnekink and Gijs Rommelse, this book focuses on international relations in early modern Europe and "provides alternative perspectives, viewing international relations as socially constructed and influenced by ideas, ideology and identities. Building on such theoretical developments, allows international relations after 1648 to be fundamentally reconsidered, by putting political and economic ideology firmly back into the picture." (Publisher's note)

REVIEW: *Engl Hist Rev* v128 no534 p1239-41 O 2013 Hamish Scott

"Ideology and Foreign Policy in Early Modern Europe (1650-1750)." "Now a leading historian of later seventeenth- and early eighteenth-century Dutch foreign policy and European diplomacy, David Onnekink, has begun to mount a concerted assault against the realist position. . . . This present volume, edited jointly with Gijs Rommelse, author of a significant monograph on the Second Anglo-Dutch War, continues the campaign. . . . Overall, this is a collection which should find a place in university libraries: the general standard of essays is higher than in many such compilations, and several are of real importance."

IDLE, MOLLY. Camp Rex; [by] Molly Idle 40 p. 2014 Viking, published by Penguin Group
1. Camping—Fiction 2. Dinosaurs—Fiction 3. Humorous stories 4. Scouting (Youth activity)—Fiction 5. Tyrannosaurus rex—Fiction
ISBN 0670785733; 9780670785735 (hardcover)
LC 2013-018234

SUMMARY: This children's book, by Molly Idle, is about "a camping trip with . . . T. Rex! It's important to set a few wilderness safety guidelines first. . . . like making sure he stays on the trail. And does not disturb the local wildlife. And knows how to build a safe campfire. But sometimes dinosaurs have a different way of doing things, and that's why it's best to be prepared . . . . for anything!" (Publisher's note)

REVIEW: *Bull Cent Child Books* v67 no9 p460 My 2014 A. A.

"Camp Rex". "Considering taking your T. rex camping? Author [Molly] Idle has some words of wisdom in this gently fanciful exploration of all that can go awry, if not completely wrong, in exploring the great outdoors with one's dino-friends. . . . Idle's winking prose makes the perfect foil to her demure but descriptive colored pencil drawings. These charming and dimensional illustrations reflect Idle's experience as an animator, inviting readers' careful consideration and quiet giggles and delivering generous and gentle humor in gorgeous full-bleed renderings. Sweet and subtle with a liberal pinch of silly, this could provide a welcome quieter interlude in an otherwise rollicking story session."

REVIEW: *Kirkus Rev* v82 no5 p67 Mr 1 2014

"Camp Rex". "Fresh from the pages of 'Tea Rex' (2013), Cordelia, her younger brother and his teddy this time join their dino pals for a camping expedition. Again limiting the text to sage words of wisdom-which sound remarkably like a true outdoorsy book about camping might-Idle lets the illustrations tell the tale. . . . While the pictures are tongue-in-cheek funny, some are difficult to make out due to the flat colors and the hugeness of the dinos—they often exceed the size of the page. Still, this is certain to raise more than a few giggles from the camping enthusiasts in any audience. What adventure's next?"

REVIEW: *Publ Wkly* v261 no11 p82 Mr 17 2014

IDLE, MOLLY.il. Camp Rex. See Idle, M.

IERONIM, IOANA. Ariadne's Veil; [by] Ioana Ieronim 2013 Contemporary Literature Press
1. Ariadne (Greek mythology) 2. Greek mythology—Poetry 3. Nature—Poetry 4. Romanian poetry 5. Theseus (Greek mythology)
ISBN 9786068366647 ebook

SUMMARY: "The story of Ariadne's thread leading Theseus out of the labyrinth is a useful metaphor for the strands that bring this book to the reader out of what had been cultural obscurity. . . . In the first half of 'Ariadne's Veil,' [author Ioana] Ieronim plays variations on the myth. . . . The book's second half, 'Songs and the Day,' refers sparingly to the myth (though an anthropomorphized laptop with erotic overtones appears in both halves)." (Publisher's note)

REVIEW: *World Lit Today* v88 no2 p68-9 Mr/Ap 2014 Robert Murray Davis

"Ariadne's Veil." "The story of Ariadne's thread leading Theseus out of the labyrinth is a useful metaphor for the strands that bring this book to the reader out of what had been cultural obscurity. . . . Although Ioana Ieronim established her reputation with poems written in Romanian--some of which, notably 'The Triumph of the Water Witch,' were translated into English--in recent years she has written in English. . . . Cristina Ioana Young's lovely photographs, which for the most part accompany rather than illustrate the poems. But Ieronim's poems are rightly the center of attention, further establishing her as a significant anglophone presence."

IGLER, DAVID. The great ocean; Pacific worlds from Captain Cook to the gold rush; [by] David Igler 272 p. 2013 Oxford University Press
1. Culture diffusion—Pacific Area—History—18th century 2. Culture diffusion—Pacific Area—History—19th century 3. East and West 4. Historical literature 5. Indigenous peoples—Pacific Area—History—18th century 6. Indigenous peoples—Pacific Area—History—19th century 7. Natural history—Pacific Area—History—18th century 8. Natural history—Pacific Area—History—19th century
ISBN 9780199914951 (alk. paper)
LC 2012-038256

SUMMARY: Written by David Igler, "'The Great Ocean' draws on hundreds of documented voyages--some painstakingly recorded by participants, some only known by archeological remains or indigenous memory--as a window into the commercial, cultural, and ecological upheavals following Cook's exploits, focusing in particular on the eastern Pacific in the decades between the 1770s and the 1840s. . . . 'The Great Ocean' is the first book to weave together American, oceanic, and world history." (Publisher's note)

REVIEW: *Am Hist Rev* v119 no2 p504-5 Ap 2014 Helen M. Rozwadowski

REVIEW: *Choice* v51 no3 p521 N 2013 J. C. Perry

REVIEW: *TLS* no5775 p10-1 D 6 2013 DAVID ARMITAGE

"The Great Ocean: Pacific Worlds From Captain Cook to the Gold Rush" and "Guano and the Opening of the Pacific World." "David Igler's 'The Great Ocean' and Gregory T. Cushman's 'Guano and the Opening of the Pacific World' are some of the first waves of a gathering tsunami of scholarship on the Pacific world. . . . 'The Great Ocean' calculates the high price of proto-globalization in the Pacific. . . . Igler's topical approach can make the chronology of Pacific history hard to follow, but the pivotal periods are tolerably clear. . . . By turns illuminating and obsessive, Cushman's book traces every thread in the modem history of nitrates and phosphates from their origins in Peru, Chile and the Pacific islands outwards to Australasia, Britain and beyond."

IGNATIEFF, MICHAEL, 1947-. Fire and ashes; success and failure in politics; [by] Michael Ignatieff 224 p. 2013 Harvard University Press

1. Memoirs 2. Political culture—Canada 3. Politicians—Canada—Biography

ISBN 9780674725997 (cloth: alk. paper)

LC 2013-021522

SUMMARY: This memoir describes how "In 2005 [author] Michael Ignatieff left his life as a writer and professor at Harvard University to enter the combative world of politics back home in Canada. By 2008, he was leader of the country's Liberal Party and poised—should the governing Conservatives falter—to become Canada's next Prime Minister. It never happened. Today, after a bruising electoral defeat, Ignatieff is back where he started, writing and teaching what he learned." (Publisher's note)

REVIEW: *Commonweal* v141 no2 p22-4 Ja 24 2014 E. J. Dionne Jr.

REVIEW: *N Y Rev Books* v51 no7 p28-30 Ap 24 2014 Paul Wilson

"Fire and Ashes: Success and Failure in Politics." "Michael Ignatieff's eighteenth book sets out to tell a tale that, in its outlines, is almost mythic. . . . The story . . . is Ignatieff's own. He left his post at Harvard and entered Canadian politics on a wave of high hopes in 2005 . . . rose to become leader of the Liberal Party . . . and then . . . led his party to the greatest defeated in its history and left the field badly beaten. In 'Fire and Ashes' he tries to understand the debacle and explain what drew him into politics in the first place."

REVIEW: *Publ Wkly* v260 no39 p60 S 30 2013

IMAGINING GERMANY IMAGINING ASIA; Essays in Asian-German Studies; vi, 279 p. 2013 Camden House

1. Comparative literature—German and Oriental 2. Comparative literature—Oriental and German 3. German literature—Oriental influences 4. Historical literature 5. National characteristics, Asian 6. National characteristics, German 7. Oriental literature—German influences

ISBN 1571135480 (hardcover: acid-free paper); 9781571135483 (hardcover: acid-free paper)

LC 2013-019460

SUMMARY: This book, edited by Veronika Fuechtner and Mary Rheil, "demonstrates that Germany and Asia have always shared cultural spaces. Indeed, since the time of the German Enlightenment, Asia served as the foil for fantasies of sexuality, escape, danger, competition, and racial and spiritual purity that were central to foundational ideas of a cohesive German national culture during crucial historical junctures such as fascism or reunification." (Publisher's note)

REVIEW: *Choice* v51 no8 p1404 Ap 2014 R. Bledsoe

"Imagining Germany Imagining Asia: Essays in Asian-German Studies". "[Veronika] Fuechtner . . . and [Mary] Rhiel . . . stake this volume's claim as the first collection of essays in the emerging field of Asian German studies. It offers new insights into the particularities of the Asian German experience and draws attention to the heterogeneity of the categories of German and Asian at different times and in different geographical locations. . . . The essays cannot cover the entirety of the field, but they model possible theoretical approaches and potential topics; in this sense, this accessible volume functions as a good introduction to the field."

IN AN INESCAPABLE NETWORK OF MUTUALITY; Martin Luther King, Jr. and the Globalization of an Ethical Ideal; 408 p. 2013 Wipf & Stock Pub

1. Civil rights—United States—History—20th century 2. Influence (Literary, artistic, etc.) 3. King, Martin Luther, Jr., 1929-1968 4. Nonviolence 5. Patriarchy

ISBN 1610974344; 9781610974349

SUMMARY: This book looks at Martin Luther King, Jr., "as both a global figure and a forerunner of much of what is currently associated with contemporary globalization theory and praxis. The contributors to this volume agree that King must be understood not only as a thinker, visionary, and social change agent in his own historical context, but also in terms of his meaning for the different generations who still appeal to him as an authority, inspiration, and model." (Publisher's note)

REVIEW: *Choice* v51 no8 p1413 Ap 2014 L. H. Mamiya

"In an Inescapable Network of Mutuality: Martin Luther King Jr. and the Globalization of an Ethical Ideal". "Editors [Lewis W.] Baldwin and [Paul R.] Dekar offer an outstanding collection of essays that focus on the global and international impact of Martin Luther King Jr.'s life and thought, captured in his phrase, 'in an inescapable network of mutuality.' Since most books and studies on Martin Luther King Jr. have elaborated on his domestic influence through the accomplishments of the civil rights movement in the US, this collection is a significantly new addition to the literature. Both Baldwin and Dekar contribute important essays. However, two chapters that this reviewer believes will be of particular interest to readers are those by Linda Wynn and Mary Elizabeth King."

IN TIME'S EYE; Essays on Rudyard Kipling; 320 p. 2013 Manchester University Press

1. English authors—Political & social views 2. English poets 3. Kipling, Rudyard, 1865-1936 4. Literature—History & criticism 5. Racism—Great Britain—History

ISBN 0719095751; 9780719095757

SUMMARY: Edited by Jan Montefiore, "Challenging received opinion and breaking new ground in Kipling scholarship, these essays on [author Rudyard] Kipling's attitudes to the First World War, to the culture of Edwardian England, to homosexuality and to Jewishness, bring historical, literary critical and postcolonial approaches to this perennially controversial writer. The Introduction situates the book in the context of Kipling's changing reputation and of recent

Kipling scholarship." (Publisher's note)

REVIEW: *TLS* no5782 p27 Ja 24 2014 ADAM ROBERTS

"In Time's Eye: Essays on Rudyard Kipling." "The Kipling Problem (see also: Wagner, Lovecraft) is that of the great artist with deplorable views. . . . Jan Montefiore's handsomely produced collection of essays tackles the subject straight on. The stated aim is not to try and quarantine his 'achievement as a writer' from his 'failure as an ideologue,' since the two really can't be separated, but rather to reinsert him in 'his place in history.' ' History' is the keynote, and the best pieces here bring a sophisticated and properly global perspective to bear."

INDIGENOUS IN THE CITY; contemporary identities and cultural innovation; 414 p. 2013 UBC Press

1. Indians of North America—Canada 2. Indigenous peoples—Australia 3. Indigenous peoples—Ethnic identity 4. Indigenous peoples—Urban residence 5. Social science literature
ISBN 9780774824644
LC 2012-376291

SUMMARY: "This book explores various geographical and temporal contexts within which urban indigeneity not only exists but also continues to evolve in all its complexity. . . . An introductory chapter summarizes the development of colonial discourses of difference. Four subsequent sections address the implications of urbanization on the production of distinctive indigenous identities in Canada, the US, New Zealand, and Australia." (Choice: Current Reviews for Academic Libraries)

REVIEW: *Choice* v51 no4 p732-3 D 2013 G. Bruyere

"Indigenous in the City; Contemporary Identities and Cultural Innovation." "This unique foray into a still-emerging body of academic literature contrasts the tendency to frame rural and remote communities (that is, Canadian reserves or US reservations) as the primary or even authentic emblem of indigenous identity. After all, at present, most indigenous peoples live in urban areas. . . . Instead of simply viewing urban experiences in terms of assimilation and social and cultural disruption, the chapter authors demonstrate the resilience, creativity, and complexity of the urban indigenous presence in specific cities around the world."

INDRIDASON, ARNALDUR. Strange Shores; 304 p. 2013 Harvill Secker

1. Detective & mystery stories 2. Icelandic fiction 3. Missing persons—Fiction 4. Murder—Fiction 5. Murder investigation—Fiction
ISBN 1846557119; 9781846557118

SUMMARY: In this book, "a young woman walks into the frozen fjords of Iceland, never to be seen again. But Matthildur leaves in her wake rumours of lies, betrayal and revenge. Decades later, somewhere in the same wilderness, Detective Erlendur is on the hunt. He is looking for Matthildur but also for a long-lost brother, whose disappearance in a snowstorm when they were children has coloured his entire life. He is looking for answers." (Publisher's note)

REVIEW: *Libr J* v139 no5 p66 Mr 15 2014 Barbara Hoffert

REVIEW: *Libr J* v139 no4 p66 Mr 1 2014 Barbara Hoffert

REVIEW: *Publ Wkly* v261 no20 p48-9 My 19 2014

REVIEW: *TLS* no5764 p20 S 20 2013 PAUL BINDING

"Strange Shores." "'Strange Shores' is very much Erlendur's, as the sequence's dynamics demand it should be, taking him to the frontiers of time, the portals of death. Though these nine novels have all the compelling qualities of popular Nordic noir, their close-worked presentation of the perennial difficulties of coping with flux--in self, in society, in existence--put them, especially when taken together, far beyond genre affiliation, out into the challenging domain of serious literature."

THE INFANT MIND; origins of the social brain; xvi, 367 p. 2013 Guilford Press

1. Cognition in children 2. Infants—Development 3. Psychological literature 4. Social interaction in children 5. Social perception in children
ISBN 9781462508174 (cloth : alk. paper)
LC 2012-030158

SUMMARY: Edited by Maria Legerstee, David W. Haley, Marc H. Bornstein and "Integrating cutting-edge research from multiple disciplines, this book provides a dynamic and holistic picture of the developing infant mind. Contributors explore the transactions among genes, the brain, and the environment in the earliest years of life. The volume probes the neural correlates of core sensory, perceptual, cognitive, emotional, and social capacities." (Publisher's note)

REVIEW: *Choice* v51 no1 p168-9 S 2013 J. F. Heberle

"The Infant Mind: Origins of the Social Brain." "The title is an indicator of how much things have changed in child development in 40 years. For many years, Jean Piaget's assertion that infants do not have representational capacity was the accepted wisdom and started to be challenged only in the late 1970s with the work of Elizabeth Spelke, Renee Baillargeon, and others. This volume represents the results of decades of research since. . . . The topics covered are wide ranging--older topics of infant memory, through children's theory of mind, to newer areas such as motor cognition. . . . A reader educated in advanced issues in developmental psychology during the last decades will appreciate the consistent integration of older with newer research."

INGLESE, JUDITH. I have a friend; [by] Judith Inglese 40 p. 2014 Satya House Publications

1. Bedtime 2. Children's stories 3. Imaginary companions 4. Imagination 5. Mother & child—Fiction
ISBN 9781935874225 (hardcover)
LC 2013-954003

SUMMARY: In this children's book, the young narrator Henry introduces his imaginary friend Vladimir. "Vladimir lives in Iceland—or sometimes next door—celebrates his birthday every day, likes the same foods as Henry, and owns an airplane and a forklift. He also has various pets including a dog named Hoss, who is big enough to scare wolves and 'stays with me at night when it is very dark.'" (Kirkus Reviews)

REVIEW: *Kirkus Rev* v82 no3 p116 F 1 2014

"I Have A Friend". "Staid pictures make a poor match for a child's free-flying introduction to an imaginary friend. In contrast to the art, which displays the drab palette and static compositions common to earnestly therapeutic titles, young Henry's imaginative portrait of his friend 'Vladimir' abounds in colorful details. . . . Though [Judith] Inglese admirably acknowledges the real importance of toys and imaginary friends in children's lives, Vladimir is an anemic alternative to, say, wild things, Calvin's tiger, Hobbes, or even the likes of Kevin Henkes' Jessica (1989). Aims high but misses."

REVIEW: *SLJ* v60 no3 p114 Mr 2014 Tanya Boudreau

INGLIS, FRED. Richard Hoggart; Virtue and Reward; [by] Fred Inglis 280 p. 2013 John Wiley & Sons Inc

1. Biography (Literary form) 2. Cultural studies—History 3. Great Britain—Intellectual life—1945- 4. Hoggart, Richard, 1918-2014 5. Scholars—Great Britain—Biography

ISBN 0745651712; 9780745651712

SUMMARY: "Richard Hoggart has been, perhaps, the best-known, and certainly the most affectionately acknowledged, British intellectual of the past sixty years. . . . This is the first biography of this . . . man. It seeks to tie together in a single narrative life and work, to settle Hoggart in the great happiness of a fulfilled family life and in the astonishing achievements of his public and professional career. . . . [Author] Fred Inglis tells this . . . tale." (Publisher's note)

REVIEW: *London Rev Books* v36 no8 p35-7 Ap 17 2014 Christopher Hilliard

REVIEW: *TLS* no5781 p3 Ja 17 2014

REVIEW: *TLS* no5781 p3-5 Ja 17 2014 STEFAN COLLINI

"The Life of R. H. Tawney: Socialism and History" and "Richard Hoggart: Virtue and Reward." "The appearance of these two sharply contrasting biographies ought to go some way towards disturbing . . . complacent preconceptions. . . . To say that Fred Inglis wears his heart on his sleeve would be to understate his forthrightness. His prose is characterized by what might be called exuberant lyricism. . . . In the cases of both R. H. Tawney and Richard Hoggart, the exemplary quality of their own characters stands high in all recollections and celebrations of them. Even in the face of the complacent disdain that I mentioned at the outset, it is difficult to come away from these two biographies without feeling renewed admiration for their subjects."

INGLIS, LUCY. Georgian London; Into the Streets; [by] Lucy Inglis 400 p. 2013 Viking

1. Historical literature 2. London (England)—History—18th century 3. London (England)—History—19th century 4. London (England)—Social conditions 5. London (England)—Social life & customs

ISBN 0670920134; 9780670920136

SUMMARY: In this book on London, England during the Georgian period, "Lucy Inglis takes readers on a tour of London's most formative age--the age of love, sex, intellect, art, great ambition and fantastic ruin." Readers "visit the madhouses of Hackney, the workshops of Soho and the mean streets of Cheapside." Historical figures discussed range "from dukes and artists to rent boys and hot air balloonists." (Publisher's note)

REVIEW: *Economist* v409 no8858 p87-8 O 19 2013

REVIEW: *TLS* no5769 p32 O 25 2013 JERRY WHITE

"Georgian London: Into the Streets." "Engaging and industrious. . . . Inevitably, some of her anecdotes will be over-familiar. . . . Less appealing, though, is a tendency to facile generalization. . . . In such a rich tapestry, however, it is hard to quarrel with the variety of choices [Lucy] Inglis makes here. And in a book aimed at a popular readership it is forgivable if she indulges a taste for the grisly. . . . Stories like these ensure that Lucy Inglis's prose never flags, while she rarely tries to extract too much juice from such over-ripe plums."

INNES, CHRISTOPHER. The Cambridge introduction to theatre directing; [by] Christopher Innes 2013 Cambridge University Press

1. Artistic collaboration 2. Theater—Production & direction 3. Theater literature 4. Theater rehearsals 5. Theatrical producers & directors

ISBN 9780521844499 (hardback); 9780521606226 (paperback)

LC 2012-034004

SUMMARY: This book, by Christopher Innes and Maria Shevtsova, part of the "Cambridge Introductions to Literature" series, offers a survey of "the different styles of theatre that twentieth-century and contemporary directors have created. It discusses artistic and political values, rehearsal methods and the diverging relationships with actors, designers, other collaborators and audiences, and treatment of dramatic material." (Publisher's note)

REVIEW: *Choice* v51 no6 p1016 F 2014 M. S. LoMonaco

"The Cambridge Introduction to Theatre Directing." "This history of directing and directors in Western theater is an eminently useful volume that should he a part of every serious theater library. . . . Extensive profiles of individual directors are supplemented by sidebars detailing terminology . . .quotable quotes . . . examples from director's books . . . and URLs for video examples. . . . The volume necessarily focuses on the usual European suspects of the 19th and 20th centuries, but the authors do not neglect the new crop of high-profile directors from eastern Europe . . . nor North American superstars. . . . The volume's notable omission (for lack of space), which the authors themselves decry, is Asian theater"

INOUE, IROHA. The manga guide to linear algebra; [by] Iroha Inoue ix, 247 p. 2012 No Starch Press

1. Algebra—Textbooks 2. Algebras, Linear—Comic books, strips, etc 3. Graphic novels 4. MATHEMATICS—Algebra—Linear 5. MATHEMATICS—General 6. Manga (Art)

ISBN 1593274130 (pbk.); 9781593274139 (pbk.)

LC 2012-012824

SUMMARY: In this book by Shin Takahashi and Iroha Inoue "Reiji wants two things in life: a black belt in karate and Misa. . . . Luckily, Misa's big brother is the captain of the university karate club and is ready to strike a deal: Reiji can join the club if he tutors Misa in linear algebra. . . . Reiji takes Misa from the absolute basics . . . through mind-bending operations like performing linear transformations, calculating determinants, and finding eigenvectors and eigenvalues." (Publisher's note)

REVIEW: *Choice* v50 no4 p708 D 2012 K. D. Holton

INQULSTAD, MATS.ed. Aluminum Ore. See Aluminum Ore

INSECURITY, INEQUALITY, AND OBESITY IN AFFLUENT SOCIETIES; xviii, 237 p. 2012 Oxford University Press

1. Equality—Health aspects—Congresses 2. Obesity—Congresses 3. Obesity—Social aspects—Congresses 4. Public health—Social aspects—Congresses 5. Social science literature

ISBN 0197264980 (hbk.); 9780197264980 (hbk.)

LC 2011-279406

SUMMARY: This book "proposes that growing rates of obesity are a response to stress produced by economic uncertainty and insecurity. Such stress is highest, it reasons, for the most vulnerable members of society. Whereas generous welfare states provide some protection from such uncertainty and insecurity via education, health care, and social insurance, more stingy welfare states leave people to process these stressors literally through their individual bodies." (Contemporary Sociology)

REVIEW: *Contemp Sociol* v43 no2 p247-9 Mr 2014 Abigail C. Saguy

"Insecurity, Inequality, and Obesity in Affluent Societies". "This engaging and coherent volume sensitizes readers to the various ways in which different forms of government and economic systems, as well as our place within such systems, provide varying degrees of protection from stress and how exposure to such stress gets written on the body. As such, it makes an important contribution to the literatures on obesity, inequality, and comparative welfare regimes. While identifying important and understudied aspects of obesity, this volume has its own notable blind spots, weaknesses, and inconsistencies. It often reads as if authors are selectively focusing on examples to fit their hypothesis, while ignoring those that do not."

INSERRA, ROSE. Captain of the toilet; 10 p. 2013 Barrons Educational Series, Inc.

1. Children's stories 2. Fathers & sons—Fiction 3. Imagination 4. Pirates—Juvenile fiction 5. Toilet training

ISBN 9780764166587

LC 2013-935237

SUMMARY: This children's book on potty training follows Jack, "a cute, bespectacled tot wearing a large pirate hat featuring a skull and crossbones. . . . Jack has decided that he's ready to give up the little potty and use the toilet like his father. Capt. Jack climbs aboard 'his ship,' pees into the bowl, sits down and 'does a poo,' flushes the toilet and then washes his hands. Proud Jack 'takes a bow' while 'Daddy claps and cheers,' proclaiming Jack 'Captain of the Toilet!'" (Kirkus Reviews)

REVIEW: *Kirkus Rev* v82 no1 p76 Ja 1 2014

"Captain of the Toilet". "A primer for little boys transitioning from their own potties to the toilet. Jack is a cute, bespectacled tot wearing a large pirate hat featuring a skull and crossbones. . . . Jack makes it look really easy, which may intimidate little ones, but they will probably be too busy repeatedly generating flushing sounds by pushing the book's big blue button to notice. . . . Not a standout, but it's potentially useful for allaying the anxieties of wee ones ready to make what can be a scary leap from child's potty to toilet."

REVIEW: *Kirkus Rev* v81 no22 p313 N 15 2013

INSIDE CONDUCTING; xii, 268 p. 2013 University of Rochester Press

1. Conducting 2. Conductors (Music) 3. Conductors (Musicians) 4. Music conducting 5. Music literature 6. Musicians—Attitudes 7. Orchestra

ISBN 9781580464116 (hardcover : alkaline paper)

LC 2013-005796

SUMMARY: "What does a conductor actually do? How much effect does he or she have? Can the orchestra manage without one? . . . These are some of the questions that receive lively and informative answers in this book by renowned conductor Christopher Seaman. Composed of short articles on individual topics, it is accessible and easy to consult. Each article begins with an anecdote or saying and ends with quotations from musicians, often expressing opposing views." (Publisher's note)

REVIEW: *TLS* no5788 p24 Mr 7 2014 MICHAEL DOWNES

"What We Really Do: The Tallis Scholars" and "Inside Conducting." "There are many different ways of becoming a conductor, and of being a conductor. 'What We Really Do' and 'Inside Conducting, as contrasting in content and approach as one would expect from their authors' careers, have much to say about both topics. . . . 'What We Really Do' is filled out with an anthology of [author Peter] Phillips's articles from the 'Spectator' and elsewhere, a Tallis Scholars discography, a list of everyone who has ever sung with the group and of broadcasts it has made, and a glossary of 'singers' argot.' . . . 'Inside Conducting,' which arouses slight regret that it is so short, such are the insights that [author Christopher] Seaman brings."

INSOLE, CHRISTOPHER J.ed. The Cambridge companion to Edmund Burke. See The Cambridge companion to Edmund Burke

INSOO HYUN. Bioethics and the future of stem cell research; [by] Insoo Hyun xii, 225 p. 2013 Cambridge University Press

1. Bioethics 2. Medical ethics 3. Medical literature 4. Stem cell treatment 5. Stem cells—Research—Moral and ethical aspects

ISBN 9780521127318 (paperback); 9780521768696 (hardback)

LC 2012-042727

SUMMARY: In this book, Insoo Hyun "critically examines the complexities of the bioethics involved in the ever-growing field of stem cell research. This field has gained tremendous momentum, and the push towards therapeutic uses of stem cells involves researchers, patients, and health care providers alike. . . . He demonstrates the importance and need to begin formally addressing several ethical issues regarding stem cell research now." (Choice: Current Reviews for Academic Libraries)

REVIEW: *Choice* v51 no8 p1426 Ap 2014 P. J. Yurco

"Bioethics and the Future of Stem Cell Research". "[Insoo] Hyun is well respected in the field of stem cell research ethics but also commands a thorough understanding of the science behind the research, effectively introducing the reader to several areas of stem cell research in language that is easy to understand. The author carefully considers the bioethics of this research from several points of view, including those of potential subjects, researchers, and bioethicists. . . .Although Hyun is quick to point out that stem cell research is equally important for basic science research, the book's major focus is on the impact of stem cell research in a therapeutic context."

THE INTELLECTUAL CONSEQUENCES OF RELIGIOUS HETERODOXY 1600-1750; xi, 331 p. 2012 Brill

1. Church history—17th century—Congresses 2. Church history—18th century—Congresses 3. Heresy—History—17th century—Congresses 4. Heresy—History—18th century—Congresses 5. Historical literature 6. Intellectual life—17th century—Congresses 7. Intellectual life—18th century—Congresses

ISBN 9789004221468 (hardback: alk. paper)

LC 2011-051727

SUMMARY: This book challenges the idea "that religious heterodoxy before the Enlightenment led inexorably to intellectual secularisation. . . . In their opening essay the editors argue that the critical problems for both Protestants and Catholics arose from destabilising the relation between the spheres of Nature and Revelation, and the adoption of an increasingly historical approach both to natural religion and to the Scriptual basis of Revelation." (Publisher's note)

REVIEW: *Engl Hist Rev* v129 no536 p212-4 F 2014 John Coffey

"The Intellectual Consequences of Religious Heterodoxy, 1600-1750". "This outstanding volume of essays opens with an impressive survey of the field by the two editors, Sarah Mortimer and John Robertson. . . . The essays that follow contribute to a fuller understanding of heterodoxy in all its complex vitality, though there are intriguing points of tension among the contributors. . . . The book is not flawless. The publishers have missed some typos, and the introduction is marred by several factual slips. . . . Fundamentally, though, the collection makes a convincing case for reading the heterodox in their own terms and not imposing an anachronistic secular framework on their thought. For early modern intellectual historians, this is essential reading."

THE INTERNATIONAL ENCYCLOPEDIA OF ETHICS; 6000 p. 2013 Wiley-Blackwell

1. Bioethics 2. Consequentialism (Ethics) 3. Encyclopedias & dictionaries 4. Ethics 5. Ethics—Encyclopedias

ISBN 1405186410 (hardback : alk. paper); 9781405186414 (hardback : alk. paper)

LC 2012-023052

SUMMARY: This ethics resource "includes more than 700 entries spread across nine volumes and is arranged in traditional A-Z fashion. There is an alphabetical listing of entries as well as a topical listing that categorizes the entries into broader themes, such as 'Bioethics,' 'Consequentialism,' and 'Sentiments and Attitudes.'" (Booklist)

REVIEW: *Booklist* v110 no2 p50-2 S 15 2013 Janet Pinkley

"The International Encyclopedia of Ethics." "Multiple reference works attempt to address ethics, but 'The International Encyclopedia of Ethics' is sure to become a core resource in the field. . . . The review process of each entry . . . makes for an authoritative source in ethics, while the international team of expert editors ensures diverse and comprehensive views, particularly on controversial issues. Additionally, this set is the first to incorporate metaethics, practical ethics, and normative ethics into one set. This set is highly recommended for libraries in higher education. Aimed at a broad audience, it will be particularly useful for undergraduate students, graduate students, and scholars, who will likely find it to be an invaluable resource."

REVIEW: *Choice* v51 no1 p44 S 2013 J. C. Swindal

INTERNATIONAL WOMEN STAGE DIRECTORS; ix, 327 p. 2013 University of Illinois Press

1. Theater—History 2. Theater literature 3. Theatrical producers & directors 4. Women in the theater 5. Women theatrical producers and directors

ISBN 9780252037818 (hbk.: alk. paper)

LC 2013-009259

SUMMARY: Edited by Anne Fliotsos and Wendy Vierow, "this internationally focused volume highlights women directors in a selection of 24 countries. Alphabetically arranged by country, the entries each offer an examination of the history of women's rights, followed by discussions of early women directors and the working climate of the 21st century, along with profiles of contemporary directors." (Choice: Current Reviews for Academic Libraries)

REVIEW: *Booklist* v110 no8 p32 D 15 2013 Paula Webb

REVIEW: *Choice* v51 no8 p1369 Ap 2014 M. Lawler

"International Women Stage Directors". "The countries profiled are meant to be a cross-section from throughout the world; however, the choices are sometimes curious. For instance, Ireland is included, but not England. In order to add authenticity, the editors chose contributors who were once or currently are residents of the 24 countries. . . . The entries . . . seem to be well researched and concise. Notes and bibliographies follow each entry, and many are enhanced with illustrations. Sidebars offer extra information in the form of biographies and essays, and the book includes a biographical list of contributors. It should serve as a starting point or basic overview for those interested in further study."

REVIEW: *Libr J* v139 no2 p77 F 1 2014 Susan L. Peters

INTERNET INNOVATORS; ix, 464 p. 2013 Salem Press, a division of EBSCO Publishing Grey House Publishing

1. Computer engineers—Biography 2. Google Inc. 3. Internet industry 4. Reference books 5. Women computer engineers—Biography 6. YouTube (Web resource)

ISBN 1429838078 (hardcover); 9781429838078 (hardcover)

LC 2012-045267

SUMMARY: This book presents "biographies of individuals who contributed to the development and expansion of the Internet. Fields of specialization include mathematics and logic; physics and engineering; computer software, hardware, and programming; Internet management, marketing, commerce, and security; social media; applications; news and entertainment; and ethics and policy. . . . Subjects' affiliations represent an array of most-visited sites: YouTube, Yahoo!, Google, Amazon, WebMD, and so on." (Booklist)

REVIEW: *Booklist* v110 no1 p59 S 1 2013 Kathleen McBroom

"Computer Technology Innovators" and "Internet Innovators." "In most cases, the book's contributors are well matched to their subjects and provide detailed profiles and sufficient background information to establish the importance and relevance of their subjects, whether in technological, social, economic, or political context. . . . The preface indicates that selection criteria included each individual's significance, his or her relevance to academic curriculum, and the appeal to the intended audience: high-school and undergraduate students. These volumes should serve as authoritative resources and are recommended for high-school, large public, and academic libraries."

REVIEW: *Choice* v51 no2 p229-30 O 2013 J. W. Barnes

"Computer Technology Innovators" and "Internet Innovators." "Drawing on the work of over 40 contributors, these two volumes each feature biographical essays on more than 120 men and women noted for their contributions to the development of computer technology, or its myriad applications over the Internet. Alphabetically arranged essays, each about 2,000 words long, often feature a line drawing of the subject, and conclude with a 'Further Reading' section. . . . Good indexes provide access to the many topics covered in both books. Unfortunately, in these otherwise well-planned and attractively printed publications, numerous lapses in copy editing are evident throughout. Part of the 'Great Lives from History' series, these volumes provide online access with purchase of the print version."

THE INTERNET POLICE; how crime went online, and the cops followed; 320 p. 2013 W W Norton & Co Inc

1. Computer crimes 2. Computer crimes—Investigation 3. International crimes 4. Internet—Security measures 5. Journalism

ISBN 9780393062984 (hardcover)

LC 2013-013978

SUMMARY: In this book, "Nate Anderson takes readers on a behind-the-screens tour of landmark cybercrime cases, revealing how criminals continue to find digital and legal loopholes even as police hurry to cinch them closed. . . . With each episode . . .Anderson shows the dark side of online spaces--but also how dystopian a fully 'ordered' alternative would be." (Publisher's note)

REVIEW: *Kirkus Rev* v81 no13 p123 Jl 1 2013

REVIEW: *N Y Times Book Rev* p54 N 10 2013

REVIEW: *N Y Times Book Rev* p17 N 3 2013 ROBERT KOLKER

"The Internet Police: How Crime Went Online--and the Cops Followed." "[Nate Anderson's] storytelling is brisk and lucid, often pithy but never glib. . . . Even familiar tales contain surprises and fresh insights. . . . Anderson wisely reminds ups that the struggle between security and liberty didn't start with the Internet, and that the debate may not be as Manichean as it seems. . . . He's also right when he concludes that 'the cost of total order is totalitarianism; the real challenge is making prudential judgments about how we weigh risks and rewards, costs and benefits, order and chaos.'"

REVIEW: *Publ Wkly* v260 no22 p52 Je 3 2013

INTRIAGO, PATRICIA. Dot; [by] Patricia Intriago un 2011 Farrar Straus Giroux

1. Opposites

ISBN 978-0-374-31835-2; 0-374-31835-2

LC 2010-019816

SUMMARY: Pairs of circular shapes convey opposite relationships in the arc of a day.

REVIEW: *N Y Times Book Rev* p15 N 3 2013 JUDITH MARTIN

"Dot Complicated: Untangling Our Wired Lives" and "Dot." "What both books demonstrate, rather than state, is that social media are inherently asocial. . . . 'Dot Complicated' is written in what may be called Facebook style--every idea and opportunity is 'awesome,' 'amazing' or 'incredible'; it all blows her mind or blows her away, and we hear a great deal about how much she loves her husband and how adorable their baby is. . . . 'Don't be a jerk,' she advises. . . . But people seeking to damage others are not generally swayed by etiquette. Nor has the law figured out how to police these activities."

INVENTIVE METHODS; the happening of the social; xiii, 269 p. 2012 Routledge

1. Interdisciplinary approach to knowledge 2. Lists 3. Research—Methodology 4. Social science literature 5. Social sciences—Research—Methodology

ISBN 9780203854921 (ebook); 9780415574815

LC 2011-048418

SUMMARY: "This volume provides a set of new approaches for the investigation of the contemporary world. Building on the increasing importance of methodologies that cut across disciplines, more than twenty expert authors explain the utility of 'devices' for social and cultural research—their essays cover such diverse devices as the list, the pattern, the event, the photograph, the tape recorder and the anecdote." (Publisher's note)

REVIEW: *Contemp Sociol* v43 no1 p45-9 Ja 2014 Devorah Kalekin-Fishman

"Inventive Methods: The Happening of the Social" and "The Institutional Logics Perspective: A New Approach to Culture, Structure, and Process". "Although densely theorized, each of the chapters shows how the ideas have grown out of research, and points to the many future research opportunities that the perspective implies. The perspective of institutional logics goes far beyond the context of organizational theory and research from which,ultimately, it must be seen to have been derived, in coming near to reflecting the contemporary pervasiveness of experience in institutional fields. While reading, I was impressed with the varied applicability of the institutional logics perspective for enriching the approaches of diverse schools of sociology. . . . All the methods included here evoke thought and rouse the reader to action, inviting one to try them, or provoking work on a contrasting approach."

IQBAL, MUHAMMAD, SIR, 1877-1938. The reconstruction of religious thought in Islam; [by] Muhammad Iqbal 2013 Stanford University Press

1. Communism & Islam 2. Islamic philosophy 3. Islamic poetry 4. Pakistani poetry 5. Philosophical literature

ISBN 9780804781473 paper; 9780804786867 ebook; 9780804781466 cloth

SUMMARY: Edited by M. Saeed Sheikh, this book "is Muhammad Iqbal's major philosophic work: a series of profound reflections on the perennial conflict among science, religion, and philosophy, culminating in new visions of the unity of human knowledge, of the human spirit, and of God. Iqbal's thought contributed significantly to the establishment of Pakistan, to the religious and political ideals of the Iranian Revolution, and to the survival of Muslim identity in parts of the former USSR." (Publisher's note)

REVIEW: *TLS* no5775 p24 D 6 2013 TARIQ ALI

"The Reconstruction of Religious Thought in Islam." "Muhammad Iqbal (1876-1938) was one of the great poets produced by the subcontinent, who wrote in Persian and Urdu. . . . Back in India he began to preach the virtues of a return to Islam. A set of eclectic lectures he delivered in various Indian cities were later collated and published in book form in 1934 and titled 'The Reconstruction of Religious Thought in Islam.' The aim was to convince Muslim students that their religion had always contained a dynamic element and could thus accommodate science and philosophy. . . . The book itself is . . . a mixture of valuable reflections and confused banalities. Compared to much . . . being produced today its reissue is positive, since the poet is . . . one of the founders of Pakistan."

IRANIAN-RUSSIAN ENCOUNTERS; empires and revolutions since 1800; xix, 411 p. 2013 Routledge

1. Historical literature 2. Imperialism—History 3. Revolutions—History
ISBN 9780203083758 (ebook); 9780415624336 (hbk.)
LC 2012-017577

SUMMARY: This book, edited by Stephanie Cronin, explores "the impact Russia and its people have had on Iran in the last 200 years. . . . Most of the contributions concentrate on politics, but culture and the arts recieve their due as well. . . . Part two . . . deal[s] with Iran's constitutional period, 1905-11. . . . Part three addresses various aspects of the relationship between Pahlavi Iran and the Soviet Union. . . . The book's closing section considers the modern period." (Middle East Journal)

REVIEW: *Middle East J* v67 no4 p645-6 Aut 2013 Rudi Matthee

"Iranian-Russian Encounters: Empires and Revolutions Since 1800." "The focus here is on the impact Russia and its people have had on Iran in the last 200 years. . . . Most of the contributions concentrate on politics, but culture and the arts receive their due as well. The result is a well-rounded volume that succeeds well in the stated goal of going beyond state-to-state relations to delve into various layers of society . . . so as to unearth the complex, often paradoxical relations between the two neighbors. . . . Filled with excellent studies, this volume provides much new material and points the way toward future research on an important topic in Iranian history."

IRELAND THROUGH EUROPEAN EYES; western Europe, the EEC and Ireland, 1945-1973; 2013 Cork University Press

1. European Economic Community 2. Historical literature 3. Ireland—Foreign relations—History 4. Ireland—History—20th century 5. Ireland—Politics & government—20th century
ISBN 9781859184646

SUMMARY: Essays in this book, edited by Mervyn O'Driscoll, Dermot Keogh, Jerome aan de Wiel, "reveal how Belgian, French, Italian, Luxembourg, Dutch, and West German politicians, policymakers and commentators perceived independent Ireland from the end of the Second World War until Irish accession to the European Economic Community (EEC) in 1973. The postwar analysis is placed in the context of older historical interactions." (Publisher's note)

REVIEW: *Choice* v51 no5 p913 Ja 2014 D. C. Kierdorf

"Ireland Through European Eyes: Western Europe, the EEC and Ireland, 1945-1973." "This well-written, well-organized book is a highly detailed study that provides a mine of information about a comparatively narrow subject. . . . The authors draw from diplomatic records, national archives, and press reports from Ireland as well as the member countries. They also place this in the context of geopolitical factors like the Cold War and local issues like the outbreak of the Troubles. A valuable addition to the libraries of government departments and academic libraries specializing in the history and politics of Ireland, international relations, and economics, or of the European Union."

IRENAEUS, SAINT, BISHOP OF LYON. St. Irenaeus of Lyons; Against the Heresies; [by] Saint Irenaeus 2012 Paulist Press

1. Christian heresies 2. Early Christian literature 3. Fathers of the church 4. Gnosticism 5. Religious literature
ISBN 9780809105991 hardcover

SUMMARY: Written by Christian church father Irenaeus of Lyons and translated by Dominic J. Unger, "Book 2 of this five-book [work] refutes the gnostic and Marcionite heresies the falsely so-called knowledge that Irenaeus so thoroughly exposed in Book I, convincingly and effectively stating the clear line between orthodox belief and gnostic doctrine." (Publisher's note)

REVIEW: *Classical Rev* v63 no2 p462-3 O 2013 Anthony Briggman

"St. Irenaeus of Lyons: 'Against the Heresies' Book 2." "That this edition offers the finest English translation of AH 2 hardly bears mentioning. . . . The inclusion of a fine introduction by [Michael] Slusser, which displays a thorough acquaintance with the literature on Irenaeus, and copious notes on points of translation, theology and pertinent scholarship, serves further to increase the value of this edition. . . . On occasion the translation suffers from infelicitous expressions. . . . As with every translation published by ACW the text is bolstered by substantial notes. Most often, these notes provide excellent discussions of the interpretative decisions that occupied the translator, which is especially helpful given the, at times, frustrating state of the Latin text."

IRIYE, AKIRA, 1934-. The new Cambridge history of American foreign relations.; [by] Akira Iriye 266 p. 2013 Cambridge University Press

1. Globalization 2. Historical literature 3. Modern civilization—American influences 4. United States—History—20th century
ISBN 9780521763288 (hardback v. 3); 9780521763622 (hardback v. 4); 9780521767521 (hardback v. 2); 9781107005907 (hardback v. 1); 9781107031838 (hardback set)
LC 2012-018193

SUMMARY: This book by Akira Iriye is part of a revised edition of the series "The Cambridge History of American Foreign Relations." It "describes how the United States became a global power--economically, culturally, and militarily--during the period from 1913 to 1945, from the inception of Woodrow Wilson's presidency to the end of the Second World War." (Publisher's note)

REVIEW: *Choice* v51 no5 p907 Ja 2014 L. M. Lees

"Dimensions of the Early American Empire 1754-1865," The American Search for Opportunity 1865-1913," and "The Globalizing of America 1913-1945." "The four volumes of this revision . . . feature one new author and relatively minimal changes by two of the original three authors. . . . In volume one, 'Dimensions of the Early American Empire, 1754-1865,' new author [William Earl] Weeks . . . frames his analysis around ten dimensions that characterize the American empire. . . . Weeks deftly weaves these themes into his intriguing and complex study, which is a worthy addition to the series. . . . Libraries with the original set should consider replacing volumes one and four only."

IRIZARRY, CHRISTINE.tr. About Europe. See Guenoun, D.

IRONMONGER, J. W. Coincidence; [by] J. W. Ironmonger 304 p. 2014 HarperCollins

1. Coincidence 2. Kony, Joseph, 1961- 3. Orphans—Fiction 4. Probability theory 5. Psychological fiction
ISBN 0062309897; 9780062309891

SUMMARY: This book by J. W. Ironmonger "charts Azalea Lewis and her complicated family across the British Isles and East Africa. The unlikely organizing principle is the seeming inevitability of disaster on Midsummer's Day, a fatal date across several decades. . . . The novel centers on a love story between Azalea and an academic, Thomas Post, whose research focuses on probability." (Booklist)

REVIEW: *Booklist* v110 no11 p20 F 1 2014 Kevin Clouther

REVIEW: *Kirkus Rev* v82 no3 p238 F 1 2014

"Coincidence". "[J. W.] Ironmonger . . . spins another nimble tale set on two continents, this one exploring the impact of coincidence by following a woman whose life is saturated by it and a man who studies it for a living. . . . The Isle of Man story is as wistful and charming as its setting suggests, while the sections involving Thomas Post are largely an enjoyable audit of coincidence science. But the Uganda scenes, as hinted at by the map at the beginning of the book, are the heartbeat of the novel—vivid and suspenseful even before the arrival of Joseph Kony. . . . The narration can be heavy-handed at times, but this tale is not a character study—it's a feat of cleverness. Weighty topics are seamlessly woven into this fast, captivating read."

IRVING, RON. Beyond the quadratic formula; [by] Ron Irving xvi, 228 p. 2013 The Mathematical Association of America

1. Algebra 2. Arithmetic 3. Mathematical literature 4. Polynomials 5. Root systems (Algebra)
ISBN 0883857839 (hardback); 9780883857830 (hardback)
LC 2013-940989

SUMMARY: "This book, written to enable self-study, addresses the problem of determining zeros of polynomials from their coefficients, avoiding modern abstract algebra and Calois theory. . . . Along the way, [Ron Irving] constructs the various discriminants for determining the number of distinct real roots, as well as complex arithmetic from scratch." (Choice: Current Reviews for Academic Libraries)

REVIEW: *Choice* v51 no5 p877-8 Ja 2014 S. J. Colley

"Beyond the Quadratic Forumula." "This book, written to enable self-study, addresses the problem of determining zeros of polynomials from their coefficients, avoiding modern abstract algebra and Calois theory.[Ron] Irving . . . developed this work from a course he taught to prospective and in-service secondary school teachers, and it would make welcome reading for any undergraduate interested in seeing some classical algebra that is no longer a regular part of the school curriculum. . . . Exercises form an integral part of the text and are embedded in the exposition so that the reader can be a partner in constructing the algebraic arguments."

ISAACMAN, ALLEN F. Dams, displacement, and the delusion of development; Cahora Bassa and its legacies in Mozambique, 1965/2007; [by] Allen F. Isaacman xvi, 291 p. 2013 Ohio University Press

1. Economic development projects—Mozambique 2. Forced migration—Zambezi River Valley 3. Historical literature
ISBN 9780821420331 (pb: alk. paper); 9780821444504 (electronic)́
LC 2012-049113

SUMMARY: In this book, authors Allen F. and Barbara Isaacman present an "'alternative history' . . . of the Cahora Bassa Dam on the Zambezi River, Mozambique's most important (supposedly) development project. The authors aim to recover the silenced voices of those who had to pay for 'progress,' suffering displacement and massive disturbances in their livelihoods." (African Studies Quarterly)

REVIEW: *Am Hist Rev* v119 no2 p651-3 Ap 2014 James C. McCann

REVIEW: *Choice* v51 no8 p1464-5 Ap 2014 T. P. Johnson

"Dams, Displacement, and the Delusion of Development: Cahora Bassa and Its Legacies in Mozambique, 1965/2007". "As veteran Mozambicanists, Allen Isaacman . . . and Barbara Isaacman draw on decades of research, also making use of numerous environmental assessments of the dam's ecological effects. A great strength of the book comes from presenting many voices of peasants, fisherfolk, and dam workers, who speak eloquently about lost lands, rights, and livelihoods. Essential for African and development studies collections."

ISAACMAN, BARBARA S. Dams, displacement, and the delusion of development. See Isaacman, A. F.

ISAACS, ANNE. Meanwhile back at the ranch; 56 p. 2014 Schwartz & Wade

1. Courtship—Fiction 2. Humorous stories 3. Ranch life—Texas—Fiction 4. Tall tales
ISBN 0375867457; 9780375867453
LC 2011-046490

SUMMARY: In this book, by Anne Issacs, "widow Tulip Jones of Bore, England, inherits a ranch in By-Golly Gully, Texas, and moves in with two trunks of tea, twelve pet tortoises, and three servants. The peaceful life suits the wealthy widow fine until word gets out and every unmarried man in Texas lines up to marry her. Widow Tulip and her small staff of three can't possibly run the farm and manage all the suitors, so she devises a plan." (Publisher's note)

REVIEW: *Booklist* v110 no9/10 p120-2 Ja 1 2014 Thom Barthelmess

"Meanwhile, Back at the Ranch." "English widow Tulip Jones is off to America, having inherited $35 million and an entire ranch in Texas, with a lot of tea, her three ranch hands (née house servants), and 12 pet tortoises in tow. . .

. [Anne] Isaacs' tall-tale plotting and over-the-top language are matched by [Kevin] Hawkes' bright, comic paintings, brimming with spirit and detail. An opening endpaper signpost warns against exaggeration in Texas, promising just the outsize adventure that Isaacs and Hawkes deliver."

REVIEW: *Bull Cent Child Books* v67 no6 p317 F 2014 Amy Atkinson

REVIEW: *Horn Book Magazine* v90 no1 p74-5 Ja/F 2014 BETTY CARTER

REVIEW: *Kirkus Rev* v81 no24 p90 D 15 2013

REVIEW: *Publ Wkly* v260 no48 p56 N 25 2013

REVIEW: *SLJ* v60 no1 p70 Ja 2014 Amy Seto Musser

ISAACSON, WALTER. Steve Jobs; [by] Walter Isaacson 656 2011 Simon & Schuster

1. Biography, Individual 2. Businesspeople—United States—Biography 3. Computer engineers—United States—Biography 4. Entrepreneurship 5. Executives 6. Inventors—United States—Biography
ISBN 9781451648546 (trade paperback); 1451648537; 9781451648539 (hardback); 9781451648553 (ebook); 1451648553
LC 2011-045006

SUMMARY: This book discusses the "basic outlines of [Steve] Jobs' career. . . . He was the co-creator of the personal computer. . . . [A]gainst the backdrop of [Jobs's] abrasive personality, [Walter] Isaacson's book offers an overriding message . . . he was a creative genius whose profound understanding of consumer appetites allowed him to create technology that no one else imagined or even thought feasible." (Commentary)

REVIEW: *America* v206 no18 p33-5 My 28 2012 MAURICE TIMOTHY REIDY

"Steve Jobs." "The appearance of [Walter] Isaacson's biography so soon after Jobs's death is a testament to [Jobs's] dogged determination to shape his legacy. It was Jobs who approached Isaacson to write the book, knowing full well that Isaacson's previous subjects were Benjamin Franklin and Albert Einstein. Jobs clearly saw himself as an inventor in the tradition of these pioneers. . . . Yet a close examination of his life, seen through the lens of Isaacson's impressive if unwieldy reportage, reveals a more complex story."

REVIEW: *Booklist* v108 no9/10 p62 Ja 1 2012 Sue-Ellen Beauregard

REVIEW: *Booklist* v109 no15 p72 Ap 1 2013 Ilene Cooper

REVIEW: *Choice* v49 no8 p1482 Ap 2012 K. D. Winward

REVIEW: *Commentary* v132 no5 p62-4 D 2011 DANIEL CASSE

Steve Jobs. "Published only weeks after [Steve] Jobs's death at age 56, 'Steve Jobs' is the result of two years of work during which [Walter] Isaacson was granted unlimited, unrestricted access to Jobs, his family, his friends, and his competitors. Isaacson took full advantage, and the result is a book Jobs could never possibly have fully approved. . . . [A]gainst the backdrop of this abrasive personality, Isaacson's book offers an overriding message that is more consistent with the public image of Jobs: he was a creative genius whose profound understanding of consumer appetites allowed him to create technology that no one else imagined or even thought feasible. Isaacson builds a persuasive case that, throughout his career, Jobs reshaped seven different businesses: personal computing, animated movies, music, mobile phones, tablet computing, digital publishing, and retail stores. . . . The most intriguing relationship in the book is that between Steve Jobs and Microsoft founder Bill Gates."

REVIEW: *Kirkus Rev* v79 no22 p2087 N 15 2011

REVIEW: *London Rev Books* v33 no24 p19-20 D 15 2011 Mattathias Schwartz

REVIEW: *N Y Rev Books* v59 no1 p24-6 Ja 12 2012 Sue Halpern

"Steve Jobs." "[Walter] Isaacson's biography—which is nothing if not a comprehensive catalog of Jobs's steps and missteps . . . is distinguished from previous books about Jobs by the author's relationship with his subject. This is a book that Jobs solicited in 2004, approaching Isaacson not long after being diagnosed with cancer. . . . Jobs, who considered himself special, sought out Isaacson because he saw himself on par with [Isaacson's previous subjects Benjamin] Franklin and [Albert] Einstien. By the time he was finished with the book, Isaacson seemed to think so as well . . . [T]he trouble is that Jobs comes across as such a repellant man . . . that the book is often hard to read. . . . Artists, [Jobs] seemed to believe, got a pass on bad behavior. Isaacson seems to think so too, proving that it is possible to write a hagiography even while exposing the worst in a person."

REVIEW: *New Repub* v243 no4 p18-27 Mr 15 2012 Evgeny Morozov

"Steve Jobs." "There are few traces of Jobs the philosopher in Walter Isaacson's immensely detailed and pedestrian biography of the man. Isaacson draws liberally on previously published biographies, and on dozens of interviews that Jobs gave to the national media since the early 1980s. . . . That the book contains few earth-shattering revelations is not necessarily Isaacson's fault. . . . As Isaacson makes clear, Jobs was not a particularly nice man, nor did he want to be one. The more diplomatic of Apple's followers might say that Steve Jobs — bloodthirsty vegetarian, combative Buddhist — lived a life of paradoxes. A less generous assessment would be that he was an unprincipled opportunist — a brilliant but restless chameleon."

REVIEW: *New Statesman* v140 no5078 p50 N 7 2011 Helen Lewis-Hasteley

REVIEW: *Publ Wkly* v259 no5 p53 Ja 30 2012

REVIEW: *SLJ* v59 no4 p120 Ap 2013 Rita Meade

REVIEW: *SLJ* v58 no3 p182-3 Mr 2012 John Peters

REVIEW: *Time* v178 no24 p62-3 D 19 2011 Lev Grossman Radhika Jones Mary Pols

REVIEW: *Time* v180 no2 p52 Jl 9 2012 Dambisa Moyo

REVIEW: *Time* v178 no18 p53 N 7 2011 Lev Grossman

REVIEW: *TLS* no5673/5674 p16 D 23 2011 Michael Saler

ISADORA, RACHEL. Old Mikamba had a farm; [by] Rachel Isadora 40 p. 2013 Nancy Paulsen Books, An Imprint of Penguin Group (USA) Inc.

1. Africa—Juvenile literature 2. Animals—Juvenile literature 3. Children's stories 4. Farm life—Juvenile literature 5. Farms—Juvenile literature 6. Folk songs—United States 7. Folk songs, English—United States—Texts 8. Songs
ISBN 0399257403; 9780399257407
LC 2012-049555

SUMMARY: "A familiar childhood song gets an African twist in [adaptor and illustrator Rachel] Isadora's latest picture book. She takes readers on safari to the plains of Africa to meet elephants, cheetahs, and dassies. . . . Old Mikamba's farm is a game park, so while there is some interaction between the two small children in the book and the animals, most of them are presented against a backdrop wilder and freer than any space Old MacDonald could offer his domestic stock." (Booklist)

REVIEW: *Booklist* v110 no3 p51 O 1 2013 Kara Dean

REVIEW: *Bull Cent Child Books* v67 no3 p160 N 2013 H. M.

"Old Mikamba Had a Farm." "Old Mikamba may have a farm, but it's a game farm on the African plains, and the animals on his farm are a far cry from the typical cow/pig/chicken that hang out with Old MacDonald. Here, baboons, zebras, and elephants share space with rhinos, giraffes, and cheetahs, each getting a verse in this adaptation of the traditional tune. . . . [Adaptor and illustrator] Isadora's collage work employs oil paints, printed paper, palette paper, ink, and pencil to compose the menagerie of wildlife; the cut paper is by far the most striking, incorporating elements of texture and pattern into the compositions; patterned borders are an element too many in some spreads, drawing focus from the intriguingly composed figures."

REVIEW: *Kirkus Rev* v81 no18 p60 S 15 2013

REVIEW: *Publ Wkly* v260 no36 p54 S 9 2013

REVIEW: *SLJ* v59 no8 p76 Ag 2013 Carol Connor

ISADORA, RACHEL.il. Old Mikamba had a farm. See Isadora, R.

ISENBERG, NOAH. Edgar G. Ulmer; a filmmaker at the margins; [by] Noah Isenberg 384 p. 2013 University of California Press

1. Biography (Literary form) 2. Film genres 3. Motion picture industry—United States—History—20th century 4. Motion picture producers and directors—United States—Biography

ISBN 9780520235779 (cloth : alk. paper)

LC 2013-025957

SUMMARY: In this "account of a career spent on the margins of Hollywood, Noah Isenberg provides the little-known details of [Edgar G.] Ulmer's personal life and a thorough analysis of his wide-ranging, eclectic films--features aimed at minority audiences, horror and sci-fi flicks, genre pictures made in the U.S. and abroad." (Publisher's note)

REVIEW: *Bookforum* v20 no5 p50 F/Mr 2014 HOWARD HAMPTON

"Edgar G. Ulmer: A Filmmaker at the Margins." "Well documented, a bit disheveled around the edges, but all in all a cogent treatment of a singularly unlikely career. [Noah] Isenberg's writing isn't especially stylish, but its recitative quality allows the monumental eccentricity of Ulmer's underground journey to shine through. . . . Isenberg's unembellished book about the long detour Edgar G. Ulmer's life and art took is too prosaic--too sensible, perhaps--to be a work of art, but it astonishes all the same: such stuff as hallucinations and bittersweet fever dreams were made of."

REVIEW: *Film Q* v67 no2 p92-4 Wint 2013 DAVID STERRITT

REVIEW: *TLS* no5798 p22 My 16 2014 ERIC J. IANNELLI

ISLAM, SYED MANZOORUL. Merman's prayer and other stories; [by] Syed Manzoorul Islam 293 p. 2013 Daily Star Books

1. Bengali fiction 2. Indic literature—Translations into English 3. Mermen 4. Point of view (Literature) 5. Short stories—Collections

ISBN 9789849027188

LC 2013-410681

SUMMARY: "The stories compiled in this collection constitute a very small part of Syed Manzoorul Islam's creative writing. Put together, they nonetheless show all the traits unique to his storytelling. His narrator is continuously talking to readers, preparing them for the twists and turns the stories take. . . . The stories are told with poise and humour in the great Bengali oral tradition." (Publisher's note)

REVIEW: *World Lit Today* v88 no2 p60-1 Mr/Ap 2014 Rifat Munim

"The Merman's Prayer and Other Stories." "The first thing that strikes the reader who encounters the stories in this collection is the narrator's role: how he talks to readers and plays with their expectations, dropping frequent hints in the process that this is a story he is a part of, or has received in a dream, or heard from a friend, or witnessed in his community. . . . Syed Manzoorul Islam, in his three-decade-long literary career, has mastered a style that sets him apart from many of his Bengali contemporaries. While surreal experimentation is not rare in Bengali literature, his open-endedness, self-reflexivity, and blend of pathos and humor have given a solid foundation to postmodern tendencies in Bengali fiction."

ISMAIL, YASMEEN. Time for bed, Fred!; [by] Yasmeen Ismail 32 p. 2014 Bloomsbury/Walker

1. Bedtime—Fiction 2. Children's stories 3. Dogs—Fiction 4. Parent & child—Juvenile literature 5. Sleep

ISBN 0802735983; 9780802735973 (hardcover); 9780802735980 (library reinforced)

LC 2013-010711

SUMMARY: In this children's bedtime story, written and illustrated by Yasmeen Ismail, "it's time for [the dog] Fred to go to bed . . . but Fred really, really doesn't want to! From hiding up in trees, to splashing in muddy puddles, to hiding behind bookshelves, Fred will do anything to avoid bedtime. He would even rather have a bath than go to bed . . . but all of this running couldn't possibly have possibly made Fred sleepy—could it?" (Publisher's note)

REVIEW: *Booklist* v110 no11 p71 F 1 2014 Daniel Kraus

REVIEW: *Kirkus Rev* v81 no24 p95 D 15 2013

"Time for Bed, Fred!". "A hilarious, not-ready-for-bed book starring Fred—an irrepressible and irresistible dog—and his diversionary tactics, in whose spirit parents and children will lovingly find the familiar. . . . Playful illustrations in an autumnal palette will endear the pup to readers, as he gleefully climbs, digs and splashes through mud. Ismail applies her watercolors skillfully. . . . Each mark has an energy, purpose and thought to it. The sophisticated and loose artwork is the ideal match for the simple, emotive text. A perfectly designed read-aloud for the bedtime staller. A sheer delight!"

REVIEW: *N Y Times Book Rev* p22 Mr 16 2014 SARAH HARRISON SMITH

REVIEW: *Publ Wkly* v260 no47 p51 N 18 2013

REVIEW: *SLJ* v60 no1 p70 Ja 2014 Jenna Boles

ISMAIL, YASMEEN.il. Time for bed, Fred! See Ismail, Y.

ISOL, 1972-.il. Numeralia. See Numeralia

ITZKOFF, DAVE. Mad as hell; the making of Network and the fateful vision of the angriest man in movies; [by] Dave Itzkoff 304 p. 2014 Times Books, Henry Holt & Co.

1. Film criticism 2. Motion picture producers & directors—United States—Biography 3. PERFORMING ARTS—Film & Video—Screenwriting 4. SOCIAL SCIENCE—Media Studies
ISBN 0805095691; 9780805095692 (hardback)
LC 2013-018292

SUMMARY: "In 'Mad As Hell,' Dave Itzkoff of 'The New York Times' recounts the surprising and dramatic story of how 'Network' made it to the screen. Such a movie rarely gets made any more--one man's vision of the world, independent of studio testing or market research. And that man was Paddy Chayefsky, the tough, driven, Oscar-winning screenwriter whose vision--outlandish for its time--is all too real today." (Publisher's note)

REVIEW: *Atlantic* v313 no2 p36-8 Mr 2014 JAMES PARKER

REVIEW: *Booklist* v110 no9/10 p34 Ja 1 2014 Ray Olson

REVIEW: *Commentary* v137 no4 p67-9 Ap 2014 TERRY TEACHOUT

REVIEW: *Kirkus Rev* v81 no24 p46 D 15 2013

REVIEW: *Libr J* v139 no3 p107 F 15 2014 Neil Derksen

REVIEW: *N Y Times Book Rev* p10 F 16 2014 ROB LOWE

"Mad As Hell: The Making of "Network" and the Fateful Vision of the Angriest Man in Movies." "Paddy Chayefsky's Oscar-winning screenplay for the 1976 film 'Network' was, and remains, the kind of literate, darkly funny and breathtakingly prescient material that prompts many to claim it as the greatest screenplay of the 20th century. In 'Mad As Hell: The Making of "Network" and the Fateful Vision of the Angriest Man in Movies,' Dave Itzkoff, a culture reporter for 'The New York Times,' takes us behind the curtain and shows us why. . . . Itzkoff's engrossing, unfolding narrative . . . is an inspiring, conflict-driven account of the parade of indignities and happy accidents that are always present when making a movie, even a great one."

REVIEW: *Natl Rev* v66 no5 p45-9 Mr 24 2014 PETER TONGUETTE

REVIEW: *New York Times* v163 no56423 pC6 F 25 2014 LISA SCHWARZBAUM

REVIEW: *New York Times* v163 no56407 p11 F 9 2014 MAUREEN DOWD

REVIEW: *Publ Wkly* v260 no43 p47 O 28 2013

IVES, JACK D. Sustainable mountain development; getting the facts right; [by] Jack D. Ives xv, 293 p. 2013 Himalayan Association for the Advancement of Science

1. Environmental literature 2. Environmental policy—Himalaya Mountains Region 3. Environmental protection—Himalaya Mountains Region 4. Himalaya Mountains Region—Social conditions 5. Sustainable development
ISBN 9789937261951; 9937261953
LC 2013-410820

SUMMARY: "This is an autobiographical account of the author's lifetime work in the mountains of the developing world. The book takes its title from the need to counter those who, in the 1970s, predicted catastrophic deforestation, soil erosion, and the resulting flooding and droughts in the Himalayas and other tropical mountains. The work of [Jack D.] Ives . . . and his colleagues has provided a scientific foundation that recognizes the wisdom of native populations." (Choice: Current Reviews for Academic Libraries)

REVIEW: *Choice* v51 no6 p1039 F 2014 N. Caine

"Sustainable Mountain Development: Getting the Facts Right." "The book is very attractive, since it is illustrated by more than 200 of the author's photographs; those, along with the large format, make this close to a coffee-table volume. Endnotes and appendixes support the work. The production of the text and photographs is excellent. Unfortunately, the binding failed after less than a week of use, without copying or scanning. Overall, readers interested in mountain environments and their populations will enjoy the book."

J

JACK, VIVIAN. Toco; Tales Told Through the Eyes of a Small Boy Growing Up in the Countryside of Trinidad Wi in the 30's & 40's; [by] Vivian Jack 158 p. 2012 Author Solutions

1. Autobiographical fiction 2. Caribbean Area—Fiction 3. Families—Fiction 4. Historical fiction, Trinidadian & Tobagonian (English) 5. Magic—Fiction
ISBN 147973165X; 9781479731657

SUMMARY: In this book by Vivian Jack, the narrator recalls "the years he lives in Toco, a small village on Trinidad, during the second world war. Toco's remoteness prevents Gabriel from focusing too much on European scuffles, though. . . . A mix of superstition, Caribbean Christianity and island traditions shapes Gabriel's understanding of the world, turning seemingly normal life events into exhilarating, sometimes harrowing affairs." (Kirkus Reviews)

REVIEW: *Kirkus Rev* v81 no7 p8 Ap 1 2013

REVIEW: *Kirkus Rev* p27 D 15 2013 supplemet best books 2013

"Toco: Tales Told Through the Eyes of a Small Boy Growing Up in the Countryside of Trinidad, WI in the 30s & 40s". "Readers will enjoy watching Gabriel grow into a young man, and when a rupture in family life forces him to leave Toco behind, readers may find themselves sharing in his dismay. [Vivian] Jack, a skillful writer, capably relates island parlance while injecting his tales with affecting color and passion, not to mention a few black-and-white illustrations. Most of the stories successfully fit together, and Jack's proclaimed goal to relate what life was like in rural Trinidad in the '30s and '40s has been achieved. Readers will be happily lost in this lively, engrossing book about home and family."

JACKSON, BUZZY. A bad woman feeling good; blues and the women who sing them; [by] Buzzy Jackson 2005 Norton

1. Blues music—History & criticism 2. Blues music—Social aspects 3. Music literature 4. Women blues musicians 5. Women singers
ISBN 0-393-05936-7

SUMMARY: This book by Buzzy Jackson "traces the lives and influence of female blues singers, including pioneers Mamie Desdunes, Ma Rainey, and Bessie Smith; jazz singers BiUie Holiday and Etta James; and pop singers Tina Turner, Aretha Franklin, and Janis Joplin, and explains how their music encouraged emotional freedom and forthrightness about the complicated struggles women face." (Booklist)

REVIEW: *Booklist* v110 no5 p16 N 1 2013 Donna Seaman
"A Bad Woman Feeling Good: Blues and the Women Who Sang Them," "Stomping the Blues," and "Nothing But the Blues: The Music and the Musicians." "[Buzzy] Jackson traces the lives and influence of female blues singers . . . and explains how their music encouraged emotional freedom and forthrightness about the complicated struggles women face. . . . [Albert Murray's] radiant interpretation is rich in incisive portraits of blues musicians and many telling anecdotes, all accompanied by extraordinary photographs. . . . This handsome, well-illustrated, and penetrating blues history tracks the metamorphosis of the blues from its African roots."

JACKSON, DONNA M. Every body's talking; what we say without words; [by] Donna M. Jackson 64 p. 2014 Twenty-First Century Books
1. Body language—Juvenile literature 2. Cross-cultural differences 3. Facial expression 4. Nonverbal communication—Juvenile literature 5. Science—Popular works
ISBN 1467708585; 9781467708586 (lib. bdg.: alk. paper)
LC 2013-019674

SUMMARY: This book, by Donna M. Jackson, "explores the complexities of body language. Discover what is really being expressed when people stand, sit, or move in certain ways and learn how you can use your body and facial expressions to communicate more effectively in a variety of situations." (Publisher's note)

REVIEW: *Booklist* v110 no12 p67-9 F 15 2014 Erin Anderson

REVIEW: *Bull Cent Child Books* v67 no10 p522 Je 2014 E. B.
"Every Body's Talking: What We Say Without Words". "Children's science writer Jackson offers a breezy but substantive introduction to unspoken communication. . . . Picture-book trim size, wide leading, and generous font size may initially suggest a younger audience, but the vocabulary is appropriately challenging for middle-schoolers and beyond, while both illustrations and situations of teen communication are used to highlight various points. Moreover, Jackson never overstates her case, and she frequently cautions readers that context and individual quirks impact interpersonal transactions in ways that preclude applying these generalizations universally."

REVIEW: *Kirkus Rev* v82 no6 p61 Mr 15 2014

REVIEW: *SLJ* v60 no3 p180 Mr 2014 Maryann H. Owen

REVIEW: *Voice of Youth Advocates* v37 no2 p92 Je 2014 Cynthia Winfield

JACKSON, JOHN. Tales for Great Grandchildren; [by] John Jackson 2011 JJ Books
1. Folklore—India 2. Indic mythology 3. Indic short stories 4. Mythology, Nepali 5. Tale (Literary form)—Nepal
ISBN 095692123X; 9780956921239

SUMMARY: This book is a "collection of 13 illustrated short stories aimed at children aged 7-12 years old" which "[d]raw[s] on the folklore and mythology of India and Nepal." (Publishers' note) It includes "stories such as 'The Hole in the Roof,' in which a lazy farmer's comeuppance is endured by his wise spouse, and 'The North Star,' in which the troublemaking wife of a king is banished to the forest." (School Library Journal)

REVIEW: *SLJ* v58 no5 p65 My 2012 Henrietta Thornton
"Tales for Great Grand Children." "Some of these 13 satisfying, Brothers Grimm-like stories, explains the author, are 'worked up' from fragments of folklore and mythology he came across in Nepal and the north of India, whereas others are translations of the tales as he found them. Either way, [the] stories . . . will enchant listeners, transporting them to faraway locales and teaching them about other cultures. The illustrations--one per story--are gorgeous, and feature small movements that observers will enjoy pointing out, such as a scurrying mouse or a multicolored quilt rising and falling on a snoring giant's chest. . . . The tales' presentation features a few problems that will keep readers and listeners on their toes, however."

JACKSON, KEVIN. Constellation of genius; 1922 : modernism year one; [by] Kevin Jackson 536 p. 2012 Hutchinson
1. Historical literature 2. Modernism (Aesthetics) 3. Modernism (Art) 4. Modernism (Literature) 5. Nineteen twenty-two, A.D
ISBN 0091930979 (hbk.); 9780091930974 (hbk.)
LC 2012-545938

SUMMARY: "In 'Constellation of Genius', Kevin Jackson puts the titanic achievements of Joyce and Eliot in the context of the world in which their works first appeared." He "traces an unforgettable journey through the diaries of the actors, anthropologists, artists, dancers, designers, filmmakers, philosophers, playwrights, politicians, and scientists." (Publisher's note)

REVIEW: *Atlantic* v312 no3 p39-40 O 2013 MICHAEL LEVENSON
"Constellation of Genius 1922: Modernism Year One." "British critic Kevin Jackson has his own way of putting the question, and returning to the scene of revolution. . . . 'Constellation of Genius' amounts to a tarted-up timeline that can't give us what we need--which is a sense of relationship, of modernism as works-in-dialogue, and the New as something that doesn't drop from the sky but grows out of struggle and exchange over many years. Implicitly, the book admits what it pretends to deny: that all this annus-mirabilising misses too much."

REVIEW: *Kirkus Rev* v81 no13 p162 Jl 1 2013

REVIEW: *Libr J* v138 no6 p60 Ap 1 2013 Barbara Hoffert

REVIEW: *Publ Wkly* v260 no22 p46 Je 3 2013

JACKSON, NATE. Slow getting up; a story of NFL survival from the bottom of the pile; [by] Nate Jackson 243 p. 2013 Harper
1. Football injuries 2. Football players—United States—Biography 3. Memoirs 4. National Football

League 5. Sports literature
ISBN 0062108026; 9780062108029
LC 2013-011427

SUMMARY: Author Nate Jackson presents "an unvarnished and uncensored memoir of everyday life in . . . the National Football League. From scouting combines to training camps, off-season parties to game-day routines, debilitating physical injuries--including degenerative brain conditions--to poor pensions and financial distress, he offers a . . . look at life in the NFL, and the young men who risk their health and even their lives to play the game." (Publisher's note)

REVIEW: *Booklist* v110 no1 p34 S 1 2013 Wes Lukowsky

"Slow Getting Up: A Story of NFL Survival From the Bottom of the Pile." "Somewhere along the way he learned to write, not just link words together to form a coherent narrative, which would be more than enough for most sports bios, but really write. There is a bit of the artist in Nate Jackson. For anyone who wants to experience the NFL player experience, this is the book to read. . . . This is Jackson's first book, but he's honed his skills at Slate, Deadspin, the Wall Street Journal, and the New York Times. Don't miss this one; it could very well be the best book about pro football you will ever read."

REVIEW: *Kirkus Rev* v81 no13 p311 Jl 1 2013

REVIEW: *New York Times* v162 no56258 pC19-24 S 13 2013 DWIGHT GARNER

REVIEW: *New York Times* v162 no56258 pC19-24 S 13 2013 DWIGHT GARNER

"Slow Getting Up: A Story of NFL Survival From the Bottom of the Pile." "We're int he middle of a boomlet of superb, satire-minded writing about professional football. . . . Here now is a book by Nate Jackson . . . and it's everything you want football memoirs to be but never are: hilarious, dirty, warm, human, honest, weird. . . . He's that unicorn-like rarity among former football players: he can write. . . . Mr. Jackson is . . . observant about almost everything. He is epigrammatical. . . . 'Slow Getting Up' is a sly, inquisitive, wide-awake book about what it's like to play in the N.F.L. if you're a relative nobody, if you're among the beefy proletariat. It'll make you see the game with fresh eyes."

JACKSON, PAUL R. W. The Last Guru; Robert Cohan's Life in Dance from Martha Graham to Contemporary Dance Theatre; [by] Paul R. W. Jackson 404 p. 2013 Princeton Book Co Pub

1. Biography (Literary form) 2. Choreographers—Biography 3. Cohan, Robert 4. Dance literature 5. Graham, Martha, 1894-1991 6. London Contemporary Dance Theatre (Performer)
ISBN 1852731621; 9781852731625

SUMMARY: Written by Paul Jackson, "This book is based on extensive interviews with [choreographer Robert] Cohan, his family, friends and colleagues. Drawing together his life in dance around the world it provides the first in depth study of this seminal figure in the dance world. . . . A distinguished teacher, choreographer and advocate for dance he has shaped the lives of generations of dance artists." (Publisher's note)

REVIEW: *TLS* no5780 p19 Ja 10 2014 JUDITH FLANDERS

"The Last Guru: Robert Cohan's Life in Dance, From Martha Graham to London Contemporary Dance Theatre." "Paul R. W. Jackson's decision to tell [choreographer Robert] Cohan's story entirely chronologically provides a number of challenges. . . . A thematic approach would have allowed the author to show the development of the choreographer, from his more formal, austere earlier pieces, to his later, more lyrical period. . . . In fact, there is almost no attempt to get inside Cohan's head and discover what he was thinking. . . . It is dispiriting . . . that Jackson constantly reduces . . . admiration to an aggrieved arguing back at critics long gone."

JACKSON, RICHARD.tr. The master of insomnia. See The master of insomnia

JACKSON, ROSS. Occupy World Street; a global roadmap for radical economic and political reform; [by] Ross Jackson 315 p. 2011 Chelsea Green Pub.

1. Climatic changes—Prevention 2. Economics literature 3. Gaia hypothesis 4. Human ecology 5. Political science literature 6. Sustainable development—International cooperation
ISBN 1603583882 (pbk.); 1603583890 (epub); 9781603583886 (pbk.); 9781603583893 (epub)
LC 2011-039163

SUMMARY: In this book, "[author Ross] Jackson opens with catastrophic prophecy, but nothing that we haven't heard before: We're past the point of abundant and cheap oil, and all that depends on it, including much of global agriculture, will suffer accordingly. Moreover, there is danger of falling into a "fatal energy trap" whereby fossil fuel is no longer available to manufacture renewable energy mechanisms--wind towers, solar panels and the like. Jackson does not . . . restate the Club of Rome conclusions of yore, but the approach is much the same, including abundant graphs and charts [and] a broad-ranging survey of ecological and political crises to come. . . . It is widely argued that the U.S. government has propped up bad-guy regimes around the world." (Kirkus)

REVIEW: *Kirkus Rev* v80 no4 p370 F 15 2012

"Occupy Wall Street: A Global Roadmap for Radical Economic and Political Reform." " Canadian think-tanker and philanthropist [Ross] Jackson . . . has a similarly pessimistic view, though he mixes in New Agey sentiments . . . thick enough to make a climate denier long for the homespun wisdom of Al Gore. Jackson opens with catastrophic prophecy, but nothing that we haven't heard before: We're past the point of abundant and cheap oil, and all that depends on it, including much of global agriculture, will suffer accordingly. . . . Policy wonks will want a more disciplined argument, even if the 'Gaian League' will probably have a cool flag."

REVIEW: *Publ Wkly* v259 no2 p45 Ja 9 2012

JACOB, CHRISTIAN. The web of Athenaeus; [by] Christian Jacob 150 p. 2013 Center for Hellenic Studies

1. Dinners & dining in literature 2. Greek literature—Translations into English 3. Plays on words 4. Symposium (Classical Greek drinking party)
ISBN 9780674073289 (alk. paper)
LC 2013-009762

SUMMARY: In this "reading of Athenaeus's 'Sophists at Dinner' (ca. 200 ce). [Christian] Jacob provides the reader with a map and a compass to navigate the unfathomable number of intersecting paths in this enormous work: the books, the quotations, the diners, the dishes served, and--above all--the wordplay, all within the simulacrum of an ancient Greek library." (Publisher's note)

REVIEW: *Choice* v51 no5 p829-30 Ja 2014 D. Konstan

"The Web of Athanaeus." "[Christian] Jacob surveys Athenaeus's characters and themes; the role of libraries and Athenaeus's relation to the past; the intersection of Greek symposium with Roman dinner party; how people read; why they were so passionate about words, many of them obsolete or arcane; what such a work might have meant to the original readership; and how the whole farrago hangs together. The translation is a bit wooden, and a certain lightness of touch does not always alleviate the scholarly tone. However, the book is a welcome introduction to a type of literature that has had a great influence, though it is out of favor and indeed all but incomprehensible today. . . . Recommended."

JACOB, REBEKAH. Controversy and hope. See Cox, J.

JACOBS, DIANE. Dear Abigail; the intimate lives and revolutionary ideas of Abigail Adams and her two remarkable sisters; [by] Diane Jacobs 528 p. 2014 Random House Inc

1. Adams, Abigail, 1744-1818 2. Biography (Literary form) 3. Cranch, Mary Smith 4. Peabody, Elizabeth Smith Shaw 5. Women—United States—History

ISBN 0345465067; 9780345465061

SUMMARY: This biography by Diane Jacobs "focuses on the interconnectedness of [Abigail Smith] Adams with her sisters, Mary Smith Cranch and Elizabeth 'Betsy' Smith Shaw Peabody. Jacobs bases her study on their lifelong correspondence. They shared private thoughts on everything from courtship, marriage, and child rearing to philosophical, economic, and political issues. . . . Jacobs uses the sisters' letters to show the women circumventing cultural restrictions." (Library Journal)

REVIEW: *Booklist* v110 no9/10 p37-8 Ja 1 2014 Margaret Flanagan

"Dear Abigail: The Intimate Lives and Revolutionary Ideas of Abigail Adams and Her Two Remarkable Sisters." "Though Abigail Adams is a perennially popular historical subject, little has been written about her two accomplished sisters, Mary Cranch and Elizabeth Shaw Peabody. This triple biography corrects that oversight by recounting the lives of the three Smith sisters, utilizing their private journals and the copious letters they wrote to each other over the course of their lifetimes to tell their collective story. Intelligent, well educated, opinionated, and informed, they not only provided each other with comfort, advice, and instruction but they also served as perceptive eyewitnesses to historical events on a grand scale."

REVIEW: *Choice* v52 no2 p329 O 2014 A. P. Hancock

REVIEW: *Kirkus Rev* v82 no1 p170 Ja 1 2014

"Dear Abigail: The Intimate Lives and Revolutionary Ideas of Abigail Adams and Her Two Remarkable Sisters". "Liberally excerpted by [Diane] Jacobs . . . the letters allow readers to plunge into the voices and milieus of these lively characters, who nonetheless were relegated to the sidelines, observing the great events of the new nation unfold while their husbands got to strut about the stage. . . . . Readers will cheer when [Abigail Adams] is finally goaded out of her enforced provincialism by the need to join her husband in his diplomatic mission to Paris in 1784. An intimate, deeply engaging method of following historic events."

REVIEW: *Libr J* v139 no2 p81 F 1 2014 Margaret Kappanadze

REVIEW: *Publ Wkly* v260 no51 p46 D 16 2013

JACOBS, JOHN HORNOR. The Shibboleth; [by] John Hornor Jacobs 393 p. 2014 Carolrhoda Lab

1. Ability—Fiction 2. Bullies—Fiction 3. Memory—Fiction 4. Psychiatric hospitals—Fiction 5. Speculative fiction 6. Supernatural—Fiction

ISBN 0761390081; 9780761390084 (trade hard cover : alk. paper)

LC 2013-009535

SUMMARY: This is the second book in the Twelve-Fingered Boy Trilogy, by John Hornor Jacobs. "Branded a 'candy' dealer for doling out drugs, Shreve is incarcerated in a juvenile detention center at first, but after he frightens a nurse there, he's sent to a mental hospital, where he's drugged for schizophrenia. What his keepers don't know is that he's not schizophrenic at all. Instead, he's a shibboleth, a being that can read minds and possess the bodies of others." (Kirkus Reviews)

REVIEW: *Booklist* v110 no9/10 p100 Ja 1 2014 Daniel Kraus

"The Shibboleth." "This is a dyed-in-the-wool middle book--filled with training, planning, and sinister omens, its chief achievement is to foment excitement for the finale. And in that it succeeds splendidly, courtesy of new friends and new foes, none of whom exist in either camp comfortably. As before, Shreve's appealing truculence is weighed down by the anguish of sharing the memories of too many damaged people. Jacobs works his ass off here; that's the best way to put it because you can feel the work, in the best of senses, to make each paragraph a battling push-pull of bruising toughness, electric wit, and dazzling metaphysicality. This fits uncomfortably in every box in which you'd try to put it--in other words, it's totally unique."

REVIEW: *Kirkus Rev* v82 no1 p123 Ja 1 2014

REVIEW: *SLJ* v60 no4 p168 Ap 2014 Sherry J. Mills

JACOBS, JORDAN. Samantha Sutton and the winter of the warrior queen; [by] Jordan Jacobs 368 p. 2013 Sourcebooks Jabberwocky

1. Adventure and adventurers—Fiction 2. Adventure stories 3. Archaeology—Fiction 4. Excavations (Archaeology)—Fiction 5. Uncles—Fiction

ISBN 9781402275630 (tp: alk. paper)

LC 2013-017899

SUMMARY: In this book by Jordan Jacobs, "twelve-year-old Samantha Sutton isn't sure she wants to go to England with her Uncle Jay, a brilliant, risk-taking archeologist. But the trip seems safe enough—a routine excavation in Cambridge—and Samantha has always had a love for the past. . . . But everything changes when Sam uncovers something extraordinary. Are the local legends true? Is this the site of the ancient fortress belonging to Queen Boudica, the warrior queen?" (Publisher's note)

REVIEW: *Kirkus Rev* v81 no24 p274 D 15 2013

"Samantha Sutton and the Winter of the Warrior Queen". "the archaeologist-author describes field research in loving detail, contrasting the careful work of scientists with the depredations of treasure hunters with metal detectors. But his depictions of the archaeological community, including Sir Cairn (a professor of archaeology at Cambridge) and Samantha's own family, are far less positive. . . . An enemy made in a previous story turns up again, and Samantha begins, not unreasonably, to fear for her life. An archaeological adventure with almost too much suspense."

REVIEW: *SLJ* v60 no3 p141 Mr 2014 Stacy Dillon

JACOBSEN, ANNIE. Operation Paperclip; the secret intelligence program to bring Nazi scientists to America; [by] Annie Jacobsen 544 p. 2013 Little Brown & Co

1. Biological weapons—History 2. Chemical weapons—History—20th century 3. Engineers—Germany—History—20th century 4. Engineers—United States—History—20th century 5. German Americans—History 6. Historical literature 7. Scientists—Germany—History—20th century 8. Scientists—United States—History—20th century

ISBN 031622104X; 9780316221047 (hardcover); 9780316239820 (large print)

LC 2013-028255

SUMMARY: This book by Annie Jacobsen describes how "in the chaos following World War II, the U.S. government faced many difficult decisions, including what to do with the Third Reich's scientific minds. These were the brains behind the Nazis' once-indomitable war machine. So began Operation Paperclip, a decades-long, covert project to bring Hitler's scientists and their families to the United States." (Publisher's note)

REVIEW: *Booklist* v110 no9/10 p38 Ja 1 2014 Jay Freeman

REVIEW: *Choice* v51 no12 p2254 Ag 2014 R. P. Hallion

REVIEW: *Kirkus Rev* v82 no1 p164 Ja 1 2014

"Operation Paperclip: The Secret Intelligence Program That Brought Nazi Scientists to America". "In this diligent report . . . [Annie] Jacobsen . . . expands previous material with the use of documents recently released under the Freedom of Information Act, as well as personal interviews, memoirs, trial evidence and obscure dossiers. . . . Throughout, the author delivers harrowing passages of immorality, duplicity and deception, as well as some decency and lots of high drama. How Dr. Strangelove came to America and thrived, told in graphic detail."

REVIEW: *Libr J* v139 no2 p83 F 1 2014 Evan M. Anderson

REVIEW: *Libr J* v139 no9 p41 My 15 2014 Forrest E. Link

REVIEW: *Libr J* v138 no14 p87 S 1 2013

REVIEW: *N Y Times Book Rev* p16 Mr 2 2014 WENDY LOWER

"Operation Paperclip: The Secret Intelligence Program That Brought Nazi Scientists to America." "Among the trophies of the Second World War captured by Allied intelligence agents were Nazi scientists and their research on biological and chemical weapons. . . . The journalist Annie Jacobsen's 'Operation Paperclip' is not the first unveiling of the program. . . . To her credit, Jacobsen deftly untangles the myriad American and German government agencies and personnel involved, though not without repetitious reminders of who is who. . . . What is clear is that contemporary public opinion had it right: Operation Paperclip was a bad idea."

REVIEW: *New Yorker* v90 no2 p75-1 Mr 3 2014

"Operation Paperclip: The Secret Intelligence Program That Brought Nazi Scientists to America." "This darkly picaresque account details the covert operation that brought Nazi scientists to work in the U.S. As the Third Reich collapsed, the Allied powers, in awe of its wonder weapons, scrambled to employ these scientists, even though they may have murdered or worked to death tens of thousands of people. . . . Jacobsen persuasively argues that the mindset of the former Nazi scientists who ended up working for the American government may have exacerbated Cold War paranoia."

REVIEW: *Publ Wkly* v260 no50 p61 D 9 2013

JAFFE, MICHELE. Minders; [by] Michele Jaffe 400 p. 2014 Penguin Group USA

1. Conduct of life—Fiction 2. Murder—Fiction 3. Speculative fiction 4. Telepathy—Fiction 5. Young adult fiction

ISBN 159514658X; 9781595146588

SUMMARY: In this book by Michele Jaffe, "the thoughts and decisions of individuals are observed and monitored. . . . Sadie Ames, a rich girl from the suburbs, has been accepted into the Mind Corps Fellowship program. . . . Her job is to enter the mind of Ford Winters, urban bad boy, and monitor his life from the inside out. Sadie unexpectedly finds herself deeply drawn to Ford, and when he makes a terrible decision, Sadie must choose between her duty as an Observer and her growing attachment." (School Library Journal)

REVIEW: *Booklist* v110 no11 p64 F 1 2014 Julie Trevelyan

REVIEW: *Bull Cent Child Books* v67 no5 p269 Ja 2014 K. C.

"Minders." "[Michele] Jaffe's speculative aesthetics of the way brains process experience at nonverbal levels is as fascinating as the mystery here. . . . As always, Jaffe . . . crafts a high-stakes adventure with impeccable pacing, and she even manages to inject a little comedy into this harrowing crime drama. Her evocative descriptions of the wasteland of inner-city Detroit read like a tragic love story as Ford imagines its renaissance, and while the premise of becoming a research subject in exchange for health care appears exploitative, there is almost an argument for the positive side of Big Brother here. The combination of romance, sci-fi, and crime drama makes for a splendidly well-rounded and engrossing story with broad appeal."

REVIEW: *Horn Book Magazine* v90 no3 p89 My/Je 2014 CLAIRE E. GROSS

REVIEW: *Kirkus Rev* v81 no21 p200 N 1 2013

REVIEW: *Publ Wkly* v260 no44 p68 N 4 2013

REVIEW: *SLJ* v60 no1 p100 Ja 2014 Katie Wilkinson

REVIEW: *Voice of Youth Advocates* v36 no6 p72 F 2014 Diane Colson

JAGER, ERIC. Blood royal; a true tale of crime and detection in medieval Paris; [by] Eric Jager 336 p. 2014 Little, Brown and Co.

1. Assassination—France—Case studies 2. Crime—France—History—To 1500 3. Historical literature 4. Murder investigation—France—Case studies 5. Regicide—France—Case studies

ISBN 0316224510; 9780316224512

LC 2013-028257

SUMMARY: This book, by Eric Jager, is a "true story of murder and detection in 15th-century Paris. . . . in 1407, Louis of Orleans was murdered by a band of masked men. The crime stunned and paralyzed France since Louis had often ruled in place of his brother King Charles, who had gone mad. As panic seized Paris, an investigation began. In charge was the Provost of Paris, Guillaume de Tignonville, the city's chief law enforcement officer." (Publisher's note)

REVIEW: *Booklist* v110 no12 p16 F 15 2014 Jay Freeman

REVIEW: *Kirkus Rev* v82 no1 p284 Ja 1 2014

"Blood Royal: A True Tale of Crime and Detection in Medieval Paris". "Few works of fiction will grab readers' attention as well as [Eric] Jager's . . . riveting story of a 1407 murder mystery that split the royal family of France. . . . Jager shares his extensive knowledge of medieval Paris, employing entertainingly meticulous descriptions throughout the book. . . . The author's portrayals of the perpetual stench and body parts will surely give readers shivers. . . . An impressive combination of mystery, crime story, and social and political history."

REVIEW: *N Y Times Book Rev* p30 My 25 2014 Charles Graeber

JALAL, AYESHA. The pity of partition; Manto's life, times, and work across the India-Pakistan divide; [by] Ayesha Jalal 272 p. 2012 Princeton University Press

1. Authors, Urdu—20th century—Biography 2. Historical literature 3. India-Pakistan Conflict, 1947-1949 4. Narration (Rhetoric)—Political aspects—South Asia—History—20th century 5. Short stories, Urdu—History and criticism 6. South Asia—History—20th century
ISBN 9780691153629 (hardcover: acid-free paper)
LC 2012-024142

SUMMARY: This historical work shows how writer Saadat Hasan Manto "navigated and interpreted the repression, chaos, and violence of the final years of British colonialism and the upheaval of India's 1947 partition. The book follows Manto's life from his rebellious youth . . . to his years as a struggling journalist and film writer in Bombay, where his provocative stories elicited numerous obscenity charges while building his reputation as 'the father of the Urdu short story'". (Publishers Weekly)

REVIEW: *Am Hist Rev* v119 no1 p164 F 2014 Ian Copland

"The Pity of Partition: Manto's Life, Times, and Work Across the Indo-Pakistan Divide". "The book is unusual for a professed work of history in quoting and paraphrasing so profusely from literature, but this is quite a deliberate gambit on [Ayesha] Jalal's part. She 'strives,' Jalal says,' for a new historical methodology that imaginatively connects fictional and historical narratives'. . . . Whether the book is actually as innovative as it claims is open to question; however there is no doubt it gains immensely from the richness and rawness of the [Saadat Hasan] Manto oeuvre. . . . At times, though, it seems to me that Jalal allows her strong identification with Manto . . . to blur her historical judgment."

REVIEW: *Choice* v50 no11 p2009 Jl 2013 U. Anjaria

REVIEW: *N Y Rev Books* v61 no16 p49-51 O 23 2014 Ian Jack

REVIEW: *Publ Wkly* v259 no50 p47 D 10 2012

JAMES, DAVID.ed. The Tempest. See The Tempest

JAMES, ELOISA. Three Weeks With Lady X; [by] Eloisa James 400 p. 2014 HarperCollins

1. Housing rehabilitation 2. Love stories 3. Man-woman relationships—Fiction 4. Marriage—Fiction 5. Nobility (Social class)—Fiction
ISBN 0062223895; 9780062223890

SUMMARY: In this book, by Eloisa James, "Thorn Dautry, the powerful bastard son of a duke, decides that he needs a wife. But to marry a lady, Thorn must acquire a gleaming, civilized façade, the specialty of Lady Xenobia India. Exquisite, headstrong, and independent, India vows to make Thorn marriageable in just three weeks. But neither Thorn nor India anticipate the forbidden passion that explodes between them." (Publisher's note)

REVIEW: *Booklist* v110 no13 p26 Mr 1 2014 John Charles

REVIEW: *Kirkus Rev* v82 no4 p267 F 15 2014

"Three Weeks With Lady X". " India and Thorn each have deep-seated insecurities and strong personalities, and their secretive courtship is intense and explosive. They are clearly perfect for each other but blinded by their own uncertainty and society's expectations. Star romance author James revisits her best-selling Desperate Duchesses series with this compelling and passionate book. India and Thorn . . . are complex, intriguing and endearing, and their romance enchants. Secondary characters enhance the emotional stakes, and fans will enjoy another peek at popular hero Villiers and his wife, Eleanor. Emotionally rewarding and elegantly written, with textured characters and a captivating plot, this is James at her best."

REVIEW: *Libr J* v139 no7 p66-7 Ap 15 2014 Kristin Ramsdell

REVIEW: *Publ Wkly* v261 no5 p42 F 3 2014

JAMES, J. ALISON.tr. Best foot forward. See Arndt, I.

JAMES, LAURA.il. Anna Carries Water. See Senior, O.

JAMIESON, DALE. Reason in a Dark Time; Why the Struggle Against Climate Change Failed - and What It Means for Our Future; [by] Dale Jamieson 288 p. 2014 Oxford University Press

1. Climatic changes 2. Environmental ethics 3. Human ecology 4. Reason 5. Scientific literature
ISBN 0199337667; 9780199337668

SUMMARY: In this book, Dale Jamieson "explains what climate change is, why we have failed to stop it, and why it still matters what we do. Centered in philosophy, the volume also treats the scientific, historical, economic, and political dimensions of climate change. Our failure to prevent or even to respond significantly to climate change, Jamieson argues, reflects the impoverishment of our systems of practical reason . . . and the limits of our cognitive and affective capacities." (Publisher's note)

REVIEW: *Booklist* v110 no12 p20-2 F 15 2014 Carl Hays

"Reason in a Dark Time: Why the Struggle Against Climate Change Failed--and What It Means for Our Future." "S growing number of atmospheric scientists are saying it's already too late and the real debate now is over how the earth's denizens can adapt. . . . Although not intended as a rallying cry for arresting climate change, [Dale] Jamieson's work is nonetheless an invaluable contribution to the dialogue about how to minimize the inevitable social and environmental devastation that looms large in our future."

JAMISON, LESLIE. The empathy exams; essays; [by] Leslie Jamison 256 p. 2014 Graywolf Press
1. Caring 2. Compassion 3. Empathy 4. Essay (Literary form) 5. Interpersonal relations
ISBN 1555976719; 9781555976712 (alk. paper)
LC 2013-946927

SUMMARY: "Beginning with her experience as a medical actor who was paid to act out symptoms for medical students to diagnose, Leslie Jamison's visceral and revealing essays ask essential questions about our basic understanding of others: How should we care about each other? How can we feel another's pain, especially when pain can be assumed, distorted, or performed? Is empathy a tool by which to test or even grade each other?" (Publisher's note)

REVIEW: *Am Sch* v83 no3 p114-5 Summ 2014 Gary Greenberg

REVIEW: *Atlantic* v313 no5 p44 Je 2014 Ann Hulbert

REVIEW: *Bookforum* v21 no1 p58 Ap/My 2014 JENNY DAVIDSON

REVIEW: *Booklist* v110 no13 p13 Mr 1 2014 Donna Seaman

REVIEW: *Kirkus Rev* v82 no10 p4 My 15 2014

REVIEW: *Libr J* v139 no7 p84 Ap 15 2014 Erica Swenson Danowitz

REVIEW: *N Y Times Book Rev* p26 Ap 6 2014 OLIVIA LAING

REVIEW: *N Y Times Book Rev* p26 Ap 13 2014

REVIEW: *N Y Times Book Rev* p27 O 12 2014 Cheryl Strayed Benjamin Moser

REVIEW: *New Statesman* v143 no5213 p49 Je 6 2014 Elizabeth Minkel

REVIEW: *New Statesman* v143 no5213 p49 Je 6 2014 Elizabeth Minkel

REVIEW: *New York Times* v163 no56454 pC23-9 Mr 28 2014 DWIGHT GARNER

REVIEW: *New Yorker* v90 no12 p75-1 My 12 2014

"The Empathy Exams." "'Empathy requires as much inquiry as imagination,' Jamison writes in this thoughtful collection of essays interrogating the physical and metaphorical meanings of pain. She reports from a conference on Morgellons—a syndrome in which patients believe that they suffer from infestations—and from a hellish ultramarathon, which only twelve people have ever finished. . . . About the compulsions and convictions of her subjects Jamison is compassionate without being partial: 'Empathy means realizing no trauma has discrete edges.'"

REVIEW: *Publ Wkly* v261 no4 p83-6 Ja 27 2014

REVIEW: *Publ Wkly* v261 no1 p1 Ja 6 2014

REVIEW: *TLS* no5806 p28 Jl 11 2014 CLAIRE LOWDON

JANCE, JUDITH A., 1944-. Moving Target; a novel; [by] Judith A. Jance 320 p. 2014 Simon & Schuster
1. Detective & mystery stories 2. Juvenile delinquents 3. Murder investigation—Fiction 4. Reynolds, Ali (Fictitious character)—Fiction
ISBN 1476745005; 9781476745008 (hardcover)
LC 2013-028619

SUMMARY: In this book, by J. A. Jance, "Ali Reynolds spans continents to solve a cold case murder and to figure out who wants a young juvenile offender dead. . . . Lance Tucker, an incarcerated juvenile offender doing time for expertly hacking into the San Leandro School District's computer system, is set on fire and severely burned one night. . . . The police say that he did it to himself, but . . . Ali's . . . fiancé . . . feels obligated to get to the bottom of what really happened." (Publisher's note)

REVIEW: *Booklist* v110 no9/10 p51 Ja 1 2014 Michele Leber

REVIEW: *Kirkus Rev* v82 no2 p96 Ja 15 2014

"Moving Target". "An ex-reporter, a high-tech specialist and a nun help right wrongs of the near and distant past as they circle the globe. . . . Ali Reynolds . . . hopes to see Leland [Brooks] reunited with his estranged family while she tries to find out if Leland's late father had a little help in dying. Ali's fiance, B. Simpson, head of a computer security company, is following the case of Lance Tucker. . . . Dizzying changes of locale and point of view, along with large helpings of sentimentality, weaken Ali's latest. If only Jance had focused on one plot instead of sending her characters all over creation in pursuit of two separate mysteries."

REVIEW: *Libr J* v139 no8 p43 My 1 2014 Sandra C. Clariday

REVIEW: *Publ Wkly* v260 no48 p33 N 25 2013

JANE, THOMAS.ed. Dumfries House. See Green, S.

JANEWAY, WILLIAM H. Doing capitalism in the innovation economy; markets, speculation and the state; [by] William H. Janeway pages cm 2012 Cambridge University Press
1. BUSINESS & ECONOMICS—Finance 2. Capitalism 3. Economic policy 4. Economics literature 5. Venture capital
ISBN 9781107031258
LC 2012-019852

SUMMARY: "Drawing on his professional experiences, [author] William H. Janeway provides an accessible pathway for readers to appreciate the dynamics of the innovation economy. He combines personal reflections from a career spanning forty years in venture capital, with the development of an original theory of the role of asset bubbles in financing technological innovation and of the role of the state in playing an enabling role in the innovation process." (Publisher's note)

REVIEW: *Kirkus Rev* v80 no20 p193 O 15 2012

REVIEW: *N Y Rev Books* v51 no7 p50-3 Ap 24 2014 Jeffrey Madrick

"The Entrepreneurial State: Debunking Public vs. Private Sector Myths" and "Doing Capitalism in the Innovation Economy: Markets, Speculation and the State." "'The Entrepreneurial State' . . . is one of the most incisive economic books in years. . . . In [author Mariana] Mazzucato's account of the enormous success of federal scientific and technical research as the foundation of the most revolutionary of today's technologies, the most telling example is how dependent Steve Job's Apple was on government-funded breakthroughs. . . . [Author William H.] Janeway . . . argues for the importance of government in the nation's economic growth."

JANG JI-HYANG.ed. The Arab Spring. See The Arab Spring

JANISCH, FRANCES.il. Cooking with Carla. See Hall, C.

JANSEN, J. P. M.ed. Engineering the human. See Engineering the human

JANSSEN, GEERT H.ed. The Ashgate research companion to the Counter-Reformation. See The Ashgate research companion to the Counter-Reformation

JANČAR, DRAGO. Best European Fiction 2014; [by] Drago Jančar 420 p. 2013 W W Norton & Co Inc

1. Europe—Fiction 2. Humorous stories 3. Political fiction 4. Short stories, European 5. Short story (Literary form)

ISBN 1564788989; 9781564788986

SUMMARY: "The 29 short stories collected here, many of which originate in the Balkans but also in France, Spain and Wales, place emphasis on the particular. They anatomise the human experience in order to resist the mediocritising influence of the global 'culture industry'. Drago Jancar . . . asks in his preface whether a European aesthetic exists. If it does, he supposes, it can be traced through the 'laughter, scepticism and black humour' shared by a continent emerging from a dark century." (New Statesman)

REVIEW: *Kirkus Rev* v81 no24 p189 D 15 2013

"Best European Fiction 2014". "Illuminating collection of current writing from across the pond, as different from its American counterpart as a Paris croissant is from a New York cronut. . . . The assembled collection offers a pleasing blend of realism, deconstruction and absurdism that sometimes vie for the dominant mood, as if the spirits of Slavoj Žižek and Samuel Beckett and maybe Georges Perec were fighting for first place. Sometimes all three meet, though. . . . Unlikely to touch off a wave of imitators on these shores but an interesting sampler."

REVIEW: *New Statesman* v142 no5189 p55 D 13 2013

REVIEW: *TLS* no5782 p21 Ja 24 2014 MATT LEWIS

JAPAN'S MODERN DIVIDE; the photographs of hiroshi hamaya and kansuke yamamoto; 224 p. 2013 J. Paul Getty Museum

1. Art literature 2. Experimental photography 3. Hamaya, Hiroshi 4. Photography—Japan 5. Yamamoto, Kansuke

ISBN 9781606061329 (hardcover)

LC 2012-952486

SUMMARY: This book, edited by Judith Keller and Amanda Maddox. asserts that "in the 1930s the history of Japanese photography evolved in two very different directions: one toward documentary photography, the other favoring an experimental, or avant-garde, approach strongly influenced by Western Surrealism. This book explores these two strains of modern Japanese photography through the work of two remarkable figures: Hiroshi Hamaya and Kansuke Yamamoto." (Publisher's note)

REVIEW: *Art Am* v101 no10 p75 N 2013

"Hybrid Culture: Japanese Media Arts in Dialogue With the West," "Japan's Modern Divide: The Photographs of Hiroshi Hamaya and Kansuke Yamamoto," and "From Postwar to Postmodern: Art in Japan 1945-1989: Primary Documents." "Sharing a high regard for precision, Japanese artists and engineers collaborate in ways that subtly meld Eastern and Western concepts, pure art and technical prowess, futurity and tradition. . . . Japanese photography bifurcated in the 1930s into a documentary stream, represented by Hiroshi Hamaya, and an experimental stream, exemplified by Kansuke Yamamoto. Five essayists discuss the artists' careers, illustrated by some 100 contrasting images. . . . Manifestos, essays and debates from Japan's fervent postwar era appear in English for the first time, accompanied by more than 20 new scholarly articles."

REVIEW: *Choice* v51 no2 p250 O 2013 M. Chaiklin

REVIEW: *Libr J* v138 no11 p88 Je 15 2013 Douglas F. Smith

JARRETT, GENE ANDREW. Representing the race; a new political history of African American literature; [by] Gene Andrew Jarrett xi, 263 p. 2011 New York University Press

1. African Americans—Intellectual life 2. African Americans—Political activity 3. American literature—African American authors—History and criticism 4. Historical literature 5. Politics and literature—United States—History and criticism

ISBN 0814743390 (pbk. : acid-free paper); 0814743382 (cloth : acid-free paper); 0814743404 (e-book); 9780814743386 (cloth : acid-free paper); 9780814743393 (pbk. : acid-free paper); 9780814743409 (e-book)

LC 2011-011052

SUMMARY: In this book on "the political value of African American literature, author Gene Jarrett "examines texts of every sort . . . to parse the myths of authenticity, popular culture, nationalism, and militancy that have come to define African American political activism in recent decades. He argues that unless we show the diverse and complex ways that African American literature has transformed society, political myths will continue to limit our understanding of this intellectual tradition." (Publisher's note)

REVIEW: *Am Lit* v85 no3 p593-6 S 2013 Evie Shockley

"Spectacular Blackness: The Cultural Politics of the Black Power Movement and the Search for a Black Aesthetic," "Specters of Democracy: Blackness and the Aesthetics of Politics in the Antebellum United States," and "Representing the Race: A New Political History of African American Literature." "[Amy Abugo] Ongiri adds her incisive analysis of materials both familiar and little-known to the growing body of work on Black Power and the Black Arts Movement (BAM) in their most active years. . . .[Ivy G.] Wilson's book [is] . . . more densely theoretical than Ongiri's lively work, but no less readable in its eloquence. . . . [Andrew Jarrett] makes a detailed, well-researched case for the importance of distinguishing between the longstanding practice of reading creative and intellectual writing as simply informally political. . . and his scholarship, which argues that such writing . . . does formal political work."

REVIEW: *Choice* v49 no4 p676 D 2011 Y. Kiuchi

REVIEW: *J Am Hist* v99 no2 p569 S 2012 Aldon Nielsen

JARROW, GAIL. Red madness; how a medical mystery changed what we eat; [by] Gail Jarrow 192 p. 2014 Calkins Creek

1. Epidemics—History 2. Historical literature 3. Malnutrition—History 4. Niacin 5. Pellagra
ISBN 1590787323; 9781590787328
LC 2008-049497

SUMMARY: In this book, author Gail Jarrow "tracks [a] disease, commonly known as pellagra, and highlights how doctors, scientists, and public health officials finally defeated it. Illustrated with 100 archival photographs, [it] includes stories about real-life pellagra victims and accounts of scientific investigations. It concludes with a glossary, timeline, further resources, author's note, bibliography, and index." (Publisher's note)

REVIEW: *Booklist* v110 no15 p43 Ap 1 2014 Erin Anderson

REVIEW: *Bull Cent Child Books* v67 no8 p408-9 Ap 2014 E. B.

Tilte: "Red Madness: How a Medical Mystery Changed What We Eat". "Though disease is likely not on most kids' radar, its historical prevalence and peril make it a riveting subject, and [Gail] Jarrow intersperses plenty of brief case histories and poignant photographs of sufferers throughout the text to keep the human interest angle as compelling as the medical mystery. Index, sources notes, bibliography, and timeline are included, as well as a fascinating FAQ section that delves further into the interrelationship between nicotinic acid, tryptophan, foods, and food preparation, and explores why pellagra is thankfully no longer a household word."

REVIEW: *Kirkus Rev* v82 no6 p112 Mr 15 2014

REVIEW: *Publ Wkly* v261 no7 p102 F 17 2014

REVIEW: *SLJ* v60 no4 p188 Ap 2014 Tammy Turner

JARVIS, SIMON. Night office; [by] Simon Jarvis 227 p. 2013 Enitharmon Press

1. English Christian poetry 2. English language—Versification 3. English poetry 4. Fathers & sons 5. Offices
ISBN 1907587330 (pbk.); 9781907587337 (pbk.)
LC 2013-409728

SUMMARY: Written by Simon Jarvis, "'Night Office' is the initial publication from among a small set of long poems for which the collective title is The Calendar. Each poem relates to the others as the points, not in a line, but of a star: none need be considered as first or last. Each . . . , from verse constraints upon syllable and intonation, works towards the concrete freedoms of poetic thinking." (Publisher's note)

REVIEW: *TLS* no5787 p22 F 28 2014 WILLIAM WOOTTEN

"Night Office." "When a devotee of the astringent 'difficulty' of J. H. Prynne and de facto member of the Cambridge School publishes a 7,000-line Anglican poem in formal rhyming verse, it is safe to conclude he has had something of a change of heart. Not total, perhaps. Simon Jarvis's 'Night Office,' the poem in question, echoes and alludes to Prynne and foregrounds the sort of Adorno-inspired theorizing Jarvis and others have used to justify Prynnian poetics. . . . 'Night Office' is in large part a meditative, discursive poem of answerable statement and argument, whole passages being effectively cultural or literary criticism, theology or philosophy in verse."

JAUME, LUCIEN. Tocqueville; the aristocratic sources of liberty; 356 p. 2013 Princeton University Press

1. Biographies 2. Democracy—Philosophy 3. Historians—France—Biography 4. Political science—France—History—19th century
ISBN 0691152047 (hardcover); 9780691152042 (hardcover)
LC 2012-032469

SUMMARY: This book, by Lucien Jaume, focuses on "Alexis de Tocqueville . . . , the young French aristocrat who came to early America and, enthralled by what he saw, proceeded to write an American book explaining democratic America to itself. . . . Jaume provides a . . . new interpretation of Tocqueville's book as well as a fresh intellectual and psychological portrait of the author." (Publisher's note)

REVIEW: *Choice* v51 no3 p548 N 2013 H. L. Cheek Jr.

REVIEW: *Hist Today* v64 no4 p62 Ap 2014 Hugh Brogan

REVIEW: *Libr J* v138 no5 p110 Mr 15 2013 David Keymer

REVIEW: *London Rev Books* v35 no14 p13-4 Jl 18 2013 David A. Bell

REVIEW: *Nation* v297 no18 p37 N 4 2013

"Tocqueville: The Aristocratic Sources of Liberty." "Excellent. . . . [Lucien] Jaume, a senior researcher at the Centre for Political Research at Sciences Po in Paris, sees in [Alexis de] Tocqueville a political scientist, sociologist, moralist and writer, and discusses in detail his labors in each guise, the wonderful effect of which is to reveal how unified the man was--like the country he visited, vast and containing multitudes, as if Tocqueville saw himself in his portrait of America."

REVIEW: *Publ Wkly* v260 no6 p55-6 F 11 2013

JAVAHERBIN, MINA. Soccer star; 40 p. 2014 Candlewick Press

1. Brazil—Juvenile literature 2. Brothers & sisters—Juvenile fiction 3. Brothers and sisters—Fiction 4. Brothers and sisters—Juvenile fiction 5. Picture books for children 6. Poor families—Fiction 7. Soccer—Fiction 8. Soccer stories 9. Women & sports
ISBN 0763660566; 9780763660567
LC 2013-944008

SUMMARY: This children's book, by Mina Javaherbin, tells the "story of a Brazilian boy who dreams of being a soccer star—and the sister who steps in to help his team win a game. When Paulo Marcelo Feliciano becomes a soccer star, crowds will cheer his famous name! Then his mother won't have to work long hours, and he won't have to work all day on a fishing boat. . . . But when Jose falls on his wrist, will the team finally break the rules and let a girl show her stuff?" (Publisher's note)

REVIEW: *Booklist* v110 no17 p103 My 1 2014 Linda Perkins

REVIEW: *Bull Cent Child Books* v67 no10 p522 Je 2014 E. B.

REVIEW: *Kirkus Rev* v82 no5 p85 Mr 1 2014

"Soccer Star". "There's a lull in pacing in the middle of the story, but it quickly picks up with the 'big game.' . . . [Renata] Alarcão expertly captures the motion of Maria's triumphant, scoring bicycle kick, but it's too bad there is no illustration that shows the team explicitly welcoming her into the fold. That's a minor quibble, as it's downright refreshing to see illustrations that realistically relay the diversity of shades found among Brazilians. [Mina] Javaherbin deftly handles Paulo and Maria's poverty with honesty while simultaneously refraining from sugarcoating, overemphasizing or romanticizing it. Perhaps most importantly, Javaherbin shows that being poor doesn't stop people from having lives and dreams. A lovely story about soccer, gender and hope."

REVIEW: *Publ Wkly* v261 no17 p137 Ap 28 2014

REVIEW: *SLJ* v60 no4 p124 Ap 2014 Linda L. Walkins

JAYAL, NIRAJA GOPAL. Citizenship and its discontents; an Indian history; [by] Niraja Gopal Jayal viii, 366 p. 2013 Harvard University Press

1. Citizenship—India—History 2. Civics, East Indian 3. Historical literature 4. Political science literature

ISBN 9780674066847 (alk. paper)

LC 2012-018084

SUMMARY: This book by Niraja Jayal "explores a century of contestations over citizenship from the colonial period to the present, analyzing evolving conceptions of citizenship as legal status, as rights, and as identity. The early optimism that a new India could be fashioned out of an unequal and diverse society led to a formally inclusive legal membership, an impulse to social and economic rights, and group-differentiated citizenship." (Publisher's note)

REVIEW: *Choice* v51 no1 p156 S 2013 S. D. Sharma

"Citizenship and Its Discontents: An Indian History." "[Author Niraja Gopal] Jayal . . . provides a broad, historically grounded discussion of contestations over democracy and citizenship in India from the late colonial period to the present. Specifically, the author lucidly analyzes the evolving conceptions of citizenship as legal status, as rights, and as identity. She persuasively illustrates how the early optimism that a new India could be fashioned out of a deeply hierarchical and unequal society led to a formally inclusive legal membership and group-differentiated citizenship."

JAYAWARDHANA, RAY. Neutrino hunters; the thrilling chase for a ghostly particle to unlock the secrets of the universe; [by] Ray Jayawardhana 256 p. 2013 Scientific American/Farrar, Straus and Giroux

1. Neutrino astrophysics 2. Neutrino interactions 3. Neutrinos 4. SCIENCE—Astrophysics & Space Science 5. SCIENCE—History 6. Scientific literature

ISBN 9780374220631 (hardback)

LC 2013-021506

SUMMARY: This book looks at "neutrinos, the 'pathologically shy' elementary particles that offer a window into supernovas and may help answer questions about antimatter, dark matter, dark energy, and the early universe. . . . After neutrinos were finally observed for the first time in 1956, scientists expanded the hunt from Earth to space, examining the rays emitted by the Sun." (Publishers Weekly)

REVIEW: *Booklist* v110 no4 p7 O 15 2013 Bryce Christensen

REVIEW: *Choice* v51 no10 p1828 Je 2014 K. D. Fisher

REVIEW: *Economist* v410 no8872 p71-2 F 1 2014

"Neutrino Hunters: The Thrilling Chase for a Ghostly Particle to Unlock the Secrets of the Universe" and "The Perfect Wave: With Neutrinos at the Boundary of Space and Time." "These two books complement each other. Mr. [Ray] Jayawardhana's is stronger on the history (though his accounts of the neutrino hunters' personal lives can read a little too much like a professional CV). It is also more comprehensive on the potential use of neutrinos in examining the innards of the sun, of distant exploding stars or of Earth, as well as more practical uses. . . . Mr. [Heinrich] Päs, for his part, places neutrinos within the broader context of contemporary high theory and delves deeper into the science. Physics buffs will relish his explanations, and not just of established ideas."

REVIEW: *Kirkus Rev* v81 no20 p45 O 15 2013

REVIEW: *Nat Hist* v122 no1 p46-7 F 2014 LAURENCE A. MARSCHALL

REVIEW: *Publ Wkly* v260 no34 p57 Ag 26 2013

JEFFERS, OLIVER.il. The day the crayons quit. See Daywalt, D.

JEFFERS, OLIVER.il. Stay where you are & then leave. See Boyne, J.

JEFFERSON, JUDITH A.ed. Multilingualism in Medieval Britain (c. 1066-1520). See Multilingualism in Medieval Britain (c. 1066-1520)

JEFFERSON, MARCI. Girl on the golden coin; a novel of Frances Stuart; [by] Marci Jefferson 336 p. 2014 Thomas Dunne Books

1. Courts and courtiers—Fiction 2. FICTION—Historical

ISBN 1250037220; 9781250037220 (hardback)

LC 2013-030272

SUMMARY: In this novel by Marci Jefferson, "the Restoration of Stuart Monarchy in England returns Frances Stuart and her family to favor. King Louis XIV turns vengeful when she rejects his offer to become his Official Mistress. He sends her to England with orders to seduce King Charles II and help him form an alliance with England. Frances maneuvers the political turbulence of Whitehall Palace, but still can't afford to stir a scandal, determined to keep her family from shame." (Publisher's note)

REVIEW: *Kirkus Rev* v82 no4 p293 F 15 2014

"Girl on the Golden Coin". "Famously beautiful, Frances Stuart has been remembered throughout history as the woman who twice refused to be the mistress of a king. But what if she did submit to King Charles II? Using the historical framework of the restoration of the Stuart monarchy in England, [Marci] Jefferson's debut novel imagines the romantic intrigues of the beautiful Frances Stuart. . . . Jealous women, competitive men, power struggles—the treacherous world of the court is familiar, predictable and disappointing."

JEFFRIES, RODERIC. In Search of Murder; [by] Roderic Jeffries 192 p. 2014 Severn House Pub Ltd

1. Detective & mystery stories 2. Majorca (Spain) 3. Murder investigation—Fiction 4. Police—Fiction 5. Rich people—Fiction

ISBN 0727883534; 9780727883537

SUMMARY: In this book, "relentlessly prodded by exasperated and sarcastic Superior Chief Salas, [Inspector Enrique] Alvarez tries to determine if the swimming pool drowning of Neil Picare, a rich, womanizing Englishman, was accident or murder. Alvarez interviews Picare's wife, Cecily, and members of his staff, including the housekeeper, the cook, and the cleaner, with inconclusive results. Salas also insists that Alvarez talk to a number of Picare's paramours" (Publishers Weekly).

REVIEW: *Booklist* v110 no13 p21-2 Mr 1 2014 Emily Melton

"In Search of Murder." "Inspector Enrique Alvarez . . . [is] called to investigate the suspicious death of English expat Señor Picare, who appears to have drowned in his swimming pool. . . . Alvarez, as always, must juggle the unreasonable demands of his superior (solve the crime immediately, but don't offend anyone important) while chasing down clues and still finding time for his afternoon siesta and cognac. Ah, but count on the seemingly bumbling but instinctively clever detective to overcome all obstacles and solve the case. A fun read with sharp wit, a lovable hero, and an intoxicating glimpse of Majorcan life."

REVIEW: *Kirkus Rev* v82 no6 p256 Mr 15 2014

REVIEW: *Publ Wkly* v261 no7 p82 F 17 2014

JELINEK, ARTHUR J. Neandertal lithic industries at La Quina; [by] Arthur J. Jelinek xxv, 419 p. 2013 University of Arizona Press

1. Archaeological literature 2. Mousterian culture—France—Charente 3. Neanderthals—France—Charente 4. Stone implements—France—Charente 5. Tools, Prehistoric—France—Charente

ISBN 9780816522460 (cloth: acid-free paper)

LC 2012-023954

SUMMARY: "This study of the significance of changes through time revealed by an analysis of the chipped stone at La Quina reports on the excavations of the Cooperative American–French Excavation Project from 1985 to 1994. It moves beyond the largely descriptive and subjective approaches that have traditionally been applied to this kind of evidence and applies several . . . quantitative analytical techniques. " (Publisher's note)

REVIEW: *Current Anthropology* v55 no1 p125-7 F 2014 James Sackett

"Neanderthal Lithic Industries at La Quina". "This magisterial volume pursues the attempt well beyond what I, at least, would have thought possible. . . . Now, as books go, this volume makes challenging reading in the sense that even an archaeologist from another field (let alone a lay person) would fail to find it easy going. . . . it is an exhaustive account of how innovative, knowledgeable Paleolithic archaeologists and their coworkers in the natural sciences actually go about their business. And, as such, it is a major contribution both to our knowledge of the Mousterian archaeological record and to the exacting, often novel methods of attacking it carried out by [Arthur] Jelinek and his crew."

JELLETT, TOM.il. Two tough crocs. See Bedford, D.

JEMISON, MAE, 1956-. Discovering new planets; [by] Mae Jemison 48 p. 2013 Children's Press

1. Astronomical literature 2. Discoveries in science 3. Extrasolar planets—Detection—Juvenile literature 4. Planets 5. Planets—Juvenile literature

ISBN 9780531240632 (pbk.); 9780531255032 (library binding)

LC 2012-035762

SUMMARY: This book, by Mae Jemison and Dana Meachen Rau, addresses how "Astronomers have been working for decades to locate and identify all of the planets they can. Readers will discover what methods these scientists use, how new technology has helped them see further than ever, and why some scientists think that faraway planets could be home to life forms unlike anything on Earth." (Publisher's note)

REVIEW: *SLJ* v59 no4 p98 Ap 2013 John Peters

JENKINS, DAN, 1929-. His ownself; a semi-memoir; [by] Dan Jenkins 288 p. 2014 Random House Inc

1. Authors—United States—Biography 2. Memoirs 3. Political correctness 4. Sports—Humor 5. Sportswriters—United States—Biography

ISBN 0385532253; 9780385532259

LC 2013-013822

SUMMARY: This book is a memoir by sportswriter Dan Jenkins. "from his friendship and the rounds played with Ben Hogan, to the stories swapped with New York's elite, to the corporate expense accounts abused, Dan lets loose on his experiences in journalism, sports, and showbiz." The book is a "look at politics, hypocrites, political correctness, the past, the present, Hollywood, money, and athletes." (Publisher's note)

REVIEW: *Booklist* v110 no9/10 p32 Ja 1 2014 Bill Ott

REVIEW: *Kirkus Rev* v82 no1 p235 Ja 1 2014

REVIEW: *New York Times* v163 no56431 pC1-4 Mr 5 2014 DWIGHT GARNER

"His Ownself: A Semi-Memoir." "One of the many good things in [author Dan] Jenkins's new book, 'His Ownself: A Semi-Memoir,' is the story of how that novel came to be written and published. He had the title first. . . . It's a casual and sly sportswriter's memoir, albeit with a few egregious missteps. . . . Mr. Jenkins has a gift for summing up a personality in a few comic strokes. . . . Mr. Jenkins is among those writers--P. J. O'Rourke is another--who combine an anarchic prose style and a sometimes colorful personal life with conservative politics."

JENKINS, EUGENIA ZUROSKI. A taste for China; English subjectivity and the prehistory of Orientalism; [by] Eugenia Zuroski Jenkins xi, 282 p. 2013 Oxford University Press

1. China trade porcelain 2. Chinese diaspora in literature 3. English literature—18th century—History and criticism 4. Historical literature 5. Orientalism in literature

ISBN 9780199950980 (acid-free paper); 9780199950997

LC 2012-035654

SUMMARY: "Broadly considered, 'A Taste for China' shows that prior to the nineteenth century, English culture did not necessarily organize the world in terms of the orientalist binary, defined by Edward Said. By historicizing British orientalism, [author Eugenia Zuroski] Jenkins reveals how the notion of the East as anathema to English identity is produced through various competing models of subjectivity over the course of the eighteenth century." (Publisher's note)

REVIEW: *Choice* v51 no4 p638 D 2013 S. Morgan

REVIEW: *TLS* no5783 p22 Ja 31 2014 MAXINE BERG

"A Taste for China: English Subjectivity and the Prehistory of Orientalism." "In 'A Taste for China,' Eugenia Zuroski Jenkins focuses on the problem of how . . . Asian goods were received. . . . Zuroski Jenkins focuses more narrowly . . . on some of the complexities of English literary and cultural responses to Chinese porcelain and chinoiserie. . . . There is some, but not deep, literary analysis; the discussion of Defoe contains little on China. The subject of the reception of Chinese goods and taste for chinoiserie is, however, an important one, and Eugenia Zuroski Jenkins reaches beyond the obvious literary works to diaries, design manuals and artists to build her case."

JENKINS, JANETTE. Firefly; [by] Janette Jenkins 165 p. 2013 Penguin Group USA

1. Authors—Fiction 2. Biographical fiction 3. Coward, Noël, 1899-1973 4. Jamaica—Fiction 5. Older men—Fiction

ISBN 1609451406; 9781609451400

SUMMARY: "On a secluded hillside in Jamaica lies Firefly, Noël Coward's peaceful retreat." A novel by Janette Jenkins, "Set over a series of summer days in the early 1970s, 'Firefly' flits through Coward's dreams and memories, his successes and regrets, against a sultry, seductive backdrop of blue skies and glistening water. Colorful and contemplative, this is a moving portrait of old age and friendship, and a poignant appraisal of a life well lived." (Publisher's note)

REVIEW: *Kirkus Rev* v81 no16 p313 Ag 15 2013

REVIEW: *N Y Times Book Rev* p20 Ja 26 2014 JAN STUART

"Firefly." "Oh, how taxing it is to be Noël Coward in his declining years, trundling between two homes in Jamaica with only one servant to pour the brandy. . . . If you are the British wit-of-all-trades so cunningly inhabited by [author] Janette Jenkins in her apple-crisp autumnal novel, 'Firefly,' you have devolved at 71 into a prisoner of your own branding. . . . As dramatic devices go, the gin-induced reverie is hardly novel. In this instance, however, it frees Jenkins to dart about Coward's history with an impressionistic briskness that offers a welcome respite from the flattening minutiae of doorstopper biographies."

REVIEW: *New York Times* v163 no56306 pC2 O 31 2013 John Williams

REVIEW: *New Yorker* v89 no38 p127-1 N 25 2013

JENKINS, JEFFERY A. Fighting for the speakership. See Stewart, C.

JENKINS, JESSICA KERWIN. All the time in the world; a book of hours; [by] Jessica Kerwin Jenkins 320 p. 2013 Nan A. Talese

1. ART—European 2. DESIGN—Fashion 3. HISTORY—World 4. Historical literature 5. Manners and customs—Miscellanea

ISBN 0385535414; 9780385535410 (hardback)

LC 2013-000795

SUMMARY: In this book, author Jessica Kerwin Jenkins "uses the template of the medieval book of hours, which provided readings and meditations for certain times of the day and seasons, to create an unusual look at 'how we pass the time.'" (Booklist) "Subjects covered include the daylong ceremony of laying a royal Elizabethan tablecloth; the radicalization of sartorial chic in 1890s Paris; [and] Nostradamus's belief in the aphrodisiac power of jam." (Publisher's note)

REVIEW: *Booklist* v110 no4 p4 O 15 2013 Whitney Scott

"All the Time in the World: A Book of Hours." "[Jessica Kerwin] Jenkins uses the template of the medieval book of hours, which provided readings and meditations for certain times of the day and seasons, to create an unusual look at 'how we pass the time.' Her 'hours' are vignettes exploring the curious, the beautiful, and the ephemeral, a reflective approach that counters our 'hyper-scheduled cult of Getting Things Done.' This lovely and lovingly researched literary gem encompasses diverse eras and cultures and reveals a world of 'fancies' and intriguing bits of history. . . . There is much to contemplate and marvel over in Jenkins' scholarly and highly entertaining book of exuberance."

REVIEW: *Kirkus Rev* v81 no18 p132 S 15 2013

JENKINS, STEVE.il. The Animal Book. See Jenkins, S.

JENKINS, STEVE. The Animal Book; A Collection of the Fastest, Fiercest, Toughest, Cleverest, Shyest—and Most Surprising—animals on Earth; [by] Steve Jenkins 208 p. 2013 Houghton Mifflin Harcourt

1. Animal behavior 2. Animals—Juvenile literature 3. Children's nonfiction 4. Picture books for children 5. Predatory animals

ISBN 054755799X (hardcover); 9780547557991 (hardcover)

SUMMARY: This children's picture book by Steve Jenkins provides an "introduction to the vast animal kingdom. After a chapter of definition, information is presented in sections on animal families, senses, predators, defenses, extremes and the story of life. More facts appear in the final chapter, which serves both as index (with page numbers and thumbnails) and quick reference." (Kirkus Reviews)

REVIEW: *Booklist* v110 no3 p52 O 1 2013 Kay Weisman

REVIEW: *Bull Cent Child Books* v67 no4 p218 D 2013 E. B.

REVIEW: *Horn Book Magazine* v90 no1 p110 Ja/F 2014 ROGER SUTTON

"The Animal Book: A Collection of the Fastest, Fiercest, Toughest, Cleverest, Shyest—and Most Surprising—Animals on Earth". "While this might look like yet another animal encyclopedia (albeit handsomer than most), chock-full of 'fun facts' and better browsed than read, [Steve] Jenkins has given us something much more thoughtful and coherent. . . . The paper collage art throughout is distilled from Jenkins's many previous books, but this is no clip job: each image—from a red-eyed tree frog jauntily balanced on a vine dog-earing a crisp white page to a full-bleed spread of a Siberian tiger's face—serves the book's purpose. . . . Charts and graphs throughout are as intriguing as the animals themselves."

REVIEW: *Kirkus Rev* p41 Ag 15 2013 Fall Preview

REVIEW: *Kirkus Rev* v81 no17 p98 S 1 2013

REVIEW: *Kirkus Rev* p47 2013 Guide to BookExpo America

REVIEW: *Kirkus Rev* p77 N 15 2013 Best Books

REVIEW: *Publ Wkly* p91 Children's starred review annual 2013

REVIEW: *Publ Wkly* v260 no38 p79 S 23 2013

REVIEW: *SLJ* v59 no10 p1 O 2013 Lynn Vanca

JENKINS, STEVE.il. Eye to eye. See Jenkins, S.

JENKINS, STEVE. Eye to eye; how animals see the world; [by] Steve Jenkins 32 p. 2014 Houghton Mifflin Books for Children, Houghton Mifflin Harcourt

1. Animals—Juvenile literature 2. Children's nonfiction 3. Compound eye 4. Eye—Juvenile literature 5. Vision
ISBN 0547959079; 9780547959078
LC 2013-024004

SUMMARY: In this picture book, author Steve Jenkins "explains how for most animals, eyes are the most important source of information about the world in a biological sense. The simplest eyes—clusters of light-sensitive cells—appeared more than one billion years ago, and provided a big survival advantage to the first creatures that had them. Since then, animals have evolved an amazing variety of eyes, along with often surprising ways to use them." (Publisher's note)

REVIEW: *Booklist* v110 no15 p41 Ap 1 2014 Carolyn Phelan

REVIEW: *Bull Cent Child Books* v67 no8 p409 Ap 2014 D. S.

REVIEW: *Horn Book Magazine* v90 no2 p142-3 Mr/Ap 2014 DANIELLE J. FORD

REVIEW: *Kirkus Rev* v82 no4 p115 F 15 2014

"Eye to Eye: How Animals See the World". "The evolution of the eye and the surprising ways animals see the world are displayed in a thoughtfully designed and engagingly illustrated album. The look of a [Steve] Jenkins book is unmistakable: realistic cut-and-torn-paper images set on a stark white background; short informational paragraphs; a helpful section of concluding facts with a pictorial index. But the content is always an interesting surprise. . . . A bibliography of suggestions for further reading and a glossary round out this intriguing introduction. Another impressive presentation from a master craftsman."

REVIEW: *Publ Wkly* v261 no16 p78 Ap 21 2014

REVIEW: *SLJ* v60 no3 p173 Mr 2014 Maryann H. Owen

JENKINS, STEVE.il. Eat like a bear. See Eat like a bear

JENKINS, WARD.il. Missing monkey! See Amato, M.

JENNINGS, KATHLEEN.il. The Bread We Eat in Dreams. See Valente,K.

JENNINGS, MICHAEL W. Walter Benjamin. See Eiland, H.

JENNINGS, PATRICK. Odd, weird, and little; [by] Patrick Jennings 160 p. 2014 Egmont USA

1. Bullies—Fiction 2. Eccentrics and eccentricities—Fiction 3. Friendship—Fiction 4. Middle schools—Fiction 5. School stories 6. Schools—Fiction
ISBN 1606843745; 9781606843741 (hardcover)
LC 2013-018248

SUMMARY: In this book, by Patrick Jennings, "Woodrow and his classmates are surprised at the old-fashioned clothing and the tiny, delicate appearance of Toulouse, a newly arrived student from Canada. . . . Woodrow risks regaining his place as top [bullying] victim as he decides to befriend and protect Toulouse. . . . Readers also learn about the psychology behind bullying and about self-empowerment." (Kirkus Reviews)

REVIEW: *Booklist* v110 no8 p49 D 15 2013 John Peters

REVIEW: *Bull Cent Child Books* v67 no5 p269-70 Ja 2014 K. Q. G.

REVIEW: *Horn Book Magazine* v90 no2 p121 Mr/Ap 2014 JULIE ROACH

"Odd, Weird & Little." "Ultimately, Toulouse's interesting point of view and many talents charm not only Woodrow but many others, altering the class dynamic for the better. All the while Toulouse has a secret, and though Woodrow never reveals it, it's spelled out in big clues throughout the plot as well as over and over in an acrostic of the title and the chapter headings. The voice periodically veers into a heavy-handedness that feels especially artificial for a young narrator. . . . The actions of the characters perfectly illustrate this already, and, like the title acrostic, spelling it out diminishes its power. Fortunately, there's genuine humor and heart here, with pacing well suited to elementary chapter-book readers."

REVIEW: *Kirkus Rev* v81 no20 p243 O 15 2013

REVIEW: *Publ Wkly* v260 no42 p52 O 21 2013

REVIEW: *SLJ* v60 no1 p71 Ja 2014 Wayne R. Cherry

JENSEN, KURT VILLADS.ed. Cultural encounters during the crusades. See Cultural encounters during the crusades

JERNIGAN, DANIEL KEITH.ed. Flann O'Brien. See Flann O'Brien

JEROLMACK, COLIN. The global pigeon; [by] Colin Jerolmack 2013 University of Chicago Press

1. Pigeon racing 2. Pigeons 3. Social science literature 4. Urban ecology (Biology) 5. Urban ecology (Sociology)
ISBN 9780226001890 hardcover; 9780226002088 paperback

SUMMARY: "Drawing on more than three years of fieldwork across three continents, Colin Jerolmack traces our complex and often contradictory relationship with these versatile animals in public spaces such as Venice's Piazza San Marco and London's Trafalgar Square and in working-class and immigrant communities of pigeon breeders in New York and Berlin. . . . Jerolmack shows how our interactions with pigeons offer surprising insights into city life, community, culture, and politics." (Publisher's note)

REVIEW: *Choice* v51 no3 p491 N 2013 J. A. Mather

REVIEW: *New Sci* v218 no2918 p48-9 My 25 2013 Stephanie Pain

REVIEW: *TLS* no5782 p30 Ja 24 2014 JENNIE ERIN SMITH

"The Global Pigeon." "In 'The Global Pigeon,' his ethnography of human-pigeon encounters, Colin Jerolmack makes an imaginative and convincing case against interpreting any of these activities as 'driven by a singular deep-seated need to connect to nature,' as environmental scholars persuaded by the biophilia hypothesis might. . . . The chapters on New York's rooftop flyers are the most compelling in 'The Global Pigeon,' and best support Jerolmack's forceful rejection of the biophilia trope."

JESS-COOKE, CAROLYN. The boy who could see demons; a novel; [by] Carolyn Jess-Cooke 288 p. 2012 Delacorte Press

1. Children—Death—Fiction 2. Delusions—Fiction 3. Grief—Fiction 4. Suspense fiction 5. Women psychiatrists—Fiction

ISBN 9780345536532; 9780345536549 (ebook)

LC 2012-038953

SUMMARY: In this book, "Anya Molokova, a child psychiatrist, has returned to her native Belfast hoping to help heal some of the 20 percent of Northern Ireland's children who suffer from severe mental health problems. Anya, herself both the child of a suicidal parent and the agonized mother of a schizoid daughter who died tragically four years earlier, becomes professionally and personally involved with Alex Broccoli, a tormented 10-year-old with an imaginary demon friend." (Publishers Weekly)

REVIEW: *Libr J* v138 no5 p90 Mr 15 2013 Barbara Hoffert

REVIEW: *N Y Times Book Rev* p21 S 1 2013 Marilyn Stasio

"How the Light Gets In," "The Boy Who Could See Demons," and "Sandrine's Case." "The only way to thwart the dastardly schemes (too dastardly for credibility) of that monstrous villain (too monstrous to be true) is to set up a satellite link to the outside world. . . . Once met, the delightfully quirky inhabitants of Three Pines are the kind of people you can't wait to see again. . . . But they all seem better suited to the modestly scaled subplot. . . . [A] 10-year-old boy . . . shares narrative duties with his psychiatrist in Carolyn Jess-Cooke's startling novel. . . . Although Thomas H. Cook is often praised for the clarity of his prose and the sheer drive of his storytelling, he deserves a special citation for bravery. In 'Sandrine's Case,' he not only dares to write a novel with an unpleasant protagonist, but also makes him the narrator."

REVIEW: *Publ Wkly* v260 no25 p144 Je 24 2013

JEWETT, ANDREW. Science, democracy, and the American university; from the Civil War to the Cold War; [by] Andrew Jewett xii, 402 p. 2012 Cambridge University Press

1. Democracy & science 2. Democracy and science—United States 3. HISTORY—United States—General 4. Historical literature 5. Science—United States—History 6. Science and state—United States 7. Social sciences—United States—History 8. United States—Intellectual life—History 9. Universities & colleges—United States—History

ISBN 9781107027268 (Hardback)

LC 2012-015679

SUMMARY: "This book reinterprets the rise of the natural and social sciences as sources of political authority in modern America. Andrew Jewett demonstrates the remarkable persistence of a belief that the scientific enterprise carried with it a set of ethical values capable of grounding a democratic culture. . . . The book traces the shifting formulations of this belief from the creation of the research universities in the Civil War era to the early Cold War years." (Publisher's note)

REVIEW: *Am Hist Rev* v118 no4 p1207-8 O 2013 J. David Hoeveler

"Science, Democracy, and the American University: From the Civil War to the Cold War." "In this ambitious and wide-ranging study, Andrew Jewett invites us to reconsider the parameters of American intellectual history. He offers science, in terms of its meanings and purposes, as the vehicle for doing so. . . Jewett brings a large array of thinkers into his narrative, but creating the phenomenon of scientific democracy often requires some force-feeding on his part. . . . Those who spoke for science's purity and autonomy also believed that they best served democracy and the public good. . . . Altogether, Jewett has written a book rich in ideas, fascinating to follow in the varieties of opinions about science in American life and fully worthy of our attention."

REVIEW: *Choice* v50 no10 p1857 Je 2013 P. D. Skiff

REVIEW: *J Am Hist* v100 no2 p561-2 S 2013 Daniel J. Wilson

THE JEWISH MOVEMENT IN THE SOVIET UNION; xv, 450 p. 2012 Woodrow Wilson Center Press Johns Hopkins University Press

1. Historical literature 2. Jews—Persecutions—Soviet Union—History—20th century—Congresses 3. Jews—Soviet Union—History—20th century—Congresses 4. Jews—Soviet Union—Politics and government—20th century—Congresses 5. Jews—Soviet Union—Social conditions—20th century—Congresses 6. Refuseniks—Congresses

ISBN 1421405644; 9781421405643

LC 2011-044956

SUMMARY: In this collection of essays on the Jewish movement in the Soviet Union, edited by Yaacov Ro'i, the contributors "examine the influences of a wide range of contemporary events, including the victory of Israel in the 1967 war, the Soviet dissident and human rights movements, and the general malaise of Soviet society, its self-contradictory attitude toward nationalism, and its underlying anti-Semitism." (Publisher's note)

REVIEW: *TLS* no5747 p25 My 24 2013 PATRICK WORSNIP

"The Jewish Movement in the Soviet Union." "To produce such a book nearly a quarter of a century after the decline and fall of the Soviet Union essentially resolved the problem, as emigration restrictions were lifted, may seem belated, but more evidence has continued to come to light and more research has been done. . . . Assembling conference papers can often result in disparate and disorganized insights, without a guiding theme. To counteract that risk, [Yaacov] Ro'i has himself written three introductory chapters, covering the origins of the Soviet Jewish movement, its strategy, tactics and achievements, and commissioned five new articles. Despite a strong editorial hand, there is some overlapping. . . . Nevertheless, almost every angle is covered."

JEWITT, CAREY.ed. The Sage Handbook of Digital Technology Research. See The Sage Handbook of Digital Technology Research

JIAN, GUO.ed. Tombstone. See Yang Jisheng

JIN LUXIAN. The Memoirs of Jin Luxian; 324 p. 2012 Columbia Univ Pr

1. Catholic Church 2. China—Church history 3. China—Religion 4. Church & state—China 5. Memoirs

ISBN 9789888139668; 9888139665

SUMMARY: This book presents a memoir by Chinese Catholic leader Jin Luxian. "Educated by the Jesuits, he joined the Society of Jesus and was ordained priest in 1945 before continuing his studies in Europe. In 1951 he made the dangerous decision to return to the newly established People's Republic of China. He became one of the many thousands of Roman Catholics who suffered persecution. Convicted of counter-revolutionary activities and treason, he was imprisoned for 27 years and only released in 1982." (Publisher's note)

REVIEW: *America* v210 no9 p36-8 Mr 17 2014 NICHOLAS CLIFFORD

"The Memoirs of Jin Luxian: Learning and Relearning 1916-1982". "This volume, splendidly translated by William Hanbury-Tenison, takes the story only up to Jin's return to Shanghai from jail in 1982. His accounts of his youth and education under the French Jesuits in Shanghai are very interesting, as are those of his studies abroad after the Second World War in Rome and in France. . . . Memoirs are not, properly speaking, history. . . . Jin's book, he tells us, was written entirely from memory, since he had lost all his papers at the time of his arrest and knew the dangers of keeping correspondence or a journal. Add to these uncertainties the fact that it was published in China, hardly a leading center of press freedom."

JINKS, CATHERINE. How to catch a bogle; [by] Catherine Jinks 320 p. 2013 Harcourt Children's Books

1. Apprentices—Fiction 2. Historical fiction 3. Monsters—Fiction 4. Orphans—Fiction 5. Supernatural—Fiction

ISBN 0544087089 (hardcover); 9780544087088 (hardcover)

LC 2012-045936

SUMMARY: This is the first in a historical fantasy trilogy from Catherine Jinks. Here, "child-eating bogles infest Victorian London, providing work aplenty for 'Go-Devil Man' Alfred Bunce and his intrepid young apprentice, Birdie." Birdie is kidnapped by "would-be warlock Roswell Morton, out to capture one of the monsters for his own evil uses." She also must deal with the unwanted "attentions of Miss Edith Eames," who wants "to see Birdie cleaned up and educated in the social graces." (Kirkus Reviews)

REVIEW: *Booklist* v110 no3 p53 O 1 2013 Carolyn Phelan

REVIEW: *Bull Cent Child Books* v67 no2 p97-8 O 2013 E. B.

"How to Catch a Bogle." "Ten-year-old Birdie knows she's quite well off as poor Victorian orphans go. She's apprenticed to Mr. Bunce, an intelligent and kindly, if somewhat morose, bogler, a sort of supernatural exterminator ridding households and businesses of troublesome bogles that hide in the properties' deep recesses and eat children. . . . [Author Catherine] Jinks[ʻs] subtext of the Victorian social themes--from the evils of child labor to the application of scientific thinking to host of unlikely problems--puts a smarter and funnier spin on preternatural shenanigans than a simple description of plot elements might suggest. The first entry in a planned trilogy, this title introduces a cast of secondary characters robust enough to expand the adventures in any direction."

REVIEW: *Horn Book Magazine* v89 no5 p101-2 S/O 2013 DEIRDRE F. BAKER

"How to Catch a Bogle." "This quasi-Victorian, somewhat gothic fantasy is a satisfying confection. . . . [Catherine] Jink is an assured storyteller: character, plot, and style develop with buoyant, pleasing momentum, and her rendition of working-class English dialect reads accessibly. While this is fantasy . . factual elements of the period undergird and strengthen setting and story line. Birdie is a bright, stalwart heroine whose limitless font of haunting ballads tinges the story with melancholy."

REVIEW: *Kirkus Rev* v81 no14 p21 Jl 15 2013

REVIEW: *Kirkus Rev* p77 N 15 2013 Best Books

REVIEW: *Kirkus Rev* p48 2013 Guide 20to BookExpo America

REVIEW: *Publ Wkly* p83 Children's starred review annual 2013

REVIEW: *Publ Wkly* v260 no25 p172-3 Je 24 2013

REVIEW: *SLJ* v60 no4 p60 Ap 2014 Maria Salvadore

REVIEW: *SLJ* v59 no8 p102 Ag 2013 Amanda Raklovits

JINKS, CATHERINE. Saving Thanehaven; [by] Catherine Jinks 384 p. 2013 Egmont USA

1. Computer games—Fiction 2. Knights and knighthood—Fiction 3. Science fiction 4. Video games & children 5. Virtual reality—Fiction

ISBN 1606842749; 9781606842744 (hardcover)

LC 2012-046190

SUMMARY: In this book, "Noble is just an earnest knight in the computer game 'Thanehaven Slayer' when he encounters young Rufus, who strongly suggests that he may be doomed if he doesn't drop all the heroics and start thinking for himself. With Rufus' mantra 'you don't have to do this' ringing in his ears, Noble sets out to change his computer world." (Kirkus Reviews)

REVIEW: *Booklist* v109 no21 p75 Jl 1 2013 Krista Hutley

REVIEW: *Bull Cent Child Books* v67 no1 p25-6 S 2013 K. Q. G.

"Saving Thanehaven." "Noble the Slayer is yet again slogging through treacherous terrain in the great kingdom of Thanehaven when a scrawny kid named Rufus shows up and informs him that Noble could be in charge of his own destiny if he helps Rufus take down something called the operating system. . . . The intriguing premise certainly makes for some amusing and imaginative scenarios . . . but it also backs the characters into a corner. . . . The breakneck pace, with characters jumping from one game and even computer to another, may nonetheless compel readers, and gamers will be particularly pleased with a few jargon-based jokes, so it may be worth keeping this on hand for gaming night."

REVIEW: *Kirkus Rev* v81 no10 p98 My 15 2013

REVIEW: *Publ Wkly* v260 no20 p60 My 20 2013

REVIEW: *SLJ* v59 no8 p102 Ag 2013 Jane Barrer

JOBIN, MATTHEW. The Nethergrim; [by] Matthew Jobin 368 p. 2014 Philomel Books, an imprint of Penguin

Group (USA) Inc.

1. Fantasy 2. Friendship—Fiction 3. Good & evil—Fiction 4. Magic—Fiction 5. Monsters—Fiction
ISBN 9780399159985
LC 2013-005309

SUMMARY: In this book by Matthew Jobin, "Tom is an abused slave, Katherine is a girl who resists the traditional expectations her small village places on her gender, and Edmund is boy whose wizarding interest and fascination with books have only ever caused him trouble. When the Nethergrim's minions begin to kidnap local children, however, the trio springs into action as unexpected heroes." (Bulletin of the Center for Children's Books)

REVIEW: *Booklist* v110 no15 p86 Ap 1 2014 Stacey Comfort

REVIEW: *Bull Cent Child Books* v67 no8 p409-10 Ap 2014 A. S.

"The Nethergrim". "This is a surprisingly quiet (and occasionally languid) novel for its subject, and the character development is careful and methodical, lending depth to a story that's more about people than adventure. The Nethergrim itself is indeed the stuff of nightmates, and [Matthew] Jobin judiciously doles out details about it, heightening suspense further. Patient fantasy fans will find much to enjoy in this elegant gem of a novel, and the haunting message that the monstrosity of some humans can rival even that of ageless creatures is so carefully and effectively inlaid that it will likely linger even after other details fade."

REVIEW: *Kirkus Rev* v82 no5 p108 Mr 1 2014

REVIEW: *Publ Wkly* v261 no4 p193 Ja 27 2014

REVIEW: *Quill Quire* v80 no5 p44 Je 2014 Dory Cerny

REVIEW: *SLJ* v60 no4 p148 Ap 2014 Martha Simpson

REVIEW: *Voice of Youth Advocates* v36 no6 p72 F 2014 Sherrie Williams

JOCKERS, MATTHEW L. Macroanalysis; digital methods and literary history; [by] Matthew L. Jockers 208 p. 2013 University of Illinois Press

1. Digital humanities 2. Literature—History & criticism 3. Literature—Research—Data processing 4. Literature—Research—Methodology 5. Literature—Statistical methods
ISBN 9780252037528 (hardcover); 9780252079078 (pbk.)
LC 2012-032491

SUMMARY: This book by Matthew L. Jockers "introduces readers to large-scale literary computing and the revolutionary potential of macroanalysis—a new approach to the study of the literary record designed for probing the digital-textual world as it exists today, in digital form and in large quantities. Using computational analysis to retrieve key words, phrases, and linguistic patterns across thousands of texts in digital libraries, researchers can draw conclusions based on quantifiable evidence." (Publisher's note)

REVIEW: *Choice* v51 no8 p1393 Ap 2014 G. Divay

"Macroanalysis: Digital Methods and Literary History". "[Matthew L.] Jockers . . . puts data mining and word crunching to good use in analyzing textual components across large textual databases. After addressing the tools allowing him to carry out his sweeping surveys within the field of digital humanities, he demonstrates, with revealing graphs and charts, how the data indicate trends in genres, themes, national identity, gender, style, and influence. The chapter on 800 works published in the eastern and western US by Irish American writers over 250 years is fascinating in its blend of statistics and sociolinguistic analysis. . . . Overall, Jockers advocates a happy, dialectical balance between traditional scholarship and computer-generated, macroanalytical methods."

REVIEW: *Libr J* v138 no10 p106 Je 1 2013 Patrick A. Smith

REVIEW: *Libr J* v138 no3 p32-3 F 15 2013 Margaret Heilbrun

REVIEW: *TLS* no5774 p30 N 29 2013 JENNIFER HOWARD

JOCKUSCH, LAURA. Collect and record!; Jewish Holocaust documentation in early postwar Europe; [by] Laura Jockusch xv, 320 p. 2012 Oxford University Press

1. Collective memory—Europe 2. Historical literature 3. Historiography—Europe—History—20th century 4. Holocaust survivors—Europe—History 5. Holocaust, Jewish (1939-1945)—Historiography 6. Holocaust, Jewish (1939-1945)—Personal narratives—Europe—History and criticism 7. Memorial books (Holocaust) 8. World War, 1939-1945—Historiography
ISBN 9780199764556 (hardback: acid-free paper)
LC 2012-004841

SUMMARY: "This book describes the vibrant activity of survivors who founded Jewish historical commissions and documentation centers in Europe immediately after the Second World War. In the first postwar decade, these initiatives collected thousands of Nazi documents along with testimonies, memoirs, diaries, songs, poems, and artifacts of Jewish victims. They pioneered in developing a Holocaust historiography that placed the experiences of Jews at the center". (Publisher's note)

REVIEW: *Am Hist Rev* v119 no1 p246-7 F 2014 Samuel Kassow

"Collect and Record! Jewish Holocaust Documentation in Early Postwar Europe". "This well-researched book by Laura Jokusch shows that, far from being "silent" in the aftermath of the Holocaust, Jewish survivors organized research institutes, collected documents, gathered testimonies, and left a legacy of archival treasures of unrivaled importance. . . . After the war, survivors saw documentation and research as a sacred mission. How they fulfilled that mission is a gripping story and Jokusch tells it well. . . . This excellent book should be read by anyone with a serious interest in Holocaust memory and historiography."

REVIEW: *Choice* v50 no8 p1496 Ap 2013 A. Ezergailis

REVIEW: *TLS* no5758 p5 Ag 9 2013 SAMUEL MOYN

JOHANN, ELISABETH. Science and hope; a forest history; [by] Elisabeth Johann 278 p. 2013 White Horse Press

1. Forest ecology 2. Forestry literature 3. Forests & forestry—Europe 4. Forests and forestry—History 5. Taxonomy
ISBN 1874267731; 9781874267737
LC 2013-427313

SUMMARY: This book presents "a history of forestry by discipline, looking at subfields such as taxonomy, silviculture, economics, and ecology as they developed as a 'science,' the first part of the title. 'Hope' in the title refers to the vision and promise of forestry as seen by foresters over centuries. The focus of the book is European, including European colonial empires, with some references to forestry in other regions." (Choice: Current Reviews for Academic Libraries)

REVIEW: *Choice* v51 no6 p1034-5 F 2014 B. D. Orr

"Science and Hope: A Forest History." "'Science and Hope' is one of those intriguing books that is so well written it can reach a wide range of readers. . . . The book is organized in such short, clear chapters that it could easily be used as a textbook for an introductory class in forestry, supplementing the book with a few readings from the US and Canada. For foresters with decades of experience. Science and Hope is a refreshing overview of the field and a compendium of interesting facts. This reviewer learned that the second book published in German was a forestry text; the first was the Bible. . . . Highly recommended."

JOHANNESSEN, INGÓLFUR. The virus that causes cancer. See Crawford, D. H.

JOHANSEN, MARIELA.tr. Seaweeds. See Seaweeds

JOHN, HYWEL. Rose; [by] Hywel John 83 2011 Nick Hern Books

ISBN 9781848422247 (Paper)
LC 2011-488713

SUMMARY: This play follows "a dysfunctional family of two bedsit . . . Arthur dotes on his clever young daughter, teaching her what he knows of educated English values, learned in his Middle Eastern country of origin, before coming to live in England. . . . Her mother has passed away in mysterious circumstances but is ever present in their lives because Rose constantly asks questions about her which the pained, lonely Arthur never answers properly. He enthusiastically diverts her attention into stories about Englishness, moral education, history, anything but his own history or that of her mother. . . . Rose Smith is trying to understand who she is, to find her identity as a person with a coloured skin in Britain. . . . As Rose grows up, she is more and more frustrated, in many ways, by his lifestyle and his secretive attitude to his past." (fringereport.wordpress.com)

REVIEW: *Bull Cent Child Books* v67 no3 p187 N 2013 J. H.

"Rose." "In this first title of a series imported from England, young Rose (who believes she's 'about ten') is excited to exchange St. Bridget's Home for Abandoned Girls for a housemaid position at the house of wealthy alchemist Mr. Fountain. Her magical powers, however, are making it difficult to keep her head down and make a living . . . [Author Holly] Webb pokes gentle fun at Victorian tropes here . . . and the plot offers both intrigue and adventure. Aside from Rose, however, the characters are fairly flat and predictable, and events whip by in order to tie the plot up before the end; the blood-sucking witch is also a rather jarring addition to what is otherwise a domestic historical fantasy."

REVIEW: *Kirkus Rev* v81 no15 p237 Ag 1 2013

REVIEW: *SLJ* v60 no2 p99 F 2014 Sada Mozer

JOHN NASH; Architect of the Picturesque; 250 p. 2013 David Brown Book Co.

1. Architects—Great Britain 2. Architectural literature 3. Architecture—Great Britain 4. Nash, John, 1752-1835 5. Picturesque, The, in architecture
ISBN 184802102X; 9781848021020

SUMMARY: This book, by Geoffrey Tyack, explores the aesthetics and work of John Nash, "one of the most important architects of late eighteenth - and early nineteenth-century Britain. . . . No complete study of Nash's work has been published since . . . 1980. Since then, new scholarship has . . . cast new light on several important aspects of Nash's work. The aim of this book . . . is to bring together this recent scholarship in a single volume." (Publisher's note)

REVIEW: *Burlington Mag* v156 no1332 p175-6 Mr 2014 JOCELYN ANDERSON

"John Nash: Architect of the Picturesque". "Later chapters include . . . a detailed (and at times very technical) discussion of his approach to construction with cast iron and timber. There is also an essay which attempts to place Nash in context by linking him to architects such as John Soane and Karl Frieriich Schinkel; however, this essay is not wholly successful as it has attempted to make too many links in too short a space. Finally, the closing pages of the book include sections directing readers to more information on Nash: most notable is a list of his buildings with directions as to which sources to consult for more information about each one. Ideally, this book will inspire more work on Nash, as there are certainly still questions to answer and avenues to pursue."

JOHNSON, AARON P. Religion and identity in Porphyry of Tyre; the limits of Hellenism in late antiquity; [by] Aaron P. Johnson 382 p. 2013 Cambridge University Press

1. Hellenism 2. Identity (Psychology) 3. Philosophical literature 4. Philosophy & religion
ISBN 9781107012738
LC 2012-035050

SUMMARY: In this book on the philosopher Porphyry, Aaron P. Johnson "rejects the prevailing modern approach to his thought, which has posited an early stage dominated by 'Oriental' superstition and irrationality followed by a second rationalizing or Hellenizing phase consequent upon his move west and exposure to Neoplatonism. . . . He argues for a complex unity of thought in terms of philosophical translation." (Publisher's note)

REVIEW: *Choice* v51 no5 p850 Ja 2014 P. W. Wakefield

"Religion and Identity in Porphyry of Tyre: The Limits of Hellenism in Late Antiquity." "This is a fine work, but more for its unifying exposition of Porphyry's philosophy than for its complex thesis about religion, identity, and Hellenism. It will be useful for students of Hellenistic philosophy. . . . [Aaron P.] Johnson rejects Joseph Bidez's 'Orientalizing' idea . . .that Porphyry progressed from his Eastern beginnings to a mature Hellenic philosophy. He presents a more unified view of Porphyry's philosophy than Andrew Smith's 'Porphyry's Place in the Neoplatonic Tradition' (1974), which focused on Porphyry's philosophy of soul."

JOHNSON, ANGELA, 1961-. All different now; Juneteenth, the first day of freedom; [by] Angela Johnson 40 p. 2014 Simon & Schuster Books for Young Readers

1. African Americans—Fiction 2. Family life—Texas—Fiction 3. Historical poetry 4. Juneteenth—Fiction 5. Slavery—Fiction

ISBN 068987376X; 9780689873768 (hardcover)
LC 2011-038273

SUMMARY: Written by Angela Johnson and illustrated by E. B. Lewis, "'All Different Now' tells the story of the first Juneteenth, the day freedom finally came to the last of the slaves in the South. Since then, the observance of June 19 as African American Emancipation Day has spread across the United States and beyond." (Publisher's note)

REVIEW: *Booklist* v110 no11 p61-2 F 1 2014 Courtney Jones

"All Different Now: Juneteenth, the First Day of Freedom". "On June 19, 1865, a young slave girl and her family go about their daily routine, unaware that their lives are about to change. . . . Rich, subdued watercolors convey the celebrations with dignity and awe. Each page shows the slaves as a collective people, finally seeing a brighter future within reach. [Angela] Johnson's attached verse enables younger readers to see the momentous nature of this date, while back matter appropriate for older readers provides a time line and other important factual references. A worthy addition to any collection on the topic."

REVIEW: *Bull Cent Child Books* v67 no10 p523 Je 2014 D. S.

"All Different Now: Juneteenth, the First Day of Freedom". "Although the end matter is plenty informative, the main text isn't so much about relaying facts as it is about depicting the emotion of a life-transforming, generations-transforming, epoch-transforming moment; [Angela] Johnson's quiet ragged-right prose has a credible breathlessness as it conveys the mixture of stunned amazement and sheer joy. . . . This is an emotive and effective way to take emancipation from a historic date to the experience of people whose lives changed, and it'll open kids' eyes to the impact of the transition."

REVIEW: *Horn Book Magazine* v90 no3 p67-8 My/Je 2014 ROBIN L. SMITH

REVIEW: *Kirkus Rev* v82 no6 p182 Mr 15 2014

REVIEW: *Publ Wkly* v261 no11 p87 Mr 17 2014

REVIEW: *SLJ* v60 no5 p84 My 2014 Wendy Lukehart

JOHNSON, D. B., 1944-. Magritte's marvelous hat; a picture book; [by] D. B. Johnson 32 p. 2012 Houghton Mifflin Harcourt

1. Children's literature 2. Dogs—Fiction 3. Hats—Fiction 4. Magic—Fiction 5. Painting, French—Fiction 6. Picture books for children

ISBN 9780547558646
LC 2011-012242

SUMMARY: This picture book "recasts René Magritte as a dapper, blue-eyed hound and incorporates the painter's surreal iconography. . . . The black bowler hat (a familiar, recurrent image in Magritte's paintings) is characterized as a playful muse, engaging the artist in frisky games on walks." Author/illustrator D.B. Johnson depicts the story with "surreal elements," including "four see-through acetate pages . . . [that] transform adjacent spreads," and images inspired by famous Magritte paintings. (Kirkus

REVIEW: *Booklist* v108 no15 p76 Ap 1 2012 Thom Barthelmess

REVIEW: *Kirkus Rev* v80 no4 p403 F 15 2012

"Magritte's Marvelous Hat." "Johnson recasts René Magritte as a dapper, blue-eyed hound and incorporates the painter's surreal iconography into a visual tour de force. . . . The black bowler hat (a familiar, recurrent image in Magritte's paintings) is characterized as a playful muse, engaging the artist in frisky games on walks. . . . [D. B.] Johnson zealously incorporates surreal elements to tickle both art appreciators and preschoolers. Four see-through acetate pages cleverly transform adjacent spreads. Magritte's paintings are mined for dozens of images, slyly inserted. . . . Arty, amusing and exceedingly clever."

REVIEW: *Publ Wkly* v259 no10 p69 Mr 5 2012

REVIEW: *SLJ* v58 no3 p128 Mr 2012 Wendy Lukehart

JOHNSON, DEBORAH. Stuck Is Not a Four-Letter Word; Seven Steps to Getting Un-Stuck; [by] Deborah Johnson 270 p. 2013 Author Solutions

1. Advice literature 2. Change (Psychology) 3. Self-actualization (Psychology) 4. Self-help materials 5. Success

ISBN 1475996624; 9781475996623

SUMMARY: This book presents "a personal self-help guide to becoming 'unstuck' in business and in life. [Deborah] Johnson . . . uses examples from her own life, and from the lives of savvy business executives and others, to illustrate seven steps to help readers achieve their goals. Each step (for example, 'reinvent yourself,' 'eliminate distractions,' 'play like you're in the major leagues') is explored in four or five chapters." (Kirkus Reviews)

REVIEW: *Kirkus Rev* p14 D 15 2013 supplement seasons readings

REVIEW: *Kirkus Rev* v81 no24 p9 D 15 2013

"Stuck Is Not a Four-Letter Word". "Although all the steps are quite useful, the sixth section, 'Do the Business,' is perhaps the strongest. [Deborah] Johnson asks close friend and successful real estate entrepreneur Jim Heitbrink for his best business advice—which can easily be applied to life in general. . . . Although the first three-quarters of the book unfolds at a fairly languid pace, the last few chapters have a much faster tempo, which gives the ending a rushed, almost disconnected feel. However, despite this, Johnson still manages to get important points across, including the powerful notion that we're all making an impact—although we may never know the extent of it until much later. . . . An engaging seven-step plan for tackling seemingly insurmountable problems."

REVIEW: *Kirkus Rev* v81 no20 p279 O 15 2013

JOHNSON, DIANE, 1934-. Flyover lives; a memoir; [by] Diane Johnson 288 p. 2014 Viking

1. Home—Middle West 2. Memoirs 3. Novelists, American—Biography 4. Pioneers—Middle West—Biography

ISBN 0670016403; 9780670016402 (hardback)
LC 2013-036808

SUMMARY: In this memoir, Diane Johnson asks, "Were Americans indifferent to history? Her own family seemed always to have been in the Midwest. Surely they had got there from somewhere? In digging around, she discovers letters and memoirs written by generations of stalwart pioneer ancestors that testify to more complex times than the derisive nickname 'The Flyover' gives the region credit for." (Publisher's note)

REVIEW: *Booklist* v110 no9/10 p33 Ja 1 2014 Donna Seaman

REVIEW: *Kirkus Rev* v81 no22 p59 N 15 2013

REVIEW: *N Y Rev Books* v61 no4 p25-7 Mr 6 2014 Francine Prose

REVIEW: *N Y Times Book Rev* p11 Ja 12 2014 CHRISTOPHER BENFEY

"Flyover Lives: A Memoir." "[Author Diane Johnson's] consternation has yielded 'Flyover Lives," a loosely structured quest for roots, ranging back to exotic 18th-century ancestors. . . . Johnson strikes an elegaic note in her cullings of family and national history. . . . At times, Johnson herself adopts something of a 'flyover' attitude toward her native Midwest. . . . She seems to have read little about its social history. . . . Late in 'Flyover Lives,' Johnson inserts some vivid personal essays, about her sporadic career as a screenwriter, for example."

REVIEW: *New Yorker* v89 no48 p79-1 F 10 2014

"Flyover Lives." "As a girl in sleepy Moline, Illinois, [Diane] Johnson, the author of 'Le Divorce' and other novels, took for granted the 'sweetness, stolidity, and common sense' of her forebears, while failing to understand the sacrifices they made as frontier settlers. Exploring her family tree, she finds an impoverished country doctor crippled by depression; a mother who watched seven of her nine children die; and relatives living an 'almost preindustrial' life well into the nineteen-fifties."

REVIEW: *Publ Wkly* v260 no47 p46 N 18 2013

JOHNSON, E. PATRICK.ed. Cultural struggles. See Conquergood, D.

JOHNSON, GEORGE. The cancer chronicles; unlocking medicine's deepest mystery; [by] George Johnson 304 p. 2013 Alfred A. Knopf

1. Cancer—Etiology—Popular works 2. Cancer patients—Family relationships 3. Memoirs 4. Oncology 5. Patients' families

ISBN 0307595145; 9780307595140

LC 2012-048474

SUMMARY: In this book, author George Johnson "tackles cancer on a technical and personal level. Johnson's discussion of the science of cancer is entwined with two tales of loss. Despite aggressive treatment, his youngest brother dies from cancer of the head and neck. His wife is diagnosed with uterine cancer and recovers, but their 17-year marriage ends." (Publisher's note)

REVIEW: *Booklist* v109 no21 p9-10 Jl 1 2013 Tony Miksanek

REVIEW: *Economist* v408 no8853 p90-1 S 14 2013

REVIEW: *Kirkus Rev* v81 no12 p52 Je 15 2013

REVIEW: *Libr J* v138 no5 p92 Mr 15 2013 Barbara Hoffert

REVIEW: *N Y Times Book Rev* p23 S 8 2013 DAVID QUAMMEN

"The Cancer Chronicles: Unlocking Medicine's Deepest Mystery". "Knowledge is better than ignorant dread, and good writing based on keen reporting is far better than medical jargon, garbled hearsay or misinformation from the Web. That's just one reason for reading George Johnson's graceful book, 'The Cancer Chronicles'. Another is that the biological details of just what cancer is and how it occurs are . . . fascinating. And not just fascinating but also, as handled by Johnson, revealing of certain deep truths about life itself. . . . Among a small cluster of very good recent books on cancer . . . Johnson's stands out as especially illuminating, forceful and, in its own quiet way, profound."

REVIEW: *Publ Wkly* v260 no23 p69 Je 10 2013

REVIEW: *Science* v342 no6163 p1172 D 6 2013 Mary L. Disis

"The Cancer Chronicles: Unlocking Medicine's Deepest Mystery." "George Johnson's 'The Cancer Chronicles' recounts his attempt to harness the vast amount of information concerning the origins and pathways of cancer growth in an effort to understand what is happening to loved ones affected by cancer. . . . Johnson, an award-winning science writer with the 'New York Times,' is no scientific neophyte. His labor has produced a fascinating compilation of selected discoveries in cancer research that helped shape his deeper understanding of the disease process."

REVIEW: *TLS* no5772 p27 N 15 2013 ALMUT SCHULZE

"The Cancer Chronicles". "[George] Johnson has spoken to many doctors and scientists, read scientific articles and visited conferences where scientists meet to discuss their latest findings. Coupled with his natural curiosity and his fascination with the process of scientific discovery, he is able to convey the most complicated facts in a highly readable manner. . . . It is to Johnson's credit that the scientific facts conveyed in this book are highly accurate. . . . Some of his musings on the possible causes of his wife's cancer seem lengthy at times. . . . Probably the strongest parts of the book are when Johnson describes the work of scientists. . . . The result is a highly captivating book that meticulously explains the current scientific understanding of cancer."

JOHNSON, JOYCE, 1935-. The voice is all; the lonely victory of Jack Kerouac; [by] Joyce Johnson xx, 489 p. 2012 Viking

1. Authors, American—20th century—Biography 2. Beat authors 3. Beat generation—Biography 4. Biographies

ISBN 0670025100; 9780670025107

LC 2012-000603

SUMMARY: In this biography of Jack Kerouac, author Joyce Johnson "peels away layers of the Kerouac legend to show how, caught between two cultures and two languages, he forged a voice to contain his dualities. Looking . . . into how Kerouac's French Canadian background enriched his prose and gave him a unique outsider's vision of America, she tracks his development from boyhood through the phenomenal breakthroughs of 1951." (Publisher's note)

REVIEW: *Rev Am Hist* v41 no3 p525-32 S 2013 Ann Douglas

"The Typewriter is Holy: The Complete, Uncensored History of the Beat Generation," "Brother Souls: John Clellon Holmes, Jack Kerouac, and the Beat Generation," and "The Voice is All: The Lonely Victory of Jack Kerouac." "[Bill Morgan's] presentation is mainly chronological; at times he's inattentive to the demands of thematic coherence and pedestrian in style, neutering rather than demythologizing his subjects. . . . Morgan, whatever his shortcomings, is still the most trustworthy, as well as the most profoundly good-natured, of Beat scholars. . . . 'Brother Souls' is strangely, punitively, lopsided--a deliberately partial picture of one man, not two. . . . The hostility is out in the open as never before, and it diminishes an otherwise remarkable achievement. . . . [Joyce] Johnson has turned for the first time to biography, and the result is by far the best book on Kerouac to date."

JOHNSON, PAUL. Stalin; The Kremlin Mountaineer; [by] Paul Johnson 2014 Houghton Mifflin Harcourt
1. Biography (Literary form) 2. Dictators—Biography 3. Soviet Union—History 4. Stalin, Joseph, 1879-1953 5. Trotsky, Leon, 1879-1940
ISBN 0544114205; 9780544114203

SUMMARY: In this biography of Joseph Stalin, author Paul Johnson "sets out the arc of a career that took Soso Dzhugashvili from poverty in the Caucasus to mastery of an empire. We see the young Stalin as an emerging revolutionary, appreciated by [Vladimir] Lenin for his smarts, organizational skills and willingness to resort to violence. . . . He was made party general secretary a few years after the revolution, a job that contained within it . . . the path to a personal dictatorship." (Wall Street Journal)

REVIEW: *Kirkus Rev* v82 no2 p272 Ja 15 2014
"Stalin: The Kremlin Mountaineer". "Slender character study of 'one of the outstanding monsters civilization has yet produced.'. . . A monster indeed and one with whom history has yet to fully reckon, a task that this too-brief book can only begin to address. Johnson writes that his impetus for writing this short study of Stalin is that "among the young, he is insufficiently known." Whether the book can remedy that situation is unknown, as well, but as informed opinion, it's very satisfying."

JOHNSON, PEGGY. Developing and managing electronic collections; the essentials; [by] Peggy Johnson ix, 186 p. 2013 ALA Editions, an imprint of the American Library Association
1. Collection development in libraries 2. Electronic information resources—Management 3. Libraries—Special collections—Electronic information resources 4. Libraries and electronic publishing—United States 5. Library science literature
ISBN 0838911900 (paper); 9780838911907 (paper)
LC 2013-005038

SUMMARY: This book, by Peggy Johnson, discusses the "complex issues associated with developing and managing electronic collections [in libraries]." The book discusses "the evolving world of acquisition options, licenses, and contracts [as well as] budgeting and financial considerations, with guidance on how to collaborate across library organizational lines to acquire and manage e-content more efficiently." (Publisher's note)

REVIEW: *Choice* v51 no9 p1559 My 2014 M. Sylvia
"Developing and Managing Electronic Collections: The Essentials". "[Peggy] Johnson . . . offers an excellent overview of the electronic collections environment for libraries. . . . Johnson discusses these topics thoroughly but concisely, and provides excellent bibliographical references for further reading. This work would be most useful to librarians who are already well informed about collection development and management for physical formats, since some of the basic skills, e.g., identifying users and their needs, are lightly addressed."

JOHNSON, PETER. Out of eden; [by] Peter Johnson 150 p. 2013 Namelos llc
1. Families—Fiction 2. Horror tales 3. Religious fanatics 4. Vacations—Fiction 5. Violence—Fiction
ISBN 9781608981601 (hardcover: alk. paper); 9781608981618 (pbk.: alk. paper); 9781608981625 (ebk.)
LC 2013-931031

SUMMARY: A family vacation goes asunder amid notes of Deliverance, religious delusions and frighteningly plausible violence. . . . Abraham is a simple brute, but Leopold is a complex religious zealot who fancies himself an angel of death, chosen to exterminate those undeserving of life. After the tense and foreboding run-in, Stony and his family are marked and subsequently hunted by Leopold and Abraham." (Kirkus Reviews)

REVIEW: *Kirkus Rev* v82 no1 p160 Ja 1 2014
"Out of Eden". "Though the majority of the novella is told in third person from Stony's point of view, there are brief, rambling and frightening glimpses into the mind of Leopold as he calculates with Bible-based fervor why and how his victims should die. At one point, Stony's father says, 'How can you explain something so cruel and pointless?' It's the inexplicability of cruelty that makes this horrifying page-turner so effective. A compelling portrayal of inevitable, realistic violence and evil personified."

REVIEW: *Publ Wkly* v260 no49 p86 D 2 2013

REVIEW: *SLJ* v60 no2 p106 F 2014 Gerry Larson

REVIEW: *Voice of Youth Advocates* v37 no1 p67-8 Ap 2014 Suzanne Osman

JOHNSON, SCOTT A. J. Translating Maya Hieroglyphs; [by] Scott A. J. Johnson xix, 386 p. 2013 University of Oklahoma Press
1. Handbooks, vade-mecums, etc. 2. Inscriptions, Hieroglyphic 3. Inscriptions, Mayan 4. Maya language—Grammar 5. Maya language—Syntax 6. Maya language—Writing 7. Translating and interpreting
ISBN 9780806143330 (hardcover : acid-free paper)
LC 2012-041253

SUMMARY: This book "uses a hands-on approach to teach learners the current state of Maya epigraphy. Johnson shows readers step by step how to translate ancient Maya glyphs. . . . Not simply a reference volume, 'Translating Maya Hieroglyphs' is pedagogically arranged so that it functions as an introductory foreign-language textbook." (Publisher's note)

REVIEW: *Choice* v51 no4 p605 D 2013 A. Headrick
"Translating Maya Hieroglyphs." "Written by [Scott A. J.] Johnson . . . , this superb primer on Maya hieroglyphic translation is accessible to the interested public, aspiring scholars, and Mesoamerican researchers not specializing in epigraphy. Rather than becoming mired in academic minutiae, the clear, engaging explanations of complex linguistics aim at conveying key concepts. Each section of this reference work/text includes a cogent explanation of a concept, clear hieroglyphic examples, and workbook-style illustrated exercises for readers to practice the concept. Reading order, translation, linguistic rules, the numerical system, and fundamental grammar form the core topics."

JOHNSON, SCOTT FITZGERALD.ed. The web of Athenaeus. See Jacob, C.

JOHNSON, TERRY LYNN. Ice dogs; [by] Terry Lynn Johnson 288 p. 2013 Houghton Mifflin, Houghton Mifflin Harcourt

1. Adventure stories 2. Dogs—Fiction 3. Dogsledding—Fiction 4. Sled dogs—Fiction 5. Survival—Fiction 6. Wilderness areas—Fiction
ISBN 0547899262; 9780547899268
LC 2012-045061

SUMMARY: In this book, by Terry Lynn Johnson, "Victoria Secord, a fourteen-year-old Alaskan dogsled racer, loses her way on a routine outing with her dogs. With food gone and temperatures dropping, her survival and that of her dogs and the mysterious boy she meets in the woods is entirely up to her." (Publisher's note)

REVIEW: *Horn Book Magazine* v90 no1 p93-4 Ja/F 2014 BETTY CARTER

"Ice Dogs". "Thus begins a top-notch survival story as for five days the two deal with a blizzard, freezing temperatures, a burnt map, a lost compass, a charging moose, injuries to the dogs, hunger, and hypothermia. Debut novelist [Terry Lynn] Johnson links character to setting by showing how Vicky uses her knowledge of the land and copes with the elements, creates shelter, and snares animals in order to survive. But she must also depend on Chris's friendship, a convincing decision that releases her from her self-imposed loneliness and creates a believable denouement."

REVIEW: *Kirkus Rev* v81 no24 p161 D 15 2013

"Ice Dogs". "[Terry Lynn] Johnson . . . a former musher, clearly writes from a deep well of experience. She admirably depicts the emotional life of a self-reliant, introspective and angry young musher mourning the loss of her beloved father, a trapper and river guide, who died in an accident 14 months earlier. Worried about dehydration, hypothermia, and food for both dogs and themselves, Vicky draws on memories of experiences with her dad to guide them. Though Chris' ignorance of outdoor life often endangers them, their burgeoning, bantering friendship adds depth even as the well-paced suspense builds. Well-crafted, moving and gripping."

REVIEW: *Publ Wkly* v260 no45 p72 N 11 2013

REVIEW: *SLJ* v60 no2 p89 F 2014 Elizabeth Nicolai

JOHNSON, WALTER. River of dark dreams; slavery and empire in the cotton kingdom; [by] Walter Johnson 560 p. 2013 The Belknap Press of Harvard University Press

1. Capitalism—Mississippi River Valley—History—19th century 2. Cotton growing—Mississippi River Valley—History—19th century 3. Historical literature 4. Imperialism—History—19th century 5. Slave trade—History—19th century 6. Slavery—Economic aspects—Mississippi River Valley—History—19th century 7. Slavery—Mississippi River Valley—History—19th century 8. Social change—Mississippi River Valley—History—19th century
ISBN 0674045556 (hardcover); 9780674045552 (hardcover)
LC 2012-030065

SUMMARY: This book, by Walter Johnson, explores how "when Jefferson acquired the Louisiana Territory, he envisioned an 'empire for liberty' populated by self-sufficient white farmers . . . , [but] was transformed instead into a booming capitalist economy . . . dependent on the coerced labor of slaves. [The book] places the Cotton Kingdom at the center of worldwide webs of exchange and exploitation that extended across oceans and drove an insatiable hunger for new lands." (Publisher's note)

REVIEW: *Am Hist Rev* v119 no2 p462-4 Ap 2014 Philip Morgan

REVIEW: *Choice* v50 no11 p2086 Jl 2013 D. Butts

REVIEW: *Kirkus Rev* v80 no24 p235 D 15 2012

REVIEW: *Libr J* v138 no5 p116 Mr 15 2013 Randall M. Miller

REVIEW: *N Y Rev Books* v60 no15 p46-8 O 10 2013 Maya Jasanoff

REVIEW: *Nation* v298 no9 p32-6 Mr 3 2014 ROBIN EINHORN

REVIEW: *TLS* no5756 p12-3 Jl 26 2013 ARI KELMAN

"River of Dark Dreams: Slavery and Empire in the Cotton Kingdom." "'River of Dark Dreams' is at its best when it focuses on the day-to-day lives of slaves in the valley. Johnson empathizes with his subjects, allows them to speak for themselves through written records they left behind, and is a gifted enough writer to make the past come alive in his prose. . . . Aside from a few under-edited or over-written passages . . . few books have captured the lived experience of slavery as powerfully as 'River of Dark Dreams'. . . . Unfortunately, Johnson's sections on empire are not nearly as compelling as his material on slavery. . . . Rarely have the sharp contours of Indian removal been recounted so flatly. The contrast with Johnson's fleshed-out history of slavery is striking."

JOHNSON, WILLIAM P. Texas waterfowl; [by] William P. Johnson viii, 176 p. 2013 Texas A&M University Press

1. Ducks 2. Environmental literature 3. Geese 4. Swans 5. Texas—Environmental conditions 6. Waterfowl—Texas 7. Waterfowl—Texas—Identification
ISBN 1603448071 (flex : alk. paper); 1603448209 (e-book); 9781603448079 (flex : alk. paper); 9781603448208 (e-book)
LC 2012-017276

SUMMARY: This book by William P. Johnson and Mark W. Lockwood describes "the life histories of forty-five species of ducks, geese, and swans that occur in Texas. For common species and those that breed in the state, each account begins with an interesting fact . . . and provides information on Texas distribution and harvest, population status, diet, range and habitats, reproduction, and appearance." (Publisher's note)

REVIEW: *Choice* v51 no2 p295 O 2013 B. C. Thomsett-Scott

"Texas Waterfowl." "'Texas Waterfowl' by professional wildlife biologists [William P.] Johnson and [Mark W.] Lockwood follows the example set by other works in this series. The book is nicely written for both experts and novices, well researched with plentiful references offering an effective mix of current and historical sources, and well illustrated with excellent use of black-and-white images showing species distribution, graphs, and more to support the text. The introduction contains several appendix-like items including terminology, plumage, and a map displaying ecological regions in Texas."

JOHNSTON, ANN DOWSETT. Drink; the intimate relationship between women and alcohol; [by] Ann Dowsett Johnston 320 p. 2013 HarperWave

1. Social science literature 2. Women—Alcohol use 3.

Women alcoholics
ISBN 0062241796; 9780062241795 (hardback)
LC 2013-026103

SUMMARY: In this book, author "Anne Dowsett Johnston combines in-depth research with her own personal story of recovery, and delivers a[n] . . . examination of a shocking yet little recognized epidemic threatening society today: the precipitous rise in risky drinking among women and girls." (Publisher's note)

REVIEW: *Booklist* v110 no4 p4 O 15 2013 Karen Springen

REVIEW: *Booklist* v110 no3 p21 O 1 2013 KAITE MEDIATORE STOVER

REVIEW: *Kirkus Rev* v81 no18 p223 S 15 2013

REVIEW: *N Y Times Book Rev* p18 N 17 2013 IRIN CARMON

"Drink: The Intimate Relationship Between Women and Alcohol" and "Her Best-Kept Secret: Why Women Drink—and How They Can Regain Control". "A temptation for many trend journalists and headline writers (a temptation to which Johnston sometimes succumbs) is to see women's higher rates of alcohol abuse and dependency as the uneasy consequence of female liberation. . . . [Ann Dowsett] Johnson's choice to blend memoir and reporting makes her book feel unfinished, too entangled in raw heartbreak to arrive at clarity. . . . Despite its pulpy title, 'Her Best-Kept Secret' is the more substantial book, interested in hard facts and nuance rather than hand-wringing. It is strongest when detailing how the American story of addiction and recovery was shaped for and by men."

REVIEW: *Quill Quire* v79 no10 p30-1 D 2013 Stacey May Fowles

JOHNSTON, E. K. The story of Owen; dragon slayer of Trondheim; [by] E. K. Johnston 305 p. 2014 Carolrhoda Lab

1. Adventure and adventurers—Fiction 2. Bards and bardism—Fiction 3. Dragons—Fiction 4. Fame—Fiction 5. Family life—Canada—Fiction 6. Fantasy fiction 7. High schools—Fiction 8. Schools—Fiction
ISBN 1467710660; 9781467710664 (trade hard cover : alk. paper)
LC 2013-020492

SUMMARY: In this book, author E. K. Johnston, "envisions an Earth nearly identical to our own, with one key difference: dragons. . . . After 16-year-old Siobhan McQuaid agrees to become the bard for dragon-slayer-in-training Owen Thorskard, who has moved with his famous dragon-slaying family to her small Ontario town, she winds up at the center of a grassroots effort to understand an odd spike in dragon numbers." (Publishers Weekly)

REVIEW: *Booklist* v110 no13 p69 Mr 1 2014 Snow Wildsmith

REVIEW: *Bull Cent Child Books* v67 no8 p391-2 Ap 2014 E. K. Johnston

"The Story of Owen: Dragon Slayer of Trondheim". "It's a cool concept, and it is one that [E. K] Johnston explores with an impeccable eye for detail and great wit. . . . If Owen ends up being a bit of a straight man to Siobhan's sardonic commentary, dramatic observations, and musical flair, they both emerge as memorable protagonists, bound together by a refreshingly romance-free enduring friendship, and by the sacrifices each ultimately makes in the name of community. . . . The result is an excellent story, an adventure that celebrates flawed but genuinely heroic individuals and also seamlessly integrates some sharp points that will likely linger with the reader."

REVIEW: *Bull Cent Child Books* v67 no8 p410-1 Ap 2014 H. M.

"The Winter Horses". "The animal story (drawing on the real-life Ukrainian reserve and thc killing of its rare herd of Przewalski's horses) offers appealing elements in Kalinka's friendship and the horses' need for protection, resulting in an unusual wartime tale. The plot, though, is too often implausible . . . and Kalinka's exposition moves the story with a slow pace unsuited to such an adventurous survival story. Those willing to ride out the far-fetched storyline will likely enjoy the survival story, however, and the social metaphor of identifying the horses as an unfit species makes for a useful entry point to discussing World War II and the Holocaust."

REVIEW: *Horn Book Magazine* v90 no2 p122-3 Mr/Ap 2014 ANITA L. BURKAM

"The Story of Owen: Dragon Slayer of Trondheim." "[E. K.] Johnston has great fun reimagining history in a dragon-filled world and takes on carbon emissions and global warming from a different angle. Modern references live comfortably next to those from Viking sagas, often to comic effect. With dragon attacks on the rise, Owen and Siobhan get wind of a new dragon hatching ground and lure the dragons away in order to destroy the eggs--a final confrontation that, in Siobhan's wry, heroic narration, is nothing short of epic."

REVIEW: *Kirkus Rev* v82 no2 p143 Ja 15 2014

REVIEW: *N Y Times Book Rev* p25 My 11 2014 DAN KOIS

REVIEW: *Publ Wkly* v261 no3 p58 Ja 20 2014

REVIEW: *Quill Quire* v80 no3 p35-6 Ap 2014 Shannon Ozirny

REVIEW: *SLJ* v60 no7 p105 Jl 2014 Jennifer Furuyama

REVIEW: *Voice of Youth Advocates* v37 no2 p76 Je 2014 Lindy Gerdes

JOHNSTON, GREGORY S.ed. A Heinrich Schütz reader. See A Heinrich Schütz reader

JOHNSTON, JULIE. Little red lies; [by] Julie Johnston 352 p. 2013 Tundra Books

1. Brothers & sisters—Fiction 2. College & school drama 3. Historical fiction 4. Teenage girls—Fiction 5. World War, 1939-1945—Veterans—Fiction
ISBN 1770493131; 9781770493131 (hardcover); 9781770493148 (ebk.)
LC 2012-947608

SUMMARY: In this book by Julie Johnston "the war is over, but for thirteen-year-old Rachel, the battle has just begun. Putting childhood behind her, she knows what she wants--to prove she has acting talent worthy of the school drama club, and what she doesn't want--to romantically fall for someone completely inappropriate. Ultimately, she finds a way to come to terms with life as it reaches an end and life as it begins." (Publisher's note)

REVIEW: *Booklist* v110 no5 p60 N 1 2013 Frances Bradburn

"Little Red Lies." "[Julie] Johnston has crafted a beautifully written, low-key, yet emotional story of a family dealing with the return of a son at the close of war, Jamie is wracked with survivor's guilt and frustrated at returning to his adolescent way of life after having experienced the trauma of battle. His letters to Rachel, unsent but carefully saved so he can read and reread them, are painfully realistic, the antithesis of the glamour that teens too often assign to war, regardless of the decade.The family has more than its share to cope with during the year that Rachel narrates the story, but the love the characters feel for each other--and the resilience that love offers them--makes this difficult story authentic and ultimately hopeful."

REVIEW: *Bull Cent Child Books* v67 no3 p161 N 2013 E. B.

"Little Red Lies." "Although this Canadian import is a work of historical fiction, readers who favor domestic drama will be the audience most appreciative of Rachel's social missteps. Driven by her own over-emotional nature and casual attitude toward deceit, Rachel is often as shameless as the Little Red Lies crimson lipstick she sports to make herself appear sophisticated. Her mistakes have a way of making her sympathetic, though, and by the end, she's a bit more self aware; her growth--and potential for further wising up--is credibly portrayed."

REVIEW: *Horn Book Magazine* v89 no6 p96-7 N/D 2013 MARTHA V. PARRAVANO

REVIEW: *Kirkus Rev* v81 no15 p279 Ag 1 2013

REVIEW: *Kirkus Rev* p53 Ag 15 2013 Fall Preview

REVIEW: *Publ Wkly* v260 no32 p62 Ag 12 2013

REVIEW: *Quill Quire* v79 no9 p11 N 2013

REVIEW: *Quill Quire* v79 no8 p36-8 O 2013 Megan Moore Burns

"Little Red Lies." "[Author] Julie Johnston knows how to speak to her audience. Rachel McLaren, the 14-year-old protagonist of 'Little Red Lies,' is instantly relatable to any young reader struggling to find a place in his or her family, peer group, or society. The fact that the story takes place in the 1940s simply makes it that much more interesting. . . . Moving seamlessly from teenage angst to grown-up trials, 'Little Red Lies' is simultaneously a coming-of-age story and a portrait of postwar life in a small Canadian town. Readers will find themselves wrapped up in Rachel's story without even realizing that they are also being immersed in history."

REVIEW: *Voice of Youth Advocates* v36 no5 p62 D 2013 Kathleen Beck

JOHNSTON, KENNETH R. Unusual suspects; Pitt's reign of alarm and the lost generation of the 1790s; [by] Kenneth R. Johnston xxi, 376 p. 2013 Oxford University Press

1. Authors, English—18th century—Political and social views 2. English literature—18th century—History and criticism 3. English literature—18th century—Political aspects 4. Historical literature 5. Persecution—Great Britain—History—18th century 6. Politics and literature—Great Britain—History—18th century 7. Romanticism—Great Britain—History—18th century

ISBN 0199657807 (hbk.); 9780199657803 (hbk.)

LC 2012-277724

SUMMARY: In this book, Kenneth R. Johnston argues that "many lives and careers were ruined in Britain as a result of the alarmist regime [William] Pitt set up to suppress domestic dissent while waging his disastrous wars against republican France. Liberal young writers and intellectuals whose enthusiasm for the American and French revolutions raised hopes for Parliamentary reform at home saw their prospects blasted." (Publisher's note)

REVIEW: *Choice* v51 no8 p1400 Ap 2014 E. Kraft

"Unusual Suspects: Pitt's Reign of Alarm and the Lost Generation of the 1790s". "[Kenneth R.] Johnston's comparison between the [Joseph] McCarthy era in US history and the oppressive [William] Pitt government of the 1790s in England is provocative and enlightening. . . . Written in highly accessible prose and with energetic engagement in terms of applicability to later eras of suppression and oppression, this book rights many wrongs and encourages readers to view heretofore neglected works as well as works and authors who seem all too familiar as possible victims of politics and fear."

REVIEW: *London Rev Books* v36 no2 p17-9 Ja 23 2014 John Barrell

REVIEW: *TLS* no5788 p26 Mr 7 2014 JOHN BUGG

JOHNSTON, MICHAEL. Frozen. See De la Cruz, M.

JOHNSTON, PAUL. The Black Life; [by] Paul Johnston 240 p. 2013 Severn House Pub Ltd

1. Collaborationists (Traitors) 2. Detective & mystery stories 3. Holocaust survivors—Fiction 4. Holocaust, Jewish (1939-1945)—Fiction 5. Missing persons—Fiction

ISBN 1780290489; 9781780290485

SUMMARY: In this book, "Scots/Greek private eye Alex Mavros' sixth case sets him on the trail of an old man who's recently been spotted in Thessaloniki even though he died in Auschwitz. . . . Though it defies belief that Aron could have survived and then hidden himself for all these years, Eliezer knows concentration camps' records are notoriously unreliable. So he asks Alex, a well-known missing persons specialist, to fly to Thessaloniki . . . to follow the trail of the apparition." (Kirkus Reviews)

REVIEW: *Kirkus Rev* v81 no24 p65 D 15 2013

"The Black Life". "Scots/Greek private eye Alex Mavros' sixth case sets him on the trail of an old man who's recently been spotted in Thessaloniki even though he died in Auschwitz. . . . Unlike Alex, readers know from the beginning that Aron is indeed alive courtesy of alternating chapters told from his perspective that trace his story from World War II to the present. It's such a horrifying tale that the odds of Alex surviving his encounter with "the abyss of the twentieth century's greatest crime" unscathed seem negligible. Just as high a body count as Alex's last two cases, though the Holocaust back story sharpens this one to a knife point."

JOLLY, SUSIE.ed. Women, sexuality and the political power of pleasure. See Women, sexuality and the political power of pleasure

JONES, ANDREW MEIRION. Prehistoric materialities; becoming material in prehistoric Britain and Ireland; [by] Andrew Meirion Jones xi, 230 p. 2012 Oxford University Press

1. Antiquities, Prehistoric—Great Britain 2. Antiquities, Prehistoric—Ireland 3. Archaeological literature

4. Material culture—History—To 1500 5. Performance theory
ISBN 0199556423; 9780199556427
LC 2012-288267

SUMMARY: It was the author's intent to demonstrate that "archaeologists need to attend to the changing character of materials if they are to understand how past people and materials intersected to produce prehistoric societies. Rather than considering materials and societies as given, he argues that we need to understand how these entities are performed. [Andrew Meirion] Jones analyses the various aspects of materials, including their scale, colour, fragmentation, and assembly." (Publisher's note)

REVIEW: *TLS* no5753 p7-8 Jl 5 2013 PETER THONEMANN

"The Idea of Order: The Circular Archetype in Prehistoric Europe," "Prehistoric Materialities: Becoming Material in Prehistoric Britain and Ireland" and "How Ancient Europeans Saw the World: Vision, Patterns, and the Shaping of the Mind in Prehistoric Times." "Richard Bradley argues in his absorbing new book . . . that we are dealing not solely, or even primarily, with a practical choice, but with a particular way of seeing the world. . . . representation." . . . [Andrew Meirion] Jones's 'performative' approach to material culture has a lot going for it, and it is a pity that his prose is so hard going. . . . Jones could learn a thing or two from Peter Wells, whose 'How Ancient Europeans Saw the World' covers much of the same ground (and a lot more besides) in beautifully crisp and elegant English."

JONES, ANN.il. Granny's clan. See Hodson, S.

JONES, BRIAN JAY. Jim Henson; the biography; [by] Brian Jay Jones 608 p. 2013 Ballantine Books

1. BIOGRAPHY & AUTOBIOGRAPHY—Entertainment & Performing Arts 2. Puppeteers—United States—Biography 3. SOCIAL SCIENCE—Popular Culture 4. Television producers and directors—United States—Biography
ISBN 0345526112; 9780345526113 (hardback)
LC 2013-024039

SUMMARY: This book explores "the life of Muppets creator Jim Henson (1936-1990) . . . explaining how Henson grew up to become a daring puppeteer and scriptwriter, how he managed to attract so much remarkable talent to his side, and how his stressful business relationship with the Disney Company might have aggravated the bacterial infection that weakened the normally healthy Henson, who died at age 53 while trying to negotiate the planned Disney purchase of the franchise." (Kirkus Reviews)

REVIEW: *Booklist* v109 no22 p17 Ag 1 2013 Donna Seaman

REVIEW: *Kirkus Rev* v81 no14 p289 Jl 15 2013

REVIEW: *Kirkus Rev* p25 Ag 15 2013 Fall Preview

REVIEW: *N Y Times Book Rev* p68 D 8 2013 JOHN SWANSBURG

"Jim Henson: The Biography." "In his new biography, Brian Jay Jones tells the story of how Henson turned a quaint art form into an entertainment empire that. . . . Jones had excellent access, and took full advantage of it, interviewing Henson's relatives . . . as well as his many collaborators. . . . He dwelled in the vast Muppet archive and pored over Henson's diary. The result is an exhaustive work that is never exhausting, a credit both to Jones's brisk style and to Henson's exceptional life."

REVIEW: *Publ Wkly* v260 no29 p61 Jl 22 2013

JONES, DANIEL. Love illuminated; exploring life's most mystifying subject (with the help of 50,000 strangers); [by] Daniel Jones 224 p. 2014 HarperCollins

1. Emotions (Psychology) 2. Love 3. Marriage 4. Monogamous relationships 5. Newspapers—Sections, columns, etc.
ISBN 0062211161; 9780062211163

SUMMARY: This book, by Daniel Jones, is "the story of love from beginning to end (or not). . . . Drawing from the 50,000 stories that have crossed his desk over the past decade, Jones explores ten aspects of love—pursuit, destiny, vulnerability, connection, trust, practicality, monotony, infidelity, loyalty, and wisdom—and creates . . . [an] enlightening journey through this universal human experience." (Publisher's note)

REVIEW: *Atlantic* v313 no3 p40-1 Ap 2014 SANDRA TSING LOH

"Love Illuminated: Exploring Life's Most Mystifying Subject (With the Help of 50,000 Strangers)". "'Love Illuminated' . . . is less a Modern Love 'best of' than a rumination on the columns' themes. . . . [Daniel] Jones is what many Modern Love columnists aren't—funny. . . . A book whose chapter titles echo a medieval morality play . . . had to work to win me over. . . . I won't promise that we'll start reading Modern Love essays aloud for fun, but 'Love Illuminated' did leave me with a good story. . . . It's that hard-earned, occasionally rewarding last turn in every Modern Love column. Pass the coffee."

REVIEW: *Kirkus Rev* v82 no2 p259 Ja 15 2014

REVIEW: *Libr J* v138 no15 p48 S 15 2013

REVIEW: *N Y Times Book Rev* p9 F 9 2014 CAITLIN FLANAGAN

JONES, DOYLE W. Tales from the Corner Service Station; [by] Doyle W. Jones 108 p. 2013 Createspace Independent Pub

1. Arkansas—History 2. Arkansas—Social conditions 3. Communities 4. Memoirs 5. Service stations
ISBN 1482583313; 9781482583311

SUMMARY: This "memoir recalls small-town life in Arkansas in the 1950s and '60s. The corner ESSO station in [Doyle W.] Jones' hometown of Carthage, Ark., connected Main Street, the sawmill and surrounding farms. More importantly for Jones, the station also connected the community. . . . He portrays small-town Arkansas—the school, churches, local elections, hunting and haying—by recalling conversations over the ESSO lunch counter or near the hydraulic car lift. " (Kirkus Reviews)

REVIEW: *Kirkus Rev* v82 no2 p354 Ja 15 2014

"Tales from the Corner Service Station". "A concise memoir recalls small-town life in Arkansas in the 1950s and '60s. . . . Throughout his memoir . . . [Doyle W.] Jones reminds readers that he tells of different, tougher and less complicated times. He's nostalgic for the days when tales were told face to face, before email and text messages, days when community and hard work mattered. The corner station still stands in Carthage, Jones says, 'a monument to a happier and simpler time.' A feel-good memoir about rural values and the lost practice of conversation."

JONES, GARETH P. Constable & Toop; [by] Gareth P. Jones 416 p. 2013 Amulet Books

1. Future life—Fiction 2. Ghosts—Fiction 3. Speculative fiction
ISBN 9781419707827 (alk. paper)
LC 2012-047785

SUMMARY: In this book, "Sam Toop . . . has a mystical ability to speak to ghosts. He also has a big problem: his murderous uncle Jack is lying low with Sam and his father. Meanwhile, Lapsewood, a paper-pushing ghost employed by the comically bureaucratic Bureau, which regulates ghost-related matters," attempts "to find a missing officer in London. Once there, he and his companions discover an even bigger problem: the Rot, a destructive, demonic force that's hungry for ghosts." (Booklist)

REVIEW: *Booklist* v110 no3 p52 O 1 2013 Sarah Hunter

"Constable and Toop." "Young Sam Toop, son of one of the owners of the titular undertaker's shop, has a mystical ability to speak to ghosts. He also has a big problem: his murderous uncle Jack is lying low with Sam and his father. . . . [Gareth P.] Jones has crafted a menacing, spooky Victorian London full of criminals and unfinished business, which is well balanced by the biting satire and buffoonery of the Bureau. Add to that a cast of fascinating, well-wrought characters--from the smarmy and threatening Jack, to the precocious, pot-stirring aspiring journalist Clara--and it's a winning combination of macabre atmosphere, whimsical antics, and heartfelt, earnest friendship."

REVIEW: *Bull Cent Child Books* v67 no4 p218-9 D 2013 A. M.

REVIEW: *Kirkus Rev* v81 no16 p154 Ag 15 2013

REVIEW: *Publ Wkly* v260 no38 p80 S 23 2013

REVIEW: *Voice of Youth Advocates* v36 no4 p82 O 2013 Debbie Wenk

REVIEW: *Voice of Youth Advocates* v36 no4 p82 O 2013 Madeline Miles

JONES, JACQUELINE. A dreadful deceit; the myth of race from the colonial era to Obama's America; [by] Jacqueline Jones 400 p. 2013 Basic Books

1. African Americans—Biography 2. African Americans—Race identity—History 3. Historical literature 4. Race—Philosophy 5. Race awareness—United States—History
ISBN 0465036708; 9780465036707 (hardback)
LC 2013-031130

SUMMARY: "In 'A Dreadful Deceit,' . . . historian Jacqueline Jones traces the lives of [six] African Americans to illustrate the strange history of 'race' in America. In truth, Jones shows, race does not exist, and the very factors that we think of as determining it--a person's heritage or skin color--are mere pretexts for the brutalization of powerless people by the powerful." (Publisher's note)

REVIEW: *Booklist* v110 no4 p4 O 15 2013 Vanessa Bush

REVIEW: *Choice* v51 no9 p1661-2 My 2014 D. R. Jamieson

REVIEW: *Kirkus Rev* v81 no20 p118 O 15 2013

REVIEW: *N Y Times Book Rev* p19 F 16 2014 TOMMIE SHELBY

"A Dreadful Deceit: The Myth of Race From the Colonial Era to Obama's America." "This new book, a sweeping account of the role of race in American history, is structured around the stories of six extraordinary but largely unknown individuals, each of African descent. . . . Her book is a call to renounce the very idea of race as a dangerous misconception. . . . If contemporary discussions of race could be focused on the interconnections between racial ideologies, political power and economic vulnerability, as Jones would like, that would be a dramatic improvement over the 'postracial' narratives that currently reign."

JONES, JEANNETTE EILEEN. In search of brightest Africa; reimagining the dark continent in American culture, 1884-1936; [by] Jeannette Eileen Jones 296 2010 University of Georgia Press

1. Africa—Foreign relations—United States 2. African Americans 3. Colonies—Africa—History 4. Congo (Democratic Republic)
ISBN 9780820333205; 0820333204
LC 2009-047895

SUMMARY: "This book interweaves two familiar and contrasting motifs to present the idea of Africa as a source of identity for African Americans and as an object of caricature for white Americans. For African Americans, the struggle to wrest the image of Africa from colonial hegemony is the same as the campaign for black liberation from slavery and the search for a usable past. It is that link between the colonization of Africa and black subjugation in America that the book sets out to explore in five chapters, with an introduction and a conclusion." (Journal of American History)

REVIEW: *J Am Hist* v98 no3 p858-9 D 2011 Lamin Sanneh

In Search of Brightest Africa: Reimagining the Dark Continent in American Culture, 1884-1936. "This book interweaves two familiar and contrasting motifs to present the idea of Africa as a source of identity for African Americans and as an object of caricature for white Americans. . . . Jeannette Eileen Jones sees the Congo as the crucible for forging the terms of engagement with Africa and the test of America's position on the European partition of the continent. . . . Despite a slow start, there is much to commend in Jones's book. The early sections are too congested to easily track the central organizing structure of the work, and I found the historical references to the scramble for Africa and the sequel of partition somewhat scattered."

JONES, NICHOLAS.ed. The Cambridge companion to Michael Tippett. See The Cambridge companion to Michael Tippett

JONES, NOAH Z. Moldylocks and the three beards; [by] Noah Z. Jones 80 p. 2014 Branches/Scholastic Inc.

1. Fairy tales 2. Friendship—Fiction 3. Humorous stories 4. Imaginary places 5. Three Bears (Tale)
ISBN 0545638402; 9780545638395 (pbk.); 9780545638401 (hardcover)
LC 2013-027613

SUMMARY: In this book, by Noah Z. Jones, "in the Land of Fake Believe, Princess meets a strange girl named Moldylocks. When Princess's stomach grumbles, Moldylocks takes her to the home of the Three Beards. The girls sit in the Beards' chairs, eat their chili, and jump on their beds. The Three Beards are not happy when they get home—and they are very, very hungry! Will Moldylocks and Princess go into the chili pot?" (Publisher's note)

REVIEW: *Bull Cent Child Books* v67 no10 p524 Je 2014 A. A.

"Princess Pink and the Land of Fake-Believe: Moldlylocks and the Three Beards". "Author and illustrator (and animator) [Noah Z.] Jones knows what will give his audience the giggles, and he doesn't hesitate to go for gross in going for laughs. The story itself is pretty superficial, with the prose sacrificing sustained wit in favor of the easy, smelly joke. However its accessibility and accompanying cartoonish art (which makes the dark-skinned Princess Pink's pink hair into a punky, piquant statement) will have kids guffawing with the silly puns and cheering for the ingenious Princess Pink in this subverted version of the more traditional tale."

REVIEW: *Kirkus Rev* v82 no6 p280 Mr 15 2014

JONES, SADIE. Fallout; a novel; [by] Sadie Jones 416 p. 2014 Harper

1. Adultery—Fiction 2. Dramatists—Fiction 3. Psychological fiction 4. Theater—England—London—Fiction 5. Theatrical companies—Fiction
ISBN 0062292811; 9780062292810 (hardback); 9780062292827 (paperback)
LC 2013-036944

SUMMARY: This book "follows the career of Luke Kanowski, who leaves behind his dysfunctional family in Northern England and moves to London in the late 1960s to pursue a career as a playwright. He is soon befriended by aspiring producer Paul Driscoll and Paul's girlfriend, Leigh Radley; together, the three start a small theater company. . . . The trio's fulfilling artistic life together gradually comes under the strain of Luke's compulsive womanizing and Leigh's unrequited attraction to him." (Publisher's note)

REVIEW: *Booklist* v110 no11 p24 F 1 2014 Joanne Wilkinson

"Fallout". "This intoxicating, deeply romantic novel of theater, love, and friendship is set in London during the 1970s. Luke Kanowski is desperate to escape his provincial hometown and the specter of his mentally ill mother, locked away in an asylum, and his depressed father, who numbs himself with drink. When Luke moves to London and falls in with aspiring producer Paul Driscoll and Paul's girlfriend, Leigh Radley, he finally feels that he has found a home for himself, both personally and artistically. . . . With both microscopic precision and operatic emotions, [Sadie] Jones, in her fourth novel . . . perfectly captures the exhilaration of the young and the talented as they find their footing in both art and love."

REVIEW: *Kirkus Rev* v82 no8 p157 Ap 15 2014

REVIEW: *Libr J* v139 no2 p65 F 1 2014 J. L. Morin

REVIEW: *New York Times* v163 no56481 pC4 Ap 24 2014 Carmela Ciuraru

REVIEW: *New Yorker* v90 no19 p87-1 Jl 7 2014

REVIEW: *Publ Wkly* v261 no5 p30 F 3 2014

REVIEW: *TLS* no5807 p20 Jl 18 2014 ALEX PEAKE-TOMKINSON

JONES, SHEILLA. Bankrupting physics; how today's top scientists are gambling away their credibility; [by] Sheilla Jones 288 p. 2013 Palgrave Macmillan

1. Physics—Experiments 2. Physics—Mathematical models 3. Physics—Philosophy 4. Physics literature 5. SCIENCE—Physics 6. SCIENCE—Relativity
ISBN 9781137278234 (hardback)
LC 2013-004524

SUMMARY: In this book, "theoretical physicist and neuroscientist [Alexander] Unzicker compares the current state of theoretical physics to a bubble economy. . . . While carefully separating himself from cranks who deny special relativity or quantum theory . . . the author offers a broad dismissal of modern theoretical physicists, whom he accuses of having 'gotten lost in bizarre constructs that are completely disconnected from reality'." (Kirkus Reviews)

REVIEW: *Choice* v51 no5 p879 Ja 2014 F. Potter

"Bankrupting Physics: How Today's Top Scientists Are Gambling Away Their Credibility." "In this controversial exposé of high-energy physics and cosmology, [Alexander] Unzicker insists that untestable conjectures such as superstrings and the multiverse should not be accepted as fundamental research. In addition to the book's accurate descriptions of the concepts in frontier research areas in physics, the numerous quotes from famous physicists . . . lend credence to the negative arguments. . . . Hopefully, the concerns raised in 'Bankrupting Physics' will trigger open discussions leading to greater advances in understanding physical reality. Avid science readers will benefit immensely from the insightful explanations, which can be further explored via the numerous literature references."

REVIEW: *Kirkus Rev* v81 no2 p73 Je 1 2013

REVIEW: *Publ Wkly* v260 no22 p52-3 Je 3 2013

JONES, STAN.tr. Hybrid culture. See Hybrid culture

JONES, STEPHEN A.ed. Presidents and Black America. See Freedman, E.

JONES, SUSAN. Literature, modernism, and dance; [by] Susan Jones x, 346 p. 2013 Oxford University Press

1. Arts, English—20th century 2. Historical literature 3. Literature and dance 4. Modernism (Aesthetics) 5. Modernism (Literature)
ISBN 0199565325 (hbk.); 9780199565320 (hbk.)
LC 2013-431110

SUMMARY: Written by Susan Jones, "This book explores the complex relationship between literature and dance in the era of modernism. During this period an unprecedented dialogue between the two art forms took place, based on a common aesthetics initiated by contemporary discussions of the body and gender, language, formal experimentation, primitivism, anthropology, and modern technologies such as photography, film, and mechanisation." (Publisher's note)

REVIEW: *TLS* no5787 p10-1 F 28 2014 JUDITH FLANDERS

"Literature, Modernism, and Dance." "Susan Jones . . . is ideally placed to take the subject forward, as one who can see how, 'At the still point of the turning world . . . there the dance is.' For the relationship between dance and literature is not merely 'one of the most striking but understudied features of modernism,' but one of reciprocity: dance drew on modem literature as much as modem literature was shaped by dance. . . . Jones has chosen to structure her book chronologically around the development of modernist aesthetics as writing, and thus privileges literature over movement. Given that most of her readers will have a better grasp of the history of literature than of dance, this is unfortunate, as the book dashes ahistorically through the dance world."

JONES, URSULA. Beauty and the beast; 32 p. 2014 Albert Whitman & Company

1. Beauty & the beast (Tale) 2. Fairy tales 3. Folklore—France 4. Personal beauty—Fiction 5. Sisters—Juvenile fiction

ISBN 9780807506004

LC 2013-020674

SUMMARY: In this adaptation of "Beauty and the Beast," by Ursula Jones, "Beauty's two older sisters are the villains, wanting only riches and titled husbands and wailing when their father loses his wealth and they must move to the countryside. When he returns to the city to mitigate his losses, the sisters ask for diamond tiaras and dresses, while Beauty asks for a rose, and the tale takes its traditional course." (Kirkus Reviews)

REVIEW: *Booklist* v110 no13 p60 Mr 1 2014 Edie Ching

REVIEW: *Bull Cent Child Books* v67 no7 p362 Mr 2014 J. H.

"Beauty and the Beast." "Most of the familiar elements from the classic fairy tale are present in this retelling, from the shallow, jealous sisters to Beauty's request for a rose to the Beast's near-death experience resulting from Beauty's prolonged home visit. [Ursula] Jones' iteration, though, manages to be both elegant and casual, with a refreshing sprinkling of humor throughout. . . . [Sarah] Gibbs' illustrations are effective in their compositions and ornate details, lending enough structure and weight--particularly in the spreads utilizing intricate black silhouettes accented with more minimal color--to balance the candy-colored pastels of the clothing and décor."

REVIEW: *Kirkus Rev* v82 no1 p226 Ja 1 2014

"Beauty and the Beast". "A version of the classic tale rich in color and design but less than satisfying in the telling. Beauty's two older sisters are the villains, wanting only riches and titled husbands and wailing when their father loses his wealth and they must move to the countryside. . . . Exquisite floral details, tiny patterns and cut-paper silhouettes make for much loveliness, but the touches of humor are forced, and the sisters are just silly. While one can nearly always use another gold-embossed fairy tale, this one fails to enchant."

REVIEW: *Publ Wkly* v260 no49 p82 D 2 2013

REVIEW: *SLJ* v60 no3 p173 Mr 2014 Margaret Bush

JONES, WENDY. The thoughts and happenings of Wilfred Price, purveyor of superior funerals; [by] Wendy Jones 264 p. 2012 Corsair

1. Betrothal 2. Courtship—Fiction 3. Humorous stories 4. Small cities 5. Undertakers & undertaking

ISBN 9781609451851; 1609451856; 9781780330563

LC 2012-379786

SUMMARY: In this book, by Wendy Jones, "young undertaker Wilfred Price blurts out a marriage proposal to a woman he barely knows. Much to his consternation, she says yes. As Wilfred attempts to extricate himself from the situation, his betrothed's overbearing father presents further complications. And when Wilfred meets another woman he does wish to marry, a comedy of manners ensues." (Publisher's note)

REVIEW: *Kirkus Rev* v81 no24 p335 D 15 2013

REVIEW: *N Y Times Book Rev* p26 My 4 2014 Carmela Ciuraru

REVIEW: *New Yorker* v90 no10 p77-1 Ap 28 2014

REVIEW: *Publ Wkly* v261 no4 p168 Ja 27 2014

REVIEW: *World Lit Today* v88 no2 p19 Mr/Ap 2014 Maria Johnson

"The Thoughts and Happenings of Wilfred Price, Purveyor of Superior Funerals." "Wilfred Price has established himself as a respectable, reliable member of his small and tightly woven rural community of Narberth, Wales. He performs bis duties impeccably as the town's undertaker, conveying a sense of calm and propriety. A momentary lapse of judgment, just a few unguarded words, manages to propel Wilfred into a life he doesn't want and can't quite manage to get back under control. . . . Author Wendy Jones examines the construction of an insular community, exposing both its strengths and flaws. . . . Her characters are delightfully drawn, lovingly described, and infused with life that transcends the printed page."

JONES, WILLIAM P. The March on Washington; jobs, freedom, and the forgotten history of civil rights; [by] William P. Jones 320 p. 2013 W.W. Norton & Co. Inc.

1. African Americans—Civil rights—History—20th century 2. Civil rights demonstrations—Washington (D.C.)—History—20th century 3. Civil rights movements—United States—History—20th century 4. Historical literature 5. March on Washington for Jobs and Freedom (1963 : Washington, D.C.)

ISBN 0393082857 (hardcover); 9780393082852 (hardcover)

LC 2013-006173

SUMMARY: This book by William P. Jones presents "an account of the American civil rights movement leading up to the infamous 1963 March on Washington, which 'aimed not just to end racial segregation and discrimination in the South but also to ensure that Americans of all races had access to quality education, affordable housing, and jobs that paid a living wage.' . . . Much of the book focuses on A. Philip Randolph, an African-American trade unionist." (Kirkus Reviews)

REVIEW: *Booklist* v109 no18 p6-7 My 15 2013 Vanessa Bush

REVIEW: *Choice* v51 no4 p710-1 D 2013 P. B. Levy

"The March on Washington: Jobs, Freedom, and the Forgotten History of Civil Rights." "The main question that arises upon reading this book is, 'Why did it take so long for someone to write it?' [William P.] Jones . . . has crafted a very readable study of one of the best-known events in US history, the March on Washington--except that the author makes clear that Americans have a poor understanding of it. Most provocatively, Jones contends that both the public and scholars have wrongly conceived of the march as a 'moderate' event. On the contrary, Jones argues that it reflected and grew out of A. Philip Randolph's 'egalitarian vision of social citizenship,' which emphasized the crucial nexus of jobs and freedom."

REVIEW: *Kirkus Rev* v81 no8 p58 Ap 15 2013

REVIEW: *Libr J* v138 no7 p93 Ap 15 2013 Karl Helicher

REVIEW: *N Y Times Book Rev* p17 Ag 18 2013 DAVID J. GARROW

"The March on Washington: Jobs, Freedom, and the Forgotten History of Civil Rights." "[William P.] Jones's most valuable contribution . . . is in detailing the activities of black trade unionists, women as well as men, as they fought employment discrimination across the post-war decades. He also provides a cogent account of the racial divisions that racked the A.F.L.-C.I.O. during the late 1950s. . . . Anyone who approaches 'The March on Washington' anticipating a richly detailed, book-length account of the actual march, however, will be sorely disappointed, for Jones devotes only one chapter out of six to the events of 1963. Another chapter provides an entirely competent but wholly unoriginal account of the Montgomery bus boycott of 1955-56."

REVIEW: *Publ Wkly* v260 no12 p51 Mr 25 2013 Sandra Dijkstra

JONSSON, FREDRIK ALBRITTON. Enlightenment's frontier; the Scottish Highlands and the origins of environmentalism; [by] Fredrik Albritton Jonsson 344 p. 2013 Yale University Press

1. Enlightenment—Scotland 2. Environmentalism—Scotland—History—18th century 3. Historical literature
ISBN 9780300162547 (hardback)
LC 2012-040302

SUMMARY: This book by Fredrik Albritton Jonsson "examines tbe environmental roots of tbe Scottish Enlightenment, suggesting that the mountains and moss bogs of tbe Highlands made this region fertile ground for tbe Enlightenment because of a geographical accident, enabling environmentalism to develop there, more than in the scientific societies in Edinburgb as is commonly understood." (Choice)

REVIEW: *Am Hist Rev* v119 no2 p612 Ap 2014 Roger L. Emerson

REVIEW: *Choice* v51 no4 p660-1 D 2013 J. S. Schwartz

"Enlightenment's Frontier: The Scottish Highlands and the Origins of Environmentalism." "British historian [Fredrik Albritton] Jonsson . . . examines the environmental roots of the Scottish Enlightenment, suggesting that the mountains and moss bogs of the Highlands made this region fertile ground for the Enlightenment. . . . This work discusses the role of moss husbandry in environmentalism, but ignores such Scottish botanists as James Dickson, Mungo Park, and Robert Brown, who were very interested in mosses and played a critical role in the flow of ideas between the two regions and the rest of Britain. This work should appeal to historians rather than historians of natural history."

JORDAN, CONSTANCE.ed. Reason and imagination. See Reason and imagination

JORDAN, EAMONN. From Leenane to L.a.; The Theatre and Cinema of Martin Mcdonagh; [by] Eamonn Jordan 288 p. 2013 Irish Academic Press

1. Biography (Literary form) 2. Irish drama 3. Irish dramatists 4. Irish films 5. McDonagh, Martin 6. Motion picture producers & directors—Biography
ISBN 0716532166; 9780716532163

SUMMARY: "As a playwright, screenwriter, and film director, Martin McDonagh has amassed an exceptional body of work since the premiere of the controversial, hugely successful, and career altering 'The Beauty Queen of Leenane' in 1996. . . . This wide ranging study considers the broad spectrum of influences on McDonagh's writing, his intricate dramaturgy, and complex relationships between the plays and their theatrical and broader social contexts." (Publisher's note)

REVIEW: *TLS* no5783 p26-7 Ja 31 2014 RUTH GILLIGAN

"From Leenane to L.A.: The Theatre and Cinema of Martin McDonagh." "On the cover of [author Eamonn] Jordan's most recent book, 'From Leenane to L.A.,' its subject, the Anglo-Irish playwright and filmmaker Martin McDonagh, sits in a suit, his Oscar . . . in hand. . . . In this new academic appraisal . . . Jordan sets out to cover everything . . . in what has been a fascinating, and often controversial, career. . . . Jordan has written an invaluable McDonagh companion, so that even after the stomach-churning mutilations, cot deaths, fairytale-inspired homicides and 'in-yer-face' gangster violence, we are left wanting to read more."

JORDAN, ELAINE GREENSMITH. Mrs. Ogg played the harp; memories of church and love in the high desert; [by] Elaine Greensmith Jordan 262 p. 2012 Two Harbors Press

1. Arizona—Social conditions 2. Memoirs 3. Pastoral theology 4. Women clergy 5. Women in church work
ISBN 1938690206; 9781938690204 (pbk)
LC 2012-945207

SUMMARY: In this book, author Elaine Greensmith Jordan "recounts a . . . slice of her past spent pastoring a small congregation in Arizona. Spanning five years in the 1990s when the author was in her 50s . . . she seeks emotional healing, marital restoration, knowledge of the transcendent and a way to shepherd her small flock. . . . She frames many of her youthful expectations and decisions within the zeitgeist of her relatively simple 1950s upbringing." (Kirkus Reviews)

REVIEW: *Kirkus Rev* v82 no2 p82 Ja 15 2014

"Mrs Ogg Played the Harp: Memories of Church and Love in the High Desert". " In her debut, essayist, poet and former minister [Elaine Greensmith] Jordan recounts a moving, humorous slice of her past spent pastoring a small congregation in Arizona. . . . Jordan's memoir artfully interweaves strands of her interior life. . . . Compassionate, robust descriptions of Jordan's flock highlight both foibles and strengths, ensuring the reader's emotional investment. . . . A singular window into the spiritual journey of a progressive female minister, particularly relevant as Christianity wrestles with the roles of women in the church."

JORDAN, SANDRA. The mad potter. See Greenberg, J.

JORDAN, SOPHIE. Uninvited; [by] Sophie Jordan 384 p. 2014 HarperTeen, an imprint of HarperCollinsPublishers

1. Genetics—Fiction 2. Love stories 3. Murder—Fiction 4. Psychopaths—Fiction 5. Science fiction
ISBN 0062233653; 9780062233653 (hardcover bdg.)
LC 2013-015448

SUMMARY: In this young adult science fiction novel, by Sophie Jordan, "when Davy tests positive for Homicidal

Tendency Syndrome . . . she loses everything. Once the perfect high school senior, she is uninvited from her prep school and abandoned by her friends and boyfriend. . . . Davy is thrown into a special class for HTS carriers. She has no doubt the predictions are right about them, especially Sean, . . . yet when the world turns on the carriers, Sean is the only one she can trust." (Publisher's note)

REVIEW: *Booklist* v110 no9/10 p112 Ja 1 2014 Snow Wildsmith

REVIEW: *Kirkus Rev* v81 no24 p159 D 15 2013

"Uninvited". "At this point, readers might think that terrible things happen to Davy-that she could be put into terrifying danger or might struggle against her own genetic code. But no-she goes to class, slaps her ex-boyfriend, gets tattooed as punishment for acting out and pines after another hot boy in her new school. This nonthriller is packed with more overwrought, lusty musings than a Harlequin romance. Some of the sentences actually work, while others are so preposterous they'll have readers giggling. . . . But there's no vampire here, and there's not that much action. And Davy comes off as a weak, whiny, boy-chasing protagonist who makes Bella look like Lara Croft. A schlocky bodice-ripper disguised as a dystopian romance."

REVIEW: *SLJ* v60 no4 p168 Ap 2014 Kristin Anderson

REVIEW: *Voice of Youth Advocates* v37 no1 p68 Ap 2014 Lona Trulove

JORON, ANDREW.ed. The collected poems of Philip Lamantia. See The collected poems of Philip Lamantia

JØRGENSEN, DOLLY.ed. New natures. See New natures

JØRGENSEN, FINN ARNE.ed. New natures. See New natures

JORTNER, ADAM. The gods of Prophetstown; the Battle of Tippecanoe and the holy war for the American frontier; [by] Adam Jortner x, 310 p. 2012 Oxford University Press

1. Frontier and pioneer life—United States 2. Governors—Indiana—Biography 3. Historical literature 4. Indians of North America—Wars—1750-1815 5. Shawnee Indians—Biography 6. Tippecanoe, Battle of, Ind., 1811 7. War—Religious aspects—History—19th century
ISBN 0199765294; 9780199765294 (alk. paper)
LC 2011-016857

SUMMARY: This book by Adam Jortner presents a "dual biography that also serves as a myth-busting history of Indian-Caucasian relationships within what became the continental United States." It explores "the lives of Tenskwatawa, a Shawnee Indian leader, and William Henry Harrison, a Virginia-bred aristocrat accumulating power as the governor of the Indiana Territory, leading all the way to the White House in 1840." (Kirkus Review)

REVIEW: *Choice* v49 no11 p2131 Jl 2012 R. L. Nichols

REVIEW: *J Am Hist* v99 no3 p899-900 D 2012 Gregory E. Smoak

REVIEW: *Libr J* v136 no20 p132-3 D 1 2011 John Burch

REVIEW: *Rev Am Hist* v41 no3 p431-5 S 2013 Jewel L. Spangler

"The Gods of Prophetstown: The Battle of Tippecanoe and the Holy War for the American Frontier." "This book is a (dual) biography in the best tradition of such life writing. It tells the stories of two prominent figures of the 1811 Battle of Tippecanoe, and uses the deep context of their life histories to makes sense not only of the razing of Prophetstown, but of conflict in the early-national Midwest more generally. The result is sometimes compelling, sometimes disappointing, and always genuinely entertaining reading. . . . [Adam] Jortner's framing of the battles between the Prophet and [William Henry] Harrison as a holy war is enticing. . . . On Harrison's side, however, the religious theme is far less well developed."

JOSEPH, MAY. Fluid New York; cosmopolitan urbanism and the green imagination; [by] May Joseph xii, 248 p. 2013 Duke University Press

1. Cosmopolitanism—New York (State)—New York 2. Social science literature 3. Urban ecology (Sociology)—New York (State)—New York
ISBN 9780822354604 (cloth : alk. paper); 9780822354727 (pbk. : alk. paper)
LC 2013-010099

SUMMARY: This book by May Joseph "considers New York's relation to the water that surrounds and defines it. Her reflections reach back to the city's heyday as a world-class port . . . and they encompass the devastation caused by Hurricane Sandy in 2012. They suggest that New York's future lies in the reclamation of its great water resources--for artistic creativity, civic engagement, and ecological sustainability." (Publisher's note)

REVIEW: *Choice* v51 no5 p905-6 Ja 2014 A. B. Audant

"Fluid New York: Cosmopolitan Urbanism and the Green Imagination." "Water surrounds New York City. Its narratives, whether geographic, historical, or ecological, are shaped by flows of ideas, and migrants, commuters, and tourists. [May] Joseph . . . explores these flows through a collage of perambulations that is instructive, poetic, and immensely personal. . . . Individual sections are illuminating, while others make curious assertions. . . . Although she documents and explores fluidity, Joseph's conclusions can be startlingly fixed. . . . Small inaccuracies puncture the reverie. . . . These errors are frustrating, and suggest the author has engaged more fully with her thoughts than with the concrete, vulnerable realities of the city itself."

JOST, EUGEN. Beautiful geometry. See Maor, E.

JOTISCHKY, ANDREW.ed. Norman expansion. See Norman expansion

JOWETT, LORNA. TV horror. See Abbott, S.

JOYCE, RACHEL, 1962-. Perfect; a novel; [by] Rachel Joyce 385 p. 2013 Random House

1. Children of the rich—Fiction 2. Detective & mystery stories 3. Male friendship—Fiction 4. Mothers & sons—Fiction 5. Psychological fiction
ISBN 9780812993301 (acid-free paper)
LC 2013-015786

SUMMARY: "'Perfect' tells the story of a young boy who is

thrown into the murky, difficult realities of the adult world with far-reaching consequences. . . . Rachel Joyce has imagined bewitching characters who find their ordinary lives unexpectedly thrown into chaos, who learn that there are times when children must become parents to their parents." (Publisher's note)

REVIEW: *New York Times* v163 no56390 pC1-6 Ja 23 2014 JANET MASLIN

"Perfect: A Novel." "Rachel Joyce's second novel, 'Perfect,' is better and less treacly than her first, 'The Unlikely Pilgrimage of Harold Fry.' It is eerier, too. Ms. Joyce builds her novel around two 11-year-old English boys who have heard that the year 1972 will be two seconds longer than other years and wonder about the cosmic consequences this change may have. . . . The story is told through the eyes of Byron Hemmings, a wealthy boy blessed with a dreamily beautiful mother. . . . 'Perfect: A Novel' radiates its own natural, understated foreboding, and even its title contributes to the sense of dread. . . . This is not a novel that will leave readers feeling tricked. When thought about in retrospect, everything that has happened in it, has happened for a reason."

JOYCE, WILLIAM. The mischievians; 56 p. 2013 Atheneum Books for Young Readers

1. Children's stories 2. Excuses 3. Explanation 4. Humorous stories 5. Imaginary creatures—Fiction 6. Questions and answers—Fiction
ISBN 9781442473478 (hardcover)
LC 2013-001889

SUMMARY: In this book by William Joyce, "the premise . . . is simple and kid friendly: how can we explain the things that annoy us? . . . The book's setup is brief, as two kids find themselves in Dr. Zooper's laboratory, where they're introduced to an encyclopedia explaining the Mischievians. From there the book becomes a Q&A, as the kids make queries ('Where do blisters come from?') and Dr. Zooper responds." (Publisher's note)

REVIEW: *Booklist* v109 no22 p84 Ag 1 2013 Ann Kelley

REVIEW: *Bull Cent Child Books* v67 no5 p270 Ja 2014 T. A.

"The Mischievians." "Some entries are significantly cleverer than others . . . but the encyclopedia's creative take on familiar situations will garner enthusiasm. The prose is similarly uneven, with an appealing conversational tone clashing with awkward sentence structure. The oil illustrations with their retro-inspired palette and watery detail evoke Mark Teague's, and the Mischievians themselves are cleverly designed to perfectly match their particular form of roguery. The multiple, lengthy entries will likely make this a text kids dive in and out of rather than read cover-to-cover, but those looking for a scapegoat for any sticky situation will likely find one to blame here."

REVIEW: *Kirkus Rev* v81 no16 p168 Ag 15 2013

"The Mischievians." "A guide to the elusive creatures responsible for everyday ills offers kids the ultimate book of excuses. . . . Two children plagued by a series of inexplicable events make the acquaintance of Dr. Zooper. He encourages them to read his guide, 'The Mischievians,' billed as 'An encyclopedia of things that make mischief, make mayhem, make noise, and make you CRAZY!' . . . Written for the most part in Q-and-A fashion, the book lends itself to both browsing and reading all in one fell swoop. This being [author William] Joyce, the creatures aren't half as disgusting as they could be (even when they're luring boogers out of noses or raising blisters on toes)."

REVIEW: *Publ Wkly* v260 no38 p78 S 23 2013

JOYCE, WILLIAM. The numberlys; [by] William Joyce 56 p. 2014 Atheneum Books for Young Readers

1. Alphabet—Fiction 2. Children's stories 3. Color—Fiction 4. Friendship—Fiction 5. Numerals—Fiction
ISBN 1442473436; 9781442473430 (hardcover: alk. paper)
LC 2013-032087

SUMMARY: In this children's book by William Joyce, illustrated by Christina Ellis, "Life was . . . fine. Orderly. Dull as gray paint. Very . . . numberly. But our five jaunty heroes weren't willing to accept that this was all there could be. They knew there had to be more. . . . One letter after another emerged, until there were twenty-six. Twenty-six letters—and they were beautiful. All colorful, shiny, and new. Exactly what our heroes didn't even know they were missing." (Publisher's note)

REVIEW: *Booklist* v110 no11 p51 F 1 2014 Gillian Engberg

REVIEW: *Booklist* v110 no14 p82-4 Mr 15 2014 Sarah Hunter

"The Numberlys". "[William] Joyce . . . has created an industrial city where, since only numbers exist, there are no words for colors or feelings or food. The inhabitants of the shadowy, sepia-toned city, the big-eyed Numberlys, march back and forth among retrofuturistic buildings in perfect unison until five fed-up Numberlys set out to make something different. . . . Though there isn't much of a story—it amounts to little more than a brief alphabet book nestled in a vastly realized, imaginative atmosphere—letter-learning kiddos (and their design-loving parents) will pore over the detailed spreads. Initially a popular app . . . this has the feel of an animated film, and that alone is a big appeal."

REVIEW: *Bull Cent Child Books* v67 no11 p580-1 Jl/Ag 2014 T. A.

REVIEW: *Kirkus Rev* v82 no8 p51 Ap 15 2014

REVIEW: *Publ Wkly* v261 no10 p62 Mr 10 2014

REVIEW: *SLJ* v60 no4 p124 Ap 2014 Margaret Bush

JOYCE, WILLIAM.il. The numberlys. See Joyce, W.

JUAN, ANA.il. The Girl Who Soared over Fairyland and Cut the Moon in Two. See Valente, K.

JUDAH, BEN. Fragile empire; how Russia fell in and out of love with Vladimir Putin; [by] Ben Judah 400 p. 2013 Yale University Press

1. Political science literature 2. Presidents—Russia (Federation) 3. Russia (Federation)—Economic conditions
ISBN 9780300181210 (cloth : alkaline paper)
LC 2012-048007

SUMMARY: In this book on the political career of Russian President Vladimir Putin, author "[Ben] Judah argues that Putinism has brought economic growth to Russia but also weaker institutions, and this contradiction leads to instability. The author explores both Putin's successes and his failed promises, taking into account the impact of a new middle class and a new generation, the Internet, social activism, and globalization on the president's impending leadership crisis." (Publisher's note)

REVIEW: *Atlantic* v313 no5 p46-8 Je 2014 David Frum

"Fragile Empire: How Russia Fell In and Out of Love With Vladimir Putin". "Too bad no one at the CIA was reading the astute new book on Russia by Ben Judah, a Russian-speaking British journalist who has been reporting on low life and high life in and around Moscow, as well as in the bleak cities of the hinterland, for more than a decade. Judah explains the manic self-confdence—and the insecurity—of Vladimir Putin's Russia. His core insight: the fragile empire, as his title describes Russia today, is such because it is built on a foundation of plunder."

REVIEW: *Economist* v407 no8835 p88-9 My 11 2013

REVIEW: *N Y Rev Books* v60 no14 p54-7 S 26 2013 Amy Knight

"Winter Olympics in the Subtropics: An Independent Expert Report" and "Fragile Empire: How Russia Fell In and Out of Love With Vladimir Putin." "Two of Putin's critics from the democratic opposition, Boris Nemtsov and Leonid Martynyuk, . . . have published a booklet . . .describing the folly of the choice of Sochi, the unprecedented amount of government money being spent to prepare for the games, and the vast corruption that is part of the process. . . . [Ben Judah's] excellent book provides a wide-ranging and highly critical account of the current state of Russia. . . . He also gives an insightful historical perspective on the rise of Putin."

REVIEW: *New Statesman* v142 no5155 p46 Ap 26 2013

REVIEW: *TLS* no5771 p24 N 8 2013 ANDREW MONAGHAN

"Fragile Empire: How Russia Fell in and Out of Love With Vladimir Putin" and "Can Russia Modernise? Sistema, Power Networks and Informal Governance." "'Fragile Empire' [is] a fluent and plausible account of Russian politics and society in the wake of the recent protests. . . . If this is familiar terrain, [Ben] Judah adds detail and colour by giving thumbnail accounts of the characters involved. . . . The question of 'getting things done' in Russia is at the heart of Alena Ledeneva's more academic study. . . . By drawing attention to the all-encompassing power of the system, Ledeneva shows that the role even of the president should not be overstated. . . . Not all will be convinced by her approach, but the result is an important study that weaves together numerous illuminating anecdotes."

JUDD, PETER HARING. The Akeing Heart; Passionate Attachments and Their Aftermath, Sylvia Townsend Warner, Valentine Ackland, Elizabeth Wade White; [by] Peter Haring Judd 414 p. 2013 CreateSpace Independent Publishing Platform

1. Ackland, Valentine 2. Historical literature 3. Lesbians—History—20th century 4. Warner, Sylvia Townsend, 1893-1978 5. White, Elizabeth Wade
ISBN 1484867181; 9781484867181

SUMMARY: This book relates how "in the 1930s, three well-educated women—English novelist Sylvia Townsend Warner, English poet Valentine Ackland and American heiress-turned-activist/writer Elizabeth Wade White—became tangled up in one another's lives. . . . Warner fostered an . . epistolary friendship with White. . . . However, when the philandering Ackland took the inexperienced White as her lover, the three women found themselves caught in a web of conflicting desires." (Kirkus Reviews)

REVIEW: *Kirkus Rev* v81 no19 p75 O 1 2013

REVIEW: *Kirkus Rev* p27-8 D 15 2013 supplemet best books 2013

"The Akeing Heart: Passionate Attachments and Their Aftermath: Sylvia Townsend Warner, Valentine Ackland, Elizabeth Wade White". "[Peter Haring] Judd's book is a straightforward biographical account. . . . Much of the text consists of the women's correspondence and, less frequently, their journals; these are true treasures, as Warner, Ackland and White were all superb writers. The book might have focused a bit more on their riveting interpersonal dramas, but Judd commits to telling their full stories faithfully, even to the most quotidian detail. Their missives about politics, their literary and artistic friends, and even the behaviors of their beloved pet cats are as finely wrought as their heartfelt notes on their romantic complications."

REVIEW: *Kirkus Rev* v81 no18 p363 S 15 2013

REVIEW: *TLS* no5780 p26 Ja 10 2014 MICHAEL CAINES

JUDGE, LITA. Flight school; [by] Lita Judge 40 p. 2014 Atheneum Books for Young Readers

1. Children's stories 2. Flight—Fiction 3. Penguins—Fiction 4. Self-realization—Fiction 5. Teacher-student relationships—Fiction
ISBN 1442481773; 9781442481770 (hardcover)
LC 2012-046161

SUMMARY: In this book, by Lita Judge, "a persevering penguin is determined to fly. . . . Although little Penguin has the soul of an eagle, his body wasn't built to soar. But Penguin has an irrepressible spirit, and he adamantly follows his dreams to flip, flap, fly! Even if he needs a little help with the technical parts, this penguin is ready to live on the wind." (Publisher's note)

REVIEW: *Booklist* v110 no15 p92 Ap 1 2014 Sarah Hunter

REVIEW: *Bull Cent Child Books* v67 no10 p524-5 Je 2014 J.H.

REVIEW: *Horn Book Magazine* v90 no3 p68-9 My/Je 2014 CYNTHIA K. RITTER

REVIEW: *Kirkus Rev* v82 no4 p111 F 15 2014

"Flight School". "A small round penguin with lofty aspirations finds success of a sort in a sweet, if slight, appreciation of the resourcefulness of teachers. . . . [Lita] Judge's edge-to-edge watercolor-and-pencil art is lively and amusing. Her various sea and shore birds-gulls, a pelican, a heron and a small owl among them-and their fledglings are just a little scruffy, and they are exaggeratedly, expressively funny in their anthropomorphic roles as teachers and students. . . . Though Penguin doesn't discover any of his own true talents, young listeners will probably empathize with wanting something so far out of reach."

REVIEW: *Publ Wkly* v261 no7 p98 F 17 2014

REVIEW: *SLJ* v60 no3 p115 Mr 2014 Roxanne Burg

JUHASZ, VICTOR.il. Hot dog! See Kimmelman, L.

JULIER, ALICE P. Eating together; food, friendship, and inequality; [by] Alice P. Julier ix, 237 p. 2013 University of Illinois Press

1. Dinners and dining 2. Eating (Philosophy) 3. Food habits 4. Philosophical literature 5. Social networks 6. Sociology literature 7. Table etiquette

ISBN 9780252037634 (cloth : alk. paper); 9780252079184 (pbk. : alk. paper)

LC 2012-050854

SUMMARY: "'Eating Together: Food, Friendship, and Inequality' argues that the ways in which Americans eat together play a central role in social life in the United States. Delving into a wide range of research, [author] Alice P. Julier analyzes etiquette and entertaining books from the past century and conducts interviews and observations of dozens of hosts and guests at dinner parties, potlucks, and buffets." (Publisher's note)

REVIEW: *Choice* v51 no5 p880 Ja 2014 R. R. Wilk

REVIEW: *TLS* no5775 p30 D 6 2013 FRAN BIGMAN

"Eating Together: Food, Friendship, and Inequality." "Cosmopolitan dining habits have become a form of social capital, as Alice P. Julier argues in 'Eating Together: Food, friendship, and inequality,' a study of social eating at home in America that explores the use of food to create both ties and boundaries. Julier's book contributes to the small field of sociology on friendship, often considered the least hierarchical of relationships. Yet, as 'Eating Together' illustrates, these supposedly democratic bonds are influenced by structural inequalities in class, race and gender."

JUNG CHANG, 1952-. Empress Dowager Cixi; the concubine who launched modern China; [by] 1952- Jung Chang 480 p. 2013 Alfred A. Knopf

1. Empresses—China—Biography 2. Historical literature

ISBN 0307271609; 9780307271600 (hardcover); 9780307456700 (pbk.)

LC 2013-020766

SUMMARY: Author Jung Chang "provides a revisionist biography of a controversial concubine who rose through the ranks to become a long-reigning, power- wielding dowager empress during the delicate era when China emerged from its isolationist cocoon to become a legitimate player on the international stage. [He shows how] as Cixi's power and influence grew . . . she radically shifted official attitudes toward Western thoughts, ideas, trade, and technology." (Booklist)

REVIEW: *Booklist* v110 no4 p12 O 15 2013 Margaret Flanagan

REVIEW: *Choice* v51 no7 p1282 Mr 2014 N. E. Barnes

REVIEW: *Economist* v409 no8864 p84 N 30 2013

REVIEW: *Kirkus Rev* v81 no18 p137 S 15 2013

REVIEW: *Libr J* v138 no10 p80 Je 1 2013

REVIEW: *Libr J* v138 no14 p118 S 1 2013 Charles Hayford

REVIEW: *Libr J* v139 no4 p55 Mr 1 2014 Susan G. Baird

REVIEW: *London Rev Books* v36 no8 p9-10 Ap 17 2014 Pamela Crossley

REVIEW: *N Y Rev Books* v60 no19 p18-20 D 5 2013 Jonathan Mirsky

"Empress Dowager Cixi: The Concubine Who Launched Modern China". "A largely new—and to me, mostly convincing—interpretation. . . . I have one small and two serious criticisms of Chang's usually impressive biography. She occasionally lapses into slang or uses the wrong word . . . More serious is the matter of sources. . . . It would be useful in a future edition to say something about these documents and how they are organized, and to include the Chinese characters for their names in the bibliography. . . . I liked this biography, but have been troubled as a reviewer because the sources are not easy to check. . . . But Jung Chang has written a pathbreaking and generally persuasive book."

REVIEW: *N Y Times Book Rev* p12 O 27 2013 ORVILLE SCHELL

REVIEW: *N Y Times Book Rev* p26 N 3 2013

REVIEW: *New Statesman* v142 no5177 p65-7 S 27 2013 Rana Mitter

REVIEW: *New Yorker* v89 no44 p75-1 Ja 13 2014

REVIEW: *TLS* no5780 p9-10 Ja 10 2014 JOHN KEAY

"Empress Dowager Cixi: The Concubine Who Launched Modern China." "For someone who ruled China on and off for nearly half a century, the Dowager Empress Cixi chose an odd theme for her final utterance in 1908. . . . The genius of China's last female ruler lay in managing the moment. . . . 'She was determined to hold on to the reins of the Empire until her last breath,' confirms Jung Chang in a colourful and extensively researched biography. . . . Also missing in this somewhat partisan book is any mention of the Dowager Empress's best-known folly."

JUNGERSEN, CHRISTIAN. You disappear; a novel; 352 p. 2014 Nan A. Talese/Doubleday

1. FICTION—Literary 2. FICTION—Medical 3. FICTION—Psychological 4. Marriage—Fiction 5. Medical fiction

ISBN 9780385537254 (hardback)

LC 2013-029148

SUMMARY: In this novel by Christian Jungersen, "Mia is a schoolteacher in Denmark. Her husband, Frederik, is the charismatic headmaster of a local private school. During a vacation on Majorca, they discover that a brain tumor has started to change Frederik's personality. . . . When millions of crowns go missing at the private school, Frederik is the obvious culprit, and Mia's private crisis quickly draws in the entire community." (Publisher's note)

REVIEW: *Booklist* v110 no8 p21 D 15 2013 Joanne Wilkinson

REVIEW: *Kirkus Rev* v81 no24 p321 D 15 2013

REVIEW: *New Yorker* v90 no1 p104-1 F 17 2014

"You Disappear." "Mia Halling's husband, Frederik, is not himself: he drives erratically and cries easily. After he suffers a fall, a trip to the hospital reveals a brain tumor. Then it emerges that he has embezzled millions from the school where he is headmaster. . . . If Mia is to forgive her husband's crimes because of his impaired judgment, mustn't she also discount a new tenderness he's shown her in recent years? Newly alert to the fragility of the human mind, she questions not just her husband's actions but the free will of everyone she meets."

JUNN, JANE. Asian American political participation. See Taeku Lee

JUNYK, IHOR. Foreign Modernism; Cosmopolitanism, Identity, and Style in Paris; [by] Ihor Junyk 200 p. 2013 University of Toronto Press

1. France—History—Third Republic, 1870-1940 2. France—Intellectual life—History 3. Historical literature 4. Paris (France)—History—1870-1940 5. Paris (France)—Intellectual life—History 6. Xenophobia—History

ISBN 1442645199; 9781442645196

SUMMARY: This book by Ihor Junyk "investigates this tense and transitional moment for both modernism and European multiculturalism by looking at the role of foreigners in Paris's artistic scene. Examining works of literature, sculpture, ballet and performing arts, music, and architecture, Ihor Junyk combines cultural history with contemporary work in transnationalism and diaspora studies." (Publisher's note)

REVIEW: *Choice* v51 no1 p81-2 S 2013 L. Simon

"Foreign Modernism: Cosmopolitanism, Identity, and Style in Paris." "In this fascinating cultural history, [Ihor] Junyk examines the role of émigré artists, writers, performers, and architects in Paris from the early 20th century through the 1930s. Rather than embracing and nurturing multiculturalism and diversity, Paris, Junyk asserts, was beset by national chauvinism, xenophobia, and strident conservatism arising after the Franco-Prussian War of 1870-71 and intensifying after WW I. . . . This fresh, erudite, yet accessible book contributes significantly to cultural studies, diaspora studies, art history, and critical cosmopolitanism."

JURY, WALTER. Scan. See Fine, S.

JUST WAR; authority, tradition, and practice; 328 p. 2013 Georgetown University Press

1. Authority 2. Just war doctrine—Congresses 3. Military ethics 4. Political science literature 5. Qaida (Organization)

ISBN 9781589019966 (pbk. : alk. paper)

LC 2012-042486

SUMMARY: This book "examine[s] just war's role as a moral guide for diplomacy. While the editors acknowledge the centrality of just war in international politics, they are concerned that the principle of 'proper authority' has received less attention because it has been connected to the concept of state sovereignty. To address this, the book takes a broader look at what constitutes authority, emphasizing its institutional, theoretical, and practical elements." (Choice: Current Reviews for Academic Libraries)

REVIEW: *Choice* v51 no7 p1304-5 Mr 2014 M. F. Cairo

"Just War: Authority, Tradition, and Practice." "The essays are divided into three parts. Part 1, which is the most interesting, addresses the practice of authority, specifically the conceptions and sources of authority in the contemporary world. Nahed Artoul Zehr's chapter on al Qaeda is particularly intriguing, raising issues of nonstate authority. Part 2 addresses authority in practice, including military ethics education and rules of engagement. Part 3 addresses whether the just war tradition restrains war. While some essays are stronger than others, the anthology is an important addition to the field. . . . Recommended."

K

KA YOSHIDA.tr. The reason I jump. See Higashida, N.

KABAKOFF, ERIC S. Rally Caps, Rain Delays and Racing Sausages; A Baseball Fan's Quest to See the Game from a Seat in Every Ballpark; [by] Eric S. Kabakoff 266 p. 2013 Eric Kabakoff

1. Baseball—Competitions 2. Baseball fans 3. Baseball fields 4. Memoirs 5. Sports literature

ISBN 0989547205; 9780989547208

SUMMARY: In this book, Eric Kabakoff "chronicles his quest to visit every major league ballpark. . . . From August 2005 to September 2011, Kabakoff traveled to every major league city in the U.S. and Canada, not only to watch the hometown teams, but also to explore the ballparks, sample the concessions, visit the halls of fame and meet local fans. Throughout this chatty book, he recaps memorable games, spars with mascots, collects oddball souvenirs and receives frequent sunburns. " (Kirkus Reviews)

REVIEW: *Kirkus Rev* p28 D 15 2013 supplemet best books 2013

"Rally Caps, Rain Delays and Racing Sausages: A Baseball Fan's Quest to See the Game From a Seat in Every Ballpark". "Debut author [Eric] Kabakoff chronicles his quest to visit every major league ballpark in this cheerful travelogue. . . . Throughout this chatty book, he recaps memorable games, spars with mascots, collects oddball souvenirs and receives frequent sunburns. He also expertly summarizes several team and ballpark histories along the way. There's nothing scientific about the way he compares stadiums' retractable roofs or evaluates fans' enthusiasm, but his casual metrics will likely make indelible impressions on readers nonetheless. His writing style is boyish and agreeable, informal and full of occasionally silly wit."

REVIEW: *Kirkus Rev* v81 no20 p64 O 15 2013

REVIEW: *Kirkus Rev* v81 no19 p351 O 1 2013

REVIEW: *Publ Wkly* v261 no41 p53-4 O 13 2014

KACIAN, JIM.ed. Haiku in English. See Haiku in English

KAEBNICK, GREGORY E.ed. Synthetic biology and morality. See Synthetic biology and morality

KAFKA, FRANZ, 1883-1924. See Stach, R.

KAGAN, SHELLY. The geometry of desert; [by] Shelly Kagan 688 p. 2012 Oxford University Press

1. Ethics—Mathematical models 2. Good & evil 3. Merit (Ethics) 4. Philosophical literature 5. Philosophy & ethics

ISBN 9780199895595 (alk. paper)

LC 2011-030067

SUMMARY: This book "considers both the fundamental and the complex nature of deserving. [Shelly] Kagan poses familiar questions initially (what makes one person more deserving than another?; what is it that the more deserving deserve more of?; does anyone deserve anything at all?) and then puts them aside in order to examine the underlying complexity of desert by means of graphs." (New Statesman)

REVIEW: *Choice* v50 no8 p1448 Ap 2013 H. Oberdiek

REVIEW: *Ethics* v124 no2 p417-26 Ja 2014 BRADFORD SKOW

"The Geometry of Desert". "At over six hundred pages, it is monumental in both size and achievement. . . . [Shelly] Kagan's book is so rich that I have only begun to scratch the surface, but I must stop. I I have said that I would prefer to build a theory of desert on foundations somewhat different from those Kagan uses. But a theory should be judged by the shape of the whole edifice, not just the ground it is built on. Kagan in this book has set a high standard for how much of that edifice can be revealed and how well its parts can be seen to fit together."

KAHANEY, AMELIA. The brokenhearted; [by] Amelia Kahaney 320 p. 2013 HarperTeen

1. Adventure and adventurers—Fiction 2. Adventure stories 3. Ballet dancing—Fiction 4. Family problems—Fiction 5. JUVENILE FICTION—Action & Adventure—General 6. JUVENILE FICTION—Love & Romance 7. JUVENILE FICTION—Social Issues—Adolescence 8. Love—Fiction 9. Secrets—Fiction 10. Social classes—Fiction 11. Superheroes—Fiction
ISBN 0062230921; 9780062230928 (hardback)
LC 2013-014336

SUMMARY: In this book by Amelia Kahaney, "Anthem Fleet, talented ballerina and heir to the Fleet fortune, is closely guarded by her parents. When she goes to a dangerous party in the wrong part of town, she meets the handsome Gavin and is immediately drawn into his forbidden world. Then, in a tragic accident, Anthem falls to her death. She awakes in an underground lab, with a bionic heart ticking in her chest. As she negotiates her dangerous new life, she uncovers the sinister truth." (Publisher's note)

REVIEW: *Booklist* v110 no2 p74 S 15 2013 Frances Bradburn

REVIEW: *Bull Cent Child Books* v67 no3 p162 N 2013 K. Q. G.

"The Brokenhearted." "From the similarities in name and crime statistics between Bedlam and Gotham to more subtle references, like Anthem's shady father referring to his tuxedo as his 'penguin suit,' the parallels to Batman are hard to miss here, and fans of that franchise will feel right at home with the wicked chase scenes and broody protagonist of this superhero origin story. Streetwise readers will likely catch a whiff of something foul the moment Gavin appears, but even they will be shocked by his ultimate betrayal and Anthem's willingness to do what needs to be done to rid herself and the city of him."

REVIEW: *Kirkus Rev* p66 2013 Guide 20to BookExpo America

REVIEW: *Kirkus Rev* v81 no17 p99 S 1 2013

KAKU, MICHIO. The future of the mind; the scientific quest to understand, enhance, and empower the mind; [by] Michio Kaku 400 p. 2014 Doubleday

1. Brain—Mathematical models 2. Brain-computer interfaces 3. Cognitive neuroscience 4. Neuropsychology 5. Scientific literature
ISBN 038553082X; 9780385530828
LC 2013-017338

SUMMARY: In this book, "theoretical physicist [Michio] Kaku . . . explores fantastical realms of science fiction that may soon become our reality. His futurist framework merges physics with neuroscience to model how our brains construct the future, and is loosely applied to demonstrations that 'show proof-of-principle' in accomplishing what was previously fictional: that minds can be read, memories can be digitally stored, and intelligences can be improved to great extents." (Publishers Weekly)

REVIEW: *Kirkus Rev* v82 no1 p216 Ja 1 2014

"The Future of the Mind: The Scientific Quest to Understand, Enhance, and Empower the Mind". "Having written the enthusiastic but strictly science-based 'Physics of the Impossible' (2008) and 'Physics of the Future' (2011), [Michio] Kaku . . . turns his attention to the human mind with equally satisfying results. . . . Kaku is not shy about quoting science-fiction movies and TV (he has seen them all). Despite going off the deep end musing about phenomena such as isolated consciousness spreading throughout the universe, he delivers ingenious predictions extrapolated from good research already in progress."

REVIEW: *Libr J* v138 no15 p47 S 15 2013

REVIEW: *N Y Times Book Rev* p21 Mr 9 2014 ADAM FRANK

REVIEW: *New Sci* v221 no2959 p46-7 Mr 8 2014 Alun Anderson

REVIEW: *New Sci* v221 no2950 p48 Ja 4 2014

"Neanderthal Man: In Search of Lost Genomes," "The Future of the Mind: The Scientific Quest to Understand, Enhance and Empower the Mind," and "Our Mathematical Universe: My Quest for the Ultimate Nature of Reality". "We're hoping for great things from geneticist Svante Pääbo, who in 2009 led the team that sequenced the first Neanderthal genome using DNA from 40,000-year-old bone. This is his story, which should prove to be a lens not only on pioneering scientific discovery but also on what makes us human. . . . We're keen to see what happens when the irrepressibly optimistic [Michio] Kaku turns his crystal ball to brain science and the future of human minds. His new book spans everything from smart pills that enhance cognition to placing our neural blueprint on laser beams sent out into space. . . . Max Tegmark, one of the world's leading theoretical physicists, opens up a deep and daring strand of thinking in this esoteric world."

REVIEW: *Publ Wkly* v260 no51 p48 D 16 2013

REVIEW: *TLS* no5803 p32 Je 20 2014 GREGORY RADICK

KALDIS, BYRON.ed. Encyclopedia of philosophy and the social sciences. See Encyclopedia of philosophy and the social sciences

KALERGIS, DAVID. It's Not About Sex; [by] David Kalergis 318 p. 2014 Atelerix

1. Art dealers—Fiction 2. Artists—Fiction 3. Ex-convicts—Fiction 4. New York (N.Y.) art scene 5. Psychological fiction
ISBN 0615820891; 9780615820897

SUMMARY: This book "follows longtime prisoner Ray Martin . . . who discovers a love for painting while serving 15 years behind bars on a manslaughter charge at the Lorton Correctional Facility in Washington, D.C. His oil-based, abstract work catches the eye of wealthy, world-renowned painter Leonard Hirsh, who goes to great lengths to ensure Martin's early release. . . . Things get complicated as Martin's unfamiliarity with social behavior outside prison walls clashes with his new, elite existence." (Kirkus Reviews)

REVIEW: *Kirkus Rev* v82 no1 p304 Ja 1 2014

"It's Not About Sex". "The novel is curiously narrated by James Bradley, an independent art dealer in the midst of a marital separation who's assisting Hirsh and living at his palatial country estate rent-free. As an authoritative narrative voice, Bradley capably carries the story, but his character is thin and falters somewhat toward the conclusion. Although the prose can be awkward and sluggish at times, the story has moments of genuine suspense. A better title, however, might have helped garner more attention for this intriguing debut. A fine novel with a fresh premise and finely wrought dramatic tension."

KALLEN, STUART A. K-pop; Korea's musical explosion; [by] Stuart A. Kallen 64 p. 2014 Twenty-First Century Books

1. Girls' Generation (Performer) 2. Music literature 3. Popular culture—Korea (South) 4. Popular music—Korea (South)—History and criticism—Juvenile literature 5. Psy, 1977-

ISBN 1467720429; 9781467720427 (lib. bdg.: alk. paper)

LC 2013-009293

SUMMARY: This book, by Stuart A. Kallen, "traces the journey of South Korean pop music, from the early influences of American rock 'n' roll in the 1950s to the success of a tiger-eyed sensation called Rain, who wowed American audiences in the early 2000s. Discover how this Korean Justin Timberlake, and those who came after him, rose through South Korea's star-making system through grueling hard work to seduce international audiences." (Publisher's note)

REVIEW: *Booklist* v110 no8 p37 D 15 2013 Erin Anderson

REVIEW: *Kirkus Rev* v82 no1 p162 Ja 1 2014

"K-Pop: Korea's Musical Explosion". "A breezy but flawed introduction to Korean pop music for novice fans. . . . Numerous color photos and playlists of artists' representative songs add interest for teens. However, knowledgeable readers will note that the author overstates some artists' impacts, overlooks other major musicians completely and appears to have only a rudimentary knowledge of Korean culture, perhaps due to his reliance on non-Korean, English-language sources. . . . Though English-language books on Korean pop culture are unfortunately quite rare, only complete newbies will find this overview informative. "

REVIEW: *SLJ* v60 no2 p125 F 2014 Krishna Grady

KALMAN, MAIRA. Thomas Jefferson; life, liberty and the pursuit of everything; [by] Maira Kalman 40 p. 2014 Nancy Paulsen Books

1. Biography (Literary form) 2. JUVENILE NONFICTION—Biography & Autobiography—Political 3. JUVENILE NONFICTION—History—United States—Colonial & Revolutionary Periods 4. JUVENILE NONFICTION—People & Places—United States—General 5. Presidents—United States—Biography—Juvenile literature

ISBN 0399240403; 9780399240409 (hardback)

LC 2013-034625

SUMMARY: In this biography of Thomas Jefferson, author "Maira Kalman sheds light on the fascinating life and interests of the Renaissance man who was [the United States'] third president. He played violin, spoke seven languages and was a scientist, naturalist, botanist, mathematician and architect. He doubled the size of the United States and sent Lewis and Clark to explore it." (Publisher's note)

REVIEW: *Booklist* v110 no12 p75 F 15 2014 Jeanne McDermott

REVIEW: *Bull Cent Child Books* v67 no6 p318 F 2014 Elizabeth Bush

"Thomas Jefferson: Life, Liberty and the Pursuit of Everything." "[Maira] Kalman launches right in to this attractive picture-book biography with a succinct, spot-on summary of what made Thomas Jefferson memorable. . . . Kalman . . . reprises some elements of her marvelously innovative picture-book biography 'Looking at Lincoln' . . . including an accessibly informal tone, a fruit bowl of vibrant colors, a frequent focus on a single telling artifact, and plenty of holes punched through the fourth wall to invite readers into the conversation. However, in this case there is no child guide regaling her peers with her discoveries about a Great Man, and thus the naïve comments and asides that pepper the text are a little more distracting."

REVIEW: *Horn Book Magazine* v90 no1 p111-2 Ja/F 2014 BART HELMESS

"Thomas Jefferson: Life, Liberty and the Pursuit of Everything." "On the cover of this striking picture book biography, Jefferson poses proudly in the foreground with his celebrated home standing on a hill in the distance. . . . A series of spreads, with [Maira] Kalman's familiar primitivist rendering and chromatic brilliance, details Jefferson's work as collector, architect, horticulturalist, and musician. . . Kalman . . . addresses all of this with a colloquial, occasionally arch, and whimsical narrative, heavy with historical import and dotted with trivia. . . . The vibrant imagery, frank content, and disarming language combine in a nuanced portrait that respects its subject and its audience in equal measure."

REVIEW: *Kirkus Rev* v81 no22 p105 N 15 2013

REVIEW: *N Y Times Book Rev* p22 Ja 19 2014

REVIEW: *N Y Times Book Rev* p14 Ja 12 2014 HAROLD HOLZER

REVIEW: *Publ Wkly* v260 no43 p63 O 28 2013

REVIEW: *SLJ* v60 no1 p114 Ja 2014 Jody Kopple

KALMRE, EDA. The human sausage factory; a study of post-war rumour in Tartu; [by] Eda Kalmre x, 180 p. 2013 Rodopi

1. Cannibalism—Estonia—Tartu—Folklore 2. Folklore—Estonia—Tartu 3. Historical literature 4. Sausages—Estonia—Tartu—Folklore 5. Social science literature 6. World War, 1939-1945—Estonia—Tartu—Folklore

ISBN 9042037172; 9789042037175

LC 2013-474460

SUMMARY: This book by Eda Kalmre describes how "Under certain conditions, some rumours, which were established as part of folklore already long ago, may become fixed in the memory and the subconscious of several generations. This is what happened with the rumour about a human sausage factory after the Second World War. . . . Through documents, photos and people's memories, the book offers an insight into the city of Tartu after the Second World War." (Publisher's note)

REVIEW: *TLS* no5776 p30 D 13 2013 ALEXANDER ETKIND

"The Human Sausage Factory: A Study of Post-War Rumour in Tartu." "'Rumour is a mctaphor for social truth,' explains Eda Kalmre, an anthropologist from Tartu who takes on the myth in this most unusual case study. . . . Kalmre's painstaking research has yielded dozens of pieces of oral and written evidence that show how the rumours circulated in oral tradition, the local press, and police denunciations. Historians and anthropologists have rarely--if ever--produced so complete and fully documented a picture of an archaic belief system that persisted, in a perfectly modem society, to express fear, anger and despair."

KALOF, LINDA.ed. A Cultural History of Women. See A Cultural History of Women

KAMINSKY, JEF.il. Dear santasaurus. See McAnulty, S.

KAMMERAAD-CAMPBELL, SUSAN.ed. The Other Mother. See Bruce, T.

KAMRATH, ANGELA E. The Miracle of America; [by] Angela E. Kamrath 382 p. 2013 Xulon Press

1. Freedom of religion 2. Historical literature 3. Religion & state 4. United States—Politics & government 5. United States—Religion

ISBN 1628711418; 9781628711417

SUMMARY: It was the author's intent "to illustrate how Biblical teachings influenced the social structures of the early colonies and ultimately informed the Founding Fathers and their philosophy of governance. She particularly describes how core American principles, such as freedom of conscience and restricted government, have a powerful Biblical foundation." (Kirkus Reviews)

REVIEW: *Kirkus Rev* v82 no1 p348 Ja 1 2014

"The Miracle of America: The Influence of the Bible on the Founding History and Principles of the United States of America for a People of Every Belief". "[Angela E.] Kamrath makes an impressive debut with a work that blends Judeo-Christian theology, political science and colonial American history. . . . Skeptical readers may suspect that the author is arguing for a more theocratic society or to make a case for America as a nation chosen by God, but she goes to careful lengths to avoid such polemics. . . . She makes a powerful case that the Bible mandates rather than restricts the pluralist society in American politics. . . . . In its quest to be comprehensive, the book sometimes sacrifices readability, but this is essentially an academic text."

KANDEL, ERIC R., 1929-. Memory. See Squire, L. R.

KANE, ANNE. Constructing Irish national identity; discourse and ritual during the land war, 1879-1882; [by] Anne Kane xv, 280 p. 2011 Palgrave Macmillan

1. Discourse analysis—Ireland—History—19th century 2. Ethnicity—Ireland—History—19th century 3. Land tenure—Ireland—History—19th century 4. Nationalism—Ireland—History—19th century 5. Political culture—Ireland—History—19th century 6. Ritual—Political aspects—Ireland—History—19th century 7. Social change—Ireland—History—19th century 8. Social movements—Ireland—History—19th century 9. Sociology literature

ISBN 0230120296; 9780230120297

LC 2011-017322

SUMMARY: This book "provides a theoretical and methodological model for analyzing symbolic and social transformation in major historical events. Synthesizing the strong program in cultural sociology with eventful temporality, [author] Anne Kane demonstrates the construction of political alliance and the emergence of a counter hegemonic cultural structure over the course of a political movement and campaign." (Publisher's note)

REVIEW: *Am J Sociol* v118 no4 p1140-2 Ja 2013 Bryan Fanning

REVIEW: *Contemp Sociol* v42 no5 p747-8 S 2013 Michael P. Young

"Constructing Irish National Identity: Discourse and Ritual During the Land War, 1879-1882." "Constructing Irish National Identity provides a cultural theory of social rupture and emergent nationalism through social movement. In this beautifully crafted book, Anne Kane grounds this theory in a careful empirical exploration of an historical case of such change and movement: the Land War in Ireland, 1879-1882. . . . This book provides a very sophisticated, theory-informed analysis of an historically important social movement. It advances theory and empirical research in the area of culture, historical processes of change, nationalism, and social movements. Beyond these contributions to particular fields, it is also simply an excellent work of social theory."

KANE, GIL. Gil Kane's the Amazing Spider Man; [by] Gil Kane 2012 IDW Publishing

1. Art literature 2. LSD (Drug) 3. Spider-Man (Fictitious character) 4. Superhero comic books, strips, etc. 5. Supervillains

ISBN 1613775253; 9781613775257

SUMMARY: This book, part of the Artist's Edition comic book series, presents drwawings by Gil Kanefrom the comic book "The Amazing Spider Man," "collecting issues Nos. 96 through 102, and 121." Most pages are "full-size and . . . scanned from the original art." (New York Times) Stories include "the infamous non comics code approved LSD drug issues [and]the 'six-arm' Spider-Man storyline that also introduced Morbius for the very first time." (Publisher's note)

REVIEW: *New York Times* v163 no56286 pC32 O 11 2013 Dana Jennings

"The Sky: The Art of Final Fantasy," "Conan: Red Nails," and "Gil Kane's the Amazing Spider-Man." "With his elegant and sinuous line, the Japanese artist Yoshitaka Amano understands the power of pen and ink. . . . Mr. Amano's light, deft touch defies genre conventions in a fantasy world where blood and beauty twine, where the ethereal has bite. . . . Mr. [Barry] Windsor-Smith shows his skill at creating a world on just one textured black-and-white page. The heroes in this lush, oversize book . . . are clearly Conan--and Mr. Windsor-Smith. . . . Gil Kane was one of the best unsung comic artists of the 1960s and '70s. . . . His muscular line and cinematic sense of page design served well superheroes like Green Lantern, Batman and especially Spider-Man."

KANE, YUKARI IWATANI. Haunted Empire; Apple After Steve Jobs; [by] Yukari Iwatani Kane 384 p. 2014 HarperCollins

1. Apple Inc. 2. Business literature 3. Chief executive officers 4. Cook, Timothy D., 1960- 5. Jobs, Steven, 1955-2011

ISBN 0062128256; 9780062128256

SUMMARY: In this book, journalist Yukari Iwatani Kane "delves deep inside Apple in the two years since Steve Jobs's death, revealing the tensions and challenges CEO Tim Cook and his team face as they try to sustain Jobs's vision and keep the company moving forward. . . . She explores Tim Cook's leadership and its impact on Jobs's loyal lieutenants, new product development, and Apple's relationships with Wall Street, the government, tech rivals, suppliers, the media, and consumers." (Publisher's note)

REVIEW: *Economist* v411 no8882 p87 Ap 12 2014

REVIEW: *Kirkus Rev* v82 no4 p193 F 15 2014

"Haunted Empire: Apple After Steve Jobs". "Though [Yukari Iwatani] Kane dwells too much on Apple as it was when Jobs lived, she points to some ongoing problems that Jobs might have dealt with differently from [Tim] Cook: for one, the appalling conditions under which Apple products are made in Chinese plants, and for another, the reputation-diminishing release of not-ready-for-prime-time products such as Maps and Siri. . . . Much of this book is an extended footnote to Walter Isaacson's biography of Jobs, which, though not without problems, is the first work to consult when thinking of things Apple."

REVIEW: *N Y Times Book Rev* p18 My 4 2014 BRAD STONE

REVIEW: *New York Times* v163 no56469 pA19 Ap 12 2014 JOE NOCERA

REVIEW: *Publ Wkly* v261 no4 p178 Ja 27 2014

KANEFIELD, TERI. The girl from the tar paper school; Barbara Rose Johns and the advent of the civil rights movement; [by] Teri Kanefield 56 p. 2013 Abrams Books for Young Readers

1. Civil rights movements—United States—History—20th century—Juvenile literature 2. Civil rights workers—United States—Biography—Juvenile literature 3. Historical literature 4. Segregation in education—Virginia—History—20th century—Juvenile literature 5. Women civil rights workers—United States—Biography—Juvenile literature

ISBN 1419707965; 9781419707964 (alk. paper)

LC 2012-040990

SUMMARY: This book, by Teri Kanefield, focuses on "Barbara Rose Johns. . . . In 1951, witnessing the unfair conditions in her racially segregated high school, Barbara Johns led a walkout . . . jumpstarting the American civil rights movement. Ridiculed by the white superintendent and school board . . . Barbara and her classmates held firm and did not give up. Her school's case went all the way to the Supreme Court and helped end segregation as part of Brown v. Board of Education." (Publisher's note)

REVIEW: *Booklist* v110 no3 p50 O 1 2013 Erin Anderson

REVIEW: *Bull Cent Child Books* v67 no6 p319 F 2014 Elizabeth Bush

"The Girl From the Tar Paper School: Barbara Rose Johns and the Advent of the Civil Rights Movement." "[Teri] Kanefield follows the students' strategies with an immediacy that will have readers chuckling and cheering and marveling at their clever audacity, as they lure the principal away from the building on a wild goose chase, forge notes to convene an all-school assembly, rally classmates to defy the probable censure of their parents, and call in the big guns from the NAACP to provide legal support. . . . Based largely on interviews, memoirs, and other primary source material, and liberally illustrated with photographs, this well-researched slice of civil rights history will reward readers who relish true stories of unsung heroes."

REVIEW: *Kirkus Rev* v81 no20 p240 O 15 2013

REVIEW: *Publ Wkly* v260 no42 p54 O 21 2013

REVIEW: *SLJ* v60 no3 p181 Mr 2014 Ann Welton

KANTOR, MELISSA. Maybe one day; [by] Melissa Kantor 400 p. 2014 HarperTeen, an imprint of HarperCollinsPublishers

1. Ballet dancing—Fiction 2. Best friends—Fiction 3. Family life—New Jersey—Fiction 4. Friendship—Fiction 5. High schools—Fiction 6. Leukemia—Fiction 7. Schools—Fiction 8. Sick—Fiction 9. Young adult fiction

ISBN 0062279203; 9780062279200 (hardcover bdg.)

LC 2013-008064

SUMMARY: Author Melissa Kantor "captures the joy of friendship, the agony of loss, and the unique experience of being a teenager in this . . . novel about a girl grappling with her best friend's life-threatening illness. . . . The one thing that keeps Zoe moving forward is knowing that Olivia will beat this, and everything will go back to the way it was before." (Publisher's note)

REVIEW: *Booklist* v110 no11 p64 F 1 2014 Heather Booth

REVIEW: *Horn Book Magazine* v90 no2 p123 Mr/Ap 2014 KATIE BIRCHER

REVIEW: *Kirkus Rev* v81 no24 p155 D 15 2013

"Maybe One Day". "A classic, youthful lament . . . avoids the maudlin and banal in the very capable hands of [Melissa] Kantor. . . . This high school drama goes well below the surface; faith is explored, and well-developed family members, friends and teachers play strong roles. These teens are not navigating life alone but are part of a supportive community. Readers just in it for the plot risk missing the poignant moments where Kantor's strong, graceful writing captures the innocence and sophistication of youth and the hopes and the fears of the girls and their families. Teens, heartache and acute illness: The tears will flow."

REVIEW: *Publ Wkly* v260 no49 p86 D 2 2013

REVIEW: *SLJ* v60 no3 p159 Mr 2014 Susannah Goldstein

REVIEW: *Voice of Youth Advocates* v37 no1 p68 Ap 2014 Barbara Fecteau

KANTOR, MICHAEL. Superheroes!; Capes, Cowls, and the Creation of Comic Book Culture; [by] Michael Kantor 304 p. 2013 Random House Inc

1. Comic books, strips, etc.—History 2. Literature—History & criticism 3. Periodical publishing—History 4. Superhero comic books, strips, etc. 5. Superhero films 6. Superheroes

ISBN 0385348584; 9780385348584

SUMMARY: Written by Laurence Maslon and Mchael

Kantor and "Based on the three-part PBS documentary series 'Superheroes,' this companion volume chronicles the never-ending battle of the comic book industry, its greatest creators, and its greatest creations. Covering the effect of superheroes on American culture--in print, on film and television, and in digital media--and the effect of American culture on its superheroes," this book "appeals to readers of all ages." (Publisher's note)

REVIEW: *Booklist* v110 no3 p13 O 1 2013 Sarah Hunter

REVIEW: *Kirkus Rev* v81 no20 p98 O 15 2013

REVIEW: *N Y Times Book Rev* p66 D 8 2013 GLEN WELDON

"Superheroes! Capes, Cowls, and the Creation of Comic Book Culture." "'Superheroes!' provides intriguing fodder for those of us who wonder how this age of adolescence dawned, and why it's stuck around so long. Laurence Maslon and Michael Kantor sagely pinpoint 1986, the year two landmark comics . . . found a devoted audience for gritty superhero stories. . . . The book is colorfully and copiously illustrated, and its prose lopes along like a jubilant puppy, with the occasional but spectacular stumble. . . . The book is the companion volume to the three-part PBS documentary series 'Superheroes: A Never-Ending Battle.'"

KANTOROVITZ, SYLVIE. The very tiny baby; [by] Sylvie Kantorovitz 32 p. 2014 Charlesbridge

1. Ambivalence—Juvenile fiction 2. Babies—Fiction 3. Children's stories 4. Jealousy in children—Juvenile fiction 5. Premature babies—Fiction 6. Premature infants—Juvenile fiction 7. Sibling rivalry—Fiction 8. Teddy bears—Fiction 9. Teddy bears—Juvenile fiction
ISBN 1580894453; 9781580894456 (reinforced for library use); 9781607346357 (ebook)
LC 2012-038697

SUMMARY: In this book, by Sylvie Kantorovitz, "Jacob learns that adults can be scared, too, when his new sibling is born prematurely. While Jacob has his grandma and his faithful teddy bear, Bob, with him at home while his parents are at the hospital, he still feels alone. The Book portrays the range of emotions older siblings often have about a new baby, including fear, anger, and resentment, along with the added challenges of the preemie's health concerns and parents' frequent absences." (Publisher's note)

REVIEW: *Bull Cent Child Books* v67 no9 p461 My 2014 H. M.

"The Very Tiny Baby". "This is not a book to accidentally hand to an unsuspecting soon-to-be older sibling, but it's a frank look at a common life situation not usually addressed for this age; [Sylvie] Kantotovitz deals with Jacob's very real and intense emotions with unusual honesty and a keen sense of child perspective. The pen, pencil, and gouache illustrations mimic a child's drawing style, and they're laid out with hand-lettered text captions in sequential bordered panels against contrasting backgrounds, as if they were in Jacob's scrapbook. Introduced in the right context and with the right amount of adult support, this could prove a useful story to families in a similar situation; consider purchasing this for your parent shelf rather than your picture-book collection."

REVIEW: *Kirkus Rev* v82 no3 p91 F 1 2014

REVIEW: *SLJ* v60 no3 p115 Mr 2014 Marianne Saccardi

KANTOROVITZ, SYLVIE.il. The very tiny baby. See Kantorovitz, S.

KANTROWITZ, STEPHEN.ed. All men free and brethren. See All men free and brethren

KAPADIA, PREMAL.ed. Śrīpāl Rās. See Śrīpāl Rās

KAPADIA, SUJATA P.tr. Śrīpāl Rās. See Śrīpāl Rās

KAPLAN, ALICE.ed. Algerian chronicles. See Camus, A.

KAPLAN, ALICE.tr. A box of photographs. See Grenier, R.

KAPLAN, CARLA. Miss Anne in Harlem; The White Women of the Black Renaissance; [by] Carla Kaplan 512 p. 2013 Harper

1. Harlem Renaissance 2. Historical literature 3. Racial identity of whites 4. United States—Race relations—History 5. Women's history—20th century
ISBN 0060882387; 9780060882389

SUMMARY: In this book, author Carla Kaplan "focuses on white women, collectively called 'Miss Anne,' who became Harlem Renaissance insiders. [She] focuses on six of the unconventional, free-thinking women, some from Manhattan high society, many Jewish, who crossed race lines and defied social conventions to become a part of the culture and heartbeat of Harlem." (Publisher's note)

REVIEW: *Booklist* v110 no1 p26 S 1 2013 Donna Seaman

REVIEW: *Choice* v51 no9 p1662 My 2014 K. B. Nutter

REVIEW: *Libr J* v138 no6 p61 Ap 1 2013 Barbara Hoffert

REVIEW: *N Y Times Book Rev* p13 S 22 2013 MARTHA A. SANDWEISS

"Miss Anne in Harlem: The White Women of the Black Renaissance." "In this remarkable work of historical recovery Carla Kaplan . . . does well by a group of women who got so much wrong. She resurrects Miss Anne as a cultural figure and explores the messy contradictions of her life. . . . This is really a collection of individual stories, a group biography that lets the idiosyncrasies of the individual women shine through. . . . The book is full of fresh discoveries. . . . Miss Anne makes for a messy heroine. But in Kaplan's deeply researched book, she becomes a useful cultural type, for all her inconsistencies and inability to effect broad social change."

REVIEW: *New York Times* v162 no56249 pC1-5 S 4 2013 JENNIFER SCHUESSLER

REVIEW: *Publ Wkly* v260 no22 p52 Je 3 2013

KAPLAN, FRED, 1937-. John Quincy Adams; American visionary; [by] Fred Kaplan 672 p. 2014 HarperCollins Publishers

1. Biography (Literary form) 2. Politicians—United States—Biography 3. Presidents—United States—Biography 4. United States—Politics & government—1815-1861
ISBN 0061915416; 9780061915413

LC 2013-035334

SUMMARY: This book, by Fred Kaplan, "brings into focus the . . . life of John Quincy Adams—the little known . . . sixth president of the United States and the first son of John and Abigail Adams. . . . Kaplan draws on a trove of unpublished archival material to trace Adams's evolution from his childhood during the Revolutionary War to his brilliant years as Secretary of State to his time in the White House and beyond." (Publisher's note)

REVIEW: *Am Sch* v83 no3 p103-5 Summ 2014 Annette Gordon-Reed

REVIEW: *Booklist* v110 no14 p46 Mr 15 2014 Brad Hooper

REVIEW: *Kirkus Rev* v82 no6 p122 Mr 15 2014

REVIEW: *Libr J* v139 no5 p125 Mr 15 2014 Frederick J. Augustyn Jr.

REVIEW: *Libr J* v138 no21 p68 D 1 2013 Barbara Hoffert

REVIEW: *N Y Rev Books* v61 no10 p45-7 Je 5 2014 Susan Dunn

"John Quincy Adams: American Visionary," "Louisa Catherine: The Other Mrs. Adams," and "A Traveled First Lady: Writings of Louisa Catherine Adams." "As Fred Kaplan demonstrates in his engaging, well-crafted, and deeply researched biography . . . this supremely successful diplomat and shrewd practitioner of realpolitik had a personality quite unsuited for a life in politics. . . . In 'Louisa Catherine: The Other Mrs. Adams,' Margery Heffron's insightful and entertaining though unfinished book . . . we enter deeply into the damaged family life of John Quincy and Louisa. . . . A fine new sampling of Louisa's writings, 'A Traveled First Lady: Writings of Louisa Catherine Adams' [is] edited by Margaret A. Hogan and C. James Taylor."

REVIEW: *N Y Times Book Rev* p1-16 My 4 2014 Robert W. Merry

REVIEW: *N Y Times Book Rev* p34 My 11 2014

REVIEW: *New Yorker* v90 no11 p71-1 My 5 2014

"John Quincy Adams: American Visionary" and "Louisa Catherine: The Other Mrs. Adams." "[John Quincy Adams's] latest biographer, Fred Kaplan . . . argues that Adams doesn't fully deserve his reputation for coldness, but, for all its diligence, 'John Quincy Adams: American Visionary' . . . never really succeeds in raising the sixth President's temperature. . . . [Author Margery M.] Heffron's agreeably written biography—cut short by the death of the author, in December, 2011—leaves Louisa [Catherine Adams] on the threshold of the Adamses' unhappy years in the White House. Another writer will have to finish her story."

REVIEW: *Publ Wkly* v261 no6 p74 F 10 2014

KAPLAN, GEOFF.ed. Power to the people. See Power to the people

KAPUR, AKASH. India becoming; a portrait of life in modern India; [by] Akash Kapur 292 p. 2012 Riverhead Hardcover

1. Generation gap 2. HISTORY—Asia—India & South Asia 3. HISTORY—Modern—21st Century 4. India—Economic conditions—1991- 5. India—Social conditions—1947- 6. Social change—India 7. Sociology literature 8. Technological innovations—Social aspects

ISBN 9781594488191 (hardback)

LC 2011-047588

SUMMARY: This book offers personal accounts that reflect the "rapid economic [and social] growth [of India]. . . . Sathy, a landowner in Tamil Nadu, a rich southern state, emerges as . . . [author Akash] Kapur's . . . dominant conservative voice. . . . He bemoans the fact that new wealth has brought dirt, traffic, noise, lack of respect from youngsters for rituals and authority, even violent crime. . . . [T]he reader is brought to sympathise with a second, contradictory, strand of complaint: that, for many, progress comes too slowly. Much poverty persists. Social repression lingers. . . . [The book's] characters display the ambiguity that many feel about the ongoing change." (Economist)

REVIEW: *Booklist* v108 no14 p9 Mr 15 2012 Vanessa Bush

REVIEW: *Economist* v402 no8774 p96 Mr 3 2012

"India Becoming: A Portrait of Life in Modern India." "[Akash Kapur's] new book is . . . readable, acutely observed and crammed with well-drawn characters. . . . Kapur's strength is in letting his characters display the ambiguity that many feel about the ongoing change. India too often remains an intolerable mess of corruption, inequality and squalor, and yet, overall, it is an optimistic place. The author's touch is less sure when he generalises. . . . In all, however, Mr Kapur offers a corrective to a simplistic 'new, happy narrative' of a rising India. . . .There is much debate about corruption, the need for better welfare and for economic growth to benefit Indians more widely. That debate is healthy; Mr Kapur's enjoyable book is a welcome addition to it."

REVIEW: *Kirkus Rev* v80 no4 p371 F 15 2012

"India Becoming: A Portrait of Life in Modern India." "Lively, anecdotal look at the people who have been vastly changed by the entrepreneurial explosion in India. In 2003, [Akash] Kapur, a half-American, half-Indian journalist, moved back to India, where he had been raised, after more than a decade in America. . . . On one hand, Kapur saw new Indians who dared to imagine for themselves a different kind of future; on the other, he found that development had taken a terrible toll on the environment, law and order and wealth distribution. . . . The author finds a nation gripped by an illusory sense of itself and in the throes of wrenching change. An honest, conflicted glimpse of a country 'still sorting through the contradictions of a rapid, and inevitably messy, transformation.'"

REVIEW: *Newsweek* v160 no14/15 p62 O 1 2012 Rob Verger Jacob Silverman Mythili G. Rao

KAPUR, ASHOK. Government and politics in South Asia; [by] Ashok Kapur xi, 526 p. 2014 Westview Press

1. Bangladesh—Politics & government 2. Ethnic conflict 3. National security—Pakistan 4. Political science literature

ISBN 9780813348797 (pbk.)

LC 2013-004623

SUMMARY: In this book on South Asia, "using themes such as political culture and heritage, constitutional structure, political parties and political leaders, conflict and mediation, policy issues, and problems and prospects, the contributors describe and compare the countries of the region. . . . This updated edition includes an examination of Pakistan's security challenges, ethnic tensions in Sri Lanka, and political changes in Bangladesh, among other things." (Choice:

Current Reviews for Academic Libraries)

REVIEW: *Choice* v51 no8 p1482-3 Ap 2014 A. Mazumdar

"Government and Politics in South Asia". "In its seventh, updated edition, 'Government and Politics in South Asia' continues to be an invaluable source for students and instructors engaged in the study of this dynamic region of the world. . . . The addition of new contributors provides fresh insight into the changes under way in South Asia. . . . The analytical framework followed in the book allows one to read it as a whole or focus on a particular section/country. The inclusion of a chapter on Afghanistan and a separate section on foreign policy within the discussion on each country would have served to further strengthen the book. Nevertheless, this book is a useful reference point for both undergraduate and graduate students in the field of South Asia."

KARABELL, ZACHARY. The leading indicators; a short history of the search for the right numbers; [by] Zachary Karabell 304 p. 2014 Simon & Schuster

1. Economic indicators—History 2. Economic indicators—United States—History 3. Economics—Statistical methods—History 4. Economics—United States—History 5. Economics literature
ISBN 1451651201; 9781451651201 (hardcover); 9781451651225 (trade pbk.)
LC 2013-039641

SUMMARY: "Gross national product, balance of trade, unemployment, inflation, and consumer confidence guide our actions, yet few of us know where these numbers come from. . . . In 'The Leading Indicators,' Zachary Karabell tells the . . . history of these indicators. . . . What is urgently needed, Karabell makes clear, is not that we invent a new set of numbers but that we tap into the thriving data revolution, which offers unparalleled access to the information we need." (Publisher's note)

REVIEW: *Kirkus Rev* v82 no1 p260 Ja 1 2014

"The Leading Indicators: A Short History of the Numbers That Rule Our World". "[A] lucid measurement of how the United States is faring. . . . [Zachary] Karabell emphasizes that indices measure what they were designed to measure. All exclude great swatches of life (GDP omits household work, cash transactions and free Internet services such as Google). It's a mistake to use them as mirrors of reality instead of modestly helpful tools. 'Our questions need to be specific,' he writes, 'and answers must be bounded by a sense of how to parse information, but the result should be a welcome liberation from 'the economy' defined by our leading indicators.' Readers of this intelligent introduction to iconic economic indices will agree that Karabell makes an excellent case."

REVIEW: *N Y Times Book Rev* p23 Ap 13 2014 DIANE COYLE

REVIEW: *N Y Times Book Rev* p26 Ap 20 2014

KARALES, MONICA. Controversy and hope. See Cox, J.

KARAS, G. BRIAN.il. Ant and honey bee. See McDonald, M.

KARAS, G. BRIAN.il. The apple orchard riddle. See McNamara, M.

KARAS, G. BRIAN.il. Tap tap boom boom. See Bluemle, E.

KARAS, RAAYA.il. Little Naomi, Little Chick. See Golan, A.

KARNAKOV, BORIS. Exploring quantum mechanics. See Kogan, V.

KARPIN, MICHAEL. Imperfect compromise; a new consensus among Israelis and Palestinians; [by] Michael Karpin xix, 251 p. 2013 Potomac Books

1. Arab-Israeli conflict—1993—Peace 2. Palestinian Arabs—Politics and government—1993- 3. Political science literature 4. Zionism
ISBN 9781612345451 (hardcover : alk. paper); 9781612345468 (electronic)
LC 2012-043913

SUMMARY: In this book, author "Michael Karpin claims that the Arab-Israeli conflict has never been closer to a resolution than it is today. He arguest that Israel's liberal Zionist movement is steadily overtaking the traditional right wing,a nd the Palestinian Authority is proving to be a serious partner for peace by acting reliably and responsibly to create order and combat terrorism." (Middle East Journal)

REVIEW: *Middle East J* v67 no4 p662-6 Aut 2013

"Imperfect Compromise: A New Consensus Among Israelis and Palestinians," "A City Consumed: Urban Commerce, the Cairo Fire, and the Politics of Decolonization in Egypt," and "A Documentary History of Modern Iraq." "Michael Karpin claims that the Arab-Israeli conflict has never been closer to a resolution than it is today. . . . Nancy Reynolds assesses consumption-driven tensions in colonial Egypt, which culminated in the Cairo fire of 1952 that extensively damaged the downtown shopping district. . . . Editor Stacey Holden divides the compilation roughly into decade-length chapters, and provides a brief contextualizing introduction ot each period and document."

KARRAS, RUTH MAZO. Unmarriages; women, men, and sexual unions in the Middle Ages; [by] Ruth Mazo Karras 283 p. 2012 University of Pennsylvania Press

1. Historical literature 2. Man-woman relationships—Europe—History—To 1500 3. Marriage (Canon law)—History—To 1500 4. Marriage—Europe—History—To 1500 5. Mate selection—Europe—History—To 1500 6. Unmarried couples (Canon law)—History—To 1500 7. Unmarried couples—Europe—History—To 1500
ISBN 9780812244205 (alk. paper)
LC 2011-043923

SUMMARY: This book on non-marital heterosexual relationships "draws on a wide range of sources from across Europe and the entire medieval millennium in order to investigate structures and relations that medieval authors and record keepers did not address directly. . . . Author Ruth Mazo Karras pays particular attention to the ways women and men experienced forms of opposite-sex union differently and to the implications for power relations between the genders." (Publisher's note)

REVIEW: *Am Hist Rev* v119 no1 p231-2 F 2014 David d'Avray

"Unmarriages: Women, Men, and Sexual Unions in the Middle Ages". "This lively and readable book sets out to study heterosexual unions outside of marriage in the Middle Ages. . . . The angle and emphasis are new because previous scholars have been primarily interested in the advance of the church's control over marriage, whereas Karras concentrates on unions outside those limits; that is the theory at least, although a lot of the book does in fact go over territory reasonably well-traveled in earlier studies on marriage. . . . Karras nonetheless performs a valuable service by representing it in an accessible form that will be very helpful to anyone approaching the subject for the first time."

REVIEW: *Choice* v50 no3 p560 N 2012 S. A. Throop

REVIEW: *TLS* no5719 p27 N 9 2012 JOANNA L. LAYNESMITH

KARSON, JILL. Should same-sex marriage be legal?; by Bonnie Szumski and Jill Karson; [by] Jill Karson 96 p. 2013 ReferencePoint Press

1. Constitutional law 2. Same-sex marriage—Law and legislation—United States 3. Same-sex marriage—Religious aspects 4. Same-sex parents 5. Social science literature
ISBN 1601524986 (hardback : alk. paper); 9781601524980 (hardback : alk. paper)
LC 2012-034782

SUMMARY: This reference book for young adults by Bonnie Szumski and Jill Karson is part of the "In Controversy" series. Asking the question "should same-sex marriage be legal?", it "is up-to-date as of June 2012 and gets into the thorny topics of religion, child rearing, and constitutional rights." The book "allow[s] room for different viewpoints without pretending each view is equally substantial. . . . Each chapter is followed by a box of quick facts, and each volume includes . . . source notes." (Booklist)

REVIEW: *Booklist* v110 no1 p100-1 S 1 2013 Susan Dove Lempke

"How Does Video Game Violence Affect Society?," "Should Same-Sex Marriage Be Legal?," and "Should Vaccinations for Youth Be Mandatory?" "The title of each book of the 'In Controversy' series asks a question, reflecting its attempt to provide a vigorous discussion of the pros and cons. The books are a little fairer in its coverage than some discussion books, which try to match every point tit-for-tat--these allow room for different viewpoints without pretending each view is equally substantial. . . . Each chapter is followed by a box of quick facts, and each volume includes good source notes. These make for ideal starting points for student researchers, and the interesting material with lots of quotes makes these useful for leisure reading, too."

KASHER, MOSHE. Kasher in the rye; the true tale of a white boy from Oakland who became a drug addict, criminal, mental patient, and then turned 16; [by] Moshe Kasher 300 p. 2012 Grand Central Pub.

1. Deaf parents 2. Drug abuse in literature 3. Jewish comedians—United States—Biography 4. Memoirs
ISBN 9780446584265
LC 2011-027140

SUMMARY: In this "memoir, stand-up comedian [Moshe] Kasher recounts how he and his friends inhaled and stole their way through their teens. . . . His parents—who split up—are both deaf. His mom, who raises him, is Jewish and on welfare . . . His hippieish mother means well but is out of her element as her 12-year-old son falls in with a crowd that guzzles . . . margaritas and smokes pot. . . . Kasher spends his bar mitzvah money on phone sex; then, beginning at 13, he spends time at a mental institution, drug treatment centers, and several different schools. Finally, at 16, he sobers up and becomes a good guy." (Booklist)

REVIEW: *Bookforum* v18 no5 p43 F/Mr 2012 Miriam Katz

"Kasher in the Rye." "In Los Angeles comedian Moshe Kasher's first book, the clever vitriol of the performer's fast-paced stand-up routines meets the vulnerable sincerity of a man who 'gave a f##k very much.' . . . Kasher balances the heavier content of his memoir with playful turns of phrase and continuous, effortless jokes, infusing the prose with an essential dose of levity. His writing reveals a keen ear for rhythm, perhaps the result of a youth spent listening to hip-hop without parental restrictions. . . . Having soaked in the comedian's words for the duration of the book, we come to accept his antagonistic bravado and his tender underbelly, a combination that renders his struggle both bearable and hysterical."

REVIEW: *Booklist* v108 no13 p38 Mr 1 2012 Karen Springen

REVIEW: *Kirkus Rev* v80 no5 p480 Mr 1 2012

REVIEW: *Publ Wkly* v258 no46 p41 N 14 2011

KASSNER, JOSHUA JAMES. Rwanda and the Moral Obligation of Humanitarian Intervention; [by] Joshua James Kassner 248 p. 2012 Columbia Univ Pr

1. Genocide—Prevention 2. Genocide intervention 3. International relations—Moral & ethical aspects 4. Philosophical literature 5. Rwanda—History—Civil War, 1994—Atrocities
ISBN 074864458X; 9780748644582

SUMMARY: This book by Joshua James Kassner "contends that the violation of the basic human rights of the Rwandan Tutsis morally obliged the international community to intervene militarily to stop the genocide. This . . . argument, grounded in basic rights, runs counter to the accepted view on the moral nature of humanitarian intervention. It has profound implications for our understanding of the moral nature of humanitarian military intervention." (Publisher's note)

REVIEW: *Choice* v51 no1 p157 S 2013 P. G. Conway

"Rwanda and the Moral Obligation of Humanitarian Intervention." "[Author Joshua James] Kassner . . . begins with the abysmal failure of the UN, the US, and the international community in general to respond to blatant evidence of genocide in Rwanda in 1994. Recognizing that this was a moral as well as a political failure, he proceeds to call for reform of the normative framework that shapes international relations when genocide occurs. The weakness of the present system is rooted in principles such as sovereignty and non-intervention that limit the capabilities of institutions such as the UN. Kassner presents a remarkably thorough philosophical (but very limited political) analysis before he concludes with prescriptions that are idealistic, albeit reasonable."

KATOUZIAN, HOMA. Iran; A Beginner's Guide; [by] Homa Katouzian 248 p. 2013 Pgw

1. Iran—Economic conditions 2. Iran—History 3. Iran—Politics & government 4. Iran—Social conditions 5. Political science literature
ISBN 178074272X; 9781780742724

SUMMARY: In this book on Iran, author Homa Katouzian "explor[es] how an ancient civilization at a cross road of diverse dynasties and religions grew to become an ethnically, linguistically and culturally rich nation still bound by the Persian tradition. Major political events and key figures are brought to life as centuries of authoritarian and arbitrary rule, chaos and revolution are unraveled and analyzed." (Publisher's note)

REVIEW: *Choice* v51 no7 p1300-1 Mr 2014 N. Entessar

"Iran: A Beginner's Guide." "This highly engaging and informative book is an antidote to the politically skewed writings on Iran. [Homa] Katouzian . . . a respected cultural and economic historian of Iran, places contemporary Iran in its proper historical context. He describes the evolution of the country's history from the ancient times through the present and provides a coherent analysis and a panoramic picture of the cultural, political, and historical dynamics of this complex multinational land. Beginning students of Iran will find this book invaluable. This volume is one of the few comprehensive books on Iran that can also be used as a textbook in a variety of undergraduate courses. . . . Highly recommended."

KATZ, BRIAN P. Distilling ideas. See Starbird, M.

KATZ, DANIEL. The Poetry of Jack Spicer; [by] Daniel Katz 256 p. 2013 Edinburgh University Press

1. American poets 2. Epistolary poetry 3. Poetry (Literary form)—History & criticism 4. Serial poetry 5. Spicer, Jack, 1925-1965

ISBN 0748640983; 9780748640980

SUMMARY: This book by Daniel Katz is a study of Jack Spicer's poetry that pays "particular attention to his two important innovations: the serial poem and the epistle. He illuminates the poet's literary context without dwelling" on Spicer's personal life. Topics include "Spicer's place in the San Francisco poetic world and his relationship to the work of Robert Duncan and Robert Creeley." (Choice)

REVIEW: *Choice* v51 no1 p76-7 S 2013 B. Almon

"The Poetry of Jack Spicer." "[Daniel] Katz . . . has written a concise and intelligent study of Jack Spicer's poetry, paying particular attention to his two important innovations: the serial poem and the epistle. He illuminates the poet's literary context without dwelling excessively on the rather sensational personal life of Spicer, and Katz is an excellent analyst of the words on the page. . . . This perceptive book puts too many of its insights into the footnotes, but the notes are worth reading. This book makes a solid contribution to one's better understanding of modern American poetry."

KATZ, DORI. Looking for strangers; the true story of my hidden wartime childhood; [by] Dori Katz 184 p. 2013 University of Chicago Press

1. Hidden children (Holocaust)—Belgium—Biography 2. Holocaust survivors' writings 3. Jews—Belgium—Biography 4. Memoirs 5. Righteous Gentiles in the Holocaust

ISBN 022605862X; 9780226058627 (cloth : alkaline paper)

LC 2013-003400

SUMMARY: This memoir by Dori Katz recounts how she "survived the Holocaust in Belgium; after Dori's father was deported to Auschwitz, her mother sent Dori, at age three, to hide with a Catholic family in a village near Brussels. More than 40 years later, she returns to find the family that saved her, even while her bitter mother in the U.S. tells her not to go." (Booklist)

REVIEW: *Booklist* v110 no2 p17-8 S 15 2013 Hazel Rochman

"Looking for Strangers: The True Story of My Hidden Wartime Childhood." "Now an American academic and poet, [Dori] Katz survived the Holocaust in Belgium; after Dori's father was deported to Auschwitz, her mother sent Dori, at age three, to hide with a Catholic family in a village near Brussels. . . . Spare, wry, frank about family conflict and loss, this searing memoir captures the immediacy of Dori's childhood experience as well as her present-day guilt and ambivalence. . . . While she expresses wonder at the fact of the rescuers ('the work and effort of strangers to save a child like me'), the commentary never denies the savage history."

KATZ, STEVEN T.ed. Comparative mysticism. See Comparative mysticism

KAUFMAN, AMIE. These broken stars. See Spooner, M.

KAUFMAN, SCOTT. Project Plowshare; the peaceful use of nuclear explosives in Cold War America; [by] Scott Kaufman 312 p. 2013 Cornell University Press

1. Historical literature 2. Nuclear energy—Industrial applications—United States—History 3. Nuclear excavation 4. Nuclear explosions—United States—History

ISBN 9780801451256 (cloth: alk. paper)

LC 2012-009128

SUMMARY: This book, by Scott Kaufman, "presents the story of America's failed attempt to employ the atom in engineering projects on the grandest scale." Particular focus is given to the U.S. nuclear excavation program known as Project Plowshare, which "theoretically would have enabled engineers to redesign geography at will." (American Historical Review)

REVIEW: *Am Hist Rev* v119 no1 p200 F 2014 David A. Burke

"Project Plowshare: The Peaceful Use of Nuclear Explosives in Cold War America". "[Scott] Kaufman's work is impressive as a narrative of the Plowshare program, and essential reading for those interested in nuclear history. It complements Scott Kirsch's 'Proving Grounds: Project Plowshare and the Unrealized Dream of Nuclear Earththmoving' (2005), which Kaufman cites. Kirsch's book contains more technical detail, devoting more space to ancillary Plowshare proposals such as the excavation of the Tennessee-Tombigbee waterway. This is but a minor point, Kaufman's narrative amply delivers Plowshare's bold visions and its ignominious decline; he has produced an elucidating and stimulating work that is most highly recommended to all those interested in the age of atomic utopianism."

REVIEW: *Choice* v51 no3 p496 N 2013 R. M. Ferguson

REVIEW: *J Am Hist* v100 no4 p1278-9 Mr 2014

REVIEW: *Rev Am Hist* v42 no3 p505-12 S 2014 John Krige

KAVANAGH, JULIE. The girl who loved camellias; the

life and legend of Marie Duplessis; [by] Julie Kavanagh 304 p. 2013 Alfred A. Knopf
1. Biographies 2. Courtesans—France—Paris—Biography 3. Courtesans in literature
ISBN 0307270793 (hardcover); 9780307270795 (hardcover)
LC 2012-051103

SUMMARY: This book, by Julie Kavanagh, presents a biography of "Marie Duplessis, the courtesan who inspired Alexandre Dumas fils's novel and play 'La dame aux camélias,' [and] Giuseppe Verdi's opera 'La Traviata.' . . . Drawing on new research, Julie Kavanagh . . . re-creates the short, intense, and passionate life of the tall, pale, slender girl who at thirteen fled her brute of a father and Normandy to go to Paris, where she would become one of the grand courtesans of the 1840s." (Publisher's note)

REVIEW: *N Y Rev Books* v60 no14 p8-12 S 26 2013 Julie Kavanagh

"The Girl Who Loved Camellias: The Life and Legend of Marie Duplessis" and "The Lady of the Camellias." "Liesl Schillinger's translation is notable for the fact that it succeeds in dusting off and invigorating the text without slipping into the contemporary idiom. This story, which sounded a little dated in the previous translations, can now be read with an urgency that seems wholly modern. . . . [Alexandre] Dumas blends factual details with others invented out of whole cloth. . . . [Julie] Kavanagh isn't fooled, but how can anyone resist the persuasive influence of the character depicted by the novelist? In spite of herself, Kavanagh falls under the sway of her elusive subject's charm. To her credit, she makes up for the shortage of unassailable facts by placing Marie's story within the larger setting of French gallantry in the first half of the nineteenth century, and she does so with uncommon precision."

REVIEW: *TLS* no5773 p8 N 22 2013 DAVID COWARD

"The Girl Who Loved Camellias: The Life and Legend of Marie Duplessis" and "The Lady of the Camellias." "Julie Kavanagh moves us briskly through her brief life. At first, she struggles with the lack of information about Alphonsine's early years and fills in the blanks with asides and lecturettes on alcoholism, social conditions, the Latin Quarter and the like. But once Marie appears on the historical radar, Kavanagh gains control of the narrative and paints a sympathetic but not uncritical portrait of the woman behind the legend. . . . [Liesl] Schillinger gives [Alexandre] Dumas's 'timeless, relatable [sic] and fiery story' a twenty-first-century voice which avoids the 'antiquated,' 'quaint' tone of the previous translations that she has perused. The result reads well enough, but . . . it is at times an awkward mixture which may not suit all tastes."

REVIEW: *Women's Review of Books* v31 no1 p24-5 Ja/F 2014 Carole DeSanti

KAWAMI, TRUDY S. Breath of heaven, breath of earth; ancient near eastern art from American collections; [by] Trudy S. Kawami 160 p. 2013 Hallie Ford Museum of Art, Willamette University
1. Art catalogs 2. Art history 3. Art literature 4. Middle Eastern art 5. Private art collections—United States
ISBN 9781930957688 (alk. paper)
LC 2012-947128

SUMMARY: This book by Trudy S. Kawami and John Olbrantz "encompasses the geographic regions of Mesopotamia, Syria and the Levant, and Anatolia and Iran, and explores several broad themes found in the art of the ancient Near East: gods and goddesses, men and women, and both real and supernatural animals. These art objects reveal a wealth of information about the people and cultures that produced them: their mythologies, religious beliefs, concepts of kingship, social structures, and daily lives." (Publisher's note)

REVIEW: *Choice* v51 no8 p1385 Ap 2014 L. Doumato

"Breath of Heaven, Breath of Earth: Ancient Near Eastern Art From American Collections". "This volume by [Trudy S.] Kawami . . . and [John] Olbrantz . . . begins with a general discussion of the emerging archaeologists and collectors of the ancient Near East. . . . Part 2 of this book documents, through individual catalogue entries, each of the 64 objects illustrated in color plates. A bibliography, chronology, and map supplement the texts in this beautiful volume, produced to accompany an exhibition at Willamette University."

KAWASH, SAMIRA. Candy; a century of panic and pleasure; [by] Samira Kawash 416 p. 2013 Faber & Faber
1. COOKING—History 2. Candy—Social aspects 3. Candy—United States—History 4. Candy industry—United States—History 5. Historical literature 6. SOCIAL SCIENCE—Agriculture & Food
ISBN 0865477566; 9780865477568 (hardback)
LC 2013-020053

SUMMARY: This book by Samira Kawash examines "how candy evolved from a luxury good to a cheap, everyday snack. After candy making was revolutionized in the early decades of mass production, it was celebrated as a new kind of food for energy and enjoyment. . . . And yet, food reformers and moral crusaders have always attacked candy, blaming it for poisoning, alcoholism, sexual depravity and fatal disease. " (Publisher's note)

REVIEW: *Bookforum* v20 no3 p16 S-N 2013 MELANIE REHAK

"Candy: A Century of Panic and Pleasure." "As Samira Kawash makes clear in her wonderful 'Candy: A Century of Panic and Pleasure' . . . my unabated passion for sugar isn't representative of the whole story when it comes to these United States.. . . . I've found a kindred spirit in Kawash, who not only shares my feeling but also articulates it with marvelous precision. 'Candy is the one kind of processed food that proclaims its allegiance to the artificial, the processed, the unhealthy,' she says, quite logically. 'This is something I really like about candy; it's honest.'"

REVIEW: *Booklist* v110 no3 p19 O 1 2013 Bridget Thoreson

REVIEW: *Kirkus Rev* v81 no20 p14 O 15 2013

REVIEW: *Publ Wkly* v260 no30 p58-9 Jl 29 2013

KAY, ADAH. Unfree in Palestine. See Abu-Zahra, N.

KAY, KATTY. The Confidence Code. See Shipman, C.

KAZU KIBUISHI.ed. Explorer. See Explorer

KAZZIHA, WALID.ed. Egypt's Tahrir revolution. See Egypt's Tahrir revolution

KEALEY, GREGORY S. Secret service. See Whitaker, R.

KEANE, NIALL.tr. Gadamer. See Di Cesare, D.

KEARNEY, C. PHILIP. Education reform and the limits of policy. See Addonizio, M. F.

KEATON, KELLY. A beautiful evil; [by] Kelly Keaton 287 p. 2012 Simon Pulse
1. Athena (Greek deity)—Fiction 2. Good and evil—Fiction 3. Monsters—Fiction 4. Supernatural—Fiction
ISBN 9781442409279 (hardcover)
LC 2011-016580

SUMMARY: In this "paranormal romance" young adult novel, a "gorgon and her aristocrat vampire boyfriend wage battle against the goddess Athena . . . in New 2--a futuristic, crumbling New Orleans. This follow-up to "Darkness Becomes Her" (2011) again features Ari, [a] . . . tough heroine, schooled in the techniques of bail bondsmen by her foster parents. Picking up where the first left off, Ari hurries to learn all she can about mastering her gorgon power so she can rescue both her father and Violet, one of the ragtag group of misfits with whom she lives in New 2, from Athena's realm. . . . [The book is a] reworking of Greek myth." (Kirkus)

REVIEW: *Booklist* v108 no13 p83 Mr 1 2012 Francisca Goldsmith

REVIEW: *Kirkus Rev* v80 no1 p2441 Ja 1 2012

REVIEW: *SLJ* v58 no5 p107 My 2012 Suzanne Gordon

REVIEW: *Voice of Youth Advocates* v34 no5 p514 D 2011 Gwen Amborski

REVIEW: *Voice of Youth Advocates* v34 no5 p513-4 D 2011 Adrienne Amborski

"A Beautiful Evil." "Continuing the story from the first book in the series, 'Darkness Become Her,' . . . Ari is fighting to break her curse with the help of a group of misfit teens living on the fringe of New 2, which New Orleans is now called. Ari's romance with half-vampire, half-witch Sebastian continues to develop, along with her fight to defeat the deliciously evil Athena. . . . Elements of Greek mythology are woven into this story, which is filled with action and suspense. . . . Readers will anticipate the next book and continue to root for Ari's triumph over Athena, hoping that she breaks the curse that plagues her future. Strong language and sexual tension make this novel appropriate for older teens and adults who enjoy an intriguing mix of paranormal and mythological elements."

KECK, KEVIN.ed. A Warrior's Path. See Ashura, D.

KEEFER, BRADLEY S. Conflicting memories on the "river of death"; the Chickamauga Battlefield and the Spanish-American War, 1863-1933; [by] Bradley S. Keefer xiii, 406 p. 2013 Kent State University Press
1. Battlefields—Conservation and restoration—United States—Case studies 2. Chattanooga, Battle of, Chattanooga, Tenn., 1863 3. Chickamauga, Battle of, Ga., 1863 4. Historic preservation—United States—Case studies 5. Historical literature
ISBN 9781606351260 (hardcover: alk. paper)
LC 2012-013525

SUMMARY: In this book, "Beginning with an account of the fierce fighting in 1863, author Bradley Keefer examines how the veterans of both sides constructed memories of this battle during the three decades leading to the creation of the Chickamauga and Chattanooga National Military Park. By preserving this most prominent battlefield, the former foes created a sacred, commemorative landscape that memorialized mutual valor, sacrifice, and sectional reconciliation." (Publisher's note)

REVIEW: *Am Hist Rev* v118 no5 p1529-30 D 2013 Denise D. Meringolo

REVIEW: *Parameters: U.S. Army War College* v44 no1 p160-2 Spr 2014 Richard J. Norton

REVIEW: *Rev Am Hist* v42 no2 p296-302 Je 2014 Gaines M. Foster

"Memories of War: Visiting Battlegrounds and Bonefields in the Early American Republic" and "Conflicting Memories on the 'River of Death': The Chickamauga Battlefield and the Spanish-American War, 1863-1933." "'Memories of War' and 'Conflicting Memories on the "River of Death"' . . . help historicize current American reverence for battlefields. . . . Despite their differing conceptualizations and time frames, the two books have much in common. Both are well written and solidly researched. They address some of the same issues and put the story of battlefields in larger historic and historiographical contexts, though [author Bradley S.] Keefer does a better job of that than [author Thomas A.] Chambers."

KEELE, CHRISTIE. Minerva Day; 334 p. 2013 CreateSpace Independent Publishing Platform
1. Mental illness—Fiction 2. Missing children—Fiction 3. Mothers—Fiction 4. Murder—Fiction 5. Suspense fiction
ISBN 1492239569; 9781492239567

SUMMARY: In this book, "Minerva Day is at odds with her children, thirty-two year old twins Piper and John. Their father, Henry, has just died, and they think she had something to do with it. . . . In the years following Henry's death, Piper and John also start to suspect that Minerva suffers from severe mental illness that she hasn't revealed; their beliefs are spurred on by her frequent strange, irrational comments, her hoarding tendencies and a seemingly constant lack of empathy." (Kirkus Reviews)

REVIEW: *Kirkus Rev* v82 no1 p356 Ja 1 2014

"Minerva Day". "A suspenseful thriller about mental illness, the nature of the truth and what it means to be family. . . . [Christie] Keele's well-written novel can be a page-turner at times, though it goes beyond being a simple mystery by taking a fascinating look at mental illness and how it is perceived and dealt with, both by its sufferers and those affected. While the plausibility is somewhat questionable that a person suffering from such severe mental illness would not yet be receiving care, Keele adeptly maps out realistic familial relationships, ones muddled by emotional strife but also founded on unconditional love. A well-crafted mystery that explores the challenges of mental illness."

KEEN, RAYMOND. Love Poems for Cannibals; [by] Raymond Keen 166 p. 2013 CreateSpace Independent Publishing Platform
1. Advertising 2. Humorous poetry 3. Poems—Collec-

tions 4. Popular culture 5. Satire
ISBN 1470182688; 9781470182687

SUMMARY: This collection by Raymond Keene presents "poems of war (in this case Vietnam), poems dealing with current spiritual issues (Christianity, Buddhism, spiritual doubt and the soaring-singing human spirit), dysfunctional family relationships and feelings, portraits of great figures in contemporary human history . . . poems that rage against the omnipresence of human hypocrisy and poems that present American/Western civilization under the glaring light of truth." (Publisher's note)

REVIEW: *Kirkus Rev* p30 D 15 2013 supplemet best books 2013

"Love Poems for Cannibals". "[Raymond] Keen's debut poetry collection arrives at the party already a little drunk, a bit raucous and talking a mile a minute, but the longer the night goes on, the more sense it seems to make. After all, he's not out to hurt anyone; he's just trying to figure out where it all went wrong for all of us. With considerable energy and tightly coiled wit, Keen ranges across the political, spiritual and pop-culture landscapes only to find them all a little disorienting and largely bereft. . . . Supporting the politics, satire and social commentary is a more than capable, sometimes beautiful verse that relies heavily on repetition—from anaphora to choral refrains—and startlingly precise imagery . . . for great effect."

REVIEW: *Kirkus Rev* v81 no8 p128 Ap 15 2013

KEENAN, SHEILA. Toilet. See Macaulay, D.

KEHOE, TIM, 1970-2014. Furious Jones and the assassin's secret; [by] Tim Kehoe 336 p. 2014 Simon & Schuster Books for Young Readers

1. Adventure and adventurers—Fiction 2. Assassins—Fiction 3. Authors—Fiction 4. Murder—Fiction 5. Organized crime—Fiction 6. Orphans—Fiction 7. Spies—Fiction 8. Suspense fiction
ISBN 9781442473379 (hc)
LC 2013-009281

SUMMARY: This book follows teenager Furious Jones. "Hoping to reconnect with the only parent he has left, he instead witnesses his father's murder, in a manner uncannily like his mother's. It turns out his mother had been an assassin for the CIA, and Furious' father's books were based on his mother's exploits. Now the family has been targeted by the mob, and it appears the CIA may not have their best interests at heart, either." (Kirkus Reviews)

REVIEW: *Booklist* v110 no17 p53 My 1 2014 Ilene Cooper

REVIEW: *Kirkus Rev* v82 no3 p222 F 1 2014

"Furious Jones and the Assassin's Secret". "Furious has no choice but to go on the run when his grandfather too is murdered: It's clear that Furious is next. Working from clues planted in his father's last book, the 12-year-old heads to the small town in the Midwest where his mother was gunned down, there to begin his quest for revenge. Credibility and questions of morality take a back seat to action as Furious dashes from one plot twist to the next, sparing little time for introspection. Readers caught up in the action will not mind the gaps."

REVIEW: *Publ Wkly* v261 no7 p99 F 17 2014

KEIL, MELISSA. Life in outer space; [by] Melissa Keil 320 p. 2013 published by Peachtree Publishers

1. Friendship—Fiction 2. Gays—Fiction 3. High schools—Fiction 4. Interpersonal relations—Fiction 5. Schools—Fiction 6. Young adult fiction
ISBN 1561457426; 9781561457427
LC 2013-004848

SUMMARY: This book follows "Sam . . . a geek movie-buff with a ragtag group of loser friends. . . . When the super-cool Camilla moves to town, she surprises everyone by choosing to spend time with Sam's group. . . . They become the best of friends, and Sam finds that he's happier and more comfortable in his own skin than ever before. But eventually Sam must admit to himself that he's fallen in love. If he confesses his true feelings to Camilla, will everything change again?" (Publisher's note)

REVIEW: *Horn Book Magazine* v89 no6 p97 N/D 2013 ELISSA GERSHOWITZ

"Life in Outer Space." "The further Sam tiptoes out of his comfort zone, the more he comes into his own, realizing that his and Camilla's friendship is a two-way street and not just infatuation on his part (though it is that, too). Camilla is like a John Green girl with slightly less angst; her pedestal is a bit lower than a Katherine, an Alaska, or a Margo Roth Spiegelman, so her actions seem a little more human. There's also more to the book than the will-they-or-won't-they of Sam and Camilla. The supporting characters--Mike especially--are multifaceted and real. Snappy banter and fish-out-of-water situations combine with touching moments to create an entertaining and diverting read."

REVIEW: *Kirkus Rev* v81 no14 p254 Jl 15 2013

REVIEW: *Voice of Youth Advocates* v36 no4 p64 O 2013 Johanna Nation-Vallee

KELLER, JUDITH.ed. Japan's modern divide. See Japan's modern divide

KELLERMAN, JONATHAN. Killer; an Alex Delaware novel; [by] Jonathan Kellerman 335 p. 2014 Ballantine Books

1. Delaware, Alex (Fictitious character)—Fiction 2. Detective & mystery stories 3. Mentally ill offenders—Fiction 4. Police—California—Los Angeles—Fiction 5. Psychologists—Fiction 6. Psychopaths—Fiction 7. Serial murders—Fiction 8. Sturgis, Milo (Fictitious character)—Fiction
ISBN 9780345505750 (hardback)
LC 2013-045834

SUMMARY: This thriller novel by Jonathan Kellerman is an "L.A. noir portrayal of the darkest impulses of human nature carried to shocking extremes. The City of Angels has more than its share of psychopaths, and no one recognizes that more acutely than the brilliant psychologist and police consultant Dr. Alex Delaware. Then, at the behest of the court, he becomes embroiled in a bizarre child custody dispute." (Publisher's note)

REVIEW: *Booklist* v110 no12 p33-4 F 15 2014 Christine Tran

"Killer." "Psychologist Alex Delaware's custody consultations can get ugly, but Alex enters uncharted territory when his best friend, LAPD Lieutenant Milo Sturgis, warns him that there's a contract out on Alex's life. . . . As usual, the rapport between Alex and Milo is a show-stealer, and longtime fans--some of whom may have noted an unevenness in the series recently--will love the well-executed flashbacks to Alex's professional past. This twenty-ninth entry reads like a straightforward thriller until the appropriately insane ending twist."

KELLOGG, RONALD T. The making of the mind; the neuroscience of human nature; [by] Ronald T. Kellogg 293 p. 2013 Prometheus Books

1. Brain—Physiology 2. Cognitive neuroscience 3. Human behavior 4. Neuropsychology 5. Scientific literature

ISBN 9781616147334 (pbk.)

LC 2013-010071

SUMMARY: In this book, Ronald T. Kellogg "explores in detail five distinctive parts of human cognition. These are the executive functions of working memory; a social intelligence . . . a capacity for symbolic thought and language; an inner voice that interprets conscious experiences by making causal inferences; and a means for mental time travel to past events and imagined futures. He argues that it is the interaction of these five components that results in our uniquely human mind." (Publisher's note)

REVIEW: *Choice* v51 no6 p1031-2 F 2014 C. L. Iwe

"The Making of the Mind: The Neuroscience of Human Nature." "How is the human mind so fundamentally distinctive as compared to nonhuman animals? [Ronald T.] Kellogg . . . proposes to answer this mystery of 'human revolution' via his 'ensemble hypothesis.' The author suggests that research in cognitive social neuroscience demonstrates that human cognition is made up of five component parts: executive working memory, social intelligence, language, an inner interpreter of consciousness, and mental time travel. . . . 'The Making of the Mind' offers an interesting theory about the origin and evolution of the human mind, accessible to a wide audience."

KELLOGG, STEVEN, 1941-.il. Snowflakes fall. See Mac Lachlan, P.

KELLY, CATRIONA. St Petersburg; shadows of the past; [by] Catriona Kelly 488 p. 2013 Yale University Press

1. Historical literature 2. Saint Petersburg (Russia)—Social conditions 3. Saint Petersburg (Russia)—Social life & customs

ISBN 0300169183; 9780300169188 (alk. paper)

LC 2013-018605

SUMMARY: In this book, author Catriona Kelly "shows how creative engagement with the past has always been fundamental to St. Petersburg's residents. Weaving together oral history, personal observation, literary and artistic texts, journalism, and archival materials, she traces the . . . feelings of anxiety and pride that were inspired by living in the city, both when it was socialist Leningrad, and now." (Publisher's note)

REVIEW: *Booklist* v110 no9/10 p38 Ja 1 2014 Jay Freeman

"St. Petersburg: Shadows of the Past." "In this excellent examination of the history, art, and everyday life of its citizens, she paints a much more nuanced and interesting portrait of this city on the Baltic. . . . [Catriona] . Kelly pays ample tribute to the beauty and artistic glitter, but she also covers a city plagued by a host of typical urban problems, including the squalor of the poorer neighborhoods. This is a well-written and honest look at a large, fascinating, and rapidly evolving city."

REVIEW: *Libr J* v139 no2 p84 F 1 2014 Amy Lewontin

KELLY, DEBRA.ed. Barbara Wright. See Barbara Wright

KELLY, GAVIN.ed. Two Romes: Rome and Constantinople in Late Antiquity. See Two Romes: Rome and Constantinople in Late Antiquity

KELLY, JILL. Fog of dead souls; a thriller; [by] Jill Kelly 272 p. 2014 Skyhorse Publishing

1. FICTION—Mystery & Detective—General 2. FICTION—Psychological 3. FICTION—Romance—Suspense 4. Life change events—Fiction 5. Older women—Fiction 6. Rape victims—Fiction

ISBN 9781628737721 (hardback)

LC 2013-038261

SUMMARY: This book "presents the story of a woman whose path in life takes an unexpected and vicious turn when she becomes the victim of a brutal crime. Ellie McKay . . . awakens to find. . . herself beaten and raped by an unknown assailant, and survival suddenly becomes her primary goal in life. At first, Ellie thinks she's trying to survive only the emotional and physical damage she's suffered, but soon, it becomes apparent that the psychopath who perpetrated the assault is still tracking her." (Kirkus Reviews)

REVIEW: *Kirkus Rev* v82 no3 p333 F 1 2014

"Fog of Dead Souls". "[Jill] Kelly's heroine is a refreshing 60-year-old woman portrayed as an intelligent, desirable individual, and the men in Ellie's life are also attractive, mature men; this age bracket is sorely neglected in much of modern literature. Although the title is fairly enigmatic, and there's the occasional clumsy passage, this is a solid book. Told mostly in alternating chapters that trace the genesis of the crime and Ellie's flight to New Mexico, as well as her present-day marriage to Al, readers will find Kelly's work engaging. Fresh, compelling writing throughout, although the ending seems a bit hurried and contrived."

REVIEW: *Publ Wkly* v261 no1 p37 Ja 6 2014

KELLY, MARK E., 1964-. Mousetronaut; based on a (partially) true story; [by] Mark E. Kelly 40 p. 2012 Simon & Schuster Books for Young Readers

1. Astronauts—Fiction 2. Astronauts—Juvenile fiction 3. Mice—Fiction 4. Mice—Juvenile fiction 5. Picture books for children 6. Space shuttles—Fiction 7. Space shuttles—Juvenile fiction

ISBN 1442458240; 9781442458246 (hardcover : alk. paper); 9781442458321 (ebook)

LC 2012-008497

SUMMARY: In this children's picture book, U.S. astronaut Mark Kelly "tells the story of Meteor, a lightly anthropomorphized rodent who turns his tininess into an advantage when an important key gets stuck in a crack between two monitors." The story is based on Kelly's experience "on his first Endeavor flight, [where] the research mice on board would have nothing to do with weightlessness and clung to the mesh of their cage for the entire mission," except for one mouse. (Publishers Weekly)

REVIEW: *Bull Cent Child Books* v66 no4 p199-200 D 2012 J. H.

"Moustronaut: Based on a (Partially) True Story." "Smaller than the other experimental mice chosen to accompany a group of astronauts on a space shuttle mission, little Meteor is nonetheless confident and excited to be going on such a journey. . . . The plot is pretty minimal, and there's an uneasy combination of anthropomorphism and utilitarianism in the treatment of the space-borne mice. Still, the idea of a tiny mouse astronaut will appeal to many kids, . . . and [C. F.] Payne's mixed media art excels at both providing a detailed look at the shuttle's interior and the astronauts while capitalizing on the cute factor of Meteor as fuzzy little space traveler."

REVIEW: *Kirkus Rev* v80 no18 p295 S 15 2012

REVIEW: *Publ Wkly* v259 no39 p74-5 S 24 2012

REVIEW: *SLJ* v58 no10 p99-100 O 2012 Sara Lissa Paulson

KELLY, MARY C. Ireland's great famine in Irish-American history; [by] Mary C. Kelly 288 p. 2013 Rowman & Littlefield

1. Historical literature 2. Irish—United States—History—19th century

ISBN 9781442226074 (cloth: alk. paper)

LC 2013-031223

SUMMARY: This book by Mary C. Kelly "track[s] Ireland's Great Famine within America's immigrant history, and . . . consider[s] the impact of the Famine on Irish ethnic identity between the mid-1800s and the end of the twentieth century. Moving beyond traditional emphases on Irish-American cornerstones such as church, party, and education, the book maps the Famine's legacy over a century and a half of settlement and assimilation." (Publisher's note)

REVIEW: *Choice* v51 no9 p1662 My 2014 J. M. O'Leary

"Ireland's Great Famine in Irish-American History: Enshrining a Fateful Memory". "[Mary C. Kelly] recounts with impressive detail the mind-set of the Irish American community concerning an Gorta Mór (the Great Hunger) and its linkages to ethnic identity, sociocultural constructions of victimhood, and the difficult process of remembering and internalizing such a tragic event. . . . Kelly shows the complex evolution associated with public memory and trauma and the ways political and cultural rhetoric framed this debate. Meticulously researched, the book succeeds in capturing a fresh perspective on a complicated topic."

KELLY, NATALY. Found in translation; how language shapes our lives and transforms the world; [by] Nataly Kelly p. cm. 2012 Perigee

1. Language & languages 2. Social science literature 3. Sociolinguistics 4. Translating and interpreting—Social aspects 5. Translators

ISBN 9780399537974

LC 2012-022942

SUMMARY: It was the authors' intent to "demonstrate demonstrate the crucial role that translation plays in health care, politics, business, religion, sports, technology, and even affairs of the heart. . . . The authors demonstrate the importance of understanding a culture as well as language in their accounts of simultaneous translation and attempts to preserve meaning when translations are themselves translated." (Publishers Weekly)

REVIEW: *Publ Wkly* v259 no35 p67 Ag 27 2012

REVIEW: *TLS* no5740 p25 Ap 5 2013 ROBERT GILLAN

"Found in Translation: How Language Shapes Our Lives and Transforms The World." "The text is pitched squarely at the layman and the authors' support sometimes feels a little overbearing, as they encourage you to 'think about it' or offer the comforting assurance that what they are telling you 'isn't so difficult to understand'. Yet at the same time the prose itself is occasionally rather imprecise. . . . The authors have chosen their material and their style to appeal to a broad audience, and they have put together a collection of anecdotes about working in the translation industry that are interesting, even if these stories do not develop conclusively into much more than the sum of their parts."

KELLY, SUSAN. Jimmy the joey; the true story of an amazing koala rescue; [by] Susan Kelly 32 p. 2013 National Geographic

1. Children's literature 2. Koala—Infancy—Juvenile literature 3. Koala—Juvenile literature 4. Veterinary hospitals—Australia—Juvenile literature 5. Wildlife rescue—Australia—Juvenile literature

ISBN 9781426313714 (hardcover : alkaline paper); 9781426313721 (library edition : alkaline paper)

LC 2012-039894

SUMMARY: Written by Deborah Lee Rose and Susan Kelly, with photographs by Kelly, this "picture book for ages 4 to 8 is a compelling and uplifting true story, with a sweet message about coping with loss that draws attention to an important and threatened wild animal. Jimmy is an adorable baby koala whose tender tale is sure to strike at the heartstrings of every animal lover." (Publisher's note)

REVIEW: *Booklist* v109 no21 p61 Jl 1 2013 Carolyn Phelan

REVIEW: *Bull Cent Child Books* v67 no1 p49-50 S 2013 J. H.

"Jimmy the Joey: The True Story of an Amazing Koala Rescue." "Rescued from the side of the road, a six-month-old koala is taken via Koala Ambulance to Port Macquarie Koala Hospital. Here he is placed in the home of a trained volunteer who names him Jimmy and who cares for him until he is old enough to join the other, bigger koalas in the hospital's tree yard. . . . The photos are clear and attractive, and they're generally well-positioned against the muted oranges, blues, greens, and tans of the backgrounds (inspired by the multicolored hues of eucalyptus bark). Unfortunately, readers will have to settle for descriptions rather than photos of newborn joeys and of some of the more comical moments mentioned in the text. . ."

REVIEW: *Kirkus Rev* v81 no2 p100-1 Je 1 2013

REVIEW: *Publ Wkly* v260 no16 p52 Ap 22 2013

REVIEW: *SLJ* v59 no7 p112 Jl 2013 Carol Goldman

KELLY, SUSAN.il. Jimmy the joey. See Kelly, S.

KELMAN, ARI. A misplaced massacre; struggling over the memory of Sand Creek; [by] Ari Kelman 384 p. 2012 Harvard University Press

1. Cheyenne Indians—Wars, 1864 2. Historical litera-

ture 3. Sand Creek Massacre, Colo., 1864
ISBN 9780674045859 (alk. paper)
LC 2012-012122

SUMMARY: Written by Ari Kelman, "'A Misplaced Massacre' examines the ways in which generations of Americans have struggled to come to terms with the meaning of both the attack and its aftermath, most publicly at the 2007 opening of the Sand Creek Massacre National Historic Site. . . . Native Americans, Colorado ranchers, scholars, Park Service employees, and politicians alternately argued and allied . . . around the question of whether the nation's crimes . . . should be memorialized." (Publisher's note)

REVIEW: *Am Hist Rev* v118 no5 p1529-30 D 2013 Denise D. Meringolo

REVIEW: *Choice* v50 no11 p2086 Jl 2013 M. L. Tate

REVIEW: *J Am Hist* v100 no3 p798-800 D 2013 Michael A. Elliott

REVIEW: *Kirkus Rev* v80 no22 p177 N 15 2012

REVIEW: *Rev Am Hist* v42 no2 p273-8 Je 2014 Andrew Denson

"A Misplaced Massacre: Struggling Over the Memory of Sand Creek." "In 'A Misplaced Massacre,' historian Ari Kelman examines the public memory of Sand Creek, focusing on the campaign by the National Park Service (NPS) to create a historic site interpreting the event. . . . Rather than proceed chronologically, the study moves around in time, while always eventually returning to the campaign to develop a historic site at Sand Creek. This approach may prove somewhat confusing for readers who are not well-versed in Western and Native American history, and, at times, the flashbacks seem to arrive somewhat randomly. At its most effective, however, this technique provides Kelman with an elegant method for showing how the past intrudes upon the present."

REVIEW: *TLS* no5745 p5 My 10 2013 MICK GIDLEY

KELSALL, TIM. Business, politics, and the state in Africa; challenging the orthodoxies on growth and transformation; [by] Tim Kelsall ix, 190 p. 2013 Zed Books

1. Africa—Economic conditions 2. Economic development—Africa 3. Economic development—Sociological aspects 4. Economics literature
ISBN 178032331X (hb); 1780324219 (pb); 9781780323312 (hb); 9781780324210 (pb)
LC 2012-285631

SUMMARY: Written by Tim Kelsall, "This book goes behind the headlines to examine the conditions necessary not just for growth in Africa but for a wider business and economic transformation. . . . Drawing on a variety of timely case studies--including Rwanda, Ethiopia, Tanzania and Ghana--this provocative book provides a radical new theory of the political and institutional conditions required for pro-poor growth in Africa." (Publisher's note)

REVIEW: *Choice* v51 no2 p317 O 2013 J. E. Weaver

"Business, Politics, and the State in Africa: Challenging the Orthodoxies on Growth and Economics." "The government's role in Africa's development is the primary focus of this volume, which examines government failure (rent-seeking behavior) and market failure (coordination problems and technological change), mainly in sub-Saharan Africa. [Author Tim] Kelsall, an African affairs specialist, presents a model that distinguishes between short- and long-term horizons and low and high levels of centralization of economic rent management. . . . Case studies provide a closer analysis of policies and performance in Tanzania, Ghana, Ethiopia, and Rwanda."

KELSEY, HARRY. Philip of Spain, King of England; The Forgotten Sovereign; [by] Harry Kelsey 2011 Palgrave Macmillan

1. Biographies 2. Great Britain—Foreign relations—16th century 3. Great Britain—Foreign relations—Spain 4. Historical literature 5. Mary I, Queen of England, 1516-1558 6. Philip II, King of Spain, 1527-1598 7. Spain—Foreign relations—1516-1700
ISBN 1848857160; 9781848857162

SUMMARY: This book "provides ceremonial context for Philip's time in England, and attempts to recover him as an active English sovereign." (London Review of Books) "Harry Kelsey uncovers Philip's life - from his childhood and education in Spain, to his marriage to Mary and the political maneuverings involved in the marriage contract, to the tumultuous aftermath of Mary's death, which ultimately led to hostile relations between Queen Elizabeth and Philip, culminating in the Armada. Focusing especially on the period of Philip's marriage to Mary, Kelsey shows that Philip was, in fact, an active King of England who took a keen interest in the rule of his wife's kingdom." (Publisher's note)

REVIEW: *London Rev Books* v34 no7 p23-4 Ap 5 2012 Thomas Penn

"Philip of Spain, King of England: The Forgotten Sovereign." "In his brisk and entertaining study, Harry Kelsey demonstrates thorough knowledge of the Spanish sources, provides ceremonial context for Philip's time in England, and attempts to recover him as an active English sovereign, but he doesn't look in detail at Philip's efforts to further Habsburg objectives in an increasingly crisis-ridden England or explore the conflict of interest at the heart of his kingship, as a consort who was half of a dual monarchy. . . . Unaccountably, Kelsey devotes barely a couple of lines to Philip's role in the persecutions, although other recent studies, notably Eamon Duffy's 'Fires of Faith' (2009) and Edwards's biography of Mary, have revealed it to be substantial, if not central."

REVIEW: *TLS* no5691 p10 Ap 27 2012 Henry Kamen

"Mary I: England's Catholic Queen." "John Edwards's decision to devote yet another biography to the subject is therefore nothing short of valiant. . . . His most important departure from previous biographies is in attempting to give more substance to Philip of Spain's role as husband and co-ruler, and placing Mary's reign within some of its international context. . . . The book is in some respects the fullest available survey of Mary. Edwards has produced very much a scholar's work, densely packed with facts, names and explanations that may overwhelm the general reader. . . . This is a wide-ranging and deeply researched work of scholarship, directed at professional historians, and offering more of a European perspective than is generally found in Lives of English figures."

KELTON, PHIL. Power Shift; The New No-Stress, No-Hassle Way to Get Your Best New-Car Deal—Every Time!; [by] Phil Kelton 200 p. 2013 Requisite Press

1. Automobile dealers 2. Automobile industry 3. Automobiles—Purchasing 4. Do-it-yourself literature 5.

Selling—Automobiles
ISBN 1939725003; 9781939725004

SUMMARY: This book by Phil Kelton presents "a step-by-step approach to using Internet research and sealed email bids to get the lowest prices on new vehicles from auto dealer. . . . The basic idea is to find the bottom-line, "out-the-door" price for the car of one's choice by researching credible sources, such as Consumer Reports and Edmunds.com, and then emailing seven to 10 dealers and asking each for a nonnegotiable, sealed bid." (Kirkus Reviews)

REVIEW: *Kirkus Rev* v82 no2 p180 Ja 15 2014

"Power Shift: The New No-Stress, No-Hassle Way to Get Your Best New-Car Deal—Every Time!". "Using detailed instructions, including sample email templates, Kelton gives readers everything they need to know to try his method. He also offers solid tips on watching out for tricks of the trade, such as unnecessary rustproofing, and clearly explains the minutiae of the business, including dealer holdbacks and manufacturers' cash incentives. . . . Given the vagaries of human nature—and especially of car dealers'—will his system work? Readers may find that it's worth a try, given the high cost and hassle of buying a new car the traditional way. . . . A clearly written guide, with many useful references, that could recoup its cost many times over."

KEMP, ALLAN. The Black Phoenix; [by] Allan Kemp 316 p. 2013 Createspace Independent Pub

1. Fantasy fiction 2. Magic—Fiction 3. Vampires—Fiction 4. Werewolves—Fiction 5. Wizards—Fiction
ISBN 149299667X; 9781492996675

SUMMARY: This book "takes place in a world ruled by supernatural beings threatened by a looming horde of lost souls in the heart of Atlanta. Seven years after the 'supernaturals' took the world from the humans, Mutt, a half-breed—his mother's a witch, his father a werewolf—seems to prefer solitude. But he finds himself party to an imminent war between the surviving humans . . . and the vampires, led by the queen, who's upset that Mutt refused an offer to join her clan." (Kirkus Reviews)

REVIEW: *Kirkus Rev* v82 no3 p42 F 1 2014

"The Black Phoenix". "The devastated lands—half the human population is gone—feel dystopian, and [Allan] Kemp meticulously establishes this new world with searing details. . . . Kemp fills his book with intense scenes, like the gripping battle with Mutt and his pseudo-girlfriend Celeste, and plenty of mystery, including the ominous and recurring phrase 'The Black Phoenix shall rise again.' There's humor too; it's easy to forget that Ed's a cat, until he laps up his vodka. Some questions in the story are left unanswered, though a sequel should resolve those issues. An exquisitely detailed, fantastic realm of wizards, witches, vampires and werecreatures that's begging for a series."

REVIEW: *Kirkus Rev* v82 no2 p362 Ja 15 2014

"The Black Phoenix". "The devastated lands—half the human population is gone—feel dystopian, and [Allan] Kemp meticulously establishes this new world with searing details. . . . Kemp fills his book with intense scenes, like the gripping battle with Mutt and his pseudo-girlfriend Celeste, and plenty of mystery, including the ominous and recurring phrase 'The Black Phoenix shall rise again.' There's humor too; it's easy to forget that Ed's a cat, until he laps up his vodka. Some questions in the story are left unanswered, though a sequel should resolve those issues. An exquisitely detailed, fantastic realm of wizards, witches, vampires and werecreatures that's begging for a series."

KEMP, MARTIN. The Chapel of Trinity College Oxford; 1691-94: 'a Beautiful Magnificent Structure'; [by] Martin Kemp 88 p. 2014 Antique Collectors Club Ltd

1. College buildings—Design & construction 2. College buildings—England 3. College chapels 4. Historical literature 5. University of Oxford
ISBN 1857598245; 9781857598247

SUMMARY: In this book, art historian Martin Kemp "pays tribute to the masterpiece of art and architecture within his own college's walls that has fascinated him over the years. He argues that Ralph Bathurst, the 16th-century President of the College, is the effective 'author' of the Chapel." (Publisher's note)

REVIEW: *TLS* no5793 p9 Ap 11 2014 RUTH SCURR

"The Chapel of Trinity College Oxford." "Martin Kemp's book evokes and explains the excitement surrounding a remarkable college building. Central to the story is Ralph Bathurst, a medically trained theologian and member of the Royal Society, ordained a priest in 1644 and President of Trinity from 1664 until his death in 1704. Under Bathurst, the College responded to the decline in student numbers during the Civil War with a series of building projects. . . . The new place of worship was both the climax of this period of expansion and a complex symbol of the intellectual concerns of its creator. . . . In reproducing examples of the fund-raising letters Bathurst wrote in the 1690s, Kemp notes the similarities and contrasts with modem-day equivalents."

KENAH, KATHARINE. Ferry tail; [by] Katharine Kenah 32 p. 2014 Sleeping Bear Press

1. Animal stories 2. Cats—Fiction 3. Dogs—Fiction 4. Ferries—Fiction 5. Human-animal relationships—Fiction
ISBN 1585368296; 9781585368297
LC 2013-024887

SUMMARY: In this book, written by Katharine Kenah and illustrated by Nicole Wong, "Walter the ferry dog loved to greet cars as they came on board each morning. . . . Cupcake the Cat was just about the only thing Walter disliked about being a ferry dog. One rainy day . . . [h]e decided it was time to leave the ferry! Once on land he ran, and ran, and ran. . . . Wondering who would do his jobs on the ferry, he felt a familiar poke from a familiar paw. Would Cupcake help him get back to ferry?" (Publisher's note)

REVIEW: *Booklist* v110 no13 p76 Mr 1 2014 Carolyn Phelan

REVIEW: *Kirkus Rev* v82 no4 p207 F 15 2014

"Ferry Tail". "When Walter leaves the ship and tries life on the island, he finds he isn't welcomed there by anyone, and life on land is strange and unsatisfying for a canine used to life onboard. Cupcake the cat shows up to retrieve the lost dog, and they return to the ferryboat together as friends in a satisfying conclusion. Although the plot is predictable, the text conveys genuine emotion in Walter's classic search for his true home. A large trim size and appealing illustrations in a variety of formats bring Walter's antics and the island community to life. Though a dog on the loose on a ferryboat is truly a fairy tale, Walter's story is a tale well-told."

REVIEW: *SLJ* v60 no4 p125 Ap 2014 Tanya Boudreau

KENEALLY, THOMAS, 1935-. The Daughters of Mars; [by] Thomas Keneally 544 p. 2013 Pocket Books
1. Historical fiction 2. Hospitals 3. Nurses—Fiction 4. Sisters—Fiction 5. World War, 1914-1918—Fiction
ISBN 1476734615 (hardcover); 9781476734613 (hardcover)
LC 2012-427270

SUMMARY: In this book by Thomas Keneally, "[d]uring World War I, sisters Naomi and Sally Durance leave Australia to serve as nurses, first at Gallipoli and then on the western front, where their training hardly prepares them for the carnage they witness. In a French hospital, they both have the chance at love they never thought they'd take." (Library Journal)

REVIEW: *Booklist* v109 no16 p30 Ap 15 2013 Brad Hooper

REVIEW: *Booklist* v109 no15 p4 Ap 1 2013

REVIEW: *Kirkus Rev* v81 no6 p315 Mr 15 2013

REVIEW: *Libr J* v138 no11 p82 Je 15 2013 Christine DeZelar-Tiedman

REVIEW: *N Y Times Book Rev* p15 Ag 18 2013 ALAN RIDING

REVIEW: *Publ Wkly* v260 no26 p64 Jl 1 2013

REVIEW: *TLS* no5750 p30-1 Je 14 2013 PETER McDONALD

"The Daughters of Mars." "[The book] has plenty of acute observation, strongly realized detail and a courageous geographical sweep. Indeed, there is a sense in which the novel is all sweep and swoosh--with its long roster of characters, painstaking recreations of several different theatres of war, and a constant awareness of the shadows of history. . . . The sisters at the centre of things are not particularly characters, nor especially well differentiated from one another; Thomas Keneally gives them a guilty secret to share early on and this becomes a dully recurring motif, brought in when-ever the book starts to run low on psychological fuel. . . . But none of this, colourfully painted as it is, sees 'The Daughters of Mars' fully engage with the history its stories draw on."

THE KENNAN DIARIES; 768 p. 2014 W.W. Norton & Company
1. Ambassadors—United States—Diaries 2. Cold War 3. Diary (Literary form) 4. Diplomats—United States—Diaries 5. Historians—United States—Diaries 6. World politics—1945-1989
ISBN 0393073270; 9780393073270 (hardcover)
LC 2013-045016

SUMMARY: This collection of diary entries, by American diplomat George F. Kennan and edited by Frank Costigliola, "reveal, among other things, that [Kennan] was anything but satisfied by the outward-appearing success of his life and career(s). . . . If complaint is one characteristic of the entries, melancholy is another as Kennan confesses unhappiness with many things, from sexuality to American society and democracy to the U.S. Department of State." (Booklist)

REVIEW: *Booklist* v110 no9/10 p26 Ja 1 2014 Gilbert Taylor

"The Kennan Diaries." "They reveal, among other things, that he was anything but satisfied by the outward-appearing success of his life and career(s);a querulous tone about the courses of both permeates his private writing. If complaint is one characteristic of the entries, melancholy is another as [George Frost] Kennan confesses unhappiness with many things, from sexuality to American society and democracy to the U.S. Department of State. . . . Readers familiar with Kennan's place in the hardheaded arena of international relations may be surprised to meet the fragile and often despairing personality in these diaries but will respect the searching honesty with which he examined his experiences of witnessing the turbulent twentieth century."

REVIEW: *Harper's Magazine* v328 no1967 p86-9 Ap 2014 Andrew J. Bacevich

REVIEW: *Kirkus Rev* v82 no1 p72 Ja 1 2014

"The Kennan Diaries". " One of 20th-century America's most significant diplomats offers a window into his inner life and private concerns, fears and dreams. . . . [Frank] Costigliola . . . has selected the most representative and revealing passages for this dauntingly thick but eminently readable volume. In this age of ubiquitous social networking and oversharing, it seems remarkable that [George Frost] Kennan could write so much, about so many topics, without being dull or self-absorbed, but nearly every entry contains a perspicacious observation or insight. His dry wit is evident from the earliest years."

REVIEW: *Libr J* v138 no15 p48 S 15 2013

REVIEW: *Libr J* v139 no6 p104 Ap 1 2014 Robert Nardini

REVIEW: *N Y Rev Books* v61 no4 p18-20 Mr 6 2014 Michael Ignatieff

REVIEW: *N Y Times Book Rev* p26 Mr 2 2014

REVIEW: *N Y Times Book Rev* p10-1 F 23 2014 FAREED ZAKARIA

REVIEW: *New Repub* v244 no26 p50-5 Ap 21 2014 David Greenberg

REVIEW: *Publ Wkly* v260 no48 p44 N 25 2013

KENNEDY, A. L. All the rage; stories; [by] A. L. Kennedy 224 p. 2014 New Harvest
1. Adultery—Fiction 2. Desire 3. Human sexuality—Fiction 4. Love stories 5. Short stories—Collections
ISBN 0544307046; 9780544307049 (hardback)
LC 2013-050974

SUMMARY: This book is A. L. Kennedy's "new collection, a luscious feast of language that encompasses real estate and forlorn pets, adolescents and sixty-somethings, weekly liaisons and obsessive affairs, 'certain types of threat and the odder edges of sweet things.' The women and men in these dozen stories search for love, solace, and a clear glimpse of what their lives have become." (Publisher's note)

REVIEW: *Booklist* v110 no15 p19 Ap 1 2014 Carol Haggas

REVIEW: *Kirkus Rev* v82 no7 p273 Ap 1 2014

REVIEW: *N Y Times Book Rev* p17 Jl 27 2014 MOLLY YOUNG

REVIEW: *New Statesman* v143 no5203 p51 Mr 28 2014 Philip Maughan

REVIEW: *New Yorker* v90 no15 p79-1 Je 2 2014

"All the Rage." "This short-story collection begins with a woman trying to imagine her aging lover's earliest kiss. . . . Kennedy is concerned with the fantasies that sustain and harm relationships; her characters are tormented by 'the sting of possibility,' though some do manage to find momentary satisfaction. The stories read as a kind of dialogue between writer and subject, cool narration cut through with first-person outbursts. The effect is one of sympathetic intimacy, as if Kennedy had pressed close enough to her characters to feel their breath hot against her ear."

REVIEW: *TLS* no5788 p20 Mr 7 2014 SHEENA JOUGHIN

"All the Rage." "This collection of stories is described as 'a dozen ways of looking at love,' which is . . . disingenuous. [Author A. L.] Kennedy's characters are given plenty of words and they love to use them to talk to themselves (in italics) . . . , but they lack emotional conviction. All of them are burdened with a sense that they are essentially inauthentic. . . . Kennedy is not concerned with what happens to people in particular states or situations. What is said (to oneself or out loud) is paramount here, yet all speech is solipsistic and mostly unconvincing. . . . Everyone in this book is pinned to the page, stripped of the business of living and most emphatically of love. As its bleak landscape unfolds, we are aware of the pleasure Kennedy takes in her craft."

KENNEDY, A. L. On writing; [by] A. L. Kennedy 357 p. 2013 Jonathan Cape

1. Authorship 2. Blogs 3. Creative nonfiction 4. English language—Written English 5. Writing
ISBN 9780224096973
LC 2013-376295

SUMMARY: This book by A. L. Kennedy is based on her blog written for the "Guardian." "We follow her during a three-year period when she finished one collection of stories and started another, and wrote a novel in between." Also included are "essays on character, voice, writers' workshops and writers' health ." (Publisher's note)

REVIEW: *TLS* no5765 p26 S 27 2013 KAMILA SHAMSIE

"On Writing." "A. L. Kennedy's entertaining and thoughtful 'On Writing' could well have been subtitled 'forms of short non-fiction'. . . . Reading through the entries, it is impossible not to notice the way Kennedy modulates her voice and paragraphs to fit the form in which she is working. The blog posts are conversational and therefore slightly meandering. . . . They are best appreciated over a period of time, dipped in and out of, rather than swallowed in one sitting. . . . The latter part of the book provides us with . . . more substantive forms--essays and lectures-edited-for-the-page."

KENNEDY, CAROLINE, 1944-. How the English Establishment Framed Stephen Ward. See Knightley, P.

KENNEDY, CHARLES H. Government and politics in South Asia. See Kapur, A.

KENNEDY, KOSTYA. Pete Rose; An American Dilemma; [by] Kostya Kennedy 352 p. 2014 Time Home Entertainment Inc.

1. Baseball players 2. Biography (Literary form) 3. Major League Baseball (Organization) 4. National Baseball Hall of Fame & Museum 5. Rose, Pete, 1941- 6. Sports betting 7. Sports literature
ISBN 1618930966; 9781618930965
LC 2013-949234

SUMMARY: This book on former professional baseball player Pete Rose presents a "consideration of Rose's place in baseball history 25 years after his ban from Major League Baseball (MLB) and from Hall of Fame consideration because he bet on baseball games. The narrative shifts between Rose's past—with anecdotes from family, friends, and former teammates—to his present life working the autograph circuit and filming a reality show with his young fiancée." (Library Journal)

REVIEW: *Booklist* v110 no13 p12 Mr 1 2014 Wes Lukowsky

"Pete Rose: An American Dilemma". "[Kostya] Kennedy delves deeply into Rose's life and the factors that contributed to his competitiveness and on-field success. He also looks into Rose's personal life and continuing charisma, noting that gambling was always part of Rose's life; he was a regular at horse tracks and never tried to hide his constant action on football and basketball. Kennedy isn't campaigning for Rose's induction into the Hall of Fame, but he does suggest that, in the post-performance enhancing drug era, perhaps the Rose situation should be reopened for discussion. This is a wonderful biography as well as a thoughtful examination of a moral quandary."

REVIEW: *Kirkus Rev* v82 no3 p39 F 1 2014

REVIEW: *Libr J* v139 no3 p108 F 15 2014 Brett Rohlwing

REVIEW: *Publ Wkly* v261 no3 p43 Ja 20 2014

THE KENNEDY TAPES; inside the White House during the Cuban missile crisis; lvi, 514 2002 Norton

1. Cuban Missile Crisis, 1962—Sources 2. Historical literature 3. United States—History—1961-1969 4. United States—Politics & government—1961-1963
ISBN 0-393-32259-9
LC 2001--44484

SUMMARY: This book presents President John F. Kennedy's secret recordings of "the meetings he held during the tension-filled days of the Cuban missile crisis. This book of transcriptions gives readers the opportunity to sit in as history is being made by a small group of advisers, led by a stoical president, who contronted the prospect of nuclear war and devised a strategy to avoid it." (New York Times Book Review)

REVIEW: *N Y Times Book Rev* p24 O 27 2013 JILL ABRAMSON

"The Making of a President 1960," "Four Days: The Historical Record of the Death of President Kennedy," and "The Kennedy Tapes: Inside the White House During the Cuban Missile Crisis." "The classic that gave birth to the campaign book genre provides fly-on-the-wall detail about every aspect of [John F.] Kennedy's climb to the White House. Although everyone knows how the story ends, [Theodore H.] White builds considerable narrative tension. . . . This slim coffee-table book, full of arresting photographs, covers the days of national shock, from Kennedy's assassination in Dallas to his funeral cortege in Washington, with raw intensity. . . . This book of transcriptions gives readers the opportunity to sit in as history is being made by a small group of advisers, led by a stoical president."

KENNEL, SARAH. Charles Marville; photographer of Paris; [by] Sarah Kennel xi, 265 p. 2013 National Gallery of Art

1. Art catalogs 2. Photographers—France—Biography 3. Photography, Artistic—Exhibitions
ISBN 022609278X (hardcover, alk. paper); 0894683853 (softcover, alk. paper); 9780226092782

(hardcover, alk. paper); 9780894683855 (softcover, alk. paper)
LC 2013-017771

SUMMARY: This book on photographer Charles Marville "begins with the city scenes and architectural studies Marville made throughout France and Germany in the 1850s, and also explores his landscapes and portraits, as well as his photographs of Paris both before and after many of its medieval streets were razed to make way for the broad boulevards, parks, and monumental buildings we have come to associate with the City of Light." (Publisher's note)

REVIEW: *Burlington Mag* v156 no1338 p613 S 2014

REVIEW: *Choice* v51 no9 p1582-3 My 2014 J. E. Housefield

"Charles Marville: Photographer of Paris". "Thanks to the efforts of this volume's authors, led by curator [Sarah] Kennel . . . Marville is a mystery no more. At the same time that the new material in this catalogue lays out Marville's previously unknown biography, bringing to light his work as an illustrator, each of the five essays offers new analytical insights into his commissioned photography for the city of Paris and his role in shaping the public image of the modern city. . . . Through its exceptional reproductions and new discoveries, this book confirms and expands Marville's significance. This will be a valuable addition to library collections of photography, urbanism, history, and French culture."

REVIEW: *TLS* no5790 p18 Mr 21 2014 PATRICK McCAUGHEY

KENNETT, JEANETTE.ed. Fashion. See Fashion

KENNEY, KAREN LATCHANA. Boho fashion; [by] Karen Latchana Kenney 48 p. 2014 Lerner Publications Co.

1. Bohemianism—Juvenile literature 2. Children's nonfiction 3. Do-it-yourself literature 4. Fashion—Juvenile literature 5. Girls' clothing—Juvenile literature
ISBN 1467714704; 9781467714709 (libary binding)
LC 2013-011590

SUMMARY: This book, by Karen Latchana Kenney, is part of the "What's Your Style?" series. It focuses on bohemian fashion. "Stars like Vanessa Hudgens and Mary-Kate and Ashley Olsen are known for sporting boho style. With a few key pieces in your closet, plus a dash of style know-how, you can look every bit as boho chic as the celebs. Find out about the clothes, accessories, and hairstyles that make up boho fashion--and discover how you can use them to create your own one-of-a-kind style!" (Publisher's note)

REVIEW: *Booklist* v110 no12 p72 F 15 2014 Ann Kelley

"Boho Fashion," "Hipster Fashion," and "Preppy Fashion." "Whether kids need help defining their personal style, cultivating it, or both, the books in the What's Your Style? series can help. . . . With hip images and current information, Kenney explores stars to turn to for style inspiration, as well as types of clothes, accessories, and hairstyles to fit the desired style bill. . . . The design of each title echoes the style presented (batik patterns for boho, for instance), and the information is accessible, helpful, and should inspire kids to express themselves."

REVIEW: *SLJ* v60 no4 p82 Ap 2014 Paula Willey

REVIEW: *Voice of Youth Advocates* v36 no6 p84-5 F 2014 Debbie Kirchhoff

KENNEY, KAREN LATCHANA. Hipster fashion; [by] Karen Latchana Kenney 48 p. 2014 Lerner Publications Co.

1. Children's nonfiction 2. Do-it-yourself literature 3. Fashion 4. Fashion design 5. Hipsters (Subculture)
ISBN 1467714720; 9781467714723 (lib. bdg. : alk. paper)
LC 2013-018712

SUMMARY: This book, by Karen Latchana Kenney, is part of the "What's Your Style?" series. It focuses on hipster fashion. "Stars like Miley Cyrus and Emma Watson are always pushing hipster fashion to the next level. With a few hip style staples and a splash of originality, you can create your own super trendy hipster fashion. Find out about the clothes, accessories, and hairstyles that radiate hipster fashion--and discover how you can use them to create your own eclectic style!" (Publisher's note)

REVIEW: *Booklist* v110 no12 p72 F 15 2014 Ann Kelley

"Boho Fashion," "Hipster Fashion," and "Preppy Fashion." "Whether kids need help defining their personal style, cultivating it, or both, the books in the What's Your Style? series can help. . . . With hip images and current information, Kenney explores stars to turn to for style inspiration, as well as types of clothes, accessories, and hairstyles to fit the desired style bill. . . . The design of each title echoes the style presented (batik patterns for boho, for instance), and the information is accessible, helpful, and should inspire kids to express themselves."

REVIEW: *SLJ* v60 no4 p82 Ap 2014 Paula Willey

REVIEW: *Voice of Youth Advocates* v36 no6 p84-5 F 2014 Debbie Kirchhoff

KENNEY, KAREN LATCHANA. Preppy fashion; [by] Karen Latchana Kenney 48 p. 2014 Lerner Publications Co.

1. Celebrities—Clothing 2. Children's nonfiction 3. Clothing & dress—Juvenile literature 4. Do-it-yourself literature 5. Fashion
ISBN 1467714690; 9781467714693 (lib. bdg. : alk. paper)
LC 2013-022643

SUMMARY: This book, by Karen Latchana Kenney, is part of the "What's Your Style?" series. It focuses on preppy fashion. "It's the go-to look for countless celebrities, from Taylor Swift to Zac Efron. With a few style staples in your closet and an eye for patterns and colors, you can pull together looks that are just as classy and creative. Find out about the clothes, accessories, and hairstyles that make up preppy fashion--and discover how you can put your own spin on this timeless style!" (Publisher's note)

REVIEW: *Booklist* v110 no12 p72 F 15 2014 Ann Kelley

"Boho Fashion," "Hipster Fashion," and "Preppy Fashion." "Whether kids need help defining their personal style, cultivating it, or both, the books in the What's Your Style? series can help. . . . With hip images and current information, Kenney explores stars to turn to for style inspiration, as well as types of clothes, accessories, and hairstyles to fit the desired style bill. . . . The design of each title echoes the style presented (batik patterns for boho, for instance), and the information is accessible, helpful, and should inspire kids to express themselves."

REVIEW: *Voice of Youth Advocates* v36 no6 p84-5 F 2014 Debbie Kirchhoff

KENNY, CHARLES. The Upside of Down; Why the Rise of the Rest Is Good for the West; [by] Charles Kenny 256 p. 2014 Perseus Books Group

1. East & West 2. Economics literature 3. Global Financial Crisis, 2008-2009 4. Globalization—Economic aspects 5. United States—Economic conditions
ISBN 0465064736; 9780465064731

SUMMARY: In this book, "Charles Kenny argues that America's so-called decline is only relative to the newfound success of other countries. And there is tremendous upside to life in a wealthier world: Americans can benefit from better choices and cheaper prices offered by schools and hospitals in rising countries, and, without leaving home, avail themselves of the new inventions and products those countries will produce." (Publisher's note)

REVIEW: *Kirkus Rev* v81 no24 p23 D 15 2013

"The Upside of Down: Why the Rise of the Rest is Good for the West". "A moralist might cringe, but to [Charles] Kenny, this is generally a good thing, not only since innovation will flow from such markets, but also due to the fact that it will help integrate the world economy even further. Arguing against 'declinist' views of the West, the author claims that the lifting-all-boats model is largely correct, and if the go-go growth models of the past are likely not to govern the future economy, at least some growth will be possible. . . . An optimistic view of the future economy—refreshing in that sense, but perhaps a touch too rosy, even if written with the dry detachment of an economist."

REVIEW: *Publ Wkly* v260 no43 p49 O 28 2013

KENT, CHRISTOBEL. A Darkness Descending; A Mystery in Florence; [by] Christobel Kent 400 p. 2013 W W Norton & Co Inc

1. Detective & mystery stories 2. Detectives 3. Florence (Italy)—Fiction 4. Murder—Fiction 5. Politicians—Fiction
ISBN 1605985368; 9781605985367

SUMMARY: In this mystery novel by Christopher Kent, "When the driven, charismatic leader of a Florentine political movement collapses at a rally, his young party immediately comes under threat. And when it emerges that his wife, Flavia, has disappeared, leaving behind not only a devastated husband but their newborn son, the political becomes dangerously personal--and Detective Inspector Sandro Cellini is summoned to investigate." (Publisher's note)

REVIEW: *Kirkus Rev* v81 no16 p187 Ag 15 2013

"A Darkness Descending." "A Florentine investigator seeks the reason for the suicide of a politically connected woman. . . . Sandro Cellini's life has settled down since his dismissal from the police force. . . . When party leader Rosselli's partner Flavia kills herself at a seaside hotel, leaving Rosselli with their newborn son and a bitter mother who hated Flavia, Sandro is asked to investigate. . . . Those looking for fast-paced thrills will not find them in this literate, cerebral, decorously paced mystery that nevertheless holds readers' interest to the end."

REVIEW: *N Y Times Book Rev* p23 O 20 2013 MARILYN STASIO

REVIEW: *Publ Wkly* v260 no29 p44 Jl 22 2013

KENT, GRAEME. On The Run; Deserters Through the Ages; [by] Graeme Kent 352 p. 2013 Robson Press

1. Arnold, Benedict, 1741-1801 2. Flynn, Errol, 1909-1959 3. Historical literature 4. Military deserters 5. Military desertion
ISBN 1849545707; 9781849545709

SUMMARY: This book by Graeme Kent presents a "history of deserters and desertion." It profiles "poets and pugilists, thieves and thugs, lovers and lunatics, princes and politicians, comedians and conspirators, film stars and fanatics, and even a Pope, all brought together by the simple fact that at one time or another they went on the run." (Publisher's note)

REVIEW: *TLS* no5772 p30-1 N 15 2013 NATHAN M. GREENFIELD

"On the Run: Deserters Through the Ages." "Less convincing is [Graeme Kent's] argument that Marc Antony was a deserter. . . . To include him or Benedict Arnold (who also did not desert from the line of battle), is to expand the definition of desertion beyond recognition. While many of the stories are interesting . . . the serious errors or omissions that mar others undermines one's faith in Kent's history. . . . Nor is Kent's hand sure when he writes about the American Civil War. . . . True, the war continued for a few more weeks, but everyone knew that General Lee's surrender was more than 'a sign that the Civil War was almost over.'"

KENT, HANNAH. Burial rites; a novel; [by] Hannah Kent 336 p. 2013 Little, Brown and Co.

1. Clergy—Fiction 2. Historical fiction 3. Master & servant—Fiction 4. Women murderers—Fiction
ISBN 0316243914; 9780316239806 (large print); 9780316243919 (hardcover)
LC 2013-014305

SUMMARY: This book presents "a retelling of real-life events from 1828, Iceland, when Agnes Magnusdottir and two others are convicted and sentenced to death in a brutal double murder. . . . The murderers were servants, assistants, and sometime lovers to one of the victims . . . herbalist and healer Natan Ketilsson. As Iceland's primitive prison system is ill equipped to house death row inmates, a local farm family is prevailed upon to board Agnes until the date of her execution." (Library Journal)

REVIEW: *Booklist* v110 no11 p38 F 1 2014 Mary McCay

REVIEW: *Booklist* v109 no21 p44 Jl 1 2013 Joanne Wilknson

REVIEW: *Kirkus Rev* v81 no8 p18 Ap 15 2013

REVIEW: *Kirkus Rev* p9 2013 Guide 20to BookExpo America

REVIEW: *Libr J* v138 no12 p73 Jl 1 2013 Barbara Love

REVIEW: *Libr J* v139 no2 p43 F 1 2014 Beth Farrell

REVIEW: *N Y Times Book Rev* p17 S 29 2013 Hannah Kent

"Burial Rites." "While the tensions and evolving relationships between Agnes and her host family are generally well realized, [Hannah] Kent's Reverend Toti remains a stereotype: meek, callow, indecisive and given to pious, predictable counsel. The author tries to build him into something more complex, but it's hard to tease fullness from what starts out flat. As the novel proceeds, Kent simply reverses Toti's initial generic traits . . . but these changes are too schematic to generate a layered character. . . . The most effective passages . . . are those told in Agnes's unmediated voice, at least once the narrative has picked up momentum. . . . There are other stylistic problems. . . . Kent offers a wealth of engaging detail."

REVIEW: *New York Times* v163 no56271 pC2 S 26 2013 Susannah Mendnws

REVIEW: *New Yorker* v89 no29 p115 S 23 2013

REVIEW: *Publ Wkly* v260 no24 p36 Je 17 2013

REVIEW: *TLS* no5782 p21 Ja 24 2014 RUTH GILLIGAN

KEOGH, DERMOT.ed. Ireland through European eyes. See Ireland through European eyes

KEOHANE, GEORGIA LEVENSON. Social entrepreneurship for the 21st century; innovation across the nonprofit, private, and public sectors; [by] Georgia Levenson Keohane viii, 263 p. 2013 McGraw-Hill

1. Business literature 2. Nonprofit organizations 3. Public-private sector cooperation 4. Social enterprises 5. Social entrepreneurship 6. Social innovation
ISBN 0071801677 (alk. paper); 0071801685 (ebk.); 9780071801676 (alk. paper); 9780071801683 (ebk.)
LC 2012-038431

SUMMARY: This book by Georgia Levenson Keohane "Shows how social entrepreneurship has radically transformed the nonprofit, private, and public sectors . . . Explores the promise of impact investing--what it really is and how it works," and "Illuminates the challenges of bringing billions of dollars in private capital to bear on social problems." (Publisher's note)

REVIEW: *Choice* v51 no1 p127-8 S 2013 N. E. Furlow

"Social Entrepreneurship for the 21st Century: Innovation Across the Nonprofit, Private, and Public Sectors." "[Author Georgia Levenson] Keohane . . . begins by defining social entrepreneurship and the evolution of the phenomenon grounded in the nonprofit sector. The book then examines the function of enterprise and the role of the private sector through impact investing; a section on social innovation in the public sector follows. . . . The book addresses criticisms of social entrepreneurship such as how to evaluate the impact that social entrepreneurship has on society. . . . While the growth of social entrepreneurship is definitely global in nature, Keohane focuses on examples from the US, with which she is personally familiar."

KEPHART, BETH. Going over; [by] Beth Kephart 262 p. 2014 Chronicle Books

1. Berlin Wall, Berlin, Germany, 1961-1989—Fiction 2. Family life—Germany—Fiction 3. Historical fiction 4. Love—Fiction
ISBN 1452124574; 9781452124575 (alk. paper)
LC 2012-046894

SUMMARY: In this book, by Beth Kephart, "Ada lives among the rebels, punkers, and immigrants of Kreuzberg in West Berlin. Stefan lives in East Berlin, in a faceless apartment bunker of Friedrichshain. Bound by love and separated by circumstance, their only chance for a life together lies in a high-risk escape. But will Stefan find the courage to leap? Or will forces beyond his control stand in his way?" (Publisher's note)

REVIEW: *Booklist* v110 no16 p59 Ap 15 2014 Ilene Cooper

REVIEW: *Booklist* v110 no13 p68 Mr 1 2014 Frances Bradburn

REVIEW: *Bull Cent Child Books* v67 no10 p525-6 Je 2014 D. S.

REVIEW: *Kirkus Rev* v82 no4 p175 F 15 2014

"Going Over". "Life in the grim shadow of the Berlin Wall is vividly reflected in Kephart's moving exploration in two voices. . . . Related in a swirling, second-person stream of consciousness that mimics the free-flowing colors of her nighttime art, Ada's and Stefan's alternating present-tense narratives offer a point/counterpoint on the need for escape but its daunting peril. Their story is at once compelling and challenging, perhaps limiting this book to an audience of sophisticated readers. The plight of young Savas adds depth, but its tragic outcome is muted by the building suspense of Stefan's evolving plan. While this gripping effort captures the full flavor of a trying time in an onerous place, many readers will find it hard going."

REVIEW: *SLJ* v60 no3 p160 Mr 2014 Andrea Lipinski

REVIEW: *Voice of Youth Advocates* v37 no1 p68 Ap 2014 Kristi Sadowski

KEPLINGER, KODY. The Swift boys & me; [by] Kody Keplinger 272 p. 2014 Scholastic Press

1. Best friends—Fiction 2. Best friends—Juvenile fiction 3. Brothers—Fiction 4. Brothers—Juvenile fiction 5. Desertion and non-support—Juvenile fiction 6. Dysfunctional families—Juvenile fiction 7. Family life—Fiction 8. Family problems—Fiction 9. Friendship—Fiction 10. Psychological fiction
ISBN 0545562007; 9780545562003; 9780545562027
LC 2013-034049

SUMMARY: In this middle-grade young adult story by Kody Keplinger, "eleven-year-old Nola Sutton has been best friends and neighbors with the Swift boys for practically her whole life. . . . Together, they have a summer of fun adventures planned. But then everything changes overnight. When the boys' dad leaves without even saying good-bye, it completely destroys the Swift family, and all Nola can do is watch." (Publisher's note)

REVIEW: *Booklist* v110 no18 p57 My 15 2014 Krista Hutley

REVIEW: *Bull Cent Child Books* v67 no10 p526 Je 2014 D. S.

"The Swift Boys & Me". "[Kody] Keplinger's first middle-grades novel is sweet and smooth, and sharp readers will realize that it's as much about change in general as Nola's drift from the Swift boys. . . . Nola's small Kentucky town, with kids pelting indiscriminately from yard to yard under the gently watchful eye of all the neighborhood adults, seems an old-fashioned idyll, but the multiracial cast, contemporary technology, and occasional helicopter parent put it firmly in the present day. This is the sort of solid, amiable preteen summer story there used to be a lot of; let's hope this heralds a revival."

REVIEW: *Kirkus Rev* v82 no7 p114 Ap 1 2014

REVIEW: *Publ Wkly* v261 no11 p85 Mr 17 2014

REVIEW: *SLJ* v60 no5 p112 My 2014 Eva Mitnick

KERBEL, LUCY. 100 Great Plays for Women; [by] Lucy Kerbel 224 p. 2014 Nick Hern Books

1. Drama—History & criticism 2. Women & literature

3. Women dramatists 4. Women in literature 5. Women's literature
ISBN 1848421850; 9781848421851

SUMMARY: "Lucy Kerbel's myth-busting book features compact and insightful introductions to 100 plays, each of which has an entirely or predominantly female cast, with the female characters taking an equal or decisive role in driving the on-stage action. 10 plays for solo female performers feature in this selection. The result is a personal but wide-ranging reappraisal of the theatrical canon." (Publisher's note)

REVIEW: *TLS* no5781 p26-7 Ja 17 2014 SAMANTHA ELLIS

"100 Great Plays for Women." "[Editor Lucy] Kerbel could almost, she writes, have filled the book with plays by just four women (Bryony Lavery, Churchill, Sarah Daniels and April de Angelis) but her decision to include only one play by each playwright gives '100 Great Plays for Women' impressive scope and sweep--and gives the male playwrights a chance. Her second rule--that the plays must have all- or mostly-female casts--unfortunately excludes some plays with wonderful roles for women. . . . In her vivid, concise essays on each play, from cast breakdown to analysis of style, structure and staging challenges, Kerbel includes some sobering history."

KERLEY, BARBARA. A Home for Mr. Emerson; 48 p. 2013 Scholastic Press

1. Authors, American—19th century—Biography 2. Biography (Literary form) 3. Children's nonfiction 4. Concord (Mass.)—History
ISBN 0545350883; 9780545350884
LC 2013-007482

SUMMARY: This children's book presents an "introduction to the life of Ralph Waldo Emerson. . . . Emerson grows up in Boston, but yearns to make a life closer to nature where he can surround himself with books and friends. He finds a perfect home in Concord, Massachusetts, where he and his wife raise a family. . . . A house fire later in his life devastates Emerson, but allows the town to demonstrate their affection for him as they rebuild his home." (School Library Journal)

REVIEW: *Booklist* v110 no11 p52-3 F 1 2014 Randall Enos

REVIEW: *Bull Cent Child Books* v67 no7 p363 Mr 2014 K. C.

"A Home For Mr. Emerson". "In this compact biography of [Ralph Waldo] Emerson, [Barbara] Kerley carefully selects those elements of Emerson's life that contribute to her tightly crafted narrative arc that stresses the hope, community and optimism required to create the life of one's dreams. . . . As a result, Emerson's joie de vivre explodes from the pages as the book captures his take-charge approach to crafting the kind of life he envisioned after he left his impoverished childhood in Boston. . . . The visual metaphors communicate both emotion and action in ways highly accessible to young readers, and Kerley extends the message by including a page of activities and advice to help children inventory their own spirits."

REVIEW: *Kirkus Rev* v81 no24 p143 D 15 2013

"A Home for Mr. Emerson". "The philosopher's ideas and historical context are not the focus of this visually dynamic biography. . . . The illustrations—prancing across oversized pages—are cheery, inventive, bright and busy, depicting a contented-looking man in coat and tails basking in the magnificence of life. In bold and whimsical spreads, Emerson literally dives into books, strides across a U.S. map and, most dramatically, looms as a silhouette amid the flaming ruins of his beloved house. It's hard to say whether this tale will inspire children to further investigation into the philosopher's life and work, but the author's note does help round out the portrait."

REVIEW: *Publ Wkly* v260 no49 p85 D 2 2013

REVIEW: *SLJ* v60 no2 p120 F 2014 Marian McLeod

KERMANI, S. ZOHREH. Pagan family values; childhood and the religious imagination in contemporary American paganism; [by] S. Zohreh Kermani xv, 235 p. 2013 NYU Press

1. Children—Religious life 2. Families—Religious life 3. Neopaganism—United States 4. Neopagans 5. Social science literature
ISBN 9780814769744 (cl : alk. paper); 9781479894604 (pbk. : alk. paper)
LC 2012-049432

SUMMARY: This book "explores the ways in which North American Pagan families pass on their beliefs to their children, and how the effort to socialize children influences this new religious movement. . . . Rather than seeking to pass along specific religious beliefs, Pagan parents tend to seek to instill values, such as religious tolerance and spiritual independence, which will remain with their children throughout their lives, regardless of these children's ultimate religious identifications." (Publisher's note)

REVIEW: *Choice* v51 no5 p853-4 Ja 2014 G. J. Reece

"Pagan Family Values: Childhood and the Religious Imagination in Contemporary American Paganism." "This study of the contemporary Pagan construction of childhood by [S. Zohreh] Kermani . . . is an important addition to academic collections, primarily because it covers an area of inquiry not addressed in the literature until now. . . . Unfortunately, Kermani's argument about the accompanying immaturity of Pagan adults is troublesome and weak. . . . Oddly, she seems blind to her own construction of maturity and, by not making a cohesive logical argument for it, considerably undermines aspects of her work."

KERR, MICHAEL.ed. Lebanon. See Lebanon

KERR, PHILIP. Prague fatale; [by] Philip Kerr 401 p. 2012 Marian Wood Books

1. Gunther, Bernhard (Fictitious character)—Fiction 2. Private investigators—Fiction
ISBN 9780399159022
LC 2011-051632

SUMMARY: This book is "[Philip] Kerr's . . . eighth Bernie Gunther novel" and "takes the Berlin cop to Prague in October 1941, to investigate the murder of an adjutant of feared SS Gen. Reinhard Heydrich, who's just become the Protector of Bohemia and Moravia. The morning after a drunken party attended by SS officers at Heydrich's country estate outside Prague, the adjutant, who was shaken by what he witnessed as part of a Nazi death squad in Latvia, is found dead in a locked guestroom. Heydrich wants Gunther, suicidal himself after similar experiences in Russia, to find the adjutant's killer fast, but how is one to identify the culprit amid a house full of professional murderers? A subplot involving the death of a foreigner run over by a train and Czech nationalists" is included. (Publishers Wkly)

REVIEW: *Booklist* v108 no14 p24 Mr 15 2012 Bill Ott

REVIEW: *Kirkus Rev* v80 no8 p125 Ap 15 2012

"Prague Fatale." "Good cop and confirmed Nazi-hater Bernie Gunther . . . lands in the middle of a homicidal riddle. . . . It seems someone has attempted to poison [Reinhard] Heydrich. . . Bernie, the designated Reichsprotector's detective, is required to nail the brazen culprit. At the moment, 39 high-ranking Nazis are guests at the castle. . . . in a house 'full of murderers, anything is possible.' Bernie's voice--ironic, mordantly funny, inimitable--reflects a world-weary journey. Still--and this is the entertaining heart of the matter--readers are never permitted to forget that survival is his religion."

REVIEW: *Libr J* v137 no15 p34-5 S 15 2012 Janet Martin

REVIEW: *Publ Wkly* v259 no9 p64 F 27 2012

KERR, PHILIP. The winter horses; [by] Philip Kerr 288 p. 2014 Alfred A. Knopf

1. Historical fiction 2. Holocaust, Jewish—Ukraine—Fiction 3. Holocaust, Jewish, 1939-1945—Ukraine—Juvenile fiction 4. Horses—Fiction 5. Jews—Ukraine—Fiction 6. Przewalski's horse—Fiction 7. Survival—Fiction 8. World War, 1939-1945—Ukraine—Fiction
ISBN 9780385755436 (hardback); 9780385755443 (lib. bdg.)
LC 2013-035978

SUMMARY: This book by Philip Kerr, "set in the Ukrainian steppe in 1941 . . . follows Kalinka, an orphaned Ukrainian Jew on the run, and Max, the elderly catetaker of the Askaniya-Nova State Steppe Nature Reserve. The reserve is presently occupied by a band of Nazi soldiers, whose leader orders the extermination of most of the animal population at the reserve." (Bulletin of the Center for Children's Books)

REVIEW: *Booklist* v110 no13 p72 Mr 1 2014 Michael Cart

REVIEW: *Bull Cent Child Books* v67 no8 p410-1 Ap 2014 H. M.

"The Winter Horses". "The animal story (drawing on the real-life Ukrainian reserve and the killing of its rare herd of Przewalski's horses) offers appealing elements in Kalinka's friendship and the horses' need for protection, resulting in an unusual wartime tale. The plot, though, is too often implausible . . . and Kalinka's exposition moves the story with a slow pace unsuited to such an adventurous survival story. Those willing to ride out the far-fetched storyline will likely enjoy the survival story, however, and the social metaphor of identifying the horses as an unfit species makes for a useful entry point to discussing World War II and the Holocaust."

REVIEW: *Kirkus Rev* v82 no3 p322 F 1 2014

REVIEW: *SLJ* v60 no3 p142 Mr 2014 Shelley Sommer

REVIEW: *Voice of Youth Advocates* v37 no1 p68-9 Ap 2014 Erin Wyatt

KERRIDGE, RICHARD. Cold Blood; Adventures with Reptiles and Amphibians; [by] Richard Kerridge 304 p. 2014 Chatto & Windus

1. Cold-blooded animals 2. Memoirs 3. Natural history 4. Natural history literature 5. Science—Popular works
ISBN 0701187956; 9780701187958

SUMMARY: Written by Richard Kerridge, "Part natural-history guide to these animals, part passionate nature writing, and part personal story, 'Cold Blood' is [a] . . . memoir about our relationship with nature. Through close observation, it shows how even the suburbs can seem wild when we get close to these thrilling, weird and uncanny animals." (Publisher's note)

REVIEW: *New Sci* v222 no2974 p47 Je 21 2014 Adrian Barnett

"The Hunt for the Golden Mole: All Creatures Great and Small and Why They Matter" and "Cold Blood: Adventures With Reptiles and Amphibians." "[Author Richard] Girling deftly combines broad themes with detailed content, exploring humanity's relationship with the natural world by taking wide narrative strides, and then pausing for close analysis. . . . [Author Richard] Kerridge writes no less eloquently, but the style and the focus are different. . . . Kerridge reserves some of his finest writing to describe the animals themselves."

REVIEW: *TLS* no5806 p29 Jl 11 2014 GEORDIE TORR

KERRIGAN, GENE. Dark times in the city; [by] Gene Kerrigan 305 p. 2009 Harvill Secker

1. Crime—Fiction 2. Dublin (Ireland)—Fiction 3. Ex-convicts—Fiction 4. Gangs—Fiction 5. Organized crime—Ireland—Dublin—Fiction
ISBN 1846552559 (pbk.); 1846552893 (hbk.); 9781846552557 (pbk.); 9781846552892 (hbk.)
LC 2009-396782

SUMMARY: This crime novel by Gene Kerrigan, "a CWA Gold Dagger Crime Novel finalist," "depicts an edgy city where affluence and cocaine fuel a ruthless gang culture, and a man's fleeting impulse may cost the lives of those who matter most to him. . . . With a troubled past and an uncertain future, Danny finds himself drawn into a vicious scheme of revenge." (Publisher's note)

REVIEW: *Booklist* v110 no7 p24 D 1 2013 Bill Ott

REVIEW: *Kirkus Rev* v81 no22 p148 N 15 2013

REVIEW: *N Y Times Book Rev* p19 Ja 5 2014 MARLIYN STASIO

"Dark Times in the City," "The Invisible Code," and "The Midas Murders." "In Gene Kerrigan's novel 'Dark Times in the City' . . . Kerrigan writes with a grim elegance that takes the edge off the blunt language and brutal deeds of his underworld villains and spares some grace for their hapless victims. . . . There are witches on Fleet Street in 'The Invisible Code.' . . . There are also devils and demons and ladies who lunch in Christopher Fowler's latest madcap mystery about the strange police detectives in London's Peculiar Crimes Unit. . . . In 'The Midas Murders' . . . , a new police procedural (its rhetorical excesses intact in Brian Doyle's translation) from Pieter Aspe. . . . It's all intricately plotted by Aspe.

REVIEW: *Publ Wkly* v260 no38 p58 S 23 2013

KERTZER, DAVID I., 1948-. The Pope and Mussolini; the secret history of Pius XI and the rise of Fascism in Europe; [by] David I. Kertzer 576 p. 2014 Random House

1. Church & state—Italy—History 2. Fascism and the Catholic Church—Italy 3. Historical literature
ISBN 0812993462; 9780812993462
LC 2013-019402

SUMMARY: "'The Pope and Mussolini' tells the story of

two men who came to power in 1922, and together changed the course of twentieth-century history. . . . Pius XI and 'Il Duce' had many things in common. They shared a distrust of democracy and a visceral hatred of Communism. . . . In a challenge to the conventional history of this period . . . [author David I.] Kertzer shows how Pius XI played a crucial role in making Mussolini's dictatorship possible and keeping him in power." (Publisher's note)

REVIEW: *America* v210 no11 p32-5 Mr 31 2014 KEVIN P. SPICER

REVIEW: *Booklist* v110 no8 p3-4 D 15 2013 Gilbert Taylor

REVIEW: *Commentary* v137 no4 p32-6 Ap 2014 Kevin J. Madigan

REVIEW: *Commonweal* v141 no15 p23-4 S 26 2014 James J. Sheehan

REVIEW: *Kirkus Rev* v81 no23 p59 D 1 2013

REVIEW: *Libr J* v138 no15 p47 S 15 2013

REVIEW: *New Repub* v244 no23 p54-7 Mr 3 2014 Saul FriedläNder

"The Pope and Mussolini: The Secret History of Pius XI and the Rise of Fascism in Europe". "From the outset of his new book, [David I.] Kertzer deftly reconstructs the parallel lives of Achille Ratti, who became Pius XI, and of Benito Mussolini, both men whose beginnings do not point to the historic role that they began to play in 1922.. . . In a vivid style, Kertzer describes the ups and downs of the ensuing relations between the pontiff and the dictator. . . . Kertzer's essential book reveals a window on this sordid history—a window that for a long time was shuttered, but will not be obscured anymore."

REVIEW: *New Yorker* v90 no3 p77-1 Mr 10 2014

REVIEW: *Publ Wkly* v260 no42 p43 O 21 2013

KESKIN, BIRHAN. & Silk & Love & Flame; [by] Birhan Keskin 120 p. 2013 Arc Publications

1. Loneliness 2. Love poetry 3. Nature—Poetry 4. Poems—Collections 5. Turkish poetry—Translations into English

ISBN 1904614574; 9781904614579

SUMMARY: In this poetry collection by Birhan Keskin, "her topic is love; but less the silky and ardent aspects of it than the losses, the separations, the hesitations. . . . Sometimes imagery involving landscapes stands for emotions; just as often, however, the landscape is the poet. . . . The narrator asserts her place in the world, her being-in-the-world, and more intimate feelings as well, like sorrow or loneliness." (Antioch Review)

REVIEW: *Antioch Rev* v72 no1 p184-91 Wint 2014 John Taylor

"& Silk & Love & Flame" and "From the Bridge: Contemporary Turkish Women Poets". "The engaging Birhan Keskin . . . uses simple word-pictures, yet carries off the tour de force of composing compelling poetry that leaves much to the reader's narrative imagination. . . . In her enlightening Introduction, Saliha Paker traces the history of Turkish women's verse. . . . These fine translations especially make me think of poetics. . . . Özmen's verse is often polysemous in ways that are pleasurable to work out."

KESSLER, LIZ. North of nowhere; [by] Liz Kessler 272 p. 2013 Candlewick Press

1. England—Juvenile fiction 2. Family secrets 3. Grandfathers—Fiction 4. Missing persons—Fiction 5. Time travel—Juvenile fiction

ISBN 9780763667276

LC 2012-954327

SUMMARY: In this book by Liz Kessler, "a mysterious disappearance leads 13-year-old Mia to uncover a long-held family secret. When Mia's grandfather suddenly goes missing, she grudgingly gives up time with her friends to accompany her mother to her grandparents' fishing village hometown, so they can help Mia's grandmother. . . . But when she happens upon an abandoned fishing boat--and a secret diary tucked inside--she embarks on a time-bending journey." (Publishers Weekly)

REVIEW: *Bull Cent Child Books* v67 no2 p98 O 2013 K. Q. G.

"North of Nowhere." "Eighth-grader Mia and her mother are spending spring break in the small English seaside town of Porthaven as they help Gran run the family inn and search for Mia's suddenly missing grandfather. . . . The eventual revelation of Grandad's secret is a rather delightful head-scratcher that will have readers revisiting various plot points to see just exactly how the puzzle pieces all fit together. Unfortunately, Mia exists mostly as an engine to get to the big reveal, and she's forced to make one illogical choice after another to move along the plot."

REVIEW: *Kirkus Rev* v81 no2 p90 Je 1 2013

REVIEW: *SLJ* v59 no10 p1 O 2013 Lisa Kropp

KESTIN, HESH. The Lie; a novel; [by] Hesh Kestin 240 p. 2014 Simon & Schuster

1. Arab-Israeli conflict—Fiction 2. Kidnapping—Fiction 3. Psychological fiction 4. Torture 5. Women lawyers—Fiction

ISBN 1476740097; 9781476740096

SUMMARY: In this novel, by Hesh Kestin, the "complexities of the Palestinian-Israeli conflict hit home for a hard-edged female human rights attorney when her soldier son is kidnapped by Hezbollah. Dahlia Barr, a 44-year-old . . . whose defense of Palestinians has made her an object of derision for many Israelis . . . unexpectedly is tapped by the Israel Police to serve as an arbiter in regard to interrogation methods." (Kirkus Reviews)

REVIEW: *Booklist* v110 no11 p27 F 1 2014 Thomas Gaughan

"The Lie." "What begins as a brilliant portrait of a fascinating character and the stunningly complex culture in which she lives becomes an utterly riveting thriller that is likely to rank as one of the year's best. [Hesh] Kestin, who served in the IDF for 18 years as well as working as a foreign correspondent, seasons his story with brilliant bits about Israeli society, culture, and government. . . . 'The Lie' has everything: memorable characters, a compelling plot, white-knuckle military action, and an economy and clarity of prose that is direct, powerful, and at times beautiful."

REVIEW: *Kirkus Rev* v82 no3 p139 F 1 2014

REVIEW: *Publ Wkly* v261 no4 p172 Ja 27 2014

KEUCHEYAN, RAZMIG. Left hemisphere. See Left hemisphere

KEYS, BARBARA J. Reclaiming American virtue; the human rights revolution of the 1970s; [by] Barbara J. Keys 324 p. 2014 Harvard University Press
1. Historical literature 2. Human rights—Government policy—United States 3. Human rights advocacy—United States 4. Vietnam War, 1961-1975—Influence
ISBN 9780674724853
LC 2013-015286

SUMMARY: It was the author's intent to demonstrate that "the American commitment to international human rights emerged in the 1970s not as a logical outgrowth of American idealism but as a surprising response to national trauma." Barbara J. Keys "situates this novel enthusiasm as a reaction to the profound challenge of the Vietnam War and its tumultuous aftermath." (Publisher's note)

REVIEW: *Choice* v52 no2 p346-7 O 2014 J. P. Dunn

REVIEW: *Kirkus Rev* v82 no1 p70 Ja 1 2014

"Reclaiming American Virtue: The Human Rights Revolution of the 1970s". "A genealogy of America's crusade to advance human rights in the world, its origins 'an antidote to shame and guilt.' . . . Interestingly, the cause of human rights was slow to catch on among leftist and even liberal groups—Morris Udall scarcely mentioned the matter when he was running for the presidency—while neoconservatives began to cloak their arguments for intervention in places like Iraq in the language of civil liberties. An accessible, searching study of an idea that seems to have been forgotten in favor of the steely, cost-cutting pragmatism of today."

REVIEW: *N Y Rev Books* v61 no16 p72-4 O 23 2014 Kenneth Roth

REVIEW: *Publ Wkly* v260 no43 p44-5 O 28 2013

KHALIDI, RASHID. Brokers of deceit; how the US has undermined peace in the Middle East; [by] Rashid Khalidi 208 p.
1. Arab-Israeli conflict—Peace 2. Historical literature 3. Palestine—Politics and government
ISBN 9780807044759 (alk. paper)
LC 2012-044821

SUMMARY: In this book, Rashid Khalidi "argues that since 1948 the reflexive support of the United States for Israel has sabotaged the possibility of a 'just and lasting peace' between Palestinians and Israelis. The US has presented itself as an honest broker, but at every juncture, and especially during the Oslo process of 1993 to 2000, Khalidi contends, America operated to defend Israel's interests at the expense of Palestinians." (Times Literary Supplement)

REVIEW: *Christ Century* v130 no21 p50-2 O 16 2013 Mark Braverman

REVIEW: *Kirkus Rev* v81 no2 p157 Ja 15 2013

REVIEW: *Middle East J* v67 no3 p476-8 Summ 2013 Douglas Little

REVIEW: *Publ Wkly* v260 no1 p50 Ja 7 2013

REVIEW: *TLS* no5764 p26-7 S 20 2013 VICTOR LIEBERMAN

"Brokers of Deceit: How the US has Undermined Peace in the Middle East." "At just over 200 pages, this volume is readily accessible and thoroughly engaging. As always, [Rashid] Khalidi writes with panache, passion and personal commitment. He wittily and ironically dissects repeated instances of alleged Israeli cynicism and American complicity. And yet the same passion that energizes the book limits its impact. Most problematic is Khalidi's embrace of essentialized ahistorical categories. . . . Whereas Khalidi sees occupation as the root of the problem, it is far more accurate to see both war and occupation as symptoms of a deeper process of reciprocal radicalization. . . . Khalidi's analysis of American policy has similar problems."

KHAMIS, SAHAR. Egyptian revolution 2.0. See El-Nawawy, M.

KHAN, RIAZ MOHAMMAD. Afghanistan and Pakistan; conflict, extremism, and resistance to modernity; [by] Riaz Mohammad Khan xii, 385 p. 2011 Woodrow Wilson Center Press Distributed by Johns Hopkins University Press
1. Islam and politics—Pakistan 2. Islamic fundamentalism—Afghanistan 3. Islamic fundamentalism—Pakistan 4. Political science literature 5. Taliban
ISBN 1421403846; 9781421403847
LC 2011-012027

SUMMARY: This book "surveys the conflict in Afghanistan from Pakistan's point of view and analyzes the roots of Pakistan's ambiguous policy--supporting the United States on one hand and showing empathy for the Afghan Taliban on the other." The author argues that "Pakistan reveals a deep confusion in its public discourse on issues of modernity and the challenges the country faces, an intellectual crisis that Pakistan must address to secure the country's survival." (Publisher's note)

REVIEW: *Middle East J* v66 no2 p374-5 Spr 2012 Michael Semple

REVIEW: *TLS* no5765 p12-3 S 27 2013 THOMAS BARFIELD

"Afghanistan Declassified: A Guide to America's Longest War," "War Comes to Garmser: Thirty Years of Conflict on the Afghan Frontier," and "Afghanistan and Pakistan: Conflict, Extremism, and Resistance to Modernity." "Brian Glyn Williams's . . . [book] was originally written for the US military as a guide to the country, its history and people for troops arriving there in 2007. . . . Much of what is presented is badly out of date. . . . Carter Malkasian's 'War Comes to Garmser,' by contrast, explores the war in Afghanistan from an explicitly provincial Afghan point of view, where foreigners (and even Kabul officials) are marginal actors rather than the centre of the story. . . . 'Afghanistan and Pakistan' . . . is a good guide by an insider familiar with the complexity of decision-making in Pakistan."

KHANDRO, SANGYE.tr. The epic of Gesar of Ling. See The epic of Gesar of Ling

KHOURY, DINA RIZK. Iraq in wartime; soldiering, martyrdom, and remembrance; [by] Dina Rizk Khoury xviii, 281 p. 2013 Cambridge University Press
1. Historical literature 2. Iran-Iraq War, 1980-1988—Political aspects—Iraq 3. Iran-Iraq War, 1980-1988—Social aspects—Iraq 4. Persian Gulf War, 1991—Political aspects—Iraq 5. Persian Gulf War, 1991—Social aspects—Iraq 6. Politics and war—Iraq—History—20th century 7. War and society—Iraq—History—20th century
ISBN 9780521711531 (paperback); 9780521884617 (hardback)

LC 2012-040130

SUMMARY: "Starting with the Iran-Iraq War, through the First Gulf War and sanctions, Dina Rizk Khoury traces the political, social, and cultural processes of the normalization of war in Iraq during the last twenty-three years of Ba'thist rule. Drawing on government documents and interviews, Khoury argues that war was a form of everyday bureaucratic governance and examines the Iraqi government's policies of creating consent, managing resistance . . . , and shaping public culture." (Publisher's note)

REVIEW: *Middle East J* v68 no3 p476-8 Summ 2014 Eric Davis

"Iraq in Wartime: Soldiering, Martyrdom, and Remembrance." "Dina Khoury's much anticipated study, 'Iraq in Wartime: Soldiering, Martyrdom and Remembrance,' fills an important lacuna in the history of modern Iraq. . . . To have an in-depth study of the impact of war on Iraq is to be welcomed, especially one that is conceptually nuanced, thoroughly researched and draws upon newly available archives. . . . 'Iraq in Wartime''s most important contribution is to have provided a conceptual and empirical 'bridge' that links the mid-1980s to the period leading up to the collapse of the Ba'thist regime in 2003."

KIBUISHI, KAZU.ed. Explorer. See Explorer

KIDD, CHIP. Go; a Kidd's guide to graphic design; [by] Chip Kidd 160 p. 2013 Workman Publishing Company, Inc.

1. Color 2. Design literature 3. Graphic arts—History 4. Graphic arts—Technique 5. Typographic design
ISBN 076117219X; 9780761172192 (alk. paper)
LC 2013-032394

SUMMARY: This book is an introduction to graphic design for children. It introduces "the aspiring designer to the thought processes behind typography and visual organization. Among the topics are color, juxtaposition, typography, design history, and the use of design to convey concepts such as irony and metaphor." (Library Journal)

REVIEW: *Booklist* v110 no5 p66 N 1 2013 Sarah Hunter

"Go: A Kidd's Guide to Graphic Design." "[Chip] Kidd dispenses with the boring technical jargon and instead presents a rich, colorful, and captivating overview of the things designers consider every day. He clearly and engagingly explains concepts such as form, color, typography, and scale, but he relies far more on delicious full-page visuals of book covers, advertisements, vintage posters, and photographs to illustrate his points. The chapter on typography in particular makes excellent use of images to demonstrate concepts. . . . Captivating, eye-opening, and just plain cool."

REVIEW: *Kirkus Rev* v81 no18 p239 S 15 2013

REVIEW: *Libr J* v138 no18 p85 N 1 2013 Eric G. Linderman

REVIEW: *Publ Wkly* v260 no33 p70 Ag 19 2013

REVIEW: *SLJ* v59 no10 p1 O 2013 Carol Goldman

KIDJO, ANGELIQUE. Spirit Rising; My Life, My Music; [by] Angelique Kidjo 256 p. 2014 Harper Design Intl

1. Benin—History 2. Memoirs 3. Singers—Biography 4. UNICEF 5. Women—Africa—Social conditions
ISBN 0062071793; 9780062071798

SUMMARY: In this memoir, musician Angélique Kidjo "reveals the details of her dangerous escape into France, and how she rose from poverty to become a Grammy Award-winning artist and an international sensation at the top of Billboard's World Albums chart. She also explains why it's important to give back by sharing stories from her work as a UNICEF ambassador and as founder of the Batonga Foundation, which gives African girls access to education." (Publisher's note)

REVIEW: *Booklist* v110 no5 p17-8 N 1 2013 Vanessa Bush

REVIEW: *Kirkus Rev* v81 no24 p19 D 15 2013

"Spirit Rising: My Life, My Music". "A Grammy Award-winning Beninese singer/songwriter's heartfelt memoir, coauthored by [Rachel] Wenrick, about her life as a musician and human rights activist. Kidjo began her career in entertainment at age 6, when her mother pushed her onto a theater stage and told the little girl to sing. Terrified, the author quickly overcame her fears and realized that she had arrived 'home.'. . . " Richly illustrated throughout with black-and-white photographs, Kidjo's work celebrates one woman's courage to use her musical gift 'to empower people all over the world.' Warm, lively and compassionate."

REVIEW: *Libr J* v139 no2 p77 F 1 2014 Lani Smith

REVIEW: *Publ Wkly* v260 no43 p49 O 28 2013

KIELY, BRENDAN. The gospel of winter; [by] Brendan Kiely 304 p. 2014 Simon & Schuster

1. Child sexual abuse by clergy 2. Friendship—Fiction 3. Priests 4. Teenage boys—Fiction 5. Young adult fiction
ISBN 1442484896; 9781442484894

SUMMARY: This book, by Brendan Kiely, is "about the restorative power of truth and love after the trauma of abuse. As sixteen-year-old Aidan Donovan's fractured family disintegrates around him, he searches for solace in a few bumps of Adderall, his father's wet bar, and the attentions of his local priest, Father Greg--the only adult who actually listens to him. When Christmas hits, Aidan's world collapses in a crisis of trust when he recognizes the darkness of Father Greg's affections." (Publisher's note)

REVIEW: *Booklist* v110 no8 p41 D 15 2013 Ann Kelley

REVIEW: *Bull Cent Child Books* v67 no7 p364 Mr 2014 K. C.

"The Gospel of Winter. "[Brendan] Kiely's lyrical prose is never explicit; readers will need to infer some details regarding what exactly happened between Aidan and the priest as well as between him and Josie. The sentiments and emotions he and Mark experience are sometimes overblown in their angst-ridden expression, but in this they fall into the grand tradition of fictional teens waxing eloquent in their distress, giving voice to truth even if that voice is more artful than realistic. . . . Through sensitive handling of a timely issue, Kiely charts a potential path toward healing."

REVIEW: *Kirkus Rev* v81 no22 p120 N 15 2013

REVIEW: *Publ Wkly* v260 no42 p53-4 O 21 2013

REVIEW: *SLJ* v60 no1 p100 Ja 2014 Geri Diorio

KIGHTLEY, ROSALINDA.il. Big Hug for Little Cub. See Grover, L. A.

KILCUP, KAREN L. Fallen forests; emotion, embodiment, and ethics in American women's environmental writing, 1781-1924; [by] Karen L. Kilcup 504 p. 2013 University of Georgia Press

1. American literature—Women authors—History and criticism 2. Ecology in literature 3. Environmental protection in literature 4. LITERARY CRITICISM—American—General 5. Literature—History & criticism 6. Nature conservation in literature 7. Nature in literature

ISBN 0820332860 (hardcover); 9780820332864 (hardback)

LC 2012-043938

SUMMARY: In this book on American women's environmental writing, "Karen L. Kilcup rejects prior critical emphases on sentimentalism to show how women writers have drawn on their literary emotional intelligence to raise readers' consciousness about social and environmental issues. She also critiques ecocriticism's idealizing tendency, which has elided women's complicity in agendas that depart from today's environmental orthodoxies." (Publisher's note)

REVIEW: *Choice* v51 no8 p1400 Ap 2014 D. J. Rosenthal

"Fallen Forests: Emotion, Embodiment, and Ethics in American Women's Environmental Writing". "In this wide-ranging, deeply insightful book, [Karen L.] Kilcup . . . both extends and challenges current thinking about American women's writings about the environment in the long 19th century. . . . Adding to the field of rhetorica, or women's rhetoric, this book makes a valuable contribution to making 'audible" many now-forgotten women's voices. Grounded in eco-feminist theory, the book is particularly strong in its close readings. . . The study is also valuable for the way it forces the reader to question the disjuncture of such terms as 'nature writing,' 'environmental literature,' pastoral, jeremiad, and activism."

REVIEW: *J Am Hist* v101 no1 p282 Je 2014

REVIEW: *Libr J* v138 no12 p82 Jl 1 2013 Stacy Russo

KILDAY, ANNE-MARIE. A history of infanticide in Britain, c. 1600 to the present; [by] Anne-Marie Kilday x, 338 p. 2013 Palgrave Macmillan

1. Historical literature 2. Infanticide—Great Britain—History 3. Infanticide—Law & legislation 4. Infanticide—Social aspects 5. Trials (Infanticide)—History

ISBN 9780230547070

LC 2013-019073

SUMMARY: In this book, "using case studies spanning over four centuries, [Anne-Marie] Kilday . . . examines the varied roles that men and women across Great Britain played in the criminal act of newborn child murder. . . . Kilday argues that infanticide was a crime committed both in isolation and under a network of surveillance, as early modern living and working environments were anything but private." (Choice: Current Reviews for Academic Libraries)

REVIEW: *Am Hist Rev* v119 no4 p1351 O 2014 Simon Devereaux

REVIEW: *Choice* v51 no9 p1668-9 My 2014 M. A. Riebe

"A History of Infanticide in Britain, c. 1600 to the Present". "[Anne-Marie] Kilday uses this evidence in her book's first half to examine the physical and emotional circumstances and networks of people who actively played a part in criminal acts. The final three chapters trace public responses to cases of infanticide and the history of how prosecutions and attempts at legal and moral reform evolved. More than a history of gender and crime, this book would benefit students at all levels because of its thorough methodological approach."

KILLEEN, JARLATH.ed. Bram Stoker. See Bram Stoker

KIM, PATTI. Here I am; [by] Patti Kim 40 p. 2013 Capstone

1. Cities & towns—Juvenile literature 2. Friendship—Juvenile fiction 3. Immigrants—United States—Juvenile literature 4. Picture books for children 5. Seeds—Juvenile literature

ISBN 1623700361; 9781404882997 (hardcover); 9781479519316 (pbk.); 9781479519323 (paper over board); 9781623700362

LC 2012-051009

SUMMARY: In this book by Patti Kim and illustrated by Sonia Sanchez, "newly arrived from their faraway homeland, a boy and his family enter into the lights, noise, and traffic of a busy American city. The language is unfamiliar. Food, habits, games, and gestures are puzzling. They boy clings tightly to his special keepsake from home and wonders how he will find his way. How will he once again become the happy, confident kid he used to be?" (Publisher's note)

REVIEW: *Bull Cent Child Books* v67 no5 p271 Ja 2014 D. S.

"Here I Am." "Mixed-media illustrations by Spanish illustrator [Sonia] Sánchez incorporate swift, hand-drawn lines, sweeps of saturated reds and translucent aquas, soft, smudgy textures, and occasional collaged elements, and the often-paneled result has the sophistication of a graphic novel. Some aspects of the kid's experience will take some decoding, but audiences will easily perceive the changing mood as them gloomy city becomes more colorful and eventually culminates in the soft green embrace of the park. An author's note explains the story, informing audiences that [Patti]Kim herself came to the U.S. as a child and drew on those experiences in the book."

REVIEW: *Horn Book Magazine* v89 no6 p76-7 N/D 2013 ROBIN L. SMITH

REVIEW: *Kirkus Rev* p58 N 15 2013 Best Books

REVIEW: *Kirkus Rev* v81 no16 p225 Ag 15 2013

REVIEW: *N Y Times Book Rev* p22 O 13 2013 SARAH SHUN-LIEN BYNUM

"The Voyage," "Here I Am," and "My Mom is a Foreigner, But Not To Me." "Perhaps there is no better way to evoke the universal than by enlisting the help of small forest animals, which the illustrator Camilla Engman does to delightful effect in 'The Voyage.' . . . The text, translated from Norwegian by Jeanne Eirhelm, feels slightly stiff at times, but the wit and inventiveness of the artwork make this voyage memorable. Patti Kim forgoes text altogether in her winsome 'Here I Am'. . . . Like Kim, the actress Julianne Moore sets her new picture book in a colorful, bustling . . . metropolis--but hers stretches luxuriously across double-page spreads. . . . Moore . . . offers an original twist on the immigrant narrative."

REVIEW: *Publ Wkly* p36 Children's starred review annual 2013

KIMMEL, ELIZABETH CODY. A taste of freedom; Gandhi and the great salt march; 48 p. 2014 Walker Childrens

1. Children's stories 2. Civil disobedience—Fiction 3. JUVENILE NONFICTION—Biography & Autobiography—Historical 4. JUVENILE NONFICTION—People & Places—Other 5. Nonviolence—Fiction

ISBN 9780802794673 (hardback); 9780802794703 (library reinforced)

LC 2013-019877

SUMMARY: "This account of the Salt March of 1930 is told through the eyes of a fictional Indian boy who, moved by Gandhi's words and actions, joins the protest against British rule of India. The Mahatma leads people on a nearly 250-mile march to the sea to gather the salt that is so precious but is controlled and sold by the British Empire. Gandhi promises not to fight and to use only peaceful means to achieve independence from colonial rule." (School Library Journal)

REVIEW: *Booklist* v110 no9/10 p90-2 Ja 1 2014 Thom Barthelmess

REVIEW: *Bull Cent Child Books* v67 no6 p320-1 F 2014 Elizabeth Bush

REVIEW: *Kirkus Rev* v81 no24 p89 D 15 2013

"A Taste of Freedom: Gandhi and the Great Salt March". "An old man recalls the extraordinary time when, as a young boy, he joined an older brother in following Mahatma Gandhi on his long march to gather salt from the sea. [Elizabeth Cody] Kimmel's simple storytelling is pitched for quite young listeners. . . . Though so much more than salt was at stake, even the afterword, detailing the history of Gandhi's nonviolent opposition to British rule, only hints at the full story. [Giuliano] Ferri's watercolor-and-pencil illustrations are full of warmth and immediacy-the young protagonist is on every spread. A gentle introduction to Gandhi's remarkable work."

REVIEW: *Publ Wkly* v260 no49 p85 D 2 2013

REVIEW: *SLJ* v60 no1 p72 Ja 2014 Jody Kopple

KIMMEL, MICHAEL. Angry white men; American masculinity at the end of an era; [by] Michael Kimmel 336 p. 2013 Nation Books

1. Civil rights—United States 2. Equality—United States 3. Masculinity—United States 4. Men—United States—Attitudes 5. POLITICAL SCIENCE—Political Ideologies—Conservatism & Liberalism 6. SOCIAL SCIENCE—Men's Studies 7. SOCIAL SCIENCE—Violence in Society 8. Social science literature 9. Whites—United States—Attitudes

ISBN 9781568586960 (hardback)

LC 2013-025872

SUMMARY: It was the author's intent to demonstrate that "downward mobility, increased racial and gender equality, and a tenacious clinging to an anachronistic ideology of masculinity has left many men feeling betrayed and bewildered. Raised to expect unparalleled social and economic privilege, white men are suffering today from what [Michael] Kimmel calls 'aggrieved entitlement': a sense that those benefits that white men believed were their due have been snatched away from them." (Publisher's note)

REVIEW: *Booklist* v110 no3 p4 O 1 2013 David Pitt

REVIEW: *Kirkus Rev* v81 no19 p148 O 1 2013

REVIEW: *N Y Times Book Rev* p12 N 24 2013 HANNA ROSIN

"Angry White Men: American Masculinity at the End of an Era." "[Michael] Kimmel . . . is unusually adventurous for an academic. . . . Kimmel maintains a delicate balance when handling his sources. He wants to be sympathetic to the people he interviews and yet loyal to his academic principles. . . . But Kimmel also strains a little to hard for a tidy sociological explanation. . . . Kimmel's balance of critical distance and empathy works best in his chapter on the fathers' rights movement. . . . Outside a more elite audience, Kimmel's diagnosis of aggrieved entitlement will be, I imagine, a tough sell."

KIMMELMAN, LESLIE. Hot dog!; Eleanor Roosevelt throws a picnic; 40 p. 2014 Sleeping Bear Press

1. Historical literature 2. Presidents' spouses—United States—Juvenile literature 3. Royal visitors—Great Britain—Juvenile literature 4. Royal visitors—United States—Juvenile literature 5. Visits of state—United States—Juvenile literature

ISBN 158536830X; 9781585368303

LC 2013-024897

SUMMARY: In this illustrated history book for children, "when King George and Queen Elizabeth decided to visit the U.S.--the first time a British monarch had set foot on U.S. shores--Mrs. Roosevelt decided that, among other entertainments, a picnic in Hyde Park was in order. But when she said that she wanted to serve that quintessential American food, hot dogs, her menu choice became a subject of national discussion." (Booklist)

REVIEW: *Booklist* v110 no14 p69-70 Mr 15 2014 Ilene Cooper

"Hot Dog! Eleanor Roosevelt Throws a Picnic." "This book . . . tak[es] a little-known incident from history and turn[s] it into a delightful picture book. . . . In just 40 pages, [Leslie] Kimmelman does a pithy job of presenting both this amusing incident and also what was happening in both the country and a world on the brink of war. An author's note gives more information, but there is no sourcing of quotes. The caricature-style art presents a cast larger than life, and while it will evoke smiles, it is toned down in more somber moments. A historical footnote that readers will enjoy."

REVIEW: *Kirkus Rev* v82 no3 p290 F 1 2014

"Hot Dog! Eleanor Roosevelt Throws a Picnic". "Caricature drawings capture the essence of the personalities and behaviors of the four main participants, Franklin and Eleanor Roosevelt and King George VI and Queen Elizabeth, while adding a sense of reality and amusement to the historically little-known episode. [Leslie] Kimmelman's straightforward storytelling incorporates some basic explanatory facts and deftly brings this bit of Americana to life. An author's note provides further context along with a statement that quoted correspondence can be found at Hyde Park; it is silent, however, on the authenticity of the Roosevelts' dialogue. A captivating introductory piece for budding history buffs. "

REVIEW: *New York Times* v163 no56560 p16 Jl 12 2014 SARAH HARRISON SMITH

REVIEW: *Publ Wkly* v261 no4 p192 Ja 27 2014

REVIEW: *SLJ* v60 no4 p180 Ap 2014 Joanna K. Fabicon

KIMMELMAN, LESLIE. Sam and Charlie (and Sam Too) return!; [by] Leslie Kimmelman 48 p. 2014 Albert Whitman & Company

1. Children's stories 2. Fasts & feasts—Judaism—Juve-

nile literature 3. Friendship—Fiction 4. Jews—United States—Fiction 5. Trees—Juvenile literature
ISBN 9780807572153
LC 2013-029480

SUMMARY: In this children's book, "Charlie's over-enthusiastic shoveling complicates Sam's plan of helping neighbors clear their walks on a snowy day; the three celebrate the Jewish holiday of Tu B'Shevat by planting a tree . . . Charlie searches for the Passover afikomen (hidden piece of matzah); Sam and Charlie befriend a mute neighbor kid; and the two older kids help little Sam Too be the dreidel-playing, menorah-candle-burning, latke-eating Hanukkah queen." (Children's Literature)

REVIEW: *Bull Cent Child Books* v67 no9 p461 My 2014 J. H.

REVIEW: *Kirkus Rev* v82 no2 p174 Ja 15 2014

"Sam and Charlie (and Sam Too) Return!" " This is a collection of Jewish stories that leaves out the stories. Reading this book feels a lot like listening to a vinyl LP with multiple skips that send listeners abruptly from the middle of one song to the next. . . . Readers may be forgiven for feeling that these scenes could have occurred in any order and made just as much sense. The illustrations are unfailingly gorgeous. Charlie's hair has more personality than the main characters in other books. If only the stories were as involving as the pictures around them."

KINCAID, JAMAICA, 1946-. The bridge of beyond; 272 p. 2013 New York Review Books

1. Guadeloupe literature (French) 2. Mothers & daughters—Fiction 3. Psychological fiction 4. Slavery—Fiction
ISBN 9781590176801 (alk. paper)
LC 2013-015580

SUMMARY: This novel by Simone Schwarz-Bart looks at "love and wonder, mothers and daughters, spiritual values and the grim legacy of slavery on the French Antillean island of Guadeloupe. Here long-suffering Telumee tells her life story and tells us about the proud line of Lougandor women she continues to draw strength from." (Publisher's note)

REVIEW: *TLS* no5782 p26 Ja 24 2014 BELINDA JACK

"The Bridge of Beyond." "'Pluie et vent sur Télumée Miracle' (1972), the first of Schwarz-Bart's two solo novels, was translated by Barbara Bray as 'The Bridge of Beyond' in 1974 and is now reissued with a splendid introduction by a fellow Antillean writer, Jamaica Kincaid. The novel tells of the complex lives and sensibilities of Guadeloupian women across five generations. . . . From their life stories, [narrator] Telumee draws the strength to withstand poverty and heartbreak and to share her own experience. Her story is, in part, about storytelling itself and the ways in which language can teach us to suffer the pain of loneliness or despair but to keep going."

REVIEW: *World Lit Today* v87 no5 p4 S/O 2013 Sam Wilson

"The Bridge of Beyond." "play. In this new edition . . . [Simone Schwarz-Bart's] narrative and Barbara Bray's 1974 translation from the French both hold up well, confirming the novel's status as a tour de force of Caribbean literature. . . . The effect of 'Bridge' is intoxicating, and not just because it nurses familiar blues riffs from my own American heritage--its heady prose renders a vivid, full-bodied account of life in the Antilles. . . . This is an infinite, celebratory novel, containing multitudes in the space of each rich sentence--a masterpiece of Caribbean literature that certainly deserves the badge of the classic."

KINCAID, JAMAICA, 1946-. See now then; [by] Jamaica Kincaid 192 p. 2013 Farrar, Straus and Giroux

1. Domestic fiction 2. Family—Fiction 3. Husband & wife 4. Marriage—Fiction 5. Mythology
ISBN 9780374180560 (hardcover : alk. paper); 0374180563
LC 2012-029932

SUMMARY: In this novel by Jamaica Kincaid "a marriage is revealed in all its joys and agonies. . . . Kincaid inhabits each of her characters, a mother and father and their two children living in a small village in New England, as they move, in their own minds, between the present, the past, and the future. . . . But their minds wander, trying to make linear sense of what is, in fact, nonlinear." (Publisher's note)

REVIEW: *Bookforum* v19 no5 p21 F/Mr 2013 JESS ROW

REVIEW: *Booklist* v109 no6 p20 N 15 2012 Donna Seaman

REVIEW: *Kirkus Rev* v80 no23 p226 D 1 2012

REVIEW: *Libr J* v137 no15 p47 S 15 2012 Barbara Hoffert

REVIEW: *Libr J* v138 no11 p47 Je 15 2013 Beth Farrell

REVIEW: *Libr J* v138 no2 p62 F 1 2013 Lauren Gilbert

REVIEW: *Ms* v23 no1 p57-9 Wint 2013 ERIN AUBRY KAPLAN

REVIEW: *N Y Times Book Rev* p28 Mr 2 2014 IHSAN TAYLOR

REVIEW: *N Y Times Book Rev* p9 F 24 2013 FERNANDA EBERSTADT

REVIEW: *N Y Times Book Rev* p22 Mr 3 2013

REVIEW: *New York Times* v162 no56038 pC1-5 F 5 2013 FELICIA R. LEE

REVIEW: *New York Times* v162 no56046 pC1-5 F 13 2013 DWIGHT GARNER

REVIEW: *Publ Wkly* v260 no5 p22-9 F 4 2013 SHANNON MAUGHAN

REVIEW: *Publ Wkly* v260 no12 p62 Mr 25 2013

REVIEW: *Publ Wkly* v259 no50 p36 D 10 2012

REVIEW: *TLS* no5740 p21 Ap 5 2013 ALEX CLARK

"See Now Then." "This wild imbalance between husband and wife obscures the novel's subtler currents; it hinders the reader from thinking--or even feeling--with much clarity about the terrifying roles that might be ascribed to individuals within families, and their inescapability. Where [Jamaica] Kincaid is more successful is in allowing her loosely jointed prose style, with its mesmerizing repetitions, echoes and patterns, to suggest the notion of time and its circular properties; to plant the idea that, while human relationships can only exist in time, time also works to destroy them by the weight of accumulated dissatisfactions, and by the irrepressibility of individual will."

KING, ANDREW. Hands On! Math Projects; 160 p. 2014 Cardinal Pub Group

1. Children's nonfiction 2. Classroom activities 3. Fractions 4. Mathematical literature 5. Shapes
ISBN 1770938907; 9781770938908

SUMMARY: In this book, "lots of hands-on games, activities and challenges allow readers to learn and practice some valuable math skills and concepts. Six chapters, each with its own table of contents, explore numbers, fractions, patterns, math facts, shapes, and points and position. Each double-page spread offers readers a simple introduction to a concept, such as number codes, Carroll diagrams, probability or tessellations, as well as a game or activity to cement or extend the learning." (Kirkus Reviews)

REVIEW: *Kirkus Rev* v82 no3 p325 F 1 2014

"Hands On! Math Projects". "Lots of hands-on games, activities and challenges allow readers to learn and practice some valuable math skills and concepts. . . . For the most part, the numbered steps are easy to follow, though occasionally page layout may prove confusing. While the projects mostly use common household materials, some are much more complicated than they need to be. . . . Some of the language is awkward. . . . Still it may be useful to those who work with kids in a teaching capacity."

KING, CARO. Shadow spell; [by] Caro King 308 p. 2012 Aladdin

1. Adventure and adventurers—Fiction 2. Brothers and sisters—Fiction 3. Fantasy 4. JUVENILE FICTION—Action & Adventure—General 5. JUVENILE FICTION—Family—Siblings 6. JUVENILE FICTION—Fantasy & Magic 7. Missing children—Fiction
ISBN 9781442420458 (hardback)
LC 2012-004010

SUMMARY: This fantasy book, "sequel to 'Seven Sorcerers' follows several characters including "Jibbit . . . a gargoyle with a good heart who is afraid of the ground. Skerridge is a rogue bogeyman. Strood of the Terrible House is busy raising an army of tiger-men out of disparate bodies and the ubiquitous crowsmorte vine. Ninevah Redstone is the plucky girl who may save this world, but not before many adventures, startling and icky brushes with torture and death . . . There are the Quick, the Grimm and the Fabulous (labels for, respectively, humans and two different types of nonhuman), the tombfolk and the skinkin." (Kirkus Reviews)

REVIEW: *Kirkus Rev* v80 no8 p234 Ap 15 2012

" A great deal of action is regularly stopped cold by explication, gory and funny parts and some delicious ideas in this confusing middle-grade fantasy, sequel to 'Seven Sorcerers' (2011). . . .Words are capitalized portentously, and much dialogue is communicated in aggressive dialect that's positively festooned with apostrophes. There are more dei ex machina than can be enumerated, and go round and round, and a lot of things end up where they started, only not exactly. It is difficult to know where one is in the story or where the story is going, quite, but readers captivated by the humor or the horror may not care, as everything is (kind of) tied up in the end."

REVIEW: *SLJ* p82 Jl 2012 Ricca Gaus

KING, JR., MARTIN LUTHER. See Flowers, Arthur.

KING, LAURIE R. The bones of Paris; a novel of suspense; [by] Laurie R. King 432 p. 2013 Bantam Books

1. Historical fiction 2. Murder—Fiction 3. Paraphilias 4. Paris (France)—Social life & customs—20th century
ISBN 0345531760; 9780345531766
LC 2013-010332

SUMMARY: In this book, author Laurie R. "King leads readers into the vibrant and sensual Paris of the Jazz Age. . . . As Stuyvesant follows Philippa's trail through the expatriate community of artists and writers, he finds that she is known to many of its famous--and infamous--inhabitants. . . . At the Grand-Guignol, murder, insanity, and sexual perversion are all staged to shocking, brutal effect: depravity as art, savage human nature on stage." (Publisher's note)

REVIEW: *Booklist* v110 no1 p43 S 1 2013 Bill Ott

REVIEW: *Booklist* v110 no13 p29 Mr 1 2014 Whitney Scott

REVIEW: *Kirkus Rev* v81 no16 p256 Ag 15 2013

"The Bones of Paris." "Harris Stuyvesant didn't think any more of Philippa Crosby than of most of the young women he bedded. Their five-day fling certainly wasn't long enough to count as an affair. So when Pip goes missing and her uncle Ernest . . . asks him to find her, the man's in an awkward position. . . . His suspicion that Pip's was only one of a long line of disappearances has made him a changed man who has to admit that 'the odors of life are not always pleasant'--even in 1929 Paris. Evocative period detail and challenging aesthetic adventures compensate for a mystery more suggestive than believable and a climactic sequence that seems to have been lifted from [author Laurie R.] King's last tale of Mary Russell and Sherlock Holmes ('Garment of Shadows')."

REVIEW: *Libr J* v139 no3 p60 F 15 2014 Judith Robinson

REVIEW: *Publ Wkly* v260 no28 p149 Jl 15 2013

KING, MICHAEL B. Democracy's Missing Arsenal; [by] Michael B. King 588 p. 2013 CreateSpace Independent Publishing Platform

1. Alternate histories (Fiction) 2. International relations—Fiction 3. Slavery—Fiction 4. United States—History—Fiction 5. World War, 1914-1918—Fiction
ISBN 9781484100943; 1484100948

SUMMARY: This book, the first in a series, "explores a world in which a Confederate victory in the Civil War has devastating effects on international and Great Power relations over the next century. . . . There is no united United States to serve as FDR's 'Arsenal of Democracy.' It is a nightmare world—one where slavery is neither stamped out nor fades away, and where the US cannot intervene decisively on the Western Front because it is enmeshed on the Potomac Front." (Publisher's note)

REVIEW: *Kirkus Rev* p33 D 15 2013 supplemet best books 2013

"Democracy's Missing Arsenal". " In the first of their planned three volume alternative American history, [Michael B.] King and [John M.] Bredehoft expertly plot the effects of the South's victory in the Civil War. . . . King and Bredehoft seamlessly weave genuine and conceivable historical happenings: The Dreyfus Affair and Boxer Rebellion are juxtaposed with imagined but entirely plausible assassinations or invasions. Omissions . . . come with faultless justification. Throughout, there is an impressive level of detail as the authors follow minute chronological swerves to their logical conclusions, illustrating 'the highly contingent nature of history.' A flawless blending of actual and potential events, aided by an engaging narrator."

REVIEW: *Kirkus Rev* v81 no21 p165 N 1 2013

KING, RYAN D. American memories. See Savelsberg, J. J.

KING, STEPHEN, 1947-. Doctor Sleep; a novel; [by] Stephen King 544 p. 2013 Scribner

1. Alcoholics—Fiction 2. Good and evil—Fiction 3. Horror tales, American 4. Paranormal fiction 5. Psychic ability Fiction
ISBN 1476727651; 9781451698855 (pbk.: alk. paper); 9781451698862 (mass market: alk. paper); 9781476727653 (hardcover: alk. paper)
LC 2013-000431

SUMMARY: This sequel to Stephen King's "The Shining," follows "Dan Torrence, the alcoholic son of the very dangerously alcoholic father." Dan's substance abuse problems "all trace back to the bad doings at the Overlook Hotel . . . and all those voices in poor Dan's head, which speak to (and because of) a very special talent he has. That 'shining' is a matter of more than passing interest for a gang of . . . torture-loving, soul-sucking folks who aren't quite folks at all—the True Knot." (Kirkus Reviews)

REVIEW: *Booklist* v109 no22 p50 Ag 1 2013 Daniel Kraus

REVIEW: *Booklist* v109 no17 p52 My 1 2013 Brad Hooper

REVIEW: *Kirkus Rev* p21-2 N 15 2013 Best Books

REVIEW: *Kirkus Rev* p4-7 Ag 15 2013 Fall Preview

REVIEW: *Kirkus Rev* v81 no17 p12-3 S 1 2013

REVIEW: *Kirkus Rev* p9-10 Ag 15 2013 Fall Preview

REVIEW: *Libr J* v138 no21 p55 D 1 2013 Tristan M. Boyd

REVIEW: *Libr J* v138 no15 p65 S 15 2013 Amy Hoseth

REVIEW: *Libr J* v138 no6 p59 Ap 1 2013 Barbara Hoffert

REVIEW: *N Y Times Book Rev* p24 Jl 13 2014 IHSAN TAYLOR

REVIEW: *N Y Times Book Rev* p1-26 S 22 2013 Margaret Atwood

"Doctor Sleep". "A very good specimen of the quintessential [Stephen] King blend. . . . King's good-and-evil arrangement is usually yin and yang, with a spot of darkness in every goodie and a tiny ray of sunshine in every baddie. . . . King is a pro; by the end of this book your fingers will be mere stubs of their former selves, and you will be looking askance at the people in the supermarket line. . . . King's inventiveness and skill show no signs of slacking: 'Doctor Sleep' has all the virtues of his best work."

REVIEW: *New York Times* v163 no56560 p24 Jl 12 2014 IHSAN TAYLOR

REVIEW: *New York Times* v162 no56261 pC1-4 S 16 2013 JANET MASLIN

REVIEW: *Publ Wkly* v260 no40 p14 O 7 2013

REVIEW: *Publ Wkly* v260 no32 p38 Ag 12 2013

REVIEW: *Time* v182 no14 p64 S 30 2013 Lev Grossman

KING, WELDON. The Way West; [by] Weldon King 268 p. 2012 Createspace Independent Pub

1. Frontier & pioneer life—West (U.S.) 2. Genealogy 3. Historical fiction 4. King family 5. United States—History—Civil War, 1861-1865
ISBN 1479355275; 9781479355273

SUMMARY: In this book, author Weldon King "remembers his homesteading family" and "the historical events that shaped their experience. Beginning with the westward migration of the King family from North Carolina, King describes the family moving via covered wagon in the mid-19th century, stopping in Georgia and Alabama toward their final destination of Texas." (Kirkus Reviews)

REVIEW: *Kirkus Rev* v82 no2 p350 Ja 15 2014

"The Way West". "Those looking for a sweeping history of America with personal anecdotes along the way may find something of interest here, but though [Weldon] King proves himself to be comfortable relating American history, there's not much narrative form. There are hardly any scenes: Almost everything is told in summary, with the author eventually finding more footing when he relates his personal experiences of growing up on a farm in the book's latter half. The family history will struggle to find an audience beyond descendants. Often charming but in need of more scene-setting to ground the author's knowledge of history."

KINKELA, DAVID. DDT and the American century; global health, environmental politics, and the pesticide that changed the world; [by] David Kinkela p. cm. 2011 University of North Carolina Press

1. Cold War, 1945-1989 2. DDT (Insecticide)—Environmental aspects 3. DDT (Insecticide)—History 4. DDT (Insecticide)—History—20th century 5. Environmentalism—United States—History 6. Historical literature 7. Insect pests—Control—History—20th century 8. United States—Foreign relations—20th century
ISBN 9780807835098 (cloth : alk. paper)
LC 2011-015416

SUMMARY: "In 'DDT and the American Century,' David Kinkela chronicles the use of DDT around the world from 1941 to the present with a particular focus on the United States, which has played a critical role in encouraging the global use of the pesticide. . . . DDT's function as a tool of U.S. foreign policy and its use in international development projects designed to solve problems of disease and famine made it an integral component of the so-called American Century." (Publisher's note)

REVIEW: *Am Hist Rev* v117 no5 p1619-20 D 2012 Gordon Patterson

REVIEW: *Bus Hist Rev* v87 no3 p581-3 Aut 2013 Dominique Tobbell

"DDT and the American Century: Global Health, Environmental Politics, and the Pesticide That Changed the World." "In 'DDT and the American Century,' David Kinkela examines the paradox of DDT's history, chronicling the US-promoted deployment of DDT in international development projects amidst a burgeoning environmentalist critique of DDT's ecological effects. Between 1941 and the 1970s, Kinkela argues, DDT was an exemplar of the American Century and the technological modernity that predicated America's global identity. . . . Although there is already a sizable history on DDT and on American environmentalism, Kinkela's 'DDT and the American Century' contributes a compelling new perspective to these histories, one that casts DDT as a powerful tool of US foreign policy during the Cold War."

REVIEW: *Choice* v49 no7 p1283 Mr 2012 H. E. Pence

REVIEW: *J Am Hist* v99 no2 p678-9 S 2012 Amy Hay

REVIEW: *Science* v335 no6066 p288 Ja 20 2012 Frederick R. Davis

KINSELLA, CLODAGH. tr. The Night. See Bernstein, M.

KINSELLA, SEAN.tr. Through the night. See Through the night

KINSEY, DAVID N. Climbing Mount Laurel. See Massey, D. S.

KINZER, STEPHEN. The brothers; John Foster Dulles, Allen Dulles, and their secret world war; [by] Stephen Kinzer 416 p. 2013 Time Books/Henry Holt and Company

1. Biographies 2. Cabinet officers—United States—Biography 3. Intelligence service—United States—History—20th century 4. Spies—United States—Biography 5. Statesmen—United States—Biography

ISBN 0805094970; 9780805094978 (hardcover)

LC 2013-007718

SUMMARY: This book presents "a dual biography of Secretary of State John Foster Dulles and CIA director Allen Dulles." Author Stephen Kinzer "roots their anti-Communist policies in their belief in American exceptionalism and its Wilsonian application to promote democracy in the world. Less abstractly, the Dulles brothers were politically connected Wall Street lawyers, servants of corporate power, according to Kinzer." (Booklist)

REVIEW: *Bookforum* v20 no4 p40 D 2013/Ja 2014 CHRIS BRAY

REVIEW: *Booklist* v110 no3 p5-6 O 1 2013 Gilbert Taylor

"The Brothers: John Foster Dulles, Allen Dulles, and Their Secret World War." "An author tending toward criticism of American foreign affairs, . . . [Stephen] Kinzer casts a jaundiced eye on siblings who conducted them in the 1950s. . . . Detailing American actions in Iran, Guatemala, Indonesia, and Cuba, Kinzer crafts a negative perspective on the legacy of the Dulles brothers, whom he absolves slightly from blame because their compatriots widely approved of their providential sense of America's role in world affairs. A historical critique sure to spark debate."

REVIEW: *Christ Century* v130 no25 p22 D 11 2013

REVIEW: *Kirkus Rev* p29 2013 Guide 20to BookExpo America

REVIEW: *Kirkus Rev* p28 2013 Guide 20to BookExpo America Megan Labrise

REVIEW: *Kirkus Rev* v81 no9 p54-5 My 1 2013

REVIEW: *Libr J* v138 no8 p60 My 1 2013

REVIEW: *N Y Times Book Rev* p50 N 10 2013 ADAM LEBOR

"The Brothers: John Foster Dulles, Allen Dulles, and Their Secret World War." "Anyone wanting to know why the United States is hated across much of the world need look no farther than this book. 'The Brothers' is a riveting chronicle of government-sanctioned murder, casual elimination of 'inconvenient' regimes, relentless prioritization of American corporate interests and cynical arrogance on the part of two men who were once among the most powerful in the world. . . . In his detailed, well-constructed and highly readable book, Stephen Kinzer . . . shows how the brothers drove America's interventionist foreign policy. . . . The Iranian section of Kinzer's book is especially strong."

KIRBY, DANIELLE. Fantasy and belief; alternative religions, popular narratives and digital cultures; [by] Danielle Kirby 194 p. 2013 Equinox

1. Cults 2. Mass media—Religious aspects 3. Religion and culture 4. Social science literature 5. Virtual communities

ISBN 9781908049230

LC 2012-026810

SUMMARY: This book, written by Danielle Kirby, "explores the context and implications of these types of beliefs through the example of the Otherkin community, a loosely affiliated group of individuals who believe themselves to be in some way non-human. Tracking a path through fiction and mythology, fan cultures and world creation, occulture and the Internet, Fantasy and Belief investigates . . . the popular and the sacred." (Publisher's note)

REVIEW: *Choice* v51 no4 p617-8 D 2013 J. H. Fitz

"Fantasy and Belief: Alternative Religions, Popular Narratives, and Digital Cultures." "[Author Danielle] Kirby . . . explores the Otherkin, a virtual online community whose members believe they are beings from mythology, classical literature, and fantasy fiction: elves, satyrs, fairies, dragons, aliens, vampires, or extraterrestrial humans. Kirby draws on literature related to popular culture, specifically 'occulture,' . . . to provide the broader context within which Otherkin beliefs and experience take shape. . . . The book includes a useful overview of related phenomena/trends such as the occult, witchcraft, paganism, magic, and New Age understandings of the world."

KIRBY, MATTHEW J. The lost kingdom; [by] Matthew J. Kirby 352 p. 2013 Scholastic Press

1. Adventure and adventurers—Fiction 2. Adventure stories 3. Naturalists—United States—Juvenile fiction 4. Quests (Expeditions)—Juvenile fiction 5. Voyages and travels—Fiction 6. Voyages and travels—Juvenile fiction

ISBN 0545274265; 9780545274265 (jacketed hardcover)

LC 2012-043516

SUMMARY: This alternate-history story is set in 1750s North America. "Billy Bartram is thrilled when his father allows him to come along on a westward expedition, but he never dreamed the journey would involve a secret philosophical society, a flying vessel crewed by geniuses, and a mythical kingdom founded by an ancient Welsh prince, which could hold allies against the encroaching French." (Publishers Weekly)

REVIEW: *Booklist* v110 no2 p70-1 S 15 2013 Carolyn Phelan

"The Lost Kingdom." "In 1753, noted American naturalist John Bartram and his son Billy join an expedition to search the frontier in the di Terzi, a flying ship powered by 'vacuum balloons' and wind. . . . This alternate history story, propelled by scenes of suspense and rousing action, traces Billy's growing independence from his beloved father. As the stakes grow higher, he comes to rely increasingly on his own judgment. Billy's first-person narrative offers insights into varied colonial American views on a number of topics. Inspired by history and legend, this inventive novel takes flight as a grand adventure with elements of fantasy and steampunk."

REVIEW: *Bull Cent Child Books* v67 no2 p99 O 2013 E. B.

REVIEW: *Kirkus Rev* v81 no14 p151 Jl 15 2013

REVIEW: *Publ Wkly* v260 no27 p88 Jl 8 2013

KIRBY, PETER. Child workers and industrial health in Britain, 1780-1850; [by] Peter Kirby 212 p. 2013 Boydell Press

1. Child labor—Great Britain—History 2. Children—Health and hygiene—Great Britain—History 3. Historical literature 4. Industrial hygiene—Great Britain—History 5. Industrial revolution

ISBN 1843838842; 9781843838845

LC 2012-361290

SUMMARY: This book by Peter Kirby examines "children's occupational health during the earlier part of the Industrial Revolution. . . . Kirby analyzes topics such as deformities, fevers, respiratory complaints, and physical punishment in mills and factories. Throughout, he emphasizes that the line previous scholars have drawn between occupational health and public health is detrimental to understanding the socioeconomic context of children's health." (Choice: Current Reviews for Academic Libraries)

REVIEW: *Choice* v51 no6 p1080-1 F 2014 L. E. Payne

"Child Workers and Industrial Health in Britain, 1780-1850." "This is an elegantly written exploration of children's occupational health during the earlier part of the Industrial Revolution. As [Peter] Kirby . . . notes in his introduction, historians' view of child industrial workers is overwhelmingly pessimistic. He seeks to complicate this picture through a close examination of children's illness and injuries in manufacturing districts over a 70-year period. The paucity of sources for this period leads Kirby to cast a wide net. . . . Recommended."

KIRKBY, MANDY.ed. Love Letters of the Great War. See Love Letters of the Great War

KIRKMAN, L. KATHERINE. The natural communities of Georgia. See Edwards, L.

KIRKPATRICK, KATHERINE. Between two worlds; [by] Katherine Kirkpatrick 304 p. 2014 Wendy Lamb Books, an imprint of Random House Children's Books

1. Eskimos—Fiction 2. Historical fiction 3. Inuit—Fiction 4. Inuit—Juvenile fiction 5. Race relations—Fiction

ISBN 0385740476; 9780375872211 (pbk.); 9780375989476 (lib. bdg.); 9780385740470 (trade)

LC 2013-014735

SUMMARY: In this book, by Katherine Kirkpatrick, "on the treeless shores of Itta, Greenland, as far north as humans can settle, sixteen-year-old Inuit Billy Bah spots a ship far out among the icebergs on the bay. . . . The ship carries provisions for Robert E. Peary, who is making an expedition to the North Pole. As a child, Billy Bah spent a year in America with Peary's family. . . . Winter comes on fast, and when the ship gets caught in the ice, Billy Bah sets out to find Peary." (Publisher's note)

REVIEW: *Booklist* v110 no16 p56 Ap 15 2014 Michael Cart

REVIEW: *Bull Cent Child Books* v67 no9 p462 My 2014 D. S.

"Between Two Worlds". "[Katherine] Kirkpatrick has been a sensitive explorer of history in both fiction and nonfiction . . . her fictional depiction of the real-life young woman who translated and sewed for Peary expeditions gives her an opportunity to explore some of the subtle complexities of this strange cultural intersection. Eqariusaq's narration vividly immerses readers in the warm companionship and icy physical chill of her Inuit community, with her perplexing American experiences revealed in flashbacks. . . . It's also a compelling counternarrative to exploration tales as Eqariusaq negotiates her way through intersectionality, remaining an active participant in her own fate."

REVIEW: *Kirkus Rev* v82 no6 p78 Mr 15 2014

REVIEW: *Publ Wkly* v261 no6 p91 F 10 2014

REVIEW: *SLJ* v60 no5 p133 My 2014 Madeline J. Bryant

KIRN, WALTER. Blood will out; the true story of a murder, a mystery, and a masquerade; [by] Walter Kirn 272 p. 2014 Liveright Publishing Corporation

1. Impostors and imposture—United States—Case studies 2. Memoirs 3. Murderers—United States—Case studies 4. True crime stories

ISBN 0871404516; 9780871404510 (hardcover)

LC 2013-046327

SUMMARY: This book, by Walter Kirn, is the true story of Clark Rockefeller, an "eccentric son of privilege who ultimately would be unmasked as a brazen serial impostor, child kidnapper, and brutal murderer. . . . As Kirn uncovers the truth about his friend, a psychopath masquerading as a gentleman, he also confronts hard truths about himself. Why, as a writer of fiction, was he susceptible to the deception of a sinister fantasist whose crimes, Kirn learns, were based on books and movies?" (Publisher's note)

REVIEW: *Bookforum* v21 no1 p52 Ap/My 2014 ERIC BANKS

REVIEW: *Booklist* v110 no12 p3-4 F 15 2014 Eloise Kinney

"Blood Will Out: The True Story of a Murder, a Mystery, and a Masquerade". "The highly personal story of [Walter Kirn's] being hoodwinked, professionally and emotionally, by a man he knew as Clark Rockefeller, a member of the famously wealthy industrial, political, and banking family. . . . This tale's a fascinating one (starting with Kirn's road trip with a paralyzed dog) that is covered elsewhere . . . but Kirn's reflecting, musing, and personal dealings add a killer punch to this true-crime memoir."

REVIEW: *Kirkus Rev* v82 no2 p233 Ja 15 2014

REVIEW: *Libr J* v139 no3 p119 F 15 2014 Deirdre Bray

REVIEW: *N Y Rev Books* v61 no8 p24-6 My 8 2014 Nathaniel Rich

"Blood Will Out: The True Story of a Murder, a Mystery, and a Masquerade." "'Blood Will Out' is an intimate portrait of a professional confidence man. . . . [It] is the true story of the relationship between this man—Walter Kirn—and a second con man, Christian Karl Gerhartsreiter, whom [author Walter] Kirn calls 'the most prodigious serial impostor in recent history.' . . . Kirn has created a fascinating, expertly paced, strikingly written ouroboros tale of two con artists circling each other."

REVIEW: *N Y Times Book Rev* p11 Mr 9 2014 NINA BURLEIGH

REVIEW: *New York Times* v163 no56444 pC1-6 Mr 18 2014 JANET MASLIN

REVIEW: *Publ Wkly* v261 no2 p62-3 Ja 13 2014

KIRWAN, GRÁINNE, 1978-.ed. Cyberpsychology and new media. See Cyberpsychology and new media

KISER, WILLIAM S. Dragoons in Apacheland; conquest and resistance in southern New Mexico, 1846-1861; [by] William S. Kiser xiii, 354 p. 2012 University of Oklahoma Press

1. Apache Indians—New Mexico—Government relations 2. Apache Indians—Wars—New Mexico 3. Historical literature

ISBN 9780806143149 (hardcover: alk. paper)

LC 2012-024000

SUMMARY: This book presents an "analysis of the vicious war between the United States Army and the Apaches in the years from 1846 to 1861. In particular, [William S.] Kiser focuses on the experiences of the First and Second United States Dragoons, along with the Mounted Rifles. . . . In the Southwest, the army faced a formidable enemy in the Chiricahua, Gila, and Mescalero Apaches." (Journal of Military History) The book "include[s] Apache voices and perspectives" (American Historical Review)

REVIEW: *Am Hist Rev* v119 no1 p183-4 F 2014 Thomas A. Britten

"Dragoons in Apacheland: Conquest and Resistance in Southern New Mexico, 1846-1861". "A comprehensive and meticulously researched account of the efforts of U.S. military and civilian officials to make good on [Stephen Watts] Kearny's promise using a combination of diplomacy and military force, and of the Apaches' equally determined efforts to retain their independence and traditional ways of life. The tragic but altogether predictable result was a fifteen-year period marked by violence, confusion, ignorance, treachery, and loss of life. . . . This important, well-written, and impressively researched book will appeal to students and scholars of Western history, borderlands history, Native American history, and military history. I recommend it highly."

KITCHELL, KENNETH F. Animals in the ancient world from A to Z; [by] Kenneth F. Kitchell 288 p. 2013 Routledge

1. Animals—Greece—Nomenclature (Popular)—Encyclopedias 2. Animals—Rome—Nomenclature (Popular)—Encyclopedias 3. Animals in art 4. Encyclopedias & dictionaries 5. Natural history

ISBN 9780415392433 (hardback: alk. paper)

LC 2013-015009

SUMMARY: This reference book takes an alphabetical look at the roles of animals in the ancient world. "Familiar animals such as the cow, dog, fox and donkey are treated along with more exotic animals such as the babirussa, pangolin, and dugong. The evidence adduced ranges from Minoan times to the Late Roman Empire and is taken from archaeology, ancient authors, inscriptions, papyri, coins, mosaics and all other artistic media." (Publisher's note)

REVIEW: *Choice* v51 no8 p1363-4 Ap 2014 B. Juhl

"Animals in the Ancient World From A to Z". "This latest offering in Routledge's 'The Ancient World from A to Z' series elegantly blends scholarly precision with an accessible style, making it a pleasure to browse. . . . Care is taken to provide authoritative translations from ancient terms, with full explanations of the shades of difference between, for instance, two separate Greek terms for 'monkey' or 'ape.' . . . This compendium should be a welcome addition to any library supporting collections ranging from archaeology to zoology, including classical studies. . . . Highly recommended."

KITCHER, PHILIP, 1947-. Deaths in Venice; the cases of Gustav von Aschenbach; [by] Philip Kitcher 280 p. 2013 Columbia University Press

1. Art & philosophy 2. Aschenbach, Gustav von (Fictitious character) 3. Philosophical literature 4. Philosophy in literature

ISBN 9780231162647 (cloth : acid-free paper)

LC 2013-007247

SUMMARY: In this book, "the philosopher Philip Kitcher reads [Thomas] Mann's novella ['Death in Venice'] as a work of philosophy, and amplifies this reading with reference to the film version by Luchino Visconti and the opera by Benjamin Britten. . . . Kitcher thinks that Aschenbach's obsession with Tadzio does not bring about his degradation, that he has had a long string of similar homoerotic crushes, and that his death may have nothing to do with the cholera epidemic." (New York Review of Books)

REVIEW: *N Y Rev Books* v61 no1 p56-8 Ja 9 2014 Leo Carey

"Deaths in Venice: The Gases of Gustav von Aschenbach." "[Philip] Kitcher's style of argument is breezily discursive rather than closely analytic. . . . He often works by suggestion, and states that he is more interested in sketching out new ways of thinking about the novella than in presenting a single interpretation. . . . All the same, the book contains new interpretations, and some of them are surprising. . . . Kitcher's actual readings of 'Death in Venice' don't always directly relate to . . . his assertion that the novella represents literary philosophy of the highest order. . . . Ultimately, the paradox of the book is that, even as Kitcher tries to bridge the gulf between art and philosophy, his arguments tend to underscore the distance between them."

REVIEW: *TLS* no5798 p13 My 16 2014 RITCHIE ROBERTSON

KITSIKOPOULOS, HARRY.ed. Agrarian change and crisis in Europe, 1200-1500. See Agrarian change and crisis in Europe, 1200-1500

KITTINGER, JO S. The house on Dirty-Third Street; 32 p. 2012 Peachtree

1. Buildings—Repair and reconstruction—Fiction 2. Children's literature 3. Faith—Fiction 4. Generosity 5. Home—Fiction 6. Neighborhoods—Fiction 7. Neighbors—Fiction 8. Picture books for children

ISBN 9781561456192

LC 2011-020458

SUMMARY: This picture book tells the story of "a girl and her mother [who] move into an old, run-down house and dare to dream that one day it will become a cozy home. The story is tinged with an underlying heartache from the very start: 'Mom said starting over would be an adventure, so I imagined a tropical island with palm trees and buried treasure. / Not this.' . . . . [Thomas] Gonzalez's illustrations start pale, with a few tints of color and heavily sketched details. But when a spark of hope emerges, and the tide turns, cheeks are flushed and eyes start to sparkle. The sky blazes with a warm sunset on the final full-color spread. A tale of generosity, faith and friendship." (Kirkus)

REVIEW: *Booklist* v108 no12 p60 F 15 2012 Daniel Kraus

REVIEW: *Kirkus Rev* v80 no4 p405-6 F 15 2012

"House on Dirty-Third Street." "A girl and her mother move into an old, run-down house and dare to dream that one day it will become a cozy home. The story is tinged with an underlying heartache from the very start: 'Mom said starting over would be an adventure, so I imagined a tropical island with palm trees and buried treasure. / Not this.' . . . Gonzalez's illustrations start pale, with a few tints of color and heavily sketched details. But when a spark of hope emerges, and the tide turns, cheeks are flushed and eyes start to sparkle. The sky blazes with a warm sunset on the final full-color spread. A tale of generosity, faith and friendship. Share it quietly within and with others."

REVIEW: *SLJ* v58 no12 p69-70 D 2012 Teresa Batenian

REVIEW: *SLJ* v58 no4 p138-9 Ap 2012 Kathleen Finn

KITTREDGE, CAITLIN. The nightmare garden; [by] Caitlin Kittredge 417 p. 2012 Delacorte Press

1. Adventure stories 2. Fantasy 3. Magic—Fiction 4. Steampunk fiction 5. Voyages to the otherworld 6. Young adult fiction

ISBN 9780375985690 (ebook); 9780385738316 (hardback); 9780385907217 (glb)

LC 2011-038306

SUMMARY: This book is the second novel in Caitlin Kittredge's 'Iron Codex' series. "Spoiled, inconsistent, often-thoughtless heroine Aoife Grayson nearly destroyed the world when she broke the Lovecraft Engine and sundered the gates between the worlds of human and Fae. But she's not going to let a little thing like that stop her, so she sets off on an exhausting, somewhat episodic adventure through the steampunk-horror '50s nightmare that is her world . . . The ending promises even bigger adventures to come." (Kirkus)

REVIEW: *Kirkus Rev* v80 no4 p406 F 15 2012

"The Nightmare Garden." " This second installment in the Iron Codex series is as inventive and as bloated as its predecessor. Spoiled, inconsistent, often-thoughtless heroine Aoife Grayson nearly destroyed the world when she broke the Lovecraft Engine and sundered the gates between the worlds of human and Fae. But she's not going to let a little thing like that stop her, so she sets off on an exhausting, somewhat episodic adventure through the steampunk-horror '50s nightmare that is her world. . . . There is a fan base that loved book one and will clamor for more of the same, which this certainly is. The ending promises even bigger adventures to come."

REVIEW: *SLJ* v58 no6 p125-6 Je 2012 Kristin Anderson

REVIEW: *SLJ* v59 no4 p56 Ap 2013 Necia Blundy

REVIEW: *Voice of Youth Advocates* v35 no2 p178 Je 2012 Amy Fiske

KIVY, PETER. Once-told tales; an essay in literary aesthetics; [by] Peter Kivy 202 p. 2011 Wiley-Blackwell

1. Books & reading 2. Literature—Aesthetics 3. Philosophical literature 4. Philosophy & literature 5. Silent reading

ISBN 0470657677 (hardback); 9780470657676 (hardback)

LC 2010-049388

SUMMARY: This book by Peter Kivy, "drawing comparisons with other art forms, . . . examines the role of aesthetic features in silent reading, such as narrative structure, and the core experience of reading a novel as a story rather than a scholarly exercise." It "focuses on the experience of the art form known as the novel" and "explores the different effects of a range of narrative approaches." (Publisher's note)

REVIEW: *Choice* v49 no4 p691-2 D 2011 S. Correa

REVIEW: *TLS* no5755 p22 Jl 19 2013 BEN JEFFERY

"Once-Told Tales" and "Filmspeak: How to Understand Literary Theory by Watching Movies." "Unfortunately, 'Once-Told Tales' is something of an exemplar for this kind of philosophy at its least inspiring, insofar as it leaves the reader with the impression of having been laboriously told not a great deal. . . . [Edward L.] Tomarken's 'Filmspeak' initially seems like less substantial fare. . . . It does, however, bear on some of Tomarken's more specialized work. . . . The pace means that, even on the book's own entry-level terms, he sometimes underestimates the opacity of the theory he is presenting. . . . Even so, some of his examples are wonderful."

KIZER, AMBER. A matter of days; [by] Amber Kizer 288 p. 2013 Delacorte Press

1. Brothers and sisters—Fiction 2. Dystopias 3. Epidemics—Fiction 4. Pandemics 5. Science fiction 6. Survival—Fiction 7. Virus diseases—Fiction 8. West Virginia—Fiction

ISBN 0385908040 (library); 9780375898259 (ebook); 9780385739733 (hardcover); 9780385908047 (library)

LC 2012-012200

SUMMARY: In this book, "Nadia and Rabbit's military doctor uncle, Bean, visited them and insisted on injecting them with a vaccine for a 'new bug.' Not long afterward, the disease XRD TB . . . starts ravaging the world, and 16-year-old Nadia and 11-year-old Rabbit are the only survivors in their entire town. With the assorted survival gear their uncle ordered for them, they attempt to make their way from their Seattle suburb to their grandfather in West Virginia." (Publishers Weekly)

REVIEW: *Bull Cent Child Books* v67 no2 p99-100 O 2013 A. M.

"A Matter of Days." "Over the past eight weeks, a man-made global pandemic has decimated the world's human population. Now, with their parents dead, sixteen-year-old Nadia and her younger brother, Rabbit, must set off on a cross-country journey in search of a family compound hidden deep in the West Virginia mountains, where they hope some of their Family has survived the plague. . . . Less grim than many postapocalyptic narratives currently on offer, this novel is a good fit for readers who want the suspense of a dystopian survival story without the suffering that heroines of the genre usually endure."

REVIEW: *Kirkus Rev* v81 no8 p95 Ap 15 2013

REVIEW: *Publ Wkly* v260 no30 p64 Jl 29 2013

REVIEW: *Publ Wkly* v260 no19 p70 My 13 2013

REVIEW: *SLJ* v59 no6 p128 Je 2013 Maggie Knapp

REVIEW: *SLJ* v59 no9 p70 S 2013 Maggie Knapp

REVIEW: *Voice of Youth Advocates* v36 no3 p78 Ag 2013 Alicia Abdul

KIŠ, DANILO, 1935-1989. The encyclopedia of the dead. See The encyclopedia of the dead

KLASSEN, JON.il. The unseen guest. See Snicket, L.

KLAVAN, ANDREW. Nightmare City; [by] Andrew Klavan 320 p. 2013 Thomas Nelson
1. Horror tales 2. Journalists—Fiction 3. Monsters—Fiction 4. Steroid drug abuse in sports 5. Supernatural—Fiction
ISBN 9781595547972 (Trade Paper)
LC 2013-023670

SUMMARY: In this book, "high school journalist Tom Harding wakes up to find his house deserted, his SoCal neighborhood abandoned, and mysterious creatures after him. He has occasional contact with his too-good-to-be-true girlfriend, his newspaper editor, and a mysterious man who seems to control the monsters. He also sees visions of his brother, a deceased military hero, and a medical TV show with a strangely familiar patient." (Publishers Weekly)

REVIEW: *Booklist* v110 no5 p76-7 N 1 2013 Daniel Kraus

"Nightmare City." "[Andrew] Klavan . . . delivers another stand-up ail-American teen hero in 17-year-old Tom, who wakes up one morning to find a world changed for the worse. . . . The rules of Tom's world, or lack thereof, lend the plot a fiddly quality that never allows for high tension; the tale might have functioned better as a bizarro short story. That said, Klavan retains his James Patterson-like gift for keeping pages turning, and the mystery behind it all--having to do with Tom's school-newspaper exposé on the performance-enhancing drug use of the football team--is a juicy one, and well handled."

REVIEW: *Booklist* v110 no16 p62 Ap 15 2014 Elizabeth Nelson

REVIEW: *Kirkus Rev* v81 no19 p123 O 1 2013

REVIEW: *SLJ* v60 no2 p58 F 2014 Julie Paladino

KLAY, PHIL. Redeployment; [by] Phil Klay 304 p. 2014 The Penguin Press
1. Afghan War, 2001—Fiction 2. American short stories 3. Iraq War, 2003-2011—Fiction 4. Soldiers—United States—Fiction 5. War stories
ISBN 1594204993; 9781594204999 (hardback)
LC 2013-028125

SUMMARY: This short story collection, by Phil Klay, "takes readers to the frontlines of the wars in Iraq and Afghanistan, asking us to understand what happened there, and what happened to the soldiers who returned. Interwoven with themes of brutality and faith, guilt and fear, helplessness and survival, the characters in these stories struggle to make meaning out of chaos." (Publisher's note)

REVIEW: *Bookforum* v21 no2 p17-9 Je-Ag 2014 WILLIAM T. VOLLMANN

REVIEW: *Booklist* v110 no12 p28 F 15 2014 Annie Tully

"Redeployment". "[Phil] Klay's stories are sensational, with vivid characters, biting dialogue, and life within and beyond the Afghan and Iraq wars conveyed with an addictive combination of the mundane and the horrifying. . . . 'Redeployment; is most remarkable, though, for the questions it asks about the aims and effects of war stories themselves, and Klay displays a thoughtful awareness of this literary tradition. That perspective holds these diverse tales together, as his narrators ask why and how war stories are told. . . . Those questions, and Klay's exciting new voice, may stay with the reader long after this book is back on the shelf."

REVIEW: *Kirkus Rev* v82 no1 p297 Ja 1 2014

REVIEW: *N Y Times Book Rev* p1-22 Mr 9 2014 Dexter Filkins

REVIEW: *New Statesman* v143 no5214 p50-1 Je 13 2014 Erica Wagner

REVIEW: *New York Times* v163 no56425 pC1-6 F 27 2014 MICHIKO KAKUTANI

REVIEW: *Publ Wkly* v261 no1 p29 Ja 6 2014

KLEIN, JESSIE. The bully society; school shootings and the crisis of bullying in America's schools; [by] Jessie Klein xi, 307 p. 2012 New York University Press
1. Bullying—United States 2. Bullying in schools—United States 3. Educational literature 4. School discipline—United States 5. School shootings—United States 6. Social science literature
ISBN 9780814748886 (cl : alk. paper); 9780814763704 (ebook); 9780814763711 (ebook)
LC 2011-039377

SUMMARY: In this book, author "Jessie Klein makes the provocative argument that the rise of school shootings across America, and childhood aggression more broadly, are the consequences of a society that actually promotes aggressive and competitive behavior. 'The Bully Society' is a call to reclaim America's schools from the vicious cycle of aggression that threatens our children and our society at large." (Publisher's note)

REVIEW: *Choice* v50 no2 p372 O 2012 D. E. Kelly

REVIEW: *Contemp Sociol* v42 no6 p854-6 N 2013 ANGELA STROUD

"The Bully Society: School Shootings and the Crisis of Bullying in America's Schools." "'The Bully Society,' by Jessie Klein, is a densely-packed examination of the cultural forces that make schools dangerous places for kids. . . . The greatest strength of 'The Bully Society' is that it reorients the conversation around school shootings by focusing on sociocultural forces rather than individual perpetrators. . . . Whatever is lost in theoretical depth in this book is more than made up for by the strong links Klein makes between large scale forces and the everyday lives of American teenagers."

REVIEW: *Kirkus Rev* v80 no1 p2408-9 Ja 1 2012

REVIEW: *N Y Times Book Rev* p16 Ap 29 2012 Dave Cullen

REVIEW: *Publ Wkly* v258 no51 p43 D 19 2011

REVIEW: *Voice of Youth Advocates* v35 no2 p196 Je 2012 Mary Ellen Snodgrass

KLEIN, STEFAN. Survival of the nicest; how altruism made us human and why it pays to get along; 272 p. 2014 Experiment
1. Altruism 2. Cooperation 3. Evolutionary psychology 4. Evolutionary theories 5. Scientific literature
ISBN 9781615190904 (cloth)
LC 2013-024044

SUMMARY: In this book, author Stefan Klein "transforms Darwinian interpretation of evolution and resets the conversation about how we relate to each other as individuals and communities. . . . Klein's inquiry fuses the work of neuropsychologists, neuroeconomists, geneticists, philosophers, anthropologists, a chemist, and a lion expert, with myriads of studies conducted in cultures around the world. . . . His main point . . . [is] that over time evolution has favored cooperation." (Publishers Weekly)

REVIEW: *Kirkus Rev* v81 no24 p247 D 15 2013

"Survival of the Nicest: How Altruism Made Us Human and Why It Pays to Get Along". "A middling look at some of the better angels of our nature by German science writer [Stefan] Klein. . . . Some of Klein's statements verge on hyperbolic: Do most of us really make 'selfless choices dozens of times every day'? Perhaps so, if we include holding the door open for someone or leaving a tip for the wait staff. . . . Even so, the argument seems a little diffuse and soft and would have benefited from more rigor in place of bromides such as 'selflessness makes us happy and transforms the world.' Tougher-minded readers will prefer Steven Pinker's 'The Better Angels of Our Nature' (2011) and even Prince [Pyotr] Kropotkin himself."

KLEINZAHLER, AUGUST. The Hotel Oneira; [by] August Kleinzahler 2013 Faber & Faber

1. American poetry 2. Everyday life 3. Music—Poetry 4. Poems—Collections 5. Travel

ISBN 9780374534813 paperback; 9780374172930 hardcover

SUMMARY: In this book, poet August "Kleinzahler's poetry is, as ever, concerned with permeability: Voices, places, the real and the dreamed, the present and the past, all mingle together in verses that always ring true. . . . This is a poet searching for—and finding—a cadence to suit life as it's lived today." (Publisher's note)

REVIEW: *Libr J* v138 no14 p113 S 1 2013 Fred Muratori

REVIEW: *New Statesman* v142 no5189 p53 D 13 2013 Paul Batchelor

REVIEW: *Poetry* v204 no4 p378-86 Jl/Ag 2014 WILLIAM LOGAN

REVIEW: *Publ Wkly* v260 no25 p152 Je 24 2013

REVIEW: *TLS* no5791 p23 Mr 28 2014 AINGEAL CLARE

"The Hotel Oneira." "[Author August] Kleinzahler has never been drawn to the strict forms in which the early Gunn would 'strap in doubt.' But where the acoustics of his poems are concerned, Kleinzahler is the model of scrupulousness. An epigraph quotes Kenneth Cox on the 'movement of sound,' and many of these poems combine physical movement with playful tuning-up sounds and other auditory adventures. . . . His musical ear lends Kleinzahler's work a modulating pitch, in Geoffrey Hill's distinction, rather than any more settled tone. . . . Things often look bleak in Kleinzahler's poems; but no inhibition need attach to pointing out how well these witty and enjoyable poems manage to turn out."

KLINENBERG, ERIC. Going solo; the extraordinary rise and surprising appeal of living alone; [by] Eric Klinenberg 273 p. 2012 Penguin Press

1. Living alone—United States 2. Single people—United States 3. Single people—United States—Psychology 4. Social change 5. Sociology literature

ISBN 9781594203220

LC 2011-031522

SUMMARY: This book explores why more than 50 percent of American adults are single--and why the usually prefer to live that way. . . . The author examines both ends of the age spectrum in an attempt to understand the social implication of this trend. He finds that among relatively affluent young adults in the 25-to-34 age bracket, living solo is seen as a rite of passage into adulthood--a period allowing more sexual freedom, a chance to explore relationships without commitment and a major focus on career building. A similar increase in solitary living is becoming the norm among the elderly. . . . [Eric] Klinenberg suggests that public support is needed to provide affordable, urban assisted-living facilities in which the elderly can maintain their independence for as long as possible. (Kirkus)

REVIEW: *Bookforum* v18 no4 p39 D 2011/Ja 2012 Buzzy Jackson

REVIEW: *Choice* v49 no12 p2380 Ag 2012 B. Weston

REVIEW: *Contemp Sociol* v42 no2 p193-6 Mr 2013 Naomi Gerstel

REVIEW: *Economist* v406 no8823 p83-4 F 16 2013

REVIEW: *Libr J* v136 no20 p137-8 D 1 2011 Ellen Gilbert

REVIEW: *Mon Labor Rev* v135 no12 p42-3 D 2012 Carol Boyd Leon

REVIEW: *New Yorker* v88 no9 p110-3 Ap 16 2012 Nathan Heller

"Going Solo: The Extraordinary Rise and Surprising Appeal of Living Alone." "Eric Klinenberg, a sociologist at New York University, has spent the past several years studying aloneness, and in [this] . . . book, . . . he approaches his subject as someone baffled by . . . recent trends. . . . 'Going Solo' is his attempt to see how this secret society fares outside the crucible of natural disaster. For seven years, Klinenberg and his research team interviewed more than three hundred people living alone, plus many of the caretakers, planners, and designers who help make that solitary life possible. . . . The results were surprising. Klinenberg's data suggested that single living was not a social aberration but an inevitable outgrowth of mainstream liberal values."

KLING, JEANNE. Vested. See Manrodt, K.

KLÍMA, IVAN, 1931-. My Crazy Century; 576 p. 2013 Pgw

1. Czech authors—20th century—Biography 2. Czechoslovakia—History—1938-1945 3. Czechoslovakia—History—1945-1992 4. Memoirs 5. Totalitarianism—History

ISBN 0802121705; 9780802121707

SUMMARY: "In his . . . autobiography, spanning six decades that included war, totalitarianism, censorship, and the fight for democracy, acclaimed Czech writer Ivan Klíma reflects back on his remarkable life and . . . twentieth-century history. . . . From the brief hope of freedom during the Prague Spring of 1968 to Charter 77 and the eventual collapse of the regime in 1989's Velvet Revolution, Klíma's revelatory account provides a . . . personal and national history." (Publisher's note)

REVIEW: *Booklist* v110 no3 p18 O 1 2013 Vanessa Bush

REVIEW: *Kirkus Rev* v81 no21 p26 N 1 2013

REVIEW: *Libr J* v138 no18 p86 N 1 2013 Ben Neal

REVIEW: *Libr J* v138 no11 p62 Je 15 2013 Barbara Hoffert

REVIEW: *N Y Rev Books* v61 no1 p61 3 Ja 9 2014 Paul Wilson

"My Crazy Century." "First published in two volumes running to almost a thousand pages in Czech and somewhat abridged in Craig Cravens's precise and elegant translation, the book chronicles [Ivan] Klima's life and times. . . . Klima's accounts of his several love affairs in the current book seem almost perfunctory, as though his love life, and in particular the powerful tensions he and his fictional characters felt between the lure of sexual passion and the deeper attractions of loyalty and domesticity, were a part of his story he would have preferred to omit but, for the sake of honesty, could not."

REVIEW: *N Y Times Book Rev* p32 D 15 2013 PAUL BERMAN

"My Crazy Century." "Why did people join the Communist movement back in the day? Ivan Klima, the distinguished Czech writer, raises the question in the prologue to his memoir, 'My Crazy Century.' . . . The essays that tag along somewhat oddly after the memoir, and yet, considered from an artistic standpoint, they have the effect of amplifying, as if through giant loudspeakers, an emotion that Klima is otherwise intent on expressing in a modest tone. This is a bellowing anger at what has happened to many millions of people, himself included, victims of the serial horrors that used to be known, and maybe still are known, as totalitarianism."

REVIEW: *Publ Wkly* v260 no33 p53 Ag 19 2013

KNAUSGAARD, KARL OVE. Boyhood Island; 496 p. 2014 Harvill Secker

1. Child psychology 2. Families 3. Father & child 4. Memoirs 5. Self-consciousness (Awareness)

ISBN 1846557224; 9781846557224

SUMMARY: "The third book of the 'My Struggle' cycle is set in a world where children and adults live parallel lives, ones that never meet. With insight and honesty, [author] Karl Ove Knausgaard writes of a child's growing self-awareness, of how events of the past impact on the present, and of the desire for other ways of living and other worlds within what we know." (Publisher's note)

REVIEW: *New Statesman* v143 no5203 p42-4 Mr 28 2014 Leo Robson

REVIEW: *Publ Wkly* v261 no15 p32 Ap 14 2014

REVIEW: *TLS* no5790 p3-4 Mr 21 2014 THOMAS MEANEY

"Boyhood Island." "In the past half-decade in Norway, a writer has recast the confessional novel in hyperbolic form. Karl Ove Knausgaard's six-volume, 3,600-page 'My Struggle' is a mercilessly quotidian epic of the author's journey from boyhood to fatherhood. . . . 'Boyhood Island' revisits much of the same territory as the previous two volumes but in a much more sustained fashion. Here Knausgaard looks back on his difficult childhood while only very rarely returning to the perspective of the writer and father he has now become. . . . 'Boyhood Island' reverberates with the joys and anxieties of early youth, and Knausgaard brilliantly recreates their exaggerated feel."

KNAUSGAARD, KARL OVE. My struggle; 573 p. 2013 Archipelago Books

1. Authors—Family relationships 2. Authors—Fiction 3. Friendship—Fiction 4. Love stories 5. Marriage—Fiction

ISBN 9781935744825

LC 2013-001224

SUMMARY: This is the second book in author Karl Knausgaard's series "My Struggle." "Walking away from everything he knows in Bergen, Karl Ove finds himself in Stockholm, where he waits for the next stretch of the road to reveal itself. He strikes up a deep friendship with another exiled Norwegian, a boxing fanatic and intellectual named Geir. He reconnects with Linda, a vibrant poet who had captivated him at a writers' workshop years earlier, and the shape of his world changes." (Publisher's note)

REVIEW: *London Rev Books* v36 no1 p21-2 Ja 9 2014 Sheila Heti

REVIEW: *N Y Times Book Rev* p21 Je 23 2013 LELAND DE LA DURANTAYE

REVIEW: *TLS* no5750 p19 Je 14 2013 KATE WEBB

"A Man In Love: My Struggle 2." "'A Man In Love,' the second instalment of Karl Ove Knausgaard's six-volume autobiographical series of novels, 'My Struggle,' continues the author's remarkable exploration of the modern self. . . . As before, there are forthright appraisals of people, some dismissive, others lit with imaginative sympathy. Always strong, because each is a testament to his freedom, Knausgaard's judgements are open to alteration in the light of later understanding. . . . The novel's sole obligation is to search for something different, he argues, but (perfectly in tune with the times) he's in danger of restricting the source of that difference to himself."

KNEALE, MATTHEW, 1960-. An Atheist's History of Belief; Understanding Our Most Extraordinary Invention; [by] Matthew Kneale 256 p. 2014 Pgw Counterpoint Press

1. Atheism 2. Belief & doubt 3. Faith 4. Religion—History 5. Religious psychology

ISBN 1619022354; 9781619022355

LC 2013-028207

SUMMARY: Author Matthew Kneale "methodically examines the development of specific aspects of faith through historical events, ancient texts and the commonality of the human condition. . . . Kneale touches on a range of faiths including Hinduism, Judaism, Islam and Scientology. Various chapters find the author seeking out the roots for the invention of a Christian heaven, prophecies of the end of the world, and the unkind ends of heretics and witches." (Kirkus Reviews)

REVIEW: *Kirkus Rev* v81 no24 p39 D 15 2013

"An Atheist's History of Belief". "[Matthew] Kneale . . . takes such an overwhelmingly polite look at religious history that there's little to rage about. This isn't by any means a personal journey; while the author gives a mild introduction to himself as the son of a Methodist atheist and a refugee German Jewish atheist, he doesn't paint the history of faith with a personal patina. Instead, he methodically examines the development of specific aspects of faith through historical events, ancient texts and the commonality of the human condition. . . . An intellectually interesting comparison in the same way that comparative histories of revolutions are interesting; there's blood and passion in all that madness, but it doesn't always land on the page."

REVIEW: *New Statesman* v142 no5181 p71 O 25 2013 Matthew Kneale

REVIEW: *Publ Wkly* v261 no3 p51 Ja 20 2014

KNIGHT, ROGER. Britain Against Napoleon; The Organisation of Victory, 1793-1815; [by] Roger Knight 720 p. 2013 Allen Lane

1. Great Britain—History—George III, 1760-1820 2. Great Britain—Military history—1789-1820 3. Great Britain—Politics & government—1789-1820 4. Historical literature 5. Napoleonic Wars, 1800-1815
ISBN 184614177X; 9781846141775

SUMMARY: In this book on Britain's role in the Napoleonic conflict, Roger Knight argues that "the conflict between Britain and France was a 'total' war. The scale of the mobilisation of resources on the home front, the use of blockades as economic warfare and the threat of invasion all share similarities with Britain's experience of the two world wars. The conflict was between two contrasting industrial economies and political systems, a contest Britain won through better organisation of its resources." (Economist)

REVIEW: *Economist* v409 no8863 p82 N 23 2013

"Britain Against Napoleon: The Organisation of Victory, 1793-1815." "The book's narrow focus on British elites is both a strength and a weakness. Mr. [Roger] Knight has made good use of political and government sources, but there is scant coverage of wider society, which weakens his broader case. . . . Mr. Knight should have looked at how ordinary people organised themselves to defeat Napoleon [Bonaparte], rather than just the 'politicians, public servants, naval and army officers' he focuses on. Total wars are fought by the masses--not just the political classes."

REVIEW: *New Statesman* v143 no3 p44-5 Ja 24 2014 Simon Heffer

REVIEW: *TLS* no5786 p8-9 F 21 2014 CHRIS WOOLGAR

"Wellington: The Path to Victory 1769-1814" and "Britain Against Napoleon: The Organization of Victory 1793-1815." "The first major Life of Wellington since Elizabeth Longford's work of 1969-72, Rory Muir's biography is matched by an extensive commentary online (at www.lifeofwellington.co.uk). . . . Together these books give us an exceptional insight into the struggle, the changes that were necessary to sustain British forces, and the impact made by determined and ambitious individuals. . . . Muir is perceptive on the formation of the Duke's character. . . . [Author Roger] Knight makes a convincing case that this was a remarkable combined effort."

KNIGHTLEY, PHILLIP. How the English Establishment Framed Stephen Ward; [by] Phillip Knightley 362 p. 2013 Createspace Independent Pub

1. Keeler, Christine 2. Profumo affair, 1963 3. Profumo, John, 1915-2006 4. True crime stories 5. Ward, Stephen, 1913-1963
ISBN 149093989X; 9781490939896

SUMMARY: This book presents an "exposé of the Profumo Affair, reissued for the 50th anniversary of the debacle. When it came to light in 1963, the affair between British defense secretary John Profumo and party girl and sometime prostitute Christine Keeler sparked concerns that Keeler could have passed military secrets from Profumo to Yevgeny Ivanov, a Soviet diplomat and spy who was said to be her lover. . . .At the center of the story is Stephen Ward, a London osteopath and artist." (Kirkus Reviews)

REVIEW: *Kirkus Rev* v82 no3 p365 F 1 2014

"How the English Establishment Framed Stephen Ward". "[A] yeasty exposé of the Profumo Affair, reissued for the 50th anniversary of the debacle. . . . Ward is a fascinating figure in the book. . . . Originally published under the title of 'An Affair of State' (1987), the book recounts facts that may be mostly old news to students of the Profumo Affair, but it's still a well-paced, engrossing narrative of the scandal and its political and other tendrils; it's replete with vivid sketches of the participants and their antics. . . . More than that, it's a revealing portrait of the dawn of swinging London, obsessed with new sexual freedoms—and anxieties that needed a scapegoat. A fine investigation of a legal injustice and the cultural upheaval that conjured it."

REVIEW: *Kirkus Rev* v82 no4 p68 F 15 2014

"How the English Establishment Framed Stephen Ward". "[A] yeasty exposé of the Profumo Affair, reissued for the 50th anniversary of the debacle. . . . Ward is a fascinating figure in the book. . . . Originally published under the title of 'An Affair of State' (1987), the book recounts facts that may be mostly old news to students of the Profumo Affair, but it's still a well-paced, engrossing narrative of the scandal and its political and other tendrils; it's replete with vivid sketches of the participants and their antics. . . . More than that, it's a revealing portrait of the dawn of swinging London, obsessed with new sexual freedoms—and anxieties that needed a scapegoat. A fine investigation of a legal injustice and the cultural upheaval that conjured it."

KNOBLER, PETER. A mayor's life. See Dinkins, D. N.

KNOPF, CHRIS. Cries of the Lost; [by] Chris Knopf 288 p. 2013 Permanent Pr Pub Co

1. Deception—Fiction 2. Detective & mystery stories 3. Grief—Fiction 4. Loss (Psychology)—Fiction 5. Murder—Fiction 6. Revenge—Fiction 7. Terrorism—Fiction
ISBN 1579623328; 9781579623326
LC 2013-034367

SUMMARY: This book, by Chris Knopf, "finds market researcher Arthur Cathcart still searching for clues to the actions of his murdered wife, Florencia Etxarte, and the secrets that died with her. . . . Aided by girlfriend Natsumi Fitzgerald, Cathcart retrieves the contents of Florencia's safe deposit box in the Caymans, only to be attacked when they leave the bank. That's the start of an increasingly complex and dangerous journey that takes the pair across Europe and the U.S." (Publishers Weekly)

REVIEW: *Booklist* v110 no2 p33 S 15 2013 Michele Leber

"Cries of the Lost." "After his wife, Florencia, is assassinated and he's left for dead . . . Arthur Cathcart gets revenge, but he still wants answers. . . . In an adrenaline-fueled chase across beautiful European locales, including the south of France and lake district of Italy, Cathcart and [Natsumi] Fitzgerald make canny use of their resources to remain a step ahead of their pursuers. With Cathcart as the once-nerdy everyman up against powerful adversaries and Fitzgerald as his loving sidekick, Knopf has a smart, sizzling, jet-setting series with a delightful touch of wry wit."

REVIEW: *Kirkus Rev* v81 no22 p49 N 15 2013

REVIEW: *Libr J* v138 no18 p74 N 1 2013 Teresa L. Jacobsen

REVIEW: *Publ Wkly* v260 no33 p42 Ag 19 2013

KNOWLES, ANNE KELLY. Mastering iron; the struggle to modernize an American industry, 1800-1868; 334 p. 2013 University of Chicago Press

1. Geographic information systems 2. Geography & history 3. Historical literature 4. Industrial relations—United States—History 5. Iron industry and trade—United States—History
ISBN 0226448592 (cloth: alk. paper); 9780226448596 (cloth: alk. paper)
LC 2012-006826

SUMMARY: In this book, "Anne Kelly Knowles argues that the prolonged development of the US iron industry was largely due to geographical problems the British did not face. Pairing . . . manuscript research with analysis of a detailed geospatial database that she built of the industry, Knowles reconstructs the American iron industry . . . locating . . . iron companies in their social and environmental contexts . . . [and] explaining workplace culture and social relations between workers and managers." (Publisher's note)

REVIEW: *Am Hist Rev* v119 no1 p175 F 2014 Bruce E. Seely

"Mastering Iron: The Struggle to Modernize an American Industry, 1800-1868". "The antebellum iron industry of the United States might seem to be well understood, but this volume by a historical geographer makes important contributions to the existing literature. . . . A central contribution of [Anne Kelly] Knowles's study is her demonstration of the utility of spatial analysis through geographic information systems (GIS) for historical research and interpretive historical analysis. . . . As a historian, I am a little uneasy about the relative lack of concern for chronology in Knowles's study. . . . These minor concerns do not reduce the value of Knowles's book. . . . The book is beautiful, with many color and black-and-white illustrations and maps."

REVIEW: *Choice* v50 no12 p2285 Ag 2013 T. E. Sullivan

KNOX, AMANDA, 1987-. Waiting to Be Heard; A Memoir; [by] Amanda Knox 480 p. 2013 HarperCollins

1. Kercher, Meredith, 1985-2007 2. Knox, Amanda, 1987—Trials, litigation, etc. 3. Memoirs 4. Sollecito, Raffaele, 1984- 5. Trials (Murder)—Italy
ISBN 0062217208; 9780062217202

SUMMARY: This book is a memoir by Amanda Knox. "In November 2007, 20-year-old Knox, an American studying in Perugia, Italy, was arrested for the gruesome murder of her British roommate, Meredith Kercher, resulting in sensationalist news coverage worldwide. Convicted and jailed after a deeply polarizing trial, Knox served until 2011, when an appeals court overturned the conviction. Here, she draws on journals she kept throughout her ordeal to give us her side of the story. " (Library Journal)

REVIEW: *Libr J* v138 no14 p74 S 1 2013 Victoria A. Caplinger

REVIEW: *N Y Rev Books* v60 no13 p20-1 Ag 15 2013 Nathaniel Rich

"Waiting to Be Heard: A Memoir." "After four years in prison, [Amanda] Knox is no longer naive. But it's clear from 'Waiting to Be Heard' that she--or her legal team--felt pressure to justify her whimsical, often callow behavior during the investigation and trial. This is understandable, since much of her trouble derived from observations the Italian investigators made about her actions in the hours and days following [Meredith] Kercher's murder. Still, the constant assertion of her former naivete can be exhausting. . . . These are also the sections of the book that seem to bear the heaviest imprint of an older, mildly patronizing collaborator--or a lawyer. . . . Yet the shattering of Knox's naivete is the memoir's central and most gripping narrative."

REVIEW: *N Y Times Book Rev* p12-3 My 27 2013 SAM TANENHAUS

REVIEW: *New York Times* v162 no56114 pC1-6 Ap 22 2013 Michiko Kakutani

REVIEW: *New York Times* v162 no56111 pA3 Ap 19 2013 JULIE BOSMAN

REVIEW: *New Yorker* v89 no12 p21-2 My 6 2013 Rebecca Mead

REVIEW: *Publ Wkly* v260 no19 p12 My 13 2013 Samuel R. Slaton

REVIEW: *Publ Wkly* v260 no30 p64 Jl 29 2013

KNOX, PETER E.ed. The Oxford Anthology of Roman literature. See The Oxford Anthology of Roman literature

KNUDSEN, ARE.ed. Lebanon. See Lebanon

KOBB, R. CHRISTOPHER. Fyrelocke; Jack Boomershine and the prophecy untold; [by] R. Christopher Kobb 266 p. 2013 Moonpepper Press

1. Adventure stories 2. Boys—Fiction 3. Children's stories 4. Fantasy fiction 5. Magic—Juvenile fiction
ISBN 9780989207201
LC 2013-936577

SUMMARY: In this children's book by R. Christopher Kobb, "In a cave, deep within the cliffs of Brighton, lies a curious stone. No ordinary rock, the Fyrelocke has a dark and intricate past. Twelve-year-old inventor Jack Boomershine believes it a practical joke. . . . But finding this powerful stone sets in motion an entangled clockwork of events that draws him ever deeper into an adventure. . . . As things spin out of control, Jack must find his way through a hidden world of magic." (Publisher's note)

REVIEW: *Kirkus Rev* v81 no14 p413 Jl 15 2013

REVIEW: *Kirkus Rev* v81 no16 p95 Ag 15 2013

"Fyrelocke Jack Boomershine and the Prophecy Untold." "In this debut children's book, a 12-year-old boy's journey into a fantastical world begins when he's mysteriously guided to find a strange, glowing rock. . . . For Jack, the journey turns out to be not just one of danger and adventure, but one of self-discovery and introspection. The well-drawn, memorable characters have equally memorable names. . . . The story's strength lies in these characters . . . as well as the vivid descriptions and imagery. The illustrations--realistic yet infused with a dreamlike quality--would be stronger if, like the striking cover, they appeared in color instead of black and white. Also, the story can be a bit convoluted in places."

KOCEK, SARA. Promise Me Something; [by] Sara Kocek

320 p. 2013 Albert Whitman & Co

1. Middle school students 2. School bullying 3. Suicide—Fiction 4. Teenagers—Suicidal behavior 5. Young adult literature

ISBN 0807566411; 9780807566411

SUMMARY: In this book, Reyna Fey must attend a new high school away from her friends. "Seven years earlier, Reyna's mother was killed by a drunk driver, and a recent car accident nearly did the same to her father, so Reyna is angry and scared when blunt, bossy, and painfully unpopular Olive Barton bounds into her life. . . . They begin a tentative friendship, but . . . when Olive shares a deeply held secret about herself, Reyna's reaction . . . has potentially devastating consequences." (Publishers Weekly)

REVIEW: *Kirkus Rev* v81 no16 p52 Ag 15 2013

REVIEW: *Publ Wkly* v260 no29 p70 Jl 22 2013

REVIEW: *SLJ* v59 no10 p1 O 2013 Mindy Whipple

REVIEW: *Voice of Youth Advocates* v36 no4 p66 O 2013 Riley Carter

REVIEW: *Voice of Youth Advocates* v36 no4 p66 O 2013 Kim Carter

"Promise Me Something." "School redistricting results in Reyna Fey attending a different high school from her lifelong friends, wondering if she will be able to make new friends. When Olive Barton from Mr. Murphy's history class initiates conversation, Reyna is both relieved and uncertain, since it is clear that Olive is not exactly popular. . . . When tragic news comes of her once-friend's suicide on the train tracks, Reyna is plagued by guilt, until she ultimately finds her courage and acts on her 'better nature.'"

KOCH, SHELLEY L. A theory of grocery shopping; food, choice and conflict; [by] Shelley L. Koch x, 134 p. 2012 Berg

1. Consumers—United States—Psychology 2. Food industry and trade—Social aspects—United States 3. Grocery shopping—Social aspects—United States 4. Grocery shopping—United States 5. Sociology literature 6. Supermarkets—United States

ISBN 0857851500 (hbk.); 0857851519 (pbk.); 0857851535 (ebook : Individual); 9780857851505 (hbk.); 9780857851512 (pbk.); 9780857851536 (ebook : Individual)

LC 2012-538933

SUMMARY: Written by Shelley L. Koch, "'A Theory of Grocery Shopping' explores the social organization of grocery shopping by linking the lived experience of grocery shoppers and retail managers in the US with information transmitted by nutritionists, government employees, financial advisors, journalists, health care providers and marketers, who influence the way we think about and perform the work of shopping for a household's food." (Publisher's note)

REVIEW: *Choice* v50 no11 p2061 Jl 2013 J. M. Deutsch

REVIEW: *Contemp Sociol* v42 no6 p886-7 N 2013

"A Theory of Grocery Shopping: Food, Choice, and Conflict." "'A Theory of Grocery Shopping: Food, Choice and Conflict' by Shelley L. Koch is an institutional ethnography focusing on the perspectives of grocery shoppers and how various social discourses shape the grocery shopping experience. Koch's analysis applies primarily to the United States. She seeks to capture under-theorized aspects of grocery shopping and to question assumptions of consumer sovereignty. Furthermore, the burden of this unpaid labor tends to fall on women, especially mothers. . . . 'A Theory of Grocery Shopping' covers new and interesting territory theoretically, and does so using both illustrative respondent quotations and examples from the different areas of social discourse."

KOEHLER, FRED.il. How to cheer up dad. See Koehler, F.

KOEHLER, FRED. How to cheer up dad; [by] Fred Koehler 32 p. 2014 Dial Books for Young Readers, an imprint of Penguin Group (USA) Inc.

1. Behavior—Fiction 2. Children's stories 3. Elephants—Fiction 4. Father and child—Fiction 5. Mood (Psychology)—Fiction

ISBN 0803739222; 9780803739222 (hardcover : alk. paper)

LC 2013-008514

SUMMARY: In this children's book, by Fred Koehler, "Little Jumbo's Dad is having a bad day. The cereal on the floor, the raisins stuck to the ceiling, and the game of hide-and-seek at bath time are not helping. Little Jumbo spends his time-out thinking of a way to cheer him up. A hug, a game of catch, and some ice cream start to do the trick." (School Library Journal)

REVIEW: *Booklist* v110 no13 p68-9 Mr 1 2014 Edie Ching

"How to Cheer Up Dad." "The expressive illustrations set the tone for this story demonstrating filial challenges and ongoing love. . . . Despite this kind of action, [Fred] Koehler's true focus is on the visual interchanges between these two well-defined and charming characters. With the setting's minimalist backgrounds, facial expressions are easy to observe and decipher. . . . This debut author-illustrator gets the father-son relationship just right in a story that's warm and memorable."

REVIEW: *Bull Cent Child Books* v67 no9 p463 My 2014 T. A.

"How to Cheer Up Dad". "This spices up familiar father-and-son narratives with its reversal, giving kids a new slant on familiar experiences. The text's understated comicality . . . is matched with smartly designed illustrations in digitally assembled pencil and pen. . . . Little Jumbo and Dad are comically drawn with rotund middles but boxy appendages, and Koehler uses all of the potential of the characters' trunks, ears, and great big smiles to cover the full range of pachyderm expression. With its sparkle that's accessible to both parents and kids, this is . . . a stellar book for father-and-son sharing."

REVIEW: *Kirkus Rev* v82 no7 p147 Ap 1 2014

REVIEW: *Publ Wkly* v261 no1 p55 Ja 6 2014

REVIEW: *SLJ* v60 no4 p125 Ap 2014 Kristine M. Casper

KOERTGE, RON. Coaltown Jesus; [by] Ron Koertge 128 p. 2013 Candlewick Press

1. Brothers—Fiction 2. Grief—Fiction 3. Jesus Christ—Fiction 4. Novels in verse 5. Young adult fiction

ISBN 0763662283; 9780763662288

LC 2013-931470

SUMMARY: In author Ron Koertge's book, "Walker shouldn't have been so surprised to find Jesus standing in the middle of his bedroom. After all, he'd prayed for whoever was up there to help him, and to help his mom, who hadn't stopped crying since Noah died two months ago. But since when have prayers actually been answered? And since when has Jesus been so . . . irreverent?" (Publisher's note)

REVIEW: *Booklist* v110 no2 p68 S 15 2013 Sarah Bean Thompson

REVIEW: *Bull Cent Child Books* v67 no2 p100 O 2013 K. C.

REVIEW: *Horn Book Magazine* v89 no6 p98 N/D 2013 DEAN SCHNEIDER

"Coaltown Jesus." "If the humor is broad, the life lessons are subtle, and life's big questions are wisely left as questions: "Why now?' Walker asked. 'I prayed / to God like a thousand times. And what / happened? Noah died. Didn't God look / downstairs? It's a nursing home. Half / my mom's clients are ready to check / out. But he picks a kid." Jesus replies that the philosophers and brainiacs are still working on that one. [Ron] Koertge's verse novel--in third person with short lines, plain language, and abundant white space--is a good vehicle for meditations on life, loss, and faith."

REVIEW: *Kirkus Rev* v81 no16 p141 Ag 15 2013

REVIEW: *Publ Wkly* v260 no34 p75 Ag 26 2013

REVIEW: *SLJ* v60 no1 p54 Ja 2014 Audrey Sumser

REVIEW: *Voice of Youth Advocates* v36 no4 p67 O 2013 Christina Miller

KOESTER, NANCY. Harriet Beecher Stowe; a spiritual life; [by] Nancy Koester 384 p. 2013 William B. Eerdmans Publishing Company

1. Abolitionists—United States—Biography 2. Biographies 3. Women—Religious life—History 4. Women authors, American—19th century—Biography

ISBN 0802833047; 9780802833044 (pbk. : alk. paper)

LC 2013-027100

SUMMARY: This book by Nancy Koester is a biography of writer Harriet Beecher Stowe, focusing on her spiritual life and beliefs. After marriage, Stowe "remained seriously committed to living out the Christianity all the Beechers embraced.That meant dedication to her spouse and children and also advancing the progressive Christian causes--women's education and suffrage, abolition, black civil rights." (Booklist)

REVIEW: *Booklist* v110 no6 p14 N 15 2013 Ray Olson

"Harriet Beecher Stowe: A Spiritual Life." "The subject of this accessible and absorbing interpretive biography was perhaps the most famous American woman of the nineteenth century and by far the most famous member of a family of distinguished--indeed, notorious-- clergymen and Christian educators. Naturally enough, then, the lens through which [Nancy] Koester illuminates her subject is that of the Christian life. . . . Koester engagingly and intelligently discusses each major novel, each family crisis, each journey, and each spiritual change, including a fluctuating interest in spiritualism after the deaths of two of her sons, without a whiff of academic fustiness. A top-notch read."

REVIEW: *Christ Century* v131 no9 p48-9 Ap 30 2014 Kathryn Gin Lum

KOGAN, VLADIMIR. Exploring quantum mechanics; a collection of 700+ solved problems for students, lecturers, and researchers; xiii, 881 p. 2013 Oxford University Press

1. Physics literature 2. Quantum field theory 3. Quantum mechanics 4. Quantum theory—Problems, exercises, etc 5. Schrödinger equation

ISBN 0199232717 (hbk.); 0199232725 (pbk.); 9780199232710 (hbk.); 9780199232727 (pbk.)

LC 2012-538470

SUMMARY: This book presents "700-plus problems from different subfields of quantum mechanics . . . spread over 15 chapters, starting with the easy (Schrödinger wave equation problems in one dimension) and progressing to the challenging (relativistic wave equation). Useful areas covered include spherically symmetric potentials, time-dependent Schrödinger wave equation, and perturbation theory." (Choice: Current Reviews for Academic Libraries)

REVIEW: *Choice* v51 no5 p878 Ja 2014 N. Sadanand

"Exploring Quantum Mechanics: A Collection of 700+ Solved Problems for Students, Lecturers, and Researchers." "This is a classic collection of modern physics problems/solutions from quantum mechanics. . . . Although the content dates from as far back as 1956, the material is very relevant because the essential subject has not changed. . . . Useful areas covered include spherically symmetric potentials, time-dependent Schrödinger wave equation, and perturbation theory. The solutions could have benefited from more graphs of the wave functions and related attributes."

KOHL, HERBERT R.ed. The Muses Go to School. See The Muses Go to School

KOHN, EDUARDO. How forests think; toward an anthropology beyond the human; [by] Eduardo Kohn 267 p. 2013 University of California Press

1. Anthropology literature 2. Human-animal relationships—Amazon River Region 3. Human-plant relationships—Amazon River Region 4. Indigenous peoples—Ecology—Amazon River Region 5. Philosophy of nature—Amazon River Region 6. Quechua Indians—Social life and customs 7. Quechua mythology 8. Semiotics—Amazon River Region 9. Social sciences—Amazon River Region—Philosophy

ISBN 9780520276109 (cloth: alk. paper); 9780520276116 (pbk.: alk. paper)

LC 2013-003750

SUMMARY: "Based on four years of fieldwork among the Runa of Ecuador's Upper Amazon, Eduardo Kohn draws on his rich ethnography to explore how Amazonians interact with the many creatures that inhabit one of the world's most complex ecosystems. Whether or not we recognize it, our anthropological tools hinge on those capacities that make us distinctly human. However, when we turn our ethnographic attention to how we relate to other kinds of beings, these tools . . . break down." (Publisher's note)

REVIEW: *Choice* v51 no5 p882 Ja 2014 E. N. Anderson

REVIEW: *Current Anthropology* v55 no5 p1-2 O 2014 Jean-Benoît Deville-Stoetzel

REVIEW: *TLS* no5795 p23 Ap 25 2014 BARBARA J. KING

"How Forests Think: Toward an Anthropology Beyond the Human." "Eduardo Kohn, an anthropologist at McGill University in Canada, who conducted fieldwork among the Runa . . . from 1996-2000, describes, in 'How Forests Think: Toward an anthropology beyond the human,' the surrounding forest as inhabited by 'unparalleled kinds and quantities of living selves.' . . . In the end, what's so welcome about Kohn's approach is that he walks a tightrope with perfect balance: never losing sight of the unique aspects of being human, while refusing to force those aspects into separating us from the rest of the abundantly thinking world. Pushes to broaden anthropology beyond the human, Eduardo Kohn rightly stresses, must always include the human."

KOHUTH, JANE. Anne Frank's chestnut tree; [by] Jane Kohuth 48 p. 2013 Random House

1. Children's nonfiction 2. Frank, Anne, 1929-1945 3. Holocaust, Jewish (1939-1945)—Juvenile literature 4. Jewish children in the Holocaust—Netherlands—Amsterdam—Juvenile literature 5. Jews—Netherlands—Amsterdam—Biography—Juvenile literature
ISBN 0449812553; 9780307975799 (trade : alk. paper); 9780375971150 (lib. bdg. : alk. paper); 9780375981135 (ebook : alk. paper); 9780449812556 (hardcover : alk. paper)
LC 2012-034585

SUMMARY: Author "Jane Kohuth explores Anne Frank's strong belief in the healing power of nature in this Step 3 leveled reader biography for newly independent readers ages 5-8," which is illustrated by Elizabeth Sayles. It describes how "hidden away in their Secret Annex in Amsterdam during World War II, Anne Frank and her family could not breathe fresh air or see the blue sky for years. . . . This small glimpse of nature gave Anne hope and courage." (Publisher's note)

REVIEW: *Booklist* v109 no21 p60-1 Jl 1 2013 Kay Weisman

REVIEW: *Bull Cent Child Books* v67 no3 p163 N 2013 H. M.

"Anne Frank's Chestnut Tree." "This easy-reader introduction to Anne Frank's life effectively uses . . . nature to offer an abbreviated and accessible overview of Anne's tragic and remarkable life. The summary of life events is appropriately succinct without being oversimplified; major historical factors are included, anti-Semitism is explained . . . , and the fear of living in hiding is effectively presented. The tree is an effective central symbol in a story about a young adult holding onto hope, and occasional quotes add further depth to the narrative. [Illustrator Elizabeth] Sayles' acrylic paintings offer plenty of visual support for the story; the portraits, possibly based on photographs, effectively capture the historical figures."

REVIEW: *Horn Book Magazine* v90 no1 p113 Ja/F 2014 BETTY CARTER

"Anne Frank's Chestnut Tree." "The presence of the tree throughout Anne's life in hiding not only gives her a sense of peace but also provides young readers a respite from her ordeal. . . . Illustrations are dark and somber except those depicting Anne's pre-war life or Annex visits from helpers bringing food and books. . . . Signaling a change in the narrative, a photograph of the Anne Frank House introduces an author's note. More sophisticated recommended readings (on the copyright page) and a website (AnneFrank.org) complete this abbreviated biography."

REVIEW: *Kirkus Rev* v81 no17 p100-1 S 1 2013

REVIEW: *SLJ* v59 no9 p176 S 2013 Jackie Partch

KOISTINEN, DAVID. Confronting decline; the political economy of deindustrialization in Twentieth-century New England; [by] David Koistinen 384 p. 2013 University Press of Florida

1. Deindustrialization—New England—History 2. Economics literature 3. Textile industry—Massachusetts—History 4. Textile industry—New England—History
ISBN 9780813049076 (alk. paper)
LC 2013-020087

SUMMARY: This book by David Koistinen presents a "discussion of 20th-century deindustrialization, focusing on Massachusetts (and New England). He provides a . . . typology of responses to deindustrialization, suggesting that the typical sequence begins with 'retrenchment' . . . progresses to 'federal assistance'; and culminates in local (statewide, regional) 'economic development' initiatives." (Choice: Current Reviews for Academic Libraries)

REVIEW: *Choice* v51 no9 p1647-8 My 2014 D. A. Coffin

"Confronting Decline: The Political Economy of Deindustrialization in Twentieth-Century New England". "[David] Koistinen . . . provides a thorough, readable discussion of 20th-century deindustrialization, focusing on Massachusetts (and New England). He provides a useful typology of responses to deindustrialization. . . . While it is understandable that the author would restrict his focus, it remains unclear whether generalizations from the New England experience are valid. Koistinen does not engage with the voluminous analytical literature on local economic development initiatives . . . so readers are left uninformed about whether these initiatives have had any significant impact on deindustrializing communities."

REVIEW: *N Engl Q* v87 no3 p561-3 S 2014 Robert Forrant

KOLBERT, ELIZABETH. The sixth extinction; an unnatural history; [by] Elizabeth Kolbert 336 p. 2014 Henry Holt and Co

1. Environmental disasters 2. Extinction (Biology) 3. Mass extinctions 4. Science—Popular works 5. Scientists
ISBN 0805092994; 9780805092998 (hardback)
LC 2013-028683

SUMMARY: "In 'The Sixth Extinction,' [author] Elizabeth Kolbert draws on the work of scores of researchers in half a dozen disciplines, accompanying many of them into the field: geologists who study deep ocean cores, botanists who follow the tree line as it climbs up the Andes, marine biologists who dive off the Great Barrier Reef. She introduces us to a dozen species, some already gone, others facing extinction." (Publisher's note)

REVIEW: *Am Sch* v83 no2 p104-6 Spr 2014 MARY BETH SAFFO

REVIEW: *Bookforum* v20 no5 p17 F/Mr 2014 ROBIN Marantz Henig

REVIEW: *Booklist* v110 no7 p19 D 1 2013 Donna Seaman

REVIEW: *Economist* v410 no8875 p1 F 20 2014

REVIEW: *Kirkus Rev* v82 no4 p15 F 15 2014

REVIEW: *Libr J* v139 no6 p59 Ap 1 2014 Forrest E. Link

REVIEW: *Libr J* v139 no3 p126 F 15 2014 Cynthia Lee Knight

REVIEW: *London Rev Books* v36 no9 p15-6 My 8 2014 Luke Mitchell

REVIEW: *N Y Rev Books* v61 no5 p29-30 Mr 20 2014 Verlyn Klinkenborg

REVIEW: *N Y Times Book Rev* p22 F 23 2014

REVIEW: *N Y Times Book Rev* p1-23 F 16 2014 Al Gore

REVIEW: *New York Times* v163 no56401 pC1-4 F 3 2014 MICHIKO KAKUTANI

REVIEW: *Orion Magazine* v33 no2 p67 Mr/Ap 2014 Mitchell Thomashow

REVIEW: *Publ Wkly* v261 no8 p9 F 24 2014

REVIEW: *Publ Wkly* v260 no48 p45 N 25 2013

REVIEW: *Publ Wkly* v261 no4 p120-5 Ja 27 2014

REVIEW: *Sci Am* v310 no2 p76 F 2014 Lee Billings

"The Sixth Extinction: An Unnatural History." "[Author Elizabeth] Kolbert . . . argues that we are now in the midst of a sixth extinction, one distressingly of our own making. Part travelogue, part exegesis of extinction's history and literature, each chapter focuses on a single already vanished or critically endangered species and the scientists who study it, revealing a planetary crisis through heartrending close-up portraits. . . . Fittingly, the book closes with a short chapter on Homo sapiens and an unflinching refusal to sugarcoat the ways we have broken our world."

KOLODNY, ANNETTE, 1941-. In search of first contact; the Vikings of Vinland, the peoples of the dawnland, and the Anglo-American anxiety of discovery; [by] Annette Kolodny p. cm. 2012 Duke University Press

1. Historical literature 2. Indians of North America—First contact with Europeans 3. Oral history 4. Sagas—History and criticism
ISBN 9780822352822 (cloth : alk. paper); 9780822352860 (pbk. : alk. paper)
LC 2012-011578

SUMMARY: This book by Annette Kolodny examines "two medieval Icelandic tales, known as the Vinland sagas. She contends that they are the first known European narratives about contact with North America. . . . Kolodny examines what happened after 1837, when English translations of the two sagas became widely available and enormously popular in the United States. She assesses their impact on literature, immigration policy, and concepts of masculinity." (Publisher's note)

REVIEW: *Am Hist Rev* v119 no1 p165-6 F 2014 Margaret Reid

REVIEW: *Am Q* v66 no1 p223-34 Mr 2014 Drew Lopenzina

REVIEW: *N Engl Q* v86 no1 p144-7 Mr 2013 Patricia Roylance

REVIEW: *Rev Am Hist* v41 no3 p379-84 S 2013 James Taylor Carson

"In Search of First Contact: The Vikings of Vinland, the Peoples of the Dawnland, and the Anglo-American Anxiety of Discovery." "A sprawling, insightful, and frustrating quest. . . . The meeting between the Norse and the indigenous people of present-day North America has garnered a fair bit of attention over the years, and [Annette] Kolodny's book is by far the most exhaustive and authoritative consideration of the consequences of the encounter. . . By acceding to disciplinary norms and historiographical conventions, Kolodny mutes the power of her argument and undermines her interesting exploration of Native oral histories. . . . The choices Kolodny makes in the first few pages of the book implicate everything she writes afterward and left me disappointed."

KOLODNY, NIKO.ed. Death and the afterlife. See Death and the afterlife

KOLPAN, GERALD. Magic words. See Magic words

KOMAKO SAKAI.il. Wait! wait! See Nakawaki, H.

KOMUNYAKAA, YUSEF, 1947-. Testimony, a tribute to Charlie Parker; with new & selected jazz poems; [by] Yusef Komunyakaa 140 p. 2013 Wesleyan University Press

1. American poetry—20th century 2. Jazz 3. Librettos 4. Parker, Charlie, 1920-1955 5. Poems—Collections
ISBN 9780819574299 (cloth: alk. paper)
LC 2013-026568

SUMMARY: This book presents poetry by Yusef Komunyakaa. "The centerpiece of this volume is the libretto 'Testimony.' Paying homage to Charlie Parker, 'Testimony' was commissioned for a radio drama with original music by eminent Australian composer and saxophonist Sandy Evans. . . . . Twenty-eight additional poems spanning the breadth of Komunyakaa's career are included, including two never previously published." (Publisher's note)

REVIEW: *Choice* v51 no9 p1592-3 My 2014 B. Wallenstein

"Testimony, A Tribute to Charlie Parker: With New and Selected Jazz Poems". "The present book reprints the title poem along with a healthy sampling of about 50 of this Pulitzer Prize-winning poet's other jazz poems. In a foreword, Sascha Feinstein—poet, editor, and close associate of Komuyakaa—provides a history of the Testimony project. The selected poems and the libretto follow. Jazz/poetry collaboration is explored in an interview between Komunyakaa and Feinstein. Testimony itself is best enjoyed while listening to the included CD. The book also includes an informative essay by jazz critic Miriam Zolin and a discussion between composer Sandy Evans and artistic director Christopher Williams."

REVIEW: *TLS* no5777/8 p34 D 20 2013 LOU GLANDFIELD

KONG, BELINDA. Tiananmen fictions outside the square; the Chinese literary diaspora and the politics of global culture; [by] Belinda Kong viii, 278 p. 2012 Temple University Press

1. Authors, Chinese—Foreign countries 2. Chinese diaspora in literature 3. Chinese literature—Foreign countries—History and criticism 4. Historical literature
ISBN 9781439907580 (cloth : alk. paper); 9781439907597 (pbk. : alk. paper); 9781439907603 (e-book)
LC 2011-043063

SUMMARY: This book examines "the afterlives of the [1989] Tiananmen killings in writings from the Chinese diaspora." Author Belinda Kong "reads plays and works of fiction in conjunction with various materials that explain their literary and historical contexts, including literary precursors, nonfiction writings by the authors she discusses, theories of diaspora, and extant discourses on the history of the Tiananmen demonstrations." (World Literature Today)

REVIEW: *Choice* v50 no3 p476 N 2012 J. C. Kinkley

REVIEW: *World Lit Today* v87 no6 p76-7 N/D 2013 Wen Jin

"Tianamen Fictions Outside the Square: The Chinese Literary Diaspora and the Politics of Global Culture." "Excellent. . . . [Belinda Kong] surveys writers based in the United States and in Europe (England and France) though she includes only English-language texts, some of them translations, in her analysis. . . . However, even as Kong theorizes her terms carefully for the most part, she does sometimes resort to unexplained political clichés such as totalitarianism and authoritarianism in her comments on contemporary China. Her contextualization of literary texts, as a result, slackens in rigor at certain points. A flaw like this, no doubt, should not eclipse the general high quality of the book."

KÖNIG, JASON.ed. Ancient libraries. See Ancient libraries

KONRAD, HELMUT.ed. Routes into abyss. See Routes into abyss

KONTZIAS, BILL. Look and see; a what's-not-the-same game; [by] Bill Kontzias 32 p. 2014 Holiday House

1. Differences 2. Picture books for children 3. Picture puzzles—Juvenile literature 4. Seashells (Biology) 5. Toys
ISBN 9780823428601 (hardcover)
LC 2013-019678

SUMMARY: In this book, "in a set of side-by-side scenes made with scads of small toys, buttons, stones, plastic letters or craft materials, [Bill] Kontzias invites viewers to spot which items have been moved or removed. The components in each pair of photographed scenes are thematically related, from dinosaurs in one to colored pencils, seashells, toy vehicles, or birds and blocks in others." (Kirkus Reviews)

REVIEW: *Kirkus Rev* v82 no3 p286 F 1 2014

"Look and See: A What's-Not-the-Same-Game". "Design fumbles make these tests of visual memory and counting skills even more challenging. 'Answers' at the end are only partial, as they identify the changes in each pair of photographed tableaux but not their locations within them. Moreover, though each spread offers a hint ('0 things are new, 11 are gone, 0 moved'), along with the difficulty of keeping the tallies straight—there are 28 changes on one spread!—the terminology isn't always consistent. A toy gorilla's arm that goes from partially to fully visible is designated 'New,' for instance, whereas seashells that are turned over count as 'Moved.' What's 'not-the-same' as any given I Spy title? Not much."

REVIEW: *SLJ* v60 no4 p180 Ap 2014 Jennifer Miskec

KOOP, ROYCE.ed. Parties, elections, and the future of Canadian politics. See Parties, elections, and the future of Canadian politics

KOOPS, BERT-JAAP.ed. Engineering the human. See Engineering the human

KOOSED, JENNIFER L. Gleaning Ruth; a biblical heroine and her afterlives; [by] Jennifer L. Koosed xiv, 173 p. 2011 University of South Carolina Press

1. Love in the Bible 2. Naomi (Biblical figure) 3. Religious literature 4. Ruth (Biblical figure)
ISBN 9781570039836 (cloth: alk. paper)
LC 2010-051371

SUMMARY: This book presents "a multifaceted portrait of the Old Testament character of Ruth and of the demanding agricultural world in which her story unfolds. . . . [Jennifer] Koosed explores the use of pairings to define Ruth's aspirational fortitude. Koosed also touches on the narrative's questions of sexuality, kinship, and law as well as the metaphoric activities of harvest that serve to advance the plot and illuminate the social and geographic context of Ruth's tale." (Publisher's note)

REVIEW: *J Am Acad Relig* v82 no1 p254-6 Mr 2014 Julie Galambush

"Gleaning Ruth: A Biblical Heroine and Her Afterlives". "An extraordinary book with a misleading subtitle. The subtitle suggests that Jennifer Koosed has written a history of interpretation of the book and character of Ruth, but readers expecting to learn of Ruth's reception history will be disappointed—that is, unless they are first captivated by the exuberant and learned eclecticism of the book. . . . The book does not follow a timeline of interpretive history. . . . Rather, Koosed invites the reader to join her as she reflects on—or perhaps more accurately, refracts—Ruth, considering its text and subtext from every conceivable angle. . . . 'Gleaning Ruth' is highly accessible, highly engaging, and highly informative for scholars and lay readers alike."

KOOYMAN, GERALD L. Penguins. See Lynch, W.

KOPENAWA, DAVI. The falling sky. See Albert, B.

KOPP-OBERSTEBRINK, HERBERT.ed. Hans Blumenberg, Jacob Taubes. See Hans Blumenberg, Jacob Taubes

KOPPELHUS, EVA B.ed. Tyrannosaurid paleobiology. See Tyrannosaurid paleobiology

KOPS, DEBORAH. The Great Molasses Flood; Boston, 1919; [by] Deborah Kops 102 p. 2012 Charlesbridge

1. Alcohol industry—Accidents—Massachusetts—Boston—History—20th century—Juvenile literature 2. Floods—Massachusetts—Boston—History—20th century—Juvenile literature 3. Industrial accidents—Massachusetts—Boston—History—20th century—Juvenile literature 4. Molasses industry—Accidents—Massachusetts—Boston—History—20th century—Juvenile literature
ISBN 1580893481; 9781580893480 (reinforced for library use); 9781580893497 (softcover)
LC 2011-000655

SUMMARY: This historical survey by Deborah Kops follows the events of "January 15, 1919 . . . an unseasonable warm day in Boston, Massachusetts, and a day that would go down in history. One minute it was business as usual on the waterfront and the next - KABOOM! A large tank holding molasses exploded, sending shards of metal hundreds of feet away, collapsing buildings, and coating the harborfront community with a thick layer of sticky-sweet sludge." (Publisher's note)

REVIEW: *Booklist* v108 no8 p48 D 15 2011 Randall Enos

REVIEW: *Bull Cent Child Books* v65 no7 p359 Mr 2012 E. B.

"The Great Molasses Flood: Boston, 1919." "In this accessible account, [Deborah] Kops first introduces the characters whose lives would be altered by the disaster, then describes the flood, the rescue efforts, theories on the cause of the flood, the three years of court hearings, and the final determination of liability. . . . Kops handily guides readers through a thoughtful discussion of the how the fear of anarchist activity following World War I led many to believe that the tank was bombed. . . . Relatively short sentences, slightly oversized font and wide leading, chapter subheadings, and ample illustrations make this a strong choice for reluctant or struggling readers."

REVIEW: *SLJ* v58 no2 p142-3 F 2012 Ann Welton

KORNGOLD, J. Sadie's almost marvelous menorah; 24 p. 2013 Kar-Ben Pub.

1. Accidents—Fiction 2. Hanukkah—Fiction 3. Holiday stories 4. Menorah—Fiction 5. Picture books for children

ISBN 0761364935; 0761364951; 9780761364931 (lib. bdg.: alk. paper); 9780761364955

LC 2011-029042

SUMMARY: In this book, "Sadie works hard to carefully sculpt and paint her clay menorah." She "is eager to show it to her mother on the last day of the week. In her rush, she trips and drops the menorah, which breaks into 'a million, zillion pieces.' Through tears and disappointment, Sadie and her mom realize that while the shattered menorah is not repairable, the shamas remains perfectly intact and becomes 'Sadie's Super Shammash' to light all the menorahs in the home each year." (Kirkus Reviews)

REVIEW: *Horn Book Magazine* v89 no6 p66 N/D 2013 ISSA GERSHOWITZ

"Sadie's Almost Marvelous Menorah". "Sadie is thrilled to take home her special pink and blue creation, but she trips, shattering the menorah into 'a million, zillion pieces.' Luckily the shammash remains intact—a Hanukkah miracle!—and a new tradition begins. The family from 'Sadie's Sukkah Breakfast' and 'Sadie and the Big Mountain' again demonstrates how kindness and creativity can overcome small (but they seem huge) setbacks. Illustrations filled with Hanukkah cheer capture both the bustling and the quiet times of Sadie's classroom; light infused pictures of the family at home radiate warmth."

REVIEW: *Kirkus Rev* v81 no17 p133 S 1 2013

REVIEW: *SLJ* v59 no10 p1 O 2013 Teri Markson

KORNGOLD, J. Sadie's Lag Ba'omer mystery; 32 p. 2014 Kar-Ben Publishing

1. Brothers and sisters—Fiction 2. Children's stories 3. Jews—United States—Fiction 4. Judaism—Customs and practices—Fiction 5. Lag b'Omer—Fiction

ISBN 0761390472; 9780761390473 (lib. bdg.: alk. paper)

LC 2013-002189

SUMMARY: In this children's book, written by Jamie Korngold and illustrated by Julie Fortenberry, "Sadie and Ori ask their grandfather" about the Jewish holiday Lag Ba'Omer. "They learn the surprising history and traditions behind the holiday, and invite their friends and family to a Lag Ba'Omer picnic and celebration." (Publisher's note)

REVIEW: *Kirkus Rev* v82 no4 p245 F 15 2014

"Sadie's Lag Ba'Omer Mystery". "One full moon in spring heralds a Jewish holiday that is not familiar to the savvy Sadie but has its own reason for celebration. . . . It is remembered with picnics, bonfires, singing and storytelling and usually celebrated between the holidays of Passover and Shavuot. The evenly told story is laced with mild suspense. It is coupled with cheery illustrations that include carefully placed details that indicate the centrality of faith to this suburban family. A welcoming introduction to an often overlooked minor holiday."

REVIEW: *SLJ* v60 no4 p125 Ap 2014 Heidi Estrin

KORNGOLD, JAMIE , 1965-. Seder in the desert; 32 p. 2014 Kar-Ben Publishing

1. Children's nonfiction 2. Deserts—Utah 3. Historical reenactments 4. Passover—Juvenile literature 5. Seder—Juvenile literature

ISBN 0761375015; 9780761375012 (lib. bdg.: alk. paper)

LC 2013-002180

SUMMARY: In this book, by Rabbi Jamie Korngold, with photographs by Jeff Finkelstein, "readers are taken through a re-enactment of the Israelites' desert journey as participants in the Adventure Rabbi Program celebrate Passover. The program seeks to '[combine] the ancient traditions of the Jewish Seder with the inspiration of the Red Rock Desert.'" (Kirkus Reviews)

REVIEW: *Kirkus Rev* v82 no5 p149 Mr 1 2014

"Seder in the Desert". "Author and rabbi [Jamie] Korngold, spiritual leader of the program, simply and effectively demonstrates how the traditional concepts of the holiday are maintained through this unusual event, which emphasizes experiential learning. With stunning natural scenery as a backdrop, families hike, carry Seder necessities including a torah and Haggadot for children, and set a table on the sandy ground complete with the special ceremonial foods. There, they read, learn and debate the story of the Exodus, eat together, sing and dance. . . . The focus of this distinctive approach is on examining how and why the Seder is celebrated rather than on retelling the familiar story. Lovely, different and yet familiar."

REVIEW: *Publ Wkly* v261 no7 p96 F 17 2014

REVIEW: *SLJ* v60 no4 p180 Ap 2014 Heidi Estrin

KORNMAN, ROBIN.tr. The epic of Gesar of Ling. See The epic of Gesar of Ling

KOSANKE, NICOLE. Beyond addiction. See Foote, J.

KOT, GREG. I'll take you there; Mavis Staples, the Staple Singers, and the march up freedom's highway; [by] Greg Kot 320 p. 2014 Scribner

1. African American women musicians 2. Biography (Literary form) 3. Gospel musicians—United States—Biography

ISBN 1451647859; 9781451647853 (hardback); 9781451647860 (trade paperback)
LC 2013-032633

SUMMARY: This book, by Greg Kot, is a biography of "Mavis Staples—lead singer of the Staple Singers and a major figure in the music that shaped the civil rights era. From her love affair with Bob Dylan, to her creative collaborations with Prince, to her recent revival alongside Wilco's Jeff Tweedy, this . . . account shows Mavis as you've never seen her before. . . . Readers will also hear from Prince, Bonnie Raitt, David Byrne, Marty Stuart, Ry Cooder, Steve Cropper, and many other individuals." (Publisher's note)

REVIEW: *Booklist* v110 no6 p7 N 15 2013 Vanessa Bush

REVIEW: *Kirkus Rev* v81 no22 p93 N 15 2013

REVIEW: *Nation* v299 no3/4 p36-7 Jl 21 2014 AARON COHEN

REVIEW: *New York Times* v163 no56419 pC1-4 F 21 2014 DWIGHT GARNER

"I'll Take You There: Mavis Staples, the Staple Singers, and the March Up Freedom's Highway." "In the 1960s and '70s, black entertainers, politicians and sports stars visiting Chicago knew where to go for comfort food and warm conversation: to the home of the Staples family. . . . In 'I'll Take You There,' his new book about the Stapleses and their musical legacy, the music journalist Greg Kot lingers for a bit at the family's table. . . . He is consistently good in his well-reported new book on the group's sound, and on its story, which is involving from beginning to end."

REVIEW: *Publ Wkly* v260 no42 p41-2 O 21 2013

KOTLER, STEVEN. Abundance; the future is better than you think; [by] Steven Kotler 386 p. 2012 Free Press

1. Future, The 2. Scientific literature 3. Technological forecasting 4. Technological innovations—Forecasting 5. Technology—Social aspects
ISBN 9781451614213; 1451614217
LC 2011-039926

SUMMARY: This book discusses technological innovations, looking at how they could help in "finding solutions for world problems, from poverty and disease to climate change and pollution. . . . Peter Diamandis, founder of the X Prize Foundation, and journalist Steven Kotler argue that innovation can provide 9 billion people with a world of plenty. . . . [Lowell Wood envisions a] toilet that would burn faeces to evaporate urine, thus preventing water pollution while generating surplus energy that could power cellphones and lights. . . . "Abundance" extols the potential of 3D printers to make almost any kind of product at home." (New Scientist)

REVIEW: *Booklist* v108 no13 p30 Mr 1 2012 David Siegfried

REVIEW: *Choice* v49 no12 p2302 Ag 2012 F. Potter

REVIEW: *Kirkus Rev* v80 no2 p142 Ja 15 2012

REVIEW: *New Repub* v244 no6 p46-9 Ap 29 2013 Tim Wu

REVIEW: *New Sci* v213 no2852 p50 F 18 2012 Jeff Hecht

"Abundance: The Future Is Better Than You Think." "In 'Abundance,' Peter Diamandis, founder of the X Prize Foundation, and journalist Steven Kotler argue that innovation can provide 9 billion people with a world of plenty. That sounds good in principle. Yet as a veteran technology writer, I found the book's cheerleading tone rose rapidly to a crescendo of irrational exuberance. 'Abundance' is right in pointing out that small groups who challenge conventional wisdom can be vital fonts of ideas. But successful innovation requires more. . . . After touring through many such examples, I was left wondering if this quest for 'abundance' for all makes sense at a time when Americans already have such an overflow of stuff."

REVIEW: *Publ Wkly* v259 no1 p74-5 Ja 2 2012

KOTSKO, ADAM.tr. The highest poverty. See Agamben, G.

KOU YANG.ed. Diversity in diaspora. See Diversity in diaspora

KOUDELKA, JOSEF.il. Wall. See Dolphin, R.

KOZLOV, GLENYS.tr. Khatyn. See Adamovich, A.

KOZUSKANICH, NATHAN.ed. The Second Amendment on trial. See The Second Amendment on trial

KRAMER, ERIC. Coarseness in U.S. public communication; [by] Eric Kramer v, 225 p. 2012 Fairleigh Dickinson University Press

1. Communication—Political aspects—United States 2. Communication—Social aspects—United States 3. Communication and culture—United States 4. Mass media—Social aspects—United States 5. Mass media and culture—United States 6. Social science literature 7. Vulgarity—Social aspects—United States
ISBN 9781611475036 (cloth : alk. paper); 9781611475043 (electronic)
LC 2012-020150

SUMMARY: Written by Philip Dalton and Eric Mark Kramer, "This book's contention is that the U.S. semantic environment is governed by tactics, not tact. . . . This follows the logic that the marketplace, an aggregate of hedonically motivated individuals, decides what's good. . . . Our present communication environment is one that invites the hypertrophic expression of the ego, enabling elites to erode public communication standards." (Publisher's note)

REVIEW: *Choice* v51 no1 p164 S 2013 L. J. Roselle

"Coarseness in U.S. Public Communication." "[Authors Philip] Dalton . . . and [Eric] Kramer . . . argue that public discourse in the US has become increasingly and dangerously coarser, due to market logic. . . . After a theoretical overview, more specific topics are examined, including the role of opinion leaders in fomenting anti-intellectualism, the growing coarseness in US politics. . . . All chapters relate to the central thesis that 'capitalism, as it manifests in the United States today, has helped foster and encourage a gross form of individualism, what we term "hypertrophic individualism."' . . . Some readers may want more discussion of cooperation and altruism that is also seen in the world."

KRAMER, ROBERT S. Historical dictionary of the Sudan. See Fluehr-Lobban, C.

KRASNOW, IRIS. Sex After...; Women Share How Inti-

macy Changes As Life Changes; [by] Iris Krasnow 272 p. 2014 Penguin Group USA Gotham Books
1. Advice literature 2. Human life cycle 3. Human sexuality—United States 4. Older women—Sexual behavior 5. Women—Sexual behavior
ISBN 1592408273; 9781592408276
LC 2013-037177

SUMMARY: This book, by Iris Krasnow, "holds the answers to everything from regaining sexual confidence after childbirth and breast cancer to navigating the dating scene in senior communities. As with all of Krasnow's books since her 'New York Times' bestseller 'Surrendering to Marriage,' the narrative is driven by real women's stories: raw, intimate, and, most importantly, true." (Publisher's note)

REVIEW: *Kirkus Rev* v81 no24 p192 D 15 2013

REVIEW: *Libr J* v139 no2 p87 F 1 2014 Linda Petty

REVIEW: *Libr J* v138 no14 p87 S 1 2013

REVIEW: *N Y Times Book Rev* p12 F 9 2014 SALIE TISDALE

"Sex After... Women Share How Intimacy Changes As Life Changes." "The theme of 'Sex After...'—how women's sexual lives shift over time—is a significant one, rich with possibility. The result, however, is underwhelming: a series of short, episodic chapters based on interviews with 150 women, each chapter focused on a transitional event—sex after baby, sex after divorce, sex after menopause, and so on. . . . 'Sex After' is largely about older women, and the subjects appear to be almost entirely white. . . . Most of her subjects are also heterosexual. . . . Transitions are often abrupt and sometimes confusing, and the prose does not sing."

REVIEW: *Publ Wkly* v260 no49 p75-6 D 2 2013

KRAUS, CHARLES. The Teen Magician: That's You; A Complete Guide to Booking and Preforming Party Shows; [by] Charles Kraus 176 p. 2013 Self Publisher
1. Do-it-yourself literature 2. Magic shows 3. Magic tricks 4. Magicians 5. Magicians—Vocational guidance
ISBN 1623097746; 9781623097745

SUMMARY: In this book, magician Charles Kraus "reveals the secrets behind a few nifty tricks and steers readers toward books, magazines, magic shops and clubs that will teach them the nuts and bolts of the magician's craft, but his focus is on helping neophyte magicians turn their passion into moneymaking gigs at children's birthday parties. He emphasizes showmanship as the key to a successful party business: flamboyant costumes . . . a commanding stage presence . . . and jokey patter." (Kirkus Reviews)

REVIEW: *Kirkus Rev* v81 no24 p37 D 15 2013

"The Teen Magician: That's You! A Complete Guide to Booking and Performing Party Shows". "The hard part of magic—getting paid for it—is ably demystified in this straightforward debut primer. . . . [Charles] Kraus writes in a clear, humorous style, sprinkling in his own entertaining anecdotes of stage fright, a prop that sliced open his thumb and a flash paper (highly flammable paper) incident that almost burned down the house. Magicians in the making will learn a lot from his vast experience and engaging presentation. A reassuring guide to turning a magical hobby into a profitable business."

KRAUS, KARL, 1874-1936. The Kraus Project; Essays by Karl Kraus; 336 p. 2013 Farrar Straus & Giroux
1. Critics 2. German essays 3. German satire 4. Literature & technology 5. Mass media industry
ISBN 0374182213; 9780374182212
LC 2013-015008

SUMMARY: In this book of essays by Viennese satirist Karl Kraus, editor Jonathan Franzen "presents new translations [and] annotates them . . . with supplementary notes from the Kraus scholar Paul Reitter and the Austrian author Daniel Kehlmann. . . . [Franzen takes] Kraus's . . . arguments [and explores] their relevance to contemporary America." (Publisher's note)

REVIEW: *Bookforum* v20 no3 p22-3 S-N 2013 ERIC BANKS

REVIEW: *Booklist* v110 no2 p15 S 15 2013 Brendan Driscoll

REVIEW: *Economist* v409 no8858 p88-9 O 19 2013

"Roth Unbound: A Writer and His Books" and "The Kraus Project." "[Claudia Roth Pierpont's] wise and captivating analysis of the work of Philip Roth . . . is not a conventional biography but a chronicle of the man through the 'life of his art'. . . . Her book has the sympathy of friendship, but she does not hesitate to be critical of the author's lesser work. . . The book is an illuminating companion to Mr. Roth's work. . . . Similarly unconventional but considerably less successful is 'The Kraus Project,' Jonathan Franzen's peculiar attempt to introduce a 21st-century English-speaking audience to the work of Karl Kraus, a 19th-century German critic and satirist. . . . There is no getting around the fact that Kraus's work is rebarbarative today."

REVIEW: *Kirkus Rev* v81 no17 p54 S 1 2013

REVIEW: *Libr J* v138 no8 p61 My 1 2013

REVIEW: *London Rev Books* v35 no21 p29-30 N 7 2013 Joshua Cohen

REVIEW: *N Y Rev Books* v60 no16 p46-8 O 24 2013 Michael Hofmann

REVIEW: *N Y Times Book Rev* p26 O 20 2013

REVIEW: *N Y Times Book Rev* p15 O 13 2013 EDMUND FAWCETT

"The Kraus Project; Essays by Karl Kraus." "Engrossing [and] highly original. . . . As a declared enemy of the easy response in an instant-access culture, [Jonathan] Franzen finds in the unduly neglected Kraus a model of how to provoke readers while at the same time getting them to do some work. . . . In making a present-day case for Kraus, Franzen has avoided the easy choice. Rather than a tasty serving of epigrams, he and two scholarly Germanists have chosen a pair of essays from the early 1900s that, Franzen believes, speak powerfully to us now. . . . Notes by Franzen, some wry, some somber, tell us how he first came to admire Kraus."

REVIEW: *New Statesman* v142 no5178 p48 O 4 2013 Philip Maughan

REVIEW: *New York Times* v162 no56277 pC1-6 O 2 2013 DWIGHT GARNER

REVIEW: *Publ Wkly* v260 no36 p53 S 9 2013

REVIEW: *TLS* no5776 p21 D 13 2013 RITCHIE ROBERTSON

KRAUTHAMER, BARBARA. Black slaves, Indian masters; slavery, emancipation, and citizenship in the Native American south; [by] Barbara Krauthamer xiii, 211 p.

2013 University of North Carolina Press
1. African Americans—Relations with Indians 2. Chickasaw Indians—History 3. Choctaw Indians—History 4. Historical literature 5. Slaveholders—United States—History 6. Slavery—United States—History
ISBN 9781469607108 (cloth : alk. paper)
LC 2013-004070

SUMMARY: This book examines "slavery, race relations, and tribal sovereignty in the Choctaw and Chickasaw nations. According to the author, "the enslavement of blacks transformed both nations' attitudes on property and race. [Barbara] Krauthamer further argues that the Choctaw and Chickasaw nations maintained these views well after slavery and as the freed blacks pushed for citizenship in their respective tribes." (Choice)

REVIEW: *Choice* v51 no4 p711 D 2013 D. L. Bryant

"Black Slaves, Indian Masters: Slavery, Emancipation, and Citizenship in the Native American South." "[Barbara] Krauthamer . . . tackles slavery, race relations, and tribal sovereignty in the Choctaw and Chickasaw nations. . . . Tribal sovereignty notwithstanding, Krauthamer portrays slavery in the Choctaw and Chickasaw nations as nearly identical to servitude in any southern state. She describes a postslavery society that mirrors the Jim Crow South. Although the author considers this study primarily an endeavor in African American history, the Choctaws and Chickasaws somewhat overshadow the slaves and freed people in this work, making it an equally important contribution to Native American history."

KRAUTHAMMER, CHARLES. Things That Matter; Three Decades of Passions, Pastimes, and Politics; [by] Charles Krauthammer 400 p. 2013 Random House Inc
1. Conservatism—United States 2. Journalism 3. Newspapers—Sections, columns, etc. 4. Politics & culture—United States 5. Social commentary
ISBN 0385349173; 9780385349178

SUMMARY: This book "features several of [author Charles] Krauthammer's major path-breaking essays—on bioethics, on Jewish destiny and on America's role as the world's superpower—that have profoundly influenced the nation's thoughts and policies. And finally, the collection presents a trove of always penetrating, often bemused reflections on everything from border collies to Halley's Comet, from Woody Allen to Winston Churchill." (Publisher's note)

REVIEW: *Commentary* v136 no3 p58-60 O 2013 MATTHEW CONTINETTI

REVIEW: *Kirkus Rev* v81 no19 p246 O 1 2013

REVIEW: *Nation* v298 no24 p31-4 Je 9 2014 GEORGE SCIALABBA

REVIEW: *Natl Rev* v66 no5 p43-4 Mr 24 2014 LISA SCHIFFREN

"Things That Matter: Three Decades of Passions, Pastimes, and Politics." "The astonishing popularity of what is, after all, a book of warmed-over newspaper columns has ratified the position of the cerebral Mr. Krauthammer as the most influential conservative columnist of our time. . . . Though the book contains many fascinating essays on his personal passions—science, chess, dogs, and some remarkable non-political figures—[author Charles] Krauthammer argues that we have no choice but to pay attention to politics foremost, grubby as it is, because politics inevitably shapes our world."

KREBS, JOHN. Food; a very short introduction; [by] John Krebs xiv, 130 p. 2013 Oxford University Press
1. Food—Popular works 2. Food habits—History 3. Food science 4. Food supply 5. Historical literature 6. Science—Popular works
ISBN 0199661081 (pbk.); 9780199661084 (pbk.)
LC 2012-277941

SUMMARY: "In this Very Short Introduction, Prof Lord John Krebs provides a brief history of human food, from our remote ancestors 3 million years ago to the present day. By looking at the four great transitions in human food--cooking, agriculture, processing, and preservation--he considers a variety of questions, including why people like some kinds of foods . . . ; the role of genetics in our likes and dislikes; and the differences in learning and culture around the world." (Publisher's note)

REVIEW: *Choice* v51 no10 p1824-5 Je 2014 D. M. Gilbert

REVIEW: *TLS* no5782 p27 Ja 24 2014 CLAIRE HAZELTON

"Food: A Very Short Introduction." "Considering the growing interest in food studies, 'Food: A Very Short Introduction' seems well timed and John Krebs, the first chairman of the UK Food Standards Agency and a leading government adviser on food and science, an obvious choice of author. His approach, however, is narrow. Food is presented as a strictly scientific matter. . . . This specialized approach can, however, lead to interesting and insightful discussion. . . . More serious is Kreb's mapping of the changing diets of our ancestors via chemical analysis of their dental remains."

KRENTZ, JAYNE ANN. River road; [by] Jayne Ann Krentz 352 p. 2014 G. P. Putnam's Sons
1. Detective & mystery stories 2. Inheritance & succession—Fiction 3. Man-woman relationships—Fiction 4. Murder—Investigation—Fiction 5. Women private investigators—Fiction
ISBN 9780399165122
LC 2013-036136

SUMMARY: In this book, by Jayne Ann Krentz, "thirteen years ago, . . . Mason Fletcher rescued 16-year-old Lucy Sheridan from becoming the victim of sociopathic classmate Tristan Brinker. Now Lucy is back in Summer River, CA, to fix up the . . . home she inherited from her Aunt Sara. Mason . . . is also back in town, to help out his uncle. When he and Lucy open up the old fireplace in her house, a body falls out, and things take an ominous turn." (Library Journal)

REVIEW: *Booklist* v110 no8 p29 D 15 2013 John Charles

REVIEW: *Kirkus Rev* v81 no24 p232 D 15 2013

"River Road". "Add in a power struggle for control of Lucy's shares and the future of the company, a few more mysteries, a dead body or two, and a full slate of suspects, and Lucy and Mason have their hands full. Thankfully, they're both really good at solving mysteries, since the more questions that arise, the more attention they draw from someone (or ones) who'd prefer they'd stop asking. As danger and attraction flare, Lucy and Mason are convinced they have a bright future together, if they can survive the investigation. [Jayne Ann] Krentz returns to her romantic suspense roots with an intriguing premise set in charming wine country, using her typical finesse with dialogue, characterization and storytelling in support of an intricate and engrossing plot. Another Krentz winner."

REVIEW: *Libr J* v138 no21 p84 D 1 2013 Kristin Ramsdell

REVIEW: *Libr J* v139 no5 p85 Mr 15 2014 Juleigh Muirhead Clark

REVIEW: *Publ Wkly* v260 no48 p38 N 25 2013

KRESS, W. JOHN, 1951-. The ornaments of life; coevolution and conservation in the tropics; [by] W. John Kress xii, 588 p. 2013 University of Chicago Press

1. Angiosperms—Pollination—Tropics 2. Animal-plant relationships—Tropics 3. Biological literature 4. Coevolution—Tropics 5. Conservation biology—Tropics 6. Mutualism (Biology)—Tropics 7. Pollination by animals—Tropics 8. Seed dispersal by animals—Tropics 9. Vertebrates—Tropics
ISBN 9780226253404 (cloth: alkaline paper); 9780226253411 (paperback: alkaline paper)
LC 2013-000803

SUMMARY: In this book, "synthesizing recent research by ecologists and evolutionary biologists, Theodore H. Fleming and W. John Kress demonstrate the tremendous functional and evolutionary importance of . . . tropical pollinators and frugivores. They shed light on how these mutually symbiotic relationships evolved and lay out the current conservation status of these essential species." (Publisher's note)

REVIEW: *Choice* v51 no8 p1426 Ap 2014 J. C. Kricher

"The Ornaments of Life: Coevolution and Conservation in the Tropics". "The title of this splendid, important book is taken from a paper published in 1977 that suggested animals such as birds and mammals are of little fundamental importance in plant dynamics in the tropics, and thus are mere 'ornaments' rather than integral to community function. [Theodore H.] Fleming . . . and [W. John] Kress . . . seek to dispel that notion, and they do so with great skill and fine detail. . . . The authors develop their thesis in ten well-crafted chapters that carefully examine all aspects of plant-animal mutualisms. . . . This book, well supported by tables, figures, and photographs, is an important contribution to tropical biology and deserves a wide readership."

KRETSEDEMAS, PHILIP. Migrants and race in the US; territorial racism and the alien/outside; [by] Philip Kretsedemas 220 p. 2013 Routledge

1. Americanization 2. Race discrimination—United States 3. Social science literature 4. United States—Race relations
ISBN 9780415658393
LC 2013-008377

SUMMARY: In this book, author Philip Kretsedemas "examines anti-immigrant discourses aimed at the alien minority or racialized foreigner, thus advancing a pluralist race analysis that there are many racisms. Furthermore, the author expands the historical scope of anti-immigrant racism using a concept he terms 'territotial racism'—the product of racial ideologies traceable to the origins of European imperial projects in the US" (Choice: Current Reviews for Academic Libraries)

REVIEW: *Choice* v51 no9 p1688-9 My 2014 E. Hu-DeHart

"Migrants and Race in the US: Territorial Racism and the Alien/Outside." "According to the author, a sociologist and critical race theorist, migrants to the US, particularly non-European ones such as Latinos and Asians, are often viewed as racial others. However, as foreigners or aliens, they do not fit easily into the biologically derived white/black binary categories reserved for use in the US. . . . This theory-laden treatise that lays one concept on top of another requires readers' full attention. Even then, following all the threads of the argument may be difficult. It could be a case of theory overkill."

KRISHNASWAMI, UMA. The problem with being slightly heroic; 288 p. 2013 Atheneum Books for Young Readers

1. Actors and actresses—Fiction 2. Best friends—Fiction 3. Children's stories 4. East Indian Americans—Fiction 5. Friendship—Fiction 6. Motion picture industry—India—Mumbai
ISBN 1442423285; 9781442423282 (hardcover); 9781442423305 (ebook)
LC 2012-006279

SUMMARY: In this book, readers are "reunited with Dini and her Bollywood movie star friend Dolly in this . . . sequel to 'The Grand Plan to Fix Everything.'" The plot "unites chefs, dancers, an elephant keeper, a taxi driver, and myriad other characters as Dini and Maddie orchestrate the opening night of Dolly's latest film . . . . Together they combat seemingly insurmountable odds involving lost passports, escaped elephants, broken toes, surreptitious catering endeavors, and flamboyant dance routines." (Booklist)

REVIEW: *Bull Cent Child Books* v67 no2 p100-1 O 2013 K. Q. G.

"The Problem With Being Slightly Heroic." "Eleven-year-old Dini is back in the States for an extended visit after spending the last ten months in her new home in India. . . . Besides getting to enjoy nightly sleepovers with her best pal Maddie, Dini is heading up the children's dance group that will be part of the opening reception for the Smithsonian's exhibit on Indian cinema, which will feature Dolly Singh, the biggest star of Bollywood and Dini's friend and neighbor back in India. . . . Although the characters are a bit one-note, each is immensely likable even in their less than charming moments. . . . The tone here is less programmatic than in the first installment, making this a particularly delightful return visit with Dini and company."

REVIEW: *Kirkus Rev* v81 no12 p100 Je 15 2013

REVIEW: *SLJ* v59 no9 p145 S 2013 D. Maria LaRocco

KRISTOF, AGOTA. The Illiterate; 58 p. 2014 CB Editions

1. Exiles' writings 2. Hungarian authors—20th century—Biography 3. Hungarian women authors 4. Hungary—History—20th century 5. Memoirs
ISBN 0957326629; 9780957326620

SUMMARY: Translated by Nina Bogin, "Narrated in a series of brief vignettes and translated into English for the first time, 'The Illiterate' is [author] Agota Kristof's memoir of her childhood, her escape from Hungary in 1956 with her husband and small child, her early years working in factories in Switzerland, and the writing of her first novel, 'The Notebook.'" (Publisher's note)

REVIEW: *New Statesman* v143 no5209 p51 My 9 2014 J. S. Tennant

REVIEW: *TLS* no5793 p20 Ap 11 2014 EIMEAR McBRIDE

"The Notebook" and "The Illiterate." "Successful compositions are copied out into the Big Notebook, which accounts for the elegantly direct handling of much of this novel's unflinching brutality. . . . Louring over Agota Kristof's entire narrative is the shadow of war, occupation and the ambivalent experience of liberation for the 'liberated.' . . . Kristof's slim memoir, 'The Illiterate,' which follows the author out of Soviet-occupied Hungary in 1956 aged eleven to a life-long exile in French-speaking Switzerland, is scarcely less stark. . . . Both translations—of 'The Notebook' by Alan Sheridan and 'The Illiterate' by Nina Bogin—are unobtrusive and delicately handled, and we can be grateful to CB editions for their availability to an English-speaking audience."

KRISTOF, AGOTA. The notebook; [by] Agota Kristof 2014 CB Editions

1. Children & war 2. Diary fiction 3. Hungarian fiction 4. Twins—Fiction 5. War stories 6. World War, 1939-1945—Fiction

ISBN 9780957326699 paperback

SUMMARY: Written by Agota Kristof, translated by Alan Sheridan, this novel tells how, "Sent to a remote village for the duration of the war, two children devise physical and mental exercises to render themselves invulnerable to pain and sentiment. They steal, kill, blackmail and survive; others . . . are sucked into war's brutal maelstrom. 'The Notebook' distils the experience of Nazi occupation and Soviet 'liberation' during World War II into a stark fable of timeless relevance." (Publisher's note)

REVIEW: *New Statesman* v143 no5209 p51 My 9 2014 J. S. Tennant

REVIEW: *TLS* no5793 p20 Ap 11 2014 EIMEAR McBRIDE

"The Notebook" and "The Illiterate." "Successful compositions are copied out into the Big Notebook, which accounts for the elegantly direct handling of much of this novel's unflinching brutality. . . . Louring over Agota Kristof's entire narrative is the shadow of war, occupation and the ambivalent experience of liberation for the 'liberated.' . . . Kristof's slim memoir, 'The Illiterate,' which follows the author out of Soviet-occupied Hungary in 1956 aged eleven to a life-long exile in French-speaking Switzerland, is scarcely less stark. . . . Both translations—of 'The Notebook' by Alan Sheridan and 'The Illiterate' by Nina Bogin—are unobtrusive and delicately handled, and we can be grateful to CB editions for their availability to an English-speaking audience."

REVIEW: *Voice of Youth Advocates* v36 no3 p12-3 Ag 2013 MARIA ZULMA CARDONA

KRIZ, IGOR. Introduction to mathematical analysis; [by] Igor Kriz 524 p. 2013 Springer

1. Calculus 2. Mathematical analysis 3. Mathematical literature 4. Multilinear algebra 5. Multivariable calculus

ISBN 9783034806350 (hardcover : alk. paper)

LC 2013-941992

SUMMARY: This book looks at mathematical analysis. "Part 1 is a theoretical approach to advanced calculus, proceeding from the basics . . . through metric space topology, multivariate differential calculus . . . and systems of ordinary differential equations and linear differential equations. Part 2 provides more content on metric space topology, along with multilinear algebra, differential forms, complex analysis . . . and some functional analysis." (Choice: Current Reviews for Academic Libraries)

REVIEW: *Choice* v51 no7 p1257 Mr 2014 D. Robbins

"Introduction to Mathematical Analysis." "As an introduction to analysis, this text by [Igor] Kriz . . . [Aleš] Pultr . . . is wide-ranging and highly nontrivial. In total, it goes beyond (and the authors acknowledge this) what could be covered in a year. . . . Exercises follow each chapter; most are nonroutine, i.e., in many more elementary texts, they might well be part of the exposition. It is difficult to imagine the book's use in a typical undergraduate course. Because of its breadth and sophistication, it is much more plausible as a graduate text or a convenient reference for mathematics graduate students, mathematicians, or other sophisticated users of analysis."

KROLL, FIONA GOLD. A Stone for Benjamin; [by] Fiona Gold Kroll 98 p. 2013 Iguana Books

1. Albaum, Benjamin 2. Auschwitz (Poland: Concentration camp) 3. Holocaust victims 4. Jews—France—History 5. Memoirs

ISBN 1771800070; 9781771800075

SUMMARY: In this memoir, author Fiona Gold Kroll "traces her ancestors' migration from Eastern to Western Europe before World War II. In searching for her family's lost history, Kroll becomes particularly interested in her great-uncle Benjamin, whose striking portrait captivates her. . .. After years of searching, she discovers that he died at Auschwitz in 1943. . . She becomes determined to uncover as much as she can about Benjamin and his family." (Kirkus Reviews)

REVIEW: *Kirkus Rev* v82 no3 p124 F 1 2014

"A Stone For Benjamin". "[Fiona Gold] Kroll's prose is eloquent and evocative, and her writing is admirably self-aware. At times, she acknowledges that her family might think she's obsessed with a ghost, and she wonders if she is, in fact, too rooted in the past. But the goal of her writing is both clear and incredibly important. . . . Benjamin's life story—his normal prewar life, his family's separation and his time in a concentration camp—is, like many real-life narratives, a paradox: remarkable and riveting without being terribly original. . . . A detailed examination of a Holocaust victim's life and a considerate, thought-provoking look into why Holocaust narratives are important."

REVIEW: *Kirkus Rev* v82 no1 p354 Ja 1 2014

"A Stone For Benjamin". "[Fiona Gold] Kroll's prose is eloquent and evocative, and her writing is admirably self-aware. At times, she acknowledges that her family might think she's obsessed with a ghost, and she wonders if she is, in fact, too rooted in the past. But the goal of her writing is both clear and incredibly important. . . . Benjamin's life story—his normal prewar life, his family's separation and his time in a concentration camp—is, like many real-life narratives, a paradox: remarkable and riveting without being terribly original. . . . A detailed examination of a Holocaust victim's life and a considerate, thought-provoking look into why Holocaust narratives are important."

KROONENBERG, SALOMON. Why Hell Stinks of Sulfur; Mythology and Geology of the Underworld; 352 p. 2013 University of Chicago Press

1. Geology—Mediterranean Region 2. Hell 3. Historical literature 4. Mouth of hell 5. Religion—History

ISBN 1780230451; 9781780230450

SUMMARY: This book, by Salomon Kroonenberg, "uses subterranean mythology as a point of departure to explore the vast world that lies beneath our feet. Geologist Salomon Kroonenberg takes us on an expedition that begins in Dante's Inferno and continues through Virgil, Da Vinci, Descartes, and Jules Verne. He investigates the nine circles of hell, searches a lake near Naples for the gates of hell used by Aeneas, and turns a scientific spotlight on the many myths of the underworld." (Publisher's note)

REVIEW: *Libr J* v138 no6 p98 Ap 1 2013 Betty Galbraith

REVIEW: *Publ Wkly* v259 no51 p46 D 17 2012

REVIEW: *TLS* no5784 p24 F 7 2014 ANDREW H. KNOLL

"Why Hell Stinks of Sulfur: Mythology and Geology of the Underworld." "In 'Why Hell Stinks of Sulfur,' Salomon Kroonenberg chronicles humanity's journey from one mode of explanation to the other. . . . The pleasure of joining Kroonenberg in his odyssey lies not in any fleeting glimpse of Hell, but rather in the finely wrought explanations of Mediterranean geology sprinkled throughout the text. . . . The book requires patience on the part of the reader--Kroonenberg loves digression and only slowly reveals his narrative arc. But the rewards are substantial. Kroonenberg interleaves science, history and autobiography with a light touch."

KROSOCZKA, JARRETT J. Peanut Butter and Jellyfish; [by] Jarrett J. Krosoczka 40 p. 2014 Alfred A. Knopf

1. Bullies—Fiction 2. Children's stories 3. Crabs—Fiction 4. Friendship—Fiction 5. Jellyfishes—Fiction 6. Sea horses—Fiction

ISBN 9780375870361; 9780375970368 (lib. bdg.)

LC 2013-003155

SUMMARY: In this children's book by Jarrett J. Krosoczka, "Peanut Butter, a sunny sea horse, and Jellyfish, a gleeful gelatinous blob, are best friends. They swim up, down and around, all over their ocean home. Unfortunately, every time they swim by Crabby, he has something mean to say. . . . But when Crabby finds himself caught in a lobster trap, his foul mouth falls silent. True to heroic form, Peanut Butter and Jellyfish save him." (Kirkus Reviews)

REVIEW: *Kirkus Rev* v82 no5 p77 Mr 1 2014

"Peanut Butter and Jellyfish". "A cantankerous crab lives up to his name, bullying everyone in the ocean until he realizes the importance of friendship. ,. . . When Crabby finds himself caught in a lobster trap, his foul mouth falls silent. . . . It's not startlingly original, but [Jarrett J.] Krosoczka's saturated waterscape and expressive cast brighten this familiar tale. Crabby does explain that he was jealous—a look behind bullying behavior is always appreciated. There's nothing new under the sea, but these creatures are irrepressible, even Crabby."

REVIEW: *Publ Wkly* v261 no7 p98 F 17 2014

REVIEW: *SLJ* v60 no4 p125 Ap 2014 Michelle Anderson

KROSSA, ANNE SOPHIE.ed. European cosmopolitanism in question. See European cosmopolitanism in question

KRULL, KATHLEEN. Lives of the scientists. See Lives of the scientists

KRUMBOLTZ, JOHN. Fail fast, fail often; how losing can help you win; [by] John Krumboltz 208 p. 2013 Jeremy P. Tarcher/Penguin

1. Career changes 2. Change (Psychology) 3. Failure (Psychology) 4. Self-actualization (Psychology) 5. Self-help materials 6. Success

ISBN 9780399166259

LC 2013-036563

SUMMARY: In this book, authors Ryan Babineaux and John Krumboltz "celebrate failures, referring to them as learning experiences, and encourage readers to get out into the world, try new things, and make mistakes. Although the authors spend some time discussing how to learn from one's miscues, they also emphasize the importance of building curiosity, overcoming analysis paralysis, and taking small steps when trying new things." (Library Journal)

REVIEW: *Libr J* v138 no20 p1 N 15 2013 Deborah Bigelow

REVIEW: *New York Times* v163 no56365 p7 D 29 2013 LIESL SCHILLINGER

"Mastering the Art of Quitting: Why It Matters in Life, Love, and Work," "Reset: How to Beat the Job-Loss Blues and Get Ready For Your Next Act," and "Fail Fast, Fail Often: How Losing Can Help You Win". "Shrewd, detailed, and exhortatory, ['Mastering the Art of Quitting'] breaks down obstacles to quitting, illustrated by exemplary stories of men and women who had the courage to gracefully quit jobs that did not satisfy them. . . . 'Reset' . . . is [Dwain Schenk's] blow-by-blow memoir of his struggle to restore his fortunes. . . . 'Fail Fast, Fail Often' . . . argues for an even more proactive approach to self-invention, encouraging those who are contemplating a new beginning to kick-start their dreams."

KRZHIZHANOVSKY, SIGIZMUND. Autobiography of a corpse; [by] Sigizmund Krzhizhanovsky 256 p. 2013 New York Review Books

1. Alienation (Social psychology)—Fiction 2. Circus—Fiction 3. Journalists—Fiction 4. Musicians—Fiction 5. Short stories

ISBN 1590176707; 9781590176702 (alk. paper)

LC 2013-019761

SUMMARY: In this book, translated by Joanne Turnbull, author Sigizmund Krzhizhanovsky presents "blackly comic philosophical fables. . . . A provincial journalist who moves to Moscow finds his existence consumed by the autobiography of his room's previous occupant; the fingers of a . . . pianist . . . run away to spend a night alone . . . ; a man's lifelong quest to bite his own elbow inspires both a . . . circus act and a new refutation of [Immanuel] Kant." (Publisher's note)

REVIEW: *Kirkus Rev* v81 no16 p242 Ag 15 2013

REVIEW: *N Y Times Book Rev* p23 N 24 2013 KEN KALFUS

"Autobiography of a Corpse." "The stories in this collection by the early Soviet writer Sigizmund Krzhizhanovsky are nearly as fantastic as the crashing combination of his consonants at the beginning of his surname. . . , Even with the skillful labor of the collection's translators, Joanne Turnbull and Nikolai Formozov, contemporary readers will find much of Krzhizhanovsky's writing excessively talky and his philosophizing sophomoric. Occasionally, however, readers will glimpse their own anxieties and anomie in those of his century-old 'desoulated' Russians."

REVIEW: *Publ Wkly* v260 no32 p32 Ag 12 2013

KUBLEY, ASHLEY NEWSOME.il. Boho fashion. See Kenney, K. L.

KUBLEY, ASHLEY NEWSOME.il. Hipster fashion. See Kenney, K. L.

KUBLEY, ASHLEY NEWSOME.il. Preppy fashion. See Kenney, K. L.

KUEHN, STEPHANIE. Charm & strange; [by] Stephanie Kuehn 224 p. 2013 St. Martin's Griffin

1. Fantasy fiction 2. Mental illness—Fiction 3. Psychological abuse—Fiction 4. Sexual abuse—Fiction 5. Sexually abused boys

ISBN 1250021944 (hardcover); 9781250021946 (hardcover)

LC 2013-003247

SUMMARY: This book follows Andrew Winston Winters, known as Win. Present-day "Win is smart, competitive and untrusting, estranged from his former roommate, Lex, his one ally and defender. The reasons for Win's self-loathing and keyed-up anxiety won't be fully revealed until story's end. What exactly does he expect to happen during the full moon? Why has he fallen out with Lex? Win's privileged childhood, when he was known as Drew, is another mystery." (Kirkus Reviews)

REVIEW: *Booklist* v109 no19/20 p86 Je 1 2013 Daniel Kraus

REVIEW: *Bull Cent Child Books* v67 no1 p27-8 S 2013 D. S.

"Charm & Strange." "Sixteen-year-old Win, attending a boarding school in Vermont, believes his bouts of violence and inner torment are signs of a family trait: they have inner wolves, creatures into whom they may be able to transform. . . . [Author Stephanie] Kuehn writes powerfully of Win's torment and rage, and her use of a fantasy trope . . . as a way of conceiving the horror of child sexual abuse is effectively disturbing. . . . The hook tries to do too much, however, with . . . the character of a new girl, Jordan, never developing beyond a superfluous device. . . . The suicides also lack the taut emotionality of the rest of the hook. . . . Sexual abuse at the hands of family is still an underexplored topic, though . . . and this is a creative and dramatic exploration."

REVIEW: *Horn Book Magazine* v89 no6 p98-9 N/D 2013 KATIE BIRCHER

REVIEW: *Kirkus Rev* v81 no10 p98-9 My 15 2013

REVIEW: *SLJ* v59 no10 p1 O 2013 Evelyn Khoo Schwartz

KUGELBERG, JOHAN.ed. Enjoy The Experience. See Enjoy The Experience

KUKLIN, SUSAN.il. Beyond magenta; transgender teens speak out; 192 p. 2014 Candlewick Press

1. Gender identity 2. Intersex people 3. Transgender people—Interviews 4. Transgender teenagers 5. Young adult literature

ISBN 0763656119; 9780763656119

LC 2013-943071

SUMMARY: For this book, author Susan Kuklin "met and interviewed six transgender or gender-neutral young adults . . . to represent them thoughtfully and respectfully before, during, and after their personal acknowledgment of gender preference. Portraits, family photographs, and candid images grace the pages, augmenting the emotional and physical journey each youth has taken." (Publisher's note)

REVIEW: *Booklist* v110 no11 p56 F 1 2014 Michael Cart

REVIEW: *Bull Cent Child Books* v67 no6 p321-2 F 2014 Thaddeus Andracki

REVIEW: *Horn Book Magazine* v90 no2 p143-4 Mr/Ap 2014 ROGER SUTTON

"Beyond Magenta: Transgender Teens Speak Out." "Rather than attempting to convey the spectrum of transgender experience through a multitude of voices, [Susan] Kuklin tries something different here, focusing on just six young people whose gender identity is something other than what it was labeled at birth. . . . In her edited transcriptions of the interviews, Kuklin lets her subjects speak wholly for themselves, and while their bravery is heartening, their bravado can be heartbreaking. But who expects teenagers to be tentative? Photographs (of most of the subjects) are candid and winning; and appended material, including Kuklin's explanation of her interview process, a Q&A with the director of a clinic for transgendered teens, and a great resource list, is valuable."

REVIEW: *Kirkus Rev* v81 no24 p213 D 15 2013

"Beyond Magenta: Transgender Teens Speak Out". "[Susan] Kuklin . . . brings her intimate, compassionate and respectful lens to the stories of six transgender young people. In verbal and, when the subjects have given permission, visual profiles, readers meet transgender teens with a wide range of backgrounds and experiences. . . . . Their stories are told largely in the teens' own words, with only a few italicized interpolations to clarify or contextualize a point or to describe a facial expression or inflection readers cannot see or hear. . . . The collective portrait that emerges from these narratives and pictures is diverse, complex and occasionally self-contradictory—as any true story should be. Informative, revealing, powerful and necessary."

REVIEW: *SLJ* v60 no6 p68 Je 2014 Shari Fesko

REVIEW: *Publ Wkly* v260 no47 p55 N 18 2013

REVIEW: *SLJ* v60 no2 p125 F 2014 Sarah Stone

REVIEW: *Voice of Youth Advocates* v37 no1 p93 Ap 2014 Amanda Fensch

KULIK, BRIAN W. American fascism and the new deal; the Associated Farmers of California and the pro-industrial movement; [by] Brian W. Kulik 231 p. 2013 Lexington Books

1. Anti-communist movements—California—History 2. Fascism—California—History 3. Historical literature 4. New Deal, 1933-1939

ISBN 9780739179260 (cloth : alk. paper); 9780739185759 (pbk. : alk. paper)

LC 2013-022826

SUMMARY: In this book, the authors "investigate the Associated Farmers (AF) of California during the Great Depression. The AF, an organization of elite growers founded as a pro-industrial reaction to workers, became sociopolitical by the late 1930s to counter the New Deal. The organization utilized vigilante violence to intimidate migrant agricultural workers. . . . The authors look at the difference between European fascism and what developed in the US." (Choice:

Current Reviews for Academic Libraries)

REVIEW: *Choice* v51 no7 p1293 Mr 2014 R. D. Screws

"American Fascism and the New Deal: The Associated Farmers of California and the Pro-Industrial Movement." "The authors look at the difference between European fascism and what developed in the US. . . . The AF attempted to become a national organization but was unable to gain a foothold outside the western states. The authors also take the characteristics of US fascism during the interwar years and apply them to modern examples, such as the Tea Party. Ultimately, one must decide what constitutes fascism, but the authors make a strong case that the Associated Farmers qualify. One issue with the book is that the editing and layout is shoddy at times, which impedes the flow."

KULISH, NICHOLAS. The eternal Nazi; from Mauthausen to Cairo, the relentless pursuit of SS doctor Aribert Heim; [by] Nicholas Kulish 320 p. 2014 Doubleday

1. Fugitives from justice—Egypt 2. Fugitives from justice—Germany 3. HISTORY—Europe—Germany 4. HISTORY—Holocaust 5. HISTORY—Modern—20th Century 6. Human experimentation in medicine—Germany—History—20th century 7. Journalism 8. Physicians—Germany—Biography 9. War criminals—Germany—Biography 10. World War, 1939-1945—Atrocities

ISBN 9780385532433 (hardback)

LC 2013-034604

SUMMARY: This book by Nicholas Kulish and Souad Mekhennet relates how, "having performed horrific experiments at the Mauthausen concentration camp, physician Aribert Heim settled comfortably in postwar Baden-Baden, then fled to Cairo and was eventually subject to a massive manhunt that extended beyond his death. . . . The larger story is Germany's reckoning with its past." (Library Journal)

REVIEW: *Kirkus Rev* v82 no3 p218 F 1 2014

"The Eternal Nazi: From Mauthausen to Cairo, the Relentless Pursuit of SS Doctor Aribert Heim". " An elusive Nazi doctor who escaped justice receives a thorough scouring by two journalists. . . . The authors admirably fill in many of the details of this fugitive Nazi. . . . The authors trace over many decades the vigilant research pursued by German detective Alfred Aedtner, Nazi hunter Simon Wiesenthal and others in exposing the deeds of this criminal. Haunting, doggedly researched but ultimately anticlimactic. The lack of decisive closure to the case tinges the outcome with bitterness."

REVIEW: *Libr J* v138 no16 p58 O 1 2013 Barbara Hoffert

REVIEW: *N Y Times Book Rev* p38 Je 8 2014 Dagmar Herzog

KULKA, OTTO DOV. Landscapes of the metropolis of death; reflections on memory and imagination; [by] Otto Dov Kulka 144 p. 2013 The Belknap Press of Harvard University Press

1. Holocaust, Jewish (1939-1945)—Influence 2. Holocaust, Jewish (1939-1945), in literature 3. Memoirs 4. Memory

ISBN 9780674072893 (cloth : alk. paper)

LC 2012-041721

SUMMARY: In this memoir, historian Otto Dov Kulka "draws from his own journal entries and audio monologues in describing his time at family camps inside Theresienstadt and Auschwitz, places he considers part of the Metropolis of Death. Having spent his professional career on Naziism and Holocaust studies, Kulka wrestles with the elusive nature of perception and recollection, questioning why his memories vary so drastically from others who experienced this landscape firsthand." (Publishers Weekly)

REVIEW: *N Y Rev Books* v60 no5 p56 Mr 21 2013 Simon Schama

REVIEW: *New Statesman* v142 no5142 p46-7 Ja 25 2013 Linda Grant

REVIEW: *TLS* no5747 p23 My 24 2013 JEREMY ADLER

"Landscapes of the Metropolis of Death: Reflections on Memory and Imagination." "Otto Dov Kulka has performed a minor miracle. He has written a masterpiece about his childhood in Auschwitz. . . . He comes late to his subject, and profits from long years of reflection. This lends his tone a rare richness and subtlety. . . . Kulka's well-honed writing--excellently rendered into English by Ralph Mandel--bears witness to the worst that man can do to man, and in doing so testifies to the enduring power of the human spirit. Much that he confronts is familiar, but it loses none of its power in being told again. The whole deadly apparatus shapes the narrative, but in a manner all the more effective for being understated."

KULLING, MONICA. The Tweedles Go Electric!; [by] Monica Kulling 32 p. 2014 Pgw

1. Automobile driving 2. Children's stories 3. Electric automobiles 4. Families—Juvenile fiction 5. Historical fiction

ISBN 1554981670; 9781554981670

SUMMARY: In this book, by Monica Kulling and Marie Lafrance, readers "meet the Tweedles: Papa, Mama, daughter Frances and her brother, Francis. It's the dawn of a new century—the twentieth century!—and the Tweedles have decided to buy a car. . . . Frances is the only member of her eccentric family who is not delighted when Papa decides they need an electric car. . . . But when Mr. Hamm is unable to get to the hospital because his car has run out of gas, Frances saves the day." (Publisher's note)

REVIEW: *Booklist* v110 no19/20 p118 Je 1 2014 Sarah Hunter

REVIEW: *Bull Cent Child Books* v67 no10 p527 Je 2014 A. A.

"The Tweedles Go Electric". "This charming portrayal of the eccentric, unselfconscious Tweedles winks at its audience through both its sly text and playful pictures, where [Marie] Lafrance's graphite and mixed-media drawings in a fitting palette of greens and yellows capture the family's quaint but rapidly expanding world. The characters' expressive features and body language, coupled with the authentic-feeling language and dialogue, make this perfect for a classroom readaloud, where the Tweedles can demonstrate not only the merits of environmental stewardship hut also the beauty of daring to be different."

REVIEW: *Kirkus Rev* v82 no4 p336 F 15 2014

REVIEW: *Quill Quire* v80 no3 p34-5 Ap 2014 Linda Ludke

REVIEW: *SLJ* v60 no6 p83 Je 2014 H. Islam

KUMAR, NARESH.il. Gandhi. See Quinn, J.

KUMAR, SHRAWAN.ed. Human work productivity. See Human work productivity

KÜMIN, BEAT A. The communal age in Western Europe, c.1100-1800; towns, villages and parishes in pre-modern society; [by] Beat A. Kümin x, 154 p. 2013 Palgrave Macmillan

1. Cities and towns—Europe, Western—History 2. Communities—Europe, Western—History 3. Historical literature 4. Parishes—Europe, Western—History 5. Villages—Europe, Western—History
ISBN 0230536859 (pbk.); 9780230536852 (pbk.)
LC 2012-537584

SUMMARY: This book presents an "interpretation of the significance of towns, villages and parishes in the medieval and early modern period." It "explains how local communities empowered common people through collective agency and a degree of local autonomy . . . demonstrates how communal units impacted on key historical developments, from the Reformation to state formation . . . [and] provides case studies of the Italian city, the English parish and the village in the Holy Roman Empire." (Publisher's note)

REVIEW: *Choice* v51 no7 p1297-8 Mr 2014 P. G. Wallace

"The Communal Age in Western Europe, c1100-1800: Towns, Villages and Parishes in Pre-Modern Society." "[Beat] Kümin . . . has published widely on English parishes and premodern, German-speaking village republics. Here, he argues that medieval and early modern Europe experienced a communal age during which horizontal political associations in towns, villages, and parishes provided alternatives to the hierarchical feudal order. . . . Includes images and intra-textual references to a topical bibliography. . . . Highly recommended."

KUNDNANI, ARUN. The Muslims are coming!; Islamophobia, extremism, and the domestic war on terror; [by] Arun Kundnani 256 p. 2014 Verso

1. Domestic terrorism—Great Britain 2. Domestic terrorism—United States 3. POLITICAL SCIENCE—Political Freedom & Security—Civil Rights 4. POLITICAL SCIENCE—Political Freedom & Security—Terrorism 5. Political science literature 6. Terrorism—Great Britain—Prevention 7. Terrorism—United States—Prevention
ISBN 9781781681596 (hardback)
LC 2013-041108

SUMMARY: It was the author's intent to demonstrate that "the war on terror will have no success unless the West stops blaming Islam and starts locating the roots of political dissent. . . .Scholars of 'radicalization' . . . zero in on a spurious 'cultural-psychological predisposition' toward violence and disaffection that offers intelligence and law enforcement agencies a framework to work with but does not address what [Arun] Kundnani believes is at the root of the unrest: poverty and oppression." (Kirkus Reviews)

REVIEW: *Ethn Racial Stud* v37 no10 p1957-9 O 2014 Nisha Kapoor

REVIEW: *Kirkus Rev* v82 no2 p84 Ja 15 2014

"The Muslims Are Coming! Islamophobia, Extremism, and the Domestic War on Terror". " A widely researched argument about why the war on terror will have no success unless the West stops blaming Islam and starts locating the roots of political dissent. . . . His examples of the pernicious reach of many policing tools are useful, such as the Prevent model launched in Britain in 2004, provoking questions about privacy and discrimination. [Arun] Kundnani frankly and refreshingly moves away from ideological symptoms and toward political causes in tackling extremism."

REVIEW: *Libr J* v139 no6 p104 Ap 1 2014 Nader Entessar

REVIEW: *New Statesman* v143 no5203 p51 Mr 28 2014

REVIEW: *Publ Wkly* v260 no52 p46 D 23 2013

KÜNG, HANS, 1928-. Can We Save the Catholic Church?; [by] Hans Küng 368 p. 2014 William Collins

1. Catholic Church 2. Catholic Church—Clergy—Sexual behavior 3. Church renewal 4. Religious literature 5. Women in the Catholic Church
ISBN 0007522029; 9780007522026

SUMMARY: In this book, radical theologian Hans Kung "relates how after fifty years the [Catholic] Church has only grown more conservative. Refusing to open dialogue on celibacy for priests; the role of women in the priesthood; homosexuality; or the use of contraception even to prevent AIDS, the Papacy has lost touch. Now, amid widespread disillusion over child abuse, the future of Catholicism is in crisis." (Publisher's note)

REVIEW: *Booklist* v110 no9/10 p24 Ja 1 2014 Ray Olson

"Can We Save the Catholic Church?." "[Hans] Küng's prescription for restoring the church to health Is many-faceted, but its effective ingredients derive from early Christianity; it is deeply reformist and revivalist, not revolutionary. Although the translation is idiomatically shaky here and there (e.g.,'ethician' rather than ethic/st), and Küng favors precision to scintillation, this updated revision of a 2011 German original is an invaluable summation of a great religious critic's life work."

REVIEW: *New Statesman* v142 no5180 p43 O 18 2013 Philip Maughan

KUNTH, WOLFGANG.ed. Terra Maxima. See Terra Maxima

KUPCHYNSKY, MELANIE. Strings attached. See Lipman, J.

KUPERSMITH, VIOLET. The Frangipani Hotel; [by] Violet Kupersmith 256 p. 2013 Spiegel & Grau

1. Hotels—Fiction 2. Past, The 3. Short story (Literary form) 4. Vietnam—Fiction 5. Vietnamese Americans
ISBN 0812993314; 9780812993318 (acid-free paper)
LC 2013-013169

SUMMARY: In this collection of short stories, by Violet Kupersmith, "a beautiful young woman appears fully dressed in an overflowing bathtub at the Frangipani Hotel in Hanoi. A jaded teenage girl in Houston befriends an older Vietnamese gentleman she discovers naked behind a dumpster. A trucker in Saigon is asked to drive a dying young man home to his village. A plump Vietnamese-American teenager is sent to her elderly grandmother in Ho Chi Minh City to lose weight." (Publisher's note)

REVIEW: *Booklist* v110 no13 p18 Mr 1 2014 Ellen Loughran

REVIEW: *Kirkus Rev* v82 no3 p313 F 1 2014

"The Frangipani Hotel". "The best of these short stories, such as 'Little Brother' and 'The Red Veil,' are indeed disturbing. . . . Other tales are less successful, omitting links that would explain startling metamorphoses. In 'Skin and Bones,' for example, an overweight girl is sent to visit her grandmother. She knows full well it's really fat camp, and she's willing to tell her story to a masked woman in exchange for delicious sandwiches. Her story may come at a cost, but [Violet] Kupersmith's tale leaves a lot of loose ends dangling. At her best, Kupersmith writes lyrically haunting tales; she's a writer to watch."

REVIEW: *Libr J* v138 no18 p67 N 1 2013 Barbara Hoffert

REVIEW: *N Y Times Book Rev* p18 My 25 2014 THEODORE ROSS

REVIEW: *Publ Wkly* v260 no51 p34 D 16 2013

REVIEW: *Publ Wkly* v261 no6 p24-6 F 10 2014 JULIE BUNTIN

THE KURDISH SPRING; geopolitical changes and the Kurds; xxv, 344 p. 2013 Mazda Publishers

1. Geopolitics—Middle East 2. Kurds—Foreign countries—Politics and government—21st century 3. Kurds—Iran—Politics and government—21st century 4. Kurds—Iraq—Politics and government—21st century 5. Kurds—Politics and government—21st century 6. Kurds—Syria—Politics and government—21st century 7. Kurds—Turkey—Politics and government—21st century 8. Political science literature

ISBN 1568592728; 9781568592725 (alk. paper)

LC 2013-021930

SUMMARY: Edited by Michael M. Gunter and Mohammed M. A. Ahmed, "The purpose of this edited book is to survey the Kurdish Spring in the aftermath of the Arab Spring that began in late 2010 and early 2011. Approximately 13 articles written by scholarly experts on the Kurds will analyze the overall Kurdish Spring as well as individual aspects of the Kurdish Spring in Iraq, Turkey, Iran, Syria, and the Diaspora." (Publisher's note)

REVIEW: *Middle East J* v68 no3 p479-80 Summ 2014 Hakan Özoğlu

"The Kurdish Spring: Geopolitical Changes and the Kurds." "This edited book . . . will be a very useful read for informed general public and scholars alike. The nonspecialists who want to familiarize themselves with the Kurdish affairs in several different Middle Eastern states, Europe, and beyond will not be disappointed since the contributors do an admirable job in decoding the current very intricate Kurdish movements in the world. The book also contains valuable references for academics who wish to conduct further research on this subject. . . . The reader should be mindful as some of the figures such as loss of life in certain uprisings might be subject to dispute."

KUREISHI, HANIF. The last word; [by] Hanif Kureishi 2014 Faber and Faber

1. Authors & publishers—Fiction 2. Authors—Fiction 3. Biographers—Fiction 4. Older men—Fiction 5. Satire

ISBN 9780571277537 paperback; 9780571277520 hardcover

SUMMARY: In this novel by Hanif Kureishi, "Mamoon is an eminent Indian-born writer who has made a career in England--but now, in his early 70s, his reputation is fading, sales have dried up, and his new wife has expensive taste. Harry, a young writer, is commissioned to write a biography to revitalise both Mamoon's career and his bank balance. . . . The ensuing struggle for dominance raises issues of love and desire, loyalty and betrayal, and the frailties of age versus . . youth." (Publisher's note)

REVIEW: *New Statesman* v143 no6 p48 F 14 2014 Michael Prodger

REVIEW: *TLS* no5785 p19 F 14 2014 BEN JEFFERY

"The Last Word." "Unfortunately, [author Hanif] Kureishi's fiction began to sputter after his first novel. . . . The premiss is the construction of a literary biography. . . . As the alert reader will soon realize, the template for this scenario is taken from Patrick French's authorized biography of V. S. Naipaul, 'The World Is What It Is' (2008). . . . In part, Kureishi seems to have a Wodehousian country comedy in mind. . . . But Kureishi is after more than laughs. . . . The main difficulty is that both Mamoon and, especially, Harry are too flimsy for the weight Kureishi wants them to bear."

KURIN, RICHARD. The Smithsonian's History of America in 101 Objects; [by] Richard Kurin 784 p. 2013 The Penguin Press

1. Historical literature 2. Material culture

ISBN 1594205299; 9781594205293

LC 2013-017171

SUMMARY: For this book, author Richard Kurin, "aided by a team of top Smithsonian curators and scholars, has assembled a literary exhibition of 101 objects from across the Smithsonian's museums that together offer a . . . perspective on the history of the United States. Ranging from the earliest years of the pre-Columbian continent to the digital age . . . each entry pairs the fascinating history surrounding each object with the story of its creation or discovery." (Publisher's note)

REVIEW: *Choice* v51 no7 p1192 Mr 2014 J. M. Piper-Burton

"The Smithsonian's History of America in 101 Objects." "Presenting an interesting view of American history and culture, Smithsonian undersecretary [Richard] Kurin covers prehistoric through present times by proposing 101 items within the Smithsonian collections that 'could act as signposts for larger ideas, achievements and issues that have defined America over time.' . . . This fascinating look at American history and culture is most suitable for public or school libraries, and for individuals. Academic institutions with a strong popular culture program may find the book useful."

REVIEW: *Kirkus Rev* v81 no19 p58 O 1 2013

REVIEW: *Libr J* v138 no10 p80 Je 1 2013

REVIEW: *Publ Wkly* v260 no29 p55 Jl 22 2013

KURLAND, CATHERINE L. Hotel Mariachi; urban space and cultural heritage in Los Angeles; ix, 106 p. 2003 University of New Mexico Press

1. Hispanic Americans—California—Los Angeles 2. Historic buildings—California—Los Angeles—Pictorial works 3. Popular culture—California—Los Angeles 4. Urban studies

ISBN 9780826353726 (pbk. : alk. paper)

LC 2013-000148

SUMMARY: "In Boyle Heights, gateway to East Los Angeles, sits the 1889 landmark 'Hotel Mariachi,' where musicians have lived and gathered on the adjacent plaza for more than half a century." Written by Catherine L. Kurland and Enrique R. Lamadrid, with photography by Miguel A. Gandert, "This book is a photographic and ethnographic study of the mariachis, Mariachi Plaza de Los Angeles, and the neighborhood." (Publisher's note)

REVIEW: *TLS* no5775 p31 D 6 2013 FRANK BRUCE

"Hotel Mariachi: Urban Space and Cultural Heritage in Los Angeles." "The three essays and one photo-essay in 'Hotel Mariachi' trace the overlapping urban, musical, and Hispanic and Mexican histories that have shaped the building and surrounding area up to the hotel's purchase, in 2006, by the East Los Angeles Community Corporation (ELACC) and its subsequent conversion into permanent low-cost housing for the Mariachis. . . . The writers all have a strong connection to the subject. . . . There is little of the theorizing about heritage and urban space suggested by the subtitle, but in spite of--or perhaps, because of--these authors' personal approaches, the book gives a clear sense of the typically postmodern mix of significances attached to the hotel and its plaza."

KURLAND, LYNN. River of dreams; [by] Lynn Kurland 384 p. 2014 Berkeley Sensation

1. Elves 2. Fantasy fiction 3. Imaginary wars and battles—Fiction 4. Love stories 5. Magic—Fiction

ISBN 0425262820; 9780425262825
LC 2013-037477

SUMMARY: This fantasy novel, by Lynn Kurland, is set within the author's "Nine Kingdoms" series. "Aisling of Bruadair is frantic to find both the truth about her future and a mercenary to save her country. . . . Rùnach of Ceangail has offered to help Aisling with her quest, then he fully intends to take up his life as a simple swordsman far from magic and evil mages. Unfortunately, a chance finding of a book of indecipherable spells tells him that an ordinary life is never going to be his." (Publisher's note)

REVIEW: *Booklist* v110 no7 p35 D 1 2013 Patricia Smith

REVIEW: *Kirkus Rev* v82 no1 p116 Ja 1 2014

"River of Dreams". "Aisling and Rùnach's adventure continues, as Rùnach steps more fully into his royal heritage, leading them back to his grandfather's elven kingdom, where they will seek answers as to who Aisling truly is and how they might save the Nine Kingdoms. . . . Taking up where 'Dreamspinner' (2012) left off, [Lynn] Kurland continues her romantic fantasy series with the same elegant writing—though a few oft-repeated phrases do get distracting—and imagination, taking the reader on an adventure chock full of magical beings, breathtaking descriptions, and beautifully rendered characters and situations. An enchanting, vibrant story that captures romance, fantasy and adventure with intriguing detail and an epic, fairy-tale sensibility."

REVIEW: *Publ Wkly* v260 no47 p37 N 18 2013

KURLAND, MICHAEL. Who thinks evil; Professor Moriarty novels; [by] Michael Kurland 304 p. 2014 Minotaur Books

1. Abduction—Fiction 2. FICTION—Mystery & Detective—Traditional British 3. Moriarty, Professor (Fictitious character)—Fiction 4. Murder investigation—Fiction 5. Princes—Fiction

ISBN 9780312365455 (hardback)
LC 2013-045933

SUMMARY: In this "tale of Professor James Moriarty, Sherlock Holmes once again takes a back seat to his historic nemesis as they battle sinister assassins to keep Victoria on the English throne. The plotters are too subtle to target the Queen directly. Instead, they're implicating her beloved but wild grandson, Prince Albert Victor, in a series of outrages they're actually committing themselves." (Kirkus Reviews)

REVIEW: *Booklist* v110 no9/10 p54 Ja 1 2014 David Pitt

REVIEW: *Kirkus Rev* v82 no3 p52 F 1 2014

"Who Thinks Evil". " In [Michael] Kurland's . . . latest tale of Professor James Moriarty, Sherlock Holmes once again takes a back seat to his historic nemesis as they battle sinister assassins to keep Victoria on the English throne. . . .The man immortalized by Holmes as the Napoleon of Crime springs into action, questioning witnesses and making lightning inferences in a way strongly reminiscent of his great adversary. . . . Holmes turns up in the late innings to lend encouragement even more surprising than his logistical support. Mainly, though, this is Moriarty's show. A preposterous, entertaining farrago."

REVIEW: *Libr J* v139 no2 p60 F 1 2014 Teresa L. Jacobsen

REVIEW: *Publ Wkly* v260 no49 p63 D 2 2013

KURLANSKY, MARK, 1948-. The world without fish; how could we let this happen?; [by] Mark Kurlansky 183 2011 Workman Pub.

1. Commercial fishing 2. Overfishing 3. Water pollution

ISBN 978-0-7611-5607-9; 0-7611-5607-0
LC 2011--15516

SUMMARY: It was the author's intent to communicate that "our 'enduring misconception' about nature's bounty may lead to the extinction of many of the fish we eat (such as cod, salmon, swordfish, and tuna) and the subsequent collapse of marine ecosystems . . . . To avoid the dystopia he fears, Kurlansky stresses the importance of supporting sustainable fishing and hopes to enlist his readers to act to help 'change the way we do things!'" (Science)

REVIEW: *Science* v334 no6060 p1205-6 D 2 2011 Sherman J. Suter

"World Without Fish." "Kurlansky . . .worries that our 'enduring misconception' about nature's bounty may lead to the extinction of many of the fish we eat (such as cod, salmon, swordfish, and tuna) and the subsequent collapse of marine ecosystems . . . Discussing four possible solutions (fish farming, quotas, limiting fishing time, and closing fishing grounds), he explains why 'they alone won't work.' While primarily emphasizing overfishing, the book also notes the threats posed by pollution and climate change. Its message is reinforced by Stockton's drawings, bold hand-lettering, and an interwoven short graphic novel. To avoid the dystopia he fears, Kurlansky stresses the importance of supporting sustainable fishing and hopes to enlist his readers to act to help 'change the way we do things!'"

KURTZ, JANE. Anna was here; [by] Jane Kurtz 288 p. 2013 Greenwillow Books

1. City and town life—Kansas—Fiction 2. Families—Fiction 3. Moving, Household—Fiction 4. Psychological fiction

ISBN 0060564938; 9780060564933 (trade bdg.); 9780060564940 (lib. bdg.)
LC 2010-017857

SUMMARY: In this book, "Anna, almost 10, is a worrier, so her family's temporary move from Colorado to her father's hometown in Kansas seems fraught with peril to her." She "decides the best way to handle things is to 'stay folded up' and studiously avoid getting settled in the new town. She manages to keep from starting school, doesn't get too friendly with her large extended family, tries to keep her cat inside and skips out on Sunday school." A tornado changes her perspective. (Kirkus Reviews)

REVIEW: *Booklist* v110 no5 p79 N 1 2013 Kathleen Isaacs

REVIEW: *Bull Cent Child Books* v67 no2 p101 O 2013 H. M.

REVIEW: *Kirkus Rev* v81 no14 p308 Jl 15 2013

REVIEW: *N Y Times Book Rev* p27 N 10 2013 ELISABETH EGAN

"Anna Was Here." "[A] timeless and sweetly funny middle-grade novel. . . . [Jane] Kurtz delivers a gentle, optimistic story about a devout family whose spirituality functions both as a safety net and an umbrella. . . . The Nickels may navigate change--and even disaster--with a lot less friction than the average family . . . but they're far from perfect. That's precisely what will make 'Anna Was Here' a moving-day classic, destined to sidestep its boxed-up brethren for the important job of steadying someone's shaky little hands."

REVIEW: *Publ Wkly* v260 no29 p69 Jl 22 2013

REVIEW: *SLJ* v59 no9 p145 S 2013 Kerry Roeder

KUSKIN, WILLIAM. Recursive origins; writing at the transition to modernity; [by] William Kuskin 272 p. 2013 University of Notre Dame Press

1. English literature—Middle English, 1100-1500—History and criticism—Theory, etc 2. Historical criticism (Literature)—England 3. Literature—History & criticism 4. Literature—Periodization 5. Literature and history—England 6. Literature, Medieval—History and criticism—Theory, etc

ISBN 0268033250 (pbk.: alk. paper); 9780268033255 (pbk.: alk. paper)
LC 2012-050649

SUMMARY: In this book, author William Kuskin argues that "most current literary histories of medieval and early modern English literature hew to period, presenting the Middle Ages and modernity as discrete, separated by a heterodox and unstable fifteenth century. In contrast, the major writers of the sixteenth century . . . were intense readers of the fifteenth century and consciously looked back to its history and poetry as they shaped their own." (Publisher's note)

REVIEW: *Choice* v51 no8 p1401 Ap 2014

"Recursive Origins: Writing at the Transition to Modernity". "[William] Kuskin . . . has written a timely, important book. . . . For Kuskin, the texts of the English Renaissance are 'recursive'; that is, they refer back to earlier works, mostly texts from the 15th century that were then exceedingly popular but are now decidedly noncanonical. The reader who decides to search out these foundational texts—many of which were Caxton's works, and others the work of Chaucer, Lydgate, Hoccleve, Holinshed, and various anonymous authors—will be rewarded through what best can be described as a totalizing reading experience, a continuum and also a matrix of shared texts, themes, sources, and cultural and historical topoi."

KUXHAUSEN, ANNA. From the womb to the body politic; raising the nation in enlightenment Russia; [by] Anna Kuxhausen xiii, 228 p. 2013 University of Wisconsin Press

1. Child rearing—Russia—History—18th century 2. Children—Russia—Social conditions—18th century 3. Historical literature 4. Pregnancy—History

ISBN 9780299289935 (ebook); 9780299289942 (pbk.: alk. paper)
LC 2012-013016

SUMMARY: This book presents "a cultural history of pregnancy, childbirth, infant care, early childhood, and other related matters in late eighteenth-century Russia. Anna Kuxhausen argues that as a result of the Enlightenment's influence on Russia's tiny but growing educated public, all of these ceased to be private matters . . . and became instead matters of public and especially state concern." (American Historical Review)

REVIEW: *Am Hist Rev* v119 no1 p274-5 F 2014 Barbara Alpern Engel

"From the Womb to the Body Politic: Raising the Nation in Enlightenment Russia". "[Anna] Kuxhausen adopts a comparative approach throughout and has read extensively in the relevant secondary literature. This helps her to compensate for the lack of secondary sources treating many of her topics; it also locates her subject within its international context. But she perhaps exaggerates the significance of some of her findings. . . . The book is occasionally repetitive, with the same evidence marshaled to support different points. Cultural rather than social history, this book nevertheless offers an important contribution to the history of the Enlightenment in Russia, to women's history, and to the comparative history of the Enlightenment."

KWAN, SAMANTHA. Framing fat. See Graves, J.

KWASNY, KARL.il. The year of shadows. See Legrand, C.

KWAYMULLINA, AMBELIN. The Interrogation of Ashala Wolf; [by] Ambelin Kwaymullina 384 p. 2014 Candlewick Press

1. Betrayal—Fiction 2. Paranormal fiction 3. Psychic ability—Fiction 4. Resistance to government 5. Speculative fiction

ISBN 0763669881; 9780763669881
LC 2013-944007

SUMMARY: This book, by Ambelin Kwaymullina "asks what happens when children develop inexplicable abilities—and the government sees them as a threat. . . . Ashala Wolf and her Tribe of fellow Illegals have taken refuge in the Firstwood, . . . where they do their best to survive and where they are free to practice their abilities. But when Ashala is compelled to venture outside her territory, she is betrayed by a friend and captured by an enemy." (Publisher's note)

REVIEW: *Booklist* v110 no16 p49 Ap 15 2014 Summer Hayes

REVIEW: *Bull Cent Child Books* v67 no8 p412 Ap 2014 J. H.

REVIEW: *Bull Cent Child Books* v67 no8 p412 Ap 2014

K. Q. G.

"The Interrogation of Ashala Wolf". "Once all the secrets are disclosed . . . the story loses its momentum, becoming a dialogue-heavy stream of Ashala's plans and worries and not a whole lot of action, and the romance between Ashala and Justin deflates. The dystopian world here offers a bit more nuance than the traditional fare, allowing for good guys to find themselves in bad situations, and emphasizing the idea that power can use even a message of peace and balance to corrupt. Feisty heroines looking to save the world are by no means losing their popularity, and their fans may wish to follow Ashala's adventures."

REVIEW: *Horn Book Magazine* v90 no2 p123-4 Mr/Ap 2014 DEIRDRE F. BAKER

"The Interrogation of Ashala Wolf". "[Ambelin] Kwaymullina's convoluted political plot is buoyed by the freshness of her imagery: a forest called Firstwood, which is conscious of its inhabitants; lizard-like 'saurs' that communicate telepathically; and the particular gifts and animal connections expressed by the Illegals. Ashala narrates her story with an earnest adolescent voice—not quirky or vivid, but responsible, loyal, and wholesome. While Kwaymullina's prose style doesn't sparkle, this futuristic fantasy offers an admirable heroine and a thought-provoking situation."

REVIEW: *Kirkus Rev* v82 no6 p79 Mr 15 2014

REVIEW: *Publ Wkly* v261 no5 p58 F 3 2014

REVIEW: *SLJ* v60 no4 p168 Ap 2014 Kathleen E. Gruver

REVIEW: *SLJ* v60 no7 p54 Jl 2014 Mary N. Oluonye

REVIEW: *Voice of Youth Advocates* v37 no1 p84 Ap 2014 Sarah Schmitt

KYD, THOMAS, 1558-1594. The Spanish tragedy; [by] Thomas Kyd 2013 Norton

1. English drama—Early modern, 1500-1700 2. English dramatists—Early modern, 1500-1700 3. Ghost stories 4. Influence (Literary, artistic, etc.) 5. Literature—History & criticism

ISBN 9780393934007 paperback

SUMMARY: A play by Thomas Kyd, edited by Michael Neill, "The freshly edited and annotated text comes with a full introduction and illustrative materials intended for student readers. 'The Spanish Tragedy' was well known to sixteenth-century audiences, and its central elements—a play-within-a-play and a ghost bent on revenge—are widely believed to have influenced Shakespeare's 'Hamlet.' This volume includes a generous selection of supporting materials, among them Kyd's likely sources." (Publisher's note)

REVIEW: *TLS* no5795 p8 Ap 25 2014 EMMA SMITH

"Shakespeare and Outsiders" and "The Spanish Tragedy." "The strength of [author Marianne] Novy's method is clear: it is attentive to varying audience responses and delicate in its understanding of the rhythms of sympathy. . . . Michael Neill's welcome new edition of Thomas Kyd's revenge play 'The Spanish Tragedy' also emphasizes its religious implications. . . . Michael Neill's introduction ranges with his customary elegance and learning across legal, formal and rhetorical analyses. He chooses to print the text as it appeared in editions from 1602 onwards."

KYI, TANYA LLOYD. Anywhere but here; [by] Tanya Lloyd Kyi 320 p. 2013 Simon Pulse

1. Coming of age—Fiction 2. Documentary films—Production and direction—Fiction 3. Grief—Fiction 4. Interpersonal relations—Fiction 5. Single-parent families—Fiction 6. Young adult fiction

ISBN 144248070X; 9781442480698 (pbk.); 9781442480704 (hardcover)

LC 2012-051439

SUMMARY: In this book, high-schooler Webster "dreams of moving to Vancouver after senior year to avoid the prospect of a ho-hum life with a boring job, wife and kids. Breaking up with Lauren is the first step on his new path to an exciting life as a filmmaker. As far as he's concerned, he's single, notwithstanding an 'accidental post-breakup sex scene' with Lauren." When Lauren turns out to be pregnant, things get complicated. (Kirkus Reviews)

REVIEW: *Booklist* v110 no3 p88 O 1 2013 Diane Colson

REVIEW: *Kirkus Rev* v81 no18 p22 S 15 2013

REVIEW: *Quill Quire* v79 no8 p35 O 2013 Robert J. Wiersema

"Anywhere But Here." "In her new novel, Vancouver's Tanya Lloyd Kyi delves into the battered soul and tormented psyche of a teenage boy. . . . Kyi demonstrates a certain amount of bravery in her treatment of the characters and their stories. . . . The author allows her characters room to make bad decisions and doesn't flinch from dramatizing the consequences. The novel's relatability twists inside the reader. 'Anywhere But Here' is a frank, often dark (and also often painfully funny) portrait of lives in transition. . . . While the ending is a little too pat, it doesn't take away from what is otherwise a powerful, significant, and ultimately valuable reading experience."

REVIEW: *Voice of Youth Advocates* v36 no4 p67 O 2013 Susan Allen

L

LABOR, EARLE. Jack London; an American life; [by] Earle Labor 480 p. 2013 Farrar Straus & Giroux

1. Authors, American—19th century—Biography 2. Authors, American—20th century—Biography 3. BIOGRAPHY & AUTOBIOGRAPHY—General 4. Gold mines & mining—Yukon

ISBN 0374178488; 9780374178482 (hardback)

LC 2012-050948

SUMMARY: This book presents a biography of writer Jack London. "Born in San Francisco in 1876 to an impoverished single mother, London . . . took up factory work to support his household while still a child, and by age 18 had worked as an oyster pirate, sailor, and rail-riding hobo. Omnivorous reading and sporadic education fueled his desire to write, and a year spent surviving the Yukon Gold Rush (1897-1898) provided him with inspiration for his earliest nonfiction and fiction." (Publishers Weekly)

REVIEW: *America* v210 no1 p35-6 Ja 6 2014 TIMOTHY O'BRIEN

REVIEW: *Booklist* v110 no3 p15 O 1 2013 Donna Seaman

"Jack London: An American Life." "[Earle] Labor extracts every drop of excitement, folly, romance, 'creative ecstasy,' grueling effort, and despair from the vast London archives, including the relentless press coverage of his exploits. . . . Labor's unceasingly vivid, often outright astonishing biography vibrantly chronicles London's exceptionally daring and wildly contradictory life and recovers and reassesses his complete oeuvre, including many powerful, long-neglected works of compassionate, eyewitness nonfiction. Let the Jack London revival begin."

REVIEW: *Booklist* v110 no19/20 p25 Je 1 2014 Donna Seaman

REVIEW: *Choice* v51 no7 p1214 Mr 2014 A. Hirsh

REVIEW: *Kirkus Rev* v81 no14 p75 Jl 15 2013

REVIEW: *Libr J* v138 no13 p94 Ag 1 2013 Sharon Britton

REVIEW: *London Rev Books* v36 no18 p30-2 S 25 2014 James Camp

REVIEW: *Natl Rev* v65 no24 p49-50 D 31 2013 JOHN DANIEL DAVIDSON

"Jack London: An American Life". "Here is a biographer's treasure trove, and London scholar Earle Labor sets about his task with both relish and care, ever conscious that the tale he's telling is at once outlandish and tragically real. For as much as London offers rich material for a biography, any book-length account of his life is bound to feel incomplete. He was dead at age 40, seemingly at a turning point in his prolific writing career, his life cut off abruptly at the opening of the second act. . . . Labor, to his credit, does not try to spare his readers from the difficulty London had in his personal relationships and the recklessness with which he sometimes treated those closest to him."

REVIEW: *N Y Times Book Rev* p8 D 29 2013 HENRY GIARDINA

REVIEW: *Publ Wkly* v260 no22 p46 Je 3 2013

REVIEW: *TLS* no5773 p7-8 N 22 2013 MARC ROBINSON

REVIEW: *Va Q Rev* v89 no4 p257-62 Fall 2013 Michael Dirda

LADD, LONDON.il. Under the freedom tree. See Vanhecke, S

LADWIG, TIM.il. Sansablatt Head. See Spilman, J.

LAERKE, MOGENS.ed. Philosophy and its history. See Philosophy and its history

LAFEBER, WALTER. The new Cambridge history of American foreign relations.; [by] Walter LaFeber 266 p. 2013 Cambridge University Press

1. Historical literature 2. Imperialism—History 3. Industrialization—History 4. United States—History—1865-1921

ISBN 9780521763288 (hardback v. 3); 9780521763622 (hardback v. 4); 9780521767521 (hardback v. 2); 9781107005907 (hardback v. 1); 9781107031838 (hardback set)

LC 2012-018193

SUMMARY: This book by Walter Lafeber is part of a revised edition of the series "The Cambridge History of American Foreign Relations." The author "explores the impact of post-Civil War industrialization and, in a new introduction, explains his use of the term 'informal empire' for the expansion that accompanied those economicn changes and sparked revolutions in a variety of countries." (Choice: Current Reviews for Academic Libraries)

REVIEW: *Choice* v51 no5 p907 Ja 2014 L. M. Lees

"Dimensions of the Early American Empire 1754-1865," The American Search for Opportunity 1865-1913," and "The Globalizing of America 1913-1945." "The four volumes of this revision . . . feature one new author and relatively minimal changes by two of the original three authors. . . . In volume one, 'Dimensions of the Early American Empire, 1754-1865,' new author [William Earl] Weeks . . . frames his analysis around ten dimensions that characterize the American empire. . . . Weeks deftly weaves these themes into his intriguing and complex study, which is a worthy addition to the series. . . . Libraries with the original set should consider replacing volumes one and four only."

LAFEVERS, ROBIN. Dark triumph; [by] Robin LaFevers 400 p. 2013 Houghton Mifflin Harcourt

1. Assassins—Fiction 2. Death—Fiction 3. Fantasy fiction 4. Gods—Fiction 5. Love—Fiction

ISBN 0547628382 (hardcover); 9780547628387 (hardcover)

LC 2012-033555

SUMMARY: In this novel, by Robin LaFevers, book 2 of the "His Fair Assassin Trilogy," "Sybella's duty as Death's assassin in 15th-century France forces her return home to the personal hell that she had finally escaped. . . . While Sybella is a weapon of justice wrought by the god of Death himself, He must give her a reason to live. When she discovers an unexpected ally imprisoned in the dungeons, will a daughter of Death find something other than vengeance to live for?" (Publisher's note)

REVIEW: *Booklist* v109 no9/10 p98 Ja 1 2013 Ilene Cooper

REVIEW: *Booklist* v109 no7 p44 D 1 2012 Gillian Engberg

REVIEW: *Booklist* v110 no2 p75 S 15 2013 Ann Kelley

"All Our Pretty Songs," 'Dark Triumph," and "Eleanor & Park." "In this suspenseful trilogy-starter, Aurora is sweet and flighty, while the unnamed narrator is surly. When Jack, an adult guitarist, comes into their life, the girls' differences come to a head. . . . The riveting historical adventure that began with 'Grave Mercy' (2012) follows the story of another of Death's handmaidens, Sybella. She is bound to a knight who is both the bane of her existence and her hope for the future. . . . Eleanor and Park, from opposite worlds, slowly build a relationship while riding the bus to school every day. The pure, fear-laced, yet steadily maturing relationship they develop is urgent and, of course, heartbreaking."

REVIEW: *Bull Cent Child Books* v66 no7 p339 Mr 2013 Kate Quealy-Gainer

REVIEW: *Horn Book Magazine* v89 no3 p86-7 My/Je 2013 DEIRDRE F. BAKER

REVIEW: *Kirkus Rev* v81 no6 p40 Mr 15 2013

REVIEW: *Publ Wkly* p122 Children's starred review annual 2013

REVIEW: *Publ Wkly* v260 no8 p171 F 25 2013

REVIEW: *SLJ* v59 no8 p53 Ag 2013 Elizabeth L. Kenyon

REVIEW: *SLJ* v59 no7 p95 Jl 2013 Nora G. Murphy

REVIEW: *Voice of Youth Advocates* v36 no1 p677 Ap 2013 Dawn Talbott

LAFLAUR, MARK. Elysian fields; [by] Mark LaFlaur 412 p. 2013 Mid City Books

1. Brothers—Fiction 2. Dysfunctional families—Fiction 3. Mentally ill—Fiction 4. New Orleans (La.)—Fiction 5. Psychological fiction
ISBN 9780615729862 (alk. paper)
LC 2012-954187

SUMMARY: In this book by Mark LaFlaur, "as Simpson ponders whether to kill his brother Bartholomew, he reflects upon their upbringing with mother Melba. At age 36, Simpson works in a copy shop, but fantasizes of escaping to San Francisco and being a famous poet. The obstacle is Bartholomew—as a second grader, he spent a year in a psychiatric ward—who is presented vividly as possibly autistic and 'laced with idiot savantism.' (Publishers Weekly)

REVIEW: *Booklist* v109 no22 p49 Ag 1 2013 Rebecca Vnuk

REVIEW: *Kirkus Rev* v81 no13 p75 Jl 1 2013

REVIEW: *Kirkus Rev* p35 D 15 2013 supplemet best books 2013

"Elysian Fields". "[Mark] , LaFlaur's descriptive talent shines. Fertile imagery drips like Spanish moss: the old buildings collapsing, 'as though the humidity-sodden bricks were returning to mud,' while 'cloud stacks glowed like the battlements of heaven.' Simpson's mental landscape is equally vivid, drawn with such empathy and depth that readers will forgive his perpetual indecision and may even root for him to carry out the removal of his near-deranged brother. . . . A wholly involving story with Faulkner-ian characters in a fully realized setting."

REVIEW: *Publ Wkly* v260 no7 p19 F 18 2013

LAFOLLETTE, HUGH.ed. The international encyclopedia of ethics. See The international encyclopedia of ethics

LAFRANCE, MARIE.il. The Tweedles Go Electric! See Kulling, M.

LAGO, EDUARDO. Call me Brooklyn; [by] Eduardo Lago 364 p. 2013 Dalkey Archive Press

1. Authors—Fiction 2. Brooklyn (New York, N.Y.)—Fiction 3. Epistolary fiction 4. Friendship 5. Journalists—Fiction 6. Manhattan (New York, N.Y.)—Fiction 7. Orphans—Fiction
ISBN 9781564788603 (pbk. : alk. paper)
LC 2013-022257

SUMMARY: Written by Eduardo Lago and translated by Ernesto Mestre-Reed, "'Call Me Brooklyn' follows the life of Gal Ackerman, a Spanish orphan adopted during the Spanish Civil War and raised in Brooklyn, NY. Moving from the secret tunnels that shelter the forgotten residents of Manhattan to the studio where Mark Rothko put an end to his life, . . . 'Call Me Brooklyn' draws upon a rich tradition." (Publisher's note)

REVIEW: *TLS* no5777/8 p25 D 20 2013 Eduardo Lago

"Call Me Brooklyn." "Eduardo Lago's 'Call Me Brooklyn' is the story of Nestor, an author who is constructing a novel, 'Brooklyn,' from jottings-by another- writer, Gal Ackerman. . . . 'Call Me Brooklyn' is very much writing about writing. . . . 'Call Me Brooklyn' uses epistolary sections, excerpts from newspaper articles and reproductions of Gal's marginal notes to tell love stories, family dramas and tales of the unexpected. . . . If Lago is extremely and self-referentially literary, he never fails to be human; his tone is conversational, charming where other such writing can be arch. . . . The novel, presented here in a flawlessly readable translation by Emesto Mestre-Reed, stands on its own, with no other credentials for enjoyment than a love of storytelling."

LAHIRI-DUTT, KUNTALA. Dancing with the river; people and life on the Chars of South Asia; [by] Kuntala Lahiri-Dutt 272 p. 2013 Yale University Press

1. Human beings—Effect of environment on—South Asia 2. Human ecology—South Asia 3. River life—South Asia 4. Social science literature
ISBN 9780300188301 (cloth : alk. paper)
LC 2012-041242

SUMMARY: "With this book Kuntala Lahiri-Dutt and Gopa Samanta offer an intimate glimpse into the microcosmic world of 'hybrid environments.' Focusing on chars--the part-land, part-water, low-lying sandy masses that exist within the riverbeds in the floodplains of lower Bengal--the authors show how, both as real-life examples and as metaphors, chars straddle the conventional categories of land and water, and how people who live on them fluctuate between legitimacy and illegitimacy." (Publisher's note)

REVIEW: *Choice* v51 no1 p141 S 2013 M. H. Fisher

REVIEW: *Science* v343 no6170 p488 Ja 31 2014 Charles W. Nuckolls

"Dancing With the River: People and Life on the Chars of South Asia." "As an introductory account of 'people and life' on chars--small, flood-prone bits of land within the river courses of West Bengal--'Dancing with the River' provides a much-needed overview of the marginal lands where poor immigrants and refugees have settled. . . . Geographers Kuntala Lahiri-Dutt . . . and Gopa Samanta . . . provide a richly detailed and jargon-free excursion into marginal lands and people in riparian West Bengal, not far from Kolkata and the border with Bangladesh. . . . 'Dancing with the River' offers a richly panoramic study of a unique geographical context."

LAHIRI, JHUMPA, 1967-. The lowland; a novel; [by] Jhumpa Lahiri 352 p. 2013 Alfred A. Knopf

1. Brothers—Fiction 2. Historical fiction 3. Kolkata (India)—History 4. Naxalite Movement—Fiction 5. Triangles (Interpersonal relations)—Fiction
ISBN 0307265749; 9780307265746 (hardcover); 9780385350402 (ebook)
LC 2012-043878

SUMMARY: In this book, by Jhumpa Lahiri, "Subhash and Udayan Mitra are inseparable brothers, one often mistaken for the other in the Calcutta neighborhood where they grow up. It is the 1960s, and Udayan . . . finds himself drawn to the Naxalite movement, a rebellion waged to eradicate inequity and poverty. Subhash . . . leaves home to pursue a life of scientific research in . . . America. When Subhash learns what happened to his brother . . . he goes back to India." (Publisher's note)

REVIEW: *Atlantic* v312 no3 p35 O 2013 JHUMPA LAHIRI Ann Hulbert

"The Lowland." "Divided consciousness has been [Jhumpa] Lahiri's recurrent theme: "the intense pressure to be two things, loyal to the old world, and fluent in the new," that she experienced as the daughter of Bengali immigrants. . . . This time, Lahiri daringly redraws the map. In Calcutta, one of two close-knit brothers becomes a Maoist revolutionary in the late 1960s, while the other proceeds to the U.S. For both--and for a wife and daughter, too--loyalties are tested, twisted to extremes that become appallingly clear only toward the end. Lahiri's prose is blunter, less mellifluous: here worlds, new and old, contain terrors."

REVIEW: *Booklist* v109 no21 p29 Jl 1 2013 Donna Seaman

REVIEW: *Kirkus Rev* p10 Ag 15 2013 Fall Preview

REVIEW: *Kirkus Rev* p23-4 N 15 2013 Best Books

REVIEW: *Kirkus Rev* v81 no17 p13 S 1 2013

REVIEW: *Libr J* v138 no7 p56 Ap 15 2013 Barbara Hoffert

REVIEW: *N Y Rev Books* v60 no16 p8-10 O 24 2013 Michael Gorra

"The Lowland." "Gauri may burst beyond decorum. Her creator never does. Nothing extreme, nothing unmannerly; it's all a little bit gray, as if the novel itself were as determined as Subhash to refuse any moment of emotional crisis. That makes [Jhumpa] Lahiri sound cautious, and in reading her I have in fact sometimes wished she would break her own rules, and allow herself to flower into extravagance. Yet restraint has a daring of its own, and 'The Lowland' is her finest work so far. . . . It is at once unsettling and generous, bow-string taut and much, much better than her episodic first novel. . . . This book is a determinedly apolitical writer's attempt to deal with an explosive subject, and some readers will think it quietist."

REVIEW: *N Y Times Book Rev* p16 S 29 2013 Jhumpa Lahiri

REVIEW: *New Statesman* v142 no5176 p85-6 S 20 2013 Claire Lowdon

REVIEW: *New York Times* v162 no56265 pC23-8 S 20 2013 MICHIKO KAKUTANI

REVIEW: *New York Times* v162 no56265 pC23-8 S 20 2013 MICHIKO KAKUTANI

REVIEW: *Publ Wkly* v260 no28 p146 Jl 15 2013

REVIEW: *Publ Wkly* v261 no4 p187 Ja 27 2014

REVIEW: *Time* v182 no14 p64 S 30 2013 Lev Grossman

REVIEW: *TLS* no5766 p21 O 4 2013 ANJALI JOSEPH

"The Lowland." "At times the brevity of the narration makes these incidents seem portentous; it is clear that they exist to set up later events and to create a unified world within the novel. . . . 'The Lowland,' which has been shortlisted for the Man Booker Pdze, is in a sense [Jhumpa] Lahiri's big novel: possessed of historical moment and reach. But for the most part, history is only the element in which the characters' lives unfold, and this allows Lahiri to exercise her own special talent. She is capable of great elegance, and here, as in her two fine collections of stories and novel 'The Namesake' (2003), her subject is the externally undramatic failure of relationships between characters, and the ways in which people hold back from living their lives."

REVIEW: *Women's Review of Books* v31 no2 p24-6 Mr/Ap 2014 Valerie Miner

REVIEW: *World Lit Today* v88 no1 p58-9 Ja/F 2014 Rita D. Jacobs

"The Lowland." "In this exquisite novel, Jhumpa Lahiri revisits some of her major themes--dislocation, assimilation, family connection, and the difficulties of love--but in this instance she develops her characters and circumstances in greater depth than ever before. It's no secret that Lahiri's prose can be lapidary . . . but here she also sustains a complicated narrative spanning three generations with a deft and yet profound touch. . . . Lahiri takes us into Indian life and custom just enough to have us viscerally feel the clash of cultures that Subhash encounters when he relocates to America."

LAIDLAW, ROB. Cat champions; caring for our feline friends; [by] Rob Laidlaw 64 p. 2014 Orca Book Pub

1. Animal welfare 2. Cat rescue 3. Cats—Juvenile literature 4. Child volunteers 5. Children's nonfiction
ISBN 1927485312; 9781927485316

SUMMARY: In this book, readers "meet kids who are helping at shelters, fostering kittens, volunteering with sterilization programs and caring for abandoned cats. Animal advocate Rob Laidlaw brings readers a hopeful, inspiring look at the issues facing domesticated and feral cats, and the cat champions who are working to help them." (Publisher's note)

REVIEW: *Booklist* v110 no12 p67 F 15 2014 Ilene Cooper

REVIEW: *Kirkus Rev* v82 no4 p57 F 15 2014

REVIEW: *Quill Quire* v79 no9 p38 N 2013 Emily Donaldson

"Cat Champions: Caring for Our Feline Friends." "Cats may have conquered the Internet, but every year thousands still end up homeless in shelters, sanctuaries, and feral colonies. Cat Champions is about some of the people--most of them kids--who dedicate their personal time, imagination, and resources to caring for them. . . . Written in a clear, unpreachy style and brimming with lovely full-colour photos, this is an ideal volume for any young cat lover who wants to take his or her passion a little further than simply clicking 'like' on YouTube videos."

REVIEW: *SLJ* v60 no3 p181 Mr 2014 Susan E. Murray

LAIDLAW, ROB. Saving lives & changing hearts; animal sanctuaries and rescue centres; [by] Rob Laidlaw 62 p. 2012 Fitzhenry & Whiteside

1. Animal rescue 2. Animal welfare 3. Children's nonfiction 4. Wildlife refuges 5. Wildlife rehabilitation
ISBN 1554552125; 9781554552122

SUMMARY: This book "profiles a variety of sanctuaries throughout the world and the people who work to safeguard the wildlife. . . . The author offers the . . . stories behind the founding of many of these sanctuaries and presents . . . conclusions to the many . . . stories of rescued animals. A section showing the difference between true sanctuaries and those neither meeting the needs of animals in their care nor preparing them for rehabilitation into the wild is" included. (School Library Journal)

REVIEW: *Quill Quire* v79 no4 p32 My 2013

REVIEW: *SLJ* v59 no4 p180 Ap 2013 Eva Elisabeth VonAncken

LAIDLAW, S. J. The voice inside my head; [by] S. J. Laidlaw 256 p. 2014 Tundra Books of Northern New York

1. Brothers & sisters—Fiction 2. Internship programs 3. Missing persons—Fiction 4. Psychological fiction 5. Utila Island (Honduras)
ISBN 1770495657; 9781770495654 (hardcover); 9781770495661 (ebk.)

LC 2013-936989

SUMMARY: In this book, by S.J. Laidlaw, "seventeen-year-old Luke's older sister, Pat, has always been his moral compass. . . . So when Pat disappears on a tiny island off the coast of Honduras and the authorities claim she's drowned, . . . Luke heads to Honduras to find her. . . . Once there, he meets several characters who describe his sister as a very different girl from the one he knows. Does someone have a motive for wanting her dead?" (Publisher's note)

REVIEW: *Booklist* v110 no17 p56-7 My 1 2014 Sarah Hunter

REVIEW: *Bull Cent Child Books* v67 no9 p464 My 2014 K. C.

"The Voice Inside My Head". "While the mystery here is enough to keep the pages turning, it's clumsily handled, with cliched Central American island experiences (such as run-ins with drug dealers and voodoo hoaxes) providing the MacGuffins that delay the ultimate resolution; the emotional tenor of the book misses on multiple occasions, with secondary characters such as stoner Zach oddly comic amid the tragic story. Nonetheless, the pull of the setting . . . will appeal to armchair travelers. Additionally, [S. J.] Laidlaw goes some way to dispel stereotypes about native Hondurans, providing insight into their daily lives through Luke's island love interest and her family's unfavorable attitudes toward entitled and clueless tourists."

REVIEW: *Quill Quire* v80 no2 p36-8 Mr 2014 Laura Godfrey

"The Voice Inside My Head". "The plot, offering abundant possibilities for Pat's fate, will keep readers turning the pages. [S. J.] Laidlaw also does a good job depicting the island's party scene without demonizing the idea of letting loose and having fun. . . . At the novel's heart is a message about family involving Luke's desperation to find his sister, the difficulty they both faced growing up with troubled parents, and the comfort Luke feels at being warmly accepted by Jamie's family. Homemade bread and group hugs are far removed from what Luke is used to, but while he's searching for his sister, he begins to understand what she saw in this strange, small community."

REVIEW: *Voice of Youth Advocates* v37 no1 p69 Ap 2014 Laura Woodruff

LAING IMANG. Almost an Army Cadet, Always a Forester. See Linggi, K. C.

LAING, OLIVIA. The Trip to Echo Spring; On Writers and Drinking; [by] Olivia Laing 352 p. 2014 Picador

1. Alcoholics—United States 2. Alcoholics in literature 3. Alcoholism in literature 4. American literature—20th century—History and criticism 5. Authors, American—20th century—Alcohol use 6. Authorship—Psychological aspects 7. Creative ability—Psychological aspects 8. Literature—History & criticism

ISBN 1250039568 (hbk.); 9781250039569 (hbk.)

LC 2013-038323

SUMMARY: In this book, "Olivia Laing examines the link between creativity and alcohol through the work and lives of six extraordinary men: F. Scott Fitzgerald, Ernest Hemingway, Tennessee Williams, John Berryman, John Cheever, and Raymond Carver. . . . Olivia Laing grew up in an alcoholic family herself. One spring, wanting to make sense of this ferocious, entangling disease, she took a journey across America that plunged her into the heart of these overlapping lives." (Publisher's note)

REVIEW: *Bookforum* v20 no5 p32 F/Mr 2014 GERALD HOWARD

REVIEW: *Booklist* v110 no6 p9 N 15 2013 Donna Seaman

REVIEW: *Kirkus Rev* v81 no21 p153 N 1 2013

REVIEW: *N Y Times Book Rev* p21 Ja 5 2014

REVIEW: *N Y Times Book Rev* p1-14 D 29 2013 Lawrence Osborne

REVIEW: *New Statesman* v142 no5167 p45-6 Jl 19 2013 Talitha Stevenson

REVIEW: *New York Times* v163 no56373 pC1-8 Ja 6 2014 JOHN WILLIAMS

"The Trip to Echo Spring: On Writers and Drinking." "Olivia Laing's 'The Trip to Echo Spring' [is] a combination of literary analysis, memoir and travelogue that is most beguiling and incisive when rambling through the work and lives of [John] Cheever, Raymond Carver, F. Scott Fitzgerald, Ernest Hemingway, Tennessee Williams and John Berryman. . . . . Those are complex, even impossible questions, and it's a credit to Ms. Laing's book that it succeeds despite inevitably finding more mystery and contradiction than answers. . . . But even the best stretches of Ms. Laing's book are interrupted by problematic, if not fatal, authorial choices."

REVIEW: *New Yorker* v89 no45 p75-1 Ja 20 2014

REVIEW: *TLS* no5757 p7 Ag 2 2013 PAUL QUINN

"A Trip to Echo Spring: Why Writers Drink." "Her new book again focuses on a much-chronicled group of writers. . . . Once again, however, any sense of over-familiarity with her cast is counteracted by a bold use of syncretic form. . . . When moving from clinical data to the fictional texts, [Olivia] Laing is often perceptive. . . . For the most part, however, and for all the defamiliarizing intent, there is a nagging sense reading this book that high-concept travel narratives with their allusive digressions around a central trauma (complete with badly reproduced photographs) have themselves become too familiar: a sub-genre dictated by publishing imperatives. This book is often at its best when most sedentary, when engaged in close reading of texts."

LAIRD, NICK. Go giants; [by] Nick Laird 69 p. 2013 Faber and Faber

1. English poetry—Irish authors 2. Ireland—Poetry 3. Marriage—Poetry 4. Poems—Collections 5. Rome—Poetry

ISBN 9780571288182

LC 2013-376384

SUMMARY: This collection of poetry by Nick Laird "looks back . . . to his youth in Northern Ireland, and to the modes and the literature of Ireland and the U.K. . . . The two-part collection begins with a miscellany--a . . . poem of marital love . . . and another on pregnancy . . . a . . . list of clichés (the title poem), . . . [an] anecdote about a girl bullied at school. . . . Laird ends with a . . . series in unrhymed tercets . . . touching on his own time in New York and Rome." (Publishers Weekly)

REVIEW: *N Y Rev Books* v61 no6 p62-4 Ap 3 2014 Dan Chiasson

REVIEW: *New Yorker* v89 no33 p102-1 O 21 2013

"Go Giants." " The book celebrates the jagged coexistence of the glorious and the mundane, the classical and the contemporary, the whimsical and the deadly serious. 'The Mission' takes place in a revival tent in gritty Northern Ireland, amid 'concrete slabs and a muddy lawn'; 'The Mark' considers 'pavonazzetto' sculptures at the Capitoline Museum, in Rome, and the virtues of music produced on lyres versus reed flutes. . . . The range of these scrupulous poems suggests that there is little in form or content that [Nick] Laird cannot master."

REVIEW: *Publ Wkly* v260 no29 p42 Jl 22 2013

REVIEW: *TLS* no5752 p23 Je 28 2013 RORY WATERMAN

LAKE, MARK.ed. Computational approaches to archaeological spaces. See Computational approaches to archaeological spaces

LAKER, BARBARA. Busted; a tale of corruption and betrayal in the city of brotherly love; [by] Barbara Laker 256 p. 2014 HarperCollins Publishers

1. Investigative reporting—Pennsylvania—Philadelphia—Case studies 2. Journalism 3. Police corruption—Press coverage—Pennsylvania—Philadelphia—Case studies

ISBN 0062085441; 9780062085443 (hardcover: alk. paper); 9780062085450 (pbk.: alk. paper)

LC 2013-036581

SUMMARY: This book, by Philadelphia Daily News reporters Wendy Ruderman and Barbara Laker, is the "true story of the biggest police corruption scandal in Philadelphia history, a tale of drugs, power, and abuse involving a rogue narcotics squad, a confidential informant, and two veteran journalists whose reporting drove a full-scale FBI probe, rocked the City of Brotherly Love, and earned a Pulitzer Prize." (Publisher's note)

REVIEW: *Booklist* v110 no8 p3 D 15 2013 Vanessa Bush

REVIEW: *Columbia J Rev* v52 no7 p60-1 My/Je 2014 ANNA CLARK

REVIEW: *Kirkus Rev* v82 no2 p64 Ja 15 2014

"Busted: A Tale of Corruption and Betrayal in the City of Brotherly Love". "[Wendy] Ruderman and [Barbara] Laker tell their personal stories, disclosing their workaholic habits, quirky personalities and deep friendship in a breezy writing style that occasionally borders on maudlin. Despite the stylistic distractions, however, the narrative offers an insightful view of high-risk, high-reward investigative journalism, made more poignant by recent severe cutbacks in newsrooms around the country. 'All the President's Men' it's not, but Ruderman and Laker provide a welcome addition to the shelves of books about the mechanics and logistics of journalistic exposés."

REVIEW: *Libr J* v139 no6 p102 Ap 1 2014 Chad Clark

REVIEW: *N Y Times Book Rev* p30 My 25 2014 Charles Graeber

REVIEW: *Publ Wkly* v260 no49 p72 D 2 2013

LAKIN, PATRICIA. Bruno and Lulu's playground adventures; 80 p. 2014 Dial Books for Young Readers, an imprint of Penguin Group (USA) Inc.

1. Best friends—Fiction 2. Children's stories 3. Chipmunks—Fiction 4. Friendship—Fiction 5. Imagination—Fiction 6. Play—Fiction 7. Squirrels—Fiction

ISBN 9780803735538 (hardcover)

LC 2012-043897

SUMMARY: This children's book by Patricia Lakin follows "two best friends who love to have fun at the playground. Bruno likes straight-forward adventure while Lulu uses her over-the-top imagination to play. In two short, funny episodes, readers discover why Bruno and Lulu's different personalities help them become even better friends." (Publisher's note)

REVIEW: *Booklist* v110 no16 p52 Ap 15 2014 Martha Edmundson

REVIEW: *Bull Cent Child Books* v67 no9 p464-5 My 2014 J. H.

REVIEW: *Kirkus Rev* v82 no5 p69 Mr 1 2014

"Bruno & Lulu's Playground Adventures". "The text is delivered almost entirely in color-coded speech-balloon dialogue between the friends (yellow for Lulu to match her hair bow and blue for Bruno to match his glasses). This supports the cartoonish quality of the humorous, digitally rendered art, but some pages end up looking rather cluttered with a surfeit of balloons. The final two pages incorporate the text in the illustrations, presenting the words 'THE END' in pebbles in the sandbox, but Bruno intercedes to scratch the word 'NOT' above them, suggesting that more squirrely adventures await the friends in future stories. A playful, comic romp of a book for new readers."

REVIEW: *Publ Wkly* v261 no5 p57 F 3 2014

REVIEW: *SLJ* v60 no5 p86 My 2014 Ellie Lease

LAKS, ELLIE. My gentle Barn; [by] Ellie Laks 288 p. 2014 Harmony Books

1. Animal rescue—California 2. Animal shelters—California 3. Human-animal relationships—California 4. Memoirs

ISBN 0385347669; 9780385347662

LC 2013-042589

SUMMARY: Author Ellie Laks "started The Gentle Barn after adopting a sick goat from a run-down petting zoo in 1999. Some two hundred animals later (including chickens, horses, pigs, cows, rabbits, emus, and more), The Gentle Barn has become . . . [a] nonprofit that brings together a volunteer staff of community members and at-risk teens to rehabilitate abandoned and/or abused animals." (Publisher's note)

REVIEW: *Booklist* v110 no12 p20 F 15 2014 Colleen Mondor

"My Gentle Barn: Creating a Sanctuary Where Animals Heal and Children Learn to Hope." "The saga of [Ellie] Laks and her animal sanctuary is enormously compelling. . . . With brutal honesty, she acknowledges the missteps in her first marriage that became a casualty to her rescue efforts, but then she recounts the happiness she found with a volunteer who became her soul mate. . . . Laks brings so much raw emotion to her narrative that readers will find themselves moved to tears over the lives of goats and cows. Intimate, powerful, and shocking in its revelations about the food we eat, 'My Gentle Barn' is not easily forgotten. This is a book to talk about and return to; it's a life changer, plain and simple."

REVIEW: *Kirkus Rev* v82 no3 p49 F 1 2014

LALA-CRIST, DESPINA. Emily Dickinson; Goddess of the Volcano: a Biographical Novel; 462 p. 2013 Cre-

ateSpace Independent Publishing Platform
1. Biographical fiction 2. Dickinson, Emily, 1830-1886 3. Dickinson, Susan Gilbert 4. Families—Fiction 5. Poets—Fiction
ISBN 1470147092; 9781470147099

SUMMARY: This book by Despina Lala Crist is a "a biographical novel" about poet Emily Dickinson. It focuses on Dickinson's "complicated family" and her relationship with her sister-in-law Susan Gilbert Dickinson. "Was she indeed the beloved of the Poet? Who loved more—Emily or Susan ? And who was truly the most dramatic figure in the cyclone of forbidden passions?" (Publisher's note)

REVIEW: *Kirkus Rev* v82 no1 p88 Ja 1 2014

"Emily Dickinson: Goddess of the Volcano: A Biographical Novel". ". Initially, this book seems to be far stranger than it really is: The title suggests a persona and possibly even a locale far outside how readers usually perceive the Belle of Amherst, and the opening chapters include supernatural meetings between the narrator and members of the Dickinson family. But before too long, the book settles down into a readable, though not revolutionary, portrait of the artist's life and loves. As such, it may appeal particularly to fans of her poetry (some of which is about volcanoes) but perhaps not to readers looking for a weighty biography interwoven with heavily academic analysis of her work."

LAMADRID, ENRIQUE R. Hotel Mariachi. See Kurland, C. L.

LAMANA, JULIE T. Upside down in the middle of nowhere; [by] Julie T. Lamana 320 p. 2014 Chronicle Books
1. African American families—Louisiana—New Orleans—Juvenile fiction 2. African Americans—Fiction 3. Family life—Louisiana—Fiction 4. Historical fiction 5. Hurricane Katrina, 2005—Fiction 6. Hurricane Katrina, 2005—Juvenile fiction 7. Survival—Fiction 8. Survival—Louisiana—New Orleans—Juvenile fiction
ISBN 9781452124568 (alk. paper)
LC 2013-003262

SUMMARY: In this book, "ten-year-old Armani is crushed to learn that her long-anticipated birthday party will be cancelled due to Hurricane Katrina's imminent approach. Her disappointment quickly transforms into terror as the storm hits, separating her from her parents. She must look after her two younger sisters on a journey that takes her first to the Superdome, then to a shelter, and finally back home to the ravaged Lower Ninth Ward." (School Library Journal)

REVIEW: *Booklist* v110 no15 p90 Ap 1 2014 Kathleen Isaacs

REVIEW: *Kirkus Rev* v82 no3 p228 F 1 2014

"Upside Down in the Middle of Nowhere". "A couple of false notes notwithstanding, [Julie T.] Lamana goes for and achieves realism here, carefully establishing the characters and setting before describing in brutal detail, beyond what is typical in youth literature, the devastating effects of Katrina—loss of multiple family members, reports of attacks in the Superdome, bodies drifting in the current and less-than-ideal shelter conditions. An honest, bleak account of a national tragedy sure to inspire discussion and research."

REVIEW: *SLJ* v60 no3 p142 Mr 2014 Julie Hanson

REVIEW: *Voice of Youth Advocates* v37 no1 p69 Ap 2014 Stacey Hayman

LAMB-SHAPIRO, JESSICA. Promise land; a journey through america's euphoric, soul-sucking, emancipating, hornswoggling, and irrepressible self-help culture; [by] Jessica Lamb-Shapiro 240 p. 2014 Simon & Schuster
1. BIOGRAPHY & AUTOBIOGRAPHY—Personal Memoirs 2. Memoirs 3. PSYCHOLOGY—Social Psychology 4. Psychologists—Psychology 5. SOCIAL SCIENCE—Popular Culture 6. Self-care, Health 7. Self-care, Health—Psychological aspects 8. Self-help materials 9. Self-management (Psychology)
ISBN 1439100195; 9781439100196 (hardback); 9781439100219 (trade paperback)
LC 2013-011014

SUMMARY: In this book, "through trial-and-error and historical accounts, [Jessica] Lamb-Shapiro . . . peers into the world of self-help culture, painting a . . . picture of the personalities and ideas found in this field of self-promotion and discovery. Lamb-Shapiro, whose father is a child psychologist and self-help author, addresses her own difficulties in attempting to deal with the death of her mother--whom she never knew--and how working on this book led her towards closure." (Publishers Weekly)

REVIEW: *Bookforum* v20 no4 p46 D 2013/Ja 2014 REBECCA TUHUS-DUBROW

"Promise Land: My Journey Through America's Self-Help Culture." "Most chapters are anchored by [Jessica] Lamb-Shapiro's first-person account of a self-help excursion, framed by cultural history as well as the author's tragedy-tinged autobiography. 'Promise Land' is very much a book of the publishing Zeitgeist--the gimmicky premise, the mash-up of genres--and risks coming off as clichéd. But Lamb-Shapiro's authorial presence rescues it from that fate. Her approach to the material is skeptical but not cynical; her personal disclosures feel generous rather than exhibitionistic; and she writes in a mordant, deadpan voice with impeccable economy and timing. . . . Still, for all the book's pleasures, Lamb-Shapiro's analysis, like her shifting narrative focus, sometimes feels scattered."

REVIEW: *Booklist* v110 no6 p5 N 15 2013 Bridget Thoreson

REVIEW: *N Y Times Book Rev* p10 Ja 5 2014 MARY ELIZABETH WILLIAMS

"Promise Land: My Journey Through America's Self-Help Culture." "As Jessica Lamb-Shapiro points out in her ambitious if unfulfilling new memoir-cum-odyssey, 'Promise Land,' we've been gobbling up self-help advice for nearly as long as the written word has existed. . . . Lamb-Shapiro . . . is a witty and enjoyably self-aware writer. . . . But 'Promise Land' ultimately aims for far more than it can deliver. And it's ironic for a book that casts a critical eye at the improvement industry that its greatest failing is an overeagerness to do it all."

REVIEW: *Publ Wkly* v260 no44 p60 N 4 2013

LAMB, CHRISTINA. I am Malala; The Girl Who Stood Up for Education and Was Shot by the Taliban; [by] Christina Lamb viii, 327 p. 2013 Little, Brown and Co.
1. Girls—Education 2. Memoirs 3. Taliban 4. Terrorism 5. Women—Pakistan
ISBN 0316322407 (hardcover); 9780316322409 (hardcover)
LC 2013-941811

SUMMARY: This memoir, by Malala Yousafzai, "is the . .

. tale of a family uprooted by global terrorism, of the fight for girls' education, of a father who, himself a school owner, championed and encouraged his daughter to write and attend school, and of . . . parents who have a . . . love for their daughter in a society that prizes sons." (Publisher's note)

REVIEW: *Booklist* v110 no15 p35-6 Ap 1 2014 Lynette Pitrak

REVIEW: *Booklist* v110 no14 p20 Mr 15 2014

"Brave Girl: Clara and the Shirtwaist Makers' Strike of 1909," "Double Victory: How African American Women Broke Race and Gender Barriers to Help Win World War II," and "I Am Malala: The Girl Who Stood Up for Education and Was Shot by the Taliban." "Clara Lemlich bravely protested unfair working conditions in New York and in 1909 led the largest walkout by women workers in U.S. history. . . . Many African American women overcame legal and social barriers to serve their country during WWII and helped lay the foundation for the civil rights movement. . . . Recovered from her attack, Malala Yousafzai has come back stronger than ever, engaging in consciousness-raising and serving as an inspiration to girls and women all over the world."

REVIEW: *Libr J* v139 no2 p47 F 1 2014 Anna Mickelsen

REVIEW: *Libr J* v138 no9 p55 My 15 2013 Barbara Hoffert

REVIEW: *Ms* v23 no4 p62 Fall 2013 Rafia Zakaria

REVIEW: *Publ Wkly* v261 no4 p189 Ja 27 2014

LAMONT, PRISCILLA.il. Lulu and the Cat in the Bag. See McKay, H.

LAMONT, PRISCILLA.il. Secrets of the seasons. See Zoehfeld, K. W.

LAMPERT, LAURENCE. The enduring importance of Leo Strauss; [by] Laurence Lampert 360 p. 2013 University of Chicago Press

1. Enlightenment 2. Philosophical literature 3. Philosophy—History—20th century 4. Philosophy, Ancient 5. Political science—Philosophy

ISBN 9780226039480 (cloth : alkaline paper)

LC 2013-000530

SUMMARY: In this book on philosoher Leo Strauss, "Laurence Lampert focuses on exotericism: the use of artful rhetoric to simultaneously communicate a socially responsible message to the public at large and a more radical message of philosophic truth to a smaller, more intellectually inclined audience. . . . Examining some of Strauss's most important books and essays through this exoteric lens, Lampert reevaluates not only Strauss but the philosophers . . . whom Strauss most deeply engaged." (Publisher's note)

REVIEW: *Choice* v51 no8 p1413 Ap 2014 W. P. Haggerty

REVIEW: *N Y Times Book Rev* p29 Ag 25 2013 STEVEN B. SMITH

"Crisis of the Strauss Divided: Essays on Leo Strauss and Straussianism, East and West" and "The Enduring Importance of Leo Strauss." "'Crisis of the Strauss Divided' consists of 19 essays, the most revealing of which is a semi-autobiographical 'Straussian Geography'. . . . [Harry V.] Jaffa's peculiar genius . . . was to apply Strauss's understanding of political philosophy as the study of high statesmanship to the theory and practice of American politics. . . . [Other] articles display a streak of meanness and vanity that do no credit to their author and far exceed the issues at stake. East Coast Straussianism, by contrast, lacks a geographical center or a single dominating presence, but Laurence Lampert's book . . . provides an extreme illustration of the tendency."

LANCASTER, BRAD. Rainwater Harvesting for Drylands and Beyond; Guiding Principles to Welcome Rain into Your Life and Landscape; [by] Brad Lancaster 304 p. 2013 Chelsea Green Pub Co

1. Arid regions agriculture 2. Do-it-yourself literature 3. Landscape design 4. Rainwater 5. Water harvesting

ISBN 0977246434; 9780977246434

SUMMARY: This "is the first book in a three-volume guide that teaches you how to conceptualize, design, and implement sustainable water-harvesting systems for your home, landscape, and community. The lessons in this volume will enable you to assess your on-site resources, give you a diverse array of strategies to maximize their potential, and empower you with guiding principles to create an integrated, multi-functional water-harvesting plan specific to your site and needs." (Publisher's note)

REVIEW: *Kirkus Rev* v81 no21 p25 N 1 2013

REVIEW: *Kirkus Rev* v81 no19 p340 O 1 2013

REVIEW: *Kirkus Rev* p36-7 D 15 2013 supplemet best books 2013

"Rainwater Harvesting for Drylands and Beyond". "Novices need not be intimidated by this revised edition's abundance of charts and diagrams or its lengthy appendices: The material is simple to understand, and [Brad] Lancaster's friendly, conversational tone is accessible for all readers. Using eight common-sense principles as a guide . . . the author makes a cogent case for water conservation; namely, it's ethical, and it saves money. . . . Though there are many practical ideas contained within these pages, readers shouldn't expect A to Z gardening instructions laid out in an easy-to-flip format; instead, Lancaster presents design ideas and plenty of engaging food for thought, including some personal worksheets."

LANCASTER, JEN. Twisted sisters; [by] Jen Lancaster 320 p. 2014 NAL, New American Library

1. FICTION—Humorous 2. Families—Fiction 3. Reality television programs—Fiction 4. Sisters—Fiction 5. Success—Fiction

ISBN 9780451239655 (hardback)

LC 2013-033481

SUMMARY: This book follows Reagan Bishop . . . a licensed psychologist who stars on the Wendy Winsberg cable breakout show I Need a Push, Reagan helps participants become their best selves by urging them to overcome obstacles and change behaviors. . . . Despite her overwhelming professional success, Reagan never seems to earn her family's respect. . . . When a national network buys Reagan's show, the pressures for unreasonably quick results and higher ratings mount." (Publisher's note)

REVIEW: *Booklist* v110 no9/10 p46-7 Ja 1 2014 Aleksandra Walker

REVIEW: *Kirkus Rev* v81 no24 p320 D 15 2013

"Twisted Sisters". "A TV psychologist shrinks from facing her own sibling rivalry issues. Reagan Bishop is the token talk therapist on the Chicago-based cable talk show I Need a

Push. . . . [Jen] Lancaster's unerring ear for hipster parlance and passive-aggressive family snark is on full display—but it isn't until Reagan risks her most daring body swap yet that the novel finds its narrative stride. A meandering midsection—extended digressions on Godfather shtick, anyone?—may discourage some readers from persevering until the truly satisfying closing twist."

LANCET, BARRY. Japantown; [by] Barry Lancet 416 p. 2013 Simon & Schuster

1. Antique dealers—California—San Francisco—Fiction 2. Detective & mystery stories 3. Japanese—California—San Francisco—Fiction 4. Murder investigation—Japan—Fiction 5. Murder investigation—San Francisco (Calif.)—Fiction

ISBN 1451691696; 9781451691696 (hardcover); 9781451691702 (trade pbk.)

LC 2012-049519

SUMMARY: In author Barry Lancet's book, "San Francisco antiques dealer Jim Brodie recently inherited a stake in his father's Tokyo-based private investigation firm. . . . One night, an entire family is gunned down in San Francisco's bustling Japantown neighbor-hood, and Brodie is called on by the SFPD to decipher the lone clue left at the crime scene. . . . Brodie can't read the clue. But he may have seen it before--at the scene of his wife's death in a house fire four years ago." (Publisher's note)

REVIEW: *Kirkus Rev* p10 Ag 15 2013 Fall Preview

REVIEW: *Kirkus Rev* v81 no15 p326 Ag 1 2013

REVIEW: *Libr J* v138 no12 p73 Jl 1 2013 Amy Nolan

REVIEW: *N Y Times Book Rev* p21 O 6 2013 MARILYN STASIO

"Alex," "The Double," and "Japantown." "[Pierre] Lemaitre's plot is laid out with mathematical precision. . . . If this sounds a bit like 'The Girl With the Dragon Tattoo,' it's because Stieg Larsson did much to validate sadomasochism as a plot device,, and thriller writers jumped all over it. . . . In Frank Wynne's assured translation, there's even a raffish quality to the prose. . . . But in the end, it's still a formula . . . and it has already worn thin. . . . It's astonishing all the good stuff [George] Pelecanos can pack into one unpretentious book. . . . First-time authors have a tendency to throw everything into the pot. Barry Lancet does that very thing in 'Japantown' when he gives the personal life of his private eye too much prominence in an otherwise sophisticated international thriller."

REVIEW: *Publ Wkly* v260 no30 p43 Jl 29 2013

THE LAND OF DREAMS; 344 p. 2013 University of Minnesota Press

1. Detective & mystery stories 2. Local history 3. Minnesota—Fiction 4. Murder investigation—Fiction 5. Norwegians—United States

ISBN 0816689407; 9780816689408

SUMMARY: This book, the first in a trilogy, follows "Lance Hansen . . . a police officer with the U.S. Forest Service. . . . His real passion is local history. While making his morning rounds, he finds the body of a young man who has been bludgeoned to death. . . . Hansen is just as intrigued by the story of a murdered Native American in the 1800s as he is in the current murder, and finds some ominous ties to his own family." (Booklist)

REVIEW: *Booklist* v110 no4 p18 O 15 2013 Stacy Alesi

"The Land of Dreams." "This transplanted Scandinavian thriller is set in Minnesota on the shores of Lake Superior and is the first book of a trilogy. Lance Hansen is a police officer with the U.S. Forest Service, but his real passion is local history. . . . The landscape is a big part of the story, as is the history of the area, making this a fascinating look at Minnesota as well as a suspenseful thriller. The novel will certainly appeal to Scandinavian crime-fiction fans, but the vivid Minnesota setting should expand its audience considerably. A fine mix of history and mystery."

REVIEW: *Kirkus Rev* v81 no2 p39 Je 1 2013

REVIEW: *Publ Wkly* v260 no29 p47 Jl 22 2013

LANDAU, ELAINE. Deadly high-risk jobs; [by] Elaine Landau 32 p. 2013 Lerner Publications Co.

1. Danger perception 2. Hazardous occupations—Juvenile literature 3. Occupations—Juvenile literature 4. Risk 5. Vocational guidance literature

ISBN 9781467706032 (lib. bdg. : alk. paper)

LC 2012-012237

SUMMARY: This book by Elain Landau encourages the reader to "Imagine yourself parachuting from a plane straight into a raging forest fire, or racing against the clock to disarm a ticking bomb while enemy forces lurk around you. For some people, this is just a typical day at work. They have some of the world's deadliest jobs." (Publisher's note)

REVIEW: *Voice of Youth Advocates* v36 no4 p95-6 O 2013 Mary Ellen Snodgrass

"Deadly High-Risk Jobs" and "Deadly Adorable Animals." "A compilation of twelve risky careers, [author Elaine] Landau's text juxtaposes entertainers--stunt actors, rodeo riders, and car racers--with serious risk-takers in law enforcement, the military, and space exploration. . . . A zoological gallery balancing catchy close-ups with alerts to perils, [author Nadia] Higgins's sampling presents a realistic glimpse of the animal kingdom. . . . While the two titles reviewed here are excellent resources, another title in the series, 'Deadly Danger Zones,' suffers from poor editorial guidance and mixing of fact with fiction."

LANDERS, MELISSA. Alienated; [by] Melissa Landers 352 p. 2014 Hyperion

1. Extraterrestrial beings—Fiction 2. Love—Fiction 3. Paranormal romance stories 4. Science fiction 5. Student exchange programs—Fiction

ISBN 1423170288; 9781423170280 (hardback)

LC 2013-032977

SUMMARY: In this paranormal romance novel, "high school senior Cara Sweeny plans on being the best at everything—schoolwork, debate, life. These ambitions earn her the ambiguous honor of hosting one of the first 'exchange students' from the L'eihrs, the aliens who have just initiated contact with Earth. But while Aelyx might be completely human-looking (and a total hottie), he's also cold and arrogant, with a major hatred for all of humanity." (Kirkus Reviews)

REVIEW: *Booklist* v110 no11 p63 F 1 2014 Summer Hayes

REVIEW: *Bull Cent Child Books* v67 no8 p413 Ap 2014 A. M.

"Alienated". "This emotionally driven, romance-heavy science fiction novel offers a thought-provoking take on a familiar story of integration. Told from the viewpoints of the two young people, the initially separate narrative strands become increasingly intertwined as the two grow closer, and the eventual romance provides plenty of heart-stopping moments. The conflict over human-alien relations follows convention but still manages to raise interesting questions about the value of forcing an alliance between uncooperative parties, and Cara and Aelyx's debates over their differences will give readers plenty of food for thought about a variety of scientific issues."

REVIEW: *Kirkus Rev* v81 no24 p153 D 15 2013

"Alienated". "A charming if lightweight science-fiction romance bogs down when it attempts to convey moral lessons. . . . The alternating viewpoints convey their personalities well. . . . Although there seems little beyond raging hormones to inspire their intense devotion, the romantic shenanigans are entertaining until overshadowed by the heavy-handed, simplistic message that prejudice is wrong. . . . Once the tone abruptly shifts to science-fiction thriller, the willing suspension of disbelief snaps under the weight of unbelievable behavior, nonsensical science and a 'happy ending' with profoundly disturbing implications. It's still rather fun in an after-school-special sort of way, but hardly an essential purchase or read."

REVIEW: *Voice of Youth Advocates* v36 no6 p73 F 2014 Susan Redman-Parodi

LANDRY, JUDITH.tr. The Mussolini Canal. See Pennacchi, A.

LANE, ALEX.tr. Keep Forever. See Sokolenko, A. K

LANE, GARRY RICHARD. The Brutus Conspiracy; [by] Garry Richard Lane 388 p. 2013 CreateSpace Independent Publishing Platform

1. Aircraft accidents—Fiction 2. Aircraft accidents—Investigation 3. Conspiracies—Fiction 4. Legal stories 5. Suspense fiction

ISBN 1492392545; 9781492392545

SUMMARY: In this book, "Becky Langevin, a talented young air crash investigator, must set aside her emotions to find and interpret clues to explain two plane crashes that occurred fourteen years apart. In one, Becky's father piloted the jet that crashed killing a U.S. senator and four prominent businessmen. Federal investigators attributed the crash to her dead father. In the second, federal investigators concluded that two hotshot Massachusetts trial lawyers were killed because the attorneys were intoxicated." (Publisher's note)

REVIEW: *Kirkus Rev* v81 no24 p405 D 15 2013

"The Brutus Conspiracy". "It's a solid action novel that moves at a frantic pace; for example, there are two tension-filled plane rides before the page count hits double digits. But it also reveals itself as a taut legal thriller when attorney Will goes after Brutus in court; even something as minor as a ruling on a motion is surprisingly engaging. . . . The author, an attorney and aviator himself, is unquestionably knowledgeable. . . Other scenes, however, are given only a modicum of description, with dialogue often monopolizing the narrative. . . . A fast-paced aviation thriller that sometimes reaches great heights."

LANE, JOHN FRANCIS. To Each His Own Dolce Vita; [by] John Francis Lane 402 p. 2013 Bear Claw Books

1. Gay journalists 2. Italy—History—1945-1976 3. Italy—Social life & customs—1945- 4. Memoirs 5. Motion picture industry—Italy

ISBN 0957246242; 9780957246249

SUMMARY: This memoir by John Francis Lane recounts his time as "a joumalist based in Rome where he mainly reported on showbusiness, while working in films as an extra. . . . Interspersed with this are fond memories of past pleasures--festivals, meals, five-star hotels, press conferences, encounters with famous people (Lane met practically everybody), and of am great many friends, lovers, or rent boys." (Times Literary Supplement)

REVIEW: *TLS* no5769 p28 O 25 2013 MASOLINO D'AMICO

"To Each His Own Dolce Vita.""This rather thick book offers a rich collection of anecdotes on films and filming along with vivid, almost day by day recollections of facts and atmospheres, and vivid assessments of innumerable movies and plays that [John Francis] Lane witnessed at first hand. Interspersed with this are fond memories of past pleasures--festivals, meals, five-star hotels, press conferences, encounters with famous people (Lane met practically everybody), and of a great many friends, lovers, or rent boys. Sharing such happiness with readers runs the risk of becoming tedious in the long run, but after all why not? Grievances are not necessarily more appealing than joys; and we are spared those."

LANG, ANTHONY F.ed. Just war. See Just war

LANG, BEREL. Primo Levi; the matter of a life; [by] Berel Lang 192 p. 2013 Yale University Press

1. Biography (Literary form) 2. Holocaust survivors—Italy—Biography 3. Jews—Italy—Biography 4. Philosophical literature

ISBN 9780300137231 (alk. paper)

LC 2013-018411

SUMMARY: This book presents a "biography of Italian Jewish author Primo Michele Levi (1919–87), who earned a degree in chemistry and worked as a chemist but became a writer after World War II when he survived his deportation and 11-month imprisonment in Auschwitz. Lang explains that Levi began with no writing ambitions or literary design but instead felt the need to write about his time in the concentration camp--a spontaneous rather than intended literary exercise." (Library Journal)

REVIEW: *Kirkus Rev* v81 no20 p219 O 15 2013

REVIEW: *Nation* v297 no24 p33-5 D 16 2013 VIVIAN GORNICK

"Primo Levi: The Matter of a Life." "An intellectual biography characterized by a somewhat schematic set of speculations on some of the basic elements of Levi's life. . . . If the reader is expecting to find Levi, the flesh-and-blood man, on the page, he is not here. What is here is a philosophically minded investigation into the contextual nature of Levi's life, mainly as a prisoner of Auschwitz. . . . The writing . . . is not always felicitous. A great many of Lang's sentences are awkward to the point of unintelligibility. . . . However, the book is carried by a rich and absorptive interest in the social and psychological realities that endow Primo Levi's life with a sense of largeness."

LANG, HEATHER. Queen of the track; Alice Coach, olympic high-jump champion; 40 p. 2012 Boyds Mills Press

1. Black athletes 2. Children's nonfiction 3. Coachman, Alice, 1923- 4. Olympic Games (14th : 1948 : London, England) 5. Women Olympic athletes
ISBN 1590788508; 9781590788509 (reinforced trade ed.)
LC 2011-939994

SUMMARY: Author Heather Lang tells the story of "the 1948 Olympics in London, [where] members of the U.S. Women's Track and Field team went down to defeat one by one. Any hope of winning rested on Alice Coachman. . . . She became the first African American woman to win an Olympic gold medal. . . . This book follows Coachman on her journey from rural Georgia, where she overcame adversity both as a woman and as a black athlete, to her triumph in Wembly Stadium." (Publisher's note)

REVIEW: *Booklist* v108 no19/20 p87 Je 1 2012 J. B. Petty

REVIEW: *Booklist* p30-5 Ja 1 2014 Supplement Henrietta Smith

"Art From Her Heart: Folk Artist Clementine Hunter," "Queen of the Track: Alice Coachman, Olympic High-Jump Champion," and "Daniel Hale Williams: Surgeon Who Opened Hearts and Minds." "The words and images in this moving picture-book biography show that Hunter was not stopped by self-pity, and she did not wait for 'the perfect time to paint.' . . . [Heather] Lang's descriptive text and [Floyd] Cooper's signature sepia-tone oil illustrations offer a rich, deep depiction of Coachman's determination to overcome obstacles. . . . [Mike] Venezia combines a chatty text with a mix of period photographs and playful cartoons in this history of Daniel Hale Williams, who not only performed one of the first successful open heart operations, in 1893, but also made great strides in opening up top-quality medical access to African Americans."

REVIEW: *SLJ* v58 no6 p104 Je 2012 Kathleen Kelly MacMillan

LANG, KENNETH R. The life and death of stars; [by] Kenneth R. Lang xiv, 332 p. 2013 Cambridge University Press

1. Stars—Evolution 2. Stars—Formation 3. Stellar dynamics
ISBN 110701638X; 9781107016385 (hardback)
LC 2012-033415

SUMMARY: In this book, Kenneth R. Lang "explains the life cycle of stars, from the dense molecular clouds that are stellar nurseries to the enigmatic nebulae some stars leave behind in their violent ends. . . . Lang's . . . text provides physical insights into how stars such as our Sun are born, what fuels them and keeps them bright, how they evolve, and the processes by which they eventually die." (Publishe'rs note)

REVIEW: *Choice* v51 no4 p661 D 2013 M. Takamiya

LANGDON, HELEN. Caravaggio's Cardsharps; trickery and illusion; [by] Helen Langdon 74 p. 2012 Kimbell Art Museum

1. Art and society—Italy—Rome—History—16th century 2. Art literature
ISBN 9780300185102 (pbk.)
LC 2012-017919

SUMMARY: This book by Helen Langdon "sets Caravaggio's Cardsharps within the context of contemporaneous literature, art theory, and theater and incorporates new archival research to enliven our understanding of the painter's time, place, and contemporaries. By fully analyzing one of Caravaggio's most daringly novel works, Langdon demonstrates the significant influence he had on the future of European art." (Publisher's note)

REVIEW: *Burlington Mag* v156 no1332 p179 Mr 2014 JOHN GASH

"Caravaggio's 'Cardsharps': Trickery and Illusion". "Helen Langdon's book on Caravaggio's most popular painting, 'The cardsharps,' is a welcome addition to the Kimbell Masterpiece Series. Presumably aimed at the general reader and at students, it provides a rich cultural history that helps to set Caravaggio's early masterpiece in various contexts. . . . Overall, her intertwining of social, cultural and artistic scenarios produces a satisfying mise-en-scene scenarios produces a satisfying mise-en-scène. If one has a criticism, it is that there is insufficient concentration on the style and iconography of Caravaggio's Cardsharps itself."

LANGFORD, JULIE. Maternal megalomania; Julia Domna and the imperial politics of motherhood; [by] Julie Langford xi, 203 p. 2013 The Johns Hopkins University Press

1. Historical literature 2. Ideology—Political aspects—Rome 3. Imperialism—Social aspects—Rome 4. Motherhood—Political aspects—Rome 5. Political culture—Rome 6. Popular culture—Rome 7. Public opinion—Rome
ISBN 1421408473 (hardcover : acid-free paper); 9781421408477 (hardcover : acid-free paper)
LC 2012-035555

SUMMARY: In this book, "Julie Langford unmasks the maternal titles and honors of Julia Domna as a campaign on the part of the administration to garner support for Severus and his sons. Langford looks to numismatic, literary, and archaeological evidence to reconstruct the propaganda surrounding the empress. She explores how her image was tailored toward different populations . . . and how these populations responded to propaganda about the empress." (Publisher's note)

REVIEW: *Choice* v51 no4 p701-2 D 2013 H. Chang

"Maternal Megalomania: Julia Domna and the Imperial Politics of Motherhood." "[Julie] Langford . . . questions Empress Julia Domna's power and influence in Severan politics. Her first argument is well supported by a detailed examination of Severus's career and ruling strategies. . . . Langford less successfully handles her second argument, that these authors deliberately shaped Julia Domna's depictions in the literary sources to criticize her male associates, such as Plautianus and Caracalla. The authorship, methodology, and historical reliability of these works, especially Herodian and the 'Historia,' are not sufficiently treated."

LANGHAMER, CLAIRE. The English in Love; The Intimate Story of an Emotional Revolution; [by] Claire Langhamer 320 p. 2013 Oxford University Press

1. Great Britain—History—20th century 2. Great Britain—Social life & customs 3. Historical literature 4. Love—History 5. Marriage—History
ISBN 0199594430; 9780199594436

SUMMARY: In this book, "Claire Langhamer examines attitudes to marriage from 1920 to the 1970s. Broadly speaking, she finds that couples changed in the 1950s. Never before were so many of them marrying, never so young and never with such hopes of mutual bliss. . . . Ms. Langhamer . . . argues that the sexual permissiveness of the 1960s and the subsequent decline in marriage were less a reaction to the so-called stability of the 1950s than a product of the decade's instability." (Economist)

REVIEW: *Economist* v408 no8849 p70 Ag 17 2013

"The English in Love: The Intimate Story of an Emotional Revolution." "Claire Langhamer examines attitudes to marriage from 1920 to the 1970s. Broadly speaking, she finds that couples changed in the 1950s. . . . Ms. Langhamer convincingly argues that the sexual permissiveness of the 1960s and the subsequent decline in marriage were less a reaction to the so-called stability of the 1950s than a product of the decade's instability. . . . A social scientist, Ms. Langhamer writes in the language of her discipline. This means that her rich and intimate material does sometimes chafe against the deliberate non-subjectivity of her field. Her decision to exclude 'cultural interventions'--as in novels, among other things--also seems a pity."

REVIEW: *New Statesman* v142 no5170 p38-9 Ag 16 2013 Richard Davenport-Hines

LANGUAGE MATTERS; interviews with 22 Quebec poets; 191 p. 2013 Signature Editions

1. Canadian poetry (English)—Québec (Province)—History and criticism 2. Literature—History & criticism 3. Poetics 4. Poetry—Authorship 5. Poetry—Political aspects 6. Poetry—Social aspects 7. Poets, Canadian (English)—Québec (Province)—20th century—Interviews

ISBN 9781927426197 (pbk.)

LC 2013-464621

SUMMARY: In this book, 22 English-language poets working in Quebec answer "a series of set questions. . . . The interviewers are primarily interested in how living in Quebec and writing in English has influenced each poet's work. . . . Some poets are essentially apolitical, while others believe that everything an Anglophone does in Quebec is a political act." The poets include "Stephanie Bolster, Erin Mouré, Jason Camlot, [and] Robyn Sarah, among many others." (Quill & Quire)

REVIEW: *Quill Quire* v80 no1 p41-7 Ja/F 2014 Bruce Whiteman

"Language Matters: Interviews With 22 Quebec Poets". "It is hardly surprising that poets should be articulate and thoughtful in conversation about their practice. . . . The Quebec poets featured in 'Language Matters' are almost uniformly smart and thoughtful in answering a series of set questions. . . . The responses tell us much about the poets . . . and their work, as well as providing insight into their strategies for composing poems. Anyone interested in poetry in general, and especially poetry in Quebec, will find these interviews deeply engaging."

LANIA, LEO. My road to Berlin. See Brandt, W.

LANIER, JARON. Who owns the future?; [by] Jaron Lanier xvi, 396 p. 2013 Simon & Schuster

1. Economic forecasting 2. Economics 3. Economics literature 4. Information technology—Economic aspects 5. Technological innovations—Economic aspects

ISBN 9781451654974 (paperback); 1451654960 (hardcover); 9781451654967 (hardcover)

LC 2013-007987

SUMMARY: This book, by Jaron Lanier, "is a . . . reckoning with the effects network technologies have had on our economy. Lanier asserts that the rise of digital networks led our economy into recession and decimated the middle class. . . . But there is an alternative to allowing technology to own our future. . . . Lanier charts the path toward a new information economy that will stabilize the middle class and allow it to grow." (Publisher's note)

REVIEW: *Bookforum* v20 no2 p4 Je-Ag 2013 CHOIRE SICHA

REVIEW: *Booklist* v109 no18 p8 My 15 2013 Mary Whaley

REVIEW: *Columbia J Rev* v52 no1 p49-53 My/Je 2013 LAUREN KIRCHNER

REVIEW: *Economist* v407 no8834 p80-1 My 4 2013

REVIEW: *Kirkus Rev* v81 no9 p57 My 1 2013

REVIEW: *N Y Times Book Rev* p28 Ap 20 2014 IHSAN TAYLOR

REVIEW: *New Statesman* v142 no5151/5152 p76-8 Mr 29 2013 Aditya Chakrabortty

REVIEW: *New York Times* v162 no56128 pC1-4 My 6 2013 JANET MASLIN

REVIEW: *Publ Wkly* v260 no14 p55 Ap 8 2013 Max Broekman

REVIEW: *Publ Wkly* v260 no43 p58 O 28 2013

REVIEW: *TLS* no5747 p3-4 My 24 2013 MICHAEL SALER

"To Save Everything, Click Here: Technology, Solutionism and the Urge to Fix Problems That Don't Exist" and "Who Owns the Future?." "'To Save Everything, Click Here' is perhaps the funniest and most savage critique of cyber-culture yet written. It is also frequently persuasive. . . . What is most striking about [Jaron] Lanier's diagnosis and remedy are not the specifics: his forecasts will inevitably miss certain marks, and perhaps the entire target. (Nor, unfortunately, is this stimulating book well written or organized; it is divided into very short sections and reads like a series of blog posts.) The value of 'Who Owns the Future?' rests in Jaron Lanier's willingness to rethink 'the Internet' and its core mantras . . . and propose radically different solutions."

LANSKY, SANDRA. Daughter of the King; Growing Up in Gangland; [by] Sandra Lansky 264 p. 2014 Weinstein Books

1. Criminals—Family relationships 2. Lansky, Meyer 3. Mafia—United States—History 4. Memoirs 5. Organized crime—United States—History

ISBN 160286215X; 9781602862159

SUMMARY: This book presents a memoir by Sandra Lansky, "the child of Mafia kingpin Meyer Lansky and a beautiful but unstable mother. . . . Wealth and glitz couldn't keep away all of life's tragedies: a severely disabled older brother, a chronically depressed mother, a divorce and her father's subsequent marriage to a despised stepmother, and an addiction to diet pills. Then there were the intimations of violence . . . and the whispers of her father's involvement." (Library Journal)

REVIEW: *Booklist* v110 no13 p4-5 Mr 1 2014 David Pitt

"Daughter of the King: Growing Up in Gangland". "This autobiography tells the story of a rich socialite, a party girl who lived in a world of wealth and glitz . . . but whose life was permeated with darkness: a mother suffering from mental illness, a father who wasn't exactly the warmest dad in the world, friends and pseudo-relatives from the criminal world. . . . Everything in the book . . . is filtered through [Sandra Lansky's] perceptions of her father and his world. It's not a crime story, exactly, but it is a fascinating account of a girl and her father, a man who happened to be a criminal."

REVIEW: *Kirkus Rev* v82 no4 p133 F 15 2014

"Daughter of the King: Growing Up in Gangland". " A biography of a true Mafia princess that leaves a lot to the imagination, despite assistance from veteran Hollywood chronicler [William] Stadiem. . . . The author, in what seems to be an attempt to protect her father's memory from the stain of organized crime, hasn't just whitewashed the story; she's bleached it. . . . When she does speak of her father and his associates, she is intent on convincing readers that they were honest businessmen, demonized by a cruel and unfair government. Personal details are in better supply, but even when writing about her sex life, drug use or fear over her father's legal troubles, the narrative is only surface deep. Though she writes about her past truthfully, the prose lacks revelation."

REVIEW: *Libr J* v139 no5 p129 Mr 15 2014 Deirdre Bray

REVIEW: *N Y Times Book Rev* p38 My 11 2014 DOMENICA RUTA

REVIEW: *Publ Wkly* v261 no4 p184 Ja 27 2014

LAPHAM, STEVEN SELLERS. Philip Reid saves the statue of freedom; 40 p. 2013 Sleeping Bear Press

1. African Americans—Anecdotes—Juvenile literature 2. Foundry workers—United States—Anecdotes—Juvenile literature 3. Historical literature

ISBN 1585368199; 9781585368198

LC 2013-002586

SUMMARY: This book, written by Eugene Walton and Steven Lapham and illustrated by R. Gregory Christie, describes how "Born into slavery, Philip Reid grew up on a South Carolina farm, helping various craftsmen such as the blacksmith and the potter. Eventually, he was sold to a man named Clark Mills, who was opening a foundry in Washington, D.C. Mr. Mills's foundry is contracted to cast the Freedom statue but the project is jeopardized when a seemingly unsolvable puzzle arises." (Publisher's note)

REVIEW: *Booklist* v110 no11 p61 F 1 2014 Ann Kelley

REVIEW: *Kirkus Rev* v81 no24 p266 D 15 2013

"Philip Reid Saves the Statue of Freedom". "A slave in Washington, D.C., has the expertise to make possible the casting in bronze of the statue atop the Capitol Building. . . . [Steven Sellers] Lapham and [Eugene] Walton invent dialogue in their narration, but they make Reid's work exciting and provide a good picture of what little is known of him. [R. Gregory] Christie's paintings are characteristically powerful, more impressionistic than realistic. Sources and further reading would have been a plus. A good introduction to the growing knowledge of the vital role slaves played in building Washington, D.C."

REVIEW: *SLJ* v60 no3 p174 Mr 2014 Rebecca Gueorguiev

LAPIERRE, BRIAN. Hooligans in Khrushchev's Russia; defining, policing, and producing deviance during the thaw; [by] Brian LaPierre xiii, 281 p. 2012 University of Wisconsin Press

1. Criminal justice, Administration of—Soviet Union 2. Deviant behavior—Government policy—Soviet Union 3. Historical literature 4. Hoodlums—Government policy—Soviet Union

ISBN 0299287432 (e-book); 0299287440 (pbk.: alk. paper); 9780299287436 (e-book); 9780299287443 (pbk.: alk. paper)

LC 2011-045234

SUMMARY: This book on hooliganism explores "how Soviet police, prosecutors, judges, and ordinary citizens during the Khrushchev era (1953–64) understood, fought against, or embraced this catch-all category of criminality. . . ." "It portrays the Khrushchev period . . . as an era of renewed harassment against a wide range of state-defined undesirables and as a time when policing and persecution were expanded to encompass the mundane aspects of everyday life. " (Publisher's note)

REVIEW: *Am Hist Rev* v119 no1 p279-80 F 2014 Anne E. Gorsuch

"Hooligans in Khruschev's Russia: Defining, Policing, and Producing Deviance During the Thaw". "Valuable. . . . The book includes a very interesting, if all-too-brief, section on hooliganism as a source of public fascination as well as fear. . . . The focus, however, is on hooliganism as a Soviet label used to civilize, socially engineer, and often criminalize a growing number of people. [Brian] LaPierre uses a wide range of sources with appropriate sensitivity in particular to the challenges of crime statistics. His use of letters to the press and other forms of complaint is very welcome as evidence of popular opinion, although the book would have benefited from a discussion of the context and challenges of using such sources."

LAPLANTE, ALICE. A Circle of Wives; [by] Alice Laplante 325 p. 2014 Pgw

1. Bigamy—Fiction 2. Detective & mystery stories 3. Murder investigation—Fiction 4. Physicians—Fiction 5. Physicians' spouses—Fiction

ISBN 0802122345; 9780802122346

SUMMARY: In this book, by Alice Laplante, "Dr. John Taylor is found dead in a hotel room. . . . The local police find enough incriminating evidence to suspect foul play. Detective Samantha Adams, whose Palo Alto beat usually covers small-town crimes, is innocently thrown into a high-profile murder case that is more intricately intertwined than she could ever imagine. . . . A closeted polygamist, Dr. Taylor was married to three very different women in three separate cities." (Publisher's note)

REVIEW: *Booklist* v110 no9/10 p48 Ja 1 2014 Joanne Wilkinson

REVIEW: *Kirkus Rev* v82 no2 p186 Ja 15 2014

"A Circle of Wives". "In this literary character study built on a mystery's framework, [Alice] LaPlante ingeniously constructs characters that are distinct and original. Deborah withdrew from her marriage to Taylor, but, unwilling to divorce, she acquiesced to his search for intimacy elsewhere, even managing logistics for all three marriages. MJ's a tortured, needy soul, ripe for seduction. Helen, a singularly focused physician, finds herself 'surprised by joy' and 'not in control of my destiny or my body.' Taylor became what each needed."

REVIEW: *Publ Wkly* v260 no49 p61 D 2 2013

LAREAU, KARA. No slurping, no burping!; a tale of table manners; 40 p. 2014 Disney-Hyperion Books

1. Dinners and dining—Fiction 2. Etiquette—Fiction 3. Fathers—Fiction 4. Humorous stories 5. Parent & child—Fiction

ISBN 9781423157335

LC 2012-040795

SUMMARY: In this children's book, "two kids must teach their parent how to adopt an appropriate tableside manner. Their father's a sweet fellow, but each day at dinner, Evie and Simon must work to correct his less-than-sterling conduct. . . . Unsurprisingly, Father has lost his taste for eating by the time Friday rolls around. Fortunately, a surprise guest (his own mama) shows everyone how far he has really come. Still, not even Grandma is immune from the occasional slip-up." (Kirkus Reviews)

REVIEW: *Booklist* v110 no14 p82 Mr 15 2014 Tiffany Erickson

REVIEW: *Kirkus Rev* v82 no2 p164 Ja 15 2014

"No Slurping, No Burping! A Tale of Table Manners". "Two impossibly neat and polite youngsters attempt to rein in their father's madcap (but undeniably cheery) mealtime missteps. . . . Parents hoping to instill good behavior in their own offspring will clamor for this title, and [Kara] LaReau's light touch makes it pleasant to read. The art is appealing, although clearly in the style of an animated film; the book is one of a series that showcases Disney's animation artists. In spite of Father's comical oafishness, it's clear that children's best bet for learning table manners is their own parents."

REVIEW: *Publ Wkly* v261 no1 p56 Ja 6 2014

REVIEW: *SLJ* v60 no3 p118 Mr 2014 Nora Clancy

LAREMONT, RICARDO.ed. Revolution, revolt and reform in North Africa . See Revolution, revolt and reform in North Africa

LARIMORE, WALT. The ultimate guys' body book; not-so-stupid questions about your body; [by] Walt Larimore 187 p. 2012 Zonderkidz

1. Adolescence—Juvenile literature 2. Children's reference books 3. Christian children—Conduct of life 4. Human growth—Juvenile literature 5. Puberty—Juvenile literature 6. Sex instruction for boys—Religious aspects—Christianity—Juvenile literature 7. Teenage boys—Conduct of life—Juvenile literature 8. Teenage boys—Health and hygiene—Juvenile literature 9. Teenage boys—Physiology—Juvenile literature 10. Teenage boys—Sexual behavior—Juvenile literature

ISBN 9780310723233 (pbk.)

LC 2011-034992

SUMMARY: This book by Walt Larimore is a "guide for readers wanting a Christian look at boys' physical and sexual development." The author "offers advice with a Christian perspective for boys wondering about their bodies as they enter puberty. More specifically, this is a volume aimed at Christian fathers of boys ages 10 to 13, so fathers can be ready with answers to sometimes tricky questions." Topics addressed include changes in body size, acne, sexual development, avoiding pornography, and tattoos and body piercings. (Kirkus)

REVIEW: *Voice of Youth Advocates* v35 no2 p190 Je 2012 Paula Gallagher

LARIZZIO, JOHN C. Silhouettes and Seasons; Essays and Images of a Personal Nature; [by] John C. Larizzio 188 p. 2013 Dog Ear Publishing

1. Animals 2. Essay (Literary form) 3. Natural history literature 4. Philosophy of nature 5. Seasons

ISBN 1457522705; 9781457522703

SUMMARY: In this book, author John C. Larizzio "offers deeply personal takes on the seasons, wildlife, modern-day living, sunrise and sunset, the sounds of nature, the art of writing, a place called Mt. Laurel, and the rain, snow and wind, among many other topics. He divides the work into several chapters by year of composition, beginning in 1994 and continuing through 2000, and further organizes the pieces by season and month. He includes black-and-white photographs throughout." (Kirkus Reviews)

REVIEW: *Kirkus Rev* v82 no3 p26 F 1 2014

"Silhouettes and Seasons: Essays and Images of a Personal Nature". " Poetic personal essays and reflections on life, featuring nature as a teacher, theme and metaphor. . . . He includes black-and-white photographs throughout, giving a sense of both a journey and a journal. . . . Like a book of watercolor sketches, each essay displays [John C.] LaRizzio's maturing skills as a descriptive narrator. The occasional overuse of alliteration . . . is easily forgiven as the author migrates to rhymed poetry. . . . A finely introspective work for lovers of nature and [Henry David] Thoreau.

LARKIN, ERIC SHABAZZ.il. Farmer Will Allen and the growing table. See Martin, J. B.

LARKIN, PETER. Wordsworth and Coleridge; promising losses; [by] Peter Larkin xii, 267 p. 2012 Palgrave Macmillan

1. Historical literature 2. Imagination 3. Romanticism—England

ISBN 9780230337367

LC 2011-040972

SUMMARY: This book "assembles essays spanning the last thirty years, including a selection of Peter Larkin's original verse, with the concept of promise and loss serving as the uniting narrative thread. Interpreting the ways [William] Wordsworth and [Samuel Taylor] Coleridge used the resources of imagination at crucial moments in their creative lives, this book reveals how they struggled to assimilate the intricacies of Romantic vision preoccupying their contemporary writers and critics." (Publisher's note)

REVIEW: *TLS* no5771 p10-1 N 8 2013 TOM DURNO

"Dorothy Wordsworth: Wonders of the Everyday," "Dorothy Wordsworth and Hartley Coleridge: The Poetics of Relationship," and "Wordsworth and Coleridge: Promising Losses." "Both book and exhibition testify to [Pamela] Woof's own efforts over many years to sustain and develop work on Dorothy Wordsworth. . . . Because of such admissions that she was no full poet, [Nicola] Healey's account of Hartley's verse seems more novel than her reading of Dorothy's works. Where Woof gives space to Dorothy's non-literary life alongside her texts, Healey's framing of Dorothy's writing in primarily literary terms is undermined by Dorothy's own discomfort with her poetic identity. . . . [Peter] Larkin's essays span thirty years, reflecting a careful tuning-in to the grain of these poets' respective voices, and are divided into discrete sections on them."

LAROCHELLE, DAVID. Moo!; [by] David LaRochelle 40 p. 2013 Walker

1. Automobile driving—Fiction 2. Behavior—Fiction 3. Children's stories 4. Cows—Fiction 5. Humorous stories

ISBN 080273409X; 9780802734099 (hardcover); 9780802734105 (reinforced)

LC 2013-007463

SUMMARY: Written by David LaRochelle and illustrated by Mike Wohnoutka, this book features "a complete story with just one word--MOO . . ." as an "imaginative picture book" that "will have readers laughing one moment and on the edge of their seats the next, as it captures the highs and lows of a mischievous cow's very exciting day." (Publisher's note)

REVIEW: *Booklist* v110 no1 p125 S 1 2013 Francisca Goldsmith

REVIEW: *Bull Cent Child Books* v67 no3 p165 N 2013 D. S.

"Moo!" "In this lively picture book limited almost entirely to a single word, an adventurous cow takes the farmer's shiny red car for a joyride, but her initial glee turns to horror when she fails to negotiate a sharp turn and ends up pancaking a police car. . . . The readaloud's the real fun here, since all this adventure is conveyed by various iterations of the word 'Moo'--and what a lot of possibilities it offers. . . . [Illustrator Mike] Wohnoutka's gouache illustrations have group viewing in mind, with every scene a full-spread, full-bleed streamlined image that possesses the subject focus and simple backdrops of old-school animation."

REVIEW: *Kirkus Rev* v81 no14 p137 Jl 15 2013

REVIEW: *Publ Wkly* v260 no30 p66 Jl 29 2013

REVIEW: *SLJ* v59 no8 p80 Ag 2013 Laura Scott Jess de-Courcy Hinds

LARSON, HOPE. Mercury; [by] Hope Larson 234 2010 Atheneum Books for Young Readers

1. Graphic novels 2. Paranormal fiction 3. Supernatural graphic novels 4. Treasure troves—Fiction 5. Young adult literature—Works

ISBN 978-1-4169-3585-8; 1-4169-3585-1; 978-1-4169-3588-9 pa; 1-4169-3588-6

LC 2009—903638

SUMMARY: This book, "relates two coming-of-age stories in tandem, showing how the past interweaves with the present. In the present, Tara and her mother have lost their old farmhouse in a fire, and Tara's mother is struggling to support them from far away while Tara lives with relatives. . . . In 1859, Josey, Tara's ancestor, falls in love with a gold dowser who has convinced her father to open a mine. Her mother, who has supernatural sight, is sure that the dowser means no good." (School Library Journal)

REVIEW: *Booklist* v110 no2 p76 S 15 2013 Sarah Hunter

"Mercury," "The Miseducation of Cameron Post," and "Saints of Augustine". "Graphic novel readers, regardless of age, will be drawn to [Hope] Larson's graceful story, universal themes of self-discovery, and expressive art. . . . Cam's experiences at a church camp that promises to 'cure' young people of their homosexuality are at the heart of this ambitious, multidimensional coming-of-age novel. [Emily M.] Danforth . . . vividly depicts the lifelong challenges of asserting one's identity. . . . Well-drawn characters, complicated family lives, first love, and realistic language (including some anti-gay slurs), make this a touchingly authentic and ageless story about the importance of friendship."

REVIEW: *Choice* v52 no2 p233-4 O 2014 J. R. Kraus

LARSON, KIRBY. Duke; [by] Kirby Larson 240 p. 2013 Scholastic Press

1. Dogs—Fiction 2. Dogs—War use—Fiction 3. Dogs—War use—Juvenile fiction 4. German shepherd dog—Fiction 5. German shepherd dog—Juvenile fiction 6. Historical fiction 7. Human-animal relationships—Fiction 8. Human-animal relationships—Juvenile fiction 9. World War, 1939-1945—United States—Fiction 10. World War, 1939-1945—United States—Juvenile fiction

ISBN 054541637X; 9780545416375 (jacketed hardcover)

LC 2012-046636

SUMMARY: In this World War II story by Kirby Larson, "when fifth-grader Hobie Hanson's father leaves his fishing boat in Seattle to pilot a B-24 in Europe, he tells Hobie 'to step up and do what needs to be done.' Whether it is buying war bonds, collecting rubber or simply making due with less, Hobie is giving all he can to the war effort. But when he begins to feel the pressure to lend his beloved German shepherd, Duke, to the Army, Hobie realizes he still has more to give." (Kirkus Reviews)

REVIEW: *Booklist* v110 no5 p80-1 N 1 2013 Angela Leeper

REVIEW: *Horn Book Magazine* v89 no5 p102-3 S/O 2013 BETTY CARTER

"Duke." "[Kirby] Larson's two main literary interests (historical fiction such as 'Hattie Big Sky' and informational dog books such as 'Two Bobbies') come together in her latest novel, set in Seattle during WWII. . . . The novel's strong concept is greater than its execution. Foreshadowing is heavy, and the nautical similes are overdone ("That worry wore away at Hobie like salt water on a wooden hull'). But the time period, shown through both product placement . . . and daily activities . . . unobtrusively frames this diverting read."

REVIEW: *Kirkus Rev* v81 no14 p161 Jl 15 2013

REVIEW: *Publ Wkly* p87 Children's starred review annual 2013

REVIEW: *Publ Wkly* v260 no38 p82 S 23 2013

REVIEW: *SLJ* v59 no10 p1 O 2013 Robbin E. Friedman

LARSON, MARK HENRY. Write Through Chicago. See Boone, B.

LASKY, KATHRYN. The Extra; [by] Kathryn Lasky 320 p. 2013 Candlewick Press

1. Concentration camp inmates—Fiction 2. Extras (Actors) 3. Historical fiction 4. Riefenstahl, Leni 5. Romanies—Fiction

ISBN 0763639729 (hbk.); 9780763639723 (hbk.)

LC 2012-955181

SUMMARY: This book, by Kathryn Lasky, "focus[es] on the Nazi genocide of the Roma and Sinti peoples. Lilo--a Sinti girl of 15 at the beginning of the book--is taken by the Nazis when they start rounding up the Romani of Austria. Lilo's losses mount quickly as she's separated from her father and many of her friends; only the opportunity to be an extra in the cast of a film by Nazi propagandist Leni Riefenstahl might save her." (Publishers Weekly)

REVIEW: *Booklist* v110 no4 p47-8 O 15 2013 Michael Cart

"The Extra." "The year is 1940. Lilo, 15, and her family are Gypsies (Romani) who have been rounded up by the Nazis and sent to the Maxglan internment camp. It is there that Leni Riefenstahl, Hitler's favorite film director, selects Lilo and her mother to serve as extras in her new movie, Tiefland. . . . [Kathryn] Lasky has written a harrowing and deeply moving novel that focuses attention on a seldom-told story of the Nazis' attempt to exterminate the Romani people. Thoroughly researched and insightful, the book is ideal for classroom use and discussion."

REVIEW: *Bull Cent Child Books* v67 no3 p166 N 2013 E. B.

REVIEW: *Kirkus Rev* v81 no17 p101-2 S 1 2013

REVIEW: *Publ Wkly* v260 no37 p57 S 16 2013

REVIEW: *SLJ* v60 no2 p57 F 2014 Robin Levin

REVIEW: *Voice of Youth Advocates* v36 no4 p67 O 2013 Marla Unruh

REVIEW: *Voice of Youth Advocates* v36 no4 p67 O 2013 Austin Bell

LASKY, KATHRYN. The escape; [by] Kathryn Lasky 240 p. 2014 Scholastic Press

1. Animal stories 2. Horses—Fiction 3. Horses—Juvenile fiction 4. Leadership—Juvenile fiction 5. Mothers and daughters—Juvenile fiction 6. Responsibility—Juvenile fiction

ISBN 0545397162; 9780545397162 (jacketed hardcover)

LC 2013-037215

SUMMARY: In this juvenile novel, by Kathryn Lasky, "the horses . . . were rounded up by the two-legs . . . to cross the wide ocean. The journey went badly . . . , so the two-legs forced the horses into the sea and sailed away. . . . By a miracle, the horses survived and made it to land. All but one— . . . the leader of the pack. Now it's up to her daughter, only a filly, to take charge of the terrified herd." (Publisher's note)

REVIEW: *Booklist* v110 no11 p67 F 1 2014 Magan Szwarek

REVIEW: *Kirkus Rev* v81 no24 p260 D 15 2013

"The Escape". "Born in the hold of a Spanish galleon destined for the New World, the young filly Estrella knows nothing of the feel of the earth under her hooves or the joy of the pasture, but her mother's soft murmurings hint at a greater destiny for the young horse and her friends. . . . As in works such as her Guardians of Ga'hoole series, [Kathryn] Lasky uses animals to touch on very human issues. The herd must face the cost of freedom and the adversity that comes with the pursuit of one's dreams. Complex and distinctive characters offer a fresh view of familiar historical events. A promising start to a new series."

REVIEW: *SLJ* v60 no2 p90 F 2014 Kathleen E. Gruver

LATHAM, ANYA.il. Our Lives As Caterpillars. See Briggs, C. E.

LATIMER, ALEX.il. Lion vs Rabbit. See Latimer, A.

LATIMER, ALEX. Lion vs Rabbit; [by] Alex Latimer 32 p. 2013 Peachtree Publishers

1. Animals—Fiction 2. Bullies—Fiction 3. Contests—Fiction 4. Lion—Fiction 5. Picture books for children 6. Rabbits—Fiction

ISBN 1561457094; 9781561457090

LC 2012-044982

SUMMARY: In this children's book, "Lion bullies the animals of the savanna, who politely ask him to cease and desist. They are too timid to fight back themselves, so they place an ad looking for someone to put Lion in his place. Bear, Moose, and Tiger fly in and take Lion on, but his prowess and skill is too much for each of them. It looks like the animals are stuck with Lion's bullying, when Rabbit arrives on a ship to offer his help." (Children's Literature)

REVIEW: *Kirkus Rev* v81 no14 p242 Jl 15 2013

REVIEW: *N Y Times Book Rev* p12 Ag 25 2013 BECCA ZERKIN

"Sea Monster and the Bossy Fish," "Lion vs. Rabbit," and "Llama Llama and the Bully Goat." "Though the text is heavy-handed, especially when Ernest is setting things right, [Kate] Messner . . . subtly implies that the new fish is behaving badly because he feels vulnerable. . . . Young readers will relate as they settle into the new school year. . . . Alex Latimer . . . doesn't hit us over the head with a message. . . . It's too bad that Latimer renders Lion's victims overly passive and the aggressor a changed man only because he lost a bet; it makes the resolution less satisfying. . . . Anna Dewdney . . . writes touchingly about the emotions of young children."

REVIEW: *Publ Wkly* v260 no22 p60 Je 3 2013

REVIEW: *SLJ* v59 no9 p124 S 2013 Linda Ludke

LATIMER, MIRIAM.il. The Prince's breakfast. See Oppenheim, J.

LATOUR, BRUNO, 1947-. An inquiry into modes of existence; an anthropology of the moderns; [by] Bruno Latour 486 p. 2013 Harvard University Press

1. Anthropology literature 2. Civilization, Modern—Philosophy 3. Modernity 4. Philosophical anthropology 5. Philosophical literature

ISBN 9780674724990 (alk. paper)

LC 2012-050894

SUMMARY: "In this new book, Bruno Latour offers answers to questions raised in 'We Have Never Been Modern,' a work that interrogated the connections between nature and culture. If not modern, he asked, what have we been, and what values should we inherit? . . . This systematic effort of building a new philosophical anthropology presents a completely different view of what Moderns have been." (Publisher's note)

REVIEW: *TLS* no5780 p7-8 Ja 10 2014 JONATHAN RÉE

"An Inquiry Into Modes of Existence: An Anthropology of the Moderns." "In his magnificent new book [Bruno] Latour returns to the problem of modernity, but he replaces actor-network theory, which now strikes him as monotonous, with a polyphonic account of 'modes of existence.' . . . Latour describes his book as a provisional report, and he wants to be taken at his word: he has launched a 'Modes of Existence' website which he intends as a platform for 'collaborative research' where his findings will be elaborated, confuted or amended. . . . Latour's main message--that rationality is 'woven from more than one thread'--is intended not just for the academic seminar, but for the public square; and the public square today is global as never before."

LAUGESEN, MALENE.il. Flying solo. See Cummins, J.

LAUGHLIN, FLORENCE. The little leftover witch; [by] Florence Laughlin 96 p. 2013 Simon & Schuster Books for Young Readers

1. Adopted children—Fiction 2. Children's stories 3. Family life—Fiction 4. Foster home care—Fiction 5. Witches—Fiction

ISBN 9781442486720 (pbk.); 9781442486775 (hardcover); 9781442486782 (e-book)

LC 2012-040276

SUMMARY: In this children's novel, "when a contrary little witch breaks her broom, she is stuck on the ground until the next Halloween. Pointy-nosed Felina shelters with the Doon family, who over the course of an eventful year come to love her. . . . She first accepts people food, a bed, and a bath; then goes to school and conquers reading; and finally gives up her witch hat and officially becomes one of the family." (Horn Book Magazine)

REVIEW: *Horn Book Magazine* v89 no5 p66 S/O 2013 MARTHA V. PARRAVANO

"The Little Leftover Witch." "Adult readers will see a metaphor for healthy, happy childrearing (the true magic is love), but kids will simply root for Felina as she first accepts people food, a bed, and a bath; then goes to school and conquers reading; and finally gives up her witch hat and officially becomes one of the family. Originally published by Macmillan in 1960, [Florence] Laughlin's brief novel reflects old-fashioned sensibilities (spanking is occasionally threatened) but is perennially fresh and genuinely affecting."

LAVDAS, KOSTAS A. Stateness and sovereign debt; Greece in the European conundrum; [by] Kostas A. Lavdas 200 p. 2013 Lexington Books

1. Debts, Public—Greece 2. Financial crises—European Union countries 3. Political science literature 4. State, The

ISBN 0739181262; 9780739181263 (cloth: alk. paper)

LC 2012-051413

SUMMARY: "This book examines the present crisis of Greece's political economy as a crisis of stateness, tackling the domestic as well as the international dimensions. It represents the first attempt by Greek academics to put forward a theoretically-informed, interdisciplinary analysis of Greece's fiscal, economic, and political crisis. . . . The book tackles the issue of the possible next steps for the EU under the influence of the crisis of the eurozone." (Publisher's note)

REVIEW: *Choice* v51 no9 p1673-4 My 2014 J. R. Strand

"Stateness and Sovereign Debt: Greece in the European Conundrum". "The chapters offer analysis of the Greek crisis from eclectic points of view that integrate disparate theories. Making extensive use of available data, the authors examine root causes of the crisis. The book provides ample details on the role of international and domestic institutions in defining and offering solutions for the sovereign debt crisis. . . . The empirical and policy analysis offered here will be of interest to scholars of the EU, as the evidence presented reveals how the deepening of integration in Europe is not a simple, linear process. Moreover, efforts to integrate Greece, and by extension other economies, are limited by the structure of and effectiveness of domestic institutions."

LAVEDRINE, BERTRAND. The Lumière autochrome; history, technology, and preservation; [by] Bertrand Lavedrine 380 p. 2012 Getty Conservation Institute

1. Color photography—Autochrome process—History 2. Color photography—France—History 3. Photography literature

ISBN 9781606061251 (pbk.)

LC 2012-029526

SUMMARY: This book looks at the history of "the autochrome, the primary medium used by commercial color photography between 1907, when it was introduced, and the early 1930s." It covers "not only the Lumière family's pioneering photographic inventions, dating to tbe mid-1880s, but also the history of color photography and technical details of processes and preservation." (Bookforum)

REVIEW: *Bookforum* v20 no5 p24-5 F/Mr 2014 Christopher Lyon

"Co-Mix: A Retrospective of Comics, Graphics and Scraps," "She Who Tells a Story: Women Photographers From Iran and the Arab World," and "Lumiere Autochrome: History, Technology, and Preservation." "'Co-Mix' perform[s] the jujitsu flip of mimicking a high-art exhibition catalogue in the quintessential low-art medium of comics. . . . Though Shirin Nesbat is well represented and an obvious inspiration for the other eleven younger artists featured, much of this work could be called post-Neshat, because it favors a less fussy approach, and is more narrative driven. . . . A kind of Swiss Army knife of a book, covering not only the Lumière family's pioneering photographic inventions, dating to the mid-1880s, but also the history of color photography and technical details of processes\ and preservation. . . . An essential resource for students and collectors of photography."

REVIEW: *Choice* v51 no9 p1583 My 2014 K. Rhodes

LAVEN, MARY.ed. The Ashgate research companion to the Counter-Reformation. See The Ashgate research companion to the Counter-Reformation

LAVERTY, ANN TAYLOR. Unraveled; A Story of Heartache and Hope; [by] Ann Taylor Laverty 488 p. 2013 Createspace Independent Pub

1. Drug addiction 2. Heroin abuse 3. Memoirs 4.

Mothers & sons 5. Parents of drug addicts
ISBN 1484167953; 9781484167953

SUMMARY: In this memoir, Ann Taylor Laverty "recounts the story of her son Matt's heroin addiction. Laverty says her purpose in writing is to show others how to prevent and cope with addiction. Her book, prefaced with the Serenity Prayer, offers detailed accounts of Matt's repetitive cycles of addiction: his numerous attempts to stay drug-free; his temporary successes; his thefts, deceptions and lies; his six in-patient rehabilitation treatments; as well as the cumulative effect on the family." (Kirkus Reviews)

REVIEW: *Kirkus Rev* v82 no2 p336 Ja 15 2014

"Unraveled: A Story of Heartache and Hope". "In a candid, unaffected style, [Ann Taylor] Laverty realistically portrays her anguish, and her feelings for her son are apparent and moving. Her sensible trepidation can be heart-wrenching: '[F]or the moment, there is a happy ending.' That said, the book could have benefited from an additional round of editing to eliminate many of the sometimes-repetitive particulars in the patterns of addiction, enabling and relapse, which, though truthful, can slow down the narrative. A poignant tale from the heart, though it could use some pruning."

LAVORATO, MARK. Serafim and Claire; [by] Mark Lavorato 336 p. 2014 Pgw

1. Dance—Fiction 2. Historical fiction 3. Montréal (Québec)—Fiction 4. Photographers—Fiction 5. Self-realization—Fiction
ISBN 1770893652; 9781770893658

SUMMARY: This novel by Mark Lavorato is "set mostly in 1920s Montreal. . . . Serafim grows up in Portugal and longs to be a photographer. Claire grows up in Montreal and longs to be a dancer. Their paths eventually cross, and the novel moves through their separate and shared stories as they struggle to earn a living and fulfill their artistic passions. Both make huge sacrifices . . . and they must learn what can and cannot be accomplished in the search for meaningful, creative lives." (Quill & Quire)

REVIEW: *Quill Quire* v80 no1 p33 Ja/F 2014 Candace Fertile

"Serafim and Claire". "Mark Lavorato delivers an engaging third novel that does a lovely job infusing history into fiction. Set mostly in 1920s Montreal, 'Serafim and Claire' is loaded with local colour and detail. The historical milieu becomes as much a character as Lavorato's fictional creations. . . . Lavorato punctuates his fictional pas de deux with descriptions of photographs that freeze moments in time. The combination of movement and stasis results in a dazzling depiction of the challenges these young people face. . . . Lavorato handles the blend of art, politics, language, religion, and power deftly,illustrating that they are inextricably linked. Above all, this novel can be read for its excellent sense of place."

LAW, IAN. Ethnicity and education in England and Europe; gangstas, geeks and gorjas; [by] Ian Law xiv, 188 p. 2011 Ashgate Pub.

1. Education—Europe 2. Education—Great Britain 3. Ethnic relations—Europe 4. Ethnic relations—Great Britain 5. Social science literature
ISBN 9781409410874 (hardback: alk. paper); 9781409410881 (ebook)
LC 2011-023631

SUMMARY: This book "analyzes the educational experiences of Gypsy, Traveller, Roma, and ethnic minority youth across national contexts, for a broad look at how ethnic differences manifest themselves in local school settings across Europe. . . . Chapters One to Three provide background material, Chapters Four to Six marshal the project's empirical data from northern England, and Chapter Seven compares the project's data from England to the data from the rest of Europe." (Contemporary Sociology)

REVIEW: *Contemp Sociol* v43 no1 p97-8 Ja 2014 Natasha Kumar Warikoo

"Ethnicity and Education in England and Europe: Gangstas, Geeks and Gorjas". "The broad ranging study, impressive in its scope, analyzes the educational experiences of Gypsy, Traveller, Roma, and ethnic minority youth across national contexts, for a broad look at how ethnic differences manifest themselves in local school settings across Europe. . . . The book will be a useful overview for those wishing to learn more about immigration and education to Britain, and especially for those who want to learn more about Gypsy, Roma, and Traveller youth in Europe. . . . More detail on the book's survey data in terms of where the data was collected, and how national, school, and ethnic group contexts influence the findings would have made the presentation of findings more compelling."

LAWLER, JUSTUS GEORGE. Were the Popes against the Jews?; tracking the myths, confronting the ideologues; [by] Justus George Lawler xviii, 387 p. 2012 William B. Eerdmans

1. Antisemitism—History 2. Christianity and antisemitism—History 3. Historical literature 4. Judaism—Relations—Catholic Church—History 5. Papacy—History
ISBN 0802866298 (alk. paper); 9780802866295 (alk. paper)
LC 2011-022240

SUMMARY: In this book, the author "poses the question in his title and answers it with a qualified yes, acknowledging that the popes were indeed against the Jews, specifically because of their alleged repudiation of Christ. . . . This theological opposition, however, does not make the popes villains, [Justus George] Lawler insists, and does not justify the vilification heaped on them by authors who portray the Vatican as 'disdainful, contemptuous, and vengeful toward Jews and their beliefs'." (Commonweal)

REVIEW: *America* v208 no15 p24-8 My 6 2013 JEROME DONNELLY

REVIEW: *Commonweal* v139 no10 p23-4 My 18 2012 Kevin P. Spicer

"Were the Popes Against the Jews? Tracking the Myths, Confronting the Ideologues." "[A] tedious, polemical, and often angry work. . . . At the heart of [Justus George] Lawler's disagreement with [David I.] Kertzer is his rejection of the essential link between the theological anti-Semitism of Christian Scripture and tradition on the one hand and, on the other, modern racial anti-Semitism, which ultimately led to the Holocaust. . . . . In the end, the problems with [the book] amount to more than just faulty scholarship. . . . From the turn of the twentieth century through the 1950s it was common to find Catholic commentary . . . permitting assaults on 'Jewish secularism' . . . while frowning on and condemning attacks against Jewish citizens based on racial anti-Semitism. Such advice, however, was rarely sustained without some form of injury and violence against Jews."

REVIEW: *N Y Rev Books* v60 no18 p75-7 N 21 2013 Kevin J. Madigan

"Were the Popes Against the Jews?: Tracking the Myths, Confronting the Ideologues." "The same critical tone, charges of fabrication, and lack of familiarity with the recent scholarship can now be found in [Justus George Lawler's] latest book. . . . He has composed a book nearly four hundred pages in length devoted largely to withdrawing that praise and dispensing criticisms of the book he once lauded. Lawler's attempt to account for his volte-face in the opening chapter is long (something like nine thousand words) and opaque; and it is difficult to find in it a clear argument. . . . In fact, readers will discover that Lawler delivers not a critique, but an unfair attack."

LAWOTI, MAHENDRA. Government and politics in South Asia. See Kapur, A.

LAWRENCE, CAROLINE. P.K. Pinkerton and the pistol-packing widows; [by] Caroline Lawrence 304 p. 2014 G.P. Putnam's Sons, an imprint of Penguin Group (USA) Inc.

1. Disguise—Fiction 2. Mystery and detective stories 3. Orphans—Fiction 4. Racially mixed people—Fiction
ISBN 0399256350; 9780399256356 (hardcover)
LC 2013-000211

SUMMARY: In this book, by Caroline Lawrence, "P.K. Pinkerton's detective agency is thriving in Virginia City—until the evening P.K. is abruptly stuffed into a turnip sack and tossed into the back of a wagon! Surfacing in Chinatown, P.K. is forced into taking a job trailing the abductor's fiancé in Carson City. Danger lurks at every turn. P.K. must battle quicksand, escape the despicable former Deputy Marshall, Jack Williams, and save Poker Face Jace from certain death." (Publisher's note)

REVIEW: *Kirkus Rev* v82 no2 p138 Ja 15 2014

"P. K. Pinkerton and the Pistol-Packing Widows". "Twelve-year-old half-Lakota 'double-orphan' detective P.K. Pinkerton heads to Carson City in the third of the disarming Western Mysteries series. . . . P.K.—the best kind of hero—navigates it all with unblinking acceptance of the salty characters he meets, straight-shooting honesty and impressive investigative work. The young detective's dryly hilarious first-person accounts keep the story at a gallop. No disguise can mask P.K. Pinkerton's stout heart and steely resolve in [Caroline] Lawrence's third (and mighty fine) Wild West adventure."

REVIEW: *SLJ* v60 no7 p51 Jl 2014 Cheryl Preisendorfer

LAWRENCE, GRANT. The Lonely End of the Rink; [by] Grant Lawrence 288 p. 2014 Pgw

1. Bullying 2. Hockey—Canada 3. Hockey goalkeepers 4. Memoirs 5. Nerds (Persons)
ISBN 1771000775; 9781771000772

SUMMARY: Written by Grant Lawrence, in this "memoir about Grant's relationship with hockey, the narrative passes back and forth between tales of Grant's life and a fascinating history of hockey, complete with lively anecdotes about the many colourful characters of the NHL. . . . For Grant, bullying and the violent game of hockey seemed to go hand-in-hand. Yet he was also enamoured with the sport." (Publisher's note)

REVIEW: *Quill Quire* v79 no9 p28 N 2013 Vit Wagner

"Keon and Me: My Search for the Lost Soul of the Leafs" and "The Lonely End of the Rink: Confessions of a Reluctant Goalie." "The author of a dozen books--all of which have been autobiographical at least to some extent, and many of which have probed our irrepressible national fixation with shinny--[Author Dave] Bidini has written a thoughtful, amusing, coming-of-age meditation on what it means, as both a child and an adult, to be a fan. 'Keon and Me' also has the virtue of dividing its focus between two subjects. . . . There is a sense that [hockey player Dave] Keon isn't much interested in reliving or revisiting the past; would that [author] Grant Lawrence shared some of Keon's reticence. . . . Lawrence leans on pop culture references to the point that it quickly feels like a lazy alternative to actual writing."

LAWRENCE, THEO. Toxic heart; a Mystic City novel; [by] Theo Lawrence 368 p. 2014 Delacorte Press

1. Love—Fiction 2. Science fiction 3. Supernatural—Fiction 4. Wealth—Fiction
ISBN 9780375990144 (glb); 9780385741620 (hardback)
LC 2013-049642

SUMMARY: "In this sequel to 'Mystic City' (2012), Aria Rose continues her evolution from clueless debutante to political activist . . . as the battle for power wages between wealthy denizens of the Aeries and mystic rebels in Manhattan's decrepit Depths. . . . When she discovers that Hunter has manipulated their private online conversations for propaganda purposes, Aria realizes she is merely a pawn that opposing sides are grappling to possess and resolves to find a solution herself." (Kirkus Reviews)

REVIEW: *Kirkus Rev* v82 no3 p226 F 1 2014

"Toxic Heart". " Aria has traded her confusion from Book 1 for determined self-empowerment this round, intensifying the narrative. Resilient though she may be, she has a fair amount of fumbles and self-doubts, maintaining her character's plausibility. Intense action and kick-ass characters will thrill fantasy and action fans. And the aerobic pace endures to an ending that will have readers clamoring to know what becomes of Aria and the revolution she has unwittingly fueled. An electric, futuristic fantasy with loads of action, heartbreak and one delicious gold-lamé cat suit."

REVIEW: *SLJ* v60 no5 p134 My 2014 Ryan P. Donovan

REVIEW: *Voice of Youth Advocates* v37 no1 p84 Ap 2014 Ava Ehde

LAWSON, RUSSELL M.ed. Encyclopedia of American Indian issues today. See Encyclopedia of American Indian issues today

LAWTON, JOHN. Then We Take Berlin; [by] John Lawton 400 p. 2013 Pgw

1. Berlin (Germany)—Fiction 2. Cold War, 1945-1989—Fiction 3. Private investigators—Fiction 4. Smuggling—Fiction 5. Spy stories
ISBN 0802121969; 9780802121967

SUMMARY: This book is the first in a series from John Lawton. It "opens on the eve of President Kennedy's 1963 Berlin visit, but the real meat lies in the . . . backstory of John Wilford Holderness, an East London Cockney who joins the

RAF in 1946. Aircraftman Wilderness . . . is cheeky to the point of risking court-martial, but an RAF colonel spots Joe's potential, sends him to Cambridge, and makes him a spy." He's posted to Berlin to identify former Nazis. (Publishers Weekly)

REVIEW: *Booklist* v109 no22 p41 Ag 1 2013 Bill Ott

REVIEW: *Kirkus Rev* v81 no18 p110 S 15 2013

REVIEW: *N Y Times Book Rev* p17 S 22 2013 MARILYN STASIO

"W is for Wasted," "Then We Take Berlin," and "Seven For a Secret." "A painstaking plot wrangler, [Sue] Grafton carefully merges both narratives in a sad but satisfying conclusion. The problems arise from her efforts to work Kinsey's personal history into the story. . . . John Lawton's stylish spy thriller . . . is a splendid introduction to John Wilfrid (Wilderness) Holderness. . . . Timothy Wilde, who rescued child prostitutes in Lyndsay Faye's rip-roaring novel 'The Gods of Gothan' returns in 'Seven for a Secret' as the protector of lovely Lucy Adams, who lost her family to slave catchers."

REVIEW: *Publ Wkly* v260 no26 p67 Jl 1 2013

LAWTOO, NIDESH. The phantom of the ego; modernism and the mimetic unconscious; [by] Nidesh Lawtoo 366 p. 2013 Michigan State University Press

1. Ego (Psychology) in literature 2. Literature—Philosophy 3. Mimesis 4. Modernism (Literature) 5. Philosophical literature

ISBN 9781611860962 (pbk.: alk. paper)

LC 2012-049425

SUMMARY: This book "shows how the modernist account of the unconscious anticipates contemporary discoveries about the importance of mimesis in the formation of subjectivity. Rather than beginning with Sigmund Freud as the father of modernism, Nidesh Lawtoo starts with Friedrich Nietzsche's antimetaphysical diagnostic of the ego, his realization that mimetic reflexes . . . move the soul, and his insistence that psychology informs philosophical reflection." (Publisher's note)

REVIEW: *Choice* v51 no9 p1586-7 My 2014 H. I. Einsohn

"The Phantom of the Ego: Modernism and the Mimetic Unconscious". "In this extraordinary study, [Nidesh] Lawtoo . . . contends that a specter is haunting modernity. . . . Using key texts of modernism by Nietzsche, Conrad, Lawrence, and Bataille, Lawtoo tells a revelatory story of how the ego becomes a protean phantom. But, as the author notes, the end of this fable is yet to be written, which leaves open the possibility that humans may in time learn to distinguish demonic possession from inspired action aimed at enhancing the commonweal."

LAZAR, ZACHARY. I pity the poor immigrant; A Novel; [by] Zachary Lazar 256 p. 2014 Little Brown & Co

1. Holocaust survivors—Fiction 2. Israel—Fiction 3. Journalists—Fiction 4. Lansky, Meyer 5. Organized crime—Fiction 6. Psychological fiction

ISBN 0316254037; 9780316254038 (hardcover)

LC 2013-954942

SUMMARY: Author Zachary Lazar "starts with Jewish American mobster Meyer Lansky, who walked away from his 1972 trial free but was denied his wish to become an Israeli citizen. In between doling out tidbits of Lansky's personal life and early years, Lazar crafts . . . fictional characters: . . . Gila Konig, Lansky's mistress and a Holocaust survivor; David Bellen, murdered Israeli poet; and Hannah Groff, an American journalist who finds herself deeply wrapped up in Lansky's story." (Booklist)

REVIEW: *Bookforum* v21 no2 p39 Je-Ag 2014 FIONA MAAZEL

REVIEW: *Booklist* v110 no16 p28 Ap 15 2014 Rebecca Hayes

REVIEW: *Kirkus Rev* v82 no3 p309 F 1 2014

"I Pity the Poor Immigrant". "A complex tale involving Meyer Lansky, Las Vegas, an investigative reporter and the murder of an Israeli poet. [Zachary] Lazar . . . brings all these elements—and more—together as he jumps across decades and intercalates different narrators. . . . It's a sign of Lazar's verisimilitude that the books his fictitious poet reviews are in fact real books. . . . The connections Lazar makes here are complex and artful, though at times bewildering even to discerning readers."

REVIEW: *Libr J* v139 no6 p81 Ap 1 2014 Andrea Kempf

REVIEW: *N Y Times Book Rev* p14 Ap 27 2014 RICH COHEN

REVIEW: *New Yorker* v90 no17 p83-1 Je 23 2014

REVIEW: *Publ Wkly* v261 no5 p32-3 F 3 2014

LE BLANC, PAUL. A freedom budget for all Americans. See Yates, M.

LE CLÉZIO, J.-M. G. (JEAN-MARIE GUSTAVE), 1940-. The African; 128 p. 2012 David R. Godine, Publisher

1. Authors, French—20th century—Biography 2. Memoirs 3. Nigerian literature (English)

ISBN 1567924603 (alk. paper); 9781567924602 (alk. paper)

LC 2012-005141

SUMMARY: "'The African' is a short autobiographical account of a pivotal moment in Nobel-Prize-winning author J. M. G. Le Clezio's childhood. In 1948, young Le Clezio, with his mother and brother, left behind a still-devastated Europe to join his father, a military doctor in Nigeria, from whom he'd been separated by the war. . . . His reflections on the nature of his relationship to his father become a chapeau bas." (Publisher's note)

REVIEW: *Choice* v51 no5 p838 Ja 2014 E. A. Vanborre

REVIEW: *Kirkus Rev* p30 2013 Guide 20to BookExpo America

REVIEW: *Kirkus Rev* v81 no8 p59 Ap 15 2013

REVIEW: *Libr J* v138 no9 p79 My 15 2013 Lonnie Weatherby

REVIEW: *World Lit Today* v88 no1 p78-9 Ja/F 2014 Michelle Bailat-Jones

"The African." "In this slender memoir. 'The African,' J. M. G. Le Clézio writes of his childhood in Nigeria and the experience of meeting his father for the first time at the age of eight. While the book is very much about Le Clézio himself and his desire to transform his wordless childhood memories--the impressions and images that still haunt and delight him--into an interpretive account, it is also an attempt to transform his father into a man Le Clézio can understand and even embrace. . . . Despite the intimate feel of 'The African,' it very subtly goes beyond a simple story of a father, a son, and their deep-rooted disconnect. The specter of colonialism ghosts through this memoir, of great men adrift of purpose, of irreconcilable worlds."

LE CORBUSIER AND THE POWER OF PHOTOGRAPHY; 256 p. 2013 Thames & Hudson Inc.

1. Architectural literature 2. Architectural photography 3. Architecture & photography 4. Historical literature 5. Le Corbusier, 1887-1965 6. Urban planning—History
ISBN 0500544220; 9780500544228 (hardback)
LC 2012-939685

SUMMARY: This book, edited by Nathalie Herschdorfer, Tim Benton, and Lada Umstatter, looks at Charles-Édouard Jeanneret, aka Le Corbusier. Here the editors "focus on the architect's visual impact, collecting a wide range of photos, film stills, and other ephemera to give readers a greater appreciation of Le Courbusier's artistic scope and lasting impact on the visual arts and architecture." (Publishers Weekly)

REVIEW: *Burlington Mag* v155 no1327 p718 O 2013 COLIN AMERY

"Le Corbusier and the Power of Photography." "This striking book . . . deals with the intricate connections between the rise in popularity of photography during the twentieth century and the development of modern architecture. Six internationally known art historians and critics contribute essays on aspects of Le Corbusier's visual and architectural imagination. . . . There is much visual and architectural pleasure to be had from this book. It is well designed and uses colour as Le Corbusier did--to enliven his concrete world."

REVIEW: *Choice* v50 no11 p2004-5 Jl 2013 J. Quinan

REVIEW: *Libr J* v138 no9 p76 My 15 2013 Amy Trendler

REVIEW: *Publ Wkly* v260 no8 p158 F 25 2013

LE MORTE DARTHUR; 984 p. 2013 D.S. Brewer

1. Arthurian romances 2. English literature—Middle English, 1100-1500 3. Knights and knighthood—Great Britain—Fiction 4. Tales, Medieval
ISBN 1843843145 (hbk.); 9781843843146 (hbk.)
LC 2013-404412

SUMMARY: Several textual "discoveries should make it possible to produce an edition of [author Thomas] Malory's book that comes closer than ever before to what Malory intended to write. The present edition [by P. J. C. Field] aims to do that, basing itself on the Winchester manuscript, but treating it merely as the most important piece of evidence for what Malory intended, and the default text where no other reading can be shown to be more probable." (Publisher's note)

REVIEW: *Choice* v51 no11 p1980 Jl 2014 J. J. Doherty

REVIEW: *TLS* no5797 p13 My 9 2014 CAROLYNE LARRINGTON

"Le Morte Darthur" and "Malory and His European Contemporaries." "[Editor P. J. C.] Field has, in Volume One, produced a wonderfully clean reading text. All the manuscript and print variants, and his comments about editorial choices, are contained in the second volume. The discussion of the different witnesses to the text yields fascinating insights into compositors' practice at the very birth of English printing. . . . All over late medieval Europe—in the Netherlands, Italy, Germany and France—as Miriam Edlich-Muth's new study 'Malory and His European Contemporaries' shows, writers or teams of writers were putting together large Arthurian compendia for their patrons."

LE VAY, DAVID.tr. Flight without end. See Roth, J.

LEADER, DARIAN. Strictly Bipolar; [by] Darian Leader 112 p. 2013 Hamish Hamilton

1. Bipolar disorder 2. Bipolar disorder—Treatment 3. People with bipolar disorder 4. Psychiatric drugs 5. Psychological literature
ISBN 0241146100; 9780241146101

SUMMARY: This book looks at bipolar disorder. "Moodstabilising medication is routinely prescribed to adults and children alike, with child prescriptions this decade increasing by 400%. . . . What could explain this explosion of bipolarity? Is it a legitimate diagnosis or the result of Big Pharma marketing? . . Darian Leader challenges the rise of 'bipolar' as a catch-all solution to complex problems, and argues that we need to rethink the highs and lows of mania and depression." (Publisher's note)

REVIEW: *TLS* no5759 p26 Ag 16 2013 BALAJI RAVICHANDRAN

"Strictly Bipolar." "[Darian] Leader writes clearly and engagingly, often with great sympathy for those who suffer from the more extreme forms of the illness, and frequently offers genuine insights into the behaviours that underlie the condition. . . . Those looking for a more well-rounded treatment of bipolar illness, however, will be disappointed. From the very first sentence, the author wears his prejudices openly. The increase in diagnoses and prescriptions for the spectrum of bipolar conditions, he must know, cannot alone amount to a conspiracy on the part of the pharmaceutical industry."

LEAVE YOUR SLEEP; 48 p. 2012 Frances Foster Books

1. Children in literature 2. Children's poetry 3. Parents in literature 4. Poetry—Collections 5. Songbooks
ISBN 0374343683; 9780374343682 (hardcover)
LC 2011-047064

SUMMARY: This book is a children's poetry collection. "For her 2010 hit album with the same title, [Natalie] Merchant composed music for 30 19th- and 20th-century British and American poems, some written for children and some written about childhood. For this volume, she's selected 19 of those poems (18 from the CD set and one other), describing them as 'representing the long conversation I had with my daughter during the first six years of her life.'" (Kirkus Reviews)

REVIEW: *Booklist* v108 no22 p60 Ag 1 2012 Gillian Engberg

REVIEW: *Booklist* v109 no4 p42 O 15 2012 Ann Kelley

REVIEW: *Horn Book Magazine* v89 no1 p98 Ja/F 2013 LOLLY ROBINSON

"Leave Your Sleep: A Collection of Classic Children's Poetry." "In a classy bit of bookmaking, this volume looks as if it could have been produced about a century ago--except for the CD embedded in the inside back cover. Showcasing nineteen of the twenty-six poems that provided lyrics for Natalie Merchant's 2010 album of the same name . . . the book works just as well on its own. In fact, while the songs on the CD are a welcome extra, experiencing both at once could prove problematic as Merchant's vocals take liberties with the original texts, sometimes skipping or inverting the order of the words."

REVIEW: *Kirkus Rev* v80 no20 p46 O 15 2012

REVIEW: *SLJ* v59 no1 p94 Ja 2013 Julie Roach

LEAVELL, LINDA. Holding on upside down; the life and work of Marianne Moore; [by] Linda Leavell 480 p. 2013 Farrar, Straus and Giroux

1. Biographies 2. Mothers & daughters 3. Poets—Biography 4. Women poets

ISBN 9780374107291 (hardcover)

LC 2013-006521

SUMMARY: In this book, author Linda Leavell "draws from the archive and private estate of American poet Marianne Moore (1887–1972) to illustrate how the modernist poet evolved from writing carefully crafted, cutting-edge poetry to producing the more prolific poems of her later years. Correspondence reveals that Moore's mother, Mary, used emotional manipulation, money, and a secret family vernacular to control both her son, Warner (John), and Marianne." (Library Journal)

REVIEW: *Bookforum* v20 no3 p38 S-N 2013 PARUL SEHGAL

REVIEW: *Booklist* v110 no3 p15 O 1 2013 Donna Seaman

"Holding on Upside Down: The Life and Work of Marianne Moore". "[A] superb, recalibrating biography, the result of three decades of intense effort. . . . [Linda] Leavell's cogent interpretations of Moore's poetry and chronicling of how diligently she pursued startling artistic innovation under her mother's watchful eye in Greenwich Village and Brooklyn while teaching, working in a library, and serving as editor for The Dial, are equally revelatory. Like a sculptor working in clay, Leavell steadily builds up contour and texture."

REVIEW: *Choice* v51 no8 p1401 Ap 2014 R. Mulligan

REVIEW: *Economist* v409 no8863 p83 N 23 2013

"Holding On Upside Down: The Life and Work of Marianne Moore". "A thorough examination of a remarkable life. . . . Ms. [Linda] Leavell's biography is in many ways a joy to read. With a keen eye for detail, she describes how Moore would often have on the side of the bath to eat dinner. . . . She is also one of the few biographers to address Mary Moore's lesbianism and to unpick the strange narrative of their domestic life. Her passages describing Moore's friendship with Elizabeth Bishop, a younger poet, are particularly illuminating."

REVIEW: *Kirkus Rev* v81 no17 p63 S 1 2013

REVIEW: *Libr J* v138 no13 p94 Ag 1 2013 Nerissa Kuebrich

REVIEW: *N Y Rev Books* v60 no17 p46-50 N 7 2013 Helen Vendler

"Holding on Upside Down: The Life and Work of Marianne Moore". "Linda Leavell . . . .has chosen, in her new and revelatory biography, to focus mainly on Moore's family life, in part because she has gained access to new sources. . . . Leavell's remarks on the poems are—as Moore might say with her characteristic double negative—'not unhelpful': they point out the main theme of a poem, trace it to a person it may be describing, or mention the event that occasioned the poem in question, but they do not equal the longer accounts of the poems in [Charles] Molesworth. . . . One must take Leavell's offering as yet another tile in the Moore mosaic, valuable for its rendering in detail both the extreme pathos and the dreadful pathology of two generations of the Moore household."

REVIEW: *N Y Times Book Rev* p30 Ap 20 2014 Daisy Fried

REVIEW: *New York Times* v163 no56411 pC1-4 F 13 2014 HOLLAND COTTER

"Holding on Upside Down: The Life and Work of Marianne Moore." "Half a century or so ago, when literate Americans still read poetry or thought they should, everyone knew about Marianne Moore, the white-haired, great-auntish New York writer who loved polysyllables, exotic animals and the Brooklyn Dodgers, and turned up around town in a signature Paul Revere hat. . . . The moment is ripe for her to be restored to us, depixified and complex. And so she has been in a swift, cool but empathetic new biography called 'Holding On Upside Down: The Life and Work of Marianne Moore,' by Linda Leavell. . . . It says much for Ms. Leavell's account of Moore's life that for all the hard and hard-to-fathom facts it marshals, it leaves the miracles intact."

REVIEW: *New Yorker* v89 no36 p72-1 N 11 2013

REVIEW: *Publ Wkly* v260 no24 p52 Je 17 2013

REVIEW: *TLS* no5809 p7-8 Ag 1 2014 FIONA GREEN

REVIEW: *Women's Review of Books* v31 no4 p30-1 Jl/Ag 2014 Robin G. Schulze

LEAVIS, F. R. (FRANK RAYMOND), 1895-1978. Two cultures? See Collini, S.

LEAVITT, DAVID. The two Hotel Francforts; a novel; [by] David Leavitt 272 p. 2013 Bloomsbury

1. Historical fiction 2. Life change events—Fiction 3. Man-woman relationships—Fiction 4. Marital conflict—Fiction

ISBN 1596910429; 9781596910423 (hc : alk. paper)

LC 2013-015952

SUMMARY: In this book, by David Leavitt, "it is the summer of 1940, and Lisbon, Portugal, is the only neutral port left in Europe. . . . Awaiting safe passage to New York on the SS Manhattan, two couples meet: Pete and Julia Winters, expatriate Americans fleeing their sedate life in Paris; and Edward and Iris Freleng, sophisticated, independently wealthy, bohemian, and beset by the social and sexual anxieties of their class. . . . This journey will change their lives irrevocably." (Publisher's note)

REVIEW: *Booklist* v109 no22 p46 Ag 1 2013 Brad Hooper

REVIEW: *Kirkus Rev* v81 no17 p16 S 1 2013

REVIEW: *Libr J* v138 no8 p59 My 1 2013

REVIEW: *N Y Times Book Rev* p13 O 6 2013 MICHAEL PYE

"The Two Hotel Francforts." "What David Leavitt tells . . . is a small story set against the big one, which is brave and risky. He's using this history as a backdrop. . . . It's the two men who embark on a quite violent affair. . . . They're too busy filling in their own back stories to be convincingly obsessed with each other. . . . Only Pete's life is changed entirely: from Buick salesman to heroic resistance driver, a change that happens in a single page of afterthought. Leavitt is a fluent, clever writer with a habit of playing with historical fact--which explains what might seem the failings of this curious and yet absorbing book. It isn't so much a story as it is a piece of writing about the writing of the story of people in a situation like this."

REVIEW: *New Yorker* v89 no40 p89-1 D 9 2013

"The Two Hotel Francforts." "Set in 1940, this novel follows a stylish American expatriate couple who have fled occupied Paris for Lisbon. . . . A self-conscious glee in literary genre hangs over the novel, not with good effects. There is a levity to the way in which very consequential actions--homosexual flings, broken marriages, suicide--flit through the narrative frame; credibility suffers. [Author David] Leavitt draws such delight from the procedures of fiction that he neglects one of its most basic pleasures--the inquiry into why people behave as they do."

REVIEW: *Publ Wkly* v260 no31 p45-6 Ag 5 2013

LEAVY, PATRICIA. Fiction as research practice; short stories, novellas, and novels; [by] Patricia Leavy 316 p. 2013 Left Coast Press, Inc.

1. Fiction—Social aspects 2. Literature—Research—Methodology 3. Qualitative research—Methodology 4. Social science literature 5. Social science research
ISBN 9781611321531 (hardback : alk. paper); 9781611321548 (pbk. : alk. paper)
LC 2012-050528

SUMMARY: This book on fiction and qualitative research by Patricia Leavy "explores the overlaps and intersections between these two ways of understanding and describing human experience. She demonstrates the validity of literary experimentation to the qualitative researcher and how to incorporate these practices into research projects. Five short stories and excerpts from novellas and novels show these methods in action." (Publisher's note)

REVIEW: *Choice* v51 no4 p630-1 D 2013 S. Batcos

"Fiction as Research Practice: Short Stories, Novellas, and Novels." "Sociologist Patricia Leavy. . . aims to assist social researchers in their fictionalizations of professional observations and experiences. The end result of this effort seems to lean heavily in the direction of encouraging writers to sway an audience's response to social issues by way of literature. Evoking contrived responses and assuming a set of shared values unfortunately tends to run hand in hand with such endeavors. Researchers interested in using their knowledge and experience in a more creative manner would be better served studying literary guides written by the greatest practitioners of the art form, of which there are many. . . . Not recommended."

LEBANON; After the Cedar Revolution; 323 p. 2012 C Hurst & Co Publishers Ltd

1. Hariri, Rafiq Baha, 1944-2005 2. Lebanon 3. Lebanon—History 4. Lebanon—Politics & government 5. Political science literature
ISBN 1849042497; 9781849042499

SUMMARY: This book of essays on Lebanon "examines the country's recent past since 2005--when a mass movement agitated against Syrian dominance in the wake of the assassination of Rafik Hariri, the then President of the country--and also details the roles of Hezbollah and other political groups. . . . The authors examine the changes that recent events have brought to Lebanon . . . and the challenges they represent for a state, which . . . remains hotly contested and unconsolidated." (Publisher's note)

REVIEW: *TLS* no5763 p24 S 13 2013 T. J. GORTON

"Lebanon: A History, 600-2011" and "Lebanon: After the Cedar Revolution." "Two new books provide timely historical context and up-to-date analysis of the endemic and external troubles afflicting the tiny state. . . . [William] Harris's book shows no signs of bias and is certainly not superficial. Harris displays an intimate knowledge of Arabic. . . . This book will provide scholars with a useful and overdue reference: but it is a pity that, like too many books of academic history, it is written in a pedestrian prose that does not do justice to Lebanon's colourful drama. . . . 'Lebanon: After the Cedar Revolution' is a collection of essays focusing on the country before and since the assassination in 2005 of the former Prime Minister, Rafiq Hariri, and several dozen others. . . . Overall, there is a deft balance between scholarly discourse and the personal observation of an insider."

LEBOW, KATHERINE. Unfinished utopia; Nowa Huta, Stalinism, and Polish society, 1949-56; [by] Katherine Lebow xiv, 233 p. 2013 Cornell University Press

1. Communism and culture—Poland—Kraków—History 2. Historical literature 3. Work-life balance—Poland—Kraków—History—20th century
ISBN 9780801451249 (cloth : alk. paper)
LC 2012-048678

SUMMARY: This book presents "a social and cultural history of Nowa Huta, dubbed Poland's 'first socialist city' by Communist propaganda of the 1950s. . . . Nowa Huta was intended to model a new kind of socialist modernity and to be peopled with 'new men'. . . . Focusing on Nowa Huta's construction and steel workers, youth brigade volunteers, housewives, activists, and architects, Katherine Lebow explores their various encounters with the ideology and practice of Stalinist mobilization." (Publisher's note)

REVIEW: *TLS* no5765 p27 S 27 2013 UILLEAM BLACKER

"Unfinished Utopia: Nowa Huta, Stalinism, and Polish Society, 1949-56." "Rich yet concise. . . . The identification of this room for manoeuvre at the heart of Stalinist social control is a key strength of 'Unfinished Utopia'. Through careful reference to memoirs, cultural representations and archival documentation, [Katherine] Lebow demonstrates how Nowa Huta's social, economic, cultural and political spheres were created through complex interactions between citizens and power. . . . 'Unfinished Utopia' offers many revealing details. . . . By placing them in a broader cultural perspective, it also provides important general insights into the intricate processes by which modernist urban spaces, despite their aspiration to control, became powerful sites of negotiation and resistance."

LECKER, ROBERT. Keepers of the code; English-Canadian literary anthologies and the representation of nation; [by] Robert Lecker 388 p. 2013 University of Toronto Press

1. Anthologies—Editing 2. Anthologies—History and criticism 3. Canadian literature (English)—History and criticism—Theory, etc 4. Canon (Literature) 5. Literary critiques 6. Literature publishing—Canada—History 7. National characteristics, Canadian, in literature
ISBN 1442613963 (pbk.); 1442645717 (bound); 9781442613966 (pbk.); 9781442645714 (bound)
LC 2012-285390

SUMMARY: This book "explores the complex network of associations and negotiations that influenced the development of literary anthologies in English Canada from 1837 to the present. [Robert A.] Lecker shows that these anthologies are deeply conflicted narratives that embody the tensions and anxieties felt by their editors when faced with the challenge of constructing or rejecting national ideals." (Publisher's note)

REVIEW: *Choice* v50 no12 p2230 Ag 2013 T. Ware

REVIEW: *TLS* no5746 p26 My 17 2013 FAYE HAMMILL

"Keepers of the Code: English-Canadian Literary Anthologies and the Representation of the Nation." "Robert Lecker reads the anthologies he surveys in 'Keepers of the Code' as 'anxious expressions of the desire for place and identity'. Canadian critics have always gone in for anxiety. . . . Lecker, however, uses the cultural myth of 'creative schizophrenia' to narrow interpretation. He attributes the anthologies' internal tensions less to the fractured ideologies of nation-building than to the 'divided personalities' of editors. Equating each anthology with its editor, he locates the conflicts of the text in an individual mind. Lecker's account of anthologies as marketable objects is more compelling."

LEDENEVA, ALENA V. Can Russia modernise?; sistema, power networks and informal governance; [by] Alena V. Ledeneva 327 p. 2013 Cambridge University Press

1. POLITICAL SCIENCE—Government—International 2. Political culture—Russia (Federation) 3. Political science literature 4. Power (Social sciences)—Russia (Federation) 5. Social change—Russia (Federation) 6. Social networks—Political aspects—Russia (Federation)

ISBN 9780521110822 (hardback); 9780521125635 (paperback)

LC 2012-030784

SUMMARY: In this book on Russian politics, Alena V. Ledeneva "investigates the informal power networks that 'account for the failure to implement leaders' will and the unfortunate outcomes of well-intentioned modernization programmes'. The centrepiece of her argument is what she calls sistema--a constraining, non-transparent and informal set of rules that bind those in official positions by blurring the boundaries between friendship, its professional abuse, and recruitment." (Times Literary Supplement)

REVIEW: *Choice* v51 no4 p721 D 2013 Y. Polsky

REVIEW: *Economist* v407 no8835 p88-9 My 11 2013

REVIEW: *TLS* no5771 p24 N 8 2013 ANDREW MONAGHAN

"Fragile Empire: How Russia Fell in and Out of Love With Vladimir Putin" and "Can Russia Modernise? Sistema, Power Networks and Informal Governance." "'Fragile Empire' [is] a fluent and plausible account of Russian politics and society in the wake of the recent protests. . . . If this is familiar terrain, [Ben] Judah adds detail and colour by giving thumbnail accounts of the characters involved. . . . The question of 'getting things done' in Russia is at the heart of Alena Ledeneva's more academic study. . . . By drawing attention to the all-encompassing power of the system, Ledeneva shows that the role even of the president should not be overstated. . . . Not all will be convinced by her approach, but the result is an important study that weaves together numerous illuminating anecdotes."

LEDGARD, J. M. Submergence; a novel; [by] J. M. Ledgard 209 p. 2013 Coffee House Press

1. Hostages—Fiction 2. Love stories 3. Qaida (Organization) 4. Undercover operations—Fiction 5. Women marine biologists—Fiction

ISBN 1566893194; 9781566893190 (pbk.)

LC 2012-036524

SUMMARY: "In a room with no windows on the eastern coast of Africa, an Englishman, James More, is held captive by jihadist fighters. Posing as a water engineer to spy on al-Qaeda activity in the area, he now faces extreme privation, mock executions and forced marches through arid Somali badlands. Thousands of miles away on the Greenland Sea, Danielle Flinders, a biomathematician, prepares for a dive to the ocean floor to determine the extent and forms of life in the deep. Both are drawn back, in their thoughts, to the Christmas of the previous year, and to a French hotel on the Atlantic coast, where a chance encounter on the beach led to an intense and enduring romance." (Publisher's note)

REVIEW: *Booklist* v109 no15 p25 Ap 1 2013 Michael Autrey

REVIEW: *Kirkus Rev* v81 no4 p181 F 15 2013

REVIEW: *Libr J* v138 no5 p104 Mr 15 2013 Barbara Hoffert

REVIEW: *N Y Times Book Rev* p11 Je 9 2013 FLOYD SKLOOT

"Submergence." "'Submergence' shows [J. M. Ledgard] has gained control over a full range of skills. . . . Ledgard writes from deep immersion in his well-imagined characters and setting, telling a strong central story involving a terrorist hostage-taking and a perilous deep-sea dive, and deploying language at once precise and flexible. . . . 'Submergence' is a hard-edged, ultracontemporary work about people a reader cares for, apart and together, through extraordinarily precarious conditions."

REVIEW: *New York Times* v162 no56162 p11 Je 9 2013 FLOYD SKLOOT

REVIEW: *Publ Wkly* v260 no5 p40 F 4 2013

LEE, AUDREY S. Flex. See Hyun, J.

LEE CHANG-RAE, 1965-. On such a full sea; [by] 1965-Lee Chang-rae 368 p. 2014 Riverhead Books

1. Chinese Americans—Fiction 2. Dystopias 3. Dystopias in literature 4. Regression (Civilization)—Fiction 5. Social stratification—Fiction

ISBN 1594486107; 9781594486104

LC 2013-036600

SUMMARY: This book "tells the mythic story of young, small, yet mighty Fan, a breath-held diver preternaturally at home among the farmed fish she tends to. When her boyfriend inexplicably disappears, Fan escapes from B-Mor to search for him, embarking on a daring, often surreal quest in a violent, blighted world. She encounters a taciturn healer bereft of all that he cherished, a troupe of backwoods acrobats, and a disturbing cloister of girls creating an intricate mural of their muffled lives." (Booklist)

REVIEW: *Booklist* v111 no1 p138 S 1 2014 Kaite Mediatore Stover

REVIEW: *Booklist* v110 no6 p22 N 15 2013 Donna Seaman

"On Such a Full Sea". "[Chang-rae] Lee . . . always entrancing and delving, has taken fresh approaches to storytelling in each of his previous four novels, but he takes a truly radical leap in this wrenching yet poetic, philosophical, even mystical speculative odyssey. . . . In a third-person plural narrative voice that perfectly embodies the brutal and wistful communities he portrays. Lee tells the mythic story of young, small, yet mighty Fan. . . . Lee brilliantly and wisely dramatizes class stratification and social disintegration, deprivation and sustenance both physical and psychic, reflecting, with rare acuity, on the evolution of legends and how, in the most hellish of circumstances, we rediscover the solace of art."

REVIEW: *Economist* v410 no8871 p71-2 Ja 25 2014

REVIEW: *Kirkus Rev* v81 no22 p193 N 15 2013

REVIEW: *Libr J* v138 no13 p54 Ag 1 2013 Barbara Hoffert

REVIEW: *Libr J* v139 no6 p58 Ap 1 2014 Nann Blaine Hilyard

REVIEW: *Ms* v24 no1 p57-8 Wint/Spr 2014 Juile Phillips

REVIEW: *N Y Rev Books* v61 no10 p22-4 Je 5 2014 Diane Johnson

"On Such a Full Sea." "Chang-rae Lee's 'On Such a Full Sea' is both a quest and a love story—a girl searches for her lover and for her brother, and so on. There's no missing the appeal, especially for adolescents, of another common structure of these tales: a protagonist, often a teen, somehow preserved from the brainwashed docility of most people in his or her society—a rebel—solves some personal or social problem afflicting everyone ('Hunger Games'), and escapes from the future into what we recognize as a more normal world."

REVIEW: *N Y Times Book Rev* p1-18 Ja 5 2014 Andrew Sean Greer

"On Such a Full Sea." "Watching a talented writer take a risk is one of the pleasures of devoted reading, and 'On Such a Full Sea' provides all that and more. It's a wonderful addition not only to Chang-rae Lee's body of work but to the ranks of 'serious' writers venturing into the realm of dystopian fantasy. . . . 'On Such a Full Sea' takes place in an almost familiar world, one whose cities were long ago rendered unlivable by polluted air and water, forcing whole societies to relocate. . . . With 'On Such a Full Sea,' [Lee] has found a new way to explore his old preoccupation: the oft-told tale of the desperate, betraying, lonely human heart."

REVIEW: *N Y Times Book Rev* p22 Ja 12 2014

REVIEW: *New York Times* v163 no56381 pC1-6 Ja 14 2014 MICHIKO KAKUTANI

"On Such a Full Sea." "Chang-rae Lee's new novel is part folk tale, part picaresque adventure, part dystopian satire. It signals a bold departure from both the carefully observed realism that distinguished Mr. Lee's powerful earlier books. . . . In eschewing one of his most potent gifts as a writer—his ability to map the inner lives of his characters with sympathy and precision—Mr. Lee has produced an ungainly and strangely inert novel. . . . 'On Such a Full Sea' often reads like a ham-handed mash-up of Aldous Huxley's 'Brave New World' and Suzanne Collins's 'The Hunger Games.' . . . Windy philosophical musings lend this novel a decidedly lugubrious tone and hobble the story."

REVIEW: *Publ Wkly* v260 no50 p2 D 9 2013

REVIEW: *Va Q Rev* v90 no2 p227-30 Spr 2014 Jiayang Fan

LEE, H. CHUKU. Beauty and the beast; a retelling; 32 p. 2014 Harper, an imprint of HarperCollinsPublishers

1. Africa, West—Fiction 2. Fairy tales 3. Folklore—France 4. Magic—Fiction 5. Picture books for children
ISBN 0688148190; 9780688148195 (hardcover bdg.)
LC 2013-021852

SUMMARY: This book, by H. Chuku Lee and illustrated by Pat Cummings, is a retelling of the Beauty and the Beast fairy tale. The book creates a "fairy-tale world flavored by the art, architecture, and culture of West Africa. . . . When her father is taken prisoner by a fearsome Beast, Beauty begs the captor to take her instead. . . . Though he will give her whatever her heart desires . . . she is forbidden to leave. Over time, however, Beauty sees the gentler side of the Beast, and an unexpected bond forms." (Publisher's note)

REVIEW: *Booklist* v110 no12 p83 F 15 2014 Amina Chaudhri

REVIEW: *Horn Book Magazine* v90 no1 p104 Ja/F 2014 ROGER SUTTON

"Beauty and the Beast." "Giving [Pat] Cummings's lushly detailed paintings center stage, [H. Chuku] Lee . . . simplifies Madame de Villeneuve's fairy tale and puts it into Beauty's first-person voice, a choice that accords well with the intense close-up perspectives of the pictures. . . . princess-crazed children of all colors should enjoy the lavish outfits and hairstyles of Beauty and her three older sisters (one more sister than the original provides, and nicer girls at that). . . . The retelling is crisp, the drafting is skillful, and the compositions are dramatic; while purists might sniff at the anachronistic setting, it's really not so much Africa as it is fairyland."

REVIEW: *Kirkus Rev* v81 no24 p96 D 15 2013

REVIEW: *Publ Wkly* v260 no49 p82 D 2 2013

REVIEW: *SLJ* v60 no1 p115 Ja 2014 Susan Scheps

LEE, HERMIONE. Penelope Fitzgerald; a life; [by] Hermione Lee xix, 508 p. 2013 Chatto & Windus

1. Authors—Biography 2. English authors—Family relationships 3. English women authors 4. European literature—20th century—History & criticism 5. Fitzgerald, Penelope, 1916-2000 6. Novelists, English—20th century—Biography 7. Women novelists, English—20th century—Biography
ISBN 0385352344; 0701184957 (hbk.); 9780385352345; 9780701184957 (hbk.)
LC 2013-487362

SUMMARY: This biography of writer Penelope Fitzgerald, by Hermione Lee, examines her life "from her childhood in a bookish Hampstead household, through . . . her years as a dazzling student at Oxford University. During the second world war she worked at the Ministry of Food, did a stint at the BBC and met a dashing young Irish army officer. . . . After their marriage came three children, a series of homes . . . years of teaching, thwarted ambitions and financial travails." (Economist)

REVIEW: *Economist* v409 no8860 p91 N 2 2013

"Penelope Fitzgerald: A Life". "A few years after Fitzgerald died in 2000, Ms. [Hermione] Lee was approached by the novelist's daughter to write her mother's biography. The result, even at 508 pages, is a little more than half the length of the Virginia Woolf book, but is just as adroitly executed and meticulously researched. . . . Ms. Lee, a notable critic, devotes whole chapters to Fitzgerald's works in which she expertly evaluates each book. . . . Ms. Lee's shrewd examination makes this a riveting biography, and gloriously illuminates the separate talents of two distinguished ladies of letters."

REVIEW: *Kirkus Rev* v82 no20 p4 O 15 2014

REVIEW: *Libr J* v139 no17 p92 O 15 2014 Morris Hounion

REVIEW: *Libr J* v139 no10 p72 Je 1 2014 Barbara Hoffert

REVIEW: *London Rev Books* v35 no24 p3-8 D 19 2013 Jenny Turner

REVIEW: *New Statesman* v142 no5184 p51 N 15 2013 Neel Mukherjee

REVIEW: *Publ Wkly* v261 no19 p52 My 12 2014

REVIEW: *TLS* no5784 p3-4 F 7 2014 A. N. WILSON

"Penelope Fitzgerald: A Life." "Penelope Fitzgerald poses a number of insuperable problems for a biographer. . . . Hermione Lee is not to be blamed for failing to write a Penelope Fitzgerald-style biography. She has written, instead, a very readable and honest account of the incomprehensible facts. . . . Fitzgerald told us things without spelling them out. Lee is a mortal, and so she has to spell things out, in a way which does not always catch fire. . . . 'Penelope Fitzgerald: A Life' is the sort of tribute which is nowadays paid by publishers, by professors, by the literary world, when a considerable figure leaves us."

LEE, JASON. The psychology of screenwriting; theory and practice; [by] Jason Lee vi, 191 p. 2013 Bloomsbury Academic

1. Characters & characteristics in motion pictures—Psychology 2. Dialogue—Psychological aspects 3. Motion picture authorship 4. Motion picture authorship—Psychological aspects 5. Motion picture literature
ISBN 9781441104984 (hardcover: alk. paper); 9781441128478 (pbk.: alk. paper); 9781623562519 (e-pdf); 9781623564735 (e-pub)
LC 2013-004540

SUMMARY: This book on screenwriting by Jason Lee "combines in-depth critical and cultural analysis with an elaboration on practice. . . . It explores how people, such as those in the Dogme 95 movement, have tried to overcome traditional screenwriting, looking in detail at the psychology of writing and the practicalities of how to write well for the screen." (Publisher's note)

REVIEW: *Choice* v51 no8 p1406-7 Ap 2014 D. A. Schmitt

"The Psychology of Screenwriting: Theory and Practice". "[Jason] Lee . . . explores the philosophical roots of psychology as they pertain to screenwriting, interweaving schools and branches of psychology with references to hundreds of European (including British) and American films. Going beyond the screenplay, the author examines the mind of the screenwriter and then the minds of the director and others involved in creating the production. . . . His advice about the editing process is brief and to the point, and he includes several handy checklists. Each chapter has extensive endnotes, but the index includes principally people and only a handful of philosophical and psychological terms."

LEE, PATRICK. Runner; [by] Patrick Lee 336 p. 2014 Minotaur Books

1. Escapes—Fiction 2. Girls—Fiction 3. Prisoners—Fiction 4. Retired military personnel—Fiction 5. Special forces (Military science)—Fiction
ISBN 1250030730; 9781250030733 (hardback)
LC 2013-032586

SUMMARY: In this book, by Patrick Lee, "ex-soldier Sam Dryden is easing into a midnight run when a young girl darts from the shadows, fleeing a shadowy group of men following close behind. She's desperate but begs Sam to trust that she has a good reason not to go to the police. . . . Rachel's memory has been clouded by interrogation drugs, so she doesn't know exactly whom her pursuers are, but it's soon evident that their motives are connected to Rachel's powerful ability to read minds." (Booklist)

REVIEW: *Booklist* v110 no6 p24 N 15 2013 Christine Tran

"Runner". "Hunted by an enemy with seemingly infinite resources, including the world's most advanced satellite technology, [Sam] Dryden strategically employs skills from his past in covert ops, taking Rachel from forest hideout to high-speed chases to track down the tidbits emerging from her memory. But the game changes when Dryden discovers why Rachel is being hunted, and he'll have to weigh his feelings for her against national security. Thriller fans, especially those drawn to conspiracies and espionage, will enjoy the cutting-edge weapons development, the anxiety-ridden showdown between cunning and technology,and the compellingly connected characters."

REVIEW: *Booklist* v110 no17 p64 My 1 2014 Candace Smith

REVIEW: *Kirkus Rev* v81 no21 p199 N 1 2013

REVIEW: *Libr J* v138 no16 p66 O 1 2013 Michele Leber

REVIEW: *Publ Wkly* v260 no49 p61 D 2 2013

LEE, SHELLEY SANG-HEE. A new history of Asian America; [by] Shelley Sang-Hee Lee 365 p. 2013 Routledge

1. Asian Americans—Cultural assimilation 2. Asian Americans—History 3. Asian Americans—Politics and government 4. Historical literature
ISBN 9780415879538 (hardback); 9780415879545 (pbk.)
LC 2013-001775

SUMMARY: In this book, Shelley Sang-Hee Lee . . . attempts to bring together older and more recent literature to provide readers with an updated overview of Asian American history. The author also analyzes key events in the history of Asian Americans, with a particular emphasis upon interethnic tension and competition as well as economic, racial, and gender inequality in US society." (Choice: Current Reviews for Academic Libraries)

REVIEW: *Choice* v51 no6 p1076-7 F 2014 M. E. Pfeifer

"A New History of Asian America." "[Shelley Sang-Hee] Lee . . . attempts to bring together older and more recent literature to provide readers with an updated overview of Asian American history. While primarily intended for undergraduates, this work will prove useful for graduate students, researchers, and community members looking for a broad overview of Asian American history. In addition to Asian American studies, the work will be of likely interest to ethnic studies, history, and multicultural education classes. . . . Recommended."

LEECH, KITTY.il. The Dollies. See Leech, K.

LEECH, KITTY. The Dollies; Scenes from Shakespeare; 32 p. 2013 The Home Press

1. Doll clothes 2. Dolls 3. Juliet (Fictitious character) 4. Picture books for children 5. Shakespeare, William, 1564-1616—Characters
ISBN 0984913378; 9780984913374

SUMMARY: This book by Kitty Leech presents "tableaux of scenes from a variety of Shakespeare plays for the picture-book crowd. Each spread features a photograph of the actors—18-inch dolls—in richly detailed dress against luscious backgrounds on the right, with a quote from a play on the left." The book includes scenes from "Romeo and Juliet," "The Taming of the Shrew," "The Tempest," and "Macbeth". (Kirkus Reviews)

REVIEW: *Kirkus Rev* v82 no3 p128 F 1 2014

"The Dollies: Scenes From Shakespeare". "Costume designer [Kitty] Leech . . . has created engaging tableaux of scenes from a variety of Shakespeare plays for the picture-book crowd. Each spread features a photograph of the actors—18-inch dolls—in richly detailed dress against luscious backgrounds on the right, with a quote from a play on the left. . . . While the picture-book age group is too young to appreciate the plots and meanings of Shakespeare's plays, this confection will give them a good taste of Shakespeare's world and the desire to explore it more fully when they are older. One of the few books about Shakespeare that children and adults can equally enjoy sharing."

LEEDER, KAREN.ed. Durs Grünbein. See Durs Grünbein

LEES, ANDREW. The hurricane port; a social history of Liverpool; [by] Andrew Lees 295 p. 2011 Mainstream Publishing

1. England—Description & travel 2. Historical literature 3. Liverpool (England)—Social conditions
ISBN 1845967267; 9781845967260
LC 2011-508309

SUMMARY: This book by Andrew Lees presents a "peregrination through Liverpool and its history. . . . He begins the story with sugar and colonial trade in the seventeenth century, tracking the city's fortunes to the present day. In the process, the book distils a history of the slave trade, migration and the development of the port, establishing Liverpool's peculiar character via familiar themes: football, sectarianism, music, dialect, violence, dockers and the Militant tendency." (Times Literary Supplement)

REVIEW: *TLS* no5748 p26 My 31 2013 CLARE GRIFFITHS

"Liverpool: The Hurricane Port." "Andrew Lee's melancholic peregrination through Liverpool and its history was first published in 2011; this paperback edition, 'Liverpool: The hurricane port,' comes with a new foreword, reflecting on how the Hillsborough enquiry may mark a shift in the city's reputation . . . and on the dilemmas posed by cultural regeneration. . . . Adopting a poetic tone, the approach is heavily allusive, with hints at connections to the author's own biography. . . . Anecdotes occur without warning and with little explanation, often proving rather baffling to the reader. The book starts to come alive when Lees sets off on journeys of exploration, walking the city's streets to find ghosts of the past in the contemporary landscape."

LEES, GRAHAM V. The future of drug discovery. See Bartfai, T.

LEFT HEMISPHERE; mapping critical theory today; 264 p. 2013 Verso

1. Critical theory 2. Philosophical literature 3. Postmodernism 4. Right and left (Political science)—History—20th century 5. Right and left (Political science)—History—21st century
ISBN 1781681023; 9781781681022 (alk. paper)
LC 2013-013995

SUMMARY: This book, by Razmig Keucheyan, "offers the first global cartography of the expanding intellectual field of critical contemporary thought. More than thirty authors and intellectual currents of every continent are presented. . . . A history of critical thought in the twentieth and twenty-first centuries is also provided, helping situate current thinkers in a broader historical and sociological perspective." (Publisher's note)

REVIEW: *Choice* v51 no8 p1489-90 Ap 2014 H. G. Reid

"Left Hemisphere: Mapping Critical Theory Today". "This is a challenging and important study both for its sweep of coverage and its depth of analytic inquiry. The book will advance the understanding of 'the new critical theories' it takes up. . . . At the same time, these impressive accomplishments ate qualified by certain paradoxical omissions. . . . The penultimate chapter may leave some readers wondering how much recent theory is caught in a 'postmodern depthlessness.' . . . Perhaps the 'the defeat of critical thinking' did not end in 1993 as [Razmig] Keucheyan . . . suggests."

LEGACIES OF THE WAR ON POVERTY; 309 p. 2013 Russell Sage Foundation

1. Domestic economic assistance—United States 2. Political science literature 3. Poverty—Government policy—United States 4. Public welfare—United States
ISBN 9780871540072 (pbk.: alk. paper); 9781610448147 (ebook)
LC 2013-009876

SUMMARY: It was the authors' intent to demonstrate "that poverty and racial discrimination would likely have been much greater today if the War on Poverty had not been launched. . . . The volume . . . examines the significant consequences of income support, housing, and health care programs." Topics discussed include the Head Start education program, Title I legislation, and Medicaid. (Publisher's note)

REVIEW: *Choice* v51 no8 p1456-7 Ap 2014 C. Apt

"Legacies of the War on Poverty". "Editors [Martha J.] Bailey and [Sheldon] Danziger . . . have compiled a comprehensive analysis of what the War on Poverty was and was not by analyzing such key components as Head Start, Title I . . . and the Older Americans Act of 1965. . . .The volume includes a section on the economic background that led to Johnson's War on Poverty as well as analyses from individuals of different disciplines as to why some of his programs worked and some did not. The existing economic and social legacies of Johnson's policies are discussed and debated by scholars from several perspectives in this interesting volume."

LEGERSTEE, MARIA.ed. The infant mind. See The infant mind

LEGRAND, CLAIRE. The year of shadows; 416 p. 2013 Simon & Schuster Books for Young Readers

1. Conductors (Musicians) 2. Family problems—Fiction 3. Fathers and daughters—Fiction 4. Ghost stories 5. Ghosts—Fiction 6. Haunted places—Fiction 7. Orchestra—Fiction
ISBN 9781442442948 (hardcover)
LC 2012-034667

SUMMARY: In this book, by Claire Legrand, illustrated by Karl Kwasny, "Olivia Stellatella is having a rough year. Her mother's left, her neglectful father--the maestro of a failing orchestra--has moved her and her grandmother into the city's dark, broken-down concert hall to save money, and her only friend is Igor, an ornery stray cat. Just when she thinks life couldn't get any weirder, she meets four ghosts who haunt the hall." (Publisher's note)

REVIEW: *Booklist* v110 no3 p92 O 1 2013 Sarah Hunter

REVIEW: *Bull Cent Child Books* v67 no2 p101-2 O 2013 K. Q. G.

"The Year of Shadows." "Nine months after her mother took off for parts unknown, Olivia Stellatella is forced to move into the back of a rundown music hall so her broody, cash-strapped father--whom Olivia refers to as Maestro--can continue to conduct the orchestra and make what little money the family has stretch further. . . . The blend of spooky but mostly harmless thrills, and family drama makes for a compelling storyline, and Olivia's grief over her mother's departure and her subsequent anger at her father are both realistic and relatable. Olivia is likable even at her snarkiest, and the ways in which she comes to care for the ghosts and even a few living people are sometimes touching."

REVIEW: *Kirkus Rev* v81 no2 p92 Je 1 2013

LEHMAN, DAVID, 1948-. New and selected poems; [by] David Lehman 320 p. 2013 Scribner Poetry

1. American Jews 2. American poetry 3. Humorous poetry 4. Poems—Collections 5. Poetry (Literary form)—Translations
ISBN 147673187X; 9781476731872 (pbk.)
LC 2013-031847

SUMMARY: This book presents new and selected poetry from David Lehman. "A gathering of . . . new poems, prose poems, and translations from modern French masters ushers in the book. Selections from each of Lehman's seven full-length books of poetry follow and are capped off by a coda of important early and previously uncollected works." (Publishers Weekly)

REVIEW: *Booklist* v110 no6 p9 N 15 2013 Ray Olson

"New and Selected Poems." "The presiding editor of The Best American Poetry heavily seasons his own work with . . . poetry. His lines echo others from [William] Blake, [John] Donne, [Robert] Frost . . . and many others, usually not in poems that cite them by name and never to flout his knowledge. He's formally various, essaying the sonnet, the villanelle, the sestina, and many less demanding forms, though he tweaks each a bit. Perhaps his happiest bouts of allusiveness are in his journals in poetry. . . . [David] Lehman's no reactionary, though, but thoroughly modernist. His matter is personal, his language common, and his manner surrealist. But the fact that he's so heavily steeped in poetry makes him a poetry lover's poet supreme."

REVIEW: *Publ Wkly* v260 no38 p54 S 23 2013

LEHMANN BENCH, ALEYA. Appraising art; the definitive guide to appraising the fine and decorative arts; 2013 Appraisers Association of America, Inc.

1. Art—Conservation & restoration 2. Art—Expertising 3. Art—Sales & prices 4. Art appraisal 5. Art literature
ISBN 9780965505321 (hardcover : alk. paper); 9780965505338 (softcover : alk. paper), 9780965505345 (e-bk.)
LC 2013-944926

SUMMARY: This book presents a "guide to appraising fine and decorative art, antiques and collectibles--from connoisseurship and appraisal methodology to legal considerations and beyond." Topics include "everything from American Paintings and Drawings to Baseball Memorabilia, plus Appraising Works of art for Tax Purposes, Resolving Art Disputes, and a Guide to Appraisal Contracts, as well as Conservation Issues, Title Insurance, and more." (Publisher's note)

REVIEW: *Choice* v51 no6 p974 F 2014 J. M. Nowakowski

"Appraising Art: The Definitive Guide to Appraising the Fine and Decorative Arts." "One striking thing about this book is that it is--not surprisingly, given the subject matter--remarkably attractive. The design is reassuring to anyone who might have misgivings about the content. Once opened, the text does not disappoint. From the reproductions included to illustrate topics, or perhaps just to entertain, to the broad coverage of appraisals of a wide variety of artistic forms, this book is sure to be worthwhile for professionals or those inclined to become professional appraisers. Plenty of the material will interest lay readers as well, but the target audience likely will be those involved in appraisals as practitioners or clients."

LEHRER, ERICA T. Jewish Poland revisited; heritage tourism in unquiet places; [by] Erica T. Lehrer xvi, 274 p. 2013 Indiana University Press

1. Collective memory—Poland 2. Holocaust memorial tours—Poland 3. Jewish diaspora 4. Jews—History 5. Jews—Poland—History—21st century 6. Social science literature
ISBN 0253008808 (hardback); 0253008867 (paperback); 9780253008800 (hardback); 9780253008862 (paperback)
LC 2012-474502

SUMMARY: In this book, " Erica T. Lehrer explores the intersection of Polish and Jewish memory projects in the historically Jewish neighborhood of Kazimierz in Krakow. Her own journey becomes part of the story as she demonstrates that Jews and Poles use spaces, institutions, interpersonal exchanges, and cultural representations to make sense of their historical inheritances." (Publisher's note)

REVIEW: *Choice* v51 no5 p898 Ja 2014 R. K. Byczkiewicz

"Jewish Poland Revisited: Heritage Tourism in Unquiet Places." "With the few remaining Polish Jews whose backgrounds were ignored or hidden since the Holocaust, [Erica T.] Lehrer explores the challenges that those who have only recently rediscovered their 'Jewishness' face. The author also discusses the controversies sparked by segregated Jewish mission tours, but voices hope in the individual avenues that she sees helping to break down mutually held stereotypes. Passionate and sensitive to the varieties of 'Jewishness' and the role of the Shabbas goyim, Lehrer offers a fresh and delightful portrait of Jewish renewal in Poland."

LEHRER, JIM, 1934-. Top down; a novel; [by] Jim Lehrer 208 p. 2013 Random House

1. Historical literature 2. Journalists—United States—Fiction 3. Secret service

ISBN 1400069165; 9781400069163 (alk. paper)

LC 2013-007984

SUMMARY: In this book, "five years after [John F.] Kennedy's death, reporter Jack Gilmore is approached by Marti Walters, the daughter of former Secret Service Agent Van Walters, the man responsible for assessing the weather and making the decision on whether to keep the presidential limo's plastic bubble top up or down on that fateful day. Plagued by guilt and suffering from debilitating post-traumatic stress syndrome. Van is physically and psychologically on his last legs." (Booklist)

REVIEW: *Booklist* v110 no2 p41 S 15 2013 Margaret Flanagan

"Top Down." "[Jim] Lehrer has crafted a uniquely focused novel about the assassination of John F. Kennedy and the ripple effect it had on both individuals and the nation as a whole. Utilizing his firsthand knowledge and experience--he was actually a reporter in Dallas on November 22, 1963--the author shifts away from the big-picture event in order to zero in on two seemingly minor players in the national tragedy. Five years after Kennedy's death, reporter Jack Gilmore is approached by Marti Walters, the daughter of former Secret Service Agent Van Walters, the man responsible for assessing the weather and making the decision on whether to keep the presidential limo's plastic bubble top up or down on that fateful day."

REVIEW: *Kirkus Rev* v81 no17 p16 S 1 2013

REVIEW: *Kirkus Rev* p11 Ag 15 2013 Fall Preview

REVIEW: *Kirkus Rev* v81 no17 p60 S 1 2013 Ian Floyd

REVIEW: *Publ Wkly* v260 no33 p40-1 Ag 19 2013

LEHRMAN, LEWIS E. Money, gold and history; [by] Lewis E. Lehrman ix, 251 p. 2013 The Lehrman Institute

1. Gold standard 2. Historical literature 3. Inflation (Finance)—United States 4. Monetary policy—United States 5. Money—History

ISBN 9780984017836

LC 2013-375213

SUMMARY: In this book, Lewis E. Lehrman "argues that not only is the gold standard the best way to maintain monetary stability, but it was pivotal to the formation of modern civilization. He argues that the British and American industrial revolution could not have happened without it. Its widespread adoption, he holds, was crucial to the first wave of globalization in the latter half of the 19th century." (National Review)

REVIEW: *Natl Rev* v66 no2 p39-41 F 10 2014 DAVID BECKWORTH

"Money, Gold, and History". "Is an international gold standard the correct path to improved monetary stability and increased global economic growth? I wish I could say yes and share [Lewis E.] Lehrman's certainty. The reason I cannot is that the history of the gold standard, the reason it worked, and the world we live in all seem far more complicated to me than their portrayal in Money, Gold, and History. . . . Though Lehrman claims that the gold standard is 'the historic common currency of civilization' and the 'proven guarantor of one hundred years of price stability,' the history of gold is much more nuanced."

LEIBERMAN, JON. Whitey on Trial. See McLean, M.

LEIBOVICH, MARK. This town; two parties and a funeral--plus, plenty of valet parking!--in America's gilded capital; [by] Mark Leibovich 386 p. 2013 Blue Rider Press

1. POLITICAL SCIENCE—Government—National 2. Political culture—Washington (D.C.) 3. Political science literature 4. Politicians—United States

ISBN 0399161309; 9780399161308 (hardback); 9780399170683 (paperback)

LC 2013-009796

SUMMARY: This book, by Mark Leibovich, presents an "account of the uncomfortably cozy relationship between the Washington press corps and the politicians they cover--along with all the spokespeople, lobbyists, cocktail-party hosts, unelected power brokers, and logrollers in between. . . . Leibovich profiles, among others, former U.S. Senator Christopher Dodd . . . [and] lawyer-agent Bob Barnett." (Booklist)

REVIEW: *America* v210 no6 p35-6 F 24 2014 JOHN P. McCARTHY

"This Town: Two Parties and a Funeral—Plus Plenty of Valet Parking!—in America's Gilded Capital". "[Mark] Leibovich, chief national correspondent for The New York Times Magazine and a former Washington Post reporter, admits to being ensconced in the old-media wing of The Club. He is acutely aware that 'This Town' exemplifies several of the phenomena it describes. The book is a piece of meta-journalism, by which he hopes to raise his own profile and profit financially. He meticulously reveals his connections to the individuals and institutions under scrutiny. Along with demonstrating how incestuous Washington is, these disclaimers are disarming—but only up to a point. They don't guarantee he's telling the whole story."

REVIEW: *Bookforum* v20 no3 p12 S-N 2013 JIM NEWELL

"This Town: Two Parties and a Funeral--Plus Plenty of Valet Parking!--In America's Gilded Capital." "A puckish satire of the Washington political class's steady retreat into its own gilded navel. . . . [Mark] Leibovich is a talented writer, and he resists the trap that more insecure, bloviating political writers . . . might fall into: affirmatively spoon-feeding their own political judgments to readers at all turns. Leibovich just documents what he sees, and whom he talks to, wittily mimicking the so-what tone that these glib, dismal samples of humanity use to describe their controversial waking lives."

REVIEW: *Booklist* v110 no5 p40 N 1 2013 Alan Moores

REVIEW: *Economist* v408 no8850 p73 Ag 24 2013

"This Town: Two Parties and a Funeral--Plus, Plenty of Valet Parking!--in America's Gilded Capital." "'This Town' may be the most pitiless examination of America's permanent political class . . . that has ever been conducted. With a wry touch, Mark Leibovich . . . chronicles the tawdry work of Washington's insiders and aspiring insiders. He refrains from presenting big thoughts about what is wrong with American politics and how it might be fixed. But it is impossible to read this book without concluding that something must be done. . . . Mr. Leibovich observes Washington's failings brilliantly. . . . But it is nevertheless impossible to finish this book without feeling a bit cheated. 'This Town' is more a symptom of the problems that it describes than a cure."

REVIEW: *Kirkus Rev* v81 no16 p283 Ag 15 2013

REVIEW: *N Y Rev Books* v60 no14 p30-2 S 26 2013 Michael Tomasky

REVIEW: *New Repub* v244 no15 p41-5 S 16 2013 Nicholas Lemann

REVIEW: *New York Times* v162 no56191 pC1-4 Jl 8 2013 DAVID M. SHRIBMAN

REVIEW: *New Yorker* v89 no21 p75 Jl 22 2013

LEIBOVITZ, LIEL. A Broken Hallelujah; Rock 'n' Roll, Redemption, and the Life of Leonard Cohen; [by] Liel Leibovitz 256 p. 2014 W W Norton & Co Inc

1. Cohen, Leonard 2. Composers—Canada—Biography 3. Folk music—History & criticism 4. Music literature 5. Redemption 6. Singers—Biography 7. Singers—Canada—Biography
ISBN 0393082059; 9780393082050
LC 2013-047874

SUMMARY: In this book on Leonard Cohen, author Liel Leibovitz "examines the musician's life and work through the angles of Jewish eschatology, Zen Buddhism, Canadian poetry, and American rock and toll, as well as 'lust and lucre.' . . . He explores the evolution of Cohen's public persona as the Poet, and states that the one theme that has consistently preoccupied Cohen is redemption, which he describes as 'a discretely Jewish affair.'" (Booklist)

REVIEW: *Bookforum* v21 no2 p55 Je-Ag 2014 RHETT MILLER

REVIEW: *Booklist* v110 no14 p40 Mr 15 2014 June Sawyers

"A Broken Hallelujah: Rock and Roll, Redemption, and the Life of Leonard Cohen" and "Leonard Cohen on Leonard Cohen: Interviews and Encounters". "[Liel] Leibovitz a thoughtful examination of the music of Leonard Cohen . . . through a strong Jewish perspective. . . . Yes, there are biographical details here, but 'A Broken Hallelujah' offers something else: a finely etched musical portrait of a complicated man . . . and the often exquisite music that he has created over many decades. . . . Leibovitz himself has a distinctive voice and approach to Cohen's work. . . . A sparkling and psychologically insightful perspective on a unique artist. . . . Many of these pieces have not previously appeared in print. Cohen is endlessly quotable and endlessly entertaining, and there is great joy in reading his words."

REVIEW: *Kirkus Rev* v82 no6 p38 Mr 15 2014

REVIEW: *Libr J* v138 no18 p68 N 1 2013 Barbara Hoffert

REVIEW: *Publ Wkly* v261 no4 p92-6 Ja 27 2014

LEIGHTON, M. Down to you; [by] M. Leighton 291 p. 2012 Berkley Books

1. Brothers—Fiction 2. Business enterprises—Fiction 3. Love stories 4. Triangles (Interpersonal relations)—Fiction 5. Twins—Fiction
ISBN 9780425269848 (alk. paper)
LC 2013-007805

SUMMARY: In this book, "when college student Olivia Townsend returned home to help her father run his business, she never imagined a complication like Cash and Nash Davenport--twin brothers different in so many ways but with one thing in common: an uncontrollable desire for Olivia. . . . However, Olivia is in for a surprise. These boys have a secret that should make her run away as far and as fast as she can. If only it wasn't too late." (Publisher's note)

REVIEW: *Booklist* v110 no2 p46 S 15 2013 John Charles

"Beautiful Disaster," "Down to You," and "Easy." "Big-man-on-campus Travis Maddox bets campus good-girl Abby Abernathy that he can abstain from sex for 30 days. If Travis wins, Abby must live with him for a month. Often cited as one of the books that kick-started the NA romance genre. 'Beautiful Disaster' is followed by 'Walking Disaster'. . . . Olivia Townsend returns home from college to help run the family business only to become caught up in a love triangle with twin brothers Cash and Nash Davenport. [M.] Leighton delivers sexy soap-opera- style plot twists in the first installment of her sizzling Bad Boys series. . . . When an overly aggressive frat boy won't take no for an answer, Lucas saves Jackie's life in more ways than one. Before being picked up by Berkley, [Tammara] Webber's debut sold more than 150,000 copies as a self-published e-book and spent nine weeks on the New York Times best-seller list."

LEIGHTON, ROBERT.il. Bugged. See Albee, S.

LEINHARDT, ZOE.ed. Beauty. See Beauty

LEIRIS, MICHEL, 1901-1990. Aurora / Cardinal Point; [by] Michel Leiris 176 p. 2014 Atlas Press

1. French fiction—20th century 2. French fiction—Translations into English 3. Novellas (Literary form) 4. Surrealism (Literature) 5. Young women—Fiction
ISBN 1900565463; 9781900565462

SUMMARY: Translated by Anna Warby, "This volume collects two classics of Surrealist fiction, both long out of print, by the writer and ethnographer Michel Leiris (1901-1990). . . . In 'Aurora,' Leiris pursues his eponymous heroine through a visionary landscape shot through with catastrophe. . . . 'Cardinal Point' is Leiris' first prose work. Written in 1925 . . . it employs 'automatic writing' to excavate the hidden meanings of ordinary words." (Publisher's note)

REVIEW: *TLS* no5795 p27 Ap 25 2014 LAUREN ELKIN

"'Aurora' and 'Cardinal Point'." "Written in 1927-8, when Leiris was twenty-six, but only published in 1946, Aurora is the story of an 'un-repression.' . . . The novella is essentially a philosophical investigation in the form of a pseudo-autobiography-cum-travelogue. The chief question is: what can we ever know of ourselves? . . . The short novella 'Cardinal Point' (1921) is a similarly oneiric traveller's tale. The strange power of these stories carries the hint of work to come from Georges Perec and Angela Carter."

LEITCH, MAURICE. Seeking Mr Hare; [by] Maurice Leitch 312 p. 2013 The Clerkenwell Press

1. Adventure stories 2. Fugitives from justice—Fiction 3. Hare, William 4. Ireland—Fiction 5. Serial murderers—Fiction
ISBN 1846689376; 9781846689376

SUMMARY: This book by Maurice Leitch follows a former serial killer on the run. "Making his way on foot through the English countryside, obtaining a passage to Ireland, he undergoes many adventures and narrow squeaks. Early in his Odyssey, he meets a mute farm girl called Hannah, who sticks to him like a burr. And hard on his heels is an ex-Bow Street Runner, Mr Speed, whose account of the ensuing events alternates with Hare's." (Times Literary Supplement)

REVIEW: *TLS* no5765 p19 S 27 2013 PATRICIA CRAIG

"The Spinning Heart," "Arimathea," and "Seeking Mr. Hare." "A cacophony of aggrieved and outspoken voices, male and female, moves the narrative forwards, bit by bit. . . .The book's succession of monologues is orchestrated by the author with cunning and authenticity. . . . The strength of this first novel lies in its insights into the rougher aspects of the Irish psyche. . . . Like 'The Spinning Heart,' Frank McGuinness's debut novel 'Arimathea' is made up of monologues. As an acclaimed playwright, McGuinness has the form at his fingertips, and he gives us a series of adept impersonations. . . . An engaging contribution to the pursuit-cum-picaresque genre is Maurice Leitch's 'Seeking Mr Hare'."

LELIC, SIMON. The child who; a novel; [by] Simon Lelic 303 p. 2012 Penguin Books

1. Children—Crimes against—Fiction 2. FICTION—Literary 3. FICTION—Suspense 4. Juvenile delinquents—Fiction 5. Legal stories 6. Missing persons—Fiction
ISBN 0143120913 (pbk.); 9780143120919 (pbk.)
LC 2011-045210

SUMMARY: In this book, "Felicity was a bright, bouncy, much-liked preteen. Adults doted on her, schoolmates clustered around her, and her future seemed unlimited--until Daniel Blake, barely a year older, assaulted her, tortured her, bound her hands with wire and left her to drown. County solicitor Leo Curtice happens to answer the phone call requesting representation for Daniel. From the moment he agrees, his life spirals out of control. . . . Leo needs to understand why Daniel became Daniel. The boy has nothing to say. . . . But Leo keeps asking why: why did this happen, what's in Daniel's past? When menacing letters arrive threatening Leo's family, he downplays the danger. . . . Then Leo's daughter goes missing, and he and his wife suffer the anguish of Felicity's family." (Kirkus)

REVIEW: *Kirkus Rev* v80 no4 p351 F 15 2012

"The Child Who." " Who deserves your sympathy most: the 11-year-old victim, the 12-year-old who killed her or the lawyer handling the case? . . . Then Leo's daughter goes missing, and he and his wife suffer the anguish of Felicity's family. Did the letter writer abduct her? No one can be sure. His marriage disintegrates. Should he have abandoned Daniel and protected his family? It will take 10 years and even more tragedy before he gets answers to any of these questions. Jarring, disturbing and not for the emotionally squeamish. [Simon] Lelic ('A Thousand Cuts,' 2010, etc.) faces thorny issues of guilt and responsibility head on, and no one comes out unscathed."

REVIEW: *Publ Wkly* v259 no2 p32 Ja 9 2012

LEMASTER, MICHELLE.ed. Creating and contesting Carolina. See Creating and contesting Carolina

LEMON, ALEX. The Wish Book; Poems; [by] Alex Lemon 113 p. 2014 Milkweed Editions

1. American poetry 2. Fatherhood 3. Grief 4. Mortality 5. Poems—Collections
ISBN 9781571314505 (pbk. : acid-free paper)
LC 2013-026960

SUMMARY: In this poetry collection, "whether in unrestrained descriptions of sensory overload or tender meditations on fatherhood and mortality, [Alex] Lemon blurs that nebulous line between the personal and the pop-cultural." Images in his poems include "jigsaws and bathtubs and kung-fu and X-rays." (Publisher's note)

REVIEW: *Booklist* v110 no9/10 p36-7 Ja 1 2014 Diego Bdez

"The Wish Book." "[Alex] Lemon shines in his new collection, composed of tightly coiled, fast-paced lines and persistently unexpected images. . . . In freewheeling sequences of seeming non sequiturs, Lemon blends the energy of a carnival barker with the precise prosody of a master craftsman, creating a literary Tilt-a-Whirl of touch-and-go emotions. . . . A wordsmith of invented verbs and odd adjectives . . . Lemon proves a unique and lively vocalist. . . . Lemon has been likened to Lucia Perillo, Ariana Reines, and Laura Kasischke."

REVIEW: *Libr J* v139 no7 p90-1 Ap 15 2014 Chris Pusateri

LENNON, J. MICHAEL. Norman Mailer; a double life; [by] J. Michael Lennon 928 p. 2013 Simon & Schuster

1. American authors—20th century—Family relationships 2. Authors—Biography 3. Authors, American—20th century—Biography 4. Journalists—United States—Biography 5. Mailer, Norman, 1923-2007
ISBN 1439150192; 9781439150191
LC 2013-005097

SUMMARY: In this biography of Norman Mailer, author J. Michael Lennon depicts his subject "as a dual-natured personality: a passive observer and an activist, a family man and a philanderer,. . . . While Lennon treats readers to accounts of Mailer's celebrity and his relations with stars such as Muhammad Ali . . . he also explores the writer's seamier side, including his stabbing of Adele Morales, his second wife, and his support of Jack Abbott, who committed murder after being paroled." (Library Journal)

REVIEW: *America* v210 no14 p34-7 Ap 21 2014 EUGENE C. KENNEDY

REVIEW: *Bookforum* v20 no4 p36-7 D 2013/Ja 2014 CHRISTIAN LORENTZEN

"Norman Mailer: A Double Life" and "Mind of an Outlaw: Selected Essays." "'The White Negro' . . . is the core of . . . a new selection of essays edited by Phillip Sipiora. . . . There are about a dozen major essays among the many 'more obscure gems' chosen by Sipiora. Not to knock the 'gems'. . . but a selection that stuck to the major pieces might have served Mailer better. . . . J. Michael] Lennon gives detailed, if apologetic, accounts of the three great crises in Mailer's life: his stabbing of his second wife, Adele, in November 1960; tbe 1981 murder committed by Jack Henry Abbott, after Mailer bad petitioned for Abbott's release from prison; and the revelation of his rampant infidelity to his last wife, Norris Church, in the early 1990s. The stabbing, in Lennon's account, was the result not only of drunkenness but of temporary mental illness."

REVIEW: *Booklist* v110 no4 p10-1 O 15 2013 Brad Hooper

"Norman Mailer: A Double Life." "Any writer of a serious biography of Mailer who hopes to contain the excesses of the man within the covers of a book must know that since Mailer in his own lifetime grated on people's taste and nerves, he could easily grate on the reader, even when presented within the pages of a biography. [J. Michael] Lennon . . . performs a great task, letting Mailer's obnoxiousness have free rein in balance with the biographer's easygoing narrative style, which coaxes the reader into accepting and even enjoying all sides of Mailer. . . . Understanding Mailer is only half the object of this welcome biography; its other intention is for readers to be enticed into reading or rereading Mailer's works."

REVIEW: *Choice* v51 no9 p1593 My 2014 A. M. Bain

REVIEW: *Kirkus Rev* p27 Ag 15 2013 Fall Preview

REVIEW: *Kirkus Rev* v81 no16 p159 Ag 15 2013

"Norman Mailer: A Double Life." "Norman Mailer (1923-2007), writes archivist and authorized biographer Lennon, grew up in a reasonably happy family, with a strong mother and dapper father, who, as Mailer wrote, 'had the gift of speaking to each woman as if she was the most important woman he'd ever spoken to.' . . . Lennon ably reveals the always-contentious Mailer but also a man who could be generous and very smart. Lennon is also a shrewd literary critic, commenting on the origins and fortunes of Mailer's works, notably his study of Marilyn Monroe, which laid bare 'his narcissism, born of early spectacular success.'"

REVIEW: *Libr J* v138 no18 p88 N 1 2013 William Gargan

REVIEW: *Libr J* v138 no9 p55 My 15 2013 Barbara Hoffert

REVIEW: *London Rev Books* v35 no21 p3-7 N 7 2013 Andrew O'Hagan

REVIEW: *N Y Rev Books* v60 no18 p22-5 N 21 2013 Edward Mendelson

"Norman Mailer: A Double Life" and "Mind of an Outlaw: Selected Essays." "J. Michael Lennon's biography is the first that interprets Mailer from within, not as a public spectacle. . . . He shepherds a prodigious variety of events into well-organized chapters, sometimes cluttered with irrelevant details. . . . Lennon is the also first biographer to see that Mailer's prolific thoughts about gods, devils, and divine forces were at the heart of his work. . . . He wrote about books and films with an unforced enthusiasm unlike anything else in his work. The selected essays in 'Mind of an Outlaw' include splendid examples such as his joyful bumper-car collisions with rival novelists in 'Quick Evaluations on the Talent in the Room'."

REVIEW: *N Y Times Book Rev* p1-19 O 20 2013 Graydon Carter

"Norman Mailer: A Double Life." J. Michael Lennon's sweeping full-scale biography . . . is a mighty undertaking befitting Mailer's lifetime of protean output. . . . Lennon is a fluid writer, and he's done his homework. There's not a paragraph in this enormous book that doesn't contain a nugget of something you should have known or wish you had known. Lennon has it all, and he has it down. And despite being his subject's literary executor, he has not sanded the corners of a career and life, each of which has plenty of texture and lots of sharp edges."

REVIEW: *New Statesman* v142 no5183 p46-7 N 8 2013 Daniel Swift

REVIEW: *New York Times* v163 no56330 p8 N 24 2013 ALEX WILLIAMS

REVIEW: *Publ Wkly* v260 no31 p57 Ag 5 2013

REVIEW: *TLS* no5777/8 p5-7 D 20 2013 ELAINE SHOWALTER

LENZ, RICK. The Alexandrite; [by] Rick Lenz 243 p.

1. Actors—Fiction 2. Gemologists 3. Monroe, Marilyn, 1926-1962 4. Reincarnation—Fiction 5. Time travel—Fiction

ISBN 0984844244; 9780984844241

SUMMARY: This book "follows Jack Cade, a 40-year-old struggling actor who's inexplicably given a valuable alexandrite ring by an unknown benefactor. . . . Maggie Partridge, who claims to be a psychophysicist, contacts the down-and-out actor. . . . She believes that Cade used to be a man named Richard Blake, a gemologist who lived in the San Fernando Valley in the 1950s—and she has a way to send him back in time to prove it. " (Kirkus Reviews)

REVIEW: *Kirkus Rev* p37 D 15 2013 supplemet best books 2013

"The Alexandrite". "[Rick] Lenz's mesmerizing, multi-faceted debut novel is both an intriguing timetravel/past-life adventure and a subtle homage to Marilyn Monroe. . . . Along the way, this fascinating look at the underbelly of Hollywood offers an intriguing glimpse into Monroe's tragic life and death. . . . Like Monroe, the novel is impressively complex. Lenz—himself a veteran actor—cunningly blends time travel, LA noir, Hollywood glitz and self-discovery, making for a uniquely appealing read."

REVIEW: *Kirkus Rev* v81 no22 p89 N 15 2013

REVIEW: *Publ Wkly* v260 no51 p18 D 16 2013

LEO, MAXIM. Red Love; The Story of an East German Family; [by] Maxim Leo 272 p. 2014 Pushkin Press

1. Communism—Germany (East) 2. Families 3. Germany (East)—Politics & government 4. Germany (East)—Social conditions 5. Historical literature

ISBN 1908968516; 9781908968517

SUMMARY: "Growing up in East Berlin, [author] Maxim Leo knew not to ask questions. All he knew was that his rebellious parents, Wolf and Anne, with their dyed hair, leather jackets, and insistence he call them by their first names, were a bit embarrassing. . . . In 'Red Love' he captures, with warmth and unflinching honesty, why so many dreamed the German Democratic Republic would be a new world and why, in the end, it fell apart." (Publisher's note)

REVIEW: *Booklist* v110 no14 p45 Mr 15 2014 Brendan Driscoll

REVIEW: *Kirkus Rev* v82 no5 p142 Mr 1 2014

REVIEW: *London Rev Books* v36 no1 p23-4 Ja 9 2014 Neal Ascherson

"Red Love: The Story of an East German Family" and "The Jew Car". "These two excellent books show that passion and commitment were often present too: not just fanatical excitement, but the genuine subjective passion to contribute to the systems' goals, beneath the outer show of marching, chanting and resolution-signing demanded by the dictatorships. . . . 'To read The Jew Car' is to be reminded that the precondition for mass belief in Hitlerism was a degree of ignorance and credulity perhaps impossible today. . . . It's unlikely that everything happened just as he describes it, and there are some very large omissions. . . . But this is, even so, one of the most honest and revealing accounts of the long rearguard action conducted by blind faith in Fatherland and Führer against disenchantment. . . . 'Red Love' is a silly title for a serious, very moving book."

REVIEW: *New Statesman* v142 no5176 p84-5 S 20 2013

Marina Benjamin

REVIEW: *New York Times* v163 no56471 pC4 Ap 14 2014 WILLIAM GRIMES

REVIEW: *TLS* no5789 p9 Mr 14 2014 PETER GRAVES

LEO STRAUSS'S DEFENSE OF THE PHILOSOPHIC LIFE; reading "What is political philosophy?"; 222 p. 2013 University of Chicago Press

1. Philosophical literature 2. Political philosophy 3. Political science—Philosophy 4. Political science literature 5. Strauss, Leo, 1899-1973

ISBN 0226924203 (cloth : alkaline paper); 0226924211 (paperback : alkaline paper); 9780226924205 (cloth : alkaline paper); 9780226924212 (paperback : alkaline paper)

LC 2012-020623

SUMMARY: This book, edited by Rafael Major, "addresses almost every major theme in [Leo Strauss] life's work and is often viewed as a defense of his overall philosophic approach. Included are treatments of Strauss's esoteric method of reading, his critique of behavioral political science, and his views on classical political philosophy. Key thinkers whose work Strauss responded to are also analyzed in depth: Plato, Al-Farabi, Maimonides, Hobbes, and Locke." (Publisher's note)

REVIEW: *Choice* v51 no1 p161-2 S 2013 M. Harding

"Leo Strauss's Defense of the Philosophic Life: Reading 'What Is Political Philosophy.'" "[Editor Rafael] Major . . . has put together a fitting tribute to the thought of Leo Strauss. Leo Strauss's 'Defense of the Philosophic Life' brings together excellent essays by major scholars on each of the chapters of Strauss's book. Of the recent works on Strauss, this is among the best. It approaches Strauss's book as a coherent and deliberately ordered whole rather than a grab bag of essays, and it admirably displays the way in which the individual essays relate to each other and contribute to that whole."

LEON, DONNA. By Its Cover; A Commissario Guido Brunetti Mystery; [by] Donna Leon 288 p. 2014 Pgw

1. Detective & mystery stories 2. Libraries 3. Murder investigation—Fiction 4. Rare books 5. Venice (Italy)—Fiction

ISBN 0802122647; 9780802122643

SUMMARY: In this book, by Donna Leon, "Commissario Guido Brunetti gets a frantic call from the director of a prestigious Venetian library. Someone has stolen pages out of several rare books. After a round of questioning, the case seems clear: the culprit must be the man who requested the volumes, an American professor from a Kansas university. The only problem—the man fled the library earlier that day, and after checking his credentials, the American professor doesn't exist." (Publisher's note)

REVIEW: *Booklist* v110 no11 p26 F 1 2014 Bill Ott

"By Its Cover." "Think of [Donna] Leon's latest Guido Brunetti novel as a love letter to her fans, many of whom are librarians. . . . Her books, despite employing the structure of traditional mysteries, are so very different from most crime novels, even those characterized as character-driven. . . . She shows what a skilled interrogator her detective is, but between the lines, there is so much more. . . . Above all, Brunetti is a careful reader, of people, of places, of situations, and he never stops at surface meanings. That's why we bookish types adore him the way we do, and why this will likely be one of his most-loved adventures."

REVIEW: *Kirkus Rev* v82 no7 p58 Ap 1 2014

REVIEW: *Libr J* v139 no4 p75 Mr 1 2014 Dan Forrest

REVIEW: *N Y Times Book Rev* p30 Ap 6 2014 MARILYN STASIO

REVIEW: *Publ Wkly* v261 no5 p37-8 F 3 2014

LEON, DONNA. Beastly Things; [by] Donna Leon 304 p. 0 Atlantic Monthly

1. Detective & mystery stories 2. Restaurants—Italy 3. Slaughtering & slaughterhouses 4. Venice (Italy) 5. Veterinarians—Fiction

ISBN 9780802120236

SUMMARY: This detective novel, a volume of the Guido Brunetti series, offers a "tale of the murder of a quiet veterinarian. . . . One painfully human mistake, a simple act of hubris, draws an ordinary man into an inescapable trap that leaves him dead in a Venetian canal, carrying no identification and wearing only one shoe. Gradually, Commissario Brunetti and his colleague Inspector Vianello follow the trail to the town of Mestre, on the mainland near Venice, and to a slaughterhouse, where the animals that provide the meat which adorns the plates of the finest Venetian restaurants (and Brunetti's own table) are killed and "dressed" in . . . [a] barbaric manner." (Booklist)

REVIEW: *Booklist* v108 no12 p21 F 15 2012 Bill Ott

Beastly things. "Throughout the 21 novels in her much-loved Guido Brunetti series, [Donna] Leon has tackled various social issues . . . always with great sensitivity toward not only the criminal aspects of the issue but also the more ambiguous toll that societal malfunction takes on individual human lives. So it is again in this wrenching tale of the murder of a quiet veterinarian, the victim of a tragedy of almost classical dimensions. . . . [Leon] leaves us here with a small but moving moment of hope, a sense that acts of kindness, from both humans and animals, are our only salvation. A seemingly straightforward mystery written with such delicacy and emotional force that we can't help but be reminded of Greek tragedy."

REVIEW: *Kirkus Rev* v80 no5 p460 Mr 1 2012

REVIEW: *Publ Wkly* v259 no8 p149 F 20 2012

THE LEONARD BERNSTEIN LETTERS; 624 p. 2013 Yale University Press

1. BIOGRAPHY & AUTOBIOGRAPHY—Composers & Musicians 2. Composers—United States—Correspondence 3. Conductors (Music)—United States—Correspondence 4. LITERARY COLLECTIONS—Letters 5. Letters 6. MUSIC—Individual Composer & Musician 7. Musicians—United States—Correspondence

ISBN 030017909X; 9780300179095 (hardback)

LC 2013-033122

SUMMARY: This book, edited by Nigel Simeone, presents letters written by musician Leonard Bernstein. "His . . . correspondents encompassed, among others, Aaron Copland, Stephen Sondheim, Jerome Robbins, Thornton Wilder, Boris Pasternak, Bette Davis, Adolph Green, Jacqueline Kennedy Onassis, and family members including his wife Felicia and his sister Shirley." (Publisher's note)

REVIEW: *Choice* v51 no8 p1409 Ap 2014 J. Behrens

REVIEW: *Commentary* v136 no3 p66-9 O 2013 TERRY TEACHOUT

"The Leonard Bernstein Letters." "Yale University Press has just published a fat volume of his correspondence, 'The Leonard Bernstein Letters,' but it was edited not by a prominent American academic but by Nigel Simeone, a British musicologist whose dust-jacket bio identifies him merely as a 'well-known as a writer and speaker on music.' . . . Whatever the ultimate value of Bernstein's work as a composer and performer, the historical value of the 650 letters reprinted here is incontestable."

REVIEW: *Kirkus Rev* v81 no18 p220 S 15 2013

REVIEW: *N Y Rev Books* v60 no20 p24-8 D 19 2013 Robert Gottlieb

"The Leonard Bernstein Letters." "Surely the letters of such a well-educated and literate man, a practiced and effective writer . . . will be revealing? Alas, it is not so. Despite his cleverness and charm--which definitely come through--we're left knowing no more, really, than we knew before. . . . The smartest decision made by Nigel Simeone was to include scores of letters to Lenny. Again and again they're more interesting than his own letters--possibly because so many of them seem refreshingly direct and sincere, in contrast to his performances. . . . And Simeone's editorial apparatus is erratic. . . . The results are uneven, but the basic problem stems not from the editor but from Lenny himself: he so often comes across as fatally facile rather than deeply probing."

REVIEW: *N Y Times Book Rev* p18 D 15 2013 JOHN ROCKWELL

"The Leonard Bernstein Letters." "Bernstein's subjects offer more about love and affection and concert triumphs than deep insights. They open up a window into his dazzling personality and his close relations with an expansive range of friends, and a smaller circle of truly close friends . . . and, above all, family. . . . As editor, Nigel Simeone had to winnow this trove, and without reading all the letters it is impossible to judge his selection. . . . The footnotes are a mess--sometimes coming long after a first mention of a name, sometimes redundant, sometimes confusing; one relies on the index to sort things out."

REVIEW: *N Y Times Book Rev* p22 D 22 2013

REVIEW: *New York Times* v163 no56303 pC4 O 28 2013 ZACHARY WOOLFE

REVIEW: *New Yorker* v89 no39 p69-1 D 2 2013

LEONARD COHEN ON LEONARD COHEN; interviews and encounters; 624 p. 2014 Chicago Review Press

1. Composers—Canada—Interviews 2. Music literature 3. Poets, Canadian—20th century—Interviews 4. Singers—Canada—Interviews

ISBN 1613747586; 9781613747582 (cloth)

LC 2013-034568

SUMMARY: This book, edited by Jeff Burger, "collects interviews from various sources to present the singular Leonard Cohen in his own voice. The earliest piece is an interview on Canadian television in 1966; the most recent is an article in the Guardian from January of [2014]. Editor Burger divides the book into four parts: the 1960s and 1970s . . . the 1980s . . . the 1990s . . . and the new millennium." (Booklist)

REVIEW: *Booklist* v110 no14 p40 Mr 15 2014 June Sawyers

"A Broken Hallelujah: Rock and Roll, Redemption, and the Life of Leonard Cohen" and "Leonard Cohen on Leonard Cohen: Interviews and Encounters". "[Liel] Leibovitz a thoughtful examination of the music of Leonard Cohen . . . through a strong Jewish perspective. . . . Yes, there are biographical details here, but 'A Broken Hallelujah' offers something else: a finely etched musical portrait of a complicated man . . . and the often exquisite music that he has created over many decades. . . . Leibovitz himself has a distinctive voice and approach to Cohen's work. . . . A sparkling and psychologically insightful perspective on a unique artist. . . . . Many of these pieces have not previously appeared in print. Cohen is endlessly quotable and endlessly entertaining, and there is great joy in reading his words."

REVIEW: *Libr J* v139 no3 p112 F 15 2014 Elizabeth D. Eisen

REVIEW: *New Statesman* v143 no5220 p69 Jl 25 2014 Stuart Maconie

REVIEW: *Publ Wkly* v261 no2 p61 Ja 13 2014

LEONARD, ELMORE, 1925-2013. Get Shorty; [by] Elmore Leonard 292 1990 Delacorte Press

1. Crime—Fiction 2. Hollywood (Calif.)—Fiction 3. Motion picture producers & directors—Fiction 4. Motion pictures—Fiction 5. Suspense fiction

ISBN 0-385-30141-3

LC 89-2-5816

SUMMARY: When Chili Palmer, a Miami extortionist, "agrees to help a fellow mobster track down a movie producer trying to evade his Las Vegas debts, a new world of opportunities opens up before him." (Quill & Quire) "Following a bad debt from Miami to Las Vegas and on to Beverly Hills, Chili hooks up with Harry Zimm, once a leading director of grade-B horror flicks, now trying to make a comeback." (Publishers Weekly)When Chili Palmer, a Miami extortionist, "agrees to help a fellow mobster track down a movie producer trying to evade his Las Vegas debts, a new world of opportunities opens up before him." (Quill Quire)

REVIEW: *Booklist* v110 no5 p88 N 1 2013

"Stick," "LaBrava," and "Get Shorty." "The thing about [Elmore] Leonard's novels from 'Stick' onward is that the comedy is always threatening to turn tragic, as characters try to scratch itches they can't quite reach. Anyone who thinks Quentin Tarantino invented the idea of juxtaposing bursts of graphic violence against the comic ordinariness of daily life needs to do a little homework. . . . Leonard found his milieu in 'Stick'--and in its successor, LaBrava (1983), which won Leonard's only Edgar Award for best novel. . . . And let's not forget 1990's 'Get Shorty' . . . in which Leonard offered his skewed take on Hollywood."

LEONARD, ELMORE, 1925-2013. LaBrava; [by] Elmore Leonard 283 1983 Arbor House

1. Actresses—Fiction 2. Crime—Fiction 3. Extortion—Fiction 4. Mystery fiction

ISBN 0-87795-527-1

LC 83-7-2676

SUMMARY: This book follows "Joe LaBrava . . . a former Secret Service agent turned free-lance photographer. A friend of his has been taking care of Jean Shaw, a middle-aged beauty who was once a movie actress. LaBrava fell in love with Jean's image when he was 12. She played the spider-woman role: she enticed second leads to their deaths and never married the hero. Now in real life the predator may be cast as the victim: a psychotic extortionist and his creepy Cuban sidekick are looking for her." (Newsweek)"The time is now; the scene, Miami's South Beach area. Joe LaBrava is a former Secret Service agent turned free-lance photographer. A friend of his has been taking care of Jean Shaw, a middle-aged beauty who was once a movie actress. LaBrava fell in love with Jean's image when he was 12. She played the spider-woman role: she enticed second leads to their deaths and never married the hero. Now in real life the predator may be cast as the victim: a psychotic extortionist and his creepy Cuban sidekick are looking for her. Jean receives a crudely typed note demanding that she pay $600,000 for the privilege of remaining alive." (Newsweek)

REVIEW: *Booklist* v110 no5 p88 N 1 2013

"Stick," "LaBrava," and "Get Shorty." "The thing about [Elmore] Leonard's novels from 'Stick' onward is that the comedy is always threatening to turn tragic, as characters try to scratch itches they can't quite reach. Anyone who thinks Quentin Tarantino invented the idea of juxtaposing bursts of graphic violence against the comic ordinariness of daily life needs to do a little homework. . . . Leonard found his milieu in 'Stick'--and in its successor, LaBrava (1983), which won Leonard's only Edgar Award for best novel. . . . And let's not forget 1990's 'Get Shorty' . . . in which Leonard offered his skewed take on Hollywood."

LEONARD, ELMORE, 1925-2013. Stick; [by] Elmore Leonard

1. Crime—Fiction 2. Drug traffic—Fiction 3. Ex-convicts—Fiction 4. Florida—Fiction 5. Suspense fiction

SUMMARY: In this book, "after serving time for armed robbery, Ernest 'Stick' Stickley is back on the outside and trying to stay legit. But it's tough staying straight in a crooked town--and Miami is a pirate's paradise, where investment fat cats and lowlife drug dealers hold hands and dance. And when a crazed player chooses Stick at random to die for another man's sins, the struggling ex-con is left with no choice but to dive right back into the game." (Publisher's note)

REVIEW: *Booklist* v110 no5 p88 N 1 2013

"Stick," "LaBrava," and "Get Shorty." "The thing about [Elmore] Leonard's novels from 'Stick' onward is that the comedy is always threatening to turn tragic, as characters try to scratch itches they can't quite reach. Anyone who thinks Quentin Tarantino invented the idea of juxtaposing bursts of graphic violence against the comic ordinariness of daily life needs to do a little homework. . . . Leonard found his milieu in 'Stick'--and in its successor, LaBrava (1983), which won Leonard's only Edgar Award for best novel. . . . And let's not forget 1990's 'Get Shorty' . . . in which Leonard offered his skewed take on Hollywood."

LEONARD, R. L. (RICHARD LAWRENCE) The Great Rivalry; Gladstone and Disraeli; [by] R. L. (Richard Lawrence) Leonard 240 p. 2013 Palgrave Macmillan

1. Biography (Literary form) 2. Disraeli, Benjamin, Earl of Beaconsfield, 1804-1881 3. Gladstone, W. E. (William Ewart), 1809-1898 4. Great Britain—Politics & government—1837-1901 5. Prime ministers—Great Britain—Biography

ISBN 1848859252; 9781848859258

SUMMARY: This dual biography of Benjamin Disraeli and William Ewart Gladstone traces "their rivalry and its origins, comparing the upbringing, education and personalities of the two leaders, as well as their political careers. Dick Leonard considers the impact of religion on the two men, their contrasting oratorical skills, their attitudes to political and social reform, foreign affairs and imperialism as well as their relations with Queen Victoria." (Publisher's note)

REVIEW: *Choice* v51 no10 p1878 Je 2014 P. Stansky

REVIEW: *Hist Today* v63 no11 p61 N 2013 ROLAND QUINAULT

REVIEW: *London Rev Books* v35 no23 p34-6 D 5 2013 John Pemble

"Disraeli: Or, the Two Lives," "The Great Rivalry: Gladstone and Disraeli," and "Disraeli; The Romance of Politics". "Douglas Hurd and Edward Young's 'Disraeli;or, the Two Lives,' and Robert O'Kell's 'Disraeli: The Romance of Politics' diverge when they come to [Benjamin] Disraeli's Byronism. Hurd and Young wave it aside. . . . O'Kell's interpretation is fundamentally different. . . . O'Kell pushes his argument too far by reading Byronic 'psychological romance' into virtually everything Disraeli wrote. . . . Dick Leonard's 'The Great Rivalry' . . . uses the old compare and contrast formula, hopping between the two protagonists, but updating the story with the recent work of Colin Matthew, Roy Jenkins, Richard Shannon, John Vincent, Sarah Bradford and Stanley Weintraub. Essentially it's drybones parliamentary history . . . and its verdict on the falling out hardly deepens our understanding."

REVIEW: *New Statesman* v142 no5167 p38-40 Jl 19 2013 David Marquand

REVIEW: *TLS* no5768 p10 O 18 2013 ROBERT SAUNDERS

"The Great Rivalry: Gladstone and Disraeli: A Dual Biography" and "Disraeli: Or the Two Lives". "[Dick] Leonard's dual biography is essentially a distillation of older, more authoritative studies, and offers very little that is new. There are so many quotations from previous writers that the early chapters, in particular, feel like the literary equivalent of a mix tape. . . . [Douglas] Hurd and [Edward] Young have a clearer sense of purpose and a stronger controlling argument. They present their biography of [Benjamin] Disraeli as a myth-busting exercise, intended to strip away the inflated claims made for Disraeli as a One Nation Conservative and a 'Tory Democrat'. . . . The result is a respectable and competent survey, but one that is unlikely to displace the competition."

LEOPARDI, GIACOMO, 1798-1837. Zibaldone; 2502 p. 2013 Farrar Straus & Giroux

1. Christianity 2. Italy—Intellectual life 3. Modernity 4. Patriotism 5. Philosophical literature

ISBN 9780374296827 (alk. paper)

LC 2012-023322

SUMMARY: This book presents an annotated translation of the notebooks of Giacomo Leopardi. "Originally comprising some 4,500 handwritten pages, this . . . text is a methodical dissection of the ruling myths of the new world that was emerging around the solitary young man. Much of it was written when he was in his early twenties, in his family home in the small hill town of Recanati." (New Statesman)

REVIEW: *N Y Rev Books* v60 no15 p28-30 O 10 2013 Tim Parks

REVIEW: *N Y Times Book Rev* p31 Mr 16 2014 Leslie Jamison Adam Kirsch

REVIEW: *New Repub* v244 no18 p42-7 N 11 2013 Adam Kirsch

"Zibaldone." "As he read his way voraciously through ancient and modern literature, [Giacomo] Leopardi developed a philosophical understanding of human life and civilization that ranks as one of the most profound, and profoundly disquieting, of modern times.. . . To get a sense of the sheer scope of Leopardi's intellect, the range of subjects that engaged him and the bodies of knowledge he mastered, consider how many scholars it took to translate and annotate this enormous book. . . . All this intermediation suggests that the Zibaldone is not exactly reader-friendly. Its sheer size is formidable: more than two thousand closely printed pages in English translation, with another five hundred or so pages of apparatus."

REVIEW: *New Statesman* v142 no5176 p76-8 S 20 2013 John Gray

LEPCZYK, CHRISTOPHER A.ed. Urban bird ecology and conservation. See Urban bird ecology and conservation

LEPORE, JILL. Book of ages; the life and opinions of Jane Franklin; [by] Jill Lepore 464 p. 2013 Alfred A. Knopf

1. Biographies 2. Women—United States—Social conditions—18th century

ISBN 0307958345; 9780307958341

LC 2013-001012

SUMMARY: This book on Jane Franklin Mecom by Jill Lepore tells "the story of Benjamin Franklin's youngest sister . . . using only a few of her letters and a small archive of births and deaths." (Kirkus Reviews) "Jane's surviving letters are . . . the correspondence of a smart, witty, hardworking woman who 'loved best books about ideas,' reveled in gossip, expressed 'impolite' opinions on religion and politics, and shared piquant observations of the struggle for American independence." (Booklist)

REVIEW: *Booklist* v110 no1 p28 S 1 2013 Donna Seaman

"Book of Ages: The Life and Opinions of Jane Franklin." "[A] zestfully rigorous portrait. . . . In spite of the tragedies she endured, Jane's surviving letters are 'gabby, frank, and vexed,' the correspondence of a smart, witty, hardworking woman who 'loved best books about ideas,' reveled in gossip, expressed 'impolite' opinions on religion and politics, and shared piquant observations of the struggle for American independence. By restoring Jane so vividly to the historical record, [Jill] Lepore also provides a fresh, personal perspective on Benjamin [Franklin]. And so extraordinarily demanding was her research, even the appendixes in Lepore's vibrantly enlightening biography are dramatic."

REVIEW: *Choice* v51 no6 p1077 F 2014 T. K. Byron

REVIEW: *Christ Century* v130 no25 p22 D 11 2013

REVIEW: *Kirkus Rev* p27 Ag 15 2013 Fall Preview

REVIEW: *Kirkus Rev* v81 no15 p316 Ag 1 2013

REVIEW: *Libr J* v139 no7 p48-9 Ap 15 2014 Nancy R. Ives

REVIEW: *Libr J* v138 no9 p55 My 15 2013 Barbara Hoffert

REVIEW: *N Y Rev Books* v60 no16 p26-8 O 24 2013 Susan Dunn

"Book of Ages: The Life and Opinions of Jane Franklin." "In her eloquent [book] . . . Jill Lepore . . . imaginatively weaves together the lives of Benjamin Franklin and his favorite sister Jane. . . . Lepore compensates for the absence of historical evidence with interesting excursions into eighteenth-century commerce, publishing, literature, and law, and also with her own diverse ruminations, associations, speculations--and inventions. . . . Mixing genres of biography and fiction as she told us she would, Lepore creates a novelistic tableau of a heartsick young woman, pitifully recognizing that her future has evaporated."

REVIEW: *N Y Times Book Rev* p14 O 20 2013 MARY BETH NORTON

"Book of Ages: The Life and Opinions of Jane Franklin." "Jill Lepore . . . is addicted to short, dramatic sentences and occasional contradictions. . . . Lepore's diligent search for Jane's 'remains'--belongings bequeathed to her descendants, her books and those remaining letters--constitutes a fascinating coda. . . . Jane Franklin Mecom's early life is sparsely documented. . . . To fill out those initial years . . . Lepore adopts several inventive narrative strategies. . . . Lepore's distinctive prose style can be remarkably evocative. . . . But the text can also be self-indulgent. . . . The most effective parts of the book explicitly contrast the lives of brother and sister."

REVIEW: *New York Times* v163 no56272 pC31 S 27 2013 DWIGHT GARNER

"Book of Ages: The Life and Opinions of Jane Franklin." "To stare at these siblings is to stare at sun and moon. But in Jill Lepore's meticulously constructed biography . . . recently placed on the long list of nominees for the National Book Award in nonfiction, this moon casts a beguiling glow. . . . [Lepore] has had to marshal her talents as historian and writer in the making of 'Book of Ages,' for a simple reason. About Jane Franklin Mecom . . . the author admits, the 'paper trail is miserably scant.' . . . The pleasures in 'Book of Ages' are real if sometimes mild. Among them is the sound a writer-historian makes when doing an elegant write-around."

REVIEW: *Publ Wkly* v260 no31 p58 Ag 5 2013

REVIEW: *Smithsonian* v44 no5 p98-9 S 2013 Chloë Schama

REVIEW: *Women's Review of Books* v31 no1 p5-6 Ja/F 2014 Martha Saxton

LEPPANEN, DEBBIE. Trick-or-treat!; a happy haunter's Halloween poems; 40 p. 2013 Beach Lane Books

1. Ghosts 2. Halloween—Juvenile poetry 3. Limericks 4. Lists 5. Poems

ISBN 1442433981; 9781442433984 (hardcover); 9781442433991 (ebook)

LC 2012-004906

SUMMARY: This book, by Debbie Leppanen and illustrated by Tad Carpenter presents a "collection of Halloween poems. In this collection of . . . rhyming poems, young readers will meet hungry ghouls, sneaky ghosts, and frisky skeletons, all who love partying in the moonlight." (Publisher's note)

REVIEW: *Booklist* v109 no22 p70 Ag 1 2013 Daniel Kraus

REVIEW: *Bull Cent Child Books* v67 no1 p28-9 S 2013 H. M.

"Trick-or-Treat: A Happy Hunter's Halloween." "This collection of fifteen original Halloween-themed poems offers a playful variety of rhyming verses that mix longer descriptive pieces in with limericks and lists. . . . Poems from the point of view of ghosts, ghouls, and mummies are intermixed with tales about ordinary humans interacting with creatures of the night, and the varying perspectives add to the entertainment value. [Illustrator Tad] Carpenter's high-contrast digital compositions are somewhat flat and slick, hut they're amusingly imbued with a retro graphic fee. . . . The occasional clunky rhyme makes a read-through mandatory before little listeners arrive for storytime, but overall the poems scan smoothly, and they'll be accessible to a crowd."

REVIEW: *Horn Book Magazine* v89 no5 p66 S/O 2013 KATRINA HEDEEN

REVIEW: *Kirkus Rev* v81 no15 p301 Ag 1 2013

REVIEW: *Publ Wkly* v260 no29 p67 Jl 22 2013

REVIEW: *SLJ* v59 no7 p109 Jl 2013 Mary Jean Smith

LEPPER, VERENA M.ed. Ancient Egyptian literature. See Ancient Egyptian literature

LESCH, DAVID W.ed. The Arab Spring. See The Arab Spring

LESLEA, NEWMAN. October mourning; a song for Matthew Shepard; [by] Newman Leslea xi, 111 p. 2012 Candlewick

1. Gays—Fiction 2. Hate crimes—Fiction 3. Murder—Fiction 4. Novels in verse 5. Poems—Collections
ISBN 0763658073; 9780763658076 (hardback)
LC 2011-048358

SUMMARY: In this book "lesbian literary icon [Lesléa] Newman offers a 68-poem tribute to Matthew Shepard, . . . [who] was lured from a bar by two men who drove him to the outskirts of town, beat him mercilessly, tied him to a fence and left him to die. This cycle of poems, meant to be read sequentially as a whole, incorporates Newman's reflections on Shepard's killing and its aftermath, using a number of . . . literary devices to portray. . . that fateful night and the trial that followed." (Kirkus Reviews)

REVIEW: *Booklist* v109 no2 p68 S 15 2012

REVIEW: *Bull Cent Child Books* v66 no2 p105-6 O 2012 C. G.

"October Mourning: A Song for Matthew Shepard." "[T] his cycle of poems . . . offers poignant commentary on the tragedy. Verses explore various perspectives . . . on the attack, the investigation and vigils, and the aftermath. Lesléa] Newman deploys a wide range of poetic forms, including pantoums, villanelles, haiku, and concrete poems, but all share jagged rhythms and a biting sense of grief and helplessness. While the writing quality dips at times, some poems are deeply emotional."

REVIEW: *Horn Book Magazine* p112-3 S/O 2012 Dean Schneider

REVIEW: *Kirkus Rev* v80 no16 p31 Ag 15 2012

REVIEW: *Publ Wkly* v259 no31 p66 Jl 30 2012

REVIEW: *SLJ* v59 no3 p70 Mr 2013 Bernie Morrissey

REVIEW: *SLJ* v58 no11 p124 N 2012 Jill Heritage Maza

REVIEW: *Voice of Youth Advocates* v35 no5 p472-3 D 2012 Dianna Geers

LESSER, WENDY. Why I Read; a Book Lover's Investigations; [by] Wendy Lesser 240 p. 2014 Farrar, Straus and Giroux

1. Books and reading 2. LITERARY CRITICISM—Books & Reading 3. Literature—History and criticism 4. Memoirs
ISBN 9780374289201 (hardback)
LC 2013-033000

SUMMARY: In this book by Wendy Lesser, "the reader will discover a definition of literature that is as broad as it is broad-minded. In addition to novels and stories, Lesser explores plays, poems, and essays along with mysteries, science fiction, and memoirs. As she examines these works from such perspectives as 'Character and Plot,' 'Novelty,' 'Grandeur and Intimacy,' and 'Authority,' 'Why I Read' sparks an overwhelming desire to put aside quotidian tasks in favor of reading." (Publisher's note)

REVIEW: *Bookforum* v20 no4 p42 D 2013/Ja 2014 CLAIRE MESSUD

REVIEW: *Booklist* v110 no7 p4 D 1 2013 Donna Seaman

REVIEW: *Economist* v410 no8870 p83 Ja 18 2014

"Why I Read: The Serious Pleasure of Books." "Fifty years after [Henry] Miller published 'The Books in My Life,' Wendy Lesser has brought out an equally personal reading memoir. . . . Her new book . . . is a model for the modern age, with a list of 100 books to read for pleasure and a notice at the back advertising an online guide for reading groups. But her instincts are those of her literary forebears. . . . 'Reading literature,' she says, 'is a way of reaching back to something bigger and older and different.' How very consoling."

REVIEW: *Kirkus Rev* v81 no19 p99 O 1 2013

REVIEW: *N Y Times Book Rev* p19 Ja 26 2014 WILLIAM GIRALDI

REVIEW: *New Statesman* v143 no10 p44-7 Mr 14 2014 Leo Robson

REVIEW: *New Yorker* v90 no1 p104-1 F 17 2014

"Why I Read." "This elegant manifesto distills more than five decades of thinking about books, from [author Wendy] Lesser's perspective as a critic, novelist, memoirist, biographer, and editor. Discussion encompasses everything from science fiction to Scandinavian mystery writers, but it is robust nineteenth-century fiction--Tolstoy, Dostoyevsky, Dickens, James--that clearly arouses Lesser's greatest passion. In chapters that aspire toward the qualities she admires in her subject matter . . . , she shows the inextricability of plot and character."

REVIEW: *Publ Wkly* v260 no42 p44 O 21 2013

REVIEW: *TLS* no5782 p27 Ja 24 2014 CHRISTINA PETRIE

LESTER, ANNE E. Creating Cistercian nuns; the women's religious movement and its reform in thirteenth-century Champagne; [by] Anne E. Lester xxii, 261 p. 2011 Cornell University Press

1. Church renewal 2. Cistercian nuns—France—Champagne-Ardenne—History—To 1500 3. Historical literature 4. Monastic and religious life of women—France—Champagne-Ardenne—History—To 1500
ISBN 0801449898 (cloth: alk. paper); 9780801449895 (cloth: alk. paper)
LC 2011-022953

SUMMARY: In this book, "Anne E. Lester addresses a central issue in the history of the medieval church: the role of women in the rise of the religious reform movement of the thirteenth century. Focusing on the county of Champagne in France, Lester reconstructs the history of the women's religious movement and its institutionalization within the Cistercian order." (Publisher's note)

REVIEW: *Am Hist Rev* v118 no4 p1238-9 O 2013 Fiona J. Griffiths

REVIEW: *Choice* v50 no1 p162 S 2012 J. M. B. Porter

REVIEW: *Engl Hist Rev* v129 no536 p181-2 F 2014 Henrietta Leyser

One hundred years ago (in 1912), Joseph Greven, in his Die Anfänge der Beginen, took it for granted that the Cistercian legislation of 1228 forbidding the acceptance of any more women into the order was so effective that henceforth women who had a religious vocation either joined the friars or became beguines. This view was for long barely questioned, but now Anne E. Lester challenges it with compelling force, at least as far as Champagne is concerned. . . . Lester's trawl offers a striking example of a particular catch."

REVIEW: *J Relig* v93 no1 p94-6 Ja 2013 CONSTANCE B. BOUCHARD

LESY, MICHAEL. Repast; dining out at the dawn of the new American century, 1900-1910; [by] Michael Lesy 264 p. 2013 W.W. Norton & Company

1. Dinners and dining—United States—History—20th century 2. Gastronomy—History—20th century 3. Historical literature 4. Restaurants—United States—History—20th century
ISBN 9780393070675 (hardcover)
LC 2013-009410

SUMMARY: This book by Michael Lesy and Lisa Stoffer "takes readers on a culinary tour of early-twentieth-century restaurants and dining. The innovations introduced at the time--in ingredients, technologies, meal service, and cuisine--transformed the act of eating in public in ways that persist to this day." (Publisher's note)

REVIEW: *Bookforum* v20 no4 p6 D 2013/Ja 2014 MELANIE REHAK

"Repast: Dining Out at the Dawn of the New American Century, 1900-1910." "Sumptuous. . . . That they manage to make discussions of awful meals both charming and interesting is in no small part due to Repast's kaleidoscopic mix of contemporary news stories, research, and gorgeous reproductions of menus from the era, festooned with illustrations of everything from bluebirds to rakish swimmers. . . . [Michael] Lesy and [Lisa] Stoffer tell at pleasing length of utterly over-the-top feasts and balls thrown by the nation's upper crust. . . . They are lively and illuminating on this crowd as well."

LETHBRIDGE, LUCY. Servants; a downstairs history of Britain from the nineteenth century to modern times; [by] Lucy Lethbridge 400 p. 2013 W. W. Norton & Company

1. Household employees—Great Britain—Attitudes 2. Household employees—Great Britain—History—20th century 3. Social classes—Great Britain—History—20th century
ISBN 0393241092; 9780393241099 (hardcover)
LC 2013-028069

SUMMARY: In this book, author Lucy Lethbridge "explores the culture of 20th-century British domestic service workers, the families that employed them, and the practice's sudden collapse after WWII. She discusses the implications of the upstairs vs. downstairs arrangement in which servants were expected to be invisible and inaudible.Lethbridge also outlines the specific nature of many positions" (Publishers Weekly)

REVIEW: *Bookforum* v21 no1 p38-9 Ap/My 2014 DAPHNE MERNIN

REVIEW: *Booklist* v110 no4 p14 O 15 2013 Margaret Flanagan

REVIEW: *Economist* v407 no8831 p83 Ap 13 2013

REVIEW: *Kirkus Rev* v81 no20 p18 O 15 2013

REVIEW: *Libr J* v138 no14 p125 S 1 2013 Kathleen McCallister

REVIEW: *Libr J* v138 no10 p82 Je 1 2013

REVIEW: *N Y Times Book Rev* p24 D 1 2013 LEAH PRICE

REVIEW: *N Y Times Book Rev* p80 D 8 2013

REVIEW: *New Yorker* v89 no37 p83-1 N 18 2013

REVIEW: *Publ Wkly* v260 no33 p54 Ag 19 2013

REVIEW: *TLS* no5745 p7 My 10 2013 PAUL ADDISON

"Servants: A Downstairs View of Twentieth-Century Britain." "Anecdotes flow freely and there is no schematic framework of the kind an academic would impose, but the evidence is deftly organized into a panorama of topics tracing the history of domestic service from its zenith in Edwardian England through two world wars to its decline and fall. Beautifully written, sparkling with insight, and a pleasure to read, 'Servants' is social history at its most humane and perceptive. In broad terms the world [Lucy] Lethbridge describes is a familiar one, but she nails it all down with the kind of detail that still has the power to astonish, outrage or amuse."

LETHEM, JONATHAN. Dissident Gardens; [by] Jonathan Lethem 384 p. 2013 Random House Inc.

1. American historical fiction 2. Communism—United States—History 3. Communists—United States 4. Counterculture—History 5. New York (N.Y.)—Fiction
ISBN 0385534930 (hardcover); 9780385534932 (hardcover)

SUMMARY: This book "begins with the case of Rose Zimmer, in Queens, New York, who was officially ousted from the [American Communist] party in 1955 for sleeping with a black cop. Rose's daughter, Miriam, is a teenager at the time, and she soon discovers the pull of Greenwich Village bohemians. Rose's and Miriam's stories are interwoven, as the narrative moves back and forth in time." (Publishers Weekly)

REVIEW: *Bookforum* v20 no3 p33 S-N 2013 JESS ROW

REVIEW: *Booklist* v109 no21 p24 Jl 1 2013 Donna Seaman

REVIEW: *Booklist* v110 no11 p38 F 1 2014 Magan Szwarek

REVIEW: *Commentary* v136 no4 p53-4 N 2013 FERNANDA MOORE

REVIEW: *Economist* v410 no8872 p72 F 1 2014

REVIEW: *Kirkus Rev* p10-1 2013 Guide 20to BookExpo America

REVIEW: *Kirkus Rev* v81 no2 p21-2 Je 1 2013

REVIEW: *Kirkus Rev* p8 2013 Guide 20to BookExpo America Alex Heimbach

REVIEW: *Libr J* v138 no7 p56 Ap 15 2013 Barbara Hoffert

REVIEW: *Libr J* v138 no12 p73 Jl 1 2013 Lisa Block

REVIEW: *Libr J* v139 no2 p44 F 1 2014 Joyce Kessel

REVIEW: *London Rev Books* v36 no4 p24-5 F 20 2014 Marco Roth

"Dissident Gardens". "In 'Dissident Gardens,' his ninth novel, he strives to put more distance between himself and his earlier woolly cultural politics: this time, his characters are all animated by explicitly political ideas and define themselves by their political loyalties. . . . Those hoping to find patient and detailed descriptions of Queens like those that marked [Jonathan] Lethem's writing about his native Brooklyn in 'The Fortress of Solitude,' where it seemed that every sidewalk crack of Boerum Hill received its due attention, will be disappointed. . . . 'Dissident Gardens' is a kitsch reliquary of the totems of America's East Coast left."

REVIEW: *N Y Rev Books* v51 no7 p47-8 Ap 24 2014 Michael Greenberg

REVIEW: *N Y Times Book Rev* p28 Je 29 2014 IHSAN TAYLOR

REVIEW: *N Y Times Book Rev* p1-26 S 8 2013 Yiyun Li

REVIEW: *New Statesman* v143 no4 p51 Ja 31 2014 Helen Lewis

REVIEW: *New York Times* v162 no56257 pC1-6 S 12 2013 JANET MASLIN

REVIEW: *Publ Wkly* v260 no43 p55-6 O 28 2013

REVIEW: *Publ Wkly* v260 no20 p33 My 20 2013

REVIEW: *Quill Quire* v79 no6 p29-31 Jl/Ag 2013

REVIEW: *TLS* no5781 p19 Ja 17 2014 KATE WEBB

"Dissident Gardens." "In [Jonathan] Lethem's new novel, 'Dissident Gardens,' [the] theme of political instrumentalism is developed in a critique of the American Left, exploring the path from the New Deal to the Occupy movement through the lives of two intertwined families. . . . This double view allows Lethem to have fun with the drama of revolutionary politics while remaining wary of its self-intoxications, to argue for the Left's sometimes overlooked role in the American story while considering its many illusions and failures. . . But this is not to say that Lethem's is a work of apostasy. Rather, it is a reckoning that pays the compliment of taking these defiant people as seriously as they took themselves. . . . It is a novel long overdue."

LETHEM, JONATHAN.ed. Fridays at Enrico's. See Carpenter, D.

LETTER FROM A LIFE; The Selected Letters of Benjamin Britten 1913-1976: Volume 6: 1966-1976; 880 p. 2012 Boydell Press

1. Britten, Benjamin, 1913-1976 2. Composers—Correspondence 3. Composers—History—20th century 4. Letters 5. Pears, Peter, Sir, 1910-1986

ISBN 1843837250 (hbk.); 9781843837251 (hbk.)

SUMMARY: This book, "the sixth and final volume of the annotated selected letters of Benjamin Britten, edited by Philip Reed and Mervyn Cooke, coversd the composer's last decade. . . . Britten's letters to his life partner and principal interpreter, the tenor Peter Pears, remain central. Other significant correspondents include the Queen and Queen Mother; librettists William Plomer and Myfanwy Piper; [and] artistic collaborators Frederick Ashton, Colin Graham and John Piper." (Publisher's note)

REVIEW: *N Y Rev Books* v60 no13 p34-6 Ag 15 2013 Leo Carey

"Benjamin Britten: A Life in the Twentieth Century," "Letters From a Life: The Selected Letters of Benjamin Britten, 1913-1976: Volume Six, 1966-1976," and "Britten's Unquiet Pasts: Sound and Memory in Postwar Reconstruction." "An authoritative new biography by Paul Kildea and the last of six huge, exhaustively annotated volumes of Britten's selected correspondence. . . . Kildea's account improves on [Humphrey] Carpenter's in two notable ways--sketching in the social background of Britten's career and offering a surer assessment of the music. . . . Heather Wiebe's astute new monograph 'Britten's Unquiet Pasts' shows how Britten's patriotic project dovetailed both with a nostalgic turn in postwar English tastes and with the nation's more forward-looking cultural enterprises."

LETTERS FROM THE EAST; Crusaders, pilgrims and settlers in the 12th-13th centuries; 188 2010 Ashgate

1. Crusades (Middle Ages)—13th-15th centuries 2. Historical literature 3. Latin Orient 4. Letters 5. Pilgrims & pilgrimages

ISBN 9780754663560

SUMMARY: This book "comprises eighty-two documents addressed to Western Europe from the Levant, supplemented by a brief introduction, two maps, a chronology (1095–1312), a contents list and an index. . . . The letters are arranged chronologically . . . opening in June 1097, with Stephen of Blois' optimistic letter to his wife about the First Crusade prior to Antioch, and ending on 20 April 1306 with a letter from James of Molay, the ill-fated Templar Master, to James II of Aragon." (English Historical Review)

REVIEW: *Engl Hist Rev* v129 no536 p176-8 F 2014 Kevin Lewis

"Letters From the East: Crusaders, Pilgrims and Settlers in the 12th-13th Centuries" and "The chanson d'Antioche: An Old French Account of the First Crusade". "Ashgate's flourishing Crusade Texts in Translation series grows with two very different volumes. . . . The translations are readable without compromising on accuracy and, where potential ambiguity or controversy exists, original terms are supplied in parentheses. . . . The introduction outlines concisely how the letters should, and could, be read. . . . As the translators [of The Chanson d'Antioche] admit, their conclusions often cannot go beyond informed guesswork, but their hypotheses are nonetheless convincing. . . . A structural problem with the book is that the three introductory chapters often tread similar ground, albeit with differing nuances. . . . Nevertheless, this accomplished translation and its thoughtful introduction will certainly prove useful to researchers and undergraduates alike."

LETTERS HOME TO SARAH; the Civil War letters of Guy C. Taylor, Thirty-sixth Wisconsin Volunteers; xxix, 328 p. 2012 University of Wisconsin Press

1. Historical literature 2. Soldiers—Wisconsin—Correspondence

ISBN 9780299291204 (cloth : alk. paper); 9780299291235 (e-book)
LC 2012-015329

SUMMARY: This book presents "the letters of Guy Carlton Taylor, a farmer who served in the Thirty-Sixth Wisconsin Volunteer Infantry Regiment in the American Civil War. From March 23, 1864, to July 14, 1865, Taylor wrote 165 letters home to his wife Sarah and their son Charley. . . . While at war, he contracts measles, pneumonia, and malaria, and he writes about the hospitals, treatments, and sanitary conditions that he and his comrades endured during the war." (Publisher's note)

REVIEW: *Rev Am Hist* v41 no3 p462-6 S 2013 Louis P. Masur

"Letters Home to Sarah: The Civil War Letters of Guy C. Taylor, 36th Wisconsin Volunteers" and "A Punishment on the Nation: An Iowa Soldier Endures the Civil War." "[Guy C. Taylor's] letters offer a Midwestern perspective on the Eastern front. They also illuminate an issue that has only recently begun to gain attention among historians: how illness affected soldiers and how at least some soldiers used illness to secure positions as non-combatants. In her introduction to this well-edited collection, Kathryn Shively Meier points out that Taylor 'parlayed his skills, as well as his relationships with medical personnel,' to escape combat. . . . In this richly annotated volume, [Brian Craig] Miller situates [Silas] Haven within the ongoing discussion of why soldiers enlisted."

THE LETTERS OF C. VANN WOODWARD; 480 p. 2013 Yale University Press

1. Historians—United States 2. Historians—United States—Biography 3. Letters 4. Scholars—United States 5. United States—Intellectual life—20th century 6. Woodward, C. Vann (Comer Vann), 1908-1999
ISBN 9780300185348 (hardcover : alk. paper)
LC 2013-011897

SUMMARY: Editor Michael O'Brien describes how "C. Vann Woodward was one of the most prominent and respected American historians of the twentieth century. . . . For the first time, his sprightly, wry, sympathetic, and often funny letters are published, including those he wrote to figures as diverse as John Kennedy, David Riesman, Richard Hofstadter, and Robert Penn Warren." (Publisher's note)

REVIEW: *Am Sch* v82 no4 p105-7 Aut 2013 William S. McFeeley

"The Letters of C. Vann Woodward." "[Editor Michael] O'Brien's 36-page introduction--the grace of its prose worthy of its subject--is a learned and excellent intellectual study of the preeminent historian of the South. It is particularly useful because [C. Vann] Woodward only rarely tells us in his letters about his writings, which so altered our view of the region. . . . The letters give rare insight into the evolution and complexity of Woodward's thought. . . . O'Brien is a sly editor. Aware of how Woodward cherished his privacy, he nevertheless includes remarkable letters the historian wrote to his former lover, Antonina Jones Hansell."

REVIEW: *TLS* no5793 p11 Ap 11 2014 TOM F. WRIGHT

THE LETTERS OF WILLIAM GADDIS; 545 p. 2013 Dalkey Archive Press

1. Authors, American—20th century—Correspondence 2. Authorship 3. Letters 4. Publishers & publishing
ISBN 9781564788047 (cloth : alk. paper)
LC 2012-048555

SUMMARY: This book, edited by Steven Moore, presents the correspondence and personal writings of the American fiction author William Gaddis. "Beginning in 1930 when Gaddis was at boardingschool and ending in September 1998, a few months before his death, these letters function as a kind of autobiography." (Publisher's note)

REVIEW: *N Y Rev Books* v60 no15 p43-5 O 10 2013 Jonathan Raban

"The Letters of William Gaddis." "For the first two hundred pages of this book, his mother is his chief--almost his only--correspondent; not because he was short of friends, but because mothers are better than most people at saving their children's letters. . . . he sent her lively commentaries on his life and its frequent changes of scenery. . . . He sounds young for his age . . . and rather priggish in his moralism, but these qualities served him well as a writer who would remain productively surprised and offended by ordinary American life. . . . They add up to a complicated, rather somber self-portrait of the novelist who always felt himself to be misunderstood."

REVIEW: *New York Times* v163 no56335 pC31 N 29 2013 DWIGHT GARNER

LETTING ANA GO; 304 p. 2013 Simon Pulse

1. Anexoria nervosa—Fiction 2. Diaries—Fiction 3. Diet—Fiction 4. Family problems—Fiction 5. Food habits—Fiction 6. Self-perception—Fiction 7. Young adult fiction
ISBN 1442472235; 9781442472235
LC 2012-037458

SUMMARY: This book provides an "account of one girl's battle with anorexia. . . . The unnamed narrator begins her story as a healthy, well-adjusted teen from a privileged family. Her overweight mother struggles with food issues on a daily basis and receives little emotional support from her husband. . . . Witnessing the deterioration of her parents' marriage, the teen becomes overwhelmed by a flood of conflicting emotions and channels her need for order into restricting what she eats." (School Library Journal)

REVIEW: *Booklist* v109 no21 p68 Jl 1 2013 Daniel Kraus

REVIEW: *Bull Cent Child Books* v67 no1 p5 S 2013 K. C.

"Letting Ana Go." "Slowly, subtly, Jill and Jill's mother feed the narrator the lies of anorexia--that thin is synonymous with attractive, that people encouraging you to eat are just jealous that your self-discipline exceeds their own, that being thin is the only way to ensure that you will be loved. . . . This title, part of a new diary series, echoes 'Go Ask Alice' in presentation and appeal, but it's a sounder exploration of its focus problem. . . . What is left unexplained and somewhat troubling is how Jill survives, given that her commitment was the stronger of the two, suggesting to the vulnerable that only some girls are at risk while others can live well at that knife's edge."

REVIEW: *Kirkus Rev* v81 no9 p71-2 My 1 2013

REVIEW: *Publ Wkly* v260 no17 p134 Ap 29 2013

REVIEW: *SLJ* v59 no7 p87 Jl 2013 Audrey Sumser

LETTRICK, ROBERT. Frenzy; [by] Robert Lettrick 304 p. 2014 Disney-Hyperion

1. Animals—Fiction 2. Camps—Fiction 3. Horror stories 4. Survival—Fiction 5. Virus diseases—Fiction

ISBN 9781423185383 (alk. paper)
LC 2013-025622

SUMMARY: In this book, "normal camp routines of horseback riding and postcard writing come to a screeching halt when the small (and not so small) woodland creatures suddenly all turn rabid. . . . Heath, Will and several others escape to the nearby river, since exposure to water seems to kill the animals on contact. . . .They travel down the river in hopes of reaching the nearest town, but the animals follow along on the riverbank, keeping the campers in sight." (Kirkus Reviews)

REVIEW: *Booklist* v110 no15 p86 Ap 1 2014 Paula Willey

REVIEW: *Bull Cent Child Books* v67 no9 p465 My 2014 A. S.

"Frenzy". "The backstory on how the animals got infected doesn't actually add much—this book is all about a group of memorable young kids trying to cope with a series of events that is completely outside the scope of their barely formed social, survival, and ethical toolkits. The death count is slightly startling for a book aimed at this age range, but it makes sense given the ferocity of the animals and the boys' understandable lack of preparation for maddened woodland creatures. Offer this to adventure fans and budding horror buffs, sure, but realistic fiction fans may also find the effective character development and thoughtful pacing as worthwhile as the monstrous foaming-mouthed squirrels."

REVIEW: *Kirkus Rev* v82 no4 p135 F 15 2014

"Frenzy". "Summer camp turns deadly: fluffy, foaming, frenzied and deadly. . . . [Robert] Lettrick's middle-grade debut is most successful during the many action scenes and in the slow reveal of certain facts about the characters. That it takes the old wives' tale that rabid animals are afraid of water and runs with it is acceptable, but the premise disintegrates at the end as the author forces events to reach his desired end. The character deaths are predictable, and the end, too tidy. Never achieves the scare it intends."

REVIEW: *SLJ* v60 no6 p104 Je 2014 Mara Alpert

REVIEW: *Voice of Youth Advocates* v37 no2 p76 Je 2014 Kelly Czarnecki

LEVACK, BRIAN P. The Devil within; possession and exorcism in the Christian West; [by] Brian P. Levack 360 p. 2013 Yale University Press

1. Demoniac possession—Europe—History 2. Exorcism—Europe—History 3. Historical literature 4. Performance theory 5. Reformation
ISBN 0300114729; 9780300114720 (cl : alk. paper)
LC 2012-042933

SUMMARY: This book "focuses on possession and exorcism in the Reformation period, but also reaches back to the fifteenth century and forward to our own times. . . . Challenging the commonly held belief that possession signals physical or mental illness, the author argues that demoniacs and exorcists--consciously or not--are following their various religious cultures, and their performances can only be understood in those contexts." (Publisher's note)

REVIEW: *Choice* v51 no1 p153-4 S 2013 J. W. McCormack

"The Devil Within: Possession and Exorcism in the Christian West." "Historian [Brian P.] Levack . . . has written what will likely become the starting point for all students and scholars interested in the history of demonic possession. The author synthesizes a wide range of local studies from early modern Europe to show the poverty of anachronistic medical and psychological explanations of possession and the cultural specificity of the details of individual cases. . . . Levack's broad claim should spur further research and make this book a classic reference work."

REVIEW: *Hist Today* v63 no6 p55 Je 2013 RONALD HUTTON

REVIEW: *London Rev Books* v35 no9 p8-9 My 9 2013 Terry Eagleton

REVIEW: *TLS* no5756 p7-8 Jl 26 2013 PETER MARSHALL

"The Devil Within: Possession and Exorcism in the Christian West." "Brian P. Levack, a distinguished historian of early modem witchcraft, now sets exorcism in a long historical perspective, providing the most comprehensive and scholarly overview of the theme yet published. . . . Underpinned by deep and empathetic learning, and an enviable knowledge of the sources, Levack's cultural 'script' theory of possession and exorcism is an attractive one. But an unintended consequence of this book may be to encourage us to view the phenomenon too narrowly through the lens of learned demonology, and to give insufficient consideration to how the meanings of possession were forged in encounters between learned and popular cultures."

LEVAN, KRISTINE. Prison violence; causes, consequences, and solutions; [by] Kristine Levan ix, 155 p. 2012 Ashgate

1. Corrections (Criminal justice administration) 2. Prison violence 3. Prisoners 4. Social science literature 5. Violence—Social aspects
ISBN 1409433900; 9781409433903 (alk. paper); 9781409433910 (ebk. - PDF); 9781409471776 (ebk. - ePUB)
LC 2012-020717

SUMMARY: Author Kristine Levan, "drawing on a range of research and media sources to provide an international perspective on the topic of prison violence, . . . focuses on the impact of such violence on the individual both while he or she is incarcerated and upon his or her release from prison, as well as on society as a whole. [The book] explores the various systems that exist to combat the problem, whilst also considering public perceptions of offenders and punishment." (Publisher's note)

REVIEW: *Choice* v51 no1 p173 S 2013 P. Lorenzini

REVIEW: *Contemp Sociol* v43 no1 p136 Ja 2014

"Prison Violence: Causes, Consequences, and Solutions". "Kristine Levan's book 'Prison Violence' is a comprehensive and compelling description of an often overlooked problem. Her concise, detailed, yet highly readable analysis makes this book an important contribution to criminologists and sociologists alike. . . . Although this book provides a comprehensive look at individual as well as collective violence perpetrated by groups or gangs, it does not focus on the larger forms of violence such as prison riots, facility-wide disturbances, or even violence that occurs between staff and inmates. This book would benefit any criminologist, but would be particularly important for those interested in penology and violence."

LEVENE, ALYSA. The childhood of the poor; welfare in eighteenth-century London; [by] Alysa Levene xii, 250 p. 2012 Palgrave Macmillan

1. Child welfare—England—London—History—18th century 2. Children—History—18th century 3. Historical literature 4. Poor children—England—London—History—18th century 5. Poor families—England—London—History—18th century
ISBN 0230354807 (hardback); 9780230354807 (hardback)
LC 2012-011159

SUMMARY: In this book, "Alysa Levene explores how far new attitudes to childhood in the eighteenth century . . . penetrated into and informed the policies of welfare providers and seekers in London." She argues "that the image of the child as innocent and deserving did affect both policy and thinking. She also demonstrates that those seeking aid, mostly women, had some power to influence what happened to their children." (American Historical Review)

REVIEW: *Am Hist Rev* v119 no1 p251-2 F 2014 Hugh Cunningham

"The Childhood of the Poor: Welfare in Eighteenth-Century London". "With careful analysis and an admirable refusal to push the evidence further than it will go, she mounts a plausible case that the image of the child as innocent and deserving did affect both policy and thinking. . . . Levene's research is most strikingly novel in her examination of the impact of the two Acts of Parliament in the 1760s that set up a new system of parish nursing. . . . [Alysa] Levene's book is based on a wide range of difficult sources, subtle and nuanced in its interpretation of them, and carefully references the extensive recent scholarship on the topics that concern her. It makes an important contribution to the histories of childhood and poverty in the long eighteenth century."

REVIEW: *Choice* v50 no6 p1126 F 2013 J. A. Jaffe

LEVI-SETTI, RICCARDO. The trilobite book; a visual journey; [by] Riccardo Levi-Setti 288 p. 2014 University of Chicago Press

1. Animals—Pictorial works 2. Natural history—Pictorial works 3. Science—Popular works 4. Trilobites—Pictorial works 5. Trilobites—Type specimens
ISBN 9780226124414 (cloth: alkaline paper)
LC 2013-028730

SUMMARY: This illustrated book by Riccardo Levi-Setti describes how as "Distant relatives of modern lobsters, horseshoe crabs, and spiders, trilobites swam the planet's prehistoric seas for 300 million years, from the Lower Cambrian to the end of the Permian eras—and they did so very capably. Trilobite fossils have been unearthed on every continent, with more than 20,000 species identified by science." (Publisher's note)

REVIEW: *New Sci* v222 no2972 p47 Je 7 2014 Adrian Barnett

"The Trilobite Book: A Visual Journey." "'The Trilobite Book' is a tour-de-force, spanning the Cambrian to the Devonian, and roaming from Newfoundland to Morocco. It's hard to know whether to be more impressed by the diversity of trilobite forms, the quality of fossil preservation or the skills of those who prepared the specimens. That task must have taken a deft touch and an uncanny ability to visualise in 3D when you consider the species with spines or defensive protrusions. The text and photographs, all taken by the author, work beautifully together to build a picture of the intricacy and complexity of trilobites."

LEVI-STRAUSS, MONIQUE. Cashmere; [by] Monique Levi-Strauss 320 p. 2013 Thames & Hudson

1. Cashmere shawls 2. Clothing & dress—History—19th century 3. Historical literature 4. Shawls—France 5. Textile industry—France
ISBN 9780500517123 (hardcover)
LC 2013-932076

SUMMARY: This book by Monique Levi-Strauss presents "the story of French cashmere shawls of the nineteenth century. At first, the shawl-makers strove to imitate the traditional hand-made designs using modern techniques of mass production, but then they began to explore and innovate. As weaving technology evolved, motifs grew increasingly complex, expanding from the decorative borders and extending across the whole surface of the shawl and filling it with jewel-like colors." (Publisher's note)

REVIEW: *Booklist* v110 no8 p12 D 15 2013 Brad Hooper

REVIEW: *Burlington Mag* v156 no1335 p401 Je 2014 SONIA ASHMORE

REVIEW: *Choice* v51 no9 p1578-9 My 2014 C. B. Cannon

"Cashmere: A French Passion, 1800-1880". "[Monique] Lévi-Sttauss draws on yeats of extensive research in European museums, private collections, and archives to present the history of French shawl production during the 19th century. . . . The author's research includes detailed descriptions of Kashmir's role in fashion and the European textile industry during the 19th century, as well as French production of shawls inspired by those woven in Kashmir. The numerous full-color illustrations include design drawings; historical invoices and other business documents; fashion plates and other images showing the art of shawl draping; and richly detailed images of shawls from Kashmir and France."

LEVI, MICHAEL. Power surge; energy, opportunity, and the battle for America's future; [by] Michael Levi 260 p. 2013 Oxford University Press

1. Energy industries—United States 2. Energy policy—United States 3. Fossil fuels 4. Political science literature 5. Renewable energy—United States
ISBN 0199986169; 9780199986163 (hardback : alk. paper)
LC 2012-043264

SUMMARY: In this book, author Michael Levi "takes on the big claims made by both sides in the fight over American energy, showing what the changes underway mean for the United States and the world. Both unfolding revolutions in American energy offer big opportunities for the country to strengthen its economy, bolster its security, and protect the environment. Levi shows how to seize those with a new strategy that blends the best of old and new energy while avoiding the real dangers." (Publisher's note)

REVIEW: *Choice* v51 no5 p870-1 Ja 2014 J. Tavakoli

"The Power Surge: Energy, Opportunity, and the Battle for America's Future." "A well-rounded account of the growing controversy between conventional and nonconventional/renewable energy sources. . . . The book also provides a good review of developments in electric cars, noting that their electricity is derived from existing power sources which mainly run on fossil fuels. Without ignoring the facts provided by supporters and opponents of fossil fuels, [Michael] Levi presents his extensive research on energy-driven technologies and suggests that the coexistence of these two camps cannot be avoided in the near future."

REVIEW: *Economist* v407 no8840 p82 Je 15 2013

REVIEW: *Kirkus Rev* v81 no6 p76 Mr 15 2013

REVIEW: *Publ Wkly* v260 no6 p52-3 F 11 2013

REVIEW: *Sci Am* v308 no5 p82 My 2013 Anna Kuchment David Biello

LEVIN, YUVAL. The great debate; Edmund Burke, Thomas Paine, and the birth of right and left; [by] Yuval Levin 296 p. 2013 Basic Books

1. Historical literature 2. Political science—Philosophy 3. Right and left (Political science)
ISBN 0465050972; 9780465050970 (hardback)
LC 2013-032088

SUMMARY: In this book, "Yuval Levin explores the origins of the left/right divide by examining the views of the men who best represented each side of that debate at its outset: Edmund Burke and Thomas Paine. In . . . [an] exploration of the roots of our political order, Levin shows that American partisanship originated in the debates over the French Revolution, fueled by the fiery rhetoric of these ideological titans." (Publisher's note)

REVIEW: *Booklist* v110 no6 p4 N 15 2013 Gilbert Taylor

REVIEW: *Commentary* v137 no1 p49-52 Ja 2014 JONAH GOLDBERG

"The Great Debate: Edmund Burke, Thomas Paine, and the Birth of Right and Left". "'The Great Debate' stands apart from many conservative books of the last decade because it is aimed almost quaintly above the current debates of the day. . . . While it is obvious that [Yuval] Levin's deeper affection is for Burke, he is never heavy-handed about it. Indeed, by the end of the book, it is clear that Levin is not really interested in selling the argument in his subtitle. Instead, he simply lets the men speak for themselves and trusts the reader to provide the context as needed. . . . The Great Debate is a masterful and loving piece of work, the kind of solo performance that commands mute attention."

REVIEW: *Commonweal* v141 no7 p22-5 Ap 11 2014 George Scialabba

REVIEW: *Kirkus Rev* v81 no21 p48 N 1 2013

REVIEW: *N Y Times Book Rev* p30 Ja 26 2014 Noah Millman

REVIEW: *Natl Rev* v65 no24 p41-2 D 31 2013 DAVID PRYCE-JONES

"The Great Debate: Edmund Burke, Thomas Paine, and the Birth of Right and Left". "At the outset of this perceptive essay in politics, Yuval Levin states that it is a case study in how ideas move history. Levin is . . . a combatant in policy debates, and, above all, a conservative, but he bends over backwards to be fair to both of these men, whom he calls 'two giants of the age of revolutions.' The central chapters of 'The Great Debate' are rather briskly theoretical. . . . In spite of Levin's best efforts to be impartial, Paine looks like his own victim, possibly psychotic, whose inhuman dream of enforced happiness gets what it deserves."

REVIEW: *Publ Wkly* v260 no38 p67 S 23 2013

LEVINA, MARINA.ed. Monster culture in the 21st century. See Monster culture in the 21st century

LEVINE, BRUCE. The fall of the house of Dixie; how the Civil War remade the American South; [by] Bruce Levine xix, 439 p., [16] p. of plates 2013 Random House

1. Elite (Social sciences)—Southern States—History—19th century 2. Historical literature 3. Slavery—Economic aspects—Southern States—History—19th century 4. Slavery—Social aspects—Southern States—History—19th century
ISBN 1400067030; 9780679645351 (ebook); 9781400067039
LC 2011-048310

SUMMARY: In this book Bruce Levine tells the "story of how [the American Civil War] upended the economic, political, and social life of the old South, utterly destroying the Confederacy and the society it represented and defended. Told through the words of the people who lived it, 'The Fall of the House of Dixie' illuminates the way a war undertaken to preserve the status quo became a second American Revolution whose impact on the country was as strong and lasting as that of our first." (Publishing note)

REVIEW: *America* v208 no13 p36-9 Ap 22 2013 JOHN MATTESON

REVIEW: *Booklist* v109 no7 p11 D 1 2012 Jay Freeman

REVIEW: *Choice* v51 no1 p148 S 2013 S. C. Hyde

"The Fall of the House of Dixie: The Civil War and the Social Revolution That Transformed the South." "The dramatic change in character imposed upon the US South as a result of the Civil War has long been the subject of serious scholarship. The destruction of the slave system, fall from power of the prewar elite, and transformation in identity of the common folk are all well-considered issues. [Bruce] Levine . . . may not offer a great deal of new material or groundbreaking analysis of these same subjects, but he does provide an easy read. The author relies heavily on secondary sources to support his conclusions, revealing the limits of this volume's usefulness in advanced coursework or graduate studies."

REVIEW: *Christ Century* v130 no9 p42-3 My 1 2013 Paul Harvey

REVIEW: *Kirkus Rev* v80 no21 p61 N 1 2012

REVIEW: *Libr J* v138 no9 p45 My 15 2013 Scott DiMarco

REVIEW: *Publ Wkly* v259 no39 p62-3 S 24 2012

LEVINE, DANIEL. Hyde; [by] Daniel Levine 416 p. 2014 Houghton Mifflin Harcourt

1. Hyde, Edward (Fictitious character) 2. Jekyll, Henry (Fictitious character) 3. Missing persons—Investigation—Fiction 4. Self-experimentation in medicine—Fiction 5. Speculative fiction
ISBN 0544191188; 9780544191181 (hardback)
LC 2013-044255

SUMMARY: This book, "narrated by Dr. Henry Jekyll, Robert Louis Stevenson's classic embodiment of the dark side of the human consciousness . . . provides an alternate perspective on Jekyll's chemical experiments on the split personality. Edward Hyde first emerges independent of Jekyll on the streets of London in 1884—not as the malevolent brute that Stevenson conjured, but as a member of the lower classes who is fiercely protective of his and Hyde's friends and interests." (Publishers Weekly)

REVIEW: *Kirkus Rev* v82 no1 p266 Ja 1 2014

"Hyde". "[Daniel] Levine's characters are fully realized, but many are abandoned in narrative cul-de-sacs. . . . Levine's masterful in his surrealistic observations of Hyde subsuming Jekyll. . . . The fracture comes with Hyde's murder of Jekyll's acquaintance, Sir Danvers X. Carew, MP, part of the London Committee for the Suppression of Traffic in Young English Girls, after which Hyde-Jekyll retreat to an abandoned surgery with a dwindling supply of the chemical catalyst. Cleverly imagined and sophisticated in execution, this book may appeal to those who like magical realism and vampire stories, but the latter should know that the book is more intellectual than thriller."

REVIEW: *N Y Times Book Rev* p34 Je 8 2014

REVIEW: *N Y Times Book Rev* p10 Je 1 2014 WALTER KIRN

LEVINE, DONALD N.tr. The view of life. See Simmel, G.

LEVINE, SARA. Bone by bone; comparing animal skeletons; [by] Sara Levine 32 p. 2014 Millbrook Press

1. Anatomy, Comparative—Juvenile literature 2. Bone—Juvenile literature 3. Children's nonfiction 4. Comparative anatomy 5. Human anatomy—Juvenile literature 6. Skeleton—Juvenile literature

ISBN 9780761384649 (lib. bdg. : alk. paper)

LC 2012-048894

SUMMARY: In this children's book, author Sara "Levine takes a unique approach to comparative anatomy. The purpose of the book is to illustrate differences between human and animal bone structures. . . . The bright, stylized, color illustrations match each question, portraying cartoon children with distorted anatomy, such as a girl with a neck like a giraffe's, or a snake with a human head." (School Library Journal)

REVIEW: *Booklist* v110 no4 p43 O 15 2013 J. B. Petty

REVIEW: *Bull Cent Child Books* v67 no3 p166 N 2013 E. B.

"Bone by Bone: Comparing Animal Skeletons." "This engaging introduction to vertebrate anatomy encourages children to regard themselves as close kin to fellow vertebrates and imagine the results of small tweaks to their own bony framework. . . . The Q & A format of this title lends itself well to group sharing and discussion, and perhaps even some acting out by the less inhibited members of the class. Spookytooth's humorous artwork supports the imaginative musings over each transformation, white his diagrams have both depth and texture to assist viewers in understanding the structures beneath the skin."

REVIEW: *Kirkus Rev* v81 no17 p103 S 1 2013

REVIEW: *SLJ* v59 no9 p177 S 2013 Jeffrey Meyer

LEVINGSTON, STEVEN. Little demon in the city of light; a true story of murder and mesmerism in Belle Epoque Paris; [by] Steven Levingston 352 p. 2014 Doubleday

1. Historical literature 2. Murder—France—Paris—Case studies 3. Paris (France)—Social life and customs—19th century

ISBN 0385536038; 9780385536035 (hardback)

LC 2013-020525

SUMMARY: This book by Steven Levingson examines the case of "Gabrielle Bompard, a young woman who became infamous as the accomplice in a garish and notorious murder in 1889 Paris. Mistress of the con man Michel Eyraud, Bompard and her tragic story became a historical footnote; her case at trial rested on a precedent-setting hypnotism defense." (Publishers Weekly)

REVIEW: *Booklist* v110 no11 p6 F 1 2014 Eloise Kinney

REVIEW: *Kirkus Rev* v81 no24 p193 D 15 2013

"Little Demon in the City of Light: A True Story of Murder and Mesmerism in Belle Eqpoque Paris". "The author foregoes the tabloid excesses and exploitation of lurid details from that time and focuses on the debate as to whether a person is capable of committing a crime under hypnosis or even post-hypnotic suggestion. . . . [Gabrielle] Bompard believed that no one could ever blame her and relished her fame as the newspapers of the time reveled in sensationalistic reporting. What could have been a silly exposé of Paris, hypnotism and detection is instead a well-constructed, informative work by a talented author."

REVIEW: *Libr J* v139 no9 p41 My 15 2014 Linda Sappenfield

REVIEW: *Libr J* v139 no4 p105 Mr 1 2014 Amelia Osterud

REVIEW: *N Y Times Book Rev* p30 My 25 2014 Charles Graeber

REVIEW: *Publ Wkly* v260 no51 p51-2 D 16 2013

LEVINSON, MARC. The great A&P and the struggle for small business in America; [by] Marc Levinson 384 2011 Hill and Wang

1. Chain stores—History 2. Corporate history 3. Great Atlantic & Pacific Tea Co. 4. Small business—United States 5. Supermarkets—History

ISBN 9780809095438

LC 2011-003811

SUMMARY: "In 'The Great A&P and the Struggle for Small Business in America,' . . . historian Marc Levinson tells the story of a struggle between small business and big business that tore America apart. George and John Hartford took over their father's business and reshaped it again and again, turning it into a vertically integrated behemoth that paved the way for every big-box retailer to come." (Publisher's note)

REVIEW: *Antioch Rev* v70 no3 p585-6 Summ 2012 Milton Ezrati

REVIEW: *Bus Hist Rev* v87 no3 p572-4 Aut 2013 Susan V. Spellman

"The Great A&P and the Struggle for Small Business in America." "According to independent scholar Marc Levinson, A&P's rise and subsequent free fall represent the advantages and disadvantages of Schumpeterian creative destruction. The same forces that enabled the Great Atlantic & Pacific Tea Company to grow . . . also led to its decline. . . . Levinson's economic focus at times overlooks the social and cultural costs of efficiency and economies of scale. While Levinson acknowledges that chain stores eventually drove 'mom and pop' from the marketplace and local communities, he portrays small businessmen primarily as reactionary figures despite their persistence in the market for nearly a hundred years after A&P's founding."

REVIEW: *J Econ Lit* v50 no3 p818-9 S 2012

LEVITT, ALEXANDRA M. Deadly Outbreaks; How Medical Detectives Save Lives Threatened by Killer Pandemics, Exotic Viruses, and Drug-resistant Parasites; [by] Alexandra M. Levitt 256 p. 2013 W W Norton & Co Inc

1. Communicable diseases—Prevention 2. Epidemics—History 3. Medical literature 4. Parasites 5. Virus diseases
ISBN 1626360359; 9781626360358

SUMMARY: This book by Alexandra M. Levitt "discusses seven episodes of American epidemiologic intrigue occurring between 1976 and 2007. Old bacteria recently discovered, medical mix-ups, evolving organisms, animal vectors, and other factors drive the narrative." (Choice: Current Reviews for Academic Libraries)

REVIEW: *Booklist* v110 no1 p22 S 1 2013 Tony Miksanek

REVIEW: *Choice* v51 no9 p1629-30 My 2014 J. P. Bourgeois

"Deadly Outbreaks: How Medical Detectives Save Lives Threatened By Killer Pandemics, Exotic Viruses, and Drug-Resistant Parasites". "While the investigations follow similar patterns, each case has unique nuances, difficulties, and intricacies. The storytelling is clear, though not always concise. . . . The style lends a personal touch, revealing details about the investigators' diets, families, and experiences. These details can quagmire the exposition, but they ease the transition into subsequent public health jargon that emerges as the medical investigation develops."

REVIEW: *Libr J* v138 no18 p111 N 1 2013 Cynthia Fox

LEVITT, MATTHEW. Hezbollah; the global footprint of Lebanon's party of god; [by] Matthew Levitt 416 p. 2013 Georgetown University Press
1. Historical literature 2. Hizballah (Lebanon) 3. Shiites—Lebanon 4. Terrorism—History
ISBN 9781626160132 (hardcover: alk. paper)
LC 2013-002933

SUMMARY: "'Hezbollah: The Global Footprint of Lebanon's Party of God' is the first thorough examination of Hezbollah's covert activities beyond Lebanon's borders, including its financial and logistical support networks and its criminal and terrorist operations worldwide. . . . [Author] Matthew Levitt examines Hezbollah's beginnings, its first violent forays in Lebanon, and then its terrorist activities and criminal enterprises abroad." (Publisher's note)

REVIEW: *Choice* v51 no10 p1882 Je 2014 Y. Polsky

REVIEW: *Libr J* v138 no12 p93 Jl 1 2013 Nader Entessar

REVIEW: *TLS* no5791 p28 Mr 28 2014 GERARD RUSSELL

"Hezbollah: The Global Footprint of Lebanon's Party of God" and "Hezbollah and Hamas: A Comparative Study." "[Author Matthew] Levitt's book is comprehensive, and attempts to leaven its forensic detail by having each chapter (all of them dealing with a separate part of the world) plunge us straight into the middle of events, in the style of a thriller. So the book jumps confusingly about in time: a chronology would have been helpful. More significantly, this hampers a proper discussion of causality and development over time. . . . [Editors] Joshua L. Gleis and Benedetta Berti provide some context and a clearer narrative in their short book comparing Hamas and Hezbollah."

LEVITT, RAYMOND E.ed. Global projects. See Global projects

LEVY, DEBBIE. Imperfect spiral; [by] Debbie Levy 352 p. 2013 Walker & Company
1. Babysitters—Fiction 2. Blame—Fiction 3. Illegal aliens—Fiction 4. Traffic accidents—Fiction 5. Young adult fiction
ISBN 9780802734419 (hardback)
LC 2012-027329

SUMMARY: Written by Debbie Levy, this book describes how "Danielle Snyder's summer of babysitting turns into one of overwhelming guilt and sadness when Humphrey, her five-year-old charge is killed suddenly. Danielle gets caught up in the machinery of tragedy: police investigations, neighborhood squabbling, and, when the driver of the car that struck Humphrey turns out to be an undocumented alien, a politically charged immigration debate." (Publisher's note)

REVIEW: *Booklist* v109 no21 p67 Jl 1 2013 Diane Colson

REVIEW: *Bull Cent Child Books* v67 no1 p29-30 S 2013 K. C.

"Imperfect Spiral." "A panic attack at her bat mitzvah shakes Danielle's confidence to the core, so she foregoes the opportunity to be a camp counselor and chooses the seemingly safer option of babysitting a five-year-old boy named Humphrey for her summer job. She and Humphrey develop a deeply caring friendship that sustains them both until one day, when walking home from the park, Humphrey darts into the road to retrieve a ball and is struck and killed by a car. . . . There are threads throughout that explore the painful, messy, but sometimes quite wonderful nature of relationships. Readers will laugh and cry, but perhaps most importantly, they will think their way through important personal and social issues as they grieve along with Danielle."

REVIEW: *Horn Book Magazine* v89 no5 p103 S/O 2013 KATIE BIRCHER

REVIEW: *Kirkus Rev* v81 no10 p99 My 15 2013

REVIEW: *SLJ* v59 no9 p161 S 2013 Brandy Danner

LEVY, DEBBIE. We Shall Overcome; The Story of a Song; 32 p. 2013 Disney Press
1. African Americans—Civil rights—Songs & music 2. African Americans—Music 3. Historical literature 4. Slaves—Songs & music 5. We Shall Overcome (Music)
ISBN 1423119541; 9781423119548

SUMMARY: This book, written by Debbie Levy and illustrated by Vanessa Brantley-Newton, focuses on the song "We Shall Overcome." "From the song's roots in America's era of slavery through to the civil rights movement of the 1960s and today, 'We Shall Overcome' has come to represent the fight for equality and freedom around the world." (Publisher's note)

REVIEW: *Booklist* v110 no7 p45 D 1 2013 Connie Fletcher

REVIEW: *Bull Cent Child Books* v67 no5 p272 Ja 2014 E. B.

"We Shall Overcome: The Story of a Song". "At its best, this title directs listeners to take notice of the way new stages in the civil rights movement influence subtle changes in the lyrics of the song. . . . Unfortunately, unsourced details of the song's international performance are shuffled into an annotated timeline in the end matter, undercutting the song's supposed impact. Digital and mixed-media artwork sports considerable energy in composition, but there's an awkward flatness in the portraiture. Sources aligned to the lyrical change-ups are included, as a list of recordings (several available on the internet) and a list for further reading."

REVIEW: *Kirkus Rev* v81 no21 p86 N 1 2013

REVIEW: *Publ Wkly* v260 no41 p61 O 14 2013

LEVY, JANICE. Thomas the toadilly terrible bully; [by] Janice Levy 34 p. 2014 Eerdmans Books for Young Readers

1. Animal stories 2. Bullying—Fiction 3. Children's stories 4. Friendship—Fiction 5. Toads—Fiction
ISBN 9780802853738
LC 2013-024834

SUMMARY: In this book, "Thomas the toad hates being ignored, so he decides to become a bully. The trouble with this plan is that Thomas isn't particularly good at bullying. . . . Even [when] he confronts Gomer, the weakest toad around, it turns out that what made Gomer cry" was "a much bigger bully. . . . After cleverly tricking the big bully into picking a fight with his own reflection, Thomas realizes that he makes a much better friend than a bully." (Bulletin of the Center for Children's Books)

REVIEW: *Bull Cent Child Books* v67 no6 p322 F 2014 Thaddeus Andracki

"Thomas the Toadilly Terrible Bully." "Thomas' strategies not to be ignored by his peers will be familiar to kids, and Thomas' change from bully to friend becomes a plot point rather than a lesson. The illustrations, acrylic on gessoed paper, take on a texture reminiscent of fresco painting, and the swatches of tan, chartreuse, and vermilion call to mind fall foliage. The big-eyed toad caricatures capture mood perfectly through dramatic facial expressions. . . . This is a slightly more serious take than [Mo] Willems' 'Leonardo the Terrible Monster' . . . but the similarities are striking, and it might be interesting to pair the two as explorations of the failures of being mean."

REVIEW: *Kirkus Rev* v81 no24 p197 D 15 2013

"Thomas the Toadily Terrible Bully". "The serious topic of bullying gets a light treatment in this tale of limited social skills and accidental friendship. The brisk introduction of Thomas, a newcomer to town, may leave readers, like his new acquaintances, cold. Cocky, pushy and clearly impatient, Thomas quickly decides that if his first approach doesn't work, he'll "be a bully instead." Unfortunately, he's just not cut out for the role. . . . Paintings in acrylics on gessoed paper have a pleasingly textural look, well-suited to the warty characters and woodland setting. . . . Unfortunately, none of this quite manages to compensate for the slim storyline and pat resolution."

REVIEW: *SLJ* v60 no2 p75 F 2014 Roxanne Burg

LEVY, PETER.tr. A civil war. See Pavone, C.

LEWIN, TED. Can you see me?; [by] Ted Lewin 32 p. 2014 Holiday House

1. Camouflage (Biology)—Juvenile literature 2. Habitat (Ecology) 3. Picture books for children 4. Rain forest animals—Juvenile literature 5. Rain forests—Juvenile literature
ISBN 0823429407; 9780823429400 (hardcover)
LC 2013-009555

SUMMARY: In this children's book, by Ted Lewin, "readers are invited to spot various animals in the Costa Rican rain forest. Lewin . . .. displays . . . mammals, birds and reptiles in their natural habitats. Camouflage is the unspoken theme. . . . A pictorial guide identifies each of the animals by name." (Kirkus Reviews)

REVIEW: *Booklist* v110 no16 p45 Ap 15 2014 Paula Willey

REVIEW: *Kirkus Rev* v82 no3 p204 F 1 2014

"Can You See Me?". "[Ted] . Lewin, an intrepid world traveler, once again displays his skill at depicting mammals, birds and reptiles in their natural habitats. . . . Simple declarative sentences encourage emerging readers to explore and, at the same time, develop a kinship for these creatures who 'are still here.' Lewin uses watercolors to brilliantly showcase the play of light and dark in the dense foliage. Sunlight shimmers, shines and fades into darkness. A pictorial guide identifies each of the animals by name. An inviting exploration of a beautiful biome for budding nature lovers."

REVIEW: *SLJ* v60 no4 p181 Ap 2014 Catherine Callegari

LEWIN, TED.il. Can you see me? See Lewin, T.

LEWIS, CATHERINE M.ed. Museums in a global context. See Museums in a global context

LEWIS, EARL B., 1956-.il. All different now. See Johnson, A.

LEWIS, JEFF. Crisis in the global mediasphere; desire, displeasure and cultural transformation; [by] Jeff Lewis ix, 244 p. 2011 Palgrave Macmillan

1. Discourse theory (Communication) 2. Mass media—Political aspects 3. Mass media—Social aspects 4. Mass media and culture 5. Social science literature
ISBN 0230247423 (alk. paper); 9780230247420 (alk. paper)
LC 2010-033962

SUMMARY: This book, by Jeff Lewis, "engages . . . with the discourses constructing-and constructed through-the anxieties and desires that permeate contemporary society. Focusing on the (re)constructions of crisis and a (collective) crisis consciousness within a 'global mediasphere', Lewis touches on issues as diverse as the current financial turmoil, sexual desire and relationships, growing global inequalities, widespread ecological destruction, and continued warfare and terrorism." (Cultural Studies Review)

REVIEW: *Contemp Sociol* v43 no1 p100-2 Ja 2014 Sarah Amsler

"Crisis in the Global Mediasphere: Desire, Displeasure and Cultural Transformation". "Jeff Lewis paints a convincing picture of societies that are not only characterized by long-cumulative effects of capitalism, penetrating technologies, rapidly expanding populations, and militarized forms of governance, but shaped by a dense atmosphere of knowledge systems and cultural mediations which represent this world as a place of perpetual possibility and immanent anxiety. . . . The book charts quite an original path as Lewis brings these sociological ideas into conversation with cultural theory, psychoanalysis, and evolution. . . . The geographical and historical scope of the book's theoretical inspiration is both dazzling and dizzying."

LEWIS, JOHN R., 1940-. March; Book One; [by] John R.

Lewis 121 p. 2013 Top Shelf Productions
1. Boycotts 2. Civil rights demonstrations 3. Civil rights movements—United States—Comic books, strips, etc 4. Graphic nonfiction 5. Historical literature
ISBN 9781603093002 (acid-free paper)
LC 2013-218903

SUMMARY: This graphic novel, by U.S. congressman John Lewis, "in collaboration with co-writer Andrew Aydin and New York Times best-selling artist Nate Powell . . . spans John Lewis' youth in rural Alabama, his life-changing meeting with Martin Luther King, Jr., the birth of the Nashville Student Movement, and their battle to tear down segregation through nonviolent lunch counter sit-ins, building to a . . . climax on the steps of City Hall." (Publisher's note)

REVIEW: *Booklist* v109 no19/20 p57 Je 1 2013 Ray Olson

REVIEW: *Horn Book Magazine* v90 no1 p114-5 Ja/F 2014 SAM BLOOM

"March: Book One." "Congressman John Lewis--the last surviving member of the 'Big Six' civil rights leaders--recounts his formative years in this first volume of a planned trilogy. . . . There's something extraordinary about reading a firsthand account of a seminal moment in history from one who not only lived through it but also led it, and this is what ultimately makes this book so essential. The volume is well-designed and the story expertly paced. . . . [Nate] Powell re-creates the time period vividly through his black-and-white art, but the artist's true gift is in his ability to capture emotion with deft use of line and shadow. His nuanced visual storytelling complements Lewis's account beautifully."

REVIEW: *Kirkus Rev* p54 Ag 15 2013 Fall Preview

REVIEW: *Kirkus Rev* v81 no14 p306 Jl 15 2013

REVIEW: *Libr J* v138 no12 p69 Jl 1 2013 M. C.

REVIEW: *N Y Times Book Rev* p38 N 24 2013 Ken Tucker

REVIEW: *Publ Wkly* v260 no28 p154 Jl 15 2013

REVIEW: *SLJ* v59 no9 p171 S 2013 Benjamin Russell

REVIEW: *Voice of Youth Advocates* v37 no1 p28-9 Ap 2014 AMANDA FOUST JACK BAUR

LEWIS, MICHAEL. Flash boys; a Wall Street revolt; [by] Michael Lewis 288 p. 2014 W.W. Norton & Co Inc.
1. Finance—United States—History—21st century 2. High-frequency trading (Securities) 3. Historical literature 4. Stockbrokers—United States 5. Stocks (Finance)
ISBN 0393244660; 9780393244663 (hardcover: alk. paper)
LC 2014-003208

SUMMARY: Written by Michael Lewis, "'Flash Boys' is about a small group of Wall Street guys who figure out that the U.S. stock market has been rigged for the benefit of insiders and that, post-financial crisis, the markets have become not more free but less, and more controlled by the big Wall Street banks. Working at different firms, they come to this realization separately; but after they discover one another, the flash boys band together and set out to reform the financial markets." (Publisher's note)

REVIEW: *Choice* v52 no2 p310 O 2014 W. S. Curran

REVIEW: *Economist* v411 no8881 p73 Ap 5 2014

REVIEW: *Kirkus Rev* v82 no9 p60 My 1 2014

REVIEW: *Libr J* v139 no13 p50 Ag 1 2014 Kelly Sinclair

REVIEW: *London Rev Books* v36 no11 p7-9 Je 5 2014 John Lanchester

REVIEW: *N Y Rev Books* v61 no12 p37-8 Jl 10 2014 James Surowiecki

REVIEW: *N Y Times Book Rev* p12-3 Ap 20 2014 JAMES B. STEWART

REVIEW: *N Y Times Book Rev* p34 My 11 2014

REVIEW: *New York Times* v163 no56462 pA21 Ap 5 2014 JOE NOCERA

REVIEW: *New York Times* v163 no56458 pC1-4 Ap 1 2014 JANET MASLIN

REVIEW: *Publ Wkly* v261 no30 p87 Jl 28 2014

REVIEW: *Time* v183 no14 p59 Ap 14 2014 Lev Grossman

"Flash Boys: A Wall Street Revolt." "[Author] Michael Lewis possesses two virtues that are rarely united in a single writer: he has no fear of talking to engineers about technical issues and he's a top-flight story-teller. In his new book, 'Flash Boys,' Lewis applies both skills to the rise of high-speed trading in the 2000s and the way its enormous complexity was being used to do something pretty simple—make a huge amount of money for people in the know, without those not in the know realizing it."

REVIEW: *TLS* no5802 p7 Je 13 2014 HOWARD DAVIES

LEWIS, PAUL. Undercover. See Evans, R.

LEWIS, RICHARD D. Fish can't see water; how national culture can make or break your corporate strategy; [by] Richard D. Lewis 312 p. 2013 John Wiley & Sons Ltd.
1. Business literature 2. Corporate culture—Cross-cultural studies 3. National characteristics 4. Organizational behavior—Cross-cultural studies 5. Strategic planning
ISBN 9781118608562 (cloth)
LC 2013-013592

SUMMARY: It was the author's intent to demonstrate that "national culture, through its influence on corporate culture, has a powerful but often-invisible impact on the success of global companies. What's more, the very same national traits that accelerate growth at one stage of the corporate life cycle may derail that growth at a different stage or when an inevitable crisis hits." (Publisher's note)

REVIEW: *Choice* v51 no9 p1643 My 2014 D. W. Huffmire

REVIEW: *Economist* v409 no8857 p99-100 O 12 2013

"Fish Can't See Water: How National Cultures Can Make or Break Your Corporate Strategy." "It is easy to poke fun at trying to capture human civilisation in a three-pointed diagram and producing a guide to business strategy from it. Cultures are hard to pin down . . . and businesses frequently defy national stereotypes. . . . Messrs [Kai] Hammerich and [Richard] Lewis try to have it both ways. . . . They also overestimate the originality of their insight. . . . But in focusing on culture they are clearly onto something important. . . . 'Fish Can't See Water' is full of interesting insights into modern business."

LEWIS, SARAH. The rise; creativity, mastery, and the gift of failure; [by] Sarah Lewis 272 p. 2014 Simon & Schuster
1. Creative ability 2. Expertise 3. Failure (Psychology) 4. Persistence (Personality trait) 5. Psychological

literature
ISBN 1451629230; 9781451629231 (hardcover: alk. paper); 9781451629248 (pbk.: alk. paper)
LC 2013-028434

SUMMARY: "The gift of failure is a riddle." Written by Sarah Lewis, "'The Rise' . . . makes the case that many of our greatest triumphs come from understanding the importance of this mystery. 'The Rise' explores the inestimable value of often ignored ideas—the power of surrender for fortitude, the criticality of play for innovation, the propulsion of the near win on the road to mastery, and the importance of grit and creative practice." (Publisher's note)

REVIEW: *Kirkus Rev* v82 no2 p62 Ja 15 2014

"The Rise: Creativity, the Gift of Failure, and the Search for Mastery". "In her nonfiction debut, curator and arts consultant [Sarah] Lewis . . . takes on the broad topic of creativity. Ranging across an expansive historical landscape, the author considers artists, scientists, writers, entrepreneurs and even an intrepid explorer, investigating the sources of their creativity. . . . Creativity, like genius, is inexplicable, but Lewis' synthesis of history, biography and psychological research offers a thoughtful response to the question of how new ideas happen."

REVIEW: *Libr J* v139 no9 p41 My 15 2014 Donna Bachowski

REVIEW: *Libr J* v139 no1 p1 Ja 2014

REVIEW: *N Y Times Book Rev* p18 Ap 6 2014 SCOTT A. SANDAGE

REVIEW: *Publ Wkly* v260 no49 p71-2 D 2 2013

LEWISOHN, MARK. The Beatles; all these years; [by] Mark Lewisohn 944 p. 2013 Crown Archetype

1. Beatles (Performer) 2. Music—20th century—History & criticism 3. Music literature 4. Musicians—Biography 5. Rock musicians—England—Biography
ISBN 9781400083053
LC 2013-031654

SUMMARY: "'Tune In' is the first volume of 'All These Years'--a highly-anticipated, groundbreaking biographical trilogy by the world's leading Beatles historian. Mark Lewisohn uses his unprecedented archival access and hundreds of new interviews to construct the full story of the lives and work of John Lennon, Paul McCartney, George Harrison, and Ringo Starr." (Publisher's note)

REVIEW: *Bookforum* v20 no5 p48 F/Mr 2014 CHRISTOPHER SORRENTINO

"Tune In--The Beatles: All These Years." "Beatles enthusiasts enthusiasts . . . seem especially susceptible to what could be called Mystical Completism--the belief that each newly discovered document, each unpublished photo, each additional outtake, represents another step along the path to ultimate enlightenment. . . . Mark Lewisohn is the most rigorous practitioner of that literal-minded pursuit, which he attempts to take to its outer limits with his new biography. . . . The reader is . . . awed by the magnitude of Lewisohn's efforts. . . . More sturdy than transcendent, his prose is designed to support the bus routes, street-name etymologies, installment-plan terms, payroll deductions, and other factoids that fascinate even as they overwhelm."

REVIEW: *N Y Times Book Rev* p74-5 D 8 2013 TIM RILEY

"Tune In: The Beatles: All These Years, Volume 1." "[Author] Mark Lewisohn [provides] the widest possible angle on an extensive and engrossing group biography built on a well-raked mountain of exacting new research. In the first of a projected three-volume work--803 pages of text that take the story up to the end of 1962--he retells this epic tale in a manner that, while ambitious, and at times even indulgent, also manages to be expertly controlled and propelling. . . . Many, many other books will be written about the Beatles. But 'Tune In,' despite its bland title, will always hold an honored place among them."

REVIEW: *New Yorker* v89 no42 p121-1 D 23 2013

"Duke: A Life of Duke Ellington" and "Tune In." "Terry Teachout's searching new biography, 'Duke: A Life of Duke Ellington' . . . touches on the mystique of the great bandleader's music as much as on its notes and measures. . . . Teachout is a sensitive writer, and one reason his biographies are moving is that he has obviously been giving himself an education in the realities of American racial history as he writes them. . . . Mark Lewisohn's new book, 'Tune In' . . . the first volume of a promised three-volume history of the Beatles--tells the story of their lives up to 1962, when they had yet to make an LP."

LI, JUDITH L. Ellie's log; 112 p. 2013 Oregon State University Press

1. Diaries—Authorship 2. Forests & forestry—Juvenile literature 3. Nature study 4. Picture books for children 5. Science—Juvenile literature
ISBN 0870716964 (paperback); 9780870716966 (paperback)
LC 2012-043665

SUMMARY: In this book, "after a huge tree falls in the forest behind her home, fifth-grader Ellie explores the area with her classmate Ricky, mapping and sketching and learning about what lives, dies and changes there. Each [chapter] opens with a spread illustrating the part of the woods they visit and closes with two pages from Ellie's field notebook." (Kirkus Reviews)

REVIEW: *Kirkus Rev* v81 no4 p190 F 15 2013

REVIEW: *Science* v342 no6162 p1045 N 29 2013 Sherman J. Suter

LICHTENHELD, TOM. Exclamation mark. See Rosenthal, Amy Krouse

LICHTMAN, ROBERT M. The Supreme Court and McCarthy-era repression; one hundred decisions; [by] Robert M. Lichtman 285 p. 2012 University of Illinois Press

1. Anti-communist movements 2. Civil rights—United States—Cases 3. Historical literature
ISBN 9780252037009 (hard cover : alk. paper); 9780252094125 (e-book)
LC 2011-052767

SUMMARY: In this book, "Robert M. Lichtman provides a a . . . history of the U.S. Supreme Court's decisions in 'Communist' cases during the McCarthy era. Lichtman shows the Court's vulnerability to public criticism and attacks by the elected branches during periods of political repression. The book describes every Communist-related decision of the era (none is omitted), placing them in the context of political events and revealing the range and intrusiveness of McCarthy-era repression." (Publisher's note)

REVIEW: *Am Hist Rev* v118 no4 p1212-4 O 2013 Robert Justin Goldstein

REVIEW: *J Am Hist* v100 no3 p895 D 2013 Alex Goodall

REVIEW: *Rev Am Hist* v41 no3 p533-9 S 2013 M. J. Heale

"The Supreme Court and McCarthy-Era Repression: One Hundred Decisions" and "The Second Red Scare and the Unmaking of the New Deal Left." "In broad terms, there is little here that is new. . . . But, with access to the justices' unpublished papers, [Robert M.] Lichtman's analysis helps to explain the various decisions, in terms both of the formal published opinions and of private considerations, as he also guides us through the friendships and frictions on the Court. . . . [Landon R. Y.] Storrs' research in this brilliant book is prodigious, including recently declassified records of the federal loyalty program, the private papers of many of the subjects, and interviews with surviving subjects or witnesses. Through careful collation across a wide range of sources, she has discovered vital relationships and connections that had been unknown to scholarship."

LIDEGAARD, BO. Countrymen; The Untold Story of How Denmark's Jews Escaped the Nazis, of the Courage of Their Fellow Danes & of the Extraordinary Role of the SS; [by] Bo Lidegaard 396 p. 2013 Alfred A. Knopf

1. Historical literature 2. Holocaust, Jewish (1939-1945)—Denmark 3. Jews—Denmark—History—20th century 4. Jews—Persecutions—Denmark 5. World War, 1939-1945—Jews—Rescue—Denmark

ISBN 0385350155; 9780385350150 (hardcover); 9780385350167 (ebook)

LC 2013-006349

SUMMARY: This book by Bo Lidegaard chronicles "the protection and eventual rescue of the approximately 7,000 Danish Jews by their fellow Gentile Danish citizens, escaping a scheduled roundup by Nazi occupiers. . . . The Danish government, including the king, had advance notice of the Nazi plan. A policy of delay and obstruction bought time, which allowed ordinary citizens to organize transport of almost all of the Jews to Sweden." (Booklist)

REVIEW: *Bookforum* v20 no3 p53 S-N 2013 ALLEN BARRA

REVIEW: *Booklist* v110 no2 p16-7 S 15 2013 Jay Freeman

"Countrymen." "One of the few feel-good stories to emerge from the Holocaust was the protection and eventual rescue of the approximately 7,000 Danish Jews by their fellow Gentile Danish citizens, escaping a scheduled roundup by Nazi occupiers. . . . [Bo] Lidegaard uses diaries, letters, and memoirs of the participants to provide a day-to-day narrative that proceeds on two tracks: the Nazi plans for roundup and the Danish plans to defeat it. The Danish government, including the king, had advance notice of the Nazi plan. A policy of delay and obstruction bought time, which allowed ordinary citizens to organize transport of almost all of the Jews to Sweden. This is a tense, inspiring story of the resistance to oppression by a united people."

REVIEW: *Kirkus Rev* v81 no16 p206 Ag 15 2013

REVIEW: *New Repub* v244 no20 p37-9 D 9 2013 Michael Ignatieff

"Countrymen: The Untold Story of How Denmark's Jews Escaped the Nazis, of the Courage of Their Fellow Danes—and of the Extraordinary Role of the SS". "Magnificent. . . . An intensely human account of one episode in the persecution of European Jews that ended in survival. . . . [Bo] Lidegaard's central insight is that human solidarity in crisis depended on the prior consolidation of a decent politics, on the creation of a shared political imagination. . . . Lidegaard is an excellent guide to this story when he sticks close to Danish realities. When he ventures further and asks bigger questions, he goes astray."

REVIEW: *New Statesman* v143 no10 p55 Mr 14 2014 Bo Lidegaard

REVIEW: *Publ Wkly* v260 no28 p158 Jl 15 2013

LIEBER, ROCHELLE. The Oxford reference guide to English morphology. See Plag, I.

LIEBERMAN, DANIEL, 1964-. The story of the human body; evolution, health, and disease; [by] Daniel Lieberman 464 p. 2013 Pantheon Books

1. Adaptation (Biology) 2. Health—Social aspects 3. Human body 4. Human evolution 5. Nutrition 6. Scientific literature

ISBN 0307379418; 9780307379412

LC 2013-011811

SUMMARY: This book, by Daniel E. Lieberman, presents the "story of human evolution consisting of five biological transformations (walking upright, eating a variety of different foods, accumulating physical traits aligned to hunting and gathering, gaining bigger brains with larger bodies, and developing unique capacities for cooperation and language) and two cultural ones (farming and reliance on machines)." (Booklist)

REVIEW: *Booklist* v110 no2 p12 S 15 2013 Tony Miksanek

REVIEW: *Choice* v51 no10 p1830 Je 2014 J. N. Muzio

REVIEW: *Kirkus Rev* v81 no16 p131 Ag 15 2013

"The Story of the Human Body." "Six million years of biological evolution have produced a human body ill-adapted to the diets and lifestyles that cultural evolution has wrought since modern humans emerged. That is the core message of this massive review of where we came from and what ails us now. [Author Daniel E.] Lieberman . . . writes authoritatively about the fossil record, crediting bipedalism as the driver that freed hands to learn new skills, enabled foraging for diverse diets and chasing prey, and ultimately built bigger brains. . . . The repeated emphasis on all the bad things humans do is wearying. By no means does Lieberman discount all the good that modern society has achieved, but that message is nearly drowned by the constant admonition to do right by your body."

REVIEW: *Libr J* v139 no4 p56 Mr 1 2014 Forrest E. Link

REVIEW: *Libr J* v138 no8 p61 My 1 2013

REVIEW: *Publ Wkly* v260 no30 p55 Jl 29 2013

LIEBERMAN, LAYNE. Beyond the mediterranean diet; european secrets of the super-healthy; [by] Layne Lieberman 280 p. 2013 WorldRD LLC

1. Advice literature 2. Food habits 3. French cooking 4. Italian cooking 5. Swiss cooking

ISBN 9780989181211 (softcover: alk. paper); 9780989181228

LC 2013-946453

SUMMARY: This book looks at food habits in "Switzerland,

Italy and France," [which] have some of the longest average life spans in the world, as well as low rates of obesity, heart disease and other markers of ill health. The book examines each country one by one and lays out the government's official dietary recommendations, akin to the U.S. food pyramid, along with detailed descriptions of a typical day in the eating life of its citizens." (Kirkus Reviews)

REVIEW: *Kirkus Rev* v82 no2 p384 Ja 15 2014

"Beyond the Mediterranean Diet". "Much of [Layne] Lieberman's background and advice will be familiar to anyone paying attention to the news. . . . But Lieberman's descriptions of the daily eating habits of her chosen European countries are downright inspiring. . . . It all sounds too romantic to be true, but Lieberman has lived it and brings an infectious enthusiasm to her writing. She concludes each chapter with a list of actionable tips for a European makeover of stateside eating habits and concludes the book with 70 pages of simple recipes, heavy on the whole grains, veggies and lean meats. While not a game-changer, this book repackages familiar diet advice in a friendly, inspiring and practical format."

REVIEW: *Kirkus Rev* v82 no3 p138 F 1 2014

"Beyond the Mediterranean Diet". "Much of [Layne] Lieberman's background and advice will be familiar to anyone paying attention to the news. . . . But Lieberman's descriptions of the daily eating habits of her chosen European countries are downright inspiring. . . . It all sounds too romantic to be true, but Lieberman has lived it and brings an infectious enthusiasm to her writing. She concludes each chapter with a list of actionable tips for a European makeover of stateside eating habits and concludes the book with 70 pages of simple recipes, heavy on the whole grains, veggies and lean meats. While not a game-changer, this book repackages familiar diet advice in a friendly, inspiring and practical format."

LIEBERMAN, MATTHEW D. Social; [by] Matthew D. Lieberman 384 p. 2013 Crown Publishers

1. Cognitive neuroscience 2. Scientific literature 3. Social interaction 4. Social networks 5. Social psychology
ISBN 9780307889096; 9780307889119 (ebook)
LC 2013-006226

SUMMARY: This book by Matthew D. Lieberman "shows readers how their brains may be wired . . . to harmonize and connect with others, rather than simply to act in their own interests. With the help of new functional MRI technology, Lieberman . . . investigat[es] how our perceptions of others affect our cognition and, even more elementally, how social interaction and its absence can produce the same mental responses as physical pain and pleasure." (Publishers Weekly)

REVIEW: *Booklist* v110 no1 p18 S 1 2013 Bridget Thoreson

REVIEW: *Kirkus Rev* v81 no16 p196 Ag 15 2013

REVIEW: *N Y Times Book Rev* p22 N 3 2013 ROBIN MARANTZ HENIG

"Social: Why Our Brains Are Wired to Connect." "[Matthew D.] Lieberman seems to be a pretty social guy himself, and he generously shares stories from his life . . . even when they're not especially flattering, in the service of making a point. Along the way, he offers a good deal of evidence, most of it M.R.I.-based, supporting the adaptive value of brain systems that give us insights into others. . . . All this scanning leads to some cool findings, even if you're not inclined to follow them as far as the author does."

REVIEW: *Publ Wkly* v260 no30 p54 Jl 29 2013

REVIEW: *Publ Wkly* v261 no8 p180 F 24 2014

LIFECYCLE EVENTS AND THEIR CONSEQUENCES; 2013 Stanford University Press

1. Cost & standard of living 2. Life change events 3. Social science literature 4. United States—Economic conditions 5. Well-being
ISBN 9780804785853

SUMMARY: This book, edited by Kenneth Couch, Mary Daly, and Julie Zissimopoulos, focuses on "the impact of unexpected life course events on economic welfare. The contributions in this volume explore how job loss, the onset of health limitations, and changes in household structure can have a pronounced influence on individual and household well-being across the life course. Although these events are typically studied in isolation, they frequently co-occur or are otherwise interrelated." (Publisher's note)

REVIEW: *Choice* v51 no6 p1061 F 2014 D. J. Conger

"Lifecycle Events and Their Consequences: Job Loss, Family Change, and Declines in Health." "With recovery from the great recession under way, it is an auspicious time for a fine scholarly work examining the consequences of job loss, family change, and health declines among Americans. . . . In unpacking each event, the authors provide guidance to the latest research and data sources, and they suggest future research agendas. Throughout, the text remains accessible to a general readership while also informing experts. . . . Recommended."

LIGHT, STEVE. Have you seen my dragon?; [by] Steve Light 48 p. 2014 Candlewick Press

1. Children's stories 2. Chinatown (New York, N.Y.) 3. Counting 4. Dragons—Juvenile fiction 5. New York (N.Y.)—Fiction
ISBN 0763666483; 9780763666484
LC 2013-943993

SUMMARY: In this children's book, by Steve Light, readers "help a boy find his dragon while counting objects from hot dogs to traffic lights. In the heart of the city, among the taxis and towers, a small boy travels uptown and down, searching for his friend. . . . Is the dragon taking the crosstown bus, or breathing his fiery breath below a busy street? Maybe he took a taxi to the zoo or is playing with the dogs in the park." (Publisher's note)

REVIEW: *Booklist* v110 no15 p93 Ap 1 2014 Jesse Karp

REVIEW: *Bull Cent Child Books* v67 no10 p528 Je 2014 T. A.

"Have You Seen My Dragon?" "The simple journey and even the counting are merely excuses, however, to take in the lavish cityscapes of the pen and ink illustrations: each spread features detailed black and white drawings using thick and thin nib techniques to achieve a calligraphic effect. The countable elements are washed over with a single colorful pigment, setting them apart for easy picking out. . . . The intricate penwork will get lost in busyness if shared with an audience; this is one for poring over, so that youngsters can not only count the color-coded hot dogs, balloons, and subway cars but also spot the dragon sneakily hiding just out of our narrator's view each step of the way."

REVIEW: *Kirkus Rev* v82 no4 p119 F 15 2014

"Have You Seen My Dragon?" "Black line pen-and-ink drawings in finely patterned detail depict a vital, lively New York City of the imagination. Colored-pencil images on each double-page spread are reserved for the city-specific items to be counted along the way, and the endpapers depict a loosely interpreted map indicating the sites. . . . If this is an attempt at reminding young readers that the dragon is imaginary, it's a bit of an anticlimax, and it takes a great deal of the fun out of the previous travels around the city. But the visual appeal overcomes it all. Lots for young readers to see and count."

REVIEW: *N Y Times Book Rev* p24 Ap 6 2014 SARAH HARRISON SMITH

REVIEW: *Publ Wkly* v261 no5 p53 F 3 2014

REVIEW: *SLJ* v60 no4 p127 Ap 2014 Roxanne Burg

LIGHT, STEVE.il. Have you seen my dragon? See Light, S.

LIMA, MANUEL. The book of trees; visualizing branches of knowledge; [by] Manuel Lima 208 p. 2014 Princeton Architectural Press

1. Communication in learning and scholarship—History 2. Graphic methods—History 3. Historical literature 4. Knowledge, Theory of—History 5. Learning and scholarship—History 6. Trees—Symbolic aspects—History 7. Visual communication—History
ISBN 9781616892180 (alkaline paper)
LC 2013-026128

SUMMARY: In this book, "Manuel Lima examines the . . . history of the tree diagram, from its roots in the illuminated manuscripts of medieval monasteries to its current resurgence as an elegant means of visualization. Lima presents two hundred intricately detailed tree diagram illustrations on a remarkable variety of subjects—from some of the earliest known examples from ancient Mesopotamia to the manuscripts of medieval monasteries to contributions by leading contemporary designers." (Publisher's note)

REVIEW: *Choice* v51 no11 p1967-8 Jl 2014 S. Skaggs

REVIEW: *New Sci* v221 no2963 p48-9 Ap 5 2014 Jonathon Keats

"The Book of Trees: Visualizing Branches of Knowledge." "[Author Manuel] Lima, a digital designer and information guru, thinks visual literacy, including the ability to express ourselves graphically, is as important as reading and writing. True to this visual orientation, he has provided us with a fine field guide to tree forms past and present in a sumptuous book that places pictures firmly in the foreground. Full-colour reproductions of charts from many of the world's great library collections graphically connect 2014 with the 1000-year evolution of using trees as a mode of visual communication."

REVIEW: *Publ Wkly* v261 no11 p77 Mr 17 2014

LIMA, ZEULER ROCHA MELLO DE ALMEIDA. Lina Bo Bardi; [by] Zeuler Rocha Mello de Almeida Lima 239 p. 2013 Yale University Press

1. Architects—Brazil—Biography 2. Architectural literature 3. Architecture—Brazil 4. Architecture—Italy 5. Women architects—Brazil—Biography
ISBN 9780300154269 (clothbound: alk. paper)
LC 2013-013065

SUMMARY: "'Lina Bo Bardi' is the first comprehensive study of Bo Bardi's career and showcases author Zeuler Lima's extensive archival work in Italy and Brazil. . . . The book examines how considerations of ethics, politics, and social inclusiveness influenced Bo Bardi's intellectual engagement with modern architecture and provides an authoritative guide to her experimental, ephemeral, and iconic works of design." (Publisher's note)

REVIEW: *N Y Rev Books* v61 no9 p12-5 My 22 2014 Martin Filler

"Lina Bo Bardi," "Lina Bo Bardi: The Theory of Architectural Practice," and "Stones Against Diamonds." "'Lina Bo Bardi,' the first full-length life-and-works, by Zeuler R. M. de A. Lima . . . is a feat of primary-source scholarship and thoughtful analysis. Lima does a masterful job of candidly assessing his brilliant, somewhat erratic, and not always truthful subject. . . . Cathrine Veikos's 'Lina Bo Bardi: The Theory of Architectural Practice' [is] the first English translation of . . . Bo Bardi's fullest exposition of a design philosophy. . . . 'Stones Against Diamonds,' a collection of Bo Bardi's writings, was recently issued by London's Architectural Association, part of its commendable Architecture Words series."

LIN, GRACE. Ling & Ting share a birthday; [by] Grace Lin 48 p. 2013 Little, Brown Books for Young Readers

1. Birthdays—Fiction 2. Children's stories 3. Chinese Americans—Fiction 4. Sisters—Fiction 5. Twins—Fiction
ISBN 0316184055; 9780316184052
LC 2012-040965

SUMMARY: In this book by Grace Lin "Ling & Ting are twins. They share a birthday. They bake cakes, and they make birthday wishes. They tell stories and wrap gifts. They also share a birthday secret." (Publisher's note) "In six stories, the girls receive birthday shoes, shop for presents, . . . open their gifts, and read a story." (Publishers Weekly)

REVIEW: *Horn Book Magazine* v89 no5 p104 S/O 2013 JENNIFER M. BRABANDER

"Ling & Ting Share a Birthday." "The terrific twins from 'Ling & Ting: Not Exactly the Same!' . . . are back in a second easy reader, this one just as well conceived as the first. . . . Once again, young readers will enjoy spotting the differences (both big and small) between the identical twins. . . . While the book has a sweetly retro feel to it, Ling and Ting's adventures will appeal to contemporary audiences. [Grace] Lin gets a lot of mileage out of the simple concept of sharing--a birthday, a cake, wishes, presents, and 'the same secret smiles'; let's hope Lin continues to share with readers the further adventures of this dynamic duo."

REVIEW: *Kirkus Rev* v81 no12 p102 Je 15 2013

REVIEW: *Publ Wkly* p72 Children's starred review annual 2013

REVIEW: *Publ Wkly* v260 no27 p87-8 Jl 8 2013

REVIEW: *SLJ* v60 no5 p63 My 2014 Terri Perper

REVIEW: *SLJ* v59 no8 p80 Ag 2013 Gloria Koster

LIND, COLENE J. Political tone. See Hart, R. P.

LINDEN, KAYE. Tales from Ma's Watering-Hole; [by] Kaye Linden 162 p. 2013 Lightning Source Inc

1. Aboriginal Australians—Fiction 2. Australian short stories 3. Boundaries 4. Coffeehouses 5. Rural-urban relations
ISBN 1626464340; 9781626464346

SUMMARY: In this collection of stories, "Ma, the 99-year-old shaman who runs a cafe on the border between a city and Aboriginal lands, dishes out stories, laughter, beer and biscuits together with healings and body decoration to her local regulars. . . . Culture clashes between city people and locals . . . manifest in Ma's teasing of her tourist visitors and in the harsher tales of city girls lost and tribal law succeeding where city law fails." (Kirkus Reviews)

REVIEW: *Kirkus Rev* v82 no3 p371 F 1 2014

"Tales From Ma's Watering Hole". "A debut collection of stories about a traditional Australian tribal community, told in the voices of shamans, elders and tricksters. . . . The stories' language is simple, and they mostly come from the characters' own lives; although there may be lessons here, the stories are meant to entertain. . . . The net effect is rough yet magical, practical yet playful, with an internally consistent authenticity that comes more from the author's modern imagination than from tradition. A fine collection evoking nostalgia for a simpler way of life."

REVIEW: *Kirkus Rev* v82 no6 p32 Mr 15 2014

LINDHARDT, MARTIN. Power in powerlessness; a study of Pentecostal life worlds in urban Chile; [by] Martin Lindhardt 270 p. 2012 Brill

1. City churches—Chile—Valparaíso 2. Pentecostalism—Chile—Valparaíso 3. Pentecostals 4. Social science literature
ISBN 9789004216006 (hardback: alk. paper)
LC 2011-042135

SUMMARY: This book presents "an ethnographic study of a traditional Pentecostal church in the city of Valparaiso in Chile. Through detailed descriptions and examination of Pentecostal rituals and everyday practices, the author wishes to uncover how people leam to think and live as Pentecostals. The author raises the question: 'how—or through what processes—are Pentecostal life worlds and self-identities constituted, reproduced, and modified?" (Pneuma: The Journal of the Society for Pentecostal Studies)

REVIEW: *Contemp Sociol* v43 no2 p285-6 Mr 2014

"Power in Powerlessness: A Study of Pentecostal Life Worlds in Urban Chile". "Expanding the study of religion and conversion, Martin Lindhardt uses Chilean Pentecostalism to explore how, rather than why, believers come to view the world through the denomination's point of view and how they live out this interpretation in their circumstances of poverty and disadvantage. . . . 'Power in Powerlessness,' though written about religious adherents, can be useful to a broader audience interested in topics beyond religion. Although the book's focus is on a specific religious denomination in a particular Latin American country, Lindhardt's findings may be applied in multiple settings, contributing to conversations on identity formation, responses to inequality, and political development."

LINDSEY, MARY. Ashes on the waves; [by] Mary Lindsey 384 p. 2013 Philomel Books

1. Gothic fiction (Literary genre) 2. Islands—Fiction 3. Love—Fiction 4. Mythology, Celtic—Fiction 5. People with disabilities—Fiction 6. Supernatural—Fiction 7. Superstition—Fiction
ISBN 0399159398; 9780399159398
LC 2012-026920

SUMMARY: In this book, "which draws from Edgar Allan Poe's poem 'Annabel Lee,' Liam MacGregor has lived his entire life on . . . an isolated island surrounded by otherworldly sea beings. The islanders, whose society is goverend by Celtic superstition, shun Liam because of his paralyzed arm and rumors that he is cursed. Liam has always loved his childhood companion Anna. . . . Yet when the island's strange creatures are threatened by Liam and Anna's love, they set a trap to destroy it." (Publishers Weekly)

REVIEW: *Bull Cent Child Books* v67 no1 p30-1 S 2013 K. Q. G.

"Ashes on the Waves." "Inspired by Poe's classic poem 'Annabel Lee', this gothic tale is dramatic and romantic, and it will be entirely irresistible to those teens drawn to stories of doomed love. Liam's narration leans toward hyperbole at times, but both his palpable loneliness and his total enchantment with Anna echo Poe. Anna, on the other hand, is a thoroughly modern girl, and her confidence and no-nonsense attitude provide a nice counter to Liam's more gloomy charm. . . . Elements of Celtic lore are skillfully woven in, recalling other tales of tragic loves, and the Otherworlders themselves are a mysterious, fickle bunch whose actions only heighten the significance of Anna and Liam's relationship and its us-against-the-world romance."

REVIEW: *Kirkus Rev* v81 no9 p91 My 1 2013

REVIEW: *SLJ* v59 no7 p96 Jl 2013 Nancy Menaldi-Scanlan

LINDSEY, ROD. Troubleshooter; [by] Rod Lindsey 286 p. 2012 Ravenhaven

1. Murder—Fiction 2. Revenge—Fiction 3. Suspense fiction 4. United States marshals—Fiction 5. Vietnam veterans—Fiction
ISBN 061561244X; 9780615612447

SUMMARY: This book "opens in the Pacific Northwest in the present time with Ezra Hooten, a U.S. marshal . . . following a hot tip about his boyhood best friend, Norman Carpenter, a scalp-collecting psychopath Hoot has spent the bulk of his career pursuing. . . . But the tie that truly binds them is their connection to the girl both loved since middle school. . . . Soon as Norman got home from the war he married Donna, and a year later he brutally murdered her." (Publisher's note)

REVIEW: *Kirkus Rev* v82 no3 p379 F 1 2014

"Troubleshooter". "[Rod] Lindsey's potent novel is dark, opening with Hoot under fire, his partner dead (the third in five years) and a nearby officer bleeding to death. Hoot is a curious but deeply flawed protagonist who blames himself as much as Norman for Donna's death and becomes obsessed with the search for his former pal, which ultimately ruins his relationships with his ex-wife, Linda, and their children. . . . Some readers may not appreciate the novel's portrayal of women, who are typically depicted in physical terms, especially since Angela and her new lover, Liz, work as strippers. . . . Heavy in its despondence and bleakness but a story that readers are unlikely to forget."

LINGGI, K. C. Almost an Army Cadet, Always a Forester; [by] K. C. Linggi 44 p. 2013 TraffordSG

1. Forests & forestry—Malaysia 2. Memoirs 3. Rain

forests—Malaysia 4. Samling Corp. 5. Surveyors
ISBN 1490702156; 9781490702155

SUMMARY: This book is "an as-told-to memoir written by [K. C.] Linggi about his colleague Laing Imang. . . . Both worked for Samling Corporation, which, since the 1970s, has logged virgin rain forest in East Malaysia on the northern coast of Borneo. . . . [Laing] often negotiated with indigenous tribes who set up blockades to protest the destruction of the forests—not only their source of food and livelihood but a habitat unrivaled for its biodiversity." (Kirkus Reviews)

REVIEW: *Kirkus Rev* v82 no3 p399 F 1 2014

"Almost an Army Cadet, Always a Forester". " This slender debut, an as-told-to memoir written by Linggi about his colleague Laing Imang, offers a rare peek inside a controversial industry in an exotic locale. . . . Throughout, the writing is crisp and grammatical but too compact. The summary approach—10 chapters and three appendices in 37 pages—stifles character development and narrative flow. Despite the cover and preface, promising the "trials and tribulations" that Linggi and Laing shared, the brevity, pace and tone tend to mute conflicts and flatten personal experiences. Some passages read like a corporate report or company newsletter."

LINIERS, 1973-. The big wet balloon; a Toon book; [by] 1973- Liniers 32 p. 2013 Toon Books
1. Balloons—Fiction 2. Graphic novels 3. Play 4. Rain and rainfall—Fiction 5. Sisters—Fiction
ISBN 1935179322; 9781935179320 (alk. paper)
LC 2012-047662

SUMMARY: This book by Ricardo Liniers "shows several tableaus of two little girls who wake up in the room they share and spend the day together. The older sister suggests fun things to do, like shouting at the top of their lungs while they run through a rain shower. Though they have one small misunderstanding, these siblings are loving and thoughtful--good companions whatever the weather." (New York Times Book Review)

REVIEW: *Booklist* v110 no2 p59-30 S 15 2013 Josse Karp

REVIEW: *Horn Book Magazine* v89 no5 p104-5 S/O 2013 CYNTHIA K. RITTER

REVIEW: *Kirkus Rev* p41-2 Ag 15 2013 Fall Preview

REVIEW: *Kirkus Rev* v81 no15 p225 Ag 1 2013

REVIEW: *N Y Times Book Rev* p42 N 10 2013 SARAH HARRISON SMITH

"You Were the First," "Dee Dee and Me," and "The Big Wet Balloon." "In the hands of [Patricia] MacLachlan, the sweetly detailed text and pictures of a biracial family living somewhere that looks a lot like Brooklyn are a comforting reminder of how special all those 'firsts' can be. . . . [Amy] Schwartz wisely withholds comment, but there's inspiration here--as well as some cheerful pictures--for those siblings who always get stuck playing the butler, rather than the duchess, at dress-up time. . . . [Ricardo] Liniers, a cartoonist . . . based this miniature graphic novel on his daughters. . . . Though they have one small misunderstanding, these siblings are loving and thoughtful--good companions whatever the weather."

REVIEW: *Publ Wkly* v260 no29 p71 Jl 22 2013

REVIEW: *SLJ* v59 no9 p168 S 2013 Sarah Stone

LINIERS, 1973-.il. The big wet balloon. See Liniers, 1973-

LINK, WILLIAM A. Atlanta, cradle of the New South; race and remembering in the Civil War's aftermath; [by] William A. Link 251 p. 2013 University of North Carolina Press
1. African Americans—Georgia—Atlanta—Social conditions 2. Memory—Social aspects—Georgia—Atlanta
ISBN 146960776X; 9781469607764 (cloth : alk. paper)
LC 2012-044361

SUMMARY: Author William A. Link examines "the broader meaning of the Civil War in the modern South, with no place embodying the region's past and future more clearly than Atlanta. Link frames the city as both exceptional--because of the incredible impact of the war there and the city's phoenix-like postwar rise--and as a model for other southern cities. He shows how . . . freedpeople in Atlanta built a cultural, economic, and political center that helped to define black America." (Publisher's note)

REVIEW: *Choice* v51 no2 p257 O 2013 D. Stuber

REVIEW: *Choice* v51 no2 p335 O 2013 T. F. Armstrong

REVIEW: *TLS* no5762 p23 S 6 2013 LAUREN ARRINGTON

"At the Violet Hour: Modernism and Violence in England and Ireland." "[Sarah] Cole focuses almost exclusively on English and Irish literature . . . but her close readings of 'Portrait' and 'To the Lighthouse' resonate powerfully across Anglo-American modernism. . . . In Cole's dynamite reading of [Joseph] Conrad's 'The Secret Agent,' meanwhile, she playfully argues that the unfortunate Stevie's body is history. . . . Cole's close readings of violence in the work of some of the major modernists are superb. Yet in her long chapter 'The Irish Insurrection and the Limits of Enchantment', she loses purchase because of factual errors that compound superficial glosses."

LINKER, DAVID.ed. Pottytime for chickies. See Trasler, J.

LIPMAN, JOANNE. Strings attached; life lessons from the world's toughest teacher; [by] Joanne Lipman 352 p. 2013 Hyperion
1. Memoirs 2. Music teachers—United States—Biography 3. Refugees 4. Ukrainians—United States
ISBN 1401324665; 9781401324667
LC 2012-036233

SUMMARY: This book, by Joanne Lipman and Melanie Kupchynsky, tells the story of "Jerry Kupchynsky, known as Mr. K--a Ukrainian-born taskmaster . . . who drove his students harder than anyone had ever driven them before. Through sheer force of will, he made them better than they had any right to be. . . . Recounted by two former students . . . [the book] spans from his days as a forced Nazi laborer and his later home life as a husband to an invalid wife, to his . . . search for his missing daughter." (Publisher's note)

REVIEW: *Kirkus Rev* v81 no17 p63 S 1 2013

REVIEW: *N Y Times Book Rev* p72 D 8 2013 KATIE HAFNER

"Play It Again: An Amateur Against the Impossible" and "Strings Attached: One Tough Teacher and the Gift of Great Expectations." "At age 56, after hearing a fellow amateur play the G minor ballade beautifully . . . , [author Alan Rusbridger] was inspired to learn and perform the piece himself. . . . Rusbridger is especially heartened to have discovered that well into middle age the brain remains plastic enough to learn new and complicated tasks. His triumph is an inspiration. . . . An entirely different musical journey is recounted in 'Strings Attached,' a very fine dual memoir by Joanne Lipman, a journalist, and Melanie Kupchynsky, a professional musician."

REVIEW: *Publ Wkly* v260 no24 p49 Je 17 2013

LIPPITT, JOHN.ed. The Oxford handbook of Kierkegaard. See The Oxford handbook of Kierkegaard

LIPPMAN, LAURA. After I'm gone; [by] Laura Lippman 352 p. 2014 William Morrow, An Imprint of HarperCollinsPublishers

1. Detective & mystery stories 2. Marriage—Fiction 3. Missing persons—Fiction 4. Murder investigation 5. Personal beauty—Fiction
ISBN 0062083392 (hbk.); 0062298496 (pbk. Large Print); 9780062083395 (hbk.); 9780062298492 (pbk. Large Print)
LC 2013-018550

SUMMARY: Written by Laura Lippman, this book tells a "story that explores how one man's disappearance echoes through the lives of the wife, mistress, and daughters he left behind. When Julie disappears . . . everyone assumes she's left to join her old lover—until her remains are eventually found. Now, twenty-six years after Julie went missing, Roberto 'Sandy' Sanchez, a retired Baltimore detective working cold cases for some extra cash, is investigating her murder." (Publisher's note)

REVIEW: *Booklist* v111 no4 p59 O 15 2014 Mary McCay

REVIEW: *Booklist* v110 no6 p22 N 15 2013 Donna Seaman

REVIEW: *Kirkus Rev* v81 no21 p196 N 1 2013

REVIEW: *Libr J* v139 no11 p52 Je 15 2014 Joyce Kessel

REVIEW: *Libr J* v138 no15 p49 S 15 2013

REVIEW: *New York Times* v163 no56415 pC4 F 17 2014 JANET MASLIN

"After I'm Gone". "The characters in Laura Lippman's 'After I'm Gone' are so well drawn that it's easy to forget why they happen to be connected. . . . Ms. Lippman is able to sustain a remarkable degree of detail about all these characters and still keep them sharply distinct and interesting. The one back story that she overworks is Sandy's: He is a widower, and there are endless, similar descriptions of what a paragon his wife was, how neat and dainty, how much more capable than he of dealing with their troubled child."

REVIEW: *Publ Wkly* v261 no4 p56-61 Ja 27 2014

REVIEW: *Publ Wkly* v261 no26 p57 Je 30 2014

REVIEW: *Publ Wkly* v260 no52 p35 D 23 2013

LIPSCOMBE, NICK. Wellington's guns; the untold story of Wellington and his artillery in the Peninsula and at Waterloo; [by] Nick Lipscombe 456 p. 2013 Osprey Publishing

1. Artillery—Great Britain—History—19th century 2. Military history 3. Napoleonic wars, 1800-1815—Artillery operations, British 4. Peninsular War, 1807-1814—Artillery operations, British 5. Peninsular War, 1807-1814—Campaigns 6. Waterloo, Battle of, Waterloo, Belgium, 1815
ISBN 9781780961149 (hbk.)
LC 2012-277983

SUMMARY: "Wellington's somewhat disparaging comments resulted in the mistaken belief that the Gunners performed badly at Waterloo." Written by Nick Lipscombe, "'Wellington's Guns' is the long overdue story of the often stormy relationship between Wellington and his artillery, the frustrations, the characters and the achievements of the main protagonists as well as a detailed account of the British artillery of this period." (Publisher's note)

REVIEW: *TLS* no5782 p25 Ja 24 2014 JOHN URE

"Wellington's Guns." "This is a meticulously researched account of the performance of almost every artillery unit that served under Wellington in the Peninsular campaign and at Waterloo, and of the commanding general's--often strained--relations with them. It is written by a retired artillery colonel who is a fervent defender of his old arm of the service. . . . For those whose military enthusiasm is centred on the gun carriages, this will rightly and permanently remain the definitive view from the breech."

LIPSITZ, GEORGE. The fierce urgency of now; improvisation, rights, and the ethics of cocreation; [by] George Lipsitz xxxiv, 292 p. 2013 Duke University Press

1. African Americans—Political activity 2. Human rights movements 3. Improvisation (Music) 4. Music literature 5. Politics and culture
ISBN 9780822354642 (cloth : alk. paper); 9780822354789 (pbk. ; alk. paper)́
LC 2013-003137

SUMMARY: This book "links musical improvisation to struggles for social change, focusing on the connections between the improvisation associated with jazz and the dynamics of human rights struggles and discourses. . . . By analyzing the dynamics of particular artistic improvisations, mostly by contemporary American jazz musicians, the authors reveal improvisation as a viable and urgently needed model for social change." (Publisher's note)

REVIEW: *TLS* no5764 p31 S 20 2013 LOU GLANDFIELD

"The Fierce Urgency of Now: Improvisation, Rights, and the Ethics of Cocreation." "'The Fierce Urgency of Now' is primarily concerned with contemporary directions in African American music, although the authors acknowledge the universality of improvisation. . . . It is the stated aim of the authors to formulate a critical language for today's worldwide interaction of improvised musics. In this they are only partially successful, as a tendency to abstruse and academic language may put off some readers; a pity, as this is a book which deserves to be widely read."

LIPSKY, SETH. The rise of Abraham Cahan; [by] Seth Lipsky 240 p. 2013 Schocken Books

1. Authors, Yiddish—United States—Biography 2. Biography (Literary form) 3. Jewish journalists—United States—Biography 4. Yiddish newspapers—United States
ISBN 9780805242102
LC 2013-006773

SUMMARY: This book by Seth Lipsky, part of the Jewish Encounters series, presents a biography of writer and political activist Abraham Cahan, "a man of profound contradictions: an avowed socialist who wrote fiction with transcendent sympathy for a wealthy manufacturer; an internationalist who turned against the anti-Zionism of the left; an assimilationist whose final battle was against religious apostasy. . . . Abraham Cahan revolutionized our idea of what newspapers could accomplish." (Publisher's note)

REVIEW: *Commentary* v136 no4 p44-6 N 2013 EDWARD KOSNER

REVIEW: *Kirkus Rev* v81 no17 p64 S 1 2013

REVIEW: *N Y Times Book Rev* p34 N 17 2013 Anna Altman

REVIEW: *Nation* v298 no7 p31-3 F 17 2014 D. D. GUTTENPLAN

"The Rise of Abraham Cahan." "Reading Seth Lipsky's biography, it is all too easy to forget why anyone should care about Cahan, a serial espouser of lost causes who died more than half a century ago. . . . In theory, Lipsky . . . ought to be an ideal match for his illustrious predecessor. . . . Yet as a biographer, Lipsky is small-minded, preachy, dull and inattentive, trampling over the twists and turns of Cahan's often capricious political evolution in a rush to fit the epic contours of his unruly life into the cookie-cutter confines of wised-up American neoconservatism. . . . Abraham Cahan is far more interesting than that. It's a shame that Lipsky seems more eager to recruit him than to understand him."

THE LISZT/D'AGOULT CORRESPONDENCE; English translations and commentaries; 400 p. 2011 Pendragon Press

1. Authors, French—19th century—Correspondence 2. Composers—Correspondence 3. Letters
ISBN 9781576471654 (alk. paper)
LC 2011-029075

SUMMARY: This book "offers English translations of letters between [Franz] Liszt and the Comtesse Marie d'Agoult, the first great love of his life and mother of his three children. . . . The present volume contains 473 of those letters, with some items omitted for space, according to [Michael] Short." It includes "notes explaining references to people and events." (Choice: Current Reviews for Academic Libraries)

REVIEW: *Choice* v51 no7 p1224-5 Mr 2014 B. J. Murray

"The Liszt-d'Agoult Correspondence: English Translations and Commentaries." "The translations are clear and idiomatic, and there is a fine scholarly apparatus: thorough notes explaining references to people and events; a useful index; a list of sources; and a running concordance with the Gut-Bellas edition and with an earlier edition. This is another valuable entry in Pendragon's ongoing [Franz] Liszt series. It represents an impressive scholarly investment in which a broad swath of Liszt's aesthetic perspective is revealed about as plainly as it is revealed anywhere else. . . . Highly recommended."

A LITERATURE OF RESTITUTION; critical essays on W. G. Sebald; 2013 Palgrave Macmillan

1. Adler, H. G., 1910-1988 2. English literature—20th century 3. German literature—20th century 4. Literature—History & criticism 5. Sebald, Winfried Georg, 1944-2001
ISBN 9780719088520

SUMMARY: This book, edited by Jeannette Baxter, Valerie Henitiuk, and Ben Hutchinson, "investigates the crucial question of 'restitution' in the work of W. G. Sebald. . . . The essays collected in this volume place Sebald's oeuvre within the broader context of European culture in order to better understand his engagement with the ethics of aesthetics . . . whilst opening up his work to a range of . . . areas including dissident surrealism, Anglo-Irish relations, . . . and the writings of H. G. Adler." (Publisher's note)

REVIEW: *TLS* no5784 p26 F 7 2014 CAROLIN DUTTLINGER

"A Literature of Restitution: Critical Essays on W. G. Sebald." "Restitution . . . provides an intriguing but elliptical entry point into Sebald's oeuvre, one which the present volume sets out to explore. The assembled essays discuss familiar issues--including intertextuality, photography, memory and architecture--but often from original perspectives, focusing on lesser-known aspects such as Sebald's poetry and his unfinished 'Corsica project.' . . . The majority of . . . essays cite Sebald in both German and English. . . . Integrating the voice of Sebald the critic into our understanding of his prose is an undertaking which this volume gestures towards; it is an ongoing, open-ended project."

LITHGOW, JOHN, 1945-. Never play music right next to the zoo; 40 p. 2013 Simon & Schuster Books for Young Readers

1. Children's songs, English—United States—Texts 2. Children's stories 3. Concerts—Songs and music 4. Music—Songs and music 5. Orchestra—Songs and music 6. Songs 7. Zoo animals—Songs and music
ISBN 1442467436; 9781442467439 (hardcover); 9781442467446 (ebook)
LC 2012-013516

SUMMARY: In this children's book written by John Lithgow and illustrated by Leeza Hernandez, "A concert gets out of hand when the animals at the neighboring zoo storm the stage and play the instruments themselves in this hilarious picture book based on one of John Lithgow's best-loved tunes. This package includes a CD of John and an orchestra performing the song." (Publisher's note)

REVIEW: *Booklist* v109 no22 p87-8 Ag 1 2013 Kay Weisman

REVIEW: *Booklist* v109 no19/20 p60 Je 1 2013

REVIEW: *Kirkus Rev* v81 no18 p38 S 15 2013

REVIEW: *N Y Times Book Rev* p15 D 22 2013 SARAH HARRISON SMITH

"Herman and Rosie," "Frog Trouble: Deluxe Songbook," "Never Play Music Right Next to the Zoo." "Music is the food of love for Herman, a crocodile who plays oboe, and his neighbor Rosie, a doe who sings jazz at the Mangy Hound. . . . You might have been so distracted by [author Sandra] Boynton's prolific literary production that you missed her musical endeavors . . . In 'Frog Trouble,' she illustrates 12 witty children's country songs with pictures of the adorably smiley animals who ostensibly sing them. . . . In [author John] Lithgow's zany and toe-tapping song, illustrated with comic abandon by [illustrated by Leeza] Hernandez, all sorts of unexpected things happen when a boy and his family attend an outdoor concert at a city zoo."

REVIEW: *Publ Wkly* v260 no33 p64 Ag 19 2013

REVIEW: *SLJ* v59 no8 p80 Ag 2013 Brooke Rasche

LITKE, JUSTIN B. Twilight of the republic; empire and exceptionalism in the American political tradition; [by] Justin B. Litke 214 p. 2013 University Press of Kentucky

1. Exceptionalism—United States—History 2. Imperialism 3. National characteristics, American—History 4. Political culture—United States—History 5. Political science literature

ISBN 9780813142203 (hardcover: alk. paper)

LC 2013-010407

SUMMARY: In this book on American exceptionalism, Justin B. Litke makes his arguments by "celebrating John Winthrop's Puritan founding, downplaying the Founders' claim that all men are created equal, and above all by charging Abraham Lincoln with a sort of political heresy in emphasizing precisely that 'abstract' claim—and thus derailing the Winthropian-Christian American tradition." (Choice: Current Reviews for Academic Libraries)

REVIEW: *Choice* v51 no8 p1490 Ap 2014 W. Morrisey

"Twilight of the Republic: Empire and Exceptionalism in the American Political Tradition". "This lively scholarly polemic takes what is often called a 'paleoconservative' view of American political history. . . . Paleoconservatives typically differ from other conservatives in denying universal natural rights, damning these as dangerous 'abstractions' tending toward all things violent and French. [Justin B.] Litke . . . follows this line, celebrating John Winthrop's Puritan founding, downplaying the Founders' claim that all men are created equal, and above all by charging Abraham Lincoln with a sort of political heresy in emphasizing precisely that 'abstract' claim. . . . Litke's case may not persuade many, but it is enthusiastically argued."

LITMAN, ELLEN. Mannequin girl; a novel; [by] Ellen Litman 304 p. 2014 W.W. Norton & Company

1. Bildungsromans 2. Jews, Russian—Moscow (Russia)—Fiction 3. Parent and child—Moscow (Russia)—Fiction 4. Scoliosis in adolecen—Moscow (Russia)—Fiction 5. Successful—Fiction 6. Young women—Moscow (Russia)—Fiction

ISBN 0393069281; 9780393069280 (hardcover)

LC 2013-041207

SUMMARY: In this book, by Ellen Litman, when Kat is diagnosed "with rapidly-progressing scoliosis, the trajectory of her life changes and she finds herself at . . . a school-sanatorium for children with spinal ailments. . . . Kat embarks on a quest to prove that she can be as exceptional as her parents: a beauty, an intellect, and free spirit despite her physical limitations, her Jewishness, and her suspicion that her beloved parents are in fact flawed." (Publisher's note)

REVIEW: *Booklist* v110 no13 p18-9 Mr 1 2014 Donna Seaman

"Mannequin Girl." "With surgical humor and supple sensitivity, [Ellen] Litman illuminates the struggles of both the spinally challenged and the straight-backed within a microcosm of the twisted, ailing, malignantly anti-Semitic Soviet state, in which typical coming of-age angst is amplified. As teen Kat rebels, certain that no one will ever love her, Litman scrupulously traces a web of social and family conundrums in this strikingly lucid and affecting novel. . . . Told from Kat's evolving point of view, this tale of young outsiders in a hostile world will intrigue teen readers of literary fiction."

REVIEW: *Kirkus Rev* v82 no1 p290 Ja 1 2014

"Mannequin Girl". "A shrewd, observant coming-of-age tale set in the twilight years of the Soviet Union. . . . [Ellen] Litman traces her bumpy progress from 1980 to 1988 entirely without sentimentality, showing Kat capable of being as mean as the kids who persecute her and revealing her parents (who join Kat's school in 1984) as too wrapped up in their own problems to be much help to their troubled daughter. Litman is equally sharp on the shifting alliances of childhood. . . . Smart, highly readable fiction propelled by a vulnerable and crankily appealing heroine."

REVIEW: *Libr J* v139 no4 p84 Mr 1 2014 Jan Blodgett

REVIEW: *Publ Wkly* v260 no51 p35-6 D 16 2013

LITSAS, SPYRIDON N. Stateness and sovereign debt. See Lavdas, K. A.

LITTELL, ROBERT. A Nasty Piece of Work; [by] Robert Littell 272 p. 2013 St. Martin's Press

1. Bail bond agents 2. Detective & mystery stories 3. Love stories 4. Missing persons—Fiction 5. Private investigators—Fiction

ISBN 1250021456; 9781250021458

SUMMARY: In this detective novel, "the action begins when the very comely Ornella Neppi, who is trying to manage her uncle's bail-bonding agency, hires [Lemuel] Gunn to track down Emilio Gava, who has jumped the bail Ornella posted for him. Gunn quickly learns that Gava seems not to exist; even his mug shot has disappeared from the police department. But Gunn is clever and resourceful, and romance blossoms during the hunt." (Booklist)

REVIEW: *Booklist* v110 no5 p30-1 N 1 2013 Thomas Gaughan

"A Nasty Piece of Work." "[Robert] Littell, whose mastery of the espionage novel . . . brings comparisons with le Carré, steps into a new genre with private eye Lemuel Gunn. . . . If Littell's superb espionage novels are a figurative blazing fastball, Gunn's debut is a tantalizing changeup. He's a twentieth-century man who listens to Nat Cole LPs, drives a 1950 Studebaker Starlight Coupe, and shuns cell phones. Littell's espionage fans might be disappointed, but fans of quirky gumshoes will love Lemuel."

REVIEW: *Kirkus Rev* v81 no17 p31-2 S 1 2013

REVIEW: *Libr J* v138 no18 p74 N 1 2013 Teresa L. Jacobsen

REVIEW: *Libr J* v138 no10 p76 Je 1 2013

REVIEW: *Publ Wkly* v260 no35 p33-4 S 2 2013

LITTLE, THOMAS J. The origins of southern evangelicalism; religious revivalism in the South Carolina lowcountry, 1670-1760; [by] Thomas J. Little 280 p. 2013 University of South Carolina Press

1. Evangelicalism—Southern States—History—17th century 2. Evangelicalism—Southern States—History—18th century 3. Historical literature

ISBN 9781611172744 (hardback)

LC 2013-013550

SUMMARY: In this book, Thomas Little "argues that evangelicalism developed in the lower South earlier than most historians have recognized. Rejecting claims that southern revivals can be traced only from the 1740s, Little explicates patterns in the South Carolina Lowcountry of religious pluralism and revivalism from the 1670s, which eventually produced an evangelical faith that became the dominant religious expression of the 19th-century South." (Choice: Current Reviews for Academic Libraries)

REVIEW: *Am Hist Rev* v119 no4 p1254-5 O 2014 Sylvester Johnson

REVIEW: *Choice* v51 no8 p1474 Ap 2014 W. B. Bedford

"The Origins of Southern Evangelicalism: Religious Revivalism in the South Carolina Lowcounry, 1670-1760". "With impressive documentation and analysis, [Thomas] Little makes a convincing case that Lowcountry Carolina enjoyed religious toleration from initial settlement, had a strong majority who dissented from the Church of England and contested the Anglican establishment, and embraced the evangelical emphasis of the Holy Spirit's work in salvation. . . . By 1760, a religious base had been established for the further expansion of revivalism to the Carolina backcountry and, remarkably, ultimate conversion of the large African American population to evangelical Christianity."

LITTLEFIELD, SOPHIE. House of Glass; [by] Sophie Littlefield 304 p. 2014 Harlequin Books

1. Families—Fiction 2. Home invasion 3. Hostages—Fiction 4. Murder—Fiction 5. Suspense fiction
ISBN 0778314782; 9780778314783

SUMMARY: In this book, author Sophie Littlefield "draws facts from a true crime to create a novel about vicious intruders, who invade an upper-class family's home in Calumet, Minn. . . . Jen and Ted assume the men will take the loot and the family's valuables and leave. However, the criminals remain in their home. . . When the older thug, Dan, drops nuggets of information about the family that only an insider would know, Jen . . . suspects their captivity is more than just a random occurrence." (Kirkus Reviews)

REVIEW: *Booklist* v110 no14 p60 Mr 15 2014 Susan Maguire

REVIEW: *Kirkus Rev* v82 no3 p278 F 1 2014

"House of Glass". "[Sophie] Littlefield pens a mechanically sound narrative by altering the family structure and adding her own twists to elements of the source material. But readers who recall the brutal attack suffered by a Connecticut family in 2007—and who empathize with family members and the lone survivor who must cope with very genuine memories every single day—may find it difficult to cast aside the true story and embrace the author's fictionalized version. While a solidly constructed book, certain headlines deserve respect and distance, and some may consider Littlefields's account exploitative."

REVIEW: *Publ Wkly* v261 no4 p172 Ja 27 2014

LITTLEWOOD, ALISON. A cold season; [by] Alison Littlewood 304 p. 2013 Quercus

1. Blizzards 2. Good & evil—Fiction 3. Mothers & sons 4. Single mothers—Fiction 5. Speculative fiction
ISBN 9781623650223 (hardcover); 9781623650230 (ebk.)
LC 2013-937739

SUMMARY: In this book, "having lost her husband to the battlefields of Afghanistan, Cass retreats with her son, Ben, to the village of Darnshaw. There she expects an idyllic life of comforting smalltown safety. What she actually gets is less a community and more a moral infestation. Ben rapidly transforms under the influence of the malevolent architect at work in Darnshaw; once a lovable young boy, he becomes rude, cold, and menacing." (Publishers Weekly)

REVIEW: *Booklist* v110 no1 p52-3 S 1 2013 Alison Downs

"A Cold Season." "Once you open the pages of [Alison] Littlewood's debut novel, the hairs on the back of your neck are not safe. This classic supernatural story with gothic undertones opens with Cass and her son, Ben, leaving behind the tragedy of losing a husband and father for a place Cass remembers fondly from childhood. Once they arrive in Darnshaw, Cass soon realizes it is no longer the idyllic town she remembers. . . . Littlewood's story isn't perfect, and some themes are overdone, but it certainly hits some very high and scary notes."

REVIEW: *Kirkus Rev* v81 no14 p344 Jl 15 2013

REVIEW: *Libr J* v139 no7 p118 Ap 15 2014

REVIEW: *Publ Wkly* v260 no26 p71 Jl 1 2013

LITWIN, MIKE. Lost in Bermooda; 144 p. 2014 Albert Whitman & Co

1. Animal stories 2. Children's stories 3. Cows 4. Friendship—Fiction 5. Islands—Fiction
ISBN 0807587184; 9780807587188

SUMMARY: Written and illustrated by Mike Litwin, this children's book describes how "Bermooda is a tropical island that is undiscovered by the outside world and is primarily populated by walking, talking cows of human intelligence. . . . Bermooda has no 'outsiders,' and most prefer to keep it that way. That is, until Chuck ventures into the boneyard alone and discovers a young human boy who has been washed up unconscious on the sandbar!" (Publisher's note)

REVIEW: *Booklist* v110 no14 p79 Mr 15 2014 John Peters

REVIEW: *Bull Cent Child Books* v67 no7 p365 Mr 2014 T. A.

"Lost in Bermooda." "Though some of the vocabulary will prove to be a challenge for transitioning readers, the deluxe-size print, brief chapters, and goofy but painterly digital artwork of the chunky, tropical characters increase the readability of this friendship tale. Litwin packs a lot of action into a little book through the pair's attempts to get Dakota home, while still making both Chuck and Dakota well-rounded and adding bumps along the way in their relationship. Although the conclusion is a little puzzling . . . it is fulfilling, and young readers will wonder if we might return to this island paradise in future books after this moo-ving story about friendship across difference."

REVIEW: *Kirkus Rev* v81 no24 p288 D 15 2013

"Lost in Bermooda". " In the cow paradise of Bermooda the only things to fear are the legendary monsters known as hu'mans. . . . [Mike] Litwin's light tale of friendship is full of Hawaii-inspired cow puns and reads like the intro to a series, since it introduces a large cast of characters, few of whom get to do much. Chuck and Dakota are nicely rounded characters, and the promised illustrations look to be endearingly cartoony. New-to-chapters readers will gladly join the herd and say 'Lo'hai' (hello) to Bermooda and its denizens."

REVIEW: *Publ Wkly* v261 no1 p57 Ja 6 2014

REVIEW: *SLJ* v60 no5 p87 My 2014 Meg Smith

LITWIN, MIKE.il. Lost in Bermooda. See Litwin, M.

LIU, JULIA. Gus, the dinosaur bus; 32 p. 2013 Houghton

Mifflin Harcourt
1. Dinosaurs—Fiction 2. Picture books for children 3. School buses—Fiction 4. Swimming pools 5. Traffic congestion—Fiction
ISBN 9780547905730
LC 2012-018091

SUMMARY: In this book, "when a long-necked dinosaur serves as the bus, none of the kids want to miss school. Though everyone loves Gus . . . the principal finally tires of complaints about him knocking down traffic lights and getting tangled in phone wires and removes him from the road. Relegated to the school gym, Gus makes a swimming pool with his tears and finds a new life as the school's playground, with a swing on his tail and his long neck serving as a slide." (School Library Journal)

REVIEW: *Bull Cent Child Books* v67 no1 p31 S 2013 D. S.

REVIEW: *Horn Book Magazine* v89 no5 p75-6 S/O 2013 ELISSA GERSHOWITZ

"Gus, the Dinosaur Bus." "For lots of little kids, riding a school bus is excitement in itself. The schoolchildren in this Taiwanese import are lucky enough to have for their mode of transport . . . a dinosaur. The story's mild suspense is just right for the book's audience, with the solution likely to have kids wishing their own play spaces were so much fun. Scribbly watercolor and pencil illustrations on creamy paper are just how a child-drawn city might look, all shaky-lined rectangular buildings and imperfect-circle-headed people. And the kindly pea-green dino steals the show with his huge smile and even bigger heart."

REVIEW: *Kirkus Rev* v81 no2 p108-9 Je 1 2013

REVIEW: *N Y Times Book Rev* p17 Ag 25 2013 SARAH HARRISON SMITH

REVIEW: *Publ Wkly* v260 no19 p68 My 13 2013

REVIEW: *SLJ* v59 no7 p65 Jl 2013 Kathleen Kelly MacMillan

LIULEVICIUS, VEJAS GABRIEL. The German myth of the East; 1800 to the present; [by] Vejas Gabriel Liulevicius 292 2009 Oxford University Press
1. Europe—Foreign relations—Germany 2. Europe, Eastern—Civilization 3. Germany—Intellectual life
ISBN 9780199546312
LC 2009-024505

SUMMARY: In this book, a "survey of German ideas and attitudes about Eastern Europe, Vejas Gabriel Liulevicius argues that Germans developed an overarching myth of the East, according to which Poland, Russia, and the lands between formed a disorganized, backward, and potentially dangerous region that required German assistance and invited German intervention. This region was also destined to be the main outlet for German energies and the locus of German national self-realization. Liulevicius bases his analysis on the often negative or condescending views of Eastern European culture, economics, and hygiene expressed by more or less prominent representatives of Germany's 'chattering classes' during the past 250 years." (American Historical Review)

REVIEW: *Am Hist Rev* v116 no5 p1585-6 D 2011 Richard Blanke

The German Myth of the East: 1800 to the Present "In his survey of German ideas and attitudes about Eastern Europe, Vejas Gabriel Liulevicius argues that Germans developed an overarching myth of the East, according to which Poland, Russia, and the lands between formed a disorganized, backward, and potentially dangerous region that required German assistance and invited German intervention. This region was also destined to be the main outlet for German energies and the locus of German national self-realization. Liulevicius bases his analysis on the often negative or condescending views of Eastern European culture, economics, and hygiene expressed by more or less prominent representatives of Germany's 'chattering classes' during the past 250 years. . . . Because it does not presume much prior knowledge of German or European history on the part of its readership, it breaks away frequently from its main theme to supply background on topics ranging from the revolutions of 1848 to trench warfare to the Cold War that would be more appropriate to a textbook survey. . . . The result falls short of being comprehensive, or balanced, but it is well-written, accessible, and generally a pleasure to read."

LIVELY, PENELOPE, 1933-. Dancing fish and ammonites; a memoir; [by] Penelope Lively 224 p. 2014 Viking Adult
1. Autobiographical memory 2. BIOGRAPHY & AUTOBIOGRAPHY—Literary 3. BIOGRAPHY & AUTOBIOGRAPHY—Personal Memoirs 4. English literature—Women authors—Biography 5. HISTORY—Modern—20th Century 6. Memoirs 7. Novelists, English—20th century—Biography
ISBN 0670016551; 9780670016556 (hardback)
LC 2013-036818

SUMMARY: This memoir "traces the arc of [author Penelope] Lively's life, stretching from her early childhood in Cairo to boarding school in England to the sweeping social changes of Britain's twentieth century. She reflects on her early love of archeology . . . [and] also writes insightfully about aging and what life looks like from where she now stands." (Publisher's note)

REVIEW: *Booklist* v110 no11 p11 F 1 2014 Donna Seaman

REVIEW: *Kirkus Rev* v81 no21 p110 N 1 2013

REVIEW: *N Y Times Book Rev* p18 F 2 2014 LOUISA THOMAS

REVIEW: *New Yorker* v90 no6 p77-1 Mr 31 2014

"Dancing Fish and Ammonites: A Memoir." "The author, eighty years old and with more than fifty books behind her, provides a 'view from old age' in this engaging but uneven memoir. [Author Penelope] Lively takes readers through childhood in Egypt, life in a cold and isolating English boarding school, the Blitz, and the social change wrought by the feminist movement. . . . Lively's writing shines brightest when her discursive remarks demonstrate the methods and preoccupations that have shaped her fiction."

REVIEW: *Publ Wkly* v261 no1 p46 Ja 6 2014

LIVERS, PAULETTE. Cementville; [by] Paulette Livers 304 p. 2014 Pgw
1. Historical fiction 2. Kentucky—Fiction 3. Murder—Fiction 4. Vietnam War, 1961-1975—Fiction 5. Vietnam veterans—Fiction
ISBN 1619022435; 9781619022430

SUMMARY: In this book, "it's 1969, and seven young men from the most well-respected families of Cementville, Ky., are coming home from Vietnam in body bags. Also returning home is still-breathing Lt. Harlan O'Brien, the town's former football star." Author Paulette Livers "ups the ante by putting a killer on the loose in the small town. And with townsfolk already on edge, mutual respect and tradition are replaced by fear and suspicion." (Publishers Weekly)

REVIEW: *Booklist* v110 no4 p26 O 15 2013 Lynn Weber

REVIEW: *Kirkus Rev* v82 no2 p248 Ja 15 2014

"Cementville". "The chief flaw of the book is that's it's stuffed full of characters who are hard to differentiate, consistently possessed as they are of [Paulette] Livers' eloquent if down-home voice. The episodic, character-sketch arrangement undercuts the central drama of the novel, involving the murder of the Vietnamese wife of another war vet. Livers means to explore the ways that perception and reality often fail to overlap in small-town life, and there are moments where the novel sings in that regard, particularly in one section where the supposed bad girl of the Ferguson clan finds a refuge in the home of an elderly resident. But the overall tone is curiously muted. An earnest and sober portrait of the homefront, filled a bit past capacity."

REVIEW: *Publ Wkly* v260 no48 p28-9 N 25 2013

LIVINGSTONE, ANGELA.tr. Phaedra. See Livingstone, A.

LIZARRALDE, ROBERTO. The ecology of the Bari. See Beckerman, S.

LJUBLJANA TALES; A Literary Guide to the City; 144 p. 2012 New Europe Writers

1. Anthologies 2. Autonomy & independence movements 3. Ljubljana (Slovenia) 4. Prostitutes—Fiction 5. Slovenia—Social conditions

ISBN 095685981X; 9780956859815

SUMMARY: This book presents a collection of stories and poems about Ljubljana, Slovenia. "In Miroslav Slana's 'The Scarlet Frog,' . . . a prostitute who cannot find other work in post-independence Slovenia fantasizes, while waiting for a client, about prehistoric times and the scarlet frogs that inhabited the marsh. . . . in Evald Flisar's 'An Incident in Ljubljana,' . . . the narrator's Uncle Schweik . . . attacks an approaching Yugoslav tank." (World Literature Today)

REVIEW: *World Lit Today* v87 no6 p66-7 N/D 2013 Robert Murray Davis

"Ljubljana Tales: A Collection of Central European Contemporary Writing." "It is difficult to get a coherent sense of Ljubljana from the sixty-six items in 'Ljubljana Tales,' but a few things are clear. First, Ljubljana itself does not seem to provide enough material to fill a whole book, confirming some local writers' view that it is too small to be a real capital city. . . . In the collection as a whole, Ljubljana itself seems almost empty, especially on a Sunday. . . . The prevailing mood is melancholic. . . . there is little energy to offset the prevailing somber mood. Had the anthology been compiled a few years earlier, in the brief period of euphoria occasioned by EU membership . . . the mood might have been different."

LLOYD-JONES, ANTONIA.tr. The assassin from Apricot City. See Szablowski, W.

LLOYD-JONES, SALLY. Poor Doreen; a fishy tale; 40 p. 2013 Schwartz & Wade

1. Animal stories 2. Children's stories 3. Fishes—Fiction 4. Fishing—Juvenile literature 5. Herons

ISBN 0375869182; 9780375869181; 9780375969188 (glb)

LC 2012-047195

SUMMARY: In this children's book, written by Sally Lloyd-Jones and illustrated by Alexandra Boiger, "an Ample Roundy Fish called Mrs. Doreen Randolph-Potts is on a mission: to visit her second cousin twice removed who's just welcomed 157 babies. But when she spies what she thinks is a yummy dragonfly—and is actually bait—poor Doreen is lifted out of the water on a fishing pole. Luckily, Doreen is, shall we say, a wee bit clueless about the dire situation." (Publisher's note)

REVIEW: *Bull Cent Child Books* v67 no10 p529 Je 2014 J. H.

"Poor Doreen: A Fishy Tale". "The cautionary narrative asides, sonorous language . . . and Doreen's complete (but enthusiastic) misunderstanding of her situation make this a boatload of fun to read aloud. [Alexandra] Boiger's watercolor, gouache, pencil, and colored pencil illustrations are pleasantly watery, but some of the paler tones and contrasts might not translate well to larger crowds. Still, one can't help but like the oblivious and rotund Doreen in her jaunty red headscarf and inexplicably toting a red umbrella, and her tale will likely make a splash, either as the silly story it is or as a lesson in perspective."

REVIEW: *Kirkus Rev* v82 no3 p88 F 1 2014

"Poor Doreen: A Fishy Tale". "Laced with panicky warnings from the narrator alerting Doreen to her impending mortal danger, the alliterative text tracks her perilous journey in humorous detail while its typographic placement visually follows her up, down and across double-page spreads. Rendered in pencil, watercolor, gouache and colored pencil, the fluid illustrations effectively rely on light and arresting perspectives to highlight Doreen's precarious situations. Ignorance equals bliss in this amusing, cleverly executed tale."

REVIEW: *Publ Wkly* v260 no52 p51 D 23 2013

REVIEW: *SLJ* v60 no10 p88 O 2014 Maryann H. Owen

LLOYD, NATALIE. A snicker of magic; [by] Natalie Lloyd 320 p. 2014 Scholastic Press

1. Family life—Fiction 2. Fantasy fiction 3. Friendship—Fiction 4. Magic—Fiction 5. Mothers and daughters—Fiction 6. Single-parent families—Tennessee

ISBN 0545552702; 9780545552707

LC 2013-027779

SUMMARY: In this book by Natalie Lloyd "Midnight Gulch used to be a magical place, a town where people could sing up thunderstorms and dance up sunflowers. But that was long ago, before a curse drove the magic away. Twelve-year-old Felicity knows all about things like that; her nomadic mother is cursed with a wandering heart. . . . But when she arrives in Midnight Gulch, Felicity thinks her luck's about to change." (Publisher's Note)

REVIEW: *Booklist* v110 no12 p83 F 15 2014 Martha Edmundson

REVIEW: *Bull Cent Child Books* v67 no9 p466 My 2014 J. H.

"A Snicker of Magic". "Sure, there are so many coincidences here that you can't swing a cat without hitting one, but this cozy fantasy reveals its secrets in a satisfyingly folkloric way and the particular manifestations of the town's magic are intriguing. Language-loving middle-graders will also be enchanted by Felicity's gift of being able to see words and may be inspired to begin their own "word collections." The colorful characters and the town's magical, memory-inducing ice cream will appeal to fans of Law's Savvy."

REVIEW: *Kirkus Rev* v81 no24 p144 D 15 2013

REVIEW: *N Y Times Book Rev* p23 Ap 6 2014 ELISABETH EGAN

REVIEW: *Publ Wkly* v261 no2 p67 Ja 13 2014

REVIEW: *SLJ* v60 no6 p63 Je 2014 Anne Bozievich

REVIEW: *SLJ* v60 no1 p84 Ja 2014 Mara Alpert

LO BELLO, ANTHONY, 1947-. The origins of mathematical words; a comprehensive dictionary of Latin, Greek, and Arabic roots; [by] Anthony Lo Bello 350 p. 2013 The Johns Hopkins University Press

1. Arabic language—Terms & phrases 2. Encyclopedias & dictionaries 3. Etymology 4. Greek language—Terms & phrases 5. Latin language—Terms & phrases 6. Mathematics—Terminology

ISBN 1421410982 (pbk.: alk. paper); 9781421410982 (pbk.: alk. paper)

LC 2013-005022

SUMMARY: This etymological dictionary by Anthony Lo Bello "identifies the original language of each mathematical term, describes combinations of root terms, provides explanatory definitions, and notes historical references of word usage." (Library Journal)

REVIEW: *Choice* v51 no8 p1374 Ap 2014 A. Megwalu

"The Origins of Mathematical Words: A Comprehensive Dictionary of Latin, Greek, and Arabic Roots". "This fascinating work by [Anthony] Lo Bello . . . is an etymological dictionary of popular mathematical terms of Latin, Greek, and Arabic origin. . . . Teaching the origins of mathematical words helps bridge the gap between everyday language and mathematical language. In this regard, this dictionary is a valuable addition to any collection for high school and college students. . . . Highly recommended."

REVIEW: *Libr J* v139 no2 p95 F 1 2014 M. S. Lary

LO, MALINDA. Inheritance; [by] Malinda Lo 470 p. 2013 Little, Brown and Co.

1. Conspiracies—Fiction 2. Extraterrestrial beings—Fiction 3. Genetic engineering—Fiction 4. Kidnapping—Fiction 5. Love—Fiction 6. Science fiction 7. Sexual orientation—Fiction 8. Speculative fiction

ISBN 0316198005; 9780316198004

LC 2012-048433

SUMMARY: In this book, by Malinda Lo, "after a car accident, mortally injured Reese and David are revived by an injection of alien DNA that has given the teens special abilities. They are kidnapped by brutal government forces. . . . Returned home, Reese and David are caught in a web of intrigue and lies. . . . The fate of the world seems to be at risk as the government, a secret faction of the government, and the aliens square off at the United Nations." (School Library Journal)

REVIEW: *Bull Cent Child Books* v67 no3 p167 N 2013 T. A.

REVIEW: *Horn Book Magazine* v89 no5 p105 S/O 2013 APRIL SPISAK

"Inheritance." "The inside look at the Imria, only peripherally understood in the previous novel, is intriguing--they are the stars here as much as Reese, who isn't always likable as she flings herself through most events impulsively rather than with wisdom or analysis. The graceful, thoughtful look at polyamorous relationships is an unexpected twist, and for this reason alone readers may find Reese (and her ex- and new boyfriends) just as memorable as the clever plot and strong world-building that are the strengths of this novel."

REVIEW: *Kirkus Rev* v81 no15 p127 Ag 1 2013

LOADER, WILLIAM R. G., 1944-. Making sense of sex; attitudes towards sexuality in early Jewish and Christian literature; [by] William R. G. Loader 168 p. 2013 William B. Eerdmans Publishing Company

1. Christian literature, Early—History and criticism 2. Historical literature 3. Rabbinical literature—History and criticism 4. Sex—Biblical teaching

ISBN 9780802870957 (pbk. : alk. paper)

LC 2013-022586

SUMMARY: "This volume systematically reviews biblical, apocryphal, and pseudepigraphal texts that reveal attitudes toward sexuality between approximately 300 BCE and 100 CE. [William] Loader divides the information into four sections that address the creation story, marriage and family issues, the temple and ritual purity, and lastly, Jewish and early Christian attitudes toward sexuality in the Greco-Roman world." (Choice: Current Reviews for Academic Libraries)

REVIEW: *Choice* v51 no6 p1023-4 F 2014 M. Y. Spomer

"Making Sense of Sex: Attitudes Towards Sexuality in Early Jewish and Christian Literature." "Biblical scholar [William] Loader . . . distills five volumes of research into one. . . . This volume systematically reviews biblical, apocryphal, and pseudepigraphal texts that reveal attitudes toward sexuality between approximately 300 BCE and 100 CE. . . . He largely succeeds in providing an impartial analysis of the materials from antiquity that address sexuality. . . . Though serious researchers most likely will want to consult the five volumes upon which this new book is based, 'Making Sense of Sex' is a valuable introduction to the topic of sexuality and to the most important writings on this issue."

LOADES, DAVID. The religious culture of Marian England; [by] David Loades viii, 209 p. 2010 Pickering & Chatto

1. Catholic Church—Great Britain—History 2. Christianity & culture—History 3. England—Church history—1485- 4. Great Britain—History—Mary I, 1553-1558 5. Historical literature

ISBN 9781851969210; 1851969217; 9781851965984; 185196598X

LC 2010-537254

SUMMARY: In this book, author David "Loades explores England's religious culture during the reign of Mary Tudor. He investigates how conflicting traditions of conformity and dissent negotiated the new spiritual, political and legal landscape which followed her reintroduction of Catholicism to England. Overall the clergy and laity remained largely acquiescent. Loades investigates religious practices in the high church and the parishes." (Publisher's note)

REVIEW: *Engl Hist Rev* v128 no534 p1208-11 O 2013 Alexander Samson

"The Religious Culture of Marian England." "This book is a response to Eamon Duffy's positive reassessment of the Marian church and its 'actual impact on the religious lives of the people' in his seminal 'Fires of Faith: Catholic England under Mary Tudor.' . . . A useful account of the structures and functioning of the late medieval church on the eve of the Reformation is included, along with a discussion of the operation of ecclesiastical courts after the Act of Appeals severed their links to Rome. . . . For [author David] Loades, in 'a culture dominated by magic and the supernatural, there was a submerged yearning for rational explanations' that the church could not provide."

LOBBAN, RICHARD A. Historical dictionary of the Sudan. See Fluehr-Lobban, C.

LOBEL, ANITA. Lena's sleep sheep; a going-to-bed book; [by] Anita Lobel 24 p. 2013 Alfred A. Knopf

1. Bedtime—Fiction 2. Children's stories 3. Sheep—Fiction 4. Wakefulness

ISBN 0449810259; 9780449810255; 9780449810262 (library binding); 9780449810279 (ebook)

LC 2012-028378

SUMMARY: In this children's picture book by Anita Lobel, "every evening Lena counts her sheep to help her fall asleep, but tonight they are afraid of the 'round monster' in the window. Lena tries to explain that it's just the Moon, but those silly creatures won't listen, so she convinces them to dress up in disguises to scare it away. When a bit of cloud covers it, the sheep finally line up so she can count them properly." (School Library Journal)

REVIEW: *Booklist* v109 no22 p87 Ag 1 2013 Carolyn Phelan

REVIEW: *Bull Cent Child Books* v67 no2 p102-3 O 2013 J. H.

"Lena's Sleep Sheep." "Little Lena's usual bedtime routine of sheep-counting hits a hitch when the sheep panic at the full moon. . . . The gentle plot and quiet cadence of the text make this bedtime book a effective soporific that may actually induce slumber in its young audience. There are occasional moments of lyricism . . . in [author and illustrator Anita] Lobel's streamlined text, and the fairly simple vocabulary and generally short sentences may even make it accessible to older brothers or sisters who are helping put smaller siblings to bed. The gouache and watercolor art is cozy and attractive, with a folk-art solidity, and Lobel's slightly smudgy layering and blending of colors gives depth and richness to the pictures."

REVIEW: *Kirkus Rev* v81 no12 p102-3 Je 15 2013

REVIEW: *N Y Times Book Rev* p20 Ag 25 2013 SARAH HARRISON SMITH

"Lena's Sleep Sheep: A Going-To-Bed Book," "The Snuggle Sandwich," and "On My Way To Bed." "[Anita] Lobel . . . tells the sweet and funny story of a little girl who is helped to sleep by a flock of sheep. . . . Full of singsong rhymes and scenes of cheerfully chaotic family life, this bedtime book [by Malachy Doyle] starts in the morning. . . . Seen in [Michael] Paraskevas's bright, action-packed illustrations, Livi's high jinks include juggling toys, playing zoo dentist and piloting an imaginary rocket."

REVIEW: *Publ Wkly* v260 no22 p58 Je 3 2013

REVIEW: *SLJ* v59 no7 p66 Jl 2013 Kathleen Kelly MacMillan

LOBEL, ANITA. Taking care of Mama Rabbit; Selected and Illustrated by Lisbeth Zwerger; [by] Anita Lobel 24 p. 2014 Alfred A. Knopf

1. Animal stories 2. Children's stories 3. Mother and child—Fiction 4. Rabbits—Fiction 5. Sick—Fiction

ISBN 0385753683; 9780385753685; 9780385753692 (lib. bdg.)

LC 2013-003154

SUMMARY: In this book by Anita Lobel, "Mama Rabbit is too sick to leave her bed. When Papa Rabbit leaves home to get her some medicine, the ten little rabbit children take it upon themselves to help her feel better. One by one they bring her treats from around the house, including a steaming cup of hot chocolate, a cuddly toy, a good book, and a shiny necklace. Before long, Mama Rabbit begins to feel better even without the help of medicine." (Publisher's note)

REVIEW: *Booklist* v110 no9/10 p122 Ja 1 2014 Carolyn Phelan

REVIEW: *Bull Cent Child Books* v67 no6 p322-3 F 2014 Jeannette Hulick

"Taking Care of Mama Rabbit." "The story is sweet and the message of everyone pitching in to try to help Mama feel better is a good-hearted one, but the premise that the children cure the mother's illness through their actions alone, without pharmaceutical help, might also be problematically wishful, particularly for kids with seriously ill parents. [Anita] Lobel's vibrantly hued gouache and watercolor illustrations are warm and cozy, though, and the kids who prefer their stuffed animals to dolls will be drawn to the cute, clothes-wearing little bunnies."

REVIEW: *Horn Book Magazine* v90 no1 p75-6 Ja/F 2014 MARTHA V. PARRAVANO

"Taking Care of Mama Rabbit." "The ten little rabbit siblings from [Anita] Lobel's '10 Hungry Rabbits' . . . are back, once again working toward a common goal. This time, Mama Rabbit is sick and needs care. With Papa Rabbit off fetching her medicine, the little rabbits spring into action. One at a time, they bring her small palliative items . . . Vibrant colors in a typically lush palette send a reassuring message of cheer and optimism, and the small trim size is just right for the intimate story."

REVIEW: *Kirkus Rev* v81 no24 p134 D 15 2013

REVIEW: *N Y Times Book Rev* p24 N 10 2013 MARIA TATAR

"Tales From the Brothers Grimm," "Michael Hague's Read-To-Me Book of Fairy Tales," and "Fairy TAle Comics." "Lisbeth Zwerger's 'Tales From the Brothers Grimm' and Michael Hague's 'Read-to-me Book of Fairy Tales' draw children into nostalgic fairy-tale worlds with the seductive beauty of their illustrations. 'Fairy Tale Comics,' edited by Chris Duffy and animated by 17 cartoonists and illustrators, by contrast, refashions classic tales with bold creativity. . . . Though Zwerger's watercolors are sometimes disturbing, the decorative beauty of her work also functions as an antidote to the violent content of the tales. This dynamic is reversed in Hague's 'Read-to-Me Book of Fairy Tales'."

REVIEW: *Publ Wkly* v260 no47 p51 N 18 2013

REVIEW: *SLJ* v60 no2 p75 F 2014 Yelena Alekseyeva-Popova

LOBELLO, KAREN. The Great Pj Elf Chase; A Christmas Eve Tradition; 40 p. 2013 CreateSpace Independent Publishing Platform

1. Christmas stories 2. Elves 3. Magic—Juvenile fiction 4. Pajamas 5. Picture books for children
ISBN 1482724626; 9781482724622

SUMMARY: "In this picture book, two boys plan to catch Santa's elves on Christmas Eve when they deliver new sets of pajamas. Santa's elves are on a mission to give all the good children of the world not toys, as one might expect, but new pairs of pajamas. . . . But brothers Jack and Ben are determined to finally catch an elf. They concoct a daring plan to capture one through traps and a net, luring it with cheese and using their dog as a lookout." (Kirkus Reviews)

REVIEW: *Kirkus Rev* v82 no1 p326 Ja 1 2014

"The Great PJ Elf Chase: A Christmas Eve Tradition". "The story is written using a simple rhyming structure, which adds a musical touch. . . . Colorful illustrations vividly bring the action to life through detailed characters and elaborate backgrounds. The elves, hidden on all the pages . . . have playful, impish smiles, and where text appears, touches of red and green and holiday decorations adorn the pages. The downside of the rhyme scheme is its impact on dialogue: No dialogue tags are used, and two speakers are often found in the same stanza, so it can be unclear who's speaking. While the text is sparse on action—the only exciting scene being Ben chasing the elves outside—the charming illustrations make up for the lack of plot. A magical, wholesome Christmas read."

LOBENTHAL, JOEL. Dancing on water. See Tchernichova, E.

LOCHBAUM, DAVID L. Fukushima. See Lyman, E.

LOCK, MARGARET. The Alzheimer conundrum; entanglements of dementia and aging; [by] Margaret Lock 328 p. 2013 Princeton University Press

1. Alzheimer's disease 2. Alzheimer's disease—Age factors 3. Alzheimer's patients 4. Brain—Aging—Molecular aspects 5. Medical literature 6. Older people—Mental health
ISBN 069114978X; 9780691149783
LC 2013-011850

SUMMARY: "Based on a careful study of the history of Alzheimer's disease and extensive in-depth interviews with clinicians, scientists, epidemiologists, geneticists, and others, Margaret Lock highlights the limitations and the dissent implicated in this approach. She stresses that one major difficulty is the . . . absence of behavioral signs of Alzheimer's disease in a significant proportion of elderly individuals, even when Alzheimer neuropathology is present in their brains." (Publisher's note)

REVIEW: *Choice* v51 no10 p1841 Je 2014 L. R. Barley

REVIEW: *N Y Rev Books* v61 no9 p23-5 My 22 2014 Jerome Groopman

"Memory: From Mind to Molecules," "The Alzheimer Conundrum: Entanglements of Dementia and Aging," and "The Answer to the Riddle Is Me: A Memoir of Amnesia." "Written in accessible language for a lay reader, [authors Larry R. Squire and Eric R. Kandel] illustrate fundamental discoveries about memory using works of art. . . . [Author Margaret] Lock's question is a fundamental one in all of medicine: Why do some individuals develop full-blown disease and others do not, despite sharing the same causative agent? . . . [Author David Stuart MacLean] collapsed at a train station while traveling in India. . . . MacLean ultimately asserts that Lariam, a drug prescribed to prevent malaria, is the culprit."

REVIEW: *Publ Wkly* v260 no33 p52 Ag 19 2013

REVIEW: *TLS* no5797 p24 My 9 2014 W. F. BYNUM

LOCKWOOD, ALISON R. The Arsonist's Last Words; [by] Alison R. Lockwood 308 p. 2012 Mansfield House Books

1. Arson—Fiction 2. Arson investigation—Fiction 3. Experimental fiction 4. Journalists—Fiction 5. Terrorism—Fiction
ISBN 0985535806; 9780985535803

SUMMARY: This book "follows the morally wrenching aftermath of a major urban catastrophe. . . . A massive fire consumes the Parramore Plaza in Orlando, Fla., killing 115 people and emotionally scarring untold more. Marko Abissi, a recently fired janitor, immediately falls under suspicion. . . . Juni Bruner, a grizzled veteran reporter, tirelessly investigates every lead, desperately trying to make sense of the despairingly senseless." (Kirkus Reviews)

REVIEW: *Kirkus Rev* v81 no12 p136 Je 15 2013

REVIEW: *Kirkus Rev* p38 D 15 2013 supplemet best books 2013

"The Arsonist's Last Words". "The book's startlingly innovative structure powerfully captures the city's madness in response to the disaster. Instead of a traditional novel told from a single perspective, the book is more like a heap of archival documents—including newspaper articles, personal correspondence, transcripts of telephone conversations and even a worker's compensation report. The reader becomes a proactive participant in the investigation, poring over the dark mystery's disjointed evidence. . . . It's a testament to the author's skill that the narrative remains a seamless whole, even as it unfolds in fractured parts."

LOCKWOOD, MARK W. Texas waterfowl. See Johnson, W. P.

LOEWEN, MARK A.ed. At the top of the grand staircase. See At the top of the grand staircase

LOFTUS, SIMON. The Invention of Memory; An Irish Family Scrapbook; [by] Simon Loftus 360 p. 2014 Daunt Books

1. Families—Ireland 2. Ireland—History 3. Memory 4. Protestants—Ireland 5. Scrapbooks
ISBN 1907970525; 9781907970528

SUMMARY: "In 'The Invention of Memory' Simon Loftus presents us with a heady blend of family memoir with a history of Ireland, foregrounding the story of the Protestant Ascendancy families. What emerges however, is also a meditation on the nature of memory, as the tall tales, legends and ghost stories combine to form a narrative of shifting moods and viewpoints." (Publisher's note)

REVIEW: *TLS* no5786 p13 F 21 2014 TOBY BARNARD

"The Invention of Memory: An Irish Family Scrapbook

1560-1934." "Auctions, fires or carelessness have left [author Simon] Loftus only with random mementoes. From these he reconstructs lives of earnest endeavour, noblesse oblige, profligacy and crime. Only occasionally does he intrude himself between the motley cast and the reader. . . . Both individuals and communities sometimes prefer to be nourished by myths rather than by proven facts. How exactly those myths are constructed and function frequently defies precise explanation. Simon Loftus's account offers useful clues."

LOGSDON, GENE. Gene everlasting; a contrary farmer's thoughts on living forever; [by] Gene Logsdon 192 p. 2014 Chelsea Green Publishing

1. American essays 2. Cancer—Patients—Psychology 3. Death—Psychological aspects 4. Longevity—Psychological aspects

ISBN 1603585397; 9781603585392 (hardcover)

LC 2013-040398

SUMMARY: Author Gene Logsdon "turns his attention here to his own, and everyone else's, unavoidable demise. In 21 . . . essays, the author ruminates over a wide variety of religious and materialistic ideas about death and finds the greatest comfort in the notion that, when his body returns to the soil, it will provide sustenance for new life. . . . Related pieces review his mother's last week of life, the reasons people commit suicide, and an 'immortal' herbicide-resistant weed." (Booklist)

REVIEW: *Booklist* v110 no12 p19-20 F 15 2014 Carl Hays

"Gene Everlasting: A Contrary Farmer's Thoughts on Living Forever". "In 21 contemplative and often trenchantly witty essays, the author ruminates over a wide variety of religious and materialistic ideas about death and finds the greatest comfort in the notion that, when his body returns to the soil, it will provide sustenance for new life. . . . While his legion of fans may pale at the thought that [Gene] Logsdon has just written his swan song, his recent remission from cancer offers hope that his writing days are far from over."

REVIEW: *Kirkus Rev* v82 no1 p234 Ja 1 2014

"Gene Everlasting: A Contrary Farmer's Thoughts on Living Forever". "Though [Gente] Logsdon . . . loves nature as much as the next writer and more than most, he refuses to indulge in the usual sentimentality and poetics of nature writing in this series of interconnected essays that combine plainspoken prose, cleareyed observation and provocative thought. There is plenty here to annoy environmental alarmists, Christians, Republicans, agribusiness, vegetarians (or anyone else bothered by the detailed, don't-read-before-dinner description of killing and butchering) and others who subscribe to various forms of conventional wisdom. . . . Wisdom and experience permeate this perceptive and understatedly well-written meditation."

REVIEW: *Publ Wkly* v260 no51 p56 D 16 2013

LOMAZZO, GIOVANNI PAOLO. Idea of the temple of painting. See Idea of the temple of painting

LOMBARDO, ROBERT M. Organized crime in Chicago; beyond the Mafia; [by] Robert M. Lombardo p. cm. 2012 University of Illinois Press

1. Criminals—Illinois—Chicago 2. Gangs—Illinois—Chicago 3. Historical literature 4. Italians—Illinois—Chicago 5. Organized crime—Illinois—Chicago

ISBN 9780252037306 (cloth); 9780252078781 (pbk.)

LC 2012-017778

SUMMARY: In this book on organized crime in Chicago, Illinois, author Robert M. Lombardo "deflates the theory that organized crime in the United States was imported from Italy, and he provides ample evidence to prove that organized crime in the city evolved from social structure, frontier immorality, and political corruption." Black American criminal organizations are also discussed. (American Historical Review)

REVIEW: *Am Hist Rev* v119 no1 p195 F 2014 Robert C. Donnelly

"Organized Crime in Chicago: Beyond the Mafia". "Readers will be attracted to Organized Crime in Chicago for its thorough treatment of 'The Syndicate,' infamously led by Johnny Torrio and later Al Capone, and 'The Outfit,' most notoriously led by Sam Giancana. These chapters are incredibly important and informative, but [Robert M.] Lombardo's chapter 'Explaining Organized Crime' is a real gem. . . . 'Organized Crime in Chicago' should be on the reading lists for true crime enthusiasts and students of Chicago history and criminal history. That recommendation, however, comes with only one criticism. Lombardo and the University of Illinois Press should be aware of and more sensitive to language that is jarring to a more contemporary ear."

REVIEW: *Booklist* v109 no5 p6 N 1 2012 Rick Roche

REVIEW: *Choice* v50 no11 p2110 Jl 2013 R. D. McCrie

REVIEW: *Contemp Sociol* v43 no4 p550-2 Jl 2014 James Finckenauer

LONDON, ALEX. Proxy; [by] Alex London 379 p. 2013 Philomel

1. Children of the rich—Fiction 2. Dystopias 3. Gays—Fiction 4. Science fiction 5. Social classes—Fiction

ISBN 0399257764; 9780399257766

LC 2012-039704

SUMMARY: In this book, "Knox is a 'patron,' a privileged and wealthy citizen of Mountain City. His only concerns are hacking, scoring with girls, and causing trouble while angering his bigwig dad. His proxy, a person who is contractually obligated to serve out Knox's punishments, is a gay teen. In exchange for working as a proxy, Syd is able to pay off his debts. When Knox accidentally kills a girl, 16 years at the Old Sterling Work Colony is too great a punishment for Syd to bear, so he escapes." (School Library Journal)

REVIEW: *Bull Cent Child Books* v67 no1 p32 S 2013 A. M.

"Proxy." "A science fiction adventure that packs an emotional punch, this novel pairs well-crafted storytelling with solid character development. The true power here lies less in the sometimes slight world-building than in the story's philosophical underpinnings and the personalities of the main characters. The narrative manages to redeem the seemingly irredeemable and to cast the abused as more than a victim, at the same time creating a gay action hero whose sexuality is only one facet of his character. While the novel draws heavily from the historical precedent of whipping boys and the moral journey at the heart of Dickens' 'A Tale of Two Cities', readers unfamiliar with the historical and literary contexts will still appreciate the story's deeper implications."

REVIEW: *Kirkus Rev* p67 2013 Guide 20to BookExpo America

REVIEW: *Kirkus Rev* v81 no2 p87 Je 1 2013

REVIEW: *Kirkus Rev* v81 no9 p92 My 1 2013

REVIEW: *Libr J* v138 no7 p84 Ap 15 2013 Annalisa Pesek

REVIEW: *Publ Wkly* v260 no17 p134 Ap 29 2013

REVIEW: *SLJ* v59 no8 p113 Ag 2013 Adrienne L. Strock

REVIEW: *Voice of Youth Advocates* v36 no3 p78 Ag 2013 Elaine Gass Hirsch

REVIEW: *Voice of Youth Advocates* v36 no2 p80 Je 2013 Elaine Gass Hirsch

LONDON, TODD.ed. An ideal theater. See An ideal theater

LONG, DAVID E.ed. The government and politics of the Middle East and North Africa. See The government and politics of the Middle East and North Africa

LONG, ETHAN.il. The contest. See Long, E.

LONG, ETHAN. The contest; [by] Ethan Long 72 p. 2013 Blue Apple Books

1. Artists—Fiction 2. Cats—Fiction 3. Children's stories 4. Contests—Fiction 5. Friendship—Fiction 6. Mice—Fiction

ISBN 1609053516; 9781609053512 (hardcover)

LC 2013-007807

SUMMARY: In this book, by Ethan Long, "Scribbles the cat and Ink the mouse are buddies and fellow artists. Ink is excited for them to enter a "Draw a Dinosaur" contest. Next, Ink draws...an egg--and insists there's a dinosaur inside it. He's right! As the egg-drawing hatches, a baby dino crawls out, and starts wailing for his mommy. Suddenly, the Chick-a-saurus comes in and scoops the baby into her feathery arms. Realizing that they won't win the contest, Ink creates a "Best Buddy" trophy for Scribbles." (Publisher's note)

REVIEW: *Kirkus Rev* v81 no16 p211 Ag 15 2013

"The Contest." "Scribbles and Ink fumble a contest entry, with amusing results. Scribbles, a cat with scribble-style fur, and Ink, a mouse with clean edges that sometimes drip ink, aspire to win a competition--'Draw a Dino! Win a Prize!'--so they can go to Mudsplash Mountain, the muddiest place on Earth. . . . Three hue sets and visual styles work well together: the mobile, black bodies of Scribbles and Ink themselves, the casual blue and red lines of their simple artwork, and the gleamingly realistic detail of their pencil and paintbrush. The pages are slightly cramped, given all the motion, but then again, Long's playing with cartoon conventions and frame breaks. A giggle-inducing romp about making mud while the sun shines."

REVIEW: *Kirkus Rev* p42 Ag 15 2013 Fall Preview

LONG, SUSAN HILL. Whistle in the dark; [by] Susan Hill Long 192 p. 2013 Holiday House

1. Coming of age—Fiction 2. Fathers & sons—Fiction 3. Friendship—Fiction 4. Historical fiction 5. Lead mines and mining—Fiction

ISBN 1467709344; 9780823428397 (hardcover)

LC 2012-034507

SUMMARY: In this book, by Susan Hill Long, "it's the 1920s in Leadanna, Missouri, and money is tight in the Harding household. So, Clem, a gifted student and talented writer, must leave school and join Pap in the lead mines. . . . Clem meets Lindy, the daughter of a local moonshiner. . . . The two become friends, but soon a series of disasters strike, including a devastating tornado." (Publisher's note)

REVIEW: *Booklist* v110 no2 p71 S 15 2013 Gail Bush

REVIEW: *Bull Cent Child Books* v67 no2 p103 O 2013 H. M.

REVIEW: *Horn Book Magazine* v90 no1 p94-5 Ja/F 2014 BETTY CARTER

"Whistle in the Dark." "It's 1924, and with his beloved sister sick, thirteen-year-old Clem must quit school and join his father deep in the Missouri lead mines in order to help pay the doctor's bill. . . . Clem hates every moment underground, a feeling [Susan Hill] Long skillfully conveys by re-creating the deep, dark, claustrophobic setting, contrasting the tunnel atmosphere beautifully with the prayer 'To grass' that miners offer when coming to the surface. . . . Although the many plot threads tie up overly conveniently, the nicely integrated setting and main characters are strong enough to carry readers to another time and place."

REVIEW: *Kirkus Rev* v81 no17 p103 S 1 2013

REVIEW: *Publ Wkly* p90-1 Children's starred review annual 2013

REVIEW: *SLJ* v59 no10 p1 O 2013 Denise Moore

LONG, THOMAS G. The good funeral; death, grief, and the community of care; [by] Thomas G. Long 252 p. 2013 Westminster John Knox Press

1. Bereavement—United States 2. Death—United States 3. Funeral rites and ceremonies—United States 4. Mourning customs—United States 5. Religious literature

ISBN 066423853X; 9780664238537 (alk. paper)

LC 2013-003068

SUMMARY: Authors Thomas G. Long and Thomas Lynch "discuss the current state of the funeral. Through their different lenses--one as a preacher and one as a funeral director--Thomas G. Long and Thomas Lynch alternately discuss several challenges facing 'the good funeral,' including the commercial aspects . . ., the sometimes tense relationship between pastors and funeral directors, the tendency of modern funerals to exclude the body from the service, and the rapid growth in cremation." (Publisher's note)

REVIEW: *Christ Century* v130 no22 p36-7 O 30 2013 William H. Willimon

REVIEW: *Commonweal* v140 no16 p21-2 O 11 2013 Thomas Baker

"The Good Funeral: Death, Grief, and the Community of Care." "It is not only our talk about the dead that has been bowdlerized, but, increasingly, the rituals at which we remember them. 'The Good Funeral' is an extended conversation on what has been lost in the process, and especially on what its authors feel is our most egregious death-avoidance tactic: the gradual disappearance of the dead themselves from the rituals at which their presence is indispensable. . . . 'The Good Funeral' suffers from some tiresome repetition. . . . But despite these flaws, this passionate, highly readable primer is an effective reminder of what funerals, at their best, do for the living."

REVIEW: *Publ Wkly* v260 no32 p54 Ag 12 2013

LONGDEN, KATE. Come into the Light; [by] Kate Longden 326 p. 2013 Createspace Independent Pub

1. Chief executive officers—Fiction 2. Conduct of life—Fiction 3. Love stories 4. Widows—Fiction 5. Women household employees—Fiction

ISBN 1489582134; 9781489582133

SUMMARY: In this book, "a young widow becomes the housekeeper to a wealthy, difficult man—and realizes her potential. Californian Sydney Holmes had been performing odd, temporary jobs for years following the deaths of her husband and children, when she applies to be a personal secretary and housekeeper for Jason Jamieson. Sydney is beautiful, with a propensity for wearing low-backed dresses, and a slow simmer of tension starts to build between her and her employer, a prominent corporate executive." (Kirkus Reviews)

REVIEW: *Kirkus Rev* v82 no2 p344 Ja 15 2014

"Come Into the Light". "The novel tells an age-old story (rich man, poor woman who teaches him virtues) through a string of anecdotes, which, while sometimes touching, lacks the specifics that would ground the story or distinguish it from previous, similar iterations. . . . Other exchanges, however, bristle with playful yet demure sexiness; it's in those moments that the chemistry between Sydney and Jason becomes unmistakable—and thoroughly enjoyable. The message of redemption through love is an admirable one, but that message too often becomes overshadowed by episodes and language that cause stumbling rather than smooth progression toward the end. A vague relationship saga with a commonplace plot."

LONGLEY, MICHAEL, 1939-.ed. Selected poems. See Graves, R.

LONGMAN, FRANES.tr. Khatyn. See Adamovich, A.

LOOK, LENORE. Brush of the gods; [by] Lenore Look 40 p. 2013 Schwartz & Wade Books

1. Artists—Fiction 2. Painting—Fiction 3. Picture books for children

ISBN 0375870016 (hardcover); 9780375870019 (hardcover); 9780375970016 (library)

LC 2012-006442

SUMMARY: In this children's picture book, Lenore Look "blends mystical realism and biography to create a magical portrait of one of ancient China's famous artists, Wu Daozi. As a boy during the T'ang Dynasty in the seventh century, Daozi is unable to conform in calligraphy class. . . . Later known for his dynamic murals, Daozi paints subjects so realistically they seem to come alive." (Publishers Weekly)

REVIEW: *Booklist* v110 no5 p65 N 1 2013 Sarah Hunter

"Brush of the Gods," "Diego Rivera: An Artist for the People," and "Henri's Scissors. "Wu Daozi is an artist with magic in his brush. As a boy in the late seventh century, Daozi was taught calligraphy, but instead of letters, worms and horsetails fall from the bristles. . . . With engaging prose that is beautifully illustrated with Rivera's paintings and murals, this spacious volume introduces the great Mexican artist to young people. . . . [Jeannette] Winter offers an elegant, accessible portrait of Matisse as an old man when, unable to paint, he begins cutting shapes from paper and dives into the art of collage."

REVIEW: *Booklist* v109 no18 p54 My 15 2013 Ilene Cooper

REVIEW: *Bull Cent Child Books* v67 no1 p32-3 S 2013 D. S.

REVIEW: *Horn Book Magazine* v89 no4 p107-8 Jl/Ag 2013 JENNIFER M. BRABANDER

REVIEW: *Kirkus Rev* v81 no9 p92 My 1 2013

REVIEW: *Kirkus Rev* p59 N 15 2013 Best Books

REVIEW: *N Y Times Book Rev* p16 Ag 25 2013 DAN YACCARINO

"Brush of the Gods," "Ike's Incredible Ink," and "The Day the Crayons Quit." "Four new books on art and white inspires it are just right for children who dream of being artists. . . . 'Brush of the Gods' [is] written by the veteran author Lenore Look, with illustrations by Meilo So evoking sumi ink paintings. . . . A blot of ink creating its own ink to write a story? Although I found the illustrations endearing, the narrative's lack of internal logic was a stumbling block I had a hard time getting over. . . . Although the crayons' wacky voices are believably the kind of thing creative kids come up with when they're daydreaming, [Drew] Daywalt's clever conceit seems stretched to its limit."

REVIEW: *Publ Wkly* p31 Children's starred review annual 2013

REVIEW: *Publ Wkly* v260 no15 p61 Ap 15 2013

REVIEW: *SLJ* v59 no5 p80 My 2013 Carol Connor

LOPEZ, DIANA. Ask my mood ring how I feel; [by] Diana Lopez 324 p. 2013 Little, Brown and Co.

1. Cancer—Fiction 2. Christian life—Fiction 3. Family life—Texas—Fiction 4. Friendship—Fiction 5. Fundraising—Fiction 6. Hispanic Americans—Fiction 7. Promises—Fiction 8. Young adult literature, American

ISBN 0316209961 (hardcover); 9780316209960 (hardcover)

LC 2012-029856

SUMMARY: In this book, Chia's "mother is diagnosed with breast cancer, which spurs . . . changes throughout their family. . . . After visiting the Basilica of Our Lady of San Juan del Valle in southern Texas, Chia dedicates herself to a promesa, vowing to secure 500 sponsors for a Walk for the Cure in exchange (she hopes) for her mother's recovery." (Publishers Weekly)

REVIEW: *Bull Cent Child Books* v67 no1 p33 S 2013 D. S.

"Ask My Mood Ring How I Feel." "Eighth grade was supposed to be about ruling middle school and drawing the attention of all the right boys, but Chia finds a different priority when her mother is diagnosed with breast cancer. . . . The family story is the strongest thread here . . . an additional subplot about the support Chia receives from an old pal who might like to be more is also well done. Characterization, though, is generally weak and shallow, with Chia's friends largely flat and her sister more of a device to convey information about cancer and its treatment than a real person. . . . The book therefore isn't a deep exploration of anything, but Chia's a relatable character, and her story offers use as an accessible treatment of an intimidating subject."

REVIEW: *Kirkus Rev* v81 no2 p81 Je 1 2013

REVIEW: *Kirkus Rev* v81 no8 p97 Ap 15 2013

REVIEW: *Publ Wkly* v260 no19 p69 My 13 2013

LOPEZ, DONALD S., 1923-2008. The Princeton dictionary of Buddhism; [by] Donald S. Lopez 1304 p. 2013 Princeton University Press

1. Buddhism—Dictionaries 2. Buddhism—Terminology 3. Buddhist literature 4. Encyclopedias & dictionaries 5. Language & languages—Religious aspects—Buddhism
ISBN 0691157863 (cloth: alk. paper); 9780691157863 (cloth: alk. paper)
LC 2012-047585

SUMMARY: This dictionary of Buddhism "covers figures, works, and terminology across a range of traditions and languages, including the canonical languages . . . as well as some Southeast Asian languages. . . . The dictionary also includes maps, a list of Asian historical periods, and a time line of Buddhism, each broken down by country." (Choice: Current Reviews for Academic Libraries)

REVIEW: *Booklist* v110 no9/10 p74-8 Ja 1 2014 Christopher McConnell

REVIEW: *Choice* v51 no9 p1566-7 My 2014 A. L. Folk

"The Princeton Dictionary of Buddhism". "This encyclopedic dictionary by [Robert E.] Buswell [Jr.] . . . and [Donald S.] Lopez [Jr.] . . . likely will become an essential resource for students and scholars of Buddhism. It has over 5,000 entries varying in length from a paragraph to a full page, and the authors acknowledge that 'this is the largest dictionary of Buddhism ever produced in the English language.' . . . Students enrolled in introductory courses probably will find this dictionary overwhelming. However, schools with advanced offerings will find it a most worthwhile investment."

REVIEW: *Libr J* v138 no18 p118 N 1 2013 Ray Arnett

LORCH, STEPHEN. Off the Top of My Head; An Alphabetical Odyssey; [by] Stephen Lorch 352 p. 2013 Pathway Book Service

1. Essay (Literary form) 2. Imagination 3. Melanoma 4. Opera 5. Robinson, Jackie, 1919-1972
ISBN 0989884007; 9780989884006

SUMMARY: In this essay collection by Stephen Lorch, "letters of the alphabet prompt ruminations on a wide range of subjects, from the pragmatic to the metaphorical—G for gestalt, I for imagine . . . etc. The project originated with a series of emails Lorch sent to friends and acquaintances while he recovered from surgery. . . . The entries mainly consider different aspects of Lorch's medical experience, but they invariably branch out from that initial starting point." (Kirkus Reviews)

REVIEW: *Kirkus Rev* v82 no3 p389 F 1 2014

"Off the Top of My Head". "In [Stephen] Lorch's richly personal, utterly beguiling book, letters of the alphabet prompt ruminations on a wide range of subjects, from the pragmatic to the metaphorical. . . . The essays exhibit considerable variation. . . . It's a fascinatingly wide-ranging feast of autobiographical musings filled with thoughts on numerous authors—from W.H. Auden to Jorge Luis Borges to Dylan Thomas to David Lodge and Daniel Dennett—all of it served with a good deal of humor. An absorbing, winning tour of one indomitable man's life and mind."

LORD, EMERY. Open road summer; [by] Emery Lord 352 p. 2014 Bloomsbury/Walker

1. Best friends—Fiction 2. Country music—Fiction 3. Friendship—Fiction 4. Love—Fiction 5. Road fiction 6. Singers—Fiction
ISBN 9780802736109 (hardback)
LC 2013-025427

SUMMARY: In this book, by Emery Lord, "Reagan joins her best friend Delilah's summer concert tour to escape some poor decisions and break some bad habits, finding romance and complication instead. When Reagan finds herself attracted to soulful musician Matt, romance seems inevitable-but the record company has hired him to pose as Delilah's wholesome boyfriend." (Kirkus Reviews)

REVIEW: *Booklist* v110 no15 p86-7 Ap 1 2014 Anne O'Malley

REVIEW: *Bull Cent Child Books* v67 no10 p530 Je 2014 K. C.

"Open Road Summer". "The erudition of Reagan's narration is initially suspicious for such a hard-partying character, but it both hints at depths in her character that unfold as the novel progresses and makes what could be a sappy romance for the celebrity-obsessed into a smartly realized, engrossing love, friendship, and redemption story. There are moments that read like a Southern-fried Hollywood rom-com, with Matt as a thinly veiled version of Matthew McConaughey (oh, those dimples!) and Lilah channeling Taylor Swift, but there is also real emotion here, keyed to contemporary teen concerns about coming back after overexposure and lost reputation, deserved or not."

REVIEW: *Kirkus Rev* v82 no5 p101 Mr 1 2014

"Open Road Summer". "These characters are predictable, and the happily-ever-after ending is really never in doubt, but romance fans will undoubtedly still enjoy the developing relationships. [Emery] Lord also deserves credit for plausibly explaining the lack of adult supervision: Their chaperone, Delilah's 26-year-old aunt, is distracted by her involvement with a new tour boyfriend. Even without adult supervision, Reagan and Matt's physical relationship is passionate but, refreshingly, restrained. Lord successfully adapts classic elements of adult romance novels into a love story gentle enough for younger readers."

REVIEW: *Publ Wkly* v261 no5 p58 F 3 2014

REVIEW: *Voice of Youth Advocates* v37 no1 p69-70 Ap 2014 Ed Goldberg

REVIEW: *Voice of Youth Advocates* v37 no1 p70 Ap 2014 Rachelle David

LORD, MICHELLE. Nature recycles; how about you?; [by] Michelle Lord 32 p. 2013 Sylvan Dell Publishing

1. Ecology—Juvenile literature 2. Ecology textbooks 3. Environmentalism—Juvenile literature 4. Recycling (Waste, etc.)—Juvenile literature 5. Salvage (Waste, etc.)
ISBN 1607186152 (reinforced); 9781607186151 (reinforced); 9781607186274 (paperback); 9781607186397 (ebook); 9781607186519 (ebook); 9781607187110 (hardcover)
LC 2012-031349

SUMMARY: In this children's picture book, "from decorator sea urchin, protected by his collection of ocean refuse, to an Asian elephant's meal of the banana leaf she first used as a fan, the text and . . . illustrations offer varied images of adaptive reuse." The quiz at the end of the book notes that "animals 'recycle for nests or shelters, camouflage or protection, as tools, or as nutrients.'" (Kirkus Reviews)

REVIEW: *Kirkus Rev* v81 no1 p82 Ja 1 2013

REVIEW: *SLJ* v59 no8 p120 Ag 2013 Anne Barreca

LORENZ, STEVEN A. When the Fates Whisper; [by] Steven A. Lorenz 210 p. 2012 CreateSpace Independent Publishing Platform

1. Families—Fiction 2. Fathers & sons—Fiction 3. Friendship—Fiction 4. Historical fiction 5. Teenagers—Fiction

ISBN 1479242659; 9781479242658

SUMMARY: This book, by Steven A. Lorenz, is "a debut novel about a young man's hijinks with his neighborhood friends. Steven, the story's 65-year-old narrator, reflects on his Midwestern childhood in Good Town. The only son of a 'grain man' and a 'fragile, timid poet,' Steven tells jovial tales of his teenage scrapes and capers, including stealing his grandfather's car, sneaking beer into soda bottles and making an underage visit to a local saloon." (Kirkus Reviews)

REVIEW: *Kirkus Rev* v82 no1 p316 Ja 1 2014

"When the Fates Whisper". "A debut novel about a young man's hijinks with his neighborhood friends. Steven, the story's 65-year-old narrator, reflects on his Midwestern childhood in Good Town. . . .The novel invites readers to admire Steven, but its tone is often boastful. That said, its clearest moments of awareness arrive when [Steven A.] Lorenz ventures into Good Town's darker aspects. . . . In such moments, Lorenz almost approaches satire, but most of the novel asks to be taken at face value. A sometimes-engaging novel of nostalgic Americana and small-town celebrations."

LOSTY, J. P. Mughal India; Art, Culture and Empire; [by] J. P. Losty 256 p. 2013 University of Chicago Press

1. Art literature 2. Historical literature 3. Mogul Empire—History 4. Mogul Empire—Social life & customs 5. Mogul art

ISBN 0712358706; 9780712358705

SUMMARY: This book by J. P. Losty and Malini Roy "showcases the British Library's extensive collection of illustrated manuscripts and paintings commissioned by Mughal emperors and other officials. . . . The lavish artworks cover a variety of subject matter, from scenes of courtly life to illustrations of works of literature. The development of a Mughal style of art can be traced through the illustrations and paintings, as can the influence of European styles." (Publisher's note)

REVIEW: *Choice* v51 no2 p245-6 O 2013 N. Dinkar

"Mughal India: Art, Culture, and Empire: Manuscripts and Paintings in the British Library." "This is a beautifully illustrated catalogue for a 2012-13 British Library exhibition of Mughal art featuring over 200 objects from the library's extensive collections. The Mughals, whose lavish courts and grandiose vision included architectural splendors such as the Taj Mahal, were also active patrons of miniature painting. [Authors J. P.] Losty . . . and [Malini] Roy . . . track the distinctive style of this art from its Persian origins to the later, Westernized elements it incorporated. . . . Where the book excels, however, is in the meticulous visual analysis of over 150 paintings."

LOTT, JOHN. Great Expectations; The Lost Toronto Blue Jays Season; [by] John Lott 220 p. 2013 ECW Press

1. Baseball—Canada 2. Baseball players 3. Baseball teams 4. Sports literature 5. Toronto Blue Jays (Baseball team)

ISBN 1770411879; 9781770411876

SUMMARY: This book by Shi Davidi and John Lott looks at the 2013 season of the baseball team the Toronto Blue Jays. It "begins with a detailed look at how general manager Alex Anthopoulos . . . acquired flashy shortstop Jose Reyes, potential pitching ace Josh Johnson and steady left-hander Mark Buehrle. Then came . . . knuckleballer R.A. Dickey. . . . The book examines the challenges that Reyes, Buehrle and Dickey faced in their formative years and during the rocky 2013 season." (Publisher's note)

REVIEW: *Quill Quire* v80 no1 p41 Ja/F 2014 Jacob McArthur Mooney

Title:"Great Expectations: The Lost Toronto Blue Jays Season". "A first pass at the history of the 2013 Toronto Blue Jays, written by two of the team's best beat reporters, Sportsnet's Shi Davidi and the National Post's John Lott. . . . Davidi and Lott have leveraged their close knowledge of the team into a handful of well-drawn character profiles placed alongside an ongoing narrative that begins with the 2012 off-season. . . . Still, 'Great Expectations' never overcomes its two-headed narrative problem. The 2013 season is both well-remembered recent history and devoid of a climax. . . . The book struggles to be interesting. . . . Frustrated fans might grow restless with the authors' refusal to assign even the outline of blame for the team's dismal showing."

LOTT, JOHN R. Dumbing down the courts; how politics keeps the smartest judges off the bench; [by] John R. Lott 354 p. 2013 Bascom Hill Pub. Group

1. Courts—United States 2. Judges—Selection & appointment 3. Judges—Selection & appointment—Political aspects 4. Political science literature 5. United States—Politics & government

ISBN 9781626522497 (pbk)

LC 2013-942834

SUMMARY: In this book, John Lott "says the pitched battles over court nominations are having real-world consequences. He argues that our federal courts are being intellectually degraded as politicians in both parties try to keep the brightest and most articulate lawyers from becoming judges. . . . Even after highly qualified judges get on the federal bench, they may not wish to shine too brightly if they wish to be promoted." (National Review)

REVIEW: *Natl Rev* v65 no20 p61-2 O 28 2013 JOHN FUND

"Dumbing Down the Courts: How Politics Keeps the Smartest Judges Off the Bench." "John Lott, an economist who has written thought-provoking books on everything from gun control to the federal budget, says the pitched battles over court nominations are having real-world consequences. . . . Bold claims, but Lott has done statistical analysis on federal court nominations that bears out his thesis. . . . It is ironic that as the federal government has grown bigger, it has become 'dumber' in finding solutions to the problems it tries to address. And as Lott shows, the federal judges who are supposed to oversee that vast expansion of power are becoming part of the problem, not part of the solution."

LOUNSBURY, MICHAEL. The institutional logics perspective; a new approach to culture, structure, and process; [by] Michael Lounsbury xiv, 234 p. 2012 Oxford Univer-

sity Press
1. Associations, institutions, etc.—Philosophy 2. Culture—Research 3. Organizational sociology 4. Social institutions 5. Social science literature
ISBN 0199601933 (hbk.); 0199601941 (pbk.); 9780199601936 (hbk.); 9780199601943 (pbk.)
LC 2011-944134

SUMMARY: This book looks at the institutional logics perspective on how "institutions influence and shape cognition and action in individuals and organizations." It "analyzes seminal research, illustrating how and why influential works on institutional theory motivated a distinct new approach to scholarship on institutional logics." (Publisher's note)

REVIEW: *Choice* v50 no4 p767 D 2012 L. L. Hansen

REVIEW: *Contemp Sociol* v43 no1 p45-9 Ja 2014 Devorah Kalekin-Fishman

"Inventive Methods: The Happening of the Social" and "The Institutional Logics Perspective: A New Approach to Culture, Structure, and Process". "Although densely theorized, each of the chapters shows how the ideas have grown out of research, and points to the many future research opportunities that the perspective implies. The perspective of institutional logics goes far beyond the context of organizational theory and research from which,ultimately, it must be seen to have been derived, in coming near to reflecting the contemporary pervasiveness of experience in institutional fields. While reading, I was impressed with the varied applicability of the institutional logics perspective for enriching the approaches of diverse schools of sociology. . . . All the methods included here evoke thought and rouse the reader to action, inviting one to try them, or provoking work on a contrasting approach."

LOURIE, BRUCE. Toxin toxout. See Smith, R.

LOVE LETTERS OF THE GREAT WAR; 240 p. 2014 Macmillan
1. Historical literature 2. Love letters 3. Military spouses 4. Soldiers' letters 5. World War, 1914-1918—Sources
ISBN 0230772838; 9780230772830

SUMMARY: Edited by Mandy Kirkby, "'Love Letters of the Great War' brings together . . . eloquent declarations of love and longing; others contain wrenching accounts of fear, jealousy and betrayal; many share sweet dreams of home. But in all the correspondence--whether from British, American, French, German, Russian, Australian and Canadian troops in the height of battle, or from the heartbroken wives and sweethearts left behind--there lies a truly human portrait of love and war." (Publisher's note)

REVIEW: *TLS* no5787 p27 F 28 2014 KATE McLOUGHLIN

"Love Letters of the Great War." "'Love Letters of the Great War,' sensitively edited by Mandy Kirkby and with an insightful foreword by Helen Dunmore, is more than a touching anthology. It shows that letters gave men the chance to reflect on their transformation into soldiers, allowed absent husbands and fathers to participate in family life, formed a point of physical contact between separated lovers (so many were carried in breast pockets and damaged alongside their owners' bodies) and, in spite of the censors, provided a forum for sexual fantasy."

LOVELACE, EARL, 1935-. Is just a movie; [by] Earl Lovelace 355 p. 2011 Faber & Faber
1. Extras (Actors) 2. Friendship—Fiction 3. Motion pictures—Production and direction—Trinidad and Tobago—Fiction 4. Psychological fiction
ISBN 0571255671 (pbk.); 9780571255672 (pbk.)
LC 2011-379732

SUMMARY: This book by Earl Lovelace is set in Trinidad. "Sonnyboy Apparicio and Kangkala" earn small roles "in a movie produced by an American film company that held tryouts for local talent. . . . Sonnyboy and Kangkala sense an affinity when both want their cinematic death to be something greater than a keeling over at the first shot fired. The film director, however, cuts their extravagant death scenes." (World Literature Today)

REVIEW: *World Lit Today* v87 no5 p58-9 S/O 2013 Robert H. McCormick Jr.

"Is Just A Movie." "Key to 'Is Just a Movie' is [Earl] Lovelace's deft positioning of his narrator amid his characters. . . . The language of Lovelace is the spoken language of the community. . . .The novel's title shows how the magic of Lovelace's concreteness is manifested in his language, a language not learned in school. . . . With chapters like 'Franklyn Batting,' an homage to West Indian cricket, Dorlene's miraculous 'Funeral,' and 'Arlene's Zipper,' Lovelace demonstrates his narrative wizardry in transforming concrete detail into something greater."

LOVELL, JULIA.tr. The Matchmaker, the Apprentice, and the Football Fan. See Zhu Wen

LOVELL, STEPHEN. The shadow of war. See The shadow of war

LOVELOCK, BRIAN.il. Flight of the honey bee. See Huber, R.

LOVERIDGE, MATT.il. Stranger things. See Lubar, D.

LOWE, SHELLY C.ed. Beyond the asterisk. See Beyond the asterisk

LOWELL, ELIZABETH. Reckless love; [by] Elizabeth Lowell 379 p. 2013 Severn House Publishers
1. Horses—Fiction 2. Indian captivities—Fiction 3. Love stories 4. Mistaken identity—Fiction 5. Utah—Fiction
ISBN 0373772521 (pbk.) :; 072788316X; 9780373772520 (pbk.); 9780727883162
LC 2007-585364

SUMMARY: In this book by Elizabeth Lowell, "no one who roamed the steep green mountains . . . of Utah Territory was safe from El Cascabel and his renegade warriors--not Janna Wayland, not the wild stallion Lucifer--not even Ty MacKenzie, the stranger who had come for the stallion, and stayed to capture Janna's heart. Now all three must join forces and make their escape, or die trying." (Publisher's note)

REVIEW: *Booklist* v110 no6 p27 N 15 2013 Shelley Mosley

"Reckless Love." "[Elizabeth] Lowell is an exceptional

writer, and her colorful tale of romance, danger, adventure, and mistaken identity, all set against the stunning background of the American West, will satisfy her longtime fans as well as entice a whole new readership. Fans of western romances, especially such classics as Maggie Osborne's 'The Promise of Jenny Jones' (1997), Rosanne Bittner's 'Follow Your Heart' (2013); and Johanna Lindsey's 'Savage Thunder' (1998), will especially enjoy this talented author's colorful tale of love in an untamed land."

REVIEW: *Libr J* v138 no21 p86 D 1 2013 Kristin Ramsdell

LOWERY, DAVID. Interest groups and health care reform across the United States; [by] David Lowery 236 p. 2013 Georgetown University Press

1. Federal Government—United States 2. Health Care Reform—United States 3. Health Policy—United States 4. Political science literature 5. Politics—United States 6. Public Opinion—United States 7. State Government—United States

ISBN 9781589019898 (pbk. : alk. paper)
LC 2012-037462

SUMMARY: This book "assesses the impact of interest groups to determine if collectively they are capable of shaping policy in their own interests or whether they influence policy only at the margins. . . . The fact that state governments took action in health policy in spite of opposing interests, where the national government could not, offers a compelling puzzle that will be of special interest to scholars and students of public policy, health policy, and state politics." (Publisher's note)

REVIEW: *Choice* v51 no6 p1095 F 2014 B. W. Monroe

"Interest Groups and Health Care Reform Across the United States." "[Virginia] Gray . . . [David] Lowery . . . and [Jennifer K.] Benz . . . provide a valuable addition to the very timely debate on health care policy in the US. The main focus is on the impact of interest groups in whether or not state governments choose to enact a wide range of health care reforms. . . . The book is clearly best suited for the so-called 'policy wonks' rather than general readers because it is incredibly comprehensive in its scope (which is a credit to the author); provides huge amounts of data; and is filled with exhaustive terminology and advanced statistics so that it is very easy to get lost in the details."

LOWINGER, KATHY. Shifting sands; life in the times of Moses, Jesus, and Muhammad; [by] Kathy Lowinger 118 p. 2014 Firefly Books Ltd

1. Historical fiction 2. Jesus Christ 3. Moses (Biblical leader) 4. Muhammad, Prophet, d. 632, in art 5. Religious leaders

ISBN 155451617X; 9781554516179

SUMMARY: This book by Kathy Lowinger introduces readers to "the lives and times of Jesus, Moses, and Muhammad," with a focus on "the experiences of young adults growing up in brutal times and facing difficult choices. . . . Lowinger uses her young characters to provide a glimpse of how everyday people may have been affected by Moses leading the Hebrews out of Egypt, Jesus helping those suffering under Roman Rule,a nd Muhammad promoting equality among his people." (Quill & Quire)

REVIEW: *Kirkus Rev* v82 no12 p224 Je 15 2014

REVIEW: *Quill Quire* v80 no1 p44 Ja/F 2014 Sarah Sawler

"Shifting Sands: Life in the Times of Moses, Jesus, and Muhammad". "Kathy Lowinger takes readers on thoroughly researched adventures through Egypt, Nazareth, and Mecca, paying plenty of attention to historical detail and handling her subject matter respectfully. At first glance, the book appears to be about the lives and times of Jesus, Moses, and Muhammad, but it soon becomes clear that it is more concerned with the experiences of young adults growing up in brutal times and facing difficult choices. . . . Lowinger masterfully conveys the violence and beauty of these eras. . . . 'Shifting Sands' is a great option for school libraries looking for well-balanced religious-studies titles."

LOWNDES, VIVIEN. Why institutions matter. See Roberts, M.

LOWRY, LOIS, 1937-. Gooney Bird and all her charms; [by] Lois Lowry 160 p. 2014 Houghton Mifflin Harcourt

1. Charm bracelets—Fiction 2. Human anatomy—Fiction 3. School stories 4. Schools—Fiction 5. Skeleton—Fiction

ISBN 0544113543; 9780544113541
LC 2012-041887

SUMMARY: In this book, by Lois Lowry, "Gooney Bird and her second-grade classmates are studying the human body. The students are in for a surprise when her uncle, Dr. Walter Oglethorpe, an anatomy professor, loans them a skeleton to help them with their research. The skeleton, on display outside the school to show the location of the respiratory system, goes missing, and Gooney Bird becomes head detective, leading her class on an investigation to solve the mystery." (Publisher's note)

REVIEW: *Booklist* v110 no5 p75 N 1 2013 Carolyn Phelan

REVIEW: *Bull Cent Child Books* v67 no6 p323-4 F 2014 Amy Atkinson

"Gooney Bird and All Her Charms". "Gooney Bird . . . amuses and inspires again in this latest installment of her series. . . . By the time this entertaining chapter book ends, she has found a way to interweave the seemingly disparate charms with the story of the skeleton and all the class learned during his stay at the school, thus modeling for young readers how the pieces of a story come together and providing ample opportunity for reader prediction in both independent and readaloud encounters. With apt jokes, recognizable classroom curriculum, and comfortably familiar characters, not to mention sly jabs at censorship, [Lois] Lowry's Gooney Bird and her skeletal adventures will satisfy readers who appreciate a humerus tale."

REVIEW: *Kirkus Rev* v81 no22 p145 N 15 2013

REVIEW: *SLJ* v60 no1 p73 Ja 2014 Sarah Polace

LOXTON, DANIEL. Abominable science! See Prothero, D. R.

LOXTON, DANIEL. Plesiosaur Peril; 32 p. 2014 Kids Can Pr

1. Animal young 2. Children's stories 3. Dinosaurs—Juvenile fiction 4. Plesiosauria 5. Predatory animals

ISBN 1554536332; 9781554536337

SUMMARY: In this book, part of the "Tales of Prehistoric Life" series, "we follow the tale of a baby Cryptoclidus, a type of plesiosaur, whose curiosity about her new world in the ocean leads her to wander away from her mother and the rest of her protective pod. As the baby happily explores and plays, she is suddenly confronted by an enormous Liopleurodon, a predatory and much larger plesiosaur." (Publisher's note)

REVIEW: *Kirkus Rev* v82 no1 p270 Ja 1 2014

"Plesiosaur Peril". "Another prehistoric predicament from the creators of 'Ankylosaur Attack' (2011) and 'Pterosaur Trouble' (2013), with similarly nongory but otherwise photorealistic illustrations. Gliding sinuously through shallow, sunlit waters crowded with tentacled ammonites and early fish, a young Cryptoclidus follows her mother and the rest of the plesiosaur pod. . . . [Daniel] Loxton stirs current theories about plesiosaur behavior and physiology into his melodramatic episode, expanding on them in an informative afterword."

LOYD, AMY GRACE. The Affairs of Others; A Novel; [by] Amy Grace Loyd 272 p. 2013 St. Martin's Press

1. Apartment buildings—Fiction 2. Apartment dwellers—Fiction 3. Brooklyn (New York, N.Y.)—Fiction 4. Interpersonal relations—Fiction 5. Landlord & tenant—Fiction 6. Man-woman relationships—Fiction 7. Neighbors—Fiction 8. Psychological fiction 9. Widows—Fiction

ISBN 1250041295; 9781250041296

LC 2013-012628

SUMMARY: In this book, by Amy Grace Loyd, "Celia Cassill is still in mourning for her young husband, who died five years earlier after a grueling illness. Fortunately, he left enough money for her to buy a small apartment building in Brooklyn. But even though she is doing all right financially, Celia is isolated and withdrawn. Now she finds herself pulled into the problems of her tenants." (Library Journal)

REVIEW: *Booklist* v109 no22 p26 Ag 1 2013 Cortney Ophoff

REVIEW: *Kirkus Rev* v81 no6 p287 Mr 15 2013

REVIEW: *New Yorker* v89 no32 p113-1 O 14 2013

"The Affairs of Others." "This moody, sensual début centers on a Brooklyn landlady named Celia, a recent widow in her late thirties. Grief has led her to wall herself off from her tenants and from her own interior life . . . but the carapace she has built begins to fracture when she allows a sultry older woman to sublet one of her apartments. Soon she must contend with the woman's abusive ex-husband, and with the various domestic crises of her other tenants. Loyd succeeds at the most difficult task for such a circumscribed setting--making the granular details of her characters' travails feel as though they added up to more than the sum of their parts. Celia's emotional breakthrough, when it comes, reads as both important and true."

REVIEW: *Publ Wkly* v260 no24 p36 Je 17 2013

LUBAR, DAVID. Stranger things; 96 p. 2013 Scholastic

1. Children's literature 2. Coins—Fiction 3. Coins—Juvenile fiction 4. Friendship—Fiction 5. Friendship—Juvenile fiction 6. Magic—Fiction 7. Magic—Juvenile fiction

ISBN 9780545496018 (reinforced hardcover library binding : alk. paper); 9780545496025 (pbk. : alk. paper); 9780545496858 (ebook)

LC 2012-024838

SUMMARY: Written by David Lubar and illustrated by Matt Loveridge, this book has a story in which protagonist "Ed finds a coin bearing the words 'strange, stranger.' Once this coin comes into his life, strange things start happening all around him. One of his friends gets stuck in midair, his brother turns into a pool float, and his sister's food makes its way off her plate! Even more bizarre events all lead up to a surprise ending. . . ." (Publisher's note)

REVIEW: *Bull Cent Child Books* v67 no1 p34 S 2013 T. A.

"Stranger Things." "This transitional chapter book is the start of a series, and it gets off to a slow start--Ed's plight in figuring out who the Stranger is never feels urgent enough to maintain an engaging plot, and the mixing of the merely bizarre (Ed's brother writes down a thousand words in exchange for a picture) with the outright preposterous (Ed's sister dances through the living room with hundreds of mice and a soda-straw flute after he reads her the story of the Pied Piper) muddles what exactly the book means by "strange." Still, Ed's straightforward explanation and earnest questioning make him likable enough as a narrator in spite of his seriousness and self-consciousness. . . . Upbeat, light-hearted sketches help lighten the chapter length. . . ."

REVIEW: *Kirkus Rev* v81 no6 p187 Mr 15 2013

REVIEW: *SLJ* v59 no7 p64 Jl 2013 Elizabeth Swistock

LUCAS, BILL. A history of the English language in 100 places; [by] Bill Lucas 256 p. 2013 Robert Hale

1. English language—Dialects 2. English language—Great Britain 3. English language—History 4. Historical literature 5. Lingua francas

ISBN 0709095708; 9780709095705

SUMMARY: "'A History of the English Language in 100 Places' is a joyous ride through time, where readers can criss-cross the British Isles and the world at large to land in a hundred contrasting places and light on a hundred wonderful topics that bring the extraordinary story of the English language alive. . . . Some places represent historic firsts, some are tied to significant people and some have seen events that have shaped the future of English." (Publisher's note)

REVIEW: *TLS* no5782 p26-7 Ja 24 2014 MICHAEL THOMAS

"A History of the English Language in 100 Places." "'A History of the English Language in 100 Places' is a fascinating gazetteer from the University of Winchester's ongoing English Project. The language's 'global reach has no parallel,' David Crystal observes in the introduction, and this handsome volume justifies his words. . . . Individual entries allow the reader to contextualize the emergence of each new form of English, a process in which power and expediency are much to the fore. . . . The title may insist on 100 places but richly, carefully, the book gives the impression of many more."

LUCIER, MAKIIA. A death-struck year; [by] Makiia Lucier 288 p. 2014 Houghton Mifflin Harcourt

1. Historical fiction 2. Influenza Epidemic, 1918-1919—Fiction 3. Influenza Epidemic, 1918-1919—Oregon—Portland—Juvenile fiction 4. Nurses—Fiction

ISBN 0544164504; 9780544164505 (hardback)

LC 2013-037482

SUMMARY: In this novel, by Makiia Lucier, "the Spanish influenza is devastating . . . Pacific Northwest. Schools, churches, and theaters are shut down. The entire city [of Portland, Oregon] is thrust into survival mode—and into a panic. Seventeen-year-old Cleo is told to stay put in her quarantined boarding school, but when the Red Cross pleads for volunteers, she cannot ignore the call for help," (Publisher's note)

REVIEW: *Booklist* v110 no16 p57 Ap 15 2014 Daniel Kraus

REVIEW: *Bull Cent Child Books* v67 no8 p414 Ap 2014 A. A.

"A Death-Struck Year". "[Makiia] Lucier has done her research, creating a compelling work of historical fiction alongside a more timeless journey of self-discovery. She includes thoughtful details of the time period (a new pamphlet on birth control circulates among the women), rounding out the reader's understanding of Cleo's world. The sickbed depictions are sobering but not gratuitous, and the romance, while pleasing, takes a backseat to the more pressing details of life and death and to Cleo's personal direction. Readable and informative, this is for . . . general historical fiction fans who appreciate a touch of romance with their world events."

REVIEW: *Horn Book Magazine* v90 no4 p99 Jl/Ag 2014 JONATHAN HUNT

REVIEW: *Kirkus Rev* v82 no5 p181 Mr 1 2014

REVIEW: *SLJ* v60 no4 p169 Ap 2014 Etta Anton

LUCKHURST, MARY.ed. A concise companion to contemporary British and Irish drama. See A concise companion to contemporary British and Irish drama

LUDERS, JOSEPH E. The civil rights movement and the logic of social change; [by] Joseph E. Luders 246 2010 Cambridge University Press

1. African Americans—Civil rights 2. Civil rights movements—United States 3. Civil rights movements—United States—History—20th century 4. Protest movements—United States 5. Social change—United States 6. Social change—United States—History—20th century 7. Social science literature

ISBN 9780521133395; 0521133394

LC 2009-014706

SUMMARY: In this book on the effectiveness of social movements, author Joseph E. Luders introduces "an analytical framework that begins with a shift in emphasis away from the characteristics of movements toward the targets of protests and affected bystanders, their interests, and why they respond as they do. Such a shift brings into focus how targets and other interests assess both their exposure to movement disruptions as well as the costs of conceding to movement demands." (Publisher's note)

REVIEW: *Contemp Sociol* v43 no1 p16-29 Ja 2014 Edwin Amenta

"The Fifth Freedom:Jobs, Politics, and Civil Rights in the United States, 1941-1972," "Doctors and Demonstrators: How Political Institutions Shape Abortion Law in the United States, Britain, and Canada," and "The Civil Rights Movement and the Logic of Social Change". "[Joseph E.] Luders analyzes a series of civil rights campaigns and policy debates, with business as well as government targets. His cost perspective yields insights about the influence of protest generally. . . With its combination of historical sophistication, astute political analysis, and quantitative examinations of lower-level political battles, this study's venal sins are mainly of omission. . . . [Drew] Halfmann demonstrates his arguments by comparative analyses, process tracing, and within-case analyses across three countries and several decades with meticulous and impressive archival research. His comparative approach cries out for imitation."

LUJÁN, JORGE. Numcralia; 32 p. 2014 Pgw

1. Children's poetry 2. Counting 3. Imagination 4. Numerals 5. Picture books for children

ISBN 1554984440; 9781554984442

SUMMARY: "In this poem, [Jorge] Luján reinvents numbers through a fanciful lens. Number one looks like a tiny flag; two is a duck gliding across the water." (School Library Journal)

REVIEW: *Kirkus Rev* v82 no4 p337 F 15 2014

"Numeralia". "An imagination stretcher disguised as a 1-10 counting book. . . . While she does present an appropriate number of objects to count in each illustration, the emphasis is on appreciation of the surreal rather than building skills. "8 for sand counting out the hours" features one boy digging in the sand in the top half of an hourglass, while below, another boy holds up an umbrella against the falling grains; eight turtles swim, almost as an afterthought, across the facing page. The overall atmosphere is, properly, one of mild abstraction. A whimsical invitation for children to become likewise "lost in daydreams.""

REVIEW: *SLJ* v60 no2 p75 F 2014 Jess deCourcy Hinds

LUKACS, PAUL. Inventing wine; a new history of one of the world's most ancient pleasures; [by] Paul Lukacs 384 p. 2012 W.W. Norton & Co.

1. Historical literature 2. Wine & wine making—Social aspects 3. Wine and wine making—History 4. Wine and wine making—History—To 1500 5. Wine industry—History

ISBN 0393064522; 9780393064520 (hardcover)

LC 2012-027151

SUMMARY: This book by Paul Lukacs tells the "story of wine's transformation from a source of spiritual and bodily nourishment to a foodstuff valued for the wide array of pleasures it can provide. . . . Drinking wine can be traced back 8,000 years, yet the wines we drink today are radically different from those made in earlier eras. While its basic chemistry remains largely the same, wine's social roles have changed fundamentally." (Publisher's note)

REVIEW: *Booklist* v110 no3 p27 O 1 2013 Brad Hooper

"Drink This: Wine Made Simple," "Inventing Wine: A New History of One of the World's Most Ancient Pleasures," and "Unquenchable: A Tipsy Quest for the World's Best Bargain Wines." "[Dara Moskowitz Grumdahl] carefully explains how to negotiate wine lists in restaurants, how to build your own wine collections, how and with what to serve wines, and how to comprehend the layouts of wine shops. . . . The book's format is both attractive and comfortable. . . . In highly readable prose, [Paul] Lukacs tells the story of winemaking's worldwide history, recounting such ever-fascinating stories as the discovery of champagne. . . . This is a lively, entertaining tour of wines and a personal look at some of [Natalie] MacLean's favorite wines."

REVIEW: *Booklist* v109 no3 p22 O 1 2012 Mark Knoblauch

REVIEW: *Kirkus Rev* v80 no20 p39 O 15 2012

REVIEW: *New York Times* v162 no56039 pD6 F 6 2013 ERIC ASIMOV

REVIEW: *New Yorker* v88 no42 p77 Ja 7 2013

REVIEW: *Publ Wkly* v259 no44 p46 O 29 2012

REVIEW: *TLS* no5743 p27 Ap 26 2013 ANNE McHALE

LUM, KATE. Princesses are not just pretty; 32 p. 2014 Bloomsbury

1. Beauty contests 2. Beauty, Personal—Fiction 3. Children's stories 4. Conduct of life—Fiction 5. Princesses—Fiction

ISBN 159990778X; 9781599907789 (hardback); 9781619630451 (reinforced)

LC 2013-025922

SUMMARY: In this children's book, by Kate Lum, "princesses Mellie, Allie, and Libby are back in another . . . royal adventure. When the girls begin to argue about which princess is the prettiest in the land, they decide to hold a contest. But of course, the girls get side-tracked helping others on their way to the contest leaving Princess Mellie as the muddiest, Princess Allie as the yuckiest, and Princess Libby as the drippiest. But due to their kindness, the princesses win in the end!" (Publisher's note)

REVIEW: *Kirkus Rev* v82 no4 p48 F 15 2014

"Princesses Are Not Just Pretty". "The text's playful language pokes good-natured fun at the princesses' self-absorption with their looks, as each tries to outdo the others in primping. On their separate ways to the contest, however, each spunky princess happens upon an emergency and does not hesitate to help—with the result that their carefully crafted ensembles are ruined. When they are lauded by the judges for being the "yuckiest," "drippiest" and "muddiest," readers understand that pretty may not be so important after all. . . . The witty narrative is supported and enhanced by the artfully froufrou watercolor illustrations in pastel colors."

REVIEW: *Publ Wkly* v261 no2 p69 Ja 13 2014

REVIEW: *SLJ* v60 no3 p118 Mr 2014 Melissa Smith

LUNA, CARI. The Revolution of Every Day; [by] Cari Luna 392 p. 2014 Tin House Books

1. Abandoned buildings 2. Drug addicts—Fiction 3. Psychological fiction 4. Squatters—Fiction

ISBN 9781935639640

LC 2013-011948

SUMMARY: This book by Cari Luna is set in 1994. Mayor "Rudy Giuliani wants to oust a group of hardworking homesteaders from their makeshift home in an abandoned building on New York's Lower East Side. Led by Dutch immigrant Gerrit, a veteran squatter who Bed Amsterdam after a violent eviction, and Steve, a tough-talking, philandering handyman of Puerto Rican heritage, the community readies for a fight to save Thirteen House (so-called for its address on Thirteenth Street)." (Booklist)

REVIEW: *Booklist* v110 no4 p28-30 O 15 2013 Diego Bdez

"The Revolution of Every Day." "[Cari] Luna portrays the thorny, complicated relationships among addicts and runaways in various stages of recovery with riveting passion and heartrending realism. Luna's narrator moves with omniscient ease into the minds of Steve and Gerrit, as well as young, pregnant Amelia and the feline rehabilitation expert. Cat, an especially sympathetic character. . . . Luna's forceful, unflinching debut is a love song for a Manhattan long lost to high-end boutiques and high-rise condos"

REVIEW: *Kirkus Rev* v81 no18 p146 S 15 2013

REVIEW: *Publ Wkly* v260 no27 p61 Jl 8 2013

LUNDE, STEIN ERIK. My father's arms are a boat; 40 p. 2013 Enchanted Lion Books

1. Death—Fiction 2. Fathers and sons—Fiction 3. JUVENILE FICTION—Boys & Men 4. JUVENILE FICTION—Family—General (see also headings under Social Issues) 5. JUVENILE FICTION—Social Issues—Death & Dying 6. JUVENILE FICTION—Social Issues—Emotions & Feelings 7. Picture books for children

ISBN 1592701248; 9781592701247 (hardback)

LC 2012-022767

SUMMARY: In author Stein Erik Lunde's book, "it's quieter than it's ever been. Unable to sleep, a young boy climbs into his father's arms. Feeling the warmth and closeness of his father, he begins to ask about the birds, the foxes . . . and whether his mother will ever wake up. Even in the face of absence and loss, the cycles of life continue unabated. We know in the end everything will somehow be all right." (Publisher's note)

REVIEW: *Horn Book Magazine* v89 no5 p56-62 S/O 2013 Thom Barthelmess

"Nana Upstairs & Nana Downstairs," "The Tenth Good Thing About Barney," and "My Father's Arms Are A Boat." "[Tomie dePaola . . . fills the text and illustrations with fond, personal, sometimes humorous details . . . giving the story a tender immediacy that is perfectly suited to the nostalgic subject matter and establishing family love as life's central theme--and death as one of its necessary components. . . . Judith Viorst's 'The Tenth Good Thing About Barney . . . employs direct prose and spare etchings to recount the death of a boy's cat. . . . [In 'My Father's Arms Are A Boat'] only passing reference is made to the death of the boy's mother. Instead, the lyrical language and still, dioramic illustrations observe the evening's simple spectacle, with all the intimacy of warm detail."

REVIEW: *Horn Book Magazine* v89 no2 p87-8 Mr/Ap 2013 ROGER SUTTON

REVIEW: *Kirkus Rev* v81 no1 p82-3 Ja 1 2013

REVIEW: *Kirkus Rev* p59 N 15 2013 Best Books

REVIEW: *Publ Wkly* v259 no49 p76 D 3 2012

REVIEW: *SLJ* v59 no2 p79-80 F 2013 Julie Roach

LUNDESTAD, GEIR. The rise and decline of the american empire; power and its limits in comparative perspective; [by] Geir Lundestad p. cm. 2012 Oxford University Press

1. Great powers (International relations) 2. Imperialism 3. International relations literature 4. State power 5. United States—Foreign relations

ISBN 9780199646104 (hardback)

LC 2011-945231

SUMMARY: "'The Rise and Decline of the American Empire' explores the rapidly growing literature on the rise and fall of the United States. The author argues that after 1945 the US has definitely been the most dominant power the world has seen and that it has successfully met the challenges from, first, the Soviet Union and, then, Japan, and the European Union." (Publisher's note)

REVIEW: *Engl Hist Rev* v128 no534 p1321-3 O 2013 Kathleen Burk

"The Rise and Decline of the American Empire: Power and Its Limits in Comparative Perspective." "The question as to whether or not the United States was an empire, is an empire, and, if so, will continue to be an empire, has, over the past decades, exercised the minds of hundreds of historians, journalists and commentators. Geir Lundestad . . . established some time ago one of the more long-lived conceptual approaches to the subject. . . . It is possible to characterise the book by means of a few adjectives: it is general, it is comparative, it is historiographical, it is lucid and it is short. . . . The book is very clearly written. It provides a good deal of information, and summarises a good many arguments."

LURY, CELIA.ed. Inventive methods. See Inventive methods

LUSH, PAIGE. Music in the Chautauqua movement; from 1874 to the 1930s; [by] Paige Lush vii, 231 p. 2013 McFarland & Company, Inc., Publishers

1. Chautauquas 2. Historical literature 3. Music—Instruction and study—New York (State)—Chautauqua—History 4. Popular culture—United States—History

ISBN 9780786473151 (softcover : alk. paper)
LC 2013-020811

SUMMARY: "This study profiles several famous musicians and introduces the reader to lesser-known musical acts that traveled the chautauqua circuits. In addition, it explores music's role in defining the chautauqua movement as 'high culture,' legitimizing the movement in the eyes of community leaders and setting it apart from vaudeville and other competing amusements. Finally, it addresses music's role in establishing chautauqua's identity as an American institution." (Publisher's note)

REVIEW: *Choice* v51 no5 p840 Ja 2014 R. Sugarman

"Music in the Chautauqua Movement: From 1874 to the 1930s." "Although musical stars like Ernestine Schumann-Heink sometimes performed at Chautauqua events, [Paige] Lush . . . notes that the general standard was lower since the audiences did not demand excellence. Strict decorum, onstage and offstage, was required of performers, and the emphasis on traditional, conservative values led Chautauqua to abhor innovations like jazz. The need for Chautauqua grew out of civic pride in isolated communities. Lush contends that as newspapers, radios, and automobiles ended rural isolation, the movement disintegrated. . . . A solid resource for those interested in popular culture."

LÜTHY, CHRISTOPH H.ed. Engineering the human. See Engineering the human

LYCETT, ANDREW. Wilkie Collins; A Life of Sensation; [by] Andrew Lycett 368 p. 2014 Windmill

1. Biography (Literary form) 2. Collins, Wilkie, 1824-1889 3. English authors—19th century—Biography 4. English authors—19th century—Family relationships 5. Scandals—England

ISBN 0099557347; 9780099557340

SUMMARY: Written by Andrew Lycett, "'Wilkie Collins: A Life of Sensation' is the first definitive biography of this brilliant, conflicted, complex man and an unforgettable portrait of a life lived in a cant-ridden Victorian world. . . . The famous author living secretly with two women, juggling a host of family problems and the possibility of scandal worthy of the racy Sensation fiction he penned." (Publisher's note)

REVIEW: *Choice* v51 no7 p1214-5 Mr 2014 W. Baker

REVIEW: *New Statesman* v142 no5173 p43 S 6 2013 Michael Prodger

REVIEW: *TLS* no5785 p10-1 F 14 2014 JOHN STOKES

"Wilkie Collins: A Life of Sensation." "Andrew Lycett's new biography takes Victorian doubleness for granted, finding a predictable irony in the relation between Collins's 'compromised' domestic situation and novels that were 'based on exposing the double standards and hypocrisy beneath the surface of Victorian society.' . . . Andrew Lycett has given the creator of sensation fiction a workmanlike but distanced treatment. His approach has the virtue of providing what documentary evidence exists, yet the biography of a writer like Collins doesn't have to be confined to prosaic detail."

LYDERSEN, KARI. Mayor 1%; Rahm Emanuel and the rise of Chicago's 99%; [by] Kari Lydersen 220 p. 2013 Haymarket Books

1. HISTORY—Social History 2. Mayors—Illinois—Chicago—Biography 3. POLITICAL SCIENCE—Government—General 4. POLITICAL SCIENCE—Government—Local 5. Political science literature

ISBN 9781608462223 (pbk.)
LC 2013-030408

SUMMARY: This book presents "a study of charismatic Chicago Mayor Rahm Emanuel. . . . Once he was elected, Emanuel critics worried that the mayor was spending a disproportionate amount of time with rich and influential movers and shakers, and not enough time on city politics. . . . The author examines Emanuel's career from a Chicago-centric perspective, paying particular attention to his tenuous relationship with the city's unions." (Publishers Weekly)

REVIEW: *Booklist* v110 no5 p14 N 1 2013 Vanessa Bush

"Mayor 1%: Rahm Emanuel and the Rise of Chicago's 99%." "[Kari] Lydersen chronicles the tempestuous Emanuel administration, focused on privatization of the public sector and facing fierce push-back from citizens who see themselves as representing the 99 percent. Drawing on interviews with community activists and vivid scenes of confrontation with the mayor, Lydersen also offers a portrait of resistance to privatization. This is a fascinating look at a fascinating political figure and the broader issues of a changing Democratic Party."

LYMAN, EDWIN. Fukushima; the story of a nuclear disaster; [by] Edwin Lyman 320 p. 2014 The New Press

1. Fukushima Nuclear Disaster, Japan, 2011 2. Nuclear energy—Government policy 3. Nuclear power plants—Accidents—Japan—Fukushima-ken 4. Nuclear reactors 5. Scientific literature

ISBN 1595589082; 9781595589088 (hc.: alk. paper)
LC 2013-035284

SUMMARY: Authors David Lochbaum, Edwin Lyman, and Susan Q. Stranahan present an "account of the Fukushima disaster. [It] combines a fast-paced . . . account of the tsunami and the nuclear emergency it created with an explanation of the science and technology behind the meltdown as it unfolded in real time." (Publisher's note)

REVIEW: *Booklist* v110 no7 p18 D 1 2013 Donna Seaman

REVIEW: *Kirkus Rev* v82 no2 p30 Ja 15 2014

"Fukushima: The Story of a Nuclear Disaster". "Technical reports written by committee are almost always dull affairs; this is an exception. The book is a gripping, suspenseful page-turner finely crafted to appeal both to people familiar with the science and those with only the barest inkling of how nuclear power works. Even with the broad outlines of the story in the public record, the authors have uncovered many important details that never came to light during the saturation-level media coverage. . . . Its criticisms are balanced, insightful and impossible to dismiss."

REVIEW: *Libr J* v139 no2 p93 F 1 2014 Michal Strutin

REVIEW: *Publ Wkly* v260 no47 p43 N 18 2013

LYNCH, BRIAN. Teenage Mutant Ninja Turtles; Micro-Series Volume 1; 104 p. 2012 IDW Publishing

1. Crime—Fiction 2. Graphic novels 3. Ninja 4. Robbery 5. Teenage Mutant Ninja Turtles (Fictitious characters)

ISBN 1613772327 (pbk.); 9781613772324 (pbk.)

SUMMARY: This graphic novel featuring the teenage mutant ninja turtles "features the turtle brothers, who each get a solo adventure. Raphael likes to go trouble-hunting with pal Casey Jones--and finds some; Michelangelo crashes a New Year's Eve party and finds himself in the middle of a heist; Donatello attends a New Worlds Expo, where he meets up with an online-forum 'enemy' . . . ; and Leonardo reminisces about the turtles' past human lives as he hunts the Foot Clan in a quest to save Splinter." (Voice of Youth Advocates)

REVIEW: *Voice of Youth Advocates* v35 no6 p556-7 F 2013 KAT KAN

"Godzilla," "Teenage Mutant Ninja Turtles Micro-Series," and "Pinocchio, Vampire Slayer: Of Wood and Blood." "'Godzilla, Volume 1' is rather disappointing. For starters, the title is a lie, at least for this volume, because you hardly get to see him. He's in a few panels, but that's just about it. Instead, we follow a group of mercenaries who hunt down the 'kaiju' one by one, and they're actually effective. That's another problem because whole military forces can't take down one of these monsters, but we're meant to believe that four individuals can do it with a sci-fi headache-inducing thingy and explosives. . . . The fun continues with 'Teenage Mutant Ninja Turtles Micro-Series,' in which the turtles and their friends star in side-stories that shed additional light on the plot in the main comics series. The first volume features the turtle brothers, who each get a solo adventure. . . . The final part of the 'Pinocchio, Vampire Slayer' story appears in two parts: 'Pinocchio, Vampire Slayer: Of Wood and Blood,' Part 1 and Part 2. Pinocchio's wish to become a real boy was granted at a most disadvantageous time: he ended up marooned in the middle of the Mediterranean with the remnants of the Great Puppet Theater, while Carlotta was dragged away by the vampires. . . . What started as a high-concept joke has become an action-packed adventure with serious underlying questions about what it means to be human."

LYNCH, CHRIS, 1962-. Little blue lies; [by] Chris Lynch 217 p. 2014 Simon & Schuster Books for Young Readers

1. Dating (Social customs)—Fiction 2. Honesty—Fiction 3. Humorous stories 4. Organized crime—Fiction

ISBN 9781442440081 (hardcover: alk. paper); 9781442440104 (ebook: alk. paper)

LC 2012-041877

SUMMARY: In this book by Chris Lynch, "Oliver is devastated when his beloved Junie Blue breaks off their relationship after high school graduation. But that doesn't stop him from trying to intervene when he hears that Junie may be in possession of a winning lottery ticket that is being sought by the local mob boss. Since their relationship was built on the outrageous lies they used to tell each other, Oliver can't figure out if Junie is telling the truth about not having the ticket." (Kirkus Reviews)

REVIEW: *Booklist* v110 no9/10 p108 Ja 1 2014 Daniel Kraus

REVIEW: *Bull Cent Child Books* v67 no7 p366 Mr 2014 E. B.

REVIEW: *Kirkus Rev* v82 no1 p220 Ja 1 2014

"Little Blue Lies". " A lovelorn teen messes with the mob in order to save his blue-collar girlfriend in this unusual comedy of social class. . . . Though secondary characters that aren't integral to the story sometimes sidetrack the plot, [Chris] Lynch's dialogue is consistently funny and sharp. Inventive descriptions—'The sun is just starting to work an orange cigarette burn through the gray fabric of the clouds'—set off the long riffs of humorous banter nicely. A worthwhile romp, if not quite a jackpot.

REVIEW: *SLJ* v60 no3 p160 Mr 2014 Joy Piedmont

REVIEW: *Voice of Youth Advocates* v36 no6 p62 F 2014 Hilary Crew

LYNCH, THOMAS, 1948-. The good funeral. See Long, T. G.

LYNCH, WAYNE. Penguins; the animal answer guide; [by] Wayne Lynch xiv, 147 p. 2013 The Johns Hopkins University Press

1. Penguins—Behavior 2. Penguins—Ecology 3. Penguins—Miscellanea 4. Penguins—Physiology 5. Scientific literature

ISBN 1421410508 (hardcover: alk. paper); 1421410516 (pbk.: alk. paper); 9781421410500 (hardcover: alk. paper); 9781421410517 (pbk.: alk. paper)

LC 2012-050455

SUMMARY: "In 'Penguins: The Animal Answer Guide,' Gerald L. Kooyman and Wayne Lynch inform readers about all seventeen species, including the emperor penguin featured in the film. Do you know why penguins live only in the Southern Hemisphere? Or that they can be ferocious predators? Why are penguins black and white? Do they play? This book answers these questions and many more." The book is part of the Animal Answer Guides: Q&A for the Curious Naturalist series. (Publisher's note)

REVIEW: *Choice* v51 no10 p1834 Je 2014 D. Flaspohler

LYNETTE, RACHEL. Three-toed sloths; [by] Rachel Lynette 24 p. 2013 Bearport Pub. Co.

1. Biology—Juvenile literature 2. Bradypus 3. Bradypus tridactylus—Juvenile literature 4. Life sciences literature 5. Sloths

ISBN 1617727563 (library binding); 9781617727566

(library binding)
LC 2012-039867

SUMMARY: Written by Rachel Lynette, "this coming-of-age introduction to these fascinating mammals" discusses "baby three-toed sloths and how most of what they do--eat and sleep--is done high up in the treetops of the Amazon jungle. The colorful interior spreads and gorgeous photos of three-toed sloth babies are sure to delight emergent readers." (Publisher's note)

REVIEW: *SLJ* v59 no4 p90 Ap 2013 Grace Oliff

LYONS, CLAIRE L.ed. Sicily. See Sicily

LYSTRA, DONALD. Something that feels like truth; stories; [by] Donald Lystra 290 p. 2013 Switchgrass Books/Northern Illinois University Press
1. Man-woman relationships—Fiction 2. Marriage—Fiction 3. Middle West 4. Short stories 5. Truth
ISBN 0875806937; 9780875806938 (paperback : acid-free paper)
LC 2013-012982

SUMMARY: This book presents short stories by Donald Lystra. "Set in and around the Midwest, from Chicago's glittering lakefront to Michigan's frigid Upper Peninsula, Lystra's tales follow ordinary people as they experience extraordinary wonder through events large and small. A widower confronts the realities of his marriage during a pickup-bar flirtation in 'Rain Check,' while a recently separated husband navigates the perilous new world of building relationships in 'Speaking of Love Abstractedly.'" (Booklist)

REVIEW: *Booklist* v110 no2 p31-2 S 15 2013 Carol Haggas
"Something That Feels Like Truth." "[A] luminous collection of short stories. . . . Set in and around the Midwest, from Chicago's glittering lakefront to Michigan's frigid Upper Peninsula, [Donald] Lystra's tales follow ordinary people as they experience extraordinary wonder through events large and small. . . . Lystra is a discerning observer of the human condition and a deft communicator of the myriad ways in which best intentions may not always achieve satisfying results. Fans of Richard Russo's and Richard Ford's short fiction will find a kindred spirit in this stellar collection of masterfully crafted gems."

M

MA, JOHN. Statues and cities; honorific portraits and civic identity in the Hellenistic world; [by] John Ma xxv, 378 p. 2013 Oxford University Press
1. Architectural inscriptions—Greece 2. City-states—Greece—History 3. Historical literature 4. Monuments—Greece—History 5. National characteristics in art 6. Portrait sculpture, Hellenistic
ISBN 0199668914; 9780199668915
LC 2012-277722

SUMMARY: "This book combines two different and quite specialized fields, archaeology and epigraphy, to explore the phenomenon of portraits in ancient art within the historical and anthropological context of city-states honouring worthy individuals through erecting statues, and the development of families imitating this practice." (Publisher's note)

REVIEW: *Choice* v51 no6 p1067-8 F 2014 J. J. Gabbert
"Statues and Cities: Honorific Portraits and Civic Identity in the Hellenistic World." "This book is probably of use to specialists, those already familiar with art and archaeology and much more. It is a very thorough look at what kinds of statues were set up, where, by whom, at what cost, and why. . . . The text is jargon laden at times, and often quite dense, but at other times rather informal and chatty. Intended readers are either fellow specialists or novices who know nothing of this and need to be told; it is uneven. . . . His book is well illustrated . . . and contains 17 plans at the end. There are 20 pages of bibliography. For researchers and faculty; novices will need their help to get through it."

MAAT, JAAP.ed. The making of the humanities. See The making of the humanities

MABERRY, JONATHAN. Code Zero; a Joe Ledger novel; [by] Jonathan Maberry 480 p. 2014 St. Martin's Griffin
1. Biological weapons—Fiction 2. FICTION—Horror 3. FICTION—Thrillers 4. International relations—Fiction 5. Military art and science—Fiction
ISBN 9781250033437 (pbk.)
LC 2013-032097

SUMMARY: In this book, part of Jonathan Maberry's Joe Ledger series, "Joe Ledger and Echo Team are scrambled when a highly elite team of killers breaks the unbreakable security and steals the world's most dangerous weapons. Within days there are outbreaks of mass slaughter and murderous insanity across the American heartland. Can Joe Ledger stop a brilliant and devious master criminal from turning the Land of the Free into a land of the dead?" (Publisher's note)

REVIEW: *Booklist* v110 no11 p35 F 1 2014 David Pitt
"Code Zero." "Sure, the series follows a pretty strict formula--Joe and his DMS team encounter a seemingly supernatural threat that has a twisted scientific explanation; they go up against a fiendishly clever supervillain; they save the world; and they do it all in about 450 pages--but when a formula is this entertaining, is anyone going to complain about it? Like Lee Child's Jack Reacher, Ledger is a hard-edged military man with a deep moral core and a razor-sharp mind; in a series of books about zombies and vampires and biblical plagues, he's the human center, a comforting, familiar face in a world of unfamiliar things. Top-grade horror fiction."

REVIEW: *Publ Wkly* v261 no4 p170-1 Ja 27 2014

MACAULAY, DAVID. Toilet; how it works; [by] David Macaulay 28 p. 2013 Roaring Brook Press
1. Bathrooms 2. Children's nonfiction 3. Sewerage 4. Toilets 5. Water treatment plants
ISBN 1596437790; 9781596437791 (hardcover); 9781596437807 (pbk.)
LC 2012-947300

SUMMARY: This book, by David Macaulay and Sheila Keenan, "takes readers on a tour of the bathroom and the sewer system, from the familiar family toilet to the mysterious municipal water treatment plant. Everyone knows what a toilet is for, right? But what exactly happens after you flush? Where does our waste go, and how is it made safe?" (Publisher's note)

REVIEW: *Booklist* v110 no1 p99 S 1 2013 Daniel Kraus

REVIEW: *Bull Cent Child Books* v67 no3 p167-8 N 2013 E. B.

"Toilet: How It Works." "[Author David] Macaulay adds to his fine and growing collection of nonfiction easy readers with a topic everyone can and does use. . . . The watercolor illustrations, though, do the heavy lifting, and kids who pore over carefully marked diagrams will find the text can serve simply as support to a largely visual experience. Information and illustrated waste flow smoothly in tandem across the page turns, with pipes color coded and arrows directing movement through the facilities. Macaulay fans will surely be alert to his signature humor. . . ."

REVIEW: *Horn Book Magazine* v89 no6 p118 N/D 2013 BETTY CARTER

"Toilet: How It Works". "Clear step-by-step directions and unobstructed diagrams and cross sections outline how waste is produced by the body, disposed of through the inner workings of a toilet, sent to either a septic tank or urban sewer system, and purified. . . . If diagrams are the language of science, then [David] Macaulay reminds readers that while such language is precise, it can also be lively. A fascinating exploration of design, both human and mechanical. Appended with a glossary, index, and recommended further reading and websites."

REVIEW: *Kirkus Rev* v81 no15 p72 Ag 1 2013

REVIEW: *Kirkus Rev* p59 N 15 2013 Best Books

REVIEW: *SLJ* v59 no10 p1 O 2013 Trina Bolfing

MACCARONE, GRACE.tr. Little Benguin. See Spagnol, E.B.

MACDONALD, ALLISON GRACE. Michael Hague's read-to-me book of fairy tales. See Michael Hague's read-to-me book of fairy tales

MACDONNELL, JULIA. Mimi Malloy at last; a novel; [by] Julia MacDonnell 288 p. 2014 Picador

1. FICTION—Cultural Heritage 2. FICTION—Family Life 3. FICTION—General 4. Family life.—Fiction 5. Life change events—Fiction 6. Memories—Fiction 7. Psychological fiction 8. Retirement—Fiction
ISBN 9781250041548 (hardback)
LC 2013-021147

SUMMARY: This book follows "Mimi Malloy, a daughter of Irish immigrants now in her late 60s. . . . Mimi's memory seems to be failing—an MRI shows deterioration—until she finds a pendant with a blue stone in the back of her closet. When she shows it to her sisters, they all say that it was their mother's. The pendant serves as a catalyst for Mimi to remember the childhood she has so well repressed, revealing the ugly truth and solving a poignant family mystery. " (Library Journal)

REVIEW: *Booklist* v110 no13 p19 Mr 1 2014 Deborah Donovan

REVIEW: *Kirkus Rev* v82 no3 p311 F 1 2014

"Mimi Malloy, At Last!" "Nearly 60 years ago, little Fagan Sheehan was sent back to Ireland, away from her sisters, father and stepmother. Whatever happened to Fagan? [Julia] MacDonnell . . . returns with her sophomore novel, following Mimi Malloy, a 68-year-old woman recently pushed into retirement. She was also pushed into divorce 15 years ago, when Jack, her husband of 30 years, eloped with his bookkeeper. A mostly charming story of feisty women reconnecting and healing old wounds, but this has a few uncomfortably disturbing secrets at its core."

REVIEW: *Libr J* v138 no18 p79 N 1 2013 Nancy H. Fontaine

REVIEW: *Publ Wkly* v260 no40 p26 O 7 2013

MACDOUGALL, JOHN A., D. MIN. Being Sober and Becoming Happy; The Best Ideas from The Director of Spiritual Guidance at Hazelden; [by] John A. MacDougall 216 p. 2013 John MacDougall

1. Alcoholics Anonymous 2. Alcoholism 3. Hazelden Foundation 4. Self-help materials 5. Temperance & religion
ISBN 0615847374; 9780615847375

SUMMARY: This book by John A. MacDougall is informed by his experiences as "alcoholic and a spiritual director at an addiction recovery center. . . . He explores the connection between sobriety, spirituality and happiness, placing an emphasis on not just avoiding alcohol but on creating a new life. . . . He sees addiction as being ultimately self-centered and views AA's emphasis on a higher power as a way to move beyond selfish thinking and into a new relationship with the self, others and reality." (Kirkus Reviews)

REVIEW: *Kirkus Rev* v81 no24 p361 D 15 2013

"Being Sober and Becoming Happy: The Best Ideas From the Director of Spiritual Guidance at Hazelden". "The work serves as an original, readable primer for those unfamiliar with AA and a fresh take on spirituality in AA for those who may be struggling with it. MacDougall writes from a Christian standpoint, though he never pushes a particular belief system, and his broad view of faith may prove useful for those with a range of views about religion. His writing is clear and accessible without being dumbed down, and his respect and compassion for readers and for anyone struggling with addiction clearly shines through. A heartfelt, worthwhile read for anyone who is struggling with or who knows someone struggling with addiction."

REVIEW: *Kirkus Rev* v82 no1 p95 Ja 1 2014

MACDOUGALL, PAULEENA M. Fannie Hardy Eckstorm and her quest for local knowledge, 1865-1946; [by] Pauleena M. MacDougall xxv, 153 p. 2013 Lexington Books

1. Biography (Literary form) 2. Ethnology—Maine 3. Historians—Maine—Biography 4. Women anthropologists—Maine—Biography 5. Women folklorists—Maine—Biography
ISBN 9780739179109 (cloth ; alk. paper); 9780739179116 (electronic)
LC 2013-011819

SUMMARY: This book presents a biography of writer and anthropologist Fannie Hardy Eckstorm. "Eckstorm's life and work illustrate the constant tension between local lay knowledge and the more privileged scientific production of academics that increasingly dominated the field from the early twentieth century. . . . As increasing specialization defined the academy, indigenous knowledge systems were dismissed as unscientific and born of ignorance." (Publisher's note)

REVIEW: *Choice* v51 no10 p1754 Je 2014 J. B. Wolford

REVIEW: *Choice* v51 no5 p883 Ja 2014 J. B. Wolford

"Fannie Hardy Eckstorm and Her Quest For Local Knowledge, 1865-1946." "Anthropologist [Pauleen M.] MacDougall . . . thoroughly mines the astounding amount of primary documentation Eckstorm left behind--personal letters, journals, notes, etc.--which provides a detailed, uncompromising comprehension of the woman and her rightful place in the nascent disciplines she helped shape. More books like this excellent biography need to be written documenting the country's definitely undervalued, if not invisible, intellectual forbears from the early 20th century."

MACEY, DAVID.tr. Emile Durkheim. See Fournier, M.

MACGREGOR, ROY. The highest number in the world; 32 p. 2014 Tundra Books of Northern New York

1. Fortune 2. Grandmothers—Juvenile fiction 3. Hockey—Juvenile literature 4. Sports stories 5. Women hockey players

ISBN 1770495754; 9781770495753 (hardcover); 9781770495760 (ebk.)
LC 2013-940755

SUMMARY: In this book, by Roy MacGregor, "9-year-old Gabe (Gabriella) Murray lives and breathes hockey. She's the youngest player on her new team . . . and she shares a lucky number with her hero, Hayley Wickenheiser: number 22. But when her coach hands out the team jerseys, Gabe is stuck with number 9. Crushed, Gabe wants to give up hockey altogether. How can she play without her lucky number?" (Publisher's note)

REVIEW: *Booklist* v110 no12 p74 F 15 2014 Carolyn Phelan

REVIEW: *Bull Cent Child Books* v67 no7 p366 Mr 2014 E. B.

"The Highest Number in the World." "Gabriella, who insists on being called Gabe, has just achieved her nine-year-old heart's desire: 'Today, Gabe had made The Spirit, the best hockey team in town.' . . .[Geneviève] Després' chipper gouache paintings nail the humor in Gabe's drama-queen meltdown—scarlet-faced, and hauling her be-jerseyed sock monkey around mercilessly by the leg--while demonstrating through the diverse gallery of teammates just how far girls have come in the sport since Grandma's day. Hockey never gets the same picture-book love as baseball, and when an excellent title like this comes along, scoop it right up."

REVIEW: *Kirkus Rev* v82 no2 p310 Ja 15 2014

"The Highest Number in the World". " You play a sport. You have a hero. You want that number on your jersey. Period. . . .[Roy] MacGregor doesn't pull his punches in the imagery department, though [Genevieve] Després brings as much honey as ice to the proceedings. . . . Grandma doesn't belabor the point, but she does offer a short history of No. 9, replete with names like Rocket Richard, Gordie Howe, Bobby Hull, the 'Great One'—Wayne Gretzky, No. 99—and Grandma herself. OK, maybe No. 9's got some mojo after all. As pleasing as a warm memory."

REVIEW: *SLJ* v60 no4 p127 Ap 2014 Diane McCabe

MACHALE, D. J. SYLO; [by] D. J. MacHale 416 p. 2013 Penguin Group USA

1. Detective & mystery stories 2. Islands—Fiction 3. Islands—Maine 4. Maine—Fiction 5. Teenagers—Fiction

ISBN 1595146652 (hardcover); 9781595146656 (hardcover)

SUMMARY: This is the first book in a proposed trilogy from D.J. MacHale. Here, Tucker Pierce has a small but satisfying life on a small island. But when the island is quarantined by the U.S. Navy, things start to fall apart. . . . People start dying. The girl he wants to get to know a whole lot better, Tori, is captured along with Tucker and imprisoned behind barbed wire." They must escape to the mainland and try to figure out what this SYLO organization that is imprisoning them is. (Kirkus Reviews)

REVIEW: *Booklist* v109 no19/20 p101 Je 1 2013 Charli Osborne

REVIEW: *Bull Cent Child Books* v67 no1 p35 S 2013 E. B.

"SYLO." In this first installment of a trilogy, Pemberwick's peace is shattered by several mysterious deaths of otherwise healthy residents, che appearance of a dealer in performance-enhancing crystals, and the sudden occupation of the island by a U.S. military organization called SYLO, ostensibly there to quarantine the islanders while the CDC isolates an unnamed contagion. . . . [Author D. J.] MacHale is off to a powerhouse start in this well-paced thriller. Taking the time in his ample page count to establish islander relationships and the state of normal on Pemberwick pays off when the action kicks in, and readers are not only entertained by the pyrotechnics but emotionally invested in the characters and their quirky piece of home turf."

REVIEW: *Kirkus Rev* p68-9 2013 Guide 20to BookExpo America

REVIEW: *Kirkus Rev* v81 no2 p93 Je 1 2013

REVIEW: *Publ Wkly* v260 no23 p78 Je 10 2013

REVIEW: *SLJ* v60 no1 p60 Ja 2014 John R. Clark

REVIEW: *SLJ* v59 no9 p161 S 2013 Eric Norton

REVIEW: *Voice of Youth Advocates* v36 no4 p84 O 2013 Bonnie Kunzel

MACHAT, LISA DOMINIQUE. A walk in the sun; [by] Lisa Dominique Machat 198 p. 2012 Vampire Vineyards Pub.

1. Families—Fiction 2. Good & evil—Fiction 3. Love stories 4. Paranormal fiction 5. Vampires—Fiction

ISBN 9780615653051 (trade pbk: alk. paper)
LC 2012-942046

SUMMARY: In this vampire novel by Lisa Dominique Machat, "Nicholas Justine was born into money but neglected by his family. At age 17, he's attacked by a vampire and, as a result, turned into one himself. As he struggles to comprehend and deal with his new fate as an immortal, supernatural being, he still desires his human love, Elena. . . . He also encounters the story's villain, Count Victor Du Fay, a practitioner of the dark arts who is driven by his ambition and greed." (Kirkus Reviews)

REVIEW: *Kirkus Rev* v81 no24 p29 D 15 2013

"A Walk in the Sun". "The novel's suspense comes as a result of this battle between good and evil, as readers wonder which will win out: . . . The vampire genre appears to be boundless in its appeal; [Lisa Dominique] Machat's entry may satisfy avid genre fans, with its briskly paced story and direct, engaging style. . . . The novel may especially please readers familiar with the classic horror from such practitioners as Ann Radcliffe and Matthew Lewis. Although the plot

. . . is fairly standard fare, and the setting recalls 19th-century Gothic romance more than modern horror, fans looking for a familiar tale with appropriate chills may find much to satisfy them in this thriller. A fast-moving, romantic vampire story that convincingly harks back to Gothic conventions."

MACIAG, DREW. Edmund Burke in America; the contested career of the father of modern conservatism; [by] Drew Maciag 285 p. 2013 Cornell University Press

1. Conservatism—United States—History 2. Political science—United States—Philosophy 3. Political science literature 4. United States—Politics & government
ISBN 9780801448959 (cloth : alk. paper)
LC 2012-040406

SUMMARY: In this book, "Drew Maciag traces [Edmund] Burke's reception and reputation in the United States, from the contest of ideas between Burke and Thomas Paine in the Revolutionary period, to the Progressive Era (when Republicans and Democrats alike invoked Burke's wisdom), to his apotheosis within the modern conservative movement." (Publisher's note)

REVIEW: *Choice* v51 no6 p1092 F 2014 R. J. Meagher

Title:"Edmund Burke in America: The Contested Career of the Father of Modern Conservatism." "Historian [Drew] Maciag claims that 'American opinions about Edmund Burke provide unique insights into the history of political thinking in the United States.' As proof, he offers this wide-ranging survey of American thinkers and politicians from John Adams through the American Whig Party to today's conservative movement. Strangely, though, much of the book involves the exploration of what Maciag claims to be Burkean themes and ideas in otherwise unrelated political figures and currents. . . . In the end, the book works better as an exploration of intellectual currents that countered liberalism in America, more suited for scholars of American political thought . . . than generalists."

REVIEW: *Natl Rev* v65 no13 p40-2 Jl 15 2013 YUVAL LEVIN

MACIEL, AMANDA. Tease; [by] Amanda Maciel 336 p. 2014 Balzer + Bray, an imprint of HarperCollinsPublishers

1. Bullying—Fiction 2. Guilt—Fiction 3. High schools—Fiction 4. Schools—Fiction 5. Suicide—Fiction 6. Young adult fiction
ISBN 0062305301; 9780062305305 (hardback)
LC 2013-043067

SUMMARY: This book, by Amanda Maciel, is "about a teenage girl who faces criminal charges for bullying after a classmate commits suicide. Emma Putnam is dead, and it's all Sara Wharton's fault. At least, that's what everyone seems to think. . . . Now Sara is the one who's ostracized, already guilty according to her peers, the community, and the media. In the summer before her senior year . . . Sara is forced to reflect on the events that brought her to this moment." (Publisher's note)

REVIEW: *Booklist* v110 no17 p98 My 1 2014 Michael Cart

REVIEW: *Bull Cent Child Books* v67 no11 p584 Jl/Ag 2014 K. C.

REVIEW: *Kirkus Rev* v82 no4 p147 F 15 2014

"Tease". "An intense examination of bullying from a seldom-heard-from side: the bully's. . . . After Emma's death, the bully becomes the bullied, and Sara finds herself being made fun of, ignored and called a slut herself. She finds a friend in summer school classmate Carmichael, who is sympathetic to both Sara and Emma and who reminds readers there are two sides to every story. The moving story is informed by the 2010 bullying and suicide of Massachusetts teen Phoebe Prince and is bound to open up debate on who is to blame when a bullied teen commits suicide. [Amanda] Maciel includes an author's note describing her decision to write the book as well as a list of anti-bullying resources. An emotional, deftly paced and heartbreaking first novel."

REVIEW: *Publ Wkly* v261 no10 p67 Mr 10 2014

REVIEW: *SLJ* v60 no4 p170 Ap 2014 Allison Tran

REVIEW: *Voice of Youth Advocates* v37 no2 p61 Je 2014 Twila A. Sweeney

REVIEW: *Voice of Youth Advocates* v37 no2 p61 Je 2014 Lisa Hazlett

MACKENZIE, SALLY. Loving Lord Ash; [by] Sally MacKenzie 352 p. 2014 Kensington Pub Corp

1. Love stories 2. Man-woman relationships—Fiction 3. Marriage—Fiction 4. Nobility (Social class)—Fiction 5. Women artists—Fiction
ISBN 1420123238; 9781420123234

SUMMARY: In this book, part of the Duchess of Love series, "Kit, Marquis of Ashton, discovered his groom's daughter, Jess, embracing a naked man. Kit . . . married Jess to save her reputation, and immediately fled without consummating the marriage. For the next eight years, Jess lives the artist's life and provides safe refuge for 'sodomites' at Kit's country manor, all the while pining away for her husband. When Kit arrives . . . seeing Jess embrace another naked man sends him running once more." (Publishers Weekly)

REVIEW: *Booklist* v110 no13 p25 Mr 1 2014 Shelley Mosley

"Loving Lord Ash." "Now, just as he enters the castle for the first time in years, he finds her in the arms of a naked man she'd apparently been painting. In fact, the whole castle is filled with men. But these men are living with Jess for a very good reason, and there's no truth to any of the plethora of rumors surrounding either her or Kit. In fact, the ultimate truth is an ironic surprise. Readers will love being treated to this lively, hilarious Regency romp in [Sally] MacKenzie's Duchess of Love series."

REVIEW: *Publ Wkly* v261 no3 p37 Ja 20 2014

MACKRELL, JUDITH. Flappers; Six Women of a Dangerous Generation; [by] Judith Mackrell 480 p. 2014 Sarah Crichton Books

1. Artists—United States—Biography 2. Baker, Josephine, 1906-1975 3. Bankhead, Tallulah 4. Celebrities—United States—Biography 5. Fitzgerald, Zelda, 1900-1948 6. Flappers (Women) 7. Historical literature 8. Popular culture—United States—History—20th century 9. Sex customs—United States—History—20th century 10. Sex role—United States—History—20th century 11. Women—United States—Biography 12. Women—United States—Social life and customs—20th century
ISBN 0374156085; 9780374156084
LC 2013-035397

SUMMARY: This book by Judith Mackrell profiles "six women, Zelda Fitzgerald, Diana Cooper, Nancy Cunard,

Tallulah Bankhead, Josephine Baker and Tamara de Lempicka, whose careers as drinking, smoking, jazzing party creatures reached their critical mass in 1925. . . . Mackrell draws an analogy between the experimental freedoms of the Roaring Twenties and those of the Swinging Sixties." (Times Literary Supplement)

REVIEW: *Bookforum* v20 no5 p49 F/Mr 2014 KERRY HOWLEY

REVIEW: *Booklist* v110 no9/10 p37 Ja 1 2014 Donna Seaman

REVIEW: *Kirkus Rev* v81 no21 p232 N 1 2013

REVIEW: *N Y Times Book Rev* p11 F 16 2014 JESSICA KERWIN JENKINS

REVIEW: *Publ Wkly* v260 no44 p59 N 4 2013

REVIEW: *TLS* no5752 p5 Je 28 2013 FRANCES WILSON

"Careless People: Murder, Mayhem and the Invention of The Great Gatsby" and "Flappers: Six Women of a Dangerous Generation." "A handful of [F. Scott] Fitzgerald scholars. . . have explored the connections between the once-famous murders and the meanings of Gatsby, but [Sarah] Churchwell takes the ball and runs with it. . . . what makes 'Careless People' so suggestive is that Churchwell . . . avoids drawing what she calls 'literal-minded, simplistic equations between fiction and reality'. . . . Re-invention is the subject of Judith Mackrell's 'Flappers,' a sober and sure-footed picture of six women, Zelda Fitzgerald, Diana Cooper, Nancy Cunard, Tallulah Bankhead, Josephine Baker and Tamara de Lempicka, whose careers as drinking, smoking, jazzing party creatures reached their critical mass in 1925."

MACLACHLAN, PATRICIA, 1938-. Snowflakes fall; 32 p. 2013 Random House

1. Loss (Psychology) 2. Picture books for children 3. Seasons 4. Snow—Fiction 5. Snowflakes

ISBN 0375973281; 9780375973284 (library binding); 9780385376938 (hardcover)

LC 2013-008622

SUMMARY: This book, by Patricia MacLachlan and illustrated by Steven Kellogg "portray[s] life's natural cycle: its beauty, its joy, and its sorrow. Together, the words and pictures offer the promise of renewal that can be found in our lives—snowflakes fall, and return again as raindrops so that flowers can grow." (Publisher's note)

REVIEW: *Booklist* v110 no1 p104-5 S 1 2013 Jeanne McDermott

"Snowflakes Fall". "This peaceful offering begins on the endpapers with a happy scene of children peeking-out amid flowers and trees. . . . The book begins its powerful meditation on the cycle of life. Readers will savor the beautifully paced descriptions as well as the delightful panoramas of children playing in the snow. Together, the poem and evocative watercolors tug at deeper emotions. . . . Youngsters are left with joyful memories of snow angels and winter fun. This is a graceful homage to the inevitable seasons of life and remembrances of loved ones and times past. Whether or not they are familiar with loss and grief, children will feel the healing power of this hopeful, uplifting book."

REVIEW: *Horn Book Magazine* v89 no6 p78 N/D 2013 ROGER SUTTON

"Snowflakes Fall". [Patricia] MacLachlan lets fly a string of snowy moments and metaphors about falling snow, scary snow, sledding snow, and finally melting snow, rain, and renewal. It's lovely if meandering, and the text of the poem is arranged imaginatively within [Steven] Kellogg's dancing paintings of frolicking children and skies of snow. A note on the dedication page explains that the impulse for the book came from a desire to commemorate the children lost in the 2012 Newtown, Connecticut, school shooting, but the connection is tenuous."

REVIEW: *Kirkus Rev* v81 no16 p155 Ag 15 2013

"Snowflakes Fall." "Falling snowflakes highlight the beauties and joys of winter in this celebration of the uniqueness of not only every snowflake, but every child. [Author Patricia] MacLachlan's lyrical free verse is set on the pages, sometimes drifting like the flakes in a storm, sometimes stacked up like so much snow on the ground. . . . Boot prints and sled tracks are not the only evidence of children in these pages, which are filled with the wonders and delights of childhood, wonderfully captured in [illustrator Steven] Kellogg's detailed and perfectly colored illustrations."

REVIEW: *Kirkus Rev* p42 Ag 15 2013 Fall Preview

REVIEW: *Publ Wkly* v260 no35 p57 S 2 2013

REVIEW: *SLJ* v59 no9 p126 S 2013 Joy Fleishhacker

MACLACHLAN, PATRICIA, 1938-. You were the first; 40 p. 2013 Little Brown & Co

1. Babies—Fiction 2. Birth order—Fiction 3. Children's stories 4. Families—Juvenile fiction 5. Parent and child—Fiction

ISBN 0316185337; 9780316185332 (alk. paper)

LC 2012-039910

SUMMARY: In this children's picture book, by Patricia MacLachlan, "two doting parents celebrate the many milestones of their first child. Very proud parents . . . narrate . . ., taking time to spell out all of the special moments they have shared with baby. They croon to the little one that he or she . . . was first to smile, cry, coo, look at the trees and flowers, go to the beach, crawl, dig in the garden, throw a ball and more." (Kirkus Reviews)

REVIEW: *Booklist* v110 no2 p67 S 15 2013 Ilene Cooper

REVIEW: *Kirkus Rev* v81 no16 p72 Ag 15 2013

REVIEW: *N Y Times Book Rev* p42 N 10 2013 SARAH HARRISON SMITH

"You Were the First," "Dee Dee and Me," and "The Big Wet Balloon." "In the hands of [Patricia] MacLachlan, the sweetly detailed text and pictures of a biracial family living somewhere that looks a lot like Brooklyn are a comforting reminder of how special all those 'firsts' can be. . . . [Amy] Schwartz wisely withholds comment, but there's inspiration here--as well as some cheerful pictures--for those siblings who always get stuck playing the butler, rather than the duchess, at dress-up time. . . . [Ricardo] Liniers, a cartoonist . . . based this miniature graphic novel on his daughters. . . . Though they have one small misunderstanding, these siblings are loving and thoughtful--good companions whatever the weather."

REVIEW: *Publ Wkly* v260 no26 p87 Jl 1 2013

REVIEW: *SLJ* v59 no9 p127 S 2013 Julie Roach

MACLAVERTY, BERNARD. Collected stories; [by] Bernard MacLaverty 2013 Jonathan Cape

1. Belfast (Northern Ireland)—Fiction 2. English fic-

tion—Irish authors 3. Northern Ireland—Fiction 4. Short stories—Collections 5. Short story (Literary form) ISBN 9780224097802 hardcover

SUMMARY: Written by Bernard MacLaverty, "these tales attend to life's big events: love and loss, separation and violence, death and betrayal. But the stories teem with smaller significant moments too--private epiphanies, chilling exchanges, intimate encounters. The Collected Short Stories includes most of 'Secrets,' 'A Time to Dance,' 'The Great Profundo,' 'Walking the Dog' and 'Matters of Life & Death.'" (Publisher's note)

REVIEW: *London Rev Books* v35 no12 p3-6 Je 20 2013 James Meek

REVIEW: *TLS* no5780 p20 Ja 10 2014 KEITH HOPPER

"Collected Stories." "In a genial and nostalgic introduction to his 'Collected Stories,' Bemard MacLaverty reflects on the accidents and enlightenments that have shaped him as a writer. . . . For MacLaverty, writing is a privileged occupation, and throughout his oeuvre there is a productive tension between creativity and craft (a tension shared by many of his protagonists). . . . In this lyrical depiction of a fragile humanity, there is a danger of becoming too cosy and formulaic. However, to keep things fresh, MacLaverty subverts the familiar with sudden shifts in direction and subject matter."

REVIEW: *TLS* no5748 p19-20 My 31 2013 MICHAEL SALER

"All That Is" and "Collected Stories." "Such extravaganzas more commonly serve as a novel's climax, but here they are merely the prologue to a narrative of everyday experience, which appears as no less significant than global conflict. Since the beginning of his literary career in the 1950s, Salter's genius has been to invoke the ancient muses to chant about modern existence making the ordinary revelatory of heroism, tragedy and mystery in a secular world. . . . The often dark tales in his 'Collected Stories,' also gesture towards an occult dimension while never departing from a naturalistic register."

MACLEAN, DAVID STUART. The answer to the riddle is me; a memoir of amnesia; [by] David Stuart Maclean 304 p. 2014 Houghton Mifflin Harcourt

1. Authors, Canadian—20th century—Biography 2. Fulbright scholars 3. Mefloquine 4. Memoirs
ISBN 0547519273; 9780547519272 (hardback)
LC 2013-026337

SUMMARY: In this memoir, by David Stuart MacLean, "a young writer reckons with his life after amnesia. On Oct. 17, 2002, first-time author MacLean came to while standing in a crush of people on a train platform in India. He had no passport and no clue where he was or what his name was. . . . The 28-year-old . . . was in Hyderabad, India, studying on a Fulbright scholarship. . . . In episodic bursts, the author relates moments he recalls from that day forward." (Publisher's note)

REVIEW: *Booklist* v110 no7 p12 D 1 2013 Carl Hays

REVIEW: *Kirkus Rev* v82 no1 p26 Ja 1 2014

"The Answer to the Riddle Is Me". "A young writer reckons with his life after amnesia. On Oct. 17, 2002, first-time author [David Stuart] MacLean came to while standing in a crush of people on a train platform in India. He had no passport and no clue where he was or what his name was. He then panicked and blacked out again. When he regained consciousness, he was still standing on the platform, utterly confused and terrified, when a kindly police officer found and took him under his protection. . . . Many of the scenes describing his wild hallucinations and slow return to relative sanity powerfully convey an immediacy. . . . A mesmerizing debut. MacLean spares no detail in tracing his formidable reconstruction."

REVIEW: *N Y Rev Books* v61 no9 p23-5 My 22 2014 Jerome Groopman

REVIEW: *N Y Times Book Rev* p14 F 16 2014 SALLY SATEL

"The Answer to the Riddle Is Me: A Memoir of Amnesia" and "I Forgot to Remember: A Memoir of Amnesia." "David Stuart MacLean . . . wandered dazed and frightened on a train platform in Hyderabad, India. . . . 'The Answer to the Riddle Is Me' is his vivid reflection on the 10 years following the Lariam-induced break with reality and the memory problems that persisted in its wake. . . . Su Meck, who was 22 when she was hit by a kitchen fan that fell from her ceiling, has spent the last two decades trying to inhabit a completely new person. . . . Her understated book, 'I Forgot to Remember,' is more an account than a memoir. The matter-of-fact delivery makes the harrowing details of her ordeal stand out all the more."

REVIEW: *New York Times* v163 no56416 pD6 F 18 2014 GREGORY COWLES
LC 2013-026337

REVIEW: *N Y Rev Books* v61 no9 p23-5 My 22 2014 Jerome Groopman

"Memory: From Mind to Molecules," "The Alzheimer Conundrum: Entanglements of Dementia and Aging," and "The Answer to the Riddle Is Me: A Memoir of Amnesia." "Written in accessible language for a lay reader, [authors Larry R. Squire and Eric R. Kandel] illustrate fundamental discoveries about memory using works of art. . . . [Author Margaret] Lock's question is a fundamental one in all of medicine: Why do some individuals develop full-blown disease and others do not, despite sharing the same causative agent? . . . [Author David Stuart MacLean] collapsed at a train station while traveling in India. . . . MacLean ultimately asserts that Lariam, a drug prescribed to prevent malaria, is the culprit."

MACLEAN, NATALIE. Unquenchable; a tipsy quest for the world's best bargain wines; [by] Natalie MacLean xx, 344 p. 2011 Penguin Group

1. COOKING—Beverages—Wine & Spirits 2. Food & wine pairing 3. Food writing 4. Wine and wine making 5. Wine industry
ISBN 9780399537073 (hbk.)
LC 2011-024632

SUMMARY: This book by Natalie MacLean "focuses on finding a wine to pair with a typical dinner each day of the week. Her overriding goal, however, is introducing readers to less familiar wine-producing regions of the world. In the process, MacLean introduces an array of colorful vintners and teaches readers how to choose good representative wines. She supplements the chapters with URLs to further information on her website." (Library Journal)

REVIEW: *Booklist* v110 no3 p27 O 1 2013 Brad Hooper

"Drink This: Wine Made Simple," "Inventing Wine: A New History of One of the World's Most Ancient Pleasures," and "Unquenchable: A Tipsy Quest for the World's Best Bargain Wines." "[Dara Moskowitz Grumdahl] carefully explains how to negotiate wine lists in restaurants, how to build your own wine collections, how and with what to serve wines, and how to comprehend the layouts of wine shops. . . . The book's format is both attractive and comfortable. . . . In highly readable prose, [Paul] Lukacs tells the story of winemaking's worldwide history, recounting such ever-fascinating stories as the discovery of champagne. . . . This is a lively, entertaining tour of wines and a personal look at some of [Natalie] MacLean's favorite wines."

MACLEOD, ALISON. Unexploded; [by] Alison MacLeod 352 p. 2013 Hamish Hamilton Ltd

1. Adultery—Fiction 2. Brighton (England)—History 3. Historical fiction 4. Royal Pavilion, Museums & Libraries 5. World War, 1939-1945—Fiction 6. World War, 1939-1945—Great Britain

ISBN 0241142636; 9780241142639

SUMMARY: This novel by Alison MacLeod describes "May 1940, Brighton, wartime, the constant threat of invasion. Geoffrey and Evelyn Beaumont and their eight-year-old son Philip are struggling to keep their small family together in the most uncertain of times. Geoffrey, a banker, is doing his bit for the war effort as the head of an internment camp, Evelyn is bored and listless and volunteering at the camp, largely against her husband's wishes (although he is too pathetic to stop her)." (The Guardian)

REVIEW: *London Rev Books* v35 no17 p21-2 S 12 2013 Adam Mars-Jones

REVIEW: *Quill Quire* v79 no9 p25 N 2013 Alison Broverman

"Unexploded." "In 'Unexploded,' which was longlisted for the 2013 Man Booker Prize, life in 1940 Brighton is tense and terrifying. . . . Simultaneously, former debutante Evelyn Beaumont begins to second-guess her 13-year marriage to middle-class bank manager Geoffrey, after he unhesitatingly accepts a position as superintendent of a local internment camp. . . . Amid this oppressive atmosphere, the Second World War becomes an effective backdrop for the book's inexorably unfolding domestic betrayals. The novel proceeds with a palpable sense of dread, but when MacLeod introduces the biblical story of David and Bathsheba as a comment on the Beaumonts' strained relationship, the comparison feels inappropriately grandiose."

REVIEW: *TLS* no5763 p21 S 13 2013 LESLEY CHAMBERLAIN

MACMILLAN, MARGARET. The war that ended peace; the road to 1914; [by] Margaret MacMillan 784 p. 2013 Random House Inc

1. Europe—History—1871-1918 2. Europe—Politics & government—1871-1918 3. Historical literature 4. International relations—History 5. World War, 1914-1918—Causes

ISBN 140006855X; 9781400068555 (alk. paper)

LC 2013-009274

SUMMARY: This book, by Margaret MacMillan, "brings. . . . to life the military leaders, politicians, diplomats, bankers, and the extended, interrelated family of crowned heads across Europe who failed to stop the descent into [World War I]. [It] is also a . . . cautionary reminder of how wars happen in spite of the near-universal desire to keep the peace." (Publisher's note)

REVIEW: *Booklist* v110 no1 p29 S 1 2013 James Orbesen

REVIEW: *Choice* v51 no6 p1083 F 2014 A. M. Mayer

REVIEW: *Economist* v409 no8861 p86 N 9 2013

REVIEW: *Hist Today* v64 no2 p63-4 F 2014 Vernon Bogdanor

"The War That Ended Peace: How Europe Abandoned Peace for the First World War." "Few works are likely to match the calm and measured judgement of 'The War that Ended Peace'. Margaret Macmillan's book is less a work of research or scholarship than a synthesis of what is known based almost entirely on secondary sources. She should not be criticised for this, since the archives have been thoroughly combed by others and it is unlikely that there are any 'secrets' still to be found. She has read widely in the English language sources and her conclusions are, on the whole, well-founded. 'The War that Ended Peace' is an ideal book for the general reader who wants to know how and why the war occurred. It has the first virtue of such works of synthesis, being both clear and accurate."

REVIEW: *Kirkus Rev* v81 no15 p212 Ag 1 2013

REVIEW: *Libr J* v138 no8 p60 My 1 2013

REVIEW: *Libr J* v138 no18 p53 N 1 2013 Edwin B. Burgess Margaret Heilbrun

REVIEW: *London Rev Books* v35 no16 p3-6 Ag 29 2013 Christopher Clark

REVIEW: *N Y Rev Books* v61 no2 p14-7 F 6 2014 R. J. W. Evans

REVIEW: *N Y Times Book Rev* p16 O 27 2013 RICHARD ALDOUS

REVIEW: *Nation* v297 no22 p31-4 D 2 2013 TARA ZAHRA

REVIEW: *New Statesman* v142 no5177 p58-63 S 27 2013 Richard Overy

REVIEW: *Publ Wkly* v260 no36 p48 S 9 2013

REVIEW: *Parameters: U.S. Army War College* v44 no2 p96-102 Summ 2014 Douglas V. Mastriano

REVIEW: *Quill Quire* v80 no1 p37-8 Ja/F 2014 Megan Moore Burns

"The War That Ended Peace: The Road to 1914". "Wonderful. . . . [Margaret MacMillan] addresses questions not often raised, such as how Germany became Britain's enemy, even though the two seemed like natural allies. . . . She clearly breaks down complex historical events, paints vivid portraits of key personalities, and brings an entire era to life. . . . MacMillan's focus on keeping the peace rather than avoiding war is welcome, and the book's accessibility will ensure that it appeals to anyone seeking guidance on how to avoid repeating some of the worst mistakes of our past."

REVIEW: *Quill Quire* v79 no6 p25-8 Jl/Ag 2013

REVIEW: *TLS* no5772 p3-4 N 15 2013 WILLIAM PHILPOTT

"The War That Ended Peace: How Europe Abandoned Peace for the First World War," "Catastrophe: Europe Goes to War 1914," and "1914: Fight the Good Fight: Britain, the Army and the Coming of the First World War." "In Britain, the centenary wars are already raging between government and historians, largely over whether we should still be wearing the patriotic cloak that nations donned in the face of aggression by traditional enemies. Max Hastings and Allan Mallinson still wear it. For Hastings the guilt of Germany is firmly established. . . . Margaret Macmillan's judgement in 'The War that Ended Peace' is more balanced, although

German intentions and action remain central to the war's origins. . . . Mallinson dissects military affairs (and political deficiencies) with a trained soldierly eye."

MACMILLAN, PAUL. The solution revolution. See Eggers, W. D.

MACNEICE, LOUIS, 1907-1963. Louis MacNeice; the classical radio plays; vi, 436 p. 2013 Oxford University Press

1. Drama—Collections 2. Radio plays, English
ISBN 0199695237 (hbk.); 9780199695232 (hbk.)
LC 2012-286456

SUMMARY: "This volume presents eleven radio scripts written and produced by the poet and writer Louis MacNeice (1907-1963) over the span of his twenty-year career at the BBC. . . . This volume's selection of scripts . . . illustrates the various ways that MacNeice re-worked one particular and recurrent source of material for radio broadcast--ancient Greek and Roman history and literature." (Publisher's note)

REVIEW: *TLS* no5773 p26 N 22 2013 KATE CLANCHY

"The Classic Radio Plays." "This excellent volume picks out several of [Louis MacNeice's] most interesting struggles with the Classics, and sets them in context with elegant introductory essays, full and informative footnotes, and records of contemporary reception, including, delightfully, the listeners' reports. . . . All the pieces here are either adaptations of comedies . . . or ambitious conceptual dramas. . . . MacNeice's intention was to reach a wide audience: unfortunately, according to the Listener, the common man often found it a bit much."

MACRI, FRANCO DAVID. Clash of empires in South China; the Allied nations' proxy war with Japan, 1935-1941; [by] Franco David Macri xiii, 465 p. 2012 University Press of Kansas

1. China, Southeast 2. Historical literature 3. Hong Kong (China)—History—1842-1997 4. Sino-Japanese War, 1937-1945 5. Sino-Japanese War, 1937-1945—Campaigns—China, Southeast 6. World War, 1939-1945—Campaigns—China, Southeast 7. World War, 1939-1945—China
ISBN 9780700618774 (cloth : alk. paper)
LC 2012-026191

SUMMARY: "In the first book to cover this southern theater in detail, [author Franco] David Macri closely examines strategic decisions, campaigns, and operations and shows how they affected Allied grand strategy. Drawing on documents of U.S. and British officials, he reveals . . . how the Sino-Japanese War served as a 'proxy war' for the Allies: by keeping Japan's military resources focused on southern China." (Publisher's note)

REVIEW: *Am Hist Rev* v118 no4 p1158-9 O 2013 Steven I. Levine

"Clash of Empires in South China: The Allied Nations' Proxy War With Japan, 1935-1941." "One of the considerable virtues of Franco David Macri's richly textured military-diplomatic history is to refocus scholarly attention in two respects: first, temporally, by emphasizing the importance of what he rightly calls the proxy war against Japan that long preceded the start of the Pacific War on December 7-8, 1941; and second, spatially, by emphasizing the importance of the relatively neglected South China theater of conflict. At the center of his analysis is the British colony of Hong Kong, which served as the main entry point for military supplies purchased by the Chinese government."

REVIEW: *Choice* v50 no10 p1900 Je 2013 M. D. Erickson

REVIEW: *Libr J* v137 no17 p89-90 O 15 2012 Claire Houck

MADDEN, JAMES D. Mind, matter, and nature; a Thomistic proposal for the philosophy of mind; [by] James D. Madden xiii, 307 p. 2013 Catholic University of America Press

1. Dualism 2. Materialism 3. Naturalism 4. Philosophical literature 5. Philosophy of mind 6. Philosophy of nature
ISBN 9780813221410 (pbk. : alk. paper)
LC 2012-043720

SUMMARY: In this book, "arguing that one is unlikely to make progress in the philosophy of mind tmtil one makes progress in the philosophy of nature, [James D.] Madden outlines and defends a version of Aristotelian hylomorphism. Then, drawing heavily on the work of Saint Thomas Aquinas, he applies this metaphysical picture to the philosophy of mind." (Choice: Current Reviews for Academic Libraries)

REVIEW: *Choice* v51 no7 p1228-9 Mr 2014 A. Kind

"Mind, Matter & Nature: A Thomistic Proposal for the Philosophy of Mind." "An introductory text in philosophy of mind that stands apart from most others on the market in its sustained attention to and defense of a Thomistic hylomorphism. Whether this is seen as a plus or a minus for course adoption purposes will undoubtedly depend on instructors' aims for their philosophy of mind courses; certainly for anyone wishing to cover hylomorphism, this volume would be an excellent choice. . . . Recommended."

MADDOX, AMANDA.ed. Japan's modern divide. See Japan's modern divide

MADE IN AUSTRALIA; The Future of Australian Cities; 328 p. 2013 University of Western Australia Press

1. Architecture—Australia 2. Cities and towns—Australia—Growth 3. City planning—Australia 4. City planning literature 5. Population
ISBN 1742584926; 9781742584928
LC 2012-537482

SUMMARY: In this book, Richard Weller and Julian Bolleter set "the stage for the growth of eight Australian cities and their respective infrastructures." Then they "examine population trends and resource needs for each metropolitan area through 2056. They consider geographical and resource limitations on each city, along with specific population growth estimates, in a . . . discussion of options available to these cities if they are to adequately support the needs of a growing population." (Choice)

REVIEW: *Choice* v51 no1 p123-4 S 2013 J. R. Bailey

"Made in Australia: The Future of Australian Cities." "Anyone interested in population studies, land use planning, natural resources, or urban studies likely will find this book useful. After setting the stage for the growth of eight Australian cities and their respective infrastructures, [Richard] Weller and [Julian] Bolleter . . . examine population trends and resource needs for each metropolitan area through 2056.

They consider geographical and resource limitations on each city, along with specific population growth estimates. . . . The second half of the book looks forward to 2101--the furthest into the future the Australian Bureau of Statistics goes with its population projections--and concludes with a series of topical essays by Australian experts in their respective fields."

MADER, C. ROGER. Lost cat; [by] C. Roger Mader 32 p. 2013 Houghton Mifflin Books for Children

1. Cats—Fiction 2. Cats—Juvenile fiction 3. Children's stories 4. Lost and found possessions—Fiction 5. Lost pets 6. Pet adoption—Fiction
ISBN 0547974582 (hbk.); 9780547974583 (hbk.)
LC 2012-041891

SUMMARY: In this children's picture book, "Slipper lives a happy life with Mrs. Fluffy Slippers. When the old woman moves, the poor tabby is left behind in the commotion. Chasing after the moving van, she gets lost and decides that she will adopt a new owner. . . . Slipper rejects Ms. Muddy Boots, High Tops, and Mr. Big Boots and finally runs into Miss Shiny Shoes, whom she accepts, and who serendipitously reunites her with Mrs. Fluffy Slippers." (School Library Journal)

REVIEW: *Booklist* v110 no5 p85 N 1 2013 Connie Fletcher

REVIEW: *Bull Cent Child Books* v67 no3 p168 N 2013 J. H.

"Lost Cat." "There are dozens of lost pet stories but this one skillfully utilizes an intriguing cat's-eye-perspective, vivid illustrations, and a happy (if unrealistic) ending to satisfying effect. Succinct, sonorous text . . . also makes for smooth reading aloud. [Author and illustrator C. Roger] Mader's almost photorealistic illustrations (done in deftly blended pastels on paper) are compelling in their detailing, composition, and lighting. . . . The attractive cat pictures and the circular storyline make this a fine addition to a cat- or pet-themed storytime; providing a real cat for furry snuggles will undoubtedly enhance the reading experience."

REVIEW: *Kirkus Rev* v81 no16 p160 Ag 15 2013

REVIEW: *N Y Times Book Rev* p24 O 13 2013 SARAH HARRISON SMITH

REVIEW: *Publ Wkly* v260 no38 p78 S 23 2013

REVIEW: *SLJ* v59 no8 p82 Ag 2013 Yelena Alekseyeva-Popova

MADER, C. ROGER.il. Lost cat. See Mader, C. R.

MADERTHANER, WOLFGANG.ed. Routes into abyss. See Routes into abyss

MADIKIZELA-MANDELA, WINNIE. 491 days; prisoner number 1323/69; [by] Winnie Madikizela-Mandela 264 p. 2014 Ohio University Press

1. Anti-apartheid movements—South Africa 2. Diary (Literary form) 3. Government, Resistance to—South Africa 4. Politicians' spouses—South Africa—Biography 5. Women political activists—South Africa—Biography
ISBN 9780821421017 (pb: alk. paper); 9780821421024 (hc: alk. paper); 9780821444924 (pdf)
LC 2013-049174

SUMMARY: This book presents the journal of "Winnie Madikizela-Mandela, activist and wife of the imprisoned Nelson Mandela," written after she was "rounded up in a group of other antiapartheid activists under Section 6 of the Terrorism Act, designed for the security police to hold and interrogate people for as long as they wanted." The book also includes"some of the letters written between several affected parties at the time, including Winnie and Nelson Mandela." (Publisher's note)

REVIEW: *Kirkus Rev* v82 no3 p331 F 1 2014

"491 Days: Prisoner Number 1323/1969". "Although footnotes provide perfunctory information, readers unfamiliar with anti-apartheid history may find some names and references confusing. Nelson Mandela's letters, on the other hand, are richer in detail and carefully crafted. He clearly knew that others besides the recipients would read them, and he calculated their effect. . . . Taken together, these documents afford a chilling perspective on the Mandelas' personal and political struggles."

REVIEW: *Ms* v24 no1 p59-60 Wint/Spr 2014 Erin Aubry Kaplan

MADSBJERG, CHRISTIAN. The moment of clarity; using the human sciences to solve your hardest business problems; [by] Christian Madsbjerg 224 p. 2014 Harvard Business Review Press

1. Business literature 2. Business planning 3. Human behavior 4. Management—Psychological aspects 5. Social sciences and management
ISBN 9781422191903 (hardback)
LC 2013-031648

SUMMARY: In this book, "Christian Madsbjerg and Mikkel Rasmussen examine the business world's assumptions about human behavior and show how these assumptions can lead businesses off track. But the authors chart a way forward. Using theories and tools from the human sciences--anthropology, sociology, philosophy, and psychology--'The Moment of Clarity' introduces a practical framework called sensemaking." (Publisher's note)

REVIEW: *Booklist* v110 no9/10 p28 Ja 1 2014 Barbara Jacobs

"The Moment of Clarity: Using the Human Sciences to Solve Your Toughest Business Problems." "Their statements of assumptions will have every head nodding: among others, that people are rational and fully informed, that tomorrow will look like today, and that hypotheses are objective and unbiased. Yet what they do is so innately smart and practical that it's a real surprise more corporations haven't adopted it. . . . Strong, seductive arguments that hopefully will sway the logic and process makers among us."

MAESTRIPIERI, DARIO.ed. Animal personalities. See Animal personalities

MAFI, TAHEREH. Ignite me; [by] Tahereh Mafi 416 p. 2014 HarperCollins

1. Love stories 2. Paranormal fiction 3. Resistance to government 4. Science fiction 5. Triangles (Interpersonal relations)—Fiction
ISBN 0062085573; 9780062085573 (hardcover)
LC 2013-951749

SUMMARY: In this book, part of the Shatter Me series by Tahereh Mafi, "with Omega Point destroyed, Juliette doesn't know if the rebels, her friends, or even Adam are alive. But that won't keep her from trying to take down The Reestablishment once and for all. Now she must rely on Warner, the handsome commander of Sector 45. The one person she never thought she could trust. The same person who saved her life. He promises to help Juliette master her powers and save their dying world." (Publisher's note)

REVIEW: *Kirkus Rev* v82 no2 p188 Ja 15 2014

"Ignite Me". "Fighting an oppressive regime is an afterthought in this conclusion to [Tahereh] Mafi's romantic trilogy. . . . Broad strokes—Warner: good, Adam: bad—destroy any complexity, mystery or tension in the love triangle. Many of the most interesting and difficult moments, such as a conversation between Adam and Warner about their parentage, are glossed over in favor of the repetitive sharing of emotions. A high page count gives the novel physical if not psychological weight and includes such padding as Juliette's lengthy musings on a bar of soap. After all this, the end is all too easy, for characters anyway. Well, most people are probably reading these books for Warner anyway."

REVIEW: *Voice of Youth Advocates* v37 no1 p85 Ap 2014 Johanna Nation-Vallee

MAGID, BARRY. Nothing is hidden; the psychology of Zen koans; [by] Barry Magid 232 p. 2013 Wisdom Publications

1. Buddhist ethics 2. Buddhist literature 3. Koan 4. Subconsciousness 5. Zen Buddhism—Psychology
ISBN 1614290822 (pbk. : alk. paper); 9781614290827
LC 2013-000339

SUMMARY: This book by Barry Magin presents an "examination of the nexus of Zen koan analysis and the interplay between the conscious and subconscious forces of human psychology. Brief chapters use a specific koan as a starting point from which Magid juxtaposes the history of its tradition in Zen Buddhist practice with contemporary reflections of what can be unpacked from its underlying interpretive possibilities." (Booklist)

REVIEW: *Booklist* v110 no3 p4-5 O 1 2013 Francisca Goldsmith

"Nothing Is Hidden: The Psychology of Zen Koans." "An accessible and thorough examination of the nexus of Zen koan analysis and the interplay between the conscious and subconscious forces of human psychology. . . . Readers unfamiliar with Buddhism will be drawn in by the artful explication of Zen morality. Zen practitioners, current and lapsed, will be interested in the discussion of how foibles of Zen masters should not be conflated with the underlying psychological truths Buddhist awareness and presence offer. While valuable to cultural observers, this small book can also serve as a guide for the contemplative and/or psychiatrically perplexed."

REVIEW: *Publ Wkly* v260 no32 p53 Ag 12 2013

MAGILL'S LITERARY ANNUAL 2013; 894 p. 2013 Salem Press

1. Books & reading 2. Literature—History & criticism 3. Modern literature—21st century 4. Readers' advisory services 5. Reference books
ISBN 1429838094; 9781429838092

SUMMARY: This book "critically evaluates 200 major examples of serious literature published during the previous calendar year. The philosophy behind our selection process is to cover works that are likely to be of interest to general readers, that are written by authors being taught in literature programs, and that will stand the test of time." This 2013 issue covers works published in 2012. (Publisher's note)

REVIEW: *Choice* v51 no5 p800 Ja 2014 H. Corbett

"Magill's Literary Annual, 2013: Essay-Reviews of 200 Outstanding Books Published in the United States During 2012: With an Annotated List of Titles:. "Although the print edition of 'Magill's Literary Annual' is billed as a reader's advisory tool, the online archive is vastly superior for this purpose. The online archive, via Salem Literature . . . gathers all content from 37 years of the print edition, from 1977 to 2013, and gives users the capability of searching across years. This experience is a vast improvement over browsing the older annuals, or the cumulative print indexes (last published in 2010)."

MAGNER, MIKE. A trust betrayed; the untold story of Camp Lejeune and the poisoning of generations of marines and their families; [by] Mike Magner 328 p. 2014 Da Capo Press

1. Drinking water—Contamination—North Carolina—Camp Lejeune—History 2. Environmentally induced diseases—North Carolina—Camp Lejeune—History 3. Families of military personnel—Health and hygiene—North Carolina—Camp Lejeune—History 4. Groundwater—Pollution—North Carolina—Camp Lejeune—History 5. Journalism 6. Marines—Health and hygiene—North Carolina—Camp Lejeune—History 7. Poisoning—North Carolina—Camp Lejeune—History
ISBN 9780306822575 (hardback)
LC 2013-045263

SUMMARY: This book examines "the poisoning of the water supply with toxic chemicals at Camp Lejeune, the large U.S. Marine Corps base in North Carolina, [which] began in the 1950s, exposing as many as a million Marines and their families to dangerously contaminated water over the next three decades. It wasn't until the 1980s, though, that the extent of the danger to the health of untold numbers of Camp Lejeune families first came to light." (Publishers Weekly)

REVIEW: *Kirkus Rev* v82 no3 p260 F 1 2014

"A Trust Betrayed: The Untold Story of Camp Lejeune and the Poisoning of Generations of Marines and Their Families". "[Mike] Magner . . . chronicles the resulting catastrophe—heartbreaking stories of infant deaths, a wide range of grisly birth defects and an alarming array of cancers—by interleaving his narrative with intimate portraits of affected Marines and their families. Nearly as shocking, though, is his tale of the Marine Corps' slow awakening to the problem, its unconscionable foot-dragging, its unwillingness to answer questions or to study the adverse health effects linked to the chemicals found in the water. A fast-moving, smartly detailed story of an environmental disaster compounded by the Corps' broken promise . . . to the men who served and suffered."

REVIEW: *Publ Wkly* v261 no5 p48 F 3 2014

MAGNET, MYRON. The founders at home; the building of America, 1735-1817; [by] Myron Magnet 480 p. 2014 W W Norton & Co Inc

1. Domestic architecture—Social aspects 2. Founding

Fathers of the United States—Biography 3. Historical literature 4. Statesmen—United States—Biography
ISBN 9780393240214 (hardcover)
LC 2013-020095

SUMMARY: This book on the lives and homes of America's founding fathers"shows how each founder's ideas about the structure of the new republic grew out of, and informed, his home life and the houses he constructed."According to author Myron Magnet, "'because they were trying to create a new nation where Americans would be truly at home, the houses they themselves inhabited . . . offer a vivid glimpse . . . into the ideal of life they imagined for themselves and for their countrymen.'" (Publishers Weekly)

REVIEW: *Booklist* v110 no3 p17-8 O 1 2013 Margaret Flanagan

"The Founders at Home: The Building of America, 1735-1817." "The Founding Fathers have provided plenty of fodder for fiction and nonfiction alike. In this series of biographical sketches. [Myron] Magnet has taken a different and wholly original tack. In addition to reviewing what this group of luminaries said and wrote about the concepts of life, liberty, and the pursuit of happiness, he also shows how they lived and how the homes they designed, cherished, and inhabited reflected the values and ideals they claimed for themselves and desired for their fellow countrymen. . . . This collective biography has crossover appeal, featuring enough new information to satisfy both Revolutionary-era enthusiasts and architectural buffs."

REVIEW: *Choice* v51 no7 p1291 Mr 2014 A. E. Krulikowski

REVIEW: *Commentary* v137 no1 p54-5 Ja 2014 JOHN STEELE GORDON

"The Founders at Home: The Building of America, 1735-1817". "Myron Magnet . . . tells the story of several of these men in a novel way: He focuses his attention on the homes they built or lived in. . . . An excellent and fluid writer, Magnet succeeds in proving his point that these were more than residences; they were an expression of the personalities of their remarkable owners. 'The Founders at Home' provides an interesting, entertaining, and informative way of looking at their lives and their world."

REVIEW: *Kirkus Rev* v81 no19 p27 O 1 2013

REVIEW: *Natl Rev* v65 no24 p42-6 D 31 2013 RICHARD BROOKHISER

REVIEW: *Publ Wkly* v260 no35 p46 S 2 2013

MAGOON, SCOTT. Breathe; [by] Scott Magoon 40 p. 2014 Simon & Schuster Books for Young Readers

1. Animal stories 2. Animals—Infancy—Fiction 3. Mother & child—Fiction 4. Whales—Fiction 5. White whale—Fiction 6. White whale—Juvenile fiction
ISBN 1442412585; 9781442412583 (hardcover)
LC 2013-017696

SUMMARY: This children's book, by Scott Magoon, "follows a young whale on a journey of discovery as he experiences his first day at sea on his own! He swims, explores, and makes friends in his marine habitat. After a day of independence, this little whale delights in returning home to his mother." (Publisher's note)

REVIEW: *Booklist* v110 no15 p91 Ap 1 2014 Lolly Gepson

REVIEW: *Kirkus Rev* v82 no5 p57 Mr 1 2014

"Breathe". "[Scott] Magoon's digital art captures the colors and crisp, airy light of the Arctic setting; cartoon lines and wide eyes present creatures above and under the ice as friendly, rounded and smiling. Even the polar bear—seen against the sky through an ice hole as a dark shadow, possibly threatening—is fairly benign. . . . The simple adventure concludes with an anthropomorphic yet welcome invitation: 'Most of all, love / and be loved.' Richly composed and sweetly appealing-just right for baby storytimes as well as one-to-one sharing."

REVIEW: *Publ Wkly* v261 no5 p56 F 3 2014

REVIEW: *SLJ* v60 no3 p120 Mr 2014 Laura J. Giunta

MAGOON, SCOTT.il. Breathe. See Magoon, S.

MAGRITTE, RENÉ, 1898-1967.il. Magritte. See Magritte

MAGRITTE; the mystery of the ordinary; 256 p. 2013 Museum of Modern Art

1. Art catalogs 2. Art literature 3. Art technique 4. Modern painting—20th century 5. Surrealism
ISBN 9780870708657 (cloth)
LC 2013-941520

SUMMARY: This book "focuses on the breakthrough Surrealist years of René Magritte. . . . Bringing together nearly 80 paintings, collages and objects with a selection of photographs, periodicals and early commercial work, it offers fresh insight into Magritte's identity as a modern artist and one of Surrealism's greatest painters. Beginning in 1926 . . . and concluding in 1938 . . . the publication traces central strategies and themes from this seminal period." (Publisher's note)

REVIEW: *Choice* v51 no7 p1202 Mr 2014 E. K. Mix

"Magritte: The Mystery of the Ordinary, 1926-1938." "Featuring works from more than 50 collections, this exhibition catalogue reproduces and contextualizes René Magritte's development as a surrealist artist from 1926, when he began his quest, until 1938, when he presented a lecture that summarized his accomplishments in this genre. . . . While this book does not replace the five-volume catalogue raisonné, it provides a reasonably priced alternative containing both well-known and lesser-known works, including Magritte's work for periodicals ranging from Variétés and Le Centaure to La Révolution Surréaliste."

MAGUIRE, MUIREANN.tr. Red Spectres; Russian Gothic tales from the twentieth century; 224 p. 2013 Penguin Group USA

1. Anthologies 2. Ghosts in literature 3. Gothic literature 4. Mental illness in literature 5. Russian literature—Translations into English
ISBN 1468303481; 9781468303483

SUMMARY: This collection of 20th century Russian gothic fiction "includes eleven vintage tales by seven writers of the period: Valery Bryusov, Mikhail Bulgakov, Aleksandr Grin and Sigizmund Krzhizhanovsky;. . . Aleksandr Chayanov, . . . and the emigres Georgy Peskov and Pavel Perov. Through the traditional gothic repertoire of ghosts, insanity, obsession, retribution and terror, Red Spectres conveys the turbulence and dissonance of life in Russia in these years." (Publisher's note)

REVIEW: *Kirkus Rev* v81 no7 p213 Ap 1 2013

REVIEW: *London Rev Books* v35 no17 p33-4 S 12 2013 Greg Afinogenov

REVIEW: *TLS* no5761 p9 Ag 30 2013 ELIOT BORENSTEIN

"Stalin's Ghosts: Gothic Themes in Early Soviet Literature" and "Red Spectres: Russian 20th-century Gothic Fantastic Tales'. "To make her case, [Muireann] Maguire is obliged to revisit familiar debates about the definition of the Gothic. As she argues, quite persuasively, the Gothic is all about the stubborn return of the past. . . . Given the lively insights of 'Stalin's Ghosts,' one would expect 'Red Spectres: Russian 20th-century Gothic-fantastic tales,' edited and translated by Maguire, to be even more entertaining. After, all, it is a collection of fiction rather than an academic study. Maguire is a fine translator who has rendered these dozen or so neo-Gothic tales in clear and elegant English that is neither too exotic nor unduly idiomatic. Footnotes are kept to a minimum, and undereducated Russian characters do not speak Cockney. But Maguire is at the mercy of her material here, far more than she is in 'Stalin's Ghosts'."

MAGUIRE, MUIREANN. Stalin's ghosts; Gothic themes in early Soviet literature; [by] Muireann Maguire viii, 331 p. 2012 Peter Lang Pub Inc

1. Ghosts in literature 2. Gothic fiction (literary genre), Russian 3. Literary critiques 4. Russian literature—20th century—History and criticism

ISBN 303430787X (pbk.); 9783034307871 (pbk.)
LC 2012-951852

SUMMARY: This book by Muireann Maguire "examines the impact of the Gothic-fantastic on Russian literature in the period 1920-1940. It shows how early Soviet-era authors, from well-known names including Fedor Gladkov, Mikhail Bulgakov, Andrei Platonov and Evgenii Zamiatin, to niche figures such as Sigizmund Krzhizhanovskii and Aleksandr Beliaev, exploited traditional archetypes of this genre: the haunted castle, the deformed body, vampires, villains, madness and unnatural death." (Publisher's note)

REVIEW: *London Rev Books* v35 no17 p33-4 S 12 2013 Greg Afinogenov

REVIEW: *TLS* no5761 p9 Ag 30 2013 ELIOT BORENSTEIN

"Stalin's Ghosts: Gothic Themes in Early Soviet Literature" and "Red Spectres: Russian 20th-century Gothic Fantastic Tales'. "To make her case, [Muireann] Maguire is obliged to revisit familiar debates about the definition of the Gothic. As she argues, quite persuasively, the Gothic is all about the stubborn return of the past. . . . Given the lively insights of 'Stalin's Ghosts,' one would expect 'Red Spectres: Russian 20th-century Gothic-fantastic tales,' edited and translated by Maguire, to be even more entertaining. After, all, it is a collection of fiction rather than an academic study. Maguire is a fine translator who has rendered these dozen or so neo-Gothic tales in clear and elegant English that is neither too exotic nor unduly idiomatic. Footnotes are kept to a minimum, and undereducated Russian characters do not speak Cockney. But Maguire is at the mercy of her material here, far more than she is in 'Stalin's Ghosts'."

MAHAN, DONNA J. 20 day trips in and around the Shawnee National Forest; [by] Donna J. Mahan xvi, 140 p. 2013 Southern Illinois University Press

1. Excursions (Travel) 2. Historic sites—Illinois 3. Travel—Guidebooks

ISBN 0809332558 (pbk. : alk. paper); 9780809332557 (pbk. : alk. paper)
LC 2012-033579

SUMMARY: This travel book by Larry P. Mahan and Donna J. Mahan was named the "Best Travel Series of the Year" for 2013 by "Booklist." It features "20 trips all around the [Shawnee] national forest and the surrounding area, by which visitors can appreciate the natural beauty and the historical importance of this part of Illinois." Sites include "waterfallls . . . caves . . . historic sites . . . [and] architecture." (Booklist)

REVIEW: *Booklist* v110 no2 p20 S 15 2013 Brad Hooper

"20 Day Trips in and around the Shawnee National Forest." "Best Travel Series of the Year, 2013. . . . The husband-and-wife authors of this handy, highly informative guide have traversed southern Illinois what seems like a million times. . . . Most of the day trips require some walking; ideal users of this guide are 'persons who are able-bodied and reasonably fit.' From waterfalls to caves to wonderful vistas overlooking the Ohio River, and from historic sites to calm lakes to interesting architecture, the Mahans take you everywhere you need to go to gain an intense appreciation of southern Illinois as a vacation spot. An enthusiastic guide to an overlooked place."

MAHAN, LARRY P. 20 day trips in and around the Shawnee National Forest. See Mahan, D. J.

MAHAWATTE, ROYCE. George Eliot and the Gothic Novel; Genres, Gender, Feeling; [by] Royce Mahawatte 260 p. 2013 University of Chicago Press

1. Characters & characteristics in literature 2. Eliot, George, 1819-1880 3. Fiction genres 4. Gothic fiction (Literary genre), English 5. Literature—History & criticism

ISBN 0708325769; 9780708325766

SUMMARY: In this book, Royce Mahawatte "tracks George Eliot's reading of gothic and sensational literature and her responses to them in her own works. Mahawatte argues that suspenseful and popular tropes play a significant role in Eliot's literary ethics and creativity and that our understanding of the author's writing needs to be broadened to include her extensive and complex engagement with the gothic tradition." (Publisher's note)

REVIEW: *Choice* v51 no2 p259-60 O 2013 W. Baker

"George Eliot and the Gothic Novel: Genres, Gender, Feeling." "This work by [Royce] Mahawatte . . . aims to redress an omission in Eliot criticism by examining what he refers to as Gothic 'genres of feeling.' . . . Mahawatte writes that 'the nuances of George Eliot's creative method remain intriguing,' thereby admitting that not everything in her creative artistry can be encompassed within the Gothic straightjacket. Despite some slips in scholarship (there are instances of page references and subjects cited that do not match up with their sources), Mahawatte's interweaving of textual reading and critical discourse makes an interesting contribution."

MAHON, BASIL. Faraday, Maxwell, and the electromagnetic field; how two men revolutionized physics; [by] Basil Mahon 300 p. 2014 Prometheus Books

1. Electromagnetic fields 2. Historical literature 3. Physics
ISBN 1616149426; 9781616149420 (hardback); 9781616149437 (ebook)
LC 2013-039969

SUMMARY: Science writers Nancy Forbes and Basil Mahon "explore the lives of physicists Michael Faraday and James Clerk Maxwell. . . . Faraday's [experimentation] led to the first electric motor, the first generator, and the idea that electricity and magnetism travel as waves. . . . [B]ut his lack of mathematical ability meant few took him seriously. Then Maxwell, a young professor from Marischal College in Aberdeen, Scotland, developed the math to back up Faraday's ideas." (Publishers Weekly)

REVIEW: *Choice* v52 no2 p300 O 2014 K. L. Schick

REVIEW: *Kirkus Rev* v82 no2 p182 Ja 15 2014

Faraday, Maxwell, and the Electromagnetic Field: How Two Men Revolutionized Physics". "A compelling new interpretation of the seminal importance of the discoveries of Michael Faraday (1791-1861) and James Clerk Maxwell (1831-1879). . . .The authors explain 'the way that Faraday and Maxwell's concept of the electromagnetic field transformed scientists' view of the physical world,' beginning with Faraday's anticipation of a unified field theory that would include the force of gravity as well as electromagnetism and the propagation of light. . . . A lively account of the men and their times and a brilliant exposition of the scientific circumstances and significance of their work."

REVIEW: *Libr J* v139 no3 p126 F 15 2014 Sara R. Tompson

REVIEW: *Publ Wkly* v261 no1 p44 Ja 6 2014

MAI JIA. Decoded; [by] Mai Jia 320 p. 2014 Farrar Straus & Giroux
1. China—Fiction 2. Chinese fiction—Translations into English 3. Spy stories, Chinese
ISBN 0374135800; 9780374135805 (hardback)
LC 2013-039911

SUMMARY: This novel by Mai Jia, translated by Olivia Milburn and Christopher Payne, "reveals the mysterious world of Unit 701, a top-secret Chinese intelligence agency whose sole purpose is counterespionage and code breaking. Rong Jinzhen, an autistic math genius with a past shrouded in myth, is forced to abandon his academic pursuits when he is recruited into Unit 701. . . . Rong discovers that the mastermind behind the maddeningly difficult Purple Code is his former teacher and best friend." (Publisher's note)

REVIEW: *Booklist* v110 no8 p22 D 15 2013 Bryce Christensen

REVIEW: *Economist* v410 no8879 p84 Mr 22 2014

REVIEW: *Libr J* v138 no15 p47 S 15 2013

REVIEW: *Libr J* v139 no5 p112 Mr 15 2014 Shirley Quan

REVIEW: *London Rev Books* v36 no17 p40-1 S 11 2014 Sheng Yun

REVIEW: *N Y Times Book Rev* p13 My 4 2014 PERRY LINK

REVIEW: *New Yorker* v90 no7 p73-1 Ap 7 2014

"Decoded." "This unusual spy thriller has neither page-turning plot twists nor a master villain. Instead, it fastidiously traces the childhood, the career, and the subsequent mental breakdown of a Chinese code-breaker named Rong Jinzhen, who is abandoned by his birth family in the early years of the last century and then recruited into China's counter-intelligence service. . . . Mai plays adroitly with literary genre and crafts a story of Borgesian subtlety and complexity that also feels specific to the politics and pathologies of revolutionary-era China."

REVIEW: *Publ Wkly* v260 no51 p36-7 D 16 2013

REVIEW: *TLS* no5782 p21 Ja 24 2014 FRANCE WOOD

MAILER, NORMAN, 1923-2007. Mind of an outlaw; selected essays; [by] Norman Mailer 656 p. 2013 Random House Inc
1. American essays
ISBN 9780812993479 (acid-free paper)
LC 2013-015716

SUMMARY: This book, edited by Phillip Sipiora, collects 50 essays by Normain Mailer. It includes "'The White Negro,' which equates the mindset of white hipster rebels with the sensibility of American blacks, who have 'been living on the margin between totalitarianism and democracy for two centuries.' Here, Mailer also draws parallels between outlaw minds and criminal psychopaths, a thread that winds through several essays, notably 'Until Dead,' prompted by the execution of Gary Gilmore." (Publishers Weekly)

REVIEW: *Bookforum* v20 no4 p36-7 D 2013/Ja 2014 CHRISTIAN LORENTZEN

"Norman Mailer: A Double Life" and "Mind of an Outlaw: Selected Essays." "'The White Negro'. . . is the core of . . . a new selection of essays edited by Phillip Sipiora. . . . There are about a dozen major essays among the many 'more obscure gems' chosen by Sipiora. Not to knock the 'gems' . . . but a selection that stuck to the major pieces might have served Mailer better. . . . J. Michael] Lennon gives detailed, if apologetic, accounts of the three great crises in Mailer's life: his stabbing of his second wife. Adele, in November 1960; tbe 1981 murder committed by Jack Henry Abbott, after Mailer bad petitioned for Abbott's release from prison; and the revelation of his rampant infidelity to his last wife, Norris Church, in the early 1990s. The stabbing, in Lennon's account, was the result not only of drunkenness but of temporary mental illness."

REVIEW: *Kirkus Rev* v81 no20 p30 O 15 2013

REVIEW: *Libr J* v138 no18 p88 N 1 2013 Patrick A. Smith

REVIEW: *Libr J* v138 no9 p55 My 15 2013 Barbara Hoffert

REVIEW: *N Y Rev Books* v60 no18 p22-5 N 21 2013 Edward Mendelson

"Norman Mailer: A Double Life" and "Mind of an Outlaw: Selected Essays." "J. Michael Lennon's biography is the first that interprets Mailer from within, not as a public spectacle. . . . He shepherds a prodigious variety of events into well-organized chapters, sometimes cluttered with irrelevant details. . . . Lennon is the also first biographer to see that Mailer's prolific thoughts about gods, devils, and divine forces were at the heart of his work. . . . He wrote about books and films with an unforced enthusiasm unlike anything else in his work. The selected essays in 'Mind of an Outlaw' include splendid examples such as his joyful bumper-car collisions with rival novelists in 'Quick Evaluations on the Talent in the Room'."

REVIEW: *Publ Wkly* v260 no35 p52 S 2 2013

MAIZES, SARAH. On my way to bed; [by] Sarah Maizes 40 p. 2013 Bloomsbury/Walker

1. Bedtime—Fiction 2. Children's stories 3. Imagination—Fiction 4. JUVENILE FICTION—Action & Adventure—General 5. JUVENILE FICTION—Bedtime & Dreams 6. JUVENILE FICTION—Family—General (see also headings under Social Issues)
ISBN 9780802723666 (hardback); 9780802723673 (reinforced edition)
LC 2013-001363

SUMMARY: In this book, "making bedtime avoidance and delay into a high art, Livi calls upon a number of strategies when her mother informs her that it is time for bed. Assuring readers that she isn't even remotely sleepy . . . she finds creative ways to slow the bedtime process down to a crawl. . . . When, at long last, an understandably frazzled mom gets her offspring under the sheets, Livi sleeps like an angel." (Kirkus Reviews)

REVIEW: *Kirkus Rev* v81 no13 p279 Jl 1 2013

REVIEW: *N Y Times Book Rev* p20 Ag 25 2013 SARAH HARRISON SMITH

"Lena's Sleep Sheep: A Going-To-Bed Book," "The Snuggle Sandwich," and "On My Way To Bed." "[Anita] Lobel . . . tells the sweet and funny story of a little girl who is helped to sleep by a flock of sheep. . . . Full of singsong rhymes and scenes of cheerfully chaotic family life, this bedtime book [by Malachy Doyle] starts in the morning. . . . Seen in [Michael] Paraskevas's bright, action-packed illustrations, Livi's high jinks include juggling toys, playing zoo dentist and piloting an imaginary rocket."

REVIEW: *SLJ* v59 no7 p66 Jl 2013 Martha Link Yesowitch

MAJD, HOOMAN. The Ministry of Guidance invites you to not stay; an American family in Iran; [by] Hooman Majd 272 p. 2013 Doubleday

1. Americans—Iran—Biography 2. Iranian Americans—Iran—Biography 3. Memoirs
ISBN 0385535325; 9780385535328 (alk. paper)
LC 2013-002552

SUMMARY: This book is U.S.-born Iranian Hooman Majd's memoir about the year he and his wife and son lived in Tehran, Iran. Topics include "attending parties both traditional and alcohol fueled; observing the resigned, yet loyal mores of the Iranians whose reformist Green Movement was crushed two years before; and recording a tale of a survivor of Evin prison." (Publishers Weekly)

REVIEW: *Booklist* v110 no2 p24 S 15 2013 Hazel Rochaman

REVIEW: *Kirkus Rev* v81 no19 p63 O 1 2013

REVIEW: *N Y Times Book Rev* p21 Ja 5 2014

REVIEW: *N Y Times Book Rev* p10 D 29 2013 LAILA LALAMI

"The Ministry of Guidance Invites You to Not Stay." "It was partly in an attempt to gain a wider perspective on the country of a birth that [author Hooman] Majd, who lives in Brooklyn, took his American wife and infant son to live in Tehran for one year. 'The Ministry of Guidance Invites You to Not Stay' is a memoir of 2011, spent reconnecting with the homeland he left as a baby. . . . That life is constrained by the political and societal restrictions of the Islamic Republic. . . . As interesting as Majd's anecdotes about life in Tehran are, they remain just that--anecdotes."

REVIEW: *Publ Wkly* v260 no31 p55 Ag 5 2013

MAJOR, F. G. Quo vadis; evolution of modern navigation; [by] F. G. Major 400 p. 2013 Springer

1. Artificial satellites in navigation 2. Electronics in navigation 3. Historical literature 4. Navigation 5. Navigation (Aeronautics)
ISBN 9781461486718
LC 2013-945533

SUMMARY: This book by F. G. Major "provides a wide-ranging, historic survey of terrestrial and space navigation. The author's goal is to help general readers understand the workings of the most modern and very accurate methods of locating the precise position of objects in space and time, the global positioning system (GPS)." (Choice: Current Reviews for Academic Libraries)

REVIEW: *Choice* v51 no9 p1614-5 My 2014 N. Sadanand

"Quo Vadis: Evolution of Modern Navigation: The Rise of Quantum Techniques". "A wide-ranging, historic survey of terrestrial and space navigation. . . . The book documents well the tremendous advances in navigation from the time of the Phoenicians and provides a good review of how navigation has evolved in nature (e.g., birds) and in human exploration. . . . However, the book is weak in trying to explain, in summary fashion, the physics of modern navigation. . . . The final third of the book presents the operations of radio and satellite navigation reasonably well. The book contains good references and illustrations, but needs better editing."

MAJOR, JUDITH K. Mariana Griswold Van Rensselaer; a landscape critic in the gilded age; [by] Judith K. Major xii, 285 p. 2013 University of Virginia Press

1. Historical literature 2. Landscape architecture—United States 3. Landscape architecture—United States—Philosophy—History 4. Van Rensselaer, Mariana Griswold 5. Women—United States—History 6. Women architectural critics
ISBN 0813933927 (cloth : alk. paper); 9780813933924 (cloth : alk. paper)
LC 2012-037883

SUMMARY: This book, by Judith K. Major, identifies "over 330 previously unattributed editorials and unsigned articles authored by [Mariana Griswold] Van Rensselaer in the influential journal 'Garden and Forest'--for which she was the sole female editorial voice-- . . . Major offers insight into her ideas about the importance of botanical nomenclature, the similarities between landscape gardening and idealist painting, design in nature, and many other significant topics." (Publisher's note)

REVIEW: *Choice* v51 no4 p623 D 2013 A. R. Michelson

"Mariana Griswold Van Rensselaer: A Landscape Critic in the Gilded Age." "[Author Judith K.] Major . . . took 15 years researching and writing this chronological study of Mariana Griswold Van Rensselaer's seminal, prolific criticism on landscape design during the 1880s and 1890s. . . . Major identified 333 . . . articles by Van Rensselaer, making her one of the most significant late-19th-century critics of landscape, art, and architecture in the US. . . . Previous scholarship, mostly articles, on Van Rensselaer's remarkable oeuvre considered her art and architectural critiques, but this monographic study sets the foundation for future examinations of her landscape writings."

MAJOR, PAUL.ed. Enjoy The Experience. See Enjoy The Experience

MAJOR, RAFAEL.ed. Leo Strauss's defense of the philosophic life. See Leo Strauss's defense of the philosophic life

MAJOR, WILFRED E. The court of comedy; Aristophanes, rhetoric, and democracy in fifth-century Athens; [by] Wilfred E. Major viii, 232 p. 2013 Ohio State University Press

1. Athens (Greece)—Politics & government 2. Greek drama (Comedy)—History and criticism 3. Historical literature 4. Rhetoric, Ancient—History
ISBN 0814212247 (cloth : alk. paper); 9780814212240 (cloth : alk. paper)
LC 2013-001523

SUMMARY: This book by Wilfred E. Major "analyzes how writers of comedy in Classical Greece satirized the emerging art of rhetoric and its role in political life. In the fifth century BCE, the development of rhetoric proceeded hand in hand with the growth of democracy both on Sicily and at Athens. In turn, comic playwrights in Athens, most notably Aristophanes, lampooned oratory as part of their commentary on the successes and failures of the young democracy." (Publisher's note)

REVIEW: *Choice* v51 no6 p1001 F 2014 D. Konstan

"The Court of Comedy: Aristophanes, Rhetoric, and Democracy in Fifth-Century Athens." "[Wilfred E.] Major . . . argues convincingly that there was no such rhetorical science in Aristophanes's day. . . . Major does not impose a single stance on Aristophanes but traces stages in his development; nevertheless, Aristophanes 'consistently dramatizes a faith in the core processes of the Athenian democracy, even as he sharply attacks its institutions when they fail to function properly.' The book is an important, sensible contribution to the recent reassessment of Aristophanes as a democrat."

MAJUMDAR, SAIKAT. Prose of the world; modernism and the banality of empire; [by] Saikat Majumdar 232 p. 2013 Columbia University Press

1. Banality (Philosophy) in literature 2. Commonwealth fiction (English)—20th century—History and criticism 3. Literature and society—Commonwealth countries—History—20th century 4. Narration (Rhetoric) 5. Philosophical literature 6. Place (Philosophy) in literature
ISBN 9780231156943 (cloth : alk. paper); 9780231527675 (e-book)
LC 2012-014234

SUMMARY: This book "surveys the novels, stories and selected non-fiction of four quite disparate anglophone writers who are drawn from the edges of empire and of former empires: James Joyce (Ireland), Katherine Mansfield (New Zealand), Zoe Wicomb (South Africa) and Amit Chaudhuri (India)." It makes "the argument that 'the mundane and the marginal,' as expressed in 'quotidian' prose, should be read as 'a pertinent index of subaltem consciousness'." (Times Literary Supplement)

REVIEW: *Choice* v50 no11 p2014 Jl 2013 K. Lynass

REVIEW: *TLS* no5755 p23 Jl 19 2013 MADELINE CLEMENTS

"Prose of the World: Modernism and the Banality of Empire." "[Saikat] Majumdar's detailed study of modem world literature in English surveys the novels, stories and selected non-fiction of four quite disparate anglophone writers who are drawn from the edges of empire and of former empires. . . . It considers their works alongside an interesting range of historical, anthropological and literary theories in order to make the compelling argument that 'the mundane and the marginal,' as expressed in 'quotidian' prose, should be read as 'a pertinent index of subaltern consciousness'. . . . Thorough and challenging."

THE MAKING OF THE HUMANITIES; From early modern to modern disciplines; 2013 Amsterdam University Press

1. Academic discourse—History—19th century 2. Historical literature 3. Humanities—History 4. Intellectual life—History 5. Modernity 6. Universities & colleges—Curricula—History 7. Universities & colleges—History—19th century
ISBN 9789089644558 paperback

SUMMARY: Edited by Rens Bod, Jaap Maat and Thijs Weststeijn, "This much-awaited second volume investigates the changes in subject, method and institutional context of the humanistic disciplines around 1800, offering a wealth of insights for specialists and students alike. Point of departure is the pivotal question whether there was a paradigm shift in the humanities around 1800 or whether these changes were part of a much longer process." (Publisher's note)

REVIEW: *Choice* v51 no1 p59 S 2013 L. A. Brewer

"The Making of the Humanities: From Early Modern to Modern Disciplines." "Few collections of conference proceedings rival the erudite scope of this second installment of a three-part project; the first volume, subtitled 'Early Modern Europe' . . . appeared in 2011. Originating from a gathering of predominantly European specialists in linguistics, history, mathematics, science, musicology, literature, and other disciplines, the essayists embrace broad topics and those more narrowly defined. Tracing the development of theories, some to their origins in the 17th century, each selection offers innovative perspectives about the precursors of prevailing intellectual movements in the 19th century, with which the volume is primarily concerned."

MAKSIK, ALEXANDER. A marker to measure drift; [by] Alexander Maksik 240 p. 2013 Alfred A. Knopf

1. Aegean Islands (Greece & Turkey) 2. Liberians 3. Memory—Fiction 4. Psychological fiction 5. Refugees—Fiction
ISBN 0307962571 (hardcover); 9780307962577 (hardcover); 9780307962584 (ebook); 9780345803863 (paperback)
LC 2012-038249

SUMMARY: This novel, written by Alexander Maksik, focuses on Jacquelin, a young Liberian woman living alone in a cave on a remote island in the Aegean Sea. She experiences "the euphoric obliteration of memory and, with it, the unspeakable violence she has seen and from which she has miraculously escaped. Slowly, irrepressibly, images from a life before this violence begin to resurface. Jacqueline must find the strength to contend with what she has survived or tip forward into . . . madness." (Publisher's note)

REVIEW: *Kirkus Rev* v81 no10 p19 My 15 2013

REVIEW: *Libr J* v138 no11 p84 Je 15 2013 Gwen Vredevoogd

REVIEW: *Libr J* v138 no4 p56 Mr 1 2013 Barbara Hoffert

REVIEW: *N Y Times Book Rev* p24 Ag 25 2013 NORMAN RUSH

"A Marker To Measure Drift." "[Alexander] Maksik has produced a bold book, and an instructive one. . . . Maksik writes, credibly, across the boundaries of gender and, in this book, race. . . . Is Maksik's grueling depiction of a woman in torment successful as a work of fiction? I think it is. The point of view is convincing. . . . The mechanics of trying to stay fed and sheltered are given plausibly enough. Maksik's narrative style, using short, declarative sentences and sentence fragments, fits the story's tenor and pace. The sustained representation of Jacqueline's search for release, for haven, has moments of bleak poetry."

REVIEW: *Publ Wkly* v260 no17 p2 Ap 29 2013

REVIEW: *World Lit Today* v87 no4 p62 Jl/Ag 2013 W. M. Hagen

MALENFANT, ISABELLE.il. Once upon a balloon. See Galbraith, B.

MALIK, SAEED. A Perspective on the Signs of Al-Quran; Through the Prism of the Heart; [by] Saeed Malik 300 p. 2009 Createspace Independent Pub

1. Faith & reason—Islam 2. Islam 3. Muhammad, Prophet, d. 632 4. Qur'an 5. Religious literature
ISBN 1439239622; 9781439239629

SUMMARY: This book presents a "devotional guide to Islamic spirituality." Author Saeed Malik "sees Islam not as a religion but as one path to spirituality-the difference being that any sincere faith leads to God. . . . Malik refutes dogmas that have long twisted the Abrahamic faiths: He proposes heaven and hell as states of mind rather than physical locations, and he argues that since Islam respects the sanctity of life, God never supports aggressors." (Kirkus Reviews)

REVIEW: *Kirkus Rev* v82 no4 p76 F 15 2014

"A Perspective on the Signs of Al-Quran: Through the Prism of the Heart". "[Saeed] Malik approaches mystical lyricism in his eloquent devotional guide to Islamic spirituality. . . . A section on Muhammad as a historical figure goes into a level of detail that might not be necessary for a spiritual guidebook, but only occasionally does the mystical tone veer into New Ageism. For the most part, Malik sticks to practical, heartfelt scriptural commentary. One could even imagine the 100 names of Allah (comprising one-third of the text) serving any member of any faith in a devotional context. . . . A useful, articulate spiritual commentary on the Quran."

REVIEW: *Kirkus Rev* v82 no3 p370 F 1 2014

MALIK, YOGENDRA K. Government and politics in South Asia. See Kapur, A.

MALITSKY, JOSHUA. Post-revolution nonfiction film; building the Soviet and Cuban nations; [by] Joshua Malitsky xi, 273, [274] p. 2013 Indiana University Press

1. Cuba—History—Revolution, 1959 2. Documentary films—Political aspects—Cuba 3. Documentary films—Political aspects—Soviet Union 4. Motion picture literature 5. Soviet Union—History
ISBN 9780253007643 (cl: alk. paper); 9780253007667 (pbk. : alk. paper)
LC 2012-037385

SUMMARY: This book "undertakes a comparative analysis of the state-sponsored nonfiction films (primarily newsreels and documentaries) that arose following two communist revolutions: the Russian Revolution of 1917 and the Cuban Revolution of 1959. The study focuses on the work of Dziga Vertov and Esfir Shub in the USSR and Santiago Alvarez in Cuba. [Joshua] Malitsky . . . argues that nonfiction films served the public as revolutionary models of everyday life." (Choice: Current Reviews for Academic Libraries)

REVIEW: *Choice* v51 no7 p1221-2 Mr 2014 A. J. DeBlasio

"Post-Revolution Nonfiction Film: Building the Soviet and Cuban Nations." "The book is arranged chronologically and broken into three parts that correspond to three comparable periods in both country's cinematic history: the immediate postrevolutionary period; a period of development and expansion of aesthetic strategies; and a period of heightened rhetorical clarity as leaders recognized that previous approaches had failed. Each of the three parts includes a chapter on the Soviet Union and a chapter on Cuba. A book that analyzes Soviet cinema side-by-side with Cuban film is welcome, even though the two countries are represented here in parallel. . . . Highly recommended."

MALKASIAN, CARTER. War comes to Garmser; thirty years of conflict on the Afghan frontier; [by] Carter Malkasian 336 p. 2013 Oxford University Press

1. Afghan War, 2001—Campaigns—Afghanistan—Helmand 2. Afghan War, 2001—Personal narratives, American 3. Historical literature 4. Postwar reconstruction—Afghanistan—Helmand
ISBN 019997375X (hardcover); 9780199973750 (hardcover)
LC 2012-045788

SUMMARY: This book, by Carter Malkasian, tells the story of "Garmser, a community in . . . Helmand province, [Afghanistan] . . . through the jihad, the rise and fall of Taliban regimes, and American and British surge. Based on his conversations with hundreds of Afghans, including government officials, tribal leaders, . . . and . . . Taliban, and drawing on extensive primary source material, Malkasian takes readers into the world of the Afghans." (Publisher's note)

REVIEW: *Kirkus Rev* v81 no2 p201 Ja 15 2013

REVIEW: *TLS* no5765 p12-3 S 27 2013 THOMAS BARFIELD

"Afghanistan Declassified: A Guide to America's Longest War," "War Comes to Garmser: Thirty Years of Conflict on the Afghan Frontier," and "Afghanistan and Pakistan: Conflict, Extremism, and Resistance to Modernity." "Brian Glyn Williams's . . . [book] was originally written for the US military as a guide to the country, its history and people for troops arriving there in 2007. . . . Much of what is presented is badly out of date. . . . Carter Malkasian's 'War Comes to Garmser,' by contrast, explores the war in Afghanistan from an explicitly provincial Afghan point of view, where foreigners (and even Kabul officials) are marginal actors rather than the centre of the story. . . . 'Afghanistan and Pakistan' . . . is a good guide by an insider familiar with the complexity of decision-making in Pakistan."

MALLACH, DAVID AUSTIN. Myth; A Wall Street Novel; [by] David Austin Mallach 260 p. 2013 Penhurst Books

1. Financial Industry Regulatory Authority 2. Financial services industry—United States—Corrupt practices 3. Investment advisors 4. Legal stories 5. Wall Street (New York, N.Y.)—Fiction

ISBN 0578122952; 9780578122953

SUMMARY: This book presents a courtroom drama "involving a retired couple in dire distress. Their income has been decimated, the result of depending on fixed income over years of declining interest rates. Their options are few and their future bleak. How will they survive? They turn to Lucien Marat for help. Armed with a passion to help others, Lucien Marat takes on Wall Street in a trial that he hopes can save millions of retirees from certain ruin." (Publisher's note)

REVIEW: *Kirkus Rev* v82 no2 p14 Ja 15 2014

"Myth: A Wall Street Novel". "A courtroom drama that indicts the dominant strategies of the financial planning industry, telling an enjoyable story at the same time. . . . [David Austin] . Mallach keeps the intricacies of investment strategy at a level the average reader can understand, using his characters, rather than infodumps, to explain concepts through fast-paced dialogue. . . . Mallach succeeds in keeping the story moving, despite the relatively dry subject matter, thanks to multidimensional characters who can't make it to the end of the page without arguing with each other. The highly descriptive style of writing, though occasionally overstuffed with colorful turns of phrase . . . continues to keep the pages turning and the conflict crackling."

MALLINSON, ALLAN. 1914; Fight The Good Fight: Britain, the Army & the Coming of the First World War; [by] Allan Mallinson 400 p. 2013 Bantam Press

1. Great Britain—Military history 2. Great Britain. Army—History 3. Historical literature 4. World War, 1914-1918—Campaigns—Western Front 5. World War, 1914-1918—Causes

ISBN 0593067606; 9780593067604

SUMMARY: In this book on World War I, Allan Mallinson "examines the century-long path that led to war, and the vital first month of fighting in Belgium and France--a conflict of movement before the stalemate of the trenches--and speculates . . . on what might have been had wiser political and military counsels prevailed." (Publisher's note)

REVIEW: *TLS* no5772 p3-4 N 15 2013 WILLIAM PHILPOTT

"The War That Ended Peace: How Europe Abandoned Peace for the First World War," "Catastrophe: Europe Goes to War 1914," and "1914: Fight the Good Fight: Britain, the Army and the Coming of the First World War." "In Britain, the centenary wars are already raging between government and historians, largely over whether we should still be wearing the patriotic cloak that nations donned in the face of aggression by traditional enemies. Max Hastings and Allan Mallinson still wear it. For Hastings the guilt of Germany is firmly established. . . . Margaret Macmillan's judgement in 'The War that Ended Peace' is more balanced, although German intentions and action remain central to the war's origins. . . . Mallinson dissects military affairs (and political deficiencies) with a trained soldierly eye."

MALLORY, J. P. The origins of the Irish; [by] J. P. Mallory 320 p. 2013 Thames & Hudson Inc.

1. Historical literature 2. Ireland—History 3. Irish—Origin

ISBN 0500051755; 9780500051757 (hardback)

LC 2012-939689

SUMMARY: This book is a study of earliest Ireland. J.P. Mallory "reports that 38 billion years ago, molten magma on the Earth's crust split apart into some 29 plates that began floating away. Later, perhaps 450 million years ago, two such parts collided to form Ireland." He discusses Celtic language, Roman invasions, and Christianity, and addresses the contentious issue of "how much of Irish culture was local invention and how much was influenced by neighbors." (Choice)

REVIEW: *Choice* v51 no1 p154 S 2013 E. J. Kealey

"The Origins of the Irish." "This major achievement is the best, most gracefully written new study of earliest Ireland. [Author J. P.] Mallory . . . reports that 38 billion years ago, molten magma on the Earth's crust split apart into some 29 plates that began floating away. Later . . . two such parts collided to form Ireland. . . . By 4000 BCE, a warming trend encouraged farming, animal domestication, ceramic technology, megalithic architecture, golden ornamentation, and possibly warfare. By 1500 BCE, there were hill forts and offerings to gods in watery places. . . . Within this exciting parade there remains a contentious issue that Mallory bravely ponders: how much of Irish culture was local invention and how much was influenced by neighbors, especially Britain?"

REVIEW: *Hist Today* v63 no4 p58-9 Ap 2013 FRANCIS PRYOR

MAN, JOHN. Samurai; A History; [by] John Man 352 p. 2014 HarperCollins

1. Historical literature 2. Japan—History 3. Japan—Politics & government 4. Samurai 5. Takamori, Saigo, 1828-1877

ISBN 0062202677; 9780062202673

SUMMARY: This book by John Man focuses on "Saigo Takamori (1828–77) . . . famed in history, fiction, and legend as 'the last samurai' for his roles in the Meiji Restoration and his leadership of the 1877 Satsuma Rebellion. Man . . . peppers his biography of Saigo with additional chapters on the samurai as a whole (with the expected discussion of bushido—the samurai honor code—and seppuku, a form of its ritual suicide) and on the development of the samurai's appeal in popular culture." (Library Journal)

REVIEW: *Kirkus Rev* v82 no2 p12 Ja 15 2014

"Samurai: A History". "[John] Man, a crack biographer of Asian historical figures . . . tenders a survey of the samurai, the equivalent of Japan's feudal knights. This is a well-written piece of history with an easy storyteller's rhythm and plenty of intrigue. Readers will quickly realize that the author . . . is well-versed in Far Eastern history, but he also accommodates new discoveries and insights. . . . Mann intricately describes the shift in the orientation of the Japanese government after the post-1600 revolution. . . . Smooth, sophisticated history writing."

REVIEW: *Publ Wkly* v260 no44 p56 N 4 2013

MANCEAU, ÉDOUARD. The race; 64 p. 2014 Owlkids Books, Inc.

1. Animal stories 2. Children's stories 3. Running races 4. Sportsmanship 5. Success

ISBN 9781771470551
LC 2013-949120

SUMMARY: In this children's book, "six bipedal caribou arrive at the starting line for a race. These competitors will do anything to win, from throwing banana peels to hitching a ride; whoever is in first place is viewed with obvious malice. In an existential twist, some runners decide to quit: 'They wonder why they started running like that in the first place. So they decide to settle down and enjoy life.'" (School Library Journal)

REVIEW: *Bull Cent Child Books* v67 no9 p467 My 2014 T. A.

"The Race". "It's a whimsy-filled ride with a straightforward message, and there's real pleasure in watching these little dudes scheme their way to the finish line and in the celebration of a laid-back lifestyle. . . . [Édouard] Manceau's signature paper collage is on full display in warm earth tones, with the guys in a snappy vermilion against an ivory background. The dinner-plate eyes, contorting antlers, and stick limbs of the racing figures convey a remarkable range of expression, and their half-moon muzzles add to the deadpan effect of the narration. After meeting these guys, one might expect kids to want to set up a race of their own, but it's just as likely they'll want to copy the loafing guy and stretch out in the sun."

REVIEW: *Kirkus Rev* v82 no5 p59 Mr 1 2014

"The Race". "While the jacket blurb calls the protagonists 'caribou,' the text refers to them as 'guys' in this tale translated from French. . . . There's a bit of misdirection, as with the pistol, and a bit more reflection about who really wants to be in this race after all, so in the end, the story might be aimed more at adults than the children they are reading it to. The collage shapes are pleasing and funny, however, and the googly eyes and placement of the stick limbs convey a surprising amount of emotion. Add this winsome fable to the shelves of slightly odd picture books."

REVIEW: *Publ Wkly* v261 no5 p53 F 3 2014

REVIEW: *SLJ* v60 no4 p128 Ap 2014 Anna Haase Krueger

MANDEL, RALPH.tr. Landscapes of the metropolis of death. See Kulka, O. D.

MANDLER, PETER.ed. From plunder to preservation. See From plunder to preservation

MANI, MUTHUKUMARA, 1964-.ed. Greening India's growth. See Greening India's growth

MANKOFF, BOB. How about never--is never good for you?; my life in cartoons; [by] Bob Mankoff 304 p. 2014 Henry Holt and Company

1. BIOGRAPHY & AUTOBIOGRAPHY—General 2. COMICS & GRAPHIC NOVELS—General 3. Cartoonists—United States—Biography 4. Memoirs 5. Periodical editors—United States—Biography
ISBN 9780805095906 (hardback)
LC 2013-021129

SUMMARY: In this memoir, cartoonist and editor Bob Mankoff "allows us into the hallowed halls of 'The New Yorker' to show us the soup-to-nuts process of cartoon creation, giving us a detailed look not only at his own work, but that of the other talented cartoonists who keep us laughing week after week. For desert, he reveals the secrets to winning the magazine's caption contest." (Publisher's note)

REVIEW: *Booklist* v110 no13 p11 Mr 1 2014 Donna Seaman

REVIEW: *Kirkus Rev* v82 no4 p14 F 15 2014

"How About Never-Is Never Good for You? My Life in Cartoons". " Part glib memoir and part cartoon anthology from the cartoon editor for the New Yorker. The most fascinating part takes readers inside the process of just how these cartoons are inspired, created and selected for publication. . . . Breezy text alternates with lots of cartoons—the author's own and others'—as he details how he went from years of being rejected by the New Yorker to his early acceptances to his current role as a gatekeeper. . . . Those who aspire to a career drawing for the New Yorker will find this essential reading-or just give up."

REVIEW: *New York Times* v163 no56446 pC1-7 Mr 20 2014 JANET MASLIN

"How About Never--Is Never Good Enough for You? My Life in Cartoons" "If anyone is entitled to pepper his memoir with 'New Yorker' cartoons, it's the cartoon editor of 'The New Yorker.' So Bob Mankoff's new book is half prose, half illustrations and tirelessly playful. But the artwork and text work together to tell a fizzy, jokey story about a long and busy career. . . . Mr. Mankoff is wise enough to know that his readers have more interest in how 'The New Yorker' picks and edits cartoons than in his childhood. . . . This book presents itself as a guide for aspiring cartoonists."

RREVIEW: *N Y Times Book Rev* p16 Je 1 2014 BRUCE HANDY

REVIEW: *Publ Wkly* v260 no51 p47-8 D 16 2013

MANN, JENNIFER K.il. Turkey Tot. See Shannon, G.

MANOS, JOHN K. Dialogues of a Crime; [by] John K. Manos 300 p. 2013 Amika Press

1. Cold cases (Criminal investigation) 2. Detective & mystery stories 3. Murder investigation—Fiction 4. Organized crime—Fiction 5. Prisons—Fiction
ISBN 1937484130; 9781937484132

SUMMARY: In this book, "Michael Pollitz, a nineteen-year-old with connections to the Outfit," is arrested on drug charges and subsequently raped and beaten in a correctional facility." Later, in 1994, "Job-weary CPD Detective Larry Klinger becomes obsessed with a cold case from that pivotal moment twenty-two years ago. In the course of his investigation, he encounters questions of ethics, guilt, and justice that make him doubt certainties that have sustained him for decades." (Publisher's note)

REVIEW: *Kirkus Rev* v81 no21 p46 N 1 2013

REVIEW: *Kirkus Rev* p39 D 15 2013 supplemet best books 2013

"Dialogues of a Crime". "[John K.] Manos is extremely deft at allowing the characters to reveal the story and what motivates them. Klinger captures this particularly well; he ponders his role in the reality of crime and punishment, and Manos allows him to grow in the process: 'Interviewing scumbags has to be the most tedious damn thing in the world, Klinger thought, as Bobby Andrews jumped back and forth over the same explanations, tripping over one lie after another.' The characters are rich in their speech, experiences and motivations, which the measured, purposeful writing only enhances."

MANRODT, KARL. Vested; how P&G, McDonald's, and Microsoft are redefining winning in business relationships; [by] Karl Manrodt 2012 Palgrave Macmillan

1. Business literature 2. Business networks 3. Contracting out 4. Strategic alliances (Business) 5. Success in business
ISBN 9780230341708; 0230341705
LC 2012-004640

SUMMARY: In this book "consultant [Kate] Vitasek . . . and performance management expert [Karl] Manrodt . . . argue that the answer [to successful companies] is the ability to work in a highly strategic manner with business partners—suppliers, customers, stakeholders, or employees. . . . The authors break down the best practices of winning companies and their strategies for improvement. These strategies break cleanly into five Vested Rules." (Publishers Weekly)

REVIEW: *Booklist* v108 no21 p19 Jl 1 2012 Mary Carroll

REVIEW: *Publ Wkly* v259 no23 p45 Je 4 2012

"Vested: How Procter & Gamble, McDonald's, and Microsoft Are Redefining Winning in Business Relationships." "What's the secret of successful companies? In this solid and thought-provoking book, consultant [Kate] Vitasek . . . and performance management expert [Karl] Manrodt . . . argue that the answer is the ability to work in a highly strategic manner with business partners—suppliers, customers, stakeholders, or employees. . . . These strategies break cleanly into five Vested Rules. . . . Though the concept is simple, the rules provide a framework to effectively redefine the reader's business relationships and way of thinking about the synergy in partnerships."

MANSBACH, ADAM. The Dead Run; [by] Adam Mansbach 304 p. 2013 HarperCollins

1. Aztec mythology 2. Detective & mystery stories 3. Horror tales 4. Mexican-American Border Region—Fiction 5. Noir fiction
ISBN 006219965X; 9780062199652

SUMMARY: In this book by Adam Mansbach, "on both sides of the border, girls are going missing and bodies are beginning to surface. It's a deadly epidemic of crime that plunges a small-town police chief into a monster of an investigation he's not equipped to handle. An ancient evil has returned, and now everyone—the innocent and the guilty—must face their deepest terrors." (Publisher's note)

REVIEW: *Booklist* v109 no22 p50 Ag 1 2013 David Pitt

REVIEW: *Kirkus Rev* v81 no16 p248 Ag 15 2013

"The Dead Run." "A badass convict and a jaded Texas sheriff go head-to-head with an ancient Aztec demon in the latest from [author Adam] Mansbach. . . . The novel is just as screwball and even more propulsive than the author's previous works. . . . Mansbach's enormous gift for language and a dedicated understanding of the genres involved--noir, horror, thriller and other tropes come into play here--make this wobbly machine work surprisingly well. . . . A head-spinning mashup of genres, with a cast that includes bikers, hookers, demons and corrupt cops. It works."

REVIEW: *Libr J* v138 no12 p73 Jl 1 2013 Peter Petruski

REVIEW: *Libr J* v138 no8 p59 My 1 2013

REVIEW: *Publ Wkly* v260 no32 p36 Ag 12 2013

MANSFIELD, NICK. Buildings of the Labour Movement; [by] Nick Mansfield 164 p. 2013 David Brown Book Co

1. Architectural literature 2. Historic buildings—Great Britain 3. Historical literature 4. Labor movement—Great Britain 5. Labour Party (Great Britain)—History
ISBN 1848021291; 9781848021297

SUMMARY: This book on buildings associated with the British labour movement "ranges from the communal buildings of the early 19th- century political radicals, Owenites and Chartists, through Arts and Crafts influenced socialist structures of the late Victorian and Edwardian period to the grand union 'castles' of the mid twentieth century. There are also chapters of the ubiquitous co-operative architecture." (Publisher's note)

REVIEW: *Hist Today* v63 no9 p64 S 2013 CHARLOTTE CROW

"Buildings of the Labour Movement." "With this wide-ranging survey of the premises and locations in which the labour movement evolved, from the trade societies of the 18th century to Owenism, Chartism and the Labour Party, Nick Mansfield has filled a void in the history of the world's oldest labour movement. . . . Mansfield describes the book as 'a conventional labour history' and he hopes to inspire readers to 'contribute at a local level to the ongoing processes of researching, recording, preserving and even interpreting the built heritage of working people'. . . . It is just a pity that such a volume has been priced so highly."

MANTLER, GORDON K. Power to the poor; Black-Brown coalition and the fight for economic justice, 1960-1974; [by] Gordon K. Mantler 362 p. 2013 University of North Carolina Press

1. African Americans—Economic conditions—20th century 2. Coalitions—United States—History—20th century 3. Ethnicity—Political aspects—United States—History—20th century 4. Hispanic Americans—Economic conditions—20th century 5. Historical literature 6. Political activists—United States—Biography 7. Poverty—Political aspects—United States—History—20th century 8. Social justice—United States—History—20th century 9. Social movements—United States—History—20th century
ISBN 9780807838518 (cloth: alk. paper)
LC 2012-031383

SUMMARY: This book by Gordon K. Mantler "uses the 1968 multiracial antipoverty Poor People's Campaign (PPC) to argue that race-based identity politics and class-based multiracial coalition politics were mutually reinforcing rather than mutually exclusive, as others have maintained. . . . In this way, he rehabilitates the late 1960s and early 1970s as an era significant to both coalitional politics and community empowerment." (American Historical Review)

REVIEW: *Am Hist Rev* v119 no1 p209-11 F 2014 Shana Bernstein

"Power to the Poor: Black-Brown Coalition and the Fight for Economic Justice, 1960-1974". "'Power to the Poor' is at its best when discussing the actual Poor People's Campaign . . . [Gordon K.] Mantler convincingly shows the PPC was a formative experience for a significant portion of the Chicano movement, while his discussion of the moment as a multiracial possibility for collaboration between not only blacks and Mexican Americans, but also Native Americans and poor whites from Appalachia . . . is fascinating. . . . However, while the main focus on African and Mexican Americans, the nation's two largest minorities, makes sense to an extent, exploring the other two ethno-racial communities in more depth would have enriched the book."

REVIEW: *Choice* v50 no11 p2087 Jl 2013 D. O. Cullen

REVIEW: *J Am Hist* v100 no4 p1282-3 Mr 2014

MANUALI, TANYA BASTIANICH. Lidia's common-sense Italian cooking. See Bastianich, L. M.

MANUWALD, GESINE. Roman republican theatre; [by] Gesine Manuwald xii, 390 p. 2011 Cambridge University Press

1. Historical literature 2. Latin drama—History and criticism 3. Literature and history—Rome 4. Theater—History—To 500 5. Theater—Rome

ISBN 0521110165 (hardback); 9780521110167 (hardback)

LC 2010-054277

SUMMARY: Written by Gesine Manuwald, this book is "A comprehensive 2011 history of Roman drama from its beginnings until the end of the Republican period. . . . It discusses the origins of Roman drama and the historical, social and institutional backgrounds of all the dramatic genres . . . during the Republic (tragedy, praetexta, comedy, togata, Atellana, mime and pantomime). Possible general characteristics are identified, and attention is paid to the nature of . . . various genres." (Publisher's note)

REVIEW: *Classical Rev* v63 no2 p415-7 O 2013 Peter Barrios-Lech

"Roman Republican Theatre: A History." "[Author Gesine Manuwald's] aim is to provide a synoptic overview of the tradition of Roman republican drama, built up from a careful consideration of testimonia, fragments and extant plays. . . . The volume achieves its aim of providing a synoptic overview of the tradition. This is especially impressive since [Manuwald] deals mainly with fragments of plays from genres which are often otherwise poorly attested. . . . [Manuwald's] book will undoubtedly become an indispensable resource for students and scholars: it offers updated treatments on many topics and its discussions provide useful points of departure for further investigation."

MAOR, ELI. Beautiful geometry; [by] Eli Maor 208 p. 2014 Princeton University Press

1. Geometry—History 2. Geometry—History—Pictorial works 3. Geometry in art 4. MATHEMATICS—Geometry—General 5. MATHEMATICS—History & Philosophy 6. Mathematical literature

ISBN 0691150990 (cloth : acid-free paper); 9780691150994 (cloth : acid-free paper)

LC 2013-033506

SUMMARY: This book "presents more than sixty . . . color plates illustrating a wide range of geometric patterns and theorems, accompanied by brief accounts of the . . . history and people behind each. With artwork by Swiss artist Eugen Jost and text by . . . math historian Eli Maor, this . . . celebration of geometry covers numerous subjects, from straightedge-and-compass constructions to intriguing configurations involving infinity." (Publisher's note)

REVIEW: *Sci Am* v309 no6 p80 D 2013 Lee Billings

"Beautiful Geometry." "In this book, [Eli] Maor, a math historian, teams with [Eugen] Jost, an artist, to reveal some of that mathematical majesty using jewel-like visualizations of classic geometric theorems. Often the pictures are actually puzzles to be solved, containing clues for perceptive readers to follow. Mixing equal parts math, history and philosophy, the authors begin with some basics . . . before expanding to introduce more baroque and contemporary theorems. The result is a book that stimulates the mind as well as the eye."

MARA, WIL. The gunsmith; [by] Wil Mara 48 p. 2013 Marshall Cavendish

1. Gunsmithing—United States—History—17th century—Juvenile literature 2. Gunsmithing—United States—History—18th century—Juvenile literature 3. Gunsmiths—United States—History—17th century—Juvenile literature 4. Gunsmiths—United States—History—18th century—Juvenile literature 5. Historical literature

ISBN 9781608704149 (print); 9781608709854 (ebook)

LC 2011-028342

SUMMARY: This book on gunsmiths in colonial America, by Wil Mara, is part of the Colonial People series. It "traces the increasing use of guns and their manufacture in the colonies from the early 1600s to the late 1700s. . . . The informative text is illustrated with tinted engravings and paintings from earlier eras as well as . . . color photos of artifacts and replicas and reenactments of historical trades in Colonial Williamsburg." (Booklist)

REVIEW: *Booklist* v110 no4 p45 O 15 2013 Carolyn Phelan

"The Gunsmith," "The Merchant," and "The Shipbuilder." "Attractively designed, the books in the Colonial People series present and discuss the roles of individual trades from colonial America. . . . The publisher indicates the reading level as four, and while the books' relatively large type and square format are consistent with a fourth-grade audience, the readability level appears to be several grades higher. . . . In each book, the informative text is illustrated with tinted engravings and paintings from earlier eras as well as excellent color photos of artifacts and replicas and reenactments of historical trades in Colonial Williamsburg."

REVIEW: *SLJ* v60 no2 p117 F 2014 Lucinda Snyder Whitehurst

MARAK, ANDRAE M. At the border of empires; the Tohono O'odham, gender, and assimilation, 1880—1934; [by] Andrae M. Marak xiii, 209 p. 2013 University of Arizona Press

1. Tohono O'odham Indians—Cultural assimilation 2. Tohono O'odham Indians—History 3. Tohono O'odham Indians—Social life and customs 4. Tohono O'odham women—Social conditions

ISBN 9780816521159 (cloth: alk. paper)

LC 2012-034715

SUMMARY: This "history of the Tohono O'odham peoples of southern Arizona and northern Sonora" presents an "analysis of how Tohono O'odham gender norms and their social roles in relation to American and Mexican assimilation and reform efforts amongst their peoples. . . . After . . . [an] introduction to Tohono O'odham history, the authors present four topical chapters, followed by a comparative look at the experiences of individuals on the Mexican side of the line." (Catholic Historical Review)

REVIEW: *Am Hist Rev* v119 no1 p184-5 F 2014 Sheila

McManus

"At the Border of Empires: The Tohono O'odham, Gender, and Assimilation, 1880-1934". "What the book does provide is a very strong analysis of the many ways that the Tohono O'odham's experiences living at the southern edge of the American West were remarkably similar to the experiences of other indigenous peoples across the region, particularly when it came to external authorities trying to use Euro-American gender norms to reshape everything that the outsiders thought was 'wrong' about Native American culture. . . . This monograph is an excellent addition to the historiographies of settler colonialism in North America."

REVIEW: *Choice* v50 no12 p2298 Ag 2013 T. P. Bowman

REVIEW: *J Am Hist* v101 no1 p287-8 Je 2014

MARANTO, ROBERT. President Obama and education reform; the personal and the political; [by] Robert Maranto pages cm. 2012 Palgrave Macmillan

1. Education and state United States 2. Educational change—United States 3. Obama, Barack, 1961—Political & social views 4. Political science literature
ISBN 9781137030917; 9781137030924
LC 2012-010434

SUMMARY: This book "offers a comprehensive description and analysis of President Obama's education agenda." Authors "Robert Maranto and Michael Q. McShane . . . believe that the Obama-era reforms reflect long-term changes in ideology and technology which have led to successful innovation in both the private and public sector, and that Obama's personal background as a community organizer has informed his reform strategies for the better." (Publisher's note)

REVIEW: *Choice* v51 no2 p355-6 O 2013 R. L. Welch

"President Obama and Education Reform: The Personal and the Political." "[Authors Robert] Maranto . . . and [Michael Q.] McShane . . . provide an enlightening look at education policy and reform in the US, with a particular focus on the efforts undertaken by President Obama. Their discussion includes chapters on recent developments, such as the No Child Left Behind Act and Race to the Top, and examines the development of Obama's beliefs on education, the history of education in the US, and other relevant issues. Maranto and McShane present competing arguments clearly and fairly and use data and social science literature to examine these various views."

MARCIANO, JOHN BEMELMANS. The 9 lives of Alexander Baddenfield; 144 p. 2013 Viking Published by Penguin Group

1. Cats—Fiction 2. Conduct of life—Fiction 3. Death—Fiction 4. Humorous stories 5. Orphans—Fiction 6. Reincarnation—Fiction 7. Wealth—Fiction
ISBN 0670014060; 9780670014064 (hardcover)
LC 2012-048448

SUMMARY: In this book, "Alexander Baddenfield is a horrible boy . . . who is the last in a long line of lying, thieving scoundrels. One day, Alexander has an astonishing idea. Why not transplant the nine lives from his cat into himself? Suddenly, Alexander has lives to spare, and goes about using them up, attempting the most outrageous feats he can imagine. Only when his lives start running out, and he is left with only one just like everyone else, does he realize how reckless he has been." (Publisher's note)

REVIEW: *Booklist* v110 no4 p52 O 15 2013 Angela Leeper

REVIEW: *Bull Cent Child Books* v67 no3 p169 N 2013 T. A.

"The 9 Lives of Alexander Baddenfield." "[Author John Bemelmans] Marciano has a wry voice in this darkly comic tale, but the exposition is somewhat clumsy; the narrative asides and sarcastic commentary are reminiscent of Lemony Snicket but unfortunately aren't as witty. [Illustrator Sophie] Blackall's black and white watercolor illustrations--mostly full-page, with a few splashes of spot art--add to the book's atmosphere with their soft cartoonishness and their creepy content (each of the later chapters is capped by an full page of the grim reaper hovering over a negative picture illustrating Alexander's death), making this an original story that could please young fans of wicked humor."

REVIEW: *Horn Book Magazine* v89 no5 p105-6 S/O 2013 SARAH ELLIS

REVIEW: *Kirkus Rev* v81 no16 p128 Ag 15 2013

REVIEW: *Publ Wkly* v260 no35 p61 S 2 2013

REVIEW: *SLJ* v59 no8 p103 Ag 2013 Miriam Lang Budin

MARCIONETTE, JAKE. Just Jake; [by] Jake Marcionette 160 p. 2014 Penguin Group USA

1. Bullying 2. Families—Fiction 3. Moving, Household 4. Popularity 5. School stories
ISBN 0448466929; 9780448466927

SUMMARY: In this book, "sixth-grader Jake Mathews' popularity has just fallen 'off a cliff and [sunk] to the bottom of the ocean.' That's what happens when your dad gets a new job and you're forced to change schools in the middle of the year. . . . But despite an older sister with a propensity for going ballistic and an intimidating search for a regular lunch table, Jake is determined to make the steep climb back up the social ladder." (Kirkus Reviews)

REVIEW: *Bull Cent Child Books* v67 no7 p366-7 Mr 2014 T. A.

REVIEW: *Kirkus Rev* v81 no24 p117 D 15 2013

"Just Jake". "This high-concept middle-grade novel appears to be aimed directly at fans of series like Diary of a Wimpy Kid. . . . Jake's first-person narrative looks and feels like a sixth-grader's real-time memoir, complete with . . . doodles. . . . Though Jake's bravado is grating at first, readers will easily relate to his desire to fit in and avoid the social land mines that litter most middle school landscapes. Unfortunately, readers are only given a brief introduction to the band of 'Misfit Toys' that Jake ultimately befriends. The novel would have benefited had Jake spent a little less time on his own awesomeness and a little more time letting readers get to know his new posse. It's an eye-catching read without a whole lot of depth."

REVIEW: *Publ Wkly* v260 no48 p57 N 25 2013

REVIEW: *SLJ* v60 no2 p93 F 2014 Megan McGinnis

MARCONI, CLEMENTE.ed. Sicily. See Sicily

MARCUS, BEN, 1967-. Leaving the sea; stories; [by] Ben Marcus 288 p. 2014 Alfred A. Knopf

1. Disillusionment 2. Dystopias 3. Families—Fiction 4. Short stories—Collections 5. Sick—Fiction
ISBN 0307379388; 9780307379382 (hardcover);

9780307739988 (trade pbk.)
LC 2013-004576

SUMMARY: This book, by Ben Marcus, is a collection of short "stories of strange worlds and estranged men, frequently tempered by inexplicable illness. In 'Rollingwood,' a corporate manager is left stranded when the mother of his asthmatic son disappears. . . . In 'The Dark Arts,' an American 'medical tourist' travels to Europe for stem-cell therapy." (Booklist)

REVIEW: *Booklist* v110 no7 p22 D 1 2013 Diego Báez

REVIEW: *Kirkus Rev* v81 no20 p85 O 15 2013

REVIEW: *Libr J* v138 no14 p105 S 1 2013 Robert E. Brown

REVIEW: *N Y Rev Books* v61 no2 p22-5 F 6 2014 Mark Ford

"Leaving the Sea." "Admirers of the experimental fiction of Ben Marcus are likely to find themselves somewhat baffled by the four stories that make up the first section of 'Leaving the Sea'--although not, perhaps, as baffled as the uninitiated reader who picked up Marcus's previous collection of stories. . . . "I Can Say Many Nice Things" . . . couldn't be called strange or hard or outside the realm of familiarity. It's pretty good, though. . . . 'Leaving the Sea' . . . is more stylistically varied than Marcus's previous three books would have led us to expect."

REVIEW: *N Y Times Book Rev* p12 Ja 26 2014 JIM KRUSOE

"Leaving the Sea: Stories." "The stories of [author Ben Marcus's] new collection, 'Leaving the Sea,' still contain peculiar linguistic and perceptual tics, but he has added to his arsenal narratives that are less relentlessly unfamiliar, less rigorously dis-enchanted, populated by characters full of longing and visible regret, though for what is not always clear. . . . In the end Marcus presents a deeper range of identification for the reader, more emotional complexity, but still plenty of the chair-gripping alienation that marked his previous books."

REVIEW: *Publ Wkly* v260 no29 p35 Jl 22 2013

REVIEW: *TLS* no5795 p22 Ap 25 2014 CLAIRE LOWDON

MARCUS, GEORGE H. The houses of Louis Kahn. See Whitaker, W.

MARCUS, LEONARD S., 1950-. Randolph Caldecott; the man who could not stop drawing; [by] Leonard S. Marcus 64 p. 2013 Farrar, Straus & Giroux (BYR)

1. Biographies 2. Illustration (Art)—History 3. Illustrators—England—Biography—Juvenile literature 4. Picture books for children—History & criticism
ISBN 0374310254; 9780374310257 (hardcover)
LC 2012-050406

SUMMARY: This book is a biography of Randolph Caldecott, "the illustrator for whom the Caldecott Medal is named." Leonard S. Marcus begins by "describing the changes wrought in 19th-century Great Britain by the steam engine, which eased travel and greatly expanded distribution of media. He details Caldecott's early days clerking in a bank and his search for freelance illustration work, then describes how diligence and charm lead to his first book-illustrating assignment" and then to a career in illustration. (Publishers Weekly)

REVIEW: *Booklist* v110 no2 p66 S 15 2013 Michael Cort

"Randolph Caldecott: The Man Who Could Not Stop Drawing." "[Leonard S.] Marcus does a superb job of summarizing Caldecott's busy life while focusing much of his attention on the work that defined him. In his acute analysis of the artist's work, Marcus, not surprisingly, gives major attention to the picture books, a form 'invented' by this 'incomparable innovator.' This beautifully designed and illustrated large-format volume is a worthy tribute to the man who remains a giant in the world of children's literature."

REVIEW: *Bull Cent Child Books* v67 no6 p341 F 2014

REVIEW: *Horn Book Magazine* v89 no6 p121-2 N/D 2013 KATHLEEN T. HORNING

REVIEW: *Kirkus Rev* v81 no16 p316 Ag 15 2013

REVIEW: *Publ Wkly* v260 no29 p71 Jl 22 2013

REVIEW: *Publ Wkly* p92-3 Children's starred review annual 2013

REVIEW: *SLJ* v59 no10 p1 O 2013 Wendy Lukehart

MARENTES, KATHLEEN. The Shadows Breathe; [by] Kathleen Marentes 602 p. 2013 CreateSpace Independent Publishing Platform

1. Adventure stories 2. Animal welfare—Fiction 3. Horse trainers 4. Horses—Fiction 5. Ranches
ISBN 1492862894; 9781492862895

SUMMARY: In this book, by Kathleen Marentes, "a young Nebraskan horse trainer and her friends try to thwart misdeeds by the ranch's new head trainer in this adventure novel. . . . Ryan Jackson has very different ideas about how to treat horses; in fact, he may be abusing them, using drugs and other means. . . . Kara and her friends gather evidence to prove that horses are being mistreated and try to find a way to rescue them." (Kirkus Reviews)

REVIEW: *Kirkus Rev* v82 no3 p349 F 1 2014

"The Shadows Breathe". "In her debut, [Kathleen] Marentes offers an appealingly brave, resourceful and compassionate lead character with an important task to accomplish. Other, secondary characters (including the horses) appealingly add to the story. Animal lovers may find some scenes unpleasant to read, but Marentes doesn't shamelessly tug heartstrings. . . .The novel effectively complicates the plot with more and more elaborate escapades, but all the postponements may begin to feel contrived, as when Kara loses evidence or fails to get it at a crucial moment. When the plans finally come together, however, the novel provides a satisfying denouement. An often entertaining, suspenseful novel that may particularly interest readers who love horses."

MARENTETTE, MEGHAN. The stowaways; 240 p. 2014 Orca Book Pub

1. Adventure stories 2. Families—Juvenile fiction 3. Family secrets 4. Grandparents—Fiction 5. Mice—Juvenile fiction
ISBN 1927485339; 9781927485330

SUMMARY: In this book, by Meghan Marentette and illustrated by Dean Griffiths, "the Stowaways aren't like the other Weedle mice. They are inventive and curious, they go on adventures, and they are much too clever for their own good. In fact, everyone knows that Grampa Stowaway was killed in a trap on one of his adventures. . . . There's something else about the Stowaways. They keep secrets." (Publisher's note)

REVIEW: *Booklist* v110 no16 p52 Ap 15 2014 Carolyn Phelan

REVIEW: *Bull Cent Child Books* v67 no10 p531 Je 2014 J. H.

"The Stowaways". "While the plot moves along at a nice clip, there's minimal character development here, and the writing is sometimes flat. The details of the mice's environment (Morgan constructs a bicycle from bits and bobs after riding a dollhouse version, for example) may nonetheless capture the imaginations of kids with a love for miniature worlds. . . . [Dead] 11). Griffiths' occasional, naturalistic illustrations in monochromatic tones have an endearing warmth, although the mice tend to be more skillfully depicted than the humans."

REVIEW: *Kirkus Rev* v82 no4 p170 F 15 2014

REVIEW: *Quill Quire* v79 no8 p38 O 2013 Deirdre Baker

REVIEW: *SLJ* v60 no3 p120 Mr 2014 Stacy Dillon

MARGIOTTA, KRISTEN.il. Gustav Gloom and The Nightmare Vault. See Castro, Adam-Troy.

MARGULIES, DONALD. Collected stories; [by] Donald Margulies 2010 Dramatist's Play Service, Inc.
ISBN 9780822216407 (pbk.)
LC 2012-533867

SUMMARY: This play, by Donald Margulies, "takes place in the early 90's in Greenwich Village. A young writer and student (Debra) has applied for a job as an assistant/gopher to an elderly teacher and successfully published writer, Ruth Steiner. She undergoes tutorials with Ruth and they develop a friendship." (Amazon)

REVIEW: *London Rev Books* v35 no12 p3-6 Je 20 2013 James Meek

REVIEW: *TLS* no5748 p19-20 My 31 2013 MICHAEL SALER

"All That Is" and "Collected Stories." "Such extravaganzas more commonly serve as a novel's climax, but here they are merely the prologue to a narrative of everyday experience, which appears as no less significant than global conflict. Since the beginning of his literary career in the 1950s, Salter's genius has been to invoke the ancient muses to chant about modern existence making the ordinary revelatory of heroism, tragedy and mystery in a secular world. . . . The often dark tales in his 'Collected Stories,' also gesture towards an occult dimension while never departing from a naturalistic register."

MARK, LISA GABRIELLE.ed. Mike Kelley. See Mike Kelley

MARKEY, DANIEL S. No exit from Pakistan; America's tortured relationship with Islamabad; [by] Daniel S. Markey xii, 248 p. 2013 Cambridge University Press
1. Anti-Americanism—Pakistan 2. Political science literature
ISBN 9781107045460 (hardback: alkaline paper); 9781107623590 (paperback)
LC 2013-019456

SUMMARY: "This book explores the main trends in Pakistani society that will help determine its future; traces the wellsprings of Pakistani anti-American sentiment through the history of U.S.-Pakistan relations from 1947 to 2001; assesses how Washington made and implemented policies regarding Pakistan since the terrorist attacks on the United States on September 11, 2001; and analyzes how regional dynamics, especially the rise of China, will likely shape U.S.-Pakistan relations." (Publisher's note)

REVIEW: *Choice* v51 no12 p2266 Ag 2014 M. L. Keck

REVIEW: *N Y Rev Books* v61 no5 p26-8 Mr 20 2014 Anatol Lieven

"No Exit From Pakistan: America's Tortured Relationship With Islamabad," "The Way of the Knife: The CIA, a Secret Army, and a War at the Ends of the Earth," and "Magnificent Delusion: Pakistan, the United States, and an Epic History of Misunderstanding". "'The Way of the Knife' . . . [is a] powerful exposé. . . . It would . . . be a pity if Pakistanis simply dismiss [Husain] Haqqani's book, because if it does not contain nearly enough that Americans need to hear, it contains a great deal that Pakistanis badly need to hear, and that they very rarely do hear from their own media. . . . [Daniel] Markey has little to suggest beyond the development of new drone technology, and the possible extension of missile attacks to new parts of Pakistan."

MARKO, CYNDI. Bok! bok! boom!; [by] Cyndi Marko 80 p. 2014 Branches Scholastic Inc.
1. Chickens—Fiction 2. Chickens—Juvenile fiction 3. Humorous stories 4. Rescues—Fiction 5. Rescues—Juvenile fiction 6. Superheroes—Fiction 7. Superheroes—Juvenile fiction 8. Supervillains—Fiction 9. Supervillains—Juvenile fiction
ISBN 054561063X (pbk. : alk. paper); 0545610648 (hardcover : alk. paper)
LC 2013-027608

SUMMARY: In this book, by Cyndi Marko, "Gordon Blue's mom drags him to a night at the opera. The show turns fowl though when its star singer, Honey Comb, is chicknapped! The evil Dr. Screech plans to turn the singer's super-high voice into a . . . weapon. It's up to Kung Pow Chicken to rescue Honey!" (Publisher's note)

REVIEW: *Bull Cent Child Books* v67 no7 p367 Mr 2014 J. H.

"Kung Power Chicken: Let's Get Cracking" and "Kung Pow Chicken: Bok! Bok! Boom!" "The combination of chickens and kid superheroes is absurdly compelling; primary-graders will chortle over all the poultry puns, elementary-school humor . . . and Benny's smart-aleck asides. . . . [Cyndi] Marko's art is as playful as her text. . . .The simple vocabulary and small chunks of text make this extremely accessible to the primary-grade crowd, and kids who want something short and funny . . . will find this just their speed."

MARKO, CYNDI.il. Let's get cracking! See Marko, C.

MARKO, CYNDI. Let's get cracking!; [by] Cyndi Marko 72 p. 2014 Branches Scholastic Inc.
1. Chickens—Fiction 2. Chickens—Juvenile fiction 3. Cookies—Fiction 4. Cookies—Juvenile fiction 5. Humorous stories 6. Superheroes—Fiction 7. Superheroes—Juvenile fiction
ISBN 9780545610612 (pbk.); 9780545610629 (hardcover)

LC 2013-018130

SUMMARY: In this book, by Cyndi Marko, "Gordon Blue transforms into Kung Pow Chicken, an avian superhero who fights crime in the city of Fowladelphia. The first book in the series kicks off when Gordon's birdy senses lead him to a festival. Suddenly, POOF! Feathers fill the air and shivering naked chickens are everywhere. Why have all these chickens lost their feathers? Forced to wear wooly sweaters, the city itches for a hero. Kung Pow Chicken hops into his Beakmobile to save the day!" (Publisher's note)

REVIEW: *Bull Cent Child Books* v67 no7 p367 Mr 2014 J. H.

"Kung Power Chicken: Let's Get Cracking" and "Kung Pow Chicken: Bok! Bok! Boom!" "The combination of chickens and kid superheroes is absurdly compelling; primary-graders will chortle over all the poultry puns, elementary-school humor . . . and Benny's smart-aleck asides. . . . [Cyndi] Marko's art is as playful as her text. . . . The simple vocabulary and small chunks of text make this extremely accessible to the primary-grade crowd, and kids who want something short and funny . . . will find this just their speed."

MARKOVA, EUGENIA. Undocumented workers' transitions. See McKay, S.

MARKS, ALAN, 1957-.il. Behold the beautiful dung beetle. See Bardoe, C.

MARKWYN, ABIGAIL M.ed. Gendering the fair. See Gendering the fair

MARMELL, ARI. False covenant; a Widdershins adventure; [by] Ari Marmell 281 p. 2012 Pyr

1. Fantasy 2. Gods—Fiction 3. Magic in literature 4. Robbers and outlaws—Fiction 5. Thieves in literature

ISBN 1616146214; 9781616146214 (cloth)

LC 2012-000416

SUMMARY: In this book, by Ari Marmell, "street-rat-turned-noble-turned-thief–and now turned bar owner–Widdershins and her deity Olgun . . . are trying their hand at honest living, but it's not working out. When they go back to the criminal life, they stumble into another big conspiracy of crime and dark magic, find themselves allied with . . . Major Bouniard of the city Guard and, more reluctantly, with a disgraced nobleman out to destroy Widdershins in revenge." (Kirkus Reviews)

REVIEW: *Kirkus Rev* v80 no8 p137 Ap 15 2012

"False Covenant." "[Ari] Marmell's occasionally florid writing and hackneyed dialogue can't detract from the gory adventures (including a wonderfully macabre bad guy), but beneath the action lies a deeper, if unsubtle, tale of loss and love. Secondary characters may be types and primary characters tropes, but genuinely adolescent (including occasional idiotic and immature behavior) high fantasy is rare enough that this stands out. A romp with an edge and a feisty female lead: Fans will rejoice at the indication that this series has even more to come."

REVIEW: *SLJ* v58 no8 p109 Ag 2012 Wendy M. Scalfaro

MAROH, JULIE. Blue Is the Warmest Color; [by] Julie Maroh 160 p. 2013 Arsenal Pulp Press

1. Dating (Social customs)—Comic books, strips, etc 2. Lesbians—Comic books, strips, etc 3. Lesbians—Fiction 4. Lesbians—Identity—Comic books, strips, etc 5. Love stories

ISBN 1551525143; 9781551525143

LC 2013-432454

SUMMARY: In this graphic novel by Julie Maroh, "a young woman named Clementine discovers herself and the elusive magic of love when she meets a confident blue-haired girl named Emma: a lesbian love story . . . that bristles with the energy of youth and rebellion and the eternal light of desire." (Publisher's note)

REVIEW: *Kirkus Rev* v81 no17 p104 S 1 2013

REVIEW: *N Y Times Book Rev* p20-1 D 15 2013 Douglas Wolk

"Nowhere Men, Vol. 1: Fates Worse Than Death," "Blue Is the Warmest Color," "Woman Rebel: The Margaret Sanger Story." "Thanks to the imminent 50th anniversary of the British Invasion, we're seeing a small wave comics inspired by the Beatles, none more inventive than Eric Stephenson and Nate Bellegarde's 'Nowhere Men, Vol. 1: Fates Worse Than Death.' . . . Julie Maroh's first graphic novel, 'Blue Is the Warmest Color,' was published in France in 2010. . . . Her delicate linework and ink-wash effects illuminate the story's quiet pauses and the characters' fraught silences and wordless longing. . . . 'Woman Rebel: The Margaret Sanger Story' . . , a biography of the birth-control activist . . . , is an unlikely but inspired pairing of author and subject."

REVIEW: *Publ Wkly* v260 no37 p34 S 16 2013

MAROUAN, MAHA. Witches, goddesses, and angry spirits; the politics of spiritual liberation in African diaspora women's fiction; [by] Maha Marouan 180 p. 2013 Ohio State University Press

1. African American women authors 2. African American women in literature 3. African diaspora in literature 4. American fiction—African American authors—History and criticism 5. American fiction—Women authors—History and criticism 6. Literary critiques

ISBN 0814212190 (cloth : alk. paper); 9780814212196 (cloth : alk. paper); 9780814293201 (cd)

LC 2012-039927

SUMMARY: This book "explores the construction of African diaspora female spirituality in works by three contemporary black writers of the Americas: Edwidge Danticat ('Breath, Eyes, Memory'), Toni Morrison ('Paradise'), and Maryse Conde ('Tituba, Black Witch of Salem'). In particular, [Maha] Marouan argues that these three writers use diasporic religious practices to empower their female characters and celebrate African diaspora womanbood while challenging essentialist identities and stereotypes." (Choice)

REVIEW: *Choice* v51 no4 p638-9 D 2013 D. E. Magill

"Witches, Goddesses, and Angry Spirits: The Politics of Spiritual Liberation in African Diaspora Women's Fiction." "[Maha Marouan] draws on scholarship and theory from religion, history, literature, gender studies, and postcolonialism, balancing them nicely to support her interpretations of the central works. . . . This volume contributes usefully to African diaspora studies, American literary studies, and feminist religious thought; its transnational focus allows Marouan to enrich and challenge understanding of the cultural narratives that define black diasporic womanhood and spirituality. . . . Highly recommended."

MARR, MELISSA. Desert tales; a Wicked lovely novel; [by] Melissa Marr 272 p. 2013 Harper, an imprint of HarperCollinsPublishers

1. Deserts—Fiction 2. Fairies—Fiction 3. Fantasy 4. Love—Fiction 5. Mojave Desert
ISBN 0062287567; 9780062287564 (pbk.)
LC 2013-032158

SUMMARY: In this book, a companion to author Melissa Marr's "Wicked Lovely" series, "the Mojave Desert was a million miles away from the plots and schemes of the Faerie Courts--and that's exactly why Rika chose it as her home. . . . But her seclusion--and the freedom of the desert fey--is threatened by the Summer King's newfound strength. And when the manipulations of her trickster friend, Sionnach, thrust Rika into a new romance, she finds new power within herself." (Publisher's note)

REVIEW: *Booklist* v110 no1 p65 S 1 2013 Gillian Engberg

"Dangerous," "Desert Tales," and "The Edge of the Water." "The acclaimed, best-selling author [Shannon Hale] takes a new direction in this fantasy adventure, in which an unsuspecting heroine discovers a terrifying plot against society-and falls in love along the way. . . . In this new companion to the blockbuster Wicked Lovely series, [Melissa] Marr focuses on faery Rika, whose free, isolated existence in the Mojave Desert is transformed by both a king's power and a new romance. . . . The second YA title from best-selling adult crime novelist [Elizabeth] George is the first entry in a new paranormal mystery series set on Washington state's Whidbey Island."

REVIEW: *Booklist* v110 no4 p47 O 15 2013 Frances Bradburn

MARRA, ANTHONY. A constellation of vital phenomena; a novel; [by] Anthony Marra 400 p. 2013 Hogarth

1. Hospitals—Russia—Fiction 2. Refugees—Fiction 3. War stories 4. Women physicians—Fiction
ISBN 0770436404; 9780770436407
LC 2012-017444

SUMMARY: This novel "intertwines the stories of a handful of characters at the end of the second, war in bleak, apocalyptic Chechnya. Though the novel spans 11 years, the story traces five days in 2004 following the arrest of Dokka, a villager from the small Muslim village of Eldar. His eight-year-old daughter escapes, and is rescued by Dokka's friend Akhmed, the village doctor, who entrusts her to the care of Sonja, the lone remaining doctor at a nearby hospital." (Publishers Weekly)

REVIEW: *Booklist* v109 no15 p21 Ap 1 2013 Joanne Wilkinson

REVIEW: *Economist* v408 no8843 p79 Jl 6 2013

REVIEW: *Kirkus Rev* p25 N 15 2013 Best Books

REVIEW: *Kirkus Rev* v81 no5 p242 Mr 1 2013

REVIEW: *Libr J* v138 no6 p75 Ap 1 2013 Michael Pucci

REVIEW: *N Y Times Book Rev* p13 Je 9 2013 MADISON SMARTT BELL

REVIEW: *N Y Times Book Rev* p28 Je 16 2013

REVIEW: *New York Times* v162 no56130 pC1-4 My 8 2013 DWIGHT GARNER

REVIEW: *New York Times* v162 no56162 p13 Je 9 2013 MADISON SMARTT BELL

REVIEW: *New Yorker* v89 no19 p69 Jl 1 2013

REVIEW: *Publ Wkly* v260 no44 p20-34 N 4 2013

REVIEW: *Publ Wkly* v260 no7 p36 F 18 2013

REVIEW: *TLS* no5753 p21 Jl 5 2013 LUKE NEIMA

REVIEW: *World Lit Today* v87 no5 p60-1 S/O 2013 W. M. Hagen

"A Constellation of Vital Phenomena." "I can only echo the amazement of other reviewers: that such an accomplished novel is Anthony Marra's first and that he visited Chechnya, the setting, only after he had all hut completed it. . . . Centering on the characters' stories and their attempts to cope with an unstable political/military situation. Marra keeps the style straightforward and informative. The texture of their experience comes primarily from character interchanges . . . Some readers may be disappointed that political history is slighted, that there is not more on the religious fervor of the Chechen rebels. But the novel reminds us that such wars entangle many who are not impelled to fight and want nothing more than a return to something approaching normalcy."

MARRIN, ALBERT, 1936-. A volcano beneath the snow; John Brown's war against slavery; [by] Albert Marrin 256 p. 2014 Alfred A. Knopf

1. Abolitionists—United States—Biography—Juvenile literature 2. Harpers Ferry (W. Va.)—History—John Brown's Raid, 1859 3. Historical literature 4. Violence—Moral & ethical aspects
ISBN 0307981525; 9780307981523 (trade); 9780307981530 (lib. bdg.)
LC 2012-043231

SUMMARY: This book, by Albert Marrin, focuses on John Brown. "Deeply religious, Brown believed that God had chosen him to right the wrong of slavery. He was willing to kill and die for something modern Americans unanimously agree was a just cause. And yet he was a religious fanatic and a staunch believer in 'righteous violence,' an unapologetic committer of domestic terrorism." (Publisher's note)

REVIEW: *Booklist* v110 no14 p73 Mr 15 2014 Michael Cart

REVIEW: *Bull Cent Child Books* v67 no8 p415 Ap 2014

"A Volcano Beneath the Snow: John Brown's War Against Slavery". "By the time young adults teach for this lengthy, double-columned text on John Brown, they will likely be familiar with the 1859 debacle at Harpers Ferry. . . . [Albert] Marrin refuses to take an easy way out by writing Brown off as a religious fanatic or a madman or even a common criminal, and in so doing forces readers into the maelstrom of mid-nineteenth century debate, to determine the most expeditious road to justice, unaided by twenty-first century hindsight. This is a rewarding work for serious adolescent readers, and educators who are equally serious about nurturing informed social criticism within their students will welcome this challenging title."

REVIEW: *Horn Book Magazine* v90 no2 p144 Mr/Ap 2014 DEAN SCHNEIDER

REVIEW: *Kirkus Rev* v82 no4 p162 F 15 2014

REVIEW: *SLJ* v60 no3 p181 Mr 2014 Carol S. Surges

REVIEW: *Voice of Youth Advocates* v37 no1 p93 Ap 2014 Sharon Martin

MARRIOTT, JAMES. The oil road; journeys from the Caspian Sea to the city of London; [by] James Marriott xiv, 362 p. 2012 Verso

1. Petroleum industry—Social aspects 2. Petroleum industry and trade—Azerbaijan—Baku 3. Petroleum industry and trade—Europe 4. Petroleum pipelines 5. Travelers' writings
ISBN 9781844676453; 9781844676460 (hardback : alk. paper); 9781844679270 (ebook)
LC 2012-019763

SUMMARY: This book on the oil industry "takes the form of a travelogue tracing . . . [the authors'] 1,100-mile journey in 2005 along the oil export pipline from Baku on the Caspian Sea to Turkey's Mediterranean port of Ceyhan. . . . The book argues that unlike the romantic Silk Road of medieval times, the new Oil Road tramples on the health and security of local denizens." (Times Literary Supplement)

REVIEW: *TLS* no5750 p10 Je 14 2013 PETER RUTLAND

"Wheel of Fortune: The Battle for Oil and Power in Russia" and "The Oil Road: Journeys From the Caspian Sea to the City of London." "Thane Gustafson has produced what will surely be the definitive work on this subject. . . . Having been present at the creation, he is uniquely placed to combine an insider's knowledge of how the industry works with academic analytical skills and a sophisticated understanding of Russian culture and politics. . . . In contrast to Gustafson's highly sympathetic account, James Marriott and Mika Minio-Paluello's book seeks to expose a sinister 'carbon web' of oilmen and their political cronies. . . . The authors try to evoke the richness of the places en route and the people whose lives are affected. Unfortunately, they have neither the local knowledge nor vivid enough personal encounters to pull this off."

MARRON, CATIE. City Parks; Public Places, Private Thoughts; 304 p. 2013 HarperCollins

1. Black & white photography 2. Grant Park (Chicago, Ill.) 3. Photography of parks 4. Presidio of San Francisco (Calif.) 5. Urban parks
ISBN 0062231790; 9780062231796

SUMMARY: "Catie Marron's 'City Parks' captures the spirit and beauty of eighteen of the world's most-loved city parks. Zadie Smith, Ian Frazier, Candice Bergen, Colm Tóibín, Nicole Krauss, Jan Morris, and a dozen other . . . contributors reflect on a particular park that holds special meaning for them. . . . Oberto Gili's color and black-and-white photographs unify the writers' unique and personal voices." (Publisher's note)

REVIEW: *N Y Times Book Rev* p53 D 8 2013 ALIDA BECKER

"City Parks: Public Places, Private Thoughts," "Private Gardens of the Hudson Valley," and "Quiet Beauty: The Japanese Gardens of North America." "The 18 contributors to Catie Marron's 'City Parks: Public Places, Private Thoughts' have . . . [created] an eloquent reminder of the way shard landscapes can provide intimate inspiration. . . . In 'Private Gardens of the Hudson Valley,' Jane Garmey and John M. Hall's follow-up . . . There's also some interesting whimsy. . . . Just flipping through the pages of 'Quiet Beauty: The Japanese Gardens of North America' will instantly lower your blood pressure."

MARSA, LINDA. Fevered; why a hotter planet will hurt our health and how we can save ourselves; [by] Linda Marsa 256 p. 2013 Rodale

1. Environmental policy literature 2. Environmentally induced diseases 3. Extreme weather—Health aspects 4. Fever—Etiology 5. Global warming—Health aspects 6. Medical literature
ISBN 9781605292014 (hardcover)
LC 2013-009887

SUMMARY: In this book, "journalist Linda Marsa blends compelling narrative with cutting-edge science to explore the changes in Earth's increasingly fragile support system and provide a blueprint--a 'medical Manhattan Project'--detailing what we need to do to protect ourselves from this imminent medical meltdown. . . . Marsa . . . argues why preparedness for the health effects of climate change is the most critical issue affecting our survival in the coming century." (Publisher's note)

REVIEW: *Booklist* v109 no21 p10 Jl 1 2013 Tony Miksanek

REVIEW: *Kirkus Rev* v81 no12 p57 Je 15 2013

REVIEW: *N Y Times Book Rev* p26 Ja 12 2014 Coral Davenport

"The Climate Casino: Risk, Uncertainty, and Economics for a Warming World," "Fevered: Why a Hotter Planet Will Hurt Our Health--And How We Can Save Ourselves," and "The Melting World: A Journey Across America's Vanishing Glaciers." "'The Climate Casino' reads like a highly engaging college textbook. [Author William] Nordhaus's tone is conversations . . . , but too many passages bog down in technical jargon. . . . Crammed with statistics, interviews and gruesome but fund facts, 'Fevered' makes its case with plenty of hard evidence. . . . 'The Melting World' takes readers to the glacial peaks with [scientist Daniel] Fagre and his team. . . . The book would have benefited from a tighter edit. . . . Despite that, a moving story emerges."

REVIEW: *Publ Wkly* v260 no19 p57 My 13 2013

MARSDEN, GEORGE M., 1939-. The twilight of the American enlightenment; the 1950s and the crisis of liberal belief; [by] George M. Marsden 264 p. 2013 Basic Books

1. Alienation (Social psychology)—United States—History—20th century 2. Cold War—Social aspects—United States 3. Group identity—United States—History—20th century 4. HISTORY—United States—20th Century 5. Historical literature 6. POLITICAL SCIENCE—Po
ISBN 9780465030101 (hardback); 9780465069774 (ebook)
LC 2013-032100

SUMMARY: In this book, George Marsden "employs historical analysis to suggest why the United States is so badly split between secular-oriented intellectuals and religiously doctrinaire church leaders. . . . Marsden criticizes the secularists who received attention in the 1950s for failing to recognize the sincerity and depth of religion-based intellectuals, but he also criticizes the religionists for failing to advocate for inclusive pluralism." (Kirkus Reviews)

REVIEW: *Bookforum* v20 no5 p40 F/Mr 2014 STEPHEN PROTHERO

REVIEW: *Christ Century* v131 no9 p40-2 Ap 30 2014 Kevin M. Schultz

REVIEW: *Commonweal* v141 no8 p31-2 My 2 2014 Andrew J. Bacevich

REVIEW: *Kirkus Rev* v82 no1 p110 Ja 1 2014

REVIEW: *Nation* v298 no8 p27-33 F 24 2014 CHRIS LEHMANN

"Apostles of Reason: The Crisis of Authority in American Evangelicalism" and "The Twilight of the American Enlightenment: The 1950s and the Crisis of Liberal Belief." "[Molly] Worthen, who is not an evangelical herself but takes the intellectual struggles of the community quite seriously as a scholar, depicts the movement in a light that is at once far more nuanced and sympathetic than what passes for serious analysis on the left, while also supplying an intellectual profile of modern evangelical thought that's at least as damning as the far more visceral secular denunciations of the religious right. . . . [George] Marsden is persuasive here--until he overreaches. . . . It's difficult, in surveying the arc of Marsden's argument, to avoid the conclusion that the author is imposing his own set of theological presuppositions on the scene before him."

REVIEW: *Publ Wkly* v260 no50 p62 D 9 2013

MARSH, DAVID. For Who the Bell Tolls; [by] David Marsh 304 p. 2013 Guardian Faber Publishing

1. Comparative grammar 2. Editors 3. English wit & humor 4. Linguistic usage 5. Literature—History & criticism

ISBN 1783350121; 9781783350124

SUMMARY: In this book on grammar and usage, David Marsh critiques "sloppy syntax, a disregard for grammar or a fundamental misunderstanding of what grammar is." He also critiques "an adherence to 'rules' that have no real basis and get in the way of fluent, unambiguous communication at the expense of ones that are actually useful." (Publisher's note)

REVIEW: *TLS* no5772 p36 N 15 2013 J. C.

"Alien Hearts," "Biteback Dictionary of Humorous Literary Quotations," and "For Who the Bell Tolls." "It is a wonderful novel, written as the author's fatal sickness was taking grip. . . . 'Notre Coeur' is available in English as 'Alien Hearts,' in a translation by Richard Howard . . . which claims to be 'the first in more than a hundred years,' but this overlooks Marjorie Laurie's 1929 version. . . . Of the 'Biteback Dictionary of Humorous Literary Quotations' we ask only two things: that it be humorous, and that we know where the jokes are coming from. . . . We delved to the index, to find that the Dictionary doesn't have one. . . . The grammar may be correct under a precise anatomical gaze, but Mr [David] Marsh illustrates how proper usage is not always best usage."

MARSHACK, KATHY J. Out of Mind - Out of Sight; Parenting With a Partner With Asperger Syndrome; [by] Kathy J. Marshack 294 p. 2013 Createspace Independent Pub

1. Advice literature 2. Asperger's syndrome 3. Autistic people—Family relationships 4. Parenting 5. Parents of autistic children

ISBN 1481930885; 9781481930888

SUMMARY: This book by Kathy J. Marshack offers "advice for dealing effectively with a spouse or child diagnosed with Asperger's syndrome. . . . In Part 1, she discusses common behaviors of people suffering from Asperger's and of 'neurotypical' family members. . . . In Part 2, Marshack reveals the condition as essentially an empathy disorder. . . . Parts 3 and 4 offer additional insights into the lives of neurotypicals, who often feel invisible and ignored." (Kirkus Reviews)

REVIEW: *Kirkus Rev* v82 no2 p340 Ja 15 2014

"Out of Mind—Out of Sight: Parenting With a Partner With Asperger Syndrome (ASD)". "The author mercifully keeps the clinical jargon to a minimum, and the prose is cogent and well-organized throughout. At the end, she provides links to online support groups, websites, phone numbers and other helpful resources. Her personal accounts of her family life and clinical practice should resonate with readers seeking to understand Asperger's and may help to assure them that they are not alone. A useful, enlightening guide to understanding and coping with Asperger's syndrome."

MARSHALL, ASHLEY. The practice of satire in England, 1658-1770; [by] Ashley Marshall xviii, 430 p. 2013 Johns Hopkins University Press

1. English literature—17th century—History and criticism 2. English literature—18th century—History and criticism 3. Literature—History & criticism 4. Satire—History 5. Satire, English—History and criticism

ISBN 1421408163 (hdbk. : alk. paper); 1421408171 (electronic); 9781421408163 (hdbk. : alk. paper); 9781421408170 (electronic)

LC 2012-025275

SUMMARY: "In 'The Practice of Satire in England, 1658-1770,' Ashley Marshall explores how satire was conceived and understood by writers and readers of the period. Her account is based on a reading of some 3,000 works ranging from one-page squibs to novels. The objective is not to recuperate particular minor works but to recover the satiric milieu--to resituate the masterpieces amid the hundreds of other works alongside which they were originally written and read." (Publisher's note)

REVIEW: *Choice* v51 no9 p1593-4 My 2014 C. S. Vilmar

REVIEW: *TLS* no5788 p3-4 Mr 7 2014 CLAUDE RAWSON

"The Practice of Satire in England 1658-1770." "[Author Ashley] Marshall courts a danger [poet T. S.] Eliot saw in the old genre histories, of lapsing into mere 'chronicle.' Her narrative is so crammed with titles of works of every kind that it is sometimes hard to see what else to call it. Her purpose is to classify the varied writings into types, and she seems to believe that taxonomy is a sufficient relief from mere enumeration. She has a point, though her taxonomic categories are sometimes too crude to provide intellectual sustenance. . . . This strong and wide-ranging book is nevertheless the work of a learned and energetic scholar. It earns its authority from the wealth of information it provides, rather than from its taxonomic skills or from interpretative performances."

MARSHALL, JEANNIE. The lost art of feeding kids; what Italy taught me about why children need real food; [by] Jeannie Marshall 240 p. 2013 Beacon Press

1. Children—Nutrition—Italy 2. Children—Nutrition—United States 3. Food habits—Italy 4. Food habits—United States 5. Food industry and trade—Health aspects 6. Social science literature

ISBN 0807032999; 9780807032992 (hardback); 9780807033005 (ebook)

LC 2013-001973

SUMMARY: In this book, "a Canadian journalist living in Rome shares her experience of trying to feed her baby in the traditional Italian style and segues into an exploration of why European food culture is giving way to Americanized processed, packaged, and industrially produced foods. . . . Not only does [Jeannie] Marshall see the U.S. exporting obesity and reduced crop diversity, she sees cultural traditions being lost abroad." (Publishers Weekly)

REVIEW: *Kirkus Rev* v81 no24 p7 D 15 2013

"The Lost Art of Feeding Kids: What Italy Taught Me About Why Children Need Real Food". ". "[Jeannie] Marshall also examines the public relations machine that offers a solution for harried mothers and fathers who go into parenting with the best of intentions but find their resolve eroded by a constant message from the food industry to buy cereal bars, crackers, cookies and yogurt and feel satisfied about it—maybe it's organic or doesn't contain high-fructose corn syrup, and it's 'packed with nutrients.' Marshall's clear, direct book ably captures the frustrations of trying to find the healthiest path and inspiring kids to do the same.

REVIEW: *Publ Wkly* v260 no40 p47 O 7 2013

MARSHALL, MICHAEL. We Are Here; [by] Michael Marshall 320 p. 2014 Little Brown & Co

1. Mind & reality 2. New York (N.Y.)—Fiction 3. Paranormal fiction 4. Stalking—Fiction 5. Suspense fiction
ISBN 0316252573; 9780316252577

SUMMARY: In this book by Michael Marshall, "people are being stalked on the streets of New York but not in the usual fashion. The stalkers are part of a strange underworld of rejected 'shadow people' who disappear as suddenly as they appear. First-person narrator John Henderson, a former lawyer now working in a restaurant, discovers that the shadow people are not easy to tail." (Kirkus Reviews)

REVIEW: *Booklist* v110 no9/10 p53-4 Ja 1 2014 Don Crinklaw

"We Are Here". "For the first half of this novel, readers will believe they're in a tingly thriller. . . . Some fine scenes, suspenseful and witty, ensue as John and his girlfriend mount their own surveillance. They walk fast, maintaining cell-phone contact, and notice that, yes, someone is tracking their friend of a friend. Odd, though: whoever it is can disappear as quickly as that person on the platform. Here's where the thriller dead-ends, and the fantasy begins. Or maybe it's magic realism. Suddenly there's a new mystery to solve. When the dreamer forgets the dream, does it live on anyway? Readers comfortable with mixing genres will enjoy the ride, while others may want to get off at the first stop."

REVIEW: *Kirkus Rev* v82 no1 p230 Ja 1 2014

"We Are Here". "Is this book a ghost story? A Stephen King-style shocker? An allegory about the neglected underclass? [Michael] Marshall takes so long to reveal the most basic details, and his writing can be so obtuse, readers may lose interest by the time they find their footing. But in the final third, Marshall puts the pieces together to unsettling effect. It helps that John and Kristina, who share an East Village apartment, are such a winning duo. Though laborious at times, Marshall's novel rewards the reader's patience with its edgy storytelling and ambition."

REVIEW: *Publ Wkly* v260 no50 p48 D 9 2013

REVIEW: *TLS* no5752 p27 Je 28 2013 TIM PASHLEY

MARSHALL, NATALIE. Numbers; [by] Natalie Marshall 12 p. 2013 Little Brown & Co

1. Bears—Juvenile literature 2. Board books 3. Counting 4. Learning 5. Picture books for children
ISBN 031625164X; 9780316251648
LC 2012-953545

SUMMARY: Written by Natalie Marshall and part of the My Turn to Learn series, this book "uses simple, colorful images and bold, lively scenes to teach early counting concepts. The tabbed edges and thick, strong pages make it easy for young readers to flip through the book by themselves, revealing fun, colorful answers on every spread." (Publisher's note)

REVIEW: *Kirkus Rev* v81 no18 p340 S 15 2013

REVIEW: *Kirkus Rev* v82 no1 p16 Ja 1 2014

"My Turn to Learn Numbers". "This simple counting book starring a sweet brown bear is perfect for little hands. . . . the number words are in large capital letters, and the nouns that follow them appear in cursive, an unusual choice for a board book and one that adds a touch of whimsy to the sweet, digitally produced illustrations. . . . Numbers six to 10 are grouped together on a final page spread. Large tabs labeled 1 through 5 run down the length of the rightmost edge of this sturdy selection, making it a cinch for little hands to grasp and open. . . . The deceptively simple and visually appealing My Turn to Learn series is a great tool for introducing basic concepts to the littlest readers."

REVIEW: *Kirkus Rev* p60 N 15 2013 Best Books

MARSICO, KATIE. Saltwater crocodiles; [by] Katie Marsico 48 p. 2013 Children's Press, an Imprint of Scholastic Inc.

1. Children's nonfiction 2. Crocodiles—Juvenile literature 3. Crocodylus porosus—Juvenile literature 4. Ecology—Juvenile literature 5. Food chains (Ecology)
ISBN 9780531233610 (library binding); 9780531251591 (pbk.)
LC 2013-000094

SUMMARY: This book on saltwater crocodiles by Katie Marsico is part of the Nature's Children series, which "provide[s] . . . introductions to wild animals around the world." It "spotlights a crocodile at the top of its food chain in Southeast Asia and northern Australia." Topics include "the animal's features, behaviors, life cycle, relatives, [and] contributions to its ecosystem." (Booklist)

REVIEW: *Booklist* v110 no6 p37-8 N 15 2013 Carolyn Phelan

"Geckos," "Saltwater Crocodiles," and "Snow Leopards." "Books in the long-running Nature's Children series provide informative introductions to wild animals around the world. . . . Features of particular interest to students include the range map in each volume and the opening, one-page 'Fact File' feature, which briefly lays out basic information such as the animal's species, distribution around the world, habitats, physical characteristics, habits, and diet. . . . With their clear organization, colorful photos, and straightforward presentation of facts, these books are well designed for students researching and writing reports on specific animals."

MARTIN, ANTHONY J. Dinosaurs Without Bones; Dinosaur Lives Revealed by Their Trace Fossils; [by] Anthony J. Martin 368 p. 2014 W W Norton & Co Inc

1. Dinosaurs—Behavior 2. Dinosaurs—Physiology 3. Ichnology 4. Scientific literature 5. Trace fossils

ISBN 160598499X; 9781605984995

SUMMARY: This book by Anthony J. Martin explores the field of "ichnology—the study of trace fossils and features left by organismal behavior, such as tracks, nests, and burrows. These yield evidence that is both more abundant than the bones, which Martin playfully disparages as 'body fossils,' and reveal more about how, where, and when dinosaurs live, moved, ate, and raised their young." (Publishers Weekly)

REVIEW: *Choice* v52 no2 p290-1 O 2014 S. L. Brusatte

REVIEW: *Kirkus Rev* v82 no3 p122 F 1 2014

"Dinosaurs Without Bones: Dinosaur Lives Revealed by Their Trace Fossils". "Paleontologist [Anthony J.] Martin . . . has written textbooks, but this is his first work for a popular audience, and his choice to use humor as an educational tool meets with mixed results. . . . A pioneer in the field, Martin delivers an expert, if overly effervescent, account of what trace fossils reveal about their environment as well as dinosaur social behavior, movement, quarrels, sex lives and care of their young. . . . Most scholarly attempts at comedy, including this one, make for a painful experience, but readers who can tolerate the relentlessly glib, jokey prose will learn a great deal about these fascinating, long-dead creatures."

REVIEW: *Publ Wkly* v261 no4 p120-5 Ja 27 2014

REVIEW: *Publ Wkly* v261 no1 p43 Ja 6 2014

MARTIN, BARNABY. Hanging man; the arrest of Ai Weiwei; [by] Barnaby Martin 256 p. 2013 Faber and Faber, Inc.

1. BIOGRAPHY & AUTOBIOGRAPHY—Artists, Architects, Photographers 2. China—Politics and government—2002- 3. China—Social conditions—2000- 4. Dissenters, Artistic—China—Social conditions—21st century 5. HISTORY—Asia—China 6. Political science literature

ISBN 0374167753; 9780374167752 (hardback)

LC 2013-015010

SUMMARY: This book focuses on the arrest of Chinese artist and activist Ai Weiwei. Journalist Barnaby Martin interviewed "the artist about his experience, to inform the larger world of his treatment, to learn why he was arrested and ultimately released, and, finally, to shed light on the current state of the Chinese government itself. . . . Martin covers . . . the political trajectory of China through the 20th century, contemporary art movements in the post-Mao era, and Ai Weiwei's own life." (Library Journal)

REVIEW: *Booklist* v110 no1 p24 S 1 2013 Donna Seaman

REVIEW: *Kirkus Rev* v81 no15 p59 Ag 1 2013

REVIEW: *Libr J* v138 no14 p106 S 1 2013 Michael Dashkin

REVIEW: *New Yorker* v89 no36 p83-1 N 11 2013

REVIEW: *Publ Wkly* v260 no29 p56 Jl 22 2013

REVIEW: *TLS* no5749 p28 Je 7 2013 MAURA CUNNINGHAM

"Hanging Man: The Arrest of Ai Weiwei." "A detailed look at dissent and control in contemporary China. . . . [Barnaby] Martin (who first came to China in 1990, only a year after the Tiananmen Square demonstrations had been crushed) appears primed to believe the worst about the Chinese government, describing the country as a totalitarian state in terms that imply a much more ominous and repressive atmosphere than the one I encounter living in Shanghai. China undeniably lacks the rule of law, and vocal dissent regularly provokes state retaliation. Many artists and writers engage in self-censorship to avoid trouble. . . . Yet at the same time, these groups do have some freedom to act . . . and their movements do not automatically provoke a crackdown by the state."

MARTIN, DANIELLA. Edible; an adventure into the world of eating insects and the last great hope to save the planet; [by] Daniella Martin 272 p. 2014 New Harvest, Houghton Mifflin Harcourt

1. COOKING—Essays 2. Cookbooks 3. Edible insects 4. Entomophagy 5. Food habits 6. Food supply 7. SOCIAL SCIENCE—Agriculture & Food 8. Sustainable agriculture

ISBN 9780544114357 (hardback)

LC 2013-045484

SUMMARY: In this book, Daniella Martin "expounds upon the 'ecological, nutritional, economic, global and culinary' benefits of consuming insects. The author's interest in eating insects began when she was studying pre-Columbian food and medicine in Mexico. . . . The author deconstructs the various tastes and textures encountered while munching on insects. . . . Martin includes helpful tips for raising bugs at home, an essential list of edible insects, cooking basics, and recipes." (Kirkus Reviews)

REVIEW: *Booklist* v110 no9/10 p30 Ja 1 2014 Nancy Bent

REVIEW: *Kirkus Rev* v82 no1 p252 Ja 1 2014

"Edible: An Adventure in the World of Eating Insects and the Last Great Hope to Save the Planet:. " The author's conversational style blends science, popular culture and personal insights, and she chronicles her interviews with a host of bug-cuisine promoters, including chefs, environmental consultants and entomologists. . . . Never didactic, [Daniella] Martin gently nudges readers toward open-mindedness at the prospect of eating bugs. . . . Regardless of readers' culinary proclivities, Martin's lively book poses timely questions while offering tasty solutions."

REVIEW: *Libr J* v139 no2 p93 F 1 2014 Mahnaz Dar

MARTIN, FÉLIX. Money; the unauthorised biography; [by] Félix Martin 336 p. 2014 Alfred A. Knopf

1. Global Financial Crisis, 2008-2009 2. Historical literature 3. International economic relations 4. Money—History 5. Risk—Economic aspects

ISBN 9780307962430

LC 2013-047572

SUMMARY: In this book, "Felix Martin . . . describes how the Western idea of money emerged from interactions between Mesopotamia and ancient Greece and was shaped over the centuries by tensions between sovereigns and the emerging middle classes. . . . Martin shows that money has always been a deeply political instrument, and that it is our failure to remember this that led to the crisis in our financial system and so to the Great Recession." (Publisher's note)

REVIEW: *Booklist* v110 no11 p7 F 1 2014 Vanessa Bush

REVIEW: *Choice* v51 no11 p2035 Jl 2014 R. T. Sweet

REVIEW: *Economist* v407 no8836 p88 My 18 2013

REVIEW: *Kirkus Rev* v82 no3 p12 F 1 2014

"Money: The Unauthorised Biography". "[An] improbably lively account. . . . All this talk can get quite heady, and that's not to mention the ancient Chinese proverb that 'the fish is the last to know water'—i.e., those of us who use money are so deeply steeped in it that it's hard to think about, let alone answer the more important question: How much power should money have to govern our lives? Refreshingly free of jargon and long on ideas—including the thought that if it's money that got us into our current mess, it's money that can get us out of it."

REVIEW: *Libr J* v139 no2 p82 F 1 2014 Caroline Geck

REVIEW: *Libr J* v139 no15 p38 S 15 2014 Cynthia Jensen

REVIEW: *N Y Times Book Rev* p12 Ap 13 2014 HEIDI N. MOORE

REVIEW: *N Y Times Book Rev* p26 Ap 20 2014

REVIEW: *New Statesman* v142 no5186 p13 N 22 2013 Supplement Alex Brummer

REVIEW: *New Statesman* v142 no5161 p44 Je 7 2013 Alex Brummer

REVIEW: *New Yorker* v90 no12 p75-1 My 12 2014

"Money." "Money is often held to have arisen as a solution to the shortcomings of barter: traders needed a universally acceptable 'medium of exchange.' In this lively history-cum-polemic, [author Felix] Martin says that the theory is 'entirely false,' and that the essence of monetary exchange is not 'the swapping of goods and services for this commodity medium' but a 'system of credit accounts and their clearing.' . . . Martin believes that, armed with this knowledge, we should be able to develop 'an economic system to deliver peace, prosperity, freedom, and fairness.' But exactly how this can be done remains unclear."

REVIEW: *Publ Wkly* v260 no49 p72 D 2 2013

REVIEW: *TLS* no5789 p23 Mr 14 2014 TYLER COWEN

MARTIN, IAIN. Making It Happen; Fred Goodwin, RBS and the Men Who Blew Up the British Economy; [by] Iain Martin 352 p. 2013 Simon & Schuster UK

1. Global Financial Crisis, 2008-2009 2. Goodwin, Frederick Anderson, 1958- 3. Great Britain—Economic conditions 4. Historical literature 5. Royal Bank of Scotland

ISBN 147111354X; 9781471113543

SUMMARY: This book on the collapse of the Royal Bank of Scotland (RBS) centers on "Fred Goodwin, the former chief executive known as 'Fred the Shred' who terrorized some of his staff and beguiled others. Not a banker by training, he nonetheless was given control of RBS and set about trying to make it one of the biggest brands in the world. . . . Treasury insiders, and regulators reveal how the bank's mania for expansion led it to take enormous risks its leaders didn't understand." (Publisher's note)

REVIEW: *Economist* v409 no8859 p95-6 O 26 2013

"Making It Happen: Fred Goodwin, RBS and the Men Who Blew Up the British Economy." "Every crisis needs a scapegoat. Few have been more reviled than Fred Goodwin, the former chief executive of the Royal Bank of Scotland (RBS). . . . Yet his complex character . . . continues to fascinate. Iain Martin . . . does a good job of capturing this in his new book. . . . He vividly illustrates the drama that surrounded the 2008 collapse of RBS, as well as the astonishing ascent and transformation of Mr. Goodwin. . . . 'Making It Happen' is rich in anecdotes. . . . Mr. Martin's book also captures the way in which Mr. Goodwin ruled his bank with a mixture of terror and charm."

MARTIN, JACQUELINE BRIGGS. Farmer Will Allen and the growing table; [by] Jacqueline Briggs Martin 32 p. 2013 Readers to Eaters

1. Allen, Will 2. Basketball players 3. Children's nonfiction 4. Urban agriculture 5. Vegetable gardening

ISBN 0983661537; 9780983661535

LC 2013-937817

SUMMARY: In this book, Jacqueline Briggs Martin "shares the real-life story of Will Allen, innovative farmer and founder of Growing Power, an urban farm in Milwaukee. 'Will Allen can see / what others can't see. / When he sees kids, he sees farmers.' Martin begins and ends with this positive premise. In between, she sketches salient events that stoked Allen's commitment to empowering people to grow their own food." (Kirkus Reviews)

REVIEW: *Booklist* v110 no8 p44 D 15 2013 Ilene Cooper

REVIEW: *Booklist* v110 no5 p58 N 1 2013 Kara Dean

"Farmer Will Allen and the Growing Table." "Basketball-player-turned-urban-farmer Will Allen is the subject of this inspiring picture book. . . . cultivate. The idea of farming as a community builder, rather than a solitary vocation, comes across clearly in the book. Martin's spare, purposeful language covers a great deal of territory, and a large time frame, but it never overwhelms or sounds preachy. The illustrations represent diverse individuals working together and enjoying the bounty of their labor. An amiable note from Will Allen concludes, as well as a list of resources to help kids start their own gardens."

REVIEW: *Kirkus Rev* v81 no18 p158 S 15 2013

REVIEW: *Nat Hist* v121 no9 p43 N 2013 Dolly Setton

MARTIN, JOHN.il. Time travel trouble. See Time travel trouble

MARTIN, PAUL. Play, playfulness, creativity and innovation. See Bateson, P.

MARTIN, RANDY. Under new management; universities, administrative labor, and the professional turn; [by] Randy Martin xviii, 253 pages 2011 Temple University Press

1. College personnel management—United States 2. Educational literature 3. Higher education administration 4. Universities and colleges—United States—Administration 5. Universities and colleges—United States—Faculty

ISBN 1439906955 (cloth); 9781439906958 (cloth)

LC 2010-046506

SUMMARY: In this book, author Randy Martin "imagines a political future for academic labour based on a critical understanding of the administrative work that faculty already undertake. He considers the differences between self-rule and specialized expertise and provides a case study of a New York City public school to show how kids and families respond to the demands of managerial productivity that is part of preparing students for college." (Publisher's note)

REVIEW: *Contemp Sociol* v43 no1 p55-7 Ja 2014 Gaye Tuchman

"Under New Management: Universities, Administrative Labor, and the Professional Turn". "I slogged through Randy Martin's 'Under New Management,' which I regard as a discursive text. That said, I'm glad I read it. . . . Martin not only understands how higher education has been transformed worldwide, but he shows us that some administrators—clearly not all—understand their work to be cutting across the grain of the bureaucratic forest being erected by professional managers. . . . Martin's book is over-flowing with pithy sentences that show he understands well how students, professors, and administrators experience higher-education today."

MARTIN, ROBERT.tr. Primates of the world. See Primates of the world

MARTIN, RUSSELL E. A bride for the Tsar; bride-shows and marriage politics in early modern Russia; [by] Russell E. Martin 380 p. 2012 NIU Press

1. Bride shows—Russia—History—16th century 2. Bride shows—Russia—History—17th century 3. Historical literature 4. Marriage customs and rites—Russia—History—16th century 5. Marriage customs and rites—Russia—History—17th century 6. Marriages of royalty and nobility—Political aspects—Russia 7. Marriages of royalty and nobility—Russia—History—16th century 8. Marriages of royalty and nobility—Russia—History—17th century

ISBN 9780875804484 (hardcover: alkaline paper); 9781609090548 (electronic)
LC 2011-043203

SUMMARY: This book examines the Russian ritual of the bride-show. It "offers an analysis of the show's role in the complex politics of royal marriage in early modern Russia. Russell E. Martin argues that the nature of the rituals surrounding the selection of a bride for the tsar tells us much about the extent of his power, revealing it to be limited and collaborative, not autocratic." (Publisher's note)

REVIEW: *Am Hist Rev* v119 no1 p273-4 F 2014 Valerie A. Kivelson

"A Bride for the Tsar: Bride-Shows and Marriage Politics in Early Modern Russia". "[Russell E.] Martin has produced a book that is engrossing and fun to read, and through the lens of royal marriage he provides a clear picture of the way that tsarist court politics functioned. . . . Martin sets out several goals for the book and delivers on each one. . . . It is striking that a book on marriage practices avoids any consideration of gender. . . . As a good historical study should, this book leaves the reader wanting more, full of questions and ideas for further research."

REVIEW: *Choice* v50 no5 p940 Ja 2013 M. E. Weisner

MARTIN, VALERIE. The ghost of the Mary Celeste; a novel; [by] Valerie Martin 320 p. 2014 Nan A. Talese/ Doubleday

1. Doyle, Arthur Conan, Sir, 1859-1930 2. FICTION—Historical 3. FICTION—Sea Stories 4. FICTION—Visionary & Metaphysical 5. Ghost stories 6. Mediums 7. Paranormal fiction

ISBN 0385533500; 9780385533508 (hardback)
LC 2013-029153

SUMMARY: This historical novel, by Valerie Martin, "delves into the lingering questions surrounding the Mary Celeste, an American brig found drifting, intact but abandoned, in the open Atlantic in 1872. . . . Arthur Conan Doyle, who wrote a sensationalist tale about the ship's fate in his youth, appears at several different points in his life, and a journalist crosses paths several times with an enigmatic medium she hopes to debunk." (Booklist)

REVIEW: *Booklist* v110 no4 p20-1 O 15 2013 Sarah Johnson

"The Ghost of the Mary Celeste." "Eschewing a traditional linear narrative for an unconventional yet far more effective structure, Martin creates what seem at first to be loosely connected vignettes. . . . Characterization is first-rate, as is the historical sensibility. Subtle undercurrents of impending tragedy create a disquieting effect throughout, a fitting atmosphere for a work about a society preoccupied with making contact with deceased loved ones. The scenes of maritime disasters are realistically terrifying. A haunting, if sometimes slowly paced, speculative look at a long-unsolved maritime mystery and the unsettling relationships between writers and their subjects."

REVIEW: *Kirkus Rev* v81 no21 p108 N 1 2013

REVIEW: *Libr J* v139 no8 p44 My 1 2014 Kristen L. Smith

REVIEW: *N Y Times Book Rev* p14 Ja 26 2014 JOHN VERNON

"The Ghost of the Mary Celeste." "'The Ghost of the Mary Celeste' is a sly and masterly historical novel, a page-turner written with intelligence and flair. . . . The result is a novel that feels both more and less real than a conventionally written work of fiction--more because of its historical provenance, less because we experience the story as if through shattered glass whose fragments can't be pieced back together. . . . [Author Valerie] Martin's novel, with its cacophony of points of view and its sometimes contradictory personal accounts, stirs uncertainties--these accounts could be hoaxes."

REVIEW: *New Statesman* v143 no7 p49 F 21 2014 Jane Shilling

MARTIN, WILLIAM. A prophet with honor; the Billy Graham story; [by] William Martin 735 1991 Morrow

1. Biography, Individual 2. Evangelists 3. Inspirational writers 4. Revivals—United States—History

ISBN 0-688-06890-1
LC 91-1-7437

SUMMARY: This is a biography of the American evangelist. Index.This is a biography of the American evangelist. Index.

REVIEW: *Booklist* v110 no6 p41-3 N 15 2013 Ilene Cooper

"Prophet With Honor: The Billy Graham Story." "[William] Martin, an experienced writer on both the topics of religion and politics, brings Billy Graham to a new audience. As he tells Graham's story, Martin pays equal attention to his evangelism and his evolution as a man of God. . . . Throughout, Martin hits on plot points that will appeal to teen readers, like how acutely the five Graham children missed their father as he constantly traveled. . . . With the writing so fine, it's too bad about the paper quality and the paucity of photographs. Still, this is a fascinating story well told."

MARTINEZ, CAROLE. The Castle of Whispers; [by] Carole Martinez 192 p. 2014 Penguin Group USA

1. Faith 2. Hermits 3. Historical fiction 4. Mother & child—Fiction 5. Women's history—Middle Ages,

500-1500
ISBN 1609451821; 9781609451820

SUMMARY: Rather than marry a brute, a 12th-century damsel opts for the life of an anchoress, walled up in a cell. . . . Esclarmonde . . . evades the powerlessness of most of her gender by refusing the hand of a rough nobleman, choosing faith instead and a life bricked up inside a cell attached to a chapel forevermore. . . . However, just prior to her entombment, Esclarmonde was raped, and . . . she can't conceal the resultant baby, a son, Elzéar." (Kirkus Reviews)

REVIEW: *Kirkus Rev* v81 no24 p334 D 15 2013

"The Castle of Whispers". " Rather than marry a brute, a 12th-century damsel opts for the life of an anchoress, walled up in a cell, in this mystical French story infused with fairy tale and feminism. . . . Deftly blurring the line between reality and mystery, [Carole] Martinez . . . keeps the reader guessing about the story's miraculous events and its characters' powers, including Elzéar's—the son who may be capable of delivering powerful visions, allowing his mother to glimpse the terrible suffering of her father's army, which is heading to the Crusades. This and other tragedies intensify Esclarmonde's fate, leading to a cataclysmic yet transcendent conclusion. Transient in impact, but a powerfully visualized magic-realist fable."

MARTINEZ, OSCAR. The beast; riding the rails and dodging narcos on the migrant trail; [by] Oscar Martinez 224 p. 2013 Verso

1. Central Americans—Mexico 2. Illegal aliens—Mexico 3. Immigrants—Mexico 4. Social science literature
ISBN 1781681325; 9781781681329 (hardback : alk. paper)
LC 2013-020580

SUMMARY: Author Oscar Martinez presents "stories he garnered from two years spent traveling up and down the migrant trail from Central America and across the US border. [He tells how] 300 migrants were kidnapped between the remote desert towns of Altar, Mexico, and Sasabe, Arizona. A local priest got 120 released, many with broken ankles and other marks of abuse, but the rest vanished." (Publisher's note)

REVIEW: *Columbia J Rev* v52 no4 p55-7 N/D 2013 MARCELA VALDES

"Narcoland: The Mexican Drug lords and Their Godfathers" and "The Beast: Riding the Rails and Dodging Narcos on the Migrant Trail." "How did the Mexican government lose control of its traffickers? An answer can be found in two new books: [Anabel] Hernández' 'Narcoland: The Mexican Drug Lords and Their Godfathers' and Óscar Martínez' 'The Beast: Riding the Rails and Dodging Narcos on the Migrant Trail.' Together they provide a top-down, bottom-up view of how Mexican cartels have consolidated and corporatized in the past two decades."

REVIEW: *Economist* v409 no8859 p94-5 O 26 2013

REVIEW: *Kirkus Rev* v81 no17 p65 S 1 2013

REVIEW: *New York Times* v163 no56354 pC4 D 18 2013 LARRY ROHTER

MARTINI, JOHN A. Sutro's glass place; the story of sutro baths; [by] John A. Martini 140 p. 2013 Hole In The Head Press

1. Historical literature 2. Modern ruins 3. San Francisco (Calif.)—History 4. Sutro, Adolph 5. Tourist attractions—History
ISBN 9780976149460
LC 2013-944852

SUMMARY: In this book, John A. Martini "relates the history of a now-defunct California attraction." It "tells the story of how Adolph Sutro, a German-born businessman and politician, conceived and built the Baths, their eventual decline (mostly due to the high cost of maintenance) and plans for their future." The book includes "period photographs" and "new architectural illustrations". (Kirkus Reviews)

REVIEW: *Kirkus Rev* v82 no3 p82 F 1 2014

"Sutro's Glass Palace: The Story of Sutro Baths". "[John A.] Martini relates the history of a now-defunct California attraction in this lavishly illustrated volume. . . . Martini tells this story clearly and well, providing not just period photographs, but also new architectural illustrations which greatly illuminate the Baths' complicated structure. He also provides contemporary photos of the now-skeletal ruins alongside artist's renderings of the complex when it was first built, which may help readers relate the past to the present day. Martini also offers many lively anecdotes from newspaper accounts, court documents and other sources to bring this past wonder to life. A beautiful resource about a mysterious San Francisco landmark."

MARTINSON, BARBARA.ed. Color and design. See Color and design

MARTÍNEZ, LUIS. The violence of petro-dollar regimes; Algeria, Iraq, and Libya; [by] Luis Martínez 202 p. 2012 Columbia University Press

1. Economics literature 2. Petroleum industry and trade—Algeria 3. Petroleum industry and trade—Iraq 4. Petroleum industry and trade—Libya
ISBN 9780231703024 (alk. paper); 9780231800808
LC 2012-003967

SUMMARY: This book describes how "The creation of oil 'rents' in the 1970s put Algeria, Iraq, and Libya on the fast track to modernization. . . . Offering the first global evaluation of these issues, [author] Luis Martinez considers the nature of oil-sponsored violence in Algeria, Iraq, and Libya and its ability both to weaken and bolster their respective regimes." (Publisher's note)

REVIEW: *Choice* v51 no1 p132-3 S 2013 M. Akacem

"The Violence of Petro-Dollar Regimes: Algeria, Iraq, and Libya." "[Author Luis] Martinez offers fresh insight and analysis on the issue of the 'resource curse' and its impact on economic development, focusing on three countries, Algeria, Libya, and Iraq. . . . An oil privatization scheme whereby oil revenues are distributed directly to the citizens would address the key problems Martinez outlines in Algeria, Iraq, and Libya. This is not addressed in the book, which nevertheless is well written and argued and very accessible to a wide audience, including undergraduate students. Martinez has made an important contribution to the literature on the role of oil in economic development. . . ."

MARWICK, ALICE E. Status update; celebrity, publicity, and branding in the social media age; [by] Alice E. Marwick 368 p. 2013 Yale University Press

1. Branding (Marketing) 2. Celebrities 3. Publicity 4.

Social media 5. Social science literature 6. Social status 7. Web 2.0
ISBN 9780300176728 (cloth: alkaline paper)
LC 2013-017042

SUMMARY: In this book on social media technologies and Silicon Valley culture, author Alice E. Marwick "analyzes status-building techniques—such as self-branding, micro-celebrity, and life-streaming—to show that Web 2.0 did not provide a cultural revolution, but only furthered inequality and reinforced traditional social stratification, demarcated by race, class, and gender." (Publisher's note)

REVIEW: *Choice* v51 no9 p1631-2 My 2014 P. L. Kantor

"Status Update: Celebrity, Publicity, and Branding in the Social Media Age". "It seems a sort of summary follow-up to the history of the discussions about the social media inclinations of Silicon Valley, with its always on, always connected, self-branded approach to life. This seemingly minor contribution makes it a worthwhile hook. But it goes one better. [Alice E.] Marwick . . . both reports on these cultural assumptions that have become the norm in the IT industry and actively questions them. The end result is a description of a culture where anyone can succeed with a generous dose of initiative and a willingness to work and learn—at least as long as one is a capable white male who is willing to sacrifice the rest of his work-life balance for getting ahead."

REVIEW: *Kirkus Rev* v81 no22 p65 N 15 2013

REVIEW: *N Y Times Book Rev* p14 N 3 2013 WALTER KIRN

REVIEW: *New Statesman* v143 no5205 p44-5 Ap 11 2014 Helen Lewis

REVIEW: *Science* v342 no6161 p933-4 N 22 2013 William H. Dutton

MARWIL, JONATHAN. Visiting modern war in Risorgimento Italy; [by] Jonathan Marwil p. cm. 2010 Palgrave Macmillan

1. Historical literature 2. Italy—History—1815-1870 3. Italy—Military history 4. Sardinia (Italy)—History—1708-1861 5. War & society
ISBN 9780230108134
LC 2010-018391

SUMMARY: Written by Jonathan Marwil, "This book examines the social and cultural consequences of a war normally looked at for its role in the story of Italian unification--the convergence of French, Austrian, and Piedmont-Sardinian armies in northern Italy in 1859, referred to in Italy as the 'Second War for Independence.' In doing so it focuses on a series of individuals who visited these battlefields during the war and in the years afterwards, coming right down to 1959." (Publisher's note)

REVIEW: *Am Hist Rev* v118 no4 p1280 O 2013 Axel Körner

"Visiting Modern War in Risorgimento Italy." "The recent commemorations for the 150th anniversary of the Unification of Italy paid relatively little attention to the so-called Second War of Liberation in 1859, which enabled Piedmont-Sardinia to expand into the Italian peninsula, a process that led to the creation of the Kingdom of Italy in 1861. . . . Rather than being a traditional military or diplomatic history of the war, Jonathan Marwil's book makes an important contribution to our understanding of its cultural and symbolic significance. . . . Regrettably, Marwil largely abstains from connecting his work to related research. . . . The publisher allowed for only ten illustrations, almost absurd for a book on the representation of war in the early age of photography."

MARWOOD, ALEX. The wicked girls; a novel; [by] Alex Marwood 384 p. 2013 Penguin Books

1. FICTION—Literary 2. FICTION—Mystery & Detective—General 3. FICTION—Suspense 4. Secrecy—Fiction 5. Women journalists—Fiction
ISBN 0143123866; 9780143123866 (pbk.)
LC 2013-002347

SUMMARY: In this novel by Alex Marwood "two . . . girls meet for the first time. By the end of the day, they will both be charged with murder. [25] years later, journalist Kirsty Lindsay is reporting on . . . attacks on young female[s] in a . . . vacation town when her investigation leads her to interview . . . Amber Gordon. For Kirsty and Amber, it's the first time they've seen each other since that dark day. . . . Will they really be able to keep their . . . secret?" (Publisher's note)

REVIEW: *Kirkus Rev* v81 no13 p274 Jl 1 2013

REVIEW: *Libr J* v138 no12 p73 Jl 1 2013 Amy Hoseth

REVIEW: *Libr J* v138 no21 p57 D 1 2013 Kristen L. Smith

REVIEW: *N Y Times Book Rev* p31 Ag 25 2013 Marilyn Stasio

"A Tap on the Window," "The Wicked Girls," and "The Crooked Maid: A Novel." "[Linwood] Barclay's convoluted 'now you see me, now you don't' plot opens on such a low-key note that it's a shock when it takes off for the narrative badlands. But even when he's tending to the gruesome details of the bad stuff, he never loses touch with the fundamental fear of people who live in nice communities like Griffon--that their children are beyond their control. . . . Alex Marwood . . . demonstrat[es] a deep, warm feeling for the shabby seaside town where she sets her harrowing first novel. . . . [In 'The Crooked Maid' the lives of . . . two strangers become intricately (if much too expediently) entwined in a complicated but gracefully executed narrative."

REVIEW: *Publ Wkly* v260 no19 p44 My 13 2013

MARY PICKFORD; queen of the movies; p. cm. 2012 University Press of Kentucky

1. Historical literature 2. Motion picture actors and actresses—United States—Biography 3. Motion picture industry—United States—History 4. Motion picture producers and directors—United States—Biography
ISBN 9780813136479 (hardcover : alk. paper); 9780813136677 (pdf); 9780813140551 (epub)
LC 2012-019015

SUMMARY: This book on actress Mary Pickford presents essays from a "group of film historians . . . on this icon's incredible life and legacy. . . . She is revealed as a gifted actress, a philanthropist, and a savvy industry leader who fought for creative control of her films and ultimately became her own producer." The book "features more than two hundred color and black and white illustrations, including photographs and stills." (Publisher's note)

REVIEW: *Libr J* v137 no16 p80 O 1 2012 Teri Shiel

REVIEW: *Sight Sound* v23 no10 p105 O 2013 Bryony Dixon

REVIEW: *TLS* no5749 p26 Je 7 2013 MARILYN ANN MOSS

"Mary Pickford: Queen of the Movies." "[Christel]

Schmidt's book is a handsome (and huge) collection of photographs and essays that aims to be the last word on all things Pickford. He has assembled an excellent group of experts who together give a well-rounded view of Pickford's career, her work as a first-rate producer and an exploration of contemporary issues such as the racial tension in her films, her impact on the film industry and her cinematic legacy. Pickford's business prowess is set alongside other, equally important aspects of her life and career--such as her use of costume to emphasize aspects of both her on- and off-screen personas."

MARÍAS, JAVIER, 1951-. The Infatuations; 352 p. 2013 Knopf

1. Experimental fiction 2. Imagination 3. Man-woman relationships—Fiction 4. Murder—Fiction 5. Time—Fiction

ISBN 0307960722; 9780307960726

LC 2013-016429

SUMMARY: In this book by Javier Marias, "the narrator, María Dolz, eavesdrops on a conversation that undoes all she thinks she knows about Javier, her lover, and his dear friend, the victim of an apparently brutal and senseless murder. What she believed was a tragedy may be the result of a conspiracy." (Booklist)

REVIEW: *Art Am* v102 no4 p29 Ap 2014

REVIEW: *Bookforum* v20 no2 p37 Je-Ag 2013 ERIC BANKS

REVIEW: *Booklist* v109 no21 p26 Jl 1 2013 Michael Autrey

REVIEW: *Kirkus Rev* v81 no14 p94 Jl 15 2013

REVIEW: *Kirkus Rev* p25 N 15 2013 Best Books

REVIEW: *Libr J* v138 no4 p55 Mr 1 2013 Barbara Hoffert

REVIEW: *N Y Times Book Rev* p32 My 18 2014 IHSAN TAYLOR

REVIEW: *N Y Times Book Rev* p22 Ag 18 2013

REVIEW: *N Y Times Book Rev* p1-9 Ag 11 2013 Edward St. Aubyn

REVIEW: *Newsweek Global* v161 no29 p1 Ag 16 2013 Benjamin Lytal

"The Infatuations." "Reading Javier Marías is like a conversation that you didn't want to have. But the speaker is so elegant, so puissant beneath his Old World clothes, so innocently macho with all his philosophical conundrums, that you let him talk. . . . 'The Infatuation' may not have the grandiosity of his preceding book, the three-volume 'Your Face Tomorrow'. . . . The Infatuations is more formally balanced. It feels like Marías is headed toward a late style, brainy and lean and a little dry. The tinge of blood that flavors all of Marias's novels is here, but the use of a female narrator slightly inhibits Marías's boyish relish. Perhaps that is for the best. The book teaches us to somehow dread the idea that life belongs to the living."

REVIEW: *Publ Wkly* v260 no25 p143 Je 24 2013

REVIEW: *TLS* no5736 p19-20 Mr 8 2013 ADAM THIRLWELL

"The Infatuations." "The author has often noted the influence of Henry James on his snaking sentences (which have been translated with gorgeous consistency across his oeuvre by Margaret Jull Costa) but the real larceny is much grander. He has borrowed James's 'supersubtle' narrators and observers, who 'convert the very pulses of the air into revelations'. And he has also inherited James's luminous belief in art. . . . This makes for a reading experience that is sometimes urbanely sensual . . . and sometimes abstractly philosophical."

MASANI, ZAREER. Macaulay; [by] Zareer Masani 288 p. 2013 The Bodley Head Ltd

1. Biographies 2. Education—India—History 3. India—History—British occupation, 1765-1947 4. India—Politics & government—1765-1947 5. Macaulay, Thomas Babington Macaulay, Baron, 1800-1859

ISBN 1847922716; 9781847922717

SUMMARY: This book, by Zareer Masani, presents a biography of politican and historian Thomas Babington Macaulay. Masani "maintains that English was the glue that held together multilingual India. . . . Unlike the Orientalists, who doubted the Indians' capacity for understanding, Macaulay saw them as capable of becoming completely immersed in imperial society, and though English was better suited to learning than the vernacular languages." (Economist)

REVIEW: *TLS* no5764 p12-3 S 20 2013 DAVID ARNOLD

"Macaulay and Son: Architects of Imperial Britain" and "Macaulay: Britain's Liberal Imperialist." "[An] insightful and compelling dual biography of Thomas Babington Macaulay and his father Zachary. . . . In this subtle book, intimacies of home and empire are never far apart. . . . Without losing empathy, even compassion, for her subjects, [Catherine] Hall is able to make the Macaulays illuminate many different historical themes and purposes-manliness and otherness, gender and race, politics and history, family and empire. . . . [Zareer] Masani's book has none of the historiographical nuances and social insights that inform Hall's biography. The past is read, with Whiggish insistence, through the prism of the present, so that even the 1848 revolutions in Europe require comparison with the 'Arab Spring'."

MASLON, LAURENCE. Superheroes! See Kantor, M.

MASON, MIKE. Global Shift; Asia, Africa, and Latin America, 1945-2007; [by] Mike Mason 349 p. 2012 McGill Queens Univ

1. Cold War, 1945-1989 2. Developing countries—Economic integration 3. Developing countries—Foreign relations—History 4. Historical literature 5. International relations—History 6. International relations literature

ISBN 0773540628; 9780773540620

SUMMARY: This book by Mike Mason addresses "the emergence of the Third World--a zone of competition and contention ultimately engulfed by the rising tide of capitalist development. . . . Drawing on history, comparative politics, and development studies, Global Shift traces the contours of state histories from Asia, Africa, and Latin America to create a comprehensive portrait of the current state of global politics that is breathtaking in scope." (Publisher's note)

REVIEW: *Choice* v51 no1 p160 S 2013 M. Amstutz

"Global Shift: Asia, Africa, and Latin America, 1945-2007." "[Author Mike] Mason . . . describes the rise, evolution, and demise of the international order that emerged at the end of WW II. The system divided the global society into three parts: a 'First World' of capitalist democracies, a 'Second World' of communist-aligned states, and a 'Third

World' of Asia, Africa, and Latin America. . . . Mason devotes chapters to China, Vietnam, India, Indonesia, South Korea, Iran, Pakistan, and Afghanistan, as well as to the regions of Africa and Latin America. . . . Although the book provides an overview of political and economic changes in the Third World, its broad historical and geographical scope results in simplistic generalizations and dubious claims."

MASON, NICHOLAS. Literary advertising and the shaping of British romanticism; [by] Nicholas Mason 202 p. 2013 The Johns Hopkins University Press

1. Advertising—Great Britain—History—18th century 2. Advertising—Great Britain—History—19th century 3. Authors and publishers—Great Britain—History—18th century 4. Authors and publishers—Great Britain—History—19th century 5. Historical literature 6. Literature publishing—Great Britain—History—18th century 7. Literature publishing—Great Britain—History—19th century 8. Romanticism—Great Britain

ISBN 1421409984 (hardcover: alk. paper); 9781421409986 (hardcover: alk. paper); 9781421410715 (electronic)

LC 2012-045506

SUMMARY: In this book, author Nicholas Mason "explores the integration of marketing and literature from 1750 to 1850. These 'entangled histories' . . . encompass the birth of advertising alongside Romantic literature, the rise of the middle-class voracious reader, and the 'commodification' of literature as a natural symbiosis between complementary facets of print culture." (Choice: Current Reviews for Academic Libraries)

REVIEW: *Am Hist Rev* v119 no4 p1357-8 O 2014 Lori Loeb

REVIEW: *Choice* v51 no8 p1401 Ap 2014 G. Shivel

"Literary Advertising and the Shaping of British Romanticism". "A book that has an entire chapter on Lord Byron and 'branding'—who would not be intrigued? . . . [Nicholas] Mason provides an illuminating comparison of the Blackwood's circle and the founders of Amazon.com, pointing out how each group, in its own way and beginning with the best intentions, was soon enough dealing with authors' reviewing their own work. . . . Book history is a solid and growing humanities discipline today. Publishers and booksellers who, after much experience, can discern a value proposition through the mist of their ideals may become profitable enough to be remembered and one day written about by scholars. Mason sets a fine example here."

MASON, PETER. The Colossal; From Ancient Greece to Giacometti; [by] Peter Mason 208 p. 2013 University of Chicago Press

1. Colossus (Sculpture) 2. Historical literature 3. Megalithic monuments—Easter Island 4. Obelisks 5. Symbolism in art

ISBN 1780231083; 9781780231082

SUMMARY: This book presents an "account of the idea of the colossal in culture. [Peter Mason] gathers instances of the colossal throughout history . . . using historical and archaeological evidence to position them within the context of time and culture. Mason establishes a vision of the colossal that encompasses both the colossal in scale and another, overlooked sense of the word: the archaic Greek kolossos, a ritual effigy, and its modern equivalents. " (Publisher's note)

REVIEW: *TLS* no5766 p28 O 4 2013 LLEWELYN MORGAN

"The Colossal: From Ancient Greece to Giacommeti." "This is an attractive book, nicely illustrated, and it covers some fascinating territory. . . . But for all the wealth of illustration and the breadth of reference, [Jean-Pierre] Vernant's kolossos theory just isn't adequate to hold it all together. [Peter] Mason's taste is for isolated, unheimlich monoliths, solidly present yet also unearthly. . . . But while he may value the 'splendid isolation' of a moai in a museum in Brussels (in actual fact a copy), the fact is that moai were not typically erected in isolation, and anyway we simply don't know enough about these remarkable sculptures to hazard any kinship to the concept of the kolossos."

MASS, ROBERT.tr. Countrymen. See Lidegaard, B.

MASSEY, DOUGLAS S. Climbing Mount Laurel; the struggle for affordable housing and social mobility in an American suburb; [by] Douglas S. Massey 269 p. 2013 Princeton University Press

1. Housing—New Jersey—Mount Laurel (Township) 2. Low-income housing—New Jersey—Mount Laurel (Township) 3. Social mobility—New Jersey—Mount Laurel (Township) 4. Social science literature 5. Zoning, Exclusionary—New Jersey—Mount Laurel (Township)

ISBN 0691157294 (cloth : alk. paper); 9780691157290 (cloth : alk. paper)

LC 2012-047549

SUMMARY: This book looks at "the Ethel Lawrence Homes (ELH) project, an affordable housing project for low- and moderate-income minority residents in an affluent white suburb in Mount Laurel Township, New Jersey." The authors "argue that the development of affordable housing projects for low-income minorities in affluent suburbs is an effective means to reduce race and class segregation, increase social mobility, reduce dependency, create better human capital, and achieve family well-being." (Choice)

REVIEW: *Choice* v51 no3 p557 N 2013 D. A. Chekki

REVIEW: *New York Times* v162 no56295 p3 O 20 2013 DAVID L. KIRP

"Climbing Mount Laurel: The Struggle for Affordable Housing and Social Mobility in an American Suburb." "'Climbing Mount Laurel,' co-written by the Princeton sociologist Douglas S. Massey and several colleagues, concludes that . . . affordable housing has had zero impact on the affluent residents of that community . . . while the lives of the poor and working-class families who moved there have been transformed. . . . 'Climbing Mount Laurel' makes good use of what social scientists call a natural experiment."

MASSIE, ALLAN. Cold Winter in Bordeaux; [by] Allan Massie 280 p. 2014 Quartet Books Ltd

1. Crime—Fiction 2. France—Politics & government—1940-1945 3. War stories 4. World War, 1939-1945—France—Fiction 5. World War, 1939-1945—Underground movements—France

ISBN 0704373289; 9780704373280

SUMMARY: In this crime novel by Allan Massie, "The investigation will lead Lannes into dangerous territory. . . . His own disaffection is sharpened by Vichy's complicity in the deportation of the city's Jews. Things, he fears, will get worse before they get better, as divisions between Vichy and the Resistance threaten civil war. The third instalment in Allan Massie's acclaimed crime series continues the story of dogged detection in a world seemingly gone mad." (Publisher's note)

REVIEW: *TLS* no5794 p20 Ap 18 2014 SEAN O'BRIEN

"Cold Winter in Bordeaux." "'Cold Winter in Bordeaux' is continually absorbing: Lannes is the kind of character and his the kind of world the reader wants to spend time with. Even as the climate chills and darkens and conditions become irrevocably set for barbarism, the odd exchange with a waiter, the taste of a dish or the sight of a familiar street sustains a sense that things might be otherwise. This third instalment does, though, feel like a transitional work, with the endgame grimly in prospect, and new readers would be wise to begin at the start of the series."

MASTER, DANIEL M.ed. The Oxford encyclopedia of the Bible and archaeology. See The Oxford encyclopedia of the Bible and archaeology

MATA, LINDA SUE. Understanding Workplace Bullying; [by] Linda Sue Mata 118 p. 2012 Author Solutions

1. Bullying—Law & legislation 2. Bullying in the workplace 3. Harassment—Prevention 4. Social science literature 5. Work environment

ISBN 1477268073; 9781477268070

SUMMARY: In this book, author Linda Sue Mata "analyzes the phenomenon of bullying at work. She differentiates bullying from harassment or incivility and discusses organizations' cultures, and how the roles of organizational leaders in allowing or preventing bullying situations. . . . The book asserts that 'more legislation needs to be enacted to enforce laws outlawing bullying and incivility in the workplace'". (Kirkus Reviews)

REVIEW: *Kirkus Rev* v81 no24 p345 D 15 2013

"Understanding Workplace Bullying". "A timely look at issues surrounding bullying in the workplace. . . . However, although this book is well-intentioned, it doesn't provide well-thought-out arguments. For example, there's no widely accepted, standard definition of bullying; however, the book chooses one definition . . . without explaining why it's better than others. Later, the book introduces the idea that a power imbalance between bully and victim is a "key component" of bullying—but doesn't revise the previous definition to include it. The prose can also be confusing at times. . . . A well-meaning but unclear overview."

REVIEW: *Kirkus Rev* p15 D 15 2013 supplement seasons readings

MATHEW, THECKEDATH M. Joshua the odyssey of an ordinary man; [by] Theckedath M. Mathew 596 p. 2013 Odyssey Press, Inc.

1. Ancient philosophy 2. Historical fiction 3. Jesus Christ—Biography 4. Jesus Christ—Fiction 5. Religious leaders

ISBN 9780988713000

LC 2012-955661

SUMMARY: This novel by Theckedath Mathew is "historical fiction that questions whether Jesus was the Son of God, and details what he was doing in the eighteen years that followed his eviction from the temple." It "reveals that the prophet gained invaluable insights from the philosophers of the East and thinkers from the West during an odyssey that lasted eighteen years." (Publisher's note)

REVIEW: *Kirkus Rev* v81 no16 p19 Ag 15 2013

"Joseph: The Odyssey of an Ordinary Man." "A compelling look at the adolescent life of Jesus Christ. In the New Testament, there's an 18-year gap in Jesus' life story, which this work attempts to fill. . . . [Author Theckedath M.] Mathew has poured over hundreds of documents to fill in the blanks, so to speak, of Joshua's life. The work is impeccably researched--perhaps even a bit too much: At times, the philosophizing seems to roll on for pages as it struggles to reach a point. While this dry ruminating may inspire thinkers, average readers might find it burdensome. . . . An impassioned, thought-provoking work of biblical fiction. "

MATLIN, DANIEL. On the corner; African American intellectuals and the urban crisis; [by] Daniel Matlin 350 p. 2013 Harvard University Press

1. African American intellectuals—Biography 2. African American intellectuals—History—20th century 3. African Americans—Social conditions—1964-1975 4. Historical literature 5. Inner cities—United States—History—20th century 6. Urban policy—United States—History—20th century

ISBN 9780674725287 (alkaline paper)

LC 2013-009716

SUMMARY: This book, by Daniel Malin, "revisits the volatile moment when African American intellectuals were thrust into the spotlight as indigenous interpreters of black urban life to white America, and examines how three figures—Kenneth B. Clark, Amiri Baraka, and Romare Bearden—wrestled with the opportunities and dilemmas their heightened public statures entailed." (Publisher's note)

REVIEW: *Choice* v51 no9 p1663-4 My 2014 W. Glasker

"On the Corner: African American Intellectuals and the Urban Crisis". "In this fascinating account of how black intellectuals and artists found themselves acting as indigenous interpreters of black life and culture to white America, [Daniel] Matlin . . . examines the roles of Kenneth Clark, Amiri Baraka, and Romare Bearden from this perspective. . . . Those who celebrated resilience and joy while minimizing damage and oppression risked romanticizing the urban condition and reinforcing the myth of the 'happy darky.' It remains a daunting challenge to get the balance right and not distort black life by reducing it to one stereotype or the other. . . . Highly recommended."

REVIEW: *J Am Hist* v101 no2 p648 S 2014

REVIEW: *Libr J* v138 no18 p103 N 1 2013 Molly McArdle

MATSON, LYNNE. Nil; [by] Lynne Matson 376 p. 2014 Henry Holt and Company

1. Islands—Fiction 2. Love—Fiction 3. Science fiction 4. Survival—Fiction 5. Teenagers—Fiction

ISBN 9780805097719 (hardback)

LC 2013-042357

SUMMARY: In this book by Lynne Matson, "a mysterious portal transports 17-year-old Charley to the possibly sentient and certainly capricious island of Nil, where she encounters a community of teens who have also been stolen from the lives they once knew. While circumstances remain clouded in uncertainty, Charley quickly learns the chief rule: she has one year to find and catch a portal home (these 'gates' appear and vanish at will), or she will die." (Publishers Weekly)

REVIEW: *Bull Cent Child Books* v67 no10 p533 Je 2014 A. S.

"Nil". "Their romance is fiery and desperate, befitting the dire situation in which they find themselves, and the urgency with which Charley commits herself to Thad's escape is believable (if a little exasperatingly self-sacrificing). There is much left unexplained about what the island actually is (although there are intriguing hints sprinkled throughout), but it doesn't really matter—the reader is swept along with the characters in just rooting for survival in a setting where taking too long to ponder answers could mean you don't live long enough to do anything with your newfound revelations. The range of characters . . . is effectively diverse—nearly every reader will spot a response that might mirror their own if thrown into this scenario."

REVIEW: *SLJ* v60 no5 p135 My 2014 Erik Knapp

REVIEW: *Voice of Youth Advocates* v37 no3 p84 Ag 2014 Hilary Crew

MATTERN, SUSAN P. Prince of medicine; Galen in the Roman world; [by] Susan P. Mattern 368 p. 2013 Oxford University Press

1. Biography (Literary form) 2. History of Medicine 3. History, Ancient 4. Physicians—Biography 5. Roman World

ISBN 019976767X; 9780199767670

LC 2012-035656

SUMMARY: Susan P. Mattern presents a "biography of Galen of Pergamum (circa 130-212 C.E.), a Greek who practiced medicine and philosophy in the Roman-dominated Mediterranean, first rising to fame at home in Asia Minor before becoming preeminent in Rome during the reign of Marcus Aurelius." (Library Journal)

REVIEW: *Am Hist Rev* v119 no1 p228-9 F 2014 John Wilkins

"The Prince of Medicine: Galen in the Roman Empire". "Susan P. Mattern has addressed this impossible task with acumen, panache, and great success. She is by trade an ancient historian, with all the methodologies that that entails. . . . Mistress of the case study and Galen's period, the second and early third centuries A.D., Mattern has framed this book around Galen's own material, using many of those anecdotes. . . . She places him beautifully and convincingly in his own world, concluding that he was arrogant and possibly misogynistic, but also passionate and a good doctor."

REVIEW: *Choice* v51 no6 p1044-5 F 2014 R. D. Arcari

"The Prince of Medicine: Galen in the Roman Empire." "A well-written, well-documented biography of the single physician who dominated Western medicine for 1,300 years. . . . [Susan P.] Mattern traces Galen's career and life from his birthplace in Pergamum to his peripatetic medical education, his service as a doctor to the gladiators in Pergamum, and finally his time as physician to the Roman emperor Marcus Aurelius. . . . The vivid descriptions of the competitiveness among doctors in imperial Rome add interest to the narrative. A valuable resource for classics and history of medicine collections. . . . Recommended."

REVIEW: *Hist Today* v63 no11 p60 N 2013 ANDREW ROBINSON

REVIEW: *Libr J* v138 no11 p98 Je 15 2013 Evan M. Anderson

REVIEW: *London Rev Books* v35 no22 p35-6 N 21 2013 James Romm

REVIEW: *Publ Wkly* v260 no20 p47 My 20 2013

MATTHEWS, JOHN H. This Is Where It Gets Interesting; [by] John H. Matthews 202 p. 2012 Six Slug Books

1. Authority 2. Death—Fiction 3. Ghost stories 4. Near-death experiences 5. Short story (Literary form)

ISBN 0615644759; 9780615644752

SUMMARY: This short story collection by John H. Matthews deals with themes of "death, government and authority, [and] smoking. . . . In 'The Black Tornado,' a man's deceased father visits him in the form of a tornado; the dead convene at a bowling alley for a meet and greet in 'Johnny Heart Attack'; and 'Ghostlike' follows a spirit who leaves notes in a shopping mall. Elsewhere in the collection, an authoritarian regime takes over a retirement community and builds a wall." (Kirkus Reviews)

REVIEW: *Kirkus Rev* v82 no2 p364 Ja 15 2014

"This Is Where It Gets Interesting". "[John H.] Matthews' marvelously entertaining debut short story collection is equal parts hysterically zany and forebodingly dark. Matthews presents the best of his short-form work in a debut collection that is as funny and witty as it is scary and menacing. Nearly all of the stories have a fantastical bent, and each contains an ending successfully surprising or unexpectedly poignant. . . . The straightforward, short sentences can grow tiresomely simple . . . but the author succeeds at telling tales that pack either a salient message or uproarious punch line (sometimes both)."

REVIEW: *Kirkus Rev* v82 no3 p43 F 1 2014

REVIEW: *Publ Wkly* v261 no21 p23 My 26 2014

MATTHEWS, OWEN. Glorious misadventures; Nikolai Rezanov and the dream of a Russian America; [by] Owen Matthews 400 p. 2013 Bloomsbury USA

1. Diplomats—Russia—Biography 2. Historical literature 3. Russians—North America—History 4. Statesmen—Russia—Biography

ISBN 1620402394; 9781620402399 (hardback)

LC 2013-031042

SUMMARY: Author Owen Matthews presents a profile of "Nikolai Rezanov, courtier and adventurer, [who] had grand plans to expand the Russian Empire in America at the dawn of the nineteenth century. His rise and fall in an age when exploration and exploitation were inextricably intertwined encompass fascinating figures from the period, including Catherine the Great, and spans the wilds of Siberia to the fledgling outpost of San Francisco." (Booklist)

REVIEW: *Booklist* v110 no2 p17 S 15 2013 Bridget Thoreson

REVIEW: *Kirkus Rev* v81 no19 p9 O 1 2013

REVIEW: *New York Times* v163 no56321 pC26 N 15 2013 WILLIAM GRIMES

REVIEW: *Publ Wkly* v260 no34 p58-9 Ag 26 2013

REVIEW: *TLS* no5781 p10 Ja 17 2014 ALEXANDER ETKIND

"Glorious Misadventures: Nikolai Rezanov and the Dream of a Russian America." "While the Russian tsars preoccupied themselves with European politics, Rezanov almost single-handedly led the imperial expansion to the Pacific East. . . . Rezanov rode to St Petersburg to report to the Tsar about his undeclared war with Japan, only to die en route in the heart of Siberia. . . . Interestingly, the counterfactual fantasies are as vivid as explanations why the world could be no different are abstract, even reductionist. But the facts, as [author] Owen Matthews renders them, are amazing."

MATTHIESSEN, PETER, 1927-2014. In Paradise; A Novel; [by] Peter Matthiessen 240 p. 2014 Riverhead Hardcover

1. Auschwitz (Poland : Concentration camp) 2. Family secrets—Fiction 3. Holocaust survivors 4. Holocaust, Jewish (1939-1945) 5. Jewish women—Fiction 6. Psychological fiction 7. Teachers—Fiction
ISBN 1594633177; 9781594633171
LC 2013-046176

SUMMARY: In this novel, author Peter Matthiessen "leaps into the big questions raised by the horrors of the Holocaust. What is the nature of good and evil? Can we bear to bear witness? Can beauty endure after the smokestacks of Auschwitz? These questions are pondered by a group gathering for a weeklong meditation retreat at the site of a World War II concentration camp." (Library Journal)

REVIEW: *Booklist* v110 no12 p26 F 15 2014 Ben Segedin

"In Paradise." "After participating in three Zen retreats at Auschwitz, [Peter] Matthiessen addresses that experience with what, at 86, may very well be his final novel. . . . The two-time National Book Award-winner doesn't shy away from boldly tackling the most profound of subjects. . . . Matthiessen expertly raises the challenges and the difficulties inherent in addressing this subject matter, proving, as the muralist Malan says, that the creation of art 'is the only path that might lead toward the apprehension of that ultimate evil ... [that] the only way to understand such evil Is to reimagine it.'"

REVIEW: *Booklist* v110 no11 p3 F 1 2014 Brad Hooper

"The Corsican Caper," "High Crime Area: Tales of Darkness and Dread," and "In Paradise." "[Peter] Mayle sends his popular sleuth Sam Levitt out on further investigative pursuits around the lovely South of France, Sam's focus this time on Russian tycoon Oleg Vronsky. . . . Eight tense, powerful short stories testify to [Joyce Carol] Oates' talent in the short form. . . . This author's esteemed reputation is deep and widespread, and his complicated, intelligent new novel--about a group of women and men gathering for meditations and reflection at the site of a former German concentration camp--will reward his followers."

REVIEW: *Kirkus Rev* v82 no3 p277 F 1 2014

REVIEW: *Libr J* v139 no5 p112 Mr 15 2014 Jim Coan

REVIEW: *Libr J* v138 no18 p69 N 1 2013 Barbara Hoffert

REVIEW: *New Statesman* v143 no5213 p49 Je 6 2014

REVIEW: *N Y Rev Books* v61 no6 p37-9 Ap 3 2014 Tim Parks

"In Paradise." "Reading the opening pages of 'In Paradise,' we're not aware that it's Auschwitz we're headed for. . . . [Author Peter] Matthiessen's work has always carried a powerful moral message. . . . 'In Paradise' is a logical conclusion to a long writing career, for Matthiessen, now in his eighties has said that this will be his last book. . . . But in a scene that I imagine Matthiessen must have witnessed himself, since it seems to bizarre to be invented, an oddly positive note is struck. . . . Matthiessen is no doubt aware that his powerful book will likely provoke the same heated disagreement."

REVIEW: *N Y Times Book Rev* p22 Ap 27 2014 DONNA RIFKIND

REVIEW: *Publ Wkly* v261 no2 p45 Ja 13 2014

REVIEW: *TLS* no5810 p19 Ag 8 2014 ALEX CLARK

MATTU, AYESHA.ed. Salaam, love. See Salaam, love

MAUDET, Y.tr. The key of Braha. See Perro, B.

MAUPASSANT, GUY DE, 1850-1893. Alien hearts; 177 2009 New York Review Books

1. France—Fiction 2. French fiction—Translations into English 3. Love stories, French 4. Man-woman relationships—Fiction 5. Salons
ISBN 1-590-17260-4; 9781590172605
LC 2009-004537

SUMMARY: This book follows "Andre Mariolle . . . a rich, handsome, gifted young man who cannot settle on what to do with himself. Madame de Burne, a glacially dazzling beauty, wants Mariolle to attend her exclusive salon. . . . At first Mariolle keeps his distance, but then he hits on the solution to all his problems: caring for nothing in particular, he will devote himself to being in love; Madame de Burne will be his everything. Soon lover and beloved are equally lost." (Publisher's note)

REVIEW: *TLS* no5772 p36 N 15 2013 J. C.

"Alien Hearts," "Biteback Dictionary of Humorous Literary Quotations," and "For Who the Bell Tolls." "It is a wonderful novel, written as the author's fatal sickness was taking grip. . . . 'Notre Coeur' is available in English as 'Alien Hearts,' in a translation by Richard Howard . . . which claims to be 'the first in more than a hundred years,' but this overlooks Marjorie Laurie's 1929 version. . . . Of the 'Biteback Dictionary of Humorous Literary Quotations' we ask only two things: that it be humorous, and that we know where the jokes are coming from. . . . We delved to the index, to find that the Dictionary doesn't have one. . . . The grammar may be correct under a precise anatomical gaze, but Mr [David] Marsh illustrates how proper usage is not always best usage."

MAUPIN, ARMISTEAD, 1944-. The Days of Anna Madrigal; [by] Armistead Maupin 304 p. 2014 HarperCollins

1. American fiction 2. Burning Man (Festival) 3. Landladies 4. San Francisco (Calif.)—Fiction 5. Transgender people—Fiction
ISBN 0062196243; 9780062196248

SUMMARY: This novel, by Armistead Maupin, book 9 in the author's "Tales of the City" series, "follows . . . Anna Madrigal, the legendary transgender landlady of 28 Barbary Lane . . . as she embarks on a road trip that will take her deep into her past. . . . With Brian and his beat-up RV, she journeys into the dusty troubled heart of her Depression childhood to unearth a lifetime of secrets and dreams and attend to unfinished business she has long avoided." (Publisher's note)

REVIEW: *Booklist* v110 no3 p4 O 1 2013

REVIEW: *Booklist* v110 no6 p21 N 15 2013 Brad Hooper

REVIEW: *Kirkus Rev* v81 no22 p79 N 15 2013

REVIEW: *Libr J* v138 no18 p80 N 1 2013 Devon Thomas

REVIEW: *Libr J* v138 no14 p82 S 1 2013

REVIEW: *N Y Times Book Rev* p10 Ja 19 2014 JESSICA BRUDER

"The Days of Anna Madrigal." "The ['Tales of the City'] series's ninth and final novel, 'The Days of Anna Madrigal . . . spotlights on of [author Armistead] Maupin's most beloved characters: the spliff-smoking, wisecracking transgender landlady who presided over 28 Barbary Lane through most of 'Tales.' . . . 'The Days of Anna Madrigal' is a genial fable. Like the earlier 'Tales,' it's riddled with outlandish coincidence and best enjoyed under the willing suspension of disbelief. Told in Maupin's roving style--call it third-person kaleidoscope--the narrative braids Anna's story, childhood flashbacks and scenes of her adopted kin, many of whom are preparing to attend Burning Man."

REVIEW: *Publ Wkly* v260 no45 p47 N 11 2013

REVIEW: *TLS* no5790 p19 Mr 21 2014 RUPERT SHORTT

"The Days of Anna Madrigal." "'The Days of Anna Madrigal' is [author Armistead] Maupin's finest work to date. One index of its success is that it seems as indispensable to the whole drama as it is unexpected. Uniquely among the nine volumes, it includes lengthy flashbacks to the remote past—1936—when the teenage Anna Madrigal, then Andy Ramsey, is struggling with his complex identity and seeking an escape from Winnemucca. . . . Is the nine-volume journey worth it? Emphatically so. . . . Maupin's pageant would have been richer still had a little space been given to rebellion against rebellion. That Christians do not get a good press in the Tales of the City is in many ways understandable. But it also made me wish for greater nuance at times."

MAVOR, CAROL. Black and blue; the bruised passion of Camera lucida, la Jetée, Sans soleil, and Hiroshima mon amour; [by] Carol Mavor 193 p. 2012 Duke University Press

1. Black 2. Blue 3. Motion picture literature 4. Philosophical literature
ISBN 0822352710; 9780822352525 (cloth : alk. paper); 9780822352716 (pbk. : alk. paper)
LC 2011-053303

SUMMARY: In this book, by Carol Mavor, "Roland Barthes and Marcel Proust are inspirations for and subjects of Carol Mavor's . . . rumination on efforts to capture fleeting moments and to comprehend the incomprehensible. At the book's heart are one book and three films" by Roland Barthes, Chris Marker, and Marguerite Duras, each 'postwar' French works that register disturbing truths about loss and regret, and violence and history, through aesthetic refinement." (Publisher's note)

REVIEW: *Choice* v50 no6 p1033 F 2013 E. A. Vanborre

REVIEW: *TLS* no5755 p19 Jl 19 2013 LUCY SCHOLES

"Black and Blue: The Bruising Passion of Camera Lucida, La Jetée, Sans Soleil, and Hiroshima mon amour." "Carol Mavor's 'Black and Blue' is less a book and more an experiment in montage. The resulting text is a mixture of film stills, reproduced images, personal memoir, theoretical analysis, and film and literary criticism. . . . The overall effect is hypnotic, aided by the stunning visual affect of the book, its elegant typesetting and the variety of the images that litter the text--meaning that some of Mavor's distinctive turns of phrase only leave one puzzling over them after the fact. . . . If you're not as avid a Barthesian as Mavor, Black and Blue can be difficult to decipher, but a joy to read nonetheless; a veritable feast for the eyes."

MAXWELL, ELIZABETH. Happily Ever After; [by] Elizabeth Maxwell 336 p. 2014 Touchstone

1. Characters & characteristics 2. Divorced women—Fiction 3. Love stories 4. Self-realization in women—Fiction 5. Women novelists—Fiction
ISBN 1476732663; 9781476732664 (trade paper)
LC 2013-017339

SUMMARY: This book is "about an erotic-romance author whose fictional characters come to life. Sadie Fuller is a slightly frumpy divorced mom with an 11-year-old daughter, gay ex-husband, and a no-strings-attached weekly date with fun-but-flabby Jason. With K. T. Briggs as her pen name, she plumbs women's wildest fantasies in her racy novels. Things get interesting when a strange passage appears in her latest manuscript, followed by the materialization of the hero, Aidan, at the local Target." (Booklist)

REVIEW: *Booklist* v110 no11 p32 F 1 2014 Aleksandra Walker

REVIEW: *Kirkus Rev* v82 no4 p291 F 15 2014

"Happily Ever After". "What if a novelist's characters object to their storylines? Worse, what if they hijack the plot? While other mothers in her posh neighborhood fill their days with Bikram yoga classes, Sadie Fuller secretly writes steamy romance novels. . . . Yet one morning, Sadie discovers an extra 1,500 words have mysteriously appeared in the novel she's writing. . . . Debut novelist Maxwell and Sadie herself deftly bend the rules of genre fiction, letting the boundaries between reality and fiction shimmy and shimmer. Clever, engaging and sparkling with wit."

MAXWELL, GLYN, 1962-. Pluto; [by] Glyn Maxwell 64 p. 2013 Picador Paperbacks

1. English poetry 2. Loss (Psychology) 3. Lyric poetry 4. Pluto (Dwarf planet) 5. Poetry (Literary form)
ISBN 1447231589; 9781447231585

SUMMARY: "Pluto--the non-planet, the ex-planet--is the dominant celestial influence in Glyn Maxwell's new collection: 'Pluto' is a book about change, the before-and-after of love, the aftermath of loss: change of status and station, home and place, of tense and pronoun. It also marks a radical departure for one of our most celebrated English poets." (Publisher's note)

REVIEW: *Economist* v407 no8830 p99 Ap 6 2013

REVIEW: *TLS* no5776 p28 D 13 2013 BEN WILKINSON

"Pluto." "Glyn Maxwell's ninth collection, 'Pluto,' is the work of a writer who properly subscribes to this ethos, and who figures poetry as that fresh look and listen which might . . . smash the frozen sea within--or at least throw the self into serious doubt. . . . 'Pluto' frequently echoes the loneliness of the decommissioned planet it is named after. . . . But what is striking is how successfully Maxwell merges genuine, often painful emotion with a postmodern embrace of ironic cross-examination and reflexiveness. . . . Formally crafted, yet forever on the brink of metrical collapse; earnest and echt, but with an eye for poetry's artifice and contradictions: Maxwell excels at casual delivery of complex thinking. . . . It is poetry that few of his contemporaries can rival."

MAXWELL, GLYN, 1962-.ed. The Poetry of Derek Walcott 1948-2013. See The Poetry of Derek Walcott 1948-2013

MAXWELL, GLYN, 1962-. On Poetry; Oberon masters; [by] Glyn Maxwell 160 p. 2012 Harvard University Press

1. English language—Versification 2. Literary form 3. Literature—History & criticism 4. Poetics 5. Poetry (Literary form)—History & criticism

ISBN 0674725662; 1849430853; 9780674725669; 9781849430852

SUMMARY: This book, by Glyn Maxwell, "is a collection of short essays and reflections on poetry. . . . These essays illustrates Maxwell's poetic philosophy, that the greatest verse arises from a harmony of mind and body, and that poetic forms originate in human necessities breath, heartbeat, footstep, posture. He speaks of his inspirations, his models, and takes us inside the strange world of the Creative Writing Class, where four young hopefuls grapple with love, sex, cheap wine and hard work." (Publisher's note)

REVIEW: *Choice* v51 no9 p1594 My 2014 M. F. McClure

REVIEW: *Commonweal* v141 no10 p24-9 Je 1 2014 Anthony Domestico

REVIEW: *N Y Rev Books* v60 no20 p83-6 D 19 2013 Nick Laird

"On Poetry." "[Glyn Maxwell's] approach is both thrilling and frustrating: it is heartening to read his assurance and enthusiasm, but his dictums shut down interesting questions and his certainty occasionally feels like camouflage for its opposite. . . . I like the urgency and stringency of Maxwell's advice, and it should be useful to students coming to a poem. . . . Maxwell is at his best when he discusses particulars, coming at well-worn poems from unusual angles. . . . Arguing with this book is part of the joy of it: it's provocative and opinionated and personal and urgent; by turns good-humored and intemperate; and full of earned advice on the writing and reading of poems."

REVIEW: *Poetry* v202 no1 p55-9 Ap 2013 Gwyneth Lewis Michael Lista Ange Mlinko

REVIEW: *TLS* no5721 p10-1 N 23 2012 WILLIAM WOOTTEN

REVIEW: *Yale Rev* v101 no4 p160-73 O 2013 STEPHEN YENSER

MAXWELL, JULIE. These are Our Children; [by] Julie Maxwell 304 p. 2013 Quercus Publishing Plc

1. Adultery—Fiction 2. English fiction 3. Neonatal intensive care 4. Nurses—Fiction 5. Stillbirth

ISBN 1780877129; 9781780877129

SUMMARY: In this novel by Julie Maxwell, "Florence believes that she can love two men at the same time. . . . Thomas . . . has invented a new incubator that promises to save the lives of very premature babies. But the implications for parents--and politics--are fraught with controversy. Then Thomas clashes with Helen: a nurse grieving for her own baby, miscarried just before the new technology was introduced." (Publisher's note)

REVIEW: *TLS* no5776 p19 D 13 2013 CLAIRE LOWDON

"These Are Our Children." "'These Are Our Children' opens the door on a whole ward full of pre- and neonatal complications. This largely uncharted subject matter brings its own complications, not least the danger of slipping into reportage or polemic. . . . But fiction can go anywhere, as long as the writer is sufficiently skilled and brave; [author Julie] Maxwell is totally unafraid, and her precision-tooled descriptive powers make her an invaluable guide. . . . This unlimited access is Maxwell's chief triumph. But in a quieter way. 'These Are Our Children' is also a formally inventive novel. . . . The innovation lies in the tonal contrast between the two storylines."

MAY, ALLYSON N. The fox-hunting controversy, 1781-2004; class and cruelty; [by] Allyson N. May viii, 209 p. 2013 Ashgate

1. Animal welfare—Great Britain 2. Fox hunting—Great Britain 3. Foxes—Great Britain 4. Historical literature 5. Social classes—Great Britain

ISBN 1409442209 (hardcover: alk. paper); 1409442217 (ebook); 140946069X (ebk - ePUB); 9781409442202 (hardcover: alk. paper); 9781409442219 (ebook); 9781409460695 (ebk - ePUB)

LC 2012-028960

SUMMARY: Written by Allyson N. May, "This study explores the attacks made on fox hunting from 1781 to the legal ban achieved in 2004, as well as assessing the reasons for its continued appeal and post-ban survival. Chapters cover debates in the areas of: class and hunting; concerns over cruelty and animal welfare; party politics; the hunt in literature; and nostalgia." (Publisher's note)

REVIEW: *TLS* no5790 p24 Mr 21 2014 CLAIRE HAZELTON

"The Fox-Hunting Controversy, 1781-2004." "Allyson N. May's 'The Fox-Hunting Controversy, 1781-2004' . . . demonstrates the sport's complex and ever-changing place in English culture, making the implications of the ban more multifaceted and far-reaching than might at first appear. . . . May captures . . . changing attitudes by viewing the hunt as a theme in literature. The fox hunter protagonist, she asserts, undergoes a drastic transformation. . . . May concludes with speculations about why hunting has survived for so long. . . . The hunt, says Allyson May, will continue as long as such complacent images of the English past remain potent."

MAY, ERNEST R.ed. The Kennedy tapes. See The Kennedy tapes

MAYAKOVSKY, VLADIMIR, 1893-1930. Selected poems; [by] Vladimir Mayakovsky 2013 Northwestern University Press

1. Agitprop 2. Futurism (Literary movement) 3. Poems—Collections 4. Political poetry, Russian 5. Soviet poetry

ISBN 9780810129078 paperback

SUMMARY: "James McGavran's new translation of Vladimir Mayakovsky's poetry is the first to fully capture the Futurist and Soviet agitprop artist's voice. Because of his work as a propagandist for the Soviet regime, and because of his posthumous enshrinement by Stalin as 'the best and most talented poet of our Soviet epoch,' Mayakovsky has most often been interpreted—and translated—within a political context." (Publisher's note)

REVIEW: *TLS* no5796 p24 My 2 2014 PETER FRANCE

"Selected Poems." "James H. McGavran III writes that his

new collection of translations 'is designed with the goal of . . . reintroducing Mayakovsky to the anglophone world, focusing instead on his gifts and achievements as a poet.' He is by no means the first in the field, but his volume contains a great deal of poetry, not all of it familiar. . . . McGavran says regretfully that while he hopes to recreate in English the powerful metaphors and innovative language, he has generally sacrificed rhythm and rhyme to 'semantic fidelity,' attempting to compensate for this by 'drawing attention in notes to effects that are particularly important or unusual in the original.' I am not convinced that this sacrifice is justified."

MAYER, JOHN D. Personal intelligence; the power of personality and how it shapes our lives; [by] John D. Mayer 288 p. 2014 Scientific American / Farrar, Straus and Giroux

1. Emotional intelligence 2. PSYCHOLOGY—Interpersonal Relations 3. PSYCHOLOGY—Personality 4. Personality 5. Psychological literature 6. SELF-HELP—Personal Growth—General
ISBN 9780374230852 (hardback); 9780374708993 (ebook)
LC 2013-033926

SUMMARY: In this book, author John D. Mayer "coined the term 'personal intelligence' in order to describe our inherent need to understand the people around us. Personal intelligence includes a spectrum of proficiencies, and there is a degree to which it can be learned and cultivated. Any apt assessment of others begins, or at least is correlated with, an ability to know one's self, and Mayer explores patterns of personal intelligence from adolescence to adulthood." (Publishers Weekly)

REVIEW: *Choice* v51 no12 p2275 Ag 2014 D. S. Dunn

REVIEW: *Kirkus Rev* v82 no1 p94 Ja 1 2014

"The Power of Personality and How It Shapes Our Lives". "[An] astute exploration of a different form of intelligence: the ability to understand the personalities of other human beings as well as our own. . . . [John D.] Mayer fills his book with ingenious studies of how people judge others. . . . Those looking to win friends and influence people should turn to Dale Carnegie and his cheerful disciples. Mayer confines himself to invariably stimulating insights backed by solid scientific research, so readers looking to understand the human condition will certainly enjoy this book."

REVIEW: *Publ Wkly* v260 no45 p59-60 N 11 2013

MAYER, PAMELA. Don't sneeze at the wedding; 32 p. 2013 Kar-Ben Pub.

1. Children's stories 2. Flower girls 3. Jewish marriage customs & rites 4. Jews—United States—Fiction 5. Sneezing—Fiction 6. Weddings—Fiction 7. Weddings—Humor
ISBN 1467704296; 9781467704298
LC 2012-029188

SUMMARY: In this book by Pamela Mayer, "it's the morning of Aunt Rachel's wedding, and Anna is going to be the flower girl. Everything is not perfect, however, because she wakes up with a sneeze and continues to sneeze as she puts on her fancy dress, her family arrives at the temple, she gets her hair done, and she watches Uncle Matt sign the ketubah. With each sneeze, well-meaning adults offer tips for halting it, which Anna incorporates into a six-step process." (School Library Journal)

REVIEW: *Booklist* v110 no6 p44 N 15 2013 Ilene Cooper

REVIEW: *Kirkus Rev* v81 no16 p71 Ag 15 2013

"Don't Sneeze at the Wedding." "This is two books in one, but it's not as much of a bargain as it sounds like. Children may feel as though they're reading two stories at once. The first is a step by step guide to a Jewish wedding. . . . That book is practical, although it may seem a little dull to children who aren't obsessed with brides or pink shoes or flower girls' dresses. The second book is a story about Anna, a flower girl who's dressed in pink from head to toe, including a pink wreath of flowers on her head. . . . The second book is much more amusing than the first. The problem is that the educational book and the humor book never quite mesh."

REVIEW: *Publ Wkly* v260 no33 p71 Ag 19 2013

REVIEW: *SLJ* v59 no9 p128 S 2013 Martha Link Yesowitch

MAYFIELD, JOHN E. The engine of complexity; evolution as computation; [by] John E. Mayfield 398 p. 2013 Columbia University Press

1. Biological control systems—Mathematical models 2. Biology—Mathematical models 3. Computational complexity 4. Evolution (Biology)—Mathematical models 5. Scientific literature
ISBN 9780231163040 (cloth : alk. paper); 9780231535281 (ebook)
LC 2013-005728

SUMMARY: In this book, John E. Mayfield "uses the phrase 'engine of complexity' to describe the basic cycle of evolution--mutate, replicate, select. He presents this paradigm as a form of iterative computation and ties it to the concept that everything in the universe (biological and otherwise) is input data, computation, or output data. From this foundation, Mayfield addresses the origins of biological complexity." (Choice: Current Reviews for Academic Libraries)

REVIEW: *Choice* v51 no5 p862-3 Ja 2014 R. M. Denome

"The Engine of Complexity: Evolution as Computation." "The book is organized as a series of questions; under each question, the writing is engaging, if a bit long-winded. The book works best as the ruminations of someone who has thought deeply and broadly about the origins of complexity in all its forms. Unfortunately, the book's large-scale organization is impenetrable. [John E.] Mayfield also falls into the trap of trying to explain some extremely complex systems (e.g., brain function) in layperson's terms. The results are nebulous at best. A significant part of the book is speculative (e.g., origins of consciousness) or digressive (e.g., relationship of entropy to information content). Despite these shortcomings, 'The Engine of Complexity' is enjoyable and thought provoking."

MAYLE, PETER. The Corsican caper; a novel; [by] Peter Mayle 176 p. 2014 Knopf

1. Businesspeople—Fiction 2. Detective & mystery stories 3. Real property—Fiction 4. Rich people—Fiction
ISBN 0307962865; 9780307962867 (hardback); 9780345804563 (trade paperback)
LC 2013-037049

SUMMARY: In this book, by Peter Mayle, "billionaire Francis Reboul owns the Palais du Pharo, which was 'originally built for Napoleon III' and is 'the biggest private residence in Marseille.' . . . Russian businessman Oleg Vronsky, accustomed to getting whatever he desires by fair means or foul, covets the Palais du Pharo, which Reboul has no interest in selling. Vronsky's machinations and Reboul's responses, mostly engineered by his American detective friend, Sam Levitt" drive the plot. (Publishers Weekly)

REVIEW: *Booklist* v110 no14 p51 Mr 15 2014 Connie Fletcher

REVIEW: *Booklist* v110 no11 p3 F 1 2014 Brad Hooper

"The Corsican Caper," "High Crime Area: Tales of Darkness and Dread," and "In Paradise". "[Peter] Mayle sends his popular sleuth Sam Levitt out on further investigative pursuits around the lovely South of France, Sam's focus this time on Russian tycoon Oleg Vronsky. . . . Eight tense, powerful short stories testify to [Joyce Carol] Oates' talent in the short form. . . . This author's esteemed reputation is deep and widespread, and his complicated, intelligent new novel—about a group of women and men gathering for meditations and reflection at the site of a former German concentration camp—will reward his followers."

REVIEW: *Kirkus Rev* v82 no7 p272 Ap 1 2014

REVIEW: *Publ Wkly* v261 no9 p45 Mr 3 2014

MAYOR, ARCHER. Three can keep a secret; [by] Archer Mayor 336 p. 2013 Minotaur Books

1. Burglars—Fiction 2. Detective & mystery stories 3. Gunther, Joe (Fictitious character)—Fiction 4. Murderers—Fiction 5. Police—Vermont—Fiction
ISBN 125002613X; 9781250026132 (hardcover)
LC 2013-016673

SUMMARY: In this book, Joe Gunther and his team . . . are usually called in on major cases by local Vermont enforcement whenever they need expertise and back-up. But after the state is devastated by Hurricane Irene, the police from one end of the state are taxed to their limits, leaving Joe Gunther involved in an odd, seemingly unrelated series of cases. . . . A seventeen year old gravesite is exposed, revealing a coffin that had been filled with rocks instead of the expected remains." (Publisher's note)

REVIEW: *Booklist* v110 no1 p48 S 1 2013 Thomas Gaughan

"Three Can Keep a Secret." "Settling in with a new Joe Günther novel is like catching up with old friends. It's a chance to check on Joe's love life (looking up),Willy Kunkel's socialization (Sammy Martens' love, fatherhood, and even the case of the rock-filled coffin are mellowing the once reliably abrasive Willy). Even Joe's former lover, Governor Gail Zigman, appears, navigating the partisan political minefield created by Irene's destruction. This twenty-fourth entry in a wonderful series is very close to Mayor's best."

REVIEW: *Kirkus Rev* v81 no18 p270 S 15 2013

REVIEW: *Publ Wkly* v260 no33 p42-3 Ag 19 2013

MAZNAVI, NURA.ed. Salaam, love. See Salaam, love

MAZZEO, TILAR J. The Hotel on Place Vendome; Life, Death, and Betrayal at the Hotel Ritz in Paris; [by] Tilar J. Mazzeo 320 p. 2014 HarperCollins

1. Collaborationists (Traitors) 2. Elite (Social sciences)—France—History 3. France—History—German occupation, 1940-1945 4. Historical literature 5. Ritz Hotel (Paris, France)
ISBN 0061791083; 9780061791086

SUMMARY: This book "tells the story of the Paris Ritz . . . as the epicenter of Hitler's occupied Paris. . . . The author chronicles a destination frequented by the upper crust, or gratin, of an increasingly international Parisian society. The focus of Mazzeo's . . . narrative is less on the hotel itself than on the various personages, from novelists Marcel Proust and F. Scott Fitzgerald to the Duke and Duchess of Windsor to actresses Arletty and Marlene Dietrich, who made it their home." (Library Journal)

REVIEW: *Booklist* v110 no13 p14-5 Mr 1 2014 Annie Bostrom

"The Hotel on Place Vendôme: Life, Death, and Betrayal at the Hotel Ritz in Paris." "[Tilar J.] Mazzeo's latest threads a great many strands . . . through a single bead: Paris' Hotel Ritz. In a narrative style, Mazzeo holds a dizzying cast of persons of interest under glass as they sleep and work, meet and seek refuge in the then-Swiss-owned hotel. Truly, fiction could not write betrayal, resistance, collaboration, or celebration with more robustness or with a more alluring who's-who of writers, artists, and military powers than history did in this single hotel. Amid chilling tales of the terrible ambiguities of war and the treatment and purging of enemies on all sides, Mazzeo offers lightness in her biography of an inarguably dark time through obvious care for her subjects."

REVIEW: *Kirkus Rev* v82 no2 p61 Ja 15 2014

REVIEW: *Libr J* v139 no8 p88 My 1 2014 Kelsey Berry

REVIEW: *Publ Wkly* v260 no48 p40 N 25 2013

MAZZOLA, ELIZABETH. Learning and literacy in female hands, 1520-1698; [by] Elizabeth Mazzola 141 p. 2013 Ashgate

1. English literature—Early modern, 1500-1700—History and criticism 2. English literature—Women authors—History and criticism 3. English women authors 4. Historical literature 5. Literacy—History 6. Literacy in literature 7. Women—Education—Great Britain 8. Women—Education—History 9. Women and literature—England—History—16th century 10. Women and literature—England—History—17th century
ISBN 9781409453758 (hardcover : alk. paper)
LC 2013-004320

SUMMARY: "Focusing on the unusual learning and schooling of women in early modern England, this study explores how and why women wrote, the myriad forms their alphabets could assume, and the shape which vernacular literacy acquired in their hands. Elizabeth Mazzola argues that early modern women's writings often challenged the lessons of their male teachers, since they were designed to conceal rather than reveal women's learning and schooling." (Publisher's note)

REVIEW: *TLS* no5788 p30-1 Mr 7 2014 JOHANNA HARRIS

"Learning and Literacy in Female Hands, 1520-1698." "This new study by Elizabeth Mazzola exemplifies the current fashion for reading early modem women's writing as 'resistant,' 'wresting language away' from the reader, both then and now. Mazzola extends this criticism to women's education and literacy, focusing on a range of female writers. . . . Mazzola's book is engaging--and the call to explore the literacy of illiterate men and women in early modem England is enticing--but its brevity is disappointing for a study that claims to address women's literacy across 178 years."

MAZZUCATO, MARIANA. The entrepreneurial state; debunking public vs. private sector myths; [by] Mariana Mazzucato 237 p. 2013 Anthem Press

1. Diffusion of innovations 2. Economics literature 3. Entrepreneurship—Government policy 4. Research, Industrial 5. Technological innovations—Government policy
ISBN 9780857282521 (pbk.: alk. paper)
LC 2013-017536

SUMMARY: Written by Mariana Mazzucato and part of the Anthem Other Canon Economics series, "This book . . . debunks the myth of the state as a large bureaucratic organization that can at best facilitate the creative innovation . . . in the dynamic private sector. Analysing various case studies of innovation-led growth. . . it describes the opposite situation, whereby the private sector only finds the courage to invest after the entrepreneurial state has made the high-risk investments." (Publisher's note)

REVIEW: *Choice* v51 no6 p1061 F 2014 J. Bhattacharya

REVIEW: *Economist* v408 no8851 p59 Ag 31 2013

REVIEW: *N Y Rev Books* v51 no7 p50-3 Ap 24 2014 Jeffrey Madrick

"The Entrepreneurial State: Debunking Public vs. Private Sector Myths" and "Doing Capitalism in the Innovation Economy: Markets, Speculation and the State." "'The Entrepreneurial State' . . . is one of the most incisive economic books in years. . . . In [author Mariana] Mazzucato's account of the enormous success of federal scientific and technical research as the foundation of the most revolutionary of today's technologies, the most telling example is how dependent Steve Job's Apple was on government-funded breakthroughs. . . . [Author William H.] Janeway . . . argues for the importance of government in the nation's economic growth."

REVIEW: *New York Times* v163 no56450 pA20 Mr 24 2014 TERESA TRITCH

REVIEW: *Newsweek Global* v161 no29 p1 Ag 16 2013 Christopher Dickey

REVIEW: *Science* v345 no6199 p883 Ag 22 2014 Davide Consoli

MCAFEE, ANDREW. The second machine age. See Brynjolfsson, E.

MCANULTY, STACY. Dear santasaurus; 32 p. 2013 Boyds Mills Press

1. Children—Conduct of life 2. Christmas gifts 3. Christmas stories for children 4. Dinosaurs—Juvenile fiction 5. Santa Claus—Juvenile fiction
ISBN 1590788761; 9781590788769
LC 2013-931087

SUMMARY: In this children's picture book, tiny purple dinosaur Ernest B. Spinosaurus "writes 16 letters to the dinosaur in the red suit over the course of a year. Throughout, Ernest never fails to emphasize his good behavior, downplay his mischievous habits, and remind Santasaurus that he'd love a Jurassic Turbo Scooter X9." (Publishers Weekly)

REVIEW: *Horn Book Magazine* v89 no6 p67 N/D 2013 SHARA L. HARDESON

"Dear Santasaurus". "On January 1st, young dinosaur Ernest B. Spinosaurus begins writing letters to Santasaurus thanking him for recent Christmas presents and vowing to stay on the nice list for the whole rest of the year. Subsequent letters are filled with wish lists and confessions of progressively outrageous mischief. . . . Visual irony augments the comedy: illustrations clearly show that Ernest doesn't always tell Santasaurus the whole truth about his trouble-making. Bold black outlines and vibrant colors mark Ernest as a fitting cartoon stand-in for unruly but well-intentioned children."

MCARDLE, MEGAN. The Up Side of Down; Why Failing Well Is the Key to Success; [by] Megan McArdle 304 p. 2014 Penguin Group USA Viking Adult

1. Business failures 2. Failure (Psychology) 3. Self-help materials 4. Success 5. Success in business
ISBN 067002614X; 9780670026142
LC 2013-036820

SUMMARY: "If you want to succeed in business and in life, Megan McArdle argues in this . . . book, you have to learn how to harness the power of failure. . . . McArdle argues that America is unique in its willingness to let people and companies fail, but also in its determination to let them pick up after the fall. Failure is how people and businesses learn." (Publisher's note)

REVIEW: *Economist* v411 no8882 p85 Ap 12 2014

REVIEW: *Kirkus Rev* v82 no2 p36 Ja 15 2014

"The Up Side of Down: Why Failing Well Is the Key to Success". "An illuminating look at the psychology behind rebounding from defeat. . . . [Megan] McArdle states her points in prose saturated with a self-effacing lightheartedness, lending levity to the crestfallen reality of loss. A detour into her mother's disastrous treatment for a ruptured appendix, however, feels odd when buttressed against chapters on the government bailout of General Motors and the art of self-identifying a recurring problem. . . . Sage counsel on how to learn from failure with humor and grace."

REVIEW: *Libr J* v139 no1 p1 Ja 2014

REVIEW: *Libr J* v138 no14 p87 S 1 2013

REVIEW: *N Y Times Book Rev* p18 Ap 6 2014 SCOTT A. SANDAGE

REVIEW: *Natl Rev* v66 no3 p44-5 F 24 2014 ROBERT VERBRUGGEN

REVIEW: *Publ Wkly* v260 no48 p47 N 25 2013

MCBETH, COLETTE. Precious thing; [by] Colette McBeth 304 p. 2014 Minotaur Books

1. Bullying 2. Detective & mystery stories 3. Female friendship—Fiction 4. Missing persons—Fiction 5. Television journalists
ISBN 1250041198; 9781250041197 (hardback)
LC 2013-032859

SUMMARY: In this book, by Colette McBeth, "Rachel and Clara promised [their friendship] would last forever. . . . Now in their late twenties Rachel has the television career, the apartment and the boyfriend, while Clara's life is spiraling further out of control. . . . Then Rachel's news editor assigns her to cover a police press conference, and she is shocked when she arrives to learn that the subject is Clara, reported missing. Is it abduction, suicide or something else altogether?" (Publisher's note)

REVIEW: *Booklist* v110 no9/10 p53 Ja 1 2014 Christine Tran

REVIEW: *Kirkus Rev* v82 no3 p224 F 1 2014

"Precious Thing". "TV journalist Rachel Walsh has been summoned to a press conference to cover the disappearance of a young woman. It's all standard operating procedure until she sees the poster of the missing woman: Clara O'Connor, her best friend. . . . Clara's disappearance is just the first of many mysteries. A former BBC crime reporter, [Colette] McBeth crafts a twisty tale in this debut novel that abounds with stalkers, secrets, betrayals, missing persons and grainy CCTV images. A darkly fraught friendship lies at the heart of this spellbinding thriller."

REVIEW: *Libr J* v139 no4 p84 Mr 1 2014 Robin Nesbitt

REVIEW: *Publ Wkly* v261 no3 p33-4 Ja 20 2014

MCBRATNEY, SAM. There, there; 40 p. 2013 Candlewick Press

1. Bears—Juvenile fiction 2. Caring 3. Children's stories 4. Fathers & sons—Fiction 5. Hugging
ISBN 9780763667023
LC 2012-954336

SUMMARY: In this book by Sam McBratney, "Little Hansie Bear loves to pretend, but walking like a duck can be hazardous, especially when he falls into a deep-down ditch and has to be helped out by his dad. With a 'There, there' and a hug, Hansie is soon off to play again. So when Dad hurts his foot, Hansie knows just what to do--a 'There, there,' a big hug, and everything is all right again." (Publisher's note)

REVIEW: *Booklist* v110 no2 p73 S 15 2013 Mary Anne Owen

REVIEW: *Bull Cent Child Books* v67 no2 p104 O 2013 J. H.

"There, There." "Little Hansie Bear is not having an easy day: he falls into a deep ditch and bangs his knee while trying to walk like a duck, gets sand blown into his eyes while digging a hole, and bumps his head on a branch while pushing his pal on the swing. . . . This could have been overly sentimental, but [author Sam] McBratney keeps it real with concise and natural language. . . . The soft: autumnal tones and softly scribbled detail in the flora and fauna of [illustrator Ivan] Bates' mixed-media illustrations effectively echo the gentleness of the text."

REVIEW: *Kirkus Rev* v81 no13 p278 Jl 1 2013

REVIEW: *Publ Wkly* p55 Children's starred review annual 2013

REVIEW: *Publ Wkly* v260 no29 p63 Jl 22 2013

REVIEW: *SLJ* v59 no9 p125 S 2013 Roxanne Burg

MCBRIDE, DAMIAN. Power Trip; A Decade of Policy, Plots and Spin; [by] Damian McBride 448 p. 2013 Biteback

1. Blair, Tony, 1953- 2. Brown, Gordon, 1951- 3. Great Britain—Politics & government 4. Memoirs 5. Political corruption
ISBN 1849545960; 9781849545969

SUMMARY: This book is a political memoir by Damian McBride. "He was [British Prime Minister] Gordon Brown's spin doctor during Brown's time at the Treasury and his first two years at No 10, in which capacity he schmoozed, bullied, berated, lied and not-quite-lied relentlessly in the service of his 'brilliant' boss." (New Statesman)

REVIEW: *London Rev Books* v35 no19 p15 O 10 2013 David Runciman

REVIEW: *New Statesman* v142 no5178 p48-9 O 4 2013 Helen Lewis

REVIEW: *TLS* no5773 p23 N 22 2013 MICHAEL WHITE

"Power Trip: A Decade of Policy, Plots and Spin." "This is a much better book than was conveyed by the brutal imperatives of tabloid serialization and sensationalization during the recent party conference season. In its boisterous fashion, it is well written, full of shrewd insights and dark humour. But it is also a shocking book in ways the tabloids were bound to miss, because it reflects what they too often regard as normal behaviour. . . . All this is self-consciously confessional. . . . But how sincere is it? [Damian] McBride gives the impression of confessing to what was known while covering up worse. He denies lying, yet admits fabrication a few pages later."

MCBRIDE, JAMES, 1957-. The good lord bird; [by] James McBride 432 p. 2013 Riverhead Books

1. Abolitionists—Fiction 2. Fugitive slaves—United States—Fiction 3. Harpers Ferry (W. Va.)—History—John Brown's Raid, 1859—Fiction 4. Historical fiction
ISBN 1594486344; 9781594486340
LC 2013-004014

SUMMARY: In this novel, by James McBride, "Henry Shackleford is a young slave living in the Kansas Territory in 1857, when the region is a battleground between anti- and pro-slavery forces. When John Brown, the legendary abolitionist, arrives in the area, an argument between Brown and Henry's master quickly turns violent. Henry is forced to leave town--with Brown, who believes he's a girl. Eventually [Henry] finds himself with Brown at the historic raid on Harpers Ferry in 1859." (Publisher's note)

REVIEW: *Booklist* v109 no19/20 p43 Je 1 2013 Carol Haggas

REVIEW: *Booklist* v110 no9/10 p68 Ja 1 2014 Joyce Saricks

REVIEW: *Christ Century* v131 no6 p40-1 Mr 19 2014 Amy Frykholm

REVIEW: *Christ Century* v130 no25 p22-3 D 11 2013

REVIEW: *Commentary* v137 no2 p53-4 F 2014 FERNANDA MOORE

"The Good Lord Bird: A Novel". "After [James] McBride's many cynical postmodern literary hijinks—the mannered and cinematic violence, the self-referential talk of tragic mulattos and the 'mental dependency' of slaves, the heretical depiction of Frederick Douglass as a lecherous drunk—a hackneyed message of teenaged self-actualization is saccharine and trite. Just when he should be ramping up for his novel's brutal, inevitable climax in Harpers Ferry, McBride seems determined to turn his protagonist into something very close to a fool. This new earnestness, moreover, undermines the tone of the rest of his book—which, for better or worse, is self-consciously arch."

REVIEW: *Kirkus Rev* v81 no2 p23 Je 1 2013

REVIEW: *Kirkus Rev* p26 N 15 2013 Best Books

REVIEW: *Libr J* v138 no21 p55 D 1 2013 Heather Malcolm

REVIEW: *Libr J* v138 no5 p90 Mr 15 2013 Barbara Hoffert

REVIEW: *N Y Times Book Rev* p34 Ag 25 2013

REVIEW: *N Y Times Book Rev* p1-16 Ag 18 2013 Baz Dreisinger

"The Good Lord Bird." "[A] brilliant romp of a novel about [John] Brown, narrated by a freed slave boy who passes as a girl. . . . [James] McBride--with the same flair for historical mining, musicality of voice and outsize characterization that made his memoir, 'The Color of Water,' an instant classic--pulls off his portrait masterfully, like a modern-day Mark Twain: evoking sheer glee with every page. . . . Delicious zingers . . . come by the paragraph, part of what makes the novel such a rollicking good time. . . . Henry's peripatetic adventures . . . make Huck Finn's seem tame. . . . For all his play, McBride studiously honors history, perhaps more than many previous portraits of Brown have done."

REVIEW: *New York Times* v162 no56243 pC6 Ag 29 2013 John Williams

REVIEW: *Publ Wkly* v260 no22 p34 Je 3 2013

MCCABE, JANET.ed. TV's Betty goes global. See TV's Betty goes global

MCCABE, VINTON RAFE. Death in Venice, California; [by] Vinton Rafe McCabe 192 p. 2014 The Permanent Press

1. Authors—Fiction 2. California—Fiction 3. Gay men—Fiction 4. Infatuation 5. Pornography 6. Psychological fiction

ISBN 9781579623524

LC 2013-040051

SUMMARY: In this book, "Jameson Frame, an educated, even revered, middle-aged man of letters, flees the cold canyons of Manhattan for Venice, California, where he is soon surrounded by all that this Bedouin village has to offer: wiccans, vegans, transients, artists, drummers, muscle men, skateboarders, plastic surgeons, pornographers, tarot card readers and ghouls. And an arrestingly beautiful young man named Chase, the subject and object of his yearning." (Publisher's note)

REVIEW: *Kirkus Rev* v82 no3 p98 F 1 2014

"Death in Venice, California". "[Vinton Rafe] McCabe's literary fiction debut reimagines Thomas Mann's 'Death in Venice,' setting it in glimmering Southern California. . . McCabe writes no heavy, dense drama; his gift is constructing intriguing characters to remodel Thomas Mann's original Death in Venice. . . . In Venice, [Jameson] Frame encounters . . . Chase, a skateboarding nude-and-underwear model, the 'perfection of the human form.' . . In this homoerotic paean, there's much symbolism. . . . An engaging allegorical pursuit of the mirage that is beauty's transcendence."

MCCANNA, TIM. Teeny Tiny Trucks; 24 p. 2013 Pathway Book Service

1. Children's stories 2. Gardens—Fiction 3. Size 4. Traffic congestion 5. Trucks—Juvenile fiction

ISBN 0989668819; 9780989668811

SUMMARY: This children's picture book, by Tim McCanna, "hits the road with a convoy of micro-sized rigs as they trek through a treacherous garden, down a grassy landscape, across a wide stretch of sidewalk and into the great beyond. Will they deliver their teeny tiny cargo on time?" (Publisher's note)

REVIEW: *Kirkus Rev* v81 no24 p349 D 15 2013

"Teeny Tiny Trucks". " In [Tim] McCanna and [Keith] Frawley's cheery picture-book debut, miniscule vehicles drive into supersized action. Accompanied by a bouncy rhyme, several brightly colored trucks rumble through the garden. . . . Though the color palette and cartoon appearance of the nameless vehicles may seem like a carbon copy of Disney's Cars (2006), illustrator Frawley has included humorous details for each truck. . . . The illustrations help tell a hilarious story, most notably of a traffic jam featuring a frog, slug and worm who are clearly not amused by the crowded garden path. McCanna similarly handles the text well. . . . The rhythmic pattern is clear, most of the rhyme is spot-on."

REVIEW: *Kirkus Rev* v82 no1 p244 Ja 1 2014

MCCARNEY, ROSEMARY. Every Day Is Malala Day; [by] Rosemary McCarney 32 p. 2014 Orca Book Pub

1. Children's nonfiction 2. Children's rights 3. Girls—Education 4. Girls—Social conditions 5. Yousafzai, Malala, 1997-

ISBN 1927583314; 9781927583319

SUMMARY: This book, by Rosemary McCarney, is "a letter of sisterhood to Malala Yousafzai. . . . After being shot for the simple act of going to school in her native Pakistan, Malala has become an international girls' rights icon and a contender for the Nobel Peace Prize. The book is written as a letter from girls around the world to Malala. . . These girls, too, know the barriers that stand in the way of a girl going to school." (Publisher's note)

REVIEW: *Booklist* v110 no18 p47 My 15 2014 Amina Chaudhri

REVIEW: *Kirkus Rev* v82 no4 p243 F 15 2014

"Every Day Is Malala Day". "An uplifting letter of tribute to Malala Yousafzai, the Pakistani teenager made famous by her determined advocacy for girls' education, illustrated with photos of her and other young people from around the world. . . . . Strong personal and collective statements of solidarity ('Instead of living in fear . . . / . . .we must shout for change') encourage readers to join Yousafzai. . . . A brief but moving manifesto that will spark both sympathy and heightened awareness of an endemic global outrage."

REVIEW: *SLJ* v60 no5 p148 My 2014 Toby Rajput

MCCARRY, SARAH. All our pretty songs; [by] Sarah McCarry 234 p. 2013 St. Martin's Griffin

1. Best friends—Fiction 2. Friendship—Fiction 3. Love—Fiction 4. Musicians—Fiction 5. Speculative fiction 6. Supernatural—Fiction

ISBN 1250040884; 9781250027085 (paperback); 9781250040886 (hardcover)

LC 2013-003451

SUMMARY: This novel by Sarah McCarry is about "two best friends who grew up like sisters: charismatic, mercurial, and beautiful Aurora, and the devoted, watchful narrator. Their unbreakable bond is challenged when a mysterious and gifted musician named Jack comes between them. They're not the only ones who have noticed Jack's gift; his music has awakened an ancient evil--and a world both above and below which may not be mythical at all." (Publisher's note)

REVIEW: *Booklist* v110 no1 p103 S 1 2013 Francisca Goldsmith

"All Our Pretty Songs." "An enigmatic, nameless narrator and her best friend, Aurora, have known each other since birth. . . . [Sarah] McCarry's beautifully rich narrative is as smooth and seductive as Aurora and Jack can be, effortlessly dropping references to authors from [Jean-Jaques] Rousseau to [Francesca Lia] Block. Goths and romantics both will eagerly await the second installment of a planned trilogy to find out what becomes of the girls, Jack, and the other well-drawn players in this magic-tinged cast."

REVIEW: *Booklist* v110 no2 p75 S 15 2013 Ann Kelley

"All Our Pretty Songs," 'Dark Triumph," and "Eleanor & Park." "In this suspenseful trilogy-starter, Aurora is sweet and flighty, while the unnamed narrator is surly. When Jack, an adult guitarist, comes into their life, the girls' differences come to a head. . . . The riveting historical adventure that began with 'Grave Mercy' (2012) follows the story of another of Death's handmaidens, Sybella. She is bound to a knight who is both the bane of her existence and her hope for the future. . . . Eleanor and Park, from opposite worlds, slowly build a relationship while riding the bus to school every day. The pure, fear-laced, yet steadily maturing relationship they develop is urgent and, of course, heartbreaking."

REVIEW: *Bull Cent Child Books* v67 no1 p36 S 2013 K. C.

"All Our Pretty Songs." "This sensually rich, richly sensual urban fairy tale channels 'Weetzie Bat' . . . as its unnamed narrator and her friend Aurora move through the music and party scene in the Pacific Northwest. . . . The decadent glamour of this world as the narrator portrays it hardly needs a hell to haunt it, but [author Sarah] McCarry takes the plunge anyway, painting word pictures that rival a Hieronymus Bosch painting in their manic intensity. The narrator is an adept foil for this world of overstimulated angst and unwise compromise. . . ."

REVIEW: *Kirkus Rev* v81 no12 p104 Je 15 2013

REVIEW: *SLJ* v59 no10 p1 O 2013 Carol A. Edwards

REVIEW: *Voice of Youth Advocates* v36 no4 p84 O 2013 Kaitlin Connors

MCCLASKEY, A. J.il. Aesop's fables. See Aesop's fables

MCCLELLAN, BRIAN. The Crimson Campaign; [by] Brian McClellan 608 p. 2014 Orbit

1. Betrayal—Fiction 2. Fantasy fiction 3. Imaginary places—Fiction 4. Imaginary wars and battles—Fiction 5. Kings and rulers—Fiction

ISBN 0316219088; 9780316219082 (hardcover); 9780316219099 (ebook); 9781478979456 (audio download)

LC 2013-024412

SUMMARY: In this book, by Brian McClellan, "Field Marshal Tamas of Adro, coup leader and powder mage, returns to the field to fend off the invasion from neighboring Kez that he hoped to provoke. Unexpected magic and the resurrection of the dead god Kresimir force Tamas and his troops to fight their way home through the army of his nemesis, Duke Nikslaus. In his absence, Inspector Adamat uncovers a network of spies in Adro's capital and learns that its patron has plans to co-opt the new democracy." (Publishers Weekly)

REVIEW: *Kirkus Rev* v82 no2 p288 Ja 15 2014

"The Crimson Campaign". "Second entry in the Powder Mage trilogy . . . something like a fantasy French Revolution with seriously weird wizards. The narrative follows the fortunes of three key figures. Field Marshal Tamas, a powder mage, one who eats or snorts gunpowder in order to gain magic powers, overthrew the monarchy and slaughtered the aristocracy and the Cabal of evil wizards that sustained them. Adamat . . .investigates conspirators and traitors. Tamas' disaffected son, Taniel, [is] a powder mage and master marksman. . . . This book is less relentlessly inventive than the inaugural volume but still impressively distinctive and pungent, with solid plotting and exceptional action sequences. A reliably rewarding installment that will keep appetites whetted for the conclusion."

REVIEW: *Libr J* v139 no7 p61 Ap 15 2014 Megan M. McArdle

REVIEW: *Publ Wkly* v260 no51 p43 D 16 2013

MCCLINTOCK, NORAH. Hit and run; [by] Norah McClintock 232 p. 2014 Darby Creek

1. Hit & run drivers 2. Murder investigation—Fiction 3. Mystery and detective stories 4. Teacher-student relationships—Fiction 5. Teachers—Fiction

ISBN 9781467726054 (lib. bdg. : alk. paper)

LC 2013-017548

SUMMARY: In this book, the first of Norah McClintock's Mike & Riel Mysteries series, "Mike was 11 when his mother was killed in a hit-and-run. Now 15, he lives with his uncle Billy, a hard partying mechanic who is more older brother than guardian. Upon discovedng that his new history teacher, Mr. Riel, is not only a retired cop but also one of the investigators who worked on his mom's case, Mike badgers Riel into reopening the case, a decision with far-reaching consequences." (Booklist)

REVIEW: *Booklist* v110 no14 p74-5 Mr 15 2014 Magan Szwarek

"Hit and Run." "This first entry in the Mike & Riel Mysteries series, originally published in Canada a decade ago, includes some dead technology references (VHS tapes, portable phones) that may distract contemporary readers. That aside, this well-crafted mystery is a real page-turner with plenty of twists and a hero kids can get behind. Mike's unacknowledged despair and his determination to uncover the truth make him a very appealing hero. This is marketed for reluctant readers, but mystery fans of all sorts will be glad to find out there are four more titles to come."

REVIEW: *Kirkus Rev* v82 no3 p323 F 1 2014

"Hit and Run". "Bad seed wars with good in an orphaned teenager who finds out that his mother's death wasn't an accident. Originally published a decade ago in Canada, this series opener set in Toronto hooks Michael—a troubled teen surrounded by poor companions and role models— up with his history teacher, quiet ex-cop John Riel. . . . The electrifying discovery that his new teacher had been in charge of his mom's never-solved case . . . leads to new questions and clues that implicate both the uncle who is his sole remaining family member and a pair of shady associates. . . .The rescue of an at-risk adolescent with light and dark sides takes center stage, but the unfolding mystery adds a dramatic subplot."

REVIEW: *Voice of Youth Advocates* v37 no2 p62 Je 2014 Kim Carter

REVIEW: *Publ Wkly* v261 no3 p57 Ja 20 2014

REVIEW: *Voice of Youth Advocates* v37 no2 p62 Je 2014 Robbie Carter

MCCLURE, NIKKI.il. Sinful Folk. See Hayes, N.

MCCONACHIE, BRUCE A., 1944-. Theatre and mind; [by] Bruce A. McConachie 82 p. 2013 Palgrave Macmillan
1. Acting—Psychological aspects 2. Actors—Psychology 3. Theater—Semiotics 4. Theater audiences—Psychology 5. Theater literature
ISBN 9780230275836
LC 2012-032290

SUMMARY: This book by Bruce McConachie "provides an introduction to the cognitive foundations of theatre studies and argues that key developments in cognitive science actually challenge some of the major assumptions about what takes place in the theatre." (Publisher's note) McConachie's arguments are "based on cognitive literary theory and Literary Darwinism." (Times Literary Supplement)

REVIEW: *Choice* v50 no12 p2241 Ag 2013 K. Tancheva

REVIEW: *TLS* no5764 p29 S 20 2013 WILLIAM FLESCH
"Theatre and Mind." "Theatre is so deeply embedded in human culture in some form or other it is probably a human universal, so it is not surprising that [Bruce] McConachie's new terminology does not give rise to particularly novel insights. What is new, or newish, besides the terminology, is the natural history that McConachie invokes to explain how and why theatre works. . . . McConachie's account, by celebrating theatre as a badge of the human achievement of co-operative culture, seems to miss what may be its most central aspect, which is that it is not only the depiction but the enactment of conflict"

MCCORMICK, CARLO.ed. City as canvas. See City as canvas

MCCORMICK, JOHN P.ed. Weimar thought. See Weimar thought

MCCRACKEN, JOHN. A history of Malawi, 1859-1966; [by] John McCracken xviii, 485 p. 2012 James Currey Boydell & Brewer
1. Great Britain—Colonies—Africa—Administration 2. Great Britain—Colonies—Africa—History 3. Historical literature 4. Malawi—Politics & government
ISBN 1847010504 (James Currey: Cloth); 9781847010506 (James Currey: Cloth)
LC 2012-288354

SUMMARY: This book is a history of Malawi, "drawing on all the major historical literature dealing with pre-independence Malawi and its environs, through the 'Cabinet Crisis' of 1964-65. . . . Specifically, [John] McCracken draws on [archival sources] to tell the story of how Malawi came to be—the political, social, economic, cultural, and environmental forces that shaped its creation, as well as the triumphs and struggles of its people." (Choice)

REVIEW: *Am Hist Rev* v119 no1 p289 F 2014 Melvin E. Page
"A History of Malawi, 1859-1966". "This book is a fitting capstone to a career spent studying and teaching the history of Malawi. . . . The book is largely successful in considering cultural, economic, demographic, ecological, as well as political spheres within the relatively small territory known to scholars of colonialism as Nyasaland. . . . it seems destined to be the history of the country for some years to come and a starting point for much future research into Malawi's past. Yet there are at least two ways in which this otherwise impressive effort may not serve students and scholars as well as it might."

REVIEW: *Choice* v50 no7 p1309 Mr 2013 J. R. Kenyon

MCCRACKEN, PEGGY.ed. From beasts to souls. See From beasts to souls

MCCUAIG, WILLIAM.tr. Spinoza for our time. See Spinoza for our time

MCCULLY, EMILY ARNOLD, 1939-.il. Dare the wind. See Fern, T.

MCCULLY, EMILY ARNOLD, 1939-.il. Little ducks go. See McCully, E. A.

MCCULLY, EMILY ARNOLD, 1939-. Little ducks go; [by] Emily Arnold McCully 32 p. 2014 Holiday House
1. Animals—Infancy—Fiction 2. Children's stories 3. Ducks—Fiction 4. Urban life—Juvenile fiction 5. Wildlife rescue
ISBN 0823429415; 9780823429417 (hardcover)
LC 2013-009559

SUMMARY: In this children's picture book, written and illustrated by Emily Arnold McCully, "when a mother duck's ducklings fall through a grate and into a storm sewer, she follows the sound of their cheeping from grate to grate. Her commotion alerts a human to her problem. The man opens a manhole cover and successfully retrieves the ducklings while a young girl watches; then the girl takes them to a nearby pond and releases the happily reunited birds." (Bulletin of the Center for Children's Books)

REVIEW: *Booklist* v110 no13 p76 Mr 1 2014 Connie Fletcher

REVIEW: *Bull Cent Child Books* v67 no9 p468 My 2014 J. H.
"Little Ducks Go". "The minimal text of this beginning reader helpfully uses repetition of words and phrases, very short sentences . . . and a large, clear sans serif font to support novice readers, especially those still at the sounding-out level. The story is more hinted at by the text than fluidly told, but the personable, detailed line and watercolor illustrations add interest to the restricted text. It's hard to go wrong with ducklings in danger, and while this is not as stellar as Moore's similarly themed 'Lucky Ducklings' . . . it's quite useful, and it would be a fitting selection for a beginning reading group to tackle after a readaloud session with Moore's book."

REVIEW: *Kirkus Rev* v82 no4 p108 F 15 2014

REVIEW: *SLJ* v60 no3 p118 Mr 2014 Megan Egbert

MCCULLY, EMILY ARNOLD, 1939-.il. Pete won't eat. See McCully, E. A.

MCCULLY, EMILY ARNOLD, 1939-. Pete won't eat, [by] Emily Arnold McCully 32 p. 2013 Holiday House
1. Animals—Juvenile fiction 2. Food habits—Fiction 3. Mothers & sons—Fiction 4. Pigs—Fiction 5. Swine
ISBN 0823428532; 9780823428533 (hardcover)
LC 2012-039209

SUMMARY: In this book, by Emily Arnold McCully, "Pete can't eat that green slop that Mom made for lunch. He won't even taste it! His siblings want Pete to eat so they can go out to play. But Pete stands firm, and his siblings desert him. Mom makes Pete stay, but she is feeling sad about it. She is about to make him a sandwich when Pete decides to try the slop. He likes it! In addition to enjoying the yummy slop, Pete has learned the benefits of keeping an open mind and trying new things." (Publisher's note)

REVIEW: *Bull Cent Child Books* v67 no2 p93-4 O 2013 H. M.
"Come Back, Ben" and "Pete Won't Eat." "These two offerings from the Holiday House 'I Like to Read' series offer simple storylines, lots of vowel sound repetition, and an extra-large font size to make reading more approachable for new readers. In [author Ann] Hassett's 'Come Back, Ben', a boy flies off on a balloon past a series of passers-by until eventually landing on the moon, where he fills his pocket with moon rocks and sends himself floating back to earth. . . . In [author and illustrator Emily Arnold] McGully's 'Pete Won't Eat', a pig named Pete refuses to eat his bowl of green slop. . . . McGully's line and watercolor illustrations feature . . . plenty of text-to-image pairing within the story to guide young readers."

REVIEW: *Bull Cent Child Books* v67 no2 p104-5 O 2013 K. Q. G.

REVIEW: *Horn Book Magazine* v90 no1 p73 Ja/F 2014 JULIE ROACH

REVIEW: *Kirkus Rev* v81 no15 p123 Ag 1 2013

REVIEW: *SLJ* v59 no10 p1 O 2013 Kristine M. Casper

MCCUNE, JOSHUA. Talker 25; [by] Joshua McCune 432 p. 2014 Greenwillow Books, an imprint of HarperCollins Publishers
1. Adventure and adventurers—Fiction 2. Dragons—Fiction 3. Human-animal communication—Fiction 4. Science fiction 5. Telepathy—Fiction 6. War—Fiction
ISBN 006212191X; 9780062121912 (hardback)
LC 2013-046186

SUMMARY: This novel, by Joshua McCune, is a "reimagining of popular dragon fantasy lore set in a militaristic future. . . . [It] imagines a North America where dragons are kept on reservations, where strict blackout rules are obeyed no matter the cost, where the highly weaponized military operates in chilling secret, and where a gruesome television show called Kissing Dragons unites the population." (Publisher's note)

REVIEW: *Booklist* v110 no18 p67 My 15 2014 Frances Bradburn

REVIEW: *Bull Cent Child Books* v67 no10 p534 Je 2014 A. S.
"Talker 25". "The book treats the situation with satisfying complexity. . . . There's some startling viciousness here, and readers expecting noble dragons (or noble humanity) will be quickly disabused of those notions as the dragons snap up children for a snack and people retaliate by utilizing extended torture tactics, only loosely under the guise of trying to get information. A slightly too sharp social comment about reality television and how it is used to exploit individuals wears thin, but this is a minor concern in what is overall an edgy, dark glimpse into a world that decides the best way to handle terrorists is terrorism."

REVIEW: *Horn Book Magazine* v90 no4 p101 Jl/Ag 2014 ANITA L. BURKAM

REVIEW: *Kirkus Rev* v82 no5 p115 Mr 1 2014
"Talker 25". "[Joshua] McCune's debut starts off with great promise, as readers get to know narrator Melissa and this terrifying world. . . . The story starts to unravel as the book moves from 'Part I: Kissing Dragons' into 'Part II: Reconditioning.' Ultimately, its early potential devolves into a chaotic mess, derailed by ambition (a trilogy's worth of plot in just over 400 pages) and gratuitous dragon torture. Left with a score of largely unlikable, unengaging human characters, readers may reach the abrupt ending hoping that the dragons are the only survivors. Intense but unsatisfying."

REVIEW: *SLJ* v60 no3 p160 Mr 2014 Laura Falli

REVIEW: *Voice of Youth Advocates* v37 no2 p78 Je 2014 Katie Mitchell

MCCUTCHEON, RUSSELL T.ed. Failure and nerve in the academic study of religion. See Failure and nerve in the academic study of religion

MCDERMID, VAL. Cross and Burn; [by] Val McDermid 416 p. 2013 Pgw
1. Detective & mystery stories 2. Kidnapping—Fiction 3. Murder investigation—Fiction 4. Police—Fiction 5. Serial murderers
ISBN 0802122043; 9780802122049

SUMMARY: In this book by Val McDermid, "a psychopath is intent on kidnapping and training the perfect wife--and beating to death and disfiguring his 'mistakes.' When [Paula] McIntyre's decision to seek help from [Tony] Hill takes a drastic, unexpected turn, she's forced to turn to the reclusive [Carol] Jordan instead." (Publishers Weekly)

REVIEW: *Booklist* v110 no2 p34 S 15 2013 Allison Block
"Cross and Burn." "In [Val] McDermid's eighth entry to feature Detective Chief Inspector Carol Jordan and psychologist Tony Hill, the once-crackerjack crime-fighting team has gone their separate ways. . . . But when a woman is found murdered in an abandoned London flat, the two wind up back within each other's orbit again. . . . Soon, more women go missing, and a disturbing trend emerges: they all eerily resemble blonde-haired, blue-eyed Jordan. Is she next on the killer's list? . . . Connoisseurs of the crime novel will happily devour veteran thriller-writer McDermid's masterful blend of crisp prose, complex characters, and relentless suspense."

REVIEW: *Kirkus Rev* v81 no19 p244 O 1 2013

REVIEW: *Libr J* v138 no9 p51 My 15 2013 Barbara Hoffert

REVIEW: *Publ Wkly* v260 no35 p35-6 S 2 2013

MCDERMID, VAL. Northanger Abbey; [by] Val McDermid 368 p. 2014 Grove Press

1. Austen, Jane, 1775-1817—Characters 2. Friendship—Fiction 3. Gothic fiction (Literary genre) 4. Suspense fiction 5. Teenage girls—Fiction
ISBN 0802123015; 9780802123015

SUMMARY: "In 'Northanger Abbey,' [author Val McDermid] delivers her own . . . updated take on Austen's classic novel about a young woman whose visit to the stately home of a well-to-do acquaintance stirs her most macabre imaginings. . . . A . . . modern update of the Jane Austen classic, 'Northanger Abbey' tells a timeless story of innocence amid cynicism, the exquisite angst of young love, and the value of friendship." (Publisher's note)

REVIEW: *Booklist* v110 no16 p15-6 Ap 15 2014 Amber Peckham

REVIEW: *Hist Today* v64 no7 p61 Jl 2014 Jerome de Groot

REVIEW: *Kirkus Rev* v82 no6 p327 Mr 15 2014

REVIEW: *Libr J* v139 no6 p81 Ap 1 2014 Liz French

REVIEW: *Libr J* v138 no21 p69 D 1 2013 Barbara Hoffert

REVIEW: *N Y Times Book Rev* p9 Je 15 2014 JO BAKER

REVIEW: *New Statesman* v143 no5205 p47 Ap 11 2014 John Mullan

REVIEW: *TLS* no5794 p20 Ap 18 2014 SARAH CURTIS

"Northanger Abbey." "'It is not the function of fiction to offer lessons in life,' is the crisp conclusion of Val McDermid's twenty-first-century version of Jane Austen's 'Northanger Abbey.' This book is the second contribution to the Austen Project. . . . McDermid has set aside her own ability to create suspense in crime novels, and meticulously follows Austen's parody of a Gothic horror story to its predictable happy ending. . . . There is plenty to be admired in McDermid's transposition. It is an amusing intellectual exercise to spot the numerous parallels in this parody of a parody and her version may encourage readers to return not only to the original but also to Radcliffe's novel."

MCDERMOTT, ALICE. Someone; A Novel; [by] Alice McDermott 224 p. 2013 Farrar, Straus and Giroux

1. Bildungsromans 2. Brooklyn (New York, N.Y.)—Fiction 3. Catholics—Fiction 4. Families—Fiction 5. Irish American women—Fiction
ISBN 0374281092 (hardcover); 9780374281090 (hardcover)
LC 2013-014938

SUMMARY: This historical novel, by Alice McDermott, follows "Marie's first heartbreak and her eventual marriage; her brother's brief stint as a Catholic priest, subsequent loss of faith, and eventual breakdown; the Second World War; her parents' deaths; the births and lives of Marie's children; [and] the changing world of her Irish-American enclave in Brooklyn." (Publisher's note)

REVIEW: *America* v209 no16 p28-30 N 25 2013 J. GREG PHELAN

REVIEW: *Booklist* v110 no7 p38 D 1 2013 Neal Wyatt

REVIEW: *Booklist* v109 no21 p30 Jl 1 2013 Donna Seaman

REVIEW: *Commonweal* v140 no18 p31-2 N 15 2013 Dominic Preziosi

REVIEW: *Kirkus Rev* p27 N 15 2013 Best Books

REVIEW: *Kirkus Rev* p11 2013 Guide 20to BookExpo America

REVIEW: *Kirkus Rev* v81 no8 p21-2 Ap 15 2013

REVIEW: *Libr J* v138 no6 p59 Ap 1 2013 Barbara Hoffert

REVIEW: *Libr J* v138 no21 p57 D 1 2013 Claire Abraham

REVIEW: *N Y Times Book Rev* p12 S 8 2013 LEAN HAGER COHEN

"Someone." "Such is the crisp purposefulness of [Alice] McDermott's prose. Her sentences know themselves so beautifully: what each has to deliver and how best to do it, within a modicum of space, with minimal fuss. . . . In the most deceptively ordinary language, she evokes both the world of light and that of darkness. . . . Aspects of this new novel might disappoint some readers. The middle-aged and elderly Marie is less vividly drawn than her younger iterations. . . . Still, McDermott's excellence is on ample display here."

REVIEW: *New York Times* v162 no56282 pC1-4 O 7 2013 JANET MASLIN

REVIEW: *New Yorker* v89 no34 p79-1 O 28 2013

REVIEW: *Publ Wkly* v260 no43 p56 O 28 2013

REVIEW: *Publ Wkly* v260 no24 p40 Je 17 2013

REVIEW: *TLS* no5776 p19 D 13 2013 MIKA ROSS-SOUTHALL

MCDONALD, ABBY. Getting over Garrett Delaney; [by] Abby McDonald 319 p. 2012 Candlewick Press

1. Fiction 2. Friendship—Fiction 3. Love—Fiction 4. Summer employment—Fiction 5. Youths' writings
ISBN 9780763655075
LC 2011-018621

SUMMARY: In this book by Abby McDonald, protagonist "Sadie recounts how she has been "madly, hopelessly, tragically in love with Garrett" . . . for two years believing that, eventually, the Gods of Unrequited Crushes would smile on her. But Garrett's confession of love never comes. . . . Heartbroken, Sadie takes a job as a barista and comes up with a 12-step program, which . . . punctuates the book, to wean herself from Garrett. But withdrawal is . . . tough, and Sadie hits rock-bottom when . . . she sprawls face-down on the floor at work just to take a call from him. Sadie needs a support group. Enter the Totally Wired crew . . . to help." (Kirkus)

REVIEW: *Booklist* v108 no12 p55 F 15 2012 Ann Kelley

REVIEW: *Bull Cent Child Books* v65 no6 p313-4 F 2012 K. C.

"Getting Over Garrett Delaney." "The realism here is refreshing and affirming, as Sadie gradually realizes just how entangled she has allowed herself to become in Garrett's worldview. . . . She's reluctant to give him up as a friend, however, and this too offers a site for realistic conflict resolution, as she has to . . . work out a way of protecting her heart and her newfound sense of self from the magnetic pull that attracted her to Garrett in the first place. [Abby] McDonald moves with sure-footed grace through Sadie's heartbreak and recovery, adding in the perfect pinch of schadenfreude for readers when Garrett finally realizes what a great girl he's been missing all along. Sadie's self-work is quietly inspirational and satisfying, offering genuine hope for the unrequited romantic."

REVIEW: *Kirkus Rev* v79 no24 p2330 D 15 2011

REVIEW: *Publ Wkly* v258 no49 p75 D 5 2011

REVIEW: *SLJ* v58 no2 p125-6 F 2012 Shawna Sherman

REVIEW: *Voice of Youth Advocates* v34 no6 p596 F 2012 Katie Mitchell

MCDONALD, LEE MARTIN.ed. The world of the New Testament. See The world of the New Testament

MCDONALD, MEGAN, 1959-. Ant and honey bee; a pair of friends in winter; 64 p. 2013 Candlewick Press

1. Ants—Juvenile literature 2. Bees—Juvenile literature 3. Children's stories 4. Friendship—Juvenile fiction 5. Winter—Juvenile literature
ISBN 0763657123; 9780763657123
LC 2012-947754

SUMMARY: "Can Ant brave the cold for one last surprise visit before the snow flies? And will Honey Bee welcome an interruption of her peace and quiet? The author of the Judy Moody series [Megan McDonald] teams up again with award-winning illustrator G. Brian Karas to show that true friends can weather whatever comes their way--even if one is feeling antsy and the other has . . . hibernation in mind." (Publisher's note)

REVIEW: *Bull Cent Child Books* v67 no3 p170 N 2013 J. H.

"Ant and Honey Bee: A Pair of Friends in Winter." "Best bug buds Ant and Honeybee (from 'Ant and Honey Bee: What a Pair!' . . .) are back, getting ready to hunker down for winter in their respective houses. . . . The interplay between the two insect pals is engaging, while the humorous text is accessible and appropriately jokey. A large, clear typeface, repeated words and phrases, and short, direct sentences will help support novice chapter book readers. [Illustrator G. Brian] Karas' gouache, acrylic, and pencil art is as charming as always, with muted tones effectively evoking the winter setting."

REVIEW: *Kirkus Rev* v81 no15 p276 Ag 1 2013

REVIEW: *SLJ* v59 no9 p126 S 2013 Laura Stanfield

MCDONALD, MEGAN, 1959-. Judy Moody and stink and the big bad blackout; [by] Megan McDonald 144 p. 2014 Candlewick Press

1. Children's stories 2. Electric power failures 3. Games 4. Grandparent & child—Fiction 5. Hurricanes—Fiction
ISBN 0763665207; 9780763665203
LC 2013-943995

SUMMARY: In this book, by Megan McDonald, "Judy and Stink and the whole Moody family hunker down with beans and batteries, ready to wait out the storm. But along with massive rain and strong winds, Hurricane Elmer throws down ghosts, squirrels, and aliens. Spooky! Just when things couldn't possibly get any freakier—flicker, flicker, gulp!—the lights go O-U-T out. The Moodys are smack-dab in the middle of a big bad blackout!" (Publisher's note)

REVIEW: *Kirkus Rev* v82 no5 p97 Mr 1 2014

"The Big Bad Blackout". "It's hurricane season in Virginia, and Stink and Judy Moody are in for some dark nights. The Moodys are stuck in their house with no electricity when Hurricane Elmer strikes. What could be challenging turns into an enjoyable few days. . . . Readers of this fine series will enjoy the full-color illustrations and the little rain clouds above the page numbers. New fans can join in the fun-no need to have read the earlier books to enjoy this newest one. A cozy, comfortable book for a rainy night."

REVIEW: *SLJ* v60 no6 p135 Je 2014 Staff

REVIEW: *SLJ* v60 no8 p49 Ag 2014 Jessica Gilcreast

MCDONALD, MEGAN, 1959-. Shoe dog; [by] Megan McDonald 40 p. 2014 Atheneum Books for Young Readers

1. Cats—Fiction 2. Children's stories 3. Dog adoption—Fiction 4. Dogs—Fiction 5. Dogs—Training—Fiction
ISBN 1416979328; 9781416979326 (hardcover)
LC 2012-051499

SUMMARY: In this book, by Megan McDonald, illustrated by Katherine Tillotson, "Shoe Dog likes to chew. And chew and chew. But he doesn't chew a boring old bone. Not a squeaky old toy. Not a smelly old sock. Nope. Shoe Dog chews well, take a guess! Chewing shoes poses a problem, however, and Shoe Dog needs help to solve it. Good thing there's...Shoe Cat!" (Publisher's note)

REVIEW: *Booklist* v110 no11 p70-1 F 1 2014 Daniel Kraus

REVIEW: *Kirkus Rev* v82 no3 p64 F 1 2014

"Shoe Dog". " An irrepressible dog can't resist falling into the same type of mischief over and over again, until something surprising changes his pattern. . . . [Katherine] Tillotson uses thick black lines for Shoe Dog's scribbly, coiled-spring body, smudging charcoal inside his shape to give him substance; scraps of pink and beige mark his pointy ears and muzzle. Motion lines show how he scampers and bounds. The visual angle varies, and shoe-box tissue paper flies through the air. Totally ebullient."

REVIEW: *N Y Times Book Rev* p22 Mr 16 2014 SARAH HARRISON SMITH

REVIEW: *Publ Wkly* v260 no51 p57-9 D 16 2013

REVIEW: *SLJ* v60 no2 p76 F 2014 Sara Lissa Paulson

MCDONNELL, EVELYN. Queens of noise; the real story of the Runaways; [by] Evelyn McDonnell viii, 342 p. 2013 Da Capo Press

1. Historical literature 2. Rock groups—United States—Biography 3. Rock musicians—United States—Biography 4. Women rock musicians—United States—Biography
ISBN 0306820390; 9780306820397
LC 2013-565042

SUMMARY: This book examines the history of the rock band the Runaways, who "did what no other group of female rock musicians before them could: they released four albums for a major label and toured the world. The Runaways busted down doors for every girl band that followed. Joan Jett, Sandy West, Cherrie Currie, lead guitarist Lita Ford, and bassists Jackie Fox and Vicky Blue were pre-punk bandits, fostering revolution girl style decades before that became a riot grrrl catchphrase." (Publisher's note)

REVIEW: *N Y Times Book Rev* p11 O 6 2013 ANDY WEBSTER

"Queens of Noise: The Real Story of the Runaways." "The band remains cruelly underrated, a perception Evelyn McDonnell seeks to rectify in her scrupulously researched. . . . McDonnell, a longtime music journalists, cites literary figures . . . and scholars to add intellectual heft to a rock'n roll story. She has done her legwork, gaining access to almost all of the surviving Runaways . . . and their colleagues. The result is more diffuse, impartial than [Cherie] Currie's memoir, 'Neon Angel'. . . . McDonnell has rightly rehabilitated a pioneering band's reputation."

MCDOUGALL, WARREN.ed. The Edinburgh History of the Book in Scotland. See The Edinburgh History of the Book in Scotland

MCDOWELL, MARTA. Beatrix Potter's gardening life; the plants and places that inspired the classic children's tales; [by] Marta McDowell 340 p. 2013 Timber Press

1. Gardens—England 2. Gardens in literature 3. Gardens, English 4. Historical literature
ISBN 9781604693638
LC 2013-001143

SUMMARY: This book "explore[s] the origins of Beatrix Potter's love of gardening and plants and show how this passion came to be reflected in her work. The book begins with a gardener's biography, highlighting the key moments and places throughout her life that helped define her, including her home Hill Top Farm in England's Lake District. Next, the reader follows Beatrix Potter through a year in her garden." (Publisher's note)

REVIEW: *Booklist* v110 no8 p10-2 D 15 2013 Donna Seaman

"Beatrix Potter's Gardening Life: The Plants and Places That Inspired the Classic Children's Tales." "In this sumptuously illustrated 'gardening biography,' horticultural consultant [Marta] McDowell, who is fascinated by writers who garden . . . fully illuminates Potter's deep botanical knowledge and joy in cultivation. . . . With wit and expertise, McDowell highlights the stamp of Potters horticultural know-how on her indelible books and chronicles a year in her exuberant gardens to create a visually exciting, pleasurably informative appreciation of Potter's devotion to art and nature."

REVIEW: *N Y Times Book Rev* p52 D 8 2013 DEBORAH NEEDLEMAN

MCELHONE, JOHN.tr. The Lumière autochrome. See Lavedrine, B.

MCELMURRY, JILL.il. The tree lady. See Hopkins, H. J.

MCFARLAND, DENNIS. Nostalgia; [by] Dennis McFarland 336 p. 2013 Pantheon Books

1. Disabled veterans—Fiction 2. Historical fiction 3. Soldiers—Fiction 4. Whitman, Walt, 1819-1892
ISBN 9780307908346
LC 2013-003361

SUMMARY: In this Civil War novel by Dennis McFarland, set "in winter 1864, 19-year-old Brooklynite Summerfield Hayes joins the fighting but soon finds himself abandoned by his comrades during the Wilderness Campaign. At a military hospital, Walt Whitman becomes his advocate" when he is accused of malingering and desertion. (Library Journal)

REVIEW: *Booklist* v110 no5 p34 N 1 2013 Mark Levine

REVIEW: *Kirkus Rev* v81 no17 p19 S 1 2013

REVIEW: *Libr J* v138 no9 p55 My 15 2013 Barbara Hoffert

REVIEW: *N Y Times Book Rev* p22 N 17 2013 DAVID GOODWILLIE

"Nostalgia." "[A] searing, poetic and often masterly new Civil War novel. . . . The novel moves gracefully back and forth through time. . . . [Dennis] McFarland's descriptions of 19th-century life, from the intricacies of musket warfare to the formative years of our national pastime, are stunning in their lyricism and detail. . . . As the narrative moves to Hayes' time at the front, McFarland's prose all but lifts off the page. . . . Shifting from the adrenaline-fueled battlefront to the Victorian-like domesticity of the home front can make for jarring reading, but that's the point; imagine how jarring it was in real life. . . . That McFarland can make such difficult subject matter both entertaining and essential is a tribute to his evident literary talents."

REVIEW: *Publ Wkly* v260 no28 p143 Jl 15 2013

MCFARLANE, FIONA. The night guest; a novel; [by] Fiona McFarlane 256 p. 2013 Farrar Straus & Giroux

1. Caregivers—Fiction 2. FICTION—Literary 3. Suspense fiction 4. Widows—Fiction
ISBN 0865477736; 9780865477735
LC 2013-022511

SUMMARY: This novel, by Fiona McFarlane, is "about trust, dependence, and fear. . . . Ruth is widowed, her sons are grown, and she lives in an isolated beach house outside of town. . . . One day a stranger arrives at her door, looking as if she has been blown in from the sea. This woman—Frida—claims to be a care worker sent by the government. Ruth lets her in. . . . How far can she trust this mysterious woman, Frida, who seems to carry with her own troubled past? And how far can Ruth trust herself?" (Publisher's note)

REVIEW: *Booklist* v110 no1 p40 S 1 2013 Allison Block

REVIEW: *Kirkus Rev* v81 no2 p23 Je 1 2013

REVIEW: *Kirkus Rev* p27 N 15 2013 Best Books

REVIEW: *Libr J* v138 no9 p54 My 15 2013 Barbara Hoffert

REVIEW: *N Y Times Book Rev* p15 O 20 2013 PATRICK McGRATH

REVIEW: *New Statesman* v143 no5 p52 F 7 2014 Philip Maughan

REVIEW: *New York Times* v163 no56306 pC2 O 31 2013 John Williams

REVIEW: *New Yorker* v89 no35 p104-1 N 4 2013

REVIEW: *Publ Wkly* v260 no27 p61-2 Jl 8 2013

REVIEW: *TLS* no5782 p20 Ja 24 2014 CATHERINE SCOTT

"The Night Guest." "Accustomed as our society may be to hearing horror stories about gullible elderly people drawn in and exploited by seductive con men (and women), we rarely experience the perspective of the elderly themselves. . . . The third-person narrative that Fiona McFarlane uses is deceptive, implying a neutral observer when really the reader is being drawn into the fears and uncertainties of the elderly mind. This seductive immersion means that while the reader feels compelled to follow Ruth to what they fear will be an unpleasant conclusion, one is always subconsciously aware, sometimes frustratingly so, that the objective truth of what really happened will remain elusive."

MCFARLANE, JUDY. Writing with Grace; A Journey Beyond Down Syndrome; [by] Judy McFarlane 208 p. 2014 Douglas & McIntyre

1. Authors with disabilities 2. Authorship 3. Down syndrome 4. Memoirs 5. Mentoring

ISBN 1771620250; 9781771620253

SUMMARY: In this book, author Judy McFarlane "addresses issues of intellectual disability and what it means to be a writer. Although the young woman McFarlane mentors self-identifies as Cinderella-Princess-Grace, the rest of the world is more inclined to see her solely as someone with Dwown syndrome. . . . Grace's focus is on writing a book about romance and, just as importantly, experiencing it." (Quill & Quire)

REVIEW: *Quill Quire* v80 no2 p33 Mr 2014 Julie Devaney

"Writing With Grace: A Journey Beyond Down Syndrome". "Recent literature and practice have brought the voices of people with disabilities to the fore, but [Judy] McFarlane misses this opportunity, instead affording more authority to medical, legal, and academic accounts of living with Down syndrome. . . . McFarlane frankly describes her own stereotypical ideas about Down syndrome, and frames this acknowledgement as a bold exposé of collective social attitudes. But as Grace consistently subverts this caricature of disability, the author's repetition of her early prejudices becomes jarring. Her offensive languages and images of intellectual disability no longer read as self-reflexive, but instead become evocative of the very discrimination the book purports to challenge."

MCGANN, DON. Stilettos in Vegas. See Diamond, V. L.

MCGARRY, NEIL. The Fall of Ventaris; [by] Neil McGarry 442 p. 2013 Peccable Productions

1. Fantasy fiction 2. Guilds 3. Race relations—Fiction 4. Social marginality 5. Thieves—Fiction

ISBN 0985014911; 9780985014919

SUMMARY: This book, the second in the Grey City series, follows the "Duchess of the Shallows . . . the newest member of the secret society of thieves and spies known as the Grey. Yet even as she exorcises the ghosts of her old life, new enemies threaten from all sides. Her struggle to survive will take her from the temples of the imperial cults, through the workshops of the great guilds and finally to the court of the empress herself." (Publisher's note)

REVIEW: *Kirkus Rev* p40 D 15 2013 supplemet best books 2013

"The Fall of Ventaris". "Readers unfamiliar with the series' first book may find some details of the world's social structure to be unclear, but the intricately plotted schemes stand alone in most other respects, and newcomers will likely find them easy to follow. The authors, through their powerful portrayals of strong-willed characters, skillfully examine and confront issues of race, class, gender and sexual orientation in a way that's rarely, if ever, done in medieval fantasy. In a manner that's both modern and timeless, they examine the ways that strong women forego niceties to fight for the respect so easily granted to men. Overall, the novel is an engaging account of a young woman's quest to succeed because of her outsider status, rather than in spite of it."

MCGAVRAN, JAMES.tr. Selected poems. See Mayakovsky, V.

MCGEE, KRISTA. Luminary; [by] Krista McGee 320 p. 2014 Thomas Nelson

1. Christian life—Fiction 2. Emotions—Fiction 3. Families—Fiction 4. Love—Fiction 5. Science fiction 6. Young adult fiction

ISBN 9781401688745 (pbk.)

LC 2013-029517

SUMMARY: "In the second installment of the Anomaly Trilogy, naïve musician Thalli and her friends, newly escaped from the evil Scientists and the underground State . . . arrive at New Hope, a small agricultural community that survived the Nuclear War 40 years ago. But alas, New Hope finds itself constantly threatened by Athens, a whole city that survived the War largely by developing . . . 'pharmaceuticals.' Thalli goes to Athens to convince evil King Jason not to attack." (Kirkus Reviews)

REVIEW: *Booklist* v110 no8 p46 D 15 2013 Frances Bradbum

REVIEW: *Kirkus Rev* v81 no24 p209 D 15 2013

"Luminary". " This simplistic dystopia delivers formulaic romance and a large dose of religious faith. . . . [Krista] McGee appears to have two goals here: to write an entertaining dystopian novel and to promote religious faith. She mostly meets her first goal, although frequent sudden storyline reversals, such as Alex's transformation, can cause whiplash. She relies, clearly intentionally, on frequent deus ex machina plot turns to promote the second goal. The roughly third-grade-level prose, dialogue that mostly avoids contractions, avoidance of necessary description and cardboard-cutout characterizations seem to pitch the book toward an expected audience of poor readers. The faithful may enjoy it."

REVIEW: *SLJ* v60 no1 p102 Ja 2014 Eric Norton

MCGILL, SCOTT. Plagiarism in Latin literature; [by] Scott McGill xiv, 241 p. 2013 Cambridge University Press

1. Ancient literature 2. Historical literature 3. Imitation in literature 4. LITERARY COLLECTIONS—Ancient, Classical & Medieval 5. Latin literature 6. Latin literature—History and criticism 7. Plagiarism 8. Plagiarism—History

ISBN 9781107019379 (hbk.); 9781108035552 (pbk.)

LC 2011-049116

SUMMARY: This book by Scott McGill "explores important questions such as, how do Roman writers and speakers define the practice? And how do the accusations and denials function? . . . McGill moves between varied sources, including Terence, Martial, Seneca the Elder and Macrobius' Virgil criticism to explore these questions. In the process, he offers new insights into the history of plagiarism and related issues, including Roman notions of literary property, authorship and textual reuse." (Publisher's note)

REVIEW: *Choice* v51 no3 p453 N 2013 M. J. Johnson

REVIEW: *Classical Rev* v63 no2 p438-40 O 2013 Boris Kayachev

"Plagiarism in Latin Literature." "[Author Scott McGill's] monograph explores the concept of plagiarism and the various uses of this concept (rather than actual cases of plagiarism as one might surmise from the title) in the Latin literary world of classical antiquity. . . . There is no doubt that [Mc-

Gill's] monograph will deservedly become a standard work on the subject of plagiarism in Latin antiquity, and all interested in different modes of literary reuse can greatly benefit from reading it. The book will also be consulted with profit by those approaching individual (con)texts discussed in it from other perspectives, for [McGill's] close readings are always illuminating and original."

MCGINNIS, J. MICHAEL.ed. Best care at lower cost. See Best care at lower cost

MCGOVERN, ANN. Aesop's fables. See Aesop's fables

MCGRATH, ALISTER E., 1953-. Darwinism and the divine; evolutionary thought and natural theology; [by] Alister E. McGrath 320 2011 Wiley-Blackwell

1. Darwin, Charles, 1809-1882 2. Evolutionary theories 3. Natural theology 4. Paley, William, 1743-1805 5. Religious literature

ISBN 9781444333435; 9781444333442

LC 2010-039893

SUMMARY: It was the author's intent "'to identify the forms of natural theology that emerged in England over the period 1690–1850 and how these were affected by the advent of [Charles] Darwin's theory,' and 'to explore and assess twenty-first-century reflections on the relation of evolutionary thought and natural theology'. . . . The book thus has both historical and contemporary foci, with the former intended to inform the latter." (Journal of the American Academy of Religion)

REVIEW: *J Am Acad Relig* v82 no1 p283-6 Mr 2014 Timothy Shanahan

"Darwinism and the Divine: Evolutionary Thought and Natural Theology". "The writing in 'Darwinism and the Divine' is clear, elegant, and well informed throughout, is distinguished by a balanced and nonpolemical style, and is a pleasure to read. Every chapter in this rich volume includes extensive endnotes guiding the reader to further study. Addressed to a general readership, the book seldom delves very deeply into the many important issues it discusses, but because the author is equally conversant in the history of science, contemporary science, and theology, this volume should be of interest especially to a diverse nonscholarly audience. In short, this book is highly recommended."

MCGRATH, PATRICK, 1950-. Constance; a novel; [by] Patrick McGrath 240 p. 2013 Bloomsbury

1. Dysfunctional families—Fiction 2. Family secrets—Fiction 3. Fathers and daughters—Fiction 4. Psychological fiction

ISBN 1608199436; 9781608199433 (hardcover : alk. paper)

LC 2012-025657

SUMMARY: In this novel, by Patrick McGrath, "Constance Schuyler . . . [is] tortured by memories of the bitterly unhappy childhood she spent with her father in a dilapidated house upstate. When she learns devastating new information about that past, Constance's fragile psyche suffers a profound shock. Her marriage, already tottering, threatens to collapse completely. Frightened, desperate and alone, Constance makes a disastrous decision, then looks on as her world rapidly falls apart." (Publisher's note)

REVIEW: *Booklist* v109 no14 p46 Mr 15 2013 Donna Seaman

REVIEW: *Kirkus Rev* v81 no2 p275 Ja 15 2013

REVIEW: *Libr J* v138 no10 p99 Je 1 2013 James Coan

REVIEW: *N Y Times Book Rev* p7 My 19 2013 JULIE MYERSON

REVIEW: *Publ Wkly* v260 no9 p49 Mr 4 2013

REVIEW: *TLS* no5753 p21 Jl 5 2013 JONATHAN BARNES

"Constance." "This is [Patrick] McGrath at his most subtle and restrained. The novel is told in carefully paced chapters by Sidney and Constance herself, their versions of events agreeing in outline only, their interpretations utterly different. Neither character is likeable--Constance is an unfaithful neurotic, Sidney a manipulative prig--yet both are scintillating narrators. Most intriguing of all is the persistent sense that the spirit of the neophyte McGrath still haunts the older artist. . . . In synthesizing the best of his earliest writing with those strengths acquired during the evolution of his work, McGrath has proved himself once again to be among the most resourceful of our contemporary novelists."

MCGRAW, PETER. The humor code; a global search for what makes things funny; [by] Peter McGraw 256 p. 2014 Simon & Schuster

1. Journalism 2. Laughter 3. Stand-up comedy 4. Wit & humor—Research 5. Wit and humor—Psychological aspects

ISBN 1451665415; 9781451665413 (hardcover : alk. paper); 9781451665420 (pbk. : alk. paper)

LC 2013-031454

SUMMARY: In this book, "[Peter] McGraw, founder of the Humor Research Lab at the University of Colorado, teams up with journalist [Joel] Warner to find, not just the source of some jokes but the answer to the Big Question, What makes something funny? It "takes the researchers around the world, asking experts (other humor researchers, comedians, writers), conducting hands-on experiments (taking improv classes, performing stand-up), trying to nail down why things make us laugh." (Booklist)

REVIEW: *Atlantic* v313 no3 p42 Ap 2014 WAYNE CURTIS

REVIEW: *Booklist* v110 no13 p4 Mr 1 2014 David Pitt

Title:"The Humor Code: A Global Search for What Makes Things Funny." "It's a lively book, taking the researchers around the world, asking experts (other humor researchers, comedians, writers), conducting hands-on experiments (taking improv classes, performing stand-up), trying to nail down why things make us laugh. You'd think this would be a no-brainer--we laugh because something is funny--but it's actually a very complicated and important subject. . . . It's not often you can say a book about comedy can teach us some serious lessons. This one does--and entertains us in the process."

REVIEW: *Kirkus Rev* v82 no3 p7 F 1 2014

REVIEW: *Publ Wkly* v260 no52 p41 D 23 2013

MCGRUTHER, JENNIFER. The nourished kitchen; farm-to-table recipes for the traditional foods lifestyle : featuring bone broths, fermented vegetables, grass-fed meats, wholesome fats, raw dairy, and kombuchas; [by]

Jennifer McGruther 320 p. 2014 Ten Speed Press
1. COOKING—Health & Healing—General 2. COOKING—Methods—Canning & Preserving 3. COOKING—Specific Ingredients—Natural Foods 4. Cookbooks 5. Cooking (Natural foods) 6. Cooking, American 7. Nutrition
ISBN 9781607744689 (paperback)
LC 2013-043368

SUMMARY: In this cookbook, "following the precepts of dentist-nutritionist Weston Price, [Jennifer] McGruther has developed a system for healthy eating based on lots of vegetables and grains as cooked and preserved on early twentieth-century American farms. . . . McGruther advocates sustainable agriculture, and she enthusiastically preserves summer's bounty through fermentation for pickles, sauerkraut, and relishes." (Booklist)

REVIEW: *Booklist* v110 no14 p39-40 Mr 15 2014 Mark Knoblauch
"The Nourished Kitchen: Farm-to-Table Recipes for the Traditional Foods Lifestyle." "What differentiates [Jennifer] McGruther's approach from other regimens is her unabashed advocacy of animal fats. She is especially fond of cooking foods in lard. . . . Her meat dishes will satisfy carnivores, whether with a rich rabbit pie studded with bacon and chanterelles or with a rare-roasted elk steak. McGruther advocates sustainable agriculture, and she enthusiastically preserves summer's bounty through fermentation for pickles, sauerkraut, and relishes."

REVIEW: *Publ Wkly* v261 no1 p46 Ja 6 2014

MCGUINNESS, FRANK. Arimathea; [by] Frank McGuinness 256 p. 2013 Brandon
1. Donegal (Ireland : County) 2. Ireland—Fiction 3. Italians—Foreign countries 4. Painters—Fiction 5. Psychological fiction
ISBN 1847175783; 9781847175786

SUMMARY: In this book, set in 1950s Ireland, "various streams of consciousness merge into a complicated outpouring centred on the arrival of a young Italian painter named Gianni. He has come to paint the Stations of the Cross in a local church, and his presence causes something of a stir. Among those intrigued or obsessed by the young Italian are a child, her mother, her father, a Protestant canon and his niece." (Times Literary Supplement)

REVIEW: *TLS* no5765 p19 S 27 2013 PATRICIA CRAIG
"The Spinning Heart," "Arimathea," and "Seeking Mr. Hare." "A cacophony of aggrieved and outspoken voices, male and female, moves the narrative forwards, bit by bit. . . .The book's succession of monologues is orchestrated by the author with cunning and authenticity. . . . The strength of this first novel lies in its insights into the rougher aspects of the Irish psyche. . . . Like 'The Spinning Heart,' Frank McGuinness's debut novel 'Arimathea' is made up of monologues. As an acclaimed playwright, McGuinness has the form at his fingertips, and he gives us a series of adept impersonations. . . . An engaging contribution to the pursuit-cum-picaresque genre is Maurice Leitch's 'Seeking Mr Hare'."

MCGUIRE, ERIN.il. The Real Boy. See The Real Boy

MCGUIRE, JAMIE. Beautiful disaster; a novel; [by] Jamie McGuire 418 p. 2012 Atria Paperback
1. College students—Fiction 2. College students—Sexual behavior 3. Love stories 4. Man-woman relationships—Fiction 5. Sexual abstinence
ISBN 9781476712048 (pbk. : alk. paper); 9781476712055 (ebook)
LC 2012-027866

SUMMARY: In this book by Jamie McGuire, "Abby believes she has enough distance from the darkness of her past, but when she arrives at college with her best friend, her path to a new beginning is quickly challenged by Eastern University's Walking One-Night Stand." (Publisher's note) "Big-man-on-campus Travis Maddox bets . . . Abby . . . that he can abstain from sex for 30 days. If Travis wins, Abby must live with him for a month." (Booklist)

REVIEW: *Booklist* v110 no2 p46 S 15 2013 John Charles
"Beautiful Disaster," "Down to You," and "Easy." "Big-man-on-campus Travis Maddox bets campus good-girl Abby Abernathy that he can abstain from sex for 30 days. If Travis wins, Abby must live with him for a month. Often cited as one of the books that kick-started the NA romance genre. 'Beautiful Disaster' is followed by 'Walking Disaster'. . . . Olivia Townsend returns home from college to help run the family business only to become caught up in a love triangle with twin brothers Cash and Nash Davenport. [M.] Leighton delivers sexy soap-opera- style plot twists in the first installment of her sizzling Bad Boys series. . . . When an overly aggressive frat boy won't take no for an answer, Lucas saves Jackie's life in more ways than one. Before being picked up by Berkley, [Tammara] Webber's debut sold more than 150,000 copies as a self-published e-book and spent nine weeks on the New York Times best-seller list."

MCGURL, MARK. The program era; postwar fiction and the rise of creative writing; [by] Mark McGurl 466 2009 Harvard University Press
1. Academic programs 2. American authors 3. American literature—20th century 4. Authors—Education 5. Creative writing—Study & teaching (Higher) 6. Historical literature
ISBN 978-0-674-03319-1; 0-674-03319-1
LC 2008--50588

SUMMARY: In this book, author "Mark McGurl offers a fundamental reinterpretation of postwar American fiction, asserting that it can be properly understood only in relation to the rise of mass higher education and the creative writing program. McGurl asks both how the patronage of the university has reorganized American literature and--even more important--how the increasing intimacy of writing and schooling can be brought to bear on a reading of this literature." (Publisher's note)

"McGurl argues that far from occasioning a decline in the quality or interest of American writing, the rise of the creative writing program has instead generated a complex and evolving constellation of aesthetic problems that have been explored with energy and at times brilliance by authors ranging from Flannery O'Connor to Vladimir Nabokov, Philip Roth, Raymond Carver, Joyce Carol Oates, and Toni Morrison." (Publisher's note) Index.

REVIEW: *Am Lit* v83 no4 p836-66 D 2011 Leonard Cassuto

REVIEW: *London Rev Books* v34 no22 p39-42 N 22 2012 Fredric Jameson

REVIEW: *N Y Rev Books* v60 no17 p77-80 N 7 2013 Diane

Johnson

"The Program Era: Postwar Fiction and the Rise of Creative Writing." "[Mark] McGurl's book on the rise of creative writing programs at American universities . . . points out that the teaching of creative writing, and indeed even the whole concept of 'creative writing,' are relatively new, and originally American. . . . Part of McGurl's contention is that now--because except in a few cases, study at a university is a requirement for a job teaching writing--American writers have been co-opted into a system of professional formation that, far from encouraging creativity, could perpetuate the opposite. . . . At bottom, McGurl believes, our creative writing expresses American anti-intellectualism; elsewhere, intellectuals are admired. And of course, our anxiety about race."

MCHUGH, JAMES. Sandalwood and carrion; smell in premodern Indian religion and culture; [by] James McHugh xix, 322 p. 2013 Oxford University Press

1. Historical literature 2. Odors—India 3. Rites and ceremonies—India 4. Smell 5. Smell—Religious aspects

ISBN 9780199916306 (hardcover: alk. paper); 9780199916313 (ebook); 9780199916320 (pbk.: alk. paper)

LC 2012-003121

SUMMARY: This book, by James McHugh, "explores smell in pre-modern India from many perspectives, covering such topics as philosophical accounts of smell perception, odors in literature, the history of perfumery in India, the significance of sandalwood in Buddhism, and the divine offering of perfume to the gods." (Publisher's note)

REVIEW: *Am Hist Rev* v119 no2 p502-3 Ap 2014 Martha Ann Selby

REVIEW: *Choice* v50 no7 p1265 Mr 2013 C. A. Barnsley

REVIEW: *J Am Acad Relig* v82 no1 p257-9 Mr 2014 David Howes

'Sandalwood and Carrion: Smell in Indian Religion and Culture". "The publication of James McHugh's fine study of the sense of smell and aromatics in premodern (i.e., early and medieval) South Asia represents a major advance in the history of the senses, and religion. While the focus of McHugh's book is on the topic of smell, his approach is distinguished by its attention to issues of materiality, intersensoriality, and the contingency of perception. . . . A book that will long stand out for bringing the text back in after the embodied turn in the history of religion, and doing so with the utmost erudition and nuance."

MCHUGH, JOSHUA.il. Murals of New York City. See Palmer-Smith, G.

MCHUGH, LAURA. The weight of blood; a novel; [by] Laura McHugh 320 p. 2014 Spiegel & Grau

1. Families—Fiction 2. Human trafficking—Fiction 3. Mothers and daughters—Fiction 4. Psychological fiction

ISBN 0812995201; 9780812995206 (alk. paper)

LC 2013-021292

SUMMARY: This novel, by Laura McHugh, is set "deep in the Ozark Mountains. Folks there still whisper about Lucy Dane's mother, a bewitching stranger who appeared long enough to marry Carl Dane and then vanished when Lucy was just a child. Now on the brink of adulthood, Lucy['s] . . . friend Cheri . . . is . . . found murdered. . . . When Cheri disappears, Lucy is haunted . . . and sets out with the help of a local boy, Daniel, to uncover the mystery behind Cheri's death." (Publisher's note)

REVIEW: *Booklist* v110 no4 p32 O 15 2013 Joanne Wilkinson

REVIEW: *Kirkus Rev* v82 no3 p186 F 1 2014

"The Weight of Blood". "A teenager investigates a friend's murder and learns much more than she bargained for. [Laura] McHugh's debut interweaves two parallel stories, set almost two decades apart. . . . McHugh's evocation of the rugged setting and local speech patterns starkly reveals the menace lurking beneath Henbane's folksy facade. However, a misguided authorial attempt to find the good in Crete only muddies the novel's moral waters, since nothing can mitigate or redeem the evil he inflicts. An accomplished literary thriller."

REVIEW: *Libr J* v139 no13 p47 Ag 1 2014 Lisa Youngblood

REVIEW: *Libr J* v138 no18 p79 N 1 2013 Amy Hoseth

REVIEW: *Publ Wkly* v260 no45 p45-6 N 11 2013

MCKAY, DOC. New World Tribe; Faces of Sacrifice; [by] Doc McKay 332 p. 2012 LOCEM Books

1. Aztecs—Fiction 2. Culture conflict 3. First contact of aboriginal peoples with Westerners 4. Historical fiction 5. Missionaries—Fiction

ISBN 0615702228; 9780615702223

SUMMARY: This novel, by Doc McKay Jr., deals with cultural contact and conflict. "In present-day Honduras, an assorted group (church members, others) sets out to make contact with a remote jungle tribe. Before long, their expedition runs into trouble. . . . Meanwhile, in the Aztec year One-Reed (1519 to readers), young villager Atl, just coming into manhood, travels with a few others from his small village to trade in a larger town, where they get their first glimpse of Europeans." (Kirkus Reviews)

REVIEW: *Kirkus Rev* p41 D 15 2013 supplemet best books 2013

"New World Tribe: Faces of Sacrifice". ". In [Doc] McKay's novel, trust, love and sacrifice are things you do, not just feel, as when looking after the sick, crossing a shaky bridge, offering food. Both timelines use well-researched, authentic, vivid details. The author has a gift for dialogue; each character sounds unique, often amusingly so. His writing is rich, complex and beautiful, whether describing a complicated battle scene or a heartfelt conversation, and his characters are equally rich, revealing layers of complexity and closely held secrets as the book develops. Deeply felt, humane, with every emotion and insight well-earned, this is a thick, rich, satisfying novel that deserves a wide audience."

REVIEW: *Kirkus Rev* v80 no24 p35 D 15 2012

MCKAY, HILARY, 1959-. Binny for short; [by] Hilary McKay 291 p. 2013 Margaret K. McElderry Books

1. Border collie 2. Children's stories 3. Dogs—Fiction 4. Dysfunctional families—Fiction 5. Family life—Fiction 6. Loss (Psychology)—Fiction 7. Moving, Household—Fiction

ISBN 1442482753; 9781442482753 (hardcover)

LC 2013-000053

SUMMARY: In this book, by Hilary McKay and illustrated by Micah Player, "Aunty Violet has died, and left Binny and her family an old house in a seaside town. Binny is faced with a new crush, a new frenemy, and a ghost. It seems Aunty Violet may not have completely departed. [For Binny] it's odd being haunted by her aunt, but there is also the warmth of a busy and loving mother, a musical older sister, and a hilarious little brother, who is busy with his experiments." (Publisher's note)

REVIEW: *Bull Cent Child Books* v67 no2 p105 O 2013 D. S.

"Binny for Short." "It's been three years since Binny's father died, leaving Binny, her brother and sister, and her mother in tight financial straits. Now eleven, Binny has only dim memories of her father; her greatest grief is still for the subsequent loss of her beloved border collie. Max, who was rehomed, much to her rage, by her great-aunt Violet when it became clear that Binny's grandmother could no longer care for him. . . . As usual, [author Hilary] McKay brings a warm dimensionality to all the members of her cast, with Binny's chicken-mad and dreamily manipulative little brother, James, a particularly fine comic turn. . . . The monochromatic art, thickly lined with gray washes, has a contemporary design flair and a youthful appeal."

REVIEW: *Horn Book Magazine* v90 no1 p96 Ja/F 2014 JENNIFER M. BRABANDER

"Binny For Short." "Binny and Gareth's final adventure of the summer nearly ends in catastrophe, the story of which is meted out in italicized chapters that alternate with the main narrative. The cartoony art, which suits the book's funnier aspects if not the seriousness of the emotion, may smooth the way for younger middle-graders challenged by the book's time shifts. . . . [Hilary] McKay's masterful control of the mayhem is ingenious; may the Cornwallis family, like the Conroys and the Cassons before them, have many adventures to come."

REVIEW: *Kirkus Rev* v81 no16 p376 Ag 15 2013

REVIEW: *Publ Wkly* p80 Children's starred review annual 2013

MCKAY, HILARY. Lulu and the Cat in the Bag; 112 p. 2011 Scholastic

1. Animal rescue 2. Cats—Juvenile fiction 3. Children's stories 4. Grandparent & child 5. Pets
ISBN 0807548057; 1407117904; 9780807548059; 9781407117904

SUMMARY: In this children's book, by Hilary McKay, "Lulu's and cousin Mellie's parents are on a grownups-only holiday, so grandmother Nan is taking care of the girls. They're staying at Lulu's house, naturally, so they can tend to her many rescued pets. But kindhearted Lulu can always save another animal. Opportunity knocks when she finds a knotted-up bag on her front doorstep containing a large cat." (Horn Book Magazine)

REVIEW: *Booklist* v109 no21 p69 Jl 1 2013 Carolyn Phelan

REVIEW: *Horn Book Magazine* v89 no5 p106 S/O 2013 BETTY CARTER

"Lulu and the Cat in the Bag". "Having already established her characters in the previous two books, here [Hilary] McKay develops new ones. Nan is particularly strong. She's patient with the girls, mindful of their manners, and a teeny bit vain. Charlie, the young neighborhood tagalong, is also spot on, especially in his inability to understand tone. . . . In a plot twist that's a little precious, the cat (described in particularly visual language . . .) gifts Nan with flowers. But the best present comes from McKay: another solid entry in this fine series."

REVIEW: *Kirkus Rev* v81 no13 p272 Jl 1 2013

REVIEW: *SLJ* v60 no2 p76 F 2014 Sada Mozer

MCKAY, SONIA. Undocumented workers' transitions; legal status, migration, and work in Europe; [by] Sonia McKay 187 p. 2011 Routledge

1. Foreign workers—Europe—Case studies 2. Illegal aliens—Europe—Case studies 3. Illegal employment 4. Precarious employment 5. Social science literature
ISBN 0415889022 (hardback); 9780415889025 (hardback)
LC 2010-053533

SUMMARY: In this book on foreign workers in Europe, "the authors suggest moving away from the dichotomies of 'documented' and 'undocumented' migrants. As they argue, migration status is not fixed, and many migrants experience changes in their status throughout their period of migration. Accordingly, the authors propose using the concept of 'status transitions,' which allows for identifying the 'the real pathways of migrants as not being fixed but as part of a changing process'." (Contemporary Sociology)

REVIEW: *Contemp Sociol* v43 no1 p103-5 Ja 2014 Rebeca Raijman

"Undocumented Workers' Transitions: Legal Status, Migration, and Work in Europe". "The weakest point of the book is the lack of balance between the macro- and micro-levels of analysis. . . Finally, although the authors assert in the first chapter that they found no differences in the situation of undocumented migrants in each of the seven countries, a more systematic presentation of the (many) similarities and (few) differences by country would have allowed us to learn more about how the context of reception prevalent in these countries . . . affects the lives of undocumented migrants. These gaps notwithstanding, the book contributes to the literature on undocumented migration in general, shedding light on the lives of migrants in many European countries."

REVIEW: *Ethn Racial Stud* v37 no5 p892-4 Ap 2014 Shannon Gleeson

MCKEE, SHARON.tr. Khatyn. See Adamovich, A.

MCKENZIE, PRECIOUS.ed. Winning by giving. See Allen, N.

MCKENZIE, PRECIOUS.ed. Winning by teamwork. See Hicks, K. L.

MCKENZIE, PRECIOUS.ed. Winning by waiting. See Winning by waiting

MCKENZIE, STEVEN L.ed. The Oxford encyclopedia of biblical interpretation. See The Oxford encyclopedia of biblical interpretation

MCKEOWN, J. C.ed. The Oxford Anthology of Roman literature. See The Oxford Anthology of Roman literature

MCKERNAN, LUKE. Charles Urban; Pioneering Non-Fiction Film in Britain and America, 1897-1925; [by] Luke McKernan 256 p. 2013 University of California Press

1. Biography (Literary form) 2. Documentary films—History 3. Motion picture producers & directors 4. Propaganda films 5. Urban, Charles

ISBN 0859898822; 9780859898829

SUMMARY: This book "examines the career and legacy of . . . Anglo-American film producer" Charles Urban. Urban is a well known and crucial figure in early film history for his development of Kinemacolor, the world's first successful natural color moving picture system. But Urban's influence was even more far-reaching, according to Luke McKernan. As McKernan reveals, Urban's deep belief in film as an educational tool led him to become an innovator of wartime propaganda." (Publisher's note)

REVIEW: *Hist Today* v64 no1 p64 Ja 2014 Taylor Downing

"Charles Urban: Pioneering the Non-Fiction Film in Britain and America, 1897-1925." "Luke McKernan's fascinating new hook establishes . . . that Charles Urban, a maverick American who settled in Britain in 1897 was the true founder of the documentary movement. . . . McKernan shows how the First World War brought out the best and the worst in Urban. . . . Luke McKernan has written a scholarly, important book on a little-known pioneer in the early documentary movement. It deserves to be widely read."

REVIEW: *TLS* no5771 p26-7 N 8 2013 ERIC J. IANNELLI

MCKINLAY, DEBORAH. That part was true; [by] Deborah McKinlay 240 p. 2013 Grand Central Publishing

1. Authors, American—Fiction 2. Epistolary fiction 3. Fan mail—Fiction 4. Friendship—Fiction 5. Love stories

ISBN 1455573655; 9781455573653 (hardcover); 9781455576104 (large print hardcover)

LC 2013-017540

SUMMARY: "When Eve Petworth writes to Jackson Cooper to praise a scene in one of his books, they discover a mutual love of cookery and food. Their friendship blossoms against the backdrop of Jackson's colorful, but ultimately unsatisfying, love life and Eve's tense relationship with her soon-to-be married daughter." (Publisher's note)

REVIEW: *Kirkus Rev* v81 no24 p308 D 15 2013

"That Part Was True". "British novelist [Deborah] McKinlay . . . offers a not-quite love affair through letters and emails between a wildly successful American writer and a lonely, well-to-do British woman. Long-divorced Eve Petworth has lived a reclusive if privileged life (driving a Bentley and never holding a job) in the English countryside. . . . Approaching 50 and recently divorced for the second time, Jack is emotionally shaky and having trouble starting his next novel. Attracted to Eve's straightforwardness and love of food, he responds to her note, and a correspondence begins. . . . While mousy Eve and sensitive Marlborough Man Jack never quite grab the reader's imagination, McKinlay wisely eschews easy romantic clichés."

REVIEW: *Libr J* v138 no15 p46 S 15 2013

REVIEW: *N Y Times Book Rev* p22 F 9 2014 ELINOR LIPMAN

"That Part Was True." "'That Part Was True' is part epistolary, beginning with a fan letter sent by Eve Petworth to Jackson Cooper, . . . best-selling American novelist. . . . Cooking earns a starring role in their correspondence. . . . [Author Deborah] McKinlay can dip into preciousness. . . . Yet almost every page offers delicious, offbeat descriptions. . . . I worried that invitations to rendezvous in Paris were premature and unearned, or, as Eve's housekeeper warns, 'dodgy.' But mercifully, Jack and Eve think so too."

REVIEW: *Publ Wkly* v260 no45 p48 N 11 2013

MCKISSACK, PAT, 1944-. Ol' Clip-Clop; a ghost story; [by] Pat McKissack 32 p. 2013 Holiday House

1. American ghost stories 2. Conduct of life—Fiction 3. Ghosts—Fiction 4. Landlord & tenant 5. Misers—Fiction

ISBN 0823422658; 9780823422654 (hardcover)

LC 2010-029448

SUMMARY: In this ghost story, "an 18th-century miser, John Leep, rides on horseback to evict a woman from her residence. But as darkness falls over the forest . . . Leep hears the 'Clip, Clop' of a ghostly rider behind him. After cruelly deceiving his desperate tenant ('You're short. This isn't everything you owe me!'), he journeys home, again pursued by the invisible horseman." (Publishers Weekly)

REVIEW: *Booklist* v110 no3 p102 O 1 2013 Randall Enos

REVIEW: *Horn Book Magazine* v89 no5 p66 S/O 2013 SHARA L. HARDESON

"Ol' Clip-Clop: A Ghost Story." "[In] 1741, Heartless moneygrubber John Leep sets out to evict the Widow Mayes from one of his properties. After being chased by a ghostly echo of horses' hooves, John arrives at the widow's front door visibly shaken and nastier than ever--he steals a coin from her rent payment to ensure that she loses her home. Little does he know it's the last cruel deed he'll ever commit. The dark, muted shades of [Eric] Velasquez's oil paintings enhance the hair-raising text."

REVIEW: *Kirkus Rev* v81 no15 p164 Ag 1 2013

REVIEW: *Publ Wkly* v260 no29 p67 Jl 22 2013

REVIEW: *Publ Wkly* p70 Children's starred review annual 2013

REVIEW: *SLJ* v59 no9 p126 S 2013 Lucinda Snyder Whitehurst

MCKITTERICK, DAVID. Old books, new technologies; the representation, conservation and transformation of books since 1700; [by] David McKitterick x, 286 p. 2013 Cambridge University Press

1. Book industries and trade—History 2. Book industries and trade—Technological innovations 3. Books—Conservation and restoration—History 4. Historical literature 5. LANGUAGE ARTS & DISCIPLINES—Publishing 6. Publishers and publishing—History 7. Publishers and publishing—Technological innovations

ISBN 9781107035935 (hardback)

LC 2012-038444

SUMMARY: This book "explores how old books have been represented and interpreted from the eighteenth century to the present day. Conservation of these texts has taken many forms. . . . Using a comprehensive range of examples, [David] McKitterick reveals these practices and their effects to address wider questions surrounding the value of printed books, both in terms of their content and their status as historical objects." (Publisher's note)

REVIEW: *Choice* v51 no10 p1776 Je 2014 J. K. Bracken

REVIEW: *TLS* no5773 p28 N 22 2013 G. THOMAS TANSELLE

"Old Books, New Technologies: The Representation, Conservation and Transformation of Books Since 1700." "This study is a learned, sensible and well-written piece of historical scholarship. [David] McKitterick takes our experiences of reading texts, new and old, on electronic screens simply as the occasion for examining other moments, primarily in eighteenth- and nineteenth-century Britain, when people were encountering new technologies. . . . Each of these accounts is remarkable for its detail, telling the stories of numerous individuals and events, sometimes referring to other classes of artefact, and drawing on a notably wide range of sources. The result is something new: a fascinating evocation of the worlds in which earlier decisions about old books were made."

MCKITTERICK, ROSAMOND.ed. Old Saint Peter's, Rome. See Old Saint Peter's, Rome

MCLACHLAN, CLAY.il. Modern art desserts. See Duggan, T.

MCLEAN, IAN W. Why Australia prospered; the shifting sources of economic growth; [by] Ian W. McLean xiv, 281 p. 2013 Princeton University Press

1. Australia—Economic conditions—History 2. Australia—Economic policy 3. Economic development—Australia 4. Economics literature 5. Historical literature 6. Imperialism—Economic aspects

ISBN 9780691154671 (hardcover)

LC 2012-008056

SUMMARY: Written by Ian McLean, "This book is the first comprehensive account of how Australia attained the world's highest living standards within a few decades of European settlement, and how the nation has sustained an enviable level of income to the present. . . . McLean also considers how the country's notorious origins as a convict settlement positively influenced early productivity levels, and how British imperial policies enhanced prosperity during the colonial period." (Publisher's note)

REVIEW: *Am Hist Rev* v118 no4 p1170-1 O 2013 Simon Ville

"Why Australia Prospered: The Shifting Sources of Economic Growth." "In a series of articles written over many years, Ian W. McLean has addressed the dual questions of how Australia attained high levels of prosperity less than a century after European settlement and why it has since remained amongst the wealthiest of nations. Although this book is not a comprehensive study of Australian economic history, it builds on this earlier body of work and brings together his answers to these questions. . . . Most important of all is McLean's impressive use of the comparative approach. . . . Besides omissions necessary to eschew some of the detail of economic development, there are also missing aspects of the story that do not form part of the author's approach to economic history."

REVIEW: *Choice* v50 no8 p1490 Ap 2013 E. L. Whalen

REVIEW: *J Econ Lit* v51 no3 p908-11 S 2013

MCLEAN, MARGARET. Whitey on Trial; Secrets, Corruption, and the Search for Truth; [by] Margaret McLean 368 p. 2014 St Martins Pr

1. Bulger, Whitey, 1929-—Trials, litigation, etc. 2. Criminal investigation 3. Informers 4. Organized crime 5. True crime stories

ISBN 0765337762; 9780765337764

SUMMARY: This book by Margaret McLean and Jon Lieberman looks at "the recent Whitey Bulger trial, which ended in the murderous Boston mobster's imprisonment in August 2013, and the events that set it in motion. . . . Their account indicts a broader pattern of the use of high-end informants to snitch on other high-end informants, which flies in the face of received police wisdom." (Kirkus Reviews)

REVIEW: *Kirkus Rev* v82 no2 p256 Ja 15 2014

"Whitey on Trial: Secrets, Corruption, and the Search for Truth". "Alternately vivid and limping yarn about the recent Whitey Bulger trial. . . . The blow-by-blow approach lends the book a curious gait: Sometimes the narrative flows swiftly, but when it doesn't, it grinds down in legal minutiae. Perhaps only John Grisham or Jeffrey Toobin could have done the events literary justice, but sensitive readers will wince. . . . Indifferent writing aside, the authors deliver some newsworthy revelations that, if proven, would make it difficult to distinguish the good guys from the bad."

MCLEAN, POLLY.tr. A curse on Dostoevsky. See Rahimi, A.

MCLEISH, TODD. Narwhals; Arctic whales in a melting world; [by] Todd McLeish x, 206 p. 2013 University of Washington Press

1. Animals—Population biology—Climatic factors 2. Arctic Ocean—Environmental conditions 3. Effect of global warming on animals 4. Narwhal 5. Scientific literature

ISBN 0295992646 (hardcover); 9780295992648 (hardcover)

LC 2012-037685

SUMMARY: In this book, Todd McLeish "relates his childhood discovery of [narwhals] via 'World Book Encyclopedia,' then brings us to the Canadian Arctic and Greenland as he recounts time spent on the water among Native hunters and international groups of researchers. As McLeish tries to form a picture of the narwhal's place in the modern world, he quickly discovers there is little consensus on most aspects of the narwhal's existence from current population figures to the impact of global warming." (Booklist)

REVIEW: *Booklist* v109 no12 p21-2 F 15 2013 Colleen Mondor

REVIEW: *N Y Rev Books* v60 no8 p28 My 9 2013

REVIEW: *Orion Magazine* v32 no4 p69-70 Jl/Ag 2013 Elizabeth Bradfield

M'CLOSKEY, KAREN. Unearthed; the landscapes of Hargreaves Associates; [by] Karen M'Closkey xii, 235 p. 2013 University of Pennsylvania Press

1. Architectural literature 2. Public spaces—United States 3. Urban landscape architecture—United States—20th century 4. Urban landscape architecture—United States—21st century
ISBN 081224480X (hardcover : alk. paper); 9780812244809 (hardcover : alk. paper)
LC 2012-046478

SUMMARY: This book "uses Hargreaves Associates' portfolio to illustrate the key challenges and opportunities of designing today's public spaces." It "explores the methods behind canonical Hargreaves Associates sites, such as San Francisco's Crissy Field, Sydney Olympic Park, and the Louisville Waterfront Park. M'Closkey outlines how Hargreaves and his longtime associate Mary Margaret Jones approach the design of public places . . . on sites that require significant remaking." (Publisher's note)

REVIEW: *Choice* v51 no5 p857 Ja 2014 S. Hammer

"Unearthed:The Landscapes of Hargreaves Associates." "This offers a fine example for today's designers, who may strive to engage the heady theories articulated here. However, [George] Hargreaves's focus on process does not preclude product, something that would seem obvious by the scale and intelligence of the projects. To a scientist, the idea of a landscape 'evolving into something complex' sounds a bit Lamarckian, but this mild misusage can be overlooked in favor of a solid body of landscape thought and its realization in physical reality."

MCLOUGHLIN, KATE.ed. The Modernist party. See The Modernist party

MCMAHON, JENNIFER. The winter people; a novel; [by] Jennifer McMahon 336 p. 2014 Doubleday
1. Horror tales 2. Missing persons—Fiction 3. Mothers & daughters—Fiction 4. Undead 5. Women—Fiction
ISBN 0385538499; 9780385538497
LC 2013-026385

SUMMARY: This book, by Jennifer McMahon, is a "thriller about . . . the unbreakable bond between mothers and daughters. . . . West Hall, Vermont, has always been a town of strange disappearances and old legends. The most mysterious is that of Sara Harrison Shea, who, in 1908, was found dead in the field behind her house just months after the . . . death of her daughter. . . . Now, in present day, nineteen-year-old Ruthie lives in Sara's farmhouse with her mother, Alice, and her younger sister, Fawn. " (Publisher's note)

REVIEW: *Booklist* v110 no8 p25 D 15 2013 Christine Tran

REVIEW: *Kirkus Rev* v81 no24 p310 D 15 2013

"The Winter People". "[Jennifer] McMahon, a masterful storyteller who understands how to build suspense, creates an ocean of tension that self-implodes in the last two-thirds of the book. That's when her characters make implausible decisions that cause them to behave like teens in low-budget horror films who know there's a mad killer on the loose, yet when they hear noises in the basement, they go down alone to investigate anyway. Although she writes flawless prose, McMahon's characters' improbable choices derail her story."

REVIEW: *Libr J* v138 no15 p47 S 15 2013

REVIEW: *N Y Times Book Rev* p30-1 Je 1 2014 TERRENCE RAFFERTY

REVIEW: *Publ Wkly* v260 no48 p33 N 25 2013

MCMAHON, SEAN F.ed. Egypt's Tahrir revolution. See Egypt's Tahrir revolution

MCMANAMON, JOHN M. The text and contexts of Ignatius Loyola's autobiography; [by] John M. McManamon xv, 230 p. 2013 Fordham University Press
1. Autobiography 2. Christian saints—Spain—Biography 3. Historical literature 4. Jesuits—History
ISBN 9780823245048 (cloth : alk. paper); 9780823245055 (pbk. : alk. paper)
LC 2012-028211

SUMMARY: This book "situates Ignatius[of Loyola]'s 'Acts' against the backgrounds of the spiritual geography of Luke's New Testament writings and the culture of Renaissance humanism. . . . In this study, John M. McManamon, S.J., persuasively argues that an appreciation of the two Lukan New Testament writings likewise helps interpret the theological perspectives of Ignatius." (Publisher's note)

REVIEW: *Choice* v51 no2 p281-2 O 2013 E. S. Steele

"The Text and Contexts of Ignatius of Loyola's Autobiography." "Ignatius of Loyola, founder of the Society of Jesus (the Jesuits), comes alive in a remarkably concise volume that will be accessible and helpful to interested readers ranging from advanced high school students to accomplished scholars. Focused on providing the historical and literary contexts of Ignatius's autobiographical 'Acta,' [author John M.] McManamon . . . provides a compellingly human portrait of a most significant figure in Western Christianity and the period in which he lived. In doing so, the author also offers a rich, nuanced account of the founding and early years of the Society of Jesuits and a clear, insider's description of Ignatian spirituality in action."

MCMILLAN, TERRY. Who asked you?; [by] Terry McMillan 400 p. 2013 Viking
1. African American women—Fiction 2. Dysfunctional families—fiction 3. FICTION—African American—Contemporary Women 4. FICTION—Contemporary Women 5. FICTION—Family Life 6. Psychological fiction
ISBN 0670785695; 9780670785698 (hardback)
LC 2013-016963

SUMMARY: Terry McMillan "weaves her tale of a black Los Angeles family's disharmony around the narratives of bickering sisters Betty Jean, Arlene, and Venetia . . . . BJ's drug-addled daughter, Trinetta . . . dumps two sons on her." Arlene, "a single mom who has a master's in psychology and harbors a painful secret, struggles with overprotecting her long-closeted gay son, Omar. And wealthy, God-fearing Venetia [has] been ignoring her own needs and her crumbling marriage." (Publishers Weekly)

REVIEW: *Booklist* v109 no21 p32 Jl 1 2013 Vanessa Bush

REVIEW: *Booklist* v110 no15 p37 Ap 1 2014 Magan Szwarek

REVIEW: *Kirkus Rev* v81 no2 p23 Je 1 2013

REVIEW: *Kirkus Rev* p12 2013 Guide 20to BookExpo America

REVIEW: *Kirkus Rev* p10 2013 Guide 20to BookExpo America Joshunda Sanders

REVIEW: *N Y Times Book Rev* p34 S 8 2013 Alex Kuczynski

"Who Asked You?" "[Terry] McMillan is a high practitioner of commerical fiction whose personal life has been so spectacularly messy, it's difficult to separate her travails from the woes of her characters. . . . In 'Who Asked You?'--and yes, the title is alarmingly accusatory--the apparently altogether fictional Betty Jean is a family matriarch who works room service at a hotel. When her drug-addict daughter, Trinetta, skips town, Betty Jean is left in charge of Trinetta's two sons. . . . At the same time, she's supporting her own dying husband, who's being sexually abused by his day nurse. . . . In the end, of course, the powerful mother figure prevails."

REVIEW: *Publ Wkly* v260 no29 p38 Jl 22 2013

MCMILLIAN, JOHN. Beatles Vs. Stones; [by] John McMillian 288 p. 2013 Simon & Schuster

1. Beatles (Performer) 2. Music literature 3. Rock musicians 4. Rock musicians 5. Rolling Stones
ISBN 1439159696; 9781439159699

SUMMARY: Author "John McMillian explores the multifaceted relationship between "two biggest bands in the world--the lovable Beatles and the bad-boy Rolling Stones. . . . Both groups liked to maintain that they weren't really 'rivals'--that was just a media myth, they politely said--but on both sides of the Atlantic, they plainly competed for commercial success and aesthetic credibility." (Publisher's note)

REVIEW: *Booklist* v110 no3 p10-2 O 1 2013 June Sawyers

"Beatles vs. Stones." "In this pleasurable romp through popular-music history, [John] McMillian discusses what set the two groups apart and what brought them together. The rivalry between the two groups was real enough, but so was their mutual respect. And despite appearances to the contrary . . . their recording output wasn't always tit for tat either. Eventually each band went its own way. The Beatles broke up while at the top of their game, while the Stones continue to tour. Fans of both groups will enjoy this musical duel."

REVIEW: *Kirkus Rev* v81 no18 p129 S 15 2013

REVIEW: *N Y Times Book Rev* p14 D 1 2013 ANTHONY DECURTIS

REVIEW: *Publ Wkly* v260 no32 p47-8 Ag 12 2013

REVIEW: *Publ Wkly* v260 no35 p20 S 2 2013 H. L. C

MCMURTRY, LARRY, 1936-. The Last Kind Words Saloon; a novel; [by] Larry McMurtry 256 p. 2014 W W Norton & Co Inc Liveright Publishing Corp.

1. Bars (Drinking establishments)—Fiction 2. Earp, Wyatt, 1848-1929 3. Holliday, John Henry, 1851-1887 4. Texas—Fiction 5. Western stories
ISBN 0871407868; 9780871407863
LC 2014-002279

SUMMARY: "With 'The Last Kind Words Saloon' [author Larry McMurtry] returns again to the vivid and unsparing portrait of the nineteenth-century and cowboy lifestyle made so memorable in his classic 'Lonesome Dove.' Evoking the greatest characters and legends of the Old Wild West, here McMurtry tells the story of the closing of the American frontier through the travails of two of its most immortal figures: Wyatt Earp and Doc Holliday." (Publisher's note)

REVIEW: *N Y Rev Books* v61 no10 p29-30 Je 5 2014 Joyce Carol Oates

"The Last Kind Words Saloon." "[Author Larry McMurtry] admiringly alludes to John Ford's famous remark about life and legend. . . . But the novel seems to subvert the director's dictum: it isn't the inflated legends of western gunslingers with which it is concerned but the less-than-heroic lives behind the legends. . . . When the celebrated gunslingers have died, or have lapsed into the oblivion of age and senility, Larry McMurtry tell us in his coruscating antiheroic work of fiction, the 'legend' may yet endure—a battered sign haphazardly rescued from a dump heap by a tabloid journalist."

REVIEW: *N Y Times Book Rev* p23 Je 29 2014 MAX BYRD

MCNAMARA, MARGARET. The apple orchard riddle; 40 p. 2013 Schwartz & Wade

1. Apples—Fiction 2. Children's stories 3. Orchards 4. Riddles—Fiction 5. School field trips—Fiction
ISBN 0375847448; 9780375847448; 9780375957444 (glb)
LC 2011-008742

SUMMARY: This book, by Margaret McNamara and illustrated by G. Brian Karas, is "about a school trip to an apple orchard! The students learn a lot about apples and apple orchards--including how apples are harvested, how cider is made, and what the different varieties of apples are--while trying to solve a riddle. The book also celebrates how some children learn differently than others." (Publisher's note)

REVIEW: *Booklist* v109 no22 p86 Ag 1 2013 Carolyn Phelan

REVIEW: *Bull Cent Child Books* v67 no1 p37 S 2013 E. B.

"The Apple Orchard Riddle." "When Mr. Tiffin cakes his class to the apple orchard for a field trip, he throws a riddle out to his students to solve during the day. . . . As the kids poke around the orchard, they continually test observations against Mr. Tiffin's riddle. . . . Thus [author Margaret] McNamara pulls off the double trick of an informative hook about commercial apple cultivation, and a sensitive lesson on learning differences. As always, [illustrator G. Brian] Karas' paint and pencil smudge kiddie cast is diverse, adorable, and believable, and the focus on trees and machinery clarifies several apple-processing activities. With its solid storyline and additional 'Apple Orchard Facts', this will make a wonderful prelude to autumn trips to the orchard."

REVIEW: *Horn Book Magazine* v89 no4 p110 Jl/Ag 2013 JULIE ROACH

REVIEW: *Kirkus Rev* v81 no2 p96 Je 1 2013

REVIEW: *N Y Times Book Rev* p41 N 10 2013 SARAH HARRISON SMITH

"How Big Could Your Pumpkin Grow?," "The Apple Orchard Riddle," and "Thanksgiving Day Thanks." "While the pie's in the oven, savor [Wendell] Minor's mighty vocabulary, silly humor and intriguing facts. . . . [G. Brian Karas], who lives in the Hudson Valley, boosts the flavor of this sweet story with soft pencil line and rich, muted colors. . . . [Laura Malone] Elliott includes facts about the Pilgrims and their friends, the Wampanoag; [Lynn] Munsinger's adorable illustrations show little animals at work on holiday crafts that readers may want to try, too."

REVIEW: *Publ Wkly* v260 no19 p68 My 13 2013

REVIEW: *SLJ* v59 no6 p92 Je 2013 Linda Ludke

MCNENLY, LINDA SCARANGELLA. Native performers in wild west shows; from Buffalo Bill to Euro Disney;

[by] Linda Scarangella McNenly xviii, 254 p. 2012 University of Oklahoma Press

1. Circus performers—West (U.S.)—History 2. Historical literature 3. Indian cowboys—West (U.S.)—History 4. Indians in popular culture 5. Wild west shows—West (U.S.)—History

ISBN 9780806142814 (hardcover: alk. paper)

LC 2012-001794

SUMMARY: In this book on Wild West shows, "focusing on the experiences of Native performers and performances, Linda Scarangella McNenly begins her examination of these spectacles with Buffalo Bill's 1880s pageants. She then traces the continuing performance of these acts, still a feature of regional celebrations in both Canada and the United States—and even at Euro Disney." (Publisher's note)

REVIEW: *Am Hist Rev* v119 no1 p186-7 F 2014 David M. Wrobel

"Native Performers in Wild West Shows: From Buffalo Bill to Euro Disney". "[Linda] Scarangella McNenly explores the themes of transculturation and expressive agency quite effectively. . . . The brief conclusion and concluding statement . . . are less developed than they might be. Also, a little more research into Natives' wages for show work would have strengthened the narrative. . . . Still, Scarangella McNenly's use of traditional archival sources, as well as oral histories, photographs, and material culture, and her effective synthesis of the pertinent scholarship in a range of connected fields make 'Native Performers in Wild West Shows' a significant addition to the field."

MCPHAIL, DAVID. Bad dog; 32 p. 2014 Holiday House

1. Behavior—Fiction 2. Children's stories 3. Dogs—Fiction 4. Human-animal relationships—Fiction 5. Pets—Juvenile literature

ISBN 0823428524; 9780823428526 (hardcover)

LC 2012-038836

SUMMARY: "Forgiveness and love triumph at the end of this . . . easy-to-read story of a family dog who is rarely on his best behavior," written and illustrated by David McPhail, and part of the I Like to Read series. (Publisher's note)

REVIEW: *Booklist* v110 no14 p80 Mr 15 2014 Martha Edmundson

REVIEW: *Kirkus Rev* v82 no4 p107 F 15 2014

"Bad Dog". "A preschool-age boy narrates this short early reader, a straightforward story about a mischievous dog and the boy who loves him. . . . This short but complete story is told in succinct sentences with just a few words per page, often the repeated admonishment 'Bad dog, Tom!' set in a speech balloon. Though this is intended for new readers, toddlers who are just transitioning into real stories will also appreciate the simple plot with its subtle message of unconditional love that endures even when someone is naughty. [David] McPhail's gentle illustrations in pen and ink with watercolor washes are appealing as always, conveying both humor and emotion."

REVIEW: *SLJ* v60 no3 p119 Mr 2014 Meg Smith

MCPHAIL, DAVID.ed. My Mother Goose. See My Mother Goose

MCPHERSON, ALAN.ed. Encyclopedia of U.S. military interventions in Latin America. See Encyclopedia of U.S. military interventions in Latin America

MCQUERRY, MAUREEN DOYLE. Beyond the door; [by] Maureen Doyle McQuerry 384 p. 2014 Amulet Books

1. Adventure and adventurers—Fiction 2. Adventure stories 3. Animals, Mythical—Fiction 4. Brothers and sisters—Fiction 5. Magic—Fiction 6. Mythology, Celtic—Fiction 7. Space and time—Fiction

ISBN 1419710168; 9781419710162

LC 2013-025513

SUMMARY: This book, by Maureen Doyle McQuerry, "weaves a . . . coming-of-age story with fantasy and mythology. With his love of learning and the game of Scrabble, Timothy James feels like the only person who understands him is his older sister, Sarah. . . . One night, while his parents and sister are away, the door opens, and mythical creatures appear in his own living room! Soon, a mystery of unparalleled proportions begins to unfold, revealing an age-old battle of Light against Dark." (Publisher's note)

REVIEW: *Booklist* v110 no18 p60 My 15 2014

REVIEW: *Booklist* v110 no17 p93 My 1 2014 Thom Barthelmess

REVIEW: *Bull Cent Child Books* v67 no8 p416 Ap 2014 K. Q. G.

"Beyond the Door". "While the elements here are familiar to the point of being derivative . . . they still make for a sometimes exciting ride through British and Welsh mythology. Characterization is also quite rich. . . . The book, however, is oddly divided: the first part covets Timothy's learning of his destiny and initial battle with Balor, offering a self-contained and concluded story, while the second half is rushed, introducing several new characters and ending rather abruptly and with no real payoff save its promise of a sequel. Nonetheless, the tale of an underdog hero is a perennial favorite, and this may well find an audience among fans of Percy Jackson, Harry Potter, and 'Gregor the Overlander'."

REVIEW: *Kirkus Rev* v82 no4 p72 F 15 2014

"Beyond the Door". " A promising start to a fantasy series mines the rich ore of Celtic mythology and propels a young boy into cosmic battle. . . . References to quantum physics and to the way that time might seem "like water pouring off a tabletop, flowing in all directions at once," emphasize the simultaneous presence of the mythic and everyday life. An Ogham-based code explained in an opening note runs along the bottoms of the pages for readers to decipher. Sure-handed and page-turning, this series opener leaves plenty to be resolved."

REVIEW: *SLJ* v60 no5 p114 My 2014 Jane Barrer

REVIEW: *Voice of Youth Advocates* v36 no6 p74-5 F 2014 Lucy Schall

REVIEW: *Voice of Youth Advocates* v37 no3 p84 Ag 2014 Morgan Brickey

MCQUINN, ANNA. Leo loves baby time; 24 p. 2014 Charlesbridge

1. Babies—Fiction 2. Infants—Juvenile fiction 3. Picture books for children 4. Play—Fiction 5. Play—Juvenile fiction 6. Play groups—Fiction 7. Play groups—Juvenile fiction

ISBN 1580896650; 9781580896658 (reinforced for library use); 9781607346654 (ebook)

LC 2013-004292

SUMMARY: In this children's picture book, "Leo . . . attends a baby program with his mother. He and his fellow sitting-up babes enjoy singing and playing on their grown-ups' laps, as well as exploring books and toys. The single- and double-page spreads include one or two sentences describing the action written in a bold, black type. . . . The setting of this program is left unclear, but it could easily be a public library or a community center in a very diverse neighborhood." (Kirkus Reviews)

REVIEW: *Kirkus Rev* v82 no2 p192 Ja 15 2014

"Leo Loves Baby Time". "[Ruth] Hearson effectively channels the style of Rosalind Beardshaw, who illustrated the previous Lola titles, and creates cozy cartoon scenes in warm jewel tones. . . . Organizations offering such events will want to stock up on this title, since it offers a perfect introduction for babies and their caregivers alike. While the ending feels a bit abrupt, little ones will find much to recognize here, and their grown-ups will appreciate the baby-friendly book design with its thicker-than-normal pages, jacketless cover and rounded corners. Like Leo and his friends, this book is a buoyant and bouncy delight."

REVIEW: *Publ Wkly* v260 no48 p54 N 25 2013

REVIEW: *SLJ* v60 no4 p128 Ap 2014 Brooke Rasche

MCSHANE, ANGELA J. Political broadside ballads of seventeenth-century England; a critical bibliography; [by] Angela J. McShane 591 p. 2011 Pickering & Chatto

1. Bibliography (Documentation) 2. Broadsides 3. Great Britain—History—Sources 4. Great Britain—History—Stuarts, 1603-1714 5. Political ballads & songs

ISBN 1848930143; 9781848930148

SUMMARY: "Political broadsides are a fascinating window on . . . the seventeenth century. . . . They took as their subject matter political heroes and villains, war and peace, and the divisions and harmonies of the Civil War, the Interregnum, the Restoration, the Popish Plot, the Exclusion Crisis and the Glorious Revolution." Written by Angela J. McShane, "This is the first truly accurate bibliography of its kind providing correct publication dates for many of the texts for the first time." (Publisher's note)

REVIEW: *Engl Hist Rev* v128 no534 p1234-6 O 2013 Ian Archer

"Political Broadside Ballads of Seventeenth-Century England: A Critical Bibliography." "As Angela McShane notes in her introduction, historians have been deterred from making extensive use of political broadside ballads in the seventeenth century because of doubts about provenance and publication details, reinforced perhaps by a disdain for the vernacular poetry in which they were couched. The appearance of this comprehensive bibliographic survey, which often corrects previous errors on dating and in its notes offers invaluable contextual information, will open up new research pathways. . . . It is perhaps a pity that her entries do not tell us where the appropriate digital copy can be found, and this is problematic in view of the dispersal of the digital ballad collections."

MCSHANE, MICHAEL Q. President Obama and education reform. See Maranto, R.

MEAD, REBECCA. My life in Middlemarch; [by] Rebecca Mead 304 p. 2014 CrownCrown Publishers

1. Books & reading 2. Creation (Literary, artistic, etc.) 3. Creative nonfiction 4. Eliot, George, 1819-1880

ISBN 0307984761; 9780307984760

LC 2013-011477

SUMMARY: In this "hybrid work of literary criticism, biography, and memoir," author Rebecca Mead discusses her relationship with the book "Middlemarch" by George Eliot. She " identifies strongly with aspects of Eliot's life and that of the characters in Middlemarch, [and] returns to the novel during various stages of her life: as a young Englishwoman finding her way in New York; in relationships with difficult men; as a stepmother and wife; and eventually as the mother of a son." (Publishers Weekly)

REVIEW: *Atlantic* v313 no1 p43 Ja/F 2014 Ann Hulbert

"My Life in Middlemarch". "Folding memoir into a blend of literary biography, journalism, and criticism, [Rebecca] Mead keeps ego and epigrammatic moralism under admirable control. She's wry about her own early, total identification with Dorothea Brooke, Middlemarch's heroine, so full of earnest striving. She's also wise about the painfully pretentious letters written by the teenage Mary Ann Evans ([George] Eliot's real name). Mead's middle-aged rediscovery of Middlemarch—and her insights into Eliot's rich middle age—is not to be missed. Her portrait of Eliot's love for George Henry Lewes . . . couldn't be more astute."

REVIEW: *Bookforum* v20 no4 p42 D 2013/Ja 2014 CLAIRE MESSUD

REVIEW: *Booklist* v110 no19/20 p130 Je 1 2014 Neal Wyatt

REVIEW: *Booklist* v110 no8 p8 D 15 2013 Donna Seaman

REVIEW: *Commonweal* v141 no12 p23-5 Jl 11 2014 Mollie Wilson O'Reilly

REVIEW: *Kirkus Rev* v81 no23 p246 D 1 2013

REVIEW: *Libr J* v139 no9 p42 My 15 2014 Beth Farrell

REVIEW: *Libr J* v138 no13 p58 Ag 1 2013 Barbara Hoffert

REVIEW: *Libr J* v138 no21 p101 D 1 2013 Meagan Lacy

REVIEW: *N Y Rev Books* v51 no7 p59-60 Ap 24 2014 Ruth Bernard Yeazell

REVIEW: *N Y Times Book Rev* p1-23 Ja 26 2014 Joyce Carol Oates

"My Life in Middlemarch." "Rarely attempted, and still more rarely successful, is the bibliomemoir—a subspecies of literature combining criticism and biography with the intimate, confessional tone of autobiography. . . . There is no irony or postmodernist posturing in Mead's forthright, unequivocal and unwavering endorsement of George Eliot as both a great novelist and a role model. . . . 'My Life in Middlemarch' is a poignant testimony to the abiding power of fiction. . . . Admirable and endearing as 'My Life in Middlemarch' is, there are virtually no surprises here that have not been uncovered by Eliot biographers."

REVIEW: *Publ Wkly* v260 no40 p38 O 7 2013

MEAD, WENDY. The Merchant; [by] Wendy Mead 48 p. 2013 Marshall Cavendish

1. Historical literature 2. Merchants—United States—History—17th century 3. Merchants—United States—History—18th century

ISBN 9781608704156 (print); 9781608709861 (ebook)

LC 2011-028343

SUMMARY: This book on merchants in colonial America, by Wendy Mead, is part of the Colonial People series. It "looks at the varied roles of colonial merchants, who dealt in imports, exports, and banking, as well as sales. The role of women as merchants is also discussed." The book "is illustrated with tinted engravings and paintings from earlier eras as well as . . . color photos of artifacts and replicas." (Booklist)

REVIEW: *Booklist* v110 no4 p45 O 15 2013 Carolyn Phelan

"The Gunsmith," "The Merchant," and "The Shipbuilder". "Attractively designed, the books in the Colonial People series present and discuss the roles of individual trades from colonial America. . . . The publisher indicates the reading level as four, and while the books' relatively large type and square format are consistent with a fourth-grade audience, the readability level appears to be several grades higher. . . . In each book, the informative text is illustrated with tinted engravings and paintings from earlier eras as well as excellent color photos of artifacts and replicas and reenactments of historical trades in Colonial Williamsburg."

MEANEY, GERARDINE. Reading the Irish Woman. See Whelan, B.

MEASURING THE REAL SIZE OF THE WORLD'S ECONOMY; the framework, methodology, and results of the International Comparison Program--ICP; xxxiv, 659 p. 2013 World Bank

1. Economics—Statistical methods 2. Economics literature 3. Gross domestic product—Statistical methods 4. National income—Statistical methods 5. Purchasing power parity

ISBN 0821397281; 9780821397282

LC 2012-286316

SUMMARY: This book, created by the World Bank, "is the most comprehensive accounting ever presented by the International Comparison Program (ICP) of the theory and methods underlying the estimation of purchasing power parities (PPPs). . . . By disclosing the theory, concepts, and methods underlying the estimates, this book increases the transparency of the ICP process." (Publisher's note)

REVIEW: *Choice* v51 no2 p318 O 2013 R. M. Ramazani

"Measuring the Real Size of the World Economy: The Framework, Methodology, and Results of the International Comparison Program (ICP)." "Since its inception in the 1960s, the International Comparison Program (ICP) has become one of the most comprehensive international statistical resources of comparative economic data, with participation of 146 countries. This volume clearly explains the theory and methods that are the basis of the estimates of purchasing power parities (PPPs) developed by the ICP. The PPPs provide valuable information about the relative size of the economy of various countries by converting their gross domestic product (GDP) . . . into a common currency. . . . This volume will be a valuable resource for researchers, government officials, and policy makers."

MEATLOAF (PERFORMER) To hell and back. See Dalton, D.

MEBANE, DONNA. Tomorrow Comes; An Emma Story; [by] Donna Mebane 266 p. 2013 Starshine Galaxy

1. Death—Fiction 2. Families—Fiction 3. Future life—Fiction 4. Grief—Fiction 5. Teenagers—Fiction

ISBN 098576080X; 9780985760809

SUMMARY: In this book, "a teenager dies and discovers a new world on the other side. . . . After she awakens with her late Aunt Patsy, Grandpa and other loved ones in a place that she calls 'After,' she finds that she can invisibly observe and move among her mourning family members. . . . With help from her late relatives and other old and new friends, Emma learns that love doesn't end when life does but in fact grows stronger." (Kirkus Reviews)

REVIEW: *Kirkus Rev* v82 no2 p378 Ja 15 2014

"Tomorrow Comes: An Emma Story". "This book was inspired by the story of [Donna] Mebane's real-life daughter, also named Emma. It's truly a labor of love, and readers can easily imagine Emma's vivacious love of life. The novel, however, is not without flaws, as the structure can be a bit confusing. . . . The work also contains many long, hard-to-follow sections of italicized thoughts, mostly Emma's. Overall, however, the characters are well fleshed out, and each family member offers a different perspective on the process of mourning. It's shown to be a distinctive experience for every individual, but the stirring moral of each journey remains the same: It will all be OK. An emotional novel about grief and the enduring power of love after death."

MECK, SU. I forgot to remember. See De Vise, D.

MEDDEB, ABDELWAHAB,ed. A history of Jewish-Muslim relations. See A history of Jewish-Muslim relations

MEDIA DISPARITY; a gender battleground; xviii, 292 p. 2013 Lexington Books

1. Mass media & women 2. Social science literature 3. Women in mass media 4. Women in popular culture 5. Women in the mass media industry

ISBN 9780739181874 (cloth: alk. paper)

LC 2013-030882

SUMMARY: This book, edited by Cory L. Armstrong, "highlights the progress—or lack thereof—in media regarding portrayals of women, across genres and cultures within the twenty-first-century. Blending both original studies and descriptive overviews of current media platforms, top scholars evaluate the portrayals of women in contemporary venues, including advertisements, videogames, political stories, health communication, and reality television." (Publisher's note)

REVIEW: *Choice* v51 no9 p1584-5 My 2014 T. E. Adams

"Media Disparity: A Gender Battleground". "[Cory L.] Armstrong . . . has assembled an impressive collection of original research studies, theoretical essays, and literature reviews that, taken together, investigate not only stereotypical, harmful, and progressive representations of women and men but also contexts of media production, representation, and usage still in need of improvement. . . . Limitations of the collection include a lack of attention to the ways in which gender representations intersect with representations of other identities . . . and a reliance on and perpetuation of the traditional female-male binary. . . . These criticisms notwithstanding, the collection will be an important resource for anyone interested in media criticism, history, and production."

MEDIEVAL ENGLISH LYRICS AND CAROLS; xiv, 466 p. 2013 D. S. Brewer

1. Anthologies 2. Carols, English (Middle)—Texts 3. Carols, English—Texts 4. English poetry—Middle English, 1100-1500 5. Songs—Texts

ISBN 1843843412 (pbk.); 9781843843412 (pbk.)

LC 2012-286363

SUMMARY: Edited by Thomas G. Duncan, "This anthology provides a generous and wide-ranging selection . . . The texts are edited anew, accompanied with a textual apparatus detailing manuscript readings where emendations have been made to restore sense, metre and rhyme. The language of pre-Chaucerian poems has been normalised to accord with the dialect of late fourteenth-century London ('Chaucerian English'), and unfamiliar spellings in later lyrics have been regularized." (Publisher's note)

REVIEW: *Choice* v51 no1 p77-8 S 2013 A. P. Church

"Medieval English Lyrics and Carols." "[Editor Thomas G.] Duncan offers the present anthology as a comprehensive, single-volume edition covering the same periods. He arranges the selected texts in two parts, the first devoted to the expected range of 13th- and 14th-century lyrics, and the second presenting material from the 15th and early-16th century. . . . In an introductory essay, the author explains his editorial choices and his classification of the lyrics and their themes, forms, meter, manuscripts, and pronunciation. . . . Although some specialists may prefer original complexity rather than redaction, novices will likely appreciate the greater accessibility that results from such choices."

REVIEW: *TLS* no5777/8 p35 D 20 2013 JAMES WADE

MEDIEVAL SHAKESPEARE; pasts and presents; 263 p. 2013 Cambridge University Press

1. English drama—Early modern and Elizabethan, 1500-1600—Medieval influences 2. Historical literature 3. LITERARY CRITICISM—European—English, Irish, Scottish, Welsh 4. Middle Ages in literature

ISBN 9781107016279

LC 2012-035061

SUMMARY: This book, edited by Ruth Morse, Helen Cooper, and Peter Holland, "present[s] new perspectives on Shakespeare and his medieval heritage. . . . The collection explores Shakespeare and his work in the context of the Middle Ages, medieval books and language, the British past, and medieval conceptions of drama and theatricality, together showing Shakespeare's work as rooted in late medieval history and culture." (Publisher's note)

REVIEW: *TLS* no5763 p26 S 13 2013 MIKA ROSS-SOUTHALL

"Medieval Shakespeare: Pasts and Presents." "There is a lively essay from Tom Bishop on how [William] Shakespeare responds to the habit and history of 'playing' in late medieval and Early Modern theatre. . . . An interesting essay comes from A. E. B. Coldiron, about the conditions and effects of early printing. . . . But the best essay in this book is devoted to graphic gore. Michael O'Donnell argues that Shakespeare's complex use of blood is inherited from the English mystery plays, where its appearance carried a nuanced, emotional impact and significance. . . . Lapses in style sometimes mar the persuasiveness of arguments . . . and abstract musings can meander around the crux. Nonetheless, this collection offers a fascinating dialogue between two literary periods."

MEDLOCK, STEPHANIE WILSON. The Lives of Things; [by] Stephanie Wilson Medlock 378 p. 2013 Createspace Independent Pub

1. Art—Expertising 2. Art objects 3. Detective & mystery stories 4. Speculative fiction 5. Truthfulness & falsehood

ISBN 1482008319; 9781482008319

SUMMARY: This book "tells a story of a woman with an unusual and dangerous talent. Rebecca Katz is no ordinary heroine. Poised, confident and controlled, she's an expert art authenticator who's known for precision and professionalism. But her secret ability remains secret: the power to communicate with objects. This is particularly useful in her line of work, in which potentially valuable ancient artifacts show up on her desk regularly, but also in her personal life." (Kirkus Reviews)

REVIEW: *Kirkus Rev* v82 no2 p374 Ja 15 2014

"The Lives of Things". "Whimsical. . . . . This suspenseful novel tells the tale of Rebecca's physical and emotional journey in a unique, often captivating manner. Her story quickly transcends the conventions of a mere mystery novel to become a story full of depth and meaning, as her unusual gift comes to symbolize an approach to life that she must leave behind. Her growth as a character plays against the intriguing backdrop of the antiques world, and the story delves into details of psychology, history and art along the way. A well-written tale of adventure and drama about a woman struggling to save herself."

MEDSGER, BETTY. The burglary; the discovery of J. Edgar Hoover's secret FBI; [by] Betty Medsger 608 p. 2014 Alfred A. Knopf

1. Burglary—United States—Case studies 2. Historical literature 3. Intelligence service—Moral and ethical aspects—United States 4. Leaks (Disclosure of information)—United States—Case studies 5. Whistle blowing—United States—Case studies

ISBN 9780307962959 (hardcover : alk. paper)

LC 2013-024540

SUMMARY: This book by Betty Medsger contains "the never-before-told full story of the history-changing break-in at the FBI office in Media, Pennsylvania, by a group of unlikely activists--quiet, ordinary, hardworking Americans--that made clear the shocking truth and confirmed what some had long suspected, that J. Edgar Hoover had created and was operating, in violation of the U.S. Constitution, his own shadow Bureau of Investigation." (Publisher's note)

REVIEW: *Booklist* v110 no9/10 p24-5 Ja 1 2014 Gilbert Taylor

"The Burglary: The Discovery of J. Edgar Hoover's Secret FBI." "In discursive detail, [Betty] Medsger recounts the protester-burglars' movements. . . . Besides dramatizating the incident, Medsger pursues its historical significance--the documents' revelation of extensive domestic surveillance by the FBI--into the congressional investigations of the 1970s. Medsger also discusses J. Edgar Hoover's appointment in 1924 and NSA activities in the present. Though it could have been more tightly organized, this work encapsulates an important event of interest to readers of the history of the antiwar movement."

REVIEW: *Choice* v51 no10 p1874-5 Je 2014 A. Theoharis

REVIEW: *Kirkus Rev* v82 no1 p98 Ja 1 2014

"The Burglary: The Discovery of J. Edgar Hoover's Secret FBI". "Ambitious, meticulous account of a successful burglary of the FBI, during a different time of controversy regarding governmental surveillance. . . . As the author points out, comparisons to post-9/11 America and recent revelations about the National Security Administration are inescapable. [Betty] Medsger captures the domestic political ferment of the 1970s on a large canvas, though the narrative's extreme detail and depth occasionally make for slow going or repetitive observations."

REVIEW: *N Y Times Book Rev* p10 F 2 2014 DAVID OSHINSKY

"The Burglary: The Discovery of J. Edgar Hoover's Secret FBI." "On a March evening in 1971, eight antiwar protesters burglarized an F.B.I. office in Media, Pa., just outside Philadelphia, with astonishing ease. . . . [Author Betty Medsger] dined with two old acquaintances who told her, without prompting, of their role in the burglary. With their aid, Medsger found and interviewed all but one of the other burglars. . . . The stolen material included the secret case histories of thousands of Americans. . . . Personal stories, impeccably researched and elegantly presented . . . , are the best parts of an engaging but overstuffed book."

REVIEW: *N Y Rev Books* v61 no16 p61-3 O 23 2014 Aryeh Neier

REVIEW: *Publ Wkly* v260 no45 p61 N 11 2013

MEIER, KATHRYN SHIVELY. Nature's Civil War; common soldiers and the environment in 1862 Virginia; [by] Kathryn Shively Meier 219 p. 2013 University of North Carolina Press

1. Historical literature 2. Military life—United States—History—19th century 3. Military life—Virginia—History—19th century 4. Self-care, Health—United States—History—19th century 5. Self-care, Health—Virginia—History—19th century

ISBN 9781469610764 (cloth : alk. paper)

LC 2013-015620

SUMMARY: In this book, Kathryn Shively Meier "focuses on how soldiers stayed healthy during a very specific historical moment and place, Virginia in 1862. She compares the swampy Peninsula Campaign with the Shenandoah Campaign, the latter perceived as a healthier environment because of the mountainous region. The book's five chapters cover such topics as the ways in which the public viewed health and healing . . . and the expansion of military health care during the war." (Choice: Current Reviews for Academic Libraries)

REVIEW: *Choice* v51 no7 p1291-2 Mr 2014 H. Aquino

"Nature's Civil War: Common Soldiers and the Environment in 1862 Virginia." "The most important chapter (5) focuses on self-care, or how common soldiers tended to their health in a particularly taxing environment. Throughout the book, but especially in chapter 5, [Kathryn Shively] Meier reveals the soldiers' thoughts through their letters home. The main focus is on physical health. The briefer discussion of mental health, although weaker, does introduce an important subject. The book is thoroughly researched, contributing to the burgeoning body of literature on environmental history in the Civil War era. It is well written and accessible to undergraduates, enhanced by figures and tables as well as an extensive bibliography. . . . Highly recommended."

MEISEL, PAUL.il. Swamp chomp. See Schaefer, L. M.

MEISEL, PAUL.il. Vampire baby. See Bennett, K.

MEISSNER, DAVID. Call of the Klondike; a true gold rush adventure; [by] David Meissner 168 p. 2013 Calkins Creek

1. Bond, Marshall 2. Gold mines & mining—Yukon 3. Historical literature 4. Klondike Gold Rush, 1896-1899 5. Pearce, Stanley

ISBN 1590788230 (reinforced); 9781590788233 (reinforced)

LC 2013-931060

SUMMARY: Here, the authors share the experience of two 20-something Yale graduates from 1897, Stanley Pearce and Marshall Bond, who participated in the Klondike gold rush. Their letters are offered along with "diary entries, telegrams and Pearce's articles for the Denver Republican." The book also incorporates "pull-out quotes, maps, posters, documents and many . . . captioned photographs, including one of Jack London, who camped near Pearce and Bond's cabin." (Kirkus Reviews)

REVIEW: *Booklist* v110 no2 p61 S 15 2013 J. B. Petty

REVIEW: *Bull Cent Child Books* v67 no5 p274 Ja 2014 E. B.

"Call of the Klondike: A True Gold Rush Adventure." "[David] Meissner pieces together the account mainly from letters, journal entries, and newspaper dispatches the men sent back to the States throughout their adventure, and the emotional highs and lows of hope and disappointment come vividly through their accessible writings. Plenty of period photos, many of notable detail and clarity, augment the text, and a bibliography and list of further resources are included. U.S. History teachers will appreciate the deft integration of primary sources, but kids who love adventure stories will simply appreciate an exciting personal account."

REVIEW: *Kirkus Rev* p37 Ag 15 2013 Fall Preview

REVIEW: *Kirkus Rev* p80 N 15 2013 Best Books

REVIEW: *Kirkus Rev* v81 no17 p105 S 1 2013

REVIEW: *Kirkus Rev* p50 2013 Guide 20to BookExpo America

REVIEW: *SLJ* v59 no8 p128 Ag 2013 Ann Welton

MEISSNER, SUSAN. A fall of marigolds; [by] Susan Meissner 400 p. 2014 NAL Trade

1. FICTION—Historical 2. FICTION—Romance—Contemporary 3. Immigrants—United States—Fiction 4. September 11 Terrorist Attacks, 2001—Fiction 5. Widows—Fiction

ISBN 045141991X; 9780451419910 (pbk.)

LC 2013-033477

SUMMARY: In this book by Susan Meissner, "a scarf ties together the stories of two women as they struggle with personal journeys 100 years apart. . . . In 1911, Clara Wood witnesses the traumatic death of the man she loves in the Triangle Shirtwaist Fire and chooses to bury her grief and guilt while ministering to sick immigrants on Ellis Island. . . . Interwoven into Clara's tale is the story of widow Taryn

Michaels, whose life 100 years later in some ways parallels Clara's." (Kirkus Reviews)

REVIEW: *Booklist* v110 no14 p60 Mr 15 2014

"The Apple Orchard," "The Bookstore," and "A Fall of Marigolds." "Art specialist Tess has a successful professional life but is lacking in the family department. When she's named heir to one-half of an estate and discovers the other half goes to the sister she never knew she had, her life gets turned upside-down. . . . Between studying art history at Columbia University on a prestigious scholarship and a two-week fling with a magnetic, wealthy man, 23-year-old Esme Garland from England is happily settling into life in Manhattan when she discovers she's pregnant. This character-driven novel is witty and poetic. . . . The heartbreaks of two women, separated by decades, come together in the history of a scarf that holds special meaning to each woman. Christian fiction author [Susan] Meissner's first mainstream women's fiction novel hits all of the right emotional notes without overdoing the two tragedies."

REVIEW: *Booklist* v110 no12 p24 F 15 2014 Susan Maguire

"A Fall of Marigolds." "Taryn Michaels specializes in hard-to-find patterns at an Upper West Side fabric shop. She is haunted by her failure to find a match for a scarf covered in bright marigolds, the same scarf she was holding v^ihen the Twin Towers fell in 2001, killing her husband. . . . [Susan] Meissner's first mainstream women's fiction novel, after more than a dozen Christian-fiction titles, hits all of the right emotional notes without overdoing the two tragedies; instead, she seamlessly weaves a connection between two women whose broken hearts have left them in an in-between place. A good choice for Christian-fiction readers, for book groups, or for readers looking for a book of hope without schmaltz."

REVIEW: *Kirkus Rev* v81 no24 p329 D 15 2013

MEISTER, CARI. Doctors; [by] Cari Meister 24 p. 2014 Jump!

1. Cancer—Juvenile literature 2. Children's nonfiction 3. Medicine—Juvenile literature 4. Physicians—Juvenile literature 5. Surgeons
ISBN 9781620310748 (hardcover : alk. paper)
LC 2012-044148

SUMMARY: This book on doctors is part of the "Community Helpers" series, which "introduces adult professions to the youngest readers." Author Cari Meister "show[s] the unpleasant sides of the job" as well as its rewarding aspects and doctors' important roles. Topics discussed include surgery and cancer. (Booklist)

REVIEW: *Booklist* v110 no12 p71 F 15 2014 Daniel Kraus

"Doctors," "Mail Carriers," and "Police Officers." "What sets this package apart from similar series is a particularly clean and stylish design and a willingness to show the unpleasant sides of the job--an unusual but welcome approach. Doctors is especially sobering. Sensitive readers may be disturbed by those flecks of blood on the surgeon's coat, and that close-up of stitches going in may cause even adults to blanch, too. . . . Police Officers doesn't flinch from shots of a criminal being cuffed, cops in riot gear, and an officer approaching a car crash. For balance, there are K-9 units! . . . An impressive blend of comforting tones plus realistic content."

MEISTER, CARI. Mail carriers; [by] Cari Meister 24 p. 2014 Jump!

1. Children's nonfiction 2. Letter carriers—Juvenile literature 3. Letter mail handling 4. Mail sorting 5. Postal service
ISBN 9781620310779 (hardcover : alk. paper)
LC 2012-044152

SUMMARY: This book on mail carriers is part of the "Community Helpers" series, which "introduces adult professions to the youngest readers." Author Cari Meister "follows the mail from the sorting shelves to the bin, to the truck, and to your door, mentioning along the way fun details (the red flag on a mailbox) as well as differences between city and country routcs." (Booklist)

REVIEW: *Booklist* v110 no12 p71 F 15 2014 Daniel Kraus

"Doctors," "Mail Carriers," and "Police Officers." "What sets this package apart from similar series is a particularly clean and stylish design and a willingness to show the unpleasant sides of the job--an unusual but welcome approach. Doctors is especially sobering. Sensitive readers may be disturbed by those flecks of blood on the surgeon's coat, and that close-up of stitches going in may cause even adults to blanch, too. . . . Police Officers doesn't flinch from shots of a criminal being cuffed, cops in riot gear, and an officer approaching a car crash. For balance, there are K-9 units! . . . An impressive blend of comforting tones plus realistic content."

MEISTER, CARI. Police officers; [by] Cari Meister 24 p. 2014 Jump!

1. Children's nonfiction 2. Law enforcement 3. Police—Juvenile literature 4. Police dogs 5. Police services
ISBN 9781620310786 (hardcover : alk. paper)
LC 2012-044153

SUMMARY: This book on police officers is part of the "Community Helpers" series, which "introduces adult professions to the youngest readers." Author Cari Meister "show[s] the unpleasant sides of the job," including "shots of a criminal being cuffed, cops in riot gear, and an officer approaching a car crash. For balance, there are K-9 units!" (Booklist)

REVIEW: *Booklist* v110 no12 p71 F 15 2014 Daniel Kraus

"Doctors," "Mail Carriers," and "Police Officers." "What sets this package apart from similar series is a particularly clean and stylish design and a willingness to show the unpleasant sides of the job--an unusual but welcome approach. Doctors is especially sobering. Sensitive readers may be disturbed by those flecks of blood on the surgeon's coat, and that close-up of stitches going in may cause even adults to blanch, too. . . . Police Officers doesn't flinch from shots of a criminal being cuffed, cops in riot gear, and an officer approaching a car crash. For balance, there are K-9 units! . . . An impressive blend of comforting tones plus realistic content."

MEKHENNET, SOUAD. The eternal Nazi. See Kulish, N.

MELICAN, BRIAN. Germany; Beyond the Enchanted Forest: A Literary Anthology; [by] Brian Melican 256 p. 2013 Signal Books Ltd

1. Anthologies 2. British—Germany 3. Germany—De-

scription & travel 4. Germany—In literature 5. International visitors—Germany
ISBN 1908493771 (pbk.); 9781908493774 (pbk.)

SUMMARY: "By following Leigh Fermor, and over eighty other British and North American literary visitors to Germany, this original anthology shows how different generations of English-speakers have depicted this country. Starting in the sixteenth century with some of the earliest travel accounts in English, [editor] Brian Melican presents a wide range of writing about, or set in, Germany." (Publisher's note)

REVIEW: *TLS* no5784 p8 F 7 2014 JANE YAGER

"Germany: Beyond the Enchanted Forest." "'Germany: Beyond the enchanted forest,' Brian Melican's breezily broad-ranging anthology of English-language writing about Germany, spans half a dozen centuries and at least as many literary genres. The book ranges from Romantic poets' letters about Rhine steamboat journey to journalists' dispatches from Nazi-era Berlin and Cold War spy novels. . . . The books best sections are devoted to dark periods of the twentieth century. . . . 'This work wants to allow readers to go beyond the forest and start seeing the wood for the trees,' Melican writes in his introduction. The book most succeeds at this at Germany's most troubled moments."

MELINA, VESANTO. Becoming vegan express edition. See Davis, B.

MELLANDER, CHARLOTTA.ed. The creative class goes global. See The creative class goes global

MELO, ESPERANÇA.il. Thomas the toadilly terrible bully. See Levy, J.

MELTZER, BRAD. I am Abraham Lincoln; 40 p. 2014 Dial Books for Young Readers, an imprint of Penguin Group (USA) Inc.
1. Children's nonfiction 2. Presidents—United States—Biography—Juvenile literature
ISBN 9780803740839 (hardcover: acid-free paper)
LC 2013-016424

SUMMARY: This book is part of Brad Meltzer's "Ordinary People Change the World" series. "Each book focuses on a particular character trait that made that role model heroic. For example, Abraham Lincoln always spoke up about fairness, and thus he led the country to abolish slavery. This book follows him from childhood to the presidency, including the Civil War and his legendary Gettysburg Address." (Publisher's note)

REVIEW: *Bull Cent Child Books* v67 no5 p274-5 Ja 2014 E. B.

REVIEW: *Kirkus Rev* v81 no24 p199 D 15 2013

"I Am Abraham Lincoln". "Lincoln resembles a doll with an oversized head as he strides through a first-person narrative that stretches the limits of credulity and usefulness. From childhood, Abe, bearded and sporting a stovepipe hat, loves to read, write and look out for animals. He stands up to bullies, noting that 'the hardest fights don't reveal a winner—but they do reveal character.' He sees slaves, and the sight haunts him. When the Civil War begins, he calls it a struggle to end slavery. Not accurate. The text further calls the Gettysburg ceremonies a 'big event' designed to 'reenergize' Union supporters and states that the Emancipation Proclamation 'freed all those people.' Not accurate."

REVIEW: *SLJ* v60 no4 p181 Ap 2014 Maggie Chase

MELVILLE, HERMAN, 1819-1891. Moby Dick; [by] Herman Melville
1. Adventure stories 2. Ahab, Captain (Fictitious character) 3. Good & evil—Fiction 4. Whaling—Fiction 5. Whaling ships—Fiction

SUMMARY: This novel by Herman Melville recounts "the voyage of the whaling ship Pequod and its embattled, monomaniacal Captain Ahab. Ishmael quickly learns that the Pequod's captain sails for revenge against the elusive Moby Dick, a sperm whale with a snow-white hump and mottled skin that destroyed Ahab's former vessel and left him crippled. As the Pequod sails deeper through the nights and into the sea, the divisions between man and nature begin to blur—so do the lines between good and evil." (Publisher's note)

REVIEW: *Kirkus Rev* v80 no16 p58 Ag 15 2012

REVIEW: *Natl Rev* v66 no2 p36-8 F 10 2014 RICHARD LOWRY

"Moby-Dick". "Moby-Dick outstrips its ponderous reputation in almost every way. Outside the occasional treatises on marine biology, it is a crackling good read. I marveled at the wit and whimsy; the lush descriptive language; the Shakespearean soliloquies; the haunting sense of foreboding that builds from the first pages. . . . The major—and many of the not-so-major—episodes of Moby-Dick had stuck with me for a couple of decades, such is their vividness and power. . . . And with that, back 'Moby Dick' goes on the shelf, with awe and enduring admiration."

REVIEW: *SLJ* v58 no9 p116 S 2012 Moby Dick

REVIEW: *SLJ* v60 no3 p166 Mr 2014 Peter Blenski

MENAKER, DANIEL. My mistake; [by] Daniel Menaker 256 p. 2013 Houghton Mifflin Harcourt
1. BIOGRAPHY & AUTOBIOGRAPHY—Editors, Journalists, Publishers 2. BIOGRAPHY & AUTOBIOGRAPHY—Personal Memoirs 3. Book editors—United States—Biography 4. Editors—United States—Biography 5. Memoirs
ISBN 0547794231; 9780547794235 (hardback)
LC 2013-019213

SUMMARY: This book is Daniel Menaker's memoir "of wrong turns, both in and out of publishing. . . . As a young man, he goaded his older brother during a game of touch football, leading to his brother's fatal injury and leaving himself with a lifetime of guilt. He smoked, quit and got lung cancer years later. He began working for the New Yorker, where it was easy to sweat the small stuff under the famously idiosyncratic editorship of William Shawn." (Kirkus Reviews)

REVIEW: *Booklist* v110 no6 p4 N 15 2013 Donna Seaman

REVIEW: *Kirkus Rev* v81 no18 p123 S 15 2013

REVIEW: *N Y Times Book Rev* p29 D 15 2013 MERYL GORDON

"My Mistake: A Memoir." "Daniel Menaker loves words, and you can see it in every clause, in the rhythms of his language, even in the length of the sentences in his bracing memoir, 'My Mistake.' A veteran editor at 'The New Yorker' and Random House, an insider who has always felt like an outsider, he was jolted by lung cancer several years ago into re-examining his past. . . . Menaker's memoir braids together three narratives: family history, literary life, cancer. . . . There are times in this volume when one wishes Daniel Menaker, the writer, had been edited by Daniel Menaker, the incisive editor. . . . But these are quibbles."

MENGESTU, DINAW, 1978-. All our names; [by] Dinaw Mengestu 272 p. 2014 Alfred A. Knopf

1. African Americans—Fiction 2. Alienation (Social psychology)—Fiction 3. Identity (Psychology)—Fiction 4. Psychological fiction 5. Students, Foreign—United States—Fiction

ISBN 038534998X; 9780345805669 (pbk.); 9780385349987 (hardcover)

LC 2013-031632

SUMMARY: Author Dinaw Mengestu presents a "love story about a searing affair between an American woman and an African man in 1970s America and an unflinching novel about the fragmentation of lives that straddle countries and histories. Yet this idyll is inescapably darkened by the secrets of his past: the acts he committed and the work he left unfinished. Most of all, he is haunted by the beloved friend he left behind, the charismatic leader who first guided him to revolution." (Publisher's note)

REVIEW: *America* v211 no10 p30-4 O 13 2014 JON M. SWEENEY

REVIEW: *Booklist* v110 no12 p23 F 15 2014 Brendan Driscoll

REVIEW: *Kirkus Rev* v82 no3 p152 F 1 2014

"All Our Names". "[An] elegiac, moving novel. . . . Himself an immigrant, [Dinaw] Mengestu is alert to the nuances of what transplantation and exile can do to the spirit. Certainly so, too, is his protagonist—or, better, one of two protagonists who just happen to share a name, for reasons that soon emerge. One narration is a sequence set in and around Uganda, perhaps in the late 1960s or early 1970s, in a post-independence Africa. . . . Weighted with sorrow and gravitas, another superb story by Mengestu, who is among the best novelists now at work in America."

REVIEW: *Libr J* v138 no16 p59 O 1 2013 Barbara Hoffert

REVIEW: *Libr J* v139 no12 p43 Jl 1 2014 Wendy Galgan

REVIEW: *Libr J* v139 no5 p112 Mr 15 2014 Barbara Hoffert

REVIEW: *London Rev Books* v36 no11 p36 Je 5 2014 Elizabeth Lowry

REVIEW: *N Y Times Book Rev* p26 Mr 30 2014

REVIEW: *N Y Times Book Rev* p1-22 Mr 23 2014 MALCOLM JONES

"All Our Names." "Superficially, 'All Our Names' is a book about an immigrant, but more profoundly it is a story about finding out who you are, about how much of you is formed by your family and your homeland, and what happens when those things go up in smoke. There is great sadness and much hard truth in this novel, as there is everywhere in [author Dinaw] Mengestu's fiction. . . . The victories in this beautiful novel are hard fought and hard won, but won they are, and they are durable."

REVIEW: *New York Times* v163 no56430 pC1-9 Mr 4 2014 MICHIKO KAKUTANI

REVIEW: *Publ Wkly* v260 no47 p1 N 18 2013

REVIEW: *World Lit Today* v88 no5 p8 S/O 2014

MENGONI, LUISA E. The economic development process in the Middle East and North Africa; [by] Luisa E. Mengoni xi, 268 p. 2014 Routledge/Taylor & Francis Group

1. Economic development—Africa, North 2. Economic development—Middle East 3. Economics literature

ISBN 9780415594059 (hardback: alk. paper)

LC 2013-012118

SUMMARY: This book, by Alessandro Romagnoli and Luisa Mengoni, presents an "analysis of the development of economies in the Middle East and North Africa over the past half century." It charts the progress of these countries through an examination of an Islamic model of economic development, reform processes, and economic integration." (Publisher's note)

REVIEW: *Choice* v51 no9 p1649 My 2014 P. Clawson

"The Economic Development Process in the Middle East and North Africa". "The subsequent six chapters are particularly strong on demography, labor, migration, and social welfare, each the subject of its own chapter. The demography chapter nicely lays out the start of the demographic transition to lower population growth but is skimpier about the next phase, namely, the region's rapidly increasing older population. The labor chapter analyzes the low contribution of human capital to growth, a by-product of low-quality education. This point could have been reinforced by highlighting the explosive growth of the numbers of students in school. . . . More could have been made of the sharp difference between the relatively open Gulf States and the rest of the region."

MENNER, SIMON, 1978-. Top Secret; Images from the Archives of the Stasi; [by] Simon Menner 128 p. 2013 Distributed Art Pub Inc

1. Germany (East)—History 2. Germany (East). Ministerium für Staatssicherheit 3. Intelligence service—Germany (East) 4. Photograph collections 5. Undercover operations

ISBN 3775736204; 9783775736206

SUMMARY: "Almost 300,000 people worked for the STASI, the East German secret police. . . . Berlin Wall was erected, German photographer Simon Menner (born 1978) unearthed an extraordinary cache of photographs in the STASI archives that document the agency's surveillance work. . . . Until now, nobody has attempted a visual study of the activities of the State Security. For Simon Menner, the undertaking is more suited to artists and philosophers than to historians." (Publisher's note)

REVIEW: *Bookforum* v20 no4 p43 D 2013/Ja 2014 ALBERT MOBILIO

REVIEW: *N Y Times Book Rev* p38-9 D 8 2013 LUC SANTE

"Wall," "Top Secret: Images From the Stasi Archives," and "George Hurrell's Hollywood: Glamour Portraits 1925-1992." "An appreciation of stony texture . . . marks 'Wall' . . . , by the veteran Czech photographer Josef Koudelka . . . a remarkable collection of panoramic photos . . . of the barrier that has been erected over the past decade in defiance of the internationally recognized border. . . . Simon Menner's 'Top Secret: Images From the Stasi Archives' . . . might be a primer on the banality of evil. . . . 'George Hurrell's Hollywood: Glamour Portraits 1925-1992' by Mark A. Vieira . . . presents rapture upon rapture."

MENTAL HEALTH CARE ISSUES IN AMERICA; an encyclopedia; xxix, 925 p. 2013 ABC-CLIO

1. Mental health—United States—Encyclopedias 2. Mental health literature 3. Mental health services—United States—Encyclopedias 4. Mental illness—United States—Encyclopedias 5. Psychiatry—United States—Encyclopedias
ISBN 9781610690133 (hard copy : alk. paper); 9781610690140 (ebook)
LC 2012-023911

SUMMARY: This book, edited by Michael Shally-Jensen, "covers major mental disorders, theories, and treatments; delves into major advances and ongoing controversies in the field; and shares the most current research on the subject in varied disciplines, including ethnic studies, criminal justice, education, and social work. Each entry features a clear definition of the issue along with a brief review of its history." (Publisher's note)

REVIEW: *Choice* v50 no11 p1986 Jl 2013 J. J. Elder

"Mental Health Care Issues in America: An Encyclopedia." "This encyclopedia provides a balanced and compassionate introduction to the full range of psychological issues that people experience today by examining how mental health care is administered in the largely outpatient US mental health care system. . . . Although the chapters are written by experts in the fields of psychiatry, psychology, criminal justice, ethnic studies, and related areas, the writing contains little jargon and will be readily understood by college students.

MERCHANT, NATALIE.ed. Leave your sleep. See Leave your sleep

MERCHANTS, MARKETS, AND EXCHANGE IN THE PRE-COLUMBIAN WORLD; vii, 472 p. 2013 Dumbarton Oaks Research Library and Collection

1. Historical literature 2. Indians of Central America—Antiquities 3. Indians of Central America—Commerce 4. Indians of Central America—Economic conditions 5. Indians of Mexico—Antiquities 6. Indians of Mexico—Commerce 7. Indians of Mexico—Economic conditions 8. Indians of South America—Andes Region—Antiquities 9. Indians of South America—Andes Region—Commerce 10. Indians of South America—Andes Region—Economic conditions
ISBN 0884023869 (alk. paper); 9780884023869 (alk. paper)
LC 2012-022302

SUMMARY: This book examines the structure, scale, and complexity of economic systems in the pre Hispanic Americas, with a focus on the central highlands of Mexico, the Maya Lowlands, and the central Andes. . . . Essays in this volume examine various dimensions of these ancient economies, including the presence of marketplaces, the operation of merchants . . . . the role of artisans . . . and the trade and distribution networks through which goods were bought, sold, and exchanged." (Publisher's note)

REVIEW: *Choice* v51 no5 p899 Ja 2014 K. Cleland-Sipfle

"Merchants, Markets, and Exchange in the Pre-Columbian World." "The papers all present more complexity in the nature of goods production and distribution in these regions than can be adequately explained or accommodated by earlier models of their exchange systems (e.g., the Aztec merchant economy, Mayan palace economy, and Andean vertical archipelago). This change has occurred over recent decades, but the emphasis and scope of the current volume is unique. . . . This well-illustrated volume includes helpful maps. . . . Essential."

THE MERCK INDEX; An encyclopedia of chemicals, drugs, and biologicals; 2013 RSC Publishing

1. Bibliography (Documentation) 2. Biologicals 3. Chemical research 4. Chemicals—Dictionaries 5. Drugs—Dictionaries 6. Encyclopedias & dictionaries
ISBN 9781849736701 hardcover
LC 2013-444070

SUMMARY: This book, edited by Maryadele J. O'Neil, "is the definitive reference work for scientists and professionals looking for authoritative information on chemicals, drugs and biologicals. . . . The 15th edition, available from RSC Publishing for the first time, is fully revised and updated and contains over 500 new monographs. Over 35% of the existing entries have been updated since the last edition." (Publisher's note)

REVIEW: *Choice* v51 no2 p230-1 O 2013 R. E. Buntrock

"The Merck Index." "The 15th edition of this well-known reference . . . now features 10,000-plus monographs covering 18,000 chemical substances, along with 50,000 synonyms. More than 500 monographs have been added since the 14th edition; 3,500-plus entries feature updated information and data. . . . Alongside pharmaceuticals, coverage includes, when available, biological agents, laboratory chemicals, and commercial chemicals. Entries include chemical or material name, synonyms, trade names, CAS Registry Number, molecular weight, molecular formula/analysis, toxicity data or references, and references to preparation and patent data. . . . A staple for over a century, 'The Merck Index' is a crucial resource for a wide range of scientists and students."

MERKEL, MARKUS. One-dimensional finite elements; [by] Markus Merkel 400 p. 2012 Springer

1. Finite element method 2. Mathematical literature 3. Shear (Mechanics) 4. Structural mechanics 5. Torsion
ISBN 3642317960; 9783642317965
LC 2012-943954

SUMMARY: Written by Andreas Öchsner and Markus Merkel, "This textbook presents finite element methods using exclusively one-dimensional elements. The aim is to present the complex methodology in an easily understandable but mathematically correct fashion. The approach of one-dimensional elements enables the reader to focus on the understanding of the principles of basic and advanced mechanical problems." (Publisher's note)

REVIEW: *Choice* v51 no1 p113 S 2013 R. Kolar

"One-Dimensional Finite Elements: An Introduction to the FE Method." "This book is an excellent addition to course resources on finite elements. [Authors Andreas] Öchsner . . . and [Marcus] Merkel . . . use one-dimensional finite elements to introduce the subject, avoiding the complexity of 2-D and 3-D finite elements and yet retaining the mathematical rigor. . . . The authors rigorously, yet lucidly, present nonlinear elasticity, plasticity, and buckling using the one-dimensional element. This unique approach makes for a clear understanding of the methodology for such difficult problems."

MERLIN, MARK D. Cannabis. See Clarke, R. C.

MERRICK, LEONARD. Mr. Bazalgette's Agent; [by] Leonard Merrick 144 p. 2013 University of Chicago Press

1. Adventure stories 2. Detective & mystery stories, English 3. English fiction—19th century 4. Private investigators—England—Fiction 5. Women detectives—England—Fiction

ISBN 0712357025; 9780712357029

SUMMARY: "Born Leonard Miller in Belsize Park, London, in 1864 to wealthy Jewish parents, Leonard Merrick began his career as an actor before abandoning the stage in 1884 to try his luck as a novelist. His first novel, 'Mr. Bazalgette's Agent,' was published in 1888 and features a determined and resourceful heroine in the figure of Miriam Lea, who grapples with some very modern dilemmas of female virtue and vice." (Publisher's note)

REVIEW: *Publ Wkly* v260 no33 p46 Ag 19 2013

REVIEW: *TLS* no5788 p28 Mr 7 2014 DAVID MALCOLM

"Miss Nobody," "Weep Not My Wanton: Selected Short Stories," and "Mr. Bazalgette's Agent." "[Author Ethel] Carnie's 'Miss Nobody,' her first published novel, came out in 1913. . . . The novel's rich material involves the conflict between the two women. . . . [Leonard] Merrick's Mr Bazalgette's Agent marks an important text in the evolution of detective fiction. As the editor of this new edition, Mike Ashley, notes, 'this book is almost certainly the first ever British novel to feature a professional female detective.' . . . The seven stories republished in 'Weep Not My Wanton' are among [A. E.] Coppard's best known and provide a good, if fragmentary, introduction to his work. They are mostly about the rural poor sometime in the early twentieth century."

MERRIDALE, CATHERINE. Red fortress; history and illusion in the Kremlin; [by] Catherine Merridale 528 p. 2013 Metropolitan Books

1. HISTORY—Europe—Russia & the Former Soviet Union 2. Historical literature

ISBN 0805086803; 9780805086805 (hardback)

LC 2013-026769

SUMMARY: This book by Catherine Merridale "looks at the development of the Muscovy region and the Kremlin's growth in context of Russia's evolution. She discusses the architecture, purpose, and design of the Kremlin, which arguably predates the city of Moscow around it. She follows the intertwined paths of the region's history and the Kremlin's, using the Kremlin as metaphor for the spirit of Russia: constantly changing yet always stalwart and identified with glory and consistency." (Library Journal)

REVIEW: *Booklist* v110 no4 p14 O 15 2013 Jay Freeman

REVIEW: *Economist* v409 no8863 p81 N 23 2013

"Red Fortress: History and Illusion in the Kremlin." "The walls of the Kremlin keep foreigners out and secrets in. But Catherine Merridale has managed to get into this famous citadel and unpick at least some of its mysteries. Nobody reading her vivid and meticulous book . . . is likely to come away with much affection for Russia's rulers. Nor are they going to wish they were transported back in time to the often squalid, mad and brutal eras she depicts. But they will begin to see why Russian history exerts such fascination on those who catch even a whiff of it. 'Red Fortress' would be remarkable as an architectural history alone. . . . Ms. Merridale is a historian by training, but she has a detective's nose and a novelist's way with words."

REVIEW: *Kirkus Rev* v81 no16 p200 Ag 15 2013

REVIEW: *New Statesman* v142 no5181 p71 O 25 2013 Catherine Merridale

REVIEW: *Publ Wkly* v260 no38 p72 S 23 2013

MERRITT, GREG. Room 1219; the life of Fatty Arbuckle, the mysterious death of Virginia Rappe, and the scandal that changed Hollywood; [by] Greg Merritt 440 p. 2013 Chicago Review Press

1. BIOGRAPHY & AUTOBIOGRAPHY—Entertainment & Performing Arts 2. Historical literature 3. Motion picture actors and actresses—United States—Biography 4. Murder—California—Los Angeles 5. Murder victims—California—Biography 6. TRUE CRIME—General

ISBN 9781613747926 (hardback)

LC 2013-015168

SUMMARY: In this book, author Greg Merritt "follows [Roscoe 'Fatty'] Arbuckle from his impoverished origins and meteoric rise through his arrest; three trials for manslaughter; and banishment from Hollywood." Merrit "examines . . . the scandal responsible for the morality code that followed. What emerges is a multifaceted portrait of not only Arbuckle but the early days of a burgeoning industry and the players . . . who helped shape it a century ago. " (Publishers Weekly)

REVIEW: *Kirkus Rev* v81 no12 p58-9 Je 15 2013

REVIEW: *N Y Times Book Rev* p58 N 10 2013 Anita Gates

"Jack Be Nimble: The Accidental Education of an Unintentional Director," "Room 1219: The Life of Fatty Arbuckle, the Mysterious Death of Virginia Rappe, and the Scandal That Changed Hollywood," and "Still Foolin' 'Em: Where I've Been, Where I'm Going, and Where the Hell Are My Keys? "Most of this gracefully written book is about [Jack O'Brien's] early days, and the influence of . . . Ellis Rabb and . . . Rosemary Harris. . . . Some scenes are quite personal, even invasive, but O'Brien's admiration for both comes through. . . . [Greg] Merritt's account of the crime . . . the three trials and the people involved is admirably evenhanded, meticulously researched and compelling. . . . [A] breezy memoir. . . . Sometimes the humor is bright. . . . Crystal is at his authorial finest when he switches into mean mode and mouths off about people and things that annoy him."

REVIEW: *Publ Wkly* v260 no27 p80-1 Jl 8 2013

MERSKY, ROY M. Landmark Supreme Court cases; the most influential decisions of the Supreme Court of the United States; [by] Roy M. Mersky 3 v., xx, 1224 p. 2012 Facts on File

1. Actions & defenses (Law)—United States 2. Law—United States—Cases 3. Legal literature 4. Reference books

ISBN 9780816069576 (hardbound : alk. paper); 0816069573 (hardbound : alk. paper)

LC 2010-048195

SUMMARY: Authors Richard A. Leiter and Roy M. Mersky's book discusses landmark U.S. Supreme Court "cases on such issues as freedom of speech, freedom of the press, civil rights, labor unions, abortion, antitrust and competition, due process, search and seizure, executive privilege, and more. Organized chronologically by issue, each entry includes the case title and legal citation, year of decision, key issue, historical background, legal arguments, decision (majority and dissenting opinions), aftermath and significance, related cases, and recommended reading." (Publisher's note)

REVIEW: *Booklist* v108 no16 p40 Ap 15 2012 Rebecca Vnuk

REVIEW: *Choice* v49 no10 p1848-9 Je 2012 C. B. Thurston

"Landmark Supreme Court Cases: The Most Influential Decisions of the Supreme Court of the United States." "Although readers will recognize prominent case names ('Bush v. Gore,' 'Gideon v. Wainwright'), few without a legal education could identify the constitutional issues raised. 'Landmark Supreme Court Cases' [2nd edition] identifies the key issues in each of 600-plus decisions. . . . Currency is a minor problem; the latest decision featured dates from 2009. However, this set updates 'Landmark Decisions of the United States Supreme Court,' edited by P. Finkleman and M. I. Urofsky. . . . The excellent index in volume 3 combines subjects and case names. Summing Up: Highly recommended."

REVIEW: *Libr J* v137 no5 p131 Mr 15 2012 Laurie Selwyn

REVIEW: *SLJ* v58 no6 p73 Je 2012 Mary Mueller

MERVEILLE, DAVID. Hello Mr. Hulot; 32 p. 2013 Ingram Pub Services

1. Hulot, Monsieur (Fictitious character) 2. Humorous stories 3. Imagination 4. Picture books for children 5. Stories without words

ISBN 0735841357; 9780735841352

SUMMARY: This wordless graphic novel-style picture book looks at "mid-20th century French cinema icon Monsieur Hulot, created and portrayed by actor Jacques Tati. More than 20 stories appear, told in groups of panels on a single page, followed by a page turn that supplies the punch line." (Publishers Weekly)

REVIEW: *Booklist* v110 no4 p55 O 15 2013 Jesse Karp

REVIEW: *Horn Book Magazine* v90 no1 p76-7 Ja/F 2014 SARAH ELLIS

"Hello, Mr. Hulot." "Monsieur Hulot, a character invented and played by French filmmaker Jacques Tati . . . is one part schlemiel, one part everyman, one part existentialist, and all parts kindness. He seems an odd choice for a picture book, given that his most recognizable characteristic is the way he moves--a slopey, optimistic half-run--and that much of the humor in the films is physical. But [David] Merveille cleverly captures the essential Hulot in every episode of this collection of short, largely wordless, comic-strip vignettes, with small visual puns that make us smile, sometimes one beat after we've turned the page, and sometimes sadly."

REVIEW: *Kirkus Rev* v81 no14 p241 Jl 15 2013

REVIEW: *Publ Wkly* v260 no25 p175 Je 24 2013

REVIEW: *SLJ* v60 no1 p108 Ja 2014 Joy Piedmont

MERVEILLE, DAVID.il. Hello Mr. Hulot. See Merveille, D.

MESHON, AARON. Tools rule!; [by] Aaron Meshon 40 p. 2014 Atheneum Books for Young Readers

1. Building—Juvenile literature 2. Children's stories 3. Sheds 4. Teams 5. Tools—Fiction

ISBN 1442496010; 9781442496019 (hardcover)

LC 2013-009361

SUMMARY: This children's book, by Aaron Meshon, "features animated tool characters, each with its own individual traits. T Square rounds up a crew of tools to clean up a messy yard and build a tool shed. T Square and Pencil draft plans; Wheelbarrow gathers materials; Saw saws Wood; Drill drills Screws; Level inspects; Glue glues on Roof Tiles, etc. Together, they work hard, and when the project is finished, they go to sleep in an organized toolshed feeling satisfied." (Kirkus Reviews)

REVIEW: *Booklist* v110 no13 p79 Mr 1 2014 Thom Barthelmess

REVIEW: *Bull Cent Child Books* v67 no8 p416-7 Ap 2014 H. M.

REVIEW: *Horn Book Magazine* v90 no2 p103 Mr/Ap 2014 ELISSA GERSHOWITZ

"Tools Rule!" "[Aaron] Meshon's lively text is packed full of tool-centric wordplay . . . sound effects . . . and occasional rhyme (plus a minor inconsistency or two: how do they lift the too-heavy-to-move workbench to pour the concrete?). The illustrations, too, have a lot going on. Some are double-page spreads; some are single pages with borders; some bleed off the edges. One helpful spread shows the tools, still strewn about the lawn, but with captionlike arrows to identify what's what; not exactly a sea of calm in this freewheeling story, but useful nonetheless. A detailed note on the copyright page describes Meshon's process for creating his digitally colored mixed-media illustrations showing smiley tools with a can-do attitude."

REVIEW: *Kirkus Rev* v82 no1 p208 Ja 1 2014

"Tools Rule!". "This appealing and inventive story features animated tool characters, each with its own individual traits. . . . The colored digital illustrations are imaginative (each tool has eyes, and some have legs), with sound effects offering opportunities for participation. . . . Diagrammatic arrows with large letters nail down the interchange among the tools and cleverly enforce the concept of working together. [Aaron] Meshon's animated style in this story could easily be turned into a short film cartoon. Buy it along with a wooden tool set as a gift for an enterprising young carpenter."

REVIEW: *Publ Wkly* v260 no49 p81 D 2 2013

REVIEW: *SLJ* v60 no2 p76 F 2014 Nora Clancy

MESHON, AARON.il. Tools rule! See Meshon, A.

MESSENGER, SHANNON. Let the storm break; [by] Shannon Messenger 400 p. 2014 Simon Pulse

1. Love—Fiction 2. Orphans—Fiction 3. Paranormal romance stories 4. Spirits—Fiction 5. Storms—Fiction 6. Supernatural—Fiction 7. Winds—Fiction

ISBN 1442450444; 9781442450448

LC 2013-007403

SUMMARY: In this sequel to "Let the Sky Fall," by Shannon Messenger, "Vane Weston is haunted. By the searing pull of his bond to Audra. By the lies he's told to cover for her disappearance. . . . But Audra's still running. From her past. From the Gales. Even from Vane, who she doesn't believe she deserves. . . . She possesses the secret power her enemy craves, and protecting it might be more than she can handle—especially when she discovers Raiden's newest weapon." (Publisher's note)

REVIEW: *Booklist* v110 no13 p70-1 Mr 1 2014 Julie Trevelyan

REVIEW: *Kirkus Rev* v82 no4 p319 F 15 2014

"Let the Storm Break". "The sylph army known as the Gales desperately wants to use Vane and his Westerly winds as a weapon against power-hungry, one-note Raiden, but Vane knows the Westerly nature is too peaceful. . . . Conveying so much information causes the first act to progress slowly, resulting in weak tension until the vague stakes become specific and immediate. Tasked with many expository reveals, Audra's narration doesn't shine as brightly as Vane's chapters. . . . Once characters deal with the ends-justify-the-means idea of sinking to Raiden's level to fight him and reach the fight scenes, the story becomes a page-turner right to a cliffhanger. Witty, romantic and filled with personality-after the slow start."

MESSER-KRUSE, TIMOTHY. The trial of the Haymarket Anarchists; terrorism and justice in the Gilded Age; [by] Timothy Messer-Kruse viii, 236 p. 2011 Palgrave Macmillan

1. Anarchists—History 2. Chicago (Ill.)—History 3. Haymarket Square Riot, Chicago, Ill., 1886 4. Historical literature 5. Trials (Anarchy)—Illinois—Chicago—History—19th century

ISBN 0230116604 (hardback); 0230120776 (pbk.); 9780230116603 (hardback); 9780230120778 (pbk.)

LC 2011-011011

SUMMARY: "In this controversial and groundbreaking new history, Timothy Messer-Kruse rewrites the standard narrative of the most iconic event in American labor history: the Haymarket Bombing and Trial of 1886. Using thousands of pages of previously unexamined materials, Messer-Kruse demonstrates that, contrary to longstanding historical opinion, the trial was not the 'travesty of justice' it has commonly been depicted as." (Publisher's note)

REVIEW: *Rev Am Hist* v42 no2 p309-16 Je 2014 Marcella Bencivenni

"The Trial of the Haymarket Anarchists: Terrorism and Justice in the Gilded Age" and "The Haymarket Conspiracy: Transatlantic Anarchist Networks." "[Author Timothy] Messer-Kruse pursues his provocative arguments in two interrelated books. The first, 'The Trial of the Haymarket Anarchists,' . . . focuses almost exclusively on the trial from a legal view. Espousing a transnational perspective, the second, 'The Haymarket Conspiracy,' is instead concerned with the ideological and political background that shaped the ideas and the events leading to the Haymarket riot. Although released separately to meet the demands of the publishing industry, the books were originally conceived as one manuscript and are meant to complement each other."

MESSNER, KATE. Marty McGuire has too many pets!; 168 p. 2014 Scholastic Press

1. Animal sanctuaries—Fiction 2. Animal sanctuaries—Juvenile fiction 3. Children's stories 4. Money-making projects—Fiction 5. Money-making projects for children—Juvenile fiction 6. Pet sitting—Fiction 7. Pet sitting—Juvenile fiction

ISBN 054553559X; 9780545535595 (hc); 9780545535601 (pb)

LC 2013-010371

SUMMARY: In this book, written by Kate Messner and illustrated by Brian Floca, "Marty McGuire really has her hands full this time. . . . After visiting a sanctuary for retired lab chimpanzees, Marty wants to follow in the footsteps of her idol Jane Goodall and help with their care. But 'adopting a chimp' is expensive, so Marty and her third-grade pals hatch a plan to raise money by holding a talent show at school and opening a pet-sitting business in Marty's basement." (Publisher's note)

REVIEW: *Bull Cent Child Books* v67 no8 p417 Ap 2014 J. H.

"Marty McGuire Has Too Many Pets!" "Generous-hearted but a bit impulsive, third-grader Marty McGuire cooks up a pet-sitting scheme to raise money for a sanctuary for retired laboratory chimpanzees, but soon runs into trouble. . . . Clear, crisp writing, elementary vocabulary, and a large font make the book a quick read and help ease the way for young chapter-book readers. The tidy lines and subtle shadings of [Brian] Floca's frequent monochromatic illustrations enhance the casually but carefully told narrative. Likable no-frills Marty will appeal to both boys and girls."

MESSNER, KATE. Sea Monster and the bossy fish; [by] Kate Messner 40 p. 2013 Chronicle Books

1. Bullies—Fiction 2. Bullying—Juvenile fiction 3. Fishes—Fiction 4. Fishes—Juvenile fiction 5. Picture books for children 6. Schools—Fiction 7. Schools—Juvenile fiction 8. Sea monsters—Fiction 9. Sea monsters—Juvenile fiction

ISBN 9781452112534 (alk. paper)

LC 2012-042447

SUMMARY: In this children's picture book by Kate Messner, "Ernest the sea monster . . . welcomes a newcomer to fish school who has trouble making friends. The new fish doles out unwelcome nicknames and hogs the dress-up clothes. . . . The last straw comes when he starts an exclusive club. . . . Ernest, taking the high road, starts a new club that welcomes all." (New York Times Book Review)

REVIEW: *Kirkus Rev* v81 no2 p109-10 Je 1 2013

REVIEW: *N Y Times Book Rev* p12 Ag 25 2013 BECCA ZERKIN

"Sea Monster and the Bossy Fish," "Lion vs. Rabbit," and "Llama Llama and the Bully Goat." "Though the text is heavy-handed, especially when Ernest is setting things right, [Kate] Messner . . . subtly implies that the new fish is behaving badly because he feels vulnerable. . . . Young readers will relate as they settle into the new school year. . . . Alex Latimer . . . doesn't hit us over the head with a message. . . . It's too bad that Latimer renders Lion's victims overly passive and the aggressor a changed man only because he lost a bet; it makes the resolution less satisfying. . . . Anna Dewdney . . . writes touchingly about the emotions of young children."

REVIEW: *SLJ* v59 no8 p84 Ag 2013 Roxanne Burg

MESSO, GEORGE.tr. & Silk & Love & Flame. See Keskin, B.

MESTRE-REED, ERNESTO.tr. Call me Brooklyn. See Lago, E.

METAXAS, ERIC. Bonhoeffer; pastor, martyr, prophet, spy: a Righteous Gentile vs. the Third Reich; [by] Eric Metaxas 591 2010 Thomas Nelson

1. Biography, Individual 2. Clergy 3. Dissenters 4. Spies 5. Theologians 6. Writers on religion
ISBN 1595551387; 1595552464 pa; 9781595551382; 9781595552464
LC 2009-013944

SUMMARY: This is a biography of the German Lutheran pastor and theologian executed by the Nazis for plotting to overthrow Hitler.

REVIEW: *Commonweal* v138 no21 p30-1 D 2 2011 James Martin

Sense and Sensibility and Bonhoeffer "Even on an e-reader, it's a delightful tale. The romantic fervor of Marianne Dashwood, who longs for the most unsuitable of men, stands in contrast to the intelligent reserve of her older sister, Elinor. [Jane] Austen compares Marianne's 'sensibility,' a word that at the time meant either romanticism, sentiment, or a refined aestheticism, with Elinor's 'sense,' the capacity to make rational, moral decisions. . . . Austen's darting wit is a highlight, particularly when the two worldviews clash. . . . Eric Metaxas's 'Bonhoeffer' . . . was a thrilling read for two reasons. First, it is the best written of the biographies I've read of the great German theologian, anti-Nazi activist, and martyr. . . . Jumping into Metaxas's colorful prose was a relief. Second, the story is unfailingly inspiring. . . . Particularly striking for me was Bonhoeffer's return from the United States in 1939 after having left Nazi Germany only a few weeks before."

METCALF, DAWN. Indelible; [by] Dawn Metcalf 2013 Paw Prints

1. Fantasy fiction 2. Monsters—Fiction 3. Stab wounds 4. Victims of violent crimes 5. Young adult fiction
ISBN 1480606073; 9781480606074

SUMMARY: Written by Dawn Metcalf, in this book, "Joy Malone learns this the night she sees a stranger with all-black eyes across a crowded room--right before the mystery boy tries to cut out her eye. Instead, the wound accidentally marks her as property of Indelible Ink, and this dangerous mistake thrusts Joy into an incomprehensible world--a world of monsters at the window, glowing girls on the doorstep and a life that will never be the same." (Publisher's note)

REVIEW: *Bull Cent Child Books* v67 no1 p38 S 2013 K. Q. G.

"Indelible." "A knife attack that eventually leads to romance between the two parties is only one of many unbelievable plot points here, and even readers who readily suspend disbelief for the fey Folk and other such supernatural happenings will find their credulity stretched by the countless contrivances that must occur to move the action forward. Thankfully, the prose is more successful than the plotting, and [author Dawn] Metcalf imaginatively employs metaphor as she describes the various beasts and creatures Joy meets."

REVIEW: *Kirkus Rev* v81 no12 p105 Je 15 2013

REVIEW: *Voice of Youth Advocates* v36 no4 p85 O 2013 Sarah Cofer

METCALF, FRED. The Biteback Dictionary of Humorous Literary Quotations; [by] Fred Metcalf 288 p. 2013 Biteback

1. Anthologies 2. Authors & critics 3. Authorship—Quotations, maxims, etc. 4. Quotation (Literary form) 5. Wit & humor
ISBN 1849542260; 9781849542265

SUMMARY: This book, edited by Fred Metcalf, presents an anthology of humorous literary quotations. Authors and subjects range "from [Charles] Dickens to Dictionaries and [Mark] Twain to Twitter." Other authors include Evelyn Waugh, Virginia Woolf, Henry James, Clive James, Jane Austen, and T. S. Eliot. (Publisher's note)

REVIEW: *TLS* no5772 p36 N 15 2013 J. C.

"Alien Hearts," "Biteback Dictionary of Humorous Literary Quotations," and "For Who the Bell Tolls." "It is a wonderful novel, written as the author's fatal sickness was taking grip. . . . 'Notre Coeur' is available in English as 'Alien Hearts,' in a translation by Richard Howard . . . which claims to be 'the first in more than a hundred years,' but this overlooks Marjorie Laurie's 1929 version. . . . Of the 'Biteback Dictionary of Humorous Literary Quotations' we ask only two things: that it be humorous, and that we know where the jokes are coming from. . . . We delved to the index, to find that the Dictionary doesn't have one. . . . The grammar may be correct under a precise anatomical gaze, but Mr [David] Marsh illustrates how proper usage is not always best usage."

METIVIER, GARY. Until Daddy comes home; [by] Gary Metivier 32 p. 2014 Pelican Publishing Company

1. Children of military personnel—Fiction 2. Children's stories 3. Families—Juvenile fiction 4. Fathers and daughters—Fiction 5. Patriotism—Fiction
ISBN 9781455618903 (hardcover: alk. paper)
LC 2013-024517

SUMMARY: In this children's story by Gary Metivier, "Ashley misses her daddy. He's gone away to protect the nation, but knowing how brave her father is doesn't make his absence any easier. Ashley and her father make a secret pledge that they whisper every day after saying the Pledge of Allegiance, ending by throwing a kiss to the American flag. The pledge is supposed to keep Ashley strong until her father returns, but every little thing reminds her that he isn't home." (Publisher's note)

REVIEW: *Kirkus Rev* v82 no3 p327 F 1 2014

"Until Daddy Comes Home". "Muddled intent and sloppy sentiment turn this soldier's daughter's vigil into a gooey slog. . . . Cast in a thick golden haze, [Robert] Rath's illustrations offer frequent views of a waving American flag behind vaguely delineated figures with clumsily drawn facial features. With no discernable justification aside from general boosterism, a tribute written for older readers to the work of the USO and particularly one of its posts in Illinois has been tacked on after Ashley's narrative."

METTLER, SUZANNE. Degrees of inequality; how the politics of higher education sabotaged the American dream; [by] Suzanne Mettler 272 p. 2014 Basic Books, a member of the Perseus Books Group

1. Educational change—United States 2. Educational literature

ISBN 0465044964; 9780465044962 (hardback)

LC 2013-043678

SUMMARY: In this book, political scientist Suzanne Mettler "explains why the . . . American Dream is increasingly out of reach for so many. . . . She illuminates how political partisanship has overshadowed America's commitment to equal access to higher education. As politicians capitulate to corporate interests, owners of for-profit colleges benefit, but for far too many students, higher education leaves them with little besides crippling student loan debt." (Publisher's note)

REVIEW: *Booklist* v110 no13 p5 Mr 1 2014 Eloise Kinney

REVIEW: *Kirkus Rev* v82 no2 p194 Ja 15 2014

"Degrees of Inequality: How the Politics of Higher Education Sabotaged the American Dream". "The author spent eight years researching and writing her withering attack, and her data is devastating. . . . Among her most damning discoveries: The majority of the for-profits receive more than 80 percent of their revenue from the federal government, and their administrators earn far more than their counterparts in brick-and-mortar universities. She notes that for-profits focus on recruitment, not on education. The GOP receives most of her fire, but the Democrats do not escape unscathed. Basically, she writes, the rich go to 'real' schools, the poor to the for-profits, exacerbating inequality. A thorough and deeply troubling analysis of a quiet but ominous threat to democracy."

REVIEW: *N Y Times Book Rev* p28 Je 8 2014 GARY RIVLIN

REVIEW: *Publ Wkly* v261 no1 p45 Ja 6 2014

METZGER, GILLIAN E.ed. The health care case. See The health care case

MEUTH, ELSBETH. Sexual Enlightenment; How to Create Lasting Fulfillment in Life, Love, and Intimacy; [by] Elsbeth Meuth 142 p. 2013 Balboa Pr

1. Emotions (Psychology) 2. Human sexuality—Religious aspects 3. Intimacy (Psychology) 4. Self-help materials 5. Sex education

ISBN 1452585431; 9781452585437

SUMMARY: "In this guidebook for sexual awareness and enjoyment, the authors deliver narrative stories and explanations to help demystify sex and bring depth and meaning to readers' sexual lives. [Elsbeth] Meuth and [Freddy Zental] Weaver present compelling information about what it means to have sexual experiences that involve mental, emotional and physical engagement." They argue "that creative, sexual energy comes from within, not from the validation and acknowledgment of others." (Kirkus Reviews)

REVIEW: *Kirkus Rev* v82 no5 p31 Mr 1 2014

"Sexual Enlightenment: How to Create Lasting Fulfillment in Life, Love, and Intimacy". "[Elsbeth] Meuth and [Freddy Zental] Weaver present compelling information about what it means to have sexual experiences that involve mental, emotional and physical engagement. . . . Written conversationally, the book dives into not only definitions of an enlightened sexual life but also ways to strive toward awareness. . . . These kinds of lessons and reinforcements make the book a valuable read for anyone seeking a deeper relationship with his or her sexual self. An informed, dynamic exploration of sexual history and energy."

REVIEW: *Kirkus Rev* v82 no3 p380 F 1 2014

MEUWESE, MARK.ed. Atlantic biographies. See Atlantic biographies

MEYER-HERMANN, EVA.ed. Mike Kelley. See Mike Kelley

MEYER, CAROLYN. Beauty's daughter; the story of Hermione and Helen of Troy; [by] Carolyn Meyer 352 p. 2013 Houghton Mifflin Harcourt

1. Beauty, Personal—Fiction 2. Helen of Troy (Greek mythology)—Fiction 3. Hermione (Greek mythology)—Fiction 4. Hermione (Greek mythology)—Juvenile fiction 5. Interpersonal relations—Fiction 6. JUVENILE FICTION—Family—Parents 7. JUVENILE FICTION—Girls & Women 8. JUVENILE FICTION—Historical—Ancient Civilizations 9. JUVENILE FICTION—Legends, Myths, Fables—Greek & Roman 10. JUVENILE FICTION—Love & Romance 11. Kings, queens, rulers, etc.—Fiction 12. Love—Fiction 13. Mythology, Greek—Fiction 14. Trojan War—Fiction 15. Young adult fiction

ISBN 9780544108622 (hardback)

LC 2013-003923

SUMMARY: This book is "Narrated by Hermione, daughter of Helen of Troy and King Menelaus of Sparta. . . . The novel transpires from the time Helen leaves for Troy with Paris, through the Trojan War, and ends when Hermione marries Orestes. Hermione grows in strength and deals with atrocities to women. . . . She also deals with the fact that she has an absent mother who is known as the most beautiful woman in the world, and that she looks nothing like her." (School Library Journal)

REVIEW: *Bull Cent Child Books* v67 no5 p275 Ja 2014 K. C.

"Beauty's Daughter: The Story of Hermione and Helen of Troy." "As Hermione, Helen of Troy's daughter, notes in this title's prologue, this is her chance to tell her side of her mother's story. It is also, however, a recitation of the many stories found throughout Greek history and mythology, with Hermione inserted, often somewhat clumsily, as observer and narrator. . . . The events of the plot are always foregrounded over emotional development or exploration. Fortunately, these particular stories have captured the imaginations of readers for millennia, and they hold up well here even without the kind of emotional investment and development one might expect from Hermione's initial insistence that she would be at the center of this tale."

REVIEW: *Kirkus Rev* v81 no15 p216 Ag 1 2013

REVIEW: *Voice of Youth Advocates* v36 no6 p75 F 2014 Ann McDuffie

MEYER, PHILIPP. The Son; [by] Philipp Meyer viii, 561 p. 2013 HarperCollins

1. Fathers & sons—Fiction 2. Frontier & pioneer life—Fiction 3. Historical fiction 4. Indian captivities—Fiction 5. Texas—Fiction

ISBN 0062120395 (hardcover); 9780062120397 (hardcover)

SUMMARY: This historical family novel, by Philipp Meyer, presents "an epic of the American West and a multigenerational saga of power, blood, land, and oil that follows the rise of one [prominent] . . . Texas family, from the Comanche raids of the 1800s to the to the oil booms of the 20th century." (Publisher's note)

REVIEW: *Booklist* v109 no17 p69 My 1 2013 John Mort

REVIEW: *Commentary* v136 no2 p61-2 S 2013 FERNANDA MOORE

REVIEW: *Kirkus Rev* p28 N 15 2013 Best Books

REVIEW: *Kirkus Rev* v81 no2 p24 Je 1 2013

REVIEW: *Libr J* v138 no6 p75 Ap 1 2013 Keddy Ann Outlaw

REVIEW: *Libr J* v138 no1 p62 Ja 1 2013

REVIEW: *N Y Times Book Rev* p13 Je 16 2013 WILL BLYTHE

REVIEW: *New York Times* v162 no56173 pC1-4 Je 20 2013 JANET MASLIN

REVIEW: *Publ Wkly* v260 no11 p53 Mr 18 2013

REVIEW: *TLS* no5759 p23 Ag 16 2013 CLIVE SINCLAIR

"The Son." "In his imperious new novel . . . [Philipp Meyer] takes on his former mentor, who also produced an epic about the Lone Star state. . . . Meyer is craftier than the average historical reconstructionist. . . . It is remarked throughout the novel that whereas white boys are easily acclimatized to Comanche ways, the reverse rarely happens. It is true of the author, too. His heart clearly belongs to the outrageous Eli. Fortunately, thanks to the novel's structure, Eli refuses to lie down, and keeps popping up, just like John Travolta in 'Pulp Fiction'. 'The Son' is pulp fiction, but with a very high IQ."

REVIEW: *TLS* no5757 p32 Ag 2 2013 J. C.

REVIEW: *World Lit Today* v88 no1 p60-1 Ja/F 2014 Kevin Pickard

"The Son." "Chronologically, Philipp Meyer's 'The Son' starts in 1849 with Eli McCullough--one of the three perspectives presented in the book--being captured by Comanches. But the book doesn't move linearly. . . . For a writer with less subtlety than Meyer, this would come off as bloated. The great success of 'The Son' is that Meyer adequately chews exactly as much as he bites off. . . . Also important in not making the story feel overtly grandiose is Meyer's stunning facility with details. . . . There are many important American standards that one might compare 'The Son' to. . . . All these comparisons would be correct, but what makes Meyer's book extraordinary is that, as a reader, one never gets the sense that Meyer has a Bloomian weight of these giants on his shoulders."

MEYER, STEPHEN C. Darwin's doubt; the explosive origin of animal life and the case for intelligent design; [by] Stephen C. Meyer 498 p. 2013 HarperOne

1. Evolution (Biology) 2. Intelligent design (Teleology) 3. Life—Origin 4. Scientific literature

ISBN 0062071475; 9780062071477; 9780062071484 (pbk)

LC 2013-004594

SUMMARY: In this book on evolutionary theory, Stephen C. Meyer examines "the 'sudden' appearance of diverse animal phyla . . .in the Cambrian period. . . . According to most paleontologists today, the Cambrian explosion, or radiation, lasted at least 20 million years, but probably longer. But Meyer contends that it was a much shorter time period. . . . And that's an explosion of diversity that is too sudden, too rapid to be adequately explained by Darwinian evolution." (National Review)

REVIEW: *Natl Rev* v65 no16 p35-7 S 2 2013 JOHN FARRELL

"Darwin's Doubt: The Explosive Origin of Animal Life and the Case for Intelligent Design." "At no point in the book does [Stephen C.] Meyer ever actually discuss these issues with [Charles R.] Marshall, or [Eric H.] Davidson, or any of the scientists working deeply in the field. He simply lifts quotes from their papers as they seem convenient to his point. This is the most disappointing aspect of Meyer's book. . . . In the end, 'Darwin's Doubt' boils down to a fundamentally weak argument--the argument from personal incredulity about the origin and evolution of life on earth."

MEYLER, DEBORAH. The bookstore; [by] Deborah Meyler 352 p. 2013 Gallery Books

1. Antiquarian booksellers—New York (State)—New York—Fiction 2. Bookstores—New York (State)—New York—Fiction 3. Love stories 4. Self-realization in women—Fiction 5. Single mothers—Fiction

ISBN 147671424X (alk. paper); 9781476714240 (alk. paper)

LC 2012-050505

SUMMARY: In this book by Deborah Meyler "Esme Garland moves to Manhattan armed with a prestigious scholarship at Columbia University. When Mitchell van Leuven . . . captures her heart . . . life seems truly glorious. Before she has a chance to tell Mitchell about her pregnancy, he suddenly . . . ends it all. Esme starts work at a small West Side bookstore. . . . When Mitchell recants his criticism, his passion and promises are hard to resist." (Publisher's note)

REVIEW: *Booklist* v109 no22 p26 Ag 1 2013

REVIEW: *Booklist* v110 no14 p60 Mr 15 2014

"The Apple Orchard," "The Bookstore," and "A Fall of Marigolds." "Art specialist Tess has a successful professional life but is lacking in the family department. When she's named heir to one-half of an estate and discovers the other half goes to the sister she never knew she had, her life gets turned upside-down. . . . Between studying art history at Columbia University on a prestigious scholarship and a two-week fling with a magnetic, wealthy man, 23-year-old Esme Garland from England is happily settling into life in Manhattan when she discovers she's pregnant. This character-driven novel is witty and poetic. . . . The heartbreaks of two women, separated by decades, come together in the history of a scarf that holds special meaning to each woman. Christian fiction author [Susan] Meissner's first mainstream women's fiction novel hits all of the right emotional notes without overdoing the two tragedies."

MFA VS NYC; the Two Cultures of American Fiction; 320 p. 2014 Faber and Faber, Inc. / n+1 Foundation, Inc.

1. Authors and publishers—United States 2. Authorship—Vocational guidance 3. Creative writing (Higher education)—United States 4. Essay (Literary form) 5. Fiction—Authorship 6. Fiction—Publishing—United States 7. Master of fine arts degree

ISBN 0865478139; 9780865478138 (pbk.)
LC 2013-048115

SUMMARY: This book, edited by Chad Harbach, describes and engages with how "the American literary scene has split into two cultures: New York publishing versus university MFA programs. This book brings together established writers, MFA professors and students, and New York editors, publicists, and agents to talk about these overlapping worlds, and the ways writers make (or fail to make) a living within them." (Publisher's note)

REVIEW: *Kirkus Rev* v82 no3 p303 F 1 2014

"MFA vs NYC: The Two Cultures of American Fiction". "A cast of literary professionals offers an entertaining bounty of experience, opinions and advice. . . . The editor's shrewd if pessimistic essay launched what he calls 'a kind of jointly written novel—one whose composite hero is the fiction writer circa 2014'—in which perceptions from a wide spectrum of struggling authors, skilled teachers, students, agents, editors and publicists comingle with essays from best-selling literary luminaries. . . . Collectively thought-provoking and provocative, this . . . publication . . . inches readers further toward understanding the often complex, political machine that transforms an idea into a published product. . . . Essential insights, masterfully assembled."

REVIEW: *Libr J* v139 no5 p120 Mr 15 2014 Patrick A. Smith

REVIEW: *New York Times* v163 no56424 pC1-4 F 26 2014 DWIGHT GARNER

"MFA vs. NYC: The Two Cultures of American Fiction." "Now comes 'MFA vs NYC,' edited by the gifted novelist . . . and n + 1 editor Chad Harbach, an even better volume that asks whether fiction writing can, or should, be taught. . . . This book is an elaboration, with contributions from many other writers, on Mr. Harbach's much-discussed original essay under this title, which appeared in n + 1 in 2010. It mapped the two most likely roads an aspiring writer can walk in this country, the mossy turf of a graduate-level writing program or the steaming asphalt of the big city, while trying to make it. . . . 'MFA vs NYC' will appeal to many young writers, not merely for its insider perspective but also for its gossip and confessional essays."

MICA, ADRIANA.ed. Sociology and the unintended. See Sociology and the unintended

MICHAEL HAGUE'S READ-TO-ME BOOK OF FAIRY TALES; 128 p. 2013 Harper, an imprint of HarperCollins Publishers

1. Beauty & the beast (Tale) 2. Cinderella (Tale) 3. Fairy tales 4. Folklore 5. Picture books for children

ISBN 9780688140106 (hardcover bdgs)
LC 2012-050674

SUMMARY: "This collection brings together 14 folk- and fairy tales, including 'Beauty and the Beast,' 'Cinderella,' 'The Little Mermaid,' and 'The Three Little Pigs,' retold simply and in a large format for sharing aloud. Many of the more violent plot points have been dampened down or omitted completely, though the girl in 'The Seven Ravens' does cut off her own finger and Snow White's stepmother 'feasted on what she thought was Snow White'." (School Library Journal)

REVIEW: *Kirkus Rev* v81 no19 p256 O 1 2013

REVIEW: *N Y Times Book Rev* p24 N 10 2013 MARIA TATAR

"Tales From the Brothers Grimm," "Michael Hague's Read-To-Me Book of Fairy Tales," and "Fairy TAle Comics." "Lisbeth Zwerger's 'Tales From the Brothers Grimm' and Michael Hague's 'Read-to-me Book of Fairy Tales' draw children into nostalgic fairy-tale worlds with the seductive beauty of their illustrations. 'Fairy Tale Comics,' edited by Chris Duffy and animated by 17 cartoonists and illustrators, by contrast, refashions classic tales with bold creativity. . . . Though Zwerger's watercolors are sometimes disturbing, the decorative beauty of her work also functions as an antidote to the violent content of the tales. This dynamic is reversed in Hague's 'Read-to-Mc Book of Fairy Tales'."

REVIEW: *SLJ* v60 no1 p114 Ja 2014 Julie Roach

MICHALAK, JAMIE. Joe and Sparky go to school; [by] Jamie Michalak 48 p. 2013 Candlewick Press

1. Children's stories 2. Friendship—Juvenile fiction 3. Giraffe—Juvenile fiction 4. High interest-low vocabulary books 5. School stories 6. Turtles—Juvenile fiction

ISBN 076366278X; 9780763662783
LC 2012-943657

SUMMARY: In this children's book by Jamie Michalak, "Joe Giraffe and Sparky, a turtle, live in Safari Land, 'the famous cageless zoo.' In four chapters they see a school bus and climb on to satisfy their curiosity; end up at school with the 'noisy short people'; try to blend in but the 'magic pond' (the toilet) provides some silliness; and Joe attempts to get a star for good work since Sparky has earned several. The animals experience the ups and downs of friendship." (School Library Journal)

REVIEW: *Bull Cent Child Books* v67 no1 p39 S 2013 J. H.

"Joe and Sparky Go to School." "In this easy reader, Joe the giraffe and Sparky the turtle ('Joe and Sparky Get New Wheels' . . .) investigate a visiting school bus and end up unintentionally riding it back to the students' school, where the nearsighted teacher fails to note that her pupils now include a giraffe and a turtle. . . . The vocabulary is within range for primary-graders who are above the level of Elephant and Piggie but not quite ready for lengthier chapter books; the book's humor, ably emphasized by [illustrator Frank] Remkiewicz's comic watercolor and prismacolor pencil illustrations, makes this a joyous readaloud as well. The art is bright and buoyant, and kids will get a kick out of the animal pair's antics. . . ."

REVIEW: *Horn Book Magazine* v89 no3 p90 My/Je 2013 ROBIN L. SMITH

REVIEW: *Kirkus Rev* v81 no2 p110 Je 1 2013

REVIEW: *SLJ* v59 no5 p82 My 2013 Susan Lissim

MICHALAK, JAMIE. Show's over; [by] Jamie Michalak 48 p. 2014 Candlewick Press

1. Australia—Juvenile literature 2. Children's stories 3. Dogs—Juvenile fiction 4. Ships—Juvenile literature 5. Television game show hosts

ISBN 0763672785; 9780763672782

SUMMARY: In this children's story, "Ruff Ruffman is having a bad day. First, his fancy pants get stolen, then he gets a message from his boss that seems to say he's been fired! There's only one way for him to find out: visit his boss in

Australia. To do this, of course, Ruff turns his doghouse into a 'green' vehicle (powered by cooking oil from a Chinese restaurant) and adds pineapples to keep it from sinking." (Publisher's note)

REVIEW: *Bull Cent Child Books* v67 no9 p469 My 2014 T. A.

"Fetch! With Ruff Ruffman: Show's Over". "This hits the right marks with respect to chapter length, print size, and goofy appeal to make transitional readers comfortable, and the familiar media face is likely to snag a broad audience. However, the science content is overplayed, being limited in actuality to a couple of facts tossed out by Blossom and the nicely designed activity about buoyancy in the end matter, and plot points stray willy-nilly. The highly saturated digital illustrations that closely follow the TV show's animation style are also uneven, with some of them evincing interesting dimensionality, but others disappointingly flat and repetitive."

REVIEW: *Kirkus Rev* v82 no5 p71 Mr 1 2014

"Show's Over". "Ruff Ruffman's second literary outing is much lighter than the first . . . especially in the science department. Whereas his first foray onto the page included many science facts and a cool experiment involving filtering water, this episode is a dud. . . . Those who love the show love it for Ruff's tone of voice, Blossom's sassy attitude and quiet intelligence, the many sound effects, and the cool things that the human guests get to do in exploring science and solving problems. Almost all of that is missing in print editions of the TV show. Rarely will a book review recommend watching TV over reading a book, but in this case, find the remote."

MICHEL, JEAN-BAPTISTE. Uncharted; big data as a lens on human culture; [by] Jean-Baptiste Michel 288 p. 2013 Riverhead Hardcover, A member of Penguin Group (USA)

1. Big data—Social aspects 2. Culture 3. HISTORY—Social History 4. Internet—Social aspects 5. SCIENCE—History 6. SOCIAL SCIENCE—Popular Culture 7. Social criticism

ISBN 9781594487453 (hardback)

LC 2013-036592

SUMMARY: "What is emerging is a new way of understanding our world, our past, and possibly, our future. In 'Uncharted,' Erez Aiden and Jean-Baptiste Michel tell the story of how they tapped into this sea of information to create a new kind of telescope. . . . By teaming up with Google, they were able to analyze the text of millions of books. The result was a new field of research and a scientific tool, the Google Ngram Viewer." (Publisher's note)

REVIEW: *Booklist* v110 no7 p17 D 1 2013 Carl Hays

REVIEW: *Kirkus Rev* v81 no22 p164 N 15 2013

REVIEW: *New Repub* v244 no27 p44-9 My 12 2014 Adam Kirsch

REVIEW: *New York Times* v163 no56361 pC1-C17 D 25 2013 WILLIAM GRIMES

"Uncharted: Big Data As a Lens on Human Culture." "[Authors Erez Aiden and Jean-Baptiste Michel] argue that just as Galileo's telescope opened new, previously unimagined worlds, the powerful lens of culturomics 'is going to change the humanities, transform the social sciences and renegotiate the relationship between the world of commerce and the ivory tower.' Judging by the evidence on offer in 'Uncharted,' the claim seems a tad boastful. . . . The Ngram Viewer delivers the what and the when but not the why. . . . 'Uncharted' began life as an article in 'Science' magazine in December 2010, and the authors have huffed and puffed to inflate it to book length. They digress at every turn and, to add weight at the back end, they have appended nearly 50 ngram searches."

REVIEW: *New York Times* v163 no56344 p3 D 8 2013 NATASHA SINGER

MICHELAKIS, PANTELIS.ed. The ancient world in silent cinema. See The ancient world in silent cinema

MICHELAKIS, PANTELIS. Greek tragedy on screen; [by] Pantelis Michelakis 2013 Oxford University Press ISBN 9780199239078

SUMMARY: This book, by Pantelis Michelakis, "considers a wide range of films which engage openly with narrative and performative aspects of Greek tragedy. . . . Michelakis argues that film adaptations of Greek tragedy need to be placed between the promises of cinema for a radical popular culture, and the divergent cultural practices and realities of commercial films, art-house films, silent cinema, and films for television, home video, and DVD." (Publisher's note)

REVIEW: *Choice* v51 no9 p1600-1 My 2014 W. A. Vincent

"Greek Tragedy on Screen". "[Pantelis] Michelakis . . . identified an astonishing number of films based on Greek tragedies, work dating back to the earliest days of cinema. He is little interested, however, in straight adaptations. . . . What interests Michelakis are films in which Greek tragedy interacts with the modern, threatening to subvert or be subverted by politics . . . generic hybridization . . . and experiments with time, space, and intermediality. . . . Michelakis writes incisively and passionately. . . . Recommended."

MICHELMORE, DAVID L., 1947-.ed. Louisa Catherine. See Heffron, M. M.

MICHIO HAYASHI.ed. From postwar to postmodern. See From postwar to postmodern

MICHÉ, MARY. Nature's patchwork quilt; understanding habitats; [by] Mary Miché 32 p. 2012 Dawn Publications

1. Habitat (Ecology)—Juvenile literature 2. Life sciences literature 3. Natural history—Juvenile literature 4. Nature—Juvenile literature 5. Nature study—Activity programs—Juvenile literature

ISBN 1584691700 (paperback); 9781584691693 (hardcover); 9781584691709 (paperback)

LC 2011-048064

SUMMARY: This "concept book compares the interdependence of the Earth's flora and fauna to the intricate structure of a quilt. Each spread features a drawing of a habitat framed by quiltlike strips featuring the various birds, mammals, amphibians, reptiles, plants, and insects to be found there." (School Library Journal)

REVIEW: *Booklist* v109 no12 p78 F 15 2013 Carolyn Phelan

REVIEW: *SLJ* v58 no12 p106 D 2012 Frances E. Millhouser

MIDDLETON, CHRISTOPHER.ed. Thirty poems. See Thirty poems

MIDTHUN, JOSEPH. The endocrine and reproductive systems; 2014 World Book, a Scott Fetzer Company

1. Children's nonfiction 2. Endocrine glands—Juvenile literature 3. Generative organs—Juvenile literature 4. Human reproduction—Juvenile literature 5. Stress (Physiology)

ISBN 9780716618447

LC 2013-025432

SUMMARY: This book on the endocrine and reproductive systems by Joseph Midthun is part of the "Building Blocks of Science" series, in which "cells and organs are occasionally depicted as friendly little characters . . . [which] cavort through the comics-style panels as they demonstrate their jobs and make occasional comments in speech balloons." It offers a "presentation of matters as varied as glands, the body's responses to stress, and the reproductive system." (Booklist)

REVIEW: *Booklist* v110 no13 p66 Mr 1 2014 Carolyn Phelan

"The Circulatory System," "The Endocrine and Reproductive Systems," and "The Skeletal and Muscular Systems." "In this engaging and surprisingly informative series, digital drawings offer visual tours inside the human body. Using correct terminology, the clearly written text conveys information in small, easy-to handle word boxes that relate directly to the simplified but clearly delineated drawings of body parts. . . . The latest additions to the Building Blocks of Science series, these books are only available as part of the full eight-book set. But the combination of simple text, clear illustrations, and cartoonlike characters makes this a useful and uncommonly accessible series."

MIDTHUN, JOSEPH. The skeletal and muscular systems; 2014 World Book, a Scott Fetzer company

1. Children's nonfiction 2. Human body—Juvenile literature 3. Human skeleton—Juvenile literature 4. Muscles 5. Musculoskeletal system—Juvenile literature

ISBN 9780716618485

LC 2013-023500

SUMMARY: This book on the skeletal and muscular systems by Joseph Midthun is part of the "Building Blocks of Science" series, in which "cells and organs are occasionally depicted as friendly little characters . . . [which] cavort through the comics-style panels as they demonstrate their jobs and make occasional comments in speech balloons." It "includes information about the parts, functions, and workings of these vital systems." (Booklist)

REVIEW: *Booklist* v110 no13 p66 Mr 1 2014 Carolyn Phelan

"The Circulatory System," "The Endocrine and Reproductive Systems," and "The Skeletal and Muscular Systems." "In this engaging and surprisingly informative series, digital drawings offer visual tours inside the human body. Using correct terminology, the clearly written text conveys information in small, easy-to handle word boxes that relate directly to the simplified but clearly delineated drawings of body parts. . . . The latest additions to the Building Blocks of Science series, these books are only available as part of the full eight-book set. But the combination of simple text, clear illustrations, and cartoonlike characters makes this a useful and uncommonly accessible series."

MIGRATION, DIASPORA, AND INFORMATION TECHNOLOGY IN GLOBAL SOCIETIES; xviii, 271 p. 2012 Routledge

1. Communication and technology 2. Identity (Psychology) and mass media 3. Information technology—Social aspects 4. Internet and immigrants 5. Social science literature

ISBN 9780203148600 (ebk.); 9780415887090

LC 2011-025196

SUMMARY: This book "primarily looks into how ICT [information and communication technology]—a new ecosystem in both external and internal (mainly economic) migrants' everyday lives—influences their communication. . . . ICT tools have become affordable for low-income migrant groups. Consequently, their growing use has changed migrants' attitude toward the media and, more importantly, migrants have become the co-creators and creators of the media." (Contemporary Sociology)

REVIEW: *Contemp Sociol* v43 no1 p86-8 Ja 2014 Franc Trček

"Migration, Diaspora, and Information Technology in Global Societies". "The analysis of concretem worlds of migrants and their narratives is this book's main feature, although individual chapters differ by their methodological approaches and emphasis as well as the depth of research into a specific subject. However, this cannot be regarded as a serious weakness; it is in many respects a pioneering work that brings new insights and poses a number of challenges for future research. The readers become aware of the everyday difficulties faced by migrants which they overcome with the help of ICT."

MIKE KELLEY; 399 p. 2013 Prestel Publishing

1. ART—Individual Artists—General 2. Art catalogs 3. Art literature 4. Installation art

ISBN 9783791352411 (hardback)

LC 2013-003821

SUMMARY: This book on artist Mike Kelley, edited by Eva Meyer-Hermann and Lisa Gabrielle Mark, "demonstrates his full range of media, from drawing, painting, and photography to video and performance—often combined in multimedia installations. Kelley reacted to what he felt was elitist minimalism with frequently shocking and sometimes scatological abjection." (Choice: Current Reviews for Academic Libraries)

REVIEW: *Choice* v51 no8 p1387 Ap 2014 E. K. Mix

"Mike Kelley". "Kelley's performance work is contextualized more thoroughly by the essays in the 1993 Whitney retrospective and catalogue 'Mike Kelley: Catholic Tastes'; however, his music, with art bands Destroy All Monsters (1973), The Poetics (1978), and Idiot Bliss (1985), receives much-needed attention in this new volume. Branden Joseph carefully contextualizes both published and unpublished live performance tapes. Although capturing the complexity of installation art typically is difficult, here readers will find a wealth of high-quality large photographs from various angles, along with detail shots that illuminate textures brilliantly."

REVIEW: *Libr J* v139 no3 p103 F 15 2014 Michael Dashkin

MIKICS, DAVID. Slow reading in a hurried age; [by] David Mikics 336 p. 2013 Belknap Press

1. Books & reading 2. Books and reading—Philosophy 3. Psychology of reading 4. Reading comprehension 5. Reading speed 6. Self-help materials
ISBN 0674724720; 9780674724723 (alk. paper)
LC 2013-009375

SUMMARY: Author David Mikics presents a "practical guide for anyone who yearns for a more meaningful and satisfying reading experience, and who wants to sharpen reading skills and improve concentration. Mikics, a noted literary scholar, demonstrates exactly how the tried-and-true methods of slow reading can provide a more immersive, fulfilling experience." (Publisher's note)

REVIEW: *Booklist* v110 no2 p9 S 15 2013 Bryce Christensen

REVIEW: *Choice* v51 no8 p1382 Ap 2014 J. A. Saklofske

REVIEW: *Kirkus Rev* v81 no15 p205 Ag 1 2013

REVIEW: *Publ Wkly* v260 no31 p57-8 Ag 5 2013

REVIEW: *TLS* no5779 p26 Ja 3 2014 LEAH PRICE

"Slow Reading in a Hurried Age." "In 'Slow Reading in a Hurried Age,' David Mikics explains how we can put on the brakes for ourselves. . . . What sets Mikics apart are not his precepts, but his examples. . . . The rules themselves are sensible, and the examples grant a glimpse into the classroom of a gifted teacher. His only mistake was to shackle them to prematurely aged platitudes about the superiority of epics to emoticons. . . . Mikics sometimes treats his readers as if they were 'slow' in the colloquial sense. . . . None of this is to say that 'Slow Reading' is any less pithy or surprising than the average book."

MILBURN, OLIVIA.tr. Decoded. See Mai Jia

MILDER, ROBERT. Hawthorne's habitations; a literary life; [by] Robert Milder xiv, 295 p., [16] p. of plates 2012 Oxford University Press

1. Biographies 2. Melancholy in literature 3. Mood (Psychology) in literature 4. Place (Philosophy) in literature
ISBN 0199917256 (hardcover); 9780199917259 (hardcover)
LC 2012-025139

SUMMARY: This book, Robert Milder's "study of the intersection between Nathanial Hawthorne's life and work, is a biography that's equal parts close reading and psychological portrait. Drawing heavily on the 'Scarlet Letter' author's notebooks, as well as his published writings and third-person primary sources, the book relentlessly presents both the author's mind and work as hot-beds of unresolved dichotomies." (Publishers Weekly)

REVIEW: *America* v208 no16 p34-5 My 13 2013 FRANKLIN FREEMAN

REVIEW: *Booklist* v109 no7 p9 D 1 2012 Bryce Christensen

REVIEW: *Choice* v50 no10 p1834-5 Je 2013 M. S. Stephenson

REVIEW: *N Engl Q* v86 no4 p709-12 D 2013 Leland S. Person

REVIEW: *Publ Wkly* v259 no40 p83 O 1 2012

REVIEW: *TLS* no5763 p12 S 13 2013 CHRISTOPHER J. KNIGHT

"Hawthorne's Habitations: A Literary Life." "[Robert] Milder has surprisingly little respect for romance as a genre. . . . As impressive as Milder is as a [Nathaniel] Hawthorne scholar, he often appears insensitive to the author's humour, and he sometimes seems to bring to his study the zeal of the prosecutor. The charges against Hawthorne are many. . . . It should also be said that Milder demonstrates a remarkable familiarity with the lives of Hawthorne and his contemporaries. Ordinarily, this should count as a great virtue, but the sense is that Milder has pried too deeply into Hawthorne's privacy, to the point that he has lost whatever respect he once had for this magnificent writer."

MILES, BARRY. Call Me Burroughs; A Life; [by] Barry Miles 736 p. 2014 Twelve

1. Authors—Biography 2. BIOGRAPHY & AUTOBIOGRAPHY—Literary 3. HISTORY—Modern—20th Century 4. HISTORY—United States—21st Century 5. Novelists, American—20th century—Biography
ISBN 9781455511952 (hardback)
LC 2013-032565

SUMMARY: Writer William "Burroughs was the original cult figure of the Beat Movement, and with the publication of his novel 'Naked Lunch,' which was originally banned for obscenity, he became a guru to the 60s youth counterculture. In 'Call Me Burroughs,' biographer and Beat historian Barry Miles presents the first full-length biography of Burroughs to be published in a quarter century." (Publisher's note)

REVIEW: *Atlantic* v313 no3 p32-4 Ap 2014 JAMES PARKER

REVIEW: *Booklist* v110 no9/10 p34 Ja 1 2014 Donna Seaman

"Call Me Burroughs." "On the centennial of [William Seward] Burroughs' birth, accomplished biographer [Barry] Miles turns in a torrentially detailed, explicit, and dramatic chronicle of Burroughs' wild life as outlaw, social critic, writer, performer, and artist. . . . Miles illuminates every facet of Burroughs' life, from his passions for guns and the occult to his depthless hunger for drugs and boys, visual and audio art, and crucial friendships with Allen Ginsberg and artist Brion Gysin. . . . [A] forthrightly definitive biography."

REVIEW: *Kirkus Rev* v81 no23 p121 D 1 2013

REVIEW: *Libr J* v138 no21 p100 D 1 2013 Benjamin Brudner

REVIEW: *London Rev Books* v36 no9 p25-6 My 8 2014 Gary Indiana

REVIEW: *N Y Times Book Rev* p17 F 23 2014 ANN DOUGLAS

"Call Me Burroughs: A Life." "In 'Call Me Burroughs,' his authoritative new biography, Barry Miles avoids unduly romanticizing Burroughs's outlaw status. . . . Miles's book is emphatically not, however, the familiar story of a gifted writer's substance-soaked decline, probably for the simple reason that Burroughs's genius for surreal black comedy tempered with hard, practical thought never deserted him. . . . Miles rightly finds Burroughs's enduring literary significance in his high-wire reinvention of the picaresque."

REVIEW: *New Yorker* v89 no47 p70-1 F 3 2014

REVIEW: *Publ Wkly* v260 no50 p64 D 9 2013

MILES, JONATHAN. Want Not; [by] Jonathan Miles 400 p. 2013 Houghton Mifflin Harcourt

1. Conduct of life—Fiction 2. Desire 3. New York (N.Y.)—Fiction 4. Psychological fiction 5. Thanksgiving Day
ISBN 0547352204; 9780547352206
LC 2013-027142

SUMMARY: This novel, by Jonathan Miles, tells "a three-pronged tale of human excess that sifts through the detritus of several disparate lives—lost loves, blown chances, countless words and deeds misdirected or misunderstood—all conjoined in their come-hell-or-high-water search for fulfillment." (Publisher's note)

REVIEW: *Booklist* v110 no3 p35 O 1 2013 Diego Báez

REVIEW: *Kirkus Rev* p29 N 15 2013 Best Books

REVIEW: *Kirkus Rev* v81 no16 p245 Ag 15 2013

REVIEW: *Libr J* v138 no11 p60 Je 15 2013 Barbara Hoffert

REVIEW: *Libr J* v138 no13 p88 Ag 1 2013 Lauren Gilbert

REVIEW: *N Y Times Book Rev* p11 N 10 2013 DAVE EGGERS

REVIEW: *New York Times* v163 no56360 pC6 D 24 2013 DAVID HAGLUND

"Want Not". "Jonathan Miles's second novel opens with an immensely satisfying first paragraph in which a city dweller named Talmadge looks at snow-covered trash bags along the sidewalk and, being thoroughly stoned, sees them as 'alpine peaks.' . . . That early glimpse into his pleasantly imaginative inner life has given him heft as a character and won part of our affections. This is an essential trick for any good novelist, and Mr. Miles pulls it off again and again . . . with increasing degrees of difficulty. . . . His gift as a writer is not for story but for back story. . . . There's not much forward motion. . . . While he is presumably capable of writing a bad sentence, he doesn't do so here, despite the big swings he often takes with his prose."

REVIEW: *New Yorker* v89 no40 p89-1 D 9 2013

REVIEW: *Publ Wkly* v260 no34 p42-3 Ag 26 2013

MILES, LISA. How to survive being dumped; [by] Lisa Miles 48 p. 2013 Rosen Publishing

1. Advice literature 2. Rejection (Psychology) in adolescence 3. Separation (Psychology) 4. Social dating 5. Teenage girls—Conduct of life
ISBN 1477707042; 1477707166; 9781477707043; 9781477707166
LC 2013-370674

SUMMARY: This book "incorporates quizzes, lists, Q&As, and blurbs from young women who have been in the same position as those staring down the barrel of first-time heartbreak. The authors explore common reasons why young couples break up and how to tell if a partner might be about to end the relationship. The old coping standbys remain. . . . However . . . care is also taken to help process emotions and potential pitfalls, such as seeking revenge or dating someone on the rebound." (Booklist)

REVIEW: *Booklist* v110 no3 p54-64 O 1 2013 Courtney Jones

"How to Survive Being Dumped." "Taking more than a few cues from glossy women's magazines, this entry into the Girl Talk series incorporates quizzes, lists, Q&As, and blurbs from young women who have been in the same position as those staring down the barrel of first-time heartbreak. . . . Great care is also taken to help process emotions and potential pitfalls, such as seeking revenge or dating someone on the rebound. Additionally, girls on the other side of the breakup fence will find advice geared to ending a relationship respectfully, A fresh and positive take on dating perils."

MILESTONES OF SCIENCE AND TECHNOLOGY; Making the Modern World; 270 p. 2013 KWS Publishers

1. Historical literature 2. Medicine—Great Britain—History 3. Science—Great Britain—History 4. Science—History 5. Technological innovations—History
ISBN 0981773656; 9780981773650

SUMMARY: "This second edition . . . has been expanded and revised to include 112 artifacts from the Science Museum, London, presenting key developments in science, technology, and medicine. . . . The artifacts date from 520 CE to 1999, predominantly related to Anglo-American developments in science, medicine, or technology, along with a few items from continental Europe and the Near East that made their way to England." (Choice: Current Reviews for Academic Libraries)

REVIEW: *Choice* v51 no6 p1028-9 F 2014 S. A. Curtis

"Making the Modern World: Milestones of Science and Technology." "This second edition of 'Making the Modern World' . . . has been expanded and revised to include 112 artifacts from the Science Museum, London, presenting key developments in science, technology, and medicine. . . . The well-written essays place each artifact into historical context and provide perspective on its contemporary and future impacts on society.. . . Not intended as comprehensive, this work is reminiscent of other interesting, highly informative museum catalogs highlighting the importance of their collections"

REVIEW: *Libr J* v138 no21 p121 D 1 2013 Talea Anderson

MILEY, MARY. The impersonator; [by] Mary Miley 368 p. 2013 Minotaur Books

1. American historical fiction 2. Detective & mystery stories 3. Fraud—Fiction 4. Heirs—Fiction 5. Impersonation—Fiction 6. Inheritance and succession—Fiction 7. Missing persons—Fiction 8. Substitution of heirs—Fiction
ISBN 1250028167; 9781250028167 (hardcover)
LC 2013-013931

SUMMARY: In this book, in "1917, a young heiress went missing from her family's Oregon manor, and seven years later, her fortune will be distributed if she doesn't return soon to claim it. A con artist—Uncle Oliver—finds a charming vaudevillian actress willing to tackle the role of impersonating Jessie Carr; the deal is they will split the money. . . . But the orphan actress gradually realizes how much she likes this new lifestyle and family, and she finds the web of deceit a struggle." (Library Journal)

REVIEW: *Booklist* v110 no1 p44 S 1 2013 Allison Block

REVIEW: *Kirkus Rev* v81 no16 p260 Ag 15 2013

"The Impersonator." "In a mystery set during the Roaring '20s, an actress takes on the role of a lifetime--if someone doesn't kill her first. . . . Leah is presented as brave, appealing, self-sufficient and smart, but the story depends on her making stupid choices. A late-entry hero, an obligatory house of doom, plot devices like a lucky train ticket and an unlucky bee sting, and a penultimate revelation worthy of Tom Jones also work against plausibility, though not necessarily against enjoyment. Historian [Mary] Miley . . . presents a colorfully detailed mystery that partially succeeds and a heroine whom readers will want to see succeed even more."

REVIEW: *Libr J* v138 no14 p92 S 1 2013 Teresa L. Jacobsen

REVIEW: *Publ Wkly* v260 no28 p150 Jl 15 2013

MILLAR, MARTIN. The Anxiety of Kalix the Werewolf; Number Three; [by] Martin Millar 624 p. 2014 Pgw

1. Anxiety 2. Eating disorders 3. Friendship—Fiction 4. Urban fantasy fiction 5. Werewolves—Fiction

ISBN 1593765371; 9781593765378

SUMMARY: In this book, part of a series by Martin Millar, "Kalix MacRinnalch, the titular fretful lycanthrope, is 18 years old, directionless, unhappy, and borderline bulimic. Empress Kabachetka of Hainusta wants to kill Kalix and her family. . . . Much of the book is devoted to Kalix and her friends hanging out, going to the movies, and shopping." (Publishers Weekly)

REVIEW: *Booklist* v110 no11 p34 F 1 2014 Diana Tixier Herald

REVIEW: *Kirkus Rev* v82 no1 p140 Ja 1 2014

"The Anxiety of Kalix the Werewolf". "Life is tough. It's tougher when you're a werewolf, or so this lumbering yarn, the third installment in [Martin] Millar's . . . Kalix Werewolf series, assures us. Even allowing for all the pop-culture slyness . . . and pomo irony, there's not much stuffing in this overstuffed book; the action scenes, though suitably bloody, come too few and too far between, and the principal characters are much too talky for the busily disruptive creatures they are. Fans of Millar's work, who are legion, won't object, but newcomers may want to take in their werewolvery by other means."

REVIEW: *Publ Wkly* v260 no45 p53-4 N 11 2013

MILLER-LACHMANN, LYN. Rogue; [by] Lyn Miller-Lachmann 240 p. 2013 Nancy Paulsen Books, an imprint of Penguin Group (USA) Inc.

1. Asperger's syndrome—Fiction 2. Autism—Fiction 3. Friendship—Fiction 4. Interpersonal relations—Fiction 5. Racially mixed people—Fiction 6. Young adult fiction

ISBN 0399162259 (hardcover); 9780399162251 (hardcover)

LC 2012-036570

SUMMARY: In this teen novel, by Lyn Miller-Lachmann, "Kiara has Asperger's syndrome, and . . . has a difficult time with other kids. They taunt her and she fights back. Now she's been kicked out of school. . . . When Chad moves in across the street, Kiara hopes that, for once, she'll be able to make friendship stick. When she learns his secret, she's so determined to keep Chad as a friend that she agrees not to tell. But being a true friend is more complicated." (Publisher's note)

REVIEW: *Bull Cent Child Books* v67 no1 p40-1 S 2013 K. C.

"Rogue." "While the issues here are challenging--child abuse, illegal drug activity, underage drinking--Kiara's perspective and the hopeful outcome keep the narrative on target for a junior-high age group. . . . The only clues to both her (and the author's) Asperger's are a sometimes overly straightforward and indiscriminate attention to detail in the writing, as well as allusions to past behavior problems such as tantrums, language loss, and a currently flourishing obsessive attachment to the X-Men (especially Rogue, hence the title); because Kiara is not officially diagnosed, her improvised methods of coping add a unique perspective to the portrayals of young people on the spectrum."

REVIEW: *Horn Book Magazine* v89 no5 p106-7 S/O 2013 SHARA L. HARDESON

REVIEW: *Kirkus Rev* v81 no8 p101 Ap 15 2013

REVIEW: *SLJ* v59 no6 p136 Je 2013 Alison Follos

MILLER, BRIAN CRAIG.ed. A punishment on the nation. See A punishment on the nation

MILLER, DONALD L. Supreme city; How Jazz Age Manhattan gave birth to modern America; [by] Donald L. Miller 784 p. 2014 Simon & Schuster

1. Historical literature

ISBN 1416550194; 9781416550198

LC 2013-020154

SUMMARY: This book, by Donald L. Miller, "is the story of Manhattan's growth and transformation in the 1920s and the brilliant people behind it. . . . As mass communication emerged, the city moved from downtown to midtown through a series of engineering triumphs—Grand Central Terminal . . . the Holland Tunnel, and the modern skyscraper. In less than ten years Manhattan became the social, cultural, and commercial hub of the country. The 1920s was the Age of Jazz and the Age of Ambition." (Publisher's note)

REVIEW: *Booklist* v110 no12 p16 F 15 2014 Mark Levine

"Supreme City: How Jazz Age Manhattan Gave Birth to Modern America". "In what amounts to a social history of an extraordinary place and time (though there is no attempt to explicitly demonstrate the premise of the subtitle, [Donald L.] Miller offers portraits of outsized individuals who altered New York, most of them not native New Yorkers. . . . Miller's prose is workmanlike but his scope prodigious, even if the book's focus blurs amidst the deluge of minutiae. Predominantly relying on previous publications, Miller usefully attaches a 50-page bibliography that, perhaps as much as the text itself, will become an essential resource for future historians."

REVIEW: *Kirkus Rev* v82 no6 p10 Mr 15 2014

REVIEW: *N Y Times Book Rev* p18 Jl 27 2014 BEVERLY GAGE

REVIEW: *New York Times* v163 no56491 p3 My 4 2014 SAM ROBERTS

REVIEW: *Publ Wkly* v261 no6 p75-6 F 10 2014

MILLER, EDWARD.il. Triangles. See Adler, D. A.

MILLER, ELIZABETH CAROLYN. Slow print; literary radicalism and late Victorian print culture; [by] Elizabeth Carolyn Miller ix, 378 p. 2013 Stanford University Press

1. English literature—19th century—Political aspects 2. Historical literature 3. Journalism—Political aspects—Great Britain—History—19th century 4. Mass media—Great Britain—History—19th century 5. Press

and politics—Great Britain—History—19th century 6. Printing—Great Britain—History—19th century 7. Radicalism and the press—Great Britain—History—19th century
ISBN 9780804784085 (cloth : alk. paper)
LC 2012-020621

SUMMARY: "This book explores the literary culture of Britain's radical press from 1880 to 1910, a time that saw a flourishing of radical political activity as well as the emergence of a mass print industry. . . . Socialist, anarchist and other radicals . . .suspected that a mass public could not exist outside the capitalist system. In response, they purposely reduced the scale of print by appealing to a small, countercultural audience." (Publisher's note)

REVIEW: *Choice* v50 no10 p1826 Je 2013 R. C. Cottrell

REVIEW: *TLS* no5747 p28 My 24 2013 LEAH PRICE

"Slow Print: Literary Radicalism and Late Victorian Print Culture." "Elizabeth Miller is the first scholar to succeed in connecting those dots. Her missing link lies in a fresh and revealing archive: the now-dusty mass of late-nineteenth-century British periodicals that took up the political mantle of earlier radicals while inventing coterie distribution methods . . . . Miller's own reading, while careful, must have been anything but slow: she commands a dauntingly deep reservoir of sources, and her argument overflows with incisive analyses of interminable novels, poems and essays. The traces of their own origin in literary-critical journals make some chapters feel more like individual case studies than parts of a continuous argument."

MILLER, EVE-MARIE.ed. Magill's Literary Annual 2013. See Magill's Literary Annual 2013

MILLER, GEORGE.tr. Nothing holds back the night. See De Vigan, D.

MILLER, HOWARD. American cocktail; a "colored girl" in the world; 352 p. 2014 Harvard University Press

1. African American psychologists—Biography 2. African American women—Biography 3. African American women entertainers—Biography 4. Memoirs 5. Motion picture actresses—United States—Biography
ISBN 0674073053; 9780674073050 (hardcover : alk. paper)
LC 2013-032113

SUMMARY: This book presents a memoir by Anita Reynolds with Howard Miller, edited by George Hutchinson. Reynolds was an "actress, dancer, model, literary critic, psychologist, but above all free-spirited provocateur. . . . One of the first black stars of the silent era, . . . she moved to New York in the 1920s and made a splash with both Harlem Renaissance elites and Greenwich Village bohemians. An émigré in Paris, she fell in with the Left Bank avant garde." (Publisher's note)

REVIEW: *Booklist* v110 no11 p17 F 1 2014 Donna Seaman

"American Cocktail: A 'Colored Girl' in the World." "A dancer, actor, psychologist, and teacher, [Anita] Reynolds recorded this archly witty, sexually frank, nonchalantly confident, yet curiously humble memoir in the mid-1970s, and it is published now for the first time, thanks to Its discovery by Cornell professor George Hutchinson. . . . Dizzying tales of famous artists and writers, escapades and affairs, sojourns inTangiers and London, and harrowing moments as WWII begins are punctuated by confrontations with prejudice and hate. Kudos to Hutchinson for bringing this independent and intrepid citizen of the world back to shimmer and shine among us."

MILLER, IAN JARED. The nature of the beasts; empire and exhibition at the Tokyo Imperial Zoo; [by] Ian Jared Miller 352 p. 2013 University of California Press

1. Historical literature 2. Nature and civilization—Japan—History 3. Philosophy of nature—Japan—History 4. Zoos—Social aspects—Japan—History
ISBN 9780520271869 (cloth : alk. paper)
LC 2013-002001

SUMMARY: "In this eye-opening study of Japan's first modern zoo, Tokyo's Ueno Imperial Zoological Gardens, opened in 1882, Ian Jared Miller offers a refreshingly unconventional narrative of Japan's rapid modernization and changing relationship with the natural world. . . . As the Japanese empire grew, Ueno became one of the primary sites of imperialist spectacle, a microcosm of the empire that could be traveled in the course of a single day." (Publisher's note)

REVIEW: *Choice* v51 no7 p1283 Mr 2014 P. L. Kantor

REVIEW: *TLS* no5783 p23 Ja 31 2014 JULIA ADENEY THOMAS

"The Nature of the Beasts: Empire and Exhibition at the Tokyo Imperial Zoo." "In the hands of a less accomplished historian, Japan's Great Zoo Massacre might be a simple tragedy, an evil perpetrated by warmongers against defenseless creatures. . . . But Ian Jared Miller's close reading of this horrific event unlocks its potential for understanding the cross-currents of Japanese politics and society as the war situation went from bad to worse. . . . What makes 'The Nature of the Beasts' a triumph, beyond its archival richness, analytical dexterity and elegant writing, is that the killing of elephants is framed . . . by the complex global processes simultaneously distancing nature while absorbing it ever more completely within human society."

MILLER, JEFFREY. The structures of law and literature; duty, justice, and evil in the cultural imagination; [by] Jeffrey Miller xi, 242 p. 2013 McGill-Queen's University Press

1. Law and literature 2. Law in literature 3. Legal literature—History 4. Social science literature 5. Sociological jurisprudence
ISBN 9780773541627 (cloth); 9780773541634 (pbk. : alk. paper)
LC 2013-433527

SUMMARY: It was the author's intent to demonstrate "that Western literature and law share a common deep cultural structure, a persisting set of archetypes and tropes guiding literary and legal imagination. This structure has four basic archetypes repeated in different variations--'Heaven,' 'Earthly Paradise,' the 'World of Experience,' and the 'Underworld'." (Choice: Current Reviews for Academic Libraries)

REVIEW: *Choice* v51 no5 p920-1 Ja 2014 J. Church

"The Structures of Law and Literature: Duty, Justice, and Evil in the Cultural Imagination." "not a run-of-the-mill interdisciplinary work; it is epic in its scope and ambition. [Jeffrey] Miller interprets a staggering number of diverse literary works from ancient Greece to contemporary South

Africa. . . . Despite the impressive erudition and charming wit displayed throughout the book. Miller's argument, executed in only 200 pages, is simply too sweeping and diffuse to be convincing. His readings of some texts such as the Old Testament are controversial, but he does not engage with the relevant scholarly discussion about these texts. Finally, Miller's writing style, though frequently conversational, is at the same time meandering, dense, and elliptical."

MILLER, JOHN. Winston & George; 56 p. 2014 Enchanted Lion Books

1. Animal stories 2. Crocodiles—Fiction 3. Friendship—Fiction 4. Plovers—Fiction 5. Symbiosis
ISBN 1592701450; 9781592701452 (hardback)
LC 2014-000087

SUMMARY: This book, by John Miller and illustrated by Giuliano Cucco, "is the story of a crocodile and a crocodile bird. These animals exist in a symbiotic relationship. Crocodile birds pick leeches and lice from the crocodile's skin and cry out whenever they see danger. In this story, Winston is a patient crocodile, George is a prankster, and their story is both sweet and dramatic." (Publisher's note)

REVIEW: *Kirkus Rev* v82 no4 p279 F 15 2014

"Winston & George". "The amusing tale plays out in energetic watercolor cartoons reminiscent of Tomi Ungerer, laid out in an expansive landscape orientation. The book was first written in the 1960s but remained unpublished until now, and that story is worth the price of admission all by itself. There's also a helpful informative page about real crocodile birds and crocodiles. [Giuliano] Cucco's vibrant illustrations, published posthumously, make [John] Miller's simple tale with its valuable message something special."

REVIEW: *SLJ* v60 no4 p128 Ap 2014 Maryann H. Owen

MILLER, JON S.ed. Alcohol and drugs in North America. See Alcohol and drugs in North America

MILLER, KRISTINE F. Almost home; the public landscapes of Gertrude Jekyll; [by] Kristine F. Miller 176 p. 2012 University of Virginia Press Published by arrangement with Architectura & Natura

1. Gardens, English—History 2. Historical literature 3. Landscape architects—Great Britain—Biography 4. Landscape architecture—Great Britain 5. Public spaces—Great Britain—History
ISBN 9780813933658 (cloth : alk. paper)
LC 2012-023752

SUMMARY: "While numerous biographers, garden historians, and critics have described and analyzed Jekyll's private commissions, her public work has received little attention." Written by Kristine F. Miller, "'Almost Home' is the first book to address these projects by one of the world's most recognized and celebrated English garden designers. . . . Jekyll's public designs reveal the garden's function as a symbol of complex themes and as an inspiration for complex emotions." (Publisher's note)

REVIEW: *Choice* v51 no4 p624 D 2013 M. Nilsen

"Almost Home: The Public Landscapes of Gertrude Jekyll." "British horticulturist Gertrude Jekyll (1843-1932) is known primarily for her private design commissions, her regular contributions to horticultural magazines, her influential books, and her collaborations with British architect Edwin Lutyens. Lesser-known are Jekyll's public commissions that include the King Edward VII Sanatorium in Midhurst (Sussex) and WW I memorials in England or on the Continent. . . . [Author Kristine F.] Miller . . . demonstrates how judicious designs and plantings transcend visual gratification. . . . With numerous, beautiful color photographs, the book will interest nonspecialists; technical descriptions of plantings add significance for practitioners."

MILLER, MARY. The Last Days of California; a novel; [by] Mary Miller 256 p. 2014 Liveright Publishing Corporation

1. Christians—Fiction 2. Families—Religious life—Fiction 3. Rapture (Christian eschatology)—Fiction 4. Road fiction 5. Teenage girls—Fiction
ISBN 0871405881; 9780871405883 (hardcover)
LC 2013-039350

SUMMARY: In this book, "fourteen-year-old Jess Metcalf is traveling with her family across the country from Alabama to California in preparation for the Rapture. Her devout father is convinced that his family will be among the chosen ones, thus redeeming his life of sporadic employment and mounting disappointment. Jess' beautiful sister, Elise, is openly rebellious. . . . Meanwhile, Jess allays her anxiety about the end-time by obsessing over boys, her weight, and her appearance." (Booklist)

REVIEW: *Booklist* v110 no5 p26 N 1 2013 Joanne Wilkinson

"The Last Days of California." "All the while, Jess keeps up an alternately hilarious and heartbreaking running commentary on, among other things, her parents' flaws, which in no way mitigate her deep love for them; her painful self-consciousness; and her growing suspicion that the Rapture is not going to happen. In her debut. [Mary] Miller captures, in a fresh and funny voice, one young teen's simultaneous desire to both belong and escape. Sending up religious extremism in deadpan prose. Miller makes this coming-of-age tale work as both a poignant portrait of a bright but vulnerable teen and a biting social critique. Supersmart fiction from an arresting new talent."

REVIEW: *Kirkus Rev* v81 no22 p194 N 15 2013

REVIEW: *N Y Times Book Rev* p15 F 2 2014 LAURIE MUCHNICK

"The Last Days of California." "Mary Miller's terrific first novel, 'The Last Days of California,' never quite makes it to the Golden State. . . . Jess Metcalf, the 15-year-old narrator, is road-tripping with her family from their home in Montgomery, Ala., to the Pacific Ocean, where they hope to witness the rapture; or at least some of them do. . . . Miller crawls so deep into Jess's skin her own voice almost disappears. . . . Miller's impressive control of her material occasionally leads her to hit a point too hard."

MILLER, RON. Chasing the storm; tornadoes, meteorology, and weather watching; [by] Ron Miller 64 p. 2014 Twenty-First Century Books

1. Children's nonfiction 2. Climatic changes 3. Meteorology—Juvenile literature 4. Storm chasers—Juvenile literature 5. Tornadoes—Juvenile literature
ISBN 9781467712842 (lib. bdg. : alk. paper)
LC 2013-009291

SUMMARY: This book "offers a window into the world of scientists and lay enthusiasts who follow violent storms, particularly tornadoes." Author Ron Miller "explains how tornadoes are formed, discusses climate change and its probable connection to the increase in extreme weather events, describes the work of meteorologists and others who watch the weather . . . and concludes by suggesting ways readers can prepare to become storm chasers themselves." (Kirkus Reviews)

REVIEW: *Booklist* v110 no11 p51-2 F 1 2014 J. B. Petty

"Chasing the Storm: Tornadoes, Meteorology, and Weather Watching." "[Ron] Miller cites global warming and increased carbon dioxide levels as major contributors to extreme weather, and he outlines the role of meteorologists and the role meteorology plays in storm prediction. Accessible text, engaging diagrams, and dynamic photographs make this a surefire hit for budding scientists and their teachers. Back matter includes instructions for creating a weather station and what's needed for a weather emergency kit."

REVIEW: *Kirkus Rev* v82 no3 p59 F 1 2014

REVIEW: *SLJ* v60 no3 p182 Mr 2014 Heather Acerro

MILLER, TOM. China's urban billion; the story behind the biggest migration in human history; [by] Tom Miller vii, 192 p. 2012 Zed Books Distributed in the U.S. exclusively by Palgrave Macmillan

1. Journalism 2. Rural-urban migration—Economic aspects—China 3. Rural-urban migration—Social aspects—China 4. Urban-rural migration—China 5. Urbanization—China
ISBN 1780321414 (pbk.); 1780321422; 9781780321417 (pbk.); 9781780321424
LC 2012-474296

SUMMARY: This book by Tom Miller "explains why China has failed to reap many of the economic and social benefits of urbanization, and suggests how these problems can be resolved. If its leaders get urbanization right, China will surpass the United States and cement its position as the world's largest economy. But if they get it wrong, China could spend the next twenty years languishing in middle-income torpor, its cities pockmarked by giant slums." (Publisher's note)

REVIEW: *Choice* v50 no11 p2071 Jl 2013 R. P. Gardella

REVIEW: *Science* v343 no6167 p138-9 Ja 10 2014 Xin Meng

"China's Urban Billion: The Story Behind the Biggest Migration in Human History." "How can we learn more about the second-largest economy in the world? One first step on that fascinating knowledge journey of 1000 li is to read Tom Miller's balanced, insightful, and detailed 'China's Urban Billion.' . . . Journalist Miller . . . tells the story of the movement of 200 million rural Chinese to the cities, which has fed the extraordinary Chinese growth. 'China's Urban Billion' offers something for everyone, lay reader and expert alike, to think about."

MILLER, WHITNEY A. The Violet Hour; [by] Whitney A. Miller 312 p. 2014 Flux

1. Cults—Fiction 2. Fathers and daughters—Fiction 3. Horror stories 4. Love—Fiction 5. Supernatural—Fiction 6. Visions—Fiction
ISBN 9780738737218
LC 2013-038454

SUMMARY: This book follows "the adopted daughter of the Patriarch of VisionCrest, a new religion so successful it claims one-quarter of the world's population as followers. . . .Harlow believes her father has simply invented the whole thing. As the story progresses, Harlow begins to understand that her father, if anything, has toned things down. As the presumed goddess that began it all decides to reassert herself, Harlow keeps hearing a female voice telling her to kill." (Kirkus Revews)

REVIEW: *Booklist* v110 no12 p82 F 15 2014 Daniel Kraus

REVIEW: *Kirkus Rev* v82 no1 p238 Ja 1 2014

"The Violet Hour". "It all comes together in the end in this exploration of a cult, but readers may wonder where this story is going until that point. . . . [Whitney A.] Miller presents an interesting, if gruesome, premise and leaves readers with a nifty ending that may just make the whole thing worth it. The path to that point seems a bit slippery, though, as she never really immerses readers in the cult, leaving readers without a solid anchor to the story. It takes a while, but this should please horror fans."

MILLGATE, MICHAEL.ed. The Collected Letters of Thomas Hardy. See The Collected Letters of Thomas Hardy

MILLIOT, JIM. The book publishing industry; [by] Jim Milliot 485 p. 2013 Routledge

1. Book industry 2. Business literature 3. Electronic publishing—United States 4. Literature publishing 5. Publishers and publishing—United States
ISBN 9780415887243 (pbk.); 9780415887250 (hardback)
LC 2012-044864

SUMMARY: This book on the book publishing industry "focuses on consumer books (adult, juvenile, and mass market paperbacks) and reviews all major book categories to present a comprehensive overview of this diverse business. In addition to the insights and portrayals of the U.S. publishing industry, this book includes an appendix containing historical data on the industry from 1946 to the end of the twentieth century." (Publisher's note)

REVIEW: *Choice* v51 no6 p973 F 2014 D. Orcutt

"The Book Publishing Industry." "This edition revises and updates the previous editions (1997; 2005), especially to reflect recent e-book developments. The revisions and shared authorship unquestionably aid the relevance and authoritativeness of many portions, even if the seams are sometimes visible (e.g., large portions of a previously separate chapter on copyright are shoehorned into a historical section). The generally textbook-style tone and treatment make for a work that is informative but not very engaging for undergraduates or general readers. Jarringly, some sections evince apparent pro-publisher bias. . . . Despite its shortcomings, this is the best, most up-to-date book on its topic."

MILLS, SAM. The Quiddity of Will Self; [by] Sam Mills 2012 Corsair

1. Authors—Societies, etc. 2. Cults—Fiction 3. Detective & mystery stories 4. Fiction 5. Human sexuality—Fiction
ISBN 1780331134; 9781780331133

SUMMARY: In this novel, "Sylvie's dead body is found by her neighbour, Richard. . . . [It thus] opens with a familiar fictional set-up - a murder mystery - in a city recognizable as London. Neither is the case, however, for this . . . story tak[es] place in a . . . world where the 'essences' of novelists have been extracted through a scientific process, and can be used as a cure for criminality, or consumed as contemplative aids by author-worshipping death cults. Richard, already sexually obsessed with Sylvie, becomes equally preoccupied with the clique of successful young authors she befriended, despite suspecting them of involvement in her murder. . . . [H]e investigates her affiliation with something called the Will Self Club (WSC) and her fixation with Self." (Times Literary Supplement)

REVIEW: *TLS* no5689 p22 Ap 13 2012 Tadzio Koelb

"The Quiddity of Will Self." "Sylvie's dead body is found by her neighbour, Richard. . . . [It thus] opens with a familiar fictional set-up - a murder mystery - in a city recognizable as London. Neither is the case, however, for this is a different kind of story, taking place in a strange world where the 'essences' of novelists have been extracted through a scientific process, and can be used as a cure for criminality, or consumed as contemplative aids by author-worshipping death cults. . . . [This is] an exercise in metafiction. The last section of Mills's novel is about a woman named Sam Mills writing a novel called 'The Quiddity of Will Self' and starts with a transcription of a letter Mills wrote to Self describing the project. . . . [I]t is . . . a form that tires easily."

MILLWARD, GWEN.il. The Snuggle Sandwich. See Doyle, M.

MILNER, DONNA. Somewhere in-between; [by] Donna Milner 256 p. 2014 Partners Pub Group

1. British Columbia—Fiction 2. Country life—Fiction 3. Grief—Fiction 4. Marriage—Fiction 5. Psychological fiction

ISBN 1927575389; 9781927575383

SUMMARY: In this book, "following tragic events, from which Julie O'Dale believes she and her husband, Ian, will never recover, Julie buys into Ian's dream to give up their comfortable city lives and retreat to the Chilcotin area of British Columbia. . . . . As both Julie and Ian wrestle with their deteriorating marriage, and . . . individual guilt and sorrow . . . they have to contend with the wilderness at their doorstep—and the mysterious tenant, Virgil Blue." (Publisher's note)

REVIEW: *Quill Quire* v80 no2 p30 Mr 2014 Candace Fertile

"Somewhere In-Between". "[Donna] Milner keeps the character count relatively small, which is fitting given the remote setting and the O'Dales' self-imposed seclusion. The author effectively describes the beauty of the Chilcotin, and explores some weighty issues. . . . But a significant suspension of disbelief is required to accept one particular first-person narrative thread, and the excursion into native culture seems forced. Milner tries to create vibrant native characters, but they tend to appear as noble and misunderstood victims. Too often it feels like the novel is being driven by themes and lessons, instead of something more organic. And the pacing doesn't quite work; by the time the nature of the tragedy is revealed, the foreshadowing has become intrusive."

MIN HYOUNG SONG. The children of 1965; on writing, and not writing, as an Asian American; [by] Min Hyoung Song 284 p. 2013 Duke University Press

1. Adult children of immigrants 2. American literature—Asian American authors 3. American literature—Asian American authors—History and criticism 4. Asian Americans 5. Literary critiques

ISBN 9780822354383 (cloth : alk. paper); 9780822354512 (pbk. : alk. paper)
LC 2012-044770

SUMMARY: In this book, "having scrutinized more than one hundred works by emerging Asian American authors and having interviewed several of these writers, Min Hyoung Song argues that collectively, these works push against existing ways of thinking about race, even as they demonstrate how race can facilitate creativity. Some of the writers eschew their identification as ethnic writers, while others embrace it as a means of tackling the uncertainty that many people feel about the near future." (Publisher's note)

REVIEW: *Choice* v51 no4 p640-1 D 2013 K. Liu

"The Children of 1965: On Writing, and Not Writing, as an Asian American." "Applying an impressive battery of data from social studies. [Min Hyoung] Song deftly moves his argument toward a poststructuralist close reading of works by Maxine Hong Kingston, Jhumpa Lahiri, Cbang-rae Lee, Hisaye Yamamoto, and Nam Le, among others, informed by an awareness that expectations based on the race of the author often creep into the unconscious of both writer and reader. The book makes a welcome contribution to the study of contemporary American literature by giving credence to the powerful force engendered by Asian Americans."

MINCHIN, ELIZABETH.ed. Orality, literacy and performance in the ancient world. See Orality, literacy and performance in the ancient world

MINIO-PALUELLO, MIKA. The oil road. See Marriott, J.

MINOR, WENDELL.il. Galapagos George. See George, J. C.

MINOR, WENDELL.il. How big could your pumpkin grow? See Minor, W.

MINOR, WENDELL. How big could your pumpkin grow?; [by] Wendell Minor 32 p. 2013 Nancy Paulsen Books

1. Monuments—Fiction 2. Natural monuments—Fiction 3. Picture books for children 4. Pumpkin—Fiction

ISBN 0399246843; 9780399246845
LC 2012-031027

SUMMARY: In this children's picture book, author Wendell Minor answers the question "How Big Could Your Pumpkin Grow?" "With each page, the pumpkins grow bigger, becoming gigantic jack-o'-lanterns. Ranging from comically spooky to downright scary, they loom over American landmarks. Some of the places are instantly recognizable, such as the Mt. Rushmore National Memorial or the U.S. Capitol, others less so, like a Yosemite Park waterfall." (School Library Journal)

REVIEW: *Booklist* v110 no1 p124-5 S 1 2013 Carolyn Phelan

"How Big Could Your Pumpkin Grow?" "After introducing giant pumpkins and giant pumpkin festivals, [Wendell] Minor asks, 'What can you do with an ENORMOUS pumpkin?' He offers a number of memorable answers (some factual, others fanciful) based on real sites in America and amplified by his wonderfully visual imagination. . . . Kids will enjoy the increasing absurdity as much as the challenge of guessing the locations pictured. . . . Minor's watercolor-and-gouache paintings are well composed, richly colored, and (best of all) just plain fun. With a text that asks leading questions, this picture book makes a fine, imaginative read-aloud choice for classrooms in the fall."

REVIEW: *Horn Book Magazine* v89 no5 p67 S/O 2013 ROGER SUTTON

REVIEW: *Kirkus Rev* v81 no15 p13 Ag 1 2013

REVIEW: *N Y Times Book Rev* p41 N 10 2013 SARAH HARRISON SMITH

"How Big Could Your Pumpkin Grow?," "The Apple Orchard Riddle," and "Thanksgiving Day Thanks." "While the pie's in the oven, savor [Wendell] Minor's mighty vocabulary, silly humor and intriguing facts. . . . [G. Brian Karas], who lives in the Hudson Valley, boosts the flavor of this sweet story with soft pencil line and rich, muted colors. . . . [Laura Malone] Elliott includes facts about the Pilgrims and their friends, the Wampanoag; [Lynn] Munsinger's adorable illustrations show little animals at work on holiday crafts that readers may want to try, too."

REVIEW: *Publ Wkly* v260 no29 p64 Jl 22 2013

REVIEW: *SLJ* v59 no7 p67 Jl 2013 Yelena Alekseyeva-Popova

MINTER, ADAM. Junkyard planet; travels in the billion-dollar trash trade; [by] Adam Minter 304 p. 2013 Bloomsbury Press

1. Journalism 2. Recycling (Waste, etc.) 3. Refuse and refuse disposal 4. Refuse disposal industry 5. Scrap materials

ISBN 1608197913; 9781608197910 (hardcover)

LC 2013-011750

SUMMARY: This book by Adam Minter "travels deeply into a vast, often hidden, multibillion-dollar industry that's transforming our economy and environment." It "traces the export of America's recyclables and the massive profits that China and other rising nations earn from it. What emerges is an engaging, colorful, and sometimes troubling tale of consumption, innovation, and the ascent of a developing world that recognizes value where Americans don't." (Publisher's note)

REVIEW: *Booklist* v110 no4 p4 O 15 2013 Carol Haggas

REVIEW: *Choice* v51 no10 p1857 Je 2014 K. L. Carriveau Jr.

REVIEW: *Economist* v410 no8869 p70 Ja 11 2014

"Junkyard Planet: Travels in the Billion-Dollar Trash Trade." "After years spent travelling the junk heaps of the world, and a decade living in China, [Adam] Minter is keen to give the scrap-dealers their due. Son of an American scrapyard owner, he approaches the industry with affectionate curiosity, marvelling at the 'groan and crunch' of machines that turn rubbish into usable goods. . . .Mr. Minter is not blind to the grim realities of the industry. Wen'an county in China, a place once known for its fertile soil, clear streams and peach trees, was the 'most polluted place' he ever visited because of its role int he plastics trade."

REVIEW: *Kirkus Rev* v81 no20 p20 O 15 2013

REVIEW: *Publ Wkly* v260 no36 p50-1 S 9 2013

MINTZBERG, HENRY, 1939-. Simply managing; what managers do and can do better; [by] Henry Mintzberg viii, 202 p. 2013 Berrett-Koehler Publishers, Inc.

1. Business literature 2. Corporate culture 3. Executives 4. Management 5. Management science

ISBN 9781609949235 (pbk.: alk. paper)

LC 2013-016851

SUMMARY: This book presents a "'substantially condensed and somewhat revised version'" of Henry Mintzberg's award-winning publication "Managing". It looks at "contemporary management practices and their behavioral and cultural influence on those impacted by the management elite." Topics include "common misconceptions about managing . . . overreliance on analytic standards, management selection, and management effectiveness." (Choice: Current Reviews for Academic Libraries)

REVIEW: *Choice* v51 no9 p1644 My 2014 S. R. Kahn

"Simply Managing: What Managers do and Can Do Better". "[Henry] Mintzberg . . . draws on his award-winning classic 'Managing' . . . to produce a 'substantially condensed and somewhat revised version.' . . . Designed for busy practitioners, this abbreviated edition's six easy-to-read chapters explore contemporary management practices and their behavioral and cultural influence on those impacted by the management elite. Throughout the book, Mintzberg presents excellent vignettes based on his research of 29 managers in diverse organizational settings. . . .Mintzberg provides unique, challenging, often controversial, and always thought-provoking insights and perspective on contemporary management practitioners and their practice of management."

MIODOWNIK, MARK. Stuff matters; exploring the marvelous materials that shape our manmade world; [by] Mark Miodownik 272 p. 2014 Houghton Mifflin Harcourt

1. Materials 2. Materials science—Popular works 3. Physical sciences 4. Science—History 5. Science—Popular works

ISBN 9780544236042 (hardback)

LC 2013-047575

SUMMARY: In this book, author Mark Miodownik "entertainingly examines the materials he encounters in a typical morning, from the steel in his razor and the graphite in his pencil to the foam in his sneakers and the concrete in a nearby skyscraper. He offers a compendium of the most astounding histories and marvelous scientific breakthroughs in the material world." (Publisher's note)

REVIEW: *Booklist* v110 no17 p70 My 1 2014 Colleen Mondor

REVIEW: *Kirkus Rev* v82 no9 p63-4 My 1 2014

REVIEW: *Libr J* v139 no13 p120 Ag 1 2014 John Kromer

REVIEW: *N Y Times Book Rev* p23 Jl 27 2014 ROSE GEORGE

REVIEW: *Publ Wkly* v261 no10 p51-2 Mr 10 2014

REVIEW: *Sci Am* v310 no5 p76 My 2014 Clara Moskowitz

"Stuff Matters: Exploring the Marvelous Material That Shape Our Man-Made World." "Pick up this book during a meal, and you might find yourself pausing to marvel at the amazing properties of the steel in your fork, the ceramic of your plate, the textiles on your chair and myriad other materials. [Author Mark] Miodownik, a materials scientist, explains the history and science behind things such as paper, glass, chocolate and concrete with an infectious enthusiasm. He explores the microscopic reasons 'why some materials smell and others are odorless.'"

MIRANDA, MEGAN. Vengeance; [by] Megan Miranda 352 p. 2014 Bloomsbury/Walker

1. Blessing and cursing—Fiction 2. Death—Fiction 3. Interpersonal relations—Fiction 4. JUVENILE FICTION—Love & Romance 5. JUVENILE FICTION—Mysteries & Detective Stories 6. JUVENILE FICTION—Social Issues—Emotions & Feelings 7. Supernatural—Fiction

ISBN 9780802735034 (hardback)

LC 2013-024937

SUMMARY: In this sequel to Megan Miranda's "Fracture," "Delaney, who fell in a frozen lake and woke up able to sense when people were on the verge of dying. Delaney's true love, Decker, picks up the narration, and watches as his father has a heart attack in the kitchen. Did Delaney know? As Decker deals with Delaney's possible betrayal, their friends are still spooked by the death of their friend Carson in the last book." (VOYA)

REVIEW: *Booklist* v110 no7 p64 D 1 2013 Frances Bradburn

REVIEW: *Kirkus Rev* v82 no1 p134 Ja 1 2014

"Vengeance". "As the teens reinforce one another's beliefs in the curse, the narration becomes increasingly paranoid, largely ignoring the ample evidence indicating that natural, rather than paranormal, explanations exist for the vandalism. In this way, [Megan] Miranda cleverly leads readers down the same path of misdirection, encouraging them to anticipate a supernatural reveal, making the final uncloaking of the human villains more surprising. However, Delaney's 'death sense' remains largely unresolved, perhaps leaving room for another installment. The realistic mystery wrapped in an eerie supernatural atmosphere will appeal to fans of both genres."

REVIEW: *SLJ* v60 no3 p161 Mr 2014 Jenny Berggren

REVIEW: *Voice of Youth Advocates* v36 no5 p63 D 2013 Matthew Weaver

MIRROR FOR THE MUSLIM PRINCE; Islam and the theory of statecraft; 448 p. 2013 Syracuse University Press

1. Islam and state—History 2. Islamic countries—Politics and government 3. Islamic law—Political aspects 4. Kings & rulers (Islamic law) 5. Political science literature

ISBN 9780815632894 (cloth : alk. paper)

LC 2013-003949

SUMMARY: In this book, the authors "reinterpret concepts and canons of Islamic thought in Arab, Persian, South Asian, and Turkish traditions. They demonstrate that there is no unitary 'Islamic' position on important issues of statecraft and governance. They recognize that Islam is a discursive site marked by silences, agreements, and animated controversies." (Publisher's note)

REVIEW: *Choice* v51 no6 p1092-3 F 2014 J. S. Parens

"Mirror for the Muslim Prince: Islam and the Theory of Statecraft." "An exemplary edited collection. Nearly every chapter is superb, and the collection as a whole is even better. 'Mirror' challenges the received scholarly notions that Islamic political thought is ultimately derivative from the Quran and all of it that deserves the name has been written in Arabic. . . . Of the four parts into which [Mehrzad] Boroujerdi divides the book, the second (chapters 3-7) offers the most striking series of studies of mirrors for princes, which give the lie to this received narrative. These contributors show that Persian political thought was not the foreign agent dooming Islam to decline that scholars, Islamists, and Salafists would have people believe. . . . Highly recommended."

REVIEW: *N Y Rev Books* v60 no8 p31 My 9 2013

MISKELLY, MATTHEW.ed. Encyclopedia of major marketing strategies. See Encyclopedia of major marketing strategies

MITAL, ANIL.ed. Human work productivity. See Human work productivity

MITCHELL, ARTHUR H. Understanding the Korean War; the participants, the tactics and the course of conflict; [by] Arthur H. Mitchell viii, 300 p. 2013 McFarland & Company, Inc., Publishers

1. Historical literature 2. Korean War, 1950-1953 3. Korean War, 1950-1953—United States 4. Macarthur, Douglas, 1880-1964 5. Truman, Harry S., 1884-1972

ISBN 9780786468577 (softcover : acid-free paper)

LC 2013-020993

SUMMARY: "This is a study of the Korean War of 1950-1953 from the inside--the nuts and bolts of armed conflict. The perspective is American, with the principal focus on the relationships of the people involved: North and South Koreans, the Chinese and Soviets, and how the U.S. and its allies engaged with them all. The lives of ordinary soldiers are examined--U.S. forces, with attention paid to the other side as well." (Publisher's note)

REVIEW: *Choice* v51 no7 p1278 Mr 2014 M. O'Donnell

"Understanding the Korean War: The Participants, the Tactics and the Course of Conflict." "Of the many works on the Korean Conflict, this may be among the most balanced, at least politically. . . . [Arthur H.] Mitchell . . . is highly critical of the [Harry] Truman administration for huge military cuts following WW II and for failing to make clear that the US would defend South Korea. . . . He is equally devastating in his attack on Republicans, including Douglas MacArthur and Dwight Eisenhower. . . . High praise must also go to Mitchell for his analyses. A lucid writing style, thorough documentation, and a superb up-to-date bibliography make this a required purchase for university and college libraries."

MITCHELL, DAVID.tr. The reason I jump. See Higashida, N.

MITCHELL, JOSHUA. Tocqueville in Arabia; dilemmas in a democratic age; [by] Joshua Mitchell 208 p. 2013 University of Chicago Press

1. Political science—Study and teaching—Qatar 2. Political science—Study and teaching—United States 3. Political science literature

ISBN 9780226087313 (cloth: alkaline paper)
LC 2013-011348

SUMMARY: This book describes how author Joshua Mitchell "spent years teaching [Alexis de] Tocqueville's classic account, 'Democracy in America,' in America and the Arab Gulf. . . . While Mitchell's American students tended to value the individualism of commercial self-interest, his Middle Eastern students had grave doubts about individualism and a deep suspicion for capitalism, which they saw as risking the destruction of long-held loyalties and obligations." (Publisher's note)

REVIEW: *Choice* v51 no9 p1680 My 2014 C. P. Waligorski

"Tocqueville in Arabia". "[Alexis de] Tocqueville is employed as a deus ex machina to support [Joshua] Mitchell's occasionally perceptive impressions of his American and Middle Eastern students' beliefs, unsupported by empirical evidence, deeper probing, or sufficient specifics. . . . His simplistic model of how capitalism and modern economies operate largely ignores their impact on the education, values, and practices he cherishes. . . . Moreover, in praising aristocratic and traditional societies he ignores oppression, what they allow and forbid, and why so many flee such societies."

MITCHELL, MARK D. Crafting history in the northern plains; a political economy of the Heart river region, 1400-1750; [by] Mark D. Mitchell xv, 269 p. 2013 University of Arizona Press

1. Ethnohistory—North Dakota—Heart River Region 2. Historical literature 3. Indians of North America—Colonization—North Dakota—Heart River Region 4. Indians of North America—First contact with Europeans—North Dakota—Heart River Region 5. Indians of North America—North Dakota—Heart River Region—Antiquities 6. Social archaeology—North Dakota—Heart River Region 7. Social change—North Dakota—Heart River Region
ISBN 9780816521296 (cloth : acid-free paper)
LC 2012-028164

SUMMARY: In this book, "Mark D. Mitchell illustrates the crucial role archaeological methods and archaeological data can play in producing trans-Columbian histories. Combining an in-depth analysis of the organization of stone tool and pottery production with ethnographic and historical data, Mitchell synthesizes the social and economic histories of the native communities located at the confluence of the Heart and Missouri rivers, home for more than five centuries to the Mandan people." (Publisher's note)

REVIEW: *Choice* v51 no1 p148-9 S 2013 P. J. O'Brien

"Crafting History in the Northern Plains: A Political Economy of the Heart River Region, 1400-1750." "This archaeological history of the Heart River region on the Missouri River in North and South Dakota is derived from materials dated from ca. 1400 CE to the historic fur trade, data ancestral to the Mandan, Hidatsa, and Arikara Indians. . . . From 1400 into the 18th century, warfare, craft specialization, resource control, developing elite families, and the continued importance of trade became more and more elaborated, culminating in the large historic Indian towns reported by explorers like Lewis and Clark."

MITCHELL, STEPHEN.tr. The illiad. See Homer (Poet)

MITFORD, NANCY, 1904-1973. Christmas Pudding & Pigeon Pie; [by] Nancy Mitford xiv, 354 p. 2013 Vintage Books, A division of Random House LLC

1. FICTION—Family Life 2. FICTION—Humorous 3. FICTION—Literary 4. Heiresses 5. World War, 1939-1945—Fiction
ISBN 034580662X (paperback); 9780345806628 (paperback)
LC 2013-024214

SUMMARY: This book presents two novels by Nancy Mitford. "Christmas Pudding" "follows the further adventures of Walter and Sally at another country retreat with another romance-minded heiress . . . named Philadelphia Bobbins. Delphie must choose between a stuffy old lord and a soupy young novelist named Paul Fotheringay." (Newsweek) In "Pigeon Pie, "Lady Sophia Garfield dreams of becoming a beautiful spy but manages not to notice a nest of German agents right under her nose." (Publisher's note)

REVIEW: *Newsweek Global* v161 no33 p1 S 20 2013 Liesl Schillinger

"Highland Fling," "Christmas Pudding," and "Pigeon Pie." "Reading Nancy Mitford's first foray into fiction, the novel 'Highland Fling,' I positively exulted. The book had an ingenuousness to it, an unchecked enthusiasm, that surprised me; and if it was less polished than her later novels, this seemed to me not a flaw but an asset. . . . Much sadness and resignation underlie Mitford's gaiety in these two maiden efforts, but you scarcely notice, given the author's precocious knack for disguising philosophy as repartée. . . . Her war novel, Pigeon Pie, stands apart . . . from the rest of her oeuvre. In it, she attempts sheer invention."

MITFORD, NANCY, 1904-1973. Highland fling; [by] Nancy Mitford 208 p. 2013 Vintage Books

1. FICTION—Family Life 2. FICTION—Literary 3. Families—Fiction 4. Marriage—Fiction
ISBN 9780345806956 (paperback)
LC 2013-024209

SUMMARY: In this book by Nancy Mitford, "a besotted young married couple named Walter Monteath (a poet) and Sally Dalloch Monteath (a cash-challenged heiress) accept an invitation to castle-sit a Scottish estate (and its grouse moor) for two months. . . . At the castle, they entertain a passel of tedious hunting fanatics and desiccated toffs while matchmaking between Jane and Albert." (Newsweek)

REVIEW: *Newsweek Global* v161 no33 p1 S 20 2013 Liesl Schillinger

"Highland Fling," "Christmas Pudding," and "Pigeon Pie." "Reading Nancy Mitford's first foray into fiction, the novel 'Highland Fling,' I positively exulted. The book had an ingenuousness to it, an unchecked enthusiasm, that surprised me; and if it was less polished than her later novels, this seemed to me not a flaw but an asset. . . . Much sadness and resignation underlie Mitford's gaiety in these two maiden efforts, but you scarcely notice, given the author's precocious knack for disguising philosophy as repartée. . . . Her war novel, Pigeon Pie, stands apart . . . from the rest of her oeuvre. In it, she attempts sheer invention."

MITHEN, STEVEN J. Thirst; water and power in the ancient world; [by] Steven J. Mithen 384 p. 2012 Harvard University Press

1. Civilization, Ancient 2. Historical literature 3. Wa-

ter consumption—History 4. Water supply—History 5. Water use—History
ISBN 9780674066939 (cloth : alk. paper)
LC 2012-027504

SUMMARY: In this book on water management in the ancient world, Steven Mithen argues that "though we may think that the rise of complex social and economic networks enabled ancient cultures to manage their water, the reverse may well be true: only when a society had reliable access to water could it turn itself into an economic or cultural power." Topics include "water storage in ancient Sumeria . . . and the aqueducts of Rome." (New York Times)

REVIEW: *Choice* v50 no9 p1686 My 2013 L. L. Johnson

REVIEW: *New York Times* v163 no56283 pD6 O 8 2013 CORNELIA DEAN

"Drinking Water: A History," "Empire of Water: An Environmental and Political History of the New York City Water Supply," and "Thirst: Water and Power in the Ancient World." "Though he ranges widely, Mr. [James] Salzman . . . focuses on what one might call social justice. Access to water may be viscerally regarded as a 'right,' but he points out that the best way to ensure a reliable supply of pure water, especially in poor regions, is often to privatize it. . . . [Steven Mithen's] tone is academic and at times highly technical, but he builds to a striking conclusion. . . . David Soll describes how the city transformed its notoriously unsanitary water system in the early 20th century by buying up watersheds in the Catskill mountains."

REVIEW: *TLS* no5745 p28 My 10 2013 W. V. HARRIS

MITTER, RANA. China's War With Japan 1937-1945; [by] Rana Mitter 480 p. 2013 Allen Lane

1. Chiang, Kai-shek, 1887-1975 2. Historical literature 3. Mao, Zedong, 1893-1976 4. Sino-Japanese War, 1937-1945 5. Wang, Jingwei, 1883-1944
ISBN 1846140102; 9781846140105

SUMMARY: "Rana Mitter's new book draws on a huge range of new sources to recreate this terrible conflict. He writes both about the major leaders (Chiang Kaishek, Mao Zedong and Wang Jingwei) and about the ordinary people swept up by terrible times. Mitter puts at the heart of our understanding of the Second World War that it was Japan's failure to defeat China which was the key dynamic for what happened in Asia." (Publisher's note)

REVIEW: *Hist Today* v63 no11 p62 N 2013 BARAK KUSHNER

REVIEW: *TLS* no5787 p24 F 28 2014 JEREMY BROWN

"China's War With Japan 1937-1945: The Struggle for Survival" and "The Tragedy of Liberation: A History of the Chinese Revolution 1945-1957." "'China's War with Japan' aims to present a comprehensive narrative of the war from the perspective of the three main political forces in China: Chiang Kai-shek's Nationalists, Mao Zedong's Communists and Wang Jingwei's collaborationist regime. [Author Rana] Mitter achieves his three-pronged goal, but Chiang's voice dominates the book. . . . In 'The Tragedy of Liberation,' Frank Dikötter agrees that terror was the foundation of Mao's regime. . . . But the mostly nameless victims . . . have been reduced to caricatures. . . . Portraying only the most terrible stories . . . as the norm . . . gives a distorted picture of everyday life in 1950s China."

MITTER, RANA. Forgotten Ally; China's World War II, 1937-1945; [by] Rana Mitter 416 p. 2013 Houghton Mifflin Harcourt

1. HISTORY—Asia—China 2. HISTORY—Military—World War II 3. Historical literature 4. Sino-Japanese War, 1937-1945 5. World War, 1939-1945—China
ISBN 061889425X; 9780618894253
LC 2013-026746

SUMMARY: Author Rana Mitter presents the "story of China's devastating eight-year war of resistance against Japan [and] focuses his . . . narrative on three towering leaders: Chiang Kai-shek, the . . . head of China's Nationalist government; Mao Zedong, the Communists' fiery ideological stalwart, . . . and the lesser-known Wang Jingwei, who collaborated with the Japanese to form a puppet state in occupied China." (Publisher's note)

REVIEW: *Choice* v51 no9 p1656 My 2014 K. E. Stapleton

REVIEW: *Economist* v407 no8841 p83-4 Je 22 2013

REVIEW: *Kirkus Rev* v81 no17 p66 S 1 2013

REVIEW: *Libr J* v138 no6 p61 Ap 1 2013 Barbara Hoffert

REVIEW: *N Y Times Book Rev* p16 S 8 2013 GORDON G. CHANG

"Forgotten Ally: China's World War II, 1937-1945." "Superb'. . . . As [Rana] Mitter says, 'the war's legacy is all over China today, if you know where to look.' . . . Still, anti-Japanese sentiment is prevalent in China today largely because of indoctrination ordered by fundamentally weak leaders seeking to bolster their rule. . . . And even if the more tolerant Communists Mitter describes had won out, it is unlikely that any for of Chinese Communism would have been liberal or benign. . . . Mitter did not have to wade into the complications of present-day China, but having done so he should have put his judgments into firmer context."

REVIEW: *New Yorker* v89 no38 p121-1 N 25 2013

MITTON, JACQUELINE. From dust to life; the origin and evolution of our solar system; [by] Jacqueline Mitton 320 p. 2013 Princeton University Press

1. Interplanetary dust 2. Origin of life 3. Science—History 4. Scientific literature 5. Solar system—Origin
ISBN 9780691145228 (alk. paper)
LC 2013-944898

SUMMARY: In this book, John Chambers and Jacqueline Mitton "trace the development of Western theories about the makeup of the solar system, from the Earth-centric model—which couldn't account for such problems as the retrograde movement of the planets—to the current eight-planet model. . . . They also briefly address the evolution of life on Earth and why we're not likely to find complex forms on other planets in our vicinity." (Publishers Weekly)

REVIEW: *Choice* v51 no9 p1618 My 2014 C. Palma

REVIEW: *New Sci* v221 no2950 p46-7 Ja 4 2014 Marcus Chown

REVIEW: *Publ Wkly* v260 no41 p52 O 14 2013

MIYARES, DANIEL.il. Prisoner 88. See Prisoner 88

MIZIELINSKA, ALEKSANDRA. The World of Mamoko in the year 3000. See Mizielinski, D.

MIZIELINSKI, DANIEL. The World of Mamoko in the year 3000; [by] Daniel Mizielinski 16 p. 2014 Candlewick Press

1. Cities & towns—Fiction 2. Extraterrestrial life—Fiction 3. Future, The 4. Imaginary places 5. Picture books for children
ISBN 9780763671259
LC 2013-943097

SUMMARY: "In this companion to 'Welcome to Mamoko' (2013), the wordless, hunt-and-find scenes depict the next millennium. Only the settings are futuristic, however; the daily dramas are universal. The opening spread names 32 animals and extraterrestrials, inviting readers to follow a unique thread for each one and to invent a narrative: 'You tell the story!'" (Kirkus Reviews)

REVIEW: *Kirkus Rev* v81 no24 p300 D 15 2013

"The World of Mamoko in the Year 3000". "In this companion to 'Welcome to Mamoko' (2013), the wordless, hunt-and-find scenes depict the next millennium . . . . Fans of the first title will recognize animal types and family names; they may speculate on relationships. An 'old world' part of the city, with its adorned buildings and familiar military statue, will send close lookers back to the original to compare the effects of time. The Mizielinskis have crafted a civilization that is clever and compassionate, hardworking and fun-loving; it is a pleasure to inhabit and visit."

MIZRUCHI, MARK S. The fracturing of the American corporate elite; [by] Mark S. Mizruchi 384 p. 2013 Harvard University Press

1. Business and politics—United States—History 2. Business literature 3. Chief executive officers—United States—History 4. Corporations—Political aspects—United States—History 5. Social responsibility of business—United States—History
ISBN 9780674072992 (alk. paper)
LC 2012-044933

SUMMARY: In this book, Mark S. Mizruchi "argues that America's corporate elites have 'abdicated responsibility' for leadership on national problems. Still wielding enormous power, they have abandoned 'enlightened self-interest' for narrow and short-term interests. Thus, they paradoxically resist regulations and policies that could preserve their firms' stability and the nation's well-being." (Choice: Current Reviews for Academic Libraries)

REVIEW: *Bookforum* v20 no2 p10 Je-Ag 2013 DANIEL GROSS

REVIEW: *Choice* v51 no5 p886 Ja 2014 P. W. Laird

"The Fracturing of the American Corporate Elite." "Sociologist [Mark S.] Mizruchi refers frequently to the business elite's 'undoing,' even as he documents its members' ongoing power. Aggressive lobbying and political contributions assure policies favorable to business leaders' short-term interests, but he believes that were they again to collaborate within professional organizations, their influence would be more benign. No evidence justifies that conclusion, however, either in the book or historically. Although the mid-century cohesion that Mizruchi praises coincided with the nation's greatest affluence, the cohesion itself deserves little credit. Extensively documented and clearly and vigorously written, this book deserves broad discussion."

REVIEW: *J Econ Lit* v51 no4 p1202-3 D 2013

REVIEW: *Kirkus Rev* v81 no6 p164 Mr 15 2013

REVIEW: *Libr J* v138 no10 p118 Je 1 2013 Susan Hurst

REVIEW: *N Y Rev Books* v61 no1 p32-4 Ja 9 2014 Andrew Hacker

"Double Down: Game Change 2012," "The Gamble: Choice and Chance in the 2012 Presidential Election," and "The Fracturing of the American Corporate Elite." "While 'Double Down' makes for intriguing reading, it tells us little about the election. . . . 'The Gamble'--a title never fully explained--argues that a complex of 'structural conditions' meant that Mitt Romney never had a chance. . . . Mark Mizruchi, in 'The Fracturing of the American Corporate Elite,' explains why corporations have become less openly political. . . . Mizruchi makes a convincing case."

REVIEW: *Publ Wkly* v260 no11 p75 Mr 18 2013

MIZUMURA MINAE, 1951-. A true novel; 880 p. 2013 Other Press

1. Gothic fiction (Literary genre) 2. Japanese—United States—Fiction 3. Love stories 4. Rich people—Fiction
ISBN 9781590512036 (pbk. original : acid-free paper)
LC 2012-046090

SUMMARY: Written by Minae Mizumura, this novel is "A remaking of Emily Brontë's 'Wuthering Heights' set in post-war Japan. 'A True Novel' begins in New York in the 1960s, where we meet Taro, a relentlessly ambitious Japanese immigrant trying to make his fortune. . . . 'A True Novel' then widens into an examination of Japan's westernization and the emergence of a middle class." (Publisher's note)

REVIEW: *Booklist* v110 no1 p42 S 1 2013 Bryce Christensen

REVIEW: *Kirkus Rev* v81 no21 p15 N 1 2013

REVIEW: *Libr J* v138 no14 p101 S 1 2013 Terry Hong

REVIEW: *N Y Times Book Rev* p14 D 15 2013 SUSAN CHIRA

"A True Novel." "'A True Novel' is a riveting tale of doomed lovers set against the backdrop of postwar Japan. . . . So how does the Gothic excess of 'Wuthering Heights' translate to a culture better known for emotional restraint, even repression? That is the larger concern of the novel, by the Japanese writer Minae Mizumura, who in adapting Emily Brontë's classic has composed a fascinating meditation on cultural borrowing and the dislocation of modernity. . . . Mizumura has triumphed in taking a quintessential Western Gothic and making it wholly Japanese."

REVIEW: *Publ Wkly* v260 no33 p40 Ag 19 2013

REVIEW: *TLS* no5779 p18 Ja 3 2014 ERI HOTTA

"A True Novel." "'A True Novel' ('Honkaku Shosetsu'), originally published in 2002 and now deftly translated by Juliet Winters Carpenter, is the only one of Mizumura's novels currently available in English, and it is modelled on Emily Bronte's 'Wuthering Heights'--'a miraculous work,' according to Mizumura. Set in Tokyo and Karuizawa, a hill station in the Nagano mountains, the main story revolves around the intense love affair between two childhood sweethearts, starting in the post-war period and spanning four decades. . . . 'A True Novel' leaves little to the reader's imagination; we are painstakingly instructed, as though by a brilliant but tyrannical professor, how best to read the story, right down to the final line of the epilogue."

MLYNOWSKI, SARAH. Don't even think about it; [by] Sarah Mlynowski 336 p. 2014 Delacorte Press

1. Extrasensory perception—Fiction 2. High schools—Fiction 3. Schools—Fiction 4. Science fiction
ISBN 0385737386; 9780385737388 (hc: alk. paper); 9780385906623 (glb: alk. paper)
LC 2012-050777

SUMMARY: This book, by Sarah Mlynowski, follows three girls who "used to be average New York City high school sophomores" but develop "telepathic powers." The girls use their powers to find about "romance, secrets, [and] scandals" involving their friends, boyfriends and students at their high school. (Publisher's note)

REVIEW: *Booklist* v111 no1 p140 S 1 2014 Heather Booth

REVIEW: *Booklist* v110 no9/10 p105-6 Ja 1 2014 Ann Kelley

REVIEW: *Kirkus Rev* v82 no3 p84 F 1 2014

"Don't Even Think About It". " Welcome to the worst fear of the anti-vaccination movement: A group of teens develop telepathy from flu shots. . . . The multiple characters are remarkably distinctive, and the plot moves along briskly, combining family drama, complicated romance and friendship turmoil into a compelling view of teen dynamics. When the group comments like a Greek chorus on one character's thoughts or actions, it's somewhat jarring, but that's a minor quibble. Overall, a solid, comical sci-fi romp."

REVIEW: *Publ Wkly* v261 no1 p57-8 Ja 6 2014

REVIEW: *SLJ* v60 no4 p171 Ap 2014 Liz Overberg

REVIEW: *SLJ* v60 no6 p68 Je 2014 Elizabeth L. Kenyon

REVIEW: *Voice of Youth Advocates* v36 no6 p75 F 2014 Jen McIntosh

M'MBOGORI, FREDA NKIROTE.ed. Humans and the environment . See Humans and the environment

MOCH, LESLIE PAGE. The pariahs of yesterday; Breton migrants in Paris; [by] Leslie Page Moch xii, 255 p. 2012 Duke University Press

1. Bretons 2. Bretons—France—Paris—History 3. Historical literature 4. Immigrants—France—Paris—History 5. Internal migration—France 6. Linguistic minorities 7. Migration, Internal—France—History 8. Paris (France)—History 9. Rural-urban migration 10. Rural-urban migration—France—History
ISBN 9780822351696 (cloth : alk. paper); 9780822351832 (pbk. : alk. paper)
LC 2011-030979

SUMMARY: In this book, "Tracing the changing status of Bretons in Paris since 1870, Leslie Page Moch demonstrates that state policy, economic trends, and the attitudes of established Parisians and Breton newcomers evolved as the fortunes of Bretons in the capital improved. . . . She interprets marriage records, official reports on employment, legal and medical theses, memoirs, and writings from secular and religious organizations in the Breton community." (Publisher's note)

REVIEW: *Am Hist Rev* v118 no4 p1259-60 O 2013 Caroline Ford

"The Pariahs of Yesterday: Breton Migrants in Paris." "In documenting the arrival of the 'pariahs of Paris,' the Breton men and women who came to do the jobs that others would not in the capital, Leslie Page Moch has provided a unique perspective on the migrants' family networks and friendships, and on the realities of working life. . . . Moch takes the story of the gradual integration of Bretons into the melting pot of Paris through the present. It is a compelling story and one that will interest historians of migration, immigration, and the Breton diaspora."

THE MODERNIST PARTY; 240 p. 2013 Columbia Univ Press

1. Authors—History—20th century 2. Historical literature 3. Literary movements—History 4. Modernism (Literature) 5. Parties 6. Parties in literature
ISBN 0748647317; 9780748647316

SUMMARY: This book, edited by Kate McLoughlin, "explore[s] the party both as a literary device and as a social setting in which the [Modernist] movement's creative values were developed. . . . Mrs. Ramsay drowns in anguish at the dinner-party she gives in Woolf's 'To The Lighthouse'. Death is a guest in Katherine Mansfield's 'The Garden Party'. Politics sour the evening party in Joyce's 'The Dead'. . . . Proust, Joyce, Picasso, Stravinsky and Diaghilev met at a post-ballet party." (Publisher's note)

REVIEW: *Choice* v51 no1 p70 S 2013 J. W. Moffett

REVIEW: *TLS* no5777/8 p29 D 20 2013 ALEXANDRA LAWRIE

"The Modernist Party." "'The Modernist Party,' edited by Kate McLoughlin, might seem like just another needless take on an already too familiar topic. Yet many of the essays collected here offer lively insights, while the book as a whole is vigorous in its handling of a range of real and imagined social gatherings, from dinner parties, to wakes, to ritualistic drug-fuelled debauchery. . . . It is unfortunate that some of the contributors to 'The Modernist Party' feel the need to justify their sideways approach to various writers. . . . This feels like special pleading, and it isn't necessary; this often thoughtful, although occasionally uneven volume of essays offers wit, entertainment and considerable interest."

MODIANO, RENZO. Of Jewish race; a boy on the run in Nazi-occupied Italy; [by] Renzo Modiano ix, 121 p. 2013 Vagabond Voices

1. Holocaust, Jewish—Italy—Personal narratives 2. Jewish children in the Holocaust—Italy—Biography 3. Jews—Italy—Biography 4. Memoirs
ISBN 1908251131; 9781908251138
LC 2013-475262

SUMMARY: "It took over sixty years for Renzo Modiano, a successful novelist, to write about this disturbing childhood experience. His school report issued in 1943, the twenty-first year of the short-lived 'Fascist Era,' contains the contemptible bureaucratic classification 'of Jewish race' immediately after his name. The enormity of this crime is known to us, but the day-to-day horrors and fears of being on the run . . . are perhaps less known." (Publisher's note)

REVIEW: *TLS* no5779 p23 Ja 3 2014 IAN THOMSON

"Of Jewish Race." "Renzo Modiano, an Italian Jew, was seven years old when the Germans occupied his native Rome on September 10, 1943. . . . Modiano's memoir of those perilous times, 'Of Jewish Race' (first published in Italy in 2005 as 'Di raiza ebraica'), is distinguished by its lucid moral candour. . . . When Rome is liberated in June 1944, he watches in disbelief as German trucks and buses move out of the city in an endless convoy along the Via Salaria. 'Of Jewish Race,' an affecting account of Jewry's plight in wartime

Italy, absorbs from start to finish."

MOGILNER, MARINA. Homo imperii; a history of physical anthropology in Russia; [by] Marina Mogilner xiv, 486 p. 2013 University of Nebraska Press

1. Historical literature 2. Imperialism—History 3. Physical anthropology—Russia—History—20th century 4. Physical anthropology—Soviet Union—History 5. Race—Study & teaching—History
ISBN 9780803239784 (cloth : alkaline paper)
LC 2013-005803

SUMMARY: This book presents a "history of racial science in prerevolutionary Russia and the early Soviet Union. Marina Mogilner places this story in the context of imperial self-modernization, political and cultural debates of the epoch, different reformist and revolutionary trends, and the growing challenge of modern nationalism." (Publisher's note)

REVIEW: *Choice* v51 no4 p704-5 D 2013 E. Pappas

"Homo Imperii: A History of Physical Anthropology in Russia." "[Marina] Mogilner . . . has produced a singular monograph on race science and physical anthropology as it was practiced in imperial Russia and the early Soviet Union. This English-language edition is more than a simple translation of the 2008 Russian-language original. It contains new material, analysis, and interpretation, as well as the reactions of Mogilner's Russian contemporaries to her research. . . . Given that this subject has received little attention in contexts beyond the Russophone world, and even there confined to a limited number of specialists, this work will be of interest to scholars of science, history, and the production of expert knowledge."

MOGK, MARJA EVELYN.ed. Different bodies. See Different bodies

MOHAMED, NADIFA. The orchard of lost souls; a novel; [by] Nadifa Mohamed 352 p. 2014 Farrar Straus & Giroux

1. FICTION—Literary 2. FICTION—War & Military 3. Somalia—History 4. Triangles (Interpersonal relations)—Fiction 5. Women, Somali—Fiction
ISBN 0374209146; 9780374209148 (hardback)
LC 2013-034411

SUMMARY: In this book, "a brutal confrontation in pre-civil war Somalia intertwines three women's lives. . . . The story opens in 1987 in the city of Hargeisa, as the widow Kawsar and the orphan Deqo prepare for a pro-government rally that all locals are required to attend. . . . When Kawsar saves Deqo from a beating for forgetting her dance steps, a female soldier, Filsan, arrests Kawsar and beats her so severely that she can never walk again." (Publishers Weekly)

REVIEW: *Booklist* v110 no9/10 p44 Ja 1 2014 Kristine Huntley

"The Orchard of Lost Souls." "The lives of three Somalian women intersect in Hargesia in the days before the 1987 revolution in [Nadifa] Mohamed's powerful, transcendent novel. . . . As the country tips over into a full-scale revolution, the three women find their paths converging under very different circumstances. Mohamed evokes the burgeoning unrest of a city on the brink of chaos with vibrant, evocative language and imagery, crafting a story that will stay with readers long after the final page is turned. . . . The lives of young women in Somalia in the 1980s as evinced by Deqo and Filsan will intrigue teens."

REVIEW: *Kirkus Rev* v82 no1 p287 Ja 1 2014

REVIEW: *Libr J* v138 no16 p57 O 1 2013 Barbara Hoffert

REVIEW: *Nation* v299 no3/4 p32 Jl 21 2014 AARON THIER

REVIEW: *N Y Times Book Rev* p11 Mr 23 2014 AMINATTA FORNA

REVIEW: *N Y Times Book Rev* p26 Mr 30 2014

REVIEW: *New Yorker* v90 no10 p77-1 Ap 28 2014

"The Orchard of Lost Souls." "In this brooding novel about three women in Somalia, Deqo, an orphan, runs away from her refugee camp and learns to stay alive. . . Kawsar, a widow, reckons with loneliness as her neighbors emigrate; Filsan, a female soldier, builds a military career as civil war tears the country apart. . . . Mohamed captures the proud spirits of the women and the chaos of nation-building in a totalitarian state, but, all too often, the characters are uneven and weighed down by their representational burden."

REVIEW: *Publ Wkly* v260 no41 p37 O 14 2013

REVIEW: *TLS* no5771 p21 N 8 2013 NABEELAH JAFFER

MOHR, MELISSA. Holy shit; a brief history of swearing; [by] Melissa Mohr x, 316 p. 2013 Oxford University Press

1. English language—History 2. English language—Obscene words—History 3. English language—Slang—History 4. English language—Social aspects—History 5. Historical literature 6. Swearing—History
ISBN 9780199742677 (hardcover)
LC 2012-034513

SUMMARY: This book is a study on swearing by Melissa Mohr. "Approaching the subject from a variety of angles—linguistic, historical, sociological, and even physiological (swearwords can help us endure pain and even increase heart rate)—Mohr gives readers a . . . report on the little words that can mean so much." (Publishers Weekly)

REVIEW: *Kirkus Rev* v81 no8 p62-3 Ap 15 2013

REVIEW: *London Rev Books* v35 no18 p25-7 S 26 2013 Colin Burrow

"Holy Shit: A Brief History of Swearing." "[Author Melissa Mohr's] argument is straightforward. It is that there are two main sources of bad language. One is the holy, which encompasses making oaths in the name of God or parts of his body. . . . The other . . . encompasses taboo bodily activities from buggery and beyond. . . . Passing over the minor errors that are inevitable in a work that draws together secondary sources about a very long period of time . . . , the larger problem with the book is its thesis that monotheism transformed obscenity for good."

REVIEW: *Publ Wkly* v260 no12 p58 Mr 25 2013 Veritas Literary

MOHR, TIM.tr. Why we took the car. See Herrndorf, W.

MOLINA, ANTONIO MUNOZ. In the Night of Time; 656 p. 2013 Houghton Mifflin Harcourt

1. Architects—Fiction 2. College teachers—Fiction 3. Historical fiction 4. Man-woman relationships—Fiction 5. Spain—History—Civil War, 1936-1939
ISBN 0547547846; 9780547547848

SUMMARY: This book, by Antonio Muñoz Molina, was the winner of the 2012 Prix Méditerranée Étranger. Set in 1936, "Spanish architect Ignacio Abel arrives at Penn Station, the final stop on his journey from war-torn Madrid, where he has left behind his wife and children, abandoning them to uncertainty. Crossing the fragile borders of Europe, he reflects on months of fratricidal conflict in his embattled country . . . and the all-consuming love affair with an American woman that forever alters his life." (Publisher's note)

REVIEW: *Booklist* v110 no5 p35 N 1 2013 Brendan Driscoll

"In the Night of Time." "[Antonio Muñoz] Molina is Interested in the legacy of violence and the messy interplay between the past and the present. Although more traditional in its form than some of his earlier works, this selection covers a lot of ground rather slowly . . . and tends to circle back repeatedly to key events and images. Readers who persist will be rewarded with a large rough-cut gem of a story that lingers in one's mind. Molina recently won the Jerusalem Prize and the Asturias Prize, and he appears to be finally getting the international attention he deserves."

REVIEW: *Economist* v410 no8873 p78 F 8 2014

REVIEW: *Kirkus Rev* v81 no23 p22 D 1 2013

REVIEW: *Libr J* v138 no12 p54 Jl 1 2013

MOLNAR, RALPH E.ed. Tyrannosaurid paleobiology. See Tyrannosaurid paleobiology

MOLZ, JENNIE GERMANN. Travel connections; tourism, technology, and togetherness in a mobile world; [by] Jennie Germann Molz 198 p. 2012 Routledge

1. Culture and tourism 2. Online social networks 3. Social science literature 4. Tourism—Social aspects 5. Tourism—Technological innovations

ISBN 9780415682855 (hardback)

LC 2011-040534

SUMMARY: In this book, "Jennie Germann Molz examines the ways networking technologies impact how travelers negotiate different forms of sociality. Her qualitative study involves a variety of cases to apply some important correctives to the sociology of tourism and in doing so, Molz demonstrates mobile technologies' impact on our ability to be present and authentic—both of which affect not only the arena of tourism and travel but everyday life more generally." (Contemporary Sociology)

REVIEW: *Choice* v50 no7 p1293 Mr 2013 S. A. Mason

REVIEW: *Contemp Sociol* v43 no2 p241-3 Mr 2014 George Sanders

"Travel Connections: Tourism, Technology and Togetherness in a Mobile World". "[Jennie Germann] Molz aptly demonstrates that novel technologies shape how we navigate quotidian life. . . . While Molz offers us an inviting and engaging perspective into tourism studies, and the book makes a compelling addition to the literature on the sociology of travel, it is the way that Molz grapples with the salient tropes of contemporary culture that make this book such a worthwhile venture. Her insights into authenticity, distraction, compassion, consumerism, and intimacy make the book relevant to social scientists of all stripes."

MONAHAN, TORIN. SuperVision. See Gilliom, J.

MONETA, GIOVANNI B. Positive psychology; a critical introduction; [by] Giovanni B. Moneta xvi, 299 p. 2014 Palgrave Macmillan

1. Optimism 2. Positive psychology 3. Psychological literature 4. Psychotherapy 5. Well-being

ISBN 9780230242937

LC 2013-044196

SUMMARY: This book on positive psychology by Giovanni B. Moneta looks at "well-being in terms of its definition and measurement, how it is impacted by self-concept, how personality traits foster or hinder its expression, how it is influenced by dynamic variables such as optimism or metacognition, and finally how 'flow' fosters various expressions of well-being." Later sections "focus on the application of this information." (Publisher's note)

REVIEW: *Choice* v51 no9 p1685-6 My 2014 R. B. Stewart Jr.

"Positive Psychology: A Critical Introduction". "Offering a unifying summary of positive psychology, this book comprises chapters on a variety of specific topics. [Giovanni B.] Moneta . . . presents theoretical and empirical approaches and explores the distinction between the hedonic and eudaemonic approaches to well-being. The reader is thus given the necessary elements to permit a thoughtful and critical analysis of each topic. . . . Each chapter concludes with lists of seminal readings and websites in the area. The closing section addresses the future of positive psychology in a succinct and intriguing manner."

MONGER, GEORGE P. Marriage customs of the world; an encyclopedia of dating customs and wedding traditions; [by] George P. Monger 2 v. (xxxiii, 743 p.) 2013 ABC-CLIO

1. Dating (Social customs) 2. Encyclopedias & dictionaries 3. Marriage customs and rites—Encyclopedias 4. Marriage law 5. Religion & marriage

ISBN 1598846639; 9781598846638 (hard copy : alk. paper); 9781598846645 (ebook)

LC 2012-031375

SUMMARY: This book, by George P. Monger, "examines historical context, social significance, and current trends and controversies of matrimony in the Western world as well as other cultures. Apart from detailing the ceremonies from specific countries, the book identifies specific elements of the wedding event and discusses them in a comparative manner, showcasing the similarities across cultures." (Publisher's note)

REVIEW: *Booklist* v110 no2 p52 S 15 2013 Maren Ostergard

"Marriage Customs of the World: An Encyclopedia of Dating Customs and Wedding Traditions." "This updated edition offers more than 340 A-Z entries . . . on courtship and marriage around the world. Almost 200 entries from the first edition (2004) were revised and updated for this edition, along with the addition of more than 150 new entries. . . . The entries are well written and easily accessible, making this suitable for high-school students. In addition, a wide variety of countries are covered, which students, will find useful. . . . As little is published on this subject, this set would be a good addition to public and academic libraries."

REVIEW: *Choice* v51 no2 p239 O 2013 S. Clerc

MONLONGO, JORGE. Hello Kitty. See Hello Kitty

MONOD, PAUL KLÉBER, 1957-. Solomon's Secret Arts; The Occult in the Age of Enlightenment; [by] Paul Kléber Monod 440 p. 2013 Yale University Press

1. Alchemy 2. BODY, MIND & SPIRIT—Occultism 3. Enlightenment 4. Europe—Intellectual life—18th century 5. HISTORY—Europe—Great Britain 6. HISTORY—Modern—17th Century 7. Historical literature 8. Magic 9. Occultism 10. Occultism—History 11. PHILOSOPHY—History & Surveys—Modern 12. Science—History—Miscellanea
ISBN 0300123582; 9780300123586 (hardback)
LC 2012-043028

SUMMARY: This book is a "study of the pursuit of the occult in England from the Restoration through 1815." Author Paul Monod "argues that occult studies—alchemy and astrology particularly—flourished in the late 17th century, then declined, only to revive in the late 18th century. In the latter period, however, those who pursued the occult played a diminished role in mainline discourse because the major intellectual figures . . . no longer expressed interest in it." (Library Journal)

REVIEW: *Choice* v51 no3 p507 N 2013 D. A. Harvey

REVIEW: *Libr J* v138 no10 p121 Je 1 2013 David Keymer

REVIEW: *N Y Rev Books* v61 no6 p68-72 Ap 3 2014 Keith Thomas

"The Enlightenment: And Why It Still Matters" and "Solomon's Secret Arts: The Occult in the Age of Enlightenment." "Anthony Pagden is a distinguished historian of early modern thought, but he too is defeated by the problem of definition. He begins his learned, eloquent, and sometimes passionate book by describing the Enlightenment as 'that period of European history between, roughly, the last decade of the seventeenth century and the first of the nineteenth.' . . . [Author Paul Kléber Monod has written a] thoroughly researched and highly informative account of the revival in late-eighteenth-century England of occult ideas and practices that are usually thought to have been effectively sidelined by the natural scientists a hundred years earlier."

MONSMAN, GERALD.ed. Sleeping Waters. See Henham, E. G.

MONSTER CULTURE IN THE 21ST CENTURY; a reader; 344 p. 2013 Bloomsbury Academic

1. Monsters in motion pictures 2. Monsters on television 3. Social science literature
ISBN 9781441178398 (paperback); 9781441187970 (hardback)
LC 2012-048383

SUMMARY: "The major contention of [Marina] Levina and [Diem-My T.] Bui's reader is that monstrosity is a condition ofthe 21st century, a result ofthe rapid change brought on by a number of social, economic, political, and environmental factors, among them terrorism, epidemics, climate change, huge natural disasters, and new communication technologies." (Choice: Current Reviews for Academic Libraries)

REVIEW: *Choice* v51 no5 p827 Ja 2014 J. A. Lent

"Monster culture in the 21st Century: A Reader." "The work included here deals with representations of monstrosity in a postracial, postgender world; technology as achieving monstrous status and capability in its own right; and the reflection of anxieties and fears in popular representations of monstrosity. Though some essays are mired too deeply in theory, most do a good job of sticking with reality. Notable in the latter respect is Jeffrey Mantz's chapter on zombification of Congo, where mining for coltan, an ore essential to digitization, has led to the world's deadliest war since 1945, full of indescribably monstrous acts. Though sometimes a difficult read, this volume pulls together a full array of modern monstrosities."

MONT, EVE MARIE. A Phantom Enchantment; [by] Eve Marie Mont 273 p. 2014 Paw Prints

1. Boarding school stories 2. Fantasy fiction 3. Love stories 4. Paris (France)—Fiction 5. Phantom of the Opera (Fictitious character)
ISBN 0758269501; 1480646539; 9780758269508; 9781480646537

SUMMARY: In this young adult novel, by Eve Marie Mont, the "conclusion to the Unbound trilogy, Emma Townsend journeys to Paris and discovers her own choices echoed within the labyrinthine love story 'The Phantom of the Opera.' . . . But no matter how busy her days, Emma Townsend misses her Coast Guard boyfriend, Gray. That lonely ache might explain the unsettling whispers Emma hears in the school's empty corridors, and the flickering images in her room's antique mirror." (Publisher's note)

REVIEW: *Kirkus Rev* v82 no4 p215 F 15 2014

"A Phantom Enchantment". "Lightweight but amusing, the Unbound Trilogy's conclusion takes on Gaston Leroux's 1910 novel, The Phantom of the Opera, and its myriad variations. . . . Emma's Paris life and creepy adventures in the mirror are vivid and thrilling, but there's not enough substance beneath the overwrought melodrama to support Emma's sturdy coming-of-age complexity. The pivotal character is the phantom, not his protégée, Christine/Emma. His choices, his fate—not hers—matter most, so that tracking the original inevitably renders Emma a bystander in her own story. Keep expectations in check, sit back and enjoy Paris (the most memorable character) vicariously."

REVIEW: *Voice of Youth Advocates* v37 no1 p71 Ap 2014 Maria Unruh

MONTALE, EUGENIO. Poetic diaries 1971 and 1972; xvi, 215 p. 2012 W.W. Norton & Co.

1. Free verse 2. Italian poetry—20th century 3. Italian poetry—Translations into English 4. Lyric poetry 5. Poetry (Literary form)
ISBN 9780393344196 (pbk.)
LC 2012-029599

SUMMARY: "'Poetic Diaries 1971 and 1972' is one of the Nobel Prize-winning poet Eugenio Montale's final works, and it reveals the last act of the twentieth-century master to be one of splendid negation. 'Poetic Diaries 1971 and 1972' is ruled by a brusque economy, and Montale's is, here, a poetics of magnificent reduction. The poet meditates on the very conditions of his art: language reveals itself to be madness, and poetry a broken promise." (Publisher's note)

REVIEW: *Yale Rev* v102 no1 p141-50 Ja 2014 ROBERT BOYERS

"Poetic Diaries, 1971 and 1972" and "Poetic Notebook, 1974-1977." "The pleasures on offer in the Arrowsmith versions of the late poems have much to do with our sense that the journey here will be less forbidding, the attendant voice more forthcoming, the reflections more vagrant and accessible. . . . [William] Arrowsmith, as translator, is clearly alert to the tensions and ambivalences that inform [author Eugenio] Montale's poetic stance. . . . And yet the suspicion does persist that Arrowsmith's versions, even in the late poems, are somehow less than they might be."

MONTALE, EUGENIO. Poetic notebook, 1974-1977; xviii, 254 p. 2012 W.W. Norton & Co.

1. Aging 2. Death—Poetry 3. Human life cycle 4. Italian poetry—20th century 5. Italian poetry—Translations into English
ISBN 9780393344189 (pbk.)
LC 2012-029600

SUMMARY: "'Poetic Notebook 1974-1977,' one of the final volumes assembled by Eugenio Montale before his death, shows the last act of the twentieth-century master to be one of splendid negation. 'Poetic Notebook 1974-1977' evokes a magnificent savagery, an attack on the poet himself and on the nihilistic squalor that he observes around him. An old man, Montale remembers his youth and recalls the dead." (Publisher's note)

REVIEW: *Yale Rev* v102 no1 p141-50 Ja 2014 ROBERT BOYERS

"Poetic Diaries, 1971 and 1972" and "Poetic Notebook, 1974-1977." "The pleasures on offer in the Arrowsmith versions of the late poems have much to do with our sense that the journey here will be less forbidding, the attendant voice more forthcoming, the reflections more vagrant and accessible. . . . [William] Arrowsmith, as translator, is clearly alert to the tensions and ambivalences that inform [author Eugenio] Montale's poetic stance. . . . And yet the suspicion does persist that Arrowsmith's versions, even in the late poems, are somehow less than they might be."

MONTEFIORE, JAN.ed. In Time's eye. See In Time's eye

MONTGOMERY, BEN. Grandma Gatewood's walk; the inspiring story of the woman who saved the Appalachian Trail; [by] Ben Montgomery 288 p. 2014 Chicago Review Press

1. Biography (Literary form) 2. Hikers—Appalachian Trail—Biography 3. Women conservationists—Appalachian Trail—Biography
ISBN 9781613747186 (cloth)
LC 2013-037551

SUMMARY: This book presents "a journalist's biography of the unassuming but gutsy 67-year-old Ohio grandmother who became the first person to walk all 2,050 miles of the Appalachian Trail three times. When Emma Gatewood (1887-1983) first decided she would hike the A.T., she told no one what she planned to do. . . [Ben] Montgomery tells the story of Gatewood's first hike and those that followed, interweaving the story with the heartbreaking details of her earlier life." (Kirkus Reviews)

REVIEW: *Booklist* v110 no13 p12 Mr 1 2014 Vanessa Bush

REVIEW: *Kirkus Rev* v82 no3 p164 F 1 2014

"Grandma Gatewood's Walk: The Inspiring Story of the Woman Who Saved the Appalachian Trail". " A journalist's biography of the unassuming but gutsy 67-year-old Ohio grandmother who became the first person to walk all 2,050 miles of the Appalachian Trail three times. . . . [Emma] Gatewood's exploits, which would later include walking the Oregon Trail, not only brought national attention to the state of hikers' trails across a nation obsessed with cars and newly crisscrossed with highways; it also made Americans more aware of the joys of walking and of nature itself. A quiet delight of a book."

MONTGOMERY, CHARLES. Happy city; transforming our lives through urban design; [by] Charles Montgomery 368 p. 2013 Farrar, Straus and Giroux

1. BUSINESS & ECONOMICS—Urban & Regional 2. City dwellers—Psychology 3. City planning—Psychological aspects 4. City planning literature 5. Environmental psychology 6. POLITICAL SCIENCE—Public Policy—City Planning & Urban Development 7. PSYCHOLOGY—Applied Psychology 8. Urban beautification—Psychological aspects
ISBN 9780374168230 (hardback)
LC 2013-022587

SUMMARY: Written by Charles Montgomery, "'Happy City' is a . . . tool for understanding and improving our own communities. The message is as surprising as it is hopeful: by retrofitting our cities for happiness, we can tackle the urgent challenges of our age. The happy city, the green city, and the low-carbon city are the same place, and we can all help build it." (Publisher's note)

REVIEW: *Booklist* v110 no3 p6 O 1 2013 Carol Haggas

REVIEW: *Columbia J Rev* v52 no4 p58-9 N/D 2013 TOM VANDERBILT

REVIEW: *Kirkus Rev* v81 no19 p52 O 1 2013

REVIEW: *N Y Times Book Rev* p25 Ja 5 2014 ALAN EHRENHALT

"Happy City: Transforming Our Lives Through Urban Design." "It was only a matter of time before someone figured out that if there were new things to say about happiness and a new interest in the evolution of urban life, the two subjects could be linked together. That is what Charles Montgomery . . . has set out to do in a book titled, logically enough, 'Happy City.' To an admirable extent, he succeeds. . . . Taken as a whole, 'Happy city' is not only readable but stimulating. It raises issues most of us have avoided for too long."

REVIEW: *N Y Times Book Rev* p22 Ja 12 2014

REVIEW: *Publ Wkly* v260 no36 p50 S 9 2013

MONTGOMERY, DAVID.ed. Black workers' struggle for equality in Birmingham. See Black workers' struggle for equality in Birmingham

MONTGOMERY, SCOTT L. Does science need a global language?; English and the future of research; [by] Scott L. Montgomery xiii, 226 p. 2013 The University of Chicago Press

1. English language—Social aspects 2. Intellectual cooperation 3. Lingua francas 4. Science—International cooperation 5. Science—Language 6. Scientific literature
ISBN 0226535037 (hardcover : alkaline paper); 9780226535036 (hardcover : alkaline paper)
LC 2012-027704

SUMMARY: "'In Does Science Need a Global Language?,' Scott L. Montgomery seeks to answer this question by investigating the phenomenon of global English in science, how and why it came about, the forms in which it appears, what advantages and disadvantages it brings, and what its future might be. He also examines the consequences of a global tongue . . . where research is still at a relatively early stage and English is not yet firmly established." (Publisher's note)

REVIEW: *Choice* v51 no5 p858 Ja 2014 V. V. Raman

REVIEW: *Science* v343 no6168 p250-1 Ja 17 2014 Yael Peled

"Does Science Need a Global Language? English and the Future of Research." "Scott Montgomery's 'Does Science Need a Global Language?' examines the changing linguistic landscape of science and the contemporary undisputed and unrivaled status of English as the common language of international communication. The book makes a timely contribution to the emerging literature on English as a (global) lingua franca (ELF). . . . Montgomery . . . undertakes the task of unpacking the evidently complex issue of ELF in science, particularly international science. . . . The book makes it clear from the outset that the answer to the question in its own title is emphatically positive."

MONTGOMERY, SY. Chasing cheetahs; the race to save Africa's fastest cats; 80 p. 2014 Houghton Mifflin Harcourt

1. Cheetah—Africa—Juvenile literature 2. Children's nonfiction 3. Wildlife conservation—Juvenile literature 4. Wildlife conservationists
ISBN 0547815492; 9780547815497
LC 2013-017611

SUMMARY: This book, by Sy Montgomery, focuses on cheetahs. "At the Cheetah Conservation Fund's (CCF) African headquarters in Namibia, Laurie Marker and her team save these . . . creatures from extinction. Since the organization's start in 1990, they've rescued more than 900 cheetahs. . . . But this arduous challenge continues. For most African livestock farmers, cheetahs are the last thing they want to see on their properties. In the 1980s, as many as 19 cheetahs per farmer died each year." (Publisher's note)

REVIEW: *Booklist* v110 no18 p47 My 15 2014 John Peters

REVIEW: *Bull Cent Child Books* v67 no9 p470 My 2014 D. S.

"Chasing Cheetahs: The Race to Save Africa's Fastest Cats". "Activist readers will be intrigued to hear about the American high-schoolers doing volunteer work on a class trip to Namibia, but there are plenty of other kinds of jobs woven into the process as well that will, in keeping with the series' practice, offer some possibilities for scientific work that young people may not have realized. [Nic] Bishop's photographs can't capture the cheetahs' blinding speed, but the cats' movie-star glamour is on prominent display, especially in a few breathtaking extreme closeups. . . . Interspersed special features . . . provide crisply focused informative overviews, while those looking to see a cheetah run will be amused by the flipbook art sequence in the book's corner."

REVIEW: *Horn Book Magazine* v90 no3 p110-1 My/Je 2014 DANIELLE J. FORD

REVIEW: *Kirkus Rev* v82 no4 p282 F 15 2014

REVIEW: *SLJ* v60 no5 p156 My 2014 Patricia Manning

MONTGOMERY, SY. The tapir scientist; 80 p. 2013 Houghton Mifflin Harcourt

1. Biologists 2. Endangered species—Juvenile literature 3. Science—Popular works 4. Tapirs—Brazil—Juvenile literature 5. Tapirs—Research—Brazil—Juvenile literature
ISBN 0547815484; 9780547815480
LC 2012-018678

SUMMARY: In this book, author Sy Montgomery and photographer Nic Bishop "experience long, hot days, cramped conditions, nervous waiting and itchy tick bites while searching for [tapirs]. . . . In less than a week, they see tapirs in the wild, find their tracks, take photographs, locate them through radio telemetry, collect 'samples of tapir poop, skin, fur, and blood,' and capture and collar two new tapirs, with more to come. This research matters, and the author . . . explains why." (Kirkus Reviews)

REVIEW: *Booklist* v109 no22 p74-5 Ag 1 2013 Gail Bush

REVIEW: *Bull Cent Child Books* v67 no1 p41-2 S 2013 D. S.

"The Tapir Scientist." "The indefatigable pairing of author [Sy] Montgomery and photographer [Nic] Bishop now heads to southwestern Brazil, where biologist Pati Medici and her crew study the indigenous lowland tapir amid the wildness of the Patanal wetlands. Montgomery is always good at conveying how laborious biological work can be, and that challenge is a strong focus here. . . . The book therefore offers a clear-eyed picture of the challenges and the joys of pioneering fieldwork, and the long wait for the actual tapir encounters allows readers to understand the field crew's excitement when they manage to tag and study some new animals."

REVIEW: *Horn Book Magazine* v89 no6 p119 N/D 2013 DANIELLE J. FORD

REVIEW: *Kirkus Rev* v81 no12 p105-6 Je 15 2013

REVIEW: *Publ Wkly* p93-4 Children's starred review annual 2013

REVIEW: *Publ Wkly* v260 no22 p62 Je 3 2013

REVIEW: *SLJ* v59 no9 p188 S 2013 Meaghan Darling

MONTIJO, RHODE. Chews your destiny; [by] Rhode Montijo 128 p. 2013 Disney-Hyperion Books

1. Bubble gum—Fiction 2. Children's stories 3. Girls—Fiction 4. Hispanic Americans—Fiction 5. Superheroes—Fiction
ISBN 1423157400; 9781423157403 (alk. paper)
LC 2012-036706

SUMMARY: In this book by Rhode Montijo, "Gabby Gomez loves to chew bubble gum even though her mother has warned her against it. It's not like she will turn into gum . . . except, that's exactly what happens! With her new, stretch-tastic powers Gabby can help save the day, but she will have to keep her gummy alter-ego a secret from her mother or else she'll find herself in a really sticky situation." (Publisher's note)

REVIEW: *Bull Cent Child Books* v67 no2 p106-7 O 2013 T. A.

"The Gumazing Gum Girl: Chews Your Destiny." "Gabby must discover how to hide her powers from her classmates and family (peanut butter turns her back to normal) and how to get them back so that she can stop planes from crashing (popping a bubble allows her to metamorphose). The chapter book-cum-graphic novel is an exploding format, and [author and illustrator Rhode] Montijo's tale fits right in, with lines of text alternating with full-page art that moves the story along with speech bubbles, comics-style omniscient narrations, and mood-setting sound effects. . . . Montijo's thickly outlined and stylistically simple drawings are playful, pleasing, and easy to parse, making them a foil for the detailed text and rich vocabulary."

REVIEW: *SLJ* v59 no12 p1 D 2013 Tim Wadham

MONTOYA, CELESTE. From global to grassroots; the European Union, transnational advocacy, and combating violence against women; [by] Celeste Montoya x, 278 p. 2013 Oxford University Press

1. Activism 2. Political science literature 3. Violence against women—Prevention 4. Women—Violence against—European Union countries
ISBN 9780199927197 (alk. paper); 9780199927203
LC 2012-031267

SUMMARY: This book by Celeste Montoya "looks at how transnational activism aimed at combating violence against women is used to instigate changes in local practice. Focusing on the case of the European Union, this book provides empirical and intersectional feminist analysis to demonstrate the transnational processes that connect global and grassroots advocacy efforts." Emphasis is given to the "roles played by regional organizations and networks in efforts to address violence against women." (Publisher's note)

REVIEW: *Choice* v51 no8 p1484 Ap 2014 K. Staudt

"From Global to Grassroots: The European Union, Transnational Advocacy, and Combating Violence Against Women". "[Celeste] Montoya . . . provides readers with one of the most thorough cross-national studies to yet emerge of transnational advocacy to combat violence against women. . . . Montoya's methodology is sound, rigorous, and comprehensive, from historical documents and discourse analysis to interviews and social network graphs that trace the density of ties among network actors over three time periods. . . . The book contributes rich theoretical insights that add to the knowledge of regional institutions (like the EU) and transnational activism."

MOODY, FRED. Unspeakable Joy; [by] Fred Moody 258 p. 2013 CreateSpace Independent Publishing Platform

1. Catholic Church 2. Catholic Church—Clergy—Sexual behavior 3. Catholic theological seminaries 4. Child sexual abuse by clergy 5. Memoirs
ISBN 1490354409; 9781490354408

SUMMARY: This book by Fred Moody presents "a memoir of the disillusionment and growth by a lapsed Catholic who learned of the church's failings. . . . As the clergy sex-abuse scandals came to public light in the 1990s, he learned, to his alarm, that at a seminary he attended, 11 priests had abused hundreds of students for more than a quarter-century. The revelations prompted him to re-examine the life he once led and the men he respected." (Kirkus Reviews)

REVIEW: *Kirkus Rev* v82 no3 p385 F 1 2014

"Unspeakable Joy". "A memoir of the disillusionment and growth by a lapsed Catholic who learned of the church's failings. . . . In this memoir, he interweaves reminiscences with snippets from notes he took and letters he sent to his family while in seminary. Together, they describe his growing awareness of horrifying memories with searing candor and a dawning sense of complicity that cut to the core of his feelings. A brave and eye-opening memoir by a writer who has stood on both sides of the wall between the public and the Catholic Church."

MOODY, TREY. Thought that nature; [by] Trey Moody ix, 77 p. 2014 Sarabande Books

1. Climatic changes 2. Consciousness 3. Human ecology 4. Nature—Poetry 5. Poems—Collections
ISBN 9781936747672 (paperback)
LC 2013-024626

SUMMARY: In this book, the winner of the Kathryn A. Morton Prize, poet Try Moody "uses pace and subtle reflections to consider the realities of climate change." It "questions the state of the climate and the biosphere and humanity's place within and upon it," (Booklist) The book also "identifies and captures moments when the border between personal consciousness and the otherness of the physical become porous." (Publisher's note)

REVIEW: *Booklist* v110 no9/10 p36 Ja 1 2014 Mark Eleveld

"Thought That Nature." "[Trey] Moody's title pays tribute to Emily Dickinson's poem, 'I thought that nature was enough.' Winner of the Kathryn A. Morton Prize, this is an ambitious and smart first book, in which the poet uses pace and subtle reflections to consider the realities of climate change. The collection begins powerfully, culminating in a 10-section piece, 'Dear Ghosts.' . . . In all, Moody has written a timely collection that questions the state of the climate and the biosphere and humanity's place within and impact upon it."

MOON, DAVID. The plough that broke the steppes; agriculture and environment on Russia's grasslands, 1700-1914; [by] David Moon xvii, 319 p. 2013 Oxford University Press

1. Agricultural history 2. Agriculture—Russia 3. Agriculture—Russia—History 4. Environmental literature 5. Historical literature 6. Steppes—Russia—History 7. Steppes ecology—Russia—History
ISBN 0199556431; 9780199556434
LC 2012-554446

SUMMARY: "This is the first environmental history of Russia's steppes." Author "David Moon analyses how naturalists and scientists came to understand the steppe environment, including the origins of the fertile black earth. . . . Farmers, and the scientists who advised them, tried different ways to deal with the recurring droughts: planting trees, irrigation, and cultivating the soil in ways that helped retain scarce moisture." (Publisher's note)

REVIEW: *Am Hist Rev* v119 no2 p641-2 Ap 2014 Mark Bernard Tauger

REVIEW: *Choice* v51 no2 p330 O 2013 N. M. Brooks

"The Plough That Broke the Steppes: Agriculture and Environment on Russia's Grasslands, 1700-1914." "This stimulating book is the first environmental history of the Russian steppe, a flat plain that stretches from Western Russia to Mongolia, north of the Black and Caspian Seas. The author focuses his attention on the 18th and 19th centuries, when colonists from northern Russia and abroad displaced the nomadic inhabitants of the steppe and began to introduce settled agriculture. [Author David] Moon . . . argues that these colonists at first tried to use agricultural techniques they were familiar with from wetter and more forested regions. . . . The author analyzes a wide variety of methods that the Russians studied, including irrigation, tree planting, and cultivating the soil."

MOONEY, LINNE R., 1949-. Scribes and the City; London Guildhall Clerks and the Dissemination of Middle English Literature, 1375-1425; [by] Linne R. Mooney 168 p. 2013 Boydell & Brewer Inc

1. English literature—Middle English, 1100-1500—History & criticism 2. Great Britain—History 3. Historical literature 4. Medieval manuscripts 5. Scribes
ISBN 1903153409; 9781903153406

SUMMARY: "This book is the first to identify the scribes responsible for the copying of the earliest manuscripts. . . . The authors reveal these revolutionary copyists as clerks holding major bureaucratic offices at the London Guildhall, working for the mayor and aldermen, officiating in their courts, and recording London business in their day jobs--while copying medieval English literature as a sideline." (Publisher's note)

REVIEW: *TLS* no5750 p29 Je 14 2013 RALPH HANNA

"Scribes and the City: London Guildhall Clerks and the Dissemination of Middle English Literature 1375-1425." "Much of this general argument depends on what I would describe as a sequence of logical leaps, in which a variety of options are left unconsidered. . . . Moreover, [Linne R.] Mooney and [Estelle] Stubbs seem to see their scribes merely as pen-wielders, but there was much more to their art than that. Here Mooney and Stubbs are perhaps at their weakest. . . . There are many unanswered questions here; but Mooney and Stubbs's study will certainly stimulate further discussion of an important stage of London book production."

MOORE, A. W. The evolution of modern metaphysics; making sense of things; [by] A. W. Moore xxi, 668 p. 2012 Cambridge University Press

1. Analytic philosophy 2. Metaphysics—History 3. Philosophical literature 4. Philosophy—History 5. Philosophy, Modern
ISBN 9780521616553 (pbk.); 9780521851114 (hardback)
LC 2011-023535

SUMMARY: "This book is concerned with the history of metaphysics since Descartes. Taking as its definition of metaphysics 'the most general attempt to make sense of things', it charts the evolution of this enterprise through various competing conceptions of its possibility, scope, and limits. The book is divided into three parts, dealing respectively with the early modern period, the late modern period in the analytic tradition, and the late modern period in non-analytic traditions. " (Publisher's note)

REVIEW: *Choice* v49 no10 p1888 Je 2012 R. T. Lee

REVIEW: *TLS* no5765 p22-3 S 27 2013 KEVIN MULLIGAN

"The Evolution of Modern Metaphysics: Making Sense of Things." "By returning again and again to the distinction between propositional and non-propositional knowledge, to variations on his three questions, to his own views and those of [Ludwig] Wittgenstein, [A. W.] Moore manages to illuminate an astonishing amount of philosophy. . . . It not only imposes a very readable and enjoyable order on the story told; it also allows him to discover order and connections often overlooked. . . . Moore is lucid, judicious, extraordinarily wide-ranging and, whatever his views about the nature of philosophy, he is an exemplar of all the cognitive virtues. Terminologies are explained, distinctions are defended or demolished, arguments reconstructed and evaluated. There is no poetry here."

MOORE, ADAM. Peacebuilding in practice; local experience in two Bosnian towns; [by] Adam Moore xii, 225 p. 2013 Cornell University Press

1. International agencies—Bosnia and Hercegovina—Brčko 2. International agencies—Bosnia and Hercegovina—Mostar 3. Peace-building—Bosnia and Hercegovina—Brčko 4. Peace-building—Bosnia and Hercegovina—Mostar 5. Political science literature
ISBN 9780801451997 (cloth: alk. paper)
LC 2013-008334

SUMMARY: In this book, "by comparing two cases in Bosnia—Mostar, where ethnic conflict still flares intermittently, and Brcko, where public institutions are models of effective multiethnic functioning—[Adam] Moore . . . identifies an interrelated set of four factors that explain the success and failure of peace building. . . . On the basis of his research, Moore argues that peace-building practices need to be reconceptualized." (Choice: Current Reviews for Academic Libraries)

REVIEW: *Choice* v51 no8 p1488 Ap 2014 R. P. Peters

"Peacebuilding in Practice: Local Experience in Two Bosnian Towns". "On the basis of his research, [Adam] Moore argues that peace-building practices need to be reconceptualized. Most importantly, he urges, there should be a shift from the ethno-territorial political framework of peace building adopted for Mostar in favor of the integrative political framework that was established in Brcko. The book is strongly recommended for those interested in peace building in the wake of international intervention, as well as those interested in applicable research methodology."

MOORE, CHARLES. Margaret Thatcher; The Authorized Biography: From Grantham to the Falklands; [by] Charles Moore 896 p. 2013 Knopf

1. BIOGRAPHY & AUTOBIOGRAPHY—Historical 2. BIOGRAPHY & AUTOBIOGRAPHY—Political 3. BIOGRAPHY & AUTOBIOGRAPHY—Women 4. Biographies 5. Prime ministers—Great Britain—Biography 6. Women prime ministers—Great Britain—Biography
ISBN 0307958949 (hbk.); 0713992824 (hbk.); 9780307958945 (hbk.); 9780713992823 (hbk.)
LC 2013-020670

SUMMARY: This "authorized biography of Margaret Thatcher reveals . . . the early life, rise to power, and first years as prime minister of the woman who transformed Britain and the world in the late twentieth century. [Author Charles] Moore has had unique access to all of Thatcher's private and governmental papers, and interviewed her and her family extensively for this book." (Publisher's note)

REVIEW: *Booklist* v109 no19/20 p23 Je 1 2013 Brad Hooper

REVIEW: *Choice* v51 no3 p536 N 2013 G. M. Stearns

REVIEW: *Choice* v51 no10 p1755 Je 2014 G. M. Stearns

REVIEW: *Commentary* v136 no1 p59-60 Jl/Ag 2013 ANDREW ROBERTS

REVIEW: *Economist* v407 no8834 p81 My 4 2013

REVIEW: *Kirkus Rev* v81 no2 p67 Je 1 2013

REVIEW: *London Rev Books* v35 no11 p13-8 Je 6 2013 David Runciman

REVIEW: *N Y Rev Books* v60 no14 p66-70 S 26 2013 Jonathan Freedland

REVIEW: *Natl Rev* v65 no14 p39-40 Ag 5 2013 CHARLES CRAWFORD

REVIEW: *New Repub* v244 no14 p40-5 S 2 2013 John Gray

"Margaret Thatcher: The Authorized Biography: From Grantham to the Falklands." "Covering the time from Thatcher's birth up to her role in the Falklands war in 1982, 'Margaret Thatcher: From Grantham to the Falklands' is one of two projected volumes; but this is already a major study of a pivotal leader--indeed, it is already one of the greatest biographies in the English language. A former newspaper editor and Conservative insider but 'never part of her "gang,"' Charles Moore brings a detached and inquiring perspective to Thatcher's life that she never thought of adopting herself. . . . A profound study of Thatcher as a human being and not just as a politician, Moore's book contains a number of revelations about her personal life."

REVIEW: *New Statesman* v142 no5156 p40-1 My 3 2013 David Owen

REVIEW: *New Yorker* v89 no23 p68-72 Ag 5 2013 John Lanchester

MOORE, CHRISTOPHER, 1957-. The Serpent of Venice; a novel; [by] Christopher Moore 336 p. 2014 HarperCollins William Morrow

1. Attempted murder—Fiction 2. Avarice—Fiction 3. Deception—Fiction 4. Humorous stories 5. Merchants—Italy—Venice—Fiction 6. Naval officers—Italy—Venice—Fiction 7. Revenge—Fiction 8. Senators—Italy—Venice—Fiction

ISBN 0061779768; 9780061779763

LC 2014-002826

SUMMARY: This book, [Christopher] Moore's mash-up of Othello and The Merchant of Venice with [Edgar Allan] Poe's 'The Cask of Amontillado' is a . . . sequel to 'Fool,' his twisted retelling of King Lear. . . . After a dastardly trio of Venetians (including Iago) plot to bury alive Pocket the fool for thwarting an attempt to cook up a new Crusade from which they'd hoped to profit. . . . He washes up in Venice's Jewish ghetto and is rescued by Shylock's lovably abrasive daughter, Jessica." (Publishers Weekly)

REVIEW: *Booklist* v110 no11 p31 F 1 2014 David Pitt

"The Serpent of Venice." "What do you get when you stitch 'Othello,' 'The Merchant of Venice,' and 'The Cask of Amontillado' together? Well, you get this rollickin' adventure in which Pocket, the royal fool introduced in [Christopher] Moore's 'Fool' (2009), is lured to Venice . . . where three men . . . are actually planning to murder him. To some, the idea of combining two Shakespeare plays and an Edgar Allan Poe short story might be vaguely chilling. . . . If you're the kind of reader who insists Shakespeare is untouchable, then this novel will probably annoy you on general principles. On the other hand, if you're a fan of Moore's brand of history-mangling humor, you'll dive right in with a big grin on your face. The grins win in the end."

REVIEW: *Kirkus Rev* v81 no22 p201 N 15 2013

REVIEW: *Libr J* v138 no21 p91 D 1 2013 Elisabeth Clark

REVIEW: *Publ Wkly* v261 no2 p45 Ja 13 2014

MOORE, CLEMENT CLARKE, 1779-1863. The night before Christmas; 40 p. 2013 Little, Brown & Co.

1. Children's poetry, American 2. Christmas poetry 3. Christmas stories for children 4. Picture books for children 5. Santa Claus—Juvenile poetry

ISBN 0316070181; 9780316070188

LC 2012-049185

SUMMARY: In this book, by Clement C. Moore and illustrated by Holly Hobbie, "a toddler awakens, looks out the window, and sees a flying sleigh. He makes his way downstairs, where he peeks around a chair to watch St. Nicholas at work. . . . An appended section offers some historical background on Moore and the poem, first published in 1823, while an artist's note comments on Hobbie's technique and her approach to the work." (Booklist)

REVIEW: *Booklist* v111 no4 p51 O 15 2014 Carolyn Phelan

REVIEW: *Horn Book Magazine* v89 no6 p67-8 N/D 2013 KATRINA HEDEEN

"The Night Before Christmas". In [Holly] Hobbie's treatment of the beloved Christmas poem, a toddler and a father . . . look on as Saint Nick pays a visit to the family's . . . home and goes about his work. The watercolor, pen-and-ink, and gouache illustrations successfully tell the story visually, and they capture light wonderfully—the cool dimness of the snow-colored landscape, the stark moonlight, the warm glow of the Christmas tree. Notes on [Clement C.] Moore and the origin of the poem as well as on Hobbie's artistic interpretation add depth."

REVIEW: *Horn Book Magazine* v90 no6 p52 N/D 2014 MARTHA V. PARRAVANO

REVIEW: *Kirkus Rev* v82 no17 p131 S 1 2014

REVIEW: *Publ Wkly* v261 no37 p58 S 15 2014

REVIEW: *Publ Wkly* v261 no37 p63 S 15 2014

REVIEW: *SLJ* v60 no10 p67 O 2014 Joanna K. Fabicon

MOORE, CYD.il. Willow. See Brennan, R.

MOORE, ELAINE A. Encyclopedia of Alzheimer's disease. See Encyclopedia of Alzheimer's disease

MOORE, JIM. The Six Trillion Dollar Man; [by] Jim Moore 242 p. 2013 Inkwater Press

1. American political fiction 2. Heirs 3. Public debts 4. Rich people—Fiction 5. Scottish Americans—Fiction

ISBN 1629010235; 9781629010236

SUMMARY: In this book, "Duncan Stuart-Bruce, of half-Scottish ancestry but born in America, is heir to an enormous fortune. . . . One day, he catches sight of the U.S. national debt clock and realizes he 'can pay off the national debt for the United States of America and have some left over for a rainy day.' And in return, all he'd ask is to become president. A character acknowledges that Duncan's plan could cause 'confusion' but is also 'a lifelong dream come true' for the country." (Kirkus Reviews)

REVIEW: *Kirkus Rev* v82 no3 p373 F 1 2014

"The Six Trillion Dollar Man". "One day, he catches sight of the U.S. national debt clock and realizes he 'can pay off the national debt for the United States of America and have some left over for a rainy day.' And in return, all he'd ask is to become president. A character acknowledges that Duncan's plan could cause "confusion" but is also 'a lifelong dream come true' for the country. That's arguable, to say the least, as are several other contentions. Much of this book does read like someone's wish-fulfillment fantasy, with idealized beautiful women, exotic vacations, private airplanes and worshipful encounters with the powerful—yet no woman, destination, possession or politician holds as much allure for Moore as the idea of paying off the national debt."

MOORE, JULIANNE. My mom is a foreigner, but not to me; [by] Julianne Moore 40 p. 2013 Chronicle Books

1. Immigrants—Fiction 2. Immigrants—United States—Juvenile fiction 3. Mother and child—Fiction 4. Mother and child—Juvenile fiction 5. Mothers—Fiction 6. Mothers—Juvenile fiction 7. Picture books for children 8. Stories in rhyme

ISBN 9781452107929 (alk. paper)

LC 2013-008426

SUMMARY: In this children's book, "a chorus of children with foreign-born mothers join voices to express their side of the immigrant experience. Having a mom who's a foreigner can be tough. 'She makes me do stuff foreign ways,' like taking soup to school and kissing people hello. Child and mom don't always look alike, and her accent--not to mention the silly foreign nicknames--attracts unwanted attention. But 'compared to OTHER Moms, / I know that she's the best.'" (Kirkus Reviews)

REVIEW: *Kirkus Rev* v81 no17 p106 S 1 2013

REVIEW: *N Y Times Book Rev* p22 O 13 2013 SARAH SHUN-LIEN BYNUM

"The Voyage," "Here I Am," and "My Mom is a Foreigner, But Not To Me." "Perhaps there is no better way to evoke the universal than by enlisting the help of small forest animals, which the illustrator Camilla Engman does to delightful effect in 'The Voyage'. . . . The text, translated from Norwegian by Jeanne Eirhelm, feels slightly stiff at times, but the wit and inventiveness of the artwork make this voyage memorable. Patti Kim forgoes text altogether in her winsome 'Here I Am'. . . . Like Kim, the actress Julianne Moore sets her new picture book in a colorful, bustling . . . metropolis--but hers stretches luxuriously across double-page spreads. . . . Moore . . . offers an original twist on the immigrant narrative."

REVIEW: *Publ Wkly* v260 no32 p58 Ag 12 2013

MOORE, KELLY. Neverwas; [by] Kelly Moore 320 p. 2014 Arthur A. Levine Books

1. Dwellings—Fiction 2. Family life—Maryland—Fiction 3. Love—Fiction 4. Psychic ability—Fiction 5. Supernatural—Fiction 6. Visions—Fiction

ISBN 0545434181; 9780545434188 (hardback); 9780545434195 (paperback)

LC 2013-020546

SUMMARY: In this book by Kelly Moore, Tucker Reed, and Larkin Reed, "Sarah Parsons has settled in at . . . the stately Maryland home that's been in her family for generations. But the world surrounding the House feels deeply wrong to Sarah. It's a place where the colonists lost the 1776 Insurrection, where the American Confederation of States still struggles with segregation, and where Sarah is haunted by echoes of a better world." (Publisher's note)

REVIEW: *Booklist* v110 no18 p66 My 15 2014 Krista Hutley

REVIEW: *Bull Cent Child Books* v67 no7 p368-9 Mr 2014 K. Q. G.

"Neverwas". "This second installment of the Amber House trilogy requires a bit more world-building and explanation than its predecessor, but the plotting remains sophisticated and intricate, with a careful and deliberate unspooling of events that manages to effectively portray how the smallest of actions might change the course of world events. Amber House as a setting is deliciously creepy, with ghost children running rampant, doors opening and closing at random, and hidden passages leading to even more secrets. This version of Sarah might trust the visions Amber House reveals to her, but readers of the previous installment will know there is something more sinister in the air and wait with bated breath for the conclusion."

REVIEW: *Kirkus Rev* v81 no22 p136 N 15 2013

REVIEW: *SLJ* v60 no2 p110 F 2014 Heather Miller Cover

MOORE, KEVIN. Elena Dorfman. See Elena Dorfman

MOORE, LORRIE, 1957-. Bark; stories; [by] Lorrie Moore 208 p. 2014 Alfred A. Knopf

1. American short stories 2. Dating (Social customs)—Fiction 3. Friendship—Fiction 4. Marriage—Fiction 5. Parent & child—Fiction

ISBN 0307594130; 9780307594136 (hardcover: alk. paper)

LC 2013-014777

SUMMARY: This book presents eight short stories by Lorrie Moore. "Here are people beset, burdened, buoyed; protected by raising teenage children; dating after divorce; facing the serious illness of a longtime friend; setting forth on a romantic assignation abroad, having it interrupted mid-trip, and coming to understand the larger ramifications and the impossibility of the connection." (Publisher's note)

REVIEW: *Atlantic* v313 no2 p44-5 Mr 2014 NATHANIEL RICH

"Bark". "[Lorrie] Moore, puzzlingly, is often compared to Alice Munro, a considerably more sober, ponderous presence. A much closer literary cousin is Jane Bowles, whose acerbic, neurotic characters take wild risks, constantly confound the reader's expectations (as well as their own), and—the rarest virtue of all— are reliably funny. At her most inventive, Moore also channels Barry Hannah's delirious spontaneity. . . . Moore is not merely a brilliant noticer. She is also brilliant at noticing those things that 'one was supposed not to notice'."

REVIEW: *Bookforum* v20 no5 p27 F/Mr 2014 PARUL SEHGAL

REVIEW: *Economist* v410 no8877 p87 Mr 8 2014

REVIEW: *Kirkus Rev* v82 no1 p120 Ja 1 2014

"Bark: Stories". "One of the best short story writers in America resumes her remarkable balancing act with a collection that is both hilarious and heartbreaking, sometimes in the same paragraph. With the announced retirement and Nobel coronation of Alice Munro, Moore (Birds of America, 1998, etc.) seems peerless in her command of tone and her virtuosity in writing stories that could never be mistaken for anyone else's. . . . Every one of these stories has a flesh-tearing bite to it, though all but one ('Referential') are also fiendishly funny. In stories both dark and wry, Moore wields a scalpel with surgical precision."

REVIEW: *Libr J* v138 no21 p93 D 1 2013 Sue Russell

REVIEW: *N Y Rev Books* v61 no6 p14-6 Ap 3 2014 Joyce Carol Oates

REVIEW: *N Y Times Book Rev* p1-18 F 23 2014 David Gates

"Bark: Stories." "'Bark' is the first collection of stories in 16 years by Lorrie Moore. . . . The uncrowded format of 'Bark' allows each story the chance it deserves for leisurely examination and appreciation. . . . Moore didn't invent the breed—Beckett, among others, got there before her—but she may be the chief contemporary chronicler of those whose dread makes them unable to turn off the laugh machine. . . . Moore is an anatomist of funny. . . . Certainly Moore's characters' lives are studies in disconnection."

REVIEW: *New Statesman* v143 no5201 p49 Mr 14 2014 Jane Shilling

REVIEW: *New York Times* v163 no56418 pC1-6 F 20 2014 MICHIKO KAKUTANI

REVIEW: *Publ Wkly* v260 no51 p34 D 16 2013

REVIEW: *TLS* no5788 p19-20 Mr 7 2014 SAM BYERS

"Bark." "'Bark,' [author Lorrie] Moore's latest collection, billed as her first in fifteen years (though four of the eight stories gathered here are already available in the Collected Stories), seems more preoccupied than ever with exactly this kind of interruption. At almost every tum, the surreal, the uncanny and the downright threatening press their way into the failing, drifting lives of her protagonists. . . . Moore's brilliance lies not only in these eerie intrusions into the everyday, but also in her unerring ability to force the everyday into places it does not belong. In Moore's world, the quotidian, the domestic, the apparently harmless, are transmuted into uncanny, unwelcome forms, largely through their appearance at unexpected moments."

REVIEW: *Va Q Rev* v90 no2 p222-6 Spr 2014 Elliott Holt

MOORE, MARK H. Recognizing public value; [by] Mark H. Moore xiii, 473 p. 2013 Harvard University Press

1. Government executives—Professional ethics—United States—Case studies 2. Municipal services 3. Political science literature 4. Public administration 5. Public administration—Moral and ethical aspects—United States—Case studies

ISBN 0674066952; 9780674066953 (alk. paper)

LC 2012-022228

SUMMARY: Author Mark H. Moore describes "a philosophy of performance measurement that will help public managers name, observe, and sometimes count the value they produce, whether in education, public health, safety, crime prevention, housing, or other areas. Blending case studies with theory, he argues that private sector models built on customer satisfaction and the bottom line cannot be transferred to government agencies." (Publisher's note)

REVIEW: *Choice* v51 no1 p166 S 2013 M. E. Ethridge

"Recognizing Public Value." "Many reformers and politicians insist that managers should identify the 'customers' for public services and measure agency performance. [Author Mark H.] Moore's new book examines the difficulties in applying this approach to public services, particularly with respect to performance measurement. He argues that private sector methods do not measure the 'public value' created by a wide range of state and local agencies. . . . His case studies demonstrate that it is possible for public managers to incorporate helpful elements of private sector performance measurement, but that it is essential to recognize the special nature of the public value created by public service agencies."

MOORE, ROWAN. Why we build; power and desire in architecture; [by] Rowan Moore 392 p. 2013 Harper Design Intl

1. Architects 2. Architectural literature 3. Architecture 4. Dubai (United Arab Emirates) 5. Hadid, Zaha, 1950-

ISBN 0062277537; 9780062277534

SUMMARY: In this book, author Rowan Moore provides an "eclectic and far-ranging tour of the history of architecture. Along the way, he demonstrates a keen understanding of architecture and history by interweaving contemplations of design, form, and function–from ancient Rome to cathedrals of the European Middle Ages to the Louvre, and Soviet-era buildings. . . . [He also] explores the relationship between the act of building and the human condition over many centuries." (Library Journal)

REVIEW: *Kirkus Rev* v81 no13 p205 Jl 1 2013

REVIEW: *Libr J* v138 no18 p85 N 1 2013 John Creech

REVIEW: *N Y Rev Books* v61 no10 p12-6 Je 5 2014 Martin Filler

"Why We Build: Power and Desire in Architecture." "Rarely do architecture writers convey a sense of place with the observational acuity, physical immediacy, and (on occasion) moral outrage of the British journalist Rowan Moore. . . . In one of the most absorbing portions of 'Why We Build,' Moore relates his complicated experiences with [architect Zaha] Hadid . . . in his capacity as director, from 2002 to 2008, of the Architecture Foundation. . . . What matters is that Moore is unafraid to raise uncomfortable questions about the practice and ramifications of the building art."

REVIEW: *Publ Wkly* v260 no26 p76-7 Jl 1 2013

REVIEW: *TLS* no5764 p31 S 20 2013 ALAN POWERS

MOORE, STEPHANIE PERRY. Forever Hot/ Truly Fine; [by] Stephanie Perry Moore 32 p. 2013 Turtleback Books

1. Flip books 2. High school football 3. High school students—Fiction 4. Stepfamilies—Fiction 5. Students' families 6. Young adult fiction

ISBN 0606318771; 9780606318778

SUMMARY: In this flip book by Stephanie Perry Moore and Derrick Moore, "'Forever Hot' follows Grovehill High transfer student Skylar Cross. Her mother just died, and already her father has found a new wife with a seven-year-old in tow. . . . Flip the book over and meet Ford Frost--he's the star of the football team, but his life is hardly perfect. Between his mother's romance with his coach and his deadbeat dad, Ford might just lose his cool and everything he's worked for." (Publisher's note)

REVIEW: *Booklist* v110 no1 p108 S 1 2013 John Peters

REVIEW: *Publ Wkly* v260 no32 p59 Ag 12 2013

REVIEW: *SLJ* v60 no1 p102 Ja 2014 Traci Glass

REVIEW: *Voice of Youth Advocates* v36 no4 p68 O 2013 Valerie Burleigh

"Forever Hot/Truly Fine." "The first of two stories in Grove Hill Giants, a new series by [author Stephanie Perry] Moore, includes two points of view for the same story. Rather than altering the viewpoint, they are presented as two separate books in a flip format. Readers can choose which book they prefer to read first--the story from Skylar's point of view or from Ford's. While these two characters are telling their side of the same story, they share their personal lives and family dynamics. . . . The stories ring true of the pain and trust issues that teens feel trying to grow up among adults who are not their parents, unexpected siblings, and new children born to their parent."

MOORE, STEVEN, 1779-1852. See The Unpublished Letters of Thomas Moore

MOORE, STEVEN, 1978-.ed. The letters of William Gaddis. See The letters of William Gaddis

MORAFF, KEN. It happened in Wisconsin; [by] Ken Moraff 268 p. 2013 Amazon Pub

1. Baseball stories 2. Baseball teams—Fiction 3. Depressions—Fiction 4. Historical fiction 5. Wisconsin—Fiction

ISBN 1477848185; 9781477848180

SUMMARY: This book, by Ken Moraff, follows "the Racine Robins . . . a traveling baseball team that raises money for local soup kitchens and striking workers" during the Great Depression. "An appreciative fan decides to treat the team to dinner when a freak April snowstorm waylays the Robins at a posh Wisconsin hotel, but the wealthy benefactor ends up having a much bigger impact on the club than anyone expected." (Booklist)

REVIEW: *Booklist* v110 no4 p28 O 15 2013 Stephanie Turza

"It Happened In Wisconsin." "Fans of Chad Harbach's 'The Art of Fielding' (2011) and Joe Schuster's 'The Might Have Been' (2012) will appreciate this new addition to baseball fiction, as first-novelist [Ken] Moraff's obvious love for the game is evident in his impassioned descriptions of the sport and its trappings. Moraff enlists the team's best pitcher to serve as narrator, and some well-placed flashbacks and a twist of romance save the novel from sports-centered monotony. Reverent and nostalgic without being mawkish or sappy, 'It Happened in Wisconsin,' winner of the 2013 Amazon Breakthrough Novel Award, is a paean to the populist cause, the colorful characters of Depression-era baseball, and the enduring power of idealism."

REVIEW: *Kirkus Rev* v82 no1 p64 Ja 1 2014

"It Happened in Wisconsin". " First-time novelist Moraff swings and occasionally hits in this homespun tale about a plucky baseball team during the Depression. This book won the 2013 Amazon Breakthrough award in general fiction. . . . Moraff's prose doles out its pleasures sporadically. . . . But too often the novel drifts aimlessly in its own warm bath of nostalgia, circling among a series of flashbacks that diffuse the impact of its class conflict. The narrator's thwarted romance with a cafe waitress further thins the plot, leaving the sense that this novel might have worked better as a pared-down short story. A likable if rambling debut that never quite gels."

MORAN, JOE. Armchair Nation; An Intimate History of Britain in Front of the TV; [by] Joe Moran 352 p. 2013 Profile Books Ltd

1. British Broadcasting Corp. 2. Historical literature 3. Television—Social aspects 4. Television broadcasting—Great Britain—History 5. Television programs—Great Britain

ISBN 1846683912; 9781846683916

SUMMARY: This book by Joe Moran explores the history of television in Great Britain, "from the first demonstration of television by John Logie Baird (in Selfridges) to the fear and excitement that greeted its arrival in households (some viewers worried it might control their thoughts), the controversies of Mary Whitehouse's 'Clean Up TV' campaign and what JG Ballard thought about Big Brother." (Publisher's note)

REVIEW: *New Statesman* v142 no5175 p48 S 13 2013 Rachel Cooke

REVIEW: *Sight Sound* v24 no3 p104-5 Mr 2014 John Wyver

REVIEW: *TLS* no5770 p34 N 1 2013 LYNSEY HANLEY

"Armchair Nation: An Intimate History of Britain in Front of the TV." "In spite of its wealth of detail, there is a fuzzy quality to 'Armchair Nation.' [Joe] Moran is, by and large, working with the impressions of diarists, memoirists and those interviewed by oral historians. The signal itself becomes a character, chided by viewers for its capriciousness and occasional disappearances, but made more magical whenever the nation tunes in and, as one, receives its messages with crystal clarity. . . . The most powerful observations throughout the book relate to the alleviation of loneliness through television - not even necessarily by watching it, simply by having it on."

MORAN, MATTHEW. The republic and the riots; exploring urban violence in French suburbs, 2005-2007; [by] Matthew Moran xii, 288 p. 2012 Peter Lang

1. Riots—France 2. Social science literature 3. Suburbs—France 4. Urban violence—France 5. Violence—France—Clichy-sous Bois 6. Violence—France—Villers-le-Bel

ISBN 3034307187 (pbk.); 9783034307185 (pbk.)

LC 2011-038768

SUMMARY: This book "explores the nature and causes of the [2005-2007] riots [in French suburbs]. . . . The book examines the relationship between the underprivileged suburbs and the French republican model. The author explores . . . interconnections: between republican ideals and the reality of daily life in the banlieues; between national projections of unity and localized realities of disunity; and between figures of authority and ordinary citizens." (Publisher's note)

REVIEW: *Contemp Sociol* v43 no1 p107-8 Ja 2014 Jennifer A. Selby

"The Republic and the Riots: Exploring Urban Violence in French Suburbs, 2005-2007". "A nuanced and contextualized portrait of how the riots materialized in the Parisian suburb of Villiers-le-Bel. . . . [Matthew] Moran's conclusions are well-informed and researched. Again, his qualitative research findings ably counter prevalent pejorative characterizations of these sociopolitical context. . . . It would have been useful had he translated the lengthy French citations he includes. . . . In addition, it is surprising that Moran includes no mention of gender. . . . Despite these two points, 'The Republic and the Riots' is a highly compelling book that effectively maps the genesis of malaise in France's banlieues."

MORAN, RUSSELL F. The Gray Ship; [by] Russell F. Moran 382 p. 2013 Coddington Press
1. Science fiction 2. Time travel—Fiction 3. United States—History—Civil War, 1861-1865—Fiction 4. Warships 5. Women military personnel—Fiction
ISBN 0989554600; 9780989554602

SUMMARY: In this book, "the USS California, under the command of Capt. Ashley Patterson, an African-American woman, is headed toward Charleston, S.C., to participate in a ceremony commemorating the first battle of the Civil War. . . . But before her ship reaches its destination, the massive cruiser—and its 630 crew members—travels through some sort of temporal wormhole and ends up near the Charleston Harbor in 1861, just hours before the Confederate assault is about to begin." (Kirkus Reviews)

REVIEW: *Kirkus Rev* v81 no23 p73 D 1 2013

REVIEW: *Kirkus Rev* p42 D 15 2013 supplemet best books 2013

"The Gray Ship"." In this stellar time-travel novel, a modern-American nuclear-powered cruiser sails through a time portal and goes back 152 years to the days just before the beginning of the Civil War. . . . Powered by a cast of well-developed characters—[Abraham] Lincoln and [Robert E.] Lee are among the prominently featured historical figures—consistently brisk pacing and a pulse-pounding (albeit slightly predictable) conclusion, the humanist themes of this novel are momentous and just as timely today as they were back in the 1860s. This provocative, intensely powerful novel is a must-read for sci-fi fans and Civil War aficionados, though mainstream fiction readers will find it heart-rending and inspiring as well."

MORBY, CONNIE STRADLING.tr. The hiccup. See Sissung, I.

MORDDEN, ETHAN. Anything goes; a history of American musical theatre; [by] Ethan Mordden 360 p. 2013 Oxford University Press
1. Actors—History 2. Historical literature 3. Musical theater 4. Musicals—United States—History and criticism 5. Theater literature
ISBN 9780199892839 (alk. paper)
LC 2013-000208

SUMMARY: Mordden looks at "such . . . innovators as Bob Fosse, Michael Bennett and Tommy Tune." He "critically chronicles Broadway's increasing reliance on revivals . . . and on jukebox musicals that use pre-existing songs." (Kirkus Reviews)

REVIEW: *Booklist* v110 no5 p18 N 1 2013 Donna Seaman

"Anything Goes: A History of American Musical Theatre," "Furious Cool: Richard Pryor and the World That Made Him," and "Kansas City Lightning: The Rise and Times of Charlie Parker." "[Ethan] Mordden traces the evolution of the musical, a quintessential American art form, and analyzes dozens of standout examples in this comprehensive, witty, and sassy history. . . . Richard Pryor drew on his difficult life and ferocious energy to create his blazing comedy, and the brothers [David Henry and Joe] Henry detail every facet of his troubled life in this superbly written account of a manic genius. . . . [Stanley] Crouch captures with novelistic verve the early years of jazz master Charlie Parker's short life in Kansas City, capturing the excitement of his artistic daring."

REVIEW: *Booklist* v110 no1 p23 S 1 2013 Ray Olson

"Anything Goes: A History of American Musical Theatre." "[Ethan] Mordden brightly differentiates those forms, citing hundreds and analyzing dozens of examples of them in a sweeping narrative that, with plenty of sass and tang, wit and even a little snark, not to mention scholarly precision, is obviously the best-ever history of the musical and likely to remain so for a very long time. Individual shows and even numbers leap to life in Mordden's colorful prose, both in the main text and the hefty bibliographical and discographical essays that propel the volume to a hilarious final bon mot."

REVIEW: *Kirkus Rev* v81 no14 p276 Jl 15 2013

MORELLI, CHRISTINE.tr. Jane, the fox & me. See Britt, F.

MORELLO, RUTH. Reading the Letters of Pliny the Younger. See Gibson, R. K.

MORGAN, BILL. The typewriter is holy; the complete, uncensored history of the beat generation; [by] Bill Morgan 291 2010 Free Press
1. American literature—20th century—History and criticism 2. American literature—History and criticism 3. Beat generation 4. Ginsberg, Allen, 1926-1997 5. Historical literature
ISBN 1-4165-9242-3; 978-1-4165-9242-6
LC 2009--42224

SUMMARY: In this book, Bill Morgan "employs a wide focus to portray the remarkable group of writers and artists that became known as the Beat Generation. He suggests that Jack Kerouac, Lawrence Ferlinghetti, Gary Snyder, Gregory Corso, William Burroughs, and others had such divergent aims and styles that they cannot properly be considered a literary movement. Instead, he sees them as a circle of friends who loved literature and were united by [Allen] Ginsberg." (Library Journal)Morgan "narrates the history of these writers as primarily a social group of friends." (Publisher's note) Bibliography. Index.

REVIEW: *Rev Am Hist* v41 no3 p525-32 S 2013 Ann Douglas

"The Typewriter is Holy: The Complete, Uncensored History of the Beat Generation," "Brother Souls: John Clellon Holmes, Jack Kerouac, and the Beat Generation," and "The Voice is All: The Lonely Victory of Jack Kerouac." "[Bill Morgan's] presentation is mainly chronological; at times he's inattentive to the demands of thematic coherence and pedestrian in style, neutering rather than demythologizing his subjects. . . . Morgan, whatever his shortcomings, is still the most trustworthy, as well as the most profoundly good-natured, of Beat scholars. . . . 'Brother Souls' is strangely, punitively, lopsided--a deliberately partial picture of one man, not two. . . . The hostility is out in the open as never before, and it diminishes an otherwise remarkable achievement. . . . [Joyce] Johnson has turned for the first time to biography, and the result is by far the best book on Kerouac to date."

MORGAN, EMILY. Next time you see a firefly; [by] Emily Morgan 32 p. 2013 National Science Teachers Association
1. Children's nonfiction 2. Fireflies—Behavior 3. Fireflies—Juvenile literature 4. Fireflies—Physiology 5.

Picture books for children
ISBN 9781936959181 (print); 9781938946165 (library binding); 9781938946790 (e-book)
LC 2013-017767

SUMMARY: In this book by Emily Morgan, part of the "Next Time You See A" series, readers can "discover why fireflies flash and how they live secret lives underground before coming out to fill the evening with their glimmers of light. . . . If you catch fireflies, you must let them go: Fireflies have a lot to do!" (Publisher's note)

REVIEW: *SLJ* v59 no10 p1 O 2013 Frances E. Millhouser

MORGAN, EMILY. Next time you see a seashell; [by] Emily Morgan 31 p. 2013 NSTA Kids
1. Children's nonfiction 2. Mollusks—Juvenile literature 3. Picture books for children 4. Seashells (Biology) 5. Shells—Juvenile literature
ISBN 9781936959150 (print); 9781936959730
LC 2012-027770

SUMMARY: This book, part of Emily Morgan's "Next Time You See A" series, "provides textual and visual explanations about these homes of the mollusk family. The book has been purposefully created to be used as a resource after young person has their first experience with seashells. . . . Clearly stated is that the purpose of this book is not to give facts to memorize but to create a sense of wonder to encourage further investigations." (SB&F: Your Guide to Science Resources For All Ages)

REVIEW: *Booklist* v110 no7 p55 D 1 2013 Kay Weisman

MORGAN, EMILY. Next time you see a sunset; [by] Emily Morgan 31 p.
1. Atmosphere—Juvenile literature 2. Children's nonfiction 3. Earth (Planet)—Rotation—Juvenile literature
ISBN 9781936959167 (pbk.)
LC 2012-026812

SUMMARY: This book by Emily Morgan, "one of four in a series, . . .provides textual and visual explanations about the impact of the earth's rotation in creating day and night. Basic earth science concepts are also introduced. The book has been purposefully created to be used as a resource after young person has begun to ask about the whys of the daily sunrise and sunsets. . . . The book gives a list of other activities to do to reinforce the concepts." (SB&F: Your Guide to Science Resources for All Ages)

REVIEW: *Booklist* v110 no4 p43 O 15 2013 Edie Ching

MORGAN, HIRAM.ed. Great Deeds in Ireland. See Great Deeds in Ireland

MORGAN, JUDE. The Secret Life of William Shakespeare; [by] Jude Morgan 448 p. 2014 St. Martin's Press
1. Biographical fiction 2. Dramatists—Fiction 3. Hathaway, Anne, 1556?-1623 4. London (England)—Fiction
ISBN 1250025036; 9781250025036 (hardback); 9781250054838 (trade paperback)
LC 2013-045690

SUMMARY: "There are so few established facts about how the son of a glove maker from Warwickshire became one of the greatest writers of all time that some people doubt he could really have written so many astonishing plays." This novel, by Jude Morgan, "pulls back the curtain to imagine what it might have really been like to be Shakespeare before a seemingly ordinary man became a legend." (Publisher's note)

REVIEW: *Booklist* v110 no13 p26 Mr 1 2014 Heather Paulson

REVIEW: *Kirkus Rev* v82 no4 p269 F 15 2014

"The Secret Life of William Shakespeare". "[Jude] Morgan writes page-turning historical fiction. . . . Morgan writes masterful characters-royals, patrons and players; Marlowe, reckless rake; Jonson, arrogant, envious, but great loyal friend; Anne, earthy, passionate, loyal, fractured after the death of their son, lost and found again after Will's dalliance with the troubled Huguenot widow Isabelle Berger; and most of all, Will himself, great, gentle genius behind a placid, circumspect exterior, implacable, unknowable, all effortless burning brilliance. In a layered narrative with a richness that rewards measured reading, Morgan re-creates Shakespeare's Elizabethan milieu, every place and person rendered with near-perfect realism. A tour de force."

REVIEW: *Libr J* v139 no4 p84 Mr 1 2014 David Keymer

MORGAN, KASS. The 100; [by] Kass Morgan 336 p. 2013 Little, Brown and Co.
1. Dystopias 2. Juvenile delinquents—Fiction 3. Romance language fiction 4. Science fiction 5. Survival—Fiction
ISBN 9780316234474 (hc)
LC 2013-016455

SUMMARY: Author Kass "Morgan's entry in the very popular dystopian, postapocalyptic YA subgenre blends science fiction, romance, and characters' shadow sides with a mostly engrossing plotline. In a future lived on spaceships, long after the earth's destruction, teenage delinquents are usually sentenced to die for their transgressions. Then 100 of them, who are deemed disposable guinea pigs, are instead sent to the ravaged earth in order to see if it is habitable for humans." (Booklist)

REVIEW: *Booklist* v110 no1 p111 S 1 2013 Julie Trevelyan

REVIEW: *Bull Cent Child Books* v67 no3 p171-2 N 2013 A. M.

"The 100." "This novel, conceived as a companion piece for a television show, reads like a pilot: all set-up and no resolution. Short chapters play out like single-event scenes, while a significant portion of the text is dedicated to backstory in the form of flashbacks. The post-apocalyptic survival narrative emerges as little more than a thin cover for the story's teen-drama heart, complete with love triangles, secret pregnancies, family dysfunction, and class-based rivalries. Still, the action here is absorbing, and the large cast provides readers with plenty of characters to love, despise, root for, and sigh over."

REVIEW: *Kirkus Rev* v81 no15 p132 Ag 1 2013

REVIEW: *Publ Wkly* v260 no31 p75 Ag 5 2013

REVIEW: *Voice of Youth Advocates* v36 no4 p85 O 2013 Bethany Martin

MORGAN, PETER. Ismail Kadare; the writer and the dictatorship, 1957-1990; [by] Peter Morgan xvi, 339 p. 2010 Legenda, Modern Humanities Research Association and Maney Pub.

1. Albanian literature—20th century—History and criticism 2. Literary critiques
ISBN 1906540519; 9781906540517
LC 2010-513895

SUMMARY: This book, by Peter Morgan, examines "the creative processes of the Albanian writer [Ismail Kadare] and the battle of wits between him and Enver Hoxha, the leader of Albania's Stalinist regime. . . . Morgan's focus is on the books that Kadare wrote during the time of the dictatorship, between 1957 and 1990, and deal, even if in oblique and allegorical terms, with the themes of power and oppression." (Times Literary Supplement)

REVIEW: *TLS* no5761 p23 Ag 30 2013 MORELLE SMITH

"Ismail Kadare: The Writer and the Dictatorship, 1957-1990." "Part history, part biography and part literary criticism, 'Ismail Kadare: The writer and the dictatorship, 1957-1990' is an enthralling book, taking us into the creative processes of the Albanian writer and the battle of wits between him and Enver Hoxha, the leader of Albania's Stalinist regime. . . . [Peter] Morgan . . . gives a profound and astute literary analysis. . . . Peter Morgan's book is immensely well researched with copious notes, which not only do justice to a great writer, but invite us to explore other Albanian writers whose work is becoming increasingly available in translation."

MORGANS, SARAH. Power. See Thorness, B.

MORIARTY, JACLYN. The cracks in the kingdom; [by] Jaclyn Moriarty 480 p. 2014 Arthur A. Levine Books, an imprint of Scholastic Inc.

1. Color—Fiction 2. Fantasy fiction 3. Interpersonal relations—Fiction 4. Magic—Fiction 5. Missing persons—Fiction
ISBN 0545397383; 9780545397384 (hardcover : alk. paper); 9780545397391 (pbk. : alk. paper)
LC 2013-022827

SUMMARY: In this book, by Jaclyn Moriarty, "Princess Ko's been bluffing about the mysterious absence of her father. . . . If she can't get him back in a matter of weeks, the consequence may be a devastating war. So under the guise of a publicity stunt she gathers a group of teens - each with a special ability - from across the kingdom to crack the unsolvable case of the missing royals of Cello." (Publisher's note)

REVIEW: *Booklist* v110 no9/10 p105 Ja 1 2014 Debbie Carton

REVIEW: *Bull Cent Child Books* v67 no6 p325-6 F 2014 Karen Coats

"The Cracks in the Kingdom." "While the first book focused more on developing the delightfully eccentric world of Cello, this book is more plot-driven, with the fascinating color storms only coming in at the most suspenseful times. Though this outing isn't quite as stylish as the first book, [Jaclyn] Moriarty still provides more frissons of delight than many other authors. . . . Alarming plot twists and welcome surprises greet readers at every turn, and enough ends are left dangling to engender anticipation for the next installment."

REVIEW: *Horn Book Magazine* v90 no2 p125-6 Mr/Ap 2014 JENNIFER M. BRABANDER

REVIEW: *Kirkus Rev* v82 no2 p133 Ja 15 2014

REVIEW: *SLJ* v60 no3 p161 Mr 2014 Elisabeth Gattullo Marrocolla

REVIEW: *Voice of Youth Advocates* v37 no1 p85-6 Ap 2014 Jan Chapman

MORIN, FRANÇOIS. A World Without Wall Street?; [by] François Morin 172 p. 2013 University of Chicago Press

1. Economics literature 2. Financial crises 3. Global Financial Crisis, 2008-2009 4. International finance 5. Securities industry
ISBN 0857420313; 9780857420312

SUMMARY: It was the author's attempt to demonstrate that "'the world is on the verge of a major economic catastrophe'. . . . The reason is that govemments have failed to address the root cause of he turmoil: the 'ultra-power of globalized finance'. [François] Morin . . . argues that, from the 1970s, financial liberalization has unleashed a cataclysmic chain of events." (Times Literary Supplement)

REVIEW: *TLS* no5761 p22 Ag 30 2013 HENRI ASTIER

"A World Without Wall Street?" "[François] Morin alternates between the tone of professor (he does a good job of explaining the securitization of debt into tradable assets and their toxic spread) and prophet of doom. . . . But even if you accept François Morin's prescriptions, the problem is putting them into practice, which by his own admission would take 'several decades'. 'A World Without Wall Street?' is pretty useless as a brief for policymakers. It seems more designed to indulge French distrust of 'les Anglo-Saxons' and free markets than to make a meaningful contribution to international debates about the crisis."

MORRILL, LAUREN. Being Sloane Jacobs; [by] Lauren Morrill 352 p. 2014 Delacorte Press

1. Camps—Fiction 2. Family problems—Fiction 3. Hockey—Fiction 4. Ice skating—Fiction 5. Interpersonal relations—Fiction 6. Young adult fiction
ISBN 9780375990243 (glb : alk. paper); 9780385741798 (hardcover : alk. paper)
LC 2012-046889

SUMMARY: This book follows two girls named Sloane Jacobs. "One is a pampered D.C. socialite who's faltering in the high-stakes world of ice skating; the other is a Philadelphia native whose hockey moves need sharpening and temper needs taming. When both Sloanes . . . accidentally meet in Canada after being shipped off to summer camps . . . they hatch a plan to switch places, thus relieving them from the pressures dogging them at home." (Publishers Weekly)

REVIEW: *Booklist* v110 no18 p69 My 15 2014 Katie Richert

REVIEW: *Booklist* v110 no9/10 p103-5 Ja 1 2014 Gail Bush

"Being Sloane Jacobs." "Rather than skating on the surface of a time-honored plot twist, [Lauren] Morrill portrays each Sloane with the grit to cross-train in a new skating sport, the perseverance to withstand the competitors' bullying and high jinks, the honesty to be true to new friends or at least struggle in the challenge, and the grace to respect each other's futures. As the Sloanes' . . . switcheroo unravels, they come together with friends and families for a sweet and satisfying resolution."

REVIEW: *Bull Cent Child Books* v67 no6 p326 F 2014

Amy Atkinson

"Being Sloane Jacobs." "Told in the voices of both Sloanes (which proves slightly confusing in shared scenes), this is a feel-good story with flashes of honesty: the two girls learn to respect each other (and each other's sport) without become besties, find themselves capable of surviving in unfamiliar territory without discovering latent genius, and ultimately make tentative peace with their families while knowing the road to healing will be long. [Lauren] Morrill understands and embraces the must-haves of satisfying teen fare; she breaks no new ground here with elements of uptown-meets-downtown and storied camp bullies, pranks, and romance, but she does strike a successful balance between the real and the rewarding."

REVIEW: *Kirkus Rev* v81 no22 p117 N 15 2013

REVIEW: *Publ Wkly* v261 no13 p62 Mr 31 2014

REVIEW: *SLJ* v60 no1 p102 Ja 2014 Liz Zylstra

REVIEW: *SLJ* v60 no4 p64 Ap 2014 Shanna Miles

REVIEW: *Voice of Youth Advocates* v36 no6 p63 F 2014 Dianna Geers

MORRIS, CHRISTOPHER.ed. Handbook of Energy, Volume I. See Handbook of Energy, Volume I

MORRIS, DESMOND. Monkey; [by] Desmond Morris 224 p. 2013 University of Chicago Press

1. Monkeys 2. Monkeys—Folklore 3. Monkeys as pets 4. Monkeys in art 5. Monkeys in literature 6. Natural history literature

ISBN 1780230966; 9781780230962

SUMMARY: This book by Desmond Morris "unpacks human attitudes toward" monkeys. "Morris reveals that our fascination with monkeys extends through many cultures and eras--ancient Egyptians revered baboons, monkey deities featured prominently in ancient Chinese and Japanese religions, and sacred status was given to the langur monkey by some groups in India. He also describes how our relationship with monkeys has changed since [Charles] Darwin, and even become more troubled." (Publisher's note)

REVIEW: *TLS* no5772 p26 N 15 2013 BARBARA J. KING

"Gorilla" and "Monkey." "Primates feature in two new volumes from Reaktion Books' Animal series. . . . Gorgeously illustrated, both books convey fascinating information about some of our closest relatives, but 'Gorilla' is by far the more successful endeavour. . . . The selection of two art experts . . . to write a book about apes does have its drawbacks. Short shrift is given to fieldwork on gorillas . . . By contrast, chapters that focus on the use of the gorilla in visual media convey stunningly how these apes have been persistently co-opted by those in power to vilify persons or social groups considered marginal or inferior. . . . The same is true for many monkeys, and a strength of Desmond Morris's 'Monkey' is his unsettling portrayal of how thoroughly our own primate species is willing to exploit its near relatives."

MORRIS, EDWARD. Public Sculpture of Cheshire and Merseyside (Excluding Liverpool); [by] Edward Morris 308 p. 2012 Univ of Chicago Pr

1. Art literature 2. Cheshire (England) 3. English sculpture 4. Merseyside (England) 5. Public sculpture

ISBN 1846314925; 9781846314926

SUMMARY: This book by Edward Morris and Emma Roberts, with photography by Reg Phillips, describes how "Cheshire and Merseyside are exceptionally rich in public sculpture. . . . The book has a catalogue section with a very detailed account of about 220 sculptures covering dating, commissioning, attribution, style, subject matter, cost, materials, dimensions, inscriptions, influence, condition, repairs, relocation, contemporary criticism and present reputation." (Publisher's note)

REVIEW: *Burlington Mag* v155 no1328 p782-3 N 2013 JOSEPH SHARPLES

"Public Sculpture of Cheshire and Merseyside (excluding Liverpool)." "The latest volume in the Public Sculpture of Britain series is complementary to the very first, which covered the city of Liverpool. Following the established gazetteer format of the series, it deals with the rest of Merseyside, from Birkenhead and the dormitory suburbs of the Wirral to old industrial towns such as Bootle and newer ones such as Runcom, plus the whole county of Cheshire. . . . This is a scholarly and highly informative guide to an area notably rich in public sculpture. Combining deep local knowledge with a broader critical perspective, the authors draw on a wealth of primary sources, from artists' papers to company records and the copious minutes of memorial committees."

MORRIS, IAN. War! What is it good for?; conflict and the progress of civilization from primates to robots; [by] Ian Morris 512 p. 2014 Farrar Straus & Giroux

1. Historical literature 2. Military history 3. War and civilization 4. War and society 5. Weapons—History

ISBN 0374286000; 9780374286002 (hardback)

LC 2013-038722

SUMMARY: This book, by Ian Morris, "tells the gruesome . . . story of fifteen thousand years of war, going beyond the battles and brutality to reveal what war has really done to and for the world. . . . War, and war alone, has created bigger, more complex societies, ruled by governments that have stamped out internal violence. Strangely enough, killing has made the world safer, and the safety it has produced has allowed people to make the world richer too." (Publisher's note)

REVIEW: *Booklist* v110 no13 p6 Mr 1 2014 Mark Levine

REVIEW: *Choice* v52 no1 p134 St 2014 K. A. Roider

REVIEW: *Kirkus Rev* v82 no4 p70 F 15 2014

"War! What Is It Good For? Conflict and the Progress of Civilization From Primates to Robots". " A profoundly uncomfortable but provocative argument that 'productive war' promotes greater safety, a decrease in violence and economic growth. . . . He recognizes—and alludes continually to—the unpleasantness of his position but charges ahead into the valley of death. . . . Drawing on the work of Jared Diamond and Steven Pinker and myriads of others, Morris relentlessly develops his thesis, which never decreases in discomfort, though it does become more convincing. . . . A disturbing, transformative text that veers toward essential reading."

REVIEW: *Libr J* v138 no18 p69 N 1 2013 Barbara Hoffert

REVIEW: *Publ Wkly* v261 no3 p43 Ja 20 2014

REVIEW: *TLS* no5817 p9-10 S 26 2014 VICTOR DAVIS HANSON

MORRIS, MITCHELL. The persistence of sentiment;

display and feeling in popular music of the 1970s; [by] Mitchell Morris ixv, 248 p. 2013 University of California Press

1. Music—History & criticism 2. Popular music—Philosophy & aesthetics 3. Popular music—United States 4. Popular music—United States—1971-1980—History and criticism 5. Popular music fans 6. Singers—United States

ISBN 9780520242852 (cloth : alk. paper); 9780520275997 (pbk. : alk. paper)

LC 2012-041528

SUMMARY: This book by Mitchell Morris "gives a critical account of a group of American popular music performers who have dedicated fan bases and considerable commercial success despite the critical disdain they have endured. . . . The complicated commercial world of pop music in the 1970s allowed the greater promulgation of musical styles and idioms that spoke to and for exactly those stigmatized audiences." (Publisher's note)

REVIEW: *Choice* v51 no2 p271-2 O 2013 M. Goldsmith

"The Persistence of Sentiment: Display and Feeling in Popular Music of the 1970s." "Musicologist [Mitchell] Morris . . . 'focuses on a group of songs in styles still significantly discounted by would-be tastemakers as they have been exalted by adoring audiences.' Recording artists and musicians considered by the author include, among others, Barry White, Barry Manilow, Karen Carpenter, Cher, and Dolly Parton. This book is an engaging exploration of dedicated music fan bases that emerged in the 1970s, unlikely commercial success, and even more unlikely revivals of the most kitsch-oriented and comical aspects of these songs. Morris includes song descriptions, musical examples, and accessible analyses of the music and song texts"

MORRIS, PATRICIA. Blue juice; euthanasia in veterinary medicine; [by] Patricia Morris 230 p. 2012 Temple University Press

1. Bonding, Human-Pet 2. Euthanasia, Animal 3. Pets—psychology 4. Professional-Patient Relations 5. Social science literature

ISBN 9781439907054 (cloth: alk. paper); 9781439907061 (paper: alk. paper); 9781439907078 (e-book)

LC 2011-047604

SUMMARY: This book "explores the emotional and ethical conflicts involved in providing a 'good death' for companion animals." Author "Patricia Morris presents . . . [an] ethnographic account of how veterinarians manage patient care and client relations when their responsibility shifts from saving an animal's life to negotiating a decision to end it." (Publisher's note)

REVIEW: *Contemp Sociol* v43 no2 p243-4 Mr 2014 Leslie Irvine

"Blue Juice: Euthanasia in Veterinary Medicine". "In 'Blue Juice,' part of the Animals, Culture, and Society series from Temple University Press, [Patricia] Morris skillfully analyzes these and other aspects of veterinary euthanasia. . . . The book enhances the research on dramaturgy and constitutes an important addition to the growing literature on human/animal relations. . . . Another of the book's strengths is its analysis of emotions. . . . In sum, Blue Juice is a thoroughly researched, clearly written, well-organized book. It offers a rich ethnographic analysis of euthanasia in veterinary medicine while reflecting on implications that extend far beyond that domain."

MORRIS, PETER.ed. Milestones of Science and Technology. See Milestones of Science and Technology

MORRIS, PETER W. G. Reconstructing project management; [by] Peter W. G. Morris xxi, 319 p. 2013 John Wiley & Sons Ltd

1. Business literature 2. Management 3. Management—Social aspects 4. Project management 5. Public administration

ISBN 9780470659076 (hardback : alk. paper)

LC 2012-037674

SUMMARY: This book on project management (PM) "begins with a presentation of the history of PM from a project, societal, and organizational perspective. The author explains the roots of formalizing or 'constructing' PM based on large US military projects. The second part of the book 'deconstructs' PM into its elements. . . . Part 3 'reconstructs' PM and offers a view of challenges and the future of PM. The final section summarizes the concepts presented." (Choice: Current Reviews for Academic Libraries)

REVIEW: *Choice* v51 no6 p1041 F 2014 M. Mehrubeoglu

"Reconstructing Project Management." "[Peter W.G.] Morris . . . shares a refreshing viewpoint on project management (PM). . . . Morris writes in down-to-earth, easily understandable language. Compared to Jack Meredith and Samuel Mantel's textbook 'Project Management: A Managerial Approach' . . . this book is more condensed, and the content is presented from a broader perspective. A strength of the book is the diverse list of PM examples in engineering and technology. The book falls short on equations and worked problems. Though not recommended as a textbook, it will be valuable as supporting material in upper-division and graduate curricula, particularly in engineering, and will be an easy but informative read for professionals interested in the history and basics of PM."

MORRIS, SEYMOUR. Supreme Commander; MacArthur's Triumph in Japan; [by] Seymour Morris 368 p. 2014 HarperCollins

1. Historical literature 2. Japan—History—Allied occupation, 1945-1952 3. Japan—Politics & government—1945- 4. World War, 1939-1945—Peace

ISBN 0062287931; 9780062287939

LC 2013-498721

SUMMARY: In this book, author Seymour Morris Jr. "combines political history, military biography, and business management to tell the story of General Douglas MacArthur's tremendous success in rebuilding Japan after World War II. . . . As the uniquely titled Supreme Commander for the Allied Powers, he was charged with transforming a defeated, militarist empire into a beacon of peace and democracy." (Publisher's note)

REVIEW: *Kirkus Rev* v82 no5 p131 Mr 1 2014

"Supreme Commander: MacArthur's Triumph in Japan". "An unabashedly admiring reappraisal of Douglas MacArthur (1880-1964) as supreme protector of a great fallen nation at the close of World War II. . . . The pursuit of the many lives of the five-star general continues in this enthusiastic breakdown of MacArthur's wildly successful five-year occupation of defeated Japan, a model to be followed and studied. . . . Most astonishing was how MacArthur's wily team managed to rewrite the Japanese Constitution-with codification of more sweeping rights for women than in any other country except Russia. A gung-ho, breezily entertaining study for lay readers."

REVIEW: *Libr J* v139 no5 p126 Mr 15 2014 Ed Goedeken

REVIEW: *N Y Times Book Rev* p27 Ap 27 2014 LYNNE OLSON

REVIEW: *Publ Wkly* v261 no6 p78 F 10 2014

MORRIS, TAYLOR. Naples! See De Laurentiis, G.

MORRIS, THERESA. Cut it out; the C-section epidemic in America; [by] Theresa Morris 256 p. 2013 New York University Press

1. Cesarean section 2. Cesarean section—Prevention 3. Childbirth—United States—Statistics 4. Medical literature 5. Surgical indications 6. Women—Health and hygiene
ISBN 0814764118; 9780814764114 (cl : alk. paper)
LC 2013-015226

SUMMARY: This book, by Theresa Morris, "examines the exponential increase in the United States of the most technological form of birth that exists: the cesarean section. While c-section births pose a higher risk of maternal death and medical complications, can have negative future reproductive consequences for the mother, increase the recovery time for mothers after birth, and cost almost twice as much as vaginal deliveries . . . [c-sections have increased] 50 percent over the past decade." (Publisher's note)

REVIEW: *Choice* v51 no9 p1630 My 2014 M. P. Tarbox

REVIEW: *N Y Times Book Rev* p26 F 2 2014 Theresa Morris

"Cut It Out: The C-Section Epidemic in America." "America's cesarean section rate was 33 percent in 2011. . . . [author Theresa] Morris . . . is determined to find out why, interviewing doctors, examining hospital protocols, and talking to women about their birth experiences. . . . Morris explains that the one surefire way for a doctor to show she has done all she can to deliver a live, healthy baby is to perform a C-section. . . . 'Cut It Out' occasionally reads too much like an academic paper. . . . But Morris's impressive research, as well as the solutions she offers to women, providers and policy planners, makes the book an important contribution to the C-section debate."

REVIEW: *Publ Wkly* v260 no30 p56 Jl 29 2013

MORRISON, CATHY.il. Nature recycles. See Lord, M.

MORRISON, SLADE. Please, Louise. See Morrison, T.

MORRISON, TONI, 1931-. Please, Louise; [by] Toni Morrison 32 p. 2013 Simon & Schuster Books for Young Readers

1. Books and reading—Fiction 2. Children's stories 3. Fear—Fiction 4. Libraries—Fiction 5. Stories in rhyme
ISBN 1416983384; 9781416983385 (hardcover: alk. paper); 9781442433106 (ebook: alk. paper)
LC 2012-026303

SUMMARY: This picture book, written by Toni Morrison and Slade Morrison and illustrated by Shadra Strickland, describes how 'on one gray afternoon, Louise makes a fateful trip to the library. With the help of a new library card and through the transformative power of books, what started out as a dull day turns into one of surprises, ideas, and fun, fun, fun!" (Publisher's note)

REVIEW: *Booklist* v110 no12 p83-4 F 15 2014 Edie Ching

REVIEW: *Kirkus Rev* v82 no4 p305 F 15 2014

"Please, Louise". "The Morrisons, mother and son, write in rhyming couplets with the message firmly hammered home: '[B]ooks can teach and please Louise.' Adult readers may find this disconcerting: A child alone on dark and scary streets finds comfort solely from books (even library staff are nowhere to be seen). Strickland's watercolor-and-gouache paintings are delicate, detailed and beautiful. Louise is a lovely child and a poster girl for reading. Still, that there appear to be no caring adults in her world is troubling. An ode to reading that raises too many concerns."

REVIEW: *Publ Wkly* v260 no51 p57 D 16 2013

REVIEW: *SLJ* v60 no3 p121 Mr 2014 Martha Link Yesowitch

MORRISON, TREVOR W.ed. The health care case. See The health care case

MORSE, RUTH.ed. Medieval Shakespeare. See Medieval Shakespeare

MORTIMER, CHARLIE. Dear Lupin. See Mortimer, R.

MORTIMER, ROGER. Dear Lupin; letters to a wayward son; [by] Roger Mortimer 192 p. 2013 Thomas Dunne Books

1. Fathers and sons 2. Great Britain—Social life & customs—20th century 3. Letters
ISBN 9781250038517 (hardcover : alk. paper)
LC 2013-017973

SUMMARY: "Nostalgic, witty, and original, 'Dear Lupin' by Roger Mortimer and Charlie Mortimer tracks the entire correspondence between a father and his only son. When the book begins, Charlie, the son, is studying at Eton, although the studying itself is not a priority, much to his father's chagrin. After Charlie graduates . . . Roger continues to write regularly, offering advice (which is rarely heeded) as well as humorous updates from home." (Publisher's note)

REVIEW: *Kirkus Rev* v81 no16 p79 Ag 15 2013

"Dear Lupin: Letters to a Wayward Son." "Epistolary commentary from a father to his son. Starting in 1967 and covering a span of more than 20 years, Mortimer reproduces the correspondence his father, Roger, sent to him throughout his life. These letters, along with brief explanations of the circumstances or context of each letter by the son, provide 'humorous insight into the life of a mildly dysfunctional English middle-class family in the 1960s, 1970s and 1980.' . . . Droll humor abounds. . . . Entertaining letters that reflect genuine concern and love despite the rarely taken advice."

REVIEW: *Publ Wkly* v260 no26 p75-6 Jl 1 2013

MORTIMER, SARAH.ed. The intellectual consequences

of religious heterodoxy 1600-1750. See The intellectual consequences of religious heterodoxy 1600-1750

MORTON, MICHAEL QUENTIN. Buraimi; The Struggle for Power, Influence and Oil in Arabia; [by] Michael Quentin Morton 304 p. 2013 Palgrave Macmillan

1. Great Britain—Foreign relations—Middle East—History 2. Historical literature 3. Oman—History—20th century 4. Saudi Arabia—History—1932- 5. Saudi Arabia—Military history—20th century 6. United Arab Emirates—History
ISBN 1848858183; 9781848858183

SUMMARY: "Buraimi is an oasis in an otherwise bleak desert on the border between Oman and the UAE. . . . In this lively account, Michael Quentin Morton tells the story of how the power of oil and the conflicting interests of the declining British Empire and the United States all came to a head with the conflict between Great Britain and Saudi Arabia, shaping the very future of the Gulf states." (Publisher's note)

REVIEW: *Middle East J* v68 no3 p490-4 Summ 2014

REVIEW: *TLS* no5792 p24 Ap 4 2014 ANDRÉ NAFFIS-SAHELY

"Buraimi: The Struggle for Power, Influence, and Oil in Arabia." "[Author Michael Quentin] Morton has produced an account of the Buraimi dispute, perhaps the choicest microcosm of how a sandy backwater emerged as a major world player. . . . As Morton tells it, the Buraimi affair encapsulates the metamorphosis of the Gulf from a 'British lake' into what it is today. . . . While Buraimi is studded with juicy anecdotes, Morton unfortunately glosses over a few complexities. . . . This is nonetheless a readable account of a turning point in recent Arabian history."

MORTON, TIMOTHY. Hyperobjects; philosophy and ecology after the end of the world; [by] Timothy Morton x, 229 p. 2013 University of Minnesota Press

1. Climatic changes 2. Future, The 3. Human ecology 4. Object (Philosophy) 5. Philosophical literature
ISBN 9780816689224 (hc : alk. paper); 9780816689231 (pb : alk. paper)
LC 2013-028374

SUMMARY: This book by Timothy Morton examines "'hyperobjects'--entities of such vast temporal and spatial dimensions that they defeat traditional ideas about what a thing is in the first place. In this book, Morton explains what hyperobjects are and their impact on how we think, how we coexist with one another and with nonhumans, and how we experience our politics, ethics, and art." (Publisher's note)

REVIEW: *Newsweek Global* v162 no1 p116-22 Ja 3 2014 Alexander Nazaryan

"Hyperobjects: Philosophy and Ecology After the End of the World." "A book of quasi- popular philosophy . . . about the very big things that have come to dominate human existence. . . . For a book concerned with hugeness, Hyperobjects is a pretty slight 200 pages. But density of ideas trumps word count. . . . Not only does Morton range from William Wordsworth . . . to Republican denialism, he does it in a way that marshals these disparate allusions in the service of a cogent idea, one that manages to come off as both intuitive and radical. . . . Hyperobjects is occasionally insane; far more frequently, though, it is brilliant. I can't pretend to have gotten the whole thing, and I suspect that few outside the university will. That shouldn't hinder the inquisitive, though."

MOSER, ELISE. Lily and Taylor; [by] Elise Moser 224 p. 2013 Pgw

1. Family violence—Fiction 2. Friendship—Fiction 3. Intimate partner violence 4. Kidnapping—Fiction 5. Sisters—Fiction
ISBN 1554983347; 9781554983346

SUMMARY: In this book, by Elise Moser, "after her older sister is murdered in a horrific incident of domestic abuse, Taylor begins a new life in a new town. She meets Lily, whose open, warm manner conceals a difficult personal life of her own. . . . But just when life seems to be smoothing out, Taylor's abusive boyfriend, Devon, arrives on the scene, and before they know it, the girls find themselves in a situation that is both scary, and incredibly dangerous." (Publisher's note)

REVIEW: *Booklist* v110 no5 p76 N 1 2013 Linda Perkins

REVIEW: *Horn Book Magazine* v90 no1 p97 Ja/F 2014 JESSICA TACKETT MACDONALD

"Lily and Taylor." "[Elise] Moser depicts violence in unnervingly poetic detail, but the moments when the girls rationalize abuse in their lives (Taylor says of Tannis, 'It seemed normal, like a kid getting spanked') are even more startling. The hostage situation is intense but never melodramatic; all attention is on Taylor as she realizes that taking action will help her escape her sister's fate, both in the cabin and for the rest of her life. Brutal and understated, Taylor's story is a powerful examination of the cycle of abuse."

REVIEW: *Kirkus Rev* v81 no15 p234 Ag 1 2013

REVIEW: *SLJ* v59 no9 p162 S 2013 Kimberly Castle-Alberts

REVIEW: *Voice of Youth Advocates* v36 no5 p63-4 D 2013 Jane Gov

MOSER, PAUL K. The severity of God; religion and philosophy reconceived; [by] Paul K. Moser xi, 218 p. 2013 Cambridge University Press

1. God (Christianity) 2. Philosophical theology 3. Philosophy and religion 4. RELIGION—Philosophy 5. Religious literature 6. Worship
ISBN 9781107023574 (hardback); 9781107615328 (paperback)
LC 2012-033990

SUMMARY: "This book explores the role of divine severity in the character and wisdom of God, and the flux and difficulties of human life in relation to divine salvation. . . . Paul K. Moser discusses the function of philosophy, evidence and miracles in approaching God. He argues that if God's aim is to extend without coercion His lasting life to humans, then commitment to that goal could manifest itself in making human life severe." (Publisher's note)

REVIEW: *Choice* v51 no4 p656-7 D 2013 F. G. Kirkpatrick

"The Severity of God: Religion and Philosophy Reconceived." "[Paul K.] Moser . . . whose philosophical credentials are impressive, invites readers into an extended (though often overly repetitive) reflection on how the trials and tribulations of the flux of everyday life are compatible with belief in a God whose love invites people into a cooperative venture that will lead to their ultimate fulfillment. . . . The author offers a particularly intriguing treatment of how divine grace is completely sufficient for human salvation, but also requires human freedom to respond it to by the active deed of trusting in it, without that deed becoming a 'work' meriting salvation."

MOSES, JONATHON W. Emigration and political development; [by] Jonathon W. Moses xvi, 295 p. 2011 Cambridge University Press

1. Emigration & immigration—Social aspects 2. Emigration and immigration—Political aspects 3. Norway—Politics & government 4. Political development 5. Social science literature

ISBN 9780521173216 (pbk.); 9780521195430 (hbk.)

LC 2011-012922

SUMMARY: "This book maps the nature of the relationship that links emigration and political development. Jonathon W. Moses explores the nature of political development, arguing that emigration influences political development. In particular, he introduces a new cross-national database of annual emigration rates and analyzes specific cases of international emigration (and out-migration within countries) under varying political and economic contexts." (Publisher's note)

REVIEW: *Choice* v49 no10 p1959 Je 2012 A. A. Caviedes

REVIEW: *Contemp Sociol* v43 no2 p245-7 Mr 2014 Natasha Iskander

"Emigration and Political Development". "Folded into Jonathon Moses' book . . . is an elegant discussion of emigration from Norway before World War I and its impact on that country's political trajectory. . . . Moses' discussion of emigration's influence on Norway's political development in the nineteenth century captures the book's greatest strengths.. . . Unfortunately, Moses' description of the political impact of Norwegian emigration, nuanced and rich as it is, nevertheless suffers from many of the same flaws that characterize, even define, the rest of the book. . . . The trouble with 'Emigration and Political Development' is that its flaws are not accidental. Rather, they are purposefully built into the research design on which the book is based."

MOSES, SHELIA P. The sittin' up; [by] Shelia P. Moses 240 p. 2014 G. P. Putnam's Sons, an imprint of Penguin Group (USA) Inc.

1. African Americans—Fiction 2. Community life—North Carolina—Fiction 3. Death—Fiction 4. Depressions—1929—Fiction 5. Historical fiction 6. Race relations—Fiction 7. Sharecroppers—Fiction

ISBN 9780399257230 (hardcover)

LC 2013-013838

SUMMARY: In this book, "when Mr. Bro. Wiley, Bean's adopted grandfather and the last slave man around, dies in the summer of 1940, Bean and his very best friend Pole are some kind of hurt. . . . Despite their grief, they are proud and excited to be included in their very first Sittin' Up--a wake for the dead. Bean and Pole know this special week will be one to remember, especially if the coming storm has its way and riles up Ole River enough to flood the Low Meadows." (Publisher's note)

REVIEW: *Booklist* v110 no7 p69 D 1 2013 Ann Kelley

REVIEW: *Booklist* v110 no16 p64 Ap 15 2014 Connie Rockman

REVIEW: *Bull Cent Child Books* v67 no5 p276 Ja 2014 K. C.

"The Sittin' Up." "The first half of the story becomes attenuated with its extended focus on spreading the news of Mr. Bro. Wiley's death and making preparations, but then the action picks up with a vengeance. . . . Nearly all of the expected Southern stereotypes are present and accounted for here. . . . Despite some mild humor in the character depictions, contemporary children will likely find Bean and Pole as bland and apple-cheeked as Dick and Jane in their unflagging desire to be obedient to the strict and arbitrary rules of their parents and to live up to the noble expectations set for them by their elders. The real value here is the evocation of the community and the carefully detailed description of funeral rites and customs from the time period."

REVIEW: *Horn Book Magazine* v90 no1 p98 Ja/F 2014 ROBIN L. SMITH

REVIEW: *Kirkus Rev* v81 no22 p122 N 15 2013

REVIEW: *Publ Wkly* v261 no17 p133 Ap 28 2014

REVIEW: *SLJ* v60 no1 p86 Ja 2014 Nancy P. Reeder

REVIEW: *SLJ* v60 no4 p61 Ap 2014 Mary Olounye

REVIEW: *Voice of Youth Advocates* v36 no6 p63 F 2014 Maria Unruh

MOSHER, STACY.tr. Tombstone. See Tombstone

MOSKOWITZ, DAVID. Wolves in the land of salmon; [by] David Moskowitz 334 p. 2013 Timber Press

1. Environmental literature 2. Environmental policy—Northwest, Pacific 3. Northwest, Pacific—Environmental conditions 4. Wolves—Northwest, Pacific 5. Wolves—Northwest, Pacific—Pictorial works

ISBN 1604692278; 9781604692273

LC 2012-025205

SUMMARY: Written by David Moskowitz, "This wide-ranging survey about wolves of the Pacific Northwest offers something for both the specialist and the curious layperson. . . . Residents of the Pacific Northwest will appreciate the specificity of this work, but any fans of wolves or wildlife biology will find this of interest." (Publishers Weekly)

REVIEW: *Choice* v51 no2 p295-6 O 2013 J. Organ

"Wolves in the Land of Salmon." "This well-researched volume discusses the natural history of wolves in the Pacific Northwest and the numerous associated sociopolitical issues. The book is very well written (except for occasional grammatical errors) in a popular style, with appropriate technical language. The photography is superb, and the maps are excellent. [Author David] Moskowitz . . . , an experienced wildlife tracker and international educator, is clearly an advocate for wolves, but he does make an attempt at illustrating views of wolf opponents."

REVIEW: *Libr J* v138 no6 p97 Ap 1 2013 Ryan Nayler

REVIEW: *Publ Wkly* v259 no43 p47-8 O 22 2012

MOSKOWITZ, HANNAH. Gone, gone, gone. See Gone, gone, gone

MOSLEY, WALTER. Devil in a blue dress; [by] Walter Mosley 219 1990 Norton

1. Detectives 2. Murder—Fiction 3. Mystery and detective stories—United States 4. Mystery fiction 5. Organized crime—Fiction

ISBN 0-393-02854-2
LC 89-2-5503

SUMMARY: In this novel "Ezekiel 'Easy' Rawlins, a young, tough black veteran living in 1948 Los Angeles, only wants respect and enough money to pay his mortgage. When fired from his factory job, however, he undertakes some paid errands for a shady white mobster. . . . As Easy plumbs his usual hangouts for clues, he relays information to the mobster, runs afoul of the police, meets the mysterious woman, discovers a murder, then investigates in self-defense." (Library Journal)

In this novel "Ezekiel 'Easy' Rawlins, a young, tough black veteran living in 1948 Los Angeles, only wants respect and enough money to pay his mortgage. When fired from his factory job, however, he undertakes some paid errands for a shady white mobster who wishes to locate a light-haired, blue-eyed beauty. As Easy plumbs his usual hangouts for clues, he relays information to the mobster, runs afoul of the police, meets the mysterious woman, discovers a murder, then investigates in self-defense." (Libr J)

REVIEW: *Hist Today* v64 no2 p61 F 2014 Jerome de Groot

"Devil in a Blue Dress," "The Shadow of Death," and "Carver's Quest." "'Devil in a Blue Dress' . . . took the hard-boiled detective novel and made it sing again. Mosley's prose is effortlessly taut and poised and he is an excellent exponent of a simple, brief, direct style that belies the sharp characterisation at the heart of his writing. . . . The series of Granchester Mysteries begin in the early 1950s with 'The Shadow of Death' . . . which takes in jazz, literariness, faith and beer, and runs gently through a neat and comfortable plot. Nick Rennison's hero is amateur archaeologist Adam Carver and his companion Quint. 'Carver's Quest' . . . takes the pair on a treasure hunt through London and Athens. The writer Rennison is echoing is mainly Arthur Conan Doyle."

MOSLEY, WALTER, 1952-. Debbie doesn't do it anymore; a novel; [by] Walter Mosley 272 p. 2014 Doubleday

1. African American actresses—Fiction 2. Pornographic film industry—Fiction 3. Psychological fiction 4. Sex workers 5. Widows—Fiction

ISBN 0385526180; 9780385526180 (alk. paper)
LC 2013-021700

SUMMARY: In this novel by Walter Mosley, "Debbie Dare, a black porn queen, has to come to terms with her sordid life in the adult entertainment industry after her tomcatting husband dies in a hot tub. . . . Burdened with massive debts that her husband incurred . . . , Debbie must reckon with a life spent in the peculiar subculture of the pornography industry. . . . She's done with porn, but her options for what might come next include the possibility of suicide." (Publisher's note)

REVIEW: *Booklist* v110 no11 p23 F 1 2014 David Pitt

"Debbie Doesn't Do It Anymore". "That's a lot of good material to work with, but, maybe just to give himself an extra challenge, [Walter] Mosley makes Sandra, better known as Debbie Dare, a porn star—and, yes, there is some graphic language and imagery in the book because Mosley's not the kind of writer who hides the truth behind a sanitized curtain. If this novel were a movie, and we were living in the early 1970s, Sandra would be played by Pam Grier:a beautiful, tough, smart woman who won't take crap from anybody This could be the best thing Mosley has written in years, a deeply affecting story of a woman whose determination to pull herself out of one life and into another is tested almost to its limits by things she can't control—until she finds a way to control them."

REVIEW: *Kirkus Rev* v82 no4 p275 F 15 2014

"Debbie Doesn't Do It Anymore" by Walter Mosley. "Prolific novelist [Walter] Mosley . . . fielded his fair share of criticism for his X-rated one-two punch of 'Killing Johnny Fry' (2006) and 'Diablerie' (2007), and readers attracted to the equally explicit nature of this novel might be expecting more of the same. In truth, readers are likely to be more surprised by the depth of protagonist Sandra Peel, whom the author treats with tremendous compassion. . . . Mosley's characteristically well-crafted cast also includes a kind police detective, a nonjudgmental shrink and a shy young architect with a crush on the non-glammed-out Sandra. A well-told redemption song about the most unlikely of heroines."

REVIEW: *Libr J* v139 no5 p114 Mr 15 2014 Ashanti White

REVIEW: *Publ Wkly* v261 no11 p59 Mr 17 2014

MOSS, CANDIDA R. The myth of persecution; how early Christians invented a Story of Martyrdom; [by] Candida R. Moss 320 p. 2013 HarperOne

1. Christianity—Relations 2. Church history 3. Martyrdom—Christianity 4. Persecution 5. RELIGION—General

ISBN 9780062104526 (hardback)
LC 2012-028405

SUMMARY: "In 'The Myth of Persecution,' Candida Moss, a leading expert on early Christianity, reveals how the early church exaggerated, invented, and forged stories of Christian martyrs and how the dangerous legacy of a martyrdom complex is employed today to silence dissent and galvanize a new generation of culture warriors." (Publisher's note)

REVIEW: *America* v208 no7 p34-5 Mr 4 2013 MARY ANN DONOVAN

REVIEW: *Booklist* v109 no11 p6 F 1 2013 Ray Olson

REVIEW: *Christ Century* v130 no9 p39-41 My 1 2013 Greg Carey

REVIEW: *Christ Today* v57 no6 p80 Jl/Ag 2013 DAVID NEFF

REVIEW: *Commonweal* v140 no13 p28-30 Ag 16 2013 Luke Timothy Johnson

"The Myth of Persecution: How Early Christians Invented a Story of Martyrdom." "Historians of Christianity routinely speak of the period from the first century to the time of Constantine as 'the age of martyrdom' or 'the age of persecution.' . . . Candida Moss, however, discerns in such formulations an insidious and pernicious myth of martyrdom, 'based in a series of inaccurate beliefs about Christian history,' which erroneously posits a Roman Empire constantly in pursuit of believers. . . . 'The Myth of Persecution' places Moss squarely in the ranks of historian-physicians who seek to heal what they perceive to be the ills of present-day Christianity through the therapy of revisionist history."

REVIEW: *Publ Wkly* v260 no2 p55 Ja 14 2013

REVIEW: *TLS* no5780 p24 Ja 10 2014 KATE COOPER

MOSS, JESSICA. Aristotle on the apparent good; perception, phantasia, thought, and desire; [by] Jessica Moss xv, 254 p. 2012 Oxford University Press

1. Aristotle, 384-322 B.C. 2. Good & evil 3. Moral motivation 4. Perception 5. Philosophical literature

ISBN 9780199656349
LC 2012-460030

SUMMARY: In this book, author "Jessica Moss argues that the notion of the apparent good is crucial to understanding both Aristotle's psychological theory and his ethics, and the relation between them. Beginning from the parallels Aristotle draws between appearances of things as good and ordinary perceptual appearances such as those involved in optical illusion, Moss argues that on Aristotle's view things appear good to us, just as things appear round or small." (Publisher's note)

REVIEW: *TLS* no5750 p32 Je 14 2013 STEPHEN MAKIN

"Aristotle on the Apparent Good: Perception, Phantasia, Thought and Desire." "In her excellent book, Jessica Moss focuses on one theme in Aristotle's reflections on the role of desire in motivation: that the object of an animal desire is 'the good or the apparent good,' as Aristotle puts it. What does this mean? And in particular, what is it for something to be an 'apparent good'? . . . This general approach promises a plausible way to understand talk of an animal 'perceiving the good,' and Moss develops the core thought wonderfully. She is very sensitive to the complexity of the issues, and both expert and sensible on the long-discussed obscurities of Aristotle's texts."

MOSS, MARISSA.il. Samantha Sutton and the winter of the warrior queen. See Jacobs, J.

MOSS, MICHAEL. Salt, sugar, fat; how the food giants hooked us; [by] Michael Moss 480 p. 2013 Random House Inc

1. Food habits—Economic aspects—United States 2. Food industry and trade—United States 3. Nutrition—Economic aspects—United States
ISBN 1400069807 (hardcover); 9780679604778 (ebook); 9781400069804 (hardcover)
LC 2012-033034

SUMMARY: Pulitzer prize winner Michael Moss offers an exposé of the U.S. food industry. He "explains the two-faced science of salt, sugar, and fat, which impart tantalizing tastes and luscious mouth-feel that light up the same neural circuits that narcotics do . . . while causing epidemic obesity, cardiovascular disease, and diabetes. But he also crafts an . . . insiders' view of the food industry, where these ingredients are the main weapons in a brutally competitive war for stomach-share." (Publishers Weekly)

REVIEW: *Choice* v50 no12 p2266 Ag 2013 J. M. Deutsch

REVIEW: *Kirkus Rev* v81 no3 p89 F 1 2013

REVIEW: *Libr J* v138 no10 p69 Je 1 2013 Donna Bachowski

REVIEW: *Libr J* v137 no17 p58 O 15 2012 Barbara Hoffert

REVIEW: *Libr J* v138 no7 p103 Ap 15 2013 Melissa Stoeger

REVIEW: *N Y Times Book Rev* p11 Mr 17 2013 DAVID KAMP

REVIEW: *N Y Times Book Rev* p22 Mr 24 2013

REVIEW: *New York Times* v162 no56079 pC4 Mr 18 2013 SCOTT MOWBRAY

REVIEW: *Publ Wkly* v260 no1 p52 Ja 7 2013

REVIEW: *TLS* no5759 p9-10 Ag 16 2013 BARBARA J. KING

"Fat Chance: The Bitter Truth About Sugar," "Salt Sugar Fat: How the Food Giants Hooked Us," and "The Metamorphoses of Fat: A History of Obesity." "These books raise powerful questions about why we become obese, what we can do about it, and how our understanding of obesity and its causes is affected by the time and place in which we live. [Robert] Lustig's approach is the most controversial. Crammed full of hard-hitting insights that may shock the reader into immediate dietary change (it did me), 'Fat Chance' makes sweeping generalizations which invite scepticism. . . . Lustig takes his championing of the power of biochemistry too far. . . . Michael Moss . . . is an ideal guide: sharp-witted but genial. . . . [Georges] Vigarello masterfully traces . . . the stigmatization of the fat person over time."

MOSSAKOWSKI, STANISLAW. King Sigismund chapel at Cracow cathedral (1515-1533); [by] Stanislaw Mossakowski 376 p. 2012 IRSA Publishing House

1. Architecture, Renaissance—Poland—Kraków 2. Art literature 3. Church decoration and ornament—Poland—Kraków
ISBN 8389831147; 9788389831149
LC 2012-514372

SUMMARY: This book by Stanislaw Mossakowski looks at the King Sigismund Chapel at Cracow Cathedral in Poland. Particular focus is given to "the precise Italian sources" for the building. "There are sections on the Hungarian marble effigies and the Polish saints who flank them; on the ideological programme; on the Virgin Mary (to whom the chapel is dedicated, and for whom Sigismund had a passionate devotion); on classical triumphalism and Neo-platonic mathematics." (Burlington Magazine)

REVIEW: *Burlington Mag* v156 no1332 p172 Mr 2014 PAUL CROSSLEY

"King Sigismund Chapel at Cracow Cathedral (1515-1533)". "This book, a slightly reduced version of its earlier Polish edition, and adapted for foreign readership, is an invaluable work of synthesis and, to date, by far the most impressive monograph on the chapel. In some sense it represents, for the author, almost a lifetime of research on the chapel (his first publication on it appeared in 1973). It answers a host of questions posed by the present building. . . . [Stanislaw] Mossakowski wears his learning lightly, transporting us into the conduct of a whole milieu, one which stretched from central Italy to the eastern borders of Christendom. The clarity of the author's exposition owes much to the book's high production values."

MOSSE, KATE, 1961-. Citadel; a novel; [by] Kate Mosse 704 p. 2014 HarperCollins

1. Anti-Nazi movement 2. Historical fiction 3. Magic realism (Literature) 4. Women guerrillas—France—Fiction 5. World War, 1939-1945—Fiction 6. World War, 1939-1945—Underground movements—France—Fiction 7. World War, 1939-1945—Women 8. World War, 1939-1945—Women—France—Fiction
ISBN 0062281259; 9780062281258 (hardback); 9780062281272 (paperback)
LC 2013-043887

SUMMARY: This book is the third in Kate Mosse's Carcassonne trilogy. She "brings the action of the novels up to the near present by setting her story of martyrdom and sacrifice during the Second World War. [The book] focuses on a group of women resisting the increasing Nazi presence in the city through the 1940s, concluding in horror and the possible end of history." (History Today)

REVIEW: *Kirkus Rev* v82 no2 p252 Ja 15 2014

"Citadel". " Yes, it's improbable in the extreme that a medieval codex should figure high on the list of priorities of both the Gestapo and the French Resistance, but, well, the Nazis were an improbable bunch, and they actually had a noted medievalist on their payroll against the odds of turning up the Holy Grail or other mysteries of the ages. Improbability doesn't get in the way of [Kate] Mosse's . . . yarn, which, though very long, is full of rousing action and intelligent character development alike. . . . The bad guys are bad, a local collaborationist particularly so; the ghouls are ghastly; the Nazis, determinedly Teutonic; and the filles de France, fetching. Suspend disbelief and enjoy the time travel and genre-blending."

REVIEW: *N Y Times Book Rev* p30 Ag 10 2014 Barbara Fisher

MOULY, FRANÇOISE.ed. Folklore & fairy tale funnies. See Folklore & fairy tale funnies

MOUNTFORD, PETER. The dismal science; a novel; [by] Peter Mountford 230 p. 2014 Tin House Books

1. Economists—Fiction 2. FICTION—Literary 3. Identity (Psychology)—Fiction 4. Loss (Psychology)—Fiction 5. Middle-aged men—Fiction 6. Widowers—Fiction

ISBN 1935639722; 9781935639725 (pbk.)

LC 2013-026627

SUMMARY: This novel, by Peter Mountford, "tells of a middle-aged vice president at the World Bank, Vincenzo D'Orsi, who publicly quits his job over a seemingly minor argument. . . . A scandal inevitably ensues, and he systematically burns every bridge to his former life. After abandoning his career, Vincenzo, a recent widower, is at a complete loss as to what to do with himself. The story follows his efforts to rebuild his identity without a vocation or the company of his wife." (Publisher's note)

REVIEW: *Booklist* v110 no11 p20-2 F 1 2014 Carol Haggas

"The Dismal Science." "Senior World Bank economist Vincenzo D'Orsi reaches a tipping point of epic proportions when a seemingly innocuous conversation with his executive director escalates into the kind of argument in which idle threats are issued and then must be acted upon. . . . Without a family, home, or career, D'Orsi is free to discover who he is and how he got there, though the answers are not always pleasing. [Peter] Mountford's wry look at middle-aged identity and transition is a sardonic yet sobering portrait of what happens when a man living life too narrowly becomes confounded when confronted with too many choices."

REVIEW: *Kirkus Rev* v81 no21 p107 N 1 2013

REVIEW: *N Y Times Book Rev* p18 Ap 13 2014 MARTHA McPHEE

REVIEW: *Publ Wkly* v260 no37 p27 S 16 2013

MOURITSEN, JONAS DROTNER.il. Seaweeds. See Mouritsen, O G

MOURITSEN, OLE G. Seaweeds; edible, available, and sustainable; 304 p. 2013 University of Chicago Press

1. Agricultural literature 2. Marine algae 3. Marine algae as food 4. Marine algae culture 5. Sustainable aquaculture

ISBN 9780226044361 (cloth : alkaline paper)

LC 2012-040240

SUMMARY: In this book, "celebrated scientist Ole G. Mouritsen, drawing on his fascination with and enthusiasm for Japanese cuisine, champions seaweed as a staple food while simultaneously explaining its biology, ecology, cultural history, and gastronomy. . . . Approaching the subject from not only a gastronomic but also a scientific point of view, Mouritsen sets out to examine the past and present uses of this sustainable resource, keeping in mind . . . the future." (Publisher's note)

REVIEW: *Choice* v51 no5 p865 Ja 2014 C. W. Schneider

REVIEW: *Libr J* v138 no3 p117 F 15 2013 Judith B. Barnett

REVIEW: *TLS* no5776 p22 D 13 2013 RICHARD SHELTON

"Seaweeds: Edible, Available, and Sustainable." "[Ole G.] Mouritsen's account of the place of seaweeds in the natural world as a diverse, highly specialized group of multi-cellular algae is brief but accurate--yet we have to wait until the final chapter before we get to what is known of the long evolutionary history and representative life cycles of the main groups of macroalgae. However, 'Seaweeds' is not primarily a botanical text. . . . Ole G. Mouritsen argues convincingly that there is abundant objective evidence in favour of making greater and more informed use of the world's coastal algae. 'Seaweeds' is an excellent book, deserving the serious attention of marine resource managers--and, certainly also, that of the more adventurous seaside cook."

MOZZI, GIULIO. This is the garden; 130 p. 2014 Open Letter Press

1. Angels—Fiction 2. Apprentices 3. Recluses—Fiction 4. Short story (Literary form) 5. Thieves—Fiction

ISBN 1934824755 (pbk.: alk. paper); 9781934824757 (pbk.: alk. paper)

LC 2013-022493

SUMMARY: This short story collection, by Giulio Mozzi, translated by Elizabeth Harris, features eight stories. "The first . . . is a love letter . . . from a professional purse-snatcher to a woman who was a victim of his predations. . . . The next story is . . . about an apprentice in a shop who tries to work his way up from messenger boy to skilled laborer. [Another] . . . concerns a woman who comes across an angel . . . [who] inadvertently . . . helps her overcome her aversion to sexuality." (Kirkus Reviews)

REVIEW: *Kirkus Rev* v81 no24 p322 D 15 2013

"This Is the Garden". " Eight elegantly translated short stories—cryptic, wry and witty. [Giulio] Mozzi tends to focus on the outré and is masterful at creating individuals in isolation. . . . 'Tana,' one of Mozzi's most cryptic stories, concerns a woman who comes across an angel, complete with wings, and this angel inadvertently (and ironically) helps her overcome her aversion to sexuality. Although Mozzi's style is crisp and straightforward, the stories themselves are beautifully nuanced and elliptical."

MUASHER, MARWAN. The second Arab awakening; and the battle for pluralism; [by] Marwan Muasher xv, 210 p. 2014 Yale University Press

1. Arab Spring, 2010- 2. Arab countries—Foreign relations 3. Arab countries—History—Arab Spring Uprisings, 2011- 4. Cultural pluralism 5. Pluralism—Arab countries 6. Political science literature 7. Religious diversity 8. Revolutions—Arab countries—History—21st century 9. Toleration

ISBN 9780300186390 (hardback)

LC 2013-029236

SUMMARY: In this book, "Marwan Muasher, former foreign minister of Jordan, asserts that all sides—the United States, Europe, Israel, and Arab governments alike—were deeply misguided in their thinking about Arab politics and society when the turmoil of the Arab Spring erupted. . . . Hope rests with the new generation and its commitment to tolerance, diversity, the peaceful rotation of power, and inclusive economic growth, Muasher maintains." (Publisher's note)

REVIEW: *Middle East J* v68 no3 p465-8 Summ 2014 I. William Zartman

"The Arab Awakening: America and the Transformation of the Middle East," "Revolution, Revolt, and Reform in North Africa: The Arab Spring and Beyond," and "The Second Arab Awakening: And the Battle for Pluralism." "'America and the Transformation of the Middle East' . . . deals with a number of forces and a number of countries. . . . Each chapter concludes with implications for the US, which is the ultimate message of the work. . . . Ricardo René Larémont . . . also offers a background setting. . . . Larémont himself provides on excellent chapter on demographics and economics. . . . The work by Marwan Muasher . . . has a more forward look."

REVIEW: *N Y Rev Books* v61 no12 p72-5 Jl 10 2014 Malise Ruthven

MUEHLBERGER, JAMES P. The Lost Cause; The Trials of Frank and Jesse James; [by] James P. Muehlberger 256 p. 2013 Westholme Pub Llc

1. Confederate States of America—History 2. Historical literature 3. James, Frank, 1844-1915 4. James, Jesse, 1847-1882 5. Outlaws—West (U.S.)—Biography

ISBN 1594161739; 9781594161735

SUMMARY: This book looks at "the murder that landed Frank and Jesse James in the headlines. . . . In December 1869, the bandit brothers walked into a bank and shot the cashier at point-blank range. Initially considered the big bang that kicked off the Jameses' spree of bank and train robberies, the murder was instead, according to [James P.] Muehlberger, a premeditated and misdirected act of retribution in response to the killing of the brothers' Confederate guerilla leader." (Publishers Weekly)

REVIEW: *Booklist* v109 no18 p8 My 15 2013 Jay Freeman

REVIEW: *Kirkus Rev* v81 no9 p61 My 1 2013

REVIEW: *Libr J* v138 no9 p90 My 15 2013 Amelia Osterud

REVIEW: *N Y Times Book Rev* p22 S 22 2013 GREG TOBIN

"The Lost Cause: The Trials of Frank and Jesse James" and "Shot All to Hell: Jesse James, the Northfield Raid, and the Wild West's Greatest Escape." "Two narratives of parallel interest and construction . . . recount the oft-told tale of the brothers and their gang. . . . Both books read like extended episodes of 'Law & Order,' set in the midwest, in the years immediately after the Civil War. Both provide detailed accountings of Jesse's and his fellows' movements. And both are equal parts violent melodrama and meticulous procedural, wrapped in vivid packages with enough bloody action to engage readers enthralled by tales of good versus evil."

REVIEW: *Publ Wkly* v260 no14 p54 Ap 8 2013

MUIR, RORY. Wellington; [by] Rory Muir 744 p. 2013 Yale University Press

1. Generals—Great Britain—Biography 2. Historical literature 3. Prime ministers—Great Britain—Biography

ISBN 9780300186659 (v. 1 : alk. paper); 9780300187861 (v. 2 : alk. paper)

LC 2013-018606

SUMMARY: "Rory Muir's . . . biography, the first of a two-volume set, is the fruit of a lifetime's research and discovery into Wellington and his times. The author brings Wellington into much sharper focus than ever before, addressing his masterstrokes and mistakes in equal measure. Muir looks at all aspects of Wellington's career. . . . The volume also revises Wellington's reputation for being cold and aloof, showing instead a man of far more complex and interesting character." (Publisher's note)

REVIEW: *Choice* v51 no10 p1878 Je 2014 J. R. Breihan

REVIEW: *Kirkus Rev* v81 no21 p254 N 1 2013

REVIEW: *New Statesman* v143 no3 p44-5 Ja 24 2014 Simon Heffer

REVIEW: *TLS* no5786 p8-9 F 21 2014 CHRIS WOOLGAR

"Wellington: The Path to Victory 1769-1814" and "Britain Against Napoleon: The Organization of Victory 1793-1815." "The first major Life of Wellington since Elizabeth Longford's work of 1969-72, Rory Muir's biography is matched by an extensive commentary online (at www.lifeofwellington.co.uk). . . . Together these books give us an exceptional insight into the struggle, the changes that were necessary to sustain British forces, and the impact made by determined and ambitious individuals. . . . Muir is perceptive on the formation of the Duke's character. . . . [Author Roger] Knight makes a convincing case that this was a remarkable combined effort."

MULDER, MICHELLE, 1976-. Brilliant!; earth-friendly energy for a healthier planet; [by] Michelle Mulder 48 p. 2013 Orca Book Publishers

1. Children's nonfiction 2. Energy development 3. Fossil fuels 4. Renewable energy sources 5. Sustainable development

ISBN 1459802217; 9781459802216 (pbk.); 9781459802223 (electronic edition; 9781459805200 (electronic edition

LC 2013-935381

SUMMARY: This book on sustainable energy "begins with a very basic explanation of how energy is created and transmitted, beginning with the moment a light switch is flicked. Our current dependence on fossil fuels is discussed, and the disadvantages of their use are laid out as the impetus for exploring alternative sources of energy. Environmental problems are treated as exciting opportunities for ingenuity, rather than a scary future menace." (Booklist)

REVIEW: *Booklist* v110 no2 p61-3 S 15 2013 Erin Anderson

"Brilliant! Shining a Light on Sustainable Energy." "[Michelle] Mulder begins with a very basic explanation of how energy is created and transmitted, beginning with the moment a light switch is flicked. . . . Environmental problems are treated as exciting opportunities for ingenuity, rather than a scary future menace. Geothermal heat, wind, hydroelectric power, and the sun are all discussed as potential alternate sources of energy, but biofuel is given the most attention. More cutting-edge approaches, such as burning human waste or creating energy through play, encourage kids to look for solutions in unexpected places."

REVIEW: *Kirkus Rev* v81 no15 p295 Ag 1 2013

REVIEW: *Quill Quire* v79 no10 p38 D 2013 Nikki Luscomhe

MULDER, MICHELLE, 1976-. Every last drop; bringing clean water home; [by] Michelle Mulder 48 p. 2014 Orca Book Pub

1. Environmental literature 2. Water—Purification 3. Water conservation 4. Water pollution 5. Water supply
ISBN 9781459802247 (electronic edition); 9781459807129 (electronic edition); 1459802233; 9781459802230 (hardcover)
LC 2013-951377

SUMMARY: This book, by Michelle Mulder, "looks at why the world's water resources are at risk and how communities around the world are finding innovative ways to quench their thirst and water their crops. Maybe you're not ready to drink fog, as they do in Chile, or use water made from treated sewage, but you can get a low-flush toilet, plant a tree, protect a wetland or just take shorter showers." (Publisher's note)

REVIEW: *Booklist* v110 no12 p77 F 15 2014 Angela Leeper

REVIEW: *Kirkus Rev* v82 no3 p242 F 1 2014

"Every Last Drop: Bringing Clean Water Home". "[Michelle] Mulder's book will make readers stop and calculate. . . . This account is particularly handy, as it goes back to the beginning, to the water cycle and the humans harvesting water: how it has been collected and distributed throughout history. . . . Lavishly illustrated with everything from woodcuts to photographs, the book is far from downbeat and scolding. . . . . Mulder writes with a clean, no-nonsense style that demonstrates that people have finally come around to realizing that only 1 percent of the water on Earth is potable and we must be careful of this resource. Informative, attractive and alarming—readers will think twice before leaving the water running as they brush their teeth."

REVIEW: *Publ Wkly* v261 no5 p55 F 3 2014

REVIEW: *SLJ* v60 no4 p190 Ap 2014 Alyson Low

MULL, BRANDON. Sky Raiders; [by] Brandon Mull 432 p. 2014 Aladdin

1. Adventure and adventurers—Fiction 2. Fantasy 3. Friendship—Fiction 4. Halloween 5. Magic—Fiction
ISBN 1442497009; 9781442497009 (hardback)
LC 2013-032734

SUMMARY: This children's novel, by Brandon Mull, is the first book in the "Five Kingdoms" series, "Cole Randolph was just trying to have a fun time with his friends on Halloween (and maybe get to know Jenna Hunt a little better). But when a spooky haunted house turns out to be a portal to something much creepier, Cole finds himself on an adventure on a whole different level." (Publisher's note)

REVIEW: *Booklist* v110 no9/10 p114 Ja 1 2014 Stacey Comfort

REVIEW: *Bull Cent Child Books* v67 no9 p471 My 2014 A. S.

"Sky Raiders". "There's a significant amount of plot to absorb in this action-packed novel, but the gripping narrative is well worth the effort. Cole is amiable and determined, and the kids with whom he allies himself, all natives of the Outskirts, are carefully developed and intriguing, offering further glimpses into the politics, cultural expectations, and social dynamics of this complex other world. Readers will be eagerly anticipating the next installment, and while they wait they'll have much to imagine about the fate of the Outskirts and how good might possibly triumph over the well-established evil that currently reigns."

REVIEW: *Kirkus Rev* v81 no24 p295 D 15 2013

REVIEW: *Publ Wkly* v261 no21 p56 My 26 2014

REVIEW: *Publ Wkly* v260 no52 p52 D 23 2013

REVIEW: *SLJ* v60 no6 p64 Je 2014 Kira Moody

REVIEW: *SLJ* v60 no3 p146 Mr 2014 April Sanders

MULLAINATHAN, SENDHIL. Scarcity. See Shafir, E.

MULLENBACH, CHERYL. Double victory; how African American women broke race and gender barriers to help win World War II; [by] Cheryl Mullenbach 272 p. 2012 Chicago Review Press

1. African American women—Civil rights—History—20th century 2. African American women—Employment—History—20th century 3. African American women—History—20th century 4. African Americans—Civil rights 5. African Americans—Employment 6. Historical literature 7. World War, 1939-1945—African Americans 8. World War, 1939-1945—Women—United States
ISBN 1569768080; 9781569768082 (hardcover)
LC 2012-021343

SUMMARY: This book, by Cheryl Mullenbach, is part of the "Women of Action" series. "African American women . . . did extraordinary things to help their country during World War II. In these pages young readers meet a range of remarkable women: war workers, political activists, military women, volunteers, and entertainers. . . . But many others fought discrimination at home and abroad in order to contribute to the war effort." (Publisher's note)

REVIEW: *Booklist* v110 no14 p20 Mr 15 2014

"Brave Girl: Clara and the Shirtwaist Makers' Strike of 1909," "Double Victory: How African American Women Broke Race and Gender Barriers to Help Win World War II," and "I Am Malala: The Girl Who Stood Up for Education and Was Shot by the Taliban." "Clara Lemlich bravely protested unfair working conditions in New York and in 1909 led the largest walkout by women workers in U.S. history. . . . Many African American women overcame legal and social barriers to serve their country during WWII and helped lay the foundation for the civil rights movement. . . . Recovered from her attack, Malala Yousafzai has come back stronger than ever, engaging in consciousness-raising and serving as an inspiration to girls and women all over the world."

REVIEW: *Kirkus Rev* v80 no23 p96 D 1 2012

REVIEW: *SLJ* v59 no1 p134 Ja 2013 Ann Welton

REVIEW: *Voice of Youth Advocates* v36 no1 p688 Ap 2013 Lindsay Grattan

MULLER, CHANDRA. Coming of political age; American schools and the civic development of immigrant youth; [by] Chandra Muller 186 p. 2013 Russell Sage Foundation

1. Children of immigrants—Education—United States 2. Children of immigrants—Political activity—United States 3. Community development—United States 4. Social science literature 5. Social sciences—Study & teaching

ISBN 9780871545787 (pb : alk. paper)

LC 2012-046069

SUMMARY: In this book, the authors "examine the relationship between social science instruction and political participation relative to the immigrant youth population and children of native-born parents in the US. The authors hypothesize that high schools significantly influence the political activity of immigrant youth as they navigate dual cultures." (Publisher's note)

REVIEW: *Choice* v51 no7 p1313 Mr 2014 A. A. Sisneros

"Coming of Political Age: American Schools and the Civic Development of Immigrant Youth." "The book employs data from the Educational Longitudinal Study of 2002, the Adolescent Health Academic Achievement Study, and the National Longitudinal Study of Adolescent Health, and requires an especially focused reading given the quantitative and qualitative presentation. Findings support the concern of curtailing social science programming relative to its impact in maintaining civil engagement and political representation. . . . Recommended."

MULLER, MARCIA. The Spook Lights Affair; A Carpenter and Quincannon Mystery; [by] Marcia Muller 256 p. 2013 Forge Books

1. Detective & mystery stories 2. FICTION—Mystery & Detective—Historical 3. Private investigators—California—San Francisco—Fiction 4. Women detectives—California—San Francisco—Fiction

ISBN 9780765331755 (hardcover)

LC 2013-024045

SUMMARY: In this mystery novel, "the wealthy parents of 18-year-old Virginia St. Ives, fearing she'll fall prey to an unsuitable fortune-hunter, have hired Sabina to keep an eye on their daughter. When Virginia gives her the slip at a debutante ball, Sabina tracks the heiress through the fog, only to see her leap from an overlook to certain death hundreds of feet below. Oddly, searches of the area where she was seen to fall fail to turn up a corpse." (Publishers Weekly)

REVIEW: *Booklist* v110 no5 p33 N 1 2013 Barbara Bibel

REVIEW: *Kirkus Rev* v81 no24 p33 D 15 2013

"The Spook Lights Affair". "The year 1895 finds the partners of Carpenter and Quincannon, Professional Detective Services . . . working another pair of cases that turn out to be closely connected. . . . . Meanwhile, a sharp-eyed lunatic calling himself Sherlock Holmes continues to bedevil the sleuthing couple. The big mystery is transparent in its outline, and the details aren't interesting enough to keep one reading. Veterans [Marcia] Muller and [Bill] Pronzini have done better work, both alone and in collaboration.

REVIEW: *Libr J* v138 no21 p75 D 1 2013 Teresa L. Jacobsen

REVIEW: *Publ Wkly* v260 no40 p31-2 O 7 2013

MULLIGAN, MARK. Environmental modelling; finding simplicity in complexity; [by] Mark Mulligan xviii, 475 p. 2013 Wiley

1. Climatology 2. Environmental sciences—Mathematical models 3. Environmental sciences—Methodology 4. Hydrology 5. Scientific literature

ISBN 9780470749111 (cloth)

LC 2012-013010

SUMMARY: This book on environmental modelling "contains four sections. . . . The first section introduces the basic characteristics of models. . . . The second section provides examples of current applications in climate science, soil mechanics, hydrology, ecology, and landscape evolution. . . . Part 3 focuses on management applications. . . . The last section summarizes current approaches, lessons learned, and future needs/trends in modeling." (Choice: Current Reviews for Academic Libraries)

REVIEW: *Choice* v51 no5 p868-9 Ja 2014 N. W. Hinman

"Environmental Modelling: Finding Simplicity in Complexity." "This new edition (1st ed., 2004) is organized in the same way as its predecessor. Some chapters are updated from those in the first edition, four chapters are entirely new, and the volume is 50-plus pages longer. Most, but not all, revised chapters are updated with more recent references. The volume contains four sections: 'Model Building,' 'The State of the Art in Environmental Modelling,' 'Models for Management,' and 'Current and Future Developments.'"

MULLIGAN, WILLIAM. The Great War for peace; [by] William Mulligan 443 p. 2014 Yale University Press

1. Historical literature 2. Peace movements—Europe—History—20th century 3. World War, 1914-1918—Diplomatic history 4. World War, 1914-1918—Peace—Social aspects 5. World War, 1914-1918—Protest movements

ISBN 9780300173772 (cl: alk. paper)

LC 2013-041983

SUMMARY: This book argues "that the first two decades of the twentieth century—and the First World War in particular—played an essential part in the construction of a peaceful new order on a global scale. Historian William Mulligan takes an entirely fresh look at the aspirations of statesmen, soldiers, intellectuals, and civilians who participated in the war and at the new ideas about peace that were forged." (Publisher's note)

REVIEW: *Natl Rev* v65 no10 p47-8 Je 2 2014 DANIEL JOHNSON

"The Great War for Peace." "[Author William] Mulligan's thesis is that the Great War was not merely the 'seminal catastrophe' of the 20th century, as George Kennan called it, but also the furnace in which the modern conception of peace . . . was forged. . . . His scholarship is broader and, in a cultural sense, deeper than that of the rest of the current crop of World War I books. Indeed, 'The Great War for Peace' may well be the most impressive and original of them all. . . . Mulligan really excels with his account of peace efforts in wartime, both by the belligerents and by neutrals such as the Vatican."

MULLIN, MIKE. Sunrise; [by] Mike Mullin 546 p. 2014 Tanglewood Publishing

1. Forgiveness—Fiction 2. Natural disasters 3. Science fiction 4. Survival—Fiction 5. Volcanoes—Fiction
ISBN 1939100011; 9781939100016 (hardback)
LC 2013-050876

SUMMARY: In this novel by Mike Mullin, the final book of the Ashfall Trilogy, "the Yellowstone supervolcano nearly wiped out the human race. Now, almost a year after the eruption, the survivors seem determined to finish the job. Communities wage war on each other, gangs of cannibals roam the countryside, and what little government survived the eruption has collapsed completely. The ham radio has gone silent. Sickness, cold, and starvation are the survivors' constant companions." (Publisher's note)

REVIEW: *Booklist* v110 no18 p65 My 15 2014 Cindy Welch

REVIEW: *Kirkus Rev* v82 no5 p159 Mr 1 2014

"Sunrise". "Throughout the novel, every decision has consequences, and characters must constantly decide what they are willing to pay. Reluctant Alex's leadership is presented as a burden rather than privilege, and his coming-of-age doesn't prevent other characters from shining. As the small community's population increases through new arrivals, everyone must learn not only trust, but how and when to forgive. The writing, even in transitory moments of peace, never lets readers forget that potential catastrophe lurks around every corner. A story about how hope is earned, as heart-pounding as it is heart-wrenching."

REVIEW: *Voice of Youth Advocates* v37 no2 p79 Je 2014 Teri Lesesne

MULTILINGUALISM IN MEDIEVAL BRITAIN (C. 1066-1520); Sources and Analysis; 242 p. 2013 Isd

1. English language—Middle English, 1100-1500 2. Great Britain—History—1066-1687 3. Historical literature 4. Macaronic literature 5. Multilingualism & literature 6. Multilingualism—History
ISBN 2503542506; 9782503542508

SUMMARY: "This book is devoted to the study of multilingual Britain in the later medieval period, from the Norman Conquest to John Skelton. It brings together experts from different disciplines--history, linguistics, and literature--in a joint effort to recover the complexities of spoken and written communication in the Middle Ages. Each author focuses on one specific text or text type." (Publisher's note)

REVIEW: *TLS* no5752 p26 Je 28 2013 GLYN S. BURGESS

"Multilingualism in Medieval Britain c. 1066-1520." "Judith A. Jefferson and Ad Putter's volume--which brings together sixteen papers given at a conference in Bristol in 2008--makes an important contribution. . . . [It] digs deeply and eruditely into the surviving sources in an attempt to tease out whatever light these documents can shed on the 'polyglot make up of medieval Britain'. The results reveal that a number of traditional views need to be revised. One such is the notion of Britain as a trilingual nation in which Latin, French (or more precisely Anglo-Norman) and English were the only languages in use. . . . The essays disentangle the processes by which, in time, English became the dominant language."

MULVEY, CHRISTOPHER. A history of the English language in 100 places. See Lucas, B.

MUNCK, RONALDO. Rethinking Latin America; development, hegemony, and social transformation; [by] Ronaldo Munck 254 p. 2013 Palgrave Macmillan

1. Historical literature
ISBN 9781137004116 (hardback : alk. paper)
LC 2013-005236

SUMMARY: This book "examines Latin America's socio-economic and political development from the 16th century through 2010 via an interpretive review of development literature. . . . A series of essays discusses five historical periods: the shift from European conquest toward conflicting visions of modernity (1510-1910); nation building (1910-64);n struggles over and for hegemony (1959-76); the hegemony of the marketplace ideal (1973 2001); and then a social countermovement (1998-2012)." (Choice: Current Reviews for Academic Libraries)

REVIEW: *Choice* v51 no5 p915-6 Ja 2014 C. H. Blake

"Rethinking Latin America: Development, Hegemony, and Social Transformation." "[Ronaldo] Munck cleanly and clearly summarizes the strengths and limitations of past development theories. Given his expressed aspiration to identify the seeds of a beneficial social transformation, a more detailed analysis of contemporary Latin American experiences would be most welcome--particularly regarding the indigenous politics that Munck emphasizes in the concluding pages but not in the main body of the book."

MUNRO, ALICE, 1931-. See Dear Life.

MUNSINGER, LYNN.il. Thanksgiving day thanks. See Elliott, L. M.

MURCHISON, WILLIAM. The cost of liberty; the life of John Dickinson; [by] William Murchison x, 252 p. 2013 ISI Books

1. Historical literature 2. Statesmen—United States—Biography
ISBN 9781933859941
LC 2013-026096

SUMMARY: In this biography, author William Jurchison argues that John Dickinson "was far more patriotic than history has credited him. . . Although reluctant to accept independence, Dickinson did ultimately believe a separation from Great Britain was required, but not at the costs that [John] Adams endorsed. For Dickinson, careful planning, both politically and economically, and deliberate negotiations with England would bring about independence in due time." (Choice: Current Reviews for Academic Libraries)

REVIEW: *Choice* v51 no8 p1474-5 Ap 2014 M. A. Byron

"The Cost of Liberty: The Life of John Dickinson". "A new biography of Dickinson—who participated in nearly every major event during the Revolutionary period, including pamphlet protests against taxation, serving on the Continental Congress, and drafting the Articles of Confederation—has long been overdue. . . . as [William] Murchison demonstrates, Dickinson was far more patriotic than history has credited him. . . . According to Murchison, Dickinson's cautious approach to liberty cost him his rightful place among the great thinkers and writers of the Revolutionary era."

MURDOCH, LYDIA. Daily life of Victorian women; [by] Lydia Murdoch xxix, 286 p. 2014 Greenwood

1. HISTORY—Europe—General 2. Historical literature 3. SOCIAL SCIENCE—Customs & Traditions 4. SOCIAL SCIENCE—Women's Studies 5. Sex role—Great Britain—History—19th century 6. Women—Great Britain—History—19th century 7. Women—Great Britain—Social conditions 8. Women's rights—Great Britain

ISBN 9780313384981 (hardback)

LC 2013-020956

SUMMARY: This book, part of the "Daily Life Through History" series, "takes a look at a wide and varied range of topics involving women living in England during the Victorian era. The book begins with a chronology covering the years from 1828 through 1903. . . . Eight chapters cover topics such as 'Women and the State'; 'Family, Home, and Leisure'; 'Childrearing, Youth, and Education'; and 'Urban Life.' Issues such as domestic violence . . . and social life are explored in depth." (Booklist)

REVIEW: *Booklist* v110 no9/10 p70 Ja 1 2014 Rebecca Vnuk

"Daily Life of Victorian Women." "This entry in Greenwood's Daily Life through History series takes a look at a wide and varied range of topics involving women living in England during the Victorian era. . . . The introduction, 'Victorian Context and Ideals of Womanhood,' does a good job laying out the reminder that there is no uniform experience or 'typical' Victorian woman. . . . The chapter on 'Health and Sexuality' is a good example of the broadness of the coverage, exploring everything from beauty rituals and fashion accessories to sewer systems and mastectomies without anesthesia. The writing is clear and should be accessible to college students or students in an advanced high-school class."

REVIEW: *Libr J* v138 no21 p122 D 1 2013 Diane Fulkerson

MURDOCK, CATHERINE GILBERT. Heaven is paved with Oreos; [by] Catherine Gilbert Murdock 208 p. 2013 Houghton Mifflin Harcourt

1. Diaries—Fiction 2. Grandmothers—Fiction 3. Interpersonal relations—Fiction 4. Pilgrims and pilgrimages—Fiction 5. Young adult fiction

ISBN 9780547625386

LC 2012-039969

SUMMARY: "This is a companion to [author Catherine Gilbert] Murdock's 'Dairy Queen' . . . and features D. J. . . . as Curtis' sister and someone Sarah admires. . . . Sarah Zorn and her similarly science-minded friend, Curtis . . . prevent classmates from teasing them about dating (which they're not). . . . But, soon, Curtis doesn't like the lying, and Sarah's . . . grandmother, Z, insists she travel with her from Wisconsin to Rome to complete a pilgrimage. . . ." (Booklist)

REVIEW: *Booklist* v110 no3 p90 O 1 2013 Ann kelley

REVIEW: *Bull Cent Child Books* v67 no3 p172-3 N 2013 K. C.

"Heaven Is Paved With Oreos." "Sarah tells her story in the form of journal entries, and her voice is authentically tween as she tries to sort through the complicated turns her life is taking. The exploration of her relationship with her grandmother (who insists, much to Sarah's dismay, that Sarah is just like her) is nuanced and reflective, allowing Sarah both to grow and to encounter complexities of adult romance that she's not quite ready for. [Author Catherine Gilbert] Murdock['s] fans will be additionally delighted at Sarah's friendship with D. J. Schwenk, protagonist of 'Dairy Queen' . . . and Curtis' sister."

REVIEW: *Horn Book Magazine* v89 no6 p100 N/D 2013 CLAIRE E. GROSS

REVIEW: *Kirkus Rev* v81 no17 p107 S 1 2013

REVIEW: *Publ Wkly* v260 no32 p61 Ag 12 2013

REVIEW: *SLJ* v59 no10 p1 O 2013 Emma Burkhart

MURPHY-AGUILAR, MOIRA.ed. Borderline slavery. See Borderline slavery

MURPHY, DERVLA. A month by the sea; encounters in Gaza; [by] Dervla Murphy xvii, 258 p. 2013 Eland

1. Arab-Israeli conflict 2. Travelers' writings

ISBN 1906011478; 9781906011475

LC 2012-551648

SUMMARY: This book chronicles author Dervla Murphy's travels in the Gaza Strip. "She met liberals and Islamists, Hamas and Fatah supporters, rich and poor. . . . Bombed and cut-off from normal contact with the rest of the world, life in Gaza is beset with structural, medical, and mental health problems, yet it is also bursting with political engagement and underwritten by an intense enjoyment of family life." (Publisher's note)

REVIEW: *Booklist* v110 no2 p24-5 S 15 2013 Adam Morgan

"A Month By the Sea: Encounters in Gaza." "Ireland's beloved octogenarian travel writer exposes harsh truths that are often stranger than fiction. Using a combination of history and her personal experiences, [Dana] Murphy uncovers the intricate social and political realities of the Gazan people that are often glossed over by headlines. . . . Although Murphy's occasional lead-thick, date-heavy lectures on history aren't the best introduction to Palestine, the light she sheds on one of the world's greatest humanitarian crises is as moving as it is invaluable."

REVIEW: *TLS* no5749 p29 Je 7 2013 JOHN URE

"A Month By the Sea: Encounters in Gaza." "Despite its ironic title, this is no account of a seaside holiday, but a highly political account of engaging with a people in dire straits. . . . She wanted to visit Gaza to empathize with a people whom, she saw as persecuted: she could hardly have claimed to arrive as an impartial observer. . . . Throughout her journeying and her long conversations it becomes abundantly clear that the residents of Gaza were moved by her sympathy and full of admiration for her courage. Readers will share the admiration for her, but many will hope that her next adventurous travel book will have more of her usual keen observation and less polemic."

MURPHY, JULIE. Side effects may vary; [by] Julie Murphy 336 p. 2014 Balzer + Bray

1. Friendship—Fiction 2. Interpersonal relations—Fiction 3. Leukemia—Fiction 4. Love—Fiction 5. Revenge—Fiction 6. Young adult fiction

ISBN 006224535X; 9780062245359 (hardcover bdg.)

LC 2013-009981

SUMMARY: In this book, by Julie Murphy, "when sixteen-year-old Alice is diagnosed with leukemia, she vows to spend her final months righting wrongs. So she convinces her best friend to help her with a crazy bucket list that's as much about revenge as it is about hope. But just when Alice's scores are settled, she goes into remission, and now she must face the consequences of all she's said and done." (Publisher's note)

REVIEW: *Booklist* v110 no13 p71-2 Mr 1 2014 Ann Kelley

"Side Effects May Vary". "Debut author [Julie] Murphy switches points of view between Harvey and Alice, and between 'Then' and 'Now'; all this back and forth gives readers much-needed insight into the complexity of Alice and Harvey's relationship. In the now, Alice's 'greatest fear in life has become expectations,' and she pushes patient, long-suffering Harvey away. What's interesting—and refreshing—about this book is that, yes, Alice has cancer, but she is not a likable girl, and readers' emotions will be all over the map even as they continue to root for her ultimate act of redemption. Alice and Harvey's relationship is raw, honest, moving, and unapologetic in its depiction of their individual, and collective, pain."

REVIEW: *Kirkus Rev* v82 no3 p58 F 1 2014

"Side Effects May Vary". " Were it not for Alice's bracing honesty (if only with herself) about her crises of confidence and her devotion to Harvey, she might come across as only a rather unpleasant and manipulative girl obsessed with having the last word before she dies. Instead, readers will, like Harvey, see Alice in all her complexity. Unlike most teens-with-cancer novels, Alice's story ends on a note of hard-won redemption and possibility. Readers will turn the last page wanting to know where the next chapter leads."

REVIEW: *Publ Wkly* v260 no52 p53-4 D 23 2013

REVIEW: *SLJ* v60 no2 p110 F 2014 Ragan O'Malley

REVIEW: *Voice of Youth Advocates* v37 no1 p71-2 Ap 2014 Jane Harper

REVIEW: *Voice of Youth Advocates* v37 no1 p72 Ap 2014 Heidi Culbertson

MURPHY, MARY.il. Say hello like this. See Murphy, M.

MURPHY, MARY. Say hello like this; [by] Mary Murphy 32 p. 2014 Candlewick Press

1. Animal sounds—Juvenile literature 2. Animals—Juvenile literature 3. Etiquette for children & teenagers 4. Picture books for children 5. Salutations

ISBN 0763669512; 9780763669515

LC 2013-943080

SUMMARY: In this children's concept book, written and illustrated by Mary Murphy, "different kinds of animals say hello in their own way. . . . Full of funny adjectives and sound words, this . . . companion to Mary Murphy's 'A Kiss Like This' is a . . . read-aloud for the very youngest of listeners." (Publisher's note)

REVIEW: *Bull Cent Child Books* v67 no6 p326-7 F 2014 Thaddeus Andracki

"Say Hello Like This!" "As with 'A Kiss Like This,' . . . the half-page flaps that reveal the salutations . . . will be extra fun layered on top of the boisterous animal noises that kids will surely want to chime in on. [Mary] Murphy's distinct ink and watercolor illustrations again pair strong shapeliness and a candy-coated color scheme to make for a friendly visual experience that matches the book's sweet, silly tone. The bold outlining of the pictures and the participatory nature makes this a winning choice for library lap-sits or storytimes on animal sounds--especially ones that enthusiastically encourage toddler noisemaking."

REVIEW: *Kirkus Rev* v81 no24 p91 D 15 2013

"Say Hello Like This". "Toddlers and their adults nationwide will welcome with open arms this clever coupling of animal sounds and lift-the-flap elements. In this book for children newly aware of the delights of saying, 'Hello,' [Mary] Murphy introduces a variety of familiar animals and describes their individual forms of greeting. . . . Murphy's thick, black outlines and bright (but never garish) colors will do well with large groups, and the half-page flaps that turn to reveal the various animal sounds will guarantee that this becomes a crowd pleaser."

REVIEW: *N Y Times Book Rev* p18 F 16 2014 SARAH HARRISON SMITH

REVIEW: *Publ Wkly* v260 no49 p81 D 2 2013

REVIEW: *SLJ* v60 no1 p74 Ja 2014 Yelena Alekseyeva-Popova

MURPHY, MONICA, 1970-. Rabid; a cultural history of the world's most diabolical virus; [by] Monica Murphy 240 p. 2012 Viking

1. Rabies—Epidemiology—History 2. Rabies—History 3. Rabies—Treatment—History 4. Rabies virus 5. Scientific literature

ISBN 0670023736; 9780670023738

LC 2011-043903

SUMMARY: This book "chart[s] four thousand years in the history, science, and cultural mythology of rabies. . . . A disease that spreads avidly from animals to humans, rabies has served throughout history as a symbol of savage madness, of inhuman possession. And today, its history can help shed light on the wave of emerging diseases, from AIDS to SARS to avian flu, that we now know to originate in animal populations." (Publisher's note)

REVIEW: *Booklist* v108 no19/20 p12 Je 1 2012 Ray Olson

REVIEW: *Choice* v50 no8 p1460 Ap 2013 M. S. Kainz

REVIEW: *Kirkus Rev* v80 no12 p1251-2 Je 15 2012

REVIEW: *Libr J* v137 no10 p119 Je 1 2012 Janet A. Crum

REVIEW: *Libr J* v137 no20 p25 D 1 2012 M. M.

REVIEW: *Nat Hist* v120 no10 p40-1 D 2012/Ja 2013 LAURENCE A. MARSCHALL

REVIEW: *New Sci* v215 no2874 p52 Jl 21 2012 Rob Dunn

"Rabid: A Cultural History of the World's Most Diabolical Virus". "In 'Rabid,' veterinary surgeon Monica Murphy and 'Wired' senior editor Bill Wasik tell the sweeping tale of the disease, one that begins in the earliest days of medicine and seems to intersect with nearly every major epoch of history. As the authors relate in compelling (and sometimes graphic) detail, rabies has affected dukes, saints and ordinary folks alike. . . . Like the virus itself, this fascinating book moves quickly, exploring both the marginalised status and deadly nature of the virus. And as the authors trace the influence of rabies through history, Rabid becomes nearly impossible to put down."

REVIEW: *Sci Am* v307 no1 p82 Jl 2012 Anna Kuchment

MURPHY, NEIL.ed. The Short Fiction of Flann O'Brien. See The Short Fiction of Flann O'Brien

MURPHY, SPORT. Everything's coming up profits. See Young, S.

MURRAY, ALBERT, 1916-2013. Stomping the blues; [by] Albert Murray 264 p. 1989 Da Capo Press

1. Blues (Music)—History and criticism 2. Blues musicians 3. Jazz—History and criticism 4. Music—United States 5. Music literature
ISBN 0306803623
LC 8901-2056

SUMMARY: This book presents an "examination of the blues spirit and blues as a cultured art form. Critic and novelist [Albert] Murray views the music not as a primitive musical expression of black suffering but as an antidote to the bad times---active good-time music, music to be danced to, music that, because of its substance and talented exponents, has emerged the most significant American music." (Library Journal)

REVIEW: *Booklist* v110 no5 p16 N 1 2013 Donna Seaman

"A Bad Woman Feeling Good: Blues and the Women Who Sang Them," "Stomping the Blues," and "Nothing But the Blues: The Music and the Musicians." "[Buzzy] Jackson traces the lives and influence of female blues singers . . . and explains how their music encouraged emotional freedom and forthrightness about the complicated struggles women face. . . . [Albert Murray's] radiant interpretation is rich in incisive portraits of blues musicians and many telling anecdotes, all accompanied by extraordinary photographs. . . . This handsome, well-illustrated, and penetrating blues history tracks the metamorphosis of the blues from its African roots."

MURRAY, CHARLES, 1943-. The bell curve; intelligence and class structure in American life; [by] Charles Murray xxvi, 845 1994 Free Press

1. Educational psychology 2. Intellect 3. Social problems 4. Social science literature
ISBN 0-02-914673-9; 0-684-82429-9 pa
LC 94-2-9694

SUMMARY: The authors argue that "low intelligence, independent of social, economic, or ethnic background lies at the root of many of our social problems. The authors also [aim to] demonstrate . . . that intelligence levels differ among ethnic groups." They also aim to "show that for a wide range of intractable social problems, the decisive correlation is between a high incidence of the problem and the low intelligence of those who suffer from it." (Publisher's note) The authors argue that "low intelligence, independent of social, economic, or ethnic background lies at the root of many of our social problems. The authors also {aim to} demonstrate . . . that intelligence levels differ among ethnic groups. . . . {They also aim to} show that for a wide range of intractable social problems, the decisive correlation is between a high incidence of the problem and the low intelligence of those who suffer from it." (Publisher's note) Bibliography. Index.

REVIEW: *TLS* no5732 p16 F 8 2013

"The Bell Curve". "A muddled offering. . . . One of this book's many curiosities is that . . . they are conspicuously unforthcoming about the operational details of this National Longitudinal Study of Youth: about who collected what evidence from whom, about attrition rates, and so on. Such insouciance is puzzling, especially in a field in which ideologically motivated misrepresentation has in the recent past been widespread. . . . The data have been heavily massaged in the interests of intelligibility and representativeness; they also contain gaps and leaps."

MURRAY, CHRISTOPHER BRENT.tr. The Gardener of Versailles. See Baraton, A.

MURRAY, THOMAS H.ed. Synthetic biology and morality. See Synthetic biology and morality

MURRIE, MATTHEW. While You Were Sleeping. See Murrie, S.

MURRIE, STEVE. While You Were Sleeping; Fun Facts That Happen at Night; 224 p. 2012 Turtleback Books

1. Children's nonfiction 2. Curiosities & wonders—Juvenile literature 3. Night 4. Sleep 5. Time perspective
ISBN 0545430283 (paperback); 0606267468 (prebind); 9780545430289 (paperback); 9780606267465 (prebind)

SUMMARY: This book "provides general observations about internal biological processes associated with sleep, nocturnal animals, nighttime jobs, and wee-hours activities—interleaved with mini-disquisitions on earthquakes, Mount Rushmore, bamboo, comets, space probes, the largest Lego tower every constructed, and an array of other subjects." (Booklist)

REVIEW: *Booklist* v109 no7 p46 D 1 2012 John Peters

THE MUSES GO TO SCHOOL; Inspiring Stories About the Importance of Arts in Education; 2014 The New Press
ISBN 9781595585394 (hardcover); 9781595589415 (paperback)

SUMMARY: In this book, edited by Herbert R. Kohl and Tom Oppenheim, "autobiographical pieces with well-known artists and performers are paired with interpretive essays by distinguished educators to produce a powerful case for positioning the arts at the center of primary and secondary school curriculums." (Publisher's note)

REVIEW: *Booklist* v108 no11 p16 F 1 2012 Whitney Scott

REVIEW: *Choice* v49 no10 p1935-6 Je 2012 L. O. Wilson

"The Muses Go to School: Inspiring Stories About the Importance of Arts in Education." "[Herbert] Kohl . . . and [Thomas] Oppenheim . . . offer readers an unusual mix of autobiographical remembrances from nine very distinguished performers and artists and commentary from educators. . . . Perhaps what makes this book truly unique is that each personal reflection is paired with an insightful commentary from a distinguished educator like Maxine Greene, Bill Ayres, or Michelle Fine, among others. . . . In this impressive collection of remembrances and commentaries, all contributors offer readers strong reasons for keeping the creative and performance arts as central components of the educational journeys of today's children."

REVIEW: *Kirkus Rev* v79 no24 p2302 D 15 2011

REVIEW: *Libr J* v137 no3 p112 F 15 2012 Rachel Owens

REVIEW: *Publ Wkly* v259 no5 p46-7 Ja 30 2012

MUSEUMS IN A GLOBAL CONTEXT; national identity, international understanding; 2013 University of Chicago Press

1. Cross-cultural communication 2. Globalization 3. Museum studies literature 4. Museums—Political aspects 5. Museums—Social aspects

ISBN 9781933253855

SUMMARY: This book, edited by Jennifer Dickey, Samir El Azhar, and Catherine M. Lewis, "looks at the way globalization has shaped museum culture, and in turn how museums have shaped the public's understanding of various local, regional, and national identities.Contributors discuss "issues of cultural patrimony and heritage tourism, and strategies for engaging both visitors and communities as a whole." They "offer case studies from around the globe, including Germany, Morocco, Saudi Arabia, South Africa, and Vietnam." (Publisher's note)

REVIEW: *Choice* v51 no5 p796-8 Ja 2014 J. Jocson-Singh

"Museums in a Global Context: National Identity, International Understanding." "Editors [Jennifer] Dickey, [Samir El] Azhar, and [Catherine] Lewis offer an insightful volume of essays that explore the global context in which museums exist, and reexamine what it means to be an institutional center of cultural value and education in an ever-changing global environment. . . . The result is a discerning, well-written volume that illuminates the need for further cross cultural research. . . . the collected essays synergize to promote further dialogue and cross cultural research about the challenges museums face in a global landscape. . . . Recommended."

MUSIC IN AMERICAN LIFE; an encyclopedia of the songs, styles, stars and stories that shaped our culture; 1270 p. 2013 Greenwood

1. Music—United States—Bio-bibliography 2. Music—United States—Encyclopedias 3. Music—United States—History & criticism 4. Music literature 5. Popular culture—United States

ISBN 9780313393471 (hardcover : alk. paper)

LC 2012-049968

SUMMARY: This encyclopedia, edited by Jacqueline Edmondson, "sets out to define and explain" the "synergistic conjunction" between music and American popular culture "and its historic roots. The bulk of the set consists of 500 alphabetically arranged entries devoted to vocalists, songwriters, genres, instruments, and places. These are augmented by a time line of American music, a general bibliography, and a discography of collected works by genre." (Booklist)

REVIEW: *Booklist* v110 no11 p48 F 1 2014 Michael Tosko

"Music in American Life: An Encyclopedia of the Songs, Styles, Stars, and Stories That Shaped Our Culture." "Opening the set to any page yields an engaging set of subjects. For example, S entries include not only artists Paul Simon and Britney Spears but also the popular children's writer Shel Silverstein, who wrote 'A Boy Named Sue,' popularized by Johnny Cash. . . . Those purchasing this book will be pleased to discover the valuable information provided. For example, there is a fine summary of the history of American theater, including Native American music, minstrel shows, and Tin Pan Alley. It is brief but informative and likely a helpful starting point for someone seeking background information. The 'Further Reading' list provides a springboard for more research."

REVIEW: *Choice* v51 no9 p1565 My 2014 D. Arnold

"Music in American Life: An Encyclopedia of the Songs, Styles, Stars, and Stories That Shaped Our Culture". "Curiously, many of the contributors, including the editor, are not primarily music specialists. Perhaps a broader cultural perspective is intended. Not surprisingly, the quality of articles varies; sometimes the lack of musical expertise shows. Still, readers will discover many excellent articles and thought-provoking perspectives. This set is appropriate for public, community college, and undergraduate libraries, and would be useful for courses in American popular music."

REVIEW: *Libr J* v139 no2 p98 F 1 2014 Michael Bemis

MUTÉN, BURLEIGH. Miss Emily; [by] Burleigh Mutén 144 p. 2014 Candlewick Press

1. Amherst (Mass.) 2. Circus—Fiction 3. Dickinson, Emily, 1830-1886 4. Historical fiction 5. Novels in verse

ISBN 0763657344; 9780763657345

LC 2013-943089

SUMMARY: This book, by Burleigh Muten, is an "adventure about Emily Dickinson, four young friends, and a traveling circus. When an invitation to join Miss Emily in the garden appears, Mattie, Ned, Sally, and Mac know they're in for some fun because Miss Emily—Emily Dickinson to the rest of us—always has a surprise in store for her young friends. And today's may be the biggest adventure yet." (Publisher's note)

REVIEW: *Booklist* v110 no14 p79 Mr 15 2014 Thom Barthelmess

REVIEW: *Bull Cent Child Books* v67 no7 p369 Mr 2014 K. C.

REVIEW: *Kirkus Rev* v82 no2 p132 Ja 15 2014

"Miss Emily". "The Belle of Amherst leads some young friends on a grand adventure. . . . With the help of [Matt] Phelan's wispy, textured drawings, [Burleigh] Mutén imagines the famously reclusive poet playfully disguised as 'Proserpina—Queen of the Night,' leading her tiny band of 'Amherst gypsies' on a midnight quest to spy the arrival of the Great Golden Menagerie and Circus at the Amherst train station. . . . Uplifting and clever, Mutén's tale also includes a layer of biographical detail sure to tantalize Dickinson lovers everywhere."

REVIEW: *N Y Times Book Rev* p26 My 11 2014 ELLEN HANDLER SPITZ

REVIEW: *SLJ* v60 no4 p131 Ap 2014 Carole Phillips

MUTH, JON J., 1960-. Koo's Haiku ABCs; [by] Jon J. Muth 32 p. 2013 Scholastic Press

1. Alphabet books 2. Children's poetry 3. Haiku 4. Pandas 5. Seasons—Juvenile poetry

ISBN 0545166683; 9780545166683 (hardcover)

LC 2012-040378

SUMMARY: In this book of children's poems, author "Jon J. Muth—and his delightful little panda bear, Koo—challenge readers to stretch their minds and imaginations with twenty-six haikus about the four seasons." This book uses the haiku form to take children through the seasons with watercolored images. (Publisher's note)

REVIEW: *Booklist* v110 no8 p37 D 15 2013 Carolyn Phelan

REVIEW: *Bull Cent Child Books* v67 no7 p369 Mr 2014 D. S.

"Hi, Koo!: A Year of Seasons". "This creative poetic sequence follows the seasons through twenty-six haiku, partnered with illustrations that feature [Jon J.] Muth's familiar anthropomorphized panda as he explores the joys of fall, winter, spring, and summer along with his child friends. The poems are deftly aimed at kid experiences . . . and the phrasing is often evocative. . . . Muth's delicate watercolors are triumphant, setting tender washes of sky and grass against the very kidlike poses of Koo the panda as he cranes his neck skyward or peers intently at ground-level action."

REVIEW: *Horn Book Magazine* v90 no4 p112-3 Jl/Ag 2014 JENNIFER M. BRABANDER

REVIEW: *Kirkus Rev* v82 no2 p52 Ja 15 2014

"Hi, Koo! A Year of Seasons". "Though light in tone and geared toward pre-reader eyes and interests, the mostly outdoor scenes [John J.] Muth depicts command serious attention from all. The first page simultaneously demonstrates both Muth's adherence to haiku's three-line form rather than its traditional five-seven-five syllabic sequence and his exquisite use of white space. . . . Muth's delicate watercolor and subtle inking deftly suggesting the forest's shifting scope. Throughout, condensed poetic image coupled with spare illustration yields huge effect; in a word, magical."

REVIEW: *N Y Times Book Rev* p18 My 11 2014 JOHN LITHGOW

REVIEW: *Publ Wkly* v260 no49 p81 D 2 2013

REVIEW: *SLJ* v60 no2 p121 F 2014 Julie R. Ranelli

MUÑOZ BOUDET, ANA MARÍA. On norms and agency. See Petesch, P.

MUÑOZ, HERALDO. Getting away with murder; Benazir Bhutto's assassination and the politics of Pakistan; [by] Heraldo Muñoz 268 p. 2014 W.W. Norton & Co. Inc.

1. Political science literature 2. Prime ministers—Assassination—Pakistan
ISBN 0393062910 (hardcover); 9780393062915 (hardcover)
LC 2013-036718

SUMMARY: In this book, Heraldo Munoz "reports on the investigation into the facts and circumstances of Benazir Bhutto's assassination. . . . [He] chronicles how the U.S. and British governments facilitated the return of Bhutto . . . in order to broaden the political base of then-dictator Gen. Pervez Musharraf. . . . After the assassination, authorities blamed Pakistan's Taliban-linked fundamentalists." (Kirkus Reviews)

REVIEW: *Booklist* v110 no4 p12 O 15 2013 Vanessa Bush

REVIEW: *Kirkus Rev* v81 no22 p17 N 15 2013

REVIEW: *Libr J* v138 no18 p106 N 1 2013 Nader Entessar

REVIEW: *Libr J* v138 no12 p55 Jl 1 2013

REVIEW: *New York Times* v163 no56391 pC30 Ja 24 2014 DECLAN WALSH

"Magnificent Delusions: Pakistan, the United States, and an Epic History of Misunderstanding" and "Getting Away With Murder: Benazir Bhutto's Assassination and the Politics of Pakistan". "Mr. [Husain] Haqqani is eminently qualified to tell this story. . . . His history relies heavily on American cables and memoirs, which serves well to illuminate some episodes. . . . But at other times, the lack of Pakistani voices feels one-sided. . . . And there is a disappointing lack of detail from the recent period when Mr. Haqqani himself was a central participant in the action. . . . As a diplo-sleuth, Mr. Heraldo [Muñoz] provides some revealing detail on this important story. But, alas, he is no Agatha Christie. A dutiful rehashing of Pakistani history is insightful but sprinkled with careless errors. And, ultimately, he fails to go much further into [Benazir] Bhutto's death than his well-regarded United Nations report."

REVIEW: *Publ Wkly* v260 no40 p43-4 O 7 2013

MUÑOZ MOLINA, ANTONIO. Winter in Lisbon; [by] Antonio Muñoz Molina 213 p. 1999 Granta Books

1. Identity (Psychology)—Fiction 2. Jazz in literature 3. Jazz musicians—Fiction 4. Love stories 5. Music—Fiction
ISBN 1862071667
LC 2001-409307

SUMMARY: In this novel by Antonio Munoz Molina, "When jazz pianist Santiago Biralbo meets the wife of an American art dealer, he begins . . . an obsessional love affair . . . [and] also an odyssey that will strip him of his identity in his quest to understand love and music." (Publisher's note) The protagonist is "a classic, contemptuous, self-conscious romantic hero; aged thirty-one but behaving like a 'lovesick teenager'." (Times Literary Supplement)

REVIEW: *TLS* no5751 p16 Je 21 2013

"Winter in Lisbon." "Although the action is set in the early 1980s, there is not one prop . . . which would be out of place in the 1940s. . . . The anomalous effect is impressively sustained. . . . It is not Sonia Soto's translation that fails in irony but the hero himself. . . . It is a pity that after eighty-nine pages, the analogy between the interwoven instruments in jazz and the interweaving parts of the story is spelt out. . . . But even if you are a fan of film noir, you finally wish that this well-written homage had said more about its own time (the 1980s)."

MY FIRST BOOK OF BABY ANIMALS; 22 p. 2013 Charlesbridge Publishing

1. Animal young—Juvenile literature 2. Animals—Infancy—Juvenile literature 3. Calves 4. Gorilla (Genus)—Juvenile literature 5. Parental behavior in animals 6. Picture books for children
ISBN 9781623540289 (alk. paper)
LC 2013-028680

SUMMARY: This children's picture book focuses on animal babies. "Each page has a . . . large photograph of a baby animal with just two words; the type of animal in bold type and then the name of the baby animal. Some pages include a photograph of the baby animal with its mother. Some animals will be familiar to young children, but others like the hippopotamus and baby calf and bison and calf may be new to them." (SB&F: Your Guide to Science Resources for All Ages)

REVIEW: *Booklist* v110 no22 p81 Ag 1 2014 Martha Edmundson

MY MOTHER GOOSE; 96 p. 2013 Roaring Brook Press

1. Children's poetry 2. Counting—Juvenile literature 3. Nursery rhymes 4. Picture books for children 5. Transportation—Juvenile literature
ISBN 9781596435261 (hardcover)

LC 2012-050296

SUMMARY: In this book, editor and illustrator David McPhail's "familiar shaggy-haired toddlers and friendly animals lend themselves to . . . [a] grouping of more than 60 Mother Goose rhymes. . . . Short sections also introduce basic concepts that include shapes, colors, getting dressed, and methods of transportation." Rhymes include "Simple Simon" and "Baa, Baa Black Sheep." (Publishers Weekly)

REVIEW: *Bull Cent Child Books* v67 no5 p273 Ja 2014 D. S.

REVIEW: *Horn Book Magazine* v90 no2 p134-5 Mr/Ap 2014 KITTY FLYNN

"My Mother Goose: A Collection of Favorite Rhymes, Songs, and Concepts." "[David] McPhail enters the crowded Mother Goose field with this affable collection of sixty-three nursery rhymes and seven interspersed short sections of concepts (e.g., counting, 'Getting Dressed,' 'Action Words'). Each spread is usually devoted to one or two mostly familiar poems, and McPhail's playful illustrations are afforded lots of room to interpret the verses, which gives the whole an uncluttered, approachable look. In general, McPhail portrays a classic, though updated, Mother Goose world. . . . This solid introduction may not be a definitive edition, but it is a welcome one."

REVIEW: *N Y Times Book Rev* p28 N 10 2013 LEONARD S. MARCUS

REVIEW: *Publ Wkly* v260 no33 p65 Ag 19 2013

MYERS, ALEX. Revolutionary; [by] Alex Myers 320 p. 2013 Simon & Schuster

1. Gender role—Fiction 2. Historical fiction 3. Women soldiers—Fiction

ISBN 1451663323; 9781451663327 (hardcover); 9781451663341 (pbk.)

LC 2013-003204

SUMMARY: This book, by Alex Myers "follows a strong-willed young woman who takes a huge gamble and fights as a male soldier for the American colonists. Deborah Sampson is a 22-year-old indentured weaver who confides in her closest friend, Jennie Newcomb, about her desperate need to escape their oppressive small Massachusetts town. After surviving a sexual assault, Deborah dresses as a young man, skips town, and reinvents herself as 'Robert D. S. Shurtliff.'" (Publishers Weekly)

REVIEW: *Booklist* v110 no6 p26-7 N 15 2013 Sarah Johnson

"Revolutionary." "In his debut, transgender author [Alex] Myers relates the story of a courageous, real-life woman. His straightforward, clear prose lets the important and complex issues he raises shine through, including gender identification, the desire for self-expression, and the meaning of freedom in an era when women's choices and actions were severely constrained. . . . Crisply rendered scenes shift from days of camaraderie and routine camp life around West Point to deadly skirmishes, the unmasking of traitors, and the discovery of unexpected love. With this thought provoking work, Myers resists modernizing Deborah/Robert's predicament and lets readers explore both the external and internal transformations of this valiant American soldier."

REVIEW: *Kirkus Rev* v81 no20 p114 O 15 2013

REVIEW: *New York Times* v163 no56380 pC6 Ja 13 2014 DAVID SHRIBMAN

REVIEW: *Publ Wkly* v260 no33 p37 Ag 19 2013

MYERS, BENJAMIN. Lapse Americana; [by] Benjamin Myers 116 p. 2013 NYQ Books

1. American poetry 2. Faith 3. Memory (Philosophy) 4. Neighbors 5. Poems—Collections

ISBN 9781935520719 (pbk.)

LC 2013-932935

SUMMARY: This book presents a collection of poems by Benjamin Myers. "Born out of the poet's childhood during the Pax Americana and situated within the war and economic lapse of the new century, these poems explore memory and amnesia, faith and doubt, presence and absence. They are rooted in rural, working class experience as well as in the poetic traditions of America, Europe, and China." (Publisher's note)

REVIEW: *World Lit Today* v87 no5 p70-1 S/O 2013 W. M. Hagen

"Lapse Americana." "Unique is the consciousness of this poet. A liberal arts education certainly matters, but more the layered awareness that occurs when one leaves and then comes back to the place of one's youth, summoning what and who is there and not there so as to hold them in the same poetic space. The poet is there, in community, and not there at the same time, even as a father. Not surprisingly, the most vivid passages are often tinged with mortality, the loss that has occurred or will occur. . . . The richness of this volume, the 'more than,' is certainly reflected in the coda, in which a lonely Pascal, here a time traveler, writes to an unresponsive beloved from different places, from a bustling nineteenth-century Paris to second-century Rome, to LA and back to France."

MYERS, MATTHEW.il. Battle Bunny. See Battle Bunny

MYERS, MATTHEW.il. E-I-E-I-O! See Sierra, J.

MYERS, WALTER DEAN, 1937-2014. All the right stuff; [by] Walter Dean Myers 213 p. 2012 HarperTeen

1. African Americans—Fiction 2. Coming of age—Fiction 3. Conduct of life—Fiction 4. Mentoring 5. Social contract—Fiction 6. Soup kitchens 7. Young adult fiction, American

ISBN 9780061960871 (tr. bdg.); 9780061960888 (lib. bdg.)

LC 2011-024251

SUMMARY: This novel tells the story of Paul DuPree, a 16-year-old boy who "has taken on two jobs: work in a soup kitchen and the required mentoring of a young basketball player. At the soup kitchen, he meets Elijah Jones, the project's driving force and resident philosopher," who helps Paul understand "how one person's decisions and actions might affect the entire community" as he mentors teenage mother Keisha and comes to terms with the death of his father." (Kirkus)

REVIEW: *Booklist* v109 no9/10 p125 Ja 1 2013 Alison O'Reilly

REVIEW: *Bull Cent Child Books* v65 no10 p520-1 Je 2012 K. C.

REVIEW: *SLJ* v58 no12 p67 D 2012 Shari Fesko

MYERS, WALTER DEAN, 1937-2014. Invasion!; [by] Walter Dean Myers 224 p. 2013 Scholastic Press

1. African American soldiers—Fiction 2. African American soldiers—Juvenile fiction 3. Historical fiction 4. Segregation—United States—History—20th century—Fiction 5. Segregation—United States—History—20th century—Juvenile fiction 6. Soldiers—Fiction 7. War—Fiction 8. World War, 1939-1945—Campaigns—France—Normandy—Fiction 9. World War, 1939-1945—Campaigns—France—Normandy—Juvenile fiction 10. World War, 1939-1945—Participation, African American—Juvenile fiction

ISBN 0545384281; 9780545384285; 9780545384292; 9780545576598

LC 2013-005595

SUMMARY: In this book by Walter Dean Myers, "old friends Josiah 'Woody' Wedgewood and Marcus Perry see each other in England prior to the invasion of Normandy. Woody is with the 29th Infantry, and Marcus, who's black, is with the Transportation Corps, the segregation of their Virginia hometown following them right into wartime. Their friendship frames the story, as the two occasionally encounter each other in the horrific days ahead." (Kirkus Reviews)

REVIEW: *Horn Book Magazine* v89 no6 p100-1 N/D 2013 BETTY CARTER

"Invasion". "The brutal battle scenes and wartime musings are vividly told. But there's also a sense of the times, such as the naive feelings Woody has for a girl back home or the racist and xenophobic attitudes among his fellow soldiers in the 29th Infantry Division. These [Walter Dean] Myers delivers, along with his themes, subtly through Woody's matter-of-fact observations as his ragged battalion fights its way through Normandy. . . . In 1944, troops were segregated and menial jobs frequently relegated to black soldiers. And this was the Good War."

MYRACLE, LAUREN, 1969-. The infinite moment of us; [by] Lauren Myracle 336 p. 2013 Amulet Books

1. Assertiveness (Psychology)—Fiction 2. Dating (Social customs)—Fiction 3. Family life—Georgia—Fiction 4. Love—Fiction 5. Romance language fiction 6. Young adult fiction

ISBN 1419707930; 9781419707933 (hardback)

LC 2013-017135

SUMMARY: This book is a love story between two high school graduates. "Poised and accomplished, Wren has always done what her parents have expected of her, while Charlie is a foster child, self-conscious about his often unpleasant upbringing, but fiercely protective of his current family." The story is an "account of two young people whose insecurities and personal histories weigh on the romance they work to build with each other." (Publishers Weekly)

REVIEW: *Booklist* v110 no1 p114 S 1 2013 Ann Kelley

REVIEW: *Bull Cent Child Books* v67 no3 p173-4 N 2013 K. Q. G.

"The Infinite Moment of Us." "The premise of an underprivileged, broken boy falling in love with an overindulged, broken girl isn't terribly new, and [author Lauren] Myracle falls back on a few too many tired tropes--the virginal heroine, the sexed-up ex of the hero, etc.--for this to stand out from the genre. The single-focus intensity of Wren and Charlie's feelings is spot-on for the age group, however, and chapters move between both their perspectives as they grow into the relationship, offering readers of both sexes a rather compelling example of the how-to's of intimacy."

REVIEW: *Kirkus Rev* p55-6 Ag 15 2013 Fall Preview

REVIEW: *Kirkus Rev* v81 no14 p338 Jl 15 2013

REVIEW: *Publ Wkly* v260 no27 p90-1 Jl 8 2013

REVIEW: *SLJ* v59 no10 p1 O 2013 Emily Moore

REVIEW: *Voice of Youth Advocates* v36 no4 p68 O 2013 Ed Goldberg

REVIEW: *Voice of Youth Advocates* v36 no4 p68 O 2013 Rachelle David

N

N., JOSÉ ÁNGEL. Illegal; reflections of an undocumented immigrant; [by] José Ángel N. 128 p. 2014 University of Illinois Press

1. Illegal aliens—Illinois—Chicago—Biography 2. Memoirs 3. Mexicans—Illinois—Chicago—Biography

ISBN 9780252038310 (hardback); 9780252079863 (paperback)

LC 2013-032194

SUMMARY: In this book, the author, an "undocumented immigrant from Mexico who must maintain anonymity, describes his years-long journey from harrowing border crossing to proud husband, father, and home owner. Humiliation and the possibility of debasement from encounters with authorities, colleagues at work, and in day-to-day living (the mere act of buying a bottle of wine is fraught) dog his every step." (Library Journal)

REVIEW: *Booklist* v110 no9/10 p26 Ja 1 2014 Vanessa Bush

REVIEW: *Kirkus Rev* v82 no3 p319 F 1 2014

"Illegal: Reflections of an Undocumented Immigrant". "While this is primarily a rather dignified personal story, between the personal passages, the author also writes angrily about the failure of the United States to reform its immigration laws. President Barack Obama comes in for especially harsh criticism, having raised hopes that have yet to be fulfilled. N.'s style often has a stilted quality, perhaps the result of his acquisition of English through formal means, but he gets his message across clearly. An utterly believable close-up picture of one illegal immigrant's life in the United States."

REVIEW: *Libr J* v139 no4 p106 Mr 1 2014 Ellen Gilbert

NADAS, PETER. Parallel stories; a novel; 1133 2011 Farrar, Straus, and Giroux

1. Communism—Europe—History—20th century 2. Historical fiction 3. Mental illness—Fiction 4. Middle classes 5. Sexual intercourse

ISBN 978-0-374-22976-4; 0-374-22976-7

LC 2010—39688

SUMMARY: This book by Péter Nádas is "the tale of a family, the Lippay-Lehrs, living in Budapest in the mid-twentieth century. . . . Each of these characters occupies center stage for a while—a few pages or a few hundred. Stories are nested within stories, time frames shift back and forth without warning. . . . The body, the condition of embodiment, is . . . Nádas's . . . subject. . . . [T]he first half of the novel is anchored by two . . . long sex scenes." (New Republic)

REVIEW: *World Lit Today* v86 no4 p60-2 Jl/Ag 2012 Ivan Sanders

"Parallel Stories". "Péter Nadas's monumental, labyrinthine novel, 'Parallel Stories,' is the first of his works of fiction not written in the first-person singular. . . . Gone are the wistful, elegiac confessions, the long and languorous sentences of 'A Book of Memories,' Nádas's previous novel. In 'Parallel Stories,' the sentences are often abrupt, jagged. But because Nádas is bent on plumbing then depths of his themes, and because more than ever eros is his perennial subject, we don't miss the languor, and don't mind the close scrutiny, the explicitness, the objectivity."

NADIN, MIHAI. Are You Stupid?; A Second Revolution Might Save America from Herself; [by] Mihai Nadin 390 p. 2013 CreateSpace Independent Publishing Platform

1. Political science literature 2. Social commentary 3. United States—Economic conditions 4. United States—Politics & government 5. United States—Social conditions

ISBN 1490525653; 9781490525655

SUMMARY: It was the author's intent to demonstrate "that America is in decline—economically, militarily, socially—but that Americans themselves are to blame. Instead of rising to the occasion and overcoming these obstacles, people remain ignorant about their history and apathetic to their current conditions. According to the author, this attitude has resulted in a somewhat ironic state of affairs: Americans are more dependent on government as their skepticism of it grows." (Kirkus Reviews)

REVIEW: *Kirkus Rev* v82 no1 p338 Ja 1 2014

"Are You Stupid? A Second Revolution Might Save America From Herself". "[Mihai Nadid\ offers especially fresh takes on the idea of attention, suggesting that while the 'public bids with its attention—on American idols, friends, movies, messages,' such action is only a pale imitation of real civic responsibility. Unfortunately, despite these positive elements, the book is unwieldy, and certain chapters feel tangential, like one on the general uselessness of lawyers. It can also be hard to gauge Nadin's tone; he seems to sympathize with the downtrodden and those on the "losing" side of America's unequal distribution of wealth, but he also has no qualms about making sweeping, insensitive generalizations about the poor."

NADON, DANIEL-RAYMOND.ed. Staging social justice. See Staging social justice

NAFF, WILLIAM E., 1929-2005. The Kiso Road; the life and times of Shimazaki Toson; [by] William E. Naff xxvi, 664 p. 2011 University of Hawaii Press

1. Japanese authors—Biography 2. Japanese literature—1868- 3. Shimazaki, Tōson, 1872-1943

ISBN 9780824832186

LC 2010-008372

SUMMARY: The book offers a biography of "[n]ovelist, poet, and essayist Shimazaki Tōson (1872–1943, born Shimazaki Haruki). . . . Using an approach that combines extensive archival research and close literary analysis, [William] Naff shows that Tōson's career is a means to understand Japanese intellectual and artistic life between the 1880s and 1940s. He analogizes Tōson's efforts to come to terms with his inner demons, family, and society to Japan's struggle to survive in the new world order of imperialism and war. In fourteen chapters arranged chronologically in a manner typical of biographies, Naff explains that Tōson's greatness lies in his broad vision of the urban and rural, self and society, old and new, which was informed by extensive self-study and personal events." (American Historical Review)

REVIEW: *Am Hist Rev* v116 no5 p1461-2 D 2011 Alisa Freedman

The Kiso Road: The Life and Times of Shimazaki Tōson. "In the late nineteenth and early twentieth centuries, Japanese authors sought to capture what they felt was a unique moment of rapid modernization, characterized by a conjuncture of historical forces that included urbanization, technological advances, educational reforms, adaption of Western practices, and study of the national past. Novelist, poet, and essayist Shimazaki Tōson (1872-1943, born Shimazaki Haruki) epitomized this quest. . . . In this book, the late William Naff (1929-2005) carefully chronicles milestones in Tōson's life. [In] this dense yet engaging biography . . . Naff shows that Tōson's career is a means to understand Japanese intellectual and artistic life between the 1880s and 1940s."

NAFFIS-SAHELY, ANDRE.tr. The Last Days. See Seksik, L.

NAFFIS-SAHELY, ANDRE.ed. The Palm Beach Effect. See The Palm Beach Effect

NAGAI, MARIKO. Dust of Eden; [by] Mariko Nagai 128 p. 2014 Albert Whitman & Company

1. Family life—Fiction 2. Japanese Americans—Evacuation and relocation, 1942-1945—Fiction 3. Japanese Americans—Evacuation and relocation, 1942-1945—Juvenile fiction 4. Novels in verse

ISBN 0807517399; 9780807517390 (hardback)

LC 2013-033074

SUMMARY: In this book, by Mariko Nagai, "thirteen-year-old Mina Masako Tagawa is a Japanese-American girl living a happy life in Seattle, . . . until that fateful day in December 1941. After the attack on Pearl Harbor, Mina's father is imprisoned for no reason, and she is hurt and confused to see that Japanese Americans have become the enemy. . . Their family is one of thousands forced to 'evacuate' . . . to an internment camp in Idaho." (Voice of Youth Advocates)

REVIEW: *Bull Cent Child Books* v67 no8 p418 Ap 2014 H. M.

"Dust of Eden". "While not all the entries shine, the verse sequence suits the subject matter; the story's fragmentation suggests that Mina too is piecing together bits and pieces of understanding in an effort to come up with a cohesive, coherent narrative for herself. The free-verse format also allows young readers to take on complex subject matter in a way that might be out of their reach in a denser prose narrative. . . . This is an honest and thoughtful exploration of a complicated chapter in American history, and the book's strong narrative voice and solid imagery will help contemporary readers understand those complexities."

REVIEW: *Kirkus Rev* v82 no4 p52 F 15 2014

"Dust of Eden". "Crystal-clear prose poems paint a heartrending picture of 13-year-old Mina Masako Tagawa's journey from Seattle to a Japanese-American internment camp during World War II. This vividly wrought story of displacement, told from Mina's first-person perspective, begins as it did for so many Japanese-Americans: with the bombs dropping on Pearl Harbor. . . . An engaging novel-in-poems that imagines one earnest, impassioned teenage girl's experience of the Japanese-American internment."

NAGAR, SACHIN.il. Gandhi. See Quinn, J.

NAGY, GREGORY. The ancient Greek hero in 24 hours; [by] Gregory Nagy 727 p. 2013 The Belknap Press of Harvard University Press

1. Civilization, Homeric 2. Greek literature—History and criticism 3. Heroes in literature 4. Historical literature

ISBN 9780674073401 (alk. paper)

LC 2012-047971

SUMMARY: "In twenty-four installments, based on the Harvard University course [author Gregory] Nagy has taught and refined since the late 1970s, 'The Ancient Greek Hero in 24 Hours' offers an exploration of civilization's roots in the Homeric epics and other Classical literature, a lineage that continues to challenge and inspire us today." (Publisher's note)

REVIEW: *Choice* v51 no6 p1001 F 2014 P. Nieto

REVIEW: *N Y Rev Books* v61 no9 p18-20 My 22 2014 Gregory Hays

"The Ancient Greek Hero in 24 Hours." "[Author Gregory] Nagy has for many years taught a large lecture course on 'the Greek hero,' both to regular Harvard undergraduates and to continuing education students. That course has now been transformed into a MOOC, to which his recent seven-hundred-page book serves as a kind of textbook. . . . For the general reader, a . . . pervasive problem is the selectivity of Nagy's interest. . . . Parts of it anyone can grasp; other parts you would probably have to be Nagy to understand."

REVIEW: *TLS* no5776 p26 D 13 2013 FRANCESCA WADE

"The Ancient Greek Hero in 24 Hours." "In 'The Ancient Greek Hero in 24 Hours' Gregory Nagy discusses the complex interactions between ancient literary depictions of the mythical hero and the religious practice of hero worship. . . . Nagy's arguments are often semantic, hinging on cultural implications teased patiently from etymologies. . . His analysis is fascinating, often ingenious. Yet, given how little is known about the context of the Homeric poems, I remain sceptical of the indirect allusions he reads. . . . 'The Ancient Greek Hero in 24 Hours' originates in a series of lectures Nagy has given at Harvard every year since the late 1970s. . . . Nagy's academic language and densely sophisticated arguments require a dedicated reader."

NAIDEN, F. S. Smoke signals for the gods; ancient Greek sacrifice from the Archaic through Roman periods; [by] F. S. Naiden 421 p. 2013 Oxford University Press

1. Animal sacrifice—Greece 2. Animal sacrifice—Rome 3. Historical literature

ISBN 9780199916405

LC 2012-008795

SUMMARY: In this book, author F. S. Naiden argues that animal sacrifice in ancient Greece "'did not depend on an animal as opposed to other offerings, or on an animal's death; it did not evoke guilt, and it did not depend on a community as opposed to an individual.' Animals were simply 'offerings that happened to be slaughtered,' which could be replaced by other kinds of offering--bronze statuettes, fig cakes, incense--without changing the meaning of the ritual." (Times Literary Supplement)

REVIEW: *Choice* v50 no11 p2033-4 Jl 2013 P. B. Harvey Jr.

REVIEW: *TLS* no5748 p9-10 My 31 2013 PETER THONEMANN

"Greek and Roman Animal Sacrifice: Ancient Victims, Modern Observers" and "Smoke Signals for the Gods: Ancient Greek Sacrifice From the Archaic Through Roman Periods." "The essays in 'Greek and Roman Animal Sacrifice struggle to come up with any real alternative. . . . No such infirmity of purpose impedes [F. S.] Naiden's Smoke Signals for the Gods, which offers a massive and sustained challenge to the Durkheimian vision of ancient sacrifice. . . . Naiden's attempt to return to a pre-Durkheimian theory of religious action, based around meaningful personal encounters and communications with the divine, fails to persuade."

NAKAMURA, FUMINORI. The thief; [by] Fuminori Nakamura 211 p. 2012 Soho

1. Crime—Fiction 2. Murder—Fiction 3. Suspense fiction 4. Thieves—Japan—Fiction

ISBN 9781616950217

LC 2011-041972

SUMMARY: This book is about Nishimura, a "Tokyo pickpocket" who "lives by his wits and other people's money. He has eyes that can spot the wealthiest person in a crowd and fingers that can swipe a wallet without raising an eyebrow. . . . All that changes when he lets Ishikawa, his former partner and mentor, rope him into a very different kind of criminal enterprise. Together with his sometime colleague Tachibana, they're hired, or rather forced, by a big fish named Kizaki to accompany some of Kizaki's regulars on a robbery. . . . Nishimura . . . is amazed to learn that after he and his mates left the house, the regulars killed their victim, a prominent politician, igniting a string of consequences that won't be over until Kizaki lures Nishimura into his net for another job." (Kirkus)

REVIEW: *Booklist* v108 no12 p27 F 15 2012 Thomas Gaughan

REVIEW: *Kirkus Rev* v80 no4 p351 F 15 2012

"The Thief." "Nakamura's first English translation takes a Tokyo pickpocket out way past his depth and makes him squirm. . . . Nishimura, who's evidently led a sheltered life that hasn't included the reading of much crime fiction, is amazed to learn that after he and his mates left the house, the regulars killed their victim, a prominent politician, igniting a string of consequences that won't be over until Kizaki lures Nishimura into his net for another job. Nishimura never wonders how this second caper will turn out, and neither will most readers. A spare but otherwise routine two rounds of larceny and betrayal fleshed out by the narrator's reflections on the Zen of picking pockets."

REVIEW: *Libr J* v137 no3 p98 F 15 2012 Terry Hong

REVIEW: *Publ Wkly* p90 My 28 2012

REVIEW: *Publ Wkly* v259 no2 p32-3 Ja 9 2012

NAOKI HIGASHIDA. The reason I jump; the inner voice

of a thirteen-year-old boy with autism; 176 p. 2013 Random House

1. Autism 2. Autistic people—Japan—Biography 3. Autistic people—Psychology 4. Autistic people's writings 5. Memoirs
ISBN 0812994868; 9780812994865 (acid-free paper)
LC 2012-045703

SUMMARY: In this book, "a 13-year-old Japanese author illuminates his autism from within. . . . The book takes the form of a series of straightforward questions followed by answers. . . . He describes the difficulty of expressing through words what the brain wants to say, the challenge of focusing and ordering experience, the obsessiveness of repetition, the comfort found in actions that others might find odd, and the frustration of being the source of others' frustration." (Kirkus Reviews)

REVIEW: *Kirkus Rev* v81 no13 p299 Jl 1 2013

REVIEW: *Libr J* v139 no7 p48 Ap 15 2014 Douglas C. Lord

REVIEW: *N Y Times Book Rev* p27 Ag 25 2013 SALLIE TISDALE

"The Reason I Jump: The Inner Voice of a Thirteen-Year-Old Boy With Autism". "The author, Naoki Higashida, was 13 years old at the time he wrote the memoir, and nonverbal. He wrote by spelling out words on a Japanese alphabet letter board. . . . Higashida is bright and thoughtful. . . . The book comes to English readers through the passionate efforts of David Mitchell . . . and his wife, KA Yoshida, [who] provided the translation. . . .'The Reason I Jump' makes for odd reading. . . . The constant presumption that he speaks for 'people with autism' and 'us kids with autism' is jarring. . . . Unfortunately, it's impossible to sort out what is Higashida here and what is Mitchell. . . . The parents of an autistic child may not be the best translators for a book by an autistic child."

REVIEW: *New Statesman* v142 no5167 p46-7 Jl 19 2013 Caroline Crampton

REVIEW: *Publ Wkly* v260 no36 p15 S 9 2013 Jessamine Chan

REVIEW: *TLS* no5766 p26-7 O 4 2013 ADAM WISHART

NAPPAALUK, MITIARJUK. Sanaaq; [by] Mitiarjuk Nappaaluk 192 p. 2014 Michigan State University Press

1. Canadian literature—Inuit authors 2. First Nations (Canada)—History 3. Human ecology 4. Inuit 5. Widows—Fiction
ISBN 0887557481; 9780887557484

SUMMARY: This book presents the "story of an Inuit family negotiating the changes brought into their community by the coming of the qallunaat, the white people, in the mid-nineteenth century. Sanaaq, a strong and outspoken young widow, and her daughter, Qumac, hunt seal, repair their kayak, and gather mussels under blue sea ice before the tide comes in. Theirs is a semi-nomadic life on the edge of the ice where . . . violence appears in the form of a fearful husband or a hungry polar bear." (Publisher's note)

REVIEW: *Quill Quire* v80 no2 p26-8 Mr 2014 Bruce Whiteman

"Sanaaq". "Written in Inukitut over a period of many years beginning in the 1950s, and first published in syllabic script in 1987, it is billed as the first Inuit novel but is, more accurately, a series of vignettes. Some of the characteristics of a traditional novel are absent, including character development and plot, although there is a great deal of incident and description and the cast is quite large. . . . If the book cannot be read for the usual pleasures of a conventional novel, it is still fascinating and has much to teach us on an anthropological and human level. . . . The translation here seems adept, although the overuse of exclamation marks in direct speech is annoying."

REVIEW: *TLS* no5790 p32 Mr 21 2014 T. E. L.

NARAYANASAMY, P. Biological Management of Diseases of Crops; Integration of Biological Control Strategies With Crop Disease Management Systems; [by] P. Narayanasamy 350 p. 2013 Springer Verlag

1. Agricultural innovations 2. Microbiology 3. Phytopathogenic microorganisms—Biological control 4. Phytopathogenic microorganisms—Management 5. Scientific literature
ISBN 940076376X; 9789400763760

SUMMARY: This book on biological management of crop diseases by P. Narayanasamy "contains seven chapters covering both cultural and physical methods related to biological management, developing and commercializing [biological control agents] , and biological management in agriculture and horticulture." (Choice: Current Reviews for Academic Libraries)

REVIEW: *Choice* v51 no7 p1245 Mr 2014 R. Frederiksen

"Characteristics of Biological Control Agents" and "Integration of Biological Control Strategies With Crop Disease Management Systems." "In this two-volume work, [P.] Narayanasamy provides a comprehensive discussion of the importance of biological management of plant pathogens in order to feed an ever-expanding population. . . . The BCAs reviewed in these volumes will inform researchers about the need to evaluate the interaction of the BCA with target hosts. Some BCAs might pose a threat to both researchers and users. There are many successes in this area; some are understood, and many remain a mystery. Every agricultural researcher who anticipates evaluating biological management for controlling diseases of any crop will find these books to be a treasure."

NARAYANASAMY, P. Biological management of diseases of crops; volume 1: characteristics of biological control agents; [by] P. Narayanasamy 600 p. 2013 Springer

1. Agricultural innovations 2. Biotechnology 3. Phytopathogenic microorganisms—Biological control 4. Plant diseases 5. Scientific literature
ISBN 9789400763791
LC 2013-932136

SUMMARY: This book on biological management of crop diseases by P. Narayanasamy "contains eight chapters with numerous appendixes within each. Topics include detecting and identifying fungal, bacterial, viral, and abiotic biological control agents (BCAs) and their mechanisms of action." (Choice: Current Reviews for Academic Libraries)

REVIEW: *Choice* v51 no7 p1245 Mr 2014 R. Frederiksen

"Characteristics of Biological Control Agents" and "Integration of Biological Control Strategies With Crop Disease Management Systems." "In this two-volume work, [P.] Narayanasamy provides a comprehensive discussion of the importance of biological management of plant pathogens in order to feed an ever-expanding population. . . . The BCAs reviewed in these volumes will inform researchers about the need to evaluate the interaction of the BCA with target hosts. Some BCAs might pose a threat to both researchers and users. There are many successes in this area; some are understood, and many remain a mystery. Every agricultural researcher who anticipates evaluating biological management for controlling diseases of any crop will find these books to be a treasure."

NARINS, BRIGHAM.ed. The Gale encyclopedia of nursing and allied health. See The Gale encyclopedia of nursing and allied health

NASAW, DAVID. The patriarch; the remarkable life and turbulent times of Joseph P. Kennedy; [by] David Nasaw xxiv, 868 p. 2012 Penguin Press

1. Ambassadors—United States—Biography 2. Biographies 3. Businesspeople—United States—Biography 4. Politicians—United States—Biography
ISBN 1594203768; 9781594203763
LC 2012-027315

SUMMARY: In this biography, "[David] Nasaw takes on Joseph P. Kennedy, businessman, Hollywood mogul, founding chair of the Securities and Exchange Commission, U.S. ambassador to Britain, and, of course, father to our 35th President. He had exclusive access to Kennedy's papers and addresses some longstanding questions." (Library Journal)

REVIEW: *Am Hist Rev* v118 no4 p1198-9 O 2013 Burton W. Peretti

"The Patriarch: The Remarkable Life and Turbulent Times of Joseph P. Kennedy." "Despite its 'WASPish condescension' . . ., Franklin D. Roosevelt's assessment of Joseph P. Kennedy encapsulates [author] David Nasaw's own take on this elusive figure. Nasaw's steadily paced, meticulously researched, and elegantly written work is the finest biography of the head of the storied Kennedy family ever to appear. . . . The book only briefly analyzes significant aspects of Kennedy's life and thought. Nasaw avoids the obsessive, time-consuming, and reductionist approach of Robert A. Caro, which boils down mountainous evidence concerning the subject into a single defining trait; on balance this is wise, but Kennedy's essential character and motives remain enigmatic."

REVIEW: *Booklist* v109 no4 p15 O 15 2012 Ilene Cooper

REVIEW: *Commonweal* v140 no8 p26-7 My 3 2013 Andrew J. Bacevich

REVIEW: *J Am Hist* v100 no3 p882-3 D 2013 Matthew Dallek

REVIEW: *Kirkus Rev* v80 no20 p137 O 15 2012

REVIEW: *Kirkus Rev* p30 D 2 2012 Best NonFiction & Teen

REVIEW: *Libr J* v138 no5 p82 Mr 15 2013 Don Wismer

REVIEW: *N Y Times Book Rev* p30 N 25 2012

REVIEW: *N Y Times Book Rev* p1 N 18 2012 CHRISTOPHER BUCKLEY

REVIEW: *N Y Times Book Rev* p28 O 6 2013 IHSAN TAYLOR

REVIEW: *New York Times* p23 N 30 2012 MICHIKO KAKUTANI

REVIEW: *Publ Wkly* v259 no40 p37 O 1 2012 WENDY SMITH

REVIEW: *Publ Wkly* v259 no40 p89-90 O 1 2012

NASSNER, ALYSSA.il. Montessori shape work. See George, B.

NASSNER, ALYSSA. Secrets of the apple tree. See Brown, C.

NASTA, DOMINIQUE. Contemporary Romanian Cinema; The History of an Unexpected Miracle; [by] Dominique Nasta 256 p. 2013 Columbia University Press

1. Motion picture industry—Finance 2. Motion picture industry—Romania 3. Motion picture literature 4. Romania—History 5. Romanian films
ISBN 023116744X; 9780231167444

SUMMARY: In this book on Romanian cinema, author Dominique Nasta "anchors her analysis in specific national historic, political, economic, and sociocultural contexts going back to the beginnings of Romania's film industry in 1911-12. She then provides . . . [an] analysis of the impact that globalization of film financing, production, and distribution has had on the revitalization of Romania's national cinema." (Choice: Current Reviews for Academic Libraries)

REVIEW: *Choice* v51 no8 p1407 Ap 2014 D. J. Goulding

"Contemporary Romanian Cinema: the History of an Unexpected Miracle". "[Dominique] Nasta . . . a native of Romania and an internationally respected published scholar, has written the essential book on Romania's complex and challenging national cinema—from the silent era to the present—which has too often been ignored or underestimated in English-language accounts. Critically astute, well informed, and engagingly written, this book provides a fascinating narrative of contemporary Romanian cinema and its rise to international prominence since the fall of communism. Nasta provides a compelling multifaceted answer to a critical question: how was the 'miracle' of the Romanian new wave possible?"

NATHAN, AMY SUE. The glass wives; [by] Amy Sue Nathan 304 p. 2013 St. Martin's Griffin

1. Domestic fiction 2. Family secrets—Fiction 3. Grief—Fiction 4. Widows—Fiction 5. Wives—Fiction
ISBN 9781250016560 (trade pbk.); 9781250040169 (hardcover)
LC 2013-003415

SUMMARY: In this book, "when a tragic car accident ends the life of Richard Glass, it also upends the lives of Evie and Nicole, and their children. There's no love lost between the widow and the ex. . . . But Evie wasn't counting on her children's bond with their baby half-brother, and she wasn't counting on Nicole's desperate need to hang on to the threads of family, no matter how frayed. . . . Evie cautiously agrees to share . . .her home . . . with Nicole and the baby." (Publisher's note)

REVIEW: *Booklist* v109 no14 p62 Mr 15 2013 Margaret Flanagan

REVIEW: *Booklist* v110 no3 p45-6 O 1 2013 Whitney Scott

"The Glass Wives." "[Joyce] Bean breezes through [Amy Sue] Nathan's first novel with a delicately shaded reading. . . . Bean voices Nicole in a deceptively wispy, little-girl manner that nicely contrasts with Evie's more solid and centered tones. Supporting players, including Evie's 10-year-old twins, Sam and Sophie, are equally believable, particularly when Bean expresses Sam's nearly unbearable anguish and withdrawal through scratchy tones, indicative of a prepubescent boy. Other characters, including friends of Evie and Nicole, are easily differentiated, especially when they take sides. Fans of domestic fiction will enjoy this story, which rings with authenticity as it touches upon such issues as familial bonds, women's friendships, and reconciliation."

NATIONAL WILDLIFE FEDERATION.comp. My first book of baby animals. See My first book of baby animals

NATSUME SOSEKI. The gate; [by] Natsume Soseki xviii, 227 p. 2013 New York Review Books

1. Brothers—Fiction 2. Japanese fiction—Translations into English 3. Tokyo (Japan)—Fiction 4. Zen monasteries

ISBN 9781590175873 (alk. paper)

LC 2012-028093

SUMMARY: This moving and deceptively simple story, a melancholy tale shot through with glimmers of joy, beauty, and gentle wit, is an understated masterpiece by one of Japan's greatest writers. At the end of his life, Natsume Sōseki declared 'The Gate,' originally published in 1910, to be his favorite among all his novels. This new translation captures the oblique grace of the original while correcting numerous errors and omissions that marred the first English version." (Publisher's note)

REVIEW: *N Y Rev Books* v60 no2 p37-40 F 7 2013 Pico Iyer

REVIEW: *TLS* no5777/8 p34 D 20 2013 LESLEY DOWNER

"The Gate." "One of Sōseki's lesser known and more difficult works. 'The Gate' is a short book, lacking the humour and lightness of touch which enliven his most famous works. . . . Written in 1910, in his middle period, it is the last of a trilogy, of which the first two are 'Sanshirō' and 'Sore Kara' ('And Then'), dealing with themes of self-knowledge and responsibility--one's accountability to society as against one's responsibility to one's own emotions. It is the low-key story of ordinary people, leading lives of quiet desperation. . . This is a jewel of book, economically written, in which every element fits perfectly. . . . [William F.] Sibley's excellent translation includes detailed notes and an introduction by Pico Iyer."

NATURAL COMPOUNDS; Plant Sources, Structure and Properties; 4000 p. 2013 Springer Verlag

1. Chemical literature 2. Chemicals—Properties 3. Chemistry—Dictionaries 4. Organic compounds 5. Reference books

ISBN 0387491406; 9780387491400

SUMMARY: Edited by Shakhnoza S. Azimova, this six-volume work "details the properties of over 7,500 chemical compounds of pharmacological interest found in plants. Each volume systematically covers occurrence of the compounds in plants, illustrations of chemical structures plus physical-chemical, spectral, and pharmacological data. Entries are indexed by plant name, subject, and pharmacological property." (Publisher's note)

REVIEW: *Choice* v51 no1 p109-10 S 2013 D. L. Jacobs

"Natural Compounds: Plant Sources, Structures, and Properties." "The ceaseless discovery and reporting of new natural products across disparate journals beseeches the development of one single, searchable repository. Indeed, this multivolume compendium features over 7,500 unique natural plant compounds; however, due to the enormity of such a task, it is not surprising that each volume is dedicated to an exceptionally specialized class of plant compounds. . . . The principal aspect that elevates this resource above similar collections is its inclusion of comprehensive IR (infrared) and ^{1}H-, and ^{13}C-NMR (nuclear magnetic resonance) data."

NAU, HENRY R. Conservative internationalism; armed diplomacy under Jefferson, Polk, Truman, and Reagan; [by] Henry R. Nau 321 p. 2013 Princeton University Press

1. HISTORY—United States—General 2. Historical literature 3. POLITICAL SCIENCE—History & Theory 4. POLITICAL SCIENCE—International Relations—Diplomacy

ISBN 9780691159317 (hardback)

LC 2013-019882

SUMMARY: It was the author's intent "to delineate and argue for a distinct historical and philosophical tradition in American foreign policy that is both internationalist and conservative. he locates this tradition in the words and actions of several U.S. presidents. . . . [Henry R.] Nau's chosen tradition is internationalist in its support for U.S. engagement abroad . . . and it is conservative in its determination to back diplomacy with force." (National Review)

REVIEW: *Natl Rev* v65 no19 p42-3 O 14 2013 COLIN DUECK

"Conservative Internationalism: Armed Diplomacy Under Jefferson, Polk, Truman, and Reagan." "The presidential case studies [Henry R.] Nau puts forward are uniformly interesting, even if some are more convincing than others. . . . Nau makes a plausible overarching case for the existence of a distinct conservative-internationalist tradition in American diplomacy, and one deserving of fresh examination in the age of [Barack] Obama. . . . I have a lingering sense that Nau's book overemphasizes democracy promotion as the one central driving purpose behind American foreign policy. . . . Still, the great strength of Nau's book is that he is right about most of the big challenges facing U.S. foreign policy right now, including challenges for conservatives."

NAVASKY, VICTOR S. The art of controversy; political cartoons and their enduring power; [by] Victor S. Navasky 256 p. 2013 Alfred A. Knopf

1. ART—Art & Politics 2. ART—Criticism & Theory 3. Art literature 4. POLITICAL SCIENCE—History & Theory 5. Political cartoons

ISBN 0307957209; 9780307957207 (hardback)

LC 2012-038247

SUMMARY: In this book, "drawing on his own encounters with would-be censors, interviews with cartoonists, and historical archives from cartoon museums across the globe, [author Victor S.] Navasky examines the political cartoon as both art and polemic over the centuries. He recounts how cartoonists and caricaturists have been censored, threatened, incarcerated, and even murdered for their art, and asks what makes this art form . . . poised to affect our minds and our hearts." (Publisher's note)

REVIEW: *America* v210 no4 p36-7 F 10 2014 ALFRED LAWRENCE LORENZ

"The Art of Controversy: Political Cartoons and Their Enduring Power". "[Victor S.] Navasky lets his readers know up front that he is an absolutist about freedom of expression, and he reproduces and defends cartoons on hair-trigger subjects like politics, sex, race and religion that have brought some readers to full boil. He maintains that they ought to be printed, if they have merit. . . . Navasky's approach throughout is somewhat like that of a memoirist. He relates his own experiences and those of cartoonists and other journalists he has known. His writing is personal, even chatty, and Navasky himself is rarely out of the reader's view. All told, 'The Art of Controversy' is a readable introduction to its subject. Unfortunately, the author does not provide footnotes or a bibliography."

REVIEW: *Bookforum* v20 no1 p36-7 Ap/My 2013 JOSH FRUHLINGER

REVIEW: *Booklist* v109 no13 p3-4 Mr 1 2013 Mark Levine

REVIEW: *Choice* v51 no2 p246 O 2013 E. K. Mix

REVIEW: *Choice* v51 no2 p328 O 2013 R. A. Callahan

REVIEW: *Columbia J Rev* v51 no6 p63 Mr/Ap 2013 JAMES BOYLAN

REVIEW: *Kirkus Rev* v81 no3 p285 F 1 2013

REVIEW: *Kirkus Rev* v81 no3 p301 F 1 2013

REVIEW: *N Y Times Book Rev* p22 Je 2 2013 DEBORAH SOLOMON

REVIEW: *Nation* v296 no22 p37 Je 3 2013 JOHN PALATTELLA

REVIEW: *New York Times* v162 no56146 pC19-21 My 24 2013 DWIGHT GARNER

REVIEW: *Publ Wkly* v260 no7 p51-2 F 18 2013

NDIBE, OKEY. Foreign Gods, Inc.; [by] Okey Ndibe 336 p. 2014 Soho Press

1. Art thefts—New York (State)—New York 2. Arts, Nigerian—New York (State)—New York 3. Nigerian Americans—Fiction 4. Nigerian fiction (English) 5. Taxicab drivers—Fiction
ISBN 1616953136; 9781616953133 (hardback)
LC 2013-025995

SUMMARY: This book, by Okey Ndibe, "tells the story of Ike, a New York-based Nigerian cab driver who sets out to steal the statue of an ancient war deity from his home village and sell it to a New York gallery." The book is "a meditation on the dreams, promises and frustrations of the immigrant life in America; the nature and impact of religious conflicts; [and] the ways in which modern culture creates or heightens infatuation with the 'exotic,'" (Publisher's note)

REVIEW: *Booklist* v110 no7 p22 D 1 2013 Bridget Thoreson

REVIEW: *Libr J* v138 no18 p81 N 1 2013 Sally Bissell

REVIEW: *New York Times* v163 no56366 pC1-4 D 30 2013 JANET MASLIN

"Foreign Gods, Inc." "Okey Ndibe's razor-sharp 'Foreign Gods, Inc.' steps into the story of a Nigerian-born New Yorker called Ike, just as everything in his life has begun to go horribly wrong. . . . 'Foreign Gods, Inc.,' which arrives early in January, will . . . . have the impact of an astute and gripping new novelist's powerful debut. . . . Throughout 'Foreign Gods, Inc.,' Ike's hard-won urban Americanness, the kind that allowed him to drive a New York taxi, slowly evaporates. . . . Mr. Ndibe invests his story with enough dark comedy to make Ngene an odoriferous presence in his own right, and certainly not the kind of polite exotic rarity that art collectors are used to. . . . In Mr. Ndibe's agile hands, he's both a source of satire and an embodiment of pure terror."

REVIEW: *Publ Wkly* v260 no42 p1 O 21 2013

REVIEW: *TLS* no5791 p20 Mr 28 2014 SAMUEL ASHWORTH

NEAL, CHRISTOPHER SILAS.il. Lifetime the amazing numbers in animal lives. See Schaefer, Lola M.

NEALE, FELICITY. The Path to Spiritual Maturity; [by] Felicity Neale 182 p. 2013 Createspace Independent Pub

1. Awareness 2. Maturation (Psychology) 3. Mindfulness (Meditation) 4. Self-help materials 5. Spirituality
ISBN 1479186996; 9781479186990

SUMMARY: This book by Felicity Neale presents "a self-help guide to spiritual development. . . . Neale provides examples of low-, middle- and high-level development. Understanding the effect of personality on awareness, cultivating mindfulness, and using different types of prayer are some of the specific techniques that Neale offers." (Kirkus Reviews)

REVIEW: *Kirkus Rev* v81 no22 p30 N 15 2013

REVIEW: *Kirkus Rev* p44 D 15 2013 supplemet best books 2013

"The Path to Spiritual Maturity". "Borrowing from many wisdom traditions from across the world and her own personal experience, [Felicity] Neale writes a warm, engaging account that gives concrete steps for reaching spiritual maturity. Penned for those who are exploring different directions and who are not concerned with doctrinaire stands, this little book should perhaps have been titled, 'The Bridge to Spiritual Maturity'. . . . Anyone who is open-minded and curious will find in this volume a wealth of information that can be applied to his or her own growth and to the inevitable pitfalls and challenges. A detailed, approachable handbook to mindfulness by a knowledgeable, experienced spiritual guide."

NEATBY, NICOLE.ed. Settling and unsettling memories. See Settling and unsettling memories

NEER, ROBERT M. Napalm; an American biography; [by] Robert M. Neer 352 p. 2013 Belknap Press of Harvard University Press

1. Historical literature 2. Incendiary bombs—Design and construction—History 3. Incendiary weapons—History 4. Napalm—History
ISBN 9780674073012 (alk. paper)
LC 2012-034926

SUMMARY: This book on napalm by Robert M. Neer "explores how a novel weapon, which appeared in the last years of the Second World War, evolved into a metaphor of destructive American excess. Neer . . . follows the story of napalm that originally empowered an often outnumbered American military to fight far abroad against the Japanese, and later. North Koreans, Chinese and Vietnamese--only to become a byword for the pathologies of the military-industrial complex of the United States." (Times Literary Supplement)

REVIEW: *Am Hist Rev* v119 no2 p551-2 Ap 2014 David Kinkela

REVIEW: *Bookforum* v20 no1 p43 Ap/My 2013 CHRIS BRAY

REVIEW: *Choice* v51 no1 p101 S 2013 H. E. Pence

REVIEW: *Kirkus Rev* v81 no2 p196 Ja 15 2013

REVIEW: *Libr J* v138 no5 p116 Mr 15 2013 Karl Helicher

REVIEW: *Nation* v297 no13 p32 S 30 2013 PETER C. BAKER

"Napalm: An American Biography" and "Extremely Loud: Sound as a Weapon." "As described by Robert Neer . . . [napalm] depended on taxpayer money and academic know-how, and required the fervent corporate desire for more products to sell. . . . Neer's closing chapters, which chronicle the decline in napalm use, are comparatively thin. . . . Juliette Volcler presents a scattered, piecemeal history of the attempts to build 'acoustic weapons.' There are examples from every swath of thee sonic spectrum."

REVIEW: *Publ Wkly* v260 no2 p49 Ja 14 2013

REVIEW: *TLS* no5755 p8-9 Jl 19 2013 VICTOR DAVIS HANSON

"Saltpeter: The Mother of Gunpowder," "Napalm: An American Biography," and "Warrior Geeks: How Twenty-First-Century Technology is Changing the Way We Fight and Think About War." "David Cressy offers a brief but fascinating history of saltpetre. . . . He has skilfully turned 200 pages on the collection of human and animal waste into a fascinating reflection on how civic liberties were often quashed by concerns for national security. . . . [Robert M.] Neer is often highly critical of the American m use of napalm; yet his narrative of its origins, production and use over the past seven decades is not a jeremiad, but learned, fair and historically accurate. . . . Do not let the almost flippant title of Christopher Coker's 'Warrior Geeks' fool you. . . . [It is] a masterly account from a very well-read humanist about the fearful advance of post-human technologies in war."

NEGRI, ANTONIO, 1933-. Spinoza for our time. See Spinoza for our time

NEILL, MICHAEL.ed. The Spanish tragedy. See Kyd, T.

NEILSON, DAVID.il. Southern Light. See Southern Light

NELIS, ANNEMIEK.ed. Engineering the human. See Engineering the human

NELMS, KATE.il. See what a seal can do! See Butterworth, C.

NELSON, CRAIG. The age of radiance; the epic rise and dramatic fall of the atomic era; [by] Craig Nelson 416 p. 2014 Scribner

1. Historical literature
ISBN 145166043X; 9781451660432 (hardcover); 9781451660449 (paperback)
LC 2013-042192

SUMMARY: This book, by Craig Nelson, is a "history of the Atomic Age. . . . From the discovery of X-rays in the 1890s, through the birth of nuclear power in an abandoned Chicago football stadium, to the bomb builders of Los Alamos, . . . Nelson illuminates a pageant of fascinating historical figures: Marie and Pierre Curie, Albert Einstein, Niels Bohr, Franklin Roosevelt, J. Robert Oppenheimer, Harry Truman, Curtis LeMay, John F. Kennedy, Robert McNamara, Ronald Reagan, and Mikhail Gorbachev." (Publisher's note)

REVIEW: *Booklist* v110 no11 p4 F 1 2014 Brendan Driscoll

REVIEW: *Choice* v52 no1 p117 St 2014 A. M. Strauss

REVIEW: *Kirkus Rev* v82 no5 p17 Mr 1 2014

"The Age of Radiance: The Epic Rise and Dramatic Fall of the Atomic Era". "[Craig] Nelson's coverage of the science underlying this saga is admirably thorough and accessible, but this is no impersonal 'march of science' story. The author also shows how the development of nuclear physics was deeply influenced by contemporary politics and the interplay of the personalities involved. He includes lively biographies of the men—Wilhelm Roentgen, Enrico Fermi, Leo Szilard and others—who created this new age and of two remarkable women: the celebrated Polish-born Marie Curie and the almost forgotten Austrian Lise Meitner. . . . An engaging history that raises provocative questions about the future of nuclear science."

REVIEW: *Libr J* v138 no16 p58 O 1 2013 Barbara Hoffert

REVIEW: *Publ Wkly* v260 no51 p46 D 16 2013

REVIEW: *Sci Am* v310 no4 p86 Ap 2014 Clara Moskowitz

REVIEW: *Science* v345 no6193 p146 Jl 11 2014 Daniel L. Sanchez

NELSON, KADIR. Baby Bear; 40 p. 2014 Balzer + Bray

1. Bears—Fiction 2. Children's stories 3. Forest animals—Fiction 4. Home 5. Lost children—Fiction
ISBN 0062241729; 9780062241726 (hardcover bdg.)
LC 2013-003083

SUMMARY: This children's book, by Kadir Nelson, is "about a lost little bear searching for home." It functions "as the tale of a bear who finds his way home with the help of his animal friends; as a reassuring way to show children how to comfort themselves and find their way in everyday life; . . . as a method of teaching readers that by listening to your heart and trusting yourself, you will always find a true home within yourself." (Publisher's note)

REVIEW: *Booklist* v110 no8 p50 D 15 2013 Ilene Cooper

REVIEW: *Bull Cent Child Books* v67 no6 p327 F 2014 Jeannette Hulick

"Baby Bear." "The gentle cadences of the animals' voices and the large, dream-like illustrations in deep twilight tones make this suitable for bedtime reading or for an evening story hour. Unfortunately, some of the animals' advice is sentimental and clichéd . . . and Baby Bear's slow progress, a result of the largely abstract advice he receives, gets a bit tedious. [Kadir] Nelson's artwork, done in oil paint on canvas, is thoughtfully composed with unusual perspectives . . . giving the pictures a fresh originality. Some illustrations are plasticky in their stiff glossiness, but others are lovely--the nearly glowing snowy owl perched in a dark tree seems almost ethereal."

REVIEW: *Kirkus Rev* v81 no22 p110 N 15 2013

REVIEW: *Publ Wkly* v260 no42 p50-1 O 21 2013

NELSON, MARILYN, 1946-. How I discovered poetry; 112 p. 2014 Dial Books

1. African American women poets 2. Authorship—Poetry 3. Poems—Collections 4. Poetry—Authorship
ISBN 0803733046; 9780803733046 (hardcover : alk. paper)
LC 2013-005289

SUMMARY: In this memoir, author Marilyn Nelson "tells the story of her development as an artist and young woman through fifty eye-opening poems. Readers are given an intimate portrait of her growing self-awareness and artistic inspiration along with a larger view of the world around her: racial tensions, the Cold War era, and the first stirrings of the feminist movement." (Publisher's note)

REVIEW: *Booklist* v110 no14 p67 Mr 15 2014 Gail Bush

REVIEW: *Bull Cent Child Books* v67 no7 p370-1 Mr 2014 D. S.

"How I Discovered Poetry." "The tightly written yet musing poems (many of them unrhymed sonnets) effectively capture single moments as slices of a larger, longer trajectory of growth, travel, and inquiry. . . . Attractive and subtle design adds appeal, with poem titles in slate blue and simple decorative spot art, usually dichromatic, neatly supplying both a retro visual quotation and contemporary currency;occasional family photographs provide additional immediacy. Use this to bring a vivid personal touch to an exploration of the era, or as a gloriously personal entry in a poetry unit that will prompt eager imitation."

REVIEW: *Horn Book Magazine* v90 no1 p105-6 Ja/F 2014 ELISSA GERSHOWITZ

"How I Discovered Poetry." "[Marilyn Nelson's] author's note calls this volume a 'late-career retrospective…a "portrait of the artist as a young American Negro Girl,"' and readers will be gratified to follow the progression of 'the Speaker' (as Nelson refers to the main character, 'whose life is very much like mine') from tentative child to self-possessed young woman on the cusp of a creative awakening. A few family photos are included, rounded out by spare 1950s–ish spot art that underscores the time period and accentuates the deeply personal nature of the remembrances."

REVIEW: *Kirkus Rev* v81 no23 p94 D 1 2013

REVIEW: *Publ Wkly* v260 no45 p73 N 11 2013

REVIEW: *Voice of Youth Advocates* v36 no5 p64 D 2013 Jennifer Rummel

NELSON, MICHAEL. Knock or ring; a novel; [by] Michael Nelson viii, 182 p. 2013 Valancourt Books

1. Book auctions—Fiction 2. Book collectors—Fiction 3. Booksellers & bookselling—Fiction 4. Popular literature 5. Price fixing
ISBN 9781939140463 (acid free paper)
LC 2013-010723

SUMMARY: This book by Michael Nelson presents a fictional account of a Ring, in which various parties "conspir[e] to keep prices low at public auctions so that valuable items could be resold at greater profit at private trade 'settlements'. . . . The plot centres on the sale of a country house and its contents." The book examines "the mechanics of the Ring in operation and the mathematics of the settlements that ensue from its activities." (Times Literary Supplement)

REVIEW: *TLS* no5746 p27 My 17 2013 A. S. G. EDWARDS

"Knock or Ring." "The plot centres on the sale of a country house and its contents. The narrative is devoid of any sense of urgency and evinces little interest in character and motivation. The novel's distinctiveness lies in the detailed presentation of the mechanics of the Ring in operation and the mathematics of the settlements that ensue from its activities. . . . John Saumarez-Smith's brief introduction offers a chatty summary of [Michael] Nelson's life, but says very little about the novel and nothing about the activities of the Ring. One might have hoped for either anecdote or historical perspective from one who describes himself as a 'bookseller since 1965'."

NELSON, MICHAEL. A room in Chelsea Square; [by] Michael Nelson 216 p. 1959 Doubleday

1. Authors—Fiction 2. Autobiographical fiction 3. Bohemianism—Fiction 4. Gay men—Fiction 5. Humorous stories 6. London (England)—Fiction
LC 5901-0688

SUMMARY: "'A Room in Chelsea Square' (1958), the semi-autobiographical second novel by Michael Nelson (1921-1990), was published anonymously both because of its frank gay content at a time when homosexuality was still illegal and because its characters were thinly veiled portrayals of prominent London literary figures." (Publisher's note)

REVIEW: *TLS* no5795 p20-1 Ap 25 2014 DAVID COLLARD

"The Prince's Boy" and "A Room In Chelsea Square." "Paul Bailey's slim novella 'The Prince's Boy' is set in the summer of 1927 when Dinu Grigorescu, a callow nineteen-year old, arrives in Paris from Bucharest in search of adventure and literary fame. . . . Bailey opts throughout for a style both formal and florid. . . . This might work well on the stage but it wears thin on the page, however true it may be to the period, and however expertly done. . . . Michael Nelson's 'A Room in Chelsea Square' is an intermittently amusing roman-à-clef first published, anonymously, in 1958. . . . 'A Room in Chelsea Square' has value as a portrait of a transitional moment in our culture."

NELSON, ROBIN. Can people count on me?; a book about responsibility; [by] Robin Nelson 32 p. 2014 Lerner Publications

1. Children's nonfiction 2. Ethics 3. Homework 4. Personality development—Juvenile literature 5. Responsibility—Juvenile literature
ISBN 9781467713634 (lib. bdg. : alk. paper)
LC 2013-018367

SUMMARY: This book by Robin Nelson is part of the Show Your Character series, which "emphasizes development traits such as responsibility, respect, honesty, and empathy and strives to help kids learn how to be good citizens and improve both their own lives and the lives of those around them." (School Library Journal) It "discusses doing the right thing and being responsible." (Booklist)

REVIEW: *Booklist* v110 no8 p39 D 15 2013 Ilene Cooper

"Can People Count on Me? A Book About Responsibility," "Does My Voice Count? A Book About Citizenship," and "How Can I Deal With Bullying? A Book Book About Respect." "Even young children can learn to be helpful, responsible citizens, and the Show Your Character series gives them a way to begin. . . . Sometimes the issues in the books overlap, but this series is a good place for children to start thinking about ways to make their world a better place. The suggestions are age appropriate, and kids are urged to talk to parents or an adult when things get to be more than they can handle (though parental discussion should be even more emphasized than it is). The book tries not to have the answers seem pat, and happily, sometimes scenarios are taken a step further."

NELSON, TIMOTHY J. Doing the best I can. See Edin, K.

NEOPLATONISM AND THE PHILOSOPHY OF NATURE; ix, 257 p. 2012 Oxford University Press

1. Ancient philosophy 2. Neoplatonism 3. Philosophical literature 4. Philosophy & science 5. Philosophy of nature

ISBN 9780199693719

LC 2012-460526

SUMMARY: Edited by James Wilberding and Christoph Horn, this book "collects essays by leading international scholars in the field which shed new light on how the Neoplatonists sought to understand and explain nature and natural phenomena. It is thematically divided into two parts, . . . directed at the explication of central Neoplatonic metaphysical doctrines . . . , and . . . showing how these same doctrines play out in individual natural sciences." (Publisher's note)

REVIEW: *Classical Rev* v63 no2 p406-8 O 2013 Giannis Stamatellos

"Neoplatonism and the Philosophy of Nature." "Despite the importance of Platonism in the history of philosophy, limited attention has been paid to the significance of the philosophy of nature in Neoplatonism. This book aims to fill this gap through a collection of essays written by eminent scholars. . . . The book is a significant contribution to Neoplatonic scholarship. It offers a well-balanced and systematic exploration of the question of physis in Neoplatonism with an excellent use of primary sources and secondary literature. The commonly held view that Neoplatonists were solely concerned with otherworldly metaphysics is excellently challenged by their philosophical insights on physis."

NEPSTAD, SHARON ERICKSON. Nonviolent revolutions; civil resistance in the late 20th century; [by] Sharon Erickson Nepstad xviii, 178 p. 2011 Oxford University Press

1. Defection 2. Government, Resistance to—History—20th century 3. Passive resistance 4. Revolutions—History—20th century 5. Social science literature

ISBN 0199778205 (hardback: alk. paper); 0199778213 (pbk.: alk. paper); 9780199778201 (hardback: alk. paper); 9780199778218 (pbk.: alk. paper)

LC 2011-015264

SUMMARY: In this book, "taking a comparative approach that includes both successful and failed cases of nonviolent resistance, [Sharon Erickson] Nepstad analyzes the effects of movements' strategies along with the counter-strategies regimes developed to retain power. She shows that a significant influence on revolutionary outcomes is security force defections, and explores the reasons why soldiers defect or remain loyal and the conditions that increase the likelihood of mutiny." (Publisher's note)

REVIEW: *Contemp Sociol* v43 no1 p108-10 Ja 2014 Celso M. Villegas

"Nonviolent Revolutions: Civil Resistance in the Late 20th Century". "Sharon Erickson Nepstad has written a timely and concise treatment of social movement strategy and political change. . . . In less than 150 pages, she crosses four continents and six countries—China, East Germany, Panama, Chile, Kenya, and the Philippines—and captures the dramatic moments of each of their nonviolent movements through her theoretical lens. As a result, the book is very accessible and the writing taut, reflecting the parsimony of her framework and analysis. . . . Despite these strengths, scholars of revolution and democratic transitions, as well as area specialists, may find the book to be dissatisfying."

NESBIT, TARASHEA. The wives of Los Alamos; a novel; [by] TaraShea Nesbit 240 p. 2014 Bloomsbury USA

1. Atomic bomb—Fiction 2. Deception (Military science)—History—20th century—Fiction 3. FICTION—General 4. Historical fiction 5. Married women—New Mexico—Los Alamos—Fiction 6. World War, 1939-1945—New Mexico—Los Alamos—Fiction

ISBN 1620405032; 9781620405031 (hardback)

LC 2013-036239

SUMMARY: This book, by TaraShea Nesbit, describes the lives of Los Alamos scientists' wives during the creation of the atomic bomb. "Hope quickly turned to hardship as they were forced to adapt to a rugged military town where everything was a secret, including what their husbands were doing at the lab. They lived in barely finished houses with P.O. box addresses in a town wreathed with barbed wire, all for the benefit of a project that didn't exist as far as the public knew." (Publisher's note)

REVIEW: *Booklist* v110 no5 p35 N 1 2013 Lynn Weber

REVIEW: *Kirkus Rev* v82 no3 p10 F 1 2014

"The Wives of Los Alamos". " The scientists' wives tell the story of daily life in Los Alamos during the creation of the atomic bomb, in Nesbit's lyrical, captivating historical debut. . . . An ominous secrecy heightens until the bomb is finally dropped. Individual women—like tough Louise, weepy Margaret, charismatic Starla and difficult Katherine—are less characters to follow than touchstones to keep the reader grounded as time passes in this insular world. Nesbit artfully accumulates the tiny facts of an important historical moment, creating an emotional tapestry of time and place."

REVIEW: *N Y Times Book Rev* p19 Ap 20 2014 GEORGE JOHNSON

REVIEW: *Publ Wkly* v260 no41 p34 O 14 2013

NESBITT, KENN. Kiss, kiss good night; 12 p. 2013 Scholastic

1. Animal stories 2. Bedtime—Juvenile literature 3. Kissing 4. Parent & child—Juvenile literature 5. Picture books for children

ISBN 0545479576; 9780545479578

SUMMARY: In this children's picture book by Kenn Nesbitt, "animal mothers tuck their babies into bed, easing them off to dreamland with snuggles and kisses. . . . The adorable animal mothers and babies—bunnies, cats, lambs and chicks, in addition to the bears—look absolutely blissful as they cuddle up and settle in for some rest. . . . The final spread incorporates all of the animal families at once." (Kirkus Reviews)

REVIEW: *Kirkus Rev* v82 no1 p42 Ja 1 2014

"Kiss, Kiss Good Night". "Soothing rhythms and apt and varied vocabulary make this goodnight book special. . . . The adorable animal mothers and babies—bunnies, cats, lambs and chicks, in addition to the bears—look absolutely blissful as they cuddle up and settle in for some rest. These sweet scenes are set against a bluish-purple night sky dotted with white stars that twinkle merrily down on the sleeping critters. . . . While this title is perfect for mother-baby bonding, it doesn't include any doting dads. . . . With large, sturdy board pages just right for tiny hands, this is a sweet selection for baby's bedtime."

REVIEW: *Kirkus Rev* v81 no20 p313 O 15 2013

NESS, PATRICK, 1971-. More than this; [by] Patrick Ness 480 p. 2013 Candlewick Press

1. Future life—Fiction 2. Gay teenagers 3. Near-death experiences—Fiction 4. Suicide victims—Fiction 5. Teenage boys—Fiction 6. Young adult fiction

ISBN 0763662585; 9780763662585

LC 2013-943065

SUMMARY: In this book, "teenage Seth is experiencing his own death in painful detail. In the next chapter, he wakes up physically weak, covered in bandages and strange wounds, and wonders if he is in Hell or the future or somewhere else entirely. . . . He is plagued by intense flashbacks of his life before he died. . . . Upon discovering two other young people . . . Seth begins to learn the Matrix-like truth about what has happened to the rest of humanity." (School Library Journal)

REVIEW: *Booklist* v109 no22 p80-1 Ag 1 2013 Daniel Kraus

REVIEW: *Bull Cent Child Books* v67 no2 p107-8 O 2013 K. Q. G.

"More Than This." "A broken heart has led sixteen-year-old Seth to suicide, but ending his life doesn't necessarily put an end to his problems. After drowning himself off the coast of his Pacific Northwest home, Seth wakes up across the world in the small English town where he spent his childhood. . . . This complex, genre-bending book opens with Seth's violent drowning death at sea, described in such spare but devastating detail that readers may feel themselves gasping for a breath as Seth draws his last. . . . Several early hints point toward the 'Matrix'-like premise that is introduced in the latter part, but Ness subverts familiar sci-fi/survival tropes and storytelling conventions, leaving readers with an ambiguous ending."

REVIEW: *Horn Book Magazine* v89 no6 p101-2 N/D 2013 JONTHAN HUNT

"More Than This." "The world-building, rather than becoming increasingly clearer, instead remains an enigma that puzzles and perplexes the characters--not to mention the reader. . . . [Patrick] Ness. . . is not only a good storyteller but an interesting prose stylist, and his latest effort is as provocative as ever. Nevertheless, the gay subplot lacks satisfactory resolution, and the overwritten third-person present-tense narration makes the novel feel more important than it really is; consequently, the audience for this book narrows considerably from Ness's previous work."

REVIEW: *Kirkus Rev* v81 no17 p107 S 1 2013

REVIEW: *Publ Wkly* v260 no27 p90 Jl 8 2013

REVIEW: *SLJ* v59 no8 p114 Ag 2013 Kyle Lukoff

REVIEW: *Voice of Youth Advocates* v36 no4 p85 O 2013 Barbara Allen

NETZLEY, PATRICIA D. How does video game violence affect society?; [by] Patricia D. Netzley 96 p. 2013 ReferencePoint Press

1. Social science literature 2. Video games—Psychological aspects—Juvenile literature 3. Video games—Social aspects—Juvenile literature 4. Violence—Juvenile literature 5. Violence in video games—Juvenile literature

ISBN 1601524900 (hbk.); 9781601524904 (hbk.)

LC 2012-031924

SUMMARY: This reference book for young adults is part of the "In Controversy" series. Written by Patricia D. Netzley, it "gives graphic descriptions of the violence, racism, and other negatives in some video games and discusses what the impact of these are upon both individuals and society at large." (Booklist)

REVIEW: *Booklist* v110 no1 p100-1 S 1 2013 Susan Dove Lempke

"How Does Video Game Violence Affect Society?," "Should Same-Sex Marriage Be Legal?," and "Should Vaccinations for Youth Be Mandatory?" "The title of each book of the 'In Controversy' series asks a question, reflecting its attempt to provide a vigorous discussion of the pros and cons. The books are a little fairer in its coverage than some discussion books, which try to match every point tit-for-tat--these allow room for different viewpoints without pretending each view is equally substantial. . . . Each chapter is followed by a box of quick facts, and each volume includes good source notes. These make for ideal starting points for student researchers, and the interesting material with lots of quotes makes these useful for leisure reading, too."

NETZLEY, PATRICIA D. Should vaccinations for youth be mandatory?; [by] Patricia D. Netzley 96 p. 2013 Publisher: ReferencePoint Press, Inc.

1. Social science literature 2. Vaccination—Public opinion 3. Vaccination of children—Law & legislation 4. Vaccination of children—Popular works 5. Vaccines—Popular works

ISBN 1601525001 (hardback); 9781601525000 (hardback)

LC 2012-034789

SUMMARY: This reference book for young adults is part of the "In Controversy" series. Written by Patricia D. Netzley, it "discusses why some people fear vaccines and how their personal choices affect society as a whole when diseases are able to spread. Each chapter is followed by a box of quick facts, and each volume includes good source notes." (Booklist)

REVIEW: *Booklist* v110 no1 p100-1 S 1 2013 Susan Dove Lempke

"How Does Video Game Violence Affect Society?," "Should Same-Sex Marriage Be Legal?," and "Should Vaccinations for Youth Be Mandatory?" "The title of each book of the 'In Controversy' series asks a question, reflecting its attempt to provide a vigorous discussion of the pros and cons. The books are a little fairer in its coverage than some discussion books, which try to match every point tit-for-tat--these allow room for different viewpoints without pretending each view is equally substantial. . . . Each chapter is followed by a box of quick facts, and each volume includes good source notes. These make for ideal starting points for student researchers, and the interesting material with lots of quotes makes these useful for leisure reading, too."

NEUBECKER, ROBERT. Winter is for snow; 32 p. 2013 Disney-Hyperion

1. Brothers & sisters—Juvenile fiction 2. Brothers and sisters—Fiction 3. Children's stories 4. Families—Juvenile fiction 5. JUVENILE FICTION—Concepts—Opposites 6. JUVENILE FICTION—Concepts—Senses & Sensation 7. JUVENILE FICTION—Holidays & Celebrations—Christmas & Advent 8. Snow—Fiction 9. Snow—Juvenile literature 10. Stories in rhyme 11. Winter—Fiction 12. Winter—Juvenile literature
ISBN 1423178319; 9781423178316 (hardback)
LC 2013-010688

SUMMARY: "In a rambunctious ode to everything winter, two siblings explore a snowy wonderland . . . and end up in the cozy warmth of family. Delve into Robert Neubecker's expressive and rejuvenating illustrations that celebrate snow and the coziness of friends and family at home. Only Robert Neubecker's magic touch could make kids love winter this much!" (Publisher's note)

REVIEW: *Booklist* v110 no5 p87 N 1 2013 Lolly Gepson

REVIEW: *Bull Cent Child Books* v67 no4 p228 D 2013 D. S.

REVIEW: *N Y Times Book Rev* p14 D 22 2013 NELL CASEY

"Big Snow," "When It Snows," and "Winter Is for Snow." "In 'Big Snow,' written and illustrated by Jonathan Bean, another child anxious to see a winter wonderland asks his mother again and again about the impending blizzard. . . . In his first picture book, 'When It Snows,' . . . illustrator Richard Collingridge dives headlong into a fantasy of the season, showing it to be a vast and mountainous expanse of white, both eerie and enchanting. . . . 'Winter Is for Snow' is a tale of two siblings--a brother who loves the icy flakes pouring down outside their apartment window and a sister who is cranky about it all--by the prolific children's book author and illustrator Robert Neubecker."

REVIEW: *Publ Wkly* v260 no36 p55 S 9 2013

REVIEW: *Publ Wkly* p40 Children's starred review annual 2013

REVIEW: *SLJ* v59 no9 p128 S 2013 Kathleen Finn

NEUBECKER, ROBERT.il. Winter is for snow. See Neubecker, R.

NEUFELD, JULIANA.il. Treasure hunters. See Treasure hunters

NEVINS, DANIEL.il. With a mighty hand. See Ehrlich, A.

NEW ARGENTINE AND BRAZILIAN CINEMA; Reality effects; 2013 Palgrave Macmillan

1. Argentine films 2. Brazilian films 3. Film criticism 4. Latin American films 5. Realism in motion pictures
ISBN 9781137304827 hardcover

SUMMARY: Edited by Jens Andermann and Álvaro Fernández Bravo, "this volume charts the emergence of a new concern with the real . . . Comparing 'New Argentine Cinema" and the Brazilian 'Retomada,' the contributors read across the boundaries between documentary and fiction and trace new modes of deploying performance and re-enactment, found footage, and the interplay between film and television and theater." (Publisher's note)

REVIEW: *Choice* v51 no2 p269-70 O 2013 D. West

"New Argentine and Brazilian Cinema: Reality Effects." "This clearly organized collection of scholarly articles, destined to be a key work in its field, examines the reality effects discerned in two prominent and recent film movements: the New Argentine Cinema and the Brazilian Retomada. . . . Editors [Jens] Andermann . . . and [Álvaro Fernández] Bravo . . . commissioned translations in order to offer an English-language readership an overview of the critical debates regarding the 'cinematic real' in these movements. . .The research for this volume proves wide-ranging and up-to-date, and insightful, innovative close readings of key films, such as 'Playing,' are offered."

NEW NATURES; joining environmental history with science and technology studies; 304 p. 2013 University of Pittsburgh Press

1. Environmental sciences—Study and teaching 2. Historical literature 3. Human ecology—History 4. Interdisciplinary approach in education 5. Nature—Effect of human beings on 6. Science—Study and teaching 7. Technology—Study and teaching
ISBN 9780822962427 (pbk.)
LC 2013-007084

SUMMARY: It was the editors' intent "to show educators of both environmental history and science and technology studies (STS) how they might broaden the scope of their research and teaching to include perspectives and analyses from the other discipline." Topics "include early natural history studies in New England; the development of corn as an important crop in Germany during the 1960s; [and] recycling oil rigs off the California coast." (Choice: Current Reviews for Academic Libraries)

REVIEW: *Choice* v51 no5 p860 Ja 2014 F. N. Egerton

"New Natures: Joining Environmental History With Science and Technology Studies." "This collection of 13 studies is the product of a workshop held in 2010. The goal is to show educators of both environmental history and science and technology studies (STS) how they might broaden the scope of their research and teaching to include perspectives and analyses from the other discipline. The volume is dominated by STS scholars interested environmental history. STS scholars emphasize theory more than many environmental historians do. . . . Fifty pages of notes support the text. The few photographs are adequate but unimpressive. Overall, an interesting and challenging read."

NEW STRATEGIST PUBLICATIONS (COMPANY) comp. Best customers. See Best customers

NEW YORK SCHOOL COLLABORATIONS; the color of vowels; 2013 Palgrave Macmillan
ISBN 9781137280565

SUMMARY: This book, edited by Mark Silverberg, explores "the alliances and artistic co-productions of New York

School poets, painters, musicians, and film-makers. Ranging from conceptual theatre to visual poetry, from experimental film to avant-garde opera, . . . [and] considering relationships between words and images, words and sounds, and words and bodies, these essays shed light on the dialogues between artists and the communities their work continues to produce." (Publisher's note)

REVIEW: *Choice* v51 no8 p1402 Ap 2014 B. Wallenstein
"New York School Collaborations: The Color of Vowels". "Each essay deals with a different aspect of these collaborations. The topics are diverse—e.g., Terence Diggory considers 'ballet, basketball, and . . . erotics,' Kimberly Lamm, 'restraint in Barbara Guest's collaborations.' The movement continues to influence contemporary aesthetics, and [Marc] Silverberg introduces readers to the second generation and beyond of NY School poets and artists. The book is enriched with illustrations by NY School artists."

NEW YORKER MAGAZINE INC.comp. The big New Yorker book of cats. See The big New Yorker book of cats

NEWELL, WALLER R. Tyranny; a new interpretation; [by] Waller R. Newell x, 544 p. 2013 Cambridge University Press
1. Despotism 2. Machiavelli, Niccolò, 1469-1527 3. Political philosophy 4. Political science literature 5. Totalitarianism
ISBN 9781107010321 (hardback)
LC 2012-028449

SUMMARY: This book presents an "exploration of ancient and modern tyranny in the history of political thought. Waller R. Newell argues that modern tyranny and statecraft differ fundamentally from the classical understanding. Newell demonstrates a historical shift in emphasis from the classical thinkers' stress on the virtuous character of rulers and the need for civic education to the modern emphasis on impersonal institutions and cold-blooded political method." (Publisher's note)

REVIEW: *Choice* v51 no8 p1491 Ap 2014 R. M. Major
"Tyranny: A New Interpretation". "[Waller R.] Newell . . . masterfully explores the phenomenon of modern tyranny, and contemporary confusion about it, with an extensive historical, philosophical, and psychological examination of older views of tyranny that were abandoned in the early-modern West. By reminding readers of the classical view of political life, Newell exposes a stunning tension within modern political thought. . . . This engaging and comprehensive study of tyranny also serves as a provocative and sometimes original history of political thought through the epochs of classical antiquity, Christianity, and modernity. Newell's argument will provoke disagreement, but it cannot be dismissed."

NEWLIN, KEITH.ed. Garland in his own time. See Garland in his own time

NEWMAN, BARBARA. Medieval crossover; reading the secular against the sacred; [by] Barbara Newman 392 p. 2013 University of Notre Dame Press
1. Historical literature 2. Holy, The, in literature 3. Literary form 4. Literature, Medieval—History and criticism 5. Secularism in literature
ISBN 026803611X (pbk. : alk. paper); 9780268036119 (pbk. : alk. paper)
LC 2013-000468

SUMMARY: In this book, Barbara Newman "argues that though the sacred was the default perspective in medieval thinking, the sacred did not exclude the secular; there was ample creative room to blend the two perspectives. In a series of . . . studies, she examines writings in French (and Picard), English, and Latin to show how medieval writers played with sacred images to create a variety of new tropes." (Library Journal)

REVIEW: *Choice* v51 no6 p998-9 F 2014 A. Castaldo
"Medieval Crossover: Reading the Secular Against the Sacred." "[Barbara] Newman . . . has written a fascinating work that offers a novel approach to medieval literature. . . . The most powerful chapter is the one on parody. Working with little-known sources, Newman convincingly illustrates how even the most sacred Christian ideals were not above parody. . . . The depth of Newman's scholarship and her engaging style strongly support her powerful, invigorating claims about medieval literature."

REVIEW: *Libr J* v138 no11 p90 Je 15 2013 David Keymer

NEWMAN, KATHERINE S., 1953-. The accordion family; boomerang kids, anxious parents, and the private toll of global competition; [by] Katherine S. Newman xxiii, 261 p. 2012 Beacon Press
1. Adult children—Family relationships 2. Competition, International 3. Generation Y 4. Parent and adult child 5. Social science literature
ISBN 0807007439; 9780807007433
LC 2011-027846

SUMMARY: This book "examines the proliferation of 'accordion families,' in which children continue to live with their parents late into their 20s and 30s. . . . [Katherine] Newman's inquiry takes her around the world to examine how family structures are responding to societal changes. She examines how high unemployment rates, the rise of short-term employment, staggered birth rates, longer life expectancies, and the high cost of living have affected the younger generation's transition to adulthood." (Publishers Weekly)

REVIEW: *Am J Sociol* v118 no3 p821-2 N 2012 Frances K. Goldscheider

REVIEW: *Contemp Sociol* v43 no4 p562-5 Jl 2014 Karrie Ann Snyder

REVIEW: *Contemp Sociol* v43 no2 p183-6 Mr 2014 Karrie Ann Snyder
"The Accordion Family: Boomerang Kids, Anxious Parents, and the Private Toll of Global Competition". "Katherine Newman's 'The Accordion Family: Boomerang Kids, Anxious Parents, and the Private Toll of Global Competition' integrates a fascinating discussion of adulthood, family life, generational ties, and globalization by drawing on 300 interviews spanning 6 countries (Denmark, Italy, Japan, Spain, Sweden, and United States) with parents and adult children. . . . Newman's book is a great starting point to consider how global economic processes filter down to a young person's family ties." relationships with parents, and even their sense of self."

REVIEW: *Libr J* v137 no10 p56-8 Je 1 2012 Rob Walsh

NEWMAN, LESLÉA. October mourning. See Leslea, N.

THE NEWS FROM SPAIN; 7 variations on a love story; 2013 Vintage Books
ISBN 9780307949295

SUMMARY: This book, by Joan Wickersham, is a "collection of stories, each a . . . parable of the power of love and the impossibility of understanding it. Spanning centuries and continents, from eighteenth-century Vienna to contemporary America, Joan Wickersham shows . . . how we never really know what's in someone else's heart--or in our own." (Publisher's note)

REVIEW: *Booklist* v109 no3 p31 O 1 2012 Meg Kinney

REVIEW: *Kirkus Rev* p41-2 N 15 2012 Best Fiction & Children's Books

REVIEW: *Kirkus Rev* v80 no18 p207 S 15 2012

REVIEW: *Libr J* v137 no17 p73 O 15 2012 Reba Leiding

REVIEW: *N Y Times Book Rev* p18 F 3 2013 TOM BARBASH

"The News From Spain: Seven Variations on a Love Story." "[Joan] Wickersham's gift is for capturing the habits of mind that lead even smart people to deceive themselves, make poor choices, slide into affairs or marriages that have little chance of succeeding. . . . Wickersham adroitly mines the small moments around which relationships shift, the places where love begins or ends or falls into that troubling middle ground that haunts sleepless nights. . . . The book holds together so well thematically that the repetition of the title phrase can feel like an unnecessary contrivance."

REVIEW: *New York Times* p4 N 29 2012 SUSANNAH MEADOWS

REVIEW: *Publ Wkly* v259 no34 p32 Ag 20 2012

REVIEW: *Women's Review of Books* v31 no1 p22-3 Ja/F 2014 Mako Yoshikawa

NEWTON AND THE ORIGIN OF CIVILIZATION; ix, 528 p. 2013 Princeton University Press

1. Chronology, Historical—History—17th century 2. Civilization, Ancient—Philosophy 3. Philosophers—England—Biography 4. Public opinion—Europe—History—17th century 5. Scientists—England—Biography
ISBN 9780691154787 (hardcover: acid-free paper)
LC 2012-024733

SUMMARY: This book examines the reception of "Isaac Newton's 'Chronology of Ancient Kingdoms Amended,' published in 1728. . . . This book tells the story of how one of the most celebrated figures in the history of mathematics, optics, and mechanics came to apply his unique ways of thinking to problems of history, theology, and mythology, and of how his radical ideas produced an uproar that reverberated in Europe's learned circles throughout the eighteenth century and beyond." (Publisher's note)

REVIEW: *London Rev Books* v35 no19 p16-8 O 10 2013 Jonathan Rée

"Newton and the Origin of Civilisation." "The exuberant new book by Jed Buchwald and Mordechai Feingold raises the stakes by arguing that Newton's biblical lucubrations are just as scientific as his theory of gravitation, and scientific in much the same way. . . . Their main concern is to demonstrate parallels between the intellectual methods of the 'Chronology' and those of Newton's contributions to natural science. Newton questioned the evidence of his historical sources, they say, just as he questioned the evidence of the senses, subjecting it to a characteristic blend of experimental manipulation and mathematical synthesis."

NEWTON, STUART. Londinium Poeta; verses from the inner city 1980-2000; [by] Stuart Newton 88 p. 2009 emp3books

1. English poetry 2. London (England)—Poetry 3. London (England)—Social conditions 4. Poems—Collections 5. Royal houses
ISBN 1907140042; 9781907140044

SUMMARY: This book of poetry on London, England presents a "tour of self and city. . . . [Stuart Newton is most interested in the social divides and tensions that define the city, with a clear sympathy for the ordinary, workaday resident. London is a place where the 'Princess waved/smiled/gestured' at a narrator taking a walk . . . but it's also the place where . . . the social pressures weigh . . . heavily." (Kirkus Reviews)

REVIEW: *Kirkus Rev* v82 no3 p28 F 1 2014

"Londinium Poeta: Verses From the Inner City". "Short, free verse poems on the psychological and sociological complexities of life in London. . . . " Like [Charles] Bukowski, whose influence is unmistakable, Newton is most interested in the social divides and tensions that define the city, with a clear sympathy for the ordinary, workaday resident. . . . At least for those readers confused by all the specific references, [Stuart] Newton provides an arbitrary, but helpful, set of notes. Perceptive and honest, Newton manages to be profound without being abstruse. Though stylistically unremarkable, this is clear-voiced and self-aware poetry that any city dweller will appreciate."

REVIEW: *Kirkus Rev* v82 no2 p327 Ja 15 2014

NEZ, JOHN.il. Diary of a worm. See Houran, L. H.

NG, JASON Q. Blocked on weibo; what gets suppressed on China's version of Twitter (and why); [by] Jason Q. Ng xxix, 224 p. 2013 The New Press

1. Censorship—China 2. Freedom of information—China 3. Internet—Censorship—China 4. Internet—Political aspects—China 5. Internet searching—China 6. Social science literature
ISBN 9781595588715 (pbk. : alk. paper)
LC 2013-010628

SUMMARY: In this book, "China specialist Jason Q. Ng" created "an innovative computer script that would make it possible to deduce just which terms are suppressed on China's most important social media site, Sina Weibo." The book "began as a highly praised blog and has been expanded here to list over 150 forbidden keywords, as well as offer possible explanations why the Chinese government would find these terms sensitive." (Publisher's note)

REVIEW: *TLS* no5768 p27 O 18 2013 JEFFREY N. WASSERSTROM

"Blocked on Weibo: What Gets Suppressed on China's Version of Twitter (and why)." "What makes his blog--and the book it has not spawned--so attractive is [Jason Q.] Ng's wit and erudition. Some entries in this Devil's Dictionary for digital times are simply descriptive, but many open surprising windows onto the wonderfully creative strategies Chinese internet users employ to circumvent blocks, such as using the imaginary date of 'May 35th' as a code word for June 4 (1989) - the date of the massacre near Tiananmen Square."

NICHOLSON, JAMES C. Never Say Die; a Kentucky colt, the Epsom Derby, and the rise of the modern thoroughbred industry; [by] James C. Nicholson xiv, 218 p. 2013 University Press of Kentucky

1. Epsom Derby, England (Horse race) 2. Historical literature 3. Horse racing—England—History—20th century 4. Horse racing—History 5. Never Say Die (Race horse)
ISBN 0813141672; 9780813141671 (hardcover : alk. paper)
LC 2012-051377

SUMMARY: In this book, James C. Nicholson "argues that the modern thoroughbred industry was heavily shaped by the 1954 Epsom Derby victory of Never Say Die, the first American bred horse to win that prestigious race since 1881. . . . The victory led to a shift in the locus of power in the sport from Great Britain to Lexington, Kentucky." The book "includes a survey of the sport's recent globalization, and biographies of" people related to the subject. (Choice)

REVIEW: *Choice* v51 no1 p120-1 S 2013 S. A. Riess

"Never Say Die: A Kentucky Colt, the Epsom Derby, and the Rise of the Modern Thoroughbred Industry." "[Author James C.] Nicholson . . . argues that the modern thoroughbred industry was heavily shaped by the 1954 Epsom Derby victory of Never Say Die, the first American bred horse to win that prestigious race since 1881. . . . The 176-page, ten-chapter book includes a survey of the sport's recent globalization, and biographies of Isaac Merritt Singer, creator of the Singer Sewing Company; Clark; the Aga Khan horseman John Bell III; and Pete Best, early Beatles drummer, whose mother's winning wager on Never Say Die went to establish the Casbah Coffee Club, the future springboard of the Beatles."

NICKERSON, JANE. The mirk and midnight hour; [by] Jane Nickerson 384 p. 2014 Alfred A. Knopf

1. African Americans—Fiction 2. Family life—Mississippi—Fiction 3. Historical fiction 4. Slavery—Fiction 5. Soldiers—Fiction 6. Vodou—Fiction
ISBN 0385752873; 9780385752862 (hard cover); 9780385752879 (library binding)
LC 2012-050893

SUMMARY: This book presents a retelling of the folktale "Tam Lin." "As if it isn't enough that Violet's twin brother was killed in the Civil War, her family's quiet Mississippi farm is changing in every way possible: before enlisting, her father remarries, giving Violet both an invalid stepmother and a spoiled stepsister. . . . Adding more complications are the mysterious Doctor VanZeldt and his African companions, as well as a wounded Union soldier tucked away in the woods." (Publishers Weekly)

REVIEW: *Bull Cent Child Books* v67 no6 p327-8 F 2014 Kate Quealy-Gainer

"The Mirk and Midnight Hour:. "While the plot is packed with significant events, there's a languid ease to the prose that invites readers to become fully immersed in the sweltering heat of a Mississippi summer, and Nickerson paints a picture of the Southern landscape that is rustic but ethereal and at times, eerie. Violet's conflicted feelings about the war and slavery are honestly but sensitively depicted. . . Unfortunately . . . most of the African-American players are reduced to being either wise templates or, as in the case of the VanZeldts, creepy others. The direct correlation to the Tam Lin folktale only shows up in the final chapters, but the blend of fairy tale tropes and the Southern Gothic setting make this a compelling, if somewhat flawed, retelling."

REVIEW: *Kirkus Rev* v82 no3 p86 F 1 2014

"The Mirk and Midnight Hour". "In this atmospheric story in which darkness houses mysteries, the VanZeldts seem to glide like shadows rather than walk as humans. . . . With rich imagery and imaginative subplots driving the storyline, the loose 'Tam Lin' connection doesn't really arrive until the end. The author is careful not to generalize all African-Americans, offering a wide variety of characters—black and white. With an inexplicable magic of her own, the ever-resilient Violet is a force against the VanZeldts' deadly rituals. Far from the typical Civil War romance."

REVIEW: *Publ Wkly* v261 no2 p71 Ja 13 2014

REVIEW: *SLJ* v60 no5 p136 My 2014 Gretchen Kolderup

REVIEW: *SLJ* v60 no6 p68 Je 2014 April Everett

REVIEW: *Voice of Youth Advocates* v36 no6 p75-6 F 2014 Matthew Weaver

NICOL, BRAN. The Private Eye; Detectives in the Movies; [by] Bran Nicol 224 p. 2013 University of Chicago Press

1. Detective & mystery films 2. Film criticism 3. Film noir 4. Love in motion pictures 5. Private investigators
ISBN 1780231024; 9781780231020

SUMMARY: In this book, author Bran Nicol "traces the history of private eye movies from the influential film noirs of the 1940s to 1970s neonoir cinema, whose slow and brilliant decline gave way to the fading of detectives into movie mythology today. Analyzing a number of classic films--including The Maltese Falcon, The Big Sleep, Chinatown, and The Long Goodbye--he reveals that while these movies are ostensibly thrillers, they are actually occupied by issues of work and love." (Publisher's note)

REVIEW: *TLS* no5762 p27 S 6 2013 OLIVER HARRIS

"The Private Eye: Detectives in the Movies." "An emphasis on the 'eye' in private eye has dominated a great deal of discussion to date, Bran Nicol notes in his valuable introduction to a busy corner of film studies. . . . [The book] focuses largely on two distinct 'moments,' the classic noir era of 1940-59 and a second wave of films produced in the late 1960s and 70s . . . in which themes of nostalgia and disillusionment contend. Nicol also discusses the stylish high school noir of 'Brick' (2005), and the Indian 'Manorama' of 2007, but ends by asking why there have not been more revisions of the template in the past twenty years."

NICOL, DAVID. Middleton and Rowley; forms of collaboration in the Jacobean playhouse; [by] David Nicol xii, 216 p. 2012 University of Toronto Press

1. Authorship—Collaboration—History—17th century 2. English drama—17th century—History and criticism 3. Historical literature
ISBN 1442643706; 9781442643703
LC 2012-532079

SUMMARY: "For Thomas Middleton and William Rowley, the playwriting team best known for their tragedy 'The Changeling,' disagreements and friction proved quite beneficial for their work.This first full-length study of Middleton and Rowley uses their plays to propose a new model for the study of collaborative authorship in early modern English drama. [Author] David Nicol highlights the diverse forms of collaborative relationships that factor into a play's meaning." (Publisher's note)

REVIEW: *Choice* v50 no8 p1432 Ap 2013 B. E. Brandt

REVIEW: *TLS* no5793 p25 Ap 11 2014 JACKIE WATSON

"Middleton and Rowley: Forms of Collaboration in the Jacobean Playhouse." "Some of the most exciting recent scholarly work on early modern theatre has arisen out of a desire to understand its social and material context. Mindful of the influence of a wide range of people on the generation and production of a play—actors, those managing, or sharing in, a playing company and patrons, as well as audiences and, of course, playwrights—we have learnt to see the process of writing drama in Jacobean London as largely a collaborative one. David Nicol's book encourages his reader to consider how exactly dramatists worked together. . . . This book ought to interest anyone with an interest in the role of drama in Jacobean society, as well as the curious nature of co-authorship."

NIEBUHR, REINHOLD, 1892-1971. The irony of American history; [by] Reinhold Niebuhr 174 2008 University of Chicago Press

1. Historical literature 2. Irony

ISBN 0-226-58398-8; 978-0-226-58398-3

LC 2007-044237

SUMMARY: This book by Reinhold Niebuhr "is a reprinting of the Protestant theologian's 1952 examination of American history and foreign policy with a new introduction." (Publisher's note)

REVIEW: *Commonweal* v141 no2 p18-9 Ja 24 2014 Andrew J. Bacevich

"The Irony of American History". "As a source of insight into the wellsprings of U.S. foreign policy, Reinhold Niebuhr's 'The Irony of American History' is an invaluable text. If you want to understand the ambitions, claims, and conceits animating the United States during its rise to power and still lingering today, then Niebuhr's your man and 'Irony' the place to look. As a policy handbook, however, 'Irony' is all but devoid of value. When it comes to concrete and immediate concerns—dealing with Iran's nuclear ambitions, winding down the Afghanistan War, or preventing another bout of North Korean bad behavior, for example—Niebuhr's not much help."

NIELSEN, JENNIFER A. The shadow throne; [by] Jennifer A. Nielsen 336 p. 2014 Scholastic Press

1. Adventure and adventurers—Fiction 2. Adventure stories 3. Battles—Fiction 4. Battles—Juvenile fiction 5. Kings and rulers—Juvenile fiction 6. Kings, queens, rulers, etc.—Fiction 7. Rescues—Fiction 8. Rescues—Juvenile fiction

ISBN 0545284171; 9780545284172 (jacketed hardcover)

LC 2013-021841

SUMMARY: This book, by Jennifer A. Nielsen, is the "finale of the Ascendance Trilogy. . . . Jaron learns than King Vargan of Avenia and allies from Gelyn and Mendenwal have invaded Carthya and captured Jaron's friend Imogen. Determined to save Imogen, Jaron attempts a rescue and fails, leaving him a prisoner and Imogen presumed dead. As he tries to cope with Imogen's death, captive Jaron discovers how much he loved her." (Kirkus Reviews)

REVIEW: *Booklist* v110 no9/10 p108-10 Ja 1 2014 Karen Cruze

REVIEW: *Horn Book Magazine* v90 no2 p126 Mr/Ap 2014 JONATHAN HUNT

"The Shadow Throne." "The plot thickens, and before everything is said and done, the Amarinda/Jaron/Imogen love triangle is sorted out, Jaron proves his leadership abilities, and Carthya emerges victorious from the war. The series, which started with a bang, has gotten a little weaker with each book. Perhaps it's that the impetuous young upstart Sage was more interesting than the king he becomes, or maybe it's that the plotting and intrigue have given way to battles and war. In any case, though, there's still plenty of adventure, mystery, and romance in this concluding volume, enough to please a variety of genre readers."

REVIEW: *Kirkus Rev* v82 no1 p133 Ja 1 2014

NIELSEN, VIBEKE LEHMANN.ed. Explaining compliance. See Explaining compliance

NIKOLOPOULOS, ANGELO. Obscenely Yours; [by] Angelo Nikolopoulos 96 p. 2013 Alice James Books

1. Desire—Poetry 2. Human sexuality in poetry 3. LGBT people—Poetry 4. Lyric poetry 5. Sexual orientation identity

ISBN 9781882295999 (pbk. : alk. paper)

LC 2012-043072

SUMMARY: "This fearless debut transcends the obscene with its self-conscious probing of sexual identity. Navigating each line with a tender awareness and a luminous honesty, [author] Angelo Nikolopoulos exposes the complex worlds of forbidden desire and vulnerability. His lyric poems boldly defy social norms with their uninhibited passion for revealing the tangled intricacies of beauty and shame." (Publisher's note)

REVIEW: *Antioch Rev* v71 no4 p818 Fall 2013 Alex M. Frankel

"Obscenely Yours." "'Obscenely Yours' lives up to its title: it's a delicious joyride through the exciting and mostly joyless territory of man-to-man sex. 'I'm logistically opposed to love,' [author Angelo] Nikolopoulos confesses in one of his untitled poems; instead of romance, he takes his readers through countless gropings, penetrations, and re-enactments of childhood trauma and fantasies, only to be left 'at day's end, holding nothing.' Virtually every poem in this book explores the body and its grim needs, but this theme never becomes monotonous."

REVIEW: *Publ Wkly* v260 no8 p142 F 25 2013

NILSSON, MARCUS.il. Lidia's commonsense Italian cooking. See Bastianich, L. M.

NIRENBERG, DAVID. Anti-Judaism; the Western tradition; [by] David Nirenberg 624 p. 2013 W. W. Norton & Company

1. Antisemitism—Europe—History 2. Christianity & antisemitism 3. Civilization, Western—Jewish influ-

ences 4. Historical literature
ISBN 0393058247; 9780393058246 (hardcover)
LC 2012-031082

SUMMARY: This book is a "history tracing how the engagement with 'Jewish questions' have shaped 3,000 years of Western thought. [David] Nirenberg . . . fashions a . . . study of how writers and thinkers from Jesus to Marx to Edward Said have recycled ideas about Jews and Jewishness in creating their own constructions of reality." (Kirkus)

REVIEW: *Am Hist Rev* v119 no3 p837-9 Je 2014 Alan T. Levenson

REVIEW: *Choice* v50 no11 p2092 Jl 2013 J. Fischel

REVIEW: *Christ Century* v130 no25 p38-40 D 11 2013 Adam Gragerman

REVIEW: *Commentary* v135 no4 p53-4 2013 PETER LOPATIN

REVIEW: *Commonweal* v140 no15 p22-5 S 27 2013 John Connelly

"Anti-Judaism: the Western Tradition." "In this monumental and brilliantly argued intellectual Jews with legalism and materialism. Jews did not even have history David Nirenberg asks how influential figures in the Western tradition have thought about Judaism over nearly three thousand years. . . . Putting aside all the methodological doubts that plague the social sciences in our day, one can safely assert, as he does, that the sources of anti-Semitism originally lie in theological ideas. . . . Still, Nirenberg's timely, erudite, and coolly passionate intervention cautions against complacency."

REVIEW: *Kirkus Rev* v80 no21 p135 N 1 2012

REVIEW: *N Y Rev Books* v61 no5 p31-3 Mr 20 2014 Michael Walzer

"Anti-Judaism: The Western Tradition". "Brilliant, fascinating, and deeply depressing. . . . What [David] Nirenberg has written is an intellectual history of Western civilization, seen from a peculiar but frighteningly revealing perspective. It is focused on the role of anti-Judaism as a constitutive idea and an explanatory force in Christian and post-Christian thought. . . . 'Anti-Judaism' is an extraordinary scholarly achievement. . . . Nirenberg's history of anti-Judaism is powerful and persuasive, but it is also unfinished. It never gets to the United States, for example, where anti-Judaism seems to have been less prevalent and less useful (less used in making sense of society and economy) than it was and is in the Old World."

REVIEW: *Nation* v296 no14 p42-5 Ap 8 2013 R.I. MOORE

REVIEW: *New Repub* v244 no17 p48-55 O 21 2013 Anthony Grafton

REVIEW: *Publ Wkly* v259 no44 p41-2 O 29 2012

NOBLE, ELIZABETH. Between a Mother and Her Child; [by] Elizabeth Noble 448 p. 2013 Penguin Group USA
1. Death—Fiction 2. Families—Fiction 3. Grief—Fiction 4. Indian Ocean Tsunami, 2004 5. Marriage—Fiction
ISBN 0425267938; 9780425267936

SUMMARY: In this book, "devastated from the death of their oldest son, Jake, killed in the 2004 tsunami while traveling on a gap year in Asia, the members of the Barrett family cope with the sudden tragedy in different but similarly isolated ways." Ultimately, father Bill moves out and meets another woman, leaving mother Maggie "to cope with even more change and further emotional repercussions." (Library Journal)

REVIEW: *Booklist* v110 no2 p27 S 15 2013 Susan Maguire

REVIEW: *Kirkus Rev* v81 no16 p207 Ag 15 2013

"Between a Mother and Her Child." "A work of fiction based on the 2004 Indonesian tsunami. British author [Elizabeth] Noble weaves multiple narrative threads into the family saga. . . . When Jake, with his father's encouragement, decides to take a year to travel the Pacific Rim countries with friends before attending university, his family is happy for him. But then he dies on a beach during a tsunami, leaving the family devastated. Maggie and Bill subsequently grow apart. . . . Sacrificed dreams and buried feelings collide in this U.K. best-seller."

REVIEW: *Libr J* v138 no14 p102 S 1 2013 Joy Gunn

NOBLIT, GEORGE W.ed. Culturally relevant arts education for social justice. See Culturally relevant arts education for social justice

NOISY FARM; 12 p. 2013 Tiger Tales
1. Animal sounds 2. Cows 3. Domestic animals—Juvenile literature 4. Farm life—Juvenile literature 5. Toy & movable books
ISBN 1589256107; 9781589256101

SUMMARY: In this children's book, "farm animals make realistic noises as youngsters press embedded tactile features. . . . Readers can press the fuzzy, black circle on a Holstein cow to hear its recorded noise. This formula is repeated on each double-page spread, one per farm critter (roosters, piglets, lambs and horses). Using stock photography, several smaller images of the animals appear on the left, and a full-page close-up dominates the right." (Kirkus Reviews)

REVIEW: *Kirkus Rev* v82 no1 p28 Ja 1 2014

"Noisy Farm". "Farm animals make realistic noises as youngsters press embedded tactile features. . . . While the layout is a little busy, the selection of photos and the tactile elements are nicely diverse. The text is simple enough for little ones, encourages interaction ("Can you baa like a lamb?") and uses animal-specific vocabulary (fleece; mane). . . . Despite the age recommendation of 3 years and up suggested on the back cover, the construction (with the battery secured by screw behind a plastic panel) looks sturdy and safe enough for younger readers. A happily multisensory exploration."

REVIEW: *Kirkus Rev* v81 no18 p375 S 15 2013

NOJ, NAHTA.il. The Lion and the mouse. See Broom, J.

NOLAN, TERRI. Glass houses; a Birdie Keane novel; [by] Terri Nolan 408 p. 2014 Midnight Ink
1. Cold cases (Criminal investigation)—Fiction 2. Detective & mystery stories 3. Murder investigation—Fiction 4. Police—Fiction 5. Women journalists—Fiction
ISBN 9780738736358
LC 2013-037365

SUMMARY: In this book, by Terri Nolan, "when investigative journalist Birdie Keane's latest story reveals the shocking truth about a famous cold case, she teams up with her cousin, homicide detective Thom Keane, to deal with the aftermath. But Thom may be in more trouble than Birdie. Assigned to a high-profile murder he should have nothing to do with, Thom suspects he's being set up by the top brass." (Publisher's note)

REVIEW: *Kirkus Rev* v82 no3 p220 F 1 2014

Glass Houses". " An investigative journalist deals with her inner demons while helping her cousin deal with a much more concrete threat. . . . Is it germane that all the victims lived in rent-stabilized homes that charged far less than Los Angeles' overheated housing market would typically command? Did foster dad Dominic Lawrence's work as a city attorney put him in someone's cross hairs? As Birdie helps Thom, her new love, Ron Hughes, helps Birdie cope with the ghost of Matt Whelan, the man she still pines over. Nolan continues what promises to be a long and lovingly crafted saga about the strains and gains of love and loyalty."

NOLLET, LEO M. L., 1948-.ed. Handbook of water analysis. See Handbook of water analysis

NOONAN, ELLEN. The strange career of Porgy and Bess; race, culture, and America's most famous opera; [by] Ellen Noonan 423 p. 2012 University of North Carolina Press

1. African Americans in popular culture—20th century 2. Historical literature 3. Music and race 4. Race in opera

ISBN 0807837164; 9780807837160 (cloth : alk. paper)
LC 2012-016635

SUMMARY: This book looks at the characters of Porgy and Bess, known from DuBose Heyward's 1925 novel 'Porgy' [and] George Gershwin's 1935 operatic adaptation 'Porgy and Bess.' Ellen Noonan's "examination of Porgy and Bess provides an abbreviated history of Charleston, SC, and places Gershwin's opera in historical, racial, and social contexts." (Library Journal)

REVIEW: *Am Hist Rev* v119 no1 p205-6 F 2014 David Monod

"The Strange Career of Porgy and Bess: Race, Culture, and America's Most Famous Opera". "[Ellen] Noonan offers interesting insights into Porgy's relationship to its creators. . . . I found Noonan's monograph a tough book to pin down. It is not a production study and pays slight attention to actual staging or performance practice. Noonan slips so quickly from the organization of shows to the reactions of critics, from the question of authenticity to its discursive underpinnings, that I felt rather like I had jumped from soup to dessert without anything substantial in between. . . . The book is a worthwhile read. It brings together art, interpretation, and social context and manages to describe their interaction. This is not easy, and Noonan has to be commended for her contribution."

REVIEW: *Choice* v50 no10 p1909 Je 2013 T. Maxwell-Long

REVIEW: *J Am Hist* v100 no3 p875-6 D 2013 Lauren Rebecca Sklaroff

REVIEW: *Libr J* v138 no2 p69-70 F 1 2013 Shannon Marie Robinson

REVIEW: *Rev Am Hist* v42 no1 p127-31 Mr 2014 Kathy Peiss

"The Strange Career of Porgy and Bess: Race, Culture, and America's Most Famous Opera." "Peggy Noonan's new book reveals the extent and depth of the cultural contradictions in Porgy and Bess by tracing its history through the thickets of American racial politics and popular culture in the twentieth century. . . . Noonan proves herself fo be a sensitive reader of the different forms of 'Porgy and Bess,' deftly charting the adaptation of [DuBose] Heyward's novel into thc play and then musical production. . . . She is less attuned to music and sound as historical sources in their own right, which oddly makes the chapter on Gershwin's opera the least satisfying in the book."

NORDHAUS, WILLIAM D. The climate casino; [by] William D. Nordhaus 392 p. 2013 Yale University Press

1. Climatic changes—Effect of human beings on 2. Climatic changes—Environmental aspects 3. Climatic changes—Social aspects 4. Economics literature 5. Environmental policy

ISBN 9780300189773 (cloth : alk. paper)
LC 2013-010722

SUMMARY: We have entered the Climate Casino and are rolling the global-warming dice, warns economist William Nordhaus. . . . Bringing together all the important issues surrounding the climate debate, Nordhaus describes the science, economics, and politics involved--and the steps necessary to reduce the perils of global warming. . . . In short, he clarifies a defining problem of our times and lays out the next critical steps for slowing the trajectory of global warming." (Publisher's note)

REVIEW: *Choice* v51 no8 p1457 Ap 2014 S. R. Steele

REVIEW: *N Y Rev Books* v60 no17 p14-8 N 7 2013 Paul Krugman

REVIEW: *N Y Times Book Rev* p26 Ja 12 2014 Coral Davenport

"The Climate Casino: Risk, Uncertainty, and Economics for a Warming World," "Fevered: Why a Hotter Planet Will Hurt Our Health--And How We Can Save Ourselves," and "The Melting World: A Journey Across America's Vanishing Glaciers." "'The Climate Casino' reads like a highly engaging college textbook. [Author William] Nordhaus's tone is conversations . . . , but too many passages bog down in technical jargon. . . . Crammed with statistics, interviews and gruesome but fund facts, 'Fevered' makes its case with plenty of hard evidence. . . . 'The Melting World' takes readers to the glacial peaks with [scientist Daniel] Fagre and his team. . . . The book would have benefited from a tighter edit. . . . Despite that, a moving story emerges."

REVIEW: *New York Times* v163 no56337 p7 D 1 2013 FRED ANDREWS

REVIEW: *Science* v343 no6169 p371-2 Ja 24 2014 Mark Jaccard

"The Climate Casino: Risk, Uncertainty, and Economics for a Warming World." "For over two decades, Bill Nordhaus . . . has been recognized as a leading climate economist, and for much of that time his work has provoked the scientist-versus-economist debate in my graduate seminar on sustainable energy. Lately, however, he has begun to disappoint--as demonstrated by 'The Climate Casino.' . . . As a hard-nosed economist, he shows that much of our economy, including food production, is highly managed and thus able to handle modest global warming, perhaps even benefit from it. . . . I was left with the impression that those polar bears don't get a fair hearing."

NORDHOLT, HENK SCHULTE.ed. Asian tigers, African lions. See Asian tigers, African lions

NORENZAYAN, ARA. Big gods; how religion transformed cooperation and conflict; [by] Ara Norenzayan xiii, 248 p. 2013 Princeton University Press

1. Conflict management—Religious aspects 2. Cooperation—Religious aspects 3. Faith development—Psychological aspects 4. Psychology—Religious aspects 5. Psychology, Religious 6. Social science literature
ISBN 0691151210 (cloth : alk. paper); 9780691151212 (cloth : alk. paper)
LC 2013-011723

SUMMARY: It was the author's intent to demonstrate that "religions that have omniscient 'Big Gods' who monitor and punish adherents for moral transgressions gave rise to large-scale societies of strangers out of small groups of related hunter-gatherers. . . . [Ara] Norenzayan . . . argues that religions with Big Gods are successful because they generate a sense of being watched and regulated, require extravagant displays of commitment . . . and encourage solidarity and trust." (Publishers Weekly)

REVIEW: *Choice* v51 no10 p1821-2 Je 2014 S. E. Forschler

REVIEW: *New Sci* v219 no2936 p52 S 28 2013 Michael Bond

"Big Gods: How Religion Transformed Cooperation and Conflict." "Ara Norenzayan's perspective is a kind of theological take on survival of the fittest. In 'Big Gods,' he argues that Islam, Christianity and other world religions prospered because they had a competitive edge over their rivals. They alone offered all-knowing, interventionist deities who judged immoral behaviour, an arrangement that encouraged cooperation among large groups of anonymous strangers--because 'watched people are nice people'. In short, they allowed groups to scale up: they paved the way for modern civilisation. It is a neat, grand theory, one that Norenzayan seems well qualified to deliver. . . . It is a convincing thesis, and whether or not you buy it, some of its implications are compelling."

NORMAN EXPANSION; connections, continuities and contrasts; xiii, 261 p. 2013 Ashgate

1. Civilization, Medieval 2. Group identity—Europe—History 3. Historical literature 4. Normans—Europe 5. Normans—Great Britain—History 6. Normans—Italy—History
ISBN 9781409448389 (hardcover: alk. paper)
LC 2013-010551

SUMMARY: This book, edited by Keith J. Stringer and Andrew Jotischky, "serves both to illustrate and to open up for fresh debate many of the salient themes concerning the Norman experience of diaspora and settlement. At the same time, it seeks to underscore how the dynamics, character and consequences of Norman expansion—and the connections, continuities and contrasts—can better be appreciated by taking the wider Norman world, or worlds, as the focus for collective study." (Publisher's note)

REVIEW: *Choice* v51 no8 p1463 Ap 2014 C. E. Beneš

"Norman Expansion: Connections, Continuities and Contrasts". "This important collection of articles is the result of a collaborative research project. . . . The authors incorporate a wide range of evidence from laws, charters, and narrative histories to archaeology and geography. The widely divergent details, however, converge to form a complex picture of state and identity formation across Europe in the central Middle Ages, replacing traditional perspectives on the Normans that were largely formed through the lens of 'national' history. . . . The authors take full advantage of the Normans' transnational, multiethnic exploits to contribute to a view of a Middle Ages that was far more complex and ambitious than is commonly thought."

NORMAN, JESSE. Edmund Burke; the first conservative; [by] Jesse Norman 325 p. 2013 Basic Books, A Member of the Perseus Books Group

1. Biography (Literary form) 2. Orators—Great Britain—Biography 3. Political scientists—Great Britain—Biography 4. Statesmen—Great Britain—Biography
ISBN 0465058973 (hardcover); 9780465058976 (hardcover)
LC 2013-935334

SUMMARY: This book, written by Jesse Norman, presents a biography of Edmund Burke "an 18th-century Irish philosopher and statesman [and] champion of human rights and the Anglo-American constitutional tradition, and a lifelong campaigner against arbitrary power. As Norman reveals, Burke was often ahead of his time, anticipating the abolition of slavery and arguing for free markets, equality for Catholics in Ireland, and responsible government in India." (Publisher's note)

REVIEW: *Choice* v51 no6 p1093 F 2014 E. J. Eisenach

"Edmund Burke: The First Conservative." "[Jesse] Norman, a British Conservative Party MP, has written an accessible, comprehensive, and instructive study of Burke. Burke's biography is canvassed through his participation in five great political battles that mark his political and intellectual career, beginning with his fight for fair treatment of Catholics in Ireland and colonial rights in North America, and ending with his epic campaign against the French Revolution. The second half of the book steps back to assess Burke's political thought that Norman says is situated at the 'hinge of our political modernity.'"

REVIEW: *Economist* v407 no8837 p85-6 My 25 2013

REVIEW: *Kirkus Rev* v81 no7 p260 Ap 1 2013

REVIEW: *Libr J* v138 no9 p84 My 15 2013 Michael O. Eshleman

REVIEW: *Natl Rev* v65 no13 p40-2 Jl 15 2013 YUVAL LEVIN

NORMAN, KIM. If it's snowy and you know it, clap your paws!; [by] Kim Norman 24 p. 2013 Sterling

1. Animals—Fiction 2. Children's stories 3. Snow—Fiction 4. Stories in rhyme 5. Winter—Fiction
ISBN 1454903848; 9781454903840 (hardcover)
LC 2012-014460

SUMMARY: Author Kim Norman presents a children's book about winter. The "variation on the classic song 'If You're Happy and You Know It' introduces a group of adorable animals playing joyfully in the snow. They tumble on the tundra, catch snowflakes on their tongues, sculpt snow-critters, and make a frosty fort. But can they go with the flow when their wild adventure drifts in a surprising direction?" (Publisher's note)

REVIEW: *Booklist* v110 no4 p55 O 15 2013 Martha Edmundson

REVIEW: *Kirkus Rev* v81 no16 p123 Ag 15 2013

"If It's Snowy and You Know It, Clap Your Paws!" "A wintry riff on the popular participation song, with a cast of appropriate cold-climate animals. A rabbit in sunglasses slides down a snowy hill, using a polar bear pal as a sled. Penguin, walrus, fox and others look on approvingly. The text faithfully follows the rhythms of the song as these characters frolic. . . . [Author Kim] Norman's solid variations on the preschool song are completely singer-friendly, supported by [illustrator Liza] Woodruff's crisply drawn, smiling animals, in watercolor, colored pencil and pastel."

REVIEW: *Publ Wkly* v260 no36 p55 S 9 2013

REVIEW: *SLJ* v59 no8 p84 Ag 2013 Kathleen Finn

NORMAN, KIM. I know a wee piggy; 32 p. 2014 Dial Books for Young Readers

1. Agricultural exhibitions—Fiction 2. Color—Fiction 3. Picture books for children 4. Pigs—Fiction 5. Stories in rhyme

ISBN 0803737351; 9780803737358 (hardcover)

LC 2011-029977

Summary: This children's book is the story of a "little piggy [who] has escaped from his owner and is running riot through the county fair, getting covered in gunk, globs, and other stuff representing nine colors: brown from the muddy pig pen, red from the tomato canning display, yellow from the broken yolks in the chicken coop . . . and so forth. By the time the wee piggy proudly wins a blue ribbon," he's very dirty indeed. Author Kimberly E. Norman's text riffs on the folk song "I Know an Old Lady." (Publishers Weekly)

REVIEW: *Booklist* v109 no1 p107 S 1 2012 Andrew Medlar

REVIEW: *Kirkus Rev* v80 no9 p978 My 1 2012

"I Know a Wee Piggy." "How can one small pig get into so much trouble? . . . This energetic, pitch-perfect riff on 'I Know an Old Lady' introduces various colors while following a spirited young piggy on a delicious romp through a county fair. . . . In a nice touch, the names of the colors are bolded and colored within the otherwise black text, making for easy recognition of the actual words. Youngsters will eagerly join in and sing along with the cumulative verse and laugh out loud with the lovable piggy as he scampers throughout the fair, wreaking havoc everywhere he goes."

REVIEW: *Publ Wkly* v259 no18 p135 Ap 30 2012

REVIEW: *SLJ* v58 no6 p92 Je 2012 Sharon Grover

NORRIS, HELEN M. Black Diamond Destiny; [by] Helen M. Norris 260 p. 2013 Author Solutions

1. Coal mines & mining—Fiction 2. Families—Fiction 3. Historical fiction 4. Mineral industries 5. West Virginia—Fiction

ISBN 1481772694; 9781481772693

SUMMARY: This book "tells the saga, based on a true story, of the Mattisons, a family of hardscrabble, mountain farmers in West Virginia who, out of desperation, develop a small outcrop of coal on their property and become miners. The novel follows the secretive, nefarious way the mining venture got its startup capital" and follows the family as their firm "grows into the world's largest coal corporation." (Kirkus Reviews)

REVIEW: *Kirkus Rev* v82 no2 p40 Ja 15 2014

"Black Diamond Destiny". " This posthumous release by first-time novelist [Helen M] Norris largely succeeds in ensnaring fans of multigenerational melodramas. . . . Norris does a marvelous job getting readers emotionally invested in the ever-expanding family, especially those members working to better the hazardous conditions for the miners. . . . Norris admirably weaves fascinating historical details into her narrative, with her exhaustive research giving context to events within her novel. . . . The book would have benefited from more thorough editing, though, to remove repetitiveness and fix typos, but the story's overall strength overcomes these shortcomings. An accessible, entrancing story that draws readers into a family's many triumphs and travails."

NORTCLIFF, STEPHEN.ed. Soil conditions and plant growth. See Soil conditions and plant growth

NORTH, CLAIRE. The first fifteen lives of Harry August; [by] Claire North 416 p. 2014 Redhook

1. Crocheting 2. End of the world—Fiction 3. Memory—Fiction 4. Reincarnation—Fiction 5. Speculative fiction 6. Time travel—Fiction

ISBN 0316399612; 9780316399616 (hardcover); 9780316399630 (ebk.); 9781478952947 (audio download)

LC 7302-0397

SUMMARY: This book by Claire North "focuses on the life of Harry August, a man who dies only to be reborn as the same person. The illegitimate son of a wealthy landowner, Harry's life is challenging not only because he is one of the kalachakra, a small group of people who have the ability to relive their lives, but also because he is a mnemonic, an individual who can remember all the details of their past lives." (Publishers Weekly)

REVIEW: *Booklist* v110 no13 p28 Mr 1 2014 David Pitt

"The First Fifteen Lives of Harry August." "This wonderful novel, narrated by Harry, ranges back and forth in time as he recounts episodes from his various lives, but it's all held together by a compelling mystery involving nothing less than the end of the world itself (a thousand years in the future). Beautifully written and structured, the book should be a big hit with SF fans. The pseudonymous author's name is being kept secret, but fans of SF and fantasy authors China Mieville, Christopher Priest, and Adam Roberts might note a stylistic similarity, especially in the novel's elegant prose. Whoever Claire North turns out to be, he or she has written a remarkable book."

A NORTH LIGHT; twenty-five years in a municipal art gallery; xxiv, 270 p. 2013 Four Courts Press

1. Art museums 2. Belfast (Northern Ireland)—History—20th century 3. Belfast (Northern Ireland)—Intellectual life 4. Hewitt, John Harold, 1907-1987 5. Irish poets 6. Northern Ireland—Politics & government—History

ISBN 1846823641 (pbk.); 9781846823640 (pbk.)

LC 2013-474260

SUMMARY: "'A North Light'--John Hewitt's own account of his life in Northern Ireland from his early years until his 'enforced exile' in Covntry in 1957--provides a [illegible] glimpse into his association with key figures from the literary and art world, including W.B. Yeats, George Orwell, Brendan

Behan, Colin Middleton and John Luke. It details Hewitt's career in the Belfast Museum and Art Gallery." (Publisher's note)

REVIEW: *TLS* no5776 p30 D 13 2013 PATRICIA CRAIG

"A North Light: Twenty-Five Years in a Municipal Art Gallery." "[Author John] Hewitt's poetry and prose are equally concerned with questions of belonging, conscience, tradition, humanist ethics and so forth, and this fascinating collection of autobiographical pieces underscores the cogency of his approach to these matters. 'A North Light' isn't just about doings and dealings in a municipal art gallery (Belfast), as its subtitle implies, but adds up to an informed commentary on cultural, social and political affairs in the North of Ireland during the middle part of the twentieth century. . . . The thirty-eight short essays that make up 'A North Light' are arranged by theme."

NORTH PACIFIC TEMPERATE RAINFORESTS; ecology & conservation; xi, 383 p. 2013 Audubon Alaska & the Nature Conservancy of Alaska in assoc. w/ Univ. of Washington Pr

1. HISTORY—United States—State & Local—Pacific Northwest (OR, WA) 2. NATURE—Ecology 3. NATURE—Ecosystems & Habitats—Forests & Rainforests 4. Natural history literature 5. Temperate rain forest conservation—Alaska 6. Temperate rain forest conservation—British Colombia 7. Temperate rain forest ecology—Alaska 8. Temperate rain forest ecology—British Colombia

ISBN 9780295992617 (hardback)

LC 2013-007835

SUMMARY: This book "examines the ecosystems that hug the West Coast of North America. The editors and contributors provide a multidisciplinary overview of what they argue are key issues associated with conservation and management of this economically, socially, and spiritually important biome. The book's ten chapters cover topics as wide-ranging as disturbance patterns, riparian ecology, conservation biology, and indigenous and commercial use of natural resources." (Choice: Current Reviews for Academic Libraries)

REVIEW: *Choice* v51 no6 p1032-3 F 2014 S. Rigg

"North Pacific Temperate Rainforests: Ecology and Conservation." "The editors and contributors provide a multidisciplinary overview of what they argue are key issues associated with conservation and management of this economically, socially, and spiritually important biome.. . . The information presented is both data based and perception oriented, providing a thoughtful discussion and analysis. The authors hope that reading this book will help impart an appreciation of the beauty and wonder of the region's ecosystems and garner support for conservation efforts. Overall, this book is aimed at anyone interested in the North Pacific temperate rainforests, especially upper-level students, practitioners, and land managers."

NORTHROP, DOUGLAS.ed. A companion to world history. See A companion to world history

NORTHRUP, DAVID. How English became the global language; [by] David Northrup xiii, 205 p. 2013 Palgrave Macmillan

1. English language—Foreign countries 2. English language—Globalization 3. English language—History 4. English language– Variation 5. Social science literature

ISBN 9781137303059 (hardcover); 9781137303066 (paperback)

LC 2012-038715

SUMMARY: In this book on the globalization of the English language, historian David Northrup examines "such contentious issues as colonialism and linguistic imperialism, including the debate about whether English is a 'killer' language; he stresses that when a minority language 'dies,' the reasons are usually complex, often involving the pragmatic interests of native speakers rather than simple coercion." (Choice)

REVIEW: *Choice* v51 no4 p631 D 2013 G. D. Bird

"How English Became the Global Language." "On beginning this book, this reviewer became irritated at the author's apparent naïvité and lack of technical linguistic knowledge, a discomfort exacerbated by frequent typos, e.g., 'Welch' for 'Welsh' and 'Claxton' for 'Caxton.' But these reservations were overcome by the author's unusual perspective on the history of the global spread of the English language. . . . He deals evenhandedly with such contentious issues as colonialism and linguistic imperialism. . . . All these considerations are refreshing and relevant as one thinks about the causes and consequences of the globalization of English."

NORWICH, JOHN JULIUS.ed. Darling monster; the letters of Lady Diana Cooper to her son John Julius Norwich 1939-1952; 520 p. 2013 Chatto & Windus

1. Letters 2. World War, 1939-1945—Personal narratives, British

ISBN 0701187794 (hbk.); 1448139112 (ebook); 9780701187798 (hbk.); 9781448139118 (ebook)

LC 2013-432039

SUMMARY: "Diana's letters to her only son, John Julius Norwich, cover the period 1939 to 1952. They take us from the rumblings of war, through the Blitz, which the Coopers spent holed up in the Dorchester . . . , to rural Sussex where we see Diana blissfully setting up a smallholding as part of the war effort. After a spell with the Free French in Algiers, Duff was appointed British Ambassador to France and the couple settled into the glorious embassy in post-Liberation Paris." (Publisher's note)

REVIEW: *TLS* no5784 p7 F 7 2014 RICHARD DAVENPORT-HINES

"Darling Monster: The Letters of Diana Cooper to Her Son John Julius Norwich 1939-1952." "Cooper . . . recounted to John Julius how she accompanied his father on a hectic propaganda tour of the United States. . . . Most remarkably of all . . . Diana Cooper accompanied her husband on a five-month tour of South-east Asia in 1941, and spent nine months with him in Algiers in 1944. Next, there were three years during which he was British ambassador in Paris, and she restored grace and style to Embassy life. But Diana Cooper's letters are at their best in conveying the atmosphere of wartime England. . . . The racial attitudes of her time are frankly revealed."

NOTHING BUT THE BLUES; the music and the musicians; 432 1993 Abbeville Press

1. African Americans—Music 2. Blues music 3. Blues music—History and criticism 4. Blues musicians 5. Music literature

ISBN 0-7892-0607-2 pa

LC 93-2-791

SUMMARY: The essays in this volume aim to: trace the metamorphosis of the blues from its African roots and the 'hollers,' work songs, and party music of the rural south to the . . . rhythms of urban blues and on to R & B and blues rock. . . . Blues styles associated with specific regions are described. . . . Other topics include the impact of radio and recording technology on the popularity of the blues, the link between gospel and blues, and the blues revival of the 1960s." (Booklist)

REVIEW: *Booklist* v110 no5 p16 N 1 2013 Donna Seaman

"A Bad Woman Feeling Good: Blues and the Women Who Sang Them," "Stomping the Blues," and "Nothing But the Blues: The Music and the Musicians." "[Buzzy] Jackson traces the lives and influence of female blues singers . . . and explains how their music encouraged emotional freedom and forthrightness about the complicated struggles women face. . . . [Albert Murray's] radiant interpretation is rich in incisive portraits of blues musicians and many telling anecdotes, all accompanied by extraordinary photographs. . . . This handsome, well-illustrated, and penetrating blues history tracks the metamorphosis of the blues from its African roots."

NOURBAKHSH, ILLAH REZA. Robot futures; [by] Illah Reza Nourbakhsh 160 p. 2013 MIT Press

1. Human-computer interaction 2. Robotics 3. Robotics—Popular works 4. Technical literature 5. Technological forecasting—Popular works

ISBN 0262018624; 9780262018623 (hardcover : alk. paper)

LC 2012-024598

SUMMARY: This book, by Illah Reza Nourbakhsh, "considers how we will share our world with [robots], and how our society could change as it incorporates a race of stronger, smarter beings. Nourbakhsh imagines a future that includes adbots offering interactive custom messaging; robotic flying toys that operate by means of 'gaze tracking'; robot-enabled multimodal, multicontinental telepresence; and even a way that nanorobots could allow us to assume different physical forms." (Publisher's note)

REVIEW: *Choice* v51 no2 p299-300 O 2013 G. Trajkovski

"Robot Futures." "In this thought-provoking work, [author Illah Reza] Nourbakhsh . . . explores what might happen in human societies and communities as technological advances continue, and as robots become ubiquitous in our daily lives. Each chapter starts with a scenario, a vignette that serves as grounds for technical and ethical discussions. Topics range from the omnipresent access to information and online analytics, to human-robot interactions, multitasking and prioritizations, nanorobots and human enhancements, and finally, the merger of the two 'species.' . . . This book is a must read for a wide audience as it provides a unique and solid vision of possibilities grounded in today's cutting-edge research and technology."

REVIEW: *New Sci* v216 no2910 p47 Mr 30 2013 George Annas

NOURSE, CAROL.il. The natural communities of Georgia. See Edwards, L.

NOURSE, HUGH.il. The natural communities of Georgia. See Edwards, L.

NOVAK, B. J. One more thing; stories and other stories; [by] B. J. Novak 288 p. 2014 Alfred A. Knopf

1. FICTION—Literary 2. FICTION—Short Stories (single author) 3. HUMOR—General 4. Humorous stories 5. Short story (Literary form)

ISBN 9780385351836 (hardback)

LC 2013-044121

SUMMARY: This collection of short stories, by B. J. Novak, "has at its heart the most human of phenomena: love, fear, hope, ambition, and the inner stirring for the one elusive element just that might make a person complete. Across a . . . range of subjects, themes, tones, and narrative voices, the many pieces in this collection . . . have one thing in common: they share the playful humor . . . of a writer with a fierce devotion to the entertainment of the reader." (Publisher's note)

REVIEW: *Booklist* v110 no9/10 p40 Ja 1 2014 Donna Seaman

"One More Thing: Stories and Other Stories"." "[B. J.] Novak's high-concept, hilarious, and disarmingly commiserative fiction debut stems from his stand-up performances and his Emmy Award-winning work on the comedy series 'The Office,' as writer, actor, director, and executive producer. Accordingly, his more concise stories come across as brainy comedy bits, while his sustained tales covertly encompass deep emotional and psychological dimensions. An adept Zeitgeist miner, Novak excels at topsy-turvy improvisations on a dizzying array of subjects, from Aesop's fables to tabloid Elvis to our oracular enthrallment to the stock market."

REVIEW: *Kirkus Rev* v82 no2 p315 Ja 15 2014

REVIEW: *Libr J* v139 no8 p44 My 1 2014 Heather Malcolm

REVIEW: *N Y Times Book Rev* p22 F 23 2014 GREGORY COWLES

REVIEW: *N Y Times Book Rev* p8 F 23 2014 TEDDY WAYNE

REVIEW: *New Statesman* v143 no16 p75 Ap 18 2014

REVIEW: *New York Times* v163 no56395 pC1-4 Ja 28 2014 MICHIKO KAKUTANI

"One More Things: Stories and Other Stories." "[Author B. J.] Novak has an idiosyncratic voice that's distinctively his own. . . . It is Mr. Novak's gift for channeling the way we talk and think today that propels many of the funnier tales here. . . . Some of the entries here are way weaker than others. Some feel like sketches for unrealized skits or undeveloped premises jotted down in a notebook; they are random musings that may give us a feel for the map of Mr. Novak's mind but are otherwise self-indulgent and annoying. . . . What redeems many of the lesser pieces in 'One More Thing' is Mr. Novak's delight in language, his precisionist eye for detail, his ability to capture the odd thoughts that burble through his characters' minds."

REVIEW: *Publ Wkly* v261 no17 p132 Ap 28 2014

REVIEW: *Publ Wkly* v260 no48 p32 N 25 2013

REVIEW: *Time* v183 no6 p56 F 17 2014 Lev Grossman

"One More Thing: Stories and Other Stories." "'One More Thing' belongs to that slightly dusty genre, the humorous collection, but it's much more interesting than that makes it sound. The line between the merely funny and the literary isn't as clear as it's made out to be. . . . [Author B. J.]

Novak has a gift for mimicry so pitch-perfect it's practically Auto-Tuned and an uncannily precise eye for where the line is and when to cross it. . . . At its best, 'One More Thing' demonstrates that sometimes if you follow the cultural logic to its logical extreme, it wraps all the way around and bites itself in the ass."

NOVAK, BORIS A.tr. The master of insomnia. See Novak, B.

NOVAK, BORIS A. The master of insomnia; selected poems; xxvi, 104 p. 2012 Dalkey Archive Press
1. Aestheticism (Literature) 2. Families—Poetry 3. Political poetry 4. Slovenian poetry—Translations into English 5. War poetry
ISBN 9781564787835 (pbk. : alk. paper)
LC 2012-021659

SUMMARY: "'The Master of Insomnia' is a collection of Slovenian poet Boris A. Novak's verse from the last fifteen years, including numerous poems never before available in English. In these sensitive translations, Novak stands revealed as both innovator and observer; as critic Ale Debeljak has written: "The poet's power in bearing witness . . . confirms . . . that what is essential hides in the marginal, negligent, and hardly observed details." (Publisher's note)

REVIEW: *World Lit Today* v88 no1 p72-3 Ja/F 2014 Robert Murray Davis

"The Master of Insomnia: Selected Poems." "[Boris A.] Novak's poems can stand on their own, but those who need information about the history of Slovenian language and literature as well as the political and cultural worlds in which Novak writes should turn to Aleš Debeljak's useful introduction. Ultimately, Novak's selection is far richer than a brief review can indicate, but perhaps the Dalkey Archive's Slovenian Literature Series will bring to Novak and other writers the wider attention they deserve."

NOVAK, MICHAEL, 1933-. Writing from left to right; from church to state, my journey from liberal to conservative image; [by] Michael Novak 336 p. 2013 Image
1. Democracy—Moral and ethical aspects 2. Memoirs 3. Political campaigns—United States
ISBN 9780385347464
LC 2013-008452

SUMMARY: In this memoir, "charting his slow drift from left to right, [Michael] Novak explains how he came to see the guiding passions of his life--fighting poverty, advocating for human rights--as better served by an enlightened capitalism and by democratic politics that restrained the well-intentioned but too often disastrously heavy hand of the state." (Kirkus Reviews)

REVIEW: *America* v209 no18 p30-3 D 9 2013 DAVID O'BRIEN

REVIEW: *Commonweal* v141 no8 p25-8 My 2 2014 Peter Steinfels

REVIEW: *Kirkus Rev* v81 no15 p271 Ag 1 2013

REVIEW: *Natl Rev* v65 no19 p38-40 O 14 2013 MARY EBERSTADT

"Writing From Left to Right: My Journey From Liberal to Conservative." "We now have his new memoir as a handy and engaging guide to at least some of the contributions of its author to America and the wider world. . . . From start to finish, 'Writing from Left to Right' throws new light onto all that activity, intellectual and otherwise. . . . Part of the appeal of 'Writing from Left to Right' is the author's charming, almost bashful sense of perspective on his former selves. . . . . To read Michael Novak's work--any of it, including this book--is to be struck by its intellectual pantheism."

NOVEL ECOSYSTEMS; intervening in the new ecological world order; xi, 368 p. 2013 John Wiley & Sons Inc.
1. Ecological disturbances 2. Ecosystem health 3. Ecosystem management 4. Environmental literature 5. Nature—Effect of human beings on
ISBN 9781118354223 (cloth)
LC 2012-031506

SUMMARY: This book, edited by Richard J. Hobbs, Eric S. Higgs, and Carol M. Hall, addresses how "Land conversion, climate change and species invasions are contributing to the widespread emergence of novel ecosystems, which demand a shift in how we think about traditional approaches to conservation, restoration and environmental management. They are novel because they exist without historical precedents and are self-sustaining." (Publisher's note)

REVIEW: *Choice* v51 no2 p291 O 2013 J. Burger

"Novel Ecosystems: Intervening in the New Ecological World Order." "'Novel Ecosystems,' despite the book's pretentious subtitle, examines the vexing challenge of ecological restoration that often foils to achieve sustainable reconstruction of ecosystems that people remember from decades past. Years of agriculture, irrigation or drainage, and invasive plants, animals, and pathogens change both the ground and the neighborhood, often thwarting restoration. This work, based on a 2011 workshop held in British Columbia, is divided into seven parts and 42 chapters. A statement in the introduction defines the work: 'It is simply impossible, or at least practically impossible, to recover historical ecosystems.'"

REVIEW: *Science* v341 no6145 p458-9 Ag 2 2013 David Moreno Mateos

NOVELLI, MARIO.ed. Global education policy and international development. See Global education policy and international development

NOVELLI, MARTIN A. The long reconstruction. See Wetta, F. J.

NOVGORODOFF, DANICA. The Undertaking of Lily Chen; [by] Danica Novgorodoff 432 p. 2014 First Second
1. Brothers—Fiction 2. China—Fiction 3. Ghost stories 4. Graphic novels
ISBN 1596435860; 9781596435865 (pbk.)
LC 2013-030816

SUMMARY: In this book, "Deshi accidentally kills his older brother, Wei, by shoving him in front of a moving jeep, and his furious mother, calling on the ancient tradition of ghost marriage, demands that he find the unmarried Wei a corpse bride, a recently deceased single woman who will accompany him in the afterlife. Guilt-ridden Deshi . . . runs into stubborn, spirited Lily, who would make a perfect bride if she weren't so alive." (Booklist)

REVIEW: *Booklist* v110 no13 p50 Mr 1 2014 Sarah Hunter

"The Undertaking of Lily Chen." "[Danica] Novgorodoff's exaggerated, cartoonish figures appear against spare, inky backgrounds resembling traditional Chinese landscape paintings, as if history and heritage loom over Deshi and Lily as they make their way forward to their futures. Deshi's grief and guilt, meanwhile, are hauntingly, gorgeously rendered in smoky, aqueous watercolor washes, which subtly suggest a gaping mouth and face hovering over Lily and spilling between panels. It's a simple, darkly comic story, but Novgorodoff's artful juxtaposition of traditional and contemporary imagery elevates it to eloquently echo a deeper, all-encompassing tension between past and progress."

REVIEW: *Publ Wkly* v261 no9 p51 Mr 3 2014

REVIEW: *Voice of Youth Advocates* v37 no1 p72 Ap 2014 Victoria Vogel

NOVY, MARIANNE. Shakespeare and outsiders; [by] Marianne Novy 2013 Oxford University Press

1. Literature—History & criticism 2. Outsiders in literature 3. Shakespeare, William, 1564-1616—Characters 4. Shakespeare, William, 1564-1616—Drama 5. Strangers in literature

ISBN 9780199642366

SUMMARY: This book, by Marianne Novy, argues that "Shakespeare's most memorable characters are treated as outsiders in at least part of their plays—Othello, Shylock, Malvolio, Katherine (the 'Shrew') , Edmund, Caliban, and many others." According to Novy, this is a "relative identity and not a fixed one, a position that characters move into and out of." She "compare[s] characters who are outsiders not just in terms of race and religion but also in terms of gender, age, poverty, illegitimate birth, psychology, morality, and other issues." (Publisher's note)

REVIEW: *TLS* no5795 p8 Ap 25 2014 EMMA SMITH

"Shakespeare and Outsiders" and "The Spanish Tragedy." "The strength of [author Marianne] Novy's method is clear: it is attentive to varying audience responses and delicate in its understanding of the rhythms of sympathy. . . . Michael Neill's welcome new edition of Thomas Kyd's revenge play 'The Spanish Tragedy' also emphasizes its religious implications. . . . Michael Neill's introduction ranges with his customary elegance and learning across legal, formal and rhetorical analyses. He chooses to print the text as it appeared in editions from 1602 onwards."

NOWAK, M. A. (MARTIN A.)ed. Evolution, games, and God. See Evolution, games, and God

NOYES, DEBORAH. Plague in the mirror; [by] Deborah Noyes 272 p. 2013 Candlewick Press

1. Black Death pandemic, 1348-1351 2. Florence (Italy)—Fiction 3. Historical fiction 4. Paranormal romance stories 5. Young adult fiction

ISBN 9780763659806

LC 2012-947257

SUMMARY: "In a sensual paranormal romance, a teen girl's doppelgänger from 1348 Florence lures her into the past in hopes of exacting a deadly trade. . . . And when later she follows the menacing Cristofana through a portale to fourteenth-century Florence, May never expects to find safety in the eyes of Marco, a soulful painter who awakens in her a burning desire and makes her feel truly seen. . . . with the Black Death ravaging Old Florence . . ." (Publisher's note)

REVIEW: *Bull Cent Child Books* v67 no1 p42-3 S 2013 K. Q. G.

"Plague in the Mirror." "Now May is wondering if the stress is also affecting her sanity when . . . she discovers a wormhole that takes her to medieval Florence. There she meets Marco, a handsome painter who sparks her as-of-yet unawakened desire, and Christofana, May's fourteenth-century doppelganger, who is willing to do anything to escape the Black Death that has taken hold of the city. . . . The real appeal here lies with the temperamental and chaotic Christofana; her bitter rage at being born during such a hopeless time is palpable, and the horrors of her world bring May's more insignificant woes into sharp contrast. Laden with atmospheric details and hits of Italian history, this is most likely to find an audience among history buffs and armchair travelers."

REVIEW: *Horn Book Magazine* v89 no4 p140-1 Jl/Ag 2013 JONATHAN HUNT

REVIEW: *Kirkus Rev* v81 no9 p97 My 1 2013

REVIEW: *SLJ* v59 no7 p99 Jl 2013 Kathy Kirchoefer

REVIEW: *SLJ* v59 no10 p1 O 2013 Julie Paladino

THE NUCLEAR RENAISSANCE AND INTERNATIONAL SECURITY; xi, 364 p. 2013 Stanford Security Studies, an imprint of Stanford University Press

1. International conflict 2. International security 3. Nuclear energy 4. Nuclear nonproliferation 5. Political science literature

ISBN 9780804784177 (cloth)

LC 2012-037023

SUMMARY: This book, edited by Adam Stulberg and Matthew Fuhrmann, addresses "critical issues relating to the nuclear renaissance, including if and how peaceful nuclear programs contribute to nuclear weapons proliferation, whether the diffusion of nuclear technologies lead to an increase in the trafficking of nuclear materials, and under what circumstances the diffusion of nuclear technologies and latent nuclear weapons capabilities can influence international stability and conflict." (Publisher's note)

REVIEW: *Choice* v51 no2 p350-1 O 2013 C. W. Herrick

"The Nuclear Renaissance and International Security." "[Adam N.] Stulberg . . . and [Matthew] Fuhrmann . . . have compiled a well-documented series of essays by 14 well-qualified analysts. These essays address three general themes: the nature of the nuclear renaissance and the factors such as strategic advantage or the desire to address the global climate change issue driving that renaissance; the potential impact of the emergent nuclear renaissance upon nuclear weapons proliferation; and the extent to which . . . the renaissance will generate . . . international conflict. Essays range from well-argued narrative analyses to descriptions of important statistical analyses that cast new light upon assumptions regarding the potential impact of an expansion of nuclear energy generation."

NUNES, PAUL. Big bang disruption. See Downes, L.

NUNEZ, ELIZABETH. Not for everyday use; a memoir; [by] Elizabeth Nunez 256 p. 2014 Akashic Books

1. Memoirs 2. Mothers & daughters 3. Mothers—Death 4. Trinidad & Tobago—Social conditions 5. Trinidadian Americans
ISBN 9781617752346 (hardcover); 9781617752780 (e-bk.); 1617752339; 9781617752339 (trade pbk. original)
LC 2013-956048

SUMMARY: In this book, "tracing the four days from the moment she gets the call that every immigrant fears to the burial of her mother, Elizabeth Nunez tells the . . . story of her lifelong struggle to cope with . . . the 'sterner stuff' of her parents' ambitions for their children and her mother's . . . conviction that displays of affection are not for everyday use. . . . But Nunez sympathizes with her parents, whose happiness is constrained by the oppressive strictures of colonialism." (Publisher's note)

REVIEW: *Booklist* v110 no13 p13 Mr 1 2014 Vanessa Bush

"Not for Everyday Use". "Her return conjures up the memories that partly inspired her novels and triggers a deeper examination of her parents' long marriage and her own (two years of real marriage, 18 more of duty before divorce). From the perspective of adulthood, marriage, and her sojourn in the U.S., [Elizabeth] Nunez ponders the cultural, racial, familial, social, and personal experiences that led to what she ultimately understands was a deeply loving union between her parents. A beautifully written exploration of the complexities of marriage and family life."

REVIEW: *Kirkus Rev* v82 no10 p5 My 15 2014

REVIEW: *Libr J* v139 no2 p76 F 1 2014 Nancy R. Ives

NUNN, KEM. Chance; a novel; [by] Kem Nunn 336 p. 2014 Scribner

1. FICTION—General 2. FICTION—Literary 3. FICTION—Thrillers 4. Neuropsychiatry—Fiction 5. Psychiatrists—California—San Francisco—Fiction 6. Psychological fiction
ISBN 9780743289245 (hardback); 9780743289290 (paperback)
LC 2013-042188

SUMMARY: In this novel by Kem Nunn, "The antihero . . . , Dr. Eldon Chance, a neuropsychiatrist, is a man primed for spectacular ruin. Into Dr. Chance's blighted life walks Jaclyn Blackstone, the abused, attractive wife of an Oakland homicide detective, a violent and jealous man. Jaclyn appears to be suffering from a dissociative identity disorder. In time, Chance will fall into bed with her--or is it with her alter ego, the voracious and volatile Jackie Black?" (Publisher's note)

REVIEW: *Booklist* v110 no8 p21 D 15 2013 Joanne Wilkinson

REVIEW: *Kirkus Rev* v81 no24 p238 D 15 2013

"Chance". "Gritty. . . . Eldon Chance sees broken people in his job, so it's almost inevitable that some of those individuals would bleed over into his personal life. . . . Eventually, [Kem] Nunn's characters cross paths, and Chance's decisions cause his life to careen from slightly off balance to out of control. Nunn, a writer with a gift for subtlety and wordplay, spins a story that is both mesmerizing and a bit confusing. Readers will find Nunn's story well-written for the most part but not always engaging. Lovers of Nunn's previous novels may discover in Chance a less than creditable antihero.

REVIEW: *N Y Times Book Rev* p10 Mr 2 2014 TERRENCE RAFFERTY

"Chance." "The tribulations (and they are legion) visited on the good doctor in the tumultuous course of 'Chance' are, virtually without exception, consequences of a midlife predilection for rash, ill-considered, idea-free life decisions. Probably the worst of these is his impulse . . . to bed one of his patients. . . . [Author Kem] Nunn, a connoisseur of slippery slopes, just gives his upright protagonist a gentle shove and watches him go down, every bump and stumble duly noted with a sort of dry relish. . . . For all the mayhem in 'Chance,' its conclusion is delicately funny."

REVIEW: *Publ Wkly* v260 no49 p63-4 D 2 2013

NUNNALLY, TIINA.tr. The Land of Dreams. See The Land of Dreams

NUSSBAUM, MARTHA CRAVEN, 1947-. Political emotions; why love matters for justice; [by] Martha Craven Nussbaum 480 p. 2013 Harvard University Press

1. Emotions (Philosophy) 2. Emotions—Political aspects 3. Philosophical literature 4. Political psychology 5. Political science—Philosophy
ISBN 0674724658; 9780674724655 (hardcover: alk. paper)
LC 2013-010890

SUMMARY: This book by Martha C. Nussbaum is a "continuation of her explorations of emotions and the nature of social justice. Amid the fears, resentments, and competitive concerns that are endemic even to good societies, public emotions rooted in love—in intense attachments to things outside our control—can foster commitment to shared goals. She offers an account of how a decent society can use resources inherent in human psychology, while limiting the damage done by the darker side of our personalities." (Publisher's note)

REVIEW: *Choice* v51 no10 p1888 Je 2014 J. E. Herbel

REVIEW: *N Y Rev Books* v61 no15 p43-4 O 9 2014 Alan Ryan

REVIEW: *Publ Wkly* v260 no32 p49-50 Ag 12 2013

REVIEW: *TLS* no5787 p26 F 28 2014 MARINA GERNER

"Political Emotions: Why Love Matters for Justice." "For [author Martha C.] Nussbaum, the liberal tradition should not cede emotion to anti-liberal forces (fascism, for example, was particularly good at using emotions for political ends). But all political principles need a proper emotional basis to ensure their stability over time, and all decent societies need to guard against division by cultivating appropriate sentiments of sympathy and love. This is why political emotions, narrative imagination and love matter for justice."

REVIEW: *TLS* no5788 p27 Mr 7 2014

NUTTING, ALISSA. Tampa; [by] Alissa Nutting 272 p. 2013 HarperCollins Publishers

1. Child sexual abuse—Fiction 2. Child sexual abuse by teachers 3. Psychological fiction 4. Sexual misconduct by teachers 5. Teacher-student relationships—Fiction
ISBN 0062280546; 9780062280541

SUMMARY: In this book by Alissa Nutting, "a middle school teacher in Tampa, Fla., goes to outrageous lengths to hide her voracious sexual appetite for adolescent boys. . . . She says that the loss of her virginity at age 14 imprinted on her, and she has been working unceasingly as a student teacher to get to the mother lode: a gig as a full-time teacher of eighth-grade boys. In her first year, she obsesses over her chosen target, young Jack Patrick." (Kirkus Reviews)

REVIEW: *Booklist* v109 no21 p32 Jl 1 2013 Kristine Huntley

REVIEW: *Kirkus Rev* v81 no7 p288 Ap 1 2013

REVIEW: *New York Times* v162 no56208 pC6 Jl 25 2013 Susannah Meadows

REVIEW: *Publ Wkly* v260 no18 p35-6 My 6 2013

REVIEW: *TLS* no5767 p20 O 11 2013 SOPHIE RATCLIFFE

"Tampa." "[Alissa] Nutting's blend of interior monologue and reportage reads like a novelized biopic, but it claims a deeper literary heritage. . . . The plot proceeds at a noirish pace, seen through Celeste's warped perspective. . . . Descriptions are graphic. . . . in a novel preoccupied with tone, tone is one of Tampa's many failures. . . . It is hard to say whether the prose style is deliberately bad--the ravings of a Humbert Humbert manque--or just inept, but the result makes Celeste feel less like flesh and blood than narrative strap-on. . . . Nutting's take on this matter is thought-provoking, but the emphasis on social satire leaves little room for the more difficult and murky questions that surround writing and reading about sexual abuse and hebephilia."

O

OAKES, JAMES. The Scorpion's Sting; Antislavery and the Coming of the Civil War; [by] James Oakes 160 p. 2014 W W Norton & Co Inc

1. Antislavery movements—United States—History 2. Historical literature 3. United States—History—Civil War, 1861-1865—Causes 4. United States—Politics & government—1783-1865 5. United States. President (1861-1865 : Lincoln). Emancipation Proclamation
ISBN 0393239934; 9780393239935
LC 2013-049978

SUMMARY: This book by James Oakes "takes an in-depth look at political attitudes toward slavery at the brink of the Civil War. His title refers to a strategy most Republicans--sometimes overtly, sometimes secretly--supported, of gradual abolition by surrounding slave states with a 'cordon of freedom' so that eventually slavery would 'sting itself to death,' like a scorpion in a circle of fire." (Publishers Weekly)

REVIEW: *Booklist* v110 no11 p16-8 F 1 2014 Brad Hooper

"The Scorpion's Sting: Antislavery and the Coming of the Civil War." "Casual American-history buffs will quietly lay this book aside, while serious students of the events and attitudes toward slave emancipation in the decades before the outbreak of the Civil War will find it, pick it up, and enthusiastically consider its provocative arguments. . . . Why that concept did not work and why, once secession pulled the nation apart, and warfare erupted, what indeed worked was military emancipation are great and greatly complicated ideas [James] Oakes airs with clear thinking and precise prose."

REVIEW: *Kirkus Rev* v82 no9 p65 My 1 2014

REVIEW: *Libr J* v138 no18 p103 N 1 2013 Molly McArdle

REVIEW: *Libr J* v139 no4 p99 Mr 1 2014 Randall M. Miller

REVIEW: *Publ Wkly* v261 no3 p41 Ja 20 2014

OAKLEY, JOHN H. The Greek vase; art of the storyteller; [by] John H. Oakley 114 p. 2013 J. Paul Getty Museum British Museum Press

1. Ancient vases 2. Art literature 3. British Museum 4. Greek vases 5. J. Paul Getty Museum 6. Vase-painting, Greek 7. Vases, Greek
ISBN 9781606061473 (hardcover)
LC 2013-005879

SUMMARY: Written by John H. Oakley, "This richly illustrated volume offers a fascinating introduction to ancient Greek vases for the general reader. It presents vases . . . as instruments of storytelling and bearers of meaning. . . . Based on the rich collections of the British Museum and the J. Paul Getty Museum, the exquisite details of the works offer the reader the opportunity for an intimate interaction with . . . ancient vases." (Publisher's note)

REVIEW: *Choice* v51 no8 p1387 Ap 2014 R. Brilliant

REVIEW: *N Y Times Book Rev* p70 D 8 2013 STEVE COATES

"The Greek Vase: Art of the Storyteller." "[John H.] Oakley's book walks through the main styles and production centers of Greek figurative pottery. . . . Oakley provides a succinct primer on the different vessel forms, a varied array of cups, pitchers, storage jars, wine-mixing bowls, sacral implements and others. . . . A limitation of Oakley's book is that it draws exclusively on the holdings of just two collections: the J. Paul Getty museum and, especially, the British Museum, London has magnificent vases, of which there is proof on every page."

OATES, JOYCE CAROL, 1938-. The Accursed; [by] Joyce Carol Oates 688 p. 2013 HarperCollins

1. Cleveland, Grover, 1837-1908 2. Horror tales 3. Princes—Fiction 4. Princeton (N.J.) 5. Wilson, Woodrow, 1856-1924
ISBN 0062231707; 9780062231703

SUMMARY: In this book by Joyce Carol Oates, "strange things start happening in peaceful, polished Princeton, NJ. Folks dream about vampires, the daughters of the town's classiest families start vanishing, and a bride-to-be runs away with a vaguely menacing European, presumably a prince and possibly the Devil. As her brother gives chase, he encounters characters from former President Grover Cleveland and future President Woodrow Wilson to authors like Upton Sinclair." (Library Journal)

REVIEW: *Booklist* v109 no21 p51 Jl 1 2013 Candace Smith

REVIEW: *Booklist* v109 no8 p23 D 15 2012 Donna Seaman

REVIEW: *Kirkus Rev* p30 N 15 2013 Best Books

REVIEW: *Kirkus Rev* v81 no2 p13 Ja 15 2013

REVIEW: *Libr J* v138 no11 p48 Je 15 2013 Deb West

REVIEW: *Libr J* v137 no19 p77 N 15 2012 Barbara Hoffert

REVIEW: *Libr J* v137 no16 p56 O 1 2012 Barbara Hoffert

REVIEW: *N Y Rev Books* v61 no8 p45-8 My 8 2014 Michael Dirda

"The Accursed" and "Carthage." "At 667 pages instead of 666, 'The Accursed' is obviously one page too long. Joyce Carol Oates's extravaganza of demons, vampires, doppelgangers, seduction, possession, murder, and terrible family secrets has been called . . . 'the world's finest postmodern Gothic novel.' In its pages the devil—or more precisely one of his 'satans'—appears in Princeton, New Jersey, in the year 1905 and . . . wreaks havoc on the town's wealthy and privileged citizens. . . . 'Carthage' is even more powerful and gripping than 'The Accursed,' if only because it's meant to shock and upset, to feel immediate, personal, contemporary. . . . 'Carthage' is, in effect, a three-part drama, set in the years 2005 to 2012."

REVIEW: *N Y Rev Books* v60 no7 p29-30 Ap 25 2013 Francine Prose

REVIEW: *N Y Times Book Rev* p22 Mr 24 2013

REVIEW: *N Y Times Book Rev* p26-8 D 8 2013

"The Accursed," "Children Are Diamonds: An African Apocalypse," "The American Way of Poverty: How the Other Half Still Lives." "['The Accursed' is Joyce Carol] Oates's extravagantly horrifying, funny prolix postmodern Gothic novel. . . . The adventure-seeking protagonist of [Edward] Hoagland's novel ['Children Are Diamonds: An African Apocalypse'] is swept up in the chaos of southern Sudan. . . . ['The American Way of Poverty'], based on [author Sasha] Abramsky's travels around the country meeting the poor, both describes and prescribes."

REVIEW: *N Y Times Book Rev* p1-17 Mr 17 2013 Stephen King

REVIEW: *Publ Wkly* v260 no17 p127 Ap 29 2013

REVIEW: *Publ Wkly* v259 no45 p47 N 5 2012

REVIEW: *Quill Quire* v79 no1 p22-3 Ja/F 2013

OATES, JOYCE CAROL, 1938-. Carthage; [by] Joyce Carol Oates 384 p. 2014 HarperCollins

1. Adirondack Mountains (N.Y.)—Fiction 2. Detective & mystery stories 3. Missing persons—Fiction 4. Veterans—United States 5. Water spirits

ISBN 0062208128; 9780062208125

SUMMARY: In this book by Joyce Carol Oates, "Zeno Mayfield's daughter has disappeared into the night, gone missing in the wilds of the Adirondacks. But when the community of Carthage joins a father's frantic search for the girl, they discover the unlikeliest of suspects--a decorated Iraq War veteran with close ties to the Mayfield family." (Publisher's note)

REVIEW: *Booklist* v110 no7 p20 D 1 2013 Donna Seaman

REVIEW: *Booklist* v111 no3 p93 O 1 2014 Laurie Hartshorn

REVIEW: *Kirkus Rev* v81 no22 p226 N 15 2013

REVIEW: *Libr J* v139 no7 p47-8 Ap 15 2014 Beth Farrell

REVIEW: *Libr J* v138 no14 p86 S 1 2013

REVIEW: *N Y Rev Books* v61 no8 p45-8 My 8 2014 Michael Dirda

"The Accursed" and "Carthage." "At 667 pages instead of 666, 'The Accursed' is obviously one page too long. Joyce Carol Oates's extravaganza of demons, vampires, doppelgangers, seduction, possession, murder, and terrible family secrets has been called . . . 'the world's finest postmodern Gothic novel.' In its pages the devil—or more precisely one of his 'satans'—appears in Princeton, New Jersey, in the year 1905 and . . . wreaks havoc on the town's wealthy and privileged citizens. . . . 'Carthage' is even more powerful and gripping than 'The Accursed,' if only because it's meant to shock and upset, to feel immediate, personal, contemporary, . . . 'Carthage' is, in effect, a three-part drama, set in the years 2005 to 2012."

REVIEW: *N Y Times Book Rev* p13 F 2 2014 LIESI SCHILLINGER

REVIEW: *New Statesman* v143 no10 p54-5 Mr 14 2014 Phil Klay

REVIEW: *New York Times* v163 no56404 pC1-6 F 6 2014 DWIGHT GARNER

"Carthage." "This somewhat cool opening makes me wish that I could, with a flamenco dancer's flourish, warm things up and report that Ms. Oates's new novel, 'Carthage,' is alive and soulful, with a freshness of purpose and attack. But it is mostly the opposite of all that. It reads as if the author were on autopilot. . . . The point of view in this entirely humorless novel skips among Cressida, Juliet, Brett, and the girls' parents. These characters' many varieties of heartbreak are difficult to take seriously, because they often speak in dialogue that could have been lifted from a script for 'Days of Our Lives,' circa 1974."

REVIEW: *Publ Wkly* v260 no47 p31 N 18 2013

REVIEW: *Libr J* v137 no7 p99 Ap 15 2012 Judith B. Barnett

REVIEW: *Publ Wkly* v259 no11 p51 Mr 12 2012

OATES, JOYCE CAROL, 1938-. High Crime Area; Tales of Darkness and Dread; [by] Joyce Carol Oates 224 p. 2014 Pgw

1. American short stories 2. Brothers & sisters—Fiction 3. Fear 4. Suspense fiction 5. Teacher-student relationships—Fiction

ISBN 0802122655; 9780802122650

SUMMARY: This book, by Joyce Carol Oates, presents "eight stories . . [that test] the bonds between damaged individuals—a brother and sister, a teacher and student, two strangers on a subway. . . . In the title story 'High Crime Area' a white, aspiring professor is convinced she is being followed. No need to panic, she has a handgun stowed away in her purse—just in case. But when she turns to confront her black, male shadow, the situation isn't what she expects." (Publisher's note)

REVIEW: *Booklist* v110 no11 p3 F 1 2014 Brad Hooper

"The Corsican Caper," "High Crime Area: Tales of Darkness and Dread," and "In Paradise". "[Peter] Mayle sends his popular sleuth Sam Levitt out on further investigative pursuits around the lovely South of France, Sam's focus this time on Russian tycoon Oleg Vronsky. . . . Eight tense, powerful short stories testify to [Joyce Carol] Oates' talent in the short form. . . . This author's esteemed reputation is deep and widespread, and his complicated, intelligent new novel—about a group of women and men gathering for meditations and reflection at the site of a former German concentration camp—will reward his followers."

REVIEW: *Booklist* v110 no12 p32-3 F 15 2014 Donna Seaman

REVIEW: *Kirkus Rev* v82 no4 p189 F 15 2014

"High Crime Area: Tales of Darkness and Dread". " From [Joyce Carol] Oates comes this collection of eight stories, seven previously published, that explore the depths of human despair and cruelty. . . . An idealistic young teacher in 1967 Detroit has to face the fears that are personified by the man following her in 'High Crime Area.' Oates is at her best here when she's writing about floundering academics thrust into situations for which they're hopelessly ill-prepared. Oates' mastery of imagery and stream of consciousness enhances the gritty settings and the frailties of her grotesque and pitiable subjects."

REVIEW: *Libr J* v139 no3 p101 F 15 2014 Sue Russell

REVIEW: *Publ Wkly* v261 no30 p85 Jl 28 2014

REVIEW: *Publ Wkly* v261 no2 p49-50 Ja 13 2014

O'BANION, PATRICK J. The sacrament of penance and religious life in golden age Spain; [by] Patrick J. O'Banion 233 p. 2013 Pennsylvania State University Press

1. Church discipline—History 2. Confession—History 3. Historical literature 4. Penance—Spain—History
ISBN 9780271058993 (cloth: alk. paper)
LC 2012-017709

SUMMARY: "Patrick J. O'Banion's book asserts that early modern Spaniards developed a distinctly vibrant culture of confession. He draws upon a variety of sources, including inquisition trial testimony, confession manuals, and official church synod and council mandates. At the heart of O'Banion's study is the contention that the sacrament of penance in early modern Spain was ubiquitous yet flexible." (American Historical Review)

REVIEW: *Am Hist Rev* v119 no1 p257-8 F 2014 David Coleman

"The Sacrament of Penance and Religious Life in Golden Age Spain". "Some scholarly specialists will likely find [Patrick J.] O'Banion's arguments in this chapter a bit too generalized given the anecdotal nature of much of the evidence employed. Criticism of this sort, though, might well be expected when attempting a study as ambitious as this one. On the whole, the book's strengths considerably outweigh the weaknesses. O'Banion's thoughtful study is on balance a skillfully executed and welcome addition to the growing literature on religious practice in early modern Spain."

OBERST, ROBERT C. Government and politics in South Asia. See Kapur, A.

O'BRIEN, FLANN, 1911-1966. Flann O'Brien; Plays and Teleplays; 300 p. 2013 Dalkey Archive Press

1. Bars (Drinking establishments) 2. Drama—Collections 3. Drinking of alcoholic beverages 4. Police—Fiction 5. Television plays
ISBN 1564788903; 9781564788900 (pbk. : acid-free paper)
LC 2013-011990

SUMMARY: This book, edited by Daniel Keith Jernegan, collects plays and teleplays by Flann O'Brien. Two versions of his play "Thirst" are "joined by three other short stage plays and six television plays, along with the first episodes of two television series which O'Brien wrote for RTÉ, the Irish national broadcaster." (Times Literary Supplement)

REVIEW: *TLS* no5771 p19 N 8 2013 HAL JENSEN

"The Short Fiction of Flann O'Brien" and "Plays and Teleplays." "Very short and slight, they have a winning exuberance. . . . Naturally, these stories lose something in translation. Not just linguistically--half the jokes are gone in English--but also typographically. . . . Flann O'Brien's two recognized masterpieces--'At Swim-Two-Birds' (1939) and 'The Third Policeman' (1967)--tear past with a satirical energy and unruly wit that leave the reader delighted while at the same time somewhat winded. Altogether different is the carefully managed charm and inspired simplicity of 'Thirst,' O'Brien's short (fifteen-page) play, commissioned for the Gate Theatre, Dublin in 1942. Despite its relative obscurity it has as much right to the title of masterpiece as the more knowingly brilliant novels."

O'BRIEN, FLANN, 1911-1966. The Short Fiction of Flann O'Brien; 157 p. 2013 Dalkey Archive Press

1. Alcoholics—Fiction 2. Ireland—Fiction 3. Language & languages 4. Mental illness—Fiction 5. Short stories
ISBN 156478889X; 9781564788894 (pbk. : acid-free paper)
LC 2013-012011

SUMMARY: This book, edited by Neil Murphy and Keith Hopper, "gathers together an expansive selection of [author] Flann O'Brien's shorter fiction in a single volume, as well as O'Brien's last and unfinished novel, 'Slattery's Sago Saga.' Also included are new translations of several stories originally published in Irish, and other rare pieces. With some of these stories appearing here in book form for the very first time, and others previously unavailable for decades." (Publisher's note)

REVIEW: *N Y Times Book Rev* p22 O 20 2013 JULIAN GOUGH

"The Short Fiction of Flann O'Brien." "In so lovingly collecting and editing Flann O'Brien's widely scattered short fiction, Neil Murphy and Keith Hopper have done the study of Irish literature a great service. . . . His juvenilia is precociously brilliant; he achieves mastery early, declines early, and by the end of his short, alcoholic life is writing material that damages rather than enhances his reputation. . . . For the dedicated Flanneur, there is much that is new and interesting. The book begins with five works originally written in ebullient, alarmingly postmodern Irish in the 1930s. . . . Jack Fennell has done an excellent job of translating them into English."

REVIEW: *TLS* no5771 p19 N 8 2013 HAL JENSEN

"The Short Fiction of Flann O'Brien" and "Plays and Teleplays." "Very short and slight, they have a winning exuberance. . . . Naturally, these stories lose something in translation. Not just linguistically--half the jokes are gone in English--but also typographically. . . . Flann O'Brien's two recognized masterpieces--'At Swim-Two-Birds' (1939) and 'The Third Policeman' (1967)--tear past with a satirical energy and unruly wit that leave the reader delighted while at the same time somewhat winded. Altogether different is the carefully managed charm and inspired simplicity of 'Thirst,' O'Brien's short (fifteen-page) play, commissioned for the Gate Theatre, Dublin in 1942. Despite its relative obscurity it has as much right to the title of masterpiece as the more knowingly brilliant novels."

O'BRIEN, GREGORY.il. The ACB with Honora Lee. See De Goldi, K.

O'BRIEN, JACK. Jack be nimble; the accidental education

of an unintentional director; [by] Jack O'Brien 368 p. 2013 Farrar Straus Giroux
1. BIOGRAPHY & AUTOBIOGRAPHY—Entertainment & Performing Arts 2. Memoirs 3. PERFORMING ARTS—Theater—General 4. Television producers and directors—United States—Biography 5. Theatrical producers and directors—United States—Biography
ISBN 9780865478985 (hardback)
LC 2012-048077

SUMMARY: This book presents a memoir by director Jack O'Brien. "Following a fairly normal Midwestern childhood, O'Brien hoped to make his mark by writing lyrics for Broadway but was instead pulled into the growing American regional theater movement by the likes of John Houseman, Helen Hayes, Ellis Rabb, and Eva Le Gallienne. He didn't intend to become a director, or to direct some of the most brilliant . . . personalities of the age, but . . . that's what happened." (Publisher's note)

REVIEW: *Kirkus Rev* v81 no7 p224 Ap 1 2013

REVIEW: *N Y Times Book Rev* p58 N 10 2013 Anita Gates

"Jack Be Nimble: The Accidental Education of an Unintentional Director," "Room 1219: The Life of Fatty Arbuckle, the Mysterious Death of Virginia Rappe, and the Scandal That Changed Hollywood," and "Still Foolin' 'Em: Where I've Been, Where I'm Going, and Where the Hell Are My Keys? "Most of this gracefully written book is about [Jack O'Brien's] early days, and the influence of . . . Ellis Rabb and . . . Rosemary Harris. . . . Some scenes are quite personal, even invasive, but O'Brien's admiration for both comes through. . . . [Greg] Merritt's account of the crime . . . the three trials and the people involved is admirably evenhanded, meticulously researched and compelling. . . . [A] breezy memoir. . . . Sometimes the humor is bright. . . . Crystal is at his authorial finest when he switches into mean mode and mouths off about people and things that annoy him."

REVIEW: *New York Times* v162 no56174 pC28 Je 21 2013 BENEDICT NIGHTINGALE

REVIEW: *Publ Wkly* v260 no12 p54 Mr 25 2013

O'BRIEN, JOHN.il. Thomas Jefferson Builds a Library. See Rosenstock, B.

O'BRIEN, MICHAEL.ed. The letters of C. Vann Woodward. See The letters of C. Vann Woodward

O'BRIEN, TIM, 1946-. The things they carried; a work of fiction; [by] Tim O'Brien 273 1990 Houghton Mifflin
1. Military personnel—Fiction 2. Short stories 3. Vietnam War, 1961-1975—Fiction 4. Vietnam veterans—Fiction 5. Vietnam veterans—Psychology 6. Vietnamese War, 1961-1975
LC 89-3-9871

SUMMARY: This book presents "a series of stories about the Vietnam experience, based on the author's recollections. [Tim] O'Brien begins by sharing the talismans and treasures his select small band of young soldiers carry into battle. The tales, ranging from a paragraph to 20 or so pages, reveal one truth after another. Sometimes the author tells the same story from different points of view, revealing the lingering, sometimes consuming, effect war leaves on the soul." (School Library Journal)

REVIEW: *N Y Times Book Rev* p14 N 24 2013 A. O. SCOTT

"The Things They Carried." "What happens in combat can be grotesque, absurd, senseless and transcendent, sometimes all at once. Capturing this in prose that upholds the post-Hemingway, Raymond Carver-era values of plainness and specificity is a challenge. . . . 'The Things They Carried' has lived in the bellies of American readers for more than two decades. . . . It sits on the narrow shelf of indispensable works by witnesses to and participants in the fighting. . . . Bryan Cranston [is] a more than suitable choice to narrate the new audiobook edition. . . . Cranston may be the most charismatic embodiment moral ambiguity we currently possess. . . . Cranston attacks O'Brien's sober, sinewy prose with slightly scary authority."

REVIEW: *Publ Wkly* v261 no13 p61 Mr 31 2014

OCASIO, WILLIAM. The institutional logics perspective. See Lounsbury, M.

OCKLER, SARAH. The Book of Broken Hearts; [by] Sarah Ockler 368 p. 2013 Simon Pulse
1. Alzheimer's patients—Family relationships 2. Argentine Americans—Fiction 3. Family life—Fiction 4. Love—Fiction 5. Love stories
ISBN 1442430389 (hardcover); 9781442430389 (hardcover)
LC 2012-033041

SUMMARY: In this romance novel, by Sarah Ockler, "Jude has learned a lot from her older sisters, but the most important thing is this: The Vargas brothers are notorious heartbreakers. . . . Now Jude is the only sister still living at home, and she's spending the summer helping her ailing father restore his vintage motorcycle--which means hiring a mechanic to help out. Is it Jude's fault he happens to be cute? And surprisingly sweet? And a Vargas?" (Publisher's note)

REVIEW: *Booklist* v110 no2 p80 S 15 2013 Alison O'Reilly

"The Book of Broken Hearts." "Jude Hernandez secretly hopes that spending the summer helping her father repair his beloved Harley Davidson motorcycle will help slow down the effects of his early-onset Alzheimer's. . . . [Zilah] Mendoza handles occasional Spanish words in the text with ease. She uses a strong accent for Jude's Argentinean parents and a slight accent when the American-born Hernandez siblings speak a Spanish word. By lowering her pitch, Mendoza creates a sexy male voice for the dangerously lovable Emilio. Fans of [Sarah] Ockler will be as drawn to this multilayered story as the Hernandez sisters are drawn to the irresistible Vargas brothers."

REVIEW: *Bull Cent Child Books* v67 no1 p43 S 2013 K. Q. G.

REVIEW: *Kirkus Rev* v81 no8 p105-6 Ap 15 2013

REVIEW: *Publ Wkly* v260 no13 p66-7 Ap 1 2013 Ted Malawer

REVIEW: *SLJ* v59 no7 p47 Jl 2013 Maggie Knapp

REVIEW: *Voice of Youth Advocates* v36 no3 p66 Ag 2013 Ava Ehde

O'CONNELL, CAITLIN. A baby elephant in the wild; [by] Caitlin O'Connell 40 p. 2014 Houghton Mifflin Har-

court
1. African elephant—Infancy—Namibia—Juvenile literature 2. Animal young 3. Children's nonfiction 4. Elephants—Behavior 5. Elephants—Juvenile literature
ISBN 0544149440; 9780544149441
LC 2013-017880

SUMMARY: "In this account of a journey into the scrub desert of Namibia, readers meet a newborn elephant and her family. Children learn about Liza's early accomplishments: walking within hours, keeping up with the herd as they travel, and learning how to use her trunk and what is safe to eat. The animals walk 10 to 20 miles a day to find food, with the babies hidden behind their mothers or under them between their legs." (School Library Journal)

REVIEW: *Booklist* v110 no13 p63 Mr 1 2014 Carolyn Phelan

REVIEW: *Bull Cent Child Books* v67 no8 p418-9 Ap 2014 J. H.

REVIEW: *Horn Book Magazine* v90 no2 p144-5 Mr/Ap 2014 DANIELLE J. FORD

"A Baby Elephant in the Wild." "Readers are invited to follow along with scientist and author [Caitlin] O'Connell's . . . observations of a newborn female elephant through the beginning of her life, starting just after her birth and moving on through her first months in the Namibian scrub desert. . . . O'Connell's account of baby Liza's development is straightforward and unsentimental yet filled with detailed and fascinating scientific information about the lifelong ties among elephants that will resonate with readers' own feelings about family. The numerous color photographs, tightly tied to the narrative, illustrate the described elephant behaviors. The back matter includes additional elephant facts and an author's note."

REVIEW: *Kirkus Rev* v81 no24 p285 D 15 2013

REVIEW: *SLJ* v60 no3 p175 Mr 2014 Cynde Suite

O'CONNELL, CAITLIN.il. A baby elephant in the wild. See O'Connell, C.

O'CONNOR, FLANNERY, 1925-1964. A Prayer Journal; [by] Flannery O'Connor 112 p. 2013 Farrar Straus & Giroux
1. Authorship—Religious aspects—Christianity 2. God—Worship & love 3. Prayer—Christianity 4. Religious literature, English 5. Spiritual journals
ISBN 0374236917; 9780374236915

SUMMARY: This book presents the personal devotional journal of author Flannery O'Connor. "Throughout, O'Connor bemoans her inability to love God as she feels she should. She also prays about writing, asking that a Christian sensibility would pervade her writing, and asking that God would help her remember that she is not the ultimate author of her work, but an 'instrument' for the words God gives her." (Publishers Weekly)

REVIEW: *America* v209 no19 p35 D 23 2013 DIANE SCHARPER

"A Prayer Journal". "This little book provides an intimate portrait of the artist as a young Catholic woman who desires to become both a saint and a famous writer. . . . The prayers show another side to O'Connor. Here she is not the hard-edged satirist stripping away at the faux piety of fictional silly old ladies or giving comeuppance to bratty kids. She's filled with doubt about her writing and her religious aspirations. She wants to succeed as a writer but does not think for a second that she can do it on her own."

REVIEW: *Bookforum* v20 no4 p33 D 2013/Ja 2014 RENÉ STEINKE

"A Prayer Journal." "Flannery O'Connor's readers either revere her fiction because it's immersed in the mystery of Christianity or admire the work in spite of this. 'A Prayer Journal' will naturally be embraced by the first group. But the book should also appeal to those who find this writer's concern with 'the action of grace' a puzzling aesthetic curiosity--because the prayer journal is also the journal of a writer scouting her own cosmology and beginning to discern its grand and peculiar design in her art. . . . There's an intimacy and rawness here that's rare even in O'Connor's outwardly autobiographical pieces. . . . These devotional writings are imprinted with the same humor, brilliance, and attention to life that one finds in her fiction."

REVIEW: *Booklist* v110 no4 p3 O 15 2013 Margaret Flanagan

REVIEW: *Christ Century* v131 no2 p9 Ja 22 2014 John Murawski

REVIEW: *Christ Century* v131 no7 p40-3 Ap 2 2014 Jill Peláez Baumgaertner

REVIEW: *Kirkus Rev* v81 no19 p57 O 1 2013

REVIEW: *Libr J* v138 no11 p62 Je 15 2013 Barbara Hoffert

REVIEW: *N Y Times Book Rev* p34 N 24 2013

REVIEW: *N Y Times Book Rev* p11 N 17 2013 MARILYNNE ROBINSON

REVIEW: *Va Q Rev* v90 no1 p218-21 Wint 2014 Carlene Bauer

O'CONNOR, JAMES.tr. The great Eurozone disaster. See The great Eurozone disaster

O'CONNOR, JANE. Almost True Confessions; Closet Sleuth Spills All; [by] Jane O'Connor 336 p. 2013 HarperCollins
1. Detective & mystery stories 2. Gossip 3. Manhattan (New York, N.Y.)—Fiction 4. Murder—Fiction 5. Women authors—Fiction
ISBN 006124094X; 9780061240942

SUMMARY: In this murder mystery by Jane O'Connor, "When Rannie arrives at the east side apartment of reclusive author Ret Sullivan, she finds more than the final draft of the manuscript waiting for her: tied to the bed and strangled with an Hermès scarf is Ret's half-naked body. Was this merely a case of rough sex that got a little too rough, as the police believe? Or was Ret murdered because someone didn't want her to meet her deadline?" (Publisher's note)

REVIEW: *Booklist* v110 no3 p35 O 1 2013 Karen Muller

REVIEW: *Kirkus Rev* v81 no16 p264 Ag 15 2013

"Almost True Confessions." "An elusive writer is murdered in spite of the tameness of her latest tell-all. . . . When Rannie shows up at Ret's and finds the reclusive writer tied to the bed and strangled, she's all the more shocked since she knows that Charlotte's family would have no reason to exact revenge on Ret. . . . [Author Jane] O'Connor . . . definitely has an insider's view of the publishing world, though she doesn't make the romantic aspects of Rannie's life nearly as interesting."

REVIEW: *N Y Times Book Rev* p10 S 29 2013 Jane O'Connor

REVIEW: *Publ Wkly* v260 no29 p42 Jl 22 2013

O'CONNOR, SCOTT. Half World; A Novel; [by] Scott O'Connor 432 p. 2014 Simon & Schuster

1. FICTION—General 2. FICTION—Literary 3. FICTION—Psychological 4. Human experimentation 5. Intelligence service—United States—Fiction

ISBN 1476716595; 9781476716596 (hardcover: alk. paper)

LC 2013-024016

SUMMARY: In this book, by Sean O'Connor, "the CIA began a clandestine operation known as Project MKULTRA, in which unwitting American citizens were subjected to insidious drug and mind-control experiments.Henry March, an unassuming 'company man' forced to spearhead MKULTRA's San Francisco branch, finds himself bridging an untenable divide between his devotion to his wife and children . . . and the brutality of his daily task." (Publisher's note)

REVIEW: *Booklist* v110 no9/10 p52 Ja 1 2014 Thomas Gaughan

REVIEW: *Kirkus Rev* v81 no24 p101 D 15 2013

"Half World". "The hunters are the haunted in a thriller from Los Angeles-based author [Scott] O'Connor that mines the depths of fact and fiction. . . . It is a world of 'ghost' that is intimately gripping. . . . O'Connor writes with fire, moving the story along briskly. Hannah, Henry's daughter, becomes the 'ghost catcher,' teamed with Dickie to find her lost father. Photography is the parallel passion between father and daughter, and in this dark world, photographs are the only handhold on reality. An invigorating historical thriller that examines the boundaries of man."

REVIEW: *Publ Wkly* v260 no48 p33 N 25 2013

O'CONNOR, TERRY. Animals as neighbors; the past and present of commensal species; [by] Terry O'Connor x, 174 p. 2013 Michigan State University Press

1. Commensalism 2. Environmental literature 3. Human ecology 4. Human-animal relationships—History 5. Urban animals

ISBN 9781611860955 (cloth: alk. paper); 9781611860986 (pbk.: alk paper)

LC 2012-049443

SUMMARY: This book by Terry O'Connor "explores the state of scientific understanding of the places of commensal species throughout human history, and assesses biological, zoological, archaeological, anthropological, and ethnographic research to develop an ethnozoological, social history. . . . The eight chapters discuss the prospects and limits of archaeological evidence . . . and the trajectory of the coevolution of commensal species with local and global cultures." (Choice: Current Reviews for Academic Libraries)

REVIEW: *Choice* v51 no8 p1447 Ap 2014 J. P. Tiefenbacher

"Animals As Neighbors: The Past and Present of Commensal Species". "Brief yet profound, this monograph examines cultural relationships with animal populations that adapt to human landscapes to advantage their nutritional needs. . . . Although he interprets evidence and often speculates on its meanings, [Terry] O'Connor carefully reasons many fascinating insights. The argument he promulgates is that awareness, analysis, attention, and management need to be more sensitive to the synanthropic vertebrates that have coevolved with humans in ancient and modern urban landscapes. . . . The result is a fresh view of the human-nature relationship conundrum."

ÖCHSNER, ANDREAS. One-dimensional finite elements. See Merkel, M.

O'DEA, SUZANNE. From suffrage to the Senate; America's political women : an encyclopedia of leaders, causes & issues; [by] Suzanne O'Dea 2 v. (xxx, 943 p.) 2006 Grey House Pub.

1. Encyclopedias & dictionaries 2. Historical literature 3. Politicians—United States 4. United States—Politics & government—History 5. Women—United States—History 6. Women in politics—United States—Encyclopedias

ISBN 1592371175 (hardcover); 1619250101; 9781619250109

LC 2007-274168

SUMMARY: This book is a 2013 update to Suzanne O'Dea's encyclopedia of America's political women leaders. O'Dea's "introduction provides an overview of the ever-expanding role of American women in politics, and the entries that follow include coverage of people, legislation, court decisions, organizations, and legal and social issues from the Colonial period to the 21st century." (Library Journal)

REVIEW: *Booklist* v110 no1 p59 S 1 2013 Becca Smith

REVIEW: *Choice* v51 no2 p240 O 2013 H. Corbett

"From Suffrage to the Senate: America's Political Women: An Encyclopedia of Leaders, Causes & Issues." "The third edition of this two-volume encyclopedia . . . comprises 937 entries on individuals, organizations, court cases, legislation, and special issues. Entries are arranged alphabetically, and appendixes include a selection of primary documents as well as facts, statistics, and a chronology about American women in politics. . . . 'From Suffrage to the Senate' is fascinating to flip through, and editor [Suzanne] O'Dea includes many lesser-known women worthy of discovery. However, the era of the expensive printed reference work has passed, and comparable information can be found easily online."

REVIEW: *Libr J* v138 no11 p112 Je 15 2013 Donald Altschiller

REVIEW: *SLJ* v59 no10 p1 O 2013 Eldon Younce

ODERA, LILIAN. Kenyan immigrants in the United States; acculturation, coping strategies, and mental health; [by] Lilian Odera ix, 186 p. 2010 LFB Scholarly Pub. LLC

1. Immigrants—United States 2. Kenyan Americans—Cultural assimilation 3. Kenyan Americans—Mental health 4. Kenyan Americans—Psychology

ISBN 9781593324131 (alk. paper)

LC 2010-019613

SUMMARY: It was the author's intent to demonstrate that "Kenyan immigrants' acculturation is determined by their gender, age, immigration status, duration of stay in the United States as well as their ties to Kenya. Acculturative stress is one of the main predictors of depressive symptoms and subjective health evaluation. Social support and religious coping styles are salient to Kenyan immigrants as they navigate American society." (Publisher's note)

REVIEW: *Contemp Sociol* v43 no1 p138 Ja 2014

"Kenyan Immigrants in the United States: Acculturation, Coping Strategies, and Mental Health". "In 'Kenyan Immigrants in the United States,' Lilian Odera illustrates the different types of acculturation Kenyans experience in the United States and how it affects their general health and happiness. . . . The book concludes with suggestions for future research on Kenyan immigrants in the United States and the implications for clinical practice. Although this research focuses specifically on Kenyan immigrants, Odera's findings are a notable contribution to immigration studies."

O'DONNELL, LISA. Closed Doors; [by] Lisa O'Donnell 256 p. 2013 William Heinemann Ltd

1. Domestic fiction 2. Family secrets—Fiction 3. Parent & child—Fiction 4. Rape victims—Fiction 5. Scotland—Fiction

ISBN 0434022551; 9780434022557

SUMMARY: This book by Lisa O'Donnell is set "on the island of Rothesay in Scotland . . . during the early 1980s" and narrated "by an eleven-year old boy, Michael. . . . Michael 'listen[s] at doors now. It's the only way to find out stuff,' and he obsessively spies on his neighbour Mrs Connor ('I only watch her dance because her windows are so low'). What begins as childish curiosity turns into unpleasant, adult reality." (Times Literary Supplement)

REVIEW: *Booklist* v110 no16 p16 Ap 15 2014 Kerri Price

REVIEW: *Publ Wkly* v261 no15 p32 Ap 14 2014

REVIEW: *TLS* no5757 p21 Ag 2 2013 MIKA ROSS-SOUTHALL

"Closed Doors." "Lisa O'Donnell was awarded the Commonwealth Book Prize for her debut novel, 'The Death of Bees'. For her second book to be published so soon afterwards creates high expectation--and 'Closed Doors' suffers for it. The close-knit neighbourhood on the island of Rothesay in Scotland . . . during the early 1980s is an interesting backdrop to a predictable plot and often tedious first-person narrative by an eleven-year old boy, Michael. . . . A plethora of clichés topped off with a sugary ending . . . make it difficult to buy into Michael's unrelenting voice--or into any of the other characters."

O'DONNELL, LISA. The death of bees; a novel; [by] Lisa O'Donnell 311 p. 2013 Harper

1. FICTION—Coming of Age 2. FICTION—Family Life 3. FICTION—Literary 4. Family secrets—Fiction 5. Neighbors—Fiction 6. Orphans—Fiction 7. Sisters—Fiction

ISBN 0062209841; 9780062209849

LC 2012-031882

SUMMARY: This novel, by Lisa O'Donnell, is "a coming-of-age story in which two young sisters attempt to hold the world at bay after the mysterious death of their parents. Marnie and Nelly, left on their own in Glasgow's Hazlehurst housing estate, attempt to avoid suspicion until Marnie can become a legal guardian for her younger sister." (Publisher's note)

REVIEW: *Booklist* v109 no5 p20 N 1 2012 Vanessa Bush

REVIEW: *Booklist* v110 no14 p8 Mr 15 2014

"The Death of Bees," "Help for the Haunted," and "The Universe Versus Alex Woods." "With their parents dead and buried in the backyard, Scottish teens Marnie and Nelly are finally free from a childhood wracked with abuse. If only the neighbors dog would quit digging in the garden. . . . Sylvie is dealing with taunting classmates, her erratic older sister, and the unsolved murder of her ghost-hunting parents. But perhaps more problematic are the cursed remnants of her parents' work still lingering in the basement. . . . It all begins when Alex is hit on the head by a meteorite, and it all ends when he is arrested trying to reenter England with several grams of marijuana, lots of cash, and the ashes of Mr. Peterson."

REVIEW: *Booklist* v110 no4 p30 O 15 2013 Donna Seaman

REVIEW: *Kirkus Rev* v80 no21 p150 N 1 2012

REVIEW: *Libr J* v137 no18 p64 N 1 2012 Nancy H. Fontaine

REVIEW: *Publ Wkly* v259 no43 p34 O 22 2012

REVIEW: *Publ Wkly* v260 no1 p10 Ja 7 2013

O'DONOVAN, GERARD. Dublin dead; a novel; [by] Gerard O'Donovan 280 p. 2012 Scribner

1. Crime—Fiction 2. Detective & mystery stories 3. Detectives—Ireland—Dublin—Fiction 4. Drug traffic—Fiction 5. Missing persons—Fiction 6. Women journalists—Fiction

ISBN 9781451610635

LC 2011-031170

SUMMARY: In this book, "it seems eminently logical that Cormac Horgan, the millionaire head of his family's chain of estate agents, would have completed his financial ruin by topping himself at a spot favored by dozens of other suicides. Nor is anyone shedding tears over the demise of Declan (Bingo) Begley in sunny Spain--except for accountant Gemma Kearney's mother. . . . Gemma was Begley's girlfriend, she tells . . . reporter Siobhan Fallon . . . [DI Mike] Mulcahy follows a tip from veteran informant Eddie McTiernan that seems to link still another death . . . to an epic consignment of drugs by sea and a well-traveled Colombian assassin. . . . Siobhan and Mulcahy realize that they're pulling opposite ends of the same tangled skein and reluctantly join forces." (Kirkus)

REVIEW: *Booklist* v108 no11 p34 F 1 2012 Thomas Gaughan

REVIEW: *Kirkus Rev* v80 no4 p341 F 15 2012

"Dublin Dead." " The deaths of an Irish drug lord who was murdered in Spain and an Irish estate agent who jumped off Bristol's storied Clifton Bridge turn out to have close and unholy connections. . . . Many dour interviews and ingenious schemes at cross-purposes later, Siobhan and Mulcahy realize that they're pulling opposite ends of the same tangled skein and reluctantly join forces. And a good thing too, because they'll both need each other to survive the denouement. Slow to gather momentum, with much checking of airline schedules. But the final bloody payoff is deeply satisfying."

REVIEW: *Publ Wkly* v259 no4 p146 Ja 23 2012

O'DOWD, MARY. Reading the Irish Woman. See Whelan, B.

O'DRISCOLL, CIAN.ed. Just war. See Just war

O'DRISCOLL, MERVYN.ed. Ireland through European eyes. See Ireland through European eyes

OFFER, AVNER.ed. Insecurity, inequality, and obesity in affluent societies. See Insecurity, inequality, and obesity in affluent societies

OFFILL, JENNY. Dept. of speculation; [by] Jenny Offill 192 p. 2014 Knopf

1. Domestic fiction 2. Family life—Fiction 3. Marriage—Fiction 4. Motherhood—Fiction 5. Women authors—Fiction
ISBN 0385350813; 9780345806871 (paperback); 9780385350815 (hardback)
LC 2013-019367

SUMMARY: In this novel, author Jenny Offill presents a "portrait of a marriage. It is also a beguiling rumination on the mysteries of intimacy, trust, faith, knowledge, and the condition of universal shipwreck that unites us all. Offill's heroine . . . once exchanged love letters with her husband postmarked Dept. of Speculation, their code name for all the uncertainty that inheres in life and in the strangely fluid confines of a long relationship." (Publisher's note)

REVIEW: *Bookforum* v20 no5 p31 F/Mr 2014 JESSICA WINTER

"Dept. of Speculation." "The arrival of 'Dept. of Speculation,' fourteen years after 'Last Things,' is exciting not only because we've waited so long for its arrival but also because it's so different from its predecessor in form, style, and tone. . . . [Jenny] Offill's mode is faster now, more streamlined, at times purposely rushed; it's episodic and mock epigrammatic in the vein of Lydia Davis, with infusions of Lorrie Moore's mordant, laughing-instead-of-screaming wit. . . . 'Dept. of Speculation' brilliantly captures the geography, ambience, and insomniac surreality of the 'small, strange town' that is the early years of motherhood."

REVIEW: *Booklist* v110 no9/10 p39-40 Ja 1 2014 Donna Seaman

"Dept. of Speculation." "This is a magnetic novel about a marriage of giddy bliss and stratospheric anxiety, bedrock alliance and wrenching tectonic shifts. . . . An exquisitely fine-tuned, journal-like account narrated by 'the wife.' Her perfect, simple sentences vibrate like violin strings. And she is mordantly funny, a wry taxonomist of emotions and relationships. Her dispatches from the fog of new motherhood are hilarious and subversive. . . . Nothing depicted in this portrait of a family in quiet disarray is unfamiliar in life or in literature, and that is the artistic magic of Offill's stunning performance. She has sliced life thin enough for a microscope slide and magnified it until it fills the mind's eye and the heart."

REVIEW: *Kirkus Rev* v81 no24 p304 D 15 2013

"Dept. of Speculation". " Scenes from a marriage, sometimes lyrical, sometimes philosophically rich, sometimes just puzzling. If Rainer Maria Rilke had written a novel about marriage, it might look something like this: a series of paragraphs, seldom exceeding more than a dozen lines, sometimes without much apparent connection to the text on either side. . . . The fragmented story, true though it may be to our splintered, too busy lives, is sometimes hard to follow, and at times, the writing is precious, even if we're always pulled back into gritty reality. . . . There are moments of literary experimentation worthy of Virginia Woolf here, but in the end, this reads more like notes for a novel than a novel itself."

REVIEW: *Libr J* v139 no9 p39 My 15 2014 Wendy Galgan

REVIEW: *Libr J* v138 no18 p81 N 1 2013 Lisa Rohrbaugh

REVIEW: *N Y Rev Books* v51 no7 p10-2 Ap 24 2014 Elaine Blair

"Dept. of Speculation." "You can read Jenny Offill's new novel in about two hours. It's short and funny and absorbing, an effortless-seeming downhill ride that picks up astonishing narrative speed as it goes. What's remarkable is that Offill achieves this effect using what you might call an experimental or avant-garde style of narration, one that we associate with difficulty and disorientation rather than speed and easy pleasure. The novel tells the story of a marital crisis in the lives of a previously more-or-less happy couple."

REVIEW: *N Y Times Book Rev* p13 F 9 2014 ROXANE GAY

REVIEW: *New York Times* v163 no56397 pC7 Ja 30 2014 MICHIKO KAKUTANI

REVIEW: *New Yorker* v90 no6 p74-1 Mr 31 2014

REVIEW: *Publ Wkly* v260 no48 p32 N 25 2013

REVIEW: *TLS* no5804 p20 Je 27 2014 NATASHA LEHRER

OFFILL, JENNY. Sparky; 40 p. 2013 Schwartz & Wade Books

1. Animal training 2. Children's stories 3. Pets—Fiction 4. Picture books for children 5. Sloths as pets
ISBN 0375870237; 9780375870231; 9780375970238 (glb)
LC 2012-047196

SUMMARY: In this book, by Jenny Offill, "a young girl desperately wants a pet but has to find one that will meet her mother's low-maintenance stipulations, so she's delighted to discover that a sloth would fill the bill nicely. . . . Know-it-all peer Mary Potts is dismissive of Sparky. . . . The girl, however, doesn't let that ruin her outlook and continues to love Sparky just as he is." (Bulletin of the Center for Children's Books)

REVIEW: *Booklist* v110 no11 p57 F 1 2014 Iline Cooper

REVIEW: *Bull Cent Child Books* v67 no7 p371-2 Mr 2014 J. H.

"Sparky!" "A young girl desperately wants a pet but has to find one that will meet her mother's low-maintenance stipulations, so she's delighted to discover that a sloth would fill the bill nicely. . . . There's a subtle dry wit to [Jenny] Offill's cogent narrative . . . which makes a clever partner to [Chris] Appelhans' endearing watercolor and pencil illustrations. The long-armed, wide-eyed Sparky has an adorably teddy bear-like posture and expression, while subdued tones of blue, brown, and gray are attractively highlighted by brighter touches of red against a creamy matte background."

REVIEW: *Horn Book Magazine* v90 no3 p69-70 My/Je 2014 SAM BLOOM

REVIEW: *Kirkus Rev* v82 no2 p156 Ja 15 2014

"Sparky!". "Quietly dry humor marks this story about a most unusual pet. . . . Even his expression's comically immobile. . . . Training sessions and a performance proceed—um—at Sparky's pace, but a beautiful closing illustration of girl and sloth together on his branch shows how close they've grown. [Chris] Appelhans uses blue and pinky-brown watercolors and pencil on creamy background to create understated humor and affection with a light touch. A serene, funny addition to the new-pet genre."

REVIEW: *Publ Wkly* v260 no51 p59 D 16 2013

REVIEW: *SLJ* v60 no3 p122 Mr 2014 Teri Markson

OFFIT, MIKE. Nothing personal; a novel of Wall Street; [by] Mike Offit 352 p. 2014 Thomas Dunne Books

1. FICTION—Crime 2. FICTION—Thrillers 3. Investment bankers—Fiction 4. Investment banking—Corrupt practices—Fiction 5. Self-realization—Fiction 6. Serial murder investigation—Fiction

ISBN 9781250035424 (hardback)

LC 2013-030271

SUMMARY: This book "tells the story of Warren Hament's journey out of business school and into the amoral abyss of top-tier investment banking In his new job, he finds crass, unhappy and unscrupulous co-workers whose only priority is making as much money as they possibly can. . . . During his meteoric rise to the top, Hament transitions from a naïve financial apprentice to a cunning manipulator of the politics of big business." (Kirkus Reviews)

REVIEW: *Kirkus Rev* v82 no3 p126 F 1 2014

"Nothing Personal". "A morally conscious business school graduate enters the cutthroat environment of 1980s Wall Street. Former trader [Mike] Offit tells the story of Warren Hament's journey out of business school and into the amoral abyss of top-tier investment banking. . . . Offit's familiarity with the characters, language and investment products allows him to deftly tell a coming-of-age story that will appeal to financial wizards and investment neophytes alike. An entertaining, well-developed work of Wall Street fiction."

REVIEW: *Publ Wkly* v260 no50 p48 D 9 2013

OFFIT, PAUL A. Do You Believe in Magic?; The Sense and Nonsense of Alternative Medicine; [by] Paul A. Offit 336 p. 2013 HarperCollins

1. Alternative medicine 2. Holistic medicine 3. Libertarianism 4. Medical literature 5. Medicine—Corrupt practices

ISBN 0062222961 (hardcover); 9780062222961 (hardcover)

SUMMARY: In this book, Paul A. Offit reveals that "half of Americans believe in the 'magic' of alternative medicine, fueling a $34 billion-a-year business that offers treatments that are at best placebos, and at worst deadly. He blasts untested, unregulated, overhyped remedies--like anti-autism creams and bogus cancer cures using 'antineoplastons'--and dares to berate celebs like" Mehmet Oz, Andrew Weil, Deepak Chopra, and Suzanne Somers. (Publishers Weekly)

REVIEW: *Choice* v51 no6 p1045 F 2014 C. L. Mejta

REVIEW: *Kirkus Rev* v81 no9 p62 My 1 2013

REVIEW: *Libr J* v138 no11 p107 Je 15 2013 Barbara Bibel

REVIEW: *New Repub* v244 no17 p64-9 O 21 2013 Jerome Groopman

"Do You Believe in Magic? The Sense and Nonsense of Alternative Medicine." "Typically absent from the claims about many 'alternative treatments' are their risks. The significant harms that they can pose form the fabric of Paul Offit's important and timely book. Offit writes in a lucid and flowing style, and grounds a wealth of information within forceful and vivid narratives. This makes his argument--that we should be guided by science--accessible to a wide audience. . . . Offit aptly quotes Isaiah Berlin on the need for limits to the libertarian creed: 'Liberty for the wolves is death for the lambs.'"

REVIEW: *New York Times* v162 no56185 pD5 Jl 2 2013 ABIGAIL ZUGER

REVIEW: *Publ Wkly* v260 no13 p54 Ap 1 2013 Gail Ross

OFFLEY, ED. The burning shore; how Hitler's U-boats brought World War II to America; [by] Ed Offley 320 p. 2014 Basic Books, a member of the Perseus Books Group

1. HISTORY—Military—Naval 2. HISTORY—Military—World War II 3. HISTORY—Modern—20th Century 4. HISTORY—United States—20th Century 5. Historical literature 6. Submarines (Ships)—Atlantic Coast (U.S.)—History—20th century 7. Submarines (Ships)—Germany—History—20th century 8. World War, 1939-1945—Atlantic Coast (U.S.) 9. World War, 1939-1945—Campaigns—Atlantic Ocean 10. World War, 1939-1945—Naval operations—Submarine 11. World War, 1939-1945—Naval operations, German

ISBN 9780465029617 (hardback)

LC 2013-038412

SUMMARY: In this book, Ed Offley "focuses on a short, early period of World War II. . . . During the course of the first six months of 1942 . . . a cluster of German U-boats marauded along the U.S. Atlantic shore, strangling the shipping lifeline to Britain, sinking scores of Allied merchant vessels, totaling more than 1 million tons of cargo, especially oil, and killing thousands of seamen." (Kirkus Reviews)

REVIEW: *Kirkus Rev* v82 no3 p56 F 1 2014

"The Burning Shore; How Hitler's U-Boats Brought World War II to America". " An authoritative work on the awful, early effectiveness of German U-boats in disrupting shipping traffic off the east coast of the United States. . . . Offley brings up the other factors that came into play for the U.S. Navy, such as the breaking of the Enigma code, interservice rivalry, taking advice from the more seasoned British, and garnering the necessary higher-level support for a convoy escort system and more effective patrol bombers. A knowledgeable overview and exciting re-creation of the final U-701 attack and defeat."

REVIEW: *Publ Wkly* v261 no2 p58 Ja 13 2014

O'FLYNN, CATHERINE. Mr. Lynch's holiday; a novel; [by] Catherine O'Flynn 272 p. 2013 Henry Holt and Company

1. British—Spain—Fiction 2. Dystopias 3. Family secrets—Fiction 4. Fathers and sons—Fiction 5. Recessions—Social aspects

ISBN 0805091815; 9780805091816

LC 2012-050500

SUMMARY: This novel, by Catherine O'Flynn, tells the story of "a father and son reconnecting in a foreign place . . . Retired bus driver and recent widower Dermot Lynch grabs his bags . . . and begins to climb the hill to his son's house. It is Dermot's first time in Spain. . . . When he finally arrives . . . Dermot learns that Eamonn, only one of a handful of settlers in the half-finished ghost town of Lomaverde, has fallen prey to an alluring vision and is upside down in a dream that is slipping away." (Publisher's note)REVIEW: *Booklist* v110 no1 p40 S 1 2013 Joanne Wilkinson

REVIEW: *Kirkus Rev* v81 no17 p21 S 1 2013

REVIEW: *Libr J* v138 no10 p99 Je 1 2013 Barbara Love

REVIEW: *Libr J* v138 no9 p55 My 15 2013 Barbara Hoffert

REVIEW: *New Yorker* v89 no43 p67-1 Ja 6 2014

"Mr. Lynch's Holiday." "When Dermot Lynch, a retired and newly widowed Englishman, decides to visit his son and daughter-in-law in a seaside village in southern Spain, he excitedly writes to say that he is looking forward to getting his first taste of abroad. But he arrives to find a development that has been deserted midway through construction, and a son deserted by his wife. Instances of disrepair and chaos are everywhere in this recession-based novel, as father and son adjust to circumstances and to one another. Most memorable are the figures of bewildered expats who have left comfortable lives in search of somewhere even better.'"

REVIEW: *New Yorker* v89 no43 p67-1 Ja 6 2014

REVIEW: *Publ Wkly* v260 no20 p30 My 20 2013

OGATA, AMY F. Designing the creative child; playthings and places in midcentury America; [by] Amy F. Ogata 293 p. 2013 University of Minnesota Press

1. ARCHITECTURE—History—Contemporary (1945-) 2. Children—United States—Social conditions—20th century 3. Creative ability in children—United States 4. Design—Human factors—United States 5. HISTORY—United States—20th Century 6. Historical literature 7. Play environments—United States 8. SOCIAL SCIENCE—Children's Studies

ISBN 9780816679607 (hardback); 9780816679614 (pb)

LC 2012-050732

SUMMARY: This book "reveals how a postwar cult of childhood creativity developed and continues to this day. Exploring how the idea of children as imaginative and naturally creative was constructed, disseminated, and consumed in the United States after World War II, Amy F. Ogata argues that educational toys, playgrounds, small middle-class houses, new schools, and children's museums were designed to cultivate imagination in a growing cohort of baby boom children." (Publisher's note)

REVIEW: *Choice* v51 no2 p246 O 2013 A. Zanin-Yost

OGDEN, DANIEL. Dragons, serpents and slayers in the classical and early Christian worlds; a sourcebook; [by] Daniel Ogden 360 p. 2013 Oxford University Press

1. Dragons—Folklore 2. Dragons—Religious aspects 3. Dragons in the Bible 4. Historical literature 5. History—Sources 6. Mythology, Classical

ISBN 9780199925094; 9780199925117

LC 2012-032468

SUMMARY: Written and edited by Daniel Ogden, this book "presents a comprehensive and easily accessible collection of dragon myths from Greek, Roman, and early Christian sources. Some of the dragons featured are well known: the Hydra, slain by Heracles; the Dragon of Colchis, the guardian of the golden fleece overcome by Jason and Medea; and the great sea-serpent from which Perseus rescues Andromeda." (Publisher's note)

REVIEW: *Choice* v51 no1 p46 S 2013 M. E. Snodgrass

"Dragons, Serpents, and Slayers in the Classical and Early Christian Worlds: A Sourcebook." "An exacting overview of serpentine lore in word and illustration, this sourcebook by [Daniel] Ogden (Univ. of Exeter, UK) applies the author's considerable expertise to differentiation of sources of monsters, dragon-slaying episodes, and their conclusions. This volume covers the more famous myths of Herakles, Jason, Laocoön, Beowulf, Medusa, and Saint George, as well as the less common herpetographic appearances in hagiography and the monster slayings by Regulus and Saint Silvester. . . . Overall, this sourcebook, with its scholarly rigor and assumptions about readers' knowledge of the classic canon, limits its accessibility to the well read."

OGLE, REX.ed. Star Wars. See Brown, J.

OHLSSON, KRISTINA. The Disappeared; a novel; 416 p. 2014 Pocket Books

1. Aging 2. Detective & mystery stories 3. Missing persons—Fiction 4. Murder investigation—Fiction 5. Police—Fiction

ISBN 1476734003; 9781476734002

SUMMARY: In this book, by Kristina Ohlsson, "Fredrika, a Stockholm detective who has returned from maternity leave too soon, lives with an emotionally fragile, much older partner, who's being targeted by a vengeful student. Recently widowed Alex Recht, a colleague of Fredrika's who became obsessed with the disappearance of Rebecca Trolle two years earlier, must contend with the discovery of Rebecca's dismembered body." (Publishers Weekly)

REVIEW: *Booklist* v110 no9/10 p52 Ja 1 2014 Stacy Alesi

"The Disappeared". "The third entry in the terrific Fredrika Bergman crime series. . . . Detective Alex Recht remembers well an earlier case involving a missing girl, so when a dismembered young woman's body is found, he realizes right away whose it is. As the site is excavated, another body is unearthed; this one is a man who has been buried for a much longer time. Then still another body is found . . . . This is a complicated yet fast-moving story, and the detectives all find themselves with personal connections to the case. [Kristina] Ohlsson excels at creating multilayered stories with substantive characters, and she does it brilliantly here; the intertwining story lines culminate with a shocking ending. Scandinavian crime-fiction fans should be enthralled."

REVIEW: *Booklist* v111 no4 p59 O 15 2014 Pam Spencer Holley

REVIEW: *Kirkus Rev* v82 no4 p196 F 15 2014

REVIEW: *Publ Wkly* v261 no1 p36 Ja 6 2014

OHLSON, KRISTIN. The soil will save us!; how scientists, farmers, and foodies are healing the soil to save the planet; [by] Kristin Ohlson 256 p. 2014 Rodale

1. Carbon dioxide 2. Global warming—Prevention 3. Scientific literature 4. Soil chemistry 5. Soils and climate

ISBN 9781609615543 (hardcover)

LC 2013-046860

SUMMARY: In this book, Kristin Ohlson "examines soil's role in countering our greenhouse-gas problem, noting how healthy soil sequesters carbon. . . . Along the way, the author touches on other subjects—genetically engineered crops, farming activities around the world, the use of leftover skim milk as a fertilizer, and the interdependence of urban planning and soil health—to provide background and local color." (Kirkus Reviews)

REVIEW: *Kirkus Rev* v82 no3 p168 F 1 2014

"The Soil Will Save Us: How Scientists, Farmers, and Foodies Are Healing the Soil to Save the Planet". "The author has a clear storytelling style, which comes in handy when drawing this head-turning portrait of lowly dirt. But dirt—or soil, if you prefer—takes on character in [Kristin] Ohlson's hands, and readers will soon become invested in its well-being, for soil is a planetary balancer, and from its goodness comes the food we eat. . . . Ohlson ably delineates this promising situation: Vital soil may well help address climate change, but it absolutely will provide for 'more productive farms, cleaner waterways, and overall healthier landscapes.'"

OHORA, ZACHARIAH.il. Tyrannosaurus wrecks! See Bardhan-Quallen, S.

OIKONOMOPOULOU, KATERINA.ed. Ancient libraries. See Ancient libraries

OJITO, MIRTA. Hunting season; immigration and murder in an all-American town; [by] Mirta Ojito 264 p. 2013 Beacon Press

1. Immigrants—New York (State)—Patchogue—Case studies 2. Journalism 3. Latin Americans—New York (State)—Patchogue—Case studies 4. Murder—New York (State)—Patchogue—Case studies 5. Racism—New York (State)—Patchogue—Case studies
ISBN 0807001813; 9780807001813 (cloth)
LC 2013-023313

SUMMARY: This book presents an "account of how attacks on Latino immigrants became a teenage sport in one suburban town, whose bigotry is seen here as typical of much of America." Author Mirta Ojito "takes an in-depth look at the entwined issues of racism and anti-immigration sentiment. . . . In this account, it was an influx of Ecuadorians to Patchogue, N.Y., that aroused hatred to the point of mayhem and manslaughter." (Kirkus Reviews)

REVIEW: *Booklist* v110 no2 p7 S 15 2013 Donna Chavez

"Hunting Season: Immigration and Murder in an All-American Town." "Pulitzer Prize-winning journalist [Mirta] Ojito achieves another award-worthy feat, this time for her treatment of the minefield issue of immigration. . . . After conducting extensive research and listening painstakingly to everyone involved who was willing to speak to her, Ojito then writes with such clarity and evenhandedness that this could be about an emotionally neutral topic. . . . In Ojito's hands, the aggregate effect of their stories is one that is far more profound than the diatribes of pundits on both sides of the complex, deeply human question of immigration reform."

REVIEW: *Kirkus Rev* v81 no18 p6 S 15 2013

REVIEW: *Libr J* v138 no18 p106 N 1 2013 Antoinette Brinkman

OKAY, ANDY; 96 p. 2014 Blue Apple Books

1. Alligators—Fiction 2. Animals—Infancy—Fiction 3. Coyote—Fiction 4. Friendship—Fiction 5. Humorous stories 6. JUVENILE FICTION—Humorous Stories 7. JUVENILE FICTION—Social Issues—Friendship
ISBN 9781609053505 (hardback)
LC 2013-043465

SUMMARY: In this children's book, "Andy and Preston are friends; Andy, the lime-green alligator, is the straight man, sober and easily annoyed, while Preston, a beige animal (whose species is never quite dcfined), is buoyantly enthusiastic and energetic. Their friendship plays off the combination of these archetypal traits as the duo meander about in their forest home looking for a rogue rabbit, learning about patience and identifying other animals' sounds." (Kirkus Reviews)

REVIEW: *Kirkus Rev* v82 no2 p218 Ja 15 2014

"Okay, Andy". "A silly buddy story about Andy the alligator and his mammalian friend Preston plods somewhat aimlessly along through three chapters of gentle, simple adventures. . . . Simple heavy lines, oversized panels and word balloons make this easy for young readers to follow. The slow-moving pace, though dotted with some bursts of humor, doesn't quite do enough to propel the action, though. With most pages containing a single panel with fewer than a half-dozen words, this offering may help burgeoning readers gain confidence in finishing a book quickly; however with many other, similar series . . . this may be passed over for more recognizable and lively selections."

OKAZAKI, KYOKO, 1963-. Helter Skelter; Fashion Unfriendly; [by] Kyoko Okazaki 320 p. 2013 Vertical Inc

1. Fashion 2. Graphic novels 3. Models (Persons)—Fiction 4. Personal beauty—Fiction 5. Plastic surgery
ISBN 1935654837; 9781935654834

SUMMARY: "In this graphic novel, Liliko has been on top of the modeling world in Japan, representing the biggest brands. But she's not getting any younger, and the cutthroat world of modeling is constantly overthrowing the reigning queen with a new, younger model. Driven hy the desire to maintain her position, Liliko decides to have a complete body makeover. The extensive plastic surgery she undergoes comes at a much higher price than she expects." (World Literature Today)

REVIEW: *World Lit Today* v87 no6 p8 N/D 2013

"Let Me Tell You a Story: A New Approach to Healing Through the Art of Storytelling," "The Silence of the Wave," and "Helter Skelter: Fashion Unfriendly." "At every session, Jorge tells Demián a tale from classic fables, folktales, or modern sagas, which help Demián better understand himself and find happiness. The author is a gestalt psychotherapist and psychodramatist. . . . 'The Silence of the Wave' tells the story of Roberto Marías and the repressed memories he must conquer. . . . In this graphic novel, Liliko has been on top of the modeling world in Japan, representing the biggest brands. But she's not getting any younger, and the cutthroat world of modeling is constantly overthrowing the reigning queen with a new, younger model."

O'KEEFFE, BRIGID. New Soviet gypsies; nationality, performance, and selfhood in the early Soviet Union; [by] Brigid O'Keeffe xvi, 328 p. 2013 University of Toronto Press

1. Historical literature 2. Romanies—Soviet Union—Politics and government—20th century 3. Romanies—Soviet Union—Social conditions—20th century 4. Romanies—Soviet Union—Social life and customs—20th century

ISBN 1442646500 (cloth : acid-free paper); 9781442646506 (cloth : acid-free paper)
LC 2012-537554

SUMMARY: In this book, author Brigid O'Keeffe argues that " Roma actively engaged with Bolshevik nationality policies, thereby assimilating Soviet culture, social customs, and economic relations. Roma proved the primary agents in the refashioning of so-called 'backwards Gypsies' into conscious Soviet citizens." (Publisher's note)

REVIEW: *Choice* v51 no6 p1070-1 F 2014 L. De Danaan

"New Soviet Gypsies: Nationality, Performance, and Selfhood in the Early Soviet Union." "The Roma or 'gypsy' population of the former Soviet Union posed a challenge to efforts to mold 'socially useful, rational, literate, cultured' citizens who would "advance the cause of the collective.' . . .Familiar stories of the trivialization and stylization of local historic cultures and their music and language abound in this fascinating account. [Brigid] O'Keeffe's book is well researched and tells an important tale of Roma history and struggle. Such histories are increasingly important as Roma face increasing prejudice, hate, and discrimination in today's Europe. . . . Highly recommended."

O'KELL, ROBERT. Disraeli; the romance of politics; [by] Robert O'Kell x, 595 p. 2013 University of Toronto Press

1. Authors, English—Biography 2. Biography (Literary form) 3. Politics and literature—Great Britain—History—19th century 4. Prime ministers—Great Britain—Biography
ISBN 9781442644595 (hbk)
LC 2012-464759

SUMMARY: This book presents a "biographical portrait of [Benjamin] Disraeli as both a statesman and a storyteller. Drawing extensively on Disraeli's published letters and speeches . . . Robert O'Kell illuminates the intimate, symbiotic relationship between his fiction and his politics. His investigation shines new light on all of Disraeli's novels, his two governments, his imperialism, and his handling of the Irish Church Disestablishment Crisis of 1868 and the Eastern Question in the 1870s." (Publisher's note)

REVIEW: *Choice* v51 no2 p261 O 2013 E. J. Jenkins

REVIEW: *Engl Hist Rev* v129 no540 p1226-8 O 2014 I. Cawood

REVIEW: *London Rev Books* v35 no23 p34-6 D 5 2013 John Pemble

"Disraeli: Or, the Two Lives," "The Great Rivalry: Gladstone and Disraeli," and "Disraeli; The Romance of Politics". "Douglas Hurd and Edward Young's 'Disraeli;or, the Two Lives,' and Robert O'Kell's 'Disraeli: The Romance of Politics' diverge when they come to [Benjamin] Disraeli's Byronism. Hurd and Young wave it aside. . . . O'Kell's interpretation is fundamentally different. . . . O'Kell pushes his argument too far by reading Byronic 'psychological romance' into virtually everything Disraeli wrote. . . . Dick Leonard's 'The Great Rivalry' . . . uses the old compare and contrast formula, hopping between the two protagonists, but updating the story with the recent work of Colin Matthew, Roy Jenkins, Richard Shannon, John Vincent, Sarah Bradford and Stanley Weintraub. Essentially it's drybones parliamentary history . . . and its verdict on the falling out hardly deepens our understanding."

REVIEW: *TLS* no5764 p23 S 20 2013 DAISY HAY

"Disraeli: The Romance of Politics". "The result is a partial portrait, shaped, and sometimes overly dominated, by [Robert] O'Kell's thesis, but which nevertheless offers an intriguing account of [Benjamin] Disraeli as statesman novelist and poetical politician. . . . At over 600 pages, O'Kell's study is long and at times his thesis feels dogmatic, even relentless. Faced with the problem of discussing novels few people have read, he permits himself long plot summaries and passages of exposition that weigh his argument down. . . . The great strength of his study, however, is the way in which it ambitiously combines readings of novels, speeches, memoranda, newspaper articles, pamphlets and letters, to produce a thorough engagement with Disraeli's voice."

OKIA, OPOLOT. Communal labor in colonial Kenya; the legitimization of coercion, 1912-1930; [by] Opolot Okia 186 p. 2012 Palgrave Macmillan

1. Colonization—History 2. Forced labor—History 3. Forced labor—Kenya—History—20th century 4. HISTORY—Africa—East 5. HISTORY—Modern—20th Century 6. Historical literature 7. Imperialism—History 8. Kenya—History 9. SOCIAL SCIENCE—Slavery
ISBN 9780230392953 (hardback)
LC 2012-002805

SUMMARY: Written by Opolot Okia, "This book describes the growth and development of communal forced labor in Kenya from 1912-1930. During the early period in Kenya's colonial history the British administration employed various forms of forced labor to make Africans work on the building of infrastructure, like roads and bridges, and also for European settlers on their plantations." (Publisher's note)

REVIEW: *Am Hist Rev* v118 no4 p1290-1 O 2013 Fred Morton

"Communal Labor in Colonial Kenya: The Legitimization of Coercion, 1912-1930." "Opolot Okia documents the persistence of coerced, unpaid communal labor in Kenya Colony in the 1920s . . . on European farms and public projects. . . . [This book] draws on a variety of sources, including reports, testimonies, newspaper editorials, and public correspondence authored by colonial office administrators, colonial officials, settlers, missionaries . . . and British-based advocates. . . . Tighter editing, and a map or two, would have improved this work. Inexcusably, the primary sources supporting Okia's argument are found only in the notes and not in the bibliography. Puzzling, contradictory, or incorrect statements appear, sometimes in close proximity."

OKIHIRO, GARY Y.ed. Encyclopedia of Japanese American internment. See Encyclopedia of Japanese American internment

OKRENT, DANIEL, 1948-.ed. American pastimes. See Smith, R.

OKSANEN, ELJAS. Flanders and the Anglo-Norman world, 1066-1216; [by] Eljas Oksanen xiii, 305 p. 2012 Cambridge University Press

1. HISTORY—Europe—General 2. Historical literature
ISBN 9780521760997
LC 2012-013650

SUMMARY: This book, written by Eljas Oksanen, "is a groundbreaking investigation of the relations and exchanges between the county of Flanders and the Anglo-Norman realm. Among other important themes, it examines Anglo-Flemish diplomatic treaties and fiefs, international aristocratic culture, the growth of overseas commerce, immigration into England and the construction of new social and national identities." (Publisher's note)

REVIEW: *Choice* v51 no2 p342-3 O 2013 S. Morillo

"Flanders and the Anglo-Norman World, 1066-1216." "[Author Eljas] Oksanen . . . knits together a number of disparate strands of Flemish and Anglo-Norman evidence into a coherent picture of a networked world that does not conform to the constraints of nationalist historiography. The author frames his study with a conventional chronological overview of the political and diplomatic relations between the Anglo-Norman realm and the County of Flanders between 1066 and 1216. . . . A careful, well-documented study whose main value is in emphasizing a trans-channel perspective on the unity of northwest European history."

REVIEW: *Engl Hist Rev* v128 no535 p1534-6 D 2013 Judith A. Green

OLBRANTZ, JOHN. Breath of heaven, breath of earth. See Kawami, T. S.

OLD SAINT PETER'S, ROME; 2013 Cambridge Univesity Press

1. Church architecture 2. Church history—Middle Ages, 600-1500 3. Historical literature 4. Old St. Peter's Basilica (Vatican City) 5. Vatican City—History
ISBN 9781107041646 (hardback)
LC 2013-013112

SUMMARY: This book, edited by Rosamond McKitterick, John Osborne, Carol M. Richardson, and Joanna Story, explores the older architecture of the Basilica of Saint Peter in Rome, Italy. "The church that is visible today is . . . only four hundred years old compared to the twelve-hundred-year-old church whose site it occupies. . . . This is the first full study of the older church, from its late antique construction to Renaissance destruction, in its historical context." (Publisher's note)

REVIEW: *Hist Today* v64 no2 p60 F 2014 David Hemsoll

"Old Saint Peter's, Rome." "This elegantly conceived volume adds considerably to our knowledge and understanding of one of the most remarkable buildings to have been constructed over the last two millennia. . . . The book examines the building and its multitudinous roles from a range of different standpoints. This results in a work of impressive richness and diversity, which at the same time displays a remarkable coherence, by being organised more-or-less chronologically and in such a way as to present the various themes as being indicative of particular historical moments and preoccupations. Thus the book treats the building as a sequence of 20 studies that In some sense parallel St Peter's changing physical state and its evolving political and cultural roles."

OLDHAM, LIZA.ed. Magill's Literary Annual 2013. See Magill's Literary Annual 2013

OLIVER, KELLY. Technologies of life and death; from cloning to capital punishment; [by] Kelly Oliver ix, 260 p. 2013 Fordham University Press

1. Bioethics 2. Biotechnology—Moral and ethical aspects 3. Derrida, Jacques, 1930-2004 4. Ethics 5. Philosophical literature
ISBN 9780823251087 (cloth : alk. paper)
LC 2012-049120

SUMMARY: "The central aim of this book is to approach contemporary problems raised by technologies of life and death as ethical issues that call for a more nuanced approach than mainstream philosophy can provide." It "analyze[s] the extremes of birth and dying insofar as they are mediated by technologies of life and death. With an eye to reproductive technologies, it shows how a deconstructive approach can change the very terms of contemporary debates over technologies of life and death." (Publisher's note)

REVIEW: *Choice* v51 no5 p850-1 Ja 2014 D. Hurst

"Technologies of Life and Death: From Cloning to Capital Punishment." "[Kelly] Oliver . . . offers a substantial review of ethical issues relating to technology, personhood, human rights, and moral obligations. Her arguments, which rest on the philosophical foundations of Derrida, help readers peer into the discursive space between accepted binaries--man/woman, human/animal, human/machine, natural/human-made (culture), fantasy/real, and sovereignty/oppression. . . . Oliver makes a final claim that deconstructionist ethics require people to become morally responsible for the actions they take, those they avoid, and the underlying fantasies and fears that drive those actions."

OLIVER, LIN. Little Poems for Tiny Ears; [by] Lin Oliver 32 p. 2013 Nancy Paulsen Books

1. Children—Poetry 2. Children's poetry 3. Parent & child 4. Picture books for children 5. Toys
ISBN 039916605X; 9780399166051
LC 2013-014049

SUMMARY: In this children's picture book, "twenty-three short poems written in the first-person viewpoints of infants and toddlers muse on the small discoveries and quietly joyful moments that are part of early childhood. Among them: learning to make new sounds; discovering one's toes, bellybutton, mouth, and nose . . . cozying up to a parent; and making messes." (Publishers Weekly)

REVIEW: *Booklist* v110 no6 p40 N 15 2013 Edie Ching

"Little Poems for Tiny Ears". "Everything about this book is child friendly, beginning with its charming cover. [Lin] Oliver has written 23 highly readable poems about almost every familiar aspect of a young child's life, from belly buttons and diapers to noises and the kitchen drawer. Almost all contain words, usually one or two syllables long, that many children have already heard. . . . The words work in perfect tandem with [Tomie] dePaola's happy art, pastels executed in his signature style. Highlighting the joy of each experience, he keeps his focus on the foreground and immediate action, creating for the listener the essence of the world they know."

REVIEW: *Kirkus Rev* v81 no24 p88 D 15 2013

REVIEW: *Publ Wkly* v260 no44 p66 N 4 2013

REVIEW: *SLJ* v60 no2 p77 F 2014 Sarah Westeren

OLIVER, LIN. How to scare the pants off your pets; [by] Lin Oliver 172 p. 2013 Scholastic Press

1. Best friends—Juvenile fiction 2. Ghost stories 3.

Pets—Juvenile fiction 4. Responsibility—Juvenile fiction 5. Schools—Juvenile fiction
ISBN 0545298849 (pbk.); 054529889X; 9780545298841 (pbk.); 9780545298896
LC 2013-371378

SUMMARY: This book is part of Henry Winkler and Lin Oliver's "Ghost Buddy" series. "Billy gets his ghost friend Hoove a pet in hopes of improving Hoove's flunking grade in Responsibility--except Hoove is too scary for most critters. It's not until the family takes in a stray cat, and she has three kittens, that Hoove steps up." (Horn Book Magazine)

REVIEW: *Horn Book Magazine* v89 no5 p126-7 S/O 2013 Katrina Hedeen

"Gustav Gloom and the Nightmare Vault," "The Sinister Sweetness of Splendid Academy," and "How to Scare the Pants Off Your Pets." "In 'Nightmare,' Fernie discovers more oddities in the spooky house, and she and Gustav go up against a new foe. The enjoyably weird and eerie stories are accompanied by suitably somber drawings. . . . This creepy modern 'Hansel and Gretel' story [The Sinister Sweetness of Splendid Academy] succeeds thanks to a well-paced plot and fluid writing. . . . ['How to Scare the Pants Off Your Pets' is part of Henry Winkler and Lin Oliver's]Ghost Buddy series. . . . There's a lesson here, but it's nicely camouflaged by this third series installment's humorous spirit and witty banter."

OLIVER, MARY. Thirst; [by] Mary Oliver 88 2006 Beacon Press

1. Gratitude 2. Nature in literature 3. Poems—Collections 4. Poetry—By individual authors 5. Religious poetry
ISBN 0-8070-6896-9

SUMMARY: This is collection of poetry by Mary Oliver "was written after the death of her beloved partner, and in the exploratory awakening of faith in God." Several poems are "a passionate and vivid celebration of life, with symbolic roots deep in the miracle of nature." Themes include "gratitude and rejoicing". (Commonweal)

REVIEW: *Commonweal* v140 no19 p27-8 D 6 2013 Tina Beattie

"How Much Is Enough? Money and the Good Life," "The Spinning Heart," and "Thirst". "[Robert Skidelsky] and Edward Skidelsky] offer a persuasive and lucid account of the 'good life' as one in which sufficiency, satisfaction, and leisure become worthy aims to pursue in common with others whose values we share (they think religion might be indispensable for this), while greed, envy, and avarice are once more recognized as the vices they are. This panoramic vision inevitably glosses the ways in which individual lives are affected by changing economic values. 'The Spinning Heart,' . . . a novel by Irish writer Donal Ryan, movingly explores the consequences of the global economic crisis in a small Irish community. . . . The best poems are a passionate and vivid celebration of life, with symbolic roots deep in the miracle of nature."

OLOPADE, DAYO. The bright continent; breaking rules and making change in modern Africa; [by] Dayo Olopade 288 p. 2014 Houghton Mifflin Harcourt

1. Social advocacy 2. Social change 3. Social commentary
ISBN 0547678312; 9780547678313
LC 2013-044254

SUMMARY: In this book, journalist Dayo Olopade "rebuts the view of Africa as mired in poverty, war, and failed aid projects, and instead offers a hopeful perspective. Olopade looks past the . . . boundaries of sub-Saharan Africa's colonial legacy and re-maps it according to categories of Family, Technology, Commerce, Natural, and Youth. Instead of dwelling on political shortcomings, corrupt leadership, and stunted infrastructure, Olopade embraces the spirit of kanju, a Yoruba word for hustle." (Publishers Weekly)

REVIEW: *Bookforum* v21 no1 p15-7 Ap/My 2014 MATT STEINGLASS

REVIEW: *Kirkus Rev* v82 no4 p55 F 15 2014

REVIEW: *N Y Times Book Rev* p21 Ap 13 2014 LYDIA POLGREEN

REVIEW: *New Yorker* v90 no9 p105-1 Ap 21 2014

"The Bright Continent." "In this upbeat study of development in Africa, Olopade identifies the great obstacle as 'formality bias'—the tendency of outsiders to recognize solutions to African problems only when they come from governments and other formal organizations. Africa's great asset is 'kanju,' a Yoruba word that Olopade defines as 'the specific creativity born from African difficulty.' . . . Despite evident exasperation at Western interventions that fail to adapt to local systems, the book is written more in wonder at African ingenuity than in anger at foreign incomprehension."

REVIEW: *Publ Wkly* v261 no4 p185 Ja 27 2014

OLSON, LYNNE. Those angry days; Roosevelt, Lindbergh, and America's fight over World War II, 1939-1941; [by] Lynne Olson 576 p. 2013 Random House Inc.

1. Historical literature 2. Intervention (International law)—History—20th century 3. Isolationism—United States—History—20th century 4. Political culture—United States—History—20th century 5. World War, 1939-1945—Diplomatic history 6. World War, 1939-1945—United States
ISBN 9781400069743 (hardcover); 1400069742 (hardcover); 9780679604716 (ebook)
LC 2012-025381

SUMMARY: This book, by Lynne Olson, offers an "account of the debate over American intervention in World War II. . . . At the center of this controversy stood the two most famous men in America: President Franklin D. Roosevelt, who championed the interventionist cause, and aviator Charles Lindbergh, who as unofficial leader and spokesman for America's isolationists emerged as the president's most formidable adversary." (Publisher's note)

REVIEW: *Booklist* v109 no11 p13 F 1 2013 Gilbert Tayler

REVIEW: *Economist* v407 no8833 p78 Ap 27 2013

REVIEW: *Kirkus Rev* v80 no24 p217 D 15 2012

REVIEW: *Libr J* v138 no5 p117 Mr 15 2013 William D. Pederson

REVIEW: *N Y Times Book Rev* p22 Ag 4 2013

REVIEW: *Publ Wkly* v260 no3 p54-5 Ja 21 2013

REVIEW: *Rev Am Hist* v42 no2 p324-31 Je 2014 Benjamin E. Varat

"Those Angry Days: Roosevelt, Lindbergh, and America's Fight Over World War II, 1939-41" and "FDR and the Jews." "'Those Angry Days' is a fun read. With a keen eye for anecdote and the perfect quote, [author Lynne] Olson, well-known for other World War II-era histories, vividly reconstructs America's internal battle over how to respond, if at all, to the Nazi victories across Europe. . . . At times, Roosevelt comes across as a schoolyard bully, using surrogates to attack his enemies rather than doing the dirty work himself. . . . This presentation is unconvincing. . . . The Franklin Roosevelt presented in Richard Breitman and Allan Lichtman's excellent 'FDR and the Jews' is a far more nuanced, complex character."

ONDAATJE, GRIFFIN. The camel in the sun; [by] Griffin Ondaatje 32 p. 2013 Groundwood Books

1. Camels 2. Children's stories 3. Hadith stories 4. Muhammad, Prophet, d. 632 5. Tales
ISBN 1554983819; 9781554983810

SUMMARY: This book, by Griffin Ondaatje, "is the story of a camel whose cruel owner only realizes what suffering he has caused when the Prophet appears and shows love to the animal. The camel has worked its entire life for a man called Halim, carrying bundles . . . on long journeys across the desert. . . . When they arrive in the . . . city of Medina, where the Prophet lives, . . . everything changes." (Publisher's note)

REVIEW: *Booklist* v110 no8 p48-9 D 15 2013 Randall Enos

"The Camel in the Sun". "In this retelling of a traditional Muslim hadith . . . a merchant learns to feel compassion for the camel that has faithfully carried him and his heavy cargo across the desert for many years. . . . The beautifully understated illustrations are monoprints, with drawings bathed in subdued colors, mostly warm and spicy browns to reflect the hot desert and occasional cool blues and greens for the night scenes. The images are simple, yet the effect is sophisticated and stylish. This will appeal to many ages, both as a peek into another culture and as an engaging story about a creature that finally gets the empathy it deserves."

REVIEW: *Bull Cent Child Books* v67 no6 p328 F 2014 Jeannette Hulick

"The Camel in the Sun". "[Griffin] Ondaatje's version of this story . . . has an elegant simplicity that allows the tale's lesson to take center stage in a non-didactic way. . . . [Linda] Wolfsgruber's art, monoprints combined with drawing and printed on matte paper, is stunning in its evocation of the desert setting (and tastefully avoids depicting the Prophet); varying tones of brown and gold are accented with cooler blues and greens while the pencil details give texture and vibrancy to the otherwise stark desert and dusty city backgrounds. This provides a solid, accessible base for some thought-provoking discussion about human-animal (or even just human) relationships, compassion, and empathy."

REVIEW: *Horn Book Magazine* v90 no2 p103-4 Mr/Ap 2014 KITTY FLYNN

REVIEW: *Kirkus Rev* v81 no19 p265 O 1 2013

REVIEW: *Publ Wkly* p31-2 Children's starred review annual 2013

REVIEW: *Publ Wkly* v260 no42 p55 O 21 2013

REVIEW: *Quill Quire* v79 no9 p35 N 2013 Shannon Ozirny ayouth

"The Camel in the Sun." "Documentary filmmaker Griffin Ondaatje (son of Michael) enters the picture-book world with a quiet, spiritual story that introduces the concept of empathy to young readers. In this thoughtful take on a traditional tale that the author first encountered in Sri Lanka, readers are given a lesson in social and emotional intelligence that is both remarkable and affecting. . . . Precise pacing and beautifully simple language keep the story from falling into a nest of cliches or overbearing morality. Ondaatje's style is deliberate and solid, creating a reverent feel that will resonate even with kindergarteners, while Linda Wolfsgruber's brilliant sun- and dust-infused illustrations lend the story its sense of place."

REVIEW: *SLJ* v60 no1 p116 Ja 2014 Linda L. Walkins

ONE THOUSAND AND ONE NIGHTS; a sparkling retelling of the beloved classic; 320 p. 2013 Pantheon Books

1. Abused women 2. Misogyny 3. Scheherazade (Legendary character) 4. Tale (Literary form) 5. Violence—Fiction
ISBN 9780307958860
LC 2012-039272

SUMMARY: In this book, Lebanese novelist Hanan al-Shaykh "takes the hundreds of stories that make up the traditional 'One Thousand and One Nights' and . . . pares them down to 19. Focusing on tales that expose misogyny—of men who kill their wives and lovers, who injure them, or who leave them for dead—al-Shaykh is interested in how women grapple with a society that is stacked against them." (Library Journal)

REVIEW: *Booklist* v109 no17 p59 My 1 2013 Mary Carroll

REVIEW: *Kirkus Rev* v81 no12 p5 Je 15 2013

REVIEW: *Libr J* v138 no11 p78 Je 15 2013 Molly McArdle

REVIEW: *N Y Rev Books* v61 no5 p37-9 Mr 20 2014 Patricia Storace

"Stranger Magic: Charmed States and the Arabian Nights" and "One Thousand and One Nights". "Two recent books by Marina Warner and the Lebanese novelist Hanan al- Shaykh confirm the continuing power of this work. . . . Stranger Magic is an unabashedly joyful work of scholarship, a study of the history of the human imagination as it shapes and reinvents reality through stories. . . . Warner's rich, diffuse, and unconventional scholarship is as much a retelling of the Arabian Nights tales as the novelist Hanan al-Shaykh's, though Warner tells the stories as they unfold in history. Al-Shaykh's charming versions were first conceived as a play. . . . The resulting book shows traces of its theatrical origin and the ingenious techniques al-Shaykh has used to maneuver the limitless scope of the tales into a form that fits the constraints \ imposed by theater."

O'NEAL, CLAIRE. Andrew Luck; [by] Claire O'Neal 32 p. 2014 Mitchell Lane Publishers

1. Children's nonfiction 2. Football players—Education 3. Football players—United States—Biography—Juvenile literature 4. Stanford University
ISBN 9781612284606 (library bound)
LC 2013-023052

SUMMARY: This book on football player Andrew Luck is part of the "Robbie Reader: Contemporary Biography" series, which presents "a brief look at each player's childhood and high-school

play before launching into their award-winning sports careers. 'Andrew Luck' reveals how this self-proclaimed 'nerd' chose an education at Stanford University over football powerhouse universities before becoming a professional quarterback." (Booklist)

REVIEW: *Booklist* v110 no16 p46 Ap 15 2014 Daniel Kraus

REVIEW: *Booklist* v110 no13 p66 Mr 1 2014 Angela Leeper

"Andrew Luck," "Buster Posey," and "Joe Flacco." "Good sports biographies are a must for any school or public library, and these titles in the Robbie Reader: Contemporary Biography series satisfy this need. Each book begins with a dramatic scene from the athlete's pro career, which ensures further reading. The large, accessible text continues with a brief look at each player's childhood and high-school play before launching into their award-winning sports careers. . . . A chronology, glossary, career statistics, and other back matter will further gratify sports enthusiasts."

O'NEAL, CLAIRE. Archimedes; [by] Claire O'Neal 48 p. 2014 Mitchell Lane Publishers

1. Biographies 2. Mathematicians—Greece—Biography—Juvenile literature 3. Mathematics—Study and teaching (Elementary) 4. Mathematics, Ancient—Juvenile literature

ISBN 9781612284378 (library bound)

LC 2013-012549

SUMMARY: This book on Archimedes by Claire O'Nea is part of the Junio Biographies From Ancient Civilizations series. "The story of Archimedes begins with his famous 'Eureka!' moment and then goes back to look at his boyhood, mathematical training, and the impact he had on ancient Greek civilization--as well as much further into the future." (Booklist)

REVIEW: *Booklist* v110 no5 p54 N 1 2013 Ilene Cooper

"Archimedes," "Leif Erikson," and "Nero." "The Junior Biographies from Ancient Civilizations series brings its subjects to life by focusing on some of history's most famous (and infamous) names. . . . The story of Archimedes begins with his famous 'Eureka!' moment and then goes back to look at his boyhood, mathematical training, and the impact he had on ancient Greek civilization. . . . The focus here is on [Leif] Erikson's voyage to Canada, where he became one of the first white men to see the new land. Roman emperor Nero was trouble almost from the beginning. . . . The books are a solid blending of art and text, with lengthy, illustrated sidebars doing the heavy lifting when it comes to explaining societies' mores."

O'NEIL, MARYADELE J.ed. The Merck index. See The Merck index

O'NEIL, MICHAEL.ed. The Oxford handbook of Percy Bysshe Shelley. See The Oxford handbook of Percy Bysshe Shelley

ONGIRI, AMY ABUGO. Spectacular blackness; the cultural politics of the Black power movement and the search for a Black aesthetic; [by] Amy Abugo Ongiri x, 223 2010 University of Virginia Press

1. African Americans—Intellectual life—20th century 2. Black Arts movement 3. Black power—United States—History 4. Historical literature

ISBN 0813928591; 0813928605; 0813929601; 9780813928593; 9780813928609; 9780813929606

LC 2009-023618

SUMMARY: In this book, "exploring the interface between the cultural politics of the Black Power and the Black Arts movements and the production of postwar African American popular culture, Amy Ongiri shows how the reliance of Black politics on an oppositional image of African Americans was the formative moment in the construction of 'authentic blackness' as a cultural identity." (Publisher's note)

REVIEW: *Am Lit* v85 no3 p593-6 S 2013 Evie Shockley

"Spectacular Blackness: The Cultural Politics of the Black Power Movement and the Search for a Black Aesthetic," "Specters of Democracy: Blackness and the Aesthetics of Politics in the Antebellum United States," and "Representing the Race: A New Political History of African American Literature." "[Amy Abugo] Ongiri adds her incisive analysis of materials both familiar and little-known to the growing body of work on Black Power and the Black Arts Movement (BAM) in their most active years. . . .[Ivy G.] Wilson's book [is] . . . more densely theoretical than Ongiri's lively work, but no less readable in its eloquence. . . . [Andrew Jarrett] makes a detailed, well-researched case for the importance of distinguishing between the longstanding practice of reading creative and intellectual writing as simply informally political . . . and his scholarship, which argues that such writing . . . does formal political work."

ONNEKINK, DAVID.ed. Ideology and foreign policy in early modern Europe (1650-1750). See Ideology and foreign policy in early modern Europe (1650-1750)

OPEN MIC; ten authors riff on growing up between cultures; 144 p. 2013 Candlewick Press

1. Cross-cultural differences 2. Cultural pluralism 3. Intergroup communication 4. Minorities 5. Young adult literature

ISBN 0763658669; 9780763658663

LC 2012-955218

SUMMARY: In this book, edited by Mitali Perkins, "ten [young adult] authors—some familiar, some new—use their own brand of humor to share their stories about growing up between cultures. Henry Choi Lee discovers that pretending to be a tai chi master or a sought-after wiz at math wins him friends for a while—until it comically backfires. A biracial girl is amused when her dad clears seats for his family on a crowded subway in under a minute, simply by sitting quietly between two uptight women." (Publisher's note)

REVIEW: *Booklist* v110 no1 p98 S 1 2013 Michael Cart

REVIEW: *Bull Cent Child Books* v67 no2 p109-10 O 2013 T. A.

"Open Mic: Riffs on Life Between Cultures in Ten Voices." "This slim collection often contemporary stories--most published here for the first time--brings together familiar and new voices in YA literature to talk candidly about race. [Editor Mitali] Perkins' smart introduction lays her framework for using humor as a method to broach a touchy subject . . . and although some stories are more humorous than others, the approach is effective. It's often said that good literature for young people can act as a mirror to one's own experiences and a window into others'--this anthology fills the bill, providing an accessible assessment of contemporary race relations, while also being as honest, refreshing, and frank as the titular open mic suggests."

REVIEW: *Horn Book Magazine* v89 no5 p122-3 S/O 2013 JENNIFER M. BRABANDER

REVIEW: *Kirkus Rev* v81 no16 p84 Ag 15 2013

"Open Mic: Riffs on Life Between Cultures in Ten Voices." "First the good news: Half the pieces in this uneven anthology are standouts. . . . The remaining pieces are significantly weaker. [Editor Mitali] Perkins salutes the value of lightening up in her introduction. . . . Yet too few pieces here reflect those rules or appear to have been conceived as humor. Undisclosed selection criteria, author bios that don't always speak to identity, and weak and dated content are problematic. The sweeping racial and cultural judgments and hostile--occasionally mean-spirited--tones of several pieces disappoint; angry venting may be justified and therapeutic, but it's seldom funny."

REVIEW: *SLJ* v60 no1 p59 Ja 2014 Toby Rajput

REVIEW: *SLJ* v59 no9 p188 S 2013 Suzanne Gordon

REVIEW: *Voice of Youth Advocates* v36 no4 p70 O 2013 Matthew Weaver

THE OPINIONS OF WILLIAM COBBETT; 214 p. 2013 Ashgate Publishing Limited

1. Journalists—Great Britain—Biography 2. Politicians—Great Britain—Biography 3. Social criticism
ISBN 9781409464327 (pbk. : alk. paper)
LC 2013-021100

SUMMARY: "Politician, journalist, reformer, convict, social commentator and all-round thorn in the side of the establishment, William Cobbett cut a swathe through late-eighteenth and early-nineteenth century British society with his copious and acerbic writings on any and every issue that caught his attention." Edited by James Grande, John Stevenson, and Richard Thomas, "this book provides a selection of his writings . . . that highlight his talents, obsessions, and concerns." (Publisher's note)

REVIEW: *TLS* no5786 p26 F 21 2014 NORMA CLARKE

"The Opinions of William Cobbett." "Nobody worked as hard or achieved as much as Cobbett, as he repeatedly pointed out, and few writers were as widely read by all classes. . . . Cobbett's hates were sometimes ugly and though this book is an avowed celebration it does not try to hide his anti-Semitism. . . . This is a timely collection of extracts from Cobbett's writings. Deftly contextualized, they make for gripping reading. . . . It would have helped if the editors had occasionally footnoted Cobbett's accuracy or otherwise in facts and figures."

OPP, SUSAN M. Local economic development and the environment; finding common ground; [by] Susan M. Opp xxiv, 322 p. 2013 CRC Press

1. Economic policy—Environmental aspects 2. Economics literature 3. Environmental policy—Economic aspects 4. Local government and environmental policy 5. Sustainable development—Environmental aspects 6. Sustainable urban development
ISBN 9781439880081 (Hardcover)
LC 2012-043731

SUMMARY: This book looks at "basic ideas concerning sustainable energy use, 'green' transportation and government procurement policies, and public-private partnerships and university-community coalitions to address sustainability. Also discussed are eminent domain and environmental remediation, tax-increment financing districts, intergovernmental grants, and the federal and state resources that are available for fostering development while protecting the environment." (Choice: Current Reviews for Academic Libraries)

REVIEW: *Choice* v51 no7 p1272 Mr 2014 R. A. Beauregard

"Local Economic Development and the Environment: Finding Common Ground." "This volume explores rationales for and local efforts to achieve 'green' or sustainable economic development. In ten substantive chapters, [Susan M.] Opp [Jeffery L.] Osgood . . . and other contributors present basic ideas concerning sustainable energy use, 'green' transportation and government procurement policies, and public-private partnerships and university-community coalitions to address sustainability. . . . This informative introduction to the topic makes a strong case for the feasibility of sustainable economic development."

OPPEL, KENNETH. The Boundless; [by] Kenneth Oppel 336 p. 2014 Simon & Schuster Books for Young Readers

1. Adventure and adventurers—Fiction 2. Circus—Fiction 3. Railroad trains—Fiction 4. Speculative fiction
ISBN 144247288X; 9781442472884 (hardcover: alk. paper); 9781442472891 (pbk.: alk. paper)
LC 2013-009879

SUMMARY: In this book, by Kenneth Oppel, "The Boundless . . . is on its maiden voyage across the country, and first-class passenger Will Everett is about to embark on the adventure of his life! When Will ends up in possession of the key to a train car containing priceless treasures, he becomes the target of sinister figures from his past. In order to survive, Will must join a traveling circus, enlisting the aid of Mr. Dorian, the ringmaster and leader of the troupe." (Publisher's note)

REVIEW: *Booklist* v110 no9/10 p96 Ja 1 2014 Carolyn Phelan

REVIEW: *Bull Cent Child Books* v67 no8 p419 Ap 2014 E. B.

"The Boundless". "The theft tales chug forward with enough life-threatening twists to keep readers involved, but the real star is the Boundless itself, which functions as a rolling city of wonders and a clever encapsulation of classism in the mid-1800s. Several luminaries associated with the actual Canadian Pacific Railroad, as well as a few cryptids from North American lore, make guest appearances, and even 'The Picture of Dorian Gray' gets a minor but significant nod. Will seems destined for a sequel, perhaps following his romantic interest, Maren, into her new life as a circus owner. If [Kenneth] Oppel can make a train this wondrous, imagine what he will do with a circus."

REVIEW: *Horn Book Magazine* v90 no3 p94 My/Je 2014 JONATHAN HUNT

REVIEW: *Kirkus Rev* v82 no6 p77 Mr 15 2014

REVIEW: *Publ Wkly* v261 no6 p88-9 F 10 2014

REVIEW: *Quill Quire* v80 no2 p16-8 Mr 2014 NATHAN WHITLOCK

"The Boundless". "[Kenneth] Oppel's newest novel, 'The Boundless' . . . is a perfect example of the sort of story he tells best. . . . It is a literally propulsive tale: most of the action takes place on an immense, moving super-train called the Boundless. . . . It's not an entirely straightforward action tale, though. . . . Oppel takes the basic facts of the [Canadian Pacific Railway's] nation-building exercise, as memorized by most Canadian students before they hit high school, and adds about a dozen surreal twists."

REVIEW: *Quill Quire* v80 no2 p35 Mr 2014 Shannon Ozirny

REVIEW: *SLJ* v60 no3 p146 Mr 2014 Alissa J. Bach

REVIEW: *SLJ* v60 no7 p52 Jl 2014 Jennifer Mann

OPPENHEIM, JOANNE. The Prince's breakfast; 32 p. 2014 Barefoot Books, Inc
1. Breakfasts—Fiction 2. Diet—Fiction 3. Food habits—Fiction 4. Princes—Fiction 5. Stories in rhyme
ISBN 9781782850748
LC 2013-029606

SUMMARY: In this book, "one young prince with a picky palate tours the world with his parents in search of the right ingredient that will make eating an enjoyable treat. . . . Alas, Indian rice cakes, Mexican tortillas, Chinese congee and even fresh African fruit are all spurned by the stubborn prince. . . . Just as they begin the trek back home, the royal family is approached by an energetic old man in Zambia, who offers the solution in the form of a red, tomato-based condiment: ketchup." (Kirkus Reviews)

REVIEW: *Kirkus Rev* v82 no3 p298 F 1 2014

"The Prince's Breakfast". "This oh-so-American solution to a familiar child-rearing dilemma may not be nutritionally preferred by more discriminating appetites, but who's to account for taste when getting kids to eat well is the ultimate goal? Brightly hued, amusing, cartoon-style drawings in acrylic paints and watercolor pencils provide international verve to complement the rhyming verse. The accompanying CD is narrated by Hugh Bonneville. The king's evident enjoyment of every new flavor as unfamiliar foods and their names are introduced makes this effort worth sampling for those fussy little diners."

REVIEW: *Publ Wkly* v261 no2 p69 Ja 13 2014

REVIEW: *SLJ* v60 no6 p62 Je 2014 Tara Hixon

OPPENHEIM, TOM.ed. The Muses Go to School. See The Muses Go to School

OPPORTUNITIES AND DEPRIVATION IN THE URBAN SOUTH; poverty, segregation and social networks in São Paulo; xii, 186 p. 2012 Ashgate
1. Segregation 2. Social networks—Brazil—São Paulo 3. Social science literature 4. São Paulo (Brazil)—Social conditions 5. Urban poor—Brazil—São Paulo
ISBN 9781409442707 (hardback: alk. paper); 9781409442714 (ebook)
LC 2012-006251

SUMMARY: This book, "contending that everyday sociability and social networks are central elements to an understanding of urban poverty, . . . draws on detailed research conducted in Sao Paulo in an examination of the social networks of individuals who identify as poor. The book uses a multi-methods approach not only to test the importance of networks, but also to disentangle the effects of networks and segregation." (Publisher's note)

REVIEW: *Contemp Sociol* v43 no2 p234-5 Mr 2014 Javier Auyero

"Opportunities and Deprivation in the Urban South: Poverty, Segregation and Social Networks in São Paulo". "In exploring these four themes, [Eduardo Cesar Leão] Marques uses, in both skillful and critical ways, extant scholarship—sometimes to confirm existing findings . . . , and other times to show how his findings either qualify or challenge established findings. . . . Scholars of poverty and marginality in the Americas, as well as those particularly interested in the effects of networks on the daily lives of those at the bottom of the socio-symbolic order and, more generally, in a truly relational approach to social phenomena, will have a lot to learn and emulate from this book."

ORALITY, LITERACY AND PERFORMANCE IN THE ANCIENT WORLD; xviii, 268 p. 2012 Brill
1. Ancient civilization 2. Ancient literature 3. Historical literature 4. Literacy—History 5. Oral communication—Greece—Congresses 6. Orality 7. Transmission of texts—Greece—Congresses 8. Written communication—Greece—Congresses
ISBN 9004217746 (hardcover : alk. paper); 9004217754; 9789004217744 (hardcover : alk. paper); 9789004217751
LC 2011-036943

SUMMARY: This collection, edited by Elizabeth Minchin, draws on "The ninth meeting in the international Orality and Literacy in the Ancient World series. . . . This volume . . . illustrate[s] . . . composition, the nature of performance, and vocalization in text. Under consideration are Homer, Hesiod, Plato, Isocrates, the orators of the Second Sophistic, and Proclus. Cross-cultural studies include . . . South Slavic epic and a text from the Sanskrit archive." (Publisher's note)

REVIEW: *Classical Rev* v63 no2 p333-5 O 2013 Thérèse De Vet

"Orality, Literacy, and Performance in the Ancient World." "This selection of papers from the ninth conference on Orality and Literacy, held in 2010 in Canberra, celebrates the 50th anniversary of the publication of Albert Lord's 'The Singer of Tales.' The book is divided into two sections. Part 1 is dedicated to pre-literate Greece (five chapters), while Part 2 presents the more literate interactive environments of later Greece and Rome (six chapters). Chapter 6, a description of an oral (but text-based) performance in contemporary India, bridges the two halves. . . . While the second half of the book provides credible evidence of oral performances in a literate environment, the first part . . . disappoints."

ORCHARD, ERIC.il. Twelve minutes to midnight. See Edge, C.

ORENSTEIN, RONALD. Ivory, horn and blood; behind the elephant and rhinoceros poaching crisis; [by] Ronald Orenstein 216 p. 2013 Firefly Books
1. African elephant—Effect of poaching on 2. Asiatic elephant—Effect of poaching on 3. Elephant hunting 4. Environmental literature 5. Illegal imports 6. Ivory industry 7. Ivory industry—Corrupt practices 8. Poaching 9. Rhinoceros (Genus) 10. Rhinoceros horn industry—Corrupt practices 11. Rhinoceroses—Effect of poaching on
ISBN 1770852271; 9781770852273
LC 2013-427986

SUMMARY: This book, by Ronald Orenstein, describes

how "today a new ivory crisis has arisen, fuelled by internal wars in Africa and a growing market in the Far East. . . . Bands of militia have crossed from one side of Africa to the other, slaughtering elephants with automatic weapons. A market surge in Vietnam and elsewhere has led to a growing criminal onslaught against the world's rhinoceroses. The situation, for both elephants and rhinos, is dire." (Publisher's note)

REVIEW: *Booklist* v110 no7 p7 D 1 2013 Nancy Bent

REVIEW: *Choice* v51 no10 p1834-5 Je 2014 B. Blossey

REVIEW: *Quill Quire* v79 no9 p33 N 2013 Matthew Behrens

"Ivory, Horn, and Blood: Behind the Elephant and Rhinoceros Poaching Crisis." "In the tradition of crusading animal lovers such as Jane Goodall and Dian Fossey, zoologist, lawyer, and wildlife conservationist Ronald Orenstein has penned a passionate call to rescue two of the planet's oldest and most recognizable species: the elephant and rhino. Both face imminent extinction . . . from an international criminal enterprise. . . . Orenstein has a tendency to overload the reader with the minutiae of international conventions and debates, but this does not detract from the forceful plea he makes. As someone repeatedly digging in his heels for another stand to save the great mammals, he writes about the fight with equal parts passion, knowledge, and commitment."

ORFALEA, GREGORY. Journey to the Sun; Junipero Serra's Dream and the Founding of California; [by] Gregory Orfalea 384 p. 2013 Simon & Schuster Scribner

1. Biography (Literary form) 2. California—History—To 1846 3. Explorers—California—Biography 4. Explorers—Spain—Biography 5. Missionaries 6. Missions—California 7. Missions, Spanish—California—History 8. Serra, Junipero, 1713-1784

ISBN 1451642725; 9781451642728

LC 2013-040181

SUMMARY: This book "offers not only a biography of the Spanish priest who fearlessly traveled the New World in the name of God, but an early history of California and its cultural origins. In 1749 under the guise of the Catholic Church, Serra left Spain to pursue missionary work in the New World. . . . He cultivated multiple societies, many of which are now major cities in California: San Diego, Santa Barbara, San Juan Capistrano, and San Francisco." (Publishers Weekly)

REVIEW: *America* v210 no9 p33-5 Mr 17 2014 THOMAS RZEZNIK

"Junípero Serra: Californias Founding Father" and "Journey to the Sun: Junípero Serra's Dream and the Founding of California". "Both authors reveal an appreciation for Serra's life and legacy, but they employ different narrative styles and differ in their characterization of their shared subject. [Steven W.] Hackel, a historian who has written about Indian-Spanish relations in the colonial missions, provides the crisper biography. Though still lively and engaging, his is the more academic study, exhibiting his broad command not just of Serra's own writings, but of the social, political and religious context of his times. [Gregory] Orfalea, in contrast, employs a more literary approach to his tale. His account can be imaginative or impressionistic at times, but he wants readers to experience the sights, sounds and spectacle of Serra's travels and ministry."

REVIEW: *Booklist* v110 no9/10 p24 Ja 1 2014 Jay Freeman

REVIEW: *Commonweal* v141 no11 p35-8 Je 13 2014 Patrick Jordan

REVIEW: *Kirkus Rev* v81 no24 p246 D 15 2013

REVIEW: *Libr J* v138 no10 p82 Je 1 2013

ORIANS, GORDON H.ed. North Pacific temperate rainforests. See North Pacific temperate rainforests

ORIENT & OCCIDENT; travelling 19th century Austrian painters; 263 p. 2013 University of Chicago Press

1. Art literature 2. East and West in art—Exhibitions 3. East and West in literature—Exhibitions 4. Painters—Austria—19th century—Exhibitions 5. Painters—Travel—Orient—Exhibitions 6. Painters—Travel—Western countries—Exhibitions 7. Painting, Austrian—19th century—Exhibitions 8. Travel in art—Exhibitions

ISBN 3777458910 (English edition : hd.bd.); 9783777458915 (English edition : hd.bd.)

LC 2012-448852

SUMMARY: This book, edited by Agnes Husslein-Arco and Sabine Grabner, presents and discusses "Austrian depictions of the Orient, including portraits, landscapes, and . . . market scenes. . . . Among the most prolific of the painters collected here was Leopold Carl Müller . . . [and] artists like August von Pettenkofen, Otto von Thoren, and Johann Gualbert Raffalt in Hungary; Rudolf Swoboda and Hermann von Königsbrunn in India and Sri Lanka; and many others." (Publisher's note)

REVIEW: *Choice* v51 no1 p64-5 S 2013 S. M. Quimby

"Orient & Occident: Travelling 19th Century Austrian Painters." "This book highlights a particular collection exhibited by the Belvedere Museum in Vienna, but it also gives a nuanced and varied discussion of 19th-century Austrian travel painting. . . . Interestingly, many Austrian painters diverged from what is considered French or English Orientalism, that of artificial colors and imaginary exotic scenery customary in studio painting. . . . Be it an attempt at humanizing or romanticizing, the works exhibit the binary opposition of the Orient and the Occident."

ORLICH, DONALD C. The school reform landscape; fraud, myth, and lies; [by] Donald C. Orlich 172 p. 2013 Rowman & Littlefield Publishers, Inc.

1. Education and state—United States 2. Educational change—United States 3. Educational literature 4. Public schools—United States 5. School improvement programs—United States

ISBN 9781475802573 (cloth : alk. paper); 9781475802580 (pbk. : alk. paper); 9781475802597 (electronic)

LC 2012-046746

SUMMARY: In this book, authors Christopher H. Tienken and Donald C. Orlich "take an in-depth and controversial look at school reform since the launch of Sputnik. They scrutinize school reform events, proposals, and policies from the last 60 years through the lens of critical social theory and examine the ongoing tensions between the need to keep a vibrant unitary system of public education and the ongoing assault by corporate and elite interests in creating a dual system." (Publisher's note)

REVIEW: *Choice* v51 no2 p322-3 O 2013 G. E. Hein

"The School Reform Landscape: Fraud, Myth, and Lies." "As the subtitle indicates, [authors Christopher H.] Tienken . . . and [Donald C.] Orlich . . . are critical of current school 'reform' efforts, especially overreliance on standardized tests, national curricula (including common core standards), and the spread of charter schools. . . . They argue that assertions that schools are failing . . . are false and put forward with little supporting evidence. . . . This summary of the liberal critique of the current state of education in the US is not particularly well written, but the authors make their case compellingly and cite much of the research and policy literature by others that supports their position."

ORMAND, KIRK.ed. A companion to Sophocles. See A companion to Sophocles

ORMSBY, LAWRENCE, 1946-.il. Sutro's glass place. See Martini, J. A.

ORR, CYNTHIA.ed. Genreflecting. See Herald, D. T.

ORR, RYAN J.ed. Global projects. See Global projects

ORT, THOMAS. Art and life in modernist Prague; Karel Čapek and his generation, 1911-1938; [by] Thomas Ort xiii, 258 p. 2013 Palgrave Macmillan

1. Arts, Czech—20th century—History and criticism 2. Czech literature—20th century—History and criticism 3. Historical literature

ISBN 0230113621 (hardcover); 9780230113626 (hardcover)

LC 2013-363626

SUMMARY: This book "highlight[s] a generation of Czech writers and artists distinguished by their affirmative encounter with the modern world in the first decades of the twentieth century. . . . Tracing the roots of [Karl] Capek's generation to cubist art and turn-of-the-century philosophy, author Thomas Ort shows that the form of modernism they championed led not into the thickets of fascism or communism but in fact closer to liberal political ideals." (Publisher's note)

REVIEW: *Choice* v51 no6 p1010-1 F 2014 P. Steiner

"Art and Life in Modernist Prague: Karel Čapek and his Generation, 1911-1938." "This lucid, well-written book on one of the leading European intellectuals of the interwar period proceeds from H. Stuart Hughes's concept of a 'generation of 1905' with the 'Čapek generation' as 'the Czech version of that wider European phenomenon.' . . . [Thomas] Ort's text should be of interest to students not only of Slavic literature and history but of European modernism in general. . . . Highly recommended."

REVIEW: *TLS* no5780 p3-5 Ja 10 2014 MARCI SHORE

"Prague, Capital of the Twentieth Century: A Surrealist History" and "Art and Life in Modernist Prague: Karel Čapek and His Generation, 1911-1938." "Their subjectivist turn inwards, Thomas Ort emphasizes in 'Art and Life in Modernist Prague,' was a free choice: it was not driven by marginality. . . . Thomas Ort is a pleasure to read for other reasons: his writing is lucid and unpretentious. These two books about Czech modernism--about what Paris meant for Prague--are alter egos of sorts: Ort's earnestness contrasts with ['Prague, Capital of the Twentieth Century' author Derek] Sayer's sarcasm. Ort's chapters are chronological; Sayer's temporality is slippery."

ORTIZ, STEPHEN R.ed. Veterans' policies, veterans' politics. See Veterans' policies, veterans' politics

ORWELL, GEORGE, 1903-1950. George Orwell; a life in letters; 542 p. 2013 W.W. Norton & Co. Inc.

1. Authors 2. Biography, Individual 3. Essayists 4. Letters 5. Novelists

ISBN 0871404621; 9780871404626 (hardcover)

LC 2013-004734

SUMMARY: Editor Peter Davison presents a collection of letters by author George Orwell, including "Orwell's message to Dwight Macdonald of 5 December 1946 explaining 'Animal Farm'; his correspondence with his first translator, R. N. Raimbault . . .and the moving encomium written about Orwell by his BBC head of department. . . . The volume concludes with [an] . . . account of the painful illness that took Orwell's life at age forty-seven. His last letter concerns his son and his estate." (Publisher's note)Selected and introduced by Peter Davison, this collection of letters written by the English author and journalist includes both personal and political correspondence and spans Orwell's entire writing career.

REVIEW: *America* v209 no10 p36-8 O 14 2013 JAMES LANG

"George Orwell: A Life in Letters." "In short, [editor Peter] Davison wants readers to catch a glimpse of the human being--born Eric Arthur Blair but known for most of his adult life, even to friends, as George Orwell--behind the celebrated author of two very famous works, 'Animal Farm' and '1984.' . . . The George Orwell that Davison presents to us is an appealing one: indefatigable writer, generous friend, champion of the poor and oppressed, avid gardener and outdoorsman. . . . The technical qualities of the book can . . . put barriers in the way of it substituting, as Davison hopes it will, for an Orwell autobiography."

REVIEW: *Choice* v51 no6 p1005-6 F 2014 D. C. Maus

"George Orwell: A Life in Letters." "Esteemed Orwell scholar Peter Davison . . . has further enhanced readers' access to this complex, idiosyncratic author's mind by editing an expansive selection of letters that span Orwell's life from his childhood years at boarding school through his myriad experiences in Burma, France, Spain, Morocco, and Great Britain. Davison's editorial hand is relatively light in the letters themselves, confined mostly to explanatory and contextual footnotes. . . . A massive epistolary archive such as this is no picnic, but it is a potential goldmine for the intensely curious reader."

REVIEW: *Commonweal* v140 no17 p40-2 O 25 2013 William H. Pritchard

"George Orwell: A Life in Letters." "Probably the most astonishing feat of editing a notable literary figure from the last century is Peter Davison's edition of George Orwell's works. Completed in 1998, its twenty volumes run to nine thousand pages; eight volumes contain his novels, with the remainder made up of essays, reviews, and letters. From the roughly seventeen hundred letters Orwell wrote, Davison has now made a generous selection, annotated with insight and without pedantry, presented in a volume that will go some way, he hopes, toward 'offering the autobiography that Orwell did not write.'"

REVIEW: *Kirkus Rev* v81 no2 p68 Je 1 2013

REVIEW: *Libr J* v138 no10 p108 Je 1 2013 Thomas Karel

REVIEW: *New York Times* v162 no56234 pC4 Ag 20 2013 LARRY ROHTER

REVIEW: *Publ Wkly* v260 no14 p53 Ap 8 2013

REVIEW: *World Lit Today* v88 no2 p73-4 Mr/Ap 2014 Daniel P. King

"A Life in Letters." "[Author George] Orwell did not live long enough to write his autobiography. 'A Life in Letters,' along with Peter Davison's editing of twenty volumes of Orwell's writings and his diaries, aptly illustrates his life and hopes. Davison's annotations and short biographies of his correspondents complement these fascinating--some momentous and others mundane--letters. . . . In distilling the 1,700 letters written by Orwell, Davison set himself two goals: the letters should illustrate his life and hopes, and 'each should be of interest in its own right.' This volume admirably fulfills this twofold mission; it is a tribute to Davison's decades-long scholarship on Orwell's life."

ORWELL, GEORGE, 1903-1950. Homage to Catalonia; [by] George Orwell 232 1952 Harcourt

1. Journalism 2. Memoirs 3. Spain—History—Civil War, 1936-1939—Foreign participation 4. Spain—History—Civil war, 1936-1939 5. Spain—Politics and government

LC 52-6-442

SUMMARY: This book by Eric Blair, writing as George Orwell, is "both a memoir of Orwell's experience at the front in the Spanish Civil War and a tribute to those who died in what he called a fight for common decency." (Publisher's note) "He blames the Republic's military defeats on its fratricidal conflicts and the suppression by the Republican government and the Communists of the social revolution he had so admired in Barcelona." (New York Review of Books)In 1936 the author went to Spain to write about Barcelona and Spain's civil war. Instead he stayed to fight and was badly wounded. On his return to England he wrote this account of the war and his experiences, which was published in England in 1938. This is the first American edition.

REVIEW: *N Y Rev Books* v60 no20 p62-4 D 19 2013 Adam Hochschild

"Homage to Catalonia:." "The book . . . is the one in which for the first time [George Orwell] fully found his voice. In 1940 he referred to it as his 'best book,' and for many of us that judgment still holds. . . . He . . . managed to write in the first person without ever sounding self-centered. You can open 'Homage' at almost any page and see how he deftly amasses rich, sensory detail, but always in the service of a larger point. . . . An unusual blend of memoir and political reportage."

OSBORNE, JOHN.ed. Old Saint Peter's, Rome. See Old Saint Peter's, Rome

OSBORNE, LAWRENCE. The ballad of a small player; A Novel; [by] Lawrence Osborne 256 p. 2014 Hogarth

1. Baccarat 2. British—China—Hong Kong—Fiction 3. Casinos—China—Hong Kong—Fiction 4. Gambling—China—Hong Kong—Fiction 5. Psychological fiction

ISBN 0804137978; 9780804137973

LC 2013-035201

SUMMARY: This novel, by Lawrence Osborne, is a "tale of risk and obsession set in the alluring world of Macau's casinos. . . . A corrupt English lawyer who has escaped prosecution by fleeing to the East, Doyle spends his nights drinking and gambling and his days sleeping off his excesses, continually haunted by his past. . . . In a moment of crisis he meets Dao-Ming, an enigmatic Chinese woman who appears to be a denizen of the casinos just like himself." (Publisher's note)

REVIEW: *Booklist* v110 no13 p16 Mr 1 2014 Carol Haggas

REVIEW: *Kirkus Rev* v82 no3 p307 F 1 2014

"The Ballad of a Small Player". " We learn that each hand is inherently short, and the drama emerges from the enormous sums won and lost on the turn of a card. We witness Doyle's status change radically from loser to winner; since a 'natural nine' is the best possible hand in baccarat, Doyle becomes something of a celebrity when he starts putting together hand after hand of these nines—and the proprietors of the casinos develop an understandable interest in this increase in his 'luck.' With his fortune mounting, Doyle plays one final hand—and decides to bet everything on the outcome. [Lawrence] Osborne masterfully recreates the atmosphere of casinos as well as the psychology of baccarat players—and leaves readers eager to try their luck at the game."

REVIEW: *Libr J* v138 no18 p69 N 1 2013 Barbara Hoffert

REVIEW: *Libr J* v139 no4 p85 Mr 1 2014 Joshua Finnell

REVIEW: *N Y Times Book Rev* p12 Ap 6 2014 TOM SHONE

REVIEW: *New Yorker* v90 no22 p69-1 Ag 4 2014

REVIEW: *Publ Wkly* v261 no5 p32 F 3 2014

OSBORNE, PETER. Anywhere or not at all; philosophy of contemporary art; [by] Peter Osborne v, 282 p. 2013 Verso

1. Aesthetics 2. Art literature 3. Art, Modern—20th century—Philosophy 4. Art, Modern—21st century—Philosophy 5. Conceptual art

ISBN 9781781680940 (pbk. : alk. paper); 9781781681138 (cloth : alk. paper)

LC 2013-003012

SUMMARY: This book by Peter Osborne discusses art philosophy. "Developing the position that 'contemporary art is postconceptual art,' the book progresses through a dual series of conceptual constructions and interpretations of particular works to assess the art from a number of perspectives: contemporaneity and its global context; art against aesthetic; the Romantic pre-history of conceptual art . . . and the institutional and existential complexities of art-space and art-time." (Publisher's note)

REVIEW: *Art Am* v102 no1 p51 Ja 2014

"Lessons From Modernism: Environmental Design Strategies in Architecture, 1925-1970," "The Filming of Modern Life: European Avant-Garde Film of the 1920s," and "Anywhere or Not at All: Philosophy of Contemporary Art." "Twenty-five buildings completed between 1925 and 1970 provide insight into how architects like Oscar Niemeyer and Le Corbusier dealt with environmental issues and influenced green building today. . . . Five classic experimental films by artists such as Hans Richter and Salvador Dalí offer contrasting--and sometimes self-contradictory--views of modernity.

. . . Drawing from philosophers like [Immanuel] Kant and the German Romantics and artists like Sol Le Witt and the Atlas Group, [Peter] Osborne critically redefines what's 'contemporary' about contemporary art."

REVIEW: *Choice* v51 no7 p1200 Mr 2014 P. Jenkins

OSBORNE, ROBERT. 85 years of the Oscar; [by] Robert Osborne 464 p. 2013 Abbeville Press Publishers
1. Academy Awards (Motion pictures) 2. Academy Awards (Motion pictures)—History 3. Academy of Motion Picture Arts & Sciences 4. Historical literature 5. Motion picture industry—United States—History 6. Motion pictures—Awards—History 7. Motion pictures—United States—History
ISBN 0789211424; 9780789211422
LC 2013-033021

SUMMARY: This book "is the official history of the Academy Awards. Following an introductory chapter on the Academy of Motion Picture Arts and Sciences and the birth of the Oscars, the book presents the story of each year's awards, beginning with . . . 1927-28. Author Robert Osborne surveys the movies in competition, recounts the speculation on various winners, and describes . . . the awards ceremony. He also provides a complete listing of . . . nominees and winners in every category." (Publisher's note)

REVIEW: *Booklist* v110 no8 p32 D 15 2013 Rebecca Vnuk

REVIEW: *N Y Times Book Rev* p15 D 8 2013 DAVID CARR

"Vanity Fair 100 Years: From the Jazz Age to Our Age" and "85 Years of the Oscar: The Official History of the Academy Awards." "'Vanity Fair 100 Years' . . . is a stunning artifact that begets staring, less for the words and publishing history than as an exercise in visual storytelling reflected through the prism of society and celebrity. . . . Visually repetitive and uninspired, with movie stills dropped willy-nilly to break up what becomes a droning year-by-year history of the Academy Awards, '85 Years of the Oscar' is sadly like the telecast itself: mildly interesting in spots, but with long stretches when nothing remarkable is seen or said."

OSGOOD, JEFFERY L. Local economic development and the environment. See Opp, S. M.

OSMAN, KHAN TOWHID. Soil degradation, conservation and remediation; [by] Khan Towhid Osman 245 p. 2013 Springer
1. Scientific literature 2. Soil conservation 3. Soil degradation 4. Soil pollution 5. Soil remediation
ISBN 9789400775893
LC 2013-950937

SUMMARY: This book by Khan Towhid Osman looks at "the extent, causes, processes and impacts of global soil degradation, and processes for improvement of degraded soils. Soil conservation measures, including soil amendments, decompaction, mulching, cover cropping, crop rotation, green manuring, contour farming, strip cropping, alley cropping, surface roughening, windbreaks, terracing, sloping agricultural land technology (SALT), dune stabilization, etc., are discussed." (Publisher's note)

REVIEW: *Choice* v51 no9 p1625-6 My 2014 M. S. Coyne

"Soil Degradation, Conservation and Remediation". "The current volume is intended for undergraduate and graduate students, but for those audiences it does not suffice. The organization of the book is good, and the illustrations are excellent. However, the extent of its coverage does not qualify it as a stand-alone text for an undergraduate-level course. There are too few examples in which the implementation of the solution has been shown to have a positive result; more case studies are needed. For graduate students, the content is superficial. . . . Some technical issues also detract from the book. It is poorly edited for grammar and style, and the data sets used are often dated."

OSSMAN, SUSAN. Moving matters; paths of serial migration; [by] Susan Ossman xi, 186 p. 2013 Stanford University Press
1. Cosmopolitanism 2. Emigration and immigration—Psychological aspects 3. Emigration and immigration—Social aspects 4. Immigrants—Social life and customs 5. Social science literature
ISBN 9780804770286 (cloth : alk. paper); 9780804770293 (pbk. : alk. paper)
LC 2012-033971

SUMMARY: This book, written by Susan Ossman, describes "the serial migrant: a person who has lived in several countries, calling each one at some point 'home.' The stories told here are both extraordinary and increasingly common. Serial migrants rarely travel freely--they must negotiate a world of territorial borders and legal restrictions--yet as they move from one country to another, they can use border-crossings as moments of self-clarification." (Publisher's note)

REVIEW: *Choice* v51 no2 p308-9 O 2013 D. W. Haines

"Moving Matters: Paths of Serial Migration." "Anthropologist [Susan] Ossman . . . aims to identify and describe a specific kind of 'serial migrant' whose experience is characterized less by the bonds of race, ethnicity, and class, and more by the nature of migration and the national borders that frame contemporary human movement. . . . Ossman's approach is, in effect, an extended essay that tries to weave together her own experiences moving among countries, her interviews with other serial migrants, and her engagement with a theoretical literature, mostly on migration and identity. . . . Readers should be warned, as the author herself notes, that the very interesting experiences of the interviewees are often elided in favor of the author's own musings."

OSSOWSKI, TAMAR. Left; a novel; [by] Tamar Ossowski 240 p. 2013 Skyhorse Pub.
1. Abandoned children—Fiction 2. Autistic children—Fiction 3. Domestic fiction 4. Mothers and daughters—Fiction 5. Mothers of autistic children—Fiction 6. Single mothers—Fiction 7. Sisters—Fiction
ISBN 1626360375; 9781626360372
LC 2013-022094

SUMMARY: In this book, by Tamar Ossowski, "single parent Therese Wolley works hard to support her two daughters financially and emotionally. Older daughter Matilda sometimes suffers from nightmares, and young Franny interprets her world from an autistic perspective, enveloping herself in letters. But an item in the newspaper and an obligation to fulfill a promise abruptly alter the family dynamics." (Kirkus Reviews)

REVIEW: *Booklist* v110 no4 p26-8 O 15 2013 Susan Maguire

"Left." "The three Wolley women narrate the story, and

each voice is as distinct as it is biased. Franny perceives the world through the lens of her autism and her youth. Matilda is plagued by strange dreams that color her daily life. Therese is ruled by her sense of touch, stubbornly relying on her impressions rather than reality, no matter how often she gets it wrong (although she doesn't always). This compact first novel is sometimes frustratingly short on details, but readers can be assured that it all makes sense in the end."

REVIEW: *Kirkus Rev* v81 no17 p20 S 1 2013

OSWALD, PETE.il. Hippos can't swim. See DiSiena, L. L.

O'TOOLE, CHRISTOPHER. Bees; A Natural History; [by] Christopher O'Toole 240 p. 2013 Firefly Books Ltd

1. Bees—Behavior 2. Bees—Folklore 3. Bees—Therapeutic use 4. Natural history literature 5. Pollination by bees

ISBN 1770852085; 9781770852082

SUMMARY: In this book, author Christopher O'Toole "addresses the basic biology of social and solitary bees, placing considerable emphasis on the pollination activities of both generalists and specialists. Chapters focus on bee enemies, conservation and management, the historical relationship with humans, bees in folklore, and bees in medicine." (Choice: Current Reviews for Academic Libraries)

REVIEW: *Booklist* v110 no7 p12 D 1 2013 Nancy Bent

REVIEW: *Choice* v51 no9 p1622-3 My 2014 P. K. Lago

"Bees: A Natural History". "Readers who wish to own one general book about bees will want to acquire this interesting, beautiful volume. . . . The numerous and exceptional photographs, half page, full page, or larger, generously scattered throughout the book might suggest that the volume was intended for the coffee table, and it will grace many. However, this is a natural history work in the truest sense, containing a wealth of information about these fascinating insects. . . . Broadly appealing."

OTTEN, WILLEMIEN.ed. The Oxford Guide to the Historical Reception of Augustine. See The Oxford Guide to the Historical Reception of Augustine

OUR MAN IN IRAQ; 280 p. 2012 Istros Books

1. Croatia—Social conditions 2. Iraq War, 2003-2011—Fiction 3. Iraq War, 2003-2011—Journalists 4. War correspondents 5. War stories

ISBN 9781908236043

LC 2012-452913

SUMMARY: In this book, "as Croatia lurches from socialism into globalized capitalism, Toni, a cocky journalist in Zagreb, struggles to balance his fragile career, pushy family, and hotheaded girlfriend. But in a moment of vulnerability he makes a mistake: volunteering his unhinged Arabic-speaking cousin Boris to report on the Iraq War. . . . But when Boris goes missing, Toni's own sense of reality--and reliability--begins to unravel." (Publisher's note)

REVIEW: *World Lit Today* v87 no5 p62-3 S/O 2013 Michele Levy

"Our Man in Iraq." "This postmodern, postcommunist picaresque hilariously skewers Croatian, Western, and global culture as it follows the rapid descent of quasi-journalist Toni, a country kid striving to make it in the big city. . . . Depicting a generation raised in 'strange Eastern European systems' who 'placed too much hope in rock 'n' roll,' this provocative satire explores both modern Croatia and its discontents and also, like Mother Courage, the human lust for power and money that still spawns war and suffering."

OUR SUPERHEROES, OURSELVES; 2013 Oxford University Press

1. Archetype (Psychology) 2. Comic books, strips, etc.—Psychological aspects 3. Social science literature 4. Superhero comic books, strips, etc. 5. Superheroes

ISBN 9780199765812 hardcover

SUMMARY: Edited by Robin S. Rosenberg, this book "ranges widely and tackles many intriguing questions. How do comic characters and stories reflect human nature? Do super powers alone make a hero super? . . . In the end, the appeal of Superman, Batman, Spiderman, and legions of others is simple and elemental. Superheroes provide drama, excitement, suspense, and romance and their stories showcase moral dilemmas, villains we love to hate, and protagonists who inspire us." (Publisher's note)

REVIEW: *Choice* v51 no6 p997 F 2014 A. W. Austin

"Our Superheroes, Ourselves" and "What is a Superhero?" "The first half of the book asks intriguing questions . . . and sets up interesting debates. The second half of the collection compares superheroes to humans. . . . Despite a few errors in various presentations of comics history and occasionally overgeneralized analysis, this is a focused effort that advances understanding of comics from a psychological perspective. . . . In their coedited volume, [Robin S.] Rosenberg and [Peter] Coogan draw from an even wider range of perspectives in attempting to answer its titular question. Each of the 25 contributors provides at least a somewhat different answer, revealing that the question is more profound than readers new to the field might expect."

OURIOU, SUSAN.tr. Jane, the fox & me. See Britt, F.

OURIOU, SUSAN.tr. Numeralia. See Lujan, J.

OVERY, RICHARD. The bombers and the bombed; Allied air war over Europe 1940-1945; [by] Richard Overy 592 p. 2013 Viking

1. Bombing, Aerial—Europe—History—20th century 2. Bombing, Aerial—Europe—Public opinion 3. Bombing, Aerial—Germany—History—20th century 4. Bombing, Aerial—Social aspects—Europe—History—20th century 5. Civil defense—Social aspects—Europe—History—20th century 6. Historical literature 7. Public opinion—Europe 8. World War, 1939-1945—Aerial operations, Allied 9. World War, 1939-1945—Aerial operations, Allied—Moral and ethical aspects 10. World War, 1939-1945—Europe 11. World War, 1939-1945—Europe—Aerial operations, Allied

ISBN 0670025151; 9780670025152

LC 2013-018405

SUMMARY: This book, by Richard Overy, presents a "comprehensive analysis of the Allied strategic bombing offensive in Europe. He addresses the subject from three interrelated perspectives: the planning and execution of the air campaign; the Axis responses; and the oft-overlooked experiences of those under Axis occupation who were 'bombed into freedom.'" (Publishers Weekly)

REVIEW: *Booklist* v110 no9/10 p37 Ja 1 2014 Jay Freeman

REVIEW: *Kirkus Rev* v81 no24 p173 D 15 2013

"The Bombers and the Bombed: Allied Air War Over Europe, 1940-1945". "This magisterial overview will not end the debate, but it skillfully illuminates all sides. . . . [Richard] Overy provides an eye-opening and often distressing account of the bombing of Europe's occupied nations, whose defenses were far less prepared than Germany's. . . . Readers looking for dramatic accounts of specific bombing missions should read a selection of books by British military historian Martin Middlebrook. For a far more expansive view that includes those on the receiving end, Overy is the choice."

REVIEW: *Libr J* v138 no14 p87 S 1 2013

REVIEW: *N Y Times Book Rev* p16 Mr 23 2014 BEN MACINTYRE

REVIEW: *Publ Wkly* v260 no48 p39 N 25 2013

OVERY, RICHARD. The Bombing War; Europe 1939-1945; [by] Richard Overy 880 p. 2013 Allen Lane

1. Aerial bombing—History 2. Air defenses 3. Historical literature 4. World War, 1939-1945—Aerial operations 5. World War, 1939-1945—Campaigns—Europe

ISBN 0713995610; 9780713995619

SUMMARY: In this book, historian Richard Overy presents an "analysis of the Allied strategic bombing offensive in Europe. He addresses the subject from three interrelated perspectives: the planning and execution of the air campaign; the Axis responses; and the oft-overlooked experiences of those under Axis occupation who were 'bombed into freedom.'" (Publishers Weekly)

REVIEW: *Economist* v408 no8854 p91-2 S 21 2013

REVIEW: *London Rev Books* v35 no22 p23-4 N 21 2013 Edward Luttwak

REVIEW: *New Statesman* v142 no5179 p42-3 O 11 2013 Gary Sheffield

REVIEW: *TLS* no5764 p8-9 S 20 2013 JOHN GOOCH

"The Bombing War: Europe 1939-1945." "[A] compendious study. . . . Readers unfamiliar with the air war have some surprises in store as the story of the war itself gets under way. . . . The bombing war in Europe involved more than just Allied aircraft battering Germany, and there is coverage here of Russia, of Italy and more besides, but Germany was and remains the big story. Richard Overy's conclusions . . . seem incontrovertible. His belief that British air chiefs engaged in subterfuge and even hypocrisy . . . will go down less comfortably. In matters of opinion this will] certainly not be the last word. In matters of fact it will be hard to surpass. If you want to know how bombing worked, what it did and what it meant, this is the book to read."

OWENS, DAVID. Shaping the normative landscape; [by] David Owens x, 260 p. 2012 Oxford University Press

1. Friendship 2. Philosophical literature 3. Promises 4. Social norms—Philosophy 5. Social sciences—Philosophy

ISBN 0199691509; 9780199691500

LC 2012-406948

SUMMARY: This book "is an investigation of the value of obligations and of rights, of forgiveness, of consent and refusal, of promise and request. David Owens shows that these are all instruments by which we exercise control over our normative environment. . . . Owens explores how we control the rights and obligations of ourselves and of those around us. We do so by making friends and . . . making promises." (Publisher's note)

REVIEW: *Choice* v50 no11 p2028 Jl 2013 S. E. Forschler

REVIEW: *Ethics* v124 no1 p201-5 O 2013 ALIDA LIBERMAN

REVIEW: *TLS* no5768 p7-8 O 18 2013 ALLAN GIBBARD

"Shaping the Normative Landscape" and "Normative Bedrock" Response-Dependence, Rationality, and Reasons." "[David] Owens's many examples convince me that this really is how we understand promises. . . . Central to Owens's book is the claim that a nonnative status can matter even apart from the good its recognition fosters. Not all acts are for goods, and some of our interests are purely normative. . . . Response-dependence has been at the centre of much discussion of normative concepts in recent decades, but understanding the response in terms of goal puzzlement is [Joshua] Gert's distinctive contribution, as far as I know. . . . Both books are models of philosophy as a cumulative enterprise that builds originally on what has been done before. Each changes one's view of an important subject."

OWENS, JOHN. Confessions of a bad teacher; the shocking truth from the front lines of American public education; [by] John Owens 272 p. 2013 Sourcebooks Inc

1. Education—United States—Anecdotes 2. Educational change—United States 3. Educational literature 4. Public schools—United States 5. Teachers—United States

ISBN 9781402281006

LC 2013-001619

SUMMARY: This book describes how author John Owens "changed careers at midlife to follow his heart and become a teacher. It took him less than one year in a South Bronx high school to be branded as 'unsatisfactory' by the 'crazed' and 'delusional' principal as well as other administrators of the 'charter style' high school. . . . Owens purports that rather than providing support and mentoring, administrators offered empty buzzwords and window dressing and pasted over problems throughout the school." (Library Journal)

REVIEW: *Booklist* v109 no22 p6-10 Ag 1 2013 Carolyn Saper

REVIEW: *Choice* v51 no9 p1651 My 2014 K. Layton

"Confessions of a Bad Teacher: The Shocking Truth From the Front Lines of American Public Education". "[John] Owens also provides the reader with insights into how high school has changed, his frustration trying to fulfill his district's expectations, how justifiable decisions placed him at odds with administrators, the limitations of teacher assessment systems, and the unfortunate truths about cheating in today's high schools. His story exposes many of the nightmares that public school teachers encounter. However, Owens develops a positive discussion about what he learned and how everyone can help. The language is rough in this challenging, emotional read, but Owens's passion for meaningful reform is real."

REVIEW: *Kirkus Rev* v81 no12 p62 Je 15 2013

REVIEW: *Libr J* v138 no15 p82 S 15 2013 Maggie Knapp

REVIEW: *Publ Wkly* v260 no21 p51 My 27 2013

OWL, WILLIAM.il. Sam and Charlie (and Sam Too) return! See Kimmelman, L.

THE OXFORD ANTHOLOGY OF ROMAN LITERATURE; 640 p. 2013 Oxford University Press
1. Latin literature—History and criticism 2. Latin literature—Translations into English
ISBN 9780195395150 (hardcover: alk. paper); 9780195395167 (pbk.: alk. paper)
LC 2012-036950

SUMMARY: This book, edited by Peter E. Knox and J. C. McKeown, is an anthology of ancient Roman literature from "between the second century BC and the second century AD. . . . Most of the authors included in the anthology wrote in Latin, but as the anthology moves forward in time, relevant Greek texts that reflect the cultural diversity of Roman literary life are also included. . . . Texts in this volume were chosen from a broad range of genres: drama, epic, philosophy, satire, lyric poetry, love poetry." (Publisher's note)

REVIEW: *Choice* v51 no9 p1590 My 2014 J. S. Louzonis
"The Oxford Anthology of Roman Literature". "Distinguished scholars [Peter E.] Knox . . . and [J. C.] McKeown . . .present this excellent anthology as a 'general introduction to the literature of the Roman world at its zenith.' The book succeeds admirably. . . . The selections are judiciously culled from the period's most distinguished authors. The brief but important chapter on the Roman world of books, including their production and their consumption—a topic not commonly addressed in anthologies of this type—is of particular contextual value. Most significantly, the editors are innovative in juxtaposing texts originally written in Latin with some composed in Greek, reflecting the dualistic linguistic and literary realities of this period of the Roman hegemony."

THE OXFORD CRITICAL AND CULTURAL HISTORY OF MODERNIST MAGAZINES; 2 p. 2009 Oxford University Press
1. Historical literature 2. Literature and society—History—19th century 3. Literature and society—History—20th century 4. Little magazines—History—19th century 5. Little magazines—History—20th century 6. North American literature
ISBN 0199211159; 9780199211159 (v. 1: hardcover: acid-free paper); 9780199545810 (v. 2: hardcover: acid-free paper); 9780199681303 (v. 3, pt. 1: hardcover: acid-free paper); 9780199681310 (v. 3, pt. 2: hardcover: acid-free paper)
LC 2009-280149

SUMMARY: This book looks at the "wide and varied range of 'little magazines' which were so instrumental in introducing the new writing and ideas that came to constitute literary and cultural modernism. This book contains forty-four original essays on the role of periodicals in the United States and Canada. Over 120 magazines are discussed." Topics include "free verse; drama and criticism; regionalism; exiles in Europe; the Harlem Renaissance; and radical politics". (Publisher's note)

REVIEW: *London Rev Books* v36 no2 p33-5 Ja 23 2014 Evan Kindley
"The Oxford Critical and Cultural History of Modernist Magazines: Britain & Ireland 1880-1955," "The Oxford Critical and Cultural History of Modernist Magazines: North America 1894-1955," "The Oxford Critical and Cultural History of Modernist Magazines: Europe 1880-1940". "A synoptic view of the modernist little magazine is very hard to come by, especially given that, on top of the sheer volume of the material, there are problems of definition. . . . 'The origins of the small review are lost in obscurity,' Ezra Pound wrote in his 1930 essay 'Small Magazines', but [Peter] Brooker and [Andrew] Thacker do their best to reconstruct them."

THE OXFORD ENCYCLOPEDIA OF BIBLICAL INTERPRETATION; 1164 p. 2013 Oxford University Press
1. Bible—Canonical criticism 2. Bible—Gay interpretations 3. Encyclopedias & dictionaries
ISBN 0199832269; 9780199832262 (set : alk. paper); 9780199993352 (v. 1 : alk. paper); 9780199993369 (v. 2 : alk. paper)
LC 2012-041156

SUMMARY: This encyclopedia, edited by Steven McKenzie, provides "detailed, comprehensive treatments of the latest approaches to and methods for interpretation of the Bible written by expert practitioners. It will provide a single source for authoritative reference overviews of scholarship on some of the most important topics of study in the field of biblical studies." (Publisher's note)

REVIEW: *Booklist* v110 no12 p41 F 15 2014 Wade Osburn
"The Oxford Encyclopedia of Biblical Interpretation." "The set offers a well-balanced mix of premodern approaches . . modern approaches . . . and the postmodern. . . . Those looking for information on how a particular religious group interprets scripture will be especially pleased. . . . The average article length throughout is 8-10 pages, which is not too much or too little for the academic crowd this series is targeting. . . . Every article also comes with a bibliography, too--all of this from the kind of top-notch contributors one expects from an Oxford published work. Highly recommended for academic libraries."

REVIEW: *Choice* v51 no9 p1566 My 2014 D. R. Stewart

THE OXFORD ENCYCLOPEDIA OF ISLAM AND WOMEN; 1428 p. 2013 Oxford University Press
1. Encyclopedias & dictionaries 2. Families—Religious aspects—Islam 3. Islam & gender 4. Women—Islamic countries 5. Women in Islam—Encyclopedias
ISBN 9780199764464; 9780199998036; 9780199998043
LC 2012-050203

SUMMARY: "This two-volume work focuses specifically on Islam and women. Issues related to women are primarily seen through the lens of contemporary gender studies. However, Islamic themes are seen not only as those related to the practice of the faith but also as those that relate to the diverse cultures of the Muslim peoples and governance of countries that have sizable Muslim populations or Muslim empires." (Booklist)

REVIEW: *Booklist* v110 no11 p48 F 1 2014 Muhammed Hassanali

REVIEW: *Choice* v51 no9 p1566 My 2014 J. Hammer
"The Oxford Encyclopedia of Islam and Women". "The collection of 450-plus alphabetically arranged entries is a

serious and impressive attempt at putting women (and gender) at the center of attention without simplistically refuting stereotypes of Muslim women and Islam or replacing them with equally problematic celebrations of women's roles and achievements. Many of the entries succeed in striking a balance between informational content and nuance as well as historical trajectory and contemporary relevance. As with most collections of this kind, the quality of the entries varies, as do the bibliographies supplied for each topic."

REVIEW: *Libr J* v139 no2 p98 F 1 2014 Amanda K. Sprochi

THE OXFORD ENCYCLOPEDIA OF THE BIBLE AND ARCHAEOLOGY; 1188 p. 2013 Oxford University Press

1. Antiquities—Social aspects 2. Encyclopedias & dictionaries 3. Excavations (Archaeology)—Palestine—Encyclopedias

ISBN 9780199846535 (set : alk. paper); 9780199996551 (v. 1 : alk. paper); 9780199996568 (v. 2 : alk. paper)

LC 2012-042595

SUMMARY: It was the authors' intent "to use archaeological evidence to provide context about the lives and culture of the writers of the biblical texts, not to reconstruct textual history or to link individual finds to specific passages. The 130 signed, alphabetically arranged articles cover individual archaeological sites, regions, and general topics such as material culture; each is followed by a bibliography and cross-references." (Library Journal)

REVIEW: *Choice* v51 no5 p812-3 Ja 2014 J. W. Wright

"The Oxford Encyclopedia of the Bible and Archaeology." "Some of this two-volume set's material appears in Oxford Biblical Studies Online . . . but these print volumes present in-depth coverage of the Bible and archaeology. . . . Two helpful innovations stand out. First, the volumes place social-historical entries alongside archaeological sites/regions; second, the entries spread geographically into the wider Mediterranean world . . . and chronologically into Hellenistic/Roman times. . . . The Persian period often is shortchanged. . . . Additionally, area editors seem to have chosen writers sympathetic to their positions. Despite these reservations, this set provides a useful entry into the changing field of the Bible and archaeology for students, scholars, and others."

THE OXFORD GUIDE TO THE HISTORICAL RECEPTION OF AUGUSTINE; 1930 p. 2013 Oxford University Press

1. Augustine, Saint, Bishop of Hippo, 354-430 2. Church history 3. Reference books 4. Religious literature 5. Theology

ISBN 0199299161; 9780199299164

SUMMARY: This is a "reference work on the thought and work of St. Augustine of Hippo (354-430). . . . Volume 1 includes a general introduction, thematic essays on broad issues of Augustinian influence, and then an entry on each of Augustine's works. Volumes 2 and 3 function as a collective encyclopedia, with 600-plus entries on individuals, themes, events, and doctrines that are relevant to the historical reception of Augustine." (Choice: Current Reviews for Academic Libraries)

REVIEW: *Choice* v51 no7 p1184 Mr 2014 J. P. Blosser

"The Oxford Guide to the Historical Reception of Augustine." "This guide is a magnificent, long-anticipated reference work on the thought and work of St. Augustine of Hippo (354-430), perhaps the most influential Christian thinker in history. . . . The present work . . . is a must for serious scholars of theology, philosophy, and the history of ideas generally. Research libraries will want to secure a copy. Its bulk, cost, and highly technical nature, however, will limit its usefulness to the general population, including undergraduate students. . . . Essential."

THE OXFORD HANDBOOK OF COGNITIVE PSYCHOLOGY; xx, 1076 p. 2013 Oxford University Press

1. Cognition 2. Cognitive psychology 3. Emotions (Psychology) 4. Memory 5. Psychological literature 6. Theory of knowledge

ISBN 0195376749; 9780195376746 (hbk.)

LC 2012-028873

SUMMARY: This book on cognitive psychology examines "all aspects of cognition, spanning perceptual issues, attention, memory, knowledge representation, language, emotional influences, judgment, problem solving, and the study of individual differences in cognition. Additional chapters turn to the control of complex actions and the social, cultural, and developmental context of cognition." (Publisher's note)

REVIEW: *Choice* v50 no12 p2322 Ag 2013 G. C. Gamst

THE OXFORD HANDBOOK OF HAPPINESS; xxx, 1097 p. 2013 Oxford University Press

1. Happiness 2. Joy 3. Psychological literature 4. Satisfaction 5. Well-being

ISBN 019955725X (hbk.); 9780199557257 (hbk.)

LC 2012-538502

SUMMARY: This book, edited by Susan David, Ilona Boniwell, and Amanda Conley Ayers, "focus[es] on psychological, philosophical, evolutionary, economic and spiritual approaches to happiness; happiness in society, education, organisations and relationships; and the assessment and development of happiness. Readers will find information on psychological constructs such as resilience, flow, and emotional intelligence." (Publisher's note)

REVIEW: *Choice* v51 no1 p169-70 S 2013 R. B. Stewart Jr.

"The Oxford Handbook of Happiness." "'The Oxford Handbook of Happiness' contains 79 chapters written by world leaders in the investigation of happiness across the fields of psychology, philosophy, economics, business administration, education, and social policy. The volume is organized into ten sections that focus on the psychological, philosophical, evolutionary, economic, and spiritual approaches to happiness; on happiness experienced at a societal level, in educational and business institutions, and in interpersonal relationships; and on various assessments of happiness and the potential to augment the experience of happiness through interventions. The handbook offers readers a coherent, multidisciplinary, and accessible book on the current study of happiness."

THE OXFORD HANDBOOK OF KIERKEGAARD; xx, 610 p. 2013 Oxford University Press

1. German philosophy—19th century 2. Kierkegaard,

Søren, 1813-1855 3. Philosophical literature 4. Philosophy, Danish 5. Theology & philosophy
ISBN 0199601305; 9780199601301
LC 2013-409402

SUMMARY: This book, edited by John Lippitt and George Pattison, explores the work of the philosopher Soren Kierkegaard. It "presents some of the philological, historical and contextual work . . . [It then] moves from context and background to the exposition of some of the key ideas and issues in Kierkegaard's writings." Conclusions examine the "impact of Kierkegaard's thought and at how it continues to influence philosophy, theology, and literature." (Publisher's note)

REVIEW: *Choice* v51 no2 p277-8 O 2013 P. K. Moser

"The Oxford Handbook of Kierkegaard." "[Editors John] Lippitt . . . and [George] Pattison . . . organized this handbook's coverage into three main parts: 'Contexts and Sources,' 'Some Major Topics in the Authorship,' and 'Kierkegaard after Kierkegaard.' Three chapters seem particularly helpful to understanding Kierkegaard: David Law's 'Kierkegaard and the History of Theology,' in part 1; Sylvia Walsh's 'Kierkegaard's Theology,' in part 2; and John Lippitt's 'Kierkegaard and Moral Philosophy,' in part 3. . . . The contributors include a number of well-established Kierkegaard scholars, and all chapters conclude with references and suggested readings. Many chapters will be helpful to students and researchers engaged with the writings of Kierkegaard."

THE OXFORD HANDBOOK OF MANAGEMENT THEORISTS; xix, 592 p. 2013 Oxford University Press
1. Business literature 2. Leadership 3. Management—History 4. Management—Philosophy 5. Management science
ISBN 0199585768; 9780199585762
LC 2012-537456

SUMMARY: This book "examines and evaluates the contributions that seminal figures, past and present, have made to the theory of management. . . . It is arranged in three parts: pioneers of management thinking from Frederick Taylor to Chester Barnard; post-war theorists, such as the Tavistock Institute and Edith Penrose; and the later phase of Business School theorists, including Alfred Chandler, Michael Porter, and Ikujiro Nonaka." (Publisher's note)

REVIEW: *Choice* v51 no6 p1058-9 F 2014 E. J. Wood

"The Oxford Handbook of Management Theorists." "Editors [Morgen] Witzel and [Malcolm] Warner, well-published UK academics, are admirably suited to compile this readable, informative handbook covering seminal 19th-21st-century management theorists. . . . In addition to recognizing pioneering theorists . . . the handbook aims to keep the work of more recent seminal figures . . . in the forefront of current management dialogue. Rigorous inclusion criteria were employed in selecting theorists. . . . Because it spotlights general management theory and covers earliest management theorists through contemporary thinkers likely to influence generations of successors, this work is at once broader and narrower in scope than similar handbooks."

THE OXFORD HANDBOOK OF PERCY BYSSHE SHELLEY; 2013 Oxford University Press
1. Biographies 2. English poets 3. Poets—Biography 4. Romanticism in literature 5. Shelley, Percy Bysshe, 1792-1822
ISBN 9780199558360

SUMMARY: This book, edited by Michael O'Neill, Anthony Howe, and Madeleine Callaghan, focuses on "the study of . . . major Romantic poet and prose-writer [Percy Bysshe Shelley]. . . . This Handbook is divided into five thematic sections: Biography and Relationships; Prose; Poetry; Cultures, Traditions, Influences; and Afterlives." (Publisher's note)

REVIEW: *Choice* v51 no2 p261-2 O 2013 D. A. Robinson

"The Oxford Handbook of Percy Bysshe Shelley." "[Editors Michael] O'Neill . . . and [Anthony] Howe . . . , with [Madeleine] Callaghan . . . , have assembled 42 essayists, some well-established experts in the field and some newly emerging scholars. They provide an astonishingly thorough examination of Shelley's literary career, which lasted a relatively short period--only a little more than ten years compared with, for example, Wordsworth's 60 years as a poet. As a collection of eminently readable essays, this volume is a splendid accomplishment, presenting a dynamic, fascinating, thoughtful, and hard-working Shelley who accomplished more, saw more, imagined and thought more in those ten years than most writers do in a lifetime."

THE OXFORD HANDBOOK OF QUAKER STUDIES; 2013 Oxford University Press
ISBN 9780199608676

SUMMARY: This book, edited by Stephen W. Angell and Pink Dandelion, a "reference work for the study of Quakerism. . . . In addition to an in-depth survey of historical readings of Quakerism, the handbook provides a treatment of the group's key theological premises and its links with wider Christian thinking. Quakerism's distinctive ecclesiastical forms and practices are analyzed, and its social, economic, political, and ethical outcomes examined." (Publisher's note)

REVIEW: *Choice* v51 no9 p1611-2 My 2014 J. H. Sniegocki

"The Oxford Handbook of Quaker Studies". "This volume is the most comprehensive interdisciplinary study of global Quakerism available. . . . Each chapter includes suggestions for further reading, and the book concludes with a very extensive bibliography. Academic in tone and style, this volume would not be the best choice for readers seeking an inspirational or devotional introduction to Quaker spirituality. It is, however, an indispensable resource for anyone interested in the academic study of Quakerism."

THE OXFORD HANDBOOK OF SHAKESPEARE'S POETRY; 2013 Oxford University Press
1. English poetry—History & criticism 2. Literature—History & criticism 3. Narrative poetry 4. Shakespeare, William, 1564-1616—Criticism & interpretation 5. Shakespeare, William, 1564-1616—Poetic works
ISBN 9780199607747

SUMMARY: This book, edited by Jonathan Post, "contains thirty-eight original essays written by leading Shakespeareans around the world. . . . The volume understands poetry to be not just a formal category designating a particular literary genre but to be inclusive of the dramatic verse as well . . . . The largest section, with ten essays, is devoted to the poems themselves: the Sonnets, plus 'A Lover's Complaint', the narrative poems, Venus and Adonis and The Rape of Lucrece, and 'The Phoenix and the Turtle'. (Publisher's note)

REVIEW: *Choice* v51 no7 p1215-6 Mr 2014 F. L. Den

"The Oxford Handbook of Shakespeare's Poetry." "Broad in scope, but focused in purpose. . . . There is a relative lack of engagement with the body of criticism that the book as a whole sets itself up against. . . . only Russ McDonald directly addresses (and takes seriously) the problems with materialist criticism hinted at in [Jonathan F. S.] Post's introduction. However, these essays will likely be quite useful in that they provide robust models of careful close reading, and a wide range of commentary that does not limit itself to Shakespeare's offstage literary activities."

REVIEW: *TLS* no5783 p12 Ja 31 2014 ELIZA BETH SCOTT-BAUMANN

THE OXFORD HANDBOOK OF THE EUROPEAN BRONZE AGE; xxxi, 979 p. 2013 Oxford University Press

1. Archaeological literature 2. Bronze Age metalwork 3. Bronze Age pottery 4. Bronze age—Europe

ISBN 0199572860; 9780199572861
LC 2012-277727

SUMMARY: This book, edited by Harry Fokkens and Anthony Harding, focuses on the Bronze Age, a "period in prehistory during which many social, economic, and technological changes took place. . . . Chapters deal with settlement studies, burial analysis, hoards and hoarding, monumentality, rock art, cosmology, gender, and trade, as well as a series of articles on specific technologies and crafts. . . . The second half of the book covers each [European] country in turn." (Publisher's note)

REVIEW: *Choice* v51 no7 p1265-6 Mr 2014 R. B. Clay

"The Oxford Handbook of the European Bronze Age." "The volume makes accessible in English summaries of work by specialists writing in many European languages, one of the book's strongest points. Each article includes an up-to-date bibliography in both English and continental languages. The individual pieces are well written, authoritative, and appropriately illustrated with geographical reference maps and photographs of artifacts, plans, and reconstructions of structures and settlements. . . . All of this makes the volume a useful tool for scholars of the period and their students."

THE OXFORD HANDBOOK OF THE PSYCHOLOGY OF WORKING; 346 p. 2013 Oxford University Press

1. Psychological literature 2. Psychotherapy—Social aspects 3. Social policy 4. Vocational guidance 5. Work—Psychological aspects 6. Work—Social aspects

ISBN 0199758794 (alk. paper); 9780199758791 (alk. paper)
LC 2012-045385

SUMMARY: In this book, the contributors "address theories informing the psychology of working; demographic, social, racial, class, gender, sexual orientation, family structure, and disabilities characteristics impacting experiences of working; the meaning of these theories/differences for work and organizations; roles, practices, and implications for working-related counseling and psychotherapy; and current/necessary public policy/reform to address working-related needs." (Publisher's note)

REVIEW: *Choice* v51 no6 p1099-100 F 2014 D. Truty

"The Oxford Handbook of the Psychology of Working." "This text is part of the 'Oxford Library of Psychology.' Per [David L.] Blustein . . . working appears to be pivotal in people's lives. Its role for those in diverse life situations and its implications for behavior lack focused psychological attention. Here scholars analyze research to expose/advance a more comprehensive perspective. . . . The book's look and feel, and the authors' writing styles, are scholarly/professional. This volume is interesting/relevant/accessible for readers beyond the psychological field. Blustein has received multiple practitioner/researcher awards and has written extensively on work-related topics."

OYEYEMI, HELEN. Boy, snow, bird; a novel; [by] Helen Oyeyemi 320 p. 2014 Riverhead Hardcover

1. FICTION—Fairy Tales, Folk Tales, Legends & Mythology 2. FICTION—General 3. FICTION—Literary 4. Fairy tales—Adaptations 5. Passing (Identity)—Fiction 6. Race relations—Fiction

ISBN 1594631395; 9781594631399 (hardback)
LC 2013-025053

SUMMARY: This novel, by Helen Oyeyemi, retells the "Snow White fairy tale . . . as a story of family secrets, race, beauty, and vanity. In the winter of 1953, Boy Novak arrives by chance in a small town in Massachusetts, . . . marries a local widower and becomes stepmother to his . . . daughter, Snow Whitman. . . . The birth of Boy's daughter, Bird, who is dark-skinned, exposes the Whitmans as light-skinned African Americans passing for white." (Publisher's note)

REVIEW: *Booklist* v110 no13 p16-8 Mr 1 2014 Kristine Huntley

"Boy, Snow, Bird." "The author of 'Mr. Fox' . . . whimsical retelling of a classic fairy tale in 1950s Massachusetts, where beautiful young Boy Novak has fled her tyrannical, abusive father to seek a fresh start. She makes two friends, glamorous Webster and ambitious Mia, and exchanges her lovelorn hometown suitor for a history teacher turned jewelry maker named Arturo Whitman, whom she marries despite not quite coming to love him. . . . [Helen] Oyeyemi delves deeply into the nature of identity and the cost of denying it in this contemplative, layered novel."

REVIEW: *Kirkus Rev* v82 no2 p207 Ja 15 2014

REVIEW: *Libr J* v139 no3 p99 F 15 2014 Lisa Block

REVIEW: *Libr J* v138 no18 p105 N 1 2013 Molly McArdle

REVIEW: *N Y Times Book Rev* p1-22 Mr 2 2014 Porochista Khakpour

REVIEW: *New Statesman* v143 no9 p45 Mr 7 2014 Helen Oyeyemi

REVIEW: *New Yorker* v90 no8 p83-1 Ap 14 2014

REVIEW: *Publ Wkly* v261 no1 p33 Ja 6 2014

REVIEW: *TLS* no5790 p20 Mr 21 2014 KATE WEBB

"Boy, Snow, Bird." "As her career progresses, [author Helen Oyeyemi] is developing into the kind of writer that A. S. Byatt described in 'Possession' (1990), one whose strong readings of stories seem 'wholly new,' while appearing to have been 'always there.' In her latest book this is even more strikingly apparent. 'Boy, Snow, Bird' reimagines 'Snow White' as a tale set in America at the birth of the Civil Rights movement. As old as this story is, and as often as it has been reworked, Oyeyemi finds meanings that we have failed to notice, even when they were staring us in the face."

ÖZBUDUN, ERGUN. Party politics & social cleavages in Turkey; [by] Ergun Özbudun x, 155 p. 2013 Lynne Rienner Publishers, Inc.

1. Core & periphery (Economic theory) 2. Political parties—Turkey 3. Political science literature 4. Social conflict—Turkey
ISBN 9781588269003 (alk. paper)
LC 2012-049139

SUMMARY: In this book, "Ergun Özbudun examines several selected aspects of party and electoral politics in Turkey. . . . The author devotes . . . two chapters to . . . the historical origins and dvelopment of the center-periphery cleavage in Turkey and its effects on the contemporary Turkish party system." Also discussed are "the electoral systems that have been used during the past 60 years of electoral politics and the current debates on electoral reforms." (Middle East Journal)

REVIEW: *Choice* v51 no4 p721-2 D 2013 R. W. Olson

REVIEW: *Middle East J* v67 no4 p653-5 Aut 2013 Sabri Sayari

"Party Politics and Social Cleavages in Turkey." "In his latest book, Ergun Özbudun examines several selected aspects of party and electoral politics in Turkey. . . . Özbudun . . . uses the center-periphery approach to explain the developments that have taken place in electoral politics since the early 1950s. . . . [The book] is informative, clearly written and provides a useful account of some of the key aspects of the country's party and electoral system. It will be an important source of reference for future studies on Turkish politics."

P

PÄÄBO, SVANTE. Neanderthal man; in search of lost genomes; [by] Svante Pääbo 288 p. 2014 Basic Books

1. Evolutionary theories 2. Genome analysis 3. Human population genetics 4. Neanderthals 5. Scientific literature
ISBN 0465020836; 9780465020836 (hardback)
LC 2013-041877

SUMMARY: Geneticist Svante Pääbo "recounts his ultimately successful efforts to genetically define what makes us different from our Neanderthal cousins. Beginning with the study of DNA in Egyptian mummies in the early 1980s and culminating in the sequencing of the Neanderthal genome in 2010, . . . we learn that Neanderthal genes offer a unique window into the lives of our hominin relatives and may hold the key to unlocking the mystery of why humans survived while Neanderthals went extinct." (Publisher's note)

REVIEW: *Booklist* v110 no11 p7 F 1 2014 Ray Olson

REVIEW: *Choice* v51 no12 p2209 Ag 2014 R. M. Denome

REVIEW: *Christ Century* v131 no9 p39 Ap 30 2014

REVIEW: *Harper's Magazine* v329 no1972 p76-81 S 1 2014 David Quammen

REVIEW: *Kirkus Rev* v82 no1 p111 Ja 1 2014

REVIEW: *Libr J* v139 no1 p1 Ja 2014

REVIEW: *N Y Rev Books* v61 no6 p48-51 Ap 3 2014 Steven Mithen

"Neanderthal Man: In Search of Lost Genomes" and "The Gap: The Science of What Separates Us From Other Animals." "Interminable academic arguments have been swept away by the revolution in studies of ancient DNA, led by [author Svante] Pääbo . . . and brilliantly recounted in his new book, 'Neanderthal Man: In Search of Lost Genomes.' Pääbo has provided us with a fabulous account of three decades of research into ancient DNA. . . . The 'prudent and cautious' analysis that [author Thomas] Suddendorf brings to the psychological evidence is lost when it comes to the Neanderthals. . . . Suddendorf's book . . . provides the most comprehensive comparison of the mentalities of humans and apes that one can imagine."

REVIEW: *N Y Times Book Rev* p30 Ap 27 2014

REVIEW: *N Y Times Book Rev* p17 Ap 20 2014 CARL ZIMMER

REVIEW: *New Sci* v221 no2950 p48 Ja 4 2014

"Neanderthal Man: In Search of Lost Genomes," "The Future of the Mind: The Scientific Quest to Understand, Enhance and Empower the Mind," and "Our Mathematical Universe: My Quest for the Ultimate Nature of Reality". "We're hoping for great things from geneticist Svante Pääbo, who in 2009 led the team that sequenced the first Neanderthal genome using DNA from 40,000-year-old bone. This is his story, which should prove to be a lens not only on pioneering scientific discovery but also on what makes us human. . . . We're keen to see what happens when the irrepressibly optimistic [Michio] Kaku turns his crystal ball to brain science and the future of human minds. His new book spans everything from smart pills that enhance cognition to placing our neural blueprint on laser beams sent out into space. . . . Max Tegmark, one of the world's leading theoretical physicists, opens up a deep and daring strand of thinking in this esoteric world."

REVIEW: *Publ Wkly* v260 no45 p59 N 11 2013

REVIEW: *Science* v345 no6194 p259 Jl 18 2014 Jeremy Chase Crawford

REVIEW: *TLS* no5797 p24 My 9 2014 GREGORY RADICK

"Neanderthal Man: In Search of Lost Genomes." "Neanderthal Man is [author Svante] Pääbo's memoir of his career as a hunter of 'ancient DNA,' culminating in the publication, in 2010, of a draft of the DNA sequence of the Neanderthal genome. . . . Like James Watson's 'The Double Helix' (1968), 'Neanderthal Man' is a coming-of-age story, as well as a somewhat disillusioning study of science in the making—though it is set in a professional world very different from the one Watson depicted. . . . Any book that gives a backstage view of a professional life risks reading like an amplified work diary. But what Svante Pääbo achieves . . . is to remove the aura of straightforwardness that clings to scientific facts like the one which he has so assiduously made his own."

PACK, JASON.ed. The 2011 Libyan uprisings and the struggle for the post-Qadhafi future. See The 2011 Libyan uprisings and the struggle for the post-Qadhafi future

PADFIELD, PETER. Hess, Hitler & Churchill; the real turning point of the Second World War : a secret history; [by] Peter Padfield xxxvi, 428 p. 2013 Icon

1. Historical literature 2. History—Errors, inventions, etc 3. World War, 1939-1945—Deception—Great Britain 4. World War, 1939-1945—Diplomatic history 5. World War, 1939-1945—Secret service—Great Britain
ISBN 184831602X (hardback); 9781848316027 (hard-

back)
LC 2013-432976

SUMMARY: This book by Peter Padfield investigates how, "when [Adolf] Hitler's deputy Rudolf Hess set off for Britain on a peace mission in May 1941, he launched one of the great mysteries of the Second World War. Had he really acted alone, without Hitler's knowledge? Who were the British he had come to see? Was British intelligence involved?" (Publisher's note)

REVIEW: *Hist Today* v64 no1 p60 Ja 2014 Roger Moorhouse

" Hess, Hitler & Churchill The Real Turning Point of the Second World War--A Secret History." "[Peter] Padfield is an accomplished writer and he has constructed a tale that rattles along with considerable pace and verve. He eschews most of the more elaborate conspiracy theories. . . . What Padfield does suggest is actually quite sensible. . . . However, in building his case, Padfield is forced to rely almost exclusively on circumstantial evidence. Understandably, perhaps, he has the barest scraps of archival sources, but the evidence that he presents is largely a melange of lost letters, missing documents, anonymous informants and unreliable witnesses. More seriously, the book tends to lean too heavily on conspiracy theories."

PAGEL, TEMPA. They danced by the light of the moon; an Andy Gammon mystery; [by] Tempa Pagel 316 p. 2014 Five Star, a part of Gale, Cengage Learning

1. FICTION—Mystery & Detective—General 2. Family secrets—Fiction 3. Historic hotels—Fiction 4. Murder—Investigation—Fiction 5. Women—Social conditions—Fiction

ISBN 1432827995 (hardcover); 9781432827991 (hardback)
LC 2013-038370

SUMMARY: This book follows "Andy Gammon, a former Detroit social studies teacher . . . [who] can't help getting involved whenever history meets mystery. . . . She can't resist sneaking through back hallways of a Victorian grand hotel and crawling through the underground tunnels of a derelict Gothic insane asylum as she seeks answers to why a woman was killed at the Grand Hotel of the Atlantic on the night of the reopening gala, why another woman disappeared from that same room a century ago." (Publisher's note)

REVIEW: *Kirkus Rev* v81 no24 p201 D 15 2013

"They Danced By the Light of the Moon". " A delightful dinner at a posh hotel ends in murder. Former social studies teacher Andy Gammon can never resist a historical mystery. But when she agrees to accompany her mother-in-law, Mayta, to the opening gala at the Grand Hotel of the Atlantic on the beautiful New Hampshire coast, she never imagines that she'll find a body or immerse herself in a turn-of-the-century mystery. . . . Like Andy's first case . . . this one is studded with flashbacks to the historical past, this time providing provocative insights into the now defunct system of asylums."

REVIEW: *Publ Wkly* v260 no52 p36-7 D 23 2013

PAINE, LINCOLN. The sea and civilization; a maritime history of the world; [by] Lincoln Paine 784 p. 2013 Knopf

1. Historical literature 2. Naval art and science—History 3. Naval history 4. Navigation—History 5. Ocean and civilization 6. Sea-power—History

ISBN 140004409X; 9781400044092 (hardback)
LC 2013-015436

SUMMARY: Author Lincoln Paine presents a "retelling of world history through the lens of maritime enterprise, revealing . . . how people first came into contact with one another by ocean and river, lake and stream, and how goods, languages, religions, and entire cultures spread across and along the world's waterways, bringing together civilizations and defining what makes us most human." (Publisher's note)

REVIEW: *Booklist* v110 no2 p26 S 15 2013 Gilbert Taylor

REVIEW: *Choice* v51 no7 p1278 Mr 2014 J. B. Richardson III

"The Sea and Civilization: A Maritime History of the World." "In 20 chapters, [Lincoln P.] Paine provides a comprehensive discussion of how the sea and inland waterways transformed long-distance communication and trade, leading to the rise and fall of a myriad of civilizations dependent on waterborne commerce for their economic gain and political control of vast regions of the globe. . . . This well-researched book (105 pages of footnotes and bibliography) will be used far into the future by students and scholars studying the importance of the oceans and waterways in the development of world civilizations from 5,000 years ago to the present . . . Highly recommended."

REVIEW: *Kirkus Rev* v81 no18 p135 S 15 2013

REVIEW: *New Statesman* v143 no5 p50-1 F 7 2014 Philip Hoare

REVIEW: *Publ Wkly* v260 no36 p48 S 9 2013

PAIVA, JOHANNAH GILMAN.ed. Hands On! Math Projects. See Hands On! Math Projects

PAK, KENARD.il. Have you heard the nesting bird? See Gray, R.

PAKKALA, CHRISTINE. Jasmine and Maddie; [by] Christine Pakkala 192 p. 2014 Boyds Mills Press

1. Friendship—Fiction 2. Middle school students 3. School stories 4. Theft 5. Truthfulness & falsehood

ISBN 9781620917398
LC 2013-956268

SUMMARY: In this book by Christine Pakkala, "Jasmine and her recently widowed mom move to Connecticut for a fresh start. As an eighth-grader living in a trailer park in an affluent community, feisty, hurting Jasmine encounters the painful pecking order of middle school. She meets wealthy, spacey, still-dressing-like-a-little-girl Maddie, who on the surface appears to be as different as possible from sarcastic, belligerent, chip-on-her-shoulder Jasmine." (Kirkus Reviews)

REVIEW: *Bull Cent Child Books* v67 no11 p588 Jl/Ag 2014 K. C.

REVIEW: *Kirkus Rev* v82 no3 p280 F 1 2014

"Jasmine and Maddie". "This friendship story is marred by contrivances. The ease and frequency of the girls' lying and stealing seem improbable, and in the span of three weeks at the beginning of school, each realizes she needs a friend. Poems interspersed throughout (both famous poems and ones penned by the students) and the message that poetry is cool are engaging touches, although the extemporaneous student poems seem far too polished to be credible. While no new ground is covered in [Christine] Pakkala's novel, the spot-on cover will entice readers who will identify with the pain of middle school, enjoy the well-developed secondary characters and applaud the girls' growth."

REVIEW: *SLJ* v60 no4 p151 Ap 2014 Kathy Cherniavsky

PALAHNIUK, CHUCK. Doomed; [by] Chuck Palahniuk 336 p. 2013 Random House Inc.

1. Dead—Fiction 2. Dystopias 3. Future life—Fiction 4. Ghosts—Fiction 5. Microblogs—Fiction

ISBN 0385533039 (hardcover); 9780385533034 (hardcover)

LC 2012-043095

SUMMARY: This book is a follow-up to Chuck Palahniuk's "Sniff, Pygmy and Tell-All." Here, Maddy continues to be trapped as a ghost in Hell. She "runs into her dead grandmother, then discovers her billionaire father shagging her rival from Hell. So there's that to fix. For better or worse, Madison is guided by Crescent City, a Ketamine-addicted paranormal detective who can see her during his frequent binges." (Kirkus Reviews)

REVIEW: *Booklist* v109 no17 p52 My 1 2013 Brad Hooper

REVIEW: *Booklist* v109 no21 p49 Jl 1 2013 David Pitt

REVIEW: *Kirkus Rev* v81 no2 p25 Je 1 2013

REVIEW: *Kirkus Rev* p13 2013 Guide 20to BookExpo America

REVIEW: *Libr J* v138 no14 p101 S 1 2013 Brooke Bolton

REVIEW: *New Yorker* v89 no42 p127-1 D 23 2013

"Doomed." "This sequel to 'Damned,' from 2011, continues the adventures of a dead thirteen-year-old girl named Madison Spencer. . . . Read generously, the narrative might be seen as a satire of contemporary materialism and spirituality. But, while satire need not necessarily be funny, it should, at least, be clever. This novel is neither: Palahniuk considers old ideas--celebrities are vacuous; liberals are intolerant; organized religion relies on hypocrisy--in a prose style that is relentlessly puerile and crass."

REVIEW: *Publ Wkly* v260 no26 p61 Jl 1 2013

REVIEW: *TLS* no5770 p20 N 1 2013 LUKE NEIMA

PALDA, FILIP. The Apprentice Economist; Seven Steps to Mastery; [by] Filip Palda 292 p. 2013 Cooper Wolfling

1. Economics literature 2. Equilibrium (Economics) 3. Game theory 4. Prices 5. Substitution (Economics)

ISBN 0987788043; 9780987788047

SUMMARY: This book by Filip Palda presents a "seven-step framework for grasping . . . economic principles. "The opening chapter" covers "substitution." The author "backs up his apprenticeship program with liberal references to a select group of economists, including a few Nobel laureates. He then considers questions of time, chance, space and equilibrium from an economic perspective, which leads to final chapters on game theory and control." (Kirkus Reviews)

REVIEW: *Kirkus Rev* v82 no3 p377 F 1 2014

"The Apprentice Economist: Seven Steps to Mastery". "A highly challenging, seven-step framework for grasping mind-bending economic principles. . . . It's distinctly disappointing . . . when the opening chapter, on the weighty subject of substitution, sinks at once into a tedious explanation of how price and budget will determine how many cans of caviar and beans a consumer may buy—which unfortunately elicits the cliché of economist-as-bean-counter. Happily, the book recovers nearly immediately, and the concept gradually emerges in its overarching splendor, ably explicated by the author. . . . That said, the book's often opaque economics jargon can be overwhelming, and whole pages may go by with average readers catching no more than smidgens of meaning."

PALIN, SARAH, 1964-. Good tidings and great joy; protecting the heart of Christmas; [by] Sarah Palin 256 p. 2013 HarperCollins

1. Christianity 2. Christmas 3. Consumption (Economics)—Religious aspects—Christianity 4. Jesus Christ—Nativity 5. Religious literature

ISBN 0062292889; 9780062292889

SUMMARY: In this book, author Sarah Palin "calls foul on the incremental disintegration of the Yuletide season by those who seek to reinvent the holiday by removing the religious element. . . . The outspoken conservative points the finger at American atheists offended by religious crosses and the presentation of Nativity scenes. Palin's ruffled feathers are due in large part to the corporatization of Christmas." (Kirkus Reviews)

REVIEW: *Kirkus Rev* v81 no24 p294 D 15 2013

"Good Tidings and Great Joy: Protecting the Heart of Christmas". "The former Alaska governor searches for the culprit leeching the joy out of Christian Christmas. . . . The author tritely dismisses the media altogether and shows great dismay toward a nation increasingly rethinking its religious allegiances. At the very least, Palin is very occasionally entertaining as she displays her conservative convictions across the diminutive pages of this stylishly produced book, which concludes with a chapter of traditional family sweet and savory recipes. A stocking stuffer for [Sarah] Palin fans."

PALKA, KURT. Clara; [by] Kurt Palka 384 p. 2014 McClelland & Stewart

1. Austria—Fiction 2. Friendship—Fiction 3. Historical fiction 4. Military spouses 5. World War, 1939-1945—Fiction

ISBN 9780771071300 (e-bk.); 9780771071324 (pbk.)

LC 2013-938801

SUMMARY: This historical novel follows " Clara Herzog . . . a privileged, intelligent, and thoughtful young woman whose world is changed forever when 1930s Vienna is swept up by the dark prelude of the Second World War. The cavalry officer she married in spite of her family's objections is soon called away to the thick of the conflict, and it falls to Clara, as to so many mothers, wives, sisters, and sweethearts through the centuries, to stay at home to provide and protect." (Publisher's note)

REVIEW: *Booklist* v110 no14 p56 Mr 15 2014 Cortney Ophoff

"Clara." "Told in flashbacks after Albert's death decades later, Clara's tale is part love story, part tribute to the women and families left behind and the terrible hardships they faced with great dignity during the war. [Kurt] Palka weaves an intimate tapestry of the Austrian home front and the philosophies and mind-sets of the time. Unflinching in its realism yet devoid of sensationalism, 'Clara' showcases Palka's great attention to detail, which enhances an already beautiful and deeply moving story of hope, love, and triumph."

PALLOTTA, JERRY. Butterfly colors and counting; 10 p. 2013 Charlesbridge

1. Butterflies—Identification 2. Butterflies—Juvenile literature 3. Colors—Juvenile literature 4. Counting 5. Picture books for children

ISBN 9781570918995 (board bk.)

LC 2012-934528

SUMMARY: "In this board book by Jerry Pallotta, award-winning author of several alphabet and counting books for young children, readers will learn how to count to ten while learning the colors of the rainbow—plus some fun patterns as a bonus. Shennen Bersani's realistic and colorful art depicts ten real butterfly species, both common and rare, from around the world." (Publisher's note)

REVIEW: *Kirkus Rev* v81 no4 p363 F 15 2013

REVIEW: *Kirkus Rev* v81 no13 p11 Jl 1 2013

REVIEW: *Publ Wkly* v260 no4 p177 Ja 28 2013

THE PALM BEACH EFFECT; Reflections on Michael Hofmann; 256 p. 2012 CB Editions

1. Hofmann, Michael, 1957- 2. Literary critiques 3. London (England)—History—1951- 4. Poets 5. University of Florida

ISBN 0957326602; 9780957326606

SUMMARY: This book, edited by André Naffis-Sahely and Julian Stannard, is a tribute to poet Michael Hofmann. It includes "essays on particular aspects of Hofmann's work, poems, memories of 1980s literary London and reports from some of Hofmann's former students at the University of Florida. . . . The book includes a bibliography and a frontispiece portrait of Michael Hofmann by Arturo Di Stefano." (Publisher's note)

REVIEW: *TLS* no5749 p26-7 Je 7 2013 SIMON POMERY

"The Palm Beach Effect: Reflections on Michael Hofmann." "This is an appropriately unorthodox celebration of Michael Hofmann . . . the influential poet, translator and critic. . . . These forty 'reflections', from poets, novelists, literary critics, translators and former students, bring focus to his career to date. . . . The enthusiasm for Hofmann would have seemed stronger, more concise (like a Hofmann poem) had this book been shorter. It is a curious editorial decision to place George Szirtes's baffiingly un-Hofmannesque "Hofmannesque" towards the end of the book, since the last poetic word becomes bathetic."

PALMER-SMITH, GLENN. Murals of New York City; 228 p. 2013 Rizzoli International Publications

1. American mural painting & decoration 2. New York (N.Y.)—Social life & customs—20th century 3. New York (N.Y.) art scene 4. Photograph collections 5. Public art

ISBN 9780847841486

LC 2013-934332

SUMMARY: Written by Glenn Palmer-Smith, with photography by Joshua McHugh, this "is the first book to curate over thirty of the most important, influential, and impressive murals found within all five boroughs. The murals featured in this volume act as both an artistic and cultural guide to New York and its citizens over the past 100+ years." (Publisher's note)

REVIEW: *N Y Times Book Rev* p42 D 8 2013 JIAYANG FAN

"The Best of New York's Public Paintings From Bemelmans to Parrish." "In 'Murals of New York City' . . . , which features more than 30 large-scale works around the city, the muralist Glenn Palmer-Smith and the photographer Joshua McHugh tutor natives and tourists alike in how these walls--and a few ceilings--can best be appreciated. . . . Unlike works of art produced in the privacy of a studio, murals are often subject to judgment--by the public and by the patrons who pay for them--from conception to completion."

PALMER, DONALD. Normal organizational wrongdoing; a critical analysis of theories of misconduct in and by organizations; [by] Donald Palmer xv, 313 p. 2012 Oxford University Press

1. Business ethics 2. Commercial crimes 3. Corporations—Corrupt practices 4. Organizational behavior

ISBN 019957359X; 9780199573592

LC 2011-942651

SUMMARY: In this book on organizational misconduct, author Donald Palmer "examin[es] wrongdoing as a normal occurrence, produced by actors with no positive inclinations to engage in this practice, but whose behaviour is shaped by the immediate social context over a period of time. The book provides a comprehensive critical review of the theory and research on organizational wrongdoing." (Publisher's note)

REVIEW: *Contemp Sociol* v43 no2 p176-80 Mr 2014 Carol A. Caronna

"Normal Organizational Wrongdoing: A Critical Analysis of Theories of Misconduct in and By Organizations". "[Donald] Palmer's book is both important and timely. . . . He provides thorough and careful descriptions and illustrations of eight specific explanations of organizational wrongdoing which he categorizes by two overarching perspectives and two ideal-typical approaches. . . . Throughout the book, Palmer makes it clear that he does not believe in the supremacy of any one theory. Thus one of the contributions of this book is a clear and comprehensive overview of each theory of wrongdoing, including those he finds less robust."

PALMISANO, JOSEPH REDFIELD. Beyond the walls; Abraham Joshua Heschel and Edith Stein on the significance of empathy for Jewish-Christian dialogue; [by] Joseph Redfield Palmisano x, 186 p. 2013 Oxford University Press

1. Christianity & other religions—Judaism 2. Christianity and other religions—Judaism 3. Empathy 4. Empathy—Religious aspects—Christianity 5. Empathy—Religious aspects—Judaism 6. Heschel, Abraham Joshua, 1907-1972 7. Holocaust, Jewish (1939-1945) 8. Interfaith dialogue 9. Judaism—Relations—Christianity 10. Religious literature 11. Stein, Edith, Saint, 1891-1942

ISBN 9780199925025 (hardcover : alk. paper); 9780199925032 (ebook)

LC 2012-002981

SUMMARY: In this book, author "Joseph Palmisano offers an in-depth examination of the significance of empathy for Jewish-Christian understanding" that draws "on the writings of Rabbi Abraham Joshua Heschel (1907-1972) and Edith Stein (1891-1942). . . . Palmisano follows Heschel's and Stein's philosophical theory and praxis through the unprecedented horrors of the Shoah." (Publisher's note)

REVIEW: *America* v209 no12 p52-3 O 28 2013 BRENNA MOORE

"Beyond the Walls: Abraham Joshua Heschel and Edith Stein on the Significance of Empathy for Jewish-Christian Dialogue." "Joseph Palmisano, S.J., advances a startling claim: Edith Stein's forced removal from her Carmelite monastery in 1942 and her subsequent murder at Auschwitz stand before us as 'a prophetic sign of our times' and a model for 'interreligious dialogue.' . . . At the center of Palmisano's deeply affecting portrait of Stein as a model of sanctity is Abraham Joshua Heschel's 'interreligiously attuned philosophy of empathy.' . . . By seeing her as a 'model for interreligious dialogue' . . . , we hear too little reflection on why for Stein . . . this dual allegiance to both Christianity and Judaism required conversion."

PALUMBI, ANTHONY R. The extreme life of the sea. See Palumbi, S. R.

PALUMBI, STEPHEN R. The extreme life of the sea; [by] Stephen R. Palumbi 256 p. 2014 Princeton University Press

1. Curiosities & wonders 2. Marine animals 3. Marine biology 4. Marine fishes—Anatomy 5. Science—Popular works

ISBN 9780691149561 (hardcover : alk. paper)
LC 2013-038174

SUMMARY: "'The Extreme Life of the Sea' takes readers to the absolute limits of the ocean world--the fastest and deepest, the hottest and oldest creatures of the oceans. . . . Coauthored by Stephen Palumbi [and Anthony Palumbi], 'The Extreme Life of the Sea' tells the unforgettable tales of some of the most marvelous life forms on Earth, and the challenges they overcome to survive." (Publisher's note)

REVIEW: *Choice* v52 no1 p106 St 2014 J. A. Mather

REVIEW: *Kirkus Rev* v82 no2 p211 Ja 15 2014

REVIEW: *Libr J* v139 no2 p94 F 1 2014 Jean E. Crampon

REVIEW: *New Sci* v221 no2961 p50 Mr 22 2014 Adrian Barnett

REVIEW: *Publ Wkly* v261 no4 p183-4 Ja 27 2014

REVIEW: *Sci Am* v310 no3 p80 Mr 2014

"The Extreme Life of the Sea." "From 'immortal jellyfish that age in reverse, to zombie bone worms that eat the skeletons of dead whales, the ocean is full of bizarre characters. Biologist Stephen Palumbi and his science writer son, Anthony, profile the most unusual [sea] specimens. Chapters cover the smallest, the oldest, the hottest and the coldest species, among others, and the landscape of strange creatures is brought to life by charming writing. . . . On the sex-switching abilities of the clownfish . . . for instance."

PAMUK, ORHAN, 1952-. The innocence of objects; [by] Orhan Pamuk 263 p. 2012 Abrams

1. Creative nonfiction 2. Istanbul (Turkey)

ISBN 9781419704567
LC 2012-008334

SUMMARY: In this book, Orhan Pamuk "uses his novel of lost love, 'The Museum of Innocence' as a departure point to explore the city of his youth. . . . He writes about things that matter deeply to him: the psychology of the collector, the proper role of the museum, the photography of old Istanbul (illustrated with Pamuk's . . . collection of . . . photographs and movie stills), and of course the customs and traditions of his beloved city." (Publisher's note)

REVIEW: *N Y Times Book Rev* p18 D 2 2012 EDMUND de WAAL

REVIEW: *Yale Rev* v101 no4 p136-47 O 2013 ANIS SHIVANI

"The Innocence of Objects." "An expansive, philosophical, meditative catalogue of the objects collected in the museum [Orhan] Pamuk worked so assiduously over the better part of a decade to assemble in connection with his novel 'The Museum of Innocence'. . . . If any novelist in contemporary times has enacted a more radical project on behalf of the innocence of writing, I don't know of it. . . . There follow seventy-four exquisite chapters, the heart of the book, one for each cabinet corresponding to a chapter in the novel. . . . It is impossible to capture on paper the stunning beauty of the images, an effect the likes of which I've never encountered in a book, all the more enhanced by the powerful juxtapositions and color contrasts."

PANGLE, THOMAS L. Aristotle's teaching in the Politics; [by] Thomas L. Pangle 343 p. 2013 University of Chicago Press

1. Philosophical literature 2. Political philosophy 3. Political science—Philosophy—Study and teaching 4. Teaching

ISBN 9780226016030 (cloth : alkaline paper)
LC 2012-036971

SUMMARY: In this book on Aristotle's text the Politics, author Thomas L. Pangle "lays out the argument of the book and brings to light Aristotle's intention or 'teaching.' Aristotle's teaching is to be understood in terms of both how he wrote or taught and what his work teaches. Understanding the literary character of the work allows readers to clearly understand its substance." (Choice: Current Reviews for Academic Libraries)

REVIEW: *Choice* v51 no7 p1306-7 Mr 2014 P. N. Malcolmson

"Aristotle's Teaching in the Politics." "In recent decades, there has been an extraordinary wave of fine scholarship on Aristotle. It has therefore become increasingly difficult to write a new book on Aristotle's Politics that is both original and good. [Thomas L.] Pangle's commentary succeeds admirably. Through a careful exegesis, Pangle . . . unpacks Aristotle's text and illuminates the work's multilayered rhetorical structure. . . . Pangle brilliantly demonstrates that Aristotle was a 'political' philosopher; he was guided by his understanding of the deep essential tension that necessarily exists between politics and philosophy. Anyone with a serious interest in understanding Aristotle and political philosophy will benefit from, and enjoy, reading this book."

PAPACONSTANTINOU, ARIETTA.tr. The web of Athenaeus. See Jacob, C.

PAPPÉ, ILAN, 1954-. The idea of Israel; a history of power and knowledge; [by] Ilan Pappé 346 p. 2014 Random House

1. Arab-Israeli conflict 2. Historical literature 3. Israel—History 4. Israel—Politics & government 5. Zionism

ISBN 1844678563; 9781844678563

SUMMARY: This book "considers the way Zionism operates outside of the government and military in areas such as the country's education system, media, and cinema, and the uses that are made of the Holocaust in supporting the state's ideological structure. In particular, [Ilan] Pappe examines the way successive generations of historians have framed the 1948 conflict as a liberation campaign, creating a foundation myth that went unquestioned in Israeli society until the 1990s." (Publisher's note)

REVIEW: *Hist Today* v64 no3 p62 Mr 2014 Colin Shindler

"Herzl: Theodor Herzl and the Foundation of the Jewish State" and "The Idea of Israel: A History of Power and Knowledge." "Herzl emerges from his diaries as a dreamer and a realist. . . . In this book [Shlomo] Avineri has reclaimed Herzl from the propagandists. . . . While [Ilan] Pappe argues that there had been a quasi-official plan, based on Zionist beliefs, to expel the Palestinian Arabs, others believe that this is not revealed by the documentation. . . . While this book gives numerous insights into the subject, Pappe also conducts a megaphone war with his Israeli academic opponents, which mars an otherwise interesting account."

PAQUETTE, AMMI-JOAN. A Ghost in the house; [by] Ammi-Joan Paquette 32 p. 2013 Candlewick Press

1. Ghost stories 2. Ghosts—Juvenile literature 3. Monsters—Juvenile fiction 4. Mummies—Fiction 5. Stories in rhyme

ISBN 9780763655297

LC 2012-943659

SUMMARY: This children's title presents a "cumulative counting book. . . that's more playful than scary," written by Ammi-Joan Paquette and illustrated by Adam Record. "When a little ghost goes slip-sliding down the hallway, he suddenly hears . . . a groan! Turns out it's only a friendly mummy, who shuffles along with the ghost . . . As the cautious explorers continue, they find a surprise at every turn--and add another adorably ghoulish friend to the count." (Publisher's note)

REVIEW: *Bull Cent Child Books* v67 no1 p44 S 2013 H. M.

"Ghost in the House." "In this cumulative rhyming story, a ghost host goes on to meet four unusual friends: a groaning mummy, a growling monster, a click-clacking skeleton, and a shrieking witch. Finally, the five creepy characters encounter the scariest creature of all: a red-headed, wide-eyed human boy in pajamas who unwittingly frightens them all away. [Author Ammi-Joan] Paquette's rhyme scheme is slightly unusual, with shifts between internal line rhymes and end rhymes, but it's but solid and lilting; once mastered, the cadence is both catchy and appealing, and the sound effects make it a natural winner for readalouds. . . . While the ending is a bit anticlimactic, this is a solid offering for preschoolers who prefer friendly over frightening at their October storytimes."

REVIEW: *Horn Book Magazine* v89 no5 p67 S/O 2013 MARTHA V. PARRAVANO

"Ghost in the House." "The cute little ghost (a benign powder blue, with wide eyes and worried-looking eyebrows) is joined, one by one, by a mummy, monster, skeleton, and witch. Then a little boy arrives, scaring them all away. The bouncy rhyme in this cumulative story is engaging, and the scariness level is just right for the very young. Digitally created illustrations, though rather pale and bland, feature clean compositions and an inventive use of type that will keep viewers focused and anticipating each new arrival."

REVIEW: *Kirkus Rev* v81 no15 p9 Ag 1 2013

REVIEW: *Publ Wkly* v260 no29 p65 Jl 22 2013

REVIEW: *SLJ* v59 no8 p86 Ag 2013 Martha Simpson

PAQUETTE, GABRIEL. Imperial Portugal in the age of Atlantic revolutions; the Luso-Brazilian world, c. 1770-1850; [by] Gabriel Paquette xiv, 450 p. 2013 Cambridge University Press

1. Decolonization—History 2. HISTORY—Europe—General 3. Historical literature 4. Imperialism—History 5. Political culture—Brazil—History 6. Political culture—Portugal—History 7. Revolutions—History

ISBN 9781107028975 (hardback : alkaline paper)

LC 2012-036034

SUMMARY: This book "examine[s] the Portuguese Atlantic World in the period from 1750 to 1850" and argues "that despite formal separation, the links and relationships that survived the demise of empire entwined the historical trajectories of Portugal and Brazil even more tightly than before. . . . Portuguese and Brazilian statesmen and political writers laboured under the long shadow of empire as they sought to begin anew and forge stable post-imperial orders on both sides of the Atlantic." (Publisher's note)

REVIEW: *Am Hist Rev* v119 no2 p632-3 Ap 2014 Anthony Disney

REVIEW: *Choice* v51 no4 p716-7 D 2013 C. Ingrao

"Imperial Portugal in the Age of Atlantic Revolutions: The Luso-Brazilian World, c. 1770-1850." "The familiar prevailing narrative of the collapse of the Ibero-American empires shows Spain and Portugal experiencing a sudden, complete, and necessary break precipitated by the Napoleonic conquest of the peninsula. [Gabriel] Paquette . . . challenges and partially modifies this account. . . . The book focuses--sometimes to the point of tedium--on the thoughts and actions of policy makers, pamphleteers, and foreign diplomats whose intrigues place Portugal's fate very much in an international context."

REVIEW: *TLS* no5774 p38 N 29 2013 FELIPE FERNÁNDEZ-ARMESTO

PARASKEVAS, MICHAEL, 1961-.il. On my way to bed. See Maizes, S.

PARASKEVOPOULOU, ANNA. Undocumented workers' transitions. See McKay, S.

PARETSKY, SARA, 1947-. Critical mass; [by] Sara Paretsky 480 p. 2013 Putnam Adult

1. FICTION—Mystery & Detective—Hard-Boiled 2. FICTION—Mystery & Detective—Women Sleuths 3. FICTION—Thrillers 4. Holocaust survivors—Fiction 5. Missing persons—Fiction 6. Warshawski, V. I. (Fictitious character)—Fiction 7. Women private investigators—Illinois—Chicago—Fiction

ISBN 0399160566; 9780399160561 (hardback)

LC 2013-025097

SUMMARY: This is Sara Paretsky's 17th novel featuring Chicago private investigator V.I. Warshawski. Here, she helps out her friend Dr. Lotty Herschel. "Lotty gets in touch with V.I. after [her friend] Kitty's drug-addicted daughter,

Judy, leaves a message claiming that she and her college-age son, Martin, whom she had left in Kitty's care, are in danger. Judy then vanishes." (Publishers Weekly)

REVIEW: *Booklist* v110 no1 p46 S 1 2013 Stephanie Zvirin

"Critical Mass." "As in previous V. I. Warshawski mysteries, [Sara] Paretsky works elements of Chicago history into the story. . . . It's clear V. I. has several puzzles to solve, and, as usual, she becomes the proverbial stick in the hornet's nest, putting herself at risk as she follows a twisted trail of ruined lives rooted in the international race to develop an atomic weapon. Vic is at her stubborn, reckless, compassionate best in this complicated page-turner about selfish secrets passed down through generations."

REVIEW: *Kirkus Rev* v81 no17 p33 S 1 2013

REVIEW: *N Y Times Book Rev* p23 N 17 2013 MARILYN STASIO

"Critical Mass," "The All-Girl Filling Station's Last Reunion," and "Country Hardball." "The drug subplot is an unnecessary complication in an already busy story told in two parallel narratives set in different countries, running on separate timelines and involving four generations of characters. But if the plot mechanics are unwieldy, the character of Martina is the serene center of this fractured universe. . . . Steve Weddle's writing is downright dazzling in 'Country Hardball'. . . . Sookie's detective work, tracing her new identity, takes her all the way to Pulaski, Wis., and into the lives of four ebullient sisters who ran their father's gas station during World War II. Honestly, who wouldn't want to be part of that family?"

REVIEW: *Publ Wkly* v260 no35 p32 S 2 2013

PARHAM, SETH. The Burning City; [by] Seth Parham 250 p. 2013 Author Solutions

1. Fantasy fiction 2. Friendship—Fiction 3. Magic—Fiction 4. Monsters—Fiction 5. Pirates—Fiction

ISBN 1491841818; 9781491841815

SUMMARY: In this book by Seth Parham, "every century, a giant creature named the Abaddon rises from the ocean and destroys a city before returning to the sea for another 100 years. . . . Ephraim, a young man from a small village, has an intense desire to fight the immortal monster. After his grandmother's death severs his remaining family ties, Ephraim sets out with Bailey, his childhood friend, for the burning city, Haydenly. His hope is to join the army and someday fight Abaddon." (Kirkus Reviews)

REVIEW: *Kirkus Rev* v82 no3 p397 F 1 2014

"The Burning City". " In between his bouts of purple prose and the formulaic plot, [Seth] Parham creates some vivid scenes and descriptions. . . . His writing is at its best when depicting action and creatures, as when the party encounters an ageless being in a decaying fortress. It's a pity that these scenes are so buried in the story, which is underdeveloped and tends to rely on unlikely happenstance. Diluted by over-affected language . . .and simple plot developments . . . this debut struggles to deliver a fulfilling story. Flashes of brilliance don't save this heroic journey."

PARIS, HARPER; The mystery of the gold coin; 118 p. 2014 Little Simon

1. Brothers and sisters—Fiction 2. Lost and found possessions—Fiction 3. Moving, Household—Fiction 4. Mystery and detective stories 5. Twins—Fiction

ISBN 9781442497184 (pbk: alk. paper); 9781442497191 (hc: alk. paper)

LC 2013-006969

SUMMARY: In this book, "Ella and Ethan Briar are devastated by their parents' announcement that the family is leaving their beloved hometown. Mrs. Briar has accepted a new job as a travel writer, a job that will send the family to new places all over the globe on a weekly basis. . . . Their grandfather . . . gives each a special gift for their travels. . . .On their last morning in town, Ethan realizes that his gold coin is missing—and they only have a few hours before they have to leave." (Kirkus Reviews)

REVIEW: *Booklist* v110 no17 p58 My 1 2014 Suzanne Harold

REVIEW: *Kirkus Rev* v82 no3 p405 F 1 2014

"The Mystery of the Gold Coin". "On their last morning in town, Ethan realizes that his gold coin is missing—and they only have a few hours before they have to leave for the airport. While their grandfather does their chores, the twins methodically determine when Ethan last had the coin—the previous day—and make a list of places he visited to retrace his steps. This allows the twins to say goodbye to friendly faces throughout the town. . . . This series-launching installment's light on mystery, but it's welcoming and accessible through expressive, frequent illustrations. . . . Not terribly remarkable, but the series has lots of growing room."

PARK, JULIE J. When diversity drops; race, religion, and affirmative action in higher education; [by] Julie J. Park 198 p. 2013 Rutgers University Press

1. Affirmative action programs in education—United States 2. Minorities—Education (Higher)—United States 3. Multiculturalism—United States 4. Social science literature

ISBN 9780813561684 (pbk.: alk. paper); 9780813561691 (hardcover: alk. paper)

LC 2012-040307

SUMMARY: This book "tracks the effects that Proposition 209, a 1996 affirmative action ban in California, has on the interaction between students." Author Julie J. Park's "case study of the InterVarsity Christian Fellowship (IVCF) at a university in California identifies the process behind successfully building ethnic diversity through displacement and intentionality, as well as subsequent setbacks after Prop. 209." (Contemporary Sociology)

REVIEW: *Contemp Sociol* v43 no2 p286-7 Mr 2014

"When Diversity Drops: Race, Religion, and Affirmative Action in Higher Education". "As race- and class-conscious admission policies continue to be contested, [Julie J.] Park's work attests to the multilevel effects that structural diversity has on enabling or limiting the cultivation of ethnic diversity. Scholars investigating the intersection between organizational structure and culture in subpopulations will certainly find Park's work useful, as will those interested in contact theory, evangelism, and race."

PARK, LINDA SUE. Xander's panda party; [by] Linda Sue Park 40 p. 2013 Clarion Books

1. Pandas 2. Pandas—Fiction 3. Parties—Fiction 4. Stories in rhyme 5. Zoo animals—Fiction

ISBN 0547558651; 9780547558653 (hardcover)

LC 2012-039662

SUMMARY: In this book by Linda Sue Park "the zoo's

paucity of pandas doesn't impede Xander's party planning for long. He decides to invite all the bears. But Koala protests. She's not a bear--she's a marsupial! Does that mean she can't come? Xander rethinks his decision to invite only bears, and 'Calling all bears' evolves into 'Calling all creatures'" (Publisher's note)

REVIEW: *Booklist* v109 no22 p88 Ag 1 2013 Ann Kelley

REVIEW: *Bull Cent Child Books* v67 no2 p108-9 O 2013 H. M.

"Xander's Panda Party." "'Xander planned a panda party. Yes, a dandy whoop-de-do!' Problem is, Xander is the only panda at his zoo, so the guest list is a bit on the slim side. . . . An author's note offers more in-depth details on some of the scientific references within the text, but really it is the jaunty cadence and spirited verses that are going to attract listeners to Xander's tale. Much of the rhyme is internal, and readers-aloud will definitely want to practice a time or two before trying the tongue-twisting verses . . . on a crowd. [Illustrator Matt] Phelan's ink and watercolor compositions offer the perfect counterpoint to the tightly wrought verses, with playfulness inherent in the fluid, inky outlines encasing broadly applied brushstrokes."

REVIEW: *Horn Book Magazine* v89 no5 p78-9 S/O 2013 CHRISTINE M. HEPPERMANN

"Xander's Panda Party." "Liberal use of internal rhyme . . . makes [Linda Sue] Park's text sing as it relates how Xander tackles each new challenge. . . . [Matt] Phelan's sprightly ink and watercolor illustrations show Xander spinning until he's prostrate, convinced his party will balloon out of control. Happily, a resourceful salamander steps up to help, and then a last-minute surprise guest turns the affair into a true celebration. Park's extensive author's note on pandas and other animals mentioned in the text seems like pedagogical overkill, but it does provide interesting further context for her characters."

REVIEW: *Kirkus Rev* v81 no14 p132 Jl 15 2013

REVIEW: *Publ Wkly* p49 Children's starred review annual 2013

REVIEW: *Publ Wkly* v260 no24 p61 Je 17 2013

REVIEW: *SLJ* v59 no8 p86 Ag 2013 Marian McLeod

PARK, TREVOR. "Nolo Episcopari"; A Life of C. J. Vaughan; [by] Trevor Park 446 p. 2013 St Bega Publications

1. Anglican priests 2. Evangelicalism—Church of England—History 3. Harrow School 4. School principals—Great Britain 5. Vaughan, Charles J.

ISBN 0950832545; 9780950832548

SUMMARY: "Trevor Park's biography is a labour of love: it took him twenty years to write, and his intention, as he puts it, is to restore Vaughan's besmirched reputation. . . . The man he describes is a devout Evangelical, an outstanding headmaster, a notable preacher, an exemplary parish priest, and a dedicated trainer of clergy. . . . The sad result is that . . . the Church of England was denied the episcopal ministry of a devout and gifted man." (Publisher's note)

REVIEW: *TLS* no5786 p24 F 21 2014 JOHN WITHERIDGE

"'Nolo Episcopari': A Life of C. J. Vaughan." "Trevor Park's biography is a labour of love: it took him twenty years to write, and his intention, as he puts it, is to restore Vaughan's besmirched reputation. Park's account of Vaughan's life is meticulous, comprehensive and admiring. The man he describes is a devout Evangelical, an outstanding headmaster, a notable preacher, an exemplary parish priest, and a dedicated trainer of clergy. . . . The sad result is that a successful headmastership was brought to an abrupt end, and the Church of England was denied the episcopal ministry of a devout and gifted man. That comes across loud and clear in Park's biography, despite the panegyric."

PARKER, CHRISTINE.ed. Explaining compliance. See Explaining compliance

PARKER, EMILY. Now I know who my comrades are; voices from the Internet underground; [by] Emily Parker 320 p. 2014 Sarah Crichton Books/Farrar, Straus and Giroux

1. Blogs—Political aspects—Communist countries 2. Blogs—Political aspects—Former communist countries 3. Intellectual freedom 4. Internet—Social aspects—Communist countries 5. Internet—Social aspects—Former communist countries 6. Political participation 7. Political science literature 8. Social change

ISBN 9780374176952 (hardcover)

LC 2013-035399

SUMMARY: In this book, Emily Parker "explores the lives of bloggers in China, Cuba, and Russia who are active criticsm of their governments.Through multiple interviews, her subjects discuss the ways in which they have challenged authority via social media. . . . Parker portrays reluctant activists drawn into action for a variety of personal reasons who are alternately bemused and surprised by their resulting renown." (Booklist)

REVIEW: *Booklist* v110 no11 p4 F 1 2014 Colleen Mondor

"Now I Know Who My Comrades Are: Voices From the Internet Underground." "Although dissident use of the Internet is already part of the twenty-first-century story,[Emily] Parker goes beyond the obvious headlines to the grinding daily battles of people and situations that receive only passing media notice. Some of what she reveals is stunning . . . but the book's greatest strength is the intimacy with which she describes the lives of her subjects. . . . Parker profiles fascinating people and effectively shows why, in hands like theirs, social media is one of the most important tools for conducting positive political and social change around the world."

REVIEW: *Kirkus Rev* v82 no2 p63 Ja 15 2014

REVIEW: *Publ Wkly* v260 no49 p76 D 2 2013

PARKER, GEOFFREY. Global crisis; war, climate change and catastrophe in the seventeenth century; [by] Geoffrey Parker 871 p. 2012 Yale University Press

1. Civil war—History—17th century 2. Climatic changes—Social aspects—History—17th century 3. Disasters—History—17th century 4. Historical literature 5. History, Modern—17th century 6. Military history—17th century 7. Revolutions—History—17th century

ISBN 0300153236; 9780300153231 (cloth: alkaline paper)

LC 2012-039448

SUMMARY: This book "presents a history of the 17th century. . . . Focusing on climate-driven unrest around the world, [Geoffrey] Parker illustrates how events such as drought can drive disease, war, and social change. . . . He traces connections between climate and population and war, factors further influencing attitudes toward education and consumption." (Publishers Weekly)

REVIEW: *America* v209 no18 p33-4 D 9 2013 ROBERT E. SCULLY

"Global Crisis: War, Climate Change and Catastrophe in the Seventeenth Century". "An exhaustive (and, at almost 900 pages, somewhat exhausting) account of this troubled century. . . . Part of what gives this book such persuasive power . . . is its often global reach. . . . In light of current concerns and debates about climate change and global warming . . . [Geoffrey] Parker's narrative and analysis manage to be relevant without being 'presentist' or an example of simplistic climate determinism. . . . In sum, this is a brilliant and multifaceted approach to the global 17th century. If at times tendentious, it nevertheless goes a long way toward demonstrating the connections between dramatic climate changes and widespread demographic and political crises."

REVIEW: *Choice* v51 no2 p325 O 2013 J. B. Richardson III

REVIEW: *Harper's Magazine* v327 no1962 p83-5 N 2013 Jane Smiley

REVIEW: *Hist Today* v63 no6 p64 Je 2013 PAUL DUKES

REVIEW: *Libr J* v138 no11 p103 Je 15 2013 Brian Odom Kelsey Berry Philpot

REVIEW: *TLS* no5746 p10-1 My 17 2013 THEODORE K. RABB

PARKER, JAKE.il. The girl who wouldn't brush her hair. See Bernheimer, K.

PARKER, RANDALL E.ed. Routledge handbook of major events in economic history. See Routledge handbook of major events in economic history

PARKS, BRAD. The player; a mystery; [by] Brad Parks 336 p. 2014 Minotaur Books

1. Detective & mystery stories 2. Environmental protection—Fiction 3. Investigative reporting—Fiction 4. Organized crime—Fiction 5. Ross, Carter (Fictitious character)—Fiction
ISBN 1250044081; 9781250044082 (hardback)
LC 2013-045900

SUMMARY: In this book, "Carter Ross looks into the outbreak of a debilitating and sometimes fatal illness within a poor neighborhood of Newark, N.J. . . . Soon Ross comes down with the same illness and . . . he discovers that a majority of the workers at a shopping center complex breaking ground nearby have exhibited the same . . . symptoms as local residents. Then the chief developer of the shopping center, Vaughn McAlister, turns up dead--the victim of a baseball bat to the skull." (Publishers Weekly)

REVIEW: *Booklist* v110 no11 p28-9 F 1 2014 Don Crinklaw

"The Player." "Carter Ross, the hero of this high-spirited novel, book five in the series, is a reporter right down to the tip of his ballpoint pen. . . . [Brad] Parks begins his story in good news-feature style--unadorned English with a pulse underneath, compulsively readable--and the topic is still fresh. . . . Readers may groan when Parks abruptly ends this narrative for a disquisition on Carter's love life. Fortunately this seems to bore Parks, too, and we're back to the good stuff: a painstaking inquiry into a real-estate scam with murder at its core. Parks tries for a high-concept finale, but the novel really ends when we learn what the moneybags are up to. Ink-stained heroes are a dying breed. Enjoy this one while you can."

REVIEW: *Kirkus Rev* v82 no4 p184 F 15 2014

REVIEW: *Publ Wkly* v261 no4 p171-2 Ja 27 2014

PARNABY, ANDREW. Secret service. See Whitaker, R.

PARNES, AMIE. HRC; state secrets and the rebirth of Hillary Clinton; [by] Amie Parnes 448 p. 2014 Crown

1. BIOGRAPHY & AUTOBIOGRAPHY—Political 2. Cabinet officers—United States—Biography 3. Journalism 4. POLITICAL SCIENCE—Political Process—Leadership 5. Presidential candidates—United States—Biography 6. Women cabinet officers—United States—Biography 7. Women presidential candidates—United States—Biography
ISBN 9780804136754 (hardback)
LC 2013-037029

SUMMARY: "'HRC' offers a rare look inside the merciless Clinton political machine, as Bill Clinton handled the messy business of avenging Hillary's primary loss while she tried to remain above the partisan fray. Exploring her friendships and alliances with Robert Gates, David Petraeus, Leon Panetta, Joe Biden, and the president himself, [Jonathan] Allen and [Amie] Parnes show how Hillary fundamentally transformed the State Department." (Publisher's note)

REVIEW: *Economist* v410 no8874 p5 F 15 2014

REVIEW: *Libr J* v139 no8 p44 My 1 2014 Kelly Sinclair

REVIEW: *N Y Times Book Rev* p9 F 23 2014 JODI KANTOR

"HRC: State Secrets and the Rebirth of Hillary Clinton." "'HRC' [is] an account of Hillary Clinton's time as Secretary of State by Jonathan Allen . . . and Amie Parnes. . . . Their Clinton is the stock version, Democratic edition. . . . Perhaps Clinton was every bit as committed, tireless and sincere as they say, but it's not easy to trust their account since they don't appear to have spoken to anyone with much distance. . . . From where we stand now . . . 'HRC' may be most valuable as a guide to future messaging, an indication of what those closest to Hillary Clinton see as her strongest moments."

REVIEW: *New York Times* v163 no56405 pC21-7 F 7 2014 MICHIKO KAKUTANI

PARNIA, SAM. Erasing death. See Young, J.

PARR, TODD. Doggy kisses 1, 2, 3; [by] Todd Parr 24 p. 2013 Little, Brown and Co.

1. Counting 2. Dogs—Juvenile literature 3. Kissing 4. Picture books for children 5. Stories in rhyme
ISBN 9780316207379
LC 2012-951024

SUMMARY: This "counting book written in rhyme features 10 different displays of doggy devotion. . . . A short snatch of text and a large numeral appear on the left-hand page with a complementary illustration on the right. . . . The illustrations are composed of simple, childlike renderings of widely smiling children and puckering pups of all shapes, sizes and colors. The final spread . . . showcas[es]. . . the numerals 1 through 10 accompanied by their adorable doggies." (Kirkus Reviews)

REVIEW: *Kirkus Rev* v82 no1 p146 Ja 1 2014

"Doggy Kisses 123". "[Todd] Parr brings his signature, toddler-friendly style to two of kids' favorite things: counting and puppies. This simple counting book written in rhyme features 10 different displays of doggy devotion. . . . The rhyming verses don't exactly trip off the tongue, but kids aren't likely to mind, focused as they'll be on counting the pooches' smooches. Sturdy, glossy pages will stand up to multiple readings—and a fair amount of slobber. Silly, sweet and simple, this counting primer is a great choice for solo exploration or group sharing in a doggy-themed storytime."

PARRISH, J. MICHAEL.ed. Tyrannosaurid paleobiology. See Tyrannosaurid paleobiology

PARSHALL, SANDRA. Poisoned ground; [by] Sandra Parshall 250 p. 2014 Poisoned Pen Press

1. Detective & mystery stories 2. Murder investigation—Fiction 3. Real estate developers—Fiction 4. Rural development 5. Virginia—Fiction

ISBN 1464202249; 9781464202247 (hardcover: alk. paper); 9781464202261 (trade pbk: alk. paper)

LC 2013-941231

SUMMARY: In this book, by Sandra Parshall, "a powerful development company sets its sights on Mason Country, Virginia, as the location for a sprawling resort for the rich. . . . Few oppose the development more vocally than veterinarian Rachel Goddard. She sides with locals reluctant to sell their land and, in the process, complicates the life of her new husband, Sheriff Tom Bridger." (Publisher's note)

REVIEW: *Kirkus Rev* v82 no2 p298 Ja 15 2014

"Poisoned Ground". "Plans to build a resort in rural Virginia start an uncivil war. Many of the locals see the new resort as Mason County's chance for much needed jobs, even if they're minimum wage with no benefits. Since some of the people whose land is required dream happily of a big payoff while others adamantly refuse to sell, it's neighbor against neighbor. . . . When a couple who refuse to sell are found shot, Tom and Rachel have to wonder if their deaths were intended to move the land deal along. But they're confounded by the murder of a woman who'd planned to sell her place. . . . [Sandra] Parshall . . . expertly maintains the tension between warring factions until the surprising conclusion."

REVIEW: *Publ Wkly* v261 no2 p51 Ja 13 2014

PARSONS, MARK HUNTLEY. Road rash; [by] Mark Huntley Parsons 352 p. 2014 Alfred A. Knopf

1. Drummers (Musicians)—Fiction 2. Fathers & sons—Fiction 3. Musicians—Fiction 4. Road fiction 5. Rock groups—Fiction

ISBN 9780385753425 (trade); 9780385753432 (lib. bdg.); 9780385753456 (pbk)

LC 2013-013578

SUMMARY: In this book by Mark Huntley Parsons, "when high school junior and drummer Zach is dumped by his current band, he's soon picked up by a group of older guys who are booked for a tour of the Rockies for the summer. Each stop on the tour opens Zach's eyes to what it means to be in a real band, as the venues range from pretty sweet to rank dive, and the interpersonal relationships among the musicians ebb and flow" (Bulletin of the Center for Children's Books)

REVIEW: *Booklist* v110 no9/10 p108 Ja 1 2014 Lexi Walters Wright

REVIEW: *Bull Cent Child Books* v67 no9 p472 My 2014 K. C.

"Road Rash". "Zach is a thoroughly likable guy's guy; kind and ethical in relationships, committed to what he feels are the best interests of the band, and diplomatic in his attempts to promote Glenn's talent and smooth over the rifts he created while doing so. His anger is justified by intolerable circumstances, and he's helped by a wise dad, who understands his son's hot temper even while he chastises Zach and advises him on how to remain politic in difficult situations. The musical terminology gets thiek on oeeasion, amping up the authenticity for readers in the know, but the play of relationships and the plot arc of dreams realized broadens the appeal."

REVIEW: *Kirkus Rev* v81 no23 p164 D 1 2013

REVIEW: *Publ Wkly* v260 no49 p84 D 2 2013

REVIEW: *SLJ* v60 no3 p161 Mr 2014 Sarah Allen

PARTHASARATHI, PRASANNAN. Why Europe grew rich and Asia did not; global economic divergence, 1600-1850; [by] Prasannan Parthasarathi 365 p. 2011 Cambridge University Press

1. Economic development—Asia—History 2. Economic development—Europe—History 3. HISTORY—Renaissance 4. Historical literature

ISBN 9780521168243 (paperback); 9781107000308 (hardback)

LC 2011-002484

SUMMARY: This book "provides a striking new answer to the classic question of why Europe industrialized from the late eighteenth century and Asia did not. Drawing significantly from the case of India, Prasannan Parthasarathi shows that in the seventeenth and eighteenth centuries, the advanced regions of Europe and Asia were more alike than different, both characterized by sophisticated and growing economies." (Publisher's note)

REVIEW: *Am Hist Rev* v117 no5 p1532-4 D 2012 Jan de Vries

REVIEW: *Bus Hist Rev* v86 no4 p809-11 Wint 2012 Larry Neal

REVIEW: *Choice* v49 no8 p1499-500 Ap 2012 R. P. Gardella

REVIEW: *Engl Hist Rev* v128 no534 p1251-4 O 2013 Victor Lieberman

"Why Europe Grew Rich and Asia Did Not: Global Economic Divergence, 1600-1850." "Prasannan Parthasarathi . . . begins by expanding the thesis that before 1750/1800 there was precious little difference between market systems, scientific and technical inquiry, and political institutions in Western Europe and in advanced sectors of Asia, as represented primarily by South Asia and China. . . . Parthasarathi is to be commended for drawing . . . attention to . . . contexts, for integrating early modern India into global comparisons, for revisiting . . . British and Chinese coal endowments, and for demonstrating . . . that competition from Indian textile imports was . . . important . . . in . . . the mechanisation of British cotton. Yet . . . many of his arguments remain unconvincing."

PARTIES, ELECTIONS, AND THE FUTURE OF CANADIAN POLITICS; 2013 UBC Press

1. Canada—Politics & government 2. Elections—Canada 3. Political parties—Canada 4. Political science literature 5. Politicians—Canada
ISBN 0774824093; 0774824085; 9780774824095; 9780774824088
LC 2013-427002

SUMMARY: This book, edited by Amanda Bittner and Royce Koop, "provides the first comprehensive account of political change in Canada over the past two decades, particularly during the 1993, 2004, and 2011 federal elections. Contributors explore the changing landscape from both historical and contemporary perspectives and speculate on the future of the national party system." (Publisher's note)

REVIEW: *Choice* v51 no7 p1301 Mr 2014 T. M. Bateman

"Parties, Elections, and the Future of Canadian Politics." "This collection of 14 essays gathers the work of new and seasoned scholars, many of whom are associated with the University of British Columbia political science department, specializing in Canadian political behavior. . . . As the book's title indicates, party politics in the last 20 years manifest both surprising demographic change and stubborn institutional continuity. Missing is an account of the mechanics of campaigning in the new age of social media and the decline of print. Also missing is an account of leadership and leaders in recent years, surprising since Canadian politics are so leader-dominated. A couple of essays are a bit opaque."

PASS, EMMA. Acid; [by] Emma Pass 384 p. 2014 Delacorte Press

1. Fugitives from justice—Fiction 2. Government, Resistance to—Fiction 3. Police—Fiction 4. Science fiction
ISBN 9780375991349 (glb); 9780385743877 (hc)
LC 2013-002923

SUMMARY: In this book, "imprisoned for the murder of her parents by the Agency for Crime Investigation and Defense, 17-year-old Jenna Strong hones her fighting skills under the tutelage of the prison medic, Dr. Fisher. Just as an altercation with an inmate lands her in the infirmary, a riot breaks out, and Jenna finds herself at the center of a covert rescue mission that ends with her escape and Dr. Fisher's death." (Kirkus Reviews)

REVIEW: *Booklist* v110 no15 p80 Ap 1 2014 Julie Trevelyan

REVIEW: *Bull Cent Child Books* v67 no10 p535 Je 2014 A. S.

"ACID". "The concept—the layering of the protagonist as she first claims a new identity and then has her memory adjusted—is admirably intriguing, but ultimately four versions (there's yet another forcible memory shift in her past that she doesn't learn about until later) of the same character makes for a muddled narrative. In addition, the resistance force is poorly described, and it's led by a character so one-sided that his evil is uninspiring rather than threatening. Nevertheless, a tough chick who can protect herself admirably, especially one who turns out to be way more sympathetic than she first appears, may still find a ready audience in character-driven YA readers."

REVIEW: *Kirkus Rev* v82 no5 p99 Mr 1 2014

"Acid". "The first-person narrative revs up quickly but slows considerably halfway through the book when Jenna is forced to make a critical and unpleasant decision. Pass draws an uneven portrait of a traumatized heroine; Jenna never regains the steeliness she had in prison after she's reintroduced into society. She falls easily for Max, a wooden character happy to remain mostly in her shadow. Devoted fans of the genre may find intrigue in a walled-off future United Kingdom but will wish for a more dynamic heroine to deliver its revolution. A dutiful dystopia that never delves below its shallow surface."

REVIEW: *Publ Wkly* v261 no2 p70 Ja 13 2014

REVIEW: *SLJ* v60 no7 p54 Jl 2014 Audrey Sumser

REVIEW: *SLJ* v60 no4 p171 Ap 2014 Gretchen Kolderup

REVIEW: *Voice of Youth Advocates* v36 no6 p76 F 2014 Sherrie Williams

PÄS, HEINRICH. The perfect wave; with neutrinos at the boundary of space and time; [by] Heinrich Päs 312 p. 2014 Harvard University Press

1. Cosmology 2. Neutrinos—Mass 3. Particles (Nuclear physics)—History 4. Scientific literature 5. Space and time
ISBN 9780674725010 (alk. paper)
LC 2013-025630

SUMMARY: In this book on the particle known as the neutrino, author Heinrich Päs "surfs the decades of dazzling research since Wolfgang Pauli first posited the particle in 1930. Päs revisits key theorists such as Ettore Majorana, and lays out the work of groundbreaking labs from Los Alamos in New Mexico, where Fred Reines and Clyde Cowan first detected neutrinos in the early 1950s, to today's vast IceCube neutrino observatory in Antarctica." (Nature)

REVIEW: *Economist* v410 no8872 p71-2 F 1 2014

"Neutrino Hunters: The Thrilling Chase for a Ghostly Particle to Unlock the Secrets of the Universe" and "The Perfect Wave: With Neutrinos at the Boundary of Space and Time." "These two books complement each other. Mr. [Ray] Jayawardhana's is stronger on the history (though his accounts of the neutrino hunters' personal lives can read a little too much like a professional CV). It is also more comprehensive on the potential use of neutrinos in examining the innards of the sun, of distant exploding stars or of Earth, as well as more practical uses. . . . Mr. [Heinrich] Päs, for his part, places neutrinos within the broader context of contemporary high theory and delves deeper into the science. Physics buffs will relish his explanations, and not just of established ideas."

REVIEW: *Publ Wkly* v260 no45 p59 N 11 2013

REVIEW: *TLS* no5788 p27 Mr 7 2014

PASSMAN, DON. The amazing Harvey; a mystery; [by] Don Passman 336 p. 2014 Minotaur Books

1. DNA fingerprinting 2. FICTION—Mystery & Detective—General 3. False imprisonment 4. Magicians—Fiction 5. Murder—Investigation—Fiction
ISBN 9781250041876 (hardback)
LC 2013-033838

SUMMARY: This book is the first in a "series starring a sleuthing magician whose greatest trick ever might just be releasing himself from a murder rap. . . . Now that he's settled in Los Angeles, serving as a substitute teacher while waiting for the big break that will write his ticket to the Vegas magic-show circuit" he gets "the news that his DNA matches the semen found in the body of Sherry Allen, a single mother who was raped and murdered." (Kirkus Reviews)

REVIEW: *Kirkus Rev* v82 no4 p183 F 15 2014

"The Amazing Harvey". "[Don] Passman . . . launches a new series starring a sleuthing magician whose greatest trick ever might just be releasing himself from a murder rap. . . . Broke, unemployable, facing eviction from his apartment and unable to afford even Hannah's cut-rate services, Harvey is desperate to clear himself. "Who's better at figuring out mysteries than a magician?" he reasons. Well, yes and no. Harvey is no great shakes as a detective, but he makes an irresistible deer in the headlights: part wiseacre, part sad-sack, all nebbish."

REVIEW: *Publ Wkly* v260 no50 p50 D 9 2013

PAST PRESENTED; archaeological illustration and the ancient Americas; xix, 498 p. 2012 Dumbarton Oaks Research Library and Collection

1. Archaeology—America—Pictorial works 2. Historical literature 3. Indians—Antiquities—Pictorial works 4. Indians—Historiography—Pictorial works
ISBN 9780884023807 (hardcover : alk. paper)
LC 2011-036487

SUMMARY: This book, "a collection of fourteen essays addressing the visual presentation of the Pre-Columbian past from the fifteenth century to the present day, explores and contextualizes the visual culture of archaeological illustration, addressing the intellectual history of the field and the relationship of archaeological illustration to other scientific disciplines and the fine arts." (Publisher's note)

REVIEW: *TLS* no5757 p12-3 Ag 2 2013 NORMAN HAMMOND

"Past Presented: Archaeological Illustration and the Ancient Americas." "[A] wide-ranging, well-written and superbly illustrated book. . . . Another chapter in which theory threatens to overcome substance is Byron Ellsworth Hamann's 'Drawing Glyphs Together'. . . . The volume is bookended by four essays: at the front is Joanne Pillsbury's splendid 'Perspectives,' bringing in a range of instructive external parallels from Ligorio's 1553 and Nolli's 1748 maps of Ancient Rome to Fuseli's 'The Artist in Despair over the Grandeur of Antique Remains' and David's 'Death of Socrates'. The essence of the enterprise is distilled into this introduction."

PASTAN, RACHEL. Alena; a novel; [by] Rachel Pastan 320 p. 2014 Riverhead Books

1. Art museum curators—Fiction 2. FICTION—Literary 3. FICTION—Psychological 4. Gothic literature 5. Women—Fiction
ISBN 9781594632471 (hardback)
LC 2013-030316

SUMMARY: "In a . . . restaging of Daphne du Maurier's classic 'Rebecca,' a young curator finds herself haunted by the legacy of her predecessor. . . . At the Venice Biennale, an aspiring assistant curator from the Midwest meets Bernard Augustin, the wealthy, enigmatic founder of the Nauk, a cutting-edge art museum on Cape Cod. . . . When Augustin offers the position to our heroine (who, like du Maurier's original, remains nameless) she dives at the chance." (Publisher's note)

REVIEW: *Booklist* v110 no8 p18 D 15 2013 Margaret Flanagan

REVIEW: *Kirkus Rev* v81 no21 p155 N 1 2013

REVIEW: *N Y Times Book Rev* p26 F 16 2014

REVIEW: *N Y Times Book Rev* p21 F 9 2014 ALEX KUCZYNSKI

"Alena." "Rachel Pastan's third novel, 'Alena,' begins with an echo of that famous opening: 'Last night I dreamed of Nauquasset again.' In this faithful, patient and occasionally hammy reimagining of Daphne du Maurier's novel ['Rebecca'], we meet a young curatorial assistant from the Midwest. . . . The writing at times is so fine you with this weren't a retold story, that Pastan would soar off on her own. . . . In fact, 'Alena' is often a brilliant take-down of the self-serious art world."

REVIEW: *Publ Wkly* v260 no43 p31 O 28 2013

PASTIS, STEPHAN.il. Timmy Failure now look what you've done. See Pastis, S.

PASTIS, STEPHAN. Timmy Failure now look what you've done; Now Look What You've Done; [by] Stephan Pastis 288 p. 2014 Candlewick Press

1. Detective & mystery stories 2. Humorous stories 3. Polar bear 4. Problem solving 5. Self-confidence
ISBN 0763660515; 9780763660512
LC 2013-944145

SUMMARY: In this book, by Stephan Pastis, "the too-smart-for-his-own-good kid detective is back for a second zany installment, along with his 1500-pound polar/bear business partner, Total. Timmy has big dreams for his crime-solving empire, fueled by his complete self-confidence, delusions of grandeur, and his assured win in a competition to find a stolen globe worth $500. But first, shenanigans are afoot and must be thwarted." (School Library Journal)

REVIEW: *Booklist* v110 no7 p69 D 1 2013 Kara Dean

REVIEW: *Kirkus Rev* v82 no1 p132 Ja 1 2014

"Timmy Failure: Now Look What You've Done". "Readers who found Timmy hard to take in his first book won't like him—or the terrible puns—any better here. (One chapter is titled 'The Lying, the Watch, and the Poor Globe.') But his many fans will speed through the pages, and they'll love [Stephan] Pastis' illustrations, which feature an adorable polar bear shaped like a bowling pin. They may even adopt Timmy's motto: 'When you lose hope, find it.' A loonily intellectual alternative to that wimpy kid."

REVIEW: *SLJ* v60 no1 p88 Ja 2014 Elly Schook

PASTORALISM IN AFRICA; Past, present, and future; 2013 Berghahn Books

1. Herding 2. Human ecology—Africa 3. Land use—Africa 4. Pastoral societies 5. Social science literature
ISBN 9780857459084 hardcover; 9780857459091 ebook

SUMMARY: Edited by Michael Bollig, Michael Schnegg, and Hans-Peter Wotzka, "this volume focuses on the emergence, diversity, and inherent dynamics of pastoralism in Africa based on research during a twelve-year period on the southwest and northeast regions. Unraveling the complex prehistory, history, and contemporary political ecology of African pastoralism, results in insight into the ingenuity and flexibility of historical and contemporary herders." (Publisher's note)

REVIEW: *Choice* v51 no6 p1055 F 2014 D. L. Browman

"Pastoralism in Africa: Past, Present and Future." "The 16 chapters in this volume are the summary of 12 years of fieldwork, beginning in 1995, of the Arid Climate, Adaptation, and Cultural Innovation in Africa project based at the Collaborative Research Center, University of Cologne, Germany. . . . While the volume will be of interest primarily to African specialists, students of pastoralism also will find it instructive. End-of-chapter reference listings, a compact index, and 100 tables, maps, and photos support the papers. . . . Recommended."

PATEL, LISA. Youth held at the border; immigration, education, and the politics of inclusion; [by] Lisa Patel xviii, 123 p. 2013 Teachers College Press

1. Children of immigrants—Education—United States 2. Immigrants—United States—Social conditions 3. Minorities—United States—Social conditions 4. Social science literature

ISBN 9780807753897 (pbk. : alk. paper); 9780807753903 (hardcover : alk. paper)

LC 2012-037135

SUMMARY: "This book explores how immigrant youth are included in, and excluded from, various sectors of American society, including education. Instead of the land of opportunity, immigrant youth often encounter myriad new borders long after their physical journey to the United States is over." Author Lisa Leigh Patel "invites readers to rethink assumptions about immigrant youth and what their often liminal positions reveal about the politics of inclusion in America." (Publisher's note)

REVIEW: *Harv Educ Rev* v83 no3 p537-9 Fall 2013

"Youth Held at the Border: Immigration, Education, and the Politics of Inclusion." "While the first half of the book consists of these rich ethnographic portraits, in its second half [Lisa] Patel raises a broader critique of the structural social apparatus underlying the lives of these young people. . . . Given the broad scope of the story she aims to tell, Patel does encounter some challenges weaving personal stories with broad currents in socioeconomics, politics, and history. She overstates some points. . . . Nonetheless, it is precisely Patel's sweeping vision and her deliberate and activist authorial voice that make this book unusually accessible and compelling to a broad audience. . . . This is a book that sounds a moral call we must heed."

PATEL, SHONA. Teatime for the Firefly; [by] Shona Patel 400 p. 2013 Harlequin Books

1. Historical fiction 2. India—Fiction 3. Love stories 4. Tea plantations—India 5. Teachers—Fiction

ISBN 0778317056; 9780778317050

SUMMARY: In this book, "because she is born under an unlucky star, Layla Roy fully expects to forgo marriage in favor of following in her grandfather Dadamoshai's footsteps to help increase educational opportunities for women in India in the 1940s.However, when Layla unexpectedly bumps into Manik Deb, an Anglo-educated Indian who has stopped by her grandfather's home to leave a message, she begins to think there might be more to life than teaching." (Booklist)

REVIEW: *Booklist* v110 no2 p39 S 15 2013 John Charles

"Teatime for the Firefly." "[Shona] Patel's remarkable debut effortlessly transports readers back to India on the brink of independence, while intriguing details about the tea industry in Assam, which Patel deftly incorporates into the story, add yet another layer of richness and depth. Fans of romantic women's fiction will be enchanted by Teatime for the Firefly's enthralling characters, exotic setting, and evocative writing style. . . . A fascinating glimpse of another time and place for teens who enjoy romantic historical fiction."

REVIEW: *Kirkus Rev* v81 no20 p158 O 15 2013

PATERSON, ANNA.tr. Fire. See Elfgren, S. B.

PATKE, RAJEEV S. Modernist literature and postcolonial studies; [by] Rajeev S. Patke xxvii, 164 p. 2013 Edinburgh University Press

1. English literature—History and criticism—Theory, etc 2. Imperialism in literature 3. Literature—History & criticism 4. Modernism (Literature) 5. Postcolonialism

ISBN 0748639926 (hardback); 0748639934 (pbk.); 9780748639922 (hardback); 9780748639939 (pbk.)

LC 2013-412449

SUMMARY: This book presents an "account of modernist writing in a perspective based on the reading strategies developed by postcolonial studies. Its basic argument is that neither modernity nor colonialism . . . can be properly understood without recognition of their intertwined development. It . . . demonstrates how the impact of Western modernism produced new developments in writing from all the former colonies of Europe and the US." (Publisher's note)

REVIEW: *Choice* v51 no4 p631-2 D 2013 D. C. Maus

REVIEW: *TLS* no5766 p26 O 4 2013 BENJAMIN POORE

"Modernist Literature and Postcolonial Studies." "This slim and attractive study by Rajeev Patke contributes to the intellectual reassessment of the ways in which modernist literary culture is inflected by colonial and imperialist history across the globe. . . . Abstruse critical debates over the nature of terms such as 'national allegory' . . . are rendered lucidly. . . The author, however, has a mildly irksome habit of interrupting discussion with a long series of questions, which on the whole go unanswered. . . . This short study is, nevertheless, impressive in its range of reference, synthesizing and translating crucial debates on texts that are necessary reading for anyone wishing to explore the field of postcolonial literature in a more than cursory manner."

PATOMAKI, HEIKKI. The great Eurozone disaster. See The great Eurozone disaster

PATRICK, ANNE E. Conscience and Calling; Ethical Reflections on Catholic Women's Church Vocations; [by] Anne E. Patrick 224 p. 2013 Bloomsbury USA Academic

1. Monastic life of women 2. Ordination of women—Catholic Church 3. Religious literature 4. Vocation 5. Women in the Catholic Church

ISBN 1441144528; 9781441144522

SUMMARY: In this book "about Catholic women religious after 1970," author Anne E. Patrick "uses historical and contemporary conflicts between Catholic sisters and Catholic institutions to illustrate a shift to what she calls the 'egalitarian-feminist paradigm,' which recognizes the equal ontological status of women. . . . She calls for women priests, but also for patience in the persistent struggle." (Choice: Current Reviews for Academic Libraries)

REVIEW: *Choice* v51 no8 p1418-9 Ap 2014 K. A. Dugan

"Conscience and Calling: Ethical Reflections on Catholic Women's Church Vocations". "[Anne E.] Patrick . . . interweaves theological, historical, and ethical questions into a poignant story about Catholic women religious after 1970. . . . Patrick makes her positions on the contentious issues she discusses overt, and she weaves her theological claims into historical realities. This creative book engages readers in the important history of Catholic sisters, but does so by making larger claims about vocation, justice, and the Catholic Church."

PATRICK, DENISE LEWIS. A matter of souls; [by] Denise Lewis Patrick 186 p. 2014 Carolrhoda Lab

1. African Americans—Southern States—Fiction 2. American short stories 3. Historical fiction 4. Race relations—Fiction

ISBN 0761392807; 9780761392804 (trade hard cover : alk. paper)

LC 2013-017597

SUMMARY: "As Elise's brother fights for his country in Vietnam, she must invade a doctor's 'Whites Only' waiting room to save her mother from dying. In another story, sixteen-year-old Hazel sees her future as one defined by white society." (Horn Book Magazine)

REVIEW: *Booklist* v110 no11 p58 F 1 2014 Michael Cart

REVIEW: *Bull Cent Child Books* v67 no9 p472 My 2014 K. C.

REVIEW: *Horn Book Magazine* v90 no2 p127 Mr/Ap 2014 BETTY CARTER

"A Matter of Souls." "This debut collection presents eight stories in which the protagonists have a moment to decide how they want to live their lives and establish the moral direction of their existence. Seven draw on the black experience in America, taking readers into the Deep South from the days of slavery through the Civil War and Jim Crow laws. The titular (and least effective) story introduces a Spanish merchant who acknowledges his part in the African slave trade. While the prose in these compelling narratives is sometimes pedestrian, the complexity of each moment marks its power."

REVIEW: *Kirkus Rev* v82 no3 p258 F 1 2014

"A Matter of Souls". "Eight short stories with long memory cut to the quick—all the more as they could be true. Patrick's tales from the distant and not-so-distant past shed fresh light on interracial and intraracial conflicts that shape and often distort the realities of African-Americans. The youthful characters possess passion and purpose, even if they remain misguided or too proud to live safely within their historically situated habitats. . . . The plots and characters change from one story to the next, but each one artfully tells a poignant truth without flinching. Shocking, informative and powerful, this volume offers spectacular literary snapshots of black history and culture."

REVIEW: *SLJ* v60 no4 p172 Ap 2014 L. Lee Butler

REVIEW: *Voice of Youth Advocates* v37 no1 p72 Ap 2014 Beth Green

PATTEN, RYAN. Hunting for "dirtbags". See Way, L. B.

PATTERSON, BRADLEY WILLIAM. Redefining Reason; The Story of the Twentieth Century Primitive Mentality Debate; [by] Bradley William Patterson 396 p. 2011 Author Solutions

1. Anthropology & history 2. Historical literature 3. Indigenous peoples—Study & teaching 4. Reason 5. Science—History

ISBN 1453589392; 9781453589397

SUMMARY: This book by Bradley William Patterson examines "science's view of reason as it relates to anthropology, from the time of Darwin to the present day. In doing so, he unveils a number of internecine arguments within the scientific community, as well as the hand-wringing in Western culture that has led to a near abandonment of the study of reason altogether." (Kirkus Reviews)

REVIEW: *Kirkus Rev* p45-6 D 15 2013 supplemet best books 2013

"Redefining Reason: The Story of the Twentieth Century 'Primitive' Mentality Debate". "[Bradley William] Patterson provides a wealth of information in an approachable but sometimes melodramatic form. . . . Though open to the general reader, Patterson's work will best lend itself to students of anthropology or sociology, and it will be a worthwhile reference for the often intractable arguments affecting such fields and the sometimes larger-than-life personalities who have shaped them. A sharp, wide-ranging historical study."

REVIEW: *Kirkus Rev* v81 no14 p62 Jl 15 2013

PATTERSON, JAMES, 1947-. Treasure hunters; 480 p. 2013 Little, Brown and Company

1. Adventure and adventurers—Fiction 2. Adventure stories 3. Brothers and sisters—Fiction 4. Buried treasure—Fiction 5. Missing persons—Fiction 6. Seafaring life—Fiction 7. Twins—Fiction

ISBN 031620756X; 9780316207560

LC 2012-040968

SUMMARY: In this book, by James Patterson, Chris Grabenstein and Mark Shulman, "the Kidd siblings have grown up diving down to shipwrecks and traveling the world, helping their famous parents recover everything from swords to gold doubloons from the bottom of the ocean. But after their parents disappear n the job, the kids are suddenly thrust into the biggest treasure hunt of their lives." (Publisher's note)

REVIEW: *Booklist* v110 no18 p72 My 15 2014 Sharton Hrycewicz

REVIEW: *Booklist* v110 no3 p98 O 1 2013 Carolyn Phelan

REVIEW: *Kirkus Rev* v81 no15 p78 Ag 1 2013

REVIEW: *N Y Times Book Rev* p37 N 10 2013 MARJORIE INGALL

"Treasure Hunters" and "The Very Nearly Honorable League of Pirates: Magic Marks the Spot." "['Treasure Hunters'] is pretty jam-packed. . . . This wild ride is narrated by Bick, 12, whose rat-a-tat descriptions of the siblings' adventures are accompanied by drawings by his twin sister, Beck. These black-and-white illustrations are delightful. . . . There isn't a lot of emotional heft, jazzy writing or deep characterization here, and the broad humor often falls flat. . . . Caroline Carlson's 'Very Nearly Honorable League of Pirates' is a more langurously paced seafaring adventure. . . . Basically, this is a drawing-room comedy set on the high seas. . . . The book is deliciously feminist but wears its politics lightly."

REVIEW: *Publ Wkly* v260 no32 p60 Ag 12 2013

REVIEW: *Publ Wkly* v260 no48 p51 N 25 2013

REVIEW: *Publ Wkly* v260 no37 p13 S 16 2013 Sally Lodge

PATTISON, GEORGE.ed. The Oxford handbook of Kierkegaard. See The Oxford handbook of Kierkegaard

PAUL, ALAN. One way out; the inside history of the Allman Brothers Band; [by] Alan Paul 416 p. 2014 St. Martin's Press

1. Music literature 2. Oral history 3. Rock musicians—United States—Biography
ISBN 1250040493; 9781250040497 (hardback)
LC 2013-030280

SUMMARY: This book traces the history of the Allman Brothers Band. "Framed as an oral history, the biography includes . . . comments not only from band members but also from players at all levels of the music business. . . . They take us through the milestones, from the early days . . . to the cusp of massive success and the deaths of bandleader and guitarist Duane Allman and bassist Berry Oakley, to the group's decision to soldier on in spite of the losses." (Booklist)

REVIEW: *Booklist* v110 no5 p21 N 1 2013 Joanne Wilkinson

"One Way Out: The Inside Story of the Allman Brothers Band". "Perhaps no music journalist has written as extensively about the Allman Brothers Band as [Alan] Paul, who has tracked the rock group's career for 25 years. And his deep familiarity with the band and its music shows everywhere in this fluid account. Framed as an oral history, the biography includes extensive, insightful comments not only from band members but also from players at all levels of the music business. . . . Augmented by photos and fascinating sidebars, this candid oral history has appeal beyond the Allman Brothers Band's loyal fan base."

REVIEW: *Kirkus Rev* v81 no24 p55 D 15 2013

"One Way Out: The Inside History of the Allman Brothers Band". "One need not share the author's belief in the band's supremacy to find its story engrossing. The majority of the book takes the form of oral history, which on other projects might sometimes seem slapdash and lazy but here proves crucial, for there are so many different perspectives—on everything from the band's name to leadership and songwriting credits—that having dozens of different voices serves readers well. . . . The author doesn't pull punches, but all involved should find it fair as well as comprehensive."

REVIEW: *Libr J* v139 no10 p62 Je 1 2014 Douglas King

REVIEW: *N Y Times Book Rev* p38-9 Je 1 2014 HOWARD HAMPTON

REVIEW: *Publ Wkly* v260 no43 p47 O 28 2013

PAUL, GREG.il. Scaly spotted feathered frilled. See Thimmesh, C.

PAULL, GREG. China Cmo; [by] Greg Paull 350 p. 2013 Whirlwind Book Consultancy

1. Business—China 2. Business literature 3. Chief marketing officers—Interviews 4. China—Social life & customs—2002- 5. Marketing—China
ISBN 9789881554239; 9881554233

SUMMARY: "As companies invest more and more in marketing, raising the country to second behind the US in advertising spending, there have been many white papers, books, and reports on how to win." Written by Greg Paull and Shufen Goh, "This book . . . comes straight from the mouths, heads, and hearts of sixteen of the leading CMOs (Chief Marketing Officers) based in China." (Publisher's note)

REVIEW: *Kirkus Rev* v81 no16 p183 Ag 15 2013

"China CMO Best Practice in Marketing Effectiveness & Efficiency in the Middle Kingdom." "[Greg] Paull and ShuFen [Goh]'s debut targets Western corporate types with capital to invest, but the accessible, conversational style makes it a compelling read for anyone interested in marketing and culture. The authors' team conducted face-to-face interviews with 17 top chief marketing officers in China, and the book begins with profiles (and color pictures) of each of these 'visionaries behind the brands.' . . . Lively chapters contain hands-on advice concerning best practices--how to build a brand around the Chinese (and not the Western) consumer--and emerging trends to watch, like China's changing demographics or the decline of foreign brand appeal."

PAVONE, CHRIS. The expats; a novel; [by] Chris Pavone 327 p. 2012 Crown Publishers

1. Americans—Luxembourg—Fiction 2. FICTION—Espionage 3. FICTION—Suspense 4. FICTION—Thrillers
ISBN 0307956350; 9780307956354 (hardback); 9780307956378 (ebook)
LC 2011-046207

SUMMARY: This book tells the story of "Kate Moore [who] is a working mother, struggling to make ends meet, to raise children, to keep a spark in her marriage . . . and to maintain an increasingly unbearable life-defining secret. So when her husband is offered a lucrative job in Luxembourg, she jumps at the chance to leave behind her double-life, to start anew. She begins to reinvent herself as an expat." (Publisher's note)

REVIEW: *New York Times* v163 no56432 pC4 Mr 6 2014 JANET MASLIN

"The Accident". "'The Accident' is a thriller about publishing, and if that sounds like an oxymoron, Mr. [Chris] Pavone is very good at rendering it wildly dramatic. He's also good at diverting close scrutiny about where any holes in his story may be. He just keeps the shocks coming and leaves the head scratching for later. . . . He lards this book with keen, bittersweet observations about the publishing world, details that become a big, poignant part of its appeal. He is clearly familiar with the trajectory of publishing careers, starting with the early years in which the word 'career' doesn't even register. . . . You will want to finish Mr. Pavone's 'The Accident' at a nice, rapid clip to see how these pieces come together."

PAVONE, CHRIS. The Accident; a novel; [by] Chris Pavone 608 p. 2014 Random House Large Print

1. Accidents—Fiction 2. Manuscripts 3. Publishers & publishing—Fiction 4. Suspense fiction 5. United States. Central Intelligence Agency
ISBN 0804121192 (pbk.); 9780804121194 (pbk.)
LC 2013-025677

SUMMARY: In this book, by Chris Pavone, "literary agent Isabel Reed is turning the final pages of a mysterious, anonymous manuscript, racing through the explosive revelations about powerful people. . . . In Copenhagen, veteran CIA operative Hayden Gray, determined that this sweeping story be buried, is suddenly staring down the barrel of an unexpected gun. And in Zurich, the author himself is hiding in a shadowy expat life, trying to atone for a lifetime's worth of lies and betrayals." (Publisher's note)

REVIEW: *Booklist* v110 no9/10 p48 Ja 1 2014 Thomas Gaughan

REVIEW: *Booklist* v111 no3 p93 O 1 2014 Kaite Mediatore Stover

REVIEW: *Kirkus Rev* v81 no24 p102 D 15 2013

REVIEW: *Libr J* v139 no8 p44 My 1 2014 Anna Mickelsen

REVIEW: *Libr J* v138 no21 p91 D 1 2013 Ron Terpening

REVIEW: *New York Times* v163 no56432 pC4 Mr 6 2014 JANET MASLIN

"The Accident". "'The Accident' is a thriller about publishing, and if that sounds like an oxymoron, Mr. [Chris] Pavone is very good at rendering it wildly dramatic. He's also good at diverting close scrutiny about where any holes in his story may be. He just keeps the shocks coming and leaves the head scratching for later. . . . He lards this book with keen, bittersweet observations about the publishing world, details that become a big, poignant part of its appeal. He is clearly familiar with the trajectory of publishing careers, starting with the early years in which the word 'career' doesn't even register. . . . You will want to finish Mr. Pavone's 'The Accident' at a nice, rapid clip to see how these pieces come together."

REVIEW: *Publ Wkly* v261 no12 p12 Mr 24 2014

REVIEW: *Publ Wkly* v260 no52 p33 D 23 2013

REVIEW: *Publ Wkly* v261 no9 p7 Mr 3 2014

PAVONE, CLAUDIO. A civil war; a history of the Italian resistance; xxiv, 744 p. 2013 Verso

1. Fascism—Italy—History 2. Historical literature 3. Italy—History—1914-1945 4. World War, 1939-1945—Underground movements—Italy
ISBN 1844677508 (alk. paper); 9781844677504 (alk. paper)
LC 2013-029227

SUMMARY: In this book, historian Claudio Pavone "combines three struggles together into the concept of a 'civil war' in Italy between 1943 and 1945. A 'patriotic war,' a 'civil war,' and a 'class war' raged simultaneously and interconnectedly." The book was translated into English by Peter Levy with David Broder. (Choice: Current Reviews for Academic Libraries)

REVIEW: *Choice* v51 no8 p1480-1 Ap 2014 D. E. Rogers

"A Civil War: A History of the Italian Resistance". "This is one of the most important and fundamental books about Italian history written in the last two decades. After appearing in Italian in 1991, it is now available for the first time in English. The book is responsible for changing the discourse about Fascism and resistance. . . . [Claudio] Pavone's decades as an archivist acquainted him with all essential official and semi-official sources, which he complements with literary and journalistic accounts. Peter Levy's translation is fluid and accessible. Indispensable for study and research concerning WW II in Italy, the fall of Fascism, and the birth of the First Italian Republic."

REVIEW: *TLS* no5797 p27 My 9 2014 JOHN FOOT

PAWEL, MIRIAM. The Crusades of Cesar Chavez; a biography; [by] Miriam Pawel 560 p. 2014 St. Martin's Press

1. Agricultural laborers—Labor unions 2. Biography (Literary form) 3. Chavez, Cesar, 1927-1993 4. Human rights workers 5. Mexican Americans—Biography
ISBN 1608197107; 9781608197101

SUMMARY: This book by Miriam Pawel presents a "biography of the innovative, daring, and persevering activist" Cesar Chavez. "Chavez (1927-93) dropped out of school to work in the fields to support his destitute, homeless family, joining the ranks of California's exploited Mexican American migrant workers. Driven by his social conscience, pragmatic genius, and motivational ardor . . . . Chavez created a scrappy and revolutionary labor union for 'the poorest, most powerless workers in the country.'" (Booklist)

REVIEW: *Booklist* v110 no19/20 p25 Je 1 2014 Donna Seaman

REVIEW: *Booklist* v110 no14 p35 Mr 15 2014 Donna Seaman

"The Crusades of Cesar Chavez". "[Miriam] Pawel, rigorous and captivating, follows her history of Cesar Chavez's crusade to protect farm workers' rights, 'The Union of Their Dreams' (2009), with a zestful, dramatic, and redefining biography of the innovative, daring, and persevering activist. . . . Pawel thoroughly chronicles every aspect of Chavez's battles against California's politically dominant produce growers, from audacious strikes to the now legendary national grape boycott to his penitential fasts. . . . Chavez's epic story, told so astutely and passionately by Pawel, is essential to understanding today's struggles for justice and equality."

REVIEW: *Choice* v52 no1 p147-8 St 2014 R. Acuña

REVIEW: *Economist* v411 no8881 p74-5 Ap 5 2014

REVIEW: *Kirkus Rev* v82 no4 p218 F 15 2014

REVIEW: *Libr J* v139 no3 p115 F 15 2014 Duncan Stewart

REVIEW: *Libr J* v138 no16 p58 O 1 2013 Barbara Hoffert

REVIEW: *N Y Times Book Rev* p26 Ap 27 2014 THOMAS GEOGHEGAN

REVIEW: *New Yorker* v90 no8 p73-1 Ap 14 2014

REVIEW: *Publ Wkly* v261 no7 p88-9 F 17 2014

PAYNE, C. F.il. To dare mighty things. See To dare mighty things

PAYNE, CHRISTOPHER.tr. Decoded. See Mai Jia

PAYTON, BRIAN. The Wind Is Not a River; [by] Brian Payton 320 p. 2014 HarperCollins

1. Airplane crash survival 2. American historical fiction 3. Journalists—Fiction 4. World War, 1939-1945—Campaigns—Alaska 5. World War, 1939-1945—United

States—Fiction
ISBN 0062279971; 9780062279972

SUMMARY: This book, by Brian Payton, is a "tale of survival and an epic love story in which a husband and wife—separated by the only battle of World War II to take place on American soil—fight to reunite in Alaska's . . . Aleutian Islands. Following the death of his younger brother in Europe, journalist John Easley is determined to find meaning in his loss. . . . He heads north to investigate the Japanese invasion of Alaska's Aleutian Islands, a story censored by the U.S. government." (Publisher's note)

REVIEW: *Booklist* v110 no6 p27 N 15 2013 Joanne Wilkinson

REVIEW: *Kirkus Rev* v81 no20 p171 O 15 2013

REVIEW: *Libr J* v138 no20 p1 N 15 2013

REVIEW: *N Y Times Book Rev* p14 F 2 2014 SARAH FERGUSON

"The Wind Is Not a River." "When Japanese forces seized the Aleutian islands of Attu and Kiska in 1942, American censors immediately ordered a news blackout to hide the invasion from a jittery public. . . . In his gripping, meditative second novel, Brian Payton explores this nearly forgotten chapter of American history. John Easley, the ironically named hero of 'The Wind Is Not a River,' is a 'National Geographic' reporter who defies the press embargo and sneaks into the Aleutians, intent on bearing witness to the heroism of American flyboys . . . only to be shot down by antiaircraft fire."

REVIEW: *Publ Wkly* v260 no42 p28-9 O 21 2013

REVIEW: *Quill Quire* v80 no2 p26 Mr 2014 Patricia Maunder

PAZ, OCTAVIO, 1914-1998. The poems of Octavio Paz; [by] Octavio Paz 606 p. 2012 New Directions

1. Art in literature 2. Mexican poetry 3. Mexico—In literature 4. Poems—Collections 5. Spanish poetry—Translations into English
ISBN 0811220435; 9780811220439 (cloth : acid-free paper)
LC 2012-016228

SUMMARY: This book edited and translated by Eliot Weinberger is "the first retrospective collection of [Octavio] Paz's poetry to span his entire writing career. . . . This edition includes many poems that have never been translated into English before, new translations based on Paz's final revisions, and a . . . capsule biography of Paz by Weinberger, as well as notes on the poems in Paz's own words, taken from various interviews he gave throughout his life." (Publisher's note)

REVIEW: *Booklist* v109 no4 p13 O 15 2012 Diego Báez

REVIEW: *London Rev Books* v35 no13 p17-8 Jl 4 2013 Michael Wood

REVIEW: *Publ Wkly* v259 no38 p33 S 17 2012

REVIEW: *TLS* no5753 p23-4 Jl 5 2013 MARTIN SCHIFINO

"The Poems of Octavio Paz." "[An] elegantly produced new selection. . . . Paz borrowed and recast many other poets' techniques, but precisely for that reason he was able to take poetry in Spanish into areas that had remained unexplored, while incorporating influences such as Sanskrit sacred texts and Japanese poetry (he was an early enthusiast for the haiku), pre-Columbian myths and the Mexican version of Spanish baroque, notably the poetry of the seventeenth-century. . . . This eclecticism is on display in [Eliot] Weinberger's parallel-text selection. . . . A lot has had to be left out in order to span that sixty-five-year arc. . . . English readers will be able to appreciate Paz's variations of tone in many well-balanced, frictionless texts presented here."

PEACE, ROGER. A call to conscience; the anti/Contra War campaign; [by] Roger Peace xiii, 307 p. 2012 University of Massachusetts Press

1. Americans—Nicaragua—History—20th century 2. Christianity and politics—United States—History—20th century 3. Historical literature 4. Nicaragua—Relations—United States 5. Peace movements—United States—History—20th century 6. Solidarity—Nicaragua—History—20th century 7. Solidarity—United States—History—20th century 8. United States—Relations—Nicaragua
ISBN 9781558499317 (library cloth: alk. paper); 9781558499324 (pbk.: alk. paper)
LC 2012-007997

SUMMARY: This book "offers the first comprehensive history of the anti-Contra War campaign and its Nicaragua connections. Roger Peace places this eight-year campaign in the context of previous American interventions in Latin America, the Cold War, and other grassroots oppositional movements. . . . This book reveals activist motivations, analyzes the organizational dynamics of the anti-Contra War campaign, and contrasts perceptions of the campaign in Managua and Washington." (Publisher's note)

REVIEW: *Am Hist Rev* v118 no3 p890-1 Je 2013 Michael J. Allen

REVIEW: *Contemp Sociol* v43 no2 p249-50 Mr 2014 Brett Heindl

"A Call to Conscience: The Anti-Contra War Campagin". "[Roger] Peace capably illustrates the intricate details and dynamics of the loose, decentralized campaign to curtail the administration's aid to the Contras, while at the same time situating that long-running struggle against the political backdrop of the late Cold War. While the book is not without its flaws, it stands as an impressive synthesis of a tremendous amount of historical information. . . . Peace provides a sometimes dizzying chronicle of the movement with fastidious attention to the details of the movement's internal dynamics: its idiosyncrasies, rivalries, and dysfunctions. A great strength of the book is its rich portrayal of the individuals and groups that made up the core of the anti-Contra movement."

REVIEW: *J Am Hist* v100 no2 p605-6 S 2013 Toby Glenn Bates

PEACEBUILDING, POWER, AND POLITICS IN AFRICA; xviii, 353 p. 2012 Ohio University Press

1. Nation building 2. Peace-building—Africa 3. Peacebuilding—Africa—International cooperation 4. Political science literature
ISBN 0821420135; 9780821420133 (pb : alk. paper); 9780821444320 (electronic)
LC 2012-019442

SUMMARY: This book, edited by Devon Curtis and Gwinyayi A. Dzinesa, "is a critical reflection on peacebuilding efforts in Africa. The authors expose the tensions and contradictions in different clusters of peacebuilding activities, including peace negotiations; statebuilding; security sector governance; and disarmament, demobilization, and reintegration." (Publisher's note)

REVIEW: *Choice* v51 no1 p158 S 2013 J. P. Smaldone

"Peacebuilding, Power, and Politics in Africa." "Editors [Devon] Curtis . . . and [Gwinyayi A.] Dzinesa . . . have done a fine job planning this volume, for which Curtis provides a useful introduction to the salient issues. Its 15 chapters focus on topical issues such as governance, security sector reform, and disarmament-demobilization-reintegration; regional institutions such as the African Union and African Development Bank; global actors like the UN Peacebuilding Commission, World Bank, International Monetary Fund, and the International Criminal Court; and country and regional case studies."

PEACOCK, KATHLEEN. Thornhill; [by] Kathleen Peacock 352 p. 2013 Katherine Tegen Books, an imprint of HarperCollins Publishers

1. Juvenile detention homes—Fiction 2. Love stories 3. Mystery and detective stories 4. Paranormal fiction 5. Rehabilitation—Fiction 6. Werewolves—Fiction
ISBN 0062048686; 9780062048684 (hardcover bdg.)
LC 2012-051734

SUMMARY: In this young adult paranormal romance novel, by Kathleen Peacock, "Mackenzie struggles to reunite with her werewolf boyfriend, Kyle, in this sequel to 'Hemlock.' . . . She hopes to find him in Denver . . . . With two of her best friends . . . , she tracks him down at a werewolf nightclub. . . . There's little time for reunions, though, as a Tracker raid quickly sends Mackenzie, Kyle and Serena to Thornhill, a model 'rehabilitation camp.'" (Kirkus Reviews)

REVIEW: *Kirkus Rev* v81 no16 p43 Ag 15 2013

"Thornhill." "The plot wallows as Mackenzie struggles to reunite with her werewolf boyfriend, Kyle, in this sequel to 'Hemlock.' She hopes to find him in Denver, something of a mecca for those infected with Lupine Syndrome. . . . Unfortunately, far too much of the plot is given over to Mackenzie's hand-wringing over having put everybody in danger and the swoony kisses she shares with Kyle in stolen moments. Real-world parallels to such issues as closeted homosexuality and the spread of HIV are quickly indicated and then dropped. A semi-climactic confrontation leaves characters poised for Book 3; only series devotees will be as well."

REVIEW: *Voice of Youth Advocates* v36 no3 p81 Ag 2013 Bethany Martin

PEARCE, PHILIPPA, 1920-2006. Amy's three best things; 40 p. 2013 Candlewick Press

1. Children's stories 2. Grandparent & child—Fiction 3. Homesickness 4. Imagination 5. Sleepovers
ISBN 9780763663148
LC 2012-947755

SUMMARY: In this children's book by Philippa Pearce, "Amy is independent enough to request an overnight at Grandma's house. . . . Fortunately, Amy has the foresight to pack, along with all the normal stuff, her three best things. . . . When she feels homesick, she takes out one of her three best things, and each object takes her on a magical journey to her home, where she is reassured by finding everyone in their rightful places." (Library Journal)

REVIEW: *Booklist* v110 no8 p50 D 15 2013 Tiffany Erickson

REVIEW: *Horn Book Magazine* v90 no1 p78-9 Ja/F 2014 SARAH ELLIS

"Amy's Three Best Things." "Amy, determined and sensible, wants to stay overnight at Grandma's--in fact, three nights--but realizes that she might need to bring with her some sustaining talismans from home. . . . [Philippa] Pearce and [Helen] Craig pack a lot of emotion and truth into this gentle story. . . . This is a world of little crosshatched cottages in pastel colors, comfortably-shaped grandmas who bake, playgrounds that still have teeter-totters, and little girls who can solve their own problems."

REVIEW: *Kirkus Rev* v81 no19 p199 O 1 2013

REVIEW: *Publ Wkly* v260 no41 p59-61 O 14 2013

PEARLMAN, JEFF. Showtime; Magic, Kareem, Riley, and the Los Angeles Lakers dynasty of the 1980s; [by] Jeff Pearlman 496 p. 2014 Gotham

1. SPORTS & RECREATION—Basketball 2. SPORTS & RECREATION—General 3. SPORTS & RECREATION—History 4. Sports literature
ISBN 1592407552; 9781592407552 (hardback)
LC 2013-026263

SUMMARY: This book, by Jeff Pearlman, profiles "the Los Angeles Lakers of the 1980s, who won five NBA championships between 1980 and 1988 with an All-Star roster that personified the decade's egotism and excess. . . . Enigmatic and aloof Kareem Abdul-Jabbar stood seven-foot-two but possessed a short emotional fuse; Spencer Haywood was dismissed from the team for excessive cocaine use . . . and Johnson dictated personnel moves and hosted extravagant . . . sex parties." (Publishers Weekly)

REVIEW: *Booklist* v110 no9/10 p33 Ja 1 2014 Mark Levine

REVIEW: *Kirkus Rev* v81 no24 p221 D 15 2013

"Showtime: Magic, Kareem, Riley, and the Los Angeles Lakers Dynasty of the 1980s". "Although Pearlman recognizes the obvious athletic supremacy of these players and the domination of the team, he delivers a number of blows to the throats of some of his principals—noting, especially, the voracious sexual appetites of [Jerry] Buss and Magic Johnson and others. He tells us that [Kareem] Abdul-Jabbar hated white people and complains that he continued playing far too long. . . . Some significant games receive sumptuous detail, and the author ends with Johnson's announcement in 1991 that he was HIV-positive. Pearlman ably demonstrates how deeply flawed human beings can nonetheless create a near-flawless beauty on the court."

REVIEW: *Libr J* v139 no10 p108 Je 1 2014 Derek Sanderson

PEARS, TIM. In the Light of Morning; [by] Tim Pears 352 p. 2014 William Heinemann

1. British—Foreign countries—Fiction 2. War stories 3. World War, 1939-1945—Fiction 4. World War, 1939-1945—Underground movements 5. World War, 1939-1945—Yugoslavia
ISBN 0434022748; 9780434022748

SUMMARY: In this novel by Tim Pears, "It is May 1944. . . . High above the mountains of occupied Slovenia an aeroplane drops three British parachutists--brash MP Major Jack Farwell, radio operator Sid Dixon, and young academic Lieutenant Tom Freedman--sent to assist the resistance in their battle against the Axis forces. . . . Greeted upon arrival by a rag-tag group of Partisans, the men are led off into the countryside." (Publisher's note)

REVIEW: *TLS* no5788 p20 Mr 7 2014 ANTHONY CUMMINS

"In the Light of Morning." "'In the Light of Morning' is narrated in the third person but from the perspective of a young English officer, Tom, parachuted into Slovenia in 1944 to assist a Partisan raid on a railway Une in the Nazi-held north. Tom, an Oxford-educated linguist, is a safe choice of protagonist. His sensitivity to his new environment allows [author Tim] Pears to write about nature, as in previous novels. . . . A fondness for clipped sentences about nightfall can't hide Pears's discomfort during the story's necessary combat scenes. He favours evasion, and it's here that Tom seems an especially useful choice of protagonist. . . . In such sidesteps there is a trace of why Tim Pears once hesitated to write this kind of novel."

PEARSON, SUSAN. Arlo Rolled; 32 p. 2014 Amazon Childrens Pub

1. Children's stories 2. Peas 3. Plants—Juvenile literature 4. Self-realization—Fiction 5. Stories in rhyme

ISBN 1477847219; 9781477847213

SUMMARY: This children's book, written by Susan Pearson and illustrated by Jeff Ebbeler, presents a "story about a pea named Arlo who wants to be free. So off he rolls...and rolls...and rolls. He meets a slug, he meets a bug—and still he rolls until . . . you'll see! . . . Told in verse, this . . . tale explores the ideas of independence and striking out on one's own." (Publisher's note)

REVIEW: *Bull Cent Child Books* v67 no10 p536 Je 2014 A. A.

"Arlo Rolled". "This lighthearted destiny quest charms with its playful rhymes and zesty acrylics depicting Arlo's journey in the bold, playful colors of a lush garden. Full-bleed double-page spreads capture the immensity of the landscape compared to a single pea while conveying the sense of boundless possibility that keeps Arlo moving. With plenty of action, accessible and engaging rhymes, and a winning pea-sized protagonist, this rollicking readaloud makes a perfect companion to an introductory unit on plants or gardening—or just a warm day when summer produce abounds."

REVIEW: *Kirkus Rev* v82 no6 p270 Mr 15 2014

REVIEW: *SLJ* v60 no5 p90 My 2014 Mary Jean Smith

PEARSON, T. R., 1956-. Nowhere Nice; [by] T. R. Pearson 288 p. 2013 Minotaur Books

1. Adventure stories 2. Crime—Fiction 3. Drug dealers—Fiction 4. Revenge—Fiction 5. Theft—Fiction

ISBN 0312583192; 9780312583194 (hardcover)

LC 2013-024713

SUMMARY: In this noir novel by Rick Gavin, "The last time Nick Reid and his pal Desmond tangled with that crazy meth-dealer Boudrot, Boudrot landed in jail and Nick and Desmond helped themselves to the several hundred grand in cash hidden in his trailer. . . . But that Boudrot is even meaner and crazier than they've bargained for, and Nick and Desmond will be lucky to make it through alive on this wild, wacky chase through the Mississippi Delta." (Publisher's note)

REVIEW: *Booklist* v110 no3 p39 O 1 2013 Thomas Gaughan

REVIEW: *Kirkus Rev* v81 no22 p11 N 15 2013

REVIEW: *Libr J* v138 no18 p72 N 1 2013 Teresa L. Jacobsen

REVIEW: *N Y Times Book Rev* p27 D 15 2013 MARILYN STASIO

"Dust," Nowhere Nice," and "City of Lies." "[Author] Patricia Cornwell's imperious forensic scientist, Kay Scarpetta, shows uncharacteristic signs of vulnerability at the beginning of 'Dust.' . . . There's plenty going on at Scarpetta's bustling lab. . . . Buckle up for a rowdy ride with [author] Rick Gavin in 'Nowhere Nice' . . . , the latest in a riotous series set in the Mississippi Delta. . . . Calling these characters colorful doesn't begin to get at the rich regional nuances that Gavin mines at every pit stop from Arkansas to Alabama. . . . A sensitive hero is a good thing to have in a tough crime novel—up to a point. That point is passed in R. J. Ellory's 'City of Lies' . . . , when the doting author allows these tender feelings to soften his protagonists's brain."

REVIEW: *Publ Wkly* v260 no31 p47 Ag 5 2013

PEASE, ALLISON. Modernism, feminism and the culture of boredom; [by] Allison Pease xiii, 159 p. 2012 Cambridge University Press

1. Boredom in literature 2. Feminism and literature 3. LITERARY CRITICISM—Women Authors 4. Literary critiques 5. Modernism (Literature) 6. Women in literature

ISBN 9781107027572 (hardback)

LC 2012-012501

SUMMARY: "In this book, Allison Pease explains how the changing meaning of boredom reshapes our understanding of modernist narrative techniques, feminism's struggle to define women as individuals, and male modernists' preoccupation with female sexuality. To this end, Pease characterizes boredom as an important category of critique against the constraints of women's lives, arguing that such critique surfaces in modernist fiction in an undeniably gendered way." (Publisher's note)

REVIEW: *Choice* v50 no10 p1835 Je 2013 J. M. Utell

REVIEW: *TLS* no5757 p8-9 Ag 2 2013 LUCY SCHOLES

"Modernism, Feminism, and the Culture of Boredom." "Boredom, by its very nature, shouldn't be interesting, but Allison Pease's recent addition to the literature on the subject . . . appear[s] to suggest otherwise. . . . Pease makes a sharp distinction between male and female literary depictions of boredom. . . This, of course, is well-trodden ground in feminist studies, but the originality of Pease's argument comes with her claim that women's boredom is a previously unrecognized 'core constituent of women's modernism'."

PECHEY, RACHEL.ed. Insecurity, inequality, and obesity in affluent societies. See Insecurity, inequality, and obesity in affluent societies

PECK, ROBERT MCCRACKEN. A glorious enterprise. See A glorious enterprise

PEDERSEN, SCOTT C.ed. Bat evolution, ecology, and

conservation. See Bat evolution, ecology, and conservation

PEDICINI, LUCIANO.il. Herculaneum. See Guidobaldi, M.P.

PEDULLA, GABRIELE. In broad daylight; movies and spectators after the cinema; 171 p. 2012 Verso

1. Motion picture audiences—History 2. Motion picture industry 3. Motion picture literature 4. Motion picture theaters—History 5. Motion pictures & television 6. Motion pictures—Electronic distribution
ISBN 9781844678532
LC 2012-003861

SUMMARY: This book "explores how the interconnected evolution of formats and devices has disrupted the relationship between cinema (as art form) and cinema (as place): 'We have become indifferent to whether we see a film on widescreen with Dolby Surround, on an eighteen or forty-two-inch TV, on a laptop, or on our mobile phones.' We are living, [Gabriele] Pedullà argues, in 'the age of individual media.'" (Times Literary Supplement)

REVIEW: *Choice* v50 no1 p90 S 2012 W. W. Dixon

REVIEW: *Sight Sound* v22 no8 p93 Ag 2012 Chris Darke

REVIEW: *TLS* no5749 p23-4 Je 7 2013 JOHN RIDPATH

"MP3: The Meaning of a Format," "In Broad Daylight: Movies and Spectators After the Cinema" and "Film After Film: Or, What Became of 21st Century Cinema." "it is clear that the story of recorded music (and audio, even) is necessarily a story of formats. Indeed, in 'MP3: The meaning of a format,' Jonathan Sterne argues that if there is such a thing as 'media theory', there should also be a 'format theory'. . . . Gabriele Pedullà's' In Broad Daylight' explores how the interconnected evolution of formats and devices has disrupted the relationship between cinema (as art form) and cinema (as place). . . . This new aesthetic of 'twenty-first century cinema' is explored more deeply in J. Hoberman's 'Film After Film'."

PEERS, ANTHONY. Birmingham town hall; [by] Anthony Peers p. cm. 2012 Lund Humphries

1. Architectural literature 2. Birmingham (England)—History 3. City halls—England 4. Historic buildings—Conservation & restoration 5. Public architecture
ISBN 9781848220744 (hardcover: alk. paper)
LC 2011-937108

SUMMARY: This book by Anthony Peers "traces the history of the [Birmingham, England] Town Hall . . . from its inception in the late 1820s to its recent programme of restoration, with an emphasis on the important bond between the building and the people of Birmingham." (Burlington Magazine)

REVIEW: *Burlington Mag* v156 no1330 p36 Ja 2014 FRANCESCA HERRICK

"Birmingham Town Hall: An Architectural History". "Anthony Peers's book offers a timely and fascinating case study of how a major civic building must be allowed to evolve if it is to meet the needs of successive generations. Lucidly written and generously illustrated, this publication traces the history of the Town Hall . . . from its inception in the late 1820s to its recent programme of restoration, with an emphasis on the important bond between the building and the people of Birmingham. . . . The author's own passion for the Town Hall is reflected in the thorough nature of his research. As the architectural historian responsible for compiling the building's 1999 Conservation Plan, Peers perhaps knows the inner workings of its design better than anyone."

PEISERT, ARKANDIUSZ.ed. Sociology and the unintended. See Sociology and the unintended

PELECANOS, GEORGE. The Double; a novel; [by] George Pelecanos 304 p. 2013 Little, Brown and Co.

1. Art thefts—Fiction 2. Detective and mystery stories 3. FICTION—Mystery & Detective—General 4. FICTION—Suspense 5. FICTION—Thrillers 6. Veterans
ISBN 0316078395 (hardcover); 9780316078399 (hardcover)
LC 2013-017709

SUMMARY: This novel, by George Pelecanos, is an entry in the "Spero Lucas" series. "The job seems simple enough: retrieve the valuable painting . . . Grace Kinkaid's ex-boyfriend stole from her. It's the sort of thing Spero Lucas specializes in: finding what's missing, and doing it quietly. But Grace wants more. She wants Lucas to find the man who humiliated her--a violent career criminal with a small gang of brutal thugs at his beck and call." (Publisher's note)

REVIEW: *Booklist* v109 no22 p36 Ag 1 2013 Bill Ott

REVIEW: *Kirkus Rev* p13 2013 Guide 20to BookExpo America

REVIEW: *Kirkus Rev* v81 no8 p23-4 Ap 15 2013

REVIEW: *Libr J* v138 no11 p84 Je 15 2013 Michael Pucci

REVIEW: *N Y Times Book Rev* p21 O 6 2013 MARILYN STASIO

"Alex," "The Double," and "Japantown." "[Pierre] Lemaitre's plot is laid out with mathematical precision. . . . If this sounds a bit like 'The Girl With the Dragon Tattoo,' it's because Stieg Larsson did much to validate sadomasochism as a plot device,, and thriller writers jumped all over it. . . . In Frank Wynne's assured translation, there's even a raffish quality to the prose. . . . But in the end, it's still a formula . . . and it has already worn thin. . . . It's astonishing all the good stuff [George] Pelecanos can pack into one unpretentious book. . . . First-time authors have a tendency to throw everything into the pot. Barry Lancet does that very thing in 'Japantown' when he gives the personal life of his private eye too much prominence in an otherwise sophisticated international thriller."

REVIEW: *Publ Wkly* v260 no34 p50 Ag 26 2013 Patrick Millikin

PELLETIER, CATHIE. The summer experiment; [by] Cathie Pelletier 288 p. 2014 Sourcebooks Jabberwocky

1. Country life—Maine—Fiction 2. Psychological fiction 3. Science projects—Fiction 4. Unidentified flying objects—Fiction
ISBN 9781402285783 (tp: alk. paper)
LC 2013-049953

SUMMARY: In this book by Cathie Pelletier, Roberta has struck upon a surefire way to win her school's upcoming science fair: she and her best friend Marilee will make contact with the UFOs spotted above their town of Allagash, Maine, in hopes of being abducted (and, of course, returned). . . .

Before they can put their plan into action, Roberta suffers the loss of her beloved grandfather, [and] Marilee runs away inn protest of her father's new girlfriend." (Bulletin of the Center for Children's Books)

REVIEW: *Booklist* v110 no15 p90 Ap 1 2014 Abby Nolan

REVIEW: *Bull Cent Child Books* v67 no9 p473 My 2014 A. A.

"The Summer Experiment". "The book uses a light but deft touch in melding the serious with the comic, creating in the spunky Roberta a balanced and believable heroine feeling the first pangs of encroaching adolescence. [Cathie] Pelletier takes familiar themes—friendship, sibling rivalries, grief—and interweaves them with an unusual but enjoyable plotline; after all, how often do middle-grade protagonists experience alien abduction? Readers will enjoy the originality and accessibility of this humorous hike through remote northern Maine—interest in UFOs not required."

REVIEW: *Horn Book Magazine* v90 no3 p94-5 My/Je 2014 ELISSA GERSHOWITZ

REVIEW: *Kirkus Rev* v82 no5 p274 Mr 1 2014

REVIEW: *Publ Wkly* v261 no5 p57 F 3 2014

REVIEW: *SLJ* v60 no3 p146 Mr 2014 Kefira Phillipe

PELONERO, CATHERINE. Kitty Genovese; a true account of a public murder and its private consequences; [by] Catherine Pelonero 352 p. 2014 Skyhorse Publishing, Inc.

1. Journalism 2. Murder—New York (State)—New York 3. Police—New York (State)—New York 4. Witnesses—New York (State)—New York
ISBN 9781628737066 (hardcover: alk. paper)
LC 2014-004232

SUMMARY: Written by Catherine Pelonero, "'Kitty Genovese: A True Account of a Public Murder and Its Private Consequences' presents the story of the horrific and infamous murder of Kitty Genovese, a young woman stalked and stabbed on the street where she lived in Queens, New York in 1964. The case sparked national outrage when the New York Times revealed that dozens of witnesses had seen or heard the attacks on Kitty Genovese and . . . had failed to come to her aid." (Publisher's note)

REVIEW: *Nation* v298 no17 p27-31 Ap 28 2014 PETER C. BAKER

"Kitty Genovese: A True Account of a Public Murder and Its Private Consequences" and "Kitty Genovese: The Murder, the Bystanders, the Crime That Changed America." "In 'Kitty Genovese: The Murder, the Bystanders, the Crime That Changed America,' journalist Kevin Cook argues that the familiar version of the story doesn't conform to what actually happened. . . . In 'Kitty Genovese: A True Account of a Public Murder and Its Private Consequences,' Catherine Pelonero insists that this brand of revisionism is ludicrous. . . . [Pelonero's] extreme irritation with the revisionists makes her a weak historian."

REVIEW: *New Yorker* v90 no3 p73-1 Mr 10 2014

PELTO, PERTTI. Applied ethnography; guidelines for field research; [by] Pertti Pelto 351 p. 2013 Left Coast Press, Inc.

1. Anthropology—Field work 2. Anthropology—Research 3. Anthropology literature 4. Applied anthropology 5. Ethnology
ISBN 1611322073 (hardback : alk. paper); 1611322081 (pbk. : alk. paper); 9781611322071 (hardback : alk. paper); 9781611322088 (pbk. : alk. paper)
LC 2012-050878

SUMMARY: This book on applied ethnography by Pertti Pelto covers topics such as "gaining entry, recording and organizing field data, a host of specialized techniques, integrating qualitativ and quantitative methods, building and training research teams, rapid assessment and focused ethnographic studies, short- and long-term ethnography, writing up results, non-Western perspectives on research, and more." (Publisher's note)

REVIEW: *Choice* v51 no6 p984-5 F 2014 M. Cedar Face

"Applied Ethnography: Guidelines for Field Research." "[Pertti] Pelto . . . does an outstanding job of covering a wide range of applied techniques, and providing contextualized examples from many countries. Clearly described methodologies like RAP (rapid assessment procedures), FES (focused ethnographic studies), social mapping, sampling, sketch mapping, free lists, pile sorting, and diaries are useful at all levels. Likewise, Pelto provides understandable guidelines for basic skills like gaining entry, training research teams, recording and organizing data, data coding and analysis, and writing the final report. . . . Equally excellent as a course text or in the field for tackling a thorny research challenge."

PENNACCHI, ANTONIO. The Mussolini Canal; 460 p. 2013 Dedalus Ltd

1. Historical fiction 2. Italy—Fiction 3. Marshes 4. Poor people—Fiction 5. Reclamation of land
ISBN 1909232246; 9781909232242

SUMMARY: This book, which won the Strega Prize in 2010, tells "the story of a generation of poverty-stricken peasants from the Veneto and Tuscany, who were enticed south in the 1930s by the promise of land in the dreaded Pontine marshes, near Rome. Until that time, nobody sane would have gone there, the place a mosquito-infested swamp. But under Mussolini's fledgling rule, the marshes were properly drained for the first time in history, allowing land to be reclaimed, and many lives with it." (Publisher's note)

REVIEW: *TLS* no5753 p19 Jl 5 2013 CAROLINE MOOREHEAD

"The Art of Joy" and "The Mussolini Canal." "Neither of these novels, on the face of it, suggests an easy read. 'The Mussolini Canal'--which won the Strega prize in 2010--is cast entirely as a monologue, recounted by an elderly member of the Peruzzi clan to a young descendant. His story takes the form of answers to unseen questions. 'The Art of Joy' switches back and forth in time and place, including set pieces and snatches of diary. . . . With both of these imaginatively and unobtrusively translated books, perseverance brings considerable rewards."

REVIEW: *TLS* no5774 p8-15 N 29 2013

PENNATHUR, ARUNKUMAR.ed. Human work productivity. See Human work productivity

PENNY, H. GLENN. Kindred by choice; Germans and American Indians since 1800; [by] H. Glenn Penny 400 p. 2013 University of North Carolina Press

1. Germans—Attitudes 2. Germans—Social life and customs 3. Indians in popular culture 4. Indians of

North America—Public opinion 5. Public opinion—Germany
ISBN 9781469607641 (cloth : alk. paper)
LC 2013-001367

SUMMARY: This book by H. Glenn Penny examines "Germans' ongoing, two-century fascination with Native American history and culture. He begins in the 18th century and continues through Alexander Humboldt's explorations and German American artists' renditions, to East Germans' reenactments of Cheyenne warriors in the 1970s-80s and present-day swarms of German tourists visiting the US Southwest." (Choice: Current Reviews for Academic Libraries)

REVIEW: *Choice* v51 no5 p913-4 Ja 2014 M. Deshmukh

"Kindred by Choice: Germans and American Indians Since 1800." "In this expansive, engaging account, [H. Glenn] Penny . . . extracts many meanings from Germans' ongoing, two-century fascination with Native American history and culture. . . . This is a big book in the best sense--punctuated with numerous thought-provoking ideas for further discussion. Penny's nuanced exploration of this multilayered German fascination is a very readable volume that will engage both European and North American students of history."

REVIEW: *TLS* no5764 p10-1 S 20 2013 PETER C. PFEIFFER

PENNY, LOUISE. How the light gets in; Chief Inspector Gamache novel; [by] Louise Penny 416 p. 2013 Minotaur Books

1. Detective & mystery stories 2. Gamache, Armand (Fictitious character)—Fiction 3. Missing persons—Fiction 4. Murder investigation—Fiction 5. Police—Québec (Province)—Fiction
ISBN 0312655479 (hardcover); 9780312655471 (hardcover)
LC 2013-013622

SUMMARY: This book is part of Louise Penny's Chief Inspector Armand Gamache series. Here, Inspector Gamache heads to "Three Pines to help therapist-turned-bookseller Myrna find out why her friend Constance Pineault didn't turn up for Christmas. . . . En route to Three Pines, Gamache happens upon a fatality at the Champlain Bridge and agrees to handle the details. But this case takes a back seat to the disappearance of Constance when she turns up dead in her home." (Kirkus Reviews)

REVIEW: *Booklist* v109 no21 p38 Jl 1 2013 Bill Ott

REVIEW: *Booklist* v110 no5 p38 N 1 2013 Joyce Saricks

"How the Light Gets In." "Through [Ralph] Cosham's masterful narration, we feel every threat to Gamache and the members of his team as well as to the residents of Three Pines. Listeners might quibble that Cosham's Gamache speaks with an English accent, rather than French, but few would deny his skill at placing listeners right with Gamache in the middle of the action. . . . As always, Cosham applies his remarkable vocal talents to channel a range of character. . . . His reading effectively captures the edgy and emotionally charged intensity as the story unfolds, building to the dramatic conclusion. . . . This ninth entry is not to be missed for series fans, but those new to [Louise] Penny should start with the first, 'Still Life'."

REVIEW: *Kirkus Rev* v81 no8 p36-7 Ap 15 2013

REVIEW: *Kirkus Rev* p14-5 2013 Guide 20to BookExpo America

REVIEW: *Libr J* v139 no4 p119 Mr 1 2014 Neal Wyatt

REVIEW: *Libr J* v138 no12 p61 Jl 1 2013 Marlene Harris

REVIEW: *N Y Times Book Rev* p21 S 1 2013 Marilyn Stasio

"How the Light Gets In," "The Boy Who Could See Demons," and "Sandrine's Case." "The only way to thwart the dastardly schemes (too dastardly for credibility) of that monstrous villain (too monstrous to be true) is to set up a satellite link to the outside world. . . . Once met, the delightfully quirky inhabitants of Three Pines are the kind of people you can't wait to see again. . . . But they all seem better suited to the modestly scaled subplot. . . . [A] 10-year-old boy . . . shares narrative duties with his psychiatrist in Carolyn Jess-Cooke's startling novel. . . . Although Thomas H. Cook is often praised for the clarity of his prose and the sheer drive of his storytelling, he deserves a special citation for bravery. In 'Sandrine's Case,' he not only dares to write a novel with an unpleasant protagonist, but also makes him the narrator."

REVIEW: *Publ Wkly* v260 no23 p55 Je 10 2013

REVIEW: *Publ Wkly* v260 no43 p57 O 28 2013

PENTLAND, ALEX. Social physics; how good ideas spread-the lessons from a new science; [by] Alex Pentland 320 p. 2014 The Penguin Press

1. Inventions—Social aspects 2. Science—Social aspects 3. Scientific literature 4. Social interaction 5. Technology transfer
ISBN 9781594205651
LC 2013-039929

SUMMARY: In this book, author Alex Pentland "claims that collecting large amounts of personal data reveals how social networks can be engineered to operate most effectively in 'our new hyperconnected world.' Hidden patterns of behavior become clear by assembling and analyzing massive amounts of data. . . . Currently, the author is studying how 'the flow of ideas and information, [translates] into changes in behavior' in a corporate setting." (Kirkus Reviews)

REVIEW: *Choice* v52 no2 p279 O 2014 R. Bharath

REVIEW: *Economist* v410 no8873 p79-80 F 8 2014

REVIEW: *Kirkus Rev* v81 no24 p175 D 15 2013

"Social Physics: How Good Ideas Spread: The Lessons From a New Science". "By analyzing this data and observing the social dynamic in small-group meetings, [Alex] Pentland demonstrates how social networking can be used to boost the collective intelligence of a group open to testing new ideas, if it is not suppressed by a hierarchical corporate structure. Though the author recognizes the threat to privacy implicit in such monitoring when it is not voluntary, 'the potential rewards of...a data-driven society,' he writes, 'are worth the effort and the risk.' A fascinating view of the future of social networks that offers intriguing possibilities but also the potential of a dystopia greater than that portrayed by George Orwell in 1984."

REVIEW: *N Y Times Book Rev* p23 My 18 2014 EVGENY MOROZOV

REVIEW: *New York Times* v163 no56478 pB6 Ap 21 2014 STEVE LOHR

REVIEW: *Publ Wkly* v260 no48 p46 N 25 2013

REVIEW: *Science* v344 no6188 p1097 Je 6 2014 William P. Butz

PEPPARD, CHRISTIANA Z. Just water; theology, ethics, and the global water crisis; [by] Christiana Z. Peppard 230 p. 2013 Orbis Books

1. Human ecology—Religious aspects—Catholic Church 2. Human rights—Religious aspects—Catholic Church 3. Religious literature 4. Right to water 5. Water supply

ISBN 9781626980563 (pbk.)

LC 2013-037515

SUMMARY: This book by Christiana Z. Peppard "reviews the scientific, social and political realities of freshwater through the . . . lens of ethics informed by faith, particularly Catholicism. . . . Peppard writes that the challenge of clean water requires the need 'to specify values that can honor both universality and particularity and to navigate carefuly their translation into norms.'" (National Catholic Reporter)

REVIEW: *America* v210 no7 p35-6 Mr 3 2014 GARY CHAMBERLAIN

"Just Water: Theology, Ethics, and the Global Water Crisis". "Although the author writes from a Roman Catholic perspective, specialists in water issues, theologians and ethicians, as well as general readers, will profit from this pointed approach. . . . Dr. [Christiana Z.] Peppard is to be commended for her foray into the arguments and analyses of water from a theological and ethical perspective. At the same time, I have several concerns that I hope she examines later. Her brief but well honed discussions of theological themes and Catholic social teaching need to be applied more fully."

PEPPE, HELEN. Pigs can't swim; a memoir; [by] Helen Peppe 2014 Da Capo Press

1. Country life—Maine—Biography 2. Farm life—Maine—Biography 3. Human-animal relationships 4. Memoirs 5. Poverty

ISBN 9780306822735

LC 2013-042048

SUMMARY: This book is "a writer and photographer's . . . account of her hardscrabble childhood and adolescence in rural New England. [Helen] Peppe grew up on an isolated Maine farm the youngest child of nine. Her housewife mother left school after eighth grade, and her ex-Army father worked as the fix-it man for the local post office. . . . She escaped the harshness of her environment by seeking the companionship of animals, especially dogs and horses." (Kirkus Reviews)

REVIEW: *Booklist* v110 no9/10 p26-7 Ja 1 2014 Bridget Thoreson

"Pigs Can't Swim." "Time has not blunted the hard edge of her anger and fear toward her family, but her brief attempts to understand their perspectives prevent this from being merely a reckoning of past wrongs. Instead her recollections make for vivid, powerful stories. They are told one by one without a larger connecting narrative, but as they are pieced together, they present a striking picture of ignorance and neglect. . . . [Helen] Peppe's past, like the book itself, is raw and brutally depicted from the perspective of a child trying to make sense of the world and her place in it."

REVIEW: *Kirkus Rev* v81 no24 p174 D 15 2013

PERCY, BENJAMIN. Red moon; [by] Benjamin Percy 544 p. 2013 Grand Central Pub.

1. Love stories 2. September 11 Terrorist Attacks, 2001—Fiction 3. Speculative fiction 4. Terrorism—Fiction 5. Werewolves—Fiction

ISBN 1455501662 (hardcover); 9781455501663 (hardcover)

LC 2012-016127

SUMMARY: In this werewolf novel, a "lycan rights group launches a terrorist attack on an airliner that shocks the nation, and the main characters deal with the aftereffects. Claire is a lycan who lives an uneventful suburban life with her parents when a post-attack government raid sends her on the run. The lone passenger who survived the attack is Patrick, whose father's National Guard unit has just shipped out as part of the U.S. peacekeeping mission in the werewolf homeland." (Library Journal)

REVIEW: *Booklist* v109 no15 p32 Ap 1 2013 David Pitt

REVIEW: *Kirkus Rev* v81 no6 p168 Mr 15 2013

REVIEW: *Libr J* v138 no4 p73 Mr 1 2013 Dan Forrest

REVIEW: *N Y Times Book Rev* p24 Je 16 2013 JUSTIN CRONIN

"Red Moon." "[Benjamin] Percy's multistranded plot resists encapsulation. . . . Percy has a lusty flair for describing destruction. Among the novel's most successful, and unnerving set pieces is the car bombing of Portland's Pioneer Courthouse Square during a Christmas tree lighting ceremony. . . . Percy is clearly enjoying himself. When Claire and Patrick take the field, the book lights up, and the writing possesses a resonant, emotional honesty. But they're not the only story here, and other figures feel more like dutiful attempts to enlarge the scope. . . . It's a bit of a tangle Percy makes for himself. Although he works gamely to weave everything together, the results, particularly in the novel's turbulent second half, are visibly effortful."

REVIEW: *N Y Times Book Rev* p24 Ja 12 2014 ISHAN TAYLOR

REVIEW: *Publ Wkly* v260 no7 p41 F 18 2013 STEFAN DZIEMIANOWICZ

PERCY, JENNIFER. Demon Camp; A Soldier's Exorcism; [by] Jennifer Percy 240 p. 2014 Simon & Schuster

1. Afghan War, 2001—Veterans 2. Creative nonfiction 3. Exorcism 4. Post-traumatic stress disorder 5. Veterans—Mental health

ISBN 1451661983; 9781451661989

SUMMARY: This work of creative nonfiction by Jennifer Percy tells "the dark story of a soldier with PTSD who is haunted by his demons. . . . The author met a young man named Caleb Daniels, a traumatized veteran of the war in Afghanistan. As the young writer unraveled the soldier's tale, she learned that Caleb's illness manifests itself as an actual demon that he alone can see, a beast he calls 'The Black Thing.' For Percy, it becomes a way into a culture that she can never fully understand." (Kirkus Reviews)

REVIEW: *Bookforum* v20 no5 p9 F/Mr 2014 JEFF SHARLET

"Demon Camp: A Soldier's Exorcism." "[A] strange and often darkly brilliant book. . . . [Jennifer] Percy can't follow Caleb . . . any more than she can be an army Night Stalker. She has no choice but to engage with much of what he tells her at face value. Much to her credit, she doesn't pretend otherwise. . . . She is coy with facts, sometimes careless (for instance, she relies for part of her narrative on former Navy SEAL Marcus Luttrell's discredited memoir 'Lone Survivor'). This can be frustrating, as when Percy tells us that Caleb's prophetic dreams so impressed his commanding officers that they decided to let the sergeant 'lead the briefings.' Who can say? But, no, not very likely. . . . Greater truth is what Percy seems to be in pursuit of. And mostly, she finds it."

REVIEW: *Booklist* v110 no6 p12 N 15 2013 David Pitt

REVIEW: *Kirkus Rev* v81 no22 p92 N 15 2013

REVIEW: *Libr J* v139 no7 p49 Ap 15 2014 Sean Kennedy

REVIEW: *N Y Times Book Rev* p11 Ja 19 2014 LEA CARPENTER

REVIEW: *Publ Wkly* v260 no45 p64 N 11 2013

PERISIC, ROBERT. Our man in Iraq. See Our man in Iraq

PERKINS, MITALI.ed. Open mic. See Open mic

PERL, ERICA S. Aces wild; [by] Erica S. Perl 224 p. 2013 Alfred A. Knopf

1. Children's stories 2. Dogs—Fiction 3. Dogs—Training—Fiction 4. Family life—Vermont—Fiction 5. Grandfathers—Fiction 6. Jews—Fiction 7. Jews—United States—Fiction 8. Sleepovers—Fiction 9. Yiddish language

ISBN 0307931722; 9780307931726; 9780307975478 (ebook); 9780375971044 (library binding)

LC 2012-023335

SUMMARY: Written by Erica S. Perl, this book describes how "Zelly Fried has finally convinced her parents to let her get a dog, with the help of her grandfather Ace. Unfortunately, said dog (also named Ace) is a shoe-chewing, mud-tracking, floor-peeing kind of dog. . . . Also wild is the other Ace in Zelly's life. Grandpa Ace has decided to begin dating again and is dining and dancing every night, against his doctor's orders." (Publisher's note)

REVIEW: *Bull Cent Child Books* v67 no1 p45-6 S 2013 J. H.

"Aces Wild." "Following their debut in 'When Life Gives You O.J.' . . . eleven-year-old Zelly Fried and her irrepressible, Yiddish-speaking, quote-spouting, retired judge of a grandfather, Ace, are back. After working hard to get a dog, Zelly finds yet another challenge in training the boisterous new puppy, named Ace after her grandpa. . . . Zelly's middle-grade friendship angst, her embarrassment at her larger-than-life grandfather, and her gentle flashes of grief for her late grandmother are deftly and believably expressed. . . . [Author Erica S.] Perl is additionally adept at naturally incorporating elements of the characters' Jewish faith while keeping Zelly's broader experiences firmly on the foreground."

REVIEW: *Kirkus Rev* v81 no7 p261 Ap 1 2013

REVIEW: *SLJ* v59 no7 p84 Jl 2013 Kerry Roeder

REVIEW: *SLJ* v59 no9 p64 S 2013 Jessica Gilcreast

PERLIS, VIVIAN. The complete Copland. See Copland, A.

PERLOV, BETTY ROSENBERG. Rifka takes a bow; 32 p. 2013 Kar-Ben Publishing

1. Jews—Social life & customs—Juvenile literature 2. Jews—United States—Fiction 3. Picture books for children 4. Theater & children 5. Theater, Yiddish—Fiction

ISBN 0761381287; 9780761381273 (lib. bdg. : alk. paper); 9780761381280

LC 2012-028985

SUMMARY: In this book, "Rifka lives in early 20th-century New York City with her glamorous, devoted parents, who are stars of the Yiddish theater. She marvels at the transformations that they undergo and revels in backstage life, with its dressing rooms filled with makeup, ribbons, and beads; its clever props . . . ; and even its rules for how to perform a kiss. . . . When Rifka accidentally ends up on stage during a performance, she blanches only for a minute." (Publishers Weekly)

REVIEW: *Booklist* v110 no2 p73 S 15 2013 Ilene Cooper

REVIEW: *Kirkus Rev* p62 N 15 2013 Best Books

REVIEW: *Kirkus Rev* v81 no13 p224 Jl 1 2013

REVIEW: *Kirkus Rev* p42-3 Ag 15 2013 Fall Preview

REVIEW: *N Y Times Book Rev* p14 Ag 25 2013 VALERIE STEIKER

"Rifka Takes a Bow," "This Is the Rope: A Story From the Great Migration," and "The Blessing Cup." "It's refreshing to find three new picture books that take as their subject the stories of human families. . . . Betty Rosenberg Perlov grew up in [the world of Yiddish theater] and it's clear she knows it well. . . . Spare and evocative as a poem, [Jacqueline] Woodson's refrain winds through the book, fastening us to the comfort of memories and the strength of family ties. . . . If 'The Blessing Cup' never quite lifts off from its history lesson as do 'Rifka Takes a Bow' and 'This Is The Rope,' it nonetheless imparts a valuable message."

REVIEW: *Publ Wkly* v260 no24 p63 Je 17 2013

REVIEW: *SLJ* v59 no8 p87 Ag 2013 Martha Link Yesowitch

PERLSTEIN, DAVID. The Boy Walker; [by] David Perlstein 254 p. 2013 Author Solutions

1. Dogs—Fiction 2. Fathers & sons—Fiction 3. Jews—Fiction 4. Psychological fiction 5. Stand-up comedy

ISBN 1491714093; 9781491714096

SUMMARY: In this book by David Perlstein, "a protective dog and the therapeutic effects of stand-up comedy help heal a wounded family. Abbie Greenbaum is a 25-year-old slacker in San Francisco who coasts through a life centered on desultory dog-walking gigs and a garage band. He still lives with his dad, Morty, an American studies professor who specializes in deep ruminations on TV comedy. Morty's English bulldog, Brutus, who's chief among Abbie's canine charges, narrates their story." (Kirkus Reviews)

REVIEW: *Kirkus Rev* v82 no1 p300 Ja 1 2014

"The Boy Walker". "In [David] Perlstein's . . . winsome fable, a protective dog and the therapeutic effects of stand-up comedy help heal a wounded family. . . . Perlstein's novel has some twee conceits that might have overwhelmed it, particularly the plummy, stentorian narrative voice of Brutus. . . . Fortunately, the author's gift for sharp, empathetic human characterizations rescues the proceedings. He steeps the story in well-observed renditions of West Coast Jewish culture, from homey dinner routines to the theory and practice of stand-up comedy, in which kvetching is the wellspring of artistic revelation. Perlstein offsets the shtick with psychological depth and nuance, keeping it charming throughout.

A funny, affecting novel about fragmented lives that slip the leash."

PERREAULT, PAMELA.ed. Aboriginal peoples and forest lands in Canada. See Aboriginal peoples and forest lands in Canada

PERRIN, CLOTILDE. At the same moment, around the world; [by] Clotilde Perrin 36 p. 2014 Chronicle Books

1. Children—Fiction 2. Everyday life 3. Picture books for children 4. Space and time—Juvenile literature 5. Time—Systems and standards—Juvenile literature

ISBN 1452122083; 9781452122083 (alk. paper)

LC 2013-028005

SUMMARY: In this children's book, by Clotilde Perrin, "discover Benedict drinking hot chocolate in Paris, France; Mitko chasing the school bus in Sofia, Bulgaria; and Khanh having a little nap in Hanoi, Vietnam! . . . Perrin takes readers eastward from the Greenwich meridian, from day to night, with each page portraying one of (the original) 24 time zones." (Publisher's note)

REVIEW: *Bull Cent Child Books* v67 no8 p420 Ap 2014 D. S.

"At the Same Moment, Around the World". "The brief views and one-line summaries are, not surprisingly, a little reductive at times, but the point about simultaneity and difference is effectively made. The book's format of tall, narrow pages tacitly echoes the divisions of the time zones, and there's cunning craftsmanship in the soft pencil and digital illustrations, with recurring motifs . . . and visual rhyming . . . connecting the atmospheric bijou scenes. The book's decision to ignore the International Date Line, though, ends up suggesting a continuum that doesn't actually exist, and one or two other locations are unclear and even questionable."

REVIEW: *Horn Book Magazine* v90 no4 p82 Jl/Ag 2014 JOANNA RUDGE LONG

REVIEW: *Kirkus Rev* v82 no3 p300 F 1 2014

REVIEW: *Publ Wkly* v261 no3 p55 Ja 20 2014

REVIEW: *SLJ* v60 no3 p122 Mr 2014 Carol Connor

PERRO, BRYAN. The key of Braha; 184 p. 2012 Delacorte Press

1. Adventure and adventurers—Fiction 2. Daragon, Amos (Fictitious character) 3. Dead—Fiction 4. Fantasy 5. Good and evil—Fiction 6. Mythology 7. Voyages to the otherworld 8. Wizards—Fiction 9. Young adult fiction, French

ISBN 0385907672; 9780375896941 (ebook); 9780385739047 (hc); 9780385907675 (glb)

LC 2011-026173

SUMMARY: This book is the second in Bryan Perro's 'Amos Daragon' young adult fantasy series, translated from French, in which a 12-year-old sorcerer named Amos, "unwittingly takes on a hazardous mission: He's killed so he can pass into and fix a netherworld crowded with dead souls who aren't being permitted to pass on to their appointed fates. . . . Once there Amos receives aid against numerous enemies from a varied cast of . . . characters, many of whom are figures from mythology (explained in a lexicon)." (Kirkus)

REVIEW: *Booklist* v108 no13 p83 Mr 1 2012 Erin Anderson

REVIEW: *Kirkus Rev* v80 no4 p417-8 F 15 2012

"The Key to Braha." "In the second of the series, 12-year-old Amos unwittingly takes on a hazardous mission: He's killed so he can pass into and fix a netherworld crowded with dead souls who aren't being permitted to pass on to their appointed fates. . . . Once there Amos receives aid against numerous enemies from a varied cast of cardboard characters, many of whom are figures from mythology (explained in a lexicon). The translation from the French is sometimes slightly awkward . . . While Amos and his best friend Beorf, a man-bear, are likable, that doesn't make up for an excess of telling instead of showing readers the fast-paced, confusing tale. Perhaps readers of the first in the series will want to continue on, but this effort neither stands alone nor compels."

PERROTTA, TOM. The wishbones; [by] Tom Perrotta 290 1997 Putnam

1. Bands (Music) 2. Betrothals 3. Humorous stories 4. Love affairs 5. Musicians 6. Musicians—Fiction 7. Suburban life

ISBN 0-399-14267-3

LC 96-2-7404

SUMMARY: This novel is about the lead guitarist in a New Jersey wedding band. "After witnessing the onstage collapse of a 73-year-old singer . . . 31-year-old Dave Raymond starts to feel intimations of his own mortality, and he does the unthinkable. He pops the question to his long-suffering girlfriend, whom he's been dating on and off for 15 years. But as soon as they set the wedding date, Dave embarks on a torrid affair with a New York City poet." (Booklist)

REVIEW: *Booklist* v110 no9/10 p42 Ja 1 2014 DAVID WRIGHT

"To Hell and Back," "The Wishbones," and "The Night Train." "Tom Perrotta captures my neighbor's vibe perfectly in his first novel, 'The Wishbones'. . . . Dave's stairway to purgatory is hilarious and familiar to pretty much everyone who isn't a rock star. . . . [James] Brown's gargantuan presence looms large over two novels that deal with the universality of music. In Clive Edgerton's 'The Night Train,' it is young Dwayne's all-consuming desire to be James Brown that lures him across the color line in 1963 North Carolina. . . . 'To Hell and Back' is truly irresistible. Imagine being stuck in an elevator with Mr. [Meat] Loaf while he tells you about the amazing, tragicomic train wreck that is his life. You can't look away. With 17 brain concussions to his name. Meat proves to be every bit the poster child for testosterone poisoning that you'd expect."

PERRY, DOUGLAS. Eliot Ness; the rise and fall of the man behind the Untouchables; [by] Douglas Perry 352 p. 2014 Viking

1. Biography (Literary form) 2. Detectives—United States—Biography 3. Law enforcement—History

ISBN 0670025887; 9780670025886

LC 2013-018406

SUMMARY: Author Douglas Perry examines the career of Eliot Ness and "follows the lawman through his days in Chicago and into his forgotten second act. As the public safety director of Cleveland, he achieved his greatest success: purging the city of corruption so deep that the mob and the police were often one and the same. It was here, too, that he faced one of his greatest challenges: a brutal, serial killer known as the Torso Murderer, who terrorized the city." (Publisher's note)

REVIEW: *Booklist* v110 no9/10 p25 Ja 1 2014 Jay Freeman

REVIEW: *Kirkus Rev* v82 no1 p106 Ja 1 2014

"Eliot Ness: The Rise and Fall of an American Hero". "A thorough recounting of the career of Eliot Ness (1903-1957), from humble beginning to humble ending, with spectacular fame in between. . . . The author ably shows that there was far more to Ness' career than just his battles with [Al] Capone, with accomplishments that may even outweigh his work during Prohibition. . . . Alongside intense and energetic investigative tales, [Douglas] Perry injects humor into the story with anecdotes. . . . Despite minor flaws, there is much to learn and enjoy for crime-solving fans and American history buffs."

REVIEW: *Libr J* v138 no21 p113 D 1 2013 Amelia Osterud

REVIEW: *Publ Wkly* v260 no44 p57 N 4 2013

PERRY, JOLENE. The summer I found you; [by] Jolene Perry 256 p. 2014 Albert Whitman & Company

1. Amputees—Fiction 2. Dating (Social customs)—Fiction 3. Diabetes—Fiction 4. Love stories 5. People with disabilities—Fiction 6. Veterans—Fiction

ISBN 0807583693; 9780807583692 (hardcover)

LC 2013-028441

SUMMARY: In this book, by Jolene Perry, "Kate's dream boyfriend has just broken up with her and she's still reeling from her diagnosis of type 1 diabetes. . . . Aidan planned on being a lifer in the army and went to Afghanistan straight out of high school. Now he's a disabled young veteran. . . . When Kate and Aidan find each other neither one wants to get attached. But could they be right for each other after all?" (Publisher's note)

REVIEW: *Booklist* v110 no13 p72 Mr 1 2014 Bethany Fort

REVIEW: *Kirkus Rev* v82 no2 p122 Ja 15 2014

"The Summer I Found You". "Chapters alternate between Kate's and Aidan's first-person narrations, and each perspective rings true as their romance progresses from awkward-but-direct conversations to kissing and eventually sleeping together. The novel's thoroughly chick-lit cover . . . will prevent most guys from picking it up, and that's a shame, as [Jolene] Perry conveys Aidan's physical and emotional journey evocatively and with authenticity. . . . The romance is sweet and believable, but the only real momentum driving the plot is readers' knowledge that Kate's disability is an invisible one that she hasn't yet revealed to Aidan, which may not be enough for many. Likable main characters, lively dialogue and a timely topic of returning soldiers fill out this low-key romance."

REVIEW: *Publ Wkly* v260 no52 p53 D 23 2013

REVIEW: *SLJ* v60 no4 p172 Ap 2014 Gerry Larson

REVIEW: *Voice of Youth Advocates* v37 no1 p72 Ap 2014 Lindy Gerdes

PERRY, MARK. The most dangerous man in America; the making of Douglas MacArthur; [by] Mark Perry 416 p. 2014 Basic Books

1. Biography (Literary form) 2. Generals—United States—Biography

ISBN 0465013287; 9780465013289 (hardcover); 9780465080670 (e-book)

LC 2014-004629

SUMMARY: "At times, even his admirers seemed unsure of what to do with General Douglas MacArthur. . . . In 'The Most Dangerous Man in America,' celebrated historian Mark Perry examines how this paradox of a man overcame personal and professional challenges to lead his countrymen in their darkest hour. As Perry shows, Franklin Roosevelt and a handful of MacArthur's subordinates made this feat possible, taming MacArthur, making him useful, and finally making him victorious." (Publisher's note)

REVIEW: *Booklist* v110 no14 p45 Mr 15 2014 Jay Freeman

REVIEW: *Kirkus Rev* v82 no3 p264 F 1 2014

"The Most Dangerous Man in America: The Making of Douglas MacArthur". "In a study of quiet authority, [Mark] Perry spotlights the presumptuous commanding general at the moment of his evolving maturity during the Pacific theater and apotheosis in the Philippines. . . . While Perry is not blind to MacArthur's overriding character issues . . . the author does suggest that the general has been judged overwhelmingly by his strong-arm tactics . . . and also underappreciated for some of his actions during his wartime command in the Pacific. . . . Perry impressively moves through each of the seminal arenas of the Pacific war. A majestic overview with an engaging sense of the nuance of character. Thankfully, Perry doesn't become mired in familiar biographical detail."

REVIEW: *Libr J* v139 no5 p131 Mr 15 2014 Ed Goedeken

REVIEW: *N Y Times Book Rev* p27 Ap 27 2014 LYNNE OLSON

REVIEW: *Publ Wkly* v261 no6 p78 F 10 2014

PERRY, S. J. Chameleon poet; R.S. Thomas and the literary tradition; [by] S. J. Perry 280 p. 2013 Oxford University Press

1. English poetry—20th century 2. English poetry—Welsh authors 3. Influence (Literary, artistic, etc.) 4. Literature—History & criticism 5. Thomas, R. S. (Ronald Stuart), 1913-2000

ISBN 9780199687336 (hardback)

LC 2013-940964

SUMMARY: "'Chameleon Poet' . . . goes against the grain of previous studies by revealing Thomas as profoundly indebted to the English literary canon. Ultimately, Thomas emerges as a classic example of what Keats famously described as the 'chameleon poet,' and through this prism [author] S.J. Perry illuminates the various dimensions of his relationship with the literary tradition." (Publisher's note)

REVIEW: *TLS* no5790 p27 Mr 21 2014 CLARE MORGAN

"Chameleon Poet: R. S. Thomas and the Literary Tradition." "S. J. Perry's claim that 'Chameleon Poet' 'goes against the grain of previous studies by revealing the extent of R. S. Thomas's debt to the English canon' might be taken as a provocative challenge to established readings of the work of Wales's foremost twentieth-century poet. Perry's study is, however, far more illuminating than it is undermining, and his extensive consideration of critics from Thomas's homeland, combined with meticulously researched and persuasively argued assessment of influences from outside Wales, have paid off richly."

PERSILY, NATHANIAL.ed. The health care case. See The health care case

PERSONAL ARCHIVING; preserving our digital heritage; xx, 299 p. 2013 Information Today, Inc.

1. Archival materials—Conservation and restoration 2. Archival materials—Digitization 3. Digital preservation 4. Do-it-yourself literature 5. Electronic records—Management 6. Personal archives 7. Records—Management
ISBN 9781573874809
LC 2013-026748

SUMMARY: This book, edited by Donald T. Hawkins, "focuses on tools and methods for archiving personal digital content in a landscape dominated by mobile devices, social networking, and cloud-based storage. It concerns preserving personal and family memories. . . . The target audience for this book includes private citizens interested in personal archiving, academic researchers, librarians, archivists, historians, and public agencies." (Choice: Current Reviews for Academic Libraries)

REVIEW: *Choice* v51 no7 p1178 Mr 2014 A. Sabharwal

"Personal Archiving: Preserving Our Digital Heritage." "The contributors are academics and information professionals from the private and public sectors who share professional experiences and personal perspectives on scanning, image quality, organizing without the benefit of metadata and indexing standards used by institutions, long-term storage, obsolescence, and legal issues. The target audience for this book includes private citizens interested in personal archiving, academic researchers, librarians, archivists, historians, and public agencies. It may also be useful to archival consultancy services. Case studies are a salient feature, covering traditional archiving, scanning, digital scrapbooks, and weeding."

PERTIERRA, RAUL.ed. Migration, diaspora, and information technology in global societies. See Migration, diaspora, and information technology in global societies

PESSL, MARISHA. Night Film; A Novel; [by] Marisha Pessl 624 p. 2013 Random House Inc.

1. Detective & mystery stories 2. Fathers and daughters—Fiction 3. Investigative reporting—Fiction 4. Subculture—Fiction 5. Suicide—Fiction
ISBN 9781400067886 (alk. paper)
LC 2012-041163

SUMMARY: In this book, "when Scott McGrath hears that the young woman found dead in an abandoned Chinatown warehouse is Ashley Cordova, his investigative journalist genes begin to percolate. He knows Ashley as the gorgeous daughter of the legendary cult horror film director Stanislas Cordova. . . . The reporter has his own previous history with the elder Cordova and almost from the first, he suspects that, whatever the coroner said, Ashley's death was no suicide." (Publishers Weekly)

REVIEW: *Booklist* v110 no7 p38 D 1 2013 Candace Smith

REVIEW: *Booklist* v109 no17 p36 My 1 2013 Bill Ott

REVIEW: *Economist* v408 no8849 p71 Ag 17 2013

"Night Film." "Marisha Pessl's follow-up to her engrossing if hyperactive 2006 debut, 'Special Topics in Calamity Physics,' is both a more intricate and far darker affair. . . . At the outset, 'Night Film' follows a tried and tested template: [Scott] Mcgrath, like Stieg Larsson's Blomkvist, is a disgraced reporter who stumbles on a scoop that could rescue his career--and which gives him more than he bargained for. But Ms. Pessl swiftly veers from the standard whodunnit to deliver a more inventive, reality-warping tale about family curses, black magic and the manipulative influence of film. . . . But there are missteps. As with her first novel, this one occasionally feels overwrought . . . and overlong. . . . Yet for all its faults, 'Night Film' is an engrossing yarn."

REVIEW: *Kirkus Rev* v81 no9 p21 My 1 2013

REVIEW: *Kirkus Rev* p31 N 15 2013 Best Books

REVIEW: *Libr J* v138 no11 p85 Je 15 2013 James Coan

REVIEW: *Libr J* v138 no18 p57 N 1 2013 Victoria A. Caplinger

REVIEW: *Libr J* v138 no5 p90 Mr 15 2013 Barbara Hoffert

REVIEW: *N Y Times Book Rev* p11 Ag 18 2013 JOE HILL

REVIEW: *New York Times* v162 no56229 pC1-6 Ag 15 2013 JANET MASLIN

REVIEW: *New Yorker* v89 no30 p1 S 30 2013

"Traveling Sprinkler," "Night Film," and "Jane Austen's England." " This tender novel finds Paul Chowder, the poet narrator of [Nicholson] Baker's previous novel 'The Anthologist,' driving around Portsmouth, New Hampshire, and speaking into a handheld recorder. . . .[Marisha] Pessl has fun elaborating the backstory . . . but the foreground isn't always sufficiently compelling. The effect is that of a finely wrought diorama, brilliantly detailed but static. . . . This enjoyable history enlarges on themes that permeate Austen's evocations of the social customs of early-nineteenth-century England."

REVIEW: *Publ Wkly* v260 no23 p48 Je 10 2013

PETCHAUER, EMERY.ed. Schooling hip-hop. See Schooling hip-hop

PETER FALLON; Poet, Publisher, Translator, Editor; 296 p. 2014 Irish Academic Press

1. Editors 2. Fallon, Peter 3. Ireland—Intellectual life 4. Irish poets 5. Publishers & publishing—Ireland
ISBN 0716531593; 9780716531593

SUMMARY: In this book, edited by Richard Rankin Russell, an "array of esteemed writers honour [poet, publisher, and editor Peter Fallon,] a man who has had an immense influence on Ireland's artistic life since 1970." Featured authors include "Seamus Heaney, Medbh McGuckian, Paul Muldoon, Derek Mahon, Ciaran Carson, Dennis O'Driscoll, [and] Conor O'Callaghan." (Publisher's note)

REVIEW: *TLS* no5781 p26 Ja 17 2014

REVIEW: *TLS* no5781 p26 Ja 17 2014 PATRICIA CRAIG

"Peter Fallon: Poet, Publisher, Editor, and Translator." "Cultural and country pursuits make an intriguing framework to Peter Fallon's life. As a publisher and founder of the Gallery Press, he is in the thick of the poetry business, and, as a sheep farmer in Co. Meath, he is in the thick of glaur, cattle feed and wicked weather. He is also a poet and translator, as the subtitle of this collection of essays and poems, edited by Richard Rankin Russell, reminds us. The tributes to Fallon assembled here are a testament to the integrity and versatility of this 'leading publisher of Irish poetry.' . . . One of Russell's objectives is to place emphasis on Fallon's poetry, and to this end he has enlisted a good variety of academics and critical commentators."

PETERS, EVELYN.ed. Indigenous in the city. See Indigenous in the city

PETERS, JOHN G. Joseph Conrad's critical reception; [by] John G. Peters xiii, 274 p. 2013 Cambridge University Press

1. Bibliography (Documentation) 2. English fiction—History & criticism 3. LITERARY CRITICISM—European—English, Irish, Scottish, Welsh 4. Literature—History & criticism 5. Polish authors
ISBN 9781107034853 (hardback)
LC 2012-036037

SUMMARY: "While tracing the general evolution of the commentary surrounding Conrad's work, John G. Peters's . . . analysis also evaluates Conrad's impact on critical trends such as the belles lettres tradition, the New Criticism, psychoanalysis, structuralist and post-structuralist criticism, narratology, postcolonial studies, gender and women's studies, and ecocriticism." (Publisher's note)

REVIEW: *Choice* v51 no6 p1006 F 2014 R. Ducharme

REVIEW: *TLS* no5790 p21 Mr 21 2014 SUSAN JONES

"Joseph Conrad's Critical Reception." "John G. Peters's 'Joseph Conrad's Critical Reception' leaves us in no doubt of the diversity of the novelist's themes, his narrative experimentation, and the depth of his philosophical and psychological exploration, by charting over a century of criticism from the period of Conrad's first novel, 'Almayer's Folly' (1895), to the most recent twenty-first-century forays into ecocriticism. . . . To structure the volume, he selects the option of a chronological overview rather than focusing on distinctive areas of criticism as the organizing principle of each chapter."

PETERS, NANCY JOYCE.ed. The collected poems of Philip Lamantia. See The collected poems of Philip Lamantia

PETESCH, PATTI. On norms and agency; conversations about gender equality with women and men in 20 countries; [by] Patti Petesch xix, 207 p. 2013 World Bank

1. Cross-cultural studies 2. Sex discrimination against women 3. Sex role 4. Social science literature 5. Women—Social conditions 6. Women's rights
ISBN 9780821398623 (paper)
LC 2013-008678

SUMMARY: This book, written by Ana María Muñoz Boudet, Patti Petesch, and Carolyn Turk, "explores some of the power dynamics of gender relations within the household and communities in different contexts. . . . Women's aspirations and empowerment to break gender barriers can be observed almost everywhere, even when economies are stagnant. . . . Yet many women around the world, the study shows, still face norms and practices that limit them." (Publisher's note)

REVIEW: *Choice* v51 no2 p362 O 2013 C. Apt

"On Norms and Agency: Conversations About Gender Equality With Women and Men in 20 Countries." "This book presents the results of a World Bank study exploring how social norms in 20 culturally diverse countries impact gender equality, which in turn encourages economic development. The premise is that allowing women to reach their full potential . . . is the single most important way to spur development. In interviews and focus groups with over 4,000 men and women, [authors Ana María Muñoz Boudet, Patti Petesch, and Carolyn Turk] provide interesting accounts of what it is like to be a male or female in a variety of cultural settings. The problem that the book glosses over is that the global status of women . . . does not seem to be improving with enough force to impact economic development."

PETIT, EMMANUEL. Irony, or, the self-critical opacity of postmodern architecture; [by] Emmanuel Petit x, 262 p. 2013 Yale University Press

1. Architects—History 2. Architectural literature 3. Architecture & philosophy 4. Architecture—Philosophy 5. Architecture, Postmodern—Themes, motives 6. Irony 7. Modern architecture—20th century 8. Postmodern architecture
ISBN 0300181515; 9780300181517 (cloth : alk. paper)
LC 2012-021492

SUMMARY: Author "Emmanuel Petit addresses the role of irony and finds a vitality and depth of dialectics largely ignored by historical critiques. A look at five individual architects--Peter Eisenman (b. 1932), Arata Isozaki (b. 1931), Rem Koolhaas (b. 1944), Stanley Tigerman (b. 1930), and Robert Venturi (b. 1925)--reveals the beginning of a phenomenology of irony in architecture." (Publisher's note)

REVIEW: *Choice* v51 no1 p66 S 2013 J. Quinan

"Irony, or, the Self-Critical Opacity of Postmodern Architecture." "If Charles Jencks was the indefatigable chronicler and polemicist of postmodernism. [Author Emmanuel] Petit . . . has plumbed the ironic heart of the movement in a brilliant study informed by a wide-ranging knowledge of philosophy and a thorough command of structuralist and post-structuralist theory. Petit's expertise is brought to bear on the work of several leading architects: [Robert] Venturi and [Denise] Scott Brown, [Stanley] Tigerman, [Arata] Isozaki, [Peter] Eisenman, and [Rem] Koolhaas. Their shared sense that modernism had run its course notwithstanding. Petit reveals the disparate intellectual paths by which each architect came to embrace the ironic."

PETRICK, JANE ALLEN. Hidden in Plain Sight; The Other People in Norman Rockwell's America; [by] Jane Allen Petrick 143 p. 2013 Informed Decisions Publishing

1. Art & race 2. Art literature 3. Historical literature 4. Race relations in art 5. Rockwell, Norman, 1894-1978
ISBN 0989260119; 9780989260114

SUMMARY: This book tells "the stories of the Asian, African, and Native Americans who modeled for Norman Rockwell. These people of color, though often hidden in plain sight, are present throughout Rockwell's more than 4000 illustrations. . . . Jane Allen Petrick explores what motivated Norman Rockwell to slip people of color "into the picture" in the first place" and "documents the famous illustrator's deep commitment to and pointed portrayals of ethnic tolerance." (Publisher's note)

REVIEW: *Kirkus Rev* v81 no23 p26 D 1 2013

REVIEW: *Kirkus Rev* p46 D 15 2013 supplemet best books 2013

"Hidden in Plain Sight: The Other People in Norman Rockwell's America". " A fresh, well-researched study of artist Norman Rockwell's treatment of race. . . . [Jane Allen] Petrick . . . , in this smart, nuanced book, encourages readers to look again at Rockwell's varied body of work . . . Petrick relays all this with clarity and insight, drawing on the portraits, Rockwell's own biography and the ample scholarship that surrounds the artist. . . . In this book, she manages to say something revealing about the artist—and about us."

PETROVIĆ, MILENKO. The democratic transition of post-communist Europe; in the shadow of communist differences and uneven EUropeanisation; [by] Milenko Petrović xx, 196 p. 2013 Palgrave Macmillan

1. Political science literature 2. Post-communism—Europe, Eastern

ISBN 9780230354319 (hardback)

LC 2013-021283

SUMMARY: This book explores "the role of communist history in setting the different regional successes in post-communist transition. It challenges the dominant view that all communist systems were the same" and shows "how certain variations in the functioning of the communist political and socio-economic systems in East Central Europe and the Balkans defined the different modes of power transfer of states in the two regions and their subsequent pathways following the fall of communism." (Publisher's note)

REVIEW: *Choice* v51 no8 p1484 Ap 2014 J. W. Peterson

"The Democratic Transition of Post-Communist Europe: In the Shadow of Communist Differences and Uneven Europeanisation". "This book contributes to general understanding of the reasons for the different postcommunist paths taken by East Central European (ECE) countries and the Balkan political systems. [Milenko] Petrovic . . . adds to theoretical understandings by demonstrating that the ECE countries experienced communist takeovers from the outside, had reform outbursts during the communist period, and replaced the communist elite with reformers after 1989. . . . He fulfills the suggestion of Asie Toje that the EU is best positioned to exert influence on a precisely defined range of security issues."

PETRYNA, ADRIANA.ed. When people come first. See When people come first

PETT, MARK.il. The girl and the bicycle. See Pett, M.

PETT, MARK. The girl and the bicycle; [by] Mark Pett 40 p. 2014 Simon & Schuster Books for Young Readers

1. Bicycles and bicycling—Fiction 2. Determination (Personality trait) 3. Friendship—Fiction 4. Money-making projects—Fiction 5. Stories without words

ISBN 1442483199; 9781442483194

LC 2013-012024

SUMMARY: This wordless picture book, by Mark Pett, is "about a little girl, a shiny bicycle, and the meaning of persistence—with an unexpected payoff. A little girl sees a shiny new bicycle in the shop window. She hurries home to see if she has enough money in her piggy bank, but when she comes up short, she knocks on the doors of her neighbors, hoping to do their yardwork. They all turn her away except for a kindly old woman." (Publisher's note)

REVIEW: *Bull Cent Child Books* v67 no9 p473 My 2014 J. H.

REVIEW: *Horn Book Magazine* v90 no3 p70-1 My/Je 2014 CLAIRE E. GROSS

REVIEW: *Kirkus Rev* v82 no4 p123 F 15 2014

"The Girl and the Bicycle". "This wordless, retro book (the girl's molded curls, turtleneck, plaid skirt and Mary Janes definitely come from another era) champions both grit and kindness, but it seems mighty bleak at times. Moody cement-gray papers, nearly colorless illustrations and a cast of cold adults make the girl's determination and her working relationship with one kind neighbor all the more moving. Much of [Mark] Pett's engrossing narrative is relayed through characters' limbs, eyes and brows, as many times they simply don't have mouths. The blank effect of a face without a smile, smirk or frown carries unexpected weight, delivering a sense that the character struggles to withhold or manage emotions."

REVIEW: *Publ Wkly* v261 no7 p95 F 17 2014

REVIEW: *SLJ* v60 no4 p132 Ap 2014 Michelle Anderson

PETTER, JEAN-JACQUES. Primates of the world. See Primates of the world

PETTIT, PHILIP. On the people's terms; a republican theory and model of democracy; [by] Philip Pettit xii, 338 p. 2012 Cambridge University Press

1. Democracy 2. POLITICAL SCIENCE—History & Theory 3. Political science—Philosophy 4. Political science literature 5. Republicanism 6. State, The

ISBN 9780521182126 (pbk.); 9781107005112 (hbk.)

LC 2012-020514

SUMMARY: This book, written by Philip Pettit, "argues that state coercion will not involve individual subjection or domination insofar as we enjoy an equally shared form of control over those in power. This claim may seem utopian but it is supported by a realistic model of the institutions that might establish such democratic control." (Publisher's note)

REVIEW: *Choice* v51 no2 p352-3 O 2013 P. R. Babbitt

"On the People's Terms: A Republican Theory and Model of Democracy.""This is a densely argued account of how the republican conception of liberty, non-domination, requires popular sovereignty. [Author Philip] Pettit . . . does not argue that liberty and democracy are the same. Instead, he argues that because government is necessary, the only way that government avoids reducing liberty is by being controlled by the people. In crafting this argument, Pettit provides a thorough, sophisticated account of contemporary republican political thought, and the book would serve as a useful introduction to the topic. The republican tradition is situated in the history of political thought generally, but Pettit pays little attention to the history of republican thought specifically."

PEVEAR, RICHARD.tr. The enchanted wanderer and other stories. See Leskov, N. S.

PFEIFER, MARK EDWARD.ed. Diversity in diaspora. See Diversity in diaspora

PHAIDON PRESS.comp. Art & Place. See Art & Place

PHAIDON PRESS.comp. Vitamin D2. See Vitamin D2

PHAM, LEUYEN.il. Alvin Ho. See Look, L.

PHAM, LEUYEN.il. Bo at Ballard Creek. See Hill, K.

PHAM, LEUYEN.il. The boy who loved math. See Heiligman, D.

PHAM, LEUYEN.il. A stick is an excellent thing. See A stick is an excellent thing

PHARMACEUTICAL PRESS (COMPANY)comp. Herbal Medicines. See Herbal Medicines

PHELAN, MATT.il. Bluffton. See Phelan, M.

PHELAN, MATT. Bluffton; my summers with Buster Keaton; 240 p. 2013 Candlewick Press

1. Actors—Fiction 2. Friendship—Fiction 3. Graphic novels 4. Traveling theater 5. Vaudeville
ISBN 076365079X (reinforced); 9780763650797 (reinforced)
LC 2012-947260

SUMMARY: In this graphic novel by Matt Phelan, set "in the summer of 1908, in Muskegon, Michigan, a visiting troupe of vaudeville performers is about the most exciting thing since baseball. Henry has a few months to ogle . . . a slapstick actor his own age named Buster Keaton. Henry longs to learn to take a fall like Buster . . . but Buster just wants to play ball with Henry and his friends." (Publisher's note)

REVIEW: *Booklist* v110 no2 p59 S 15 2013 Sarah Hunter

"Bluffton: My Summer With Buster." "[Matt] Phelan's soft, pastel watercolors perfectly depict the idyllic lakeside summer as well as the riotous circus antics and elaborate pranks Buster and his family pull, both on and off the stage. There's enough background about vaudeville, Buster Keaton, and the real-life Actors' Colony in Bluffton to make this an informative glimpse into American history, but it's compellingly, solidly centered on Henry's discovery that, though the grass on the other side may appear greener, more exciting, and full of the thrill of fame, the grass on his own side, where he's happy being himself, is just as good."

REVIEW: *Bull Cent Child Books* v67 no1 p46 S 2013 E. B.

REVIEW: *Horn Book Magazine* v89 no6 p102-3 N/D 2013 SUSAN DOVE LEMPKE

REVIEW: *Kirkus Rev* v81 no12 p109-10 Je 15 2013

REVIEW: *Kirkus Rev* p81 N 15 2013 Best Books

REVIEW: *Publ Wkly* p95 Children's starred review annual 2013

REVIEW: *SLJ* v59 no12 p1 D 2013

REVIEW: *SLJ* v59 no7 p104 Jl 2013 Peter Blenski

PHELAN, MATT.il. Miss Emily. See Mutén, B.

PHELAN, MATT.il. Xander's panda party. See Park, L. S.

PHELPS, NICOLE M. U.S.-Habsburg relations from 1815 to the Paris peace conference; sovereignty transformed; [by] Nicole M. Phelps xi, 293 p. 2013 Cambridge University Press

1. Citizenship—United States—History 2. Diplomatic and consular service, American—History 3. Diplomatic and consular service, Austrian—History 4. Historical literature 5. Immigrants—United States—History—19th century 6. Immigrants—United States—History—20th century
ISBN 9781107005662 (hardback)
LC 2013-004471

SUMMARY: "This study provides the first book-length account of U.S.-Habsburg relations from their origins in the early nineteenth century through the aftermath of World War I and the Paris Peace Conference. . . . Nicole M. Phelps demonstrates the influence of the Habsburg government on the integration of the United States into the nineteenth-century Great Power System and the influence of American racial politics on the Habsburg Empire's conceptions of nationalism and democracy." (Publisher's note)

REVIEW: *Choice* v51 no7 p1293 Mr 2014 C. Ingrao

"U.S.-Habsburg Relations From 1815 to the Paris Peace Conference: Sovereignty Transformed." "Citing the US embrace of racial science, immigration restrictions, and language-based nationhood, [Nicole M.] Phelps argues that its leaders could not appreciate the legitimacy of a multiethnic, polyglot country like Austria-Hungary. Hence, policy makers like Woodrow Wilson and the unschooled 'experts' who advised him felt that European stability and the triumph of democracy demanded monolingual societies and the dissolution of multicultural polities like Austria-Hungary. Those who see Wilson as the helpless dupe of his European allies in 1919 should read this book. . . . Highly recommended."

PHILBRICK, RODMAN. Zane and the hurricane; [by] Rodman Philbrick 192 p. 2014 The Blue Sky Press, an imprint of Scholastic Inc.

1. Adventure stories 2. African Americans—Fiction 3. Hurricane Katrina, 2005—Fiction 4. Hurricane Katrina, 2005—Juvenile fiction 5. Racially mixed people—Fiction 6. Survival—Fiction
ISBN 0545342384; 9780545342384 (hardback)
LC 2013-025489

SUMMARY: In this children's novel, by Rodman Philbrick, "Zane Dupree is a charismatic 12-year-old boy of mixed race visiting a relative in New Orleans when Hurricane Katrina hits. Unexpectedly separated from all family, Zane and his dog experience the terror of Katrina's wind, rain, and horrific flooding. Facing death, they are rescued from an attic air vent by a kind, elderly musician and a scrappy young girl." (Publisher's note)

REVIEW: *Booklist* v110 no11 p68-9 F 1 2014 Thom Barthelmess

"Zane and the Hurricane: A Story of Katrina." "Thirteen-year-old Zane Dupree and his trusted dog, Bandy, travel from their home in New Hampshire to New Orleans to visit his great-grandmother, Miss Trissy, the only link to the father who died before he was born. But almost as soon as they arrive, they are caught up in the turmoil of Hurricane Katrina, separated from family, and left on their own to survive. . . . [Rodman] Philbrick examines issues of race and class with a deft hand (Zane is of mixed race himself), letting the story unfold directly and leaving moralizing to the reader. Though the convenience of a few plot points strains credibility, the tight prose, harrowing pace, and resonant relationships will appeal to a broad audience."

REVIEW: *Bull Cent Child Books* v67 no6 p328-9 F 2014 Deborah Stevenson

REVIEW: *Kirkus Rev* v81 no24 p171 D 15 2013

"Zane and the Hurricane: A Story of Katrina". "An appropriately serious and occasionally gruesome tale of surviving Hurricane Katina, buoyed by large doses of hope and humor. . . . Careful attention to detail in representations of the storm, the city and local dialect give this tale a realistic feel. Zane's perspective as an outsider allows [Rodman] Philbrick to weave in social commentary on race, class, greed and morality, offering rich fodder for reflection and discussion. This compelling story of Katrina is like the floodwaters it describes: quickly moving, sometimes treacherous and sometimes forgiving, with a lot going on beneath the surface."

REVIEW: *N Y Times Book Rev* p17 F 16 2014 THOMAS BELLER

"Zane and the Hurricane: A Story of Katrina." "Most of Rodman Philbrick's new middle-grade novel, 'Zane and the Hurricane,' is set in a battered green canoe floating on the oily sea that covered New Orleans in the aftermath of Hurricane Katrina. The story is narrated by Zane Dupree, a mixed-race 12-year-old boy. . . . The novel's plot unfolds with the detailed precision of scrimshaw. . . . But there is something a bit studied about his display of the Louisianians' slang and gumption. . . . Still, for a young reader who knows nothing of the Katrina debacle, Philbrick does convey much information about New Orleans while the plot chugs along, and even a bit of the city's essence."

REVIEW: *Publ Wkly* v260 no48 p58 N 25 2013

REVIEW: *SLJ* v60 no2 p94 F 2014 Jennifer Schultz

PHILLIPS, ADAM. One way and another; New and selected essays; [by] Adam Phillips 2013 Penguin

1. Essay (Literary form) 2. Literature—History & criticism 3. Metaphor 4. Psychoanalysis & literature 5. Writing processes

SUMMARY: "Throughout his . . . career, Adam Phillips has lent a new and incisive dimension to the art of the literary essay, and in so doing revived the form for audiences of the new millennium. Collected here are nineteen pieces that have best defined his thinking—including 'On Tickling,' 'On Being Bored' and 'Clutter: A Case History'—along with a selection of new writings and an introduction by Man Booker Prize winner John Banville." (Publisher's note)

REVIEW: *TLS* no5794 p13 Ap 18 2014 BRIAN DILLON

"One Way and Another: New and Selected Essays." "According to the analyst Adam Phillips, writing in a coda to his new collection, Freud and the past century's Freudians have employed a telling variety of forms—or at least signalled allegiance to such forms with the titles they (or later acolytes) have given their works. . . . 'Coda: Up to a point' is an excellent defence of the essay's wandering nature at the level of content, but one longs for—and suspects that Phillips is well capable of—another sort of writing: a prose that would give up on the mere pragmatics of 'availability' and give in to his discipline's implied practice, and theory, of metaphor."

PHILLIPS, CLYDE. Unthinkable; [by] Clyde Phillips 324 p. 2013 Amazon Pub

1. Mass murder investigation—Fiction 2. Policewomen—Fiction 3. Pregnant women—Employment—Fiction

ISBN 1611098114; 9781611098112

LC 2013-901626

SUMMARY: In this book, by Clyde Phillips, "homicide lieutenant Jane Candiotti . . . and her husband are expecting their first child. . . . When a mass shooting at a local restaurant claims six victims—including her teenaged nephew, . . . Jane vows to hunt down the monster who didn't think twice about shooting an innocent kid. But every thread of evidence leads her deeper into a tangled web of deception, violence, and murder." (Publisher's note)

REVIEW: *Booklist* v109 no22 p75 Ag 1 2013 Edie Ching

REVIEW: *Booklist* v109 no21 p41 Jl 1 2013 Michel Leber

REVIEW: *Bull Cent Child Books* v67 no3 p188 N 2013 K. C.

"Unthinkable." "When Lucy Scarborough performed the three impossible tasks to break the centuries- old curse of the Scarborough women (in "Impossible" . . .), her ancestor, Fenella, thought she would be released to the death she has sought for four hundred years; however, it was not to be. It turns out that to reverse the life-spell cast on her, Fenella must perform three tasks of destruction to balance out the three tasks of creation in the original curse. . . . [Author Nancy] Werlin manages to create in Fenella a character both prickly and sympathetic; even though she was unable to break the curse that destroyed generation after generation of her family . . . , her backstory provides the necessary character development and motivation for readers to wish her success."

REVIEW: *Horn Book Magazine* v89 no5 p116 S/O 2013 LAUREN ADAMS

"Unthinkable." "Fenella's mission is complicated and confused by her own unexpectedly awakened desires--to learn about fascinating new technologies, to hold Lucy's child, to be with the beautiful, tender Walker Dobrez. The Faerie Queen's brother Ryland, sent in cat form, nudges her to stay her course of destruction, and she begins her terrible tasks. Werlin, a deft storyteller and creative world-builder, weaves a twisting strand of faerie magic through the human realm, smoldering with sparks of romance and danger, just waiting to ignite."

REVIEW: *Kirkus Rev* v81 no14 p218 Jl 15 2013

REVIEW: *Publ Wkly* v260 no24 p45 Je 17 2013

REVIEW: *SLJ* v59 no8 p107 Ag 2013 Gretchen Kolderup

REVIEW: *Voice of Youth Advocates* v36 no4 p90 O 2013 Courtney Huse Wika

PHILLIPS, CRAIG.il. Chasing Shadows. See Avasthi, S.

PHILLIPS, DAVE.il. Magic marks the spot. See Carlson, C.

PHILLIPS, JAYNE ANNE, 1952-. Quiet dell; a novel; [by] Jayne Anne Phillips 480 p. 2013 Scribner

1. Detective & mystery stories 2. Murder—Investigation—Fiction 3. Women journalists—Fiction

ISBN 1439172536; 9781439172537 (Hardcover : alk.

paper)
LC 2013-016013

SUMMARY: Author Jayne Anne Phillips presents a "novel based on a real-life multiple murder by a con man who preyed on widows. Asta Eicher, mother of three, is lonely and despairing, pressed for money after the sudden death of her husband. She begins to receive seductive letters from a chivalrous, elegant man [and] weeks later, all four Eichers are dead. Emily Thornhill, one of the few women journalists in the Chicago press, becomes deeply invested in understanding what happened to this beautiful family." (Publisher's note)

REVIEW: *Booklist* v109 no22 p44 Ag 1 2013 Brad Hooper

REVIEW: *Booklist* v110 no16 p29 Ap 15 2014 Brad Hooper

REVIEW: *Kirkus Rev* p31 N 15 2013 Best Books

REVIEW: *Kirkus Rev* p12-3 Ag 15 2013 Fall Preview

REVIEW: *Kirkus Rev* v81 no15 p308 Ag 1 2013

REVIEW: *Libr J* v138 no9 p52 My 15 2013 Barbara Hoffert

REVIEW: *N Y Times Book Rev* p10 O 13 2013 MALCOLM JONES

"Quiet Dell." "Jayne Anne Phillips . . . weaves her own convincing version of the story through quotations from the trial transcript, photographs, news accounts and letters. Had she stopped there, 'Quiet Dell' would have been a vivid historical novel, but perhaps not much more. . . . To ensure against that possibility--to haunt her readers as she herself has been haunted since childhood--Phillips avoids explaining [Harry] Powers outright. Instead, she fashions a counternarrative to his story. . . . Phillips portrays Harry Power's monstrousness through a host of indelible details."

REVIEW: *New Yorker* v89 no44 p75-1 Ja 13 2014

REVIEW: *Publ Wkly* v260 no32 p29-30 Ag 12 2013

PHILLIPS, PETER. What We Really Do; The Tallis Scholars; [by] Peter Phillips 2013 Musical Times

1. Choirs (Musical groups) 2. Choral conductors 3. Music literature 4. Part songs 5. Tallis Scholars
ISBN 0954577728; 9780954577728

SUMMARY: "Through almost 2000 concerts and 60 CDs, the Tallis Scholars have changed the status of Renaissance polyphony for millions of music-lovers. 'What We Really Do' tells the story of this peerless ensemble. Peter Phillips has written a warts and all account, with a little help from his friends." (Publisher's note)

REVIEW: *TLS* no5788 p24 Mr 7 2014 MICHAEL DOWNES

"What We Really Do: The Tallis Scholars" and "Inside Conducting." "There are many different ways of becoming a conductor, and of being a conductor. 'What We Really Do' and 'Inside Conducting, as contrasting in content and approach as one would expect from their authors' careers, have much to say about both topics. . . . 'What We Really Do' is filled out with an anthology of [author Peter] Phillips's articles from the 'Spectator' and elsewhere, a Tallis Scholars discography, a list of everyone who has ever sung with the group and of broadcasts it has made, and a glossary of 'singers' argot.' . . . 'Inside Conducting,' which arouses slight regret that it is so short, such are the insights that [author Christopher] Seaman brings."

PHILLIPS, REG.il. Public Sculpture of Cheshire and Merseyside (Excluding Liverpool). See Morris, E.

PHILLIPS, SCOTT L. Beyond sound; the college and career guide in music technology; [by] Scott L. Phillips xviii, 222 p. 2013 Oxford University Press

1. Music—Vocational guidance 2. Music and technology 3. Music industry 4. Sound recording industry 5. Vocational guidance—Handbooks, manuals, etc.
ISBN 9780199837663 (alk. paper); 9780199837687 (alk. paper)
LC 2012-042406

SUMMARY: This book "offers a vocational guidance book for those wishing to enter thc broadly described field of music technology. This field encompasses many jobs within the music business, including audio/video production in studios; live sound production; film and television; digital media; manufacturing; sales and service; and education." It includes "interviews with several working professionals about what they do and how they proceeded through their careers." (Choice: Current Reviews for Academic Libraries)

REVIEW: *Choice* v51 no5 p802 Ja 2014 J. Farrington

"Beyond Sound: The College and Career Guide in Music Technology." "These interviews (sometimes with stories that could have used a little more judicious editing or fact-checking) are some of the most useful sections in the book. The author's history of recordings is somewhat confused, and when he discusses the skills one needs for the various jobs in the music industry, he neglects to mention that perhaps the most useful tools are a well-developed set of ears and a musical background. Students and others contemplating jobs in this field that do not involve performance may wish to consider this book. It offers food for thought."

PHILOSOPHICAL TEMPERAMENTS; from Plato to Foucault; 136 p. 2013 Columbia University Press

1. Descartes, René, 1596-1650 2. Foucault, Michel, 1926-1984 3. Philosophers—Biography 4. Philosophical literature 5. Philosophy—Introductions
ISBN 9780231153720 (cloth : alk. paper); 9780231153737 (pbk. : alk. paper); 9780231527408 (e-book)
LC 2012-037921

SUMMARY: This book "comprises prefaces composed in the 1990s by Peter Sloterdijk . . .for a series of primary philosophical texts. Through the series, Sloterdijk . . . intended to circumvent the authority of secondary literature and challenge the 'rampant mindlessness' of the era with an 'alternate history' of the Western philosophical tradition for a general readership facing the challenges and opportunities of an increasingly globalized and virtually networked world." (Choice)

REVIEW: *Choice* v51 no4 p652-3 D 2013 R. A. Sica Jr.

"Philosophical Temperaments: From Plato to Foucault." "This volume is alternately incisive and obscure, bristling with insights that defy easy dismissal, despite their imperious, sometimes frustrating, brevity and suggestiveness. Compact and pungent, this little book comprises prefaces composed in the 1990s by Peter Sloterdijk, a controversial, high profile, German public intellectual, for a series of primary philosophical texts. . . . Overall, this is a scintillating introduction for Anglophone readers to a stimulating provocateur of contemporary European intellectual culture."

PHILOSOPHY AND ITS HISTORY; Aims and methods in the study of early modern philosophy; 2013 Oxford University Press

1. Books & reading 2. Charity 3. Historiography 4. Philosophical literature 5. Philosophy—History
ISBN 9780199857142 hardcover

SUMMARY: Edited by Mogens Lærke, Justin E. H. Smith, and Eric Schliesser, this volume addresses "conflicting visions of the history of philosophy as an autonomous subdiscipline of professional philosophy. . . . Among the topics discussed and debated in the volume are: the status of the principle of charity; the nature of reading texts; the role of historiography within the history of philosophy; the nature of establishing proper context." (Publisher's note)

REVIEW: *Choice* v51 no6 p1019 F 2014 S. Young

"Philosophy and its History: Aims and Methods in the Study of Early Modern Philosophy." "Most of the 15 contributors to this quality collection are committed to the value for contemporary philosophy of thorough, historically situated studies of earlier thinkers' philosophies. Their clear, persuasive articles confront Anglo-American philosophy's tendency to mine earlier philosophical works for precious argumentative nuggets that may be applied to current philosophical problems. . . . This text should be required reading for all philosophers who think mere analysis of textual meaning is sufficient for philosophical analysis."

PHILOSOPHY OF PSEUDOSCIENCE; reconsidering the demarcation problem; 480 p. 2013 University of Chicago Press

1. Philosophical literature 2. Philosophy of science 3. Pseudoscience 4. Science 5. Science & civilization
ISBN 9780226051796 (cloth : alkaline paper); 9780226051963 (paperback : alkaline paper)
LC 2013-000805

SUMMARY: In this book, editors Massimo Pigliucci and Maarten Boudry "for the unequivocal importance of reflecting on the separation between pseudoscience and sound science. . . . Pseudoscience often mimics science, using the superficial language and trappings of actual scientific research to seem more respectable. Even a well-informed public can be taken in by such questionable theories dressed up as science." (Publisher's note)

REVIEW: *Choice* v51 no6 p1027 F 2014 J. D. Martin

"Philosophy of Pseudoscience: Reconsidering the Demarcation Problem." "If the philosophical problem of demarcating science from pseudoscience has a stale reputation, this book is a revitalizing gust of fresh air. . . . These essays bring focused attention to the practice and historical development of science. Therein lies this book's strength. Although the contributions to this volume revolve around a single, well-defined problem, they provide a superb introduction to foundational questions that every philosophy student should confront. . . . Distinguished and emerging scholars . . . confront these questions through accessibly written pieces that are intellectually adventurous, appropriate for all academic audiences, and accessible to interested general readers."

PHOSPHORUS, FOOD, AND OUR FUTURE; 224 p. 2013 Oxford University Press

1. Food—Phosphorus content 2. Phosphorus 3. Phosphorus cycle (Biogeochemistry) 4. Scientific literature 5. Sustainable agriculture
ISBN 9780199916832 (alk. paper)
LC 2013-003194

SUMMARY: This book discusses the relationship between phosphorus and food production. "The first chapter will introduce the biological and chemical necessity of phosphorus. The subsequent ten chapters will explore different facets of phosphorus sustainability and the role of policy on future global phosphorus supplies. The final chapter will synthesize all of the emerging views contained in the book, drawing out the leading dilemmas and opportunities for phosphorus sustainability." (Publisher's note)

REVIEW: *Choice* v51 no7 p1248 Mr 2014 T. R. Blackburn

"Phosphorous, Food, and Our Future." "This odd little book, based on the results of an international conference, 'Sustainable Phosphorus Summit,' held in Arizona in 2011, presents the economic and environmental cycles of P. Its ten brief chapters are written at a level appropriate for undergraduate students of environmental sciences, with each chapter decorated with a sketchy bit of 'art' meant to introduce or summarize its content. . . . Conclusions are bolstered by reasonable quantitative arguments. The editing is uniform but shaky."

PIANA, RON. The great prostate hoax; how big medicine hijacked the PSA test and caused a public health disaster; [by] Ron Piana 272 p. 2014 Palgrave Macmillan

1. Early Detection of Cancer—adverse effects—United States 2. History, 20th Century—United States 3. History, 21st Century—United States 4. Medical literature 5. Prostate-Specific Antigen—adverse effects—United States 6. Prostate-Specific Antigen—history—United States 7. Prostatic Neoplasms—diagnosis—United States
ISBN 9781137278746 (alk. paper)
LC 2013-030332

SUMMARY: In this book, "Richard J. Ablin exposes how a discovery he made in 1970, the prostate-specific antigen (PSA), was co-opted by the pharmaceutical industry into a multibillion-dollar business. He shows how his discovery of PSA was never meant to be used for screening prostate cancer, and yet nonetheless the test was patented and eventurally approved by the FDA in 1994." (Publisher's note)

REVIEW: *Economist* v410 no8877 p85-6 Mr 8 2014

"The Great Prostate Hoax: How Big Medicine Hijacked the PSA Test and Caused a Public Health Disaster." "Mr. [Richard] Ablin, and his co-author, Ronald Piana, are good at describing how the many ills of American health care--from doctors' fears of malpractice suits to their fascination with new gizmos--conspired to encourage treatment. But this is a flawed book. Mr. Ablin races down tangential lines of argument making hyperbolic charges. Are the proponents of the PSA test really as bad as tobacco companies."

REVIEW: *Kirkus Rev* v82 no1 p191 Ja 1 2014

REVIEW: *Libr J* v139 no3 p122 F 15 2014 Chad Clark

PICHARDO ALMANZAR, NELSON A. American fascism and the new deal. See Kulik, B. W.

PICKERING, ANDREW. Witch Hunt; The Persecution of the Witches in England; [by] Andrew Pickering 224 p. 2013 Casemate Pub & Book Dist Llc

1. Great Britain—History 2. Historical literature 3.

Witch hunting—History 4. Witchcraft—England 5. Witchcraft—Law & legislation
ISBN 1445608618; 9781445608617

SUMMARY: "In this book, Andrew and David Pickering present a comprehensive catalogue of witch-hunts, arranged chronologically within geographical regions. The tales of persecution within these pages are testimony to the horror of witch-hunting that occurred throughout England in the hundred years after the passing of the Elizabethan Witchcraft Act of 1563." (Publisher's note)

REVIEW: *TLS* no5743 p26-7 Ap 26 2013 JAMES SHARPE

"Witch Hunt: The Persecution of Witches in England." "The book includes an introduction, which demonstrates a reasonable working knowledge of recent writing on the history of witchcraft in England. . . . There are, unfortunately, some problems with the work. The first is a worrying scatter of minor errors. . . . More annoyingly the cases in the gazetteer are frequently imperfectly referenced, which means that anyone wanting to trace an entry through to its source will often have difficulties in so doing. . . . 'Witch Hunt' remains, however, a lively and accessible book which will provide the nonspecialist reader with interesting material and a reasonably sound introduction to recent academic interpretations."

PICKFORD, SUE. Bob and Rob; [by] Sue Pickford 32 p. 2014 Pgw

1. Children's stories 2. Dogs—Juvenile fiction 3. Good & evil—Juvenile fiction 4. Loyalty 5. Thieves—Fiction
ISBN 1847803431; 9781847803436

SUMMARY: In this children's book by Sue Pickford, pet dog "Bob remains faithful to his horrible owner, helping him with robberies. One night Bob and Rob see some inviting packages through the window of a house and can't resist stealing them all. When the parcels turn out to be filled with children's toys, Bob must stand up for what's right and return the stolen goods." (Publisher's note)

REVIEW: *Kirkus Rev* v82 no4 p323 F 15 2014

"Bob and Rob". "There's not much for readers to chew on here that they haven't heard a hundred times (crime doesn't pay, being good is its own reward). Still, [Sue] Pickford's artwork is a treat, with Rob in his pink slippers and Bob with his binoculars, both as two-dimensional as possible-as if Bob has taken a good, hot iron to them-and with lots of crooked linework, which befits a couple crooks (or at least one real crook). Remember-nice dogs find a good home and bumbling burglars find the big house."

PIEN, LARK.il. Boxers. See Yang, G. L.

PIEN, LARK.il. Saints. See Yang, G. L.

PIERCE, TAMORA, 1954-. Battle magic; [by] Tamora Pierce 464 p. 2013 Scholastic Press

1. Fantasy fiction 2. Magic—Fiction 3. Magic—Juvenile fiction 4. Wizards—Fiction 5. Wizards—Juvenile fiction
ISBN 0439842972; 9780439842976 (jacketed hc)
LC 2013-013175

SUMMARY: This book is part of Tamora Pierce's Winding Circle series. It relates "the events that befell plant mages Briar and Rosethorn and Briar's student, stone mage Evvy." The trio travels from Gyongxe to Yanjing, where they learn that the Emperor "is a cruel man who keeps slaves . . . . Evvy impulsively decides to free Parahan, an enslaved prince. . . . In return Parahan lets them know that the emperor plans to invade Gyongxe." (School Library Journal)

REVIEW: *Bull Cent Child Books* v67 no4 p232-3 D 2013 K. Q. G.

REVIEW: *Horn Book Magazine* v90 no1 p98-9 Ja/F 2014 ANITA L. BURKAM

"Battle Magic." "[Tamora] Pierce achieves an epic sweep of cultures and intrigue in this wide-ranging volume, constructing her world with painstaking detail. . . . But the three mages' powers, their loyalties to one another, and their testing under the rigors of combat are the real draw here. Evvy in particular has a rough time, surviving torture, near-death, and the loss of her beloved feline companions, but she still comes back strong in the battle scenes. Add in the author's signature wry humor, and the result is another winning companion to Pierce's highly successful Circle Quartet and Circle Opens fantasy franchises."

REVIEW: *Kirkus Rev* v81 no17 p109 S 1 2013

REVIEW: *Publ Wkly* v260 no36 p58 S 9 2013

REVIEW: *SLJ* v59 no10 p1 O 2013 Eric Norton

REVIEW: *Voice of Youth Advocates* v36 no6 p76 F 2014 Beth Karpas

PIERPONT, CLAUDIA ROTH. Untitled on Philip Roth; [by] Claudia Roth Pierpont 368 p. 2013 Farrar Straus & Giroux

1. American literature—History & criticism 2. Authors—Biography 3. Biography (Literary form) 4. Jewish authors 5. Roth, Philip, 1933-
ISBN 0374280517; 9780374280512

SUMMARY: This book on writer Philip Roth "traces moments from the author's life and explores the 'life of his art.' [Claudia Roth] Pierpont develops the story of Roth's writing chronologically, summarizing the plots and critical reception of each of his many novels, from Goodbye, Columbus (1959) to Nemesis (2010)." (Publishers Weekly)

REVIEW: *Choice* v51 no8 p1402 Ap 2014 T. H. Oliviero

REVIEW: *Commonweal* v141 no5 p20-1 Mr 7 2014 William H. Pritchard

REVIEW: *Economist* v409 no8858 p88-9 O 19 2013

"Roth Unbound: A Writer and His Books" and "The Kraus Project." "[Claudia Roth Pierpont's] wise and captivating analysis of the work of Philip Roth . . . is not a conventional biography but a chronicle of the man through the 'life of his art'. . . . Her book has the sympathy of friendship, but she does not hesitate to be critical of the author's lesser work. . . . The book is an illuminating companion to Mr. Roth's work. . . . Similarly unconventional but considerably less successful is 'The Kraus Project,' Jonathan Franzen's peculiar attempt to introduce a 21st-century English-speaking audience to the work of Karl Kraus, a 19th-century German critic and satirist. . . . There is no getting around the fact that Kraus's work is rebarbarative today."

REVIEW: *Kirkus Rev* v81 no23 p240 D 1 2013

REVIEW: *Libr J* v138 no10 p80 Je 1 2013

REVIEW: *London Rev Books* v36 no2 p9-16 Ja 23 2014 Adam Mars-Jones

"Roth Unbound: A Writer and His Books". "'Roth Unbound' has his blessing but wasn'tvetted by him, and [Claudia Roth] Pierpont feels free to criticise his work, his behaviour (on special occasions) and once, even, his knowledge of Yiddish. . . . Her independence is necessarily approximate, an effort of will, and in the introduction she strikes an ominously protective and even proprietorial note, though one that rarely resurfaces in the body of the book. . . . One of the high points of Roth Unbound is the extract from the tapes (recorded on 3 November 1971) in which [Richard] Nixon considers his anti-Roth strategy."

REVIEW: *New Repub* p40-5 D 2013/Ja 2014 Adam Kirsch

"Roth Unbound: A Writer and His Books". "[Claudia Roth] Pierpont is a fine reader of Roth's books, thoughtful and sympathetic but not afraid to make criticisms. She points out that he has produced uneven work throughout his long career, and she allows the reader who has never sought out 'When She Was Good' or 'The Great American Novel' to continue to not read them with a good conscience. In turn, this makes her high opinion of Roth's best books . . . easier to trust. The structure of 'Roth Unbound' does not allow Pierpont to delve very deeply into any particular book, but then this is not an academic study. It is more in the nature of an introduction, ideal for readers who know Roth's reputation and one or two of his books but want to get the whole picture."

REVIEW: *N Y Rev Books* v60 no20 p72-4 D 19 2013 Gideon Lewis-Kraus

"Roth Unbound: A Writer and His Books." "Claudia Roth Pierpont's . . . [book] could only have been written 'with the full arc of [Philip] Roth's work completed.' She believes, then, that there is an arc to the work, and that we can only now . . . trace that arc properly. This might read as introductory biographical boilerplate, but in Roth's case it makes a real claim. . . . . She strains to have it both ways: Roth's life resembles his alter ego Nathan Zuckerman's only when it suits her purposes, which, without making the distinction clear, alternate between Roth's invincibility and his vulnerability. . . . But in her alacrity to provide for him as expansive and triumphant a life as possible, Pierpont inadvertently diminishes his real, inestimable achievements."

REVIEW: *N Y Times Book Rev* p1-17 O 20 2013 Martin Amis

REVIEW: *New Statesman* v143 no2 p46-8 Ja 17 2014 Leo Robson

REVIEW: *Publ Wkly* v260 no35 p50-1 S 2 2013

REVIEW: *TLS* no5790 p7-8 Mr 21 2014 ADAM THIRLWELL

"Roth Unbound: A Writer and His Books." "It's impossible to read this book without being aware that it is saturated in [Philip] Roth's presence, however much [author Claudia Roth] Pierpont might assure the reader that 'he has done all of this with the understanding that he would read not a single word in advance of publication.' . . . Pierpont's tender, detailed book is, in its way, another variation on the same material: from the conversations in Roth's studio, his biography emerges as a suite of parables, lessons in the self's miniature battles for its freedom."

PIERPONT, CLAUDIA ROTH. Roth unbound; [by] Claudia Roth Pierpont 2013 Farrar, Straus and Giroux

1. American fiction—20th century 2. American fiction—History & criticism 3. American fiction—Jewish authors—History & criticism 4. Authors—Biography 5. Biography in literature 6. Roth, Philip, 1933-

ISBN 9780374280512 hardcover; 9780374534936 paperback

SUMMARY: Written by Claudia Roth Pierpont, "'Roth Unbound' is not a biography . . . but something ultimately more rewarding: the exploration of a great writer through his art. . . . Here are insights and anecdotes that will change the way many readers perceive this most controversial and galvanizing writer: a young and unhappily married Roth struggling to write; a wildly successful Roth . . . Roth responding to . . . attacks on his work." (Publisher's note)

REVIEW: *Choice* v51 no8 p1402 Ap 2014 T. H. Oliviero

REVIEW: *Commonweal* v141 no5 p20-1 Mr 7 2014 William H. Pritchard

REVIEW: *Economist* v409 no8858 p88-9 O 19 2013

"Roth Unbound: A Writer and His Books" and "The Kraus Project". "[Claudia Roth Pierpont's] wise and captivating analysis of the work of Philip Roth . . . is not a conventional biography but a chronicle of the man through the 'life of his art'. . . . Her book has the sympathy of friendship, but she does not hesitate to be critical of the author's lesser work. . . The book is an illuminating companion to Mr. Roth's work. . . . Similarly unconventional but considerably less successful is 'The Kraus Project,' Jonathan Franzen's peculiar attempt to introduce a 21st-century English-speaking audience to the work of Karl Kraus, a 19th-century German critic and satirist. . . . There is no getting around the fact that Kraus's work is rebarbarative today."

REVIEW: *Kirkus Rev* v81 no23 p240 D 1 2013

REVIEW: *Libr J* v138 no10 p80 Je 1 2013

REVIEW: *London Rev Books* v36 no2 p9-16 Ja 23 2014 Adam Mars-Jones

"Roth Unbound: A Writer and His Books". "'Roth Unbound' has his blessing but wasn'tvetted by him, and [Claudia Roth] Pierpont feels free to criticise his work, his behaviour (on special occasions) and once, even, his knowledge of Yiddish. . . . Her independence is necessarily approximate, an effort of will, and in the introduction she strikes an ominously protective and even proprietorial note, though one that rarely resurfaces in the body of the book. . . . One of the high points of Roth Unbound is the extract from the tapes (recorded on 3 November 1971) in which [Richard] Nixon considers his anti-Roth strategy."

REVIEW: *N Y Rev Books* v60 no20 p72-4 D 19 2013 Gideon Lewis-Kraus

"Roth Unbound: A Writer and His Books". "Claudia Roth Pierpont's . . . [book] could only have been written 'with the full arc of [Philip] Roth's work completed.' She believes, then, that there is an arc to the work, and that we can only now . . . trace that arc properly. This might read as introductory biographical boilerplate, but in Roth's case it makes a real claim. . . . . She strains to have it both ways: Roth's life resembles his alter ego Nathan Zuckerman's only when it suits her purposes, which, without making the distinction clear, alternate between Roth's invincibility and his vulnerability. . . . But in her alacrity to provide for him as expansive and triumphant a life as possible, Pierpont inadvertently diminishes his real, inestimable achievements."

REVIEW: *N Y Times Book Rev* p1-17 O 20 2013 Martin Amis

REVIEW: *New Repub* p40-5 D 2013/Ja 2014 Adam

Kirsch

"Roth Unbound: A Writer and His Books". "[Claudia Roth] Pierpont is a fine reader of Roth's books, thoughtful and sympathetic but not afraid to make criticisms. She points out that he has produced uneven work throughout his long career, and she allows the reader who has never sought out 'When She Was Good' or 'The Great American Novel' to continue to not read them with a good conscience. In turn, this makes her high opinion of Roth's best books . . . easier to trust. The structure of 'Roth Unbound' does not allow Pierpont to delve very deeply into any particular book, but then this is not an academic study. It is more in the nature of an introduction, ideal for readers who know Roth's reputation and one or two of his books but want to get the whole picture."

REVIEW: *New Statesman* v143 no5193 p46-8 Ja 17 2014 Leo Robson

REVIEW: *Publ Wkly* v260 no35 p50-1 S 2 2013

REVIEW: *TLS* no5790 p7-8 Mr 21 2014 ADAM THIRLWELL

"Roth Unbound: A Writer and His Books." "It's impossible to read this book without being aware that it is saturated in [Philip] Roth's presence, however much [author Claudia Roth] Pierpont might assure the reader that 'he has done all of this with the understanding that he would read not a single word in advance of publication.' . . . Pierpont's tender, detailed book is, in its way, another variation on the same material: from the conversations in Roth's studio, his biography emerges as a suite of parables, lessons in the self's miniature battles for its freedom."

PIGLIUCCI, MASSIMO.ed. Philosophy of pseudoscience. See Philosophy of pseudoscience

PIKE, APRILYNNE. Sleep no more; [by] Aprilynne Pike 352 p. 2014 HarperTeen, an imprint of HarperCollins Publishers

1. Conduct of life—Fiction 2. Fantasy fiction 3. High schools—Fiction 4. Murder—Fiction 5. Oracles—Fiction 6. Prophecies—Fiction 7. Schools—Fiction 8. Serial murders—Fiction

ISBN 0061999032; 9780061999031 (hardback)

LC 2013-047722

SUMMARY: In this young adult novel, by Aprilynne Pike, "Charlotte Westing . . . is an Oracle and has the ability to tell the future. But . . . modern-day Oracles are told to fight their visions--to refrain from interfering. And Charlotte knows the price of breaking the rules. . . . But when a premonition of a classmate's death is too strong for her to ignore, Charlotte is forced to . . . risk everything . . . to stop the serial killer who is stalking her town." (Publisher's note)

REVIEW: *Booklist* v110 no12 p81-2 F 15 2014 Debbie Carton

"Sleep No More." "Sixteen-year-old Charlotte Westing is shy and not especially popular, and she has long been ostracized for her frequent health issues, including debilitating migraines that accompany her rare gift/curse--she's an Oracle and can see the future. . . . There's plenty of action, gore, and romance in this quick-paced read that will appeal to Pike's many fans. As Charlotte figures out the rather obvious solution to the mystery, she gains self-confidence and strength, leading to a satisfying conclusion."

REVIEW: *Kirkus Rev* v82 no6 p158 Mr 15 2014

REVIEW: *Publ Wkly* v261 no12 p79 Mr 24 2014

REVIEW: *SLJ* v60 no3 p162 Mr 2014 Heather Miller Cover

PIKETTY, THOMAS, 1971. Capital in the twenty-first century; 696 p. 2014 The Belknap Press of Harvard University Press

1. Capital 2. Economics literature 3. Income distribution 4. Labor economics 5. Wealth

ISBN 067443000X; 9780674430006 (alk. paper)

LC 2013-036024

SUMMARY: "In 'Capital in the Twenty-First Century,' Thomas Piketty analyzes a unique collection of data from twenty countries, ranging as far back as the eighteenth century, to uncover key economic and social patterns. . . . Piketty shows that modern economic growth and the diffusion of knowledge have allowed us to avoid inequalities on the apocalyptic scale predicted by Karl Marx. . . . Political action has curbed dangerous inequalities in the past, Piketty says, and may do so again." (Publisher's note)

REVIEW: *America* v210 no17 p5 My 19 2014

REVIEW: *America* v211 no4 p34-6 Ag 18 2014 MATTHEW CARNES

REVIEW: *Bookforum* v21 no1 p40-1 Ap/My 2014 DOUG HENWOOD

REVIEW: *Choice* v51 no12 p2238 Ag 2014 A. R. Sanderson

REVIEW: *Economist* v411 no8885 p67 My 3 2014

REVIEW: *Economist* v411 no8889 p69 My 31 2014

REVIEW: *J Econ Lit* v52 no2 p519-34 Je 2014

REVIEW: *Kirkus Rev* v82 no10 p317 My 15 2014

REVIEW: *Libr J* v139 no17 p57 O 15 2014 Kelly Sinclair

REVIEW: *London Rev Books* v36 no13 p17-20 Jl 3 2014 Benjamin Kunkel

REVIEW: *N Y Rev Books* v61 no8 p15-8 My 8 2014 Paul Krugman

REVIEW: *Nation* v298 no19 p6-8 My 12 2014 Eric Alterman

REVIEW: *Natl Rev* v65 no8 p43-4 My 5 2014 JOSHUA R. HENDRICKSON

"Capital in the Twenty-First Century." "'Capital in the Twenty-First Century' is a significant contribution to our understanding of the distribution of wealth and income—in particular, in his evidence suggesting that there is no inherent tendency for the distribution of income and wealth to become less unequal as countries grow. In addition, the sheer volume of data Piketty has compiled and summarized in this text is a significant contribution to economic science. Nonetheless, there is much work to be done in understanding the mechanisms that lead to inequality, and the policy implications thereof."

REVIEW: *Natl Rev* v65 no9 p31-4 My 19 2014 SCOTT WINSHIP

REVIEW: *New Repub* v244 no27 p50-5 My 12 2014 Robert M. Solow

"Capital in the Twenty-First Century." "This is a serious book. It is also a long book: 577 pages of closely printed text and seventy-seven pages of notes. . . . The English translation by Arthur Goldhammer reads very well. . . . Over the long span of history surveyed by Piketty, the rate of return on capital is usually larger than the underlying rate of growth. . . . As long as the rate of return exceeds the rate of growth, the income and wealth of the rich will grow faster than the typical income from work."

REVIEW: *New Statesman* v143 no5203 p38-40 Mr 28 2014 Nick Pearce

REVIEW: *New York Times* v163 no56450 pA21 Mr 24 2014 PAUL KRUGMAN

REVIEW: *New Yorker* v90 no6 p69-1 Mr 31 2014

"Capital in the 21st Century." "In the United States, the very idea of a new wealth tax looks like a nonstarter politically, as would the notion of raising the top rate of income tax to eighty per cent. That's not a knock on [author Thomas] Piketty, though. The proper role of public intellectuals is to question accepted dogmas, conceive of new methods of analysis, and expand the terms of public debate. 'Capital in the Twenty-First Century' does all these things. As with any such grand prognostication, some of it may not withstand the test of time. But Piketty has written a book that nobody interested in a defining issue of our era can afford to ignore."

REVIEW: *TLS* no5804 p3-5 Je 27 2014 DUNCAN KELLY

PILLING, DAVID. Bending Adversity; Japan and the Art of Survival; [by] David Pilling 416 p. 2014 Penguin Group USA

1. Fukushima Nuclear Accident, Fukushima, Japan, 2011 2. Japan—Politics & government 3. Japan—Social conditions 4. Journalism 5. Sendai Earthquake, Japan, 2011
ISBN 1594205841; 9781594205842

SUMMARY: This book, by David Pilling, focuses on Japan. It "begins with the 2011 triple disaster of earthquake, tsunami, and nuclear meltdown. . . . He revisits 1990--the year the economic bubble burst, and the beginning of Japan's 'lost decades'--to ask if the turning point might be viewed differently." According to the book, "while financial struggle and national debt are a reality, post-growth Japan has also successfully maintained a stable standard of living and social cohesion." (Publisher's note)

REVIEW: *Booklist* v110 no5 p13 N 1 2013 Vanessa Bush

REVIEW: *Economist* v410 no8870 p81 Ja 18 2014

"Bending Adversity: Japan and the Art of Survival." "An excellent book for which 3/11, as the event is known in Japan, is as much pretext as subject matter. For Mr. [David] Pilling's thesis is that, horrifying though it was, the triple disaster three years ago was neither a game-changing event nor truly novel. The way in which Japanese people have reacted to the disaster represents continuity with centuries of Japan's history. . . . As the book's title indicates, they may 'bend' adversity to whatever interests they have, or adversity may 'bend' them, but change is unlikely to be more radical. This will be a disappointment to all those who liked to think that 3/11 could bring about the third great transformation in the country's modern history."

REVIEW: *Kirkus Rev* v82 no4 p3 F 15 2014

REVIEW: *N Y Times Book Rev* p22 My 18 2014 JAMES FALLOWS

REVIEW: *New Statesman* v143 no4 p52-3 Ja 31 2014 Felix Martin

REVIEW: *Publ Wkly* v260 no47 p40 N 18 2013

REVIEW: *TLS* no5793 p8 Ap 11 2014 ERI HOTTA

PILLSBURY, JOANNE.ed. Merchants, markets, and exchange in the Pre-Columbian world. See Merchants, markets, and exchange in the Pre-Columbian world

PILLSBURY, JOANNE.ed. Past presented. See Past presented

PINA POLO, FRANCISCO.ed. Consuls and res publica. See Consuls and res publica

PINES, TRENT D. Life on Altamont Court; Finding the Extraordinary in the Ordinary; [by] Trent D. Pines 362 p. 2013 TD Literary Tales

1. Dwellings—Maintenance & repair 2. Memoirs 3. Morristown (N.J.) 4. Neighborhoods 5. Neighbors
ISBN 0615837956; 9780615837956

SUMMARY: This memoir by Trent D. Pines is "about his time on Altamont Court—a small, suburban cul-de-sac in Morristown, N.J.—and the neighbors who became his surrogate family. . . . The memoir's first section centers on Pines' story of renovating a 'half-million-dollar fixer-upper' home soon after he and Ken arrived in Morristown. . . . The latter, and longer, section focuses on the couple's life on Altamont Court after the renovation was complete and their relationships with their neighbors." (Kirkus Reviews)

REVIEW: *Kirkus Rev* v82 no3 p359 F 1 2014

"Life on Altamont Court: Finding the Extraordinary in the Ordinary". "[Trent D.] Pines' debut memoir offers a lighthearted, entertaining tale about his time on Altamont Court—a small, suburban cul-de-sac in Morristown, N.J.—and the neighbors who became his surrogate family. . . . Ultimately, the stories here are simply amusing, at best, but the author's voice and personality make this book highly entertaining. Pines is an honest, self-deprecating narrator . . . and reading his book feels like having a conversation with an old friend. This memoir is also notable for its real-life story of a committed gay couple living a peaceful domestic life, something rarely portrayed in the popular culture. A heartwarming memoir featuring funny stories of suburban life."

REVIEW: *Kirkus Rev* v82 no5 p21 Mr 1 2014

"Life on Altamont Court: Finding the Extraordinary in the Ordinary". "[Trent D.] Pines' debut memoir offers a lighthearted, entertaining tale about his time on Altamont Court—a small, suburban cul-de-sac in Morristown, N.J.—and the neighbors who became his surrogate family. . . . Ultimately, the stories here are simply amusing, at best, but the author's voice and personality make this book highly entertaining. Pines is an honest, self-deprecating narrator . . . and reading his book feels like having a conversation with an old friend. This memoir is also notable for its real-life story of a committed gay couple living a peaceful domestic life, something rarely portrayed in the popular culture. A heartwarming memoir featuring funny stories of suburban life."

PINKNEY, ANDREA DAVIS. Martin and Mahalia; his words, her song; [by] Andrea Davis Pinkney 40 p. 2013 Little, Brown and Co.

1. African Americans—Civil rights—History—20th century—Juvenile literature 2. Children's nonfiction 3. Civil rights movements—United States—History—20th century—Juvenile literture 4. Historical literature 5. March on Washington for Jobs & Freedom, Washington,

D.C., 1963
ISBN 0316070130 (reinforced); 9780316070133 (reinforced)
LC 2012-005499

SUMMARY: This children's picture book weaves together "the stories of two giants of the American civil rights movement," Martin Luther King, Jr. and Mahalia Jackson. "At first the stories are distinct, with alternating, dedicated spreads tracing the individuals' paths as gospel preacher and singer until they meet and combine forces at the Montgomery bus boycott in 1955 and forge a collaboration that takes them through Martin's most famous speech, at the Lincoln Memorial." (Booklist)

REVIEW: *Booklist* v109 no9/10 p77 Ja 1 2013 Gillian Engberg

REVIEW: *Booklist* v109 no15 p45-6 Ap 1 2013 Thom Borthelmess

REVIEW: *Bull Cent Child Books* v67 no1 p46 S 2013 E. B.

"Martin & Mahalia: His Words, Her Song." "This picture-book tribute to the civil rights movement focuses on two voices that stirred listeners to action: the preacher's oratory of Dr. Martin Luther King, Jr., and the powerful contralto of gospel singer Mahalia Jackson. Rather than presenting standard biographical background, author [Andrea Davis] Pinkney discusses in her own rhythmic prose the effect these two voices had on their listeners. . . . [Illustrator] Brian Pinkney's watercolor illustrations are rendered in clear, springtime hues replete with optimism; phrases from speeches, songs, signage, and exhortation wind across and through stylized scenes from the movement and the March."

REVIEW: *Kirkus Rev* v81 no2 p100 Je 1 2013

REVIEW: *Publ Wkly* v260 no24 p65-6 Je 17 2013

REVIEW: *SLJ* v59 no7 p110 Jl 2013 Wendy Lukehart

PINKNEY, BRIAN.il. Martin and Mahalia. See Pinkney, A. D.

PINKNEY, JERRY, 1939-. The tortoise & the hare; 40 p. 2013 Little, Brown and Co.

1. Animal stories 2. Fables 3. Folklore 4. Perseverance (Ethics) 5. Running races
ISBN 0316183563; 9780316183567
LC 2012-048426

SUMMARY: In this book, by Jerry Pinkney, "even the slowest tortoise can defeat the quickest hare, and even the proudest hare can learn a timeless lesson from the most humble tortoise: Slow and steady wins the race! Here is a . . . journey from starting line to finish that embodies the bravery, perseverance, and humility we can all find inside ourselves." (Publisher's note)

REVIEW: *Booklist* v109 no22 p75 Ag 1 2013 Thom Barthelmess

REVIEW: *Bull Cent Child Books* v67 no5 p277 Ja 2014 D. S.

"The Tortoise and the Hare". "etc.). Sassy touches of clothing personify the competitors and their teeming audience (Tortoise sports a denim cap and a jaunty neckerchief, while Hare is a fan of checks, even loaning his checkered scarf to Coyote for a finish flag), yet the anthropomorphism blends seamlessly with the naturalistic detail as Hare springs with power and grace over fallen objects and Tortoise clambers determinedly over rocky ground. . . The scope of the illustrations makes the book a compelling distance show. . . . While this is an oft-retold tale in picture-book land, [Jerry] Pinkney's version is faithful to the original while offering a lively and imaginative take on the ancient Greek version of 'You snooze, you lose.'"

REVIEW: *Horn Book Magazine* v89 no5 p118 S/O 2013 KATHLEEN T. HORNING

REVIEW: *Kirkus Rev* v81 no17 p110 S 1 2013

REVIEW: *Publ Wkly* v260 no33 p64 Ag 19 2013

REVIEW: *Publ Wkly* p34 Children's starred review annual 2013

REVIEW: *SLJ* v59 no9 p178 S 2013 Kristine M. Casper

PINS, ARTHUR DE. Zombillenium; Gretchen; [by] Arthur de Pins 48 p. 2013 NBM Publishing

1. Amusement parks 2. Graphic novels 3. Monsters—Fiction 4. Vampires—Fiction 5. Zombies
ISBN 1561637343; 9781561637348 (hardcover)
LC 2013-936651

SUMMARY: In this graphic novel, by Arthur de Pins, "Francis von Bloodt, a vampire and good family man, operates the one-of-a-kind theme park Zombiellenium. But this unique amusement park doesn't just hire anyone: mere mortals need not apply--only genuine werewolves, vampires, zombies, and other citizens from the undead community are employed." (Publisher's note)

REVIEW: *Booklist* v110 no2 p58-9 S 15 2013 Francisca Goldsmith

"Zombillenium." "This newly, excellently translated series opens with a volume featuring a witch turned monster-theme-park intern, Gretchen. On\ immediate glance, the theme and patter seem more reminiscent of young-adult fare, but the satirical take on a host of popular books, memes, and themes best targets the well-read, parody-appreciative culture maven. . . . The gorgeously colored tiny panels across folio-sized pages offer sly asides of their own. This award-winning, laugh-aloud, smart comic should be of high interest to those who enjoy parodies of Tintin, Posy Simmonds' reworking of nineteenth-century literature, and anything that pokes gentle fun at Harry Potter or the Twilight craze."

REVIEW: *Publ Wkly* v260 no33 p50 Ag 19 2013

REVIEW: *Voice of Youth Advocates* v36 no4 p78-9 O 2013 Kaitlin Connors

PINTO, JOHN A. Speaking ruins; Piranesi, architects and antiquity in eighteenth-century Rome; [by] John A. Pinto xxiii, 304 p. 2012 University of Michigan Press

1. ARCHITECTURE—History—General 2. ART—History—Ancient & Classical 3. ART—History—Renaissance 4. Architecture—Italy—Rome—History—18th century 5. Architecture and history—Italy—Rome 6. Architecture, Classical—Appreciation—Europe 7. Historical literature
ISBN 9780472118212 (hardback)
LC 2012-000986

SUMMARY: This book by John Pinto explores "the study of the ruins of Rome and other classical sites, archaeological or visionary recreations of them, and the relationship of both to contemporary and future architectural design ideas.

. . . The central figure is the great printmaker and polemicist Giovanni Battista Piranesi (1720-78). . . . Emphasis is given to "the tensions between the Enlightenment quest for rational principles and a proto-Romantic urge to self-expression." (Times Literary Supplement)

REVIEW: *Burlington Mag* v155 no1328 p780-1 N 2013 JONATHAN YARKER

REVIEW: *Choice* v50 no10 p1823 Je 2013 T. J. McCormicks

REVIEW: *TLS* no5751 p21 Je 21 2013 FRANK SALMON

"Speaking Ruins: Piranesi, Architects, and Antiquity in Eighteenth-Century Rome." "At its heart, 'Speaking Ruins' is about the tensions between the Enlightenment quest for rational principles and a proto-Romantic urge to self-expression. . . . [John] Pinto traces elements of . . . [Giovanni Battista Piranesi's] complex response to the ruins back to the three illustrated treatises prepared by Carlo Fontana between 1694 and 1696, which dealt (as Renaissance architects such as Palladio had not) with the present-day urban contexts of ruined Roman buildings."

PISTOIA, SARA. Fractions; [by] Sara Pistoia 24 p. 2007 Child's World

1. Children's nonfiction 2. Food 3. Fractions—Juvenile literature 4. Mathematics—Juvenile literature 5. Picture books for children

ISBN 1592966861 (lib. bdg. : alk. paper); 1623235294; 9781623235291

LC 2005-037833

SUMMARY: This children's book on fractions, by Sara Pistoia, is part of the "Simply Math" series, which "offer[s] real-world introductions to basic math concepts suited for the youngest children." This book "uses foods, such as pie, pizza, a candy bar, fruit, a sandwich, and cookies, as well as everyday objects like traffic lights, to show how a whole can be divided into even parts. (They encourage sharing, too.)" (Booklist)

REVIEW: *Booklist* v110 no12 p72-4 F 15 2014 Miriam Aronin

"Fractions," "Measurement," "Patterns." "These new books in the Simply Math series offer real-world introductions to basic math concepts suited for the youngest children. Bright photos illustrate the concept of each book clearly. The pictures and text both point toward age-appropriate real-world applications of each concept. . . . Colorful examples make these charmingly simple books accessible to even the very youngest. These are sure to engage readers and perhaps even encourage children to keep an eye out for their math concepts in the world."

PISTOIA, SARA. Patterns; [by] Sara Pistoia 24 p. 2007 Child's World

1. Animal coloration 2. Children's nonfiction 3. Mathematics—Juvenile literature 4. Pattern perception—Juvenile literature 5. Picture books for children

ISBN 159296690X; 1623235332; 9781592966905 (lib. bdg. : alk. paper); 9781623235338

LC 2005-037838

SUMMARY: This children's book on patterns, by Sara Pistoia, is part of the "Simply Math" series, which "offer[s] real-world introductions to basic math concepts suited for the youngest children." This book "focuses largely on animal markings but also includes demonstrations using calendars and colored candy." (Booklist)

REVIEW: *Booklist* v110 no12 p72-4 F 15 2014 Miriam Aronin

"Fractions," "Measurement," "Patterns." "These new books in the Simply Math series offer real-world introductions to basic math concepts suited for the youngest children. Bright photos illustrate the concept of each book clearly. The pictures and text both point toward age-appropriate real-world applications of each concept. . . . Colorful examples make these charmingly simple books accessible to even the very youngest. These are sure to engage readers and perhaps even encourage children to keep an eye out for their math concepts in the world."

PISTOIA, SARA. Shapes; [by] Sara Pistoia 24 p. 2007 Child's World

1. Geometry—Juvenile literature

ISBN 1592966918 (lib. bdg. : alk. paper); 1623235340; 9781623235345

LC 2005-037839

SUMMARY: This educational illustrated children's book, by Sara Pistoia, as part of the publisher's "MathBooks" series, presents the concept of shapes with illustrations and photographs of everyday objects and in nature, such as watermelon wedges, soccer balls, and square birthday gift boxes. The text then expands onward to teach children various related skills and activities relating mathematics to the shapes.

REVIEW: *Booklist* v110 no12 p72-4 F 15 2014 Miriam Aronin

"Fractions," "Measurement," "Patterns." "These new books in the Simply Math series offer real-world introductions to basic math concepts suited for the youngest children. Bright photos illustrate the concept of each book clearly. The pictures and text both point toward age-appropriate real-world applications of each concept. . . . Colorful examples make these charmingly simple books accessible to even the very youngest. These are sure to engage readers and perhaps even encourage children to keep an eye out for their math concepts in the world."

PITCHER, ANNABEL. Ketchup clouds; a novel; [by] Annabel Pitcher 272 p. 2013 Little, Brown and Company

1. Children's secrets—Juvenile fiction 2. Epistolary fiction 3. Families—England—Juvenile fiction 4. Family life—England—Fiction 5. Grief—Fiction 6. Grief—Juvenile fiction 7. Guilt—Fiction 8. Guilt—Juvenile fiction 9. Letters—Fiction 10. Secrets—Fiction 11. Young adult fiction

ISBN 031624676X; 9780316246767

LC 2012-044116

SUMMARY: In this book, by Annabel Pitcher, "Zoe has an unconventional pen pal-Mr. Stuart Harris, a Texas Death Row inmate and convicted murderer. But then again, Zoe has an unconventional story to tell. A story about how she fell for two boys, betrayed one of them, and killed the other." (Publisher's note)

REVIEW: *Horn Book Magazine* v89 no6 p103 N/D 2013 DEIRDRE F. BAKER

"Ketchup Clouds". "This may all sound ponderous (and it is rather rich family drama), but Zoe's original mind, turns of phrase, and sprightly narrative style give her story quick, light momentum and movements of lyricism. 'It wasn't just dancing. It was living,' she says of a photo of her grandparents dancing together. 'Really living, like imagine the width of a moment rather than the length, and two people determined to fill every last millimeter of it.' Sharp, articulate perceptions and a measure of suspense—as well as a lively thread of wit and humor—make this a very engaging read."

REVIEW: *Publ Wkly* v260 no40 p53-5 O 7 2013

PITE, REBEKAH E. Creating a common table in twentieth-century Argentina; Doña Petrona, women, and food; [by] Rebekah E. Pite xv, 326 p. 2013 University of North Carolina Press

1. COOKING—Regional & Ethnic—Central American & South American 2. Cooking—Argentina 3. Cooking, Argentine 4. Feminism—Argentina—History—20th century 5. HISTORY—Latin America—South America 6. Historical literature 7. Women—Argentina—Social conditions—20th century
ISBN 9781469606897 (hardback: alk. paper); 9781469606903 (pbk.: alk. paper)
LC 2012-034766

SUMMARY: This book by Rebekah E. Pite looks at "Dona Petrona C. de Gandulfo (c. 1896-1992), [who] reigned as Argentina's preeminent domestic and culinary expert from the 1930s through the 1980s. An enduring culinary icon thanks to her magazine columns, radio programs, and television shows, she was likely second only to Eva Peron in terms of the fame she enjoyed and the adulation she received." (Publisher's note)

REVIEW: *Am Hist Rev* v119 no1 p226-7 F 2014 Donna J. Guy

"Creating a Common Table in Twentieth-Century Argentina: Doña Petrona, Women, and Food". "Rebekah E. Pite's study of Doña Petrona's successful career from the first edition of her cookbook in 1934 until the 1970s offers many new social insights for twentieth- century Argentina. . . . A readable and fascinating history of how modernity changed domestic life during the twentieth century. . . . Her study reaffirms the centrality of mass media and gender as cultural actors in Argentina. I hope that it will encourage other scholars to explore the role of women in radio and television as purveyors of normative patterns marked by both tradition and modernity."

REVIEW: *Choice* v51 no10 p1751 Je 2014 D. M. Gilbert
REVIEW: *Choice* v51 no2 p286-7 O 2013 D. M. Gilbert

PITTAU, FRANCESCO. Birds of a feather; [by] Francesco Pittau 18 p. 2012 Chronicle Books

1. Bird habitats 2. Birds—Behavior 3. Birds—Juvenile literature 4. Lift-the-flap books 5. Picture books for children
ISBN 1452110662; 9781452110660 (alk. paper)
LC 2012-004256

SUMMARY: This book by Francesco Pittau and Bernadette Gervais is "a lift-the-flap picture album of birds. . . . Pittau and Gervais hide . . . animal portraits (some of which are small pop-ups) behind large, shaped or die-cut flaps. Each image is paired to a comment on the subject's behavior, habitat or physical features." (Kirkus Reviews)

REVIEW: *Kirkus Rev* v80 no22 p68 N 15 2012
REVIEW: *Publ Wkly* v259 no41 p59 O 8 2012
REVIEW: *SLJ* v58 no12 p106 D 2012 Patricia Manning

PITZER, ANDREA. The secret history of Vladimir Nabokov; [by] Andrea Pitzer 432 p. 2013 Pegasus Books

1. Concentration camps in literature 2. Holocaust, Jewish (1939-1945), in literature 3. Literature—History & criticism 4. Nabokov, Vladimir Vladimirovich, 1899-1977 5. Russian literature—History & criticism
ISBN 1605984116; 9781605984117

SUMMARY: This book, by Andrea Pitzer, discusses the life and work of the Russian novelist Vladimir Nabokov, who "witnessed the horrors of his century, escaping Revolutionary Russia then Germany under Hitler. . . . He repeatedly faced accusations of turning a blind eye to human suffering to write artful tales of depravity. But does one of the greatest writers in the English language really deserve the label of amoral aesthete bestowed on him by so many critics?" (Publisher's note)

REVIEW: *World Lit Today* v87 no5 p74-5 S/O 2013 Andrew Martino

"The Secret Life of Vladimir Nabokov." "The thesis of Andrea Pitzer's book on Vladimir Nabokov is an ambitious one. . . . Yet, 'The Secret Life of Vladimir Nabokov' is a beautifully written, thoroughly researched book that is sure to significantly enrich the stream of Nabokovian studies. . . . 'The Secret Life of Vladimir Nabokov' is a tremendous book, but perhaps the best thing I can say about it is that Pitzer inspires us to return to Nabokov, to go back and reread his entire oeuvre with a new, now unsentimental eye."

PIZZOLI, GREG.il. The watermelon seed. See Pizzoli, G.

PLA, JOSEP. The Gray Notebook; 656 p. 2013 New York Review Books

1. Authors, Catalan—20th century—Biography 2. Authorship 3. Diary (Literary form) 4. Spain—Description & travel
ISBN 1590176715; 9781590176719 (alk. paper)
LC 2013-028497

SUMMARY: This book presents the diary of author Joseph Pla, translated by Peter Bush. "Aspiring to be a writer, not a lawyer, he resolved to hone his style by keeping a journal. In it he wrote about his family, local characters, . . . the quips, quarrels, ambitions, and amours of his friends; writers he liked and writers he didn't; and the long . . . walks he would take in the countryside under magnificent skies." (Publisher's note)

REVIEW: *Kirkus Rev* v82 no3 p268 F 1 2014

"The Gray Notebook". "[Joseph] Pla (1897-1981) is considered one of the greatest writers of Catalan language, and this beautiful translation lets English readers glory in the quiet strength of his words. . . . This diary . . . begs to be read slowly, calmly and multiple times. . . . The author's writing is not just about description—that's too simple a word. He masterfully conveys the actual mushroom-y smell of the earth, the odors, the colors in the egg-yolk sky and the taste of spring in Muscat grapes. His lyrical stories capture the soul of his people. . . . A classic."

REVIEW: *N Y Times Book Rev* p23 Ap 20 2014 ALAN RIDING

PLACING POETRY; viii, 313 p. 2013 Rodopi

1. English poetry—History and criticism 2. Literary form 3. Poetics 4. Poetry (Literary form)—History &

criticism 5. Space in literature
ISBN 9042036141 (pbk.); 9789042036147 (pbk.)
LC 2012-532970

SUMMARY: This book, edited by Ian Davidson and Zoë Skoulding, offers "a thorough re-evaluation of the idea of place for the twenty-first century, linking across theoretical interests in space and spatialisation and in motion and mobility. . . . Placing . . . happens in different contexts, in the production of visual images, in translation, in performance and in poetry that is both 'there' and 'here'. The range of poets under consideration matches the breadth . . . of the contributors." (Publisher's note)

REVIEW: *Choice* v51 no2 p254-5 O 2013 R. K. Mookerjee

"Placing Poetry." "The spatial theme enjoyed a critical vogue in the 1980s and 1990s, but [editors Ian] Davidson . . . and [Zoë] Skoulding . . . argue for its special contemporary relevance based on the 'mobility' of spaces. These essays, by an international gathering of scholars, demonstrate the geographical mobility as well as the flexibility of the concept. Taken together, they show that a poem has never been a purely mimetic or symbolic verbal composition. . . . Serious and playful, the collection is less about the migration of poetry from lines and stanzas than the expansion of the conception of formal and experimental verse. Despite the theoretical bent, the essays remain lively and accessible throughout, grounding each instance of spatiality in specific, well-explained examples."

PLAG, INGO. The Oxford reference guide to English morphology; [by] Ingo Plag x, 691 p. 2013 Oxford University Press

1. English language—Parts of speech 2. Grammar, Comparative and general—Morphology 3. Grammar, Comparative and general—Morphology—Terminology 4. Grammar, Comparative and general—Word formation 5. Reference books
ISBN 9780199579266 (hbk.)
LC 2013-474668

SUMMARY: This book provides a reference guide to English morphology, "beginning with several chapters that define terminology, describe data collection methods, and explain spelling conventions. Next, descriptive sections are organized by category (inflection, derivation, compounding); individual chapters within each section focus on the parts of speech (nouns, verbs, adjectives, adverbs). The authors collect the theoretical chapters at the end." (Choice: Current Reviews for Academic Libraries)

REVIEW: *Choice* v51 no8 p1366 Ap 2014 P. J. Kurtz

"The Oxford Reference Guide to English Morphology". "The authors hope this handbook will reach 'the widest possible audience,' and to this end they spend an entire chapter defining their terminology. This chapter is highly useful for general readers unfamiliar with the array of linguistic terms needed for this work. The book's writing style is accessible, though the sheer volume of new terms, while unavoidable, might overwhelm some readers. The information is organized in a logical manner. . . . This comprehensive book, which covers all aspects of English morphology, is a needed reference work. It will be most useful for linguistics professionals or professors/ teachers of linguistics. General readers may struggle with the inevitable use of linguistic terms."

PLAGNOL, ANKE C.ed. Gendered Lives. See Gendered Lives

PLANKEY-VIDELA, NANCY. We are in this dance together; gender, power, and globalization at a Mexican garment firm; [by] Nancy Plankey-Videla xiv, 259 p. 2012 Rutgers University Press

1. Clothing trade—Mexico 2. Clothing workers—Labor unions—Mexico 3. Social science literature 4. Strikes and lockouts—Clothing trade—Mexico 5. Women clothing workers—Mexico
ISBN 0813553016 (hbk.: alk. paper); 0813553024 (pbk.: alk. paper); 0813553156 (e-book); 9780813553016 (hbk.: alk. paper); 9780813553023 (pbk.: alk. paper); 9780813553153 (e-book)
LC 2011-037602

SUMMARY: In this book, author Nancy Plankey-Videla "documents and analyzes events leading up to [a]female-led factory strike and its aftermath—including harassment from managers, corrupt union officials and labor authorities, and violent governor-sanctioned police actions." The book "illustrates how the women's shared identity as workers and mothers . . . became the basis for radicalization and led to further civic organizing". (Publisher's note)

REVIEW: *Am J Sociol* v119 no1 p288-90 Jl 2013 Krista M. Brumley

REVIEW: *Contemp Sociol* v43 no2 p250-1 Mr 2014 Carolina Bank Muñoz

"We Are in This Dance Together: Gender, Power, and Globalization at a Mexican Garment Firm". "A thoughtful, well-researched, and rich ethnographic study of how women workers and mothers beat the odds and went on strike against a high-end garment factory in Mexico in the early 2000s at the height of the global economic crisis. While the author clearly supports the women in their quest for dignity, respect, and a decent wage, she presents a nuanced account of the multitude of factors that led to the strike. . . . I only wish she had incorporated more of the voices of the women workers themselves. 'We Are in This Dance Together' is a must read for all of those interested in work, labor, social justice, gender, globalization, and Latin America."

PLANT, ANDREW.il. Ancient animals. See Ancient animals

PLANTE, DAVID. Becoming a Londoner; a diary; [by] David Plante 544 p. 2013 Bloomsbury

1. Americans—England 2. Gay male authors 3. Memoirs 4. Novelists, American—20th century—Biography
ISBN 9781620401880 (alk. paper)
LC 2013-018704

SUMMARY: "David Plante has kept a diary of his life for more than half a century. Both a deeply personal memoir and a fascinating and significant work of cultural history, this first volume spans his first twenty years in London, beginning in the mid-sixties, and pieces together fragments of diaries, notes, sketches, and drawings to reveal a beautiful, intimate portrait of a relationship and a luminous evocation of a world of writers, poets, artists, and thinkers." (Publisher's note)

REVIEW: *Booklist* v110 no3 p14 O 1 2013 Donna Seaman

REVIEW: *Kirkus Rev* v81 no15 p147 Ag 1 2013

REVIEW: *London Rev Books* v36 no3 p21-3 F 6 2014 Andrew O'Hagan

"Becoming a Londoner: A Diary and "The Animals: Love Letters Between Christopher Isherwood and Don Bachardy". "Early in David Plante's diaries, we find him tinkling away, dropping names in basso profundo, as if knowing people and knowing what they do in private can be the thing that makes one special. . . . Let's applaud him, though. . . . His diaries are good because they are true to his own narcissism. . . . A taste for silliness is a capital virtue when it comes to considering the Isherwoods. . . . Their letters to each other must be the silliest in modern literature and none the less entertaining for that. For five hundred pages, it's like watching two pre-adolescent girls in full spate, giving vent to an OMGfest involving sparkles, super-furry animals and lots of pink, while occasionally dropping bombshells about the teachers."

REVIEW: *Publ Wkly* v260 no28 p162 Jl 15 2013

REVIEW: *TLS* no5780 p22 Ja 10 2014 PETER PARKER

"Becoming a Londoner: A Diary." "Rather than publishing his diary of this period as written, [author David] Plante has in 'Becoming a Londoner' created a continuous narrative, adding in material from later diaries by way of explanation and embellishment, but providing no dates beyond the first one. While this makes the book very readable, it is occasionally disconcerting to find historical events tumbled together. . . . As readers of the notorious 'Difficult Women' (1983) will know, candour is also the hallmark of what Plante writes about others, and those drawn to this book for its high-calibre gossip will not be disappointed. . . . The book is not simply an often very funny portrait of an age, however: it is also a moving portrait of a marriage."

PLATER, ZYGMUNT J. B. The snail darter and the dam; how pork-barrel politics endangered a little fish and killed a river; [by] Zygmunt J. B. Plater 369 p. 2013 Yale University Press

1. Endangered species—Government policy—United States 2. Environmental legislation—United States 3. Environmental policy—United States 4. Political science literature 5. Rare fishes—Government policy—United States

ISBN 9780300173246 (hardcover : alk. paper)

LC 2012-047816

SUMMARY: This book by Zygmunt J. B. Plater looks at "the Tennessee Valley Authority's Tellico Dam project." The author "was centrally involved in the litigation that sought to stop the project by claiming that it violated the Endangered Species Act because the dam would make the snail darter (a small fish) extinct. Although the Supreme Court agreed, Congress quickly passed legislation exempting the dam from the Act." (Choice: Current Reviews for Academic Libraries)

REVIEW: *Choice* v51 no7 p1309-10 Mr 2014 M. E. Ethridge

"The Snail Darter and the Dam: How Pork-Barrel Politics Endangered a Little Fish and Killed a River." "Readers will learn about the limits and power of litigation as a policy-making tool, and about the clash between developers and conservationists, and between state and federal government. Given his role in the litigation, readers will not be surprised to find that the author does not present a work of academic neutrality, but the point of view of a deeply committed (and disappointed) advocate. Nevertheless, the book is a compelling history of a controversy that sheds light on the policy process and is fascinating in its own right."

PLAYER, MICAH.il. Binny for short. See McKay, H.

PLOTKIN, JEFFREY S. Industrial organic chemicals. See Wittcoff, H. A.

PLOURDE, LYNN, 1955-. You're wearing that to school?!; 32 p. 2013 Disney-Hyperion Books

1. First day of school—Fiction 2. Hippopotamus—Fiction 3. Individuality—Fiction 4. Mice—Fiction 5. School stories 6. Schools—Fiction

ISBN 1423155106; 9781423155102 (hardcover)

LC 2011-031614

SUMMARY: This children's picture book follows hippo Penelope, who's "excited about starting school. Her retiring friend Tiny, a mouse, is a pessimistic first-grader determined to prevent what he expects would be gaffes on her first day. Penelope plans to wear her favorite outlandish outfit, bring her well-worn stuffed toy for show-and-tell, and pack a picnic lunch. Tiny quashes her cheerful plans, dialing her down to jeans and a T-shirt, a rock, and PB&J. Undeterred, the hippo ignores Tiny." (School Library Journal)

REVIEW: *Bull Cent Child Books* v67 no1 p47 S 2013 J. H.

"You're Wearing THAT to School?!" "Vivacious hippo Penelope is excited aboue starting school, but her older mouse pal, Tiny, thinks she needs to curb some of her natural tendencies: he wants Penelope to dress low-key, take a boring lunch, and bring a rock rather than a stuffed 'baby' toy for show-and-tell. When the first day of school comes, though, a fearless Penelope . . . has a great first day without sacrificing her unique tastes. Sure, this is kind of messagey, but the message is a worthy one. . . . Clear writing, lively dialogue, and a solid story structure enhance this title's readaloud value as well. [Illustrator Sue] Cornelison's slightly soft-focus illustrations are strongly composed, with Penelope's size and verve making her dominate most of the spreads."

REVIEW: *Kirkus Rev* v81 no2 p110 Je 1 2013

REVIEW: *Publ Wkly* v260 no21 p61 My 27 2013

REVIEW: *SLJ* v59 no5 p84 My 2013 Amy Lilien-Harper

POE, DONALD B. Huh. I didn't Know That!; [by] Donald B. Poe 312 p. 2013 CreateSpace Independent Publishing Platform

1. Anecdotes 2. Curiosities & wonders 3. Etymology 4. Geographic names 5. Reference books

ISBN 1482047020; 9781482047028

SUMMARY: This book, by Donald B. Poe, Jr., presents "a varied collection of trivia and anecdotes. . . . The facts, beginning with an explanation of why the Battle of Hastings was not fought in the town from which it takes its name, are generally unaccompanied by cited evidence, although sources for some sections are given at the end of the book." (Kirkus Reviews)

REVIEW: *Kirkus Rev* v81 no24 p343 D 15 2013

"Huh. I Didn't Know That!" "A varied collection of trivia and anecdotes compiled by an enthusiast with an evident passion for his work. . . . Each factoid appears in its own brief chapter, written in a chatty style that reminds the reader that this book should not be taken too seriously while delivering on the author's promise to give the reader not just a list of trivia, but 'stories…on why I find the fact of the moment interesting.' . . . The facts . . . are generally unaccompanied by cited evidence, although sources for some sections are given at the end of the book. While readers looking for substantive documentation . . . should look elsewhere for their research, more casual readers are likely to find their interest piqued by Poe's explanations."

POHLER, EVA. The Gatekeeper's Sons; Gatekeeper's Trilogy; [by] Eva Pohler 384 p. 2012 Green Press

1. Fantasy fiction 2. Greek mythology—Fiction 3. Hypnos (Greek deity) 4. Love stories 5. Thanatos (Greek deity)

ISBN 061568596X; 9780615685960

SUMMARY: " In this teen fantasy novel and love story," the first book in Eva Pohler's Gatekeeper's Saga, "an orphaned girl finds herself at the center of a war brewing among the gods of Olympus. . . . While Therese is . . .in a coma following [an] accident, she travels through the dream world and meets two alluring young men, Hypnos, or Hip, and Thanatos, or Than, twin sons of Hades. . . . Than makes a deal with his father: 40 days among humans to try to make Therese his bride." (Kirkus Reviews)

REVIEW: *Kirkus Rev* v82 no2 p370 Ja 15 2014

"The Gatekeeper's Sons". "When a book opens with a bang like this, readers might expect great things. . . . After this fast and eventful introduction, things slow down—way, way down. . . . As Than and Therese flirt with one another, the story plods along with unnecessary subplots and minor characters, as well as turgid descriptions of everyday actions. Things pick up again about two-thirds of the way through. . . . Pohler's straightforward storytelling might not appeal to many teenagers, and the book's central metaphor, a dying tree, feels like an afterthought. Teenage readers might be swept up in the passion between Therese and Than, though the story is unlikely to inflame any sort of literary fervor."

POISSANT, DAVID JAMES. The heaven of animals; stories; [by] David James Poissant 272 p. 2014 Simon & Schuster

ISBN 1476729964; 9781476729961 (hardcover)

LC 2013-037118

SUMMARY: This collection of short stories, by David James Poissant, "explores the tenuous bonds of family—fathers and sons, husbands and wives—as they are tested by the sometimes brutal power of love. . . . From two friends racing to save the life of an alligator in 'Lizard Man' to a girl helping her boyfriend face his greatest fears in 'The End of Aaron,' . . . to a brother's surprise at the surreal, improbable beauty of a late night encounter with a wolf, Poissant creates worlds." (Publisher's note)

REVIEW: *Booklist* v110 no13 p18 Mr 1 2014 Diego Báez

REVIEW: *Kirkus Rev* v82 no1 p286 Ja 1 2014

"The Heaven of Animals: Stories". "The much-anthologized [David James] Poissant justifies his status as a favorite of the literary quarterlies with this debut collection of unsparing yet warmly empathetic stories. . . . Two short, overstylized pieces, 'Knockout' and 'The Baby Glows,' are the author's only missteps, but perhaps they were warm-ups for the delicate balance between allegory and realism achieved in 'What the Wolf Wants.' . . . Rueful and kind, akin to both Anton Chekhov and Raymond Carver in humane spirit and technical mastery."

REVIEW: *Libr J* v139 no5 p117 Mr 15 2014 Lauren Gilbert

REVIEW: *N Y Times Book Rev* p30 Jl 27 2014 Rebecca Lee

POLACCO, PATRICIA. The blessing cup; 48 p. 2013 Simon & Schuster Books for Young Readers

1. Drinking cups—Fiction 2. Family life—Fiction 3. Historical fiction 4. Jewish refugees—History 5. Jews—Fiction 6. Jews—Russia—Fiction 7. Jews—Russia—History

ISBN 1442450479; 9781442450479 (hardcover); 9781442450486 (ebook)

LC 2012-023596

SUMMARY: This book is Patricia Polacco's prequel to "The Keeping Quilt." Here, "readers learn how Polacco's great-grandmother Anna and her parents were forced from their shtetl in Czarist Russia and made their way to America. Among the few treasures the family took with them was a vibrantly painted tea set, a kind of familial talisman . . ., which also served as a reminder that they would always be rich in what matters: resilience and love." (Publishers Weekly)

REVIEW: *Booklist* v110 no3 p100 O 1 2013 Kay Weisman

REVIEW: *Bull Cent Child Books* v67 no2 p110-1 O 2013 H. M.

"The Blessing Cup." "This companion story to 'The Keeping Quilt' recounts the details of how young Anna . . . and her family are driven from their home in Czarist Russia. A kind doctor comes to their aid, offering them food, shelter, and warmth, and he proves their savior once again when, upon receiving notification from authorities that he cannot house Jews, he purchases tickets for the entire family to travel to America. . . . [Author Patricia] Polacco has a particular flair for turning family stories into universal tales. . . . The story is suffused with warmth, and while many of the events described are tragic, there is an air of familial joy (if also occasional sentimentality) that supersedes the sadness."

REVIEW: *Horn Book Magazine* v89 no5 p79-80 S/O 2013 JOANNA RUDGE LONG

REVIEW: *Kirkus Rev* v81 no2 p100 Je 1 2013

REVIEW: *N Y Times Book Rev* p14 Ag 25 2013 VALERIE STEIKER

"Rifka Takes a Bow," "This Is the Rope: A Story From the Great Migration," and "The Blessing Cup." "It's refreshing to find three new picture books that take as their subject the stories of human families. . . . Betty Rosenberg Perlov grew up in [the world of Yiddish theater] and it's clear she knows it well. . . . Spare and evocative as a poem, [Jacqueline] Woodson's refrain winds through the book, fastening us to the comfort of memories and the strength of family ties. . . . If 'The Blessing Cup' never quite lifts off from its history lesson as do 'Rifka Takes a Bow' and 'This Is The Rope,' it nonetheless imparts a valuable message."

REVIEW: *Publ Wkly* v260 no22 p58-60 Je 3 2013

REVIEW: *SLJ* v59 no8 p87 Ag 2013 Nora Clancy

POLACCO, PATRICIA.il. The blessing cup. See Polacco, P.

POLACCO, PATRICIA. Clara and Davie; [by] Patricia Polacco 40 p. 2013 Scholastic Press

1. Children's nonfiction 2. Nurses—United States—Biography—Juvenile literature
ISBN 0545354773; 9780545354776
LC 2013-011859

SUMMARY: This book, by Patricia Polacco, tells the "story of young Clara Barton. Animals and flowers were Clara's best friends. She had a special way with critters and found joy in the beauty that sprang from the soil. But whenever Clara talked, her words didn't come out right. As hard as she tried, she could not get over her lisp. Clara's older brother Davie understood that his sister was gifted. . . . [She] founded the American Red Cross." (Publisher's note)

REVIEW: *Booklist* v110 no9/10 p90 Ja 1 2014 Connie Fletcher

REVIEW: *Bull Cent Child Books* v67 no6 p329 F 2014 Elizabeth Bush

REVIEW: *Kirkus Rev* v81 no24 p133 D 15 2013

"Clara and Davie". ". The pictures are done in [Patricia] Polacco's vivid, vibrant pencil, marker and acrylics, with exaggerated gestures and abundant details. The dialogue is occasionally a bit over-the-top: 'Davie, I know you can walk. You have always told me that I have a gift of healing. Unless you try to walk, I'll never believe that again.' An author's note outlines [Clara] Barton's founding of the American Red Cross and her work with soldiers during the Civil War. The abundance of dialogue and absence of specific sources makes this book problematic for use as nonfiction. Not up to Polacco's usual standard."

REVIEW: *Publ Wkly* v260 no49 p85 D 2 2013

REVIEW: *SLJ* v60 no1 p116 Ja 2014 Sara-Jo Lupo Sites

POLISNER, GAE. The summer of letting go; [by] Gae Polisner 320 p. 2014 Algonquin

1. Best friends—Fiction 2. Brothers and sisters—Fiction 3. Dating (Social customs)—Fiction 4. Death—Fiction 5. Family problems—Fiction 6. Friendship—Fiction 7. Young adult fiction
ISBN 1616202564; 9781616202569 (alk. paper)
LC 2013-038536

SUMMARY: In this book, by Gae Polisner, "it's been four years since her little brother, Simon, drowned, but fifteen-year-old Frankie and her family are still shattered by the tragedy. . . . What changes her summer is a little boy she begins to babysit, whose eager fearlessness helps Frankie recapture some of the pre tragedy joys of having a little brother–and whose extraordinary connections to Simon suggest to Frankie that her new charge may be Simon's reincarnation." (Bulletin of the Center for Children's Books)

REVIEW: *Bull Cent Child Books* v67 no7 p372 Mr 2014 D. S.

"The Summer of Letting Go." "Frankie's guilt about Simon (she was supposed to be watching Simon when he died) and the family's subsequent dissolution are believably conveyed, and her absorption with her new charge (also called Frankie) is an understandable development. The multiplicity of plot threads overburdens the book, however, and little boy Frankie lacks authenticity; additionally, the book brushes off Frankie's serious childcare lapses (usually due to mooning over Bradley). [Rebecca] Serle's The Edge of Falling, reviewed below, is a superior story of coming to grips with the legacy of a sibling's death, but the enticing themes of forbidden romance, possible reincarnation, and expiation of guilt will likely have enough emotional pull to attract readers."

REVIEW: *Kirkus Rev* v82 no4 p47 F 15 2014

REVIEW: *N Y Times Book Rev* p26 My 11 2014 ELIZABETH DEVITA-RAEBURN

REVIEW: *Publ Wkly* v260 no52 p52-3 D 23 2013

REVIEW: *SLJ* v60 no2 p110 F 2014 Jennifer Prince

REVIEW: *Voice of Youth Advocates* v36 no6 p64 F 2014 Laura Lehner

A POLITICAL COMPANION TO SAUL BELLOW; 2013 University Press of Kentucky

1. Bellow, Saul, 1915-2005 2. Democracy in literature 3. Literature—History & criticism 4. Neoconservatism 5. Politics & literature
ISBN 9780813141855

SUMMARY: This book, edited by Gloria L. Cronin and Lee Trepanier, "examines [Saul Bellow's] novels, essays, short stories, and letters in order to illuminate his evolution from liberal to neoconservative. It investigates Bellow's exploration of the United States as a democratic system, the religious and ideological influences on his work, and his views on race relations, religious identity, and multiculturalism in the academy." (Publisher's note)

REVIEW: *Choice* v51 no5 p834-5 Ja 2014 S. Miller

"A Political Companion to Saul Bellow." "In their introduction [Gloria L.] Cronin and [Lee] Trepanier study and explain Bellow's politics in this literal way, and the essays that follow do a good job of covering Bellow's manner--as an immigrant Jew, professor, and American man of letters--of representing his characters' conflicted lives: he portrays complex individuals motivated mostly by personal, not partisan, views of society and politics. The scholarly studies in this companion are complemented by brief memoirs by Bellow's sons."

THE POLITICS OF KNOWLEDGE; vi, 211 p. 2012 Routledge

1. Information technology—Political aspects 2. Knowledge, Sociology of 3. Political science literature 4. Political sociology 5. Sociology literature
ISBN 0203877748 (ebook); 0415497108 (alk. paper); 9780203877746 (ebook); 9780415497107 (alk. paper)
LC 2011-004531

SUMMARY: Edited by Fernando Domínguez Rubio and Patrick Baert, "this book provides a novel perspective on current debates about 'knowledge societies', and offers an interdisciplinary agenda for future research. It addresses four fundamental aspects of the relation between knowledge and politics." (Publisher's note)

REVIEW: *Contemp Sociol* v42 no5 p740-2 S 2013 Steve Fuller

"The Politics of Knowledge." "'The Politics of Knowledge' would have been better conceived as the special issue of a journal, reminding the discerning reader that there is a big difference between talking about 'the politics of knowledge' and doing it. This is not to take away from the editorial efforts of Fernando Domínguez Rubio and Patrick Baert in corralling a set of prominent contemporary scholars to tackle the topic. . . . The overall value of this book lies less in its ability to tell intellectuals things that they did not already know than in its challenge to taken-for-granted views within sociology, especially if the discipline is taken to assume Durkheim's realist social ontology and positivist view of science."

POLLACK, KENNETH M. The Arab awakening; America and the transformation of the Middle East; [by] Kenneth M. Pollack xvi, 381 p. 2011 Brookings Institution

1. Democratization—Arab countries—History—21st century 2. Political science literature 3. Protest movements—Arab countries—History—21st century

ISBN 9780815722267 (pbk.: alk. paper)

LC 2011-038375

SUMMARY: "Protests born of oppression and socioeconomic frustration erupted throughout the streets; public unrest provoked violent police backlash; long-established dictatorships fell. How did this all happen? . . . In 'The Arab Awakening,' experts from the Brookings Institution tackle such questions to make sense of this tumultuous region that remains at the heart of U.S. national interests." (Publisher's note)

REVIEW: *Middle East J* v68 no3 p465-8 Summ 2014 I. William Zartman

"The Arab Awakening: America and the Transformation of the Middle East," "Revolution, Revolt, and Reform in North Africa: The Arab Spring and Beyond," and "The Second Arab Awakening: And the Battle for Pluralism." "'America and the Transformation of the Middle East' . . . deals with a number of forces and a number of countries. . . . Each chapter concludes with implications for the US, which is the ultimate message of the work. . . . Ricardo René Larémont . . . also offers a background setting. . . . Larémont himself provides on excellent chapter on demographics and economics. . . . The work by Marwan Muasher . . . has a more forward look."

POLLACK, KENNETH M. Unthinkable; Iran, the Bomb, and American Strategy; [by] Kenneth M. Pollack 560 p. 2013 Simon & Schuster

1. Containment (Political science) 2. Iran—Foreign relations—United States 3. Iran—Politics & government 4. Nuclear arms control—Government policy—United States 5. Nuclear nonproliferation—Iran 6. Nuclear weapons—Iran 7. Nuclear weapons—United States—Government policy 8. Political science literature

ISBN 1476733929; 9781476733920

LC 2013-431171

SUMMARY: In this book on U.S. relations with Iran, author Kenneth Pollack "clearly states his preference for containment but not before thoroughly exploring the pros and cons of a military attack (including one by Israel) and not without conceding the dangers of the policy he recommends. As the Cold War demonstrated, the path of nuclear deterrence and containment is a difficult slog, but this choice . . . is likely less bad than the alternative." (Kirkus Reviews)

REVIEW: *Economist* v408 no8853 p89-90 S 14 2013

REVIEW: *Kirkus Rev* v81 no15 p267 Ag 1 2013

REVIEW: *Middle East J* v68 no1 p156-8 Wint 2014 Olli Heinonen

REVIEW: *N Y Times Book Rev* p14 S 8 2013 LESLIE H. GELB

"Unthinkable: Iran, the Bomb, and American Strategy". "Inexplicably, [Michael J.] Pollack throws away the best single argument for containment: that it worked against Saddam Hussein. He argues that it failed. The facts say otherwise. . . . But the ultimate weakness of Pollack's argument is his pessimism about the possibility of negotiations with Iran. . . . Still, his book was completed before the more hopeful signals that have been coming from both capitals. . . . By playing down the chance of negotiations in favor of containment, Pollack ends up proposing too little, rather than too much. Preventative war is as dangerous as he says. But a policy of containment would probably be too fragile to succeed."

POLLAK, ELLEN.ed. A cultural history of women in the age of enlightenment. See A cultural history of women in the age of enlightenment

POLLMANN, KARLA.ed. The Oxford Guide to the Historical Reception of Augustine. See The Oxford Guide to the Historical Reception of Augustine

POLO, AMBER. Recovered; [by] Amber Polo 264 p. 2013 Blue Merle Publishing

1. Fantasy fiction 2. Libraries 3. Shapeshifting 4. Werewolves 5. Women librarians—Fiction

ISBN 0985774827; 9780985774820

SUMMARY: In this book, part of the Shapeshifters' Library series, "Bliss is a dogshifter, and her newly discovered ability to change from human form into that of a sleek white greyhound has left her yearning to know more about her true heritage. The answer to all her questions, she is certain, lies with the dogshifters' long lost Library of the Ancients and, undeterred by the fact that thousands before her have searched, she sets out to find it." (Publisher's note)

REVIEW: *Kirkus Rev* v82 no1 p336 Ja 1 2014

"Recovered". "Author [Amber] Polo does an excellent job organizing the details of her inviting series for new and returning readers. . . . The werewolves here suffer a madness not limited to urban fantasy—distaste for intellectualism. . . . Yet Bliss and Harry's adventure avoids getting bogged down in political parallels. New Age elements, snippets of cleverness—e.g., the 'bowser browser, Zoogle'—and dogs in realistic danger find an appealing balance. At its core, the narrative illustrates how some kennels and breeders abuse animals but also how kindness can heal humans and dogs—and maybe even cats. A fanciful read that remains loyal to its noble principles."

POLYNESIAN OUTLIERS; the state of the art; 226 p. 2012 University of Pittsburgh

1. Islands of the Pacific 2. Pacific Islanders—First contact with Europeans 3. Polynesia—Social life & customs 4. Social science literature 5. Traditional societies

ISBN 9780945428152 (alk. paper)

LC 2012-940015

SUMMARY: This book,edited by Richard Feinberg and Richard Scaglion, addressing Polynesian outlier societies, asking questions such as "What is their relationship to the better-known Polynesian societies?" and "Can they, in some way, be thought of as representing Polynesian society before it became permanently altered by contact with Europeans?" (Publisher's note)

REVIEW: *Choice* v51 no1 p125 S 2013 G. R. Campbell

"Polynesian Outliers: The State of the Art." "A series of widely separated islands whose inhabitants speak Polynesian languages can be found in Micronesia and Melanesia, outside the Polynesian triangle. These islands are culturally influenced by location, surrounding non-Polynesian cultural systems, and by geographical isolation, depopulation, and repopulation. . . . In these chapters arising from conference symposia, [editors Richard Feinberg and Richard Scaglion] gathered leading scholars to consider the history of research and synthesize the current state of knowledge about the Polynesian outliers. . . . The volume's significance is in being a comprehensive synthesis of ethnographic data of previous research, raising new questions and directions for future research."

PON, CYNTHIA. Music everywhere! See Ajmera, M.

POOLE, IMOGEN. The vegetation of Antarctica through geological time. See Cantrill, D. J.

POP PAGANS; 2013 Acumen Publishing

1. Music—Religious aspects 2. Music literature 3. Neopaganism 4. Popular music 5. Popular music genres
ISBN 9781844656479

SUMMARY: This book, edited by Donna Weston and Andy Bennett, "assesses the histories, genres, performances, and communities of pagan popular music." According to the book, "Over time, paganism became associated with the counter culture, satanic and gothic culture, rave and festival culture, ecological consciousness and spirituality, and new ageism. . . .It has found . . . public expressions in . . . rock, folk, techno, goth, metal, Celtic, world, and pop music." (Publisher's note)

REVIEW: *Choice* v51 no5 p855 Ja 2014 J. B. Wolford

"Pop pagans: paganism and popular music." "While pagan popular music is an emerging subfield, the 14 Australian, UK, and US contributors to this volume cover the multiplicities of paganism admirably. The editors divide the book into four sections, 'Histories,' 'Genres,' 'Performance,' and 'Community,' all equally strong. Each contributor, implicitly or overtly, showcases how paganism and popular music in whatever form share traits of individualism, community, and transcendence. This work successfully serves as a broad overview of the relationship between popular music and paganism, but can serve equally well as a general introduction to the core ideas and foci unifying diverse pagan groups."

POPE, PAUL. Battling Boy; [by] Paul Pope 208 p. 2013 First Second

1. Gods 2. Graphic novels 3. Magic—Fiction 4. Monsters—Fiction 5. Superheroes 6. Supervillains
ISBN 9781480615090 (prebind); 1596438053 (hardcover); 9781596438057 (hardcover)

SUMMARY: In this book, "the hero Haggard West helps battle the evil forces of Sadisto and his hooded ghouls. However, in a shocking turn of events, evil triumphs over good, and the metropolis is left without protection. In a world far, far away, a 13-year-old son of a god has been chosen to help Earth fight the onslaught of monsters as a rite of passage. Sent with only a few possessions, including an array of magical T-shirts, Battling Boy helps the city—but he finds he cannot do it alone." (Kirkus Reviews)

REVIEW: *Booklist* v110 no2 p59 S 15 2013 Jesse Karp

REVIEW: *Booklist* v110 no13 p54 Mr 1 2014 Sarah Hunter

REVIEW: *Bull Cent Child Books* v67 no5 p278 Ja 2014 A. M.

"Battling Boy." "This first volume in a series introduces compelling new heroes designed to please middle-school readers. Drawing on a mixture of tropes both classic and cutting-edge, the narrative offers an introduction to the darker side of superhero comics for fans who want moral and narrative complexity but aren't quite ready to tackle the pervasive gloom of Frank Miller's 'Batman' sagas. The illustrations are crisp and bright, with most scenes tightly focused on dialogue or battle (though the book is tastefully light on actual gore)."

REVIEW: *Kirkus Rev* v81 no17 p110-1 S 1 2013

REVIEW: *Kirkus Rev* p71-2 2013 Guide 20to BookExpo America

REVIEW: *N Y Times Book Rev* p38 N 24 2013 Ken Tucker

REVIEW: *N Y Times Book Rev* p30 D 1 2013

REVIEW: *Publ Wkly* v260 no28 p174 Jl 15 2013

REVIEW: *Publ Wkly* p94 Children's starred review annual 2013

REVIEW: *SLJ* v59 no9 p171 S 2013 Peter Blenski

REVIEW: *Voice of Youth Advocates* v37 no1 p28-9 Ap 2014 AMANDA FOUST JACK BAUR

REVIEW: *Voice of Youth Advocates* v36 no3 p54-5 Ag 2013 KAT KAN

POPMA, LEO. As gong der in oar; [by] Leo Popma 2013 Elikser B.V. Uitgeverij

1. Architects—Fiction 2. Dutch fiction 3. Interpersonal relations—Fiction 4. Secrecy—Fiction 5. Translators
ISBN 9085660270; 9789085660279

SUMMARY: "Leo Popma has written an intriguing story with an intriguing title, 'As gong dêr in oar' ('As if another went there'), a story that sometimes confuses and often mystifies, for there are secrets within nearly every character. . . .In fact, nearly every character in this novel suffers from estrangement and disconnection, from homesickness for the place and the people they left behind but which yet inhabit them." (Publisher's note)

REVIEW: *World Lit Today* v88 no1 p62 Ja/F 2014 Henry J. Baron

"As gong dêr in oar." "Leo Popma has written an intriguing story with an intriguing title, 'As gong dêr in oar' ('As if another went there'), a story that sometimes confuses and often mystifies, for there are secrets within nearly every character. . . . Nearly every character in this novel suffers from estrangement and disconnection, from homesickness for the place and the people they left behind but which yet inhabit them. Indeed, the reader sometimes wonders whether the author meant to write an essay on the inextricable bond between language, culture, and identity, for the theme keeps recurring. . . . The serious reader will appreciate the thought-provoking substance of this novel."

POPPER, NICHOLAS. Walter Ralegh's History of the world and the historical culture of the late Renaissance;

[by] Nicholas Popper xvi, 350 p. 2012 University of Chicago Press

1. Historical literature 2. Historiography 3. History & politics 4. Raleigh, Walter, Sir, 1552?-1618
ISBN 0226675009 (hardcover: alkaline paper); 9780226675008 (hardcover: alkaline paper)
LC 2012-001096

SUMMARY: In this book, "Nicholas Popper uses [Walter] Ralegh's 'History of the World' as a touchstone" for his "exploration of the culture of history writing and historical thinking in the late Renaissance. From Popper we learn . . . how scholars and statesmen began to see historical expertise as not just a foundation for political practice and theory, but a means of advancing their power in the courts and councils of contemporary Europe." (Publisher's note)

REVIEW: *Choice* v50 no11 p2090 Jl 2013 S. Morillo

REVIEW: *Engl Hist Rev* v129 no536 p205-7 F 2014 Mark Nicholls

"Walter Ralegh's History of the World and the Historical Culture of the Late Renaissance". "In this learned, elegant and informative study, Nicholas Popper carefully locates Ralegh's History in the high summer of the ars historica and reminds us why contemporaries and many later readers were so impressed. . . . Popper's book is full of insights. . . . Happily, Ralegh's complex character and the scope of his magnum opus still leave a few questions unresolved. . . . There is still scope to locate the book more closely within English political life."

REVIEW: *TLS* no5750 p28 Je 14 2013 ADAM SMYTH

PORTER, CATHERINE.tr. An inquiry into modes of existence. See Latour, B.

PORTER, JANE, 1964-. The good wife; [by] Jane Porter 432 p. 2013 Berkley Books

1. Adultery—Fiction 2. Baseball players—Family relationships 3. Baseball players—Fiction 4. Love stories 5. Married people—Fiction 6. Sisters—Fiction
ISBN 9780425253670
LC 2013-015207

SUMMARY: In this novel by Jane Porter, part of the Brennan Sisters Novel series, "Always considered the beauty of the family, the youngest Brennan sister, Sarah, remains deeply in love with her husband of ten years. . . . Emotionally exhausted, Sarah can't cope with yet another storm. Now, she must either break free from the past and forgive Boone completely, or leave him behind and start anew." (Publisher's note)

REVIEW: *Booklist* v110 no1 p36 S 1 2013 John Charles

REVIEW: *Kirkus Rev* v81 no16 p276 Ag 15 2013

"The Good Wife." "A novel about marriages, sibling relationships and parenting, from [author Jane] Porter. . . . This is the final book in the author's Brennan Sisters Trilogy. The story follows Sarah Brennan Walker, the youngest Brennan sister, married to a famous baseball player, and Lauren Summers, once seduced, then abandoned, by another famous baseball player. . . . The book explores themes of love and loss, anger and guilt. Too much information about Sarah and Boone's sex life sometimes interrupts the far more interesting emotional and psychological developments. On the whole, though, the story is believable, insightful and marked by witty dialogue."

REVIEW: *Libr J* v138 no14 p102 S 1 2013 Anne M. Miskewitch

PORTERFIELD, JASON. Niklas Zennström and Skype; [by] Jason Porterfield 128 p. 2014 Rosen Publishing

1. Business literature 2. Businessmen—Sweden—Biography 3. Internet telephony 4. Telecommunications engineers—Sweden—Biography
ISBN 9781448895274 (library binding)
LC 2012-039848

SUMMARY: This book on entrepreneur Niklas Zennström, by Jason Porterfield, is part of the Internet Biographies series. After "a few pages covering the early life" of the Skype founder, it introduces his "Internet-based telephone service as well as [his] lawsuit-fraught other businesses, such as Kazaa." The book "includes color photographs and sidebars on related topics." (Booklist)

REVIEW: *Booklist* v110 no4 p45 O 15 2013 Susan Dove Lempke

"Nick Swinmurn, Tony Hsieh, and Zappos," "Niklas Zennström and Skype," and "Tim Westergren and Pandora." "The titles in the Internet Biographies series feature people who are far from household names, but the Internet businesses they began should be very familiar to a young adult audience. . . . 'Tim Westergren and Pandora' has an especially lively conversational style and does a good job of helping readers understand the issues facing the Internet radio station. Each book includes color photographs and sidebars on related topics. While not the most exciting reads, these succeed in showing how ordinary people can take a good idea and turn it into a business."

REVIEW: *Voice of Youth Advocates* v36 no6 p84 F 2014 Ursula Adams

PORTRAIT OF A PATRIOT; the major political and legal papers of Josiah Quincy Junior; var 2009 Colonial Society of Massachusetts

1. Law—United States—History 2. Law reports, digests, etc.—United States 3. Quincy, Josiah, 1744-1775
ISBN 9780979466243

SUMMARY: "In these two volumes, Daniel Coquillette and Neil Longley York . . . provide an annotated reprint of . . . the 'Law Reports' of Josiah Quincy Jr. . . . These volumes provide American legal historians with four . . . resources. First among these is the reprint of the text and notes of Samuel Quincy's 1865 edition of his grandfather's 'Law Reports.' . . . Second, this reprint edition features a[n] . . . introductory essay by Daniel Coquillette. . . . The third . . . resource contained in these volumes lies in the editors' . . . annotations on the cases, in which they provide information on lawyers and judges, sources cited, and the later history of the cases. . . . Finally, these volumes contain a number of . . . appendices . . . [such as the] 'Catalogue of Books Belonging to the Estate of Josiah Quincy, Jr.'." (New England Quarterly)

REVIEW: *N Engl Q* v84 no4 p727-8 D 2011 M. H. Hoeflich

"Portrait of a Patriot: Major Political and Legal Papers of Josiah Quincy Jr.: The Law Reports." "In these two volumes, Daniel Coquillette and Neil Longley York now provide an annotated reprint of one of this field's [i.e. colonial American law] principal sources, the 'Law Reports' of Josiah Quincy Jr. Coquillette, York, and the Colonial Society of Massachusetts are to be congratulated for producing this exemplary model of both scholarship and bookmaking. . . . The third invaluable resource contained in these volumes lies in the editors' extensive annotations on the cases, in which they provide information on lawyers and judges, sources cited, and the later history of the cases. . . . The editors' notes make these volumes crucial reading not only for legal historians but for every lawyer who may have issues for which the reported eases may serve as precedent."

POST, JONATHAN.ed. The Oxford handbook of Shakespeare's poetry. See The Oxford handbook of Shakespeare's poetry

POTPARA, LILI.tr. The master of insomnia. See Novak, B.A.

POTTS, ALEX. Experiments in modern realism; world-making, politics and the everyday in postwar European and American art; [by] Alex Potts 320 p. 2013 Yale University Press

1. Art literature 2. Painting—Political aspects—Europe—History—20th century 3. Painting—Political aspects—United States—History—20th century 4. Painting, American—20th century 5. Painting, European—20th century 6. Realism in art—Europe 7. Realism in art—United States

ISBN 9780300187687 (cl : alk. paper)

LC 2012-029588

SUMMARY: It was the author's intent to demonstrate that "'many of the artists who were intensively engaged with modernist or avant-garde experimentation were at the same time committed to producing work that referred to, evoked or commented on phenomena in the world at large'. The thrust of Alex Potts' s reading, accordingly, is to seek 'reality' wherever it may be found in the work at hand." (Times Literary Supplement)

REVIEW: *TLS* no5772 p30 N 15 2013 ALEX DANCHEV

"Experiments in Modern Realism: World Making, Politics and the Everyday in Postwar European and American Art." "This makes for a rich diet and [Alex] Potts's patient rereadings have many virtues. He attends carefully to the writings and sayings of the artists themselves, lending them a significance that they too often lack. . . . In its own terms, much of the exegesis is unexceptionable. . . . But it's not clear how far this gets us. . . . 'Experiments in Modern Realism' aims to be two things at once: a treatise in its own right and an intervention in art-historical disputation. Alex Potts is adept at both, but the mix is not a happy one."

POWELL, CONSIE.il. Nature's patchwork quilt. See Miché, M.

POWELL, NATE.il. March. See Lewis, J. R.

POWELL, NEIL, 1948-. Benjamin Britten; a life for music; [by] Neil Powell 528 p. 2013 Henry Holt and Company

1. Biography (Literary form) 2. Composers—England—Biography 3. Gay male composers 4. Opera—History—20th century

ISBN 0805097740; 9780805097740

LC 2012-051536

SUMMARY: In this biography of "Benjamin Britten, the celebrated British composer . . . [Neil] Powell . . . traces the development of Britten's musical gifts from his childhood and youth in England to his travels to America, his meetings and lifelong friendship with W.H. Auden, and his crucial role in helping to establish the Alderburgh Festival. . . . He probes the genius of Britten's compositions from Sinfonietta . . . to the triptych of Peter Grimes . . . Billy Budd, and Death in Venice." (Publishers Weekly)

REVIEW: *Booklist* v109 no21 p11 Jl 1 2013 Roy Olson

REVIEW: *Economist* v406 no8825 p79-80 Mr 2 2013

REVIEW: *Kirkus Rev* v81 no15 p29 Ag 1 2013

REVIEW: *Libr J* v138 no5 p92 Mr 15 2013 Barbara Hoffert

REVIEW: *London Rev Books* v35 no24 p13-5 D 19 2013 James Wood

"Benjamin Britten: A Life in the 20th Century" and "Benjamin Britten: A Life for Music". "Two biographies, by Paul Kildea and Neil Powell, intelligently appraise this official and unofficial Britten, and are rich with contradiction. . . . Kildea, the deeper, more probing of the two biographers, describes well the deep musical immersion of Britten's early years. . . . Kildea, himself a conductor and music administrator, offers an authoritative account of the amateurism of British musical performance in the first few decades of the last century. . . . Kildea and Powell are straightforward and easy about Britten's boys."

REVIEW: *N Y Times Book Rev* p13 O 27 2013 VIVIEN SCHWEITZER

"Benjamin Britten: A Life For Music". "[Neil] Powell is not looking to uncover any prurient scandal. He writes as an unabashed fan. . . . Powell, a poet and biographer, is not a musicologist; instead of notated examples he offers elegant descriptions of Britten's music and the Suffolk countryside that inspired it. . . . Powell also writes insightfully about the relationship between the music and the texts Britten used. . . . Powell disagrees with many critiques of Britten's music, but makes relevant criticisms of his own about various works. . . . Some of Powell's psychoanalysis . . . seems tenuous. . . . Powell also speculates unnecessarily about why Britten was still unhappy after achieving fame and material success."

REVIEW: *Publ Wkly* v260 no30 p61 Jl 29 2013

POWER, ANDREW.ed. Cyberpsychology and new media. See Cyberpsychology and new media

POWER TO THE PEOPLE; the graphic design of the radical press and the rise of the counter-culture, 1964-1974; 264 p.

1. Counterculture—United States—Bibliography 2. Graphic design (Typography)—United States—History—20th century 3. Historical literature 4. Underground press publications—United States—History—20th century 5. Underground press publications—United States—History—20th century—Pictorial works 6. Youth—Books and reading—United States—History—20th century

ISBN 0226424359 (hardcover : alkaline paper); 9780226424354 (hardcover : alkaline paper)

LC 2012-024547

SUMMARY: This book on graphic design in the 1960s and

1970s "includes essays by Gwen Allen, Bob Ostertag, and Fred Turner . . . all of which comment on the critical impact of the alternative press in the social and popular movements of those turbulent years. 'Power to the People' treats the design practices of that moment as activism in its own right that offers a vehement challenge to the dominance of official media and a critical form of self-representation." (Publisher's note)

REVIEW: *Choice* v51 no5 p798 Ja 2014 R. M. Labuz

REVIEW: *Publ Wkly* v260 no4 p25-9 Ja 28 2013 MICHAEL COFFEY

REVIEW: *TLS* no5756 p32 Jl 26 2013 J. C.

"Two American Scenes," "Power to the People," and "Vagina: A Literary and Cultural History." "'Our Village'. . . is a 're-presentation' of an existing work, 'Our Village' by Sidney Brooks, Ms [Lydia] Davis's great-great-great-uncle, born in Harwich, MA, in 1837. . . . Brooks wrote in prose; Davis has intervened with line breaks. Together with her abridgements and the change of a word here and there, this is all she has done to create a companion to the original. . . . 'Our Village' appears in 'Two American Scenes'. . . . The browser leafing through 'Power to the People' . . . may expect to meet such genial old friends as Love, Peace, and Happiness. . . . But was there really such an eager interest in pubic hair? . . Among the season's most coveted prizes is the Kate Adie Award for the year's most unoriginal book title. . . On the longlist is sure to be 'The Vagina: A Literary and Cultural History' by Emma L. E. Rees."

POWERS, RICHARD. Orfeo; a novel; [by] Richard Powers 393 p. 2014 W.W. Norton & Company

1. Composers—Fiction 2. Fugitives from justice—Fiction 3. Music—Quotations, maxims, etc.—Fiction 4. Musical fiction 5. Time travel—Fiction

ISBN 0393240827; 9780393240825 (hardcover)

LC 2013-031952

SUMMARY: In this novel, author Richard Powers "tells the story of a man journeying into his past as he desperately flees the present. Composer Peter Els opens the door one evening to find the police on his doorstep. His home microbiology lab . . . has aroused the suspicions of Homeland Security. Panicked by the raid, Els turns fugitive. Through . . . help . . . Els hatches a plan to turn this disastrous collision with the security state into a work of art." (Publisher's note)

REVIEW: *Am Book Rev* v35 no4 p9 My/Je 2014 Stephen J. Burn

REVIEW: *Booklist* v110 no4 p16 O 15 2013 Keir Groff

"Orfeo." "[Peter] Els' leap from music to genetics seems forced at first, but [Richard] Powers . . . plays the long game, sure-handedly building a rich metaphor in which composition is an analog for other kinds of human invention, with all the beauty and terror that implies. Like his protagonist, he makes art that challenges rather than reassures his audience. Powers has a way of rendering the world that makes it seem familiar and alien, friendly and frightening. He is sometimes criticized as too cerebral, but when the story's strands knit fully together in the final act, the effect is heartbreaking and beautiful."

REVIEW: *Kirkus Rev* v81 no20 p120 O 15 2013

REVIEW: *Libr J* v138 no13 p56 Ag 1 2013 Barbara Hoffert

REVIEW: *Libr J* v139 no12 p44 Jl 1 2014 Claire Abraham

REVIEW: *Nation* v298 no14 p37 Ap 7 2014

"The Circle" and "Orfeo." "Very good, except that a shark . . . retrieved from the deep ocean will die of decompression sickness . . . before it can ever function as a metaphor. Eggers ignores this complication, a lapse that seems emblematic of 'The Circle''s basic problem, which is that its images, characters and long, didactic passages are illustrations of political and philosophical convictions rather than credible elements of a fictional world. . . . The issue of privacy, or rather its erosion, is also at the heart of 'Orfeo' . . . , by Richard Powers. . . . 'Orfeo' is wide and deep, concerned ultimately not with privacy or bioterrorism or unlawful detention but rather with the bigger thing, the real thing—the soul, or even The Soul."

PRAHIN, ANDREW. Brimsby's hats; [by] Andrew Prahin 40 p. 2013 Simon & Schuster Books for Young Readers

1. Children's stories 2. Creative ability—Fiction 3. Friendship—Fiction 4. Hats—Fiction 5. Loneliness—Fiction

ISBN 1442481471; 9781442481473 (hardcover : alk. paper); 9781442481480 (ebook : alk. paper)

LC 2012-024049

SUMMARY: In this picture book by Andrew Prahin, "a lonely hat maker uses quirky creativity to make friends. Brimsby is a happy hat maker--until his best friend goes off to find adventure at sea. Now Brimsby is a lonely hat maker, unsure of what to do. But since making hats is what he does best, perhaps his talents can help him find some friends." (Publisher's note)

REVIEW: *Booklist* v110 no8 p41 D 15 2013 Carolyn Phelan

REVIEW: *Bull Cent Child Books* v67 no5 p279 Ja 2014 J. H.

"Brimsby's Hats." "Handling the loss of a friend who moves away is a common theme in picture books, but this is a fresh and offbeat take that helpfully highlights kindness and proactive problem-solving. Subdued, slightly retro shades of blue, gray, green, and brown are highlighted with pops of brighter pink and scarlet, and the smooth color application and crisp edges of the digital illustrations give a clean, ordered feel to the cozy milieu. The small print and trim size may make this a challenge for group sharing, but it would be perfect for an armchair or bedtime reading session."

REVIEW: *Kirkus Rev* v81 no23 p168 D 1 2013

REVIEW: *Publ Wkly* v260 no48 p56 N 25 2013

PRAHIN, ANDREW.il. Brimsby's hats. See Prahin, A.

PRATCHETT, TERRY, 1948-. Raising Steam; a Discworld novel; [by] Terry Pratchett 384 p. 2014 Doubleday

1. Discworld (Imaginary place)—Fiction 2. Dwarves (Fictitious characters) 3. Fantasy fiction 4. Railroad stories 5. Steam engines 6. Terrorism—Fiction

ISBN 038553826X; 9780385538268 (hardback)

LC 2014-000869

SUMMARY: In this book, part of Terry Pratchett's Discworld series, "when intrepid inventor Dick Simnel comes to Ankh-Morpork looking for a backer for his revolutionary steam engine, the Iron Girder . . . Lord Vetinari . . . immediately puts master facilitator . . . Moist von Lipwig in charge of the Discworld's first railway. But while the would-be railway tycoons are busy cutting deals . . . a group of radically conservative dwarf extremists are determined to stop the railroad." (Publishers Weekly)

REVIEW: *Booklist* v110 no13 p26-7 Mr 1 2014 Carl Hays

"Raising Steam." "Here the invention of a steam-powered locomotive by an ingenious young artificer named Dick Simnel creates a stir among the citizens of Discworld's prominent metropolis, Ankh-Morpork, as well as disrupting the affairs of assorted dwarfs, trolls, and goblins in the surrounding countryside. To keep Simnel's invention properly reigned in Lord Vetinari dispatches Moist von Lipwig, his trusted minister of almost everything, including the Royal Bank, to fund and supervise the construction of a railway. Leavened with Pratchett's usual puns, philosophical quips, and Discworld in-jokes, the story offers an amusing allegory of Earthly technology's many seductions and give series fans at least one more visit with their favorite characters."

REVIEW: *Kirkus Rev* v82 no5 p226 Mr 1 2014

REVIEW: *Libr J* v139 no9 p39 My 15 2014 Tristan M. Boyd

REVIEW: *Libr J* v139 no5 p98 Mr 15 2014 Megan M. McArdle

PRATCHETT, TERRY, 1948-. Turtle Recall; the Discworld Companion. So Far; [by] Terry Pratchett 464 p. 2014 William Morrow

1. Discworld (Imaginary place)—Handbooks, manuals, etc 2. Fan mail 3. Fantasy fiction, English—History and criticism—Handbooks, manuals, etc 4. Handbooks, vade-mecums, etc. 5. Translating & interpreting
ISBN 9780062292551 (hardback); 9780062292568 (trade paperback)
LC 2014-002828

SUMMARY: This book by Terry Pratchett "references all the Discworld's 40 books and includes interviews with Pratchett, an essay on how he deals with readers and fan mail, [and] a section on the often mind-boggling difficulties of translating Discworld books . . . into other languages. . . . But the main event is, of course, the A-Z of places, people and things large and small that have at one time or another graced the pages of a Discworld yarn." (Kirkus Reviews)

REVIEW: *Kirkus Rev* v82 no3 p244 F 1 2014

"Turtle Recall: The Discworld Companion . . . So Far". "The fourth incarnation of the Discworld Companion, which is essentially an encyclopedia of a fictional world—perhaps the most popular and deservedly acclaimed fantasy creation of them all. . . . One thing leads to another, and the shorter entries lead naturally to extended meditations on such important characters as Lord Vetinari, the Machiavellian ruler of Ankh-Morpork, Commander Sam Vimes of the City Watch, the meddlesome witches Nanny Ogg and Granny Weatherwax, skeletal Death, and, yes, the Death of Rats (he also does gerbils, mice and hamsters). Won't do you much good if you haven't read any of the Discworld books. But then, if you haven't—why haven't you?"

REVIEW: *Libr J* v139 no5 p98 Mr 15 2014 Megan M. McArdle

PRATT, SARAH RODRIGUEZ. Choose Your Weapon; [by] Sarah Rodriguez Pratt 306 p. 2013 Quail School Press

1. Dragons—Fiction 2. Fantasy fiction 3. Friendship—Fiction 4. High schools—Juvenile fiction 5. School stories
ISBN 0988707500; 9780988707504

SUMMARY: In this book, part of the Helen Hollingsworth Trilogy, "when Helen suddenly receives a second chance to become a Dragonfighter, nothing can ruin her happiness—until she has to train with two arrogant jocks and a bitter 'weirdo' from her school. The teens struggle to find common ground in the grassy Erwingdonian hills . . . and pretend not to know each other in the gossipy school hallways. And when catastrophe strikes, Helen must discover who her true friends are." (Publishers Note)

REVIEW: *Kirkus Rev* p49 D 15 2013 supplemet best books 2013

"Choose Your Weapon". "The primary strength of the book . . . lies in the intersections between Erwingdon and Helen's 'real world' home of Hollingsworth, Texas. . . . Like Helen, several of her schoolmates also have parallel lives in Erwingdon, a plot device that initially seems like an eye-rolling coincidence. This conceit, however, allows the author to examine the teens' more familiar concerns—navigating the social atmosphere of high school, grappling with authority, dealing with parental expectations, worrying about the future—through the lens of life, death and saving the world. . . . A well-written, intelligent, exciting choice for readers looking to get hooked on a new fantasy series."

PRENDERGAST, GABRIELLE. Audacious; [by] Gabrielle Prendergast 336 p. 2013 Orca Book Publishers

1. Families—Fiction 2. Identity (Psychology)—Fiction 3. Moving, Household 4. Muslims—United States 5. Young adult fiction
ISBN 1459805305; 9781459802643 (pbk.); 9781459802650 (electronic edition; 9781459802667 (electronic edition; 9781459805309 (hardcover)
LC 2013-936062

SUMMARY: In this book, just "before Ella's junior year, her family moves to escape their problems--her mother's grief over the death of her baby, younger sister Kayli's learning difficulties, Ella's victimization by school bullies, and her father's unwillingness to face any of it--only to continue to wrestle with the same things. Ella falls for a Palestinian classmate, Samir, bringing up questions of identity and faith for both." (Publishers Weekly)

REVIEW: *Booklist* v110 no5 p63-4 N 1 2013 Gail Bush

"Audacious." "In [Gabrielle] Prendergast's affecting novel in verse, school life doesn't change, just the names of the bullies do, and family life doesn't change, it just unhinges at another address. . . . In deft, layered verse, Prendergast chronicles her heroine's desperate search for a positive identity. Young love, religion, politics, prejudice, and the meaning of art in society all factor into Raphaelle's acceptance of herself and her family in all its complexities. Many readers will recognize both her tendencies toward self-sabotage and her growing belief in herself, and they will likely want to continue this journey in the planned sequel."

REVIEW: *Kirkus Rev* v81 no18 p183 S 15 2013

REVIEW: *Publ Wkly* v260 no37 p56-7 S 16 2013

REVIEW: *Quill Quire* v79 no8 p34 O 2013 Grace O'Connell

REVIEW: *SLJ* v60 no2 p111 F 2014 Lindsay Cesari

REVIEW: *Voice of Youth Advocates* v36 no5 p64 D 2013 Morgan Brickey

PRESS, DAVID P. Abraham Lincoln; the great emancipator; [by] David P. Press 64 p. 2013 Crabtree Publishing Company

1. Abolitionists—United States—Biography—Juvenile literature 2. Antislavery movements—United States—History—19th century—Juvenile literature 3. Historical literature 4. Presidents— United States—Biography—Juvenile literature 5. Slaves—Emancipation—United States—Juvenile literature

ISBN 9780778710615 (reinforced library binding); 9780778710646 (pbk.)

LC 2013-007629

SUMMARY: This book, by David P. Press, is part of the "Voices for Freedom: Abolitionist Heroes" series. It "offers a . . . background on slavery in the U.S. and how it grew to divide the country. The book also looks at [Abraham] Lincoln's changing views on the end of slavery (which may surprise some readers) and his fight, once he decided that a gradual end to slavery would not work, to draft the Emancipation Proclamation and lobby for the Thirteenth Amendment." (Booklist)

REVIEW: *Booklist* v110 no1 p101-2 S 1 2013 Angela Leeper

"Abraham Lincoln: The Great Emancipator" and "Theodore Weld: Architect of Abolitionism." "Covering both well- and lesser-known abolitionists, these entries in the Voices for Freedom: Abolitionist Heroes series provide an extensive view of the nation's anti-slavery movement. While the books touch upon the subjects' childhood, education, and career successes and failures, they differ from traditional biographies as they focus on each individual's role as an abolitionist. . . . Each title concludes with the subject's legacy on race relations. Archival photos, reproductions, maps, and copious back matter add to the richness of this valuable series."

PRESSLY, PAUL M. On the rim of the Caribbean; colonial Georgia and the British Atlantic world; [by] Paul M. Pressly xii, 354 p. 2013 University of Georgia Press

1. Historical literature 2. Plantations—Georgia—History—18th century

ISBN 0820335673 (hardcover : alk. paper); 0820345032 (pbk. : alk. paper); 9780820335674 (hardcover : alk. paper); 9780820345031 (pbk. : alk. paper)

LC 2012-033964

SUMMARY: In this book, "Paul M. Pressly interprets Georgia's place in the Atlantic world in light of recent work in transnational and economic history." He "examines the ways in which Georgia came to share many of the characteristics of the sugar islands, how Savannah developed as a 'Caribbean' town, the dynamics of an emerging slave market, and the role of merchant-planters as leaders in forging a highly adaptive economic culture open to innovation." (Publisher's note)

REVIEW: *Choice* v51 no1 p149 S 2013 J. J. Rogers

"On the Rim of the Caribbean: Colonial Georgia and the British Atlantic World." "This richly documented, analytically complex, and well-written book is a major contribution to the study of Colonial Georgia and the 18th-century Atlantic world. Long viewed as tangential . . . the history of Colonial Georgia has been consistently underappreciated by historians. [Author Paul M.] Pressly corrects this oversight with a thorough examination of how the relatively new, economically stagnant colony struggled at first under the shadow of South Carolina, its wealthier neighbor, but was transformed through the lifting of the ban on slavery in 1750 and the interlinking of the young colony's economy with that of the larger Atlantic system and, in particular, the Caribbean."

PRESSMAN, STEVEN. 50 Children; One Ordinary American Couple's Extraordinary Rescue Mission into the Heart of Nazi Germany; [by] Steven Pressman 320 p. 2014 HarperCollins

1. Historical literature 2. Jews—United States—History 3. Kraus, Eleanor 4. Kraus, Gilbert 5. World War, 1939-1945—Austria 6. World War, 1939-1945—Jews—Rescue

ISBN 0062237470; 9780062237477

SUMMARY: This book by Steven Pressman describes how "in early 1939, America's rigid immigration laws made it virtually impossible for European Jews to seek safe haven in the United States. . . . Yet one brave Jewish couple from Philadelphia refused to silently stand by. Risking their own safety, Gilbert Kraus, a successful lawyer, and his stylish wife, Eleanor, traveled to Nazi-controlled Vienna and Berlin to save fifty Jewish children." (Publisher's note)

REVIEW: *Booklist* v110 no18 p10 My 15 2014 Gilbert Taylor

REVIEW: *Kirkus Rev* v82 no5 p87 Mr 1 2014

"50 Children: One Ordinary American Couple's Extraordinary Rescue Mission Into the Heart of Nazi Germany". "The astonishing story of a Philadelphia couple's resolve to help bring Jewish children out of Nazi-occupied Austria. . . . The details around selection of the children, leave-taking of their parents and the tearful travels are heart-rending, but eventually, they were safely shepherded to a summer camp in Collegeville, Pa. With a careful eye to detail and dialogue, [Steven] Pressman vividly re-creates this epic rescue."

REVIEW: *Publ Wkly* v261 no5 p44 F 3 2014

PRESTON-GANNON, FRANN. How to Lose a Lemur; [by] Frann Preston-Gannon 32 p. 2014 Sterling Pub Co Inc

1. Children's stories 2. Friendship—Juvenile fiction 3. Human-animal relationships—Fiction 4. Lemurs 5. Voyages & travels—Juvenile literature

ISBN 145491131X; 9781454911319

SUMMARY: In this book, by Frann Preston-Gannon, "some lemurs take a shine to a slightly wary boy. The boy is holding an ice cream cone, and the lemur clutches a red flower. Their eyes lock; the lemur's smile says it all: '[O]nce a lemur takes a liking to you, there is not much that can be done about it.' The boy tries to slip away, even climbing up a tree, but he can't shake the lemur, who manages to attract a few more." (Kirkus Reviews)

REVIEW: *Booklist* v110 no15 p93 Ap 1 2014 Sarah Hunter

REVIEW: *Kirkus Rev* v82 no5 p123 Mr 1 2014

"How to Lose a Lemur". "Wild adventure follows when some lemurs take a shine to a slightly wary boy. The boy is holding an ice cream cone, and the lemur clutches a red flower. Their eyes lock; the lemur's smile says it all: '[O]nce a lemur takes a liking to you, there is not much that can be done about it.' The boy tries to slip away, even climbing up a tree, but he can't shake the lemur, who manages to attract a few more. . . . [Frann] Preston-Gannon's lemurs are quite adorable. Each two-page spread is beautifully evocative, with basic shapes and shrewd use of white space. Simple but silly and satisfying."

REVIEW: *N Y Times Book Rev* p24 Ap 6 2014 SARAH HARRISON SMITH

REVIEW: *SLJ* v60 no3 p122 Mr 2014 Heather Webb

PRESTON, DONALD. The Thinking Odyssey; [by] Donald Preston 222 p. 2013 CreateSpace Independent Publishing Platform

1. Death of God theology 2. Intelligent design (Teleology) 3. Nature—Religious aspects 4. Religion & science 5. Religious literature

ISBN 1481254138; 9781481254137

SUMMARY: In this "wide-ranging discussion of the natural world," author Donald Preston "confidently credits a supreme being presiding over the whole shebang. . . . The God described here is omnipresent and omnipotent, but he doesn't intervene or answer prayers: 'God does not tinker with anything on Earth.' This view, the author says, leaves the door wide open for science and theism to happily coexist." (Kirkus Reviews)

REVIEW: *Kirkus Rev* v81 no24 p57 D 15 2013

"The Thinking Odyssey". " A wide-ranging discussion of the natural world from a dedicated but inquisitive theist. . . . Ultimately, however, the lack of a coherent or compelling focus threatens to undermine the earnestness that resides within this constantly leapfrogging treatise. Those operating outside the restrictive lens of religious dogma won't be inspired or especially challenged, but seen through a more accommodating lens, this God-fearing author's exhortations could prove notably provocative and productive. A well-crafted reflection on the place of religion in the physical world."

PREUS, MARGI. West of the moon; [by] Margi Preus 224 p. 2014 Amulet Books

1. Emigration and immigration—Fiction 2. Historical fiction 3. Human trafficking—Fiction 4. Sisters—Fiction

ISBN 1419708961; 9781419708961 (alk. paper)

LC 2013-023250

SUMMARY: Author Margi Preus "weaves original fiction with myth and folktale to tell the story of Astri, a young Norwegian girl desperate to join her father in America. After being separated from her sister and sold to a cruel goat farmer, Astri makes a daring escape. She quickly retrieves her little sister, and, armed with a troll treasure, a book of spells and curses, and a possibly magic hairbrush, they set off for America." (Publisher's note)

REVIEW: *Booklist* v111 no2 p68 S 15 2014 Connie Rockman

REVIEW: *Booklist* v110 no12 p75 F 15 2014 Sarah Hunter

REVIEW: *Bull Cent Child Books* v67 no10 p537 Je 2014 K. Q. G.

"West of the Moon". "Elements of familiar folktales, such 'The Billy Goat's Gruff' and, obviously, 'East of the Sun, West of the Moon,' blend seamlessly with historical fact; an author's note details the family history of immigrant siblings that inspired the story and explains historical and folkloric details. It's Astri's voice, however, that is most appealing. . . . The chapters have an episodic structure that makes this an ideal choice for readaloud or storytelling adaptations, while the mix of folklore, fact, and fantasy will please fans of Edith Patou's 'East'."

REVIEW: *Horn Book Magazine* v90 no3 p95-6 My/Je 2014 JENNIFER M. BRABANDER

REVIEW: *Kirkus Rev* v82 no4 p151 F 15 2014

"West of the Moon". "Folk tales from 'The Twelve Wild Ducks' to 'The Three Billy Goats Gruff' weave through Astri's often dryly humorous, suspenseful first-person account until one feels like the other. . . including her riotous escape from the violent man-troll and the rescue of her beloved little sister. . . . [Margi] Preus, who won a Newbery Honor for 'Heart of a Samurai' (2010), was inspired by her Norwegian great-great-grandmother, who immigrated to America in 1851, as she explains in an author's note, even providing reproductions of some of her great-great-grandmother's papers. Norwegian history, fiction and folklore intertwine seamlessly in this lively, fantastical adventure and moving coming-of-age story."

REVIEW: *SLJ* v60 no9 p64 S 2014 Julie Paladino

REVIEW: *SLJ* v60 no4 p152 Ap 2014 Eva Mitnick

REVIEW: *Voice of Youth Advocates* v37 no1 p73 Ap 2014 Jennifer Rummel

PREWITT, KENNETH. What is your race?; the census and our flawed efforts to classify Americans; [by] Kenneth Prewitt xiii, 271 p. 2013 Princeton University Press

1. Demography—United States 2. Ethnicity—United States—Statistics 3. Social science literature

ISBN 0691157030 (hbk. : alk. paper); 9780691157030 (hbk. : alk. paper)

LC 2012-037528

SUMMARY: In this book, Kenneth Prewitt looks at "the social construction of race and the US Census Bureau's role in that social construction. . . . In particular, he argues that the census categories, as innocuous as they seem, shape not only policy but also the very definitions and understandings of race that people use in everyday life." (Choice: Current Reviews for Academic Libraries)

REVIEW: *Choice* v51 no5 p930-1 Ja 2014 A. J. Hattery

"What is Your Race?: The Census and Our Flawed Efforts to Classify Americans." "In one of the best discussions of the social construction of race and the US Census Bureau's role in that social construction that this reviewer has seen, [Kenneth] Prewitt . . . goes way beyond the typical discussion by demonstrating the policy implications of the social construction and shifting definitions of race. . . . This discussion is especially important today as the census grapples with an ever changing racial demographic in the US . . . and the increase in individuals choosing to identify as multiracial. . . .. This detailed history and policy analysis is an absolute requirement for race scholars and policy analysts alike."

PRICE, ASHER. The great Texas wind rush. See Galbraith, K.

PRICE, F. DOUGLAS.ed. English historical documents. See English historical documents

PRICE, JANE. Underworld; exploring the secret world beneath your feet; 96 p. 2012 WeldonOwen Publishing Kids Can Pr

1. Children's nonfiction 2. Earth (Planet)—Internal structure—Juvenile literature 3. Underground areas—

Juvenile literature 4. Underground construction—Juvenile literature 5. Underground ecology—Juvenile literature
ISBN 1894786890; 9781742522852 (bound); 9781894786898
LC 2013-432120

SUMMARY: This children's book, by Jane Price, "contains topics such as underground animals, tombs, catacombs, caves filled with crystals, subterranean cities, and futuristic underground farms and laboratories. . . . Examples include artwork in the Lascaux caves, animals that live in the dark, tombs of the pharaohs, terra-cotta warriors in China, trench warfare of World War I, Cu Chi Tunnels in Vietnam, and underground Tokyo." (School Library Journal)

REVIEW: *Booklist* v110 no16 p45 Ap 15 2014 Erin Anderson

REVIEW: *Kirkus Rev* v82 no3 p206 F 1 2014

"Underworld: Exploring the Secret World Beneath Your Feet". " A scattershot but revealing dig beneath our planet's surface, illustrated with a mix of photos and schematic cutaways. . . . [Jane] Price adds introductory paragraphs and explanatory captions to each busy spread. The captions are numbered on some spreads, which compensates, at least in part, for the way the photos are often slapped down over or next to the drawings without much regard for visual unity or logical progression. Topical coverage and level of detail are likewise unsystematic. . . . Sheds plenty of light into dark places, but best for flip-through browsing, as the tunneling goes in arbitrary directions."

REVIEW: *Publ Wkly* v261 no5 p55 F 3 2014

REVIEW: *SLJ* v60 no3 p183 Mr 2014 Patricia Ann Owens

PRICE, LISSA. Starters; [by] Lissa Price 336 p. 2012 Delacorte Press
1. Brain-computer interfaces 2. Brothers and sisters—Fiction 3. Older people—Fiction 4. Orphans—Fiction 5. Science fiction 6. Young adult fiction
ISBN 9780385742481 (paperback); 0385742371 (hardcover); 9780307975232 (ebook); 9780375990601 (glb); 9780385742375 (hardcover)
LC 2011-040820

SUMMARY: In this book, "[w]hen a deadly virus wipes out the entire population of the U.S. save the elderly and the young, . . . the result is a dysfunctional society polarized between young 'Starters' and the increasingly long-lived 'Enders.' Children who are unclaimed by surviving relatives are institutionalized, and many—like Callie and her little brother, Tyler—learn to fend for themselves in virtual hiding from the law to escape that fate." (Bulletin of the Center for Children's Books)

REVIEW: *Booklist* v108 no14 p59 Mr 15 2012 Karen Cruze

REVIEW: *Bull Cent Child Books* v65 no8 p418 Ap 2012 C. G.

"Starters." "When a deadly virus wipes out the entire population of the U.S. save the elderly and the young, who were both vaccinated against it, the result is a dysfunctional society polarized between young "Starters" and the increasingly long-lived 'Enders.' . . The world-building is engaging but the character development here is flat, with neither Callie's love interests, nor Helena's friendships, nor Callie's ability to impersonate an Ender at all convincing. Still, the body-swap premise allows for plenty of twists to spice up the plot, and this latest take on dystopian resistance offers enough new ideas to the mix to make it worth a read for genre devotees."

REVIEW: *Kirkus Rev* v80 no4 p418 F 15 2012

"Starters." "In a future in which the elderly hold all of the power, the only things left for them to take are the bodies of the young. After a germ-warfare attack, America was only able to vaccinate high-risk groups--medically vulnerable children and senior citizens--in time, creating an age gulf and an orphaned generation. . . . In between living the high life as a socialite grandniece and ward of her wealthy renter, Callie learns of plots more dangerous than the renter's and that only she can stop them. Some exposition is clumsily dropped in through dialogue, and some plot aspects don't hold up to scrutiny, but the twists and turns come so fast that readers will stay hooked. Constantly rising stakes keep this debut intense."

REVIEW: *Publ Wkly* p91-2 My 28 2012

REVIEW: *SLJ* v58 no8 p58 Ag 2012 Rebecca James

REVIEW: *SLJ* p87 Jl 2012 Amy S. Pattee

REVIEW: *Voice of Youth Advocates* v35 no5 p492 D 2012 Amy Sisson

PRICE, SARA.ed. The Sage Handbook of Digital Technology Research. See The Sage Handbook of Digital Technology Research

PRIEST, CHRISTOPHER. The Adjacent; [by] Christopher Priest 384 p. 2014 Random House Inc
1. English fiction 2. Historical fiction 3. Science fiction 4. Space & time—Fiction 5. Terrorism—Fiction
ISBN 1781169438; 9781781169438

SUMMARY: This novel, by Christopher Priest, describes how "a theoretical physicist develops a new method of diverting matter, a discovery with devastating consequences that will resonate through time." It features several eras of British history, from World War I to the future, delving into implications of a dangerous scientific discovery. (Publisher's note)

REVIEW: *Booklist* v110 no13 p28 Mr 1 2014 David Pitt

REVIEW: *Libr J* v139 no3 p77 F 15 2014 Megan M. McArdle

REVIEW: *London Rev Books* v35 no19 p33-4 O 10 2013 Ned Beauman

"The Adjacent." "In general [author Christopher] Priest's prose is just dull, but sometimes it reaches new frontiers of dull. Most of his new book, 'The Adjacent,' is set during wartime, so his characters get a lot of bad news. . . . 'The Adjacent' revisits themes, characters and settings from many of his previous books. . . . 'The Adjacent's' jagged edges don't work to complicate the scientific explanation but rather seem entirely irrelevant to it. . . . Everything really good in his books comes from the sound of Priest banging on the walls of his genre."

REVIEW: *Publ Wkly* v261 no2 p54 Ja 13 2014

PRIMACK, RICHARD B. Walden warming; climate change comes to Thoreau's woods; [by] Richard B. Primack 264 p. 2014 University of Chicago Press
1. Animals—Effect of global warming on—Massachu-

setts—Concord 2. Animals—Effect of global warming on—Massachusetts—Walden Pond State Reservation 3. Climatic changes—Massachusetts—Concord 4. Climatic changes—Massachusetts—Walden Pond State Reservation 5. Plants—Effect of global warming on—Massachusetts—Concord 6. Plants—Effect of global warming on—Massachusetts—Walden Pond State Reservation 7. Science—Popular works

ISBN 0226682684; 9780226682686 (cloth: alk. paper)

LC 2013-038942

SUMMARY: "In 'Walden Warming,' Richard B. Primack uses Thoreau and Walden, icons of the conservation movement, to track the effects of a warming climate on Concord's plants and animals. Under the attentive eyes of Primack, the notes that Thoreau made years ago are transformed from charming observations into scientific data sets." (Publisher's note)

REVIEW: *Booklist* v110 no12 p22 F 15 2014 Donna Seaman

REVIEW: *Libr J* v139 no5 p136 Mr 15 2014 Susan E. Brazer

REVIEW: *N Y Rev Books* v61 no11 p50-2 Je 19 2014 Bill McKibben

"Walden Warming: Climate Change Comes to Thoreau's Woods." "Richard Primack, in 'Walden Warming,' adds to Thoreau's legacy by highlighting the increasing value of another aspect of his life, one well known to scholars but not so much to casual readers: Thoreau was a remarkable and systematic naturalist. . . . Thoreau, in Primack's words, has provided us with a valuable 'biological yardstick' against which to measure a changing climate. . . . Thanks to Primack scientists are now giving Thoreau's remarkable journals their due."

REVIEW: *New Sci* v222 no2964 p49 Ap 12 2014 Alun Anderson

"Walden Warming: Climate Change Comes to Thoreau's Woods." "[Author Richard] Primack was astonished to find that Thoreau also kept a detailed record of the flowering times of more than 300 plants around Walden, gathered over many years of walking for 4 hours a day. . . . The book tells the story of Primack's struggle to replicate Thoreau and find changes in flowering times, but soon broadens into a hymn to citizen science. . . . It is . . . extraordinary people who make the book a rich, rewarding read. And there is also the inspiring message that anyone with a keen eye for nature can make a difference, with an afterword on how to become a citizen scientist."

REVIEW: *Science* v345 no6198 p737-8 Ag 15 2014 Adam C. Schneider

PRIMATES OF THE WORLD; an illustrated guide; 192 p. 2013 Princeton University Press

1. Primate behavior 2. Primate evolution 3. Primates 4. Primates—Physiology 5. Scientific literature

ISBN 9780691156958

LC 2013-930446

SUMMARY: "This . . . illustrated guide to the world's primates covers nearly 300 species, from the feather-light and solitary pygmy mouse lemurs of Madagascar--among the smallest primates known to exist--to the regal mountain gorillas of Africa. Organized by region and spanning every family of primates on Earth, the book features 72 . . . color plates, facing-page descriptions of key features of each family, and 86 color distribution maps." (Publisher's note)

REVIEW: *Booklist* v110 no4 p35 O 15 2013 Blaire Ranucci

REVIEW: *Choice* v51 no6 p1036-7 F 2014 E. Delson

"Primates of the World: An Illustrated Guide." "This survey of living primates for a general audience combines weak text with an extensive array of beautiful artwork. . . . The French edition was published in 2010, but it is not clear if [Robert] Martin . . . has updated it in addition to providing an excellent translation. The first part of the book is a rambling review of primate adaptation, distribution, social behavior, ecology, and some morphology and paleontology, interspersed with small sketches of primates and their environments. . . . The meat of the book is a survey of most living species by region and zoological grouping. . . . The book is valuable for its illustrations, but most readers can skip the jumpy first 35 pages."

REVIEW: *Sci Am* v309 no4 p94 O 2013 Arielle Duhmime-Ross

"Primates of the World." "Woolly monkeys . . . look plump because of their thick fur, which is the densest possessed by any primate. Muriqui spider monkeys are also known as hippie monkeys for their tendency to hug one another in times of stress. In infancy, bearded saki monkeys use their prehensile tails as a 'fifth hand' but lose that grasping ability as they mature. These are but a few of the delightfully surprising facts peppered through this beautifully illustrated tour of the lives and behaviors of our closest living relatives in the animal kingdom."

PRIMIANO, JAY. Swim that rock. See Swim that rock

THE PRINCETON ENCYCLOPEDIA OF POETRY AND POETICS; xxxvi, 1639 p. 2012 Princeton University Press

1. Encyclopedias & dictionaries 2. Literary movements 3. Poetics—Dictionaries 4. Poetry—Dictionaries 5. Poetry—History and criticism

ISBN 0691133344; 0691154910; 9780691133348 (cloth : alk. paper); 9780691154916 (pbk. : alk. paper)

LC 2012-005602

SUMMARY: This is a reference book about poetry technique and terminology. This updated fourth edition "includes 250 new entries on topics such as 'Cognitive poetics,' 'Fireside poets,' 'Fractal verse,' 'Gay poetry,' 'Poetry of the indigenous Americas,' and 'Poetry slam.' . . . The work contains more than 1,100 entries, and those on major subjects, such as classical poetics, dramatic poetry, and rhetoric, among others, have all been rewritten to reflect updated scholarship." (Booklist)

REVIEW: *TLS* no5759 p25 Ag 16 2013 ROSS WILSON

"The Princeton Encyclopedia of Poetry and Poetics." "Since its first appearance in 1965, 'The Princeton Encyclopedia of Poetry and Poetics' has steadily gained admirers among poets, scholars and those semi-mythical beasts, general readers, around the world. . . . The requirement to take seriously poetries other than those emanating from Britain and the United States is still more central to the latest edition of the Encyclopedia, and its coverage of an impressive range of poetic traditions hitherto relatively unheralded in mainstream Western criticism is one of its most prominent achievements. The carefully considered but flexible principles that inform that coverage are set out in the lucid and suggestive preface."

PRINGLE, LAURENCE. Scorpions!; strange and wonderful; 32 p. 2013 Boyds Mills Press

1. Children's nonfiction 2. Human animal relationships 3. Scorpions 4. Scorpions—Behavior 5. Scorpions—Physiology

ISBN 1590784731; 9781590784730

LC 2013-931088

SUMMARY: This book, by Laurence Pringle and illustrated by Meryl Henderson, describes scorpions' "life cycle, body structure, habits, and habitat [through] realistic illustrations." (Publisher's note) "Besides briefly discussing the fossil evidence of early scorpions and the place of scorpions in ancient Greek, Mayan, and Egyptian cultures, Pringle introduces a wide variety of scorpions living around the world today." (Booklist)

REVIEW: *Booklist* v110 no4 p42 O 15 2013 Carolyn Phelan

REVIEW: *Horn Book Magazine* v90 no1 p116 Ja/F 2014 DANIELLE J. FORD

"Scorpions! Strange and Wonderful." "[Laurence] Pringle cuts through misconceptions about scorpions with no-nonsense factual information about this arachnid order. . . . Scorpion range and habitats, hunting and feeding behaviors, and reproduction are explored, often through comparisons across scorpion species to show both variations and commonalities that define the order. . . . Numerous delicate, detailed paintings of scorpions include field guide–like illustrations, often to scale, of single specimens, as well as portrayals of the scorpions in prey-or-be-preyed-upon interactions with other animals. Back matter includes a brief bibliography, websites, sources, and a pronunciation guide."

REVIEW: *Kirkus Rev* v81 no18 p59 S 15 2013

REVIEW: *SLJ* v59 no9 p190 S 2013 Patricia Manning

PRIOR, CHARLES W. A. A confusion of tongues; Britain's wars of reformation, 1625-1642; [by] Charles W. A. Prior 257 p. 2012 Oxford University Press

1. Church & state—Great Britain—History—17th century 2. Counter-Reformation 3. Historical literature 4. Pamphlets—History—17th century 5. Reformation—England

ISBN 9780199698257 (hbk. : alk. paper)

LC 2011-942658

SUMMARY: In this book, Charles W. A. Prior "presents a view of the upheavals in mid-17th-century England and Scotland that focuses on ecclesiology. . . . Prior concentrates attention on differing conceptions of the relationship between church, state, and people. The author's main source is the exhaustive polemic pamphlet literature produced in the disputes surrounding the revolt against Charles I." (Choice: Current Reviews for Academic Libraries)

REVIEW: *Am Hist Rev* v118 no4 p1244-5 O 2013 Keith M. Brown

"A Confusion of Tongues: Britain's Wars of Reformation, 1625-1642." "The focus of this thoroughly researched, clearly written, and closely argued discussion is . . . relatively narrow. . . . The wars under consideration, therefore, were not the battles of the 1640s but rather the conflicts waged on paper between writers divided over the direction of the Church of England. . . . The central argument is the connectivity among religion, law, and history in political ideas, particularly in relation to those unresolved constitutional matters inherent in Henry VIII's legacy. . . . One problem with Prior's approach is that his discussion of texts can be a little divorced from the world in which they were written, the audience to which they were directed, or even the men who wrote them."

REVIEW: *Choice* v50 no2 p352-3 O 2012 J. Berlatsky

"A Confusion of Tongues: Britain's Wars of Reformation, 1625-1642." "[Charles W. A.] Prior . . . presents a view of the upheavals in mid-17th-century England and Scotland that focuses on ecclesiology. This approach to the 'wars of Reformation' has little to do with military matters. Instead, Prior concentrates attention on differing conceptions of the relationship between church, state, and people. The author's main source is the exhaustive polemic pamphlet literature produced in the disputes surrounding the revolt against Charles I. . . . Readers will find special value in the introductory historiographical discussion and the extensive bibliography of Prior's work. Summing Up: Highly recommended."

REVIEW: *Engl Hist Rev* v128 no535 p1572-4 D 2013 Clive Holmes

PRITCHARD, SARA B.ed. New natures. See New natures

PRO MARCO CAELIO; xv, 206 p. 2013 Cambridge University Press

1. Political oratory 2. Speeches, addresses, etc., Latin

ISBN 1107014425 (hardback); 1107643481 (paperback); 9781107014428 (hardback); 9781107643482 (paperback)

LC 2012-277610

SUMMARY: This book presents a speech by Marcus Tullius Cicero, edited by Andrew R. Dyck. "Speaking in defence of the young aristocrat Marcus Caelius Rufus on charges of political violence, Cicero scores his points with wit but also with searing invective directed at a supporter of the prosecution, Clodia Metelli, whom he represents as seeking vengeance as a lover spurned by his client." (Publisher's note)

REVIEW: *TLS* no5762 p8-9 S 6 2013 MARY BEARD

"Community and Communication: Oratory and Politics in Republican Rome," "The Cambridge Companion to Cicero," and "Pro Marco Caelio." "All the main players . . . have contributed essays discussing contiones to 'Community and Communication,' and, despite the wealth of expertise on show, it is hard to resist the conclusion that the law of diminishing returns is beginning to apply. Taken together, these essays show all the signs of a debate whose groundbreaking phase is over. . . . For those starting out to explore Cicero, 'The Cambridge Companion' is a brisk and business-like guide; though I was disappointed that the final chapter is a rather plodding piece on Cicero's role in modern film, fiction and popular history. . . . I suspect that [Robert Symes] might have admired the austerity of [Andrew R.] Dyck's Pro Caelio, and its undoubted philological expertise. But as a way to introduce twenty-first-century readers to Cicero's unusually engaging speech? No."

PROCHASKA, FRANK. The memoirs of Walter Bagehot; [by] Frank Prochaska 224 p. 2013 Yale University Press

1. Biography (Literary form) 2. Economists—Great

Britain—Biography 3. Intellectuals—Great Britain—Biography 4. Journalists—Great Britain—Biography
ISBN 0300195540; 9780300195545 (cl: alk. paper)
LC 2013-010902

SUMMARY: This book, written in the first person, presents what [author Frank] Prochaska imagines [Walter] Bagehot, once dubbed 'the greatest Victorian,' might have produced. It provides a . . . glimpse of British intellectual and practical life in the mid-nineteenth century, drawing extensively on Bagehot's writings (in which he often mused on an enormous range of subjects), his letters, and the diaries of his wife." (Foreign Affairs)

REVIEW: *Hist Today* v64 no1 p64-5 Ja 2014 Ruth Dudley Edwards

REVIEW: *London Rev Books* v36 no3 p9-11 F 6 2014 Ferdinand Mount

"The Memoirs of Walter Bagehot". "'The Memoirs of Walter Bagehot' is an oddity, for Bagehot left behind no memoir when his chronically weak chest finally undid him at the age of 51. Instead, Frank Prochaska has stitched together this self-portrait out of the boxfuls of essays, letters and articles he did leave. . . . As far as I can check, pretty much everything in this little book is direct quotation, with only minimal editorial linking. So you will probably get as good a picture of what Bagehot was like and what he thought from Prochaska's two hundred pages as from St John Stevas's 15 volumes. Prochaska picks out the plums nicely, and the ripest and juiciest are usually Bagehot's remarks on the world he really knew from the inside, the world of money."

PROCHNIK, GEORGE. The Impossible Exile; Stefan Zweig at the end of the world; [by] George Prochnik 408 p. 2014 Other Press

1. Authors, Austrian—20th century—Biography 2. Biography (Literary form) 3. Europe—History—20th century—Biography 4. Jewish authors—20th century—Biography
ISBN 1590516125; 9781590516126 (hardcover)
LC 2013-025383

SUMMARY: In this book, George Prochnik "examines the life of exiled Austrian writer Stefan Zweig (1881–1942) to shed light on the affliction of exile that redefined the lives and works of many intellectuals during WWII. Perhaps best known for his novellas, Zweig, who was Jewish, fled from his native Vienna and spent time abroad (New York, Rio de Janeiro), but was never able to adjust." (Publishers Weekly)

REVIEW: *Bookforum* v21 no1 p18-20 Ap/My 2014 BENJAMIN MOSER

REVIEW: *Booklist* v110 no17 p73 My 1 2014 Donna Seaman

REVIEW: *Choice* v52 no1 p78 St 2014 C. L. Dolmetsch

REVIEW: *Kirkus Rev* v82 no5 p13 Mr 1 2014

"The Impossible Exile". "stefan Zweig (1881-1942) stands in for Europe's uprooted intellectuals in this elegiac portrait by [George] Prochnik. . . . Prochnik sensitively considers his final books—the poignant memoir 'The World of Yesterday' (1942) and 'Brazil: Land of the Future' (1941), which determinedly celebrated his adopted country's embrace of 'the humanist values his native Europe had so wretchedly betrayed.' In the end, accumulating losses and dwindling hopes of a better tomorrow drove Zweig to commit suicide not long after his 60th birthday. Intelligent, reflective and deeply sad portrait of a man tragically cut adrift by history."

REVIEW: *Libr J* v139 no2 p75 F 1 2014 Patrick A. Smith

REVIEW: *N Y Times Book Rev* p26 Je 22 2014

REVIEW: *N Y Times Book Rev* p12-3 Je 15 2014 A. O. SCOTT

REVIEW: *New Repub* v245 no14 p40-5 Ag 25 2014 Adam Kirsch

REVIEW: *New Statesman* v143 no5218 p42-4 Jl 11 2014 John Gray

REVIEW: *New Yorker* v90 no16 p107-1 Je 9 2014

REVIEW: *Publ Wkly* v261 no8 p169 F 24 2014

PROFILES OF CALIFORNIA, 2013; 500 p. 2013 Grey House Pub

1. California—Economic conditions 2. Cities & towns—California 3. Counties—California 4. Public schools—California 5. Reference books
ISBN 161925140X (pbk.); 9781619251403 (pbk.)

SUMMARY: This reference book "provides detailed demographic and statistical data on the 58 counties and 1,369 places in the state of California, including "demographics on each county & individual city or town, detailed data on school districts, hispanic & asian population statistics, informative statistics & rankings on ancestry groups, weather statistics, [and] comparative ranking charts." (Publisher's note)

REVIEW: *Choice* v51 no7 p1193-4 Mr 2014 B. D. Singleton

"Profiles of California." "Make no mistake: these are brief profiles, averaging three to four places per double-column page. One of the volume's more interesting features is the 'Ancestry and Ethnicity' section, which presents country-of-origin statistics at the state, county, and city levels as well as top ten city rankings by total number and highest percentage for each national group. Another helpful section features color photos, maps, and charts, detailing demographics and natural resources. One perplexing feature of the book is missing data. . . . All in all, though, this is a great statistical resource for California localities."

PROIMOS, JAMES.il. Year of the jungle. See Collins, S.

PROKHOROVA, IRINA.ed. 1990. See 1990

PRONZINI, BILL. The Spook Lights Affair. See Muller, M.

PROPHETIC IDENTITIES; indigenous missionaries on British colonial frontiers, 1850-75; xvi, 217 p. 2012 UBC Press

1. Christianity and culture—Colonies—Great Britain—Africa—History—19th century 2. Christianity and culture—Colonies—Great Britain—America—History—19th century 3. Cree Indians—Colonies—Great Britain—Ethnic identity—History—19th century 4. Historical literature 5. Missionaries—Colonies—Great Britain—Africa—History—19th century 6. Xhosa (African people)—Colonies—Great Britain—Ethnic identity—History—19th century
ISBN 0774822791; 9780774822794 (hbk.)
LC 2012-450203

SUMMARY: "This book is an analysis of the impacts of the conversion and commitment to Christianity by two nineteenth-century Indigenous men, Henry Budd (1812–75), a Cree in Western British North America, and Tiyo Soga (1829–71), a Xhosa man from southern Africa. . . . [Tolly] Bradford argues that these two, admittedly exceptional Indigenous missionaries created for themselves 'new' Indigenous identities." (Canadian Historical Review)

REVIEW: *Can Hist Rev* v95 no1 p101-42 Mr 2014

"Settling and Unsettling Memories: Essays in Canadian Public History," "Prophetic Identities: Indigenous Missionaries on British Colonial Frontiers," and "Aboriginal Peoples and Sport in Canada: Historical Foundations and Contemporary Issues". "This important collection maps the rapidly expanding field of collective memory in Canada, presenting a sampling of articles that usefully balances older pioneering studies by established practitioners with more recent work by emerging scholars. . . . In comparative work at its best, [Tolly] Bradford argues that these two, admittedly exceptional Indigenous missionaries created for themselves "new" Indigenous identities. What makes this study noteworthy is its framing of these men within empire and the processes of modernity. . . . 'Aboriginal Peoples and Sport in Canada' stands as an exceptional collection that demonstrates the ways in which sport studies can make Aboriginal world views accessible to a non-Aboriginal audience."

PROSE, FRANCINE. Lovers at the Chameleon Club; Paris, 1932; [by] Francine Prose 448 p. 2014 HarperCollins

1. Historical fiction 2. Lesbians—Fiction 3. Transvestism 4. World War, 1939-1945—France—Paris—Fiction

ISBN 0061713783; 9780061713781

LC 2013-048443

SUMMARY: This novel by Francine Prose describes how "Paris in the 1920s shimmers with excitement, dissipation, and freedom. It is a place of intoxicating ambition, passion, art, and discontent, where louche jazz venues like the Chameleon Club draw expats, artists, libertines, and parvenus looking to indulge. . . . It is at the Chameleon where the striking Lou Villars, an extraordinary athlete and scandalous cross-dressing lesbian, finds refuge among the club's loyal denizens." (Publisher's note)

REVIEW: *Booklist* v110 no11 p30 F 1 2014 Donna Seaman

"Lovers at the Chameleon Club, Paris 1932." "Artistically and intellectually adventurous, [Francine] Prose presents a house-of-mirrors historical novel built around a famous photograph by Brassai of two women at a table in a Paris nightclub. The one wearing a tuxedo ¡s athlete, race-car driver, and Nazi collaborator Violette Morris. So intriguing and disturbing is her story, Prose considered writing a biography, but instead she forged an electrifying union of fact and fiction. . . . In an intricately patterned, ever-morphing, lavishly well-informed plot . . . Prose intensifies our depth perception of that time of epic aberration and mesmerizing evil as she portrays complex, besieged individuals struggling to become their true selves. A dark and glorious tour de force."

REVIEW: *Booklist* v110 no9/10 p20 Ja 1 2014 Brad Hooper

"All the Light We Cannot See," "And the Dark Sacred Night," and "Lovers at the Chameleon Club, Paris 1932." "[Anthony] Doerr's brilliance as a short story writer was established by the popular 'Shell Collector' (2001), but his work in the novel form has also been exceptional; his latest one, about a young couple in Europe, will attest to that. . . . [Julia] Glass won the National Book Award for 'Three Junes' (2002), and she has been on serious fiction readers' radar ever since; they will not be disappointed in her latest novel, about family secrets. . . . One of the finest current literary-fiction writers, [Francine] Prose presents a novel focused on a Paris jazz club and its fascinating clientele in the 1920s and 1930s."

REVIEW: *Kirkus Rev* v82 no2 p283 Ja 15 2014

REVIEW: *Libr J* v138 no21 p69 D 1 2013 Barbara Hoffert

REVIEW: *Libr J* v139 no4 p85 Mr 1 2014 Barbara Hoffert

REVIEW: *N Y Times Book Rev* p34 My 11 2014 GREGORY COWLES

REVIEW: *N Y Times Book Rev* p1-22 Ap 20 2014 Edmund White

REVIEW: *New York Times* v163 no56468 pC23-31 Ap 11 2014 JANET MASLIN

REVIEW: *New York Times* v163 no56468 pC23-31 Ap 11 2014 JANET MASLIN

REVIEW: *Publ Wkly* v261 no7 p76 F 17 2014

PROST, ANTOINE. René Cassin and human rights. See Winter, J.

PROTHERO, DONALD R., 1954-. Abominable science!; origins of the Yeti, Nessie, and other famous cryptids; [by] Donald R. Prothero 432 p. 2013 Columbia University Press

1. Animals, Mythical 2. Cryptozoology 3. Historical literature 4. Loch Ness monster 5. Pseudoscience

ISBN 0231153201; 9780231153201 (cloth: alk. paper)

LC 2013-008424

SUMMARY: In this book, "after examining the nature of science and pseudoscience and their relation to cryptozoology, [Daniel] Loxton and [Donald R.] Prothero take on Bigfoot; the Yeti . . .; the Loch Ness monster . . . [and] the Congo dinosaur. They conclude with an analysis of the psychology behind the persistent belief in paranormal phenomena . . . and consider . . . the challenge it poses to clear and critical thinking in our increasingly complex world." (Publisher's note)

REVIEW: *Choice* v51 no8 p1429-30 Ap 2014 M. A. Wilson

"Abominable Science! Origins of the Yeti, Nessie, and Other Famous Cryptids". "Writer/journalist [Daniel] Loxton and noted paleontologist [Donald R.] Prothero . . . have written the best and most useful book yet on the phenomenon of illusory 'cryptids' like Bigfoot and the Loch Ness monster. . . . The illustrations are spectacular, and the book is very well referenced and up-to-date. The prose combines scientific rigor with journalistic flash. . . . This book is valuable for all libraries because interest in this topic is high in virtually all age and scholarship groups."

REVIEW: *Libr J* v138 no12 p101 Jl 1 2013 Laurie Neuerburg

REVIEW: *Publ Wkly* v260 no22 p50-1 Je 3 2013

PROTHERO, DONALD R., 1954-. Rhinoceros giants; the paleobiology of Indricotheres; [by] Donald R. Prothero 141 p. 2013 Indiana University Press

1. Animals, Fossil 2. Indricotherium—Asia, Central 3. Natural history literature 4. Paleobiology—Asia, Central 5. Paleontology—Eocene
ISBN 9780253008190 (cloth : alk. paper)
LC 2012-036059

SUMMARY: "This book introduces the giant hornless rhinoceros, Indricotherium. These massive animals inhabited Asia and Eurasia for more than 14 million years, about 37 to 23 million years ago. They had skulls 6 feet long, stood 22 feet high at the shoulder, and were twice as heavy as the largest elephant ever recorded, tipping the scales at 44,100 pounds." (Publisher's note)

REVIEW: *Choice* v51 no5 p869 Ja 2014 S. L. Brusatte

"Rhinoceros Giants: The Paleobiology of Indricotheres." " Within this slim tome . . . [Donald R.] Prothero packs in an encyclopedic summary of indricothere anatomy and biology, as well as information on where these beasts have been found, what environments they lived in, and how they evolved over time. Most refreshing, this book describes the lives and accomplishments of several little-known but fascinating, paleontologists who studied indricotheres, including the Barbados-born Guy Pilgrim, the naturalist-then-knight Clive Forster Cooper, and the czarist-trained but Bolshevik bureaucrat Aleksei Borissiak. These forgotten scientists and the animals they studied finally get their due in Prothero's book. Most useful for specialist scientists."

PRUITT, BERNADETTE. The other great migration; the movement of rural African Americans to Houston, 1900-1941; [by] Bernadette Pruitt xxi, 453 p. 2013 Texas A&M University Press

1. African Americans—Texas—Houston—Social conditions—20th century 2. African-Americans—Texas—Houston—Migrations—History—20th century 3. Community development—Texas—Houston—History—20th century 4. Historical literature 5. Migration, Internal—Texas—Houston—History—20th century 6. Rural-urban migration—Texas—Houston—History—20th century
ISBN 9781603449489 (book/cloth: alk. paper); 9781623490034 (ebook format/all ebooks)
LC 2013-017813

SUMMARY: In this book, "Bernadette Pruitt portrays the move from rural to urban homes in Jim Crow Houston as a form of black activism and resistance to racism. . . . Pruitt details who the migrants were, why they embarked on their journeys to Houston, the migration networks on which they relied, the jobs they held, the neighborhoods into which they settled, the culture and institutions they transplanted into the city, and the communities and people they transformed in Houston." (Publisher's note)

REVIEW: *Choice* v51 no8 p1475 Ap 2014 T. F. Armstrong

"The Other Great Migration: The Movement of Rural African Americans to Houston, 1900-1941". "The history of African American migration to Houston is important. Through detailed biographical sketches, oral histories, newspapers, and census records, as well as a thorough reading of the secondary literature, [Bernadette] Pruitt . . . recreates the migration of thousands of Texas and Louisiana African Americans to Houston. The reproduction of photographs depicting migrant life strengthens the narrative. . . . For its many strengths, this book suffers from more than an occasional unsupported generalization, redundancy, and a conclusion that is more of an introduction to the migrations that followed than a conclusion to the book at hand."

PRYCE, WILL.il. The library. See Campbell, J. W. P.

PRYOR, S. C.ed. Climate change in the Midwest. See Climate change in the Midwest

PUCHNER, WILLY. The ABC of Fabulous Princesses; [by] Willy Puchner 64 p. 2014 NorthSouth

1. Alphabet books 2. Children's stories 3. Gifts 4. Princes—Fiction 5. Princesses—Juvenile fiction
ISBN 0735841136; 9780735841130

SUMMARY: In this children's alphabet book, "the time has come for Prince William to choose a princess. His eager family has 'worked unwaveringly to woo princesses from around the world,' one for each letter of the alphabet. What follows is a highly alliterative compendium of 26 princesses that discloses their personalities, favorite foods and activities, and the gifts they bring for William." (Publishers Weekly)

REVIEW: *Kirkus Rev* v81 no24 p85 D 15 2013

"The ABC of Fabulous Princesses". "This is not your mother's abecedary. There is a letter on every spread, and Princess Anna does present an ambrosia apple, but that is where the similarity stops. The framing story is slim. . . . The mysterious objects and animals, the deep colors and subtle textures, and the luminous auras surrounding the princesses interact to conjure a magical atmosphere. The narrative's construction is more about alliteration than letter recognition, with three to five sentences per creature producing a variety of delicious sounds, unfamiliar words and idiosyncratic images. . . . Children who prefer more action, plot or character development may tire."

REVIEW: *Publ Wkly* v260 no42 p50 O 21 2013

REVIEW: *SLJ* v60 no1 p75 Ja 2014 Joanna K. Fabicon

PUG AND OTHER ANIMAL POEMS; 40 p. 2012 Margaret Ferguson Books, Farrar Straus Giroux

1. Animals—Juvenile poetry 2. Birds—Juvenile literature 3. Children's poetry, American 4. Poems 5. Pug
ISBN 0374350248; 9780374350246
LC 2010-034300

SUMMARY: This juvenile poetry collection, by Valerie Worth, illustrated by Steve Jenkins, "examines a wide range of animal behavior, from the fleetingness of a fly sipping spilled milk to the constant steely presence of a powerful bull; the greedy meal of a street rat to a cat's quiet gift of a dead mouse on the doorstep." (Publisher's note)

REVIEW: *Booklist* v109 no12 p64 F 15 2013 Randall Enos

REVIEW: *Bull Cent Child Books* v66 no7 p358 Mr 2013 D. S.

"Pug and Other Animal Poems." "Following up on 'Animal Poems,' [Steve] Jenkins again selects an array of elegant free verse by classic twentieth-century poet Valerie Worth, combining each of the eighteen verses with a dramatic cut-paper portrait of its animal subject. Worth's poems are precise and gemlike in their glittering compactness; some are gently playful . . . , others reach heights of grandeur. . . . Jenkins ramps up the impact with compositions of tight focus, posing animals mostly against contrasting backdrops of solid rich color (the bull's dark bulk looms across a three-quarter spread of flame red; a firefly, lacework wings in stop-motion stillness mid-flight, floats in a sea of nocturnal dark blue)."

REVIEW: *Horn Book Magazine* v89 no2 p130-1 Mr/Ap 2013 JOANNA RUDGE LONG

REVIEW: *Kirkus Rev* v81 no3 p113 F 1 2013

REVIEW: *Publ Wkly* p64 Children's starred review annual 2013

REVIEW: *Publ Wkly* v260 no1 p58 Ja 7 2013

REVIEW: *SLJ* v59 no3 p144 Mr 2013 Stephanie Whelan

PULTR, ALEŠ. Introduction to mathematical analysis. See Kriz, I.

A PUNISHMENT ON THE NATION; an Iowa soldier endures the Civil War; xii, 228 p. 2012 The Kent State University Press

1. Historical literature 2. New Englanders—Iowa—Correspondence 3. Soldiers—Iowa—Correspondence
ISBN 1606351443; 9781606351444 (hardcover)
LC 2012-037939

SUMMARY: This book presents the letters of Civil War soldier Silas W. Haven. "Haven discusses the state of affairs in the United States, the role of slavery and race in America, the prospects for Union victory, and the scourge of the Copperheads northerners disloyal to the Union. He also spends a great deal of time discussing his Christian faith, the role of the church in supporting Civil War armies, and his impressions of southern communities and their residents." (Publisher's note)

REVIEW: *Rev Am Hist* v41 no3 p462-6 S 2013 Louis P. Masur

"Letters Home to Sarah: The Civil War Letters of Guy C. Taylor, 36th Wisconsin Volunteers" and "A Punishment on the Nation: An Iowa Soldier Endures the Civil War." "[Guy C. Taylor's] letters offer a Midwestern perspective on the Eastern front. They also illuminate an issue that has only recently begun to gain attention among historians: how illness affected soldiers and how at least some soldiers used illness to secure positions as non-combatants. In her introduction to this well-edited collection, Kathryn Shively Meier points out that Taylor 'parlayed his skills, as well as his relationships with medical personnel,' to escape combat. . . . In this richly annotated volume, [Brian Craig] Miller situates [Silas] Haven within the ongoing discussion of why soldiers enlisted."

PUNTER, DAVID.ed. The encyclopedia of the gothic. See The encyclopedia of the gothic

PURDUM, TODD S., 1959-. An idea whose time has come; two presidents, two parties, and the battle for the Civil Rights Act of 1964; [by] Todd S. Purdum 416 p. 2014 Henry Holt & Co

1. Civil rights—United States—History—20th century 2. Historical literature
ISBN 9780805096729 (hardback)
LC 2013-038545

SUMMARY: In this book, "Todd S. Purdum tells the story of the Civil Rights Act of 1964, recreating the legislative maneuvering and the larger-than-life characters who made its passage possible. . . . Purdum shows how these all-too-human figures managed, in just over a year, to create a bill that prompted the longest filibuster in the history of the U.S. Senate yet was ultimately adopted with overwhelming bipartisan support." (Publisher's note)

REVIEW: *Atlantic* v313 no3 p88-98 Ap 2014 MICHAEL O'DONNELL

"We the People: The Civil Rights Revolution," "An Idea Whose Time Has Come: Two Presidents, Two Parties, and the Battle for the Civil Rights Act of 1964," and "The Years of Lyndon Johnson: The Passage of Power". "[Bruce] Ackerman's is the most ambitious; it is the third volume in an ongoing series on American constitutional history called 'We the People'. . . . [Todd S.] Purdum's . . . book is an astute, well-paced, and highly readable play-by-play of the bill's journey to become a law. . . . Purdum's version of this story is excellent, but he cannot surpass the masterful Robert A. Caro, who offers a peerless and truly mesmerizing account of Johnson's assumption of the presidency in 'The Passage of Power'."

REVIEW: *Booklist* v110 no14 p35 Mr 15 2014 Mark Levine

REVIEW: *Christ Century* v131 no14 p40-1 Jl 9 2014 Paul Harvey

REVIEW: *Kirkus Rev* v82 no7 p15 Ap 1 2014

REVIEW: *Libr J* v139 no4 p101 Mr 1 2014 Karl Helicher

REVIEW: *N Y Times Book Rev* p13 My 18 2014 KEVIN BOYLE

REVIEW: *New Yorker* v90 no20 p74-1 Jl 21 2014

REVIEW: *Publ Wkly* v261 no3 p43 Ja 20 2014

PURDY, AL, 1918-2000. We Go Far Back in Time. See Birney, E.

PURDY, JAMES, 1914-2009. The complete short stories of James Purdy; [by] James Purdy 752 p. 2013 Liveright Publishing Corporation, a Division of W. W. Norton & Company

1. Animals—Fiction 2. Gays—Fiction 3. Human sexuality—Fiction 4. Marriage—Fiction 5. Short stories, American
ISBN 0871406691; 9780871406699 (hardcover)
LC 2013-013992

SUMMARY: This book is a collection of short stories by late fiction writer James Purdy. "Purdy's themes, sometimes homoerotic and sometimes obsessive, transcend the merely sexual. . . . His characters are often argumentative, bitter, unhappy, full of malign intent. In one . . . example, a woman awakens as if from a dream to decide that after years of married life she cannot stand her husband's name--and by extension, her husband," who repays this by hitting her. (Kirkus Reviews)

REVIEW: *Kirkus Rev* v81 no14 p55 Jl 15 2013

REVIEW: *N Y Times Book Rev* p15 Ag 4 2013 JOHN LELAND

"The Complete Short Stories of James Purdy." "[This book,] which includes two novellas, brings together old and new in one twisted, occasionally surreal burlesque, spanning roughly six decades and held together by that oddly formal voice that seems to belong to none of them. Stories materialize as if from dreams. . . . This is the Purdy method: dispense with externals to get at more interior sins. He dealt in myths and universals, not daily reality. Many of the earliest stories are little more than dialogues; the later ones include cracked fairy tales involving cannibals or talking cats. This 'tell don't show' can make the prose feel antique or overeager, but it also creates space for Purdy's dark humor."

REVIEW: *New York Times* v162 no56202 pC21 Jl 19 2013 DWIGHT GARNER

REVIEW: *Publ Wkly* v260 no21 p30 My 27 2013

REVIEW: *TLS* no5762 p19 S 6 2013 BENJAMIN MARKOVITS

"The Complete Short Stories of James Purdy." "A very handsome hardback edition . . . with an introduction by John Waters. . . . Short stories are often a good place to begin a re-evaluation--they allow you to draw a fairly accurate map of a writer's tendencies, virtues and weaknesses. Purdy, however, proves to be difficult to map. His fiction works at a remove from realism, and part of what makes it hard to pin down is that this distance keeps changing. . . . Then there are the stories filled with such obvious sentimentality that they seem to be part of a deliberate attempt to make us uncomfortable. . . . What is impressive about these stories is that, in spite of their variety, they remain recognizably the work of one author, one voice."

PURDY, JAMES, 1914-2009. Eustace Chisholm and the works; [by] James Purdy

1. Chicago (Ill.)—Fiction 2. Gay men—Fiction 3. Poets—Fiction 4. Poor people—Fiction 5. Psychological fiction

ISBN 0907040330; 9780907040330

SUMMARY: This book by James Purdy was "named one of the Publishing Triangle's 100 Best Lesbian and Gay Novels of the 20th Century." (Publisher's note) It is set in "Chicago in the freezing 1930s" and follows "a penniless poet writing his epic, the eponymous works, in charcoal on old pages of the Tribune." (Times Literary Supplement)

REVIEW: *TLS* no5762 p16 S 6 2013

"Eustace Chisholm and the Works." "American fiction gets curiouser and curiouser. . . . There is a dandyish crust of style to this book, and the major bloodlettings have a garnish of minor naughtiness. . . . But once past this, the story is warmly, readily, even cheaply humane. . . . A cliché in drag is a cliché still. When Eustace Chisholm finally bums the works, admitting that he is not a writer, one can only wonder that so much suffering was necessary for such an obvious consummation. . . . 'Eustace Chisholm may delight the converted, but is unlikely to make many converts.'"

PUROHIT, TEENA. The Aga Khan case; religion and identity in colonial India; [by] Teena Purohit x, 183 p. 2012 Harvard University Press

1. Ginans 2. Historical literature 3. Identification (Religion)—History 4. Ismailites—History 5. Ismailites—Legal status, laws, etc.—India—History—19th century 6. Khojas—Legal status, laws, etc.—India—History—19th century 7. Muslims—India—History 8. Religion and state—India—History—19th century 9. Tithes (Islamic law)—India—History—19th century

ISBN 9780674066397

LC 2012-007917

SUMMARY: This book by Teena Purohit "focuses on a nineteenth-century court case in Bombay that influenced how religious identity was defined in India and subsequently the British Empire. The case arose when a group of Indians known as the Khojas refused to pay tithes to the Aga Khan, a Persian nobleman and hereditary spiritual leader of the Ismailis." (Publisher's note)

REVIEW: *Am Hist Rev* v118 no4 p1167 O 2013 Francis Robinson

"The Aga Khan Case: Religion and Identity in Colonial India." "Teena Purohit examines . . . the context of the 'Satpanthis' of Gujarat. . . . Purohit demonstrates admirably how, over the past two centuries, 'Satpanthi' religious complexity has been ironed out into what she would term 'identitarian religion.' It is research much enriched by her deep understanding of the 'ginãns.' The outcomes sit well alongside similar work on the fate of 'Satpanthi' traditions in the hegemonic Sunni world of Pakistan by Michel Boivin and Hasan Ali Khan. This book is an important contribution to understanding religious change in South Asia."

THE PUSHCART PRIZE XXXVIII; Best of the Small Presses 2014 Edition; 600 p. 2013 W W Norton & Co Inc

1. American literature—21st century 2. American poetry—21st century 3. Anthologies 4. Musicians—Fiction 5. Small presses

ISBN 1888889705; 9781888889703

SUMMARY: This anthology, the 38th in the Pushcart Prize series, "features a diverse selection of fiction, poetry, and nonfiction from hundreds of small presses. . . . Fiction includes 'A Full-Service Shelter,' Amy Hempel's tale of tireless animal shelter volunteers taking on the Sisyphean task of saving animals slated for execution, as well as Lorrie Moore's 'Wings,' in which a washed-up musician finds an unlikely companion in her elderly neighbor." (Publishers Weekly)

REVIEW: *Booklist* v110 no6 p7-8 N 15 2013 Donna Seaman

"Pushcart Prize XXVIII, 2014: Best of the Small Presses." "Each year for 38 years, a big, enticing collection of fiction, essays, and poems appears, evoking both the promise of a harvest and the awe of a celestial event. Here are more than 60 works selected from 700 diverse small-press publications. The poets are present in full force, including Afaa Michael Weaver with his beautiful if wrenching poem, 'Blues in Five / Four, the Violence in Chicago.' The fiction bounty includes edgy stories by Amy Hempel and Lorrie Moore. And a number of essays delve into the conundrums of literature.'

PUSHKIN HILLS; 160 p. 2014 Counterpoint Press

1. Alcoholics—Fiction 2. Authors—Fiction 3. FICTION—Literary 4. Soviet Union—Fiction 5. Tour guides (Persons)

ISBN 1619022451; 9781619022454 (hardback)

LC 2013-028859

SUMMARY: This novel by Sergei Dovlatov describes how "an unsuccessful writer and an inveterate alcoholic, Boris Alikhanov has recently divorced his wife Tatyana, and he is running out of money. The prospect of a summer job as a tour guide at the Pushkin Hills Preserve offers him hope of regaining some balance in life as his wife makes plans to emigrate to the West with their daughter Masha, but . . . his life continues to unravel." (Publisher's note)

REVIEW: *Booklist* v110 no12 p24 F 15 2014 Michael

Autrey

REVIEW: *Kirkus Rev* v82 no4 p98 F 15 2014

REVIEW: *N Y Rev Books* v61 no9 p16-7 My 22 2014 Masha Gessen

REVIEW: *Publ Wkly* v260 no50 p46 D 9 2013

REVIEW: *TLS* no5772 p21 N 15 2013 OLIVER READY

"Pushkin Hills." "Its great merit is to recreate, in American prose, the varied speech patterns and colloquial mode of storytelling that [Sergei] Dovlatov worked so hard to render natural in Russian (even subjecting himself to the perverse discipline of never beginning two words in one sentence with the same letter--thus inevitably shortening his sentences). Katherine Dovlatov has chosen, understandably, to leave many of the abundant allusions to Russian and Soviet culture unexplained, and there are occasional lapses of idiom; but the overall effect is convincing, amusing and richly disconcerting."

PUTTER, AD.ed. Multilingualism in Medieval Britain (c. 1066-1520). See Multilingualism in Medieval Britain (c. 1066-1520)

PUTZEL, STEVEN D. Virginia Woolf and the theater; [by] Steven D. Putzel 2013 Fairleigh Dickinson University

1. Historical literature 2. Theater & literature 3. Theater—Great Britain—History 4. Theater in literature 5. Woolf, Virginia, 1882-1941

ISBN 9781611476231

SUMMARY: This book, by Steven D. Putzel, "demonstrates that drama, theater and performance formed a continuous subtext in Virginia Woolf's art and in her life, from the plays she attended as a child, . . . to the Bloomsbury theatrical evenings, to her own studio play 'Freshwater', to her many essays discussing drama and theater, to her final novel, 'Between the Acts', which fulfills her desire to create a work that combines verse, prose and drama." (Publisher's note)

REVIEW: *Choice* v49 no12 p2280 Ag 2012 J. M. Utell

REVIEW: *TLS* no5769 p14-5 O 25 2013 AMBER K. REGIS

"Charleston and Monk's House: The Intimate House Museums of Virginia Woolf and Vanessa Bell," "In the Hollow of the Wave: Virginia Woolf and Modernist Uses of Nature," and "Virginia Woolf and the Theater." "[Nuala] Hancock understands better than most the performances required by a house museum. . . . The result is a strikingly personal, reflective account of how these houses work as memorial sites and businesses. . . . Over six chapters, [Bonnie Kime] Scott demonstrates the revisionary potential of posthuman and ecocritical approaches to literary study. . . . [Steven D.] Putzel identifies the essence of Woolf s fully developed sense of the theatre."

THE PUZZLE OF EXISTENCE; why is there something rather than nothing?; viii, 295 p. 2013 Routledge, Taylor & Francis Group

1. Analytic philosophy 2. God—Proof 3. Nothing (Philosophy) 4. Ontology 5. Philosophical literature 6. Theology

ISBN 0415624657 (hardcover : alk. paper); 9780415624657 (hardcover : alk. paper)

LC 2012-049727

SUMMARY: This book investigates the question "why is there something rather than nothing? The question is explored from diverse and radical perspectives: religious, naturalistic, platonistic and skeptical. Does science answer the question? Or does theology? Does everything need an explanation? Or can there be brute, inexplicable facts? Could there have been nothing whatsoever? Or is there any being that could not have failed to exist? Is the question meaningful after all?" (Publisher's note)

REVIEW: *Choice* v51 no5 p851 Ja 2014 H. C. Byerly

"The Puzzle of Existence: Why Is There Something Rather Than Nothing?" "The contributors are all well versed in contemporary analytic philosophy. The discussions of the puzzle of existence touch on general issues of causation and explanation that are of general philosophical interest beyond the thematic question. The editor's fine introduction illuminates the book's terminology. However, for those unfamiliar with the logic of modality, possible worlds, and distinctions between necessity and contingency, the discussions may make for heavy reading. For those with a deep interest in metaphysics, this work offers an excellent exercise in abstract philosophical reasoning. Good index, but no general bibliography."

PYLE, COLIN. The Middle Kingdom Ride; Two Brothers, Two Motorcycles, One Epic Journey Around China; [by] Colin Pyle 306 p. 2012 Createspace Independent Pub

1. Brothers 2. China—Description & travel 3. Memoirs 4. Motorcycling 5. Travelers' writings

ISBN 146815981X; 9781468159813

SUMMARY: This travel memoir is by Ryan Pyle, "a freelance photographer and journalist in China," and his brother Colin Pyle "a currency trader in Toronto. In 2010 . . . they put their jobs aside and took a self-financed road trip through China. It began in Shanghai, Ryan's new home. They traveled clockwise, to the North Korean border, west to the Mongolian border and across the Xinjiang region, south through Tibet, then east through southern China back to Shanghai." (Kirkus Reviews)

REVIEW: *Kirkus Rev* v81 no6 p85 Mr 15 2013

REVIEW: *Kirkus Rev* p47 D 15 2013 supplemet best books 2013

"The Middle Kingdom Ride". " Two brothers drove BMW motorcycles on a 65-day, 18,000-km loop around China, then co-authored this brisk, optimistic memoir about the trip. . . . Ryan narrates most of the story and his writing is professional and ripe with factoids about China. Colin interjects with entertaining journallike entries that address the same narrative with a rarely redundant, saltier voice. . . . When describing sights and events, their descriptions tend to be logistical rather than florid, and, for the most part, they eschew disparaging words about the country. . . . Enthusiastic, archetypal travelers whose informative story is worth the ride."

PYLE, KEVIN C. Bad for you. See Cunningham, S.

PYLE, RYAN. The Middle Kingdom Ride. See Pyle, C.

PYNCHON, THOMAS, 1937-. Bleeding edge; [by] Thomas Pynchon 496 p. 2013 The Penguin Press

1. Conspiracies—Fiction 2. High technology—Fiction

3. New York (N.Y.)—Fiction 4. Speculative fiction 5. Women private investigators—Fiction
ISBN 1594204233; 9781594204234
LC 2013-017173

SUMMARY: In this book, "Maxine Tarnow is, on the face of it, just another working mom in the city, but in reality, after she's packed her kids' lunches and delivered them at school, she's ferreting around with data cowboys and code monkeys, looking into various sorts of electronic fraud. . . . One track she follows leads to a genius billionaire and electronic concoctions that can scarcely be believed--but also . . . to organized crime, terrorism, big data and the U.S. government." (Kirkus Reviews)

REVIEW: *Atlantic* v312 no3 p34-6 O 2013 NATHANIEL RICH

"Bleeding Edge." "The central preoccupation of 'Bleeding Edge' is the nexus of technology and terror--not terrorism itself so much as our culture's amorphous fears about the future. . . . [Thomas] Pynchon has always been strong on story, the events that fill the narrative, but weak on plot, the causal relationship between these events. His indifference to plot reached its most flagrant expression in 'Against the Day' and 'Gravity's Rainbow', large, action-saturated novels that nevertheless unfold chaotically, often with no obvious linear connection between one episode and the next. But he has never shown more hostility to plot than in 'Bleeding Edge', where he relies almost exclusively on the hoariest of devices: the chance encounter."

REVIEW: *Bookforum* v20 no3 p31 S-N 2013 ED PARK

"Bleeding Edge." "It's the living, breathing details of Upper West Side life, circa 2001, that give 'Bleeding Edge' its humor and its heart. . . . Even as its plot grows ever more complex, 'Bleeding Edge' is reliably entertaining as a sort of cracked Zagat's, with entries ghostwritten by Ben Katchor. . . . 'Bleeding Edge' is several times the length of 'The Crying of Lot 49,' and [Thomas] Pynchon's close-third-person POV is even closer this time around. The prose is looser, the magpie high-low warblings inflected with New York attitude. . . . When Maxine ventures into DeepArcher . . . Pynchon conveys the magic sensation of entering a virtual world (be it Myst, Skyrim, Minecraft) for the first time."

REVIEW: *Booklist* v110 no2 p33 S 15 2013 Donna Seaman

REVIEW: *Kirkus Rev* v81 no17 p21-2 S 1 2013

REVIEW: *Kirkus Rev* p32 N 15 2013 Best Books

REVIEW: *Kirkus Rev* p13 Ag 15 2013 Fall Preview

REVIEW: *Libr J* v138 no21 p57 D 1 2013 Cliff Glaviano

REVIEW: *Libr J* v138 no14 p103 S 1 2013 Barbara Hoffert

REVIEW: *London Rev Books* v35 no18 p21-3 S 26 2013 Christian Lorentzen

REVIEW: *N Y Rev Books* v60 no17 p68-70 N 7 2013 Michael Chabon

"Bleeding Edge." "Irony, verbal and situational, has been the most often remarked of the tactics deployed by [Thomas] Pynchon in his fifty-year struggle against . . . Jack Kirby called 'the Anti-Life Equation': death understood as the dehumanization imposed by vast and totalizing systems of control. And in spite of the depravities, brutalities, and horrors . . . Pynchon's struggle has overarchingly been a joyful one, rooted in a profound and abiding goofiness. . . . 'Bleeding Edge' is best understood not as the account of a master of ironized paranoia coming to grips with the cultural paradigm he helped to define but as something much braver and riskier: an attempt to acknowledge, even at the risk of a melodramatic organ chord, that paradigm's most painful limitation."

REVIEW: *N Y Times Book Rev* p18-9 N 24 2013 JOHN SCHWARTZ

"Infinite Jest," Bleeding Edge," and "Billy Lynn's Long Halftime Walk." "Oliver Wyman . . . imbues each member of Bravo Company with a thoughtfully defined character: Billy is unschooled but far from stupid, and Wyman walks that line effectively. . . . Something is lost in the transition from print to sound, but Wyman manages to give each word and phrase the sensibility of the typographical tricks. . . . The heroine, Maxine Tarnow, is a street-savvy investigator of financial fraud who was born and raised in Manhattan, but [Jeannie] Berlin seems to be channeling Fran Drescher and Selma Diamond. And instead of the Crazy Eddie delivery I was hoping for, the pacing is lugubrious. . . . [Sean] Pratt is a startling good narrator, dry and expressive, with the kind of vocal control that evokes dozens of characters with only slight but very distinctive variations of accent and affect."

REVIEW: *N Y Times Book Rev* p30 S 22 2013

REVIEW: *New Statesman* v142 no5175 p56-7 S 13 2013 Leo Robson

REVIEW: *New York Times* v162 no56256 pC1-2 S 11 2013 MICHIKO KAKUTANI

REVIEW: *New Yorker* v89 no29 p115 S 23 2013

REVIEW: *Newsweek Global* v161 no32 p1 S 13 2013 Malcolm Jones

"Bleeding Edge." "The older [Thomas] Pynchon gets, the less he tries to re-create the whole world from scratch in every novel and the more fun he seems to have. . . . Vagrant passages . . . . and not his Major American Novelist cred--were what kept bringing me back. That and his sneaky, stoner humor, his bent for conspiracies that resonated more soundly with each news cycle. . . . Maybe the plot makes sense. . . . And maybe you can keep the cast of thousands straight. I couldn't. But none of that matters much when set against the way this novel nails the feeling post-9/11 that someone or something had hijacked my experience of that awful day and turned it into something that in no way squared with the jumbled reality I was trying to sort out."

REVIEW: *Publ Wkly* v260 no43 p55 O 28 2013

REVIEW: *Quill Quire* v79 no6 p29-31 Jl/Ag 2013

REVIEW: *Time* v182 no14 p64 S 30 2013 Lev Grossman

REVIEW: *TLS* no5767 p19 O 11 2013 LIDIJA HAAS

Q

QITSUALIK-TINSLEY, RACHEL. The Raven and the Loon; [by] Rachel Qitsualik-Tinsley 32 p. 2014 Inhabit Media

1. Children's stories 2. Inuit literature 3. Loons 4. Ravens 5. Tale (Literary form)—Canada
ISBN 1927095506; 9781927095508

SUMMARY: Written by Rachel Qitsualik-Tinsley and Sean Qitsualik-Tinsley and illustrated by Kim Smith, this children's book tells "cheerfully illustrated tale from traditional Inuit mythology. . . . This retelling of a pan-Arctic traditional story features lively, colorful illustrations and the whimsical storytelling of two of the Arctic's most gifted storytellers." (Publisher's note)

REVIEW: *Kirkus Rev* v82 no6 p99 Mr 15 2014

REVIEW: *Quill Quire* v79 no8 p34 O 2013 Sarah Sawler

"The Raven and the Loon." "In 'The Raven and the Loon,' acclaimed Inuit author Rachel Qitsualik-Tinsley and her husband, Sean Qitsualik-Tinsley, draw on their knowledge of the culture to retell the traditional folktale of how the titular birds, originally sporting plain white plumage, came by their current appearances. . . . The simple words and exuberant tone will make it easy for younger listeners to follow the narrative, yet the story and characters are complex enough that the book should appeal to school-aged children as well. [Illustrator] Kim Smith's playful, eye-catching illustrations add a dramatic element to the story, bringing the characters to life and reinforcing the action with visual cues."

REVIEW: *SLJ* v60 no3 p123 Mr 2014 Megan McGinnis

QITSUALIK-TINSLEY, SEAN. The Raven and the Loon. See Qitsualik-Tinsley, R.

QUARTERMAIN, PETER.ed. The collected early poems and plays. See Duncan, R.

QUATTLEBAUM, MARY. Jo Macdonald hiked in the woods; 32 p. 2013 Dawn Publications

1. Children's songs—Texts 2. Children's stories 3. Forest animals—Juvenile literature 4. Nature—Juvenile literature 5. Nursery rhymes

ISBN 9781584693345 (hardback); 9781584693352 (pbk.)

LC 2013-009249

SUMMARY: This children's book by Mary Quattlebaum, illustrated by Laura J. Bryant, invites readers to "Come along with Jo MacDonald and learn about the wild creatures in the woods at her grandfather's farm. Noisy ones, quiet ones, and a few surprises. This delightful variation on 'Old MacDonald Had a Farm' playfully introduces youngsters to the woodland habitat while engaging little ones with rhythm and wordplay." (Publisher's note)

REVIEW: *Kirkus Rev* v81 no16 p75 Ag 15 2013

"Jo MacDonald Hiked in the Woods." "[Author Mary] Quattlebaum and [illustrator Laura J.] Bryant continue their nature-themed sing-along books with one focused on the sounds of the forest animals. Jo MacDonald and her grandfather head out for a hike in the woods, the familiar childhood song inspiring the pair to describe the animal sounds they hear. . . . Bryant's watercolors are sweetly lovely, not only capturing the relationship between the girl and her grandfather (though their faces could be more expressive), but also simplifying the nature scenes in order to highlight the important parts of the ecosystem and to allow young children to easily spot the featured animal and the squirrel that appears in each spread. . . . The weakest of Jo's three adventures."

REVIEW: *SLJ* v59 no9 p178 S 2013 Gay Lynn Van Vleck

QUERCIA, HAILEY.il. Tales of Eva and Lucas / Cuentos De Eva Y Lucas. See Berlin, D.

QUICK, MATTHEW. The good luck of right now; [by] Matthew Quick 304 p. 2014 Harper

1. Buddhism 2. Family life—Fiction 3. Gere, Richard, 1949- 4. Grief therapy 5. Humorous stories 6. Orphans—Fiction

ISBN 006228553X; 9780062285539 (hardback)

LC 2013-026035

SUMMARY: In this novel, by Matthew Quick, "for thirty-eight years, Bartholomew Neil has lived with his mother. When she gets sick and dies, . . . his . . . grief counselor, Wendy, says he needs to find his flock and leave the nest. But how does a man whose whole life has been grounded in his mom, Saturday mass, and the library learn how to fly? Bartholomew thinks he's found a clue when he discovers a 'Free Tibet' letter from Richard Gere hidden in his mother's underwear drawer." (Publisher's note)

REVIEW: *Booklist* v110 no9/10 p40 Ja 1 2014 Margaret Flanagan

REVIEW: *Kirkus Rev* v81 no24 p339 D 15 2013

"The Good Luck of Right Now". "Quirky, feel-good fiction. . . . Through synchronicity (a key concept in the novel), it turns out the Girlbrarian, Elizabeth, has a brother, Max, going through grief counseling for his cat, Alice. Max, who can't get through a single sentence without using the f-word, links up with Bartholomew through Wendy, and the novel switches to a road trip to Canada, where Bartholomew can supposedly discover a father he has long thought dead and Max can visit the 'Cat Parliament' in Ottawa. A whimsical, clever narrative."

REVIEW: *Libr J* v139 no3 p135 F 15 2014 Barbara Hoffert

REVIEW: *Libr J* v139 no2 p68 F 1 2014 Jennifer B. Stidham

REVIEW: *Libr J* v138 no14 p82 S 1 2013

REVIEW: *New York Times* v163 no56409 pC1-4 F 11 2014 JANET MASLIN

"The Good Luck of Right Now." "'The Good Luck of Right Now' is only the second nominally adult novel by Matthew Quick, whose attention-getting first was 'The Silver Linings Playbook.' Mr. Quick's other books have been categorized as young adult fiction, though, in his hands, the two genres are not that different. . . . It takes the epistolary form of a series of letters to 'Dear Mr. Richard Gere.' . . . Its assortment of waifs and shut-ins begin to realize that they need one another and form a ragtag band with just enough pointless goals to turn this into a road story. . . . This book so overplays its hand that you may wish that Bartholomew had read Mr. Gere's initial letter and left it at that."

REVIEW: *Publ Wkly* v260 no52 p29 D 23 2013

QUIMBY, CHARLIE. Monument road; [by] Charlie Quimby 365 p. 2013 Torrey House Press

1. Colorado—Fiction 2. Grief—Fiction 3. Psychological fiction 4. Suicide—Fiction 5. Widowers

ISBN 9781937226251

LC 2013-952247

SUMMARY: This book "opens with widower Leonard Self desperately seeking oblivion as he heads toward the cliff he plans to jump to off. Prior to the death of his wife, he promised her he would wait exactly one year to spread her ashes. . . . We soon learn that the despair-filled Leonard has spent the past year quietly paring down what remains of his ranch, disposing of his belongings, and preparing to carry out his promise while also secretly planning on going off cliff with her." (Publishers Weekly)

REVIEW: *Booklist* v110 no4 p32 O 15 2013 Diane Holcomb

"Monument Road." "Leonard Self, an aging Colorado rancher, sets out to fulfill the promise he made to his dying wife, Inetta, to release her ashes over the highest overlook on Monument Road one year after her passing. . . . Within the novel, two powerful subplots--a teenage girl seeking her inner Joan of Arc, an abused boy giving up on himself--rear up seemingly from nowhere. But trust [Charlie] Quimby. He merges them masterfully by book's end. His love of character and the West is evident in every essential detail. Part modern western, part mystery, this first novel will appeal to fans of Louise Erdrich and Kent Haruf. Quimby's prose reads so true, it breaks the heart."

QUIN, ÉLISABETH. The killer detail. See Armanet, F.

QUINDEAU, ILKA. Seduction and desire; the psychoanalytic theory of sexuality since Freud; xix, 300 p. 2013 Karnac Books

1. Desire 2. Psychoanalysis 3. Psychological literature 4. Psychosexual development 5. Sex (Psychology)
ISBN 1780490895; 9781780490892
LC 2013-478093

SUMMARY: In this book by Ilka Quindeau, "the author gives a systematic presentation of psychoanalytic theories and develops a model of human sexuality that transgresses gender-binarities, integrates 'male' -phallic and 'female' -receptive parts, and encompasses the diversity of gender identifications and sexual varieties. She . . . argues for a universal human sexuality in which men and women differ less between the sexes but individually." (Publisher's note)

REVIEW: *Choice* v51 no5 p928-9 Ja 2014 W. P. Anderson

"Seduction and Desire: The Psychoanalytic Theory of Sexuality Since Freud." "[Ilka] Quindeau . . . has written a book for readers who are already confirmed believers in Freudian psychoanalysis as explanation for much of human behavior. . . . Heavily referenced with 333 works from the psychoanalytic literature, the book pays little attention to more recent scientific studies that rely on evolutionary theories of sex differences and studies of brain differences. . . . To a non-psychoanalyst, the reasoning often seems convoluted, but this may be partly due to translation from the original German."

QUINN, JASON. Gandhi; Apostle of Peace; 212 p. 2014 Random House Inc

1. Biography (Literary form) 2. Gandhi, Mahatma, 1869-1948 3. Graphic nonfiction 4. India—Politics & government—1919-1947 5. Nonviolence
ISBN 9380741227; 9789380741222

SUMMARY: This book by Jason Quinn, illustrated by Naresh Kumar, focuses on the life of "Mohandas Karamchand Gandhi, better known as the Mahatma or Great Soul. . . . We discover the man behind the legend, following him from his birth in the Indian coastal town of Porbandar in 1869, to the moment of his tragic death at the hands of an assassin in January 1948, just months after the Independence of India." (Publisher's note)

REVIEW: *Booklist* v110 no13 p50 Mr 1 2014 Francisca Goldsmith

REVIEW: *Kirkus Rev* v82 no2 p258 Ja 15 2014

"Gandhi: My Life is My Message". "A fictionalized graphic 'memoir' conveys bright pictures of the Great Soul's character and achievements without falling into blind hero worship. Quinn's account is written in the first person and includes invented thoughts and dialogue that sometimes have an anachronistic ring. These literary gestures notwithstanding, the author retraces Gandhi's career accurately and in relatively fine detail from childhood to assassination. More importantly, he also depicts the origins, logic and applications of Gandhi's philosophy of nonviolent disobedience (satyagraha) in deft, compelling strokes. . . . [Sachin] Nagar expertly positions panels and figures to create a visual sweep even in relatively static compositions."

REVIEW: *Publ Wkly* v261 no5 p43 F 3 2014

REVIEW: *SLJ* v60 no5 p159 My 2014 Peter Blenski

REVIEW: *Voice of Youth Advocates* v37 no1 p73 Ap 2014 Barbara Johnston

QUINN, SARAH.tr. The race. See Manceau, É.

QUON, ANNA. Low; [by] Anna Quon 287 p. 2013 Invisible Publishing

1. Canadian fiction 2. Fathers & daughters—Fiction 3. Mental illness—Fiction 4. Mothers—Death 5. Racially mixed people—Fiction
ISBN 1926743326; 9781926743325 (pbk.)
LC 2013-433371

SUMMARY: This novel by Anna Quon "is a novel about family, identity, illness, love and loss. Lyrical, personal prose draws readers into the world of Adriana Song. We feel our way through Low with her as she navigates lopsided friendships, failed romances--as she tries to to weather the storm that is her life." (Publisher's note)

REVIEW: *Quill Quire* v79 no7 p31-2 S 2013 Maria Siassina

"Low." "Anna Quon's second novel revisits themes of race and identity previously explored in her 2009 debut, 'Migration Songs.' . . . Adriana's time at the mental hospital focuses on her transformation from a doubtful, insecure teenager to a young women who sees a chance to start over. Quon highlights the bleak realities of mental illness, and does not shy away from critiquing the shortcomings of the health-care system. . . . Quon's writing is confident throughout. 'Low' is a genuine and gentle novel about family, identity, and the road to recovery."

R

RAABE, EMILY. Lost children of the far islands; [by] Emily Raabe 288 p. 2014 Alfred A. Knopf

1. Adventure and adventurers—Fiction 2. Brothers and sisters—Fiction 3. Family life—Maine—Fiction 4. Fantasy fiction 5. Selective mutism—Fiction 6. Shapeshifting—Fiction 7. Supernatural—Fiction
ISBN 9780375870910; 9780375970917 (lib. bdg.)
LC 2013-014768

SUMMARY: In this book, by Emily Raabe, "twins Gus and Leo and their little sister, Ila, live a quiet life in Maine—until their mother falls ill, and it becomes clear her strength is fading because she is protecting them from a terrible evil. Soon the children are swept off to a secret island far in the sea, where they discover a hidden grandmother and powers they never knew they had. Like their mother, they are Folk, creatures who can turn between human and animal forms." (Publisher's note)

REVIEW: *Booklist* v110 no15 p89 Ap 1 2014 Sarah Hunter

REVIEW: *Bull Cent Child Books* v67 no9 p474 My 2014 K. Q. G.

"Lost Children of the Far Islands". "There are quiet echoes of Susan Cooper and C. S. Lewis here in both mythology and structure, and [Emily] Raabe manages the difficult feat of balancing the Family drama and the epic Fantasy with surprising ease. The affection among the siblings is particularly well drawn; the third-person narration focalizes through Gus, who feels responsible for her more passive brother, and through little Ila, who struggles with Feeling left out of the twins' inherent bond. Vivid imagery makes the underwater scenes utterly captivating, as the siblings in seal form frolic with dolphins, battle off great white sharks, and, of course, eventually beat the bad guy. A cozy fantasy with a few deep-sea thrills, this would make a fine family or classroom readaloud as well."

REVIEW: *Kirkus Rev* v82 no3 p232 F 1 2014

"Lost Children of the Far Islands". "The first sentence grabs readers right away: 'On May 23, exactly one month before Gustavia and Leomaris Brennan's eleventh birthday, their mother became terribly, mysteriously ill.' The promise of the sentence is fulfilled as Gus, Leo and their selectively mute little sister, Ila, discover and battle the source of their mother's illness, simultaneously learning of their own magical powers. Filtered primarily through Gus' point of view, the third-person narration is full of action, with cliffhangers ending most chapters. In a nice feminist touch, Gus is the active twin; Leo, the bookworm. . . . A mostly strong magical adventure in the grand tradition."

REVIEW: *SLJ* v60 no4 p153 Ap 2014 Jessica Ko

RABBAN, DAVID M. Law's history; American legal thought and the transatlantic turn to history; [by] David M. Rabban xvi, 564 p. 2013 Cambridge University Press

1. HISTORY—United States—19th Century 2. Historical literature 3. Law—Study and teaching—United States—History—19th century 4. Law—United States—Interpretation and construction—History—19th century 5. Law—United States—Philosophy—History—19th century
ISBN 9780521761918 (hbk.)
LC 2012-012605

SUMMARY: Written by David M. Rabban, "This is a study of the central role of history in late-nineteenth century American legal thought. . . . Unprecedented in its coverage and its innovative conclusions about major American legal thinkers from the Civil War to the present, the book combines transatlantic intellectual history, legal history, the history of legal thought, historiography, jurisprudence, constitutional theory, and the history of higher education." (Publisher's note)

REVIEW: *Am Hist Rev* v118 no5 p1537-8 D 2013 Howard Schweber

REVIEW: *J Am Hist* v100 no2 p538-9 S 2013 Herbert Hovenkamp

REVIEW: *Rev Am Hist* v42 no1 p115-20 Mr 2014 Roman J. Hoyos

"Law's History: American Legal Thought and the Transatlantic Turn to History." "'Law's History' is a highly readable reconstruction of an important and largely overlooked segment of postbellum legal thought. [David M.] Rabban traces the transatlantic emergence of a modern and professional legal history, and its role in the emergence of historical jurisprudence in late nineteenth-century America. . . . The book's readability, however, is also due to a certain lack of causal complexity. . . . 'Law's History' is a standard work on postbellum jurisprudence and will be an essential guide to American jurisprudence for years to come."

RABER, KAREN.ed. A cultural history of women in the Renaissance. See A cultural history of women in the Renaissance

RACZKA, BOB. Joy in Mudville; 32 p. 2014 Carolrhoda Books

1. Baseball—Fiction 2. Sex role—Fiction 3. Sports—Fiction 4. Stories in rhyme 5. Women baseball players
ISBN 9780761360155 (lib. bdg.: alk. paper)
LC 2013-018619

SUMMARY: In this book, a follow up to the poem "Casey at the Bat," the Mudville baseball team is rescued by "Joy, a female rookie pitcher whom the crowd greets with mistrust, boos and catcalls. Her technique is extremely unusual. She variously emulates a football snap to the quarterback, a tennis serve and a basketball dribble and jump shot. Finally, Joy kicks a bunt back to home plate for the out to save the game. And the crowd goes wild." (Kirkus Reviews)

REVIEW: *Kirkus Rev* v82 no3 p156 F 1 2014

"Joy in Mudville". "[Bob] Raczka's sequel echoes Ernest Lawrence Thayer's original, which appears in full following the victory. Although many of his lines are choppy, and unfortunately, the rhymes are too often tortured, the repartee between the whining batter and the umpire is delightful, as is Joy's highly imaginative, definitely rule-breaking pitching style. In [Glin] Dibly's bright illustrations, the umpire steals some of the spotlight, as his attire and mannerisms match Joy's other-sport pitches, and all the characters' expressions and actions are perfectly suited to this very odd game. The old ball game is still great fun."

REVIEW: *Publ Wkly* v261 no6 p88 F 10 2014

REVIEW: *SLJ* v60 no4 p133 Ap 2014 Marilyn Taniguchi

RADFORD, GAIL. The rise of the public authority; statebuilding and economic development in Twentieth-Century America; [by] Gail Radford ix, 218 p. 2013 University of Chicago Press

1. Corporations, Government—United States—History—20th century 2. Federal land banks—United States—History—20th century 3. Government securities 4. Historical literature 5. United States—Politics & government—20th century
ISBN 9780226037691 (cloth : alkaline paper); 9780226037721 (paperback : alkaline paper)
LC 2012-047522

SUMMARY: This book by Gail Radford offers a "history of the development of public authorities, beginning with Woodrow Wilson's secretary of the treasury creating the Federal Fleet Corporation to fiind merchant ship construction. She shifts to the creation of Federal Land Banks, which were intended to provide funding to modernize agriculture, which would reduce dissatisfaction over the inflation in food prices." (Choice: Current Reviews for Academic Libraries)

REVIEW: *Choice* v51 no5 p890 Ja 2014 M. Perelman

"The Rise of the Public Authority: Statebuilding and Economic Development in Twentieth-Century America."

"This valuable study of public authorities covers a largely overlooked subject. The subtitle . . . is particularly informative about the author's approach to this curious institutional form. . . . [Gail] Radford . . . offers a fascinating history of the development of public authorities. . . . This well-researched and well-written book richly deserves interest due to the importance of its subject matter."

RADKAU, JOACHIM. The Age of Ecology; [by] Joachim Radkau 600 p. 2013 John Wiley & Sons Inc

1. Environmentalism—History 2. Environmentalists 3. Historical literature 4. Human ecology—History 5. Social movements

ISBN 0745662161; 9780745662169

SUMMARY: In this history of environmentalism, author Jachim Radkau "shows that this is not a single story of the steady ascent of environmentalism but rather a multiplicity of stories, each with its own dramatic tension: between single-issue movements and the challenges posed by the interconnection of environmental issues, between charismatic leaders and bureaucratic organizations, and between grass-root movements and global players. " (Publisher's note)

REVIEW: *Choice* v51 no12 p2209 Ag 2014 F. N. Egerton

REVIEW: *New Sci* v221 no2954 p50-1 F 1 2014 Fred Pearce

"The Age of Ecology". "A pioneering and highly readable history. . . . Author Joachim Radkau is no dispassionate outsider. He admits at the start that since his youth he felt ecology was his movement. But nor is he a firebrand or doomsayer, and his range and scholarship are impressive. . . . Sometimes, like many German greens, Radkau appears to hate anything nuclear. From Hiroshima through Chernobyl to Fukushima, atom-splitting is his number one enemy. Even so, he reflects well the environmental movement's diversity, in its causes and intellectual approaches. Jostling for space in the 500-plus pages is everything from deep ecology and guerrilla gardening to water wars and the joys of cycling."

RADNER, JOHN B. Johnson and Boswell; a biography of friendship; [by] John B. Radner xii, 415 p. 2012 Yale University Press

1. Authors, American—19th century—Biography 2. Authors, English—18th century—Biography 3. Biographies 4. Friendship

ISBN 9780300178753 (cloth : alk. paper)

LC 2012-019520

SUMMARY: This book by John Radner explores the "profound, occasionally volatile 20 year friendship between authors Samuel Johnson and James Boswell. . . . Johnson guided his protégée away from promiscuity and drinking and through many bouts of depression, often with tough love. Meanwhile Boswell gently prodded Johnson to explore the fear of death and damnation that haunted him." (Publishers Weekly)

REVIEW: *Choice* v50 no11 p2015 Jl 2013 A. W. Lee

REVIEW: *TLS* no5755 p25 Jl 19 2013 FREYA JOHNSTON

"Johnson and Boswell: A Biography of Friendship." "Mistrust of happiness is one of Samuel Johnson's signature tunes. . . . In this exhaustive study, the labour of years, John B. Radner rehearses the many occasions on which [James] Boswell interrogated his friend (and others) about happiness and free will. . . . In between those extremes of consummate union and supreme irritation, the happiness of real friendship suddenly heaves into view. Such moments are delicately restaged and painstakingly analysed by Radner."

RADZILOWSKI, JOHN.ed. American immigration. See American immigration

RAFF, ANNA.il. Things that float and things that don't. See Adler, D. A.

RAFFAELLI, LARA GOCHIN.tr. Pleasure. See D'Annunzio, G.

RAGEN, NAOMI. The sisters Weiss; [by] Naomi Ragen 336 p. 2013 St. Martin's Press

1. Family secrets—Fiction 2. Historical fiction 3. Sisters—Fiction 4. Ultra-Orthodox Jews—Fiction

ISBN 0312570198; 9780312570194 (hardback)

LC 2013-020570

SUMMARY: In this book, "growing up in a strictly Orthodox Jewish family in Brooklyn in the 1950s, Rose Weiss and her younger sister, Pearl, are very close, until Rose . . . leaves home to escape an arranged marriage. . . . Pearl follows the rules as docile daughter, dutiful wife, and breadwinner. . . . But things do not turn out as planned for either sister. . . . Pearl's daughter, Rivka, runs away from her pious husband to find her artist aunt, while Rose's daughter finds her mother's family." (Booklist)

REVIEW: *Booklist* v110 no1 p51 S 1 2013 Hazel Rochman

"The Sisters Weiss." "Readers familiar with Yiddish will love the wry idiom ('What else do you want already?'), but the intense personal drama will reach a wide audience across ethnicity Returning to her community after 40 years. Rose finds that nothing has changed--neither the prejudice nor the caring love, 'if you are one of them.' . . . The secrets hold you to the very end, when the sisters confront the universal question: Whose memory is true to what really happened? . . . The family drama, past and present, will grab older teen readers."

REVIEW: *Kirkus Rev* v81 no18 p145 S 15 2013

RAGHAVAN, SRINATH. 1971; a global history of the creation of Bangladesh; [by] Srinath Raghavan 368 p. 2013 Harvard University Press

1. Decolonization 2. Historical literature 3. India-Pakistan Conflict, 1971

ISBN 9780674728646 (alk. paper)

LC 2013-012267

SUMMARY: In this book, "Srinath Raghavan contends that far from being a predestined event, the creation of Bangladesh was the product of conjuncture and contingency, choice and chance. The breakup of Pakistan and the emergence of Bangladesh can be understood only in a wider international context of the period: decolonization, the Cold War, and incipient globalization." (Publisher's note)

REVIEW: *Choice* v51 no8 p1467-8 Ap 2014 R. D. Long

REVIEW: *Nation* v297 no23 p36-40 D 9 2013 THOMAS MEANEY

REVIEW: *New Repub* v244 no19 p44-9 N 25 2013 Sunil Khilnani

"The Blood Telegram: Nixon, Kissinger, and a Forgotten Genocide" and "1971: A Global History of the Creation of Bangladesh." "Now we have two excellent and uncannily complementary books about the crucible of 1971. [Gary J.] Bass . . . has written an account--learned, riveting, and eviscerating--of the delusions and the deceptions of [Richard] Nixon and [Henry] Kissinger. Steeped in the forensic skills of a professional academic historian, he also possesses the imaginative energies of a classical moralist, and he tells the story of the choices and the decisions that led to the slaughter in Bengal . . . appropriately as a moral saga. Srinath Raghavan, a former Indian army officer who researches and teaches in Delhi and in London, takes a more dispassionate approach. His superb analysis of the global intricacies of 1971 uses that wider lens with great precision to explain the breakup of Pakistan more convincingly than any preceding account."

REVIEW: *New Yorker* v89 no29 p109-14 S 23 2013 Pankaj Mishra

"1971: A Global History of the Creation of Bangladesh" and "The Blood Telegram: Nixon, Kissinger, and a Forgotten Genocide." "Two absorbing new books . . . describe, from different perspectives, this strangely neglected episode of the Cold War. [Srinath] Raghavan covers a range of mentalities, choices, and decisions in Islamabad, Moscow, Beijing, Washington, New Delhi, and other capitals. [Gary J.] Bass focusses mainly on American actions and inaction. . . . Bass describes the devious way that [Richard] Nixon and [Henry] Kissinger managed to bury their role in the debacle."

REVIEW: *TLS* no5780 p11 Ja 10 2014 ISAAC CHOTINER

"The Blood Telegram: Nixon, Kissinger, and a Forgotten Genocide" and "1971: A Global History of the Creation of Bangladesh." "As Gary J. Bass so astutely argues in his superb book 'The Blood Telegram,' in 1971 the Bangladesh Liberation War did not raise the question of whether Americans should try to prevent or cut short a genocide. The Nixon administration, in violation of American law, had been giving moral and material aid to Pakistan's junta as it slaughtered its own citizens. The United States was already involved--on the wrong side. . . . [Srinath] Raghavan's book focuses on the world's reaction to the crisis. . . . Raghavan generally refrains from moral judgements . . . and describes the ways in which the crisis could have been prevented."

RAHIMI, ATIQ. A curse on Dostoevsky; 272 p. 2014 Other Press

1. Guilt—Fiction 2. Murder—Fiction 3. Prostitution 4. Raskolnikov (Fictitious character)
ISBN 1590515471; 9781590515471 (pbk.: alk. paper)
LC 2013-042495

SUMMARY: In this novel, by Atiq Rahimi, "Rassoul remembers reading 'Crime and Punishment' as a student of Russian literature in Leningrad, so when, with axe in hand, he kills the wealthy old lady who prostitutes his beloved Sophia, he thinks twice before taking her money or killing the woman whose voice he hears from another room. He wishes only to expiate his crime and be rightfully punished. Out of principle, he gives himself up to the police." (Publisher's note)

REVIEW: *Booklist* v110 no11 p22 F 1 2014 Bryce Christensen

REVIEW: *Kirkus Rev* v82 no3 p190 F 1 2014

"A Curse on Dostoevsky". "While [Atiq] Rahimi frames Rassoul's experiences through a third-person recounting, Rassoul also keeps a journal of his activities and thoughts, and Rahimi offers generous glimpses into Rassoul's mind with this first-person account. The parallels to [Fyodor] Dostoevsky's novel are striking, as, like Raskolnikov, Rassoul has issues with his landlord; he first confesses his crime to Sophia; and he has a relatively clueless mother. One irony is that, in Kabul, violence is so pervasive that people are being killed almost indiscriminately, so one more "murder" shouldn't make a difference, right? But it does. Rahimi does a masterful job both in echoing Dostoevsky and in updating the moral complexities his protagonist both creates and faces."

REVIEW: *Publ Wkly* v260 no50 p46 D 9 2013

RAHMAN, SYEDUR. Government and politics in South Asia. See Kapur, A.

RAM-PRASAD, CHAKRAVARTHI. Divine self, human self; the philosophy of being in two Gita commentaries; [by] Chakravarthi Ram-Prasad xx, 148 p. 2013 Bloomsbury Academic

1. Bhagavadgita 2. Hindu philosophy 3. Hinduism—Doctrines—Comparative studies 4. Philosophical literature
ISBN 9781441154644 (pbk. ; alk. paper); 9781441182654 (alk. paper)
LC 2013-002700

SUMMARY: "This book approaches [two 'Gita'] commentaries through a study of the interaction between the abstract atman (self) and the richer conception of the human person. While closely reading the Sanskrit commentaries, [Chakravarthi] Ram-Prasad develops reconstructions of each philosophical-theological system, drawing relevant and illuminating comparisons with contemporary Christian theology and Western philosophy." (Publisher's note)

REVIEW: *Choice* v51 no7 p1229-30 Mr 2014 C. A. Barnsley

"Divine Self, Human Self: The Philosophy of Being in Two Gita Commentaries." "This work by [Chakravarthi] Ram-Prasad . . . on philosophy of being in the Gîtâ commentaries, despite what the title and table of contents might suggest, is not a study of the Bhagavad Gita. Further, the author does not seek to provide a subcommentary on the commentaries of either Sankara or Ramanuja. Rather, he borrows from Christian theology and asserts his approach as one of constructive theology. . . . While this volume does not serve as a traditional or synoptic commentary on the Gîta, it nonetheless provides a new and insightful lens through which to approach the text and its rich commentaries."

RAMAKRISHNAN, S. KARTHICK (SUBRAMANIAN KARTHICK), 1975-. Asian American political participation. See Taeku Lee

RAMALINGAM, BEN. Aid on the edge of chaos; rethinking international cooperation in a complex world; [by] Ben Ramalingam 480 p. 2014 Oxford University Press

1. Complexity (Philosophy) 2. Economic development 3. International cooperation 4. International economic assistance 5. Social science literature
ISBN 9780199578023 (hardback)

LC 2013-944498

SUMMARY: This book on foreign aid by Ben Ramalingam "explores how thinkers and practitioners in economics, business, and public policy have started to embrace new, ecologically literate approaches to thinking and acting, informed by the ideas of complex adaptive systems research. It showcases insights, experiences, and dramatic results of a growing network of practitioners, researchers, and policy makers who are applying a complexity-informed approach to aid challenges." (Publisher's note)

REVIEW: *Choice* v51 no9 p1648-9 My 2014 S. Paul

"Aid on the Edge of Chaos: Rethinking International Cooperation in a Complex World". "This timely critique of aid is divided into three parts. . . . The first describes the system of foreign aid, noting critically the shortcomings in the operations of aid agencies and their inability to provide satisfactory answers to questions about whether aid is effective and who gains from it. The second part of the book deals with the notion of complexity. . . . In the third and final part, [Ben] Ramalingam . . . explains how complexity could be employed to make aid more effective. . . . The examples presented in this work should prompt a reconsideration of how one thinks of foreign aid."

REVIEW: *Economist* v411 no8884 p83 Ap 26 2014

REVIEW: *New Sci* v220 no2947 p50-1 D 14 2013 Debora MacKenzie

"Aid on the Edge of Chaos". "[Ben] Ramalingam knows a lot about the development business. His detailed analysis might be too exhaustive for some, as he shows how aid can be more about reinforcing the power and preconceptions of the aid agency than ending poverty. But he also argues that even at its best, aid is a child of 19th-century science, with reductionist solutions for simple problems. Sometimes this works, but more often it doesn't. Aid doesn't have the expected effect. . . . Ramalingam knows enough about complex systems that his book would probably be worth reading as a non-mathematical primer on complexity theory—the science of non-linear, interlocking systems. Some of his best examples come from the way it has already been applied to banking and finance."

RAMIREZ, AINISSA G. Newton's football. See St. John, A.

RAMPRASAD, GAYATHRI. Shadows in the sun; healing from depression and finding the light within; [by] Gayathri Ramprasad 240 p. 2014 Hazelden

1. Depressed persons—United States—Biography 2. Depression, Mental—India 3. Memoirs 4. Mind and body therapies 5. Postpartum depression—India
ISBN 1616494751; 9781616494759 (softcover)
LC 2013-035456

SUMMARY: This memoir, by Gayathri Ramprasad, traces her "battle with the depression that consumed her from adolescence through marriage and a move to the United States. It was only after the birth of her first child, when her husband discovered her in the backyard . . . 'digging a grave so that I could bury myself alive' that she finally found help. After a stay in a psych ward she eventually found . . . an emotional and spiritual awakening from the darkness of her tortured mind." (Publisher's note)

REVIEW: *Kirkus Rev* v82 no4 p169 F 15 2014

"Shadows in the Sun: Healing From Depression and Finding the Light Within". "[Gayathri] Ramprasad chronicles her harrowing journey through depression, from which she emerged with the light of hope to become a mental health advocate. . . . It was in her lowest moment that the author realized that the keys to her wellness were within her, and she began searching for other remedies. Breathing techniques, meditation, exercise and openness about her illness slowly helped her climb out of that dark place. A well-written, novellike story offering hope for recovery for families in the throes of mental illness."

REVIEW: *Publ Wkly* v261 no7 p93 F 17 2014

RAMSAY, FREDERICK. Drowning Barbie; [by] Frederick Ramsay 250 p. 2014 Poisoned Pen Press

1. Adult child sexual abuse victims—Fiction 2. Detective & mystery stories 3. Drug abuse—Fiction 4. Marriage—Fiction 5. Murder investigation—Fiction
ISBN 9781464202148 (hardcover: alk. paper); 9781464202162 (trade pbk: alk. paper)
LC 2013-941227

SUMMARY: In this book, part of Frederick Ramsay's mystery series featuring sheriff Ike Schwartz, "the discovery of the corpse of meth addict Ethyl Smut in a shallow grave atop another murder victim, who was buried 10 years earlier, puts Ike on the trail of Ethyl's 17-year-old daughter, Darla." (Publishers Weekly)

REVIEW: *Kirkus Rev* v82 no1 p178 Ja 1 2014

"Drowning Barbie". " Sheriff Ike Schwartz and his longtime love, college president Ruth Harris, have to plan their wedding reception around a couple of corpses. . . . Andy Lieux's dog throws a hitch into their getting hitched by digging up not one but two dead bodies in the woods by the old spring. . . . Worst of all, Darla Smut, the one person who might know who killed her mom, disappears, and Ike knows that if he doesn't find Darla fast, deadly dangerous drug dealer George LeBrun just might beat him to her. . . . Why Picketsville's first Jewish sheriff is hellbent on a church wedding is just one of the mysteries that doesn't get solved in Ramsay's otherwise highly entertaining ninth."

REVIEW: *Libr J* v139 no2 p60 F 1 2014 Teresa L. Jacobsen

REVIEW: *Publ Wkly* v260 no51 p41 D 16 2013

RAMSEY, GUTHRIE P. The amazing Bud Powell; Black genius, jazz history, and the challenge of bebop; [by] Guthrie P. Ramsey xi, 240 p. 2013 University of California Press Center for Black Music Research, Columbia College

1. Bop music 2. Jazz—History and criticism 3. Jazz musicians 4. Music literature
ISBN 9780520243910 (cloth : alk. paper)
LC 2012-039182

SUMMARY: In this book on jazz musician Bud Powell, author Guthrie P. Ramsey Jr. explores "Powell's life, art and revolutionary contribution to the development of jazz," focusing his argument on "how [Powell's] progress 'can be interpreted through several social orders, all of which mark him as a genius and jazz as a complicated culturally heterogeneous art form'." (Times Literary Supplement)

REVIEW: *Choice* v51 no3 p470-1 N 2013 K. R. Dietrich

REVIEW: *TLS* no5750 p33 Je 14 2013 JOHN MOLE

"The Amazing Bud Powell: Black Genius, Jazz History, and the Challenge of Bebop." "A celebration of Bud Powell's life, art and revolutionary contribution to the development of jazz is at the heart of this wide-ranging academic study that sets out to demonstrate how his progress 'can be interpreted through several social orders, all of which mark him as a genius and jazz as a complicated culturally heterogeneous art form'. . . . [There are] many passages in this book where [Guthrie P.] Ramsey writes with a musician's ear, taking a break from the earnest discourse of scholarly analysis."

RANDALL, GREGORY. Snow on the Pea Soup; And Other Anecdotes; [by] Gregory Randall 164 p. 2013 Author Solutions

1. Australia—Description & travel 2. Business travel 3. Flight 4. Netherlands—Description & travel 5. Travelers' writings
ISBN 1491876263; 9781491876268

SUMMARY: This book by Gregory Randall presents " a meditation on one man's meandering about the globe. . . . In 142 pages, there are more than 150 chapters, some barely registering as a full-fledged paragraph. The themes touched upon are wide-ranging, even discontinuous: Chilean wine, groceries, actuarial communication skills, Brazil, Prince Andrew and unpleasant flights are only a tiny sampling of what the book offers." (Kirkus Reviews)

REVIEW: *Kirkus Rev* v81 no24 p351 D 15 2013

"Snow on the Pea Soup: And Other Anecdotes". "A random collection of memories, part travelogue and diary, held together by light interjections of humor. First-time author [Gregory] Randall has traveled the world as a businessman, gathering his pithy memoirs in the process. This is less a tale than an accumulation of cosmopolitan ruminations, stylistically held together by neat, aphoristic brevity. . . . Sometimes, the disjointedness can be bit grating, leaving readers unmoored from a progressing story or guiding ideas. Mostly, however, the unpretentiousness of the observations and the spirit of levity with which they're offered make up for the lack of structure and chronology."

RANDALL, MARTIN. 9/11 and the literature of terror; [by] Martin Randall 174 p. 2011 Edinburgh University Press

1. American literature—21st century 2. Literary critiques 3. Modern literature—21st century 4. September 11 Terrorist Attacks, 2001—Influence 5. September 11 Terrorist Attacks, 2001, in literature
ISBN 9780748638529; 0748638520
LC 2011-486330

SUMMARY: In this book on literature related to the September 11, 2001 terror attacks, "works by Don DeLillo, Martin Amis, Ian McEwan, Simon Armitage and Mohsin Hamid are discussed in relation to the specific problems of writing about such a visually spectacular 'event' that has had enormous global implications. Other chapters analyse initial responses to 9/11, the intriguing tensions between fiction and non-fiction, [and] the challenge of describing traumatic history." (Publisher's note)

REVIEW: *Am Lit* v85 no3 p604-6 S 2013 Hillary Chute

"9/11 and the Literature of Terror" and "After the Fall: American Literature Since 9/11." "Randall's introduction lays out compelling questions about how the event of 9/11 might be understood to place pressure on the endeavor of fiction. . . . Randall's account of the word-and-image problem plaguing novelists is fascinating, as is his assessment of the amplification of documentary after 9/11. . . . But if these authors lament what [Richard] Gray calls 'the seductive pieties' that structure much of American fiction, they also reveal what feels like their own pieties here (realism/domestic= bad; hybrid/global= good)."

REVIEW: *Choice* v49 no7 p1262 Mr 2012 E. T. Mason

RANDY, DUNCAN.ed. Icons of the American comic book. See Icons of the American comic book

RANEY, JAMES MATLACK. Jim Morgan and the Pirates of the Black Skull; [by] James Matlack Raney 342 p. 2013 Dreamfarer Press

1. Adventure stories 2. Mermaids—Fiction 3. Orphans—Fiction 4. Pirates—Fiction 5. Treasure troves—Fiction
ISBN 0985835931; 9780985835934

SUMMARY: In this book by James Matalack Raney, "young Jim Morgan returns to seek a powerful talisman and retribution against a malevolent pirate. . . . Count Cromier and his vicious son, Bartholomew," have "stolen a map that Jim's father gave him. The map shows the way to the Treasure of the Ocean, a trident that gives its wielder amazing power." (Kirkus Reviews)

REVIEW: *Kirkus Rev* v82 no3 p148 F 1 2014

"Jim Morgan and the Pirates of the Black Skull". "The book is a quick-paced pirate tale with elements that may seem derivative to some readers. However, most will enjoy the genre essentials, such as the aforementioned treasure map, mermaids—or, in this case, merpeople—and a kraken attack. The author prudently relegates the more overt pirate traits to the elderly MacGuffy, Jim's friend who has an eye patch and speaks in pirate-talk. . . . A YA adventure that will likely charm many readers, regardless of age."

REVIEW: *Kirkus Rev* v82 no1 p357 Ja 1 2014

REVIEW: *Publ Wkly* v261 no7 p74 F 17 2014

RANKIN, ALISHA. Panaceia's daughters; noblewomen as healers in early modern Germany; [by] Alisha Rankin xiv, 298 p. 2013 University of Chicago Press

1. Historical literature 2. Medicine—Germany—History—16th century 3. Pharmacy—Germany—History—16th century 4. Women—Germany—History—16th century 5. Women healers—Germany—History—16th century
ISBN 0226925382 (cloth : alkaline paper); 9780226925387 (cloth : alkaline paper)
LC 2012-021911

SUMMARY: This book, by Alisha Rankin, "provides the first book-length study of noblewomen's healing activities in early modern Europe. Rankin demonstrates that numerous German noblewomen were deeply involved in making medicines and recommending them to patients, and many gained widespread fame for their remedies. Turning a common historical argument on its head, Rankin maintains that noblewomen's pharmacy came to prominence not in spite of their gender but because of it." (Publisher's note)

REVIEW: *Choice* v51 no1 p115-6 S 2013 S. W. Moss

"Panaceia's Daughters: Noblewomen As Healers in Early Modern Germany." "The medical practitioners of 16th-century German principalities included a loose network of literate noblewomen. In this impeccably researched history, [author Alisha] Rankin . . . portrays the carefully managed herb gardens, distilleries, libraries, and apothecaries of these capable women, who were anything but dilettantes. . . . The medical practices of these noblewomen unfold in the context of the nascent Protestant Reformation, the duty of charity, the recognition of God as the supreme healer, and a growing interest in observational and experimental science among the upper classes. Rankin's extensive archival research brings to the fore a previously neglected category of healers."

RANKIN, IAN, 1960-. Saints of the shadow bible; [by] Ian Rankin 389 p. 2014 Little, Brown and Co.

1. Cold cases (Criminal investigation) 2. Criminal investigation 3. Detective & mystery stories 4. Police—Fiction 5. Traffic accidents—Fiction
ISBN 9780316224550 (hardcover)
LC 2013-955201

SUMMARY: John Rebus comes out of retirement in Edgar-winner [Ian] Rankin's . . .20th novel featuring the Edinburgh cop. . . . Malcolm Fox, the officer in charge of the Complaints department . . . leads an investigation into whether a fast and loose group of cops in the mid-1980s known as the Saints of the Shadow Bible might have tainted a murder trial back when Rebus was a young officer." (Publishers Weekly)

REVIEW: *Kirkus Rev* v82 no2 p276 Ja 15 2014

"Saints of the Shadow Bible". "When John Rebus left retirement to rejoin the Edinburgh police force, he had to take the reduced rank of detective sergeant. Siobhan Clarke, his former junior partner, is now a detective inspector and theoretically his boss in the investigation of the road accident of Jessica Traynor, a young art student. . . . Although Rebus . . . is the protagonist of this gritty procedural, you see the action through so many other eyes that the hard-living detective is less vivid a presence than in his earlier outings. But the most persistent cop in the shop will still do whatever it takes to crack a case."

REVIEW: *N Y Times Book Rev* p19 Ja 19 2014 MARILYN STASIO

RANSOM, CANDICE. Rebel McKenzie; [by] Candice Ransom 270 p. 2012 Disney Hyperion

1. Beauty contests—Fiction 2. Children's literature 3. Country life—Virginia—Fiction 4. Loss (Psychology)—Fiction 5. Nephews—Fiction 6. Trailer camps—Fiction
ISBN 1423145399; 9781423145394
LC 2011-032729

SUMMARY: In this novel by Candice Ransom "Rebel McKenzie wants to spend her summer attending . . . a camp where kids discover prehistoric bones, right alongside real paleontologists. But digs cost money, and Rebel is broker than four o'clock. When she finds out her annoying neighbor Bambi Lovering won five hundred dollars by playing a ukulele behind her head in a beauty contest, Rebel decides to win the Frog Level Volunteer Fire Department's beauty pageant." (Publisher's note)

REVIEW: *Booklist* v108 no19/20 p78 Je 1 2012 Kara Dean

REVIEW: *Kirkus Rev* v80 no9 p980 My 1 2012

"Rebel McKenzie." "Twelve-year-old Rebel McKenzie is aptly named. While the aspiring paleontologist dreams of unearthing ancient fossils, she must instead spend her summer watching her 7-year-old nephew, Rudy--who prefers hot dogs with his spaghetti, misses his absent father, and routinely saves a seat for God during lunch. . . . A beauty contest with a cash prize seems to be Rebel's golden opportunity to achieve her goal of getting out of town and into camp. [Candice] Ransom comically depicts Rebel's endeavors to prepare for the contest and dethrone local beauty queen/neighborhood nemesis Bambi. However, Ransom carefully balances the tale's humor with subtler scenes that convey Lacey Jane's poignant struggle to adjust to her mother's death and Rudy's fragile vulnerability."

REVIEW: *Publ Wkly* v259 no20 p69 My 14 2012

REVIEW: *SLJ* v58 no6 p134 Je 2012 Alison O'Reilly

RANSOME, JAMES E.il. Benny Goodman & Teddy Wilson. See Cline-Ransome, L.

RANSOME, JAMES.il. This is the rope. See This is the rope

RANSOME, JAMES E.il. Words set me free. See Cline-Ransome, L.

RAO, MADANMOHAN.ed. Global mobile. See Global mobile

RAO, MAHESH. The Smoke is Rising; [by] Mahesh Rao 288 p. 2014 Daunt Books

1. Humorous stories 2. India—Fiction 3. Indic fiction (English) 4. Modernization (Social science) 5. Mysore (India)
ISBN 1907970312; 9781907970313

SUMMARY: In this novel by Mahesh Rao, "The future is here. India has just sent its first spacecraft to the moon, and the placid city of Mysore is gearing up for its own global recognition with the construction of HeritageLand—Asia's largest theme park. From behind the formidable gates of Mahalakshmi Gardens to the shanty houses on the edge of town, the people of Mysore are abuzz as they watch their city prepare for a complete transformation." (Publisher's note)

REVIEW: *New Statesman* v143 no5205 p47 Ap 11 2014 Mahesh Rao

REVIEW: *TLS* no5791 p20 Mr 28 2014 PHILIP WOMACK

"The Smoke Is Rising." "In Mahesh Rao's debut novel, 'The Smoke is Rising,' it is not just the smoke from the city's fearsome riots that obfuscates and blots. The main narrative begins and ends at dusk, first seen 'stealing' into the city of Mysore. . . . Everything and everybody in the novel is occluded. . . . Rao's omniscient narrator employs a journalistic accuracy. . . . While this style is successful for describing place, when delving into the emotional backgrounds of characters it can seem clunky. . . . What Rao does excellently is delineate the social layers of Mysore. . . . The medieval and the modem India are depicted here as co-existing, and Rao has succeeded in capturing this with delicacy and insight."

RAPPAPORT, DOREEN, 1939-. To dare mighty things. See To dare mighty things

RAPPOLE, JOHN H. The avian migrant; the biology of bird migration; [by] John H. Rappole 464 p. 2013 Columbia University Press

1. Biological literature 2. Bird evolution 3. Bird navigation 4. Birds—Migration 5. Migratory birds
ISBN 9780231146784 (cloth : alk. paper)
LC 2012-036925

SUMMARY: This book on avian migration by John H. Rappole "clarifies key ecological, biological, physiological, navigational, and evolutionary concerns. He begins with the very first migrants, who traded a home environment of greater stability for one of greater seasonality, and uses the structure of the annual cycle to examine the difference between migratory birds and their resident counterparts." (Publisher's note)

REVIEW: *Choice* v51 no5 p867 Ja 2014 C. A. Fassbinder-Orth

REVIEW: *Science* v341 no6150 p1065-6 S 6 2013 Franz Bairlein

"The Avian Migrant: The Biology of Bird Migration." "It is not important that [John H.] Rappole's treatments of various aspects of migratory birds (such as orientation and navigation, physiology, stopover ecology, tracking methodology, climate change, and conservation) are rather cursory and fail to reflect the latest available research. The author's way of thinking, critically addressing existing hypotheses and theories, and formulating alternative hypotheses (often rather conflicting and provocative) makes the book readable, inspiring, and stimulating if challenging as well. . . . I like that the book devotes so much attention to population ecology and population regulation."

RASCHKA, CHRIS. Charlie Parker played be bop; [by] Chris Raschka 1992 Orchard Bks.

1. Children's literature—Works—Preschool through grade two 2. Composers 3. Jazz music—Juvenile literature 4. Jazz musicians 5. Jazz musicians—United States—Biography—Juvenile literature 6. Picture books for children 7. Saxophonists
ISBN 0-531-05999-5; 0-531-08599-6 lib bdg
LC 91-3-8420

SUMMARY: In this picture book biography of musician Charlie Parker, author Chris Raschka presents a "celebration of a man and a musical form. . . . 'Charlie Parker played be bop. Charlie Parker played saxophone. The music sounded like be bop. Never leave your cat alone.' And a fine, flat-eared feline he is, that cat--waiting for Charlie with a baleful glance for the reader." (Booklist)

REVIEW: *Horn Book Magazine* v89 no5 p11-8 S/O 2013 Barbara Bader

"Ruth Law Thrills a Nation," "Charlie Parker Played Be Bop," and "Roberto Clemente: Pride of the Pittsburgh Pirates." "[Don] Brown is as much a writer as an artist. A stylist, in both cases, and a wit. . . . Chris Raschka's 'Charlie Parker Played Be Bop' . . . is less a biography than an improvisation on a personality--all juicy, exuberant cartooning, bouncy scribbles, and sweeps of color . . . with a bop-along text. For kids, a rousing performance. . . . Lives of sports heroes would stand out among picture book biographies. Jonah Winter, a professed baseball nut and a wordsmith, a poet, had something to do with this. . . . In 'Roberto Clemente' . . . the vehicle is a confiding near-verse."

RASCHKA, CHRIS.il. When lions roar. See Harris, R. H.

RASH, ANDY.il. Game over, Pete Watson. See Schreiber, J.

RASH, ANDY.il. Sea Monster and the bossy fish. See Messner, K.

RASMUSSEN, MIKKEL B. The moment of clarity. See Madsbjerg, C.

RASSLER, DON. Fountainhead of jihad. See Brown, V.

RATH, ROBERT.il. Until Daddy comes home. See Metivier, G.

RATUSZNIAK, ANNETTE.ed. Elisabeth Frink catalogue raisonne of sculpture, 1947-93. See Elisabeth Frink catalogue raisonne of sculpture, 1947-93

RAU, DANA MEACHEN, 1971-. Discovering new planets. See Jemison, M.

RAU, PETRA. Our Nazis; representations of fascism in contemporary literature and film; [by] Petra Rau vii, 214 p. 2013 Edinburgh University Press

1. National socialism in art 2. National socialism in literature 3. National socialism in motion pictures 4. Nazis in motion pictures 5. Social science literature
ISBN 0748668640 (hbk.); 9780748668649 (hbk.)
LC 2013-409703

SUMMARY: In this book, Petra Rau "argues that Nazism survives partly because historians, scholars, and critics choose to probe it--looking through surviving sources in order to write judicious histories of complex Nazi and Fascist cultures. . . . In so doing, Rau observes, she and her generation support a thirst for the study of Nazism and also preserve Nazi culture in their published work, thus feeding proto-Nazi advocates and activists bent on reviving Nazism." (Choice: Current Reviews for Academic Libreries)

REVIEW: *Choice* v51 no5 p817 Ja 2014 T. Cripps

"Our Nazis: Representations of Fascism in Contemporary Literature and Film." "This brief, well-documented account of survival of Nazi and Fascist imagery and ideas in the literary, visual, rhetorical, and graphic imagery of world cultures, primarily the English speaking world, is startling in its imaginative sweep. . . . Using the trope of genetic theory, [Petra] Rau . . . rises above mere reportage in sketching a Nazi culture that lives on. . . . Rau is less persuasive in arguing that some who suffered defeat might embrace Nazism anew as a means of national redemption or revenge."

RAUSING, SIGRID. Everything Is Wonderful; Memories of a Collective Farm in Estonia; [by] Sigrid Rausing 304 p. 2014 Pgw

1. Collective farms 2. Estonia—History 3. Estonia—Social conditions 4. Memoirs 5. Postcommunist societies
ISBN 0802122175; 9780802122179

SUMMARY: This book by Sigrid Rausing offers a "look at the devastations of communism in Estonia" through the author's memories of "her fieldwork on the Noarootsi peninsula in 1993-1994. . . . She unearths . . . history of this remote area, annexed and depleted by Russia, then Germany, then the Soviet Union; all the while, she taught ninth grade in the local school, tramped through the Baltic forests and interviewed people on the farms." (Kirkus Reviews)

REVIEW: *Economist* v411 no8886 p82 My 10 2014

REVIEW: *Kirkus Rev* v82 no1 p68 Ja 1 2014

"Everything is Wonderful: Memories of a Collective Farm in Estonia". "An intimate look at the devastations of communism in Estonia. . . . A . . . sensuous, character-rich portrait of the denuded landscape, ruined economy, and erratic, alcoholic personalities she encountered as a dreamy, lonely observer and teacher. . . . She unearths fascinating history of this remote area, annexed and depleted by Russia, then Germany, then the Soviet Union. . . . A mellifluous portrait of a country slowly and painfully pulling itself into the European world."

REVIEW: *Publ Wkly* v260 no45 p57 N 11 2013

REVIEW: *TLS* no5797 p5 My 9 2014 PAUL BINDING

"Everything Is Wonderful: Memories of a Collective Farm in Estonia." "This memoir is a personal, even emotional revisiting of the material of her monograph. She herself acts as the prism through which readers can view places, routines, mores, the many physical and psychological indignities brought about by acute economic depression, and—most importantly—individuals who embody the questions and tensions of this period while stubbornly remaining themselves. She vividly conveys the terminal decline of the collective farm. . . . Subtly and convincingly Sigrid manages to convey, in Noarootsi and beyond, a sense, through all the disappointments, instabilities and poverty, of a people's continuous journey towards a firmer, more inclusive society."

RAVA, ANTONIO. Conserving contemporary art. See Chiantore, O.

RAVIPINTO, DANIEL. The Fall of Ventaris. See McGarry, N.

RAVITCH, DIANE, 1938-. Reign of Error; the hoax of the privatization movement and the danger to America's public schools; [by] Diane Ravitch 352 p. 2013 Random House Inc

1. EDUCATION—Aims & Objectives 2. Education and state—United States 3. Educational literature 4. Privatization in education—United States 5. SOCIAL SCIENCE—Children's Studies 6. School choice—United States

ISBN 0385350880; 9780345806352 (paperback); 9780385350884 (hardback); 9780385350891 (ebook)
LC 2013-015275

SUMMARY: In this book, author Diane Ravitch "argues that the crisis in American education is not a crisis of academic achievement but a concerted effort to destroy public schools in this country. She makes clear that, contrary to the claims being made, public school test scores and graduation rates are the highest they've ever been, and dropout rates are at their lowest point." (Publisher's note)

REVIEW: *America* v210 no14 p37-8 Ap 21 2014 CHARLES M. A. CLARK

REVIEW: *Atlantic* v312 no2 p38-41 S 2013 SARA MOSLE

"Reign of Error: The Hoax of the Privatization Movement and the Danger to America's Public Schools." "The survival of the school-reform movement, as it's known to champions and detractors alike, is no longer assured. . . . If one person can be credited--or blamed--for the reform movement's sudden vulnerability, it's a fiercely articulate historian, now in her 70s, named Diane Ravitch. . . . Ravitch the counterrevolutionary may be right that the reformers' cause is primed for derailment. But Ravitch the historian once foretold what typically follows a contentious drive for school improvement: 'It was usually replaced,' she observed in 2003, 'by a movement called "back to basics," or "essentialism,"' which didn't herald new progress but rather 'a backlash against failed fads.' Ravitch herself is the 'essentialist' now."

REVIEW: *Booklist* v110 no2 p8 S 15 2013 Vanessa Bush

"Reign of Error: The Hoax of the Privatization Movement and the Danger to America's Public Schools." "A well-researched and insightful critique of current efforts at public education reform. Putting the current 'privatization movement' in the broader historical context of public school reform, [Diane] Ravitch argues that there never was an ideal time when social inequities didn't fall hardest on poor and minority students. . . . Ravitch advocates for more rigorous preschools, smaller class sizes, better teacher training, and comprehensive social services, among other initiatives. In this passionate plea to protect the nation's public schools from privatization."

REVIEW: *Choice* v51 no10 p1861 Je 2014 G. Moreno

REVIEW: *Commonweal* v140 no18 p23-8 N 15 2013 Jackson Lears

REVIEW: *Educ Stud* v50 no1 p91-5 Ja/F 2014 Brigitte C. Scott

"Reign of Error: The Hoax of the Privatization Movement and the Danger to America's Public Schools". "[Diane] Ravitch makes a welcome contribution to the task of addressing damaging misconceptions about the current state of public education. She is an articulate bricoleur of history, media, qualitative and quantitative research, popular culture, politics, and policy. . . . Ravitch's solutions . . . provide viable action plans . . . . What I appreciate even more is that Ravitch does not leave out desegregation, poverty reduction, and equity as solutions for an education system at risk. . . . Considering its status as a trade book, Ravitch's 'Reign of Error' is an incredible resource for the general public."

REVIEW: *Kirkus Rev* v81 no15 p263 Ag 1 2013

REVIEW: *Libr J* v138 no6 p59 Ap 1 2013 Barbara Hoffert

REVIEW: *N Y Rev Books* v60 no15 p4-8 O 10 2013 Andrew Delbanco

"Reign of Error: The Hoax of the Privatization Movement and the Danger to America's Public Schools" and "Radical: Fighting to Put Students First." "If [Diane] Ravitch disputes prevailing assumptions, she does not gloss over the fact that school performance by the large minority of American children who grow up poor or in segregated neighborhoods is disproportionately weak. . . . The title of [Michelle] Rhee's new book . . . suggests, accurately, that her main subject is herself. . . . She tells the rest of her story as an alternating series of victories on behalf of children grateful for her gifts and setbacks at the hands of adults threatened by her smarts. . . . To read Rhee and Ravitch in sequence is like hearing a too-good-to-be-true sales pitch followed by the report of an auditor who discloses mistakes and outright falsehoods in the accounts of the firm that's trying to make the sale."

REVIEW: *N Y Times Book Rev* p21 S 29 2013 Diane Ravitch

"Reign of Error: The Hoax of the Privatization Movement and the Danger to America's Public School System." "In her new book . . . [Diane Ravitch] arrows in more directly, and polemically, on the privatization movement, which she calls a 'hoax' and a 'danger' that has fed on the myth that schools are failing. . . . Those . . . who have grown increasingly alarmed at seeing public education bartered off piece by piece, and seeing schools and teachers thrown into a state of siege, will be grateful for this cri de coeur--a fearless book, a manifesto and a call to battle."

REVIEW: *Nation* v298 no7 p34-7 F 17 2014 JOSEPH FEATHERSTONE

REVIEW: *Publ Wkly* v260 no29 p59 Jl 22 2013

RAWLE, TIM.il. The Chapel of Trinity College Oxford. See Kemp, M.

RAY, AIMEE. Aimée Ray's sweet & simple jewelry. See Aimée Ray's sweet & simple jewelry

RAY, MICHAEL.ed. Gaming. See Gaming

READ, SOPHIE. Eucharist and the poetic imagination in early modern England; [by] Sophie Read xi, 225 p. 2013 Cambridge University Press

1. English poetry—Early modern, 1500-1700—History and criticism 2. Literature—History & criticism 3. Lord's Supper in literature 4. Religion in literature 5. Transubstantiation in literature

ISBN 9781107032736 (alk. paper)

LC 2012-046417

SUMMARY: "This study of six canonical early modern lyric poets traces the literary afterlife of what was one of the greatest doctrinal shifts in English history. [Author] Sophie Read argues that the move from a literal to a figurative understanding of the phrase 'this is my body' exerted a powerful imaginative pull on successive generations." (Publisher's note)

REVIEW: *TLS* no5794 p11 Ap 18 2014 HELEN HACKETT

"Shakespeare's Unreformed Fictions" and "Eucharist and the Poetic Imagination in Early Modern England." "These new books by Gillian Woods and Sophie Read are excellent examples, and also exemplify what has been called the 'new formalism' in Renaissance studies in their use of intricate close readings and their emphasis on aesthetic questions. Woods makes clear at the outset that 'Shakespeare's Unreformed Fictions' is not about Shakespeare's personal religious position, but is unashamedly—and, as it proves, very successfully—a work of literary criticism. . . . Sophie Read has undertaken a similar project to analyse the literary effects of changing religious thinking. . . . Each chapter offers many insights."

THE REAL BOY; 288 p. 2013 Harpercollins Childrens Books

1. Boys—Fiction 2. Fairy tales 3. Magic—Juvenile fiction 4. Orphans—Fiction 5. Pinocchio (Fictitious character) 6. Social interaction in children

ISBN 0062015079 (hardcover); 9780062015075 (hardcover)

LC 2013-021861

SUMMARY: In this book, "an isolated, insecure orphan living in magical Aletheia becomes a 'real boy' when his ordered world crumbles and he must rely on himself." Oscar works for the magician Caleb. "When urgent business takes Caleb away, his apprentice is murdered, and Oscar must run Caleb's shop. Lacking social skills, Oscar longs to fold 'up, like an envelope,' but he manages the shop with help from a kindhearted girl who befriends him." More things go wrong, and Oscar must help. (Kirkus Reviews)

REVIEW: *Booklist* v110 no3 p96 O 1 2013 Sarah Hunter

REVIEW: *Bull Cent Child Books* v67 no3 p184 N 2013 K. Q. G.

"The Real Boy." "As she did with 'Breadcrumbs' . . . [author Anne] Ursu constructs an elegantly sophisticated but age-appropriate tale upon the bones of a well-known story, in this case, Pinocchio, though the hint in the tide is the only allusion until the final reel. An underdog boy saving the people who ridicule him is a familiar premise, but here it unfolds organically, echoing the fairy-tale tradition of mixing darkly sinister themes with moments of true heroism and bravery. Although most adult readers will recognize Oscar as on the spectrum, his guilelessness and bewilderment at social customs will likely ring true with plenty of children who have found themselves perplexed by the grownups' conversations."

REVIEW: *Horn Book Magazine* v89 no5 p114-5 S/O 2013 MARTHA V. PARRAVANO

"The Real Boy." "Using Pinocchio as her point of departure (with a little 'Red Riding Hood' thrown in for good measure), [Anne] Ursu skillfully implies a connection between Oscar and the little wooden puppet boy . . . which turns out to be a clever piece of misdirection. But not quite, because in fact Oscar does become more of a 'real boy' in the end. It's all highly rewarding and involving, with a tight plot, resonant themes, a gripping adventure, a clearly limned fantasy landscape, and a sympathetic main character."

REVIEW: *Kirkus Rev* v81 no14 p28 Jl 15 2013

REVIEW: *Kirkus Rev* p55 2013 Guide 20to BookExpo America

REVIEW: *N Y Times Book Rev* p33 N 10 2013 CHELSEY PHILPOT

"The Real Boy." "A lovely and sophisticated new middle-grade fantasy that asks readers to wrap their heads around abstractions and accept a lack of absolutes. There is no one bad guy, people are simultaneously greedy and miraculous, and even a monster deserves understanding. . . . 'The Real Boy' contains delicate allusions to 'The Adventures of Pinnochio' . . . and is rich with beautiful, heady notions that demand to be lingered over. . . . Readers will need to go slowly, both to savor [Anne] Ursu's descriptions and to avoid confusion."

REVIEW: *Publ Wkly* v260 no37 p55-6 S 16 2013

REARDON, CAROL. A field guide to Gettysburg; experiencing the battlefield through its history, places, and people; [by] Carol Reardon 384 p. 2013 University of North Carolina Press

1. Gettysburg (Pa.)—History 2. Gettysburg, Battle of, Gettysburg, Pa., 1863 3. Guidebooks 4. Historic sites—United States—Guidebooks
ISBN 9780807835258 (pbk : alk. paper)
LC 2013-002824

SUMMARY: This guide to Gettysburg "provide[s] 35 stops, allowing the reader to follow along on a self-guided tour. Sections for each stop contain several elements, including 'Orientation'; 'What Happened Here?'; 'Who Fought Here?'; 'Who Commanded Here?'; 'Who Fell Here?'; 'Who Lived Here?'; and 'What Did They Say About It Later?' The volume . . . discusses the consequences of victory and defeat, as well as the direct impact of the battle on the town of Gettysburg itself." (Library Journal)

REVIEW: *Booklist* v110 no2 p23 S 15 2013

"World's Ultimate Cycling Races," "A Field Guide to Gettysburg: Experiencing the Battlefield Through Its History, Places, and People," and "Antarctic Peninsula: A Visitor's Guide." "These exciting, beautifully presented guides present pertinent--and inspirational--information on a wealth of places to test one's mettle on foot or bike. . . . An attractive presentation--beautiful color photos and handsomely laid-out text--partners with a wealth of information on individuals, troop movements, and skirmishes, amounting to an indispensable guide to a major event in American history. . . . This guide will inform you of the geographical and geological conditions, indigenous flora and fauna, international governance, and history of place-names and explorations that will be necessary background for a worthwhile trip."

REVIEW: *Choice* v51 no2 p241 O 2013 R. J. Havlik

REVIEW: *Libr J* v138 no9 p92 My 15 2013 Matthew Wayman

REARICK, CHARLES. The French in love and war; popular culture in the era of the World Wars; [by] Charles Rearick 321 p. 1997 Yale University Press

1. French national characteristics 2. Historical literature 3. Popular culture—France 4. Popular culture—France—History—20th century
ISBN 0300064330
LC 96-5-0287

SUMMARY: In this book, Charles Rearick argues that "the myths and symbols of popular culture fostered a common sense of French national identity [and] . . . helped people cope and survive during the world wars. . . . He draws examples from photos, songs, placards, films, music-hall repertoires, and musical stars. During World War I, for example, patriotism was extolled through cultural representations of le poilu, the tough French soldier." (Library Journal)Rearick argues that "the myths and symbols of popular culture fostered a common sense of French national identity {and} . . . helped people cope and survive during the world wars. . . . He draws examples from photos, songs, placards, films, music-hall repertoires, and musical stars. During World War I, for example, patriotism was extolled through cultural representations of le poilu, the tough French soldier, while in the postwar years commercial culture tried to steer attention away from political causes." (Libr J) Bibliography. Index.

REVIEW: *Choice* v50 no7 p1185-94 Mr 2013 Felicia Hardison Londré

"A Companion to World War I," "European Culture in the Great War: The Arts, Entertainment, and Propaganda 1914-1918," and "The French in Love and War: Popular Culture in the Era of the World Wars." "An important volume in the 'Blackwell Companions to World History' series, 'A Companion to World War I,' edited by John Horne, includes essays on the social culture of war and on various arts, although none of the essays focuses specifically on theater. . . . The 'Companion' also offers excellent bibliographic sections on 'gender, society, culture' and on specific nations. . . . Many histories of World War I incorporate the arts. 'European Culture in the Great War: The Arts, Entertainment, and Propaganda, 1914-1918,' edited by Aviel Roshwald and Richard Stites, comprises thirteen contributed essays in which theater figures prominently. Each essay focuses on a different country, including eastern European cultures in addition to Russia, France, Belgium, and Britain. . . . France's parallel reshaping of its cultural identity during and after the Great War--with emphasis on representations of ordinary people--is the subject of Charles Rearick's 'The French in Love and War: Popular Culture in the Era of the World Wars.'"

REASON AND IMAGINATION; the selected correspondence of Learned Hand 1897-1961; xxxi, 435 p. 2013 Oxford University Press

1. Judges—United States—Correspondence 2. Law—United States—History 3. Letters 4. Segregation—United States
ISBN 9780199899104 (hbk. : alk. paper)
LC 2012-013714

SUMMARY: This book, edited by Constance Jordan, presents a "sampling of the correspondence between [judge Learned] Hand and" several "intellectual and legal giants, including Justice Oliver Wendell Holmes, Theodore Roosevelt, Walter Lippmann, Felix Frankfurter, Bernard Berenson, and many other prominent political and philosophical thinkers. The letters . . . cover almost half a century, often taking the form of brief essays on current events." (Publisher's note)

REVIEW: *N Y Rev Books* v60 no19 p38-40 D 5 2013 Lincoln Caplan

"Reason and Imagination: The Selected Correspondence of Learned Hand 1897-1961." "[Constance Jordan authored a] well-informed introduction . . . she is Hand's granddaughter and edited this sympathetic, dense, and finely annotated array of letters by and to him. . . . 'Reason and Imagination' is meant as a companion to Learned Hand: The Man and the Judge. . . . But Jordan's book is also intended as an antidote to [Gerald] Gunther's. Jordan does not say so directly, but to mend Hand's reputation, she seems to aim in particular at correcting what she considers a major misimpression left by Gunther's book: that . . . judicial restraint . . . took him outside the legal mainstream when it came to Brown v. Board of Education . . . and tarnished what he stood for as a judge."

RECKHOW, SARAH. Follow the money; how foundation dollars change public school politics; [by] Sarah Reckhow 221 p. 2013 Oxford University Press

1. Privatization in education—United States 2. Public schools—United States—Finance
ISBN 0199937737; 9780199937738
LC 2012-018098

SUMMARY: In this book, Sarah Reckhow "shows where and how foundation investment in education is occurring and provides a penetrating analysis of the effects of these investments in the two largest urban districts in the United States: New York City and Los Angeles. . . . With vast wealth and a political agenda, these foundations have helped to reshape the reform landscape in urban education." (Publisher's note)

REVIEW: *Choice* v51 no1 p166 S 2013 A. J. Nownes

"Follow the Money: How Foundation Dollars Change Public School Politics." [Author Sarah] Reckhow . . . documents how philanthropy has defined the raging and ongoing debate over education reform in the US. First, she shows readers the people behind the money--that is, the people and institutions (e.g., Bill and Melinda Gates Foundation and the Broad Foundation) who have spent millions on concocting education reform proposals and getting governments to adopt them. Next, she examines the effects of all this money. . . . Reckhow offers important conclusions about the role of philanthropy in public policy, the future of education reform, the political realities that determine the fate of reform proposals, and the issues raised by private money affecting how public money is spent."

RECONCEPTUALIZING THE LITERACIES IN ADOLESCENT'S LIVES; bridging the everyday, academic divide; p. cm. 2011 Routledge

1. Critical pedagogy—United States 2. Educational literature 3. Language arts (Secondary)—Social aspects—United States 4. Literacy—Social aspects—United States 5. Teenagers—Books & reading

ISBN 9780203817285; 9780415892919 (alk. paper); 9780415892926 (alk. paper)

LC 2011-026130

SUMMARY: In the third edition of their book, Donna E. Alvermann and Kathleen A. Hinchman "challenge today's educational culture by interrogating the ways that teens' identities are multiple, fluid, and amalgamated into their lives at school. . . . Chapters are written by various . . . researchers of adolescent literacy (e.g.. Bob Fecho, Kelly Wissman, and Margaret Hagood) on the myriad ways teens consume and construct texts in and out of school." (Choice)

REVIEW: *Choice* v49 no12 p2342-3 Ag 2012 M. B. Hopkins

"Reconceptualizing the Literacies in Adolescents' Lives: Bridging the Everyday/Academic Divide." "In this third edition of their time-honored text, [Donna E.] Alvermann . . . and [Kathleen A.] Hinchman . . . challenge today's educational culture by interrogating the ways that teens' identities are multiple, fluid, and amalgamated into their lives at school--understandings necessary for any teacher looking to reach adolescent learners. . . . The chapters written by teachers are a wonderful model of the reflective stance practitioners should assume in respect to educational research, practice, and the profession as a whole."

RECORD, ADAM.il. A Ghost in the house. See Paquette, Ammi-Joan

RECOVERING DISABILITY IN EARLY MODERN ENGLAND; 224 p. 2013 Ohio State University Press

1. Disability studies 2. England—Civilization—1066-1485 3. English literature—Early modern, 1500-1700—History and criticism 4. Historical literature 5. People with disabilities in literature

ISBN 9780814212158 (cloth : alk. paper); 9780814293164 (cd)

LC 2012-048536

SUMMARY: This book examines "disability and disabled selves in sixteenth- and seventeenth-century England. . . . The ten essays in this collection range across genre, scope, and time, including examinations of real-life court dwarfs and dwarf narrators in Edmund Spenser's poetry; disability in Aphra Behn's assessment of gender and femininity; disability humor, Renaissance jest books, and cultural ideas about difference; [and] madness in revenge tragedies." (Publisher's note)

REVIEW: *Choice* v51 no4 p639-40 D 2013 K. L. Cole

"Recovering Disability in Early Modern England." "This is a significant contribution to both early modern studies and disability studies. [Allison P.] Hobgood . . . and [David Houston] Wood . . . not only fill a lacuna in early modern studies with respect to disability but also develop a durable collection of essays, in terms of both excellent scholarship and demonstrating bow to attend to and integrate the theoretical perspective of disability. . . . . this collection will appeal to a wide audience. . . . Highly recommended."

RED PHONE BOX; A Darkly Magical Story Cycle; 368 p. 2013 Ghostwoods Books

1. Magic—Fiction 2. Murder—Fiction 3. Short story writing 4. Speculative fiction 5. Telephone booths

ISBN 0957627114 (hbk.); 9780957627116 (hbk.)

SUMMARY: This book presents "a genre-bending collection of horror-fantasy short stories set in London, centering on a red phone booth, gateway to the netherworld. Suffering from insomnia due to her recently ended love affair, Amber sets off on a midnight stroll through London, imagining that her entire body is glowing. She returns to her apartment to find a new boyfriend who can't comprehend why she doesn't know him. . . . As the anthology progresses, characters and plotlines interweave." (Kirkus Reviews)

REVIEW: *Kirkus Rev* v81 no22 p294 N 15 2013

REVIEW: *Kirkus Rev* v82 no1 p58 Ja 1 2014

"Red Phone Box: A Darkly Magical Story Cycle". " A genre-bending collection of horror-fantasy short stories set in London, centering on a red phone booth, gateway to the netherworld. . . . Particularly heart-rending are Francesca Burgon's stories. . . . he compelling Gloria Vandenbussche, despite her despair at being her father's gofer, is transcendent in the stories in which she appears. . . . Occasionally disjointed due to the abundance of plotlines, characters and settings, the collection comprises 58 short stories by 29 different authors. Nonetheless, the anthology's style works overall, a testament to skillful editing. A few of the storylines remain unresolved, leaving the door open for the promised Book 2."

RED SPECTRES; Russian Gothic tales from the twentieth century; 224 p. 2013 Penguin Group USA

1. Anthologies 2. Ghosts in literature 3. Gothic fiction (Literary genre) 4. Mental illness in literature 5. Russian literature—Translations into English

ISBN 1468303481; 9781468303483

SUMMARY: This collection of 20th century Russian gothic fiction "includes eleven vintage tales by seven writers of the period: Valery Bryusov, Mikhail Bulgakov, Aleksandr Grin and Sigizmund Krzhizhanovsky;. . . Aleksandr Chayanov, . . . and the emigres Georgy Peskov and Pavel Perov. Through the traditional gothic repertoire of ghosts, insanity, obsession, retribution and terror, Red Spectres conveys the turbulence and dissonance of life in Russia in these years." (Publisher's note)

REVIEW: *Kirkus Rev* v81 no7 p213 Ap 1 2013

REVIEW: *London Rev Books* v35 no17 p33-4 S 12 2013 Greg Afinogenov

REVIEW: *TLS* no5761 p9 Ag 30 2013 ELIOT BORENSTEIN

"Stalin's Ghosts: Gothic Themes in Early Soviet Literature" and "Red Spectres: Russian 20th-century Gothic Fantastic Tales'. "To make her case, [Muireann] Maguire is obliged to revisit familiar debates about the definition of the Gothic. As she argues, quite persuasively, the Gothic is all about the stubborn return of the past. . . . Given the lively insights of 'Stalin's Ghosts,' one would expect 'Red Spectres: Russian 20th-century Gothic-fantastic tales,' edited and translated by Maguire, to be even more entertaining. After, all, it is a collection of fiction rather than an academic study. Maguire is a fine translator who has rendered these dozen or so neo-Gothic tales in clear and elegant English that is neither too exotic nor unduly idiomatic. Footnotes are kept to a minimum, and undereducated Russian characters do not speak Cockney. But Maguire is at the mercy of her material here, far more than she is in 'Stalin's Ghosts'."

REDAK, RICHARD. Bugs rule! See Cranshaw, W.

REDZEPI, RENÉ. Rene Redzepi; A Work in Progress; [by] René Redzepi 648 p. 2013 Phaidon Inc Ltd

1. Cookbooks 2. Cooks 3. Diary (Literary form) 4. Restaurants 5. Scandinavian cooking

ISBN 0714866911; 9780714866918

SUMMARY: This "three-book collection" includes a personal journal written by [chef] René [Redzepi] himself over a full year in which he explores creativity, innovation, and the meaning and challenges of success; a . . .cookbook with 100 brand new recipes from Noma; and a pocket book of candid Instagram-style snapshots taken by the restaurant staff behind the scenes and at its annual MAD Food Symposium." (Publisher's note)

REVIEW: *Economist* v409 no8866 p90-1 D 14 2013

"A Work in Progress: Journal, Recipes and Snapshots." "Affecting the same spartan elegance of the restaurant itself, it comes as three unadorned books in a cardboard box, with recipes, photographs,and, most interestingly, [René Redzepi's] journal from 2011. Written during the year after Noma became famous, in the spare moments between finishing service and falling asleep, this diary is the best portrait yet of the intellectual and emotional challenges of delivering one of the most creative menus in the business. . . . What emerges from Mr. Redzepi's chronicles is a portrait of thrift, environmental sensitivity and ingenuity."

REVIEW: *Publ Wkly* v260 no47 p48 N 18 2013

REECE, ERIK.ed. A Guy Davenport reader. See Davenport, G.

REECE, HENRY. The Army in Cromwellian England, 1649-1660; [by] Henry Reece xv, 267 p. 2013 Oxford University Press

ISBN 0198200633; 9780198200635

LC 2012-454642

SUMMARY: This book on the Army in Cromwellian England is "split into three parts. . . . The first section looks at the size of the army, its material needs, promotion structure, and political engagement. . . . The second part considers the impact of the military presence on society. . . The final section re-evaluates the army's role in the political events from Cromwell's death to the restoration of the Stuart monarchy, and explains why the army crumbled." (Publisher's note)

REVIEW: *Am Hist Rev* v119 no1 p248-9 F 2014 Mark Charles Fissel

"The Army in Cromwellian England, 1649-1660". "[Henry] Reece establishes at least four historically and historiographically significant points.. . . 'The Army in Cromwellian England 1649–1660' is an elegant synthesis of forty years' worth of historiography, securely anchored in primary sources. Reece's conclusions lead us to reconsider long-held orthodoxies, such as the beliefs that an 'un-English' autocracy characterized the Commonwealth and Protectorate, and that the return of the Stuarts was inevitable."

REVIEW: *Choice* v51 no5 p911 Ja 2014 C. L. Hamilton

REVIEW: *History* v99 no335 p324-6 Ap 2014 Anthony Fletcher

REED, AMY. Over you; [by] Amy Reed 299 p. 2013 Simon Pulse

1. Communal living—Fiction 2. Family problems—Fiction 3. Farm life—Nebraska—Fiction 4. Friendship—Fiction 5. Mothers and daughters—Fiction 6. Young adult fiction

ISBN 1442456965 (hardcover); 9781442456969 (hardcover)

LC 2012-023492

SUMMARY: In this book, 17-year-old friends Max and Sadie spend a summer on a communal farm. "Max welcomes the hippie residents (which include Sadie's absentee mother), yurts, and grueling farm work, but Sadie--volatile, self-absorbed, and always the center of attention--quickly grows bored and irate. After Sadie is quarantined with mono, Max has even more freedom to explore her own thoughts, interests, and desires--including a love/hate crush on a surly older boy that surprises even Max." (Publishers Weekly)

REVIEW: *Booklist* v109 no21 p73 Jl 1 2013 Bethany Fort

REVIEW: *Bull Cent Child Books* v67 no1 p48-9 S 2013 K. C.

"Over You." "Teen hipsters Max and Sadie have been inseparable friends for years, but their friendship has fallen into a pattern that Max has begun to find oppressive: Sadie goes wild and does reckless things, while Max stays in control and mops up the messes. . . . [Author Amy] Reed charts her character arc through a subtle shift: in Max's narrative voice from a direct internal address to Sadie to a more inward-focused monologue as Max leaves Sadie behind both physically and emotionally. . . . The novel is more artfully written than authentic and insightful, but readers may appreciate the coils of the emo labyrinth."

REVIEW: *Kirkus Rev* v81 no9 p101 My 1 2013

REVIEW: *Publ Wkly* v260 no18 p63 My 6 2013

REVIEW: *SLJ* v59 no7 p100 Jl 2013 Nicole Knott

REED, CHRISTOPHER ROBERT. The Depression comes to the South Side; protest and politics in the Black metropolis, 1930-1933; [by] Christopher Robert Reed xiii,

178 p. 2011 Indiana University Press

1. African Americans—Civil rights—Illinois—Chicago—History—20th century 2. African Americans—Illinois—Chicago—Politics and government—20th century 3. African Americans—Illinois—Chicago—Social conditions—20th century 4. African Americans—Political activity 5. Chicago (Ill.)—History 6. Depressions—1929 7. Depressions—1929—Social aspects—Illinois—Chicago 8. Historical literature 9. South Side (Chicago, Ill.)

ISBN 0253356520 (cloth : alk. paper); 9780253356529 (cloth : alk. paper)

LC 2011-011595

SUMMARY: "In this timely book, Christopher Robert Reed explores early Depression-era politics on Chicago's South Side. The economic crisis caused diverse responses from groups in the black community, distinguished by their political ideologies and stated goals. Some favored government intervention, others reform of social services. . . . Reed examines the complex interactions among these various groups as they . . . sought to find common ground to address . . . economic stresses." (Publisher's note)

REVIEW: *Am Hist Rev* v118 no4 p1194-5 O 2013 Clare Corbould

"The Depression Comes to the South Side: Protest and Politics in the Black Metropolis, 1930-1933." "Christopher Robert Reed continues in this brief book his quest to document the history of black Chicago. Drawing on some of his earlier and longer studies, Reed offers a summary of the impact of the Depression on Chicago's South Side in the few years prior to Franklin D. Roosevelt's 1932 election, and before the New Deal began to ease the suffering of the city's African American population. . . . Reed . . . maintains that the Communists failed to recognize that black residents' primary goal was to end racial oppression. In doing so he downplays the sophistication of those black South Siders who well understood that cultural and economic circumstances could not be separated."

REED, LARKIN. Amber House. See Moore, K.

REED, LARKIN. Neverwas. See Moore, K.

REED, MARK L. A bibliography of William Wordsworth, 1787-1930; [by] Mark L. Reed 1296 p. 2013 Cambridge University Press

1. Bibliography (Documentation) 2. English poetry—Bibliography 3. Personal bibliography 4. Poems—Collections 5. Publishers & publishing—History

ISBN 9781107026377

LC 2012-039596

SUMMARY: Written by Mark L. Reed, "These two volumes set out, for the first time, a comprehensive, detailed bibliographic description of every edition of Wordsworth's writings up to 1930. The great variety of forms in which readers encountered both authorized and unauthorized texts by Wordsworth is revealed, not only as produced during his lifetime but also during the years of his largest sales, popularity and influence, the late nineteenth and early twentieth centuries." (Publisher's note)

REVIEW: *TLS* no5775 p8-9 D 6 2013 NICHOLAS ROE

"A Bibliography of William Wordsworth 1787-1930." "In two volumes and more than 1,200 pages, [author Mark L.] Reed sets out in meticulous bibliographic detail first printings of [poem William] Wordsworth's finished formal writings; editions of unfinished works and drafts; and posthumous printings of collective and selective volumes. . . . Reed's bibliography offers an overview of thc poct's entire career and its posthumous aftermath. . . . Reed's bibliography represents the remarkable achievement of a lifetime, and, inevitably, as Reed knows all too well, his poet will demand the last word."

REED, PHILIP.ed. Letter From a Life. See Letter From a Life

REED, S. ALEXANDER. Assimilate; a critical history of industrial music; [by] S. Alexander Reed xiv, 361 p. 2013 Oxford University Press

1. Denio, Amy 2. Industrial music—History and criticism 3. Kraftwerk (Performer) 4. Music literature 5. Smegma (Performer)

ISBN 9780199832583 (hardcover : alk. paper); 9780199832606 (pbk. : alk. paper)

LC 2012-042281

SUMMARY: This history of industrial music by S. Alexander Reed "starts with precursors like William S. Burroughs's tape experiments and Kraftwerk's recordings, continues through bands featured on the soundtrack of The Doom Generation (1995)--with the minor omission of The Wolfgang Press--and ends with currently active established bands, music collectives, and composers--e.g. Chrysalide, Smegma, and Amy Denio." (Choice: Current Reviews for Academic Libraries)

REVIEW: *Choice* v51 no5 p844-5 Ja 2014 M. Goldsmith

"Assimilate: A Critical History of Industrial Music." "[S. Alexander] Reed's study of industrial music is impressive in scope. Readers will appreciate Reed's attention to the scenes of creation of industrial music, his explanation of its aesthetics, and his expressions of his own fandom and experiences listening to and attending various performances of industrial music. For the benefit of those who wish to dig into the music itself, this critical history--the first on this genre of music--includes lists of 'iconic' and 'arcane' songs and singles along with the performers and dates of release. Unfortunately, the analytical examples are presented in a small, difficult-to-read font, a problem that Oxford should remedy in subsequent editions. Some musical background will be a benefit."

REED, TUCKER. Neverwas. See Moore, K.

REEKLES, BETH. The Kissing Booth; [by] Beth Reekles 2013 Paw Prints

1. High school students—Fiction 2. Jealousy 3. Kissing 4. Love stories 5. Secrecy—Fiction

ISBN 1480614769; 9781480614765

SUMMARY: In this book, "shortly after Elle and Lee plan a student-council-sponsored kissing booth for an upcoming school fair, Elle's romantic life takes an upswing when hottie Noah (Lee's older brother) becomes interested in Elle. Their rocky relationship is fraught with obstacles, including Noah's violent temper and parental disapproval." (Booklist)

REVIEW: *Booklist* v110 no2 p80 S 15 2013 Courtney Jones

"The Kissing Booth." "[Cynthia] Holloway's engaged, no-nonsense performance anchors Elle's whirlwind romance, posing the heroine as a benevolent, friendly, popular girl. Her male voices vary mostly by tonal register--older, hunkier Noah is read in deeper tones than Lee. And the best part of her reading is that she transforms the British author's English turns of phrase into something that resonates with American teens. For instance. Elle is warned not to 'strip off' while at a party, and although the phrase really means 'strip down,' it seems more comprehensible through Holloway's American accent. Seventeen-year-old Reekles' debut novel, a frilly, fun delight, is perfect for audio."

REVIEW: *Booklist* v109 no19/20 p91 Je 1 2013 Courtney Jones

REVIEW: *Kirkus Rev* v81 no10 p107 My 15 2013

REVIEW: *SLJ* v59 no7 p100 Jl 2013 Jennifer Furuyama

REVIEW: *SLJ* v59 no10 p1 O 2013 Betsy Davison

REVIEW: *Voice of Youth Advocates* v36 no3 p67 Ag 2013 Amy Wykoff

REES, EMMA L. E. The vagina; a literary and cultural history; [by] Emma L. E. Rees 352 p. 2013 Bloomsbury Academic

1. Feminist literature 2. Vagina—In art 3. Vagina in literature 4. Vagina in popular culture 5. Women—Sexual behavior

ISBN 9781623568719 (hardcover : alk. paper)
LC 2012-050836

SUMMARY: In this book by Emma L. E. Rees, "analyses of representations of the vagina in art and culture couple with feminist politics. . . . Rees coins the phrases 'covert visibility' and "autonomous anatomy," and applies this perspective to four historical motifs. . . . Examples from literature, film, television, visual and performance art draw from the U.K. and U.S., a range of historical periods, highbrow, experimental, and pop culture alike." (Publishers Weekly)

REVIEW: *Booklist* v110 no8 p32 D 15 2013 Rebecca Hayes

REVIEW: *New Statesman* v142 no5172 p47 Ag 30 2013 Helen Lewis

REVIEW: *TLS* no5756 p32 Jl 26 2013 J. C.

"Two American Scenes," "Power to the People," and "Vagina: A Literary and Cultural History." "'Our Village' . . . is a 're-presentation' of an existing work, 'Our Village' by Sidney Brooks, Ms [Lydia] Davis's great-great-great-uncle, born in Harwich, MA, in 1837. . . . Brooks wrote in prose; Davis has intervened with line breaks. Together with her abridgements and the change of a word here and there, this is all she has done to create a companion to the original. . . . 'Our Village' appears in 'Two American Scenes'. . . . The browser leafing through 'Power to the People' . . . may expect to meet such genial old friends as Love, Peace, and Happiness. . . . But was there really such an eager interest in pubic hair? . . Among the season's most coveted prizes is the Kate Adie Award for the year's most unoriginal book title. . . . On the longlist is sure to be 'The Vagina: A Literary and Cultural History' by Emma L. E. Rees."

REES, JONATHAN. Refrigeration nation; a history of ice, appliances, and enterprise in America; [by] Jonathan Rees x, 236 p. 2014 The Johns Hopkins University Press

1. Cold storage industry—Economic aspects—United States—History 2. Cold storage industry—Social aspects—United States—History 3. Cold storage industry—United States—History 4. Historical literature 5. Refrigeration and refrigerating machinery—Economic aspects—United States—History 6. Refrigeration and refrigerating machinery—Social aspects—United States—History 7. Refrigeration and refrigerating machinery—United States—History

ISBN 1421411067 (hardcover : acid-free paper); 9781421411064 (hardcover : acid-free paper)
LC 2013-006073

SUMMARY: In this book, "Jonathan Rees explores the innovative methods and gadgets that Americans have invented to keep perishable food cold--from cutting river and lake ice and shipping it to consumers for use in their iceboxes to the development of electrically powered equipment that ushered in a new age of convenience and health." (Publisher's note)

REVIEW: *Choice* v51 no7 p1239 Mr 2014 S. A. Curtis

"Refrigeration Nation: A History of Ice, Appliances, and Enterprise in America." "While the book, part of the 'Studies in Industry and Society' series, focuses primarily on the US, the author also discusses Great Britain and Germany, covering the basic technology developments as well as the development of the cold storage and transport industries, and the marketing of cold-stored foodstuffs and refrigeration units for business and the home. Extensive endnotes provide references to primary resources. . . . Recommended."

REESE, LINDA WILLIAMS. Trail sisters; freedwomen in Indian Territory, 1850-1890; [by] Linda Williams Reese 186 p. 2013 Texas Tech University Press

1. African American women—Indian Territory—History—19th century 2. African Americans—Relations with Indians 3. Ex-slaves of Indian tribes—Indian Territory—History 4. Historical literature 5. Indians of North America—Mixed descent 6. Slavery—Oklahoma—History

ISBN 9780896728103 (hardcover : alk. paper)
LC 2013-011211

SUMMARY: In this book, Linda Williams Reese "covers relationships forged between freed African American women and their Indian masters and mistresses in Indian Territory during and after the Civil War. The author focuses on the experiences of the freedwomen in the Cherokee, Chickasaw, and Creek nations, largely in Oklahoma. Throughout the five chapters, she relies heavily on interviews with former enslaved female laborers or freedwomen." (Choice: Current Reviews for Academic Libraries)

REVIEW: *Choice* v51 no7 p1293-4 Mr 2014 B. C. Ryan

"Trail Sisters: Freedwomen in Indian Territory, 1850-1890." "These stories portray how the results of enforced relocations of the Indians as well as slavery of African Americans filled the lives of women in these societies, enslaved or freed, with danger and uncertainty, and how they negotiated their relationships and lives to survive. The retelling of these individual stories of the women who were on the last rung of society, and otherwise voiceless, offers a unique, vital perspective. This book serves as a very good companion piece to other works in a similar vein that have been published recently. . . . Recommended."

REESE, WILLIAM J. Testing wars in the public schools; a forgotten history; [by] William J. Reese 298 p. 2013 Harvard University Press

1. Achievement tests—United States 2. Educational tests and measurements—United States—History—19th century 3. Historical literature 4. Mann, Horace, 1796-1859 5. Public schools—United States—History—19th century

ISBN 0674073045; 9780674073043

LC 2012-033665

SUMMARY: Author William J. Reese provides an "examination of the roots of the testing culture in American education and the ramifications for administrators, teachers, and students. Reese organizes the book into six chapters, including those that concentrate upon the origins of large-scale testing, the reform-minded reasons for using such instruments, the procedures by which testing was implemented, the effects of testing, how the content was selected, and how the culture of testing evolved." (Choice)

REVIEW: *Am Hist Rev* v119 no1 p176-7 F 2014 William W. Cutler

"Testing Wars in the Public Schools: A Forgotten History". "By examining the shift from oral to written achievement tests before 1900, [William J.] Reese has broadened and enriched our understanding of the history of testing. But the argument he makes to explain how this happened is not entirely satisfying. More than two-thirds of this book (five of seven chapters) is devoted in one way or another to [Horace] Mann's dispute with Boston's grammar school masters. Reese is to be commended for piecing together the convoluted story of this local altercation. But the leap he makes from it to the adoption of written achievement tests nationwide spans a chasm."

REVIEW: *Choice* v51 no4 p696 D 2013 S. T. Schroth

REVIEW: *J Am Hist* v100 no4 p1197 Mr 2014

REEVE, PHILIP, 1966-. Goblins; [by] Philip Reeve 2012 Marion Lloyd

1. Fairies—Juvenile fiction 2. Fantasy fiction 3. Goblins 4. Magic—Juvenile fiction 5. Wizards—Juvenile fiction

ISBN 1407115278; 9781407115276

SUMMARY: This book features "a wild world of magical creatures and heroic adventure from . . . [author] Philip Reeve. The squabbling goblins who live in the great towers of Clovenstone spend their time fighting and looting. Only clever young Skarper understands that dark magic created by a vanquished sorcerer is rising again." (Publisher's note)

REVIEW: *Booklist* v110 no3 p95 O 1 2013 Cindy Welch

REVIEW: *Bull Cent Child Books* v67 no2 p111-2 O 2013 K. Q. G.

"Goblins." "Once they're joined by three wizards, a princess, and a giant, the goblin realizes that they are already in the middle of an adventure, and it's one that will affect the future of Clovenstone. With a bit more of a wink than a nod to classic fantasy tropes, [author Philip] Reeve peppers stylized, formal prose with delightfully funny asides and wry bits of humor. . . . The characters are revised archetypes, with the princess an aging spinster with no interest in being rescued, and the giant a friendly sort who takes an interest in lost causes. The solid storytelling and careful pacing makes this an excellent intro to fantasy for those new to the genre, while avid fantasy readers will take particular delight in the inside jokes."

REVIEW: *Horn Book Magazine* v89 no5 p109-10 S/O 2013 ANITA L. BURKAM

"Goblins." "This endlessly inventive, freewheeling tale begins when young goblin Skarper is ejected . . . from Blackspike Tower into the wilds of Clovenstone, where he meets brave-but-naive Henwyn, a hero/cheesewright on his way to rescue Princess Eluned from the giant Fraddon. . . . [Philip] Reeve brings a light comedic tone to his convoluted yet satisfying plot, deftly juggling multiple story lines and characters while playing an enjoyable game of bait-and-switch with reader expectations. His imagination seems nearly bottomless (with a profligate supply of cheese monsters, rhyming boglins, and the dreaded Dragonbone Men, to name a few), creating a surprising new environment that will amply reward fantasy lovers."

REVIEW: *Kirkus Rev* v81 no14 p154 Jl 15 2013

REEVES, RICHARD. President Kennedy; profile of power; [by] Richard Reeves 798 1993 Simon & Schuster

1. Biography, Individual 2. Historical literature 3. Members of Congress 4. Presidents 5. Presidents—United States 6. Senators

ISBN 0-671-89289-4 pa

LC 93-2-4805

SUMMARY: This is an account "of John F. Kennedy's three years as president, with an emphasis on leadership techniques." (Choice) "Each chapter presents a different day in the administration. . . . The Berlin Wall, the Cuban Missile Crises, Vietnam, and the diplomacy of arms reduction illustrate how Kennedy was constrained by the unshakable Cold War fear of monolithic communism." (Library Journal)This is an account "of John F. Kennedy's three years as president, with an emphasis on leadership techniques." (Choice) Annotated bibliography. Index.

REVIEW: *N Y Times Book Rev* p1-24 O 27 2013 Jill Abramson

"If Kennedy Lived: The First and Second Terms of President John F. Kennedy: An Alternate History," "The Dark Side of Camelot," and "President Kennedy: Profile of Power." "The loathsomely titled 'If Kennedy Lived' . . . imagines a completed first Kennedy term and then a second. . . . 'President Kennedy: Profile of Power' is a minutely detailed chronicle of the Kennedy White House. As a primer on Kennedy's decision-making . . . the book is fascinating. What's missing is a picture of Kennedy's personal life. . . . In 'The Dark Side of Camelot,' [Seymour M.] Hersh wildly posits connections between the Kennedys and the mob."

REGALADO, SAMUEL O. Nikkei baseball; Japanese American players from immigration and internment to the major leagues; [by] Samuel O. Regalado 187 p. 2013 University of Illinois Press

1. Baseball—United State—History 2. Discrimination in sports—United States—History 3. Historical literature 4. Japanese American baseball players—Biography 5. Japanese Americans—History

ISBN 9780252037351 (hardcover: alk. paper); 9780252078835 (pbk.: alk. paper); 9780252094538 (e-book)

LC 2012-013875

SUMMARY: This book by Samuel O. Regalado "explores the story of the Issei (first-generation Japanese immigrants)

who carried baseball as part of their national culture in their migration to the United States and shared the sport with the Nisei (second generation) and subsequent generations. The book's seven chapters analyze the meanings those of Japanese ancestry grafted onto baseball." (American Historical Review)

REVIEW: *Am Hist Rev* v119 no1 p195-6 F 2014 Adrian Burgos

"Nikkei Baseball: Japanese American Players From Immigration and Internment to the Major Leagues". "A challenging question that Regalado does not fully address is the degree to which professional baseball's color line actually barred Japanese Americans. . . . The answer to this question would influence whether historians consider Nikkei Baseball another vital addition to the growing literature on baseball's racial integration. Nonetheless, Regalado convincingly illustrates how baseball brought generations of Japanese together and aided some in overcoming the challenges of becoming Japanese American in a land often hostile to their individual and collective presence for much of the twentieth century."

REVIEW: *Choice* v50 no12 p2272 Ag 2013 Y. Kiuchi

REVIEW: *Rev Am Hist* v42 no3 p497-504 S 2014 Daniel Borus

REGION AND STATE IN NINETEENTH-CENTURY EUROPE; nation-building, regional identities and separatism; x, 293 p. 2012 Palgrave Macmillan

1. Historical literature 2. Nation-building—Europe—History—19th century 3. Nation-state—History 4. Nationalism—Europe—History 5. Regionalism—Europe 6. Regionalism—Europe—History—19th century

ISBN 0230313949; 9780230313941

LC 2012-277304

SUMMARY: In this book, eidted by Joost Augusteijn and Eric Strom, "specialists analyze why regional identities became widely celebrated towards the end of [the 19th] century and why some considered themselves part of the new national self-image. In reaction to the centralizing nation-building efforts of states in nineteenth-century Europe, many regions began to define their own identity." (Publisher's note)

REVIEW: *Choice* v51 no1 p154 S 2013 D. A. Harvey

"Region and State in Nineteenth-Century Europe: Nation-Building, Regional Identities and Separatism." "While scholars once assumed that the advance of the nation-state supplanted more 'traditional' regional cultures . . . , the case studies presented in this collection demonstrate persuasively that the 'region' is as much a complex and contradictory construction as is the 'nation.' Like nations, regions drew upon cultural traditions and memories of the distant past . . . , with the fin de siècle appearing as a particularly vital period for the emergence of both nationalism and regionalism. . . . These case studies emphasize the contingent nature of this process and show that few universal generalizations can be made about European regionalism."

REICH, BERNARD.ed. The government and politics of the Middle East and North Africa. See The government and politics of the Middle East and North Africa

REICH, CHRISTOPHER. The Prince of Risk; a novel; [by] Christopher Reich 384 p. 2013 Doubleday

1. International finance—Fiction 2. Murder—Fiction 3. Suspense fiction 4. Terrorism—Fiction

ISBN 0385535074; 9780385535069 (hardcover)

LC 2012-041924

SUMMARY: In this book, by Christopher Reich, "Bobby Astor is a fearless New York hedge-fund gunslinger on the verge of making his biggest killing ever. But everything changes when his father, the venerable chief executive of the New York Stock Exchange, is murdered along with the head of the Federal Reserve in a brazen, inexplicable attack on the South Lawn of the White House." (Publisher's note)

REVIEW: *Booklist* v110 no17 p62 My 1 2014 Joyce Saricks

REVIEW: *Booklist* v110 no8 p24 D 15 2013 Christine Tran

REVIEW: *Kirkus Rev* v81 no24 p230 D 15 2013

"The Prince of Risk". "Most readers will be scratching their heads as well, wondering how a plot to ruin Bobby by manipulating the value of the Chinese yuan and cripple the New York Stock Exchange through 'industrial espionage as state-sponsored covert policy' might be connected to the 30 cells of well-trained mercenaries who've sneaked into the country in a fine flourish of mayhem overkill. Have no fear. [Christopher] Reich . . . supplies plenty of code-named acronyms and villains, a high body count, patient explanations of arcane financial transactions and regulations, and a heroine who prays to J. Edgar Hoover. How could the exchange, the nation and the free world possibly be in better hands?"

REVIEW: *Libr J* v138 no12 p55 Jl 1 2013

REICH, KASS.il. This little hamster. See Reich, K.

REICH, KASS. This little hamster; [by] Kass Reich 24 p. 2013 Orca Book Publishers

1. Collectors & collecting 2. Colors—Juvenile literature 3. Hamsters 4. Picture books for children 5. Stories in rhyme

ISBN 1459804104; 9781459804104

LC 2013-935389

SUMMARY: In this children's picture book by Kass Reich, "a horde of hamsters introduces little ones to colors. On the left-hand page, one, two or three hamsters express a penchant for a specific hue; they possess an odd collection of objects, everything from a bubble machine to a tire swing, in said color. On the right-hand page, the hamsters cavort among their things." (Kirkus Reviews)

REVIEW: *Kirkus Rev* v82 no1 p84 Ja 1 2014

"This Little Hamster". "Clunky verse describes the action and incorporates each color's name; this word is printed in large, quirky bubble letters as if it were colored in by hand. Some of the objects depicted seem to have been chosen because they fit the rhyme scheme. . . . As with their first outing, the critters are endearingly drawn cartoons with thick lines and goofy expressions. Design hampers the book's effectiveness: The background color of the art, a lighter shade of the featured hue, prevents the colorful objects from standing out on the page. . . . While there are some cute hamster antics going on here, it is an ineffective color concept book for the youngest readers."

REVIEW: *Kirkus Rev* v81 no22 p317 N 15 2013

REVIEW: *Publ Wkly* v260 no40 p51 O 7 2013

REICHEL, TAMMI.tr. In the river darkness. See Roder,

M.

REICHENBACH, BRUCE R. Epistemic obligations; truth, individualism, and the limits of belief; [by] Bruce R. Reichenbach 285 p. 2012 Baylor University Press

1. Belief and doubt 2. Epistemics 3. Evidentialism 4. Philosophical literature 5. Responsibility 6. Theory of knowledge—Moral & ethical aspects

ISBN 1602586233; 9781602586239 (hardcover : alk. paper)

LC 2012-007965

SUMMARY: This book by Bruce R. Reichenbach "contends that while individuals have direct control over belief, they are obligated to believe--and purposely seek--the truth. . . . These epistemic obligations are critical, as the influence of belief is evident throughout society, from law and education to religion and daily decision-making. Grounding his argument in practical case studies, Reichenbach . . . demonstrates the necessity of moral accountability and belief." (Publisher's note)

REVIEW: *Choice* v51 no1 p93-4 S 2013 L. A. Wilkinson

"Epistemic Obligations: Truth, Individualism, and the Limits of Belief." "Beginning with four well-chosen case studies involving the relationship between belief and action, [author Bruce R.] Reichenbach draws parallels between epistemic and moral obligations (chapter 2) and grounds epistemic obligations in epistemic virtues (chapter 3). From there, he moves through discussions of Richard Feldman's internalism versus Alvin Goldman's externalism (chapter 4), belief voluntarism (chapter 5), a critique of dispositional accounts of belief (chapter 6), and a final meditation on accountability (chapter 7). . . . This book does not pave much new ground. However, with its strong command of the relevant literature . . . it is an excellent introduction to the ethics of belief."

REICHMAN, DANIEL R. The broken village; coffee, migration, and globalization in Honduras; [by] Daniel R. Reichman x, 209 p. 2011 ILR Press

1. Coffee industry—Social aspects—Honduras 2. Sociology literature

ISBN 0801450128 (cloth : alk. paper); 0801477298 (pbk. : alk. paper); 9780801450129 (cloth : alk. paper); 9780801477294 (pbk. : alk. paper)

LC 2011-020007

SUMMARY: In this book, "Daniel R. Reichman tells the story of a remote village in Honduras that transformed almost overnight from a sleepy coffee-growing community to a hotbed of undocumented migration to and from the United States. The small village--called here by the pseudonym La Quebrada--was once home to a thriving coffee economy." (Publisher's note)

REVIEW: *Choice* v50 no2 p358 O 2012 C. H. Blake

REVIEW: *Contemp Sociol* v42 no6 p889-90 N 2013

"The Broken Village: Coffee, Migration, and Globalization in Honduras." "Daniel Reichman's 'The Broken Village: Coffee, Migration, and Globalization in Honduras' vividly paints the picture of 'La Quebrada,' a pseudonym used to mark a rural Honduran town whose crippled coffee economy led to a dependence on labor migration to the United States. Drawing on extensive fieldwork in Honduras and supplemental interviews with migrants and key informants in the United States, Reichman immerses the reader in the issues that face migrants, their families, and the community as a whole. . . . Thus, Reichman tells a series of very personal stories if only to portray the strong sociological influence that volatile markets, globalization, and migration have had on the town."

REID-MARR, DAVID. Emergent teaching. See Crowell, S.

REID, GREG S. Think and grow rich!; stickability, the power of perseverance; [by] Greg S. Reid 208 p. 2013 Jeremy P. Tarcher/Penguin

1. Business literature 2. Perseverance (Ethics)—Case studies 3. Self-help materials 4. Success—Case studies 5. Success in business—Case studies

ISBN 9780399165825

LC 2013-016746

SUMMARY: This business self-help book was written by entrepreneur Greg S. Reid. "The heart of the book's message is called 'stickability'--basically, having the capacity to not turn away from difficult conditions. . . . The components of stickability . . . include maintaining flexibility, overcoming fear, and acting on a desire more than just a wish." (Booklist)

REVIEW: *Booklist* v110 no1 p20-1 S 1 2013 Brad Hooper

"Think and Grow Rich Stickability: The Power of Perseverance." "[A] crisply written book full of admonishment and encouragement. . . . [Greg S.] Reid, a businessman and motivational speaker, bases this book on not only his own wisdom about the success he has gained from his business experiences but also on interviews with individuals who represent business success stories. . . . Reid's explanation of the components of stickability, which include maintaining flexibility, overcoming fear, and acting on a desire more than just a wish, are carefully articulated to apply to any reader's personal circumstances."

REVIEW: *Publ Wkly* v260 no30 p57 Jl 29 2013

REID, MEGAN H. Law and piety in medieval Islam; [by] Megan H. Reid xii, 249 p. 2013 Cambridge University Press

1. Historical literature 2. Islam—Customs and practices 3. Islamic law 4. Muslim scholars—Biography 5. Muslims—Conduct of life 6. Spiritual life—Islam

ISBN 9780521889599 (hardback)

LC 2011-008594

SUMMARY: Author "Megan H. Reid's book, which traverses three centuries from 1170 to 1500, recovers the stories of medieval men and women who were renowned not only for their intellectual prowess but also for their devotional piety. Through these stories, the book examines trends in voluntary religious practice that have been largely overlooked in modern scholarship." (Publisher's note)

REVIEW: *Am Hist Rev* v119 no4 p1393 O 2014 John P. Turner

REVIEW: *TLS* no5792 p28 Ap 4 2014 KONRAD HIRSCHLER

"Law and Piety in Medieval Islam." "Extensive fasting, celibacy, supererogatory worship, living on a rather rudimentary diet, sleeping on the floor and similar pious and ascetic practices were so common in the late medieval Middle East that historians of the region have rarely discussed them in depth before now. Megan Reid's vivid study brings the meaning of these practices in Syria and Egypt to life, most importantly by dissociating them from the vague and catch-all concept of mystical Sufism. . . . This is a well-written, thoughtful book, and after so much piety it comes as something of a relief that those who failed to live up to exemplary behaviour make at least a brief appearance."

REIDE, MACKENZIE. The Adventurers Troll Creek; [by] Mackenzie Reide 212 p. 2011 MR Books

1. Adventure stories 2. Mines & mineral resources—Fiction 3. Stepbrothers 4. Stepsisters 5. Wilderness survival—Fiction

ISBN 0986964700; 9780986964701

SUMMARY: In this book, "Twelve-year-old Dana, a city girl, arrives in the tiny town of Troll Creek . . . to spend two weeks of her summer vacation with her soon-to-be stepsiblings, Amy, 14, and Jack, 11. . . . Soon after Dana's arrival, the trio sets out on mountain bikes to camp out near an abandoned coal mine . . . . In the mine's numerous, often collapsed tunnels, the kids manage to reunite, and they also find skeletons, stolen goods and a masked man with a gun." (Kirkus Reviews)

REVIEW: *Kirkus Rev* v82 no3 p347 F 1 2014

"The Adventurers: Troll Creek". " Reide's debut YA novel, the first book in her Adventurers series, offers a little bit of conflict and a lot of escapades. . . . Although readers may find it refreshing to have girls do the fighting and a boy do the 'cooking,' the author doesn't flesh out any of the characters enough for them to be especially memorable. That said, their relationships do evolve, as their survival depends not just on smarts and spunk, but also on cooperation. Middle-grade readers will appreciate the fact that there are hardly any adults around except for the bad guys, who aren't too hard for the heroes to outwit. The fast pace, too, will keep them eagerly turning pages. An entertaining, if somewhat undemanding, YA adventure."

REIKO YAMAMOTO.tr. MacArthur in Asia. See

REILLY, BRENDAN. One doctor; close calls, cold cases, and the mysteries of medicine; [by] Brendan Reilly 352 p. 2013 Atria Books

1. Emergency physicians 2. Medical literature 3. Memoirs 4. Physician's Role—Personal Narratives 5. Physician-Patient Relations—Personal Narratives

ISBN 1476726299; 9781476726298; 9781476726366 (ebook)

LC 2013-006739

SUMMARY: In this book, phyisican Brendan Reilly "relates his most challenging cases, beginning in the present—when he sees 19 ER patients on an average day—before backtracking to his early career at Dartmouth in 1985. That year, Reilly struggled to identify the cause of an eccentric and lovable patient's delirium. By the time he figured it out, the patient—Fred—had died." (Publishers Weekly)

REVIEW: *Booklist* v110 no2 p12 S 15 2013 Tony Miksanek

REVIEW: *Libr J* v138 no5 p92 Mr 15 2013 Barbara Hoffert

REVIEW: *New York Times* v163 no56637 pD6 D 31 2013 ABIGAIL ZUGER

"One Doctor: Close Calls, Cold Cases and the Mysteries of Medicine". "Dr. Brendan Reilly . . . has done history a true service in attempting to get this landscape down on paper—first because its emotion-dense human interest belongs on the page, and second because it is all vanishing fast. . . . He is a good, fluent writer with a fine ear for dialogue, and his excursions from the particulars of his cases to the broad medical, social and economic principles are always on point. Still, the sheer press of humanity in his pages and some of the jargon may overwhelm readers. . . . Dr. Reilly deserves a resounding bravo for telling it like it is (sometimes), like it should be (always) and, increasingly, like it never will be again."

REVIEW: *Publ Wkly* v260 no27 p78 Jl 8 2013

REVIEW: *Publ Wkly* v261 no17 p133 Ap 28 2014

REILLY, DIANA HOWANSKY. Scattered; the forced relocation of Poland's Ukrainians after World War II; [by] Diana Howansky Reilly xiv, 177 p. 2013 University of Wisconsin Press

1. Forced migration—Poland 2. Historical literature 3. Lemky—Poland—Biography 4. Lemky—Poland—History—20th century 5. Ukrainians—Poland—History—20th century 6. World War, 1939-1945—Lemkivshchyna (Poland and Slovakia)

ISBN 9780299293406 (cloth : alk. paper); 9780299293437 (e-book)

LC 2012-037002

SUMMARY: In this book, "following World War II, the communist government of Poland forcibly relocated the country's Ukrainian minority by means of a Soviet-Polish population exchange and then a secretly planned action. . . . Diana Howansky Reilly recounts these events through the experiences of three siblings caught up in the conflict, during a turbulent period when compulsory resettlement was a common political tactic used against national minorities to create homogenous states." (Publisher's note)

REVIEW: *TLS* no5771 p26 N 8 2013 UILLEAM BLACKER

"Scattered: The Forced Relocation of Poland's Ukrainians After World War II." "The context for 'Scattered' is complex and remains controversial in both Poland and Ukraine. Yet [Diana Howansky] Reilly's narrative, written in short vignettes, is clear and balanced, and she successfully weaves the wider history into a rich fabric containing details of everyday life, stories of individual characters, and the rhythms and texture of Lemko speech. The result is a short, but skilfully crafted synthesis of family memoir and micro-history that is as interesting for its uncovering of a neglected, tragedy as for its portrait of a little-known culture."

REINER, JONATHAN. Heart. See Cheney, R.B.

REINERT, SOPHUS A. Translating empire; emulation and the origins of political economy; [by] Sophus A. Reinert 438 p. 2011 Harvard University Press

1. Economics—Europe—History—18th century 2. Enlightenment—Europe 3. Historical literature 4. Philosophy, European—18th century

ISBN 0674061519 (alk. paper); 9780674061514 (alk. paper)

LC 2011-017919

SUMMARY: It was the author's intent "to trace the movement of the now relatively neglected Bristol merchant John Cary's 1695 Essay on the State of England from England to France, Italy, Germany, and Scandinavia, and in the process reflect on how English political economy gradually became the main analytical and policymaking framework for nations battling for survival in an increasingly hostile European geopolitical contest." (American Historical Review)

REVIEW: *Am Hist Rev* v119 no1 p241-2 F 2014 Carl Wennerlind

"Translating Empire: Emulation and the Origins of Political Economy". "This elegantly written, impressively erudite, wonderfully rich depiction of the development and transmission of political economic ideas throughout Europe in the eighteenth century offers a crisp analytical framework that illuminates the context and content of the formation of Enlightenment political economy. . . . While [Sophus A.] Reinert might have overstated the novelty and uniqueness of [John] Cary's ideas in England during the decades following the Glorious Revolution and perhaps downplayed the relative importance of political economists who did not embrace this lineage of ideas, he deserves great praise for so carefully tracing one of the most central strands in the genealogy of political economy."

REINHARDT, DANA. We are the Goldens; [by] Dana Reinhardt 208 p. 2014 Wendy Lamb Books, an imprint of Random House Children's Books

1. Divorce—Fiction 2. High schools—Fiction 3. Schools—Fiction 4. Sexual abuse—Fiction 5. Sisters—Fiction 6. Teacher-student relationships—Fiction 7. Young adult fiction

ISBN 0385742576; 9780375990656 (lib. bdg.); 9780385742573 (trade); 9780385742580 (pbk.)
LC 2013-023351

SUMMARY: In this book, by Dana Reinhardt, 'Nell worships her older sister, Layla. They're one unit, intertwined: Nellayla. As Nell and her best friend, Felix, start their freshman year in high school, on Layla's turf, there's so much Nell looks forward to: Joining Layla on the varsity soccer team. Parties. Boys. Adventures. But the year takes a very different turn. Layla is . . . hiding something, and when Nell discovers what it is, and the consequences it might have, she struggles." (Publisher's note)

REVIEW: *Booklist* v110 no17 p98 My 1 2014 Karen Cruze

REVIEW: *Bull Cent Child Books* v67 no10 p538 Je 2014 D. S.

"We Are the Goldens". "[Dana] Reinhardt astutely structures Nell's narration as being directed entirely toward Layla, the second-person address underscoring the centrality of the older girl in her sister's life. Nell's voice is fluid yet authentic as she puzzles out Layla's changing behavior and moves to define herself. . . . Other elements are less effective, unfortunately: Nell's obsession with teenaged brothers who died within a few months of each other is narratively distracting despite its thematic relevance; while Nell's separation from Layla is important, the emphasis on her telling Layla's secret is overdramatized, with an abrupt cliffhanger ending. Nonetheless, it's an eloquent and concise story."

REVIEW: *Horn Book Magazine* v90 no3 p96 My/Je 2014 DEIRDRE F. BAKER

REVIEW: *Kirkus Rev* v82 no7 p117 Ap 1 2014

REVIEW: *Publ Wkly* v261 no8 p187 F 24 2014

REVIEW: *SLJ* v60 no3 p162 Mr 2014 Allie Bronston

REVIEW: *Voice of Youth Advocates* v37 no2 p64 Je 2014 Karen Jensen

REINHARDT, ERIC. The Victoria System; [by] Eric Reinhardt 480 p. 2013 Hamish Hamilton Ltd

1. Adultery—Fiction 2. Architects—Fiction 3. Erotic stories 4. Sex addiction 5. Women executives

ISBN 0241145589; 9780241145586

SUMMARY: This book by Eric Reinhardt was "nominated for The Prix Goncourt, The Prix Renaudot and The Grand Prix Du Roman De L'academie Francaise. David Kolski never sleeps with the same woman twice--apart from his wife. Then he meets Victoria. . . . . By day she is a ruthless executive in a lightning-paced, high-pressured whirlwind of power and productivity. By night she likes good wine, luxurious hotel rooms, and abandoning herself to her sexual fantasies. David is soon addicted." (Publisher's note)

REVIEW: *TLS* no5761 p18 Ag 30 2013 HAL JENSEN

"The Victoria System." "Shortlisted for three literary awards, including the Prix Goncourt, it is intriguingly presented as 'part erotica, part thriller, part novel of ideas.' Ultimately, however, it is none of these things, and would be better described as a straightforward morality tale, provocatively spiced up with lots of sex. . . . Perhaps it is in order to represent the unnuanced monotony of sexual obsession that the language of the sex scenes is so startlingly unsuggestive. . . . These problems beset the whole book, in which there is also much redundancy. . . . The translator--Sam Taylor--must take some blame. . . . Most damaging is the narrator's self-pitying and aggrieved tone."

REISBERG, DANIEL.ed. The Oxford handbook of cognitive psychology. See The Oxford handbook of cognitive psychology

REMKIEWICZ, FRANK.il. Joe and Sparky go to school. See Michalak, J.

RENOUARD, MADELEINE.ed. Barbara Wright. See Barbara Wright

RENWICK, ROBIN. Helen Suzman; Bright Star in a Dark Chamber; [by] Robin Renwick 256 p. 2014 Biteback

1. Biography (Literary form) 2. Human rights workers 3. South Africa—Politics & government 4. Suzman, Helen, 1917-2009 5. Women politicians

ISBN 1849546673; 9781849546676

SUMMARY: This book presents a biography of South African parliamentarian Helen Suzman.. "Armed with the relentless determination and biting wit for which she became renowned, Suzman battled the racist regime and earned her reputation as a legendary anti-apartheid campaigner. Despite constant antagonism and the threat of violence, she forced into the global spotlight the injustices of the country's minority rule." (Publisher's note)

REVIEW: *Economist* v410 no8870 p82 Ja 18 2014

"Helen Suzman: Bright Star in a Dark Chamber." "Robin Renwick . . . served as British ambassador to South Africa from 1987 until 1991. He helped in critical ways to unravel the system from within. According to this crisply lucid account, Mrs. Suzman was his closest ally. He is persuasive in presenting her as the doughtiest of fighters for human rights anywhere in the world--and one of the finest parliamentarians of her era. . . . [Nelson] Mandela and other African National Congress luminaries recognised that Mrs. Suzman's struggle within the system had, in fact, been invaluable."

RENWICK, ROBIN. A Journey with Margaret Thatcher; [by] Robin Renwick 352 p. 2013 Biteback Publishing

1. Cold War, 1945-1989 2. Great Britain—Foreign relations—1945- 3. Great Britain—Politics & government—1964-1979 4. Historical literature 5. Memoirs 6. Thatcher, Margaret, 1925-2013

ISBN 1849545332; 9781849545334

SUMMARY: This book, an account of Margaret Thatcher's role in British foreign policy, was written "by Robin Renwick, the diplomat who was at her side in Rhodesia, Washington and Brussels. . . . He depicts a demanding but entirely rational boss, eager to test any argument to the limit but seeking a stable and realistic solution." (Times Literary Supplement) Particular focus is given to "her relationship with Ronald Reagan and how they worked together to end the Cold War." (Publisher's note)

REVIEW: *TLS* no5749 p3-7 Je 7 2013 FERDINAND MOUNT

"Not for Turning: The Life of Margaret Thatcher," "A Journey With Margaret Thatcher: Foreign Policy Under the Iron Lady" and "The Real Iron Lady: Working With Margaret Thatcher." "Even her most loyal of ghosts, Robin Harris, . . . accuses her of being a naive and hopeless picker of ministers. This is surely an unrealistic criticism. . . . In his absorbing accounts of the negotiations he himself was involved in . . . [Robin Renwick] he depicts a demanding but entirely rational boss. . . .The freshest part of his account is of the encouragement she gave F. W. de Klerk and the steady pressure she exerted for the release of Nelson Mandela. . . . [Gillian] Shephard's accounts of Mrs Thatcher's encounters with unfamous cogs in the political world supplement this picture on the domestic front."

RESCEK, SANJA.il. A Bedtime Prayer. See A Bedtime Prayer

RESURRECTOR, P. R. Horny Ghost of Osama Bin Laden; Rise of the Ghost; [by] P. R. Resurrector 280 p. 2013 Createspace Independent Pub

1. Bin Laden, Osama, 1957-2011 2. Erotic stories 3. Ghost stories 4. Mediums 5. Rape

ISBN 1490372091; 9781490372099

SUMMARY: This book, centered on the ghost of al-Qaeda leader Osama bin Laden, begins with "bin Laden's rape of a deep-sea diver who recovers his corpse and unwittingly unleashes his sexually insatiable spirit upon the world. . . . Meanwhile, Janet, a young woman who can talk to ghosts, works with the U.S. government to bring him down, and she receives help from the ghost of Naughty B##ch, a dog who, after being raped by a still-living bin Laden, jumped off a cliff in order to escape him." (Kirkus Reviews)

REVIEW: *Kirkus Rev* v82 no1 p324 Ja 1 2014

"Horny Ghost of Osama Bin Laden: Rise of the Ghost". "A problematically perverse erotic thriller. As if the geopolitical situation of the Middle East were not already rife with literary possibility, this debut novel incorporates aliens, vampires, a talking dog, and page after page of disturbingly rendered nonconsensual sex into a tale centering on the titular undead al-Qaida leader. Although the industry standards of erotica usually exclude rape scenes, here they serve as incremental actions moving the plot forward. . . . Admittedly, the sheer absurdity of the novel's plot and concept may hold a sort of camp appeal, and fans of black humor may laugh at bin Laden's insecurity. . . . That said, if erotic fiction's central aim is to arouse, this book doesn't fulfill that requirement."

REUBEN, BRYAN G. Industrial organic chemicals. See Wittcoff, H. A.

REUTER, ELIZABETH.ed. The dead lands. See Hautala, R.

REVOLUTION, REVOLT AND REFORM IN NORTH AFRICA; the Arab Spring and beyond; 2013 Routledge

1. Africa, North—Politics & government 2. Arab countries—History—Arab Spring Uprisings, 2011- 3. Democratization 4. Political science literature 5. Revolutions

ISBN 9780415839471

SUMMARY: This book, edited by Ricardo Laremont, provides "an account of the recent revolutions or reform movements that constituted part of the Arab Spring . . . in a North African context. . . . Using examples from Tunisia, Egypt, Libya, Morocco and Algeria, Revolution, 'Revolt and Reform in North Africa' provides an insider scholar's account of these recent revolutions or reform movements." (Publisher's note)

REVIEW: *Middle East J* v68 no3 p465-8 Summ 2014 I. William Zartman

"The Arab Awakening: America and the Transformation of the Middle East," "Revolution, Revolt, and Reform in North Africa: The Arab Spring and Beyond," and "The Second Arab Awakening: And the Battle for Pluralism." "'America and the Transformation of the Middle East' . . . deals with a number of forces and a number of countries. . . . Each chapter concludes with implications for the US, which is the ultimate message of the work. . . . Ricardo René Larémont . . . also offers a background setting. . . . Larémont himself provides on excellent chapter on demographics and economics. . . . The work by Marwan Muasher . . . has a more forward look."

REWALD, SABINE. Balthus; Cats and Girls; [by] Sabine Rewald 192 p. 2013 Yale University Press

1. Art literature 2. Balthus, 1908-2001 3. Cats in art 4. Erotic art 5. Women in art

ISBN 0300197012; 9780300197013

SUMMARY: "Balthus (1908-2001) mingles intuition into his young sitters' psyches with overt erotic desire and forbidding austerity. . . . Often included in these scenes are enigmatic cats, possible stand-ins for the artist himself." Written by Sabine Rewald, "'Balthus: Cats and Girls' is the first book devoted to this subject, focusing on the early decades of the artist's career from the mid-1930s to the 1950s." (Publisher's note)

REVIEW: *Burlington Mag* v156 no1333 p251 Ap 2014 R.

S.

REVIEW: *Libr J* v139 no2 p72 F 1 2014 Kathryn Weekselman

REVIEW: *N Y Times Book Rev* p56 D 8 2013 JENNIFER B. MCDONALD

"Balthus: Cats and Girls" and "The Big New Yorker Book of Cats." "A great strength of [author Sabine] Rewald's catalog is its informed (if brief) reading of Balthus's confrères in the portrayal of un-self-conscious eroticism. . . . 'The Big New Yorker Book of Cats' . . . comes a year after 'The Big New Yorker Book of Dogs.' . . . Comprising 57 works of prose and poetry (with pictures!), it assembles quite a cast, both feline and human. We meet cats loitering at wine shops and book shops, a cat that stops at Sardi's on book tour, cats prone to vice."

REVIEW: *Publ Wkly* v260 no31 p62 Ag 5 2013

REX, ADAM.il. Moonday. See Rex, A.

REX, ADAM. Moonday; [by] Adam Rex 40 p. 2013 Disney-Hyperion

1. Day 2. Families—Juvenile fiction 3. Night 4. Picture books for children
ISBN 1423119207; 9781423119203
LC 2012-020301

SUMMARY: In this children's picture book by Adam Rex, "the moon follows a girl home, takes up residence in her yard and stays put--keeping the sun from rising and the town stuck in a drowsy stupor. . . . When teachers nod off and punk bands sing lullabies, the moon's family decides to drive back up the mountain, where they first picked up their round friend, in the hope it will follow." (Kirkus Review)

REVIEW: *Booklist* v110 no5 p85-6 N 1 2013 Carolyn Phelan

"Moonday." "As a girl and her parents drive home from a nearby hill, they watch the big, beautiful moon, which seems to follow them home. . . . Dreamlike, this picture book skates on thin ice with its mixture of fantasy and reality. Some narrative elements, such as the mother's gently amusing final comment, strengthen the story, while others seem a bit contrived. Still, the image of the luminous moon, which feels close enough to touch and small enough for a child to explore, is well worth seeing. A drowsy, rather surreal bedtime story."

REVIEW: *Bull Cent Child Books* v67 no2 p112 O 2013 T. A.

REVIEW: *Kirkus Rev* v81 no13 p230 Jl 1 2013

REVIEW: *Publ Wkly* v260 no27 p86 Jl 8 2013

REVIEW: *SLJ* v59 no10 p1 O 2013 Anna Haase Krueger

REYBROUCK, DAVID VAN, 1971-. Congo; The Epic History of a People; [by] David van Reybrouck 639 p. 2014 HarperCollins Publishers

1. Congo (Democratic Republic)—History 2. Congo (Democratic Republic)—Politics & government 3. Congo (Democratic Republic)—Social conditions 4. Historical literature 5. Imperialism
ISBN 0062200119; 9780062200112
LC 2013-035201

SUMMARY: This book on the Democratic Republic of the Congo by David van Reybrouck "describes the country throughout three eras: the precolonial Congo Free State privately controlled by Leopold II of Belgium, the colonial Belgian Congo, and the postindependence Democratic Republic of the Congo. Included are numerous interviews that aim to provide a 'bottom-up' view of the country." (Library Journal)

REVIEW: *Bookforum* v21 no1 p15-7 Ap/My 2014 MATT STEINGLASS

REVIEW: *Booklist* v110 no9/10 p37 Ja 1 2014 Vanessa Bush

REVIEW: *Kirkus Rev* v82 no5 p7 Mr 1 2014

"Congo: The Epic History of a People". "Sprawling portrait of a land that, by Belgian writer [David] van Reybrouck's account, has been at the center of world history as well as a continent. The subtitle is a touch off, for as the author notes, Congo is home to hundreds of peoples, even if there is 'great linguistic and cultural homogeneity' owing to the dominance of Bantu-speaking tribes. . . . Though the book is overlong, van Reybrouck makes a good case for the importance of Congo to world history and its ongoing centrality in a time of resurgent economic colonialism, this time on the part of China."

REVIEW: *Libr J* v139 no13 p108 Ag 1 2014 Sue Giffard

REVIEW: *Libr J* v138 no18 p69 N 1 2013 Barbara Hoffert

REVIEW: *N Y Times Book Rev* p10-1 My 4 2014 J. M. LEDGARD

REVIEW: *Publ Wkly* v260 no50 p55 D 9 2013

REVIEW: *TLS* no5812/5813 p12 Ag 22 2014 JASON K. STEARNS

REYNOLDS, AARON. Here comes Destructosaurus!; [by] Aaron Reynolds 32 p. 2014 Chronicle Books

1. Children's stories 2. Conduct of life—Fiction 3. Conduct of life—Juvenile fiction 4. Monsters—Fiction 5. Monsters—Juvenile fiction 6. Orderliness—Fiction
ISBN 145212454X; 9781452124544 (alk. paper)
LC 2013-015843

SUMMARY: In this children's book, written by Aaron Reynolds and illustrated by Jeremy Tankard, "a baby dinosaur emerges from the sea and goes on a rampage across New York City, tracking seaweed and dead fish all over the tourists and setting fire to every ship in the harbor. His tail the size of a small planet, Destructosauraus is chastised by the narrator for his lack of self-control and for his sassy attitude, much like a mother would speak to a wild child." (School Library Journal)

REVIEW: *Booklist* v110 no15 p93 Ap 1 2014 Kay Weisman

REVIEW: *Bull Cent Child Books* v67 no10 p538 Je 2014 H. M.

REVIEW: *Kirkus Rev* v82 no3 p282 F 1 2014

"Here Comes the Destructoaurus!" "A parent/caregiver—unseen after a glimpse at the beginning—translates a 'terrible twos'-style tantrum into a movie-monster rampage. As it turns out, it's all just a failure to communicate. . . . when the uproar turns out to have been just a search for a misplaced teddy bear, the scolding changes to repentance. . . . The silliness of the premise is nicely amplified by the mixed-media illustrations, which feature disaster-movie perspectives and lots of rubble."

REVIEW: *N Y Times Book Rev* p25 My 11 2014 SARAH HARRISON SMITH

REVIEW: *Publ Wkly* v261 no4 p190 Ja 27 2014

REVIEW: *Quill Quire* v80 no2 p34 Mr 2014 Dory Cerny

"Here Comes Destructosaurus!". "It's obvious from the tone and content of Aaron Reynolds' text that he is well acquainted with at least one of these lovable but frustrating children/ As Destructosaurus tracks seaweed and dead fish all over the freshly cleaned street and throws around skyscrapers mid-tantrum, the disapproving and chastising parental feel of the narration is hilariously bang-on and will resonate with adult readers. . . . The visual gags bring as much entertainment-value to the story as Reynolds' comic words."

REVIEW: *SLJ* v60 no4 p133 Ap 2014 Jennifer Miskec

REYNOLDS, NANCY Y. A city consumed; urban commerce, the Cairo fire, and the politics of decolonization in Egypt; [by] Nancy Y. Reynolds xvii, 355 p. 2012 Stanford University Press

1. Consumption (Economics)—Egypt—Cairo—History—20th century 2. Historical literature 3. Nationalism—Economic aspects—Egypt
ISBN 9780804781268 (cloth : alk. paper)
LC 2012-001451

SUMMARY: In this book, "Nancy Reynolds assesses consumption-driven tensions in colonial Egypt, which culminated in the Cairo fire of 1952 that extensively damaged the downtown shopping district. She explores materialism as a factor of Egyptians' perception of captivity under European rule, which persisted not only through formal legal channels, but through informal daily exposure to . . . European culture." (Middle East Journal)

REVIEW: *Middle East J* v67 no4 p662-6 Aut 2013

"Imperfect Compromise: A New Consensus Among Israelis and Palestinians," "A City Consumed: Urban Commerce, the Cairo Fire, and the Politics of Decolonization in Egypt," and "A Documentary History of Modern Iraq." "Michael Karpin claims that the Arab-Israeli conflict has never been closer to a resolution than it is today. . . . Nancy Reynolds assesses consumption-driven tensions in colonial Egypt, which culminated in the Cairo fire of 1952 that extensively damaged the downtown shopping district. . . . Editor Stacey Holden divides the compilation roughly into decade-length chapters, and provides a brief contextualizing introduction ot each period and document."

REYNOLDS, PETER H.il. Judy Moody and stink and the big bad blackout. See McDonald, M.

REYNOLDS, PETER H.il. The Smallest gift of Christmas. See Reynolds, P. H.

REYNOLDS, PETER H. The Smallest gift of Christmas; [by] Peter H. Reynolds 40 p. 2013 Candlewick Press

1. Christmas stories for children 2. Families—Juvenile fiction 3. Gifts 4. Picture books for children 5. Wishes
ISBN 0763661031; 9780763661038
LC 2012-947753

SUMMARY: In this book by Peter H. Reynolds "Roland is less than impressed with the size of his Christmas gift and wishes for something bigger. And while wishing sort of works, much to Roland's frustration, the gifts are never big enough. A journey for a truly huge present takes him on an adventure through town and into a rocket blasting off to space. Orbiting Earth, Roland realizes that the best gift, the perfectly sized gift, is back home." (School Library Journal)

REVIEW: *Horn Book Magazine* v89 no6 p68 N/D 2013 KATRINA HEDEEN

"The Smallest Gift of Christmas." "Diminutive Roland is 'not impressed' with the tiny wrapped present awaiting him on Christmas morning. So he wishes for a bigger gift, then an even bigger one, and so on until he finally sets off in a red rocket ship to search the universe for a gift large enough to please him. But soon Earth is just a tiny dot in the distance, and Roland realizes he misses his home. . . . Red- and green-heavy digital illustrations in [Peter H.] Reynolds's signature nimble style with plentiful white space propel this predictable tale of appreciating the small, simple things in life, especially around the holidays."

REVIEW: *Kirkus Rev* v81 no17 p137 S 1 2013

REVIEW: *Publ Wkly* v260 no37 p47 S 16 2013

REVIEW: *SLJ* v59 no10 p1 O 2013 Brooke Sheets

RHEE, MICHELLE A., 1969-. Radical; fighting to put students first; [by] Michelle A. Rhee 304 p. 2013 Harper

1. EDUCATION—General 2. Education—Aims and objectives—United States 3. Educational change—United States 4. Educational literature 5. Public schools—United States 6. SOCIAL SCIENCE—General 7. School improvement programs—United States
ISBN 0062203983 (hardcover); 9780062203984 (hardcover)
LC 2012-038474

SUMMARY: This book, by education reformer Michelle Rhee, "draws on her own life story and delivers her plan for better American schools. . . . Informing her critique are her . . . experiences in education. . . . Rhee draws on dozens of compelling examples from schools she's worked in and studied, from students who've left behind unspeakable home lives and thrived in the classroom to teachers whose groundbreaking methods have produced unprecedented leaps in student achievement." (Publisher's note)

REVIEW: *Booklist* v109 no12 p10 F 15 2013 Carolyn Saper

REVIEW: *Commentary* v135 no5 p38-40 2013 SOHRAB AHMARI

REVIEW: *Kirkus Rev* v81 no3 p87 F 1 2013

REVIEW: *N Y Rev Books* v60 no15 p4-8 O 10 2013 Andrew Delbanco

"Reign of Error: The Hoax of the Privatization Movement and the Danger to America's Public Schools" and "Radical: Fighting to Put Students First." "If [Diane] Ravitch disputes prevailing assumptions, she does not gloss over the fact that school performance by the large minority of American children who grow up poor or in segregated neighborhoods is disproportionately weak. . . . The title of [Michelle] Rhee's new book . . . suggests, accurately, that her main subject is herself. . . . She tells the rest of her story as an alternating series of victories on behalf of children grateful for her gifts and setbacks at the hands of adults threatened by her smarts. . . . To read Rhee and Ravitch in sequence is like hearing a too-good-to-be-true sales pitch followed by the report of an auditor who discloses mistakes and outright falsehoods in the accounts of the firm that's trying to make the sale."

REVIEW: *New Repub* v244 no8 p35-7 My 27 2013 Nicholas Lemann

RHIEL, MARY.ed. Imagining Germany Imagining Asia. See Imagining Germany Imagining Asia

RHODES, DAN. Marry Me; [by] Dan Rhodes 2014 Europa Editions

1. Adultery—Fiction 2. Families—Fiction 3. Love stories 4. Marriage—Fiction 5. Short stories—Collections
ISBN 9781609451813; 1609451813

SUMMARY: In this fiction collection, author Dan Rhodes presents an "honest look at marital life (and strife), in 79 (very) short stories. Rhodes's deft use of language spares no emotion and leaves no romantic stone unturned—husbands, wives, lovers, and all combinations thereof are ripe for the picking (and choosing)." (Publisher's note)

REVIEW: *New Yorker* v90 no5 p93-1 Mr 24 2014

"Marry Me." "The seventy-nine vignettes in this slim, addictive volume range in length from two sentences to two pages, and are concerned with the absurdities of modern marriage. In one, a couple spend all their money on their wedding and end up homeless. Memories of the special day (the calligraphy was exquisite) keep them going as they huddle together for warmth. . . . Some of the stories fall flat, but [author Dan] Rhodes's playful approach to storytelling and language beguiles."

RHODES, JESSE H. An education in politics; the origins and evolution of No Child Left Behind; [by] Jesse H. Rhodes p. cm. 2012 Cornell University Press

1. Education and state—United States—History—20th century 2. Education and state—United States—History—21st century 3. Educational change—United States 4. Educational literature
ISBN 9780801449710 (cloth: alk. paper)
LC 2011-044129

SUMMARY: This book, by Jesse H. Rhodes, "explains the uneven development of federal involvement in education. While supporters of expanded federal involvement enjoyed some success in bringing new ideas to the federal policy agenda, Rhodes argues, they also encountered stiff resistance from proponents of local control. Built atop existing decentralized policies, new federal reforms raised difficult questions about which level of government bore ultimate responsibility for improving schools." (Publisher's note)

REVIEW: *Choice* v51 no3 p551 N 2013 E. T. Jones

REVIEW: *Contemp Sociol* v43 no2 p253-5 Mr 2014 Thurston Domina

"An Education in Politics: The Origins and Evolution of No Child Left Behind". "[Jesse H.] Rhodes is by no means the first to provide a systematic overview of the evolution of American educational policy from the ESEA to NCLB. . . . But Rhodes builds on this literature in two ways: First, he introduces a theoretical perspective . . . that helps to make sense of both the profound changes that have occurred in American educational policy. . . .Second, he skillfully updates the literature on federal educational policy to reflect the important, but not well-understood policy shifts that have occurred under the [Barack] Obama administration."

RHOMBERG, CHRIS. The broken table; the Detroit Newspaper Strike and the state of American labor; [by] Chris Rhomberg x, 387 p. 2012 Russell Sage Foundation

1. Collective bargaining—Newspapers—Michigan—Detroit 2. Newspaper Strike, Detroit, Michigan, 1995-2000 3. Newspaper employees—Labor unions—Michigan—Detroit 4. Newspaper publishing—Michigan—Detroit 5. Social science literature 6. Strikes and lockouts—Newspapers—Michigan—Detroit
ISBN 9780871547170 (pbk.: alk. paper); 9781610447751 (ebook)
LC 2011-053536

SUMMARY: In this book, "Chris Rhomberg illustrates the institutional dissonance between employers and unions regarding their collective bargaining strategies. Drawing upon the Detroit newspaper strike from 1995 to 2000, the book affirms that while the unions bargained in a manner consistent with labor/management accord era practices, their employer sought to subvert the collective bargaining process." (Contemporary Sociology)

REVIEW: *Am J Sociol* v119 no3 p870-2 N 2013 Richard Sullivan

REVIEW: *Choice* v50 no4 p742 D 2012 R. A. Batch

REVIEW: *Contemp Sociol* v43 no2 p255-7 Mr 2014 Benjamin Lind

"The Broken Table: The Detroit Newspaper Strike and the State of American Labor". "Although the book retreads some familiar subjects typical among studies on contemporary, post-accord era strikes, 'The Broken Table' absolutely excels at documenting the exorbitant responses taken by the newspapers. . . . Scholars of the American labor movement and labor advocates will find that 'The Broken Table' offers compelling evidence on the limits of collective bargaining in the current era. . . . Readers from the general public will find the book relatively accessible, given the ample context provided in its first half along with the review of labor-management law."

REVIEW: *J Am Hist* v100 no1 p298-9 Je 2013 Joseph A. McCartin

RIBON, PAMELA. Notes to Boys; And Other Things I Shouldn't Share in Public; [by] Pamela Ribon 264 p. 2014 Pgw

1. Dating (Social customs) 2. Love letters 3. Memoirs 4. Teenagers
ISBN 1940207053; 9781940207056

SUMMARY: In this book, author Pamela Ribon reflects on her teenage years and her collection of love letters. "Miserably trapped in small town Texas with no invention of the internet in sight, Ribon spent countless hours of her high school years writing letters to her (often unrequited) crushes. The big question is: Why did she always keep a copy for herself?" (Publisher's note)

REVIEW: *Booklist* v110 no11 p11 F 1 2014 Kristine Huntley

REVIEW: *Kirkus Rev* v82 no1 p180 Ja 1 2014

"Notes to Boys: And Other Things I Shouldn't Share in Public". "If reading through the detritus of [Pamela] Ribon's adolescent longings is not tiresome enough, the author includes, in bold type, contemporary dissections of her previous copious correspondence and overwrought interior landscape. . . . Ribon's numerous fans should welcome this retelling of 'things she shouldn't share in public,' now twined with her adult musings. For others, it's a tedious slog through a year in the life of a teenager who, as the author herself recalled, wrote obsessively, compulsively and constantly."

RICARDO, FRANCISCO J. The engagement aesthetic; experiencing new media art through critique; [by] Francisco J. Ricardo vi, 250 p. 2013 Bloomsbury

1. Aesthetics 2. Art criticism 3. Art literature 4. Art theory 5. New media art
ISBN 9781623560409 (pbk. : alk. paper); 9781623561345 (hardcover : alk. paper)
LC 2012-044419

SUMMARY: In this book, "the author posits that digital media inspire an interaction with an audience, and that this engagement can be productively explored through the artistic process of critique (an open-ended and reflective process of exploration that begins with the senses and avoids judgments). Each aesthetic property identified (e.g., metonymy, performativity, reflexivity) is linked both to art history and theory." (Choice: Current Reviews for Academic Libraries)

REVIEW: *Choice* v51 no5 p821-2 Ja 2014 E. K. Mix

"The Engagement Aesthetic: Experiencing New Media Art Through Critique." "[Francisco J.] Ricardo . . . wisely avoids pitfalls associated with new media: the fast-changing nature of the technology that underpins it, and an unlimited array of possible examples to discuss. Instead Ricardo focuses both on the experience that new media provides and its critical difference from earlier, specifically object-based, or 'modern,' forms of art. The book's title might mislead potential readers, as Ricardo's work is not really about aesthetics per se; nor does it fit into the category of art criticism. . . . Despite the weightiness of the material, the short-chapter structure and restrained use of jargon makes this volume surprisingly accessible."

RICE, AMY. Playing with stencils; exploring repetition, pattern, and personal designs; [by] Amy Rice 144 p. 2013 Quarry Books

1. CRAFTS & HOBBIES—Stenciling 2. Do-it-yourself literature 3. Patterns for crafts 4. Stencil work 5. Stencils & stencil cutting
ISBN 9781592538294 (pbk.)
LC 2012-037756

SUMMARY: In this book, "multimedia artist [Amy] Rice explores the possibilities of stenciling in this collection of basic to intermediate-level projects. Rice shows crafters how to cut or burn custom stencils from their own artwork or photographs, then presents a variety of projects that showcase stenciling on materials ranging from fabric and wood to paper products and cake. Each project includes step-by-step illustrations with photographs." (Library Journal)

REVIEW: *Booklist* v110 no5 p10-1 N 1 2013 Barbara Jacobs

"Playing With Stencils: Exploring Repetition, Pattern, and Personal Designs." "[Amy Rice] excels at explaining the basics, beginning with the actual design of the project, and she provides step-by-step color photographs to augment her written instructions. Her aesthetic viewpoint does not depend on one era or one style. Rather, she delights in gathering inspiration from the world, including German paper cutting (Scherenschnitte), twentieth-century rustic antiques, 'mod' and 'pop,' Victorian lace, and many others. There's much to admire and choose from here, including shadowbox frames (with paper dolls inside), customer wallpaper, and a dancing-in-the-rain shower curtain."

RICH, DANIEL J. Project Gitmo; Resurrection; [by] Daniel J. Rich 344 p. 2013 CreateSpace Independent Publishing Platform

1. Iraq War, 2003-2011 2. Persian Gulf War, 1991 3. Speculative fiction 4. Vampires—Fiction 5. War stories
ISBN 1482051168; 9781482051162

SUMMARY: In this book, "eight wounded American servicemen discover their miraculous recoveries occurred because they were genetically modified with a serum stolen from the Iraqis. The modification gave them enhanced physical abilities that could finally defeat the insurgencies in Iraq and Afghanistan. Their mission changes from offense to defense when the president is briefed into the project and orders it terminated. Now the team must outwit the fanatically devoted men sent to capture them." (Publishers' note)

REVIEW: *Kirkus Rev* p48 D 15 2013 supplemet best books 2013

"Project Gitmo". "A debut sci-fi technothriller in which U.S. troops find themselves the subjects of a bizarre government experiment. . . . , [Daniel J.] Rich's extremely clever, infectiously readable narrative. . . sprawls over 10 years and two continents, but he manages it all with a confident hand. His dialogue is immediately believable, his tensely controlled action scenes build in intensity as the plot advances, and his pitch-perfect blending of sci-fi and military action will appeal equally to fans of Tom Clancy and True Blood. An ingenious, thoroughly absorbing twist on the military-fiction genre."

REVIEW: *Kirkus Rev* v81 no9 p120 My 1 2013

RICHARDS, JAMIE.tr. Shklovsky. See Shklovsky

RICHARDS, JON. The human body; [by] Jon Richards 24 p. 2013 Owlkids Books

1. Charts, diagrams, etc. 2. Children's nonfiction 3. Human anatomy—Juvenile literature 4. Human body—Juvenile literature 5. Illustrated books
ISBN 9780750278683 paperback; 9781926973937 hardcover

SUMMARY: Written by Jon Richards and illustrated by Ed Simkins, this book helps children to "Discover what goes into every drop of your blood, compare the size of your lungs to the surface area of a tennis court, find out how many pencils the carbon in your body would fill, and more! From bone structure and muscles to the senses, our central nervous systems, and reproduction, this book explores the human body using a wide variety of icons, graphics, and pictograms." (Publisher's note)

REVIEW: *Kirkus Rev* v81 no16 p127 Ag 15 2013

"The Human Body." "In single-topic spreads, [author Jon] Richards surveys the human body's insides and outsides, senses, bacterial fellow travelers, reproduction, growth and organ transplants. Though not particularly systematic--mentioning, for instance, red, white and platelet blood cells but only explaining (some of) the actual functions of whites--he does drop many impressively big numbers and also describes major parts and processes clearly. Printed in intense colors against monochromatic backgrounds, [illustrator Ed]

Simkins' images are eye-catching, but they only illustrate the arrays of quick facts and numbers rather than highlighting comparisons or contrasts."

REVIEW: *Libr J* v139 no9 p50 My 15 2014 Barbara Hoffert

RICHARDS, MICHAEL.il. Inside conducting. See Inside conducting

RICHARDSON, CAROL M.ed. Old Saint Peter's, Rome. See Old Saint Peter's, Rome

RICHARDSON, KIM. Call of the Klondike. See Meissner, D.

RICHARDSON, MATT. The queer limit of Black memory; Black lesbian literature and irresolution; [by] Matt Richardson 204 p. 2013 Ohio State University Press

1. Blacks in literature 2. Lesbianism in literature 3. Lesbians in literature 4. Literature—History & criticism
ISBN 9780814212226 (cloth: alk. paper); 9780814293232 (cd)
LC 2012-050159

SUMMARY: It was author Matt Richardson's "intent to consider 'the impact of Black vernacular culture from a queer theoretical perspective, specifically revising the function of performance, blues, and jazz as structures that enable gender transition and fluidity as well as same-sex desire.'... Richardson concludes that 'being black and queer and living in the world is a dangerous proposition'." (Choice: Current Reviews for Academic Libraries)

REVIEW: *Choice* v51 no8 p1382-3 Ap 2014 C. Machado

"The Queer Limit of Black Memory: Black Lesbian Literature and Irresolution". "This well-researched, well-argued book grew out of [Matt] Richardson's visit to San Francisco's Museum of the African Diaspora, where he noted the absence of black queer histories. . . . One of the book's persistent themes is the transgressive nature of black lesbian love and its alienation from mainstream heterosexual black experience; in fact, being black and queer can be seen as something the white dominant (former colonizer) culture has foisted on an already oppressed black community. . . . Valuable in African American history and queer/GLBT studies and literature."

RICHARDSON, MICHAEL.tr. A World Without Wall Street? See Morin, F.

RICHARDSON, ROBERT D. Splendor of heart; Walter Jackson Bate and the teaching of literature; [by] Robert D. Richardson 127 p. 2012 David R. Godine, Publisher

1. College teachers—Interviews 2. Literature teachers—United States—Biography 3. Memoirs
ISBN 1567924751; 9781567924756
LC 2012-020827

SUMMARY: This memoir focuses on the author's relationship with literature professor "Walter Jackson Bate (1918-99). Bate initially taught a sophomore-survey English class at Harvard in the 1950s. . . . [Robert D.] Richardson remembers him then and in later years, quoting from works Bate loved and rounding out his memories with interludes of walks, visits to Bate's farm, or trips through a forest in an old jeep. . . . The book concludes with a wide-ranging interview with Bate by John Paul Russo." (Booklist)

REVIEW: *Am Sch* v83 no1 p121-2 Wint 2014 MICHAEL DIRDA

"Splendor of Heart: Walter Jackson Bate and the Teaching of Literature". "Although 'Splendor of Heart' is an affectionate and winning portrait of a scholar, it could have been better. Richardson's memoir comes across as somewhat loosely written, rambling and even repetitive, which is surprising given the incisive brilliance of his own biographies. . . . By contrast, [Paul] Russo's interview, though fine, seems a little too high-minded and respectful. . . . Walter Jackson Bate believed that a good reader possesses 'intensity and empathy' and that literature was, above all else, 'an expression of human experience.' Cavils aside, to be reminded of these truths is just one of the many pleasures of 'Splendor of Heart.'"

REVIEW: *Booklist* v110 no8 p7 D 15 2013 Eloise Kinney

RICHLER, HOWARD. How happy became homosexual; and other mysterious semantic shifts; [by] Howard Richler 163 p. 2013 Ronsdale Press

1. English language—Etymology 2. English language—History 3. Historical lexicology 4. Historical literature 5. Linguistic change
ISBN 1553802306; 9781553802303 (print); 9781553802310 (ebook); 9781553802327 (pdf)
LC 2013-412948

SUMMARY: This book, written by Howard Richler, "educates and entertains us while explaining how words such as 'nice' and 'gay' have changed meanings. Surprisingly, we discover that even many of our nouns and verbs have been in a constant state of flux. . .. This morphing of meanings is ever-present, and Richler explains how, even in the last twenty years or so, words such as 'fulsome' are in the midst of a reversal of meaning." (Publisher's note)

REVIEW: *Can Lit* no220 p180-1 Spr 2014 Gabrielle Lim

REVIEW: *Choice* v51 no4 p606 D 2013 J. Adlington

"How Happy Became Homosexual: And Other Mysterious Semantic Shifts." "Students of English literature may become aware of the many changes in the meaning of common words that produce surprising and counterintuitive readings of Chaucer or Shakespeare. [Author Howard] Richler . . . uses this volume to trace the evolving meanings of some 250 words, drawn primarily from earlier centuries of British English with occasional excursions into Canadian and American usage. Richler discusses the processes involved in language change—metaphor, generalization, narrowing, strengthening, weakening, and value judgments—but provides themed chapters for only two processes, pejoration and amelioration. . . . A lively work, but not an academic one."

RICHMOND, PETER. Phil Jackson; lord of the rings; [by] Peter Richmond 352 p. 2013 Blue Rider Press, a member of Penguin Group (USA)

1. BIOGRAPHY & AUTOBIOGRAPHY—Sports 2. Basketball coaches—United States—Biography 3. Biography (Literary form) 4. SPORTS & RECREATION—Basketball
ISBN 9780399158704 (hardback : alkaline paper)

LC 2013-039592

SUMMARY: This book presents a biography of "Phil Jackson . . . the most successful coach in professional sports history. He won six NBA championships with the Chicago Bulls and another five with the Los Angeles Lakers. And he was a player on two New York Knick championship teams in the early seventies. . . . The enigmatic Phil has been the public Phil--hippie, coach, husband, teacher, seeker, friend, and father." (Booklist)

REVIEW: *Booklist* v110 no8 p6-7 D 15 2013 Wes Lukowsky

"Phil Jackson: The Lord of the Rings." "Veteran sports journalist [Peter] Richmond calls this a biography, but it's really more of a quest--Richmond in search of the real Phil Jackson, a fascinating man who has remained a bit of a mystery despite a penchant for writing books about himself and his career (four to date). Richmond spent a lot of time with those four books, but he also interviewed former players, friends, and associates in an attempt to get a sense of the man as well as the coach. . . . He's a fascinating subject, and while Richmond may not plumb Jackson's depths completely, he makes a reasonably good dive in that direction."

REVIEW: *Kirkus Rev* v81 no24 p206 D 15 2013

REVIEW: *Publ Wkly* v260 no50 p64 D 9 2013

RICKER, ANDY, 1964-. Pok Pok; food and stories from the streets, homes, and roadside restaurants of Thailand; viii, 295 p. 2013 Ten Speed Press

1. COOKING—Methods—Wok 2. COOKING—Regional & Ethnic—Asian 3. COOKING—Regional & Ethnic—Thai 4. Cookbooks 5. Cooking, Thai
ISBN 9781607742883 (hardback); 9781607742890 (eBook); 1607742888
LC 2013-012451

SUMMARY: "In this much-anticipated debut cookbook, [author Andy] Ricker shares seventy of the most popular recipes from Thailand and his Pok Pok restaurants. . . . But 'Pok Pok' is more than just a collection of favorite recipes: it is also a master course in Thai cooking from one of the most passionate and knowledgeable authorities on the subject." (Publisher's note)

REVIEW: *N Y Times Book Rev* p20-1 D 8 2013 WILLIAM GRIMES

"Cooking From the Heart: My Favorite Lessons Learned Along the Way," "Pok Pok: Food and Stories From the Streets, Homes, and Roadside Restaurants of Thailand," and "Daniel: My French Cuisine." "John Best has an interesting life story to tell in 'John Besh: Cooking From the Heart.' . . . There are a few too many usual-suspect recipes, but Besh makes an engaging guide. . . . By Andy Ricker with J.J. Goode, . . . As a tutorial on Thai cuisine and its principal regional styles, 'Pok Pok' can't be beat. . . . In 'Daniel: My French Cuisine' . . . , Daniel Boulud . . . conducts a guided tour of his life and the parts of France he know best. . . . From there it's a giant leap to the . . . drop-dead elegant dishes from Daniel that take up about half the book."

RICKINSON, ALAN. The virus that causes cancer. See Crawford, D. H.

RICKS, THOMAS E. The generals; American military command from World War II to today; [by] Thomas E. Ricks 576 p. 2012 Penguin Press

1. Command of troops—History—20th century—Case studies 2. Generals—United States—History—20th century 3. Historical literature 4. Military literature
ISBN 1594204047; 9781594204043
LC 2012-015110

SUMMARY: This book, by Thomas E. Ricks, presents an overview of U.S. military leadership since 1945. "History has been kind to the American generals of World War II--Marshall, Eisenhower, Patton, and Bradley--and less kind to the generals of the wars that followed. . . . Thomas E. Ricks sets out to explain why that is. . . . [W]e meet great leaders and suspect ones, generals who rose to the occasion and those who failed themselves and their soldiers." (Publisher's note)

REVIEW: *Booklist* v109 no2 p6 S 15 2012

REVIEW: *Choice* v51 no2 p337 O 2013 J. Tucci

REVIEW: *Kirkus Rev* v80 no18 p194 S 15 2012

REVIEW: *Libr J* v137 no16 p91 O 1 2012 Richard Fraser

REVIEW: *N Y Times Book Rev* p20 D 29 2013 IHSAN TAYLOR

"The Generals: American Military Command From World War II to Today," "The Hot Country," and "A Man of Misconceptions: The Life of an Eccentric in an Age of Change." "History has been kind to the American generals of World War II. . . . But today's Army is an entrenched bureaucracy . . . , [author Thomas E.] Ricks argues in ['The Generals']. . . . [Author Robert Olen] Butler's crime fiction debut ['The Hot Country'] is a high-spirited adventure set during the Mexican Revolution. . . . ['A Man of Misconceptions'] is told through the life of the 17th-century Jesuit priest and polymath Athanasius Kircher, who wrote sweeping (and error-filled) studies on alchemy, astronomy, optics, hieroglyphics, medicine and music."

REVIEW: *N Y Times Book Rev* p20 D 9 2012 MAX BOOT

REVIEW: *Natl Rev* v65 no4 p45-6 Mr 11 2013 MACKUBIN THOMAS OWENS

REVIEW: *Publ Wkly* v259 no34 p51-2 Ag 20 2012

RICO, MONICA. Nature's noblemen; transatlantic masculinities and the nineteenth-century American West; [by] Monica Rico 287 p. 2013 Yale University Press

1. British—West (U.S.)—History—19th century 2. Frontier and pioneer life—West (U.S.) 3. Historical literature 4. Masculinity—Great Britain—History—19th century 5. Masculinity—United States—History—20th century 6. Upper class—Great Britain—History—19th century 7. Upper class—West (U.S.)—History—19th century
ISBN 9780300136067 (hardbound : alk. paper)
LC 2012-047960

SUMMARY: This book by Monica Rico "explores the myth of the American West in the nineteenth century as a place for men to assert their masculinity by 'roughing it' in the wilderness and reveals how this myth played out in a transatlantic context. . . . Each chapter tells the story of an individual who, by traveling these transatlantic paths, sought to resolve anxieties about class, gender, and empire in an era of profound economic and social transformation." (Publisher's note)

REVIEW: *Choice* v51 no4 p712-3 D 2013 S. D. Reschly

"Nature's Noblemen: Transatlantic Masculinities and the

Nineteenth-Century American West." "This book tracks homosocial hunting expeditions led by British and American elite men. Theodore Roosevelt and Buffalo Bill hunted big game and stalked white, masculine, wealthy superiority; other explorers hailed from England, Scotland, and Anglo-Ireland. . . . Leaders such as Roosevelt worried about the "race suicide" of Anglo-Saxons, and theorized that hunting in preserved wilderness spaces could advance civilization as the closing frontier had done. [Monica] Rico is well tuned to colorful and illustrative adventurists, such as Sir William Drummond Stewart, who imported American bison to his Scottish estate."

RIDGWAY, CHRISTIE. Turn Up the Heat. See Foster, L.

RIDINGTON, JILLIAN. Where Happiness Dwells. See Ridington, R.

RIDINGTON, ROBIN. Where Happiness Dwells; A History of the Dane-zaa First Nations; [by] Robin Ridington 402 p. 2013 University of Washington Press

1. Historical literature 2. Indians of North America—Canada 3. Indians of North America—History 4. Oral history 5. Tsattine Indians

ISBN 0774822953; 9780774822954

SUMMARY: "At the request of the Doig River First Nations anthropologists Robin and Jillian Ridington present a history of the Dane-zaa people based on oral histories collected over a half century of fieldwork. Taking a poetic form that does justice to the rhythm of Dane-zaa storytelling, these powerful stories span the full length of history, from the story of creation to the fur trade, from the arrival of missionaries to cases heard in the Supreme Court of Canada." (Publisher's note)

REVIEW: *Choice* v51 no1 p149-50 S 2013 B. F. R. Edwards

"Where Happiness Dwells: A History of the Dane-Zaa First Nations." "This history of the Dane-zaa First Nations, who are also known as the Fort St. John Beaver Band, or Doig River and Blueberry River First Nations, portrays a people who within just six decades have transitioned from a traditional hunting and gathering lifestyle to learning to succeed in the modern world. . . . This history consists of elders' stories recorded and kept in an archive by anthropologists Robin Ridington and Jillian Ridington at the request of the chief and council of Doig River First Nation, based on the oral histories they had collected."

RIEGER, BERNHARD. The people's car; a global history of the Volkswagen Beetle; [by] Bernhard Rieger 416 p. 2013 Harvard University Press

1. Automobile industry—Germany (West) 2. Automobile industry—Germany—History 3. Germany (West)—History 4. Historical literature 5. Volkswagen Beetle automobile 6. Volkswagen Beetle automobile—History

ISBN 0674050916; 9780674050914 (alk. paper)

LC 2012-029928

SUMMARY: In this book, Bernhard Rieger "examines culture and technology, politics and economics, and industrial design and advertising genius to reveal how a car commissioned by Hitler and designed by Ferdinand Porsche became an exceptional global commodity on a par with Coca-Cola. Beyond its quality and low cost, the Beetle's success hinged on its uncanny ability to capture the imaginations of people across nations and cultures." (Publisher's note)

REVIEW: *Bus Hist Rev* v88 no1 p225-7 Spr 2014 Corinna Ludwig

REVIEW: *Choice* v51 no2 p287 O 2013 C. J. Myers

REVIEW: *Libr J* v138 no12 p79 Jl 1 2013 Maria Bagshaw

REVIEW: *London Rev Books* v35 no17 p35-7 S 12 2013 Richard J. Evans

"The People's Car: A Global History of the Volkswagen Beetle." "The Beetle, [author Bernhard] Rieger plausibly argues, achieved iconic status in West Germany in the 1950s by being a typical product of the 'economic miracle': not flashy or glamorous, but solid, functional, dependable, inexpensive to acquire, cheap to run and easy to maintain--everything the Third Reich was not. . . . Lacking obvious symbols of national identification. West Germany fixed on the Beetle. . . . He is very good . . . on its appeal in the United States, where it became a popular second car for many families in the expanding suburbs of the 1950s and 1960s, as American car manufacturers were unable to keep pace with rapidly rising demand."

RIEGER, SUSAN. The divorce papers; a novel; [by] Susan Rieger 496 p. 2014 Crown Publishers

1. Divorce—Fiction 2. Divorce settlements—Fiction 3. Domestic relations—Fiction 4. Legal stories 5. Women lawyers—Fiction

ISBN 0804137447; 9780804137447 (hardback)

LC 2013-027552

SUMMARY: This novel, by Susan Rieger, "tells the story of one very messy, very high-profile divorce, and the endearingly cynical young lawyer dragooned into handling it. Twenty-nine-year-old Sophie Diehl . . . must handle the intake interview for the daughter of the firm's most important client. After eighteen years of marriage, . . . Mia Meiklejohn Durkheim has just been served divorce papers. . . . She is locked and loaded to fight her eminent and ambitious husband." (Publisher's note)

REVIEW: *Booklist* v110 no11 p22 F 1 2014 Carol Gladstein

REVIEW: *Kirkus Rev* v82 no1 p236 Ja 1 2014

"The Divorce Papers". "A brutally comic chronicle of high-end divorce told through letters, emails and a huge pile of legal memorandums. . . . As Sophie gears up to battle the sleazy New York lawyer Daniel has hired, she also must contend with Fiona's ruffled feathers and office politics involving ethnic, class and gender issues brought to light in a flurry of interoffice memos. . . . Rieger pulls out every legal document connected to the case, including witness affidavits, settlement offer breakdowns and legal invoices. Extremely clever, especially the legal infighting; this book should prove hugely popular with the legal set as well as anyone who has ever witnessed a divorce in process."

REVIEW: *Libr J* v139 no3 p99 F 15 2014 Brooke Bolton

REVIEW: *N Y Times Book Rev* p45 Je 1 2014 EMILY GIFFIN

REVIEW: *N Y Times Book Rev* p34 Je 8 2014

REVIEW: *New Yorker* v90 no18 p75-1 Je 30 2014

REVIEW: *Publ Wkly* v260 no47 p32 N 18 2013

RIEGLE, ROSALIE G. Crossing the line; nonviolent resisters speak out for peace; [by] Rosalie G. Riegle xxiv, 377 p. 2013 Cascade Books

1. Civil disobedience—United States 2. Government, Resistance to—United States 3. Historical literature 4. Pacifism—United States 5. Pacifists—United States—Interviews 6. Peace movements—United States 7. Political prisoners—United States—Interviews 8. War resistance movements—United States

ISBN 1610976835; 9781610976831

LC 2012-285237

SUMMARY: In this book, "more than sixty-five peacemakers have contributed oral narratives" to a history of civil disobedience. "Many work at conventional careers; some do full-time peacemaking by living in Catholic Worker houses or in the Jonah House community; several are priests and nuns who minister worldwide. Also featured are three resisters prominent in War Resisters League history." (Publisher's note)

REVIEW: *America* v210 no2 p25-6 Ja 20 2014 ANNA J. BROWN

"Crossing the Line: Nonviolent Resister Speak Out for Peace" and "Doing Time for Peace: Resistance, Family, and Community". "[A] rather stunning collection of resistance stories. . . . [Rosalie G.] Riegle, the steward of such noble stories, has done a work of great service. . . . The text [of 'Crossing the Line'] is both challenging and inviting. . . . In 'Doing Time for Peace: Resistance, Family, and Community,' the reader has a chance, in its seven chapters, to become immersed in the stories and lives of peacemakers and of their families and communities. To have this opportunity is a delight and a gift."

RIEGLE, ROSALIE G.ed. Doing time for peace. See Doing time for peace

RIES, ALEX.il. Zoobots. See Becker, H.

RIFFENBURGH, BEAU. Pinkerton's great detective; the amazing life and times of James McParland; [by] Beau Riffenburgh 400 p. 2013 Viking Adult

1. BIOGRAPHY & AUTOBIOGRAPHY—Law Enforcement 2. HISTORY—United States—19th Century 3. HISTORY—United States—General 4. Historical literature 5. Private investigators—United States—Biography

ISBN 0670025461; 9780670025466 (hardback)

LC 2013-017204

SUMMARY: In this book, author Beau Riffenburgh "digs deep into the recently released [Pinkerton's National Detective Agency] archives to present the first biography of [James] McParland [and] brings readers along on McParland's most challenging cases: from young McParland's infiltration of the murderous Molly Maguires gang . . . to his hunt for the notorious Butch Cassidy and the Wild Bunch to his controversial investigation of the Western Federation of Mines." (Publisher's note)

REVIEW: *Kirkus Rev* v81 no22 p13 N 15 2013

REVIEW: *Libr J* v138 no10 p82 Je 1 2013

REVIEW: *Libr J* v139 no6 p59 Ap 1 2014 Stephen L. Hupp

REVIEW: *N Y Times Book Rev* p12 D 22 2013 BEN MACINTYRE

"Pinkerton's Great Detective: The Amazing Life and Times of James McParland." "Locating the real James McParland amid the invective, acclaim and invention (including his own) is no easy task, and Beau Riffenburgh . . . has made good use of the recently released Pinkerton archives to produce the fullest and fairest biography to date. Yet McParland continues to be an oddly mysterious character, obscured by his very notoriety. . . . He was the first private eye in the public eye, and yet he remains strangely private."

REVIEW: *Publ Wkly* v260 no36 p50 S 9 2013

RIGGLE, KRISTINA. The Whole Golden World; A Novel; [by] Kristina Riggle 448 p. 2013 HarperCollins

1. Domestic fiction 2. Marriage—Fiction 3. Mothers & daughters—Fiction 4. Teacher-student relationships—Fiction 5. Trials (Statutory rape)

ISBN 0062206451; 9780062206459

SUMMARY: This book, by Kristina Riggle, "follows high school senior Morgan Monetti's affair with her married calculus teacher, T.J. Hill, and how it impacts several lives in the small town of Arbor Valley, Mich. Raised by emotionally absent high school principal Joe and his overbearing wife, Dinah (whose control issues stem from living with the fear of losing her now teenage special-needs twins), 17-year-old Morgan has always been treated as though she were older than she actually is." (Publishers Weekly)

REVIEW: *Booklist* v110 no4 p17 O 15 2013 Rebecca Vnuk

"The Whole Golden World." "Dinah's world is about to fall apart--her independent coffee shop is failing, and her nemesis wants to buy it out from under her; her overly coddled twin sons are having a hard time adjusting to a new school; and, worst of all, her 17-year-old daughter, Morgan, has just been caught half-undressed in her math teacher's car. . . . [Kristina] Riggle . . . masterfully unfolds the families' stories with just the right pace, tone, and drama, uncovering plenty of family secrets and emotional struggles without making it a soap opera. Fans of Jodi Picoult and Barbara Delinsky will devour this story."

REVIEW: *Kirkus Rev* v81 no19 p154 O 1 2013

REVIEW: *Publ Wkly* v260 no38 p52-3 S 23 2013

RILEY-SMITH, JONATHAN. The Knights Hospitaller in the Levant, c.1070-1309; [by] Jonathan Riley-Smith xiii, 334 p. 2012 Palgrave Macmillan

1. Historical literature 2. Middle East—History 3. Military religious orders

ISBN 9780230290839

LC 2012-011175

SUMMARY: This book looks at the history of "the Order of the Hospital of St John . . . a major landowner and a significant political presence in most European states. . . . Themes in the book relate to the tension that always existed between the Hospital's roles as both a hospitaller and a military order and its performance as an institution that was at the same time a religious order and a great international corporation." (Publisher's note)

REVIEW: *Choice* v50 no8 p1496-7 Ap 2013 S. A. Throop

REVIEW: *Engl Hist Rev* v129 no536 p174-6 F 2014 C.J. Tyerman

"The Knights Hospitaller in the Levant, c.1070-1309".

"This is an insider's book, not so much in the crude sense of its author being a Knight Grand Cross of Grace and Devotion of the Sovereign Military Order of Malta, but because he takes vocation seriously and assesses the plentiful medieval Hospitallers' records (to an extent) on their own terms in the light of their own professed adherence to their calling. [Jonathan] Riley-Smith presents an account rich in empathy for the order and its members in their dual role. . . . The virtues of this study rest on its clarity of construction and mature control of a mass of literary, archival and archaeological material, which is presented in characteristically lucid style."

REVIEW: *History* v98 no330 p270-2 Ap 2013 Norman Housley

RILEY, BRENDAN P.tr. Hypothermia. See Enrigue, A.

RIMER, J. THOMAS.ed. The Kiso Road. See Naff, W. E.

RIOLS, NOREEN. The Secret Ministry of Ag. & Fish; [by] Noreen Riols 324 p. 2013 Macmillan

1. Great Britain. Special Operations Executive 2. Historical literature 3. Women spies 4. World War, 1939-1945—Secret service 5. World War, 1939-1945—Underground movements—France

ISBN 0230770908; 9780230770904

SUMMARY: "'My mother thought I was working for the Ministry of Ag. and Fish.' So begins Noreen Riols' compelling memoir of her time as a member of Churchill's 'secret army', the Special Forces Executive. . . . For the next four years, Noreen worked . . . to support the French Resistance. Sworn to secrecy, Noreen told no one that she spent her days meeting agents returning from behind enemy lines, acting as a decoy, passing on messages . . . and picking up codes in crossword puzzles." (Publisher's note)

REVIEW: *TLS* no5779 p9-10 Ja 3 2014 MARK SEAMAN

"She Landed by Moonlight: The Story of Secret Agent Pearl Witherington: The Real Charlotte Gray," "Priscilla: The Hidden Life of an Englishwoman in Wartime France," and "The Secret Ministry of Ag. & Fish." "'She Landed by Moonlight' is a conventional biography of a hitherto somewhat neglected heroine of E Section of the British secret service, the Special Operations Executive (SOE); 'The Secret Ministry of Ag. & Fish' is the autobiography of a very junior member of that organization's backroom staff; and 'Prisciila: The hidden life of an Englishwoman in wartime France' is a fascinating voyage of discovery into a decidedly murky family history, in which a nephew goes in search of his aunt's wartime secrets."

RIPLEY, AMANDA. The smartest kids in the world; and how they got that way; [by] Amanda Ripley 320 p. 2013 Simon & Schuster

1. Comparative education 2. Education—Finland 3. Education—Korea (South) 4. Education—Poland 5. Educational literature

ISBN 1451654421; 9781451654424

LC 2013-002021

SUMMARY: This book looks at the educational disparities between the U.S. and other world nations. Journalist Amanda Ripley "recounts the experiences of three American teens studying abroad for a year in the education superpowers. Fifteen-year-old Kim raises $10,000 so she can go to high school in Finland; Eric, 18, trades a leafy suburb in Minnesota for a 'city stacked on top of a city' in South Korea; and Tom, 17, leaves Gettysburg, Pa., for Poland." (Publishers Weekly)

REVIEW: *Choice* v51 no9 p1652 My 2014 G. A. Clark

"The Smartest Kids in the World: And How They Got That Way". "Few books are this impressive and depressing, and few authors have assessed and evaluated US education as thoroughly as [Amanda] Ripley. . . . . Ripley does not specifically address the deficient conditions of US schools, but she does address many of the reasons these conditions exist. Everyone associated with US education, from school board members and teachers to parents and interested members of the public, should read this book, and everyone concerned about US education should address and alter this reality."

REVIEW: *Economist* p9 O 19 2013 Supplement The Great Deceleration

REVIEW: *Economist* v408 no8849 p69-70 Ag 17 2013

REVIEW: *Kirkus Rev* v81 no12 p63 Je 15 2013

REVIEW: *N Y Times Book Rev* p26 S 1 2013

REVIEW: *N Y Times Book Rev* p1-22 Ag 25 2013 Annie Murphy Paul

"The Smartest Kids in the World: And How They Got That Way." "[Amanda] Ripley is offering to show how other nations educate more students so much more effectively than we do, and her opening pages hold out a promising suggestion of masochistic satisfaction. . . . But Ripley . . . has a more challenging, and more interesting, project in mind. . . . In the best tradition of travel writing . . . she gets well beneath the glossy surface of these foreign cultures, and manages to make our own culture look newly strange . . . quite a feat for an institution as familiar and fiercely defended as high school. The question is whether the startling perspective provided by this masterly book can also generate the will to make changes."

REVIEW: *New York Times* v163 no56290 pD5 O 15 2013

REVIEW: *Publ Wkly* v260 no28 p163 Jl 15 2013

RIPPIN, SALLY. Angel Creek; [by] Sally Rippin 152 p. 2013 Text Publishing Company

1. Angels—Juvenile fiction 2. Cousins—Fiction 3. Families—Juvenile fiction 4. Fantasy fiction 5. Pets—Juvenile literature

ISBN 1921758058; 9781921758058

SUMMARY: In this book by Sally Rippin, "frustrated and lonely after her family's recent move, Jelly faces the first year of high school knowing no one. She wanders down to the creek behind her house with her cousins, Gino . . . where they discover a small, waterlogged angel with a broken wing. . . . She and Gino hide it in a metal shed, a poor choice in the summer heat. Then, as the angel suffers from its captivity, things begin to go badly all around them." (Kirkus Reviews)

REVIEW: *Bull Cent Child Books* v67 no2 p112-3 O 2013 K. Q. G.

"Angel Creek." "Over the next few weeks, Jelly cares for the celestial being in a nearby shed but soon realizes that her relationship with Gino may not be the only thing suffering from the angel's presence; convinced her family's recent spate of bad luck must have something to do with the creature, she sets off to return the angel child to its mother. A gentle tale with just a hint of spookiness, this Australian import will please fans of Patricia MacLachlan's domestic dramas as well as readers of David Almond's more cerebral and fantastical works. Bits of Australian slang and local references give the story a regional flair, while Jelly's struggles with her family, anxieties about her new school, and feelings of ambiguity toward adulthood make her broadly relatable."

REVIEW: *Kirkus Rev* v81 no12 p111 Je 15 2013

RISEMAN, NOAH. Defending whose country?; indigenous soldiers in the Pacific war; [by] Noah Riseman xii, 304 p. 2012 University of Nebraska Press

1. Historical literature 2. Native American military personnel 3. Navajo Indians 4. Navajo code talkers 5. Papua New Guineans 6. World War, 1939-1945—Campaigns—Pacific Ocean 7. World War, 1939-1945—Cryptography 8. World War, 1939-1945—Participation, Aboriginal Australian 9. World War, 1939-1945—Participation, Indian 10. World War, 1939-1945—Personal narratives, Australian 11. Yolngu (Australian people) 12. Yolngu (Australian people)—Warfare

ISBN 9780803237933 (cloth : alk. paper)
LC 2012-015594

SUMMARY: This book by Noah Riseman "is a comparative study of the military participation of Papua New Guineans, Yolngu, and Navajos in the Pacific theater. . . . In the campaign against Japan in the Pacific during the Second World War, the armed forces of the United States, Australia, and the Australian colonies of Papua and New Guinea made use of indigenous peoples in new capacities." (Publisher's note)

REVIEW: *Am Hist Rev* v118 no4 p1154-5 O 2013 Timothy C. Winegard

"Defending Whose Country? Indigenous Soldiers in the Pacific War." "Noah Riseman's engaging book compares the service of Yolngu Aboriginal Australians, Navajo (Diné) Native Americans, and Papua New Guineans in the Pacific theater during World War II. The author is to be commended for tackling the always difficult comparative approach to history. While the respective two-chapter case studies offer exceptional detail and articulate prose, this framework does not lend itself to a fully integrated and interwoven contextual relationship between the three focus groups, as would structural thematic chapters. In fairness, however, Riseman does include enough comparative vignettes within the stand-alone chapters to parallel thematic elements."

RISEN, CLAY. The bill of the century; the epic battle for the Civil Rights Act; [by] Clay Risen 320 p. 2014 Bloomsbury Press

1. Civil rights—United States—History

ISBN 1608198243; 9781608198245 (hardback)
LC 2014-004662

SUMMARY: "Clay Risen shows [that] the battle for the Civil Rights Act was a . . . broad, epic struggle, a sweeping tale of unceasing grassroots activism, ringing speeches, backroom deal-making and finally, hand-to-hand legislative combat. The larger-than-life cast of characters ranges from Senate lions like Mike Mansfield and Strom Thurmond to NAACP lobbyist Charles Mitchell, called 'the 101st senator' for his Capitol Hill clout, and industrialist J. Irwin Miller, who helped mobilize a powerful religious coalition for the bill." (Publisher's note)

REVIEW: *Atlantic* v313 no3 p88-98 Ap 2014 MICHAEL O'DONNELL

"We the People: The Civil Rights Revolution," "An Idea Whose Time Has Come: Two Presidents, Two Parties, and the Battle for the Civil Rights Act of 1964," and "The Years of Lyndon Johnson: The Passage of Power". "[Bruce] Ackerman's is the most ambitious; it is the third volume in an ongoing series on American constitutional history called 'We the People'. . . . [Todd S.] Purdum's . . . book is an astute, well-paced, and highly readable play-by-play of the bill's journey to become a law. . . . Purdum's version of this story is excellent, but he cannot surpass the masterful Robert A. Caro, who offers a peerless and truly mesmerizing account of Johnson's assumption of the presidency in 'The Passage of Power'."

REVIEW: *Booklist* v110 no17 p66 My 1 2014 David Pitt

REVIEW: *Choice* v51 no12 p2256 Ag 2014 D. R. Turner

REVIEW: *Kirkus Rev* v82 no4 p217 F 15 2014

REVIEW: *Libr J* v139 no4 p101 Mr 1 2014 Karl Helicher

REVIEW: *N Y Times Book Rev* p13 My 18 2014 KEVIN BOYLE

REVIEW: *New Yorker* v90 no20 p74-1 Jl 21 2014

REVIEW: *Publ Wkly* v261 no6 p77 F 10 2014

RISSE, MATHIAS. On global justice; [by] Mathias Risse 465 p. 2012 Princeton University Press

1. Cosmopolitanism 2. Distributive justice 3. Human rights 4. Internationalism 5. Social justice

ISBN 0691142696 (cloth : alk. paper); 9780691142692 (cloth : alk. paper)
LC 2011-053393

SUMMARY: In this book, "Stressing humanity's collective ownership of the earth, Mathias Risse offers a new theory of global distributive justice--what he calls pluralist internationalism--where in different contexts, different principles of justice apply. Arguing that statists and cosmopolitans seek overarching answers to problems that vary too widely for one single justice relationship, Risse explores who should have how much of what we all need and care about." (Publisher's note)

REVIEW: *Choice* v50 no11 p2101 Jl 2013 J. E. Herbel

REVIEW: *Ethics* v124 no1 p209-13 O 2013 LUIS CABRERA

"On Global Justice." "In this long-anticipated monograph, Mathias Risse offers the most comprehensive and probably most formidable set of arguments to date for a midlevel, 'internationalist' approach to global justice. . . . The account overall is sophisticated and highly detailed. . . . The most pivotal claims are in part 1, where Risse defends strong compatriot distributive priority. These claims centrally inform the later critiques of stronger global principles of justice and thus merit close scrutiny. . . . The above should indicate how rich, detailed, and deftly theorized the overall work is. It provides a wealth of nuanced arguments to be taken up by those advocating intermediate views on global justice."

REVIEW: *London Rev Books* v35 no4 p15-7 F 21 2013 Malcolm Bull

REVIEW: *Polit Sci Q (Wiley-Blackwell)* v128 no3 p577-8 Fall 2013 ADAM HOSEIN

RISSER, NICOLE DOMBROWSKI. France under fire;

German invasion, civilian flight and family survival during World War II; [by] Nicole Dombrowski Risser xv, 312 p. 2012 Cambridge University Press

1. HISTORY—Military—General 2. Historical literature 3. War—Protection of civilians—France 4. World War, 1939-1945—Civilian relief—France 5. World War, 1939-1945—France 6. World War, 1939-1945—Refugees

ISBN 9781107025325 (hardback)

LC 2012-016904

SUMMARY: This book "offers a social, political and military examination of the origins of the French refugee crisis of 1940, a mass displacement of eight million civilians fleeing German combatants. Scattered throughout a divided France, refugees turned to German Occupation officials and Vichy administrators for relief and repatriation. Their solutions raised questions about occupying powers' obligations to civilians and elicited new definitions of refugees' rights." (Publisher's note)

REVIEW: *Am Hist Rev* v119 no1 p261 F 2014 Robert Gildea

"France Under Fire: German Invasion, Civilian Flight, and Family Survival During World War II". "Nicole Dombrowski Risser's book is very strong in a number of domains. . . . But Dombrowski Risser is very keen to frame the story of claims made by women on the French state in terms of the emergence of human rights to protection and compensation for loss. . . . This would be a powerful argument if it could be demonstrated. But letters from women tend to show that they made their claims not on the basis of human rights but by virtue either of having been wronged or of the sacrifices they had made. . . . In all other ways the book is exemplary."

RITCHIE, ANGUS. From morality to metaphysics; the theistic implications of our ethical commitments; [by] Angus Ritchie vii, 198 p. 2012 Oxford University Press

1. Ethics 2. God—Proof 3. Philosophical literature 4. Religion and ethics 5. Theism

ISBN 0199652511 (hbk.); 9780199652518 (hbk.)

LC 2012-460133

SUMMARY: This book "offers an argument for the existence of God, based on our most fundamental moral beliefs. Angus Ritchie engages with a range of the most significant secular moral philosophers of our time, and argues that they all face a common difficulty which only theism can overcome. . . . Only theism can adequately explain our capacity for knowledge of objective moral truths." (Publisher's note)

REVIEW: *TLS* no5759 p28 Ag 16 2013 JOHN COTTINGHAM

"From Morality to Metaphysics: The Theistic Implications of Our Ethical Commitments," "God and Moral Obligation," and "Good God: The Theistic Foundations of Morality." "In . . . a powerful and carefully organized study, Angus Ritchie goes systematically through the main options available to the secularist, and finds them all wanting. . . . Stephen Evans's superbly lucid book . . . provides one of the best overviews of the current debate on this matter that one could hope for. . . . David Baggett and Jerry Walls . . . work carefully and conscientiously through some of the manoeuvres in the recent literature on the Euthyphro debate. . . . The overall impression left by all four books is of a rich and fertile area of research."

RIVAS, VICTOR.il. The secret of Ferrell Savage. See Gill, J. D.

RIVERA, JONATHAN. The Dreamer; Origins; [by] Jonathan Rivera 360 p. 2013 Jonathan Rivera

1. Fantasy fiction 2. Friendship—Fiction 3. Good & evil—Fiction 4. Magic—Fiction 5. Young adult fiction

ISBN 0988739321; 9780988739321

SUMMARY: In this book, "a group of children faces off against an evil ice queen. At the novel's outset, a group of children plans a daring escape from the Ice Queen's prison. At first, the story's 11-year-old hero, John, doesn't feel up to the task, but his unlikely friendship with a talking rat teaches him that he may have latent talents, including the ability to illuminate himself and summon an otherworldly power. He eventually helps his friends out of many dire situations." (Kirkus Reviews)

REVIEW: *Kirkus Rev* v82 no2 p376 Ja 15 2014

"The Dreamer: Origins". ". It's unclear who the target audience for this book is, although it's apparently aimed at an older middle-grade or younger YA audience. There are suggestions that the young characters are in their teens (and some hints of romance), but the text repeatedly refers to them as "kids," and they speak in a somewhat hokey dialect. . . . The relationships between the boys and girls are also somewhat old-fashioned: The boys always seem to be the heroes, while the girls tend to be mere love interests. . . . However, although the book is on the long side, it moves along quickly, with lots of action and new dangers to threaten the intrepid children, and its ending leaves room for a sequel."

RIVERS-MOORE, DEBBIE. Max's magical potion; [by] Debbie Rivers-Moore 10 p. 2013 Barrons Educational Series, Inc.

1. Children's stories 2. Dragons—Juvenile fiction 3. Hiccups 4. Magic—Juvenile fiction 5. Wizards—Juvenile fiction

ISBN 9780764166471

LC 2013-934755

SUMMARY: In this children's story by Debbie Rivers-Moore, "a young wizard helps cure Dudley the dragon's hiccups. He does so after the royal family and their servants call on him to help solve the hiccup-induced wafts of smoke that keep appearing throughout the castle. Magician Max concocts a potion that quickly cures Dudley, to everyone's delight." (Kirkus Reviews)

REVIEW: *Kirkus Rev* v82 no1 p150 Ja 1 2014

"Max's Magical Potion". "On each page, there is a die-cut hole shaped like arched windows or an opening to a cellar. When the page is turned, the image framed by the hole appears on the next double-page spread. These features appear to be only an attention-getting gimmick and do little to illuminate the slight story. While there are some clever images in the jewel-toned, detailed cartoon art . . . the antics and medieval imagery are going to go over the heads of typical board-book readers. The interactive feature on the cover—a pull-tab at the top of the book that opens and closes the castle doors to reveal the hero Max—will probably interest youngsters the most. . . . Neither magical nor memorable for typical board-book readers."

RIVERS, DANIEL WINUNWE. Radical relations; lesbian mothers, gay fathers, and their children in the United States since World War II; [by] Daniel Winunwe Rivers 304 p. 2013 University of North Carolina Press

1. Children of gay parents—United States—History 2. Families—United States—History 3. Gay parents—United States—History 4. Gay rights—United States—History 5. Historical literature
ISBN 1469607182; 9781469607184 (cloth : alk. paper)
LC 2013-001366

SUMMARY: In this book, "Daniel Winunwe Rivers offers a previously untold story of the American family: the first history of lesbian and gay parents and their children in the United States. Beginning in the postwar era, a period marked by both intense repression and dynamic change for lesbians and gay men, Rivers argues that by forging new kinds of family and childrearing relations, gay and lesbian parents have successfully challenged legal and cultural definitions of family as heterosexual." (Publisher's note)

REVIEW: *Choice* v51 no6 p1078 F 2014 E. W. Carp

"Radical Relations: Lesbian Mothers, Gay Fathers, and Their Children in the United States Since World War II." "In this deeply researched social history of six decades (1945-2003) of gay fathers, lesbian mothers, and their children. [Daniel Winunwe] Rivers . . . seamlessly blends legal materials, oral histories, personal correspondence, and archival materials of grassroots organizations. . . . The book concludes with a dazzling chapter on the ongoing history of lesbian and gay activism during the last two decades of the 20th century, focusing on insemination, adoption, surrogacy, donor paternity cases, and lesbian co-mother custody cases. . . . Essential."

RIVKEES, SCOTT A. Resident on call; a doctor's reflections on his first years at Mass General; [by] Scott A. Rivkees 232 p. 2014 Lyons Press

1. Memoirs 2. Residents (Medicine)—Training of—United States 3. Residents (Medicine)—United States—Biography
ISBN 9780762794539
LC 2013-050234

SUMMARY: This memoir recounts Scott A. Rivkee's "residency at Massachusetts General Hospital," which took place after "he had recently graduated from a medical school in New Jersey. Like his fellow residents, some from austere schools like Harvard and Yale, he was not fully prepared for the demanding schedules, exhaustion and on-the-spot decisions required from a doctor on call. . . . Over time, and with the help of older doctors . . . Rivkees learned the ins and outs of pediatric care." (Kirkus Reviews)

REVIEW: *Kirkus Rev* v82 no5 p157 Mr 1 2014

"Resident on Call: A Doctor's Reflection on His First Years at Mass General". "In short, almost abrupt prose, the author recalls riveting memories of those early years of practice when he had to learn how to start IVs in veins the size of pencil leads, how to diagnose rare diseases and how to deal with the agony of losing a patient. . . . Although many patients are introduced via emergency room or in-patient scenarios, most are abandoned in lieu of another tale, leaving readers to ponder what happened to that particular person after his or her hospital visit was over. . . . Amusing medical stories as seen through the eyes of a new doctor."

ROACH, STEPHEN. Unbalanced; the codependency of America and China; [by] Stephen Roach 344 p. 2014 Yale University Press

1. BUSINESS & ECONOMICS—Exports & Imports 2. HISTORY—Modern—21st Century 3. POLITICAL SCIENCE—International Relations—Trade & Tariffs 4. Political science literature
ISBN 9780300187175 (hardback)
LC 2013-021900

SUMMARY: In this book, author Stephen Roach "lays bare the pitfalls of the current China-U.S. economic relationship. He highlights the conflicts at the center of current tensions, including disputes over trade policies and intellectual property rights, sharp contrasts in leadership styles, the role of the Internet, the recent dispute over cyberhacking, and more." (Publisher's note)

REVIEW: *Choice* v51 no10 p1858 Je 2014 D. Li

REVIEW: *Kirkus Rev* v81 no24 p217 D 15 2013

"Unbalanced: The Codependency of America and China". "Eye-opening look at a condition that wanders from the boardroom to the psychiatrist's couch: financial codependency, which enables the worst qualities of two powerful economies. . . . Roach's arguments are complex and data-packed, and it helps to have some grounding in economics in order to appreciate such matters as how Ben Bernanke, in his role as chairman of the Federal Reserve, helped keep the U.S. economy afloat during the crisis of 2007-2009. . . . Even without such background, readers will not mistake the urgency with which Roach approaches his subject—which promises economic meltdown if our bad habits are not lessened. Full of implication, well-written and of much interest, especially to fiscal policy wonks."

REVIEW: *N Y Rev Books* v61 no8 p34-6 My 8 2014 Ian Johnson

REVIEW: *New York Times* v163 no56414 p5 F 16 2014 FRED ANDREWS

ROBB, GRAHAM. Ancient Paths; [by] Graham Robb 400 p. 2013 Picador Hardbacks

1. Cartography—History 2. Celtic civilization 3. Celtic mythology 4. Celts—History 5. Historical literature
ISBN 0330531506; 9780330531504

SUMMARY: In this book, "when Graham Robb made plans to cycle the legendary Via Heraklea, he had no idea that the line he plotted--stretching from the south-western tip of the Iberian Peninsula, across the Pyrenees and towards the Alps--would change the way he saw a civilization. . . . Gradually, a lost map revealed itself. . . .Oriented according to the movements of the Celtic sun god, the map had been forgotten for almost two millennia." (Publisher's note)

REVIEW: *New Statesman* v142 no5178 p46-7 O 4 2013 Rosemary Hill

REVIEW: *TLS* no5773 p25 N 22 2013 PATRICK SIMS-WILLIAMS

"The Ancient Paths:Discovering the Lost Map of Celtic Europe." "An occasional redeeming feature of this book is its self-deprecating asides. . . . Perhaps this book is an elaborate hoax? [Graham] Robb is aware that the ley-line hunting inspired by Alfred Watkins's 'Old Straight Track' (1925), with its 'muddling of different eras,' was 'anathema to archaeologists and historians,' but he barely attempts to forestall similar objections. He seems in thrall to Celtomania but appears to have read little Celtic scholarship. . . . There is absolutely nothing here for scholars, and general readers may prefer Robert Macfarlane's 'The Old Ways' (2012)."

ROBBINS, TOM, 1932-. Tibetan Peach Pie; A True Account of an Imaginative Life; [by] Tom Robbins 28 p. 2014 HarperCollins

1. Authors—Biography 2. Drugs & authors 3. Hargrave Military Academy (Chatham, Va.) 4. Imagination 5. Memoirs

ISBN 006226740X; 9780062267405

SUMMARY: In this memoir by Tom Robbins, "we travel with Tommy Rotten—his mother's pet name for him—from his birth in Statesville, N.C., through his youth in Virginia—including a stint at Hargrave Military Academy—his meteorological training in the military, and his peripatetic pursuit of language and wonder. . . . Along the way, Robbins offers flashes of enlightenment into the writing of each of his novels." (Publishers Weekly)

REVIEW: *Booklist* v110 no14 p44 Mr 15 2014 Ben Segedin

"Tibetan Peach Pie: A True Account of an Imaginative Life". "Insisting that this tome is neither autobiography nor memoir, countercultural icon [Tom] Robbins . . . covers the significant touchstones of his life. . . . Humorous anecdotes and high jinks fill these pages. . . . Robbins continues to embody Zen coolness and bohemian charm. Famous for his clever turn of a phrase, Robbins, with such nuggets as 'Adrenaline shot through me like a crystal meth espresso through a break-dance" and 'shaking his hand was like being forced to grasp the flaccid penis of a hypothermic zombie,' certainly won't disappoint."

REVIEW: *Kirkus Rev* v82 no8 p114 Ap 15 2014

REVIEW: *Libr J* v139 no7 p84 Ap 15 2014 Meagan Lacy

REVIEW: *N Y Times Book Rev* p26 Je 15 2014 GREGORY COWLES

REVIEW: *New York Times* v163 no56508 pC1-6 My 21 2014 DWIGHT GARNER

REVIEW: *Publ Wkly* v261 no12 p74 Mr 24 2014

REVIEW: *Publ Wkly* v261 no4 p87-91 Ja 27 2014

ROBERTS, DAVID, 1943-. Alone on the ice; the greatest survival story in the history of exploration; [by] David Roberts 256 p. 2013 W. W. Norton & Company

1. Explorers 2. Historical literature 3. Wilderness survival

ISBN 0393083713; 9780393083712 (hardcover)

LC 2012-037677

SUMMARY: This book by David Roberts presents a "portrait of Aussie explorer Douglas Mawson and his arduous trek through some of the most treacherous icy Antarctic terrain. . . . Roberts parallels the courageous achievements of Mawson's team on the 1911-1913 journey along the previously uncharted regions of the landscape with those of his acclaimed peers . . . battling the bitter cold, starvation, and peril to the limits of human endurance." (Publishers Weekly)

REVIEW: *Booklist* v109 no7 p8-9 D 1 2012 Jay Freeman

REVIEW: *Kirkus Rev* v80 no21 p143 N 1 2012

REVIEW: *Libr J* v137 no19 p88 N 15 2012 Ingrid Levin

REVIEW: *Publ Wkly* v259 no44 p45-6 O 29 2012

REVIEW: *TLS* no5746 p30 My 17 2013 STEPHEN J. PYNE

"Alone on the Ice: The Greatest Survival Story in the History of Exploration." "A story so elemental would seem to tell itself David Roberts, however, argues that the AAE overall 'presents a narrative conundrum', because it dispatched those eight teams. But it's easy enough to tell those stories in sequence or syncopation; in chronology and theme, [Douglas] Mawson's Far Eastern Party serves as climax. . . . There are few rhetorical conceits or flourishes, just straight, man-hauling prose. Historical background belongs with ice axes and crampons, a tool to move the action. Events, personalities and ideas are treated like sledge dogs--left to pull, and when they are exhausted, cut out of their traces and killed off."

ROBERTS, DAVID.il. Operation Bunny. See Gardner, S.

ROBERTS, DAVID.il. Rosie Revere, engineer. See Beaty, A.

ROBERTS, KENNETH. The Tactical Option Investor; [by] Kenneth Roberts 108 p. 2013 Createspace Independent Pub

1. Exchange traded funds 2. Financial management 3. Investment instructions 4. Options (Finance) 5. Stock market index options

ISBN 148268313X; 9781482683134

SUMMARY: Written by Kenneth Roberts, "This book is written for serious investors who want to understand how to use options to enhance the return from their portfolios, not for the speculator who thinks he can get rich with a small trading account. . . . Though written for the advanced or intermediate investor, this book will also provide and introduction to basic investment concepts for neophytes." (Publisher's note)

REVIEW: *Kirkus Rev* v81 no16 p47 Ag 15 2013

"The Tactical Option Investor." "[Author Kenneth] Roberts' debut provides an insider's take on utilizing options to enhance portfolio returns while minimizing risk in bullish and bearish markets. . . . There are no guaranteed ways to minimize all risks, but Roberts offers solutions to keep them low. . . . Options are contracts written on an underlying investment vehicle--for Roberts's purposes, stock and ETF options. Most importantly, they can be used to manage stock portfolios and produce solid returns while lowering risk. . . . Roberts writes in short, declaratory sentences that are simple to follow, making market jargon easy to comprehend. Quick and concise, the book makes perfect plane reading for anyone interested in the intricacies of options-trading strategies."

ROBERTS, MARK. Why institutions matter; the new institutionalism in political science; [by] Mark Roberts x, 236 p. 2013 Palgrave Macmillan

1. Democracy 2. Institution building 3. Political science 4. Political science literature 5. Social institutions

ISBN 9780333929544 (paperback); 9780333929551 (hardback)

LC 2013-021653

SUMMARY: It was the authors' intent to demonstrate that "institutionalism . . . is essential in political science, not just to explain post hoc but also to anticipate the shape and dynamics of ongoing political projects. Starting from a constructivist ontological position, the authors make a case that beneath the apparent diversity and fragmentation of new institutionalisms . . . a single, coherent institutionalism is emerging from the central core of concepts." (Choice: Current Reviews for Academic Libraries)

REVIEW: *Choice* v51 no7 p1298-9 Mr 2014 S. Mitropolitski

"Why Institutions Matter: The New Institutionalism in Political Science." "[Vivien] Lowndes . . . who writes on local governance and citizen participation, and [Mark] Roberts . . . whose interests are in urban politics, race, and faith, coauthored this book on institutional theory. The main premise is that institutions do matter and that they matter more than anything else that could explain political decisions: social and economic structures, political ideas, or the observable behavior of individual actors."

ROBERTS, NORA, 1950-. Dark witch; [by] Nora Roberts 368 p. 2013 Berkley Books

1. Americans—Ireland—Fiction 2. Love stories 3. Magic—Fiction 4. Man-woman relationships—Fiction 5. Witches—Fiction

ISBN 0425259854; 9780425259856

LC 2013-006292

SUMMARY: In this book, by Nora Roberts, "Iona Sheehan arrives in County Mayo intent on finding out more about her family's history and legacy of magic. . . . She meets her cousins Branna and Connor O'Dwyer. . . . She tells them that she's had dreams about an evil sorcerer named Cabhan. More than 800 years earlier their ancestress, Sorcha, the original Dark Witch, thwarted Cabhan's plan to steal her powers, and he has been plotting his revenge ever since." (Booklist)

REVIEW: *Booklist* v110 no3 p41-2 O 1 2013 John Charles

"Dark Witch." "With the support of her maternal grandmother, Iona Sheehan arrives in County Mayo intent on finding out more about her family's history and legacy of magic. . . . After moving in with Branna and Connor and taking a job working for cranky but incredibly sexy stable owner, Boyle McGrath, Iona begins putting down roots in Ireland. But her newfound happiness may be short-lived unless she and her cousins can find a way to harness their powers and defeat Cabhan. Best-seller-extraordinaire Roberts works her own brand of literary magic as she begins a new trilogy featuring the cousins O'Dwyer."

REVIEW: *Kirkus Rev* v81 no21 p159 N 1 2013

REVIEW: *Libr J* v138 no21 p132 D 1 2013

ROBERTS, RICHARD. Saving the city; the great financial crisis of 1914; [by] Richard Roberts 304 p. 2013 Oxford University Press

1. Financial crises—Great Britain 2. Financial crises—History 3. Great Britain—Economic conditions—20th century 4. Historical literature 5. London (England)—Economic conditions—History

ISBN 9780199646548 (hardback)

LC 2013-938932

SUMMARY: Written by Richard Roberts, "This book tells the extraordinary, and largely unknown, story of this acute financial crisis that surged over London and around the globe. Drawing on diaries, letters, and memoirs of participants and a wide range of press coverage, as well as government and bank archives, it presents a lively and colourful account of a remarkable episode in financial and social history, outlining the drama of the collapse and the measures taken to contain it." (Publisher's note)

REVIEW: *TLS* no5788 p11 Mr 7 2014 KATHLEEN BURK

"Saving the City: The Great Financial Crisis of 1914." "In 'Saving the City,' Richard Roberts argues that the financial crisis lasting from July 23, 1914 to January 4, 1915 was the most severe systemic crisis that London has ever experienced, worse even than that of 2007-08. Unforgivably, it has been almost forgotten, and he sets out to remedy this. The book is primarily a day-by-day description of the crisis from different perspectives. . . . It is a riveting tale. . . . Richard Roberts's analysis shows the interrelationship of politics and finance: 'Saving the City' is an important book, both thought-provoking and entertaining."

ROBERTS, RUSSELL, 1953-. Joe Flacco. See Torres, J.

ROBERTSON, JOHN.ed. The intellectual consequences of religious heterodoxy 1600-1750. See The intellectual consequences of religious heterodoxy 1600-1750

ROBERTSON, ROBIN. One-dish vegan; more than 150 soul-satisfying recipes for easy and delicious one-bowl and one-plate dinners; [by] Robin Robertson viii, 200 p. 2013 The Harvard Common Press

1. Casserole cooking 2. Cookbooks 3. One-dish meals 4. Stews 5. Vegan cooking

ISBN 9781558328129 (pbk. : alk. paper)

LC 2013-001297

SUMMARY: This vegan cookbook by Robin Robertson "contains more than 150 recipes. They range from the most popular categories of one-dish dining like stews, chilis, and casseroles (and other baked dishes) to a host of stovetop sautés and stir-fries as well as substantial salads and dishes that feature pasta as well as other noodles, such as Asian noodles." (Publisher's note)

REVIEW: *Booklist* v110 no3 p29-30 O 1 2013 Mark Knoblauch

"One-Dish Vegan: More than 150 Soul-Satisfying Recipes for Easy and Delicious One-Bowl and One-Plate Dinners." "[Robin] Robertson exhibits imagination and experience in her recipes' design and execution. As do so many expert cooks, Robertson commences with stock--in this case, simple vegetable stock, which can add lots of flavor to many different dishes, not just to soups. Ethnic cuisines contribute intriguing variations on lasagna and even popular pad Thai. . . . Certain ingredients appear frequently, especially chickpeas. But Robertson covers plenty of other beans and similar protein sources to help ensure balanced nutrition."

ROBERTSON, ROLAND.ed. European cosmopolitanism in question. See European cosmopolitanism in question

ROBIN, CYNTHIA. Everyday Life Matters; Maya Farmers at Chan; [by] Cynthia Robin 256 p. 2013 University Press of Florida

1. Archaeological literature 2. Chan Site (Belize) 3. Everyday life 4. Mayas 5. Mayas—Agriculture—Belize

ISBN 0813044995; 9780813044996

SUMMARY: This book by Cynthia Robin looks at the "two-thousand-year history (800 B.C.–A.D. 1200) of the ancient farming community of Chan in Belize." It "explains why the average person should matter to archaeologists studying larger societal patterns. Robin argues that the impact of the mundane can be substantial, so much so that the study of a polity without regard to its citizenry is incomplete." (Publisher's note)

REVIEW: *Choice* v51 no8 p1450-1 Ap 2014 J. A. Hendon

"Everyday Life Matters: Maya Farmers at Chan". "[Cynthia] Robin . . . has written an important contribution to the archaeological study of daily life, based on the ancient Maya. . . . Using a variety of methods, the author presents a rich and detailed reconstruction that supports her claim that 'the seemingly ordinary things people do . . . affect their societies.' Robin presents complex social theories and the details of archaeological research in accessible language. The specifics of her Chan research provide an effective case study of how archaeological data may be applied to significant theoretical issues to make them accessible to advanced undergraduates."

ROBINSON, ANDREW C.il. The Fifth Beatle. See The Fifth Beatle

ROBINSON, CARY. The Dudley files; sold out without the hold out; [by] Cary Robinson 284 p. 2012 Two Harbors Press

1. Detective & mystery stories 2. Dogs—Fiction 3. Friendship—Fiction 4. Human-animal relationships—Fiction 5. Kidnapping—Fiction
ISBN 9781937293796 (dust jacket)
LC 2011-944843

SUMMARY: This mystery novel by Cary Robinson focuses on "Careless' caring relationship with his dog, Dudley, who clearly fills an emptiness in Careless' life. . . . When "Jake Harm, lead singer of Jake Harm and the Holdouts, is abducted by a deranged fan before a concert attended by Careless and his friends . . . a detective soon gives Careless . . . authority to direct the investigation." (Kirkus Reviews)

REVIEW: *Kirkus Rev* v81 no24 p341 D 15 2013

"The Dudley Files: Sold Out Without the Holdout". "A debut crime novel that focuses far more on comedy than mystery. . . . He narrates the story in a tone that wavers between admirable effortlessness and wearisome flippancy, but he's a well-defined, mostly entertaining character, despite the novel's relatively unfocused storyline. . . . The eventual mystery plotline is relegated to the final 50 pages or so. . . . This plotline develops much too quickly . . . and feels detached from the rest of the narrative. Careless himself suggests that the subplot is meant to introduce a new series, based on his new role as a consulting detective. If this is the case, the novel serves its purpose, if a little late. An unfocused crime novel, but an entertaining tale of companionship."

ROBINSON, FIONA.il. The abominables. See Ibbotson, E.

ROBINSON, KIM STANLEY. Red Mars; [by] Kim Stanley Robinson 519 1993 Bantam Books

1. Life on other planets 2. Planetary engineering 3. Science fiction 4. Space colonies
ISBN 0-553-09204-9; 0-553-56073-5 pa
LC 92-2-1607

SUMMARY: This book "concerns the first permanent settlement on Mars, a multinational band of 100 hardy experts, and their mission [of terraforming it]--to begin making Mars habitable for humans by releasing underground water and oxygen into the atmosphere. Unfortunately, they are divided over whether this is a desirable step in human evolution or an ecological crime." (Booklist)The story "concerns the first permanent settlement on Mars, a multinational band of 100 hardy experts, and their mission {of terraforming it}—to begin making Mars habitable for humans by releasing underground water and oxygen into the atmosphere. Unfortunately, they are divided over whether this is a desirable step in human evolution or an ecological crime." (Booklist)

REVIEW: *Economist* v409 no8866 p24 D 14 2013 Robert Macfarlane

"Red Mars." "The most compelling aspects of 'Red Mars' are not its hard-science details or political dramas, but its evocation of the awesome Martian landscape. . . . [Kim Stanley] Robinson narrates this epic journey as a kind of future history, telling it so calmly, with such particularity, that it is hard to believe it has not in fact taken place. We have never reached Mars, of course, but for centuries we have projected our dreams--political, cosmogonical, aesthetic--onto it. To me, thanks to Robinson, it represents a last true wilderness."

REVIEW: *Libr J* v138 no5 p131 Mr 15 2013 Neal Wyatt

ROBINSON, LISA. There goes gravity; a life in rock and roll; [by] Lisa Robinson 368 p. 2013 Riverhead Books

1. Memoirs 2. Music journalists—United States—Biography 3. Rock music—History and criticism 4. Rock musicians
ISBN 1594487146; 9781594487149
LC 2013-037121

SUMMARY: This book, by Lisa Robinson, discusses the history of rock music. "Lisa Robinson has interviewed the biggest names in music—including Led Zeppelin, the Rolling Stones, John Lennon, Patti Smith, U2, Eminem, Lady Gaga, Jay Z and Kanye West. . . . A keenly observed and lovingly recounted look back on years spent with countless musicians backstage, after hours and on the road, . . . [the book] documents a lifetime of riveting stories, told together here for the first time." (Publisher's note)

REVIEW: *Booklist* v110 no13 p12 Mr 1 2014 Eloise Kinney

REVIEW: *Kirkus Rev* v82 no4 p82 F 15 2014

"There Goes Gravity: A Life in Rock and Roll". "A lifetime of memories from classic rock's heyday by one of the finest rock journalists of her generation. . . . It's a fantastic collection of stories, partially due to the fact that [Lisa] Robinson is a top-notch writer and partly since she enjoyed completely unfettered access and the genuine friendship of figures ranging from John Lennon to Phil Spector. . . . All of these movements have been written about before, but the scope of Robinson's memoir lends it an extraordinary spirit. A backstage pass to the greatest circus of the 20th century."

REVIEW: *Libr J* v139 no5 p123 Mr 15 2014 Neil Derksen

REVIEW: *Libr J* v138 no18 p69 N 1 2013 Barbara Hoffert

REVIEW: *New York Times* v163 no56487 pC4 Ap 30 2014 DWIGHT GARNER

ROBINSON, MARK A.il. I Love Trouble. See Symons, K.

ROBINSON, MICHELLE. How to wash a woolly mammoth; 32 p. 2014 Henry Holt and Company

1. Baths—Fiction 2. Children's stories 3. Humorous stories 4. Pets—Juvenile literature 5. Woolly mammoth—Fiction

ISBN 9780805099669 (hardback)

LC 2013-030800

SUMMARY: In this book, "children are introduced to a gigantic, unwashed wooly mammoth and the intrepid young girl who demonstrates the proper method for bathing such a beast. . . . The girl quickly takes charge, recommending the proper level of water for the tub and methods to entice the mammoth into the bath (by brute force, scare tactics, or tempting baked goods). All ends with an invitation to a bubbly, toy-filled soak for her muddy, wooly friend." (School Library Journal)

REVIEW: *Booklist* v110 no9/10 p116 Ja 1 2014 Ann Kelley

REVIEW: *Bull Cent Child Books* v67 no5 p280-1 Ja 2014 J. H.

"How to Wash a Woolly Mammoth." "[Michelle] Robinson excels at playing out an absurd premise to amusing effect . . . and this scenario provides plenty of laughs. The art is a treat: thin, dark outlines and subtle, judicious application of color and pattern keep the bathtime action neat and tidy yet comic. The freckle-faced little girl in her mustard-colored, hooded slicker and red boots is an attractive foil for the enormous, shaggy brown mammoth. The mammoth's small, pop eyes and darker topknot of hair beam with humor, especially when he sports various shampoo-lather hairstyles."

REVIEW: *Kirkus Rev* v81 no23 p130 D 1 2013

REVIEW: *Publ Wkly* v260 no43 p59 O 28 2013

REVIEW: *SLJ* v60 no1 p76 Ja 2014 Mary Elam

ROBINSON, NICHOLAS A.ed. Dictionary of environmental and climate change law. See Dictionary of environmental and climate change law

ROBINSON, SHARON, 1950-. Under the Same Sun; 40 p. 2013 Scholastic Press

1. African American grandmothers—Juvenile fiction 2. African Americans—Fiction 3. Birthdays—Fiction 4. Birthdays—Juvenile fiction 5. Families—Tanzania—Juvenile fiction 6. Family life—Tanzania—Fiction 7. Family traditions 8. Grandmothers—Fiction 9. Safaris—Fiction 10. Safaris—Tanzania—Juvenile fiction

ISBN 9780545166720 (hardcover : alk. paper)

LC 2012-015732

SUMMARY: In this book, illustrated by A. G. Ford, "Sharon Robinson, daughter of baseball great Jackie Robinson, shares an inspirational story about her family in Tanzania. . . . Auntie Sharon and Grandmother Bibi have come to visit the family in Tanzania--all the way from America! Soon it will be Bibi's 85th birthday, and her seven grandchildren are planning a big surprise! . . . Sharon Robinson . . . gives African-American history a powerful new perspective." (Publisher's note)

REVIEW: *Booklist* v110 no12 p84 F 15 2014 Jeanne McDermott

REVIEW: *Bull Cent Child Books* v67 no6 p330 F 2014 Thaddeus Andracki

REVIEW: *Kirkus Rev* v81 no22 p102 N 15 2013

REVIEW: *N Y Times Book Rev* p16 F 16 2014 GLENDA R. CARPIO

"Mumbet's Declaration of Independence," "Under the Same Sun," and "Knock Knock: My Dad's Dream for Me." "Gretchen Woelfle's 'Mumbet's Declaration of Independence' . . . tells the story of . . . Bett or Betty [who] successfully sued her owner . . . for her emancipation, and once liberated chose to name herself Elizabeth Freeman. . . . In 'Under the Same Sun,' Sharon Robinson, the daughter of the baseball legend Jackie Robinson, also deals with the history of slavery but folds it into a story about a modern-day family reunion. . . . [In] Daniel Beaty's 'Knock Knock: My Dad's Dream for Me,' . . . a letter from the father finally arrives explaining that he will not be coming home."

REVIEW: *Publ Wkly* v260 no45 p71 N 11 2013

REVIEW: *SLJ* v60 no2 p78 F 2014 Robbin E. Friedman

ROBISON, ANDREW. Albrecht Dürer; master drawings, watercolors, and prints from the Albertina; [by] Andrew Robison xi, 315 p. 2013 National Gallery of Art Delmonico Books/Prestel

1. Drawing 2. Dürer, Albrecht, 1471-1528 3. Graphische Sammlung Albertina 4. Old Masters (Artists)

ISBN 9780894683800 (softcover : alk. paper); 9783791352879 (alk. paper)

LC 2012-041971

SUMMARY: "A panoply of the finest works by Albrecht Dürer, the master of the Northern European Renaissance, is collected in this . . . book," edited by Andrew Robison and Klaus Albrecht Schröder. "Vienna's Albertina Museum is home to the world's most comprehensive collection of works by Albrecht Dürer. Dürer's genius . . . rivaled that of his Italian contemporaries, and his exquisitely detailed and delicately colored watercolors and prints elevated these to new levels of accomplishment." (Publisher's note)

REVIEW: *Choice* v51 no4 p622-3 D 2013 A. V. Coonin

"Albrecht Dürer: Master Drawings, Watercolors, and Prints From the Albertina." "The recent Albrecht Dürer celebrations continue with the appearance of one excellent publication after another. . . . In this impressive context, the present book holds its own. It accompanies a 2013 National Gallery of Art exhibition of the same name. Edited by curators [Andrew] Robison . . . and [Klaus Albrecht] Schröder . . . , the catalogue highlights the extraordinary holdings of Dürer in the Albertina Museum. The book takes the form of three introductory essays followed by straightforward entries for 118 works, written by various contributors. . . . Catalogue entries are informative and accessible."

REVIEW: *N Y Times Book Rev* p64-5 D 8 2013 Sarah Harrison Smith

ROBISON, JOHN ELDER. Raising Cubby; a father and son's adventures with Asperger's, trains, tractors, and high explosives; [by] John Elder Robison 304 p. 2013 Random House Inc

1. Asperger's syndrome—Patients—Family relationships 2. Asperger's syndrome in children—Patients—Life skills guides 3. Asperger's syndrome in children—Patients—United States—Biography 4. BIOGRAPHY & AUTOBIOGRAPHY—Personal Memoirs 5. FAMI-

LY & RELATIONSHIPS—Children with Special Needs 6. Memoirs 7. PSYCHOLOGY—Psychopathology—Autism Spectrum Disorders 8. Parenting
ISBN 0307884848; 9780307884848 (hardback); 9780307884855 (trade paperback)
LC 2012-033979

SUMMARY: This book is a "memoir of an unconventional dad's relationship with his equally offbeat son. . . . [Author] John Robison was never a . . . model dad. Diagnosed with Asperger's syndrome at the age of forty, he approached fatherhood as a series of logic puzzles and practical jokes. . . By the time he turned seventeen, [Robinson's son] Cubby had become a brilliant chemist--smart enough to make military-grade explosives and bring state and federal agents calling." (Publisher's note)

REVIEW: *Atlantic* v313 no2 p40-3 Mr 2014 HANNA ROSIN

"Raising Cubby: A Father and Son's Adventures With Asperger's, Trains, Tractors, and High Explosives," "Thinking in Numbers: On Life, Love, Meaning, and Math," and "The Autistic Brain: Thinking Across the Spectrum." "[John Elder] Robison . . . champions the label and the tribal protection it offers in a 'neurotypical' world that he is sure will always stigmatize and misunderstand people like him--and like his son. Jack. Yet Robison's new memoir. . . . turns out to offer vivid evidence that just the opposite is true. The world his son grew up in is welcoming in ways that Robison curiously fails to recognize, even as he recounts them in great detail. . . . In his most moving chapter, [Daniel] Tammet explains how as a child he tried hard to create a 'predictive model of my mother's behavior.' . . . In [Temple Grandin's] view, settling on a diagnosis is not nearly as interesting as taking note of the many permutations of minds along the spectrum."

REVIEW: *Booklist* v109 no12 p15 F 15 2013 David Siegfried

REVIEW: *Kirkus Rev* v80 no23 p136 D 1 2012

REVIEW: *Publ Wkly* v259 no48 p39 N 26 2012

REVIEW: *Publ Wkly* v260 no4 p7 Ja 28 2013

ROBOTHAM, MICHAEL. Watching you; [by] Michael Robotham 432 p. 2014 Mulholland Books

1. Escort services 2. Missing persons—Fiction 3. Murder—Fiction 4. Psychologists—Fiction 5. Suspense fiction
ISBN 031625200X; 9780316252003 (hardback)
LC 2013-032945

SUMMARY: In this book, by Michael Robotham, "Marnie Logan often feels like she's being watched. . . . She has reason to be frightened. Her husband Daniel has inexplicably vanished, and the police have no leads in the case. Without proof of death or evidence of foul play, she can't access his bank accounts or his life insurance. Depressed and increasingly desperate, she seeks the help of clinical psychologist Joe O'Loughlin." (Publisher's note)

REVIEW: *Booklist* v110 no11 p28 F 1 2014 Don Crinklaw

REVIEW: *Kirkus Rev* v82 no1 p294 Ja 1 2014

"Watching You". "A complicated story that centers around a group of individuals who are not what they seem. Marnie is a beautiful woman who has fallen on hard times. In addition to the untimely and unexplained disappearance of her journalist husband, Daniel, she's struggling with a moody teenage daughter, a fragile young son and debts that are driving her into a demeaning lifestyle. . . . [Michael] Robotham's writing remains solid. His latest, while not his best, will convert new readers and make his fans happy."

REVIEW: *Libr J* v138 no16 p57 O 1 2013 Barbara Hoffert

REVIEW: *Libr J* v139 no2 p67 F 1 2014 Lisa O'Hara

REVIEW: *N Y Times Book Rev* p23 Mr 23 2014 MARILYN STASIO

REVIEW: *Publ Wkly* v261 no1 p34-5 Ja 6 2014

ROCCO, JOHN.il. Swim that rock. See Rocco, J.

ROCCO, JOHN. Swim that rock; 304 p. 2014 Candlewick Press

1. Debt 2. Families—Fiction 3. Family-owned business enterprises 4. Fishing stories 5. Quahoging
ISBN 0763669059; 9780763669058
LC 2013-952797

SUMMARY: In this book, by John Rocco and Jay Primiano, "a young working-class teen fights to save his family's diner after his father is lost in a fishing-boat accident. . . . In Narragansett Bay, scrabbling out a living as a quahogger isn't easy, but with the help of some local clammers, Jake is determined to work hard and earn enough money to ensure his family's security and save the diner in time." (Publisher's note)

REVIEW: *Booklist* v110 no15 p87 Ap 1 2014 John Peters

REVIEW: *Bull Cent Child Books* v67 no10 p539 Je 2014 E. B.

"Swim That Rock". "Landlubbers who think they won't give a rip for a novel about clamming have another think coming. Jake's efforts make for a dangerous business, even without loan sharks closing in, and the grab-a-buck antics of the Pirate add yet another layer of suspense to an already tightly plotted tale. There's a happy ending—perhaps a tad too tidy for the murky buildup—but it's honestly won, and, like all good maritime novels, this one will have landlocked kids pining for a strong gust of salt spray."

REVIEW: *Horn Book Magazine* v90 no2 p127-8 Mr/Ap 2014 DEAN SCHNEIDER

REVIEW: *Kirkus Rev* v82 no4 p150 F 15 2014

REVIEW: *N Y Times Book Rev* p23 Ap 6 2014 JOHN FREEMAN GILL

REVIEW: *SLJ* v60 no3 p162 Mr 2014 Liz Overberg

RODDA, EMILY. The third door; [by] Emily Rodda 288 p. 2013 Scholastic Press

1. Adventure and adventurers—Fiction 2. Brothers—Fiction 3. Magic—Fiction 4. Monsters—Fiction
ISBN 0545429943; 9780545429948 (jacketed hardcover); 9780545429955 (pbk.)
LC 2013-007883

SUMMARY: In this book, by Emily Rodda, "Three magic Doors are the only way in and out of the walled city of Weld. . . . The city of Weld is under attack by skimmers, flying beasts that terrorize the night. If Rye and Sonia can't discover the enemy sending the skimmers in time, Weld has no hope. Twice before, Rye and Sonia left Weld on a quest to save it. Twice before, they failed. Now there's just one Door left—one last chance to save the people of Weld." (Publisher's note)

REVIEW: *Booklist* v110 no4 p53 O 15 2013 Snow Wildsmith

REVIEW: *Horn Book Magazine* v89 no6 p104-5 N/D 2013 ANITA L. BURKAM

"The Third Door". "Still struggling against the skimmers, nocturnal flying predators that are attacking the walled city of Weld . . . Rye, his companion Sophie, and his two brothers Dirk and Sholto go through the third, wooden door to seek a way to drive off the skimmers and bring peace to Dorne. . . . The imaginative and diverse world-building that marked the first two books continues, though in this last book of the trilogy [Emily] Rodda adds plot twists that play with the concepts of time, perception, and 'the enemy' and that makes the triumphant conclusion that much more rewarding."

REVIEW: *Kirkus Rev* v81 no17 p112-3 S 1 2013

RODOREDA, MERCÈ. In diamond square; xiii, 206 p. 2013 Virago

1. Historical fiction 2. Man-woman relationships—Fiction 3. Marriage—Fiction 4. Mothers—Fiction

ISBN 1844088952 (hbk.); 1844089258 (pbk.); 9781844088959 (hbk.); 9781844089253 (pbk.)

LC 2013-414564

SUMMARY: This book is set in Barcelona in the early 1930s. "Natalia, a pretty shop-girl from the working-class quarter of Gracia, is hesitant when a stranger asks her to dance at the fiesta in Diamond Square. But Joe is charming and forceful, and she takes his hand. They marry and soon have two children. . . . Then the Spanish Civil War erupts, and lays waste to the city and to their simple existence." (Publisher's note)

REVIEW: *TLS* no5770 p21 N 1 2013 MATTHEW TREE

"In Diamond Square." "Natàlia is an elusive character, at once sympathetic and unprepossessing. Her first-person narrative is spun from equal measures of reported speech, direct speech and straight monologue. . . . There is nothing gratuitous about these Dali-esque details: Natàlia sees the world as cruel, senseless and bizarre; her unblinking vision heightens her--and the novel's--ambivalent take on life before, during and after the war. Peter Bush's translation is the third in English and differs from its precursors in its willingness to tackle the class setting. Bush has ventured not only to include British working-class slang in Natàlia's monologue, but even to anglicize the names of the characters (Quimet, for example, is transformed into Joe). The touches are deft."

RODRIGUEZ, JUNIUS P.ed. Slavery in the modern world. See Slavery in the modern world

RODRÍGUEZ, RICHARD. Darling; a spiritual autobiography; [by] Richard Rodríguez 256 p. 2013 Viking

1. Christian pilgrims and pilgrimages—Israel 2. Memoirs

ISBN 0670025305; 9780670025305

LC 2013-017046

SUMMARY: In this book, author Richard Rodriguez "examin[es] his continuing belief in God and in the Catholic Church in the context of his life as a gay man in the early years of the twenty-first century, years, he says, that have been defined by religious extremism, rising public atheism, and what he calis 'digital distraction.' And, yet, in the wake of September 11, Rodriguez found himself searching for commonality rather than difference between the 'religions of the desert'." (Booklist)

REVIEW: *Booklist* v110 no6 p14 N 15 2013 Bill Ott

"Darling: A Spiritual Autobiography". "Paradox has always been at the heart of [Richard] Rodriguez's brilliant personal essays. . . . While his wide-ranging, erudite, passionate, and thought-provoking essays range over a wealth of seemingly disparate topics (gay marriage, Las Vegas, women, California, newspapers, technology), they all reflect his remarkable ability to penetrate the contradictions of our lives, reveling in them as much as understanding them. 'We gather,' he says of his congregation, 'in belief of one big thing: that we matter, somehow.'"

REVIEW: *Christ Century* v130 no24 p41 N 27 2013

REVIEW: *Commonweal* v141 no9 p29-30 My 16 2014 Michael O. Garvey

REVIEW: *Kirkus Rev* v81 no17 p68 S 1 2013

REVIEW: *Libr J* v138 no13 p81 Ag 1 2013 Graham Christian

REVIEW: *N Y Times Book Rev* p28 S 14 2014 IHSAN TAYLOR

REVIEW: *N Y Times Book Rev* p10 N 17 2013 LESLIE JAMISON

"Darling: A Spiritual Autobiography". "'Darling' is both more and less than a 'spiritual autobiography,' which is how it has been marketed. It doesn't offer a continuous personal narrative of spiritual development, but its inquiries range much further than personal experience, exploring hospice care in Las Vegas and drag queen nuns in San Francisco; the crises of Mother Teresa and the emptiness that 'clings' to Jerusalem shopkeepers. . . . Sometimes these various strands of inquiry resonate in unexpected ways, while at other times they feel cobbled together for the sake of a book-length project, their points of connection forced. But the book is remarkably and consistently willing to confess its fallibilities."

REVIEW: *Publ Wkly* v260 no38 p74 S 23 2013

REVIEW: *World Lit Today* v88 no2 p74-5 Mr/Ap 2014 Spencer R. Herrera

RODWELL, T. C.il. A baby elephant in the wild. See O'Connell, C.

ROGAK, LISA. One big happy family; heartwarming stories of animals caring for one another; [by] Lisa Rogak 160 p. 2013 St. Martin's Griffin/Thomas Dunne Books

1. Adoption—Anecdotes 2. Animal behavior—Anecdotes 3. Natural history literature 4. PETS—General 5. Parenting—Anecdotes 6. Social behavior in animals—Anecdotes

ISBN 9781250035400 (trade paperback)

LC 2013-025063

SUMMARY: This book by Lisa Rogak "gathers 50 stories of animals of one species mothering (or, in several cases, fathering) babies from an entirely foreign species. . . . We see a mother cat who warms a nest of baby chicks with her own kittens, and the hen who adopts a nestful of ducklings--assisted by a goose. Even male cats get into the act when a ginger tomcat takes over the cuddling duties for a hand-reared lion cub." (Booklist)

REVIEW: *Booklist* v110 no2 p11-2 S 15 2013 Nancy Bent

"One Big Happy Family: Heartwarming Stories of Animals Caring for One Another." "This book 'sells' itself. It gathers 50 stories of animals of one species mothering (or, in several cases, fathering) babies from an entirely foreign species. . . . More than half of the stories feature dogs as the surrogate parent. Even wild animals enter the picture, as a lioness treats an antelope calf like a cub and a baboon cuddles an infant bush baby. Illustrated with irresistible color photos, this one is a charmer."

REVIEW: *Publ Wkly* v260 no29 p58 Jl 22 2013

ROGERS, DEBRA. He Did You a Favor; A Smart Girl's Guide to Breaking Up, Waking Up, and Discovering the Gift of YOU; [by] Debra Rogers 248 p. 2013 Did You A Favor, Inc.

1. Advice literature 2. Dating (Social customs) 3. Man-woman relationships 4. Romantic love 5. Separation (Psychology)

ISBN 0991063503; 9780991063505

SUMMARY: In this book, "a script analyst and writing coach offers a debut guide to help women get over breakups and regain their self-confidence. . . . She encourages women to figure out exactly what they want out of a relationship, while also emphasizing the importance of being open-minded. . . . Each chapter includes a variety of exercises ranging from a 'Date Right for Your Type' nutrition workbook to a multiple-choice test to help readers identify what kind of princess they are." (Kirkus Reviews)

REVIEW: *Kirkus Rev* v81 no24 p403 D 15 2013

"He Did You A Favor: A Smart Girl's Guide to Breaking Up, Waking Up, and Discovering the Gift of YOU". "Her ability to get through what may be many women's worst nightmare may make it easy for readers to trust her advice, and here, she dispenses it with a sassy sense of humor, focusing on building her readers up rather than lecturing them about past mistakes. The author strikes a balance between offering women no-nonsense rules to live by and helping them figure out their own personal requirements. . . . Overall, most of her suggestions are more practical than groundbreaking, but for someone suffering under a cloud of heartbreak, even a straightforward solution can feel like a ray of sunlight. A snappy, sensible guide to relationships."

ROGERS, GUY MACLEAN. The mysteries of Artemis of Ephesos; cult, polis, and change in the Graeco-Roman world; [by] Guy MacLean Rogers xii, 500 p. 2012 Yale University Press

1. Artemis (Greek deity)—Cult 2. Artemis (Greek deity)—Cult—Turkey—Ephesus (Extinct city) 3. Greece—Religion 4. Historical literature 5. Temple of Artemis (Ephesus)

ISBN 0300178638 (hbk. : alk. paper); 9780300178630 (hbk. : alk. paper)

LC 2012-011998

SUMMARY: "In this work Guy MacLean Rogers sets out the evidence for the celebration of Artemis's mysteries against the background of the remarkable urban development of the city during the Roman Empire and then proposes an entirely new theory about the great secret that was revealed to initiates into Artemis's mysteries." (Publisher's note)

REVIEW: *Choice* v51 no2 p327 O 2013 P. C. Dilley

REVIEW: *TLS* no5776 p27 D 13 2013 ROBIN OSBORNE

"The Mysteries of Artemis of Ephesos: Cult, Polis, and Change in the Graeco-Roman World." "In 'The Mysteries of Artemis of Ephesos,' Guy MacLean Rogers aims to reinterpret the mysteries and to use them to show how to write about Greco-Roman religion. A methodological purist, Rogers goes through the ancient sources, very slowly, in chronological order (or almost). . . . For Rogers what is important survives inscribed on marble. But like other official records, Ephesus's inscriptions can be understood only within a framework that they do not themselves supply. . . . Rogers cites Achilles Tatius only for drunkards at the festival and criminals seeking refuge in the sanctuary, mentions Acts only in footnotes, and passes over Ephesians in silence."

ROGERS, REBECCA. A Frenchwoman's imperial story; Madame Luce in nineteenth-century Algeria; [by] Rebecca Rogers xviii, 267 p. 2013 Stanford University Press

1. Biography (Literary form) 2. Education and state—Algeria—History—19th century 3. Muslim girls—Education—Algeria—History—19th century 4. Women—Algeria—Social conditions—19th century 5. Women teachers—France—Biography

ISBN 9780804784313 (cloth: alk. paper)

LC 2012-031058

SUMMARY: This book presents a biography of "Eugénie Luce . . . a French schoolteacher who fled her husband and abandoned her family, migrating to Algeria in the early 1830s. By the mid-1840s she had become a major figure in debates around educational policies, insisting that women were a critical dimension of the French effort to effect a fusion of the races. To aid this fusion, she founded the first French school for Muslim girls in Algiers in 1845." (Publisher's note)

REVIEW: *Am Hist Rev* v119 no1 p286-7 F 2014 James Smith Allen

"A Frenchwoman's Imperial Story; Madame Luce in Nineteenth-Century Algeria". "Rebecca Rogers has written a first-rate biography of Eugénie Allix Luce (1804–1882), a determined French schoolteacher in mid-nineteenth-century Algiers. She has also made a significant contribution to the historiography of primary education, ethnic relations, cultural patrimony, international feminism, and colonial administration, among other inherently gendered issues in the social history of French Algeria. . . . Of particular appeal is the author's own journey of discovery that opens and closes the volume."

ROGERS, SIMON. Information graphics animal kingdom; 80 p. 2014 Candlewick Press

1. Animals 2. Children's nonfiction 3. Dogs 4. Habitat (Ecology) 5. Senses & sensation

ISBN 9780763671228

LC 2013-944025

SUMMARY: This book by Simon Rogers "takes a visual approach to sharing information. Tabs help readers flip between eight chapters devoted to animal species, families, habitats, predators, and more; dogs get their own chapter, which includes a profile view of a canine skeleton, an icon-based guide to dogs' body language, and simplified portraits of a dozen breeds." (Publishers Weekly)

REVIEW: *Kirkus Rev* v82 no3 p240 F 1 2014

"Animal Kingdom". "With scattered exceptions, the trendy 'infographics' approach stops at the title in this haphazard ramble past animal types and extremes. The book is printed on stiff stock and features edge tabs bearing icons to denote each section's subject—not always well-chosen ones: Dog faces mark both the chapter on dogs and one on animal senses in general. The coverage begins with Darwin and ends abruptly (sans index or other backmatter) with a highly select gallery of canine breeds. . . . The writing sometimes reads like a bad translation. . . . the art is seldom arranged or scaled to impart information in a visual way. . . . Flashy at first glance, routine at second and subsequent looks."

RO'I, YAACOV.ed. The Jewish movement in the Soviet Union. See The Jewish movement in the Soviet Union

ROISMAN, HANNA M.ed. The encyclopedia of Greek tragedy. See The encyclopedia of Greek tragedy

ROMAGNOLI, ALESSANDRO. The economic development process in the Middle East and North Africa. See Mengoni, L. E.

ROMAN, CAROLE P. If You Were Me and Lived in ...Kenya; A Child's Introduction to Cultures Around the World; [by] Carole P. Roman 30 p. 2013 Createspace Independent Pub

1. Children's nonfiction 2. Cricket (Sport) 3. Kenya—Juvenile literature 4. Kenya—Social life & customs 5. Kenyan cooking

ISBN 1481979914; 9781481979917

SUMMARY: This book by Carole P. Roman "offers a children's primer of the geography, sports, food and vocabulary that Kenyan kids encounter in their daily lives. The latest installment in this cultural series—preceded by books on Mexico, France, South Korea and Norway—takes young readers to the African nation of Kenya, where they get a short . . . lesson on the country's culture." (Kirkus Reviews)

REVIEW: *Kirkus Rev* v82 no2 p342 Ja 15 2014

"If You Were Me and Lived In . . . Kenya: A Child's Introduction to Cultures Around the World". "[Carole P.] Roman's books are successful since she draws connections between cultures while maintaining a tone that keeps young readers engaged. Colorful illustrations further enhance the text. . . .A glossary at the end offers a pronunciation key for the unfamiliar words throughout. This series of books would be a natural fit in school classrooms and would also provide a good way for parents to teach their own kids about the cultures, languages and geography of different countries. This installment is a quick read that may help kids see the similarities between themselves and their Kenyan peers. An excellent introduction to the Kenyan culture for children."

ROMER, STEPHEN.tr. The Arriere-pays. See Bonnefoy, Y.

ROMER, STEPHEN.tr. French decadent tales. See French decadent tales

ROMERO, MARY. The maid's daughter; living inside and outside the American dream; [by] Mary Romero 265 2011 New York University Press

1. Hispanic American children—Social conditions 2. Hispanic American women—Employment 3. Household employees—Social conditions 4. Immigrant children 5. Sociology literature

ISBN 9780814776421

LC 2011-005653

SUMMARY: Author "Mary Romero's 20- year study highlights the struggles and powerlessness that children often experience as immigrants in the United States. In addition, her book highlights the experiences of immigrant youth as they struggle to adopt a new culture and still keep their own immigrant culture by following 'Olivia Salazar' as an immigrant in both a familiar and foreign setting." (Contemporary Sociology)

REVIEW: *Contemp Sociol* v43 no1 p112-4 Ja 2014 Katy M. Pinto

"The Maid's Daughter: Living Inside and Outside the American Dream". "'The Maid's Daughter' contributes to existing scholarship that examines the immigrant experience in the United States. However, it uniquely contributes to this scholarship by giving a voice to the experience of immigrant children. . . . Olivia's story alone is compelling enough to keep the reader interested as it often reads like a novel, and one cannot help but wonder about how her life will unfold. [Mary] Romero's ability to apply the sociological perspective to Olivia's life and to highlight the struggle of assimilation in America makes the book interesting."

REVIEW: *Ethn Racial Stud* v35 no9 p1700-1 S 2012 Elizabeth J. Clifford

ROMMELSE, GIJS.ed. Ideology and foreign policy in early modern Europe (1650-1750). See Ideology and foreign policy in early modern Europe (1650-1750)

RONSTADT, LINDA, 1946-. Simple dreams; a musical memoir; [by] Linda Ronstadt 208 p. 2013 Simon & Schuster

1. Autobiography—Women authors 2. California, Southern 3. Rock musicians—United States—Biography 4. Singers—United States—Biography 5. Tucson (Ariz.) 6. Women rock musicians—United States

ISBN 9781451668728 (hc : alk. paper); 9781451668735 (tp : alk. paper); 9781451668742 (ebook : alk. paper)

LC 2013-009309

SUMMARY: In this autobiography, "Tracing the timeline of her remarkable life, Linda Ronstadt, whose forty-five year career has encompassed a wide array of musical styles, weaves together a captivating story of her origins in Tucson, Arizona, and her rise to stardom in the Southern California music scene of the 1960s and '70s." (Publisher's note)

REVIEW: *Booklist* v109 no22 p19 Ag 1 2013 June Sawyers

REVIEW: *Kirkus Rev* v81 no13 p214 Jl 1 2013

REVIEW: *N Y Times Book Rev* p26 D 22 2013 Alan Light

"Americana: The Kinks, the Riff, the Road: The Story," "Simple Dreams: A Musical Memoir," and "Everybody's Brother." "Like some Kinks songs, 'Americana' can be overstuffed with distracting detail (especially the passages about the band's various record deals), but [author Ray] Davies is candid and honest about his personal and creative struggles. . . . In her slim, warmhearted memoir, 'Simple Dreams,' [author Linda Ronstadt] claims . . . that she is allergic to alcohol. . . . 'I am like a human lava lamp,' writer CeeLo Green in his affable autobiography, 'Everybody's Brother.' Moments like that are the highlights of the book."

REVIEW: *Publ Wkly* v260 no35 p18-25 S 2 2013 HENRY L. CARRIGAN JR.

REVIEW: *Publ Wkly* v260 no29 p60-1 Jl 22 2013

RODE, DANIEL.il. Moustache Up! See Ainsworth, K.

ROOSE, KEVIN. Young money; inside the hidden world of Wall Street's post-crash recruits; [by] Kevin Roose 336 p. 2014 Grand Central Publishing

1. Business literature 2. Financial services industry—United States 3. Global Financial Crisis, 2008-2009 4. Investment advisors—New York (State)—New York 5. Investment bankers—New York (State)—New York 6. Stockbrokers—New York (State)—New York

ISBN 9780446583251 (hardcover)

LC 2013-032580

SUMMARY: In this book, "Kevin Roose investigates why young people still seek jobs on Wall Street even after the crash of 2008 revealed it to be a seeping moral gutter. . . . He reports on the experiences of eight young people who have just launched their careers in finance. He charts their progress from 2010 to 2013, as they toil away in the industry's most demanding entry-level positions: junior analysts on the sell side of the biggest banks' front offices." (Bookforum)

REVIEW: *Bookforum* v20 no5 p11 F/Mr 2014 SARAH LEONARD

"Young Money: Inside the Hidden World of Wall Street's Post-Crash Recruits." "The grimmest part of 'Young Money' is [Kevin] Roose's depiction of the miserable demands that banks make on their youngest employees. The book's close-in chronicle of this process is light, but it rests on more rigorous recent work about Wall Street. . . . But 'Young Money' makes it amply clear why, in the moment, these sleep-deprived twenty-two-year-olds can't help but regard such introspection as a luxury they can't afford. All they're doing in the unyielding rounds of their junior-banking lives, Roose writes, is 'trying to keep from drowning.'"

REVIEW: *Booklist* v110 no9/10 p28-9 Ja 1 2014 Mary Whaley

REVIEW: *Kirkus Rev* v82 no3 p22 F 1 2014

REVIEW: *N Y Times Book Rev* p11 Ap 13 2014 CHRIS HAYES

REVIEW: *Publ Wkly* v261 no2 p64 Ja 13 2014

ROOSEVELT, THEODORE, 1858-1919. Selected speeches and writings of Theodore Roosevelt; 384 p. 2014 Vintage Books, A Division of Random House LLC

1. Anthologies 2. Presidents—United States—Biography 3. Presidents—United States—Messages

ISBN 9780345806116 (pbk.)

LC 2013-033547

SUMMARY: This book, edited by Gordon Hutner, is a collection of former U.S. President Theodore Roosevelt. "Organized by general categories, readers can sample writings on subjects as varied as the environment, the danger of professional sports; the famous charge of San Juan Hill, and Roosevelt's passion for literary criticism." It features writings on "travel writing, to ecological concerns, to writings on hunting, to international politics and history." (Publisher's note)

REVIEW: *Booklist* v110 no15 p15 Ap 1 2014 Gilbert Taylor

REVIEW: *Kirkus Rev* v82 no3 p196 F 1 2014

"Selected Speeches and Writings of Theodore Roosevelt". "An eclectic collection from the highly literate and scholarly president of the United States. Editor [Gordon] Hutner . . . had a difficult task: selecting representative samples from among the mountains of Roosevelt's publications. Some selections are unsurprising . . . but there are also some welcome surprises. . . . His racial ideas, though (as the editor notes), were progressive for Roosevelt's time—not ours. . . . Intriguing pieces, unobtrusively and skillfully edited, that form both a time and a timeless capsule."

ROOT, PHYLLIS. Plant a pocket of prairie; 40 p. 2014 University of Minnesota Press

1. Children's nonfiction 2. Ecology—Juvenile literature 3. Gardening—Juvenile literature 4. Prairie plants—Juvenile literature 5. Prairies—Minnesota

ISBN 9780816679805 (hc: alk. paper)

LC 2013-040345

SUMMARY: In this book, "free verse poems invite readers to plant flowers and reconstruct pockets of lost prairie in backyards and on balconies to entice insects and birds to return, such as butterfly weed to attract monarch butterflies or rough blazing star for great spangled fritillaries. A map shows the once extensive prairie in Minnesota and the less than one percent now remaining, while the plant list will inspire the planting of at least some of the 14 recommended flowers and grasses." (School Library Journal)

REVIEW: *Horn Book Magazine* v90 no3 p113-4 My/Je 2014 DANIELLE J. FORD

REVIEW: *Kirkus Rev* v82 no5 p121 Mr 1 2014

"Plant a Pocket of Prairie". "Readers won't find a definition of what a prairie actually is, but they will learn about the wealth of flora and fauna it contains—and how the loss of any of its life forms affects others tremendously. . . . The lively, simple text is poetic; the colorful illustrations of native creatures and plants are energetic. While some of the author's supplemental text and a map refer specifically to Minnesota, she emphasizes that tiny 'pockets of prairie' still exist in various-and unexpected-places elsewhere. This not-so-whimsical flight of fancy could well inspire a new generation of conservationists."

REVIEW: *Publ Wkly* v261 no4 p195 Ja 27 2014

REVIEW: *SLJ* v60 no9 p163 S 2014 Frances E. Millhouser

ROOT, ROBERT. Happenstance; [by] Robert Root 296 p. 2013 University of Iowa Press

1. Chance 2. Geology—Niagara Escarpment 3. Memoirs

ISBN 1609381912 (pbk. : alk. paper); 9781609381912 (pbk. : alk. paper)

LC 2013-007536

SUMMARY: In this book, author Robert Root "muses on the random occurrences that led to his parents' troubled marriage and its subsequent effects on his own trajectory." His account "begins with the unlikely romance between his mother, Marie, a vivacious young woman focused on marriage and movie stars, and his father, Bob, a quiet, industrious man. . . . Further segments address Root's own divorce and remarriage and the ways that we alternately repeat and reject our parents' choices." (Kirkus Reviews)

REVIEW: *Booklist* v110 no4 p12-3 O 15 2013 Rick Roche

"Happenstance." "In recounting the unpredictable course of his life, [Robert] Root recognizes the importance of happenstance, the chance circumstance. He includes stories about how the American entry into WWII stunted the growth of his parents' love, how a false accusation at school isolated him from classmates, how a girlfriend's college plans stirred his ambition, and how meeting a friend of a temporary co-worker led to his happy second marriage. Through 96 short personal essays categorized as 'The Hundred Days' for pivotal days, 'Album' for close examination of family photos, 'Literary Remains' for clues from family papers, and 'Happenstance' for the intervening of outside influences. Root cleverly reveals to readers how powerful the unexpected has been in his life."

REVIEW: *Kirkus Rev* v81 no19 p115 O 1 2013

ROOTING FOR YOU; (a moving up story); 32 p. 2013 Disney-Hyperion

1. Children's stories 2. Courage 3. Daisies 4. Growth—Fiction 5. Seeds—Fiction
ISBN 9781423152309
LC 2012-006712

SUMMARY: This children's book presents "a story about a seed's journey from sprout to bloom. A nervous daisy seed, 'safe and sound,/down/down/down/here in the ground,' finally becomes bored and decides to begin his travels through soil, meeting a helpful worm and bravely passing a menacing spider." (School Library Journal)

REVIEW: *Booklist* v110 no13 p77 Mr 1 2014 Connie Fletcher

REVIEW: *Bull Cent Child Books* v67 no7 p361 Mr 2014 T. A.

"Rooting for You: A Moving Up Story." "The story is simple, and the worm's gentle rhymes keep a pleasant rhythm going. . . . The full-page flaps that unfold as the flower sprouts add some suspense, and they also the increase the fun for use in lapsits or storytimes, as does the book's vertical format as the daisy grows and grows. Cordell's scrawling illustrations temper the earnestness of the inspiration, and the rich, earthy palette necessary for the worm and the dirt is balanced by the jellybean purples of nearby beetles and greens of the foliage above ground; the seed's round face shows just how worried two lines and a dot can make a face look."

REVIEW: *Kirkus Rev* v82 no3 p100 F 1 2014

REVIEW: *Publ Wkly* v260 no51 p57 D 16 2013

REVIEW: *SLJ* v60 no3 p114 Mr 2014 Nora Clancy

ROSANVALLON, PIERRE. The society of equals; 384 p. 2013 Harvard University Press

1. Democracy 2. Equality—Sociological aspects 3. Historical literature 4. Social structure 5. Solidarity
ISBN 9780674724594 (alk. paper)
LC 2013-009718

SUMMARY: In this book on the history of economic and political equality, author "[Pierre] Rosanvallon sees the roots of today's crisis in the period 1830-1900. . . . By the early twentieth century, progressive forces had begun to rectify some imbalances of the Gilded Age, and the modern welfare state gradually emerged from Depression-era reforms. But new economic shocks in the 1970s began a slide toward inequality that has only gained momentum in the decades since." (Publisher's note)

REVIEW: *Choice* v51 no12 p2269 Ag 2014 C. P. Waligorski

REVIEW: *N Y Rev Books* v61 no9 p33-6 My 22 2014 Paul Starr

"The Society of Equals." "'The Society of Equals' . . . is a work of both history and political philosophy: a sweeping historical analysis of equality since the American and French Revolutions and an effort to reconstruct the understanding of equality for a new 'age of singularity' when 'everyone wants to "be someone."' . . . [Author Pierre] Rosanvallon's theory lacks clear criteria for judging distributive questions; it is too vague to be wrong, although not too vague to be interesting."

ROSE, CAROL M., 1940-. Saving the neighborhood. See Brooks, R. R. W.

ROSE, DEBORAH LEE. Jimmy the joey. See Kelly, S.

ROSE, KENNETH D. Unspeakable awfulness; America through the eyes of European travelers, 1865-1900; [by] Kenneth D. Rose xiii, 288 p. 2014 Routledge

1. Historical literature 2. Travelers' writings, European
ISBN 9780415817646 (hbk.); 9780415817653 (pbk.)
LC 2013-000906

SUMMARY: This book by Kenneth D. Rose presents a "study of the impressions of European travelers in the US in the late 19th century. He examines a panoply of behaviors, settings, feelings, and so on by (mostly British) Europeans, who reveal their own prejudices as well as illuminate what Rose considers a distinct, exceptional American environment and character." (Choice: Current Reviews for Academic Libraries)

REVIEW: *Choice* v51 no5 p908 Ja 2014 R. A. Shaddy

"Unspeakable Awfulness: America Through the Eyes of European Travelers, 1865-1900." "[Kenneth D.] Rose . . . presents a thoroughly researched and documented study of the impressions of European travelers in the US in the late 19th century. . . . Most of the travelers published their observations, and these books provide much of the content and quoted material for the author's fascinating, enjoyable book. Their writings as well as Rose's are lucid, clear, and convincing. The book provides an excellent introduction to the 19th-century US following the Civil War, and thanks to the far-reaching number of topics and documented sources, inherently suggests numerous points of exploration for further study and research."

ROSE, NIKOLAS. Neuro; the new brain sciences and the management of the mind; [by] Nikolas Rose xii, 335 p. 2013 Princeton University Press

1. Brain—Physiology 2. Brain imaging 3. Neuropsychology 4. Neurosciences 5. Scientific literature
ISBN 0691149607; 9780691149608 (hardcover : acid-free paper); 9780691149615 (pbk. : acid-free paper)
LC 2012-023222

SUMMARY: It was the authors' intent to demonstrate that

"neuroscience can often answer the obvious questions but rarely the interesting ones. It can tell us how our minds are made to hear music, and how groups of notes provoke neural connections, but not why [Wolfgang Amadeus] Mozart is more profound than [Barry] Manilow. . . . They take on, and dismiss, the famous experiments by Benjamin Libet that seem to undermine the idea of free will." (New Yorker)

REVIEW: *Choice* v51 no1 p104-5 S 2013 R. Borchardt

"Neuro: The New Brain Sciences and the Management of the Mind." "'Neuro' explores the reach of neuroscience beyond its scientific roots into increasingly interdisciplinary areas such as neuroeconomics, neurophilosophy, and neuroeducation, as well as its adoption into mainstream society, policy, and even law. [Authors Nikolas] Rose . . . and [Joelle M.] Abi-Rached . . . are not part of the neuroscientific community. They . . . do a thorough job of both exploring and gently critiquing the ways in which 'neuro' has been adopted in numerous areas. The book is a dense read, similar to a scientific journal article, but is well researched and presents a good reflection on the field of neuroscience, as well as today's society."

REVIEW: *New Yorker* v89 no27 p86-8 S 9 2013 Adam Gopnik

"A Skeptic's Guide to the Mind: What Neuroscience Can and Cannot Tell Us About Ourselves," "Brainwashed: The Seductive Appeal of Neuroscience," and "Neuro: The New Brain Sciences and the Management of the Mind." "A series of new books all present watch-and-ward arguments designed to show that brain science promises much and delivers little. . . . Each author, though, has a polemical project, something to put in place of mere Bumpology. . . . [Sally Satel] and [Scott O.] Lilienfeld are worried that neuroscience will shift wrongdoing from the responsible individual to his irresponsible brain, allowing crooks to cite neuroscience in order to get away with crimes. This concern seems overwrought. . . . [Robert A.] Burton, a retired medical neurologist, seems anxious to prove himself a philosopher. . . . [Nikolas] Rose and [Joelle M.] Abi-Rached see the real problem: neuroscience can often answer the obvious questions but rarely the interesting ones."

ROSE, NIKOLAS. The politics of life itself; biomedicine, power, and subjectivity in the twenty-first century; [by] Nikolas Rose 350 2007 Princeton University Press

1. Bioethics 2. Medical innovations—Social aspects 3. Medicine 4. Medicine—Political aspects 5. Philosophical literature 6. Power (Social sciences)
ISBN 0-691-12191-5; 9780691121918

SUMMARY: This book offers an "examination of recent developments in the life sciences and biomedicine that have led to the widespread politicization of medicine, human life, and biotechnology. . . . [Nikolas] Rose analyzes contemporary molecular biopolitics, examining developments in genomics, neuroscience, pharmacology, and psychopharmacology and the ways they have affected racial politics, crime control, and psychiatry." (Publisher's note)

REVIEW: *Contemp Sociol* v43 no2 p155-60 Mr 2014 Graham Scambler

"The Future of Human Nature," "The Politics of Life Itself: Biomedicine, Power, and Subjectivity in the Twenty-First Century," and "The New Medical Sociology: Social Forms of Health and Illness". "[Jürgen Habermas's] short volume comprises three pieces of direct relevance to medical sociology dating back to 2001: the first two are expanded versions of lectures delivered at the Universities of Zurich and Marburg and the third is based on a speech he gave on receiving the Peace Prize of the German Book Trade. . . . [Nikolas] Rose traverses similar territory but takes a very different route. Drawing on explicitly Foucauldian theoretical foundations as well as his previous work, he takes off from the current and growing ambiguity around notions of the normal. . . . Bryan Turner has decisively intervened in medical sociology's development more than once. His 'The New Medical Sociology' consolidates his reputation."

ROSEN, RACHEL. Negotiating adult-child relationships in early childhood research; [by] Rachel Rosen 153 p. 2014 Routledge

1. Child development—Research 2. Children and adults 3. Early childhood education—Research 4. Research—Moral & ethical aspects 5. Social science literature
ISBN 9780415633277 (hbk); 9780415633314 (pbk)
LC 2013-004102

SUMMARY: In this book on early childhood research ethics, "the authors contend that relationships are part of a wider web of social relations and space-time configurations. They propose and develop a relational ethics of answerability and social justice, inspired by the work of [Mikhail] Bakhtin and, in addition, explore the way material bodies come to matter, the ambiguity of consent in educator-research, and the risks and possibilities of research relationships." (Publisher's note)

REVIEW: *Choice* v51 no7 p1260-1 Mr 2014 R. B. Stewart Jr.

"Negotiating Adult-Child Relationships in Early Childhood Research." "Thoughtful and provocative discussions addressing the ambiguity of consent in research and the risks and possibilities inherent in research relationships are provided in a manner not often found in the standard accounts of the ethical treatment of research participants. This book contributes to current debates about research with young children, offering an incisive and thorough exploration of the importance of relationships within the research process. It should be considered required reading for those interested in early childhood and research with children."

ROSENBERG, MORGAN D.tr. Shakespeare's The Tempest. See Shakespeare's The Tempest

ROSENBERG, ROBIN S.ed. Our superheroes, ourselves. See Our superheroes, ourselves

ROSENBERG, ROBIN S.ed. What is a superhero? See What is a superhero?

ROSENBLATT, ROGER. The Boy Detective; A New York Childhood; [by] Roger Rosenblatt 272 p. 2013 HarperCollins

1. Detectives 2. Gramercy Park (New York, N.Y.) 3. Imagination 4. Memoirs 5. New York (N.Y.)—Social life & customs—20th century
ISBN 0062241338; 9780062241337

SUMMARY: Author Roger Rosenblatt presents the story of his "childhood in New York City. . . . Resisting the deadening silence of his family home in the elegant yet stiflingly safe neighborhood of Gramercy Park, nine-year-old Roger imagines himself a private eye in pursuit of criminals. With the dreamlike mystery of the city before him, he sets off alone, out into the streets of Manhattan." (Publisher's note)

REVIEW: *Booklist* v110 no2 p16 S 15 2013 Vanessa Bush

"The Boy Detective: A New York Childhood." "Teaching a class on memoir writing, [Roger] Rosenblatt is struck by his own powerful memories of a childhood in Manhattan with fantasies ot being a boy detective. . . . Rosenblatt shares poignant memories of the landscape of his childhood: the New York Public Library, Gramercy Park, Union Square, Madison Square Garden, and long-gone tenements and movie theaters. With the beautiful, lyrical writing and thoughtful reflection for which he is known, Rosenblatt offers beautifully rendered memories of childhood and ongoing curiosity about the city he so obviously loves."

REVIEW: *Kirkus Rev* v81 no19 p5 O 1 2013

REVIEW: *N Y Times Book Rev* p34 N 24 2013

REVIEW: *N Y Times Book Rev* p15 N 17 2013 PETE HAMILL

REVIEW: *Publ Wkly* v260 no31 p55-6 Ag 5 2013

ROSENFELD, RICHARD.ed. Economics and youth violence. See Economics and youth violence

ROSENFELD, SOPHIA. Common sense; a political history; [by] Sophia Rosenfeld 337 2011 Harvard University Press

1. Common sense 2. Historical literature 3. Paine, Thomas, 1737-1809 4. Political science—History 5. United States—Politics & government—1775-1783
ISBN 9780674057814
LC 2010-038504

SUMMARY: This book on the idea of common sense "traces the turns the phrase has taken since it came into use in 18th-century urban centers. She covers London . . . Aberdeen . . . and Philadelphia, where Thomas Paine employed common sense as a means to bring down a government. Here, too, is Paris, where those against the Revolution used common sense to critique democracy. [Sophia] Rosenfeld treats the post-18th-century era more briefly in a final chapter." (Library Journal)

REVIEW: *Am Hist Rev* v117 no2 p488-9 Ap 2012 Seth Cotlar

REVIEW: *Choice* v49 no5 p947 Ja 2012 M. G. Spencer

REVIEW: *Rev Am Hist* v41 no3 p399-404 S 2013 Craig Yirush

"Common Sense: A Political History." "Sophia Rosenfeld's elegant and engaging intellectual history takes common sense seriously as a political idea central to early modern and modern democratic life. . . . Rosenfeld's sweeping history of a neglected idea has much to recommend it. . . . 'Common Sense: A Political History,' however, is not without flaws. If we are to accept Rosenfeld's argument . . . then we need to know much more about how it related to other concepts at the heart of liberal and democratic modernity. . . . Finally, while Rosenfeld wants to stress the dualism of common sense, its ability to produce both reform and reaction, the evidence she offers of its impact suggests that it was, on the whole, more likely to reify existing prejudices than to challenge them."

REVIEW: *TLS* no5667 p12 N 11 2011 JONATHAN CLARK

ROSENGREN, GAYLE. What the moon said; [by] Gayle Rosengren 224 p. 2014 G. P. Putnam's Sons, an imprint of Penguin Group (USA) Inc.

1. Depressions—1929—Fiction 2. Family life—Wisconsin—Fiction 3. Farm life—Wisconsin—Fiction 4. Historical fiction 5. Mothers and daughters—Fiction 6. Superstition—Fiction
ISBN 9780399163524 (hardcover)
LC 2013-003442

SUMMARY: In this book, set " in 1930, Esther's life changes dramatically when her family moves from Chicago to a Wisconsin farm after her father loses his job. . . . Optimistically determined to see the situation as an 'adventure,' Esther is thrilled to have horses, cows, and (best of all) a dog, and she finds beauty in the quiet landscape and excels in school. Yet what she really wants--approval, a steady best friend, and relief from poverty--are elusive." (Bulletin of the Center for Children's Books)

REVIEW: *Booklist* v110 no8 p50 D 15 2013 Kathleen Isaacs

REVIEW: *Bull Cent Child Books* v67 no7 p373-4 Mr 2014 A. A.

"What the Moon Said." "[Gayle] Rosengren's depiction of them Great Depression from a child's perspective rings true, with the direness of financial circumstances not as keenly felt as the desire for approval from one's mother. Though Esther's constant worry over her mother's love feels forced at times, the sentiment will resonate with young readers whose parents show love in ways other than constant displays. The author's keen understanding of the emotions and preoccupations of late childhood shine through Esther, including the struggle to interpret adult behavior and reconcile family rules with personal truths. Sensitive and engaging, this novel would work as an accompaniment to a classroom unit on the Great Depression."

REVIEW: *Kirkus Rev* v81 no24 p162 D 15 2013

REVIEW: *Publ Wkly* v260 no47 p53 N 18 2013

REVIEW: *SLJ* v60 no2 p96 F 2014 Beth Dobson

ROSENHEIM, JEFF L. Photography and the American Civil War; [by] Jeff L. Rosenheim 288 p. 2013 Yale Univ Pr

1. Art catalogs 2. Photography & history 3. Portraits—History 4. United States—History—Civil War, 1861-1865—Pictorial works 5. War photography—History
ISBN 0300191804; 9780300191806

SUMMARY: In this book, Jeff L. Rosenheim "argues that the rise of popular photography coincided with the onset of the Civil War to signify the beginning of the modern era. Examining the use of war images in newspapers and political campaigns, the sentimental obsession over portraiture by soldiers and their families, and the national mourning enacted through mass images, Rosenheim weaves the rhetorical and material realities of the war years by attaching them to the photographic image." (Publishers Weekly)

REVIEW: *Bookforum* v20 no3 p19 S-N 2013 CHRISTOPHER LYON

REVIEW: *Choice* v51 no2 p251 O 2013 E. Hutchinson

REVIEW: *Hist Today* v63 no7 p63 Jl 2013 NICK LIPTROT

REVIEW: *N Y Rev Books* v60 no13 p8-10 Ag 15 2013 David Bromwich

"Photography and the American Civil War." "Splendid. . . . Judicious. . . . Some of the most absorbing pages of the Met catalog recount the history of faked Civil War photographs. . . . There are omissions in the Met exhibition that come from necessity and not chance; and these bring to mind how large a part of suffering is irretrievable. . . . It must be added that a few pieces in the exhibition exhibition . . . are so cunningly indebted to the technology of the 1860s that they lose much of their charm in the flat presentation of a book. . . . Overall the exhibition catalog makes a wonderful enhancement of the show itself."

REVIEW: *New Statesman* v143 no4 p51 Ja 31 2014

ROSENSTOCK, BARBARA. Thomas Jefferson Builds a Library; 32 p. 2013 Calkins Creek

1. Books & reading—United States 2. Children's nonfiction 3. Jefferson, Thomas, 1743-1826 4. Library of Congress—History 5. Presidents—United States—Biography—Juvenile literature
ISBN 1590789326; 9781590789322
LC 2013-931061

SUMMARY: Author Barb Rosenstock "uses Thomas Jefferson's love of reading and collecting books as a lens through which to view the story of his life. Even as a young child, Tom reads through his father's library, and as a young man, he collects his own. The story concludes with Jefferson selling his beloved books to form the basis of the new collection [at the Library of Congress]." (Booklist)

REVIEW: *Booklist* v109 no22 p68 Ag 1 2013 Carolyn Phelan

REVIEW: *Bull Cent Child Books* v67 no1 p50 S 2013 E. B.

REVIEW: *Kirkus Rev* v81 no16 p59 Ag 15 2013

"Thomas Jefferson Builds a Library." "This unusual picture-book biography fosters a new understanding of Thomas Jefferson's life as viewed through his love of books and its impact on our burgeoning nation. . . . The narrative replicates the rhythm of a conversation as it provides numerous examples of his love of books. Clever spreads combine expansive full-bleed images and individual, framed pen-and-ink-and-watercolor illustrations, plus vignettes amplifying points made in the text. Throughout, fact boxes shaped like open books scattered across the pages supply additional details. . . . Sure to be enjoyed, this is an engaging study of one of our Founding Father's great legacies."

REVIEW: *Publ Wkly* v260 no30 p71 Jl 29 2013

REVIEW: *SLJ* v59 no8 p124 Ag 2013 Wendy Lukehart

ROSENTHAL, LORRAINE ZAGO. New money; a novel; [by] Lorraine Zago Rosenthal 336 p. 2013 Thomas Dunne Books/St. Martin's Press

1. Cinderella (Legendary character) 2. Love stories 3. New York (N.Y.)—Fiction 4. Upper class—Fiction 5. Wealth—Fiction 6. Women—Southern States
ISBN 9781250025357 (hardcover)
LC 2013-013484

SUMMARY: In this novel by Lorraine Zago Rosenthal, "A young Southern woman of modest means suddenly finds herself thrust into New York's high society when she discovers that she is the illegitimate daughter of a recently-deceased billionaire. . . . Putting aside her mother's disapproval, Savannah plunges into a life of wealth and luxury that is threatened by Edward's other children . . . whose joint mission is to get rid of Savannah." (Publisher's note)

REVIEW: *Kirkus Rev* v81 no16 p288 Ag 15 2013

"New Money." "A modern Cinderella finds herself the heir to a fortune, two nasty stepsiblings and a struggling writer from Queens for a Prince Charming. . . . Although Edward has two other children, Ned and Caroline, he's left the bulk of his fortune to Savannah, with the stipulation that she stay in New York and work for Stone News. Her stepsiblings are furious, but Ned's wife, Kitty (her hip fairy godmother), makes Savannah an editorial assistant at 'Femme' magazine. Savannah is given a driver, a stunning apartment and a beginning allowance of $10,000 a week. What could intrude on this fairy-tale concoction? Lots. Will her fairy godmother pull through? [Author Lorraine Zago] Rosenthal tackles some contemporary issues in the midst of an agreeable fantasy."

REVIEW: *Publ Wkly* v260 no24 p38 Je 17 2013

ROSENTHAL, NICOLAS G. Reimagining Indian country; native American migration & identity in twentieth-century Los Angeles; [by] Nicolas G. Rosenthal xi, 239 p. 2012 University of North Carolina Press

1. Historical literature 2. Indians of North America—California—Los Angeles—Migrations 3. Indians of North America—California—Los Angeles—Social conditions 4. Indians of North America—Urban residence—California—Los Angeles 5. Los Angeles (Calif.)—History—20th century 6. Rural-urban migration—California—Los Angeles
ISBN 0807835552 (cloth : alk. paper); 9780807835555 (cloth : alk. paper)
LC 2011-047233

SUMMARY: This book by Nicolas Rosenthal "reorients our understanding of the experience of American Indians by tracing their migration to cities, exploring the formation of urban Indian communities, and delving into the shifting relationships between reservations and urban areas. With a focus on Los Angeles, . . . [Rosenthal] shows how cities have played a defining role in modern American Indian life." (Publisher's note)

REVIEW: *Am Hist Rev* v118 no4 p1211-2 O 2013 Andrew H. Fisher

"Reimagining Indian Country: Native American Migration and Identity in Twentieth-Century Los Angeles." "Los Angeles easily has the biggest population of urban Indians, yet until now it lacked a substantive case study. . . . Nicholas G. Rosenthal gives the 'Urban Indian Capital of the United States' the attention it deserves. . . . As the title suggests, however, he aims for something more than a mere chronicle of Native life in Los Angeles; rather, he strives to connect it to 'larger discussions about mobility and migration, racialized power structures, and individual and community agency.' . . . In short, his book advances the ongoing intellectual project of writing Native Americans back into modern U.S. history."

REVIEW: *Choice* v50 no4 p743 D 2012 T. Maxwell-Long

ROSENTHAL, T. G. LS Lowry; The Art and the Artist;

[by] T. G. Rosenthal 320 pp. 2010 Unicorn Press

1. Art literature 2. Artists—England 3. British art 4. English painting 5. Lowry, Laurence Stephen, 1887-1976

ISBN 9781906509064

SUMMARY: In this book on artist L. S. Lowry, author T. G. Rosenthal "has devoted chapters to Lowry's technique, his visual friendship with his fellow painter David Carr; and a serious analysis and rebuttal of a theory that has advanced the view that Lowry suffered from Asperger's Disease. The book begins with teh previously unpublished transcripts of the broadcasts which cast a unique light on Lowry's art and developing reputation." (Publisher's note)

REVIEW: *N Y Rev Books* v60 no14 p26-9 S 26 2013 Sanford Schwartz

"Lowry and the Painting of Modern Life" and "L. S. Lowry: The Art and the Artist." "T. J. Clark and Anne M. Wagner, while writing as admirers, imply what many viewers have no doubt felt: that in the sheer volume of his work Lowry was something of an industrial producer himself. . . . When Clark writes that in some of Lowry's paintings 'the real energy, obduracy and confinement of working-class England are visible,' his carefully chosen words enliven our sense of the paintings and of the North West of the time. But his and Wagner's exhibition shortchanges Lowry."

ROSOFF, MEG. Picture me gone; [by] Meg Rosoff 256 p. 2013 G.P. Putnam's Sons

1. Coming of age—Fiction 2. Fathers and daughters—Fiction 3. Missing persons—Fiction 4. Mystery and detective stories 5. Young adult fiction

ISBN 0399257659; 9780399257650

LC 2012-048974

SUMMARY: This book by Meg Rosoff is a story "about the relationship between parents and children, love and loss. Mila has an exceptional talent for reading a room—sensing hidden facts and unspoken emotions from clues that others overlook. So when her father's best friend, Matthew, goes missing from his upstate New York home, Mila and her beloved father travel from London to find him. Just when she's closest to solving the mystery, a shocking betrayal calls into question her trust." (Publisher's note)

REVIEW: *Booklist* v109 no22 p78 Ag 1 2013 Ilene Cooper

REVIEW: *Bull Cent Child Books* v67 no4 p235-6 D 2013 A. M.

REVIEW: *Bull Cent Child Books* v67 no5 p292-5 Ja 2014 Deborah Stevenson

REVIEW: *Horn Book Magazine* v89 no6 p105 N/D 2013 MARTHA V. PARRAVANO

REVIEW: *Kirkus Rev* p43 Ag 15 2013 Fall Preview

REVIEW: *Kirkus Rev* v81 no16 p111 Ag 15 2013

"Picture Me Gone." "Mila, 12, a keen observer of people and events, accompanies her translator father, Gil, on a journey from London to upstate New York in search of Gil's lifelong friend, who's disappeared. Mila applies her puzzle-solving skills to the mystery of why Matthew would abandon his wife and baby, not to mention his dog. . . . [Author Meg] Rosoff respects her young character, portraying her as a complete person capable of recognizing that there are things she may not yet know. . . . The author skillfully turns to a variety of literary devices to convey this transition."

REVIEW: *Kirkus Rev* p82 N 15 2013 Best Books

REVIEW: *N Y Times Book Rev* p25 N 10 2013 SUSAN CHOI

REVIEW: *Publ Wkly* p106 Children's starred review annual 2013

REVIEW: *SLJ* v59 no10 p1 O 2013 Colleen S. Banick

REVIEW: *Voice of Youth Advocates* v36 no5 p65 D 2013 Stephanie Wilkes

ROSOFF, MEG. There is no dog; [by] Meg Rosoff 243p. 2011 G. P. Putnam's Sons

1. Fiction 2. God in literature 3. Love stories 4. Man-woman relationships 5. Teenagers in literature

ISBN 9780399257643

LC 2011-020651

SUMMARY: This book "looks at the world's natural disasters, injustices, and chaos and presents a[n] . . . explanation: God is a horny teenage boy. According to this . . . account, God, aka 'Bob,' was given Earth by his mother, who won the planet in a poker game. Bob showed flashes of brilliance during Creation, but he feels little responsibility for the planet. When he falls head-over-heels in lust with a beautiful zoo employee, Lucy, Bob's passion and growing anger toward those who would keep them apart is manifested through wildly fluctuating weather and rampant flooding." (Publishers Weekly)

REVIEW: *Booklist* v108 no6 p52 N 15 2011 Ilene Cooper

REVIEW: *Booklist* v109 no6 p56 N 15 2012 Lolly Gepson

REVIEW: *Bull Cent Child Books* v65 no6 p320 F 2012 C. G.

"There Is No Dog." "When a sweet, lonely, twenty-one-year-old zoo worker named Lucy sends a small prayer to God asking to fall in love, God gets the memo—and, being a rather feckless teenage boy named Bob, decides he will fulfill the prayer himself. . . . His single-minded focus on Lucy both flatters and unnerves her . . . and if she is a bit flat as a love interest, it is because the novel as a whole is more interested in allegory, image, and commentary than in character. The narrative threads and multitude of bit characters come together like puzzle pieces, offering thought-provoking world-building at an emotional remove. . . . Readers . . . with a fondness for satire or religious inquiry will be fascinated."

REVIEW: *Horn Book Magazine* v88 no1 p99 Ja/F 2012 Sarah Ellis

REVIEW: *Kirkus Rev* v79 no23 p2238 D 1 2011

REVIEW: *Publ Wkly* v258 no45 p68-70 N 7 2011

REVIEW: *SLJ* v59 no4 p58 Ap 2013 Stephanie A. Squicciarini

REVIEW: *SLJ* v58 no1 p126 Ja 2012 Emma Burkhart

REVIEW: *Voice of Youth Advocates* v34 no5 p500 D 2011 Walter Hogan

ROSS, CHARLES L. Inside; [by] Charles L. Ross 454 p. 2013 CreateSpace Independent Publishing Platform

1. Detective & mystery stories 2. Human sexuality—Fiction 3. Interior decoration 4. Murder—Fiction 5. Periodical publishing—Fiction

ISBN 1492237108; 9781492237105

SUMMARY: In this book, "an ambitious young man's rise in the magazine world is stymied by a secret history of murder and betrayal. When Leaf Wyks, the editor of the high-end interior design magazine Inside, is found poisoned to death in her Los Angeles home, the police immediately suspect Anthony Dimora. Before Leaf abruptly fired him, Anthony was Inside's art director and the man most likely to take her place on the masthead. Worse yet, it was Anthony who discovered Leaf's corpse." (Kirkus Reviews)

REVIEW: *Kirkus Rev* v82 no6 p13 Mr 15 2014

REVIEW: *Kirkus Rev* v82 no2 p338 Ja 15 2014

"Inside". "[Charles L.] Ross eschews the conventions of the whodunit in favor of a dishy flashback account of Anthony's rise to the top of the interior design world and the precipitous fall that preceded Leaf's death. . . . To his credit, Ross manages to pack a great deal of interest and suspense into even the most technical aspects of the magazine business. When Anthony directs a photo shoot, the stakes are high, and the sexiness of the work comes through. Despite a few belabored descriptions of rooms and their furnishings, this world is so enticing that readers might nearly forget to wonder who killed Leaf Wyks and why. A sexy, scathing insider's view of an interior design magazine that hardly needs its murder plot to keep readers enthralled."

ROSS, MICHAEL ELSOHN, 1952-. A world of her own; 24 amazing women explorers and adventurers; [by] Michael Elsohn Ross 224 p. 2014 Chicago Review Press

1. BIOGRAPHY & AUTOBIOGRAPHY—Adventurers & Explorers 2. Biography (Literary form) 3. JUVENILE NONFICTION—Adventure & Adventurers 4. JUVENILE NONFICTION—Biography & Autobiography—Women 5. JUVENILE NONFICTION—Girls & Women 6. JUVENILE NONFICTION—History—Exploration & Discovery 7. Women explorers—Biography
ISBN 9781613744383 (hardback)
LC 2013-024947

SUMMARY: This book "tells the stories of 24 brave women from different cultures, epochs, and economic backgrounds who have shared similar missions: to meet the physical and mental challenges of exploring the natural world, to protect the environment and native cultures, and to leave a mark in the name of discovery." Subjects include "Rosaly Lopes, who . . . discovered 71 volcanoes on one of Jupiter's moons; [and] Helen Thayer, the first woman to walk and ski the Magnetic North Pole." (Publisher's note)

REVIEW: *Kirkus Rev* v82 no2 p102 Ja 15 2014

"A World of Her Own: 24 Amazing Women Explorers and Adventurers". "If only the writing lived up to the subject matter. . . . Twenty-four vignettes of intrepid true-life women—exploring, adventuring and risking their lives to live fully—are recounted in passive, confusing narratives. Disjointed thoughts plague many of the accounts. . . . For a book about women, the influence of men infiltrates irritatingly. . . . While many of the women profiled knew struggle in both childhood and adulthood, the flat tone of the writing keeps readers from engaging emotionally. . . . The book's overall tone—that of a laundry list of accomplishments—does a disservice to readers who deserve to relate to and be inspired by these remarkable women."

REVIEW: *Voice of Youth Advocates* v37 no1 p94 Ap 2014 Rachel Wadham

ROSS, RON. Tales from the Sidewalks of New York; [by] Ron Ross 230 p. 2012 CreateSpace Independent Publishing Platform

1. American short stories 2. Boxers (Sports)—Fiction 3. Boxing stories 4. Immigrants—Fiction 5. New York (N.Y.)—Fiction
ISBN 1470002191; 9781470002190

SUMMARY: This book of short stories by Ron Ross focuses on boxing and street life in New York City.In "'The Journeyman,' Ross' opening story, the author portrays the weary existence of a seasoned prizefighter named Billy Dumas. . . . The succeeding trio of tales revolves around the streetwise, Brooklyn adolescence of future Jewish prizefighter Al 'Boomy' Davidoff and a gang of miscreants." (Kirkus Reviews)

REVIEW: *Kirkus Rev* p49-50 D 15 2013 supplemet best books 2013

"Tales From the Sidewalks of New York". ". The final three tales are told in rhyming verse, which detracts slightly from the power of the author's wise-guy vernacular and polished prose. For the most part, [Ron] Ross writes like a [John] Steinbeck trained as a boxing columnist on the Lower East Side. Humorous turns of phrase keep sad inevitabilities at bay: '(T]his whole world ain't made up of ditch-diggers and pugs,' says Monk—a thought that runs contrary to the world Ross handily creates. A lithe, lyrical collection that packs more than a few punches."

REVIEW: *Kirkus Rev* v81 no19 p18 O 1 2013

ROSSELL, JUDITH.il. Mice mischief. See Stills, C.

ROSSER, GERVASE. Spectacular Miracles; Transforming Images in Italy, from the Renaissance to the Present; [by] Gervase Rosser 320 p. 2013 University of Chicago Press

1. Christian art & symbolism 2. Historical literature 3. Idols & images 4. Italy—Religion 5. Miracles (Christianity)
ISBN 1780231059; 9781780231051

SUMMARY: This book by Jane Garnett and Gervase Rosser "confronts an enduring Western belief in the supernatural power of images: that a statue or painting of the Madonna can fly through the air, speak, weep, or produce miraculous cures. Although contrary to widely held assumptions, the cults of particular paintings and statues held to be miraculous have persisted beyond the middle ages into the present, even in a modern European city such as Genoa, the primary focus of this book." (Publisher's note)

REVIEW: *Apollo: The International Magazine for Collectors* v178 no612 p119 S 2013

REVIEW: *Apollo: The International Magazine for Collectors* v178 no613 p120-1 O 2013 Richard Cork

"Spectacular Miracles: Transforming Images in Italy From the Renaissance to the Present" and "The Miraculous Image in Renaissance Florence." "These two defiant books, both focused on miraculous images in Italian art, are under no illusions about the hostility which their chosen subject can provoke. Jane Garnett and Gervase Rosser, co-authors of 'Spectacular Miracles,' . . . have written an impressively researched and perceptive study of miraculous images in Italy. . . . The simultaneous publication of another deeply considered book, 'The Miraculous Image in Renaissance Florence,' proves that this ambition is shared. Although the author, Megan Holmes, focuses on a far shorter period, her text is the fruit of long, sustained and carefully considered research."

REVIEW: *Choice* v51 no4 p621 D 2013 A. V. Coonin

ROSSI, CATHARINE.ed. EP Volume 1. See EP Volume 1

ROSSI, VERONICA. Under the never sky; [by] Veronica Rossi 376 p. 2012 HarperCollins

1. Apocalyptic literature (Christian literature) 2. Dystopias 3. Science fiction
ISBN 9780062072030 (hardback)
LC 2011-044631

SUMMARY: This book tells the story of "Aria [who] knows her chances of surviving in the outer wasteland--known as The Death Shop--are slim. . . . Then Aria meets an Outsider named Perry. He's wild--a savage--and her only hope of staying alive. A hunter for his tribe in a merciless landscape, Perry views Aria as sheltered and fragile--everything he would expect from a Dweller. . . . Opposites in nearly every way, Aria and Perry must accept each other to survive." (Publisher's note)

REVIEW: *Booklist* v108 no12 p56 F 15 2012 Heather Booth

REVIEW: *Booklist* v108 no18 p72 My 15 2012 Heather Booth

REVIEW: *Bull Cent Child Books* v65 no8 p420 Ap 2012 C. G.

"Under the Never Sky." "Aria lives in a protected domed city where the monotony of existence is buried under layers of virtual reality and constant technological input. Perry lives in the harsh world outside, where Aether storms scorch the earth and imbue a select few (including Perry) with enhanced senses essential to humanity's continuing survival. . . . The differences between her and Perry are thoughtfully explored: with each raised on scary bedtime stories about the other, she finds him primitive, he finds her barely human, and their relationship . . . develops with refreshing slowness. In the meantime, it's exhilarating to watch Aria develop into a strong, purposeful heroine, discovering and reveling in her own skills as she's honed by the hardships of the real world."

REVIEW: *Horn Book Magazine* v88 no2 p119-20 Mr/Ap 2012 April Spisak

REVIEW: *Kirkus Rev* v79 no24 p2337 D 15 2011

REVIEW: *Publ Wkly* v258 no46 p55 N 14 2011

REVIEW: *SLJ* v58 no3 p172 Mr 2012 Eric Norton

REVIEW: *SLJ* v58 no6 p63-4 Je 2012 Elizabeth L. Kenyon

"Under the Never Sky." "Aria has been banished from Reverie, a pod community that was created to protect its inhabitants, the Dwellers, from the mutating storms that began wreaking havoc on the surface hundreds of years ago. . . . Veronica Rossi's debut novel . . . takes listeners to a world torn apart by violent storms and genetic mutations. Can an Outsider and a Dweller work together to help each other in their quests? This production is a pure delight. Narrator Bernadette Dunne flawlessly moves from character to character, giving each one a distinct persona. Sure to captivate listeners."

REVIEW: *Voice of Youth Advocates* v34 no5 p519 D 2011 Cynthia Winfield

ROSTAIN, MICHEL. The Son; [by] Michel Rostain 320 p. 2013 Trafalgar Square Books

1. Children—Death—Fiction 2. Domestic fiction 3. Fathers & sons—Fiction 4. Grief—Fiction 5. Regret
ISBN 0755390792; 9780755390793

SUMMARY: This book by Michel Rostain is "narrated in the first person by Lion, a twenty-one-year-old student who has just died from meningitis and is now observing from an afterlife. . . . Through Lion's one-sided, chronologically fragmented 'conversation' with his father, we see Michel struggle with his grief. He replays the days before Lion's death, the terrible madness of the emergency ward and the funeral, before moving into a future without his son." (Times Literary Supplement)

REVIEW: *TLS* no5750 p20 Je 14 2013 J. C. SUTCLIFFE

"The Son." "Choosing the dead son to tell the story of Michel's anguish helps the author to avoid self-pity. . . . [Michel] Rostain exposes the father's flaws, and the difficulties in this very human, very loving relationship. Michel must also confront other versions of his son--those of Lion's friends and girlfriend--learning to accept them with a grace and humility he could not always find during Lion's life. The colloquial, youthful register, translated with careful attention to nuance by Adriana Hunter, is both compelling and jarring."

REVIEW: *TLS* no5757 p32 Ag 2 2013 J. C.

ROSTKER, BERNARD. Providing for the casualities of war; the American experience through World War II; [by] Bernard Rostker xviii, 286 p. 2013 RAND

1. Battle casualties—Medical care—History 2. Historical literature 3. Medicine, Military—History 4. Veterans—Medical care—History 5. War casualties—Medical care—History
ISBN 9780833078353 (pbk. : alk. paper); 9780833078360 (hardcover : alk. paper)
LC 2013-009885

SUMMARY: "This book explores the history of health care for the military. . . . In the first eight chapters, [Bernard] Rostker . . . provides a . . . history of wartime casualties from ancient Greek and Roman times through WW II. . . . Advances in antibiotics, blood products, and medical evacuations are among the variables highlighted; the book also addresses neuropsychiatric conditions." (Choice: Current Reviews for Academic Libraries)

REVIEW: *Choice* v51 no5 p874 Ja 2014 P. Leung

"Providing for the Casualties of War: The American Experience Through World War II." "The well-documented chapters include interesting data and photographs that bring the past to light. . . . A plus is a well-done appendix on the number of military personnel and associated casualties from the Revolutionary War to the Persian Gulf War, which provides an interesting perspective. At the same time, the book is somewhat disappointing in terms of meeting the author's objective. The final chapter is a summary based on four broad themes, but it provides very little analysis of lessons learned or implications for the future. The work's utility appears more as a background resource."

ROTH, JOSEPH, 1894-1939. Flight without end; 144 p. 1977 Owen

1. Europe, Western—History 2. Friendship—Fiction 3. Military personnel—Fiction 4. Soviet Union—History—Revolution, 1917-1921 5. World War, 1914-1918—Austria 6. World War, 1914-1918—Fiction

ISBN 0720603242
LC 7737-9144

SUMMARY: This novel explores the story of Franz Tunda, an Austrian soldier who was captured by the Russian army and held as a prisoner of war in 1916, as he escapes and makes his way back to the West. "The rest of the book documents Tunda's failure to fit in with a much-changed system. A man removed from Western Europe during its momentous postwar development, he finds its new machinery easy to understand but impossible to esteem. . . . The synthesis Tunda makes of his opposing styles of life . . . has lived on into modern jargon as 'opting out.'" (TLS)

REVIEW: *TLS* no5681 p16 F 17 2012

"Flight Without End." ." . . Among [Roth's] earlier works are several which put into a form both stylistically and politically ominous the convictions Roth had formed about the modern world. 'Flight Without End' is one of these: characteristically abrupt, oblique, ironic and dislocated. . . . The rest of the book documents Tunda's failure to fit in with a much-changed system. A man removed from Western Europe during its momentous postwar development, he finds its new machinery easy to understand but impossible to esteem. . . . Modishly unlubricated shifts of narrative gear apart, amazingly little about this book's thinking has dated. Even the synthesis Tunda makes of his opposing styles of life . . . has lived on into modern jargon as 'opting out.'"

ROTH, JOSEPH, 1894-1939. On the end of the world; [by] Joseph Roth 2013 Hesperus Press

1. Exiles' writings, Austrian 2. Jews, Austrian 3. Journalism 4. National socialism 5. Paris (France)—History—1870-1940

ISBN 9781843916192 paperback

SUMMARY: "Having fled to Paris in 1933 following Hitler's rise to power in Germany, Joseph Roth wrote a series of articles in that 'hour before the end of the world' which he foresaw was to come and that would culminate in World War II. This collection has never before been translated into English. Incisive and ironic, the writing evokes Roth's bitterness and despair at the coming annihilation of the free world." (Publisher's note)

REVIEW: *TLS* no5785 p26-7 F 14 2014 REBECCA K. MORRISON

"On the End of the World." "As unremittingly bleak as its title suggests, this selection of Joseph Roth's journalism, written in his last years, demands its place beside Roth's other work: published predominantly in the newspapers and journals available to the exile community in Paris of the 1930s . . . the pieces excel as an act of resistance, a masterclass in channelling despair into searing prose, and showcasing a writer respecting his responsibility as a writer to the end while grappling to win back the power of the written word, and the spoken German language, from the 'evil genius' of the machine of propaganda, Joseph Goebbels. . . . 'On the End of the World' is an excellent addition to Roth's oeuvre in English, deftly translated and with comprehensive notes by Will Stone."

ROTH, MARCO, 1974-. The scientists; a family romance; [by] Marco Roth 196 p. 2012 Farrar, Straus, and Giroux

1. AIDS (Disease)—Patients—Family relationships—New York (State)—New York 2. Bereavement 3. Bisexuality 4. Fathers and sons 5. Memoirs

ISBN 0374210284; 9780374210281 (alk. paper)
LC 2011-051264

SUMMARY: This memoir, by Marco Roth, describes how as a child "Marco Roth was able to share his parents' New York, a world centered around house concerts, a private library, . . . and dinner discussions of the latest advances in medicine. That world ended when his father started to suffer . . . [from] the AIDS virus that had infected him in the early 1980s. What this family could not talk about for years came to dominate the lives of its surviving members, often in unexpected ways." (Publisher's note)

REVIEW: *Economist* v405 no8810 p86 N 10 2012

REVIEW: *Kirkus Rev* v80 no14 p1480 Jl 15 2012

REVIEW: *Libr J* v137 no20 p29 D 1 2012 Therese Purcell Nielsen

REVIEW: *London Rev Books* v35 no5 p21-2 Mr 7 2013 Jenny Diski

REVIEW: *N Y Times Book Rev* p32 S 22 2013 IHSAN TAYLOR

"The Scientists: A Family Romance," "Some Kind of Fairy Tale," and "All We Know: Three Lives." "In this memoir [Marco] Roth . . . investigates his father's troubled life through the novels he cherished. . . . Drawing faithfully on English folklore, [Graham] Joyce's novel of disruption and grief concerns Tara, who vanished from a forest when she was a teenager. . . . This group biography plunges readers into the milieu of midcentury upper-class lesbians, portraying it as a beguiling, exclusive club."

REVIEW: *New Statesman* v142 no5143 p49-50 F 1 2013 Jonathan Derbyshire

REVIEW: *New Yorker* v88 no32 p86-7 O 15 2012

REVIEW: *Publ Wkly* v259 no25 p1 Je 18 2012

REVIEW: *TLS* no5734 p30 F 22 2013 TOBY LICHTIG

ROTH, SUSAN L. Parrots over Puerto Rico; 48 p. 2013 Lee & Low Books

1. Children's nonfiction 2. Endangered species—Puerto Rico 3. Natural history—Puerto Rico 4. Puerto Rican parrot—Conservation

ISBN 1620140047; 9781620140048 (hardcover: alkaline paper)
LC 2012-048195

SUMMARY: Authors Susan L. Roth and Cindy Trumbore present "a picture book telling the intertwined histories of the Puerto Rican parrot and the island of Puerto Rico, culminating with current efforts to save the parrots from extinction. Roth and Trumbore recount the efforts of the scientists of the Puerto Rican Parrot Recovery Program to save the parrots and ensure their future. Woven into the parrots' story is a brief history of Puerto Rico itself." (Publisher's note)

REVIEW: *Booklist* v110 no6 p40 N 15 2013 Erin Anderson

"Parrots Over Puerto Rico". "Few nonfiction picture books attempt this level of ambition, and even fewer succeed. Thankfully, [Susan L.] Roth and [Cindy] Trumbore's first instinct ends up being the best one: to tell the story of the Puerto Rican parrot you must also tell the story of Puerto Ricans. . . . Roth's stunning artwork—fluttery, textural collages of fabric and paper with a three-dimensional quality—complement the high-interest narrative and are arranged vertically across dual pages to make the most of the tall trees and the related human actions taking place below. A triumphant reminder of the inescapable connection between people's actions and the animals in the wild."

REVIEW: *Bull Cent Child Books* v67 no5 p281 Ja 2014 T. A.

REVIEW: *Horn Book Magazine* v90 no1 p117 Ja/F 2014 DANIELLE J. FORD

"Parrots Over Puerto Rico". "This gorgeously illustrated history of the critically endangered Puerto Rican parrot, along with the settlement and development of Puerto Rico, underscores the environmental consequences of human populations on indigenous animal species. . . . With stunning paper-and-fabric artwork on each spread, the book is laid out vertically to best give a sense of height. . . . An afterword includes additional details about conservation efforts, several color photographs of the parrots and the people working to save them, and a timeline of historical and environmental events in Puerto Rico."

REVIEW: *Kirkus Rev* v81 no17 p113-4 S 1 2013

REVIEW: *Kirkus Rev* p63 N 15 2013 Best Books

REVIEW: *Publ Wkly* v260 no31 p75 Ag 5 2013

REVIEW: *Publ Wkly* p58-60 Children's starred review annual 2013

REVIEW: *SLJ* v59 no10 p1 O 2013 Kathy Piehl

ROTHERY, MARK. Man's estate. See French, H.

ROTMAN, JOSEPH J. Learning modern algebra. See Cuoco, A.

ROTTENBERG, JONATHAN. The depths; the evolutionary origins of the depression epidemic; [by] Jonathan Rottenberg 272 p. 2014 Basic Books

1. Depression, Mental 2. Depression, Mental—Treatment 3. Evolutionary psychology 4. Mood (Psychology) 5. PSYCHOLOGY—Emotions 6. PSYCHOLOGY—Mental Illness 7. Psychobiology 8. SCIENCE—Life Sciences—Evolution 9. SELF-HELP—Mood Disorders 10. Scientific literature

ISBN 9780465022212 (hardback); 9780465069736 (e-book)

LC 2013-036462

SUMMARY: In this book, Jonathan Rottenberg "argues that depression is a particularly severe outgrowth of our natural capacity for emotion. In other words, it is a low mood gone haywire. Drawing on recent developments in the science of mood . . . Rottenberg explains depression in evolutionary terms, showing how its dark pull arises from adaptations that evolved to help our ancestors ensure their survival. Moods, high and low, evolved to compel us to more efficiently pursue rewards." (Publisher's note)

REVIEW: *Booklist* v110 no9/10 p29 Ja 1 2014 Tony Miksanek

REVIEW: *Choice* v52 no1 p167 St 2014 A. J. Scripa

REVIEW: *Economist* v411 no8882 p83 Ap 12 2014

REVIEW: *Kirkus Rev* v81 no24 p185 D 15 2013

"The Depths: The Evolutionary Origins of the Depression Epidemic". " In [Jonathan] Rottenberg's opinion, our cultural emphasis on being upbeat can be counterproductive. The human capacity for reflection can derail this semiautomatic process when we seek to enhance pleasurable upbeat moods and worry about being depressed. By shifting our attention to our own mental processes, we risk losing sight of broader goals. Rottenberg does not dismiss the benefits of talk therapy and medications to treat depression or deny the role of genetic predisposition. His laudable aim is to broaden the discussion. An important contribution to his stated aim of promoting 'an adult national conversation about depression.'"

REVIEW: *Publ Wkly* v260 no51 p50 D 16 2013

ROUD, STEVE. New Penguin Book of English Folk Songs. See Bishop, J.

ROUSE, JOSEPH.ed. Dasein disclosed. See Haugeland, J.

ROUTES INTO ABYSS; coping with the crises in the 1930s; vi, 224 p. 2013 Berghahn Books

1. Depressions—1929 2. Economic policy 3. Europe—Economic conditions—1918-1945 4. Historical literature 5. World politics—1933-1945

ISBN 0857457853 (institutional ebook); 817594295 (hardback : alk. paper); 9780857457844 (hardback : alk. paper); 9780857457851 (institutional ebook)

LC 2012-032899

SUMMARY: This book "provides nation-focused studies of governmental responses to the Great Depression of the 1930s. Predominantly European in perspective . . . the editors include studies specifically referring to Brazil, the US, India, Japan, and China, as well as continent-straddling Turkey. . . . All regimes sought economic relief from the Depression through some mixture of public and private sector activities, whether they were promoted as fascist, socialist, nationalist, or democratic." (Choice)

REVIEW: *Choice* v51 no4 p699-700 D 2013 J. A. Young

"Routes Into Abyss: Coping With the Crises in the 1930s." "This timely, erudite collection from a symposium inspired initially by the desire to commemorate Austria's traumatic crisis of February 1934 provides nation-focused studies of governmental responses to the Great Depression of the 1930s. . . . The overall result is stimulating, and the essays emphasize clarity as well as content. Inescapably, perhaps, several authors use the concept of totalitarianism as a point of reference, despite doubts about its efficacy as an analytic tool. The various governments' responses to the crisis become apparent, as do their commonalities, irrespective of party and ideology. . . . While gaps inevitably remain, this volume provides much for all postsecondary readers."

ROUTLEDGE HANDBOOK OF MAJOR EVENTS IN ECONOMIC HISTORY; 454 p. 2013 Routledge

1. Depressions—1929 2. Economics—History 3. Economics literature 4. Global Financial Crisis, 2008-2009 5. National banks (U.S.)

ISBN 9780415677035 (hb)

LC 2012-031239

SUMMARY: This book presents "a comprehensive review of major economic events over the past 200 years. Events are divided into four periods, beginning with Alexander Hamilton's proposal for a national bank. Contributing economists provide background to major events leading up the Great Depression and the New Deal. After WW II, essays address the rise of China and the demise of the Soviet

Union." (Choice: Current Reviews for Academic Libraries)

REVIEW: *Choice* v51 no6 p1062-3 F 2014 R. T. Sweet

"Routledge Handbook of Major Events in Economic History." "Although one volume cannot cover every major event in economic history, editors [Randall E.] Parker . . . and [Robert] Whaples . . . have organized 35 essays by leading economic historians into a comprehensive review of major economic events over the past 200 years. . . . All of the essays have bibliographic references that will aid readers wishing to undertake additional research. This handbook will serve as an important historical reference as well as provide readers with insight concerning current economic affairs in the US and rising world economies. . . . These historical essays provide a valuable understanding of today's economy. . . . Highly recommended."

ROUTLEDGE HANDBOOK ON THE GLOBAL HISTORY OF NURSING; 265 p. 2013 Routledge

1. Historical literature 2. Medicine—Political aspects 3. Nursing—History—20th century 4. Nursing literature 5. Nursing services

ISBN 9780415594271 (hardback)

LC 2012-047333

SUMMARY: This book looks at "the history of nursing worldwide. The volume is divided into four sections: 'New Directions in the Global History of Nursing,' 'New Methodological Approaches in the History of Nursing,' 'The Politics of Nursing Knowledge,' and 'Nursing and the 'Practice Turn.' Contributors focus primarily on nursing in Africa, Europe, and North and South America." (Choice: Current Reviews for Academic Libraries)

REVIEW: *Choice* v51 no7 p1254-5 Mr 2014 D. B. Hamilton

"Routledge Handbook on the Global History of Nursing." "[Patricia] D'Antonio, [Julie A.] Fairman, and [Jean C.] Whelan . . . have compiled 14 articles that address the history of nursing worldwide. . . . Each article is well written and extensively documented. The editors/nurse historians have selected stellar pieces of historical research to craft a cutting-edge work that will be appreciated by undergraduates, graduates, and researchers of nursing, nursing history, and health policy. . . . Highly recommended."

ROWELL, RAINBOW. Fangirl; [by] Rainbow Rowell 448 p. 2013 St. Martin's Griffin

1. College students—Fiction 2. Fan fiction 3. Fans (Persons) 4. Loneliness—Fiction 5. Young adult fiction

ISBN 1250030951; 9781250030955 (hardcover)

LC 2013-013842

SUMMARY: This book "tells the story of a painfully shy teen who prefers the fantasy world of fanfiction to reality. Cath expected to survive her first year of college with the help of her twin sister. Wren, however, is taking full advantage of her newfound freedom from parental supervision, spending" her time partying rather than with Cath. "Feeling lost and alone, Cath scurries from class to class, hiding in her room and working on her Simon Snow fanfiction omnibus." (School Library Journal)

REVIEW: *Booklist* v110 no6 p55 N 15 2013 Edie Ching

REVIEW: *Booklist* v110 no2 p65 S 15 2013 Courtney Jones

"Fangirl." "An awakening unfolds, as Cath battles loneliness, her father's mental illness, a new writing class, and feelings for her dorm mate's friendly part-time boyfriend. This is an epic writ small; the magic here is cast not with wands but with [Rainbow] Rowell's incredible ability to build complex, vivid, troubling, and triumphant relationships. The internal lives of the characters are so well developed that it is almost surprising to remember that Rowell is writing in third person. Fans of 'Eleanor & Park' (2013) and other novels about nerdy types will thrill at finding such a fantastic and lasting depiction of one of their own."

REVIEW: *Bull Cent Child Books* v67 no3 p176-7 N 2013 A. M.

"Fangirl." "Suddenly facing the social whirl of college alone, Cath finds allies in unexpected places. . . . An engaging read, this funny, heartfelt novel conveys a touching personal journey toward self-confidence and romance. The sizable length leaves room for the introduction of many memorable characters, hut this is really Cath's story, and readers will find her worth the attention. As the supportive boyfriend, Levi is perhaps too perfectly ready-made for reader crushes, but the romance as a whole is grounded and real. [Author Rainbow] Rowell treats fanfic writers and readers with respect, making this book a treat for anyone who appreciates fan culture, hut also offers a nuanced perspective of the values and challenge of striking out on your own in writing and in life."

REVIEW: *Horn Book Magazine* v90 no2 p149 Mr/Ap 2014 CYNTHIA K. RITTER

"Fangirl." "[Rebecca] Lowman's narration draws listeners in as she transitions fluidly between different voices, her inflections and pacing reflecting an impressive familiarity with the text and sensitivity for Cath's character as she slowly matures. But it is British actor [Maxwell] Caulfield's charismatic lilt as he narrates the Simon Snow passages between the chapters that really adds something special to this audio edition. His captivating performance will leave listeners wanting more Simon Snow and sympathetic to Cath's resistance to live outside that fantasy world."

REVIEW: *Horn Book Magazine* v89 no6 p105-6 N/D 2013 CYNTHIA K. RITTER

"Fangirl." "As she did in 'Eleanor & Park' . . . [Rainbow] Rowell creates a refined narrative style that transitions seamlessly between Cath's strong interior voice and clever dialogue to fully develop Cath's complex personality. Between chapters, Rowell incorporates scenes from both the Simon Snow series and Cath's fanfiction, further connecting readers to Cath's literature-centric world. This sophisticated novel from a talented writer will captivate nerds, romantics, and book lovers alike."

REVIEW: *Kirkus Rev* p56 Ag 15 2013 Fall Preview

REVIEW: *Kirkus Rev* v81 no14 p147 Jl 15 2013

REVIEW: *N Y Times Book Rev* p34 S 22 2013 Jessica Bruder

REVIEW: *Publ Wkly* p100 Children's starred review annual 2013

REVIEW: *Publ Wkly* v260 no48 p51 N 25 2013

REVIEW: *Publ Wkly* v260 no28 p174 Jl 15 2013

REVIEW: *SLJ* v59 no8 p115 Ag 2013 Heather E. Miller Cover

ROWLAND, AMY. The transcriptionist; a novel; [by] Amy Rowland 256 p. 2014 Algonquin Books Of Chapel Hill

1. Alienation (Social psychology)—Fiction 2. Lion at-

tacks—Fiction 3. New York (N.Y.)—Fiction 4. Psychological fiction 5. Women journalists—New York—New York City—Fiction
ISBN 9781616202545
LC 2013-044719

SUMMARY: This book by Amy Rowland "centers on Lena, an employee at major New York daily the Record, where she transcribes interview tapes and takes reporting calls from foreign correspondents. . . . A story about a woman who broke into the lions' den at the Bronx Zoo and was promptly killed sparks Lena's sorrow and curiosity (they had a brief encounter), and the novel turns on her effort to learn more about the woman's life than simple journalism will deliver." (Kirkus Reviews)

REVIEW: *Booklist* v111 no3 p96 O 1 2014 Marna Rundgren

REVIEW: *Booklist* v110 no15 p24 Ap 1 2014 June Sawyers

REVIEW: *Kirkus Rev* v82 no4 p289 F 15 2014

"The Transcriptionist". "In stuffing this milieu with bits of mystery, romance and aphoristic riffs on listening and silence, [Amy] Rowland has taken on a bit too much; the novel's tone unsteadily shifts from the bluntly realistic to the fuzzily philosophical. Even so, individual scenes and characters are very well-turned. . . . Rowland has a talent for making the real world just a touch more Day-Glo and off center, but Lena's own concerns about listening and being get short shrift in the process. An appealing attempt to wed the weird and everyday in a newsroom setting . . . that never quite finds solid footing."

REVIEW: *Libr J* v139 no12 p45 Jl 1 2014 Mary Knapp

REVIEW: *Libr J* v139 no2 p68 F 1 2014 Patrick Sullivan

REVIEW: *Ms* v24 no2 p57-8 Summ 2014 Casey Cep

REVIEW: *N Y Times Book Rev* p8 Jl 27 2014 AMANDA EYRE WARD

REVIEW: *Publ Wkly* v261 no30 p86 Jl 28 2014

REVIEW: *Publ Wkly* v261 no6 p64-5 F 10 2014

ROWLAND, PHILIP.ed. Haiku in English. See Haiku in English

ROWLANDS, PENELOPE. The Beatles are here!; 50 years after the band arrived in America, writers and other fans remember; [by] Penelope Rowlands 288 p. 2014 Algonquin Books of Chapel Hill

1. Rock music fans—United States
ISBN 9781616203504
LC 2013-033601

SUMMARY: This book, edited by Penelope Rowlands, "explores the emotional impact—some might call it hysteria—of the . . . [Beatles'] February 1964 dramatic landing on . . . [U.S.] shores. Contributors, including Lisa See, Gay Talese, Renée Fleming, Roy Blount, Jr., and many others, describe in essays and interviews how they were inspired by the Beatles." (Publisher's note)

REVIEW: *Kirkus Rev* v81 no24 p215 D 15 2013

"The Beatles Are Here! 50 Years After the Band Arrived in America, Writers, Musicians & Other Fans Remember". "A collection of light-as-a-feather remembrances of the Beatles' British invasion. This latest round of idol worship is mostly harmless to the rose-colored memories of Beatles fans. . . . However, this collection is vexing in its seesawing arc among screaming tweens who remain steadfast Paul-worshipping Beatlemaniacs at 64 and beyond, all-too-clever New York intelligentsia defending careers built on iconoclasm, and the occasional superfluous blurb from the likes of Cyndi Lauper or Billy Joel (these latter bits are so bland they would be completely at home in any tribute issue of Rolling Stone)."

ROY, CARTER. The blood guard; [by] Carter Roy 288 p. 2014 Two Lions

1. Adventure stories 2. Fantasy fiction 3. Good & evil—Fiction 4. Kidnapping—Fiction 5. Secret societies—Fiction
ISBN 1477847251; 9781477847251 (trade pbk.: alk. paper)
LC 2013-958330

SUMMARY: In this book, by Carter Roy, "when thirteen-year-old Ronan Truelove's . . . mom snatches him from school, then sets off on a high speed car chase, Ronan is shocked. His . . . dad has been kidnapped? And the kidnappers are after him, too? His mom, he quickly learns, is . . . a member of an ancient order of knights, the Blood Guard, a sword-wielding secret society sworn to protect the Pure—thirty-six noble souls whose safety is crucial if the world as we know it is to survive." (Publisher's note)

REVIEW: *Booklist* v110 no14 p79 Mr 15 2014 Snow Wildsmith

REVIEW: *Kirkus Rev* v82 no2 p128 Ja 15 2014

"The Blood Guard". "[Carter] Roy's first novel is the humorous and exciting start of a new trilogy. . . . The stakes are raised with a startling revelation that will have readers eager for the next book. The pacing is quick, with important details revealed evenly throughout. It can be sentimental in places but never sappy, and Ronan (please don't call him Evelyn) is a believable protagonist, gradually moving from ordinary boy to hero. Though it's a little on the derivative side, this iteration of the hero's journey will have readers chuckling all the way to the satisfying cliffhanger."

REVIEW: *SLJ* v60 no7 p93 Jl 2014 Jane Barrer

REVIEW: *SLJ* v60 no6 p64 Je 2014 Maggie Knapp

REVIEW: *Voice of Youth Advocates* v37 no1 p86 Ap 2014 Blake Norby

ROY, MALINI. Mughal India. See Losty, J. P.

ROY, WILLIAM G. Reds, whites, and blues; social movements, folk music, and race in the United States; [by] William G. Roy 286 2010 Princeton University Press

1. Civil rights movements—Social aspects 2. Civil rights movements—United States—History—20th century 3. Folk music—Political aspects 4. Music & society 5. Social movements—United States—History—20th century 6. Sociology literature
ISBN 0-691-14363-3; 978-0-691-14363-7
LC 2009--49319

SUMMARY: This book "investigates music's role as an agent of change. . . . Roy describes how during the 1930s and 1940s, the Old, communist-inspired Left adopted music instrumentally, as a medium of information and a propaganda tool. . . . By contrast, the civil rights movement of the 1960s incorporated music into the very fabric of protest activity. . . . Through this activity, the performer/audience distinction was blurred and music's power as an agent of change was reconceived." (Contemporary Sociology)This book "is about how two North American movements, the communist-led Old Left and the civil rights movement, made use of music. The central claim is that these two collective actors differed in their approach to music, which then led to different outcomes." (Am J Sociol) Index.

REVIEW: *Contemp Sociol* v41 no4 p521-2 Jl 2012 Tia DeNora

"Reds, Whites, and Blues: Social Movements, Folk Music, and Race in the United States." "As its very clever title implies, this book investigates music's role as an agent of change. . . . This thoughtful book by William [G.] Roy goes some way toward advancing our understanding of how, as he puts it in the concluding chapter, 'social movements do culture.' Roy describes how during the 1930s and 1940s, the Old, communist-inspired Left adopted music instrumentally, as a medium of information and a propaganda tool. . . . 'Reds, Whites, and Blues' is a major contribution to the ever more audible collection of voices in sociology addressed to the dynamic relationship between music and social life."

RUBBINO, SALVATORE. A Walk in Paris; 40 p. 2014 Candlewick Press

1. Louvre (Paris, France) 2. Paris (France)—Description & travel 3. Paris (France)—History 4. Paris (France)—Social life & customs 5. Picture books for children

ISBN 0763669849; 9780763669843

LC 2013-943083

SUMMARY: This children's book, by Salvatore Rubbino, "follows a girl and her grandfather through the streets of Paris. . . . The girl narrates excitedly while her grandfather offers occasional details about the Place Saint-Michel, the Louvre, and more. Brief informational captions about Parisian landmarks, cuisine, and language are tucked throughout the mixed-media illustrations." (Publishers Weekly)

REVIEW: *Booklist* v110 no12 p70 F 15 2014 Carolyn Phelan

REVIEW: *Horn Book Magazine* v90 no3 p72 My/Je 2014 JOANNA RUDGE LONG

REVIEW; *Kirkus Rev* v82 no4 p211 F 15 2014

"A Walk in Paris". " Scattered about the pages in a distinct, smaller typeface that does not overshadow the primary text are translations of commonly used French words and terms, historical facts, trivia and even travel tips. The consciously retro illustrations in soft, muted colors are lively and expressive, and there's a nice balance between detailed images and simple silhouettes. Adults familiar with M. Sasek's 'This Is . . .' series will find this pleasantly reminiscent of those old favorites. As the book reads more like a travelogue and less a story with a captivating plot, its natural audience is older readers of picture books. Sparkling lights and lovely sights fill this whirlwind tour of Paris."

REVIEW: *Publ Wkly* v261 no2 p69 Ja 13 2014

RUBBINO, SALVATORE.il. A Walk in Paris. See Rubbino, S.

RUBEL, NICOLE.il. Rotten Ralph's rotten family. See Gantos, J.

RUBENFELD, JED. The Triple Package; How Three Unlikely Traits Explain the Rise and Fall of Cultural Groups in America; [by] Jed Rubenfeld 304 p. 2014 Penguin Group USA

1. American Dream 2. Ethnic groups—United States 3. Personality—United States 4. Social commentary 5. Success—United States 6. Temperament—United States

ISBN 1594205469; 9781594205460

LC 2013-039970

SUMMARY: Authors Amy Chua and Jed Rubenfeld "show why certain groups in the U.S. perform better than others. Studying the more material measures of success—income, occupational status, and test scores—[they] found . . . that Mormons occupy leading positions in politics and business; the Ivy League admission rates of West Indian and African immigrant groups far exceed those of non-immigrant American blacks; . . . and Indian and Jewish Americans have the highest incomes." (Publishers Weekly)

REVIEW: *Bookforum* v20 no4 p18-51 D 2013/Ja 2014 JIM NEWELL

REVIEW: *Commentary* v137 no5 p69-70 My 2014 KAY HYMOWITZ

REVIEW: *Economist* v411 no8882 p85 Ap 12 2014

REVIEW: *Kirkus Rev* v81 no24 p194 D 15 2013

REVIEW: *Libr J* v138 no14 p86 S 1 2013

REVIEW: *Libr J* v139 no11 p54 Je 15 2014 Douglas C. Lord

REVIEW: *Libr J* v139 no2 p87 F 1 2014 David Azzolina

REVIEW: *N Y Times Book Rev* p1-17 F 2 2014 Sandra Tsing Loh

REVIEW: *Natl Rev* v65 no6 p43-5 Ap 7 2014 KEVIN D. WILLIAMSON

"The Triple Package: How Three Unlikely Traits Explain the Rise and Fall of Cultural Groups in America." "Amy Chua of 'Tiger Mom' fame/infamy has written an airport book. An airport book is like an airport meal: bland and easy to consume . . . , so rarely good that a good one is memorable, and of course engineered to be consumed most frequently . . . in airports, in business travelers' hotels between airports, and in similar locales. . . . Chua offers a persuasive case for her thesis. . . . She is by no means fanatical in making her case, and is more than willing to consider non-supportive data points."

REVIEW: *New Repub* v244 no25 p40-5 Ap 7 2014 William Deresiewicz

REVIEW: *New Statesman* v143 no5200 p46 Mr 7 2014 Kwasi Kwarteng

REVIEW: *Publ Wkly* v260 no51 p51 D 16 2013

RUBIN, BARNETT R. Afghanistan From the Cold War Through the War on Terror; [by] Barnett R. Rubin 536 p. 2013 Oxford Univ Pr

1. Afghanistan—History 2. Afghanistan—Politics & government 3. Historical literature 4. Islamic fundamentalism—Afghanistan 5. War on Terrorism, 2001-2009

ISBN 0199791120; 9780199791125

SUMMARY: This collection of essays on Afghanistan by Barnett R. Rubin "address[es] a time frame from the late 1980s to the start of the Obama administration." Topics include "the need for statecraft objectives to be matched by adequate resources to achieve them, and the predictable dangers inherent in a border region as 'underdeveloped and overarmed' as the ambiguously defined Afghan-Pakistani frontier." (Publishers Weekly)

REVIEW: *Middle East J* v67 no4 p644-5 Aut 2013 Benjamin D. Hopkins

REVIEW: *New Repub* v244 no5 p48-52 Ap 8 2013 Ahmed Rashid

"Afghanistan From the Cold War Through the War on Terror." "With decision time on Afghanistan now at hand, it is a good moment to reflect on what has gone wrong, and on the historical mistakes that should not be repeated. Those are among the themes of this important new book by Barnett Rubin, the great American scholar and veteran of all things Afghanistan. Rubin's book is a compilation of his best essays on Afghanistan and the region, beginning in 1996 and ending in 2009. . . . Some of Rubin's most revealing writing in this book comes in the short links that he creates to connect his scholarly essays and the different sections of the volume."

RUBIN, SUSAN GOLDMAN. Everybody paints!; the lives and art of the Wyeth family; [by] Susan Goldman Rubin 105 p. 2013 Chronicle Books

1. American painting 2. Art literature 3. Artists—United States—Biography—Juvenile literature 4. Biography (Literary form)

ISBN 0811869849; 9780811869843 (alk. paper)

LC 2013-006595

SUMMARY: Author Susan Goldman Rubin "shares the . . . story of the Wyeths--N.C., Andrew, and Jamie--three generations of painters and arguably the First Family of American Art. The . . . text traces the events that shaped their art and the ways their art influenced them in return, while the . . . design showcases . . . reproductions of the works that have made the Wyeth family legendary." (Publisher's note)

REVIEW: *Booklist* v110 no13 p68 Mr 1 2014 Carolyn Phelan

"Everybody Paints! The Lives and Art of the Wyeth Family." "While focused primarily on the artists' lives and their work, the clearly written text also describes the Wyeth households and family dynamics from generation to generation. [Susan Goldman] Rubin adroitly meets the challenge of presenting three artists in one book, letting each story flow naturally into the next, while the occasional narrative overlap reinforces the story as a whole. The clearly written and engaging text, the well-integrated design elements, and the excellent reproductions of paintings and photos make this an informative, visually appealing presentation."

REVIEW: *Bull Cent Child Books* v67 no7 p374 Mr 2014 D. S.

REVIEW: *Kirkus Rev* v82 no2 p262 Ja 15 2014

"Everybody Paints! The Lives and Art of the Wyeth Family". "A perceptive, if undersized and overdesigned, introduction to a dynasty of American painters. Playing to her well-established strengths, [Susan Goldman] Rubin . . . does a fine job of setting selected works of N.C. Wyeth, his son Andrew and his grandson Jamie into biographical context and explicating emotional substrates in their art. . . . Though nearly every spread offers a sharply reproduced image of a painting or drawing (or an occasional photo), the volume's modest trim size cramps the often large originals. Still, Rubin's portrait of this creative clan merits at least a look by students of both book illustration and American fine art in general."

REVIEW: *SLJ* v60 no5 p157 My 2014 Nancy Menaldi-Scanlan

RUBIO, MARY HENLEY.ed. The Complete Journals of L.M. Montgomery. See The Complete Journals of L.M. Montgomery

RUBY, MICHAEL. American songbook; [by] Michael Ruby 144 p. 2013 Ugly Duckling Presse

1. American poetry 2. Music & literature 3. Music—Poetry 4. Popular music 5. Songs

ISBN 9781937027001 (pbk.)

LC 2013-026239

SUMMARY: Written by Michael Ruby, "'American Songbook' is a poetic response to the grand sweep of recorded vocal music in the 20th century. The poems are based on 75 recordings, with singers ranging from Bessie Smith to Tupac Shakur, and songs from a little-known Lomax prison recording to the last No.1 pop hit in the century. Many musical traditions inform the poems, including blues, jazz, gospel, country, folk, bluegrass, electric blues, R&B, rock, disco and hip hop." (Publisher's note)

REVIEW: *N Y Rev Books* v61 no6 p62-4 Ap 3 2014 Dan Chiasson

"American Songbook," "Go Giants," and "Nothing by Design." "American poets tend to want the benefits of song . . . without its costs. . . . This conflict drives Michael Ruby's 'American Songbook.' . . . The Irish poet Nick Laird's brilliantly titled new book is 'Go Giants.' . . . 'Go Giants' is a book about rooting for something, anything, now that the comforts of religious belief are, for Laird as for many of us, nonexistent. . . . 'Nothing by Design' is [author Mary Jo] Salter's seventh book. Its accomplishments of prosody are, by turns, vengeful, saddened, and funny."

RUDERMAN, WENDY. Busted. See Laker, B.

RUDOLF, ANTHONY. Silent Conversations; A Reader's Life; [by] Anthony Rudolf 748 p. 2013 University of Chicago Press

1. Arts 2. Authors—Biography 3. Books & reading 4. Memoirs 5. Translators

ISBN 0857420801; 9780857420800

SUMMARY: "For Anthony Rudolf, reading is a profoundly serious and intense activity, as well as a major source of pleasure and solace. At the same time, it is always interrupted by day jobs, friendships, politics and, paradoxically, by the act of writing. All of this comes together in 'Silent Conversations: A Reader's Life.' . . . 'Silent Conversations' captures Rudolf's inimitable style and his own admitted tendency to digress--with invariably fascinating and revealing results." (Publisher's note)

REVIEW: *World Lit Today* v88 no2 p74-6 Mr/Ap 2014 Daniel P. King

"Silent Conversations: A Reader's Life." "Silent conversations (the lowercase is indicative of Anthony Rudolf's aura of mystery) is an account, albeit fragmentary and digressive, of the author's seventy-year association with the printed word. Rudolf is (was) variously a psychiatrist, essayist, translator, poet, autobiographer, literary critic, editor, and occasional BBC broadcaster. His autobiography, 'The Arithmetic of Memory,' is complemented by this rambling account of his lifetime of reading. . . . Anthony Rudolf is an intense reader and writer: his opinions are dogmatically personal and revealing and reflect the extensiveness of his library. His lifetime infatuation with the printed page provides a sometimes-delightful excursion and a sometimes-frustrating read."

RUEDA, CLAUDIA.il. Here comes the Easter Cat! See Underwood, D.

RUGE, EUGEN. In times of fading light; 304 p. 2013 Graywolf Press

1. Families—Fiction 2. Germany (East)—Politics & government 3. Gulag (Soviet Union) 4. Historical fiction 5. Soviet Union—Fiction
ISBN 1555976433; 9781555976439 (alk. paper)
LC 2013-931482

SUMMARY: This historical family saga novel, by Eugen Ruge, flows back and forth through the family history of "Alexander Umnitzer, . . . creating a panoramic view of the family's history: from Alexander's grandparents' return to the GDR to build the socialist state, to his father's decade spent in a gulag for criticizing the Soviet regime, to his son's desire to leave the political struggles of the twentieth century in the past." (Publisher's note)

REVIEW: *Booklist* v109 no16 p34 Ap 15 2013 Brendan Driscoll

REVIEW: *Kirkus Rev* v81 no5 p222 Mr 1 2013

REVIEW: *Libr J* v138 no18 p57 N 1 2013 Stephen L. Hupp

REVIEW: *New York Times* v162 no56228 pC4 Ag 14 2013 ADAM LANGER

REVIEW: *Publ Wkly* v260 no10 p35-6 Mr 11 2013

REVIEW: *TLS* no5755 p21 Jl 19 2013 MAREN MEINHARDT

"In Times of Fading Light." "'In Times of Fading Light' employs a cut-and-paste technique that shines the spotlight back and forth across four generations of the Umnitzer family. Key scenes are replayed from the point of view of another character, and sometimes played again and again. The variations in perception are minute, and yet an added detail, a small shift in perspective, often changes the meaning of an event utterly. . . . Alexander's instinct, and, by implication, Eugen Ruge's, to seek out the truth of what happened, is amply rewarded: the past will be clearer, with lives emerging as the worthwhile results of choices that may have been the wrong ones, but seemed the right ones in the light of their times."

REVIEW: *World Lit Today* v87 no5 p63-4 S/O 2013 Ulf Zimmermann

RUGGIERO, CRISTINA M. Judicial power in a federal system; Canada, United States and Germany; [by] Cristina M. Ruggiero x, 334 p. 2012 LFB Scholarly Pub.

1. Federal government—Canada 2. Federal government—Germany 3. Federal government—United States 4. Judge-made law 5. Judicial review 6. Political questions and judicial power—Canada 7. Political questions and judicial power—Germany 8. Political questions and judicial power—United States 9. Political science literature
ISBN 159332443X; 9781593324438 (hbk. : alk. paper)
LC 2012-020789

SUMMARY: Author Cristina M. Ruggiero "provides a systematic evaluation of the 'interdependent nature' of judicial power within three federal systems. She seeks to answer the question: Why are some high courts more powerful than others? By integrating strategic assumptions about the behavior of courts and other political actors and by employing a comparative, historical analysis of court policy-making and legislative responses to said policy-making, Ruggiero tests and refines concepts of court influence." (Publisher's note)

REVIEW: *Choice* v51 no1 p158 S 2013 A. R. Brunello

"Judicial Power in a Federal System: Canada, United States, and Germany." "[Author Cristina M.] Ruggiero . . . demonstrates that to understand the power of high courts, and to effectively compare judicial politics across the system, scholars must account for the multidimensional structures and the complex interdependence of institutional relationships. In comparing Canada, the US, and Germany, the author has selected three of the most powerful high courts in the world. . . . Empirically cogent and densely argued, Ruggiero's book makes a valuable contribution to middle range theory of comparative judicialization."

RULE, ADI. Strange sweet song; [by] Adi Rule 336 p. 2014 St. Martin's Griffin

1. Boarding schools 2. JUVENILE FICTION—Girls & Women 3. Mythical animals 4. Paranormal fiction 5. Singers—Fiction
ISBN 1250048168; 9781250036339 (trade paperback); 9781250048165 (hardback)
LC 2013-032020

SUMMARY: In this book, "Sing da Navelli, daughter of a world-famous conductor and the late, legendary soprano Barbara da Navelli, arrives at the prestigious Dunhammond Conservatory determined to find recognition for her own talent. Surrounding the conservatory is a dark forest . . . rumored home of the Felix, a fantastical beast whose tears become wishes. Sing is drawn to the forest and to the off-putting yet strangely attractive Nathan Daysmoor, an apprentice at the conservatory." (Kirkus Reviews)

REVIEW: *Booklist* v110 no14 p78 Mr 15 2014 Stacey Comfort

REVIEW: *Bull Cent Child Books* v67 no7 p374-5 Mr 2014 K. Q. G.

"Strange Sweet Song." "The cache of standard YA elements--a girl suffocated by parental expectations, a wickedly handsome love interest, a catfight among Sing's peers--make a compelling story. A second narrative strand follows a mythical beast in the surrounding woods, from its fall from the heavens centuries ago, to its despair at killing its sibling, to its joy at birthing a cub, to its recent interest in human activity and specifically, their ability to feel joy and despair. The two storylines come together in a climactic scene that demands an accompaniment of swelling music, and the resolution manages a bittersweet blend of tragedy and happiness. Music buffs will relate to Sing's passion and insecurities, and readers who enjoy a good melodrama will be captivated."

REVIEW: *Kirkus Rev* v82 no3 p69 F 1 2014

REVIEW: *Voice of Youth Advocates* v37 no1 p86-8 Ap 2014 Kathleen Beck

RUNCIE, JAMES. Sidney Chambers and the shadow of death; [by] James Runcie 392 p. 2012 Bloomsbury

1. Art forgeries—Fiction 2. Detective & mystery stories 3. Jewelry theft—Fiction 4. Murder investigation—Fiction 5. Suicide—Fiction

ISBN 1608198561; 9781608198566

SUMMARY: This detective novel by James Runcie is set in 1953 and features "Sidney Chambers, vicar of Grantchester and honorary canon of Ely Cathedral, [who] is a thirty-two-year-old bachelor. . . . Together with his roguish friend, inspector Geordie Keating, Sidney inquires into the suspect suicide of a Cambridge solicitor, a . . . jewelry theft at a New Year's Eve dinner party, the unexplained death of a jazz promoter's daughter, and a[n] . . . art forgery that puts a close friend in danger." (Publisher's note)

REVIEW: *Hist Today* v64 no2 p61 F 2014 Jerome de Groot

"Devil in a Blue Dress," "The Shadow of Death," and "Carver's Quest." "'Devil in a Blue Dress' . . . took the hard-boiled detective novel and made it sing again. Mosley's prose is effortlessly taut and poised and he is an excellent exponent of a simple, brief, direct style that belies the sharp characterisation at the heart of his writing. . . . The series of Granchester Mysteries begin in the early 1950s with 'The Shadow of Death' . . . which takes in jazz, literariness, faith and beer, and runs gently through a neat and comfortable plot. Nick Rennison's hero is amateur archaeologist Adam Carver and his companion Quint. 'Carver's Quest' . . . takes the pair on a treasure hunt through London and Athens. The writer Rennison is echoing is mainly Arthur Conan Doyle."

RUNCIMAN, DAVID. The Confidence Trap; a History of Democracy in Crisis from World War I to the Present; [by] David Runciman 408 p. 2013 Princeton University Press

1. Democracy—History—20th century 2. Democracy—History—21st century 3. HISTORY—Modern—20th Century 4. HISTORY—Modern—21st Century 5. HISTORY—United States—General 6. HISTORY—World 7. POLITICAL SCIENCE—History & Theory 8. POLITICAL SCIENCE—Political Ideologies—Democracy 9. Political science literature 10. World politics—20th century 11. World politics—21st century

ISBN 0691148686; 9780691148687 (hardback)

LC 2013-019899

SUMMARY: Author David Runciman "shows that democracies are good at recovering from emergencies but bad at avoiding them. The lesson democracies tend to learn from their mistakes is that they can survive them . . . —a confidence trap that may lead to a crisis that is just too big to escape, if it hasn't already. The most serious challenges confronting democracy today are debt, the war on terror, the rise of China, and climate change." (Publisher's note)

REVIEW: *Choice* v51 no12 p2269 Ag 2014 R. W. Glover

REVIEW: *Economist* v409 no8856 p87-8 O 5 2013

REVIEW: *Libr J* v138 no18 p107 N 1 2013 Robert Nardini

REVIEW: *N Y Rev Books* v61 no5 p42-4 Mr 20 2014 John Gray

"The Confidence Trap: A History of Democracy in Crisis From World War I to the Present". "[David] Runciman argues that democracies survive crises without having any clear insight into how they manage this feat. . His rich and refreshing book will be of intense interest to anyone puzzled by the near paralysis that seems to afflict democratic government in a number of countries, not least the United States. . . . One of the limitations of Runciman's analysis is that he has chosen to work with a dichotomy between democracy and other forms of government. . . . The trouble with this binary typology is that it mixes distinctions in kind with differences of degree. . . . Runciman devotes comparatively little space to the European situation."

REVIEW: *New Statesman* v142 no5183 p40-1 N 8 2013 Vernon Bogdanor

REVIEW: *Publ Wkly* v260 no37 p37 S 16 2013

REVIEW: *TLS* no5794 p22 Ap 18 2014 ANDREW GAMBLE

"The Confidence Trap: A History of Democracy in Crisis From World War I to the Present" and "Democracy: All That Matters." "Why does democracy everywhere seem to be in crisis, unable to deliver what its citizens want? In 'The Confidence Trap,' David Runciman argues this is because democracy has always been like that. It invariably disappoints. . . . From Runciman's perspective, [author Steven] Beller is claiming that democracy can still bring a moment of truth, when the people gain control of their fate, decide who they are, and what they should do collectively. For Runciman, this is an illusion."

RUNDELL, KATHERINE. Rooftoppers; 288 p. 2013 Simon & Schuster Books for Young Readers

1. Guardian and ward—Fiction 2. Historical fiction 3. Homeless persons—Fiction 4. Missing persons—Fiction 5. Roofs—Fiction

ISBN 1442490586; 9781442490581 (hardcover)

LC 2012-049469

SUMMARY: In this book, by Katherine Rundell, "everyone thinks that Sophie is an orphan. . . . Her guardian tells her it is almost impossible that her mother is still alive. . . . When the Welfare Agency writes to her guardian, threatening to send Sophie to an orphanage, she takes matters into her own hands and flees to Paris to look for her mother. . . . She meets Matteo and his network of rooftoppers--urchins who live in the hidden spaces above the city. Together they scour the city in a search for Sophie's mother." (Publisher's note)

REVIEW: *Booklist* v110 no1 p104 S 1 2013 Ilene Cooper

REVIEW: *Booklist* v110 no12 p96 F 15 2014 Amanda Blau

REVIEW: *Bull Cent Child Books* v67 no3 p177-8 N 2013 J. H.

"Rooftoppers." "Baby Sophie is found floating in a cello case after the passenger ship she was on sinks in the English Channel. She's adopted and raised by Charles, a fellow survivor, but when she is twelve, the authorities determine that as a single man Charles is not a fit parent for the young girl. Sophie and Charles flee to Paris . . . then Sophie meets Matteo, a 'rooftopper.' . . . The hard-knock world of the rooftoppers is intriguing in both its grit and detail, and Matteo is an especially strong character as he refuses to cut Sophie any slack or to compromise his own rules for living. Unfortunately, the highly implausible happy ending, reuniting Sophie and her mom but giving no explanation of what will happen to Charles' role in Sophie's life, is abrupt and unsatisfying."

REVIEW: *Kirkus Rev* v81 no15 p39 Ag 1 2013

REVIEW: *Kirkus Rev* p82 N 15 2013 Best Books

REVIEW: *Kirkus Rev* p44 Ag 15 2013 Fall Preview

REVIEW: *N Y Times Book Rev* p15 D 22 2013 EMILY EAKIN

REVIEW: *Publ Wkly* p78-9 Children's starred review annual 2013

REVIEW: *Publ Wkly* v260 no30 p68 Jl 29 2013

REVIEW: *SLJ* v60 no2 p54 F 2014 Maria Salvadore

RUNNING THE WHALE'S BACK; Stories of Faith and Doubt from Atlantic Canada; 288 p. 2013 Goose Lane Editions

1. Atlantic Provinces 2. Canada—Fiction 3. Canada—Religion 4. Canadian fiction 5. Canadian short stories
ISBN 0864929137; 9780864929136

SUMMARY: Edited by Andrew Atkinson and Mark Harris, this book "presents a host of Eastern Canada's brightest literary talents, all putting pens to paper to explore the multiple facets of what we call 'faith' through a unique Atlantic vantage point. In a satisfying mixture of styles and themes, the full breadth of Atlantic Canadian spirituality is revealed. These are pieces that poke and prod, ruminate and circulate with themes of religion and cultures of spirituality." (Publisher's note)

REVIEW: *Quill Quire* v79 no8 p31-2 O 2013 Alex Good

"Running the Whale's Back: Stories of Faith and Doubt From Atlantic Canada." "'Running the Whale's Back' is an anthology of fiction (both short stories and novel excerpts) that tugs in two directions. The first is geographical: the authors all hail from Atlantic Canada (the lineup includes well-known names like Alistair MacLeod, David Adams Richards, Lynn Coady, Michael Crummey, and Michael and Kathleen Winter) and that is where most of the stories are set. But the volume also looks inward, as all of the pieces are concerned in some way with spiritual matters. . . . In any event the book's success--and it is a great read from cover to cover--comes down to the high quality of the stories themselves."

RUSCH, ELIZABETH. Eruption!; volcanoes and the science of saving lives; [by] Elizabeth Rusch 76 p. 2013 Houghton Mifflin Harcourt

1. Children's literature 2. Geologists 3. Merapi Volcano (Java, Indonesia) 4. Science—Juvenile literature 5. Volcanic eruptions—Juvenile literature
ISBN 0547503504 (hardcover); 9780547503509 (hardcover)
LC 2012-034055

SUMMARY: This book by Elizabeth Rusch contains "photographs and sidebars [which] reveals the perilous . . . life-saving work of an international volcano crisis team (VDAP) and the sleeping giants they study, from Colombia to the Philippines, from Chile to Indonesia. [It presents an] stunning account of volcanologists Andy Lockhart, John Pallister, and their group of scientists who risk their lives, investigating deadly volcanoes that remain constant threats to people around the world." (Publisher's note)

REVIEW: *Bull Cent Child Books* v67 no1 p50 S 2013 E. B.

"Eruption!: Volcanoes and the Science of Saving Lives." "This Scientists in the Field entry focuses on the work of the Volcano Disaster Assistance Program (VDAP), a cadre of scientists within the U.S. Geological Survey that trains international vulcanologists and seismologists in monitoring techniques, and joins them (by invitation only) with assistance and advice during a crisis. [Author Elizabeth] Rusch's admirably organized title begins with the tragic story of the pre-VDAP eruption of Nevado del Ruiz in Colombia in 1985, in which some 23,000 lives were lost. . . . Images of destruction may initially draw the casual browser, but far more impressive is the balance of vivid photographs that bring the international scientists into the limelight."

REVIEW: *Horn Book Magazine* v89 no6 p119-20 N/D 2013 DANIELLE J. FORD

"Eruption!: Volcanoes and the Science of Saving Lives." "This terrific addition to the Scientists in the Field series features the dedicated geologists of the Volcano Disaster Assistance Program, a U.S. agency that provides technical expertise in eruption prediction, as they work with their scientific counterparts in countries with potentially dangerous volcanoes. Gripping accounts of the team's successful work at the 1991 Mount Pinatubo (Philippines) and the 2010 Mount Merapi (Indonesia) eruptions expose the complicated scientific and social dimensions of predicting the intensity of volcanic eruptions and their potential impact on human populations, where the costs of being wrong could be devastating. The portrayal of scientific investigation is exceptional."

REVIEW: *Kirkus Rev* v81 no12 p112 Je 15 2013

REVIEW: *Science* v342 no6162 p1044 N 29 2013 Nicholas S. Wigginton

REVIEW: *SLJ* v59 no8 p129 Ag 2013 Trina Bolfing

RUSCH, ELIZABETH. Volcano rising; [by] Elizabeth Rusch 32 p. 2013 Charlesbridge

1. Children's nonfiction 2. Mountains 3. Volcanic eruptions 4. Volcanoes—Environmental aspects 5. Volcanoes—Juvenile literature
ISBN 1580894089; 9781580894081 (reinforced for library use); 9781580894098 (softcover); 9781607346166 (ebook)
LC 2012-000793

SUMMARY: This children's picture book by Elizabeth Rousch explores volcanoes. "Blowing their tops off, growing taller and wider, and forming new mountains and islands, volcanoes can be both destructive and creative. . . . A dual-level narrative provides both a simple explanation of how volcanoes work and longer paragraphs that go into greater depth." Examples of eight volcanoes from around the world are discussed. (Kirkus Reviews)

REVIEW: *Booklist* v109 no22 p70 Ag 1 2013 J. B. Petty

REVIEW: *Horn Book Magazine* v89 no5 p123-4 S/O 2013 DANIELLE J. FORD

"Volcano Rising." "The book opens with an impressive explosive eruption--a magnificent mixed-media illustration shows a volcanic vent gushing steam, rock, and lava. . . . Each spread includes one sentence in large type that provides general information (sometimes including catchy, volcano-like onomatopoeia: 'KABAMBAM-BOOM!'). Smaller-type paragraphs below both employ scientific vocabulary (some of these words are just as much fun to pronounce) and provide detailed background on the science and societal impacts of volcanic activity."

REVIEW: *Kirkus Rev* v81 no14 p121 Jl 15 2013

REVIEW: *SLJ* v59 no9 p180 S 2013 Patricia Manning

RUSH, NORMAN. Subtle bodies; [by] Norman Rush 256 p. 2013 Alfred A. Knopf

1. Friendship—Fiction 2. Male friendship 3. Marriage—Fiction 4. Psychological fiction 5. Reunions—Fiction
ISBN 140004250X; 9781400042500 (hardcover); 9781400077137 (trade pbk.)
LC 2013-013813

SUMMARY: Author Norman Rush presents "a . . . romp through the particular joys and tribulations of marriage, and the dilemmas of friendship, as a group of college friends reunites in upstate New York twenty-some years after graduation. When Douglas, the ringleader of a clique of self-styled wits of 'superior sensibility' dies suddenly, his four remaining friends are summoned to his luxe estate high in the Catskills to memorialize his life and mourn his passing." (Publisher's note)

REVIEW: *Bookforum* v20 no3 p36-7 S-N 2013 MICHELLE ORANGE

"Subtle Bodies." "'Subtle Bodies' . . . appears in size and scope to deliver on its author's promises. [Norman] Rush has proved himself a writer of grand and self-conscious ambition, possessed by a keen sense of the thing called greatness. He has also been a writer of powerful--sometimes overwhelming--sensibility. . . . Rush's exuberant, late-modern style feels as smooth and casual as freshly pressed khakis, but beneath it a sort of parasympathetic network courses with moral ambivalence. . . . Not a hack job. 'Subtle Bodies' doesn't offer a glowing likeness, either. The novel rather delicately extends Rush's interest in what he described in a 2010 Paris Review interview as 'the baffled, compromised liberalism' at the center of 'Mortals'."

REVIEW: *Booklist* v109 no22 p33 Ag 1 2013 Carol Gladstein

REVIEW: *Kirkus Rev* v81 no16 p53 Ag 15 2013

REVIEW: *Libr J* v138 no7 p56 Ap 15 2013 Barbara Hoffert

REVIEW: *N Y Rev Books* v60 no14 p71-3 S 26 2013 Francine Prose

"Subtle Bodies." "Without being heavy-handed or undermining the importance of the fictional dramas he is staging, [Norman] Rush can make us view (and measure) temporary social discomfort against the darker background of the more serious and enduring nastiness. . . . Rush endows his fictional creations with so much intelligence, complexity, and depth. . . . Their quirks, opinions, compulsions, and the cruel or considerate ways in which they treat their rivals and allies are all aspects of the personalities that keep us engrossed in 'Subtle Bodies'--along with the clarity and precision of Rush's sentences, the freshness of his observations, and our awareness that we are reading something quite rare."

REVIEW: *N Y Times Book Rev* p13 S 8 2013 GEOFF DYER

REVIEW: *New Repub* v244 no16 p48-53 O 7 2013 Ruth Franklin

REVIEW: *New York Times* v162 no56262 pC1-6 S 17 2013 MICHIKO KAKUTANI

REVIEW: *New Yorker* v89 no33 p102-1 O 21 2013

"Subtle Bodies." "[Norman] Rush's third novel is slighter than its brilliant predecessors . . . but has many of the qualities that define his best work. It is an intimate portrait of a couple, Ned and Nina, three years married and trying to conceive a baby. They arrive in the Catskills to mourn the death of Ned's friend Douglas, and end up in tough, sprawling conversations about politics and life with his estranged pals. Rush gestures toward a traditional plot at various points, but most of the important events turn out to have taken place before the novel's opening. What resonates most vividly is Nina's fierce, idiosyncratic love."

REVIEW: *Publ Wkly* v260 no27 p63 Jl 8 2013

REVIEW: *TLS* no5768 p19 O 18 2013 THOMAS MEANEY

"Subtle Bodies." "The style is more honed; the sentences more domesticated; the form almost unnaturally compressed. . . . 'Subtle' Bodies looks set to be a meditation on friendship. . . . But following Nina's unexpected arrival at the estate much of the novel retreads familiar matrimonial ground. Rush is a great writer on love, in particular on the ways two lovers colonize each others' consciousness. . . . The novel is full of well-observed light comedy. . . . But for a novel this short, the intrigues are frustratingly diffuse, and they circle like dead moons around the main star of Douglas."

RUSHIN, STEVE. The 34-ton bat; the story of baseball as told through bobbleheads, cracker jacks, jockstraps, eye black, and 375 other strange and unforgettable objects; [by] Steve Rushin 352 p. 2013 Little, Brown and Co.

1. Baseball—Equipment & supplies 2. Baseball—History—Miscellanea 3. Baseball bats 4. Baseball gloves 5. Historical literature 6. Sports literature
ISBN 031620093X; 9780316200936
LC 2013-017752

SUMMARY: This book, by Steve Rushin, "chronicles the history of baseball through the items used by players (baseball bats, sanitary socks), enjoyed by fans (beer and hot dogs), and sported by both (baseball caps). Rushin's exuberant prose describes the continuous evolution of baseball paraphernalia." (Publisher's note)

REVIEW: *Booklist* v110 no1 p30 S 1 2013 Wes Lukowsky

"The 34-Ton Bat: The Story of Baseball as Told Through Bobbleheads, Cracker Jacks, Jockstraps, Eye Black, and 375 Other Strange and Unforgettable Objects." "[Steve] Rushin approaches his passion with a mischievous gleam in his eye, a point of view captured perfectly in this anecdote-filled account of the sport's odd corners. He covers the evolution of the baseball glove, from a less-than-manly novelty in the game's earliest days to its current status as standard equipment. . . . In an era of sports literature when societal significance and statistical algorithms aren't always as fun as we'd hoped, Rushin has reintroduced readers to silliness. Read it with a smile."

REVIEW: *Kirkus Rev* v81 no18 p96 S 15 2013

REVIEW: *Publ Wkly* v260 no30 p57 Jl 29 2013

RUSHTON, MICHAEL.ed. Creative communities. See Creative communities

RUSNAK, M. F.tr. Galateo, or, The rules of polite behavior. See Galateo, or, The rules of polite behavior

RUSS, SANDRA W. Pretend play in childhood; foundation of adult creativity; [by] Sandra W. Russ ix, 241 p. 2014 American Psychological Association

1. Cognition in children 2. Creative ability 3. Imaginative play 4. Play—Psychological aspects 5. Psychological literature

ISBN 1433815613; 9781433815614 (hardcover)

LC 2013-016988

SUMMARY: This book by Sandra W. Russ "examines converging evidence from evolutionary, psychodynamic, and developmental work to look at the connections between characteristics of childhood pretend play and adult creativity at both the everyday level and the level of major artistic and intellectual innovations. . . . Concluding that children's play and adult creativity share processes, she includes a chapter about work on encouragement of pretend play for children." (Choice: Current Reviews for Academic Libraries)

REVIEW: *Choice* v51 no8 p1494-5 Ap 2014 J. Mercer

"Pretend Play in Childhood: Foundation of Adult Creativity". "[Sandra W. Russ . . . reviews her work on play and creativity, a subject to which she has devoted her career. . . . Transcripts of pretend play and an appendix describing the Affect in Play Scale will be useful for researchers, as will the extensive reference section and complete index. Thorough and simply organized, this title is an invaluable resource; however, appealing though the topic is, the book will not be accessible to general readers."

RUSSEL, MARIE.ed. Food system sustainability. See Food system sustainability

RUSSELL, DANIEL C.ed. The Cambridge companion to virtue ethics. See The Cambridge companion to virtue ethics

RUSSELL, DONALD.tr. Aeneas of Gaza. See Aeneas of Gaza

RUSSELL, NATALIE. Lost for words; 32 p. 2014 Peachtree Publishers

1. Authorship—Fiction 2. Children's stories 3. Creative ability—Fiction 4. Drawing—Fiction 5. Individuality—Fiction 6. Tapirs—Fiction

ISBN 1561457396; 9781561457397

LC 2013-032151

SUMMARY: This children's book follows "Tapir, a gray animal with a long snout and a gently curved body. . . . When he tries to write, his head feels 'empty, just like his page.'. . . Feeling insecure and wordless, Tapir wanders up a hill and gazes at the landscape. When he unpacks his pencils, he knows what to do: He draws a sun for Flamingo, a muddy pool for Hippo and a tall tree for Giraffe, and then he draws his friends into the scene." (Kirkus Reviews)

REVIEW: *Booklist* v110 no11 p70 F 1 2014 Sarah Hunter

REVIEW: *Kirkus Rev* v82 no2 p168 Ja 15 2014

"Lost for Words". "[Natalie] Russell's screen-print illustrations use simple, tidy shapes and flat, medium-intensity colors. Tapir's drawings, like his friends' work, are childlike; unlike similar books that show dramatic distinction between the primary visual narrative and the characters' in-book work, Russell provides little contrast. While blander than many available options about writer's block, mustering voice or choosing an art form, this may also be more directly encouraging for readers who need the message, as the results seem so achievable."

REVIEW: *Publ Wkly* v260 no50 p67-9 D 9 2013

REVIEW: *SLJ* v60 no3 p124 Mr 2014 Marge Loch-Wouters

RUSSELL, NATALIE.il. Lost for words. See Lost for words

RUSSELL, RICHARD RANKIN.ed. Peter Fallon. See Peter Fallon

RUSSO, MARISABINA, 1950-.il. Sophie sleeps over. See Russo, M.

RUSSO, MARISABINA, 1950-. Sophie sleeps over; [by] Marisabina Russo 32 p. 2014 A Neal Porter Book; Roaring Brook Press

1. Best friends—Fiction 2. Children's stories 3. Friendship—Fiction 4. Rabbits—Fiction 5. Sleepovers—Fiction

ISBN 1596439335; 9781596439337 (hardcover)

LC 2013-011277

SUMMARY: In this children's book, by Marisabina Russo, "Sophie is looking forward to her first sleepover. She is excited from the tops of her ears to the tips of her toes and has even made a list of all the things she wants to bring over to her best friend Olive's house. But, when she arrives, a bunny she's never seen before opens the door." (Publisher's note)

REVIEW: *Booklist* v110 no13 p78 Mr 1 2014 Carolyn Phelan

REVIEW: *Horn Book Magazine* v90 no2 p104-5 Mr/Ap 2014 ELISSA GERSHOWITZ

"Sophie Sleeps Over." "After lights-out . . . the competing bunny girls reach détente over their inability to sleep and missing their favorite dolls, paving the way for a new three-way best-friendship. [Marisabina] Russo knows her way around drawing rabbit-children . . . and in her tidy gouache illustrations these three bunnies, dressed in their birthday party best, display clear emotions that will be immediately recognizable to young readers and listeners. Friendship bliss, anticipation, hurt feelings, homesickness--all are familiar to (human) kids and are all conveyed with respect and sensitivity."

REVIEW: *Kirkus Rev* v82 no2 p159 Ja 15 2014

REVIEW: *Publ Wkly* v261 no3 p53 Ja 20 2014

REVIEW: *SLJ* v60 no3 p124 Mr 2014 Blair Christolon

RUTH, GREG. The lost boy; [by] Greg Ruth 192 p. 2013 GRAPHIX

1. Children's stories 2. Detective & mystery stories 3. Friendship—Fiction 4. Missing children—Fiction 5. Paranormal fiction

ISBN 0439823323; 9780439823319; 9780439823326; 9780545576901

LC 2013-937147

SUMMARY: This children's picture book by Greg Ruth "opens as a boy named Nate moves to a new town and discovers a tape recorder hidden underneath the floorboards of his bedroom. The action shifts back several decades as Nate listens to recordings left by Walter Pidgen, an outcast boy who disappeared without a trace. Along with a neighbor, Tabitha, Nate is drawn into a supernatural battle involving the denizens of an ancient woodland kingdom, which include talking toys and insects." (Publishers Weekly)

REVIEW: *Horn Book Magazine* v90 no1 p99-100 Ja/F 2014 JONATHAN HUNT

"The Lost Boy". "Kids are always clamoring for scary books, but far too few deliver the goods in a satisfyingly creepy way. Fortunately, that's not the case with this eerie, atmospheric graphic novel, with pen-and-brush black-and-white illustrations. . . . If the story leans a bit on cliché as it unfolds (the underlying mythology remains a vague mishmash of pop culture references), the moody artwork coupled with the promise of further adventures should be enough for readers to return for the next installment."

REVIEW: *Kirkus Rev* v81 no16 p296 Ag 15 2013

"The Lost Boy." "A mysterious reel-to-reel tape player may solve a local mystery, but it may also lead to gravest peril. . . . Nate's new friend, Tabitha, relates the local legends of Walt's disappearance. . . . As they dig deeper, the two are drawn into a frightening mystery that thrusts them into a strange world through the gate in Crow's Woods. Can they find Walt? Will they even survive? . . . Author/illustrator [Greg] Ruth creates a sinister, yet familiar urban fantasy of parallel worlds. Some lettering in the speech bubbles can be difficult to decipher, but the black-and-white panels of spirits, insects, animals and shadows are packed with action and realistic dialogue. A refreshing fantasy in which not all is spelled out, with tantalizing hints at a sequel."

REVIEW: *Publ Wkly* v260 no29 p71 Jl 22 2013

REVIEW: *SLJ* v60 no1 p109 Ja 2014 Amy Seto Musser

REVIEW: *Voice of Youth Advocates* v37 no1 p28-9 Ap 2014 AMANDA FOUST JACK BAUR

REVIEW: *Voice of Youth Advocates* v36 no5 p82 D 2013 Geri Diorio

RUTH LAW THRILLS A NATION; un 1993 Ticknor & Fields

1. Aeronautics—Flights—Juvenile literature 2. Air pilots 3. Biographies 4. Children's literature—Works—Grades two through six 5. Children's literature—Works—Preschool through grade two 6. Women air pilots

ISBN 0-395-66404-7; 0-395-73517-3 pa

LC 92-4-5701

SUMMARY: The author discusses the flight performed by Ruth Law, who in 1916 "tried to fly from Chicago to New York City in one day. She did not succeed (she landed outside Binghamton, New York), but she broke a nonstop cross-county flying record." (Booklist)

REVIEW: *Horn Book Magazine* v89 no5 p11-8 S/O 2013 Barbara Bader

"Ruth Law Thrills a Nation," "Charlie Parker Played Be Bop," and "Roberto Clemente: Pride of the Pittsburgh Pirates." "[Don] Brown is as much a writer as an artist. A stylist, in both cases, and a wit. . . . Chris Raschka's 'Charlie Parker Played Be Bop' . . . is less a biography than an improvisation on a personality--all juicy, exuberant cartooning, bouncy scribbles, and sweeps of color . . . with a bop-along text. For kids, a rousing performance. . . . Lives of sports heroes would stand out among picture book biographies. Jonah Winter, a professed baseball nut and a wordsmith, a poet, had something to do with this. . . . In 'Roberto Clemente' . . . the vehicle is a confiding near-verse."

RUTHERFORD, JOHN. The Power of the Smile; Humour in Spanish Culture; [by] John Rutherford 173 p. 2012 Francis Boutle Publishers

1. Laughter in literature 2. Literary critiques 3. Smiling in literature 4. Spanish humorous poetry 5. Spanish wit & humor

ISBN 190342769X; 9781903427699

SUMMARY: It was the author's intent "to assess the place of humour in four canonical texts--'El poema de mío Cid,' 'El Libro de buen amor,' 'La Celestina,' and 'Don Quixote.' [John] Rutherford's rereadings of these works make up the core of his book, but there is also a wide-ranging preliminary chapter on some aspects of theory . . . and a preliminary excursus into the sculpture of Santiago de Compostela's cathedral (the statue of the smiling Daniel)." (Times Literary Supplement)

REVIEW: *TLS* no5752 p11 Je 28 2013 ROBERT ARCHER

"The Power of the Smile: Humour in Spanish Culture." "A bold attempt to assess the place of humour in four canonical texts--'El poema de mío Cid,' 'El Libro de buen amor,' 'La Celestina,' and 'Don Quixote'. . . . The theoretical chapter is a lucid series of reflections on humour that the reader is likely to want to return to for its own sake. But the central part of 'The Power of the Smile' manages only to develop parts of this material. . . . [John] Rutherford works with great independence of thought. . . . But ultimately, 'The Power of the Smile' is a book to be consulted for the excellence of some of its parts, rather than the cogency of the whole."

RUTKOSKI, MARIE. The winner's curse; [by] Marie Rutkoski 368 p. 2014 Farrar Straus & Giroux

1. Fantasy fiction 2. Imperialism—Fiction 3. Love—Fiction 4. Music—Fiction 5. Slavery—Fiction

ISBN 0374384673; 9780374384678 (hardcover)

LC 2013-000312

SUMMARY: In this book, by Marie Rutkoski, "winning what you want may cost you everything you love. As a general's daughter in a vast empire that revels in war and enslaves those it conquers, seventeen-year-old Kestrel has two choices: she can join the military or get married. But Kestrel has other intentions. One day, she is startled to find a kindred spirit in a young slave up for auction. Arin's eyes seem to defy everything and everyone. Following her instinct, Kestrel buys him." (Publisher's note)

REVIEW: *Booklist* v110 no11 p67 F 1 2014 Cindy Welch

REVIEW: *Bull Cent Child Books* v67 no7 p375 Mr 2014 K. Q. G.

REVIEW: *Horn Book Magazine* v90 no2 p128 Mr/Ap 2014 DEIRDRE F. BAKER

"The Winner's Curse." "[Marie] Rutkoski's invented world and political situation are loosely inspired by Greco-Roman antiquity. The story's mechanics pivot on military strategies and a romantic relationship that is predictable and somewhat improbable. The tale reads as a confection, with forbidden love, fancy gowns, putative musical giftedness (vague in its expression), and warrior stoicism to delight teenage readers. Characterization and prose style are serviceable rather than profound, but the plot takes some satisfying twists and turns."

REVIEW: *Kirkus Rev* v82 no1 p212 Ja 1 2014

"The Winner's Curse". "Rich characterization, exquisite worldbuilding and rock-solid storytelling make this a fantasy of unusual intelligence and depth. . . . Precise details and elegant prose make this world fresh and vivid. The intricate and suspenseful plot, filled with politics, intrigue and even graphic violence, features neither heroes nor villains; every character displays a complex mixture of talents, flaws and motives. Kestrel is an especially compelling protagonist, both determined and hesitant, honest and manipulative, ferociously observant and painfully naïve. Her bond with Arin develops slowly and naturally from congruent personalities. . . . Breathtaking, tragic and true."

REVIEW: *N Y Times Book Rev* p34 Jl 20 2014 AMY ZILLIAX

REVIEW: *Publ Wkly* v261 no1 p58 Ja 6 2014

REVIEW: *Publ Wkly* v261 no21 p56 My 26 2014

REVIEW: *SLJ* v60 no6 p69 Je 2014 Shanna Miles

REVIEW: *SLJ* v60 no2 p114 F 2014 Chelsey Philpot

RYAN, DONAL. The Spinning Heart; [by] Donal Ryan 160 p. 2014 Random House Inc

1. Community life—Fiction 2. Debt 3. Financial crises 4. Ireland—Economic conditions 5. Ireland—Fiction 6. Psychological fiction
ISBN 1586422243; 9781586422240

SUMMARY: This book by Donal Ryan "takes up the theme of Celtic failure and malaise in a tight-knit community somewhere in the west of Ireland. A local builder. Pokey Burke, has absconded in a hurry, leaving his employees to their debts and disgruntlement. A cacophony of aggrieved and outspoken voices, male and female, moves the narrative forwards, bit by bit." (Times Literary Supplement)

REVIEW: *Booklist* v110 no9/10 p46 Ja 1 2014 Kerri Price

REVIEW: *Commonweal* v140 no19 p27-8 D 6 2013 Tina Beattie

"How Much Is Enough? Money and the Good Life," "The Spinning Heart," and "Thirst". "[Robert Skidelsky] and Edward Skidelsky] offer a persuasive and lucid account of the 'good life' as one in which sufficiency, satisfaction, and leisure become worthy aims to pursue in common with others whose values we share (they think religion might be indispensable for this), while greed, envy, and avarice are once more recognized as the vices they are. This panoramic vision inevitably glosses the ways in which individual lives are affected by changing economic values. 'The Spinning Heart,' . . . a novel by Irish writer Donal Ryan, movingly explores the consequences of the global economic crisis in a small Irish community. . . . The best poems are a passionate and vivid celebration of life, with symbolic roots deep in the miracle of nature."

REVIEW: *Kirkus Rev* v81 no21 p235 N 1 2013

REVIEW: *N Y Times Book Rev* p12 Mr 23 2014 DAPHNE KALOTAY

REVIEW: *Publ Wkly* v261 no1 p30 Ja 6 2014

REVIEW: *TLS* no5765 p19 S 27 2013 PATRICIA CRAIG

"The Spinning Heart," "Arimathea," and "Seeking Mr. Hare." "A cacophony of aggrieved and outspoken voices, male and female, moves the narrative forwards, bit by bit. . . .The book's succession of monologues is orchestrated by the author with cunning and authenticity. . . . The strength of this first novel lies in its insights into the rougher aspects of the Irish psyche. . . . Like 'The Spinning Heart,' Frank McGuinness's debut novel 'Arimathea' is made up of monologues. As an acclaimed playwright, McGuinness has the form at his fingertips, and he gives us a series of adept impersonations. . . . An engaging contribution to the pursuit-cum-picaresque genre is Maurice Leitch's 'Seeking Mr Hare'."

RYAN, DONAL. The thing about December; [by] Donal Ryan 207 p. 2013 The Lilliput Press

1. Bildungsromans 2. Ireland—Fiction 3. Irish fiction 4. Orphans—Fiction 5. Young men—Fiction
ISBN 1843512726; 9781843512721
LC 2013-432582

SUMMARY: In this novel by Donal Ryan, "While the Celtic Tiger rages, and greed becomes the norm, Johnsey Cunliffe desperately tries to hold on to the familiar. . . . Village bullies and scheming land-grabbers stand in his way, no matter where he turns. Set over the course of one year of Johnsey's life, 'The Thing About December' breathes with his grief, bewilderment, humour and agonizing self-doubt." (Publisher's note)

REVIEW: *Libr J* v139 no9 p74 My 15 2014 Henrietta Verma

REVIEW: *New Statesman* v143 no2 p50 Ja 17 2014 Philip Maughan

REVIEW: *TLS* no5781 p20 Ja 17 2014 RUTH GILLIGAN

"The Thing About December." "[Donal Ryan's] new novel 'The Thing About December' follows twelve months in the life of Johnsey Cunliff . . . and scrutinizes the effects of Ireland's infamous boom. . . . Through Johnsey's indirect lilt, issues of economics, racism, emigration and religion are alluded to; and despite his social alienation, his muted observations can be shrewd. . . . Just as Ireland's Celtic Tiger coming of age ended in dismay, so 'The Thing About December' offers a subtle portrait of a young man whose promotion to adulthood comes tumbling down, greed showing no mercy in its devastating wake."

RYAN, HENRIETTA. The Image of Venice. See Howard, D.

RYAN, JAMES R. Photography and Exploration; [by] James R. Ryan 192 p. 2013 University of Chicago Press

1. Discoveries in geography 2. Documentary photography 3. Photography literature 4. Scientific photography 5. Underwater photography
ISBN 1780231008; 9781780231006

SUMMARY: In this book, James R. Ryan "investigates mid-19th through early-21st-century photography by European and American explorers. . . . He discusses early state-sponsored scientific photography, survey photography, early-20th-century explorations of the North and South Poles, and space and underwater images. He emphasizes three themes: how photographs were made and in what context, form and aesthetics, and reception and circulation." (Choice: Current Reviews for Academic Libraries)

REVIEW: *Choice* v51 no6 p995 F 2014 S. Spencer

"Photography and Exploration." "[James R.] Ryan . . . investigates mid-19th through early-21st-century photography by European and American explorers. Following a brief history of travel photography, he discusses early state-sponsored scientific photography, survey photography, early-20th-century explorations of the North and South Poles, and space and underwater images. . . . As he indicates, this book is intended to launch further investigation into a little-studied area of photography. . . . Recommended."

RYAN, MARTIN J. The Anglo-Saxon world. See Higham, N. J.

RYAN, MARY MEGHAN.ed. Handbook of U.S. Labor Statistics, 2013. See Handbook of U.S. Labor Statistics, 2013

RYAN, MICHAEL W. S. Decoding Al-Qaeda's strategy; the deep battle against America; [by] Michael W. S. Ryan 368 p. 2013 Columbia University Press

1. Jihad 2. Political science literature 3. Terrorism—Religious aspects—Islam 4. Terrorism—United States—Prevention

ISBN 9780231163842 (cloth: alk. paper)

LC 2012-049506

SUMMARY: In this book, Michael W. S. Ryan "examines the Salafist roots of al-Qaeda ideology and the contributions of its most famous founders, Osama Bin Laden and Ayman al-Zawahiri, in a political-military context. He also reads the Arabic-language works of lesser known theoreticians who have played an instrumental role in framing al-Qaeda's so-called war of the oppressed. These authors readily cite the guerrilla strategies of Mao, Che Guevara, and . . . General Giap." (Publisher's note)

REVIEW: *Choice* v51 no9 p1678 My 2014 R. D. Stacey

"Decoding al-Qaeda's Strategy: The Deep Battle Against America". "[Michael W. S.] Ryan . . . has produced an outstanding and unique contribution that examines al Qaeda's strategy against the US, a remarkable achievement given the crowded marketplace of books on this topic. The author argues convincingly that al Qaeda strategy is actually a departure from mainstream Islamist military tradition. . . . Rather than a 'counterstrategy,' America must develop a 'counter-narrative' that demonstrates convincingly that al Qaeda cannot hope to win the close battle, American constitutionalism is consistent and beneficial even for Muslims, and despite its claims to the contrary, al Qaeda doctrine 'is secular in nature and is not based on Islam.'"

REVIEW: *London Rev Books* v35 no24 p19-21 D 19 2013 Owen Bennett-Jones

"Decoding Al-Qaida's Strategy: The Deep Battle Against America" and:The Terrorist's Dilemma: Managing Violent Covert Organisations". "Michael Ryan draws a useful distinction between the drawn-out or 'deep' battle of ideas and the 'close' battle of combat. . . . Ryan's survey pins down crucial elements of al-Qaida's appeal. . . . [Jacob] Shapiro sees the dilemma clearly: the mechanisms required to exert control, such as semijudicial processes to hand down punishments to wayward members, expenses claim sheets and documents in which new members commit themselves to following the leadership's policies, all make a group vulnerable."

REVIEW: *Middle East J* v68 no2 p334-5 Spr 2014 Barak Mendelsohn

RYAN, P. E. Saints of Augustine; [by] P. E. Ryan 308 p. 2007 HarperTeen

1. Best friends—Fiction 2. Conduct of life—Fiction 3. Death—Fiction 4. Friendship—Fiction 5. Homosexuality—Fiction 6. Self-acceptance—Fiction 7. Young adult literature

ISBN 0060858109 (trade bdg.); 0060858117 (lib. bdg.); 9780060858100 (trade bdg.); 9780060858117 (lib. bdg.)

LC 2006-019519

SUMMARY: In this book, "closeted journalist Sam and stoner basketballer Charlie were best friends since the age of nine, but just months before Charlie's mom died of leukemia, the two parted ways and haven't spoken since. Neither knows why one dropped the other; they simply stopped talking. Just over a year later, the two reunite at night in a park near their neighborhood. Sam's just botched his first date with a guy named Justin, and Charlie's licking the wounds of a pot-smoking habit gone to the dogs." (Kirkus Reviews)

REVIEW: *Booklist* v110 no2 p76 S 15 2013 Sarah Hunter

"Mercury," "The Miseducation of Cameron Post," and "Saints of Augustine." "Graphic novel readers, regardless of age, will be drawn to [Hope] Larson's graceful story, universal themes of self-discovery, and expressive art. . . . Cam's experiences at a church camp that promises to 'cure' young people of their homosexuality are at the heart of this ambitious, multidimensional coming-of-age novel. [Emily M.] Danforth . . . vividly depicts the lifelong challenges of asserting one's identity. . . . Well-drawn characters, complicated family lives, first love, and realistic language (including some anti-gay slurs), make this a touchingly authentic and ageless story about the importance of friendship."

RYAN, PAM MUÑOZ. Tony Baloney; school rules; 40 p. 2012 Scholastic Inc.

1. Behavior—Fiction 2. First day of school—Fiction 3. First day of school—Juvenile fiction 4. Macaroni penguin—Fiction 5. Macaroni penguin—Juvenile fiction 6. Penguins—Fiction 7. School stories 8. Schools—Fiction 9. Schools—Juvenile fiction

ISBN 054548166X; 9780545481663 (paper over board); 9780545481670 (pbk.)

LC 2012-006962

SUMMARY: This children's book, written by Pam Muñoz Ryan and illustrated by Edwin Fotheringham, describes how "Tony Baloney, a little penguin, hopes for the best as he starts school, but it's hard to follow all the new rules, and besides, accidents happen. Still, at the end of the day, he is proud to be crowned his classroom's 'Friendship Ambassador'." (Publisher's note)

REVIEW: *Bull Cent Child Books* v67 no1 p51 S 2013 J. H.

"Tony Baloney: School Rules." "Macaroni penguin Tony Baloney, from the picture book 'Tony Baloney', is back in this easy reader about Tony's school debut. Tony has a bit of trouble following his teacher's rules. . . . This will be welcomed teachers who want to instigate discussion about class or school rules with an enjoyably non-didactic text. . . . Some of the text is on the higher end of the easy-reader spectrum, but this could be easily read aloud to preschoolers and kindergarteners, who will likely most relate to Tony. [Illustrator Edwin] Fotheringham's cheery digital illustrations feature lots of black, white, and grays for the penguin cast of characters, punched up with plenty of candy-colored hues."

REVIEW: *Kirkus Rev* v81 no2 p110-1 Je 1 2013

REVIEW: *Publ Wkly* v260 no21 p59 My 27 2013

REVIEW: *SLJ* v59 no6 p98 Je 2013 Kelly Roth

RYAN, PATRICK JOSEPH. Master-servant childhood; a history of the idea of childhood in medieval English culture; [by] Patrick Joseph Ryan vii, 130 p. 2013 Palgrave Macmillan

1. Children—England—History—To 1500 2. Children—England—Social conditions 3. Children—England—Social life and customs 4. Historical literature 5. Social history—Medieval, 500-1500

ISBN 1137364785 (hardback); 9781137364784 (hardback)

LC 2012-361278

SUMMARY: This book by Patrick Joseph Ryan "offers a new understanding of childhood in the Middle Ages as a form of master-servant relation embedded in an ancient sense of time as a correspondence between earthly change and eternal order. It challenges the misnomer that children were 'little adults' in the Middle Ages and corrects the prevalent misconceptions that childhood was unimportant, unrecognized or disregarded." (Publisher's note)

REVIEW: *Choice* v51 no8 p1478-9 Ap 2014 C. Carlsmith

"Master-Servant Childhood: A History of the Idea of Childhood in Medieval English Culture". "[Patrick Joseph] Ryan advocates for the historical study of childhood, taking medieval England as his test case. In his analysis, the author borrows substantially from literary criticism—there is much about 'discourse' and 'symbols' and 'deep structures.' Ryan utilizes other disciplinary approaches to provide an anatomy of the vocabulary of childhood in Anglo-Saxon and Middle English, and argues that children, and childhood, must be viewed within the paradigm of master-servant relationships."

RYAN, VANESSA L. Thinking without thinking in the Victorian novel; [by] Vanessa L. Ryan viii, 243 p. 2012 Johns Hopkins University Press

1. Books & reading—History—19th century 2. Consciousness in literature 3. English fiction—19th century—History and criticism 4. Historical literature 5. Psychology in literature

ISBN 1421405911 (hdbk. : acid-free paper); 1421406470 (electronic); 9781421405919 (hdbk. : acid-free paper); 9781421406473 (electronic)

LC 2011-044972

SUMMARY: In this book, author "Vanessa L. Ryan demonstrates how both the form and the experience of reading novels played an important role in ongoing debates about the nature of consciousness during the Victorian era. . . . Ryan shows how the novelistic emphasis on dynamic processes and functions . . . can also be seen in some of the most exciting and comprehensive scientific revisions of the understanding of 'thinking' in the Victorian period." (Publisher's note)

REVIEW: *Choice* v50 no5 p877 Ja 2013 S. Bernardo

REVIEW: *TLS* no5755 p3-4 Jl 19 2013 GREGORY CURRIE

"The Poet's Mind: The Psychology of Victorian Poetry" and "Thinking Without Thinking in the Victorian Novel." "[Gregory] Tate, like the poets he discusses, is somewhat vague on the content of the science. . . . The science highlighted by [Vanessa L.] Ryan and Tate overlaps, but Ryan's emphasis is on 'unconscious cerebration,' so named by the zoologist William Carpenter. . . . Both speak as if science and literature at this time were engaged in complementary projects of mental discovery. . . . Perhaps we should not criticize either author for failing to investigate a question that belongs to the philosophy of knowledge and not to intellectual history. But there are times when their judgements are less guarded and less historically limited."

RYLANDER, CHRIS. Codename Zero; [by] Chris Rylander 368 p. 2014 Walden Pond Press

1. Adventure and adventurers—Fiction 2. Humorous stories 3. Middle schools—Fiction 4. Schools—Fiction 5. Spies—Fiction

ISBN 0062120085; 9780062120083 (hardback)

LC 2013-032327

SUMMARY: In this book by Chris Rylander, "Carson Fender, seventh grader and notorious prankster [has] lived in North Dakota for his entire life. Nothing ever changes, and nothing ever happens. That is, until . . . a desperate man hands him a package with a dire set of instructions. And that package is going to lead Carson to discover that there's a secret government agency operating in his small, quiet North Dakota hometown." (Publisher's note)

REVIEW: *Bull Cent Child Books* v67 no7 p375-6 Mr 2014 E. B.

"Codename Zero." "carnival. This seriocomic action story struggles to amalgamate several subgenres--spy parody . . . friendship story . . . and thriller . . . making the overall tone of this series opener somewhat chaotic. Moreover, even readers who easily suspend disbelief will find the Fender family's apparent obliviousness to Carson's leg cast and bandages (results of the big climax) hard to swallow. The central premise of a middle-school populated by undercover agents is a promising one, though, and kids who like to settle into a series will be happy to know there's more to come."

REVIEW: *Kirkus Rev* v81 no24 p158 D 15 2013

REVIEW: *SLJ* v60 no4 p153 Ap 2014 Emma Burkhart

RÖDER, MARLENE. In the river darkness; 224 p. 2014 Scarlet Voyage

1. Brothers—Fiction 2. Family secrets—Fiction 3. Neighbors 4. Triangles (Interpersonal relations)—Fiction 5. Young adult fiction

ISBN 9781623240103

LC 2013-933047

SUMMARY: This book follows "Mia . . . a big-city girl who finds herself in a country town when her family relocates for her father's job. She has brought a secret with her, one she tries to conceal beneath black clothes and goth makeup. She becomes interested in the activity of brothers Alex and Jay Stonebtook, who live next door with their father and grandmother and are at the center of a mystery themselves." (Booklist)

REVIEW: *Booklist* v110 no9/10 p106-8 Ja 1 2014 Kara Dean

"In the River Darkness." "This story starts as a fish-out-of-water tale and eventually becomes something else entirely, as each of the three main characters advance the narrative from alternating chapters. The original novel . . . was an award winner in the author's native Germany, and it has been translated by 2013 Batchelder Award winner [Tammi] Reichel. Despite this pedigree, the story is unevenly paced.

The ingredients for a tense and thoughtful piece of magic realism are in place throughout, and the characters ring true. Readers will genuinely be surprised by the reveal at the end, but they will have to he patient to get there."

REVIEW: *Kirkus Rev* v81 no22 p129 N 15 2013

REVIEW: *SLJ* v60 no1 p104 Ja 2014 Jennifer Furuyama

S

SABATO, LARRY J. The Kennedy half-century; the presidency, assassination, and lasting legacy of John F. Kennedy; [by] Larry J. Sabato 624 p. 2013 Bloomsbury USA

1. HISTORY—United States—General 2. Historical literature 3. Public opinion—United States
ISBN 9781620402801 (hardback)
LC 2013-023969

SUMMARY: This book by Larry J. Sabato examines the "[John F.] Kennedy political legacy. He . . . addresses the early Kennedy career, highlighting the hard-fought Nixon-Kennedy presidential race and the much-discussed debates. Throughout, Sabato notes the differences between politics circa 1960 and now, noting that Kennedy's Catholicism was controversial. . . . Sabato also attempts to clear the murky waters surrounding the Kennedy assassination." (Publishers Weekly)

REVIEW: *Economist* p158 N 24 2012 World in 2013 Emma Hogan

REVIEW: *Kirkus Rev* v81 no19 p67 O 1 2013

REVIEW: *Libr J* v138 no8 p60 My 1 2013

REVIEW: *Natl Rev* v65 no22 p42-6 N 25 2013 JAMES ROSEN

"The Kennedy Half-Century: The Presidency, Assassination, and Lasting Legacy of John F. Kennedy," "End of Days: The Assassination of John F. Kennedy" and "The Interloper: Lee Harvey Oswald Inside the Soviet Union." "James L. Swanson's 'End of Days,' a concise tick-tock account, and Larry J. Sabato's more ambitious 'The Kennedy Half-Century,' a multidisciplinary effort that weighs in at 603 pages . . . bring into sharp relief once again these contradictory traits in mid-century America's proudest son. Perhaps fittingly, the anniversary also brings us only one new book about the president's killer--Peter Savodnik's 'The Interloper'--but it is an important work, for it illuminates, as never before, the complexity of humanity that also graces the most wretched assassin."

REVIEW: *Publ Wkly* v260 no31 p33-40 Ag 5 2013 LENNY PICKER

REVIEW: *Publ Wkly* v260 no36 p47 S 9 2013

SABUDA, ROBERT. The Little Mermaid; 12 p. 2013 Simon & Schuster

1. Fairy tales 2. Mermaids—Fiction 3. Picture books for children 4. Pop-up books 5. Princes—Fiction
ISBN 144245086X; 9781442450868

SUMMARY: In this pop-up book adaptation of "The Little Mermaid," by Robert Sabuda, "the text closely follows the original, often echoing [Hans Christian] Andersen's phrasings and similes while streamlining events. . . .The little mermaid's heartfelt longing for her human prince, her quiet courage, and her selfless sacrifice at story's end are . . . depicted in both words and images." (School Library Journal)

REVIEW: *Booklist* v110 no6 p49-50 N 15 2013 Ann Kelley

"The Little Mermaid." "Readers will gasp when they open the first page of [Robert] Sabuda's latest pop-up adaptation. . . . It's an intricate below-sea world--the castle of the sea king extends 14 inches and is populated with merfolk, twisting trees, and brightly colored coral. The story itself plays out on side flaps and folded booklets, which also feature intricately rendered pop-ups (in one, the sea witch pops forth, moving eyebrows and all). Sabuda is faithful to Hans Christian Andersen's tale, and the text seems less abridged than most retellings of classic stories. . . . The colors are jewel-toned and lit like a stained-glass window, and it's visually splendid. Be careful with the pages, and enjoy time and again."

REVIEW: *Kirkus Rev* v81 no23 p36 D 1 2013

REVIEW: *Publ Wkly* p68 Children's starred review annual 2013

REVIEW: *Publ Wkly* v260 no35 p58 S 2 2013

REVIEW: *SLJ* v60 no1 p64 Ja 2014 Amy Lilien-Harper

SABUDA, ROBERT.il. The Little Mermaid. See Sabuda, R.

SACCHET, GREGORY. Straight Lines; A Story of Illness, Addiction and Redemption; [by] Gregory Sacchet 156 p. 2013 CreateSpace Independent Publishing Platform

1. Cocaine abuse 2. Drug addiction 3. Memoirs 4. Multiple sclerosis 5. Tourette syndrome
ISBN 1492250074; 9781492250074

SUMMARY: In this debut memoir, [Gregory] Sacchet recounts his descent into cocaine addiction." After "his diagnosis of multiple sclerosis at the age of 23 . . . the symptoms' unpredictability played a large role in what Sacchet calls his 'physical and psychological agony.' A friend 'of ill-repute' introduced him to cocaine, and under the sway of another friend, the author began using the drug more and more frequently." (Kirkus Reviews)

REVIEW: *Kirkus Rev* v81 no24 p365 D 15 2013

"Straight Lines: A Story of Illness, Addiction and Redemption". " Although this memoir is often perceptive, [Gregory] Sacchet relates some of his teenage escapades at somewhat disproportionate length, including details of street life and drug deals, as well as events in the lives of unsavory friends. Much of this material might have been omitted, and overall, this briskly paced narrative might have been strengthened by some pruning. That said, he powerfully tells of the havoc that cocaine addiction created in his life and his eventual recovery. An often engaging, if somewhat overlong, memoir."

SACCO, JOE. The Great War; July 1, 1916 : the first day of the Battle of the Somme : an illustrated panorama; [by] Joe Sacco 54 p. 2013 W.W. Norton & Co. Inc.

1. Art literature 2. Historical literature 3. Panoramas 4. Somme, 1st Battle of the, France, 1916 5. Somme, 1st Battle of the, France, 1916—Comic books, strips, etc 6. World War, 1914-1918 in art
ISBN 0393088804; 9780393088809
LC 2013-010710

SUMMARY: This art book by Joe Sacco presents "a single continuous panorama, eight inches tall and twenty-four feet long," which "illustrates, in minutely detailed black-and-white drawings, events just before and during a summer day when the British army suffered morethan fifty-seven thousand dead and wounded, its greatest single-day loss. . . . An accompanying booklet" presents a "brief account of the day by Adam Hoschchild." (Bookforum)

REVIEW: *Bookforum* v20 no4 p20-1 D 2013/Ja 2014 CHRISTOPHER LYON

"Kara Walker: Dust Jackets for the N##gerati," "Great War: July 1, 1916: The First Day of the Battle of the Somme," and "Wall: Israeli & Palestinian Landscape 20008-2012." "The artist, assisted by the design firm CoMa, has cleverly folded the dust jacket into a large artwork that includes her entire foreword and a full-scale detail of a large text piece. The fine reproductions include these boldly graphic works as well as her powerfully kinetic figurative drawings. . . , Sacco conveys an eloquent, convincing, entirely wordless story. . . . [There is an] accompanying booklet with an affecting, brief account . . . by Adam Hochschild. . . . Josef Koudelka's book of purposely ugly photos--from which we cannot turn away."

REVIEW: *Booklist* v110 no13 p36 Mr 1 2014 Sarah Hunter

REVIEW: *Booklist* v110 no4 p37 O 15 2013 Daniel Kraus

REVIEW: *Economist* v410 no8868 p66-7 Ja 4 2014

REVIEW: *Kirkus Rev* v81 no14 p323 Jl 15 2013

REVIEW: *Kirkus Rev* p29 Ag 15 2013 Fall Preview

REVIEW: *N Y Times Book Rev* p17 D 8 2013 JEFF SHESOL

"The Great War: July 1, 1916: The First Day of the Battle of the Somme: An Illustrated Panorama." "[Cartoonist Joe] Sacco's new book, 'The Great War,' is a work of history, not journalism, but its themes are resonant in our own time. It is a searing depiction of a single day--the first and bloodiest--in the nearly five-month Battle of the Somme. . . . In truth, it's not really a book at all, but a tableau in a slipcase, an extended illustration, 24 feet long when fully unfolded. . . . Sacco's illustration--exacting in every damning detail, magnificent in its tragic way--is both indictment and tribute enough."

SACHS, NELLY, 1891-1970. Glowing enigmas; 2013 Tavern Books

1. German literature—Jewish authors 2. German poetry—20th century 3. Jewish refugees 4. Melancholy 5. Women poets, German
ISBN 9781935635222 paperback; 9781935635277 hardcover

SUMMARY: "Translated from the German by Michael Hamburger. Nelly Sachs's book-length poem 'Glowing Enigmas' is widely regarded as the Nobel Laureate's finest poetic achievement and one of the essential poetic works of postwar Europe. This definitive edition is the first in English to showcase the poem in its entirety. Michael Hamburger's . . . translation captures the deep sadness, lyrical mystery, and transcendent opacity at the heart of Sachs's haunting masterpiece." (Publisher's note)

REVIEW: *Libr J* v138 no7 p89 Ap 15 2013 Barbara Hoffert

REVIEW: *TLS* no5786 p23 F 21 2014 WILL STONE

"Glowing Enigmas." "Nelly Sachs wrote 'Glowing Enigmas' in a four-metre-squared apartment in Stockholm between 1962 and 1966. Her post-war work, which made her name, was concerned with giving voice to those numberless guiltless innocents, those 'sisters' who had perished in the Nazi extermination system. Sachs's poems courageously reach for a perhaps impossible transcendence, a spiritual resurrection in the face of human cruelty and the speech-inhibiting power of the Holocaust. . . . The Enigma poems are graceful yet pumped up with a delirious fortitude and sense of mounting urgency. The late Michael Hamburger's sympathetic translation . . . is suitably pared down, swift and assured, keeping track of Sachs as she weaves in and out of light and dark."

SACHSMAN, DAVID B.ed. Sensationalism. See Sensationalism

SACKS, NATHAN. The big fix; [by] Nathan Sacks 107 p. 2014 Darby Creek

1. Boxing—Fiction 2. Conspiracies—Fiction 3. Historical fiction 4. Journalism—Fiction
ISBN 9781467714594 (lib. bdg.: alk. paper)
LC 2013-028887

SUMMARY: In this historical novel, reporter George Choogart "is assigned the task of finding a story so new as to be unfamiliar to the editor. He thinks he has found it in Lew Mayflower's Woodrat Saloon, where he goes undercover as a fighter to learn more about illegal bare-knuckle boxing matches. Politician Big Jim Dickinson finds fighters there for use in his secret and very crooked matches." (Kirkus Reviews)

REVIEW: *Kirkus Rev* v82 no3 p74 F 1 2014

"The Big Fix". "[Nathan] Sacks nicely captures the chaos of the time and place and weaves a fast-paced, action-packed tale. Detailed descriptions of the brawls and bare-knuckle fights make up the bulk of the text. Several peripheral characters, while quite colorful, appear to have little purpose. In the end, George leaves New York and heads west, thus paving the way for a series of tales set in the Woodrat with new fighters and their back stories and penned by different authors. . . . Lots of action and low page count should propel reluctant readers along."

REVIEW: *Voice of Youth Advocates* v37 no1 p58-9 Ap 2014 Jen McIntosh

SADLER, MARILYN. Alice from Dallas; 40 p. 2013 Abrams Books for Young Readers

1. Children's stories 2. Cowgirls—Fiction 3. Friendship—Fiction 4. Jealousy
ISBN 9781419707902 (alk. paper)
LC 2012-036740

SUMMARY: In this book, "Alice (from Dallas, Pennsylvania) regales her classmates with her passion for the Wild West. When a new girl comes to school with lasso tricks and cowgirl songs of her own, Alice is miffed. Feelings of jealousy lead Alice to challenge Lexis to a 'showdown . . . at high noon.' . . . But when Lexis falls and hurts her foot in the Texas-Two-Step duel, Alice feels remorse." (School Library Journal)

REVIEW: *Booklist* v110 no13 p74-5 Mr 1 2014 Sarah Hunter

"Alice From Dallas." "There's no better cowgirl in all of Dallas (Pennsylvania) than cowboy hat-wearing, cattle-herding Alice. Everyday, she puts on her boots and spurs and ties up Nellie (her hobby horse) at the hitching rail (bike rack) at school. But Alice's confidence is shaken with the arrival of a new cowgirl. Lexis, who is really from Texas!

. . . [Ard] Hoyt's ink-and-watercolor illustrations gleefully capture the girls' enthusiasm for all things western. A lively story for cowgirls everywhere, with a breezy lesson about jealousy."

REVIEW: *Bull Cent Child Books* v67 no8 p422 Ap 2014 A. A.

"Alice From Dallas". "[Ard] Hoyt's playful watercolor illustrations expand on [Marilyn] Sadler's light-hearted text, providing humor and whimsy while capturing the details of an aspiring cowgirl's world in her clothing, books, and ever-changing bandana for her dog. Swift, pale strokes of red, blue, green, and yellow in mirror Alice's rangy spirit, as does the straightforward, lively prose. Young readers will enjoy the Wild West tropes smartly used throughout, and they will delight in the expressive images that fancifully capture Alice's spunk and frankness."

REVIEW: *Kirkus Rev* v82 no3 p117 F 1 2014

REVIEW: *SLJ* v60 no3 p125 Mr 2014 Linda Ludke

SADLER, MARILYN. Ten eggs in a nest; 48 p. 2014 Random House Inc

1. Chickens—Fiction 2. Children's stories 3. Counting 4. Eggs—Fiction 5. Father & child—Fiction
ISBN 0449810828; 9780375971518 (library binding); 9780449810828 (trade)
LC 2012-051234

SUMMARY: This children's book, by Marilyn Sadler, illustrated by Michael Fleming, is a beginning reader's counting book. "Gwen the hen has laid her eggs, but just how many is anyone's guess. For now, she's quite content to sit and wait for them to hatch. Red Rooster, however, is too excited to wait." (Publisher's note)

REVIEW: *Kirkus Rev* v81 no24 p67 D 15 2013

"Ten Eggs in a Nest". "[Marilyn] Sadler manages to keep it fast-paced and lively. Repetitive phrases and plot patterns mix with delightfully descriptive language and surprise elements to keep readers and listeners agog with interest. Proud papa Red struts and puffs his chest when he tells Pinky of his newborn chicks. . . . Lots of white space surrounds heavy, black, large print with the names of numbers emphasized in all capitals. [Michael] Fleming's black-outlined, brightly colored illustrations are expressive and filled with action, aptly capturing all the excitement while allowing little readers to count along with Red and Gwen. A happy and entertaining tale."

REVIEW: *SLJ* v60 no1 p76 Ja 2014 Mary Elam

SADRAEY, MOHAMMAD H. Aircraft design; a systems engineering approach; [by] Mohammad H. Sadraey xxx, 778 p. 2013 Wiley

1. Aeronautics 2. Airplanes—Design and construction 3. Systems engineering 4. TECHNOLOGY & ENGINEERING—Aeronautics & Astronautics 5. Technical literature
ISBN 9781119953401 (hardback)
LC 2012-009907

SUMMARY: Written by Mohammad H. Sadraey, "This book presents the entire process of aircraft design based on a systems engineering approach from conceptual design phase, through to preliminary design phase and to detail design phase. . . . The basic topics that are essential to the process, such as aerodynamics, flight stability and control, aero-structure, and aircraft performance are reviewed in various chapters where required." (Publisher's note)

REVIEW: *Choice* v51 no2 p300 O 2013 M. D. Maughmer

"Aircraft Design: A Systems Engineering Approach." "As 'Aircraft Design' does not rely heavily on theoretical underpinnings, it is an excellent resource for those mechanical engineering departments that have an offering in airplane design, as well as for nonaerospace engineering students interested in entering one of the popular competitions. [Author Mohammad H.] Sadraey . . . does an excellent job of walking the reader through the design process for almost any established configuration. Using only simple algebraic formulas and plotted data, the author considers the airplane primarily from its geometrical properties and defines the relationships necessary to satisfy given mission requirement."

SAEED, MAHMOUD. Ben Barka Lane; 278 p. 2013 Interlink Books, an imprint of Interlink Publishing Group, Inc.

1. Arabic fiction—20th century 2. Arabic fiction—Iraq 3. Arabic fiction—Translations into English 4. Morocco—Fiction 5. Refugees—Fiction
ISBN 9781566569262
LC 2013-000043

SUMMARY: "In 'Ben Barka Lane' we see the Morocco of the late 1960s through the eyes of a young political exile from Iraq--its beauty and misery, its unforgettable people. In this contemporary classic, Mahmoud Saeed offers us a unique portrait of a time and place, and a tale of the passion, politics, vengeance, and betrayal that take place there." (Publisher's note)

REVIEW: *Publ Wkly* v260 no21 p29-30 My 27 2013

REVIEW: *World Lit Today* v88 no1 p64 Ja/F 2014 M. D. Allen

"Ben Barka Lane." "'Ben Barka Lane' is not set in Iraq; and the novel is not among [author Mahmoud] Saeed's latest works but rather dates from 1970, when he was in his early thirties. . . . This is the novel's first appearance in English. It is a young man's book, full of the joy of life, the allurements and satisfactions of the physical world, women's bodies, grilled lamb and alcoholic exaltation, even the delight of walking down a street in the evening. . . . 'Ben Barka Lane' provides insights into the Morocco of the 1960s and Saeed's early promise as a novelist."

SAETERBAKKEN, STIG. Through the night. See Through the night

SAGA. [VOL. 1]; 160 p. 2012 Image Comics
ISBN 1607066017 (pbk.); 9781607066019 (pbk.)

SUMMARY: This fantasy graphic novel, by Brian K. Vaughan, illustrated by Fiona Staples, presents "the sweeping tale of one young family fighting to find their place in the worlds. . . . Two soldiers from opposite sides of a never-ending galactic war fall in love. . . [and] risk everything to bring a fragile new life into a dangerous old universe." (Publisher's note)

REVIEW: *Booklist* v110 no2 p57-8 S 15 2013 Sarah Hunter

"Saga." "[Brian K.] Vaughan and [Fiona] Staples' wholly original 'Saga' (2012) won Eisner awards for best new and best continuing series, and it's no surprise. This smash hit continues to be a powerhouse: intergalactic intrigue, truly alien aliens, multifaceted characters, and a universe full of lush environments all wrapped around a compellingly told story of forbidden love in wartime. . . . Vaughan has a peculiarly wonderful world at his fingertips, and he's setting himself up for something big, but it's Staples' stunning and otherworldly art that makes Saga such a thrilling read. . . . Vaughan and Staples are seriously upping the ante for comics. Fans will be eager to pick this up, and intrigued new readers won't be far behind."

REVIEW: *Booklist* v109 no8 p38 D 15 2012 Ian Chipman

REVIEW: *Libr J* v138 no1 p79 Ja 1 2013 M. C.

REVIEW: *Publ Wkly* v259 no41 p42 O 8 2012

REVIEW: *Publ Wkly* v259 no25 p26-7 Je 18 2012

SAGAR, RAHUL. Secrets and leaks; the dilemma of state secrecy; [by] Rahul Sagar 304 p. 2013 Princeton University Press

1. Leaks (Disclosure of information) 2. Official secrets 3. POLITICAL SCIENCE—Government—Executive Branch 4. POLITICAL SCIENCE—History & Theory 5. POLITICAL SCIENCE—Political Freedom & Security—International Security 6. Political science literature 7. Whistle blowing—Political aspects
ISBN 9780691149875 (hardback)
LC 2013-007163

SUMMARY: In this book, "Rahul Sagar argues that though whistleblowing can be morally justified, the fear of retaliation usually prompts officials to act anonymously--that is, to 'leak' information. As a result, it becomes difficult for the public to discern when an unauthorized disclosure is intended to further partisan interests. Because such disclosures are the only credible means of checking the executive, Sagar writes, they must be tolerated." (Publisher's note)

REVIEW: *N Y Rev Books* v61 no2 p7-9 F 6 2014 David Cole

REVIEW: *New Repub* v244 no18 p52-5 N 11 2013 Eric A. Posner

"Secrets and Leaks." "[Rahul Sagar's] book thus amounts to a defense of the status quo--where there is an equilibrium between government efforts to stop leaks and press efforts to spring them, one that happily results in neither too many disclosures nor too few. . . . In Sagar's view it seems to balance secrecy and transparency in the best way imaginable under current conditions. . . . This is an excellent book that comes at an essential time. [Edward] Snowden's leaks, which took place after Sagar finished the book, have focused public debate on the secrecy/transparency paradox, and Sagar's book is infinitely superior to the sloganeering that dominates the media. This does not mean, of course, that it cannot be criticized."

REVIEW: *New Statesman* v142 no5184 p50 N 15 2013 Katrina Forrester

THE SAGE HANDBOOK OF DIGITAL TECHNOLOGY RESEARCH; 512 p. 2013 Sage Pubns

1. Digital electronics—Research 2. Digital technology—Research 3. Human-computer interaction 4. Social science literature 5. Technology & civilization
ISBN 1446200477; 9781446200476

SUMMARY: This book "addresses aspects of research in the digital technology field, touching on technological development, social change, and the ubiquity of computing technologies. Some of the themes include introduction to the field of contemporary digital technology research; new digital technologies, key characteristics, and considerations; research perspectives for digital technologies, theory, and analysis environments; and tools for digital research." (Computers in Libraries)

REVIEW: *Choice* v51 no6 p1047 F 2014 B. G. Turner

"The SAGE Handbook of Digital Technology Research." "This extensive, well-organized work, edited by [Sara] Price . . . [Carey] Jewitt . . . and Brown . . . is not for the faint of heart. The discipline-specific content, highly sophisticated research, and germane terminology . . . will put general readers at a disadvantage and may challenge interested professionals outside the field. Fortunately, a glossary in one chapter helps to bridge this gap in expertise. . . . Part 3 is the gold mine, identifying emergent and established theories along with theoretical origins, key concepts, major studies, and restrictions. . . . Highly recommended."

SAHLINS, MARSHALL. What kinship is - and is not; [by] Marshall Sahlins 110 p. 2012 The University of Chicago Press

1. Anthropology literature 2. Belonging (Social psychology) 3. Families 4. Kinship 5. Sociobiology
ISBN 0226925129 (cloth : alkaline paper); 9780226925127 (cloth : alkaline paper)
LC 2012-013886

SUMMARY: This book by Marshall Sahlins investigates anthropological "debates on what constitutes kinship." According to the author, "kinfolk are persons who are parts of one another to the extent that what happens to one is felt by the other. Meaningfully and emotionally, relatives live each other's lives and die each other's deaths. In the second part of his essay, Sahlins shows that mutuality of being is a symbolic notion of belonging, not a biological connection by 'blood.'" (Publisher's note)

REVIEW: *TLS* no5754 p12-3 Jl 12 2013 ADAM KUPER

"What Kinship Is--And Is Not." "It runs to just eighty-nine pages of text, divided into two overlapping and at times repetitive chapters. The first asks what kinship is, and answers that kinship is a cultural construct (ideas, symbols, not institutions or strategies for living). The second chapter asks what kinship is not, and answers that it is not biology. . . . Not an easy read for all its short span, the details of [Marshall] Sahlins's demonstration will be largely unintelligible to readers who are unfamiliar with the jargon of kinship studies in anthropology. However, the central thesis is presented clearly."

SAINT, ANDREW.ed. Survey of London. See Survey of London

SAKA, MARK SAAD. For God and revolution; priest, peasant, and agrarian socialism in the Mexican Huasteca; [by] Mark Saad Saka xxi, 186 p. 2013 University of New Mexico Press

1. Agriculture—Economic aspects—Mexico—Huasteca Region 2. Historical literature 3. Land tenure—Mexico—Huasteca Region 4. Peasant uprisings—Mexico—Huasteca Region 5. Socialism—Mexico—Huasteca Region 6. Sociology, Rural—Religious aspects—Catholic Church
ISBN 9780826353382 (cloth: alk. paper)

LC 2013-000926

SUMMARY: This book by Mark Saad Saka "traces the century-long struggle of the indigenous/peasant villagers of the Huasteca districts in the state of San Luis Potosi [Mexico] against an invading, accelerating agrarian capitalism that sought to absorb and privatize their lands, reduce them to servile laborers, and break up their aspirations for village autonomy, ending in their unsuccessful rebellion of 1879-84." (Choice: Current Reviews for Academic Libraries)

REVIEW: *Am Hist Rev* v119 no2 p570-1 Ap 2014 Matthew Butler

REVIEW: *Choice* v51 no9 p1659 My 2014 S. F. Voss

"For God and Revolution: Priest, Peasant, and Agriarian Socialism in the Mexican Huasteca". "After an introduction to the subregion's cultural geography, the author analyzes the evolution of this conflict from the colonial legacy through the independence wars, the war with the US, the liberal-conservative civil war and the French Intervention, and the early years of the Porfirian dictatorship. A final section explains the interweaving of the moral and ideological threads into the villagers' alternative national vision of agrarian socialism and municipal autonomy, and details the course of the five-year rebellion. [Mark Saad] Saka employs a rich collection of state and national archives, personal papers, and newspapers. . . . Recommended."

SALAAM, LOVE; American Muslim men on love, sex, and intimacy; 248 p. 2014 Beacon Press

1. Intimacy (Psychology)—Religious aspects—Islam 2. Muslim men—United States 3. Sex role—Religious aspects—Islam

ISBN 0807079758; 9780807079751 (pbk.); 9780807079768 (electronic)

LC 2013-035892

SUMMARY: In this book, editors Ayesha Mattu and Nura Maznavi "provide a space for American Muslim men to speak openly about their romantic lives, offering . . . glimpses into their hearts—and bedrooms. The twenty-two writers come from a broad spectrum of ethnic, racial, and religious perspectives—including orthodox, cultural, and secular Muslims." The book is an "exploration of the most intimate parts of Muslim men's lives." (Publisher's note)

REVIEW: *Kirkus Rev* v82 no1 p154 Ja 1 2014

"Salaam, Love: American Muslim Men on Love, Sex, and Intimacy". "By nature, anthologies are a little uneven, and this one is no different. Though every story is worth reading and each piece will be enjoyed for its own unique understanding of love from a Muslim man's perspective, each contributor seems to have been responsible for writing his own history. Some stories are better written than others, but editors [Ayesha] Mattu, an international development consultant, and [Nura] Maznavi, a civil rights attorney, ensure that the focus remains on the importance of the story rather than the telling, and they separate the essays into three loose categories."

SALAS, LAURA PURDIE. A leaf can be; 32 p. 2012 Millbrook Press

1. Camouflage (Biology) 2. Leaves—Fiction 3. Photosynthesis 4. Poems 5. Stories in rhyme

ISBN 0761362037; 9780761362036 (lib. bdg. : alk. paper)

LC 2011-022227

SUMMARY: In this book of poetry, by Laura Purdie Salas, "rhyming text explores the many roles a leaf can play, from providing shelter for animals in the rain . . . to housing cocoons, . . . to purifying the air, . . . to providing autumnal entertainment for children. . . . [The] book offers abundant opportunity for discussion of scientific concepts from photosynthesis ('Sun taker/ Food maker') to camouflage ('Moth matcher' and 'Snake concealer')." (Bulletin of the Center for Children's Books)

REVIEW: *Booklist* v108 no14 p66 Mr 15 2012 Carolyn Phelan

REVIEW: *Bull Cent Child Books* v65 no8 p421 Ap 2012 H. M.

"A Leaf Can Be . . . " "Playful rhyming text explores the many roles a leaf can play, from providing shelter for animals in the rain ('Rain stopper') to housing cocoons ('Soft cradle'), to purifying the air ('Air cleaner'), to providing autumnal entertainment for children ('Pile grower'). The terms are poetically focused, yet they compactly sum up some complicated processes, so the book offers abundant opportunity for discussion of scientific concepts from photosynthesis . . . to camouflage. . . . An accessible and useful explanatory note at the end of the book breaks down the meaning of each verse in detailed paragraphs, providing the lesson for each reference. . . . This is an ideal curricular introduction to a unit on leaves."

REVIEW: *Kirkus Rev* v80 no2 p200 Ja 15 2012

REVIEW: *SLJ* v58 no3 p134 Mr 2012 Roxanne Burg

SALEM PRESS INC.comp. Internet innovators. See Internet innovators

SALEM PRESS INC.comp. Computer technology innovators. See Computer technology innovators

SALERNO, SHANE. Salinger; [by] Shane Salerno 720 p. 2013 Simon & Schuster

1. Authors—Biography 2. Authors, American—20th century—Biography 3. Biographies 4. Oral history 5. Salinger, J. D. (Jerome David), 1919-2010 6. World War, 1939-1945—Veterans 7. World War, 1939-1945—Veterans—Biography

ISBN 1476744831; 9781476744834

LC 2013-372430

SUMMARY: This book, by David Shields and Shane Salerno, offers an "oral biography [of writer J. D. Salinger with] direct eyewitness accounts from Salinger's World War II brothers-in-arms, his family members, his close friends, his lovers, his classmates, his neighbors, his editors, his publishers, his New Yorker colleagues, and people with whom he had relationships that were secret even to his own family." (Publisher's note)

REVIEW: *Christ Century* v131 no10 p39-42 My 14 2014 Harold K. Bush

REVIEW: *Economist* v405 no8855 p81 S 28 2013

"Salinger." "Arranged like an oral history (awkwardly without an index), 'Salinger' draws on some previously inaccessible letters and interviews with more than 200 people. Those seeking serious scholarship will be disappointed. This is an inelegant, prurient and often fascinating smorgasbord of insight and anecdotes from historians, friends and random talking heads. . . . Full of colour and intrigue, 'Salinger' can be gripping. It is also exactly the kind of messy, unsubtle, intrusive and speculative work the man himself understandably shunned."

REVIEW: *Kirkus Rev* v81 no19 p314 O 1 2013

REVIEW: *Libr J* v139 no4 p57 Mr 1 2014 Heather Malcolm

REVIEW: *Natl Rev* v65 no21 p42-4 N 11 2013 PETER TONGUETTE

REVIEW: *New York Times* v162 no56240 pC1-4 Ag 26 2013 MICHIKO KAKUTANI

REVIEW: *Time* v182 no12 p57 S 16 2013 Lev Grossman

REVIEW: *TLS* no5777/8 p3-4 D 20 2013 JAMES CAMPBELL

"Salinger." "To David Shields and Shane Salerno, . . . the authors and compilers of this mammoth posthumous assault on Salinger's privacy, the Holden missing in action in France and the Holden underground in New York City . . . are manifestations of the author's post-traumatic stress disorder. . . . Salinger is a maddening production, compelling yet never satisfying, impertinent in its rush to judgement on the late author's renunciatory preoccupations, his human appetites and foibles, and even his single testicle. . . . Testimony from almost 300 contributors is made use of, and just about anyone who made contact with Salinger is mentioned in the book's 700 pages, yet the publishers see no need for an index."

SALES, LEILA. This song will save your life; [by] Leila Sales 288 p. 2013 Farrar Straus & Giroux

1. Disc jockeys—Fiction 2. High schools—Fiction 3. Interpersonal relations—Fiction 4. Popularity—Fiction 5. Schools—Fiction 6. Suicide—Fiction 7. Young adult fiction

ISBN 0374351384; 9780374351380 (hard)
LC 2012-050408

SUMMARY: In this book, "Elise has endured a lifetime of social isolation and bullying at school. Walking alone one night soon after a halfhearted suicide attempt, the 16-year-old inadvertently ends up at an underground nightclub. There, an aspiring musician befriends her, and she catches the eye of Char, a cute DJ who agrees to teach her to mix music. But as talented, driven Elise spends more nights sneaking out to learn how to DJ (and kiss Char), her double life spins out of control." (Publishers Weekly)

REVIEW: *Booklist* v110 no1 p105 S 1 2013 Ilene Cooper

REVIEW: *Bull Cent Child Books* v67 no4 p236 D 2013 K. C.

REVIEW: *Horn Book Magazine* v89 no5 p110 S/O 2013 RACHEL L. SMITH

REVIEW: *Kirkus Rev* p56 Ag 15 2013 Fall Preview

REVIEW: *Kirkus Rev* v81 no14 p189 Jl 15 2013

REVIEW: *N Y Times Book Rev* p35 N 10 2013 JEN DOLL

"This Song Will Save Your Life." "Elise is a mostly relatable misfit trapped by a feeling nearly everyone has experienced. . . . There are times when Elise seems almost too likable for her outcast status, but 'misfit' is in the eye of the beholder, and she may be her own harshest critic. Her struggle not just to alter what others see but also to find what she wants to see is a poignant reminder that the current presiding perspective is not everything; that there are other opinions and new opportunities for acceptance and joy; that people can and do change, no matter how hard it seems. . . . The resonance of Elise's journey . . . feels very much of the moment."

REVIEW: *Publ Wkly* v260 no29 p70 Jl 22 2013

REVIEW: *Voice of Youth Advocates* v36 no4 p71-2 O 2013 Geri Diorio

"This Song Will Save Your Life." "Elise will admit herself how precocious she is, but she has been a bullied outsider all her life. As sophomore year begins, a suicide attempt is foiled when Elise calls a classmate after realizing that she just wants attention, not death. While out for a habitual middle-of-the-night walk, Elise stumbles across a warehouse dance party and finds something new to be precocious about: DJ-ing. . . . Elise is not an easy protagonist to like. She is arrogant and stubborn and almost too precocious, but she is also smart and young and determined. . . . This novel is complicated, even messy at times, and thus, very lifelike."

REVIEW: *Voice of Youth Advocates* v36 no4 p72 O 2013 Holly Storm

SALIME, ZAKIA. Between feminism and Islam; human rights and Sharia Law in Morocco; [by] Zakia Salime xxx, 195 p. 2011 University of Minnesota Press

1. Feminism—Morocco 2. Human rights—Morocco 3. Muslim women—Political activity—Morocco 4. Social science literature 5. Women in Islam—Morocco

ISBN 0816651337 (hc: alk. paper); 0816651345 (pb: alk. paper); 9780816651337 (hc: alk. paper); 9780816651344 (pb: alk. paper)
LC 2011-003817

SUMMARY: This book by Zakia Salime looks at "two major women's movements in Morocco: the Islamists who hold shari'a as the platform for building a culture of women's rights, and the feminists who use the United Nations' framework to amend shari'a law." It "shows how the interactions of these movements over the past two decades have transformed the debates, the organization, and the strategies of each other." (Publisher's note)

REVIEW: *Br J Sociol* v64 no2 p372-4 Je 2013 Margot Badran

REVIEW: *Contemp Sociol* v43 no2 p257-9 Mr 2014 Valentine M. Moghadam

"Between Feminism and Islam: Human Rights and Sharia Law in Morocco". "What Zakia Salime does in her slender but comprehensive book is to take us back to the 1980s, reveal the evolution of the women's movement and its relationship to domestic and global politics, and uncover the 'interdependencies' and interaction\ between the rival secular and Islamist women's groups across three 'movement moments.' It is a compelling and well-written narrative. . . . The non-specialist reader will appreciate the clarity of Salime's discussion of Moroccan political parties. . . . I recommend the book to scholars of social movements and of women's movements in the Middle East and North Africa."

SALINAS, VERONICA. The voyage; 40 p. 2013 Groundwood Books

1. Deserts—Juvenile literature 2. Ducks 3. Friendship—Juvenile fiction 4. Immigrants—Fiction 5. Picture books for children

ISBN 155498386X; 9781554983865

SUMMARY: In this picture book by Veronica Salinas and illustrated by Camilla Engman "a small duck finds himself in a place full of unusual creatures who speak an unfamiliar language. Eventually, he meets an animal whose big feet are just like his own. And with a friend by his side, he soon can feel at home." (Publisher's note)

REVIEW: *Kirkus Rev* v81 no18 p312 S 15 2013

REVIEW: *N Y Times Book Rev* p22 O 13 2013 SARAH SHUN-LIEN BYNUM

"The Voyage," "Here I Am," and "My Mom is a Foreigner, But Not To Me." "Perhaps there is no better way to evoke the universal than by enlisting the help of small forest animals, which the illustrator Camilla Engman does to delightful effect in 'The Voyage'. . . . The text, translated from Norwegian by Jeanne Eirhelm, feels slightly stiff at times, but the wit and inventiveness of the artwork make this voyage memorable. Patti Kim forgoes text altogether in her winsome 'Here I Am'. . . . Like Kim, the actress Julianne Moore sets her new picture book in a colorful, bustling . . . . metropolis--but hers stretches luxuriously across double-page spreads. . . . Moore . . . offers an original twist on the immigrant narrative."

REVIEW: *Publ Wkly* v260 no36 p54 S 9 2013

SALLY, DAVID. The numbers game. See Anderson, C.

SALMENNIEMI, SUVI. Rethinking class in Russia; [by] Suvi Salmenniemi xii, 270 p. 2012 Ashgate

1. Social classes—Russia (Federation)—21st century 2. Social science literature 3. Social stratification—Russia (Federation) 4. Women—Russia (Federation)—Social conditions
ISBN 9781409421375 (hardback: alk. paper)
LC 2011-052188

SUMMARY: This book "explor[es] the manner in which class positions are constructed and negotiated in the new Russia." It "demonstrates that class is a central axis along which power and inequality are organized in Russia, revealing how symbolic, cultural and emotional dimensions are deeply intertwined with economic and material inequalities. Topics include "popular culture, politics, social policy, consumption, education, work, family and everyday life." (Publisher's note)

REVIEW: *Contemp Sociol* v43 no2 p259-61 Mr 2014 Vladimir Shlapentokh

"Rethinking Class in Russia". "The Finnish scholars who published this volume should be credited for having gathered an interesting collection of foreign researchers (Finnish, Russian, British) to discuss the role of class in contemporary Russia. . . . Unfortunately, the authors generally failed to meet these expectations. . . . Nobody in the book defines the term 'discourse,' which is so popular in postmodernist literature. The interpretation of this term varies enormously and is sometimes puzzling to the reader. . . . Still, despite the organic flaws of this book, some of the authors made a considerable contribution to our understanding of the mentality of certain groups of the population in Russia."

SALONEN, KIRSI.ed. Cultural encounters during the crusades. See Cultural encounters during the crusades

THE SALT COMPANION TO CHARLES BERNSTEIN; 377 p. 2012 Salt Publishing

1. American poetry—History & criticism 2. Language poetry 3. Literature—History & criticism—Theory, etc. 4. Literature—Philosophy
ISBN 1844714853; 9781844714858
LC 2013-414567

SUMMARY: This book presents scholarly essays on the poetry of Charles Bernstein. "Scholars explore major themes in his work, and poets present pieces inspired by his poetry. The book is intended for both scholars looking for informed critical insight into Bernstein's work as well as for students to examine his work." (Publisher's note)

REVIEW: *TLS* no5773 p21 N 22 2013 MARK FORD

"All the Whiskey in Heaven: Selected Poems," "Recalculating," and "The Salt Companion to Charles Bernstein." "That's not to say that there is no fun to be had from this 'Selected Poems,' which offers a smorgasbord of disruptive techniques, verbal distortion and extravagant pastiche, as well as much literary knockabout. . . . The essays gathered in 'The Salt Companion to Charles Bernstein' tend towards a celebration of the guerrilla tactics with which he attempts to undermine linguistic conventions rather than antithetical readings, or evaluative assessments of particular poems or books. . . . 'Recalculating' includes inventive versions of poems by Baudelaire, Mandelstam, Apollinaire, Celan and Catullus, but the finest of Bernstein's translations is a ravishingly simple rendition of Victor Hugo's elegy for his daughter Léopoldine."

SALTER, ELISABETH. Popular Reading in English; c. 1400-1600; [by] Elisabeth Salter 224 p. 2012 Palgrave Macmillan

1. Books & reading—History 2. Books—History—1450-1600 3. English literature—History & criticism 4. Historical literature 5. Manuscripts—History
ISBN 0719077990; 9780719077999

SUMMARY: This book on popular reading in the 15th and 16th centuries investigates "'service books' (primers and prayer books), 'moral reading,' 'practical texts' on husbandry and carving, and popular fictional literature dealing with the figure of Sir Gawain. [Elisabeth] Salter's objective is 'to uncover evidence for the reading practices and experiences of real . . . readers using evidence that is found within the material of book and manuscript itself." (Times Literary Supplement)

REVIEW: *TLS* no5752 p8 Je 28 2013 MARY C. FLANNERY

"Popular Reading in English c. 1400-1600." "Elisabeth Salter's book . . . deals with perhaps the most exciting period in relation to the history of reading in England. . . . Prospective readers of Salter's book might have had a clearer picture of its contents, however, if it had been given a subtitle: "Four Case Studies." . . . She brings formidable codicological expertise to bear on the texts in question. . . . Salter makes a number of valuable points in this volume, and it is a pleasure to follow the close attention she lavishes on such under-appreciated material. . . . It is a shame, however, that she so seldom attempts to move from the specific manuscripts and early printed books she discusses to the big picture."

SALTER, MARY JO, 1954-. Nothing by design; poems; [by] Mary Jo Salter 108 p. 2013 Alfred A. Knopf

1. American poetry 2. Dead 3. Divorce 4. Humorous poetry 5. Peace
ISBN 9780385349796
LC 2013-001009

SUMMARY: In this poetry collection by Mary Jo Salter, "we're asked to entertain the thought of a no-fault universe. The wary search for peace, personal and public, is a constant theme in poems as varied as 'Our Friends the Enemy,' about the Christmas football match between German and British soldiers in 1914; 'The Afterlife,' in which Egyptian tomb figurines labor to serve the dead; and 'Voice of America,' where Salter returns to the Saint Petersburg of . . . the late Joseph Brodsky." (Publisher's note)

REVIEW: *Antioch Rev* v72 no1 p193 Wint 2014 Benjamin S. Grossberg

REVIEW: *N Y Rev Books* v61 no6 p62-4 Ap 3 2014 Dan Chiasson

"American Songbook," "Go Giants," and "Nothing by Design." "American poets tend to want the benefits of song . . . without its costs. . . . This conflict drives Michael Ruby's 'American Songbook.' . . . The Irish poet Nick Laird's brilliantly titled new book is 'Go Giants.' . . . 'Go Giants' is a book about rooting for something, anything, now that the comforts of religious belief are, for Laird as for many of us, nonexistent. . . . 'Nothing by Design' is [author Mary Jo] Salter's seventh book. Its accomplishments of prosody are, by turns, vengeful, saddened, and funny."

SAMANTA, GOPA. Dancing with the river. See Lahiri-Dutt, K.

SAMPSON, HENRY T. Blacks in blackface; a sourcebook on early black musical shows; [by] Henry T. Sampson 2013 Scarecrow Press

1. African American actors 2. African American theater 3. African Americans—Music 4. Historical literature 5. Theater—United States—History
ISBN 9780810883505

SUMMARY: The 2nd edition of this book, by Henry T. Sampson, focuses on "all-African American musical comedies performed on the stage between 1900 and 1940 . . . , including show synopses, casts, songs, and production credits. Sampson also recounts the struggles of African American performers and producers to overcome the racial prejudice of white show owners, music publishers, theatre managers, and booking agents to achieve adequate financial compensation for their talents and managerial expertise." (Publisher's note)

REVIEW: *Choice* v51 no8 p1370 Ap 2014 J. C. Wanser

"Blacks in Blackface: A Sourcebook on Early Black Musical Shows". "Intending to give greater coverage to the hundreds of black musical shows beyond the few described in standard references, independent scholar Sampson has done a remarkable job. This new volume is nearly triple the size of the previous edition. . . . Coverage of musicians is spotty, but other sources provide significant treatments. . . . Rare photos supplement the entries and provide visual documentation. Sampson has done a fine job of pulling together source material for this vital reference on the history of the black entertainment industry."

SAMUELS, DETAVIO. Exist No More; The Art of Squeezing The Most Out of Life; [by] Detavio Samuels 111 p. 2013 Bare Group, Inc

1. Advice literature 2. Creative ability 3. Goal (Psychology) 4. Self-help materials 5. Self-realization
ISBN 0615817580; 9780615817583

SUMMARY: In this book, author Detavio Samuels "inspires readers to find and follow their true passions instead of simply functioning on autopilot. . . . His book is divided into three main sections: 'Unleash Your Magic,' which focuses on people's inherent potentials; 'Think Differently,' about learning new ways to perceive and act on desires and challenges; and 'Make It Happen,' which imparts tips for turning dreams into realities." (Kirkus Reviews)

REVIEW: *Kirkus Rev* v82 no2 p326 Ja 15 2014

"Exist No More: The Art of Squeezing the Most Out of Life". "In this readable, slightly spiritual volume, [Detavio] Samuels inspires readers to find and follow their true passions instead of simply functioning on autopilot. . . . The bulk of the book is passionate and well-meaning, packed with short chapters headed by inspirational quotes, but the exhortations can feel more like self-help slogans. . . . Samuels' passion and positivity are inspirational, and the book is certain to jump-start those who just need a bit of a boost, but readers looking for concrete actions might be disappointed. Bighearted and energizing advice for being your best self, but it's all a bit vague."

SAMWORTH, KATE.il. Aviary Wonders Inc. Spring Catalog and Instruction Manual. See Samworth, K.

SAMWORTH, KATE. Aviary Wonders Inc. Spring Catalog and Instruction Manual; renewing the world's bird supply since 2031; 32 p. 2014 Clarion Books, Houghton Mifflin Harcourt

1. Automata—Fiction 2. Birds—Fiction 3. Catalogs—Fiction 4. Environmental degradation—Fiction 5. Mechanical toys—Fiction 6. Picture books for children
ISBN 0547978995; 9780547978994 (hardcover)
LC 2013-020247

SUMMARY: This book, by Kate Samworth, is "a catalog of bird parts and instructions for making your own in a . . . possible future in which living birds have nearly disappeared. Feathers, beaks, legs and feet, bodies, tails and even flight styles can be ordered from this enterprising company, whose motto is 'Renewing the World's Bird Supply Since 2031.' . . . The author also enumerates actual bird threats: insecticides, habitat loss, the exotic pet trade and cats." (Kirkus Reviews)

REVIEW: *Booklist* v110 no13 p68 Mr 1 2014 Carolyn Phelan

REVIEW: *Bull Cent Child Books* v67 no7 p376 Mr 2014 E. B.

REVIEW: *Kirkus Rev* v82 no2 p118 Ja 15 2014

"Aviary Wonders Inc. Spring Catalog & Instruction Manual". " A catalog of bird parts and instructions for making your own in a sadly possible future in which living birds have nearly disappeared. . . . Written and illustrated (in oil, ink, graphite and colored pencil) in the style of traditional mail-order inventories, this weaves in a surprising amount of genuine bird information while displaying the variety of interchangeable parts. . . . For children and their bird-watching parents, who will appreciate the clever premise and the message of admiration."

REVIEW: *Publ Wkly* v261 no3 p55 Ja 20 2014

REVIEW: *SLJ* v60 no1 p90 Ja 2014 Kathy Piehl

SANCHEZ GONZALEZ, LISA.ed. The stories I read to the children. See The stories I read to the children

SANCHEZ, SONIA, 1934-.il. Here I am. See Kim, P.

SANCLEMENTS, MICHAEL. Plastic purge; how to use less plastic, eat better, keep toxins out of your body, and help save the sea turtles!; [by] Michael SanClements 256 p. 2014 St. Martin's Griffin

1. Environmental literature 2. Plastic scrap—Environmental aspects 3. Plastics—Environmental aspects 4. Plastics—Health aspects 5. Plastics—History 6. Plastics industry and trade

ISBN 9781250029393 (trade paperback)

LC 2013-033778

SUMMARY: This book by Michael SanClements tells how "he started documenting each plastic item he encountered during a typical day. Next, the author and his partner embarked on a larger experiment: to not purchase or create plastic waste for two weeks." Topics include "the history of plastics" and "the science of plastic usage. . . . The author concludes with a . . . guide to 'help you reduce plastic consumption, keep toxins out of your body, and spare Mother Nature the excess waste.'" (Kirkus Reviews)

REVIEW: *Booklist* v110 no12 p20 F 15 2014 Carol Haggas

REVIEW: *Kirkus Rev* v82 no5 p83 Mr 1 2014

"Plastic Purge: How to Use Less Plastic, Eat Better, Keep Toxins Out of Your Body, and Help Save the Sea Turtles!". " A breezy yet highly informative trek through our plasticized world coupled with tips for reducing plastic from your life. . . . [Michael] SanClements divides the narrative into four digestible sections. . . . The author concludes with a remarkably helpful guide to 'help you reduce plastic consumption, keep toxins out of your body, and spare Mother Nature the excess waste.' Thankfully, SanClements is never self-righteous or heavy-handed. . . . This worthwhile little tome packs a wallop consisting of equal portions of healthy education and pertinent entertainment."

SANDERS, ANDREW. In the olden time; the Victorians and the British past; [by] Andrew Sanders 330 p. 2013 Yale University Press

1. Arts and history—Great Britain 2. Arts, Victorian—Themes, motives 3. Historical literature 4. History in art

ISBN 0300190425; 9780300190427

LC 2012-037478

SUMMARY: In this book, Andrew Sanders "explores the essentially literary nature of Victorian history writing, and he reveals the degree to which painters were indebted to written records both fictional and factual. Starting with a . . . comparison of Queens Elizabeth I and Victoria, 'In the Olden Time' examines works by poets and painters, essayists and dramatists, architects and musicians, including Jane Austen, John Donne, William Shakespeare, and John Soane." (Publisher's note)

REVIEW: *Burlington Mag* v156 no1334 p321 My 2014 JOHN CHRISTIAN

REVIEW: *Hist Today* v63 no9 p60-1 S 2013 JAD ADAMS

"In the Olden Time: Victorians and the British Past." "[Andrew] Sanders' contribution is to explore the literary nature of Victorian history to reveal how painters were indebted to written record. . . . 'In the Olden Time' is beautifully written and illustrated, notably with little-known paintings such as Paul Delaroche's 'Strafford on his Way to Execution' and 'Cromwell Uncovering the Coffin of Charles I, showing the dictator taking a last peek at the king. One of the joys of this book is the range of material shown from private collections and neglected municipal galleries that are clearly well worth a visit."

REVIEW: *TLS* no5779 p5-7 Ja 3 2014 A. N. WILSON

"In the Olden Time: Victorians and the British Past." "As Sanders shows in this 'treasure-house of detail' about the Victorians' attitude to their own British past, as seen, chiefly, by their historians, novelists, painters and architects, Dickens was, as so often, representative of his age in his open hatred of the past, and his perky lower-middle-class joy in nowadays. . . . Andrew Sanders's book, therefore, as well as calling up a host of images from the Victorian era, challenges our own way of viewing, changing, cleansing and rose-tinting the past."

SANDERS, SHELLY. Rachel's secret; [by] Shelly Sanders 248 p. 2012 Second Story Press

1. Antisemitism in literature 2. Christianity & other religions—Judaism 3. Fiction 4. Friendship in literature 5. Pogroms in literature

ISBN 1926920376; 9781926920375

SUMMARY: This book follows "14-year-old Rachel . . . living under Russian rule in Kishinev in 1903, [she] was one of the last people to see her Christian friend Mikhail alive when she witnessed his murder at the hands of disgruntled relatives who stood to lose out on an inheritance. His death is blamed on Jews, however, and a vicious pogrom is unleashed on the city. Rachel's anguish about knowing what happened stems from a justified fear of not being believed if she comes forward, thus evoking more turmoil. She also harbors guilt that her somewhat risky friendship with a non-Jewish boy somehow triggered the calamity. . . . [W]hile Rachel does act courageously and courtroom justice is meted out, virulent anti-Semitism still rules the day." (Booklist)

REVIEW: *Can Lit* no219 p170-1 Wint 2013 Norman Ravvin

SANDERSON, BRANDON. Steelheart; [by] Brandon Sanderson 400 p. 2013 Delacorte Press

1. Guerrilla warfare—Fiction 2. Revenge—Fiction 3. Science fiction 4. Supervillains—Fiction 5. Vigilantes—Fiction

ISBN 0375991212; 0385743564; 9780375991219 (glb); 9780385743563 (hc)

LC 2012-045751

SUMMARY: This science-fiction superhero story is the first in a series from Brandon Sanderson. Here, "when David was six, an unexplained explosion in the sky caused perpetual darkness and ordinary people to gain supernatural powers. These people became known as Epics. Two years later, in a bank in what was once Chicago, now called Newcago, David witnessed Steelheart, one of the most powerful Epics of all, murder his father." David is seeking revenge. (School Library Journal)

REVIEW: *Booklist* v110 no1 p105 S 1 2013 Frances Bradburn

REVIEW: *Bull Cent Child Books* v67 no5 p281-2 Ja 2014 A. M.

"Steelheart." "Known best for his high fantasy series, [Brandon] Sanderson offers up something different here: an entertaining take on near-future science fiction that turns superhero conventions on their head. Action-packed and overflowing with imaginatively rendered villains, the narrative convincingly places humans in the role of hero and celebrates knowledge and strategy over superpowers. David's story will have special resonance for teen readers as he tries to prove his worth to more experienced adults who want to keep him on the sidelines, and he emerges as a relatable mixture of capability and naïveté."

REVIEW: *Kirkus Rev* v81 no12 p113 Je 15 2013

REVIEW: *Publ Wkly* v260 no28 p173-4 Jl 15 2013

REVIEW: *SLJ* v60 no3 p76 Mr 2014 Amanda Raklovits

REVIEW: *SLJ* v59 no7 p100 Jl 2013 Sharon Rawlins

REVIEW: *Voice of Youth Advocates* v36 no3 p83 Ag 2013 Jonathan Ryder

SANDLER, RONALD L.ed. Designer biology. See Designer biology

SANKOVITCH, NINA. Signed, sealed, delivered; celebrating the joys of letter writing; [by] Nina Sankovitch 224 p. 2014 Simon & Schuster

1. English language—Rhetoric 2. English letters—History and criticism 3. Historical literature 4. Letter writing—History 5. Letter writing—Social aspects 6. Letters in literature 7. Written communication—Social aspects

ISBN 145168715X; 9781451687156 (hardback); 9781451687163 (trade paperback)
LC 2013-023240

SUMMARY: Author Nina Sankovitch "goes on a quest through the history of letters and her own personal correspondence to discover and celebrate what is special about the handwritten letter. . . . Sankovitch uncovers and defines the specific qualities that make letters so special, examining not only historical letters but also the letters in epistolary novels, her husband's love letters, and dozens more sources, including her son's brief reports from college on the weather and his allowance." (Publisher's note)

REVIEW: *Booklist* v110 no12 p12 F 15 2014 Mark Knoblauch

REVIEW: *Kirkus Rev* v82 no4 p6 F 15 2014

"Signed, Sealed, Delivered: Celebrating the Joys of Letter Writing". "Her desire for an actual handwritten letter got the author thinking about the different ways in which correspondence connects us to others, and her agreeable narrative roams through many varieties: love letters, thank-you letters, condolence letters, letters to friends, letters of advice, etc. [Nina] Sankovitch begins with her discovery of a cache of old letters in the dilapidated house she and her husband, Jack, bought on Manhattan's Upper West Side when their four children were small. . . . There are no especially astounding insights here, but it's a sweet-natured, well-written affirmation of the time-honored role of letters as a uniquely personal way to communicate."

REVIEW: *Publ Wkly* v260 no50 p55 D 9 2013

SANTANA, CINTIA. Forth and back; translation, dirty realism, and the Spanish novel (1975-1995); [by] Cintia Santana xvi, 175 p. 2013 Bucknell University Press Copubl. w/Rowman & Littlefield Pub. Group

1. Historical literature 2. Realism in literature 3. Spanish fiction—20th century—History and criticism 4. Spanish fiction—American influences 5. Translating and interpreting—Spain

ISBN 161148460X (cloth : alk. paper); 1611484618 (electronic); 9781611484601 (cloth : alk. paper); 9781611484618 (electronic)
LC 2012-038923

SUMMARY: In this book, "[Cintio] Santana analyzes the translation 'boom' of U.S. literature that marked literary production in Spain after [Francisco] Franco's death, and the central position that U.S. writing came to occupy within the Spanish literary system. Santana examines the economic and literary motives that underlay the phenomenon, as well as the particular socio-cultural appeal that U.S. 'dirty realist' writers . . . held for Spaniards in the 1980s." (Publisher's note)

REVIEW: *Choice* v51 no5 p838-9 Ja 2014 F. J. Peas-Bermejo

"Forth and Back: Translation, Dirty Realism, and the Spanish Novel (1975-1995)." "Focusing on postdictatorship Spain, transition to democracy, and the meaning of 'nationness,' [Cintia] Santana . . . takes a welcome look at the effervescent translations of US literature in Spain, in particular of 'dirty realism.' . . . Expertly documented and soundly written, this book challenges how one reads across languages and how 'nation-ness' is constructed vis-à-vis those readings. . . . Recommended."

SANTAT, DAN.il. The adventures of Beekle. See Santat, D.

SANTAT, DAN. The adventures of Beekle; the unimaginary friend; [by] Dan Santat 40 p. 2014 Little, Brown and Co.

1. Children's stories 2. Friendship—Fiction 3. Imaginary places 4. Imaginary playmates—Fiction 5. Playgrounds

ISBN 9780316199988
LC 2013-017700

SUMMARY: In this book by Dan Santat, "an imaginary friend . . . longs for the day when a child will 'imagine' him, and thus choose and name him. As the days pass and he remains unchosen, the intrepid fellow goes in search of his intended child, leaving his imaginary home for the real world. . . . Finally a girl named Alice chooses him; once she dubs him 'Beekle' a bond is formed, and the two go on to have adventures, both real and imaginary, together." (Bulletin of the Center for Children's Books)

REVIEW: *Bull Cent Child Books* v67 no10 p540 Je 2014 J. H.

"Beekle: The Unimaginary Friend". "Pithy writing combines with the rich, slightly stylized illustrations . . . to give an elegant edge to the storytelling. Pudgy white Beekle is a lovable toylike figure (kids will particularly giggle at his 'rear' view, in which butt cheeks are subtly indicated), and the visual contrasts between the bright-hued, multi-patterned imaginary world and the darker, drabber real world are striking (especially lovely is the rainbow-scaled sea serpent he encounters). This tale could enhance multiple educational or storytime themes—friendship, imagination, journeys—and could be used to spark some imaginative writing or art activities; it might also inspire the development of some new imaginary friends."

SANTAT, DAN.il. Crankenstein. See Berger, S.

SANTAT, DAN.il. Fire! Fuego! Brave bomberos. See Elya, S. M.

SANTOMAURO, FABIO.il. The whispering town. See Elvgren, J.

SANTOSO, CHARLES.il. Max makes a cake. See Edwards, M.

SAPIENZA, GOLIARDA. The art of joy; 704 p. 2013 Farrar Straus & Giroux

1. Autobiographical fiction 2. Convents 3. Fascism—Italy 4. Historical fiction 5. Italy—Fiction
ISBN 0374106142; 9780374106140 (hardcover)
LC 2013-005477

SUMMARY: This book by Goliarda Sapienza follows "a Sicilian woman born on January 1, 1900, whose strength and character are an affront to conventional morality. Impoverished as a child, Modesta believes she is destined for a better life. She is able, through grace and intelligence, to secure marriage to an aristocrat--without compromising her own deeply felt values. Friend, mother, lover--Modesta revels in upsetting the rules of her fascist, patriarchal society." (Publisher's note)

REVIEW: *Booklist* v109 no21 p23 Jl 1 2013 Deborah Donovan

REVIEW: *Kirkus Rev* v81 no14 p11 Jl 15 2013

REVIEW: *Libr J* v138 no10 p100 Je 1 2013 Evelyn Beck

REVIEW: *Libr J* v138 no3 p70 F 15 2013 Barbara Hoffert

REVIEW: *Ms* v23 no3 p58-9 Summ 2013

REVIEW: *Publ Wkly* v260 no17 p104-6 Ap 29 2013

REVIEW: *TLS* no5753 p19 Jl 5 2013 CAROLINE MOOREHEAD

"The Art of Joy" and "The Mussolini Canal." "Neither of these novels, on the face of it, suggests an easy read. 'The Mussolini Canal'--which won the Strega prize in 2010--is cast entirely as a monologue, recounted by an elderly member of the Peruzzi clan to a young descendant. His story takes the form of answers to unseen questions. 'The Art of Joy' switches back and forth in time and place, including set pieces and snatches of diary. . . . With both of these imaginatively and unobtrusively translated books, perseverance brings considerable rewards."

SAPORITO, ANASTASIA V. Ancient furies; a young girl's struggles in the crossfire of World War II; [by] Anastasia V. Saporito 400 p. 2014 Potomac Books, an imprint of the University of Nebraska Press

1. Memoirs 2. Russians—Serbia—Belgrade—Biography 3. World War, 1939-1945—Personal narratives, Russian 4. World War, 1939-1945—Personal narratives, Yugoslav 5. World War, 1939-1945—Serbia—Belgrade
ISBN 9781612346335 (cloth: alkaline paper)
LC 2013-031943

SUMMARY: This memoir by Anastasia V. Saporito "recounts . . . the difficulties of her childhood as the daughter of White Russian aristocrats forced to flee their native Russia for refuge in Yugoslavia. . . . Saporito . . . depicts her family, her own struggles as a girl coming of age in war-torn central Europe, and the devastation incurred as a result of Nazi actions toward civilian populations of occupied countries." (Publisher's note)

REVIEW: *Kirkus Rev* v82 no1 p262 Ja 1 2014

"Ancient Furies: A Young Girl's Struggle in the Crossfire of World War II". " A haunting coming-of-age memoir by a woman who survived the traumatic experiences of war, internment in a Nazi labor camp and life as a displaced person with her faith in humanity intact. [Anastasia V.] Saporito wrote the book with her American husband, Donald, who saw it to completion after her death in 2007. They were married in 1958, two weeks after meeting in Colorado. The author began her memoir in 1967, when Vietnam brought back painful memories of her own wartime experiences, and she continued writing it sporadically thereafter. . . . A beautifully written memoir with a spellbinding immediacy."

SARASWATI, L. AYU. Seeing beauty, sensing race in transnational Indonesia; [by] L. Ayu Saraswati 173 p. 2013 University of Hawai'i Press

1. Feminine beauty (Aesthetics)—Indonesia 2. Historical literature 3. Human skin color—Indonesia—Psychological aspects 4. Indonesia—Social conditions 5. Race awareness—Indonesia 6. Racial classification 7. Racism—History 8. Social science literature
ISBN 0824836642; 9780824836641 (cloth : alk. paper); 9780824837365 (pbk. : alk. paper)
LC 2012-042310

SUMMARY: This book, by L. Ayu Saraswati, "offers a rich repertoire of analytical and theoretical tools that allow readers to rethink issues of race and gender in a global context and understand how feelings and emotions contribute to and are constitutive of transnational and gendered processes of racialization. Saraswati's ground-breaking work is a nuanced theoretical exploration of the ways in which representations of beauty and the emotions they embody travel geographically." (Publisher's note)

REVIEW: *Choice* v51 no1 p174 S 2013 T. L. Loos

"Seeing Beauty, Sensing Race in Transnational Indonesia." "In this pithy book, [author L. Ayu] Saraswati argues that contrary to the assumption that colonialism brought with it racialized understandings of skin color, transnational ideals of whiteness as a characteristic of beauty have traversed the Indonesian archipelago since the precolonial era. The author examines the positive associations with whiteness in the precolonial Javanese Ramayana. . . . The book integrates theories of affect into understandings of whiteness in historical contexts. It offers an excellent analysis of the feeling of shame linked to a woman's sense of her own dark skin, and the use of whiteners to manage feelings along gender lines."

SARGENT, ANNA K. The Legend of Juan Miguel; The

Tale of an Unlikely Texas Hero; [by] Anna K. Sargent 378 p. 2013 Violet Crown Publishers

1. Ethnic conflict 2. Historical fiction 3. Love stories 4. Outlaws—Fiction 5. Ranchers—Fiction

ISBN 1938749065; 9781938749063

SUMMARY: This book by Anna K. Sargent "starts at the end, with the funeral of Primo, an infamous outlaw whose death drew droves of mourners from around the country. Then, as the casket is lowered, a slip of the hand results in it tumbling open to reveal, for just a few seconds, what many believed to be a different man. The story then jumps back six years, when the man who became known as the legendary Primo was simply Juan Miguel, an earnest teenager with a terrible crush." (Kirkus Reviews)

REVIEW: *Kirkus Rev* v82 no2 p346 Ja 15 2014

"The Legend of Juan Miguel: The Tale of an Unlikely Texas Hero". "[Anna K.] Sargent does a fine job of showing how this unlikely love develops, and her writing has a cadence that is both elegant and charming: 'He opened her heart barely a crack. Only a sliver of light came through, but it was enough. She got a glimpse of another world, like a half line of poetry plopped down in a dry brittle tome of prose.' Budding love story aside, this is also a compelling tale of the growing tensions between whites and Hispanics over dwindling property and how the hardships of life turned that sweet young man into an outlaw. A fun Western romp with a decent balance of romance and mystery."

SARTIN, JOHN. The complete photo guide to making metal jewelry; [by] John Sartin 223 p. 2013 Creative Publishing international

1. Do-it-yourself literature 2. Jewelry—Equipment & supplies 3. Jewelry making 4. Jewelry making—Amateurs' manuals 5. Metal-work

ISBN 1589237366; 9781589237360 (pbk.)

LC 2012-051156

SUMMARY: "This how-to book includes all the techniques involved in crafting metal jewelry, including: cutting and filing, cold connections, soldering, texturing, forging and forming, setting stones, [and] applying specialty finishes." Author John Sartin also includes project instructions and a "gallery of metal jewelry pieces by experienced designers." (Publisher's note)

REVIEW: *Booklist* v110 no8 p14 D 15 2013 Brad Hooper Donna Seaman

"The Complete Photo Guide to Making Metal Jewelry," "Connect the Shapes Crochet Motifs: Creative Techniques for Joining Motifs of All Shapes," and "Journal Your Way: Designing and Using Handmade Books." "If any crafter has reservations about learning to make metal jewelry, [John] Sartin knocks those reservations out of the water in a very savvy approach to the subject. . . . This is smart publishing: a spiral-bound pattern and instructional book that actually lies flat, so that avid needleworkers can practice while reading instructions. . . . [Gwen] Diehn teaches readers how to create the blank book most suited to one's needs through a series of questions and selections from eight different personal journals."

REVIEW: *Booklist* v110 no4 p9 O 15 2013 Barbara Jacobs

SAUERLÄNDER, WILLIBALD. The Catholic Rubens; saints and martyrs; 312 p. 2014 Getty Research Institute

1. Catholic artists 2. Christianity and art—Catholic Church 3. European art—16th century 4. European art—17th century 5. Religious art

ISBN 9781606062685

LC 2013-039285

SUMMARY: This book by Willibald Sauerländer, translated by David Dollenmayer, "The art of Rubens is rooted in an era darkened by the long shadow of devastating wars between Protestants and Catholics. In the wake of this profound schism, the Catholic Church decided to cease using force to propagate the faith. Like Gian Lorenzo Bernini, Peter Paul Rubens (1577-1640) sought to persuade his spectators to return to the true faith through the beauty of his art." (Publisher's note)

REVIEW: *Burlington Mag* v156 no1333 pVIII Ap 2014

REVIEW: *Choice* v51 no12 p2170 Ag 2014 A. Golahny

REVIEW: *N Y Rev Books* v61 no8 p19-21 My 8 2014 Charles Hope

"The Catholic Rubens: Saints and Martyrs." "As [author Willibald] Sauerländer shows, Ruben's altarpieces, some of them for churches in Flanders and some for Germany, where the Thirty Years' War was still raging, need to be understood against the background of the religious divide between Catholics and various categories of Protestants. . . . Sauerländer reminds us that if we judge Rubens as a man of his times, his work acquires a consistency and depth that it lacks when we choose instead to single out those aspects of his output most accessible to modern sensibility."

SAUL, JOHN RALSTON. Dark Diversions; [by] John Ralston Saul 2013 Penguin Books

1. Humorous stories 2. Kings & rulers—Fiction 3. Murder—Fiction 4. Nobility (Social class)—Fiction 5. Rich people—Fiction

ISBN 0241964997; 9780241964996

SUMMARY: "The narrator of this series of encounters is a journalist of sorts. In the 1980s and 1990s, he interviews dictators, bankers, princesses, and other high-ranking officials from New York to Paris to Morocco to Haiti, while insinuating himself into their lives and luxurious lifestyles. Each encounter is a story in itself, sometimes tied to another vignette but often contrasting markedly, with different worlds featured from one story to the next." (Library Journal)

REVIEW: *Quill Quire* v78 no8 p25-6 O 2012 Vit Wagner

REVIEW: *TLS* no5754 p20 Jl 12 2013 EDMUND GORDON

"Dark Diversions: A Traveller's Tale." "Saul's fame outside Canada remains fairly limited, and his new book is unlikely to change this. . . . The tone is of course deliciously ironic, but there's a defensive quality to it. The metafictional flourishes add little to the stories themselves and it's hard not to feel that Saul is simply covering his back: he'd rather be thought of as pretentious than naive. 'Dark Diversions' is so self-conscious about the trenchancy of its insights, about the cleverness of its design, about its cosmopolitanism, elegance and cynicism, that it comes to seem every bit as shallow as the world it sets out to skewer."

SAUNDERS, GEORGE. Congratulations, by the way; some thoughts on kindness; [by] George Saunders 64 p. 2014 Random House Inc.

1. Advice literature 2. Baccalaureate addresses 3. Kindness 4. Love 5. Selfishness

ISBN 0812996275; 9780812996272
LC 2013-037902

SUMMARY: This book, by George Saunders, focuses on kindness. "Three months after . . . Saunders gave a convocation address at Syracuse University, a transcript of that speech was posted on the website of 'The New York Times,' where its simple, uplifting message struck a deep chord. Within days, it had been shared more than one million times. Why? Because Saunders's words tap into a desire in all of us to lead kinder, more fulfilling lives." (Publisher's note)

REVIEW: *Kirkus Rev* v82 no4 p346 F 15 2014

"Congratulations, By the Way: Some Thoughts on Kindness". " Another example of an author who might well reach a wider audience through a graduation speech than through anything else he has written. . . . This meditation on kindness that he delivered in 2013 at Syracuse (where he teaches creative writing) is transparent in its message, which, he admits, is 'a little facile, maybe, and certainly hard to implement, but I'd say, as a goal in life, you could do worse than: Try to be kinder.' . . . Its self-deprecating tone is as pitch perfect as one would expect from Saunders, and the advice it imparts seems sincere and ultimately more helpful than the usual platitudes."

REVIEW: *Kirkus Rev* v82 no4 p374 F 15 2014

SAUNDERS, ROBERT.ed. Best care at lower cost. See Best care at lower cost

SAVAL, NIKIL. Cubed; a secret history of the workplace; [by] Nikil Saval 368 p. 2014 Doubleday

1. Clerks—History 2. Historical literature 3. Office buildings—History 4. Office layout—History 5. Office management—History 6. Offices—History
ISBN 0385536577; 9780345802804 (pbk.: alk. paper); 9780385536578 (hardcover: alk. paper)
LC 2013-037635

SUMMARY: This book, by Nikil Saval, "reveals the unexplored yet surprising story of the places where most of the world's work—our work—gets done. From 'Bartleby the Scrivener' to 'The Office,' from the steno pool to the open-plan cubicle farm, 'Cubed' is a fascinating, often funny, and sometimes disturbing anatomy of the white-collar world and how it came to be the way it is—and what it might become." (Publisher's note)

REVIEW: *Am Sch* v83 no3 p107-9 Summ 2014 M. G. Lord

REVIEW: *Bookforum* v21 no1 p54-5 Ap/My 2014 JERRY STAHL

REVIEW: *Economist* v411 no8885 p75-6 My 3 2014

REVIEW: *Kirkus Rev* v82 no6 p97 Mr 15 2014

REVIEW: *Libr J* v139 no9 p88 My 15 2014 David Keymer

REVIEW: *Libr J* v139 no3 p24 F 15 2014 Mahnaz Dar Bette-Lee Fox Liz French Margaret Heilbrun Stephanie Klose Annalisa Pesek Henrietta Thornton-Verma Wilda Williams

REVIEW: *Libr J* v139 no14 p64 S 1 2014 Kristen L. Smith

REVIEW: *London Rev Books* v36 no15 p3-7 Jl 31 2014 Jenny Diski

REVIEW: *N Y Rev Books* v61 no11 p44-6 Je 19 2014 Martin Filler

"Cubed: A Secret History of the Workplace." "In 'Cubed,' his impressive but substantially flawed study of the modern office over the past two hundred years, Nikil Saval . . . develops two subthemes with particular clarity and power. The first . . . is the increasing participation of women in the office workplace. . . . The second . . . might be termed the office politics of fear. . . . Regrettably, Saval's grasp of architectural history is not nearly as secure as his command of literary criticism, popular culture, or social analysis. . . . Beyond such misinterpretations are several factual errors."

REVIEW: *N Y Times Book Rev* p11 Je 15 2014 RICHARD SENNETT

REVIEW: *New York Times* v163 no56482 pC23-31 Ap 25 2014 DWIGHT GARNER

REVIEW: *New York Times* v163 no56482 pC23-31 Ap 25 2014 DWIGHT GARNER

REVIEW: *New Yorker* v90 no12 p72-1 My 12 2014

REVIEW: *Publ Wkly* v261 no5 p46-7 F 3 2014

SAVAT, DAVID. Uncoding the digital; technology, subjectivity and action in the control society; [by] David Savat x, 246 p. 2013 Palgrave Macmillan

1. Human behavior 2. POLITICAL SCIENCE—Political Process—General 3. Philosophical literature 4. SOCIAL SCIENCE—Media Studies 5. Social control 6. TECHNOLOGY & ENGINEERING—Electronics—Digital 7. Technology—Philosophy 8. Technology—Social aspects
ISBN 0230278159 (hardback); 9780230278158 (hardback)
LC 2012-022280

SUMMARY: Written by David Savat, "This book challenges how we understand our relationship with our digital machines, and shows how they open up a new capacity for action in the world. . . . A capacity for action that produces a politics of fluids, and finds its expression not only in new forms of social control, but also in a renewed ability for people to engage with the world and each other." (Publisher's note)

REVIEW: *Choice* v51 no1 p99-100 S 2013 P. L. Kantor

"Uncoding the Digital: Technology, Subjectivity, and Action in the Control Society." "The premise of [author David] Savat . . . is that modern politics is dancing on a boundary layer that is the interface between the solid-body politics of the industrial world and the fluid politics of the digital age. Perhaps the one aspect that keeps this title from being an essential work is that it looks at these two political realms, subjects (individuals, control structures, and power) and superjects ('dividuals,' flows, and modulation), as competing political patterns, in which both have roles in the future of politics and political theory. . . . However, the book never really addresses the extent to which modern politics exists as the turbulence at the boundary between them."

SAVELSBERG, JOACHIM J. American memories; atrocities and the law; [by] Joachim J. Savelsberg xxvi, 238 p. 2011 Russell Sage Foundation

1. Atrocities—Law & legislation 2. Atrocities—United States 3. Collective memory—United States 4. Social science literature 5. War crimes—United States
ISBN 9780871547361 (alk. paper); 9781610447492 (ebook)
LC 2011-022368

SUMMARY: In this book, authors Joachim J. Savelsberg and Ryan D. King seek to answer the question "how do Americans remember atrocities committed by Americans and others? . . . Savelsberg and King argue that how a nation collectively remembers atrocities is socially constructed and that institutions play a strong role in shaping these memories. . . . The authors focus primarily on the institution of law." (Contemporary Sociology)

REVIEW: *Am J Sociol* v118 no6 p1718-20 My 2013 Sandra Ristovska Monroe Price

REVIEW: *Contemp Sociol* v42 no2 p167-76 Mr 2013 Joachim J. Savelsberg

REVIEW: *Contemp Sociol* v43 no2 p261-2 Mr 2014 Wenona Rymond-Richmond

"American Memories: Atrocities and the Law". "Joachim Savelsberg and Ryan King ask thought-provoking, challenging questions. . . . 'American Memories' is a well-written, innovative, and well-argued analysis of how the law acts as a mechanism to shape the ways in which the United States remembers its own and others' atrocities. The authors demonstrate that law plays a vital role in contributing to the collective memory of past atrocities. . . . Overall, this book provides an informative and innovative approach to collective memory scholarship and provides a much needed addition to the literature. This book should be of considerable interest to anyone studying collective memory, law, criminology, or cultural sociology."

SAVODNIK, PETER. The Interloper; Lee Harvey Oswald Inside the Soviet Union; [by] Peter Savodnik 288 p. 2013 Perseus Books Group

1. Biographies 2. Kennedy, John F. (John Fitzgerald), 1917-1963—Assassination 3. Oswald, Lee Harvey, 1939-1963 5. Soviet Union—History

ISBN 0465021816; 9780465021819

SUMMARY: This biography of Lee Harvey Oswald "emphasizes the nearly three years Oswald spent in the Soviet Union. . . . A mildly rebellious youth whose mother never provided a stable home, Oswald joined the Marines at age 17. . . .Soon after discharge, he traveled to Moscow where he requested Soviet citizenship. . . . Oswald made friends and enjoyed success with women who considered him exotic, but he became bored and dissatisfied." (Publishers Weekly)

REVIEW: *Booklist* v110 no1 p29 S 1 2013 David Pitt

REVIEW: *Commentary* v136 no3 p60-2 O 2013 MICHAEL MOYNIHAN

REVIEW: *Economist* v409 no8858 p87 O 19 2013

"The Interloper: Lee Harvey Oswald Inside the Soviet Union." "Few episodes in history have been so thoroughly picked over as the murder of John F. Kennedy in 1963. But Peter Savodnik, in his exemplary biography of Lee Harvey Oswald, has unearthed a missing chapter: the real story of the assassin's time in the Soviet Union from 1959 to 1962. . . . His finely drawn picture is of a drifter, a life-long emotional cripple, maimed by an absent father and neurotic mother. . . . A seasoned Russia hand and magazine writer, Mr. Savodnik knows how to bring to life the dull grey world of the Soviet provinces. With a knack for characterisation, he turns his subject into a real person."

REVIEW: *Kirkus Rev* v81 no17 p69 S 1 2013

REVIEW: *N Y Times Book Rev* p34 O 27 2013 Jacob Heilbrunn

"The Interloper: Lee Harvey Oswald Inside the Soviet Union," "JFK, Conservative," and "If Kennedy Lived: The First and Second Terms of President John F. Kennedy: An Alternate History." "In this penetrating study of Oswald's pivotal sojourn in the Soviet Union, [Peter] Savodnik outlines the pitiable delusions and hopes Oswald harbored both in America and abroad. Savodnik, a gifted writer, draws on archival documents and interviews . . . to explain the murderous rage that prompted him to assassinate John F. Kennedy. . . . [Ira] Stoll . . . provides a wonderfully mischievous analysis. . . . In his diverting 'If Kennedy Lived,' [Jeff] Greenfield . . . asks how things might have played out had John F. Kennedy survived."

REVIEW: *Nation* v298 no1/2 p27-31 Ja 6 2014 BEVERLY GAGE

REVIEW: *Natl Rev* v65 no22 p42-6 N 25 2013 JAMES ROSEN

"The Kennedy Half-Century: The Presidency, Assassination, and Lasting Legacy of John F. Kennedy," "End of Days: The Assassination of John F. Kennedy" and "The Interloper: Lee Harvey Oswald Inside the Soviet Union." "James L. Swanson's 'End of Days,' a concise tick-tock account, and Larry J. Sabato's more ambitious 'The Kennedy Half-Century,' a multidisciplinary effort that weighs in at 603 pages . . . bring into sharp relief once again these contradictory traits in mid-century America's proudest son. Perhaps fittingly, the anniversary also brings us only one new book about the president's killer--Peter Savodnik's 'The Interloper'--but it is an important work, for it illuminates, as never before, the complexity of humanity that also graces the most wretched assassin."

REVIEW: *Publ Wkly* v260 no32 p48-9 Ag 12 2013

SAVOY, DANIEL. Venice from the water; architecture and myth in an early modern city; [by] Daniel Savoy 143 p. 2012 Yale University Press

1. Architecture—Italy—Venice—Psychological aspects 2. Canals—Italy 3. Historical literature 4. Water and architecture—Italy—Venice

ISBN 0300167970 (cl : alk. paper); 9780300167979 (cl : alk. paper)

LC 2011-044473

SUMMARY: In this book, "by viewing the architecture and experience of the canals in relation to the production of Venetian civic mythology, the author found that the waterways of Venice and its lagoon were integral areas of the city's premodern urban space, and that their flanking buildings were constructed in an intimate dialogue with the water's visual, spatial, and metaphorical properties." (Publisher's note)

REVIEW: *Choice* v50 no5 p866 Ja 2013 D. Pincus

REVIEW: *TLS* no5756 p28-9 Jl 26 2013 BRUCE BOUCHER

"Venice From the Water: Architecture and Myth in an Early Modern City" and "Tumult and Order: Malcontenta, 1924-1939." "The ceremonial display of Venice is the subject of Daniel Savoy's perceptive new book, which draws together various strands of historical and ecological analysis into an engaging narrative about the perfection of a myth. 'Venice from the Water' is as much a reminder of what has long been known about La Serenissima as it is a multidisciplinary revelation. . . . Palladio's architecture in the Venetian Lagoon also features in Antonio Foscari's 'Tumult and Order. Malcontenta, 1924-1939'."

SAWKINS, ANNEMARIE.ed. Layton's legacy. See Layton's legacy

SAWYER, PETER. The wealth of Anglo-Saxon England; based on the Ford Lectures delivered in the University of Oxford in Hilary Term 1993; [by] Peter Sawyer xi, 155 p. 2013 Oxford University Press

1. Coins, Anglo-Saxon 2. Historical literature 3. Wealth—England—History—To 1500

ISBN 0199253935; 9780199253937

LC 2012-277334

SUMMARY: This book presents an updated version of Peter Sawyer's "1993 Ford Lectures, the foundations for which were laid in a seminal essay of 1965. This contended that on the eve of the Norman Conquest England was an extraordinarily wealthy realm and that this prosperity was due to an abundant currency powered by a flourishing export trade." (Times Literary Supplement)

REVIEW: *TLS* no5748 p23 My 31 2013 ALEX BURGHART

"The Wealth of Anglo-Saxon England." "For nearly fifty years, Professor [Peter] Sawyer has expounded on the riches of late Anglo-Saxon England. His new book is a somewhat belated write-up of his 1993 Ford Lectures, the foundations for which were laid in a seminal essay of 1965. This contended that on the eve of the Norman Conquest England was an extraordinarily wealthy realm and that this prosperity was due to an abundant currency powered by a flourishing export trade. It is a mark of the quality of Sawyer's scholarship that, nearly half a century later, his central argument not only stands, but has been bolstered. . . . Over nearly half a century, Peter Sawyer has led a generation of historians in showing just how much later England owed to its Anglo-Saxon heritage."

SAX, BORIA. Imaginary Animals; The Monstrous, The Wondrous and The Human; [by] Boria Sax 272 p. 2013 University of California Press

1. Folklore 2. Mythical animals 3. Mythical animals in art 4. Mythical animals in literature 5. Reference books

ISBN 1780231733; 9781780231730

SUMMARY: "This illustrated compendium" of imaginary animals "by independent scholar [Boria] Sax scrutinizes artistic and literary models, ranging from Chauvet cave art from 36,000 BCE to political cartoons, graphic Japanese novels, and postmodern robotics. Conclusions about the nature and purpose of fantasy animals draw on scripture, anthropology, medicine, myth, and psychology." (Choice: Current Reviews for Academic Libraries)

REVIEW: *Choice* v51 no8 p1379 Ap 2014 M. E. Snodgrass

"Imaginary Animals: The Monstrous, the Wondrous and the Human". "A thought-provoking analysis of bestial creations, this illustrated compendium by independent scholar [Boria] Sax scrutinizes artistic and literary models. . . . Sax is conversant with essential viewpoints of Dante, Lewis Carroll, Franz Kafka, Mircea Eliade, Paracelsus, Ando Hiroshige, Brendan, Homer, Dr. Seuss, Confucius, Levi-Strauss, and poster artist Max Ernst. Missing from the overview is discussion of Jewish concepts of the golem and dybbuk, Hopi kachinas, and Gothic beasts from India, Cambodia, Central America, and Pacific peoples. . . . An intriguing, highly readable reference work at a low price. Sax's multifaceted work covers a host of reference needs."

SAXONBERG, STEVEN. Transitions and non-transitions from communism; regime survival in China, Cuba, North Korea and Vietnam; [by] Steven Saxonberg 350 p. 2012 Cambridge University Press

1. China—Politics & government 2. Communism—Case studies 3. POLITICAL SCIENCE—General 4. Political science literature 5. Post-communism—Case studies

ISBN 9781107023888

LC 2012-018846

SUMMARY: In this "study of fourteen countries, Steven Saxonberg explores the reasons for the survival of some communist regimes while others fell. He also shows why the process of collapse differed among communist-led regimes in Europe, Africa, and Latin America. Based on the analysis of the different processes of collapse that has already taken place," he "discusses the future prospects for the survival of the regimes in China, Cuba, North Korea, and Vietnam." (Publisher's note)

REVIEW: *Choice* v51 no6 p1066-7 F 2014 M. D. Rothwell

"Transitions and Non-Transitions From Communism: Regime Survival in China, Cuba, North Korea, and Vietnam." "This interesting hook examines a range of factors that lead to different types of regime collapse and makes the case that these regimes tend to fall when they initiate change, or when faced with revolt. While regional specialists will doubtless at times feel that [Steven] Saxonberg has overreached, and that regime-type generalizations tend to erase the importance of particular histories and cultures, there is much of interest here, and scholars interested in exploring the similarities among regimes inspired in part by Marxism across the globe will benefit from reading this book. . . . Recommended."

SAYER, DEREK. Prague, capital of the twentieth century; a surrealist history; [by] Derek Sayer 656 p. 2013 Princeton University Press

1. Art literature 2. Czech art—20th century 3. Czechoslovakia—Intellectual life 4. Historical literature 5. Surrealism—Czech Republic—Prague

ISBN 0691043809; 9780691043807 (hardcover : alk. paper)

LC 2012-023215

SUMMARY: In this book, Derek Sayer "argues that 20th-century Prague can lay claim to witnessing the birth of the modern and postmodern world. Not only was Prague host or home to such pioneers of surrealism as André Breton and Franz Kafka, but its very history, encompassing so many transformations and conjunctions, gives it a kind of surreality itself, as the author seeks to show." (Library Journal)

REVIEW: *Choice* v51 no2 p330 O 2013 P. W. Knoll

REVIEW: *Libr J* v138 no11 p103 Je 15 2013 Kelsey Berry Philpot

REVIEW: *Publ Wkly* v260 no4 p160 Ja 28 2013

REVIEW: *TLS* no5780 p3-5 Ja 10 2014 MARCI SHORE

"Prague, Capital of the Twentieth Century: A Surrealist History" and "Art and Life in Modernist Prague: Karel Čapek and His Generation, 1911-1938." "Their subjectivist turn inwards, Thomas Ort emphasizes in 'Art and Life in Modernist Prague,' was a free choice: it was not driven by marginality. . . . Thomas Ort is a pleasure to read for other reasons: his writing is lucid and unpretentious. These two books about Czech modernism--about what Paris meant for Prague--are alter egos of sorts: Ort's earnestness contrasts with ['Prague, Capital of the Twentieth Century' author Derek] Sayer's sarcasm. Ort's chapters are chronological; Sayer's temporality is slippery."

SAYER, PHILIP.il. Milestones of Science and Technology. See Milestones of Science and Technology

SAYERS, VALERIE. The powers; a novel; [by] Valerie Sayers ix, 297 p. 2013 Northwestern University Press

1. American historical fiction 2. Baseball players—United States—Fiction 3. Baseball stories—United States 4. World War, 1939-1945—United States—Fiction

ISBN 0810152290 (hardcover); 9780810152298 (hardcover)

LC 2012-036262

SUMMARY: This novel, by Valerie Sayers, is set in "1941 . . . , Joe DiMaggio's record-breaking hitting streak enlivens the summer, and winter begins with the shock and horror of the Japanese attack on Pearl Harbor. . . . Joltin' Joe, possessing a sweet swing and range in center, also has another gift: he can see the future. And he sees dark times ahead. . . . At once magical and familiar, [the novel] is a story of witness and moral responsibility." (Publisher's note)

REVIEW: *America* v209 no8 p49-51 S 30 2013 DENNIS VELLUCCI

"The Powers." "Though icons like DiMaggio (pictured on the novel's cover) and Dorothy Day and Walker Evans appear prominently in [author Valerie] Sayers's compelling novel, 'The Powers' is at heart a coming-of-age story focusing on the idealistic Joe, his more practical friend, Bernhard Keller and, more centrally, on his sometime love interest Agnes O'Leary as they negotiate the challenges of fraught family histories and uncertain futures. . . . stylistic missteps are minor and infrequent. Sayers creates a cast of memorable characters, both real and imagined, and tells their stories with grace, understanding and affection."

REVIEW: *Booklist* v109 no16 p34 Ap 15 2013 Carol Gladstein

REVIEW: *Publ Wkly* v260 no8 p141 F 25 2013

SAYLES, ELIZABETH.il. Anne Frank's chestnut tree. See Kohuth, J.

SAYRE, APRIL PULLEY. Eat like a bear; 32 p. 2013 Henry Holt and Company

1. Bears—Fiction 2. Grizzly bear—Fiction 3. Grizzly bear—Juvenile fiction 4. JUVENILE NONFICTION—Animals—Mammals 5. JUVENILE NONFICTION—Science & Nature—Biology 6. JUVENILE NONFICTION—Science & Nature—Environmental Conservation & Protection 7. Picture books for children

ISBN 0805090398; 9780805090390 (hardback)

LC 2013-015686

SUMMARY: This children's picture book by April Pulley, a "grizzled, lumbering bear wakes up in the springtime. What is there to eat? . . . 'With long, strong claws, / dig in. Dig down. / Paw and claw and pull. / Find . . . // . . . ants! / Chew them, / sour and squirming. / Lick your lips.' As the months go by, bears eat many different types of food." (Kirkus Reviews)

REVIEW: *Booklist* v110 no5 p83-4 N 1 2013 Thom Barthelmess

"Eat Like a Bear." "[April Pulley] Sayre tells the simple tale in colorful free verse in careful patterns, rich with vocabulary. . . . [Steve] Jenkins fixes the action in the Rocky Mountains with his trademark cut- and torn-paper collage. Using a variety of materials, including handmade Mexican bark paper for the bears, he achieves a remarkable variety of line and texture, as crisp leaves and flowers contrast with fuzzy fur. This contrast is mirrored in the juxtaposition of expressive narration and careful pictorial depiction."

REVIEW: *Bull Cent Child Books* v67 no3 p178-9 N 2013 D. S.

"Eat Like a Bear." "'Can you eat like a bear?' this early nature study book asks. . . . The lilting text hovers between poetry and prose, avoiding metrically structured lines but drawing on gentle internal and end rhymes and repetition to provide shape and rhythm. . . . [Illustrator Steve] Jenkins' paper-collage art is superlative here; compositions are creative, dramatic, and even comical (a page turn after the elk chase reveals the disappointed bear peering out at the audience), and the textured blend of bristle and fur is aptly conveyed (by, according to the note, a Mexican bark paper)."

REVIEW: *Horn Book Magazine* v89 no6 p120 N/D 2013 DANIELLE J. FORD

REVIEW: *Kirkus Rev* v81 no17 p115 S 1 2013

REVIEW: *Publ Wkly* p56 Children's starred review annual 2013

REVIEW: *Publ Wkly* v260 no33 p70 Ag 19 2013

REVIEW: *SLJ* v59 no10 p1 O 2013 Sara-Jo Lupo Sites

SCADDEN, ROSEMARY. No Job for a Little Girl; [by] Rosemary Scadden 179 p. 2013 Gomer Press

1. Historical literature 2. Household employees—Great Britain 3. Household employees—History—20th century 4. Wales—History 5. Women—Employment—Great Britain

ISBN 1848517009; 9781848517004

SUMMARY: This book on domestic service in Great Britain, by Rosemary Scadden, "deals with young girls from South Wales who 'went out' during the twenty-five-year period between the two world wars. Her account is based on extended interviews with over twenty elderly women from the Cardiff area who have sharp memories of tiieir lives as housemaids, scullerymaids, parlourmaids and 'tweenies,' mostly in London households." (Times Literary Supplement)

REVIEW: *TLS* no5761 p22 Ag 30 2013 KATHRYN HUGHES

"No Job for a Little Girl: Voices From Domestic Service." "Each of the book's eleven chapters deals with different aspects of the servant experience, from finding a job to negotiating a salary, working conditions to time off. In general, [Rosemary] Scadden's interviewees are remarkably blithe in their recollections of what sounds to modem ears like a very hard life. . . . Particularly illuminating is the way that Scadden draws out the tensions of being Welsh in an English household. . . . Rosemary Scadden's careful selection and unobtrusive editing of her material allows for a nuanced approach that is not afraid to include difficult truths but steers clear of anything that might smack of 'servant gothic'."

SCAGLION, RICHARD.ed. Polynesian outliers. See

Polynesian outliers

SCALZI, JOHN. Redshirts; [by] John Scalzi 317 p. 2012 Tor

1. Human-alien encounters—Fiction 2. Interplanetary voyages—Fiction 3. Science fiction 4. Space ships—Fiction 5. Space warfare—Fiction
ISBN 0765316994 (hbk.); 1429963603 (ebk.); 9780765316998 (hbk.); 9781429963602 (ebk.)
LC 2012-009383

SUMMARY: This science fiction novel by John Scalzi follows "Ensign Andrew Dahl [as he] has just been assigned to the Universal Union Capital Ship Intrepid, flagship of the Universal Union since the year 2456. . . . Life couldn't be better . . . until Andrew begins to pick up on the fact that (1) every Away Mission involves some kind of lethal confrontation with alien forces, (2) the ship's captain, its chief science officer, and the handsome Lieutenant Kerensky always survive these confrontations, and (3) at least one low-ranked crew member is, sadly, always killed." (Publisher's note)

REVIEW: *Booklist* v108 no18 p31 My 15 2012 David Pitt

"Redshirts." "[T]his new novel is a real joy to read. Ensign Andrew Dahl, assigned to the spaceship 'Intrepid,' begins to notice that things are a bit weird. . . . As he tries to figure out what the heck is going on around him, Andy discovers a truth so staggering that he has no choice but to believe it. Although the novel does have some thematic similarities to the movie 'Galaxy Quest' (not to mention 'Visit to a Weird Planet,' a 'Star Trek'-fan short story in which key members of the 'Enterprise' crew are transported to the Hollywood set of the show), [John] Scalzi takes the reality-versus-fiction idea in a new and decidedly mind-bending direction. It's hard to imagine a reader who wouldn't enjoy this one."

REVIEW: *Christ Century* v129 no25 p23 D 12 2012

REVIEW: *Kirkus Rev* v80 no10 p1025-6 My 15 2012

REVIEW: *Libr J* v137 no9 p64 My 15 2012 Dan Forrest

REVIEW: *Publ Wkly* v259 no14 p40 Ap 2 2012

SCANLON, LIZ GARTON. The Good-Pie Party; 32 p. 2014 Arthur A. Levine Books, An Imprint of Scholastic Inc.

1. Baking—Fiction 2. Children's stories 3. Friendship—Fiction 4. Moving, Household—Fiction 5. Parties—Fiction 6. Pies—Fiction
ISBN 0545448700; 9780545448703 (hardcover: alk. paper)
LC 2013-006975

SUMMARY: In this children's book, by Liz Garton Scanlon, "Posy, Megan, and Mae have always been the best of friends—but now Posy has to move away. Only their favorite activity can comfort the girls: baking pie! And when they realize they can host a good-pie party instead of a good-bye party, the sad situation becomes a sweet gathering for their entire community." (Publisher's note)

REVIEW: *Booklist* v110 no14 p81 Mr 15 2014 Carolyn Phelan

REVIEW: *Kirkus Rev* v82 no2 p166 Ja 15 2014

"The Good-Pie Party". "[Liz Garton Scanlon] Scanlon's gentle, child's-eye view of a common challenge hits the right notes—the move will happen, but memories link people forever. [Kady MacDonald] Denton's gentle, muted watercolors get at the girls' emotions with angry scowls and somber faces and extend the spare text. The furnished house transforms into empty rooms with tan boxes and bare walls, letting readers know the inevitability of the move. The final spreads, showing the pie-shaped moon, is a reminder that these friends will always share these special memories. A must for every child who has to move away and for teachers and parents who want to help children through these times."

REVIEW: *N Y Times Book Rev* p14 Jl 13 2014 LEONARD S. MARCUS

REVIEW: *New York Times* v163 no56560 p14 Jl 12 2014 LEONARD S. MARCUS

REVIEW: *Publ Wkly* v261 no7 p98 F 17 2014

REVIEW: *SLJ* v60 no4 p135 Ap 2014 Whitney LeBlanc

SCARBOROUGH, JOE, 1963-. The right path; from Ike to Reagan, how Republicans once mastered politics— and can again; [by] Joe Scarborough xxviii, 194 p. 2013 Random House Inc

1. Political science literature 2. Presidents—United States—History
ISBN 0812996143; 9780812996142 (hardback)
LC 2013-029788

SUMMARY: In this book on the U.S. Republican Party, Joe Scarborough argues that "the GOP went astray in its steady march toward ideological purity in the post-[Ronald] Reagan years, forsaking the big-tent approach that [Dwight] Eisenhower espoused for a mean-spirited politics of 'grievance and resentment.' In the past, writes the author, purity over practicality led to the near-damnation of the GOP to 'complete political irrelevance'." (Kirkus Reviews)

REVIEW: *Kirkus Rev* v81 no24 p305 D 15 2013

REVIEW: *N Y Rev Books* v61 no1 p14-5 Ja 9 2014 Garry Wills

"The Right Path: From Ike to Reagan, How Republicans Once Mastered Politics—and Can Again". "The current Thing to Say about Republicans is that they are caught in a civil war—the Tea Party against the Establishment, 'wacko birds' against 'the adults,' fringe against mainstream. One of the most clamorous bearers of this message, on his TV show and in various other media, is Joe Scarborough. . . . Over and over, a closer look shows how skewed is this reading of political history. . . . Scarborough, born into a Thurmondized South, literally cannot see race in any part of his home region's history. . . . Scarborough's silly picture of American politics leaves out most of the things that matter—including (but not restricted to) race, religion, and money."

REVIEW: *N Y Times Book Rev* p30 Ja 26 2014 Noah Millman

SCARRY, ELAINE. Thermonuclear monarchy; choosing between democracy and doom; [by] Elaine Scarry 592 p. 2014 W W Norton & Co Inc

1. Civil society—United States 2. Constitutional law—United States 3. Democracy—United States 4. Nuclear disarmament—United States 5. Nuclear weapons—Government policy—United States 6. Nuclear weapons—Moral and ethical aspects—United States 7. Nuclear weapons—Political aspects—United States 8. Political science literature
ISBN 0393080080; 9780393080087 (hardcover)
LC 2013-037713

SUMMARY: In this book, "social theorist Elaine Scarry

demonstrates that the power of one leader to obliterate millions of people with a nuclear weapon—a possibility that remains very real even in the wake of the Cold War—deeply violates our constitutional rights, undermines the social contract, and is fundamentally at odds with the deliberative principles of democracy. . . . 'Thermonuclear Monarchy' identifies the tools that will enable us to eliminate nuclear weapons." (Publisher's note)

REVIEW: *Choice* v52 no2 p345 O 2014 J. D. Moon

REVIEW: *Commonweal* v141 no11 p29-30 Je 13 2014 Gregg Herken

REVIEW: *Kirkus Rev* v82 no2 p32 Ja 15 2014

"Thermonuclear Monarchy: Choosing Between Democracy and Doom". "[Elaine] Scarry's argument is intriguing, but its presentation is flawed. Her philosophical analyses of social contract, consent and emergencies are learned and thorough but far more extensive than necessary to support her thesis. The author's arguments about American constitutional law, though creative, suffer from superficial analysis and factual misperceptions. . . . An important discussion that deserves a more disciplined presentation."

REVIEW: *N Y Times Book Rev* p17 Mr 23 2014 RICHARD RHODES

"Thermonuclear Monarchy: Choosing Between Democracy and Doom." "'Thermonuclear Monarchy' is only the latest in a long series of efforts to think through the question of how to eliminate these terrible and useless weapons. . . . There are useful insights in 'Thermonuclear Monarchy' as well, but over all it fails to persuade. It explores the baleful political consequences of limiting the control of nuclear weapons to a select few, and the authority to launch them to even fewer—in the case of the United States, to the president alone in what amounts to his monarchical power. . . . [author Elaine] Scarry constructs a legally interesting but highly abstract argument about the consent of the governed."

SCARSBROOK, RICHARD. Nothing Man and the Purple Zero; [by] Richard Scarsbrook 240 p. 2013 Cormorant Books

1. Antique & classic cars 2. High school students—Fiction 3. School bullying 4. Superheroes 5. Young adult fiction

ISBN 1770863117; 9781770863118

SUMMARY: In this young adult novel by Richard Scarsbrook, "Marty Apostrophes and Bill Brown are from opposite sides of the tracks, but their friendship allows them to overcome bullies and scrape through classes. . . . Bill's obsession with the classic cars owned by Marty's family leads to a joyride in a 1937 Cord 812 Sportsman, and the accidental foiling of a robbery . . . which is caught on video by their friend, aspiring teen reporter Elizabeth Murphy." (Publisher's note)

REVIEW: *Quill Quire* v79 no7 p37 S 2013 Nathan Whitlock

"Nothing Man and the Purple Zero." "'Nothing Man and the Purple Zero,' by Toronto author Richard Scarsbrook, features the brief career of two accidental super-dudes who stumble their way through a novel that, frankly, does more than its share of stumbling on its own. . . . Scarsbrook can't seem to decide if he's writing a realistic story about the problems of modern teens . . . or a goofy . . . adventure farce for younger readers. . . . The novel often feels a few decades out of date. . . Though the epilogue ties up every loose thread, Scarsbrook does leave the door open to a possible sequel. What's really needed here is a reboot."

SCHACHNER, JUDY. Bits and pieces; [by] Judy Schachner 32 p. 2013 Dial Books for Young Readers, an imprint of Penguin Group (USA) Inc.

1. Cats—Fiction 2. Human-animal relationships 3. Lost and found possessions—Fiction 4. Pets—Juvenile literature 5. Picture books for children

ISBN 0803737882; 9780803737884 (hardcover)

LC 2012-042083

SUMMARY: This children's picture book focuses on Tink the cat, who "is the kitten that was raised by Simon, the elderly Siamese cat in [Judy Schachner's previous book 'The Grannyman']. The narrator speculates that perhaps this unorthodox upbringing is the source of Tink's quirky habits. . . . Schachner describes how Tink digs in the plants, sits on the newspaper, jumps into the middle of board games, stalks the bathtub and generally makes a beloved pest of himself." (Kirkus Reviews)

REVIEW: *Booklist* v110 no4 p54-5 O 15 2013 Lally Gepson

"Bits and Pieces." "[Judy] Schachner uses charcoal pencil, pan pencil, pastels, watercolor, and cut paper to glorify the antics of this beloved cat in full-bleed spreads and panels. . . . In a vibrant double-page spread, Tink strolls into the night, viewing the moon, the owls, and other nighttime creatures, and then realizes he is lost. All ends well with reassuring smiles between the two cats as they rest on the blue polka-dotted armchair. Fans of Schachner's Skippyjon Jones series should lap this one up."

REVIEW: *Bull Cent Child Books* v67 no4 p237 D 2013 J. H.

REVIEW: *Kirkus Rev* v81 no18 p209 S 15 2013

REVIEW: *Publ Wkly* v260 no35 p57 S 2 2013

REVIEW: *SLJ* v59 no9 p130 S 2013 Jenna Boles

SCHACHNER, JUDY.il. Bits and pieces. See Schachner, J.

SCHACTER, RAFAEL.ed. The World Atlas of street art and graffiti. See The World Atlas of street art and graffiti

SCHAEFER, LOLA M., 1950-. Lifetime the amazing numbers in animal lives; the amazing numbers in animal lives; 40 p. 2013 Chronicle Books Llc

1. Animals—Pictorial works—Juvenile literature 2. Children's nonfiction 3. Developmental biology—Juvenile literature 4. Life expectancy—Juvenile literature 5. Real numbers

ISBN 1452107149; 9781452107141 (alk. paper)

LC 2012-039328

SUMMARY: This book, by Lola M. Schaefer and illustrated by Christopher Silas Neal, "collects animal information not available anywhere else and shows all 30 roosting holes, all 200 spots, and, yes!, all 1,000 baby seahorses in eye-catching illustrations. A book about picturing numbers and considering the endlessly fascinating lives all around us, 'Lifetime' is [designed] to delight young nature lovers." (Publisher's note)

REVIEW: *Booklist* v110 no1 p99 S 1 2013 J. B. Petty

REVIEW: *Horn Book Magazine* v90 no1 p118-9 Ja/F 2014 DANIELLE J. FORD

"Lifetime: The Amazing Numbers in Animal Lives." "The concepts of counting and quantity are cleverly examined in the context of animal lives. . . . Bold, beautifully composed, and somewhat retro . . . [Christopher Silas] Neal's block print–like mixed-media illustrations of the eleven animals featured contain the actual number of items on each double-page spread--industrious readers can count every one of the 550 sharply defined alligator eggs or the nine hundred flowers a swallowtail visits. Significant supplemental information can be found after the main text, including scientific names and additional numerical facts about each animal, a discussion of the concept of average, and word problems to think about the mathematics behind calculating some of these numbers."

REVIEW: *Kirkus Rev* v81 no15 p249 Ag 1 2013

REVIEW: *Publ Wkly* p57 Children's starred review annual 2013

REVIEW: *Publ Wkly* v260 no38 p78 S 23 2013

REVIEW: *SLJ* v59 no10 p1 O 2013 Carol S. Surges

SCHAEFER, LOLA M., 1950-. Swamp chomp; 32 p. 2014 Holiday House

1. Alligators—Juvenile literature 2. Children's nonfiction 3. Food chains (Ecology)—Fiction 4. Swamp animals—Fiction 5. Swamps—Fiction

ISBN 9780823424078 (hardcover)

LC 2011-046561

SUMMARY: "The sounds of the swamp come alive in this look at the creatures that live and feed there. At first, 'water ripples.' Creatures are introduced with an active verb following: 'Crayfish crawl. Carry,' 'Turtles bob. Dig.' Clearly, the creatures are all deftly aware of their surroundings as the center spread reveals a sudden cacophony of sound and each creature begins to feed." (School Library Journal)

REVIEW: *Booklist* v110 no16 p55 Ap 15 2014 Carolyn Phelan

REVIEW: *Kirkus Rev* v82 no3 p284 F 1 2014

"Swamp Chomp". " The names of several animals that might inhabit a cypress swamp, along with a plethora of verbs, adorn pages full of brightly colored animals, plants and water. . . . There is a nice interruption of rhythm when the alligators emerge on land with a sudden 'Alligators CHOMP!' It is unclear until the endnote that the text and illustrations are attempting to show a cypress swamp food chain in action. The illustrations invite children to take their time finding animals and figuring out their activities; the text would sparkle equally if the author had played more with rhyme, rhythm and alliteration."

REVIEW: *SLJ* v60 no4 p135 Ap 2014 Carol Connor

SCHAFFERT, TIMOTHY. The swan gondola; [by] Timothy Schaffert 464 p. 2014 Riverhead Books

1. Circus performers—Fiction 2. FICTION—Historical 3. FICTION—Literary 4. Love stories

ISBN 9781594486098 (hardback)

LC 2013-030317

SUMMARY: This book follows Ferret Skerritt, "a one-time petty thief who's getting by as a ventriloquist at a vaudeville theater, where he meets (and promptly falls for) Cecily, an actress with an obscure history. . . . The couple perform on the midway daily . . . before meeting in the swan-shaped gondola of the title. Ferrett wants to get serious with Cecily, who has an infant daughter (the father is absent), but enter William Wakefield, a wealthy fair organizer who wants Cecily for himself." (Kirkus Reviews)

REVIEW: *Booklist* v110 no9/10 p56 Ja 1 2014 Sarah Johnson

REVIEW: *Kirkus Rev* v81 no24 p191 D 15 2013

"The Swan Gondola". "[An] entertaining if light novel. . . . [Timothy] Schaffert captures the grandeur and strangeness of the fair pavilions, as well as the political ferment of the time. (President William McKinley, in the thick of the Spanish-American War, has a cameo.) Despite the novel's widescreen setting, though, the central love story is thin and upended so quickly the reader is challenged to feel invested in Ferrett's and Cecily's fates. And though Schaffert uses fakery as an intriguing theme (ventriloquists, automatons, Spanish-American War propaganda), the closing chapters' would-be ghost story has too much stage makeup to achieve its intended Oz-like effect. A rambunctious and well-researched but ungainly historical romance."

REVIEW: *Libr J* v138 no14 p84 S 1 2013

REVIEW: *Publ Wkly* v260 no49 p58 D 2 2013

SCHALET, AMY T. Not under my roof; parents, teens, and the culture of sex; [by] Amy T. Schalet x, 298 p. 2011 University of Chicago Press

1. Parent and teenager—Netherlands 2. Parent and teenager—United States 3. Sociology literature 4. Teenagers—Sexual behavior—Netherlands 5. Teenagers—Sexual behavior—United States

ISBN 0226736180 (alk. paper); 0226736199 (pbk.: alk. paper); 9780226736181 (alk. paper); 9780226736198 (pbk.: alk. paper)

LC 2011-003357

SUMMARY: This book by Amy T. Chalet "consists of several interviews with Dutch and American parents and their teenage children about how they manage and negotiate the challenges of teenagers becoming sexually active. . . . The country-level differences extend to parenting styles and Schalet spends much of the book explaining how they are manifested and the reasons for the differences." (Contemporary Sociology)

REVIEW: *Contemp Sociol* v43 no1 p114-5 Ja 2014 Amy Adamczyk

"Not Under My Roof: Parents, Teens, and the Culture of Sex". "A fascinating, although anticipated, contrast between American and Dutch parents. . . . While 'Not Under My Roof' draws some excellent parallels between larger cultural and economic forces and differences in American and Dutch childrearing styles, at times [Amy T.] Schalet tries to make connections that her data are unable to support and misses out on at least one key cultural difference. . . . 'Not Under My Roof' does a great job of bringing into focus the clear contrasts between Dutch and American childrearing styles. This book is not just for sociologists and other academics. The writing is easily accessible and the interviews make it interesting and fun to read."

SCHAMA, SIMON, 1945-. The story of the Jews; finding the words: 1000 BC-1492 AD; [by] Simon Schama 512 p. 2014 HarperCollins

1. Historical literature 2. Jewish history 3. Jewish iden-

tity 4. Jews—Civilization 5. Jews—Spain—History—Expulsion, 1492
ISBN 0060539186; 9780060539184

SUMMARY: This book, by Simon Schama, "details the story of the Jewish experience, tracing it across three millennia, from their beginnings as an ancient tribal people to the opening of the New World in 1492. . . . It takes you to . . . a Jewish kingdom in the mountains of southern Arabia; a Syrian synagogue glowing with . . . wall paintings; [and] the palm groves of the Jewish dead in the Roman catacombs." (Publisher's note)

REVIEW: *Booklist* v110 no14 p34 Mr 15 2014 Jay Freeman

"The Story of the Jews: Finding the Words, 1000 BC-1492 AD". "This is the first of a planned two-volume work. . . . [Simon] Schama has written an unconventional but masterful and deeply felt history of his people, which seamlessly integrates themes of art, religion, and ethnicity as he illustrates how Jews both influenced and were influenced by the other people they lived among for more than 1,500 years. While Schama follows a roughly chronological approach, this is not a strictly narrative account. Rather, he focuses on particular topics to define the essence of a particular period, and he does so by examining literary and archaeological remnants that provide a human and often deeply moving touch. . . . This beautifully written chronicle is a tie-In to an upcoming PBS series."

REVIEW: *Choice* v52 no1 p134 St 2014 R. M. Seltzer

REVIEW: *Kirkus Rev* v82 no3 p210 F 1 2014

"The Story of the Jews: Finding the Words 1000 BC-1492". " Witty, nimble and completely in his element, [Simon] Schama, . . . in a book tie-in to a PBS and BBC series, fashions a long-planned 'labor of love' that nicely dovetails the biblical account with the archaeological record. Indeed, as this densely written effort accompanies the visual story, the author fixes on a tangible element (such as papyrus, shard or document) in each chapter as a point of departure in advancing the early history of the Jews. . . . Schama is relentless in faulting the break between Christianity and Judaism as the spur to the subsequent phobia against the 'pariah tribe.' A multifaceted story artfully woven by an expert historian."

REVIEW: *Libr J* v139 no5 p124 Mr 15 2014 Crystal Goldman

REVIEW: *N Y Rev Books* v51 no7 p41-3 Ap 24 2014 G. W. Bowersock

REVIEW: *N Y Times Book Rev* p16-7 Mr 30 2014 JUDITH SHULEVITZ

REVIEW: *N Y Times Book Rev* p32 Ap 6 2014 GREGORY COWLES

REVIEW: *New Statesman* v142 no5173 p40-1 S 6 2013 David Cesarani

REVIEW: *New York Times* v163 no56437 pC1-6 Mr 11 2014 DWIGHT GARNER

REVIEW: *Publ Wkly* v261 no2 p62 Ja 13 2014

SCHAUER, THOMAS.il. Daniel. See Boulud, D.

SCHEFFLER, AXEL. Flip flap farm; 26 p. 2014 Candlewick Press

1. Animals—Juvenile fiction 2. Domestic animals 3. Farms—Juvenile literature 4. Picture books for children 5. Toy & movable books
ISBN 0763670677; 9780763670672
LC 2013-943076

SUMMARY: In this flip book, by Axel Scheffler, readers can mix and match pages to create different animals. "What do you get when you cross a goat with a turkey? Why, a gurkey, of course! What about a pig with a sheep? Well, that would be a peep, naturally!" The book features "split pages and spiral binding . . . [and] 121 possible combinations." (Publisher's note)

REVIEW: *Kirkus Rev* v82 no2 p228 Ja 15 2014

"Flip Flap Farm". "[Axel] Scheffler illustrates a series of bouncy two-verse poems about animals, with verses on the left-hand page and pictures on the right. . . . . There are 11 individual animals in all, bringing the number of possible combinations to well over 100. And each crazy creature has a different name. That oinker with udders is called a pow. There's also a cabbit (cow/rabbit), a moat (mouse/goat) and a hirrel (horse/squirrel). And on and on and on. Bold colors, phonetically zippy rhymes, sturdy book construction and countless creature combinations are a winning formula for beginning readers and storytimers."

SCHEFFLER, AXEL.il. Superworm. See Donaldson, J.

SCHEFFLER, SAMUEL. Death and the afterlife; 224 p. 2013 Oxford University Press

1. Egoism 2. Future, The—Moral & ethical aspects 3. Life 4. Motivation (Psychology) 5. Philosophical literature 6. Values
ISBN 9780199982509 (alk. paper)
LC 2013-001134

SUMMARY: "In 'Death and the Afterlife,' philosopher Samuel Scheffler poses this thought experiment in order to show that the continued life of the human race after our deaths--the 'afterlife' of the title--matters to us to an astonishing and previously neglected degree. Indeed, Scheffler shows that, in certain important respects, the future existence of people who are as yet unborn matters more to us than our own continued existence and the continued existence of those we love." (Publisher's note)

REVIEW: *Choice* v51 no9 p1608 My 2014 D. R. Boscaljon

REVIEW: *N Y Rev Books* v61 no1 p26-8 Ja 9 2014 Thomas Nagel

REVIEW: *Publ Wkly* v260 no32 p50 Ag 12 2013

REVIEW: *TLS* no5786 p21 F 21 2014 DAVID OWNES

"Death and the Afterlife." "Samuel Scheffler draws our attention to a quite different afterlife, one which consists in the fact that the human race is likely to persist long after you and I are dead. That collective afterlife is, Scheffler thinks, at least as significant as the individual afterlife that has received so much attention. . . . 'Death and the Afterlife' comprises three chapters written by Scheffler, followed by incisive comments from four eminent philosophers, rounded off with a short reply from the author. . . . 'Death and the Afterlife' is a model of how to make difficult philosophy intelligible to thinking people. Perhaps it will even improve them."

SCHELL, ORVILLE. Wealth and power; [by] Orville

Schell 496 p. 2013 Random House Inc
1. Historical literature
ISBN 0679643478; 9780679643470
LC 2013-002596

SUMMARY: In this book, the authors "track the intellectual and political pursuit of fuqiang, or wealth and power, by Chinese thinkers and leaders in response to the humiliations heaped upon their country by Western powers, beginning with the Opium Wars of the mid-19th century. The work comprises chronologically ordered minibiographies, . . . with long sections devoted to Mao Zedong and Deng Xiaoping." (Publishers Weekly)

REVIEW: *Booklist* v109 no19/20 p18 Je 1 2013 Brendan Driscoll

REVIEW: *Kirkus Rev* v81 no10 p77 My 15 2013

REVIEW: *Libr J* v138 no11 p104 Je 15 2013 Joshua Wallace

REVIEW: *N Y Rev Books* v60 no18 p59-61 N 21 2013 Ian Johnson

"Wealth and Power: China's Long March to the 21st Century," "Stumbling Giant: The Threats to China's Future," and "The China Choice: Why America Should Share Power." "[Orville] Schell and [John] Delury describe a series of eleven thinkers, activists, and leaders in their stylishly written, provocative book. . . . Identifying [wealth and power]--correctly, I think--as the dominant discourse over the past nearly two hundred years allows the authors to make several important points. . . . [Timothy] Beardson's thesis is clear and succinct. . . . Perhaps the least interesting part of the book is chapter on serious issues that need fixing, but that are not unfixable. . . . Hugh White . . . writes . . . that the United States must find a way to coexist with China. In my view, however. White constructs something of a straw man by arguing that Barack Obama's 'pivot' to Asia means the United States has chosen to confront China."

REVIEW: *Publ Wkly* v260 no21 p48 My 27 2013

SCHENCK, DWAIN. Reset; how to beat the job loss blues and get ready for your next act; [by] Dwain Schenck xxvii, 242 p. 2014 Da Capo Lifelong, A Member of the Perseus Books Group
1. Job hunting 2. Memoirs 3. Unemployed—Psychology 4. Unemployment—Psychological aspects 5. Vocational guidance
ISBN 9780738216959 (pbk.)
LC 2013-029744

SUMMARY: This book is a memoir and self-help guide by Dwain Schenk, "a successful journalist and communications professional who joins the ranks of the unemployed during the most dismal job market in modern history." It details how "his initial reactions of denial and depression sabotage his morale and motivation. Then, with the assistance of friends, wisdom from experts, and good old-fashioned creativity and tenacity, Schenck turns his attitude around." (Publisher's note)

REVIEW: *New York Times* v163 no56365 p7 D 29 2013 LIESL SCHILLINGER

"Mastering the Art of Quitting: Why It Matters in Life, Love, and Work," "Reset: How to Beat the Job-Loss Blues and Get Ready For Your Next Act," and "Fail Fast, Fail Often: How Losing Can Help You Win". "Shrewd, detailed, and exhortatory, ['Mastering the Art of Quitting'] breaks down obstacles to quitting, illustrated by exemplary stories of men and women who had the courage to gracefully quit jobs that did not satisfy them. . . . 'Reset' . . . is [Dwain Schenk's] blow-by-blow memoir of his struggle to restore his fortunes. . . . 'Fail Fast, Fail Often' . . . argues for an even more proactive approach to self-invention, encouraging those who are contemplating a new beginning to kick-start their dreams."

SCHEUNEMANN, PAM. Trash to treasure; a kid's upcycling guide to crafts : fun, easy projects with paper, plastic, glass & ceramics, fabric, metal, and odds & ends; [by] Pam Scheunemann 144 p. 2013 Scarletta Junior Readers
1. CRAFTS & HOBBIES—Crafts for Children 2. Children's nonfiction 3. Handicraft—Juvenile literature 4. JUVENILE NONFICTION—Activity Books 5. JUVENILE NONFICTION—Art—General 6. JUVENILE NONFICTION—Crafts & Hobbies 7. Recycling (Waste, etc.)—Juvenile literature 8. Salvage (Waste, etc.)—Juvenile literature
ISBN 9781938063183 (pbk.)
LC 2013-010144

SUMMARY: "This book will help kids get creative and recycle and repurpose their trash into handmade treasures. All projects feature common everyday items to reuse in a fun new way. From bottle-top pop art to felted tin-can organizers, kids will . . . mak[e] useful crafts and help the environment. . . . Tips and advice on reusing, garage sales, and spotting treasures are also provided." (Publisher's note)

REVIEW: *Booklist* v110 no8 p43-4 D 15 2013 Ilene Cooper

"Trash to Treasure: A Kid's Upcycling Guide to Crafts." "What do you have around the house? Cans, glass, pieces of games? This attractive book shows you how to turn them into something interesting--though many of the finished products look like they'll take patience. The brightly colored, graphically appealing layout will draw crafters right in. . . . Instead of offering directions for a few projects in each category, the introductory spreads are taken up with suggestions. . . . But there are no relevant pictures, and as far as directions, you're on your own. . . . However, the two-page spread of an actual project in each section . . . has crisp photos and clear directions."

SCHILLINGER, LIESL.tr. The Lady of the Camellias. See Dumas, A.

SCHILLINGER, LIESL. Wordbirds; an irreverent lexicon for the 21st century; [by] Liesl Schillinger 224 p. 2013 Simon & Schuster
1. Birds 2. Encyclopedias & dictionaries 3. English language—Dictionaries 4. English language—New words 5. Twenty-first century
ISBN 9781476713489 (hardcover)
LC 2013-008365

SUMMARY: "Armed with 'Wordbirds,'" written by Liesl Schillinger and illustrated by Elizabeth Zechel, "you will be able to skillfully talk your way into, or out of, any situation the twenty-first century throws at you. With 150 gorgeous, Audubony, highly expressive bird illustrations, these neologisms will have you crowing with delight, and show you that fine feathers make fine words." (Publisher's note)

REVIEW: *N Y Times Book Rev* p19 D 22 2013 MOI-

GNON FOGARTY

"The Book of Jezebel: An Illustrated Encyclopedia of Lady Things," "The Horologicon: A Day's Jaunt Through the Lost Words of the English Language," "Wordbirds: An Irreverent Lexicon for the 21st Century." "'The Book of Jezebel' is drawn from the energetic contributors to the Jezebel.com blog, and its editor, Anna Holmes . . . takes care to note that what appears to be a colorful encyclopedia is actually a work fo both fact and opinion. . . . Once you pick up 'The Horologicon' it's hard to put down. As a devotee of useful tips, I approached Mark Forsyth's book with skepticism. . . . Liesl Schillinger's 'Wordbirds' embraces the theme of birds. . . . While 'The Horologicon' shines a light on the past, 'Wordbirds' does the same for our times."

REVIEW: *Publ Wkly* v260 no31 p57 Ag 5 2013

SCHILTHUIZEN, MENNO. Nature's nether regions; what the sex lives of bugs, birds, and beasts tell us about evolution, biodiversity, and ourselves; [by] Menno Schilthuizen 256 p. 2014 Viking

1. Comparative anatomy 2. Generative organs—Evolution 3. Genitalia 4. Science—Popular works 5. Sexual behavior in animals—Evolution

ISBN 9780670785919

LC 2013-047833

SUMMARY: In this book, author "Menno Schilthuizen invites readers to join him as he uncovers the ways the shapes and functions of genitalia have been molded by complex Darwinian struggles: penises that have lost their spines but evolved appendages to displace sperm; female orgasms that select or reject semen from males, in turn subtly modifying the females' genital shape." (Publisher's note)

REVIEW: *Kirkus Rev* v82 no8 p85 Ap 15 2014

REVIEW: *Publ Wkly* v261 no10 p56 Mr 10 2014

REVIEW: *Sci Am* v310 no5 p76 My 2014 Clara Moskowitz

"Nature's Nether Regions: What the Sex Lives of Bugs, Birds, and Beasts Tell Us About Evolution, Biodiversity, and Ourselves." "The science of genitals is a relatively new field for biologists, who have long overlooked the evolutionary important of species' private parts. Biologist [Menno] Schilthuizen balances the silly and the serious to describe researchers' latest efforts to understand how 'evolution has graced the animal kingdom with such a bewildering diversity of reproductive organs.'"

SCHINDLER, HOLLY. The junction of Sunshine and Lucky; [by] Holly Schindler 240 p. 2014 Dial Books for Young Readers, an imprint of Penguin Group (USA) Inc.

1. Domestic fiction 2. Dwellings—Fiction 3. Folk art—Fiction 4. Grandfathers—Fiction 5. Neighborhoods—Fiction

ISBN 0803737254; 9780803737259 (hardcover)

LC 2013-009134

SUMMARY: In this book, by Holly Schindler, "August 'Auggie' Jones lives with her Grandpa Gus, a trash hauler, in a poor part of town. . . . Her wealthy classmate's father starts the House Beautification Committee. . . [and] Auggie is determined to prove that she is not as run-down as the outside of her house might suggest. . . . What starts out as a home renovation project becomes much more as Auggie and her grandpa . . . redefine a whole town's perception of beauty." (Publisher's note)

REVIEW: *Booklist* v110 no11 p67 F 1 2014 Suzanne Harold

REVIEW: *Bull Cent Child Books* v67 no6 p332 F 2014 Amy Atkinson

"The Junction of Sunshine and Lucky." "In Auggie, [Holly] Schindler creates a spunky, sympathetic character young readers will engage with and enjoy. Though the voice and even elements of the plot are derivative of [Kate] DiCamillo's 'Because of Winn Dixie' . . . the lively narration is enjoyable, and the diverse cast of characters (Auggie herself is African American, though many in her neighborhood are white) brings meaningful messages of community and self-respect to the fore. Some readers may wish Schindler had provided more detailed descriptions of the sculptures, but aspiring artists and anyone else looking for their shine will appreciate this satisfying portrait of a young girl and her close-knit community."

REVIEW: *Kirkus Rev* v81 no24 p149 D 15 2013

"The Junction of Sunshine and Lucky". "There are no surprises here, but it's a heartwarming and uplifting story nonetheless. . . . Auggie's present-tense, first-person narration, rife with similes, often comes off sounding more contrived than quirky, and the story's numerous characters function more as formulaic devices rather than individual personalities. Additionally, the storyline concerning Auggie's absent mother seems more tangential than imperative, and its revelatory windup comes as no surprise. The story shines in its conclusion, however, with vibrant themes of community, self-empowerment and artistic vision delivered with a satisfying verve that forgives any predictability."

REVIEW: *Publ Wkly* v260 no48 p57 N 25 2013

REVIEW: *SLJ* v60 no3 p148 Mr 2014 Gesse Stark-Smith

SCHLABACH, ELIZABETH SCHROEDER. Along the streets of Bronzeville; black Chicago's literary landscape; [by] Elizabeth Schroeder Schlabach xxii, 167 p. 2013 University of Illinois Press

1. African Americans—Illinois—Chicago—Intellectual life 2. American literature—African American authors—History and criticism 3. American literature—Illinois—Chicago—History and criticism 4. Historical literature

ISBN 9780252037825 (cloth: acid-free paper)

LC 2013-012803

SUMMARY: This book "examines the flowering of African American creativity, activism, and scholarship in the South Side Chicago district known as Bronzeville during the period between the Harlem Renaissance in the 1920s and the Black Arts Movement of the 1960s. Poverty stricken, segregated, and bursting at the seams with migrants, Bronzeville was the community that provided inspiration, training, and work for an entire generation of diversely talented African American authors and artists." (Publisher's note)

REVIEW: *Choice* v51 no9 p1665-6 My 2014 W. Glasker

"Along the Streets of Bronzeville: Black Chicago's Literary Landscape". "Following the lead of African American literature scholar Robert Bone, [Elizabeth Schroeder] Schlabach . . . seeks to fill in the gap that neglects the Chicago Black Renaissance of the 1930s-40s. She points to the mass migration of blacks from the South to Chicago and the blossoming of music, visual arts, and literature there. . . . In the midst of debasement and suffering, some black artists found and expressed 'a grace moving beyond mere survival to [greater] possibility.' . . . Highly recommended."

SCHLAGER, MELINDA. Rethinking the reentry paradigm; a blueprint for action; [by] Melinda Schlager xviii, 342 p. 2013 Carolina Academic Press

1. Criminals—Rehabilitation—United States 2. Ex-convicts—United States—Life skills guides 3. Parole—United States—Planning 4. Prison release 5. Social science literature

ISBN 9781594609237 (alk. paper)

LC 2012-042005

SUMMARY: Written by Melinda Schlager, "The perspective that this text will take presupposes that offender reentry is not a static isolated event, but a process that occurs over time. . . . Consequently, this text will discuss the issue of offender reentry in more global terms and locate solutions to reentry issues on a continuum of service that begins at entry to prison, includes release from prison, and culminates with integration into the community." (Publisher's note)

REVIEW: *Choice* v51 no2 p362-3 O 2013 R. D. McCrie

"Rethinking the Reentry Paradigm: A Blueprint for Action." "Approximately 95 percent of all prisoners will eventually be free. Doesn't it make sense to find ways that ex-offenders can become productive, law-abiding citizens? How can the inevitable collateral punishment to indirect parties and costly burden for taxpayers be lessened? [Author Melinda] Schlager . . . provides a dry but diligent summation of research and trends on this important topic. . . . The author analyzes the 'reentry paradigm' with data and insights any policy advocate or program operator would require. . . . Schlager offers two points: provide programs that concentrate on building offenders' strengths, and nudge ex-offenders into greater civic engagement so they will be less inclined to re-offend."

SCHLESINGER, ANDREW.ed. The Schlesinger letters. See The Schlesinger letters

THE SCHLESINGER LETTERS; 624 p. 2013 Random House Inc

1. Historians—United States—Correspondence 2. Letters

ISBN 0812993098; 9780812993097

LC 2012-049922

SUMMARY: This book, edited by Andrew Schlesinger and Steven Schlesinger, presents the collected correspondence of Arthur Schlesinger Jr. "An advisor to presidents, two-time Pulitzer Prize winner, and tireless champion of progressive government, Arthur Schlesinger, Jr., was also an inveterate letter writer. . . . [This book] reveals the late historian's unvarnished views on the great issues and personalities of his time, from the dawn of the Cold War to the aftermath of September 11." (Publisher's note)

REVIEW: *Booklist* v110 no4 p13-4 O 15 2013 Gilbert Taylor

REVIEW: *Kirkus Rev* v81 no21 p236 N 1 2013

REVIEW: *Libr J* v138 no8 p60 My 1 2013

REVIEW: *N Y Times Book Rev* p9 D 22 2013 GEORGE PACKER

"The Letters of Arthur Schlesinger, Jr." "There's very little sense in 'The Letters of Arthur Schlesinger, Jr.,' selected by two of his sons, of Schlesinger as a private man. . . . When Schlesinger writes about himself and his friends, the results are often stiff and a bit smug, without psychological insight, which may be the price of the sense of belonging. The best letters--and there are many--come from the typewriter of the public Schlesinger, the fighting liberal, especially when he's jousting with a provocative antagonist like William F. Buckley."

SCHLESINGER, STEPHEN.ed. The Schlesinger letters. See The Schlesinger letters

SCHLIESSER, ERIC.ed. Philosophy and its history. See Philosophy and its history

SCHLOSSER, ERIC, 1959-. Command and control; nuclear weapons, the Damascus Accident, and the illusion of safety; [by] Eric Schlosser 640 p. 2013 The Penguin Press

1. Historical literature 2. Nuclear weapons—Accidents—Arkansas—History 3. Nuclear weapons—Accidents—United States—History 4. Nuclear weapons—Government policy—United States 5. Nuclear weapons—United States—Safety measures 6. Titan (Missile)—History

ISBN 1594202273; 9781594202278

LC 2013-017151

SUMMARY: This book "interweaves the minute-by-minute story of an accident at a nuclear missile silo in rural Arkansas with a historical narrative that spans more than fifty years. It depicts the urgent effort by American scientists, policymakers, and military officers to ensure that nuclear weapons can't be stolen, sabotaged, used without permission, or detonated inadvertently." (Publisher's note)

REVIEW: *Am Sch* v82 no4 p111-3 Aut 2013 Scott D. Sagan

REVIEW: *Booklist* v110 no1 p6-7 S 1 2013 Gilbert Taylor

REVIEW: *Choice* v51 no6 p1078 F 2014 A. O. Edmonds

REVIEW: *Economist* v405 no8855 p79 S 28 2013

REVIEW: *Kirkus Rev* v81 no15 p248 Ag 1 2013

REVIEW: *Kirkus Rev* p29-30 Ag 15 2013 Fall Preview

REVIEW: *Libr J* v138 no21 p59 D 1 2013 Dale Farris

REVIEW: *London Rev Books* v36 no2 p20-3 Ja 23 2014 Steven Shapin

"Command and Control". "Eric Schlosser's brilliant 'Command and Control' [is] a gripping, joined-up history of American nuclear strategy and nuclear accidents over the past sixty years or so. The broader story is intercut with a minute-by-minute reconstruction of an accident that took place on 18 September 1980 in Damascus, Arkansas. . . . Criticising Schlosser as a hysteric misses the point. . . . The precautionary principle more familiar from environmentalist arguments relates the quality of damage inversely to the acceptability of risk, and nuclear weapons are, as Schlosser notes, 'the most dangerous technology ever invented'."

REVIEW: *N Y Times Book Rev* p30 S 22 2013

REVIEW: *New Yorker* v89 no30 p1 S 30 2013 Louis Menand

REVIEW: *Publ Wkly* v260 no28 p157 Jl 15 2013

REVIEW: *Time* v182 no14 p65 S 30 2013 Lev Grossman

"Command and Control." "A devastatingly lucid and detailed new history of nuclear weapons in the U.S. Drawing on recently declassified documents, [Eric] Schlosser shows us nuclear bombs being 'burned, melted, sunk, blown apart, [and] smashed into the ground,' often in populated areas. Sometimes people just plain dropped them. One study found 'that at least 1,200 nuclear weapons had been involved in 'significant' incidents and accidents between 1950 and March 1968.' . . . One of the things great histories do is reawaken us to the knowledge of how easily we could and probably should have ended up with a present far worse than the one we've got."

REVIEW: *TLS* no5788 p26 Mr 7 2014 JOHN MUELLER

"Command and Control: Nuclear Weapons, the Damascus Accident, and the Illusion of Safety." "His book, some 485 pages of text and ninety-nine pages of notes followed by a twenty-nine-page bibliography, attempts to raise the alarm with a series of rather breathless anecdotes involving accidents which involve nuclear weapons in one way or another. . . . Although the record with nuclear weapons, as he acknowledges, has indeed been perfect for over two-thirds of a century now, there is no way, of course, to absolutely guarantee the condition will continue forever. . . . Nor, it appears, can anything be done to expunge the alarmism they inspire. [Author Eric] Schlosser has a great many distinguished predecessors."

SCHMID, MONIKA S.ed. Engineering the human. See Engineering the human

SCHMID, PAUL. Petunia goes wild; [by] Paul Schmid 40 p. 2012 HarperCollins

1. Behavior—Fiction 2. Children's costumes 3. Humorous stories 4. Illustrated children's books 5. Parent and child—Fiction 6. Parenting 7. Temper tantrums in children 8. Tigers as pets

ISBN 9780061963346 (trade bdg.); 9780061963353 (lib. bdg.)

LC 2011-001888

SUMMARY: In this children's book, "Petunia . . . would much rather be an animal than a human girl, a preference that she expresses by wearing a tiger tail, roaring at passersby, and pleading with her parents for a cave in which to live. As a compromise, she offers to be their pet, an offer that provokes a page-long parental lecture: "No, you may NOT! Where did you get such an idea? Of all the crazy things! That is NOT how nice little girls behave." Feeling completely misunderstood, Petunia addresses a packing box to Africa and climbs in, only to have second thoughts when she overhears her mother singing in the kitchen ("Tigers did not sing, thought Petunia. Or tickle at bedtime, neither"), and she decides to stay." (Bulletin of the Center for Children's Books)

REVIEW: *Bull Cent Child Books* v65 no7 p371 Mr 2012 J. H.

"Petunia Goes Wild." "Although the ending is a bit anticlimactic, Petunia's desire for wildness will be easily understood by kids who have similar trouble containing themselves, and her parents' overreaction to her behavior will likely resonate with obstreperous youngsters as well. They'll also be tickled by her actions, especially when 'Petunia, wearing no more than a smile, bathed in a mud puddle.' Schmid's cheerful, minimalist illustrations . . . feature scribbly lines in a childlike style against lots of white space. Petunia is irrepressibly jaunty in her striped dress and tiger tail, and she's as endearing as she is excessive."

REVIEW: *Kirkus Rev* v80 no1 p2455 Ja 1 2012

REVIEW: *Publ Wkly* v258 no51 p51 D 19 2011

REVIEW: *SLJ* v58 no1 p86 Ja 2012 Jayne Damron

SCHMID, SUSANNE. British literary salons of the late eighteenth and early nineteenth centuries; [by] Susanne Schmid xi, 252 p. 2013 Palgrave Macmillan

1. English literature—18th century—History and criticism 2. English literature—19th century—History and criticism 3. Historical literature 4. LITERARY CRITICISM—Books & Reading 5. LITERARY CRITICISM—European—English, Irish, Scottish, Welsh 6. LITERARY CRITICISM—General 7. Salons—Great Britain—History—18th century 8. Salons—Great Britain—History—19th century

ISBN 9780230110656 (hardback)

LC 2012-031260

SUMMARY: "In this comprehensive study of the British salon between the 1780s and the 1840s, [author Susanne] Schmid traces the activities of three salonnières: Mary Berry, Lady Holland, and the Countess of Blessington. Mapping out the central place these circles held in London, this study explains to what extent they shaped intellectual debate and publishing ventures." (Publisher's note)

REVIEW: *TLS* no5783 p26 Ja 31 2014 CHRISTY EDWALL

"British Literary Salons of the Late Eighteenth and Early Nineteenth Centuries." "Susanne Schmid's study of three hostesses of the long eighteenth century--Mary Berry; Elizabeth Fox, Lady Holland; and Marguerite, Countess of Blessington--is part of a larger and continuing project of reviving the memory of influential women during a period when female participation in public life was severely constrained. Coming from very different backgrounds, Schmid's subjects are united by their taste for travel, and their interest in Continental life and political affairs. . . . No matter how witty, these clever ghosts are hardly accessible to the twenty-first-century reader."

SCHMIDT, CHRISTEL.ed. Mary Pickford. See Mary Pickford

SCHMIDT, DENNIS J. Between word and image; Heidegger, Klee, and Gadamer on gesture and genesis; [by] Dennis J. Schmidt x, 187 p. 2013 Indiana University Press

1. Aesthetics 2. Image (Philosophy) 3. Philosophical literature 4. Thought and thinking

ISBN 9780253006189 (cloth: alk. paper); 9780253006202 (pbk.: alk. paper); 9780253006226 (electronic book)

LC 2012-022626

SUMMARY: In this book, Dennis J. Schmidt "develops the question of philosophy's regard of the image in thinking by considering painting—where the image most clearly calls attention to itself as an image. Focusing on [Martin] Heidegger and the work of Paul Klee, Schmidt pursues larger issues in the relationship between word, image, and truth." (Publisher's note)

REVIEW: *Choice* v51 no8 p1414 Ap 2014 J. G. Moore

"Between Word and Image: Heidegger, Klee, and Gadamer on Gesture and Genesis". "Despite a tenuous and elusive documentary trail, [Dennis J.] Schmidt expertly fills in missing parts with informed commentary drawn from lecture notes, letters, and biographical testimonia. Earlier studies of the [Martin] Heidegger-[Paul] Klee relation filled in biographical details, but Schmidt presses the inquiry into a more philosophical direction, broadening the focus to include the hermeneutic challenges presented by gesture, word, and image to Heidegger's ontological framework."

SCHMIDT, ERIC E., 1955-. The new digital age; reshaping the future of people, nations and business; [by] Eric E. Schmidt 336 p. 2013 Alfred A. Knopf

1. Computers and civilization—Forecasting 2. Digital electronics—Political aspects—Forecasting 3. Digital electronics—Social aspects—Forecasting 4. Digital media—Political aspects—Forecasting 5. Digital media—Social aspects—Forecasting 6. Information technology—Political aspects—Forecasting 7. Information technology—Social aspects—Forecasting 8. Technical literature 9. Technology and civilization—Forecasting
ISBN 0307957136; 9780307957139
LC 2013-004565

SUMMARY: This book "examines the boundaries of the physical world we currently inhabit and offers a vision into our digital future: a world where everyone is connected, and what it means for people, nations, and businesses. . . . [Eric] Schmidt and [Jared] Cohen address global connectivity and the relationships between invasion of privacy and government's control over people's private information." (Publishers Weekly)

REVIEW: *Booklist* v109 no15 p4 Ap 1 2013 Gilbert Taylor

REVIEW: *Choice* v51 no3 p501 N 2013 C. Vickery

REVIEW: *Columbia J Rev* v52 no1 p49-53 My/Je 2013 LAUREN KIRCHNER

REVIEW: *Economist* v407 no8834 p80-1 My 4 2013

REVIEW: *Kirkus Rev* v81 no8 p66 Ap 15 2013

REVIEW: *New Repub* v244 no9 p41-7 My 10 2013 Evgeny Morozov

"The New Digital Age: Reshaping the Future of People, Nations, and Business". "The goal of books such as this one is not to predict but to reassure—to show the commoners, who are unable on their own to develop any deep understanding of what awaits them, that the tech-savvy elites are sagaciously in control. . . . In the simplicity of its composition, [Eric] Schmidt and [Jared] Cohen's book has a strongly formulaic—perhaps I should say algorithmic—character. . . . The problem is that you cannot devise new concepts merely by sticking adjectives on old ones. The future depicted in 'The New Digital Age' is just the past qualified with 'virtual.' . . . Schmidt and Cohen's book consistently substitutes unempirical speculation for a thorough engagement with what is already known."

REVIEW: *New York Times* v162 no56118 pC29 Ap 26 2013 JANET MASLIN

REVIEW: *New York Times* v162 no56155 p4 Je 2 2013 JULIAN ASSANGE

REVIEW: *Sci Am* v308 no4 p84 Ap 2013 Anna Kuchment

SCHMIDT, GARY D. Making Americans; children's literature from 1930 to 1960; [by] Gary D. Schmidt 314 p. 2013 University of Iowa Press

1. Children—Books and reading—United States—History—20th century 2. Children's literature—Publishing—United States—History—20th century 3. Children's literature, American—History and criticism 4. Democracy in literature 5. Literature—History & criticism 6. National characteristics, American, in literature
ISBN 1609381920 (pbk. : acid-free paper); 9781609381929 (pbk. : acid-free paper)
LC 2013-010352

SUMMARY: In this examination of 20th-century children's books, Gary D. Schmidt "searches for the meaning of America, the American experience, and democracy. In doing so, he divides his issue-oriented study into four sections: the first addresses America as a pioneer nation; the second, otherness within a democracy; the third,American children's literature and WWII; and, fourth, positioning the American democracy globally." (Booklist)

REVIEW: *Booklist* v110 no12 p69 F 15 2014 Michael Cart

"Making Americans: Children's Literature From 1930 to 1960." "In 'Making Americans,' the celebrated children's book author [Gary D.] Schmidt has written a critical analysis of American children's literature from 1930 to 1960. In his close readings of such works as the Little House books, the Childhood of Famous Americans series, the regional novels of Lois Lenski, and more, he searches for the meaning of America, the American experience, and democracy. Though not for every reader, 'Making Americans will appeal to all those who have a serious interest in children's literature."

REVIEW: *Choice* v51 no10 p1804 Je 2014 C. E. Epple

SCHMIDT, MICHAEL, 1947-. The novel; a biography; [by] Michael Schmidt 1200 p. 2014 Harvard University Press

1. Authorship 2. English literature—History & criticism 3. Fiction—History and criticism 4. Historical literature 5. Literary form 6. Novelists
ISBN 9780674724730 (alk. paper)
LC 2013-026938

SUMMARY: In this book, Michael Schmidt "presents what he terms a 'brief' life of the novel in English, from its origins in the 14th century through 2000. Included are writers from virtually all English-speaking countries and chapters on French and Russian novelists whose works have influenced those in English. . . . The content consists largely of quotations from later authors commenting on earlier ones to whom they feel a connection." (Library Journal)

REVIEW: *Atlantic* v313 no5 p88-99 Je 2014 William Deresiewicz

"The Novel: A Biography" and "The Dream of the Great American Novel". "Michael Schmidt's 'The Novel: A Biography' . . . [contains] 45 brisk, brilliant, intimate, assured, and almost unfaggingly interesting chapters. . . . If anyone's up for the job, it would seem to be him. . . . Take a breath, clear the week, turn of the WiFi, and throw yourself in. . . . [Lawrence] Buell seems less interested in the 'dream,' the concept as a cultural phenomenon, than in constructing a taxonomy of GAN contenders—and thus, in large measure, of American fiction as a whole. This is where the ambition comes in, as well as Buell's enormous erudition. . . . Buell's book tells us a great deal about American fiction. What it also tells us, in its every line, is much of what is wrong with academic criticism. . . . The book does so much posturing, you think it's going to throw its back out."

REVIEW: *Kirkus Rev* v82 no5 p38 Mr 1 2014

REVIEW: *Libr J* v139 no6 p92 Ap 1 2014 Denise J. Stankovics

REVIEW: *N Y Times Book Rev* p17 Ag 10 2014 JOHN SUTHERLAND

REVIEW: *New Statesman* v143 no5216 p52-4 Je 27 2014 Leo Robson

REVIEW: *TLS* no5809 p21 Ag 1 2014 LINDSAY DUGUID

SCHMIDT, TIFFANY. Bright before sunrise; [by] Tiffany Schmidt 288 p. 2014 Bloomsbury/Walker

1. Emotional problems—Fiction 2. High schools—Fiction 3. Love—Fiction 4. Love stories 5. Schools—Fiction 6. Self-acceptance—Fiction
ISBN 9780802735003 (hardback)
LC 2013-025425

SUMMARY: In this book, "Prim Brighton, a high school junior, agrees to accompany sullen Jonah to a party only after the senior reluctantly promises to participate in a community-service project. Soon, sparks are flying in this opposites-attract romance. . . . Brighton begins recognizing Jonah's sensitive side. . . . Her growing understanding allows her to see his observations about her personality less as critiques and more as permission to shed the burden of pursuing her father's legacy." (Kirkus Reviews)

REVIEW: *Booklist* v110 no12 p79-80 F 15 2014 Diane Colson

"Bright Before Sunrise." "Seems like it would take a mighty strong gust of fate to bring these two together, yet over the course of one poignant Friday night, Brighton and Jonah gradually discover that they cannot pull themselves apart. Told in the teens' alternating viewpoints, the chapters use a countdown format that creates a nice tension. Fate gets a little frenzied in its machinations to bring the star-crossed lovers together, but fans of the one-crazy-night romance genre will love the budding tenderness and passion between the teens. Recommend to readers who like a lighthearted love story with serious undertones, such as those by Lauren Myracle or Deb Caletti."

REVIEW: *Bull Cent Child Books* v67 no7 p377 Mr 2014 K. C.

REVIEW: *Kirkus Rev* v81 no23 p191 D 1 2013

REVIEW: *Publ Wkly* v260 no47 p53 N 18 2013

REVIEW: *SLJ* v60 no3 p148 Mr 2014 Diana Pierce

REVIEW: *Voice of Youth Advocates* v36 no6 p64-5 F 2014 Barbara Johnston

SCHNEGG, MICHAEL.ed. Pastoralism in Africa. See Pastoralism in Africa

SCHNEIDER, GREGORY L. Rock Island requiem; the collapse of a mighty fine line; [by] Gregory L. Schneider xviii, 380 p. 2013 University Press of Kansas

1. Business failures—United States—History—20th century 2. Historical literature 3. Railroads—United States—Finance—History—20th century 4. Railroads—United States—History—20th century
ISBN 9780700619184 (cloth: alk. paper)
LC 2013-009247

SUMMARY: "In this railroad business history, [Gregory L.] Schneider . . . chronicles the course of the Rock Island Line from 1948 to its liquidation as a railroad in 1980. Schneider says that after a few prosperous postwar years, competition from trucks, airlines, and barges, coupled with hobbling government regulation and tough labor unions, depleted the Rock Island and other railroads of the revenue they needed to survive." (Publisher's note)

REVIEW: *Choice* v51 no8 p1476 Ap 2014 R. M. Hyser

"Rock Island Requiem: The Collapse of a Mighty Fine Line". "Historian [Gregory L.] Schneider . . . examines the demise of the Rock Island Line in this well-written account that draws on various government records, archival materials, and newspapers. . . . The author places the Rock Island in the context of outdated government regulatory policies that stifled innovations; mergers of larger railroads; a weak economy; and government subsidies to airports and highways that reduced costs for competitors. . . . The merger chapters skillfully explain the economic forces, the government policies, and the business decisions that affected the railroad industry in general and, specifically, the Rock Island Line."

REVIEW: *J Am Hist* v101 no2 p663-4 S 2014

REVIEW: *Libr J* v138 no20 p1 N 15 2013

SCHNEIDER, JOSH.il. Bedtime monsters. See Schneider, J.

SCHNEIDER, JOSH. Bedtime monsters; [by] Josh Schneider 32 p. 2013 Clarion Books, Houghton Mifflin Harcourt

1. Bedtime—Fiction 2. Fear of the dark—Fiction 3. Imagination 4. Monsters—Fiction 5. Picture books for children
ISBN 0544002709; 9780544002708 (hardcover)
LC 2012-036483

SUMMARY: In this book, "Arnold knows he has nothing more to be afraid of at bedtime after the winged fargle, the horrible tooth gnasher, the grozny buzzler, and other monsters with their own fears crawl into his bed. These colorful figures lurk in the darkest corners of bedrooms, but, as Arnold discovers, the scary creatures have more in common with him than he could have imagined." (School Library Journal)

REVIEW: *Horn Book Magazine* v89 no6 p81-2 N/D 2013 SUSAN DOVE LEMPKE

"Bedtime Monsters". "[Josh] Schneider's watercolor, pen-and-ink, and colored-pencil illustrations depict Arnold as a solid, ordinary-looking boy, while his imaginary world is outlined in blue around him. The funny monster names and the sight of them crowded into Arnold's bed will help get scaredy-cats to read this for the first time, and once they've seen how the story turns out, they will want this worthy successor to Mercer Mayer's classic 'There's a Nightmare in My Closet' read over and over again."

SCHNEIDER, NATHAN. God in proof; the story of a search, from the ancients to the Internet; [by] Nathan Schneider xii, 253 p. 2013 University of California Press

1. Catholic Church & philosophy 2. God—Proof 3. God—Proof—History of doctrines 4. Memoirs 5. Phil-

osophical literature 6. Religious literature
ISBN 0520269071; 9780520269071 (cloth : alk. paper)
LC 2012-033541

SUMMARY: "In this tour of the history of arguments for and against the existence of God, Nathan Schneider embarks on . . . [an] intellectual, historical, and theological journey through the centuries of believers and unbelievers--from ancient Greeks, to medieval Arabs, to today's most eminent philosophers and the New Atheists." (Publisher's note)

REVIEW: *America* v209 no13 p36-7 N 4 2013 WILLIAM REHG
"God in Proof: The Story of a Search From the Ancients to the Internet." "In his eminently readable 'God in Proof,' Nathan Schneider presents this history of proving not as a merely academic exercise but as an existential quest of the highest importance in his own life. . . . Tracing the philosophical dialectic in a manner both responsible to the issues and accessible to the ordinary reader, Schneider weaves together intellectual history with his own quest for faith. . . . In the end, Schneider hints that the practice of proving, ever inconclusive, is itself an opening on the divine."

REVIEW: *Booklist* v109 no19/20 p6 Je 1 2013 Ray Olson

REVIEW: *Choice* v51 no3 p481 N 2013 P. K. Moser

SCHOEN, JOHN W.ed. North Pacific temperate rainforests. See North Pacific temperate rainforests

SCHOENHERR, IAN.il. The Twistrose Key. See Almhjell, T.

SCHOLASTIC INC.comp. Star wars. See Star wars

SCHOLL, CHRISTIAN. Shutting down the streets. See Fernandez, L.

SCHOOLING HIP-HOP; Expanding hip-hop based education across the curriculum; 2013 Teachers College Press
1. Educational literature 2. Hip-hop 3. Teaching—Methodology 4. Teaching—Philosophy 5. Urban education
ISBN 9780807754320 hardcover; 9780807754313 paperback

SUMMARY: Edited by Marc Lamont Hill and Emery Petchauer, "this book brings together veteran and emerging scholars from a variety of fields to chart new territory for hip-hop based education. Looking beyond rap music and the English language arts classroom, innovative chapters unpack the theory and practice of hip-hop based education in science, social studies, college composition, teacher education, and other fields." (Publisher's note)

REVIEW: *Choice* v51 no9 p1652 My 2014 E. Correa

REVIEW: *Harv Educ Rev* v84 no1 p125-33 Spr 2014 E.L.E. Y.Y. A.M.N.
"Schooling Hip-Hop: Expanding Hip-Hop Based Education Across the Curriculum," "Charter Schools and the Corporate Makeover of Public Education: What's At Stake?" and "Global Education Policy and International Development: New Agendas, Issues and Policies." "The authors face a difficult challenge as they attempt to move hip-hop pedagogical scholarship beyond a conversation about lyrics and instructional content. . . . For the most part, the authors in Schooling Hip-Hop achieve this feat. . . . Michael Fabricant and Michelle Fine write with a sense of urgency. . . Their imaginative investigation reveals the intricate network of decisions . . . that have created the current charter school landscape. . . . A timely compendium of studies aimed at elucidating the specific social, historical, political, and economic conditions that have shaped global education policies (GEPs) in diverse contexts."

SCHOU, NICHOLAS. The weed runners; travels with the outlaw capitalists and modern-day bootleggers of America's medical marijuana trade; [by] Nicholas Schou 224 p. 2013 Chicago Review Press
1. BUSINESS & ECONOMICS—Industries—Agribusiness 2. Drug legalization—United States 3. Journalism 4. Lobbying—United States 5. Marijuana—Therapeutic use—United States 6. Marijuana industry—United States 7. SOCIAL SCIENCE—Agriculture & Food 8. SOCIAL SCIENCE—Criminology 9. SOCIAL SCIENCE—Disease & Health Issues
ISBN 9781613744109 (pbk.)
LC 2013-011343

SUMMARY: In this book on the marijuana industry, author "[Nicholas] Schou's investigation showed that the tensions between law enforcement and 'legal' marijuana growers and distributors in California had never truly abated" following legalization of medical marijuana. "Anti-marijuana politicians and district attorneys . . . suspected . . . that 'medical marijuana' provided an excuse for longtime drug smugglers and dealers to grow their recreational weed businesses under the color of law." (Kirkus Reviews)

REVIEW: *Booklist* v110 no1 p22-3 S 1 2013 David Pitt
"Weed Runners: Travels With the Outlaw Capitalists of America's Medical Marijuana Trade." "Focusing on the last few years, which have seen big changes in the ever-more-legitimate marijuana industry, [Nicholas] Schou tells the story by looking at its players; the Big Kahuna, owner of a medical-marijuana collective (with 30 employees and health insurance for all); Racer X, a delivery driver for the Big Kahuna who later became manager of his storefront dispensary; and Steele Smith, a highly vocal marijuana activist and tireless self-promoter. Readers expecting a Hunter Thompsonesque account of pot dealers may be surprised: this is, ultimately, a business book (although one written with panache)."

REVIEW: *Kirkus Rev* v81 no14 p100 Jl 15 2013

REVIEW: *Publ Wkly* v260 no23 p63 Je 10 2013

SCHREFER, ELIOT. Threatened; [by] Eliot Schrefer 288 p. 2014 Scholastic Press
1. Adventure stories 2. Animal rescue—Fiction 3. Chimpanzees—Fiction 4. Orphans—Gabon—Fiction 5. Wildlife rescue—Fiction
ISBN 0545551439; 9780545551434 (jacketed hardcover)
LC 2013-018599

SUMMARY: In this juvenile story, by Eliot Schrefer, "Luc and Prof head into the rough, dangerous jungle in order to study the elusive chimpanzees. There, Luc finally finds a new family—and must act when that family comes under attack. . . . [It] is the story of a boy fleeing his present, a man fleeing his past, and a trio of chimpanzees who are struggling not to flee at all." (Publisher's note)

REVIEW: *Booklist* v110 no11 p66 F 1 2014 Debbie Carton

REVIEW: *Bull Cent Child Books* v67 no7 p377 Mr 2014 E. B.

"Threatened". "[Eliot] Schrefer focuses on the delicate, fraught nature of contact between humans and their primate kin and conveys in vivid detail the individual and communal behaviors that seldom enjoy such rich, unanthropomorphized treatment in fiction. Luc's and Prof's marginalized status within their own cultures demands thoughtful comparison with the chimpanzees that struggle to define their roles in the group, but Schrefer respectfully declines to turn the chimps into mini-mes with recognizably human emotion and motivation. Readers are again treated to a thought-provoking study of endangered creatures—both the poached and hunted chimpanzees and the exploited and neglected children with little hope."

REVIEW: *Horn Book Magazine* v90 no3 p96-7 My/Je 2014 MONICA EDINGER

REVIEW: *Kirkus Rev* v82 no2 p108 Ja 15 2014

"Threatened". "A poignant demonstration of connection between chimpanzees and humans. . . . Luc's story is riveting and seldom comfortable, for him or for his readers. . . . Luc's first-person narration is so lively and detailed readers won't notice that he seems remarkably acute for a 12- or 13-year-old, even one who has watched his mother and baby sister die and lived, afterward, by his own wits. The particulars of his daily life Inside—where Gabonese believe humans shouldn't go—will enthrall those who enjoy adventure, and the intimate glimpse of chimpanzee daily life is a treat for nature lovers. Engrossing action and characters readers will keep thinking about in a splendid survival story."

REVIEW: *Publ Wkly* v260 no49 p84 D 2 2013

REVIEW: *SLJ* v60 no2 p114 F 2014 Carol A. Edwards

REVIEW: *Voice of Youth Advocates* v36 no6 p65 F 2014 Rachel Wadham

SCHREIBER, JOE. Game over, Pete Watson; 224 p. 2014 Houghton Mifflin Harcourt

1. Fathers & sons—Fiction 2. Humorous stories 3. Spies—Fiction 4. United States. Central Intelligence Agency 5. Video games—Fiction

ISBN 9780544157569 (hardback)

LC 2013-024335

SUMMARY: In this book, "after he sells a vintage console of his dad's to the neighborhood exterminator," Pete's "dad gets kidnapped before his eyes. Pete discovers that his father is a CIA agent and is now trapped in the gaming system, which also doubles as a database for government secrets. Aided by his geeky ex-best friend Wesley and Wesley's attractive older sister, Pete must stop the supervillain . . .by going into the game himself." (Bulletin of the Center for Children's Books)

REVIEW: *Booklist* v110 no21 p72 Jl 1 2014 Julia Smith

REVIEW: *Booklist* v110 no21 p72 Jl 14 2014 Julia Smith

REVIEW: *Bull Cent Child Books* v67 no9 p475 My 2014 T. A.

"Game Over, Pete Watson". "Wacky comedy carries the day, and the breathless pace, short chapters, and frequent spot art . . . make this novel zoom. However, the silliness amps up to levels that will lead those playing along at home to incredulity by the end (a monetary amount that's so large that the number will literally kill you without protection, for example), and the rushed conclusion gets lost in tired gags that even Pete's conversational narration can't surmount. Additionally, the characters remain as flat as their eight-bit counterparts in the game world. Nevertheless, the appeal to multimodality . . . is going to have reluctant reader appeal."

REVIEW: *Kirkus Rev* v82 no5 p260 Mr 1 2014

REVIEW: *SLJ* v60 no5 p116 My 2014 Andy Plemmons

SCHRIFT, MELISSA. Becoming Melungeon; making an ethnic identity in the Appalachian South; [by] Melissa Schrift x, 222 p. 2013 University of Nebraska Press

1. Ethnicity—United States 2. Ethnology—Appalachian Region 3. Melungeons—Appalachian Mountains, Southern—Ethnic identity 4. Melungeons—Appalachian Mountains, Southern—History 5. Melungeons—Appalachian Mountains, Southern—Social conditions 6. Social science literature

ISBN 9780803271548 (cloth : alk. paper)

LC 2012-038654

SUMMARY: This book, written by Melissa Schrift, "examines the ways in which the Melungeon ethnic identity has been socially constructed over time by various regional and national media, plays, and other forms of popular culture. Schrift explores how the social construction of this legend evolved into a fervent movement of a self-identified ethnicity in the 1990s." (Publisher's note)

REVIEW: *Choice* v51 no2 p311-2 O 2013 F. J. Hay

"Becoming Melungeon: Making an Ethnic Identity in the Appalachian South." "Anthropologist [Melissa] Schrift . . . explores the birth of an Appalachian ethnic group. In the popular imagination, Melungeons were considered a 'triracial isolate,' interrelated families descended from African, Native American, and European ancestors who share phenotypical features. . . . Using archival research, interviews, and a questionnaire, Schrift examines the multifaceted emergence of a new ethnicity and ethnic pride movement. Documentation and analysis are excellent, but there are problems: referring to the 1890s as the 'heyday of racial integration'; Appalachians stereotyped as 'largely Scots-Irish'; the omission of important sources in the creation of the Melungeon myth."

SCHRÖDER, KLAUS ALBRECHT. Albrecht Dürer. See Robison, A.

SCHUBERT, LEDA. Monsieur Marceau. See Monsieur Marceau

SCHUETT, STACEY.il. Hanukkah in Alaska. See Brown, B.

SCHUI, FLORIAN. Rebellious Prussians; urban political culture under Frederick the Great and his successors; [by] Florian Schui x, 221 p. 2013 Oxford University Press

1. Frederick II, King of Prussia, 1712-1786 2. Historical literature 3. Political culture—Germany—Prussia—History—18th century

ISBN 0199593965 (hbk.); 9780199593965 (hbk.)

LC 2013-431548

SUMMARY: In this book, author Florian Schui "argues that Prussians in the eighteenth century were much more willing to challenge the state than has been recognised. Schui explores several instances where urban Prussians successfully resisted government policies and forced Frederick the Great and his successors to give in to their demands." (Publisher's note)

REVIEW: *Hist Today* v63 no10 p59 O 2013 GILES MACDONOGH

"Rebellious Prussians: Urban Political Culture Under Frederick the Great and His Successors." "There is plenty here to get your teeth into. . . . I picked up this book imagining that I would find my illusions about 18th-century Prussia shattered: that the state was a hive of unruly individualists whose behaviour routed the more dictatorial rule of Frederick the Great and his father, not to mention Prussian kings before and after. In fact, [Florian] Schui confirms most of my ideas on Prussia in its golden age: the state was by no means a simple nation in arms; I had never thought it was."

SCHULMAN, DANIEL. Sons of Wichita; How the Koch Brothers Became America's Most Powerful and Private Dynasty; [by] Daniel Schulman 432 p. 2014 Grand Central Pub

1. Biography (Literary form) 2. Koch, Charles G. (Charles de Ganahl), 1935- 3. Koch, David H., 1940- 4. Libertarians 5. Rich people 6. United States—Politics & government

ISBN 1455518735; 9781455518739

SUMMARY: This book by Daniel Schulman, "traces the complicated lives and legacies of these four tycoons, as well as their business, social, and political ambitions. No matter where you fall on the ideological spectrum, the Kochs are one of the most influential dynasties of our era. . . . Based on hundreds of interviews with friends, relatives, business associates, and many others, 'Sons of Wichita' is the first major biography about this wealthy and powerful family-warts and all." (Publisher's note)

REVIEW: *Bookforum* v21 no2 p8-9 Je-Ag 2014 JIM NEWELL

REVIEW: *Kirkus Rev* v82 no12 p318 Je 15 2014

REVIEW: *Libr J* v138 no21 p69 D 1 2013 Barbara Hoffert

REVIEW: *N Y Rev Books* v61 no11 p22-4 Je 19 2014 Michael Tomasky

"Sons of Wichita: How the Koch Brothers Became America's Most Powerful and Private Dynasty." "[Author Daniel] Schulman is a senior editor at 'Mother Jones' magazine, and 'Sons of Wichita' is his first book. He writes that he conducted 'hundreds of interviews,' and in that sense the book is an impressive piece of reporting. . . . Yet for all his effort, the book, which was released under an unusually ominous embargo, contains no earth-shaking revelations or scoops that I could find. . . . Schulman can be faulted . . . for being a bit stingy in citing other journalists' work."

REVIEW: *N Y Times Book Rev* p12 My 25 2014 NICHOLAS LEMANN

REVIEW: *N Y Times Book Rev* p34 Je 8 2014 GREGORY COWLES

REVIEW: *Publ Wkly* v261 no4 p28-33 Ja 27 2014

SCHULTE, BRIGID. Overwhelmed; work, love, and play when no one has the time; [by] Brigid Schulte 368 p. 2014 Sarah Crichton Books, Farrar, Straus and Giroux

1. Leisure—Social aspects 2. Social science literature 3. Work and family 4. Working mothers 5. Working mothers—Time management

ISBN 0374228442; 9780374228446 (hardback); 9781429945875 (ebook)

LC 2013-040637

SUMMARY: In this book, author Brigid Schulte "explores the multiple levels where humans waste time and offers concrete advice on how to reclaim those lost moments. Today's workplace . . . doesn't take into account the millions of women now juggling a full-time career with family life. . . . Schulte advocates for a new system that provides flexibility in hours, paid maternal and paternal leave, and consideration of the desire for more freedom and leisure time." (Publisher's note)

REVIEW: *Bookforum* v20 no5 p5 F/Mr 2014 HEATHER HAVRILESKY

"All Joy and No Fun: The Paradox of Modern Parenthood" and "Overwhelmed: Work, Love and Play When No One Has the Time". "[Jennifer] Senior quickly demonstrates a real talent for portraying the thorniest challenges of parenting as a chilling house of horrors. . . . Yet strangely enough, the more Senior delineates the unmatched suffering of today's parents, the less sympathetic one feels. . . . Unfortunately, rather than wrapping up her book with a galvanizing critique of America's delusional embrace of the ideal mother and the ideal, child-focused home Senior retreats into generic, glowing talk of the deeply felt rewards of self-sacrifice. . . . Luckily . . . Brigid Schulte has fewer qualms about emphasizing how the American way of parenting . . .has eroded our happiness. . . . Rather than dragging us into the mire and then retreating into warm fuzzies, Schulte offers an unflinching view of overachieving and overscheduling as a pervasive American sickness."

REVIEW: *Booklist* v110 no13 p6 Mr 1 2014 Colleen Mondor

REVIEW: *Choice* v52 no1 p170 St 2014 S. K. Gallagher

REVIEW: *Commentary* v137 no6 p76-7 Je 2014 NAOMI SCHAEFER RILEY

REVIEW: *Kirkus Rev* v82 no3 p118 F 1 2014

"Overwhelmed: Work, Love, and Play When No One Has the Time". " An examination of how to change how you use your time. . . . Backed by numerous examples, [Brigid] Schulte's effective time-management ideas will be helpful in stamping out ambivalence and will empower readers to reclaim wasted moments, so life becomes a joyful experience rather than a mad dash from one task to the next. An eye-opening analysis of today's hectic lifestyles coupled with valuable practical advice on how to make better use of each day."

REVIEW: *N Y Times Book Rev* p15 Mr 30 2014 ANN CRITTENDEN

REVIEW: *New Yorker* v90 no14 p70-1 My 26 2014

REVIEW: *Publ Wkly* v261 no1 p45 Ja 6 2014

REVIEW: *Publ Wkly* v261 no4 p113-8 Ja 27 2014

REVIEW: *Time* v183 no11 p58 Mr 24 2014 Lev Grossman

"Overwhelmed: Work, Love, and Play When No One Has the Time." "'Overwhelmed' is [author Brigid] Schulte's attempt to not merely survive but also unpack and analyze the quintessentially modern and increasingly universal experience of feeling utterly unable to cope. . . . Schulte tries to figure out how we got here and how we can get out of it. She consults life coaches, neuroscientists, anthropologists and time analysts who pepper their conversation with evocative phrases like task density and contaminated time."

SCHULTZ, DEBORAH WASSERMAN, 1966-. For the Next Generation. See Fenster, J. M. (. M.

SCHUPPE, JONATHAN. A chance to win; boyhood, baseball, and the struggle for redemption in the inner city; [by] Jonathan Schuppe 288 p. 2013 Henry Holt and Co.

1. At-risk youth 2. Drug addicts—Rehabilitation—New Jersey—Newark 3. Drug dealers—New Jersey—Newark 4. Journalism 5. Little League baseball
ISBN 0805092870 (hardcover); 9780805092875 (hardcover)
LC 2012-034298

SUMMARY: In this book by Jonathan Schuppe, "when Rodney Mason, an ex-con drug dealer from Newark's rough South Ward, was shot and paralyzed, he vowed to turn his life around. A former high-school pitching ace with a 93 mph fastball, Mason decided to form a Little League team to help boys avoid the street life that had claimed his youth and mobility." (Publisher's note)

REVIEW: *Booklist* v110 no1 p32 S 1 2013 Bill Ott

"The Boys in the Boat," "A Chance to Win," and "Color Blind: The Forgotten Team That Broke Baseball's Color Line." "The Jesse Owens story will always be the big event of the 1936 Berlin Olympics, but the triumph of the University of Washington's crew team in those same games comes in a close second. [Daniel James] Brown retells the little-known story with verve. . . . [Jonathan] Schuppe follows the remarkable life story of Rodney Mason, a New Jersey baseball star and gang member who was confined to a wheelchair after a shooting and rebuilt his life around drawing young people at risk to baseball. . . . [Tom] Dunkel tells the story of a North Dakota car dealer who, more than a decade before Jackie Robinson, formed an integrated baseball team that captured the hearts of the region."

REVIEW: *Booklist* v109 no16 p14 Ap 15 2013 Wes Lukowsky

REVIEW: *Kirkus Rev* v81 no10 p78 My 15 2013

REVIEW: *N Y Times Book Rev* p38 O 13 2013 Jay Jennings

"American Pastimes: The Very Best of Red Smith," "Breaking the Line: The Season in Black College Football that Transformed the Sport and Changed the Course of Civil Rights," and "A Chance to Win: Boyhood, Baseball, and the Struggle for Redemption in the Inner City." "Smith rarely sounds dated or overwrought. Whatever the subject, the authority of his prose never flags. . . . It's probably not fair to blame the author for overstatement in a subtitle. . . . [Samuel G.] Freedman never makes the case for the latter in what is a dutiful, near-hagiographic dual biography of Eddie Robinson and Jake Gaither. . . . The sport is merely the occasion for [Jonathan] Schuppe's deep excavation into four hard-knock lives in Newark. . . The 'cycle' in the rough neighborhoods Schuppe vividly captures is not something you hit for but something that hits you, repeatedly."

REVIEW: *Publ Wkly* v260 no4 p160 Ja 28 2013

SCHWARTZ, AMY, 1954-.il. Dee Dee and me. See Schwartz, A.

SCHWARTZ, AMY, 1954-. Dee Dee and me; [by] Amy Schwartz 32 p. 2013 Holiday House

1. Families—Juvenile fiction 2. Picture books for children 3. Sharing 4. Sibling rivalry 5. Sisters—Fiction
ISBN 082342524X (reinforced); 9780823425242 (reinforced)
LC 2012-016565

SUMMARY: In this children's picture book, "Hannah is an easy target for Dee Dee. She's younger and shorter (Dee Dee says the brains are in the 5 1/2 inches of height Hannah's missing), and she longs for her sister's acceptance. But after one too many manipulations, Hannah learns to assert herself--and now she's sure her brains are growing!" (Kirkus Reviews)

REVIEW: *Booklist* v110 no6 p39 N 15 2013 Ilene Cooper

"Dee Dee and Me." "Little sister Hannah tells the story here. Dee Dee is five-and-a-half inches taller (where a person's brains are,' Dee Dee informs Hannah) and always one step ahead. . . . In both heartfelt words and sympathy-inducing art, [Amy] Schwartz captures the push-pull of sibling love. Bright ink-and-watercolor pictures juxtapose humor with indignation iced with tenderness, making way for an ending that's as lovable as its heroines. Any sister will appreciate this one, no matter where she falls in the family order."

REVIEW: *Bull Cent Child Books* v67 no4 p238 D 2013 J. H.

REVIEW: *Horn Book Magazine* v89 no5 p80-1 S/O 2013 JULIE ROACH

REVIEW: *Kirkus Rev* v81 no13 p94 Jl 1 2013

REVIEW: *Kirkus Rev* p44 Ag 15 2013 Fall Preview

REVIEW: *Kirkus Rev* p53 2013 Guide 20to BookExpo America

REVIEW: *N Y Times Book Rev* p42 N 10 2013 SARAH HARRISON SMITH

"You Were the First," "Dee Dee and Me," and "The Big Wet Balloon." "In the hands of [Patricia] MacLachlan, the sweetly detailed text and pictures of a biracial family living somewhere that looks a lot like Brooklyn are a comforting reminder of how special all those 'firsts' can be. . . . [Amy] Schwartz wisely withholds comment, but there's inspiration here--as well as some cheerful pictures--for those siblings who always get stuck playing the butler, rather than the duchess, at dress-up time. . . . [Ricardo] Liniers, a cartoonist . . . based this miniature graphic novel on his daughters. . . . Though they have one small misunderstanding, these siblings are loving and thoughtful--good companions whatever the weather."

REVIEW: *Publ Wkly* p34 Children's starred review annual 2013

REVIEW: *Publ Wkly* v260 no32 p58 Ag 12 2013

REVIEW: *SLJ* v59 no8 p89 Ag 2013 B. Allison Gray

SCHWARTZ, COREY ROSEN. Goldi Rocks and the three bears; [by] Corey Rosen Schwartz 32 p. 2014 G.P. Putnam's Sons, an imprint of Penguin Group (USA) Inc.

1. Bears—Fiction 2. Rock groups—Fiction 3. Singers—Fiction 4. Stories in rhyme 5. Three Bears (Tale)
ISBN 9780399256851 (hardcover)
LC 2012-046278

SUMMARY: "In this modernized version of the fairy tale, the bears are a jammin' rock-and-roll group, but they can't seem to draw a crowd. They really need a singer who can hit the high notes. While they're out auditioning new talent, Goldi walks into their house/studio. But this blond youngster bypasses the porridge in favor of the musical gear. Naturally, the bears are outraged when they come home to find a sleeping girl, but once they find out she has pipes of gold, they write a new song." (School Library Journal)

REVIEW: *Horn Book Magazine* v90 no5 p136-7 S/O 2014 Katrina Hedeen

REVIEW: *Kirkus Rev* v81 no24 p87 D 15 2013

"Goldi Rocks and the Three Bears". "The classic tale of a blonde house invader is given a new rock-'n'-roll spin. [Corey Rosen] Schwartz and [Beth] Coulton use light verse to trace the beginnings of a hot new band. . . . While they are out auditioning singers, Goldi stumbles upon their cottage-turned-recording studio. . . .[Nate] Wragg's pencil-and-digital cartoon illustrations match the text but add little that's new, and the limericklike verse doesn't always scan well. Cute but not much more."

REVIEW: *Publ Wkly* v260 no47 p52-3 N 18 2013

REVIEW: *SLJ* v60 no2 p79 F 2014 Amy Seto Musser

SCHWARTZ, LYNNE SHARON. This is where we came in; intimate glimpses; [by] Lynne Sharon Schwartz 272 p. 2014 Counterpoint Press

1. American essays 2. Authors, American—20th century—Biography 3. Cardiac patients 4. Grandparent & child 5. Parent & child
ISBN 9781619022461
LC 2013-029182

SUMMARY: This collection of essays by Lynne Sharon Schwartz presents "recollections of her life, beginning with her serious heart-valve surgery and ranging back in time, to going to movies as a child, her relationship with her complicated and challenging parents, her own difficulties with intimacy and anger, thoughts about long friendships, and the pure delight of grandchildren." (Publisher's note)

REVIEW: *Booklist* v110 no13 p13-4 Mr 1 2014 Deborah Donovan

"This Is Where We Came In: Intimate Glimpses." "[Lynne Sharon] Schwartz . . . offers probing and perceptive 'glimpses' into her life, past and present. She begins with her confrontations with the medical bureaucracy during her heart valve surgery, as well as the surprising camaraderie she experienced with other patients on the cardiac floor. . . . Schwartz muses on topics as varied as the bullying she experienced in the third grade and the wheelchair yoga class she took with a friend dying of cancer. While many of these essays treat familiar themes--the joy of being a grandmother--Schwartz imbues them with her signature curiosity, introspection, and insight."

REVIEW: *Kirkus Rev* v81 no24 p244 D 15 2013

SCHWARTZ, NEIL DAVID. What If Tomorrow Never Comes?; [by] Neil David Schwartz 224 p. 2013 CreateSpace Independent Publishing Platform

1. Adjustment (Psychology) 2. Cancer patients 3. Diseases—Religious aspects 4. Life change events 5. Memoirs
ISBN 1484900359; 9781484900352

SUMMARY: This book is "a memoir of a father, his family and their collective battle with his daughter's cancer. Schwartz is a father, husband and attorney experiencing spiritual galut, a Hebrew word meaning the search to gain understanding of one's existence. His faith was tested when his 26-year-old daughter was diagnosed with stage 4 lung cancer. . . . Schwartz and his wife, Joanne, accompanied Amy to every appointment and test. As Amy's health deteriorated, so did her mother's." (Kirkus Reviews)

REVIEW: *Kirkus Rev* v82 no1 p312 Ja 1 2014

"What If Tomorrow Never Comes?" "The beginning chapters of [Neil David\ Schwartz's memoir recount the family's history and their journey through galut, with an essaylike level of detail that's compelling although separate in some ways from the heart of the story. The book then moves to his daughter's battle with cancer, a story both heartbreaking and powerful. . . . An absorbing read, the heartrending memoir portrays the family's tragic but compelling story without sentimentality but with Schwartz's ample love for his family and a wish to help others. A touching memoir of dealing with two losses."

SCHWARTZBERG, MELISSA. Counting the many; the origins and limits of supermajority rule; [by] Melissa Schwartzberg xiv, 237 p. 2014 Cambridge University Press

1. Constitutional law—Cross-cultural studies 2. Democracy—Cross-cultural studies 3. Majorities—Cross-cultural studies 4. Political science literature 5. Representative government and representation—Cross-cultural studies
ISBN 9780521124492 (paperback); 9780521198233 (hardback); 9781107040427
LC 2013-007634

SUMMARY: "In this book, Melissa Schwartzberg challenges the logic underlying the use of supermajority rule as an alternative to majority decision making. She traces the hidden history of supermajority decision making, which originally emerged as an alternative to unanimous rule, and highlights the tensions in the contemporary use of supermajority rules as an alternative to majority rule." (Publisher's note)

REVIEW: *New Repub* v244 no21 p52-5 F 3 2014 Adrian Vermeule

"Counting the Many: The Origins and Limits of Supermajority Rule". "Melissa Schwartzberg's new study of supermajority rules could not be more timely. . . . This book is . . . innovative and . . . excellent. . . . Whereas mathematical social choice became increasingly self-absorbed, cramped, and baroque, the new social choice has thrown open its doors to the fresh air of the world. Schwartzberg nicely exemplies the trend. . . . Schwartzberg is at her most arresting and novel when she documents and explains the use of such non-formal methods of social choice; the contrast with the blackboard theorems can be no sharper."

SCHWARZ-BART, SIMONE. The bridge of beyond; 272 p. 2013 New York Review Books

1. Guadeloupe literature (French) 2. Mothers & daughters—Fiction 3. Psychological fiction 4. Slavery—Fiction
ISBN 9781590176801 (alk. paper)
LC 2013-015580

SUMMARY: This novel by Simone Schwarz-Bart looks at "love and wonder, mothers and daughters, spiritual values and the grim legacy of slavery on the French Antillean island of Guadeloupe. Here long-suffering Telumee tells her life story and tells us about the proud line of Lougandor women she continues to draw strength from." (Publisher's note)

REVIEW: *TLS* no5782 p26 Ja 24 2014 BELINDA JACK

"The Bridge of Beyond." "'Pluie et vent sur Télumée Miracle' (1972), the first of Schwarz-Bart's two solo novels, was translated by Barbara Bray as 'The Bridge of Beyond' in 1974 and is now reissued with a splendid introduction by a fellow Antillean writer, Jamaica Kincaid. The novel tells of the complex lives and sensibilities of Guadeloupian women across five generations. . . . From their life stories, [narrator] Telumee draws the strength to withstand poverty and heartbreak and to share her own experience. Her story is, in part, about storytelling itself and the ways in which language can teach us to suffer the pain of loneliness or despair but to keep going."

REVIEW: *World Lit Today* v87 no5 p4 S/O 2013 Sam Wilson

"The Bridge of Beyond." "play. In this new edition . . . [Simone Schwarz-Bart's] narrative and Barbara Bray's 1974 translation from the French both hold up well, confirming the novel's status as a tour de force of Caribbean literature. . . . The effect of 'Bridge' is intoxicating, and not just because it nurses familiar blues riffs from my own American heritage--its heady prose renders a vivid, full-bodied account of life in the Antilles. . . . This is an infinite, celebratory novel, containing multitudes in the space of each rich sentence--a masterpiece of Caribbean literature that certainly deserves the badge of the classic."

SCHWARZ, VIVIANE. The Sleepwalkers; [by] Viviane Schwarz 96 p. 2013 Candlewick Press

1. Animals—Juvenile fiction 2. Children—Sleep 3. Children's nightmares 4. Children's stories 5. Dreams—Fiction
ISBN 0763662305 (paperback); 9780763662301 (paperback)
LC 2012-947253

SUMMARY: This book by Viviane Schwarz offers a "tale of a band of intrepid dream warriors who rescue defenseless sleeping children from nightmares. Bonno (short for Bonifacius), a blanket transformed into a timid bear; Amali, an exuberant sock monkey; and Sophia, a crow made from a writing quill who communicates by writing, are the Sleepwalkers' newest recruits, learning the ropes from a trio of seasoned sheep." (Publishers Weekly)

REVIEW: *Booklist* v109 no16 p48 Ap 15 2013 Jesse Karp

REVIEW: *Bull Cent Child Books* v67 no1 p52 S 2013 K. Q. G.

"The Sleepwalkers." "Fear not, sleepy reader, a peaceful rest awaits you now that the Sleepwalkers are here to banish those pesky bad dreams for good. First, however, they have to undergo a major staffing change in this whimsical graphic novel, as the three incumbent Walkers (a goat, a ram, and a bison) yearn to take a rest themselves and recruit Bonno, a large but timid bear (formerly a blanket); Amali, an over-eager sock monkey; and Sophia, a crow-like creature with a pen-nib head. . . . The cheerful chaos of the plot structure and the illustrations provide cheerful buoyancy, and. . . the ultimate effect is that of a strange but enjoyable dream. The sketchy art . . . perfectly echoes the nebulous space of the inner mind. . ."

REVIEW: *Kirkus Rev* v81 no8 p110 Ap 15 2013

REVIEW: *Publ Wkly* v260 no15 p66 Ap 15 2013

REVIEW: *SLJ* v59 no7 p105 Jl 2013 Peter Blenski

SCHWENINGER, LOREN. Families in crisis in the Old South; divorce, slavery, and the law; [by] Loren Schweninger xv, 236 p. 2012 University of North Carolina Press

1. Adultery—United States 2. Divorce—Law and legislation—United States 3. Domestic relations—United States 4. Historical literature 5. Slavery—Law and legislation—United States 6. Wife abuse—United States
ISBN 9780807835692 (cloth : alk. paper)
LC 2012-002040

SUMMARY: In this book on divorce in the antebellum South, Loren Schweninger "explores the impact of divorce and separation on white families and on the enslaved and provides insights on issues including domestic violence, interracial adultery, alcoholism, insanity, and property relations. He examines how divorce and separation laws changed, how married women's property rights expanded, how definitions of inhuman treatment of wives evolved, and how these divorces challenged conventional mores." (Publisher's note)

REVIEW: *Am Hist Rev* v118 no3 p852-3 Je 2013 Mary Beth Sievens

REVIEW: *Choice* v50 no7 p1319 Mr 2013 P. D. Travis

REVIEW: *J Am Hist* v100 no1 p202-3 Je 2013 David Silkenat

REVIEW: *Rev Am Hist* v41 no3 p458-61 S 2013 Anya Jabour

"Families in Crisis in the Old South: Divorce, Slavery, and the Law." "Concise and comprehensive. . . . [Loren Schweninger] also offers provocative analyses of gender, race, and slaveholding as these factors played out in family dynamics, often coming to surprising conclusions. . . . African Americans play a minor and supporting role. . . . Here the limitations of Schweninger's otherwise revealing source base become frustratingly apparent. Schweninger's clear explanations of legal terminology and his decision to open and close each chapter with a detailed narrative of a particular family's travails save this book from becoming either an esoteric legal study or a dry recital of statistics."

SCHYFTER, PABLO. Synthetic aesthetics; investigating synthetic biology's designs on nature; [by] Pablo Schyfter 376 p. 2014 MIT Press

1. Art 2. Biotechnology—trends 3. Esthetics 4. Science—Popular works 5. Synthetic Biology—trends
ISBN 9780262019996 (hardcover: alk. paper)
LC 2013-013618

SUMMARY: "In this book, synthetic biologists, artists, designers, and social scientists investigate synthetic biology and design. After chapters that introduce the science and set the terms of the discussion, the book follows six boundary-crossing collaborations between artists and designers and synthetic biologists from around the world, helping us understand what it might mean to 'design nature.'" (Publisher's note)

REVIEW: *New Sci* v222 no2966 p50 Ap 26 2014 Alun Anderson

"Synthetic Aesthetics: Investigating Synthetic Biology's Designs on Nature." "Some of [synthetic biology's] leading scientists took the unusual step of teaming up with artists and designers to create some fresh thinking. The result is the glossy 'Synthetic Aesthetics: Investigating Synthetic Biology's Designs on Nature.' It is a freewheeling book with 20 authors and may irritate conventional scientists. . . . But it certainly explains the key ideas of the field and leads you to many lateral conversations about what it may become."

THE SCIENCE OF PHYSICS; 80 p. 2012 Britannica Educational Pub.

1. Electricity 2. Light 3. Magnetes 4. Mechanics 5. Physics—Juvenile literature 6. Physics literature
ISBN 1615306765; 9781615306763 (library binding)
LC 2011-026548

SUMMARY: This children's book, edited by Andrea R. Field, is part of the Introduction to Physics series. It "surveys some of the major branches of physics, the laws, and theories significant to each. Also chronicled are some of the historical milestones in the field by such great minds as Galileo and Isaac Newton." (Publisher's note)

REVIEW: *Booklist* v108 no22 p64 Ag 1 2012 Susan Dove Lempke

SCIESZKA, JON, 1954-. Battle Bunny. See Battle Bunny

SCIUTO, ALEX.il. Natural disasters through infographics. See Higgins, N.

SCOFIELD, TED. Eat what you kill; [by] Ted Scofield 304 p. 2014 St. Martin's Press

1. FICTION—Thrillers 2. Financial services industry 3. Investment fraud 4. Revenge—Fiction 5. Stockbrokers
ISBN 9781250021823 (hardback)
LC 2013-031861

SUMMARY: This book by Ted Scofield follows "Evan Stoess, the byproduct of a ritzy prep school education but born out of wedlock to a trailer park-trash mom who raised him in a home dominated by an abusive stepfather, envies the rich and successful to the point of obsessiveness. Evan, who works in finance, spends much of his free time scheming ways to grow rich and spying on a wealthy man and his family." (Kirkus Reviews)

REVIEW: *Booklist* v110 no12 p32 F 15 2014 Stacy Alesi
REVIEW: *Kirkus Rev* v82 no2 p284 Ja 15 2014

"Eat What You Kill". "[Ted] Scofield, an attorney, writes knowledgeably about high finance, but unless readers are familiar with the terminology, they'll find much of the book incomprehensible. This is a tale spun in staccato and somewhat lifeless prose. Scofield buries the plot under a mountain of name-dropping minutiae, to the point of regaling readers with the brand of shorts worn by a store clerk. An intriguing idea that could have been better executed but instead ends up top-heavy with dull technical detail, static writing and a hard-to-swallow conclusion."

REVIEW: *Publ Wkly* v261 no4 p169 Ja 27 2014

SCOTCH, ALLISON WINN. The Theory of Opposites; [by] Allison Winn Scotch 310 p. 2013 Camellia Press

1. Fate & fatalism 2. Life change events—Fiction 3. Man-woman relationships—Fiction 4. Married women—Fiction 5. Psychological fiction
ISBN 0989499006; 9780989499002

SUMMARY: In this book, the protagonist's "husband proposes . . . a two-month break. . . . And before Willa can sort out destiny and fate and what it all means, she's axed from her job, her 12 year-old nephew Nicky moves in, her exboyfriend finds her on Facebook, and her best friend Vanessa lands a gig writing for Dare You!, the hottest new reality TV show. And then Vanessa lures Willa into dares of her own." (Publisher's note)

REVIEW: *Booklist* v110 no6 p21-2 N 15 2013 Rebecca Vnuk

"The Theory of Opposites." "Thanks to her famous father's theory that there is no such thing as free will (as outlined in his best-selling self-help book), Willa has been told her entire life that everything that happens is fate, and people have no control over their destinies. When Willa's world comes crashing down (she loses her job, and her husband proposes a two-month separation out of the blue), she's pretty sure her dad was right, but her best friend, Vanessa, convinces her to test that theory by doing the opposite of what instinct tells her to do. . . . Readers who enjoyed [Allison Winn] Scotch's 'The Song Remains the Same' (2012) will find much to like in this similar and satisfying tale of a woman changing her fate."

REVIEW: *Libr J* v139 no9 p73 My 15 2014 ALA Rusa-Codes
REVIEW: *Publ Wkly* v261 no7 p72 F 17 2014
REVIEW: *Publ Wkly* v261 no4 p146-54 Ja 27 2014

SCOTT, ALEV. Turkish Awakening; A Personal Discovery of Modern Turkey; [by] Alev Scott 336 p. 2014 Faber & Faber Non-Fiction

1. Journalism 2. Protest movements 3. Travelers' writings 4. Turkey—Politics & government—1980- 5. Turkey—Social life & customs
ISBN 0571296572; 9780571296576

SUMMARY: "From the European buzz of modern-day Constantinople to the Arabic-speaking towns of the southeast, 'Turkish Awakening' investigates a country moving swiftly towards a new position on the world stage. Relating wide-ranging interviews and colourful personal experience, [author Alev Scott] charts the evolving course of a country bursting with surprises—none more dramatic than the unexpected political protests of 2013." (Publisher's note)

REVIEW: *TLS* no5792 p34 Ap 4 2014 JEREMY SEAL

"Turkish Awakening." "The book is not primarily an eyewitness account of [the Gezi Park] protest movement, with its park occupations, running battles and incidents of police brutality. . . . This book bespeaks a welcome grounding in personal experience, one which only occasionally resorts to newspaper cuttings or internet searches for its substance. Scott has managed to process a remarkable amount of information in her comparatively brief exposure to Turkey. . . . What further distinguishes 'Turkish Awakening' is Scott's pronounced demimonde streak. . . . The book's concluding chapter reflects on the nationwide protests which Gezi Park sparked."

SCOTT, BETHAN-ANN. Empress Fallen; [by] Bethan-Ann Scott 510 p. 2013 Createspace Independent Pub

1. Imperialism—Fiction 2. Science fiction 3. Scientists—Fiction 4. Slave insurrections—Fiction 5. Slav-

ery—Fiction
ISBN 1492187313; 9781492187318

SUMMARY: "In this debut sci-fi novel, two young women in different corners of a faraway solar system learn a secret that might save the fate of the human race. Aliya Soter has always known that she wasn't born on the slave planet on which she lives. . . . She begins to uncover the tyrannical Western Empire's secret. . . . Far away, Miriam Ferox . . . has wanted to bring down the Empress since she was 9, and she recently found the very information that could do so." (Kirkus Reviews)

REVIEW: *Kirkus Rev* v82 no3 p357 F 1 2014

"Empress Fallen: Through Darkness". "[Bethan-Ann] Scott's debut novel, the first in a planned series, explores issues such as class, oppression and the nature of freedom, drawing from classic sci-fi and other literature as it relates its story in elegant prose. . . . The story's numerous supporting characters may be hard for readers to keep track of at first, but the beautifully developed women at its center more than make up for such difficulty. Although Miriam's story is a bit slow at first, she ultimately becomes a complex, compelling character whose story is certain to grab readers' attention. A poignant tale of revolution that's much more than mere space opera."

SCOTT, DAMON. Well-structured mathematical logic; [by] Damon Scott xix, 269 p. 2013 Carolina Academic Press

1. Logic, Symbolic and mathematical 2. Mathematical literature 3. Mathematical proofs 4. Philosophy of mathematics 5. Symbolic & mathematical logic
ISBN 9781611633689
LC 2012-041322

SUMMARY: This book, written by Damon Scott, "does for logic what Structured Programming did for computation: make large-scale work possible. From the work of George Boole onward, traditional logic was made to look like a form of symbolic algebra. . . . A very important feature of the new system is that it structures the expression of mathematics in much the same way that people already do informally." (Publisher's note)

REVIEW: *Choice* v51 no2 p305-6 O 2013 D. V. Feldman

"Well-Structured Mathematical Logic." "The argument is that conventional formal logic captures only the content of informal mathematics, making formal proofs convoluted and obscure beyond human utility. The reform would be new, less-nested syntax designed to flow in the manner of informal proof, still structured sufficiently for machine verification and manipulation. [Author Damon] Scott . . . writes polemically, constantly anticipating reader negativity. . . . This book's style seems too pedantic for experts, without speaking directly to beginners hoping to learn logic correctly the first time. . . . Despite an irritating style, the book is clear, readable, and provocative in its discussion of mathematical and programming practice and pedagogy."

SCOTT, ELIZABETH. Heartbeat; [by] Elizabeth Scott 304 p. 2013 Harlequin Books

1. Brain death 2. Grief—Fiction 3. Love stories 4. Mothers—Death—Fiction 5. Stepfathers—Fiction
ISBN 0373210965; 9780373210961

SUMMARY: In this book by Elizabeth Scott, "Emma's mom lies in a hospital, brain-dead and being kept physically alive until the baby is able to be born." Her stepfather "Dan insists this is what his wife would want, but Emma is sure her mother would never want to be hooked up to machines. Her grades plummet and grief threatens to consume her when she suddenly finds herself drawn to bad boy, Caleb, whose parents still blame him for his little sister's death years before." (School Library Journal)

REVIEW: *Booklist* v110 no11 p63-4 F 1 2014 Kathryn Schleff

REVIEW: *Bull Cent Child Books* v67 no5 p282-3 Ja 2014 D. S.

"Heartbeat." "[Elizabeth] Scott is a versatile and capable writer, and here she creates a romance where the relationship ties in directly with a more central family drama. Emma's rage against her stepfather is believable in its shifts from cold and punitive to white-hot and screaming, but it's also credible that this focused fury operates as her main emotional response to a horrible and deeply conflicted situation; the book is especially effective at depicting the torturous limbo of the grieving in such a situation. Caleb is a little idealized, but that just makes the romance of the romance sweeter, and the sorrow that brings Emma and Caleb together is sensitively handled."

REVIEW: *Horn Book Magazine* v90 no3 p98 My/Je 2014 LAUREN ADAMS

REVIEW: *Kirkus Rev* p73-4 2013 Guide 20to BookExpo America

REVIEW: *Kirkus Rev* v81 no24 p2 D 15 2013

REVIEW: *SLJ* v60 no1 p104 Ja 2014 Heather Webb

REVIEW: *Voice of Youth Advocates* v36 no6 p65 F 2014 Teri Lesesne

SCOTT, JACQUELINE.ed. Gendered Lives. See Gendered Lives

SCOTT, JAMES. The kept; [by] James Scott 368 p. 2014 Harper

1. American historical fiction 2. Murder—Fiction 3. Revenge—Fiction 4. Teenage boys—Fiction 5. Upstate New York (N.Y.)
ISBN 0062236733; 9780062236654 (trade paperback); 9780062236739 (hardback)
LC 2013-027875

SUMMARY: Set in rural New York state at the turn of the twentieth century, . . . James Scott makes his literary debut with 'The Kept'--a . . . novel reminiscent of the works of Michael Ondaatje, Cormac McCarthy, and Bonnie Jo Campbell, in which a mother and her young son embark on a quest to avenge a terrible and violent tragedy that has shattered their secluded family. . . . A scorching portrait of a merciless world . . . 'The Kept' introduces an old-beyond-his-years protagonist." (Publisher's note)

REVIEW: *Booklist* v110 no6 p26 N 15 2013 Sarah Johnson

REVIEW: *Kirkus Rev* v81 no20 p172 O 15 2013

REVIEW: *N Y Times Book Rev* p23 Ja 26 2014 ALYSON HAGY

REVIEW: *New York Times* v163 no56375 pC1-C10 Ja 8 2014 IVY POCHODA

"The Kept." "James Scott's debut novel, 'The Kept,' opens on a scene of massacred children. It's daring and bleak in a novel whose daring is found in its bleakness. . . . What follows is an unrelentingly somber story of revenge played out across an austere landscape. . . . If not for the author's sparse, elegant prose, twanged with puritanical patois, 'The Kept' might be simply agonizing. Instead, it is a haunting narrative, salvaged by precise language that never overreaches or oversells. . . . 'The Kept' reaches a credible outcome, if a disturbing one."

REVIEW: *Publ Wkly* v260 no45 p48 N 11 2013

SCOTT, JUSTIN. The bootlegger. See Cussler, C.

SCOTT, LISA ANN. School of Charm; [by] Lisa Ann Scott 304 p. 2014 Katherine Tegen Books, an imprint of HarperCollins Publishers

1. Beauty contests—Fiction 2. Family life—North Carolina—Fiction 3. Historical fiction 4. Individuality—Fiction 5. Race relations—Fiction 6. Self-perception—Fiction

ISBN 006220758X; 9780062207586 (hardcover bdg.)
LC 2013-014341

SUMMARY: In this children's novel, by Lisa Ann Scott, "eleven-year-old Chip has always been her daddy's girl, so when he dies she pins her hopes on winning a beauty pageant to show her family of southern belles that she still belongs. But she'd rather be covered in mud than makeup! Can a rough-and-tumble girl ever become a beauty queen?" (Publisher's note)

REVIEW: *Booklist* v110 no11 p68 F 1 2014 Carolyn Phelan

REVIEW: *Bull Cent Child Books* v67 no6 p332-3 F 2014 Jeannette Hulick

"School of Charm." "Chip is a likable heroine, and the period setting is cozy but still realistic. . . . The family dynamics are engaging but overdrawn: Chip's grandmother is so nasty to her for so much of the book that her change of heart near the end, while a relief, is hard to swallow. Chip's willingness to participate in a pageant may be equally unbelievable, but her sorrow at the loss of her father is entirely credible. Despite the book's shortcomings, readers who like heart-warming family stories, spunky heroines, and Southern settings may still find this an entertaining read."

REVIEW: *Kirkus Rev* v81 no23 p186 D 1 2013

REVIEW: *Publ Wkly* v260 no51 p61 D 16 2013

REVIEW: *SLJ* v60 no2 p96 F 2014 Maria B. Salvadore

SCOTT, TOM. The city-state in Europe, 1000-1600; hinterland, territory, region; [by] Tom Scott xi, 382 p. 2012 Oxford University Press

1. Cities and towns, Medieval—Europe—History 2. City-states—Europe—History—16th century 3. City-states—Europe—History—To 1500 4. Historical literature

ISBN 0199274606 (hbk. : acid-free paper); 9780199274604 (hbk. : acid-free paper)
LC 2011-276781

SUMMARY: In this book, author Tom Scott "criticizes current typologies of the city-state in Europe advanced by political and social scientists to suggest that the city-state was not a spent force in early modern Europe, but rather survived by transformation and adaption. He puts forward instead a typology which embraces both time and space by arguing for a regional framework for analysis which does not treat city-states in isolation but within a wider geopolitical setting." (Publisher's note)

REVIEW: *Am Hist Rev* v118 no4 p1236-7 O 2013 David Nicholas

REVIEW: *Choice* v50 no3 p561 N 2012 K. F. Drew

REVIEW: *Engl Hist Rev* v128 no534 p1199-200 O 2013 Gianluca Raccagni

REVIEW: *History* v98 no330 p254-6 Ap 2013 Gervase Rosser

REVIEW: *TLS* no5761 p21 Ag 30 2013 LAURO MARTINES

"The City-State in Europe, 1000-1600: Hinterland, Territory, Region." "Tom Scott's 'The City-State in Europe, 1000-1600' brings a major addition to our picture of the subject. He provides a detailed cross-section of developments in Italy, Germany, Switzerland and the Low Countries. . . . In his investigative tenacity, Scott goes into the doings of two tiny Swiss cities, Schaffliausen and Solothum, at more length than he gives to Augsburg and Nuremberg, thereby putting Swiss towns on a scale with Pisa, Genoa and the main cities of the Low Countries. This tack introduces considerable diversity to the history of city-states, but threatens to distort our perspective. He is therefore driven, in his conclusion, to try to sort out conflicting definitions of the city-state."

SCOTT, VICTORIA. Fire & flood; [by] Victoria Scott 320 p. 2014 Scholastic Press

1. Adventure racing—Juvenile fiction 2. Brothers and sisters—Fiction 3. Brothers and sisters—Juvenile fiction 4. Competition (Psychology)—Fiction 5. Competition (Psychology)—Juvenile fiction 6. Contests—Fiction 7. Contests—Juvenile fiction 8. Fantasy fiction 9. Racing—Fiction 10. Survival—Fiction 11. Survival—Juvenile fiction

ISBN 9780545537469 (hardcover)
LC 2013-014732

SUMMARY: In this book, "when a mysterious blue box arrives for Tella, a small audio device invites her to compete in the Brimstone Bleed. She has less than 48 hours to report to the competition, select a Pandora companion and enter in a three-month race across four separate ecosystems—first to the finish line gets a cure for any illness. Tella seizes the chance to save her deathly ill brother's life and is tossed into a ruthless survivalist competition." (Kirkus Reviews)

REVIEW: *Booklist* v110 no12 p80 F 15 2014 Paula Willey

REVIEW: *Kirkus Rev* v82 no2 p54 Ja 15 2014

"Fire & Flood". " While the overall worldbuilding is light, the more immediate competition settings are ably exploited for dangers. The Pandoras are eggs that hatch genetically engineered, superpowered animals—not terribly realistic but so much fun that nobody will care. Everyone has a loved one to save so stakes are high, but survival necessitates teaming up, yielding hilarious dialogue. Of course, one of Tella's teammates is a handsome, broody, uber-competent love interest. The female supporting characters are less stock. Tella herself is awkward, doofy and self-consciously superficial—the combination makes her easy to root for."

REVIEW: *Publ Wkly* v261 no1 p58 Ja 6 2014

REVIEW: *SLJ* v60 no3 p163 Mr 2014 Kim Dare

REVIEW: *Voice of Youth Advocates* v36 no6 p77 F 2014 Heidi Culbertson

REVIEW: *Voice of Youth Advocates* v36 no6 p77 F 2014 Jane Harper

SCOTT, W. RICHARD.ed. Global projects. See Global projects

SCREENING LOVE AND SEX IN THE ANCIENT WORLD; viii, 278 p. 2013 Palgrave Macmillan

1. Civilization, Ancient, in motion pictures 2. Civilization, Ancient, on television 3. Film criticism 4. Love in motion pictures 5. Rome—In motion pictures 6. Sex in motion pictures 7. Sex on television 8. Television criticism
ISBN 1137299592; 9781137299598
LC 2013-409627

SUMMARY: This book, edited by Monica S. Cyrino, "addresses the provocative representation of sexuality in the ancient world on screen. Throughout the history of cinema, filmmakers have returned to the history, mythology, and literature of Greek and Roman antiquity as the ideal site for narratives of erotic adventure and displays of sexual excess. A critical reader on the creative approaches used to screen sexuality in classical settings, contributors utilize case studies." (Publisher's note)

REVIEW: *Choice* v51 no1 p85-6 S 2013 D. Konstan

"Screening Love and Sex in the Ancient World." "[Editor Monica S.] Cyrino . . . has gathered 16 original and entertaining essays by leading international film scholars and classicists exploring how images of a dissolute Rome, as well as of alternative sexualities (especially homoerotic) in ancient Greece, have influenced modern films and TV series. The first seven essays treat films that evoke classical models implicitly . . . , whereas the next nine deal with shows that recreate quasi-historical episodes. . . . Film buffs, fans of the classics, and anyone interested in ideologies of love and sex will find much to enjoy in this well-edited volume."

SCUDAMORE, JAMES. Wreaking; [by] James Scudamore 400 p. 2013 Harvill Secker

1. Abandoned buildings 2. Broadcast journalism 3. Fathers & daughters—Fiction 4. Psychiatric hospitals 5. Psychological fiction
ISBN 1846551897; 9781846551895

SUMMARY: In this book, "Jasper Scriven spends his days roaming the wards of a derelict psychiatric hospital on England's southeast coast. His daughter Cleo works in London as a news editor, making palatable stories of the world's events and trying to stay one step ahead of her demons. Meanwhile, she is watched by Roland, a hulking, silent figure who inhabits a network of railway arches, emerging at night to pound the streets and burgle homes to order." (Publisher's note)

REVIEW: *TLS* no5762 p20 S 6 2013 THEA LENARDUZZI

"Wreaking." "Not a lot happens to the characters in . . . James Scudamore's third novel. . . . Like the novel itself--cutting back and forth across time and flitting between characters--Wreaking resists closure; the institution belongs to all who have dwelt there. . . . 'Wreaking' is a self-conscious and self-reflexive novel. . . . It is this introspection that limits Wreaking's ability to move us. Having introduced a number of characters and associations . . . Scudamore fails to pay them the attention required to make them live in their own right. The airiness that defines the best of his descriptions and breathes realism into his dialogue is too often smothered by passages of neo-gothic fancy."

SEALY, JON. The whiskey baron; [by] Jon Sealy 250 p. 2014 Hub City Press

1. Distilling, Illicit—Fiction 2. Historical fiction 3. Murder—Investigation—Fiction 4. Sheriffs—Fiction
ISBN 9781891885747 (cloth: alk. paper)
LC 2013-032664

SUMMARY: This book by Jon Sealy is "set in South Carolina during Prohibition. Outside a bar that serves as a front for the lucrative whiskey operation of town heavy Larthan Tull, two boys who work for him are shotgunned to death, and a man called Mary Jane barely escapes, pellets embedded in his shoulder. . . . But Sheriff Furman Chambers is convinced Mary Jane is guilty of nothing more than chronic drunkenness." (Kirkus Reviews)

REVIEW: *Kirkus Rev* v82 no4 p16 F 15 2014

"The Whiskey Baron". "[Jon] Sealy's stunning debut novel is a potent mashup of noir, Southern fiction and period novel, set in South Carolina during Prohibition. . . . Told in pitch-perfect prose, with a rich command of time and place, Sealy's novel builds slowly but powerfully to a violent climax with deepening themes pertaining to blood ties, religion, community and American enterprise. Even the most upstanding citizens sell corn to Tull to make ends meet. Though it could use a better title, this is a near-flawless effort by a writer to watch."

REVIEW: *Libr J* v138 no21 p92 D 1 2013 Michael Pucci

REVIEW: *Publ Wkly* v260 no50 p44 D 9 2013

SEAMAN, CHRISTOPHER. Inside conducting. See Inside conducting

SEAMAN, REBECCA M.ed. Conflict in the early Americas. See Conflict in the early Americas

SEARLES, JOHN. Help for the Haunted; A Novel; [by] John Searles 368 p. 2013 William Morrow

1. Demonology 2. Murder—Fiction 3. Parent & child—Fiction 4. Parents—Death 5. Young adult fiction
ISBN 0060779632; 9780060779634

SUMMARY: In this book, "Sylvie Mason's parents are--or were--'demonologists.' Devoutly Christian, her dad zealously worked the lecture circuit while her mom had the talent to soothe the haunted humans who came to them for help. When they are both murdered in a church on a snowy night, 14-year-old Sylvie is the sole witness but doesn't fully remember what happened. . . . Sylvie struggles to reconcile her bleak new life with her slightly less-bleak former life. " (Kirkus Reviews)

REVIEW: *Booklist* v110 no14 p8 Mr 15 2014

"The Death of Bees," "Help for the Haunted," and "The Universe Versus Alex Woods." "With their parents dead and buried in the backyard, Scottish teens Marnie and Nelly are finally free from a childhood wracked with abuse. If only the neighbors dog would quit digging in the garden. . . . Sylvie is dealing with taunting classmates, her erratic older sister, and the unsolved murder of her ghost-hunting parents.

But perhaps more problematic are the cursed remnants of her parents' work still lingering in the basement. . . . It all begins when Alex is hit on the head by a meteorite, and it all ends when he is arrested trying to reenter England with several grams of marijuana, lots of cash, and the ashes of Mr. Peterson."

REVIEW: *Booklist* v109 no21 p37 Jl 1 2013 Joanne Wilkinson

REVIEW: *Kirkus Rev* v81 no10 p25 My 15 2013

REVIEW: *Libr J* v138 no7 p58 Ap 15 2013 Barbara Hoffert

REVIEW: *Libr J* v138 no12 p424 Jl 1 2013 Mahnaz Dar Bette-Lee Fox Margaret Heilbrun Barbara Hoffert Stephanie Klose Molly McArdle Annalisa Pesek Henrietta Thornton-Verma Wilda Williams

REVIEW: *Publ Wkly* v260 no22 p32 Je 3 2013

SEARLES, RACHEL. The Lost Planet; [by] Rachel Searles 384 p. 2014 Feiwel & Friends

1. Amnesia—Fiction 2. Crime—Fiction 3. Science fiction 4. Space flight—Fiction 5. Terrorism—Fiction

ISBN 1250038790; 9781250038791

SUMMARY: In this book, "when thirteen-year-old Chase Garrety suddenly appears within . . . an isolated compound on the planet Trucon, he has a blaster wound to the back of his head and no memory of his name, his life before, or how he got there. Things get even more complicated when the compound's only other resident . . .tricks him into an unauthorized trip to a nearby moon, and the boys inadvertently survive Trucon's total destruction as a result." (Bulletin of the Center for Children's Books)

REVIEW: *Booklist* v110 no9/10 p113 Ja 1 2014 Stacey Comfort

REVIEW: *Bull Cent Child Books* v67 no6 p333 F 2014 Alaine Martaus

"The Lost Planet." "A rollicking space adventure in the spirit of classic juvenile science fiction . . . this fast-paced novel will keep readers on the edge of their seats from page one. Chase and Parker are amusing, likable, authentically realized teenage boys, as likely to put their foot in their mouth as to save the day with unexpected courage. Strongly crafted alien worlds, discordant alien races, and often unsound space vehicles only add to the overall sense of strange and dangerous fun. Perfect for . . . Star Trek and Star Wars fans who want a middle-grade adventure of their own, this novel will have readers jetting across space itself for probable sequels"

REVIEW: *Publ Wkly* v260 no44 p67 N 4 2013

REVIEW: *SLJ* v60 no2 p97 F 2014 Marissa Lieberman

SEARLS, DAMION.ed. A schoolboy's diary and other stories. See A schoolboy's diary and other stories

SEARS, STEPHEN W.ed. The Civil War. See The Civil War

SEBAG-MONTEFIORE, CHARLES. A dynasty of dealers. See Armstrong-Totten, J.

SEBALD, WINFRIED GEORG, 1944-2001. A place in the country; 240 p. 2013 Random House Inc

1. Artists 2. Authors 3. Authors, German—20th century—Biography 4. Essay (Literary form)

ISBN 9781400067718 (acid-free paper)

LC 2013-012963

SUMMARY: This book by W. G. Sebald "contains essays on five German and Swiss writers, Jean-Jacques Rousseau, Johann Peter Hebel, Gottfried Keller, Eduard Mörike, and Robert Walser, and one painter, Jan Peter Tripp. Composed mainly in 1997, these essays explore familiar themes in Sebald's creations—the writer's isolation, the fading of memory, and the painstaking attention to the details in writing." (Library Journal)

REVIEW: *Bookforum* v21 no1 p42 Ap/My 2014 DAMION SEARLS

REVIEW: *Booklist* v110 no7 p10-1 D 1 2013 Michael Autrey

REVIEW: *Kirkus Rev* v81 no24 p18 D 15 2013

REVIEW: *N Y Times Book Rev* p26 Mr 30 2014

REVIEW: *N Y Times Book Rev* p10 Mr 23 2014 JOSHUA COHEN

"A Place in the Country." "'A Place in the Country,' which contains profiles of five writers and one painter, is the third volume of nonfiction Sebaldiana to appear in English, and the most casually generous, not least because it's the last. It's fitting that his English posterity ends at the beginning—with literary history, and with influence. . . . 'A Place in the Country' extends Sebald's canon deeper into the past, and into the Alemannic. . . . The book's finest essay concerns its earliest figure, Jean-Jacques Rousseau."

REVIEW: *Nation* v298 no20 p35-8 My 19 2014 BEN EHRENREICH

"A Place in the Country." "'A Place in the Country' . . . is . . . perhaps [author W. G.] Sebald's most tender and jovial book. But then it is about six men he professes to adore, a painter and five writers. . . . The five selected for tribute here are almost stock Sebaldian characters: broken and despondent, struggling to pull themselves from the crevasse of their understanding, seeking refuge in nature, solitude and silence. There is something sour in all of this, something stodgy and not quite honest."

REVIEW: *New York Times* v163 no56408 pC4 F 10 2014 JOHN WILLIAMS

"A Place in the Country". "It's tempting to say that 'A Place int he Country,' lightly connected essays in which W. G. Sebald writes about six artists he admires, will hold interest only for Sebald completists. But then, it's hard to imagine a Sebald reader who isn't an obsessive completist. . . . The artists in 'A Place in the Country,' first published in German in 1998, will most likely be unknown to American readers, except for Jean-Jacques Rousseau and possibly Robert Walser. . . . The essays include the familiar Sebaldian flourish of black-and-white photos, as well as stunning color images in two-page foldouts, and they lean on the indirect approach used in Sebald's major works."

REVIEW: *Publ Wkly* v260 no40 p38 O 7 2013

REVIEW: *TLS* no5767 p13 O 11 2013 BRIAN DILLON

SECKBACH, JOSEPH.ed. Habitability of other planets and satellites. See Habitability of other planets and satellites

THE SECOND AMENDMENT ON TRIAL; critical essays on District of Columbia v. Heller; ix, 446 p. 2013 University of Massachusetts Press

1. Firearms—Law and legislation—United States 2. Legal literature
ISBN 9781558499942 (hardcover: alk. paper); 9781558499959 (pbk.: alk. paper)
LC 2013-017812

SUMMARY: This book looks at a 2008 U.S. Supreme Court ruling "striking down the District of Columbia's stringent gun control laws as a violation of the Second Amendment. Reversing almost seventy years of settled precedent, the high court reinterpreted the meaning of the 'right of the people to keep and bear arms' to affirm an individual right to own a gun in the home for purposes of self-defense." It examines "the strengths and problems of originalist constitutional theory and jurisprudence." (Publisher's note)

REVIEW: *Choice* v51 no9 p1683-4 My 2014 J. R. Vile

"The Second Amendment On Trial: Critical Essays on District of Columbia v. Heller". "Historians [Saul] Cornell and [Nathan] Kozuskanish have compiled an excellent reader, especially designed to examine the originalist arguments of both sides of the debate. . . . Nathan Kozuskanich further questions the originalist pretensions of the majority decision, Kevin M. Sweeney examines early militia service in the states, and the editors summarize other scholarly sources since Heller and major briefs in the case."

SECORD, JAMES A. Visions of science; books and readers at the dawn of the Victorian age; [by] James A. Secord 256 p. 2014 University of Chicago Press

1. Books & reading—History 2. Great Britain—Intellectual life—19th century 3. Historical literature 4. Science—Great Britain—Historiography 5. Science—Great Britain—History—19th century
ISBN 9780226203287 (cloth: alk. paper)
LC 2014-010721

SUMMARY: "In 'Visions of Science,' James A. Secord . . . explores seven key books—among them Charles Babbage's 'Reflections on the Decline of Science,' Charles Lyell's 'Principles of Geology,' Mary Somerville's 'Connexion of the Physical Sciences,' and Thomas Carlyle's 'Sartor Resartus'—and shows how literature that reflects on the wider meaning of science can be revelatory when granted the kind of close reading usually reserved for fiction and poetry." (Publisher's note)

REVIEW: *Science* v343 no6178 p1433-4 Mr 28 2014 Bernard Lightman

"Visions of Science: Books and Readers at the Dawn of the Victorian Age." "In 'Visions of Science,' [author James A.] Secord offers answers to these questions by showing how print culture considerations illuminate the importance of seven key scientific texts from around 1830. . . . When it comes to analyzing the reactions of readers, Secord lacks the wealth of primary sources that he drew on for his earlier study of 'Vestiges.' . . . Nevertheless, his discussion of the reception of these works is always revealing. . . . One finds the payoff of the print culture perspective in the fresh interpretations of each text that Secord gives us. . . . Elegantly written, Secord's 'Visions of Science' provides its readers with fresh insights into the turbulent decade around 1830."

REVIEW: *TLS* no5805 p25 Jl 4 2014 USHASHI DASGUPTA

SEDER, RUFUS BUTLER. Santa!; a Scanimation picture book; [by] Rufus Butler Seder 24 p. 2013 Workman Publishing

1. Board books 2. Christmas stories 3. Santa Claus—Fiction 4. Stories in rhyme 5. Toy and movable books 6. Toy and movable books—Specimens
ISBN 9780761177258 (alk. paper)
LC 2013-032393

SUMMARY: In this children's picture book, "Santa swings into action, twisting that hoop around his portly waist behind an acetate overlay of thin black-and-white stripes. This gives the effect of an animated inset, achieved by technology similar to a flip book but concentrated in a small window. A simple, rhyming text describes Santa's actions as he juggles candy canes, twirls around on ice skates, does a back flip and a cartwheel, and kisses Rudolph on the nose." (Kirkus Reviews)

REVIEW: *Kirkus Rev* v81 no24 p407 D 15 2013

"Santa! A Scanimation Picture Book". "The cover has a round die cut with an illustration showing Santa with a hula hoop around his waist. As soon as the glittery white cover is opened, Santa swings into action, twisting that hoop around his portly waist behind an acetate overlay of thin black-and-white stripes. This gives the effect of an animated inset, achieved by technology similar to a flip book but concentrated in a small window. . . .The illustrations are a little dark due to the striped overlays, but the novelty is both mystifying and undeniably mesmerizing. This is a book that will interest everyone around the Christmas tree, from toddlers who use board books to older kids who will want to know how the moving pictures work. A gimmick…but one with a lot of bang for the buck."

SEEGERT, SCOTT. Time travel trouble. See Time travel trouble

SEGAL, LORE. Half the kingdom; a novel; [by] Lore Segal 176 p. 2013 Melville House

1. Dementia 2. FICTION—Literary 3. FICTION—Psychological 4. Humorous stories 5. Life change events—Fiction 6. Older people—Fiction
ISBN 1612193021; 9781612193021 (hardback)
LC 2013-018656

SUMMARY: This book, by Lore Segal, focuses on "Cedars of Lebanon Hospital, [where] doctors have noticed a marked uptick in Alzheimer's patients. People who seemed perfectly lucid just a day earlier suddenly show signs of advanced dementia. Is it just normal aging, or an epidemic? Is it a coincidence, or a secret terrorist plot?" (Publisher's note)

REVIEW: *Bookforum* v20 no3 p35 S-N 2013 EMILY COOKE

REVIEW: *Booklist* v110 no2 p30 S 15 2013 Carol Gladstein

"Half the Kingdom." "The staff of Cedars of Lebanon Hospital in New York have noticed a dramatic increase in the number of dementia patients. Apparently, people who seem perfectly clearheaded one day arrive at the hospital's emergency room the next with advanced Alzheimer's. . . . [Lore] Segal, Pulitzer Prize nominee for 'Shakespeare's Kitchen' (2007), has collected a very disparate group of people and expertly tied them together. With masterful dialogue and a good dose of black humor, she creates characters that are both easily recognizable and refreshingly new. Funny, sad, and at times deeply moving. 'Half the Kingdom' is a fascinating novel, a well-crafted, meaningful examination of life and death and all that lies in between."

REVIEW: *Kirkus Rev* v81 no18 p195 S 15 2013

REVIEW: *N Y Times Book Rev* p11 S 29 2013 Lore Segal

"Half the Kingdom." "[Lore] Segal wastes no time getting down to the excruciations. . . . Her new novel . . . opens in a hospital emergency room where a crisis is in progress. Anyone over 62 who sets foot in the E.R.--patient, relative, caregiver--goes bonkers. For lack of a better diagnosis, the disorder has been tagged 'copycat Alzheimer's.' Fans of Segal's fiction should feel right at home in this darkly comic novel. . . . Some scenes resemble high-tech horror fantasies. . . . Yet the novel's comedy beats back the darkness."

REVIEW: *Publ Wkly* v260 no32 p31-2 Ag 12 2013

REVIEW: *TLS* no5776 p20 D 13 2013 HIRSH SAWHNEY

"Half the Kingdom." "'Half the Kingdom' . . . is both funny and astute, a dialogue-driven novel about a group of loving but egotistical people who seem daunted by the ceaseless passage of time and alienated by their highly individualized, technology-driven world. . . . [Author Lore] Segal weaves together this sprawling cast and farcical plot with an omniscient and acerbic third-person narrator prone to meta-narrative musings on the art of storytelling. This guiding voice is precise and unsentimental, bringing readers closer to the mentally ill with a skilful combination of vivid language and purposefully disordered clauses. . . . Segal displays affection and warmth for her characters while ridiculing their imperfections. She is a bold satirist."

SEGAL, LYNNE. Out of time; the pleasures and perils of ageing; [by] Lynne Segal 320 p. 2013 Verso

1. Aging 2. Intergenerational relations 3. LITERARY CRITICISM—Feminist 4. Old age 5. Psychological literature 6. SOCIAL SCIENCE—Women's Studies

ISBN 9781781681398 (hardback)

LC 2013-019104

SUMMARY: This book by Lynne Segal "explores the subject of aging in this combination memoir and analysis. Segal outlines fears about growing older and discusses our culture's ingrained negative attitudes about the elderly female body, as well as men's fear of losing their masculinity as they age. The author also highlights the joys of love and sexuality as one grows older." (Publishers Weekly)

REVIEW: *Economist* v409 no8862 p86-7 N 16 2013

"Out of the Time: The Pleasures and the Perils of Ageing." "So what does it mean to age gracefully? How is this done? These questions are at the centre of a thoughtful new book from Lynne Segal. . . . It is a winding, often lyrical and occasionally muddled look at what it feels like to get older. Ms. Segal is startled to discover that her feminism did not prepare her better for the dilemmas of ageing. It was easy to disdain the dictates of youthful beauty when she was young herself, she candidly notes. It is rather less so now that she feels more likely to be ignored."

REVIEW: *Kirkus Rev* v81 no20 p23 O 15 2013

REVIEW: *Publ Wkly* v260 no35 p48 S 2 2013

REVIEW: *Women's Review of Books* v31 no2 p7-8 Mr/Ap 2014 Alix Kates Shulman

SEGEL, HAROLD B.ed. The walls behind the curtain. See The walls behind the curtain

SEGERBERG, EBBA.tr. Let the old dreams die. See Ajvide Lindqvist, J.

SEGHERS, ANNA, 1900-1983. Transit; 2013 New York Review Books Classics

1. Jewish refugees 2. Marseille (France) 3. Revolutionaries—Fiction 4. World War, 1939-1945—France—Fiction 5. World War, 1939-1945—Refugees

ISBN 9781590176252 paperback

SUMMARY: "Anna Seghers's 'Transit' is an existential, political, literary thriller that explores the agonies of boredom, the vitality of storytelling, and the plight of the exile with extraordinary compassion and insight. Having escaped from a Nazi concentration camp in Germany in 1937, and later a camp in Rouen, the nameless twenty-seven-year-old German narrator of Seghers's multilayered masterpiece ends up in the dusty seaport of Marseille." (Publisher's note)

REVIEW: *TLS* no5777/8 p26 D 20 2013 IAN THOMSON

"Transit." "In her somewhat forgotten novel 'Transit' (1944), the German writer Anna Seghers conjures a noirish, 'Casablanca'-like world of escape and flight in unoccupied Marseille. The novel unfolds in 1940, a year before the arrival of the Nazis, in a city filled with hopeful transit-seekers, cramming the consulate waiting rooms and visa departments. . . . In this excellent new translation by Margot Bettauer Dembo, 'Transit' emerges as a Kafkaesque parable of grotesquely unravelling bureaucracy and deferred transit deadlines."

SEIDEL, MAX. Father and Son; Nicola and Giovanni Pisano; [by] Max Seidel 989 p. 2012 University of Chicago Press

1. Art literature 2. Fathers & sons 3. Pisano, Giovanni, ca. 1240-ca. 1320 4. Pisano, Niccolo, 1206?-1280? 5. Sculptors

ISBN 3777451010; 9783777451015

SUMMARY: In this book on sculptors Nicola and Giovanni Pisano, author "Max Seidel offers a broad examination of both artists' styles, paying particular attention to the emergence of Giovanni Pisano's practice under his father's guidance and the social and iconographic aspects of both artists' work. . . . The second volume comprises five hundred newly-published illustrations." (Publisher's note)

REVIEW: *Burlington Mag* v156 no1332 p169 Mr 2014 BRENDAN CASSIDY

"Father and Son: Nicola and Giovanni Pisano". "Over many years Max Seidel has contributed significantly to our knowledge of Italian late medieval sculpture in a series of highly important articles. In his new book, a lavish and weighty production, he focuses his attention on the two most influential sculptors of the period, Nicola Pisano and his son Giovanni.. . . . The iconographic interpretations notwithstanding, this is an exceptional and valuable study of the Pisanos which, in its analysis of the documents and detailed account of Nicola's influence on other artists, is unlikely to be superseded. It sets a new standard for the study of Italian late medieval sculpture. The book would have benefited, however, from a tighter editorial rein."

SEIFE, CHARLES. Virtual unreality; just because the Internet told you, how do you know it's true?; [by] Charles Seife 256 p. 2014 Viking

1. Computer network resources—Evaluation 2. Electronic information resource literacy 3. Internet—Safety measures 4. Internet fraud—Prevention 5. Internet literacy 6. Journalism
ISBN 0670026085; 9780670026081
LC 2013-047849

SUMMARY: This book, by Charles Seife, "explains how to separate fact from fantasy in the digital world. . . . Digital information is a powerful tool that spreads unbelievably rapidly . . . , even when that information is actually a lie. . . . Charles Seife uses the skepticism, wit, and sharp facility for analysis . . . to take us deep into the Internet information jungle and cut a path through the trickery, fakery, and cyber skullduggery that the online world enables." (Publisher's note)

REVIEW: *Kirkus Rev* v82 no11 p140 Je 1 2014

REVIEW: *New Sci* v222 no2972 p46 Je 7 2014 Douglas Heaven

REVIEW: *New York Times* v163 no56550 pC1-6 Jl 2 2014 DWIGHT GARNER

REVIEW: *Publ Wkly* v261 no18 p53-4 My 5 2014

REVIEW: *Sci Am* v310 no6 p80 Je 2014 Clara Moskowitz

"Virtual Unreality: Just Because the Internet Told You, How Do You Know It's True?" "Modern technology, especially the World Wide Web, has profoundly altered how people find and interpret information, journalist [Charles] Seife argues, and even how we interact with the world around us. 'We now live in a world where the real and the virtual can no longer be disentangled,' he writes, illustrating his case with stories of Web hoaxes and viral falsehoods that have fooled experts, journalists and the public alike. . . . Seife demonstrates how easy it is for fallacies to become accepted truths online."

SEKSIK, LAURENT. The Last Days; 160 p. 2013 Pushkin Press

1. Austrian authors—20th century—Biography 2. Biographical fiction 3. Suicide 4. Zweig, Lotte 5. Zweig, Stefan, 1881-1942
ISBN 1908968915; 9781908968913

SUMMARY: "On the 22nd February 1942 Stefan Zweig, one of the most popular authors of his generation, committed suicide with his wife Lotte. The final, desperate gesture of this great writer has fascinated ever since. . . . Blending reality and fiction this novel tells the story of the great writer's final months. Laurent Seksik uncovers the man's hidden passions, his private suffering, and how he and his wife came to end their lives one peaceful February afternoon." (Publisher's note)

REVIEW: *TLS* no5787 p19 F 28 2014 WILL STONE

"The Last Days." "A double suicide, as in the case of Stefan and Lotte Zweig, in Brazil on February 22, 1942, exudes its own singular exoticism. So 'The Last Days' by Laurent Seksik, which describes the couple's gradual slide down the greasy deck of circumstance into a covenant of death, comes as little surprise. . . . André Naffis-Sahely's translation has settled into English without fuss and generally follows the contours of the original admirably, though the odd pothole disturbs the ride. . . . The slew of Zweig biographies, in several languages, letters and testimonies provided Seksik with the primer on to which to apply his lavish topcoat."

SELBY, SCOTT ANDREW. A serial killer in Nazi Berlin; the chilling true story of the S-Bahn murderer; [by] Scott Andrew Selby 294 p. 2013 Berkley Caliber

1. Historical literature 2. Serial murder investigation—Germany—Berlin—Case studies 3. Serial murders—Germany—Berlin—Case studies
ISBN 9780425264140
LC 2013-032412

SUMMARY: This book by Scott Andrew Selby presents an "account of the historical curiosity of a sadistic serial killer preying on women in the heart of Nazi Germany." Railroad worker Paul Orgozow "realized he could freely pursue women traveling on the blacked-out 'S-Bahn' commuter line. Selby shifts perspectives between Ogorzow's grisly misdeeds . . . , and the 'Kripo' (criminal police) detectives, determined to catch him yet kept in check" by Nazi officials worried about the country's image. (Kirkus Reviews)

REVIEW: *Kirkus Rev* v82 no1 p168 Ja 1 2014

"A Serial Killer in Nazi Berlin: The Chilling True Story of the S-Bahn Murderer". "[Scott Andrew] Selby creates verisimilitude by focusing on numerous details of daily life in the Third Reich, demonstrating how everything from rail travel to law enforcement was bent to the will of Hitler's henchmen. Yet, he rarely exploits the obvious historical irony of [Paul] Ogorzow's small-scale evil against the grander backdrop of Berliners' complicity in conquest and genocide, only noting that some of his pursuers went on to participate in war crimes. The workmanlike telling of Ogorzow's pursuit and eventual capture lacks a certain impact, though fans of serial-killer narratives will surely be engaged."

REVIEW: *Libr J* v139 no2 p86 F 1 2014 Deirdre Bray

REVIEW: *N Y Times Book Rev* p30 My 25 2014 Charles Graeber

THE SELECTED LETTERS OF ROBERT CREELEY; 512 p. 2014 University of California Press

1. LITERARY COLLECTIONS—Letters 2. LITERARY CRITICISM—American—General 3. Letters 4. POETRY—General 5. Poets, American—20th century—Correspondence
ISBN 9780520241602 (hardback)
LC 2013-026610

SUMMARY: "Robert Creeley is one of the most celebrated and influential American poets." Edited by Rod Smith, Peter Baker, and Kaplan Harris, "This first-ever volume of his letters, written between 1945 and 2005, document the life, work, and times of one of our greatest writers, and represent a critical archive of the development of contemporary American poetry, as well as the changing nature of letter-writing and communication in the digital era." (Publisher's note)

REVIEW: *TLS* no5782 p10 Ja 24 2014 JAMES CAMPBELL

"The Selected Letters of Robert Creeley." "There is little evidence in these letters of Creeley reading and enjoying a work of fiction not written by friend or associate. . . . The three editors of 'Selected Letters' suffer from a comparable lack of curiosity. While splendidly produced . . . , it has to be ranked as one of the most poorly edited books of its kind. . . . The failings are consistent throughout. . . . To omit discussion of the issues raised by 'Robert Creeley: A Biography' is to risk appearing party to an act of suppression."

SELES, MONICA. Love match; [by] Monica Seles 224 p. 2014 Bloomsbury/Walker

1. Athletes—Fiction 2. Dating (Social customs)—Fiction 3. Interpersonal relations—Fiction 4. Sports stories 5. Tennis—Fiction

ISBN 9781599909028 (pbk); 9781619631595 (hardback)

LC 2013-034320

SUMMARY: In this book, the second in a series, "Maya is settling into her stay at the Academy after enduring a few months full of drama on and off the tennis court. Jake's betrayal with her archrival was a blow, but now she is determined to improve her game as she makes her way on the professional women's tour. Despite coming up short against a veteran player, Maya's unexpectedly strong performance garners attention from the press and a possible agent." (Kirkus Reviews)

REVIEW: *Kirkus Rev* v81 no24 p125 D 15 2013

"Love Match". "[Monica] Seles returns with the second in her series about teens in training to become elite athletes and envied celebrities. . . . This installment provides a look behind the scenes as the all-important image-making of young athletes unfolds. Here, a headline can give sought-after exposure, or an influential blogger's targeted comments can bring misery. Seles does a good job of portraying the pressures of Maya's need for financial success, unlike some of her peers. Readers will find themselves pulling for this scrappy teen as she navigates fame and relationships."

REVIEW: *Voice of Youth Advocates* v36 no6 p65 F 2014 Beth E. Andersen

SELIGMANN, MATTHEW S. The Royal Navy and the German threat, 1901-1914; admiralty plans to protect British trade in a war against Germany; [by] Matthew S. Seligmann 186 p. 2012 Oxford University Press

1. Germany—Naval history 2. Great Britain—Naval history 3. Great Britain. Royal Navy—History 4. Historical literature 5. Naval strategy—History 6. Seapower—Germany—History—20th century 7. Sea-power—Great Britain—History—20th century

ISBN 0199574030; 9780199574032

LC 2012-931193

SUMMARY: Written by Matthew S. Seligmann, this book "argues that Germany emerged as a major threat at the outset of the twentieth century, not because of its growing battle fleet, but because the British Admiralty (rightly) believed that Germany's naval planners intended to arm their country's fast merchant vessels in wartime and send them out to attack British trade in the manner of the privateers of old." (Publisher's note)

REVIEW: *Am Hist Rev* v118 no4 p1250-1 O 2013 Eric W. Osborne

"The Royal Navy and the German Threat, 1901-1914: Admiralty Plans to Protect British Trade in a War Against Germany." "Matthew S. Seligmann has produced a fine re-assessment of the British navy's strategic planning versus Germany in the years before World War I. The author focuses on measures taken by the Royal Navy to guard against a German war on British commerce. . . . All told, this well-researched book challenges both traditional and revisionist thinking concerning British perceptions of the threat posed by Germany."

REVIEW: *Choice* v50 no7 p1322 Mr 2013 B. M. Gough

SELLAND, ERIC.tr. The Guest Cat. See Takashi Hiraide

SELLEN, DANIEL. Adventures in Dystopia; [by] Daniel Sellen 266 p. 2013 CreateSpace Independent Publishing Platform

1. Cultural property 2. Economists 3. Missionaries—Fiction 4. Poor people—Fiction 5. Psychological fiction

ISBN 1491068337; 9781491068335

SUMMARY: This book "interweaves a series of vignettes from across the globe to create a broad diorama of modern-day culture clashes. . . . Key personages include a Colombian cab driver . . . a pair of 20-something missionaries on a mission to Delhi; a French economist . . . and a conservationist stationed in Ivory Coast facing the twin hurdles of crime and corruption in his attempt to preserve a UNESCO World Heritage Site." (Kirkus Reviews)

REVIEW: *Kirkus Rev* v82 no3 p403 F 1 2014

"Adventures in Dystopia". "[Daniel] Sellen's debut novel interweaves a series of vignettes from across the globe to create a broad diorama of modern-day culture clashes. Lacking a centralized plot, the narrative globe-trots from one place to the next, switching among characters and places that rarely share more than a distant connection. . . . . Even the occasional far-fetched or surreal event carries a certain authenticity. . . . Though skillfully narrated, their individual trials would perhaps function better as discrete and consecutively told short stories rather than placed in this haphazardly shuffled arrangement. Missing a unifying narrative but nonetheless an intimate, intercontinental voyage through a series of disparate lives."

SEN, AMARTYA, 1933-. An uncertain glory. See Drèze, J.

SENIOR, JENNIFER. All Joy and No Fun; The Paradox of Modern Parenthood; [by] Jennifer Senior 320 p. 2014 HarperCollins

1. Division of household labor 2. Gender role 3. Happiness 4. Parenting 5. Parents—United States 6. Psychological literature

ISBN 0062072226; 9780062072221

SUMMARY: In this book, author Jennifer Senior "argues that changes in the last half century have radically altered the roles of today's mothers and fathers. . . . Recruiting from a wide variety of sources--in history, sociology, economics, psychology, philosophy, and anthropology--she dissects both the timeless strains of parenting and the ones that are brand new, and then brings her research to life in the homes of ordinary parents around the country." (Publisher's note)

REVIEW: *Bookforum* v20 no5 p5 F/Mr 2014 HEATHER HAVRILESKY

"All Joy and No Fun: The Paradox of Modern Parenthood" and "Overwhelmed: Work, Love and Play When No One Has the Time." "[Jennifer] Senior quickly demonstrates a real talent for portraying the thorniest challenges of parenting as a chilling house of horrors. . . . Yet strangely enough, the more Senior delineates the unmatched suffering of today's parents, the less sympathetic one feels. . . . Unfortunately, rather than wrapping up her book with a galvanizing critique of America's delusional embrace of the ideal mother and the ideal, child-focused home Senior retreats into generic, glowing talk of the deeply felt rewards of self-sacrifice. . . . Luckily . . . Brigid Schulte has fewer qualms about emphasizing how the American way of parenting . . .has eroded our happiness. . . . Rather than dragging us into the mire and then retreating into warm fuzzies, Schulte offers an unflinching view of overachieving and overscheduling as a pervasive American sickness."

REVIEW: *Commentary* v137 no5 p81-2 My 2014 ABBY W. SCHACHTER

REVIEW: *Kirkus Rev* v82 no2 p2 Ja 15 2014

"All Joy and No Fun: The Paradox of Modern Parenthood". "New York contributor [Jennifer] Senior delves into a broad survey of the topic, parsing out the different arenas in which children are molding the lives of their parents. . . . The author does an admirable job of reviewing the current state of affairs with technology—specifically, the reversal of roles, with parents asking their kids to friend them on Facebook. Senior could have made this book twice as long given the minefield parents and their kids face, but what she did produce is well-considered and valuable information."

REVIEW: *Libr J* v138 no14 p86 S 1 2013

REVIEW: *Libr J* v139 no5 p134 Mr 15 2014 Mindy Rhiger

REVIEW: *N Y Times Book Rev* p1-16 F 2 2014 Andrew Solomon

"All Joy and No Fun: The Paradox of Modern Parenthood." "[Author Jennifer] Senior . . . examines what it means to be a parent, through interviews with a handful of families who are neither typical nor extraordinary. . . . She supplements these vignettes with extremely impressive research, weaving in insights from philosophy, psychology, and an occasionally overwhelming mélange of social science reports. . . . Salted with insights and epigrams, the book is argued with bracing honesty and flashes of authentic wisdom. . . . If there is a downside to this excellent book, it is that Senior's tone is sometimes too breezy and often rushed."

REVIEW: *New York Times* v163 no56394 pC1-4 Ja 27 2014 JANET MASLIN

REVIEW: *New Yorker* v90 no4 p73-1 Mr 17 2014

REVIEW: *Publ Wkly* v260 no44 p63 N 4 2013

SENIOR, OLIVE. Anna Carries Water; 40 p. 2014 Tradewind Books

1. Cows 2. Families—Fiction 3. Jamaica—Fiction 4. Picture books for children 5. Water

ISBN 1896580602; 9781896580609

SUMMARY: In this book, by Olive Senior and illustrated by Laura James, "Anna fetches water from the spring every day, but she can't carry it on her head like her older brothers and sisters can. In this charming and poetic family story set in Jamaica, . . . Senior shows young readers the power of determination, as Anna achieves her goal and overcomes her fear." (Publisher's note)

REVIEW: *Kirkus Rev* v82 no1 p194 Ja 1 2014

"Anna Carries Water". "Exuberant paintings accompany . . . the simple text, ideal for reading aloud. . . . [Laura] James, of Antiguan background, allows her bold acrylic paintings in tropical colors to sprawl across wide double-page spreads of lush Caribbean landscapes. The hummingbirds and butterflies add a bit of whimsy to Anna's cover portrait. While not mentioned in the text, the Jamaican flag is seen on the wall of a country store, and the author was born there. When water easily comes out of a faucet, young readers rarely think about the difficult chore of carrying water, but they will empathize with Anna's desire to reach an important milestone."

REVIEW: *Quill Quire* v79 no10 p35 D 2013 Joanne Findon

REVIEW: *SLJ* v60 no5 p94 My 2014 Michele Shaw

SENSATIONALISM; murder, mayhem, mudslinging, scandals, and disasters in 19th-century reporting; xxxiv, 391 p. 2013 Transaction Publishers

1. Historical literature 2. Journalism—Objectivity—United States—History—19th century 3. Journalism—United States—History—19th century 4. Journalists—United States—Biography 5. Press—United States—History—19th century 6. Sensationalism in journalism—United States—History—19th century

ISBN 9781412851718 (hardcover: acid-free paper)

LC 2012-045370

SUMMARY: This book by David B. Sachsman and David W. Bulla presents a "collection of essays exploring sensationalism in nineteenth-century newspaper reporting. The contributors analyze the role of sensationalism and tell the story of both the rise of the penny press in the 1830s and the careers of specific editors and reporters dedicated to this particular journalistic style." (Publisher's note)

REVIEW: *Choice* v51 no8 p1392 Ap 2014 J. K. Chakars

"Sensationalism: Murder, Mayhem, Mudslinging, Scandals, and Disasters in 19th-Century Reporting". "Another strong chapter looks at the rise of illustration, perhaps the key facet of present-day sensationalism, as a component of 19th-century practice. Several contributions touch on the morality play that often constitutes sensational coverage; Les Sillars argues that the judgmental lessons embedded in that style of reporting were rooted in sermonizing. This book offers much food for thought, and it succeeds because of sensationalism's inherent allure."

SENZAI, N. H. Saving Kabul Corner; [by] N. H. Senzai 288 p. 2014 Simon & Schuster Books for Young Readers

1. Afghan Americans—California—San Francisco Bay Area—Juvenile fiction 2. Afghan Americans—Fiction 3. Family life—California—Fiction 4. Grocery trade—Fiction 5. Immigrants—Fiction 6. Mystery and detective stories 7. Vendetta—Fiction

ISBN 1442484942; 9781442484948 (hardcover)

LC 2013-005211

SUMMARY: In this children's book, by N. H. Senzai, "twelve-year-old Ariana couldn't be more different from her cousin Laila, who just arrived from Afghanistan with her family. Laila is a proper, ladylike Afghan girl. . . . Arianna hates her. . . . Then a rival Afghan grocery store opens near Ariana's family store. . . . The cousins . . . must ban together to help the families find a lasting peace before it destroys both businesses and everything their parents have worked for." (Publisher's note)

REVIEW: *Booklist* v110 no11 p68 F 1 2014 Amina Chaudhri

REVIEW: *Bull Cent Child Books* v67 no6 p334 F 2014 Amy Atkinson

"Saving Kabul Corner." "Though explanations of weightier issues verge on the conspicuous, the book maintains a fairly light touch when helping young readers understand Ariana and her family's culture, keeping these details in the background and wisely allowing the mystery plot to take center stage. Thoughtfully written, with just the right amount of hint-dropping to get readers guessing, this engaging story features immigrants, minorities, and complex political issues while credibly treating the thoughts and feelings of a twelve-year old girl and the bonds of family. This is one for any preteen interested in the broader world, or just navigating the one at home."

REVIEW: *Kirkus Rev* v81 no24 p145 D 15 2013

"Saving Kabul Corner". "[N. H.] Senzai successfully weaves the dynamics of Afghan culture, history and political wranglings into a classically American mystery story, unraveling who and what are really at the heart of the conflict between the two Afghani grocery stores. Readers will appreciate that young people solve all of the questions at hand and ultimately bring the two families together. An engaging mystery-that it's about Afghani families struggling and surviving in America is a plus."

REVIEW: *Publ Wkly* v260 no49 p83-4 D 2 2013

REVIEW: *SLJ* v60 no2 p97 F 2014 Ellen Norton

REVIEW: *Voice of Youth Advocates* v36 no5 p66 D 2013 Anna Foote

SEPETYS, RUTA. Between shades of gray; [by] Ruta Sepetys 344 2011 Philomel Books

1. Gulag (Soviet Union) 2. Teenage girls—Fiction 3. Young adult literature—Works

ISBN 978-0-399-25412-3; 0-399-25412-9

LC 2009--50092

SUMMARY: In this novel by Ruta Sepetys, "Fifteen-year-old Lina is a Lithuanian girl living an ordinary life--until Soviet officers invade her home and tear her family apart. Separated from her father and forced onto a crowded train, Lina, her mother, and her young brother make their way to a Siberian work camp, where they are forced to fight for their lives." (Publisher's note)In 1941, fifteen-year-old Lina, her mother, and brother are pulled from their Lithuanian home by Soviet guards and sent to Siberia, where her father is sentenced to death in a prison camp while she fights for her life, vowing to honor her family and the thousands like hers by burying her story in a jar on Lithuanian soil. Based on the author's family, includes a historical note.

REVIEW: *Voice of Youth Advocates* v34 no5 p445-7 D 2011 REBECCA A. HILL

REVIEW: *World Lit Today* v88 no2 p6 Mr/Ap 2014 J. L. Powers

"Song for Night," "Between Shades of Gray," and "Mali Under the Night Sky: A Lao Story of Home." "In this lyrical novella ['Song for Night'] narrated by a child soldier, we travel across a West African country as fifteen-year-old 'My Luck' searches for his platoon. . . . Fifteen-year-old Lina loves boys, drawing, her cousin, and her father, a professor in Soviet-occupied Lithuania. . . . [Author Ruta] Sepetys paints Lina's experiences in delicate, layered strokes, revealing the humanity of both prisoner and prison guard in unique and subtle ways. . . . In 'Mali under the Night Sky,' a true story, a young girl named Mali flees her beloved home in Laos, seeking safety on foreign soil."

SESSIONS, W. A.ed. A Prayer Journal. See O'Connor, F.

SESTERO, GREG. The disaster artist. See Bissell, T.

SETH, 1962-.il. When did you see her last? See Snicket, L.

SETTLING AND UNSETTLING MEMORIES; essays in Canadian public history; xii, 652 p. 2012 University of Toronto Press

1. Canada—History 2. Collective memory 3. Historical literature 4. History in popular culture 5. Public history—Canada

ISBN 9780802038166 (paper); 9780802038937 (cloth)

LC 2012-374761

SUMMARY: This book "analyses the ways in which Canadians over the past century have narrated the story of their past in books, films, works of art, commemorative ceremonies, and online. . . . Prominent and emerging scholars explore the ways in which Canadian memory has been put into action across a variety of communities, regions, and time periods." (Publisher's note)

REVIEW: *Can Hist Rev* v95 no1 p101-42 Mr 2014

"Settling and Unsettling Memories: Essays in Canadian Public History," "Prophetic Identities: Indigenous Missionaries on British Colonial Frontiers," and "Aboriginal Peoples and Sport in Canada: Historical Foundations and Contemporary Issues". "This important collection maps the rapidly expanding field of collective memory in Canada, presenting a sampling of articles that usefully balances older pioneering studies by established practitioners with more recent work by emerging scholars. . . . In comparative work at its best, [Tolly] Bradford argues that these two, admittedly exceptional Indigenous missionaries created for themselves "new" Indigenous identities. What makes this study noteworthy is its framing of these men within empire and the processes of modernity. . . . 'Aboriginal Peoples and Sport in Canada' stands as an exceptional collection that demonstrates the ways in which sport studies can make Aboriginal world views accessible to a non-Aboriginal audience."

REVIEW: *Can Lit* no218 p177-81 Aut 2013 Martin Kuester

REVIEW: *Choice* v50 no2 p348 O 2012 B. F. R. Edwards

SEXUALLY TRANSMITTED DISEASE; an encyclopedia of diseases, prevention, treatment, and issues; 2 volumes (xxxiii, 784 p.) 2014 Greenwood

1. Medical literature 2. Sexually transmitted diseases—Encyclopedias 3. Sexually transmitted diseases—Prevention 4. Sexually transmitted diseases—Social aspects 5. Sexually transmitted diseases—Treatment

ISBN 1440801347; 9781440801341 (hardcopy: alk. paper)

LC 2013-016319

SUMMARY: This encyclopedia, edited by Jill Grimes, MD, "contains over 230 entries that span the history and wide range of topics regarding [sexually transmitted diseases], from the birth of condoms over 3,000 years ago through discovery of the infectious agents and the invention of effective vaccines to the legal and societal implications of STDs." (Publisher's note)

REVIEW: *Booklist* v110 no14 p64 Mr 15 2014 Barbara Bibel

REVIEW: *Choice* v51 no9 p1569 My 2014 L. M. McMain

"Sexually Transmitted Disease: An Encyclopedia of Diseases, Prevention, Treatment, and Issues". "The need for a clearly written, informative, and accurate encyclopedia on the topic is clear. This book fulfills that need and more, addressing not only the basics of disease, symptoms, treatment, and prevention, but also the societal, financial, and personal aspects of STDs. . . . Articles are signed by qualified experts and include a bibliography of suggested further readings. Case studies, a few illustrations, and somc vcry informative insets and tables support the text. . . . Highly recommended."

REVIEW: *Libr J* v139 no3 p127 F 15 2014 Laurie Selwyn

SEYMOUR-JONES, CAROLE. She Landed by Moonlight; The Story of Secret Agent Pearl Witherington: the Real 'charlotte Gray'; [by] Carole Seymour-Jones 432 p. 2014 Trafalgar Square

1. Historical literature 2. Witherington, Pearl 3. Women spies 4. World War, 1939-1945—Secret service 5. World War, 1939-1945—Underground movements—France
ISBN 1444724622; 9781444724622

SUMMARY: This book by Carole Seymour-Jones describes how "On the night of the September 22, 1943, Pearl Witherington, a 29-year-old British secretary and agent of the Special Operations Executive (SOE), was parachuted from a Halifax bomber into occupied France. . . . As the only woman agent in the history of SOEs in France to have run a network, she became a fearless and legendary guerrilla leader, organizing, arming, and training 3,800 Resistance fighters." (Publisher's note)

REVIEW: *TLS* no5779 p9-10 Ja 3 2014 MARK SEAMAN

"She Landed by Moonlight: The Story of Secret Agent Pearl Witherington: The Real Charlotte Gray," "Priscilla: The Hidden Life of an Englishwoman in Wartime France," and "The Secret Ministry of Ag. & Fish." "'She Landed by Moonlight' is a conventional biography of a hitherto somewhat neglected heroine of E Section of the British secret service, the Special Operations Executive (SOE); 'The Secret Ministry of Ag. & Fish' is the autobiography of a very junior member of that organization's backroom staff; and 'Prisciila: The hidden life of an Englishwoman in wartime France' is a fascinating voyage of discovery into a decidedly murky family history, in which a nephew goes in search of his aunt's wartime secrets."

SEYMOUR, GERALD. The dealer and the dead; [by] Gerald Seymour 464 p. 2014 Thomas Dunne Books

1. Assassins—Fiction 2. Illegal arms transfers—Croatia—Fiction 3. Revenge—Fiction 4. Spy stories 5. Yugoslav War, 1991-1995—Fiction
ISBN 1250018781; 9781250018786 (hardback)
LC 2013-038811

SUMMARY: In this book, by Gerald Seymour, "Croatian villagers pooled together their worldly goods to buy weapons to use against advancing Serb forces, only to be left defenseless by a shadowy arms dealer who took the money and ran. Nearly 20 years later, survivors of the brutal attack discover his identity and pay to have him killed to avenge the deaths. Harvey Gillot, the still-active, internationally successful arms dealer, regards this betrayal as the only blot on his record." (Kirkus Reviews)

REVIEW: *Booklist* v110 no9/10 p50 Ja 1 2014 Thomas Gaughan

REVIEW: *Kirkus Rev* v82 no2 p198 Ja 15 2014

"The Dealer and the Dead". "[Gerald] Seymour's 25th novel, published in England in 2010, has its share of nail-biting moments, gaining intensity down the stretch. But it largely eschews action scenes in favor of a simmering, multilayered account of the past catching up to the present. [Harvey] Gillot is in a classic melancholic mode; readers who like more adrenalized thrillers might do better to look elsewhere. Those who are drawn to densely woven, slowly unfolding plots and thoughtful writing will rate this book a winner. Decades after establishing himself as a master of British spy fiction with 'Harry's Game,' Seymour shows no signs of slowing down or losing relevance."

REVIEW: *Publ Wkly* v260 no50 p50 D 9 2013

SEYMOUR, MIRANDA. Noble Endeavours; The Life of Two Countries, England and Germany, in Many Stories; [by] Miranda Seymour 512 p. 2013 Simon & Schuster

1. Germans—Great Britain 2. Germany—Foreign relations—Great Britain—History 3. Historical literature 4. Wettin, House of 5. Windsor, House of
ISBN 1847378250; 9781847378255

SUMMARY: This book describes how "German monarchs ruled over England for three hundred years--and only ceased to do so through a change of name. [Author] Miranda Seymour has written a . . . history--told through the lives of kings and painters, soldiers and sailors, sugar-bakers and bankers, charlatans and saints--of two countries so entwined that one man, asked for his allegiance in 1916, said he didn't know because it felt as though his parents had quarrelled." (Publisher's note)

REVIEW: *Hist Today* v64 no1 p63 Ja 2014 Clare Mulley

REVIEW: *TLS* no5775 p31 D 6 2013 CAROLINE MOOREHEAD

"Noble Endeavours: The Life of Two Countries, England and Germany, in Many Stories,". "Writing in the mid-nineteenth century, Carlisle famously remarked that history is but the 'biography of great men'--a view taken to heart by Miranda Seymour in 'Noble Endeavours.' Starting from the premiss that over many centuries--with a notable break 'of monstrous meditated evil' between 1933 and 1945--Germany and Britain felt towards each other mutual affection, admiration and trust. It is time, she argues, for them to do so again. . . . Miranda Seymour's research is meticulous, and many of her vignettes are lively and perceptive. Her biographical portraits, however, are dizzying in number. . . . Rather than as a narrative, 'Noble Endeavours' might best be consulted as a work of reference."

SHACOCHIS, BOB. The Woman Who Lost Her Soul; [by] Bob Shacochis 640 p. 2013 Atlantic Monthly Press

1. Americans—Haiti 2. Haiti—Fiction 3. Political fiction 4. Special operations (Military science) 5. Spy stories
ISBN 0802119824; 9780802119827

SUMMARY: Author Bob Shacochis presents a "novel of sex, lies, and American foreign policy, [where] 1990s Haiti, Nazi-occupied Croatia, and Cold War–era Istanbul are shown as places where people are pulled into a vortex of personal and political destruction. Shacochis details how espionage not only reflects a nation's character but can also endanger its soul." (Publishers Weekly)

REVIEW: *Booklist* v109 no22 p32 Ag 1 2013 John Mort

REVIEW: *Kirkus Rev* v81 no15 p262 Ag 1 2013

REVIEW: *Kirkus Rev* p14 Ag 15 2013 Fall Preview

REVIEW: *Kirkus Rev* p34 N 15 2013 Best Books

REVIEW: *Libr J* v138 no7 p56 Ap 15 2013 Barbara Hoffert

REVIEW: *N Y Times Book Rev* p16 S 22 2013 AMY WILENTZ

REVIEW: *Publ Wkly* v260 no30 p40 Jl 29 2013

REVIEW: *TLS* no5770 p20 N 1 2013 MARK KAMINE

"The Woman Who Lost Her Soul." "An ambitiously wide-ranging examination of the people who conduct overt and covert operations abroad, and those caught up in their execution. . . . [Bob] Shacochis employs genre elements, including a private investigator and a host of aliases and red herrings, to keep the plot moving while his rich portrait of Dottie unfolds non-sequentially, her mysterious murder only fully explained near the novel's end. . . . Each locale provides ground for trenchant insights into the soul of the crusading nation. . . . Along the way he shows a Graham Greene-like ability to dramatize the moral issues of individuals sent overseas to carry out hastily conceived initiatives."

SHAFIR, ELDAR. Scarcity; why having too little means so much; [by] Eldar Shafir 304 p. 2013 Times Books, Henry Holt and Company

1. Decision making 2. Poor people—Psychology 3. Scarcity 4. Social science literature 5. Supply and demand
ISBN 0805092641; 9780805092646
LC 2013-004167

SUMMARY: In this book, authors Sendhil Mullainathan and Eldar Shafir "discuss how scarcity affects our daily lives, recounting anecdotes of their own foibles and making . . . connections that bring this research alive. Their book provides a new way of understanding why the poor stay poor and the busy stay busy, and it reveals not only how scarcity leads us astray but also how individuals and organizations can better manage scarcity for greater satisfaction and success." (Publisher's note)

REVIEW: *Economist* v408 no8851 p71 Ag 31 2013

"Scarcity: Why Having Too Little Means So Much." "By making people slower witted and weaker willed, scarcity creates a mindset that perpetuates scarcity, the authors argue. . . . The authors discuss a range of solutions to the psychological pratfalls of scarcity. . . . Some of these practical antidotes are not new. But the book's unified theory of the scarcity mentality is novel in tis scope and ambition. This theory has a lot of moving parts, perhaps too many. . . . It is, however, easy to enjoy the book's many vignettes and insights, leaving it to others with more bandwidth to fit it all together."

REVIEW: *Kirkus Rev* v81 no13 p169 Jl 1 2013

REVIEW: *N Y Rev Books* v60 no14 p47-9 S 26 2013 Cass R. Sunstein

"Scarcity: Why Having Too Little Means So Much." "In their extraordinarily illuminating book, the behavioral economist Sendhil Mullainathan and the cognitive psychologist Eldar Shafir explore . . . the feeling of scarcity, and the psychological and behavioral consequences of that feeling. They know that the feeling of scarcity differs across various kinds of experiences. . . . But their striking claim, based on careful empirical research, is that across all of those categories, the feeling of scarcity has quite similar effects. . . . In providing a unified treatment of those consequences, Mullainathan and Shafir have made an important, novel, and immensely creative contribution. But there is an immediate question, which is whether their real topic is stress rather than scarcity."

REVIEW: *New Sci* v220 no2937 p48-9 O 5 2013 Debora MacKenzie

REVIEW: *New Sci* v220 no2945 p55 N 30 2013

REVIEW: *New Statesman* v142 no5172 p44-6 Ag 30 2013 Felix Martin

REVIEW: *Publ Wkly* v260 no23 p63 Je 10 2013

SHAHAN, SHERRY. Skin & bones; [by] Sherry Shahan 240 p. 2014 Albert Whitman & Company

1. Anorexia nervosa—Fiction 2. Eating disorders—Fiction 3. Friendship—Fiction 4. Hospitals—Fiction 5. Young adult fiction
ISBN 0807573973; 9780807573976 (hardcover)
LC 2013-028442

SUMMARY: This book follows a teenage boy hospitalized for anorexia. "Bones is a stubborn patient, exercising like crazy and trying to cheat the weigh-ins; his recovery is hindered further when he falls for Alice, a pro-ana dancer who makes Bones her secret rehearsal partner and applauds his dangerously underweight form. Bones is unable to resist Alice's increasingly self-destructive requests, and he struggles to find a way to please her even as he moves toward health." (Bulletin of the Center for Children's Books)

REVIEW: *Booklist* v110 no14 p78 Mr 15 2014 Lexi Walters Wright

REVIEW: *Bull Cent Child Books* v67 no7 p378 Mr 2014 D. S.

"Skin and Bones." "The writing is simple and accessible, and Bones' warped self-image is effectively conveyed; it's also clear to the reader that Alice is more in love with her disease than with any boy, and that Bones is just a convenient means to an end for her. However, characterization is generally scanty and sometimes puzzling (sixteen-year-old Bones is bewildered by what's apparently his first wet dream), motivations are fairly stock, and the details of the EDU vary from credible to dubious, making the journey ultimately superficial and message-focused. The subject remains compelling, however, and the camaraderie between Bones and Lard is endearing."

REVIEW: *Kirkus Rev* v82 no1 p210 Ja 1 2014

"Skin and Bones". "[Sherry] Shahan tackles eating disorders in a fast-paced, contemporary coming-of-age novel. . . . The pace quickens as Alice manipulates all in her quest to lose more weight, a joy ride turns dark, and Jack's life depends on the choices he makes. Adult characters are well-meaning but somewhat distant; the edgy banter may help readers refrain from questioning a residential rehab program where teens roam at night and have easy access to cars. A quick read with a worthy message: We are all recovering from something, and the right companions can help you heal. The wrong ones could kill you."

REVIEW: *SLJ* v60 no4 p173 Ap 2014 Eden Rassette

REVIEW: *Voice of Youth Advocates* v36 no6 p65 F 2014 Lindy Gerdes

SHAKESPEARE AND ME; 528 p. 2014 Oneworld Publications

1. Actors 2. Authors 3. Literature—History & criticism

4. Motion picture producers & directors 5. Shakespeare, William, 1564-1616—Influence
ISBN 1780744269; 9781780744261

SUMMARY: In this book, edited by Susannah Carson, "scholars and writers . . . share stories of their own personal relationship with Shakespeare. We hear from Ralph Fiennes on interpreting Coriolanus for a modern filmic audience, James Earl Jones on reclaiming Othello as a tragic hero, Sir Ben Kingsley on communicating Shakespeare's ideas through performance, Julie Taymor on turning Prospero into Prospera, Brian Cox on social conflict in Shakespeare's time and ours." (Publisher's note)

REVIEW: *TLS* no5795 p10 Ap 25 2014 LAURIE MAGUIRE

"Shakespeare and Me: 38 Great Writers, Actors, and Directors on What the Bard Means to Them—And Us." "There are gems tucked away in this collection of essays, in which 'great writers, actors and directors' recount their relationship with Shakespeare. . . . But 'Celebrities on Shakespeare' is a precarious way of thematizing and unifying a book, and the result is an uneven and often reductive survey. It is also a book in which carelessness and inaccuracy abound. . . . The essays range from short to very short. Brevity is not a problem except that here it tends to become skimpy and summary. . . . 'Shakespeare & Me' was first published in the US last year. In simply reprinting the original, without updating, this British edition creates new errors."

SHAKESPEARE BEYOND DOUBT; evidence, argument, controversy; 304 p. 2013 Cambridge University Press

1. English literature—History & criticism 2. Historical literature 3. Shakespeare, William, 1564-1616—Authorship—Baconian theory 4. Shakespeare, William, 1564-1616—Authorship—Marlowe theory
ISBN 9781107017597
LC 2012-040135

SUMMARY: This book, edited by Paul Edmondson and Stanley Wells, "sets the debate [over the authorship of William Shakespeare's works] in its historical context and provides an account of its main protagonists and their theories. Presenting the authorship of Shakespeare's works in relation to historiography, psychology and literary theory, . . . scholars reposition and develop the discussion. The book explores the issues in the light of biographical, textual and bibliographical evidence." (Publisher's note)

REVIEW: *New Statesman* v142 no5155 p44 Ap 26 2013 Jonathan Bate

REVIEW: *TLS* no5754 p24 Jl 12 2013 EMMA SMITH

"Shakespeare Beyond Doubt: Evidence, Argument, Controversy." "These contributors use a creative and broadly empathetic literary hermeneutic to interpret the genre of authorship contention as text, rather than merely to repudiate it. Elsewhere, though, the rhetoric is more emphatically evidential. . . . The language of Shakespeare's defenders shuttles between headmasterly. . . . But the main rhetorical technique is bathos. . . . The authorship question is acknowledged as silly, even as the form of the book takes it deeply seriously."

SHAKESPEARE, NICHOLAS, 1957-. Priscilla; The Hidden Life of an Englishwoman in Wartime France; [by] Nicholas Shakespeare 448 p. 2014 HarperCollins

1. Aunts 2. British—France—Paris 3. Historical literature 4. World War, 1939-1945—Collaborationists—France 5. World War, 1939-1945—Women
ISBN 0062297031; 9780062297037

SUMMARY: This book shows how "When [author] Nicholas Shakespeare stumbled across a trunk full of his late aunt's personal belongings . . . The glamorous, mysterious figure he remembered from his childhood was very different from the morally ambiguous young woman who emerged from the trove of love letters, journals and photographs . . . living the precarious existence of a British citizen in a country controlled by the enemy during World War II." (Publisher's note)

REVIEW: *Economist* v409 no8862 p86 N 16 2013

REVIEW: *Kirkus Rev* v81 no23 p252 D 1 2013

REVIEW: *N Y Times Book Rev* p6 Ja 19 2014 ALAN RIDING

"Priscilla: The Hidden Life of an Englishwoman in Wartime France." "Priscilla Thompson was long dead when her nephew Nicholas Shakespeare was moved to find an answer to that question. He knew she had lived in France during the German occupation. . . . The result makes for gripping reading, not least because his findings on how his blond, blue-eyed relative survived four years of Nazi rule were not what he expected. . . . Shakespeare was lucky to locate a trove of love letters and photographs and a draft of his aunt's unpublished memoir."

REVIEW: *New Statesman* v142 no5183 p43 N 8 2013 Michael Prodger Philip Maughan

REVIEW: *New York Times* v163 no56363 pC27 D 27 2013 ANNA SHAPIRO

REVIEW: *TLS* no5779 p9-10 Ja 3 2014 MARK SEAMAN

"She Landed by Moonlight: The Story of Secret Agent Pearl Witherington: The Real Charlotte Gray," "Priscilla: The Hidden Life of an Englishwoman in Wartime France," and "The Secret Ministry of Ag. & Fish." "'She Landed by Moonlight' is a conventional biography of a hitherto somewhat neglected heroine of E Section of the British secret service, the Special Operations Executive (SOE); 'The Secret Ministry of Ag. & Fish' is the autobiography of a very junior member of that organization's backroom staff; and 'Prisciila: The hidden life of an Englishwoman in wartime France' is a fascinating voyage of discovery into a decidedly murky family history, in which a nephew goes in search of his aunt's wartime secrets."

SHAKESPEARE, WILLIAM, 1564-1616. Shakespeare's The Tempest; a modern English translation; 2013 Algora Publishing

ISBN 9781628940244 (soft cover: alk. paper); 9781628940251 (hard cover: alk. paper)
LC 2013-027402

SUMMARY: This play, translated by Morgan D. Rosenberg, is "a line-by-line translation of [William] Shakespeare's play, 'The Tempest,' translated into modern English. The original play's five act structure has been preserved, with a one-to-one correspondence between each original line and each translated line. . . . The present book provides a natural language translation for each line, one which could easily be performed on stage." (Publisher's note)

REVIEW: *TLS* no5742 p9-10 Ap 19 2013 RAPHAEL LYNE

"The Tempest". "The new pages are a sound and worthwhile addition to an edition that was good already. They are not mould-breaking enough to make someone who already owned it need to buy another, but a pleasing reassurance for the first-time buyer. They may also be a sign of an interesting phenomenon: the competition among series of Shakespeare editions may lead to more such updates. The economic advantage for the publisher is apparent, but here the editors' scholarly scruples lead the way. The performance section of this revised Arden Tempest clearly benefits from Virginia Vaughan's immersion in the subject, which manifests itself in her volume on The Tempest in Manchester's Shakespeare in Performance series. The play is ideal for this treatment."

SHAKESPEARE, WILLIAM, 1564-1616. The most excellent and lamentable tragedy of Romeo & Juliet. See The most excellent and lamentable tragedy of Romeo & Juliet

SHAKESPEARE, WILLIAM, 1564-1616. The Tempest; 2014 Oxford University Press
ISBN 9780199009978 (paperback)

SUMMARY: This book is a critical edition of the play by William Shakespeare with an introduction by Daniel Fischlin. "In additional to a scholarly edition of the playtext complete with original new annotation, . . . [it includes] both short introductions by noted scholars and prefaces by well-known Canadians who have experience with Shakespeare . . . [as well as] act and scene summaries, dramatis personae, quick reference notes on reading Shakespeare, and recommended reading/resources." (Publisher's note)

REVIEW: *TLS* no5742 p9-10 Ap 19 2013 RAPHAEL LYNE

"The Tempest." "The new pages are a sound and worthwhile addition to an edition that was good already. They are not mould-breaking enough to make someone who already owned it need to buy another, but a pleasing reassurance for the first-time buyer. They may also be a sign of an interesting phenomenon: the competition among series of Shakespeare editions may lead to more such updates. The economic advantage for the publisher is apparent, but here the editors' scholarly scruples lead the way. The performance section of this revised Arden Tempest clearly benefits from Virginia Vaughan's immersion in the subject, which manifests itself in her volume on The Tempest in Manchester's Shakespeare in Performance series. The play is ideal for this treatment."

SHAKESPEARE'S STATIONERS; studies in cultural bibliography; viii, 374 p. 2013 University of Pennsylvania Press

1. Canon (Literature) 2. Drama—Publishing—England—History—16th century 3. Drama—Publishing—England—History—17th century 4. Historical literature 5. Transmission of texts

ISBN 0812244540 (hardcover : alk. paper); 9780812244540 (hardcover : alk. paper)
LC 2012-016198

SUMMARY: This book, edited by Marta Straznivcky, "explore[s] the multiple and intersecting forms of agency exercised by Shakespeare's stationers in the design, production, marketing, and dissemination of his printed works. Nine critical studies examine the ways in which commerce intersected with culture and how individual stationers engaged in a range of cultural functions and political movements through their business practices." (Publisher's note)

REVIEW: *TLS* no5767 p23-4 O 11 2013 H. R. WOUDHUYSEN

"Shakespeare and the Book Trade" and "Shakespeare's Stationers: Studies in Cultural Bibliography." "The two books under review are part of a further line of investigation which seeks to see the poet and playwright in relation to the book trade and the stationers with whom he or his theatrical colleagues dealt. Lukas Erne and the contributors to the volume that Marta Straznicky has edited share an interest in many of the same sorts of questions. . . . [Erne's] argument . . . is essentially straightforward, clearly argued, with plenty of supporting evidence, and written in an elegant and eminently reasonable style. . . . These appendices are useful and fuller than the account of '[William] Shakespeare's publishers, 1593-1622' that Erne offers, but could still be improved. There is almost no mention of modem editions of Shakespeare's plays and poems in either Erne's book or Straznicky's collection."

SHALEV-EYNI, SARIT. Jews among Christians; Hebrew book illumination from Lake Constance; [by] Sarit Shalev-Eyni xi, 227 p. 2010 Harvey Miller

1. Christianity & other religions—Judaism 2. Historical literature 3. Illumination of books and manuscripts, German—Germany—Konstanz 4. Illumination of books and manuscripts, Medieval—Constance, Lake, Region 5. Illumination of books and manuscripts, Medieval—Germany—Konstanz 6. Jewish art and symbolism 7. Jewish illumination of books and manuscripts—Constance, Lake, Region 8. Jewish illumination of books and manuscripts—Germany—Konstanz

ISBN 1905375093; 9781905375097
LC 2011-383193

SUMMARY: This book "focuses on a south-west German workshop active in the Lake Constance region in the first decades of the fourteenth century which produced both Christian and Jewish manuscripts. This is a rich . . . resource for research on Jewish-Christian relationships. . . . The book's five chapters focus on the context, structure, liturgy and decoration programmes of the south-west-German Hebrew manuscripts, the Jewish-Christian visual dialogue, and the urban workshop in which these books were produced as a collaborative venture between commissioners, Jewish scribes and Christian illuminators." (Burlington Magazine)

REVIEW: *Burlington Mag* v154 no1311 p420 Je 2012 Karl-Georg Pfändtner

"The Medieval Haggadah: Art Narrative, and Religious Imagination" and "Jews Among Christians: Hebrew Book Illumination from Lake Constance." "This group of manuscripts offers material suitable for the questions Epstein raises. . . . In the introduction, the author acknowledges that his analysis of medieval manuscripts and their illumination is conditioned by modem-day approaches. . . . Despite this modest and apt observation, the study of each of the manuscripts is informed by a profound knowledge of Jewish customs, history and art history. Epstein offers major new insights into the Bird's Head Haggadah. . . . The other chapters give comparably fresh insights into the material. . . . Sarit Shalev-Eyni's book focuses on a south-west German workshop active in the Lake Constance region in the first decades of the fourteenth century which produced both Christian and Jewish manuscripts. . . . In their detailed research and scholarly analysis of the material, both publications demonstrate an impressive amount of background knowledge and interpretation free of ideological prejudice that sheds light on old problems."

SHALEV, ERAN. American Zion; the Old Testament as a political text from the Revolution to the Civil War; [by] Eran Shalev 256 p. 2013 Yale University Press

1. Bible and politics—United States—History 2. Historical literature 3. Nationalism—United States—History 4. Political culture—United States—History
ISBN 9780300186925 (cloth: alkaline paper)
LC 2012-026939

SUMMARY: "In this original book, historian Eran Shalev closely examines how this powerful predilection for Old Testament narratives and rhetoric in early America shaped a wide range of debates and cultural discussions—from republican ideology, constitutional interpretation, southern slavery, and more generally the meaning of American nationalism to speculations on the origins of American Indians and to the emergence of Mormonism." (Publisher's note)

REVIEW: *Choice* v50 no12 p2300 Ag 2013 M. S. Hill

REVIEW: *J Am Hist* v100 no4 p1190-1 Mr 2014

REVIEW: *N Engl Q* v87 no1 p154-8 Mr 2014 Reiner Smolinski

REVIEW: *Publ Wkly* v260 no6 p61 F 11 2013

REVIEW: *Rev Am Hist* v42 no2 p242-7 Je 2014 Curtis D. Johnson

"American Zion: The Old Testament As a Political Text From the Revolution to the Civil War." "'American Zion' is intellectual history at its finest. In this volume, Eran Shalev deftly traces the Old Testament's impact on republican thought, from its European origins through its flourishing in the American Revolutionary and early national periods, to its eventual decline in the decades before the Civil War. While other distinguished historians have alluded to the many themes, ideas, and images in 'American Zion,' this study is unique in its singular book-length focus on and chronological description of the Old Testament's impact on American government and identity."

SHALLY-JENSEN, MICHAEL.ed. Mental health care issues in America. See Mental health care issues in America

SHANE, KUHN. The Intern's handbook; a thriller; [by] Kuhn Shane 288 p. 2014 Simon & Schuster

1. Assassins—Fiction 2. Humorous stories 3. Impersonation—Fiction 4. Internship programs—Fiction 5. Law firms—Fiction
ISBN 1476733805; 9781476733807 (hardback); 9781476733845 (trade paperback)
LC 2013-034014

SUMMARY: In this novel by Shane Kuhn, "John Lago is a very bad guy. But he's the very best at what he does. And what he does is infiltrate top-level companies and assassinate crooked executives while disguised as an intern. . . . Part confessional, part DIY manual, 'The Intern's Handbook' chronicles John's final assignment, a twisted thrill ride in which he is pitted against the toughest—and sexiest—adversary he's ever faced: Alice, an FBI agent." (Publisher's note)

REVIEW: *Booklist* v110 no15 p29 Ap 1 2014 Michele Leber

REVIEW: *Booklist* v110 no21 p54 Jl 1 2014 JOYCE SARICKS

REVIEW: *Kirkus Rev* v82 no3 p276 F 1 2014

"The Intern's Handbook". "Couched as a piece of evidence in an FBI investigation, this debut novel by B-movie screenwriter [Shane] Kuhn is an inventive, profane and violent comedy. . . . It's a propulsive, well-written black comedy that apes a variety of other killer comedies . . . while also exploring tender subjects like what happens to children who are raised without parents. Believable dialogue, a whip smart and cynical central character, clever reversals and an entertaining amount of bone-crunching violence help wrap up this nasty package with a pretty little bow. An entertaining, ferociously violent romp about a morally bankrupt killer trying to find his way home."

REVIEW: *Libr J* v139 no6 p83 Ap 1 2014 Emily Byers

REVIEW: *Publ Wkly* v261 no7 p79 F 17 2014

SHANNON, GEORGE. Turkey Tot; 32 p. 2013 Holiday House

1. Animals—Fiction 2. Children's stories 3. Determination (Personality trait)—Fiction 4. Inventions 5. Turkeys—Fiction
ISBN 0823423794; 9780823423798 (hardcover)
LC 2011-022103

SUMMARY: In this picture book, written by George Shannon and illustrated by Jennifer K. Mann, "Turkey Tot thinks outside the box. He's hopeful, imaginative, and persistent, refusing to let his Debbie Downer friends in the farmyard discourage him. He's determined to retrieve juicy blackberries that hang just out of reach, but he needs a little help to implement the plans he makes to get within range." (School Library Journal)

REVIEW: *Bull Cent Child Books* v67 no3 p180 N 2013 D. S.

"Turkey Tot." "The text's simplicity and careful, folkloric structure, including audience-appealing phrases and plot patterns, will draw young audiences in; Turkey Tot's gleeful, overoptimistic take on the possibilities of detritus will ring true to anybody who's known an ambitious collector/tinkerer, and his enthusiastic exploratory approach is heroic as well as comic. [Illustrator Jennifer K.] Mann's art assembles pencil and watercolor figures in layered digital collage; there's a breath of Jules Feiffer to her vigorous scrawls but also a sly contemporary edge to the critters' wide, dubious eyes and slightly skewed comic poses."

REVIEW: *Horn Book Magazine* v90 no1 p79-80 Ja/F 2014 SUSAN DOVE LEMPKE

"Turkey Tot." "[George] Shannon's comically gangly turkey is a creative thinker and excellent problem-solver, unlike pessimistic Pig, Hen, and Chick, who immediately give up on reaching some high-growing blackberries. . . . [Jennifer K.] Mann uses loose black lines with bright watercolors and digital collage in her illustrations. Big, comic-style thought balloons show the friends imagining each of the turkey's schemes failing, their round eyes with black dots somehow giving away their thoughts. With its short words and sentences and humorous repetition, this makes a good early reader as well as an entertaining storytime book."

REVIEW: *Kirkus Rev* v81 no15 p182 Ag 1 2013

REVIEW: *SLJ* v60 no4 p46 Ap 2014 Alyson Low

REVIEW: *SLJ* v59 no8 p90 Ag 2013 Alyson Low

SHAPIRO, JACOB N. The terrorist's dilemma; managing violent covert organizations; [by] Jacob N. Shapiro 352 p. 2013 Princeton University Press

1. Political science literature 2. Qaida (Organization) 3. Terrorism—Finance 4. Terrorism—History 5. Terrorist organizations—Management

ISBN 9780691157214 (hardcover: alk. paper)

LC 2013-937553

SUMMARY: In this book, Jacob N. Shapiro "explores the management" of terrorists groups, " beginning with the nineteenth-century Russian progenitors of contemporary terrorist groups and ending with al Qaeda. Some of the groups he examines, such as the Palestinian organization Fatah . . . were substantial operations, and their size made it more difficult to retain cohesion among their distinct factions, especially when opportunities arose to move into more mainstream political activity." (Foreign Affairs)

REVIEW: *London Rev Books* v35 no24 p19-21 D 19 2013 Owen Bennett-Jones

"Decoding Al-Qaida's Strategy: The Deep Battle Against America" and:The Terrorist's Dilemma: Managing Violent Covert Organisations". "Michael Ryan draws a useful distinction between the drawn-out or 'deep' battle of ideas and the 'close' battle of combat. . . . Ryan's survey pins down crucial elements of al-Qaida's appeal. . . . [Jacob] Shapiro sees the dilemma clearly: the mechanisms required to exert control, such as semijudicial processes to hand down punishments to wayward members, expenses claim sheets and documents in which new members commit themselves to following the leadership's policies, all make a group vulnerable."

SHAPIRO, SUSAN. The Bosnia list. See Trebincevic, K.

SHAPTON, LEANNE. Sunday night movies; [by] Leanne Shapton 96 p. 2013 Drawn & Quarterly

1. Canadian painting 2. Motion pictures in art 3. Picture books 4. Stills (Motion pictures) 5. Watercolor painting

ISBN 1770461272; 9781770461277

SUMMARY: This book by author and artist Leanne Shapton "a collection of stills from black-and-white films remembered and recaptured in an arresting series of watercolors. The book itself is structured like a movie, its pages like frames on a celluloid reel. It begins . . . with illustrations of studio logos . . . and opening credits. . . . Some of the artworks are immediately recognizable . . . or evoke romantic ideas about 'the movies' in general." (Bookforum)

REVIEW: *Bookforum* v20 no3 p43 S-N 2013 ELIZABETH GUMPORT

"Sunday Night Movies" and "Swimming Studies." "[Leanne Shapton is] an artist, author, and designer as skillful with words and images as she was in the pool. . . . 'Swimming Studies' . . . won the National Book Critics Circle Award for autobiography. . . . In this memoir of a solitary coming of age, the watercolors and photographs are not there to defer to or serve the writing, or to disrupt or challenge it. Rather than being illustrations or examples of what she's said, they're another way of saying it. . . . 'Sunday Night Movies' is a collection of stills from black-and-white films remembered and recaptured in an arresting series of watercolors. The book itself is structured like a movie, its pages like frames on a celluloid reel."

SHAPTON, LEANNE. Swimming studies; [by] Leanne Shapton 320 p. 2012 Blue Rider Press

1. Illustrated books 2. Memoirs 3. Teenage girls 4. Women swimmers—Canada—Biography

ISBN 0399158170 (hbk.); 9780399158179 (hbk.)

LC 2012-011506

SUMMARY: This memoir by Leane Shapton "explores the worlds of competitive and recreational swimming. From her training for the Olympic trials as a teenager to enjoying pools and beaches around the world as an adult, . . . Shapton offers a fascinating glimpse into the private, often solitary, realm of swimming. . . . [The book] reveals an intimate narrative of suburban adolescence, spent underwater in a discipline that continues to inspire Shapton's work as an artist and author." (Publisher's note)

REVIEW: *Bookforum* v20 no3 p43 S-N 2013 ELIZABETH GUMPORT

"Sunday Night Movies" and "Swimming Studies." "[Leanne Shapton is] an artist, author, and designer as skillful with words and images as she was in the pool. . . . 'Swimming Studies' . . . won the National Book Critics Circle Award for autobiography. . . . In this memoir of a solitary coming of age, the watercolors and photographs are not there to defer to or serve the writing, or to disrupt or challenge it. Rather than being illustrations or examples of what she's said, they're another way of saying it. . . . 'Sunday Night Movies' is a collection of stills from black-and-white films remembered and recaptured in an arresting series of watercolors. The book itself is structured like a movie, its pages like frames on a celluloid reel."

REVIEW: *Kirkus Rev* v80 no10 p1052 My 15 2012

REVIEW: *New York Times* p37 N 23 2012 DWIGHT GARNER

REVIEW: *New Yorker* v88 no22 p79 Jl 30 2012

REVIEW: *Smithsonian* v43 no3 p82 Je 2012 Chloë Schama

REVIEW: *TLS* no5713 p30 S 28 2012 Elizabeth Lowry

SHARAFEDDINE, FATIMA.tr. The servant. See Sharafeddine, F.

SHARMA, AKHIL. Family Life; a novel; [by] Akhil Sharma 224 p. 2014 W W Norton & Co Inc

1. American fiction 2. East Indians—United States 3. Families—Fiction 4. Fathers and sons—Fiction 5. Grief—Fiction

ISBN 0393060055; 9780393060058

LC 2013-041222

SUMMARY: In this novel by Akhil Sharma, readers "meet the Mishra family in Delhi in 1978, where eight-year-old Ajay and his older brother Birju [are] waiting for the day when their plane tickets will arrive and they and their mother can fly across the world and join their father in America. Life is extraordinary until tragedy strikes, leaving one brother severely brain-damaged and the other lost and virtually orphaned in a strange land." (Publisher's note)

REVIEW: *Booklist* v110 no14 p48 Mr 15 2014 Donna Chavez

REVIEW: *Economist* v411 no8886 p80 My 10 2014

REVIEW: *Kirkus Rev* v82 no2 p303 Ja 15 2014

REVIEW: *Libr J* v138 no18 p67 N 1 2013 Barbara Hoffert

REVIEW: *N Y Times Book Rev* p1-28 Ap 6 2014 Sonali Deraniyagala

REVIEW: *N Y Times Book Rev* p26 Ap 13 2014

REVIEW: *New Statesman* v143 no5210 p51 My 16 2014 Philip Maughan

REVIEW: *Publ Wkly* v260 no50 p44 D 9 2013

REVIEW: *TLS* no5797 p20 My 9 2014 DAISY HILDYARD

"Family Life." "Ajay is eight years old when his family moves from Delhi to New York in the late 1970s. More than once, as 'Family Life' follows him through childhood and adolescence, he makes a distinction between an early wave of Indian immigrants who are skilled workers . . . and the later, larger influx of arrivals . . . who work as cleaners or gas-pump attendants. In this, 'Family Life' inhabits an American tradition of pioneer fiction. . . , Like other pioneer books, 'Family Life' is also a novel about work. . . . 'Family Life' is not romantic about what happens to daring, free-spirited settlers of an expansive land. It ends with a disturbing and inconclusive scene, and another, quieter narrative that reminds us of a different truth about the life of a pioneer."

SHARMA, SURESH. The 3rd American Dream; ... That Is Global in Reach; [by] Suresh Sharma 262 p. 2013 CreateSpace Independent Publishing Platform

1. Economics literature 2. Education—United States 3. Information technology—Economic aspects 4. Infrastructure (Economics) 5. United States—Economic conditions

ISBN 1484873327; 9781484873328

SUMMARY: In this book, "an entrepreneur offers a vision for a new wave of American economic success. Drawing on history, economic theory and his own experience as an immigrant, an employee and an entrepreneur, [Suresh] Sharma . . . lays out a road map for American prosperity based on innovation and a high-tech infrastructure that allows the best and brightest to both collaborate and compete." (Kirkus Reviews)

REVIEW: *Kirkus Rev* v82 no2 p26 Ja 15 2014

"The 3rd American Dream . . . That Is Global In Reach". ". It is clear that [Suresh] Sharma has thought through the details of his fundamental reorganization of the economy, as the book offers not only big-picture theoretical explanations for his advice, but also itemized discussions of how his proposed structures, such as a Cabinet-level innovation department and an integrated system of in-person and remote education, should be set up, funded and operated. Although the book is at times overly enthusiastic about American exceptionalism . . . Sharma does point out that he reached this conclusion after years of international experience. A unique recommendation for the economic future of the United States, offering well-thought-out proposals sure to spark discussion."

REVIEW: *Kirkus Rev* v81 no24 p359 D 15 2013

"The 3rd American Dream . . . That Is Global In Reach". ". It is clear that [Suresh] Sharma has thought through the details of his fundamental reorganization of the economy, as the book offers not only big-picture theoretical explanations for his advice, but also itemized discussions of how his proposed structures, such as a Cabinet-level innovation department and an integrated system of in-person and remote education, should be set up, funded and operated. Although the book is at times overly enthusiastic about American exceptionalism . . . Sharma does point out that he reached this conclusion after years of international experience. A unique recommendation for the economic future of the United States, offering well-thought-out proposals sure to spark discussion."

SHARP, NANCY. Both Sides Now; A True Story of Love, Loss and Bold Living; [by] Nancy Sharp 320 p. 2014 Innovative Logistics Llc

1. Bereavement 2. Cancer patients—Family relationships 3. Marriage 4. Memoirs 5. Widows

ISBN 0983937869; 9780983937869

SUMMARY: This book is Nancy Sharp's "debut memoir about losing her young husband to cancer and the struggle to rebuild her life. . . . For two and a half years, Sharp was brutally squeezed between managing new motherhood and caring for a rapidly declining spouse. . . .. Through dating, and eventually marrying, a widower with experiences so like her own, and then learning how to live in a blended family, Sharp came to her most powerful realization." (Kirkus Reviews)

REVIEW: *Kirkus Rev* v81 no24 p83 D 15 2013

"Both Sides Now: A True Story of Love, Loss and Bold Living". "A blogger and speechwriter's debut memoir about losing her young husband to cancer and the struggle to rebuild her life. . . . Through dating, and eventually marrying, a widower with experiences so like her own, and then learning how to live in a blended family, Sharp came to her most powerful realization: While it would never be possible to completely 'balance the scales' after a loss of the kind she suffered, she could still rededicate herself to living life to the fullest. Wrenching yet eloquent and fiercely hopeful."

SHARPE, TESS. Far from you; [by] Tess Sharpe 352 p. 2014 Hyperion Books

1. Best friends—Fiction 2. Drug abuse—Fiction 3. Friendship—Fiction 4. Lesbians—Fiction 5. Murder—Fiction 6. Mystery and detective stories

ISBN 1423184629; 9781423184621 (hardback)

LC 2013-037960

SUMMARY: In this young adult novel by Tess Sharpe, "Sophie Winters nearly died. Twice. The first time, she's fourteen, and escapes a near-fatal car accident with . . . an addiction to Oxy that'll take years to kick. The second time, she's seventeen, and . . . Sophie and her best friend Mina are confronted by a masked man in the woods. Sophie survives, but Mina is not so lucky. . . . No one is looking in the right places and Sophie must search for Mina's murderer on her own." (Publisher's note)

REVIEW: *Booklist* v110 no17 p53 My 1 2014 Kara Dean

REVIEW: *Bull Cent Child Books* v67 no9 p476 My 2014 K. Q. G.

"Far From You". "Between Sophie's addiction, Mina's death, and their hidden affair, this could have easily veered off into melodrama, but [Tess] Sharpe instead wrings the hurt out of each of these elements in slow but deliberate strokes, creating a lacerating picture of grief and regret. . . . Secondary characters are credibly nuanced, particularly Mina's older brother, whose attraction to Sophie is tangled up in his guilt about causing the car crash that left her in chronic pain. The murder mystery is compelling (and, thankfully, unconnected to Mina's sexuality), and its resolution serves as a reminder that love is irrevocably tied to loss and that few people get out of it unscathed."

REVIEW: *Kirkus Rev* v82 no5 p127 Mr 1 2014

"Far From You". "This beautifully realized debut delves into the emotions of a girl recovering from drug addiction and grief, all wrapped up in a solid mystery. . . . [Tess] Sharpe writes in chapters alternating between scenes from the past and present as she moves the story forward. Within the mystery plot, she focuses mostly on Sophie's battle against drugs and against those who refuse to believe her—and on an emotional secret the two girls shared. She doesn't settle for simplistic, one-dimensional characters, giving each flaws and virtues, strengths and weaknesses, from Sophie's parents to her friends. An absorbing story full of depth and emotion."

REVIEW: *SLJ* v60 no4 p173 Ap 2014 Genevieve Feldman

REVIEW: *Voice of Youth Advocates* v37 no2 p65 Je 2014 Mary Ann Darby

SHAVIT, ARI, 1957-. My promised land; [by] Ari Shavit 464 p. 2013 Spiegel & Grau

1. Arab-Israeli conflict 2. Historical literature 3. Israel—History 4. Zionism

ISBN 9780385521703; 9780812984644 (ebook)

LC 2012-046122

SUMMARY: In this book, "Israeli journalist [Ari] Shavit . . . presents a history of and meditation on Zionism's successes and failures. . . .He traces the rise and demise of the kibbutzim, the 1948 displacement of Palestinians, the shock of 1967's Six-Day War victory, and the near defeat in the 1973 Yom Kippur War." He asks, "Can Israel fully integrate its Arab citizens, do justice to the Palestinians, and assure security in the face of looming military and demographic threats? " (Library Journal)

REVIEW: *America* v210 no13 p37-8 Ap 14 2014 BILL WILLIAMS

REVIEW: *Booklist* v109 no18 p13 My 15 2013 Jay Freeman

REVIEW: *Christ Century* v131 no11 p42 My 28 2014

REVIEW: *Commentary* v137 no1 p52-4 Ja 2014 ELLI FISCHER

REVIEW: *Economist* v409 no8865 p85-8 D 7 2013

REVIEW: *Economist* v409 no8866 p88-9 D 14 2013

"My Promised Land: The Triumph and Tragedy of Israel". "The lone voice of the cantor is often more haunting than the chorus. So it is with Ari Shavit in this spellbinding book. Rather than set out Israel's history in a densely scored chronicle, he presents it in solos. . . . Mr. Shavit subtly builds his stories with a mix of individual portraits, historical detail and personal memoir. . . . The music of this book is laced with mournful notes. . . . Mr. Shavit is that rare person who can listen as intensely as he can think. . . . He transcends tribal politics. . . . He manages to reach conclusions without lapsing into narrow judgements. . . . Inevitably, perhaps, his vision clouds slightly as he draws near to the present day. . . . But these flaws are small."

REVIEW: *Kirkus Rev* v81 no8 p68 Ap 15 2013

REVIEW: *Kirkus Rev* p34-5 2013 Guide to BookExpo America

REVIEW: *Libr J* v139 no6 p56 Ap 1 2014 Ilka Gordon

REVIEW: *Libr J* v138 no13 p108 Ag 1 2013 Joel Neuberg

REVIEW: *London Rev Books* v36 no19 p29-34 O 9 2014 Nathan Thrall

REVIEW: *N Y Times Book Rev* p30 D 1 2013

REVIEW: *N Y Times Book Rev* p1-30 N 24 2013 Leon Wieseltier

"My Promised Land: The Triumph and Tragedy of Israel". "It is one of the achievements of Ari Shavit's important and powerful book to recover the feeling of Israel's facticity and to revel in it, to restore the grandeur of the simple fact in full view of the complicated facts. 'My Promised Land' startles in many ways, not least in its relative lack of interest in providing its readers with a handy politics. Shavit . . . comes not to praise or to blame, though along the way he does both, with erudition and with eloquence; he comes instead to observe and to reflect. This is the least tendentious book about Isral I have ever read. It is a Zionist book unblinkered by Zionism. It is about the entirety of the Israeli experience."

REVIEW: *New York Times* v163 no56356 pC23-9 D 20 2013 JANET MASLIN

"The Goldfinch," "Life After Life," and "My Promised Land: The Triumph and Tragedy of Israel". "In this astonishing Dickensian Novel, Ms. [Donna] Tartt uses her myriad talents—her tactile prose, her knowledge of her characters' inner lives, her instinct for suspense—to immerse us in a fully imagined fictional world that reminds us of the wonderful stay-up-all-night pleasures of reading. . . . In her best novel thus far, Ms. [Kate] Atkinson is a wonderful liar. . . . . The book's many mysteries keep it riveting and intense. And Ms. Atkinson, always haunting, has never seemed more artfully in control of her storytelling. . . . This book—it's a gale of conversation, of feeling, of foreboding, of ratiocination—combines road trips, interviews, memoir and straightforward history to relate Israel's past and present."

REVIEW: *New York Times* v163 no56326 pC1-4 N 20 2013 DWIGHT GARNER

SHEA, DANIEL M. Presidential campaigns; documents decoded; [by] Daniel M. Shea xxii, 305 p. 2013 ABC-CLIO, LLC

1. Communication in politics—United States—History 2. English language—United States—Discourse analysis 3. Mass media—Political aspects—United States—History 4. Political campaigns—United States—History 5. Political science literature 6. Presidential candidates—United States—Language 7. Presidents—United States—Election—History 8. Rhetoric—Political aspects—United States—History 9. Speeches, addresses, etc., American—History and criticism

ISBN 9781610691925 (hardcover: alk. paper)

LC 2013-006048

SUMMARY: This book "examines key moments during modern presidential campaigns, based on unedited excerpts from speeches, interviews, public addresses, and other documents. [Daniel M.] Shea . . . and [Brian M.] Harward . . . offer analysis and commentary on politicians, political campaigning, and other political matters that they have determined to be especially important in American history as understood through the lens of documentary evidence." (Choice: Current Reviews for Academic Libraries)

REVIEW: *Choice* v51 no9 p1574 My 2014 R. V. Labaree

"Presidential Campaigns: Documents Decoded". "The

format is easy to follow; considered collectively, the chapters provide important insights into the campaign. . . . End matter includes a helpful narrative time line that summarizes each campaign and a list of further readings for each campaign. The authors state that they used no predetermined set of objective measures to select issues to analyze; how the documents were chosen to represent various issues is unclear. However, this work provides important insights into the frequently unpredictable and sometimes unruly dynamics of presidential campaigning in the US."

REVIEW: *Libr J* v139 no2 p95 F 1 2014 Beth Bland

SHEBAN, CHRIS.il. The lonely book. See Bernheimer, K.

SHEEHAN-DEAN, AARON.ed. The Civil War. See The Civil War

SHEEPSHANKS, MARY. Wild Writing Granny; A Memoir; [by] Mary Sheepshanks 285 p. 2012 Stone Trough Books

1. Eton College 2. Memoirs 3. Poets—Biography 4. Rich people 5. School principals
ISBN 0954454278; 9780954454272

SUMMARY: This book presents the memoir of Mary Sheepshanks, who was "born in the early 1930s . . , the daughter of an Eton housemaster and then married a headmaster of a prep school in Berkshire. She now lives in Yorkshire where she writes novels and poetry. . . . Mary Sheepshanks, or Mary Nickson as she was then, mixed with aristocracy and royalty, even attending dancing lessons and Guide classes with the royal princesses." (Times Literary Supplement)

REVIEW: *TLS* no5769 p30 O 25 2013 MARION SHAW

"Wild Writing Granny: A Memoir." "To anyone who is at Eton College or has been, or hopes to go, or has family in any of these categories, 'Wild Writing Granny' will be a welcome book. . . . To the vast majority of people who have nothing to do with Eton, the experience of reading this book will be like looking into an bubble in which numerous figures move with little reference to the outside world. . . . If this rather coy knowingness is accepted, you will find her book clearly and diligently written within its narrow confines; and the poems scattered throughout it add a touching emotional dimension."

SHEHABI, DEEMA.ed. Al-mutanabbi street starts here. See Al-mutanabbi street starts here

SHEIKH, M. SAEED.ed. The reconstruction of religious thought in Islam. See Iqbal, M.

SHEINKIN, STEVE. The Port Chicago 50; disaster, mutiny, and the fight for civil rights; [by] Steve Sheinkin 208 p. 2014 Roaring Brook Press

1. African American sailors 2. African Americans—Civil rights 3. Historical literature 4. Port Chicago Mutiny, Port Chicago, Calif., 1944 5. World War, 1939-1945
ISBN 1596437960; 9781596437968 (hardcover: alk. paper)
LC 2013-013452

SUMMARY: Author Steve Sheinkin tells how "on July 17, 1944, a massive explosion rocked the segregated Navy base at Port Chicago, California. On August 9th, 244 men refused to go back to work until unsafe and unfair conditions at the docks were addressed. Fifty were charged with mutiny.[It is the story] of the prejudice that faced black men and women in America's armed forces during World War II." (Publisher's note)

REVIEW: *Booklist* v110 no19/20 p128 Je 1 2014 Elizabeth Nelson

REVIEW: *Booklist* v110 no11 p58 F 1 2014 Sarah Hunter

REVIEW: *Bull Cent Child Books* v67 no6 p334-5 F 2014 Elizabeth Bush

"The Port Chicago 50: Disaster, Mutiny and the Fight for Civil Rights". "[Steve] Sheinkin handily sketches in the background of segregation at the time period and allows much of the episode to unfold through first-hand accounts and extensive excerpts from the trial itself, supplying commentary to assist readers in following the prosecution and defense strategies. The result is a gripping narrative that underscores the tragic fallout from misguided military policy, while involving readers in the courtroom debate and the exact meaning of 'mutiny.'"

REVIEW: *Horn Book Magazine* v90 no2 p146-7 Mr/Ap 2014 ROGER SUTTON

REVIEW: *Kirkus Rev* v81 no24 p219 D 15 2013

"The Port Chicago 50: Disaster, Mutiny, and the Fight for Civil Rights". "In this thoroughly researched and well-documented drama, [Steve] Sheinkin lets the participants tell the story, masterfully lacing the narrative with extensive quotations drawn from oral histories, information from trial transcripts and archival photographs. The event, little known today, is brought to life and placed in historical context, with Eleanor Roosevelt, Thurgood Marshall and Jackie Robinson figuring in the story. An important chapter in the civil rights movement, presenting 50 new heroes."

REVIEW: *Publ Wkly* v260 no45 p74 N 11 2013

REVIEW: *Publ Wkly* v261 no17 p133 Ap 28 2014

REVIEW: *SLJ* v60 no4 p64 Ap 2014 Patricia Ann Owens

REVIEW: *SLJ* v60 no2 p128 F 2014 Jody Kopple

SHELDON, DYAN. One or two things I learned about love; [by] Dyan Sheldon 288 p. 2013 Candlewick Press

1. Abusive relationships 2. Diary fiction 3. First loves—Fiction 4. Jealousy 5. Love stories
ISBN 9780763666651
LC 2012-950623

SUMMARY: In this book, "Hildy D'Angelo's . . . summer becomes a rush of kisses and romantic dates with the seemingly perfect Connor. The teen finds herself blowing off her friends and trying to justify her actions by telling herself (and her friends) that it's normal to want to spend all your time with your boyfriend. But then Connor starts acting jealous. . . . As his behavior becomes more possessive and unpredictable, Hildy wonders if this is what love is really all about." (School Library Journal)

REVIEW: *Booklist* v110 no8 p45-7 D 15 2013 Ann Kelley

"One or Two Things I Learned about Love." "Writing diary style, sarcastic Hildy chronicles (with funny asides in parentheses) her daily life with two high-maintenance sisters, wacky parents, and a bunch of fun-loving friends, all of whom seem younger and more naive than their age suggests.

Of course, she also dishes on falling for sweet and sensitive Connor. The flip side of his personality is revealed slowly but nonetheless alarmingly. . . . A somewhat rushed final awakening makes the pacing feel off in [Dyan] Sheldon's humorous yet cautionary tale of first love; on the upside, there's plenty of time for readers to scream, 'Dump him!'."

REVIEW: *Bull Cent Child Books* v67 no5 p283-4 Ja 2014 K. C.

"One or Two Things I Learned About Love." "The diary format keeps the reader firmly inside Hildy's viewpoint as Connor goes from ideal boyfriend to jealous stalker, but the book provides enough reported conversation . . . to give readers perspective on what's really happening. The negative opinions start to feel programmatic, however, especially when Hildy's enthusiasm and excuses for Connor's behavior persist in the face of the clues her friends and family are giving her. . . . The high-energy narration, though, is reminiscent of that of Georgia Nicolson . . . and the warm antics of Hildy's close circle of friends leaven this cautionary tale that readers will enjoy visiting even as they cringe at Hildy's naïveté."

REVIEW: *SLJ* v60 no2 p97 F 2014 Heather Webb

SHELDON, KATHY. Aimée Ray's sweet & simple jewelry. See Aimée Ray's sweet & simple jewelry

SHELLEY, FRED M. Nation shapes; the story behind the world's borders; [by] Fred M. Shelley xix, 634 p. 2013 ABC-CLIO

1. Boundaries 2. Citizenship 3. Political geography 4. Political science literature 5. Sovereignty (Political science)

ISBN 9781610691055 (hardcopy : alk. paper); 9781610691062 (ebook)

LC 2012-035416

SUMMARY: This book by Fred M. Shelley explores "the origins, effects, and meanings of individual country borders. . . . Broad chapters are organized more by cultural than physical geography. . . . Entries are subdivided into three sections: 'Overview,' 'Historical Context,' and 'Contemporary Issues' (where relevant). . . . The . . . introduction covers topics such as systems of governance, citizenship, sovereignty, exclaves/enclaves, and the history of state symbols and flags." (Booklist)

REVIEW: *Booklist* v110 no1 p59 S 1 2013 Michael Tasko

"Nation Shapes: The Story Behind the World's Borders." "The origins, effects, and meanings of individual country borders are summarized succinctly in this collection by geography professor Shelley. Broad chapters are organized more by cultural than physical geography. . . . Although the information provided is of the 'quick and dirty' variety, the history of complex border disputes in a region like Eritrea is explained with care and clarity, still giving the reader enough to form an accurate overview. The informative and interesting introduction covers topics such as systems of governance, citizenship . . . and the history of state symbols and flags. Overall, this is a handy and useful resource aimed at the high-school and lower-level undergraduate audience."

REVIEW: *Choice* v51 no4 p615 D 2013 E. A. Scarletto

REVIEW: *Libr J* v138 no12 p104 Jl 1 2013 Judy Quinn

SHELLEY, JOHN.il. Stone giant. See Stone giant

SHELLEY, MARY WOLLSTONECRAFT, 1797-1851. Gris Grimly's Frankenstein, or, The modern Prometheus; 208 p. 2013 Balzer + Bray

1. Canon (Literature) 2. Graphic novels 3. Horror stories 4. Monsters—Fiction 5. Scientists—Fiction

ISBN 0061862975; 9780061862977 (trade bdg.)

LC 2010-046237

SUMMARY: This is a graphic novel version of Mary Shelley's "Frankenstein" by Gris Grimly. "Spidery ink lines and a palette of jaundiced yellows and faded sepias plumb the darkness of the writer's imaginings. Frankenstein's bone-embellished military jacket and pop-star shock of hair turn him into a sort of anachronistic punk scientist." Focus is given to "the monster's self-loathing and Frankenstein's ruin." (Publishers Weekly)

REVIEW: *Bull Cent Child Books* v67 no2 p113-4 O 2013 K. C.

"Gris Grimly's Frankenstein." "While most everyone knows the story of Frankenstein and his monstrous creation, approaching the original text can be a daunting prospect. [Adaptor and illustrator Gris] Grimly succeeds admirably, following the novel by first setting the scene through letters from Captain Walton (the eventual finder of the monster) reproduced in a sepia font resembling handwriting on parchment, before moving into a more recognizable graphic narrative format. . . . Grimly proves himself a more adept assembler of parts than his subject proved to be; his product is no monster, but a pastiche of style and substance that will reanimate the original for yet another generation of readers."

REVIEW: *Horn Book Magazine* v89 no5 p68 S/O 2013 KATIE BIRCHER

"Gris Grimly's 'Frankenstein, or, the Modern Prometheus'". "Adeptly 'assembled from the original text,' this graphic novel adaptation abridges [Mary] Shelley's tale while staying true to its spirit. The inventive illustrations relocate Frankenstein and his creation to a goth-y, Tim Burton-esque time-out-of-time with a mix of modern, nineteenth-century, and steampunk sensibilities. A muted palette of sepia, gray, and olive tones is effectively punctuated by black, pinks, and purples, and, in more gruesome moments, bilious green. Grimly makes excellent use of his format with dynamic shapes, sizes, and pacing of panels."

REVIEW: *Kirkus Rev* v81 no14 p341 Jl 15 2013

REVIEW: *Publ Wkly* v260 no22 p63 Je 3 2013

REVIEW: *Publ Wkly* p134-6 Children's starred review annual 2013

REVIEW: *SLJ* v59 no7 p105 Jl 2013 Peter Blenski

REVIEW: *Voice of Youth Advocates* v36 no4 p86 O 2013 Stacy Holbrook

"Gris Grimly's Frankenstein." "'Gris Grimiy's Frankenstein' is an illustrated version of the original 1818 work by Mary Shelley. . . . Using most of Shelley's original text. Grimly breathes life into this classic by telling the tale simultaneously through his gothic illustrations. Any text omitted from the original work is instead told through comic-style panels; though no text appears in these panels, the artwork stands on its own to represent the story. . . . Grimly's version has a whimsical quality that will draw teens in and allow them to better access this classic novel."

SHEPHARD, GILLIAN, 1940-. The real Iron Lady; working with Margaret Thatcher; [by] Gillian Shephard x, 273 p. 2013 Biteback Publishing

1. Historical literature 2. Prime ministers—Great Britain—Biography 3. Women prime ministers—Great Britain—Biography
ISBN 1849544018 (hbk.); 9781849544016 (hbk.)
LC 2013-376294

SUMMARY: This book by Gillian Shephard, the British Education Secretary under Prime Minister Margaret Thatcher, collects "reminiscences of what she was like to work with, often from unsung Conservative Party officers and apparatchiks." (Times Literary Supplement). Particular focus is given to "her thoroughness, her extraordinary capacity for hard work, and her rare ability to combine attention to detail with a grasp of strategic issues." (Publisher's note)

REVIEW: *TLS* no5749 p3-7 Je 7 2013 FERDINAND MOUNT

"Not for Turning: The Life of Margaret Thatcher," "A Journey With Margaret Thatcher: Foreign Policy Under the Iron Lady" and "The Real Iron Lady: Working With Margaret Thatcher." "Even her most loyal of ghosts, Robin Harris, . . . accuses her of being a naive and hopeless picker of ministers. This is surely an unrealistic criticism. . . . In his absorbing accounts of the negotiations he himself was involved in . . . [Robin Renwick] he depicts a demanding but entirely rational boss. . . .The freshest part of his account is of the encouragement she gave F. W. de Klerk and the steady pressure she exerted for the release of Nelson Mandela. . . . [Gillian] Shephard's accounts of Mrs Thatcher's encounters with unfamous cogs in the political world supplement this picture on the domestic front."

SHEPHERD, STEPHEN H. A.ed. Le Morte Darthur. See Le Morte Darthur

SHEPPARD, GILDA L.ed. Culturally relevant arts education for social justice. See Culturally relevant arts education for social justice

SHERIDAN, ALAN.tr. The notebook. See Kristof, A.

SHERIF, ANN.tr. A true novel. See Mizumura Mi.

SHERMAN, CASEY. The finest hours; the true story of a heroic sea rescue; [by] Casey Sherman 176 p. 2014 Christy Ottaviano Books/Henry Holt and Company
1. Historical literature 2. Shipwreck survival—History—Juvenile literature 3. Shipwrecks—Massachusetts—Chatham—History—Juvenile literature
ISBN 0805097643; 9780805097641 (hardback); 9781250044235 (paperback)
LC 2013-030661

SUMMARY: This nonfiction novel, by Michael J. Tougias and Casey Sherman, "tells the story of a harrowing Coast Guard rescue when four men in a tiny lifeboat overcame insurmountable odds and saved more than 30 stranded sailors." In this book, the events of the February 18, 1952 wreck of two oil tankers near Cape Cod are adapted for middle-grade readers. (Publisher's note)

REVIEW: *Booklist* v110 no8 p35 D 15 2013 Daniel Kraus

REVIEW: *Bull Cent Child Books* v67 no5 p286 Ja 2014 E. B.

"The Finest Hours: The True Story of a Heroic Sea Rescue." "The author unquestionably knows how to spin a suspenseful yarn, following the perilous attempts by the Coast Guard to retrieve men clinging to four different ship sections, often without power or communication devices and tossed near drifting shoals, while upping the emotional ante with background on some of the lead rescuers. Although the text focuses mainly on the rescue itself, results of the official inquiry are included, as well as a robust selected bibliography and updates on the Pendleton rescuers who were awarded the Gold Lifesaving Medal. True adventure readers appreciate a dark and stormy night as much as any gothic fan; just add thick wool socks, a heavy sweater, and a mug of hot chocolate."

REVIEW: *Kirkus Rev* v81 no23 p136 D 1 2013

REVIEW: *SLJ* v60 no3 p183 Mr 2014 Bob Hassett

SHERMAN, CHARLES S. The broken and the whole; discovering joy after heartbreak: lessons from a life of faith; [by] Charles S. Sherman 224 p. 2013 Scribner
1. Faith 2. Memoirs 3. Providence and government of God—Judaism 4. Rabbis—New York (State)—Syracuse—Biography 5. Suffering
ISBN 1451656165; 9781451656169
LC 2013-037360

SUMMARY: This book, by Charles S. Sherman, is a "memoir about a rabbi's search for understanding and his discovery of hope and joy after his young son suffered a catastrophic brain-stem stroke that left him a quadriplegic and dependent on a ventilator for each breath. . . . The ground had shifted beneath the Sherman family's feet, yet over the next thirty years, they were able to find comfort, pleasure, and courage in one another, their community, their faith, and in the love they shared." (Publisher's note)

REVIEW: *Booklist* v110 no13 p3-4 Mr 1 2014 Francisca Goldsmith

REVIEW: *Kirkus Rev* v82 no2 p50 Ja 15 2014

"The Broken and the Whole: Discovering Joy After Heartbreak". "A meaningful portrayal of how tragedy affected and transformed one family and especially one religious leader. . . . Throughout, [Charles S.] Sherman ties his narrative to his faith, exploring how everything he has experienced, from anger to joy, is mirrored in Scripture. 'When I heard Eyal's terrible prognosis, my life was shattered,' he writes. 'But eventually, as Moses did, I got up and climbed the mountain again.' Deeply moving, extraordinarily thought-provoking and entirely humane."

REVIEW: *Publ Wkly* v261 no3 p50 Ja 20 2014

SHERMAN, GABRIEL. The Loudest Voice in the Room; Fox News and the Making of America; [by] Gabriel Sherman 336 p. 2013 Random House Inc
1. Ailes, Roger, 1940- 2. Cable television networks—Officials & employees 3. Executives—United States—Biography 4. Fox News 5. Journalism
ISBN 0812992857; 9780812992854

SUMMARY: Author Gabriel "Sherman chronicles the rise of [Roger] Ailes, a sickly kid from an Ohio factory town who . . . built the most influential television news empire of our time. Drawing on hundreds of interviews with Fox News insiders past and present, Sherman documents Ailes's tactical acuity as he battles the press, business rivals, and countless real and perceived enemies inside and outside Fox." (Publisher's note)

REVIEW: *Columbia J Rev* v52 no6 p63 Mr/Ap 2014 JAMES BOYLAN

REVIEW: *Kirkus Rev* v82 no4 p332 F 15 2014

REVIEW: *Libr J* v137 no20 p61 D 1 2012 Barbara Hoffert

REVIEW: *N Y Rev Books* v61 no6 p8-12 Ap 3 2014 Steve Coll

"The Loudest Voice in the Room: How the Brilliant, Bombastic Roger Ailes Built Fox News—and Divided a Country." "A limitation of [author Gabriel] Sherman's biography is that he makes too many breezy claims about Ailes's singular importance. . . . Such hype isn't necessary; Ailes is a fascinating subject, and plenty important. . . . For all of Sherman's admirably persistent reporting and the hundreds of interviews he has conducted, there is something about Ailes's character that remains elusive in his pages."

REVIEW: *N Y Times Book Rev* p12-3 Ja 19 2014 JACOB WEISBERG

"The Loudest Voice in the Room: How the Brilliant, Bombastic Roger Ailes Built Fox News and Divided a Country." "What drives this need to create conflict? In his actually fair and balanced, carefully documented biography, [author Gabriel] Sherman . . . struggles to come up with an answer. . . . In Sherman's telling, [media executive Roger] Ailes was driven more by money than by any fixed set of political beliefs. . . . His identification with the right was mostly a matter of opportunities. . . . After Rupert Murdoch gave him the keys to Fox News, Ailes had a 24-hour megaphone to express both his personal feelings and his populist views."

REVIEW: *N Y Times Book Rev* p22 F 2 2014 GREGORY COWLES

REVIEW: *New York Times* v162 no56068 pC4 Mr 7 2013 BRIAN STELTER

REVIEW: *New York Times* v163 no56387 pC1-4 Ja 20 2014 JANET MASLIN

SHERMER, ELIZABETH TANDY.ed. Barry Goldwater and the remaking of the American political landscape. See Barry Goldwater and the remaking of the American political landscape

SHEVTSOVA, MARIA. The Cambridge introduction to theatre directing. See Innes, C.

SHIELDS, CAROL DIGGORY. Baby's got the blues; [by] Carol Diggory Shields 32 p. 2014 Candlewick Press

1. Blues music 2. Brothers & sisters—Juvenile fiction 3. Children's stories 4. Infants—Juvenile fiction 5. Picture books for children

ISBN 0763632600; 9780763632601

LC 2013-943085

SUMMARY: This book, by Carol Diggory Shields, illustrated by Lauren Tobia, is a "tale of soggy diapers, mushy meals, and sleepin' behind bars. . . . Babies can't talk, can't walk, can't even really chew. It's enough to make the baby in this story blue, blue, blue." The book "gives a tip of the fedora to B.B. King in an ode to babyhood." (Publisher's note)

REVIEW: *Booklist* v110 no14 p80 Mr 15 2014 Ilene Cooper

REVIEW: *Bull Cent Child Books* v67 no6 p335 F 2014 Deborah Stevenson

"Baby's Got the Blues." "It's both funny and accurate in the details of infant frustration (some of which continue well beyond babyhood). The art gives viewers a hook in the form of baby's older sister, who's squirming away from the diaper change and zipping around with the freedom that the baby yearns for, thereby cleverly turning the book into a celebration of all the things post-baby kids can do that babies can't. Figures in the ink, pencil, and digital illustrations have a combination of flow and rotundity that recalls Patricia Polacco at times, though the compositions are cleaner and more rhythmic and the linework crisper. Kids plagued by attention-grabbing new babies will find this a sly and lively reminder of their own superiority and their siblings' lovability."

REVIEW: *Kirkus Rev* v82 no1 p223 Ja 1 2014

REVIEW: *Publ Wkly* v260 no51 p57 D 16 2013

REVIEW: *SLJ* v60 no2 p79 F 2014 Marianne Saccardi

SHIELDS, DAVID. Salinger. See Salerno, S.

SHINN, GENE. Bootstrap geologist; my life in science; [by] Gene Shinn xii, 297 p. 2013 University Press of Florida

1. Autobiographies 2. Geologists—United States—Biography 3. Geology—Study & teaching 4. Geology—United States—History

ISBN 9780813044361 (alk. paper)

LC 2012-039464

SUMMARY: This book is a memoir by geologist Gene Shinn. "Though initially handicapped by a lack of advanced degrees, Shinn's drive, hard work, and dedication allowed him to rise to the top of his profession and receive the Twenhofel Medal--the highest award given by the International Society for Sedimentary Geology." Shinn "shares the highs and lows of his remarkable career." (Publisher's note)

REVIEW: *New York Times* v163 no56311 pD5 N 5 2013 MICHAEL POLLAK

"Boostrap Geologist: My Life in Science." "In his autobiography . . . Mr. [Gene] Shinn recounts his life and research, dispensing advice and anecdotes--some hilarious--starting from his boyhood . . . all the way to his receiving the top award in his field, sedimentary geology. . . . Mr. Shinn invites the reader along in a conversational, enthusiastic style that it is impressively free of rancor for a scientist whose views were sometimes in the minority. He keeps jargon to a minimum, explaining unavoidable terminology in highly readable notes. Generous to a fault in giving credit to his mentors, colleagues and friends, Mr. Shinn has apparently felt the need to throw in their names as often as possible. . . . But that is a minor distraction."

SHINODA, ANNA. Learning not to drown; [by] Anna Shinoda 352 p. 2013 Atheneum Books for Young Readers

1. Brothers and sisters—Fiction 2. Criminals—Fiction 3. Drug abuse—Fiction 4. Family life—Fiction 5. Secrets—Fiction 6. Self-actualization (Psychology)—Fiction 7. Young adult fiction

ISBN 1416993932; 9781416993933 (hardback)

LC 2012-051502

SUMMARY: In this young adult novel by Anna Shinoda,

"no closet is going to contain Clare's 'Skeleton.' Her older brother Luke's drug and criminal transgressions guarantee that she will never be far from scorn in her small hometown. Clare's parents and brother Peter all suffer in their own individual ways, while Luke calls the shots that define the family. Clare has strong friendships, college dreams, an affinity for swimming and knitting, and an unabashed love for wayward Luke." (Publisher's note)

REVIEW: *Booklist* v110 no16 p49 Ap 15 2014 Gail Bush

REVIEW: *Bull Cent Child Books* v67 no10 p541 Je 2014 K. C.

"Learning Not to Drown". "The mother and father are psychologically if maddeningly credible in their denial of the extent of their son's problems, and Clare's dawning understanding of how their cover-ups have allowed many people, including herself and her other brother, to be hurt is painful to read. Ultimately, Clare has to come to terms with the fact that no amount of compassion and forgiveness on her part can change her brother, and that her responsibility must be to herself first; that she gradually realizes this through experience rather than through adult supports and guidance relieves the book of any message-y pretense."

REVIEW: *Kirkus Rev* v82 no3 p219 F 1 2014

REVIEW: *SLJ* v60 no6 p129 Je 2014 Vicki Reutter

SHIPMAN, CLAIRE. The Confidence Code; The Art and Science of Self-assurance - and What Women Need to Know; [by] Claire Shipman 256 p. 2014 HarperCollins

1. Advice literature 2. Self-confidence 3. Self-esteem in women 4. Sexism 5. Women—Attitudes

ISBN 006223062X; 9780062230621

SUMMARY: Authors Katty Kay and Claire Shipman "provide an informative and practical guide to understanding the importance of confidence—and learning how to achieve it—for women of all ages and at all stages of their career. . . . Combining . . . research in genetics, gender, behavior, and cognition—with examples from their own lives and those of other successful women in politics, media, and business—Kay and Shipman . . . offer the . . . advice women need to close the gap." (Publisher's note)

REVIEW: *Kirkus Rev* v82 no5 p153 Mr 1 2014

"The Confidence Code: The Science and Art of Self-Assurance: What Women Should Know". "BBC World News America Washington correspondent [Katty] Kay and Good Morning America contributor [Claire] Shipman address how a lack of self-confidence hinders women's career advancement. . . . Through these interviews, Kay and Shipman confirmed their beliefs about the significant contrast between the typical male approach of pushing forward aggressively (e.g., shouting out questions or making unsubstantiated assertions in order to dominate meetings) and that of women, who instinctively hold back for fear of seeming pushy and aggressive. . . . An insightful look at how internalizing cultural stereotypes can hold women back from competing with men."

REVIEW: *N Y Times Book Rev* p34 My 18 2014 Erin Gloria Ryan

REVIEW: *Publ Wkly* v261 no4 p28-33 Ja 27 2014

REVIEW: *Publ Wkly* v261 no6 p77-8 F 10 2014

REVIEW: *Publ Wkly* v261 no17 p10 Ap 28 2014

SHIPMAN, TALITHA.il. You are my little pumpkin pie. See Sklansky. A. E.

SHKLOVSKII, VIKTOR, 1893-1984. Bowstring; on the dissimilarity of the similar; xii, 467 p. 2011 Dalkey Archive Press

1. Art 2. Artistic collaboration 3. Creative ability 4. Literature—History and criticism—Theory, etc 5. Philosophical literature

ISBN 9781564784254 (pbk. : alk. paper)

LC 2011-012936

SUMMARY: This book "focuses on innovation in art--what it means and requires. To [Viktor] Shklovsky, an 'innovator is a guide who changes the tracks but who also knows the old pathways,' and he surveys history and the present moment to identify those crucial points where innovation occurs, when 'the similar turns out to be dissimilar.'" (Publishers Weekly)

REVIEW: *TLS* no5756 p9-10 Jl 26 2013 ZINOVY ZINIK

"Shklovsky: Witness to an Era," "Bowstring: On the Dissimilarity of the similar" and "A Hunt for Optimism." "[Serena] Vitale creates her witty and moving minimalist portrait by unobtrusively observing [Viktor] Shklovsky's daily routine. . . . Dalkey Archive Press, which over the past decade and more has performed the heroic task of bringing out all the key works of Shklovsky in English, should have appointed a Russian-speaker and editor to supervise the work of its translators. Successful in transposing the ironical voice of Shklovsky's analytical passages in 'Bowstring,' Shushan Avagyan is sometimes defeated by the idiosyncratic collation of hackneyed colloquialisms that mark 'A Hunt for Optimism'."

SHKLOVSKII, VIKTOR, 1893-1984. A hunt for optimism; vi, 175 p. 2012 Dalkey Archive Press

1. Authors, Russian—Soviet Union—Fiction 2. Experimental literature 3. Jews—Russia—Fiction 4. Soviet Union—Fiction 5. Trials in literature

ISBN 9781564787903 (paperback : alkaline paper)

LC 2012-029207

SUMMARY: This book "circles obsessively around a single scene of interrogation in which a writer is subjected to a show trial for his unorthodoxy. Using multiple perspectives, fragments, and aphorisms, and bearing the vulnerability of both the Russian Jewry and the anti-Bolshevik intelligentsia--who had unwittingly become the 'enemies of the people'--'Hunt' satirizes Soviet censorship and the ineptitude of Soviet leaders " (Publisher's note)

REVIEW: *Nation* v296 no8 p33-6 F 25 2013 BEN EHRENREICH

REVIEW: *TLS* no5756 p9-10 Jl 26 2013 ZINOVY ZINIK

"Shklovsky: Witness to an Era," "Bowstring: On the Dissimilarity of the similar" and "A Hunt for Optimism." "[Serena] Vitale creates her witty and moving minimalist portrait by unobtrusively observing [Viktor] Shklovsky's daily routine. . . . Dalkey Archive Press, which over the past decade and more has performed the heroic task of bringing out all the key works of Shklovsky in English, should have appointed a Russian-speaker and editor to supervise the work of its translators. Successful in transposing the ironical voice of Shklovsky's analytical passages in 'Bowstring,' Shushan Avagyan is sometimes defeated by the idiosyncratic collation of hackneyed colloquialisms that mark 'A Hunt for Optimism'."

SHOEMAKE, JOSH. Tangier; A Literary Guide for Travellers; [by] Josh Shoemake 288 p. 2013 St. Martin's Press

1. Authors—Homes & haunts 2. Expatriate authors 3. Historical literature 4. Literary landmarks 5. Tangier (Morocco)

ISBN 1780762763; 9781780762760

SUMMARY: In this book, author "Josh Shoemake's first chapter is devoted to the port of Tangier and the arrival there of assorted literary figures, including Samuel Pepys, Hans Christian Andersen, Truman Capote and Jack Kerouac. . . . Thereafter, Shoemake continues to eschew chronology, as he proceeds from port to plage to Kasbah, then to Medin and Petit Socco, and on to various cafés, bars and hotels, logging the various celebrities who might have assembled there over the decades." (Times Literary Supplement)

REVIEW: *TLS* no5762 p27 S 6 2013 ROBERT IRWIN

"Tangier: A Literary Guide for Travelers." "An excellent book in its own right and more lively than its predecessors. . . . Time is compressed to whimsical effect. . . . [Paul] Bowles is clearly Josh Shoemake's hero--the dominant figure in literary Tangier--and the city's Arabs are almost invisible except as informants, collaborators or proxy authors. The pervading impression one gets from this seedy version of Fitzrovia on the Mediterranean is of louche despair, something of which is captured in Bowles's remark that 'Tangier doesn't make a man disintegrate but it does attract people who are going to disintegrate anyway'."

SHOOK, DAVID.tr. Shiki Nagaoka. See Bellatin, M.

SHORT, MICHAEL.ed. The Liszt/D'Agoult correspondence. See The Liszt/D'Agoult correspondence

SHORT, PHILIP. A taste for intrigue; The multiple lives of François Mitterrand; [by] Philip Short 2014 Henry Holt and Co.

1. Biography (Literary form) 2. France—Politics & government—1945- 3. Mitterrand, François, 1916-1996 4. Politicians—France—Biography 5. Presidents—France—Biography

ISBN 9780805088533 hardcover

SUMMARY: This biography by Philip Short tells how "In 1981, François Mitterrand became France's first popularly elected socialist president. By the time he completed his mandate, he had led the country for 14 years, longer than any other French head of state in modern times. Mitterrand mirrored France in all its imperfections and tragedies, its cowardice and glory, its weakness and its strength." (Publisher's note)

REVIEW: *Booklist* v110 no14 p46 Mr 15 2014 Jay Freeman

REVIEW: *Libr J* v139 no3 p115 F 15 2014 Linda Frederiksen

REVIEW: *N Y Rev Books* v61 no10 p39-41 Je 5 2014 Louis Begley

"A Taste for Intrigue: The Multiple Lives of François Mitterrand." "François Mitterrand [is] the subject of Philip Short's engrossing, authoritative, and fair biography, which is chock-full of previously unavailable information. . . . Mitterrand became the Socialist president of the French Republic, thus breaking the right's more than forty-five-year hold on power. After he completed his second seven-year term as president, he became the third-longest-serving head of the French state. . . . Short has [exhibited] throughout his book a fine understanding of French society."

REVIEW: *Publ Wkly* v260 no52 p40-1 D 23 2013

SHORTO, RUSSELL. Amsterdam; a history of the world's most liberal city; [by] Russell Shorto 368 p. 2013 Doubleday

1. Amsterdam (Netherlands)—Social life & customs 2. Historical literature 3. Liberalism—Netherlands—Amsterdam—History 4. Netherlands—Politics & government

ISBN 0385534574; 9780385534574

LC 2013-003544

SUMMARY: Author Russell Shorto's book presents a history of the city of Amsterdam. "Weaving in his own experiences of his adopted home, Shorto provides" a "story of Amsterdam from the building of its first canals in the 1300s, through its brutal struggle for independence, its golden age as a vast empire, to its complex present in which its cherished ideals of liberalism are under siege." (Publisher's note)

REVIEW: *Booklist* v110 no1 p28 S 1 2013 Dane Carr

REVIEW: *Economist* v409 no8859 p95 O 26 2013

REVIEW: *Kirkus Rev* p30 Ag 15 2013 Fall Preview

REVIEW: *Kirkus Rev* v81 no15 p207 Ag 1 2013

REVIEW: *Libr J* v139 no3 p63 F 15 2014 Denis Frias

REVIEW: *N Y Times Book Rev* p12-3 D 29 2013 PICO IYER

"Amsterdam: A History of the World's Most Liberal City." "The author's method in his new book is to take us on a very brisk tour across the highlights of Dutch history. . . . Much of this has little to do with Amsterdam or with liberalism. . . . So much has to be packed into so little space that quite often one is left with the feeling of ingesting an entire turkey with every mouthful. . . . The effect, inevitably, is of an old-style documentary, at once sonorous and excitable, that someone has mistakenly set on fast forward. . . . The looseness of the language seems to speak for an imprecision in the thinking. . . . The problem is that [author Russell] Shorto's grand ideas seem to be superimposed upon his material rather than to flow out of it."

REVIEW: *New York Times* v163 no56317 pC6 N 11 2013 JANET MASLIN

REVIEW: *Publ Wkly* v260 no32 p43 Ag 12 2013

REVIEW: *TLS* no5796 p5 My 2 2014 PHILIPP BLOM

"Amsterdam: A History of the World's Most Liberal City." "With great narrative flair, if not always entirely convincingly, [author Russell] Shorto ties this particular social climate from which modernity would grow to the history of Amsterdam. . . . It is perhaps impossible for a work of narrative history to do justice to questions of such complexity; Shorto's argument frequently remains mired in assertions. But the author is a perceptive observer of his adopted home and often draws together salient points about the nature of the city's liberal culture."

SHOTTON, HEATHER J.ed. Beyond the asterisk. See Beyond the asterisk

SHOURD, SARAH. A sliver of light. See Bauer, S.

SHRAYER, MAXIM D. I Saw It; Ilya Selvinsky and the Legacy of Bearing Witness to the Shoah; [by] Maxim D. Shrayer 340 p. 2014 Academic Studies Press

1. Holocaust, Jewish (1939-1945)—Personal narratives—History & criticism 2. Holocaust, Jewish (1939-1945)—Ukraine 3. Jewish poets 4. Literature—History & criticism 5. Selvinsky, Ilya 6. Soviet poetry

ISBN 1618113070; 9781618113078

SUMMARY: In this book, author "Maxim D. Shrayer introduces the work of Ilya Selvinsky, the first Jewish-Russian poet to depict the Holocaust (Shoah) in the occupied Soviet territories. In January 1942, while serving as a military journalist, Selvinsky witnessed the immediate aftermath of the massacre of thousands of Jews outside the Crimean city of Kerch, and thereafter composed and published poems about it." (Publisher's note)

REVIEW: *Choice* v51 no3 p464 N 2013 E. R. Baer

REVIEW: *TLS* no5794 p25 Ap 18 2014 KATHARINE HODGSON

"I Saw It: Ilya Selvinsky and the Legacy of Bearing Witness to the Shoah." "It was the site of the mass murder by shooting of most of the Jewish population of Kerch. . . . 'I Saw It' explores Selvinsky's poetic response to what he saw at this site as an act of witness that was to cost him a great deal. . . . Against this background, carefully researched by the author using a wide range of rare contemporary resources, some of which are reproduced in the text, Shrayer sets Selvinsky's wartime poems about the mass killings in Crimea in late 1941. . . . Through the example of Ilya Selvinsky, Maxim Shrayer has made an important contribution to our understanding of the workings of Soviet literary life at the intersection of poetry and policy."

SHRIVER, LIONEL. Big Brother; [by] Lionel Shriver 384 p. 2013 HarperCollins

1. Brothers & sisters—Fiction 2. Children of celebrities 3. Domestic fiction 4. Obesity 5. Reducing diets

ISBN 0061458570 (hardcover); 9780061458576 (hardcover)

SUMMARY: In this book by Lionel Shriver, "Pandora Halfdanarson . . . lives an apparently tranquil life as a successful businesswoman in Iowa with her 'nutritional Nazi' husband and stepchildren, until the arrival of her glamorous jazz pianist brother Edison. Edison has grown fat: appallingly, stinkingly, suicidally, repellently so. . . . [Pandora] decide whether she is prepared to sacrifice her family to save her brother." (Times Literary Supplement)

REVIEW: *Booklist* v109 no15 p18 Ap 1 2013 Deborah Donovan

REVIEW: *Economist* v407 no8834 p82-3 My 4 2013

REVIEW: *Kirkus Rev* v81 no7 p16 Ap 1 2013

REVIEW: *Kirkus Rev* v81 no2 p15 Je 1 2013

REVIEW: *Libr J* v138 no1 p62 Ja 1 2013

REVIEW: *Libr J* v138 no7 p77 Ap 15 2013 Lisa Block

REVIEW: *London Rev Books* v35 no12 p34 Je 20 2013 Deborah Friedell

REVIEW: *N Y Times Book Rev* p11 Je 30 2013 JINCY WILLETT

REVIEW: *New York Times* v162 no56177 pC1-4 Je 24 2013 JANET MASLIN

REVIEW: *Publ Wkly* v260 no10 p35 Mr 11 2013

REVIEW: *Time* v181 no19 p50 My 20 2013 Lev Grossman

REVIEW: *TLS* no5750 p20 Je 14 2013 LISA HILTON

"Big Brother." "A sly and startling work of fiction. . . . Pandora's reactions to her brother's self-inflicted condition are sometimes brutally delineated, but 'Big Brother' is engaged with something more subtle than the social and personal question of obesity. [Lionel] Shriver can produce virtuoso passages . . . yet the dense intelligence of her writing is most evidently displayed in the accumulation of subtle observations. The strength of this haunting and at times horribly comic novel lies in its depiction of appetite in all its forms."

SHTEYNGART, GARY. Little failure; a memoir; [by] Gary Shteyngart 368 p. 2014 Random House Inc

1. Authors, American—21st century—Biography 2. Immigrant families 3. Immigrants—United States 4. Jews, Soviet 5. Memoirs 6. Russians—United States

ISBN 0679643753; 9780679643753 (acid-free paper)

LC 2013-013217

SUMMARY: "After three acclaimed novels, Gary Shteyngart turns to memoir in a candid, witty, deeply poignant account of his life so far. Shteyngart shares his American immigrant experience, . . . with self-deprecating humor, moving insights, and literary bravado. . . . Swinging between a Soviet home life and American aspirations, Shteyngart found himself living in two contradictory worlds, all the while wishing that he could find a real home in one." (Publisher's note)

REVIEW: *Bookforum* v20 no4 p35 D 2013/Ja 2014 KATE CHRISTENSEN

REVIEW: *Economist* v410 no8868 p67-8 Ja 4 2014

REVIEW: *Kirkus Rev* v81 no23 p250 D 1 2013

REVIEW: *Libr J* v138 no21 p101 D 1 2013 Audrey Snowden

REVIEW: *Libr J* v139 no7 p49 Ap 15 2014 Heather Malcolm

REVIEW: *N Y Rev Books* v61 no3 p4-6 F 20 2014

REVIEW: *N Y Times Book Rev* p9 Ja 5 2014 ANDY BOROWITZ

"Little Failure: A Memoir." "Early in his hilarious and moving memoir, Gary Shteyngart reveals that his mother's post-collegiate nickname for him is Little Failure, which would seem more insulting if his father didn't already call him Snotty. In this Russian Jewish family--the Shteyngarts moved from Leningrad to Queens in 1979, when Gary was 7--barbed jokes, or shutki, are tokens of love. . . . 'Little Failure' is so packed with humor, it's easy to overlook the rage, but it's there, and it's part of what makes the book so compelling."

REVIEW: *New Statesman* v143 no7 p44-5 F 21 2014 Erica Wagner

REVIEW: *New York Times* v163 no56734 pC1-C14 Ja 7 2014 MICHIKO KAKUTANI

REVIEW: *Publ Wkly* v260 no43 p48 O 28 2013

REVIEW: *TLS* no5790 p9 Mr 21 2014 AMELIA GLASER

SHUBERT, BETTY KREISEL. Out-of-style; a modern perspective of how, why and when vintage fashions evolved; 372 p. 2012 Flashback Pub

1. Clothing & dress—History 2. Clothing & dress—History—19th century 3. Clothing & dress—History—20th century 4. Fashion—History 5. Historical literature
ISBN 9780983576167 (hard cover: alk. paper); 9780983576198 (paper back: alk. paper)
LC 2012-952901

SUMMARY: In this book by Bettie Kreisel Shubert, "the author presents a broad overview of 19th- and 20th-century dress. . . . Descriptions of each era's dominant silhouettes, hats, sleeves and fabric details are illustrated by the author's line drawings, hundreds of which appear throughout the book. These sketches are essential to understanding the difference between a toque and a cloche or the posture produced by the evolving corset in the early 20th century." (Kirkus Reviews)

REVIEW: *Kirkus Rev* v81 no14 p6 Jl 15 2013

REVIEW: *Kirkus Rev* v81 no13 p324 Jl 1 2013

REVIEW: *Kirkus Rev* p34-5 D 15 2013 supplemet best books 2013

"Out-of-Style: A Modern Perspective of How, Why and When Vintage Fashions Evolved". "Her book, which targets genealogists, would be especially helpful for nonexperts who may want to learn more about their historic family photographs. . . . The author's deep knowledge of fashion, the book's greatest strength, is evident in her cataloging of a broad range of men's, women's and children's styles. . . . The book's forays into social history and analysis, however, are less compelling. . . . There's also, at times, a note of disdain for women who don't conform to the author's sense of taste. . . . The descriptions of historic styles and their accompanying illustrations, however, constitute a useful resource that outweighs the book's shortcomings."

SHUBERT, BETTY KREISEL.il. Out-of-style. See Shubert, B. K.

SHUBIN, NEIL H., 1960-. The universe within; discovering the common history of rocks, planets, and people; [by] Neil H. Shubin 240 p. 2012 Pantheon Books

1. Geology 2. Human body 3. Petrology 4. Scientific literature
ISBN 0307378438; 9780307378439
LC 2012-007541

SUMMARY: This book by Neil Shubin addresses "how . . . the events that formed our solar system billions of years ago [are] embedded inside each of us. . . . Starting . . . with fossils, [Shubin] turns his gaze skyward, showing us how the entirety of the universe's fourteen-billion-year history can be seen in our bodies. As he moves from our very molecular composition . . . to the workings of our eyes, Shubin makes clear how the evolution of the cosmos has profoundly marked our own bodies." (Publisher's note)

REVIEW: *Booklist* v109 no7 p19 D 1 2012 Ray Olson

REVIEW: *Choice* v50 no12 p2262 Ag 2013 L. T. Spencer

REVIEW: *Kirkus Rev* v80 no20 p138 O 15 2012

REVIEW: *Libr J* v138 no3 p117-8 F 15 2013 Jeffrey Beall

REVIEW: *Libr J* v138 no3 p118 F 15 2013

REVIEW: *New Sci* v217 no2898 p41 Ja 5 2013 Colin Barras

"The Universe Within." " In 'The Universe Within,' evolutionary biologist Neil Shubin shares the findings of some of the great scientific specialists--as well as those of a few unsung heroes. But he also explains how a generalist's appreciation of their work is still possible, simply by looking inside the human body. . . . Shubin's book is filled with . . . sweeping scientific stories, sewn into a broader narrative--the tale of his first palaeontological exploration of Greenland. He often begins with tales from his first experiences of Arctic life, making chapters impressively broad in scope--but also prone to meandering. Still, one take-home message is clear throughout: just how much we can learn about the complex scientific world outside by looking within."

REVIEW: *Publ Wkly* v259 no41 p46 O 8 2012

REVIEW: *Sci Am* v308 no1 p76 Ja 2013 Anna Kuchment

REVIEW: *TLS* no5748 p25 My 31 2013 RICHARD HAMBLYN

"The Universe Within: A Scientific Adventure." "An illuminating account of how life on earth is shaped by the rhythms of the cosmos. . . . It's an ambitious thesis--that our biology, including our consciousness, was shaped by the birth of stars and the movements of celestial bodies--but [Neil] Shubin unearths plenty of supporting evidence. . . . Shubin's gift for storytelling is rooted in such shifts of scale, from the cosmic to the quotidian, with some of his best stories concerning the antics of his scientific forebears."

SHUGAAR, ANTONY.tr. On earth as it is in heaven. See Enia, D.

SHUKERT, RACHEL, 1980-. Love me; [by] Rachel Shukert 325 p. 2014 Delacorte Press

1. Actors and actresses—Fiction 2. Conduct of life—Fiction 3. Fame—Fiction 4. Historical fiction
ISBN 0385741103; 9780375989858 (glb: alk. paper); 9780385741101 (hardcover: alk. paper)
LC 2012-047071

SUMMARY: In this historical novel, by Rachel Shukert, sequel to "Starstruck," "Amanda is heartbroken. She's tried, but she can't get over her breakup with hotshot writer Harry Gordon. . . . Margo has to pinch herself: there's talk of her getting an Oscar nom for her first film role, and she's living with the Dane Forrest, the gorgeous movie star. . . . [And] Gabby's drinking is out of control, but who cares? She's bored and depressed." (Publisher's note)

REVIEW: *Kirkus Rev* v81 no24 p113 D 15 2013

"Love Me". " In this scintillating sequel to Starstruck (2013), the stakes are higher, the fights are cattier, and the drama soars sky-high. . . . [Amanda Farraday] makes a rash decision that sets off a chain of events that affects all three girls. Their interwoven narratives of Hollywood in the 1930s have more twists and turns than Mulholland Drive. Secrets abound, and enough is held back to ensure that the next volume will have plenty left to reveal. This sizzling sequel definitely delivers the goods: think Valley of the Dolls meets Gossip Girl."

SHULEVITZ, URI. Dusk; [by] Uri Shulevitz 32 p. 2013 Farrar, Straus & Giroux (BYR)

1. City and town life—Fiction 2. Holiday stories 3. Light 4. Night—Fiction 5. Picture books for children
ISBN 0374319030; 9780374319038 (hardcover)
LC 2012-045967

SUMMARY: In this companion to Uri Shulevitz's Caldecott Honor-winning book "Snow," a boy and his dog who are "out for a walk with his 'grandfather with beard,' comes to realize that a city (especially if it's New York City) can come alive in magical ways at dusk. The sidewalks and streets fill with people (and one extraterrestrial) headed home or out for a night's adventure." (Publishers Weekly)

REVIEW: *Horn Book Magazine* v89 no6 p82-3 N/D 2013 JOANNA RUDGE LONG

"Dusk". "Text here is minimal, with a nice lilt featuring irregular rhyme; the figures carry the action—whether the Old-Country sturdy, stylishly debonair, or as zany as a 'visitor from planet Zataplat'. . . . The city itself is deftly sketched, with energetically skewed buildings and wholesome signage. . . . [Uri] Shulevitz's palette is similar to yet brighter than that in 'Snow' (his more authoritatively drawn figures livelier without that subtle scrim of snow) and luminous indeed in the last few pages' celebration of light. A lovely companion piece."

SHULMAN, DAVID. More than real; a history of the imagination in south India; [by] David Shulman xi, 333 p. 2012 Harvard University Press

1. Culture diffusion—India—History 2. Historical literature 3. Imagination—History 4. India, South—History 5. Indic literature—To 1500

ISBN 0674059913 (alk. paper); 9780674059917 (alk. paper)

LC 2011-038131

SUMMARY: It was the author's intent to demonstrate that "from the fifteenth to the eighteenth centuries, the major cultures of southern India underwent a revolution in sensibility reminiscent of what had occurred in Renaissance Italy. During this time, the imagination came to be recognized as the defining feature of human beings. . . . David Shulman illuminates this distinctiveness and shows how it differed radically from Western notions of reality and models of the mind." (Publisher's note)

REVIEW: *TLS* no5747 p11 My 24 2013 ROSINKA CHAUDHURI

"More than Real: A History of the Imagination in South India." "The patient unravelling of the complex articulations of select Indian poets and commentators is the job that David Shulman has undertaken in this pioneering effort towards the production of a history of the imagination in South India. . . . Apart from advancing a thesis about early modem south India and the attainment there of a transfiguration comparable to the Italian Renaissance . . . Shulman interprets for us some of the major works of the pre-modern period. . . . The ancient and early modem imagination . . . leaps out of its contexts and finds its place in Shulman's argument with a luminous and, crucially, a present-day life of its own."

SHULMAN, MARK. Treasure hunters. See Patterson, James

SHULMAN, ROBERT G. Brain imaging; what it can (and cannot) tell us about consciousness; [by] Robert G. Shulman 173 p. 2013 Oxford University Press

1. Brain—Imaging 2. Consciousness 3. Mind & body 4. Neurosciences 5. Psychological literature

ISBN 0199838720 (hardcover); 9780199838721 (hardcover)

LC 2012-046107

SUMMARY: This book, written by Robert G. Shulman, "traces how assumptions about the nature of brain function made in planning scientific experiments are the consequences of philosophical positions. Experiments that relate brain activities to observable behavior are shown to avoid the philosophical and psychological assumptions about mental processes that have been proposed to underlie these behaviors. This analysis establishes the conditions necessary for reproducible brain responses." (Publisher's note)

REVIEW: *Choice* v51 no2 p358-9 O 2013 K. G. Akers

"Brain Imaging: What It Can (and Cannot) Tell Us About Consciousness." "As brain imaging techniques are increasingly employed to investigate human thought and emotion, [author Robert G.] Shulman . . . cautions against using measurements of brain physics and chemistry to explain psychological concepts. Believing that mental processes like memory and consciousness are metaphysical properties that cannot be reduced to brain mechanisms, the author urges a 'black box' approach to neuroscience that links changes in brain energy metabolism only to observable behaviors. Shulman presents a mostly philosophical argument that draws upon his lifetime of research in chemical and biological physics. For most readers, however, that argument may be difficult to understand and therefore unconvincing."

SHUMWAY, REBECCA. The Fante and the transatlantic slave trade; [by] Rebecca Shumway xii, 232 p. 2011 University of Rochester Press

1. Fanti (African people)—History—18th century 2. Historical literature 3. Slave trade—Ghana—History—18th century 4. Slave trade—History

ISBN 1580463916 (hardcover: alk. paper); 9781580463911 (hardcover: alk. paper)

LC 2011-010288

SUMMARY: In this book on the transatlantic slave trade, "focusing on the Gold Coast (roughly, present-day Ghana) in the eighteenth century, Rebecca Shumway . . . . argues that what she calls a decentralised 'coastal coalition' of interdependent Fante polities arose which controlled the ports of the Gold Coast, and played a substantial role both in shaping African–European relations and in developing Fante identities that have subsequently endured." (English Historical Review)

REVIEW: *Engl Hist Rev* v129 no536 p217-9 F 2014 Toby Green

"The Fante and the Transatlantic Slave Trade". "[Rebecca] Shumway makes excellent use of oral sources in Fanteland, combined with written sources, to pull together a very convincing argument as to the long-term influences of the trade on Fante society. . . . Her book offers an important new analysis of the interaction of Fante and European societies over the course of the long eighteenth century. . . . . While at times Shumway does overstate the macro-importance of her case-study . . . this is a significant contribution to the literature which all serious scholars of the subject will want to engage with."

SHUSTERMAN, NEAL, 1962-. Ship out of luck; a companion to The Schwa was here; [by] Neal Shusterman 256 p. 2013 Dutton Books, an imprint of Penguin Group (USA) Inc.

1. Adventure and adventurers—Fiction 2. Children's

stories 3. Cruise ships—Fiction 4. Sea stories
ISBN 0525422269; 9780525422266 (hardcover : alk. paper)
LC 2013-000031

SUMMARY: In this book, "Old Man Crawley, a filthy-rich irascible codger with a soft spot for his blind, 16-year-old granddaughter, Lexie, is about to turn 80. To celebrate, he invites--commands, really--Antsy and his family to join him and Lexie for a week aboard the incredibly fabulous cruise ship Plethora of the Deep." During the trip, Antsy meets and tries to help "Tilde, who claims she's a stowaway and smuggler of illegal immigrants." (Kirkus Reviews)

REVIEW: *Booklist* v109 no19/20 p94-5 Je 1 2013 Frances Bradburn

REVIEW: *Bull Cent Child Books* v67 no1 p53-4 S 2013 T. A.

"Ship Out of Luck." "Antsy Bonano, the wisecracking eighth-grade Brooklynite from 'The Schwa Was Here' . . . and 'Antsy Does Time', is back for an adventure on the high seas. . . . The plot gets a little ahead of itself by the end, with one too many pieces falling too niftily into place, but the story . . . is alternately hilarious and thought-provoking. [Author Neal] Shusterman deftly circumvents questions about the ethics of undocumented immigration by instead foregrounding more accessible questions of why Antsy--or anyone--does any of the harebrained things he does, rather than whether he should have done them. Obviously a treat for those who've been taken in by Antsy's antics in the past, this is a rollicking summer read that's also more contemplative than most."

REVIEW: *Horn Book Magazine* v89 no4 p147-8 Jl/Ag 2013 SARAH ELLIS

REVIEW: *Kirkus Rev* v81 no9 p103-4 My 1 2013

REVIEW: *SLJ* v59 no7 p86 Jl 2013 Liz Overberg

REVIEW: *Voice of Youth Advocates* v36 no3 p68 Ag 2013 Christina Miller

SHUSTERMAN, NEAL, 1962-. Tesla's attic. See Elfman, E.

SHYAM, BHAJJU.il. Alone in the forest. See Wolf, Gi.

SIBBICK, JOHN.il. Scaly spotted feathered frilled. See Thimmesh, C.

SICIARZ, STEPHANIE. Left at the Mango Tree; [by] Stephanie Siciarz 294 p. 2013 Pink Moon Press
1. Detective & mystery stories 2. Imaginary places 3. Islands—Fiction 4. Pineapple 5. Race relations—Fiction
ISBN 0989686302; 9780989686303

SUMMARY: In this book, narrator Almondine Orlean "will reconstruct the efforts of her grandfather—a book-loving, magic-hating, Customs and Excise Officer named Raoul—to explain his new white grandbaby, a case of island magic if ever there was. As Raoul struggles to prove otherwise (for surely otherwise it has to be!), Oh's pineapples begin to disappear. Acres without a trace, and Officer Raoul must find out how and why." (Publisher's note)

REVIEW: *Kirkus Rev* v81 no19 p65 O 1 2013

REVIEW: *Kirkus Rev* p50-1 D 15 2013 supplemet best books 2013

"Left at the Mango Tree". " In this remarkable debut . . . a young girl named Almondine narrates the mystery of her own birth on the whimsical island of Oh. . . . The novel is built upon Almondine's incredible narration, as she coyly pulls the reader along on these tandem mysteries, weaving in and out of her family's stories and secrets. Her witty, pun-filled language and swift storytelling imbue the novel with charm, yet for all the back stories and interweaving, Almondine is careful to keep readers by her side as she unravels the detailed story of her grandfather and his friends. [Stephanie] Siciarz has a talent as plentiful as Oh's pineapples, and readers will hunger for more. A tropical feast of charming, clever characters, smart storytelling and just the right amount of magic."

SICILY; art and invention between Greece and Rome; 254 p. 2013 J. Paul Getty Museum
1. Arts, Classical—Italy—Sicily 2. Greeks—Italy—Sicily—History 3. Historical literature
ISBN 160606133X; 9781606061336 (hardcover)
LC 2012-033738

SUMMARY: This book, edited by Claire L. Lyons, Michael Bennett, and Clemente Marconi, covers "Sicily's classical and early Hellenistic periods and hold the island up as a cultural rival to Athens. . . . New opportunities for trade and natural resources such as rich volcanic soils and warm temperatures drew immigrants from Greece to the island." (Library Journal)

REVIEW: *Choice* v51 no1 p140-1 S 2013 B. A. Ault

REVIEW: *Hist Today* v63 no9 p58 S 2013 PAUL LAY

"Sicily: Art and Invention Between Greece and Rome." "Sicily, or Sikelia, came under Greek domination between 480 and 212 BC, during which it became a dynamic cultural centre, producing not only great art but also such figures as Theocritus, the creator of pastoral poetry, and the scientist and mathematician Archimedes. The riches of this volume are abundant. Excellent essays by leading scholars accompany illustrations of extraordinary objects such as the Gold Phiale of Damarchos . . . a magnificent libation bowl of the late fourth century BC. The exhibition travels to Cleveland for three months from September before returning to Palermo."

REVIEW: *Libr J* v138 no9 p78 My 15 2013 Nancy J. Mactague

REVIEW: *TLS* no5754 p23 Jl 12 2013 A. J. BOYLE

SICKELS, ROBERT C.ed. 100 entertainers who changed America. See 100 entertainers who changed America

SIDDIQUI, MONA. Christians, muslims, and jesus; [by] Mona Siddiqui 296 p. 2013 Yale University Press
1. Christianity & other religions—Islam 2. Jesus Christ—Crucifixion 3. Jesus Christ—Islamic interpretations 4. Mary, Blessed Virgin, Saint—Islamic interpretations 5. Mysticism—Islam 6. Religious literature
ISBN 0300169701 (hardcover); 9780300169706 (hardcover)
LC 2013-934407

SUMMARY: In this book, Mona Siddiqui "examines how Muslims and Christians view Jesus from within their religious traditions as well as how they interpret others' views of him. Drawing extensively from medieval and modern scholars, Siddiqui outlines mainstream Islamic and Christian perspectives on Jesus, Mary, mysticism, religious doctrine, and the crucifixion." (Library Journal)

REVIEW: *Choice* v51 no4 p657 D 2013 J. Hammer

REVIEW: *Libr J* v138 no11 p96 Je 15 2013 Muhammed Hassanali

REVIEW: *TLS* no5783 p13 Ja 31 2014 JONATHAN BENTHALL

"Christians, Muslims, and Jesus." "Mona Siddiqui is a notable practitioner of interfaith dialogue from a Muslim standpoint, and one might expect her 'Christians, Muslims, and Jesus' to make a self-assured case . . . that Muslims and Christians worship the same God. . . . Her book concentrates on the life and death of Jesus according to both Christianity and Islam--literally the crux of the matter. . . . She deserves recognition as one of the most imaginative leaders of contemporary Islamic thought."

SIDES, JOHN. The gamble. See Vavreck, L.

SIDMAN, JOYCE. What the Heart Knows; chants, charms, and blessings; [by] Joyce Sidman 80 p. 2013 Houghton Mifflin Harcourt

1. Blessing & cursing 2. Children's poetry, American 3. Friendship—Poetry 4. Shame 5. Time
ISBN 0544106164; 9780544106161
LC 2012-047836

SUMMARY: This book, by Joyce Sidman and illustrated by Pamela Zagarenski, "is a collection of poems to provide comfort, courage, and humor at difficult or daunting moments in life. It conjures forth laments, spells, invocations, chants, blessings, promises, songs, and charms. Here are pleas on how to repair a friendship, wishes to transform one's life or to slow down time, charms to face the shame of a disapproving crowd, invocations to ask for forgiveness, [and] to understand the mysteries of happiness." (Publisher's note)

REVIEW: *Booklist* v110 no6 p45 N 15 2013 Ilene Cooper

"What the Heart Knows: Chants, Charms, and Blessings." "A beautiful and meaningful book. . . . While not every celebration might seem of the highest order--for instance, 'Blessing on the Curl of a Cat'--the words make you see things differently. If pictures can be poetic, then [Pamela] Zagarenski's surely are. Her signature stylized mixed-media pictures can be intricately designed, but some are spare: a teddy bear and a crown hugging the bottom of a tall page. An evocative book that pulls readers to a special place--their hearts."

REVIEW: *Bull Cent Child Books* v67 no3 p180 N 2013 D. S.

REVIEW: *Horn Book Magazine* v90 no1 p106 Ja/F 2014 ROBIN L. SMITH

REVIEW: *Kirkus Rev* v81 no18 p163 S 15 2013

REVIEW: *Publ Wkly* p133 Children's starred review annual 2013

REVIEW: *Publ Wkly* v260 no31 p73 Ag 5 2013

SIEBURGH, C. H., 1969-.ed. Engineering the human. See Engineering the human

SIEDENTOP, LARRY. Inventing the Individual; The Origins of Western Liberalism; [by] Larry Siedentop 416 p. 2014 Belknap Press

1. Historical literature 2. Intellectual life—History 3. Liberalism—History 4. Social history 5. Western civilization
ISBN 0674417534; 9780674417533

SUMMARY: Written by Larry Siedentop, "'Inventing the Individual' tells how a new, equal social role, the individual, arose and gradually displaced the claims of family, tribe, and caste as the basis of social organization. Asking us to rethink the evolution of ideas on which Western societies and government are built, Siedentop contends that the core of what is now the West's system of beliefs emerged earlier than we commonly think." (Publisher's note)

REVIEW: *Hist Today* v64 no6 p2 Je 2014 Paul Lay

REVIEW: *New Statesman* v143 no5227 p36-8 S 12 2014 David Marquand

REVIEW: *TLS* no5793 p7-8 Ap 11 2014 JEFFREY COLLINS

"Inventing the Individual: The Origins of Western Liberalism." "[Author Larry Siedentop's] new book attempts a 'very long view' (millennially long) at the 'origins of Western liberalism.' It is an intellectual history of the old school, an effort to trace a fundamental concept—in this case liberal individualism—as far back in time as the historical data will bear. There are perils in such an approach. . . . But make no mistake, Siedentop's confidence in his own approach is merited. 'Inventing the Individual' is a thoroughly interesting and fundamentally convincing book."

SIEGEL, ERIC. Predictive analytics; the power to predict who will click, buy, lie, or die; [by] Eric Siegel 302 p. 2013 Wiley

1. Economic forecasting 2. Human behavior 3. Information science literature 4. Prediction (Psychology) 5. Social prediction 6. Social sciences—Forecasting
ISBN 1118356853; 9781118356852 (cloth)
LC 2012-047252

SUMMARY: This book, by Eric Siegel, examines "the power of data. With this technology, the computer literally learns from data how to predict the future behavior of individuals. Rather than a 'how to' for hands-on techies, the book entices lay-readers and experts alike by covering new case studies and the latest state-of-the-art techniques." (Publisher's note)

REVIEW: *Choice* v51 no1 p117-8 S 2013 J. Beidler

"Predictive Analytics: The Power to Predict Who Will Click, Buy, Lie, or Die." "The first sentence in the foreword by Thomas Davenport says it all: 'This book deals with quantitative efforts to predict human behavior.' Readers should start with the foreword and continue sequentially through the introductory information and seven somewhat self-contained chapters. [Author Eric] Siegel . . . presents a range of interesting applications in business/finance, science/health, politics, and other areas to explain how data are used to make predictions. . . . Beside a well-formed index, the book includes an excellent collection of chapter notes that consume over 60 pages."

SIEGEL, FRED. The revolt against the masses; how liber-

alism has undermined the middle class; [by] Fred Siegel xii, 225 p. 2013 Encounter Books
1. Liberalism—United States—History—20th century 2. Middle class—United States—History—20th century 3. Political science literature
ISBN 9781594036989 (hardcover: alk. paper)
LC 2013-007444

SUMMARY: In this book, "Fred Siegel insists that the essence of liberalism has always been snobbery. Liberalism's eternal enemy, in his view, is the American middle class and its traditional views of capitalism and mass democracy. President Barack Obama's 'top-and-bottom coalition,' pitting the rich and poor against the middling sorts, is no new innovation but has defined liberalism since its origins." (First Things: A Monthly Journal of Religion & Public Life)

REVIEW: *N Y Times Book Rev* p30 Ja 26 2014 Noah Millman

REVIEW: *Natl Rev* v66 no4 p39-40 Mr 10 2014 RONALD RADOSH

"The Revolt Against the Masses: How Liberalism Has Undermined the Middle Class". "A tour de force of reinterpretation. . . . [Fred] Siegel's book is nothing less than a brilliant frontal assault on our understanding of the very nature of liberalism. . . . Liberalism is not, as some conservatives would have it, a continuation of Progressivism into the mid 20th century and beyond . . . Rather, it is an ideology of elite intellectuals, who believe that the ideas they pronounce are not only inherently profound, but are in fact the roadmap to a good society. . . . It is the power of Fred Siegel's dazzling intellectual history to have shown us how we got here from the beginning of the modern era. The 1920s, it seems, are still with us."

SIERRA, JUDY. E-I-E-I-O!; how Old MacDonald got his farm with a little help from a hen; 32 p. 2014 Candlewick Press
1. Domestic animals—Juvenile Fiction 2. Farms—Juvenile literature 3. Gardening—Juvenile Fiction 4. Human-animal relationships—Fiction 5. Stories in rhyme
ISBN 0763660434 (hbk.); 9780763660437 (hbk.)
LC 2013-934306

SUMMARY: In this book, by Judy Sierra, "Little Red Hen gives old MacDonald some pointers on composting—and a legendary farm is born. . . . Once upon a time, Old MacDonald didn't have a farm. He just had a yard—a yard he didn't want to mow. But under the direction of . . . Little Red Hen, Mac learns to look at the environment in a very different way, and whole new worlds start to bloom with the help of some mud, garbage, horse poop, and worms!" (Publisher's note)

REVIEW: *Booklist* v110 no11 p69 F 1 2014 Connie Fletcher

REVIEW: *Kirkus Rev* v81 no24 p97 D 15 2013

"E-I-E-I-O: How Old Macdonald Got His Farm (with a Little Help from a Hen)". "[Matthew] Myers' inventive acrylic-on-illustration board paintings add a bushel of laugh-out-loud details, from documents attesting to Red's impressive horticultural credentials to an in-your-face depiction of horse poop. . . . Bits of [Judy] Sierra's text can be sung to the familiar tune, rendering this a good choice for spring storytimes and family read-alouds. Sierra's upbeat look at small-scale local farming, fulsomely fertilized by Myers, yields a harvest of good fun. "

REVIEW: *Publ Wkly* v260 no47 p51-2 N 18 2013

REVIEW: *SLJ* v60 no2 p79 F 2014 Martha Link Yesowitch

SIEVERT, FRED. God Revealed; Revisit Your Past to Enrich Your Future; [by] Fred Sievert 252 p. 2014 Morgan James Publishing
1. Businesspeople 2. Faith 3. Memoirs 4. New York Life Insurance Co. 5. Religious literature
ISBN 1614486999; 9781614486992

SUMMARY: "In this debut memoir, a life insurance executive retires early and focuses his life on family and faith. Executive-turned-inspirational writer [Fred] Sievert tells how he went from running the rat race to living a life of grace. . . . After marrying, climbing the corporate ladder and becoming president of New York Life Insurance, Sievert left a successful career to attend divinity school and pursue 'things that really mattered.'" (Kirkus Reviews)

REVIEW: *Kirkus Rev* v82 no3 p369 F 1 2014

"God Revealed: Revisit Your Past to Enrich Your Future". "The book starts slowly, but the stories soon gather momentum. [Fred] Sievert's prose is crisp and clear, and his tales about his family are particularly moving. Although he was clearly a power player during his business career, he never comes off as arrogant, instead modestly and honestly relating his faults and struggles. (One story, about how he worked to change tax law, delves a bit too deeply into insurance company workings, but otherwise, the book is free of business jargon.) . . . A memoir with practical and often powerful inspirational advice."

SIGAL, JANET A.ed. Violence against girls and women. See Violence against girls and women

SIGLER, SCOTT. Pandemic; a novel; [by] Scott Sigler 592 p. 2014 Crown Publishers
1. Biological warfare—Fiction 2. Death—Fiction 3. Parasites—Fiction 4. Science fiction 5. Zombies
ISBN 0307408973; 9780307408976 (hardback)
LC 2013-021173

SUMMARY: In this horror novel by Scott Sigler "to some, Doctor Margaret Montoya is a hero—a brilliant scientist who saved the human race from an alien intelligence determined to exterminate all of humanity. To others, she's a monster—a mass murderer single-handedly responsible for the worst atrocity ever to take place on American soil. . . . Part Cthulhu epic, part zombie apocalypse and part blockbuster alien-invasion tale, 'Pandemic' completes the Infected trilogy." (Publisher's note)

REVIEW: *Booklist* v110 no7 p35 D 1 2013 David Pitt

REVIEW: *Kirkus Rev* v81 no24 p47 D 15 2013

"Pandemic". "Yeah, yeah. Space zombies have taken over the world, courtesy of [Scott] Sigler . . . and his capable if derivative Infected series, which winds down with this volume. Fans of the series will know that it started as a kind of police procedural that got increasingly supernatural and sci-fi-ish, a kind of Childhood's End with oodles of mayhem. . . . Sigler excels at snappy dialogue, but the story itself is too familiar for anyone who grew up on a diet of The Omega Man and Aliens. Still, for those who can't get enough of must-eat-brains yellow monster types with extremely bad attitudes, this is just the book."

REVIEW: *Publ Wkly* v260 no48 p35 N 25 2013

SIK, AHMET. İmamin Ordusu; [by] Ahmet Sik 2011 Postaci Publishing House

1. Gülen movement 2. Gülen, Fethullah, 1941- 3. Journalism 4. Police—Turkey 5. Turkcy—Politics & government

SUMMARY: "At the time of his arrest, [author] Ahmet Sik had almost completed work on a new book that was supposed to be published in May. The book, titled 'İmamin Ordusu' ('The Imam's Army'), contains explosive material. It describes in detail how followers of the Islamic theologian Fethullah Gülen have allegedly infiltrated the Turkish police since the mid-1980s." (Publisher's note)

REVIEW: *N Y Rev Books* v61 no6 p18-22 Ap 3 2014 Christopher de Bellaigue

"The Rise of Turkey: The Twenty-First Century's First Muslim Power," "Gülen: The Ambiguous Politics of Market Islam in Turkey and the World," and "İmamin Ordusu." "'The Rise of Turkey: The Twenty-First Century's First Muslim Power' . . . might have struck one as triumphal. . . . 'Gülen: The Ambiguous Politics of Market Islam in Turkey and the World' is . . . a helpful and detailed account of a movement that is defined . . . by obfuscation. . . . In 2011, a journalist called Ahmet Şik brought out a book . . . that shows how the Gülenists took control of the police force over a period of two decades. 'The Imam's Army' is full of fascinating details."

SIKKA, MADHULIKA. A breast cancer alphabet; [by] Madhulika Sikka 224 p. 2014 Crown Publishers

1. Breast—Cancer—Miscellanea 2. Breast cancer—Patients—Attitudes 3. Breast cancer—Patients—Family relationships 4. Breast cancer patients' writings 5. Memoirs

ISBN 0385348517; 9780385348515

LC 2013-003652

SUMMARY: In this book, Madhulika Sikka "has gathered together her reflections and discoveries of being in 'Cancerland' in an A-to-Z guidebook to the entire process of cancer diagnosis, treatment and life afterward. The author examines the process of coping with the waves of feelings one will experience (anxiety, guilt, indignity and others), the need for pampering and the odds of a diagnosis—one in eight women in the United States will get breast cancer." (Kirkus Reviews)

REVIEW: *Booklist* v110 no12 p10 F 15 2014 Karen Springen

"A Breast Cancer Alphabet". "Breast-cancer patients will fall in love with [Madhulika] Sikka, executive producer of NPR's Morning Edition and a funny, chatty, and honest storyteller. . . . She succeeds in writing the kind of book she wanted: 'A little pick-me-up that I could turn to—nothing too long or scientific or self-indulgent A short book that wouldn't tax my chemo-addled brain.' . . . She comes across as a loving mom (to two daughters), wife (to a Georgetown history professor, who was diagnosed with cancer in 2000), and friend. Just what the doctor ordered."

REVIEW: *Kirkus Rev* v82 no2 p216 Ja 15 2014

"A Breast Cancer Alphabet". "A compilation of thoughts by a woman with breast cancer. . . . Whether you want to Quit, need Kindness from a friend, or long for a Vacation, [Madhulika] Sikka gives counsel. Sometimes humorous, always honest and straightforward, this little book offers the perfect combination of practical advice and personal musings to help any woman, her family and her friends handle the complicated road through Cancerland. Insightful, helpful comments on living with breast cancer."

REVIEW: *Libr J* v138 no14 p134 S 1 2013 Bette-Lee Fox

SILBERMAN, JAMES.ed. Collision 2012. See Balz, D.

SILVA, DORSIA SMITH.ed. Feminist and critical perspectives on Caribbean mothering. See Feminist and critical perspectives on Caribbean mothering

SILVER, KATHERINE.tr. The End of Love. See Torrente, M. G.

SILVERBERG, MARK.ed. New York School collaborations. See New York School collaborations

SILVERMAN, ERIC. A cultural history of Jewish dress; [by] Eric Silverman xxv, 259 p. 2013 Bloomsbury Academic, an imprint of Bloomsbury Publishing Plc

1. Clothing & dress—Symbolic aspects 2. Historical literature 3. Jewish clothing & dress 4. Jewish clothing and dress—History 5. Jewish history 6. Jews—Social life & customs 7. Judaism & culture

ISBN 0857852094 (ebook); 0857852108 (ebook); 1845205138 (hbk.); 1847882862 (pbk.); 9780857852090 (ebook); 9780857852106 (ebook); 9781845205133 (hbk.); 9781847882868 (pbk.)

LC 2012-491597

SUMMARY: Author Eric Silverman presents an "account of how Jews have been distinguished by their appearance from Ancient Israel to today. This lively work explores the rich history of Jewish dress, examining how Jews and non-Jews alike debated and legislated Jewish attire in different places, as well as outlining the big debates on dress within the Jewish community today." (Publisher's note)

REVIEW: *Choice* v51 no2 p326 O 2013 B. B. Chico

"A Cultural History of Jewish Dress." "Anthropologist [Eric] Silverman . . . provides a valuable update to the classic 'A History of Jewish Costume' . . . by British scholar Alfred Rubens. Rubens fused Jewish traditions with Western archaeological findings and developments in Central Asia, India, and China. In contrast, Silverman stresses tensions between authoritative Biblical proscriptions and community clothing practices in recent times. He emphasizes US culture with its gender implications related to political individualism, changing social roles, and legal freedoms--an important approach, since Jews have been predominant players in US clothing history. . . . His chapter on the yarmulke, a small cap whose name and origin have been contested by scholars, is noteworthy."

SILVERMAN, M. E.ed. The Bloomsbury anthology of contemporary Jewish American poetry. See The Bloomsbury anthology of contemporary Jewish American poetry

SILVERTOWN, JONATHAN. The long and the short of

it; the science of life span and aging; [by] Jonathan Silvertown 208 p. 2013 The University of Chicago Press

1. Aging 2. Life spans (Biology) 3. Longevity 4. Mortality 5. Scientific literature

ISBN 9780226757896 (cloth: alk. paper)

LC 2013-021536

SUMMARY: This book by Jonathan Silvertown examines " the scientific study of longevity and aging. Dividing his daunting subject by theme—death, life span, aging, heredity, evolution, and more—Silvertown draws on the latest scientific developments to paint a picture of what we know about how life span, senescence, and death vary within and across species." (Publisher's note)

REVIEW: *Choice* v51 no8 p1427 Ap 2014 R. A. Hoots

REVIEW: *Harper's Magazine* v327 no1962 p85-9 N 2013 Bee Wilson

REVIEW: *New Sci* v220 no2945 p54 N 30 2013 Jonathon Keats

REVIEW: *New York Times* v163 no56423 pD6 F 25 2014 ABIGAIL ZUGER

"The Long and the Short of It: The Science of Life Span and Aging". "Jonathan Silvertown has managed to distill the thousands of years of thought and research behind this and many related biologic questions into a small book so captivating and enlightening that—unusual for a volume packed with difficult scientific concepts—you will read it for pure pleasure, even though it provides remarkably few solid answers. . . . It is a glorious, mysterious cycle Mr. Silvertown presents, one that demands enthusiastic rereading."

SIM, B. A. K. Double Rainbow at Full Moon; Surviving the Collapse of Zimbabwe; [by] B. A. K. Sim 284 p. 2013 Agio Publishing House

1. Diplomats 2. Historical fiction 3. Scarcity 4. Zimbabwe—Economic conditions—1980- 5. Zimbabwe—Fiction

ISBN 1897435908; 9781897435908

SUMMARY: "In this novel set in Zimbabwe in the early 2000s, a Danish former diplomat and her Canadian husband cope with hardships as the country's economy collapses in the wake of Robert Mugabe's disastrous land reforms. . . . Clyde and Bodie must endure the subsequent hyperinflation, food shortages, power outages and the harassment of whites. . . . Bodie's story unfolds as a series of episodes." (Kirkus Reviews)

REVIEW: *Kirkus Rev* v82 no2 p320 Ja 15 2014

"Double Rainbow at Full Moon: Surviving the Collapse of Zimbabwe". "Told in the first person, [B. A. K.] Sim's novel unfolds in crisp, matter-of-fact prose. She has a keen eye for cultural differences, and she presents life in Zimbabwe in clear detail. Her character sketches bring the people suffering under [Robert] Mugabe's rule into sharp focus, the only exception being Clyde, who never seems to come fully to life in the way other characters do. But that's only a minor quibble in this otherwise excellent and informative book. A well-written, fascinating look at day-to-day life in a nation on the brink of collapse."

REVIEW: *Kirkus Rev* v82 no3 p18 F 1 2014

"Double Rainbow at Full Moon: Surviving the Collapse of Zimbabwe". "Told in the first person, [B. A. K.] Sim's novel unfolds in crisp, matter-of-fact prose. She has a keen eye for cultural differences, and she presents life in Zimbabwe in clear detail. Her character sketches bring the people suffering under [Robert] Mugabe's rule into sharp focus, the only exception being Clyde, who never seems to come fully to life in the way other characters do. But that's only a minor quibble in this otherwise excellent and informative book. A well-written, fascinating look at day-to-day life in a nation on the brink of collapse."

SIM, STUART. Fifty key postmodern thinkers; [by] Stuart Sim x, 252 p. 2013 Routledge

1. Anthropology—Philosophy 2. Literature—Philosophy 3. Philosophers 4. Philosophical literature 5. Postmodernism

ISBN 9780415525848 (pbk.: alk. paper); 9780415525855 (hardback: alk. paper)

LC 2012-049726

SUMMARY: This book on postmodern theory and theorists "frames postmodernism as a diverse intellectual tradition, skeptical about modernity's emancipatory potential, given its complicity with authoritarian sociopolitical systems." Stuart Sim "includes thinkers active across many fields: poststructuralist philosophy, of course, but also literature, the arts, architecture, anthropology, sociology, politics, religion, history, gender studies, and . . . math and science." (Choice: Current Reviews for Academic Libraries)

REVIEW: *Choice* v51 no8 p1383 Ap 2014 E. D. Rasmussen

"Fifty Key Postmodern Thinkers". "Despite inevitable omissions—some startling . . . others merely regrettable . . . it is difficult to find fault with the inclusions, especially considering the collection's scope. A joy to read, [Stuart] Sim's 2,000-word essays provide concise, cogent glosses of complex concepts. . . . Sim's cross-referenced critical commentary enables readers to perceive transdisciplinary conceptual constellations, chart major and minor theoretical trajectories, and orient postmodernism in relation to current real-world debates about surveillance, neoliberalism, fundamentalism, and the global financial crisis. Intelligently designed, this informative book will not induce information overload."

SIMBER, CHRIS. Personal Finance Simply Understood; Prudent Strategies for Setting and Achieving Financial Goals and the Reasons Behind Them; [by] Chris Simber 222 p. 2013 Author Solutions

1. Advice literature 2. Financial planning 3. Goal (Psychology) 4. Personal finance 5. Saving & investment

ISBN 1491705221; 9781491705223

SUMMARY: This book by Chris Simber presents "common-sense advice about living reasonably and planning for the future. . . . It covers everything from weekly budgets and emergency funds to IRAs and life insurance, leaving few stones unturned. Simber" highlights "what average people might overlook, such as the fees associated with mutual funds and the fact that an average month is actually 4.33 weeks long, not four." (Kirkus Reviews)

REVIEW: *Kirkus Rev* v82 no4 p181 F 15 2014

"Personal Finance Simply Understood: Prudent Strategies for Setting and Achieving Financial Goals and the Reasons Behind Them". " A straightforward debut guidebook to securing good financial health. In [Chris] Simber's highly accessible book about smart financial planning, his first lesson is to proceed with caution. . . . Unsurprisingly, then, his book is replete with common-sense advice about living reasonably and planning for the future. Its breadth is its strongest aspect. . . . Other books feature flamboyant, overly opinionated authors, but Simber is matter-of-fact without being judgmental, and there's nothing preachy about his style. Instead, he explains his subject to his readers respectfully and without hyperbole."

REVIEW: *Kirkus Rev* p4 D 15 2013 supplement seasons readings

REVIEW: *Kirkus Rev* v82 no3 p398 F 1 2014

SIMBERLOFF, DANIEL. Invasive species; what everyone needs to know; [by] Daniel Simberloff 329 p. 2013 Oxford University Press

1. Conservation biology 2. Evolution (Biology) 3. Introduced organisms 4. Plants—Evolution 5. SCIENCE—Life Sciences—Ecology 6. Scientific literature
ISBN 9780199922017 (hardback : acid-free paper); 9780199922031 (pbk. : acid-free paper)
LC 2012-046577

SUMMARY: This book on invasive species "addresses 36 interdisciplinary questions on biological invasions. Ecologist Daniel Simberloff . . . enriches his responses with more than 500 examples from a broad array of taxa, ecosystem types, and geographic regions. He notes the major progress achieved since the early 1990s." (Science)

REVIEW: *Choice* v51 no6 p1033 F 2014 B. R. Shmaefsky

REVIEW: *Science* v342 no6157 p424 O 25 2013 Montserrat Vila

"Invasive Species: What Everyone Needs to Know." "In the realm of applications, the book provides compelling information for improving conservation of native species and ecosystems threatened by invasive species. . . . [Daniel] Simberloff devotes a third of the book to aspects of effective management of invasive species. He describes not only technological improvements but also policy options, cultural perceptions, citizen- science initiatives, and controversies surrounding biological invasions. . . . Written for nonexpert but educated readers, 'Invasive Species' will reward those who demand well-documented information without requiring the scientific details."

SIMEONE, NIGEL.ed. The Leonard Bernstein letters. See The Leonard Bernstein letters

SIMKINS, ED.il. The human body. See Richards, J.

SIMMEL, GEORG, 1858-1918. The view of life; four metaphysical essays, with journal aphorisms; xxxiv, 203 p. 2010 The University of Chicago Press

1. Death 2. Individuality 3. Life 4. Metaphysics 5. Sociology—Philosophy 6. Sociology literature
ISBN 0226757838 (cloth : alk. paper); 9780226757834 (cloth : alk. paper)
LC 2010-004863

SUMMARY: "This book is the belated translation--more than ninety years after its publication in German immediately following his untimely death at the age of 60--of Georg Simmel's last 'testament': a wide-ranging intellectual meditation on 'life' in its most general aspects. . . . The essence of life is thus--as Simmel argues in a[n] . . . attempt to marry Darwinism to vitalism--to persevere in its continuity (life is always 'more-life')." (Contemporary Sociology)

REVIEW: *Contemp Sociol* v41 no3 p302-4 My 2012 Omar Lizardo

"The View of Life: Four Metaphysical Essays, With Journal Aphorisms." "This book is the belated translation--more than ninety years after its publication in German immediately following his untimely death at the age of 60--of Georg Simmel's last 'testament': a wide-ranging intellectual meditation on 'life' in its most general aspects. . . . The essence of life is thus--as Simmel argues in a groundbreaking attempt to marry Darwinism to vitalism--to persevere in its continuity (life is always 'more-life'). . . . This argument as laid out in the first chapter is intuitive and innovative. However, this is not to say that the rest of the book is easy going."

SIMMONS, DAN. The abominable; [by] Dan Simmons 672 p. 2013 Little, Brown and Co.

1. Everest, Mount (China & Nepal) 2. FICTION—Action & Adventure 3. FICTION—Historical 4. FICTION—Horror 5. FICTION—Suspense 6. FICTION—Thrillers 7. Missing persons—Fiction 8. Mountaineering 9. Racers (Persons)—Fiction
ISBN 0316198838; 9780316198837 (hardback)
LC 2013-017754

SUMMARY: This book by Dan Simmons, set in 1924, focuses on three climbers on Mount Everest. "The three climbers--joined by [a] missing boy's female cousin--find themselves being pursued through the night by someone . . . or something. This nightmare becomes a matter of life and death at 28,000 feet - but what is pursuing them? And what is the truth behind the 1924 disappearances on Everest?" (Publisher's note)

REVIEW: *Booklist* v110 no2 p38-9 S 15 2013 Daniel Kraus

"The Abominable." "Required reading for anyone inspired or terrified by high-altitude acrobatics; sudden avalanches, hidden crevasses, murderous temperatures, mountainside betrayals, and maybe--just maybe--a pack of bloodthirsty yeti. Though the first 200 pages of climbing background might have readers pining for the big climb. it is nearly always interesting, and, later, [Dan] Simmons excels at those small but full-throated moments of terror when, for example, a single bent screw might mean death for everyone. Exhausting in all the best ways; maybe read this while it's still warm out?"

REVIEW: *Kirkus Rev* v81 no19 p102 O 1 2013

REVIEW: *Libr J* v138 no14 p103 S 1 2013 Liza Oldham

REVIEW: *Publ Wkly* v260 no32 p1 Ag 12 2013 Clare Swanson

SIMON, ALONZO.ed. Teenage Mutant Ninja Turtles. See Lynch, B.

SIMON, CLEA. Grey Howl; [by] Clea Simon 208 p. 2014 Severn House Pub Ltd

1. Cats—Fiction 2. College teachers—Fiction 3. Detective & mystery stories 4. Murder investigation—Fiction 5. Theft
ISBN 0727883461; 9780727883469

SUMMARY: In this book, part of Clea Simon's Dulcie Schwartz Feline Mystery series, "when a paper that Stella

Roebuck had planned to read vanishes from her computer, professor Roebuck, blaming her former lover Barnes, demands that Dulcie's boyfriend, Chris, a computer expert, find it. Then Marco Telsa, Roebuck's newest lover, falls off a balcony at an evening party, and the police suspect murder." (Kirkus Reviews)

REVIEW: *Kirkus Rev* v82 no2 p292 Ja 15 2014

"Grey Howl". "Dulcie, who often seeks advice from the ghost of her deceased cat Mr. Grey and her new cat, Esmé, is worried about Thorpe, who appeared to be drunk at the party, and Chris, who's acting strangely. Although she's survived several murder investigations . . . her immersion in all things gothic gives her a distinctive slant on sleuthing that puts her in peril. Though Dulcie's rather scatterbrained approach to sleuthing may put readers off, her seventh provides a plethora of suspects that keeps them guessing."

REVIEW: *Publ Wkly* v261 no3 p35 Ja 20 2014

SIMON, PHILIP.ed. The Fifth Beatle. See Tiwary, V.

SIMONS, RAE. Fashion math; [by] Rae Simons 48 p. 2014 Mason Crest

1. Clothing & dress—Sales & prices 2. Clothing & dress—Sizes 3. Estimates 4. Fashion—Mathematics—Juvenile literature 5. Mathematical literature

ISBN 9781422229019 (series); 9781422229064 (hardcover)

LC 2013-015665

SUMMARY: This book by Rae Simons is part of the Math 24/7 series, which "emphasizes how math skills come into play at all times and in all places, from the kitchen to the soccer field. . . . Guided questions walk readers through the process and provide practice problems. . . . In 'Fashion Math,' a budding fashion designer uses math to convert sizes, choose enough fabric for a pattern, and determine prices to make a profit." (Booklist)

REVIEW: *Booklist* v110 no5 p56 N 1 2013 Angela Leeper

"Culinary Math," "Fashion Math," and "Game Math." "The Math 24/7 series emphasizes how math skills come into play at all times and in all places, from the kitchen to the soccer field. Each book centers on a young person who is involved in a series of scenarios that requires real-world math to solve a problem. . . . In 'Culinary Math,' a culinary student uses estimating to budget his grocery shopping, multiplication to determine a food's calorie content, and fractions to measure ingredients. In 'Fashion Math,' a budding fashion designer uses math to convert sizes, choose enough fabric for a pattern, and determine prices to make a profit. In Game Math, Mason is surprised to discover that many of his favorite games incorporate such concepts as probability, coordinates, estimation, and logic."

SIMONSON, MARY. Body knowledge; performance, intermediality, and American entertainment at the turn of the twentieth century; [by] Mary Simonson x, 278 p. 2013 Oxford University Press

1. Historical literature 2. Intermediality 3. Revues—United States—20th century—History and criticism 4. Women dancers—United States—History—20th century 5. Women entertainers—History

ISBN 9780199898015 (alk. paper); 9780199898039 (alk. paper)

LC 2013-005314

SUMMARY: It was the author's intent to demonstrate that "while female performers in the early 20th century were regularly advertised as dancers, mimics, singers, or actresses, they wove together techniques and elements drawn from a wide variety of genres and media. Onstage and onscreen, performers borrowed from musical scores and narratives, referred to contemporary shows, films, and events, and mimicked fellow performers." (Publisher's note)

REVIEW: *Choice* v51 no8 p1405-6 Ap 2014 M. D. Whitlatch

"Body Knowledge: Performance, Intermediality, and American Entertainment at the Turn of the Twentieth Century". "[Mary] Simonson . . . delves into scholarship that has been either ignored or misinterpreted by other researchers. . . . In fascinating fashion, this book also exposes how white artists pilfered black artists' talents by not acknowledging their creative contributions to productions such as the Ziegfeld Follies and the musical revue The Passing Show. But the book's real contribution is the discussion of how female performers created new trends in dance, musical reviews, opera, and the budding film industry The superior research and clear prose make this book a welcome addition to the scholarship on this era."

SIMPSON, BROOKS D.ed. The Civil War. See The Civil War

SIMPSON, EMILE. War from the ground up; twenty-first century combat as politics; [by] Emile Simpson 285 p. 2012 Emile Simpson

1. Afghan War, 2001—Political aspects 2. Counterinsurgency—Afghanistan 3. Counterinsurgency—Political aspects—Case studies 4. Insurgency—Case studies 5. Military literature 6. Politics and war 7. Strategy 8. War (Philosophy) 9. World politics—21st century

ISBN 9780231704069 (alk. paper)

LC 2012-031599

SUMMARY: This book by Emile Simpson "offers a distinctive perspective on contemporary armed conflict: . . . the author looks up from the battlefield to consider the concepts that put him there, and how they played out on the ground. Simpson argues that in the Afghan conflict, and in contemporary conflicts more generally, liberal powers and their armed forces have blurred the line between military and political activity." (Publisher's note)

REVIEW: *Choice* v51 no1 p160 S 2013 E. Chenoweth

"War From the Ground Up: Twenty-First Century Combat As Politics." "[Author Emile] Simpson argues that the typical approach to war--a means to achieving political solutions--needs rethinking. Blending academic theory and personal accounts of his experiences in Afghanistan, Simpson makes the case that contemporary counterinsurgency is different from Carl von Clausewitz's conception of war in several fundamental ways. . . . The book's combination of theory and practice is refreshing, although the writing is a quite dense in places. Additionally, the author could have done more to identify more clearly how precisely counterinsurgency strategy could change to better reflect the conditions he describes."

REVIEW: *Parameters: U.S. Army War College* v43 no2 p132-3 Summ 2013 Richard M. Swain

REVIEW: *TLS* no5740 p9 Ap 5 2013 MICHAEL HOW-

ARD

SIMPSON, MONA. Casebook; a novel; [by] Mona Simpson 336 p. 2014 Alfred A. Knopf

1. Boys—Fiction 2. Detective & mystery stories 3. Divorce—Fiction 4. Eavesdropping—Fiction 5. Family secrets—Fiction

ISBN 0385351410; 9780345807281 (trade paperback); 9780385351416 (hardback)

LC 2014-006222

SUMMARY: This novel, by Mona Simpson, is "about a young boy's quest to uncover the mysteries of his unraveling family. . . . Miles Adler-Hart starts eavesdropping to find out what his mother is planning for his life. When he learns instead that his parents are separating, his investigation deepens, and he enlists his best friend, Hector, to help. . . . Their amateur detective work starts innocently but quickly takes them to the far reaches of adult privacy." (Publisher's note)

REVIEW: *Booklist* v110 no13 p18 Mr 1 2014 Donna Seaman

REVIEW: *Commentary* v137 no5 p85-6 My 2014 FERNANDA MOORE

REVIEW: *Kirkus Rev* v82 no5 p251 Mr 1 2014

REVIEW: *Libr J* v139 no5 p115 Mr 15 2014 Sally Bissell

REVIEW: *Libr J* v138 no18 p69 N 1 2013 Barbara Hoffert

REVIEW: *N Y Times Book Rev* p42 Je 1 2014 JOHN WILLIAMS

REVIEW: *New York Times* v163 no56472 pC1-6 Ap 15 2014 MICHIKO KAKUTANI

REVIEW: *New Yorker* v90 no12 p75-1 My 12 2014

"Casebook." "On the cusp of adolescence, the narrator of this novel, Miles Adler-Hart, sees himself as a sleuth, but his attempts at surveillance are hapless. When he tries to rig a walkie-talkie under his parents' bed, he overhears a marriage breaking down. Much of the rest of the novel charts his concerns about his mother's new boyfriend, whose visits make him feel 'as if wolves were biting at our walls.' . . . [Author Mona] Simpson manipulates the tropes of suspense fiction astutely, and the touches of noir are delicate. Miles's snooping is considerate and his voice frank, more often than not in pursuit of 'the lit, apparent side' of life."

REVIEW: *Publ Wkly* v261 no6 p67 F 10 2014

SIMSION, GRAEME. The Rosie project; a novel; [by] Graeme Simsion 304 p. 2013 Simon & Schuster

1. Asperger's syndrome 2. College teachers—Australia—Fiction 3. Genetics—Research—Fiction 4. Love stories 5. Marriage—Fiction

ISBN 1476729085; 9781476729084 (hardcover); 9781476729091 (trade pbk.)

LC 2013-000364

SUMMARY: This book focuses on genetics professor Don Tillman's search for a wife. His "devised solution is the Wife Project: dating only those who 'match' his idiosyncratic standards as determined by an exacting questionnaire. His plans take a backseat when he meets Rosie, a bartender who wants him to help her determine her birth father's identity. His rigidity and myopic worldview prevents him from seeing her as a possible love interest, but he nonetheless agrees to help." (Publishers Weekly)

REVIEW: *Booklist* v110 no1 p40 S 1 2013 Bridget Thoreson

"The Rosie Project." "Diagnosis is not the issue here, as the reader is rooting for Don as he searches for ways to fit in. . . . The protagonist is passingly similar to that of [Mark] Haddon's 'The Curious Incident of the Dog in the Night-Time' (2003), but [Graeme] Simsion's first novel is not as dark, focusing instead on the humor and significance of what makes us human. . . . Funny, touching, and hard to put down, 'The Rosie Project' is certain to entertain even as readers delve into deep themes. For a book about a logic-based quest for love, it has a lot of heart."

REVIEW: *Kirkus Rev* v81 no2 p28 Je 1 2013

REVIEW: *Kirkus Rev* p35 N 15 2013 Best Books

REVIEW: *Kirkus Rev* p16 2013 Guide 20to BookExpo America Chelsea Langford

REVIEW: *Kirkus Rev* p17 2013 Guide 20to BookExpo America

REVIEW: *Libr J* v138 no9 p54 My 15 2013 Barbara Hoffert

REVIEW: *Libr J* v138 no14 p104 S 1 2013 Robin Nesbitt

REVIEW: *N Y Times Book Rev* p22 O 20 2013 GABRIEL ROTH

REVIEW: *Publ Wkly* v260 no26 p60-1 Jl 1 2013

SINCLAIR, CLIVE, 1940-. Death & Texas; [by] Clive Sinclair 240 p. 2014 Halban Publishers

1. Families—Fiction 2. Loss (Psychology)—Fiction 3. Love stories 4. Short stories—Collections 5. Texas—Fiction

ISBN 1905559631; 9781905559633

SUMMARY: In the short stories found in this collection by Clive Sinclair, "Their subjects are loss, the fear of loss, and love, most especially that between husbands and wives, fathers and sons. Their cast includes the quick and the dead, the real and the imagined: Davy Crockett, Kinky Friedman, Captain Haddock, Princess Diana, and Shylock." (Publisher's note)

REVIEW: *TLS* no5795 p22 Ap 25 2014 MICHAEL LAPOINTE

"Death & Texas." "In these cosmopolitan stories, which roam freely from Israel to Machu Picchu, Venice to New Orleans, [author] Clive Sinclair takes up his vigorous themes—art, religion, sex and sex—with a new, elegiac temper, an awareness of time's passage and the toll it takes. . . . Throughout 'Death & Texas,' Sinclair displays the range of his interests. . . .shrewd essayist, Sinclair plugs . . . narratives into their broader historical and cultural contexts, but his love of the tale never lets the drama falter, and both of these carefully constructed, intellectually playful pieces have the brisk momentum of detective fiction. . . . 'Death & Texas' shows Clive Sinclair, unlike so many of his hapless, hobbled characters, still testing the depth of his power."

SINCLAIR, IAIN. American smoke; journeys to the end of the light; [by] Iain Sinclair 320 p. 2014 Faber & Faber

1. Artists—United States—Biography 2. BIOGRAPHY & AUTOBIOGRAPHY—Artists, Architects, Photographers 3. BIOGRAPHY & AUTOBIOGRAPHY—Literary 4. Beat generation 5. Intellectuals—United States—Biography 6. Memoirs 7. TRAVEL—Europe—Great Britain

ISBN 9780865478671 (hardback)
LC 2013-041335

SUMMARY: In this book, "for the first time, the enigma that is Iain Sinclair lands on American shores for his long-awaited engagement with the memory-filled landscapes of the American Beats and their fellow travelers. A book filled with bad journeys and fated decisions, 'American Smoke' is an epic walk in the footsteps of Malcolm Lowry, Charles Olson, Jack Kerouac, William Burroughs, Gary Snyder and others, . . . enlivened by false memories, broken reports, and strange adventures." (Publisher's note)

REVIEW: *Kirkus Rev* v82 no4 p65 F 15 2014

REVIEW: *Libr J* v139 no4 p92 Mr 1 2014 William Gargan

REVIEW: *Publ Wkly* v261 no2 p60 Ja 13 2014

REVIEW: *TLS* no5780 p23 Ja 10 2014 JEROME BOYD MAUNSELL

"American Smoke: Journeys to the End of the Light." "Iain Sinclair is an inimitable, insatiable stylist. The stop-start rhythms of his prose--its grit and drive and lurch; the glut of referentiality and proper nouns; the street transcriptions; the itchy reiteration of obsessions; the endlessly unravelling free association--are immediately identifiable, as if trademarked. There is a tremendous hunger at the root of his work, for all its black comedy and feints of mild self-parody. The writing is dense with facts and links, opening out in several directions at once in every paragraph, as the raddled scribe follows trails, hints, ghosts, echoes, murmurs, myths--which lead to further trails, hints, echoes, myths."

SINGER, MARILYN, 1948-. Rutherford B., who was he?; poems about our presidents; 56 p. 2013 Disney-Hyperion Books

1. Children's poetry, American 2. Historical poetry, American 3. Poems—Collections 4. Political poetry 5. Presidents—United States—Biography—Juvenile poetry
ISBN 1423171004; 9781423171003
LC 2013-010690

SUMMARY: In this collection of children's poetry, author Marilyn Singer and illustrator John Hendrix bring "the presidents of the United States to life--from [George] Washington to [Barack] Obama and contextualizes them in their time. Backmatter enriches the experience with short biographies, quotes by each president, and more." (Publisher's note)

REVIEW: *Booklist* p21 S 1 2013 Book Links Supplement

REVIEW: *Booklist* v110 no7 p45 D 1 2013 Carolyn Phelan

REVIEW: *Bull Cent Child Books* v67 no4 p239-40 D 2013 D. S.

REVIEW: *Horn Book Magazine* v90 no1 p106-7 Ja/F 2014 BETTY CARTER

"Rutherford B., Who Was He? Poems About Our Presidents." "Unlike Susan Katz's 'The President's Stuck in the Bathtub' . . . which focused on quirky traits, this volume touches on more sophisticated subjects such as political ideology, foreign policy, and domestic programs. . . . The richly colored art overwhelms the text; for example, William Henry Harrison's poem is lost in the swirling storm that surrounds him as he delivers his inaugural address (but then again, that weather also overpowered the man, causing the pneumonia that killed him). Brief biographical notes of each president give pertinent, but abbreviated, background information; sources are included."

REVIEW: *Kirkus Rev* v81 no19 p233 O 1 2013

REVIEW: *SLJ* v60 no1 p122 Ja 2014 Marilyn Taniguchi

SINGER, MARILYN, 1948-. The superheroes' employment agency; 39 p. 2012 Clarion Books

1. Children's poetry 2. Employment agencies 3. Paranormal fiction 4. Picture books for children 5. Superheroes—Juvenile poetry
ISBN 0547435592 (hardcover); 9780547435596 (hardcover)
LC 2011-025722

SUMMARY: Author Marilyn Singer's book features "underemployed B-list superheroes. . . . Got rats and mice? Call on the . . . Verminator! Supernatural foes will flee from the garlic foam wielded by Muffy the Vampire Sprayer. . . . Along with having distinct individual powers and abilities, several of these eager job seekers combine to offer enhanced services. Armored Sir Knightly and The Masked Man, both aging veterans, can team up to entertain at children's parties, for instance." (Kirkus Reviews)

REVIEW: *Booklist* v108 no21 p50 Jl 1 2012 Daniel Kraus

"The Superheroes Employment Agency." "Need a superhero? Batman out of your budget? Then head on down to the Superheroes Employment Agency, where you can rent the services of such B-listers as Blunder Woman, the Verminator, and Stuporman. [Marilyn] Singer introduces each wannabe via a comic poem. . . . Singer relates some stories with comic strips or fake advertisements and even finds ways to have two characters meet for transactions of business (or romance). . . . Meanwhile, [Noah Z.] Jones' exaggerated cartoon interpretations of these bumblers keeps things super-duper silly."

REVIEW: *SLJ* v58 no6 p106 Je 2012 Rita Meade

SINGER, MARILYN, 1948-. Tallulah's Nutcracker; 48 p. 2013 Clarion Books

1. Ballet dancing—Fiction 2. Christmas—Fiction 3. Picture books for children 4. Stage fright
ISBN 054784557X; 9780547845579 (hardcover)
LC 2012-034744

SUMMARY: In this book by Marilyn Singer, "it's Christmastime, and Tallulah finally gets what she's been wishing for—a part in a real ballet, a professional production of The Nutcracker. She's only a mouse, but she works as hard as if she had been cast as the Sugar Plum Fairy. On the night of the show, everything is perfect. But then disaster strikes! Does Tallulah have what it takes to become a real ballerina?" (Publisher's note)

REVIEW: *Horn Book Magazine* v89 no6 p69 N/D 2013 KATIE BIRCHER

"Tallulah's Nutcracker". "Dancing in the Nutcracker is not what Tallulah expected: rehearsals are tiring (and a bit boring); she misses out on pre-Christmas activities; and her mouse costume is not at all 'elegant.' Worst of all, on the big night, a stage fright-stricken Tallulah inadvertently causes a pile-up of mice and toy soldiers. Backstage, her teacher, the Sugar Plum Fairy, and Clara regale her with their own performance mistakes. . . . Gentle text and warm watercolor and gouache (mixed with egg yolk) illustrations together offer an un-sugarcoated, but humorous, portrayal of life in the theater for young dancers—and an encouraging example for any reader."

SINGH, BHARAT P.ed. Biofuel crops. See Biofuel crops

SINGH, KELVIN. British-controlled Trinidad and Venezuela; a history of economic interests and subversion, 1830-1962; [by] Kelvin Singh xiii, 294 p. 2010 University of the West Indies Press

1. Aussenpolitik 2. Historical literature 3. Imperialism—History 4. Subversive activities 5. Trinidad—History 6. Venezuela—Foreign economic relations 7. Venezuela—History
ISBN 976640237X; 9789766402372
LC 2011-523263

SUMMARY: Written by Kelvin Singh, this book "assesses the diplomatic, commercial and political consequences of the conflicting interests of the British imperial government and colonial Trinidad on Venezuela. Imperial interests predominated and the British turned a blind eye to the use of Trinidad by opponents of Venezuelan regimes as a base for the overthrow of Venezuelan governments. The island colony played an important role in the politics of destabilization in Venezuela." (Publisher's note)

REVIEW: *Am Hist Rev* v118 no4 p1234-5 O 2013 Victor Bulmer-Thomas

"British Controlled Trinidad and Venezuela: A History of Economic Interests and Subversion, 1830-1962." "Kelvin Singh's excellent book has been meticulously researched and very well written. Although dedicated to a relatively narrow topic, it sheds light on broader issues including informal empire, center-periphery relationships, and Anglo-American rivalry before World War I. It also draws out the strategic nature of oil, which is found in abundance in Trinidad and Venezuela. It will be read with pleasure not only by those interested in Latin America and the Caribbean, but also by others with more thematic interests."

SINGH, LATA. Popular translations of nationalism; Bihar, 1920-1922; [by] Lata Singh xiii, 277 p. 2012 Primus Books

1. Bihar (India)—History 2. Historical literature 3. India—History—Non-cooperation movement, 1920-1922 4. Nationalism—India 5. Nationalism—India—Bihar—History 6. Social movements—India—History
ISBN 9789380607139
LC 2012-354190

SUMMARY: Written by Lata Singh, "This study on Bihar highlights the fact that nationalism was not a monolithic movement, but was constituted of diverse facets and streams which unleashed a variety of protests. Once people's desires and aspirations were linked to nationalism, the movement developed its own rhythm and dynamics, throwing up its own agenda." (Publisher's note)

REVIEW: *Am Hist Rev* v118 no4 p1167-8 O 2013 John McLeod

"Popular Translations of Nationalism: Bihar, 1920-1922." "In Popular Translations of Nationalism, Lata Singh studies mass participation in Non-Cooperation in the province of Bihar, where Gandhi rose to prominence in an agrarian campaign in 1917. Her book, which is based largely on the records of the police and civil authorities, includes three substantive chapters. . . . This monograph has one overriding weakness: poor editing. . . . Much of the book consists of more or less undigested primary sources. . . . Such detail is unnecessary and distracting. All this mars a fine study that adds considerably to our understanding of a turning point in Indian history."

SINGLETON, LINDA JOY. Snow dog, sand dog; 32 p. 2014 Albert Whitman & Company

1. Allergy—Juvenile literature 2. Children's stories 3. Dogs—Fiction 4. Imagination 5. Seasons—Fiction
ISBN 0807575364; 9780807575369
LC 2013-029482

SUMMARY: This children's book by Linda Joy Singleton, illustrated by Jess Golden, asks readers: "What would you do if you were allergic but really wanted a dog? . . . A young girl uses her crafty nature and imagination to create four-legged friends each season as the weather changes. She builds a dog out of snow in winter, sand in summer, leaves in fall, and flowers in spring!" (Publisher's note)

REVIEW: *Booklist* v110 no13 p78 Mr 1 2014 Carolyn Phelan

REVIEW: *Kirkus Rev* v82 no3 p110 F 1 2014

"Snow Dog, Sand Dog". "The boundaries between imagination and reality are creatively blurred in the pictures, as the realistic dogs each play with Ally, following her faithfully and engaging in seasonal activities. Charming illustrations in a loose, playful style bring the dogs to life, whether they are real or not. An open-ended conclusion shows Ally drawing all her dogs at play and Snow Dog returning with the first snow of the winter, even as the text indicates the other dogs also return. A final, unnecessary page gives directions for making a dog sculpture out of common household items. Ally is a clever and creative character that kids with similar afflictions will relate to."

REVIEW: *Publ Wkly* v260 no52 p49 D 23 2013

REVIEW: *SLJ* v60 no3 p126 Mr 2014 Julie Roach

SIPIORA, PHILLIP.ed. Mind of an outlaw. See Mailer, N.

SISMAN, ADAM.ed. One hundred letters from Hugh Trevor-Roper. See One hundred letters from Hugh Trevor-Roper

SISSON, STEPHANIE ROTH.il. Princess Posey and the Christmas magic. See Greene, S.

SISSUNG, INGRID. The hiccup; 32 p. 2014 Skyhorse Publishing, Inc.

1. Bears—Fiction 2. Children's stories 3. Forest animals—Fiction 4. Friendship—Juvenile fiction 5. Hiccups—Fiction
ISBN 9781626363878 (hardcover : alk. paper)
LC 2013-033588

SUMMARY: In this children's book, written and illustrated by Ingrid Sissung, "The hiccups are annoying. They come on quickly and refuse to go away. Just ask Elliot. There he was, having a nice picnic with his cousin Lutz, when he accidentally ate too fast. Now, he's stuck hiccupping around the forest, and Elliot's unbearable situation couldn't be any funnier to Lutz. . . . But will Lutz learn his lesson about not making fun of his friend's hiccups?" (Publisher's note)

REVIEW: *N Y Times Book Rev* p16 Ja 12 2014 SARAH HARRISON SMITH

"Cub's Big World," "The Hiccup," and "Please Bring Balloons." "Pleasingly realistic yet reassuringly sweet, 'Cub's Big World' follows a young polar bear on her first trip out of the cozy snow cave the shares with her mother. . . . '[Author and illustrator Ingrid] Sissung's freewheeling story ['The Hiccup'] delivers justice in the end for the teaser and the teased. . . . [Author and illustrator Lindsay] Ward, a cut-paper artist, gives her book great visual appeal with snippets of colorful origami paper, calendars and maps."

REVIEW: *SLJ* v60 no3 p126 Mr 2014 Tanya Boudreau

SISSUNG, INGRID.il. The hiccup. See Sissung, I.

SITTON, ROBERT. Lady in the dark; Iris Barry and the art of film; [by] Robert Sitton 496 p. 2014 Columbia University Press

1. Archivists—United States—Biography 2. Biography (Literary form) 3. Motion picture film—Preservation—United States—History 4. Motion picture film collections—United States—Archival resources 5. film critics—England—Biography

ISBN 9780231165785 (cloth: alk. paper)

LC 2013-044123

SUMMARY: This book presents a biography of film critic Irish Barry, who founded the Museum of Modern Art's "film department and became its first curator, assuring film's critical legitimacy. She convinced powerful Hollywood figures to submit their work for exhibition, creating a new respect for film and prompting the founding of the International Federation of Film Archives." (Publisher's note)

REVIEW: *Film Q* v67 no4 p85-7 Summ 2014 JAN-CHRISTOPHER HORAK

REVIEW: *Kirkus Rev* v82 no2 p86 Ja 15 2014

"Lady in the Dark: Iris Barry and the Art of Film". "[Robert] Sitton exhaustively traces Barry's career from aspiring poet to playwright, biographer and film critic. . . . Life at MOMA, the involvement in wartime propaganda, the gossipy tale of [Alfred] Barr's replacement by [John] Abbott and the easing out of Iris from her life's work all help reduce the ennui of Sitton's name-dropping, long quotes and abundance of information in general. Film students will enjoy this book; however, to learn criticism, they should read Barry's 'Let's Go to the Pictures' (1926)."

REVIEW: *Libr J* v139 no3 p112 F 15 2014 Peter Thornell

REVIEW: *Sight Sound* v24 no7 p107 Jl 2014 Henry K. Miller

SJÖBERG, FREDRIK. The Fly Trap; A Book About Summer, Islands and the Freedom of Limits; [by] Fredrik Sjöberg 288 p. 2014 Particular Books

1. Hoverflies 2. Insect traps 3. Memoirs 4. Naturalists 5. Swedish literature—Translations

ISBN 184614776X; 9781846147760

SUMMARY: "'The Fly Trap' begins with Fredrik Sjöberg's own experiences collecting hoverflies on a remote island in Sweden. His curiosity about the inventor of his fly trap leads him to rediscover the extraordinary life of a near-forgotten Naturalist, René Malaise. The tale that Sjöberg unravels . . . leads him to reflect on life itself, on the natural world and how we learn to interpret it, on slowness, freedom and the bliss of limitation." (Publisher's note)

REVIEW: *New Sci* v222 no2971 p47 My 31 2014 Bob Holmes

"The Fly Trap." "The great passion of [author Fredrik Sjöberg's] life—and the ostensible subject of 'The Fly Trap'—is collecting and studying hoverflies. . . . The book unfolds like a leisurely after-dinner conversation, as Sjöberg meanders through the pleasure of collecting hoverflies on a summer's day, the eccentricities of entomologists and the surprising intimacy of conversations between strangers on a ferry. . . . But the real message of the book, published in Swedish a decade ago and now translated into English, is the quiet pleasure to be found in reading the fine print of knowledge."

SKAFF, JONATHAN KARAM. Sui-Tang China and its Turko-Mongol neighbors; culture, power and connections, 580-800; [by] Jonathan Karam Skaff xix, 400 p. 2012 Oxford University Press

1. Balance of power—History—To 1500 2. Borderlands—Asia, Central—History—To 1500 3. Borderlands—China—History—To 1500 4. China—Foreign relations—History 5. China—History—Tang dynasty, 618-907 6. Eurasia—History 7. Historical literature 8. Mongols—Asia, Central—History—To 1500 9. Mongols—History 10. Nomads—Asia, Central—History—To 1500 11. Turkic peoples—Asia, Central—History—To 1500 12. Turks—History

ISBN 0199734135 (hbk. : acid-free paper); 9780199734139 (hbk. : acid-free paper)

LC 2011-041069

SUMMARY: This book "challenges readers to reconsider China's relations with the rest of Eurasia. Investigating interstate competition and cooperation between the successive Sui and Tang dynasties and Turkic states of Mongolia from 580 to 800, [author] Jonathan Skaff upends the notion that inhabitants of China and Mongolia were irreconcilably different and hostile to each other." (Publisher's note)

REVIEW: *Am Hist Rev* v118 no4 p1157-8 O 2013 Wang Zhenping

"Sui-Tang China and Its Turko-Mongol Neighbors: Culture, Power, and Connections, 580-800." "This work, with its copious maps, figures, and tables, makes a significant contribution to a growing English-language literature on Tang China's relations with its Asian neighbors. Jonathan Karam Skaff's core argument is that Tang China should be considered as part of a broader 'Eastern Eurasian' region that included Korea in the east and Byzantium and Iran in the West. . . . Methodologically innovative and empirically dense, this book enriches our understanding of the ways Eastern Eurasian rulers formed power relationships at home and abroad."

REVIEW: *Choice* v50 no9 p1690 My 2013 V. C. Xiong

SKIADAS, DIMITRIOS V. Stateness and sovereign debt. See Lavdas, K. A.

SKIDELSKY, EDWARD. How much is enough? See Skidelsky, R. J. A.

SKIDELSKY, ROBERT JACOB ALEXANDER, 1939-. How much is enough?; money and the good life; [by] Robert Jacob Alexander Skidelsky p. cm. 2012 Other Press

1. Avarice 2. Economics—Sociological aspects 3. Phil-

osophical literature 4. Self-realization 5. Wealth
ISBN 9781590515075 (hbk.); 9781590515082 (ebook)
LC 2012-008052

SUMMARY: In this book, authors Robert and Edward Skidelsky "argue that modern Western societies have lost the concept of the good life, which has shaped the values of every previous culture. Central to the idea of the good life is the ability to distinguish between needs and wants. While the satisfaction of needs is an attainable and worthwhile goal, religious and ethical traditions recognize that human wants are insatiable." (Commonweal)

REVIEW: *Choice* v50 no5 p931-2 Ja 2013 R. B. Emmett

REVIEW: *Commonweal* v140 no19 p27-8 D 6 2013 Tina Beattie

"How Much Is Enough? Money and the Good Life," "The Spinning Heart," and "Thirst". "[Robert Skidelsky] and Edward Skidelsky] offer a persuasive and lucid account of the 'good life' as one in which sufficiency, satisfaction, and leisure become worthy aims to pursue in common with others whose values we share (they think religion might be indispensable for this), while greed, envy, and avarice are once more recognized as the vices they are. This panoramic vision inevitably glosses the ways in which individual lives are affected by changing economic values. 'The Spinning Heart,' . . . a novel by Irish writer Donal Ryan, movingly explores the consequences of the global economic crisis in a small Irish community. . . . The best poems are a passionate and vivid celebration of life, with symbolic roots deep in the miracle of nature."

REVIEW: *Economist* v404 no8794 p70 Jl 21 2012

REVIEW: *New Statesman* v141 no5116 p70-1 Jl 30 2012 Will Hutton

REVIEW: *New Yorker* v88 no24 p93 Ag 13 2012

SKIDMORE, CHRIS. Bosworth; [by] Chris Skidmore 464 p. 2013 Weidenfeld & Nicolson

1. Bosworth Field, Battle of, England, 1485 2. Great Britain—History—Wars of the Roses, 1455-1485 3. Henry VII, King of England, 1457-1509 4. Historical literature 5. Tudor, House of
ISBN 0297863762; 9780297863762

SUMMARY: This book by Chris Skidmore focuseson the Battle of Bosworth and the history of the Tudor dynasty. "To unpick the story of Bosworth, Skidmore delves far into the histories of both the Wars of the Roses and the Tudor family. His book begins nearly 60 years before Henry VII's coronation: in the late 1420s, when the widowed Queen of England, Katherine de Valois, secretly took up with the Welsh squire Owain ap Maredudd ap Tudur (aka Owen Tudor)." (telegraph.co.uk)

REVIEW: *TLS* no5759 p36 Ag 16 2013 PAUL CAVILL

"Bosworth: The Dawn of the Tudors." "The first half has so much to include that, while he skilfully recounts the Wars of the Roses, [Chris] Skidmore can add little that is distinctive. . . . . Contradictions tend not to be resolved. . . . Much of the excitement of Skidmore's tale lies, of course, in Henry Tudor's triumph over adversity against long odds; but a balanced account of Yorkist England is probably sacrificed in the telling. Skidmore's book becomes more gripping as he turns to the Bosworth campaign. The author now has the space to interpret and distinguish between sources. . . . The book also benefits from recent archaeological work. . . . 'Bosworth' is a well-executed and well-informed book."

SKINNER, RICHARD. The Mirror; [by] Richard Skinner 336 p. 2014 Faber & Faber Fiction

1. Composers—Fiction 2. Future life—Fiction 3. Historical fiction 4. Nuns—Fiction 5. Satie, Erik, 1866-1925
ISBN 0571305075; 9780571305070

SUMMARY: In this novel by Richard Skinner, "Erik Satie--composer, dandy, eccentric--is dead. . . . In the convent of Sant' Alvise, Oliva is about to take the veil and become a bride of Christ. . . . Told with playful elegance, these are two utterly original tales of art and devotion, of religious and creative fervour. They contemplate the eternal in different ways--one examining a life only just beginning, tentatively; the other a life lived without compromise as it reaches its close." (Publisher's note)

REVIEW: *TLS* no5783 p20 Ja 31 2014 STUART KELLY

"The Mirror." "This diptych of novellas . . . is a rather curious proposition. . . . The first half, 'The Mirror,' is about a novice, Oliva, in early sixteenth-century Venice who is due to be painted by Signor Avilo before she takes the veil; the second, 'The Velvet Gentleman' imagines the composer Erik Satie in limbo. . . On the level of the word, the sentence, the paragraph, the narrative arc and the intellectual architecture, these seemed hobbled by convention and unwilling to dare. They are written as if the avant-garde never happened, let along is still happening. 'The Mirror,' in a melancholy way, is not writing: it's Creative Writing."

SKLANSKY, AMY E. You are my little pumpkin pie; 16 p. 2013 Little, Brown and Co.

1. Families—Juvenile literature 2. Love 3. Parent & child—Juvenile literature 4. Picture books for children 5. Pies
ISBN 9780316207140
LC 2012-937347

SUMMARY: In this children's picture book by Amy E. Slansky, "smitten adults gush over the attributes of their little ones by comparing them to the goodness of sweet pumpkin pie. . . . The illustrations depict different families on each page spread, and the multiethnic cast of characters includes both women and men cuddling with their little ones." (Kirkus Reviews)

REVIEW: *Kirkus Rev* v82 no1 p14 Ja 1 2014

"You Are My Little Pumpkin Pie". "The simple rhyming text is jovial, celebratory and just a little silly. . . . The interactions between adult and baby that the text invites will make sharing this an enjoyable experience and help keep baby's attention. In a nice touch, the illustrations depict different families on each page spread, and the multiethnic cast of characters includes both women and men cuddling with their little ones. The warm tones, pumpkin-pie theme, and orange and gold-leafed trees featured in the illustrations make this a natural choice for fall reading. A shiny corrugated pie plate and glittery whipped cream add a little zip to the cover, inviting readers to dig in. Share this sweet treat with baby for some serious bonding time."

REVIEW: *Kirkus Rev* v81 no15 p379 Ag 1 2013

REVIEW: *Publ Wkly* v260 no24 p62 Je 17 2013

SKORO, MARTIN.ed. Baba Yaga. See Baba Yaga

SKOULDING, ZOË.ed. Placing poetry. See Placing poetry

SKOVRON, JON. Man made Boy; [by] Jon Skovron 368 p. 2013 Viking

1. Frankenstein's monster (Fictitious character) 2. Human beings—Fiction 3. Monsters—Fiction 4. Runaways—Fiction 5. Science fiction
ISBN 0670786209; 9780670786206 (hardcover)
LC 2012-043217

SUMMARY: This novel by Jon Skovron describes how "When you're the son of Frankenstein's monster and the Bride, it's tough to go out in public, unless you want to draw the attention of a torch-wielding mob. And since Boy and his family live in a secret enclave of monsters hidden under Times Square, it's important they maintain a low profile. . . . When conflict erupts at home, Boy runs away and embarks on a cross-country road trip. . . ." (Publisher's note)

REVIEW: *Booklist* v110 no3 p91 O 1 2013 Sarah Hunter

REVIEW: *Bull Cent Child Books* v67 no3 p181 N 2013 K. Q. G.

"Man Made Boy." "Suffused with warmth and humor, this homage pokes fun more at the pop-culture tropes that have sprung up around Frankenstein than the actual classic work, with the digital version of a creation gone awry a particularly brilliant and contemporary twist. The plot is pieced together in episodic bits as Boy encounters different creatures at each pit stop, and both the various settings and the individual characters provide depth and complexity; the awe and wonder of the Southwestern desert, for example, is on full display here, while the painful loneliness of the Chupacabra, the last of its kind, is equally powerful."

REVIEW: *Kirkus Rev* v81 no16 p145 Ag 15 2013

REVIEW: *Publ Wkly* v260 no38 p81 S 23 2013

REVIEW: *Publ Wkly* v260 no48 p51 N 25 2013

REVIEW: *SLJ* v60 no1 p58 Ja 2014 Chani Craig

SKRABEC, QUENTIN R. The green vision of Henry Ford and George Washington Carver; two collaborators in the cause of clean industry; [by] Quentin R. Skrabec 211 p. 2013 McFarland & Company, Inc., Publishers

1. Business literature 2. Chemurgy—History—20th century 3. Industries—Environmental aspects—United States—History—20th century 4. Manufacturing industries—Environmental aspects—United States—History—20th century
ISBN 9780786469826 (softcover : alk. paper)
LC 2013-005775

SUMMARY: "Henry Ford and George Washington Carver had a unique friendship and a shared vision." Written by Quentin R. Skrabec, Jr., "This book details their paths to 'green' manufacturing and the start of the chemurgic movement in America. It covers a number of little known projects such as their efforts to use ethanol as a national fuel, the use of soybeans for plastic production, and the use of waterpower for factories." (Publisher's note)

REVIEW: *Choice* v51 no2 p287-8 O 2013 S. A. Curtis

"The Green Vision of Henry Ford and George Washington Carver: Two Collaborators in the Cause of Clean Industry." "[Author Quentin R.] Skrabec[, Jr.] . . . frames the development of the 'chemurgical' movement through the parallel lives of George Washington Carver and Henry Ford, who met in 1937 toward the end of their long careers. 'Chemurgy' refers to the use of organic products, chiefly of agricultural origin, in industrial products and processes. . . . This biography presents a primarily business, economics, and policy perspective and is one of the works the author wrote to fulfill his goal of 'building a literary pantheon of American capitalists and businesspersons.'"

SKUY, DAVID, 1963-. Striker; [by] David Skuy 216 p. 2014 Orca Book Pub

1. Bullying—Juvenile fiction 2. Cancer patients—Family relationships 3. Cancer patients—Fiction 4. Soccer stories 5. Soccer teams
ISBN 1459405129; 9781459405127

SUMMARY: In this book, by David Skuy, "thirteen-year-old soccer player and cancer survivor Cody is determined to get back on the field. Having completed treatment, Cody longs to regain his equilibrium, both at home and on the soccer field. While an opportunity to try out for the Lions—a team just moving up to the division he played in before he got sick—seems ideal, Cody encounters several obstacles." (Kirkus Reviews)

REVIEW: *Kirkus Rev* v82 no3 p200 F 1 2014

"Striker". "[David] Skuy subtly explores the emotional aspects of Cody's recovery, portraying family dynamics in the wake of a child's critical illness and addressing Cody's struggles to establish new friendships after his illness. He also presents the issue of domineering sports parents, whose enthusiasm for their child's success sometimes eclipses good sportsmanship. . . . Invigorating, detailed game descriptions capture the kinetic energy of soccer while illuminating the skills and strategies essential to the sport. Skuy adeptly combines exhilarating sports with a thoughtfully engrossing storyline that will inspire readers."

SKYE, CHRISTINA. The accidental bride; [by] Christina Skye 376 p. 2012 Harlequin

1. Deception—Fiction 2. Love stories 3. Man-woman relationships—Fiction 4. Summer resorts—Fiction 5. Women cooks—Fiction
ISBN 0373776594; 9780373776597

SUMMARY: In this book by Christina Skye, "when her friends order her to take a vacation, successful chef Jilly O'Hara is less than enthused. She may be overworked, but a trip to the mountains is not her idea of fun. Especially when she's roped into an outrageous scheme to pose as a happy bride--all to fulfill the kindly resort owner's dreams of once again hosting a lavish wedding. But the ruggedly handsome make-believe groom may just make it tolerable." (Publisher's note)

REVIEW: *Booklist* v110 no2 p49 S 15 2013 Donna Seaman

"The Accidental Bride," "Any Duchess Will Do," and "Cowboy Take Me Away." "Jilly loves being a chef, but the stress is killing her. Off she goes to the Lost Creek Resort in Wyoming for a calming knitting retreat, but instead, she meets Walker Hale. . . . With just one day to select a bride, the future Duchess of Halford, Griffin chooses serving girl Pauline, as RITA Award-winning [Tessa] Dare continues her sparkling and sexy Spindle Cove series. . . . Graves launches a new series with this charming, emotionally rich novel about the return to Rainbow Valley, Texas, of champion bull rider Luke Dawson and Shannon North, who left her big-city career to run a no-kill animal shelter."

REVIEW: *Booklist* v109 no2 p38 S 15 2012

SLACK, MICHAEL.il. How do you burp in space? See Goodman, S. E.

SLAVERY AND THE BRITISH COUNTRY HOUSE; 208 p. 2013 David Brown Book Co

1. Country homes—Great Britain 2. Country homes—History 3. Historical literature 4. Slave trade—History 5. Slavery—Great Britain—History
ISBN 1848020643; 9781848020641

SUMMARY: "This book . . . grew out of a 2009 conference on 'Slavery and the British Country house: mapping the current research'. . . . It asks what links might be established between the wealth derived from slavery and the British country house and what implications such links should have for the way such properties are represented to the public today." (Publisher's note)

REVIEW: *TLS* no5768 p30 O 18 2013 MIRANDA KAUFMANN

"Slavery and the British Country House." "The genesis of this volume can be traced back to the surge of research prompted by the bicentenary of the abolition of the slave trade in 2007, via a conference hosted by English Heritage, the University of the West of England ' and the National Trust in 2009. Whether surveying areas near slave ports such as Bristol and Liverpool; connections with colonies such as Antigua or St Vincent; or focusing on particular houses such as Brodsworth Hall in Yorkshire or Normanton Hall in Rutland, these studies both break the silence and provoke further questions."

SLAVERY IN THE MODERN WORLD; a history of political, social, and economic oppression; 2 v. (xi, 859 p.) 2011 ABC-CLIO

1. Exploitation of humans 2. Forced labor 3. Reference books 4. Slave labor 5. Slavery 6. Slavery—History—20th century 7. Slavery—History—21st century
ISBN 9781851097838 (hardcopy : alk. paper); 9781851097883 (ebook)
LC 2011-019834

SUMMARY: This book examines slavery in the modern world, focusing on "modern forms of exploitation that encompass more than 27 million individuals. . . . The work is comprised of 5 introductory essays, 450 individually signed "A-Z" entries, and 60 primary source documents. . . . The introductory essays cover the topics of "Slavery and Abolition in the 20th Century," "Coercion and Migration," "Enslavement," "Organized Crime and Enslavement," and "Sweatshop Labor." . . . The individual entries, contributed by 125 subject specialists, canvass a . . . diversity of subjects" for example, "Abolitionism and prostitution," "Child Rights Information Network," "Dred Scott v. Sandford," "Sudan Peace Act (2002)," "William Wilberforce," and "World Trade Organization."" (Booklist)

REVIEW: *Booklist* v108 no12 p34 F 15 2012 Brian Odom

Slavery in the modern world: A history of political, social, and economic oppression. ." . . Rodriguez reminds us in his expansive, enlightening look at more modern forms of exploitation that encompass more than 27 million individuals—slavery has more of an impact on our own time than at any other time in the past. . . . The variety of primary documents is one of the great strengths of the work, drawing from a rich tapestry of attempts by both governments and the private sector to battle all forms of illegal labor exploitation. . . .Overall, this a solid work of vast importance that works well in supporting the existing social-science curriculum and could become a go-to resource for AP classes addressing the socioeconomic issues that arise in the era of globalization."

REVIEW: *Libr J* v137 no1 p130-2 Ja 1 2012 Annette Haldeman

REVIEW: *SLJ* v58 no4 p70 Ap 2012 Kathleen Kelly MacMillan

SLAVICK, ELIN O'HARA.il. After Hiroshima. See Elkins, J.

SLAVIN, BILL.il. Thomas the toadilly terrible bully. See Levy, J.

SLAYTON, REBECCA. Arguments that count; physics, computing, and missile defense, 1949-2012; [by] Rebecca Slayton 325 p. 2013 The MIT Press

1. Ballistic missile defenses—United States—History 2. Computer science—Political aspects—United States—History 3. Computer scientists—Political activity—United States—History 4. Historical literature 5. National security—United States—History—20th century 6. National security—United States—History—21st century 7. Physicists—Political activity—United States—History 8. Physics—Political aspects—United States—History 9. Software engineering—Political aspects—United States—History 10. Technological complexity—Political aspects—United States—History
ISBN 9780262019446 (hardcover : alk. paper)
LC 2012-051748

SUMMARY: This book presents an "account of how scientists came to terms with the unprecedented threat of nuclear-armed intercontinental ballistic missiles (ICBMs)." Author Rebecca Slayton "compares how two different professional communities--physicists and computer scientists--constructed arguments about the risks of missile defense, and how these arguments changed over time." (Publisher's note)

REVIEW: *Choice* v51 no10 p1892 Je 2014 J. C. Hickman

REVIEW: *Science* v342 no6160 p800-1 N 15 2013 Cyrus C. M. Mody

"Arguments That Count: Physics, Computing, and Missile Defense, 1949-2012." "[Rebecca] Slayton finds an ingenious and novel way to tell the history of missile defense systems anew: as a stage on which physicists and computing experts--computer professionals? software engineers? this group's muddled identity is part of Slayton's point--performed for one another and for policy-makers and the public, while using those performances to forward their individual and community objectives. . . . One of Slayton's major contributions is to tease out the continuities and discontinuities between air defense and BMD."

SLEGERS, LIESBET. Take a Look, Buzz; [by] Liesbet Slegers 12 p. 2013 Clavis Publishing

1. Animals—Juvenile literature 2. Bees—Juvenile literature 3. Birds—Juvenile literature 4. Picture books for children 5. Toy & movable books
ISBN 1605371688; 9781605371689

SUMMARY: In this children's picture book, "youngsters are encouraged to explore a garden through brightly painted cartoons and sliding panels. Every other page is split down the middle; something unexpected is revealed on an inner panel when the two halves of the page are pulled apart. A 'little bird' pops out of an apple tree, a worm slithers out of the grass, a chick hatches out of an egg, a bee buzzes at the heart of a flower and so on." (Kirkus Reviews)

REVIEW: *Kirkus Rev* v81 no18 p347 S 15 2013

REVIEW: *Kirkus Rev* v82 no1 p20 Ja 1 2014

"Take a Look, Buzz". "Youngsters are encouraged to explore a garden through brightly painted cartoons and sliding panels. Every other page is split down the middle; something unexpected is revealed on an inner panel when the two halves of the page are pulled apart. . . . While the panels are relatively easy to slide, toddlers will likely need some assistance opening and closing them to make sure pages stay on track and no fingers are pinched. With some adult supervision, readers will encounter many engaging surprises."

REVIEW: *Publ Wkly* v260 no31 p70 Ag 5 2013

SLIFKIN, ROBERT. Out of time; Philip Guston and the refiguration of postwar American art; [by] Robert Slifkin 304 p. 2013 University of California Press

1. American painting—20th century 2. Art and society—United States—History—20th century 3. Art literature 4. Figurative painting, American—20th century
ISBN 9780520275294 (hardback)
LC 2013-018305

SUMMARY: This book, part of the Phillips Book Prize series, is a "monograph on the postwar American painter Philip Guston, who was associated with Abstract Expressionism. [Robert] Slifkin (NYU) focuses on Guston's return to figurative painting in his 1970 exhibition at New York's Marlborough Gallery. . . . Slifkin counters the common reading of the paintings as a return to a politically inflected, figurative art. He argues that they should instead be regarded as figural." (Choice: Current Reviews for Academic Libraries)

REVIEW: *Burlington Mag* v156 no1333 p250 Ap 2014 DAVID KAUFMANN

REVIEW: *Choice* v51 no8 p1388 Ap 2014 C. N. Robbins

"Out of Time: Philip Guston and the Refiguration of Postwar American Art". "The reading of the paintings that this cross-referencing produces is quite esoteric at moments, relying heavily on an interpretive methodology that allows [Robert] Siifkin to analogize Guston's works to contemporary sociohistorical and theoretical concerns. These include the historicization of Abstract Expressionism, postwar political events, and poststructuralist literary theory. This volume's theoretical and historical examples are presented in clear language, but they are directed toward a knowing audience. Accordingly, the book likely will be most useful for advanced students and established scholars."

SLINGERLAND, EDWARD. Trying not to try; the art and science of spontaneity; [by] Edward Slingerland 304 p. 2014 Crown Publishers

1. Nothing (Philosophy) 2. Philosophical literature 3. Philosophy, Chinese 4. Spontaneity (Philosophy) 5. Struggle
ISBN 9780770437619 (hardcover); 9780770437633 (pbk.)
LC 2013-023431

SUMMARY: This book "introduces broad strategies for attaining and instilling the ancient Taoist art of wu-wei ('no trying'), a clear unselfconsciousness of the self. Developed by early Chinese philosophers such as Confucius, Laozi and Xunzi, wu-wei induces de, the simultaneous harmony of the mind, body and spirit, producing a calm outward posture that's palpably reassuring and trusting to others." (Kirkus Reviews)

REVIEW: *Kirkus Rev* v82 no3 p36 F 1 2014

"Trying Not to Try: The Art and Science of Spontaneity". "Richly fortified with Daoist parables and anecdotes, the narrative offers examples of the history and consistent effectiveness of wu-wei, including the author's own attainment of it while penning this book within the coveted 'writing zone.' Delivered via clever and convincing explanation, [Edward] Slingerland advocates for the adoption of wu-wei into daily life, and in doing so, true contentment and serenity should follow. 'In addition to helping us get beyond strong mind-body dualism,' he writes, 'the Chinese concepts of wu-wei and de reveal important aspects of spontaneity and human cooperation that have slipped through the nets of modern science.' A studious and fluent appeal for the benefits of a sound mind."

REVIEW: *Publ Wkly* v260 no51 p50 D 16 2013

SLOAN, BARBARA BELLE. Resplendent dress from Southeastern Europe. See Barber, E. W.

SLOAN, HOLLY GOLDBERG. Counting by 7s; [by] Holly Goldberg Sloan 384 p. 2012 Dial Books for Young Readers

1. Eccentrics and eccentricities—Fiction 2. Gardening—Fiction 3. Genius—Fiction 4. High schools—Fiction 5. Orphans—Fiction 6. School stories 7. Schools—Fiction
ISBN 0803738552; 9780803738553 (hardcover)
LC 2012-004994

SUMMARY: This book follows "Willow Chance . . . an extremely precocious and analytical 12-year-old 'genius'. . . . Despite Willow's social difficulties, she makes an impression on everyone around her--whether it's Dell Duke, a lonely and ineffectual school district counselor, or Jairo Hernandez, the taxi driver Willow hires to drive her to her meetings with Dell. After Willow's parents die in a car crash, her new friend Mai Nguyen persuades her mother to take Willow in." (Publishers Weekly)

REVIEW: *Booklist* v109 no22 p72 Ag 1 2013 Sarah Hunter

REVIEW: *Bull Cent Child Books* v67 no1 p54-5 S 2013 D. S.

"Counting by 7s." "There are echoes of Horvath's 'Everything on a Waffle' in this quirky story of life after tragedy, but it's still a deeply original tale; Willow's narration effectively conveys both her outlier tendencies, with her fierce focus on scientific details of botany and her love of the number seven, and the utter, flooding grief she suffers in the wake of her loss. Characterization is sharp yet joyful, with Willow and Mai bonding over not only their racial outsiderhood (Willow is mixed race and Mai Vietnamese) but also their ability to take charge of a situation or an inept adult, while the secondary cast is also afforded nuance and development."

REVIEW: *Horn Book Magazine* v89 no5 p111-2 S/O 2013 MARTHA V. PARRAVANO

REVIEW: *Kirkus Rev* v81 no14 p177 Jl 15 2013

REVIEW: *Publ Wkly* v261 no4 p188 Ja 27 2014

REVIEW: *Publ Wkly* v260 no27 p88-90 Jl 8 2013

REVIEW: *SLJ* v59 no9 p148 S 2013 Cheryl Ashton

SLOAN, ROBERT H. Unauthorized access. See Warner, R.

SLONIM, DAVID.il. Digger, dozer, dumper. See Vestergaard, H.

SLONIM, DAVID. Patch; [by] David Slonim 32 p. 2013 Roaring Brook Press

1. Children's stories 2. Dogs—Fiction 3. Human-animal relationships—Fiction 4. Loyalty 5. Pets—Juvenile literature

ISBN 9781596436435 (hardcover)

LC 2012-029545

SUMMARY: In this children's book by David Slonim, "Patch is a good dog. At least he tries to be--but sometimes he finds it hard to remember commands or resist chasing rabbits. Three very short stories of a boy and his dog are combined in this . . . illustrated picture book that honors the special bond between dogs and their people and between friends of all species." (Publisher's note)

REVIEW: *Booklist* v109 no21 p80 Jl 1 2013 Angela Leeper

REVIEW: *Bull Cent Child Books* v67 no2 p114-5 O 2013 D. S.

"Patch." "This gentle chapter-divided, picture book-format title offers three brief stories featuring the narrator's adventures with his beloved dog, Patch. . . . The text is spare, with short simple sentences that gain energy from the narrator's informal voice, and the chapter format makes this a promising title for youngsters oscillating between readalouds and readalones. [Author and illustrator David] Slonim's line and watercolor art is lighter in tone and intensity than his goofy cartoons for books such as Goodman's 'It's a Dog's Life'. . . . While touches of visual hyperbole add humor, the illustrations, with their soft blurs of watercolor and casual penciled textures, are at heart comradely more than comic."

REVIEW: *Kirkus Rev* v81 no2 p102 Je 1 2013

REVIEW: *SLJ* v59 no7 p71 Jl 2013 Anna Haase Krueger

SLOTERDIJK, PETER. Philosophical temperaments. See Philosophical temperaments

SLOTKIN, RICHARD, 1942-. Long Road to Antietam; how the Civil War became a revolution; [by] Richard Slotkin 512 p. 2012 Liveright Publishing Corporation

1. Antietam, Battle of, Md., 1862 2. Historical literature 3. McClellan, George Brinton, 1826-1885

ISBN 0871404117; 9780871404114 (hardcover)

LC 2012-007795

SUMMARY: This book looks at the germination of the U.S. Civil War which "became a revolution in summer 1862, when Lincoln acknowledged that peaceful compromise was at that point impossible and thoroughly committed himself to war. First up in this new strategy: the Emancipation Proclamation. As Lincoln clashed with ambitious general George McClellan, the country started on the bloody road to Antietam." (Library Journal)

REVIEW: *Rev Am Hist* v42 no1 p84-8 Mr 2014 Michael P. Gray

"The Long Road to Antietam: How the Civil War Became a Revolution." "[Author Richard] Slotkin now contributes to Civil War historiography with 'The Long Road To Antietam: How the Civil War Became a Revolution,' a timely evaluation that will leave readers intrigued but also asking questions. . . . Slotkin contends in 'The Long Road To Antietam' that a combination of political and military maneuvers drove leaders on each side to adopt increasingly radical and even revolutionary military policies that remained in place long after the conflict."

SMALLMAN, STEVE. Bear's Big Bottom; [by] Steve Smallman 32 p. 2014 Capstone Pr Inc

1. Animal stories 2. Bears—Juvenile fiction 3. Friendship—Juvenile fiction 4. Humorous stories 5. Teasing

ISBN 162370118X; 9781623701185

SUMMARY: In this children's book, "after his friends scold him, the devastated Bear runs away into the woods. His friends search high and low; for once, they can't find him, not-so-cleverly concealed as part of a tree. Things take a dangerous turn when they call into a cave and a fox leaps out, chasing them and trying to bite their bottoms. Bear hears their cries for help, but he's kind of stuck. Luckily, his silhouette against the tree looks like a monster, and that's enough to scare away the fox. " (Kirkus Reviews)

REVIEW: *Bull Cent Child Books* v67 no6 p336 F 2014 Jeannette Hulick

REVIEW: *Kirkus Rev* v82 no1 p200 Ja 1 2014

"Bear's Big Bottom". " Sometimes, good things come in big packages. He's friendly and sweet, with "little paws and little feet." But Bear's big bottom gets him into all kinds of trouble. When he plays on the seesaw, he sends smaller animal friends into outer space. He fills the couch from side to side, threatening to squish them all, and empties the pool with a single splash. . . .[Steve] Smallman's crisp rhyming text is in tune with [Emma] Yarlett's bright and sometimes goofy illustrations. It's hard not to laugh at the difference in scale, and snippets of dialogue incorporated into the illustrations add to the fun. Solid lesson neatly presented."

SMILEY, DAVID. Pedestrian modern; shopping and American architecture, 1925-1956; [by] David Smiley xi, 357 p. 2013 University of Minnesota Press

1. ARCHITECTURE—History—General 2. ARCHITECTURE—Urban & Land Use Planning 3. Architectural literature 4. Architecture and society—United States—History—20th century 5. Commercial buildings—United States—History—20th century 6. Consumer behavior—United States—History—20th century 7. HISTORY—United States—20th Century

ISBN 9780816679294 (hardback); 9780816679300 (pb)

LC 2013-003504

SUMMARY: "This is a history of mercantile design from the 1920s through the 1950s told through six theme-based chapters. In the first . . . one sees how modernist storefronts opened up the intransigent facades of conventional urban buildings. The second features four designers . . . who transformed merchandizing through modernist design. The third treats traffic congestion as the impetus for new strategies for planning around parking." (Choice: Current Reviews for Academic Libraries)

REVIEW: *Choice* v51 no6 p993-4 F 2014 J. Quinan

"Pedestrian Modern: Shopping and American Architecture, 1925-1956." "[David] Smiley . . . offers an invaluable alternative to the canonical history of modernism in the US, understood as a collection of iconic buildings. This is a history of mercantile design from the 1920s through the 1950s told through six theme-based chapters. . . . This study elevates and elucidates an underappreciated, ubiquitous aspect of American culture through meticulous research in the books, magazines, journals, and archival resources of those several tumultuous decades. . . . Highly recommended."

SMILEY, JANE, 1949-. Pie in the Sky; Book Four of the Horses of Oak Valley Ranch; 257 p. 2012 Alfred A. Knopf Books for Young Readers

1. Christian life—Fiction 2. Family life—California—Fiction 3. High schools—Fiction 4. Horses—Training—Fiction 5. JUVENILE FICTION—Animals—Horses 6. JUVENILE FICTION—Family—General (see also headings under Social Issues) 7. JUVENILE FICTION—Social Issues—Friendship 8. Ranch life—California—Fiction 9. Schools—Fiction 10. Sports stories

ISBN 0375869689; 9780375869686 (hardback); 9780375969683 (library binding); 9780375985324 (e-book)

LC 2011-044104

SUMMARY: In this book, by Jane Smiley, "Abby Lovitt doesn't realize how unprepared she is when she takes her beloved horse, True Blue, to a clinic led by the most famous equestrian anyone knows. The biggest surprise, though, is that Sophia . . . stops riding. Who will ride her horse? Abby's dad seems to think it will be Abby. Pie in the Sky is the most expensive horse Abby has ever ridden. But he is proud and irritable, and he takes Abby's attention away from the continuing mystery that is True Blue." (Publisher's note)

REVIEW: *Horn Book Magazine* p106-7 S/O 2012 Anita L. Burkam

"Pie in the Sky." "As in previous volumes, Abby's believable, engaging voice and her low-key demeanor, along with [Jane] Smiley's finely tuned sense of place, make the story a standout for horse-book fans (although the details of advanced jumping may elude less technical readers). What's exciting in this book (and accessible to any level horse-lover) is Abby's in-depth analysis of the animals' behavior and her step-up to even greater achievements in 'horse-whispering'--actions that will deeply gratify anyone who's ever wished to become one with a horse."

REVIEW: *Kirkus Rev* v80 no15 p173 Ag 1 2012

REVIEW: *SLJ* v58 no9 p156 S 2012 Lisa Crandall

REVIEW: *Voice of Youth Advocates* v35 no3 p271 Ag 2012 Sara Martin

REVIEW: *Voice of Youth Advocates* v35 no3 p272 Ag 2012 Raluca Topliceanu

SMITH-READY, JERI. This side of salvation; [by] Jeri Smith-Ready 384 p. 2014 Simon Pulse

1. Cults—Fiction 2. End of the world—Fiction 3. Family life—Pennsylvania—Fiction 4. Grief—Fiction 5. High schools—Fiction 6. Missing persons—Fiction 7. Schools—Fiction 8. Young adult fiction

ISBN 1442439483; 9781442439481 (hardcover)

LC 2013-019948

SUMMARY: In this book, by Jeri Smith-Ready, "when his older brother was killed, David got angry. . . . But his parents . . . got religious. David's still figuring out his relationship with a higher power, but there's one thing he does know for sure: The closer he gets to new-girl Bailey, the better . . . he feels. Then his parents start cutting all their worldly ties in to prepare for the Rush, the divine moment when the faithful will be whisked off to Heaven...and they want David to do the same." (Publisher's note)

REVIEW: *Booklist* v110 no13 p69 Mr 1 2014 Daniel Kraus

REVIEW: *Bull Cent Child Books* v67 no10 p542 Je 2014 K. C.

"This Side of Salvation". "Through the use of flashbacks that alternate with the present, the story of the four years between his brother's death and his parents' disappearance unfolds with remarkable grace and sensitivity. David's sincere belief is balanced by his girlfriend Bailey's skepticism, with their love (and, frankly, their steamy sexual desire) for each other forcing them to talk honestly and with respect about their differences. . . . His multi-dimensionality, as a baseball player, a devoted son, a strong Christian, an anxious boyfriend, and a sometimes impulsive little brother make him a standout character with unexpected depths in this unusual and insightful family story."

REVIEW: *Kirkus Rev* v82 no4 p138 F 15 2014

REVIEW: *Publ Wkly* v261 no7 p102 F 17 2014

REVIEW: *SLJ* v60 no5 p140 My 2014 Shelley Diaz

REVIEW: *Voice of Youth Advocates* v37 no1 p74-5 Ap 2014 Kristi Sadowski

SMITH, AMINDA M. Thought reform and China's dangerous classes; reeducation, resistance, and the people; [by] Aminda M. Smith xi, 255 p. 2013 Rowman & Littlefield Publishers

1. China—Politics & government—1949- 2. Communism—China—History—20th century 3. Education—Social aspects—China—History—20th century 4. Education and state—China—History—20th century 5. Historical literature 6. Political culture—China—History—20th century 7. Reformatories 8. Tramps 9. Underclass

ISBN 9781442218376 (cloth : alk. paper)

LC 2012-032389

SUMMARY: This book by Aminda Smith "takes readers inside the early-PRC reformatories where the new state endeavored to transform socially marginalized 'vagrants' into socially integrated members of the laboring masses. . . . Her book explores reformatories as institutions dedicated to molding new socialist citizens and as symbolic spaces. . . . She offers . . . answers . . . about . . . the 1950s, especially with respect to the development and future of PRC political culture." (Publisher's note)

REVIEW: *Am Hist Rev* v118 no4 p1159-60 O 2013 Jeffrey C. Kinkley

"Thought Reform and China's Dangerous Classes: Reeducation, Resistance, and the People." "Aminda M. Smith faithfully and in many ways imaginatively addresses a lacuna in our understanding of the Chinese Communist Party's (CCP) attitudes toward the social underclass, first during the revolution that brought the party to power, and later after the party assumed control in the 1950s. This monograph sheds new light on the origins of the CCP's extrajudicial ways of dealing with a wide range of social types it deemed not fully supportive of the revolution, and with alleged offenders against the old and new social orders. . . . This book's strength is in depicting changes in how the Chinese revolutionaries saw the 'dangerous classes' and the social forces that motivated them, and sometimes how those 'classes' viewed their own reformation."

SMITH, ANDREW.ed. The encyclopedia of the gothic. See The encyclopedia of the gothic

SMITH, ANDREW F.ed. Food and drink in American history. See Food and drink in American history

SMITH, APRIL. A Star for Mrs. Blake; a novel; [by] April Smith 352 p. 2014 Alfred A. Knopf

1. Cemeteries—France—Verdun—Fiction 2. FICTION—Contemporary Women 3. FICTION—Historical 4. FICTION—Romance—General 5. Mothers and sons—Fiction 6. Parental grief—Fiction 7. United States—History—1919-1933—Fiction 8. World War, 1914-1918—Fiction

ISBN 0307958841; 9780307958846 (hardcover)

LC 2013-023987

SUMMARY: This novel, by April Smith, focuses on five mothers of fallen soldiers from World War I. These "very different Gold Star Mothers travel to the Meuse-Argonne American Cemetery to say final good-byes to their sons and come together along the way to face the unexpected: a death, a scandal, and a secret revealed." (Publisher's note)

REVIEW: *Kirkus Rev* v81 no24 p109 D 15 2013

"A Star for Mrs. Blake". "The fifth member of the party, Wilhelmina Russell, does not respond to Cora's letters, but Mrs. Russell does show up to travel on the train from Boston to New York. Only this is Selma Russell, a black seamstress, stereotypically large and comic-discomforting whiffs of race and class snobbery filter throughout the novel. A snafu has mixed up the two Mrs. Russells, and Wilhelmina, a deeply disturbed middle-class housewife recently released from a mental hospital for the journey, has ended up in Harlem. . . . While the line-by-line writing is engaging, this take on historic events is made shallow by broad brush strokes and lots of heartstring pulling."

SMITH, BARDWELL L. Narratives of sorrow and dignity; Japanese women, pregnancy loss, and modern rituals of grieving; [by] Bardwell L. Smith xvii, 410 p. 2013 Oxford University Press

1. Abortion—Religious aspects—Buddhism 2. Buddhist women—Religious life—Japan 3. Fetal propitiatory rites—Buddhism 4. Fetal propitiatory rites—Japan 5. Social science literature

ISBN 9780199942138 (alk. paper); 9780199942152 (pbk. : alk. paper)

LC 2012-042673

SUMMARY: In this book, "Bardwell L. Smith examines the way the Japanese deal with death and mourning, particularly the death of aborted foetuses. . . . He looks at the changing role of women in Japanese society and at death and grieving in folk custom and literature. . . . His book opens out further to discuss exorcism as a means of getting rid of pain." (Times Literary Supplement)

REVIEW: *Choice* v51 no4 p687 D 2013 A. Y. Lee

REVIEW: *TLS* no5768 p26 O 18 2013 LESLEY DOWNER

"Narratives of Sorrow and Dignity: Japanese Women, Pregnancy Loss, and Modern Rituals of Grieving." "For [Bardwell L.] Smith this book is clearly a labour of love. Deeply immersed in Japanese and Buddhist culture, he has spent some twenty-five years researching, interviewing, studying notebooks in temples where bereaved mothers anonymously record their feelings, and examining Japanese and Western feminist literature. . . . 'Narratives of Sorrow and Dignity' offers gripping, often extraordinary, insights into worlds we know very little of, together with pointers towards how we might learn to deal with loss and grieving and come to terms with our own mortality."

SMITH, CARL. City water, city life; water and the infrastructure of ideas in urbanizing Philadelphia, Boston, and Chicago; [by] Carl Smith xii, 327 p. 2013 University of Chicago Press

1. Boston (Mass.) 2. Chicago (Ill.)—History 3. Municipal water supply—United States—History—19th century 4. Philadelphia (Pa.)—History 5. Urban planning 6. Urbanization 7. Urbanization—United States—History—19th century 8. Waterworks 9. Waterworks—United States—History—19th century

ISBN 022602251X (cloth : alkaline paper); 9780226022512 (cloth : alkaline paper)

LC 2012-043193

SUMMARY: In this book, Carl Smith explores the concept of the city as "an infrastructure of ideas that are a support for the beliefs, values, and aspirations of the people who created the city." The book offers an "examination of the development of the first successful waterworks systems in Philadelphia, Boston, and Chicago between the 1790s and the 1860s." (Publisher's note)

REVIEW: *Am Hist Rev* v119 no1 p175-6 F 2014 David Soll

REVIEW: *Choice* v51 no3 p484 N 2013 W. K. Bauchspies

REVIEW: *Hist Today* v63 no8 p64-5 Ag 2013 FRANK TRENTMANN

"City Water, City Life: Water and the Infrastructure of Ideas in Urbanizing Philadelphia, Boston, and Chicago." "[Carl] Smith's focus is on ideas rather than on the material culture of everyday life. The mindset of civic leaders and engineers is beautifully recreated, but some readers may have wanted a more intimate sense of what happened inside the home, the taps and tubs, cooking and cleaning. What this elegantly written history does accomplish is to take the reader into the liquid revolution of modern life."

SMITH, CHLOE WIGSTON. Women, work and clothes in the eighteenth-century novel; [by] Chloe Wigston Smith x, 260 p. 2013 Cambridge University Press

1. Clothing and dress in literature 2. English fiction—18th century—History and criticism 3. Historical literature 4. Women in literature 5. Work in literature 6. Working class in literature

ISBN 9781107035003 (hardback: alk. paper)

LC 2013-004680

SUMMARY: This book by Chloe Wigston Smith "examines the vexed and unstable relations between the eighteenth-century novel and the material world. Rather than exploring dress's transformative potential, it charts the novel's vibrant engagement with ordinary clothes in its bid to establish new ways of articulating identity and market itself as a durable genre." (Publisher's note)

REVIEW: *Choice* v51 no6 p1007 F 2014 M. E. Burstein

"Women, Work, and Clothes in the 18th-Century Novel". "Intriguing. . . .[Chloe Wigston] Smith . . . is not interested in simply representations of changing fashions (copiously illustrated here). She argues that representations of clothes do not 'reflect' their aterial context but instead 'redefine' what such objects meant and how they functioned discursively. . . . In the book's second half. Smith unpacks links between women's bodies and women's labor as makers of clothes, cloth, and paper. . . . A book for collections strong in 18th-century studies, fashion history, and material culture. . . . Highly recommended."

SMITH, DENNISON. Eye Of The Day; [by] Dennison Smith 288 p. 2014 HarperCollins Publishers Ltd

1. Friendship—Fiction 2. Fugitives from justice—Fiction 3. Historical fiction 4. Photographers—Fiction 5. World War, 1939-1945—Fiction

ISBN 1443411876; 9781443411875

SUMMARY: In this book by Dennison Smith, "when a brutal explosion in a summer-cottage town in Vermont brings together Amos, a disfigured handyman, and Aubrey, the cosseted son of a wealthy New England family, neither has any idea that this one event will shape them forever. As their lives touch again and again over the years, these two unlikely friends forge a bond that survives war and peace, love and loss." (Publisher's note)

REVIEW: *Quill Quire* v80 no1 p34 Ja/F 2014 Dana Hansen

"The Eye of the Day". "The world young Aubrey Brown inhabits in B. C. writer Dennison Smith's accomplished second novel is one of privilege and leisure. . . . But history has determined that this coddled existence cannot last forever. . . . 'The Eye of the Day' is surprisingly beautiful in its sheer coldness, from its description of the heartless Vermont winter to the chilly and dysfunctional relationships among Aubrey and his family. Smith's novel is a riveting narrative of survival, self-knowledge, and the possibility of second chances."

SMITH, EMILIE.tr. Victoria. See Goldemberg, S.

SMITH, GREGORY WHITE, 1951-2014. Van Gogh. See Naifeh, S.

SMITH, HEATHER. Baygirl; [by] Heather Smith 288 p. 2013 Orca Book Pub

1. Alcoholic fathers 2. Children of alcoholics 3. Newfoundland & Labrador—Fiction 4. Rural-urban migration 5. Young adult fiction

ISBN 9781459802742 (pbk.); 9781459802759 (electronic edition; 9781459802766 (electronic edition

LC 2013-935299

SUMMARY: In this young adult novel by Heather Smith, "Growing up in a picturesque Newfoundland fishing village should be idyllic for sixteen-year-old Kit Ryan, but living with an alcoholic father makes Kit's day-to-day life unpredictable and almost intolerable. When the 1992 cod moratorium forces her father out of a job, the tension between Kit and her father grows. Forced to leave their rural community, the family moves to the city." (Publisher's note)

REVIEW: *Kirkus Rev* v81 no16 p91 Ag 15 2013

"Baygirl." "In the Newfoundland fishing village of Parsons Bay, Kitty has her refuges all staked out, for when she needs to hide from her father's nearly incessant drunken belligerence. . . . But it's 1992, and the cod fishery is subject to a moratorium, leaving her father suddenly without work. Hoping to find work, the family moves to live with Uncle Iggy in St. John's. The bigger city and foreign environment require that Kitty find new friends and new ways to cope. . . . Kitty's initial belligerence and anger, so predominant early on, modulates to a more nuanced point of view; given her growth, it's a shame the mother remains a nonentity. This first-person tale gently illustrates change, both good and bad."

REVIEW: *Quill Quire* v79 no9 p35 N 2013 Dory Cerny

REVIEW: *SLJ* v60 no2 p114 F 2014 Lisa Gieskes

SMITH, JENNIFER E. The geography of you and me; [by] Jennifer E. Smith 352 p. 2014 Little, Brown & Co.

1. Electric power failures—Fiction 2. Love—Fiction 3. Love stories 4. Social classes—Fiction 5. Voyages and travels—Fiction

ISBN 0316254770; 9780316254779 (hardcover)

LC 2013-022845

SUMMARY: In this book, by Jennifer E. Smith, "Lucy lives on the 24th floor. Owen lives in the basement. It's fitting, then, that they meet in the middle–stuck between two floors of a New York City apartment building, on an elevator rendered useless by a citywide blackout. After they're rescued, Lucy and Owen spend the night wandering the darkened streets. . . . But once the power is back, so is reality. Lucy soon moves abroad with her parents, while Owen heads out west with his father." (Publisher's note)

REVIEW: *Booklist* v110 no14 p72 Mr 15 2014 Daniel Kraus

REVIEW: *Booklist* v111 no2 p63 S 15 2014 Ilene Cooper

REVIEW: *Bull Cent Child Books* v67 no9 p477 My 2014 K. C.

"The Geography of You and Me". "The romance is a fluffy bit of froth floating on top of a more substantive exploration of finding one's literal and figurative place in the world; both Lucy and Owen have to adjust their ideas of home to include new configurations of family and their places therein. . . . Readers on the verge of moving on to new territories, emotionally or physically, will find new ways to think about anchors here, or maybe they'll just indulge in the pleasures of a sweetly predictable love story."

REVIEW: *Horn Book Magazine* v90 no3 p99 My/Je 2014 RACHEL L. SMITH

REVIEW: *Kirkus Rev* v82 no6 p209 Mr 15 2014

REVIEW: *Publ Wkly* v261 no7 p100-1 F 17 2014

REVIEW: *SLJ* v60 no3 p148 Mr 2014 Tiffany Davis

REVIEW: *Voice of Youth Advocates* v37 no2 p66 Je 2014 Kate Neff

SMITH, JIM W. W.il. Plesiosaur Peril. See Loxton, D.

SMITH, JUSTIN E. H.ed. Philosophy and its history. See Philosophy and its history

SMITH, KIM.il. The Raven and the Loon. See Qitsualik-Tinsley, R.

SMITH, LINDSAY. Sekret; [by] Lindsay Smith 352 p. 2014 Roaring Brook Press

1. Paranormal romance stories 2. Psychic ability—Fiction 3. Spies—Fiction

ISBN 1596438924; 9781596438927 (hardback)

LC 2013-027913

SUMMARY: In this book, by Lindsay Smith, "Yulia's father always taught her to hide her thoughts and control her emotions to survive the harsh realities of Soviet Russia. But when she's captured by the KGB and forced to work as a psychic spy with a mission to undermine the U.S. space program, she's thrust into a world of suspicion, deceit, and horrifying power." (Publisher's note)

REVIEW: *Booklist* v110 no16 p60 Ap 15 2014 Sarah Bean Thompson

REVIEW: *Bull Cent Child Books* v67 no9 p477 My 2014 A. S.

REVIEW: *Kirkus Rev* v82 no5 p111 Mr 1 2014

"Sekret". "Cold War espionage smoothly blended with psychic romance. . . . Yulia narrates with prose that ably reflects the sometimes-discordant cacophony of these disparate musical styles, as she seeks the simple melody that will explain family secrets and earn her freedom. [Lindsay] Smith strikes an inexpert contextualizing balance, teetering between unexplained Russian and giving Yulia an outsider's view of her own culture. Still, the Soviet setting (uncannily similar to many a sci-fi dystopian future) is a flavorful backdrop for psychic espionage. A sudden cliffhanger sets up this fast-paced thriller (full of blaring brass and pounding drums) for a sequel."

REVIEW: *Publ Wkly* v261 no7 p101 F 17 2014

REVIEW: *SLJ* v60 no5 p140 My 2014 Jamie-Lee Schombs

REVIEW: *Voice of Youth Advocates* v37 no1 p89 Ap 2014 Jessica Miller

SMITH, MARK D.ed. Best care at lower cost. See Best care at lower cost

SMITH, MARTIN CRUZ. Tatiana; An Arkady Renko Novel; [by] Martin Cruz Smith 304 p. 2013 Simon & Schuster

1. Detective & mystery stories 2. Organized crime—Fiction 3. Political corruption—Fiction 4. Russia (Federation)—Fiction 5. Women journalists—Fiction

ISBN 1439140219; 9781439140215

SUMMARY: In this novel by Martin Cruz Smith "Tatiana Petrovna falls to her death from a sixth-floor window in Moscow the same week that a mob billionaire, Grisha Grigorenko, is shot. No one makes the connection, but Arkady [Renko] is transfixed by the tapes he discovers of Tatiana's voice. His only link is a notebook written in the personal code of a translator whose body is found in the dunes. Arkady's only hope of decoding the symbols lies in Zhenya, a teenage chess hustler." (Publisher's note)

REVIEW: *Booklist* v110 no13 p30-1 Mr 1 2014 Renee Young

REVIEW: *Booklist* v110 no5 p34 N 1 2013 Bill Ott

"Tatiana." "That [Martin Cruz] Smith has kept this series going for more than 30 years, finding through decades of change more and more reasons for Arkady to justify his cynicism, says much about the modern world--and much about Arkady's bedrock humanity in the face of snowballing absurdity. If a man believes in self-immolation, Tatiana asks Arkady, what doesn't he believe in? 'I don't believe in saints,' Arkady replies. 'They get people killed.'"

REVIEW: *Kirkus Rev* p36 N 15 2013 Best Books

REVIEW: *Kirkus Rev* v81 no9 p23 My 1 2013

REVIEW: *Libr J* v139 no6 p58 Ap 1 2014 Victoria A. Caplinger

REVIEW: *Libr J* v138 no11 p60 Je 15 2013 Barbara Hoffert

REVIEW: *Libr J* v138 no14 p104 S 1 2013 Barbara Conaty

REVIEW: *N Y Times Book Rev* p12 N 17 2013 LIESL SCHILLINGER

"Tatiana: An Arkady Renko Novel." "It would be a treat to watch the evening news with Martin Cruz Smith's fabulist's eyes and see current events colorized through [Arkady] Renko's dramatic filter. In 'Tatiana,' Smith continues the tradition he began at the end of the Brezhnev era with 'Gorky Park,' using Russia as his game board to make geopolitical conspiracy, well . . . fun. 'Tatiana' ought to come with a decoder ring so readers who share the author's fondness for brainteasers can try to crack the translator's code on their own. Then again, struggling slowly from benighted dread into the glimmering dawn of fictional resolution is the reward of reading an Arkady Renko thriller. Figuring everything out too quickly would only spoil the game."

REVIEW: *Publ Wkly* v260 no36 p37-8 S 9 2013

SMITH, MATTHEW J.ed. Icons of the American comic book. See Icons of the American comic book

SMITH, MERINA. Revelation, resistance, and Mormon polygamy; the introduction and implementation of the principle, 1830-1853; [by] Merina Smith 267 p. 2013 Utah State University Press

1. Historical literature 2. Mormon Church—Doctrines 3. Polygamy—Illinois—Nauvoo—History—19th century 4. Polygamy—Religious aspects—Church of Jesus Christ of Latter-day Saints—History—19th century 5. Polygamy—Religious aspects—Mormon Church—History—19th century

ISBN 9780874219173 (cloth)

LC 2013-015080

SUMMARY: In this book, Merina Smith "argues that Mormons succeeded in instituting plural marriage in the face of massive cultural and internal opposition because they managed to resacralize marriage and link it to the theology of family and the restoration of all things. The book consists of seven chapters that cover millenarian expectations, secrets and salvation narrative, resistance integration, internal dissent, the succession crisis, and open living." (Choice: Current Reviews for Academic Libraries)

REVIEW: *Choice* v51 no5 p856 Ja 2014 T. G. Alexander

"Revelation, Resistance, and Mormon Polygamy: The Introduction and Implementation of the Principle, 1830-1853." "By linking the practice with theology, [Merina Smith] clears up some previously difficult historical problem. . . . In addition to extensive research in primary sources, the author has spent considerable time in secondary literature. This includes not only the excellent scholarly work by writers who work in Mormon history, but also those who have written on general US religious history. Smith argues that Mormons succeeded in instituting plural marriage in the face of massive cultural and internal opposition because they managed to resacralize marriage and link it to the theology of family and the restoration of all things."

SMITH, MICHAEL FARRIS. Rivers; [by] Michael Farris Smith 352 p. 2013 Simon & Schuster

1. Dystopias 2. Gulf Coast (U.S.) 3. Southern States—Fiction 4. Wilderness survival—Fiction
ISBN 9781451699425 (hardcover); 9781451699432 (trade pbk.)
LC 2012-049521

SUMMARY: In this dystopian novel by Michael Farris Smith, "Following years of catastrophic hurricanes, the Gulf Coast--stretching from the Florida panhandle to the western Louisiana border--has been brought to its knees. . . . Eerily prophetic in its depiction of a southern landscape ravaged by extreme weather, 'Rivers' is a masterful tale of survival and redemption in a world where the next devastating storm is never far behind." (Publisher's note)

REVIEW: *Booklist* v109 no22 p32 Ag 1 2013 Carl Hays

REVIEW: *Kirkus Rev* p18 Ag 15 2013 Fall Preview

REVIEW: *Kirkus Rev* v81 no16 p231 Ag 15 2013

"Rivers." "[Author Michael Farris] Smith's vision of a post-apocalyptic society left behind by civilization is expertly executed. This world is chilling--all the more so for its believability--and it is peopled by compelling, fully realized characters, some of whom only exist in the form of ghosts. In contrast to this bleak world, Smith's prose is lush, descriptive and even beautiful. A compelling plot, fueled by a mounting sense of tension and hope in the face of increasing hopelessness, will keep readers engrossed to the very end. Tense, moving and expertly executed."

REVIEW: *Libr J* v138 no7 p56 Ap 15 2013 Barbara Hoffert

REVIEW: *N Y Times Book Rev* p42 D 15 2013 Michael Farris Smith

"Rivers." "In the haunted Gulf Coast region of this debut novel, hurricane season never relents. . . . Out of these stark circumstances a kind of dystopian reality rises up, largely driven by survival, grief, hunger, and redemption. Moving among third-person perspectives, the well-paced narrative charts the journey of Cohen, a young man who has lost his beloved wife and their unborn daughter during an evacuation. . . . Combined with [author Michael Farris] Smith's incantatory prose, their adventures and will for survival propel this apocalyptic narrative at a compelling clip until the very last page."

SMITH, ORIANNE. Romantic women writers, revolution and prophecy; rebellious daughters, 1786-1826; [by] Orianne Smith x, 278 p. 2013 Cambridge University Press

1. English fiction—19th century—History and criticism 2. English fiction—Women authors—History and criticism 3. Historical literature 4. Prophecy in literature 5. Romanticism—Great Britain
ISBN 9781107027060 (hardback : alk. paper)
LC 2012-040695

SUMMARY: In this book, "Orianne Smith explores the work of prominent women writers--from Hester Piozzi to Ann Radcliffe, from Helen Maria Williams to Anna Barbauld and Mary Shelley--through the lens of their prophetic influence. As this book demonstrates, Romantic women writers not only thought in millenarian terms, but they did so in a way that significantly alters our current critical view of the relations between gender, genre, and literary authority in this period." (Publisher's note)

REVIEW: *Choice* v51 no5 p835-6 Ja 2014 J. Coghill

"Romantic Women Writers, Revolution, and Prophecy: Rebellious Daughters, 1786-1826." "This excellent study discusses these writers who, along with their male counterparts, formed the intellectual vanguard of the period. Though not as well-known as the men, these women were prolific, and the importance of their work has been overlooked. . . . The volume opens with an extensive introduction; the six chapters that follow provide an excellent overview of the women. . . . The meticulous notes are a gold mine for period research; the bibliography is extensive, the index outstanding. In sum, the volume is outstanding in every way. . . . Essential."

SMITH, RED, 1905-1982. American pastimes; the very best of Red Smith; 560 p. 2013 Library of America

1. Ali, Muhammad, 1942- 2. Athletes 3. Baseball 4. Ruth, Babe, 1895-1948 5. Sports literature
ISBN 1598532170; 9781598532173 (alk. paper)
LC 2013-930950

SUMMARY: This book, edited by Daniel Okrent, is a collection of sportswriter Red Smith's columns. "Accounts of historic occasions--Bobby Thompson's Shot Heard 'Round the World, Don Larsen's perfect game in the 1956 World Series, the first Ali-Frazier fight--are joined by more offbeat stories . . . Here, too, are more personal glimpses into Smith's life and work, revealed in stories about his lifelong passion for fishing and in 'My Press-Box Memoirs,' a 1975 reminiscence." (Publisher's note)

REVIEW: *N Y Times Book Rev* p38 O 13 2013 Jay Jennings

"American Pastimes: The Very Best of Red Smith," "Breaking the Line: The Season in Black College Football that Transformed the Sport and Changed the Course of Civil Rights," and "A Chance to Win: Boyhood, Baseball, and the Struggle for Redemption in the Inner City." "Smith rarely sounds dated or overwrought. Whatever the subject, the authority of his prose never flags. . . . It's probably not fair to blame the author for overstatement in a subtitle. . . . [Samuel G.] Freedman never makes the case for the latter in what is a dutiful, near-hagiographic dual biography of Eddie Robinson and Jake Gaither. . . . The sport is merely the occasion for [Jonathan] Schuppe's deep excavation into four hard-knock lives in Newark. . . . The 'cycle' in the rough neighborhoods Schuppe vividly captures is not something you hit for but something that hits you, repeatedly."

SMITH, RICK. Toxin toxout; getting harmful chemicals out of our bodies and our world; [by] Rick Smith 304 p. 2014 St. Martin's Press

1. Detoxification (Health) 2. Environmental health 3.

Environmentally induced diseases—Nutritional aspects 4. Scientific literature 5. Toxins
ISBN 1250051339; 9781250051332 (hardcover)
LC 2013-049688

SUMMARY: This book presents a "guide to the toxins in our everyday environment and how best to avoid them or get them out of our bodies. . . . The authors . . . focus on providing practical advice on how to avoid toxins (the short answer is to buy organic and natural products) and eliminate those that have accumulated from our bodies. . . . Toward the end of their book, [Bruce] Lourie and [Rick] Smith discuss some of the broader implications of their findings." (CCPA Monitor)

REVIEW: *Booklist* v110 no12 p22 F 15 2014 Colleen Mondor

"Toxin Toxout: Getting Harmful Chemicals Out of Our Bodies and Our World". "In a collegial, straightforward style, [Bruce] Lourie and [Rick] Smith quiz doctors and researchers, converse with wellness activists, visit organic stores and companies and, most interestingly, engage in a variety of experiments to track how the more than 80,000 synthetic chemicals in use today got into our bodies and what it will take to get them out. . . . Scrupulously researched and sourced with thorough chapter notes, 'Toxin Toxout' is remarkable both for its content and appealing narrative voice. Simply put, this is a book no one in the industrialized world has the luxury of ignoring."

REVIEW: *Kirkus Rev* v82 no9 p60-1 My 1 2014

SMITH, ROD.ed. The selected letters of Robert Creeley. See The selected letters of Robert Creeley

SMITH, RON. Public relations; the basics; [by] Ron Smith ix, 268 p. 2014 Routledge

1. Business literature 2. Public relations 3. Public relations—Vocational guidance 4. Public relations consultants 5. Public relations firms
ISBN 9780415675833 (pbk: alk. paper); 9780415675840 (hbk: alk. paper)
LC 2013-005178

SUMMARY: This book by Ron Smith, part of the book series "The Basics," is "a knowledge-based look at the industry and practice of public relations. . . . Included in the first section is a brief history of the profession . . . and the various types of public relations and skills needed to be successful in the field. The second half of the book . . . addresses the steps necessary to effectively develop a PR plan in a 'how-to workshop' format." (Choice: Current Reviews for Academic Libraries)

REVIEW: *Choice* v51 no8 p1453-4 Ap 2014 N. E. Furlow

"Public Relations: The Basics". "An addition to Routledge's 'The Basics' series, this comprehensive handbook is a knowledge-based look at the industry and practice of public relations. . . . As the author is a professor of public communication, it is only fitting that the book includes an appendix offering guidance for career seekers. Chapters are peppered with examples of effective PR. A thorough glossary is included, as is a substantial list of recommended readings. This book would appeal to students considering a career in public relations or business owners looking to develop a PR strategy."

SMITH, SANDRA.tr. Outsider. See Camus, A.

SMITH, WINTHROP H. Catching Lightning in a Bottle; How Merrill Lynch Revolutionized the Financial World; [by] Winthrop H. Smith 609 p. 2013 Prestige Publishing

1. Business literature 2. Finance—United States—History 3. Merrill Lynch & Co. (1973-) 4. Merrill Lynch Pierce Fenner & Smith Inc. 5. Securities industry—History
ISBN 0989854310; 9780989854313

SUMMARY: This book on the financial firm Merrill Lynch traces its "impact on the world of finance from the day Charlie Merrill opened his one-man shop on January 6, 1914, to the final shareholder meeting prior to its acquisition by Bank of America on December 5, 2008. Win Smith also weaves in his personal experiences and observations. As the son of a founding partner, the author has known every Merrill Lynch CEO from the first, Charlie Merrill, to the last, John Thain." (Publisher's note)

REVIEW: *Economist* v410 no8868 p68 Ja 4 2014

"Catching Lighting in a Bottle: How Merrill Lynch Revolutionised the Financial World." "The sheer magnitude of Merrill's fall is hard to take on-board. The book sheds vital light on two eras: the early years that saw the expansion of the firm and of populist finance and on the bleak-post-millennial decade when its confidence and vision collapsed along with much of Wall Street's reputation. . . . [Winthrop Smith Jr.] provides a wrenching picture of the ensuing multi-billion-dollar crackup. As part of an elegant exit, Mr. [Stanley] O'Neal received a $160m package. Wall Street and Main Street were left to suffer. As Mr. Smith's book shows, Merrill's success had broad implications. Sadly, so did its travails."

SMITH, ZADIE, 1975-. The Embassy Of Cambodia; [by] Zadie Smith 80 p. 2013 Hamish Hamilton

1. Cambodia—History—1975-1979 2. Embassy buildings—England 3. English fiction 4. London (England)—Fiction 5. Willesden (London, England)
ISBN 0241146526; 9780241146521

SUMMARY: Written by Zadie Smith, "'The Embassy of Cambodia' is a . . . story that takes us deep into the life of a young woman, Fatou, domestic servant to the Derawals and escapee from one set of hardships to another. Beginning and ending outside the Embassy of Cambodia, which happens to be located in Willesden, NW London, Zadie Smith's . . . story suggests how the apparently small things in an ordinary life always raise larger, more extraordinary questions." (Publisher's note)

REVIEW: *TLS* no5777/8 p25 D 20 2013 STUART KELLY

"The Embassy of Cambodia." "'The Embassy of Cambodia' begins as if there is a chorus, speaking in the first person plural. . . . [Author Zadie] Smith has fashioned a significant little parable which may confound her critics. This is the real Zadie Smith--humane, Chekhovian, tentative, surprising, stammering, reluctant, revolutionary. Her narrator poses a question that novelists will have to ask themselves: 'Surely there is something to be said for drawing a circle around our attention and remaining within that circle. But how large should that circle be?'"

SMITHERS, ANDREW. The road to recovery; how and

why economic policy must change; [by] Andrew Smithers 360 p. 2013 John Wiley & Sons Ltd

1. Economic policy 2. Economics literature 3. Executive compensation 4. Financial crises—Prevention 5. Incentives in industry

ISBN 9781118515662 (cloth)

LC 2013-026697

SUMMARY: In this book, economist Andrew Smithers argues that "there has been a dramatic change in the way managements are paid in the UK and the US. . . . This key problem is being ignored. The current management incentives are not only the reason for the massive gap between high and average pay but also for our economic stagnation. Attempts to generate growth, while ignoring the cause of this inaction, threaten to create another financial crisis." (Publisher's note)

REVIEW: *Economist* v409 no8856 p74 O 5 2013

"The Road to Recovery: How and Why Economic Policy Must Change." "In the early 1970s American companies invested 15 times as much cash as they distributed to shareholders; in recent years the ratio has dropped back to below two. . . . What has driven this exchange? In his new book, 'The Road to Recovery: How and Why Economic Policy Must Change,' Andrew Smithers, an economist, argues that the main cause has been management incentives. . . . Mr. Smithers is something of a maverick in financial and economic circles but he makes a powerful case--just as he did in 2000, when his book,'Valuing Wall Street,' pointed to the excesses of the dot-com bubble. Few listened to him then. More should do so now."

SMITHERS, GREGORY D. Slave breeding; sex, violence, and memory in African American history; [by] Gregory D. Smithers xii, 257 p. 2012 University Press of Florida

1. African Americans—Southern States—History 2. Historical literature 3. Slavery—United States—History 4. Slaves—United States—Sexual behavior—History 5. Slaves—United States—Social conditions

ISBN 9780813042381 (alk. paper)

LC 2012-018876

SUMMARY: "In this bold and provocative book, historian Gregory Smithers investigates how African Americans have narrated, remembered, and represented slave-breeding practices. He argues that while social and economic historians have downplayed the significance of slave breeding, African Americans have refused to forget the violence and sexual coercion associated with the plantation South." (Publisher's note)

REVIEW: *Am Hist Rev* v118 no5 p1527-8 D 2013 Emily West

REVIEW: *Choice* v50 no9 p1701 My 2013 J. D. Smith

REVIEW: *J Am Hist* v100 no3 p830 D 2013 R. Blakeslee Gilpin

REVIEW: *Rev Am Hist* v42 no2 p255-64 Je 2014 Kendra Field

"Help Me to Find My People: The African American Search for Family Lost in Slavery" and "Slave Breeding: Sex, Violence, and Memory in African American History." "Heather Williams' 'Help Me to Find My People' documents the 'thoughts and feelings' of enslaved people and former slaves in the midst of the forced separation of African American families that characterized Southern slavery in the United States. Gregory Smithers' 'Slave Breeding' considers the history and memory of constant interventions by white Southerners' into the sexual and reproductive lives of enslaved women and men, including the use of forced and coerced 'breeding' practices. . . . At their best, Williams and Smithers offer a complex history of chattel slavery, while locating an intellectual history of this system among slaves and former slaves."

SMOLIN, LEE. Time Reborn; from the crisis of physics to the future of the universe; [by] Lee Smolin 352 p. 2013 Houghton Mifflin Harcourt

1. Physics literature 2. Quantum cosmology 3. Quantum field theory 4. Space & time 5. Time—Philosophy

ISBN 0547511728 (hardcover); 9780547511726 (hardcover)

LC 201-3000389

SUMMARY: In this book, theoretical physicist Lee Smolin offers a "re-evaluation of the role of time in the universe. [He] points out that no one doubts that space is real. If the cosmos were empty, space would exist, but there would be no time. So time is . . . a real phenomenon at the heart of nature. This turns out to be controversial since the great thinkers from Plato to Newton to Einstein taught that time is an illusion that humans must transcend to achieve true understanding." (Kirkus Reviews)

REVIEW: *Booklist* v109 no14 p35 Mr 15 2013 Bryce Christensen

REVIEW: *Choice* v51 no2 p288 O 2013 E. Kincanon

REVIEW: *Economist* v407 no8837 p84-5 My 25 2013

REVIEW: *Kirkus Rev* v81 no4 p222 F 15 2013

REVIEW: *London Rev Books* v36 no3 p27-8 F 6 2014 David Kaiser

"Time Reborn: From the Crisis in Physics to the Future of the Universe". "Lee Smolin has picked up [Ernst] Mach's mantle and begun to criticise the metaphysical obscurities he detects in the latest multiverse theories. . . .The legacy of such a project remains difficult to predict. I suspect that few physicists will commit an about-face on reading 'Time Reborn,' just as few physicists dropped what they were doing when Mach's learned volumes appeared. But then again, it was reading Mach's 'Science of Mechanics,' a generation after it was published, that fired the imagination of a young Albert Einstein."

REVIEW: *N Y Rev Books* v60 no10 p46-9 Je 6 2013 James Gleick

REVIEW: *N Y Times Book Rev* p16 My 5 2013 ALAN LIGHTMAN

REVIEW: *Publ Wkly* v260 no7 p54 F 18 2013

REVIEW: *Quill Quire* v79 no3 p32 Ap 2013 Alex Good

REVIEW: *Science* v341 no6149 p960-1 Ag 30 2013 Huw Price

"Time Reborn: From the Crisis in Physics to the Future of the Universe." "[Lee] Smolin is a classic time snob, in [D. C.] Williams's terms. When he says that he is defending the unpopular view that time is real, he means time in the time snobs' proprietary sense. This makes him sound like a defender of common sense--'of course time is real,' the reader is being invited to think--whereas in fact the boot is on the other foot. It is Smolin's view that trips over common and scientific sense, denying the reality of what both take for granted. . . . So I have grave doubts whether Smolin's version of the Heraclitan view is any more plausible than its predecessors. And yet it has a tragic quality that other versions of the view mostly lack."

REVIEW: *TLS* no5763 p23 S 13 2013 DAVID PAPINEAU

SNEDEKER, REBECCA. Unfathomable city, a New Orleans atlas. See Solnit, R.

SNEED, BRAD.il. Washday. See Bunting, E.

SNEGIREV, ALEXANDER. Petroleum Venus; [by] Alexander Snegirev 208 p. 2013 GLAS New Russian Writing

1. Art thefts—Fiction 2. Down syndrome 3. Fathers & sons—Fiction 4. Psychological fiction 5. Single fathers
ISBN 571720096X; 9785717200967

SUMMARY: This book focuses on "the tender, loving relationship between the narrator, Fyodor, and his seventeen-year-old son, Vanya, who has Down's syndrome. After Vanya's mother abandons them and Fyodor's parents die, the two are left alone in the world. . . . [A] purloined painting sets off a series of coincidences, leading Fyodor through many encounters." (World Literature Today)

REVIEW: *World Lit Today* v87 no6 p68-9 N/D 2013 Bradley Gorski

"Petroleum Venus." "Alexander Snegirev's 'Petroleum Venus' stands out against the backdrop of Russia's contemporary literary scene, where conceptual postmodernism is still in vogue. In contrast, this slightly absurd but character-driven novel seems positively realistic. . . . Even as Snegirev builds a world where oil takes on mythic status . . . he never loses sight of his characters. . . . This well-observed portrait of single parenthood unfolds in a Moscow charged with symbolic potential. . . . At times, the plot's peregrinations expose Snegirev's youth and inexperience, but the power of his imagery saves the novel."

SNELL, DANIEL C. Ancient Near East; the basics; [by] Daniel C. Snell xi, 161 p. 2014 Routledge

1. Alexander, the Great, 356 B.C.-323 B.C. 2. Historical literature 3. Intellectual life—History
ISBN 9780415656979 (hardback : alkaline paper); 9780415656986 (paperback : alkaline paper)
LC 2013-004790

SUMMARY: This book by Daniel C. Snell "surveys the history of the ancient Middle East from the invention of writing to Alexander the Great's conquest. The book introduces both the physical and intellectual environment of those times, the struggles of state-building and empire construction, and the dissent from those efforts. Topics covered include . . . the rise and fall of powerful states and monarchs" and "daily life in the cities and out in the fields." (Publisher's note)

REVIEW: *Choice* v51 no5 p895-6 Ja 2014 M. Van De Mieroop

"Ancient Near East: The Basics." "This book is the first devoted to the ancient Near East in the now-popular genre of short introductions. [Daniel C.] Snell . . . has exacerbated the challenge to summarize in a few pages what elsewhere generates massive tomes by casting a very wide net. . . . Throughout, he discusses highlights that derive from such a wide spectrum of concerns that one wonders how much a novice will retain. The treatment of ancient Egypt is so summary that it becomes almost meaningless. Some statements are outdated or will raise a specialist's eyebrows. The writing style is vivid, but at times it feels like the author is addressing infants. He has not succeeded in providing die tools needed to understand the history and study of the ancient Near East."

SNELLING, LAURAINE. An untamed heart; [by] Lauraine Snelling 352 p. 2013 Bethany House

1. Families—Fiction 2. Farm life—Fiction 3. First loves—Fiction 4. Historical fiction 5. Single women—Fiction 6. Widowers—Fiction
ISBN 9780764202032 (pbk.); 9780764211515 (cloth : alk. paper)
LC 2013-023297

SUMMARY: In this book, set "in 1878 Norway, women are expected to marry, but Ingeborg Strand is more interested in becoming a midwife than a wife. . . . Then Nils, a university student, comes into her life, and Ingeborg knows she's found a love that will last forever. Alas, their happiness is short-lived. The only cure for Ingeborg's overwhelming grief is radical change, which might include widower Roald Bjorklund, his son, and America." (Booklist)

REVIEW: *Booklist* v110 no3 p40-1 O 1 2013 Shelley Mosley

"An Untamed Heart." "In 1878 Norway, women are expected to marry, but Ingeborg Strand is more interested in becoming a midwife than a wife. . . . This faith-based novel of a strong woman made even stronger by surviving a tragedy will appeal to a broad audience. It is a prequel to [Lauraine] Snelling's popular Red River of the North saga ('An Untamed Land,' 1996; 'A New Day Rising,' 1997; 'A Land to Call Home,' 1997), but would also work well as a standalone title. . . . This tale of a young, tragic love will appeal to teens."

REVIEW: *Publ Wkly* v260 no34 p45 Ag 26 2013

REVIEW: *Publ Wkly* p21 Children's starred review annual 2013

REVIEW: *Publ Wkly* v260 no3 p65 Ja 21 2013

REVIEW: *Quill Quire* v79 no5 p34-5 Je 2013 Kerry Clare

REVIEW: *SLJ* v59 no4 p144 Ap 2013 Joy Fleishhacker

SNEYD, LYNN WIESE. The horse lover. See Day, H. A.

SNICKET, LEMONY, 1970-. When did you see her last?; 288 p. 2013 Little Brown & Co

1. Chemists 2. Criminal investigation 3. Detective & mystery stories 4. Missing persons—Fiction 5. Private investigators—Fiction
ISBN 0316123056; 9780316123051 (hardcover); 9780316251952 (electronic bk. - library edition)
LC 2012-955921

SUMMARY: In this book, author Lemony Snicket "has a new case to solve when he and his chaperone are hired to find a missing girl. Is the girl a runaway? Or was she kidnapped? Was she seen last at the grocery store? Or could she have stopped at the diner? Is it really any of your business? These are All The Wrong Questions." (Publisher's note)

REVIEW: *Booklist* v109 no21 p75 Jl 1 2013 Ilene Cooper

REVIEW: *Booklist* v109 no19/20 p60 Je 1 2013

REVIEW: *Horn Book Magazine* v89 no5 p112 S/O 2013 SARAH ELLIS

"When Did You See Her Last?" "While dropping more hints about his own mysterious family background; demonstrating his gift for deadpan; and musing on such topics as the zen of lockpicking and the pointlessness of honeydew melons, [Lemony] Snicket also confronts the bad guy and solves the mystery. Reading this second adventure is like playing a combination of Clue . . . and a children's literature version of Trivial Pursuit, as the text is peppered with references to classic children's books. Final art unseen."

REVIEW: *Kirkus Rev* v81 no16 p147 Ag 15 2013

"When Did You See Her Last?" "The duo is searching for Miss Cleo Knight, daughter of the heirs of Ink Inc. . . . [Author Lemony] Snicket's second of four All the Wrong Questions is more sly noir for preteens. Chock-full of linguistic play and literary allusions to children's and classic literature, this is adventure mystery for young readers who like to think as they read. Little is answered definitively, but fans won't mind; they'll just be pleased there are two more young Snicket adventures to come."

REVIEW: *SLJ* v59 no9 p148 S 2013 Liz Overberg

SNICKET, LEMONY, 1970-. 29 Myths on the Swinster Pharmacy; 32 p. 2014 Pgw

1. Buses 2. Cities & towns—Juvenile literature 3. Drugstores 4. Humorous stories 5. Picture books for children

ISBN 1938073789; 9781938073786

SUMMARY: In this children's book, author Lemony Snicket and illustrator by Lisa Brown "examine [an] emporium of enigma, the Swinster Pharmacy. . . . Two children are fascinated by the store and what it might sell, and their 29 notes and comments comprise the narrative. This isn't a book about solving a mystery—entering the pharmacy would, after all, basically put the matter to rest. Instead, Snicket and Brown let readers dwell in the gray, desolate weirdness of the downtown." (Publishers Weekly)

REVIEW: *Booklist* v110 no11 p69 F 1 2014 Thom Barthelmess

REVIEW: *Kirkus Rev* v82 no2 p190 Ja 15 2014

"29 Myths on the Swinster Pharmacy". "There's an implication of nonspecific sinister happenings: Much is unexplained and slightly surreal (and the richer for it). From the title . . . [Lemony] Snicket channels the slightly awkward, odd syntax of children. Some of the sleuths' 29 numbered statements are a little spooky—'Dogs bark at it all the time'—while some are slyly funny: 'I was going to write a poem about the Swinster Pharmacy.' A sign in the window declares 'Included.' [Lisa] Brown's simple, cartoon-style artwork against a dark background is just right: It's direct and not overly edgy; her characters are distinctive and expressive."

REVIEW: *Publ Wkly* v260 no48 p56-7 N 25 2013

REVIEW: *SLJ* v60 no3 p148 Mr 2014 Sara Lissa Paulson

SNODGRASS, MARY ELLEN. Isabel Allende; a literary companion; [by] Mary Ellen Snodgrass 351 p. 2013 McFarland & Company, Inc., Publishers

1. Chilean literature 2. Historical fiction—History & criticism 3. Literature—History & criticism 4. Women authors

ISBN 0786471271; 9780786471270 (softcover: alk. paper)

LC 2013-004082

SUMMARY: "This reference work," part of the McFarland Literary Companion series, by Mary Ellen Snodgrass, "provides an introduction to [Isabel] Allende's life as well as a guided overview of her body of work. Designed for the fan and scholar alike, this text features an alphabetized, fully annotated listing of major terms in the Allende canon, including fictional characters, motifs, historical events and themes. A comprehensive index is included." (Publisher's note)

REVIEW: *Booklist* v110 no14 p63-4 Mr 15 2014 Art A. Lichtenstein

"Isabel Allende: A Literary Companion". "Part of the McFarland Literary Companion series, this is an expertly crafted study guide and tribute to the works of Isabel Allende. . . . Author [Mary Ellen] Snodgrass . . . clearly both understands and treasures great literature. . . . These entries are rich in relevant historical detail, insightful literary criticism, and reflections on Allende's place among contemporary writers of serious fiction. . . . In addition to thematic entries, Snodgrass provides her readers with engaging essays on specific Allende writings. . . . An erudite, affectionate, and wonderfully rich treatment of Isabel Allende and her work. Any academic or public library that offers her literature should add it to the circulating collection."

REVIEW: *Choice* v50 no12 p2234 Ag 2013 F. Colecchia

SNOW, SARAH.il. These rocks count! See Formento, A.

SO, MEILO.il. Brush of the gods. See Look, L.

SO, MEILO.il. My mom is a foreigner, but not to me. See Moore, J.

SOCIAL WELFARE IN EAST ASIA AND THE PACIFIC; x, 292 p. 2013 Columbia Univ Press

1. Human services—Asia 2. Human services—Pacific Area 3. Social science literature 4. Social service—Asia 5. Social service—Pacific Area

ISBN 0231157142; 9780231157148 (cloth : alk. paper); 9780231157155 (pbk. : alk. paper); 9780231530989 (e-book)

LC 2012-028190

SUMMARY: In this book, edited by Sharlene B.C.L. Furuto, "experts describe the social welfare systems of fifteen East Asian and Pacific Island nations and locales. Vastly understudied, these lands offer key insight into the successes and failures of Western and native approaches to social work, suggesting new directions for practice and research in both local and global contexts." (Publisher's note)

REVIEW: *Choice* v51 no1 p175 S 2013 J. C. Altman

"Social Welfare in East Asia and the Pacific." "[Editor Sharlene B. C. L.] Furuto has assembled an admirable collection of knowledge about social welfare policies and practices in 10 East Asian/Pacific Rim countries. . . . The book was written by indigenous authors, and its strength is in the comprehensive but contextual way they describe their unique social welfare histories; current social problems or issues; governmental, NGO, and indigenous social solutions and responses; and the status of both social work education and the social work profession in that political entity. Readers should find their social welfare worldviews considerably enlarged and perhaps challenged through this text."

THE SOCIETY OF EQUALS; 384 p. 2013 Harvard University Press

1. Democracy 2. Equality—Sociological aspects 3. Historical literature 4. Social structure 5. Solidarity
ISBN 9780674724594 (alk. paper)
LC 2013-009718

SUMMARY: In this book on the history of economic and political equality, author "[Pierre] Rosanvallon sees the roots of today's crisis in the period 1830-1900. . . . By the early twentieth century, progressive forces had begun to rectify some imbalances of the Gilded Age, and the modern welfare state gradually emerged from Depression-era reforms. But new economic shocks in the 1970s began a slide toward inequality that has only gained momentum in the decades since." (Publisher's note)

REVIEW: *Bookforum* v20 no3 p50 S-N 2013 CHRIS LEHMANN

"The Society of Equals." "French political theorist Pierre Rosanvallon takes fresh stock of the ideal of equality in 'The Society of Equals,' an ambitious bid to revive egalitarian thought in a global economy that no longer recognizes any moral or political legitimacy in schemes to redistribute wealth. . . . Rosanvallon deftly traces the slow collapse of the egalitarian tradition, mainly in the counterposed trajectories of French and American political thought. . . . Unfortunately, though, 'The Society of Equals' isn't nearly as strong in sketching a vision of social equality untethered from the destructive dogmas of blood and soil."

REVIEW: *N Y Rev Books* v61 no9 p33-6 My 22 2014 Paul Starr

SOCIOLOGY AND THE UNINTENDED; Robert Merton revisited; 387 p. 2011 Peter Lang

1. Merton, Robert King, 1910-2003 2. Social action 3. Social impact 4. Social policy 5. Sociology literature
ISBN 3631621205; 9783631621202
LC 2012-406430

SUMMARY: "This collection of essays aims to revive the sociological debate on the unintended, unanticipated and unexpected consequences of social action, as started by Robert K. Merton in a classic study of 1936. The contributing authors provide insights on both Merton's work and the reception it received in the academia." Topics discussed include "education, law, politics, financial markets, consumption, . . . organizations and institutional work . . . and Polish studies." (Publisher's note)

REVIEW: *Contemp Sociol* v43 no2 p239-40 Mr 2014 Charles Crothers

"Sociology and the Unintended: Robert Merton Revisited". "'Sociology and the Unintended' is remarkable for its quick publishing turnaround, being issued in the same year as the conference. . . . Editors Adriana Mica, Arkadiusz Peisert, and Jan Winczorek organized the book reasonably successfully into three parts. . . . While the book's intentions are to extend work in this area, the unintended consequence is a rich but rather undigested volume which defies ready retrieval of its material into broader conceptual structures. The\ editors provide a useful introduction, however the introductions to each of three parts merely summarize the forthcoming chapters—and the lack of an index hinders accessibility."

SOCKEN, PAUL.ed. The edge of the precipice. See The edge of the precipice

SOHN, TANIA. Socks!; [by] Tania Sohn 2014 Kane Miller, A Division of EDC Pub.

1. Children's stories 2. Clothing & dress—Juvenile literature 3. Clothing & dress—Korea 4. Picture books for children 5. Socks
ISBN 9781610672443 (h)
LC 2013-939409

SUMMARY: In this children's book, "a little girl just loves her many-colored socks. . . . Some are colored green or yellow. One pair has holes. They are different sizes, from 'baby socks' to 'daddy socks.' One pair fits at the ankle, and one pair is knee-high. 'Christmas socks' hang by the tree. She plays with her puppet socks and then opens a box with a very special pair of socks. These are 'Beoseon! Traditional Korean socks, from Grandma.'" (Kirkus Reviews)

REVIEW: *Booklist* v110 no13 p78 Mr 1 2014 Carolyn Phelan

REVIEW: *Kirkus Rev* v82 no4 p205 F 15 2014

"Socks!". "A little girl just loves her many-colored socks. With her cat by her side, the preschooler struts about in her patterned socks of polka dots and stripes. . . . The brief text unfortunately does not scan smoothly, making it unappealing as a read-aloud despite the child-friendly subject. The collaged artwork, though appropriately colorful, lacks charm. A pronunciation guide and a brief note about Korean socks would have been helpful to a general audience. A concept book that falls short."

SOIKA, AYA. Max Pechstein. See Fulda, B.

SOIL CONDITIONS AND PLANT GROWTH; 472 p. 2012 Wiley-Blackwell

1. Agricultural literature 2. Crops and soils 3. Plant growth 4. Plant-soil relationships 5. Soil science 6. Soils
ISBN 9781118337288 (epub); 9781118337295 (obook); 9781118337301 (emobi); 9781118337318 (epdf/ebook); 9781405197700 (hardback : alk. paper)
LC 2012-024777

SUMMARY: In this book, edited by Peter J. Gregory and Stephen Nortcliff, "Subject areas covered range from crop science and genetics; soil fertility and organic matter; nitrogen and phosphoros cycles and their management; properties and management of plant nutrients; water and the soil physical environment and its management; plants and change processes in soils; management of the soil/plant system; and new challenges including food, energy and water security in a changing environment." (Publisher's note)

REVIEW: *Choice* v51 no2 p298 O 2013 M. S. Coyne

"Soil Conditions and Plant Growth." "This new edition lives up to the reputation of its predecessor . . . , and provides a needed resource for cross-disciplinary studies in plant and soil sciences. [Editors Peter] Gregory and [Stephen] Nortcliff . . . have done an excellent job selecting the authors and content for each of the 13 chapters. The presentation style is uniform, the organization clear. The introductory chapter nicely describes the necessity of integrating plant and soil science study. . . . The coverage of topics gives plants and soils each fair treatment, and includes soil-plant systems;

chemical, biological, and physical properties of soil; plant growth properties; and the management of adverse soil conditions to promote plant growth.

SOINTU, EEVA. Theorizing complementary and alternative medicines; self, gender, class; [by] Eeva Sointu 253 p. 2012 Palgrave Macmillan

1. Complementary Therapies 2. Holistic Health 3. Self Care 4. Sex Factors 5. Social Class 6. Social science literature
ISBN 9780230309319
LC 2012-011341

SUMMARY: This book by Eeva Sointu, "addressing the increasing proliferation of complementary and alternative medicines . . . explores the meanings that people attach to non-biomedical health practices and of the therapeutic experiences that emerge through holistic medicines, arguing that these medicines are intimately connected with the changing configurations of selfhood, gender and class." (Publisher's note)

REVIEW: *Choice* v50 no6 p1147-8 F 2013 A. H. Koblitz

REVIEW: *Contemp Sociol* v43 no1 p117-9 Ja 2014 Dana Fennell

"Theorizing Complementary and Alternative Medicines: Wellbeing, Self, Gender, Class". "This book is worth examining for readers interested in health and illness more generally, not just those interested in CAM. . . . [Eeva] Sointu's language speaks of broad claims, but the scope of her work is limited (as she notes near the end of the introduction). At times, the book seemed to reinforce an image of CAM users as stereotypical New-Agers. . . . The vocabulary used . . . gears it toward a scholarly audience rather than a popular one. In terms of organization, some theories and claims repeat within various parts of the book and not all of the arguments are completely new. Nonetheless, the book provides intriguing arguments meriting further examination and consideration."

SOKOLENKO, ALEKSANDR KONSTANTINOVICH. Keep Forever; Gulag Memoirs; 156 p. 2012 CreateSpace Independent Publishing Platform

1. Correctional personnel 2. Gulag (Soviet Union) 3. Memoirs 4. Political prisoners 5. Soviet Union—Politics & government—1936-1953
ISBN 1475246897; 9781475246896

SUMMARY: In this memoir, "a former prisoner recounts his years in the Soviet gulag. . . . [Aleksandr Konstantinovich] Sokolenko shares stories from his years of imprisonment for political offenses during the Stalin regime. . . . The narrative does not follow Sokolenko's imprisonment chronologically but is made up of a series of vignettes, with Sokolenko blending his own experiences into the stories of his fellow prisoners and their guards." (Kirkus Reviews)

REVIEW: *Kirkus Rev* p52 D 15 2013 supplemet best books 2013

"Keep Forever: Gulag Memoirs". "These true stories capture both the horrific experience and bitter humor of Russia under [Joseph] Stalin, as committed socialists, black-market businessmen and ordinary people struggled with the changing definition of 'enemy of the state.' [Aleksandr Konstantinovich] Sokolenko's narrative clearly demonstrates that the corruption and absurdity of the Soviet system confronted prisoners inside the gulag as well as outside. . . . Throughout the book, the tone is matter-of-fact, allowing the events described, rather than any elegant prose, to work on readers' emotions. This was a wise decision by the author, who does not overwhelm the prisoners' anecdotes with unnecessary commentary."

REVIEW: *Kirkus Rev* v81 no6 p352 Mr 15 2013

REVIEW: *Kirkus Rev* v81 no24 p1 D 15 2013

"Keep Forever: Gulag Memoirs". "These true stories capture both the horrific experience and bitter humor of Russia under Stalin. . . . Throughout the book, the tone is matter-of-fact, allowing the events described, rather than any elegant prose, to work on readers' emotions. This was a wise decision by the author, who does not overwhelm the prisoners' anecdotes with unnecessary commentary. . . . The result is a clear, bracing depiction, but not a maudlin one. . . . Skillfully portrays the bleakness of the prison system with an appreciation for the dark humor that allowed the author to survive it."

SOLL, DAVID. Empire of water; an environmental and political history of the New York City water supply; [by] David Soll x, 283 p. 2013 Cornell University Press

1. Historical literature 2. Water-supply—Environmental aspects—New York (State)—New York—History 3. Water-supply—Political aspects—New York (State)—New York—History 4. Water-supply engineering—New York (State)—New York—History 5. Watershed management—New York (State)—New York—History
ISBN 9780801449901 (cloth : alk. paper)
LC 2012-033792

SUMMARY: In this book, "David Soll describes how [New York City] transformed its notoriously unsanitary water system in the early 20th century by buying up watersheds in the Catskill Mountains and building a large network of resevoirs, pipes, tanks, sambling stations and other devices that deliver a billion gallons a day of excellent water into the city's homes and businesses." (New York Times)

REVIEW: *New York Times* v163 no56283 pD6 O 8 2013 CORNELIA DEAN

"Drinking Water: A History," "Empire of Water: An Environmental and Political History of the New York City Water Supply," and "Thirst: Water and Power in the Ancient World." "Though he ranges widely, Mr. [James] Salzman . . . focuses on what one might call social justice. Access to water may be viscerally regarded as a 'right,' but he points out that the best way to ensure a reliable supply of pure water, especially in poor regions, is often to privatize it. . . . [Steven Mithen's] tone is academic and at times highly technical, but he builds to a striking conclusion. . . . David Soll describes how the city transformed its notoriously unsanitary water system in the early 20th century by buying up watersheds in the Catskill mountains."

SOLNIT, REBECCA. Unfathomable city, a New Orleans atlas; [by] Rebecca Solnit 1 atlas (166 p.) 2013 University of California Press

1. ART—American—General 2. Atlases 3. New Orleans (La.)—Social life & customs 4. SCIENCE—Earth Sciences—Geography
ISBN 9780520274037 (hardback); 9780520274044 (paper)
LC 2013-014799

SUMMARY: Written by Rebecca Solnit and Rebecca Snedeker, "this book is a . . . reinvention of the traditional atlas, one that provides a vivid, complex look at the multi-faceted nature of New Orleans. . . . More than twenty essays assemble a chorus of vibrant voices, including geographers, scholars of sugar and bananas, the city's remarkable musicians, prison activists, environmentalists, Arab and Native voices, and local experts, as well as the coauthors' . . . contributions." (Publisher's note)

REVIEW: *N Y Times Book Rev* p26 Ja 5 2014 Daniel Brook

"Unfathomable City: A New Orleans Atlas." "In the second volume of her planned trilogy of deliciously eccentris atlases, [author Rebecca] Solnit . . . amasses a team led by [Rebecca] Snedeker . . . to plumb the Crescent City's admittedly 'unfathomable' depths. . . . This objet d'art is as infectious as a second line. . . . With 'Unfathomable City,' Solnit and Snedeker have produced an idiosyncratic, luminous tribute to the greatest human creation defined by its audience participants: the city itself."

REVIEW: *Orion Magazine* v33 no2 p67-8 Mr/Ap 2014 Matthew Battles

SOLOMON, ALISA. Wonder of wonders; a cultural history of Fiddler on the roof; [by] Alisa Solomon x, 433 p. 2013 Metropolitan Books

1. Historical literature 2. Jewish theater—New York (State)—New York—History—20th century 3. Musicals—New York (State)—New York—20th century—History and criticism 4. Theater, Yiddish—New York (State)—New York—History—20th century
ISBN 9780805092608
LC 2013-003900

SUMMARY: In this book, "Alisa Solomon traces how and why the story of Tevye the milkman, the creation of the great Yiddish writer Sholem-Aleichem, was reborn as blockbuster entertainment and a cultural touchstone, not only for Jews and not only in America. It is a story of the theater, following Tevye from his humble appearance on the New York Yiddish stage, through his adoption by leftist dramatists as a symbol of oppression, to his Broadway debut in one of the last big book musicals." (Publisher's note)

REVIEW: *Commentary* v136 no4 p50-3 N 2013 TERRY TEACHOUT

REVIEW: *Kirkus Rev* v81 no22 p7 N 15 2013

REVIEW: *N Y Times Book Rev* p29 D 8 2013 MARJORIE INGALL

REVIEW: *Nation* v298 no6 p41-4 F 10 2014 JULIA M. KLEIN

"The Worlds of Sholem Aleichem: The Remarkable Life and Afterlife of the Man Who Created Tevye" and "Wonder of Wonders: A Cultural History of 'Fiddler on the Roof'." "Two new books, complementary in their aims and conclusions, manage these daunting tasks with aplomb, even if they're nowhere near as much fun as reading the writer himself. In 'The Worlds of Sholem Aleichem,' Jeremy Dauber . . . offers a sometimes irreverent--but also deeply serious--literary biography that attempts to channel his subject's antic spirit. Episodic in feel, it is most effective as a work of criticism that identifies Sholem Aleichem's affinities with literary modernism and postmodernism. . . . [Alisa] Solomon . . . finds her footing with the wonderfully gossipy creation tale of the long-running Broadway musical."

REVIEW: *New Repub* v244 no28 p44-7 My 26 2014 Jenna Weissman Joselit

REVIEW: *Publ Wkly* v260 no34 p61 Ag 26 2013

SOLOMON, DEBORAH, 1957-. American mirror; the life and art of Norman Rockwell; [by] Deborah Solomon 512 p. 2013 Farrar Straus & Giroux

1. ART—American—General 2. BIOGRAPHY & AUTOBIOGRAPHY—Artists, Architects, Photographers 3. Biographies 4. Illustrators—United States—Biography 5. Painters—United States—Biography
ISBN 9780374113094 (hardback)
LC 2013-021682

SUMMARY: This biography of Norman Rockwell "reveals an enormously complicated man whose wholesome vision of America was not merely commercial kitsch, but art that sprung from an emotional life fraught with anxiety, depression, and self-doubt. This sympathetic portrait depicts a repressed and humble Rockwell. . . . Thrice married and an apathetic husband, he clearly preferred the companionship of male friends and was likely a closeted homosexual." (Publishers Weekly)

REVIEW: *America* v210 no11 p35-7 Mr 31 2014 JAMES P. MCCARTIN

REVIEW: *Atlantic* v312 no5 p1 D 2013 James Parker

REVIEW: *Booklist* v110 no5 p20 N 1 2013 Donna Seaman

"American Mirror: The Life and Art of Norman Rockwell". "Esteemed art critic and biographer [Deborah] Solomon turns our perception of Norman Rockwell inside out in this fast-paced yet richly interpretative inquiry. . . . As Solomon points out manifestations of 'homoerotic desires' in Rockwell's brilliantly composed paintings, her sensitivity to his struggles deepen appreciation for his virtuosic artistry and for his valor in using his work to champion civil rights and nuclear disarmament. Solomon's penetrating and commanding biography is brimming with surprising details and provocative juxtapositions, just like Rockwell's mesmerizing paintings."

REVIEW: *Booklist* v110 no19/20 p130 Je 1 2014 Brian Odom

REVIEW: *Kirkus Rev* v81 no22 p10 N 15 2013

REVIEW: *Libr J* v138 no11 p62 Je 15 2013 Barbara Hoffert

REVIEW: *Libr J* v139 no11 p55 Je 15 2014 Susan Herr

REVIEW: *Libr J* v138 no16 p73 O 1 2013 Paula Frosch

REVIEW: *N Y Rev Books* v60 no20 p14-20 D 19 2013 Christopher Benfey

REVIEW: *N Y Times Book Rev* p1-18 D 22 2013 Garrison Keillor

"American Mirror: The Life and Art of Norman Rockwell." "In 'American Mirror,' [author Deborah] Solomon pays honest respect to Rockwell for his clear sense of calling and his dedication through periods of self-doubt, exhaustion, depression and marital tumult, and she offers the word 'masterpiece' to numerous pictures. . . . She does seem awfully eager to find homoeroticism—poor Rockwell cannot go on a fishing trip with other men without his biographer finding sexual overtones. . . . Rockwell painted 323 covers for 'The Saturday Evening Post.'"

REVIEW: *N Y Times Book Rev* p18 D 29 2013

REVIEW: *New York Times* v163 no56307 pC29-31 N 1 2013 JOHN WILMERDING

REVIEW: *Publ Wkly* v260 no25 p21-6 Je 24 2013 JAMES H. MILLER

REVIEW: *Publ Wkly* v260 no32 p47 Ag 12 2013

REVIEW: *TLS* no5792 p11-2 Ap 4 2014 PAULA MARANTZ COHEN

"American Mirror: The Life and Art of Norman Rockwell." "Norman Rockwell was and remains the premier artist of a comforting America of the imagination. But if Rockwell's art doesn't conform to a postmodern idea, this biography most certainly does. . . . [Author Deborah] Solomon doesn't re-evaluate the art, only the life, and here she is in full postmodern mode: not out to prove anything but to imply a lot, she sees patterns in events and images where other patterns could as easily fit. Her approach could be viewed as creative interpretation or irresponsible speculation, depending on your perspective. Rockwell's family, who gave Solomon generous access to archives . . ., take the latter view and are understandably irked. . . . Solomon's argument seems more prurient than persuasive."

SOLOMON, DIANA. Prologues and epilogues of Restoration theater; gender and comedy, performance and print; [by] Diana Solomon 263 p. 2013 University of Delaware Press

1. English drama—Restoration, 1660-1700—History and criticism 2. Gender role in the theater 3. Historical literature 4. Human sexuality in the theater 5. Prologues and epilogues—History and criticism 6. Theater—England—History—17th century

ISBN 9781611494228 (cloth: alk. paper)

LC 2012-047557

SUMMARY: "Accompanying over ninety per cent of all performed and printed plays between 1660 and 1714, these customized comic verses that promoted the play evolved into essential theatrical elements, and they both contributed to and reflected a performer's success. Once dismissed by scholars as formulaic, prologues and epilogues should be included in scholars' analyses of Restoration and eighteenth-century plays in order for us to understand how Restoration audiences consumed plays." (Publisher's note)

REVIEW: *Choice* v51 no3 p472 N 2013 A. Castaldo

REVIEW: *TLS* no5790 p22 Mr 21 2014 ROS BALLASTER

"Prologues and Epilogues of Restoration Theatre: Gender and Comedy, Performance and Print." "Diana Solomon's work promises to treat prologues and epilogues 'systematically, analytically, culturally, and theoretically.' . . . Prologues and epilogues have tended to be classified by tone. Solomon defines them rather by type. . . . The majority of Solomon's discussion is of the exposed epilogue delivered by the actress for comic effect. . . . Solomon is on stronger and more convincing ground in the final two chapters, which offer fine, illuminating and insightful readings of two usefully contrasted case-studies."

SOLOVEY, MARK.ed. Cold War social science. See Cold War social science

SOMJEE, SULTAN. Bead Bai; [by] Sultan Somjee 466 p. 2013 Createspace Independent Pub

1. Africa, East—Fiction 2. Beads 3. Canadian fiction 4. East Indians—Africa 5. Ismailites—History 6. Women, East Indian

ISBN 1475126328; 9781475126327

SUMMARY: Written by Sultan Somjee, "'Bead Bai' is one woman's story inspired by lives of Asian African women who sorted out, arranged and generally looked after huge quantities of ethnic beads in urban and isolated rural parts of the British East African Empire. . . . This is a historical novel drawn from domestic and community lives evolving around women's art." (Publisher's note)

REVIEW: *World Lit Today* v88 no1 p65-6 Ja/F 2014 J. Roger Kurtz

"Bead Bai." "To the growing list of East African literature focusing on the heritage of that region's Asian population we may now add the title 'Bead Bai,' a historical novel about thc Ismaili community in Kenya during the first part of the twentieth century. . . . This is the first novel published by Sultan Somjee, whose career as an anthropologist began in Kenya and continues in his present home in western Canada. . . . 'Bead Bai' links that material culture to the stories which lie behind it, ultimately offering a thoughtful window into an important part of East Africa's cultural heritage, through the eyes of the young bride Saki."

SONES, SONYA. To be perfectly honest; a novel based on an untrue story; [by] Sonya Sones 496 p. 2013 Simon and Schuster Books for Young Readers

1. Brothers and sisters—Fiction 2. Dating (Social customs)—Fiction 3. Fame—Fiction 4. Honesty—Fiction 5. Single-parent families—Fiction 6. Young adult fiction

ISBN 0689876041; 9780689876042 (hardcover)

LC 2012-048563

SUMMARY: In this novel, by Sonya Sones, "Fifteen-year-old Colette is addicted to lying. Her shrink says this is because she's got a very bad case of Daughter-of-a-famous-movie-star Disorder—so she lies to escape out from under her mother's massive shadow. When her mother drags her away from Hollywood to spend the entire summer on location in a boring little town in the middle of nowhere, Colette is less than thrilled. But then she meets a sexy biker named Connor. So what if she lies to him about her age, and about who her mother is?" (Publisher's note)

REVIEW: *Booklist* v110 no2 p77 S 15 2013 Gail Bush

REVIEW: *Bull Cent Child Books* v67 no2 p115-6 O 2013 K. C.

"To Be Perfectly Honest: A Novel Based on an Untrue Story." "Colette, whom readers may remember as the heroine's friend in [author Sonya] Sones' previous verse novel 'One of Those Hideous Books Where the Mother Dies . . ., takes center stage here as her movie-star mother insists that Colette and her seven-year-old brother, Will, accompany her on location for her latest movie. . . . Characterization is weak--Colette is all surface, Connor is a mean-spirited cliché, and Will's lisp is overplayed--and the plot becomes messagey when Colette is distressed to find a mirror of herself in Connor. The non-rhyming verse of varying forms and the well-paced plot make this a quick read, though. . . ."

REVIEW: *Kirkus Rev* v81 no14 p178 Jl 15 2013

REVIEW: *SLJ* v59 no8 p116 Ag 2013 Teresa Pfeifer

REVIEW: *Voice of Youth Advocates* v36 no4 p74 O 2013 Amy Cummins

SONNEBORN, LIZ. North Korea; [by] Liz Sonneborn 144 p. 2014 Children's Press; an imprint of Scholastic Inc.
1. Children's nonfiction 2. Kim, Chŏng-ŭn, 1984- 3. Korea (North)—Politics & government 4. Korea (North)—Social conditions
ISBN 0531236781; 9780531236789 (library binding)
LC 2013-003650

SUMMARY: This book, by Liz Sonneborn, is part of the Enchantment of the World Series. "Each volume has been completely rewritten from a previous edition. . . . 'North Korea' has a new author and a strong political focus, discussing life under the new leader, Kim Jong-un. . . . Each volume in this . . . series includes extensive back matter with a detailed index." (Booklist)

REVIEW: *Booklist* v110 no9/10 p94 Ja 1 2014 Susan Dove Lempke

"Brazil," "Ireland," "North Korea." "For reliably accurate, attractively presented and well-calibrated information, the longstanding 'Enchantment of the World' series remains a superior choice. . . . Although the basic structure holds true to past versions, the updated photographs are truly eye-popping and take care to portray the countries as modern. . . . 'Brazil' . . . conveys an excitement about the country and its people as well as its plentiful animals and plants. It might not be necessary for libraries to replace 'Ireland,' since it hasn't changed radically, but this is a solid offering with updated statistics. 'North Korea' has a new author and a strong political focus, discussing life under the new leader, Kim Jong-un."

SONNENBLICK, JORDAN. Are You Experienced?; [by] Jordan Sonnenblick 304 p. 2013 Feiwel & Friends
1. Drug overdose 2. Fathers & sons—Fiction 3. United States—Social life & customs—1945-1970 4. Woodstock Festival 5. Young adult literature, American
ISBN 1250025648; 9781250025647

SUMMARY: Author Jordan Sonnenblick's book centers around Rich, who is "fifteen and plays guitar. When his girlfriend asks him to perform at protest rally, he jumps at the chance. Unfortunately, the police show up, and so does Rich's dad. He's in big trouble. Again. To make matters worse, this happens near the anniversary of his uncle's death from a drug overdose years ago. Rich's dad always gets depressed this time of year, but whenever Rich asks questions about his late uncle, his dad shuts down." (Publisher's note)

REVIEW: *Booklist* v110 no1 p112 S 1 2013 Daniel Kraus

REVIEW: *Bull Cent Child Books* v67 no2 p116 O 2013 K. C.

"Are You Experienced?" "As a cultural history, Rich's experience captures the mood and magic of the [Woodstock Festival] from a distinctly contemporary perspective. . . . However, this is a family story as well, and Rich must come to terms with the fact that he can't change history. . . . The backstory Rich uncovers is one of abuse and neglect that leads to tragic circumstances, but the message is an inverted story of resilience, where a teen helps his father overcome the pain of abuse, which proves that the magic of Woodstock might not be a thing of the past after all."

REVIEW: *Kirkus Rev* v81 no16 p303 Ag 15 2013

REVIEW: *Publ Wkly* v260 no31 p73 Ag 5 2013

REVIEW: *SLJ* v59 no9 p148 S 2013 Ryan P. Donovan

REVIEW: *Voice of Youth Advocates* v36 no4 p86 O 2013 Jan Chapman

SONTAG, SUSAN, 1933-2004. Growing up absurd. See Goodman, P.

SOO AH KWON. Uncivil youth; race, activism, and affirmative governmentality; [by] Soo Ah Kwon xi, 169 p. 2013 Duke University Press
1. Asian American youth 2. Democracy and education—United States 3. Minorities—Political activity—United States 4. Nonprofit organizations 5. Social science literature 6. Youth—Political activity—United States
ISBN 0822354055; 9780822354055 (cloth : alk. paper); 9780822354239 (pbk. : alk. paper)civil education
LC 2012-044747

SUMMARY: In this book, author Soo Ah Kwon "explores youth of color activism as linked to the making of democratic citizen-subjects. . . . She draws on several years of ethnographic research with an Oakland-based, panethnic youth organization that promotes grassroots activism among its second-generation Asian and Pacific Islander members (ages fourteen to eighteen)." (Publisher's note)

REVIEW: *Choice* v51 no2 p361-2 O 2013 D. E. Kelly

"Uncivil Youth: Race, Activism, and Affirmative Governmentality." "In this definitive text examining youth engagement among Asian American youth, [author Soo Ah] Kwon . . . takes readers on an ethnographic journey to explore afterschool initiatives and other community-based projects, and shows how these initiatives serve as protective factors against juvenile delinquency. Set in the community of Oakland, California, the book helps readers understand grassroots activism among second-generation Asian American youth. Much of this activism takes the form of vocal and political activism in organizing institutes, workshops, and political rallies to raise awareness of juvenile delinquency in the local Asian American community."

SORIANO, LORENA.il. The Great Pj Elf Chase. See Lo-Bello, K.

SORKIN, MICHAEL, 1948-.ed. The architecture of change. See The architecture of change

SOTO, GARY, 1952-. Accidental love; [by] Gary Soto 179 2006 Harcourt
1. Hispanic Americans—Fiction 2. Love stories 3. School stories 4. Self-realization 5. Young adult literature—Works
ISBN 0-15-205497-9
LC 2004--29900

SUMMARY: In this book by Gary Soto, "Marisa is in her first year of high school, a little overweight and always ready to pick a fight. After punching her best friend's cheating boyfriend in an elevator, she gets home to find she has someone else's cell phone-and realizes she must have switched phones with the nerdy kid who was in the elevator with them. When she meets Rene, she immediately notices his white socks and flood pants, and yet, she can't help wanting to hang around him." (Kirkus Reviews)

REVIEW: *Booklist* v110 no2 p80 S 15 2013 Heather Booth

"Accidental Love." "[Barrie] Kreinik is generous in her portrayal of Marisa, warts and all, by giving her a soft and gentle vibe, although the rough edges Marisa shows to others emerge in dialogue and self-talk scenes laced with Spanish slang. Rene is portrayed with a charming earnestness that seems almost too earnest at times, but this matches descriptions of the 'genuine nerd' chess player, who attends a magnet school. Kreinik lowers her voice for other males, giving teens and adults gender-appropriate tones. This gentle romance, which shows the importance of overlooking first impressions, is a comfortable listen."

REVIEW: *SLJ* v59 no9 p64 S 2013 Toby Rajput

SOTO, SONIA.tr. Winter in Lisbon. See Muñoz Molina, A.

SOUAID, CAROLYN MARIE.ed. Language matters. See Language matters

SOUEIF, AHDAF. Cairo; memoir of a city transformed; [by] Ahdaf Soueif 256 p. 2013 Pantheon Books

1. Memoirs
ISBN 9780307908100
LC 2013-003190

SUMMARY: This book presents author Ahdaf Soueif's account of the Egyptian revolution of 2011. It comprises "her diary of the decisive first 18 days, which is followed by accounts tracking later events during the year, such as the elections. Her grown children and nephews and nieces raced home. . . .They participated in spontaneous street demonstrations and provided aid to protestors, as well as setting up film and Internet stations." (Publishers Weekly)

REVIEW: *Bookforum* v20 no4 p38 D 2013/Ja 2014 HUSSEIN IBISH

"Cairo: Memoir of a City Transformed." "Stylistically, her book is a mash-up of genres. It includes detours into confessional personal memoir as well as stretches of quasi political reportage. It is primarily structured around entries from a daily diary that lapse all too often into purely mundane personal detail. . . . These passages are linked together by . . . forays into social commentary that only gain full traction in Cairo's outstanding postscript. . . . While the book's individual parts can make for an incomplete and frustrating vantage . . . Cairo is nonetheless greater than the sum of its diary entries. It offers an invaluable window into the mind-set of a large proportion of the engaged Egyptian population."

REVIEW: *Booklist* v110 no6 p10 N 15 2013 Margaret Flanagan

REVIEW: *Kirkus Rev* v81 no22 p9 N 15 2013

REVIEW: *Publ Wkly* v260 no30 p52 Jl 29 2013

SOUTHALL, ROGER. Liberation Movements in Power; Party and State in Southern Africa; [by] Roger Southall xv, 384 p. 2013 James Currey Ltd

1. National liberation movements—Namibia 2. National liberation movements—South Africa 3. National liberation movements—Zimbabwe 4. Political science literature
ISBN 1847010660; 9781847010667
LC 2013-431508

SUMMARY: "This work comparatively chronicles the progress of liberation movements in South Africa (African National Congress), Namibia (South West Africa People's Organization), and Zimbabwe (Zimbabwe African National Union--Patriotic Front, ZANU-PF) from challengers. [Roger] Southall argues that following the collapse of the settler regimes, the liberation movements gained power through democratic elections only to establish 'political machine' type of governance." (Choice: Current Reviews for Academic Libraries)

REVIEW: *Choice* v51 no6 p1087-8 F 2014 R. M. Fulton

"Liberation Movements in Power: Party and State in Southern Africa." "[Roger] Southall . . . writes extensively on Southern Africa and is editor of the Journal of Contemporary African Studies. . . . With meticulous detail and extensive documentation, Southall analyzes the theoretical and political environment of Southern Africa and the growth and development of the liberation movements. The thesis of the work is that the liberation movements are slowly succumbing to the complexities of the societies they have tried to mold and their own corruption. . . . Highly recommended."

SOUTHERDEN, FRANCESCA. Landscapes of desire in the poetry of Vittorio Sereni; [by] Francesca Southerden xii, 291 p. 2012 Oxford University Press

1. Desire in literature 2. Liminality in literature 3. Literature—History & criticism 4. Self in literature
ISBN 0199698457; 9780199698455
LC 2011-939889

SUMMARY: This book by Francesca Southerden looks at "Vittorio Sereni (1913-83), one of the major figures of Italian twentieth-century poetry. It argues that a key innovation of Sereni's poetry is constituted in the way in which . . . he reworks the boundaries of poetic space to construct a lyric 'I' radically repositioned in the textual universe with respect to its predecessors: an 'I' that is decentred, in limine, and struggles to subordinate the world to its point of view." (Publisher's note)

REVIEW: *TLS* no5766 p9 O 4 2013 PETER ROBINSON

"Through the Looking Glass: Landscapes of Desire in the Poetry of Vittorio Sereni." "[Francesca] Southerden's closely researched account of [Vittorio] Sereni's affinities with Eugenio Móntale, Petrarch and Dante treats them in a reverse chronological sequence. . . . Only thirty-five of Sereni's some 170 poems are discussed. Southerden makes no mention of works from 'Stella variablie' (1981) that address Sereni's wife ('Di tagho e cucito') and daughters Silvia ('Crescita') and Giovanna ('Giovanna e i Beaties'), or his granddaughter Laura ('Sara noia')."

SOUTHERN LIGHT; Images from Antarctica; 306 p. 2013 Abbeville Press

1. Antarctic Peninsula (Antarctica) 2. East Antarctica (Antarctica) 3. Macquarie Island (Tas.) 4. Photography of polar regions 5. Ross Sea (Antarctica) 6. South Georgia (South Georgia & South Sandwich Islands)
ISBN 0789211556; 9780789211552

SUMMARY: "Between 1990 and 2009, veteran wilderness photographer David Neilson made six journeys to Antarctica and the subantarctic, in a quest to capture the exquisite light of these southernmost lands. This oversized volume presents . . . his efforts; its 130 color and 100 duotone plates portray . . . the Antarctic Peninsula; . . . East Antarctica; the Ross Sea region . . . ; and the subantarctic islands of South Georgia and Macquarie." (Publisher's note)

REVIEW: *N Y Times Book Rev* p8 D 8 2013 REBECCA PEPPER SINKLER

"Southern Light: Images From Antarctica" and "The Last Ocean: Antarctica's Ross Sea Project: Saving the Most Pristine Ecosystem on Earth." "'Southern Light' is a blast of beauty. . . . [Author] David Neilson, an Australian photographer, spreads before us myriad majestic peaks and plains in images that seem lit from within. . . . 'The Last Ocean' uses images as the hook to pull us more deeply into the science, lore and heroic history of the place and its people. [Author] John Weller is alarmed by never preachy. It helps that he is as fine a writer as he is a photographer. . . . He goes to intrepid lengths to get his underwater images."

SOWERBY, SCOTT. Making toleration; the repealers and the Glorious Revolution; [by] Scott Sowerby 404 p. 2013 Harvard University Press

1. Historical literature 2. Religion and politics—Great Britain—History—17th century 3. Religion and state—England—History—17th century 4. Religious tolerance—England—History—17th century

ISBN 9780674073098

LC 2012-034734

SUMMARY: This book by Scott Sowerby "turns traditional interpretations of the rise of religious toleration and the reign of James II on their heads. Sowerby reconstructs the repealer movement from a variety of printed and archival sources, demonstrating that the Glorious Revolution of 1688 was, in fact, a counter-revolutionary movement opposing the political movement for toleration of nonconformists that James himself sponsored." (Choice)

REVIEW: *Choice* v50 no12 p2303 Ag 2013 J. W. McCormack

REVIEW: *TLS* no5750 p28 Je 14 2013 JONATHAN CLARK

"Making Toleration: The Repealers and the Glorious Revolution." "Scott Sowerby's able and important work, drawn from an impressive array of primary sources, tells a story quite different from the. conventional, but still repeated, version of this short reign. . . . Sowerby is clear in his verdict: the Revolution 'was not primarily a crisis provoked by political repression. It was, in fact, a conservative counter-revolution against the movement for enlightened reform that James himself encouraged and sustained'."

SPAGNOL, ESTELLE BILLON. Little Benguin; 32 p. 2014 Holiday House

1. Animal stories 2. Animals—Fiction 3. Bullying—Juvenile fiction 4. Individuality—Fiction 5. Racially mixed children

ISBN 9780823429349 (hardcover)

LC 2013-008049

SUMMARY: In this book, "hatched from the happy, mixed-species union of penguin (dad) and rabbit (mom)—Little Benguin greets the world—only to be instantly rejected. . . . Unispecies age mates jeer at his looks; his self-esteem plummets ('I am an alien. I am a monster'); his parents worry uselessly. He longs to be 'normal.' When a hungry wolf shows up, Little Benguin leads him away, using super-skills—running, swimming—his mixed-species heritage has given him." (Kirkus Reviews)

REVIEW: *Booklist* v110 no14 p82 Mr 15 2014 Connie Fletcher

REVIEW: *Kirkus Rev* v82 no3 p160 F 1 2014

"Little Benguin". "Manifestly good intentions and charming illustrations can't rescue this high-concept, lead-footed tale, burdened with wince-inducing subtext. . . . Throughout, the plot relies on dated, offensive plant- and animal-breeding stereotypes. . . . (Disconnected from the grim content, the sunny art seems to have wandered in from a different story.) Questions are begged: Why is it assumed that being mixed will prompt universal rejection? What if the wolf hadn't shown up? Why is it up to Little Benguin to prove himself acceptable to the majority? Who gets to define what is 'normal'? Tackling xenophobia, racial and otherwise, in a picture book is a worthy goal, but replacing negative with positive stereotypes doesn't achieve it."

REVIEW: *Publ Wkly* v260 no52 p49-51 D 23 2013

REVIEW: *SLJ* v60 no3 p126 Mr 2014 Jenna Boles

SPANIER, SANDRA.ed. The Letters of Ernest Hemingway. See Hemingway, E.

SPARGO, R. CLIFTON. Beautiful Fools; The Last Trip of Zelda and Scott Fitzgerald; [by] R. Clifton Spargo 368 p. 2013 Penguin Group USA

1. Authors—Travel 2. Cuba—Fiction 3. Fitzgerald, F. Scott (Francis Scott), 1896-1940 4. Fitzgerald, Zelda, 1900-1948 5. Historical fiction

ISBN 1468304925; 9781468304923

SUMMARY: This historical novel about F. Scott Fitzgerald and Zelda Fitzgerald "focuses on the pair's ill-fated final trip to Cuba--the last of the Fitzgeralds' parties. The known details of the Cuban trip are sparse. Fitzgerald drank heavily and was badly beaten up when he tried to stop a cockfight. Zelda, despite being barely able to care for herself, brought him home to a hospital in New York. It was the last time they ever saw one another." (Times Literary Supplement)

REVIEW: *Booklist* v109 no17 p69 My 1 2013 Cynthia-Marie O'Brien

REVIEW: *Kirkus Rev* v81 no6 p322 Mr 15 2013

REVIEW: *TLS* no5749 p17-8 Je 7 2013 PAULA BYRNE

"Melting the Snow on Hester Street," "Z: A Novel of Zelda Fitzgerald," and "Beautiful Fools: The Last Affair of Zelda and Scott Fitzgerald." "[Daisy] Waugh creates the early Hollywood world with verve and conviction in this taut, clever and moving novel. . . . Capturing that voice is no easy feat and [Therese Anne] Fowler does not succeed. Nor does she believe that Zelda was insane, although a cursory glance at the family lineage reveals a long history of mental illness and suicide on both sides. . . . To underplay this, as Fowler's novel does, is to deny her painful and courageous struggle to come to terms with her pitiful condition. . . . R. Clifton Spargo's 'Beautiful Fools' . . . is historical fiction at its best, imaginatively filling the gaps and bringing us intimately into a portrait of a marriage."

SPARKS, SIMON.tr. Proust as philosopher. See Proust as philosopher

SPARROW, ELIZABETH. Phantom of the Guillotine; The Real Scarlet Pimpernel, Louis Bayard - Lewis Duval 1769

- 1844; [by] Elizabeth Sparrow 264 p. 2013 Carn Press

1. Bayard, Louis 2. Biography (Literary form) 3. France—History—Revolution, 1789-1799 4. Napoleonic Wars, 1800-1815 5. Spies—History

ISBN 095764650X; 9780957646506

SUMMARY: This book presents a biography of "Louis Bayard . . . one of the most important French spies of the Revolutionary and Napoleonic eras who led a life of adventure privileged access and ultimately treachery. Elizabeth Sparrow . . . believes Bayard to have been a double if not triple agent, but by the end of this . . . study she provides enough evidence to convict him of being that rarest of beasts a quadtriple agent." (History Today)

REVIEW: *Hist Today* v64 no1 p65 Ja 2014 Andrew Roberts

" Phantom of the Guillotine: The Real Scarlet Pimpernel: Louis Bayard-Lewis Duval 1769-1844." "Elizabeth Sparrow believes Bayard to have been a double if not triple agent, but by the end of this well-researched study she provides enough evidence to convict him of being that rarest of beasts a quadruple agent. . . . Inevitably with espionage history. Sparrow is occasionally forced to rely on what she calls credible speculation. Yet pieces of paperwork that spy agencies do tend to retain are expenses claims and receipts for the vast wads of cash secretly handed over--what Bayard called 'the delicacy' --and which Sparrow has put to good detective use."

SPEARING, A. C. Medieval autographies; the "I" of the text; [by] A. C. Spearing viii, 347 p. 2012 University of Notre Dame Press

1. Autobiography in literature 2. English literature—Middle English, 1100-1500—History and criticism 3. First person narrative 4. Literary critiques 5. Medieval poetry

ISBN 0268017824 (pbk. : alk. paper); 9780268017828 (pbk. : alk. paper); 9780268092801 (ebook)

LC 2012-030897

SUMMARY: In this book, author "A. C. Spearing develops a new engagement of narrative theory with medieval English first-person writing, focusing on the roles and functions of the 'I' as a shifting textual phenomenon, not to be defined either as autobiographical or as the label of a fictional speaker or narrator. Spearing identifies and explores a previously unrecognized category of medieval English poetry, calling it 'autography.'" (Publisher's note)

REVIEW: *Choice* v50 no11 p2016 Jl 2013 D. W. Hayes

REVIEW: *TLS* no5750 p24 Je 14 2013 HELEN COOPER

Medieval Autographies: The 'I' of the Text." "The core argument of his book--at places it becomes almost a polemic--is that scholars of medieval literature have too often mistaken this 'supergenre' for autobiography, whether nonfictional (as with [Geoffrey] Chaucer's follower Thomas Hoccleve) or as a full fictional simulacrum. . . . If it seems that that might leave literary critics with rather little to say, they could find abundant compensation by becoming as accurate and nuanced readers as [A. C.] Spearing is, and it would be a very good exchange."

SPEECH BEGINS AFTER DEATH; 81 p. 2013 University of Minnesota Press

1. LITERARY CRITICISM—Semiotics & Theory 2. PHILOSOPHY—General 3. Philosophical literature 4. Writing—Philosophy—Interviews

ISBN 9780816683208 (hardback)

LC 2012-043834

SUMMARY: This book presents an interview with theorist Michel Foucault by critic Claude Bonnefoy. "Bonnefoy wanted a dialogue with Foucault about his relationship to writing rather than about the content of his books. . . . In this . . . exchange, Foucault reflects on how he approached the written word throughout his life, from his school days to his discovery of the pleasure of writing." (Publisher's note)

REVIEW: *TLS* no5746 p27 My 17 2013 NEIL BADMINGTON

"Speech Begins After Death: In Conversation With Claude Bonnefoy." "'I don't want', Bonnefoy begins, 'to ask you to repeat differently what you've expressed so well in your books.' Seeking instead a 'secret texture', he elicits a surprisingly biographical account of 'the pleasure of writing'. . . . While the book casts new light on Foucault's work, it has been prepared carelessly. . . . More disappointing still is the quality of the translation. . . . Foucault refers often to 'speech' and 'language', and distinguishes firmly between them. Given the nuances in French of 'parole', 'langue' and 'langage', the absence' of the original terms limits the pleasure of reading."

SPEER, ROGER.il. A Warrior's Path. See Ashura, D.

SPELLBERG, DENISE A. Thomas Jefferson's Qur'an; Islam and the founders; [by] Denise A. Spellberg viii, 392 p. 2013 Alfred A. Knopf

1. Constitutional history—United States 2. Freedom of religion—United States—History—18th century 3. Historical literature 4. Islam and politics—United States 5. Muslims—Civil rights—United States—History—18th century

ISBN 0307268225; 9780307268228 (hardcover); 9780307388391 (pbk.)

LC 2013-010153

SUMMARY: Author Denise A. Spellberg "recounts how a handful of the Founders, [Thomas] Jefferson foremost among them, drew upon Enlightenment ideas about the toleration of Muslims (then deemed the ultimate outsiders in Western society) to fashion out of what had been a purely speculative debate a practical foundation for governance in America. In this way, Muslims, who were not even known to exist in the colonies, became the imaginary outer limit for an unprecedented, uniquely American religious pluralism." (Publisher's note)

REVIEW: *Booklist* v110 no2 p18-9 S 15 2013 Brenan Driscoll

REVIEW: *Choice* v51 no6 p1079 F 2014 M. S. Hill

REVIEW: *Kirkus Rev* v81 no18 p131 S 15 2013

REVIEW: *Kirkus Rev* v81 no16 p271 Ag 15 2013

"Thomas Jefferson's Qur'an: Islam and the Founders." "[Author Denise A.] Spellberg . . . is straightforward about Jefferson's numerous contradictions of thought throughout his political career. . . . In this fascinating and timely study, Spellberg exposes the early American views about Muslims. . . . Spellberg reveals Jefferson's tortuous thought processes regarding religious freedom, as he could not envision how the 'universal' legislation regarding liberty of conscience could extend to the West African slaves, who happened to be the only Muslims in America at the time. . . . Meticulous research and a well-structured text combine in this important study of the early American political leaders and their convictions regarding religious and social tolerance."

REVIEW: *N Y Times Book Rev* p17 N 17 2013 KIRK DAVIS SWINEHART

REVIEW: *New Repub* v244 no26 p46-9 Ap 21 2014 Abbas Milani

"Thomas Jefferson's Qur'an: Islam and the Founders." "Jefferson would have commended [author Denise A.] Spellberg for unearthing a fascinating moment of American history and for showing how the Founding Fathers defended the rights of a minority that they knew little about. Yet it is not less important to remember that the Founding Fathers, and Jefferson in particular, made no effort to stop the publication of sometimes scurrilous books. . . . His message is that any society that wants democracy . . . must limit the realm of religion in public life."

REVIEW: *New Yorker* v89 no39 p69-1 D 2 2013

REVIEW: *Publ Wkly* v260 no38 p75-6 S 23 2013

SPELLER, ELIZABETH. The First of July; [by] Elizabeth Speller 352 p. 2013 W W Norton & Co Inc

1. Historical fiction 2. Military personnel—Fiction 3. Somme, 1st Battle of the, France, 1916 4. War stories 5. World War, 1914-1918—Fiction

ISBN 1605984973; 9781605984971

SUMMARY: This book, by Elizabeth Speller, "tracks the life experiences of four disparate Allied soldiers fighting in the bloody Battle of the Somme. The four soldiers encounter each other on occasion [and] each young man is swept into the First World War's maelstrom and serves in a different capacity." (Publisher's note)

REVIEW: *Booklist* v110 no4 p21 O 15 2013 Jen Baker

"The First of July." "Utterly gripping and completely immersing, [Elizabeth] Speller's historical novel of WWI captures the experience of four very different young men during the war's early years, leading up to one of the grimmest campaigns, the Battle of the Somme. . . . Elegant writing steeped in atmospheric realism describes a journey undertaken by men with a mistrustful reluctance. The moody, melancholy tone of the novel is signature for Speller. . . . Gritty, disturbing, moody, and intensely real, the novel's psychological impact is like those of Mary Doria Russell's 'A Thread of Grace' (2005) and Denis Johnson's 'Tree of Smoke' (2007) and asks readers to consider war's high costs. Great book-club fare."

REVIEW: *Kirkus Rev* v81 no19 p152 O 1 2013

REVIEW: *Libr J* v138 no18 p83 N 1 2013 Mara Bandy

REVIEW: *Publ Wkly* v260 no32 p28-9 Ag 12 2013

SPENCER-FLEMING, JULIA. Through the Evil Days; a Clare Fergusson/Russ van Alstyne mystery; [by] Julia Spencer-Fleming 368 p. 2013 Minotaur Books

1. Detective & mystery stories 2. Episcopalians—Fiction 3. FICTION—Mystery & Detective—Women Sleuths 4. Fergusson, Clare (Fictitious character)—Fiction 5. Missing persons—Fiction 6. Murder—Investigation—Fiction 7. Police chiefs—Fiction 8. Van Alstyne, Russ (Fictitious character)—Fiction 9. Women clergy—Fiction

ISBN 0312606842; 9780312606848 (hardback)

LC 2013-025276

SUMMARY: In this book, by Julia Spencer-Fleming, "newly married (and pregnant) Episcopal priest Clare Fergusson and Miller's Kill Police Chief Russ van Alstyne are grateful for the solitude of their ice-fishing honeymoon. . . . But soon after they arrive, a snowstorm begins burying the region. As the honeymooners make preparations to depart, . . . Miller's Kill is left without Russ to solve the murders of local foster parents and the disappearance of their foster child." (Booklist)

REVIEW: *Booklist* v110 no2 p36 S 15 2013 Christine Tran

"Through the Evil Days." "This novel, the eighth starring Glare Fergusson and Russ van Alstyne, is among the best in the series, combining steady action with complex, sympathetic characters and an immersive setting. Glare and Russ are an unusual but fitting pair, and [Julia] Spencer-Fleming perfectly captures the contrasting emotions of love and frustration that define marriage. Readers seeking tales of city crime reaching small towns will love the well-crafted setting and story but shouldn't expect a cozy; there's plenty of grit here."

REVIEW: *Booklist* v110 no13 p31 Mr 1 2014 Renee Young

REVIEW: *Kirkus Rev* v81 no22 p38 N 15 2013

REVIEW: *Libr J* v139 no3 p60 F 15 2014 Donna Bachowski

REVIEW: *N Y Times Book Rev* p27 D 1 2013 MARILYN STASIO

REVIEW: *Publ Wkly* v260 no37 p29 S 16 2013

SPENCER, ELIZABETH. Starting Over; Stories; [by] Elizabeth Spencer 208 p. 2014 Liveright

1. Divorce—Fiction 2. Families—Fiction 3. Parent & child—Fiction 4. Short stories 5. Weddings—Fiction

ISBN 0871406810; 9780871406811 (hardcover)

LC 2013-033483

SUMMARY: In this short story collection, author Elizabeth Spencer explores "the deep emotional fault lines and unseen fractures that lie just beneath the veneer of happy family life. In 'Sightings,' a troubled daughter suddenly returns to the home of the father she accidently blinded during her parents' bitter separation; in 'Blackie,' the reappearance of a son from a divorcee's first marriage triggers a harrowing confrontation with her new family." (Publisher's note)

REVIEW: *Booklist* v110 no6 p22 N 15 2013 Brad Hooper

"Starting Over." "[Elizabeth] Spencer's first work of fiction . . . was published in 1948, and, as affirmed by her new collection of short fiction, these many years have not dulled the sharpness of her prose nor inched her into out-of-date perceptions of the world. Grand dame of southern letters that Spencer is, she remains a vital, passionate, contemporary-issues writer. She writes especially well about lives ostensibly like anyone's neighbors, but, like everyone's neighbors, peculiarities lurk behind closed doors. . . . Each story has superb qualities of artistry and social relevance."

REVIEW: *Kirkus Rev* v81 no22 p195 N 15 2013

REVIEW: *Libr J* v139 no1 p1 Ja 2014

REVIEW: *N Y Rev Books* v61 no9 p26-8 My 22 2014 Michael Gorra

REVIEW: *N Y Times Book Rev* p9 Ja 12 2014 MALCOLM JONES

"Starting Over: Stories." "Given that [author Elizabeth]

Spencer is 92, it's tempting to call the title audacious, but since there seems to be nothing this extraordinary writer can't do, maybe she's just being realistic. Like most of her work, the nine stories in this collection are set in the South, and they concentrate on families, most from small towns, and the bonds that characterize, constrict and sometimes sustain the people who claim kin with one another. Spencer recounts the details and doings of her characters in such spare, unfussy, almost conversational prose that she sounds at first like nothing no much as a shrewd family storyteller."

REVIEW: *N Y Times Book Rev* p22 Ja 19 2014

REVIEW: *New York Times* v163 no56397 pC7 Ja 30 2014 John Williams

REVIEW: *Publ Wkly* v260 no42 p30 O 21 2013

SPENCER, SALLY. Blackstone and the Endgame; [by] Sally Spencer 192 p. 2013 Severn House Pub Ltd

1. Detective & mystery stories 2. Historical fiction 3. Intelligence service—Fiction 4. Police—Fiction 5. Russia—Fiction

ISBN 0727882899; 9780727882899

SUMMARY: In this book, by Sally Spencer, "the new head of Special Branch . . . tells [Sam] Blackstone to deliver £25,000 in cash to a German known only as Max in exchange for information on U-boats. Max has asked for Blackstone by name, and he's forbidden Blackstone to have any backup. As Blackstone fears, the exchange late one night at a London dockyard doesn't come off as planned. Now a fugitive, Blackstone embarks on an unlikely journey that reunites him with a Russian spy from a previous outing." (Publishers Weekly)

REVIEW: *Booklist* v110 no2 p32 S 15 2013 Emily Melton

"Blackstone and the Endgame." "A broken man, he's living rough when an old acquaintance from his past, the mysterious Vladimir, comes to his rescue, offering to take [Sam] Blackstone to Russia until thirds cool down. Blackstone is sure there's a catch, especially since Russia is on the brink of revolution, with Czar Nicholas losing his power. But even Blackstone's vivid imagination cannot predict the horrifying and incredible things that will happen while he's in St. Petersburg--things that will ultimately lead to an astonishing discovery. [Sally] Spencer has outdone herself in this latest Blackstone adventure. With its vivid characters, far-fetched but compelling plot, and fanciful twists, it's a gripping page-turner that will appeal to a wide range of fans."

REVIEW: *Kirkus Rev* v81 no19 p176 O 1 2013

REVIEW: *Publ Wkly* v260 no36 p40 S 9 2013

SPENCER, SALLY. Death's Dark Shadow; a DCI Paniatowski mystery; [by] Sally Spencer 208 p. 2014 Severn House Pub Ltd

1. Detective & mystery stories 2. Franco, Francisco, 1892-1975 3. Murder investigation—Fiction 4. Spain—Fiction 5. Spain—History—Civil War, 1936-1939

ISBN 072788347X; 9780727883476

SUMMARY: In this book, by Sally Spencer, "before she can even begin to track down the killer of the old woman dumped by the lonely canal, Monika Paniatowski needs to find out who she is--and no one seems to know. Even when her daughter Louisa provides the vital clue, it only makes life more difficult, because the Chief Constable--intent on making Paniatowski's life difficult--refused to let her follow the obvious trail." (Publisher's note)

REVIEW: *Booklist* v110 no9/10 p50 Ja 1 2014 Emily Melton

"Death's Dark Shadow." "Despite DCI Monika Paniatowski being a more than worthy successor to DCI 'Cloggin' It' Charlie Woodend when he retires, fans of the likable curmudgeon will be delighted that Charlie makes an encore appearance in [Sally] Spencer's latest. . . . The plot shows just how ruthless Franco was and what horrors his regime perpetrated--horrors that have echoed down through the years and resulted in the Whitebridge murder case Monika is trying to solve. . . . A final bombshell will leave readers shocked in this brutal, dark, gripping, and sometimes touching tale that is Spencer at her very best. A must-read."

REVIEW: *Kirkus Rev* v82 no4 p311 F 15 2014

"Death's Dark Shadow". "A family trip to Spain has far-reaching consequences for DCI Monika Paniatowski. . . . She's been on her boss's bad list ever since Chief Constable George Baxter's wife, who was pathologically jealous of Monika, killed herself in a car crash. Now the pressure to find Elena's killer is intense. Monika knows that Elena was in England to see Robert Martinez, Whitebridge's first-ever Hispanic MP. But she suspects that the roots of Elena's murder date back to her involvement with anti-Franco forces in Spain. . . . What looks like an open-and-shut case ends with twists nobody will see coming in Spencer's most in-your-face outing for Monika yet."

REVIEW: *Libr J* v139 no4 p74 Mr 1 2014 Teresa L. Jacobsen

REVIEW: *Publ Wkly* v261 no4 p173 Ja 27 2014

SPERBER, JONATHAN. Karl Marx; a nineteenth-century life; [by] Jonathan Sperber 512 p. 2013 W W Norton & Co Inc

1. Biographies 2. Communists—Germany—Biography 3. Journalists—Biography 4. Philosophers—Germany—Biography

ISBN 0871404672; 9780871404671 (hardcover)

LC 2012-044951

SUMMARY: This book by Jonathan Sperber is a biography of "Karl Marx, the German philosopher and political firebrand turned London émigré journalist. . . . Sperber demonstrates that Marx had more in common with Robespierre than with twentieth-century Communists. Using the complete Marx and Engels database . . . Sperber juxtaposes the private man against the public agitator who helped foment the 1848-49 Revolution and whose incendiary books inflamed the dissident world of Europe." (Publisher's note)

REVIEW: *Booklist* v109 no11 p7 F 1 2013 Gilbert Taylor

REVIEW: *Choice* v50 no12 p2306 Ag 2013 S. Bailey

REVIEW: *Harper's Magazine* v326 no1955 p96-102 Ap 2013 Terry Eagleton

REVIEW: *Kirkus Rev* v81 no5 p4 Mr 1 2013

REVIEW: *Libr J* v137 no20 p91 D 1 2012 Jessica Moran

REVIEW: *London Rev Books* v35 no10 p17-20 My 23 2013 Richard J. Evans

REVIEW: *N Y Rev Books* v60 no8 p38-40 My 9 2013 John Gray

REVIEW: *Nation* v297 no17 p27-32 O 28 2013 SAM STARK

"Karl Marx: A Nineteenth-Century Life." "How could

such a backward, remote place have shaped an author of 'The Communist Manifesto'? The way Jonathan Sperber answers this question . . . illustrates and vindicates the historical method suggested in his subtitle, showing just how badly we needed a new life of Marx and why it needed to be written by a historian. . . . The idea of a 'nineteenth-century life' determines Sperber's simple and brilliant three-part structure. The titles of its three parts . . . suggest three different stages of life as well as three different ways of relating to history. . . . This elegant form, with its slowly shifting perspective, captures the incredible scale of the changes that Marx lived through without lapsing into the picaresque."

REVIEW: *New Repub* v244 no7 p36-41 My 13 2013 Peter E. Gordon

REVIEW: *New York Times* v162 no56092 p14 Mr 31 2013 JONATHAN FREEDLAND

REVIEW: *New Yorker* v89 no9 p77 Ap 15 2013

REVIEW: *Publ Wkly* v260 no4 p115-21 Ja 28 2013 JESSAMINE CHAN

REVIEW: *Publ Wkly* v259 no43 p51 O 22 2012

SPICER, JOHN. Intervention in the modern UK brewing industry. See Walters, J.

SPIEGELMAN, ART, 1948-. Co-Mix; A Retrospective of Comics, Graphics, and Scraps; [by] Art Spiegelman 120 p. 2013 Farrar Straus & Giroux

1. Art criticism 2. Art literature 3. Artists 4. Comic books, strips, etc. 5. Sendak, Maurice, 1928-2012
ISBN 1770461140; 9781770461147

SUMMARY: This book, "a companion piece to a retrospective exhibition . . . collects some of [Art] Spiegelman's best work spanning nearly six decades along with biographical information and critical essays. The editors trace his career from commercial work for Playboy to his underground, experimental work, including the Raw anthology where he first serialized 'Maus'. . . . The book also features many of Spiegelman's controversial 1990's New Yorker covers and autobiographical comics." (Publishers Weekly)

REVIEW: *Bookforum* v20 no5 p24-5 F/Mr 2014 Christopher Lyon

"Co-Mix: A Retrospective of Comics, Graphics and Scraps," "She Who Tells a Story: Women Photographers From Iran and the Arab World," and "Lumiere Autochrome: History, Technology, and Preservation." "'Co-Mix' . . . perform[s] the jujitsu flip of mimicking a high-art exhibition catalogue in the quintessential low-art medium of comics. . . . Though Shirin Nesbat is well represented and an obvious inspiration for the other eleven younger artists featured, much of this work could be called post-Neshat, because it favors a less fussy approach, and is more narrative driven. . . . A kind of Swiss Army knife of a book, covering not only the Lumière family's pioneering photographic inventions, dating to the mid-1880s, but also the history of color photography and technical details of processes\ and preservation. . . . An essential resource for students and collectors of photography."

REVIEW: *Booklist* v110 no4 p37 O 15 2013 Gordon Flagg

"Co-Mix: A Retrospective of Comics, Graphics, and Scraps." "[Art] Spiegelman is best known for his Pulitzer Prize-winning graphic novel, 'Maus' (1986), but the comics cognoscenti laud him for a five-decade body of work that includes some of the most formally daring efforts the medium has seen. Based on a museum retrospective, this lavish coffee-table compilation encompasses Spiegelman's 1970s commercial work . . . but his comics output is appropriately at the fore. . . . Combining brazen experimentation with lowbrow yuks, Spiegelman pulls off the hat trick of being simultaneously intelligent, graphically compelling, and entertaining."

REVIEW: *World Lit Today* v88 no3/4 p124-5 My-Ag 2014 Rita D. Jacobs

SPIEGELMAN, ART, 1948-.ed. Folklore & fairy tale funnies. See Folklore & fairy tale funnies

SPIELER, MIRANDA FRANCES. Empire and underworld; captivity in French Guiana; [by] Miranda Frances Spieler 284 p. 2011 Harvard University Press

1. Captivity—French Guiana—History 2. Historical literature 3. Marginality, Social—French Guiana—History 4. Minorities—French Guiana—History 5. Political violence—French Guiana—History 6. Power (Social sciences)—French Guiana—History
ISBN 9780674057548 (alk. paper)
LC 2011-017838

SUMMARY: In this book on French Guiana, " Miranda Spieler chronicles the encounter between colonial officials, planters, and others, ranging from deported political enemies to convicts, ex-convicts, vagabonds, freed slaves, non-European immigrants, and Maroons. . . . She finds that at a time when France was advocating the revolutionary principles of liberty, equality, and fraternity, Guiana's exiles were stripped of their legal identities and unmade by law, becoming nonpersons living in limbo." (Publisher's note)

REVIEW: *Am Hist Rev* v119 no1 p223-4 F 2014 John Savage

"Empire and Underworld: Captivity in French Guiana". "Although Miranda Frances Spieler's remarkable book concerns a marginal place, its insights and implications should be of compelling interest to historians across a wide range of subfields and regional specialties. It is precisely because Guiana was such a marginal territory within the French Empire that Spieler is able to articulate a provocative new perspective on central and critical issues, especially how the changing relationship between forms of legal subjectivity and imperial sovereignty shaped the transition from subjecthood to modern citizenship. . . . Refreshingly original, deeply researched, and elegantly argued, Spieler's study could also be seen as a call for further research."

SPIELHAGEN, FRANCES R. Debating single-sex education; separate and equal; [by] Frances R. Spielhagen 2013 Rowman & Littlefield Publishers

1. Education—United States 2. Educational literature 3. Gender differences in education 4. Single sex classes (Education) 5. Single sex schools
ISBN 9781610488693

SUMMARY: The 2nd edition of this book, edited by Frances R. Spielhagen, "provides a balanced summary of the context, concerns, and findings about single sex education in 21st Century United States. . . . This book examines the history of single-sex classes and legislation that has over time evolved to render the reform legal, even though it continues to be subject to public scrutiny. . . . It explains controversial brain-based research and addresses the problem of bullying in single-sex classes." (Publisher's note)

REVIEW: *Choice* v51 no9 p1651 My 2014 L. O. Wilson

"Debating Single-Sex Education: Separate and Equal?". "In this revised and expanded second edition, 11 veteran educators continue the debate on both the efficacy and the value of single-sex education. Beyond the statistical data from Africa and the US, the authors offer case studies, student interviews, and well-aimed comments on the evidence of effectiveness on student achievement. . . . [Frances R.] Spielhagen . . . has done an admirable job of compiling an array of articulate and interesting voices. The ten surprising conclusions in chapter 14, plus the recommendations offered there, are worth the price of the book and are must reads on this topic."

SPIELMANN, YVONNE. Hybrid culture; Japanese media arts in dialogue with the West; viii, 267 p. 2013 MIT Press

1. Art—Japan 2. Art literature 3. Cultural fusion and the arts—Japan 4. Modernity—In art 5. New media art—Japan

ISBN 9780262018371 (hardcover : alk. paper)

LC 2012-014485

SUMMARY: "This book grew out of Yvonne Spielmann's 2005--2006 and 2009 visits to Japan, where she explored the technological and aesthetic origins of Japanese new-media art. . . . Spielmann discovered an essential hybridity in Japan's media culture: an internal hybridity, a mixture of digital-analog connections together with a non-Western development of modernity . . . and external hybridity, produced by the international, transcultural travel of aesthetic concepts." (Publisher's note)

REVIEW: *Art Am* v101 no10 p75 N 2013

"Hybrid Culture: Japanese Media Arts in Dialogue With the West," "Japan's Modern Divide: The Photographs of Hiroshi Hamaya and Kansuke Yamamoto," and "From Post-war to Postmodern: Art in Japan 1945-1989: Primary Documents." "Sharing a high regard for precision, Japanese artists and engineers collaborate in ways that subtly meld Eastern and Western concepts, pure art and technical prowess, futurity and tradition. . . . Japanese photography bifurcated in the 1930s into a documentary stream, represented by Hiroshi Hamaya, and an experimental stream, exemplified by Kansuke Yamamoto. Five essayists discuss the artists' careers, illustrated by some 100 contrasting images. . . . Manifestos, essays and debates from Japan's fervent postwar era appear in English for the first time, accompanied by more than 20 new scholarly articles."

REVIEW: *Choice* v50 no12 p2214 Ag 2013 E. K. Mix

SPILMAN, JOAN. Sansablatt Head; 312 p. 2013 Createspace Independent Pub

1. Fantasy fiction 2. Imaginary places 3. Imagination 4. Middle school students 5. Parent & child—Fiction

ISBN 1482668955; 9781482668957

SUMMARY: This book follows "seventh-grader Alec Mulroon," who "acts out for the attention he doesn't get at home. His father is deceased, and his mother travels the world, concerned mainly with her tan. . . . Alec resents his mother's attempts to buy his affection. Then, incredibly, in the mail he receives a carved wooden head, which soon begins talking to Alec in private, calling itself Sansablatt and telling him fanciful bedtime tales about a place called Quelle." (Kirkus Reviews)

REVIEW: *Kirkus Rev* v82 no3 p24 F 1 2014

"Sansablatt Head". "[Joan] Spilman's playful story will have readers racing for the answer. And even before the magic begins, fiendishly animated prose casts a spell. . . . When Spilman fully unleashes her imagination, the result is often splendid chaos. . . . But perhaps this novel's most miraculous feat is the way it finds tenderness amid the cacophonies of silliness: 'Alec already knew that Sansablatt was quarrelsome, impatient, and demanding. He also knew that he couldn't live without him.' As the world within a world builds in complexity, readers will wonder if any canvas is large enough for Spilman's imagination. A masterfully weird adventure, likely to leave fantasy lovers in awe."

SPINOZA FOR OUR TIME; politics and postmodernity; 125 p. 2013 Columbia University Press

1. Philosophical literature 2. Philosophy—History 3. Political theology 4. Postmodernism (Philosophy)

ISBN 9780231160469 (cloth: alk. paper)

LC 2012-051155

SUMMARY: In this book on Baruch Spinoza, author Antonio Negri "defends his understanding of the philosopher as a proto-postmodernist, or a thinker who is just now, with the advent of the postmodern, becoming contemporary. Negri also connects Spinoza's theories to recent trends in political philosophy, particularly the reengagement with Carl Schmitt's 'political theology,' and the history of philosophy." (Publisher's note)

REVIEW: *Choice* v51 no9 p1607-8 My 2014 M. J. Latzer

"Spinoza For Our Time: Politics and Postmodernity". "This small, attractively produced volume consists of four essays delivered by [Antonio] Negri . . . at various colloquia between 2005 and 2009, as well as an introduction. . . . What is particularly intriguing is his claim that 'the political thought of [Baruch] Spinoza is to be found in his ontology . . . much more than in any parallel or posterior work'. . . . The essays do presume specialist knowledge of Spinoza's metaphysics and his political writings, as well as familiarity with the writings of those thinkers with whom Negri brings Spinoza into dialogue. . . . And while the translation is lucid and elegant, Negri's analysis is subtle and couched in the philosophical grammar of contemporary Continental philosophy."

SPIRES, ASHLEY.il. The Most Magnificent Thing. See Spires, A.

SPIRES, ASHLEY. The Most Magnificent Thing; [by] Ashley Spires 32 p. 2014 Kids Can Press

1. Anger—Juvenile literature 2. Children's stories 3. Dogs—Juvenile fiction 4. Friendship—Juvenile fiction 5. Human-animal relationships—Fiction

ISBN 1554537045; 9781554537044

SUMMARY: "Award-winning author and illustrator Ashley Spires has created a charming picture book about an unnamed girl and her very best friend, who happens to be a dog. The girl has a wonderful idea. . . . But making her magnificent thing is anything but easy, and the girl tries and fails, repeatedly. Eventually, the girl gets really, really mad." (Publisher's note)

REVIEW: *Booklist* v110 no15 p94 Ap 1 2014 Shelle Rosenfeld

REVIEW: *Kirkus Rev* v82 no6 p56 Mr 15 2014

REVIEW: *Publ Wkly* v261 no4 p191 Ja 27 2014

REVIEW: *Quill Quire* v80 no2 p35 Mr 2014 Katherine Pedersen

"The Most Magnificent Thing". "[Ashley] Spires includes some clever visual twists to engage early readers. . . . The text hums with description, as Spires employs a rich vocabulary to tell readers what the girl is up to. . . . The overall impression is positive, but the pace suffers from the flurry of words, and the story is too long and didactic to earn favoured-book status. still, Spire's buddy tale of overcoming obstacles and learning to manage expectations will likely find an appreciative audience, especially in a classroom setting."

REVIEW: *SLJ* v60 no4 p136 Ap 2014 Melissa Smith

SPIRIN, GENNADY.il. The greatest dinosaur ever. See Guiberson, B. Z.

SPOO, ROBERT. Without copyrights; piracy, publishing, and the public domain; [by] Robert Spoo 384 p. 2013 Oxford University Press

1. Copyright—United States—History 2. Copyright, International—History 3. Historical literature 4. Law and literature 5. Publishers & publishing—United States—History

ISBN 9780199927876; 9780199927883

LC 2012-040019

SUMMARY: This book "tells the story of how the clashes between authors, publishers, and literary 'pirates' influenced both American copyright law and literature itself." Author "Robert Spoo recounts efforts by James Joyce, Ezra Pound, Bennett Cerf--the founder of Random House--and others to crush piracy, reform U.S. copyright law, and define the public domain." (Publisher's note)

REVIEW: *Choice* v51 no7 p1310 Mr 2014 J. D. Graveline

"Without Copyrights: Piracy, Publishing, and the Public Domain." "[Robert] Spoo . . . does a masterful job of exploring the intersection between European and American publishing, economics, and copyright law in the late 19th and early 20th centuries. . . . Spoo demonstrates that trade courtesy survived on a 'quiet, subterranean' level. . . . Spoo's book is a must for anyone interested in the history of copyright law or the publishing industry. His clear writing style makes the book accessible to every audience. . . . Highly recommended."

REVIEW: *Libr J* v138 no10 p108 Je 1 2013 Nerissa Kuebrich

REVIEW: *Nation* v297 no16 p34-6 O 21 2013 CALEB CRAIN

"Without Copyrights: Piracy, Publishing, and the Public Domain." "In his new scholarly book 'Without Copyrights,' the legal and literary historian Robert Spoo tells the remarkable tale, which Spoo doesn't necessarily deem a pretty one. . . . Spoo rather sympathizes, in fact, with the character many observers would consider the villain. . . . .Samuel Roth. . . . The aspersions seem to me a bit unfair. . . . Whatever my reservations about Spoo's assessment of [James] Joyce's motives, his account of the case of Joyce v. Roth is careful and definitive."

REVIEW: *TLS* no5789 p3-4 Mr 14 2014 ERIC BULSON

SPOOKYTOOTH, T. S.il. Bone by bone. See Levine, S.

SPOONER, MEAGAN. These broken stars; [by] Meagan Spooner 384 p. 2013 Disney-Hyperion

1. Interplanetary voyages—Fiction 2. Love– Fiction 3. Outer space—Exploration 4. Science fiction 5. Survival—Fiction

ISBN 1423171020; 9781423171027

LC 2013-010334

SUMMARY: In this book by Amie Kaufman and Meagan Spooner, a "massive luxury spaceliner is yanked out of hyperspace and plummets into the nearest planet. Lilac LaRoux and Tarver Merendsen survive. Tarver comes from nothing, a young war hero who learned long ago that girls like Lilac are more trouble than they're worth. But with only each other to rely on, Lilac and Tarver must work together." (Publisher's note)

REVIEW: *Booklist* v110 no5 p62 N 1 2013 Frances Bradburn

REVIEW: *Booklist* v110 no16 p64 Ap 15 2014 Katie Richert

REVIEW: *Bull Cent Child Books* v67 no6 p320 F 2014 Alaine Martaus

"These Broken Stars." "This engaging read offers a compelling survival story andn science fiction adventure with a heavy dose of romance. Narration in alternating points of view gives insight into Tarver and Lilac's miscommunications while allowing readers to revel in the slow burn of their growing attraction. At the same time, brief snippets of Tarver's eventual debrief provide evocative hints about the characters' futures but manage not to spoil any of the plot's twists or surprises. As class-line-crossing lovers and deserted-island stories go, no new ground is being broken here, but the novel brings together a strong mix of familiar tropes and popular storylines for a thoroughly entertaining result."

REVIEW: *Kirkus Rev* v81 no19 p129 O 1 2013

REVIEW: *Libr J* v138 no18 p107 N 1 2013 Dale Farris

REVIEW: *Publ Wkly* v260 no33 p54 Ag 19 2013

REVIEW: *SLJ* v60 no3 p74 Mr 2014 Betsy Davison

REVIEW: *Voice of Youth Advocates* v36 no5 p76 D 2013 Shanna Miles

SPOTSWOOD, JESSICA. Born wicked; [by] Jessica Spotswood 330 p. 2012 G. P. Putnam's Sons

1. American alternate histories (Fiction) 2. Children's literature 3. Family life—New England—Fiction 4. Governesses—Fiction 5. New England—Fiction 6. Sisters—Fiction 7. Witchcraft—New England 8. Witches—Fiction

ISBN 9780399257452 (hardcover)

LC 2011-026818

SUMMARY: This children's book offers an "alternative version of the late nineteenth century, [in which] the Brotherhood rules New England with an iron fist, punishing any hint of witchcraft with death and limiting the fate of young girls to either marriage or the Sisterhood. With her seventeenth birthday just weeks away, Cate Cahill must declare her future intentions in a mandatory ceremony, but she's not prepared to become either a wife or a Sister. Instead, she's determined to keep the promise she made to her dying mother to protect her younger sisters, who, like Cate, happen to be witches." (Bulletin of the Center for Children's Books)

REVIEW: *Booklist* v108 no9/10 p102 Ja 1 2012 Frances Bradburn

REVIEW: *Bull Cent Child Books* v65 no7 p373 Mr 2012 K. Q. G.

"Born Wicked." "In this alternative version of the late nineteenth century, the Brotherhood rules New England with an iron fist, punishing any hint of witchcraft with death and limiting the fate of young girls to either marriage or the Sisterhood. . . . Disorienting in an intriguing kind of way, Spotswood's world is vaguely familiar, and it alludes more than once to current oppressions under certain religious oligarchies. Cate is a product of her times and culture—her belief in the wickedness of both her ability to do magic and her own femininity is authentically drawn, and her reluctance to concede that anything good can come from her gift is heartbreakingly credible."

REVIEW: *Kirkus Rev* v80 no1 p2456 Ja 1 2012

REVIEW: *Publ Wkly* v258 no51 p54 D 19 2011

REVIEW: *SLJ* v58 no4 p176-7 Ap 2012 Janice M. Del Negro

REVIEW: *Voice of Youth Advocates* v35 no1 p81 Ap 2012 Lindsey Weaver

SPRING, JOEL. Common core; a story of school terrorism; [by] Joel Spring 186 p. 2013 CreateSpace Independent Publishing Platform

1. Common Core State Standards 2. Satire 3. School stories 4. Standardized tests 5. Terrorism—Fiction
ISBN 0615873545 (trade pbk: alk. paper); 9780615873541 (trade pbk: alk. paper)
LC 2013-948992

SUMMARY: This book presents "a novel of intrigue centered on standardized school testing. . . . First, the U.S. secretary of education keels over dead at his podium. . . . Second, an explosion rocks the Booker T. Washington Charter School in Cincinnati. . . . During the investigation, the FBI exposes connections among the Cincinnati school system, Brightstone, and Kiwi, a China-based tech company that manufactures computers and tablets loaded with Brightstone testing materials." (Kirkus Reviews)

REVIEW: *Kirkus Rev* v82 no3 p30 F 1 2014

"Common Core: A Story of School Terrorism". "[Joel] Spring . . . starts his over-the-top satirical novel with two plot twists to hook readers. . . . The high-spirited, engaging plot eventually branches into governmental conspiracies, financial misdeeds and international skullduggery—mostly involving scheming Chinese businessmen intent on using Kiwi technology and Brightstone greed to make a killing in the impending global robot-teacher market. The real enemy throughout, however, is the Common Core agenda itself—a stance that educators may find drolly entertaining but may somewhat limit the novel's appeal. A sharp, tongue-in-cheek adventure set in a world of testing run amok."

SPRUILL, MATT. Summer Lightning; A Guide to the Second Battle of Manassas; [by] Matt Spruill 324 p. 2013 The University of Tennessee Press

1. Bull Run, 2nd Battle of, Va., 1862 2. Guidebooks 3. Historical literature 4. United States—History—Civil War, 1861-1865—Battlefields 5. United States—Military history
ISBN 9781572339989 (pbk.)
LC 2013-018590

SUMMARY: This book on the 1862 Second Battle of Manassas is a "battlefield guide that sequentially follows the fighting from Brawner's Farm on August 28 to the final Confederate attacks against Union positions at Henry Hill on August 30. 'Summer Lightning' uses a series of twenty 'stops' with multiple positions to guide the reader through the battlefield and to positions and routes used by both armies, thus providing a 'you are there' view of the engagement." (Publisher's note)

REVIEW: *Choice* v51 no7 p1194-5 Mr 2014 B. S. Exton

"Summer Lightning: A Guide to the Second Battle of Manassas." "This volume is a guided tour of the Second Battle of Manassas, or Second Battle of Bull Run, which took place August 28-30, 1862. The book does not follow the National Parks Service's map of battlefield tour stops, but has created stops based on the chronological order of the battle. . . . This reviewer has not been to the battlefield described here, but recommends the book as a very in-depth guide for Civil War scholars and enthusiasts as well as academic and public libraries with Civil War sections."

SPRUNK, JON. Blood and iron; [by] Jon Sprunk 445 p. 2014 Pyr

1. FICTION—Fantasy—Epic 2. FICTION—Fantasy—General 3. Imaginary wars and battles 4. Magic—Fiction 5. Slavery—Fiction
ISBN 9781616148935 (pbk.)
LC 2013-037702

SUMMARY: In this book, "Ship's carpenter Horace is bound for the crusade to fight the Akeshian Empire when a strange storm wrecks the Bantu Ray and Horace finds himself marooned in Erugash, a city-state in Akeshia. He's immediately captured and enslaved; his fortunes and his danger rise during another storm, which reveals that Horace possesses zoana, or elemental magic. Unchained and whisked to Queen Byleth's court, Horace must quickly learn to master his previously unknown magic." (Kirkus Reviews)

REVIEW: *Kirkus Rev* v82 no1 p292 Ja 1 2014

"Blood and Iron". "The assimilation of a white man into a dark-skinned alien culture and his superior mastery of an ability intrinsic to that culture whiffs faintly (and vaguely unpleasantly) of Dances With Wolves or The Last Samurai. And perhaps a bit too much is made of Horace's nobility of character, used to explain why queen's handmaiden (and foreign spy) Alyra and closeted-gay, enslaved soldier Jirom are both so drawn to him. But it's undeniable that this novel is also sheer fun, with engaging, pulse-quickening action, sympathetic characters and intricate intrigue. Despite some flaws, definitely a series to follow."

REVIEW: *Libr J* v139 no3 p78 F 15 2014 Megan M. McArdle

REVIEW: *Publ Wkly* v261 no2 p54 Ja 13 2014

SPUFFORD, FRANCIS. Unapologetic; why, despite everything, Christianity can still make surprising emotional sense; [by] Francis Spufford 221 p. 2013 HarperCollins

1. Apologetics 2. Christian life 3. Emotions (Psychology)—Religious aspects 4. Faith 5. Religious literature
ISBN 0062300458; 9780062300454

SUMMARY: This book, by Francis Spufford, is a "defense

of Christianity. Refuting critics such as Richard Dawkins, Sam Harris, and the 'new atheist' crowd, Spufford, a former atheist and Fellow of the Royal Society of Literature, argues that Christianity is recognizable, drawing on the . . . vocabulary of human feeling, satisfying those who believe in it by offering a ruthlessly realistic account of the grown-up dignity of Christian experience." (Publisher's note)

REVIEW: *Booklist* v110 no2 p6-7 S 15 2013 Christoher McConnell

REVIEW: *Christ Century* v130 no25 p21 D 11 2013

REVIEW: *Christ Today* v57 no8 p67 O 2013 WESLEY HILL

REVIEW: *Commonweal* v140 no19 p34-6 D 6 2013 Paul Elie

"Soil and Sacrament: A Spiritual Memoir of Food and Faith" and "Unapologetic". "The book, about [Fred] Bahnson's efforts to open new portals in the soil, also becomes a soil of sorts where the reader's interior life can find space and light and nourishment with which to grow. . . . I've been describing ['Unapologetic'] to people as an account of Christian belief as David Foster Wallace might have written it, but that's not quite right. It's probably closer to Julian Barnes. . . . Spufford's attention to emotion is original and remarkable. . . . Spufford asks these questions—asks them colorfully and dramatically. I would say his book, beautifully written as it is, reads like a novel, but it doesn't. It is unapologetically not a fiction."

REVIEW: *Kirkus Rev* v81 no17 p71 S 1 2013

REVIEW: *London Rev Books* v35 no2 p26-7 Ja 24 2013 Adam Phillips

REVIEW: *Publ Wkly* v260 no32 p53 Ag 12 2013

REVIEW: *TLS* no5712 p28 S 21 2012 Theo Hobson

SQUIRE, LARRY R. Memory; from mind to molecules; [by] Larry R. Squire 256 2009 Roberts & Co.

1. Biological literature 2. Memory 3. Neurobiology 4. Psychological literature 5. Psychology of learning
ISBN 0981519415; 9780981519418
LC 2008-016888

SUMMARY: "What is memory and where in the brain is it stored? How is memory storage accomplished?" Written by Larry R. Squire and Eric R. Kandel, "This book touches on these questions and many more, showing how the recent convergence of psychology and biology has resulted in an exciting new synthesis of knowledge about learning and remembering." (Publisher's note)

REVIEW: *N Y Rev Books* v61 no9 p23-5 My 22 2014 Jerome Groopman

"Memory: From Mind to Molecules," "The Alzheimer Conundrum: Entanglements of Dementia and Aging," and "The Answer to the Riddle Is Me: A Memoir of Amnesia." "Written in accessible language for a lay reader, [authors Larry R. Squire and Eric R. Kandel] illustrate fundamental discoveries about memory using works of art. . . . [Author Margaret] Lock's question is a fundamental one in all of medicine: Why do some individuals develop full-blown disease and others do not, despite sharing the same causative agent? . . . [Author David Stuart MacLean] collapsed at a train station while traveling in India. . . . MacLean ultimately asserts that Lariam, a drug prescribed to prevent malaria, is the culprit."

ŚRĪPĀL RĀS; 5 volumes (1110 p.) 2011 Harshadray Pvt. Ltd.

1. Jaina art 2. Jaina legends 3. Jaina literature 4. Jainism 5. Legends
ISBN 8192009467 (set); 8192009475 (v. 1); 8192009483 (v. 2); 8192009491 (v. 3); 9788192009469 (set); 9788192009476 (v. 1); 9788192009483 (v. 2); 9788192009490 (v. 3)
LC 2013-407424

SUMMARY: In this illustrated retelling of a Jain legend, edited by Premal Kapadia, "an egotistical King marries off his daughter to a leper as punishment for her refusal to acknowledge his greatness, and for her insistence on seeing all of life's pleasures and pains as the ripening of karma. What appears as a cruel act of a spiteful father turns out to be a cosmic event, and a fantastical tale begins, told in over one thousand two hundred verses." (Journal of the American Academy of Religion)

REVIEW: *J Am Acad Relig* v82 no1 p286-9 Mr 2014 Anne Vallely

"Śrīpāl Rās". "The tale has been published widely, but none with the majesty and dedication (nay, devotion) of the recent publication by Mumbai-based Jain philanthropist and editor of the volume, Premal Kapadia. . . . The legend of a leper who becomes a king is a captivating story of destiny and devotion. . . . The narrative of Śrīpāl Rās meanders over five oversized volumes, interspersed among a treasure of magnificent paintings and border decorations. Not a single page is left unadorned. The experience of reading a book of this size and splendor is unique in that it informs the way the story is received."

ST. CROW, LILI. Wayfarer; a tale of beauty and madness; [by] Lili St. Crow 348 p. 2014 Razorbill, a division of Penguin Young Readers Gropu

1. Characters in literature—Fiction 2. Child abuse—Fiction 3. Fantasy 4. Magic—Fiction 5. Stepfamilies—Fiction
ISBN 1595146202; 9781595146205 (pbk.)
LC 2013-047603

SUMMARY: This novel, by Lili St. Crow, presents a paranormal retelling of the fairy tale of Cinderella. "Newly orphaned, increasingly isolated from her friends, and terrified of her violent stepmother, Ellen Sinder . . . has a plan for surviving and getting through high school. . . . But when a train arrives from over the Waste beyond New Haven, carrying a golden boy and a new stepsister, all of Ellie's plans begin to unravel, one by one." (Publisher's note)

REVIEW: *Bull Cent Child Books* v67 no9 p478 My 2014 K. Q. G.

"Wayfarer: A Tale of Beauty and Madness". "The dark and magical world of this reworking of Cinderella was better established in [Lili] St. Crow's last fairy-tale revision, 'Nameless' . . . and readers unfamiliar with that title might be confused by New Haven and the threat presented by twisted magic. The realistic elements here are more successful than the fantasy ones. . . . Unfortunately, her hesitancy to act makes for an agonizingly slow first half, and her sudden ability to trust the mother of her love interest at the book's conclusion seems more convenient than authentic. Still, the combination of dark magic, a vulnerable heroine, and a handsome hero is likely to please readers reluctant to let go of their copy of Twilight."

ST. GERMAIN, TONIA.ed. Conflict-related sexual violence. See Conflict-related sexual violence

ST. JAMES PRESS.comp. Encyclopedia of global brands. See Encyclopedia of global brands

ST. JOHN, ALLEN. Newton's football; the science behind America's game; [by] Allen St. John 272 p. 2013 Ballantine Books

1. Football 2. POLITICAL SCIENCE—Public Policy—General 3. Physics 4. SCIENCE—Physics 5. SPORTS & RECREATION—Football 6. Sports literature 7. Sports sciences
ISBN 0345545141; 9780345545145 (hardback)
LC 2013-031521

SUMMARY: In this book, authors Allen St. John and Ainissa Ramirez "explore the unexpected science behind [football]. 'Newton's Football' illuminates football—and science—through . . . stories told by some of the world's sharpest minds. St. John and Ramirez address topics that have long beguiled scientists and football fans alike, including: the unlikely evolution of the football, what Vince Lombardi has in common with Isaac Newton [and] how better helmets actually made the game more dangerous." (Publisher's note)

REVIEW: *Booklist* v110 no7 p17 D 1 2013 Bryce Christensen

REVIEW: *Kirkus Rev* v81 no21 p146 N 1 2013

REVIEW: *Publ Wkly* v260 no41 p50-1 O 14 2013

STAALESEN, GUNNAR. Cold Hearts; 300 p. 2013 Dufour Editions

1. Detective & mystery stories 2. Missing persons—Fiction 3. Murder investigation—Fiction 4. Private investigators—Fiction 5. Prostitutes—Fiction
ISBN 1908129433; 9781908129437

SUMMARY: In this book, by Gunnar Staalesen, "social worker turned private investigator Varg Veum" is hired to find a missing prostitute. "He begins exploring multiple avenues: the prostitute's menacing pimp, the pair of violent johns she refused, and the minefield of her troubled childhood. When bodies begin stacking up with connections to all three scenarios, Veum is certain Maggi's disappearance is related, but each clue creates a new layer of questions." (Booklist)

REVIEW: *Booklist* v110 no5 p28 N 1 2013 Christine Tran

"Cold Hearts." "'Cold Hearts' is top-tier Scandinavian crime fiction; straightforward dialogue drives the plot, and tough but sympathetic Veum is equally comfortable in a fistfight, probing for secrets behind Bergen's closed doors, or examining crime's sociological roots. Those attracted to the grudgingly humanistic investigators created by Michael Connelly . . . Anne Holt, and Ken Bruen will embrace Varg Veum. Although this novel can stand alone, some American readers may be frustrated by having to read the series out of order; this is the fourteenth of 20 Varg Veum novels, but only the third released in the U.S."

REVIEW: *Publ Wkly* v260 no36 p40 S 9 2013

STACEY, FRANK D. The earth as a cradle for life; [by] Frank D. Stacey 308 p. 2013 World Scientific

1. Earth sciences—Textbooks 2. Environmental protection 3. Environmental sciences—Textbooks 4. Renewable energy sources 5. Scientific literature
ISBN 9789814508322 (alk. paper)
LC 2013-007925

SUMMARY: This book by Frank D. Stacey and Jane H. Hodgkinson "aims to fill the gap between readers who have a strong and informed scientific interest in the environment (but no access to the journal literature), and their desire for a basic understanding of the environment. . . . It draws attention to observations that have been neglected or discounted for reasons the authors found invalid." (Publisher's note)

REVIEW: *Choice* v51 no6 p1039-40 F 2014 B. M. Simonson

"The Earth as a Cradle for Life: The Origin, Evolution and Future of the Environment." "[Frank D.] Stacey and [Jane H.] Hodgkinson . . . hope to clarify for general audiences how Earth's environments have evolved through deep time to better understand the crises the world currently faces. However, this laudable goal is largely unfulfilled. Before outlining human influences on today's environments in 3 brief chapters, the authors devote 12 chapters to summaries of a broad range of processes they deem necessary as background information. . . . Some claims are even outside the scientific mainstream. . . . There are elegant explanations of some processes, but the treatment is unfocused and too technical for wide appeal."

STACH, REINER. Kafka; the decisive years; vi, 581 p. 2013 Princeton University Press

1. Authors—Relations with women 2. Authors, Austrian—20th century—Biography 3. Biographies 4. Literature—History & criticism
ISBN 0691147418; 9780691147413 (pbk. : acid-free paper)
LC 2013-930936

SUMMARY: This book is the second volume of Reiner Stach's three-part biography of Franz Kafka. "He picks up Kafka's life not in childhood, but in 1910, the fitful beginning of his literary career, and follows it only until 1915. But these were the years when Kafka produced some of his greatest works, including 'The Metamorphosis' and The Trial. We see the writer in all his torments, but also his moments of triumph, however fleeting." (Publishers Weekly)

REVIEW: *N Y Rev Books* v60 no16 p17-9 O 24 2013 John Banville

"Kafka: The Decisive Years," "Kafka: The Years of Insight," and "Franz Kafka: The Poet of Shame and Guilt." "It is to [Saul] Friedländer's credit that he notes 'the ongoing influence of Expressionism' and contemporary works of fantastic literature . . . on Kafka's literary sensibility.. . . . Reiner Stach, in his ongoing biography of Kafka, strives for a similarly intimate knowledge of his subject, and of the time and place in which he lived and worked. Stach is at once highly ambitious and admirably unassuming. . . . On the evidence of the two volumes that we already have, this is one of the great literary biographies."

REVIEW: *New Repub* v244 no26 p36-45 Ap 21 2014 Cynthia Ozick

STACH, REINER. Kafka, the years of insight; 720 p. 2013 Princeton University Press

1. Authors—Family relationships 2. Authors—Health

3. Authors, Austrian—20th century—Biography 4. Biographies
ISBN 0691147515 (hardcover); 9780691147512 (hardcover)
LC 2012-042048

SUMMARY: This book is part of Reiner Stach's three-part biography of author Franz Kafka. This volume "covers the period from 1916 to 1924, his terminal years." Topics include "his father's disapprobation, his job at the Worker's Accident Insurance Institute, his turbulent courtships with Felice Bauer, Milena Jesenská, and Dora Diamant, and finally his encounter with malignant and fatal tuberculosis." (Library Journal)

REVIEW: *Choice* v51 no6 p1009 F 2014 E. Williams

REVIEW: *N Y Rev Books* v60 no16 p17-9 O 24 2013 John Banville

"Kafka: The Decisive Years," "Kafka: The Years of Insight," and "Franz Kafka: The Poet of Shame and Guilt." "It is to [Saul] Friedländer's credit that he notes 'the ongoing influence of Expressionism' and contemporary works of fantastic literature . . . on Kafka's literary sensibility. . . . Reiner Stach, in his ongoing biography of Kafka, strives for a similarly intimate knowledge of his subject, and of the time and place in which he lived and worked. Stach is at once highly ambitious and admirably unassuming. . . . On the evidence of the two volumes that we already have, this is one of the great literary biographies."

REVIEW: *New Repub* v244 no26 p36-45 Ap 21 2014 Cynthia Ozick

STACHNIAK, EVA. Empress of the night; a novel of Catherine the Great; [by] Eva Stachniak 400 p. 2013 Bantam Books
1. Courts & courtiers—Fiction 2. Historical fiction 3. Nobility (Social class)—Fiction 4. Russia—Fiction
ISBN 9780553808131
LC 2013-010159

SUMMARY: In this book, the second in a series by Eva Stachniak, "Catherine the Great suffers a debilitating stroke and reflects back on her life, loves and country. . . . Unbeknownst to those holding vigil, Catherine is still in control of her mental faculties and aware of the activities around her in the hours before she dies. Although she is paralyzed and appears lifeless, she retains her ability to remember her rise from humble beginnings in Prussia." (Kirkus Reviews)

REVIEW: *Kirkus Rev* v82 no4 p295 F 15 2014

"Empress of the Night". "Catherine the Great suffers a debilitating stroke and reflects back on her life, loves and country in [Eva] Stachniak's second in her series . . . about the Russian empress. . . . Although Stachniak creates a noteworthy representation of life at the Russian court during Catherine's rule, she fails to draw readers into the political and personal intrigues. Rather than a vibrant, earthy, intelligent woman, Catherine seems disappointingly mundane, and her court contains an endless succession of names and nicknames with few distinguishing features. An unremarkable account of a remarkable reign."

REVIEW: *Libr J* v139 no3 p98 F 15 2014 Catherine Lantz

REVIEW: *Quill Quire* v80 no3 p28-9 Ap 2014 Patricia Maunder

STACKHOUSE, CHRISTOPHER. Kara Walker. See Als, H.

STADIEM, WILLIAM. Daughter of the King; Growing Up in Gangland; [by] William Stadiem 264 p. 2014 Weinstein Books
1. Criminals—Family relationships 2. Lansky, Meyer 3. Mafia—United States—History 4. Memoirs 5. Organized crime—United States—History
ISBN 160286215X; 9781602862159

SUMMARY: This book presents a memoir by Sandra Lansky, "the child of Mafia kingpin Meyer Lansky and a beautiful but unstable mother. . . . Wealth and glitz couldn't keep away all of life's tragedies: a severely disabled older brother, a chronically depressed mother, a divorce and her father's subsequent marriage to a despised stepmother, and an addiction to diet pills. Then there were the intimations of violence . . . and the whispers of her father's involvement." (Library Journal)

REVIEW: *Booklist* v110 no13 p4-5 Mr 1 2014 David Pitt

"Daughter of the King: Growing Up in Gangland." "This autobiography tells the story of a rich socialite, a party girl who lived in a world of wealth and glitz . . . but whose life was permeated with darkness: a mother suffering from mental illness, a father who wasn't exactly the warmest dad in the world, friends and pseudo-relatives from the criminal world. . . . Everything in the book . . . is filtered through [Sandra Lansky's] perceptions of her father and his world. It's not a crime story, exactly, but it is a fascinating account of a girl and her father, a man who happened to be a criminal."

REVIEW: *Kirkus Rev* v82 no4 p133 F 15 2014

REVIEW: *Libr J* v139 no5 p129 Mr 15 2014 Deirdre Bray

REVIEW: *N Y Times Book Rev* p38 My 11 2014 DOMENICA RUTA

REVIEW: *Publ Wkly* v261 no4 p184 Ja 27 2014

STAFFORD, KIM. 100 tricks every boy can do; how my brother disappeared; [by] Kim Stafford 202 p. 2012 Trinity University Press
1. Authors, American—20th century—Biography 2. Brothers—Oregon—Biography 3. Memoirs
ISBN 1595341366 (pbk.); 9781595341365 (pbk.)
LC 2012-019210

SUMMARY: This book by Kim Stafford presents a "memoir of oss and guilt about the suicide of his beloved brother, Bret, at age forty. . . . Told in small chunks of narrative anecdotes, it becomes both an exhaustive catalog of memories of the brothers' shared moments of intimacy and isolation and a valiant attempt to understand the talented Bret's descent into darkness." (World Literature Today)

REVIEW: *World Lit Today* v87 no5 p76-7 S/O 2013 Marvin J. LaHood

"100 Tricks Every Boy Can Do: How My Brother Disappeared." "Kim Stafford's moving memoir of loss and guilt about the suicide of his beloved brother, Bret, at age forty is brilliantly conceived and fascinatingly written. Told in small chunks of narrative anecdotes, it becomes both an exhaustive catalog of memories of the brothers' shared moments of intimacy and isolation and a valiant attempt to understand the talented Bret's descent into darkness. . . . Kim Stafford spent years thinking this haunting story to its sad end, but like all authors and thinkers and teachers, he did it for others:

his brother, himself, and for all of us. 'For the work of memoir is to put personal memory in a form that may serve the memories of others.' This poignant book will serve well."

STAGING SOCIAL JUSTICE; collaborating to create activist theatre; xxiv, 299 p. 2013 Southern Illinois University Press

1. Community theater—Social aspects 2. Social justice 3. Theater and society 4. Theater—Political aspects 5. Theater literature
ISBN 0809332388 (pbk. : alk. paper); 9780809332380 (pbk. : alk. paper)
LC 2012-039092

SUMMARY: This book, edited by Norma Bowles and Daniel-Raymond Nadon, focuses on "Fringe Benefits, an award-winning theatre company . . . [that] collaborates with schools and communities to create plays that promote constructive dialogue about diversity and discrimination issues." The book describes "Fringe Benefits' script-devising methodology and their collaborations in the United States, Australia, Canada and the United Kingdom." (Publisher's note)

REVIEW: *Choice* v51 no5 p847-8 Ja 2014 M. A. Brennan

"Staging Social Justice: Collaborating to Create Activist Theatre." "Contributors to the present collection explain the democratic process used to elicit the narratives; how to create a safe place for interaction; and how the script is developed. They also provide numerous examples of where this program has been used and the reactions of the facilitators, participants, and community. And they note the challenges in this process. . . . Through this unique form of transformational theater attitudes began to change. A great resource for anyone interested in social justice issues and effective means of addressing them through theater. . . . Highly recommended."

STAINCLIFFE, CATH. Dead to me; [by] Cath Staincliffe 400 p. 2014 Minotaur Books

1. Drug abuse—Fiction 2. FICTION—Mystery & Detective—Police Procedural 3. FICTION—Mystery & Detective—Women Sleuths 4. Murder—Investigation—Fiction 5. Women detectives—Fiction
ISBN 9781250038548 (hardback)
LC 2013-038926

SUMMARY: In this book, "two female detectives form an uneasy partnership in the grim back streets of Manchester. DC Rachel Bailey is thrilled when golden girl DCI Gill Murray invites her to join an elite unit for major crimes. However, the street-wise Bailey is less pleased with her partner, middle-class DC Janet Scott, especially since Scott doesn't hesitate to put Bailey in her place when they investigate the murder of Lisa Finn." (Kirkus Reviews)

REVIEW: *Booklist* v110 no7 p25 D 1 2013 Stacy Alesi

REVIEW: *Kirkus Rev* v82 no1 p188 Ja 1 2014

"Dead to Me". "[Rachel] Bailey, [Janet] Scott and [Gill] Murray all have their own pasts, which affect their judgments and make them more human—but also put the brakes on the pace. A grudging trust between Bailey and Scott provides a stronger payoff for the tale than the solution of the mystery. [Cath] Staincliffe . . . devotes nearly as much attention to her three leads' struggles with their personal lives as she does to the procedural itself. Sympathetic though they are, one keeps wanting them to stop agonizing and just get on with the case."

REVIEW: *Publ Wkly* v260 no44 p49 N 4 2013

STALEY, ERIN. Nick Swinmurn and Tony Hsieh and Zappos; [by] Erin Staley 128 p. 2013 Rosen Publishing

1. Business literature 2. Businesspeople—United States—Biography 3. Electronic commerce—United States—History 4. Entrepreneurship—Moral and ethical aspects
ISBN 9781448895298 (library binding)
LC 2012-040916

SUMMARY: This book on entrepreneurs Nick Swinmurn and Tony Hsieh, by Erin Staley, is part of the Internet Biographies series. After "a few pages covering the early life of each entrepreneur," the book introduces their business, Zappos, and "discusses the popular online shoe business and its employee culture, which emphasizes delivering 'WOW through service.'" (Booklist)

REVIEW: *Booklist* v110 no4 p45 O 15 2013 Susan Dove Lempke

"Nick Swinmurn, Tony Hsieh, and Zappos," "Niklas Zennström and Skype," and "Tim Westergren and Pandora." "The titles in the Internet Biographies series feature people who are far from household names, but the Internet businesses they began should be very familiar to a young adult audience. . . . 'Tim Westergren and Pandora' has an especially lively conversational style and does a good job of helping readers understand the issues facing the Internet radio station. Each book includes color photographs and sidebars on related topics. While not the most exciting reads, these succeed in showing how ordinary people can take a good idea and turn it into a business."

REVIEW: *Voice of Youth Advocates* v36 no6 p84 F 2014 Ursula Adams

STAMP, GAVIN. Anti-ugly; Excursions in English Architecture and Design; [by] Gavin Stamp 272 p. 2013 Motorbooks Intl

1. Architectural literature 2. Architecture—England 3. Design 4. Design literature 5. English architecture
ISBN 1781311234; 9781781311233

SUMMARY: "Since 2004 Gavin Stamp, one of Britain's most eminent and readable architectural historians, has written a monthly column for Apollo, the esteemed architecture and fine art magazine. The subject is simply whatever in design or architecture happens to take his fancy." This book is a collection of those columns. (Publisher's note)

REVIEW: *Apollo: The International Magazine for Collectors* v178 no614 p121 N 2013

"Anti-Ugly: Excursions in English Architecture and Design," "Islamic and Oriental Arms and Armour: A Lifetime's Passion," and "The Image of Venice: Fialetti's View and Sir Henry Wotton." "Some 50 . . . pieces are collected in ['Anti-Ugly'], which focuses on English architecture. A reminder, if one were needed, of [author Gavin] Stamp's . . . wit. . . . After discovering antique weaponry in the mid 1960s, [author] Robert Hales went on to spend almost 30 years as a highly respected dealer. . . . ['Islamic and Oriental Arms and Armour'] reproduces many of the daggers, swords, firearms and armour that passed through his hands. . . . Odoardo Fialetti's early 17th-century view of Venice has spent 400 years in relative obscurity. . . . Its recent restoration and public exhibition have inspired ['The Image of Venice']."

STANARD, MATTHEW G. Selling the Congo; a history of European pro-empire propaganda and the making of Belgian imperialism; [by] Matthew G. Stanard 387 p. 2012 University of Nebraska Press

1. Belgium—Politics & government—20th century 2. Congo (Democratic Republic)—History—1908-1960 3. HISTORY—Africa—Central 4. HISTORY—Europe—Western 5. Historical literature 6. Imperialism—History—20th century 7. POLITICAL SCIENCE—Colonialism & Post-Colonialism 8. Propaganda, Belgian 9. Propaganda, Belgian—History—20th century 10. Public opinion—Belgium—History—20th century
ISBN 9780803237773 (hardback : alk. paper)
LC 2011-023628

SUMMARY: This book "is a study of European pro-empire propaganda in Belgium, with particular emphasis on the period 1908-60. [Author] Matthew G. Stanard questions the nature of Belgian imperialism in the Congo and considers the Belgian case in light of literature on the French, British, and other European overseas empires. Comparing Belgium to other imperial powers, the book finds that pro-empire propaganda was a basic part of European overseas expansion and administration during the modern period." (Publisher's note)

REVIEW: *Am Hist Rev* v118 no4 p1263-4 O 2013 David Ciarlo

"Selling the Congo: A History of European Pro-Empire Propaganda and the Making of Belgian Imperialism." "Despite the vast scholarly literature on imperialism, there is little English-language work on Belgium's relationship to empire. Matthew G. Stanard offers a welcome addition to studies of the imperial metropole. The book offers a survey of 'pro-empire propaganda,' with substantive chapters devoted to imperial expositions, museums of empire, educational/curricular efforts by the colonial office, monuments, and colonial filmmaking. . . . The book is written in a clear and very direct style, which makes it accessible to a broad audience, including undergraduates. Such directness of prose has its costs, however: colonial theory can be oversimplified."

REVIEW: *Choice* v50 no1 p163 S 2012 J. M. Rich

STANDAGE, TOM. Writing on the wall; Social Media - the First 2,000 Years; [by] Tom Standage 288 p. 2013 St. Martin's Press

1. Graffiti 2. Historical literature 3. Mass media & history 4. Social media 5. Social networks
ISBN 1620402831; 9781620402832

SUMMARY: In this book, author Tom Standage "draws comparisons between modern social media and the forms of communication and information dissemination used over 2,000 years to show how, in fact, 'History retweets itself.' Examples include ancient Roman graffiti that bears a strong resemblance to a Facebook status update . . . and Martin Luther's 95 theses, perhaps the first document to go viral." (Publishers Weekly)

REVIEW: *Booklist* v110 no1 p5 S 1 2013 Vanessa Bush

"Writing on the Wall: Social Media--the First 2,000 Years." "[Tom] Standage . . . explores the human impulse to socialize and the earlier technologies, from papyrus to printing press, that accommodated that impulse. Standage offers historical perspective on such concerns about evolving social media as faddishness, coarsening of discourse, distraction from serious work, and erosion of social skills. Still, the social media evolution marched on, influencing politics and religion and aiding revolution in Europe and the Americas. A thoroughly fascinating look at the evolution of social media."

REVIEW: *Kirkus Rev* v81 no14 p231 Jl 15 2013

REVIEW: *N Y Times Book Rev* p21 N 3 2013 FRANK ROSE

"Writing on the Wall: Social Media--The First 2,000 Years." "A provocative book that asks us to look at media less in terms of technology . . . than in terms of the role they invite us to play. . . . This observation has been made before, but never with such a wealth of information to back it up. [Tom] Standage . . . makes a convincing case. . . . Standage gives us a fascinating account of the early days of radio. . . . Even when Standage considers social media on their own terms, he can be a bit short on insight. . . . Nonetheless, Standage makes a crucial point: Social media, whether of the digital or the preindustrial variety, fill a universal human need for connectedness."

STANDIFORD, NATALIE. The secret tree; [by] Natalie Standiford 245 p. 2012 Scholastic Press

1. Coming of age 2. Detective & mystery stories 3. Forests & forestry—Juvenile literature 4. Friendship 5. Haunted houses
ISBN 0545334799; 9780545334792

SUMMARY: This coming of age story combines "[m]iddle-school dynamics, pesky sibling relations, a rumored haunted house, . . . and a mystery. . . . When 10-year-old Minty discovers a hollow tree in the woods . . . [and] find[s] a secret written on a scrap of paper stashed inside, it sets the stage for a . . . mystery. . . . [W]hile Minty tries to figure out what's going on, she . . . befriend[s] an apparently parentless kid, Raymond, who seems to live in an abandoned spec house." (Kirkus)

REVIEW: *Booklist* v108 no17 p58 My 1 2012 Courtney Jones

REVIEW: *Kirkus Rev* v80 no7 p752 Ap 1 2012

"The Secret Tree." "Middle-school dynamics, pesky sibling relations, a rumored haunted house, some truly heart-wrenching situations and a mystery all combine to make this coming-of-age novel an engrossing read. When 10-year-old Minty discovers a hollow tree in the woods that seems to be literally buzzing with secrets, actually finding a secret written on a scrap of paper stashed inside, it sets the stage for a slightly creepy, good old-fashioned mystery. . . . Minty is a satisfying everygirl--just mischievous enough to seem real--and her interactions with Paz . . . recall universal coming-of-age experiences. The neat ending gratifies, with many of the issues having been resolved by the resourceful preteens themselves."

REVIEW: *N Y Times Book Rev* p33 D 2 2012

REVIEW: *Publ Wkly* v259 no11 p61 Mr 12 2012

REVIEW: *SLJ* p89 Jl 2012 Maria B. Salvadore

STANLEY, WILLIAM. Enabling peace in Guatemala; the story of MINUGUA; [by] William Stanley 341 p. 2012 Lynne Rienner Publishers, Inc.

1. Historical literature 2. Human rights—Guatemala 3. Peace-building—Guatemala
ISBN 9781588266569 (hc : alk. paper); 9781588266811 (pb : alk. paper)
LC 2012-044241

SUMMARY: This book by William Stanley is part of the "Histories of UN Peace Operations" series. It "describes the ten-year endeavor of the UN Mission for the Verification of Human Rights (MINUGUA) as an important example of the limits of 'United Nations' power to reshape war-torn societies.' From 1994 to 2004, MINUGUA faced serious challenges in its peacekeeping and peace-building activities designed to correct the conditions that sparked the then recently concluded 30-year civil war in Guatemala." (Choice)

REVIEW: *Choice* v51 no4 p722-3 D 2013 S. L. Rozman

"Enabling Peace in Guatemala: The Story of MINUGUA." "[William] Stanley (Univ. of New Mexico) describes the ten-year endeavor of the UN Mission for the Verification of Human Rights (MINUGUA) as an important example of the limits of 'United Nations' power to reshape war-torn societies.' . . . He observes that 'Guatemalan officials periodically bullied the United Nations on nationalist grounds for allegedly exceeding its mandate,' but points out that MINUGUA did have some leverage since Guatemala risked the loss of major foreign grants and loans if it failed to cooperate. This book is part of the International Peace Institute series 'Histories of UN Peace Operations.'"

STANNARD, JULIAN.ed. The Palm Beach Effect. See The Palm Beach Effect

STAPLES, FIONA.il. Saga. [Vol. 1]. See Saga. [Vol. 1]

STAR WARS; Colors; 26 p. 2013 Scholastic

1. Colors—Juvenile literature 2. Picture books for children 3. Skywalker, Luke (Fictitious character) 4. Star Wars fiction 5. Vader, Darth (Fictitious character)

ISBN 0545609194; 9780545609197

SUMMARY: In this children's book on colors, "creatures, characters and objects from the Star Wars saga represent different hues. Each double-page spreads focuses on one color and features stills from the nine films. The iconic characters are here—Luke Skywalker in an orange flight suit, brown-furred Chewbacca, green Yoda, white-armored stormtroopers and black-garbed Darth Vader." (Kirkus Reviews)

REVIEW: *Kirkus Rev* v82 no1 p148 Ja 1 2014

"Star Wars: Colors". " Little ones unfamiliar with the Star Wars universe will find many of the masked and extreme close-up faces (Yoda reaches menacingly out of the page) scary in this 9-inch-square offering. While many of the colors are bold and true, particularly gold C-3PO, others are a bit of stretch. Queen Amidala's ship looks more purple than silver, and the MagnaGuard's electrostaff does not look purple at all. While the book is not an effective color primer, the youngest Star Wars fans will enjoy the large images of their favorite characters."

STARBIRD, MICHAEL. Distilling ideas; an introduction to mathematical thinking; [by] Michael Starbird xvi, 171 p. 2013 Mathematical Association of America

1. Calculus 2. Graphic methods 3. Mathematical literature 4. Mathematics 5. Number theory

ISBN 1939512034; 9781939512031

LC 2013-945470

SUMMARY: In this book on mathematics by Brian P. Katz and Michael Starbird, "the authors focus on four topical areas—graphs, groups, calculus, and number theory—and include narrative text for each. . . .The book also contains statements of definitions, lemmas, theorems, and corollaries typically presented in first- and second-year undergraduate mathematics courses treating these four topics. Proof exercises are suggested." (Choice: Current Reviews for Academic Libraries)

REVIEW: *Choice* v51 no8 p1441-2 Ap 2014 W. R. Lee

"Distilling Ideas: An Introduction to Mathematical Thinking". "[Brian P.] Katz . . . and [Michael] Starbird . . . wrote this book to assist professors in teaching mathematical reasoning through an 'inquiry based learning method.' It can supplement other materials used in courses in which proof is introduced, but cannot serve as a textbook for an introductory proofs course. . . . Proof exercises are suggested, but the book lacks examples, background information, guidance, and follow-up. The authors do not discuss the nature of proof or types of proof. The difficulty of the exercises varies without warning."

STARK, PETER. Astoria; John Jacob Astor and Thomas Jefferson's lost Pacific empire: a story of wealth, ambition, and survival; [by] Peter Stark 366 p. 2014 HarperCollins Publishers

1. Astor, John Jacob, 1763-1848 2. Astoria (Or.) 3. Historical literature 4. Jefferson, Thomas, 1743-1826 5. United States—Discovery & exploration

ISBN 0062218298; 9780062218292

SUMMARY: This book, by Peter Stark, relates how "in 1810, entrepreneur John Jacob Astor proposed to Thomas Jefferson that Astor start a trading colony in what is now Oregon. . . . [Peter] Stark . . . chronicles Astor's mad dash to establish a fur-trading company, Astoria, which would capture the territory's wealth and allow Jefferson to inaugurate his vision of a democracy from sea to shining sea." (Publishers Weekly)

REVIEW: *Booklist* v110 no8 p8 D 15 2013 Vanessa Bush

REVIEW: *Choice* v51 no12 p2256 Ag 2014 P. T. Sherrill

REVIEW: *Kirkus Rev* v82 no2 p42 Ja 15 2014

"Astoria: Astor and Jefferson's Lost Pacific Empire: A Story of Wealth, Ambition, and Survival". "If the character of [John Jacob] Astor remains indistinct, not so the horrors faced by the Astorians. Their various ordeals give [Peter] Stark the chance to comment on cold water immersion and hypothermia, the efficacy of pounded, dried wild cherries in combating scurvy, and the intriguing role of what we would today call PTSD in the early exploration of North America. Near the end of his life, Astor employed Washington Irving to tell the astonishing story of Astoria. With Stark, this almost unbelievable tale remains in expert hands. A fast-paced, riveting account of exploration and settlement, suffering and survival, treachery and death."

REVIEW: *Libr J* v139 no4 p100 Mr 1 2014 Nathan Bender

REVIEW: *N Y Times Book Rev* p38 Ap 6 2014 Jessica Loudis

REVIEW: *Publ Wkly* v260 no52 p44 D 23 2013

STARMER, AARON. The Riverman; [by] Aaron Starmer 320 p. 2014 Farrar Straus Giroux

1. Fantasy 2. Friendship—Fiction 3. Imaginary places 4. Missing children—Fiction 5. Space & time—Fiction

ISBN 0374363099; 9780374363093 (hardback)

LC 2013-027900

SUMMARY: In this book, by Aaron Starmer, "Fiona Loomis shows up at Alistair's door asking him to pen her biography and begins to tell him of a strange land she's visited called Aquavania. . . . Fiona warns Alistair that the Riverman is stealing the souls of children and that she is next. Alistair, drawn into Fiona's story, wants to protect her—if only he can discover the full truth." (Booklist)

REVIEW: *Booklist* v110 no11 p65-6 F 1 2014 Sarah Bean Thompson

REVIEW: *Bull Cent Child Books* v67 no7 p379-80 Mr 2014 K. Q. G.

"The Riverman." "This blend of magical realism and mystery blurs the line between reality and fantasy, setting up a creepy unease that both disturbs and propels the reader forward. While it is awash with familiar tropes--the steady, humble protagonist, the sleepy small town with secrets, the manic pixie dreamgirl, the menacing male relative, etc.--the deliciously tangled web of a plot defies categorization and leaves each character utterly untrustworthy while ultimately questioning the act of storytelling altogether. The events of the ambiguous ending can be interpreted in a few different ways, but each is so tragic that readers will be left pondering Alistair's fate long after closing the book."

REVIEW: *Kirkus Rev* v82 no3 p80 F 1 2014

"The Riverman". "Convinced Fiona's bizarre story hides something bad in her real life, Alistair's determined to protect her and unearth the truth. But what is the truth, especially when Fiona vanishes after warning Alistair about Charlie and swearing him to secrecy? Alistair's first-person voice lends immediacy and realism to a haunting story, progressing in intensity from October 13 through November 20, as he discovers people are not who they seem to be and reality is much more than he imagined. Lines between reality and fantasy blur in this powerful, disquieting tale of lost children, twisted friendship and the power of storytelling."

REVIEW: *SLJ* v60 no3 p149 Mr 2014 Sara Lissa Paulson

REVIEW: *SLJ* v60 no8 p52 Ag 2014 Kira Moody

REVIEW: *SLJ* v60 no9 p65 S 2014 Kira Moody

REVIEW: *Voice of Youth Advocates* v36 no6 p78 F 2014 Barbara Johnston

STARR, AMORY. Shutting down the streets. See Fernandez, L.

STASHOWER, DANIEL. The hour of peril; the secret plot to murder Lincoln before the Civil War; [by] Daniel Stashower 368 p. 2013 St. Martin's Minotaur

1. American historical fiction 2. Pinkerton, Allan, 1819-1884 3. Presidents—Assassination attempts—United States

ISBN 0312600224; 9780312600228 (hardcover)

LC 2012-042103

SUMMARY: This book by Daniel Stashower chronicles "the first major plot to assassinate Abraham Lincoln . . . in 1861 in anticipation of the then president-elect's . . . inauguration. Stashower . . . explains how Allan Pinkerton, a temperamental Scottish cooper turned 'fierce and incorruptible lawman' and founder of the Pinkerton Agency, sought to infiltrate and obfuscate a murderous group led by Cypriano Ferrandini, an outspoken Italian barber in Baltimore." (Publishers Weekly)

REVIEW: *Booklist* v109 no9/10 p32 Ja 1 2013 Jay Freeman

REVIEW: *Booklist* v109 no19/20 p120 Je 1 2013 Alan Moores

REVIEW: *Libr J* v138 no1 p97-8 Ja 1 2013 John Carver Edwards

REVIEW: *N Y Times Book Rev* p24 F 23 2014 IHSAN TAYLOR

""The Hour of Peril: The Secret Plot to Murder Lincoln Before the Civil War," "Frances and Bernard," and "Ghana Must Go." "['The Hour of Peril'] is a swift and detailed rendering of the little-known Baltimore-based plot to assassinate Abraham Lincoln in February 1861. . . . Inspired by the lives of Flannery O'Connor and Robert Lowell, Bauer's epistolary novel concerns kindred spirits who meet at an artists' colony in 1957. . . . In [Taiye] Selasi's daring first novel, the of Kweku Sai, a renowned Ghanaian surgeon and failed husband, sends a ripple around the world.

REVIEW: *N Y Times Book Rev* p15 F 17 2013 GREG TOBIN

REVIEW: *Publ Wkly* v259 no41 p44 O 8 2012

STATE AND METROPOLITAN AREA DATA BOOK 2013; 468 p. 2013 Rowman & Littlefield Publishers, Inc.

1. Cities & towns—United States—Statistics 2. Families—United States—Statistics 3. Industrial statistics—United States 4. Statistics 5. United States—Statistics

ISBN 1598886274; 9781598886276

SUMMARY: This book presents a "summary of statistics on the social and economic characteristics of the US as well as the sources for these statistics. . . The data for this first Bernan Press edition were gathered from the 2010 Census and enhanced with the one-year and three-year estimates of the American Community Survey. Data on health insurance, commuting, union membership, and other topics are included." (Choice: Current Reviews for Academic Libraries)

REVIEW: *Booklist* v110 no11 p48 F 1 2014 Danise Hoover

REVIEW: *Choice* v51 no8 p1380 Ap 2014 L. M. Stuart

"State and Metropolitan Area Data Book, 2013". "The data for this first Bernan Press edition were gathered from the 2010 Census and enhanced with the one-year and three-year estimates of the American Community Survey. Data on health insurance, commuting, union membership, and other topics are included. Bernan has added data on causes of death, the number of prisoners removed from death row, and more to this edition. . . . Bernan Press's experience publishing the 'County and City Extra' . . . and recently the Statistical Abstract of the United States provides continuity for those who have relied on these compendiums over the years."

REVIEW: *Libr J* v139 no2 p96 F 1 2014 Judy Quinn

THE STATESMAN'S YEARBOOK 2014; The Politics, Cultures and Economies of the World; 1608 p. 2013 Palgrave Macmillan

1. Almanacs 2. International economic relations 3. Political science—Dictionaries 4. World politics 5. Yearbooks

ISBN 0230377696 (hardcover); 9780230377691 (hardcover)

SUMMARY: This reference book "presents a political,

economic and social account of every country of the world together with facts and analysis. The 2014 edition includes revised and updated biographical profiles of all current leaders," "revised economic overviews for every country," and a "chronology of key political events from April 2010 to March 2011." (Publisher's note)

REVIEW: *Libr J* v138 no21 p124 D 1 2013 Donald Altschiller

REVIEW: *TLS* no5776 p32 D 13 2013 ANDREW GAMBLE

"The Statesman's Yearbook 2014: The Politics, Cultures and Economics of the World." "Barry Turner, the current editor, contributes a short and engaging history of the 'Yearbook.' Its origins reflect the Victorian passion for facts, and for reference books of all kinds. . . . While the 'Yearbook' is primarily a reference book, to be consulted when you would like to find out the population of a particular country, the name of its President, or the number and size of its religious denominations, it is also a delight to leaf through it, discovering unexpected facts about some of the more obscure as well as some of the less obscure nations. Its wealth of information is arranged in a logical and consistent manner."

STAUNTON, TED. Who I'm not; [by] Ted Staunton 208 p. 2013 Orca Book Publishers

1. Deception 2. False personation—Fiction 3. Foster children 4. Impostors & imposture—Fiction 5. Missing children—Fiction 6. Young adult fiction

ISBN 1459804341; 9781459804340 (pbk.); 9781459804357 (electronic edition; 9781459804364 (electronic edition

LC 2013-935300

SUMMARY: In this novel by Ted Staunton, "Danny has been bounced from foster home to foster home ever since he was born. He cannot remember his name, he's been given too many. . . . Danny decides he will do anything to avoid being sent to yet another foster home and assumes the identity of a missing teen from Canada. Much to Danny's surprise, the family quickly accepts him as their own, but a retired cop has his suspicions." (School Library Journal)

REVIEW: *Bull Cent Child Books* v67 no3 p182 N 2013 D. S.

"Who I'm Not." "After a youth of foster homes, assumed identities, and scams, our narrator isn't sure what his real name actually is. He knows who he plans to be, however: Danny Dellomondo, an Ontario boy who disappeared a few years ago, and who would now be fifteen. . . . [Author Ted] Staunton . . . brings an engaging solidity to the currently popular impostor plot, and fake Danny is an intriguing character--a genuinely talented, compulsive grifter who's great at understanding everybody's behavior but his own, and who's more of a lost soul than he realizes."

REVIEW: *Kirkus Rev* v81 no18 p65 S 15 2013

REVIEW: *Publ Wkly* v260 no35 p62 S 2 2013

REVIEW: *Quill Quire* v79 no10 p35 D 2013 Grace O'Connell

REVIEW: *SLJ* v59 no10 p1 O 2013 Tiffany Davis

REVIEW: *Voice of Youth Advocates* v36 no4 p74 O 2013 Debbie Wenk"Who I'm Not." "'Danny' is not his real name--he has had so many names that he does not remember his real one, or his real birth date. Bounced between multiple miserable foster homes, . . . He takes on the identity of Danny, a Canadian teen who has been missing for three years. Danny's family readily accepts him as Danny, although one retired cop remains skeptical, and Danny must be extra cautious until he can amass enough money and figure out a plan to flee. . . . The story moves at a rapid pace, and most of the characters have no real depth. . . . The ending is abrupt, with no resolution to his identity, but this serves to enhance the mystery surrounding the boy and somehow makes the reader care even more about him."

STECKEL, JOSHUA. Hold fast to dreams. See Zasloff, B.

STEEL, CATHERINE.ed. The Cambridge companion to Cicero. See The Cambridge companion to Cicero

STEEL, CATHERINE.ed. Community and Communication. See Community and Communication

STEELE, BRIAN. Thomas Jefferson and American nationhood; [by] Brian Steele xiii, 321 p. 2012 Cambridge University Press

1. HISTORY—United States—19th Century 2. Historical literature

ISBN 1107020700; 9781107020702

LC 2012-013662

SUMMARY: This book "emphasizes the centrality of nationhood to Thomas Jefferson's thought and politics, envisioning Jefferson as a cultural nationalist whose political project sought the alignment of the American state system with the will and character of the nation. Jefferson believed that America was the one nation on earth able to realize in practice universal ideals to which other peoples could only aspire." (Publisher's note)

REVIEW: *Am Hist Rev* v119 no1 p172-3 F 2014 Rosemarie Zagarri

"Thomas Jefferson and American Nationhood". "[Brian] Steele's effort succeeds brilliantly. By focusing on Jefferson's understanding of the meaning of nationhood and national identity, Steele brings to light continuities that help resolve some of the apparent inconsistencies in Jefferson's political thought and career. . . . One of Steele's most significant contributions is the integration of gender into his conceptual framework. . . . At times, Steele's decision to organize the book thematically rather than chronologically obscures important changes in Jefferson's ideas over time. Nonetheless, Steele has produced a closely argued, highly nuanced, and original interpretation of Jefferson's thought-one that succeeds in allowing us to see Jefferson in a startling new light."

REVIEW: *J Am Hist* v100 no1 p189-90 Je 2013 Kevin J. Hayes

REVIEW: *Rev Am Hist* v42 no2 p227-36 Je 2014 R. B. Bernstein

"Thomas Jefferson and American Nationhood," "Jefferson's Shadow: The Story of His Science," and "Thomas Jefferson: The Art of Power." "In 'Thomas Jefferson and American Nationalism,' Brian Steele addresses the central role of American nationalism in Jefferson's thought. . . . Steele's tightly reasoned, well-researched study sets Jefferson in historical context while examining unique aspects of his thought. . . In his gracefully written (though digressive) thematic biography 'Jefferson's Shadow: The Story of His

Science,' [author Keith] Thomson extends the path blazed by [other] scholars. . . . Jefferson's strengths and weaknesses as a politician deserve the extended study and analysis that [author Jon] Meacham offers. Indeed, this smoothly written biography illuminates in many ways our understanding of Jefferson."

STEIN, CAMILLA.ed. Khatyn. See Adamovich, A.

STEIN, DAVID EZRA. Dinosaur kisses; [by] David Ezra Stein 32 p. 2013 Candlewick Press

1. Children's stories 2. Dinosaurs—Behavior 3. Dinosaurs—Infancy 4. Dinosaurs—Juvenile fiction 5. Kissing

ISBN 076366104X (reinforced); 9780763661045 (reinforced)

LC 2012-954335

SUMMARY: In this book, written and illustrated by David Ezra Stein, "an energetic young dinosaur figures out her own way to give a kiss. For newly hatched dinosaur Dinah, the world is an exciting place. After a few disastrous attempts, can she figure out how to give someone a kiss without whomping, chomping, or stomping them first?" (Publisher's note)

REVIEW: *Bull Cent Child Books* v67 no1 p55-6 S 2013 J. H.

"Dinosaur Kisses." "[Author and illustrator David Ezra] Stein's pithy, amusing narration is adroitly coupled with his humorous illustrations; the pen and ink, watercolor, charcoal, and crayon illustrations are bold and childlike, with stocky, boxy earth-toned dinosaurs cavorting around with all the vigor--and sonorous exclamations--of a Batman fight scene. The large, blocky black font will visually carry the text to a crowd as well as to individuals; the short, simple, action-centered sentences will hold the attention of even the restless preschool crowd, who will also find the various situations hilarious, and doubtless (to the chagrin of nearby adults) want to imitate Dinah's moves."

REVIEW: *Horn Book Magazine* v89 no5 p81-2 S/O 2013 KITTY FLYNN

"Dinosaur Kisses." "[David Ezra] Stein's engaging illustrations work hand in hand with his simple, energetic text. The bare, but not barren, landscape features pink and yellow skies and a lush green foreground dotted with occasional plants and a few primordial pools of water. Friendly Dinah takes center stage; her silly antics never look threatening. She finally meets her match when one of her nestmates hatches, and the two 'kiss'-- a.k.a. chomp and stomp and whomp--to their hearts' content. Preschool humor at its finest."

REVIEW: *Kirkus Rev* v81 no2 p103 Je 1 2013

REVIEW: *Publ Wkly* p44 Children's starred review annual 2013

REVIEW: *Publ Wkly* v260 no20 p56 My 20 2013

REVIEW: *SLJ* v59 no9 p132 S 2013 Alison Donnelly

REVIEW: *SLJ* v60 no1 p54 Ja 2014 Jennifer Verbrugge

STEIN, DAVID EZRA.il. Dinosaur kisses. See Stein, D. E.

STEIN, DEBORAH JIANG. Prison baby; a memoir; [by] Deborah Jiang Stein 176 p. 2014 Beacon Press

1. Adopted children—United States—Biography 2. Children of women prisoners—United States—Biography 3. Drug addicts—Rehabilitation—United States—Biography 4. Female juvenile delinquents—United States—Biography 5. Memoirs 6. Racially mixed children—United States—Biography

ISBN 9780807098103 (pbk.: alk. paper)

LC 2013-039396

SUMMARY: In this book by Deborah Jiang Stein, " the author recalls how, as a 12-year-old girl of mixed, uncertain race adopted into an academic family and a life of the arts, she found a letter that devastated her. Her adoptive mother had long ago made a request that the author's birth certificate be altered so that she would never learn that she had been born in prison to a heroin-addicted mother." (Kirkus Reviews)

REVIEW: *Kirkus Rev* v82 no1 p90 Ja 1 2014

"Prison Baby: A Memoir". "Perhaps the revelation comes too early in the narrative, before readers have gotten a chance to get to know the writer, but such overwriting (and overdramatizing) initially seems to undermine a story that is powerful enough on its own. Through the first half of the memoir, it remains difficult to get to know Stein due to the fact that she doesn't really know herself. . . . The redemptive second half of the memoir explains much of the first, as she learns what heroin in utero can cause, follows a paper trail back to her prison origin, comes to terms with both her birth mother and her adoptive family, and devotes her life to helping and raising consciousness about women in prison. A book of hope for lives that need turning around."

STEINBERG, DOMINIQUE MOYSE. Blanche; World Class Musician, World Class Mother: Noteworthy Lessons for Living in Harmony With Self, Others, & the Universe; [by] Dominique Moyse Steinberg 144 p. 2013 Createspace Independent Pub

1. Biography (Literary form) 2. Choruses 3. Conduct of life 4. Holocaust survivors 5. Moyse, Blanche

ISBN 1490425667; 9781490425665

SUMMARY: This book by Dominique Moyse Steinberg looks at the author's mother, Blanche Moyse. "Through the metaphor of music as she coaches the Blanche Moyse Chorale in preparation for performance, Blanche Moyse offers lessons on living the good and honest life. Seen through the eyes of her youngest daughter, she teaches us about living, loving, being honest, and staying real." (Publisher's note)

REVIEW: *Kirkus Rev* v82 no2 p4 Ja 15 2014

"Blanche: World Class Musician, World Class Mother: Noteworthy Lessons for Living in Harmony With Self, Others, & the Universe". " Though it's immediately evident that Blanche was a remarkable woman with insightful commentary, this volume tends to be a bit scattered. At times, it resembles a family scrapbook instead of a narrative. The jumps back and forth between story and advice can be a bit jarring, which could be alleviated by separating the text into lengthier chunks and giving each tale a longer arc. Despite these organizational issues, Blanche shines through as a worthy central figure."

STEINER, ROBERT. Nothing lasts forever; three novellas; [by] Robert Steiner 288 p. 2014 Counterpoint

1. Coma—Patients—Fiction 2. Couples—Fiction 3.

FICTION—Literary 4. Infidelity (Couples) 5. Marriage—Fiction
ISBN 9781619022317 (hardback)
LC 2013-028858

SUMMARY: This book, by Robert Steiner, presents three novellas in which "spouses and lovers are at the edge of themselves, saying the unsayable, doing the undoable." (Publisher's note)

REVIEW: *Kirkus Rev* v82 no2 p244 Ja 15 2014

"Nothing Lasts Forever: Three Novellas". "A trio of stubbornly relentless fictions on sex and death and infidelity and sex and death and infidelity. Also: sex, death and infidelity. . . . The prose is marked by its gynecological and scatological candor and a repetitive style that might tire Gertrude Stein. . . . [Robert] Steiner knows what he's doing, and he's in firm command of his style, but his assurance doesn't make these stories any less tedious and distancing. . . .. If Steiner means to explore the fragile nature of our lives, let alone the flickers of love we get to enjoy within them, he's done it with a dispiriting lack of humor and empathy. Pretentious, cold and exhausting."

REVIEW: *Libr J* v139 no10 p98 Je 1 2014 Barbara Hoffert

REVIEW: *Publ Wkly* v260 no49 p56 D 2 2013

STEINHAUER, OLEN. The Cairo affair; [by] Olen Steinhauer 416 p. 2014 Minotaur Books
1. Adultery—Fiction 2. Arab countries—History—Arab Spring Uprisings, 2011- 3. Diplomats—Fiction 4. Murder—Investigation—Fiction 5. Spy stories
ISBN 1250036135; 9781250036131 (hardback)
LC 2013-033452

SUMMARY: In this suspense novel, by Olen Steinhauer, "minutes after [a woman] confesses to her husband, a mid-level diplomat at the American embassy in Hungary, that she had an affair while they were in Cairo, he is shot in the head and killed. . . . Omar Halawi has worked in Egyptian intelligence for years, and he knows how to play the game. . . . But the murder of a diplomat in Hungary has ripples all the way to Cairo, and Omar must follow the fall-out wherever it leads." (Publisher's note)

REVIEW: *Booklist* v110 no17 p4-5 My 1 2014 Bill Ott

REVIEW: *Booklist* v110 no7 p23 D 1 2013 Keir Graff

REVIEW: *Booklist* v111 no2 p66 S 15 2014 Joyce Saricks

REVIEW: *Kirkus Rev* v82 no3 p154 F 1 2014

"The Cairo Affair". "In the new novel by the well-traveled [Olen] Steinhauer . . . the death of an American diplomat in Hungary sets wheels spinning across North Africa. . . . As the Egyptians cope with their own version of the Arab Spring, more contestants vie for the Betrayal of the Month prize, and the body count climbs. In the end, it's a question of which will win out: misguided nationalism or plain old greed. Could easily dispense with a third of the pages in this [John] le Carré wannabe."

REVIEW: *Libr J* v138 no16 p57 O 1 2013 Barbara Hoffert

REVIEW: *N Y Times Book Rev* p13 Mr 23 2014 JAMES MCBRIDE

"The Cairo Affair." "When a spy novel reels from espionage to murder mystery to love story gone sour, forcing you to spin back pages to check names as if you're thumbing through the phone directory, the story becomes less of a novel and more of a grocery list of action items. . . . That's the handicap represented by the latest offering from the spymaster Olen Steinhauer, 'A Cairo Affair,' a work that will surely have his fans clamoring for more—and the rest of us trying to figure out a nice way to reach for the bar bill and exit. It's not that it's a bad book. It's just that the handicaps to reading it loom pretty large."

REVIEW: *New York Times* v163 no56439 pC1-4 Mr 13 2014 JANET MASLIN

"The Cairo Affair." "'The Cairo Affair' . . . has only the C.I.A., the Bosnian War and the most inflamed parts of the Middle East on its playing field. For a writer of [Olen] Steinhauer's skills, this practically qualifies as Tradecraft 101, even though 'The Cairo Affair' has a large cast of suspicious characters. Under ordinary circumstances, a dramatis personae at the front of the book might be helpful in telling them apart. But not one person in this story—O.K., maybe one—is who he or she pretends to be. So stay on your toes and enjoy the guessing game. . . . Mr. Steinhauer also lets a streak of black humor run through this tight, expert book.

REVIEW: *Publ Wkly* v261 no1 p35 Ja 6 2014

STEINKELLNER, TEDDY. Trash can days; a middle school saga; [by] Teddy Steinkellner 352 p. 2013 Disney-Hyperion
1. Family life—California—Fiction 2. Interpersonal relations—Fiction 3. Maturation (Psychology)—Fiction 4. Middle schools—Fiction 5. School stories 6. Schools—Fiction
ISBN 1423166329; 9781423166320
LC 2012-015327

SUMMARY: In this book, "Jake Schwartz is not looking forward to middle school. Puberty feels light years away, he's not keen on the cool clothes or lingo. Since Danny's summer growth spurt, there's been a growing distance between him and Jake. Meanwhile, Hannah is dealing with her own problems; being Queen Bee is not easy. Dorothy Wu could not care less about junior high drama. In the course of one year . . . these four lives will intersect in unique and hilarious ways." (Publisher's note)

REVIEW: *Kirkus Rev* v81 no12 p117-17 Je 15 2013

REVIEW: *N Y Times Book Rev* p18 Ag 25 2013 JESSICA GROSE

"Runt" and "Trash Can Days: A Middle School Saga." "'Runt' has a straightforward message to impart: Don't sink to the level of the mean girl. 'Trash Can Days' has a more nuanced, more entertaining take on the socially powerful--one that doesn't fit into the tidy parameters of an 'After-school Special'-style lesson. . . . [Nora Raleigh] Baskin uses the animals Elizabeth's mother looks after to make a heavy-handed, book-long metaphor about alpha dogs . . . and submissive dogs. . . . [Teddy] Steinkellner has a sharp grasp of the insult-laden dialogue middle schoolers use with obnoxious abandon. Just as he doesn't sugarcoat the way his characters express themselves, the relationship between Danny and Jake doesn't resolve itself neatly or painlessly."

REVIEW: *Publ Wkly* v260 no24 p64 Je 17 2013

STEINMETZ, ANDREW. This Great Escape; The Case of Michael Paryla; [by] Andrew Steinmetz 256 p. 2013 Biblioasis
1. Biographies 2. Great Escape, The (Film) 3. Jewish actors 4. Jewish refugees 5. Jews—Biography 6. Paryla, Michael
ISBN 1927428335; 9781927428337

SUMMARY: This biography by Andrew Steinmetz "reconstructs the life of a man seen by millions yet recognized by no one, whose history--from childhood flight from Nazism to suspicious death twenty years later--intersects bitterly, ironically, and often movingly with the plot of Sturges's great war film. Splicing together documentary materials with correspondence, diary entries, and Steinmetz's own travel journal, 'This Great Escape' does more than reconstruct the making of a cinema classic." (Publisher's note)

REVIEW: *Quill Quire* v79 no8 p33 O 2013 Andrew Wilmot

"This Great Escape: The Case of Michael Paryla." "With the most sprawling POW film ever produced as its backdrop, 'This Great Escape' details the short but eventful life of Michael Paryla, a part-Jewish refugee from Nazi Germany who moved to Canada with his mother in 1949, only to return to Germany seven years later to become an actor. . . . Part biography, part memoir, and part mystery, [author] Andrew Steinmetz's follow-up to his 2008 novel, 'Eva's Threepenny Theatre,' is, like its predecessor, a genre-bending exploration. . . . It is clear that, for Steinmetz, this is a personal journey; however, he struggles to find a clear narrative through-line for his story. . . .The book has an erratic, sometimes manic feel that hampers the reader's immersion in the material."

STEINMETZ, JENA M. Codename; Sob Story: The Tale of a Picket Line Sailor During Wwii; [by] Jena M. Steinmetz 312 p. 2013 CreateSpace Independent Publishing Platform

1. Memoirs 2. Steinmetz, Robert J. 3. World War, 1939-1945—Naval operations 4. World War, 1939-1945—Personal narratives 5. World War, 1939-1945—Veterans
ISBN 1480031070; 9781480031074

SUMMARY: This memoir recounts how, "ten months after Pearl Harbor, young but gung-ho Robert J. Steinmetz convinced his parents to sign off on his Navy enlistment. . . .The Navy issued these sailors only Marine knives for their assignment to plug holes in sinking ships. 'Not even worth real weapons,' he concludes—'the lowest of the low.' He survived seven invasions and battles that forever changed him, hiding his anguish from family members for nearly 70 years." (Kirkus Reviews)

REVIEW: *Kirkus Rev* v81 no8 p134 Ap 15 2013

REVIEW: *Kirkus Rev* p53 D 15 2013 supplemet best books 2013

"Codename: Sob Story: The Tale of a Picket Line Sailor During World War II". " In this notable debut penned by his granddaughter, a World War II veteran recalls action in the Pacific fleet. . . . Jena Steinmetz, who began this as-told-to memoir as a project for her English degree, deftly captures her grandfather's language and personality, as if readers are listening across the kitchen table. Despite a number of typos and editorial lapses that seem to have survived the production process, she demonstrates skill and judgment in transforming extemporaneous talk into fluid prose. Sentence fragments fill the book yet enhance conversational tone rather than hinder readability."

STENT, ANGELA E. The limits of partnership; U.S.-Russian relations in the twenty-first century; [by] Angela E. Stent 384 p. 2014 Princeton University Press

1. HISTORY—Europe—Russia & the Former Soviet Union 2. HISTORY—Modern—21st Century 3. HISTORY—United States—General 4. POLITICAL SCIENCE—International Relations—General 5. Political science literature
ISBN 9780691152974 (hardback)
LC 2013-024484

SUMMARY: In this book on U.S.-Russian relations, author Angela Stent "argues that the same contentious issues--terrorism, missile defense, Iran, nuclear proliferation, Afghanistan, the former Soviet space, the greater Middle East--have been in every president's inbox, Democrat and Republican alike, since the collapse of the USSR." (Kirkus Reviews)

REVIEW: *Economist* v410 no8872 p74 F 1 2014

"The Limits of Partnership: U.S.-Russian Relations in the Twenty-First Century." "[A] magisterial survey of the subject since December 1991, when the Soviet Union was abolished. . . . Ms. [Angela] Stent tells the story clearly and dispassionately. . . . One point that emerges strongly from this book is that the Russians did not crave agreement so much as respect. Had successive American presidents reassured Russia's leaders that they still counted in the world, the relationship surely would have been easier. The problem is that, with a sinking economy, a demographic decline and almost no exports beyond oil and gas, Russia genuinely matters less than it once did. And that may be the hardest truth for Mr. [Vladimir] Putin to learn."

REVIEW: *Kirkus Rev* v81 no24 p74 D 15 2013

STEPHEN, LYNN. We are the face of Oaxaca; testimony and social movements; [by] Lynn Stephen 368 p. 2013 Duke University Press

1. Oral communication—Mexico—Oaxaca (State) 2. Social movements—Mexico—Oaxaca (State) 3. Social science literature 4. Testimony (Theory of knowledge)
ISBN 9780822355199 (cloth : alk. paper);
9780822355342 (pbk. : alk. paper)
LC 2013-012815

SUMMARY: In this book on a 2006 uprising in Oaxaca, Mexico, "Lynn Stephen emphasizes the crucial role of testimony in human rights work, indigenous cultural history, community and indigenous radio, and women's articulation of their rights to speak and be heard. She also explores transborder support for APPO, particularly among Oaxacan immigrants in Los Angeles." (Publisher's note)

REVIEW: *Choice* v51 no7 p1316 Mr 2014 C. M. Kovic

"We Are the Face of Oaxaca: Testimony and Social Movements." "In a detailed study based on long-term ethnographic research with social activists in Oaxaca, anthropologist [Lynn] Stephen . . . explores oral testimony's role in constructing human rights claims and political agency. . . . Stephen centers the book around the knowledge, leadership, and agency of indigenous communities and women, groups that are still marginalized in dominant political narratives. . . . The analysis of testimony and human rights is valuable well beyond the case of Oaxaca. Woven throughout the text are segments of testimonies from the activists involved in the APPO, and links to a bilingual website containing video clips, maps, and photos, which will be particularly useful for university classes."

STEPHENS, HELEN. How to hide a lion; [by] Helen Stephens 32 p. 2013 Henry Holt and Company

1. Children's stories 2. Friendship—Juvenile fiction 3.

Kindness 4. Lion—Fiction 5. Secrecy—Fiction
ISBN 0805098348; 9780805098341 (hardcover)
LC 2013-001930

SUMMARY: "In this children's picture book, a girl named Iris secretly cares for a lion she knows to be kind--a lion who eventually saves the town from burglary. All the lion wants as he strolls into town is to purchase a hat, but he soon finds himself fleeing from terrified, broom-and-rolling-pin-armed townspeople. . . . Iris recognizes his gentleness, but it isn't easy to hide him." (Kirkus Reviews)

REVIEW: *Booklist* v110 no8 p52-4 D 15 2013 Ann Kelley

REVIEW: *Horn Book Magazine* v90 no1 p81 Ja/F 2014 JULIE ROACH

"How to Hide a Lion." "When a bright yellow lion strolls into town to buy a hat, the townspeople don't react well at all. A little girl named Iris offers the lion refuge, and the two become fast friends. . . . The art, both single pages and double-page spreads, moves the story along at a jaunty pace. Text and art pay homage to classic picture books both indirectly and directly, including a nod to Judith Kerr's 'The Tiger Who Came to Tea' (1968). Heavy stock, detailed endpapers, and a second cover illustration hiding under the book jacket complete this story-hour special."

REVIEW: *Kirkus Rev* v81 no18 p288 S 15 2013

REVIEW: *N Y Times Book Rev* p34 N 10 2013 CAROLYN JURIS

STEPHENS, HELEN.il. How to hide a lion. See Stephens, H.

STEPHENS, MITCHELL. Beyond news; the future of journalism; [by] Mitchell Stephens 256 p. 2014 Columbia University Press

1. Business literature 2. Journalism—History—21st century 3. Journalism—Technological innovations 4. Online journalism 5. Reporters and reporting
ISBN 9780231159388 (cloth: alk. paper); 9780231536295 (ebook)
LC 2013-038840

SUMMARY: In this book, Mitchell Stephens "questions what should be next for modern journalism in the demanding digital age. He explores options for a news industry to revamp and retool. . . . With the Internet, the news business requires not only collecting facts and details of events, and opinionated views, but a need to practice 'wisdom journalism'—thoughtful judgment, insight, and informed argument—which is sometimes lacking in current media." (Publishers Weekly)

REVIEW: *Kirkus Rev* v82 no5 p133 Mr 1 2014

"Beyond News: The Future of Journalism". "A professor makes what will seem to some a radical suggestion to disconnect journalism from news, but he belabors the obvious in making the argument and offers little suggestion for a business model that might support his vision of journalism's future. . . . [Mitchell] Stephens' confidence that readers 'haven't had all that much difficulty filtering out the foolishness' isn't necessarily warranted, as spin becomes increasingly polarized and lies go viral. . . . Like the news itself, an analysis that must be read with a critical eye."

REVIEW: *Libr J* v139 no9 p88 My 15 2014 Barbara Kundanis

STEPHENS, MITCHELL. Imagine there's no heaven; how atheism helped create the modern world; [by] Mitchell Stephens 336 p. 2014 Palgrave Macmillan

1. Atheism—History 2. Atheism—Influence 3. Historical literature 4. Human rights 5. Religion & science
ISBN 9781137002600 (alk. paper)
LC 2013-035039

SUMMARY: This book by Mitchell Stephens "explores the role of disbelief in shaping Western civilization. At each juncture common themes emerge: by questioning the role of gods in the heavens or the role of a God in creating man on earth, nonbelievers help move science forward. By challenging the divine right of monarchs and the strictures of holy books, nonbelievers, including Jean- Jacques Rousseau and Denis Diderot, help expand human liberties." (Publisher's note)

REVIEW: *Kirkus Rev* v82 no1 p174 Ja 1 2014

"Imagine There's No Heaven". "[Mitchell] Stephens . . . has not composed yet another screed but, for the most part, a reasonable summary and analysis of the phenomenon of atheism. He does have a pro-atheism position, however, that becomes increasingly prominent—or more difficult to disguise—as the text progresses. . . . Ultimately, he gives heavy credit to atheists for social advances (abortion, gay rights, women's rights) that many religions opposed most desperately. A text sure to give atheists some data and believers another annoyance."

REVIEW: *Libr J* v139 no2 p80 F 1 2014 David Keymer

REVIEW: *New Yorker* v90 no1 p107-1 F 17 2014

STEPHENS, RANDALL J. The anointed. See Giberson, K. W.

STEPHENSON, ERIC. Nowhere men; Fates worse than death; 184 p. 2013 Image Comics

1. Fame—Fiction 2. Graphic novels 3. Human experimentation 4. Science fiction comic books, strips, etc. 5. Scientists—Fiction
ISBN 1607066912; 9781607066910 paperback

SUMMARY: In this graphic novel, written by Eric Stephenson and illustrated by Nate Bellegarde and Jordie Bellair, "Dade Ellis, Simon Grimshaw, Emerson Strange, and Thomas Walker . . . became the most celebrated scientists of all time. They changed the world–and we loved them for it. But where did it all go wrong? And when progress is made at any and all cost, who ultimately pays the price?" (Publisher's note)

REVIEW: *Libr J* v139 no5 p104 Mr 15 2014 Steve Raiteri

REVIEW: *N Y Times Book Rev* p20-1 D 15 2013 Douglas Wolk

"Nowhere Men, Vol. 1: Fates Worse Than Death," "Blue Is the Warmest Color," "Woman Rebel: The Margaret Sanger Story." "Thanks to the imminent 50th anniversary of the British Invasion, we're seeing a small wave comics inspired by the Beatles, none more inventive than Eric Stephenson and Nate Bellegarde's 'Nowhere Men, Vol. 1: Fates Worse Than Death.' . . . Julie Maroh's first graphic novel, 'Blue Is the Warmest Color,' was published in France in 2010. . . . Her delicate linework and ink-wash effects illuminate the story's quiet pauses and the characters' fraught silences and wordless longing. . . . 'Woman Rebel: The Margaret Sanger Story' . . . , a biography of the birth-control activist . . . , is an unlikely but inspired pairing of author and subject."

REVIEW: *New York Times* v163 no56369 pC6 Ja 2 2014 GEORGE GENE GUSTINES

"Nowhere Men: Fates Worse than Death" and "The Fifth Beatle: The Brian Epstein Story". "The scientists, like the Beatles, are celebrities with an outsize influence on culture, which allows Mr. [Eric] Stephenson and the illustrator, Nate Bellegarde, to explore the love-hate relationship we have with our idols in the context of a richly complex, created world.... When a writer-artist team is truly clicking, something magical can happen, and it does here. Mr. Stephenson and Mr. Bellegarde juggle multiple characters and locations . . . yet personalities and appearances remain distinct. . . . 'The Fifth Beatle' is maddeningly uneven. It abounds with emotional moments, but they would be more resonant if balanced with additional facts about [Brian] Epstein's life. In some ways, this book feels like a teaser or the movie version."

STERK, DARRYL.tr. The man with the compound eyes. See The man with the compound eyes

STERN, DANIEL. Swingland; between the sheets of the secretive, sometimes messy, but always adventurous swinging lifestyle; [by] Daniel Stern 320 p. 2013 Simon & Schuster

1. Free love 2. Group sex 3. Memoirs 4. Sex customs 5. Single men
ISBN 9781476732534
LC 2013-005231

SUMMARY: In this book, author Daniel Stern "initiates readers into the world of swinging, sharing his experiences, often in graphic detail, and instructions" for behavior in swinging communities. "Stern decided he needed 'sexual batting practice' and joined a Web site for those seeking casual encounters. . . . Stern provides advice for single men about being respectful to women and impervious to rejection, and about how to create the ideal online profile." (Publishers Weekly)

REVIEW: *Kirkus Rev* v81 no19 p36 O 1 2013

REVIEW: *N Y Times Book Rev* p30 O 6 2013 Emily Witt

"Swingland: Between the Sheets of the Secretive, Sometimes Messy, But Always Adventurous Swinging Lifestyle." "Half memoir, half instruction manual, the book offers particularly focused advice on how to gain acceptance as a single male in a community dominated by couples. . . . Despite lessons in humility [Daniel] Stern claims to have learned, certain chapters read as boastful. . . . Other stories are more fun, but single women looking for advice on how to become a swinger will find almost no practical or emotionally gender-specific lessons . . . There's little inquiry here into the politics of . . . fetishes coded by race. A sexual freedom that organizes humans into porn search terms seems to trade one kind of confinement for another."

REVIEW: *Publ Wkly* v260 no30 p56 Jl 29 2013

STERN, JOSEF. The matter and form of Maimonides' guide; [by] Josef Stern 448 p. 2013 Harvard University Press

1. Jewish philosophy 2. Judaism—Doctrines 3. Philosophical literature 4. Philosophy, Medieval
ISBN 9780674051607 (alk. paper)
LC 2012-039313

SUMMARY: In this book on Moses Maimonides' "Guide of the Perplexed," author "Josef Stern argues that the perplexity addressed in this famously enigmatic work is not the conflict between Athens and Jerusalem but the tension between human matter and form, between the body and the intellect. . . . Stern articulates Maimonides' skepticism about human knowledge of metaphysics and his heterodox interpretations of scriptural and rabbinic parables." (Publisher's note)

REVIEW: *Choice* v51 no6 p1025 F 2014 E. Halper

"The Matter and Form of Maimonides' Guide." "[Josef] Stern closely examines [Moses] Maimonides's interpretations of biblical parables, and the parables Maimonides himself constructed. Following Jewish interpretative tradition, he identifies four layers of meaning. Specific interpretations are not always convincing. Moreover, Stern makes too much of the conflict of matter and form in the Aristotelian tradition, and his Maimonides is too close to Augustine. Nonetheless, this linking of parables with other parables, and with biblical and Talmudic passages, is invaluable."

STERNBERG, JULIE. Like carrot juice on a cupcake; 183 p. 2014 Amulet Books

1. Best friends—Fiction 2. Friendship—Fiction 3. Novels in verse 4. Schools—Fiction 5. Stage fright
ISBN 9781419710339
LC 2013-023276

SUMMARY: In this book by Julie Sternberg, "a new girl, Ainsley, seems to be taking Eleanor's place with Eleanor's long-term best friend, Pearl; additionally, Eleanor, the stage-averse, has been cast as a lead rabbit, complete with a song, in the class production of 'A Tale of Two Bunnies'. The more Eleanor tries to fix things, the worse they seem to get, especially when she blurts out Ainsley's secret crush to a taunting crowd." (Bulletin of the Center for Children's Books)

REVIEW: *Bull Cent Child Books* v67 no9 p479 My 2014 D. S.

"Like Carrot Juice on a Cupcake". "[Julie] Sternberg again displays her talent at putting Eleanor on the horns of a common youthful dilemma in accessible prose, while her perceptive portrayal of the way a misstep can turn into a downward spiral . . . conveys a lifelong truth about the ways relationships start to deteriorate. . . . Eleanor has a good heart and good counsel, fortunately. So she manages to repair her damaged friendship as well as overcome her theatrical fears; even kids who share Eleanor's stage fright will see the former as the real victory here."

REVIEW: *SLJ* v60 no6 p93 Je 2014 Amy Commers

STERNBERGH, ADAM. Shovel ready; A Novel; [by] Adam Sternbergh 240 p. 2014 Crown Publishers

1. Assassins—Fiction 2. Dystopias 3. New York (N.Y.)—Fiction 4. Street life 5. Terrorism—Fiction
ISBN 0385348991; 9780385348997
LC 2013-012901

SUMMARY: This book, by Adam Sternbergh, is "about a garbage man turned kill-for-hire. Spademan used to be a garbage man . . . before the dirty bomb hit Times Square, before his wife was killed, and before the city became a blown-out shell of its former self. Now he's a hitman. In a near-future New York City split between those who are wealthy enough to 'tap in' to a sophisticated virtual reality, and those who are left to fend for themselves in the ravaged streets, Spademan chose the streets." (Publisher's note)

REVIEW: *Booklist* v110 no5 p33 N 1 2013 Bill Ott

REVIEW: *Kirkus Rev* v81 no20 p123 O 15 2013

REVIEW: *Libr J* v138 no21 p93 D 1 2013 Kristin Centorcelli

REVIEW: *N Y Times Book Rev* p30 F 16 2014 Tom LeClair

REVIEW: *New Yorker* v89 no48 p79-1 F 10 2014

"Shovel Ready." "In this dystopian thriller, Manhattan is largely deserted after a dirty-bomb attack. The taxi-drivers who remain keep Geiger counters on their dashboards. The wealthy spend their days getting nutrition through I.V.s, and the poor are in thrall to a post-apocalyptic evangelist named T. K. Harrow. . . . [Adam] Sternbergh's writing is sometimes stripped down to the point of obfuscation, but he skillfully blends elements of noir, sci-fi, and speculative fiction, and keeps the action and the dialogue energetic."

REVIEW: *Publ Wkly* v260 no44 p48-9 N 4 2013

REVIEW: *Quill Quire* v80 no2 p30 Mr 2014 Steven W. Beattie

STERNE, JONATHAN. MP3; the meaning of a format; [by] Jonathan Sterne xv, 341 p. 2012 Duke University Press

1. Historical literature 2. MP3 (Audio coding standard) 3. Psychoacoustics 4. Sound recording & reproducing 5. Sound recordings

ISBN 0822352877 (hardcover); 9780822352839 (hardcover); 9780822352877 (paperback)

LC 2011-053340

SUMMARY: This book, by Jonathan Sterne, examines the history of the MP3 digital recording format. "Understanding the historical meaning of the MP3 format entails rethinking the place of digital technologies in the larger universe of twentieth-century communication history, from hearing research conducted by the telephone industry in the 1910s, through the mid-century development of perceptual coding . . . , to the format's promiscuous social life since the mid 1990s." (Publisher's note)

REVIEW: *Am Hist Rev* v118 no4 p1227-8 O 2013 David Suisman

REVIEW: *Am Q* v65 no2 p447-55 Je 2013 Aaron Trammell

REVIEW: *Art Am* v101 no8 p47-50 S 2013 Alexander Provan

"MP3: The Meaning of a Format." "To [Jonathan] Sterne, a musician and professor of media studies at Montreal's McGill University, the story of the MP3 reveals much about the politics of media today. . . . Sterne's primary concern is not that anyone has been wronged by the MP3, but rather that standards in general should be regarded as a potent force for reshaping social and political life. . . . Rooting the MP3 within the broader history of psychoacoustic research, Sterne provides an extensive chronicle of experiments, methodological shifts and innovations in telegraph and telephone technology."

REVIEW: *Bus Hist Rev* v87 no3 p564-6 Aut 2013 JoAnne Yates

REVIEW: *Choice* v50 no6 p1062 F 2013 D. B. Thornblad

REVIEW: *J Am Hist* v100 no2 p609 S 2013 Joseph Schloss

REVIEW: *TLS* no5749 p23-4 Je 7 2013 JOHN RIDPATH

"MP3: The Meaning of a Format," "In Broad Daylight: Movies and Spectators After the Cinema" and "Film After Film: Or, What Became of 21st Century Cinema." "it is clear that the story of recorded music (and audio, even) is necessarily a story of formats. Indeed, in 'MP3: The meaning of a format,' Jonathan Sterne argues that if there is such a thing as 'media theory', there should also be a 'format theory'. . . . Gabriele Pedullà's' In Broad Daylight' explores how the interconnected evolution of formats and devices has disrupted the relationship between cinema (as art form) and cinema (as place). . . . This new aesthetic of 'twenty-first century cinema' is explored more deeply in J. Hoberman's 'Film After Film'."

STEVENS, PAT. White Bird Under the Sun; [by] Pat Stevens 230 p. 2011 CreateSpace Independent Publishing Platform

1. Autobiographical fiction 2. Brothers & sisters—Fiction 3. Parent & child—Fiction 4. South Africa—Fiction 5. Whites—South Africa

ISBN 1463726821; 9781463726829

SUMMARY: "In this semiautobiographical novel, [Pat] Stevens . . . recounts his adventurous childhood in South Africa and Northern Rhodesia (now Zambia). Beginning with his earliest memories as a twin in the womb, Stevens uses tongue-in-cheek humor to describe the relatively carefree childhood he enjoyed as the son of middle-class white parents in 1940s and 1950s South Africa." (Kirkus Reviews)

REVIEW: *Kirkus Rev* v82 no3 p363 F 1 2014

"White Bird Under the Sun". "[Pat] Stevens colorfully describes the many antics he played as a rascal child, including a trial drive of his father's car, with wry humor and descriptive stage-setting. . . . In lush detail, Stevens describes the new terrain and wildlife. The nostalgic, vividly described memories of adventures in the Rhodesian bush with friends transport the reader to a time before video games and the Internet. . . . he prose is at times politically incorrect; black Africans are simply called "the blacks," and the historic struggles are but lightly acknowledged. . . . Readers should beware of some politically incorrect, off-color humor. A somewhat tone-deaf depiction of a white child's picturesque childhood in mid-20th-century Northern Rhodesia."

STEVENSON, JOHN.ed. The opinions of William Cobbett. See The opinions of William Cobbett

STEWART, AMY. The drunken botanist; the plants that create the world's great drinks; [by] Amy Stewart 400 p. 2013 Algonquin Books of Chapel Hill

1. Alcoholic beverages 2. Botanical literature 3. Cocktails 4. Plants, Edible 5. Plants, Useful

ISBN 1616200464; 9781616200466

LC 2012-041725

SUMMARY: This book by Amy Stewart "explores the botanical beginnings of our favorite drinks. . . . Each plant description includes history, propagation, and usage details. Stewart includes sidebars with recipes, field guides, planting instructions, a description of the role of bugs in getting from seed to plant to table, and in-depth historical details. She includes archaeological finds such as the presence of barley beer on clay pot fragments dated to 3400 B.C.E." (Library Journal)

REVIEW: *Kirkus Rev* v81 no2 p140 Ja 15 2013

REVIEW: *Libr J* v138 no3 p116 F 15 2013 Ann Wilberton

REVIEW: *New York Times* v162 no56082 pD3 Mr 21 2013

REVIEW: *Science* v341 no6144 p347-8 Jl 26 2013 Daniela Hernandez

"The Drunken Botanist: The Plants That Create the World's Great Drinks." "Her excitement about the biological heritage of the various spirits is almost intoxicating. . . . Although it's usually hard to get excited about taxonomy, somehow in the context of potions we drink on a regular basis, [Amy] Stewart breathes some life into the often arcane subject. . . . Unfortunately, the remainder of the book leaves one thirsty for the kind of adventure story Stewart had in Portland. Instead, it generally reads like a mash-up of botanical history tome; cocktail-recipe book; do-it-yourself agriculture guide; and an abridged encyclopedia of the trees, roots, leaves, fruits, flowers, and seeds that come in contact with, flavor, or are made into your booze of choice."

STEWART, BARBARA. The in-between; [by] Barbara Stewart 256 p. 2013 St. Martin's Griffin

1. Best friends—Fiction 2. Friendship—Fiction 3. Grief—Fiction 4. JUVENILE FICTION—Social Issues—General (see also headings under Family) 5. Moving, Household—Fiction 6. Near-death experiences—Fiction 7. Single-parent families—Fiction 8. Supernatural—Fiction 9. Young adult fiction

ISBN 1250030161; 9781250030160 (pbk.)

LC 2013-025064

SUMMARY: In this book by Barbara Stewart, "when a car terrible accident changes [Elanor's] life forever, her near-death experience opens a door to a world inhabited by Madeline Torus . . . Madeline is everything Elanor isn't: beautiful, bold, brave. . . . But Madeline is not like other girls, and Elanor has to keep her new friend a secret or risk being labeled 'crazy.' Soon, though, even Elanor starts to doubt her own sanity." (Publisher's note)

REVIEW: *Booklist* v110 no6 p46-7 N 15 2013 Debbie Carton

"The In-Between." "[Barbara] Stewart's tightly constructed ghost story is tantalizingly creepy with completely believable twists. We meet Ellie's twin, Madeline, who was not a miscarriage but mysteriously disappeared in utero. Her eerie power over Ellie leads to dark places, including a unique take on near-death experiences. Ellie's dad suffered from severe depression, and her mother recognizes Ellie needs help and gets her therapy and hospitalization. But it's a steep spiral down into Ellie's mind as she succumbs to mental illness. Stewart's debut novel is a riveting page-turner with real empathy and compassion. The journal format clarifies Ellie's different stages and lends a wonderful voyeuristic appeal."

REVIEW: *Bull Cent Child Books* v67 no5 p284-5 Ja 2014 D. S.

"The In-Between." "Mood and style make this story: [Barbara] Stewart keeps readers off-balance, never pinning Madeline down as either a supernatural presence or a product of Ellie's disordered mind; to Ellie, Madeline is absolutely real, while the rest of the world sees Madeline's destructive actions--assaulting one of Ellie's friends, for instance--as Ellie herself in the grip of something troubling. Madeline's seductive, insistent pull on Ellie is deeply creepy. . . .. There's an inventive touch in the culmination, which involves Ellie's mother's current pregnancy (again twins, with one lost prior to birth) and which will have readers tensely guessing as to Ellie's self-destruction or survival."

REVIEW: *Kirkus Rev* v81 no17 p119 S 1 2013

REVIEW: *SLJ* v60 no2 p115 F 2014 Jennifer Prince

REVIEW: *Voice of Youth Advocates* v36 no5 p66-7 D 2013 Erin E. Forson

STEWART, CHARLES. Fighting for the speakership; the House and the rise of party government; [by] Charles Stewart 476 p. 2012 Princeton University Press

1. Historical literature 2. Political parties—United States—History 3. Political science literature 4. United States—Politics & government—History 5. United States. Congress—History 6. United States. Congress. House—Speakers

ISBN 0691118124; 9780691118123 (hardback : alk. paper); 9780691156446 (pbk. : alk. paper)

LC 2012-010959

SUMMARY: This book by Jeffrey A. Jenkins and Charles Stewart III "provides a comprehensive history of how Speakers have been elected in the U.S. House since 1789, arguing that the organizational politics of these elections were critical to the construction of mass political parties in America and laid the groundwork for the role they play in setting the agenda of Congress today." (Publisher's note)

REVIEW: *Choice* v51 no1 p165 S 2013 W. K. Hall

"Fighting for the Speakership: The House and the Rise of Party Government." "This is a study of the evolution of the election of the Speaker of the US House of Representatives and the effort to establish majority party control in the House. . . . [Authors Jeffery A.] Jenkins . . . and [Charles] Stewart [III] . . . have organized House history into five eras, the present era running from 1891 until now. They review the evolution of the election of the Speaker through each of these five eras. . . . An excellent look at the history of majority party leadership in the House."

REVIEW: *Polit Sci Q (Wiley-Blackwell)* v128 no4 p768-9 Wint 2013/2014 CHRIS DEN HARTOG

STEWART, CHRISTOPHER S. Jungleland; A Mysterious Lost City, a Wwii Spy, and a True Story of Deadly Adventure; [by] Christopher S. Stewart 288 p. 2013 HarperCollins

1. Adventure stories 2. Journalism 3. Mosquitia (Nicaragua & Honduras) 4. Spies 5. World War, 1939-1945—Secret service

ISBN 0061802549; 9780061802546

SUMMARY: "Armed with the personal notebooks of the mysterious World War II spy Theodore Morde, an adventurer who attempted to assassinate Adolf Hitler, journalist Christopher S. Stewart sets out in search of the lost White City, buried somewhere deep in the Mosquito Coast of Honduras. Stewart pieces together the whirlwind life and peculiar death of Morde . . . as he tries to verify Morde's claim of having discovered the 'Lost City of the Monkey God.'" (Publisher's note)

REVIEW: *Booklist* v109 no9/10 p31 Ja 1 2013 Gilbert Taylor

REVIEW: *Kirkus Rev* v80 no23 p106 D 1 2012

REVIEW: *N Y Times Book Rev* p24 F 2 2014 IHSAN TAYLOR

"The Real Jane Austen: A Life in Small Things," "Tenth of December," and "Jungleland: A Mysterious Lost City, a WWII Spy and a True Story of Deadly Adventure." "[Author

Paula] Byrne's vividly persuasive biography shirks chronological constraints, using objects of special significance to Austen . . . to depict her as an exuberant, worldly woman of fierce convictions. . . . [Author George] Saunders's wickedly entertaining collection . . . veers from the deadpan to the flat-out demented. . . . [Author Christopher S.] Stewart sets out in search of the fabled White City, buried deep in the Mosquito Coast of Honduras."

REVIEW: *Publ Wkly* v259 no49 p69-70 D 3 2012

STEWART, ELIZABETH. Blue Gold; [by] Elizabeth Stewart 296 p. 2014 Firefly Books Ltd

1. Child labor—Fiction 2. Electronics—Social aspects 3. Refugees—Fiction 4. Technology & civilization 5. Young adult fiction

ISBN 1554516358; 9781554516353

SUMMARY: In this book, "the human price of technology is explored from the perspectives of three teen girls. . . . Fiona [is] a middle-class Canadian teen. . . . Sylvia is a Congolese refugee. . . . Coltan, a mineral used in the technology that helps power cell phones and computers, is a resource that her people have killed and died for. . . . In China, Laiping works long hours in a factory assembling cell phones." (School Library Journal)

REVIEW: *Kirkus Rev* v82 no4 p321 F 15 2014

"Blue Gold". " The human costs of modern technology are explored through the alternating third-person narratives of three girls from different countries. Canadian Fiona sends her boyfriend a risqué selfie. In Africa, fighting in the Democratic Republic of Congo has forced Sylvie to Tanzania's Nyarugusu Refugee Camp. . . . In China, Laiping joins her cousin in the city to work for a better life in a factory that manufactures electronics. . . . The stories converge (though not seamlessly) at the conclusion. The prose is strongest when closest to the characters, weakest in didactic moments. In the afterward, [Elizabeth] Stewart explains the real-world situation and provides further research resources. Fictional characters make an important story accessible."

REVIEW: *Quill Quire* v80 no1 p45 Ja/F 2014 Nathan Whitlock

"Blue Gold". "[Elizabeth Stewart] manages to cram an enormous amount of geopolitical strife into her brisk and eventful novel without violating a YA novelist's more fundamental requirement to entertain. . . . 'Blue Gold' is very much in the Deborah Ellis vein of issue-driven fiction, though Stewart . . . doesn't' have Ellis's gift for simultaneously creating suspense and raising awareness. The inevitable chunks of exposition force Stewart to compensate by suddenly revving up the action, leading to occasionally narrative whiplash. . . . The sections of the book that feature Laiping and Sylvie are especially vivid and disturbing, so much so that even the most jaded teen readers may find themselves stealing a guilty glance at the phone or laptop sitting nearby."

REVIEW: *SLJ* v60 no4 p174 Ap 2014 Samantha Lumetta

STEWART, MELISSA. Feathers; not just for flying; 32 p. 2014 Charlesbridge

1. Avian anatomy 2. Birds—Behavior—Juvenile literature 3. Children's nonfiction 4. Feathers—Juvenile literature 5. Natural history literature

ISBN 1580894313; 9781580894302 (reinforced for library use); 9781580894319 (softcover)

LC 2012-038694

SUMMARY: In this book by Melissa Stewart, readers "meet sixteen birds in this elegant introduction to the many uses of feathers. A concise main text highlights how feathers are not just for flying. Informative sidebars, which underscore specific ways each bird uses its feathers for a variety of practical purposes [are included]. A scrapbook design showcases life-size feather illustrations." (Publisher's note)

REVIEW: *Booklist* v110 no11 p53 F 1 2014 Erin Anderson

REVIEW: *Bull Cent Child Books* v67 no7 p380-1 Mr 2014 E. B.

"Feathers: Not Just for Flying." "Compact, consistent entries, most set in attractively composed double-page spreads, focus on the many ways in which birds benefit from their feathers. . . . Each bird gets a lovely portrait set in its habitat, captioned with its identity and a precise geographic location. A brief paragraph, just the right length for classroom or storytime sharing, explains the utility of the bird's plumage, and the entries are unified by a line of oversized font that runs across the tops of the spreads and compares feathers to a familiar human device."

REVIEW: *Horn Book Magazine* v90 no3 p115-6 My/Je 2014 DANIELLE J. FORD

REVIEW: *Kirkus Rev* v82 no2 p105 Ja 15 2014

REVIEW: *Publ Wkly* v260 no51 p58 D 16 2013

REVIEW: *SLJ* v60 no2 p122 F 2014 Meaghan Darling

STEWART, MELISSA. No monkeys, no chocolate; [by] Melissa Stewart 32 p. 2013 Charlesbridge

1. Cacao—Diseases and pests—Juvenile literature 2. Cacao—Juvenile literature 3. Cacao beans—Juvenile literature 4. Children's nonfiction 5. Chocolate—Juvenile literature 6. Cocoa processing—Juvenile literature

ISBN 9781580892872; 9781580892889

LC 2012-000789

SUMMARY: This children's picture book explores "the rain forest microhabitat of the cocoa tree. In each spread, the authors take children backward through the life cycle of the tree: pods, flowers, leaves, stems, roots and back to beans. The interdependence of plants and animals is introduced in the process: Midges carry pollen from one flower to another; aphids destroying tender stems are kept in check by an anole." (Kirkus Reviews)

REVIEW: *Bull Cent Child Books* v67 no1 p56-7 S 2013 E. B.

"No Monkeys, No Chocolate." "Here [author's Melissa] Stewart [and Allen Young] trace . . . the journey to chocolate treats in reverse, starting with cocoa beans, which develop in pods, which 'can't form without flowers,' which can't bloom without leaves, etc., all the way back to the monkeys that scatter the beans that produce the trees. It's initially an elegant framework, with each step explained in a couple of short, accessible paragraphs. However, the narrative gets tangled several times when insects come into play and explanations lengthen to fully explain the process. . . . [Illustrator Nicole] Wong's watercolor illustrations . . . offer detailed close-ups of important stages of cocoa development and of the critters that various aid or impede its growth."

REVIEW: *Horn Book Magazine* v90 no1 p119 Ja/F 2014 BETTY CARTER

REVIEW: *Kirkus Rev* p64-5 N 15 2013 Best Books

REVIEW: *Kirkus Rev* v81 no14 p115 Jl 15 2013

REVIEW: *SLJ* v59 no9 p190 S 2013 Patricia Manning

STIEFVATER, MAGGIE. The Curiosities; a collection of stories; [by] Maggie Stiefvater 2014 Carolrhoda Books
ISBN 9781467716239; 1467716235

SUMMARY: Authors Maggie Stiefvater, Tessa Gratton, and Brenna Yovanoff presents a collection of short stories. Plots include "a vampire locked in a cage in the basement, for good luck, bad guys, clever girls, and the various reasons why the guys have to stop breathing, [and] a world where fires never go out." (Publisher's note)

REVIEW: *Booklist* v108 no22 p72 Ag 1 2012 Daniel Kraus

REVIEW: *Bull Cent Child Books* v66 no5 p264-5 Ja 2013 K. C.

"The Curiosities: A Collection of Stories." "In 2008, [Maggie] Stiefvater, [Tessa] Gratton, and [Brenna] Yovanoff agreed to start a blog wherein they'd take turns posting short fiction that would enable them to experiment with their craft and critique one another's work. This book includes some of the pieces from the blog as well as other original short stories that highlight the process of a writing group. . . . The end result of the combination of stories and formal and informal commentary is that readers will feel a stronger, more intimate connection with these writers as people, as well as gain insight into the kinds of support and critique that are useful in story-making and story-sharing. . . . The stories themselves are good, too, some even bordering on exquisite."

REVIEW: *Horn Book Magazine* p88 S/O 2012 Sarah Ellis

REVIEW: *Kirkus Rev* v80 no10 p65 My 15 2012

REVIEW: *Kirkus Rev* v80 no18 p5 S 15 2012

REVIEW: *Publ Wkly* v259 no38 p57 S 17 2012

REVIEW: *SLJ* v58 no9 p157-8 S 2012 Cindy Wall

REVIEW: *Voice of Youth Advocates* v35 no5 p494 D 2012 Heidi Uphoff

STIEFVATER, MAGGIE. The dream thieves; [by] Maggie Stiefvater 416 p. 2013 Scholastic

1. Dreams—Fiction 2. Dreams—Juvenile fiction 3. Family secrets—Juvenile fiction 4. Fantasy fiction 5. Magic—Fiction 6. Magic—Juvenile fiction 7. Occultism—Fiction 8. Paranormal fiction 9. Secrets—Fiction
ISBN 0545424941; 9780545424943 (jacketed hardcover)
LC 2013-018731

SUMMARY: This is the second book in Maggie Stiefvater's Raven Cycle series. Here, after "the transformative events at Cabeswater . . . , the context in which Gansey, Blue, Adam, Ronan, and Noah operate is further altered by the arrival of the Gray Man, a self-described hit man. . . . The Gray Man brings with him the machinations of larger, previously unknown forces as he takes orders from a voice on the phone to hunt the Greywaren, the identity of which is revealed early on." (Publishers Weekly)

REVIEW: *Booklist* v110 no1 p103 S 1 2013 Michael Cart

"The Dream Thieves." "In this continuation of 'The Raven Boys' (2012), Printz Honor Book recipient [Maggie] Stiefvater continues the compelling story, keeping the focus once again on the Raven Boys themselves. . . . Visceral suspense builds as the characters pursue answers to these and other questions, and a palpable sense of foreboding and danger increasingly permeates the novel. Richly written and filled with figurative language . . . this story of secrets and dreams, of brothers, and of all-too-real magic is an absolute marvel of imagination and an irresistible invitation to wonder."

REVIEW: *Booklist* v110 no12 p96 F 15 2014 Lynn Rutan

REVIEW: *Bull Cent Child Books* v67 no2 p117 O 2013

"The Dream Thieves." "At the end of The Raven Boys . . . , readers learned that Ronan, the sarcastic private-school student, is the new Greywaren, having inherited his father's gift for bringing objects out of dreams. . . . After having so deftly introduced and developed this constellation of characters in the first novel, [author Maggie] Stiefvater plies their strengths and weaknesses into an ever more complex web of magical intrigue and heartstopping action. In this sequel, every character . . . has an increasingly important role to play, and the new characters the author introduces are just right for . . . drawing out productive tensions between the ordinary world of rural Virginia and the wild, magical world they have awakened. . . ."

REVIEW: *Horn Book Magazine* v90 no1 p100-1 Ja/F 2014 CYNTHIA K. RITTER

"The Dream Thieves." "Sound overly complex? It is, but in [Maggie] Stiefvater's capable hands the mysteries unravel authentically, with new questions invariably arising with every answer to continually ratchet up suspense. Her descriptive prose reveals a complicated plot, multiple viewpoints, and detailed character backstories that necessitate patient, thoughtful reading. In this darker second book, Gansey, Blue, their love-triangle-turned-square, and the search for Glendower take a backseat to the exploration of Ronan and Adam's tortured personalities. Many mysteries remain, but the (over-the-top) cliffhanger ending makes it clear that Glendower will resurface as the main focus of book three."

REVIEW: *Kirkus Rev* p57 Ag 15 2013 Fall Preview

REVIEW: *Kirkus Rev* v81 no15 p235 Ag 1 2013

REVIEW: *Publ Wkly* p122-3 Children's starred review annual 2013

REVIEW: *Publ Wkly* v261 no4 p189 Ja 27 2014

REVIEW: *Publ Wkly* v260 no29 p71 Jl 22 2013

REVIEW: *SLJ* v60 no1 p54 Ja 2014 Alissa Bach

REVIEW: *SLJ* v59 no10 p1 O 2013 Maggie Knapp

REVIEW: *Voice of Youth Advocates* v36 no4 p87 O 2013 Lisa A. Hazlett

STILL, TODD D.ed. Tertullian and Paul. See Tertullian and Paul

STILLS, CAROLINE. Mice mischief; math facts in action; 24 p. 2014 Holiday House

1. Addition—Juvenile literature 2. Children's stories 3. Chores 4. Circus—Juvenile literature 5. Counting—Juvenile literature 6. Mice—Juvenile literature
ISBN 0823429474; 9780823429479 (hardcover)
LC 2013-017150

SUMMARY: In this children's picture book, written by Caroline Stills and illustrated by Judith Rossell, "ten colorful and acrobatic circus mice demonstrate the different ways that the numbers from 1 to 9 can add up to 10." (Publisher's note)

REVIEW: *Booklist* v110 no12 p70 F 15 2014 Carolyn

Phelan

REVIEW: *Bull Cent Child Books* v67 no9 p479 My 2014 E. B.

REVIEW: *Kirkus Rev* v82 no4 p92 F 15 2014

"Mice Mischief: Math Facts in Action". "The mice are differentiated enough so careful observers can see that the diligent mice are always the same ones. . . . [Judith] Rossell's delightful pencil, liquid acrylic and collage illustrations are the stars here. . . . While the math is there on every page, the learning is painless, as preschoolers will likely be more focused on the antics of the mice; repeat readings will keep exposing children to the math facts. Though these mice are rather tame in the mischief department, preschoolers get some good practice in counting down, adding up to 10 and recognizing addition sentences."

REVIEW: *Publ Wkly* v261 no9 p64 Mr 3 2014

REVIEW: *SLJ* v60 no3 p177 Mr 2014 Nancy Jo Lambert

STITES, RICHARD. The four horsemen; riding to liberty in post-Napoleonic Europe; [by] Richard Stites 456 p. 2014 Oxford University Press

1. HISTORY—Europe—Western 2. HISTORY—Modern—19th Century 3. Historical literature 4. Revolutionaries—Europe—Biography 5. Revolutions—Europe—History—19th century

ISBN 9780199978083 (hardback)

LC 2013-040021

SUMMARY: This book by Richard Stites describes how "In a series of revolts starting in 1820, four military officers rode forth on horseback from obscure European towns to bring political freedom and a constitution to Spain, Naples, and Russia; and national independence to the Greeks. The men who launched these exploits from Andalusia to the snowy fields of Ukraine . . . all hoped to overturn the old order. Over the next six years, their revolutions ended in failure." (Publisher's note)

REVIEW: *Choice* v52 no1 p135 St 2014 G. P. Cox

REVIEW: *Publ Wkly* v260 no51 p50-1 D 16 2013

REVIEW: *TLS* no5797 p9 My 9 2014 GABRIEL PAQUETTE

"The Four Horsemen: Riding to Liberty in Post-Napoleonic Europe." "In Richard Stites's marvellous, posthumously published book, the lives of four remarkable, if unlikely, rebels are chronicled: a Spanish colonel, Rafael del Riego; a Neapolitan general, Guglielmo Pepe; a Greek general in the service of Russia, Alexandros Ypsilanti, and a Russian colonel. Serge Muraviev-Apostol. . . . Richard Stites's astute and engagingly written book helps to recover the importance of these men and their lost causes, both for their time as well as ours."

STOCKMAN, NATHAN.il. I Love Trouble. See I Love Trouble

STOCKTON, FRANK.il. The world without fish. See Kurlansky, M.

STOFFER, LISA. Repast. See Lesy, M.

STOHR, KAREN. On manners; [by] Karen Stohr x, 183 p. 2012 Routledge

1. Conduct of life 2. Ethics 3. Etiquette 4. Everyday life 5. Philosophical literature

ISBN 9780203859803 (e-book); 9780415875370 (hardback : alk. paper); 9780415875387 (pbk. : alk. paper)

LC 2011-019899

SUMMARY: In this book, Karen Stohr argues "that the scope of manners is much broader than most people realize and that manners lead directly to the roots of enduring ethical questions. Stohr suggests that though manners are mostly conventional, they are nevertheless authoritative insofar as they . . . carry out important moral goals. Drawing . . . on Aristotle and Kant and . . . cultural examples . . . the author ultimately concludes that good manners are essential to moral character." (Publisher's note)

REVIEW: *Ethics* v124 no1 p214-7 O 2013 KRISTJÁN KRISTJÁNSSON

"On Manners." "Karen Stohr's new book on manners and etiquette forms part of the Routledge series Thinking in Action that is meant to take philosophy to the public and to cover salient contemporary topics in a clear and accessible--but still academically grounded--way. This book seems to be eminently well pitched at its target readership and, hence, destined for a positive reception. It provides sufficient substance and subtlety (and enough learned references to Plato, Aristotle, Hobbes, Hume, and Kant) to satisfy the philosophically discerning reader, but it also shifts effortlessly, wittily, and imaginatively to issues and examples from popular culture)Seinfeld and Starbucks, Facebook and Twitter)."

STOLL, IRA. JFK, conservative; [by] Ira Stoll 288 p. 2013 Houghton Mifflin Harcourt

1. Conservatism—United States—History—20th century 2. Historical literature 3. United States—Politics & government—1961-1963

ISBN 0547585985; 9780547585987

LC 2013-001595

SUMMARY: It was the author's intent to demonstrate that "John F. Kennedy's priorities as president . . . were not to promote large government and federally funded social programs but to seek tax reductions, maintain a strong department of defense, fight communism, and reduce federal spending. . . . [Ira] Stoll posits that Ronald Reagan is the true inheritor of the Kennedy legacy because . . . he advocated the same priorities as JFK and made similar fiery, anticommunist speeches." (Library Journal).

REVIEW: *Commentary* v136 no5 p44-6 D 2013 JAMES PETHOKOUKIS

REVIEW: *Kirkus Rev* v81 no17 p72 S 1 2013

REVIEW: *Libr J* v138 no8 p61 My 1 2013

REVIEW: *Libr J* v138 no12 p93 Jl 1 2013 Karl Helicher

REVIEW: *N Y Rev Books* v61 no3 p19-22 F 20 2014 Frank Rich

REVIEW: *N Y Times Book Rev* p34 O 27 2013 Jacob Heilbrunn

"The Interloper: Lee Harvey Oswald Inside the Soviet Union," "JFK, Conservative," and "If Kennedy Lived: The First and Second Terms of President John F. Kennedy: An Alternate History." "In this penetrating study of Oswald's pivotal sojourn in the Soviet Union, [Peter] Savodnik outlines the pitiable delusions and hopes Oswald harbored both in America and abroad. Savodnik, a gifted writer, draws on archival documents and interviews . . . to explain the murderous rage that prompted him to assassinate John F. Kennedy. . . . [Ira] Stoll . . . provides a wonderfully mischievous analysis. . . . In his diverting 'If Kennedy Lived,' [Jeff] Greenfield . . . asks how things might have played out had John F. Kennedy survived."

REVIEW: *Natl Rev* v65 no22 p46-7 N 25 2013 JAMES PIERESON

REVIEW: *Publ Wkly* v260 no25 p155-6 Je 24 2013

REVIEW: *Publ Wkly* v260 no31 p33-40 Ag 5 2013 LENNY PICKER

STOLZENBERG, DANIEL. Egyptian Oedipus; Athanasius Kircher and the secrets of antiquity; [by] Daniel Stolzenberg 307 p. 2013 The University of Chicago Press

1. Egyptian language—Writing, Hieroglyphic 2. Egyptology—History 3. Europe—Intellectual life—17th century 4. Historical literature 5. Italy—Intellectual life—17th century 6. Occultism—History 7. Orientalism—History—17th century

ISBN 0226924149 (cloth : alk. paper); 9780226924144 (cloth : alk. paper)

LC 2012-022898

SUMMARY: "In 1655, after more than two decades of toil, Kircher published his solution to the hieroglyphs, 'Oedipus Aegyptiacus', a work that has been called 'one of the most learned monstrosities of all times.' Here Daniel Stolzenberg presents a new interpretation of Kircher's hieroglyphic studies, placing them in the context of seventeenth-century scholarship on paganism and Oriental languages." (Publisher's note)

REVIEW: *Choice* v51 no1 p139-40 S 2013 R. Fritze

"Egyptian Oedipus: Athanasius Kircher and the Secrets of Antiquity." "Athanasius Kircher (1601/2-1680) was a German Jesuit and polymath who produced a succession of massive tomes on a variety of subjects. Most famously, he claimed to have deciphered Egyptian hieroglyphs, although most of his contemporaries doubted his success. . . . [Author Daniel] Stolzenberg's book is a study of Kircher's 'Egyptian Oedipus' (1652-54), which appeared as three books in four volumes. It is the magnum opus of Kircher's claims to have deciphered hieroglyphs. . . . A fine study of Kircher's Egyptological writings and the world of scholarship in the second half of the 17th century."

REVIEW: *London Rev Books* v35 no21 p25-7 N 7 2013 Anthony Grafton

REVIEW: *TLS* no5765 p30 S 27 2013 ALASTAIR HAMILTON

"Egyptian Oedipus: Athanasius Kircher and the Secrets of Antiquity." "Thoroughly researched and informative. . . . To rehabilitate Kircher entirely is impossible, and [Daniel] Stolzenberg is well aware of his shortcomings--his absolute confidence in his own judgement, his ingenuousness in assessing ancient texts, and his rejection of the more recent critical methods. Yet, even in the domain of Egyptology in which he committed some of his greatest mistakes, Kircher made contributions which have remained valid through the ages."

STOMMEL, JON.il. Summer at the Z House. See Zanville, H.

STONE, BRAD. The everything store; jeff bezos and the age of amazon; [by] Brad Stone 320 p. 2013 Little Brown & Co.

1. Amazon.com Inc. 2. Bezos, Jeffrey, 1964- 3. Businesspeople—Biography 4. Electronic commerce 5. Journalism

ISBN 9780316219266; 9780316239905 (large print)

LC 2013-941813

SUMMARY: This book on Amazon founder Jeff Bezos and his company "explores Amazon's technology breakthroughs with its Kindle e-reader and cloud-computing initiatives, but mainly tells a surprisingly traditional story about monopolistic retail, hinging on price wars over diapers, disputes with toy suppliers, carefully cultivated economies of scale, and the nuts and bolts of getting goods into customers' hands." (Publishers Weekly)

REVIEW: *Bookforum* v20 no4 p8 D 2013/Ja 2014 ASTRA TAYLOR

REVIEW: *Choice* v51 no8 p1454 Ap 2014 S. A. Schulman

REVIEW: *Economist* v409 no8862 p84-5 N 16 2013

"Hatching Twitter: A True Story of Money, Power, Friendship, and Betrayal" and "The Everything Store: Jeff Bezos and the Age of Amazon." "'Hatching Twitter' by Nick Bilton . . . is a made-for-the-movies account of the personal rivalries that fuelled several epic boardroom battles at the fast-growing startup. . . . Mr. Bilton is at his best when describing the turmoil at the top of Twitter. He also captures the thrill of being at a startup whose 140-character messages captivate high-profile people. . . . There is little boardroom drama to liven up Mr. [Brad] Stone's pages. But his book has triggered a bust-up online. . . . Such controversy will do doubt be good for sales of a tome that paints a fascinating picture of a remarkable tech entrepreneur."

REVIEW: *Kirkus Rev* v81 no22 p220 N 15 2013

REVIEW: *Libr J* v139 no6 p60 Ap 1 2014 Mark John Swails

REVIEW: *Libr J* v138 no9 p56 My 15 2013 Barbara Hoffert

REVIEW: *London Rev Books* v35 no23 p17-9 D 5 2013 Deborah Friedell

REVIEW: *N Y Times Book Rev* p19 N 3 2013 DUFF McDONALD

"The Everything Store: Jeff Bezos and the Age of Amazon." "Engrossing. . . . [Brad] Stone obviously admires his subject, but it's hard to tell if he likes him. . . . Stone's long tenure covering both Bezos and Amazon . . . gives his retelling a sureness that keeps the story moving swiftly, even in passages where Amazon's ever-present (and apparently intentional) internal chaos threatens to spill out onto the pages of the book itself. Stone does know when to provide a breather with entertaining anecdotes about Amazon's competitive jujitsu."

REVIEW: *New York Times* v162 no56304 pC1-5 O 29 2013 MICHIKO KAKUTANI

REVIEW: *New Yorker* v89 no38 p68-1 N 25 2013

REVIEW: *Publ Wkly* v260 no25 p28-33 Je 24 2013 JIM MILLIOT

STONE, MICHEL. The iguana tree; [by] Michel Stone 224 p. 2012 Hub City Press

1. Families—Mexico—Fiction 2. Fiction 3. Human smuggling—Fiction 4. Illegal aliens—Crimes against—

Mexican-American Border Region—Fiction 5. Illegal aliens—Mexican-American Border Region—Fiction 6. Missing persons—Fiction
ISBN 9781891885884
LC 2011-037779

SUMMARY: This book focuses on people "braving the deadly trail across our southern border, seeking only to find work, living only to be pursued as illegal immigrants. Héctor has set out from Puerto Isadore, a bucolic village near Oaxaca, Mexico, paying a coyote to smuggle him into America. Héctor has left his wife Lilia and baby daughter Alejandra, who live with Lilia's beloved grandmother, Crucita. . . . Héctor's plans to save money to bring Lilia and Alejandra to America collapse when Crucita dies, and lonely Lilia defies Héctor's demands she wait. With the help of a childhood friend, Emanuel, Lilia begins an illicit journey that soon descends into horror." (Kirkus)

REVIEW: *Booklist* v108 no12 p18 F 15 2012 Deborah Donovan

REVIEW: *Kirkus Rev* v80 no4 p343 F 15 2012

"The Iguana Tree." "Stone's debut literary fiction gives face and spirit, emotion and character, to those braving the deadly trail across our southern border, seeking only to find work, living only to be pursued as illegal immigrants. . . . Each character resonates authentically, and the contrasts between idyllic but circumscribed life in Mexico, the bloody border and the welcome success hard work can bring to an appreciative immigrant is empathetically rendered. Stone has done exceptional work in making real the struggles and despair, the resolute discipline and hope, driving the desire to find a better life while also illuminating unexpected connections of near-familial love among people of difference cultures who live and work together."

REVIEW: *Libr J* v137 no2 p60 F 1 2012 Lisa Rohrbaugh

STONE, ROBERT, 1937-. Death of the black-haired girl; [by] Robert Stone 288 p. 2013 Houghton Mifflin Harcourt

1. Adultery—Fiction 2. Murder—Fiction 3. Psychological fiction 4. Teacher-student relationships—Fiction 5. Women college students—Fiction
ISBN 0618386238 (hardcover); 9780618386239 (hardcover)
LC 2013-001597

SUMMARY: This novel, written by Robert Stone, focuses on college professor Steven Brookman who "has determined that for the sake of his marriage, and his soul, he must extract himself from his relationship with Maud Stack, his . . . student." It is a "tale of infidelity, accountability, the allure of youth, the promise of absolution, and the notion that madness is everywhere, in plain sight." (Publisher's note)

REVIEW: *America* v210 no14 p38-40 Ap 21 2014 DIANE SCHARPER

REVIEW: *Booklist* v110 no1 p36 S 1 2013 Ben Segedin

"Death of the Black-Haired Girl." "Set on campus, [Robert] Stone's novel features Maud, smart, beautiful, and full of passion for her convictions and her married professor. . . . Although Stone . . . introduces a cast of menacing and motivated characters, he is interested less in whodunit than in questions of fate and of faith. . . . Stone's world, full of ominous forebodings, is populated by characters familiar to readers of his novels: the disaffected, the politically naive, and the world weary--lost souls who have lost their faith and others with false faith."

REVIEW: *Booklist* v109 no19/20 p4 Je 1 2013

REVIEW: *Kirkus Rev* v81 no17 p25 S 1 2013

REVIEW: *Kirkus Rev* p15 Ag 15 2013 Fall Preview

REVIEW: *Libr J* v138 no10 p78 Je 1 2013

REVIEW: *Libr J* v138 no14 p104 S 1 2013 James Coan

REVIEW: *N Y Rev Books* v60 no20 p53-4 D 19 2013 Adam Kirsch

"Death of the Black-Haired Girl." "Everything about Maud--from her name. . . to her poetic description as 'the black-haired girl'—makes her seem more like a figure out of a folk legend than a three-dimensional novelistic character. . . . This is not how any living college-age American talks, but Stone is not interested in realism. He is creating a desperate, fateful mood. . . . The result is a book missing some of its center, in which the religious themes never quite find a focus in the actual plot."

REVIEW: *N Y Times Book Rev* p16 N 17 2013 CLAIRE MESSUD

"Death of the Black-Haired Girl." "Robert Stone . . . tackles a genre . . . and twists it to his purposes in ways that surprise and provoke. A subtle writer, he demands an attentive reader as he explores, through superficially familiar narratives, substantial themes. . . . It soon becomes clear that Stone isn't really interested in a whodunit--this very structure proves a MacGuffin--but rather is addressing greater, even spiritual, questions. . . . Stone turns his considerable powers of concrete evocation to describing Amesbury's almost mythically dystopian landscape, populated by the indigent and mentally unstable."

REVIEW: *New York Times* v163 no56332 pC1-6 N 26 2013 MICHIKO KAKUTANI

REVIEW: *New Yorker* v89 no39 p69-1 D 2 2013

REVIEW: *Publ Wkly* v260 no20 p30 My 20 2013

REVIEW: *Publ Wkly* v261 no8 p178 F 24 2014

STONE, WILL.tr. Nietzsche. See Nietzsche

STOPPATO, CATERINA. Regular functions of a quaternionic variable. See Gentili, G.

STORA, BENJAMIN.ed. A history of Jewish-Muslim relations. See A history of Jewish-Muslim relations

STORACE, PATRICIA. The book of heaven; a novel; [by] Patricia Storace 384 p. 2014 Pantheon

1. Astrology—Fiction 2. BODY, MIND & SPIRIT—Astrology—General 3. FICTION—Fantasy—Historical 4. FICTION—Literary 5. Women—Fiction
ISBN 9780375408069 (hardback)
LC 2013-022316

SUMMARY: In this novel by Patricia Storace, "we begin with Eve, who tells a tale of evading rape and discovering a zodiac of constellations that we usually cannot see from Earth. The constellations offer archaic feminine images, such as a giant cooking pot, and hold the tales of archetypal women (some biblical, some invented by Storace)." (Publishers Weekly)

REVIEW: *Booklist* v110 no9/10 p39 Ja 1 2014 Amber Peckham

REVIEW: *Kirkus Rev* v82 no1 p138 Ja 1 2014

"The Book of Heaven". "In her visionary first novel, [Patricia] Storace . . . gives voice to the stories behind four of them, tales of women dwelling in different yet not unfamiliar worlds of oppression and submission. Stupendously imagined and detailed, occasionally didactic and dense, Storace's descriptions of the four women's lives that inspired these unknown star formations are filled with distantly recognizable tribes, beliefs, dynasties and social systems. . . . Storace's striking feminist mythopoeic work offers provocative alternatives in beautifully crafted prose."

REVIEW: *Libr J* v138 no15 p49 S 15 2013

REVIEW: *Publ Wkly* v260 no50 p47-8 D 9 2013

STOREY, MARK. Rural fictions, urban realities; a geography of Gilded Age American literature; [by] Mark Storey viii, 200 p. 2013 Oxford University Press

1. American fiction—19th century—History and criticism 2. City and town life in literature 3. Farm life in literature 4. Pastoral fiction, American—History and criticism 5. Rural conditions in literature

ISBN 9780199893188

LC 2012-015367

SUMMARY: In this study of American literature, "Mark Storey proffers a capacious, trans-regional version of rural fiction that contains and coexists with urban-industrial modernity. To remap literary representations of the rural, Storey pinpoints four key aspects of everyday life that recur with surprising frequency in late nineteenth-century fiction: train journeys, travelling circuses, country doctors, and lynch mobs." (Publisher's note)

REVIEW: *Choice* v50 no11 p2017 Jl 2013 D. E. Sloane

REVIEW: *N Engl Q* v86 no4 p698-9 D 2013 Stephanie Foote

REVIEW: *TLS* no5776 p24 D 13 2013 ALEXANDRA MANGLIS

"Rural Fictions, Urban Realities: A Geography of Gilded Age American Literature." "Mark Storey's 'Rural Fictions, Urban Realities: A geography of Gilded Age American literature' draws attention to some hitherto unnoticed alternative histories and narratives in American literature. Instead of concentrating on the city, modernity's main locus, Storey leads the reader into the strange and alluring terrain of the rural, postbellum US. . . . In this ambitious first book, Storey demonstrates the importance of rural fictions as the means of complicating and refreshing our mostly one-eyed view of America's literary development. . . . Mark Storey's book . . . provides . . . a compelling reason to begin reading postbellum rural American literature."

THE STORIES I READ TO THE CHILDREN; the life and writing of Pura Belpré, the legendary storyteller, children's author, and New York Public librarian; xii, 285 p. 2013 Center for Puerto Rican Studies

1. Anthologies 2. Belpré, Pura, 1899-1982 3. Children's literature—Authorship 4. Hispanic American librarians 5. Tales—Puerto Rico 6. Women authors, Puerto Rican

ISBN 9781878483805 (pbk.)

LC 2012-041664

SUMMARY: Edited by Lisa Sánchez González, this book "documents, for the very first time, Pura Belpré's contributions to North American, Caribbean and Latin American literary and library history. Thoroughly researched but clearly written, this study is scholarship that is also accessible to general readers, students and teachers. Pura Belpré (1899-1982) is one of the most important public intellectuals in the history of the Puerto Rican diaspora." (Publisher's note)

REVIEW: *Bull Cent Child Books* v67 no2 p128 O 2013 T. A.

"The Stories I Read to the Children: The Life and Writing of Pura Belpré, the Legendary Storyteller, Children's Author, and New York Public Librarian." "Pura Belpré, the first Latina librarian at the New York Public Library and author of the first known Latina/o children's book from a mainstream publisher, has received a strikingly small amount of scholarly attention. This book, a collection of Belpré's stories and essays . . . seeks to fill that gap. . . . [Editor Lisa] Sánchez González provides a brief biographical sketch of Belpré, drawing from . . . archival sources and accessibly situating Belpré's life and work within larger contexts. . . . She also has carefully selected thirty-two of Belpré's Puerto Rican folktales, . . . all of which are wondrous in their simple magic."

REVIEW: *SLJ* v59 no8 p131 Ag 2013 Margaret Bush

THE STORIES THEY TELL; artifacts from the National September 11 Memorial & Museum; 160 p. 2013 Skira Rizzoli, A Division of Rizzoli International Publications

1. Historical literature 2. National September 11 Memorial & Museum at the World Trade Center 3. September 11 Terrorist Attacks, 2001 4. Terrorism victims' families 5. Victims of terrorism

ISBN 9780847841332 (pbk. : alk. paper); 9780847841714 (hardcover : alk. paper)

LC 2013-934955

SUMMARY: Edited by Alice M. Greenwald and Clifford Chanin, "This . . . selection of artifacts--and their stories--from September 11 provides an official, lasting record of that day's experience. In both text and photography, the story of September 11 is told through a selection of powerfully moving artifacts from the 9/11 museum's collection that serve as touchstones to the day and its aftermath." (Publisher's note)

REVIEW: *N Y Times Book Rev* p85 D 8 2013 Clyde Haberman

"The Stories They Tell: Artifacts From the National September 11 Memorial Museum: A Journey of Remembrance," "The Nature of Urban Design: A New York Perspective on Resilience," and "Mapping Manhattan: A Love (and Sometimes Hate) Story in Maps by 75 New Yorkers." "Artifacts in this handsome 'journey of remembrance' are drawn from the museum that is part of New York's Sept. 11 memorial. The book matches photos with essays by museum staff members. . . . For [author Alexandros] Washburn . . . the ruination inflicted by Hurricane Sandy was intensely personal. . . . This book may appeal more to students of urban policy than to general readers. . . . [Author Becky] Cooper, a cartographer, takes us on an entertaining journey."

STORLI, ESPEN, 1975-.ed. Aluminum Ore. See Aluminum Ore

STORM, ERIC.ed. Region and state in nineteenth-century Europe. See Region and state in nineteenth-century Europe

STORY, JOANNA.ed. Old Saint Peter's, Rome. See Old Saint Peter's, Rome

STOSSEL, SCOTT. My age of anxiety; fear, hope, dread, and the search for peace of mind; [by] Scott Stossel 416 p. 2014 Alfred A. Knopf

1. Anxiety 2. Anxiety—Chemotherapy 3. Anxiety disorders—Epidemiology 4. Memoirs 5. Tranquilizing drugs—Social aspects
ISBN 0307269876; 9780307269874 (hardcover); 9780307390608 (pbk.)
LC 2013-006336

SUMMARY: This book, by Scott Stossel, presents an "account of the author's struggles with anxiety, and of the history of efforts by scientists, philosophers, and writers to understand the condition. . . . He ranges from the earliest medical reports of Galen and Hippocrates, through later observations by Robert Burton and Soren Kierkegaard, to the investigations by great nineteenth-century scientists, such as Charles Darwin, William James, and Sigmund Freud." (Publisher's note)

REVIEW: *Am Sch* v83 no2 p102-4 Spr 2014 GARY GREENBERG

REVIEW: *Bookforum* v20 no4 p47 D 2013/Ja 2014 GEORGE SCIALABBA

REVIEW: *Booklist* v110 no7 p19 D 1 2013 Tony Miksanek

REVIEW: *Choice* v51 no12 p2275 Ag 2014 A. L. Bizub

REVIEW: *Kirkus Rev* v81 no22 p82 N 15 2013

REVIEW: *Libr J* v139 no7 p49-50 Ap 15 2014 Laurie Selwyn

REVIEW: *Libr J* v138 no12 p56 Jl 1 2013

REVIEW: *N Y Times Book Rev* p13 Ja 26 2014 NATHAN HELLER

REVIEW: *New Sci* v221 no2955 p49-50 F 8 2014 Bob Holmes

"Anxiety: A Short History" and "My Age of Anxiety: Fear, Hope, Dread, and the Search for Peace of Mind". "[Allan V.] Horwitz, a sociologist of mental illness and mental health at Rutgers University in New Jersey, and [Scott] Stossel, editor of The Atlantic magazine, give remarkably similar historical overviews. They seem to have read the same sources, cite identical quotes from The Iliad, and come to the same conclusions. It's almost as if they had shared a desk at the library. Despite that, they have written very different books. Horwitz's book gives an objective, somewhat detached look at anxiety through the ages. . . . It's one thing to read a dispassionate discussion of whether social and economic pressures have medicalised anxiety, and quite another to read of Stossel's lifelong torture from overpowering anxiety, despite trying 20 different therapies and 28 different anti-anxiety drugs, none of which gave lasting relief."

REVIEW: *New Statesman* v143 no5223 p40-2 Ag 15 2014 Lisa Appignanesi

REVIEW: *New Yorker* p64-1 Ja 27 2014

REVIEW: *Publ Wkly* v260 no42 p43 O 21 2013

REVIEW: *Publ Wkly* v261 no5 p13 F 3 2014

REVIEW: *Publ Wkly* v261 no8 p179-80 F 24 2014

STOTT, ANDREW MCCONNELL. The Vampyre Family; The Curse of Byron; [by] Andrew McConnell Stott 464 p. 2013 Canongate Books Ltd

1. Byron, George Gordon Byron, Baron, 1788-1824 2. English poets—19th century 3. Geneva (Switzerland)—History—19th century 4. Historical literature 5. Romanticism—History 6. Shelley, Percy Bysshe, 1792-1822
ISBN 1847678718; 9781847678713

SUMMARY: This book by Andrew McConnell Stott describes how "In the spring of 1816, Lord Byron . . . sought refuge in Europe, taking his young doctor with him. As an inexperienced medic with literary aspirations of his own, Dr Polidori could not believe his luck. That summer another literary star also arrived in Geneva. With Percy Bysshe Shelley came his lover, Mary and her step-sister Claire Clairmont." (Publisher's note)

REVIEW: *New Statesman* v142 no5189 p52 D 13 2013 John Mullan

REVIEW: *TLS* no5796 p22 My 2 2014 MIKA ROSS-SOUTHALL

"The Vampyre Family: Passion, Envy, and the Curse of Byron" and "Lord Byron's Best Friends: From Bulldogs to Boatswain and Beyond." "The effect of Byron was not just felt by women; the Romantic age was feverishly obsessed with him. But those who came closest to the poet and his fame discovered that what they had hoped would improve their own lives turned out to destroy them, as Andrew McConnell Stott shows us in his biography, 'The Vampyre Family: Passion, envy and the curse of Byron.' . . 'Lord Byron's Best Friends: From bulldogs to Boatswain and beyond' also concentrates on peripheral characters in Byron's life. . . . [Author Geoffrey] Bond narrates the story of Byron's life plainly, with help from paintings."

STOTT, ANNE. Wilberforce; family and friends; [by] Anne Stott viii, 338 p. 2012 Oxford University Press

1. Abolitionists—Great Britain—Biography 2. Historical literature 3. Legislators—Great Britain—Biography 4. Philanthropists—Great Britain—Biography
ISBN 9780199699391 (hbk.: acid-free paper)
LC 2012-372743

SUMMARY: This book "presents an interwoven account of three marriages and families—those of William and Barbara Wilberforce, Henry and Marianne Thornton, and Zachary and Selina Macaulay—set amidst the well-known stories of Evangelical philanthropy and political activism. [Anne] Stott's stated intention is . . . to piece together the inner life of the 'Clapham Sect' as it unfolded for them, bringing to the fore the ways in which they themselves understood their life stories." (English Historical Review)

REVIEW: *Engl Hist Rev* v129 no536 p226-8 F 2014 Roshan Allpress

"Wilberforce: Family and Friends". "Anne Stott is a talented biographer. This book should further her reputation, as she presents an interwoven account of three marriages and families . . . set amidst the well-known stories of Evangelical philanthropy and political activism. . . . Stott has amassed a vast body of material for this task, and anyone who has ever struggled to read the scrawled and blotched handwriting of a hasty correspondent with poor eyesight will appreciate her achievements in primary research. . . . It is this meticulously researched and engagingly written movement between broad themes and intimate detail that makes Stott's book an important contribution to the history of the Clapham Sect, telling the very human story of these much-studied humanitarians."

REVIEW: *Hist Today* v62 no11 p58 N 2012 IAN BRADLEY

STOTT, REBECCA. Darwin's Ghosts; In Search of the First Evolutionists; [by] Rebecca Stott 2012 Bloomsbury UK

1. Darwin, Charles, 1809-1882 2. Evolution (Biology)—History 3. Naturalists 4. Scientific literature 5. Scientists—Biography

ISBN 1408809087; 9781408809082

SUMMARY: This book "draws for readers stories of the people who came before [Charles] Darwin and who presented ideas that were precursors to the theory of evolution. . . . Many of the thinkers and ideas presented in this book . . . Darwin was not aware of until after the publication of 'On the Origin of Species.' After receiving a critical letter, he compiled a list of his scientific predecessors to be included in the foreword of later editions . . . including Aristotle, Al-Jahiz, Leonardo da Vinci, and Denis Diderot." (Library Journal)

REVIEW: *TLS* no5743 p7 Ap 26 2013 ANGELIQUE RICHARDSON

"Darwin's Ghosts: In Search of the First Evolutionists." "Rebecca Stott's story . . . indefatigably researched and deftly plotted, plunges us into a kaleidoscope of rivals and revolutions, fantastic ideas, worlds enormous and small, connections, and failures to connect. . . . Brave new ideas can need many thinkers, and years, taking shape gradually (if not uniformly). Spanning the globe, and more than 2,000 years, 'Darwin's Ghosts' tells an original story about what was, of necessity, not original about the 'Origin'. It is a book to like, and learn from, immensely."

STOTZ, KAROLA. Genetics and philosophy. See Griffiths, P.

STOVALL, TYLER. Paris and the spirit of 1919; consumer struggles, transnationalism, and revolution; [by] Tyler Stovall xii, 342 p. 2012 Cambridge University Press

1. Anti-imperialist movements 2. Consumerism—History 3. Consumption (Economics)—Social aspects—France—Paris—History—20th century 4. France—History—20th century 5. HISTORY—Europe—General 6. Historical literature 7. Labor movement—France—Paris—History—20th century 8. Paris (France)—History—20th century 9. Popular fronts—France—Paris—History—20th century 10. Strikes and lockouts—France—Paris—History—20th century 11. Working class—France—Paris—History—20th century

ISBN 9781107018013 (hardback)

LC 2011-030735

SUMMARY: Written by Tyler Stovall, "This transnational history of Paris in 1919 explores the global implications of the revolutionary crisis of French society at the end of World War I. As the site of the Peace Conference, Paris was a victorious capital and a city at the centre of the world. . . . The book takes as its central point the eruption of political activism in 1919, using the events of that year to illustrate broader tensions in working class, race and gender politics." (Publisher's note)

REVIEW: *Am Hist Rev* v118 no4 p1260-1 O 2013 Keith Mann

"Paris and the Spirit of 1919: Consumer Struggles, Transnationalism, and Revolution." "Tyler Stovall has produced a work of social and labor history that incorporates recent scholarly insights on postcolonialism, transnationalism, and consumer struggles. . . . The book focuses on the year 1919 and the city of Paris and its industrial suburbs to examine the ways that a number of local, national, and international processes came together to reshape what it meant to be working class in post--World War I France. Paris in 1919 was a focal point for these processes and the conflicts they generated. . . . All in all, this far-reaching study greatly expands the scope of social and labor history and demonstrates the continued vitality of the subfield of French labor history."

REVIEW: *Choice* v50 no4 p748 D 2012 D. A. Harvey

STOVER, TIM. Epic and empire in Vespasianic Rome; a new reading of Valerius Flaccus' Argonautica; [by] Tim Stover x, 244 p. 2012 Oxford University Press

1. Argonautica (Poem) 2. Argonauts (Greek mythology) 3. Flaccus, Valerius 4. Latin epic poetry 5. Rome—History—Vespasian, 69-79

ISBN 019964408X; 9780199644087

LC 2011-942661

SUMMARY: This book by Tim Stover "offers a new interpretation of Valerius Flaccus' 'Argonautica,' a Latin epic poem written during the reign of . . . Vespasian (70-79 AD). Recounting the famous voyage of Jason and the Argonauts as they set off to retrieve the Golden Fleece, the poem depicts . . . epic adventure. In this volume, Stover shows how Flaccus' epic reflects the restorative ideals of Vespasianic Rome, which attempted to restore order following the . . . civil war of 68-69 AD." (Publisher's note)

REVIEW: *Classical Rev* v63 no2 p445-7 O 2013 Nikoletta Manioti

"Epic and Empire in Vespasianic Rome: A New Reading of Valerius Flaccus' 'Argonautica.'" "In this very interesting book, a revised version of his 2006 doctoral thesis, [author Tim Stover] reads the Roman 'Argonautica' in two, often intertwined, ways. . . . This interpretation is unusually optimistic . . . , but nevertheless highly convincing. [Stover's] book, a 'new reading' indeed, is an important contribution to the field of Latin literature and Flavian epic in particular. A brief introduction consisting of an outline of the argument and the contents of the book is followed by six chapters."

STOWER, ADAM. Slam!; A Tale of Consequences; [by] Adam Stower 32 p. 2014 Pgw

1. Accidents 2. Boys—Fiction 3. Causation (Philosophy) 4. Cities & towns—Juvenile literature 5. Picture books for children

ISBN 1771470070; 9781771470070

SUMMARY: This picture book depicts a "calamity of epic and silly proportions, all thanks to a slammed door that dislodges a red ball. As the ball bounces through the neighborhood, it unleashes an escalating series of slapstick events that involve animals and people thrown off course and into the air, traffic jams and near-collisions, a fire-breathing dragon, tiny alien creatures—and a boy completely oblivious to the chaos he has caused." (Publisher's note)

REVIEW: *Bull Cent Child Books* v67 no7 p381 Mr 2014 D. S.

REVIEW: *Kirkus Rev* v82 no1 p228 Ja 1 2014

"Slam! A Tale of Consequences". "Meanwhile, the door-slammer is oblivious, walking just a step ahead of the tide of chaos, ears safely protected from the din by earphones. It is all a cumulative contagion of catastrophe, with few words to interrupt the proceedings, just an eyeful of cockamamie consequences. This story will be left up to the teller's panache, aided and abetted by [Adam] Stower's crazy art happenings, strangely but effectively drawn with a palette of candy-heart colors and with teeming action on every page. Not a lullaby by any stretch, but good for a guffaw."

REVIEW: *Publ Wkly* v261 no2 p65 Ja 13 2014

REVIEW: *SLJ* v60 no3 p128 Mr 2014 Mary Elam

STRALEY, JOHN. Cold storage, Alaska; [by] John Straley 304 p. 2014 Soho Crime

1. Detective & mystery stories 2. Ex-convicts—Fiction 3. Paranormal fiction 4. Small cities—Alaska—Fiction
ISBN 1616953063; 9781616953065 (hardback)
LC 2013-019796

SUMMARY: In this novel, by John Straley, "Clive 'The Milkman' McCahon returns to his tiny Alaska hometown after a seven-year jail stint for dealing coke. He has a lot to make up to his younger brother, Miles, who has dutifully been taking care of their ailing mother. . . . His vengeful old business partner is hot on his heels, a . . . State Trooper is dying to bust Clive for narcotics, and, to complicate everything, Clive might be going insane—lately, he's been hearing animals talking to him." (Publisher's note)

REVIEW: *Booklist* v110 no9/10 p48 Ja 1 2014 Thomas Gaughan

"Cold Storage, Alaska". "After seven years in prison, Clive McCahon heads home to Cold Storage, Alaska. On the way, he liberates a pile of cash from his drug-dealer former boss and adopts a dog as big as a wolf. . . . [John] Straley . . . has created a wonderfully evocative place in Cold Storage. His evocation of nature and human nature approaches the lyrical, and he seems guided by [William] Faulkner's dictum that the only thing truly worth writing about is the human heart in conflict with itself."

REVIEW: *Kirkus Rev* v81 no23 p173 D 1 2013

REVIEW: *Libr J* v138 no18 p83 N 1 2013 Dan Forrest

REVIEW: *N Y Times Book Rev* p19 F 2 2014 MARLYN STASIO

REVIEW: *Publ Wkly* v260 no49 p61-2 D 2 2013

STRANAHAN, SUSAN Q. Fukushima. See Lyman, E.

STRAND, JEFF. I have a bad feeling about this; [by] Jeff Strand 256 p. 2014 Sourcebooks Fire

1. Adventure stories 2. Camps—Fiction 3. Self-confidence—Fiction 4. Survival—Fiction 5. Teenage boys—Fiction
ISBN 9781402284557 (tp: alk. paper)
LC 2013-045600

SUMMARY: In this book, "sixteen-year-old nerd (or geek, but not dork) Henry Lambert has no desire to go to Strongwoods Survival Camp. . . . When they arrive at the shabby camp in the middle of nowhere and meet the possibly insane counselor (and only staff member), Max, Henry's bad feelings multiply. . . . When a trio of gangsters drops in on the camp Games to try to collect the debt owed by the owner, the boys suddenly have to put their skills to the test." (Kirkus Reviews)

REVIEW: *Booklist* v110 no14 p75 Mr 15 2014 John Peters

REVIEW: *Bull Cent Child Books* v67 no10 p543 Je 2014 T. A.

REVIEW: *Kirkus Rev* v82 no3 p158 F 1 2014

"I Have A Bad Feeling About This". "[Jeff] Strand's summer-camp farce is peopled with sarcastic losers who're chatty and wry. It's often funny, and the gags turn in unexpected directions and would do Saturday Night Live skits proud. However, the story's flow is hampered by an unnecessary and completely unfunny frame that takes place during the premier of the movie the boys make of their experience. The repeated intrusions bring the narrative to a screeching halt. Without that frame, this would have been a fine addition to the wacked-out summer-camp subgenre."

REVIEW: *Publ Wkly* v261 no2 p70 Ja 13 2014

REVIEW: *SLJ* v60 no3 p163 Mr 2014 Kimberly Castle-Alberts

REVIEW: *Voice of Youth Advocates* v37 no1 p75 Ap 2014 Julia Bowersox

STRANDBERG, MATS. The Circle. See Elfgren, S. B.

STRANDBERG, MATS. Fire. See Elfgren, S. B.

STRANGE SHORES; an Inspector Erlendur novel; 304 p. 2014 Minotaur Books

1. Detective & mystery stories 2. Erlendur Sveinsson (Fictitious character)—Fiction 3. Family secrets—Fiction 4. Icelandic fiction 5. Missing persons—Fiction 6. Murder—Fiction 7. Murder investigation—Fiction
ISBN 1250000408; 9781250000408 (hardcover)
LC 2014-007876

SUMMARY: This detective novel by Arnaldur Indridason, part of the Inspector Erlendur Series, "begins when a young woman disappears from the frozen fjords of Iceland. . . . Detective Erlendur is on the hunt. He is looking for the missing woman but also for his long-lost brother. . . . Slowly, the past begins to surrender its secrets. But as Erlendur uncovers a story about the limits of human endurance, he realizes that many people would prefer their crimes to stay buried." (Publisher's note)

REVIEW: *Booklist* v110 no19/20 p48 Je 1 2014 Thomas Gaughan

REVIEW: *Kirkus Rev* v82 no16 p112 Ag 15 2014

REVIEW: *Libr J* v139 no5 p66 Mr 15 2014 Barbara Hoffert

REVIEW: *Libr J* v139 no4 p66 Mr 1 2014 Barbara Hoffert

REVIEW: *Libr J* v139 no11 p89 Je 15 2014 Edward Goldberg

REVIEW: *Publ Wkly* v261 no20 p48-9 My 19 2014

REVIEW: *TLS* no5764 p20 S 20 2013 PAUL BINDING

"Strange Shores". "'Strange Shores' is very much Erlendur's, as the sequence's dynamics demand it should be, taking him to the frontiers of time, the portals of death. Though these nine novels have all the compelling qualities of popular Nordic noir, their close-worked presentation of the perennial difficulties of coping with flux—in self, in society, in existence—put them, especially when taken together, far beyond genre affiliation, out into the challenging domain of serious literature."

STRASSER, TODD. Fallout; [by] Todd Strasser 272 p. 2013 Candlewick Press

1. Alternate histories (Fiction) 2. Cuban Missile Crisis, 1962 3. Families—Fiction 4. Nuclear bomb shelters 5. Racism—Fiction

ISBN 0763655341; 9780763655341

LC 2012-955123

SUMMARY: This book is an alternate history novel by Todd Strasser. "In the summer of 1962, the possibility of nuclear war is all anyone talks about. But Scott's dad is the only one in the neighborhood who actually prepares for the worst. . . . . When the unthinkable happens," their neighbors "force their way into the shelter. . . . With not enough room, not enough food, and not enough air, life inside the shelter is filthy, physically draining, and emotionally fraught." (Publisher's note)

REVIEW: *Booklist* v110 no1 p119 S 1 2013 Krista Hutley

REVIEW: *Bull Cent Child Books* v67 no2 p117-8 O 2013 E. B.

REVIEW: *Horn Book Magazine* v89 no6 p107 N/D 2013 JONATHAN HUNT

"Fallout." "Alternating chapters tell the story of the months leading up to that tense week and a half in the bomb shelter, allowing the author to vividly depict the 1960s setting, create complex characters, and build the backstory. An interesting author's note describes the inspiration for this novel: his own family's backyard bomb shelter. [Todd] Strasser has crafted a memorable piece of alternative history that will leave readers pondering the characters and their choices long after the last page is turned."

REVIEW: *Kirkus Rev* v81 no14 p319 Jl 15 2013

REVIEW: *N Y Times Book Rev* p29 N 10 2013 EDWARD LEWINE

"Fallout." "Exciting, harrowing. . . . [Todd] Strasser has reimagined the Cuban missile crisis and set 'Fallout' in a realistic John F. Kennedy America. . . . The one unhistorical detail is that in this story the Soviets don't back down. They strike. . . . For all its horror, this is a superb entertainment suitable for any tough-minded kid over the age of 10. It thrums along with finely wrought atmosphere and gripping suspense. If the characters aren't exactly overburdened with complexity, they're better drawn than many of the people one bumps into in the average thriller. . . . Strasser, a prolific writer for children and teenagers, writes with purpose and economy and structures his book intelligently."

REVIEW: *Publ Wkly* v260 no32 p61-2 Ag 12 2013

REVIEW: *Publ Wkly* p87-8 Children's starred review annual 2013

REVIEW: *SLJ* v59 no9 p148 S 2013 Diana Pierce

REVIEW: *SLJ* v60 no5 p66 My 2014 Necia Blundy

REVIEW: *Voice of Youth Advocates* v36 no4 p74 O 2013 Rebecca Moore

REVIEW: *Voice of Youth Advocates* v36 no4 p74 O 2013 Tapan Srivastava

STRASSER, TODD. No place; [by] Todd Strasser 272 p. 2014 Simon & Schuster Books for Young Readers

1. Friendship—Fiction 2. Homeless persons—Fiction 3. Homeless teenagers 4. Poverty—Fiction 5. Young adult fiction

ISBN 144245721X; 9781442457218 (hardcover)

LC 2012-043701

SUMMARY: In this novel, by Todd Strasser, "It seems like Dan has it all. . . . Then his family loses their home. Forced to move into the town's Tent City, Dan feels his world shifting. . . . As Dan struggles to adjust to his new life, he gets involved with the people who are fighting for better conditions and services for the residents of Tent City. But someone wants Tent City gone, and will stop at nothing until it's destroyed." (Publisher's note)

REVIEW: *Booklist* v110 no5 p77 N 1 2013 Daniel Kraus

REVIEW: *Bull Cent Child Books* v67 no5 p285 Ja 2014 E. B.

"No Place." "Responding to a sharp spike in homelessness, a community mayor establishes a temporary tent village, Dignityville, with basic sanitation, a heated dining tent, and a few electrical generators. . . . The ham-fisted messaging makes the book read more like a polemic than a novel, with characters weighing in on the homeless question as if reading from scripts. Nonetheless, teen readers who recognize that their own families may be just a paycheck or two away from a similar fate may rightly regard this as a gripping horror story, with fall from social grace as terrifying as cold nights and hungry mornings."

REVIEW: *Kirkus Rev* v81 no23 p98 D 1 2013

REVIEW: *Publ Wkly* v260 no42 p53 O 21 2013

REVIEW: *Voice of Youth Advocates* v36 no6 p66 F 2014 Jamie Hansen

STRAZNICKY, MARTA.ed. Shakespeare's stationers. See Shakespeare's stationers

STREEP, PEG. Mastering the art of quitting. See Bernstein, A.

STREVENS, MICHAEL. Tychomancy; inferring probability from causal structure; [by] Michael Strevens xii, 265 p. 2013 Harvard University Press

1. Causation (Philosophy) 2. Empiricism 3. Inference 4. Probabilities 5. Scientific literature

ISBN 9780674073111 (alk. paper)

LC 2012-042985

SUMMARY: This book "presents a set of rules for inferring the physical probabilities of outcomes from the causal or dynamic properties of the systems that produce them. Probabilities revealed by the rules are wide-ranging: they include the probability of getting a 5 on a die roll, the probability distributions found in statistical physics, and the probabilities that underlie many prima facie judgments about fitness in evolutionary biology." (Publisher's note)

REVIEW: *Choice* v51 no4 p659-60 D 2013 R. Paul Thompson

"Tychomancy: Inferring Probability From Causal Structure." "[Michael Strevens'] exploration is part philosophy of science, part history of science, and part psychology. It is wide ranging, encompassing the inferring of probabilities--using the system of rules--regarding the behavior of physical objects, organisms, minds, social groups, and the like. His construction of equidynamics is a fascinating and captivating journey; his examples of the employment of equidynamics are convincing. . . . This book will interest historians and philosophers of science, psychologists, physicists, and biologists."

STRICKLAND, SHADRA.il. Please, Louise. See Morrison, T.

STRINGER, KEITH J.ed. Norman expansion. See Norman expansion

STROBY, WALLACE. Shoot the woman first; [by] Wallace Stroby 288 p. 2013 Minotaur Books

1. Drug traffic—Fiction 2. Ex-police officers—Fiction 3. FICTION—Crime 4. FICTION—Mystery & Detective—Hard-Boiled 5. FICTION—Mystery & Detective—Women Sleuths 6. Female offenders—Fiction 7. Stone, Crissa (Fictitious character)—Fiction
ISBN 1250000386; 9781250000385 (hardback)
LC 2013-029818

SUMMARY: This book, by Wallace Stroby, centers on "professional thief Crissa Stone. . . . When [a] split goes awry in a blaze of gunfire, Crissa finds herself on the run with a duffel bag of stolen cash. . . . In pursuit are the drug kingpin's lethal lieutenants and a former Detroit cop with his own deadly agenda. They think the money's there for the taking, for whoever finds her first. But Crissa doesn't plan to give it up without a fight." (Publisher's note)

REVIEW: *Booklist* v110 no5 p32-3 N 1 2013 Don Crinklaw

"Shoot the Woman First." "The shootouts have been staged in many a gangster--and western--tale. But when they're done as skillfully as this, who cares? We first meet Burke as he beats up a prostitute and robs her. Crissa [Stone] is attempting to deliver the stolen money to her dead partner's family, who are down on their luck. The moral order is thus established, and as the finale approaches and the writing style burns down to its hard essence, even jaded readers will hope Burke is right about that 'smarter, faster, meaner, and deadlier.'"

REVIEW: *Kirkus Rev* v81 no24 p202 D 15 2013

REVIEW: *Libr J* v138 no21 p74 D 1 2013 Teresa L. Jacobsen

STROUD, JONATHAN, 1970-. The screaming staircase; [by] Jonathan Stroud 400 p. 2013 Disney-Hyperion

1. Ghost stories 2. Ghosts—Fiction 3. Haunted houses—Fiction 4. Psychic ability—Fiction 5. Supernatural—Fiction
ISBN 1423164911; 9781423164913
LC 2013-000352

SUMMARY: This is the first book in Jonathan Stroud's Lockwood & Co. series. Lucy Carlyle has joined the Lockwood & Co. firm to help with England's ghost problem. "As its third member, she teams with glib, ambitious Anthony Lockwood and slovenly-but-capable scholar George Cubbins to entrap malign spirits for hire. The work is fraught with peril, not only because a ghost's merest touch is generally fatal, but also, as it turns out, as none of the three is particularly good at careful planning." (Kirkus Reviews)

REVIEW: *Booklist* v109 no19/20 p100-1 Je 1 2013 Carolyn Phelan

REVIEW: *Bull Cent Child Books* v67 no2 p118 O 2013 K. Q. G.

"The Screaming Staircase." "In an alternative England plagued by hauntings, ghostbusting agencies are staffed mostly by Sensitive kids and teens, since only people under the age of eighteen have the psychic abilities to deal with the spirits properly. . . . [Author Jonathan] Stroud brings together the seemingly disparate plot points together with his usual combination of thrilling adventure and snarky humor. Fans of his Bartimaeus Trilogy will recognize Lockwood's assistant, George, as a kindred (albeit human) soul to that series' wise-cracking djinni. . . . The ghosts themselves are scary but not gory, and the descriptions are vivid without being intense. . . ."

REVIEW: *Horn Book Magazine* v89 no5 p113 S/O 2013 CLAIRE E. GROSS

"The Screaming Staircase." "With a morbidly cheery tone and sure-footed establishment of characters and setting, [Jonathan] Stroud . . . kicks off a new series that is part procedural and part ghost story, with a healthy dash of caper thrown in for good measure. . . . The setup is classic and is executed with panache. Lucy's wry, practical voice counterpoints the suspenseful supernatural goings-on as she, agency owner Anthony Lockwood, and dour associate George attempt to stiff-upper-lip their way through the ultimate haunted house. Tightly plotted and striking just the right balance between creepiness and hilarity, this rollicking series opener dashes to a fiery finish but leaves larger questions about the ghost Problem open for future exploration."

REVIEW: *Kirkus Rev* v81 no12 p117-8 Je 15 2013

REVIEW: *N Y Times Book Rev* p23 O 13 2013 ALEXANDRA MULLEN

REVIEW: *Publ Wkly* v261 no4 p187 Ja 27 2014

REVIEW: *Publ Wkly* v260 no26 p90 Jl 1 2013

REVIEW: *SLJ* v59 no9 p148 S 2013 Janice M. Del Negro

REVIEW: *Voice of Youth Advocates* v36 no6 p11 F 2014 Rachel Anne Bradbury

STROUD, PATRICIA TYSON. A glorious enterprise. See A glorious enterprise

STROUP, SARAH S. Borders among activists; international NGOs in the United States, Britain, and France; [by] Sarah S. Stroup x, 246 p. 2012 Cornell University Press

1. Activism 2. International cooperation 3. Non-governmental organizations—France 4. Non-governmental organizations—Great Britain 5. Non-governmental organizations—United States 6. Social science literature
ISBN 9780801450730 (cloth : alk. paper)
LC 2011-042190

SUMMARY: "In 'Borders among Activists,' Sarah S. Stroup challenges the notion that political activism has gone beyond borders and created a global or transnational civil society. Instead, at the most globally active . . . groups in the world--international nongovernmental organizations (INGOs)--organizational practices are deeply tied to national environments, creating great diversity in the way these groups organize themselves, engage in advocacy, and deliver services."

(Publisher's note)

REVIEW: *Am J Sociol* v118 no6 p1710-2 My 2013 Mark Frezzo

REVIEW: *Choice* v50 no4 p754 D 2012 M. L. Keck

REVIEW: *Contemp Sociol* v42 no5 p723-5 S 2013 Judith Blau

"Borders Among Activists: International NGOs in the United States, Britain, and France." "Sarah Stroup's thesis is incredulous and her title enigmatic. She asserts that International Non-governmental Organizations (INGOs) are by and large more like multinationals than charitable organizations. . . . The problem is her limited sample. . . . On the other hand, her conclusion that American, English, and French INGOs are fundamentally different from one another is convincing. . . . Confining oneself to library and even survey research on NGOs and INGOs does not do justice to them. . . . The researcher of NGOs and INGOs has to get out in the field rather than rely on websites, newspaper accounts, and secondary sources, which is the approach Professor Stroup uses."

REVIEW: *Polit Sci Q (Wiley-Blackwell)* v128 no1 p180-1 Spr 2013 CLAUDE WELCH

STROUT, ELIZABETH.ed. The Stories of Frederick Busch. See Busch, F.

STRUGATSKIĬ, ARKADIĬ NATANOVICH, 1925-1991. Definitely maybe; a manuscript discovered under strange circumstances; 149 p. 2014 Melville House Publishing

1. Experimental fiction, Soviet 2. Russian fiction—Translations into English 3. Satire 4. Social criticism 5. Soviet science fiction
ISBN 9781612192819 (pbk.)
LC 2013-038567

SUMMARY: "Boris and Arkady Strugatsky were the greatest science fiction writers of the Soviet era: their books were intellectually provocative and riotously funny, full of boldly imagined scenarios and veiled—but clear—social criticism. Which may be why 'Definitely Maybe' has never before been available in an uncensored edition, let alone in English," now translated by Antonina W. Bouis. (Publisher's note)

REVIEW: *TLS* no5795 p26 Ap 25 2014 MUIREANN MAGUIRE

"Definitely Maybe." "Antonina W. Bouis originally translated Arkady and Boris Strugatsky's novella in 1978; this revised version is based on the unexpurgated Russian text, finally published by Boris in 2001. 'Definitely Maybe' exemplifies Russian science fiction's crucial role as independent social critique. Boris Strugatsky's afterword, published in English for the first time, explains how he and his brother intended this book to satirize the Soviet regime's clumsy but inexorable oppression of intellectual culture. . . . Bouis's style is authentic and engrossing. Regrettably, no footnotes identify the titles of poems cited in the text. . . . These omissions mask some of the brothers' subtler developments of the themes of professional compromise and intellectual cowardice."

REVIEW: *World Lit Today* v88 no5 p81-3 S/O 2014 Michael A. Morrison

STRUGATSKIĬ, BORIS NATANOVICH, 1933-2012. Definitely maybe. See Strugatskii, A.

STRUPPA, DANIELE C. Regular functions of a quaternionic variable. See Gentili, G.

STRUYK-BONN, CHRIS. Whisper; [by] Chris Struyk-Bonn 352 p. 2014 Orca Book Publishers

1. Alienation (Social psychology)—Fiction 2. Cities & towns—Fiction 3. Cleft palate children 4. People with disabilities—Fiction 5. Young adult fiction
ISBN 1459804759; 9781459804753 (pbk.); 9781459804760 (electronic edition; 9781459804777 (electronic edition
LC 2013-954148

SUMMARY: In this young adult novel by Chris Struyk-Bonn, "sixteen-year-old Whisper, who has a cleft palate, lives in an encampment with three other young rejects and their caregiver, Nathanael. They are outcasts from a society . . . that kills or abandons anyone with a physical or mental disability. . . . Whisper's father comes to claim her, and she becomes his house slave. . . . But when she proves rebellious, she is taken to the city to live with other rejects." (Publisher's note)

REVIEW: *Bull Cent Child Books* v67 no10 p544 Je 2014 A. S.

"Whisper". "This is a complex novel, and Whisper's trajectory from forest to village to city is intense and often anguishing; readers will likely be so sympathetic to the protagonist that they will be more than willing to endure her painful life lessons right along with her. The innate musical talent is more romantic than plausible, but Whisper is clearly brimming with passions that could, perhaps, lead to her being able to write extraordinary pieces with no training or musical context. Offer this to character-driven dystopia fans who will likely relish this glimpse into a multi-layered society that as well-developed and plausible as it is troubling."

REVIEW: *Kirkus Rev* v82 no6 p141 Mr 15 2014

REVIEW: *SLJ* v60 no4 p174 Ap 2014 Nina Sachs

REVIEW: *Voice of Youth Advocates* v37 no1 p75 Ap 2014 Susan Redman-Parodi

STUBBS, ESTELLE. Scribes and the City. See Mooney, L. R.

STUCKHARDT, LEIGH.ed. Best care at lower cost. See Best care at lower cost

STUCKLER, DAVID. The body economic. See Basu, S.

STULBERG, ADAM N.ed. The nuclear renaissance and international security. See The nuclear renaissance and international security

SUDDENDORF, THOMAS. The gap; the science of what separates us from other animals; [by] Thomas Suddendorf 368 p. 2013 Basic Books

1. Animal psychology 2. Comparative psychology 3. Human evolution 4. Psychology 5. Psychology, Com-

parative 6. Science—Popular works
ISBN 0465030149; 9780465030149 (hardcover)
LC 2013-017538

SUMMARY: Author Thomas Suddendorf "provides a definitive account of the mental qualities that separate humans from other animals. Drawing on . . . research on apes, children, and human evolution, he surveys the abilities most often cited as uniquely human—language, intelligence, morality, culture, theory of mind—and finds that two traits account for most of the ways in which our minds appear so distinct: [the] ability to imagine . . .and our insatiable drive to link our minds together." (Publisher's note)

REVIEW: *Choice* v52 no2 p288 O 2014 J. A. Mather

REVIEW: *Kirkus Rev* v81 no21 p22 N 1 2013

REVIEW: *N Y Rev Books* v61 no6 p48-51 Ap 3 2014 Steven Mithen

"Neanderthal Man: In Search of Lost Genomes" and "The Gap: The Science of What Separates Us From Other Animals." "Interminable academic arguments have been swept away by the revolution in studies of ancient DNA, led by [author Svante] Pääbo . . . and brilliantly recounted in his new book, 'Neanderthal Man: In Search of Lost Genomes.' Pääbo has provided us with a fabulous account of three decades of research into ancient DNA. . . . The 'prudent and cautious' analysis that [author Thomas] Suddendorf brings to the psychological evidence is lost when it comes to the Neanderthals. . . . Suddendorf's book . . . provides the most comprehensive comparison of the mentalities of humans and apes that one can imagine."

REVIEW: *New Sci* v221 no2953 p48-9 Ja 25 2014 Anil Ananthaswamy

REVIEW: *Publ Wkly* v260 no34 p58 Ag 26 2013

REVIEW: *Science* v344 no6185 p695 My 16 2014 Bryan Sim

REVIEW: *TLS* no5799 p22 My 23 2014 RAYMOND CORBEY

SUEN, ANASTASIA. Downloading and online shopping safety and privacy; [by] Anastasia Suen 64 p. 2014 Rosen Central

1. Children's nonfiction 2. Computer network resources—Evaluation—Juvenile literature 3. Computer security—Juvenile literature 4. Downloading of data 5. Electronic commerce—Juvenile literature 6. Internet—Security measures—Juvenile literature 7. Money—Juvenile literature
ISBN 1448895715; 9781448895717
LC 2013-427623

SUMMARY: This book on downloading and online shopping is part of the "21st Century Safety and Privacy" series, which "focuses on safe use of the Internet and social media, explaining each activity, noting pleasures as well as perils, and offering suggestions for minimizing risk. The information is organized into short chapters . . . laced with . . . subheadings, photographs of young users, and boxes to break up then text." (Booklist)

REVIEW: *Booklist* v110 no12 p71 F 15 2014 Kathleen Isaacs

"Downloading and Online Shopping Safety and Privacy," "Facebook Safety and Privacy," and "Twitter Safety and Privacy: A Guide to Microblogging." "This timely series focuses on safe use of the Internet and social media, explaining each activity, noting pleasures as well as perils, and offering suggestions for minimizing risk. The information is organized into short chapters liberally laced with appropriate subheadings, photographs of young users, and boxes to break up the text and presented in an oversize, easy-to-read font. . . . In spite of similarities across the titles, there is enough specific information in each to justify purchasing the full series. There are older teen faces on the covers, but this would be most useful for middle-schoolers just entering the social media world."

SUEN, ANASTASIA. Winning by waiting; 24 p. 2013 Rourke Educational Media

1. Children—Conduct of life—Juvenile literature 2. Children's nonfiction 3. Patience 4. Plants—Juvenile literature 5. Saving & investment
ISBN 9781621699088
LC 2013-937303

SUMMARY: This book on patience by Anastasia Suen is part of the Social Skills series, which "takes one aspect of a winning attitude and explains why it might be a worthy goal. . . . 'Winning by Waiting' teaches a lesson well suited to impatient children to appreciate the strategy of the tortoise. Saving money is roped in, and growing plants serves as an overarching metaphor." (Booklist)

REVIEW: *Booklist* v110 no5 p56 N 1 2013 Daniel Kraus

"Winning By Giving," "Winning By Teamwork," and "Winning By Waiting." "Each cheerful title in the Social Skills series takes one aspect of a winning attitude and explains why it might be a worthy goal. 'Winning by Giving' defines philanthropy and then suggests that readers give their kindness, talents, and time to family, friends, and the community. 'Winning by Teamwork' is the series standout, alternating modern examples of good sportsmanship with photos of a U.S. Olympics team, Babe Ruth, and a famous college basketball handshake between a white and black player. 'Winning by Waiting' teaches a lesson well suited to impatient children to appreciate the strategy of the tortoise. . . . Though the text can be a bit cornball, the clean design and bright full-bleed photos of giddy kids make these books suitable and approachable tools in addressing those, shall we say, character quirks out there."

SUK-YOUNG CHWE, MICHAEL. Jane Austen, game theorist; [by] Michael Suk-Young Chwe 276 p. 2013 Princeton University Press

1. Austen, Jane, 1775-1817 2. Game theory—Social aspects 3. Game theory in literature 4. Literature—History & criticism 5. Rational choice theory
ISBN 0691155763; 9780691155760 (hardcover: acid-free paper)
LC 2012-041510

SUMMARY: Author Michael Suk-Young Chwe's book looks at author Jane Austen and how she focused on game theory in her books. The book looks at "how this beloved writer theorized choice and preferences, prized strategic thinking, argued that jointly strategizing with a partner is the surest foundation for intimacy, and analyzed why superiors are often strategically clueless about inferiors." (Publisher's note)

REVIEW: *Choice* v51 no1 p122 S 2013 A. R. Sanderson

"Jane Austen, Game Theorist." "Game theory, developed by mathematician John von Neumann and economist Oskar

Morgenstern in the 1940s, is about strategic decision making. UCLA social scientist [Michael Suk-Young] Chwe . . . argues that 19th-century English novelist Jane Austen may have beaten them to the punch. His book's first several chapters introduce basic game theory concepts and constructs and provide a CliffsNotes-like review of Austen's six major works. . . . Well researched and with an excellent index, the book will appeal to Austen fans who can see her characters in another light, and to students of game theory who will see vindication for the Nobel committees having awarded economic prizes . . . to game theorists."

REVIEW: *J Econ Lit* v51 no4 p1187-90 D 2013

REVIEW: *New Repub* v244 no21 p44-7 F 3 2014 William Deresiewicz

"Jane Austen, Game Theorist". "There is only one problem with this approach: it is intellectually bankrupt. Actually, there are a lot of problems, as Michael Suk-Young Chwe's abominable volume shows. If this is the sort of thing that we have to look forward to, as science undertakes to tutor the humanities, the prospect isn't bright. . . . What we really get, once we fight through Chwe's meandering, ponderous, frequently self-contradictory argument, is only the claim that [Jane] Austen wants her characters to think in game-theoretic ways: to reflect upon the likely consequences of their choices, to plan out how to reach their goals, to try to intuit what the people around them are thinking and how they in turn are likely to act. But this is hardly news."

REVIEW: *New Statesman* v142 no5160 p43 My 31 2013 Philip Maughan

REVIEW: *New York Times* v162 no56115 pC1-6 Ap 23 2013 JENNIFER SCHUESSLER

REVIEW: *TLS* no5758 p27 Ag 9 2013 JONATHAN SACHS

SULLIVAN, DANA.il. Digger and Daisy go on a picnic. See Young, J.

SULLIVAN, HANNAH. The work of revision; [by] Hannah Sullivan 349 p. 2013 Harvard University Press

1. American literature—20th century—Criticism, Textual 2. Authorship 3. Editing 4. English literature—20th century—Criticism, Textual 5. Intertextuality 6. Literature—History & criticism 7. Modernism (Literature)—English-speaking countries
ISBN 9780674073128 (alk. paper)
LC 2012-042986

SUMMARY: Author "Hannah Sullivan argues that we inherit our faith in the virtues of redrafting from early-twentieth-century modernism. Closely examining changes made in manuscripts, typescripts, and proofs by T. S. Eliot, Ezra Pound, Ernest Hemingway, James Joyce, Virginia Woolf, and others, she shows how modernist approaches to rewriting shaped literary style, and how the impulse to touch up, alter, and correct can sometimes go too far." (Publisher's note)

REVIEW: *TLS* no5794 p24 Ap 18 2014 WILLIAM VINEY

"The Work of Revision." "In 'The Work of Revision,' Hannah Sullivan shows herself to be a critic willing to go through the bins. . . . Sullivan's case histories unsettle the safe passage from draft to bound copy. She reminds us of the laborious transformations that can occur before and after publication, and the mixed fortunes of those who revise and revise again. . . . 'The Work of Revision' is carefully organized around writings by authors such as Henry James, Pound, Eliot, Joyce, Virginia Woolf and Ernest Hemingway. . . . Provocative, timely and a welcome contribution to the study of Modernist writing. 'The Work of Revision' goes to great lengths to show just how difficult it can be to elucidate the social life of texts whose use and meaning remain a work in progress."

SULLIVAN, JAY. Raising Gentle Men; Lives at the Orphanage Edge; [by] Jay Sullivan 354 p. 2013 Apprentice House

1. Boys—Social conditions 2. Boys' schools 3. Jamaica—Social conditions 4. Memoirs 5. Orphanages 6. Orphans—Social conditions
ISBN 9781934074817; 1934074810

SUMMARY: In this book, Jay Sullivan describes how "For more than 100 years, a small band of nuns have run Alpha Boys School in Kingston, caring for the abandoned, abused and delinquent boys of Jamaica. From 1984-1986, they allowed the author to share their world. He was one of many people during those years who lived on the periphery of the boys' lives, trying to help, and trying to understand." (Publisher's note)

REVIEW: *America* v209 no9 p37-8 O 7 2013 ELIZABETH REAVEY

"Raising Gentle Men: Lives at the Orphanage Edge." "Jay Sullivan's 'Raising Gentle Men: Lives at the Orphanage Edge' is real, and serving others is complicated. Sullivan spent two years between undergraduate and law school teaching in Kingston, Jamaica, in the 1980s. But his real Jamaican experience came during his time living at an orphanage for young boys. The structure of the book is more or less a series of vignettes about life at the orphanage and Jay's desperate attempts to understand God's will for him. . . . The power of Jay's story is in the small details: a bed-time story, a brief moment holding hands."

SULLIVAN, KATE. On Linden Square; [by] Kate Sullivan 40 p. 2013 Sleeping Bear Press

1. Neighborhoods—Fiction 2. Picture books for children 3. Snow—Fiction 4. Snow sculpture—Fiction 5. Youths' writings
ISBN 9781585368327
LC 2013-004097

SUMMARY: In this book, "the neighbors of Stella Mae Culpepper keep to themselves, listening to their own music, riding their bikes, and playing with their dogs. And Stella remains aloof, too, as an observer. But a snowstorm brings them all out at once, first to wonder at Stella's snow sculpture creation and then to join in, adding unique features including horns and dancing feet. Ultimately, they create . . . a reflection of their varied cultures and interests." (Booklist)

REVIEW: *Booklist* v110 no2 p72-3 S 15 2013 Edie Ching

"On Linden Square." "While there are many books about building friendships, this one celebrates the creation of a community. . . . [Kate] Sullivan's watercolor illustrations, which leave plenty of white space on the page, are lively and fluid, with few straight lines outlining soft colors. The cartoonlike humans are more realized by their actions than their features, but the text and illustrations individualize them all, showing their unique interests. A glossary at the conclusion explains many of the musical terms interspersed in the text, along with cultural references. Move over. Frosty, more imaginative snow sculptures are on the way."

REVIEW: *Kirkus Rev* v81 no15 p228 Ag 1 2013

REVIEW: *SLJ* v59 no9 p132 S 2013 Lynn Vanca

SULLIVAN, KATE.il. On Linden Square. See Sullivan, K.

SULLIVAN, MARY.il. Ball. See Sullivan, M.

SULLIVAN, STEVE. Encyclopedia of great popular song recordings; [by] Steve Sullivan 2 volumes (1016 p.) 2013 Scarecrow Press, Inc.

1. Encyclopedias & dictionaries 2. Music literature 3. Popular music—Discography 4. Popular music—History and criticism 5. Sound recording industry—History
ISBN 9780810882959 (cloth : alk. paper); 9780810882966 (ebook)
LC 2012-041837

SUMMARY: In this book, Steve Sullivan "explores the diversity of popular music in one- to three-page entries covering some 1,000 recordings from 1889 to 2012. Selections are chosen from well-known lists such as those of the Grammy Hall of Fame. . . . Popular music herein includes rock, soul, country, jazz, blues, gospel, and ethnic music. Entries are chronological within ten 'playlists,' providing charting/list information, performer, writer, recording specifics, and documented history." (Choice)

REVIEW: *Booklist* v110 no9/10 p70 Ja 1 2014 Steven York

"Encyclopedia of Great Popular Song Recordings." "Each entry is exceptionally detailed with historical backstories, quotes from artists and authors, and [Steve] Sullivan's own fresh take on the song's importance. Most entries are at least several paragraphs long, and many are quite lengthy. . . . Sullivan admirably accomplishes his goal of bringing together important pieces of our musical past into a form that lets readers learn historical details about these songs and reminisce about their meaning in their own lives. Highly recommended for most academic and public libraries."

REVIEW: *Choice* v51 no8 p1370-1 Ap 2014 R. A. Aken

"Encyclopedia of Great Popular Song Recordings". "This well-documented encyclopedia draws on many respected sources, including Music Trades www.musictrades.com, which is particularly pertinent for earlier works. . . . The ten playlists are labeled with a song title from the pertinent section, but the groupings' relevance is nor stated or obvious (e.g., playlist 'Crazy Blues' includes 'Take Me Out to the Ball Game' and 'Smells like Teen Spirit'); a single chronological presentation would serve as well. The indexes are superb. For breadth of coverage and currency, this set (also available electronically through ProQuest and EBSCO) is a useful, superior complement to David Ewen's 'American Popular Songs'."

SUN, ANNA. Confucianism as a world religion; contested histories and contemporary realities; [by] Anna Sun xix, 244 p. 2013 Princeton University Press

1. China—Religion 2. Civilization, Confucian 3. Confucianism 4. Confucianism—China 5. Confucianism—History 6. Historical literature
ISBN 9780691155579 (hardcover)
LC 2012-036448

SUMMARY: This book by Anna Sun claims that "Contested histories of Confucianism are vital signs of social and political change. Sun also examines the revival of Confucianism in contemporary China and the social significance of the ritual practice of Confucian temples. While the Chinese government turns to Confucianism to justify its political agenda, Confucian activists have started a movement to turn Confucianism into a religion." (Publisher's note)

REVIEW: *Choice* v51 no2 p283 O 2013 C. Schirokauer

"Confucianism As a World Religion: Contested Histories and Contemporary Realities." "Part 1 of this admirable book presents a fascinating, well-researched, historical account of the establishment of Confucianism as a world religion in tandem with the emergence of comparative religion as a discipline. [Author Anna] Sun's keen sense of history serves her equally well as she turns to contemporary issues. In part 2, she asks, 'who are the Confucians in China?', and concludes, 'there will always be new ways of becoming a Confucian.' Part 3 . . . considers the present revival of Confucianism in China. . . . Throughout, Sun . . . makes excellent use of current scholarship, employs theory with a sure and delicate touch while avoiding jargon, and displays excellent judgment."

REVIEW: *J Am Acad Relig* v82 no2 p570-3 Je 2014 Rodney L. Taylor

SUN, SHIRLEY HSIAO-LI. Population policy and reproduction in Singapore; making future citizens; [by] Shirley Hsiao-Li Sun xiv, 189 p. 2012 Routledge

1. Family policy—Singapore 2. Fertility, Human—Singapore 3. Singapore—Politics & government 4. Social science literature
ISBN 0203146182 (ebook); 0415670683 (hardback); 9780203146187 (ebook); 9780415670685 (hardback)
LC 2011-025864

SUMMARY: "Using the case study of Singapore, this book examines the relationship between population policies and individual reproductive decisions in low fertility contexts. It demonstrates that the effectiveness of population policy is a function of globalization processes, competing notions of citizenship, and the gap between seemingly neutral policy incentives and the perceived and experienced disparate effects." (Publisher's note)

REVIEW: *Contemp Sociol* v43 no1 p121-2 Ja 2014 Rachel Sullivan Robinson

"Population Policy and Reproduction in Singapore: Making Future Citizens". "Although rich in detail about the population policy, as well as the various funds set up by the Singaporean government for retirement, education, housing, and health, the book's ultimate contribution to citizenship studies could have been more fully expressed. . . . while Sun's interviews reveal Singaporean's desires for greater government support for childbearing, and that many feel their jobs are threatened by foreign workers, they speak very little to questions of national identity or citizenship."

SUNDARAM, ANJAN. Stringer; a reporter's year in the Congo; [by] Anjan Sundaram 265 p. 2014 Doubleday

1. Journalism 2. Memoirs
ISBN 0385537751; 9780345806321 (hardcover : alk. paper); 9780385537759; 9780385537766 (electronic)
LC 2013-000980

SUMMARY: Author Anjan "Sundaram exchanged mathematics for journalism, starting out as a stringer in dangerous Congo with little in the way of experience or contacts. This memoir sees him struggling to learn his craft while battling malaria, isolation, financial woes, and the tendency of editors to send in name reporters when a big story breaks. In addition, Sundaram offers an intensely rendered account of the immeasurable sadness of Congo through the tumultuous 2006 elections. " (Library Journal)

REVIEW: *Booklist* v110 no4 p14 O 15 2013 Vanessa Bush

"Stringer: A Reporter's Journey in the Congo." "[Anjan] Sundaram left the calm, logical world of mathematics and a job offer from Goldman Sachs for the chaos of the Congo and the uncertainties of journalism. The combination was unpromising, as 'few cared ... for news' of the Congo. Then he lucked into a position as a stringer with the Associated Press. . . . Excerpts from his notebooks chronicle personal reflections as he struggles to learn how to report from an unruly land, harboring doubts and misgivings and a feverish desperation to make sense of one of the deadliest places in the world. A breathtaking look at a troubled nation exploited by greedy forces within and without."

REVIEW: *Economist* v410 no8871 p70-1 Ja 25 2014

REVIEW: *Kirkus Rev* v81 no21 p73 N 1 2013

REVIEW: *Publ Wkly* v261 no4 p184 Ja 27 2014

SUNDSTØL, VIDAR. The Land of Dreams. See The Land of Dreams

SUNSTEIN, CASS R. (CASS ROBERT), 1954-. Conspiracy theories and other dangerous ideas; [by] Cass R. (Cass Robert) Sunstein 288 p. 2014 Simon & Schuster

1. Conspiracy theories 2. Environmental policy 3. Government policy 4. Political science literature 5. Same-sex marriage

ISBN 9781476726625 (hardcover: alk. paper); 9781476726632 (trade paper: alk. paper)

LC 2013-012476

SUMMARY: This book presents a collection of essays on public policy by Cass R. Sunstein. Topics include "why cost-benefit analysis promotes effective and humane regulation; why juries should award more compensation for lower back pain than for lost limbs; why animals should get their day in court; why gay marriage is right; and why spending to abate greenhouse emissions may be wrong." (Publishers Weekly)

REVIEW: *Atlantic* v313 no4 p36-8 My 2014 DAVID COLE

"Conspiracy Theories and Other Dangerous Ideas". "[Cass R. Sunstein] has collected 11 of his most controversial articles—on subjects as diverse as conspiracy theories, climate change, same-sex marriage, animal rights, and 'new progressivism'—in one volume. . . . Sunstein often seems to go out of his way to avoid controversy. He is careful, deliberative, and painstaking. . . . And he is virtually always ready to identify counterarguments, not simply to knock them down but to credit them for raising important caveats and concerns. These are all good qualities in a lawyer and a law professor, to be sure, but it's a good bet that he won't be leading a revolution anytime soon."

REVIEW: *Kirkus Rev* v82 no3 p21 F 1 2014

REVIEW: *N Y Rev Books* v61 no15 p21-3 O 9 2014 Jeremy Waldron

REVIEW: *Publ Wkly* v261 no3 p44 Ja 20 2014

SURPLICE, HOLLY. Peek-a-boo bunny; [by] Holly Surplice 32 p. 2014 Harper, an imprint of HarperCollinsPublishers

1. Animals—Fiction 2. Hide-and-seek—Fiction 3. JUVENILE FICTION—Animals—Rabbits 4. JUVENILE FICTION—Imagination & Play 5. JUVENILE FICTION—Social Issues—Friendship 6. Rabbits—Fiction 7. Stories in rhyme

ISBN 9780062242655

LC 2013-021834

SUMMARY: In this children's story, "as his friends hide, Bunny counts to 10, slyly peeking out from behind his paws. A little mole pops up to help Bunny, trying to point out the hiding characters during the ensuing search, but Bunny is so excited to be playing the game that he bounds right past the hiding places. Finally, Bunny slumps down under a tree, dejected—but on the final, joyous spread, the animal friends all jump out shouting, 'PEEK-A-BOO!'" (Kirkus Reviews)

REVIEW: *Booklist* v110 no11 p70 F 1 2014 Maryann Owen

REVIEW: *Kirkus Rev* v82 no2 p260 Ja 15 2014

"Peek-A-Boo Bunny". " A gray rabbit plays hide-and-seek with his forest friends in this delightfully illustrated, simple story with a bouncy, rhyming text. . . . Vibrant illustrations in mixed media and collage use stylized shapes for the animals against juicy lime and lavender backgrounds that burst with flowers, leaves and trees. The wildflowers and grasses often stretch across the foreground of a full spread in an impressionistic blur, complemented by delicate leaves that hang from the overarching boughs, together framing the animal action in a distinctive, theatrical way. Preschoolers who are just beginning to understand the game of hide-and-seek will find this irresistible."

REVIEW: *Publ Wkly* v260 no45 p71 N 11 2013

REVIEW: *SLJ* v60 no1 p76 Ja 2014 Linda Ludke

SURPLICE, HOLLY.il. Peek-a-boo bunny. See Surplice, H.

SURVEY OF LONDON; Battersea; 1040 p. 2014 Yale University Press

1. Architectural history 2. Architecture—England—London 3. Battersea (London, England) 4. Historical literature 5. London (England)—History

ISBN 0300198132; 9780300198133

SUMMARY: Edited by Andrew Saint and Colin Thom, "The two latest volumes of the 'Survey of London,' 49 and 50, trace Battersea's development from medieval times to the present day. Offering detailed analysis of its streets and buildings both thematically and topographically, and including copious original in-depth research and investigation, the books are a trove of architectural history and British history." (Publisher's note)

REVIEW: *TLS* no5794 p3-4 Ap 18 2014 JERRY WHITE

"Survey of London: Battersea." "'The Survey' is an institution unique in the urban world. Nothing like it has been attempted elsewhere and perhaps could never be. It is both testimony to and commemoration of London's patchwork complexity where the distinctive character of small neighbourhoods has defined in large part the living history of the city. . . . It is salutary to reflect that this charting of the history of London parish by parish, though 120 years old in 2014, has only just begun and will never be finished. . . . These are volumes forty-nine and fifty of the parish surveys. The half-century in volumes has taken just 113 years to accomplish. . . . Certainly excellence has been an enduring feature of the 'Survey' volumes."

SUSSMAN, RACHEL. The oldest living things in the world; [by] Rachel Sussman 304 p. 2014 University of Chicago Press

1. Longevity 2. Longevity in art 3. Nature photography 4. Organisms—Pictorial works 5. Plants—Longevity
ISBN 9780226057507 (cloth: alkaline paper)
LC 2013-048562

SUMMARY: "'The Oldest Living Things in the World' is [a] . . . journey through time and space. Over the past decade, artist Rachel Sussman has . . . traveled the world to photograph continuously living organisms that are 2,000 years old and older. Spanning from Antarctica to Greenland, the Mojave Desert to the Australian Outback, the result is a . . . visual collection of ancient organisms unlike anything that has been created in the arts or sciences before." (Publisher's note)

REVIEW: *New Statesman* v143 no5224 p44 Ag 22 2014

REVIEW: *Sci Am* v310 no4 p86 Ap 2014 Clara Moskowitz

REVIEW: *Science* v344 no6185 p694-5 My 16 2014 Jared Farmer

"The Oldest Living Things in the World." "Rachel Sussman, a photographer who first earned wide attention through a 2010 TED talk, spent ten years taking portraits of organisms that have lived longer than two millennia. The result, 'The Oldest Living Things in the World,' is not a Guinness Book of Longevity. . . . Her photographs, shot in natural light with a medium-format film camera, are more evocative than informational. . . . Sussman believes that '[t]he best art and science projects enhance and extend each other, bringing something new to both; they are not about simply making the research pretty, or making artworks using novel scientific tools.' By this measure, 'The Oldest Living Things in the World' is a work for the ages."

SUSTAINING HUMAN RIGHTS IN THE TWENTY-FIRST CENTURY; strategies from Latin America; 424 p. 2010 Woodrow Wilson Center Press John Hopkins University Press

1. Citizenship 2. Human rights—Latin America 3. Latin America—Politics & government 4. Political accountability 5. Social science literature
ISBN 9781421410128
LC 2013-005974

SUMMARY: This book, edited by Katherine Hite and Mark Ungar, examines " human rights strategies rooted in the last century's struggles against brutally repressive dictators. Those struggles continue today across Latin America. Augmented by the pursuit of broader political, cultural, labor, and environmental rights, they hold accountable a much wider cast of national governments, local governments, international agencies, and multinational corporations." (Publisher's note)

REVIEW: *Choice* v51 no4 p724 D 2013 C. E. Welch

"Sustaining Human Rights in the Twenty-First Century: Strategies From Latin America." "Of the dozen contributors, the overwhelming majority come from the US. All are well regarded for their own publications and policy advocacy. They argue that Latin America's human rights movements started with struggles against military dictatorships in the late 1970s. . . . Two chapters are derived from other books. With exception of one chapter focused on Chile, individual states are discussed only briefly in select chapters or simply mentioned. The book is comparable to books such as Margaret Keck and Kathryn Sikkink, 'Activists beyond Borders'."

SUTCLIFFE, JANE. Stone giant; Michelangelo's David and how he came to be; 32 p. 2013 Charlesbridge

1. Children's nonfiction 2. Florence (Italy)—History 3. Michelangelo Buonarroti, 1475-1564 4. Sculpture
ISBN 1580892957; 9781580892957 (reinforced for library use); 9781607346142 (ebook)
LC 2012-024579

SUMMARY: In this book, by Jane Sutcliffe, "no one wanted the 'giant.' The hulking block of marble lay in the work yard, rained on, hacked at, and abandoned—until a young Michelangelo saw his David in it. This is the story of how a neglected, discarded stone became a masterpiece for all time. It is also a story about art—about an artist's vision and process, and about the ways in which we humans see ourselves reflected in art." (Publisher's note)

REVIEW: *Booklist* v110 no14 p69 Mr 15 2014 J. B. Petty

REVIEW: *Bull Cent Child Books* v67 no9 p480 My 2014 E. B.

REVIEW: *Kirkus Rev* v82 no4 p127 F 15 2014

"Stone Giant: Michelangelo's David and How He Came to Be". "[Jane] Sutcliffe make a big impression with this eye-catching introduction to one of Western civilization's most iconic sculptures. . . . Sutcliffe limns the lively details of this multiyear project, and her tale of Michelangelo's talent and industry is considerably enhanced by the thoughtful pen, ink and watercolor work of British illustrator [John] Shelley. He makes the finely modeled realism of the statue the real standout here. . . . Shelley wondrously juxtaposes this cool, nuanced marble hero with a crowded city, brimming with the bright colors and lively action of Renaissance book illuminations. . . . Sadly missing? An artist's note to help curious readers place all the highly researched imagery and background."

REVIEW: *SLJ* v60 no3 p177 Mr 2014 Carol Goldman

SUTCLIFFE, JOHN. The Colours of Rome; [by] John Sutcliffe 32 p. 2013 The Old School Press

1. Architectural literature 2. Color in architecture 3. Paint 4. Rome (Italy)—Buildings, structures, etc. 5. Rome (Italy)—Description & travel
ISBN 1899933336; 9781899933334

SUMMARY: "To illustrate [this] essay [author] John [Sutcliffe] made several trips to Rome, returning finally with twenty sheets of colours copied directly from the buildings themselves. His carefully chosen selection is designed to demonstrate the diversity of the palette and also to draw together two very different strands of tradition that have created the appearance of the streets of Rome today." (Publisher's note)

REVIEW: *TLS* no5788 p22 Mr 7 2014 DAVID WATKIN

"The Colours of Rome." "This highly unusual and beautifully produced book attempts to recreate and explain the colours--often a warm ochre like fresh pasta--that we find on the exterior of buildings in the centre of Rome. John Sutcliffe's text is only twenty-six pages long but is accompanied by a bound folder of twenty loose pages, on heavier paper, to each of which a large patch of colour has been applied with water-based paints. The de luxe edition even includes bottled samples of nine of the most important pigments, mostly in powder form, presumably for home use."

SUTCLIFFE, WILLIAM. The Wall; [by] William Sutcliffe 304 p. 2013 Walker Childrens

1. Arab-Israeli conflict—Fiction 2. Coming of age—Fiction 3. Walls—Fiction 4. West Bank 5. Young adult literature

ISBN 0802734928; 9780802734921

LC 2012-032047

SUMMARY: In this novel by William Sutcliffe "Joshua lives . . . in Amarias, an isolated town. Amarias is surrounded by a high wall, guarded by soldiers, which can only be crossed through a heavily fortified checkpoint. Joshua has been taught that the Wall is the only thing keeping his people safe from a brutal and unforgiving enemy. Joshua stumbles across a tunnel that leads underneath the Wall. He's heard plenty of stories about the other side, but nothing has prepared him for what he finds." (Publisher's note)

REVIEW: *TLS* no5747 p20 My 24 2013 TOM SPERLINGER

"The Wall." "[William] Sutcliffe has an acute ear for dialogue, and the family conflicts are convincingly evoked. But they can feel schematic, with Liev representing 'extreme' religious settlers, Joshua the 'liberal' Israeli Left, and his mother the damaged pragmatist caught between. As a depiction of Israeli society, this is simplistic, and potentially evasive. Despite its limitations as an allegory, Sutcliffe's novel remains an impressive piece of fiction--for adult or younger readers. . . . His story reminds us that to imagine the suffering of others is an act of courage in itself."

SUTHERLAND, DANIEL E. Whistler; a life for art's sake; [by] Daniel E. Sutherland 440 p. 2014 Yale University Press

1. Artists—United States—Biography 2. Biography (Literary form) 3. Painters 4. Self-doubt

ISBN 9780300203462 (cl: alk. paper)

LC 2013-027646

SUMMARY: This biography of painter James McNeill Whistler "dispels the popular notion of Whistler as merely a combative, eccentric, and unrelenting publicity seeker, a man as renowned for his public feuds with Oscar Wilde and John Ruskin as for the iconic portrait of his mother. The Whistler revealed in these pages is an intense, introspective, and complex man, plagued by self-doubt and haunted by an endless pursuit of perfection in his painting and drawing." (Publisher's note)

REVIEW: *Am Sch* v83 no2 p116-7 Spr 2014 ELEANOR JONES HARVEY

REVIEW: *Apollo: The International Magazine for Collectors* v179 no617 p85 F 2014

"Dumfries House: An Architectural Story," "Piero della Francesca: Artist and Man," and "Whistler: A Life for Art's Sake". "This study, which draws on previously unpublished archival material, opens up the house and its history as never before—apt for a building and collection that has recently been saved for the public. . . . James Banker couches the Tuscan painter's achievements carefully within the social and artistic contexts of his time, making compelling claims about the dating of certain works, and offering a new interpretation of the enigmatic Flagellation of Christ. . . This is the first full biography of [James] Whistler for more than 20 years. Making use of the painter's private correspondence, historian Daniel Sutherland presents a more introspective figure than the truculent eccentric who has entered the public consciousness."

REVIEW: *Apollo: The International Magazine for Collectors* v179 no618 p196-7 Mr 2014 J. B. Bullen

"Whistler: A Life for Art's Sake". "[Daniel E.] Sutherland has risen to the task, creating the most factually dense of Whistler's biographies to date. . . . He has worked minutely through the personal documents and has sifted the secondary literature to produce a text that is so extensively annotated that the references occupy 67 pages of small print. . . . For the general reader, he stages the climactic moments in Whistler's life with engaging vitality. . . . The art historian will also find Sutherland's book a valuable tool. . . . But has Sutherland's ambition to reveal the 'covert myth' been achieved? Again and again, he amasses and marshals the facts of Whistler's life, but the narrative continues to raise more questions than it answers."

REVIEW: *Choice* v51 no12 p2170 Ag 2014 W. S. Rodner

REVIEW: *Kirkus Rev* v82 no2 p291 Ja 15 2014

REVIEW: *N Y Times Book Rev* p16 Jl 6 2014 DEBORAH SOLOMON

REVIEW: *Nation* v298 no10/11 p33-6 Mr 10 2014 BARRY SCHWABSKY

REVIEW: *New Statesman* v143 no5200 p46-7 Mr 7 2014 Alex Danchev

REVIEW: *TLS* no5792 p8-10 Ap 4 2014 MATTHEW STURGIS

SUTTON, DEBORAH. Other landscapes; colonialism and the predicament of authority in nineteenth-century South India; [by] Deborah Sutton xvi, 239 p. 2011 Orient Blackswan

1. British—India, South—History—19th century 2. Colonization—History 3. Historical literature 4. Imperialism—History 5. India—History—British occupation, 1765-1947 6. Nilgiri Hills (India)—History

ISBN 8125042024; 9788125042020

LC 2013-319132

SUMMARY: This book by Deborah Sutton describes how "European settlement of India was never seriously considered apart from in selected upland areas with cooler climates and sparse native populations. One such area was the Nilgiri Hills of South India which, from the early 19th century, saw concerted efforts at European colonization and displacement of the local population as well as an attempt to visualize and recreate an English landscape in the area." (Publisher's note)

REVIEW: *Am Hist Rev* v118 no4 p1166 O 2013 Sanjukta Das Gupta

"Other Landscapes: Colonialism and the Predicament of Authority in Nineteenth-Century South India." "The unfamiliar landscape of India had evoked . . . reactions from British colonizers who . . . believed the country to be capable of environmental amelioration through adoption of measures that would make the land fit for European settlement. . . . [This book] explores the story of one such transformation, i.e., the gradual British colonization of the Nilgiri Hills of South India from the second decade of the nineteenth century onward. . . . [Author Deborah] Sutton's analysis of the colonial linking up of ethnicity to topography is one of the novel arguments of the book."

SWAN, SUSAN.il. Cheers for a dozen ears. See Chernesky, F. S.

SWAN, SUSAN.il. Volcano rising. See Rusch, E.

SWANN, SARAH. Ethnicity and education in England and Europe. See Law, I.

SWANSON, JAMES L. End of Days; The Assassination of John F. Kennedy; [by] James L. Swanson 416 p. 2013 HarperCollins

1. Historical literature 2. Kennedy, John F. (John Fitzgerald), 1917-1963—Assassination 3. Oswald, Lee Harvey, 1939-1963 4. Presidents—Assassination—United States 5. Ruby, Jack, 1911-1967

ISBN 0062083481; 9780062083487

SUMMARY: This book, by James L. Swanson, on the assassination of U.S. President John F. Kennedy "follows the event hour-by-hour, from the moment Lee Harvey Oswald conceived of the crime three days before its execution, to his own murder two days later at a Dallas Police precinct at the hands of Jack Ruby, a two-bit nightclub owner." (Publisher's note)

REVIEW: *Kirkus Rev* v81 no20 p223 O 15 2013

REVIEW: *Natl Rev* v65 no22 p42-6 N 25 2013 JAMES ROSEN

"The Kennedy Half-Century: The Presidency, Assassination, and Lasting Legacy of John F. Kennedy," "End of Days: The Assassination of John F. Kennedy" and "The Interloper: Lee Harvey Oswald Inside the Soviet Union." "James L. Swanson's 'End of Days,' a concise tick-tock account, and Larry J. Sabato's more ambitious 'The Kennedy Half-Century,' a multidisciplinary effort that weighs in at 603 pages . . . bring into sharp relief once again these contradictory traits in mid-century America's proudest son. Perhaps fittingly, the anniversary also brings us only one new book about the president's killer--Peter Savodnik's 'The Interloper'--but it is an important work, for it illuminates, as never before, the complexity of humanity that also graces the most wretched assassin."

SWANSON, JAMES L. The President Has Been Shot!; The Assassination of John F. Kennedy; [by] James L. Swanson 336 p. 2013 Scholastic Press

1. Historical literature 2. Oswald, Lee Harvey, 1939-1963 3. Presidents—Assassination—United States 4. Young adult literature

ISBN 0545490073 (hbk.); 9780545490078 (hbk.); 9780545496544 (ebook)

LC 2012-041167

SUMMARY: This book by James L. Swanson is a "young-adult book on the Kennedy assassination" in which the author "transport[s] readers back to one of the most shocking, sad, and terrifying events in American history. . . . The book [is] illustrated with archival photos, . . . diagrams, source notes, bibliography, places to visit, and index." (Publisher's note)

REVIEW: *Booklist* v110 no3 p50 O 1 2013 Gail Bush

REVIEW: *Horn Book Magazine* v90 no1 p119-20 Ja/F 2014 DEAN SCHNEIDER

"The President Has Been Shot!' The Assassination of John F. Kennedy." "The assassination of John F. Kennedy on November 22, 1963, was 'the great American tragedy,' according to [James L.] Swanson, whose clear and concisely written narrative highlights the key events of the Kennedy administration before focusing on the moment-by-moment details of the assassination. . . . With riveting text and well-selected photographs, the narrative proceeds with an account of the assassination, weaving in information from the now-famous Abraham Zapruder film and culminating with grisly hospital scenes. Everything is here but the matter of [Lee Harvey] Oswald's motive."

REVIEW: *Kirkus Rev* v81 no17 p120 S 1 2013

REVIEW: *Publ Wkly* v260 no35 p63 S 2 2013

REVIEW: *Publ Wkly* p133 Children's starred review annual 2013

REVIEW: *SLJ* v59 no9 p191 S 2013 Jeffrey Meyer

REVIEW: *Voice of Youth Advocates* v36 no4 p94 O 2013 Alicia Abdul

SWANSON, PETER. The girl with a clock for a heart; a novel; [by] Peter Swanson 304 p. 2013 William Morrow

1. Criminals—Fiction 2. Disappeared persons—Fiction 3. Man-woman relationships—Fiction 4. Mistaken identity—Fiction 5. Suspense fiction

ISBN 9780062267498 (hardcover); 9780062267504 (trade pbk.)

LC 2012-050454

SUMMARY: This book follows accountant George Foss. "One night in his local bar, he spots his long-lost first love from college, a woman whom he knew as Audrey. Her real name, he's since discovered, is Liana Decter. . . . Soon, she's pressed her loyal sap into service as a go-between in returning some stolen money to a wealthy and shady man with whom she's been involved." (Kirkus Reviews)

REVIEW: *Booklist* v110 no7 p26 D 1 2013 Michele Leber

REVIEW: *Kirkus Rev* v82 no3 p4 F 1 2014

"The Girl With a Clock for a Heart". "The pace is fast, the prose mostly smooth, and the plot genuinely twisty. But the characters aren't quite fully fleshed; George is sometimes too one-note in his role as helplessly enamored milquetoast, and Liana—who has great potential, possibly to be explored in the sequel this book points toward—is a little too purely a femme fatale, with the emphasis—as usual—on the second word rather than the first. We know her almost exclusively by her effect on men. Seemingly pre-measured for the movies, sometimes to its detriment but often to good effect; all in all, a quick, deft, promising first crime novel."

REVIEW: *Publ Wkly* v260 no43 p37 O 28 2013

SWARTZ, DAVID R. Moral minority; the evangelical left in an age of conservatism; [by] David R. Swartz 376 p. 2012 University of Pennsylvania Press

1. Christian conservatism—United States—History—

20th century 2. Christianity and politics—United States—History—20th century 3. Church & politics—Evangelical churches 4. Evangelicalism—History—20th century 5. Evangelicalism—United States—History—20th century 6. Historical literature 7. Religious right—United States
ISBN 9780812244410 (hardcover : alk. paper)
LC 2012-014396

SUMMARY: "How did the evangelical right gain a moral monopoly and why were evangelical progressives, who had shown such promise, left behind? In 'Moral Minority,' the first comprehensive history of the evangelical left, David R. Swartz sets out to answer these questions, charting the rise, decline, and political legacy of this forgotten movement. . . . Swartz chronicles the efforts of evangelical progressives who expanded the concept of morality from the personal to the social." (Publisher's note)

REVIEW: *Am Hist Rev* v118 no4 p1222 O 2013 J. Brooks Flippen

REVIEW: *Choice* v50 no12 p2300 Ag 2013 B. F. Le Beau

REVIEW: *Christ Century* v130 no2 p37-9 Ja 23 2013 Heath W. Carter

REVIEW: *J Am Hist* v100 no1 p267 Je 2013 Mark Edwards

REVIEW: *Rev Am Hist* v42 no1 p174-80 Mr 2014 Mark A. Lempke

"The Anointed: Evangelical Truth in a Secular Age" and "Moral Minority: The Evangelical Left in an Age of Conservatism." "Collectively, these two books do their readers a great service, challenging the stereotypical perception of evangelicals in ways that may surprise even the evangelical community itself. . . . 'Moral Minority' turns its gaze to the Evangelical Left that formed in conversation with, rather than opposition to, the social movements of the late 1960s and early 1970s. 'The Anointed,' meanwhile, is decidedly presentist, exploring how some contemporary evangelicals acquire their understanding of science, American history, child rearing, and other topics through a litany of dubious authorities."

SWARUP, BOB. Money mania; booms, panics, and busts from Ancient Rome to the Great Meltdown; [by] Bob Swarup 320 p. 2014 Bloomsbury Press
1. Economics literature 2. Finance—History 3. Investments—History 4. Money—History 5. Speculation—History
ISBN 9781608198412 (alk. paper)
LC 2013-041928

SUMMARY: In this book, author Bob Swarup "takes a very long view of the economic cycles that define both modern and ancient societies. He traces the same foibles of human nature that caused financial disaster in the Roman Empire to those that contributed to the most recent global economic woes." (Library Journal)

REVIEW: *Bookforum* v20 no5 p10 F/Mr 2014 BETHANY MCLEAN

REVIEW: *Choice* v52 no1 p130 St 2014 H. Mayo

REVIEW: *Kirkus Rev* v82 no2 p212 Ja 15 2014

"Money Mania: Booms, Panics, and Busts From Ancient Rome to the Great Meltdown". "[Bob] Swarup's evaluative efforts rely heavily on his discussion of money. He is a monetarist who believes that 'money is a commodity' and has an intrinsic value of its own, which can be traded. . . . Thus he supports virtual monies like Bitcoin or the Linden of Second Life. The author doesn't accept that the differences also undermine his own attempt to unify the disparate cases and that pop psychology and trendy behavioral economics don't fill the void. There are many good books on this subject; this is not one of them."

REVIEW: *Libr J* v139 no3 p116 F 15 2014 Carol Elsen

SWEENEY, MATTHEW. Horse Music; [by] Matthew Sweeney 96 p. 2013 Bloodaxe Books
1. Death—Poetry 2. Infants 3. Irish poetry 4. Lyric poetry 5. Poetry (Literary form)
ISBN 1852249676 (pbk.); 9781852249670 (pbk.)
LC 2013-431944

SUMMARY: "Matthew Sweeney's tenth collection of poems is as sinister as its dark forebears, but the notes he hits in 'Horse Music' are lyrical and touching as well as disturbing and disquieting. This is not only Sweeney's most adventurous book to date, it is also his most varied, including not only outlandish adventures and macabre musings, but also moving responses to family deaths." (Publisher's note)

REVIEW: *TLS* no5776 p29 D 13 2013

"Horse Music." "[Author Matthew] Sweeney has become particularly adept at producing rhetorically unadorned mini-narratives, often in single verse paragraphs and encapsulating semi-surreal shots of alternative realities populated by the hopeful and the disenchanted. . . . There is a bit too much 'Horse Music' for its own good. Some of the seventy poems lack polish and others are a little inconsequential. But with Sweeney one must always be willing to read between the lines; most of the poems in this distinctively Sweeneyish collection give readers plenty to get their teeth into."

SWEET DREAMS; the world of Patsy Cline; 198 p. 2013 University of Illinois Press
1. Country music—History and criticism 2. Country music—Social aspects 3. Country musicians 4. Music literature
ISBN 9780252037719 (cloth : alk. paper); 9780252079306 (pbk. : alk. paper)
LC 2012-050575

SUMMARY: This book "examines the regional and national history that shaped [Patsy] Cline's career and the popular culture that she so profoundly influenced with her music. . . . Contributors provide an account of Cline's early performance days in Virginia's Shenandoah Valley, analyze the politics of the split between pop and country music, and discuss her strategies for negotiating gender in relation to her public and private persona." (Publisher's note)

REVIEW: *Choice* v51 no6 p1014-5 F 2014 K. S. Todd

"Sweet Dreams: The World of Patsy Cline." "Of interest is George Hamilton IV's story of meeting Cline when he was a 19-year-old beginner: '"What kind of country singer are you?.. Where are your cowboy boots? . . Who do you think you are, Hoss?--the Pat Boone of country music?" From that moment onward, we were good friends!' In the afterword, [Warren R.] Hofstra synthesizes everything offered and ruminates on the durability and permanence of Cline's legacy, determining that 'the iconic Cline' will continue to survive changes in cultural paradigms and social media."

SWEET, MELISSA.il. Little Red Writing. See Holub, J.

SWEETENHAM, CAROL.tr. The Chanson d'Antioche. See The Chanson d'Antioche

SWENSON, ASTRID.ed. From plunder to preservation. See From plunder to preservation

SWENSON, JAMIE A. Big rig; [by] Jamie A. Swenson 32 p. 2014 Disney-Hyperion Books

1. Children's stories 2. Citizens band radio 3. Delivery of goods 4. Tractor trailers—Fiction 5. Trucks—Fiction
ISBN 1423163303; 9781423163305
LC 2013-012223

SUMMARY: In this book, by Jamie A. Swenson, readers "come along for the ride as Frankie the big rig truck takes us on the job, driving past kiddie cars (school buses) and land yachts (RVs). [After] a blow-out . . . a service truck saves the day so we can get the job done and make a very special delivery." (Publisher's note)

REVIEW: *Booklist* v110 no8 p50-2 D 15 2013 Paula Willey

"Big Rig". "There's lots to look at as Frankie takes on cargo and then hits the road, passing a waterpark, a farm, and a retro diner before reaching his destination—Dinosaur Land! Speckled with convincing onomatopoeia and sound effects . . . and jazzy CB slang (handily defined in a glossary),the text has an unpredictable edge, making it a vibrant read-aloud, while sharp realistic paintings with lots of background detail will capture prereaders' attentions. A friendly, peppy addition to the canon of books for truck-obsessed."

REVIEW: *Kirkus Rev* v81 no24 p131 D 15 2013

"Big Rig". "A big rig gets up close and personal in [Jamie A.] Swenson's latest, and young vehicle lovers will be enthralled. Frankie pulls no punches in this down-to-earth look at semis. He speaks directly to readers, and his voice is definitely that of a truck. (Those who read this aloud may be thrown off by the rhyme that comes and goes.) . . . Frankie's surroundings are slightly retro, but all is shiny and spiffed, just like the big rig himself. Youngsters who meet Frankie will be looking for him on every highway, as he's a friend they won't soon forget."

REVIEW: *Publ Wkly* v260 no45 p69 N 11 2013

REVIEW: *SLJ* v60 no3 p128 Mr 2014 Judith Constantinides

SWIFT, WILL. Pat and Dick; the Nixons, an intimate portrait of a marriage; [by] Will Swift 496 p. 2014 Threshold Editions

1. Historical literature 2. Married people—United States—Biography 3. Presidents—United States—Biography 4. Presidents' spouses—United States—Biography
ISBN 1451676948; 9781451676945 (hardcover); 9781451676952 (trade paper)
LC 2013-024650

SUMMARY: This book by Will Swift draws on "recently released love letters and other private documents" to describe the marriage of former U.S. President Richard "Dick" M. Nixon and his wife Pat Nixon. "From Dick's unrelenting crusade to marry the glamorous teacher he feared was out of his league through the myriad crises of his political career, the Nixons' story is filled with hopes and disappointments, both intimate and global." (Publisher's note)

REVIEW: *Booklist* v110 no8 p9 D 15 2013 Margaret Flanagan

REVIEW: *Kirkus Rev* v81 no23 p125 D 1 2013

REVIEW: *Libr J* v139 no2 p81 F 1 2014 Lisa Guidarini

REVIEW: *N Y Times Book Rev* p14 F 9 2014 THOMAS MALLON

"Pat and Dick: The Nixons: An Intimate Portrait of a Marriage." "Now comes 'Pat and Dick,' Will Swift's fair-minded and thorough attempt to trace the long, jagged arc of the Nixons' marriage, a devoted and sometimes strained journey that ended when Richard Nixon, convulsed with sobs, helped bury his wife in 1993. . . . Swift . . . sometimes sounds like a gentle couples therapist. He occasionally gets tangled up in the jargon of his trade . . . and too many overjudicious qualifiers sometimes render his presentation more cautious than bold, but 'Pat and Dick' remains highly intelligent and far more sophisticated than the decades' worth of quick takes from self-satisfied sharpies who dismissed Plastic Pat and Tricky Dick as a couple of squares."

SWINBURNE, STEPHEN R. Sea turtle scientist; [by] Stephen R. Swinburne 65 p. 2013 Houghton Mifflin Books for Children, Houghton Mifflin Harcourt

1. Environmental literature 2. Leatherback turtle—Research—Saint Kitts and Nevis—Juvenile literature 3. Science—Popular works 4. Sea turtles—Juvenile literature 5. Wildlife veterinarians
ISBN 0547367554; 9780547367552
LC 2012-034045

SUMMARY: This middle grades book by Stephen R. Swinburne describes how "Dr. Kimberly Stewart, also known as the Turtle Lady of St. Kitts, is already waiting at midnight when an 800-pound leatherback sea turtle crawls out of the Caribbean surf and onto the sandy beach. The mother turtle has a vital job to do: dig a nest in which she will lay eggs that will hatch into part of the next generation of leatherbacks." (Publisher's note)

REVIEW: *Booklist* v110 no15 p43 Ap 1 2014 Carolyn Phelan

REVIEW: *Bull Cent Child Books* v67 no9 p480-1 My 2014 D. S.

"Sea Turtle Scientist". "There's plenty of information here about various sea turtles and the way they're being affected by environmental changes, and the 'ridealong' descriptions of [Kimberly] Scott and her companions' attendance at egg-layings and hatchings are particularly involving. . . . The photos here are not overall as impressive as the sea horse gallery, but the occasional closeup of a venerable-looking turtle mother or a scuttling wee hatchling is still compelling. Neophytes to this classic series who thought science was always conducted in old buildings on lab benches will be delighted to find it can take place in an island paradise."

REVIEW: *Horn Book Magazine* v90 no3 p116-7 My/Je 2014 BETTY CARTER

REVIEW: *SLJ* v60 no5 p158 My 2014 Patricia Manning

SWINDALL, LINDSEY R. Paul Robeson; a life of activism and art; [by] Lindsey R. Swindall 212 p. 2013 Rowman & Littlefield Pub Inc

1. African American athletes—Biography 2. African American authors—Biography 3. African American political activists—Biography 4. African American singers—Biography 5. African Americans—Biography 6. Biographies 7. Harlem Renaissance
ISBN 1442207930 (hardcover); 9781442207936 (hardcover)
LC 2012-046652

SUMMARY: This book, by Lindsey R. Swindall, profiles Paul Robeson as part of the "Library of African-American Biography" series. "Paul Robeson was, at points in his life, an actor, singer, football player, political activist and writer, one of the most diversely talented members of the Harlem Renaissance. Swindall centers Robeson's story around the argument that . . . a Pan-African perspective is fundamental to understanding his life as an artist and political advocate." (Publisher's note)

REVIEW: *Booklist* v109 no11 p18-9 F 1 2013 Vanessa Bush

REVIEW: *Choice* v51 no2 p337-8 O 2013 G. R. Butters Jr.

"Paul Robeson: A Life of Activism and Art." "[Author Lindsey R.] Swindall's concise biography is a great introduction to this iconic African American artist, athlete, and activist. Swindall . . . contextualizes Robeson's life within larger global, political, and racial spheres. . . . The author draws heavily on existing secondary sources, including biographies by Martin Duberman . . . and Paul Robeson Jr. . . . , as well as from earlier works and primary sources, but does not footnote in a traditional academic way. This is problematic at times. Swindall relies heavily on the 'Daily Worker' and other communist or communist-influenced publications, yet fails to identify this political affiliation."

SWOPE, KENNETH M. The military collapse of China's Ming Dynasty, 1618-44; [by] Kenneth M. Swope viii, 291 p. 2014 Routledge, Taylor & Francis Group

1. Civil-military relations—China 2. Historical literature
ISBN 9780415449274 (hardback)
LC 2013-008015

SUMMARY: In this "study of the fall of the Ming Dynasty from a military perspective," author Kenneth M. Swope "finds that political leaders failed to maintain the balance between civil and military leaders. This led to an inability to deal with the mounting military crises represented by the Jurchens in the northeast and peasant rebellions in the northwest and Shandong, which hastened the Ming's military collapse." (Choice: Current Reviews for Academic Libraries)

REVIEW: *Choice* v51 no9 p1657 My 2014 J. Li

"The Military Collapse of China's Ming Dynasty, 1618-44". "[Kenneth M.] Swope . . . offers the first systematic study of the fall of the Ming Dynasty from a military perspective, arguing that although political and economic dynamics should not be underestimated, the fall of the Ming was largely a result of its military collapse. . . . Not an easy read for undergraduates, the book is required reading for historians of the Ming and Qing. Military historians in general will find the book engaging as well."

SYLVIA, POLLY. Cultural messaging in the U.S. war on terrorism; a performative approach to security; [by] Polly Sylvia vii, 151 p. 2013 LFB Scholarly Pub.

1. Advertising—United States 2. Mass communication—United States 3. Social control—United States 4. Social science literature 5. Terrorism—Prevention—United States 6. War on Terrorism, 2001-2009—Social aspects—United States
ISBN 9781593325350 (hardcover : alk. paper)
LC 2012-040192

SUMMARY: This book by Polly Sylvia is part of the "Criminal Justice: Recent Scholarship" series. It discusses "the application of critical theory and Foucaultian social criticism to a particular advertising campaign conducted by New York Metropolitan Transit Authority (MTA). Sylvia argues that the 'If You See Something, Say Something' campaign of 2002-08 slyly 'branded' notions of 'suspicion' and 'security' and served as a mechanism of social control." (Choice)

REVIEW: *Choice* v51 no4 p726-7 D 2013 R. D. Stacey

"Cultural Messaging in the U.S. War on Terrorism: A Performative Approach to Security." "[Polly] Sylvia . . . offers a most curious volume on the War on Terror. Though the book is part of a publisher's series, 'Criminal Justice: Recent Scholarship,' it is really more about the application of critical theory and Foucaultian social criticism to a particular advertising campaign conducted by New York Metropolitan Transit Authority (MTA). . . . While there may be some utility here for students of Michel Foucault, the overall objectivity of the work is dubious. . . . The scholarly analysis will be of interest to a rarefied group of academics. The value of the memoir portion remains unclear."

SYMONS, KEL. I Love Trouble; 160 p. 2014 Image Comics

1. Assassins—Fiction 2. Graphic novels 3. Runaway teenagers—Fiction 4. Swindlers & swindling 5. Teleportation
ISBN 1607068486; 9781607068488

SUMMARY: In this graphic novel, "Felicia Castillo is a small-time grifter on the run from a nasty New Orleans gangster she just ripped off when she discovers she has the amazing ability to teleport. This lands her in the crosshairs of the nefarious Mars Corporation, which exploits supernatural gifts of people like Felicia. They make her an offer she can't refuse: use her unique talent to become an assassin that can get close to anyone, anywhere." (Publisher's note)

REVIEW: *Booklist* v110 no13 p36-7 Mr 1 2014 Candice Mack

"I Love Trouble." "A former stripper and teenage runaway, Felicia Castro's no angel. No matter how far she runs, though, trouble always seems to find her. While trying to escape gangsters who she ripped off, Felicia discovers she has the power to teleport when she mysteriously survives a plane crash unscathed. . . [Mark A.] Robinson and [Nathan] Stockman's street-art inspired exaggerated figures and soft-focus coloring recall Rob Cuillory's expressive line work in Chew. This stylized urban tale of the adventures of a sassy, imperfect, and mentally ill antihero would appeal to adult fans of Frank Miller's Sin City, Scott Snyder's American Vampire, or Denise Mina's graphic novel The Girl with the Dragon Tattoo."

SYNTHETIC BIOLOGY AND MORALITY; artificial life and the bounds of nature; vi, 214 p. 2013 The MIT Press

1. Artificial life—Moral and ethical aspects 2. Bioengineering—Moral and ethical aspects 3. Bioethics 4.

Biological literature 5. Synthetic biology—Moral and ethical aspects
ISBN 0262019396 (alk. paper); 0262519593 (pbk.: alk. paper); 9780262019392 (alk. paper); 9780262519595 (pbk.: alk. paper)
LC 2012-049083

SUMMARY: In this essay collection, edited by Gregory E. Kaebnick and Thomas H. Murray, "the contributors consider the basic question of the ethics of making new organisms, with essays that lay out the conceptual terrain and offer opposing views of the intrinsic moral concerns; discuss the possibility that synthetic organisms are inherently valuable; and address whether, and how,moral objections to synthetic biology could be relevant to policy making and political discourse." (Publisher's note)

REVIEW: *Choice* v51 no8 p1427 Ap 2014 M. C. Pavao

"Synthetic Biology and Morality: Artificial Life and the Bounds of Nature". "With contributors from several fields including philosophy, medical ethics, sociology, and physics, in addition to systems and synthetic biology, this book should surely stimulate discussions around these three areas, including whether synthetic life-forms have the same intrinsic value as natural organisms, whether an intrinsic objection to synthetic biology is a good basis for legislating policy, and whether scientists should try to accommodate those who reasonably reject the technology. Valuable for genetics, genomics, or bioethics classes."

SZABLOWSKI, WITOLD. The assassin from Apricot City; reportage from Turkey; xvii, 210 p. 2013 Stork Press Ltd
1. Journalism
ISBN 0957391250 (pbk.); 9780957391253 (pbk.)
LC 2013-487103

SUMMARY: "As he travels across this fascinating and beautiful country, [author Witold] Szabłowski heads for the most remote villages and towns to meet young women who have run away from honour killings, . . . a family of immigrants from Africa who dream of a better life, and Kurdish journalists and freedom fighters. A polyphonic portrait of contemporary Turkey, 'The Assassin from Apricot City' masterfully evokes the present-day dreams and hopes of ordinary people." (Publisher's note)

REVIEW: *TLS* no5792 p30-1 Ap 4 2014 WILLIAM ARMSTRONG

REVIEW: *World Lit Today* v88 no2 p76-7 Mr/Ap 2014 Jacob Daniels

"The Assassin From Apricot City: Reportage From Turkey." "Witold Szabłowski is a Polish journalist who has written extensively about Turkey. Twelve pieces of nonfiction have been arranged into his newly translated book, 'The Assassin from Apricot City.' Each story can stand alone, but Szabłowski weaves them loosely into a larger work of art. . . . Sometimes Szabłowski makes awkward generalizations. Too many sentences start with phrases like 'Turkish boys are obsessed with . . .' or 'That's how the Turks behave whenever . . .' These statements feel lazy and run contrary to his theme of human complexity. But when he tells poignant stories about tangible men and women, a broader picture begins to emerge--baffling as the image may be."

SZABLYA, HELEN M.tr. Mind Twisters. See Töttösy, E.

SZE, SARAH.il. Sarah Sze. See Burton, J.

SZUMSKI, BONNIE. Should same-sex marriage be legal? See Karson, J.

T

TO DARE MIGHTY THINGS; the life of Theodore Roosevelt; 48 p. 2013 Disney-Hyperion
1. Biography (Literary form) 2. Children's nonfiction 3. Presidents—United States—Biography—Juvenile literature 4. United States—History—Juvenile literature
ISBN 142312488X (hardback); 9781423124887 (hardback)
LC 2013-010691

SUMMARY: This picture book, by Doreen Rappaport and illustrated by C. F. Payne, is a biography of American president Theodore Roosevelt. "As an American president, he left [a] . . . mark upon his country. He promised a 'square deal' to all citizens, he tamed big businesses, and protected the nation's wildlife and natural beauty. His . . . leadership assured that he would always be remembered." (Publisher's note).

REVIEW: *Booklist* v110 no8 p42 D 15 2013 Ilene Cooper

REVIEW: *Bull Cent Child Books* v67 no5 p253-4 Ja 2014 Elizabeth Bush

"To Dare Mighty Things: The Life of Theodore Roosevelt." "Roosevelt was arguably the most frenetic of U.S. Presidents, and his renowned energy and multitudinous enthusiasms--both personal and political--are admirably conveyed in the litany of efforts and accomplishments compressed into this fast-moving text. . . . The very speed at which political appointments and elected offices fly past is a vital characteristic of TR's life, and if readers are left a bit breathless, so much the better. . . . Political bluster and bravado are balanced with attention to TR's domestic life, though, and here readers meet a down-to-earth kid to whom they can relate. . . . A strong current of humor also runs through Payne's grittily textured mixed-media paintings."

REVIEW: *Horn Book Magazine* v90 no2 p145-6 Mr/Ap 2014 JONATHAN HUNT

"To Dare Mighty Things: The Life of Theodore Roosevelt." "In her latest picture book biography, [Doreen] Rappaport capably distills Theodore Roosevelt's life with the help of her trademark primary source quotations interspersed throughout the main text. . . . Rappaport's account of Roosevelt's political career is balanced with brief but intimate glimpses into his two marriages and family life. As good as Rappaport's text is, however, [C. F.] Payne's illustrations--which seem to straddle the worlds of fine art and political cartoon--are even better, and allow him to capture Roosevelt's multifaceted, larger-than-life personality."

REVIEW: *Kirkus Rev* v81 no20 p76 O 15 2013

REVIEW: *N Y Times Book Rev* p14 Ja 12 2014 HAROLD HOLZER

TACKLEY, CATHERINE. Benny Goodman's famous 1938 Carnegie Hall jazz concert; [by] Catherine Tackley xviii, 223 p. 2012 Oxford University Press
1. Jazz—New York (State)—New York—1931-1940—History and criticism 2. Music literature
ISBN 9780195398304 (hardcover : alk. paper);

9780195398311 (pbk. : alk. paper)
LC 2011-030910

SUMMARY: In this analysis of jazz musician Benny Goodman's landmark 1938 concert, author Catherine Tackley "strips back the accumulated layers of interpretation and meaning to assess the performance in its original context, and explore what the material has come to represent in its recorded form." She "analyzes the compositions, arrangements and performances themselves, before discussing the immediate reception, and lasting legacy and impact of this storied event and album." (Publisher's note)

REVIEW: *Choice* v50 no10 p1844 Je 2013 K. R. Dietrich

REVIEW: *TLS* no5744 p25 My 3 2013 JOHN MOLE

"Benny Goodman's Famous 1938 Carnegie Hall Jazz Concert." "[A] fascinating study of Goodman's canonical 1938 concert at Carnegie Hall. It is the evidently joyous combination of enthusiasm, scholarly discipline and musical expertise that makes this contribution to the Oxford Studies in Recorded Jazz intriguing for the analyst, particularly companionable for those of us who have grown up with this landmark recording (not released until 1950) and an entertaining narrative for the general reader interested in the place of jazz in American culture."

TADROS, SAMUEL. Motherland Lost; The Egyptian and Coptic Quest for Modernity; [by] Samuel Tadros 262 p. 2013 Hoover Inst Pr

1. Christianity & other religions—Islam 2. Copts 3. Egypt—Politics & government 4. Egypt—Religion 5. Historical literature
ISBN 081791644X; 9780817916442

SUMMARY: This book by Samuel Tadros looks at "Copts--the native Egyptian Christians--and their crisis of modernity in conjunction with the overall developments in Egypt as it faced its own struggles with modernity. He argues that the modern plight of Copts is inseparable from the crisis of modernity and the answers developed to address that crisis by the Egyptian state and intellectuals, as well as by the Coptic Church and laypeople." (Publisher's note)

REVIEW: *Natl Rev* v65 no17 p42-4 S 16 2013 PAUL MARSHALL

"Motherland Lost: The Egyptian and Coptic Quest for Modernity." "In the first two chapters of his excellent new book, Samuel Tadros gives us a much-needed succinct survey of earlier Coptic history. . . . But this survey is only a prolegomenon to his two major interrelated themes. One is Egypt's struggle with modernity. . . . The other major theme is the Copts' own struggle with modernity. . . . Tadros's historically informed description of Egypt's ongoing failure to come to terms with modernity reveals the shallowness of most contemporary American commentary, rooted as it is in the categories of parochial Western modernity. . . . His depiction is not despairing, but it is acutely sobering."

TAEKU LEE. Asian American political participation; emerging constituents and their political identities; [by] Taeku Lee xv, 372 p. 2011 Russell Sage Foundation

1. Asian Americans—Political activity 2. Asian Americans—Politics and government 3. Asian Americans—Societies, etc. 4. Political participation 5. Political science literature
ISBN 9780871549624 (pbk.: alk. paper); 9781610447553 (ebook)
LC 2011-022380

SUMMARY: This book presents "a detailed examination of political involvement among Asian Americans, now the fastest-growing racial group in the United States." The authors "seek to document patterns and explain why some Asian Americans participate in political life and some do not, and among those who participate, why some individuals engage in political activity such as voting while others choose to contact government officials or work within the context of community organizations." (Contemporary Sociology)

REVIEW: *Contemp Sociol* v43 no2 p282-3 Mr 2014 Dina G. Okamoto

"Asian American Political Participation: Emerging Constituents and Their Political Identities". "Makes a significant contribution to the literature by providing a detailed examination of political involvement among Asian Americans, now the fastest-growing racial group in the United States. . . . 'Asian American Political Participation' is a must read for scholars, students, and policy makers alike who are interested in learning more about the political attitudes and behaviors among Asian Americans and immigrant populations. Students of immigration, race/ethnicity, and politics will also discover that the book holds important insights about identity, intergroup attitudes, and civic engagement."

REVIEW: *Ethn Racial Stud* v35 no11 p2022-3 N 2012 Russell Jeung Holly Raña Lim

TAGLIACOZZO, ERIC. The longest journey; Southeast Asians and the pilgrimage to Mecca; [by] Eric Tagliacozzo 356 p. 2013 Oxford University Press

1. Historical literature 2. Islam & state 3. Muslim pilgrims & pilgrimages—Saudi Arabia—Mecca 4. Muslim pilgrims and pilgrimages—Saudi Arabia—Mecca 5. Muslims—Southeast Asia 6. Pilgrims & pilgrimages—History 7. Southeast Asia—History
ISBN 9780195308273 (alk. paper); 9780195308280 (alk. paper)
LC 2012-039784

SUMMARY: "By the end of the nineteenth century, and the beginning of the twentieth, fully half of all pilgrims making the journey in any given year could come from Southeast Asia." This book by Eric Tagliacozzo, "spanning eleven modern nation-states and seven centuries, is the first book to offer a history of the Hajj from one of Islam's largest and most important regions." (Publisher's note)

REVIEW: *Am Hist Rev* v119 no2 p490-1 Ap 2014 Henri Chambert-Loir

REVIEW: *Choice* v51 no2 p328-9 O 2013 P. B. Guingona

"The Longest Journey: Southeast Asians and the Pilgrimage to Mecca." "More comprehensive than his edited 'Southeast Asia and the Middle East' . . . , Cornell historian [Eric] Tagliacozzo's excellent new monograph outlines the social and economic exchange that accompanied the journey to Mecca of Southeast Asian Muslims. Starting with the first 13th century mention to the present, this transnational history engages with scholarship of an impressive chronological and geographical scope. . . . Tagliacozzo argues that the Hajj, a pilgrimage that maintained the connection between Southeast Asia and the Middle East, changed from privately financed, small-scale journeys early on into a state-regulated endeavor. . . . Overall, this is a concise, erudite monograph."

TAIT, ARCH.tr. Snow Germans. See Snow Germans

TAIT, ARCH.tr. 1990. See 1990

TAKAHASHI, MUTSUO. Twelve views from the distance. See Twelve views from the distance

TAKAHASHI, SHIN. The manga guide to linear algebra. See Inoue, I.

TAKAKI, RONALD T., 1939-2009. A different mirror for young people. See Stefoff, R.

TAKASHI HIRAIDE. The Guest Cat; 144 p. 2014 New Directions Books

1. Cats—Fiction 2. Human-animal relationships—Fiction 3. Marriage—Fiction 4. Married people—Fiction 5. Psychological fiction

ISBN 0811221504; 9780811221504 (acid-free paper)

LC 2013-046516

SUMMARY: This novel, by Takahashi Hiraide, winner of Japan's Kiyama Shohei Literary Award, is "about a visiting cat who brings joy into a couple's life in Tokyo. . . . A couple in their thirties . . . no longer have very much to say to one another. But one day a cat invites itself into their small kitchen. It leaves, but the next day comes again, and then again and again. Soon they are buying treats for the cat and enjoying talks about the animal and all its little ways." (Publisher's note)

REVIEW: *Kirkus Rev* v81 no24 p240 D 15 2013

"The Guest Cat". "The simplest of relationships often elicit the most complex emotions, as two freelance editors discover in an eloquent tale written by poet and essayist [Takashi] Hiraide and translated by [Eric] Selland. . . . One day, a small cat appears in the couple's garden. . . . Though the cat doesn't belong to them, the couple develops a proprietary feeling for the cat as their lives become more centered around its visits. They begin to take joy in small pleasures as the cat, always on its own terms, slips between their neighbors' home and theirs. . . A multifaceted tale that explores love and the fragility of life; the author creates an introspective, poetic story that's deeply moving. Cat lovers may be especially moved."

REVIEW: *N Y Times Book Rev* p30 Mr 9 2014 Takashi Hiraide

REVIEW: *N Y Times Book Rev* p26 Mr 23 2014 GREGORY COWLES

REVIEW: *Publ Wkly* v260 no49 p2 D 2 2013

TALKINGTON, AMY. Liv, forever; [by] Amy Talkington 288 p. 2014 Soho Teen

1. Artists—Fiction 2. Ghosts—Fiction 3. High schools—Fiction 4. JUVENILE FICTION—Horror & Ghost Stories 5. JUVENILE FICTION—Love & Romance 6. JUVENILE FICTION—Mysteries & Detective Stories 7. Murder—Fiction 8. Schools—Fiction 9. Supernatural—Fiction

ISBN 9781616953225 (hardback)

LC 2013-038270

SUMMARY: In this book, "sixteen-year-old Liv . . . wins a scholarship to attend New Hampshire's uber-exclusive Wickham Hall. . . . The school has an elite secret society, the Victors. It also has ghosts, spirits of various girls who were murdered on campus over a span of many decades. When the same fate befalls her, Liv begins, as a ghost, to investigate the mystery of the deaths, which somehow may be tied to the Victors." (Kirkus Reviews)

REVIEW: *Booklist* v110 no14 p75 Mr 15 2014 Ilene Cooper

REVIEW: *Kirkus Rev* v82 no3 p198 F 1 2014

"Liv, Forever". " A ghost story set at a posh boarding school hits plenty of buttons for school-conspiracy and romance fans. . . . As usual for the genre, the school has an elite secret society, the Victors. It also has ghosts, spirits of various girls who were murdered on campus over a span of many decades. . . . While the narrator-as-ghost adds an interesting twist, the book remains primarily a mystery surrounding the school's secret society. The romance elements come across as bittersweet, of course, considering the fact that Liv's dead. Average, but satisfying enough for paranormal fans still engaged by the genre."

REVIEW: *Publ Wkly* v261 no2 p71 Ja 13 2014

REVIEW: *SLJ* v60 no3 p164 Mr 2014 Audrey Sumser

REVIEW: *Voice of Youth Advocates* v37 no1 p89 Ap 2014 Deborah L. Dubois

TALLBEAR, KIM. Native American DNA; tribal belonging and the false promise of genetic science; [by] Kim Tallbear xi, 252 p. 2013 University of Minnesota Press

1. DNA fingerprinting—North America 2. Genetic genealogy—North America 3. Human population genetics—North America 4. Indians of North America—Anthropometry 5. Social science literature

ISBN 9780816665853 (hc : alk. paper); 9780816665860 (pb : alk. paper)

LC 2013-012526

SUMMARY: This book by Kimberly TallBear "provides an anthropological and Native American perspective of the interplay between DNA testing and multiple views of Native American tribal identity and status. The author critiques 'direct to consumer' genotyping companies, private molecular genealogists, and National Geographic's Genographic Project." (Choice: Current Reviews for Academic Libraries)

REVIEW: *Choice* v51 no7 p1243-4 Mr 2014 R. M. Dename

"Native American DNA: Tribal Belonging and the False Promise of Genetic Science. "Unfortunately, [Kimberly] Tallbear's critiques are frequently statements on broad swaths of science and society, supported by few data points. Many of her arguments take on the tenor of jargon-filled polemics. However, her conclusion is not in this mold; it is an insightful, balanced analysis of concerns and opportunities for indigenous peoples, scientists, and policy makers. The book's strengths include a good alternative viewpoint for human population geneticists and generally good referencing. Drawbacks are a sometimes strident, personal tone and the use of jargon in the text."

TALLON, LEAH.ed. Don't start me talkin'. See Don't start me talkin'

TAMMET, DANIEL. Thinking in numbers; on life, love, meaning, and math; [by] Daniel Tammet 288 p. 2013 Lit-

tle, Brown and Co.
1. Autism 2. Essay (Literary form) 3. Mathematics 4. Savants (Savant syndrome) 5. Synesthesia
ISBN 0316187372; 9780316187374
LC 2013-935728

SUMMARY: This is a book of essays by Daniel Tammet. "His topics include the concept of zero, the calendar, prime numbers, chess, time and statistics. . . . Several of his pieces have an autobiographical component. His essay on infinity shows him as a young boy discovering the infinity of fractions between two points on his walk home from school, and readers learn of his amazing memory in his account of reciting aloud the decimals of pi to 22,514 places at the University of Oxford's Pi Day." (Kirkus Reviews)

REVIEW: *Atlantic* v313 no2 p40-3 Mr 2014 HANNA ROSIN

"Raising Cubby: A Father and Son's Adventures With Asperger's, Trains, Tractors, and High Explosives," "Thinking in Numbers: On Life, Love, Meaning, and Math," and "The Autistic Brain: Thinking Across the Spectrum." "[John Elder] Robison . . . champions the label and the tribal protection it offers in a 'neurotypical' world that he is sure will always stigmatize and misunderstand people like him--and like his son. Jack. Yet Robison's new memoir. . . . turns out to offer vivid evidence that just the opposite is true. The world his son grew up in is welcoming in ways that Robison curiously fails to recognize, even as he recounts them in great detail. . . . In his most moving chapter, [Daniel] Tammet explains how as a child he tried hard to create a 'predictive model of my mother's behavior.' . . . In [Temple Grandin's] view, settling on a diagnosis is not nearly as interesting as taking note of the many permutations of minds along the spectrum."

REVIEW: *Booklist* v109 no21 p9 Jl 1 2013 Bryce Christensen

REVIEW: *Kirkus Rev* v81 no12 p69 Je 15 2013

REVIEW: *New York Times* v162 no56255 pD6 S 10 2013 KATIe HAFNER

"Thinking in Numbers: On Life, Love, Meaning, and Math." "Mr. [Daniel] Tammet . . . is a 'prodigious savant'-someone who combines developmental disabilities, in this case autism, with the skills of a prodigy. Happily . . . he has a rare ability to describe what he sees in his head. His new book is, in part, a description of an intimate relationship with numbers. . . . His description of the shape and character the digits took as they rolled across his brain, past his tongue and out of his mouth, is at once eerie and poetic. . . . Yet in 'Thinking in Numbers' Mr. Tammet fails to sustain these revelatory glimpses into his highly unusual brain Many of his connections between humanity, art, the brain and numbers are something of a stretch."

REVIEW: *Publ Wkly* v260 no17 p120 Ap 29 2013

REVIEW: *Sci Am* v308 no7 p90 Jl 2013 Anna Kuchment

REVIEW: *Smithsonian* v44 no3 p103 Je 2013 Chloë Schama

REVIEW: *TLS* no5733 p30 F 15 2013 ADAM FEINSTEIN

"Thinking in Numbers: How Maths Illuminates Our Lives." "By his own admission, [Daniel] Tammet's Asperger's syndrome meant that numbers--and books--were his only friends when he was younger, and his highly literate enthusiasm shimmers on every page of 'Thinking in Numbers.' . . Tammet's analysis of an extract from Dante is startlingly perceptive. . . . Tammet's account of being brought up in the East End of London as the eldest of nine children, and of finding a second home in local libraries, is full of endearing honesty."

TAN, AMY, 1952-. The Valley of Amazement; [by] Amy Tan 608 p. 2013 HarperCollins
1. China—Fiction 2. Historical fiction 3. Mothers & daughters—Fiction 4. Prostitutes—Fiction 5. San Francisco (Calif.)—Fiction
ISBN 0062107313; 9780062107312

SUMMARY: In this novel, Amy Tan "explores the complex relationships between mothers and daughters, control and submission, tradition and new beginnings. Jumping from bustling Shanghai to an isolated village in rural China to San Francisco at the turn of the 19th century, the epic story follows three generations of women pulled apart by outside forces. The main focus is Violet, once a virgin courtesan in one of the most reputable houses in Shanghai, who faces a series of crippling setbacks." (Publishers Weekly)

REVIEW: *Booklist* v110 no2 p40 S 15 2013 Donna Seaman

"The Valley of Amazement." "Reaching back to Lulu's San Francisco childhood and forward to Violet's operatic struggles and traumas and reliance on her smart, loyal mento,. Magic Gourd, this scrolling saga is practically a how-to on courtesan life and a veritable orgy of suspense and sorrow. Ultimately,Tan's prodigious, sumptuously descriptive, historically grounded, sexually candid, and elaborately plotted novel counters violence, exploitation, betrayal, and tragic cultural divides with beauty, wit, and transcendent friendships between women."

REVIEW: *Kirkus Rev* p15 Ag 15 2013 Fall Preview

REVIEW: *Kirkus Rev* v81 no14 p346 Jl 15 2013

REVIEW: *Libr J* v139 no10 p61 Je 1 2014 Susan G. Baird

REVIEW: *Ms* v23 no4 p59-60 Fall 2013 Erin Aubry Kaplan

REVIEW: *N Y Times Book Rev* p10 N 10 2013 LESLEY DOWNER

"The Valley of Amazement." "[A] long and ultimately heart-wrenching narrative that covers more than four decades and moves from Shanghai in the 1920s and '30s to the Hudson River Valley to a mountain village in rural China, with an interlude of backtracking in late-19th-century San Francisco. The epic history of these times is woven into the complex background of the story of three generations of women. . . . Written in [Amy] Tan's characteristically economical and matter-of-fact style, 'The Valley of Amazement' is filled with memorably idiosyncratic characters. And its array of colorful multilayered stories is given further depth by Tan's affecting depictions of mothers and daughters."

REVIEW: *New Yorker* v89 no38 p127-1 N 25 2013

REVIEW: *Publ Wkly* v261 no8 p178 F 24 2014

REVIEW: *Publ Wkly* v260 no30 p38 Jl 29 2013

TANGHERLINI, TIMOTHY R.tr. Danish folktales, legends, and other stories. See Danish folktales, legends, and other stories

TANKARD, JEREMY.il. Here comes Destructosaurus! See Reynolds, A.

TANPINAR, AHMET HAMDI. The Time Regulation Institute; 464 p. 2014 Penguin Books
1. Bureaucracy 2. Clocks & watches 3. FICTION—Classics 4. FICTION—Literary 5. Time—Fiction 6. Turkey—Fiction
ISBN 9780143106739 (pbk.)
LC 2013-033709

SUMMARY: In this book by Ahmet Hamdi Tanpinar, "the narrator, Hayri Irdal, presents his life story in the guise of a memoir about his (along with others') creation of the Time Regulation Institute, charged with changing the clocks of Turkey to Western time. The institute is given the freedom to use an elaborate series of fines for those who fail to comply, and Irdal delights in the . . . system of synchronization." (Kirkus Reviews)

REVIEW: *Bookforum* v20 no4 p31 D 2013/Ja 2014 NIKIL SAVAL

"The Time Regulation Institute." "Despite [Ahmet Hamdi] Tanpinar's hopes for a novel centered around psychologically rich characters, his own work consists almost entirely of minor figures sketched out in deft strokes. . . . But rather than a failure, this turns into a source of strength. Instead of emphasizing the rational, hierarchical nature of the Institute, Tanpinar evokes the persistence of human activities within it. . . . 'The Time Regulation Institute,' by contrast, with its multiple registers, fugue-like plot, and granular attention to everyday life in a time of upheaval, proves to be the synthesis he had sought: a truly pathbreaking novel, at once nostalgic and modernist, contemporary and out of its time."

REVIEW: *Kirkus Rev* v81 no20 p212 O 15 2013

REVIEW: *N Y Times Book Rev* p11 Ja 5 2014 MARTIN RIKER

REVIEW: *Publ Wkly* v260 no42 p29 O 21 2013

TAO LIN. Taipei; a novel; [by] Tao Lin 272 p. 2013 Random House Inc
1. Authors—Fiction 2. Drug abuse—Fiction 3. Man-woman relationships—Fiction 4. Popular literature 5. Taipei (Taiwan)
ISBN 0307950174; 9780307950178
LC 2013-005675

SUMMARY: In this book, "protagonist Paul is still prowling Brooklyn parties and bars. He's made a quick trip home to Taiwan, but little happened there either. Back in the borough, Paul has moved from one maybe-a-girlfriend to another, met dealer friends who trade in recreational pharmaceuticals--Xanax, Adderall, cocaine, 'shrooms and MDMA--and ruminated a bit about his novel, soon to be released." (Kirkus Reviews)

REVIEW: *Booklist* v109 no18 p16 My 15 2013 Sarah Grant

REVIEW: *Kirkus Rev* v81 no5 p226 Mr 1 2013

REVIEW: *N Y Rev Books* v60 no19 p13-6 D 5 2013 Zadie Smith

REVIEW: *N Y Times Book Rev* p8 Je 30 2013 CLANCY MARTIN

REVIEW: *New York Times* v162 no56158 pC1-5 Je 5 2013 DWIGHT GARNER

REVIEW: *New Yorker* v89 no25 p69 Ag 26 2013 Tao Lin Mara Faye Lethem Jon Mooallem Karen Green

REVIEW: *Publ Wkly* v260 no8 p138 F 25 2013

REVIEW: *TLS* no5752 p21 Je 28 2013 SAM BYERS

"Taipei." "His new novel, 'Taipei,' reads like a consolidation and vindication of everything he has produced to date. . . . Many of [Tao] Lin's similes and metaphors--usually more concerned with 'making-strange' than they are with demystification--involve space. . . . The book is not without its problems, but it is testament to Lin's commitment to his aesthetic that these, stem in part from its success. Lin is so convincing at representing the depressed lives of his characters that the reader begins to feel rather depressed too. . . . But perseverance is advised because, in its final third, 'Taipei' becomes extremely moving. . . . Here, Lin emerges as a novelist of compassion; one who recognizes the value and risk of intimacy."

TARNOPOLSKI, MICHELLE.tr. Soft soil, black grapes. See Cinotto, S.

TARO MIURA. The tiny king; [by] Taro Miura 32 p. 2013 Candlewick Press
1. Families—Juvenile fiction 2. Happiness 3. Kings & rulers—Fiction 4. Picture books for children 5. Stature, Short
ISBN 0763666874; 9780763666873
LC 2012-955151

SUMMARY: In this children's picture book by Taro Miura "the Tiny King lives all alone in his big castle with too much space, accompanied only by an army. When he falls in love with a big princess, they soon have 10 children who share his massive table, ride in a carriage pulled by his giant white horse, splash in the gigantic bathtub, and fill up the once-empty bed. The king is so happy that he sends his army marching home for a holiday." (School Library Journal)

REVIEW: *Horn Book Magazine* v89 no6 p80 N/D 2013 SARAH ELLIS

"The Tiny King". "The story in pictures has the same clear simplicity, with geometric cut-paper collage in bright colors with decorated papers, touches of old-timey clip art, and Bruna-stylized figures. As the tiny king finds domestic happiness, the background of the pages changes from matte black to matte white to a gorgeous raspberry pink (followed by lemon yellow, pumpkin orange, etc.), and even the bathwater explodes into color. This graphically cheerful, quietly amusing Japanese import is a celebration of family life in the key of C major."

TARTT, DONNA, 1963-. The goldfinch; [by] Donna Tartt 784 p. 2013 Little Brown & Co
1. Artists—Fiction 2. Loss (Psychology)—Fiction 3. Self-realization—Fiction 4. Young men—Fiction
ISBN 0316055433; 9780316055437 (hardback); 9780316242370 (international)
LC 2013-028907

SUMMARY: In this book, "Theo Decker . . . miraculously survives an accident that kills his mother. Abandoned by his father, Theo is taken in by the family of a wealthy friend. . . . Disturbed by schoolmates who don't know how to talk to him, and tormented above all by his unbearable longing for his mother, he clings to one thing that reminds him of her: a small, mysteriously captivating painting that ultimately draws Theo into the underworld of art." (Publisher's note)

REVIEW: *Booklist* v110 no1 p38 S 1 2013 Donna Seaman

"The Goldfinch". "[Donna] Tartt writes from Theo's point of view with fierce exactitude and magnetic emotion as, stricken with grief and post-traumatic stress syndrome, he seeks sanctuary with a troubled Park Avenue family. . . . Drenched in sensory detail, infused with Theo's churning thoughts and feelings, sparked by nimble dialogue, and propelled by escalating cosmic angst and thriller action, Tartt's trenchant, defiant, engrossing, and rocketing novel conducts a grand inquiry into the mystery and sorrow of survival, beauty and obsession, and the promise of art."

REVIEW: *Christ Century* v131 no9 p3 Ap 30 2014 John M. Buchanan

REVIEW: *Commentary* v136 no5 p53-4 D 2013 FERNANDA MOORE

REVIEW: *Economist* v409 no8859 p93 O 26 2013

"The Goldfinch". "The explosion, the sudden, awful deaths, the painting and the ring are the mechanisms that set this big, complex novel in motion. It is a testament to Ms. [Donna] Tartt's Dickensian skill that she is able to make this extraordinary situation, and every one that follows, feel both true and lived. . . . [Theo Decker is] a subtle mouthpiece for Ms. Tartt's acute observations about the lives her protagonist finds himself leading. . . . It is in Vegas that Theo meets Boris, the sidekick every good hero needs and one of the book's most appealing creations. . . . 'The Goldfinch' is a startling accomplishment, bringing a truly Victorian tale . . . right up against the explosive device of a postmodern thriller. But Ms. Tartt has the true storyteller's gift."

REVIEW: *Kirkus Rev* v81 no17 p26 S 1 2013

REVIEW: *Kirkus Rev* p37 N 15 2013 Best Books

REVIEW: *Libr J* v138 no8 p59 My 1 2013

REVIEW: *London Rev Books* v35 no24 p22-3 D 19 2013 Christopher Tayler

REVIEW: *N Y Rev Books* v61 no1 p10-2 Ja 9 2014 Franane Prose

REVIEW: *N Y Times Book Rev* p20 My 4 2014

REVIEW: *N Y Times Book Rev* p31-6 Ap 6 2014

REVIEW: *N Y Times Book Rev* p12 D 15 2013

REVIEW: *N Y Times Book Rev* p28 Ap 27 2014

REVIEW: *N Y Times Book Rev* p1-30 O 13 2013 Stephen King

REVIEW: *N Y Times Book Rev* p32 My 11 2014

REVIEW: *New Statesman* v142 no5180 p43-5 O 18 2013 Jane Shilling

REVIEW: *New York Times* v163 no56356 pC23-9 D 20 2013 JANET MASLIN

"The Goldfinch," "Life After Life," and "My Promised Land: The Triumph and Tragedy of Israel". "In this astonishing Dickensian Novel, Ms. [Donna] Tartt uses her myriad talents—her tactile prose, her knowledge of her characters' inner lives, her instinct for suspense—to immerse us in a fully imagined fictional world that reminds us of the wonderful stay-up-all-night pleasures of reading. . . . In her best novel thus far, Ms. [Kate] Atkinson is a wonderful liar. . . . The book's many mysteries keep it riveting and intense. And Ms. Atkinson, always haunting, has never seemed more artfully in control of her storytelling. . . . This book—it's a gale of conversation, of feeling, of foreboding, of ratiocination—combines road trips, interviews, memoir and straightforward history to relate Israel's past and present."

REVIEW: *New York Times* v163 no56356 pC23-9 D 20 2013 JANET MASLIN

REVIEW: *New York Times* v162 no56283 pC1-6 O 8 2013 MICHIKO KAKUTANI

REVIEW: *Publ Wkly* v260 no30 p38 Jl 29 2013

REVIEW: *TLS* no5770 p19 N 1 2013 ALEX CLARK

TASAKI, SUSAN.ed. Sutro's glass place. See Martini, J. A.

TATE, DON.il. The Cart that carried Martin. See Bunting, E.

TATE, GREGORY. The Poet's Mind; The Psychology of Victorian Poetry 1830-1870; [by] Gregory Tate 224 p. 2013 Oxford Univ Pr

1. English poetry—19th century 2. English poetry—History & criticism 3. Historical literature 4. Poetry (Literary form)—Psychological aspects 5. Psychology—History

ISBN 0199659419; 9780199659418

SUMMARY: This book by Gregory Tate examines "how Victorian poets thought and wrote about the human mind. It argues that Victorian poets, inheriting from their Romantic forerunners the belief that subjective thoughts and feelings were the most important materials for poetry, used their writing both to give expression to mental processes and to scrutinise and analyse those processes." (Publisher's note)

REVIEW: *Choice* v51 no2 p263 O 2013 T. Hoagwood

REVIEW: *TLS* no5755 p3-4 Jl 19 2013 GREGORY CURRIE

"The Poet's Mind: The Psychology of Victorian Poetry" and "Thinking Without Thinking in the Victorian Novel." "[Gregory] Tate, like the poets he discusses, is somewhat vague on the content of the science. . . . The science highlighted by [Vanessa L.] Ryan and Tate overlaps, but Ryan's emphasis is on 'unconscious cerebration,' so named by the zoologist William Carpenter. . . . Both speak as if science and literature at this time were engaged in complementary projects of mental discovery. . . . Perhaps we should not criticize either author for failing to investigate a question that belongs to the philosophy of knowledge and not to intellectual history. But there are times when their judgements are less guarded and less historically limited."

TATSURO, FUZIKURA. The noodle narratives. See Gewertz, D.

TAVARES, MATT.il. Becoming Babe Ruth. See Tavares, M.

TAYLOR, A. R. Sex, Rain, and Cold Fusion; [by] A. R. Taylor 348 p. 2013 Ridgecrest House

1. Love stories 2. Murder—Fiction 3. Physics 4. Satire 5. Scientists—Fiction

ISBN 0615818447; 9780615818443

SUMMARY: In this book, "30-year-old hotshot physicist David Oster find[s] himself fed up with teaching physics to undergraduates . . . He manages to wrangle an appointment at the prestigious, deep-pocketed Larson Kinne Institute for Applied Physics at Western Washington State University.

Once there, he embraces the change, despite the eccentric reputation of the institute's enigmatic founder and namesake." (Kirkus Reviews)

REVIEW: *Kirkus Rev* v82 no4 p88 F 15 2014

"Sex, Rain, and Cold Fusion". "A surreal novel about a promising young academic trying to change his life. [A. R.] Taylor's funny, meticulously controlled fiction debut opens with 30-year-old hotshot physicist David Oster finding himself fed up with teaching physics to undergraduates . . . . Taylor so skillfully blends David Lodge-style academic farce with Thomas Pynchon-style weird science (mostly of the aquatic variety) that it's impossible to spot the dividing line between the two. In David Oster, she crafts a perfect, hapless Everyman. . . . he interdisciplinary rivalries at Kinne are particularly well-done. . . . An unpredictable, winningly bizarre academic satire."

REVIEW: *Kirkus Rev* v82 no3 p382 F 1 2014

TAYLOR, ABBIE. The stranger on the train; a novel; [by] Abbie Taylor 352 p. 2014 Atria Paperback/Atria Books

1. Infants—Crimes against—Fiction 2. Kidnapping—Fiction 3. Mothers of kidnapped children—Fiction 4. Single mothers—England—Fiction 5. Suspense fiction
ISBN 9781476754970 (paperback)
LC 2014-009092

SUMMARY: In this book,"single mom Emma Turner watches in horror as her one-year-old son, Ritchie, somehow gets on a train that leaves without her. . . . The police assigned to Emma's missing person's case have little sympathy. . . . Dirt poor, she's overwhelmed by the responsibility of raising a child, the spawn of a quick fling. Worse, in a fit of desperation, she earlier confessed to her GP that she wished Ritchie were dead. So everybody doubts whether the tot was really kidnapped." (Publishers Weekly)

REVIEW: *Booklist* v110 no14 p54-5 Mr 15 2014 Michele Leber

"The Stranger on the Train." "Emma Turner is struggling to get home on the London underground with her 13-month-old son, Ritchie, in his buggy, along with shopping bags and a purse, when the train takes off without her. A woman on the same car takes Ritchie in hand, waiting for Emma at the next station and offering further help--until she takes off with the child when Emma is in the bathroom. . . . Readers may occasionally want to slap Emma, to keep her from behaving against her own best interests, although her background provides some explanation. But this first novel is driven less by character than plot, and the roller-coaster ride, starting with an all-too-plausible incident, is compelling enough to grab and hold interest."

REVIEW: *Kirkus Rev* v82 no6 p341 Mr 15 2014

REVIEW: *Publ Wkly* v261 no9 p47 Mr 3 2014

TAYLOR, ANNETTE KUJAWSKI.ed. Encyclopedia of human memory. See Encyclopedia of human memory

TAYLOR, C. JAMES.ed. A traveled first lady. See A traveled first lady

TAYLOR, FREDERICK. The Downfall of Money; Germany's Hyperinflation and the Destruction of the Middle Class; [by] Frederick Taylor 432 p. 2013 St Martins Pr

1. Financial crises—Germany 2. Germany—Economic conditions—1918-1945 3. Germany—Politics & government—1918-1933 4. Historical literature 5. Inflation (Finance)—Germany
ISBN 162040236X; 9781620402368

SUMMARY: This book presents an "account of the human face of hyperinflation in the 1920s Weimar Republic. Many blame the collapse of the German mark on the reparations imposed by the Treaty of Versailles, yet [Frederick] Taylor argues that it was the Second Empire's decision to finance WWI primarily by borrowing that led to the economic catastrophe. Postwar uprisings on the left and right further destabilized the country's fragile, young government." (Publishers Weekly)

REVIEW: *Choice* v51 no8 p1458 Ap 2014 T. R. Weeks

REVIEW: *Economist* v408 no8853 p91 S 14 2013

"The Downfall of Money: Germany's Hyperinflation and the Destruction of the Middle Class." "Frederick Taylor, who has written several books on this era, is careful to blame no one--except perhaps the French. He is quick to offer parallels with the recent financial crisis, when many governments turned to quantitative easing (buying assets with newly created money) to avoid recession or even depression. And his book has suggestions about where the world may be heading if it is not careful. . . . Mr. Taylor notes similarities between the Treaty of Versailles and European economic and monetary union. Both, broadly, were attempts to die down Europe's giant and help prevent another war. Versailles failed."

REVIEW: *Kirkus Rev* v81 no16 p156 Ag 15 2013

REVIEW: *N Y Times Book Rev* p16 Ja 5 2014 CATHRINE RAMPELL

REVIEW: *Publ Wkly* v260 no26 p80 Jl 1 2013

REVIEW: *TLS* no5789 p23 Mr 14 2014 TYLER COWEN

TAYLOR, JAMES. Precision Agriculture for Grain Production Systems; [by] James Taylor 208 p. 2013 Stylus Pub Llc

1. Agricultural literature 2. Agriculture—Environmental aspects 3. Agriculture—Management 4. Grain trade 5. Precision farming
ISBN 0643107479; 9780643107472

SUMMARY: In this book on precision agriculture, "readers will gain an understanding of the magnitude, spatial scale and seasonality of measurable variability in soil attributes, plant growth and environmental conditions. They will be introduced to the role of sensing systems in measuring crop, soil and environment variability, and discover how this variability may have a significant impact on crop production systems." (Publisher's note)

REVIEW: *Choice* v51 no7 p1245-6 Mr 2014 M. K. Swan

"Precision Agriculture for Grain Production Systems." "This well-designed book presents technical information on precision agriculture (PA) in a logical and efficient manner. Educators/practitioners [Brett] Whelan . . . and [James] Taylor . . . begin by providing a meaningful understanding of precision farming for both novice and experienced readers. They use graphics, diagrams, and pictures throughout the book to enhance comprehension of the concepts. The color in the map layers is a great asset for illustrating the interactions between items being evaluated. . . . This book is a must have for the instructor of any PA course, regardless of country/location."

TAYLOR, K. W. A history of the Vietnamese; [by] K. W. Taylor xv, 696 p. 2013 Cambridge University Press
1. HISTORY—Asia—Southeast Asia 2. Historical literature 3. Vietnamese—History
ISBN 9780521699150 (paperback); 9780521875868 (hardback)
LC 2012-035197

SUMMARY: "The history of Vietnam prior to the nineteenth century is rarely examined in any detail. In this groundbreaking work, K. W. Taylor takes up this challenge, addressing a wide array of topics from the earliest times to the present day--including language, literature, religion and warfare --and themes--including Sino-Vietnamese relations, the interactions of the peoples of different regions within the country, and the various forms of government adopted by Vietnam." (Publisher's note)

REVIEW: *TLS* no5783 p28 Ja 31 2014 GRANT EVANS
"A History of the Vietnamese." "[Author Keith W.] Taylor's massive new book, running from ancient times to the present . . . is deliberately entitled 'A History of the Vietnamese,' emphasizing the people rather than the nation. . . . The main weakness of the book . . . is that Taylor deliberately eschews any perspective whatsoever. . . . Taylor justifies his approach by arguing that there is a need to sort out 'a basic sequence of events because this has never been done with the detail and method enabled by surviving evidence and recent scholarship.' And indeed, he accomplishes this through his extraordinary mastery of the sources."

TAYLOR, KARA. Wicked little secrets; a Prep school confidential novel; [by] Kara Taylor 320 p. 2014 Thomas Dunne Books, St. Martin's Griffin
1. Boarding schools—Fiction 2. JUVENILE FICTION—Girls & Women 3. JUVENILE FICTION—Mysteries & Detective Stories 4. JUVENILE FICTION—School & Education 5. Mystery and detective stories 6. Schools—Fiction 7. Youths' writings
ISBN 9781250033604 (pbk.)
LC 2013-032065

SUMMARY: This "sequel to 'Prep School Confidential' (2013) continues this series set in yet another hyperexclusive prep school as Anne tries to solve some mysteries left over from the opening installment only to encounter more intrigue. Intrepid 17-year-old sleuth Anne just can't let go of an unsolved mystery she thinks may be related to the murder of her roommate, which occurred in the first book." (Kirkus Reviews)

REVIEW: *Kirkus Rev* v82 no3 p134 F 1 2014
"Wicked Little Secrets". " Along the way, old and new relationships evolve, making the romance elements of the novel a bit different from the genre norm. [Kara] Taylor stuffs the story with characters that mostly come across as believable, and she includes enough romance to satisfy readers looking for it while keeping the mystery complex enough to challenge. Though familiarity with the first book is assumed, she provides enough background to allow new readers to follow the action, and a nifty surprise will whet their appetites for the third book. A solid investigative mystery."

REVIEW: *Voice of Youth Advocates* v37 no1 p75 Ap 2014 Shanna Miles

TAYLOR, LAUREN A. The American health care paradox. See Bradley, E. H.

TAYLOR, MICHAEL A. Hippocrates cried; the decline of American psychiatry; [by] Michael A. Taylor 296 p. 2013 Oxford University Press
1. Medical literature 2. Neurosciences—United States—History 3. Psychiatry—United States—History 4. Psychoanalysis
ISBN 9780199948062 (hardcover : alk. paper)
LC 2012-030771

SUMMARY: In this book, Michael A. Taylor "writes . . . about patients, doctors, and the training of young psychiatrists. He criticizes pharmaceutical companies for their role as profiteers, and the American Psychiatric Association for what he calls its pseudo-scientific Diagnostic and Statistical Manual. . . . Taylor would delegate the study of [psychoanalysis] to nonphysicians while training neuropsychiatrists who diagnose and treat syndromes traceable to the brain." (Library Journal)

REVIEW: *Choice* v51 no7 p1255 Mr 2014 M. L. Charleroy
"Hippocrates Cried: The Decline of American Psychiatry." "Using vignettes and data from his 45 years of practice, [Michael Allan] Taylor argues that patients with mental illness are no longer receiving the care they need. . . . In relying too heavily on the DSM, the author argues, psychiatrists fail to properly identify patients with mental illness. Taylor's previous writings have appeared mostly in peer-reviewed professional journals; 'Hippocrates Cried' is written for a general audience. The language is conversational and accessible for nonpractitioners. . . . Recommended."

REVIEW: *Libr J* v138 no5 p119 Mr 15 2013 E. James Lieberman

REVIEW: *Publ Wkly* v260 no11 p74 Mr 18 2013

TAYLOR, PATRICK.ed. The Encyclopedia of Caribbean Religions. See The Encyclopedia of Caribbean Religions

TAYLOR, ROGER. God Bless the Nhs; [by] Roger Taylor 352 p. 2013 Faber & Faber
1. Great Britain—Politics & government 2. Great Britain. National Health Service 3. Health care reform—Great Britain 4. Medical databases 5. Political science literature
ISBN 0571303641; 9780571303649

SUMMARY: This book on Great Britain's National Health Service (NHS) "looks at the ideology behind the current reforms and the reasons why the government decided to take on the nation's most treasured institution. Roger Taylor looks equivocally at those who support and oppose the new system, and at the patchy history of attempts to reform the NHS and the likelihood of the success this time round. Finally, it addresses the political failure at the heart of the problem." (Publisher's note)

REVIEW: *New Statesman* v142 no5149 p44 Mr 15 2013 Nicholas Timmins

REVIEW: *TLS* no5754 p25 Jl 12 2013 K. BISWAS
"God Bless the NHS: The Truth Behind the Current Crisis." "[Roger] Taylor uses his fairly tepid polemic to argue that the sharing of data would greatly benefit patients. . . . His argument is not entirely convincing, especially given that we know that his organization makes its money from the collation and publication of healthcare data. . . . The details he presents are shocking . . . but it is rather disingenuous to imply that better information-gathering would have pre-

vented their occurrence. . . . Conscious that the reader could struggle with the technical aspects of his subject, Taylor uses a series of stretched metaphors in an attempt to make things more palatable. . . . In trying to make sense of Britain's most treasured national institution, Taylor falls short."

TAYLOR, SAM.tr. The Victoria System. See Reinhardt, E.

TCHERNICHOVA, ELENA. Dancing on water; a life in ballet, from the Kirov to the ABT; [by] Elena Tchernichova 328 p. 2013 Northeastern University Press

1. Autobiographies 2. Ballerinas—Russia (Federation)—Biography 3. Ballerinas—United States—Biography 4. Dance teachers—United States—Biography
ISBN 9781555537920 (cloth : alk. paper)
LC 2012-046385

SUMMARY: This book, "part historical portrait of Leningrad in the 20th century, part ballet primer, and part nostalgic coming-of-age story . . . tells the story of world renowned ballerina and coach Elena Tchernichova. From her tragic beginnings in the Soviet Union to her success with the American Ballet Theatre, Tchernichova chronicles her trials and triumphs from poverty to prosperity." (Library Journal)

REVIEW: *N Y Rev Books* v60 no15 p31-3 O 10 2013 Robert Gottlieb

"Dancing on Water: A Life in Ballet, From the Kirov to the ABT." "'Dancing on Water' is an important account of 'A Life in Ballet,' as its subtitle has it: a book as illuminating as it is interesting, revelatory about how ballet works, and fascinating as an account of a life devoted to an art--and to survival. The immediate interest stems from the extraordinary arc her life has followed, and the clearheaded intelligence with which she (and her excellent coauthor, Joel Lobenthal) recount it. For someone who has experienced the tragedies that have fallen her way, she's remarkably free of self-pity and, more remarkable, of self-dramatization."

TEACHOUT, TERRY. Duke; a life of Duke Ellington; [by] Terry Teachout 496 p. 2013 Gotham Books

1. Artistic collaboration 2. Biographies 3. Jazz—History & criticism 4. Jazz musicians—United States—Biography
ISBN 1592407498; 9781592407491
LC 2013-011138

SUMMARY: This book presents a biography of musician Duke Ellington. "The grandson of a slave, he dropped out of high school to become one of the world's most famous musicians, a showman of incomparable suavity who was as comfortable in Carnegie Hall as in the nightclubs where he honed his style. He wrote some fifteen hundred compositions, many of which . . . remain beloved standards, and he sought inspiration in an endless string of transient lovers." (Publisher's note)

REVIEW: *Booklist* v110 no1 p24 S 1 2013 Mark Levine

"Duke: A Life of Duke Ellington." "One might have thought yet another life, admittedly a 'synthesis,' 40 years after the subject's death might be superfluous. In this addition to our music literature, however, [terry] Teachout . . . abundantly justifies the effort. Though respectful and musically knowing,Teachout presents the famously evasive and not altogether admirable Ellington . . . scars and all, including the rarely photographed one (rectified here) on his left cheek, inflicted by his jealous wife. . . . Included is a list of 'key recordings,' all currently downloadable, a perfect accompaniment to one's reading of this entertaining and valuable biography."

REVIEW: *Choice* v51 no9 p1603-4 My 2014 K. R. Dietrich

REVIEW: *Economist* v409 no8861 p89 N 9 2013

REVIEW: *Kirkus Rev* v81 no22 p6 N 15 2013

REVIEW: *Libr J* v138 no14 p113 S 1 2013 James E. Perone

REVIEW: *N Y Times Book Rev* p50 D 8 2013 JAMES GAVIN

REVIEW: *Natl Rev* v65 no22 p49-50 N 25 2013 THOMAS S. HIBBS

REVIEW: *New Yorker* v89 no42 p121-1 D 23 2013

"Duke: A Life of Duke Ellington" and "Tune In." "Terry Teachout's searching new biography, 'Duke: A Life of Duke Ellington' . . . touches on the mystique of the great bandleader's music as much as on its notes and measures. . . . Teachout is a sensitive writer, and one reason his biographies are moving is that he has obviously been giving himself an education in the realities of American racial history as he writes them. . . . Mark Lewisohn's new book, 'Tune In' . . . the first volume of a promised three-volume history of the Beatles--tells the story of their lives up to 1962, when they had yet to make an LP."

REVIEW: *Publ Wkly* v260 no29 p57 Jl 22 2013

REVIEW: *TLS* no5796 p10 My 2 2014 JOHN MOLE

"Duke: A Life of Duke Ellington." "[Author Terry] Teachout is well placed to examine with equal authority Ellington's methods of composition and the individual contributions of many other great musicians who brought out the unique tone colour of his orchestration. Teachout integrates his analysis with a vivid exploration of character. . . . Teachout gives full attention to the range of Ellington's ambition and achievement, and the trajectory of his career. . . . The final chapter, which describes Ellington's seventieth birthday celebrations at the White House . . . , as well as his loneliness and decline, is a particularly moving last act, reminding us, as so often in this book, of Terry Teachout's ability to bring his experience of theatre to bear on the story he tells."

TEAGUE, DAVID. Saving Lucas Biggs; [by] David Teague 288 p. 2014 Harper, an imprint of HarperCollinsPublishers

1. Company towns 2. Hydraulic fracturing 3. Mystery and detective stories 4. Time travel—Fiction 5. Whistleblowers
ISBN 0062274627; 9780062274625 (hardback)
LC 2013-043189

SUMMARY: This "time-travel story from husband-and-wife team Marisa de los Santos and David Teague follows one girl's race to change the past in order to save her father's future. Thirteen-year-old Margaret knows her father is innocent, but that doesn't stop the cruel Judge Biggs from sentencing him to death. Margaret is determined to save her dad, even if it means using her family's secret—and forbidden—ability to time travel." (Publisher's note)

REVIEW: *Booklist* v110 no17 p100 My 1 2014 Snow Wildsmith

REVIEW: *Bull Cent Child Books* v67 no11 p568 Jl/Ag

2014 A. A.

REVIEW: *Kirkus Rev* v82 no5 p95 Mr 1 2014

"Saving Lucas Biggs". " The authors, a husband-and-wife writing team, seamlessly incorporate heavy social-justice issues—fracking for natural gas in 2014 and a coal-mining protest in 1938—into a riveting time-travel adventure story. . . Two stories set in the company town of Victory, Ariz., told in alternating voices—Margaret's in 2014 and 13-year-old Josh's in 1938—run parallel and then converge. . . .Strong storytelling, suspense, lyrical writing, high drama, weighty matters made accessible and a bit of humor add up to a terrific and heartwarming read."

REVIEW: *SLJ* v60 no4 p142 Ap 2014 Cheryl Ashton

TEAL, THOMAS.tr. The Fly Trap. See Sjöberg, F.

TECKENTRUP, BRITTA. Busy bunny days; in the town, on the farm, at the port; [by] Britta Teckentrup 56 p. 2014 Chronicle Books LLC

1. Cities and towns—Fiction 2. Cities and towns—Juvenile fiction 3. Families—Juvenile fiction 4. Family life—Fiction 5. Farms—Fiction 6. Farms—Juvenile fiction 7. Harbors—Fiction 8. Harbors—Juvenile fiction 9. Picture books for children 10. Rabbits—Fiction 11. Rabbits—Juvenile fiction

ISBN 9781452117003 (alk. paper)

LC 2013-022000

SUMMARY: In this children's picture book, "young readers join the Bunny Family for a busy day in their home town, on a fun-filled farm adventure, and at the port. . . . From the time they wake up until the time they go to sleep, there is so much to see and do. Don't forget to keep an eye out for that pesky Benny Badger—he is always up to no good!" (Publisher's note)

REVIEW: *Booklist* v110 no11 p69 F 1 2014 Carolyn Phelan

REVIEW: *Kirkus Rev* v82 no1 p268 Ja 1 2014

"Busy Bunny Days: In the Town, On the Farm & At the Port". "Bright-eyed, neatly drawn little animals in human dress crowd three successive settings from morning to night in this low-key seek-and-find import originally published in Germany as three separate, stand-alone titles. . . . Viewers who keep looking will see plenty of other activity, though aside from the odd small fire or other minor mishap, the action runs to easily identifiable playtimes, farm chores, meals, sightseeing and other quotidian occupations. There's plenty to reward nose-to-page viewing, but even Richard Scarry fans may find this a little dull. "

REVIEW: *Publ Wkly* v260 no51 p60 D 16 2013

REVIEW: *SLJ* v60 no4 p137 Ap 2014 Blair Christolon

TECKENTRUP, BRITTA. The Odd one out; [by] Britta Teckentrup 32 p. 2014 Candlewick Press

1. Animals—Juvenile literature 2. Children's poetry 3. Differences 4. Picture books for children 5. Picture puzzles

ISBN 9780763671273

LC 2013-943095

SUMMARY: This picture book by Britta Teckentrup "asks readers to scan . . . patterned images for an 'odd one out.' More than 50 pandas tumble across a page, for instance, all but one clutching a stick: 'In among all of/ this hullaballoo,/ which panda has lost/ its shoot of bamboo?' Identically posed two-hump camels stand in five measured rows: 'Can you see a camel/ with just one bump?'" (Publishers Weekly)

REVIEW: *Kirkus Rev* v82 no3 p90 F 1 2014

"The Odd One Out: A Spotting Book". "In this classic take on a hunt for the odd one out, [Britta] Teckentrup creates elegant Escher-like wallpapers of prints depicting a varied selection of interesting animals. . . . Subtle coloration and textures and thoughtfully chosen background colors give the pages a hand-printed feel, in spite of the repetitive nature of the illustrations. . . .The wallpaper-pattern format determines the size of the illustrations, thus limiting readership to individuals or smaller groups. Although the verses tend toward doggerel rather than fine poetry, and are at times grammatically questionable, the very young and their adult readers will improve their differentiation skills while having fun spotting the odd ones out."

REVIEW: *SLJ* v60 no3 p128 Mr 2014 Laura Stanfield

TECKENTRUP, BRITTA. Run home, little mouse; [by] Britta Teckentrup 36 p. 2013 Kids Can Press

1. Animal stories 2. Forests & forestry—Juvenile literature 3. Mice—Juvenile fiction 4. Predation (Biology) 5. Toy & movable books

ISBN 1771380330; 9781771380331

SUMMARY: In this children's picture book, "Little Mouse has gotten lost in the big, dark forest, and he must avoid some scary predators as he makes his way back home. In the first three spreads, poor lost Little Mouse is pictured in a simple forest scene featuring a few trees, a small moon and a winding gray path. Next, he appears tiny and frightened against a black background, while two yellow eyes peek through cat's-eye-shaped die cuts." (Kirkus Reviews)

REVIEW: *Kirkus Rev* v82 no1 p40 Ja 1 2014

"Run Home, Little Mouse". "Though Little Mouse's big eyes convey fright, the predators all have a rather friendly appearance, which tones down the potential fear factor. The black background and strategic die cuts make for dramatic images, and children will enjoy guessing which animals the different eyes belong to as they watch Little Mouse find his way back to the safety of his family. This simple, repetitive tale with vivid images and a comforting ending is a good choice for one-on-one or group sharing."

REVIEW: *Kirkus Rev* v81 no18 p384 S 15 2013

TEGMARK, MAX. Our mathematical universe; my quest for the ultimate nature of reality; [by] Max Tegmark 432 p. 2013 Alfred A. Knopf

1. Cosmology—Mathematics 2. MATHEMATICS—General 3. Mathematical literature 4. Physics—Mathematics 5. Plurality of worlds 6. SCIENCE—Cosmology 7. SCIENCE—Physics

ISBN 0307599809; 9780307599803 (hardback); 9780307744258 (paperback)

LC 2013-016020

SUMMARY: In this book, author Max Tegmark "leads us . . . through the physics, astronomy and mathematics that are the foundation of his work, most particularly his hypothesis that our physical reality is a mathematical structure and his theory of the ultimate multiverse. He . . . shares with us some of the often surprising triumphs and disappointments that have shaped his life as a scientist." (Publisher's note)

REVIEW: *Booklist* v110 no5 p8 N 1 2013 Bryce Christensen

"Our Mathematical Universe: My Quest for the Ultimate Nature of Reality." "The rare intellectual daring in this claim emerges as [Max] Tegmark teases out its stunning implications not only for the visible universe but also for countless, unseen, parallel universes (on four levels!) in which all conceivable possibilities become realities. . . . Lively and lucid, the narrative invites general readers into debates over computer models for brain function, over scientific explanations of consciousness, and over prospects for finding advanced life in other galaxies. . . . An exhilarating adventure for bold readers."

REVIEW: *Choice* v51 no10 p1829 Je 2014 E. Kincanon

REVIEW: *Commonweal* v141 no8 p33-5 My 2 2014 John F. Haught

REVIEW: *New Sci* v221 no2950 p48 Ja 4 2014

"Neanderthal Man: In Search of Lost Genomes," "The Future of the Mind: The Scientific Quest to Understand, Enhance and Empower the Mind," and "Our Mathematical Universe: My Quest for the Ultimate Nature of Reality". "We're hoping for great things from geneticist Svante Pääbo, who in 2009 led the team that sequenced the first Neanderthal genome using DNA from 40,000-year-old bone. This is his story, which should prove to be a lens not only on pioneering scientific discovery but also on what makes us human. . . . We're keen to see what happens when the irrepressibly optimistic [Michio] Kaku turns his crystal ball to brain science and the future of human minds. His new book spans everything from smart pills that enhance cognition to placing our neural blueprint on laser beams sent out into space. . . . Max Tegmark, one of the world's leading theoretical physicists, opens up a deep and daring strand of thinking in this esoteric world."

REVIEW: *New Sci* v221 no2952 p45-6 Ja 18 2014 Mark Buchanan

"Our Mathematical Universe: My Quest for the Ultimate Nature of Reality". "Is this still science? Or has inflationary cosmology veered towards something akin to religion? Some physicists wonder. The enthusiasts, of course, see it very differently. Max Tegmark, a physicist at the Massachusetts Institute of Technology, certainly does. His new book . . . is an impassioned defence of the theory, especially its implications for parallel universes. The book is an excellent guide to recent developments in quantum cosmology and the ongoing debate over theories of parallel universes. Tegmark tries hard to make the seemingly outlandish sound almost obvious and unavoidable, and offers a taxonomy to help organise a zoo of imagined parallel universes."

REVIEW: *New York Times* v163 no56570 pD6 Jl 22 2014 GEORGE JOHNSON

REVIEW: *New York Times* v163 no56479 pD5 Ap 22 2014 AMIR ALEXANDER

REVIEW: *N Y Times Book Rev* p21 F 16 2014 EDWARD FRENKEL

"Our Mathematical Universe: My Quest for the Ultimate Nature of Reality." "[Max Tegmark's] new book, 'Our Mathematical Universe,' . . . can be divided into two parts. . . . One, by Dr. Tegmark, is an informative survey of exciting recent developments in astrophysics and quantum theory. The other, by Mr. Tegmark, is a discussion of his controversial idea that reality itself is a mathematical structure. . . . There is nothing wrong with contemplating speculative ideas, but the problem is that while pretending to stay in the realm of science, . . . part of the book crosses over to what I must consider science fiction and mysticism."

REVIEW: *Publ Wkly* v260 no39 p57 S 30 2013

TEITELBAUM, MICHAEL S. Falling behind?; boom, bust, and the global race for scientific talent; [by] Michael S. Teitelbaum 280 p. 2014 Princeton University Press

1. Historical literature 2. Labor market—United States—History 3. Science & state—History 4. Science & state—United States 5. Science—United States—History 6. Scientists—United States

ISBN 9780691154664 (alk. paper)

LC 2013-957467

SUMMARY: "Is the United States falling behind in the global race for scientific and engineering talent? . . . Examining historical precedent, Michael Teitelbaum highlights five episodes of alarm about 'falling behind' that go back nearly seventy years to the end of World War II. In each of these episodes the political system responded by rapidly expanding the supply of scientists and engineers, but only a few years later political enthusiasm or economic demand waned." (Publisher's note)

REVIEW: *Science* v344 no6183 p471-2 My 2 2014 Adam B. Jaffe

"Falling Behind? Boom, Bust, and the Global Race for Scientific Talent." "Having rejected simplistic crisis diagnoses, [author Michael S.] Teitelbaum turns to more nuanced discussion of what ails U.S. science. While not new, his discussion usefully pulls together previous work by him and others that shows that the existing funding model and practices of universities have uncoupled the supply of new scientists from the need for new scientists, particularly in the life sciences. . . . 'Falling Behind?' also illuminates a bigger picture: Scientists must recognize that the solution to low grant acceptance rates and poor job prospects for new scientists is not increased public funding for research."

TEJPAL, TARUN J., 1963-. The valley of masks; [by] Tarun J. Tejpal 336 p. 2014 Melville House

1. Assassins—Fiction 2. Conformity—Fiction 3. FICTION—Literary 4. FICTION—Political 5. India—Fiction

ISBN 9781612192628

LC 2013-034222

SUMMARY: This book presents an "allegory of wisdom and enlightenment but ultimately of corruption and the struggle for power. Although [Tarun] Tejpal starts the story with his narrator under siege, his life threatened by the Wafadars (a warrior clan to be feared), most of the narrative is recounted in a long flashback as the narrator reviews his life and explains how he got into his current perilous situation." (Kirkus Reviews)

REVIEW: *Kirkus Rev* v81 no24 p337 D 15 2013

"The Valley of Masks". "An intricate allegory of wisdom and enlightenment but ultimately of corruption and the struggle for power. Although [Tarun J.] Tejpal starts the story with his narrator under siege, his life threatened by the Wafadars (a warrior clan to be feared), most of the narrative is recounted in a long flashback as the narrator reviews his life and explains how he got into his current perilous situation. . . . Tejpal puts demands on the reader both through the entanglements of his narrative and through the specialized vocabulary (e.g., the Mausoleum of Our Egos, the Kiln of

Inevitable Impulses) he generates. The narrative will appeal to readers who delight in allegory that is political, philosophical and convoluted."

TEMPLEMAN, MCCORMICK. The glass casket; [by] McCormick Templeman 352 p. 2014 Delacorte Press

1. Community life—Fiction 2. Fairy tales 3. Love—Fiction 4. Murder—Fiction 5. Supernatural—Fiction 6. Witches—Fiction

ISBN 0385743459; 9780375991134 (glb); 9780385743457 (hc)

LC 2013-001970

SUMMARY: In this young adult fantasy novel, by McCormick Templeman, "one bleak morning, . . . five horses and their riders thunder into [Rowan's] village and through the forest, disappearing into the hills. Days later, the riders' bodies are found. . . . Something has followed the path those riders made and has come down from the hills, through the forest, and into the village. Beast or man, it has brought death to Rowan's door." (Publisher's note)

REVIEW: *Booklist* v110 no8 p45 D 15 2013 Daniel Kraus

REVIEW: *Bull Cent Child Books* v67 no6 p337-8 F 2014 Kate Quealy-Gainer

"The Glass Casket". "There's a quiet stillness to the prose as Rowan and her friends essentially wait to discover who will be killed next. The cool aloofness of the folkloric narration manages to simultaneously mute the graphic horror of the attacks and ratchet up the tension as the situation escalates. Plot layers twist upon plot layers and the relationships among the characters prove increasingly complex. . . .The titular allusion to 'Snow White' is accompanied by several other nods to classic fairy tales, and indeed, this has both the stylish beauty of those tales and the chilling darkness that makes them timeless."

REVIEW: *Kirkus Rev* v81 no23 p159 D 1 2013

REVIEW: *SLJ* v60 no2 p115 F 2014 Maggie Knapp

TEMPLIN, STEPHEN. I am a SEAL Team Six warrior. See Wasdin, H. E.

TENNIEL, JOHN.il. Writers in Wonderland. See Camp, K. P.

TEPPER, STEVEN J. Not here, not now, not that!; protest over art and culture in America; [by] Steven J. Tepper 361 2011 The University of Chicago Press

1. Arts & religion 2. Arts—Political aspects 3. Culture conflict 4. Protest movements 5. Social science literature

ISBN 9780226792866; 0226792862; 9780226792873; 0226792870

LC 2010-037424

SUMMARY: This book "examines a wide range of controversies over films, books, paintings, sculptures, clothing, music, and television in dozens of cities across the country to find out what turns personal offense into public protest. What Steven J. Tepper discovers is that these protests are always deeply rooted in local concerns. Furthermore, they are essential to the process of working out our differences in a civil society." (Publisher's note)

REVIEW: *Contemp Sociol* v43 no1 p122-4 Ja 2014 Diane Grams

"Not Here, Not Now, Not That!: Protest Over Art and Culture In America". "[Steven J. Tepper] builds a big empirical dataset and then offers cool analysis. With this approach, Tepper makes an important contribution to our understanding of cultural conflict at the end of the twentieth century. . . . His use of multiple datasets in his analysis is both a strength and a weakness. It is a strength because it allows access to data on a host of issues that are not found in the data drawn from news accounts, but this is also a weakness which does not allow him to test rigorously some of his conclusions."

TERCIO, RICARDO.il. Aesop's fables. See Aesop's fables

TERHUNE, TORI RANDOLPH. Land your dream career. See Hays, B. A.

TERRA MAXIMA; The Records of Humankind; 576 p. 2013 Firefly Books Ltd

1. Cities & towns 2. Civilization 3. Reference books 4. Technological innovations 5. World records

ISBN 1770852425; 9781770852426

LC 2013-456556

SUMMARY: This book, edited by Wolfgang Kunth, "is comprised of more than 3,000 full-color photographs . . . that showcase the biggest and the best religious, cultural, and technological marvels of the world. The work is broken down into 10 sections: 'Countries and Nations,' 'Languages and Scripts,' 'Faith and Religion,' 'Cities and Metropolises,' 'Urban Megastructures,' 'Transportation and Traffic,' 'Aviation and Space Travel,' 'Art and Culture,' 'Science and Research,' and 'Sports and Leisure.'" (Booklist)

REVIEW: *Booklist* v110 no7 p40 D 1 2013 Rebecca Vnuk

REVIEW: *Choice* v51 no9 p1559-60 My 2014 S. Markgren

"Terra Maxima: The Records of Humankind". "A tantalizing display of photographs and facts, and data and descriptions of civilization's most outstanding achievements. From countries and languages, to religion, cities, structures, and transportation—as well as culture, science, and sports—this big compendium documents the largest, tallest, oldest, and fastest. Its 10 chapters provide readers with a highly enjoyable and thoroughly informative hybrid that combines the facts and figures of a record book with the visual beauty of a coffee-table book. . . . This book allows for easy reading and browsing."

TERRAZZINI, DANIELA JAGLENKA.il. Tales for Great Grandchildren. See Jackson, J.

TERRY, WILL.il. Skeleton for Dinner. See Cuyler, M.

TERTULLIAN AND PAUL; 2013 Bloomsbury USA

1. Bible—Criticism, interpretation, etc. 2. Bible. Epistles of Paul 3. Paul, the Apostle, Saint 4. Religious literature 5. Tertullian, ca. 160-ca. 230

ISBN 9780567008039; 0567008037

SUMMARY: This book, edited by Todd D. Still and David Wilhite, "presents a collaborative attempt to understand, critique, and appreciate [Tertullian,] one of the earliest and most influential interpreters of Paul, and thereby better understand and appreciate both the dynamic event of early patristic exegesis and the Pauline texts themselves. Each chapter takes a two pronged approach, beginning with a patristic scholar considering the topic at hand, before a New Testament response." (Publisher's note)

REVIEW: *Choice* v51 no5 p856 Ja 2014 J. C. Hanges

"Tertullian and Paul." "This volume focuses both New Testament (NT) and Patristic scholars on the second/third-century Christian scholar Tertullian as a reader of the apostle Paul. This juxtaposition provides an almost comprehensive survey of Tertullian's vast theological competency, too often unfamiliar to NT scholars. . . . Although slightly unsure of their audience, most of the essays transliterate Greek; the Greek that does appear exhibits a number of typos. Overall, the volume's coherent inclusion of wide-ranging content and current debate commends it to both specialists and students."

TESH, JANE. Bad reputation; [by] Jane Tesh 250 p. 2014 Poisoned Pen Press

1. Commercial art galleries 2. Detective & mystery stories 3. Murder investigation—Fiction 4. North Carolina—Fiction 5. Women private investigators—Fiction
ISBN 9781464202308 (hardcover : alk. paper); 9781464202322 (trade pbk : alk. paper)
LC 2013-941458

SUMMARY: In this book, "when Wendall Clarke announces plans to open a new art gallery downtown, it's both the talk of Celosia, North Carolina and the envy of its residents. But the news is upstaged when Clarke is found murdered, prompting beauty queen turned private investigator Madeline Maclin to take on the case. Faced with a laundry list of suspects . . . Madeline's also struggling to keep her con man husband, Jerry Fairweather, out of handcuffs." (Publisher's note)

REVIEW: *Booklist* v110 no9/10 p47-8 Ja 1 2014 Barbara Bibel

"A Bad Reputation." "Former beauty queen Madeline Maclin and her reforming con-man husband, Jerry Fairweather, are renovating their home in Celosia, North Carolina. Madeline is building her PI business and trying to keep Jerry on the straight and narrow by having him use his musical talent in the community-theater production of Oklahoma. It seems to be working until he gets a mysterious letter from Honor Perkins, a former partner in crime, who is trying to lure him back into the game. . . . This humorous mystery will appeal to those who enjoy small-town crime."

REVIEW: *Kirkus Rev* v81 no24 p253 D 15 2013

TESH, JANE. Now you see it; [by] Jane Tesh 250 p. 2013 Poisoned Pen Press

1. Detective & mystery stories 2. Jewelry theft—Fiction 3. Magicians—Fiction 4. Murder—Fiction 5. Private investigators—Fiction
ISBN 9781464201967 (hardcover : alk. paper); 9781464201981 (trade pbk : alk. paper)
LC 2013-933203

SUMMARY: In this book, "North Carolina PI David Randall has a new client; stage magician Lucas Finch, who wants Randall to find a missing prop that was once owned by Houdini. Randall is already working for Sandy Olaf, a local socialite, looking for some lost jewelry, but he can always use some new clients. Although when Finch's brother, also a stage magician, turns up dead, Randall wonders if perhaps he should have stuck to the missing-jewelry case." (Booklist)

REVIEW: *Booklist* v110 no1 p47-8 S 1 2013 David Pitt

"Now You See It." "North Carolina PI David Randall has a new client; stage magician Lucas Finch, who wants Randall to find a missing prop that was once owned by Houdini. . . . Randall is a good character, a struggling PI with some serious personal issues--he's avoiding dealing with his young daughter's death in a car accident four years ago--and he's surrounded by some nifty supporting players (including friend Camden, a professional psychic). This is the third Randall mystery . . . should be encouraged to crack this one open."

REVIEW: *Kirkus Rev* v81 no17 p36 S 1 2013

REVIEW: *Publ Wkly* v260 no32 p37 Ag 12 2013

THACKER, ANDREW, ed. The Oxford critical and cultural history of modernist magazines. See The Oxford critical and cultural history of modernist magazines

THAMES, FRANK C. Contagious representation. See Williams, M. S.

THATTE, SID. GRE/ GMAT Math; A Systematic Approach; [by] Sid Thatte 326 p. 2010 Createspace Independent Pub

1. College entrance examinations—Study guides 2. Graduate Management Admission Test 3. Graduate Record Examination 4. Mathematical literature 5. Study guides
ISBN 1453633987; 9781453633984

SUMMARY: This book by Sid Thatte presents "a systematic approach to solving math problems on the Graduate Record Examinations and Graduate Management Admission Test" as well as "strategies to help readers do so as quickly and easily as possible." The book includes "practice problems to help reinforce each new concept and problem-solving strategy." (Kirkus Reviews)

REVIEW: *Kirkus Rev* v82 no2 p44 Ja 15 2014

"GRE/GMAT Math: A Systematic Approach". "[Sid] Thatte's first study guide provides not just a systematic approach to solving math problems on the Graduate Record Examinations and Graduate Management Admission Test, but also the strategies to help readers do so as quickly and easily as possible. Thatte's greatest accomplishment here may be breaking down word problems—often a bane for math test takers—and clearly explaining the intuitive, comprehension-heavy process that goes into solving them. But before he teaches readers how to translate words into mathematical equations and vice versa, Thatte lays a solid groundwork of mathematical concepts. . . . His experience in prepping students for competitive exams shines through with spare, to-the-point explanations."

THEALL, MICHELLE. Teaching the Cat to Sit; A Memoir; [by] Michelle Theall 288 p. 2013 Simon & Schuster

1. Catholic lesbians 2. Coming out (Sexual orientation) 3. Homosexuality—Religious aspects—Catholic Church 4. Lesbian mothers 5. Memoirs
ISBN 1451697295; 9781451697292

SUMMARY: Author Michelle Theall's "memoir of alienation and discrimination alternates between the past and present as she recounts her experiences growing up gay in a strict, Catholic Texas family and her adult life. Throughout her adolescent turmoil and atrocious coming out to her parents . . . Theall's driving need for church-certified acceptance persisted, affecting her relationships with her partner and their adopted, biracial son as well as her sense of self." (Booklist)

REVIEW: *Booklist* v110 no9/10 p27 Ja 1 2014 Whitney Scott

REVIEW: *Kirkus Rev* v82 no2 p18 Ja 15 2014

"Teaching the Cat to Sit". "In a narrative that deftly moves between past and present, [Michelle] Theall tells the moving story of how she found self-acceptance as a lesbian mother of faith. . . . In the journey away from Catholicism and the need for maternal approval that followed, Theall eventually found peace. She also came to understand that the 'raging love' between her and her mother was part of what made them 'something more.' A searingly honest memoir of faith, sexuality and motherhood."

REVIEW: *Libr J* v138 no5 p93 Mr 15 2013 Barbara Hoffert

REVIEW: *Publ Wkly* v260 no47 p44 N 18 2013

THELEN, ALBERT VIGOLEIS, 1903-1989. The island of second sight; from the applied recollections of Vigoleis; [by] Albert Vigoleis Thelen 816 p. 2012 Penguin Group USA

1. German fiction—20th century 2. Historical fiction 3. Majorca (Spain)—History 4. Refugees—Fiction
ISBN 1468301160; 1903385067; 9781468301168; 9781903385067
LC 2011-379493

SUMMARY: This novel by Albert Vigoleis Thelen is "set on Mallorca in the 1930s in the years leading up to World War II. . . . Pursued by both the Nazis and Spanish Francoists, Vigoleis and Beatrice embark on a series of the most unpredictable and surreal adventures in order to survive. Low on money, the couple seeks shelter in a brothel for the military, serves as tour guides to groups of German tourists, and befriends such literary figures as Robert Graves and Harry Kessler." (Publisher's note)

REVIEW: *Booklist* v109 no4 p24 O 15 2012 Bryce Christensen

REVIEW: *Kirkus Rev* v80 no18 p284 S 15 2012

REVIEW: *Libr J* v137 no17 p70 O 15 2012 Patrick Sullivan

REVIEW: *N Y Times Book Rev* p40 D 15 2013 IHSAN TAYLOR

"I am the Change: Barack Obama and the Future of Liberalism," "The Island of Second Sight: From the Applied Recollections of Vigoleis," and "Going Clear: Scientology, Hollywood, and the Prison of Belief." "[Charles R.] Kesler . . . sees President Obama as 'the latest embodiment of the visionary prophet-statesman'--the fourth phase of the Progressive experiment begun at the turn of the 20th century. . . . 'The Island of Second Sight' . . . , this fictionalized memoir . . . recounts [author Albert Vigoleis] Thelen's picaresque adventures in Majorca in the 1930s. . . . Armed with years of archival research and hundreds of interviews, [Lawrence] Wright . . . takes a calm and cleareyed stance toward Scientology."

REVIEW: *Publ Wkly* v259 no35 p47-8 Ag 27 2012

THEROUX, MARCEL. Strange bodies; a novel; [by] Marcel Theroux 292 p. 2014 Farrar, Straus and Giroux

1. Forgery 2. Forgery—Fiction 3. Identity (Philosophical concept)—Fiction 4. Identity (Psychology)—Fiction 5. Psychiatric hospital patients—Fiction 6. Psychotherapy patients—Fiction 7. Suspense fiction 8. Transmigration 9. Transmigration—Fiction
ISBN 0374270651; 9780374270650
LC 2013-034018

SUMMARY: This book follows an inmate of a psychiatric hospital "who insists that he is Dr. Nicholas Slopen, failed husband and impoverished Samuel Johnson scholar. Slopen has been dead for months. Yet nothing can make this man change his story. What begins as a tale of apparent forgery, involving unseen letters by the great Dr. Johnson, grows to encompass a conspiracy between a Silicon Valley mogul and his Russian allies to exploit the darkest secret of Soviet technology: the Malevin Procedure." (Publisher's note)

REVIEW: *Kirkus Rev* v81 no24 p43 D 15 2013

"Strange Bodies". " A labyrinthine exploration of identity and mortality, filled with big ideas that transcend the occasionally clunky plotting. As one of the more literary-minded of science-fiction novelists (or vice versa), [Marcel] Theroux . . . challenges summary in a novel that encompasses literary criticism (the protagonist is a Samuel Johnson scholar, or perhaps he was); a conspiracy between a record company mogul and Russian scientists that involves shifting an individual's consciousness into a new body (or 'carcass'); and a couple of possible love stories that may include romance between the living and the dead. . . . Often enthralling and occasionally maddening, the novel expands the reader's sense of possibility even as it strains credulity."

REVIEW: *Libr J* v138 no14 p84 S 1 2013

REVIEW: *N Y Times Book Rev* p12 Mr 2 2014 STEVE ALMOND

"Strange Bodies." "The academic who narrates [author Marcel] Theroux's new book, 'Strange Bodies' . . . has trouble running together a string of thoughts without citing one writer or another, most often the subject of his scholarly labors, the revered English critic Samuel Johnson. . . . Our collective fear of death, and the hovering possibility of resurrection, tug the reader through this ingenious if sometimes vexing novel far more than the protagonist's personality. . . . For all its laudable aims, Theroux's novel never made me feel deeply for Nicholas Slopen, or his experimental twin."

REVIEW: *New York Times* v163 no56412 pC25-9 F 14 2014 DWIGHT GARNER

REVIEW: *New York Times* v163 no56412 pC25-9 F 14 2014 DWIGHT GARNER

"Strange Bodies". "It's a pop narrative with a payload of plot contrivance. I wouldn't call it genre fiction exactly; it's too eccentric for that. But its machinations snap together like something bought at Ikea. Mr. [Marcel] Theroux's novel is a techno-thriller with echoes of both 'Frankenstein' and a Sherlock Holmes whodunit. It's the kind of book in which people fall and bonk their heads on doorknobs at inopportune moments. It's got brain implants and reincarnation and Russian bad guys and sneaky murders. It's all pretty baroque. The good news about 'Strange Bodies' is that Mr. Theroux, when he can extricate himself from the Silly String of his plot and find some open ground, is a superb writer."

REVIEW: *Publ Wkly* v260 no42 p28 O 21 2013

REVIEW: *TLS* no5744 p20 My 3 2013 M. JOHN HARRISON

"Strange Bodies". "A convoluted tale; difficulties—especially of time, memory and point of view—abound. . . . This gives rise to the dense, juicy writing about consciousness that lies at the centre of this novel. . . . The idea that anything resembling the 'consciousness' of Samuel Johnson can he reconstituted, however imperfectly, from his texts seems flimsy and wilful, a joke carried too far. In the end this hardly matters. The unconvincing foundations of the process . . . are precisely what make it so entertaining. . . . 'Bodies' is an examination of contemporary consciousness. But from its robust hook, through its comic set-up, to its dark if hopeful conclusions, it is also a kindly, intelligently entertaining thriller."

THEROUX, PAUL, 1941-. Last train to Zona Verde; my ultimate African safari; [by] Paul Theroux 368 p. 2013 Houghton Mifflin Harcourt

1. Travelers' writings
ISBN 061883933X; 9780618839339
LC 2013-000388

SUMMARY: In this book, by Paul Theroux, the author "sets out on a new journey through the continent he knows and loves best. Theroux first came to Africa as a twenty-two-year-old Peace Corps volunteer. . . . Now he returns, after fifty years on the road, to explore the little-traveled territory of western Africa and to take stock both of the place and of himself." (Publisher's note)

REVIEW: *Am Sch* v82 no3 p110-2 Summ 2013 Graeme Wood

REVIEW: *Kirkus Rev* v81 no2 p59 Je 1 2013

REVIEW: *Kirkus Rev* v81 no7 p88 Ap 1 2013

REVIEW: *N Y Times Book Rev* p24-5 Je 2 2013 JOSHUA HAMMER

REVIEW: *Natl Rev* v65 no16 p39-40 S 2 2013 SARAH RUDEN

"The Last Train to Zona Verde: My Ultimate African Safari." " Today, however, the sort of confrontation he cherishes is less illuminating. . . . In this book, for as far as he travels . . . [Paul] Theroux seems rhetorically stuck even while still on the go. . . . Ordinary tourism--of which Theroux is not a fan--with its demands for at least functional relationships up and down the social scale, is in fact a very positive force in a place like Africa, but to acknowledge that, you'd have to at least understand what a 'people person' is, if not be one. Africans are the ultimate 'people people.' I suspect that some of his despair comes not from the admittedly appalling things he encounters but from his perception that, whatever happens, Africans will continue to be themselves."

REVIEW: *New Statesman* v142 no5159 p40-2 My 24 2013 Hedley Twidle

REVIEW: *Publ Wkly* v260 no8 p152 F 25 2013

REVIEW: *Publ Wkly* v260 no4 p141-5 Ja 28 2013 LOUISA ERMELINO

THESING, JIM. U-9; a damned un-English weapon; [by] Jim Thesing 272 p. 2013 Merriam Press

1. Historical fiction 2. Naval officers 3. Submarines (Ships)—Germany 4. World War, 1914-1918—Fiction 5. World War, 1914-1918—Naval operations
ISBN 9781482644852
LC 2013-941176

SUMMARY: In this book, "in the summer of 1914, Lt. Henry Fischer enjoys a cushy position in Great Britain's Royal Navy On the other side is Johannes Speiss, a young sailor in the German naval fleet. . . . It's simply a matter of time until both Britain and Germany—and Fischer and Speiss—are in the thick of what will become the first world war. Later, Speiss gets an assignment as an officer aboard one of the infamous German 'undersea boats': U-9." (Kirkus Reviews)

REVIEW: *Kirkus Rev* v81 no24 p357 D 15 2013

"U-9: A Damned Un-English Weapon". "Much of the novel's appeal is in its documentation of the great naval battles of WWI, particularly the day in September 1914 when a lone German U-boat felled three British cruisers. History buffs, particularly those with a passion for the sea, will enjoy this in-depth look at the early days of submarine warfare. Beyond that, the prose is steady enough but doesn't distinguish itself from the many other novels that crowd this historical fiction genre. Readers looking for an exciting yarn may not find unique, realistic characters, but they will appreciate the novel's fast pace. A thoroughly researched submarine novel that sails along smoothly despite underdeveloped characters."

THICK, MALCOLM. Sir Hugh Plat; the search for useful knowledge in early modern London; [by] Malcolm Thick 432 2010 Prospect Books

1. Alchemists 2. Biography, Individual 3. Courtiers 4. Historical literature 5. Inventors
ISBN 9781903018651

SUMMARY: This book by Malcolm Thick offers "an investigation of the life and work of Sir Hugh Plat (1552-1611), an English author, alchemist, speculator and inventor whose career touched on the fields of alchemy, general scientific curiosity, cookery and sugar work, cosmetics, gardening and agriculture, food manufacture, victualling, supplies and marketing." (Publisher's note)

REVIEW: *Engl Hist Rev* v129 no536 p198-200 F 2014 Margaret Pelling

"Sir Hugh Plat: The Search for Useful Knowledge in Early Modern London". "Malcolm Thick, who adopts a down-to-earth and realistic approach to his subject's motives and achievements, emphasises Plat's economic aims as reflected in his publications and surviving manuscripts. . . . The methodology that Thick applies to texts is as down-to- earth as his conclusions, but is eminently serviceable in preventing a literal reading of materials constructed for particular purposes. . . . Thick does not overburden his book with structure. . . . Like Plat himself, the book is a treasure trove of intriguing and often surprising information. . . . Thick writes in a straightforward and accessible style which gives the reader easy access to his content."

THIEDE, TODD M. Lies to Die for; [by] Todd M. Thiede 258 p. 2013 CreateSpace Independent Publishing Platform

1. Detective & mystery stories 2. Murder investigation—Fiction 3. Serial murderers—Fiction 4. Serial murders—Fiction 5. Truthfulness & falsehood
ISBN 1492166472; 9781492166474

SUMMARY: This book is the second book in the Max Larkin detective series. "A few weeks after the brutal slayings that took place in the previous novel, Detective Larkin and his partner, Jesse Fairlane, are assigned to a grizzly case involving the double homicide of a professor and his much younger girlfriend. As in [Todd M.] Thiede's previous novel, a pattern emerges, and the detectives soon realize they're looking at the handiwork of another serial killer." (Kirkus Reviews)

REVIEW: *Kirkus Rev* v82 no1 p352 Ja 1 2014

"Lies to Die For". "Max and Jessie will instantly feel familiar to readers who've read the first entry in the series, but despite that instant recognition, the characters don't develop as richly this time around. While the two heroes experience some growing pains in their partnership . . . too much time is spent on the procedural elements of the story, and much of the chemistry that was so palpable in their first outing is missing here. Still, both characters remain likable, and while the bloody trail leads the duo down some dark paths, readers will find themselves guessing at every turn. . . . As with [Todd M.] Thiede's previous work, readers can expect plenty of black humor and gruesome murder scenes. Although the action ends rather abruptly, the stage is set for more sleuthing."

THIEL, JOHN E. Icons of hope; the "last things" in Catholic imagination; [by] John E. Thiel 223 p. 2013 University of Notre Dame Press

1. Eschatology 2. Judgment Day 3. Religious literature 4. Saints

ISBN 026804239X (pbk.: alk. paper); 9780268042394 (pbk.: alk. paper)

LC 2013-022549

SUMMARY: This book by John Thiel "presents an interpretation of heavenly life, the Last Judgment, and the communion of the saints that is shaped by a view of the activity of the blessed dead consistent with Christian belief in the resurrection of the body, namely, the view that the blessed dead in heaven continue to be eschatologically engaged in the redemptive task of forgiveness." (Publisher's note)

REVIEW: *America* v210 no1 p34-5 Ja 6 2014 THOMAS P. RAUSCH

"Icons of Hope: The 'Last Things' in Catholic Imagination". "John Thiel's creative effort to explore Christian belief in eternal life, is clearly the work of a major theological thinker. . . . While highly speculative, Thiel's vision is both imaginative and deeply Catholic. His fascinating analysis of Catholic and Protestant artistic representations of the Last Judgment . . . enriches his narrative. . . . Some of his points I find more problematic. . . . This is not an easy book to read, but because it opens up a new vision of the life to come, it is well worth the effort."

REVIEW: *Commonweal* v141 no17 p34-6 O 24 2014 Leo J. O'Donovan

THIMMESH, CATHERINE. Scaly spotted feathered frilled; how do we know what dinosaurs really looked like?; 64 p. 2013 Houghton Mifflin Books for Children, Houghton Mifflin Harcourt

1. Children's nonfiction 2. Dinosaurs—Juvenile literature 3. Dinosaurs in art—Juvenile literature 4. Paleoart—Juvenile literature 5. Paleontology—Juvenile literature

ISBN 0547991347; 9780547991344

LC 2012-048466

SUMMARY: Author Catherine Thimmesh "explores the border between science and speculation in this [book about] how paleontologists . . . reconstruct prehistoric creatures from fossil evidence. . . . [She] explains how surviving evidence—including fossilized bone fragments, plant matter, bits of skin and, recently, feathers, prehistoric 'trackways' (preserved pathways of dino footprints) and similar physical features in modern animals—is assembled and interpreted by scientists." (Kirkus Reviews)

REVIEW: *Booklist* v110 no4 p42 O 15 2013 Carolyn Phelan

REVIEW: *Bull Cent Child Books* v67 no3 p183 N 2013 E. B.

"Scaly Spotted Feathered Frilled: How Do We Know What Dinosaurs Really Looked Like?" "Six paleoartists are featured here as they make informed decisions how to portray, in illustration and in three-dimensional art, what may be unknowable--what dinosaurs exactly looked like. . . . This is the kind of information that can lure in readers beyond the usual dino hounds, so casual museumgoers and kids with an interest in forensic reconstructions should find the topic of interest too. However, specialized vocabulary can be challenging for general readers (even the glossary and index aren't much help if you don't know what a dino frill is, or that Paul Sereno is something of a big deal) and terms such as 'ginormous,' 'colossal,' and 'gigantic' are too imprecise to be useful."

REVIEW: *Horn Book Magazine* v89 no5 p124 S/O 2013 DANIELLE J. FORD

REVIEW: *Horn Book Magazine* v90 no1 p12-20 Ja/F 2014

"Have You Seen My New Blue Socks?" "The Thing About Luck." "The Thing About Luck," and "Scaly Spotted Feathered Frilled: How Do We Know What Dinosaurs Really Looked Like?" "With the help of his friends, Duck . . . searches for his lost socks in this child-centered, funny, read-it-again picture book. [Eve] Bunting's jaunty Seuss-inspired rhyming text is a seamless match for [Sergio] Ruzzier's sweetly surreal illustrations. . . . [Cynthia] Kadohata displays her deft hand with characterization and setting in this poignant, funny, and insightful coming-of-age novel set in the contemporary Midwest. . . . Rather than adding to the panoply of dino-guides, [Catherine] Thimmesh instead looks at how new discoveries in paleontology require sometimes-drastic revisions by paleoartists. Is that a job? Yes! Copious illustrations by leading artists add much appeal to the book's unique approach."

REVIEW: *Kirkus Rev* v81 no15 p203 Ag 1 2013

REVIEW: *Nat Hist* v121 no9 p45 N 2013 Dolly Setton

REVIEW: *SLJ* v59 no10 p1 O 2013 Alyson Low

THINGS LOOK DIFFERENT IN THE LIGHT AND OTHER STORIES; 272 p. 2014 Pushkin Press

1. Anthologies 2. Everyday life 3. Short stories—Collections 4. Spanish fiction—20th century 5. Spanish fiction—Translations into English

ISBN 1908968184; 9781908968180

SUMMARY: This collection of short stories by Medardo Fraile, translated by Margaret Jull Costa, is based on Fraile's "Cuentos de verdad" collection, which "won him the 1965 Premio Nacional de la Crítica. . . . Medardo Fraile is a chronicler of the minor tragedies and triumphs of ordinary life, and each short tale opens up an entire exquisite world." (Publisher's note)

REVIEW: *TLS* no5795 p21 Ap 25 2014 MICHAEL KERRIGAN

"Things Look Different in the Light." "Like [Medardo] Fraile's far-flung Scottish home, the short story affords him a place to stand outside the run of everyday Spanish life: unfamiliar perspectives, alternative ways of seeing. Formally conservative, quiet and correct in style, his fictions break out chiefly in their unexpected ironies and quirky humour—yet they really do show things in a different light. . . . The 'stultifying inertia' Fraile finds in the schoolroom can too easily, for the author, become the standard for our existence as a whole. The imaginative order against which he rebels hinges on a fundamental poetic failure of humanity. . . . Unassuming as they may immediately appear, Fraile's stories represent a radical challenge, to make us see the world with a fresh eye."

THINKING POETRY; philosophical approaches to nineteenth-century French poetry; 2013 Palgrave Macmillan

1. Baudelaire, Charles, 1821-1867 2. French poetry—19th century 3. Literature—History & criticism 4. Mallarmé, Stéphane, 1842-1898 5. Philosophy & literature
ISBN 9781137303639; 1137303638

SUMMARY: This book, edited by Joseph Acquisto, attempts to answer "why have poets played such an important role for contemporary philosophers? How can poetry link philosophy and political theory? How do formal considerations intersect with philosophical approaches? These essays seek to establish a dialogue between poetry and philosophy. Each essay contributes to our understanding of the relationships between theory and lived experience while providing new insight into important poets." (Publisher's note)

REVIEW: *Choice* v51 no2 p266 O 2013 W. Edwards

"Thinking Poetry: Philosophical Approaches to Nineteenth-Century French Poetry." "This collection of 12 substantial essays by a variety of junior and senior Anglophone scholars is, like much of late-19th-century French poetry itself, dominated by Charles Baudelaire and Stéphane Mallarmé, two poets described in the introduction as those 'who did the most to transform poetry's relation to metaphysics, ethics, and other avenues of philosophical inquiry.' . . . To a much lesser degree, Hugo and Rimbaud also receive sustained analysis. Yet, while the literary focus of this volume--ably assembled by [editor Joseph] Acquisto . . . --appears narrow, the breadth of theoretical approaches is noteworthy and enriching."

THISTLE, ALARIC.ed. The Watergate Memoirs of Gordon Walter. See The Watergate Memoirs of Gordon Walter

THOM, COLIN.ed. Survey of London. See Survey of London

THOMAS, AUDREY. Local Customs; [by] Audrey Thomas 208 p. 2014 Dundurn

1. Ghana—History—19th century 2. Historical fiction 3. L. E. L. (Letitia Elizabeth Landon), 1802-1838 4. Slavery—Fiction 5. Women poets—Fiction
ISBN 1459707982; 9781459707986

SUMMARY: In this novel, "almost 40 years after visiting the graves of British authoress-poet Letitia Landon and her husband George Maclean," author Audrey Thomas "crafts a story of what might have transpired between 1836 and 1838, in London and the Gold Coast. Landon, from a 'shabby-genteel' family with a past that brought 'malicious whispers,' sets her sights on marrying George, governor of Cape Coast Castle on the Gold Coast of West Africa." (Publishers Weekly)

REVIEW: *Quill Quire* v80 no1 p39 Ja/F 2014 Jim Bartley

"Local Customs". "[Audrey] Thomas constructs a romantic, sometimes comic adventure spiced up with vivid images, tropical redolence, and the lurking spectre of violence. The period ambiance and conversational rhythms are deftly captured. Thomas is especially good on the solitudes of Victorian marriage. . . . Given the time frame, the brutal African slave trade must enter this story. Thomas calibrates our sympathies, making George not an open abolitionist, but an abstainer during the slave years, then active in chasing down rogue traders after the passage of the 1833 abolition laws."

THOMAS, BILL. Second wind; navigating the passage to a slower, deeper, and more connected life; [by] Bill Thomas 336 p. 2014 Simon & Schuster

1. Advice literature 2. Baby boom generation—Social aspects—United States 3. Conduct of life 4. Longevity—United States—Social aspects 5. Older people—United States—Social conditions
ISBN 1451667566; 9781451667561 (hardcover); 9781451667578 (trade pbk.)
LC 2013-035558

SUMMARY: In this book, Bill Thomas "posits that baby boomers, his intended audience, are heading for a second coming-of-age in a new stage of adulthood. Thomas creates four composite characters—Tom, Flo, Rita, and Melanie—to serve as examples and sets a framework according to 'Crucibles': 'a test or severe trial brought about by the confluence of cultural, economic, and political forces within a society.'" (Publishers Weeklyl)

REVIEW: *Kirkus Rev* v82 no4 p18 F 15 2014

"Second Wind: Navigating the Passage to a Slower, Deeper, and More Connected Life". "[Bill] Thomas, possibly unaware of criticisms of the egocentrism of the baby boomer generation, suggests that the dynamics that gave rise to the cultural shift of baby boomers have also engendered a unique imbalance as their late adulthood sets in. . . . Thomas explores possible paradigms that might enable us, as we transition through adulthood and beyond, to expand those ideas of identity. A mostly nuanced look at the challenges of growing old gracefully for a generation that aches to see youth in the mirror."

REVIEW: *Publ Wkly* v260 no50 p59 D 9 2013

THOMAS, DEBORAH A. Exceptional violence; embodied citizenship in transnational Jamaica; [by] Deborah A. Thomas xiii, 298 p. 2011 Duke University Press

1. Reparations for historical injustices—Jamaica 2. Slavery—Jamaica—History 3. Social classes—Jamaica 4. Social science literature 5. Violent crimes—Jamaica
ISBN 9780822350682 (cloth: alk. paper); 9780822350866 (pbk.: alk. paper)
LC 2011-015703

SUMMARY: It was the author's intent to demonstrate that

"violence in Jamaica is the complicated result of a structural history of colonialism and underdevelopment, not a cultural characteristic passed from one generation to the next. . . . Suggesting that U.S. anthropology should engage more deeply with history and political economy, [Deborah A.] Thomas mobilizes a concept of reparations as a framework for thinking, a rubric useful in its emphasis on structural and historical lineages." (Publisher's note)

REVIEW: *Contemp Sociol* v43 no2 p271-3 Mr 2014 Bowen Paulle

"Exceptional Violence: Embodied Citizenship in Transnational Jamaica". "Deborah Thomas' investigation of embodied citizenship in transnational Jamaica has—to put it mildly—a lot to offer. Whether or not readers have particular interests in Caribbean or Africana studies, they will find invigorating insights on nearly every page of this thoroughly researched study. . . . Although the multiple strands of analysis pose a problem for the reviewer, they are woven together with such acumen that they remain a joy for the reader. . . . Not least because it can help promote (institutionalized) reflexivity, this book should become a classic in sociology as well as in anthropology."

REVIEW: *Ethn Racial Stud* v35 no8 p1505-7 Ag 2012 Ralph Premdas

THOMAS, EDWARD, 1878-1917. Selected poems and prose; [by] Edward Thomas 270 p. 2013 Paw Prints

1. Anthologies 2. Diary (Literary form) 3. English poetry 4. Soldiers' writings, English 5. World War, 1914-1918—Literature & the war

ISBN 1480625736; 9781480625730

SUMMARY: This book is a reissue of editor David Wright's 1981 selection of poetry and prose by Edward Thomas. It includes the essay 'Ghost' by Robert MacFarlane. "Because Wright maintains a chronological approach, the first 140 pages are all prose (except for a single 'translation' from a 'bard' who is in fact one of Thomas's 'imaginary selves')." (Times Literary Supplement)

REVIEW: *TLS* no5769 p23 O 25 2013 JOHN GREENING

"Like Sorrow or a Tune: A New Selection of Poems" and "Selected Poems and Prose." "[Eleanor Farjeon's] own poems about [Edward Thomas] are the serious heart of 'Like Sorrow or a Tune,' and may be considered very successful sonnets, but the bulk of her work is for children. . . . For all [Anne] Harvey's advocacy . . . this verse does require modem adult readers to make allowances. Where she reaches for greater depths, she is too often remarking on a mystery, rather than recreating it. In the end, it is Harvey ' s own commentary and the relationship with Thomas that give this book its interest. . . . Although there has been no lack of recent editions, [David] Wright's judicious selection . . . is certainly worth reviving. . . . With Wright's succinct notes, this might be considered the most fully representative edition of Thomas's work."

THOMAS, GLENN.il. Flights and chimes and mysterious times. See Trevayne, E.

THOMAS, GORDON. The Pope's Jews; the Vatican's secret plan to save Jews from the Nazis; [by] Gordon Thomas xx, 314 p.

1. Christianity and antisemitism—History—20th century 2. Historical literature 3. Holocaust, Jewish (1939-1945) 4. Jews—Italy—Rome—History—20th century 5. Judaism—Relations—Catholic Church 6. World War, 1939-1945—Jews—Rescue 7. World War, 1939-1945—Religious aspects—Catholic Church

ISBN 9780312604219 (hardcover); 0312604211

LC 2012-028222

SUMMARY: "Investigating assassination plots, conspiracies, and secret conversions, [author Gordon] Thomas unveils faked documentation, quarantines, and more extraordinary actions taken by Catholics and the Vatican. 'The Pope's Jews' finally answers the great moral question of the War: Why did Pope Pius XII refuse to condemn the genocide of Europe's Jews?" (Publisher's note)

REVIEW: *Booklist* v109 no1 p29 S 1 2012 Gilbert Taylor

REVIEW: *Hist Today* v63 no8 p58-9 Ag 2013 DANIEL SNOWMAN

REVIEW: *Kirkus Rev* v80 no15 p335 Ag 1 2012

REVIEW: *Libr J* v137 no13 p108 Ag 1 2012 Maria C. Bagshaw

REVIEW: *London Rev Books* v35 no18 p13-5 S 26 2013 Eamon Duffy

"The Life and Pontificate of Pope Pius XII: Between History and Controversy," "The Pope's Jews: The Vatican's Secret Plan to Save Jews from the Nazis," and "Soldier of Christ: The Life of Pope Pius XII." "These welcome new biographies by Frank Coppa and Robert Ventresca make telling use of the newly available papers of Pius XI. The detailed picture that emerges of Pacelli's diplomatic career and years as secretary of state brings a new depth to our understanding of this austere and complicated man. . . . Gordon Thomas's account of Pacelli's response to the Final Solution, for instance, is a tendentious exercise in exculpation and hagiography that implausibly depicts Pacelli as a papal pimpernel, actively masterminding a campaign to save European Jewry."

REVIEW: *Publ Wkly* v259 no26 p159 Je 25 2012

THOMAS, MARY E. Multicultural girlhood; racism, sexuality, and the conflicted spaces of American education; [by] Mary E. Thomas viii, 204 p. 2011 Temple University Press

1. Minority teenagers—United States 2. Multiculturalism—United States 3. Racism—United States 4. Social interaction in adolescence—United States 5. Social science literature 6. Teenage girls—United States

ISBN 1439907315 (cloth: alk. paper); 1439907323 (pbk.: alk. paper); 1439907331 (e-book); 9781439907313 (cloth: alk. paper); 9781439907320 (pbk.: alk. paper); 9781439907337 (e-book)

LC 2011-015414

SUMMARY: In this book, Mary E.Thomas "interviewed 26 African American, Anglo, Armenian, Filipina, and Latina girls in 2005 at a Los Angeles high school after a race riot ended in a police lock-down. As the young women wondered why they all could not 'just get along,' Thomas listened closely to their narratives and detected an underlying racism and sexism in their comments. Thomas deployed psychoanalytic theory to interpret these seeming contradictions." (Contemporary Sociology)

REVIEW: *Choice* v49 no10 p1974 Je 2012 P. A. Quiroz

REVIEW: *Contemp Sociol* v43 no2 p273-5 Mr 2014 Laurie

Schaffner

"Multicultural Girlhood: Racism, Sexuality, and the Conflicted Spaces of American Education". "In this carefully crafted and theoretically sophisticated study, Mary E. Thomas offers a much-needed critique of the limitations of multiculturalism to fight racism, sexism, misogyny, and violence in schools. . . . . Thomas offers a refreshing critique of two mainstays of neoliberal thought, multiculturalism and agency. . . . This challenging text may be useful in advanced undergraduate seminars but definitely in graduate courses in gender and women's studies, education, sociology of race and ethnicities, qualitative methodology, and contemporary theory. . . .Thomas adds an exceptional and provocative study to our research on the politics in the urban U.S. schoolyard setting."

THOMAS, MIDDY.il. Gooney Bird and all her charms. See Lowry, L.

THOMAS, NICHOLAS.ed. Art in Oceania. See Art in Oceania

THOMAS, P. L.ed. De-testing and de-grading schools. See De-testing and de-grading schools

THOMAS, PAUL. Youth, multiculturalism and community cohesion; [by] Paul Thomas vii, 219 p. 2011 Palgrave Macmillan

1. Multiculturalism—Great Britain 2. Racism—Great Britain 3. Social science literature 4. Violence—Great Britain—Prevention 5. Youth—Great Britain

ISBN 0230251951 (hardback); 9780230251953 (hardback)

LC 2011-004349

SUMMARY: In this book, "Paul Thomas examines [British] New Labour's community cohesion policy that was introduced following the riots in Oldham, Burnley, and Bradford in the summer of 2001. Thomas' central argument is that community cohesion agenda does not represent a knee jerk assimilationist reversal against multiculturalism but rather, a progressive shift toward a new phase in multiculturalism that deals with the reality and complexity of modern diverse identities." (Contemporary Sociology)

REVIEW: *Contemp Sociol* v43 no1 p124-6 Ja 2014 Steven Loyal

"Youth, Multiculturalism and Community Cohesion". "[Paul] Thomas' use of empirical evidence to question academic speculations about community cohesion is undoubtedly justified. . . . However, the book only vaguely describes the evidence it draws on. . . . This is a shame since the chapters quoting interviews are among the most interesting parts of the book. Second, the book uncritically converts what [Pierre] Bourdieu calls 'social problems into sociological problems.' . . . Third, although the book acknowledges the rise of neo-liberalism and especially some of its economic effects, it fails to look at the political aspect of this process. . . . Fourth, and perhaps most importantly, the book fails to look at issues of power, and places too much importance on contact theory."

THOMAS, RICHARD.ed. The opinions of William Cobbett. See The opinions of William Cobbett

THOMAS, RICHARD F.ed. The Virgil encyclopedia. See The Virgil encyclopedia

THOMAS, ROY. Conan; Red Nails; [by] Roy Thomas 36 p. 2013 Genesis West

1. Art literature 2. Comic books, strips, etc. 3. Conan (Fictitious character) 4. Extinct cities 5. Pirates—Fiction

ISBN 1467572152 (hbk.); 9781467572156 (hbk.)

SUMMARY: This book, the first in the Original Art Archives series, "features the classic [Conan the Barbarian] tale 'RED NAILS' as adapted in 1973 by Roy Thomas and Barry Windsor-Smith. The entire story, as well as additional feature materials, are presented in a deluxe 136 page slipcased hardcover edition measuring roughly 14x19 inches." (Publisher's note)

REVIEW: *New York Times* v163 no56286 pC32 O 11 2013 Dana Jennings

"The Sky: The Art of Final Fantasy," "Conan: Red Nails," and "Gil Kane's the Amazing Spider-Man." "With his elegant and sinuous line, the Japanese artist Yoshitaka Amano understands the power of pen and ink. . . . Mr. Amano's light, deft touch defies genre conventions in a fantasy world where blood and beauty twine, where the ethereal has bite. . . . Mr. [Barry] Windsor-Smith shows his skill at creating a world on just one textured black-and-white page. The heroes in this lush, oversize book . . . are clearly Conan--and Mr. Windsor-Smith. . . . Gil Kane was one of the best unsung comic artists of the 1960s and '70s. . . . His muscular line and cinematic sense of page design served well superheroes like Green Lantern, Batman and especially Spider-Man."

THOMAS, SAM. The harlot's tale; a Bridget Hodgson mystery; [by] Sam Thomas 320 p. 2014 Minotaur Books

1. Detective & mystery stories 2. Serial murderers—England—Fiction 3. Women detectives—England—Fiction

ISBN 1250010780; 9781250010780 (hardback)

LC 2013-032884

SUMMARY: This historical mystery novel, by Sam Thomas, volume two of "The Midwife's Tale," begins "August, 1645, one year since York fell into Puritan hands. As the city suffers through a brutal summer heat, Bridget Hodgson and Martha Hawkins are drawn into a murder investigation. . . . First a prostitute and her client are found stabbed to death, then a pair of adulterers are beaten and strangled. York's sinners have been targeted for execution." (Publisher's note)

REVIEW: *Booklist* v110 no8 p22 D 15 2013 Barbara Bibel

REVIEW: *Kirkus Rev* v81 no24 p245 D 15 2013

"The Harlot's Tale". " There's no dearth of suspects for the murder, including one uncomfortably close to home. Bridget often gets help from her nephew, Will, whose physical disability has always placed him below his brother Joseph in his father's affections. As a soldier, Joseph has often killed, and he's fanatical about ridding York of sinners—exactly the profile that makes him an obvious suspect. As the killings continue, Bridget does everything in her power to discover the killer from among far too many candidates. The second adventure for [Sam] Thomas' midwife uses a mystery with plenty of twists, turns and suspects to illuminate a difficult period in British history."

REVIEW: *Publ Wkly* v260 no47 p34 N 18 2013

THOMAS, SHERRY. The Luckiest Lady in London; [by] Sherry Thomas 304 p. 2013 Berkley Pub Group

1. Courtship—Fiction 2. Historical fiction 3. London (England)—Fiction 4. Love stories 5. Secrecy—Fiction
ISBN 0425268888; 9780425268889

SUMMARY: In this book, by Sherry Thomas, "Felix Rivendale, the Marquess of Wrenworth, is . . . a man all men want to be and all women want to possess. . . . But underneath is a damaged soul soothed only by public adulation. Louisa Cantwell needs to marry well to support her sisters. She does not, however, want Lord Wrenworth—though he seems inexplicably interested in her. . . . Still, when he is the only man to propose at the end of the London season, she reluctantly accepts." (Publisher's note)

REVIEW: *Booklist* v110 no5 p36 N 1 2013 John Charles

REVIEW: *Kirkus Rev* p37 N 15 2013 Best Books

REVIEW: *Kirkus Rev* v81 no21 p136 N 1 2013

REVIEW: *N Y Times Book Rev* p30 F 9 2014 Sarah MacLean

"The Luckiest Lady in London," "The Perfect Match," and "The Last Man on Earth." "[Author Sherry] Thomas is known for a lush style that demonstrates her love of her second language, and ['The Luckiest Lady in London'] edges into historical fiction with its transporting prose even as it delivers on heat and emotion and a well-earned happily ever after. . . . In 'The Perfect Match' . . . [author Kristan] Higgins offers readers a journey filled with tears and laughter and the best kind of sighs. . . . Few things are more fun than an enemies-to-lovers romance, and [author Tracy Anne] Warren delivers with 'The Last Man on Earth.'"

THOMAS, WYN.il. The Pubs of Dylan Thomas. See The Pubs of Dylan Thomas

THOMPSON, ANNE. The $11 billion year; from Sundance to the Oscars, an inside look at the changing Hollywood system; [by] Anne Thompson 320 p. 2014 Newmarket Press

1. Digital cinematography 2. Motion picture industry—United States 3. Motion picture literature 4. Motion pictures & technology 5. Motion pictures—United States—History—21st century
ISBN 9780062218018 (hardcover); 9780062218025 (pbk.); 9780062218032 (ebook)
LC 2013-036507

SUMMARY: This book by Anne Thompson presents "a yearlong chronicle of 2012's major films—from Sundance to Oscar night—highlighting the many challenges currently dogging the industry." Particular focus is given to "digitization," which "is at once propelling the industry to untold revenues, while at the same time making it more difficult for the industry to stake out easy gains in a rapidly shifting and unpredictable landscape." (Kirkus Reviews)

REVIEW: *Booklist* v110 no13 p11 Mr 1 2014 Kristine Huntley

REVIEW: *Film Q* v67 no4 p88-90 Summ 2014 LISA DOMBROWSKI

REVIEW: *Kirkus Rev* v82 no5 p129 Mr 1 2014

"The $11 Billion Year: From Sundance to the Oscars, an Inside Look at the Changing Hollywood System". "In [Anne] Thompson's . . . dissection of the film year, she provides an interesting case study for the future of the industry. . . . While the author undoubtedly understands the prevailing industry trends and how they are changing, she remains a reporter at heart. Rich with anecdotes and gossip, Thompson presents Hollywood as a living, breathing community. . . .Thompson's journalistic flair makes her analysis of the film industry a compelling and page-turning read. An insider investigation into the ways in which Hollywood is changing that will certainly prove invaluable in the coming years."

THOMPSON, CAROL. One, Two, Three... Crawl!; 12 p. 2013 Childs Play Intl Ltd

1. Crawling & creeping 2. Infants—Juvenile literature 3. Picture books for children 4. Play 5. Stories in rhyme
ISBN 1846436141; 9781846436147

SUMMARY: This children's picture book by Carol Thompson is an "ode to crawling. The only signs of grown-ups in this title are a few pairs of shoes under a table; the low-to-the-ground universe presented here belongs to the wee ones. An adorable cast of multiethnic tots crawls, wobbles and falls. They wind their way through tunnels, climb over one another and scurry under tables." (Kirkus Reviews)

REVIEW: *Kirkus Rev* v81 no21 p315 N 1 2013

REVIEW: *Kirkus Rev* v82 no1 p82 Ja 1 2014

"One, Two, Three . . . Crawl!". "Spare text and dynamic illustrations pair well in this ode to crawling. The only signs of grown-ups in this title are a few pairs of shoes under a table; the low-to-the-ground universe presented here belongs to the wee ones. An adorable cast of multiethnic tots crawls, wobbles and falls. . . . Thompson's collage illustrations create a textured world of sweet, slightly quirky-looking babies rejoicing in their newfound mobility. . . . A simple but effective celebration of the thrill that comes with moving under one's own steam. Get ready for repeat readings."

THOMPSON, CLIVE. Smarter Than You Think; How Technology Is Changing Our Minds for the Better; [by] Clive Thompson 352 p. 2013 Penguin Group USA

1. Information technology—Psychological aspects 2. Information technology—Social aspects 3. Internet—Psychological aspects 4. Internet—Social aspects 5. SOCIAL SCIENCE—General 6. Social media 7. Social science literature 8. TECHNOLOGY & ENGINEERING—General 9. Thought and thinking
ISBN 1594204454; 9781594204456
LC 2013-017155

SUMMARY: In this book "about the advent of technology and its influence on humans, journalist [Clive] Thompson . . . admits that we often allow ourselves to be used by facets of new technologies and that we must exercise caution to avoid this; yet, he demonstrates, digital tools can have a huge positive impact on us, for they provide us with infinite memory, the ability to discover connections . . . previously unknown to us, and new and abundant avenues for communication and publishing." (Publishers Weekly)

REVIEW: *Booklist* v109 no22 p13 Ag 1 2013 Gilbert Taylor

REVIEW: *Choice* v51 no6 p1027 F 2014 K. D. Winward

REVIEW: *Kirkus Rev* v81 no14 p297 Jl 15 2013

REVIEW: *Libr J* v138 no14 p129 S 1 2013 Jim Hahn

REVIEW: *N Y Times Book Rev* p54 N 10 2013

REVIEW: *N Y Times Book Rev* p11 N 3 2013 WALTER ISAACSON

"Smarter Than You Think: How Technology is Changing Our Minds for the Better." "[A] judicious and insightful book on human and machine intelligence. . . . What [Clive Thompson] provides . . . are some interesting current examples of how human-computer symbiosis is enlarging our intellect. . . . Thompson avoids both the hype and the handwringing so common among digital age pontificators by sidestepping most of the topics that agitate the geekosphere. . . . He comes across as a sensible utopian. . . . In debunking the doomsayers, Thompson has pleasant sport poking fun at history's procession of pessimists."

REVIEW: *New Yorker* v89 no35 p104-1 N 4 2013

REVIEW: *Publ Wkly* v260 no26 p79-80 Jl 1 2013

REVIEW: *Quill Quire* v79 no10 p28 D 2013 Alex Good

THOMPSON, HELEN. Culinary math; [by] Helen Thompson 48 p. 2014 Mason Crest

1. Budget 2. Cooking—Mathematics—Juvenile literature 3. Fractions 4. Mathematical literature 5. Multiplication

ISBN 9781422229019 (series); 9781422229057 (hardcover)

LC 2013-015662

SUMMARY: This book by Helen Thompson is part of the Math 24/7 series, which "emphasizes how math skills come into play at all times and in all places, from the kitchen to the soccer field. . . . Guided questions walk readers through the process and provide practice problems. In 'Culinary Math,' a culinary student uses estimating to budget his grocery shopping, multiplication to determine a food's calorie content, and fractions to measure ingredients." (Booklist)

REVIEW: *Booklist* v110 no5 p56 N 1 2013 Angela Leeper

"Culinary Math," "Fashion Math," and "Game Math." "The Math 24/7 series emphasizes how math skills come into play at all times and in all places, from the kitchen to the soccer field. Each book centers on a young person who is involved in a series of scenarios that requires real-world math to solve a problem. . . . In 'Culinary Math,' a culinary student uses estimating to budget his grocery shopping, multiplication to determine a food's calorie content, and fractions to measure ingredients. In 'Fashion Math,' a budding fashion designer uses math to convert sizes, choose enough fabric for a pattern, and determine prices to make a profit. In Game Math, Mason is surprised to discover that many of his favorite games incorporate such concepts as probability, coordinates, estimation, and logic."

THOMPSON, JAMES. Helsinki white; [by] James Thompson 326 p. 2012 G. P. Putnam's Sons

1. Detective & mystery stories 2. Emigration & immigration 3. Helsinki (Finland) 4. Homicide investigation—Fiction 5. Murder investigation—Fiction 6. Police—Finland—Fiction 7. Police corruption—Fiction

ISBN 9780399158322

LC 2011-047679

SUMMARY: In this book "[d]esperate to hide the ultra-compromising video Inspector Kari Vaara has of him, Jyri Ivalo, Finland's national chief of police, offers him a free hand assembling a dream team, financed by whatever it can steal from the bad guys, to go after international traffickers in human flesh. . . . Kari and his mates, dirty cops in all but name, are already getting sucked into a cesspool of corruption. Ironically, the tipping point comes with the order to close a pair of high-profile cases . . . the recent beheading of pro-immigration activist Lisbet Söderlund and the year-old kidnapping of Antti and Kaarina Saukko, son and daughter of megalomaniac industrialist Veikko Saukko, and Kaarina's murder three days after she was ransomed and returned unharmed." (Kirkus)

REVIEW: *Booklist* v108 no12 p26 F 15 2012 Jessica Moyer

REVIEW: *Kirkus Rev* v80 no4 p352 F 15 2012

"Helsinki White." " Finland's top cop gets to run his very own black-ops unit--and rue the day he ever took what looked like a dream job. Desperate to hide the ultra-compromising video Inspector Kari Vaara has of him, Jyri Ivalo, Finland's national chief of police, offers him a free hand assembling a dream team, financed by whatever it can steal from the bad guys, to go after international traffickers in human flesh. Determined 'to help people' now that he's a new father, Kari ('Lucifer's Tears,' 2011, etc.) brings in his loose-cannon partner Milo Nieminien and his protégé Sulo (Sweetness) Polvinen and hits the bricks. . . . Enough violent felonies for a Sunday newspaper--and, as a depressingly informative epilogue intimates, that's exactly where they've come from."

REVIEW: *Libr J* v137 no2 p58 F 1 2012 Annabelle Mortensen

REVIEW: *Publ Wkly* v259 no3 p38 Ja 16 2012

THOMPSON, JERRY L. Why photography matters; [by] Jerry L. Thompson 104 p. 2013 The MIT Press

1. Art & literature 2. Art literature 3. Logic 4. Photography—Philosophy 5. Photography—Psychological aspects

ISBN 9780262019286 (hardcover : alk. paper)

LC 2012-044048

SUMMARY: This book "argues on behalf of photography as a medium for creating a dialectic between the self and the world. [Jerry L.] Thompson . . . constructs his argument out of both his experience creating images and the Western literary tradition. He favors a style of photography that he considers more robust than the style in which the medium is commonly used and described by contemporary artists and thinkers." (Publisher's note)

REVIEW: *Choice* v51 no7 p1204 Mr 2014 E. Baden

REVIEW: *TLS* no5767 p30-1 O 11 2013 DAVID COLLARD

"Why Photography Matters." "Jerry L. Thompson's slim and gently eccentric volume delves deeper, through an engaging series of reflections on the art, and offers a belated but vigorous response to Susan Sontag's essay 'America, Seen through Photographs, Darkly'. . . . His approach is refreshingly informal and this book . . . is the product of a lifetime's professional engagement with the subject. His reasoning is subtle but there is none of the opaque critical language that characterizes much academic writing about photography, just plenty of good sense and good taste, based on a generous and cultivated intelligence. . . . Of particular value is the author's quietly passionate defence of the small-scale in the face of what he disparagingly calls 'studio art'."

THOMPSON, KATRINA DALY. Zimbabwe's cinematic arts; language, power, identity; [by] Katrina Daly Thompson xii, 237 p. 2013 Indiana University Press

1. Mass media and language—Political aspects—Zimbabwe 2. Motion picture industry—Zimbabwe—Foreign influences 3. Motion pictures and television—Social aspects—Zimbabwe 4. Social science literature
ISBN 0253006465 (cloth : alk. paper); 0253006511 (pbk. : alk. paper); 0253006562 (electronic book); 9780253006462 (cloth : alk. paper); 9780253006516 (pbk. : alk. paper); 9780253006561 (electronic book)
LC 2012-028173

SUMMARY: In this book, author Katrina Daly Thompson "analyzes identity discourses through cinematic arts . . . consumed (whether or not produced) in Zimbabwe. She examines Zimbabwean diachronic and ideological aspects at the intersection of indigenousness . . . and 'foreign,' with foreign nebulously construed as white, Western, colonial, and inauthentic. She contrasts these during two phases: Unilateral Declaration of Independence (UDI) and post-independence." (Choice)

REVIEW: *Choice* v51 no4 p645 D 2013 K. M. Kapanga

"Zimbabwe's Cinematic Arts: Language, Power, Identity." "[Katrina Daly] Thompson . . . analyzes identity discourses through cinematic arts--films, documentaries, television programs, videos--consumed (whether or not produced) in Zimbabwe. . . . The fear of seeing the colonial past return or of yielding to cultural imperialism has often obfuscated the debate. Thompson makes viewers' choices and motivations relevant. She relies on research, interviews, and her interpretations of bow power controls the art of representation."

THOMPSON, KEN, 1943-. Where Do Camels Belong?; The story and science of invasive species; [by] Ken Thompson 272 p. 2014 Profile Books Ltd

1. Biological invasions 2. Biological literature 3. Camels 4. Introduced organisms 5. Natural history
ISBN 1781251746; 9781781251744

SUMMARY: "In 'Where Do Camels Belong?' Ken Thompson puts forward a fascinating array of narratives on invasive and natural plants and animals to explore what he sees as the crucial question—why only a minority of introduced species succeed, and why so few of them go on to cause trouble. He discusses, too, whether fear of invasive species could be getting in the way of conserving biodiversity." (Publisher's note)

REVIEW: *Libr J* v139 no16 p108 O 1 2014 Gretchen Kolderup

REVIEW: *New Sci* v221 no2962 p54 Mr 29 2014 Bob Holmes

REVIEW: *TLS* no5795 p26 Ap 25 2014 MARK WILLIAMS

"Where Do Camels Belong? The Story and Science of Invasive Species." "Ken Thompson explores how we define invasive species and what we should do about them. . . . Thompson applies these fluctuating criteria to the camel, a species which originated in North America, but became extinct there 8,000 years ago. What was once a natural species would now, were it reintroduced, be considered an invasive one. . . . 'Where Do Camels Belong?' is a thought-provoking book, a bit righteous in places, but nonetheless full of interesting examples of invasive species and how their populations are shaped by the ecological, social and political concerns of our own."

THOMPSON, MARK. Birth certificate; the story of Danilo Kiš; [by] Mark Thompson 368 p. 2013 Cornell University Press

1. Authors—Biography 2. Authors, Serbian—20th century—Biography 3. Biographies 4. Jews—Europe, Eastern—History
ISBN 9780801448881 (cloth : alk. paper)
LC 2012-027625

SUMMARY: This book by Mark Thompson offers "a careful and sensitive telling of a life that experienced some of the last century's greatest cruelties. [author Danilo] Kiš' father was a Hungarian Jew, his mother a Montenegrin of Orthodox faith. . . . Thompson's book pays tribute to Kiš' experimentalism by being itself experimental in form. It is patterned as a series of commentaries on a short autobiographical text that Kiš called 'Birth Certificate.'" (Publisher's note)

REVIEW: *Choice* v51 no2 p266-7 O 2013 D. C. Maus

"Birth Certificate: The Story of Danilo Kiš." "This book easily could have gone terribly wrong. British writer [Mark] Thompson pays homage to one of the 20th century's most innovative and difficult writers in the very form of this immense autobiography that simultaneously moonlights as an attempt to rekindle interest in Kiš's work and as a cultural history of Jews in south central Europe. Thompson divides his analysis into 33 chapters, each of which is headed by and framed around fragments taken from a brief autobiographical sketch . . . that Kiš wrote in 1983. . . . Thompson risks overloading and confusing his reader with this initially odd structure, hut he ultimately succeeds brilliantly by using this patchwork approach to put Kiš and his works into a wide range of contexts."

REVIEW: *N Y Rev Books* v60 no9 p40-1 My 23 2013 Charles Simic

REVIEW: *Publ Wkly* v259 no51 p48 D 17 2012

REVIEW: *TLS* no5767 p3-5 O 11 2013 ADAM THIRLWELL

"Birth Certificate: The Story of Danilo Kiš." "[A] comprehensive, erudite and stylish new biography. . . . Some readers of [Mark] Thompson's biography . . . might perhaps prefer a more traditional, less zigzagging form. There are moments when it causes problems of comprehension, when, faced with pile-ups of parentheses, the reader is sent forwards or backwards to other chapters for explanation. But in the end, this essayistic method is powerfully convincing. . . . Thompson's method of close readings, commenting on Kiš's sentences, clause by clause, becomes a delicate way of illuminating these various repressions and deletions--Kiš's oblique approaches to catastrophe."

THOMPSON, N. S.tr. Deliverance of evil. See Costantini, R.

THOMPSON, SIMON. A Long Walk with Lord Conway; An Exploration of the Alps and an English Adventurer; [by] Simon Thompson 320 p. 2013 Signal Books Ltd

1. Alps 2. Biography (Literary form) 3. Conway, William Martin 4. Memoirs 5. Mountaineers—Great Britain—Biography

ISBN 1908493801; 9781908493804

SUMMARY: "In 'A Long Walk with Lord Conway,' Simon Thompson retraces Conway's long journey over the peaks, passes and glaciers of the Alps and rediscovers the life of a complex and remarkable English adventurer. . . . In 1894, Martin Conway became the first man to walk the Alps 'from end to end' when he completed a 1,000-mile journey from the Col de Tende in Italy to the summit of the Ankogel in Austria." (Publisher's note)

REVIEW: *TLS* no5781 p27 Ja 17 2014 IAN THOMSON

"A Long Walk With Lord Conway: An Exploration of the Alps and an English Adventurer." "Born in provincial Rochester in 1856, Conway was a socially ambitious if somewhat roguish individual. . . . [Author Simon] Thompson follows in Conway's footsteps across the Alps, quoting from his notebooks of 'Ruskinian prose' as he goes, and recreating the expedition that set out from Turin. . . . 'A Long Walk with Lord Conway,' an absorbing amalgam of travel, biography and history, will help to rehabilitate one of the more 'colourful' late Victorian personalities."

THOMSON, KEITH. Jefferson's shadow; the story of his science; [by] Keith Thomson p. cm. 2012 Yale University Press

1. Historical literature 2. Science—History—18th century 3. Science—History—19th century

ISBN 9780300184037 (cloth: alk. paper)
LC 2012-022590

SUMMARY: "This new and original study of Jefferson presents him as a consummate intellectual whose view of science was central to both his public and his private life. [Author] Keith Thomson reintroduces us in this remarkable book to Jefferson's eighteenth-century world and reveals the extent to which Jefferson used science, thought about it, and contributed to it, becoming in his time a leading American scientific intellectual." (Publisher's note)

REVIEW: *Choice* v50 no9 p1648-9 My 2013 J. S. Schwartz

REVIEW: *Kirkus Rev* v80 no20 p200 O 15 2012

REVIEW: *Rev Am Hist* v42 no2 p227-36 Je 2014 R. B. Bernstein

"Thomas Jefferson and American Nationhood," "Jefferson's Shadow: The Story of His Science," and "Thomas Jefferson: The Art of Power." "In 'Thomas Jefferson and American Nationalism,' Brian Steele addresses the central role of American nationalism in Jefferson's thought. . . . Steele's tightly reasoned, well-researched study sets Jefferson in historical context while examining unique aspects of his thought. . . . In his gracefully written (though digressive) thematic biography 'Jefferson's Shadow: The Story of His Science,' [author Keith] Thomson extends the path blazed by [other] scholars. . . . Jefferson's strengths and weaknesses as a politician deserve the extended study and analysis that [author Jon] Meacham offers. Indeed, this smoothly written biography illuminates in many ways our understanding of Jefferson."

THOMSON, LORRIE. Equilibrium; [by] Lorrie Thomson 336 p. 2013 Kensington Pub Corp

1. Domestic fiction 2. Man-woman relationships—Fiction 3. Mental illness—Fiction 4. Parent & child—Fiction 5. Suicide—Fiction

ISBN 0758285779; 9780758285775

SUMMARY: In this book, by Lorrie Thomson, "one year after Laura's husband, Jack, killed himself, she is finally learning to live with the guilt and grief of his death. Her main concern now is taking care of their two children, but just as her own life is getting back on track, theirs seem to be jumping the rails. While Laura is busy watching her pubescent son for signs of the manic depression that drove Jack to suicide, her teenage daughter, Darcy, is falling in love with the wrong guy." (Booklist)

REVIEW: *Booklist* v110 no2 p27-8 S 15 2013 Cortney Ophoff

"Equilibrium." "Written alternately from the mother's and daughter's viewpoints, [Lorrie] Thomson's first novel treats issues of loss, mental illness, adolescence, and sexuality with great openness and sensitivity. Fans of Kristin Hannah and Holly Chamberlin will similarly appreciate this hopeful, uplifting story about family, friendships, and a second chance at love. . . . Darcy's turbulent relationships with family and friends and her conflicting emotions about sex may strike a chord with older teens."

THOMSON, RUPERT. Secrecy; [by] Rupert Thomson 312 p. 2013 Granta

1. Artists—Fiction 2. Florence (Italy)—History—1737-1860 3. Historical fiction 4. Love stories 5. Murder—Fiction

ISBN 1590516850; 9781590516850; 9781847081636 (hbk.); 9781847087652 (pbk.)
LC 2013-375913

SUMMARY: This historical novel follows "Gaetano Zummo, a sculptor of wax images. . . . Zummo is commissioned by the lovelorn Duke Cosimo to produce a sculpture of a beautiful woman. . . . Zummo uncovers the murder of a young woman, and preserves her drowned body; he falls in love with Faustina, an apothecary's daughter with a secret connection to the Duke's wife. Their relationship appears doomed, threatened by the Duke's meddling and malign agents." (Times Literary Supplement)

REVIEW: *Booklist* v110 no13 p25-6 Mr 1 2014 Cortney Ophoff

"Secrecy." "Florence is a dangerous place for freethinkers, lovers, and artists at the end of the seventeenth century. An atmosphere of repression has settled over the region, and people are held in check by religious figures in powerful places. . . . Though some anachronistic details occasionally interrupt the realism, [Rupert] Thomson brings Renaissance-era Florence to life with rich descriptions and scenic locales. Readers who have toured Florence will enjoy revisiting the sites in the mind's eye, and historical fiction fans in general will relish the virtual trip brimming with mystery and intrigue."

REVIEW: *Kirkus Rev* v82 no4 p203 F 15 2014

"Secrecy". "[Rupert] Thomson . . . takes us to 17th-century Florence, which by definition seems to be full of corrupt politicians, unscrupulous clergy and aspiring artists-and this, of course, long after the Renaissance has ended. . . . Through some detective work, Zummo eventually discovers that Faustina is in fact the daughter of the Grand Duchess, but this knowledge does not protect her, and Zummo comes up with a plan to forever rid their lives of Stufa. . . . Thomson succeeds on a number of levels here, for the novel works as a mystery, as a love story, as a historical novel and, more abstractly, as an exploration of aesthetic theory."

REVIEW: *Libr J* v139 no2 p69 F 1 2014 Joshua Finnell

REVIEW: *London Rev Books* v35 no8 p19-20 Ap 25 2013 Adam Mars-Jones

REVIEW: *New Yorker* v90 no22 p69-1 Ag 4 2014

REVIEW: *Publ Wkly* v261 no6 p66-7 F 10 2014

REVIEW: *TLS* no5738 p21 Mr 22 2013 STEPHEN ABELL

"Secrecy." "An exquisitely written historical mystery. It is also an artful meditation on art itself. . . . Zummo . . . is consistently preoccupied with a sense of his own artistry, and its relationship with the surrounding world. This allows [Rupert] Thomson to fill the narration with the beautifully mannered, patterned description that adorns so much of 'Secrecy'. . . . Thomson arguably allows this artistic approach to dominate excessively. We see this in his occasional ungainly spasms of metaphor, suggesting a superfluous desire to conjure imagery from nothing. . . . Thankfully, the author recognizes that genre novels also rely on plotting, and 'Secrecy,' while pretty, is also pacy."

THOMSON, SARAH L. Ancient animals. See Ancient animals

THOMSON, SARAH L. Cub's big world; 32 p. 2013 Harcourt Children's Books, Houghton Mifflin Harcourt

1. Animals—Infancy—Fiction 2. Bears—Fiction 3. Children's stories 4. Mother and child—Fiction 5. Polar bear—Fiction

ISBN 0544057392; 9780544057395

LC 2012-045056

SUMMARY: In this picture book, by Sarah L. Thomson, "Cub knows all about the familiar world in the snow den where she was born. When she follows Mom out of their den, tumbling into the Arctic wilderness, she finds that the world under the wide blue sky is big, big, BIG! It's easy to be curious when there's so much to explore—and when Mom is nearby. But when she thinks she's all alone, can Cub be brave?" (Publisher's note)

REVIEW: *Booklist* v110 no6 p51 N 15 2013 Karen Cruze

REVIEW: *Horn Book Magazine* v89 no6 p83 N/D 2013 CLAIRE E. GROSS

REVIEW: *Kirkus Rev* v81 no20 p77 O 15 2013

REVIEW: *N Y Times Book Rev* p16 Ja 12 2014 SARAH HARRISON SMITH

"Cub's Big World," "The Hiccup," and "Please Bring Balloons." "Pleasingly realistic yet reassuringly sweet, 'Cub's Big World' follows a young polar bear on her first trip out of the cozy snow cave the shares with her mother. . . . '[Author and illustrator Ingrid] Sissung's freewheeling story ['The Hiccup'] delivers justice in the end for the teaser and the teased. . . . [Author and illustrator Lindsay] Ward, a cut-paper artist, gives her book great visual appeal with snippets of colorful origami paper, calendars and maps."

THOREAU, HENRY DAVID, 1817-1862. See The Correspondence of Henry D. Thoreau

THORNESS, BILL. Power; how J.D. Power III became the auto industry's adviser, confessor, and eyewitness to history; [by] Bill Thorness 399 p. 2013 Fenwick Publishing Group, Inc.

1. Automobile industry and trade—Public relations—United States 2. Biography (Literary form) 3. Consumer satisfaction—United States 4. Marketing research companies—United States 5. Selling—Automobiles—United States

ISBN 9780981833675

LC 2013-003414

SUMMARY: This book presents "an authorized biography of J.D. Power, who built an eponymous business that revolutionized the relationship between automobile manufacturers and consumers. . . . [Sarah] Morgans and [Bill] Thorness lift the curtain, showing Power's individuality as a slowly developing business tycoon who eventually sold his creation to a much larger corporation yet remained active in management." (Kirkus Reviews)

REVIEW: *Kirkus Rev* v82 no2 p314 Ja 15 2014

"Power: How J.D. Power III Became the Auto Industry's Adviser, Confessor and Eyewitness to History". "A clearly written account of how Power quit a stable job to invent a new kind of market research company in 1968. Power was a partner in the composition of the book, referred to by his nickname 'Dave' throughout the text. The narrative often reads like a valentine, and thus it is difficult to discern whether the co-authors found any negative information on their subject. However, the evidence is convincing that Power is both a visionary and a moral, nice human being. . . . An occasionally hagiographic but surprisingly captivating biography."

THORNTON, PATRICIA H. The institutional logics perspective. See Lounsbury, M.

THORPE, ADAM.tr. Therese Raquin. See Zola, E.

THROUGH THE NIGHT; 150 p. 2013 Dalkey Archive Press

1. Fathers & sons—Fiction 2. Grief—Fiction 3. Mental illness—Fiction 4. Psychological fiction 5. Suicide—Fiction

ISBN 9781564788740 (pbk. : alk. paper)

LC 2013-003454

SUMMARY: This book presents "a philosophical horror story charting the madness of a father whose son has committed suicide. Dentist Karl Meyer's worst nightmare comes true when his son, Ole-Jakob, takes his own life." The book asks "questions about human experience: What does sorrow do to a person? How can one live with the pain of unbearable loss? How far can a man be driven by the grief and despair surrounding the death of a child?" (Publisher's note)

REVIEW: *N Y Times Book Rev* p30 S 1 2013 Alison McCulloch

"Through the Night," "The Matchmaker, the Apprentice, and the Football Fan," and "The Sinistra Zone." "[Stig] Saeterbakken entices the reader along some dark paths from which, in the end, there is no easy escape. . . . Even in this grim tale, Zhu [Wen] manages to inject some of the sly humor that suffuses these stories, which, unlike some of the lives he describes, are never dreary. . . . Like everything else in this cryptic novel, its main character is a bit of a mystery. . . . Adding to its perplexity is the book's structure: 15 overlapping chapters that could double as independent short stories."

THUBRON, COLIN, 1939-.ed. The Broken Road. See The Broken Road

THURLO, AIMÉE. Ghost medicine. See Thurlo, D.

THURLO, AIMÉE. The pawnbroker. See Thurlo, D.

THURLO, DAVID. Ghost medicine; [by] David Thurlo 320 p. 2013 Forge Books

1. FICTION—Mystery & Detective—General 2. Murder—Investigation—Fiction 3. Navajo Indians—Fiction 4. Paranormal fiction 5. Spirits—Fiction

ISBN 0765334038; 9780765334039 (hardback)

LC 2013-022085

SUMMARY: This book, by Aimée Thurlo and David Thurlo, part of the Ella Clah book series, follows "a Navajo police special investigator. . . . The discovery of the body of a former Navajo police officer who has undergone ritualistic-looking mutilations leads Ella and her team to suspect that this may be the work of 'skinwalkers,' Navajo witches who try to control through intimidation. The retired cop-victim had been working as a private eye, hunting down stolen Navajo artifacts." (Booklist)

REVIEW: *Booklist* v110 no3 p36-8 O 1 2013 Connie Fletcher

"Ghost Medicine." "The Ella Clah novels (this is the seventeenth) stand apart from the other series, thanks to the complexity of Ella, a Navajo Police special investigator, who faces down opposing Anglo and Navajo cultures in her work and home life. . . . The skinwalker angle is especially creepy here, with vivid descriptions of the way they leave their calling card of body mutilation at staged scenes. The Thurlos [Aimée Thurlo and David Thurlo] mix in a great deal of knowledge about trafficking in Native American antiquities with a well-constructed investigation steered by a believable and admirable heroine."

REVIEW: *Kirkus Rev* v81 no20 p101 O 15 2013

REVIEW: *Publ Wkly* v260 no37 p28-9 S 16 2013

THURLO, DAVID. The pawnbroker; [by] David Thurlo 304 p. 2014 Minotaur Books

1. Detective & mystery stories 2. Murder—Investigation—Fiction 3. Pawnbroking 4. Post-traumatic stress 5. Retired military personnel—United States—Fiction

ISBN 9781250027986 (hardcover)

LC 2013-032887

SUMMARY: This book follows "Charlie Henry, a Navajo who was formerly a special-ops agent in Afghanistan and Iraq. Henry returns to civilian life in Albuquerque, hoping for a quieter life as co-owner of a pawnshop with his best army, 'got your back' buddy. . . . The mystery centers on what is in the pawnshop that so many people are desperately searching for." (Booklist)

REVIEW: *Booklist* v110 no8 p23-4 D 15 2013 Connie Fletcher

"The Pawnbroker." "The entire novel moves at a breakneck pace through burglaries, stakeouts, and car chases, always aggravating Charlie's residual PTSD. The mystery centers on what is in the pawnshop that so many people are desperately searching for. Henry's hard-won street smarts and informal contacts allow him access to a detective within the Albuquerque Police Department, giving this book more authenticity and punch than if he worked alone. This is a promising debut for a very contemporary character."

REVIEW: *Kirkus Rev* v81 no24 p264 D 15 2013

"The Pawnbroker". " Two war veterans find that their special ops skills come in unexpectedly handy back stateside in Albuquerque, N.M. Only after purchasing the Three Balls pawnshop do Navajo Charlie Henry and his Anglo buddy Gordo Sweeney discover that former owner Diego Baza has wiped the computers. . . .The dangerous duo soon become involved in gunfights with rival gangs as they track down the mystery woman and try to discover the motive for the pawnbroker's murder. Fans of the Sister Agatha and Ella Clah mysteries . . . will find . . . [David and Aimee] Thurlos' new series kickoff more thriller than mystery, though there's still a touch of the trademark Navajo lore."

REVIEW: *Libr J* v139 no1 p1 Ja 2014 Teresa L. Jacobsen

REVIEW: *Publ Wkly* v260 no47 p33 N 18 2013

THURMAN, CHRIS. Intervention in the modern UK brewing industry. See Walters, J.

TIANO, SUSAN.ed. Borderline slavery. See Borderline slavery

TIENKEN, CHRISTOPHER H. The school reform landscape. See Orlich, D. C.

TIERNAN, CATE. Darkest fear; [by] Cate Tiernan 368 p. 2014 Simon Pulse

1. Families—Fiction 2. JUVENILE FICTION—Social Issues—Friendship 3. JUVENILE FICTION—Social Issues—New Experience 4. Jaguar—Fiction 5. Orphans—Fiction 6. Paranormal romance stories 7. Shapeshifting—Fiction 8. Supernatural—Fiction

ISBN 9781442482456 (pbk.); 9781442482463 (hardcover)

LC 2013-025046

SUMMARY: In this paranormal romance story, "Vivi Neves has known she's one of the haguari, an ancient race of shapeshifting jaguar people, since she was 13. . . . She and her parents are attacked during a family picnic. Her parents end up dead, her father's heart missing. . . . Vivi uncovers evidence of an aunt she never knew existed and heads to New Orleans to find her. Instead, she meets her 20-something cousin, Matéo, whose parents died a year and a half before, their hearts also taken." (Kirkus Reviews)

REVIEW: *Booklist* v110 no9/10 p105 Ja 1 2014 Annie Miller

REVIEW: *Bull Cent Child Books* v67 no5 p286 Ja 2014 K. Q. G.

REVIEW: *Kirkus Rev* v81 no24 p195 D 15 2013

"Darkest Fear". "The first book in [Cate] Tiernan's Birthright series . . . is both predictable and unoriginal. . . . Vivi's first-person narration is an exhausting mix of back story and summary that prevents the plot from developing. She thinks and speaks in ellipses and speculative questions, and her snarky voice is whiny rather than quirky. Her jaguar voice is a stream-of-consciousness jumble of broken and run-on sentences in present tense, and the move from one voice to the other is jarring. The anticlimactic ending will leave readers too frustrated to read subsequent installments to find out who is kidnapping haguari and taking their hearts. This lackluster addition to the bloated teen-paranormal-romance genre has nothing new to offer."

REVIEW: *SLJ* v60 no3 p164 Mr 2014 Jennifer Furuyama

TIERNEY, JIM.il. The Boundless. See Oppel, K.

TIGER TALES.comp. Noisy Farm. See Noisy Farm

TIGER TALES.comp. 100 First Words. See 100 First Words

TILLMAN, LYNNE. What would Lynne Tillman do?; [by] Lynne Tillman 192 p. 2013 Red Lemonade/Cursor

1. Art 2. Authorship 3. Baker, Chet, 1929-1988 4. Bowles, Paul, 1910-1999 5. Essay (Literary form)
ISBN 9781935869214 (alk. paper)
LC 2013-932435

SUMMARY: In this collection of short writings, Lynne Tillman "studies subjects as varied as President Obama, art, language, literature, film, and music (from Chet Baker to the Rolling Stones). Consciousness, time, and desire, as well as problems of authenticity, ideology, and taste emerge as leitmotifs, though Tillman's real subject is the making of art." (Publishers Weekly)

REVIEW: *Bookforum* v21 no1 p57 Ap/My 2014 JOHANNA FATEMAN

REVIEW: *Booklist* v110 no14 p44 Mr 15 2014 Donna Seaman

REVIEW: *Kirkus Rev* v82 no2 p230 Ja 15 2014

"What Would Lynne Tillman Do?" "These are shorter works by Tillman . . . but it's a generous set, allowing one essay for each letter of the alphabet. . . . 'White Cool' gives a heartbreaking flash of famed jazz musician Chet Baker. Tillman is a fantastic writer in long-form or short, and the exercise of turning that famous intellect on herself seems to make her more abrupt yet more focused. . . . The collection doesn't even really serve as an introduction to Tillman's work, although it certainly represents her wit. . . . In short, it's a nonessential pastiche of book reviews and other miscellaneous writings that reads less as a collage and more like someone handed you one drawer of a great writer's file cabinet. The world's culture dissected, one cunning, bemused essay at a time."

REVIEW: *Libr J* v139 no8 p78 My 1 2014 Joyce Sparrow

REVIEW: *New Yorker* v90 no15 p79-1 Je 2 2014

"What Would Lynne Tillman Do?" "This witty compendium of essays and interviews is arranged alphabetically . . . and its subjects are wide-ranging. [Author Lynne] Tillman writes of Barack Obama's media savvy, of hearing the Rolling Stones play in New York in 1965, of the pitfalls of defining New York's 'downtown' arts scene. . . . Taken together, the pieces express an abiding curiosity in the commitment to making art and a willingness to read carefully and think deeply about other artists' work."

REVIEW: *Publ Wkly* v261 no4 p178 Ja 27 2014

TILLOTSON, KATHERINE.il. Shoe dog. See McDonald, M.

TIME TRAVEL TROUBLE; 192 p. 2013 Egmont USA

1. Children's stories 2. Heroes—Juvenile fiction 3. Humorous stories 4. Supervillains 5. Supervillains—Fiction 6. Time travel—Fiction 7. Time travel—Juvenile fiction 8. Wit & humor
ISBN 9781606844618 (hardcover)
LC 2012-045853

SUMMARY: In this juvenile time travel story in the Vordak the Incomprehensible series by Scott Seegert, illustrated by John Martin, "After having yet another evil plan to rule the world foiled by Commander Virtue, Vordak travels back in time in an attempt to defeat his archnemesis at the point of his greatest vulnerability--his childhood." (Publisher's note)

REVIEW: *Kirkus Rev* v81 no16 p39 Ag 15 2013

"Time Travel Trouble." "This book might be the definition of 'Your mileage may vary.' A lot of people like to say, 'The stupidest jokes are always the best,' but this book may test their patience levels. . . . It might help to think of this book as a psychological test. Older readers can use it as a dating service: If two people both laugh at the grammar joke, they might be perfect for each other. But even fans of dumb jokes may get frustrated with the narrator. Vordak is one of the least sympathetic characters in children's literature."

TIMM, MAXIMILIAN A. The WishKeeper; Book One of The Paragonia Chronicles; [by] Maximilian A. Timm 354 p. 2013 Lost King Entertainment

1. Fairies—Fiction 2. Fantasy fiction 3. Magic—Fiction 4. People with disabilities—Fiction 5. Self-realization—Fiction
ISBN 0991063201; 9780991063208

SUMMARY: This book, the first in Maximilian A. Timm's "Patagonia Chronicles" series, "follows Shea, a stubborn fairy with a tumultuous past whose present reality includes a lot of disappointment and bullying. . . . She begins taking risks to make her own wishes come true: 'All she ever asked or wished for was a chance. But she might just need to create that chance on her own and she was done feeling sorry for herself.'" (Kirkus Reviews)

REVIEW: *Kirkus Rev* v82 no1 p136 Ja 1 2014

"The WishKeeper". "An imaginative take on pursuing dreams. [Maximilian A.] Timm masterminds a fantastical setting, rife with inventive terminology. . . . Due to all the unfamiliar language in the foreign land of Paragonia, the first 15 of 48 chapters paint a curious world with numerous questions that are answered later in the relatively lengthy book. . . . Timm takes on the fantasy gamut with finesse, including everything from high jinks to romance. . . . Parents will appreciate the book's inspiring message and the courage it might stir in young readers. An action-packed, dramatic tale with a nonstandard relationship and a winning message."

TINDALL, D. B.ed. Aboriginal peoples and forest lands in Canada. See Aboriginal peoples and forest lands in Canada

TIPLING, DAVID.il. Birds & People. See Cocker, M.

TIPPINS, SHERILL. Inside the Dream Palace; the life and times of New York's legendary Chelsea Hotel; [by] Sherill Tippins 448 p. 2013 Houghton Mifflin Harcourt

1. ART—Art & Politics 2. Apartment dwellers—New York (State)—New York—Biography 3. Artists—New York (State)—New York—Biography 4. Arts, American—New York (State)—New York—History 5. Eccentrics and eccentricities—New York (State)—New York—Biography 6. HISTORY—United States—20th Century 7. Historical literature 8. MUSIC—General 9. PERFORMING ARTS—Film & Video—General 10. PERFORMING ARTS—General 11. PHOTOGRAPHY—History
ISBN 0618726349; 9780618726349 (hardback)
LC 2013-026747

SUMMARY: Author Sherill Tippins "delivers a masterful and endlessly entertaining history of the Chelsea [Hotel in New York] and of the successive generations of artists who have cohabited and created there, among them John Sloan, Edgar Lee Masters, Thomas Wolfe, Dylan Thomas, Arthur Miller, Allen Ginsberg, Bob Dylan, Janis Joplin, Leonard Cohen, Patti Smith, Robert Mapplethorpe, Andy Warhol, Sam Shepard, Sid Vicious, and Dee Dee Ramone." (Publisher's note)

REVIEW: *Booklist* v110 no5 p20-1 N 1 2013 Donna Seaman

REVIEW: *Kirkus Rev* v81 no19 p28 O 1 2013

REVIEW: *Libr J* v138 no21 p111 D 1 2013 Richard Drezen

REVIEW: *Libr J* v138 no12 p56 Jl 1 2013

REVIEW: *N Y Times Book Rev* p84 D 8 2013 ADA CALHOUN

REVIEW: *New Yorker* v89 no43 p67-1 Ja 6 2014

"Inside the Dream Palace: The Life and Times of New York's Legendary Chelsea Hotel." "This history explores the ups and downs of the Chelsea Hotel, where scores of the twentieth century's greatest artists and writers lived. . . . Opened in 1884 . . . , it began as a community-minded, affordable residence where people from various classes and professions (but particularly artists) could live and create. [Author Sherill] Tippins tells riveting stories about the Chelsea's artists, but she also captures a much grander, and more pressing, narrative: that of the ongoing battle between art and capitalism in the city."

REVIEW: *New Yorker* v89 no43 p67-1 Ja 6 2014
REVIEW: *Publ Wkly* v260 no31 p55 Ag 5 2013

TITUS, ALAN L.ed. At the top of the grand staircase. See At the top of the grand staircase

TIWARY, VIVEK J., 1973-. The Fifth Beatle; The Brian Epstein Story; 144 p. 2013 Dark Horse

1. Beatles (Performer) 2. Concert agents 3. Epstein, Brian, 1934-1967 4. Gay men—Great Britain—Biography 5. Graphic novels
ISBN 1616552565; 9781616552565

SUMMARY: This graphic novel, by Vivek Tiwary, edited by Philip Simon, and illustrated by Andrew C. Robinson and Kyle Baker, "is the untold true story of Brian Epstein, the visionary manager who discovered and guided the Beatles—from their gigs in a tiny cellar in Liverpool to unprecedented international stardom." (Publisher's note)

REVIEW: *New York Times* v163 no56369 pC6 Ja 2 2014 GEORGE GENE GUSTINES

"Nowhere Men: Fates Worse than Death" and "The Fifth Beatle: The Brian Epstein Story". "The scientists, like the Beatles, are celebrities with an outsize influence on culture, which allows Mr. [Eric] Stephenson and the illustrator, Nate Bellegarde, to explore the love-hate relationship we have with our idols in the context of a richly complex, created world. . . . When a writer-artist team is truly clicking, something magical can happen, and it does here. Mr. Stephenson and Mr. Bellegarde juggle multiple characters and locations . . . yet personalities and appearances remain distinct. . . . 'The Fifth Beatle' is maddeningly uneven. It abounds with emotional moments, but they would be more resonant if balanced with additional facts about [Brian] Epstein's life. In some ways, this book feels like a teaser or the movie version."

REVIEW: *Publ Wkly* v260 no47 p39 N 18 2013

TOBIA, LAUREN.il. Baby's got the blues. See Shields, C. D.

TOBIN, JIM. The very inappropriate word; 40 p. 2013 Christy Ottaviano Books

1. Obscene words 2. School stories 3. Schools—Fiction 4. Swearing (Profanity) 5. Swearing—Fiction 6. Vocabulary—Fiction
ISBN 0805094741; 9780805094749 (hardcover)
LC 2012-021084

SUMMARY: In this children's picture book, "Michael is a budding logophile: 'He picked up new words at practice and downtown and even in school, where Mrs. Dixon gave the kids one new spelling word every day.' But when Michael picks up an 'inappropriate' word (albeit one that grownups use with impunity) on the school bus, he can't resist helping it go viral ('Michael could see there was some thing kind of bad about it. But there was also something about it that he kind of liked')." (Publishers Weekly)

REVIEW: *Booklist* v110 no3 p103 O 1 2013 Daniel Kraus

REVIEW: *Bull Cent Child Books* v67 no2 p119 O 2013 H. M.

"The Very Inappropriate Word." "Michael loves words, loves them so much that he collects them and keeps them in a box under his bed. His logophilic tendencies get him into trouble, however, when he collects a rather inappropriate word on the bus (uttered by a student examining his report card). . . . The text shifts from prose to verse in the library section, and the transition is somewhat startling and the rhyme forced despite the creative highlighting of Michael's found words. . . . Cartoonist [Dave] Coverly plays fast and free with the abstract elements of the tale, and the art breathes life into the idea of collecting words, ranging from the literal . . . to the metaphorical. . . ."

REVIEW: *Kirkus Rev* v81 no12 p120 Je 15 2013

REVIEW: *Publ Wkly* p49 Children's starred review annual 2013

REVIEW: *Publ Wkly* v260 no22 p60 Je 3 2013

REVIEW: *SLJ* v59 no7 p72 Jl 2013 Lucinda Snyder Whitehurst

TODD, CHARLES. Hunting shadows; an Inspector Ian

Rutledge Mystery; [by] Charles Todd 336 p. 2014 William Morrow

1. Detective & mystery stories 2. Police—Scotland—Fiction 3. Rutledge, Ian (Fictitious character)—Fiction 4. World War, 1914-1918—Fiction

ISBN 0062237187; 9780062237187 (hardback)

LC 2013-021319

SUMMARY: "A dangerous case with ties leading back to the battlefields of World War I dredges up dark memories for Scotland Yard Inspector Ian Rutledge in" this "historical mystery set in 1920s England," written by Charles Todd. "A society wedding at Ely Cathedral in Cambridgeshire becomes a crime scene when a man is murdered. After another body is found, the baffled local constabulary turns to Scotland Yard." (Publisher's note)

REVIEW: *Booklist* v110 no8 p22 D 15 2013 David Pitt

REVIEW: *Kirkus Rev* v82 no1 p190 Ja 1 2014

"Hunting Shadows". "Inspector Rutledge returns for another painstaking investigation of murders in the aftermath of World War I. . . . The mother-and-son team [Charles] Todd . . . may be letting up on their tortured hero: The ghostly voice of Hamish MacLeod, the soldier whom Rutledge had to shoot in the Great War, is a bit less prominent than in earlier installments. Less from ghost Hamish? That change may be as welcome to some fans as to the inspector himself, though others may miss the inspector's invisible partner and conscience."

REVIEW: *N Y Times Book Rev* p19 F 2 2014 MARLYN STASIO

REVIEW: *Publ Wkly* v260 no49 p62 D 2 2013

TODD, JANET M.ed. The Cambridge companion to Pride and prejudice. See The Cambridge companion to Pride and prejudice

TODD, MICHELLE.il. Max's magical potion. See Rivers-Moore, D.

TÓIBÍN, COLM, 1955-. The testament of Mary; [by] Colm Tóibín 81 p. 2012 Scribner

1. Apostles—Fiction 2. Bible—History of Biblical events—Fiction 3. Historical fiction

ISBN 1451688385; 9781442354944 (eAudio); 9781451688382; 9781451690750 (ebook); 9781451692389 (trade paper)

LC 2012-007578

SUMMARY: This novel, by Colm Tóibín, portrays the Virgin Mary "as a solitary older woman still seeking to understand the events that become the narrative of the New Testament and the foundation of Christianity. In the ancient town of Ephesus, Mary lives alone, years after her son's crucifixion. She has no interest in collaborating with the authors of the Gospel. . . . She does not agree that her son is the Son of God; nor that his death was 'worth it.'" (Publisher's note)

REVIEW: *America* v208 no1 p29-30 Ja 7 2013 DIANE SCHARPER

"The Testament of Mary." "Colm Tóibín's 'The Testament of Mary' tells an intriguing, though not always convincing story. Its main character, and to an extent its only character, is an old woman fretting about her past as she tries to get the facts straight. Given the book's title and story line, one assumes that the woman is Mary, the mother of Jesus of Nazareth, although the identity of the characters is not clearly defined. If this were just any old woman, the book would probably garner no interest. But since this old woman is central to Christianity, she is inherently interesting. . . . As it is, despite Tóibín's poetic writing, Mary never quite comes across in her role as mother of Christ, which is what this story is or should be all about."

REVIEW: *Booklist* v110 no13 p31 Mr 1 2014 Brian Odom

REVIEW: *Booklist* v109 no1 p56 S 1 2012 Brad Hooper

REVIEW: *Kirkus Rev* v80 no18 p224 S 15 2012

REVIEW: *Libr J* v137 no14 p95 S 1 2012 Susanne Wells

REVIEW: *Libr J* v139 no5 p85 Mr 15 2014 I. Pour-El

REVIEW: *N Y Rev Books* v60 no1 p43-6 Ja 10 2013 Hermione Lee

"New Ways to Kill Your Mother: Writers and Their Families" and "The Testament of Mary." "Every so often, in his captivating new collection of essays, 'New Ways to Kill Your Mother,' Colm Tóibín allows himself moments of general (and perhaps also personal) meditation and commentary. . . . Not all these essays are equally acute: Tóibín's unsympathetic treatment of the remarkable novelist Brian Moore . . . is disappointing. But his thinking about writers on the edge is always interesting. . . . But imagining himself into Mary's interior life is his boldest jump yet, and his most extreme form of self-disguise and self-dramatization. . . . The high intensity of this short book draws its tension--and also a tinge of sensational theatricality--from its stage origins."

REVIEW: *N Y Times Book Rev* p22 N 24 2013 CHARLES ISHERWOOD

REVIEW: *N Y Times Book Rev* p26 N 18 2012

REVIEW: *N Y Times Book Rev* p14 N 11 2012 MARY GORDON

REVIEW: *New Statesman* v141 no5127 p48 O 12 2012 Linda Grant

REVIEW: *New York Times* p4 N 29 2012 SUSANNAH MEADOWS

REVIEW: *New York Times* p5 N 29 2012 ALASTAIR MACAULAY

REVIEW: *New Yorker* v88 no40 p81 D 17 2012

REVIEW: *Publ Wkly* v260 no48 p49 N 25 2013

REVIEW: *Publ Wkly* v259 no30 p29 Jl 23 2012

REVIEW: *TLS* no5717 p19 O 26 2012 JOHN CORNWELL

TOLKIEN, J. R. R. (JOHN RONALD REUEL), 1892-1973. The hobbit; or, There and back again; [by] J. R. R. (John Ronald Reuel) Tolkien 310 1937 Houghton

1. Dragons—Fiction 2. Dwarves (Fictitious characters) 3. Elves 4. Fantasy fiction 5. Hobbits (Fictitious characters)

LC (W) -38-5859

SUMMARY: This book presents "a tale of the adventures of Bilbo Baggins, the hobbit, in a land inhabited by dwarfs, elves, goblins, dragons, and humans---tho the last named play only a small part in the story. Bilbo's adventures begin when he is persuaded to join a band of dwarfs, led by Gandalf, the Wizard, who are off on an expedition to recover the treasure stolen by Smaug, the Dragon, and hidden in the depths of the Lonely Mountain." (Publisher's note)

REVIEW: *Choice* v50 no9 p1623 My 2013 C. Holt-Fortin

REVIEW: *Libr J* v137 no14 p101 S 1 2012 Jennifer Harris

REVIEW: *TLS* no5752 p16 Je 28 2013

"The Hobbit, or There and Back Again." "[This book] admits us to a world of its own--a world that seems to have been going on before we stumbled into it but which, once found by the right reader, becomes indispensable for him. . . . You cannot anticipate it before you go there, as you cannot forget it once you have gone. . . . No common recipe for children's stories will give you creatures so rooted in their own soil and history as those of Professor [J. R. R.] Tolkien Still less will the common recipe prepare us for the curious shift from the matter-of-fact beginnings of his story . . . to the saga-like tone of the later chapters. . . . Prediction is dangerous: but 'The Hobbit' may well prove a classic."

TOLSTOY, LEO, GRAF, 1828-1910. The death of Ivan Ilyich and Confession; 224 p. 2013 Liveright Publishing Corporation

1. Death—Fiction 2. Death—Religious aspects 3. Despair 4. Memoirs 5. Russian fiction

ISBN 0871404265; 9780871404268 (hardcover)

LC 2013-018533

SUMMARY: In this book, translator Peter Carson presents English versions of fiction and nonfiction works by Leo Tolstoy. "Unlike so many previous translations that have tried to smooth out Tolstoy's rough edges, Carson presents a translation that captures the verisimilitude and psychological realism of the original Russian text." (Publisher's note)

REVIEW: *Atlantic* v312 no4 p46 N 2013 Ann Hulbert

"The Death of Ivan Ilyich & Confession." "It's perhaps little wonder that these two short works seem never to have been published as a pair before: a double dose of memento mori is a lot to take. But putting them back-to-back, with the fiction first--rendered in Peter Carson's stunning, unvarnished translation--is a brilliantly timed stroke. . . . Tolstoy's own discovery of faith after his long turmoil may not be for everyone. But the master's self-scrutinizing example is: When the author of 'War and Peace' doubts the meaning of his life, who dares to be complacent?"

REVIEW: *Christ Today* v57 no9 p72 N 2013

REVIEW: *Publ Wkly* v260 no31 p47 Ag 5 2013

REVIEW: *TLS* no5773 p5 N 22 2013 DONALD RAYFIELD

"The Death of Ivan Ilyich and Confession." "'The Death of Ivan Ilyich' (1886) crowns [Leo] Tolstoy's many attempts to describe the one experience nobody can personally report. Like 'Confession' (1884) it also shows him fighting, not always successfully, the influence . . . of Arthur Schopenhauer, an enormous portrait of whom hung over the couch in Tolstoy ' s study. . . . Over the past hundred years we have had numerous versions, from serviceable to excellent, of the major works. This volume, however, is arguably the best so far, not just because Peter Carson makes no mistakes, but because he has found the perfect balance in English, which tolerates repetition less than Tolstoy did, to provide a text retaining all the hypnotic power of the original."

REVIEW: *Va Q Rev* v90 no1 p212-7 Wint 2014 William Giraldi

TOMARKEN, EDWARD. Filmspeak; How to Understand Literary Theory by Way of Movies; [by] Edward Tomarken 208 p. 2012 Continuum Intl Pub Group

1. Criticism 2. Film theory 3. Literature—History & criticism—Theory, etc. 4. Motion picture literature 5. Philosophical literature

ISBN 0826428924; 9780826428929

SUMMARY: It was the author's intent to demonstrate "how once arcane literary and cultural theory has infiltrated popular culture. . . . Edward L. Tomarken explains how it is possible to study the rudiments of literary theory by watching and analyzing contemporary mainstream movies--from 'The Dark Knight' to 'Kill Bill'. . . . Theorists discussed include [Michel] Foucault . . . [and Hélène] Cixous." (Publisher's note)

REVIEW: *Choice* v50 no6 p1034 F 2013 W. W. Dixon

REVIEW: *TLS* no5755 p22 Jl 19 2013 BEN JEFFERY

"Once-Told Tales" and "Filmspeak: How to Understand Literary Theory by Watching Movies." "Unfortunately, 'Once-Told Tales' is something of an exemplar for this kind of philosophy at its least inspiring, insofar as it leaves the reader with the impression of having been laboriously told not a great deal. . . . [Edward L.] Tomarken's 'Filmspeak' initially seems like less substantial fare. . . . It does, however, bear on some of Tomarken's more specialized work. . . . The pace means that, even on the book's own entry-level terms, he sometimes underestimates the opacity of the theory he is presenting. . . . Even so, some of his examples are wonderful."

TOMKINS, CALVIN. Marcel Duchamp; The Afternoon Interviews; [by] Calvin Tomkins 110 p. 2013 Distributed Art Pub Inc

1. Artists—Attitudes 2. Artists—Interviews 3. Dadaism 4. Duchamp, Marcel, 1887-1968 5. Interviews 6. Modern art—20th century

ISBN 1936440393; 9781936440399

SUMMARY: This book presents a series of interviews with artist Marcel Duchamp, conducted in 1964 by Calvin Tomkins. "Casual yet insightful, Duchamp reveals himself as a man and an artist whose playful principles toward living freed him to make art that was as unpredictable, complex, and surprising as life itself." The book "includes an introductory interview with Tomkins reflecting on Duchamp as an artist, guide and friend." (Publisher's note)

REVIEW: *Art Am* v101 no9 p64 O 2013

"Dada and Beyond," "Generation Dada: The Berlin Avant-Garde and the First World War," and "Marcel Duchamp: The Afternoon Interviews." "Paying particular attention to lesser-known Dada figures, sixteen essayists explore the movement's links to Surrealism and a host of later art developments featuring chance operations and automatism. . . . While Berlin Club Dada members such as George Grosz, John Heartfield and Raoul Hausmann espoused the topical, transitory and inane, they also worked tirelessly to spread and preserve the influence of their art. . . . These previously unreleased interviews, conducted in [Marcel] Duchamp's New York home in 1964, reveal the master at his playful, ever-provocative ease."

REVIEW: *Art Am* v101 no2 p20 F 2013

TOPOL, JÁCHYM, 1962-. The Devil's Workshop; [by] Jáchym Topol 160 p. 2013 Portobello Books

1. Concentration camps—Fiction 2. Czechoslovakia 3. Holocaust survivors—Fiction 4. Memory—Fiction 5.

Psychological fiction
ISBN 1846274176; 9781846274176

SUMMARY: In this book, "the concentration camp may have been liberated years ago, but its walls still cast their long shadows . . . . When the camp is marked for demolition, one of the survivors begins a campaign to preserve it. . . . But before long, the authorities impose a brutal crack-down, leaving only an 'official' memorial and three young collaborators whose commitment to the act of remembering will drive them ever closer to the evils they hoped to escape." (Publisher's note)

REVIEW: *Booklist* v110 no17 p30 My 1 2014 Connie Fletcher

REVIEW: *Kirkus Rev* v82 no8 p185 Ap 15 2014

REVIEW: *Libr J* v139 no7 p80 Ap 15 2014 Andrea Tarr

REVIEW: *TLS* no5765 p20 S 27 2013 DANIEL MEDIN

"The Jew Car" and "The Devil's Workshop." "[Franz] Fühmann pairs phases of his youth with key moments in the Third Reich's rise and fall--a set of parallel narratives that justify calling the book a novel and allow the story of a life to stand in for the story of a nation. . . . Driven by [Jáchuym] Topol's ingenuity and mischief, these commercial passages are easily the funniest of the novel. . . . In the novel's second part, the humour grows corrosive. . . . 'The Devil's Workshop' is a miracle of compression, its scope greater than ought to be possible for a book of its length. It should help to cement Jáchym Topol's reputation as one of the most original and compelling European voices at work today."

TORDAY, PIERS. The last wild; [by] Piers Torday 322 p. 2014 Viking, an imprint of Penguin Group (USA) Inc.
1. Animals—Fiction 2. Diseases—Fiction 3. Human-animal communication—Fiction 4. Science fiction 5. Selective mutism—Fiction
ISBN 0670015547; 9780670015542; 9780670015559 (hardcover)
LC 2013-011240

SUMMARY: Author Piers Torday "introduces 12-year-old Kester Jaynes, a prisoner at Spectrum Hall Academy for Challenging Children. Kester's world was turned upside down by the death of his mother six years earlier. . . . The larger world is . . . wrecked by global warming and 'the red-eye,' which killed off most animal life and threatens humans. . . . One day, Kester is stunned to discover he can communicate with cockroaches, pigeons, and other 'varmints,' who ask him for help." (Publishers Weekly)

REVIEW: *Booklist* v111 no4 p60 O 15 2014 Amanda Blau

REVIEW: *Bull Cent Child Books* v67 no8 p423 Ap 2014 K. Q. G.

"The Last Wild". "His subsequent journey—to find the research left: behind by his veterinarian father and thwart the company behind Formula-A and the redeye—is equal parts thrilling and poignant; Kester revels in new friendships, escapes dastardly bad guys, grieves for lost companions, and dares to hope that perhaps he can make a difference. A few dashes of humor, in the forms of a confused pigeon, a dance-obsessed mouse, and a comically arrogant wolf, add levity to the seriousness of Kester's situation, and Kester himself is an appealing Everykid. Animal lovers are the obvious audience here, but so are middle-graders intrigued by post-apocalyptic worlds but not quite ready for the grimness of YA dystopias."

REVIEW: *SLJ* v60 no8 p52 Ag 2014 Deanna Romriell

REVIEW: *Voice of Youth Advocates* v37 no2 p85 Je 2014 Liz Sundermann

TORRENTE, MARCOS GIRALT. The End of Love; 176 p. 2013 McSweeney's
1. Divorce—Fiction 2. Love stories 3. Short stories 4. Social classes—Fiction 5. Travelers—Fiction
ISBN 1938073568; 9781938073564

SUMMARY: This book presents four short stories by Marcos Giralt Torrente. "Two tourists visit a remote island off the coast of Africa and are undone by a disconcerting encounter with another couple. A young man, enchanted by his bohemian cousin and her husband, watches them fall into a state of resentful dependence over the course of decades. A chaste but all-consuming love affair between a troubled boy and a wealthy but equally troubled girl leaves a scar that never heals." (Publisher's note)

REVIEW: *Bookforum* v20 no4 p24 D 2013/Ja 2014 BENJAMIN ANASTAS

"The End of Love." "The four stories that make up 'The End of Love' are so good at evoking absences that I would call them elliptical machines, but that would create the wrong associations and do this prizewinning writer from Madrid an injustice. Thanks to Katherine Silver's translations, which hardly break a sweat, . . . Giralt Torrente's first publication in the United States arrives with the force of the unexpected, the nervous excitement of a first encounter. The sense of loss pervading the stories only makes them linger more potently in the mind. . . . There is a balance to these stories that suggests they were conceived of as a book, rather than being merely collected, a formal and thematic unity that makes it feel, at times, as if you're reading a novel."

REVIEW: *Booklist* v110 no4 p16 O 15 2013 Diego Bdez

REVIEW: *Kirkus Rev* v81 no18 p119 S 15 2013

REVIEW: *Publ Wkly* v260 no28 p144 Jl 15 2013

TORRES, JOHN. Joe Flacco; [by] John Torres 32 p. 2014 Mitchell Lane Publishers
1. Children's nonfiction 2. Determination (Personality trait) 3. Football players—United States—Biography—Juvenile literature 4. Super Bowl (Football game)
ISBN 9781612284569 (library bound)
LC 2013-027509

SUMMARY: This book on football player Joe Flacco is part of the "Robbie Reader: Contemporary Biography" series, which presents "a brief look at each player's childhood and high-school

play before launching into their award-winning sports careers. . . . 'Joe Flacco' describes how determination helped this football quarterback achieve many goals, including a Super Bowl championship." (Booklist)

REVIEW: *Booklist* v110 no13 p66 Mr 1 2014 Angela Leeper

"Andrew Luck," "Buster Posey," and "Joe Flacco." "Good sports biographies are a must for any school or public library, and these titles in the Robbie Reader: Contemporary Biography series satisfy this need. Each book begins with a dramatic scene from the athlete's pro career, which ensures further reading. The large, accessible text continues with a brief look at each player's childhood and high-school play before launching into their award-winning sports careers. .

. . A chronology, glossary, career statistics, and other back matter will further gratify sports enthusiasts."

TORREY, E. FULLER (EDWIN FULLER), 1937-. American psychosis; how the federal government destroyed the mental illness treatment system; [by] E. Fuller (Edwin Fuller) Torrey 224 p. 2014 Oxford University Press

1. Medical literature 2. Mental health policy—United States 3. Mental health services—United States—Evaluation 4. Mentally ill—Care—United States—History 5. Mentally ill—Services for—United States

ISBN 0199988714; 9780199988716

LC 2013-017565

SUMMARY: This book, by E. Fuller Torrey, is "about the inability of government agencies and private institutions to care well for the severely mentally ill. . . . Torrey focuses . . . on the historical reasons for the . . . situation, with special emphasis on the family of President John F. Kennedy. . . . [He] explains how community jails and state prisons have become the new centers for warehousing severely mentally ill individuals." (Kirkus Reviews)

REVIEW: *Choice* v51 no8 p1439-40 Ap 2014 R. L. Jones

"American Psychosis: How the Federal Government Destroyed the Mental Illness Treatment System". "Here, [E. Fuller] Torrey . . . draws on his personal experience at the National Institute of Mental Health when the federal mental health program was being developed. . . . He examines how mental health ideology, politics, underfunding, and outright neglect has prevented this program from reaching its potential and has actually caused harm. Torrey connects the closing of state mental hospitals with increased community violence, homelessness, and incarceration of the mentally ill. He does provide a chapter on suggested solutions, but it is clear that unless the public better understands the issues confronting the mental health system, improvement will be slow and limited."

REVIEW: *Kirkus Rev* v81 no15 p334 Ag 1 2013

REVIEW: *Natl Rev* v65 no19 p44-5 O 14 2013 THEODORE DALRYMPLE

REVIEW: *New York Times* v163 no56381 pD2 Ja 14 2014 RICHARD A. FRIEDMAN

"American Psychosis: How the Federal Government Destroyed the Mental Illness Treatment System". "That subtitle is the opening shot across the bow in this jeremiad of a book by the psychiatrist Dr. E. Fuller Torrey. . . . The sorry of what happened to the half-million Americans who were deinstitutionalized over the past 50 years is the subject of this unsparing and lively takedown of American psychiatry. . . . Curiously, he does not explore the possibility that better psychiatric treatment might well reduce the risk of suicide. . . . Dr. Torrey's solutions for our broken mental health care system are mostly thoughtful, though not everyone will like them. . . . This wise and unflinching book is an object lesson in good intentions gone awry on a grand scale. It should be widely read."

TORREY, E. FULLER (EDWIN FULLER), 1937-. The martyrdom of abolitionist Charles Torrey; [by] E. Fuller (Edwin Fuller) Torrey 239 p. 2013 Louisiana State University Press

1. Abolitionists—Maryland—Biography 2. Abolitionists—United States—Biography 3. Antislavery movements—Maryland—History—19th century 4. Clergy—New England—Biography 5. Fugitive slaves—Maryland—History—19th century 6. Historical literature 7. Underground Railroad—Maryland

ISBN 9780807152317 (cloth: alk. paper)

LC 2013-008666

SUMMARY: In this book, E. Fuller Torrey argues that "Charles Torrey pushed the abolitionist movement to become more political and active. He helped advance the faction that challenged the leadership of William Lloyd Garrison, provoking an irreversible schism in the movement and making Torrey and Garrison bitter enemies. Torrey played an important role in the formation of the Liberty Party and in the emergence of political abolitionism." (Publisher's note)

REVIEW: *Choice* v51 no8 p1476-7 Ap 2014 L. B. Gimelli

"The Martyrdom of Abolitionist Charles Torrey". "The author, who has kinship ties with his subject, contends that Torrey's active years in the abolitionist movement were often contentious but significant. This is particularly true of his opposition to the increasing presence of women in the movement, a presence that William Lloyd Garrison and his followers championed. In addition, together with like-minded abolitionists, Torrey shifted the focus of abolition from the moral suasion tactics of the Garrisonians to political activism, which gained the acrimony of the Garrisonians. . . . Both African American and white abolitionists memorialized Torrey. Readers interested in the abolitionist movement and its internal disputes should find this an appealing and enlightening book."

TORSELLO, DAVIDE. The new environmentalism?; civil society and corruption in the enlarged EU; [by] Davide Torsello viii, 206 p. 2011 Ashgate

1. Corruption—European Union countries 2. Environmentalism—Europe 3. Political participation—European Union countries 4. Social movements—Europe 5. Social science literature

ISBN 9781409423645 (hardback: alk. paper); 9781409423652 (ebook)

LC 2011-031611

SUMMARY: This book, "focusing on environmental movements across Central Europe and Northern Italy . . . explores the ways in which environmental movements deal with tensions between the local nature of environmental problems and global and transnational dimensions of environmental politics. . . . It examines the development of civil society in postsocialist contexts . . . [and] focuses on the ways in which narratives of corruption intersect with environmental agendas and activism." (Contemporary Sociology)

REVIEW: *Contemp Sociol* v43 no2 p275-6 Mr 2014 Diana Mincyte

"The New Environmentalism? Civil Society and Corruption in the Enlarged EU". "While [Davide] Torsello brings an important contribution to the scholarship on environmentalism in Central Europe, his book would have, nevertheless, benefitted from a deeper engagement with the existing literature on this topic. . . . Making use of direct quotes from the interviews and including more ethnographic materials would strengthen the analysis of the environmental agendas. . . . Combining a sophisticated theoretical framework with case study analyses, 'The New Environmentalism?' is a timely book which will be of interest to scholars and students in environmental studies, social anthropology, political sociology, human geography, mobility studies, and

European studies."

TORSETER, ØYVIND. The hole; 64 p. 2013 Enchanted Lion Books

1. Apartment buildings—Fiction 2. Cities & towns—Fiction 3. Holes—Fiction 4. Laboratories 5. Picture books for children

ISBN 9781592701438 (hardback)

LC 2013-029591

SUMMARY: In this book, "the human-like main character with a strange shaped head trips on the hole as he is unpacking in the kitchen of his new apartment. The hole then moves from place to place. Finally upset by this, the person character traps the hole in a box and takes it to a laboratory where the interested scientists test it and ask to keep it 'for the moment.' But the hole has a mind of its own." (Children's Literature)

REVIEW: *Horn Book Magazine* v89 no6 p84 N/D 2013 JOANNA RUDGE LONG

"Hole." "[Øyvind] Torseter's spare pen drawings exude a quiet humor as this everyman seeks the meaning of what is, after all, a ubiquitous nothing—or anything. Other figures, including oblivious bystanders, are amusingly varied, while economically suggested interiors and cityscapes offer amusing details as well as scope for the imagination. Occasional areas of color--sunlight, cardboard tan, twilight blue--focus attention and enhance mood. A peruse-more-than-once conversation-starter that may also appeal to older graphic novel fans."

REVIEW: *Kirkus Rev* v81 no16 p300 Ag 15 2013

"The Hole." "The Norwegian illustrator [and author Oyvind Torseter] pokes a pencil-sized hole through both covers and all 64 pages of this outing--but then doesn't do much with it. In very plain, nearly wordless line drawings with pale monochromatic highlights, Torseter depicts a cartoon figure (a lanky creature with a face like a hippo) who spots the hole in the wall of his new apartment. . . . Though the hole may take a moment to spot in some scenes, it is too small to have any significant visual impact. . . . A one-trick pony--and the trick's not all that great."

REVIEW: *Publ Wkly* v260 no31 p69 Ag 5 2013

TORSETER, ØYVIND.il. My father's arms are a boat. See Lunde, S.

TOTALLY UNOFFICIAL; the autobiography of Raphael Lemkin; 328 p. 2013 Yale University Press

1. Autobiographies 2. BIOGRAPHY & AUTOBIOGRAPHY—Historical 3. BIOGRAPHY & AUTOBIOGRAPHY—Political 4. Genocide—Prevention 5. HISTORY—Holocaust 6. Human rights workers—Poland—Biography 7. Human rights workers—United States—Biography 8. Lawyers—Poland—Biography 9. Lawyers—United States—Biography 10. World War, 1939-1945—Atrocities

ISBN 9780300186963 (hardback)

LC 2012-051175

SUMMARY: This book presents the autobiography of activist Raphael Lemkin, who "lived an extraordinary life of struggle and hardship, yet altered international law and redefined the world's understanding of group rights. He invented the concept and word 'genocide' and propelled the idea into international legal status. An uncommonly creative pioneer in ethical thought, he twice was nominated for the Nobel Peace Prize." (Publisher's note)

REVIEW: *Kirkus Rev* v81 no2 p62-3 Je 1 2013

REVIEW: *New Repub* v244 no15 p46-51 S 16 2013 Michael Ignatieff

"Totally Unofficial: The Autobiography of Raphael Lemkin." "Donna-Lee Frieze, an Australian scholar, spent four years in the New York Public Library, where the Lemkin papers are deposited, reading faded typescripts, collating different drafts, deciphering illegible scribbles, and occasionally filling in gaps between or within sentences. Now she has published Lemkin's autobiography under his chosen title. . . . Frieze has performed a labor of love with the materials that Lemkin left behind, but her best efforts cannot manage to turn the fragments into a complete and coherent book. Important chunks of the narrative are missing. . . . It is at its most alive when he evokes his childhood in the Jewish world of Eastern Europe before World War I."

TOTEN, TERESA. The Unlikely Hero of Room 13B; [by] Teresa Toten 272 p. 2013 Doubleday Canada

1. Love stories 2. Mentally ill youth 3. Obsessive-compulsive disorder in adolescence 4. Support groups 5. Young adult fiction

ISBN 0385678347; 9780385678346

SUMMARY: In this young adult novel by Teresa Toten, "When Adam meets Robyn at a support group for kids coping with obsessive-compulsive disorder, he is drawn to her almost before he can take a breath. . . . But when you're fourteen and the everyday problems of dealing with divorced parents and step-siblings are supplemented by the challenges of OCD, it's hard to imagine yourself falling in love." (Publisher's note)

REVIEW: *Quill Quire* v79 no7 p35 S 2013 Cara Smusiak

"The Unlikely Hero of Room 13B." "The frenetic compulsions of (almost) 15-year-old Adam Spencer Ross vibrate off the pages of Toronto author Teresa Toten's latest YA novel. In the space of a heart-beat, Adam falls for Robyn, the newest member of his support group for adolescents with obsessive-compulsive disorder. . . . Toten masterfully portrays the turbulent emotions and deep-seated fears of someone suffering from mental illness. . . . Ultimately, the book draws the reader in with its emotional intensity and sophistication."

TOTH, SUSAN ALLEN. No saints around here; a caregiver's days; 64 p. 2014 University of Minnesota Press

1. Death 2. Husband & wife 3. Memoirs 4. Parkinson's disease 5. Women caregivers

ISBN 9780816692866 (pb: alk. paper)

LC 2013-034893

SUMMARY: This memoir by Susan Allen Toth records "her time as a caregiver during the last 18 months of her husband's life." He "had Parkinson's disease. . . . Once a successful architect, he declined both physically and mentally as the disease ravaged his body. The author was determined to care for him at home in the house he had designed for them. . . . Toth jotted down her thoughts, feelings and uncertainties, and she recorded the intimate details of caring for a helpless person." (Kirkus Reviews)

REVIEW: *Kirkus Rev* v82 no5 p137 Mr 1 2014

"No Saints Around Here: A Caregiver's Days". "A wife's frank memoir of her time as a caregiver during the last 18 months of her husband's life. . . . They do what has to be done. While [Susan Allen] Toth makes it clear that she dearly loved the man she was caring for, she lets her fatigue, guilt, frustrations, fraying patience and even exasperation show. . . . That may be the book's greatest value—that caregivers of loved ones reading it will take comfort in knowing that what they are going through has been shared by many others. An inward-looking account with an important take-home message: Caring for a dying loved one is a demanding task, and caregivers are only human."

TÖTTÖSY, ERNEST. Mind Twisters; Memories for the Future; 192 p. 2012 CreateSpace Independent Publishing Platform

1. Hungary—Politics & government 2. Memoirs 3. Political prisoners 4. Schizophrenia 5. Torture

ISBN 147816817X; 9781478168171

SUMMARY: "[Ernest] Töttösy's first memoir, translated by [Helen M.] Szablya, delves into his psyche under the extreme stress of torture, as well as his mental destabilization as a result of hallucinogenic drugs he ingested under duress in 1952 and '53. During Stalin's reign, the Hungarian secret police, the AVH, were utterly ruthless in extracting confessions from their political prisoners." (Kirkus Reviews)

REVIEW: *Kirkus Rev* p54 D 15 2013 supplemet best books 2013

"Mind Twisters: Memories for the Future". "[Ernest] Töttösy's resilience will stagger even the most stoic reader. . . . The fact that his memory remained so sharp in the grip of mental illness and abuse is miraculous. [Helen M.] Szablya's fluid translation carries the weight of historical importance, providing deep insights into the hidden brutality of the AVH. More information and research about the Hungarian regime may have strengthened the work's readability to those unfamiliar with the surrounding history, but this unflinching portrayal of inhumanity will capture anyone's attention."

REVIEW: *Kirkus Rev* v81 no9 p122 My 1 2013

TOUGIAS, MICHAEL J. The finest hours. See Sherman, C.

TOWNS, JEFF. The Pubs of Dylan Thomas; 192 p. 2014 Dufour Editions

1. Alcoholics 2. Bars (Drinking establishments) 3. Poets—Biography 4. Thomas, Dylan, 1914-1953 5. Welsh poets

ISBN 1847716938; 9781847716934

SUMMARY: "One of the main experts on the life of Dylan Thomas, Jeff Towns, is launching a brand new and revealing book, 'Dylan Thomas: The Pubs.' Tired of the lazy clichéd description of Dylan as a Bohemian drunken poet, scrounger and womaniser, Jeff Towns and artist Wyn Thomas decided to investigate exactly what role pubs and alcohol had played in his remarkable life. . . . A pictoral tour of some of the pubs Dylan Thomas attended in Swansea, west Wales, Oxford, London and the USA." (Publisher's note)

REVIEW: *TLS* no5780 p26 Ja 10 2014 MATT STURROCK

"Dylan Thomas: The Pubs." "What follows is a curious biography-cum-travel guide, in which we are presented with twenty short chapters, each devoted to an establishment the great man once roistered and declaimed in. . . . The result is slightly shambolic, with occasional lapses into idle speculation, and the winking prose, thick with exclamation marks, may be fatiguing for some readers. But Towns, a Wales-based bookseller who specializes in Dylan Thomas-related publications and ephemera, does have unquestionable expertise, and effectively marshals here an array of primary and secondary sources. . . . Appealing illustrations by his collaborator, Wyn Thomas, lend additional colour to the overall production."

TOWNSEND, ANTHONY M., 1973-. Smart cities; big data, civic hackers, and the quest for a new utopia; [by] Anthony M. Townsend 400 p. 2013 W W Norton & Co Inc

1. Cities and towns—History 2. City planning—Technological innovations 3. City planning literature 4. Information technology—Economic aspects 5. Regional planning—Technological innovations 6. Technological innovations—Economic aspects

ISBN 0393082873; 9780393082876 (hardcover)

LC 2013-012755

SUMMARY: In this book, author Anthony M. Townsend "takes a broad historical look at the forces that have shaped the planning and design of cities and information technologies from the rise of the great industrial cities of the nineteenth century to the present. As technology barons, entrepreneurs, mayors, and an emerging vanguard of civic hackers are trying to shape this new frontier, 'Smart Cities' considers the motivations, aspirations, and shortcomings of them all." (Publisher's note)

REVIEW: *Booklist* v110 no2 p9-10 S 15 2013 Carl Hays

"Smart Cities: Big Data, Civic Hackers, and the Quest for a New Utopia." "In this far-reaching overview of all the ways computer technology is transforming life for today's metropolitan dwellers, urban planning specialist [Anthony] Townsend takes a look at how modern cities around the world are upgrading their infrastructure for the Internet age. . . . Although the omnipresent surveillance that accompanies this interconnectivity may make some readers nervous, Townsend persuasively demonstrates how ubiquitous information resources can provide more protection, as it did in the Boston marathon bombing case, and facilitate a more comfortable, less stress-inducing city-living experience."

REVIEW: *Choice* v51 no6 p1103-4 F 2014 P. Gamsby

REVIEW: *Kirkus Rev* v81 no20 p10 O 15 2013

REVIEW: *N Y Times Book Rev* p26 Ja 5 2014 Daniel Brook

"Smart Cities: Big Data, Civic Hackers, and the Quest for a New Utopia." "Guiding us through the nexus of urbanization and digital technology is [author Anthony M.] Townsend, the rare technologist who is in the know without being in the tank. . . . Rather than again turning over our collective future to the 'paternalistic philosophy' of multinational corporations, 'Smart Cities' endorses 'civic hackers' who create public-interest apps tailored to their hometowns. . . . Less a to-do list than a framework and a sensibility, 'Smart Cities' is a timely and necessary guide to this age of the Franken-city."

REVIEW: *Nation* v298 no5 p35-7 F 3 2014 CATHERINE TUMBER

"Smart Cities: Big Data, Civic Hackers, and the Quest for a New Utopia." "Those who enjoy the convenience of social media, smartphones and GPS but are uneasy about being data-tracked--and perhaps are befuddled by what's at stake in the apparent war between Silicon Valley titans and hipster hacker heroes--could do worse than turn to Townsend for guidance. . . . he has written a generous book in clean prose, one that will engage both advanced geeks and cyberdolts--willful and otherwise--who merely tolerate terms like 'open source' and are only dimly aware of how the Internet works."

REVIEW: *Publ Wkly* v260 no33 p59 Ag 19 2013

TOWNSEND, JACINDA. Saint monkey; a novel; [by] Jacinda Townsend 352 p. 2104 W W Norton & Co Inc

1. African-Americans—Kentucky—Fiction 2. Friendship in children—Kentucky—Fiction 3. Historical fiction 4. Singers—Kentucky—Fiction 5. Successful people—Kentucky—Fiction
ISBN 9780393080049 (hardcover)
LC 2013-041186

SUMMARY: This book "chronicles the lives of two black girls growing up in the dusty Appalachian mountains of Kentucky in the era of segregation. As children, Audrey and Caroline are bound together by their unpopularity, They grow apart during high school" and Audrey later becomes "a jazz musician in Harlem. . . . . Back home, Caroline struggles to take care of her ailing grandmother and bring some money into the house." (Publishers Weekly)

REVIEW: *Booklist* v110 no9/10 p56 Ja 1 2014 Donna Seaman

"Saint Monkey." "The women take turns narrating, and stellar first novelist [Jacinda] Townsend renders their opposite lives with stunningly sensuous and revelatory detail. Her characters' struggles form one long dance of need and denial, jealousy and longing that embodies the anguish of women's lives compounded by brutal racial prejudice. As Townsend intimately and indelibly illuminates the psychological traumas of the times, she asks profoundly personal questions about staying and going, sacrifice and ambition. This is a breathtakingly insightful, suspenseful, and gorgeously realized novel of cruelty and sorrow, anger and forgiveness, improvisation and survival, and the transcendent beauty of nature and art."

REVIEW: *Kirkus Rev* v81 no24 p178 D 15 2013

REVIEW: *N Y Times Book Rev* p9 Ap 20 2014 AYANA MATHIS

REVIEW: *New York Times* v163 no56425 pC6 F 27 2014 Carmela Ciuraru

REVIEW: *Publ Wkly* v260 no51 p37 D 16 2013

TOWNSEND, TIM. Mission at Nuremberg; An American Army Chaplain and the Trial of the Nazis; [by] Tim Townsend 400 p. 2014 HarperCollins

1. Gerecke, Henry 2. Goering, Hermann, 1893-1946 3. Historical literature 4. Nuremberg War Crime Trials, Nuremberg, Germany, 1945-1949 5. World War, 1939-1945—Chaplains
ISBN 0061997196; 9780061997198

SUMMARY: In this book, author Tim Townsend tells the "story of the American Army chaplain sent to save the souls of the Nazis incarcerated at Nuremberg. . . . Lutheran minister Henry Gerecke was fifty years old when he enlisted as am Army chaplain during World War II. . . . At the war's end, when other soldiers were coming home, Gerecke was recruited for the most difficult engagement of his life: ministering to the twenty-one Nazis leaders awaiting trial at Nuremburg." (Publisher's note)

REVIEW: *Booklist* v110 no11 p6 F 1 2014 Eloise Kinney

REVIEW: *Kirkus Rev* v82 no2 p184 Ja 15 2014

"Mission at Nuremberg: An American Army Chaplain and the Trial of the Nazis". "Passages recalling the middle-aged St. Louis preacher's counseling of [Hermann] Goering (and the decision to deny the Luftwaffe commander Holy Communion) and Gerecke's first meeting with Rudolf Hess are especially well-done. [Tim] Townsend authoritatively addresses the excruciating moral and religious issues confronting wartime chaplains and deftly explains the role of a spiritual adviser in bringing the wrongdoer, even one seemingly beyond redemption, back to 'a place of restoration.' [Henry] Gerecke's story is only a footnote to 'the trial of the century,' but Townsend thoroughly understands and skillfully handles the rich, potentially explosive material it contains."

REVIEW: *Libr J* v138 no16 p58 O 1 2013 Barbara Hoffert

REVIEW: *Publ Wkly* v261 no4 p184-5 Ja 27 2014

TOWNSHEND, CHARLES. The Republic; [by] Charles Townshend 560 p. 2013 Allen Lane

1. Historical literature 2. Home rule—Ireland 3. Ireland—History—Civil War, 1922-1923 4. Ireland—Military history—20th century 5. Irish question
ISBN 0713999837; 9780713999839

SUMMARY: "Charles Townshend's 'Easter 1916' opened up the astonishing events around the Rising for a new generation and in 'The Republic' he deals, with the same unflinchingly wish to get to the truth behind the legend, with the most critical years in Ireland's history. . . . The picture painted by Townshend . . . never loses sight of the ordinary forms of heroism performed by Irish men and women trapped in extraordinary times." (Publisher's note)

REVIEW: *TLS* no5793 p24 Ap 11 2014 CLAIR WILLS

"The Republic: The Fight for Irish Independence." "Charles Townshend's last book, his authoritative and fast-paced history of the Easter Rising of 1916, ended with the suppression of the rebellion by the British commander General Sir John Maxwell. . . . Townshend picks up the story in 1918. . . . He is strongest on the military campaigns, and offers a fascinating account of the development of guerrilla-style fighting, which was unfamiliar to both sides. . . . Charles Townshend has written a wonderfully readable and yet comprehensive history which accounts for that messy and intractable situation."

TOYE, RICHARD. The Roar of the Lion; The Untold Story of Churchill's World War II Speeches; [by] Richard Toye 336 p. 2013 Oxford University Press

1. Churchill, Winston, Sir, 1874-1965 2. Great Britain—Politics & government—1936-1945 3. Historical literature 4. Political oratory—History 5. World War, 1939-1945—Great Britain
ISBN 0199642524; 9780199642526

SUMMARY: In this book on the World War II speeches of British Prime Minister Winston Churchill, author Richard Toye argues that "mass enthusiasm sat side-by-side with considerable criticism and dissent from ordinary people" in response to the speeches. "There were speeches that stimulated, invigorated, and excited many, but there were also speeches which caused depression and disappointment in many others and which sometimes led to workplace or family arguments." (Publisher's note)

REVIEW: *Choice* v51 no9 p1669 My 2014 R. A. Callahan

REVIEW: *Hist Today* v63 no10 p63-4 O 2013 TAYLOR DOWNING

"The Roar of the Lion: The Untold Story of Churchill's World War II Speeches." "Ther are few national myths as enduring as those surrounding [Winston] Churchill's legendary, wartime speeches. . . . So Richard Toye appears to take on the mantle of an angry iconoclast by arguing that the impact they had at the time was far more mixed than posterity allows for. . . . Toye's scholarly arguments, however, are largely convincing. . . . The flaw with much of what Toye argues is that he does not distinguish clearly enough between how people took in the speeches. . . . Toye is at his best when he follows the trail of the collaborative process through which many speeches were written."

REVIEW: *Libr J* v138 no11 p103 Je 15 2013 Randall M. Miller

REVIEW: *N Y Times Book Rev* p12-3 D 1 2013 BENJAMIN SCHWARZ

REVIEW: *TLS* no5780 p10 Ja 10 2014 RICHARD OVERY

TRACY, KRISTEN. Hung up; [by] Kristen Tracy 288 p. 2014 Simon Pulse

1. Dating (Social customs)—Fiction 2. Friendship—Fiction 3. Love stories 4. Telephone calls—Fiction

ISBN 144246075X; 9781442460751 (hardback)

LC 2013-042272

SUMMARY: In this book, "Lucy's trying to leave messages about an order she placed but is actually leaving them on James' voicemail; when James finally picks up and explains, the two begin to banter, and a telephone relationship is born. That relationship becomes close and confessional, but as it moves toward meeting in person Lucy begins to worry, because she hasn't been honest with James about who she really is." (Bulletin of the Center for Children's Books)

REVIEW: *Booklist* v110 no14 p75 Mr 15 2014 Jeanne Fredriksen

REVIEW: *Bull Cent Child Books* v67 no7 p381 Mr 2014 D. S.

"Hung Up." "[Kristen] Tracy musters a rapid-fire banter for her conversants (in dialogue ormatted like a playscript) that's mannered yet witty and funny. . . . The eventual revelations are foreshadowed rather than coming as surprises, so the pleasure here is watching the protagonists gradually trust each other with more of the truth. While it's overall somewhat more artful than authentic, the play between James and Lucy is rhythmic and entertaining, and the format could prompt a readers' theater performance or serve as an inspiration for young writers to create their own dialogue narratives."

REVIEW: *Kirkus Rev* v82 no3 p66 F 1 2014

"Hung Up". "n a narrative rendered entirely in voice mails, text messages and transcribed phone conversations, James and Lucy gradually go from strangers to romance. Lucy starts it off by calling what she thinks is the customer-service number of a company she's ordered a plaque from, but it's actually James' new phone number. . . . Once they get past the initial confusion, their conversations are full of teasing, casual and funny. As the back and forth continues, more serious subjects gradually arise, and eventually they become confidants, more candid with each other in this mediated relationship than they might be in person. . . . Appealing characters stand out in a quick read that is a lighthearted look at how real friendships develop, grow and deepen."

REVIEW: *Publ Wkly* v260 no51 p62 D 16 2013

TRAMMELL, REBECCA. Enforcing the convict code; violence and prison culture; [by] Rebecca Trammell ix, 157 p. 2012 Lynne Rienner Publishers

1. Prison administration—United States 2. Prison conditions 3. Prison gangs 4. Prison violence—United States 5. Prisoners—United States 6. Sociology literature

ISBN 158826808X; 9781588268082 (hc : alk. paper)

LC 2011-028656

SUMMARY: In this book, author "Rebecca Trammell illuminates the social code that prisoners enforce--in defiance of official rules and regulations--to maintain a predictable order. Trammell also compares the experiences of male and female prisoners, underscoring the role of gender and sexual assault in shaping life behind bars. Equally important, she explores the significance of prison culture for the fate of convicts when they leave the prison environment." (Publisher's note)

REVIEW: *Contemp Sociol* v42 no5 p753-5 S 2013 Thomas Ugelvik

"Enforcing the Convict Code: Violence and Prison Culture." "According to [author Rebecca] Trammell, the convict code, an informal yet highly influential set of subcultural norms governing everyday life in prisons, works as a tool which prisoners use to make their environment controllable by curbing the disruptive behavior of others. By organizing their lives and controlling each other, the gang members retain or reconstruct some semblance of autonomy and control. . . . Trammell's aim is to examine how inmates socially and collectively construct the prison reality, and what effects this particular construction may have on prison violence. . . . In my view, she ends up not writing about how inmates construct reality, but how former inmates construct reality after release."

THE TRANSFORMATION OF SOLIDARITY; changing risks and the future of the Welfare state; 214 p. 2012 Amsterdam University Press

1. Netherlands—Social conditions 2. Social science literature 3. Welfare state—Economic aspects—European Union countries 4. Welfare state—European Union countries

ISBN 9089643834 (print); 9089643842; 9789048515318 (pdf); 9789048515530 (e-Pub); 9789089643834 (print); 9789089643841

LC 2012-424718

SUMMARY: In this book, the authors "ask whether globalization and individualization . . . have undermined support for the post-WWII welfare state and significantly altered the relationship between workers and firms." They also present "an examination of the Dutch welfare state and changes that it has undergone as part of the changes that have affected all developed economies." (Contemporary Sociology)

REVIEW: *Contemp Sociol* v43 no2 p276-8 Mr 2014 Ronald Angel

"The Transformation of Solidarity: Changing Risks and

the Future of the Welfare State". "The analyses in this book add empirical corroboration to other findings that document important changes in support for the welfare state. As in most other countries, the demand for individual accountability has grown. 'No rights without responsibilities' is a clear message of new third way solutions generally. Given the unique nature of this particular corporatist state, comparisons with other more liberal nations would have been useful. Nonetheless, one leaves the book with the sense that it reflects more than the idiosyncrasies of a particular system and reveals processes that are widespread in a globalized economic environment."

TRASLER, JANEE. Pottytime for chickies; 24 p. 2014 HarperFestival

1. Animal stories 2. Chicks 3. Parent & child—Juvenile literature 4. Picture books for children 5. Toilet training
ISBN 9780062274694 (board bk.)
LC 2013-938787

SUMMARY: In this children's story by Janee Trasler, "a pig, cow and sheep attempt to toilet train a brood of boisterous chicks. . . . The three Chickies tell each of their caregivers that they know what the potty is for and can use it independently. This assertion proves to be false, as the chicks splash in the water, play with the toilet paper and jump on the towels. With loving patience, their barnyard companions gently correct this behavior." (Kirkus Reviews)

REVIEW: *Kirkus Rev* v82 no13 p22 Jl 1 2014

REVIEW: *Kirkus Rev* v82 no3 p387 F 1 2014

"Pottytime for Chickies". "In lighthearted dialogue rendered in verse, the three Chickies tell each of their caregivers that they know what the potty is for and can use it independently. This assertion proves to be false, as the chicks splash in the water, play with the toilet paper and jump on the towels. With loving patience, their barnyard companions gently correct this behavior. . . . [Janee] Trasler employs a shaky line to create bold, droll cartoons on flecked and muted backgrounds. The chicks are pleasing in their simplicity: round yellow circles with dots for eyes and sideways V's for beaks. Spritely entertainment and gentle encouragement for toddlers."

TRASLER, JANEE.il. Pottytime for chickies. See Trasler, J.

A TRAVELED FIRST LADY; writings of Louisa Catherine Adams; 416 p. 2014 The Belknap Press of Harvard University Press

1. Letters 2. Politicians' spouses 3. Presidents' spouses—United States—Biography
ISBN 9780674048010 (alk. paper)
LC 2013-031131

SUMMARY: This book, by Louisa Catherine Adams, edited by Margaret A. Hogan and C. James Taylor, presents excerpts from the personal writings of the U.S. first lady Louisa Catherine Adams. "These excerpts from diaries and memoirs recount her early years in London and Paris . . . , her courtship and marriage to John Quincy Adams, her time in the lavish courts of Berlin and St. Petersburg as a diplomat's wife, and her years aiding John Quincy's political career in Washington." (Publisher's note)

REVIEW: *Choice* v51 no12 p2249 Ag 2014 T. K. Byron

REVIEW: *N Y Rev Books* v61 no10 p45-7 Je 5 2014 Susan Dunn

"John Quincy Adams: American Visionary," "Louisa Catherine: The Other Mrs. Adams," and "A Traveled First Lady: Writings of Louisa Catherine Adams." "As Fred Kaplan demonstrates in his engaging, well-crafted, and deeply researched biography . . . this supremely successful diplomat and shrewd practitioner of realpolitik had a personality quite unsuited for a life in politics. . . . In 'Louisa Catherine: The Other Mrs. Adams,' Margery Heffron's insightful and entertaining though unfinished book . . . we enter deeply into the damaged family life of John Quincy and Louisa. . . . A fine new sampling of Louisa's writings, 'A Traveled First Lady: Writings of Louisa Catherine Adams' [is] edited by Margaret A. Hogan and C. James Taylor."

REVIEW: *Publ Wkly* v261 no3 p45 Ja 20 2014

TREADWELL, HENRIE M. Beyond stereotypes in black and white; how everyday leaders can build healthier opportunities for African American boys and men; [by] Henrie M. Treadwell xxvi, 259 p. 2013 Praeger

1. African American boys—Health and hygiene 2. African American boys—Social conditions 3. African American men—Health and hygiene 4. African American men—Social conditions 5. Community leadership—United States 6. Leadership—United States 7. Social science literature
ISBN 1440803994; 9781440803994 (hbk. : alk. paper); 9781440804007 (ebook)
LC 2012-036575

SUMMARY: Author Henrie M. Treadwell's book "spotlights the plight of African American boys and men, examining multiple systems beyond education, incarceration, and employment to assess their impact on the mental and physical health of African American boys and men--and challenges everyday citizens to help start a social transformation." (Publisher's note)

REVIEW: *Choice* v51 no1 p175 S 2013 G. Parangimalil

"Beyond Stereotypes in Black and White: How Everyday Leaders Can Build Healthier Opportunities for African American Boys and Men." "Drawing from a repertoire of experience as a researcher and scholar, [author Henrie M.] Treadwell . . . presents a passionate account of the health crisis encountered by the underserved, particularly black men and boys. With poignant case studies and real-life examples, Treadwell demonstrates how a mostly lethargic leadership at both the national and local levels in conjunction with an array of inadequate and often indifferent public policies have had a devastating impact on this vulnerable segment of the population. . . . A compelling resource for advocacy groups and social service agency specialists; a good read for the general public."

TREBINCEVIC, KENAN. The Bosnia list; a memoir of war, exile, and return; [by] Susan Shapiro 336 p. 2014 Penguin Books

1. Bosnian Americans—Biography 2. Escapes—Bosnia and Hercegovina—History—20th century 3. Memoirs 4. Yugoslav War, 1991-1995—Bosnia and Hercegovina—Personal narratives
ISBN 0143124579; 9780143124573 (paperback)
LC 2013-035345

SUMMARY: In this memoir, author Kenan Trebincevic

"blends his childhood experience of Bosnia's tragedy with a return to his original home in Brcko after nearly 20 years in the United States. The titular list is of goals the author intends to accomplish. They include seeking out surviving friends and relatives as well as confronting Serbs guilty of crimes against Trebincevi's defenceless Muslim family." (Library Journal)

REVIEW: *Booklist* v110 no7 p11 D 1 2013 Vanessa Bush

REVIEW: *Kirkus Rev* v82 no1 p104 Ja 1 2014

"The Bosnia List: A Memoir of War, Exile, and Return". "[Kenan] Trebincevic returns to the scene of childhood trauma during the Bosnian War of the early 1990s. The author fled the bloody civil war in his native Bosnia in 1993 with his father, mother and older brother, Eldin, and settled in Connecticut. Just 11 years old when the war broke out, the author observed the sudden hostility of the Serbs toward him and his family, native Muslims, as ethnic tensions flared in their diverse town of Brcko and the Muslims were persecuted in the name of Serbian supremacy. . . . An engaging memoir of war trauma and the redemption to be found in confronting it."

REVIEW: *Libr J* v139 no6 p98 Ap 1 2014 Zachary Irwin

REVIEW: *N Y Times Book Rev* p25 Ap 6 2014 JANINE DI GIOVANNI

REVIEW: *Publ Wkly* v260 no51 p48 D 16 2013

TREFIL, JAMES. Space atlas; mapping the universe and beyond; [by] James Trefil 335 p. 2012 National Geographic

1. Astronomy—Charts, diagrams, etc 2. Galaxies—Atlases 3. Science—Popular works 4. Stars—Atlases

ISBN 1426209711; 9781426209710 (hardback); 9781426210914 (deluxe)

LC 2012-020000

SUMMARY: Author James Trefil presents a "guide to the planets, stars and outer reaches of the universe." The book "explains the nature of planets, stars, galaxies and exotic objects such as black holes alongside photos and art . . . In addition to the latest imagery coming from space telescopes and diagrams explaining key astronomical concepts, this atlas also includes more than 90 pages of detailed maps." (Publisher's note)

REVIEW: *Booklist* v109 no8 p29 D 15 2012 David Tyckoson

REVIEW: *Choice* v50 no11 p1986-8 Jl 2013 R. J. Havlik

"Space Atlas: Mapping the Universe and Beyond." "[Author James] Trefil . . . is the author/editor of numerous works on science for nonscientists . . . His latest contribution is a beautifully printed coffee-table atlas, mapping the universe and beyond. . . . This volume is masterfully done. A foreword by astronaut Buzz Aldrin sets the stage for a lavishly visual review of the universe. . . . Several appendixes and indexes likely will be valuable to amateur astronomers. With the incredible pace of technical change in the fields of physics and astronomy, this is a movable feast for those interested in journeying through the heavens."

REVIEW: *Libr J* v138 no2 p79 F 1 2013 Frances Eaton Millhouser

REVIEW: *SLJ* v59 no6 p70 Je 2013 Kathleen Kelly MacMillan

TREGLOWN, JEREMY. Franco's crypt; Spanish culture and memory since 1936; [by] Jeremy Treglown 336 p. 2013 Farrar, Straus and Giroux

1. Architecture, Spanish—20th century 2. Art, Spanish—20th century 3. Collective memory—Spain 4. Historical literature 5. Motion pictures—Spain—History—20th century 6. Spanish literature—20th century—History and criticism

ISBN 9780374108427 (alk. paper)

LC 2012-048086

SUMMARY: In this book, Jeremy Treglown argues that "Spain under Nationalist dictator Francisco Franco was not a mute, traumatized wasteland, but a country with a complex, imaginative culture that deserves to be remembered, according to this probing study. Treglown . . . surveys an eclectic range of cultural artifacts from the Spanish Civil War, the Franco period, and Spain's modern democratic era." (Publishers Weekly)

REVIEW: *Booklist* v109 no21 p15 Jl 1 2013 Brendan Driscoll

REVIEW: *Choice* v51 no6 p1084 F 2014 E. Colecchia

REVIEW: *Commonweal* v140 no17 p38-40 O 25 2013 James J. Sheehan

REVIEW: *Kirkus Rev* v81 no12 p70 Je 15 2013

REVIEW: *N Y Rev Books* v61 no10 p61-3 Je 5 2014 Jeremy Adelman

"Franco's Crypt: Spanish Culture and Memory Since 1936." "[Author] Jeremy Treglown has ventured into . . . controversies and exposed some of the limits of using historical memory or forgetting to reconcile bitter social divisions caused by civil wars and dictatorships. 'Franco's Crypt,' his most recent book, is a fascinating journey into Spain's little-known, sometimes underground, literary and artistic recent history. . . . Behind the lines, Treglown observes, many artists and writers refused to act as propagandists or to be silenced. This is where his book is especially powerful. His inquiries into the Spanish past recover experiences and efforts that don't fit neatly into the rival rhetorics."

REVIEW: *Nation* v298 no3 p33-6 Ja 20 2014 JONATHAN BLITZER

REVIEW: *New York Times* v162 no56267 pC8 S 23 2013 VALERIE MILES

"Franco's Crypt: Spanish Culture and Memory Since 1936." "A discerning, provocative book, part travelogue, part reflection on how memory passes into history, and part cultural narrative, 'Franco's Crypt' establishes that much more was going on during [Francisco] Franco's regime than is usually credited. Touching on prickly issues with the pragmatic detachment of a foreigner, Mr. [Jeremy] Treglown shows that subversive elements were at play in art, literature and cinema, and that a cautious yet irreversible process of modernity had begun long before Franco's death. . . . An unflinching edition to the literature on contemporary Spanish history. . . . It also serves as a thought-provoking study on artistic expression under authoritarian regimes."

REVIEW: *Publ Wkly* v260 no20 p44-5 My 20 2013

REVIEW: *TLS* no5772 p10-1 N 15 2013 FELIPE FERNÁNDEZ-ARMESTO

TREML, MARTIN.ed. Hans Blumenberg, Jacob Taubes. See Hans Blumenberg, Jacob Taubes

TREND-PRO CO. LTD.comp. The manga guide to linear algebra. See Inoue, I.

TRENEMAN, ANN. Finding the Plot!; 100 Graves To Visit Before You Die; [by] Ann Treneman 320 p. 2013 Robson Press

1. Cemeteries 2. Dead—Great Britain 3. Memorials 4. Tombs 5. Travel—Guidebooks
ISBN 1849541957; 9781849541954

SUMMARY: In this book, "Ann Treneman . . . has branched out--to graveyards. In this riveting book she takes you to the most interesting graves in Britain. . . . This unique book is made up of a hundred entries, each telling the story of one or more graves. Some are chosen for who is in them, others for the grave itself. Some of the entries are humorous, some are poignant, but all tell us something about the British way of death." (Publisher's note)

REVIEW: *TLS* no5776 p34 D 13 2013 DAVID WALLER

"Finding the Plot: 100 Graves to Visit Before You Die." "Ann Treneman, parliamentary sketchwriter for 'The Times,' has written a book about her favourite hundred graves, an eclectic selection which includes a dog, a horse, and an owlet, but very few politicians. Everyone on the list had to be interesting, she explains. . . . Half should be in or close to London, as many readers will be visiting London and London has more interesting dead people than most other places. . . . She delights in serendipity and incongruity."

TREPANIER, LEE.ed. A political companion to Saul Bellow . See A political companion to Saul Bellow

TRESCH, JOHN. The romantic machine; Utopian Science and Technology after Napoleon; [by] John Tresch xvii, 449 p. 2012 University of Chicago Press

1. France—History—19th century 2. France—Intellectual life—19th century 3. Historical literature 4. Machinery—Social aspects—19th century 5. Romanticism—France 6. Science & the arts 7. Science—France—History 8. Science—Social aspects—France—19th century 9. Technology—Philosophy—19th century 10. Technology—Social aspects—France—19th century 11. Utopias—France—History—19th century
ISBN 0226812200 (cloth : alkaline paper); 9780226812205 (cloth : alkaline paper)
LC 2011-038172

SUMMARY: This book by John Tresch "reveals how thoroughly entwined science and the arts were in early nineteenth-century France and how they worked together to unite a fractured society. Focusing on a set of celebrated technologies, including steam engines, electromagnetic and geophysical instruments, early photography, and mass-scale printing, Tresch looks at how new conceptions of energy, instrumentality, and association fueled . . . diverse developments." (Publisher's note)

REVIEW: *Am Hist Rev* v118 no4 p1258 O 2013 Jeff Horn

"The Romantic Machine: Utopian Science and Technology After Napoleon." "This dense, multifaceted book links epistemology, theories of nature, and technology during the Restoration and July Monarchy through what John Tresch terms 'mechanical romanticism.' A well-produced book with attractive plates helps him tell the tale. Tresch seeks to rescue the notion and practice of romanticism and especially romantic science from what he describes as the dustbin of history. Based on a set of interconnected case studies, Tresch's work contains many interesting and provocative insights, but his account provides only a partial portrayal of 'utopian science and technology after Napoleon.'"

REVIEW: *Choice* v50 no4 p690-1 D 2012 P. D. Skiff

TREVAYNE, EMMA. Flights and chimes and mysterious times; 320 p. 2014 Simon & Schuster Books for Young Readers

1. Escapes—Fiction 2. Fairy tales 3. Kings & rulers—Fiction 4. London (England)—Fiction 5. Steampunk fiction
ISBN 1442498773; 9781442498778 (hardcover); 9781442498792 (pbk.)
LC 2013-019389

SUMMARY: "In this steampunk fantasy, Jack Foster, the oft-ignored son of affluent socialites in Victorian England, finds himself trapped in the land of Londonium after following an evil magician named Lorcan through a door at the base of Big Ben. Londonium, a land of metal automatons, sooty skies, and humanoid citizens with gear-augmented bodies, is run by a temperamental, ageless Lady who is desperate for a 'perfect' (human) son." (School Library Journal)

REVIEW: *Booklist* v110 no18 p67-8 My 15 2014 Carolyn Phelan

REVIEW: *Bull Cent Child Books* v67 no10 p545 Je 2014 A. S.

"Flights and Chimes and Mysterious Times". "Jack is interesting rather than likable—he is spoiled and demanding from the start, and he knowingly commits actions that lead to executions of the innocent—but his character adds edge to the folkloresque plot. Additionally, Trevayne surrounds Jack with deeply sympathetic characters on both sides of the good/evil spectrum, with even the reprehensible Lorcan, who has done horrific things for his beloved Lady, clearly motivated by desperate love. Steampunk novels for the young set are fairly uncommon, and this creaking, smoky, dangerous world fits the bill elegantly."

REVIEW: *Horn Book Magazine* v90 no4 p107 Jl/Ag 2014 ANITA L. BURKAM

REVIEW: *Kirkus Rev* v82 no6 p196 Mr 15 2014

REVIEW: *SLJ* v60 no3 p149 Mr 2014 Elisabeth Gattullo Marrocolla

TREVENA, JOHN. Sleeping Waters. See Henham, E. G.

TREVOR-ROPER, H. R. (HUGH REDWALD), 1914-2003. One hundred letters from Hugh Trevor-Roper; 2014 Oxford University Press

1. Great Britain—Intellectual life—1945- 2. Historians—Great Britain—History—20th century 3. Letters 4. Nobility (Social class)—Great Britain 5. University of Oxford—History
ISBN 9780198703112 hardcover

SUMMARY: Edited by Richard Davenport-Hines and Adam Sisman, "The one hundred letters brought together for this book illustrate the range of Hugh Trevor-Roper's life and preoccupations: as an historian, a controversialist, a public intellectual, an adept in academic intrigues, a lover of literature, a traveller, a countryman. They depict a life of rich diversity; a mind of intellectual sparkle and eager curiosity; . . . and the absurdities . . . and vanities of his contemporaries." (Publisher's note)

REVIEW: *TLS* no5785 p5 F 14 2014 A. N. WILSON

"One Hundred Letters From Hugh Trevor-Roper." "The reader becomes quickly used to [Hugh] Trevor-Roper's prejudices. . . . As these letters show, Trevor-Roper road not two horses but at least four. There was the serious intellectual. . . . Then there was the public man. . . . One was the journalist. . . . The fourth Trevor-Roper was the mischief-maker of genius. . . . The quality of the prose is so sparkling, the wit is so sharp, and the Enlightenment standpoint so carefully nourished, that the book serves not only as entertainment, but as a manifesto for the intellectual values that were Hugh Trevor-Roper's lodestar."

TRIFKOVIĆ, MAK. Algebraic theory of quadratic numbers; [by] Mak Trifković xi, 197 p. 2013 Springer

1. Algebraic number theory 2. Factorization (Mathematics) 3. Mathematical literature 4. Quadratic fields 5. Ring theory

ISBN 1461477166 (alk. paper); 9781461477167 (alk. paper); 9781461477174 (ebk.)

LC 2013-941873

SUMMARY: In this book on quadratic numbers, "the techniques of elementary arithmetic, ring theory and linear algebra are shown working together to prove important theorems, such as the unique factorization of ideals and the finiteness of the ideal class group. The book concludes with two topics particular to quadratic fields: continued fractions and quadratic form." (Publisher's note)

REVIEW: *Choice* v51 no9 p1634 My 2014 D. V. Feldman

"Algebraic Theory of Quadratic Numbers". "[Mark] Trifkovic . . . introduces algebraic number theory with all the usual abstractions, except limited to whatever proves necessary just for extensions of degree two. Degree two, in particular, makes the role of Galois theory 'invisible,' as the author terms it. Though many books offer study of quadratic forms and Pell's equation by purely elementary means, the approach here strikes a perfect balance, achieving legible results while preparing students for deeper study. A 'crash course' in ring theory obviates abstract algebra prerequisites, and the author gives a similarly generous review and amplification of linear algebra tools. Degree two allows for many illuminating diagrams, an algebraic number theory rarity."

TRINER, GAIL D. Mining and the State in Brazilian Development; [by] Gail D. Triner 253 p. 2011 Ashgate Pub Co

1. Brazil—Politics & government 2. Historical literature 3. Mineral industries 4. Mines & mineral resources—Brazil 5. Property rights

ISBN 1848930682; 9781848930681

SUMMARY: It was the author's intent to demonstrate that "the Brazilian state played a central role in creating the conditions for the exploration and exploitation of minerals by changing the property rights framework for subsoil resources. While the chronological focus of the book lies in the twentieth century, it traces the history of property rights regimes back to colonial times." (American Historical Review)

REVIEW: *Am Hist Rev* v119 no1 p225-6 F 2014 Oliver Dinius

"Mining and the State in Brazilian Development". "As in any good work of the new economic history, the text moves back and forth between historical narrative and economic analysis. The problem is that [Gail D.] Triner never develops either fully. The historical narrative is not specific enough to support original insights into the role of institutions in economic development, and the economic analysis is not precise enough to cast new light on the meaning of historical events. . . . The study does ask important questions about the role of the state in Brazil's industrialization and presents diligent research on the impact of the changing legal environment."

REVIEW: *Bus Hist Rev* v87 no1 p168-70 Spr 2013 Anne Hanley

TRINH, T. MINH-HA (THI MINH-HA), 1952-. D-passage; the digital way; [by] T. Minh-Ha (Thi Minh-Ha) Trinh 224 p. 2013 Duke University Press

1. Digital cinematography 2. Motion picture literature

ISBN 9780822355250 (cloth: alk. paper); 9780822355403 (pbk.: alk. paper)

LC 2013-013828

SUMMARY: In this book, T. Minh-ha Trinh "discusses the impact of new technology on cinema culture and explores its effects on creative practice. Less a medium than a 'way,' the digital is here featured in its mobile, transformative passages. Trinh's reflections shed light on several of her major themes: temporality; transitions; transcultural encounters; ways of seeing and knowing; and the implications of the media used, the artistic practices engaged in, and the representations created." (Publisher's note)

REVIEW: *Choice* v51 no8 p1408 Ap 2014 J. Belton

"D-Passage: The Digital Way". "[T. Miha-ha] Trinh's book is designed to accompany her narrative film 'Night Passage' (2004, co-directed with Jean-Paul Bourdier), which is based on a 1927 children's story by Kenji Miyazawa (Night Train to the Stars). The book consists of an introduction to the film project by Trinh; the film's screenplay; four interviews with Trinh on the film; and a discussion of the museum installation based on the film by Trinh and Bourdier at the Musée de Quai Branly in Paris. . . . Recommended."

TRIPATHI, DEEPAK. Imperial designs; war, humiliation & the making of history; [by] Deepak Tripathi xxix, 175 p. 2013 Potomac Books

1. Historical literature

ISBN 1612346243 (hardcover : alk. paper); 9781612346243 (hardcover : alk. paper)

LC 2012-049625

SUMMARY: In this book on "the Middle East and South Asia . . . Deepak Tripathi offers an . . . analysis of how this volatile region has endured the manipulation and humiliation" of imperial wars. He "argues that these foreign invasions to gain access to others' wealth and the consequent ignominy of the defeated peoples of the regions have had far-reaching consequences." He explains "how the shame of defeat radicalizes nations and societies, and often makes future conflict inevitable." (Publisher's note)

REVIEW: *Choice* v51 no5 p919 Ja 2014 F. S. Pearson

"Imperial Designs: War, Humiliation and the Making of History." "Former BBC correspondent [Deepak] Tripathi . . . here completes his trilogy . . . on regional violence, using a meandering yet readable approach to illuminate historical alienation for today's Western audiences. . . . This brief book, focused on contemporary policy, with illustrative appendixes, alerts readers to the problem, but affords few precise distinctions or clear remedies. Policy makers may yet learn from these experiences: show respect and, as consistently as possible, reverse the sense of victimization."

REVIEW: *Middle East J* v68 no2 p343 Spr 2014 T. P.

TRITTO, STEPHEN. Taking Flight; [by] Stephen Tritto 464 p. 2013 CreateSpace Independent Publishing Platform

1. Americans in foreign countries—Fiction 2. El Salvador 3. Marriage—Fiction 4. Psychological fiction 5. Self-realization—Fiction

ISBN 1482662469; 9781482662467

SUMMARY: In this book, "Anthony is blindsided when he loses his job, which leaves him casting about for what he wants to do with his life. . . . A member of their group dies while doing charitable work in El Salvador, and Anthony, the only one with time on his hands, volunteers to retrieve his remains. In fact, he selfishly does so without consulting Bernadette, further threatening their crumbling relationship. Anthony's worldview changes once he lands in the Central American country." (Kirkus Reviews)

REVIEW: *Kirkus Rev* v82 no1 p308 Ja 1 2014

"Taking Flight". "[Stephen] Tritto's sparkling debut novel succeeds as a gripping tale of one man's self-discovery. . . . Anthony is blindsided when he loses his job, which leaves him casting about for what he wants to do with his life. Such ruminations could come off as whiny, but in Tritto's capable hands, Anthony blossoms. . . . Tritto helps Anthony evolve from a self-absorbed yuppie to a man more empathetic to those around him, a man readers can root for even if he still doesn't truly know himself. A novel that artfully spans two cultures, from a talented new author ready to take wing."

TROGDON, ROBERT W.ed. The Letters of Ernest Hemingway. See Hemingway, E.

TROLLOPE, ANTHONY, 1815-1882. The warden; xxix, 294 p. 2008 Oxford University Press

1. Almshouses—Fiction 2. Barsetshire (England : Imaginary place)—Fiction 3. Clergy—Fiction 4. Psychological fiction 5. Trusts & trustees

ISBN 9780199537785 (pbk.)

LC 2008-482153

SUMMARY: This book examines "the ethical dilemma of a virtuous man. The Reverend Harding is the warden of a small home providing quarters for 12 retired, indigent workers. . . . Income off the land provides revenue for the maintenance of the home and a living for the warden. . . . Reverend Harding is a gentle, honest man who has never given thought to his 800 pound annual revenue until a young reformer files suit, claiming the intent of the will is being violated." (Publisher's note)

REVIEW: *Booklist* v110 no9/10 p66 Ja 1 2014 Joyce Saricks

"[Anthony] Trollope's eloquent and satiric prose is made to be heard, to be read aloud and savored in company. In his splendid reading of this first of the Barsetshire series, [David] Shaw-Parker skillfully inhabits the role of the companionable omniscient narrator, assuming a tone of mock pomposity as he guides listeners through the tangle of social and ecclesiastical issues and introduces his audience to a community of gossipy parishioners, pensioners, and the ecclesiastical hierarchy. . . . Shaw-Parker excels in capturing Trollope's humorous asides and pointed barbs at the sins of society and the frailties of its members. His care in creating memorable characters is also notable. He deftly varies tones and speech patterns to reflect the large cast."

TROOST, J. MAARTEN. Headhunters on My Doorstep; A True Treasure Island Ghost Story; [by] J. Maarten Troost 304 p. 2013 Penguin Group USA

1. Oceania—Description & travel 2. Oceania—History 3. Recovering alcoholics' writings 4. Stevenson, Robert Louis, 1850-1894 5. Travelers' writings

ISBN 1592407897; 9781592407897

SUMMARY: This book "chronicles [J. Maarten] Troost's return to the South Pacific after his struggle with alcoholism and time in rehab left him numb to life. Deciding to retrace the path once traveled by the author of Treasure Island, Troost follows Robert Louis Stevenson to the Marquesas, the Tuamotus, Tahiti, the Gilberts, and Samoa, tumbling from one comic misadventure to another as he confronts his newfound sobriety." (Publisher's note)

REVIEW: *Booklist* v110 no2 p25 S 15 2013 David Pitt

"Headhunters on My Doorstep: A True Treasure Island Ghost Story." "This travel memoir charts the author's own South Pacific voyage, replicating (to a degree) [Robert Louis] Stevenson's. . . . [J. Maarten] Troost deftly combines humor, commentary, and education (an aside about the Marquesas episode of Survivor, sparked by the author's discovery that he's standing on a beach that featured in the show, leads smoothly into a look at 'old Marquesas' and its odd mixture of wealth and poverty). Troost is a very funny guy, but he also has a lot of serious things to talk about. A splendid travel memoir."

REVIEW: *Kirkus Rev* v81 no13 p132 Jl 1 2013

REVIEW: *Kirkus Rev* p31 Ag 15 2013 Fall Preview

TROPIANO, STEPHEN. Saturday night live FAQ; everything left to know about television's longest-running comedy; [by] Stephen Tropiano 476 p. 2014 Applause Theatre & Cinema Books

1. Encyclopedias & dictionaries 2. Television comedies 3. Television hosts 4. Television programs—History

ISBN 9781557839510

LC 2013-038849

SUMMARY: This book looks at the television show "Saturday Night Live". "Most of the chapters are devoted to recounting the show's genesis and providing a season-by-season or eta-by-era overview of its many highs and occasionally too frequent lows. Othet chapters recount 'memorable characters, sketches and moments'; provide an SNL cast directory; discuss SNL hosts and musical guests, SNL film shorts, and the 'Weekend Update' segment." (Choice: Current Reviews for Academic Libraries)

REVIEW: *Booklist* v110 no16 p34 Ap 15 2014 Rebecca Vnuk

REVIEW: *Choice* v51 no9 p1568 My 2014 D. Highsmith

"Saturday Night Live FAQ: Everything Left to Know About Television's Longest-Running Comedy". "This volume by [Stephen] Tropiano . . . is the latest addition to the list, and a worthy one. But the first thing to note is that some readers may find the title 'Saturday Night Live FAQ' somewhat misleading since the book does not follow the question-and-answer format traditionally associated with FAQs. Instead, it is organized along the lines of a more traditional history or overview. . . . Given its subject, this book likely will appeal more to public libraries than to academic ones; however, it is a well-researched and well-organized effort that should be of interest to academic libraries with strong holdings in broadcasting and media history."

TROSPER, RONALD L.ed. Aboriginal peoples and forest lands in Canada. See Aboriginal peoples and forest lands in Canada

TROTTER, DAVID. Literature in the first media age; Britain between the wars; [by] David Trotter 352 p. 2013 Harvard University Press

1. English literature—20th century—History and criticism 2. Great Britain—Intellectual life—20th century 3. Literature—History & criticism 4. Mass media and literature—Great Britain—History—20th century 5. Technology in literature
ISBN 9780674073159 (alk. paper)
LC 2013-006906

SUMMARY: "Interwar literature, [author] David Trotter argues, stood apart by virtue of the sheer intelligence of the enquiries it undertook into the technological mediation of experience. After around 1925, literary works began to portray communication by telephone, television, radio, and sound cinema—and to examine the sorts of behavior made possible for the first time by virtual interaction." (Publisher's note)

REVIEW: *Choice* v51 no11 p1982 Jl 2014 M. DelloBuono

REVIEW: *TLS* no5793 p26-7 Ap 11 2014 CALUM MECHIE

"Literature in the First Media Age: Britain Between the Wars." "[Author David] Trotter is fascinated by things and the processes by which they are produced and operated and so, he argues, compellingly, were the writers who came of age in 'Britain between the wars.' . . . 'I have consistently sought to distinguish the literary meta-attitude I have defined in this book from Modernism,' Trotter writes in conclusion. He has achieved that, and more. . . . Trotter's new history takes the things with which we fill our lives—our books, our films and the technical and then social protocols dictating their uses—as its focalizing issues. What emerges is a compelling and often uplifting study, the spatial and temporal boundaries of which extend far beyond Britain between the wars."

TROUT, NICK. Dog gone, back soon; [by] Nick Trout 336 p. 2014 Hyperion

1. Family-owned business enterprises 2. Human-animal relationships—Fiction 3. Psychological fiction 4. Veterinarians—Fiction 5. Veterinary hospitals
ISBN 9781401310899 (trade pbk.)
LC 2013-038782

SUMMARY: This book, the second in Nick Trout's "Bedside Manor" series, opens with Cyrus Mills, a former veterinarian pathologist, back in his hometown trying to pull his deceased father's veterinary clinic out of financial ruin. . . . Cyrus is facing increasing pressure from the ruthless corporate chain Healthy Paws, which is trying to run him out of business. Will Cyrus be able to make his clinic thrive and still provide pets, and their owners, with the most exceptional treatment available?" (Library Journal)

REVIEW: *Kirkus Rev* v82 no3 p315 F 1 2014

"Dog Gone, Back Soon"."In the second of his Bedside Manor series, [Nick] Trout . . . highlights another week in the life of the newest veterinarian in Eden Falls, Vt. . . . Trout, a staff surgeon at the Angell Animal Medical Center in Boston, Mass., once again hits the mark with a wholesome, heartwarming story that ends on an optimistic note. He creates a homey community full of compassion, charm and humorous characters typical of many small towns. No doubt many animal lovers are panting in anticipation of the next Bedside Manor installment. Pawsitively delightful."

REVIEW: *Libr J* v139 no6 p85 Ap 1 2014 Susan Moritz

TROY, TEVI. What Jefferson Read, Ike Watched, and Obama Tweeted; 200 Years of Popular Culture in the White House; [by] Tevi Troy 416 p. 2013 Perseus Distribution Services

1. Historical literature 2. Popular culture—United States—History 3. Presidents—United States—Attitudes 4. Presidents—United States—History 5. Presidents—United States—Knowledge & learning
ISBN 1621570398; 9781621570394

SUMMARY: This book presents "a history of American presidents' interactions with popular culture. Can a president show that he has the gravitas to govern the nation and still reveal that he knows who Snooki is? The question animates this . . . view of presidents from George Washington to Barack Obama and their efforts to find the right distance for the leader of a republic to keep between himself and the people." (Kirkus Reviews)

REVIEW: *Kirkus Rev* v81 no15 p83 Ag 1 2013

REVIEW: *Natl Rev* v65 no18 p52-3 S 30 2013 BETSY WOODRUFF

"What Jefferson Read, Ike Watched, and Obama Tweeted: 200 Years of Popular Culture in the White House." "In this new book, Tevi Troy . . . explores the fascinating, messy, and often amusing connections between presidents and pop culture. In the process, Troy has probably written the unsexiest pop-culture book imaginable--and that's not a bad thing. He seems to have limited interest in appealing to readers' lesser angels. The book is straightforward and linear, with extensive notes. Condensing a 200-year narrative into just about 250 pages of text isn't an easy feat, but Troy succeeds admirably. The book is an entertaining refresher course on the personalities who have filled the White House."

REVIEW: *Publ Wkly* v260 no28 p158 Jl 15 2013

TRUBETA, SEVASTI. Physical anthropology, race and eugenics in Greece (1880s-1970s); [by] Sevasti Trubeta xii, 337 p. 2013 Brill

1. Anthropology literature 2. Eugenics—Greece—History 3. Physical anthropology—Greece—History 4. Racism in anthropology—Greece—History
ISBN 9789004257665 (hardback : alk. paper); 9789004257672 (e-book)
LC 2013-026491

SUMMARY: In this book, Sevasti Trubeta "identifies the origins and evolution of Greek anthropological concepts and institutional trajectories, paying special attention first to Hellenism and then to the Greek fili, or community, in racial, eugenic, and nationalistic terms. Trubeta frames her investigation around the work of Greece's two anthropological pioneers--Clon Stephanos (1854- 1915) and Ioannis Koumaris (1879-1970)." (Choice: Current Reviews for Academic Libraries)

REVIEW: *Choice* v51 no6 p1056 F 2014 J. D. Smith

"Physical Anthropology, Race and Eugenics in Greece (1880s-1970s)." "[Sevasti] Trubeta . . . examines the rise of modern anthropology in Greece. Her book's rigid, formulaic organization, structure, and dense, theoretical language hetray its origins, figuratively and literally, as a heavily researched German doctoral thesis. . . . In assessing the influence of Greek anthropological science, especially eugenics, since WW II, Trubeta identifies biologistic, racial, and racist models that continue to holster the country's racial nationalism today. . . . Recommended."

TRUEIT, DONNA. Grasshoppers; [by] Donna Trueit 23 2009 Marshall Cavendish Benchmark

1. Children's nonfiction 2. Grasshoppers 3. Grasshoppers—Behavior 4. Insect anatomy 5. Insects—Identification

ISBN 978-0-7614-3964-6 lib bdg; 0-7614-3964-1

LC 2008--24210

SUMMARY: This book on grasshoppers is part of the "Backyard Safari series," which provides "a hands-on, practical point of view on discovering local insects. . . . The first part of each book offers information on the life cycle and anatomy of the title creatures." The book also includes "three hands-on sections" offering "practical instructions and tips for finding and observing the title creatures . . . characteristics and about a dozen pictures . . . and a final section suggest[ing] additional projects." (Booklist)

REVIEW: *Booklist* v110 no11 p54 F 1 2014 Miriam Aronin

"Beetles," "Dragonflies," and "Grasshoppers." "These new books in the Backyard Safari series offer a hands-on, practical point of view on discovering local insects, mollusks, and worms. The first part of each book offers information on the life cycle and anatomy of the title creatures, so brief that it sometimes feels abbreviated. In 'Beetles,' fascinating facts, such as those about how beetles lay their eggs in dung, could have used more fleshing out. Likewise, in 'Dragonflies,' various cultures' interpretations of dragonflies could use a bit more explanation. In 'Grasshoppers,' on the other hand, the description of the insects' noise making and hearing feels sufficient. . . . these hooks offer an accessible, engaging introduction to these elements of science."

TRUEIT, TRUDI STRAIN. Beetles; [by] Trudi Strain Trueit 23 2010 Marshall Cavendish Benchmark

1. Beetles 2. Beetles—Behavior 3. Children's nonfiction 4. Insect anatomy 5. Insects—Identification

ISBN 978-0-7614-3962-2 lib bdg; 0-7614-3962-5

LC 2008--23153

SUMMARY: This book on beetles is part of the "Backyard Safari series," which provides "a hands-on, practical point of view on discovering local insects. . . . The first part of each book offers information on the life cycle and anatomy of the title creatures." The book also includes "three hands-on sections" offering "practical instructions and tips for finding and observing the title creatures . . . characteristics and about a dozen pictures . . . and a final section suggest[ing] additional projects." (Booklist)

REVIEW: *Booklist* v110 no11 p54 F 1 2014 Miriam Aronin

"Beetles," "Dragonflies," and "Grasshoppers." "These new books in the Backyard Safari series offer a hands-on, practical point of view on discovering local insects, mollusks, and worms. The first part of each book offers information on the life cycle and anatomy of the title creatures, so brief that it sometimes feels abbreviated. In 'Beetles,' fascinating facts, such as those about how beetles lay their eggs in dung, could have used more fleshing out. Likewise, in 'Dragonflies,' various cultures' interpretations of dragonflies could use a bit more explanation. In 'Grasshoppers,' on the other hand, the description of the insects' noise making and hearing feels sufficient. . . . these hooks offer an accessible, engaging introduction to these elements of science."

TRUMBORE, CINDY. Parrots over Puerto Rico. See Roth, S L.

TSCHIRGI, DAN.ed. Egypt's Tahrir revolution. See Egypt's Tahrir revolution

TUCH, STEVEN A. Religion, politics, and polarization. See D'Antonio, W. V.

TUCHOLKE, APRIL GENEVIEVE. Between the devil and the deep blue sea; [by] April Genevieve Tucholke 368 p. 2013 Dial Books

1. Devil—Fiction 2. Good & evil—Fiction 3. Horror tales 4. Love stories 5. Supernatural—Fiction

ISBN 0803738897 (hardcover); 9780803738898 (hardcover)

LC 2012-035586

SUMMARY: In this horror novel, "Violet White and her 17-year-old twin brother are living in the dilapidated glory of their family's coastal estate while their parents traipse Europe. To help pay the bills, Violet places an ad for a boarder for their guesthouse; it's quickly answered by River West, a mysterious boy who cannily avoids giving straight answers about his past. Violet doesn't typically pay boys much mind, but she's soon spending the night with River, both drawn to and wary of him." (Publishers Weekly)

REVIEW: *Booklist* v110 no4 p57 O 15 2013 Ilene Cooper

"Between the Devil and the Deep Blue Sea." "[April Genevieve] Tucholke paints this moody, gothic romance with a languid brush. Moments of horror nestle against warm, dreamy kisses. Though the text could have been tighter--and the number of important characters fewer--there are unexpected twists that make the story a surprise. That, and the faded elegance that permeates almost every page, elevates this above more generic offerings of its type. Violet, too, has a quirky uniqueness that will draw readers, just as it draws River--for better or worse."

REVIEW: *Bull Cent Child Books* v67 no2 p120-1 O 2013 K. Q. G.

"Between the Devil and the Deep Blue Sea." " After her bohemian artist parents skip town for Europe, seventeen-year-old Violet White is facing down a long, hot summer with her hostile twin brother in the family's decaying old mansion, with no AC and dwindling funds. . . . Like any good gothic fare, this is as much about morality as it is about atmosphere, and [author April Genevieve] Tucholke strikes just the right balance between the windswept, seaside setting and Violet's interior struggles with right and wrong (and wrong-but-oh-so-right feelings toward dangerous River)."

REVIEW: *Kirkus Rev* v81 no13 p88 Jl 1 2013

REVIEW: *Kirkus Rev* p75-6 2013 Guide 20to BookExpo America

REVIEW: *Publ Wkly* v260 no21 p62-3 My 27 2013

REVIEW: *SLJ* v59 no7 p102 Jl 2013 Danielle Serra

REVIEW: *Voice of Youth Advocates* v36 no3 p86 Ag 2013 Amy Fiske

TUCKER, BRIAN A. An Essential Deception; [by] Brian A. Tucker 726 p. 2013 CreateSpace Independent Publishing Platform

1. Missing persons—Fiction 2. Prime ministers 3. Secret societies—Fiction 4. Supernatural 5. Suspense fiction

ISBN 1481187740; 9781481187749

SUMMARY: In this book by Brian A. Tucker, "the British Prime Minister is missing. Vanished without trace. Government security has launched an urgent investigation. Former Scotland Yard detective, Dr. Hanson Shaw, is drawn into the mystery. Guarding the secret of his own remarkable abilities, Shaw is quickly thrust into the center of a shocking conspiracy of global dimensions." (Publisher's note)

REVIEW: *Kirkus Rev* v82 no1 p169 Ja 1 2014

REVIEW: *Kirkus Rev* v81 no24 p401 D 15 2013

"An Essential Deception: "[Brian A.] Tucker's blandly titled but brilliantly executed debut. . . . With an amazingly assured narrative style, Tucker takes readers from the machinations of his nefarious, multicultural bad guys to the dogged sleuthing of Shaw and his allies, punctuated by vivid descriptions of Shaw's painful attacks and incredible deductive visions. Before long, the plot expands to a global scale involving the Syrians, the Americans, and al-Qaida and half a dozen other volatile groups. Tucker handles it all with extremely lively pacing and frequent glints of Shaw's wry outlook on life. As long as this book is, readers will likely wish it were longer. A truly impressive thriller debut in the vein of Dan Brown's 'The Da Vinci Code'."

TUCKER, PATRICK. The naked future; what happens in a world that anticipates your every move; [by] Patrick Tucker 288 p. 2014 Current

1. Big data—Social aspects 2. Forecasting 3. Information technology—Social aspects 4. Privacy, Right of 5. Technical literature 6. Technological innovations—Social aspects

ISBN 9781591845867

LC 2013-040374

SUMMARY: In this book, Patrick Tucker "provides an anecdote-filled account of the many ways in which massive sets of data . . .can be used by individuals to 'live much more healthily, realize more of your own goals in less time [and] avoid inconvenience and danger.' . . . The author argues that a "thrilling and historic transformation" lies ahead in our ability to predict the future using continuously sourced streams of information accessed via smartphones." (Kirkus Reviews)

REVIEW: *Kirkus Rev* v82 no4 p94 F 15 2014

"The Naked Future: What Happens in a World That Anticipates Your Every Move?". "[Patrick] Tucker's exploration of computer-aided forecasting shows the growing role of big data in aspects of American life, including education, online dating, predictive policing and customer loyalty programs. . . . A well-written consideration of how, 'in the next two decades, we will be able to predict huge areas of the future with far greater accuracy than ever before in human history, including events long thought to be beyond the realm of human interference.'"

REVIEW: *N Y Times Book Rev* p23 My 18 2014 EVGENY MOROZOV

REVIEW: *Publ Wkly* v261 no5 p45-6 F 3 2014

TUCKER, PHILLIP THOMAS, 1953-. George Washington's surprise attack; a new look at the battle that decided the fate of America; [by] Phillip Thomas Tucker 656 p. 2014 Skyhorse Publishing

1. Historical literature 2. Rall, Johann 3. Trenton, Battle of, Trenton, N.J., 1776 4. United States—History—Revolution, 1775-1783—Campaigns

ISBN 9781628736526 (alk. paper)

LC 2013-047083

SUMMARY: This book by Phillip Thomas Tucker presents "a blow-by-blow re-creation of George Washington's 1776 Christmas crossing of the Delaware and the capture of Trenton. Washington's shocking victory over the Hessian garrison occupying Trenton gave teeth to the Declaration of Independence, greatly enhanced his own and his discouraged army's reputations, sobered public opinion in Britain and fueled hope that France might intervene to aid the struggling young nation." (Kirkus Reviews)

REVIEW: *Kirkus Rev* v82 no3 p166 F 1 2014

"George Washington's Surprise Attack: A New Look at the Battle That Decided the Fate of America". "[Phillip Thomas] Tucker . . . appears to have missed no detail: the varying intensity of the snow, sleet and wind; every feature of the topography; the positioning of each cannon; the nuances of the attack and the counterattack. . . . . Although marred by far too many repetitions, hackneyed locutions and a tedious insistence upon his various theses, Tucker's account brims with colorful information . . . that vivifies this pivotal episode in American history. Of most interest to military historians and Revolutionary War buffs."

REVIEW: *Publ Wkly* v261 no3 p44 Ja 20 2014

TUCKER, SPENCER C.ed. American Civil War. See American Civil War

TUCKER, WILLIAM, 1942-. Marriage and civilization; [by] William Tucker 289 p. 2014 Regnery Publishin, Inc.

1. Civilization—Philosophy 2. Civilization, Modern 3. Marriage—Philosophy 4. Marriage—Social aspects 5. Social commentary

ISBN 1621572013; 9781621572015

LC 2013-051314

SUMMARY: "In 'Marriage and Civilization,' [author William] Tucker takes readers on a journey through the history of the human race to demonstrate how a pattern of life-long, monogamous pairings has enabled humans to build modern civilization. Drawing extensively on biological, anthropological, and historical evidence, Tucker makes the case that marriage is not only a desirable institution for societies, it's actually the bedrock of civilization." (Publisher's note)

REVIEW: *Natl Rev* v65 no9 p41-3 My 19 2014 RYAN T. ANDERSON

"Marriage and Civilization: How Monogamy Made Us Human." "[Author William] Tucker is not himself an academic, but he is a smart journalist, and 'Marriage and Civilization' is the result of some 20 years of reading through the scholarly literature on marriage and thinking through the implications. . . . Tucker comes to some rather politically incorrect views. . . . Tucker goes through human history at blazing speed. . . . On Mormonism and Islam, I fear he moves too quickly and paints with too broad a brush.

TUENNERMAN, LAURA. At the border of empires. See Marak, A. M.

TULLOCH, JANET H.ed. A Cultural History of Women. See A Cultural History of Women

TUMULT AND ORDER; La Malcontenta: 1924-1939; 160 p. 2012 Lars Muller

1. Historic buildings—Conservation & restoration 2. Historical literature 3. Italy—Intellectual life 4. Landsberger, Albert Clinton 5. Villa Foscari (Mira, Italy)

ISBN 3037782978 (hbk.); 9783037782972 (hbk.)

SUMMARY: This book examines the history of "the Villa Foscari in Venice, better known as La Malcontenta, [which] became a meeting place for intellectuals, artists, and members of the nobility. . . . Antonio Foscari recounts this lively period in the building's history and talks about its then owner, Albert Clinton Landsberger . . . who not only lovingly renovated the villa, but made it such a lively place for the first time." (Publisher's note)

REVIEW: *TLS* no5756 p28-9 Jl 26 2013 BRUCE BOUCHER

"Venice From the Water: Architecture and Myth in an Early Modern City" and "Tumult and Order: Malcontenta, 1924-1939." "The ceremonial display of Venice is the subject of Daniel Savoy's perceptive new book, which draws together various strands of historical and ecological analysis into an engaging narrative about the perfection of a myth. 'Venice from the Water' is as much a reminder of what has long been known about La Serenissima as it is a multidisciplinary revelation. . . . Palladio's architecture in the Venetian Lagoon also features in Antonio Foscari's 'Tumult and Order. Malcontenta, 1924-1939'."

TUNICK, MICHAEL H. The science of cheese; [by] Michael H. Tunick xvii, 281 p. 2014 Oxford University Press

1. Cheese 2. Cheese—History 3. Cheese industry—Law & legislation 4. Cheesemaking 5. Scientific literature

ISBN 0199922306 (hardcover: acid-free paper); 9780199922307 (hardcover: acid-free paper)

LC 2013-010729

SUMMARY: "This book is a detailed account of the biology, chemistry, and physics of cheese and its formation for the nonscientific reader. . . . Author [Michael H.] Tunick . . . takes the reader back 8,000 years looking at the history of cheese from the Fertile Crescent to the present day. Outside of the technical details, broad topics are covered, from etymology . . . to dietary issues to laws and regulations on cheese and cheese making." (Booklist)

REVIEW: *Booklist* v110 no14 p64 Mr 15 2014 Diana Shonrock

"The Science of Cheese". "This book is a detailed account of the biology, chemistry, and physics of cheese and its formation for the nonscientific reader; however, this is definitely not light reading. . . . Some sections feature highly academic writing, but [Michael H.] Tunick has intentionally placed the bulk of that technical information in boxes. . . . Recommended for academic and large public libraries, although smaller libraries where there is interest in the topic will want to take note of the reasonable price and consider adding this to their collections."

REVIEW: *Choice* v51 no11 p2003 Jl 2014 M. Kroger

TUNNELL, MICHAEL. Candy bomber; the story of the Berlin airlift's chocolate pilot; [by] Michael Tunnell 110 2010 Charlesbridge

1. Air force officers 2. Air pilots 3. Biography, Individual—Juvenile literature 4. Bomber pilots 5. Candy 6. Children's literature—Works—Grades two through six 7. Halvorsen, Gail 8. Historical literature 9. World War, 1939-1945—Children

ISBN 1-58089-336-8; 1-58089-337-6; 978-1-58089-336-7; 978-1-58089-337-4 pa

SUMMARY: This book takes place "[i]n 1948, after World War II, [in] Berlin, . . . [where Michael] Tunnell tells us that pilot Gail Halvorsen spent a night in the city, noticing kids behind a fence watching the planes land. He offered sticks of Doublemint gum to two of the kids, who passed them around so their pals could get a whiff. . . . Soon people all over began sending candy-and-handkerchief parachutes to Halvorsen and other pilots to drop over Berlin." (School Library Journal)

REVIEW: *SLJ* v58 no4 p16 Ap 2012 KATHLEEN BAXTER

"The Candy Bomber: The Story of the Berlin Aircraft's Chocolate Pilot." "Michael Tunnell's latest book did something amazing to my brain. Now I can't hear the word 'candy' without thinking of the word 'hero.' This is a delectable combination that I'm certain my booktalk audiences make daily, but I'm also certain they haven't heard the amazing story found in Tunnell's [book]. . . . Tunnell tells us that pilot Gail Halvorsen spent a night in the city, noticing kids behind a fence watching the planes land. He offered sticks of Doublemint gum to two of the kids, who passed them around so their pals could get a whiff. . . . He asked the kids if they would agree to share candy and gum if he dropped more of it from his plane."

TUNNEY, RUSS.ed. The Wolves of Willoughby Chase. See Aiken, J.

TÜRCKE, CHRISTOPH. Philosophy of dreams; 304 p. 2013 Yale University Press

1. Civilization 2. Dream interpretation 3. Dreams—Philosophy 4. Dreams—Psychological aspects 5. Philosophical literature

ISBN 9780300188400 (cloth: alk. paper)

LC 2013-015739

SUMMARY: In this book, author Christoph Türcke examines "the phenomenon of the dream, using it as a psychic fossil connecting us with our Stone Age ancestors. . . . He argues that both civilization and mental processes are the results of a compulsion to repeat early traumas, one to which hallucination, imagination, mind, spirit, and God all developed in response." (Publisher's note)

REVIEW: *Choice* v51 no9 p1608-9 My 2014 B. G. Murchland

"Philosophy of Dreams". "This densely written, speculatively bold, and imaginatively provocative book at times borders on the fictional. . . . His book is largely an extended commentary on [Sigmund] Freud's 'Interpretation of Dreams'. But in the final chapter he does a kind of Marxist volte-face, arguing that, with the advent of modern technology and capitalism, 'traumatic repetition became removed from the human organism and hence objectified.' . . . This is an updated version of [Karl] Marx's theory of alienation. But in the end [Christoph] Türcke holds out a faint hope that people's alienation can be overcome."

REVIEW: *J Am Acad Relig* v82 no1 p250-4 Mr 2014 Benjamin Y. Fong

TURK, A. First Do No Harm; [by] A. Turk 420 p. 2013 A. Turk LLC

1. Lawyers 2. Legal stories 3. Physicians—Corrupt practices 4. Physicians—Malpractice 5. Trials (Law)
ISBN 0989266303; 9780989266307

SUMMARY: " In this novel, based in part on the author's legal experiences, a lawyer goes after two crooked doctors who have been performing unnecessary surgeries at a small-town hospital in Tennessee. . . . [Dr.] Herman informs patients that they need to have their gall bladders removed, then refers the patients to [Dr.] English, who performs the surgeries. Both doctors get paid handsomely, and the patients never realize there wasn't anything wrong with their gall bladders in the first place." (Kirkus Reviews)

REVIEW: *Kirkus Rev* v81 no24 p41 D 15 2013

"First Do No Harm: A Benjamin Davis Novel". " Written in crisp, clear prose, [A.] Turk's debut novel is rich with legal detail. Sometimes, those details are a bit too rich, as the courtroom scenes seem to include every motion, question, instruction to the jury, etc. While fascinating from a legal perspective, these details cause pacing issues and, at times, drag the narrative to a crawl. The subplot involving the thugs who terrorize Davis and his team feels tacked on, and it never properly resolves. However, the quality of the writing coupled with the insider's view of the cases—Turk is a retired attorney, and the novel is based on actual cases from his career—mostly make up for these shortfalls. Sometimes slow but always well-written and full of detail."

TURK, CAROLYN. On norms and agency. See Petesch, P.

TURK, EVANY.il. Grandfather Gandhi. See Gandhi, A.

TURNAGE, SHEILA. The ghosts of Tupelo Landing; [by] Sheila Turnage 368 p. 2014 Kathy Dawson Books

1. Community life—North Carolina—Fiction 2. Foundlings—Fiction 3. Ghosts—Fiction 4. Haunted places—Fiction 5. Hotels—Fiction 6. Identity—Fiction 7. Mystery and detective stories
ISBN 0803736711; 9780803736719 (hardcover)
LC 2013-019376

SUMMARY: In this book, by Sheila Turnage, "when Miss Lana makes an Accidental Bid at the Tupelo auction and winds up the mortified owner of an old inn, she doesn't realize there's a ghost in the fine print. Naturally, Desperado Detective Agency (aka Mo and Dale) opens a paranormal division to solve the mystery of the ghost's identity. But Mo and Dale start to realize . . . [p]eople can also be haunted by their own past." (Publisher's note)

REVIEW: *Booklist* v110 no18 p69 My 15 2014 Karen Cruze

REVIEW: *Booklist* v110 no18 p47 My 15 2014 Gillian Engberd

REVIEW: *Booklist* v110 no8 p41 D 15 2013 Carolyn Phelan

REVIEW: *Bull Cent Child Books* v67 no7 p382 Mr 2014 K. C.

REVIEW: *Horn Book Magazine* v90 no1 p102 Ja/F 2014 BETTY CARTER

"The Ghosts of Tupelo Landing." "Those who visited Tupelo Landing previously (in Newbery Honor book 'Three Times Lucky' . . .) are familiar with the numerous colorful inhabitants of this small North Carolina town. Newcomers, though, will need more than a smidgen of time and patience to sort them all out, time that would be more enjoyably spent reading the first book. But once readers get the lay of the land, their efforts will be rewarded. . . . Mo's distinctive voice, full of humor and Southern colloquialisms, narrates a tale with as many twists and turns as North Carolina's own Tar River, giving readers a sweet, laid-back story that reveals a ghost who, bless her heart, just wants to set the record straight about her death."

REVIEW: *Kirkus Rev* v81 no23 p184 D 1 2013

REVIEW: *Publ Wkly* v260 no45 p72 N 11 2013

REVIEW: *SLJ* v60 no1 p92 Ja 2014 Kathy Cherniavsky

TURNBULL, JOANNE.tr. Autobiography of a corpse. See Krzhizhanovsky, S.

TURNER, ALEXIS, 1963-. Taxidermy; [by] Alexis Turner 256 p. 2013 Rizzoli International Publications

1. Art literature 2. Art museums 3. Fashion 4. Interior decoration 5. Taxidermy
ISBN 9780847840977 (hardcover)
LC 2013-930106

SUMMARY: This book, by Alexis Turner, considers "taxidermy as an art form, and it balances showcasing classic work (such as pieces by Walter Potter) alongside innovative and modern contemporary pieces by various practitioners, from traditional taxidermists to interior designers, fashionistas, stylists, and fine artists. Collected here in one volume are . . . examples of taxidermy, freshly photographed in situ, from contemporary apartments and rarely seen private interiors to luxury fashion shoots, hipster lounges and restaurants, and museums and galleries." (Publisher's note)

REVIEW: *N Y Times Book Rev* p30 D 8 2013 MELISSA MILGROM

"Taxidermy." "The 337 images in 'Taxidermy' are artful and immaculate. . . . This book is eye candy . . . , which makes sense because [author] Alexis Turner is the founder of London Taxidermy, a business that supplies natural history artifacts to the fashion and film industries, among other clients. . . . Generally, his taste is as au courant as it is idiosyncratic. . . . He doesn't want to disturb us too much, though, which leads to some significant inaccuracies, like his assertion that 'modern taxidermy is primary derived from animals that have died from natural or accidental deaths.'"

TURNER, BARRY.ed. The Statesman's Yearbook 2014. See The Statesman's Yearbook 2014

TURNER, BRYAN. The new medical sociology; social forms of health and illness; [by] Bryan Turner xxviii, 356 p. 2004 W W Norton & Co Inc

1. Globalization 2. Sick 3. Social cohesion 4. Social medicine 5. Sociology literature

ISBN 0393975053 (pbk.)

LC 2004-043475

SUMMARY: In this book, Bryan Turner "examines how macro processes like globalization, risk, economic deregulation, and technological change shape personal experiences of health and illness. Addressing key topics in contemporary sociology such as the body, power, and knowledge, Turner sets out to rethink medical sociology as an exciting perspective on the principal transformations of modern society." (Publisher's note)

REVIEW: *Contemp Sociol* v43 no2 p155-60 Mr 2014 Graham Scambler

"The Future of Human Nature," "The Politics of Life Itself: Biomedicine, Power, and Subjectivity in the Twenty-First Century," and "The New Medical Sociology: Social Forms of Health and Illness". "[Jürgen Habermas's] short volume comprises three pieces of direct relevance to medical sociology dating back to 2001: the first two are expanded versions of lectures delivered at the Universities of Zurich and Marburg and the third is based on a speech he gave on receiving the Peace Prize of the German Book Trade. . . . [Nikolas] Rose traverses similar territory but takes a very different route. Drawing on explicitly Foucauldian theoretical foundations as well as his previous work, he takes off from the current and growing ambiguity around notions of the normal. . . . Bryan Turner has decisively intervened in medical sociology's development more than once. His 'The New Medical Sociology' consolidates his reputation."

TURNER, CHRIS. The War on Science; Muzzled Scientists and Wilful Blindness in Stephen Harper's Canada; [by] Chris Turner 176 p. 2014 Pgw

1. Canada—Politics & government 2. Federal aid to environmental research 3. Harper, Stephen, 1959- 4. Political science literature 5. Science & state 6. Science—Political aspects

ISBN 1771004312; 9781771004312

SUMMARY: "In this arresting and passionately argued indictment, award-winning journalist Chris Turner contends that Stephen Harper's attack on basic science, science communication, environmental regulations, and the environmental NGO community is the most vicious assault ever waged by a Canadian government on the fundamental principles of the Enlightenment. . . . Drawing on interviews with scientists," this book "paints a vivid and damning portrait of a government." (Publisher's note)

REVIEW: *Quill Quire* v79 no9 p31-2 N 2013 Jan Dutkiewicz

"The War on Science: Muzzled Scientists and Wilful Blindness in Stephen Harper's Canada." "[Author] Chris Turner is angry. . . . In 'The War on Science,' the veteran journalist lays out the federal Conservatives' systematic efforts to remove science from Canadian politics. His argument is as simple as it is frightening: under Stephen Harper, Canada has gone from being a world leader in scientific research and a beacon of environmental stewardship to an embarrassment on the international stage. . . . Turner's work is certainly polemical, but, in the political climate Harper has created, a bit of vitriol may be exactly what is needed."

TURNER, DENYS. Thomas Aquinas; a portrait; [by] Denys Turner 300 p. 2013 Yale University Press

1. Biography (Literary form) 2. Saints 3. Theologians 4. Theology

ISBN 9780300188554 (alk. paper)

LC 2012-044497

SUMMARY: In this book on Thomas Aquinas, Denys Turner "schews a traditional biographical approach and attempts to develop a 'portrait' or 'caricature' of the saint's mind by analyzing his thoughts on various theological and philosophical topics including the soul, God, Christ, friendship, and grace. . . . He observes that it is a mistake to try separately to understand his thought, spirituality, and sanctity; rather, these are all intrinsically intertwined." (Library Journal)

REVIEW: *America* v209 no10 p34-6 O 14 2013 JAMES R. KELLY

REVIEW: *Choice* v51 no4 p657-8 D 2013 J. C. Swindal

REVIEW: *Christ Century* v130 no18 p41-3 S 4 2013 Lawrence S. Cunningham

REVIEW: *Commonweal* v141 no9 p26-8 My 16 2014 Gary Gutting

REVIEW: *Libr J* v138 no9 p83 My 15 2013 Fred Poling

REVIEW: *London Rev Books* v35 no23 p39-40 D 5 2013 Terry Eagleton

"Thomas Aquinas: A Portrait". "His materialism was not some kind of brutal reductionism, any more than [Karl] Marx's was. On the contrary, as Denys Turner points out in this superb study, he understood that 'there is a lot more to matter itself than meets the eye of today's average materialist.' . . . Modern-day materialists, Turner complains, talk about matter, but unlike Thomas they cannot hear matter talking. . . . Turner makes much of what one might call the anonymity of Aquinas, the fact that he effaces himself in his deadpan, meticulous, unfussy writing so as not to allow personality to obtrude between the reader and the truth."

TUROW, SCOTT, 1949-. Identical; [by] Scott Turow 416 p. 2013 Grand Central Pub.

1. Detective & mystery stories 2. Ex-convicts—Fiction 3. Murder investigation—Fiction 4. Political candidates 5. Twins—Fiction

ISBN 9781455527205 (hardcover); 9781455576081 (large print hardcover)

LC 2013-939287

SUMMARY: In this book, "State Senator Paul Giannis is a candidate for Mayor of Kindle County. His identical twin brother Cass is newly released from prison, 25 years after pleading guilty to the murder of his girlfriend, Dita Kronon.

When Evon Miller, an ex-FBI agent who is the head of security for the Kronon family business, and private investigator Tim Brodie begin a re-investigation of Dita's death, a complex web of murder, sex, and betrayal . . . unfolds." (Publisher's note)

REVIEW: *Booklist* v109 no22 p39 Ag 1 2013 Connie Fletcher

REVIEW: *Kirkus Rev* p18 2013 Guide 20to BookExpo America

REVIEW: *Kirkus Rev* v81 no2 p31 Je 1 2013

REVIEW: *Libr J* v138 no14 p104 S 1 2013 Jerry P. Miller

REVIEW: *Libr J* v138 no8 p59 My 1 2013

REVIEW: *N Y Times Book Rev* p10 O 20 2013 ADAM LIPTAK

"Identical." "It is always a pleasure to visit Kindle County, Scott Turow's shadow version of greater Chicago. . . . But not every trip to Kindle County is equally rewarding. This latest one . . . is stuffed with so many themes and reversals that readers may end up feeling the way you do after a long family meal with too much talk and food: disoriented, logy and a little nostalgic. Turow has many gifts. He might consider being a little more parsimonious in doling them out. Yes, he wants to stretch, and who can blame him? . . . So he has set himself new challenges, touching on areas of the law where he is less sure-footed and working with a classical template apparently meant to give his tale literary weight. The stew gets awfully rich."

REVIEW: *Publ Wkly* v260 no26 p65-6 Jl 1 2013

TURVEY, MALCOLM. The filming of modern life; European avant-garde film of the 1920s; [by] Malcolm Turvey 213 2011 MIT Press

1. Art and motion pictures 2. Art and society—Europe—History—20th century 3. Avant-garde (Arts) 4. Experimental films—Europe—History—20th century 5. Motion picture literature
ISBN 9780262015189; 0-262-01518-8
LC 2010-020908

SUMMARY: In this book, "Malcolm Turvey examines five films from the avant-garde canon and the complex, sometimes contradictory, attitudes toward modernity they express. . . . Turvey argues that these films share a concern with modernization and the rapid, dislocating changes it was bringing about. He critically addresses major theories of the avant-garde and its relation to modern life . . . and he challenges the standard view of the avant-garde as implacably opposed to bourgeois modernity." (Publisher's note)"Turvey argues for a reassessment and regrouping of the radical cinematic works of European avant-garde artists in the 1920." (Times Lit Suppl) Index.

REVIEW: *Art Am* v102 no1 p51 Ja 2014

"Lessons From Modernism: Environmental Design Strategies in Architecture, 1925-1970," "The Filming of Modern Life: European Avant-Garde Film of the 1920s," and "Anywhere or Not at All: Philosophy of Contemporary Art." "Twenty-five buildings completed between 1925 and 1970 provide insight into how architects like Oscar Niemeyer and Le Corbusier dealt with environmental issues and influenced green building today. . . . Five classic experimental films by artists such as Hans Richter and Salvador Dalí offer contrasting--and sometimes self-contradictory--views of modernity. . . . Drawing from philosophers like [Immanuel] Kant and the German Romantics and artists like Sol Le Witt and the Atlas Group, [Peter] Osborne critically redefines what's 'contemporary' about contemporary art."

REVIEW: *Film Q* v65 no2 p84-5 Wint 2011 Leo Charney

TUSHNET, MARK. In the balance; law and politics on the Roberts Court; [by] Mark Tushnet 352 p. 2013 W W Norton & Co Inc

1. Judges—United States 2. Law—Political aspects—United States 3. Political questions and judicial power—United States 4. Political science literature
ISBN 0393073440; 9780393073447 (hardcover)
LC 2013-012744

SUMMARY: In this book, "constitutional law expert Mark Tushnet clarifies the lines of conflict and what is at stake on the Supreme Court as it hangs 'in the balance' between its conservatives and its liberals." He "cover[s] the legal philosophies that have informed decisions on major cases such as the Affordable Care Act, the political structures behind Court appointments, and the face-off between John Roberts and Elena Kagan for intellectual dominance of the Court." (Publisher's note)

REVIEW: *Booklist* v109 no22 p11-2 Ag 1 2013 Jay Freeman

REVIEW: *Choice* v51 no6 p1097-8 F 2014 H. J. Knowles

"In the Balance: Law and Politics on the Roberts Court." "[Mark] Tushnet covers ground that will be familiar to many students of the contemporary Court. However, unlike some scholars he provides analysis that is refreshingly objective. He draws upon insights from both law and politics, and he avoids popular, reductionist tendencies that settle for easy (and oftentimes partisan) labels such as 'conservative' and 'liberal.' 'In the Balance' will be a valuable and well-received addition to reading lists for undergraduate courses about the Supreme Court and judicial decision making."

REVIEW: *Kirkus Rev* v81 no14 p70 Jl 15 2013

TUTTLE, BETH. Magnetic; the art and science of engagement; [by] Beth Tuttle 224 p. 2013 AAM Press of American Alliance of Museums

1. Business literature 2. Engagement (Philosophy) 3. Management 4. Museums—Management 5. Service learning
ISBN 9781933253831
LC 2013-006506

SUMMARY: In this book, authors Anne Bergeron and Beth Tuttle "analyze ten years of qualitative museum data and interviews with museum professionals about customer service, management, and innovation from six museums. . . . The book outlines six practices that make these institutions 'magnetic.' All of the examples used have three commonalities: investing in relationships, forging connections, and creating meaningful experiences for everyone involved." (Choice: Current Reviews for Academic Libraries)

REVIEW: *Choice* v51 no5 p795 Ja 2014 A. Zanin Yost

"Magnetic: The Art and Science of Engagement." "[Anne] Bergeron . . . and [Beth] Tuttle . . . analyze ten years of qualitative museum data and interviews with museum professionals about customer service, management, and innovation from six museums:Their examples provide a model for corporations and nonprofits on how to think more creatively and effectively in response to the changing needs and demographics of their respective clients and constituencies. . . . The book is clearly written and documented with many ideas that other institutions may apply. It will make an excellent addition to any art or business collection. . . . Recommended."

TUTU, DESMOND, 1931-. The book of forgiving; the fourfold path for healing ourselves and our world; 240 p. 2014 HarperOne

1. Apartheid 2. Forgiveness 3. Reconciliation 4. Self-help materials 5. Spirituality

ISBN 0062203568; 9780062203564; 9780062203571 (pbk)

LC 2013-033890

SUMMARY: In this book, Desmond Tutu and his daughter Mpho "lay out the simple but profound truths about the significance of forgiveness, how it works, why everyone needs to know how to grant it and receive it, and why granting forgiveness is the greatest gift we can give to ourselves when we have been wronged." (Publisher's note)

REVIEW: *Christ Century* v131 no20 p42-3 O 1 2014 Arianne Braithwaite Lehn

REVIEW: *Kirkus Rev* v82 no4 p78 F 15 2014

"The Book of Forgiving: The Fourfold Path for Healing Ourselves and Our World". "The book is almost entirely practical in focus, geared toward helping people come to grips with issues of anger, grief and loss. It includes meditations, rituals and journal exercises after each chapter. While potentially useful, the text is lightweight in relation to some of the examples of superhuman forgiveness punctuating the work-victims of grave crimes pardoning those who have caused such anguish. There is a disconnect between the gravitas of the surname Tutu in relationship to what is basically a self-help book. [Desmonend] Tutu's 'No Future Without Forgiveness' (1999) is a far weightier and more worthy discussion of the topic."

REVIEW: *Libr J* v139 no3 p87 F 15 2014 Graham Christian

REVIEW: *Publ Wkly* v261 no3 p49 Ja 20 2014

TUTU, MPHO A., 1963-. The book of forgiving. See Tutu, D.

TV'S BETTY GOES GLOBAL; from telenovela to international brand; xv, 259 p. 2013 I.B. Tauris

1. Telenovelas 2. Television and globalization 3. Television criticism 4. Television programs—Plots, themes, etc 5. Yo Soy Betty la Fea (TV program)

ISBN 1780762674 (pbk.); 9781780762678 (pbk.)

LC 2012-285399

SUMMARY: This book, edited by Janet McCabe and Kim Akass, is "about how television formats go global [and] asks what the ['Ugly] Betty' phenomenon can tell us about the international circulation of locally produced TV fictions as the Latin American telenovela is sold to, and/or re-made for, different national contexts. The contributors explore what 'Betty' says about the tensions between multimedia conglomerates' commercial demands and the regulatory forces of national broadcasters." (Publisher's note)

REVIEW: *Choice* v51 no4 p627-8 D 2013 A. N. Valdivia

"TV's Betty Goes Global: From Telenovela to International Brand." "Joining a growing body of scholarship on global television hit 'Ugly Betty,' this elegantly crafted collection brings together . . . of scholars who analyze this bit television show from such specific locations as Colombia (where the program was born as a telenovela, 'Yo soy Betty, la fea,' in 1999), India, Spain, the US, Greece, the People's Republic of China, the Czech Republic, Russia, Israel, Germany, and Flanders. Contributors explore . . . transnational cultural flow, cultural proximity, global commodification, franchise deployment, gender and ethnic politics, and hybridization of genres. Methods include representational analysis, audience and ethnographic studies, production, and political economic studies."

TWELVE VIEWS FROM THE DISTANCE; xx, 243 p. 2012 University of Minnesota Press

1. Gay male poets 2. Japan—History—20th century 3. Memoirs 4. Poets, Japanese—20th century—Biography

ISBN 9780816672776 (hc : acid-free paper); 9780816679362 (pb : acid-free paper)

LC 2012-022567

SUMMARY: This memoir by Mutsuo Takahashi, which was nominated for a 2013 Lambda Literary award, "traces a boy's childhood and its intersection with the rise of the Japanese empire and World War II. . . . Growing up poor in rural southwestern Japan, far from the urban life that many of his contemporaries have written about, Takahashi experienced a reality rarely portrayed in literature. In addition to his personal remembrances, the book paints a . . . portrait of rural Japan." (Publisher's note)

REVIEW: *World Lit Today* v87 no5 p78 S/O 2013 Takeshi Kimoto

"Twelve Views From the Distance." "This superb translation of [Mutsuo] Takahashi's autobiography--nominated for the 2013 Lambda Literary Award--is an excellent companion to the poet's other translated works. . . . In his autobiography, he adopts a plainer prose style to narrate his family history, one that is filled with unhappy episodes. Yet for the reader, the is somewhat mitigated because of Takahashi's optics of the weak that looks at this worldly cruelty as if from another world. . . . At the end of the book, he presents a poem in which he promiscuously melts into the crowds becomes anonymous, and is no longer present. This imagery affirms absence as such and represents a commentary on Takahashi's politics."

TWIGGER, ROBERT. Red Nile; The Biography of the World's Greatest River; [by] Robert Twigger 600 p. 2014 Phoenix

1. Burton, Richard Francis, Sir, 1821-1890 2. Egypt—History 3. Historical literature 4. Nile River 5. Nile River—In literature

ISBN 1780220936; 9781780220932

SUMMARY: This book by Robert Twigger is "a chronicle of the White Nile and Blue Nile and the stories attached to those great tributaries. Though the silt carried by the Nile flows red until it is deposited on land . . . the 'Red' of the title really refers to the bloodiness of so many of the stories Twigger has to tell: the murder of the Pharaoh Seqenenre . . . the alleged suicide of John Hanning Speke in 1864, the bodies of countless Tutsis seen drifting down the Nile in 1994." (Times Literary Supplement)

REVIEW: *TLS* no5754 p10 Jl 12 2013 ROBERT IRWIN

"Red Nile: A Biography of the World's Greatest River." "'Red Nile' is described on the dust jacket as 'idiosyncratic'. It certainly is that. . . . In itself the wealth of misinformation present here (and there is far more than I can be troubled to list) did not bother me, for I am fairly familiar with the real history of medieval Egypt and I enjoyed [Robert] Twigger's colourful stories. But then I became doubtful, for, if the chapter on medieval Egypt contains so much misinformation, then how much else can be relied on?"

TWO LAMENTABLE TRAGEDIES; 2013 Manchester University Press

1. English drama (Tragedy) 2. English drama—17th century 3. European drama—Renaissance, 1450-1600 4. Fathers & sons—Drama 5. Murder—Drama
ISBN 9780719090622 hardcover

SUMMARY: "This edition of 'Two Lamentable Tragedies,' a quarto printed in 1601 by Richard Read for Matthew Law, and ascribed on the title-page to Robert Yarington, is the first to be published since 1913. . . . The introduction [by Chiaki Hanabusa] contains an up-to-date consideration of many aspects of the text, including a detailed bibliographical analysis of types, page dimensions, headlines, watermarks and paper." (Publisher's note)

REVIEW: *TLS* no5785 p27 F 14 2014 HANNAH AUGUST

"Two Lamentable Tragedies." "'Two Lamentable Tragedies' . . . the 1601 play by Robert Yarington . . . has recently been added to the corpus of Malone Society Reprints, in a facsimile edition prepared by Chiaki Hanabusa. Hanabusa's edition provides easy access to a play notable primarily for its insouciant juxtaposition of two entirely unrelated plotlines, and infamous early modern stage directions. . . . The ordering of topics treated by the introduction . . . is potentially confusing for the reader in search of context, and Hanabusa's arguments are occasionally hampered by a lack of clarity in his expression."

TWO PROSPECTORS; The Letters of Sam Shepard and Johnny Dark; 304 p. 2013 University of Texas Press

1. Authors—Correspondence 2. Dark, Johnny 3. Fathers-in-law 4. Letters 5. Shepard, Sam, 1943-
ISBN 0292735820; 9780292735828

SUMMARY: This book, edited by Chad Hammett, presents "a decades-long friendship between the writer and his former father-in-law, revealed in a collection of letters, notes and transcripts. Only three years separate [Johnny] Dark and [Sam] Shepard, and in this engaging correspondence, we see the evolution of their relationship. They were buddies earlier, and they remained close despite Shepard's rise to celebrity as a playwright and actor." (Kirkus Reviews)

REVIEW: *Choice* v51 no9 p1594-5 My 2014 K. Tancheva

"2 Prospectors: The Letters of Sam Shepard & Johnny Dark". "This volume comprises the extraordinarily prolific exchange between Sam Shepard and his friend Johnny Dark, often his first reader, critic, sounding board, and adviser. . . . The letters offer an unexpectedly candid look at Shepard, and the book will surely be much appreciated by his current and future biographers. [Chad] Hammett edited the letters to create a 'compelling story,' and the book is well illustrated. . . . It has been published with both Shepard's and Dark's approval, which probably explains its rather reverent tone."

REVIEW: *Kirkus Rev* v81 no13 p271 Jl 1 2013

TWO ROMES: ROME AND CONSTANTINOPLE IN LATE ANTIQUITY; xiii, 465 p. 2012 Oxford University Press

1. City and town life—Rome—History 2. City and town life—Turkey—Istanbul—History—To 1500 3. Historical literature 4. Social change—Rome—History 5. Social change—Turkey—Istanbul—History—To 1500
ISBN 9780199739400
LC 2011-017620

SUMMARY: In this book, edited by Lucy Grig and Gavin Kelly "prominent international scholars examine the changing roles and perceptions of Rome and Constantinople in Late Antiquity from a range of different disciplines and scholarly perspectives. . . . These studies present important revisionist arguments and new interpretations of significant texts and events." (Publisher's note)

REVIEW: *Choice* v50 no3 p545 N 2012 R. I. Frank

REVIEW: *Classical Rev* v63 no2 p555-7 O 2013 David Woods

REVIEW: *TLS* no5748 p5 My 31 2013 PETER FRANKOPAN

"Two Romes: Rome and Constantinople in Late Antiquity.""In this collection of seventeen essays, written by some of the most eminent figures in the field, the cities of Rome and New Rome--as Constantinople was often called--get a thorough going-over. One long-accepted view after another is taken on and exposed. . . . The results revolutionize how we should understand Rome and Constantinople, as well as the relationship between them. . . . 'Two Romes,' which brings together the latest archaeological material and a consistently subtle and intelligent handling of complex and nuanced written sources, is a treat--if not always easy reading."

TWOHY, MIKE. Wake up, Rupert!; [by] Mike Twohy 32 p. 2014 Simon & Schuster

1. Children's stories 2. Farm life—Fiction 3. Morning 4. Roosters—Fiction 5. Sheep—Fiction
ISBN 1442459980; 9781442459984 (hardcover : alk. paper)
LC 2012-047857

SUMMARY: In this book by Mike Twohy, "Rupert the rooster knows that every morning when the sun comes up he must cock-a-doodle-do--no matter what. But Rupert is terrible at waking up! And even worse, he can never, ever sleep in. Life just isn't fair. When his friend Sherman the Sheep volunteers for the job, everything is perfect. Or is it?" (Publisher's note)

REVIEW: *Booklist* v110 no11 p71-2 F 1 2014 Paula Willey

"Wake Up, Rupert!" "Rupert the rooster is just not a morning person. He doesn't think it's fair that he has to get up before everyone else, and who can blame him? Certainly not his pal Sherman the sheep, who volunteers to take over Rupert's job. . . . Sharp-lined, cartoonish ink drawings with lots of color complement the action-packed text. It seems a shame that Rupert is the only man for the job, due solely to his species, but he resumes his duties cheerfully and with a newfound sense of responsibility."

REVIEW: *Kirkus Rev* v81 no23 p148 D 1 2013

REVIEW: *Publ Wkly* v260 no45 p69 N 11 2013

REVIEW: *SLJ* v60 no3 p128 Mr 2014 Linda Ludke

TWOHY, MIKE.il. Wake up, Rupert! See Twohy, M.

TWOMEY, RYAN. The child is father of the man; the importance of juvenilia in the development of the author; [by] Ryan Twomey 164 p. 2012 H&DG, Hes & De Graaf Publishers
1. Ainsworth, William Harrison, 1805-1882 2. Authorship 3. Brontë, Emily, 1818-1848 4. Child authors 5. Children's writings 6. Edgeworth, Maria, 1768-1849 7. Eliot, George, 1819-1880 8. Literary critiques
ISBN 9061945216; 9789061945215
LC 2012-455454

SUMMARY: Author "Ryan Twomey's study of nineteenth-century juvenilia argues that 'many of the advances writers make that are praised in their adult work can be shown to have been established in their juvenilia'. This point is made in a series of chapters that examine the juvenilia of four disparate writers: Maria Edgeworth, William Harrison Ainsworth, George Eliot and Emily Brontë." (Times Literary Supplement)

REVIEW: *TLS* no5751 p26 Je 21 2013 CHRISTINA PETRIE

"The Child Is Father of The Man: The Importance of Juvenilia in the Development of the Author." " Unfortunately, [Ryan] Twomey gets bogged down in pursuing arguments that seem unnecessary to his project. . . . Such distracting reflections on the value of juvenilia 'as a literary genre worthy of the critic's attention' are a strong feature of the book and suggest a lack of editorial support to develop the more compelling aspect of Twomey's research: his interest in how nineteenth-century child writers developed a relationship with a genre, such as the historical novel. In trying to prove how seriously juvenilia should be taken, he misses the opportunity to expand on the unique aspects of these very unusual childhood writings, educations and lives."

TYACK, GEOFFREY.ed. John Nash. See John Nash

TYRANNOSAURID PALEOBIOLOGY; 294 p. 2013 Indiana University Press
1. Dinosaur anatomy 2. Natural history literature 3. Paleobiology 4. Paleontology—Cretaceous 5. Tyrannosauridae
ISBN 9780253009302 (cl : alk. paper)
LC 2013-002879

SUMMARY: This book on tyrannosaurid paleobiology "includes studies of the tyrannosaurids Chingkankousaurus fragilis and 'Sir William' and the generic status of Nanotyrannus; theropod teeth, pedal proportions, brain size, and craniocervical function; soft tissue reconstruction . . . paleopathology and tyrannosaurid claws . . . and tyrannosaur feeding and hunting strategies." (Publisher's note)

REVIEW: *Choice* v51 no7 p1250 Mr 2014 J. C. Kricher

"Tyrannosaurid Paleobiology." "This work, part of the outstanding 'Life of the Past' series, is based on a 2005 symposium held at the Burpee Museum of Natural History. . . . Much content is technical, requiring a strong knowledge . of vertebrate anatomy. Likely the last section will be of most interest to general readers as it considers whether adult tyrannosaurs were primarily scavengers (as has often been suggested) or active predators. The evidence presented, including a wonderful analogy between 'cow tipping' and 'ceratopsian tipping' (how tyrannosaurs might have attacked these large dinosaurs), argues forcefully for viewing tyrannosaurs as just how they seemed: scary predators. . . . Highly recommended."

TYRRELL, TOBY. On Gaia; a critical investigation of the relationship between life and earth; [by] Toby Tyrrell 320 p. 2013 Princeton University Press
1. Coevolution 2. Gaia hypothesis 3. Geobiology 4. Philosophy of nature 5. Scientific literature
ISBN 9780691121581 (hardcover : alk. paper)
LC 2013-005823

SUMMARY: This book presents an "evaluation and rebuttal" of James Lovelock's Gaia hypothesis, which posits "that life is not just a casual occupant of this planet, but instead that life has controlled the environment of the planet." Toby Tyrrell "examines alternative arguments about the long-term characteristics of the Earth, considering geological and coevolutionary effects." (Choice: Current Reviews for Academic Libraries)

REVIEW: *Choice* v51 no5 p870 Ja 2014 D. Bardack

"On Gaia: A Critical Investigation of the Relationship Between Life and Earth." "This is the first full-scale evaluation and rebuttal of [James] Lovelock's argument. . . . [Toby Tyrrell's] examination of physical and chemical forces is thorough. He investigates how oceanic acidity, greenhouse gases, and glaciation have affected the planet and its organisms. This is a comprehensive exploration of what--to some people--has been an attractive idea. The book is well documented with 52 pages of detailed notes and 21 pages of references. Overall, a useful examination of the changing nature of Earth and the biologic/physical factors that affect the planet's organisms."

TZUCHIEN THO.ed. Badiou and the philosophers . See Badiou and the philosophers

U

UFBERG, ROSS.tr. Beautiful Twentysomethings. See Hlasko, M.

UGAZ, DANIELA MARIA.tr. The beast. See Martinez, O.

UHLMAN, TOM.il. Eruption! See Rusch, E.

ULIJASZEK, STANLEY.ed. Insecurity, inequality, and obesity in affluent societies. See Insecurity, inequality, and obesity in affluent societies

UMOJA, AKINYELE OMOWALE. We will shoot back; armed resistance in the Mississippi Freedom Movement; [by] Akinyele Omowale Umoja xii, 339 p. 2013 New York University Press
1. African Americans—Civil rights—Mississippi—History—20th century 2. African Americans—Suffrage—Mississippi—History—20th century 3. Civil rights movements—Mississippi—History—20th century 4. Civil rights workers—Mississippi—History—20th cen-

tury 5. Historical literature 6. Self-defense—Political aspects—Mississippi—History—20th century
ISBN 9780814725245 (cl: alk. paper)
LC 2012-046909

SUMMARY: "In 'We Will Shoot Back: Armed Resistance in the Mississippi Freedom Movement,' Akinyele Omowale Umoja argues that armed resistance was critical to the efficacy of the southern freedom struggle and the dismantling of segregation and Black disenfranchisement. . . . Armed self-defense was a major tool of survival in allowing some Black southern communities to maintain their integrity and existence in the face of White supremacist terror." (Publisher's note)

REVIEW: *Am Hist Rev* v119 no1 p207-8 F 2014 Christopher Strain

REVIEW: *Choice* v51 no2 p338 O 2013 W. T. Howard

REVIEW: *Ethn Racial Stud* v37 no5 p895-7 Ap 2014 Matthew W. Hughey

REVIEW: *J Am Hist* v101 no1 p337 Je 2014

REVIEW: *Rev Am Hist* v42 no2 p341-5 Je 2014 Jason Morgan Ward

"We Will Shoot Back: Armed Resistance in the Mississippi Freedom Movement." "By stressing the primacy of armed self-defense to everyday activists and local struggles, [author Akinyele Omowale] Umoja does more than simply broaden the cast of characters and list of locales in the civil rights narrative. Emphasizing continuity, he places the interaction between armed resistance and black activism at the heart of his study. . . . 'We Will Shoot Back' is a model of careful, serious, and compelling scholarship. The fruit of more than two decades of study, Umoja's book combines deep archival research, extensive oral history work, and an impressive command of the existing scholarship on the Black Freedom Movement."

UMSTÄTTER, LADA.ed. Le corbusier and the power of photography. See Le corbusier and the power of photography

UNDERWOOD, DEBORAH. Here comes the Easter Cat!; 80 p. 2014 Dial Books for Young Readers

1. Animal stories 2. Cats—Fiction 3. Easter—Juvenile literature 4. Easter Bunny—Fiction 5. Humorous stories
ISBN 0803739397; 9780803739390 (hardcover)
LC 2012-038134

SUMMARY: This book, by Deborah Underwood and illustrated by Claudia Rueda, tells the story of a cat that attempts to deliver eggs on Easter. "He dons his sparkly suit, jumps on his Harley, and roars off into the night. But it turns out delivering Easter eggs is hard work. And it doesn't leave much time for naps (of which Cat has taken five--no, seven). So when a pooped-out Easter Bunny shows up, and with a treat for Cat, what will Cat do?" (Publisher's note)

REVIEW: *Booklist* v110 no11 p70 F 1 2014 Jesse Karp

REVIEW: *Bull Cent Child Books* v67 no5 p287 Ja 2014 J. H.

REVIEW: *Horn Book Magazine* v90 no2 p106 Mr/Ap 2014 CYNTHIA K. RITTER

"Here Comes the Easter cat." "The text addresses Cat directly throughout the book, and he responds using placards, humorous expressions, and body language to convey his emotions to great effect. . . . [Claudia] Rueda expertly uses white space, movement, and page turns to focus attention on Cat and the repartee. The combination of Underwood's knowledgeable authorial voice and Rueda's loosely sketched, textured ink and colored-pencil illustrations make this an entertaining, well-paced tale for interactive story hours. And if he isn't going to usurp the Easter Bunny, then clever Cat will just have to take over another ho-ho-holiday."

REVIEW: *Kirkus Rev* v82 no5 p145 Mr 1 2014

"Here Comes the Easter Cat". "Quirky colored-pencil illustrations complement the whimsical story, with a minimalist illustration on each spread facing a short question or comment from the narrator. The design uses an interesting, old-fashioned typeface and plenty of white space, creating a playful but sophisticated mood that plays on Cat's contrary personality. After his success at assisting the Easter Bunny, Cat comes up with another idea for the final spread: He tries on a Santa Claus costume that just might predict a sequel. Utterly endearing."

REVIEW: *Publ Wkly* v261 no7 p96 F 17 2014

REVIEW: *SLJ* v60 no1 p77 Ja 2014 Brooke Rasche

UNDSET, SIGRID (1882-1949). Marta Oulie; a novel of betrayal; 128 p. 2014 University of Minnesota Press

1. Adultery—Fiction 2. Diary fiction 3. Married women—Fiction 4. Norwegian fiction—20th century
ISBN 9780816692521 (pbk.)
LC 2013-046280

SUMMARY: "'Marta Oulie,' written in the form of a diary, intimately documents the inner life of a young woman disappointed and constrained by the conventions of marriage as she longs for an all-consuming passion. Set in Kristiania (now Oslo) at the beginning of the twentieth century, [author Sigrid] Undset's book is an incomparable psychological portrait of a woman whose destiny is defined by the changing mores of her day—as she descends, inevitably, into an ever-darker reckoning." (Publisher's note)

REVIEW: *New Yorker* v90 no8 p83-1 Ap 14 2014

"Marta Oulie: A Novel of Betrayal." "This novella, about a woman who has committed adultery, caused a minor scandal when it was published, in 1907. The core of Marta's dissatisfaction is her husband's disregard for her intellect and her interior life. The attentions of an appreciative cousin enable her to see herself anew, though she cares for him no more 'than for the mirror on my dressing table.' Her inability to navigate the needs of family, faith, and self is rather tentatively portrayed, and the narrative structure, a series of diary entries, feels contrived."

UNGAR, MARK.ed. Sustaining human rights in the twenty-first century. See Sustaining human rights in the twenty-first century

UNGER, DOMINIC J.tr. St. Irenaeus of Lyons. See Irenaeus, S.

UNITED PRESS INTERNATIONAL INC.comp. Four days. See Four days

THE UNPUBLISHED LETTERS OF THOMAS MOORE; 864 p. 2013 Ashgate Pub Co

1. Authors & publishers 2. Authors—Correspondence 3. Irish authors 4. Letters 5. Moore, Thomas, 1779-1852

ISBN 1848930747; 9781848930742

SUMMARY: This collection of letters by Thomas Moore "presents over seven hundred previously unpublished letters from numerous libraries, archives and other sources in the UK, Ireland and America. Also included are excerpts from hundreds of Moore's letters written to his music publisher, James Power, which have not been published since 1854." (Publisher's note)

REVIEW: *TLS* no5773 p10-1 N 22 2013 H. J. JACKSON

"The Unpublished Letters of Thomas Moore." "Jeffrey W. Vail has . . . performed a significant service to scholarship by collecting, collating, correcting and organizing these letters. . . . Moore was not one of the great Romantic letter-writers. . . . He turned reluctantly to correspondence, so most of the entries here are short and businesslike. . . . Nevertheless, there are many gems here. . . . A scholarly edition with a reliable text and annotation based on original research is such a labour-intensive, time-consuming and consequently expensive project that all parties have reason to hope that it will become standard and last for ever, or at least for the foreseeable future. This one will; every library that holds [Wilfred] Dowden should now add Vail."

UNSWORTH, TANIA. The one safe place; a novel; [by] Tania Unsworth 304 p. 2014 Algonquin Young Readers

1. Abandoned children—Fiction 2. Orphanages 3. Orphans—Fiction 4. Science fiction 5. Survival—Fiction

ISBN 1616203293; 9781616203290

LC 2013-043145

SUMMARY: This book, by Tania Unsworth, is a "near-future dystopia. . . . Devin doesn't remember life before the world got hot; he has grown up farming the scorched earth with his grandfather in their remote valley. When his grandfather dies, Devin heads for the city. Once there, among the stark glass buildings, he finds scores of children, just like him, living alone on the streets. They tell him rumors of a place for abandoned children, . . . but only the luckiest get there." (Publisher's note)

REVIEW: *Booklist* v110 no18 p64 My 15 2014 Daniel Kraus

REVIEW: *Kirkus Rev* v82 no3 p252 F 1 2014

"The One Safe Place". "A group of orphans uncovers a sinister plot in this chilling and engrossing tale filled with detailed, sharply drawn characters. . . . There are many familiar tropes here, the dystopian setting and the uncanny perfection of the orphanage among them. Yet [Tania] Unsworth's use of unadorned but vivid language . . . is incredibly effective. Likewise, the straightforward third-person narration and the gradual resistance that builds among the children to the unique horrors at the home are convincingly well-paced. A standout in the genre's crowded landscape."

REVIEW: *Publ Wkly* v261 no6 p91 F 10 2014

REVIEW: *SLJ* v60 no7 p55 Jl 2014 Jessica Moody

REVIEW: *SLJ* v60 no3 p150 Mr 2014 Kathy Cherniavsky

REVIEW: *Voice of Youth Advocates* v37 no1 p90 Ap 2014 Janice M. Del Negro

UNZICKER, ALEXANDER. Bankrupting physics. See Jones, S.

UPDIKE, JOHN. Updike; [by] Adam Begley 576 p. 2014 Harper

1. Authors, American—20th century—Biography 2. BIOGRAPHY & AUTOBIOGRAPHY—General 3. BIOGRAPHY & AUTOBIOGRAPHY—Literary 4. LITERARY CRITICISM—American—General

ISBN 9780061896453 (hardback)

LC 2013-039246

SUMMARY: This biography of John Updike "explores the stages of the writer's pilgrim's progress: his beloved home turf of Berks County, Pennsylvania; his escape to Harvard; his brief, busy working life as the golden boy at The New Yorker; his family years in suburban Ipswich, Massachusetts; his extensive travel abroad; and his retreat to another Massachusetts town, Beverly Farms, where he remained until his death in 2009." (Publisher's note)

REVIEW: *Am Sch* v83 no2 p100-2 Spr 2014 ROBERT WILSON

REVIEW: *Booklist* v110 no14 p41-4 Mr 15 2014 Brad Hooper

"Updike." "A keen appreciation for literary criticism is a prerequisite for reader interest in this thoroughly researched and rigorously presented biography of one of the most honored and respected American writers of the twentieth century. . . . It is [Adom] Begley's primary goal to stitch [John] Updike's writing to the realities of his existence. He does so meaningfully but too often intrusively, at the expense of a smoothly flowing pursuit of the events in Updike's life. Nevertheless, this is an important view of a giant literary figure."

REVIEW: *Kirkus Rev* v82 no3 p318 F 1 2014

REVIEW: *Libr J* v139 no5 p118 Mr 15 2014 Lonnie Weatherby

REVIEW: *Libr J* v138 no20 p1 N 15 2013 Barbara Hoffert

REVIEW: *N Y Rev Books* v61 no8 p6-8 My 8 2014 Hermione Lee

REVIEW: *N Y Times Book Rev* p10-1 Ap 20 2014 ORHAN PAMUK

REVIEW: *N Y Times Book Rev* p30 Ap 27 2014

REVIEW: *New Statesman* v143 no17 p42-4 My 2 2014 David Baddiel

REVIEW: *New Statesman* v143 no17 p44-5 My 2 2014 Jeffrey Meyers

REVIEW: *New York Times* v163 no46466 pC1-6 Ap 9 2014 DWIGHT GARNER

REVIEW: *New Yorker* v90 no10 p70-1 Ap 28 2014

REVIEW: *Publ Wkly* v261 no7 p89-90 F 17 2014

REVIEW: *Va Q Rev* v90 no2 p216-21 Spr 2014 John Freeman

UPDIKE, JOHN, 1932-2009. Collected later stories; ix, 994 p. 2013 Library of America

1. American fiction 2. Short stories—Collections 3. Short stories, American 4. Updike, John, 1932-2009

ISBN 1598532529 (hc.); 9781598532524 (hc.)

LC 2012-954952

SUMMARY: Written by John Updike, edited by Christopher

Carduff, "The Library of America presents the second of two volumes in its definitive Updike collection. Here are 84 classic stories that display the virtuosic command of character, dialogue, and sensual description that was Updike's signature. Based on new archival research, each story is presented in its final definitive form and in order of composition, established here for the first time." (Publisher's note)

REVIEW: *N Y Rev Books* v61 no8 p6-8 My 8 2014 Hermione Lee

"Updike" and "The Collected Stories: Collected Early Stories," and "The Collected Stories: Collected Later Stories." "[Author Adam] Begley is quiet, careful, self-effacing, and steady. He is especially good and revealing on how others see Updike: friends, fellow writers, mother, first wife, children, lovers, editors. . . . The childhood stories—stories of 'family, family without end'—shine out of the two-volume Library of America 'Collected Stories.' This has been excellently edited by Christopher Carduff, whose very full chronology makes a useful aid to set alongside the biography, which has no family tree, timeline, or bibliography."

UPDIKE, JOHN, 1932-2009. Collected early stories; x, 955 pages 2013 Library of America

1. American fiction 2. American short stories 3. Short stories—Collections 4. Short stories, American
ISBN 1598532510 (hbk.); 9781598532517 (hbk.)
LC 2012-954899

SUMMARY: In this collection by John Updike, edited by Christopher Carduff, "The Library of America presents the first of two volumes in its definitive Updike collection. Here are 102 classic stories that chart Updike's emergence as America's foremost practitioner of the short story, 'our second Hawthorne,' as Philip Roth described him. Based on new archival research, each story is presented in its final definitive form and in order of composition, established here for the first time." (Publisher's note)

REVIEW: *N Y Rev Books* v61 no8 p6-8 My 8 2014 Hermione Lee

"Updike" and "The Collected Stories: Collected Early Stories," and "The Collected Stories: Collected Later Stories." "[Author Adam] Begley is quiet, careful, self-effacing, and steady. He is especially good and revealing on how others see Updike: friends, fellow writers, mother, first wife, children, lovers, editors. . . . The childhood stories—stories of 'family, family without end'—shine out of the two-volume Library of America 'Collected Stories.' This has been excellently edited by Christopher Carduff, whose very full chronology makes a useful aid to set alongside the biography, which has no family tree, timeline, or bibliography."

URBAN BIRD ECOLOGY AND CONSERVATION; xiv, 326 p. 2012 University of California Press

1. Birds—Conservation 2. Birds—Ecology 3. Environmental literature 4. Urban animals—Conservation 5. Urban animals—Ecology
ISBN 9780520273092 (cloth: alk. paper)
LC 2012-011732

SUMMARY: This book on urban bird ecology and conservation was edited by Christopher A. Lepczyk and Paige S. Warren. "Areas of particular focus include the processes underlying patterns of species shifts along urban-rural gradients, the demography of urban birds and the role of citizen science, and human-avian interaction in urban areas." (Publisher's note)

REVIEW: *Choice* v50 no10 p1864 Je 2013 D. Flaspohler

URQUHART, JANE. Sanctuary line; [by] Jane Urquhart 278 2010 McClelland & Stewart

1. Butterflies—Fiction 2. Canadian fiction 3. Family—Canada—Fiction 4. Farm life—Fiction
ISBN 0-7710-8646-6; 0-7710-8648-2; 978-0-7710-8646-5; 978-0-7710-8648-9; 978-1-59692-366-9
LC 2010-039517

SUMMARY: "Set in the present day on a farm at the shores of Lake Erie, Jane Urquhart's . . . novel weaves elements from the nineteenth-century past, in Ireland and Ontario, into a gradually unfolding contemporary story of events in the lives of the members of one family that come to alter their futures irrevocably. There are ancestral lighthouse-keepers, seasonal Mexican workers; the migratory patterns and survival techniques of the Monarch butterfly; the tragedy of a young woman's death during a tour of duty in Afghanistan; three very different . . . love stories." (Publisher's note)

REVIEW: *Booklist* v110 no1 p41 S 1 2013 Carol Haggas

REVIEW: *Can Lit* no213 p187-9 Summ 2012 Beverley Haun

REVIEW: *Kirkus Rev* v81 no16 p292 Ag 15 2013

"Sanctuary Line." "In Canadian [author Jane] Urquhart's latest . . . , a grown woman returns to the abandoned family farm where she experienced her happiest and most emotionally troubling moments. A year after her cousin Mandy's death while serving in the military in Afghanistan, 40-ish Liz returns to the Ontario farm once owned by Mandy's father, Liz's maternal uncle Stanley, until he disappeared 20 years ago. . . . While Liz's own adulthood remains mostly a blank, Urquhart sensitively portrays her limited perceptions in childhood. Heavy with literary allusions and overt symbolism, Liz's ruminations make for a ponderously slow if finely tuned read."

REVIEW: *TLS* no5685 p20 Mr 16 2012 Sarah Curtis

URQUHART, RACHEL. The Visionist; [by] Rachel Urquhart 400 p. 2014 Simon & Schuster Ltd

1. American historical fiction 2. Collective settlements 3. Female friendship—Fiction 4. Shakers 5. Women mystics
ISBN 1471113329; 9781471113321

SUMMARY: In this novel by Rachel Urquhart, "After 15-year-old Polly Kimball sets fire to the family farm, killing her abusive father, she and her young brother find shelter in a Massachusetts Shaker community called the City of Hope. It is the Era of Manifestations, when young girls in Shaker enclaves all across the Northeast are experiencing extraordinary mystical visions, earning them the honorific of 'Visionist' and bringing renown to their settlements." (Publisher's note)

REVIEW: *Booklist* v110 no3 p41 O 1 2013 Margaret Flanagan

REVIEW: *Kirkus Rev* v81 no8 p28 Ap 15 2013

REVIEW: *N Y Rev Books* v51 no7 p24-5 Ap 24 2014 Cathleen Schine

"The Visionist." "'The Visionist,' Rachel Urquhart's fine first novel, follows the intersecting paths of two fifteen-year-old girls in the early-nineteenth-century New England of spiritual enthusiasm, in this case a Shaker community in Massachusetts. . . . 'The Visionist' is a remarkably sensitive journey into an utterly foreign land. . . . Urquhart reveals the truly exotic nature of Shaker culture without relying on that exoticism for effect—her eye is fresh and alert. The novel explores the lies we tell ourselves, the fantasies we weave to protect ourselves from a harsh and unyielding reality."

REVIEW: *N Y Times Book Rev* p11 Ja 26 2014 AMBER DERMONT

REVIEW: *New Yorker* v89 no47 p79-1 F 3 2014

"The Visionist." " In this début novel, set in New England in the eighteen-forties, a young woman, Polly Kimball, helps her family escape an abusive father by setting fire to their farm. Fearing repercussions, her mother sends Polly and her brother to a Shaker settlement. There the girl is mistaken for a visionist--someone capable of mystical visions--and she becomes the object of both admiration and suspicion. . . . Although the narrative wanders, it contains many exciting twists."

REVIEW: *Publ Wkly* v260 no27 p61 Jl 8 2013

URRU, FRANCO.il. Teenage Mutant Ninja Turtles. See Lyncb, B.

URSU, ANNE. The Real Boy. See The Real Boy

URWAND, BEN. The collaboration; Hollywood's pact with Hitler; [by] Ben Urwand 320 p. 2013 The Belknap Press of Harvard University Press

1. Historical literature 2. Motion picture industry—United States—History—20th century 3. National socialism and motion pictures

ISBN 0674724747; 9780674724747 (hardcover: alk. paper)

LC 2013-013576

SUMMARY: This book looks at the "alliance Hollywood made with the Nazis, which allowed both to keep packing movie theaters in Germany up until the outbreak of war. Concomitant with Hollywood's golden era of the 1930s was the rise of the Nazi Party, whose chief officials admired American films. . . . The result of this complicated and slippery relationship . . . was the absolute disappearance from film of Nazis and Jews until the end of the decade." (Kirkus Reviews)

REVIEW: *Am Hist Rev* v119 no2 p545-7 Ap 2014 M. Todd Bennett

REVIEW: *Bookforum* v20 no4 p45 D 2013/Ja 2014 NOAH ISENBERG

REVIEW: *Choice* v51 no5 p909-10 Ja 2014 J. Fischel

"The Collaboration: Hollywood's Pact With Hitler". "In this now controversial book, [Ben] Urwand . . . has uncovered documentation that describes how the Hollywood movie studios of the 1930s, to protect their German markets, allowed the Nazis to censor US films. . . . One concludes from this important study that its title is an exaggeration, inasmuch as the Hollywood studios were motivated more by profits than a desire to collaborate with the Third Reich. Nevertheless, despite criticism of the book, it is a welcome addition to understanding of Hollywood's response to the rise of Nazism."

REVIEW: *Film Q* v67 no1 p86-7 Fall 2013 JOHANNES VON MOLTKE

REVIEW: *Hist Today* v64 no9 p62 S 2014 Taylor Downing

REVIEW: *J Am Hist* v101 no2 p632-3 S 2014

REVIEW: *Kirkus Rev* v81 no14 p307 Jl 15 2013

REVIEW: *London Rev Books* v35 no24 p25-6 D 19 2013 J. Hoberman

"Hollywood and Hitler: 1933-39" and "The Collaboration: Hollywood's Pact With Hitler". "Thomas Doherty's 'Hollywood and Hitler' and Ben Urwand's 'The Collaboration' cover much the same ground while emphasising different aspects of the Hollywood-Hitler connection. Doherty sees the moguls who founded and ran most of the large movie studios as only one part of Hollywood and is sensitive to the pressures both on and within the industry. . . . He concludes, with some generosity, that when it came to dealing with the Nazis, Hollywood was 'no worse than the rest of American culture in its failure of nerve and imagination, and often a good deal better in the exercise of both'. Urwand has dug deep in the German archives and found evidence that the Nazis' business dealings with some of the studios were much closer than previously realised.. . . Urwand . . . is far less interested than Doherty in the American cultural climate of the 1930s and far more accusatory."

REVIEW: *Nation* v297 no23 p42 D 9 2013 AKIVA GOTTLIEB

"The Collaboration: Hollywood's Pact With Hitler". "The product of exhaustive research in US and German archives, [this book] clearly intends to disturb readers with the force of its promised revelations. . . . 'The Collaboration' sounds a righteous lament about Hollywood's inability to marshal the willpower to alarm the world about Nazism's unspeakable horrors. But given Hitler's own talent for selective perception, would it even have mattered? . . . [Ben] Urwand wants to tell a tale of tragic historical cowardice, but even if we take his slipshod book at its word—and several scholars have strongly suggested that we shouldn't—it remains unclear why, in the final analysis, movies could have accomplished something that newspapers, say, could not."

REVIEW: *New Yorker* v89 no28 p1 S 16 2013 David Denby

"The Collaboration: Hollywood's Pact With Hitler," and "Hollywood and Hitler 1933-1939". "[Thomas] Doherty's book is much the better of the two. A witty writer familiar with Hollywood history and manners, Doherty places the studios' craven behavior within a general account of the political culture of the movies in the thirties and forties. He finds both greed and fear in studio practice, but in a recent Times report on the controversy he strongly objects to [Ben] Urwand's use of the word 'collaboration.' Urwand, an Australian, and the grandson of Hungarian Jews who spent the war years in hiding, flings many accusations. He speaks of [Adolf] Hitler's victory 'on the other side of the globe,' by which he means Hollywood, and he claims to see 'the great mark that Hitler left on American culture.' Throughout the book, he gives the impression that the studios were merely doing the Nazis' bidding."

REVIEW: *Publ Wkly* v260 no29 p53-4 Jl 22 2013

REVIEW: *TLS* no5774 p3-5 N 29 2013 FREDERIC RAPHAEL

THE U.S. SOUTH AND EUROPE; transatlantic relations in the nineteenth and twentieth centuries; 307 p. 2013 University Press of Kentucky

1. Historical literature
ISBN 9780813143088 (hardcover: alk. paper); 9780813143194 (pdf)
LC 2013-030209

SUMMARY: In this book on relations between the U.S. South and Europe, "the authors cover four main themes. The first considers how Europeans and southerners interacted with one another, and the second, how those interactions helped facilitate identity formation on both sides of the Atlantic. The last two themes explore how those interactions helped bolster or undermine racial and ethnic identities." (Choice: Current Reviews for Academic Libraries)

REVIEW: *Am Hist Rev* v119 no2 p660-1 Ap 2014

REVIEW: *Choice* v51 no8 p1464 Ap 2014 L. Stacey

"The U.S. South and Europe: Transatlantic Relations in the Nineteenth and Twentieth Centuries". "[Cornelis A.] Van Minnen and [Manfred] Berg have edited a fine collection of essays that cover various interactions between the southern US and Europe in the 19th and 20th centuries. . . . The quality of the essays in anthologies is often uneven. However, all of these essays are crisply written, well argued, supported through primary research, and cognizant of extant historiography. . . . Highly recommended."

REVIEW: *J Am Hist* v101 no1 p292-3 Je 2014

UTTARO, ROBERT. To the Survivors; One Man's Journey As a Rape Crisis Counselor With True Stories of Sexual Violence; [by] Robert Uttaro 268 p. 2013 CreateSpace Independent Publishing Platform

1. Attitudes toward rape 2. Memoirs 3. Rape crisis centers 4. Rape victims 5. Volunteers
ISBN 149093166X; 9781490931661

SUMMARY: This book presents "a debut memoir about a man working as a rape crisis counselor. . . . In college, he was inspired by a classroom visit from the center's staff, during which he found himself 'called' to work there. He chronicles his service as a counselor and occasionally includes the poetry of some of the rape survivors with whom he worked. He frequently addresses readers directly and offers compassionate advice." (Kirkus Reviews)

REVIEW: *Kirkus Rev* v82 no3 p401 F 1 2014

"To the Survivors; One Man's Journey As A Rape Crisis Counselor With True Stories of Sexual Violence". "He frequently addresses readers directly and offers compassionate advice. Occasionally, the memoir reads more like a journal, particularly when [Robert] Uttaro reflects on feelings of nervousness: 'Dude relax. . . . Chill out,' he tells himself. His use of expletives may jar some readers, and the book's tone often shifts between personal and professional. At times, he wanders off track, as when he vents about the lack of enthusiasm at a 'pathetic rally,' but for the most part, he focuses on his admiration and respect for survivors and counselors alike. . . . An engaging examination of a painful subject, with a focus on healing and forgiveness."

V

VACHEDIN, DMITRY. Snow Germans; 300 p. 2013 GLAS New Russian Writing

1. Germans—Russia (Federation) 2. Immigrants—Fiction 3. Russian fiction—Translations into English 4. Russians—Germany 5. Transnationalism
ISBN 5717200978; 9785717200974

SUMMARY: In this novel, translated by Arch Tait, "The characters exist in the cross-cultural space between Russia and Germany." Through a novel, author "Dmitry Vachedin describes his personal experiences of growing up as a German in Russia and then moving to Germany to find himself an alien again." (Publisher's note)

REVIEW: *World Lit Today* v88 no2 p62 Mr/Ap 2014 Bradley Gorski

"Snow Germans." "'Snow Germans' is built on three beautifully differentiated narrative voices, conveying diverse and moving transnational experiences between Russia and Germany. . . . The novel's plot brings these characters into one anothers' orbits, but Vachedin resists the temptation to herd them into one room for a grand culmination. Instead, the narrators remain loosely connected nodes in a greater phenomenon that this novel only starts to explore. . . . Vachedin's prose style and his ability to understand and convey diverse experiences make 'Snow Germans' a pleasure to read and Dmitry Vachedin an author to follow."

VAIL, JEFFERY W.ed. The Unpublished Letters of Thomas Moore. See The Unpublished Letters of Thomas Moore

VAILL, AMANDA. Hotel Florida; Truth, Love, and Death in the Spanish Civil War; [by] Amanda Vaill 464 p. 2014 Farrar Straus & Giroux

1. Capa, Robert, 1913-1954 2. Gellhorn, Martha, 1908-1998 3. Hemingway, Ernest, 1899-1961 4. Historical literature 5. Spain—History—Civil War, 1936-1939
ISBN 0374172994; 9780374172992

SUMMARY: In this book on the Spanish Civil War, author Amanda Vaill "follows three leftist couples caught up in the heroic but doomed Loyalist cause. Most prominent are literary lion Ernest Hemingway and his new girlfriend, reporter Martha Gellhorn." Vaill also looks at "photographer Robert Capa and his partner, Gerda Taro. The only Spaniard in the bunch is writer Arturo Barea, who managed the Madrid press office with Viennese Ilsa Kulcsar." (Library Journal)

REVIEW: *Am Sch* v83 no2 p106-9 Spr 2014 CHARLES TRUEHEART

REVIEW: *Booklist* v110 no15 p14-5 Ap 1 2014 Vanessa Bush

REVIEW: *Kirkus Rev* v82 no2 p232 Ja 15 2014

"Hotel Florida: Truth, Love, and Death in the Spanish Civil War". "Among the many popping up for cameos are Stephen Spender, Eric Blair (George Orwell) and John Dos Passos. Although it will be difficult for readers to turn their eyes away from the power couple ([Ernest] Hemingway and [Martha] Gellhorn), [Amanda] Vaill does a good job of getting us deeply interested in the lives, experiences and, sadly, the deaths of some of the others. It helps her cause, too, that she elected to portray Hemingway in the most unflattering (and deserved?) light."

REVIEW: *Libr J* v138 no18 p69 N 1 2013 Barbara Hoffert

REVIEW: *Libr J* v139 no3 p118 F 15 2014 Stewart Desmond

REVIEW: *N Y Times Book Rev* p23 Je 22 2014 JESSICA KERWIN JENKINS

REVIEW: *New Yorker* v90 no15 p79-1 Je 2 2014

REVIEW: *Publ Wkly* v261 no3 p42-3 Ja 20 2014

REVIEW: *TLS* no5805 p7 Jl 4 2014 JEREMY TREGLOWN

VALENCIUS, CONEVERY BOLTON. The lost history of the New Madrid earthquakes; [by] Conevery Bolton Valencius 472 p. 2013 University of Chicago Press

1. Earthquakes—Mississippi River Valley—History 2. Earthquakes—Social aspects 3. Historical literature 4. New Madrid Earthquakes, 1811-1812 5. Paleoseismology

ISBN 9780226053899 (cloth: alkaline paper)

LC 2013-007013

SUMMARY: In this book, Conevery Bolton Valencius "weaves together scientific and historical evidence to demonstrate the vast role the New Madrid earthquakes played in the United States in the early nineteenth century, shaping the settlement patterns of early western Cherokees and other Indians, heightening the credibility of Tecumseh and Tenskwatawa for their Indian League in the War of 1812, giving force to frontier religious revival, and spreading scientific inquiry." (Publisher's note)

REVIEW: *Choice* v51 no8 p1434 Ap 2014 T. L. T. Grose

"The Lost History of the New Madrid Earthquakes". "In this most beautifully written book, [Conevery Bolton] Valencius . . . integrates prodigious research about how the history of the central US, including its economy, society, and environment, were shaped by seismicity and geology. While a few recent books deal skillfully with the ramifications of the New Madrid earthquakes, this book in particular delves deeply into the larger cultural meaning and influence of the value of deep scientific reanalysis and application to modern social and environmental problems. And, it is worth repeating, the writing is superb. Referencing is extensive and annotated."

VALENTE, CATHERYNNE M. The Bread We Eat in Dreams. See The Bread We Eat in Dreams

VALENTE, CATHERYNNE M. The Girl Who Soared over Fairyland and Cut the Moon in Two; 256 p. 2013 Feiwel & Friends

1. Fairies—Fiction 2. Fantasy fiction 3. Friendship—Fiction 4. Moon—Fiction 5. Yeti

ISBN 1250023505; 9781250023506

SUMMARY: In this book, by Catherynne M. Valente, September is "tasked with delivering a package to the moon, which has begun to shudder and shake with moonquakes because a . . . yeti is trying to break it to pieces. September and her friends traverse the moon, meet their fates, encounter older and younger versions of themselves, and wonder what, exactly, makes them who they are—all while trying to find the speedy yeti and stop him from his destructive plans." (Booklist)

REVIEW: *Booklist* v110 no2 p65 S 15 2013 Sarah Hunter

"The Girl Who Soared Over Fairyland and Cut the Moon in Two". "Plucky September makes her way back to [Catherynne M.] Valente's marvelous, mesmerizing fairyland, following her previous trip, in 'The Girl Who Fell beneath Fairyland and Led the Revels There' (2012). . . . As usual, Valente enlightens readers with pearly gleams of wisdom about honesty, identity, free will, and growing up. September often worries who she should be and what path she should follow, but the lovely truth, tenderly told, is that it's all up to her. Thanks to a dramatic cliff-hanger ending, there is sure to be more empowerment and whimsy to come."

REVIEW: *Horn Book Magazine* v89 no6 p108 N/D 2013 KATIE BIRCHER

"The Girl Who Soared Over Fairyland and Cut the Moon in Two". "Now a wiser, somewhat sadder girl, September longs for autonomy and choice even as she fears that these 'grown-up' attributes will bar her from Fairyland forever. Likewise, Fairyland itself and its inhabitants are darker, more adult: while September (a 'professional revolutionary') has fought childish tyrants before, this is the first time she's encountered such systemic, casual oppression. But [Catherynne M.] Valente's Fairyland is terrible and beautiful—with a circus made out of stationery, a city populated with photographic negatives, and glimpses of Septembers and Saturdays past and future just a few of the strange wonders introduced in this volume."

REVIEW: *Kirkus Rev* v81 no18 p166 S 15 2013

REVIEW: *Publ Wkly* v261 no1 p53 Ja 6 2014

VALENTE, STEFANO.ed. I lessici a Platone di Timeo Sofista e Pseudo-Didimo. See I lessici a Platone di Timeo Sofista e Pseudo-Didimo

VALENTINE, MADELINE. The bad birthday idea; [by] Madeline Valentine 40 p. 2013 Alfred A. Knopf Books for Young Readers

1. Behavior—Fiction 2. Birthdays—Fiction 3. Brothers and sisters—Fiction 4. Children's stories 5. Robots—Fiction 6. Toys—Fiction

ISBN 0449813312; 9780449813317 (hardcover); 9780449813324 (library binding); 9780449813331 (ebook)

LC 2012-042634

SUMMARY: In this book, by Madeline Valentine, "Ben likes to play with robots. His little sister, Alice, would like to play with Ben. But when she and her doll try to join Ben's games, Ben says, 'No dolls allowed. This is a robot game.' That's why Alice asks for a robot for her birthday. Not just any robot. The exact robot Ben has been wanting forever!" (Publisher's note)

REVIEW: *Bull Cent Child Books* v67 no5 p287 Ja 2014 J. H.

"The Bad Birthday Idea". "[Madeline] Valentine's clear, succinct text is effective at conveying the complexity of some sibling interactions. . . . Additionally, the brevity of the text will put this within range of kids who can work their way through primary-level easy readers. The graphite, gouache, and colored pencil art on watercolor paper is warm and affectionate. . . . Freckled Ben's apprehension, shame, and regret are palpably communicated through his facial expressions and body posture. This would be a strong family readaloud . . . or even a useful classroom story to share, as the relationship and jealousy issues easily transfer to friendships as well."

REVIEW: *Kirkus Rev* v81 no20 p78 O 15 2013

REVIEW: *Publ Wkly* v260 no40 p49-50 O 7 2013

VALIANT, LESLIE. Probably Approximately Correct; Nature's Algorithms for Learning and Prospering in a Complex World; [by] Leslie Valiant 208 p. 2013 Perseus Books Group

1. Algorithms 2. Ecology—Mathematical models 3. Human behavior—Mathematical models 4. Mathematical literature 5. Mathematics in nature
ISBN 0465032710; 9780465032716

SUMMARY: It was the author's intent to demonstrate "how both individually and collectively we not only survive, but prosper in a world as complex as our own. The key is 'probably approximately correct' algorithms, a concept Valiant developed to explain how effective behavior can be learned. The model shows that pragmatically coping with a problem can provide a satisfactory solution in the absence of any theory of the problem." (Publisher's note)

REVIEW: *Choice* v51 no5 p876 Ja 2014 P. Cull

REVIEW: *New York Times* v163 no56276 pD5 O 1 2013 EDWARD FRENKEL

REVIEW: *Publ Wkly* v260 no13 p58 Ap 1 2013

REVIEW: *Sci Am* v308 no6 p88 Je 2013 Anna Kuchment

REVIEW: *TLS* no5772 p32 N 15 2013 CHRISTOPHER MOLE

"Probably Approximately Correct: Nature's Algorithms for Learning and Prospering in a Complex World." "Concepts like 'consciousness' must, [Leslie Valiant] thinks, be vague, and the questions raised in philosophers' thought experiments may have no determinate answer. Valiant's argument on this point is rather too quick. The lack of a theory within which 'consciousness' is defined need not entail that that concept is a vague one. The concept might instead get a precise meaning from our acquaintance with consciousness itself, in our own experience. Such qualms do little to compromise the importance of Leslie Valiant's research to our understanding of intelligent life. This book makes some of that research accessible to a broad audience."

VALLAT, CHRISTELLE. Celia; 36 p. 2014 Peter Pauper Press, Inc.

1. Children's stories 2. Listening—Fiction 3. Magic—Juvenile fiction 4. Sadness—Fiction 5. Seeds—Fiction
ISBN 9781441315366 (hardcover: alk. paper)
LC 2013-040045

SUMMARY: This book by Christelle Vallat presents a "story about a wise old woman who listens to the sadnesses of many neighbors. In return, the people give her seeds of sorrow, which she turns into beautiful balloons, frosted cupcakes, flowers on a hill, sparkling stars, and apples on a tree. On her journey to plant beauty, she discovers a lost seed and learns that it belongs to an unhappy child named Julian. Together they plant it, and over time, the seed grows into a tiny flower." (School Library Journal)

REVIEW: *Kirkus Rev* v82 no4 p281 F 15 2014

"Celia". " Celia is a listener. Every Sunday, people line up to tell the old woman their problems, and in exchange for her kind service, they each give her a seed. However, this is no gardening tale. . . .The cover gives a clue to the yin-yang of the artwork, which salvages this quirky import from Belgium. Aside from a few rosy cheeks, the only colors are the eruptions of the seeds into vivid hues, contrasting sharply against the sketchily drawn figures in black and white. Imaginative? Yes. Metaphoric? Yes. Broadly appealing? Probably not, but readers who do respond will probably think it's too bad there aren't any real Celias in the world."

REVIEW: *SLJ* v60 no3 p129 Mr 2014 Melissa Smith

VALLIN, ROBERT W. The elements of Cantor sets; with applications; [by] Robert W. Vallin 248 p. 2013 John Wiley & Sons, Inc.

1. Cantor sets 2. Mathematical analysis 3. Mathematical literature 4. Measure theory
ISBN 9781118405710 (hardback)
LC 2013-009452

SUMMARY: This book by Robert W. Vallin presents an "introduction to Cantor Sets and applies these sets as a bridge between real analysis, probability, topology, and algebra." It includes "chapter coverage of fractals and self-similar sets, sums of Cantor Sets, the role of Cantor Sets in creating pathological functions, p-adic numbers, and several generalizations of Cantor Sets." (Publisher's note)

REVIEW: *Choice* v51 no7 p1258 Mr 2014 D. V. Feldman

"The Elements of Cantor Sets: With Applications." "Despite an exotic focus, basing a capstone course on this book will mainly recapitulate rather than exalt core undergraduate content. It is a first-of-its-kind volume, but one immediately imagines a more comprehensive, systematic tome, including perspectives from dynamics, harmonic analysis, logic, group theory, category theory, complex analysis, etc. Readers might also wish for a stronger sense of some kind of core Cantor set theory, whatever that may mean, paying off in diverse applications."

VAN CREVELD, MARTIN. Wargames; from gladiators to gigabytes; [by] Martin Van Creveld x, 332 p. 2013 Cambridge University Press

1. Computer war games—History 2. Military art & science—History 3. Military technology 4. Social science literature 5. War games—History
ISBN 9781107036956; 9781107684423 (pbk.)
LC 2012-039203

SUMMARY: In this book, author Martin van Creveld asks "Where did wargames come from? Who participated in them, and why? How is their development related to changes in real-life warfare? Which aspects of war did they capture, which ones did they leave out, how, and why? What do they tell us about the conduct of war in the times and places where they were played?" (Publisher's note)

REVIEW: *Choice* v51 no6 p1053-4 F 2014 P. L. de Rosa

"Wargames: From Gladiators to Gigabytes." "[Martin] Van Creveld (emer., Hebrew Univ., Israel) surveys the history of war games, defined as strategy games, from prehistory to modern times. The games' purpose is to simulate aspects of warfare for religious, training, and entertainment purposes, and to settle disputes. . . . Overall, the sheer range of this work makes it an important contribution to simulation studies, although a bibliography would have been welcome. . . . Highly recommended."

VAN DEN BERG, LAURA. The Isle of Youth; stories; [by] Laura Van den Berg 256 p. 2013 Farrar, Straus and Giroux

1. FICTION—Literary 2. FICTION—Psychological 3. FICTION—Short Stories (single author) 4. Marriage—Fiction 5. Women—United States—Fiction
ISBN 9780374177232 (pbk.)
LC 2013-022588

SUMMARY: This book of short stories, by Laura van den

Berg, an NPR Best Book of 2013, "explores the lives of women mired in secrecy and deception. From a newlywed caught in an inscrutable marriage, to private eyes working a . . . case in South Florida, to a teenager who assists her magician mother and steals from the audience, the characters in these . . . stories . . . will do what it takes to survive." (Publisher's note)

REVIEW: *Booklist* v110 no6 p20-1 N 15 2013 Annie Bostrom

"The Isle of Youth." "In strange and overwhelming locales . . . [Laura] van den Berg . . . explores the lonely, triumphant sorrow of love and family in this new collection. . . . In the squirming, electric title story, a woman impersonates her twin sister as a favor, with vertiginous results. . . . Van den Berg sends her characters along the undulations of extraordinary familial relationships--navigating their understood strength and, at the same time, arbitrariness--and gathers their piercingly true, hauntingly single voices in this memorable collection."

REVIEW: *Kirkus Rev* v81 no15 p310 Ag 1 2013

REVIEW: *Kirkus Rev* p16 Ag 15 2013 Fall Preview

REVIEW: *N Y Times Book Rev* p24 N 24 2013 NATALIE SERBER

REVIEW: *New York Times* v163 no56334 pC4 N 28 2013 John Williams

REVIEW: *Publ Wkly* v260 no28 p143 Jl 15 2013

REVIEW: *TLS* no5781 p21 Ja 17 2014 TADZIO KOELB

VAN DER BLOM, HENRIETTE.ed. Community and Communication. See Community and Communication

VAN DER MAAREL, EDDY.ed. Vegetation ecology. See Vegetation ecology

VAN DER VEEN, ROEL.ed. Asian tigers, African lions. See Asian tigers, African lions

VAN DER VEEN, ROMKE.ed. The transformation of solidarity. See The transformation of solidarity

VAN DUSEN, CHRIS.il. President taft is stuck in the bath. See Barnett, M.

VAN ES, BART. Shakespeare in Company; [by] Bart Van Es 371 p. 2013 Oxford University Press

1. English drama—History & criticism 2. Historical literature 3. Shakespeare, William, 1564-1616—Biography 4. Shakespeare, William, 1564-1616—Friends & associates 5. Theatrical companies

ISBN 0199569312; 9780199569311

SUMMARY: In this book, author "Bart van Es argues that Shakespeare's decision, in 1594, to become an investor (or 'sharer') in the newly formed Chamberlain's acting company had a transformative effect on his writing, moving him beyond the conventions of Renaissance dramaturgy. On the basis of the physical distinctiveness of his actors, Shakespeare developed 'relational drama', something no previous dramatist had explored." (Publisher's note)

REVIEW: *Choice* v51 no3 p472 N 2013 F. L. Den

REVIEW: *London Rev Books* v36 no3 p7-8 F 6 2014 Michael Neill

REVIEW: *TLS* no5776 p3-4 D 13 2013 CHARLES NICHOLL

"Shakespeare in Company." "[Author Bart van Es] seeks to show that Shakespeare's achievement as a writer was in crucial ways communal; that the contributions of his playhouse colleagues, indeed his whole immersion in the business and practice of the theatre, are woven into the fabric of his plays; and that in a broadly chronological framework one can see his literary skills evolving in response to certain changes in his working conditions. These are not in themselves new ideas, but they are pursued with great vigour and clarity, and with much telling documentary detail, and the book moves us yet further away from that daft but tenacious construct of Shakespeare the lofty genius, 'seated' (as Coleridge put it) among the 'glory-smitten summits of the poetic mountain.'"

VAN FLEET, MARA. Night-Night, Princess; [by] Mara Van Fleet 16 p. 2014 Simon & Schuster

1. Bedtime 2. Children's stories 3. Play 4. Princesses—Juvenile fiction 5. Sisters—Juvenile fiction

ISBN 1442486465; 9781442486461

SUMMARY: In this children's book, "it's long past time for bed, but a certain little princess is not one bit sleepy. The text describes . . . two sisters' valiant efforts to ease their wide-awake sibling toward slumber, including hugs and kisses, fairy-dust wishes, playtime and dress-up, dancing, a snack of milk and honey buns, a warm bath and wrapping her up in her soft blanket. Nothing seems to slow the princess down until the sisters put her in a comfy chair with a big stack of books." (Kirkus Reviews)

REVIEW: *Kirkus Rev* v82 no13 p7 Jl 1 2014

REVIEW: *Kirkus Rev* v82 no2 p324 Ja 15 2014

"Night-Night, Princess". "The uninspiring illustrations, which feature lots of pinks and purples and silver glitter for the fairy dust, are partly rescued by a couple of interactive elements. The front cover depicts the three sisters in bed with the youngest sister holding a baby doll; it features a tab that, when pulled, moves the baby back and forth as though the girl is rocking it. The final page includes a large flap in the shape of pillows and blankets that when pulled back reveals the little princess sound asleep. The topic of getting reluctant little ones to bed is a perennial favorite, but the execution here is lackluster at best. Not worth losing sleep over."

REVIEW: *Publ Wkly* v260 no51 p60 D 16 2013

VAN FLEET, MARA.il. Night-Night, Princess. See Van Fleet, M.

VAN LEEUWEN, JOKE. The Day My Father Became a Bush; [by] Joke Van Leeuwen 104 p. 2014 Gecko Press

1. Camouflage (Military science) 2. Children of military personnel 3. Refugees—Fiction 4. War & families 5. War stories

ISBN 1877579483; 9781877579486

SUMMARY: The narrator of this story" by Joke van Leeuwen "describes two terrible results of her country's war. One is that her father 'becomes a bush' (she imagines him in various forms of camouflage); the other is that she's sent with other refugees across the border to live with her estranged mother in a neighboring country." (Horn Book Magazine)

REVIEW: *Booklist* v110 no4 p51 O 15 2013 Thom Barthelmess

REVIEW: *Bull Cent Child Books* v67 no3 p184-5 N 2013 K. C.

REVIEW: *Horn Book Magazine* v90 no1 p103 Ja/F 2014 DEIRDRE F. BAKER

"The Day My Father Became a Bush." "This popular Dutch author/illustrator has a gift for writing of serious matters while maintaining a deceptively light, quirky sense of humor. . . . [Joke] Van Leeuwen presents vagaries of personality, bureaucracy, and nationalism with a gentle form of Brechtian absurdity; and the narrator's naive clarity of voice and affection creates an engaging critique on the idiocies of conflict and bureaucracy. At the same time, this fable is warm, intelligent, and funny, arriving at a conclusion that is emotionally satisfying, if not secure. Liberally endowed with van Leeuwen's comic, ironic cartoon drawings."

REVIEW: *Kirkus Rev* v81 no24 p10 D 15 2013

REVIEW: *Publ Wkly* v260 no33 p32-4 Ag 19 2013 SALLY LODGE

REVIEW: *Publ Wkly* v261 no5 p58 F 3 2014

VVAN LEEUWEN, JOKE.il. The Day My Father Became a Bush. See Van Leeuwen, J.

VAN LEMMEN, HANS. 5000 years of tiles; [by] Hans Van Lemmen 304 p. 2013 Smithsonian Books

1. ANTIQUES & COLLECTIBLES—Art 2. ARCHITECTURE—Decoration & Ornament 3. Art literature 4. DESIGN—Decorative Arts 5. Decoration and ornament, Architectural—History 6. Tile industry—History 7. Tiles—History
ISBN 9781588343987 (pbk.)
LC 2013-023242

SUMMARY: This book by Hans van Lemmen "focuses on European clay tiles, but also takes a look at Egyptian, Chinese, Islamic, and American tile history Hundreds of color photographs of unique and mass-produced floor, wall, stove, flue, and roof tiles from numerous collections and museums illustrate the narrative that examines how tiles have influenced daily life and the economy." (Choice: Current Reviews for Academic Libraries)

REVIEW: *Choice* v51 no6 p977 F 2014 C. A. Ventura

"5000 Years of Tiles." "[Hans] Van Lemmen . . . has written an authoritative and fascinating book that focuses on European clay tiles, but also takes a look at Egyptian, Chinese, Islamic, and American tile history. . . . The detailed historic scholarship is excellent, but the technical information contains several minor errors. For instance, the Chinese did not paint cobalt blue oxide onto biscuit-fired porcelain in Jingdezhen, but painted it onto bone-dry clay, then sprayed clear glaze over it before the first firing. Metric measurements and British spelling and vocabulary are used throughout. Few references are mentioned in the text, and there are no endnotes. A technical glossary is included."

VAN MINNEN, CORNELIS A.ed. The U.S. South and Europe. See The U.S. South and Europe

VAN TUYLL, DEBRA REDDIN. The Confederate press in the crucible of the American Civil War; [by] Debra Reddin Van Tuyll xvi, 344 p. 2012 Peter Lang International Academic Publishers

1. American newspapers—Southern States—History—19th century 2. Historical literature 3. Journalism—Confederate States of America—History 4. Press and politics—Confederate States of America—History
ISBN 1433116294; 9781433116292 (hardcover : alk. paper); 9781453909287 (e-book)
LC 2012-032466

SUMMARY: This book, by Debra Reddin van Tuyll, places "its focus on the press as a social, political, and economic institution that both shaped and was shaped by the Confederacy's experience in the Civil War. It expertly documents how the press changed, how it stayed the same, and how it evolved by examining the role of the press in Confederate society, social and demographic characteristics of journalists and their audiences, legal regulation of the industry, and how the war influenced the business side of journalism." (Publisher's note)

REVIEW: *Choice* v51 no1 p68-9 S 2013 R. Ray

"The Confederate Press in the Crucible of the American Civil War." "As the war progressed, worker shortages, financial challenges, limited resources, and restricted opportunities impacted many Southern papers, yet some benefited from advancements, as did their Northern counterparts. [Author Debra Reddin] Van Tuyll . . . discusses how these changes affected the Southern press, which became a viable force of persuasion. Unlike previous studies of Civil War newspapers, 'The Confederate Press' examines the social, political, economic, and legal environments that shaped the Confederate press. In this cultural study, the author discusses the Confederate community of news producers and consumers, and also examines the social, political, and business roles Southern newspapers filled."

VAN UDEN, MARISSA.ed. The Casquette Girls. See Arden, A.

VAN WAGENEN, MAYA. Popular; Vintage wisdom for a modern geek; [by] Maya Van Wagenen 272 p. 2014 Dutton Juvenile

1. Life skills—Humor 2. Memoirs 3. Popularity 4. Self-confidence—Juvenile literature 5. Teenage girls—Juvenile literature
ISBN 9780525426813 (hardback)
LC 2014-000236

SUMMARY: This memoir by Maya Van Wagenen tells how "stuck near the bottom of the social ladder at 'pretty much the lowest level of people at school who aren't paid to be here,' Maya has never been popular. But before starting eighth grade, she decides to begin a unique social experiment: spend the school year following a 1950s popularity guide, written by former teen model Betty Cornell." (Publisher's note)

REVIEW: *Bull Cent Child Books* v67 no10 p546 Je 2014 K. C.

"Popular: Vintage Wisdom for a Modern Geek". "The results of her makeover, adorned with photos and related in a style replete with dry humor and deadpan observations, are a complete hoot. . . . Her early years as a socially abused nerd seem to have strengthened her skills of critical observation and rendered her fearless in the face of ridicule, but it may be her unwavering ambition to be a writer that carries her through her year with the admirable tenacity of a budding social researcher; clearly, this fifteen-year-old author is a talent to watch."

REVIEW: *Kirkus Rev* v82 no8 p212 Ap 15 2014

VAN WRIGHT, CORNELIUS. When an alien meets a swamp monster; [by] Cornelius Van Wright 32 p. 2014 Nancy Paulsen Books, an imprint of Penguin Group (USA) Inc.

1. Alligators—Juvenile literature 2. Children's stories 3. Fear 4. Friendship—Fiction 5. Mistaken identity—Fiction
ISBN 9780399256233
LC 2013-014046

SUMMARY: In this book, "J.T. Boi sets out on an adventure wearing a helmet and goggles and riding his scooter. . . . He speeds down the hill and lands in a muddy swamp, where he comes face to face with a terrifying monster. Alik is really an alligator who was reading his comic book, Attack of the Aliens, when he was interrupted and frightened out of his wits by what looked to be the very alien he was reading about." (Kirkus Reviews)

REVIEW: *Booklist* v110 no12 p84 F 15 2014 Daniel Kraus

REVIEW: *Kirkus Rev* v82 no1 p112 Ja 1 2014

"When an Alien Meets a Swamp Monster". "[Cornelius] Van Wright turns the whole silly affair into a hilarious romp with easy, breezy language that captures the essence of little boys (or little alligators). The type's font is varied to reflect the levels of hysteria and panic, and it is set in the delightfully named 'Delicious and Dynamo.' Large-scale watercolor-and-pencil illustrations are appropriately goofy and perfectly depict the high-speed action and the rampant emotions of the characters. Small details add to the fun as young readers notice Boi's low-slung shorts, Alik's brother's science book by Dr. Spekulate and Boi's sister's popped bubble gum. Total laugh-out-loud joy."

REVIEW: *Publ Wkly* v260 no45 p69 N 11 2013

REVIEW: *SLJ* v60 no2 p80 F 2014 Julie R. Ranelli

VANASSE, DEB. No Returns. See Giles, G.

VANCE, NORMAN. Bible and novel; narrative authority and the death of God; [by] Norman Vance x, 233 p. 2013 Oxford University Press

1. Bible and literature—History—19th century 2. English fiction—19th century—History and criticism 3. Literature—History & criticism 4. Religion and literature—Great Britain—History—19th century
ISBN 0199680574; 9780199680573
LC 2012-277840

SUMMARY: In this book, Norman Vance "argue[s] that the Victorian period was notable not so much for 'the disappearance of God' . . . . but for its transformative attitude to the Bible. . . . Vance approaches his subject from two directions: first he surveys biblical 'authority' from the beginnings to the 19th century; then he provides close . . . analyses of his four novelists [George Eliot, Thomas Hardy, Mrs. Humphry Ward, and H. Rider Haggard]." (Choice: Current Reviews for Academic Libraries)

REVIEW: *Choice* v51 no7 p1217-8 Mr 2014 M. E. Burstein

"Bible and Novel: Narrative Authority and the Death of God." "In keeping with his title, [Norman] Vance approaches his subject from two directions: first he surveys biblical 'authority' from the beginnings to the 19th century; then he provides close, graceful analyses of his four novelists. The first half of the book treads ground covered elsewhere, but will be useful to those unacquainted with the topic; the most striking chapter in the latter part is on Rider Haggard, a novelist rarely studied in the light of his religious experimentalism. Accessible, despite sometimes difficult material. . . . Recommended."

REVIEW: *TLS* no5789 p24 Mr 14 2014 STEPHEN PRICKETT

VANDERBES, JENNIFER. The Secret of Pigeon Point; [by] Jennifer Vanderbes 320 p. 2013 Simon & Schuster

1. Brothers & sisters—Fiction 2. Families of military personnel 3. Historical fiction 4. Nurses—Fiction 5. World War, 1939-1945—Fiction
ISBN 1439167001; 9781439167007

SUMMARY: In this book, "when seventeen-year-old Juliet Dufresne receives a cryptic letter from her enlisted brother and then discovers that he's been reported missing in action, she lies about her age and travels to the front lines as an army nurse, determined to find him. Shy and awkward, Juliet is thrust into the bloody chaos of a field hospital, a sprawling encampment north of Rome where she forges new friendships and is increasingly consumed by the plight of her patients." (Publisher's note)

REVIEW: *Booklist* v110 no8 p26-7 D 15 2013 Joanne Wilkinson

"The Secret of Raven Point." "When her brother goes missing in Italy during WWII, young Juliet Dufresne signs up to he an army nurse. . . . In her third novel, [Jennifer] Vanderbes . . . graphically depicts the gruesome nature of battlefield injuries, both to the body and to the psyche, even as she shows Juliet's courage and strength. The skillful Vanderbes' aching depiction of Juliet's struggle to maintain her humanity amid the army's callous bureaucracy and the horrors of war works as both an homage to our armed forces and a moving personal story of emotional growth."

REVIEW: *Kirkus Rev* v81 no21 p140 N 1 2013

REVIEW: *Libr J* v138 no14 p86 S 1 2013

REVIEW: *Libr J* v139 no8 p44 My 1 2014 Linda Sappenfield

REVIEW: *Libr J* v138 no20 p1 N 15 2013

VANDERLAAN, ANN. A flame in the wind of death. See Danna, J. J.

VANDERPOOL, CLARE. Navigating Early; [by] Clare Vanderpool 320 p. 2013 Delacorte Press

1. Adventure and adventurers—Fiction 2. Adventure stories 3. Boarding schools—Fiction 4. Eccentrics and eccentricities—Fiction 5. JUVENILE FICTION—Historical—United States—20th Century 6. Schools—Fiction
ISBN 0385742096; 9780307974129 (ebook); 9780375990403 (glb); 9780385742092

LC 2012-014973

SUMMARY: In this children's novel, by Clare Vanderpool, "Jack Baker, . . . after his mother's death, . . . [is] placed in a boy's boarding school in Maine. There, Jack encounters Early Auden. . . . Newcomer Jack feels lost yet can't help being drawn to Early. . . . When the boys find themselves unexpectedly alone at school, they embark on a quest on the Appalachian Trail in search of the great black bear. But what they are searching for is sometimes different from what they find." (Publisher's note)

REVIEW: *Booklist* v109 no16 p71 Ap 15 2013 Heather Booth

REVIEW: *Booklist* v109 no8 p43 D 15 2012 Thom Borthelmess

REVIEW: *Bull Cent Child Books* v66 no7 p355 Mr 2013 E. B.

"Navigating Early." "With World War II finally over, young Jack Baker is forced to move from Kansas to a private boys school in Maine, where he will be closer to the naval base of his captain father. Landlubber Jack knows nothing of the sea-oriented culture of his new environs, and his first attempts at handling a boat are pitiful indeed. . . . This story of a poignant friendship of two heartbroken boys shifts quickly among genres, beginning with a fairly routine problem-novel trajectory and then moving into territory more often claimed by high fantasy quests, heroic epics, wilderness adventures, and even mysteries. The incorporation of these familiar tropes give the book broad and fascinating appeal."

REVIEW: *Horn Book Magazine* v89 no2 p123 Mr/Ap 2013 ROGER SUTTON

"Navigating Early." "While the writing [in 'Navigating Early'] is as minutely observant as it was in the author's Newbery-winning debut, 'Moon over Manifest,' this book has a stronger trajectory, developed by the classic quest structure that emerges when [Clare] Vanderpool sends the boys into the Maine wilderness, on a search that Jack thinks is metaphorical but is gradually revealed to be real—and life-changing—for both of them. Interspersed episodes from a story Early tells about a wanderer named Pi sit uneasily; and Jack's narration can be to self-aware and self-explanatory, leaving the reader with perhaps not enough to do, but the same attentiveness also gives the book a rich texture and envelopment."

REVIEW: *Kirkus Rev* p85 N 15 2013 Best Books

REVIEW: *Kirkus Rev* v80 no22 p133 N 15 2012

REVIEW: *N Y Times Book Rev* p17 Ja 13 2013 JERRY GRISWOLD

REVIEW: *Publ Wkly* p78 Children's starred review annual 2013

REVIEW: *Publ Wkly* v259 no47 p55-8 N 19 2012 Andrea Cascardi

REVIEW: *SLJ* v59 no4 p56 Ap 2013 Deanna Romriell

REVIEW: *SLJ* v59 no3 p176 Mr 2013 Jessica Miller

VANDERWARKER, TONY. Writing With the Master; How One of the World's Bestselling Authors Fixed My Book and Changed My Life; [by] Tony Vanderwarker 208 p. 2014 Skyhorse Publishing

1. Authorship 2. Grisham, John, 1955- 3. Memoirs 4. Prewriting (Writing process) 5. Revision (Writing process)
ISBN 1626365520; 9781626365520

SUMMARY: In this combination memoir and how-to book, aspiring novelist Tony Vanderwarker "discovers that writing a novel is hard work, even harder when his taskmaster mentor is his friend John Grisham. . . . He ultimately found his mentor criticizing his characters, plotting, organization and pretty much everything else about a novel that is presented here in chunks of various drafts, with Grisham's notes, and then revisions, with notes." (Kirkus Reviews)

REVIEW: *Booklist* v110 no11 p11 F 1 2014 Carl Hays

REVIEW: *Kirkus Rev* v82 no1 p246 Ja 1 2014

"Writing With the Master: How One of the World's Best-selling Authors Fixed My Book and Changed My Life". "[John] Grisham would later remark of the manuscript that the "dialogue doesn't sound real." Neither does it here, as [Tony] Vanderwarker purports to remember paragraphs of conversation from a time that he wouldn't have been taking notes. . . . If nothing else, the book convinces readers that the prolific Grisham works methodically on his fiction, as the author's experience confirms that it isn't as easy to write a best-seller as some might think. Not only did the collaboration result in this, the author's first published book, but the same publisher has agreed to issue the novel that had been rejected, for which this how-to guide serves as an extended promotion."

VANHECKE, SUSAN. Under the freedom tree; 32 p. 2013 Charlesbridge

1. Children's nonfiction 2. Children's poetry, American 3. Fugitive slaves—Juvenile poetry 4. Slavery—United States—History—Juvenile literature 5. United States—History—Civil War, 1861-1865—Juvenile literature
ISBN 1580895506; 9781580895507 (reinforced for library use); 9781607346340 (ebook)
LC 2012-038698

SUMMARY: This book, by Susan Vanhecke and illustrated by London Ladd, "illuminates . . . [a] slice of Civil War history: runaway slaves' establishment of a settlement in newly seceded Virginia. In 1861, three slaves--Frank Baker, James Townsend, and Shepard Mallory--escape by boat from a Confederate camp. . . . The three men land at a Union camp whose commander declares them 'contraband of war' and refuses to return them to the Confederates." (Publishers Weekly)

REVIEW: *Horn Book Magazine* v90 no2 p147-8 Mr/Ap 2014 ROBIN L. SMITH

"Under the Freedom Tree." "Told in a spare, poetic voice, this story is filled with bravery, luck, and timing. . . . Realistic acrylic paintings depict the everyday life of the 'enemy property,' as the growing community builds a new town near the old oak tree that serves as shade for the school and place of joy to celebrate the Emancipation Proclamation. The lengthy author's note fills in the details left out by the brief verse, making this one a story to read more than once. Slavery is a challenging topic to introduce to young readers, but they have to start somewhere."

REVIEW: *Kirkus Rev* v81 no21 p227 N 1 2013

REVIEW: *Publ Wkly* v260 no44 p69 N 4 2013

REVIEW: *SLJ* v60 no3 p177 Mr 2014 Stephanie Whelan

VANHEE, JASON. Engines of the broken world; [by] Jason Vanhee 272 p. 2013 Henry Holt and Company

1. Ghost stories 2. Horror tales 3. Science fiction 4.

Spirit possession 5. Supernatural—Fiction
ISBN 0805096299; 9780805096293 (hardcover)
LC 2013-026768

SUMMARY: In this book, by Jason Vanhee, "Merciful Truth and her brother, Gospel, have just pulled their dead mother into the kitchen and stowed her under the table. It was a long illness, and they wanted to bury her—they did—but it's far too cold outside, and they know they won't be able to dig into the frozen ground. The Minister who lives with them, who preaches through his animal form, doesn't make them feel any better about what they've done." (Publisher's note)

REVIEW: *Booklist* v110 no6 p41 N 15 2013 Angela Leeper

REVIEW: *Bull Cent Child Books* v67 no4 p241-2 D 2013 K. Q. G.

REVIEW: *Horn Book Magazine* v90 no2 p130 Mr/Ap 2014 KATIE BIRCHER

"Engines of the Broken World." "Reading between the lines of Merciful's naive but evocative first-person narration reveals Auntie's weird and surprising origins. The setting of this ghost-story-meets- apocalyptic-story is unusually domestic, even claustrophobic; Merciful and Gospel's shrinking world and dwindling options heighten the immediacy of the horrors they face. In dense, lyrical language, the novel raises questions of religion, morality, and free will as it builds toward a dark and ambiguous ending."

REVIEW: *Kirkus Rev* v81 no20 p108 O 15 2013

REVIEW: *Voice of Youth Advocates* v36 no5 p83 D 2013 Mark Flowers

VANITY FAIR 100 YEARS; 456 p. 2013 Abrams

1. Crowninshield, Frank 2. Historical literature 3. Periodical publishing 4. Periodicals—History—20th century 5. Popular culture—United States—History
ISBN 9781419708633
LC 2013-935981

SUMMARY: This book by Graydon Carter traces the history of the magazine "Vanity Fair" "from its inception in 1913, through the Jazz Age and the Depression, to its reincarnation in the boom-boom Reagan years, to the image-saturated Information Age." It "takes a decade-by-decade look at the world as seen by the magazine." Topics include "editor Frank Crowninshield . . . the magazine's controversial rebirth in 1983, and the history of the glamorous Vanity Fair Oscar Party." (Publisher's note)

REVIEW: *N Y Times Book Rev* p15 D 8 2013 DAVID CARR

"Vanity Fair 100 Years: From the Jazz Age to Our Age" and "85 Years of the Oscar: The Official History of the Academy Awards." "'Vanity Fair 100 Years' . . . is a stunning artifact that begets staring, less for the words and publishing history than as an exercise in visual storytelling reflected through the prism of society and celebrity. . . . Visually repetitive and uninspired, with movie stills dropped willy-nilly to break up what becomes a droning year-by-year history of the Academy Awards, '85 Years of the Oscar' is sadly like the telecast itself: mildly interesting in spots, but with long stretches when nothing remarkable is seen or said."

REVIEW: *New Yorker* v89 no33 p103-1 O 21 2013

"Vanity Fair 100 Years: From the Jazz Age to Our Age." "This lavish book opens with an image of Kate Moss adopting a Marlene Dietrich pose--a cunning allusion to Vanity Fair's bifurcated history. . . . [Graydon] Carter's introduction identifies 'a tone, a style of writing, a form of humor, and a stance toward the culture' that bind these two eras of the magazine together. . . . . Wandering over so many iconic images of the famous, the eye is drawn to people for whom celebrity never quite happened--like Alice White or Judith Wood--and who arc captured in their brief moment of beauty and promise."

VANN, DAVID. Goat Mountain; A Novel; [by] David Vann 256 p. 2013 Harper

1. Hunting accidents 2. Hunting stories 3. Masculinity 4. Psychological fiction 5. Violence—Fiction
ISBN 006212109X; 9780062121097

SUMMARY: In author David Vann's book, "an 11-year-old boy at his family's annual deer hunt is eager to make his first kill [in the fall of 1978]. His father discovers a poacher on the land, a 640-acre ranch in Northern California, and shows him to the boy through the scope of his rifle. With this simple gesture, tragedy erupts, shattering lives irrevocably." (Publisher's note)

REVIEW: *Booklist* v109 no22 p29 Ag 1 2013 Carl Hays

REVIEW: *Kirkus Rev* v81 no16 p227 Ag 15 2013

"Goat Mountain." "[Author David] Vann's third novel is his most visceral yet: a grinding examination of killing, God and the unnamable forces that create a dynasty of violence. An 11-year-old boy, his father, grandfather, and his father's best friend, Tom, make the trip to Goat Mountain, a vast family ranch, for their annual deer hunt. . . . The narrator meditates on the Bible and its glorification of violence, of our inescapable murderous legacy, and that '[t]he act of killing might even be the act that creates god.' Nothing that begins so badly can end well, yet there is also something comforting in the inevitable; when a gun is loaded, the bullet yearns for a home. This book is as all of Vann's fiction: provocative and unforgiving."

REVIEW: *Libr J* v138 no7 p56 Ap 15 2013 Barbara Hoffert

REVIEW: *Libr J* v138 no12 p75 Jl 1 2013 Patrick Sullivan

REVIEW: *Publ Wkly* v260 no26 p1 Jl 1 2013

REVIEW: *TLS* no5767 p20 O 11 2013 ALISON KELLY

"Goat Mountain." "'Goat Mountain' is more than a contribution to a masculinist tradition of hunting literature; it has epic and neobiblical dimensions. [David] Vann is a daring writer, as bold in his plot developments as he is unflinching in his prose. . . . [John] Steinbeck . . . springs to mind, specifically 'East of Eden,' with its biblical determinism and preoccupation with patriarchy and intergenerational male conflict. . . . Vann's biblical referencing can feel oppressive, and there is perhaps too frequent recourse to irregular sentences designed to create a sense of preordination. . . . Nevertheless, 'Goat Mountain' is a compelling and morally challenging novel by one of America's most powerful writers."

VANORSDELL, JOHN. Angelesis; [by] John VanOrsdell 516 p. 2013 Author Solutions

1. Angels—Fiction 2. Extraterrestrial life—Fiction 3. Politicians—Fiction 4. Speculative fiction 5. Terrorism—Fiction
ISBN 149170649X; 9781491706497

SUMMARY: In this book, "a large alien spacecraft announces its imminent arrival in Earth's orbit and seeks to open communications with the United States, claiming to come in peace. American president Bryce and his advisers . . . frantically plan their approach, including whether to let space shuttle astronauts attempt to board the alien vessel once it appears. . . . The aliens want to warn Earth of impending crisis and announce the advent of a divine being called the Holy Daughter." (Kirkus Reviews)

REVIEW: *Kirkus Rev* v82 no5 p27 Mr 1 2014

"Angelesis: A Divine Incarnation". ". The world of [John] VanOrsdell's immensely enjoyable fiction debut is completely normal . . . when everything suddenly receives a gigantic, fundamental disruption: A large alien spacecraft announces its imminent arrival in Earth's orbit. . . .VanOrsdell moves his plot forward at such a brisk pace through terrorist threats, belligerent Russians, Peter Klein's love life, etc., that readers will wonder how he's going to further complicate an already complicated story. Some of VanOrsdell's readers may be nonplussed by his aliens-are-angels concept, but even the hardest to please will enjoy his exuberant, dramatic storytelling. A spirited new take on the old story of Earth making first contact with aliens."

REVIEW: *Kirkus Rev* v82 no2 p381 Ja 15 2014

VAPNYAR, LARA. The scent of pine; [by] Lara Vapnyar 208 p. 2014 Simon & Schuster

1. College teachers—Fiction 2. FICTION—Cultural Heritage 3. FICTION—General 4. FICTION—Literary 5. Love stories
ISBN 147671262X; 9781476712628 (hardback); 9781476712635 (paperback)
LC 2013-025893

SUMMARY: In this book, by Lara Vapnyar, "Lena is only thirty-eight, [but] she finds herself in the grip of a midlife crisis. She feels out of place in her adoptive country, her career has stalled, and her marriage has tumbled into a spiral of apathy and distrust. . . . But then she meets Ben, a failed artist turned reluctant academic, who is just as lost as she is. They strike up a . . . friendship and soon surprise themselves by embarking on an impulsive weekend adventure." (Publisher's note)

REVIEW: *Booklist* v110 no7 p23 D 1 2013 Susan Maguire

REVIEW: *Kirkus Rev* v81 no20 p113 O 15 2013

REVIEW: *N Y Times Book Rev* p12 Ja 12 2014 ANDREA WALKER

"The Scent of Pine." "Lena, the 38-year-old protagonist of [author Lana Vapnyar's sly and seductive second novel . . . tells stories to pass the time, about the moment in her life when she was happiest. This was the summer she was 18, when she worked as a counselor at a Soviet youth camp. . . . 'The Scent of Pine' shares many characteristics with Vapnyar's two story collections and her first novel: a buoyant wit, a sharp-edged Russian melancholy, a fascination with outsiders who long to be insiders and a blunt reckoning with the costs of that transition for those who achieve it. This slender but provocative novel advances those concerns, skillfully questioning the notion that age brings wisdom, at least in matters of the heart."

REVIEW: *New York Times* v163 no56368 pC6 Ja 1 2014 JON FASMAN

REVIEW: *Publ Wkly* v260 no37 p25 S 16 2013

VARTY, BOYD. Cathedral of the wild; an African journey home; [by] Boyd Varty 304 p. 2014 Random House Inc

1. Memoirs 2. Wildlife conservation—South Africa—Londolozi Game Reserve—History
ISBN 1400069858; 9781400069859 (acid-free paper)
LC 2013-022706

SUMMARY: Author Boyd Varty presents a "memoir of his life in [Londolozi Game Reserve in South Africa]. At Londolozi, Varty gained the confidence that emerges from living in Africa. It was there that young Boyd and his equally adventurous sister learned to track animals, raised leopard and lion cubs, followed their larger-than-life uncle on his many adventures filming wildlife, and became one with the land. An intense spiritual quest takes him across the globe and back again." (Publisher's note)

REVIEW: *Booklist* v110 no7 p14 D 1 2013 Rick Roche

REVIEW: *Kirkus Rev* v82 no1 p66 Ja 1 2014

"Cathedral of the Wild: An African Journey Home". "Scion of a South African wildlife preserve recounts somewhat canned yet poignant memories of growing up in the wild. . . . . A visit to Londolozi from Nelson Mandela in 1990 is a highlight, as was [Boyd] Varty's accompanying his uncle to film the migration of the wildebeest across the Serengeti, while some of the horrors included contracting malaria, getting held up in their Johannesburg home by knifepoint and being bitten by a crocodile. The final chapters chronicle the author's youthful, inchoate 'seeking' in India and Arizona, until, by his late 20s, he recognized that Londolozi was home. He's no Isak Dinesen, but Varty writes for a stirring cause."

REVIEW: *Libr J* v139 no9 p42 My 15 2014 Joyce Kessel

REVIEW: *New York Times* v163 no56461 pC27 Ap 4 2014 JANET MASLIN

REVIEW: *Publ Wkly* v260 no49 p70-1 D 2 2013

VARTZIOTI, OLGA. Quintus Horatius Flaccus; [by] Olga Vartzioti 2010 TYPIS Humanities Publishing House

1. Historical literature 2. Horace, 65 B.C.-8 B.C. 3. Inspiration 4. Latin poetry 5. Philosophy & literature
ISBN 9789609808569 paperback

SUMMARY: "In her introduction [author Olga Vartzioti] clearly states the aim of her study: the examination of Horace's innovative treatment of traditional motifs of poetic inspiration under the influence of philosophical, mainly Hellenistic, theories about the origin, the unity and the reception of poetry. . . . Each chapter follows the same pattern: an introductory note . . . , a section on the poet's persona . . . , poetic inspiration, and two or three sections on specialised issues." (Publisher's note)

REVIEW: *Classical Rev* v63 no2 p425-7 O 2013 Charilaos N. Michalopoulos

"Quintus Horatius Flaccus." "[Author Olga Vartzioti] book is a new and welcome contribution to the study of Horatian poetics. The book, a revised version of [Vartzioti's] 2004 doctoral thesis . . . , is divided into a prologue, an introduction, five chapters, conclusions and an English summary. The well-researched and up-to-date bibliography is followed by three useful indexes: Latin terms, Greek terms and ancient writers. . . . In her introduction [Vartzioti] clearly states the aim of her study: the examination of Horace's innovative treatment of traditional motifs of poetic inspiration under the influence of philosophical, mainly Hellenistic, theories about the origin, the unity and the reception of poetry."

VASTA, GIORGIO. Time on my hands; 320 p. 2013 Faber and Faber

1. Historical fiction 2. Terrorists—Italy—Fiction 3. Youth—Political activity
ISBN 9780865479371 (pbk. : alk. paper)
LC 2012-034574

SUMMARY: This novel looks at "the 1978 kidnapping of Italy's former Prime Minister, Aldo Moro, by a leftist terrorist group. . . . Three11-year-old friends experience radio broadcasts of the terrorists' violent demands as a thrilling strike at bourgeois Italian society. They shave their heads, create a private system for communicating with each other, and form their own brigade. . . . When Moro is murdered, they must decide how far their mimicry will go." (Publishers Weekly)

REVIEW: *Kirkus Rev* v81 no3 p222 F 1 2013

REVIEW: *N Y Times Book Rev* p34 Je 9 2013 Tom LeClair

REVIEW: *New York Times* v162 no56162 p34 Je 9 2013 Tom LeClair

REVIEW: *Publ Wkly* v260 no7 p38-9 F 18 2013

REVIEW: *TLS* no5745 p19-20 My 10 2013 THEA LENARDUZZI

REVIEW: *World Lit Today* v87 no5 p64-5 S/O 2013 Maurizio Vito

"Time on My Hands." "Although carefully crafted, [Giorgio] Vasta's allegory of Italian terrorism as an immature, brutal, and purposeless undertaking, an outdated and ominously excessive rite of passage, is perhaps a portrayal less sophisticated than the reader would expect. Then again, the implausible middle-schoolboys' catabasis does not ring completely untrue because of the aloofness between them and the adults. . . . 'Time on My Hands' pits the visible apathy of the adults and the invisible anger of the boys against each other, producing a generational clash fought by means of violent actions and puzzled reactions, as incommunicability rules and splits."

VÁSQUEZ, JUAN GABRIEL, 1973-. The sound of things falling; 288 p. 2013 Riverhead Books, a member of Penguin Group (USA) Inc.

1. Colombian literature 2. Drug traffic—Colombia—Fiction 3. Fathers & daughters—Fiction 4. Male friendship—Fiction 5. Murder—Fiction
ISBN 1594487480; 9781594487484
LC 2013-009330

SUMMARY: In this book by Juan Gabriel Vasquez, set "around 1996, when murder and bloody mayhem fueled by the drug trade were commonplace in Bogotá, the young law professor Antonio Yammara befriends enigmatic stranger Ricardo Laverde. One night, assassins on motorbikes open fire on the two, killing Laverde and seriously wounding Yammara. Conflicted and at a loss to understand the damage Laverde has wrought, Yammara looks into his life story." (Publishers Weekly)

REVIEW: *Booklist* v109 no21 p31 Jl 1 2013 Bryce Christensen

REVIEW: *Kirkus Rev* v81 no12 p30 Je 15 2013

REVIEW: *Libr J* v138 no12 p75 Jl 1 2013 Lawrence Olszewski

REVIEW: *Libr J* v138 no5 p92 Mr 15 2013 Barbara Hoffert

REVIEW: *N Y Times Book Rev* p1-8 Ag 4 2013 Edmund White

"The Sound of Things Falling." "Juan Gabriel Vásquez's brilliant new novel rejects the vivid colors and mythical transformations of his older countryman's [Gabriel García Márquez's] Caribbean masterpiece . . . in favor of the cold, bitter poetry of Bogotá and the hushed intensity of young married love. . . . A gripping novel, absorbing right to the end. . . . 'The Sound of Things Falling' may be a page turner, but it's also a deep meditation on fate and death. Even in translation, the superb quality of Vásquez's prose is evident, captured in Anne McLean's idiomatic English version. All the novel's characters are well imagined original and rounded. Bogotá and the colombian countryside are beautifully if grimly described."

REVIEW: *New York Times* v162 no56214 pC1-4 Jl 31 2013 DWIGHT GARNER

REVIEW: *Publ Wkly* v260 no23 p47-8 Je 10 2013

REVIEW: *Time* v182 no6 p55 Ag 5 2013 Lev Grossman

"The Sound of Things Falling." "This could easily be the setup for a Hitchcockian thriller, but [Juan Gabriel] Vàsquez has subtler, less obvious intentions; he's playing a deeper, longer game. The story drifts and tacks like a sailboat beating upwind. . . . Only . . . 180-something pages in--do we feel as if we've come to the seed around which the book crystallizes: the drug trade that's so central to Colombia's recent history. But once you see that, you realize it's been there from the first page. . . . Vàsquez lacks [Roberto] Bolaño's total immunity from cliché. . . . But like Bolaño, he's a master stylist and a virtuoso of patient pacing and intricate structure."

REVIEW: *TLS* no5738 p22 Mr 22 2013 NICK CAISTOR

"The Sound of Things Falling." "The central part of the novel is entirely given over to Ricardo Laverde's background and family, and as the reader is taken on increasingly wide loops into the past, this becomes a problem for the story's forward thrust: we almost lose sight of the central character and his particular situation. . . . Despite its shortcomings, there is much to enjoy in Vásquez's latest book (admirably rendered in English by Anne McLean). His intense, intricate prose is far removed from the pyrotechnics of an earlier generation of Latin American novelists."

VAUGHAN, BRIAN K., 1976-. Saga. [Vol. 1]. See Saga. [Vol. 1]

VAUGHT, SUSAN. Insanity; [by] Susan Vaught 384 p. 2014 Bloomsbury

1. Haunted places—Fiction 2. Horror stories 3. Paranormal fiction 4. Psychiatric hospitals—Fiction 5. Teenagers—Fiction
ISBN 9781599907840 (hardback)
LC 2013-034321

SUMMARY: In this book, "a psychiatric hospital in Never, Ky., forms the locus for all sorts of occult and paranormal activities. Forest . . . is new on the job at Lincoln Psychiatric, hoping to earn enough money to get to college. Darius has also just taken a job at Lincoln to save money for college. Trina is Darius' girlfriend. . . . And Levi . . . has haunted the halls of Lincoln. . . . Though born at and living in different times, the four teens converge for a series of paranormal adventures." (Kirkus Reviews)

REVIEW: *Booklist* v110 no11 p64 F 1 2014 Daniel Kraus

REVIEW: *Bull Cent Child Books* v67 no5 p288 Ja 2014 K. Q. G.

REVIEW: *Kirkus Rev* v82 no1 p122 Ja 1 2014

"Insanity". "In four linked novellas, each teen tells a story of utmost creepiness, but aside from the locale and atmosphere, there is little overarching logic. The paranormal knack that comes with 'Madoc blood'—descent from the Welsh prince who, according to folklore, came to the New World in 1170—is one element, but there's also witchcraft and plenty of garden-variety evil. The central question of exactly what makes Lincoln such a magnet for ghosts, haints, shades and whatnot is never satisfactorily addressed. Readers content to do without the plotted throughline of a novel will find plenty of effective horror set pieces here."

VAVRECK, LYNN. The gamble; choice and chance in the 2012 presidential election; [by] Lynn Vavreck xviii, 331 p. 2013 Princeton University Press

1. Elections—United States—Demographic aspects 2. Political campaigns—United States—History—21st century 3. Political science literature 4. Presidents—United States—Election—2012 5. Voting—United States—Religious aspects

ISBN 9780691156880 (hardcover : alk. paper)

LC 2013-942892

SUMMARY: This book on the 2012 U.S. presidential election argues that "Barack Obama's reelection was assured even before the campaign began. . . . A complex of 'structural conditions' meant that Mitt Romney never had a chance. One such condition was the president's 'unexpected popularity'. . . . Another was "partisan polarization'. . . . In addition a 'slow recovery' was underway, with people still blaming George W. Bush for the state of the economy." (New York Review of Books)

REVIEW: *N Y Rev Books* v61 no1 p32-4 Ja 9 2014 Andrew Hacker

"Double Down: Game Change 2012," "The Gamble: Choice and Chance in the 2012 Presidential Election," and "The Fracturing of the American Corporate Elite." " While 'Double Down' makes for intriguing reading, it tells us little about the election. . . . 'The Gamble'--a title never fully explained--argues that a complex of 'structural conditions' meant that Mitt Romney never had a chance. . . . Mark Mizruchi, in 'The Fracturing of the American Corporate Elite,' explains why corporations have become less openly political. . . . Mizruchi makes a convincing case."

VAZSONYI, NICHOLAS. Richard Wagner; self-promotion and the making of a brand; [by] Nicholas Vazsonyi 222 2010 Cambridge University Press

1. Biographies 2. Branding (Marketing) 3. Composers 4. Self-promotion

ISBN 0521519969 (hardback : alk. paper); 9780521519960 (hardback : alk. paper)

LC 2009-048047

SUMMARY: "In his monograph, Nicholas Vazsonyi demonstrates that Richard Wagner employed an unprecedented variety of means to win acceptance for his art; or, to rephrase this in the 'business speak' he adopts throughout, Wagner undertook a multi-fronted advertising campaign to establish and promote his brand. . . [The book] highlights the extent to which Wagner's activities can be interpreted as deliberate efforts at self-promotion." (Notes)

REVIEW: *Notes* v68 no4 p802-4 Je 2012 David Larkin Stephen Luttmann

"Richard Wagner: Self Promotion and the Making of a Brand." "This accessibly written study highlights the extent to which [Richard] Wagner's activities can be interpreted as deliberate efforts at self-promotion. . . . [Nicholas] Vazsonyi's study thus marks a vigorous response to the 'lack of interest, if not discomfort, in examining Wagner's marketing tactics' he diagnosed in the existing literature. . . . He has taken a deliberately provocative tone throughout, starting with the cover design which features a Warholesque sequence of differently tinted portraits of Wagner."

VEAL, MICHAEL E. Tony Allen. See Allen, T.

VECSEY, CHRISTOPHER. Jews and Judaism in the New York Times; [by] Christopher Vecsey 397 p. 2013 Lexington Books

1. Historical literature 2. Jews—Press coverage—New York (State)—New York 3. Journalism—Objectivity—United States 4. Judaism—Press coverage—New York (State)—New York

ISBN 9780739184691 (cloth : alk. paper); 9780739184707 (electronic); 9780739184912 (pbk. : alk. paper)

LC 2013-016967

SUMMARY: This book by Christopher Vecsey examines portrayals of Jews and Jewish topics in the newspaper the "New York Times." "Ten chapters discuss and analyze coverage of events, personalities, institutions, and issues of both local Jewish concern and national and international impact." (Choice: Current Reviews for Academic Libraries).

REVIEW: *Choice* v51 no5 p804 Ja 2014 D. Mizrachi

"Jews and Judaism in the New York Times." "[Christopher] Vecsey . . . aims 'to compile a multi-detailed, encyclopedic portrait of Jews and Judaism, as they have appeared on the pages of the Times over three decades and beyond.' In this book, sharp analysis and an accessible style turn what could have been a dull accounting into a lively, engaging read. A meticulous bibliography and helpful index complete the book, which will be useful for anyone interested in contemporary Jewish history."

VEGETATION ECOLOGY; 2013 Wiley-Blackwell

1. Biotic communities 2. Ecosystems 3. Life sciences literature 4. Plant ecology 5. Plants—Adaptation

ISBN 9781444338898 paperback; 9781444338881 hardcover

SUMMARY: Edited by Eddy van der Maarel and Janet Franklin, this book "covers the composition, structure, ecology, diversity, distribution and dynamics of plant communities, with an emphasis on functional adaptations to the abiotic and biotic processes governing plant communities." It "tackles applied aspects of vegetation ecology, notably nature management, restoration ecology and global change studies." (Publisher's note)

REVIEW: *Choice* v51 no2 p294 O 2013 R. Schmid

"Vegetation Ecology." "This new edition . . . is divided into 17 chapters and is more than 150 pages longer than the original work. [Editors Eddy] Van der Maarel . . . and [Janet] Franklin . . . condensed the first chapter, resequenced and substantially updated the other original chapters, and added three new chapters--2, 12, and 16--covering, respectively, classification of vegetation, plant functional types, and mapping vegetation. . . . Overall, the book is comprehensive and multifaceted. The sparse, often complicated illustrations . . . , the paucity of color . . . , the numerous tables (34), the lack of a glossary, the lengthy chapter bibliographies, and the dense text are hallmarks of a technical book aimed at professionals and advanced students."

VEIDLINGER, JEFFREY. In the shadow of the shtetl; small-town Jewish life in Soviet Ukraine; [by] Jeffrey Veidlinger 424 p. 2013 Indiana University Press

1. Historical literature 2. Jews—Ukraine—Social life and customs—20th century 3. Jews—Ukraine—Vinnyt□s□□ka oblast□—Social life and customs—20th century 4. Shtetls—Ukraine—History—20th century 5. Shtetls—Ukraine—Vinnyt□s□□ka oblast□—History—20th century
ISBN 9780253011510 (cloth: alk. paper)
LC 2013-014359

SUMMARY: "The recollections of some 400 returnees in Ukraine provide the basis for [author] Jeffrey Veidlinger's reappraisal of the traditional narrative of 20th-century Jewish history. These elderly Yiddish speakers relate their memories of Jewish life in the prewar shtetl, their stories of survival during the Holocaust, and their experiences living as Jews under Communism." (Publisher's note)

REVIEW: *Choice* v51 no12 p2246 Ag 2014 R. M. Shapiro

REVIEW: *N Y Rev Books* v61 no10 p64-71 Je 5 2014 Marci Shore

"In the Shadow of the Shtetl: Small-Town Jewish Life in Soviet Ukraine." "What is disconcerting about [author Jeffrey] Veidlinger's book is that these people existed in the twenty-first century at all. The recovery of these Yiddish-speaking Jews and their stories was made possible by the eccentric charm of Dov-Ber Kerler, a linguist who grew up in Soviet Russia. . . . What is impressive about [Veidlinger's] writing is his sobriety. The people Veidlinger and Kerler found were, for the most part, born in the 1910s and 1920s in the last years of the Russian Empire or the early Soviet Union."

VEIKOS, CATHRINE. Lina Bo Bardi; the theory of architectural practice; [by] Cathrine Veikos x, 269 p. 2014 Routledge

1. Architectural literature 2. Architecture—Brazil 3. Architecture—Philosophy 4. Architecture—Study and teaching
ISBN 9780415689120 (hardback); 9780415689137 (pb)
LC 2012-023432

SUMMARY: Translated by Cathrine Veikos, "This book contains the first English-language translation of 'Propeadeutic Contribution to the Teaching of Architecture Theory,' (Habitat, Ltd. São Paulo, 1957), a seminal text, published in Portuguese by the Italo-Brazilian Bo Bardi. It is arguably the first published writing on architecture theory by a practicing woman architect." (Publisher's note)

REVIEW: *Choice* v51 no10 p1793 Je 2014 L. E. Carranza

REVIEW: *N Y Rev Books* v61 no9 p12-5 My 22 2014 Martin Filler

"Lina Bo Bardi," "Lina Bo Bardi: The Theory of Architectural Practice," and "Stones Against Diamonds." "'Lina Bo Bardi,' the first full-length life-and-works, by Zeuler R. M. de A. Lima . . . is a feat of primary-source scholarship and thoughtful analysis. Lima does a masterful job of candidly assessing his brilliant, somewhat erratic, and not always truthful subject. . . . Cathrine Veikos's 'Lina Bo Bardi: The Theory of Architectural Practice' [is] the first English translation of . . . Bo Bardi's fullest exposition of a design philosophy. . . . 'Stones Against Diamonds,' a collection of Bo Bardi's writings, was recently issued by London's Architectural Association, part of its commendable Architecture Words series."

VELASQUEZ, ERIC.il. Ol' Clip-Clop. See McKissack, P.

VELLEKOOP, MARIJE. Van gogh at work; [by] Marije Vellekoop 304 p. 2013 Yale University Press

1. Art catalogs 2. Art literature 3. Art technique 4. Gogh, Vincent van, 1853-1890 5. Painting technique
ISBN 9780300191868 (paper over board)
LC 2013-936998

SUMMARY: This book "follows [Vincent] Van Gogh's quest to perfect his skills and the way he adopted various drawing and painting techniques; acquired information about materials; learned about the physical characteristics of canvasses, paint, paper, chalk, and other materials; how he approached working on paper and canvas and which factors influenced his working practice. Van Gogh's working methods are explored along with his most famous works." (Publisher's note)

REVIEW: *Choice* v51 no6 p992 F 2014 L. R. Matteson

"Van Gogh at Work." "Of the catalogue's four sections, the most accessible is curator [Marije] Vellekoop's chronological survey of the artist's oeuvre. While her discussion is not new, her matching--with such specificity--of manuals, paints, canvases, and more to [Vincent] Van Gogh's evolving style is. The sections that follow are much more technical in nature ('Van Gogh's Cobalt Blue Analyzed' and 'Reused Canvases' are two chapters that give a flavor of its content). . . . A crucial and innovative contribution to Van Gogh studies."

VENEZIA, MIKE, 1945-. Daniel Hale Williams; surgeon who opened hearts and minds; 32 2010 Children's Press

1. African Americans—Biography 2. Children's nonfiction 3. Physicians 4. Surgeons 5. Writers on medicine
ISBN 0-531-23729-X; 978-0-531-23729-8 lib bdg

SUMMARY: This book by Mike Venezia, part of the "Getting to Know the World's Greatest Inventors and Scientists" series, looks at "Daniel Hale Williams, founder of the first non-segregated hospital in the United States. . . . One of Williams' most significant contributions to the field of medicine was being one of the first surgeons to operate on the area around the heart." (Children's Literature)

REVIEW: *Booklist* p30-5 Ja 1 2014 Supplement Henrietta Smith

"Art From Her Heart: Folk Artist Clementine Hunter," "Queen of the Track: Alice Coachman, Olympic High-Jump Champion," and "Daniel Hale Williams: Surgeon Who Opened Hearts and Minds." "The words and images in this moving picture-book biography show that Hunter was not stopped by self-pity, and she did not wait for 'the perfect time to paint.' . . . [Heather] Lang's descriptive text and

[Floyd] Cooper's signature sepia-tone oil illustrations offer a rich, deep depiction of Coachman's determination to overcome obstacles. . . . [Mike] Venezia combines a chatty text with a mix of period photographs and playful cartoons in this history of Daniel Hale Williams, who not only performed one of the first successful open heart operations, in 1893, but also made great strides in opening up top-quality medical access to African Americans."

VENEZIA, MIKE, 1945-.il. Daniel Hale Williams. See Venezia, M.

VENTER, J. CRAIG, 1946-. Life at the Speed of Light; From the Double Helix to the Dawn of Digital Life; [by] J. Craig Venter 240 p. 2013 Penguin Group USA

1. Artificial life 2. Biology—Philosophy 3. Genomics 4. Science—Popular works 5. Science—Social aspects

ISBN 0670025402; 9780670025404

LC 2013-017049

SUMMARY: In this book author J. Craig Venter "presents a fascinating and authoritative study of [synthetic genomics]—detailing its origins, current challenges and controversies, and projected effects on our lives. This scientific frontier provides an opportunity to ponder anew the age-old question 'What is life?' and examine what we really mean by 'playing God.'" (Publisher's note)

REVIEW: *Booklist* v110 no2 p11 S 15 2013 Bryce Christensen

REVIEW: *Choice* v51 no7 p1237 Mr 2014 R. M. Denome

REVIEW: *Kirkus Rev* v81 no17 p73 S 1 2013

REVIEW: *Libr J* v138 no9 p55 My 15 2013 Barbara Hoffert

REVIEW: *Publ Wkly* v260 no32 p44-5 Ag 12 2013

REVIEW: *Sci Am* v309 no4 p94 O 2013 Michael Lemonick

REVIEW: *Science* v342 no6156 p312-3 O 18 2013 Sophia Roosth

REVIEW: *Smithsonian* v44 no6 p110 O 2013 Chloë Schama

REVIEW: *TLS* no5797 p22 My 9 2014 RICHARD P. NOVICK

"Life at the Speed of Light: From the Double Helix to the Dawn of Digital Life." "'In Life at the Speed of Light,' J. Craig Venter lays claim to Schrödinger's scientific heritage and to this modem holy grail. His book is, in essence, an extensive and dramatic presentation of the work that he thinks empowers him to make this claim. . . . While the insertion of novel genes, native or synthetic, into existing cells has been practised for many years, producing genetically modified organisms, the possibilities do seem to increase with Craig Venter's technological wizardry. Although his work may thus represent an industrial breakthrough, it is certainly not a scientific one."

VENTURA, GABRIELA BAEZA.tr. The missing chancleta and other top-secret cases. See Vicente, A.

VERBA, CYNTHIA. Dramatic expression in Rameau's Tragédie en musique; between tradition and enlightenment; [by] Cynthia Verba xi, 327 p. 2013 Cambridge University Press

1. Enlightenment—France 2. Music—France—Philosophy and aesthetics 3. Music literature 4. Opera—France—18th century

ISBN 1107021561 (hardback); 9781107021563 (hardback)

LC 2012-016542

SUMMARY: In this book, author Cynthia Verba "builds on decades of study of Jean-Phillipe Rameau's musical practice, taking a two-directional approach--theory and musical practice. She provides a . . . quick summary of general operatic style leading to Rameau, especially as influenced by Jean-Baptiste Lully and the pre-Ramistes. She then considers Rameau (1683-1764) as a microcosm of musical practice of his time, providing an overview and comparison of Rameau's tragedies." (Choice)

REVIEW: *Choice* v51 no4 p647 D 2013 C. A. Traupman-Carr

"Dramatic Expression in Rameau's tragédie en musique: Between Tradition and Enlightenment." "The study is important in showing how [Jean-Phillipe] Rameau melded the well-established national design, highly emotionally charged texts, and Enlightenment principles. Detailed musical study focuses on three types of scenes--scenes of forbidden love, of intense conflict, and of conflict resolution--important in Rameau's tragédie en musique and key to understanding Rameau's practice. The three chapters discussing these three types of scenes are replete with musical examples; appendixes offer French text and English translation, and there is brief summary analysis of the scenes."

VERBRUGGE, MARTHA H. Active bodies; a history of women's physical education in twentieth-century America; [by] Martha H. Verbrugge xi, 391 p. 2012 Oxford University Press

1. Discrimination in sports—United States 2. Educational equalization—United States 3. Historical literature 4. Physical education for women—United States 5. Physical education teachers—United States 6. Women—Education—United States 7. Women physical education teachers—United States

ISBN 0195168798 (alk. paper); 9780195168792 (alk. paper)

LC 2011-030958

SUMMARY: In this book, Martha H. Verbrugge provides a "review of physical activity and physical education for women across the 20th century. The changes in physical education mirror numerous societal changes. The author devotes the first six chapters to the period from 1890 to 1950. The last three chapters bring the discussion to 2005." (Choice)

REVIEW: *Am Hist Rev* v118 no4 p1201-2 O 2013 Amy Erdman Farrell

REVIEW: *Choice* v50 no7 p1290 Mr 2013 K. H. Weiller

REVIEW: *J Am Hist* v100 no1 p228-9 Je 2013 Lynne Curry

REVIEW: *Rev Am Hist* v41 no3 p496-500 S 2013 Susan Ware

"Active Bodies: A History of Women's Physical Education in Twentieth-Century America." "[An] insightful and comprehensive survey of the history of women's physical education over the past century. . . . This is cultural and social history at its best, moving the topic of physical education from the margins of historical inquiry to the center of twentieth-century debates about gender, race, class, and sexuality. . . . Martha Verbrugge has demonstrated remarkable skill and endurance in patiently gathering a huge amount of evidence and then presenting it in such a complete and comprehensive fashion. At times, the narrative gets a bit bogged down in detail. . . . The writing is clear but probably could have been enlivened by a few more quotes from some of the major players."

REVIEW: *Women's Review of Books* v30 no1 p24-6 Ja/F 2013 Laura Pappano

VERDI, JESSICA. The summer I wasn't me; [by] Jessica Verdi 352 p. 2014 Sourcebooks Fire

1. Camps—Fiction 2. Lesbians—Fiction 3. Mothers and daughters—Fiction 4. Sexual reorientation programs 5. Young adult fiction

ISBN 1402277881; 9781402277887 (tp: alk. paper)

LC 2013-049957

SUMMARY: In this novel, by Jessica Verdi, "summer camp promise[s] a new life for seventeen-year-old Lexi. Ever since her mom found out she was in love with a girl, her . . . family has been pulled even further apart. But Lexi swears she can change. . . . [Yet] when she falls heads over heels for one of her fellow campers, Lexi will have to risk her mother's approval for the one person who might love her no matter what." (Publisher's note)

REVIEW: *Bull Cent Child Books* v67 no8 p425 Ap 2014 A. S.

"The Summer I Wasn't Me". "The question of how to balance personal needs with those of one's parents will resonate for many readers, and Lexi's earnest efforts to protect her mom from further grief (they are both still reeling from the death of Lexi's dad) are poignant and powerfully conveyed. . . . Unfortunately, the additional subplot surrounding sexual abuse actually reinforces stereotypes about closeted gay men and adds unnecessary horror to what was already a pretty grim situation. In addition, the emotional growth of minor characters tends to happen at a convenient rate rather than an authentic one, making them foils for Lexi's big changes rather than humans in their own right."

REVIEW: *SLJ* v60 no4 p175 Ap 2014 Georgia Christgau

REVIEW: *Voice of Youth Advocates* v37 no2 p68 Je 2014 Dianna Geers

VERGER, ANTONI.ed. Global education policy and international development. See Global education policy and international development

VERHOEVEN, MARIËTTE. The Early Christian Monuments of Ravenna; Transformations and Memory; [by] Mariëtte Verhoeven 343 p. 2011 lsd

1. Art literature 2. Christian art & symbolism—Italy 3. Church architecture—Italy 4. Italy—Religion 5. Ravenna (Italy)

ISBN 2503541151; 9782503541150

SUMMARY: "This study takes the transformations of the monuments of Ravenna as a starting point to explore the city's attitude towards its religious cultural heritage throughout the centuries. Together with the local historiographical sources, dating from Medieval and the Early Modern times, they provide a picture of the manner in which Ravenna experienced, appropriated and imagined its past." (Publisher's note)

REVIEW: *Burlington Mag* v156 no1332 p170-1 Mr 2014 DEBORAH M. DELIYANNIS

"The Early Christian Monuments of Ravenna: Transformations and Memory". "There is an extremely interesting book to be written about the later history of Ravenna's early Christian past, and Mariëtte Verhoeven has attempted to write it. I say 'attempted' because while many of the points she makes are unexceptionable, the organisation of the book makes it difficult to discern the guiding principles or themes of her study. . . . If the entire book had focused on this material and had developed it better, then it would be a valuable study. Unfortunately, the rest of the book does not serve to advance these theses."

REVIEW: *Engl Hist Rev* v128 no533 p921-3 Ag 2013 David Rollason

VERMOND, KIRA. Inside and out; 104 p. 2013 Owlkids Books

1. Puberty 2. Self-help materials 3. Sex differences (Biology) 4. Teenagers—Health 5. Teenagers—Sexual behavior

ISBN 1771470046 (pbk.); 1926973895 (hbk.); 9781771470049 (pbk.); 9781926973890 (hbk.)

LC 2013-930985

SUMMARY: In this book for preteens, Kira Vermond "discusses bodily and hormonal changes, body image, emotional ups and downs, cliques, attraction, dating, and sex. Throughout, the author encourages readers to do what's right for them, rather than fall prey to what society, entertainment, or peers have to say about how bodies should look or how relationships should work." (Publishers Weekly)

REVIEW: *Kirkus Rev* v81 no18 p55 S 15 2013

REVIEW: *Publ Wkly* v260 no28 p172 Jl 15 2013

REVIEW: *Quill Quire* v79 no8 p38 O 2013 Cynthia O'Brien

"Growing Up, Inside and Out." "[Author] Kira Vermond's excellent 'Growing Up' is a straight-talking guide to the roller coaster of puberty, from the first physical changes to what it means to have a healthy sexual relationship. . . . At first glance, the two-colour, understated design and text-heavy pages seem a little dry, even with the inclusion of a few quirky illustrations by Carl Chin. However, this sophisticated visual approach lends the material more authority, and allows Vermond's good-humoured, conversational style and abundance of great advice to take centre stage."

VERMÈS, GÉZA, 1924-2013. Christian beginnings; from Nazareth to Nicaea, (AD 30-325); [by] Géza Vermès xvi, 271 p. 2012 Allen Lane

1. Christianity 2. Church history—Primitive and early church, ca. 30-600 3. Dogma 4. Religious literature

ISBN 1846141508 (hbk); 9781846141508 (hbk)

LC 2012-494589

SUMMARY: This book "traces the evolution of the figure of Jesus from the man he was—a prophet recognizable as the successor to other Jewish holy men of the Old Testament—to what he came to represent: a mysterious, otherworldly being at the heart of a major new religion. As Jesus's teachings spread across the eastern Mediterranean . . . they were transformed in the space of three centuries into a centralized, state-backed creed worlds away from its humble origins."

(Publisher's note)

REVIEW: *America* v209 no11 p35-7 O 21 2013 CAROLYN OSIEK

REVIEW: *Commonweal* v140 no20 p28-30 D 20 2013 Michael Peppard

"Christian Beginnings: From Nazareth to Nicaea, A.D. 30-325". "From the opening . . . the late Géza Vermes's approach to the history of early Christianity perplexed me. In this, his last book, the eminent scholar . . . turned his attention to later centuries to show that 'by the early fourth century, the practical, charismatic Judaism preached by Jesus was transformed into an intellectual religion defined and regulated by dogma.' Yes, early Christianity had a few world-class intellectuals, and important dogmas were developing over time. But Christianity, then as now, can be described primarily as intellectual and dogmatic only if one sets aside lots of evidence. That's precisely what Vermes does in this book."

REVIEW: *TLS* no5730 p12 Ja 25 2013 JOHN BARTON

VERNICK, AUDREY. Bogart and Vinnie; a completely made-up story of true friendship; 40 p. 2013 Walker & Company

1. Children's stories 2. Dogs—Fiction 3. Friendship—Fiction 4. Rhinoceroses—Fiction 5. Wildlife refuges—Fiction

ISBN 0802728227; 9780802728227 (hardback); 9780802728234 (reinforced)

LC 2012-027335

SUMMARY: In this children's picture book, "when Vinnie, a crazy-happy dog, gets lost while visiting a nature preserve with his family, he finds comfort in the company of Bogart, a big, lazy rhinoceros. Vinnie loves his new friend, but Bogart would rather just take a nap. . . . When word of their unique situation spreads, Bogart and Vinnie are a worldwide sensation! But as soon as their fifteen seconds of fame ends, what's left is a bond even Bogart can't ignore." (Publisher's note)

REVIEW: *Bull Cent Child Books* v67 no1 p58 S 2013 D. S.

"Bogart and Vinnie: A Completely Made-Up Story of True Friendship." "[Author Audrey] Vernick, author of 'Brothers at Bat' . . . takes a sly poke here at the popularity of animal-friendship stories, and kids with pesky siblings will likely see something of themselves in Bogart and Vinnie's relationship. . . . The ending loses a bit of steam, but the manically eager Vinnie . . . is a giggleworthy protagonist throughout. [Illustrator Henry] Cole's illustrations, a luminous mix of acrylic paints, ink, and colored pencil, are classically cartoonish, usually broken into fast-moving panels thick with speech-balloon dialogue (mostly from goofy, enthusiastic Vinnie)."

REVIEW: *Kirkus Rev* v81 no9 p106 My 1 2013

REVIEW: *Publ Wkly* p42 Children's starred review annual 2013

REVIEW: *SLJ* v59 no5 p88 My 2013 Roxanne Burg

VERNICK, AUDREY. Screaming at the ump; [by] Audrey Vernick 272 p. 2014 Clarion Books, Houghton Mifflin Harcourt

1. Baseball—Fiction 2. Baseball umpires—Fiction 3. Fathers and sons—Fiction 4. Journalism—Fiction 5. Mothers and sons—Fiction 6. Single-parent families—Fiction 7. Sports stories

ISBN 9780544252080 (hardback)

LC 2013-036213

SUMMARY: In this book by Audrey Vernick, Casey's "plans to cover sports for his school newspaper are stonewalled by the unwritten rule that sixth-graders must pay their dues by selling ad space before they can become journalists. He stumbles across a big story, however, while helping out at the umpire academy and begins to investigate the mystery behind ump-in-training J-Mac, who retired from the big leagues after a drug scandal." (Bulletin of the Center for Children's Books)

REVIEW: *Bull Cent Child Books* v67 no9 p481-2 My 2014 E. B.

"Screaming at the Ump". "Subplots involving Casey's relationship with his divorced mother, and the irksome presence of an eight-year-old girl who tags along with Casey and his pal Zeke, are amiable, but it's the peek into the world of professional umpire training that carries the interest here, culminating in the fictional but tantalizing event, You Suck, Ump! Day, in which students perform under intense pressure of a local crowd recruited to heckle them on the field. The briefest of notes on umpire academies is provided, but any kid who can find the way to the Major League Baseball website can begin to fill in the intriguing blanks."

REVIEW: *Kirkus Rev* v82 no5 p261 Mr 1 2014

REVIEW: *SLJ* v60 no5 p118 My 2014 Geri Diorio

VESETH, MIKE. Extreme wine; searching the world for the best, the worst, the outrageously cheap, the insanely overpriced, and the undiscovered; [by] Mike Veseth 248 p. 2013 Rowman & Littlefield

1. Food writing 2. Wine & wine making—History 3. Wine and wine making 4. Wine industry 5. Wine industry—Economic aspects

ISBN 9781442219229 (cloth : alk. paper); 9781442219243 (electronic)

LC 2013-006779

SUMMARY: In this book, author Mike Veseth examines "wine's outliers, revealing those wines that have unusual histories, are particularly expensive or cheap, or are made under the most difficult conditions. . . . He chronicles booms and busts, relating how Prohibition actually became a boon for vineyards. . . . Veseth also details why the cheapest wines aren't necessarily the worst nor the most expensive the best." (Booklist)

REVIEW: *Booklist* v110 no3 p22-6 O 1 2013 Mark Knoblauch

"Extreme Wine: Searching the World for the Best, the Worst, the Outrageously Cheap, the Insanely Overpriced, and the Undiscovered." "No wine-making or wine-selling professional can afford to ignore [Mike] Veseth's blog, which illuminates wine's often murky economics. Here he expounds on wine's outliers, revealing those wines that have unusual histories, are particularly expensive or cheap, or are made under the most difficult conditions. Taking what could be an esoteric subject and making it compelling for any wine drinker, Veseth probes the best and worst that the world's vineyards produce. . . . Not just for geeky wine snobs."

VESS, CHARLES.il. Seven wild sisters. See De Lint, C.

VESTERGAARD, HOPE. Digger, dozer, dumper; 32 p. 2013 Candlewick Press

1. Building—Juvenile literature 2. Building sites—Juvenile literature 3. Children's poetry 4. Construction equipment 5. Motor vehicles—Juvenile literature

ISBN 0763650781 (reinforced); 9780763650780 (reinforced)

LC 2012-947724

SUMMARY: In this children's picture book, Hope Vestergaard "offers 16 poetic tributes to big machines and trucks," where she "celebrates not only the jobs these machines perform but also their marvelous mechanics (the garbage truck's hydraulic arms; the levers of the agile skid-steer loader)." (Publishers Weekly)

REVIEW: *Booklist* v109 no21 p61 Jl 1 2013 Carolyn Phelan

REVIEW: *Bull Cent Child Books* v67 no2 p121-2 O 2013 E. B.

"Digger, Dozer, Dumper." "Muddy wheels, hefty loads, thrumming engines, and automotive grunt work inspire [author Hope] Vestergaard's poetic paeans, praising the humble hard work and civic contributions of sixteen awesomely loud and impressively tough trucks. Although [illustrator David] Slonim's perky accompanying cartoon illustrations play to a younger crowd, Vestergaard's careful wordsmithery, precise terminology, and sly humor assure that the poems themselves will be appreciated by even more sophisticated listeners. . . . Vestergaard changes up her rhyme and meter enough to keeps things interesting, and the scansion is reliable enough to coax even poetry-shy adults into trying a read aloud."

REVIEW: *Horn Book Magazine* v89 no5 p119 S/O 2013 KITTY FLYNN

"Digger, Dozer, Dumper." "These playful verses sing the praises of sixteen trucks and the work they do. The lighthearted acrylic and charcoal illustrations enhance the poems' humor and give their subjects loads of personality. There's some refreshing gender equality, too, as six of the trucks are female. . . . The poems, at their best, not only describe the trucks' jobs but also reveal something of their spirit. . . . The final scene reveals that the kids are actually playing with toy trucks, and while that toys-are-real conceit may not be new, it never gets old for a child audience. 'Digger, Dozer, Dumper' will make light work of even the toughest storytimes."

REVIEW: *Kirkus Rev* v81 no12 p121 Je 15 2013

REVIEW: *Publ Wkly* v260 no21 p63 My 27 2013

REVIEW: *Publ Wkly* p62-3 Children's starred review annual 2013

REVIEW: *SLJ* v59 no7 p112 Jl 2013 Teresa Pfeifer

VETERANS' POLICIES, VETERANS' POLITICS; new perspectives on veterans in the modern United States; xiv, 318 p. 2012 University Press of Florida

1. Historical literature 2. Veterans—Employment—United States 3. Veterans—Services for—United States 4. Veterans—United States

ISBN 9780813042077 (alk. paper)

LC 2012-018869

SUMMARY: "'Veterans' Policies, Veterans' Politics' is the first multidisciplinary, comprehensive examination of the American veteran experience. [Author] Stephen Ortiz has compiled some of the best work on the formation and impact of veterans' policies, the politics of veterans' issues, and veterans' political engagement over the course of the twentieth and twenty-first centuries in the United States." (Publisher's note)

REVIEW: *Choice* v50 no9 p1701 My 2013 E. A. Goedeken

REVIEW: *J Am Hist* v100 no2 p581-2 S 2013 David A. Gerber

REVIEW: *Rev Am Hist* v42 no2 p379-85 Je 2014 Beth Bailey

"Veterans' Policies, Veterans' Politics: New Perspectives on Veterans in the Modern United States" and "Those Who Have Borne the Battle: A History of America's Wars and Those Who Fought Them." "[Author James] Wright calls his work a 'meditation' . . . , and the mix of autobiographical context, emotional engagement, and concrete proposals for action he offers moves his work beyond the traditional realm of historical analysis. . . . Wright's emotional commitment gives this book its power, but it also sometimes undermines its logic. . . . [Editor] Stephen R. Ortiz envisions his readers as scholars. . . . The fundamental claim of this smart, well-edited collection is historiographical: we cannot fully understand U.S. political history . . . without paying significant attention to the changing historical roles of veterans."

VIANO, HANNAH. S is for salmon; [by] Hannah Viano 32 p. 2014 Sasquatch Books

1. Alphabet books 2. English language—Alphabet 3. Natural history—Northwest, Pacific—Juvenile literature 4. Nature—Juvenile literature 5. Northwest, Pacific

ISBN 9781570618734

LC 2013-030908

SUMMARY: This alphabet book by Hannah Viano "mirrors the natural wonders of the Pacific Northwest. . . . Each Northwest entity is allotted one . . . page, showing the capital and lowercase versions of each letter. The artwork resembles woodcuts, but Viano carves away black paper to shape her images." (Kirkus Reviews)

REVIEW: *Kirkus Rev* v82 no2 p98 Ja 15 2014

"S is for Salmon: A Pacific Northwest Alphabet". "This elegant alphabet book mirrors the natural wonders of the Pacific Northwest. . . . Each Northwest entity is allotted one gift-card-perfect page, showing the capital and lowercase versions of each letter. The artwork resembles woodcuts, but [Hannah] Viano carves away black paper to shape her images. A soothing palette—creams, robin's-egg blue, pale greens, warm rose—sets a reflective mood in keeping with the quiet, still illustrations of close-up objects and landscapes alike. The text—sometimes factual, sometimes more whimsical—is best for reading aloud to wee ones, as the sentence structure can be somewhat convoluted."

VIANO, HANNAH.il. S is for salmon. See Viano, H.

VICENTE, ALIDIS. The missing chancleta and other top-secret cases; 64 p. 2013 Pinata Books, An Imprint of Arte Publico Press

1. Allergies—Fiction 2. Bilingual books 3. Food allergy—Fiction 4. Hispanic Americans—Fiction 5. Lost and found possessions—Fiction 6. Mystery and detective stories 7. Salsa (Dance)—Fiction 8. Spanish language materials—Bilingual

ISBN 9781558857797 (alk. paper)

LC 2013-029355

SUMMARY: In this book, "the eight-year-old narrator" recounts "her first case as a gumshoe trying to locate her missing chancleta (flip-flop). . . . Flaca tells readers about two other cases she's taken on: the time she faced an assassination attempt when a fruit cup someone slid into her lunch box contained oranges (she's allergic), and the case of her missing salsa when her mother signs her up for dance lessons in preparations for her sister's quinceañera." (Bulletin of the Center for Children's Books)

REVIEW: *Bull Cent Child Books* v67 no6 p338 F 2014 Thaddeus Andracki

"The Missing Chancleta and Other Top-Secret Cases/La chancleta perdida y otros casos secretos." "This collection of three brief short stories, peppered with both with Spanish vocabulary, as well as some more difficult English phrasing . . . that might push it toward stronger readers or a readaloud, is followed by a parallel Spanish translation. Flaca is delightfully smart-alecky for an eight-year-old . . . and her insistence in her sleuthing skills despite the anticlimactic nature of what she usually uncovers will be endearing to aspirant investigators. A hardboiled, bilingual version of 'Nate the Great,' Flaca and her age-appropriate grit will likely spur new interest in the whodunit."

REVIEW: *Kirkus Rev* v81 no20 p197 O 15 2013

VIEIRA, MARK A. George Hurrell's hollywood; glamour portraits, 1925-1992; [by] Mark A. Vieira 416 p. 2013 Running Press Book Publishers

1. Glamour photography 2. Hurrell, George 3. Motion picture industry—United States—History—20th century 4. Photograph collections 5. Photography of actors

ISBN 9780762450398

LC 2013-937706

SUMMARY: "George Hurrell (1904-1992) was the creator of the Hollywood glamour portrait, the maverick artist who captured movie stars of the most exalted era in Hollywood history with bold contrast and seductive poses." Written by Mark A. Vieira, this "book spans Hurrell's entire career, from his beginnings as a society photographer to his finale as the celebrity photographer who was himself a celebrity, and a living legend." (Publisher's note)

REVIEW: *Libr J* v138 no21 p103 D 1 2013 Teri Shiel

REVIEW: *N Y Times Book Rev* p38-9 D 8 2013 LUC SANTE

"Wall," "Top Secret: Images From the Stasi Archives," and "George Hurrell's Hollywood: Glamour Portraits 1925-1992." "An appreciation of stony texture . . . marks 'Wall' . . . , by the veteran Czech photographer Josef Koudelka . . . a remarkable collection of panoramic photos . . . of the barrier that has been erected over the past decade in defiance of the internationally recognized border. . . . Simon Menner's 'Top Secret: Images From the Stasi Archives' . . . might be a primer on the banality of evil. . . . 'George Hurrell's Hollywood: Glamour Portraits 1925-1992' by Mark A. Vieira . . . presents rapture upon rapture."

VIEROW, WENDY.ed. International women stage directors. See International women stage directors

VIGAN, DELPHINE DE. Nothing holds back the night. See De Vigan, D.

VIGARELLO, GEORGES. The metamorphoses of fat; a history of obesity; 296 p. 2013 Columbia University Press

1. Body image 2. Historical literature 3. Obesity—Public opinion 4. Obesity—Social aspects—History 5. Overweight persons

ISBN 0231978159760 (cloth : alk. paper)

LC 2012-029197

SUMMARY: This book by Georges Vigarello "maps the evolution of Western ideas about fat and fat people from the Middle Ages to the present, paying particular attention to the role of science, fashion, fitness crazes, and public health campaigns in shaping these views. While hefty bodies were once a sign of power, today those who struggle to lose weight are considered poor in character and weak in mind." (Publisher's note)

REVIEW: *Choice* v51 no3 p500 N 2013 R. A. Hoots

REVIEW: *Publ Wkly* v260 no12 p59 Mr 25 2013

REVIEW: *TLS* no5759 p9-10 Ag 16 2013 BARBARA J. KING

"Fat Chance: The Bitter Truth About Sugar," "Salt Sugar Fat: How the Food Giants Hooked Us," and "The Metamorphoses of Fat: A History of Obesity." "These books raise powerful questions about why we become obese, what we can do about it, and how our understanding of obesity and its causes is affected by the time and place in which we live. [Robert] Lustig's approach is the most controversial. Crammed full of hard-hitting insights that may shock the reader into immediate dietary change (it did me), 'Fat Chance' makes sweeping generalizations which invite scepticism. . . . Lustig takes his championing of the power of biochemistry too far. . . . Michael Moss . . . is an ideal guide: sharp-witted but genial. . . . [Georges] Vigarello masterfully traces . . . the stigmatization of the fat person over time."

VIGILANTE, DANETTE. Saving Baby Doe; [by] Danette Vigilante 240 p. 2014 G.P. Putnam's Sons, an imprint of Penguin Group (USA) Inc.

1. Best friends—Fiction 2. Conduct of life—Fiction 3. Foundlings—Fiction 4. Friendship—Fiction 5. Hispanic Americans—Fiction 6. Neighbors—Fiction 7. Psychological fiction 8. Single-parent families—Fiction

ISBN 039925160X; 9780399251603 (hardback)

LC 2013-022728

SUMMARY: In this book, by Danette Vigilante, "a cry in a building-site portable toilet leads thirteen-year-old Lionel and his friend Anisa to the discovery of an abandoned newborn baby. . . . Lionel, himself abandoned by his father, fears that Baby Doe will be hurt by a similar loss, so he schemes to bring her home with him. Realizing baby supplies cost money, a rare commodity around his house, he reluctantly agrees to take on some work for a local drug dealer." (Bulletin of the Center for Children's Books)

REVIEW: *Booklist* v110 no14 p79-80 Mr 15 2014 Erin Anderson

REVIEW: *Bull Cent Child Books* v67 no7 p382 Mr 2014 D. S.

"Saving Baby Doe." "[Danette] Vigilante returns here to the same minority-dominated Brooklyn neighborhood (Lionel and Anisa are Latino) and group of kids featured in 'The Trouble with Half a Moon' . . . and offers a similar straightforward and accessible narrative style. The plot unfortunately spirals out of control with a multitude of final tragedies, and the unlikely resolution to the Baby Doe story (the baby's teenaged mother is identified and gets to take her baby home) is hardly as happy as the book paints it. However, Vigilante writes about tough subjects with an engaging clarity and a tender touch, making this story a gentle younger version of urban lit that might also appeal to reluctant older readers."

REVIEW: *Horn Book Magazine* v90 no2 p131-2 Mr/Ap 2014 SUSAN DOVE LEMPKE

REVIEW: *Kirkus Rev* v82 no3 p76 F 1 2014

REVIEW: *SLJ* v60 no5 p118 My 2014 Lalitha Nataraj

VILE, JOHN R. The men who made the Constitution; lives of the delegates to the Constitutional Convention; [by] John R. Vile xxxvi, 447 p. 2013 The Scarecrow Press, Inc.

1. Biography (Literary form) 2. Constitutional conventions—United States—History—18th century 3. Constitutional history—United States 4. Founding Fathers of the United States—Biography

ISBN 9780810888647 (cloth: alkaline paper)

LC 2013-014081

SUMMARY: This book by John R. Vile looks at "the 55 men who served as delegates to the [U.S.] Constitutional Convention—whether or not they signed the document on September 17, 1787. Vile adds biographical information and detailed descriptions of each delegate's documented actions and opinions on the issues debated in the convention." (Choice: Current Reviews for Academic Libraries)

REVIEW: *Choice* v51 no8 p1380 Ap 2014 D. A. Lincove

"The Men Who Made the Constitution: Lives of the Delegates to the Constitutional Convention". "Among his sources, [John R.] Vile relies heavily on Max Farrand's edited 'The Records of the Federal Convention of 1787' (rev. ed., 1966), a key compilation of documents, notes, and proceedings of the convention written by James Madison. He does not provide much interpretation or evaluation concerning delegates' influence, but instead offers a unique, descriptive guide to their convention participation and sources for further study."

VILLA, VICTOR RIVAS.il. Just Jake. See Marcionette, J.

VILLALOBOS, JUAN PABLO. Quesadillas; A Novel; 160 p. 2013 And Other Stories

1. Mexican cooking 2. Mexican fiction 3. Poor families—Fiction 4. Poor people—Mexico 5. Social classes—Fiction

ISBN 0374533954; 1908276223 (pbk.); 9780374533953; 9781908276223 (pbk.)

SUMMARY: In this book, author Juan Pablo Villalobos "writes of a poor family that thinks of itself as middle class. . . . This figures into the narration of a man remembering his boyhood of 25 years earlier, when he was 13 and the second oldest in a family subsisting totally on quesadillas. The cheap meal provides the titular metaphor for the family's condition and has a wide range of quality and implications." (Kirkus Reviews)

REVIEW: *Booklist* v110 no8 p19-20 D 15 2013 Brendan Driscoll

"Quesadillas." "Orestes, the irreverent adolescent narrator of this surrealist sociopolitical satire, struggles to come to terms with his Mexican family's poverty. . . . Orestes veers toward profanity and hyperbole, and the story's plot pivots upon comic absurdities, including invading extraterrestrials and the sexual proclivities of cows; at times, the entire narrative seems in danger of spiraling out of control. But in the end such devices underscore, rather than distract from, this novel's caustic critique of Mexican politics under the Carlos Salinas regime."

REVIEW: *Kirkus Rev* v81 no23 p75 D 1 2013

REVIEW: *N Y Times Book Rev* p23 Mr 9 2014 RACHEL NOLAN

REVIEW: *New York Times* v163 no56426 pC21-9 F 28 2014 DWIGHT GARNER

"Quesadillas." "Both of [author Juan Pablo] Villalobos's novels are short, dark, comic, ribald and surreal. They aren't so much manic-depressive as they are, to borrow Delmore Schwartz's phrasing, manic-impressive. This writer stares down serious issues--poverty, class, systemic violence--and doesn't analyze them so much as sneeze all over them. . . . The comedy in 'Quesadillas' has a moral dimension. Conquered people, Saul Bellow told us, tend to be witty. So do long-oppressed people. . . . Orestes is a great noticer of things, especially when they concern his stomach."

REVIEW: *New York Times* v163 no56426 pC21-9 F 28 2013 DWIGHT GARNER

REVIEW: *TLS* no5761 p22 Ag 30 2013 MATT LEWIS

REVIEW: *World Lit Today* v88 no2 p64-5 Mr/Ap 2014 Arthur Dixon

"Quesadillas." "'Quesadillas' searches for the identity of a place that is anything but normal. Juan Pablo Villalobos invokes the weird and the random as he questions what it means to be Mexican, to be poor, and to be poor in Mexico. His second novel can be read as a picaresque adventure, imparting social criticism through a poor boy's travels in a decaying country. . . . 'Quesadillas' is fast-paced and colloquial; it is troubling and funny all at once. . . . Rosalind Harvey's English translation--while noticeably more British than American--maintains the verve of the original and offers readers a chance to realign their perceptions of Mexico and Mexicans. 'Quesadillas' is an unusual and important novel that deserves to be read."

VINCENT, JANE.ed. Migration, diaspora, and information technology in global societies. See Migration, diaspora, and information technology in global societies

VIOLENCE AGAINST GIRLS AND WOMEN; international perspectives; 549 p. 2013 Praeger, An Imprint of ABC-CLIO, LLC

1. Girls—Crimes against 2. Girls—Violence against 3. Social science literature 4. Women—Crimes against 5. Women—Violence against

ISBN 9781440803352 (hardcover: alk. paper)

LC 2013-002150

SUMMARY: In this book on violence against girls and women, edited by Janet A. Sigal and Florence L. Denmark, the authors "posit that institutional and social policy needs to protect the rights of females and change historical and cultural norms. The essays examine the history and cultural context of sexual violence and aggression against females—from female genital mutilation, trafficking, and cyber bullying to physical abuse." (Choice: Current Reviews for Academic Libraries)

REVIEW: *Choice* v51 no9 p1639 My 2014 S. M. Valente

"Violence Against Girls and Women: International Perspectives". "Gendered violence against women and girls is a major international public health and human rights issue. Understanding and remedying it requires a multidisciplinary and coordinated response from community stakeholders and advocates. . . . The contributors encourage readers to reflect on the resilience and suffering of the survivor victims, and offer practical suggestions for changing policy and practices concerning violence against girls and women. Case vignettes offer poignant illustrations. This book adds an international perspective that was absent in earlier works."

VIORST, JUDITH, 1931-. Lulu's mysterious mission; 192 p. 2014 Atheneum Books for Young Readers

1. Babysitters—Fiction 2. Behavior—Fiction 3. Children's stories 4. Conduct of life—Juvenile fiction 5. Spies—Fiction

ISBN 1442497467; 9781442497467 (hardcover); 9781442497474 (pbk.)

LC 2013-004350

SUMMARY: In this book, by Judith Viorst, "Lulu has put her tantrum-throwing days behind her. That is, until her parents announce that they are going on vacation—WITHOUT LULU. Not only that, but they are leaving her with the formidable Ms. Sonia Sofia Solinsky. . . . The second her parents are out of the house, Lulu tries out several elaborate schemes to bring them straight back. But just when she seems to finally be making some headway, her babysitter reveals an astonishing secret." (Publisher's note)

REVIEW: *Booklist* v110 no16 p51 Ap 15 2014 Karen Cruze

REVIEW: *Horn Book Magazine* v90 no2 p132 Mr/Ap 2014 JOANNA RUDGE LONG

"Lulu' Mysterious Mission." "Astute readers may wonder: is Ms. Solinsky truly a spy? No matter; craving her tutelage, Lulu is hooked into behaving with uncommon decorum, at least for the duration, though she retains plenty of panache. Farce, slapstick, tall tale; punctuated with authorial asides, leavened with scads of white space and the many energetic sweeps of [Kevin] Cornell's comic illustrations--a tad more light-hearted than previous illustrator Lane Smith's--this is a book to tickle younger listeners as well as emerging readers."

REVIEW: *Kirkus Rev* v82 no4 p155 F 15 2014

"Lulu's Mysterious Mission". "Another wild adventure featuring the exasperating and inexplicably lovable Lulu. . . . As hard as it may be to believe, Lulu's doting parents have decided to take a vacation without their precious darling. What's worse, they have hired a professional babysitter to care for her while they are gone. . . .Throughout the text, [Judith] Viorst weaves in an authorial voice that speaks directly to readers, offering witty metafictional commentary sure to induce giggles. Black-and-white drawings depicting a spirited Lulu in action and a good deal of white space keep the text from becoming overwhelming to readers new to chapter books. Great fun for Lulu fans old and new."

REVIEW: *SLJ* v60 no3 p129 Mr 2014 Marian McLeod

VIORST, JUDITH, 1931-. The tenth good thing about Barney; 25 p. 1987 Aladdin Books

1. Cats—Fiction 2. Death—Fiction 3. Pet funeral rites & ceremonies 4. Pets—Juvenile literature 5. Picture books for children

ISBN 068970416X (pbk.)

LC 8602-5948

SUMMARY: This children's picture book by Judith Viorst presents a story about the loss of a pet. "'My cat Barney died this Friday. I was very sad. My mother said we could have a funeral for him, and I should think of ten good things about Barney so I could tell them.' . . . . But the small boy who loved Barney can only think of nine. Later, while talking with his father, he discovers the tenth." (Publisher's note)

REVIEW: *Horn Book Magazine* v89 no5 p56-62 S/O 2013 Thom Barthelmess

"Nana Upstairs & Nana Downstairs," "The Tenth Good Thing About Barney," and "My Father's Arms Are A Boat." "[Tomie dePaola . . . fills the text and illustrations with fond, personal, sometimes humorous details . . . giving the story a tender immediacy that is perfectly suited to the nostalgic subject matter and establishing family love as life's central theme--and death as one of its necessary components. . . . Judith Viorst's 'The Tenth Good Thing About Barney . . . employs direct prose and spare etchings to recount the death of a boy's cat. . . . [In 'My Father's Arms Are A Boat'] only passing reference is made to the death of the boy's mother. Instead, the lyrical language and still, dioramic illustrations observe the evening's simple spectacle, with all the intimacy of warm detail."

THE VIRGIL ENCYCLOPEDIA; 1600 p. 2014 Wiley Blackwell

1. Classical literature—History & criticism 2. Encyclopedias & dictionaries 3. Latin literature—Appreciation 4. Latin poetry 5. Latin poets

ISBN 9781405154987 (hardback : alk. paper)

LC 2012-037003

SUMMARY: Edited by Richard F. Thomas and Jan M. Ziolkowski, "Featuring over 2,200 entries, 'The Virgil Encyclopedia' represents the first comprehensive reference volume to be published in English on Virgil, a poet whose works and thoughts have been at the center of Western literary, cultural, artistic, and pedagogical traditions for more than two millennia. [It] offers readers a new accessibility not previously available on Virgil scholarship." (Publisher's note)

REVIEW: *Choice* v51 no9 p1568 My 2014 F. W. Jenkins

REVIEW: *Libr J* v139 no2 p98 F 1 2014 Julie Seifert

REVIEW: *TLS* no5783 p10-1 Ja 31 2014 EMILY GOWERS

"The Virgil Encyclopedia." "Trim, at a mere 1,526 pages and appropriately tripartite, Wiley-Blackwell's long-heralded 'Virgil Encyclopedia' has been brought to birth, larger than its equivalent three-volume forerunner on Homer . . . and with considerably more headings and voices. . . . The 'Encyclopedia's' editors present their remarkable achievement in translating, digesting and updating so much Virgiliana in modest enough terms. . . . Their ideal reader is the student seeking basic orientation, but there is plenty here for those interested in more esoteric material such as classical scholarship, inaugural presidential addresses or postage stamps."

THE VIRILIO DICTIONARY; 228 p. 2013 Edinburgh Universary Press

1. Encyclopedias & dictionaries 2. France—Intellectual

life 3. Social criticism 4. Social theory 5. Virilio, Paul, 1932-
ISBN 0748646833; 0748646841; 9780748646838 (pbk.); 9780748646845 (hbk.)
LC 2013-412213

SUMMARY: This book, edited by John Armitage, is "The first dictionary dedicated to the pioneering work of French art and technology critic Paul Virilio. . . . This dictionary guides you through his concepts with headwords including Accident, Body, Cinema, Deterritorialization and Eugenics. Explore the very edge of Virilio's pioneering thought in cultural and social theory with the entries on Foreclosure, Grey Ecology, Polar Inertia and the Overexposed City." (Publisher's note)

REVIEW: *Choice* v51 no4 p616 D 2013 H. G. Reid

"The Virilio Dictionary." "The editor of this timely, useful volume modestly describes Paul Virilio as a leading critic of art and technology. This reviewer would claim that Virilio's work as political theorist insightfully carries readers into the 21st century as few others have. . . . Here, six contributions by Eric Wilson brilliantly account for Virilio's key theme of the political and ontological loss of reality. . . . Editor [John] Armitage's introduction astutely points to Virilio's 'A Landscape of Events' . . . and the present era of 'temporal crash,' examined by Nicholas Michelson. . . . This is an extremely useful volume."

VISCHER, FRANS. A Very Fuddles Christmas; [by] Frans Vischer 32 p. 2013 Simon & Schuster

1. Cats—Juvenile fiction 2. Christmas stories for children 3. Pets—Juvenile literature 4. Picture books for children 5. Squirrels
ISBN 1416991565; 9781416991564

SUMMARY: This book continues Frans Vischer's Fuddles series. Here, when "Fuddles follows the delectable aromas to the dining room and spies a fancy, feast-laden table, he can't contain himself. . . . But an authoritative voice shoos him from the dinner, presents, gingerbread house, and decorated tree, sending him scurrying right out the front door." (Publishers Weekly)

REVIEW: *Horn Book Magazine* v89 no6 p69 N/D 2013 SHARA L. HARDESON

"A Very Fuddles Christmas". "Fat and spoiled as ever, Fuddles the cat is back . . . in this comical holiday sequel. Fuddles can't help but investigate the many holiday decorations and treats that surround him. When he accidentally knocks over the Christmas tree, he bolts through an open door and finds himself locked out in the snow. A rowdy squirrel chase sends him tumbling down the chimney and back inside. . . . The digitally rendered illustrations capture Fuddles's frantic feline physicality, as well as his contented expressions."

VISCHER, FRANS.il. A Very Fuddles Christmas. See Vischer, F.

VISWANATHAN, PADMA. The Ever After of Ashwin Rao; [by] Padma Viswanathan 384 p. 2014 Random House Canada

1. Air-India Flight 182 Bombing Incident, 1985 2. East Indians—Canada 3. Grief—Fiction 4. Psychological fiction 5. Psychologists—Fiction
ISBN 0307356345; 9780307356345

SUMMARY: In this book, set "almost 20 years after the fatal bombing of an Air India flight from Vancouver, 2 suspects—finally—are on trial for the crime. Ashwin Rao, an Indian psychologist trained in Canada, comes back to do a 'study of comparative grief,' interviewing people who lost loved one in the attack. What he neglects to mention is that he, too, had family members who died on the plane." (Publisher's note)

REVIEW: *Quill Quire* v80 no2 p25 Mr 2014 Piali Roy

"The Ever After of Ashwin Rao". "Padma Viswanathan chronicles the impact of the crash on the lives of survivors in her ambitious second novel. . . . Viswanathan shuffles voices, narrative styles, and time periods as Ashwin retells his subjects' stories, as well as his own. . . . Viswanathan's writing is most vivid in relating these stories. It becomes less so when she turns to an overt examination of some big ideas. . . . A lack of immediacy in these areas notwithstanding, 'The Ever After of Ashwin Rao' does surprise, especially with an ending that finds redemption for the works-in-progress that constitute our lives."

VITA-FINZI, CLAUDIO. Planetary geology; an introduction; [by] Claudio Vita-Finzi 176 p. 2013 Dunedin Academic Press

1. Gravity 2. Orbits 3. Planetary tectonics (Astrogeology) 4. Planets—Geology 5. Scientific literature
ISBN 1780460155 (pbk.); 9781780460154 (pbk.)
LC 2013-444025

SUMMARY: In this book, the authors "survey what happens inside, on, and around planetary bodies, especially rocky and icy ones. Topics include internal processes and structures; the actions of ice, water, wind, etc., on surfaces; tectonics and volcanism; orbital motions and their cycles; magnetic and gravitational fields; atmospheric variations; collisions between celestial objects; and theories of how it all originated." (Choice: Current Reviews for Academic Libraries)

REVIEW: *Choice* v51 no7 p1240-1 Mr 2014 B. M. Simonson

"Planetary Geology: An Introduction." "Although this second edition has the same 12 chapters as the original . . . it is a much improved version of what was already a good book. The new text is some 20 percent longer; moreover, attractive color illustrations have been dispersed throughout (not restricted to a separate section), and the information presented is brought right up to the minute with numerous injections of new scientific results from the many space missions that have been conducted since the first edition appeared. . . . Given its extreme breadth, explanations are terse and probably not always sufficient for general readers. The book includes a short glossary and a bibliography, but most of the references are intended for specialists."

VITALE, SERENA. Shklovsky; witness to an era; p. cm. 2012 Dalkey Archive Press

1. Authors, Russian—Interviews 2. Avant-garde (Arts) 3. Interviews 4. Soviet Union—Politics & government
ISBN 9781564787910 (pbk. : alk. paper)
LC 2012-029352

SUMMARY: This book presents "interviews with Viktor Shklovsky conducted by scholar Serena Vitale in the '70s, toward the end of the great critic's life, and in the face of interference and even veiled threats of violence from the

Soviet government. Shklovsky's answers . . . focus . . . particularly on the years of the early Soviet avant-garde." (Publisher's note)

REVIEW: *N Y Rev Books* v51 no7 p63-6 Ap 24 2014 Keith Gessen

REVIEW: *Nation* v296 no8 p33-6 F 25 2013 BEN EHRENREICH

REVIEW: *Publ Wkly* v259 no36 p57 S 3 2012

REVIEW: *TLS* no5756 p9-10 Jl 26 2013 ZINOVY ZINIK

"Shklovsky: Witness to an Era," "Bowstring: On the Dissimilarity of the similar" and "A Hunt for Optimism." "[Serena] Vitale creates her witty and moving minimalist portrait by unobtrusively observing [Viktor] Shklovsky's daily routine. . . . Dalkey Archive Press, which over the past decade and more has performed the heroic task of bringing out all the key works of Shklovsky in English, should have appointed a Russian-speaker and editor to supervise the work of its translators. Successful in transposing the ironical voice of Shklovsky's analytical passages in 'Bowstring,' Shushan Avagyan is sometimes defeated by the idiosyncratic collation of hackneyed colloquialisms that mark 'A Hunt for Optimism'."

VITAMIN D2; New Perspectives in Drawing; 352 p. 2013 Phaidon Inc Ltd

1. Art literature 2. Drafting (Illustration) 3. Drawing 4. Modern aesthetics—21st century 5. Modern art—21st century

ISBN 0714865281; 9780714865287

SUMMARY: Edited by Craig Garrett, this book "presents the work of 115 artists who are currently emerging on the world stage, have become established since the first volume was published in 2005, or who have made a significant contribution to the medium of drawing in this time." It "features practices ranging from highly accomplished figurative drawing to abstract explorations of the medium, in materials including pencil, charcoal, crayon, pastel, ink, watercolour and digital drawing." (Publisher's note)

REVIEW: *Choice* v51 no4 p621-2 D 2013 J. H. Heinieke

"Vitamin D2: New Perspectives in Drawing." "This valuable treasury of text and imagery presents the responses of today's emerging artists to issues and ideas in the first quarter of a new century. The statement 'drawing is part of life and life is an occasion to draw' appears in an introductory essay by Christian Rattemeyer (MoMA) and sums up the intent of the work of the 115 artists who contributed to this volume. . . . Regardless of where they live at present. the artists--seeing and feeling the first years of the new millennium--respond, translate, alter, and interpret fearlessly and forcibly. This book could be a valuable tool for emerging artists, experienced draftspersons, and serious art appreciators. It is the sequel to 'Vitamin D.'"

REVIEW: *Publ Wkly* v260 no17 p122-3 Ap 29 2013

VITASEK, KATE. Vested. See Manrodt, K.

VITELLO, SUZY. The Moment Before; [by] Suzy Vitello 216 p. 2014 Diversion Books

1. Bereavement—Fiction 2. Death—Fiction 3. Secrecy—Fiction 4. Sisters—Fiction 5. Young adult fiction

ISBN 1626811679; 9781626811676

SUMMARY: In this book by Suzy Vitello, "after Sabine dies in a horrific cheerleading accident, grief unravels Brady and her family. Once recognized for her artistic talent, 17-year-old Brady finds herself questioning the value of everything she once held dear. Her best friend betrays her. Her parents' marriage is crumbling. And the boy everyone blames for the accident seems to be her only ally in the search for answers in the wake of her sister's death. " (Publisher's note)

REVIEW: *Kirkus Rev* v81 no24 p276 D 15 2013

"The Moment Before". " The question of what Brady will do with this information is complicated by the underdeveloped subplots of her parents' deteriorating marriage, her loss of a prestigious school art prize, and her best friend Martha's decision to date Sabine's abusive ex. All of this leads to a bizarre climax in which Brady hurls some of Sabine's cremains at Nick after he drugs and kidnaps Martha, obliterating any suspension of disbelief. While the initial premise is intriguing, the story is crippled by self-conscious dialogue, abrupt transitions and the fact that all relevant information is spelled out instead of shown. Overwrought and half baked."

REVIEW: *Voice of Youth Advocates* v36 no6 p66-7 F 2014 Lisa Hazlett

VIVIAN, SIOBHAN. Fire with fire. See Han, J.

VLAHOS, LEN. The Scar Boys; a novel; [by] Len Vlahos 256 p. 2014 Egmont USA

1. Bands (Music)—Fiction 2. Disfigured persons—Fiction 3. Family life—Fiction 4. Friendship—Fiction 5. Near-death experiences—Fiction 6. Road fiction

ISBN 1606844393; 9781606844397 (hardcover ; alk. paper)

LC 2013-018265

SUMMARY: In this book, by Len Vlahos, "Harry is used to making people squirm. When others see his badly scarred face, there is an inevitable reaction that ranges from forced kindness to primal cruelty. In this first-person tale written as an extended college entrance essay, . . . he recounts the trauma of his young life spent recuperating from the act of childhood bullying that left him a burn victim. In middle school, he meets Johnny McKenna, the first person to seem to offer him genuine friendship." (Kirkus Reviews)

REVIEW: *Booklist* v110 no9/10 p108 Ja 1 2014 Sarah Hunter

REVIEW: *Bull Cent Child Books* v67 no6 p338-9 F 2014 Karen Coats

"The Scar Boys." "The '80s setting and reflective tone impose a problematically adult sensibility on what's supposed to be an extended college-entrance essay; the retrospective wisdom strips the immediacy of emotion from Harry's narration and makes the book read more like a vehicle for adult nostalgia than teen investment. Some readers will appreciate the additional insight, though, and while the familiar elements of realistic boy fiction here--strong language, cruel bullying, a traumatized underdog hero, an enigmatic and untouchable girl, an eventful road trip, and a redemptive moment with a friend--aren't surprising, they're popular for a reason."

REVIEW: *Kirkus Rev* v81 no21 p212 N 1 2013

REVIEW: *N Y Times Book Rev* p15 Ja 12 2014 PETER BEHRENS

"The Scar Boys" and "Why We Took the Car." "In Len

Vlahos's debut novel, the Scar Boys are a punk band from Yonkers that hits the road riding a rusty van and working out personal problems while playing gigs in college towns. . . . Playing and touring demand creativity and commitment, forcing the Scar Boys--actually three guys and a girl--to come of age in this wry, stylish tale. . . . In Wolfgang Herrndorf's 'Why We Took the Car,' originally published in German and ably translated by Tim Mohr, the title question never really gets answered. . . . By no means a wholesome story, 'Why We Took the Car' is exuberant and without a mean bone in its narrative. American teenagers shouldn't have trouble relating to Mike and Tschick."

REVIEW: *Publ Wkly* v260 no44 p68 N 4 2013

REVIEW: *SLJ* v60 no1 p105 Ja 2014 Leah Krippner

VLAUTIN, WILLY. The Free; a novel; [by] Willy Vlautin 320 p. 2014 HarperCollins

1. American fiction 2. Brain injury patients—Rehabilitation 3. Medical fiction 4. Nurses—Fiction 5. Social realism in literature

ISBN 0062276743; 9780062276742

SUMMARY: This novel, by Willy Vlautin, follows "veteran Leroy Kervin, [who] suffered a traumatic brain injury. . . . Freddie McCall works two jobs and still can't make ends meet. He's lost his wife and kids, and the house is next. . . . Pauline Hawkins is a nurse at the local hospital. Though she attends to others' needs . . . , she remains emotionally removed. . . . The lives of these characters intersect as they look for meaning in desperate times." (Publisher's note)

REVIEW: *Booklist* v110 no12 p24 F 15 2014 Bill Ott

REVIEW: *Kirkus Rev* v81 no22 p188 N 15 2013

REVIEW: *Libr J* v139 no15 p53 S 15 2014 Megan M. McArdle

REVIEW: *N Y Times Book Rev* p21 Mr 23 2014 MARISA SILVER

"The Free." "Some novels are so wedded to a blunt rendition of reality that they seem, paradoxically, less real than life, which after all is studded with moments of poetry and metaphoric resonance. The challenge for the writer of social realism is to enlist the plastic qualities of fiction to produce something lifelike, in which artifice creates the shimmer of recognition. In his fourth novel, 'The Free,' [author] Willy Vlautin demonstrates an impressive ability to navigate this challenge. . . . Vlautin's unadorned narrative is affecting; these unassuming characters bore into us in surprising ways."

REVIEW: *N Y Times Book Rev* p26 Mr 23 2014 GREGORY COWLES

REVIEW: *New Statesman* v143 no5201 p54-5 Mr 14 2014 Phil Klay

REVIEW: *Publ Wkly* v261 no34 p83 Ag 25 2014

REVIEW: *Publ Wkly* v260 no40 p26 O 7 2013

VNUK, REBECCA. Women's fiction; a guide to popular reading interests; [by] Rebecca Vnuk xv, 233 p. 2013 Libraries Unlimited, an imprint of ABC-CLIO, LLC

1. American fiction—20th century—Bibliography 2. American fiction—21st century—Bibliography 3. American fiction—Women authors—Bibliography 4. Fiction in libraries—United States 5. Library science literature 6. Public libraries—United States—Book lists 7. Readers' advisory services—United States 8. Women—Books and reading—United States 9. Women—Fiction—Bibliography

ISBN 9781598849202 (hardback : acid-free paper)

LC 2013-023685

SUMMARY: This book on women's fiction is part of the Libraries Unlimited Genreflecting Advisory series. "Nine chapters gather titles under such categories as 'Grande Dames of Women's Fiction,' 'Gentle Reads,' 'Chick Lit and Beyond,' and 'Multicultural Women's Fiction.' Each chapter begins with a brief explanation of the subgenre or classificadon; for each title presented within each chapter, a two-to- three-sentence annotation highlights plot, theme, and characters." (Booklist)

REVIEW: *Booklist* v110 no14 p62 Mr 15 2014 Brad Hooper

"Women's Fiction: A Guide to Popular Reading Interests." "Women's fiction is a popular reading interest that continues to grow in appeal and scope but is sometimes difficult to define. Those in need of clarity on this issue should turn to . . . Rebecca] Vnuk's book [which] is part of the estimable Libraries Unlimited Genreflecting Advisory series, and it not only follows the series format but also lives up to the series' high standards of information presentation and readers'-advisory guidance. . . . Anyone interested in reading, or charged with recommending, women's fiction should consult this book. It's expertly done."

VOGEL, ERIC. Layton's legacy; a historic american art collection, 1888-2013; 480 p. 2013 Layton Art Collection, Inc

1. Art—Collectors & collecting 2. Art catalogs 3. Art literature 4. Layton, Frederick 5. Milwaukee (Wis.)—History

ISBN 9780982381014

LC 2013-942341

SUMMARY: This book "recounts the story of Frederick Layton (1827-1919), an immigrant butcher who became one of Milwaukee's first serious art collectors. It offers the first major publication on the Layton Art Collection's history from its establishment in 1888 to the present day. After introducing Layton's early biography, the book focuses on the story of the gallery." (Choice: Current Reviews for Academic Libraries)

REVIEW: *Choice* v51 no7 p1198-9 Mr 2014 J. Decker

"Layton's Legacy: A Historic American Art Collection, 1888-2013." "With copious notes, 700-plus illustrations, and a compilation of the art collection since its inception, this volume makes available detailed information about individual works in the collection, closely documenting 40 of them. It pays tribute to the Art Gallery's formative place in the development of the American art museum, ensuring the collection and its narrative a place in exhibition, museum, and art history. . . . Essential."

VOGEL, SEAN. Chicago bound; a Jake McGreevy novel; [by] Sean Vogel 176 p. 2013 MB Pub., LLC

1. Art forgeries—Fiction 2. Art historians—Fiction 3. Chicago (Ill.)—Fiction 4. Detective & mystery stories 5. Missing persons—Fiction

ISBN 9780985081454 (softover); 9780985081461 (epub); 9780985081478 (mobi)

LC 2013-943391

SUMMARY: In this book, part of Sean Vogel's Jake McGreevy series, "Jake's plan for a carefree holiday at a musical performing arts camp in the Windy City hits a sour note when he stumbles upon a long-hidden message from his late mother, art historian Karen McGreevy. She had traveled to Chicago thirteen years earlier on a dream assignment, never to return home. . . . Jake . . . will follow the clues and uncover the truth about a missing masterpiece." (Publisher's note)

REVIEW: *Kirkus Rev* v81 no24 p375 D 15 2013

"Chicago Bound". "Jake is a likable and sympathetic hero—intelligent but impulsive, easygoing and funny with his pals but a little nervous with girls. His friends are well-developed, creating a fun cast of secondary characters as well as a strong support system for Jake. Many scenes are set in famous Chicago landmarks, including a thrilling chase sequence in the Museum of Science and Industry and a suspenseful moment in Macy's Walnut Room that kicks off the story's action-packed climax. It's not necessary to read the first Jake McGreevy book in order to follow this one, but readers who enjoy Jake's Chicago adventures will likely want to pick up the earlier novel as well. A rollicking, fun mystery with a young, charismatic hero."

REVIEW: *Kirkus Rev* v82 no3 p13 F 1 2014

VOGELSTEIN, FRED. Dogfight; how Apple and Google went to war and started a revolution; [by] Fred Vogelstein 272 p. 2013 Sarah Crichton Books/Farrar, Straus & Giroux

1. Business literature 2. Competition 3. Computer industry

ISBN 0374109206; 9780374109202 (hardback)

LC 2013-021855

SUMMARY: This book, by Fred Vogelstein, examines the rivalry between Apple and Google, focusing particularly on competition between their iPhone and Android smartphones. According to Vogelstein, the importance of his subject is "not just that two of the biggest, most influential corporations in their worlds . . . are fighting each other to the death. . . . It's that the mobile revolution they set off has suddenly put nearly $1 trillion in revenue from half a dozen industries up for grabs." (Kirkus Reviews)

REVIEW: *Bookforum* v20 no4 p9 D 2013/Ja 2014 CHRIS WILSON

"Dogfight: How Apple and Google Went to War and Started a Revolution." "Dogfight: How Apple and Google Went to War and Started a Revolution." "'Dogfight' . . . draws heavily from [Fred] Vogelstein's reporting for 'Wired' . . . Like many military histories. Dogfight sees the war that ensued between the companies through the eyes of the battlefield commanders. And here any Silicon Valley raconteur faces an uphill battle. Google and Apple are remarkably ungossipy companies that leak very little information. . . . Hard-pressed to deliver much in the way of genuine corporate drama, [Fred] Vogelstein strings together a central narrative about two companies with very different attitudes to control. . . . But Vogelstein never quite closes the loop on these themes."

REVIEW: *Booklist* v110 no6 p4 N 15 2013 David Siegfried

REVIEW: *Choice* v51 no10 p1855 Je 2014 E. J. Szewczak

REVIEW: *Kirkus Rev* v81 no21 p147 N 1 2013

REVIEW: *N Y Times Book Rev* p18 N 3 2013 SIVA VAIDHYANATHAN

REVIEW: *New Yorker* v89 no38 p68-1 N 25 2013

VOGT, HELLE.ed. Cultural encounters during the crusades. See Cultural encounters during the crusades

VOICES FROM THE OREGON TRAIL; 48 p. 2014 Dial Books for Young Readers, an imprint of Penguin Group (USA) Inc.

1. Frontier and pioneer life—West (U.S.)—Juvenile literature 2. Historical fiction 3. Overland journeys to the Pacific—Juvenile literature 4. Pioneers—Oregon National Historic Trail—History—Juvenile literature

ISBN 9780803737754 (hardcover)

LC 2013-000034

SUMMARY: In this book on the Oregon Trail, "fifteen overlanders and a Sioux scout comment in free-verse poems about personal episodes that illuminate typical occurrences along the wagon route from Missouri to Oregon in the mid 1800s. Patience Mills has no choice but to follow her husband once he sells the family farm. . . . Carl Hawks, son of the wagon master, embraces the excitement of the journey . . . even as he worries about repeats of previous disasters." (Bulletin of the Center for Children's Books)

REVIEW: *Booklist* v110 no12 p69 F 15 2014 Carolyn Phelan

REVIEW: *Bull Cent Child Books* v67 no6 p340 F 2014 Elizabeth Bush

"Voices From the Oregon Trail." "Many stories interconnect and the voices are lively and engaging, although each individual is given only a single hearing, leaving readers unable to gauge changes in attitude along the way. Copious endnotes expand on various aspects of wagon train organization, and [Larry] Day's detailed watercolor artwork nimbly switches mood from the grief of a mother making a last visit at her child's tombstone, to the cowpie-slinging antics of kids inventing their own fun to shake off boredom. This format will enliven middle grades history classes as a readaloud or, better still, as an adaptable script for readers theater."

REVIEW: *Kirkus Rev* v81 no23 p146 D 1 2013

REVIEW: *SLJ* v60 no2 p128 F 2014 Kathy Piehl

VOIGT, JUDY. The Great Pj Elf Chase. See LoBello, K.

VOINIGESCU, SORIN. High-frequency integrated circuits; [by] Sorin Voinigescu xviii, 902 p. 2013 Cambridge University Press

1. Computer logic 2. Impedance matching 3. Radio frequency integrated circuits 4. Scientific literature 5. Very high speed integrated circuits

ISBN 9780521873024 (hardback)

LC 2012-028115

SUMMARY: This book on high-frequency integrated circuits by Sorin Vonigescu "covers high-speed, RF, mm-wave, and optical fibre circuits using nanoscale CMOS, SiGe BiCMOS, and III-V technologies. Step-by-step design methodologies, end-of chapter problems, and practical simulation and design projects are provided." (Publisher's note)

REVIEW: *Choice* v51 no7 p1252 Mr 2014 L. McLauchlan

"High-Frequency Integrated Circuits." "[Sorin] Voinigescu . . . has written a relatively easy-to-read book on the subject of high-frequency circuits. He provides many of the basic concepts required for understanding these high-frequency circuits, starting with basic transceiver circuits;

two-port parameter models such as ABCD-parameters; Z-, Y-, or H-parameters; and S-parameters and the Smith chart. . . . End-of-chapter problems illustrate or help students to practice concepts. Part of the 'Cambridge RF and Microwave Engineering' series."

VOLCLER, JULIETTE. Extremely loud; sound as a weapon; [by] Juliette Volcler x, 198 p. 2013 The New Press, Perseus Distribution

1. Journalism 2. Military weapons—Research—History 3. Noise—Physiological effect—Research 4. Nonlethal weapons 5. Psychological torture 6. Sound—Physiological effect—Research 7. Sound—Psychological aspects

ISBN 1595588736 (hardcover); 9781595588739 (hardcover); 9781595588883 (ebook)

LC 2012-047132

SUMMARY: This book looks at how sound is used "as a tool of subjugation and control in modern warfare. French journalist [Juliette] Volcler postulates that these developments 'scramble the boundaries between war, culture, and games,' and, in a media-saturated environment, they have become palatable nonlethal methods of repression and aggression. Indeed, many of the world's major powers, including the U.S., Germany, and the former Soviet Union, have sought to develop acoustic weapons." (Publishers Weekly)

REVIEW: *Kirkus Rev* v81 no10 p81 My 15 2013

REVIEW: *Nation* v297 no13 p32 S 30 2013 PETER C. BAKER

"Napalm: An American Biography" and "Extremely Loud: Sound as a Weapon." "As described by Robert Neer . . . [napalm] depended on taxpayer money and academic know-how, and required the fervent corporate desire for more products to sell. . . . Neer's closing chapters, which chronicle the decline in napalm use, are comparatively thin. . . . Juliette Volcler presents a scattered, piecemeal history of the attempts to build 'acoustic weapons.' There are examples from every swath of thee sonic spectrum."

REVIEW: *Publ Wkly* v260 no9 p58 Mr 4 2013

VOLK, CAROL.tr. Extremely loud. See Volcler, J.

VON BISMARCK, HELENE. British policy in the Persian Gulf, 1961-1968; conceptions of informal empire; [by] Helene Von Bismarck xx, 269 p. 2013 Palgrave Macmillan

1. Great Britain—Politics & government—1945- 2. Historical literature 3. Imperialism—History

ISBN 1137326719; 9781137326713

LC 2013-431629

SUMMARY: This book examines "Great Britain's policy in the oil-rich Persian Gulf region during the last years of British imperialism in the area, covering the period from the independence of Kuwait in 1961 to the decision of the Wilson Government in January 1968 to withdraw from the Gulf by 1971. Helene von Bismarck explains the motivation and methods of British imperialism in an area which was of great strategic and economic value to Great Britain." (Publisher's note)

REVIEW: *Choice* v51 no6 p1085 F 2014 K. M. Zaarour

REVIEW: *Middle East J* v67 no4 p659-60 Aut 2013 Nigel J. Ashton

"British Policy in the Persian Gulf, 1961-1968: Conceptions of Informal Empire." "Helene von Bismarck's study shows that for much of the decade the British government and its representatives on the ground in the Gulf did not contemplate such a retreat. . . . This study fills an important gap in the existing literature by providing considerably greater detail about Britain's attempts to develop and defend its position in the Gulf during the 1960s. For von Bismarck, the story of the British role in the Gulf in the 1960s was principally one of the intensification of British imperialism, rather than its gradual disappearance."

VON BREMZEN, ANYA. Mastering the art of Soviet cooking; a memoir of love and longing; [by] Anya Von Bremzen 352 p. 2013 Crown Publishers

1. Cooking, Russian—History—20th century 2. Food habits—Soviet Union 3. Food writers—United States—Biography 4. Memoirs 5. Russian Americans—Biography 6. Women cooks—Soviet Union—Biography

ISBN 0307886816; 9780307886811

LC 2013-007787

SUMMARY: This book by Anya von Bramzen presents "a memoir of life in Soviet Russia. The book is subdivided by decade, and von Bremzen . . . weaves her own memories together with stories from her grandmother and mother, beginning in 1910. The common denominator--and recurring touchstone--is food. . . . Von Bremzen concludes with nine recipes." (Library Journal)

REVIEW: *Booklist* v110 no2 p12-3 S 15 2013 Mark Knoblauch

REVIEW: *Kirkus Rev* v81 no15 p218 Ag 1 2013

REVIEW: *N Y Rev Books* v60 no18 p10-2 N 21 2013 Masha Gessen

"Mastering the Art of Soviet Cooking: A Memoir of Food and Longing." "'Mastering the Art of Soviet Cooking' is an unfortunate title, for it makes the work sound like a cookbook . . . but this is something else entirely. Nor is it, as the subtitle indicates, solely 'A Memoir of Food and Longing.' It is a painstakingly researched and beautifully written cultural history but also the best kind of memoir: one with a self-aware narrator who has mastered the art of not taking herself entirely seriously. It is also a breathtaking balancing act inasmuch as it tells the story of [Anya] von Bremzen's relationship with her mother, Larisa, a love story told with enough candor to trouble the reader--but not Larisa herself, who emerges as both a character and a collaborator in the book."

REVIEW: *New York Times* v163 no56270 pD1-6 S 25 2013 JULIA MOSKIN

REVIEW: *New Yorker* v89 no32 p113-1 O 14 2013

"Mastering the Art of Soviet Cooking." " This memoir by a James Beard Award-winning food and travel writer explores the culinary history of the country she left at the age of eleven, in 1974. We see Soviet food change from decade to decade: the relative abundance of the thirties . . . couldn't be more different from the meagreness of the sixties. . . . [Anya] Von Bremzen blends her research with a history of her family, including her grandfather, a daring intelligence officer whose missions yielded forbidden delicacies from abroad."

REVIEW: *Publ Wkly* v260 no34 p61 Ag 26 2013

REVIEW: *Time* v182 no21 p57 N 18 2013 Howard Chua-Eoan

REVIEW: *TLS* no5777/8 p13 D 20 2013 LESLEY CHAMBERLAIN

"Mastering the Art of Soviet Cooking: A Memoir of Food and Longing." "In 'Mastering the Art of Soviet Cooking: A memoir of food and longing,' Anya von Bremzen sets aside the legendary queues, which have featured so productively in fiction. . . . Ingenious confections and luscious textures defined the Soviet food scene just as much in the desperate, terrifying 1940s as in the stagnant, cynical 1970s. Von Bremzen writes about each period with energy and originality. . . . 'Mastering the Art of Soviet Cooking' is much more a work of family memory than a practical cookbook or a historical survey. . . . There are a few recipes included in this would-be primer, but what 'Mastering the Art of Soviet Cooking' truly offers is Russian tragedy and absurdity by the ladleful."

VON TOBEL, ALEXA. Financially fearless; the learnvest guide to worry-free finances; [by] Alexa Von Tobel 336 p. 2013 Crown Business

1. BUSINESS & ECONOMICS—Personal Finance—Money Management 2. BUSINESS & ECONOMICS—Public Finance 3. Finance, Personal 4. Personal budgets 5. Self-help materials
ISBN 9780385347617 (hardback)
LC 2013-025103

SUMMARY: This book on personal financial planning offers to help readers "create your customized 50/20/30 plan. 50/20/30 simply refers to the percentage breakdown of how to spend your take-home pay each month. The 50 gets the essentials out of the way so you don't have to stress about them. The 20 sets your foundation for the future, then the 30 is left to spend on the things that bring happiness to your life." (Publisher's note)

REVIEW: *New York Times* v163 no56379 p17 Ja 12 2014 PAUL B. BROWN

"Financially Fearless" and "Keynes's Way to Wealth". "If improving your net worth made your list of New Year's resolutions, two books . . . could help. . . . In her book, seemingly aimed at those in their 20s and early 30s—and people who haven't' gotten around to planning their finances—Ms [Alexa]. Von Tobel argues that take-home pay should be divided into three parts. . . . This is not exactly a new idea. . . . But what is intriguing are her percentages. . . . Because she gives it so little attention, the investing advice is extremely general. . . . But if the book convinces people who've never mapped out a financial future to start doing so, it will have done its job. . . . And people looking for specific investing advice for 2014 and beyond could turn to . . . Keynes's Way to Wealth. . . . Mr. [John F. Wasik's] distillation of how Keynes made—and then remade—his fortune is instructive."

REVIEW: *Publ Wkly* v260 no43 p53-4 O 28 2013

VONNEGUT, KURT, 1922-2007. Kurt Vonnegut; letters; [by] Kurt Vonnegut 436 p. 2012 Delacorte Press

1. Authors—Economic conditions 2. Dresden (Germany)—History—Bombardment, 1945 3. Letters 4. Prisoners of war
ISBN 0385343752; 9780345535399 (ebook); 9780385343756
LC 2012-001544

SUMMARY: Author Kurt Vonnegut and editor Dan Wakefield present Vonnegut's "collection of personal correspondence." It includes "the letter a twenty-two-year-old Vonnegut wrote home immediately upon being freed from a German POW camp" and "wry dispatches from Vonnegut's years as a struggling writer slowly finding an audience and then dealing with sudden international fame in middle age." (Publisher's note)

REVIEW: *Booklist* v109 no3 p12 O 1 2012 Carl Hays

REVIEW: *Kirkus Rev* v80 no18 p54 S 15 2012

REVIEW: *Kirkus Rev* p42 D 2 2012 Best NonFiction & Teen

REVIEW: *Libr J* v137 no16 p78-9 O 1 2012 Lonnie Weatherby

REVIEW: *N Y Times Book Rev* p27 O 28 2012 KURT ANDERSEN

REVIEW: *New Statesman* v142 no5157 p47 My 10 2013 Daniel Swift

REVIEW: *Publ Wkly* v259 no27 p55-6 Jl 2 2012

REVIEW: *TLS* no5763 p5 S 13 2013 ALLAN MASSIE

"Letters." "Some of the letters in this collection are hurtful, were even written to hurt, and this is true of letters to friends and members of his family who had disappointed him or let him down, not to mention reproofs directed to reviewers. A number were doubtless written late at night when he was in liquor, and quickly regretted. . . . [Kurt] Vonnegut's affectionate and admiring editor, Dan Wakefield, claims that these letters 'tell the story of a writer's life'. Though this collection may indeed serve as a substitute for the autobiography he never wrote (though several of his books, notably Timequake, draw on his own life), one should remember that letters are written to particular individuals at a particular time and represent a particular mood."

VORA, NEHA. Impossible citizens; Dubai's Indian diaspora; [by] Neha Vora xi, 245 p. 2013 Duke University Press

1. East Indians—United Arab Emirates—Dubayy (Emirate) 2. Social science literature
ISBN 9780822353782 (cloth : alk. paper); 9780822353935 (pbk. : alk. paper)
LC 2012-044774

SUMMARY: In this book, Neha Vora "examines the experiences of Dubai's most typical and entrenched residents: the middle-class, working-class, and elite Indians who populate the downtown neighborhoods. . . . Vora argues that while Indians cannot become legal citizens of the UAE, their everyday practices, forms of belonging, and claims to the city make them Dubai's quintessential, yet impossible, citizens." (Middle East Journal)

REVIEW: *Middle East J* v67 no4 p656-8 Aut 2013 Noora Anwar Lori

"Impossible Citizens: Dubai's Indian Diaspora." "Neha Vora's first book is a rich and comprehensive ethnography of Dubai's Indian community that sets new standards for writing about 'guest workers' in the Gulf. . . . Accessible to both lay and academic audiences, her work uses Dubai's largest community to push the study of citizenship and diaspora in new directions while dismantling the three dominant myths about immigration in the GCC:that migrants are temporary, economically driven, and ancillary to the politics or governance structures of the Gulf States."

VOROS, RIA. The Opposite of Geek; [by] Ria Voros 240

p. 2013 Scholastic Canada
1. Haiku 2. High school students—Fiction 3. School stories 4. Teenage girls—Fiction 5. Young adult fiction
ISBN 1443104841; 9781443104845

SUMMARY: In this young adult novel by Ria Voros, "Gretchen Meyers doesn't know exactly what went wrong, but life in the eleventh grade is beginning to suck. . . . Bewildered by harsh new emotions of grief and love, Gretchen realizes she must now decide who she wants to be and what it means to be loyal. Written partly in verse, as self-confessed poetry geek Gretchen finds new ways of expressing herself, 'The Opposite of Geek' is a tale of haiku, high school, and heartache." (Publisher's note)

REVIEW: *Quill Quire* v79 no9 p36 N 2013 Natalie Samson

"The Opposite of Geek." "Suddenly cast in the role of uncool loner, Gretchen discovers friends in the keeners and geeks she has previously written off--in particular her math tutor, a bullied senior named James. . . . The novel is structured as a sort of poetic journal kept by Gretchen, and the inclusion of haikus . . . inject playfulness and might convince young readers that not all poetry has to rhyme or be heavy and boring. 'The Opposite of Geek' is Ria Voros's first foray into YA fiction . . . , and she does a good job capturing the realities of teen life. However, the book's underlying messages of trusting in yourself and valuing actions over appearances may strike readers deep in the trenches of high school as easier said than done."

VOSS, R. A. We Never Travel Alone; A Collection of Essays on Journeys Near and Far; [by] R. A. Voss 266 p. 2013 Createspace Independent Pub
1. Germany—Description & travel 2. Iowa—Description & travel 3. Memoirs 4. Spain—Description & travel 5. Travelers' writings
ISBN 1482610892; 9781482610895

SUMMARY: In this book, R.A. Voss, "a 50-something registered nurse, mediates upon her life's trajectory in the context of what she has identified as key travel moments, encompassing childhood and adult experiences. In particular, she details trips within her native state of Iowa to the Mines of Spain Recreation Area; her visit to . . . Germany, the land of her descendants . . .; and to Spain . . . as part of her process of obtaining a later-in-life graduate degree in creative writing." (Kirkus Reviews)

REVIEW: *Kirkus Rev* v82 no2 p390 Ja 15 2014

"We Never Travel Alone: A Collection of Essays on Journeys Near and Far". "Her most affecting stories are often those of treks more near than far; for instance, a treacherous sailboat experience in Canada that she endures with a soon-to-be ex-husband, who she realizes cares more about adventure than her safety, and her connection to Iowa eagles and their shared 'history of endocrine disruptor chemicals that led to the eagles' near extinction and to the total extinction of my dreams of motherhood.' The autobiographical details are sometimes intense. . . . Still, [R.A.] Voss' largely elliptical approach in unfolding her life stories is elegantly executed and effective. Readers may be left wanting more from this engaging author."

REVIEW: *Kirkus Rev* v82 no6 p48 Mr 15 2014

VOSSLER, TOM. A field guide to Gettysburg. See Reardon, C.

VUKIĆEVIĆ, DANICA. Visoki fabrički dimnjaci; [by] Danica Vukićević 2013 Narodna Biblioteka Stefan Provovenčani
1. Feminist poetry 2. Free verse 3. Serbian poetry—Translations into English 4. Social commentary 5. Social criticism
ISBN 9788681355374

SUMMARY: "Danica Vukićević, a Serbian poet from Belgrade, offers us feminist social criticism in an often-fragmented free-verse form in 'Visoki fabrički dimnjaci' ('High smokestacks'), her short sixth collection of poems. . . . Most of the poems seem to be social commentary. . . . Besides having several poems composed of lists, she also writes an elegy about her grandfather." (Publisher's note)

REVIEW: *World Lit Today* v88 no2 p70 Mr/Ap 2014 Biljana D. Obradović

"Visoki fabrički dimnjaci." "Danica Vukićević, a Serbian poet from Belgrade, offers us feminist social criticism in an often-fragmented free-verse form in 'Visoki fabrički dimnjaci' ('High smokestacks'), her short sixth collection of poems. . . . Besides having several poems composed of lists, she also writes an elegy about her grandfather, about visiting bis grave for All Saint's Day. . . . These are intriguing poems, although the book's title doesn't seem to fit the collection as a whole. The feminist background of the author is clear. This is provocative material that begs for attention from its audience."

VYLETA, DAN. The Crooked Maid; A Novel; [by] Dan Vyleta 448 p. 2013 St. Martin's Press
1. Austria—Fiction 2. Family secrets—Fiction 3. Historical fiction 4. Marriage—Fiction 5. World War, 1939-1945—Fiction
ISBN 160819809X; 9781608198092

SUMMARY: This book by Dan Vyleta is set in post-WWII Vienna, Austria. "Anna Beer returns to the city she fled nine years earlier after discovering her husband's infidelity. She has come back to find him and, perhaps, to forgive him. Traveling on the same train from Switzerland is 18-year-old Robert Seidel, a schoolboy summoned home to his stepfather's sickbed and the secrets of his family's past." (Publisher's note)

REVIEW: *Booklist* v109 no21 p43 Jl 1 2013 Lynn Weber

REVIEW: *Kirkus Rev* v81 no14 p222 Jl 15 2013

REVIEW: *N Y Times Book Rev* p31 Ag 25 2013 Marilyn Stasio

"A Tap on the Window," "The Wicked Girls," and "The Crooked Maid: A Novel." "[Linwood] Barclay's convoluted 'now you see me, now you don't' plot opens on such a low-key note that it's a shock when it takes off for the narrative badlands. But even when he's tending to the gruesome details of the bad stuff, he never loses touch with the fundamental fear of people who live in nice communities like Griffon--that their children are beyond their control. . . . Alex Marwood . . . demonstrat[es] a deep, warm feeling for the shabby seaside town where she sets her harrowing first novel. . . . [In 'The Crooked Maid' the lives of . . . two strangers become intricately (if much too expediently) entwined in a complicated but gracefully executed narrative."

REVIEW: *Publ Wkly* v260 no25 p143 Je 24 2013

W

WACHTEL, ANDREW.tr. The master of insomnia. See Novak, B.A.

WACHTEL, NATHAN. The faith of remembrance; Marrano labyrinths; xiv, 390 p. 2013 University of Pennsylvania Press

1. Crypto-Jews—Latin America—History 2. Historical literature 3. Inquisition—Latin America 4. Marranos—Latin America—Biography 5. Marranos—Latin America—History
ISBN 9780812244557 (hardcover: alk. paper)
LC 2012-036989

SUMMARY: In this book, "Nathan Wachtel traces the journeys of the seventeenth- and eighteenth-century Marranos—Spanish and Portuguese Jews who were forcibly converted to Catholicism but secretly retained their own faith. Fleeing persecution in their Iberian homeland, some sought refuge in the Americas, where they established transcontinental networks linking the New World to the Old." (Publisher's note)

REVIEW: *Am Hist Rev* v119 no1 p216-7 F 2014 Yirmiyahu Yovel

"The Faith of Remembrance: Marrano Labyrinths". "In this outstanding book, Nathan Wachtel takes a deep and illuminating look at the Marranos in Central and South America during the seventeenth and eighteenth centuries. . . . Beyond such types of Marrano duality, Wachtel's eight chapters provide rich details of the times and places in which they are set. Each life (and death) embodies the broader Marrano situation within a particular person or chain of events; and since Wachtel is also a master narrator with a fine sense of drama, he turns the dry records of the Inquisition, his main source, into an engaging human story and a superb piece of work."

WAGNER, ANNE M. Lowry and the Painting of Modern Life. See Clark, T. J.

WAGNER, BRUCE. The Empty Chair; Two Novellas; [by] Bruce Wagner 304 p. 2013 Penguin Group USA Blue Rider Press

1. Big Sur (Calif.) 2. Buddhists 3. Gurus 4. Novellas (Literary form) 5. Spirituality—Fiction
ISBN 0399165886; 9780399165887
LC 2013-037030

SUMMARY: This book, by Bruce Wagner, is "composed of two companion novellas. . . . In 'First Guru,' a fictional Wagner narrates the tale of a Buddhist living in Big Sur, who achieves enlightenment in the horrific aftermath of his child's suicide. In 'Second Guru,' Queenie, an aging wild child, returns to India to complete the spiritual journey of her youth." (Publisher's note)

REVIEW: *Booklist* v110 no4 p16 O 15 2013 Carol Haggas

REVIEW: *Kirkus Rev* v81 no14 p342 Jl 15 2013

REVIEW: *Libr J* v138 no12 p55 Jl 1 2013

REVIEW: *N Y Times Book Rev* p8 D 22 2013 DANI SHAPIRO

REVIEW: *New York Times* v163 no56353 pC1-4 D 17 2013 MICHIKO KAKUTANI

"The Empty Chair: Two Novellas." "In his unsettling new novel, Bruce Wagner exchanges his usual stomping ground of Hollywood for Big Sur and India. . . . 'The Empty Chair' consists of two dovetailing novellas, both told in the guise of confessional monologues, both served up to a fictional version of the author, called Bruce. . . . The strange and terrible connection between the two tales that is eventually revealed not only reminds us of Mr. Wagner's love of coincidence but also makes us ponder, as his characters do, big existential questions about fate (versus randomness), destiny (versus free will) and the patterning (or lack of patterning) in the universe."

REVIEW: *Publ Wkly* v260 no43 p32-3 O 28 2013

WAGNER, GÜNTER P. Homology, genes, and evolutionary innovation; [by] Günter P. Wagner 478 p. 2014 Princeton University Press

1. Biological literature 2. Developmental genetics 3. Evolution (Biology) 4. Genetic regulation 5. Homology (Biology)
ISBN 9780691156460 (hardcover: alk. paper)
LC 2013-025386

SUMMARY: Written by Günter P. Wagner, "The first major synthesis of homology to be published in decades, 'Homology, Genes, and Evolutionary Innovation' reveals how a mechanistically based theory can serve as a unifying concept for any branch of science concerned with the structure and development of organisms, and how it can help explain major transitions in evolution and broad patterns of biological diversity." (Publisher's note)

REVIEW: *Choice* v52 no2 p284-5 O 2014 R. M. Denome

REVIEW: *Science* v344 no6189 p1234-5 Je 13 2014 Carl Simpson Douglas H. Erwin

"Homology, Genes, and Evolutionary Innovation." "The developmental origin of novel traits is the central focus of Günter Wagner's rich and insightful 'Homology, Genes, and Evolutionary Innovation.' Wagner, an evolutionary biologist at Yale, has been studying evolutionary novelty empirically and conceptually for over two decades. This deep engagement is evident in the rigor of his arguments for a new approach to the study of developmental evolution. . . . 'Homology, Genes, and Evolutionary Innovation' makes a seminal contribution to evolutionary biology. As Wagner argues, his view provides an opportunity for a major research program on the study of novelty as distinct from adaptation."

WAGNER, ROBERT, 1930-. You must remember this; life and style in Hollywood's golden age; [by] Scott Eyman 272 p. 2014 Viking

1. Memoirs 2. Motion picture actors and actresses—United States—Biography 3. Motion picture industry—United States—History—20th century 4. Motion picture producers and directors—United States—Biography
ISBN 0670026093; 9780670026098
LC 2013-036970

SUMMARY: In this memoir, Robert J. Wagner "revisits the architecture, fashion, restaurants and pastimes of Hollywood's golden age through anecdotes and personal memories." He presents an "account of early Los Angeles and Beverly Hills, their surrounding neighborhoods and the silver screen notables who frequented them, including James Cagney, Gloria Swanson, Frank Sinatra, James Stewart and many others." (Kirkus Reviews)

REVIEW: *Booklist* v110 no11 p10 F 1 2014 David Pitt

REVIEW: *Booklist* v111 no3 p95 O 1 2014 Sue-Ellen Beauregard

REVIEW: *Kirkus Rev* v82 no2 p80 Ja 15 2014

"You Must Remember This: Life and Style in Hollywood's Golden Age". "[Robert J.] Wagner presents a brisk account of early Los Angeles and Beverly Hills, their surrounding neighborhoods and the silver screen notables who frequented them, including James Cagney, Gloria Swanson, Frank Sinatra, James Stewart and many others. Topical chapters provide generous vistas on a world marked by exclusivity. . . . A few mild, curmudgeonly laments on current realities . . . underscore the actor's nostalgia for the studio days, yet they stop short of idealizing. . . . Ultimately, the book is a charmed and mostly charming tribute to off-screen lives during a period many may regard as Hollywood's finest. A diverting ancillary note to heavier biographies."

REVIEW: *Libr J* v139 no3 p112 F 15 2014 Roy Liebman

REVIEW: *Libr J* v139 no10 p63 Je 1 2014 Theresa Horn

REVIEW: *Publ Wkly* v260 no50 p58 D 9 2013

WAGNER, TONY. Creating innovators; the making of young people who will change the world; [by] Tony Wagner p. cm. 2012 Scribner

1. Curricula (Courses of study)—Aims & objectives 2. Education, Secondary—Aims and objectives—United States 3. Educational change—United States 4. Educational literature 5. Technological innovations—United States

ISBN 9781451611496 (hardcover : alk. paper); 9781451611519 (trade paper : alk. paper)

LC 2012-007162

SUMMARY: In this book on U.S. education, "former Gates Foundation senior advisor [Tony] Wagner . . . believes one of the solutions is redirecting classroom emphasis toward more 'college-ready' curriculums. The author . . . advocates for more progressive skill building to better prepare students for life beyond the classroom. . . . Wagner . . . [offers] advice on how early educational coaching and motivational mentorship can facilitate success in today's competitive marketplace." (Kirkus Reviews)

REVIEW: *Choice* v50 no1 p144 S 2012 W. A. Garrett

REVIEW: *Harv Educ Rev* v83 no3 p532-4 Fall 2013

"Creating Innovators: The Making of Young People Who Will Change the World." "'Creating Innovators' itself is innovative. [Tony] Wagner not only explores his subject matter through the written word, but he also sprinkles throughout the text approximately sixty Microsoft Tags (variants of QR codes) linked to professionally produced videos that directly connect readers to the individuals interviewed in the text.. . . . I was perplexed by the disconnect between the case studies of young innovators earlier in the book and the emphasis on collaboration over individual achievement in chapter 5. . . . Despite these shortcomings, 'Creating Innovators' is a powerful text that not only articulates the need to foster innovation through education but embodies the spirit of innovation."

REVIEW: *Kirkus Rev* v80 no7 p719 Ap 1 2012

"Creating Innovators: The Making of Young People Who Will Change the World." "In the face of the current global recession, Harvard fellow and former Gates Foundation senior advisor [Tony] Wagner . . . believes one of the solutions is redirecting classroom emphasis toward more 'college-ready' curriculums. . . . Wagner's thesis derives its strength from expertly structured content. He focuses less on the problem (America's lack of innovators) and more on a remedy supported by testimonials from an impressive array of young minds gainfully employed in STEM fields . . . or civic-minded entrepreneurships. . . . A seminal analysis promising hope for the future through small wonders in the classroom."

WAINER, HOWARD. Medical illuminations; using evidence, visualization and statistical thinking to improve healthcare; [by] Howard Wainer 192 p. 2013 Oxford University Press

1. Computer visualization 2. Evidence-based medicine 3. Information visualization 4. Medical literature 5. Medical statistics

ISBN 9780199668793 (hardback)

LC 2013-938497

SUMMARY: Written by Howard Wainer, "'Medical Illuminations' presents thirteen contemporary medical topics, from the diminishing value of mammograms to how to decide if a hip needs to be replaced, to understanding cancer maps. In each case it illustrates how modern tools of statistical thinking and statistical graphics can illuminate our understanding." (Publisher's note)

REVIEW: *Science* v343 no6171 p614 F 7 2014 Ben Shneiderman

"Medical Illuminations: Using Evidence, Visualizations, and Statistical Thinking to Improve Healthcare." "Howard Wainer's insight-filled 'Medical Illuminations' continues his agenda of promoting statistical thinking and visualization, here with a focus on healthcare. His sensitivities are well aligned with the huge upswing in interest in these topics, but once again he leads the way with fresh ideas, compelling examples, wise generalizations, and clever phrases. . . . 'Medical Illuminations' offers ample substance along with sufficient piquant comments to ensure that readers reflect on every sentence."

WAINWRIGHT, JOHN. Environmental modelling. See Mulligan, M.

WAJNBERG, ERIC.ed. Chemical ecology of insect parasitoids. See Chemical ecology of insect parasitoids

WAKEFIELD, DAN.ed. Kurt Vonnegut. See Vonnegut, K.

WAKEFIELD, VIKKI. Friday never leaving; [by] Vikki Wakefield 336 p. 2013 Simon & Schuster Books for Young Readers

1. Coming of age—Fiction 2. Homeless children 3. Homeless persons—Fiction 4. Orphans—Fiction 5. Street children

ISBN 144248652X; 9781442486522 (hardcover); 9781442486539 (pbk.)

LC 2012-036386

SUMMARY: This book by Vikki Wakefield follows "Friday Brown, [who] has never had a home. She and her mother live on the road, running away from the past. . . . So when her mom succumbs to cancer, the only thing Friday can do is keep moving. Her journey takes her to an abandoned house where a bunch of street kids are squatting, and an intimidating girl named Arden holds court. Friday gets initiated into the group, but her relationship with Arden is precarious." (Publisher's note)

REVIEW: *Booklist* v110 no5 p58 N 1 2013 Diane Colson

REVIEW: *Bull Cent Child Books* v67 no3 p185 N 2013 K. C.

"Friday Never Leaving." "Artfully written, this story ranges from a sensitive portrait of broken kids trying to survive on their own and create the family they need, to depictions of life in urban and outback Australia, to a breathtaking action/adventure with outcomes both heartbreaking and chilling. Friday emerges as a character who is vulnerable to the machinations of others because she doesn't yet understand her own needs or power, and [author Vikki] Wakefield surely but subtly charts how Friday escapes the thrall of Arden to embrace the legacy of her mother, who has taught her many practical things as well as how to survive by staying mobile and knowing your own stories."

REVIEW: *Horn Book Magazine* v89 no6 p108-9 N/D 2013 JESSICA TACKETT MACDONALD

REVIEW: *Kirkus Rev* v81 no14 p216 Jl 15 2013

REVIEW: *SLJ* v60 no1 p105 Ja 2014 Denise Ryan

REVIEW: *Voice of Youth Advocates* v36 no4 p75 O 2013 Dawn Talbott

WAKEFORD, NINA.ed. Inventive methods. See Inventive methods

WAKS, LEONARD J. Education 2.0; the learningweb revolution and the transformation of the school; [by] Leonard J. Waks 270 p. 2013 Paradigm Publishers

1. Educational literature 2. Internet in education 3. Public schools 4. Web 2.0 5. Web-based instruction
ISBN 9781612050355 (hardcover : alk. paper)
LC 2012-042273

SUMMARY: In this book, Leonard J. Waks "calls for 'a new network learning paradigm to replace the factory school.' This network might include Judy Breck's hand-schooling model, which envisions learning primarily on mobile devices, and Curtis Bonk's education 2.0 vision, with more personalized learning; teachers skilled in guiding eLearning emerging as a distinct professional group." (Choice: Current Reviews for Academic Libraries)

REVIEW: *Choice* v51 no7 p1276-7 Mr 2014 D. L. Stoloff

"Education 2.0: The Learningweb Revolution and the Transformation of the School." "[Leonard J.] Waks . . . defines education 2.0 as 'a networked, learner-centric model' in which the Internet's 'learningweb,' with its 'knowledgeweb,' open courses and textbooks, and informal learning, serves as the centerpiece. He posits that current schooling has failed as a result of 'academic underperformance and administrative inefficiency' and 'social irrelevance and the loss of political legitimacy.' . . . Recommended."

WALCOTT, DEREK, 1930-. The Poetry of Derek Walcott 1948-2013; 640 p. 2014 Farrar Straus & Giroux

1. Caribbean Area—Poetry 2. Caribbean poetry (English) 3. Poems—Collections 4. Saint Lucian poetry (English) 5. Sea poetry
ISBN 9780374125615 (hardcover)
LC 2013-034997

SUMMARY: "'The Poetry of Derek Walcott 1948-2013' draws from every stage of the poet's storied career. . . . Across sixty-five years, Walcott has grappled with the themes that have defined his work as they have defined his life. . . . This collection, selected by Walcott's friend the English poet Glyn Maxwell, will prove as enduring as the questions, the passions, that have driven Walcott to write for more than half a century." (Publisher's note)

REVIEW: *Economist* v411 no8884 p81-2 Ap 26 2014

REVIEW: *Libr J* v138 no18 p105 N 1 2013 Molly McArdle

REVIEW: *N Y Times Book Rev* p12 F 23 2014 TEJU COLE

REVIEW: *N Y Times Book Rev* p26 Mr 2 2014

REVIEW: *New Yorker* v89 no47 p75-1 F 3 2014

"The Poetry of Derek Walcott 1948-2013." "A poet who comes to consciousness on a small island--like Derek Walcott, who was born on St. Lucia in 1930--is doomed, or privileged, to spend a lifetime writing about the sea. . . . But, like so many great poets before him, he shows that constraints do not have to starve the imagination; they can also nourish it. What is the sea to Walcott? In the more than six decades covered by 'The Poetry of Derek Walcott' . . . a rich and beautiful new selection of his life's work, edited by Glyn Maxwell--it can be anything, like matter itself."

WALDEN, DANIEL.ed. Chaim Potok. See Chaim Potok

WALDMAN, ADELLE. The Love Affairs of Nathaniel P.; A Novel; [by] Adelle Waldman 256 p. 2013 Henry Holt and Co.

1. Authors—New York (State)—New York—Fiction 2. Man-woman relationships—Fiction 3. Psychological fiction 4. Self-realization—Fiction 5. Young men—New York (State)—New York—Fiction
ISBN 0805097457 (hardcover); 9780805097450 (hardcover)
LC 2012-040366

SUMMARY: In this novel, by Adelle Waldman, "Nate Piven is a rising star in Brooklyn's literary scene. . . . He has his pick of both magazine assignments and women: . . . the hotshot business reporter . . . , his gorgeous ex-girlfriend, . . . and Hannah, . . . who is lively, fun and holds her own in conversation with his friends. [The novel is a] tale of one young man's search for happiness--and an inside look at how he really thinks about women, sex and love." (Publisher's note)

REVIEW: *Booklist* v109 no17 p66 My 1 2013 Joanne Wilkinson

REVIEW: *Kirkus Rev* v81 no7 p259 Ap 1 2013

REVIEW: *Libr J* v138 no10 p102 Je 1 2013 Julie Elliott

REVIEW: *N Y Times Book Rev* p9 Jl 14 2013 JESS WALTER

REVIEW: *New York Times* v162 no56219 pC4 Ag 5 2013 MARIA RUSSO

REVIEW: *New Yorker* v89 no21 p75 Jl 22 2013

REVIEW: *Publ Wkly* v260 no14 p36 Ap 8 2013 Elyse Cheney

REVIEW: *TLS* no5768 p12 O 18 2013 JESSICA LOUDIS

"An exploration of the kind of entitlement that can arise from being a reasonably attractive single male in a place as insular and demographically skewed as the New York publishing world. It is also a more subtle account of the machinations of desire, and the difficulty of recognizing the difference between feeling that one should want something--or rather, somebody--and actually wanting them. . . . Not much happens in 'Love Affairs,' so the plot is structured around Nate's relationships with women. . . . There is no grand revelation, just a vague sense of missed opportunity. Even so, 'Nathaniel P.' avoids tipping into self-indulgence: [Adelle] Waldman doesn't moralize, and she has ultimately produced an intelligent and entertaining experiment in literary sympathy."

REVIEW: *World Lit Today* v88 no2 p65-6 Mr/Ap 2014 Kevin Pickard

WALDRON, KEVIN. Panda-Monium at Peek zoo; [by] Kevin Waldron 40 p. 2014 Candlewick Press

1. Animal young—Juvenile fiction 2. Children's stories 3. Pandas 4. Parades 5. Zoos—Juvenile literature
ISBN 0763666580; 9780763666583
LC 2013-946621

SUMMARY: In this book, by Kevin Waldron, "Peek Zoo is holding an animal parade to celebrate the birth of their baby panda. But when the day arrives, nothing is ready. As Mr. Peek races around preparing, he leaves a trail of chaos—including an escaped baby panda heading for the lion's den! Thank goodness Mr. Peek's son, Jimmy, is there to save the day and ensure the crowd gets the best animal parade ever." (Publisher's note)

REVIEW: *Booklist* v110 no16 p54 Ap 15 2014 Thom Barthelmess

REVIEW: *Bull Cent Child Books* v67 no11 p603-4 Jl/Ag 2014 J. H.

REVIEW: *Kirkus Rev* v82 no4 p117 F 15 2014

"Panda-Monium At Peek Zoo". "A parade, a party and a panda veer tenuously close to a disastrous fiasco in this charming sequel. . . . The story comes shockingly, delightfully close to true horror (the baby panda is at one point within a hair's breadth of becoming lion food) but wraps up neatly by the end. The accompanying digital art resonates with the influence of 1960s designers and fizzes with energy. It's a true shame, though, that the attending hordes of visitors are disconcertingly, universally white. In spite of this misfire, few will be able to resist this sweet tale of adult incompetence and youthful problem-solving skills."

REVIEW: *Publ Wkly* v261 no11 p83 Mr 17 2014

REVIEW: *SLJ* v60 no3 p129 Mr 2014 Gay Lynn Van Vleck

WALDRON, KEVIN.il. Panda-Monium at Peek zoo. See Waldron, K.

WALDRON, MARY ANNE. Free to believe; rethinking freedom of conscience and religion in Canada; [by] Mary Anne Waldron 298 p. 2013 University of Toronto Press

1. Canada. Canadian Charter of Rights & Freedoms 2. Freedom of religion—Canada—Cases 3. Law—Canada 4. Liberty of conscience—Canada—Cases 5. Political science literature
ISBN 144261384X (pbk.); 1442645555 (cloth: alk. paper); 9781442613843 (pbk.); 9781442645554 (cloth: alk. paper)
LC 2013-363937

SUMMARY: This book on Canadian law "investigates the protection for freedom of conscience and religion . . . and its interpretation in the courts. Through an examination of decided cases that touches on the most controversial issues of our day . . . Mary Anne Waldron examines how the law has developed in the way that it has, the role that freedom of conscience and religion play in our society, and the role it could play in making it a more open, peaceful, and democratic place." (Publisher's note)

REVIEW: *Choice* v51 no8 p1485 Ap 2014 A. F. Johnson

"Free to Believe: Rethinking Freedom of Conscience and Religion in Canada". "This uniquely brilliant contribution to the study of diverse social values is also timely as the Quebec government endeavors to inscribe Quebec society's putative values in a controversial charter. . . . The author claims that her oeuvre is not philosophy while still raising many significant but practical philosophical questions. She also claims that it is not a legal text although legal scholars and practitioners would benefit greatly from this eloquently written and insightful tome, as would public policy analysts."

WALDROP, HOWARD. Horse of a different color; stories; [by] Howard Waldrop 216 p. 2013 Small Beer Press

1. FICTION—Fantasy—Short Stories 2. FICTION—Science Fiction—General 3. FICTION—Science Fiction—Short Stories 4. FICTION—Short Stories (single author) 5. Grail—Fiction 6. Science fiction, American 7. Vaudeville
ISBN 9781618730732 (hardback)
LC 2013-028910

SUMMARY: This book is a collection of short stories by Howard Waldrop. "From 'The Wolfman of Alcatraz' to a horrifying Hansel and Gretel, from 'The Bravest Girl I Ever Knew' to the sixth Marx brother's story of a vaudeville act tracking down the Holy Grail, this new collection . . . [presents] keys to the secrets of the stories behind the stories." (Publisher's note)

REVIEW: *New York Times* v163 no56349 pC30 D 13 2013 DANA JENNINGS

"Horses of a Different Color" and "The Bread We Eat in Dreams". "Two fine collections of short stories. . . . Mr. [Howard] Waldrop, 67, is the sly old pro here, while Ms. [Catherynne M.] Valente, 34, is the incandescent young star, but both are steeped in American pop-cultural myth. . . . And they leaven these legends with the off-kilter literary shrewdness of writers like [Jorge Luis] Borges . . . and Donald Barthelme to forge a dark Americana where life tends to suddenly skid sideways. . . . At least half the 10 tales in his new collection are prime eccentric Waldrop, though some feel more like extended jokes than fully realized stories. . . . Ms. Valente, too, is adept at updating the tall tale, but also writes with grace and power. She was a poet first, and her precise and lyrical ear is apparent thoughout."

WALKER, ANNA. Peggy; a brave chicken on a big adventure; 32 p. 2014 Clarion Books, Houghton Mifflin Harcourt

1. Adventure and adventurers—Fiction 2. Chickens—Fiction 3. Children's stories 4. City and town life—Fiction 5. Homesickness
ISBN 0544259009; 9780544259003 (hardback)

LC 2013-034562

SUMMARY: In this book, by Anna Walker, "Peggy the hen is contented with her quiet existence and daily routine. When a powerful gust of wind sweeps her up and deposits her in the midst of a busy city, she explores her new surroundings, makes new friends, and cleverly figures out how to get home—with a newly kindled appetite for adventure." (Publisher's note)

REVIEW: *Horn Book Magazine* v90 no3 p76-7 My/Je 2014 CYNTHIA K. RITTER

REVIEW: *Kirkus Rev* v82 no4 p239 F 15 2014

"Peggy: A Brave Chicken on a Big Adventure". "A charmer of a chicken has a big adventure in this import from Australia. . . . Understated text reveals her daily routine of breakfast, play in the backyard and pigeon watching, and accompanying ink-and-photo-collage illustrations humorously depict her eating from a bowl, jumping on a trampoline and gazing at pigeons. . . . In a pitch-perfect resolution, Peggy resumes her routine, but instead of just watching the pigeons, she now chats with them, and the final page turn assures readers that she sometimes catches 'the train to the city.' Here's hoping that Peggy has many more big adventures."

REVIEW: *SLJ* v60 no4 p137 Ap 2014 Tanya Boudreau

WALKER, DAVID.il. Time for a hug. See Gershator, P.

WALKER, GABRIELLE. Antarctica; an intimate portrait of the world's most mysterious continent; [by] Gabrielle Walker 416 p. 2013 Houghton Mifflin Harcourt

1. Antarctic research stations 2. Cold (Temperature)—Physiological effect 3. Scientists—Antarctica 4. Travel writing

ISBN 0151015201; 9780151015207

LC 2012-014248

SUMMARY: Author Gabrielle Walker attempts to answer "who travels to Antarctica, and why? [She] addresses her curiosity to the scientists and support personnel at stations various nations maintain on [Antarctica]. During several separate journeys, she stayed at a half-dozen outposts operated by the U.S., the UK, Russia, France, Italy, and Argentina and learned the protocols of cold-weather survival, accompanied scientists on their fieldwork, and observed how people cope with the environmental extremes." (Booklist)

REVIEW: *Booklist* v109 no2 p16 S 15 2012

REVIEW: *Choice* v51 no2 p298-9 O 2013 A. C. Prendergast

"Antarctica: An Intimate Portrait of a Mysterious Continent." "[Author Gabrielle] Walker . . . has achieved the near impossible with Antarctica--she made this reviewer want to visit the region. The author admits her own fascination with the environment, animals, and people of the Antarctic continent and with the scientific work being conducted there. Through her descriptions and narrative, she makes these aspects almost equally alluring to the reader. Walker explains the geologic history as well as the history of the human presence on Antarctica, and describes some of the fascinating investigations that have been carried out."

REVIEW: *Kirkus Rev* v80 no20 p37 O 15 2012

REVIEW: *Libr J* v137 no16 p97 O 1 2012 Jean E. Crampon

REVIEW: *Publ Wkly* v259 no38 p43 S 17 2012

REVIEW: *TLS* no5743 p8-9 Ap 26 2013 RICHARD HAMBLYN

WALKER, JAN. The Whiskey Creek Water Company; [by] Jan Walker 336 p. 2013 Plicata Press

1. Cities & towns—Fiction 2. Depressions—Fiction 3. Distilling, Illicit 4. Families—Fiction 5. Historical fiction

ISBN 0984840052; 9780984840052

SUMMARY: This book "opens in November 1932" in "Burke Bay, on the banks of Washington state's Puget Sound. . . . Seeking work and a chance to cash in on the area's lucrative distilleries, a dapper Farley Price arrives in his fancy automobile with his timid wife, Eleanor, and their young daughter, Hannah. . . . But when Price's violent drunkenness and underhanded business plans threaten the community's stability, Burke Bay residents rally to protect Eleanor and Hannah." (Kirkus Reviews)

REVIEW: *Kirkus Rev* v82 no2 p365 Ja 15 2014

REVIEW: *Kirkus Rev* v82 no3 p44 F 1 2014

"The Whiskey Creek Water Company". "[Jan] Walker deftly reveals his story as Blevins struggles to balance his desire to continue his family's traditional livelihood with his wife's demands that he adjust to the post-Prohibition marketplace and devise a suitable business for their son, Theodore, to inherit. . . . Walker's characters and keen observations bring the town alive, leaving readers with a deep understanding of the people and the challenges they faced during a tumultuous era. The author also intriguingly shows how the production and consumption of alcohol influences individual people, families and the community at large. A solidly researched, artfully written novel that's both entertaining and educational."

WALKER, MARTIN. The Resistance Man; a Bruno, Chief of Police novel; [by] Martin Walker 336 p. 2014 Alfred A. Knopf

1. Detective & mystery stories 2. Food habits—Fiction 3. Police—France—Fiction 4. Theft 5. World War, 1939-1945—Underground movements—France

ISBN 0385349548; 9780385349543 (hardcover)

LC 2013-022876

SUMMARY: This book, by Martin Walker, is the sixth in the series. "Bruno Courrèges . . . is back in another . . . tale of mystery and suspense. . . . A veteran of the Resistance dies, and among his possessions are documents that connect him to a notorious train robbery. A former British spymaster's estate is burglarized. . . . An academic's home is broken into just as she is finishing a revelatory book on France's nuclear weapons program. An antiques dealer is found brutally murdered." (Publisher's note)

REVIEW: *Booklist* v110 no9/10 p52 Ja 1 2014 Connie Fletcher

REVIEW: *Kirkus Rev* v82 no4 p62 F 15 2014

"The Resistance Man". "The passing of an 86-year-old Resistance fighter opens another can of worms (and stocks of truffles and pâté de fois gras) for chief of police Bruno Courrèges. . . . Amid all the hustle and bustle, however, there's still plenty of time for good friends to share good food and make new memories. As usual, the tale of crime and detection is mainly a pretext for a gentle celebration of la belle France. But this time, Bruno, who's required to act as enforcer, sleuth, diplomat, comforter, impersonator, hostage negotiator and rescuer, reveals unsuspected resources."

REVIEW: *Libr J* v139 no2 p60 F 1 2014 Teresa L. Jacobsen

REVIEW: *Publ Wkly* v260 no52 p33-4 D 23 2013

WALKER, MELISSA. Ashes to ashes; [by] Melissa Walker 356 p. 2014 Katherine Tegen Books, an imprint of HarperCollinsPublishers

1. Future life—Fiction 2. Ghosts—Fiction 3. Love—Fiction 4. Paranormal romance stories 5. Supernatural—Fiction

ISBN 0062077341; 9780062077349 (hardcover)
LC 2013-005069

SUMMARY: Author Melissa Walker presents a romantic ghost story. "When Callie's life is cut short by a tragic accident in her hometown of Charleston, South Carolina, her spirit travels to another dimension called the Prism. Here she meets a striking and mysterious ghost named Thatcher, who guides her as she learns how to bring peace to those she left behind. But Callie soon uncovers a dark secret about the spirit world: Some of the souls in it are angry, and they desperately want revenge." (Publisher's note)

REVIEW: *Booklist* v110 no8 p45 D 15 2013 Debbie Carton

REVIEW: *Bull Cent Child Books* v67 no5 p288-9 Ja 2014 K. C.

"Ashes to Ashes." "A gentle didacticism aimed squarely at risky teen behavior pervades the story as Cassie learns to appreciate her father's style of care, and her glaringly bad judgment will have readers shaking their heads; the lure of an after-death romance on top of the tried-and-true premise of a teen's imagining what will happen to friends and family after her death, though, will keep readers enthralled. [Melissa] Walker has chosen a perfect setting in Charleston, SC, where ghosts are a matter of course and steamy summers heighten the gothic atmospherics of teens courting danger. The ending is a bit of a tease—sequel, or just a wink to resist closure? Either way, readers will be intrigued by this entry in the paranormal romance genre."

REVIEW: *Kirkus Rev* v81 no16 p361 Ag 15 2013

REVIEW: *Kirkus Rev* v81 no20 p26 O 15 2013

REVIEW: *Kirkus Rev* p58 Ag 15 2013 Fall Preview

REVIEW: *SLJ* v60 no1 p92 Ja 2014 Natalie Struecker

WALKER, SALLY M. Boundaries; how the Mason-Dixon line settled a family feud and divided a nation; [by] Sally M. Walker 208 p. 2014 Candlewick Press

1. Boundaries 2. Historical literature 3. Mason, Charles 4. Mason-Dixon Line 5. Surveying (Engineering)—History

ISBN 0763656127; 9780763656126
LC 2013-946612

SUMMARY: This book, by Sally M. Walker, details the "Mason-Dixon Line's history, replete with property disputes, persecution, and ideological conflicts. . . . Walker traces the tale of the Mason-Dixon Line through family feuds, brave exploration, scientific excellence, and the struggle to define a cohesive country. But above all, this [is a] . . . story of surveying, marking, and respecting lines of demarcation." (Publisher's note)

REVIEW: *Booklist* v110 no11 p51 F 1 2014 Carolyn Phelan

REVIEW: *Bull Cent Child Books* v67 no8 p425-6 Ap 2014 E. B.

REVIEW: *Horn Book Magazine* v90 no3 p117 My/Je 2014 JONATHAN HUNT

REVIEW: *Kirkus Rev* v82 no1 p224 Ja 1 2014

"Boundaries". "In this richly layered, thoroughly researched history of the Mason-Dixon Line, [Sally M.] Walker crisscrosses the boundaries of geography, culture, economics, science, mathematics, politics and religion to reveal that drawing lines is as likely to cause conflict as settle it. . . . Abundant use is made of quotations from primary sources, and many photographs and archival images enrich the narrative. A thoughtful, insightful, challenging and extensively researched chronicle of United States history and the shaping of national identity from a unique perspective."

REVIEW: *Publ Wkly* v261 no3 p59 Ja 20 2014

REVIEW: *SLJ* v60 no3 p183 Mr 2014 Mary Mueller

REVIEW: *Voice of Youth Advocates* v37 no1 p94 Ap 2014 Rebecca O'Neil

WALKER, SUSAN.tr. Of Jewish race. See Modiano, R.

WALKER, WICKLIFFE W. Goat Game; Thirteen Tales from the Afghan Frontier; [by] Wickliffe W. Walker 168 p. 2013 CreateSpace Independent Publishing Platform

1. Afghan War, 2001- 2. American short stories 3. Counterterrorism 4. Fort Bragg (N.C.) 5. Qaida (Organization)

ISBN 1479320471; 9781479320479

SUMMARY: These short stories follow "Special Forces Officer Col. Bailey and his counterpart and friend from Pakistan. Though fictional, the episodes are based on real events. . . . Danger is always present as Bailey . . . tries to befriend the Pashtuns and Afghans while chasing al-Qaida and all manner of nasty terrorists. With his Pakistani colleague, he goes into a remote area to establish the truth of a claim that a tribal sect has captured a Soviet chemical-weapons truck." (Kirkus Reviews)

REVIEW: *Kirkus Rev* v81 no10 p131 My 15 2013

REVIEW: *Kirkus Rev* v81 no7 p378 Ap 1 2013

REVIEW: *Kirkus Rev* p55 D 15 2013 supplemet best books 2013

"Goat Game: Thirteen Tales From the Afghan Frontier". "The author is well-aware of the trickery and chicanery in Afghanistan, but he has great respect for the people and the region. Vivid details abound; [Wickliffe W.] Walker's description of a character's 'lean, sunken cheeks, one eye the milky white of advanced cataracts, and a voluminous white turban accented with a tall gold-colored brush' brings him to life. Military tactics play against the background of the thousands of years of history that have produced the Afghanistan of today. Insightful, striking portrayal of the Afghan culture and people."

WALLACE, ALFRED RUSSEL, 1823-1913. Island life, or, The phenomena and causes of insular faunas and floras; including a revision and attempted solution of the problem of geological climates; [by] Alfred Russel Wallace lxxxvii, 526 p. 2013 University of Chicago Press

1. Biogeography 2. Evolutionary theories 3. Glacial epoch 4. Island ecology 5. Scientific literature

ISBN 022604503X (paperback : alkaline paper); 9780226045030 (paperback : alkaline paper)
LC 2013-003830

SUMMARY: This book by Alfred Russel Wallace, first published in 1880, "extends studies on the influence of the glacial epochs on organismal distribution patterns and the characteristics of island biogeography. . . . The book includes history's first theory of continental glaciation based on a combination of geographical and astronomical causes, a discussion of island classification, and a survey of worldwide island faunas and floras." (Publisher's note)

REVIEW: *Choice* v51 no6 p1033-4 F 2014 E. J. Sargis

"Island Life, or, The Phenomena and Causes of Insular Faunas and Floras, Including a Revision and Attempted Solution of the Problem of Geological Climates." "Fortunately, the first edition (1880) has been reissued to commemorate the centennial of [Alfred Russel] Wallace's death. This new version begins with a brief foreword by author David Quammen and a thorough 60-page introduction by Lawrence Heaney . . . one of the foremost modern scholars on island biogeography, especially for Southeast Asia. Heaney's detailed commentary is a wonderful addition that updates the original book. . . . Highly recommended."

WALLACE, CAREY. The ghost in the glass house; [by] Carey Wallace 240 p. 2013 Clarion Books, Houghton Mifflin Harcourt

1. Aristocracy (Social class)—Fiction 2. Ghosts—Fiction 3. Historical fiction 4. Mothers and daughters—Fiction
ISBN 0544022912; 9780544022911 (hardback)
LC 2012-051330

SUMMARY: This young adult historical novel, by Carey Wallace, is set "in a 1920s seaside town, [where] Clare discovers a mysterious glass house in the backyard of her new summer home. There she falls in love with Jack, the ghost of a boy who can't remember who he was before he died. Their romance is a haven for her from the cruel pranks of her society friends . . . in a world where every character is haunted by lingering ghosts of love." (Publisher's note)

REVIEW: *Bull Cent Child Books* v67 no3 p186 N 2013 K. Q. G.

"The Ghost in the Glass House." "In the three years since her father's death, twelve-year-old Clare has been forced to tag along behind her high-society mother, flitting from resort to resort as her mother uses her wealth and freedom to fully enjoy the height of the Roaring Twenties. At their latest temporary home, Clare finds comfort with Jack, a ghostly boy who haunts a mysterious locked glass house behind the estate. . . . She attempts to negotiate the shark-infested waters between childhood and adulthood. The plot rambles quite a bit, however, with an ambiguously violent episode serving as the climax and a sudden, completely unmotivated turnaround by Clare's mother providing an unexpected resolution."

REVIEW: *Horn Book Magazine* v89 no6 p109 N/D 2013 RUSSELL PERRY

"The Ghost in the Glass House". "Clare is a refreshingly thoughtful heroine, a quiet, keen observer of others even as she harbors her own insecurities about growing up. While her mother finds solace in social gatherings and her peers experiment with adolescent romance, Clare is reluctant to cross the 'boundaries of childhood'—just as Jack fears moving on to the afterlife. [Carey] Wallace deftly uses the Spiritualist fervor of the 1920s period setting to populate her novel with characters who are paralyzed by ghosts of the past, both real and metaphorical, and demonstrates the need to balance honoring the past and living in the present."

WALLACE, DAVID FOSTER, 1962-2008. Infinite jest; [by] David Foster Wallace

1. American wit & humor 2. Compulsive behavior 3. Drug addicts—Fiction 4. Halfway houses 5. Speculative fiction
ISBN 0316066524; 9780316066525

SUMMARY: This book by David Foster Wallace presents a "comedy about the pursuit of happiness in America. Set in an addicts' halfway house and a tennis academy . . . 'Infinite Jest' explores essential questions about what entertainment is and why it has come to so dominate our lives; about how our desire for entertainment affects our need to connect with other people; and about what the pleasures we choose say about who we are." (Publisher's note)

REVIEW: *N Y Times Book Rev* p18-9 N 24 2013 JOHN SCHWARTZ

"Infinite Jest," Bleeding Edge," and "Billy Lynn's Long Halftime Walk." "Oliver Wyman . . . imbues each member of Bravo Company with a thoughtfully defined character: Billy is unschooled but far from stupid, and Wyman walks that line effectively. . . . Something is lost in the transition from print to sound, but Wyman manages to give each word and phrase the sensibility of the typographical tricks. . . . The heroine, Maxine Tarnow, is a street-savvy investigator of financial fraud who was born and raised in Manhattan, but [Jeannie] Berlin seems to be channeling Fran Drescher and Selma Diamond. And instead of the Crazy Eddie delivery I was hoping for, the pacing is lugubrious. . . . [Sean] Pratt is a startling good narrator, dry and expressive, with the kind of vocal control that evokes dozens of characters with only slight but very distinctive variations of accent and affect."

WALLACE, RICH. Babe conquers the world; the legendary life of Babe Didrikson Zaharias; [by] Rich Wallace 272 p. 2014 Calkins Creek

1. Biography (Literary form) 2. Children of immigrants 3. Olympic athletes 4. Women athletes 5. Zaharias, Babe Didrikson, 1911-1956
ISBN 1590789814; 9781590789810
LC 2013-953471

SUMMARY: This book, by Rich Wallace and Sandra Neil Wallace, is a biography of Babe Didrikson Zaharias. "A champion basketball player, an Olympic track-and-field star, and career golfer, Babe didn't let obstacles stand in the way of her success. The authors detail her trajectory from the daughter of a Norwegian immigrant born in a working-class Texas neighborhood to record wins at the 1932 Olympics (still not broken to this day) to her last days as she fought cancer." (School Library Journal)

REVIEW: *Booklist* v110 no13 p58-60 Mr 1 2014 Erin Anderson

"Babe Conquers the World: The Legendary Life of Babe Didrickson Zaharias." "Babe Didrikson Zaharias is perhaps the most accomplished athlete that young people have never heard of. . . . Her life story as drawn from contemporary news articles and interviews is fascinating and inspirational, and it is punctuated with photographs like Zaharias shooting targets with Amelia Earhart and giving Sam Snead tips on his golf swing. This is part sports journalism, part narrative nonfiction, and part proof that professional athletes can be exemplary role models for young people."

REVIEW: *Bull Cent Child Books* v67 no9 p482 My 2014 E. B.

REVIEW: *Kirkus Rev* v82 no4 p212 F 15 2014

REVIEW: *SLJ* v60 no2 p128 F 2014 Shelley Diaz

WALLACE, RICH. Wicked cruel; [by] Rich Wallace 208 p. 2013 Knopf Books for Young Readers

1. Folklore—New Hampshire—Fiction 2. Ghost stories 3. Halloween—Fiction 4. JUVENILE FICTION—Holidays & Celebrations—Halloween 5. JUVENILE FICTION—Social Issues—Bullying 6. New England—Fiction 7. School stories 8. Schools—Fiction 9. Supernatural—Fiction

ISBN 0375867481; 9780375865145 (paperback); 9780375867484 (hardback); 9780375967481 (library binding)

LC 2012-042504

SUMMARY: This book of three "ghostly stories explore urban legends--actually rural New England legends--and how they changed lives. A bullied boy moves away and dies from a brain injury, yet he is seen in a music video after his death. A team of horses drowns in a flooded brickyard, but on certain rainy nights, they run free. Five farm children die young, but one mysteriously communicates with a young boy who may be as afraid of girls as of ghosts." (Kirkus Reviews)

REVIEW: *Booklist* v109 no22 p93 Ag 1 2013 Daniel Kraus

REVIEW: *Bull Cent Child Books* v67 no2 p122 O 2013 K. Q. G.

"Wicked Cruel." "A small New England town with a ghostly history serves as the setting for this trio of spooky stories. . . . Each story runs about eighty or so pages, making this frightening fare that will appeal to readers who've enjoyed Alvin Schwartz's stories but who'd prefer a bit more meat on the bones of their scares. [Author Rich] Wallace knows his pacing and utilizes genre tropes for maximum impact, pairing the sordid past of an aging town with the perils of modern society and technology to create atmospheric chills. The protagonists are aren't deeply drawn, but they're not there to be memorable characters; they're average everyday kids . . . dealing with average everyday problems . . . like bullies, sibling conflicts, and confusion with the opposite sex."

REVIEW: *Kirkus Rev* v81 no2 p105 Je 1 2013

REVIEW: *SLJ* v59 no9 p151 S 2013 Jenny Berggren

WALLACE, SANDRA NEIL. Babe conquers the world. See Wallace, R.

WALLACE, SANDRA NEIL. Muckers; [by] Sandra Neil Wallace 288 p. 2013 Alfred A. Knopf

1. Copper mines and mining—Fiction 2. Fathers and sons—Fiction 3. Football—Fiction 4. Grief—Fiction 5. High schools—Fiction 6. Mexican Americans—Fiction 7. Race relations—Fiction 8. Schools—Fiction 9. Sports stories

ISBN 0375867546; 9780375867545 (hardback); 9780375967542 (hardcover library binding)

LC 2013-003537

SUMMARY: In this book, "Felix 'Red' O'Sullivan is the best hope to lead his team to a statewide football championship. Unlike other teams in 1950 in Arizona, whites and Latinos play together on the Hartley Muckers. Nevertheless, both groups are aware of the dividing lines." Red must also deal with an alcoholic father and a mother grieving for Red's older brother, killed in World War II. "For Red, this season will be his last chance to return glory to 'Bobby's school.'" (Kirkus Reviews)

REVIEW: *Booklist* v111 no1 p104 S 1 2014 Daniel Kraus

REVIEW: *Booklist* v110 no1 p109-10 S 1 2013 Sarah Hunter

"Muckers". "Muckers football is the only thing the small Arizona town has to look forward to. . . . Based on a true story, Wallace's novel follows the tough-as-nails, desegregated Muckers as they dig their heels into the slag and face impossible odds, all while the threat of racial tensions, anti-Communist sentiments, and the Korean War simmer in the background. Wallace, a former ESPN correspondent, captures a vivid sense of atmosphere and well-wrought characters, all while showcasing balls-to-the-wall football action."

REVIEW: *Bull Cent Child Books* v67 no3 p186-7 N 2013 E. B.

REVIEW: *Kirkus Rev* v81 no18 p15 S 15 2013

REVIEW: *Publ Wkly* v260 no38 p81 S 23 2013

WALLERSTEIN, IMMANUEL MAURICE, 1930-. Centrist liberalism triumphant, 1789/1914; [by] Immanuel Maurice Wallerstein xvii, 377 p. 2011 University of California Press

1. Capitalism 2. Economic history 3. Historical literature 4. Ideology 5. Liberalism 6. World history

ISBN 9780520267602 (cloth : alk. paper); 9780520267619 (pbk. : alk. paper)

LC 2010-040366

SUMMARY: This book "is the fourth volume in Immanuel Wallerstein's 'The Modern World-System,' with at least two more volumes promised. . . . Wallerstein argues that, 'in the late fifteenth and early sixteenth century, there came into existence what we may call a European world-economy' linked by economic forces. . . . Unlike earlier empires such as China, Persia, and Rome, the world-economy functions without 'a unified political structure.'" (Reviews in American History)

REVIEW: *Contemp Sociol* v41 no1 p20-3 Ja 2012 Michael Mann

REVIEW: *Contemp Sociol* v41 no1 p23-6 Ja 2012 George Steinmetz

REVIEW: *Rev Am Hist* v40 no3 p415-8 S 2012 Stanley L. Engerman

"The Modern World System: Centrist Liberalism Triumphant 1789-1914." "It is rather impressive that some thirty-seven years after the publication of the first of this quartet, [Immanuel Maurice] Wallerstein is still providing as high a level of intellectual studies as the volume presented here. It is one that has the power to stimulate with its insights and arguments. With its broad coverage, some of this work may seem inaccurate or incomplete, but that is the price paid for its great ambition. We readers await the next volumes of the series--hopefully in less time than we waited for the current book."

THE WALLS BEHIND THE CURTAIN; East European prison literature, 1945-1990; x, 436 p. 2012 University of Pittsburgh Press
1. Anthologies 2. LITERARY COLLECTIONS—Continental European 3. LITERARY CRITICISM—European—Eastern (see also Russian & Former Soviet Union) 4. Prisoners' writings, East European—Translations into English
ISBN 9780822962021 (pbk.)
LC 2012-022364

SUMMARY: This book "is an anthology of texts produced by writers who were imprisoned in Eastem Europe between 1945 and 1990. Perceived (or constructed) as 'inimical elements' by their countries' Communist regimes, they spent anything from months to decades in prisons or labour camps. . . . Harold B. Segel collects the voices of almost fifty authors from Albania, Bulgaria, Czechoslovakia, Hungary, Poland, Romania and Yugoslavia." (Times Literary Supplement)

REVIEW: *Choice* v50 no8 p1426 Ap 2013 B. K. Beynen

REVIEW: *TLS* no5762 p22 S 6 2013 COSTICA BRADATAN

"The Walls Behind the Curtain: East European Prison Literature, 1945-1990." "Occasionally, one might wish that [Harold B. Segal] had recruited more expert translators for some of the languages outside his primary fields of expertise (Polish and Russian), but the erudition and passion underlying this collection are nevertheless impressive. . . . With its extensive linguistic, literary, and geographic range, 'The Walls Behind the Curtain' is a very ambitious project. Too ambitious perhaps, for the book's flaws appear to derive from an inability to manage its enormous proportions. Insightfully designed, it appears to have been hastily executed. . . . The real problems begin when Segel's narrative almost collapses, under the weight of contradictory information."

WALLS, JERRY L. Good God. See Baggett, D.

WALSER, KARL, 1877-1943.il. A schoolboy's diary and other stories. See Walser, R.

WALSER, ROBERT, 1878-1956. Microscripts; 159 2010 New Directions
1. German fiction—Translations into English 2. Jealousy 3. Marriage—Fiction 4. Short stories—By individual authors 5. Urban life—Fiction
ISBN 0-811-21880-5; 9780811218801

SUMMARY: "Selected from the six-volume German original, these twenty-five short pieces address schnapps, rotten husbands, small-town life, elegant jaunts, the radio, swine, . . . jealousy, and marriage proposals. This is the first English translation of [Robert] Walser's work to be accompanied by facsimiles of the original microscripts and the original German texts." (Publisher's note)

REVIEW: *TLS* no5753 p11-2 Jl 5 2013 CHARLIE LOUTH

"Microscripts," "The Walk," and "Thirty Poems." "Of the 526 small slips of paper that make up the microscripts, twenty-one of which are finely reproduced in this edition, about half, when they were eventually puzzled out, proved to have a fair-copy equivalent or to have been published by Walser already in newspapers and magazines. . . . 'The Walk' is a good place to start reading [Robert] Walser, and offers a kind of bridge between the novels and the microscripts.. . . Walser started off as a poet entirely in the Romantic vein. . . . The poems also give us Walser's manner in concentrated miniature."

WALSER, ROBERT, 1878-1956. A schoolboy's diary and other stories; 208 p. 2013 New York Review Books
1. Children—Fiction 2. German literature—Translations into English 3. Modernism (Literature) 4. Short story (Literary form) 5. Swiss literature (German)
ISBN 9781590176726 (alk. paper)
LC 2013-011577

SUMMARY: This book, by Robert Walser, "brings together more than seventy of [the author's] . . . stories, most never before available in English. Opening with a sequence from Walser's first book, . . . the complete classroom assignments of a fictional boy who has met a tragically early death, this selection ranges from sketches of uncomprehending editors, overly passionate readers, and dreamy artists to tales of . . . sexual encounters on a train, and Walser's service in World War I." (Publisher's note)

REVIEW: *New Statesman* v142 no5180 p43 O 18 2013 Philip Maughan

REVIEW: *Publ Wkly* v260 no21 p27-8 My 27 2013

REVIEW: *TLS* no5779 p23 Ja 3 2014 SCOTT ESPOSITO

"A Schoolboy's Diary and Other Stories." "Robert Walser's writing never fully lost touch with the fresh, at times naive aspect with which the young observe their fellow men. . . . The blessings, trials and fragility of youth tie together the short prose selected by Damion Searls for his new translation of 'A Schoolboy's Diary: And other stories.' . . . Walser's affection for the marginalized shines through; awkward youths, young ladies, soldiers, poets, and the handicapped. . . . In the hands of Searls, Walser's prose manifests a glassy precision."

WALSER, ROBERT, 1878-1956. Thirty poems; 62 p. 2012 Christine Burgin/New Directions
1. German poetry 2. Illustrated books 3. Poems—Collections 4. Romanticism in literature 5. Swiss literature (German)—20th century
ISBN 9780811220019 (alk. paper)
LC 2011-048682

SUMMARY: This book of poetry by Robert Walser "collects famed translator Christopher Middleton's favorite poems from the more than five hundred Walser wrote. The illustrations range from an early poem in perfect copperplate handwriting, to one from a 1927 Czech-German newspaper, to a microscript." (Publisher's note) Most of the poems "fall into the period 1925-30, so from the end of Walser's writing life, half of them from the microscripts." (Times Literary Supplement)

REVIEW: *TLS* no5753 p11-2 Jl 5 2013 CHARLIE LOUTH

"Microscripts," "The Walk," and "Thirty Poems." "Of the 526 small slips of paper that make up the microscripts, twenty-one of which are finely reproduced in this edition, about half, when they were eventually puzzled out, proved to have a fair-copy equivalent or to have been published by Walser already in newspapers and magazines. . . . 'The Walk' is a good place to start reading [Robert] Walser, and offers a kind of bridge between the novels and the microscripts.. . . Walser started off as a poet entirely in the Romantic vein. .

. . The poems also give us Walser's manner in concentrated miniature."

WALSH, JOHN PATRICK. Free and French in the Caribbean; Toussaint Louverture, Aimé Césaire, and narratives of loyal opposition; [by] John Patrick Walsh x, 193 p. 2013 Indiana University Press

1. Caribbean, French-speaking—History—Autonomy and independence movements 2. Decolonization in literature 3. Historical literature 4. Martinican literature (French)—History and criticism 5. Nationalism—Caribbean, French speaking—History 6. Nationalism—Haiti—History 7. Nationalism in literature
ISBN 9780253006271 (cloth: alk. paper); 9780253006301 (pbk.: alk. paper)
LC 2013-002202

SUMMARY: In this book, "John Walsh studies the writings of Toussaint Louverture and Aimé Césaire to examine how they conceived of and narrated two defining events in the decolonializing of the French Caribbean: the revolution that freed the French colony of Saint-Domingue in 1803 and the departmentalization of Martinique and other French colonies in 1946." (Publisher's note)

REVIEW: *Choice* v51 no8 p1469-70 Ap 2014 L. W. Yoder

"Free and French in the Caribbean: Toussaint Louverture, Aimé Césaire, and Narratives of Loyal Opposition". "By linking the Haitian Revolution and the 1946 law of departmentalization, along with the legacies of Toussaint Louverture and Aimé Césaire, [John Patrick] Walsh . . . has opened a fascinating and fruitful line of study, not only of the writings of these two leaders, but also of the ambiguous colonial and postcolonial relationship between the French Republic and the French Caribbean."

WALSH, KENNETH T. Prisoners of the White House; the isolation of America's presidents and the crisis of leadership; [by] Kenneth T. Walsh 256 p. 2013 Paradigm Publishers

1. Political leadership—United States 2. Political science literature 3. Presidents—United States 4. Presidents—United States—Social life and customs
ISBN 161205160X; 9781612051604 (hardcover : alk. paper)
LC 2013-002152

SUMMARY: This book is an "account of the American presidency since FDR." Author Kenneth T. Walsh reveals that the Executive Mansion is a space of power and privilege but "it is also a space that keeps the politically entitled at a distance from their fellow Americans. . . . Walsh suggests that the problem stems from several factors, not the least of which is that the White House was designed 'to serve the material needs and desires of one man.'" (Kirkus Reviews)

REVIEW: *Choice* v51 no7 p1311 Mr 2014 J. E. Walsh

"Prisoners of the White House: The Isolation of America's Presidents and the Crisis of Leadership." "[Kenneth T.] Walsh . . . documents ways that presidents strive to stay connected with the opinions of 'average' Americans despite the social and political isolation experienced by modern presidents. . . . Walsh argues that presidents must stay informed about public opinion while serving time within the White House prison if they hope to be successful. . . . Walsh advises presidents to stay connected with voters and to avail themselves of sophisticated polling data that can help illuminate public opinion. . . . Recommended."

REVIEW: *Kirkus Rev* v81 no12 p72 Je 15 2013

REVIEW: *Libr J* v138 no9 p93 My 15 2013 Marcus Kieltyka

REVIEW: *Polit Sci Q (Wiley-Blackwell)* v129 no1 p163-4 Spr 2014 MARK NEVIN

REVIEW: *Publ Wkly* v260 no15 p54 Ap 15 2013

WALSH, RODOLFO. Operation massacre; 252 p. 2013 Seven Stories Press

1. Executions & executioners 2. Nonfiction novel 3. Police—Argentina—Buenos Aires (Province)
ISBN 1609805135; 9781609805135 (pbk.)
LC 2013-012770

SUMMARY: This book, a "true crime narrative first published in Spanish in 1957 and . . . translated here by [Daniella] Gitlin, is Argentinian political journalist [Rodolfo] Walsh's account of "the [secret] execution, on June 9, 1956, of five men suspected of participating in a failed coup against the military government designed to return [deposed Argentine leader Juan Domingo] Peron to power.'" (Publishers Weekly)

REVIEW: *Kirkus Rev* v81 no14 p320 Jl 15 2013

REVIEW: *London Rev Books* v35 no21 p13-4 N 7 2013 Michael Wood

REVIEW: *Publ Wkly* v260 no30 p59 Jl 29 2013

REVIEW: *TLS* no5761 p17 Ag 30 2013 JULIUS PURCELL

"Operation Massacre." "One of the first and most significant non-fiction novels from Latin America. . . . Exasperated by the incurious Argentine press, [Rudolfo] Walsh--then aged thirty--went to ground to research and write his masterwork, its precision all the more remarkable for the conditions in which it was written. . . . Moved by the urgency of the present,Walsh makes few concessions to later, non-Latin American readers. . . . A foreword by Michael Greenberg helps to orientate the reader. So do samples of Walsh's later writings, revealing the way in which this by now 'lesser' atrocity became a symbol for the even-bloodier drift of 1970s Argentina. . . . And for all its spare style, the writing is not without moments of eloquence."

WALSH, THERESE. The moon sisters; a novel; [by] Therese Walsh 336 p. 2013 Crown Publishers

1. Families—Fiction 2. Forgiveness—Fiction 3. Mothers and daughters 4. Psychological fiction 5. Sisters—Fiction
ISBN 9780307461605
LC 2013-018032

SUMMARY: In this book, "after their mother's probable suicide, sisters Olivia and Jazz take steps to move on with their lives. Jazz, logical and forward-thinking, decides to get a new job, but spirited, strong-willed Olivia—who can see sounds, taste words, and smell sights—is determined to travel to the remote setting of their mother's unfinished novel to lay her spirit properly to rest." (Publisher's note)

REVIEW: *Booklist* v110 no12 p28 F 15 2014 Kristine Huntley

REVIEW: *Kirkus Rev* v82 no4 p101 F 15 2014

"The Moon Sisters". "This second novel by [Therese] Walsh . . . centers on two sisters—one with synesthesia and one with a pragmatic outlook—as they recover from the suicide of their mother. . . . hen their van breaks down on the way to the Glade, Olivia hops a train, and Jazz furiously follows. . . . Though Walsh creates a vivid journey for the two sisters, they both speak and act, as does Hobbs, far older than their years, resulting in a less-than-believable coming-of-age tale. An uneven mix of magic and sorrow, from a promising writer."

REVIEW: *Libr J* v139 no5 p114 Mr 15 2014 Mara Dabrishus

REVIEW: *Publ Wkly* v260 no51 p36 D 16 2013

WALT DISNEY'S MICKEY MOUSE COLOR SUNDAYS; Robin Hood Rides Again" Robin Hood rides again; 278 p. 2013 W W Norton & Co Inc

1. American wit & humor 2. Comic books, strips, etc. 3. Donald Duck (Fictitious character) 4. Mickey Mouse (Fictitious character) 5. Robin Hood (Legendary character)

ISBN 160699686X; 9781606996867

SUMMARY: This book presents "full-color Sunday newspaper strips" by artist Floyd Gottfredson featuring the character Mickey Mouse. (Booklist) "Stories in this volume include 'The Robin Hood Adventure,' in which Mickey joins the Merry Men: swordfighting, jousting, and risking his life to rob the rich! Then Mickey faces Gold Rush gunslingers as the 'Sheriff of Nugget Gulch'--and outwits the ever-sneaky Mortimer Mouse in 'Mickey's Rival!'" (Publisher's note)

REVIEW: *Booklist* v110 no9/10 p80-1 Ja 1 2014 Gordon Flagg

"Walt Disney's Mickey Mouse Color Sundays: Robin Hood Rides Again." "This second volume of full-color Sunday newspaper strips by artist [Floyd] Gottfredson sees Mickey entering a more genteel phase in the late 1930s. . . . In contrast to the daily episodes, which largely featured adventure-oriented story lines that extended for weeks, these Sunday installments are mostly self-contained gags. Welcome exceptions are serialized tales in which Mickey joins Robin Hood in Sherwood Forest, becomes a sheriff in the Wild West, and portrays the Brave Little Tailor in an adaptation of his then current film. . . . With their retro appeal, Gottfredson's buoyant drawings might just look even better now than they did when they were fresh."

WALTERS, ERIC. The rule of three; [by] Eric Walters 416 p. 2014 Farrar Straus & Giroux

1. Electric power failures—Fiction 2. Neighborhoods—Fiction 3. Speculative fiction 4. Survival—Fiction 5. Technology & civilization

ISBN 0374355029; 9780374355029 (hardback)

LC 2013-022077

SUMMARY: In this book, by Eric Walters, "computers around the globe shut down in a viral catastrophe. At sixteen-year-old Adam Daley's high school, the problem first seems to be a typical electrical outage, until students discover that cell phones are down. . . . Driving home, Adam encounters a storm tide of anger and fear as the region becomes paralyzed. Soon—as resources dwindle, crises mount, and chaos descends—he will see his suburban neighborhood band together for protection." (Publisher's note)

REVIEW: *Booklist* v110 no9/10 p108 Ja 1 2014 Paula Willey

REVIEW: *Bull Cent Child Books* v67 no7 p383 Mr 2014 A. M.

REVIEW: *Kirkus Rev* v81 no24 p127 D 15 2013

"The Rule of Three". "Reticent Adam, who frequently witnesses the adults' closed-door proceedings, often gets lost in his silence, and Herb consistently steals the show. Otherwise, Adam and Herb make a good team, pairing youthful hope with calculating cynicism. Many of the most exciting moments involve student-pilot Adam's homemade ultralight plane—noncomputerized and therefore still functional. The prose can be clunky, reading at times like a survivalist instruction manual disguised as dialogue—but the detailed content is more than worth it, capturing the nitty-gritty of rebuilding—and defending—civilization. Perfect for aspiring doomsday preppers and survivalists."

REVIEW: *Publ Wkly* v260 no43 p61-2 O 28 2013

REVIEW: *Quill Quire* v80 no1 p43-4 Ja/F 2014 Cara Smusiak

REVIEW: *SLJ* v60 no1 p106 Ja 2014 Kristyn Dorfman

REVIEW: *Voice of Youth Advocates* v36 no6 p67 F 2014 Amy Fiske

WALTERS, JOHN. Intervention in the modern UK brewing industry; [by] John Walters xviii, 315 p. 2012 Palgrave Macmillan

1. BUSINESS & ECONOMICS—Corporate & Business History 2. BUSINESS & ECONOMICS—Government & Business 3. BUSINESS & ECONOMICS—Industries—Hospitality, Travel & Tourism 4. BUSINESS & ECONOMICS—Industries—Service Industries 5. BUSINESS & ECONOMICS—Organizational Behavior 6. Brewing industry—Great Britain 7. Business literature 8. Historical literature

ISBN 9780230298576 (hardback)

LC 2011-047527

SUMMARY: Written by John Spicer, Chris Thurman, John Walters, and Simon Ward, "This is the story of the radical intervention carried out by the Thatcher administration in response to 1986-89 Monopolies and Mergers Commission inquiry into brewing. It describes the creation of big brewers, the official investigations into what many saw as an uncompetitive structure and the damaging consequences for consumers and licensees." (Publisher's note)

REVIEW: *Bus Hist Rev* v87 no3 p611-3 Aut 2013 Terence Gourvish

"Intervention in the Modern UK Brewing Industry." "This book is a straightforward account of political intervention in the British brewing industry, undertaken in the name of competition. The authors are all brewing industry insiders with three decades of experience behind them. . . . As a result, their account is authoritative and supported by ample statistical and regulatory information. . . . Inevitably, the main thrust of the book is on the background to the Thatcher Government's Beer Orders of 1989 . . . designed to enforce competitive change on an integrated industry. . . . While the book fails to engage very much with the available academic work . . . the general outcome is a valuable case study in economic regulation."

WALTON, CALDER. Empire of Secrets; British Intelligence, the Cold War, and the Twilight of Empire; [by] Calder Walton 432 p. 2013 Overlook Hardcover

1. Cold War, 1945-1989 2. Great Britain—Colonies—History—20th century 3. Historical literature 4. Imperialism 5. Intelligence service—Great Britain
ISBN 1468307150; 9781468307153

SUMMARY: In this book, " intelligence historian Calder Walton reveals how Britain contributed largely silently yet stunningly effectively to the Cold War effort. . . . Mining recently declassified intelligence records, Walton uncovers this missing link in Britain's post-war history. He sheds new light on everything from violent counterinsurgencies fought by British forces in the jungles of Malaya and Kenya, to urban warfare campaigns conducted in Palestine and the Arabian Peninsula." (Publisher's note)

REVIEW: *Booklist* v110 no3 p6 O 1 2013 Adam Morgan

REVIEW: *Hist Today* v64 no3 p64 Mr 2014 Taylor Downing

"Empire of Secrets: British Intelligence, the Cold War and the Twilight of Empire." "Calder Walton is well suited to write such a book. . . . He has used with great flair a mountain of top secret records that were only recently declassified. . . . Walton is good at making connections. One that clearly comes across is the progression from the Government Code and Cypher School at Bletchley Park to the postwar GCHQ. . . . Walton asks some big questions. What is Intelligence for? What evidence does it generate? . . . With 'Empire of Secrets,' Calder Walton has produced a scholarly and highly readable book that provides a fascinating background to the development of the secret intelligence networks in Britain."

REVIEW: *Kirkus Rev* v81 no21 p12 N 1 2013

REVIEW: *London Rev Books* v35 no6 p21-2 Mr 21 2013 Bernard Porter

REVIEW: *Publ Wkly* v260 no38 p71 S 23 2013

WALTON, EUGENE. Philip Reid saves the statue of freedom. See Lapham, S. S.

WALTON, JO, 1947-. My real children; [by] Jo Walton 320 p. 2014 Tor

1. Alternate histories (Fiction) 2. Identity (Psychology)—Fiction 3. Memory—Fiction 4. Speculative fiction 5. Women—Fiction
ISBN 0765332655; 9780765332653 (hardcover)
LC 2013-029673

SUMMARY: In this novel by Jo Walton, "Patricia Cowan is very old. 'Confused today,' read the notes clipped to the end of her bed. She forgets things she should know—what year it is, major events in the lives of her children. But she remembers things that don't seem possible. She remembers marrying Mark and having four children. . . . Jo Walton's 'My Real Children' is the tale of both of Patricia Cowan's lives . . . and of how every life means the entire world." (Publisher's note)

REVIEW: *Kirkus Rev* v82 no7 p230 Ap 1 2014

REVIEW: *Libr J* v139 no7 p62 Ap 15 2014 Megan M. McArdle

REVIEW: *Publ Wkly* v261 no13 p45 Mr 31 2014

REVIEW: *Quill Quire* v80 no2 p31 Mr 2014 Robert J. Wiersema

"What Makes This Book So Great? Re-Reading the Classics of Science Fiction and Fantasy" and "My Real Children". "What Makes This Book So Great' follows two-and-a-half years of [Jo] Walton's rereading. The book gathers 130 mini-essays, originally appearing on the blog of her publisher, Tor. Because of their origin, the pieces are casual and conversational rather than formal. . . . This is, perhaps, the book's greatest strength. . . . It is unclear whether Walton has wrapped a literary novel around SF tropes, or crafted a subtle genre novel featuring achingly beautiful prose and carefully crafted characters. Ultimately, it doesn't matter. Walton has created an SF story focused on characters and informed by the world around them. 'My Real Children' is the rarest sort of novel—one that transcends genre."

WALTON, JO, 1947-. What Makes This Book So Great; Re-reading the classics of science fiction and fantasy; [by] Jo Walton 448 p. 2014 Tor

1. Books and reading—United States 2. Fantasy fiction, American—History and criticism 3. Fiction genres 4. Literature—History & criticism 5. Science fiction, American—History and criticism
ISBN 0765331934; 9780765331939 (hardback)
LC 2013-028170

SUMMARY: "This collection gathers 130 of [novelist Jo] Walton's blog posts from science fiction site Tor.com about her favorites works of sci-fi and fantasy. . . . The themes of the essays interweave . . . many are meditations on the genre as a whole more than reviews of specific works, and Walton often ties her points back to earlier posts." (Publishers Weekly)

REVIEW: *Booklist* v110 no8 p30 D 15 2013 Roland Green

REVIEW: *Libr J* v139 no1 p1 Ja 2014 Megan McArdle

REVIEW: *Publ Wkly* v260 no47 p46 N 18 2013

REVIEW: *Quill Quire* v80 no2 p31 Mr 2014 Robert J. Wiersema

"What Makes This Book So Great? Re-Reading the Classics of Science Fiction and Fantasy" and "My Real Children". "What Makes This Book So Great' follows two-and-a-half years of [Jo] Walton's rereading. The book gathers 130 mini-essays, originally appearing on the blog of her publisher, Tor. Because of their origin, the pieces are casual and conversational rather than formal. . . . This is, perhaps, the book's greatest strength. . . . It is unclear whether Walton has wrapped a literary novel around SF tropes, or crafted a subtle genre novel featuring achingly beautiful prose and carefully crafted characters. Ultimately, it doesn't matter. Walton has created an SF story focused on characters and informed by the world around them. 'My Real Children' is the rarest sort of novel—one that transcends genre."

WALTON, LESLYE. The Strange and beautiful sorrows of Ava Lavender; [by] Leslye Walton 320 p. 2014 Candlewick Press

1. Families—Fiction 2. Love stories 3. Mothers & daughters—Fiction 4. Speculative fiction 5. Supernatural
ISBN 0763665665; 9780763665661
LC 2013-946615

SUMMARY: In this book, by Leslye Walton, "Ava—in all other ways a normal girl—is born with the wings of a bird. . . . Sixteen-year old Ava ventures into the wider world, ill-prepared for what she might discover and naive to the twisted motives of others. Others like the pious Nathaniel Sorrows, who mistakes Ava for an angel and whose obsession with her grows until the night of the summer solstice celebration." (Publisher's note)

REVIEW: *Booklist* v110 no13 p72 Mr 1 2014 Kara Dean

REVIEW: *Bull Cent Child Books* v67 no9 p482-3 My 2014 K. C.

"The Strange & Beautiful Sorrows of Ava Lavender". "This remarkable, magic-laced family history continues and spreads to other members of Ava's Seattle neighborhood to produce a gauzy narrative of love and loss, heavily tipped toward loss as relationships flounder on the shoals of misunderstanding, greed, and obsession, with Ava herself ultimately suffering rape and mutilation. . . . Sensibility overrides sense in this intentionally artful tale; though the ethereal nature of the storytelling is appealing, it occludes narrative clarity and cohesion, and the result is a mood without an object."

REVIEW: *Kirkus Rev* v82 no4 p56 F 15 2014

"The Strange and Beautiful Sorrows of Ava Lavender". " Lyrical magical realism paints four generations of women with tragic lives until a shocking violation fixes everything. . . . The story's language is gorgeous: 'I turned and spread my wings open, as wide as they would go, feeling the wind comb its cold fingers through my feathers.' Disturbingly, a horrific assault acts as the vehicle of redemption, magically bringing people together for reasons that make sense only in the dreamlike metaphysics of literary device. Gorgeous prose for readers willing to be blindsided."

REVIEW: *Publ Wkly* v260 no52 p54 D 23 2013

REVIEW: *SLJ* v60 no2 p116 F 2014 Jill Heritage Maza

REVIEW: *SLJ* v60 no6 p69 Je 2014 Ann Weber

WALTZ, TOM. Teenage Mutant Ninja Turtles. See Lynch, B.

WALVIN, JAMES. Crossings; Africa, the Americas and the Atlantic Slave Trade; [by] James Walvin 256 p. 2013 University of Chicago Press

1. Antislavery movements 2. Emancipation of slaves 3. Historical literature 4. Slave trade—History 5. Slavery—History

ISBN 1780231946; 9781780231945

SUMMARY: In this book on the Atlantic slave trade, "the author stresses the role played by Africans during the ages of slavery and emancipation, arguing that through their agency and resistance, Africans had a tremendous impact on the development of slavery and its ensuing demise. He also examines abolition and the continued efforts to eradicate the trade throughout the 19th century." (Choice: Current Reviews for Academic Libraries)

REVIEW: *Choice* v51 no7 p1279-80 Mr 2014 J. Rankin

"Crossings: Africa, the Americas and the Atlantic Slave Trade." "[James] Walvin . . . offers a valuable synthesis of the Atlantic slave trade, the development and practice of slavery in the New World, and the challenges and motives for eventual abolition. The author takes a broad perspective, weaving the British, French, Portuguese, and US experiences, contributions, and level of involvement into a seamless narrative. . . . The monograph closes with a thought-provoking essay on slavery in the modern world. It provides one of the most thorough evaluations of slavery and emancipation, and its scope and presentation make it valuable to a wide audience, including scholars, students, and general readers."

WANG XI.ed. Dictionary of environmental and climate change law. See Dictionary of environmental and climate change law

WANG, XIAOJUE, 1973-. Modernity with a cold war face; reimagining the nation in Chinese literature across the 1949 divide; [by] Xiaojue Wang 359 p. 2013 Harvard University Asia Center

1. China—History—20th century 2. Chinese literature—20th century—History and criticism 3. Cold War in literature 4. Literature—History & criticism 5. Modernism (Literature)—China

ISBN 9780674726727 (hardcover: acid-free paper)

LC 2013-007732

SUMMARY: This book "examines the competing, converging, and conflicting modes of envisioning a modern nation in mid-twentieth century Chinese literature. Bridging the 1949 divide in both literary historical periodization and political demarcation, Xiaojue Wang proposes a new framework to consider Chinese literature beyond national boundaries, as something arising out of the larger global geopolitical and cultural conflict of the Cold War." (Publisher's note)

REVIEW: *Choice* v51 no8 p1395-6 Ap 2014 P. F. Williams

"Modernity With a Cold War Face: Reimagining the Nation in Chinese Literature Across the 1949 Divide". "[Xiaojue] Wang magnifies the importance of the Gold War to modern Chinese literary studies by focusing on post-WW II literary criticism, to the near exclusion of literary criticism in pre-war decades. She also pushes back the beginning of the Cold War six years so that it can include Mao Zedong's 1940 essay 'On New Democracy,' which—along with a 1953 Taiwan tract by Chiang Kai-shek and a 1958 Confucian manifesto in Hong Kong—serves as her fountainhead of Chinese Cold War discourse. Wang concludes with an anticlimactic call for 'de-Cold War criticism' that will not brook 'sentimental' dissent "against the state machine.""

WARBY, ANNA.tr. Aurora / Cardinal Point. See Leiris, M.

WARD, CHARLES B. Who's bigger? See Skiena, S.

WARD, JOSEPH P. London; a social and cultural history, 1550-1750; [by] Joseph P. Ward 413 p. 2012 Cambridge University Press

1. HISTORY—Europe—Great Britain 2. Historical literature

ISBN 9780521896528 (hardback)

LC 2011-050687

SUMMARY: This book presents a social and cultural history of London, England. "Between 1550 and 1750 London became the greatest city in Europe and one of the most vibrant economic and cultural centers in the world. This book is a history of London during this crucial period of its rise to world-wide prominence, during which it dominated the economic, political, social and cultural life of the British Isles." (Publisher's note)

REVIEW: *Choice* v50 no4 p745 D 2012 G. F. Steckley

REVIEW: *Engl Hist Rev* v129 no536 p209-10 F 2014 P. Gauci

"London: A Social and Cultural History, 1550-1750". "This book reflects both the insight and enjoyment which two leading scholars of early modern England have derived from their engagement with London's history. . . . Robert Bucholz and Joseph Ward have achieved their aim of writing an accessible work which will be of particular value to newcomers to metropolitan history. Although they modestly declare it to be a work of synthesis, their complementary specialist interests also ensure plenty of stimulating commentary for the more established London observer. . . . Their most welcome innovation is to encompass a period which transcends the conventional historical divides of 1660 or 1700."

WARD, LINDSAY. Please bring balloons; [by] Lindsay Ward 32 p. 2013 Dial Books for Young Readers

1. Adventure and adventurers—Fiction 2. Balloons 3. Children's stories 4. Merry-go-round—Fiction 5. Polar bear—Fiction
ISBN 9780803738782 (hardcover)
LC 2012-033588

SUMMARY: This children's book by Lindsay Ward, shows how "Every day can be an adventure. Especially if you bring balloons. Ever wondered what it would be like to ride a carousel right off its platform? As Emma discovers, all it takes is a handful of balloons and a very kind polar bear to show you the way. This soaring story of friendship . . . will take readers to the arctic and back--in time for bedtime, of course--and remind them anything is possible." (Publisher's note)

REVIEW: *Booklist* v110 no5 p86 N 1 2013 Ann Kelly

REVIEW: *Kirkus Rev* v81 no16 p150 Ag 15 2013

REVIEW: *N Y Times Book Rev* p16 Ja 12 2014 SARAH HARRISON SMITH

"Cub's Big World," "The Hiccup," and "Please Bring Balloons." "Pleasingly realistic yet reassuringly sweet, 'Cub's Big World' follows a young polar bear on her first trip out of the cozy snow cave the shares with her mother. . . . [Author and illustrator Ingrid] Sissung's freewheeling story ['The Hiccup'] delivers justice in the end for the teaser and the teased. . . . [Author and illustrator Lindsay] Ward, a cut-paper artist, gives her book great visual appeal with snippets of colorful origami paper, calendars and maps."

REVIEW: *Publ Wkly* v260 no38 p77 S 23 2013

REVIEW: *SLJ* v59 no9 p135 S 2013 Jenna Boles

WARD, SIMON. Intervention in the modern UK brewing industry. See Walters, J.

WARD, YVONNE M. Censoring Queen Victoria; How Two Gentlemen Edited a Queen and Created an Icon; [by] Yvonne M. Ward 224 p. 2014 Pgw

1. Benson, Arthur Christopher 2. Editors—History 3. Esher, Reginald Baliol Brett, Viscount, 1852-1930 4. Historical literature 5. Letters—History 6. Victoria, Queen of Great Britain, 1819-1901
ISBN 1780743637; 9781780743639

SUMMARY: This book describes how "after Victoria's death, in 1901, Reginald Brett (Lord Esher) and Arthur Benson, two eccentric, relatively minor, and fundamentally ill-suited court factotums, were assigned the task of editing the queen's voluminous correspondence. . . . [Yvonne] Ward presents the story of these men and their multilayered motivations for censoring out the all-too-human woman, wife, and mother hovering within the revered icon." (Booklist)

REVIEW: *Booklist* v110 no12 p16 F 15 2014 Margaret Flanagan

REVIEW: *Kirkus Rev* v82 no5 p45 Mr 1 2014

"Censoring Queen Victoria: How Two Gentlemen Edited a Queen and Created an Icon". "An Australian historian's study of the two men who edited Queen Victoria's letters and how their methods and choices affected posterity's view of her. . . . In her analysis of these two biographers, [Yvonne] Ward examines the complex working relationship between them. . . . Rich in intrigue, Ward's book offers not only an enlightening look at the two men who defined Queen Victoria to the future, but also the ways that notions about gender influenced early-20th-century biographical portraiture."

REVIEW: *Publ Wkly* v261 no1 p41 Ja 6 2014

WARE, CHRIS. Building stories; [by] Chris Ware p. cm. 2012 Pantheon Books

1. Apartment buildings—Fiction 2. Apartment dwellers 3. Graphic novels 4. Loneliness 5. Married people—Fiction
ISBN 9780375424335
LC 2012-007946

SUMMARY: This graphic novel by Chris Ware, assembled as separate pieces in a box, "imagines the inhabitants of a three-story Chicago apartment building: a 30-something woman who has yet to find someone with whom to spend the rest of her life; a couple, possibly married, who wonder if they can bear each other's company another minute; and the building's landlady, an elderly woman who has lived alone for decades. . . . 'Building Stories' is a book with no deliberate beginning nor end." (Publisher's note)

REVIEW: *Booklist* v109 no2 p58 S 15 2012

REVIEW: *Booklist* v109 no13 p43 Mr 1 2013

REVIEW: *Kirkus Rev* p41 N 15 2012 Best Fiction & Children's Books

REVIEW: *Kirkus Rev* v80 no15 p438 Ag 1 2012

REVIEW: *Libr J* v139 no1 p1 Ja 2014

REVIEW: *London Rev Books* v34 no23 p19-20 D 6 2012 Nick Richardson

REVIEW: *N Y Rev Books* v59 no20 p66-9 D 20 2012 Gabriel Winslow-Yost

"Building Stories." "[Chris] Ware's drawings are meticulous, even chilly, with flat, muted colors and the straight lines and perfect curves of an architectural rendering. The panels follow an orderly horizontal grid, but have a discomfiting tendency to occasionally shrink to near illegibility; or they might suddenly demand to be read from right to left, or even disappear entirely, to be replaced by pretty but unhelpful typography . . . complicated diagrams, or plans for a paper model of one of the stories' locations. . . . Throughout 'Building Stories,' Ware's attention to the awkward physicality, the constant humiliations and cruelties of human existence is as precise and as brutally funny as it is in his previous work."

REVIEW: *N Y Times Book Rev* p11 D 9 2012

REVIEW: *N Y Times Book Rev* p22 O 28 2012

REVIEW: *N Y Times Book Rev* p1 O 21 2012 DOUGLAS WOLK

REVIEW: *New York Times* p34 N 23 2012 THE NEW

YORK TIMES

REVIEW: *Publ Wkly* v259 no25 p27 Je 18 2012

REVIEW: *Publ Wkly* v259 no26 p158 Je 25 2012

REVIEW: *Time* v180 no16 p52 O 15 2012 LEV GROSSMAN DOUGLAS WOLK

REVIEW: *Yale Rev* v101 no4 p148-59 O 2013 AMY HUNGERFORD

"Building Stories." "Upon raising the lid, the reader becomes ambitious to move beyond delighted curiosity (everyone who sees the box wants to open it) to serious reading. This takes commitment: the fourteen elements entice with color and shape, but 'Building Stories' requires the same number of hours demanded by a regular novel. Readers who can't make the time to read it may find it all too easy to give the beautiful thing away. But they shouldn't be too quick to give up or give away. The rewards of reading 'Building Stories,' and reading it in a way that attends to its special form, are significant."

WARNECKE, TONIA L.ed. Handbook of research on gender and economic life. See Handbook of research on gender and economic life

WARNER, JOEL. The humor code. See McGraw, P.

WARNER, MALCOLM.ed. The Oxford handbook of management theorists. See The Oxford handbook of management theorists

WARNER, MARINA, 1946-. Stranger magic; charmed states and The Arabian nights; [by] Marina Warner xx, 540 p. 2012 Belknap Press of Harvard University Press

1. Literature—History & criticism 2. Magic in literature 3. Myth in literature 4. Orientalism
ISBN 0701173319 (hbk.); 9780701173319 (hbk.); 0674055306; 9780674055308 (alk. paper)
LC 2011-047124

SUMMARY: This book on the Arabian Nights by Marina Warner "has a double mission: On the one hand, the author traces . . . why the 'Nights' held such potent sway over figures like [Samuel Taylor] Coleridge, becoming a runaway best seller in Europe and retaining a lock grip over the Western imagination for generations. But she also shows why its themes and preoccupations remain relevant today." (Bookforum)

REVIEW: *Choice* v49 no12 p2274 Ag 2012 S. Gomaa

REVIEW: *N Y Rev Books* v61 no5 p37-9 Mr 20 2014 Patricia Storace

"Stranger Magic: Charmed States and the Arabian Nights" and "One Thousand and One Nights". "Two recent books by Marina Warner and the Lebanese novelist Hanan al- Shaykh confirm the continuing power of this work. . . . Stranger Magic is an unabashedly joyful work of scholarship, a study of the history of the human imagination as it shapes and reinvents reality through stories. . . . Warner's rich, diffuse, and unconventional scholarship is as much a retelling of the Arabian Nights tales as the novelist Hanan al-Shaykh's, though Warner tells the stories as they unfold in history. Al-Shaykh's charming versions were first conceived as a play. . . . The resulting book shows traces of its theatrical origin and the ingenious techniques al-Shaykh has used to maneuver the limitless scope of the tales into a form that fits the constraints \ imposed by theater."

REVIEW: *Women's Review of Books* v30 no3 p8-11 My/Je 2013 Rebecca Steinitz

WARNER, RICHARD. Unauthorized access; the crisis in online privacy and security; [by] Richard Warner 374 p. 2014 CRC Press, Taylor & Francis Group

1. Computer security 2. Data protection 3. Internet—Moral and ethical aspects 4. Privacy, Right of 5. Technical literature
ISBN 1439830134 (alk. paper); 9781439830130 (alk. paper)
LC 2013-003387

SUMMARY: This book by Robert H. Sloan and Richard Waner "proposes specific solutions to public policy issues pertaining to online privacy and security. . . . The authors also discuss how rapid technological developments have created novel situations that lack relevant norms and present ways to develop these norms for protecting informational privacy and ensuring sufficient information security." (Publisher's note)

REVIEW: *Choice* v51 no8 p1440-1 Ap 2014 J. Beidler

"Unauthorized Access: The Crisis in Online Privacy and Security". "A guide though the thicket of contradictions and trade-offs in this area. The book grew out of a course that the authors jointly taught to computer science students and law students, focusing on the legal issues of privacy and security for the former audience and the complexity of computer science for the latter. An overriding theme is making trade-offs, which is a central focus in the first chapter. The well-written collection of 12 chapters starts with the basics of computing, networking, and data mining, and proceeds through systems vulnerabilities, attacks, and defenses, all within the perspectives of costs (economy), law, social engineering, and public policy."

WARREN, ELIZABETH, 1949-. A fighting chance; [by] Elizabeth Warren 384 p. 2014 Metropolitan, Henry Holt & Co.

1. Biography (Literary form) 2. Legislators—United States—Biography 3. Women legislators—United States—Biography
ISBN 1627790527; 9781627790529 (hardcover)
LC 2014-000776

SUMMARY: This book by Elizabeth Warren tells the "story of the two-decade journey that taught her how Washington really works—and really doesn't. . . . She fought for better bankruptcy laws for ten years and lost. She tried to hold the federal government accountable during the financial crisis but became a target of the big banks. . . . Finally, at age 62, she decided to run for elective office and won the most competitive—and watched—Senate race in the country." (Publisher's note)

REVIEW: *Booklist* v110 no16 p5 Ap 15 2014 Vanessa Bush

REVIEW: *Christ Century* v131 no14 p43 Jl 9 2014

REVIEW: *Kirkus Rev* v82 no8 p161 Ap 15 2014

REVIEW: *Libr J* v139 no12 p46 Jl 1 2014 Heather Malcolm

REVIEW: *Libr J* v139 no9 p93 My 15 2014 Jill Ortner

REVIEW: *N Y Rev Books* v61 no9 p4-8 My 22 2014 John Cassidy

REVIEW: *N Y Times Book Rev* p34 My 11 2014 GREGORY COWLES

REVIEW: *N Y Times Book Rev* p22 My 4 2014

REVIEW: *N Y Times Book Rev* p34 My 11 2014

REVIEW: *N Y Times Book Rev* p13 Ap 27 2014 AMY CHOZICK

REVIEW: *New Yorker* v90 no9 p96-1 Ap 21 2014

"A Fighting Chance." "Elizabeth Warren has a case to make about what bankers do with other people's money; she's been making it for twenty-five years. It's hardly uncontested, but it rests on collaborative, peer-reviewed, empirical research. . . . In 'A Fighting Chance,' Warren argues that the federal government has allowed an unregulated financial industry to prey on the middle class; she also writes no small amount about peach cobbler and burned frying pans. Still, she is not adorable; instead, she's fierce in her affections. . . . Warren is also smart enough to use the conventions of political biography, old and new, to insist on the existence of a relationship between caring for other people and caring about politics."

REVIEW: *Publ Wkly* v261 no30 p87 Jl 28 2014

REVIEW: *Publ Wkly* v261 no18 p12 My 5 2014

WARREN, PAIGE S.ed. Urban bird ecology and conservation. See Urban bird ecology and conservation

WARREN, TRACY ANNE. The Last Man on Earth; [by] Tracy Anne Warren 352 p. 2014 Penguin Group USA

1. Advertising—Fiction 2. Competition (Psychology) 3. Love stories 4. Secrecy—Fiction 5. Workplace romance
ISBN 0451466004; 9780451466006

SUMMARY: This romance novel by Tracy Anne Warren describes how "When a hot promotion pops up at their company, both Zack and Madelyn wind up on the short list for the position. But as the two square off, they discover that being heated rivals in the office makes for scorching bed play behind closed doors. Will Madelyn's steamy, secret affair with Mr. Vice make her compromise her ideals--or worse, lose her heart?" (Publisher's note)

REVIEW: *Booklist* v110 no9/10 p58 Ja 1 2014 Patricia Smith

REVIEW: *N Y Times Book Rev* p30 F 9 2014 Sarah MacLean

"The Luckiest Lady in London," "The Perfect Match," and "The Last Man on Earth." "[Author Sherry] Thomas is known for a lush style that demonstrates her love of her second language, and ['The Luckiest Lady in London'] edges into historical fiction with its transporting prose even as it delivers on heat and emotion and a well-earned happily ever after. . . . In 'The Perfect Match' . . . [author Kristan] Higgins offers readers a journey filled with tears and laughter and the best kind of sighs. . . . Few things are more fun than an enemies-to-lovers romance, and [author Tracy Anne] Warren delivers with 'The Last Man on Earth.'"

REVIEW: *Publ Wkly* v260 no45 p56 N 11 2013

WARSHAW, SHIRLEY ANNE. A guide to the White House staff; [by] Shirley Anne Warshaw 488 p. 2013 CQ Press

1. Historical literature 2. Political science literature 3. Presidents—United States—History 4. Presidents—United States—Staff 5. Public administration—United States
ISBN 160426604X; 9781604266047 (cloth)
LC 2012-045661

SUMMARY: This book by Shirley Anne Warshaw "provides a study of executive-legislative relations, organizational behavior, policy making, and White House-cabinet relations. It also makes an important contribution to the study of public administration." It "explores the statutes, executive orders, and a succession of reorganization plans that have helped shape and refine the EOP [Executive Office of the President]." (Publisher's note)

REVIEW: *Booklist* v110 no1 p62 S 1 2013 Brian Odom

REVIEW: *Choice* v51 no2 p242 O 2013 R. V. Labaree

"A Guide to the White House Staff." "[Author Shirley Anne] Warshaw . . . here documents the history and composition of the staffing and advisory structures surrounding the US presidency. Part I's chapters describe White House staffing history and the president's increasing authority to appoint personnel. . . . Part 2 comprises five chapters that focus on staffing patterns from 1939 to the present. . . . This companion to 'Guide to the Presidency and the Executive Branch,' edited by Michael Nelson . . . , fills an important gap in readers' understanding of the White House's staffing and advisory structure and its evolving role in shaping policy."

REVIEW: *Libr J* v138 no10 p140 Je 1 2013 Judy Quinn

WASDIN, HOWARD E. I am a SEAL Team Six warrior; memoirs of an American soldier; [by] Howard E. Wasdin vi, 182 p. 2012 St. Martin's Griffin

1. Black Hawk Friendly Fire Incident, Iraq, 1994 2. Memoirs 3. Mogadishu (Somalia)—History 4. Persian Gulf War, 1991 5. Snipers—United States—Biography—Juvenile literature 6. United States. Navy. SEALs 7. Veterans—Wounds & injuries
ISBN 1250016436 (paperback); 9781250016430 (paperback)
LC 2012-376658

SUMMARY: This book offers an "[a]bridged, . . . young-readers version of an ex-SEAL sniper's account ('SEAL Team Six,' 2011) of his training and combat experiences in Operation Desert Storm and the first Battle of Mogadishu. . . . In later chapters he retraces his long, difficult physical and emotional recovery from serious wounds received during the 'Black Hawk Down' operation, his increasing focus on faith and family after divorce and remarriage and his second career as a chiropractor." (Kirkus Reviews)

REVIEW: *Booklist* v108 no16 p52 Ap 15 2012 Ian Chipman

REVIEW: *Kirkus Rev* v80 no7 p755 Ap 1 2012

"I Am a Seal Team Six Warrior: Memoirs of an American Soldier." "Abridged but not toned down, this young-readers version of an ex-SEAL sniper's account ('SEAL Team Six,' 2011) of his training and combat experiences in Operation Desert Storm and the first Battle of Mogadishu makes colorful, often compelling reading. . . . He tears into the Clinton administration, . . . indecisive commanders and corrupt Italian "allies" for making such a hash of the entire Somalian mission. In [a] later chapter . . . he retraces his long, difficult physical and emotional recovery from serious wounds received during the 'Black Hawk Down' operation. . . . Fans of all things martial will echo his 'HOOYAH!'--but the troubled aftermath comes in for some attention too."

REVIEW: *SLJ* v58 no8 p116 Ag 2012 Erik Carlson

WASHBURN, ALEXANDROS. The nature of urban design; a New York perspective on resilience; [by] Alexandros Washburn 264 p. 2013 Island Press

1. City planning—New York (State)—New York 2. City planning literature 3. Hurricane Sandy, 2012 4. New York (N.Y.) 5. Urban planners 6. Urban planning
ISBN 1610913809 (cloth : alk. paper); 9781610913805 (cloth : alk. paper)
LC 2013-014789

SUMMARY: "In this visually rich book, Alexandros Washburn, Chief Urban Designer of the New York Department of City Planning, redefines urban design. . . . Washburn draws heavily on his experience within the New York City planning system while highlighting forward-thinking developments in cities around the world. . . . Throughout the book, Washburn shows how a well-designed city can be the most efficient, equitable, safe, and enriching place on earth." (Publisher's note)

REVIEW: *Choice* v51 no8 p1391 Ap 2014 A. E. Lenoard

REVIEW: *N Y Times Book Rev* p85 D 8 2013 Clyde Haberman

"The Stories They Tell: Artifacts From the National September 11 Memorial Museum: A Journey of Remembrance," "The Nature of Urban Design: A New York Perspective on Resilience," and "Mapping Manhattan: A Love (and Sometimes Hate) Story in Maps by 75 New Yorkers." "Artifacts in this handsome 'journey of remembrance' are drawn from the museum that is part of New York's Sept. 11 memorial. The book matches photos with essays by museum staff members. . . . For [author Alexandros] Washburn . . . the ruination inflicted by Hurricane Sandy was intensely personal. . . . This book may appeal more to students of urban policy than to general readers. . . . [Author Becky] Cooper, a cartographer, takes us on an entertaining journey."

REVIEW: *Publ Wkly* v260 no35 p53 S 2 2013

WASHINGTON, JOHN.tr. The beast. See Martinez, O.

WASHINGTON, MARY HELEN. The Other Blacklist; the African American Literary and Cultural Left of the 1950s; [by] Mary Helen Washington 368 p. 2014 Columbia University Press

1. African Americans—Intellectual life—20th century 2. American literature—20th century—History and criticism 3. American literature—African American authors—History and criticism 4. Cold War in literature 5. Historical literature 6. Politics and literature—United States—History—20th century 7. Right and left (Political science) in literature
ISBN 0231152701; 9780231152709
LC 2013-031563

SUMMARY: This book looks at six black artists who were suspected of communist activities during the Cold War. "They were all drawn to the Left's appreciation of black folk culture and support for the ideal of self-determination. . . . [Mary Helen] Washington profiles novelist and essayist Lloyd L. Brown, visual artist Charles White, playwright and novelist Alice Childress, poet and novelist Gwendolyn Brooks, novelist Frank London Brown, and novelist and activist Julian Mayfield." (Booklist)

REVIEW: *Booklist* v110 no11 p18 F 1 2014 Vanessa Bush

"The Other Blacklist: The African American Literary and Cultural Left of the 1950s". "Very little has been written about the black artists and writers who were surveilled, investigated, and blacklisted because of their beliefs and their work. Literary scholar [Mary Helen] Washington remedies that neglect with this engrossing look at six artists. . . . Tapping archival material, biographies, interviews, and FBI files,Washington examines his subjects' aesthetic and relationships with other writers and artists and the black community as well as their frustrations with and ambivalent feelings about the Left. Photographs of the artists and their works and pages from FBI files enhance this compelling look at artists and writers who became part of the vanguard of the progressive politics."

REVIEW: *Choice* v52 no2 p259-60 O 2014 J. W. Miller

REVIEW: *Publ Wkly* v261 no4 p180 Ja 27 2014

WASIK, JOHN F. Keynes's way to wealth; timeless investment lessons from the great economist; [by] John F. Wasik 195 p. 2013 McGraw-Hill

1. BUSINESS & ECONOMICS—Personal Finance—Investing 2. Finance literature 3. Investment analysis 4. Investments 5. Portfolio management
ISBN 0071815473 (hardback); 9780071815475 (hardback)
LC 2013-020008

SUMMARY: This book on personal investing offers advice based on the theories and financial history of economist John Maynard Keynes. Author John F. Wasik "explains that Keynes learned to be an effective investor the hard way. He made and lost two fortunes speculating on commodities and currency futures. After the second setback, he became what we would now call a buy-and-hold investor." (New York Times)

REVIEW: *New York Times* v163 no56379 p17 Ja 12 2014 PAUL B. BROWN

"Financially Fearless" and "Keynes's Way to Wealth". "If improving your net worth made your list of New Year's resolutions, two books . . . could help. . . . In her book, seemingly aimed at those in their 20s and early 30s—-and people who haven't' gotten around to planning their finances—Ms [Alexa]. Von Tobel argues that take-home pay should be divided into three parts. . . . This is not exactly a new idea. . . . But what is intriguing are her percentages. . . . Because she gives it so little attention, the investing advice is extremely general. . . . But if the book convinces people who've never mapped out a financial future to start doing so, it will have done its job. . . . And people looking for specific investing advice for 2014 and beyond could turn to . . . Keynes's Way to Wealth. . . . Mr. [John F. Wasik's] distillation of how Keynes made—and then remade—his fortune is instructive."

WASSER, LAURA A. It doesn't have to be that way; how to divorce without destroying your family or bankrupting yourself; [by] Laura A. Wasser 304 p. 2013 St. Martin's Press

1. Advice literature 2. Divorce—Law and legislation—United States—Popular works 3. Divorce—So-

cial aspects 4. Divorce suits—United States—Popular works 5. Divorced people—United States—Handbooks, manuals, etc

ISBN 1250029783; 9781250029782 (hardcover)
LC 2013-014469

SUMMARY: This book is a "step-by-step guide to divorce." Lawyer Laura Wasser "guides readers on the intricate process of separating from one's spouse while minimizing the emotional and financial harm to each other or to any children in the picture. . . . She emphasizes the need for communication so that the dissolution of the relationship is amicable and fair and causes the least amount of damage to all parties." (Kirkus Reviews)

REVIEW: *Kirkus Rev* v81 no16 p199 Ag 15 2013

"It Doesn't Have to Be That Way: How to Divorce Without Destroying Your Family or Bankrupting Yourself." "With more than 20 years of expertise, especially with celebrity clients, divorce lawyer [Laura] Wasser brings her considerable knowledge to the table and guides readers on the intricate process of separating from one's spouse while minimizing the emotional and financial harm to each other or to any children in the picture. Using examples from her celebrity clients and her own life to illustrate her points, Wasser's advice is relevant to same-sex couples, mixed-race couples and heterosexual relationships."

REVIEW: *Publ Wkly* v260 no30 p54 Jl 29 2013

WASSON, SAM. Fosse; [by] Sam Wasson 672 p. 2013 Houghton Mifflin Harcourt

1. BIOGRAPHY & AUTOBIOGRAPHY—Entertainment & Performing Arts 2. Biographies 3. Choreographers—Biography 4. Choreographers—United States—Biography 5. Dance—History 6. Fosse, Bob, 1927-1987 7. Motion picture producers & directors 8. PERFORMING ARTS—Individual Director (see also BIOGRAPHY & AUTOBIOGRAPHY—Entertainment & Performing Arts) 9. PERFORMING ARTS—Theater—Broadway & Musical Revue 10. PERFORMING ARTS—Theater—History & Criticism

ISBN 0547553293; 9780547553290
LC 2013-026082

SUMMARY: This book, by Sam Wasson, presents a biography of choreographer and director Bob Fosse. "Fosse revolutionized nearly every facet of American entertainment, forever marking Broadway and Hollywood with his iconic style--hat tilted, fingers splayed--that would influence generations of performing artists. Yet in spite of Fosse's innumerable achievements, no accomplishment ever seemed to satisfy him, and offstage his life was shadowed in turmoil and anxiety." (Publisher's note)

REVIEW: *Bookforum* v20 no4 p44 D 2013/Ja 2014 BEN SCHWARTZ

"Fosse." "A well of self-serving rationalizations, [Bob] Fosse blamed those wicked strippers for the decades of sexual deception, manipulation, and harassment of women to come. It's here that readers will take Sam Wasson seriously--or elect not to. Wasson agrees with Fosse portraying the women as sexual monsters who set Fosse on his road to ruin. Wasson's done solid reporting in documenting Fosse's career over an impressive range of time. In 2013, however, Wasson's apologia for Fosse's lifetime of piggery is a hard sell. Wasson's (and Fosse's) further argument that sex with the director actually improved his dancers' work (it's that director-performer intimacy, you see) is ridiculous."

REVIEW: *Booklist* v110 no2 p13 S 15 2013 David Pitt

REVIEW: *Commentary* v137 no4 p67-9 Ap 2014 TERRY TEACHOUT

REVIEW: *Film Q* v67 no2 p99-100 Wint 2013 ED SIKOV

REVIEW: *Kirkus Rev* v81 no19 p110 O 1 2013

REVIEW: *Libr J* v138 no11 p64 Je 15 2013 Barbara Hoffert

REVIEW: *N Y Times Book Rev* p49 D 8 2013 JOHN MCWHORTER

"Fosse." "[Author Sam] Wasson . . . explains [choreographer Bob] Fosse's achievement in prose that apparently is meant to summon the spirit of a Fosse show. That spirit includes a melodramatic 'behind the music' quality that will turn off as many readers as it delights. . . But Wasson's narrative style--let's call it snazzy--often captures the theatrical feel of Fosse's work at its height. A stage choreographer was the last thing this working-class kid from Chicago, who grew up in the Depression and hid the fact that he took ballet lessons from his classmates, wanted to become."

REVIEW: *New York Times* v163 no56313 pC1-7 N 7 2013 JANET MASLIN

REVIEW: *New Yorker* v89 no41 p87-1 D 16 2013

"Fosse." "At sixteen, he became the youngest m.c. on the seedy Chicago burlesque circuit, and was both inspired and traumatized by 'the girls, the failures, and the slimeballs.' Girls are the shaping force in [Author Sam] Wasson's thorough and lively biography, and, in seven hundred pages, there are many. [Choreographer Bob] Fosse's second wife got him out of night clubs and made him a choreographer; his third pushed him to become a director. Although he pioneered a distinctive and witty style of dancing, his biggest fear was that his 'razzle-dazzle' would be exposed as a con."

REVIEW: *Publ Wkly* v260 no38 p2 S 23 2013

REVIEW: *Sight Sound* v24 no5 p106 My 2014 Nick Pinkerton

THE WATERGATE MEMOIRS OF GORDON WALTER; 178 p. 2013 Christopher Matthews Publishing

1. Agnew, Spiro T., 1918-1996 2. Humorous stories 3. Nixon, Richard M. (Richard Milhous), 1913-1994 4. United States—Politics & government—1969-1974 5. Watergate Affair, 1972-1974

ISBN 1938985095; 9781938985096

SUMMARY: This fictional memoir chronicles Richard Nixon's presidency through the eyes of his secret assistant and operative, Gordon Walter. "Walter proved his worth by helping Nixon make off with a few cases of an admiral's whiskey for a party. From that moment on, whenever he needed a little covert help behind the scenes, Nixon turned to his old friend. As Nixon's political career took off, he found himself calling on Walter's services again and again, especially after he became president." (Kirkus Reviews)

REVIEW: *Kirkus Rev* p55-6 D 15 2013 supplemet best books 2013

"The Wategate Memoirs of Gordon Walter". "The fictional, humorous life and times of Gordon Walter, Richard Nixon's top-secret right-hand man. . . . As edited by Alaric Thistle, this debut fictional memoir is an uproarious take on the [Richard] Nixon years as seen from the inside. There are ample laughs throughout the book, but some sections stand out, especially Walter and Agnew's covert trip to England and Germany to bolster the vice president's foreign policy-making skills and Walter's experience tailing Nixon's burglars while they attempt to nab Ellsberg's psychiatric file from his doctor's office. Walter and Nixon's imagined plotting lends a humorous slant to real-life historical events, and Walter himself is a great character—wry, licentious but with a stubborn loyal streak."

REVIEW: *Kirkus Rev* v81 no21 p68 N 1 2013

WATERHOUSE, MICHAEL. Edwardian Requiem; A Life of Sir Edward Grey; [by] Michael Waterhouse 448 p. 2013 Biteback

1. Biographies 2. Great Britain—Politics & government—1901-1936 3. Grey of Fallodon, Edward Grey, Viscount, 1862-1933 4. Politicians—Biography 5. World War, 1914-1918—Causes

ISBN 1849544433; 9781849544436

SUMMARY: This book presents a biography of British statesman Sir Edward Grey, who "spent nearly thirty years in Parliament and only reluctantly became Foreign Secretary. . . . Yet it was a position he filled for more than a decade, the longest anyone has ever served continuously in his or any age. . . . During this time he battled relentlessly to protect and advance the interests of his country against the volatile backdrop of a Europe in which the balance of power was tilting wildly." (Publisher's note)

REVIEW: *Hist Today* v63 no9 p59 S 2013 IAN CAWOOD

"Edwardian Requiem: A Life of Sir Edward Grey." "Michael Waterhouse . . . makes a sustained effort in his new study to cement Grey's claim to greatness. . . . Of course the book is dominated by the July Crisis of 1914. . . . It is a complex issue and Waterhouse navigates it patiently, with Grey emerging almost totally exonerated. There are problems with the book, however. The structure is sometimes frustrating, with chapters digressing far beyond the years they claim to cover. There is a lot of prurient speculation as to Grey's sex life. . . . Despite these misgivings Waterhouse is to be congratulated for presenting such a fully rounded portrait of a man unfairly accused of leading Britain into the most disastrous war in modern history."

REVIEW: *New Statesman* v142 no5155 p48-9 Ap 26 2013 Andrew Adonis

WATERMAN, STEPHANIE J.ed. Beyond the asterisk. See Beyond the asterisk

WATERS, ALYSON.tr. Take a closer look. See Arasse, D.

WATERSTON, ELIZABETH HILLMAN.ed. The Complete Journals of L.M. Montgomery. See The Complete Journals of L.M. Montgomery

WATKINS, PATRICIA. The Wayward Gentleman; John Theophilus Potter & The Smock Alley Theatre; [by] Patricia Watkins 322 p. 2012 Down Design Publications

1. Actors—Fiction 2. Historical fiction 3. Nobility (Social class)—Great Britain—Fiction 4. Sheridan, Thomas 5. Theater—Ireland—History

ISBN 0957210477; 9780957210479

SUMMARY: In this book by Patricia Watkins, "an 18th-century 'gentleman player' fights, loves and charms his way through Ireland. . . . He becomes enamored with the theater as a precocious child growing up on a country estate outside Dublin, where he's raised to be a gentleman. In 18th-century Ireland, however, propriety forbade gentlemen from performing onstage, a custom gradually being reversed by the likes of Thomas Sheridan—a real actor who features prominently in Theo's story." (Kirkus Reviews)

REVIEW: *Kirkus Rev* v82 no4 p8 F 15 2014

"The Wayward Gentleman: John Theophilus Potter & The Smock Alley Theatre". "An 18th-century 'gentleman player' fights, loves and charms his way through Ireland in [Patricia] Watkins' . . . delightful ode to the theater. . . . The novel's plot is as restless as its protagonist, resulting in a compelling narrative with a few hastily introduced and dropped characters and storylines. Like the picaresque novels this one emulates, Watkins' story isn't too concerned with psychology; readers know little about Theo's internal state. . . . But it is nonetheless a vivid historical envisioning."

REVIEW: *Kirkus Rev* v81 no24 p363 D 15 2013

"The Wayward Gentleman: John Theophilus Potter & The Smock Alley Theatre". "An 18th-century 'gentleman player' fights, loves and charms his way through Ireland in [Patricia] Watkins' . . . delightful ode to the theater. . . . The novel's plot is as restless as its protagonist, resulting in a compelling narrative with a few hastily introduced and dropped characters and storylines. Like the picaresque novels this one emulates, Watkins' story isn't too concerned with psychology; readers know little about Theo's internal state. . . . But it is nonetheless a vivid historical envisioning."

WATKINS, PHILIP C. Gratitude and the good life; toward a psychology of appreciation; [by] Philip C. Watkins 240 p. 2013 Springer Berlin Heidelberg

1. Gratitude 2. Gratitude—Psychological aspects 3. Happiness 4. Psychological literature 5. Self-realization

ISBN 9789400772526

LC 2013-949602

SUMMARY: "This volume explores the many aspects of well-being that are associated with gratitude. Moreover, experimental work has now provided promising evidence to suggest that gratitude actually causes enhancements in happiness. If gratitude promotes human flourishing, how does it do so? This issue is addressed in the second section of the book by exploring the mechanisms that might explain the gratitude/well-being relationship." (Publisher's note)

REVIEW: *Choice* v51 no7 p1312 Mr 2014 D. S. Dunn

"Gratitude and the Good Life: Toward a Psychology of Appreciation." "A comprehensive, well-organized, engaging book on gratitude as essential emotion, trait, and mood state. The work's strength lies in the author's skill at relating empirical work--his own work and that conducted by others, including luminaries from positive psychology--on gratitude, appreciation, and the good life. . . . What sets this fine book apart is [Philip C.] Watkins's scholarly generosity--he is a truly gracious person as well as a skilled writer: in virtually every chapter, he highlights the informing work done by others while also indicating issues, areas, and questions ripe for exploration by motivated readers."

WATMAN, MAX. Harvest; field notes from a far-flung pursuit of real food; [by] Max Watman 224 p. 2014 W.W. Norton & Co. Inc.

1. Family farms—Hudson River Valley Region (N.Y.

and N.J.) 2. Memoirs 3. Natural foods 4. Self-reliant living

ISBN 039306302X; 9780393063028 (hardcover)

LC 2013-036810

SUMMARY: This memoir presents author Max Watman's "quest to craft meals from scratch. . . . Invigorated by memories of his childhood in rural Virginia with foodie parents, he hunts, fishes, gardens, bakes, makes cheese, raises livestock, butchers, preserves, and pickles. All does not go as planned: his backyard paradise is invaded by a defiant chicken-killing raccoon; his homemade Camembert tastes like chalk; and for one moment it seems as if he's lost a thousand-pound steer." (Publisher's note)

REVIEW: *Bookforum* v20 no5 p6 F/Mr 2014 MELANIE REHAK

REVIEW: *Booklist* v110 no11 p8 F 1 2014 Mark Knoblauch

REVIEW: *Kirkus Rev* v82 no4 p26 F 15 2014

"Harvest: Field Notes From a Far-Flung Pursuit of Real Food". "[Max] Watman . . . charts his adventures in sourcing or producing whole foods in more direct ways, without the polemical emphasis on locavore movements, environmental politics, corporate agriculture or related issues. . . . For readers intrigued by personal back-to-the-land cooking journeys, Watman is honest in his admission of the 'deep foodie DIY production' that entailed difficult ingredients and unusual forays. . . . With an essayist's flair for careful description, this is an entertaining, if not eye-opening, look at one man's passion for the pleasures of the table. Recommended as a congenial overview of homespun ideals."

REVIEW: *Libr J* v139 no2 p40 F 1 2014 Kristi Chadwick

REVIEW: *N Y Times Book Rev* p26 Jl 13 2014 Dawn Drzal

REVIEW: *New York Times* v163 no56560 p26 Jl 12 2014 Dawn Drzal

REVIEW: *Publ Wkly* v260 no49 p70 D 2 2013

WATSON, BEN. Derek Bailey and the story of free improvisation; [by] Ben Watson 459 p. 2013 Verso

1. Bailey, Derek 2. Biography (Literary form) 3. Guitarists 4. Guitarists—England—Biography 5. Improvisation in music 6. Jazz musicians—Biography

ISBN 9781781681053 (pbk.)

LC 2013-568061

SUMMARY: This biography by Ben Watson "will likely cause you to abandon everything you thought you knew about jazz improvisation, post-punk and the avant-garde. Derek Bailey was at the top of his profession as a dance band and recordsession guitarist when, in the early 1960s, he began playing an uncompromisingly abstract form of music." (Publisher's note)

REVIEW: *TLS* no5796 p28 My 2 2014 LOU GLANDFIELD

"Derek Bailey: And the Story of Free Improvisation." "'Derek Bailey: And the story of free improvisation' was first published in 2004, a year before Bailey died. Although Ben Watson's unilateral and frequently strident critical stance may have endeared him to few, Derek Bailey, a dogged pioneer of a genuinely unpopular music, could not have wished for a more committed and enthusiastic champion. Watson clearly thrives on controversy. . . . He is especially good at explaining why and how improvisers come to do what they do. . . . The book offers a comprehensive overview of the life and work of a man who deplored the reduction of music to the status of mere commodity, sought constantly to thwart expectations and, ultimately, to dispense altogether with the whole business of genre."

WATSON, JAMES D., 1928-. The annotated and illustrated double helix; 345 p. 2012 Simon & Schuster

1. DNA 2. Franklin, Rosalind 3. Genetic Code 4. Genetics—History 5. Memoirs 6. Molecular Biology

ISBN 1476715491 (hardcover); 9781476715490 (hardcover); 9781476715506 (paperback); 9781476715513 (ebook)

LC 2012-037483

SUMMARY: This book, by James D. Watson, Alexander Gann and Jan Witkowski, was "published to mark the 50th anniversary of the Nobel Prize for Watson and Crick's discovery of the structure of DNA, an annotated and illustrated edition of . . . his 1968 memoir, 'The Double Helix,' the brash young scientist James Watson chronicled the drama of the race to identify the structure of DNA, a discovery that would usher in the era of modern molecular biology." (Publisher's note)

REVIEW: *Choice* v50 no8 p1460-1 Ap 2013 A. K. Rinehart

REVIEW: *Kirkus Rev* v80 no21 p224 N 1 2012

REVIEW: *Sci Am* v308 no1 p76 Ja 2013 Anna Kuchment

REVIEW: *Science* v339 no6120 p648 F 8 2013 Nathaniel Comfort

WATSON, JESSE JOSHUA.il. The soccer fence. See Bildner, P.

WATT, RICHARD. Going Back; [by] Richard Watt 296 p. 2013 Richard Watt

1. British—Germany 2. Memory—Fiction 3. Psychological fiction 4. School field trips 5. Teenagers—Fiction

ISBN 0991924703; 9780991924707

SUMMARY: This story by Richard Watt "traces the tangled legacies of a long-ago trip to Germany by British high school students. In 1978, when Andrew was 15, he stayed with a host family while on a field trip to Germany. Now, in 2003, as he visits that country on business, he feels compelled to stir up the past and explore long-suppressed memories. . . . Through a series of visits and conversations, Watt's characters come to new understandings of their relationships." (Kirkus Reviews)

REVIEW: *Kirkus Rev* v82 no1 p318 Ja 1 2014

"Going Back". "The novel starts out very well; its structure expertly builds tension as the reader waits to discover more information, particularly about Karla. . . . The next section, the story of Anne . . . lacks the freshness of the first, and the following section, about Matthias, is also not as strong. Watt handles his characters' realizations naturalistically and insightfully. . . . The novel provides keen observations and excellent characterization throughout, but as it continues, its focus dissipates due to so many parallel events and the logistics of simply getting people together in one room to chat."

WATTCHOW, BRIAN. A pedagogy of place. See Brown, M.

WATTS, ANDREW. Adapting Nineteenth-Century France; Literature in Film, Theatre, Television, Radio and Print; [by] Andrew Watts 288 p. 2013 University of Chicago Press

ISBN 0708325947; 9780708325940

SUMMARY: This book "draws on six canonical novelists and the ways their works have been transformed in a variety of media to reconsider our approach to the study of adaptation. Kate Griffiths and Andrew Watts examine film, theater, television, radio, and print adaptations of the works of . . . [Victor] Hugo, [Gustave] Flaubert, [Emile] Zola . . . and [Jules] Verne, and, in doing so, cast new light on their source texts and on notions of originality and authorial borrowing." (Publisher's note)

REVIEW: *Choice* v51 no6 p1009 F 2014 I. Ivantcheva-Merjanska

"Adapting Nineteenth-Century France: Literature in Film, Theatre, Television, Radio and Print." "This important book represents an interdisciplinary approach to understanding the aesthetics and ideology of adaptations (cinema, theater, radio, television, graphic novels) of the works of six major 19th-century French novelists. . . . There are revealing moments about the creative process of the writers because [Kate] Griffiths and [Andrew] Watts explore as well influences of myth, history, folklore, literature, and theater. This book leads one to comprehend how sometimes these novelists thought of their oeuvres in 'adaptive terms.' . . . The book is well documented and positions the adapted and the adaptive works in a detailed sociohistorical context."

WATTS, DUNCAN J. Everything is obvious; once you know the answer; [by] Duncan J. Watts 335 2011 Crown Business

1. Common sense 2. Marketing 3. Reasoning 4. Sociology literature 5. Thought and thinking

ISBN 978-0-385-53168-9; 0-385-53168-0

LC 2010-031550

SUMMARY: It was the author's intent to demonstrate that "while what we mean when we say 'common sense' may seem to most people like, well, common sense, it is in reality a series of complex social rules, a priori assumptions, and inaccurate instinctive responses. . . . He taps into everything from marketing (a field relying heavily on sociological concepts) to Artificial Intelligence, methodically unpacking assumptions and revealing the hidden intricacies of what we call obvious." (Publishers Weekly)This book argues that "common sense can be an unreliable guide to the social world." (N Y Times Book Rev) Bibliography. Index.

REVIEW: *Contemp Sociol* v43 no2 p278-80 Mr 2014 Jenny Trinitapoli

"Everything Is Obvious, Once You Know the Answer: How Common Sense Fails Us". "Duncan Watts . , . has written sociology's most popular book. And if you . . . have not already, you must read it. Importantly, 'Everything Is Obvious' is not a treatise by a trained sociologist on what the discipline should be . . . but an accessible description of what is going on in sociology today and what the discipline can offer the general public. . . . I would recommend that every Introduction to Sociology professor teach this book—not because it is perfect but because it makes teaching sociology easier and much more fun."

WATTS, STEVEN. Self-help Messiah; Dale Carnegie and success in modern America; [by] Steven Watts 32 p. 2013 Other Press

1. Authors, American—20th century—Biography 2. Biography (Literary form) 3. Conduct of life 4. Orators—United States—Biography 5. Success 6. Teachers—United States—Biography

ISBN 1590515021; 9781590515020

LC 2013-003227

SUMMARY: This book, by Steven Watts, "tells the story of [Dale] Carnegie's personal journey and how it gave rise to the movement of self-help and personal reinvention. His book, 'How to Win Friends and Influence People,' became a best seller worldwide. Carnegie conceived his book to help people learn to relate to one another and enrich their lives through effective communication. His success was extraordinary, so hungry was 1920s America for a little psychological insight." (Publisher's note)

REVIEW: *Economist* v409 no8860 p90 N 2 2013

REVIEW: *Kirkus Rev* v81 no24 p5 D 15 2013

"Self-Help Messiah: Dale Carnegie and Success in Modern America". ". The author goes beyond simple biography to explore the sea-change in American thought heralded by the author of How to Win Friends and Influence People (1936). . . . [Steven] Watts portrays Carnegie not as a wildly original thinker or electrifying guru figure but rather as an easygoing, avuncular, self-deprecating . . . man, a brilliant synthesizer of ideas from psychology, philosophy, advertising and his own experience. He was an intuitive savant who grasped the nature of his changing times and crafted a message that resonated with a mass culture struggling to adapt. A fascinating portrait of the father of self-help and incisive analysis of the mercurial era that produced him."

REVIEW: *Libr J* v138 no18 p97 N 1 2013 Nathan Rupp

REVIEW: *N Y Rev Books* v61 no15 p37-8 O 9 2014 Ian Frazier

REVIEW: *Natl Rev* v65 no20 p62-3 O 28 2013 FLORENCE KING

REVIEW: *Publ Wkly* v260 no33 p56 Ag 19 2013

WAUGH, DAISY. Melting the Snow on Hester Street; [by] Daisy Waugh 416 p. 1993 St. Martin's Press; Book Club

1. Deception—Fiction 2. Historical fiction 3. Immigrants—Fiction 4. Motion picture industry—Fiction 5. Triangle Shirtwaist factory fire, New York (N.Y.), 1911

ISBN 0007431740; 9780007431748

SUMMARY: This novel follows "Max Beecham . . . a famous film director, married to Eleanor, a beautiful movie star. The gilded couple appear to have it all, but their marriage is disintegrating and they have a secret which has blighted their lives. We later discover that they are Jewish immigrants, Matz and Elena Beekman, who have fled the slums of the Lower East Side of New York and remade themselves in Hollywood." (Times Literary Supplement)

REVIEW: *TLS* no5749 p17-8 Je 7 2013 PAULA BYRNE

"Melting the Snow on Hester Street," "Z: A Novel of Zelda Fitzgerald," and "Beautiful Fools: The Last Affair of Zelda and Scott Fitzgerald." "[Daisy] Waugh creates the early Hollywood world with verve and conviction in this taut, clever and moving novel. . . . Capturing that voice is no easy feat and [Therese Anne] Fowler does not succeed. Nor does she believe that Zelda was insane, although a cursory glance at the family lineage reveals a long history of mental illness and suicide on both sides. . . . To underplay this, as Fowler's novel does, is to deny her painful and courageous struggle to come to terms with her pitiful condition. . . . R. Clifton Spargo's 'Beautiful Fools' . . . is historical fiction at its best, imaginatively filling the gaps and bringing us intimately into a portrait of a marriage."

WAWRO, GEOFFREY. A mad catastrophe; the outbreak of World War I and the collapse of the Habsburg Empire; [by] Geoffrey Wawro 472 p. 2014 Basic Books

1. Austria—History—Franz Joseph I, 1848-1916 2. Historical literature 3. World War, 1914-1918—Campaigns—Balkan Peninsula 4. World War, 1914-1918—Campaigns—Galicia (Poland and Ukraine) 5. World War, 1914-1918—Causes

ISBN 0465028357; 9780465028351 (hardback)

LC 2013-039393

SUMMARY: "The Austro-Hungarian army that marched east and south to confront the Russians and Serbs in the opening campaigns of World War I had a glorious past but a pitiful present. . . . As prizewinning historian Geoffrey Wawro explains in 'A Mad Catastrophe,' the doomed Austrian conscripts were an unfortunate microcosm of the Austro-Hungarian Empire itself—both equally ripe for destruction." (Publisher's note)

REVIEW: *Choice* v52 no1 p140 St 2014 A. M. Mayer

REVIEW: *Kirkus Rev* v82 no5 p43 Mr 1 2014

"A Mad Catastrophe: The Outbreak of World War I and the Collapse of the Habsburg Empire". "A distinguished historian's takedown of the Austro-Hungarian Empire's spectacularly inept leadership, which helped usher in the 20th century's greatest tragedy. . . . [Geoffrey] Wawro offers a crucial insight into the Eastern Front, where the fecklessness of Germany's most important ally drained attention and resources, almost guaranteeing the bloody standoff in the Western trenches and the eventual capitulation of the Kaiser's army. On this centennial of the Great War's beginning, Wawro has composed a thoroughly researched and well-written account, mercilessly debunking any nostalgia for the old monarch and the deeply dysfunctional empire over which he presided."

REVIEW: *Libr J* v139 no7 p101-4 Ap 15 2014 Michael Farrell

REVIEW: *Publ Wkly* v261 no11 p74-5 Mr 17 2014

REVIEW: *Publ Wkly* v261 no19 p22-6 My 12 2014

WAY, J. T. The Mayan in the mall; globalization, development and the making of modern Guatemala; [by] J. T. Way x, 310 p. 2012 Duke University Press

1. Economic development—Latin America 2. Economic development—Social aspects—Guatemala 3. Globalization—Economic aspects 4. Globalization—Economic aspects—Guatemala 5. Globalization—Social aspects—Guatemala 6. Guatemala—History 7. Guatemala—Social conditions 8. Historical literature 9. Modernization (Social science) 10. Social science literature

ISBN 9780822351207 (cloth : alk. paper); 9780822351313 (pbk. : alk. paper)

LC 2011-038525

SUMMARY: "In 'The Mayan in the Mall,' [author] J. T. Way traces the creation of modern Guatemala from the 1920s to the present through a series of national and international development projects. Way shows that, far from being chronically underdeveloped, this nation of stark contrasts--where shopping malls and multinational corporate headquarters coexist with some of the Western Hemisphere's poorest and most violent slums--is the embodiment of globalized capitalism." (Publisher's note)

REVIEW: *Am Hist Rev* v118 no2 p560-1 Ap 2013 CARLOTA McALLISTER

REVIEW: *Bus Hist Rev* v87 no3 p561-3 Aut 2013 Cyrus Veeser

"The Mayan in the Mall: Globalization, Development, and the Making of Modern Guatemala." "'The Mayan in the Mall' is a complex and admirable work that explores how the violent world inhabited by Guatemala's poor majority came into being. Based on extensive archival research and interviews, the study combines political and economic analysis with ethnographies that drill deep into the sublayers of Guatemala's impoverished masses. Despite its title, 'The Mayan in the Mall' does not focus on the indigenous population--the Guatemalan elite's 'imagined Maya' is more present than the actual Maya. The work tends toward urban history, as [author] J. T. Way identifies the national and transnational developments that shaped the nation and . . . its capital . . . across the twentieth century."

REVIEW: *Choice* v50 no3 p550 N 2012 J. M. Rosenthal

WAY, LORI BETH. Hunting for "dirtbags"; why cops over-police the poor and racial minorities; [by] Lori Beth Way vi, 200 p. 2013 Northeastern University Press

1. Minorities 2. Police—United States—Case studies 3. Police discretion 4. Police-community relations 5. Poor 6. Social science literature

ISBN 9781555538125 (cloth: alk. paper); 9781555538132 (pbk.: alk. paper)

LC 2012-048404

SUMMARY: In this book, authors Lori Beth Way and Ryan Patten "evaluate the conditions in which police officers take discretionary action and how these policing practices affect minorities and the poor. . . . The authors argue that institutional pressure and expectations motivate police officers to fulfill certain roles, while proactive policing policies have become the method of operation in meeting those institutional goals." (Contemporary Sociology)

REVIEW: *Contemp Sociol* v43 no2 p288-9 Mr 2014

"Hunting for 'Dirtbags': Why Cops Over-Police the Poor and Racial Minorities". "This topic is of great interest today because of the aforementioned 'stop-and-frisk' policies of the NYPD. There is also concern among minority groups that the criminal justice system overemphasizes so-called 'blue collar' crime while ignoring crimes committed by wealthier people. The authors attempt to offer some explanation as to the process that leads police to behave in such a way while filling in the gaps that they understand to be present in the literature. Given the intensity of the debate recently, this work should be of interest in establishing a framework for how proactive policing becomes focused on the poor and minorities."

WAY, RICHARD. Long-term athlete development. See Balyi, I.

WAYNE, TIFFANY K.ed. Feminist writings from ancient times to the modern world. See Feminist writings from ancient times to the modern world

WEAKLAND, MARK. Hockey shapes; [by] Mark Weakland 32 p. 2014 Capstone Press

1. Children's nonfiction 2. Hockey—Juvenile literature 3. Hockey arenas 4. Shapes—Juvenile literature 5. Sports uniforms

ISBN 9781476502250 (library binding)

LC 2013-015392

SUMMARY: This hockey-themed children's book on shapes is part of the "Sports Illustrated Kids Rookie Books" series. "Stretching across each double page spread is a large, colorful photo, often showing players on the ice before, during, or after the game. A few sentences in large type comment on each picture as it relates to the concept." The book "identifies the center circle on the ice, a triangle (more or less) of players huddled around the goalie, and ovals and stars on team uniforms." (Booklist)

REVIEW: *Booklist* v110 no9/10 p94 Ja 1 2014 Carolyn Phelan

"Hockey Counting," "Hockey Patterns," and "Hockey Shapes." "Stretching across each double page spread is a large, colorful photo, often showing players on the ice before, during, or after the game. A few sentences in large type comment on each picture as it relates to the concept. Pointing out good sportsmanship at times, the tone is positive. Kids will be drawn by the quality and the sometimes dramatic action of the photos, which usually focus on the players but also include hockey equipment, rinks, and fans. . . . While there's no shortage of concept books for young children, picture books involving sports are in short supply and those showcasing large action photos are particularly hard to find. Here's one way to meet the demand from young sports fans."

WEAKLAND, MARK. Hockey counting; [by] Mark Weakland 32 p. 2014 Capstone Press

1. Children's nonfiction 2. Counting—Juvenile literature 3. Hockey—Juvenile literature 4. Hockey fans 5. Hockey players

ISBN 9781476502267 (library binding)

LC 2013-015393

SUMMARY: This hockey-themed children's counting book is part of the "Sports Illustrated Kids Rookie Books" series. "Stretching across each double page spread is a large, colorful photo, often showing players on the ice before, during, or after the game. A few sentences in large type comment on each picture as it relates to the concept." The book "offers practice in basic arithmetic." (Booklist)

REVIEW: *Booklist* v110 no9/10 p94 Ja 1 2014 Carolyn Phelan

"Hockey Counting," "Hockey Patterns," and "Hockey Shapes." "Stretching across each double page spread is a large, colorful photo, often showing players on the ice before, during, or after the game. A few sentences in large type comment on each picture as it relates to the concept. Pointing out good sportsmanship at times, the tone is positive. Kids will be drawn by the quality and the sometimes dramatic action of the photos, which usually focus on the players but also include hockey equipment, rinks, and fans. . . . While there's no shortage of concept books for young children, picture books involving sports are in short supply and those showcasing large action photos are particularly hard to find. Here's one way to meet the demand from young sports fans."

WEAKLAND, MARK. Hockey patterns; [by] Mark Weakland 32 p. 2014 Capstone Press

1. Children's nonfiction 2. Colors 3. Hockey—Juvenile literature 4. Patterns (Mathematics) 5. Shapes

ISBN 9781476502274 (library binding)

LC 2013-018449

SUMMARY: This hockey-themed children's book on patterns is part of the "Sports Illustrated Kids Rookie Books" series. "Stretching across each double page spread is a large, colorful photo, often showing players on the ice before, during, or after the game. A few sentences in large type comment on each picture as it relates to the concept." The book "points out 'repeating shapes and color' in various places, from the referee's shirt to the arena seats to the equipment shelf." (Booklist)

REVIEW: *Booklist* v110 no9/10 p94 Ja 1 2014 Carolyn Phelan

"Hockey Counting," "Hockey Patterns," and "Hockey Shapes." "Stretching across each double page spread is a large, colorful photo, often showing players on the ice before, during, or after the game. A few sentences in large type comment on each picture as it relates to the concept. Pointing out good sportsmanship at times, the tone is positive. Kids will be drawn by the quality and the sometimes dramatic action of the photos, which usually focus on the players but also include hockey equipment, rinks, and fans. . . . While there's no shortage of concept books for young children, picture books involving sports are in short supply and those showcasing large action photos are particularly hard to find. Here's one way to meet the demand from young sports fans."

WEATHERFORD, CAROLE BOSTON, 1956-. Sugar Hill; Harlem's historic neighborhood; 32 p. 2014 Albert Whitman & Company

1. African Americans—Fiction 2. African Americans—New York (State)—New York—Fiction 3. Stories in rhyme

ISBN 0807576506; 9780807576502 (hardback)

LC 2013-030748

SUMMARY: In this book, by Carole Boston Weatherford, "take a walk through Harlem's Sugar Hill and meet all the . . . people who made this neighborhood legendary. . . . Includes brief biographies of jazz [musicians] Duke Ellington, Count Basie, Sonny Rollins, and Miles Davis; artists Aaron Douglas and Faith Ringgold; entertainers Lena Horne and the Nicholas Brothers; writer Zora Neale Hurston; civil rights leader W. E. B. DuBois and lawyer Thurgood Marshall." (Publisher's note)

REVIEW: *Bull Cent Child Books* v67 no8 p426 Ap 2014 E. B.

"Sugar Hill: Harlem's Historic Neighborhood". "Essentially a poetic list of the notables who resided in the Sugar Hill section of Harlem during the Harlem Renaissance and beyond, this bouncy exercise in name-dropping introduces listeners to high profilers whose concentration in the well-to-do African-American neighborhood shone a floodlight on black cultural achievement and material prosperity. . . .

Rhyming and scansion are sometimes clunky, and for children unfamiliar with the litany of Big Names, there's little to encounter in the main text other than atmosphere. The real heft of this title is found in the end matter, which includes an author's note on the significance of the neighborhood . . . and brief paragraphs on the residents mentioned within the text."

WEATHERFORD, DORIS. Women in American politics; history and milestones; [by] Doris Weatherford v. cm. 2012 CQ Press

1. Women—Political activity—United States—History
ISBN 1608710076; 9781608710072
LC 2011-044100

SUMMARY: This book, by Doris Weatherford, "is a new reference detailing the milestones and trends in women's political participation in the United States. It offers insightful analysis on women's political achievements in the United States, including such topics as the campaign to secure nation-wide suffrage; pioneer women state officeholders; women first elected to U.S. Congress, governorships, mayoralties, and other offices." (Publisher's note)

REVIEW: *Booklist* v108 no19/20 p56 Je 1 2012 Sarah Watstein

REVIEW: *Choice* v49 no12 p2258-9 Ag 2012 T. S. Hefner-Babb

"Women in American Politics: History and Milestones." "This two-volume set compiled by [Doris] Weatherford . . . joins other reference works . . . that focus on women in United States politics. It features a preface and 18 chapters, each of which has useful tables and charts on women officeholders at all levels from federal to local government, including offices, names, dates, and political affiliation. . . . One distinctive feature of this set is its coverage, in early chapters, of the women's suffrage movement and women who held office before passage of the 19th Amendment. . . . Academic libraries supporting political science and women's studies programs will find this a useful reference resource."

REVIEW: *Libr J* v137 no9 p102 My 15 2012 Diane Fulkerson

REVIEW: *SLJ* v58 no8 p67 Ag 2012 Wayne R. Cherry Jr.

WEAVER, FREDDY ZENTAL. Sexual Enlightenment. See Meuth, E.

WEBB, HOLLY. Rose; [by] Holly Webb 2013 Sourcebooks Jabberwocky

1. Fantasy fiction 2. Historical fiction 3. Magic—Fiction 4. Missing children 5. Missing persons 6. Monsters—Fiction
ISBN 9781402285813 paperback

SUMMARY: In this fantasy novel by Holly Webb, "The grand residence of the famous alchemist Mr. Fountain is a world away from the dark orphanage Rose has left behind. The house is positively overflowing with sparkling magic, and Rose can feel it. It's not long before she realizes that maybe, just maybe, she has a little bit of magic in her, too." (Publisher's note)

REVIEW: *Bull Cent Child Books* v67 no3 p187 N 2013 J. H.

"Rose." "In this first title of a series imported from England, young Rose (who believes she's 'about ten') is excited to exchange St. Bridget's Home for Abandoned Girls for a housemaid position at the house of wealthy alchemist Mr. Fountain. Her magical powers, however, are making it difficult to keep her head down and make a living . . . [Author Holly] Webb pokes gentle fun at Victorian tropes here . . . and the plot offers both intrigue and adventure. Aside from Rose, however, the characters are fairly flat and predictable, and events whip by in order to tie the plot up before the end; the blood-sucking witch is also a rather jarring addition to what is otherwise a domestic historical fantasy."

REVIEW: *Kirkus Rev* v81 no15 p237 Ag 1 2013

REVIEW: *SLJ* v60 no2 p99 F 2014 Sada Mozer

WEBB, STEPHEN SAUNDERS, 1937-. Marlborough's America; [by] Stephen Saunders Webb p. cm. 2013 Yale University Press

1. Historical literature 2. Imperialism—History—18th century 3. Military government of dependencies
ISBN 9780300178593 (cloth : alk. paper)
LC 2012-018059

SUMMARY: It was the author's intent to demonstrate "that the American provinces, under the spur of war, became capitalist, coercive, and aggressive, owing to the vigorous leadership of career army officers, trained and nominated to American government by the captain general of the allied armies, the first duke of Marlborough, and that his influence, and that of his legates, prevailed through the entire century in America." (Publisher's note)

REVIEW: *Am Hist Rev* v119 no1 p250 F 2014 William R. Nester

"Marlborough's America". "One can learn a lot from reading Stephen Saunders Webb's fourth volume in his 'Governors-General' series. The book is packed with meticulously compiled facts throughout its 413 pages of dense narrative and 138 pages of endnotes. It is beautifully illustrated with twenty-five black-and-white and five color portraits accompanied by lengthy descriptions of these key participants in events, along with four color copies of tapestries depicting some of Marlborough's greatest victories. . . . If Webb finely describes what happened during Marlborough's military campaigns, he is less adept at explaining why things happened there or elsewhere. . . . A book for specialists rather than general readers who may get lost in the thickets of facts without contexts."

REVIEW: *Choice* v50 no10 p1914 Je 2013 J. D. Lyons

REVIEW: *J Am Hist* v100 no2 p499-500 S 2013 Jeremy Black

REVIEW: *Publ Wkly* v259 no45 p62 N 5 2012

REVIEW: *TLS* no5759 p14 Ag 16 2013 T. H. BREEN

"Marlborough's America." "[Stephen Saunders] Webb credits the Duke of Marlborough for advancing the master plan for British North America. This assertion comes as a surprise, since most of Marlborough's career centred on battling French troops on the Continent and fighting the Tories in government who schemed incessantly to undermine the Duke's political power. . . . In case modern readers fail to appreciate the Duke's military record, Webb insists on taking them on an exhaustive tour of the battlefields. . . Webb makes a valuable contribution by placing the political history of the American colonies in an Atlantic context. The great wars for empire did matter. But so too did other cultural, religious and economic developments."

WEBBER, TAMMARA. Easy; [by] Tammara Webber 310 p. 2012 Berkley Books

1. Guilt—Fiction 2. Love stories 3. Man-woman relationships—Fiction 4. Rape victims—Fiction 5. Trust
ISBN 0606269592; 9780606269599

SUMMARY: In this book by Tammara Webber, "when an overly aggressive frat boy won't take no for an answer, Lucas saves Jackie's life in more ways than one." (Booklist) The novel chronicles "one girl's struggle to regain the trust she's lost, find the inner strength to fight back against an attacker, and accept the peace she finds in the arms of a secretive boy." (Publisher's note)

REVIEW: *Booklist* v110 no2 p46 S 15 2013 John Charles

"Beautiful Disaster," "Down to You," and "Easy." "Big-man-on-campus Travis Maddox bets campus good-girl Abby Abernathy that he can abstain from sex for 30 days. If Travis wins, Abby must live with him for a month. Often cited as one of the books that kick-started the NA romance genre. 'Beautiful Disaster' is followed by 'Walking Disaster'. . . . Olivia Townsend returns home from college to help run the family business only to become caught up in a love triangle with twin brothers Cash and Nash Davenport. [M.] Leighton delivers sexy soap-opera- style plot twists in the first installment of her sizzling Bad Boys series. . . . When an overly aggressive frat boy won't take no for an answer, Lucas saves Jackie's life in more ways than one. Before being picked up by Berkley, [Tammara] Webber's debut sold more than 150,000 copies as a self-published e-book and spent nine weeks on the New York Times best-seller list."

WEBER, BRUCE. Life is a wheel; love, death, etc., and a bike ride across America; [by] Bruce Weber 352 p. 2014 Scribner

1. BIOGRAPHY & AUTOBIOGRAPHY—Personal Memoirs 2. Cycling—Psychological aspects 3. Cycling—United States 4. Memoirs 5. Middle-aged men—United States—Biography 6. Mortality—Social aspects—United States 7. SPORTS & RECREATION—Cycling 8. Self-reliance—United States 9. TRAVEL—United States—General
ISBN 9781451695014 (hardback); 9781451695021 (paperback)
LC 2013-040182

SUMMARY: In this book, "reprising a similar trip he took from California to New York City in 1993, in 2011 New York Times obituary writer and author [Bruce] Weber . . . bicycled from Oregon to Manhattan. Weber documented the trip for Times Web site, but here he has expanded on those posts to create a lengthier form that allows him to explore deeper themes. . . . His trip is . . . about the internal explorations of a 57-year-old man pushing his body to its limits." (Publishers Weekly)

REVIEW: *Booklist* v110 no9/10 p32-3 Ja 1 2014 Jay Freeman

"Life is a Wheel: Love, Death, Etc. and a Bike Ride Across America." "A delightful, insightful saga that combines the genres of travelogue and journal of self-discovery while paying tribute to the joy and value of cycling. . . . He describes the changes he saw in the nation, from the ubiquitous use of cell phones to changes in the political climate. What hasn't changed, thankfully, is [Bruce] Weber's ability to be awestruck and inspired by the power and beauty of the landscapes he traverses. This is a thoughtful and thoroughly enjoyable 'road' story that will appeal to both cyclists and the more sedentary."

REVIEW: *Kirkus Rev* v82 no4 p39 F 15 2014

REVIEW: *New York Times* v163 no56447 pC23-9 Mr 20 2014 LIESL SCHILLINGER

REVIEW: *Publ Wkly* v260 no51 p47 D 16 2013

WEBER, DAVID, 1952-. Like a Mighty Army; [by] David Weber 672 p. 2014 Tor Books

1. FICTION—Science Fiction—General 2. Imaginary wars & battles—Fiction 3. Robots—Fiction 4. Space warfare—Fiction 5. Technological innovations
ISBN 9780765321565 (hardback)
LC 2013-025525

SUMMARY: This book is the seventh in author David Weber's Safehold series. "The empire of Charis and its allies are valiantly attempting to end the corrupt Church of God Awaiting's centuries-long planetary stranglehold on all innovation. Unfortunately, even Merlin Athrawes, their swashbuckling robot ally from a more scientifically advanced past, hasn't been able to save the Charisian side from heavy losses over a brutal winter campaign." (Publishers Weekly)

REVIEW: *Booklist* v110 no5 p4 N 1 2013 Brad Hooper

"Like A Mighty Army," "A Nice Little Place on the North Side: Wrigley Field at One Hundred," and "Uganda Be Kidding Me." "The seventh volume in the best selling Safehold series of sf novels sees the heretofore unchallenged and repressive rule of the Church of God Awaiting being threatened. . . . Conservative commentator [George] Will has always held baseball in a special place in his heart, and in his new book, he gives free rein to his passion, imparting the history of Wrigley Field, home of the Chicago Cubs. . . . In comedian and best-selling author [Chelsea] Handler's new hook, she talks about her travels."

REVIEW: *Publ Wkly* v260 no49 p66 D 2 2013

WEBER, TRACY. Murder strikes a pose; a Downward Dog mystery; [by] Tracy Weber 288 p. 2014 Midnight Ink

1. Detective & mystery stories 2. Homeless men—Crimes against—Fiction 3. Women—Fiction 4. Yoga—Fiction
ISBN 9780738739687
LC 2013-030623

SUMMARY: In this book, part of the Downward Dog mystery series, "Seattle yoga teacher Kate Atkinson . . . discovers an intimidating German shepherd, Bella, outside of her studio. Also waiting at the front door is Bella's owner, a homeless man named George. . . . Kate befriends George, who is subsequently found dead in her studio's parking lot. When the police dismiss the crime as the result of a dispute between drug dealers, Kate is determined to find . . . George's murderer." (Publishers Weekly)

REVIEW: *Kirkus Rev* v81 no24 p35 D 15 2013

"Murder Strikes a Pose". " The police are certain the death is an accident and don't want to waste their time and resources on a homeless man anyway. But Kate feels that there's something more to it. Why else would George be so certain about a future cash influx? Along with her troublemaking friend Rene and her potential new boyfriend, Michael, Kate works to uncover the truth behind George's demise while also finding the perfect home for Bella, hopefully before the murderer returns for Kate. In spite of a few charmers, Weber's debut falls flat. The premise and the details are just too sad for chick-lit fare."

REVIEW: *Publ Wkly* v260 no43 p39 O 28 2013

WEBER, WILLIAM. Neither victor nor vanquished; America in the War of 1812; [by] William Weber xx, 243 p. 2013 Potomac Books

1. Great Britain—Foreign relations—United States—History 2. Historical literature 3. United States—History—War of 1812—Campaigns 4. United States—Military history

ISBN 1612346073; 9781612346076 (hardcover : alk. paper)

LC 2013-001472

SUMMARY: In this book, William Weber "builds the case for his study of the War of 1812 by investigating he ambiguity of the war's two principal narratives. One portrays the conflict as 'Mr. Madison's War,' highlighting the indecisive military campaigns that failed to capture Canada or to force Britain to respect US maritime rights. The second narrative depicts the conflict as the 'Second War for Independence,' celebrating defensive victories at Baltimore, Plattsburg, and New Orleans." (Choice)

REVIEW: *Choice* v51 no4 p713-4 D 2013 G. A. Smith

"Neither Victor Nor Vanquished: America in the War of 1812." "By offering alternative narratives, [William] Weber suggests the conflict should instead be portrayed as a 'Second Revolutionary War' and as a war for expansion that ultimately led to the Civil War. In his conjectural conclusion, Weber maintains that had the war not been fought, Andrew Jackson would not have emerged as a national figure, the South and West would have developed more slowly, and the country would have avoided the quick expansion of the cotton economy that led to sectional strife, the Civil War, and the dissolution of the Union. But would it have really happened that way?"

WEDDLE, STEVE. Country Hardball; [by] Steve Weddle 208 p. 2013 Adams Media Corp

1. Country life—Fiction 2. Crime—Fiction 3. Exconvicts—Fiction 4. Psychological fiction 5. Working class—Fiction

ISBN 1440570809; 9781440570803

SUMMARY: This book presents a "novel told in intertwined stories." It follows "Roy Alison, fresh out of prison and looking to start a new life. But things have changed since he's been away: There's no work, drugs are rampant, amilies, are breaking up, [and] people are losing their homes to the banks. . . . It doesn't take Roy long to hook up with his scary cousin Cleovis to pull off a string of crimes that somehow make him feel alive in this land of the living dead." (New York Times Book Review)

REVIEW: *Booklist* v110 no3 p31 O 1 2013 Michele Leber

REVIEW: *Kirkus Rev* v81 no19 p103 O 1 2013

REVIEW: *N Y Times Book Rev* p23 N 17 2013 MARILYN STASIO

"Critical Mass," "The All-Girl Filling Station's Last Reunion," and "Country Hardball." "The drug subplot is an unnecessary complication in an already busy story told in two parallel narratives set in different countries, running on separate timelines and involving four generations of characters. But if the plot mechanics are unwieldy, the character of Martina is the serene center of this fractured universe. . . . Steve Weddle's writing is downright dazzling in 'Country Hardball'. . . . Sookie's detective work, tracing her new identity, takes her all the way to Pulaski, Wis., and into the lives of four ebullient sisters who ran their father's gas station during World War II. Honestly, who wouldn't want to be part of that family?"

REVIEW: *Publ Wkly* v260 no35 p30 S 2 2013

WEEKS, WILLIAM EARL. The new Cambridge history of American foreign relations.; [by] William Earl Weeks 336 p. 2013 Cambridge University Press

1. Historical literature 2. Imperialism—History 3. Slavery—United States—History 4. United States—Foreign relations—History

ISBN 9780521763288 (hardback v. 3); 9780521763622 (hardback v. 4); 9780521767521 (hardback v. 2); 9781107005907 (hardback v. 1); 9781107031838 (hardback set)

LC 2012-018193

SUMMARY: This book by William Earl Weeks is part of a revised edition of the series "The Cambridge History of American Foreign Relations." The author "frames his analysis around ten dimensions that characterize the American empire. They include the relationship between expansion, unity, and security; the rhetoric of a 'redeemer nation'; technological innovations; and the conflict over slavery." (Choice: Current Reviews for Academic Libraries)

REVIEW: *Choice* v51 no5 p907 Ja 2014 L. M. Lees

"Dimensions of the Early American Empire 1754-1865," The American Search for Opportunity 1865-1913," and "The Globalizing of America 1913-1945." "The four volumes of this revision . . . feature one new author and relatively minimal changes by two of the original three authors. . . . In volume one, 'Dimensions of the Early American Empire, 1754-1865,' new author [William Earl] Weeks . . . frames his analysis around ten dimensions that characterize the American empire. . . . Weeks deftly weaves these themes into his intriguing and complex study, which is a worthy addition to the series. . . . Libraries with the original set should consider replacing volumes one and four only."

WEGMUELLER, SARAH.ed. Dictionary of environmental and climate change law. See Dictionary of environmental and climate change law

WEIGHT, RICHARD. Mod; A Very British Style; [by] Richard Weight 496 p. 2013 Bodley Head

1. Great Britain—Social life & customs—1945- 2. Historical literature 3. Mod culture (Subculture) 4. Subcultures—History—20th century 5. Youth—Great Britain—History

ISBN 0224073915; 9780224073912

SUMMARY: In this book, "Richard Weight tells the story of Britain's biggest and most influential youth cult, from its origins in the Soho jazz scene of the 1950s through to its explosion amid Beatlemania in the 1960s. Along the way he takes in the many influences that shaped it: from Be-Bop Jazz to RnB and Soul and Jamaican Ska, together with French and Italian fashion, Anglo-American Pop Art and continental Dadaism. " (Publisher's note)

REVIEW: *London Rev Books* v35 no16 p25-7 Ag 29 2013 Ian Penman

"Mod: A Very British Style." "What Richard Weight calls the 'very British style' of Mod found its initial foothold in late 1950s Soho with the arrival of the jazz 'modernists', who defined themselves in strict opposition to the reigning gatekeepers of Trad. . . . As a result of Mod, he says, 'it is true to say that more British people came to see themselves as modern than ever before.' Sure, fine, maybe, even if that 'ever before' feels a bit fudgy. . . . Weight's spayed, odourless jargonese is to real analysis what a TV makeover or a 'scooters only' weekender in Margate in 2013 are to the original modernist dare: a perfectly glossy simulation, with all risky elements stowed."

REVIEW: *New Statesman* v142 no5150 p55 Mr 22 2018 Alwyn W. Turner

WEIKOP, CHRISTIAN.ed. The Oxford critical and cultural history of modernist magazines. See The Oxford critical and cultural history of modernist magazines

WEIKUM, TARA.ed. Ignite me. See Mafi, T.

WEIMAR THOUGHT; a contested legacy; vi, 451 p. 2013 Princeton University Press

1. Historical literature 2. Humanities—Germany—History—20th century 3. Political culture—Germany—History—20th century 4. Social sciences—Germany—History—20th century

ISBN 9780691135106 (hardback : alk. paper)
LC 2012-038154

SUMMARY: This book, edited by Peter E. Gordon and John P. McCormick, discusses the intellectual developments of the Weimar Republic (1918-33), which "achievements in many areas, including psychology, political theory, physics, philosophy, literary and cultural criticism, and the arts . . . The book is divided into four thematic sections: law, politics, and society; philosophy, theology, and science; aesthetics, literature, and film; and general cultural and social themes of the Weimar period." (Publisher's note)

REVIEW: *Choice* v51 no6 p1084 F 2014 D. M. Imhoof

REVIEW: *TLS* no5771 p23 N 8 2013 JULIAN PREECE

"Weimar Thought: A Contested Legacy." "The American editors of this densely packed book of nineteen essays are interested in 'the astonishing cultural and intellectual ferment of interwar Germany . . . that helped to make Weimar a veritable birthplace of European intellectual modernity'. The contributions range over areas as diverse as sociology, film theory, cultural criticism, theology and neo-Kantian philosophy to argue that methodologies which were first properly worked out in the German language in the 1920s have exerted an unparalleled influence in the Western world up to the present day. . . . One conclusion is that Weimar's significance to us today may be broader even than the editors of this otherwise very good book allow."

WEIN, ELIZABETH. Rose under fire; [by] Elizabeth Wein 368 p. 2013 Hyperion

1. Air pilots—Fiction 2. Concentration camp inmates—Fiction 3. Diaries—Fiction 4. Historical fiction 5. Prisoners of war—Fiction 6. Ravensbrück (Germany: Concentration camp) 7. World War, 1939-1945—Prisoners and prisons, German—Fiction

ISBN 1423183096 (hardcover); 9781423183099 (hardcover)
LC 2013-010337

SUMMARY: This historical novel chronicles the experiences of American pilot Rose in a Polish concentration camp. "After being brutally punished for her refusal to make fuses for flying bombs . . . , Rose is befriended by Polish 'Rabbits,' victims of horrific medical experimentation. She uses 'counting-out rhymes' to preserve her sanity and as a way to memorize the names of the Rabbits. Rose's poetry . . . is at the heart of the story, revealing her growing understanding of what's happening around her." (Kirkus Reviews)

REVIEW: *Booklist* v109 no22 p81-2 Ag 1 2013 Ilene Cooper

REVIEW: *Bull Cent Child Books* v67 no2 p123-4 O 2013 D. S.

"Rose Under Fire." "As a young American, Rose brings a contrasting perspective from a country that's been unscathed by a war that's been raging in Europe for years. . . . Rose's love of poetry threads through the novel as she captures her own experiences and also uses the art to memorialize her blockmates; indeed, the strongest underlying theme is that of witnessing to the outside world, through poetry, prose, wall graffiti, or, in the final chapters, literally witnessing in the Doctors' Trial in post-war Nuremberg. . . . This is therefore an atypical concentration camp story but a gripping one for contemporary American readers, who will easily connect with Rose and will be eager to discuss the ethical challenges raised by her story."

REVIEW: *Horn Book Magazine* v89 no6 p109-10 N/D 2013 DEIRDRE F. BAKER

REVIEW: *Kirkus Rev* p58 Ag 15 2013 Fall Preview

REVIEW: *Kirkus Rev* p76 2013 Guide to BookExpo America

REVIEW: *Kirkus Rev* v81 no14 p41 Jl 15 2013

REVIEW: *Libr J* v138 no21 p57 D 1 2013 Stephanie Charlefour

REVIEW: *N Y Times Book Rev* p34 S 22 2013 Jessica Bruder

REVIEW: *Publ Wkly* v260 no28 p1 Jl 15 2013

REVIEW: *Publ Wkly* p129 Children's starred review annual 2013

REVIEW: *SLJ* v59 no10 p1 O 2013 Necia Blundy

REVIEW: *SLJ* v60 no2 p59 F 2014 Julie Paladino

REVIEW: *Voice of Youth Advocates* v36 no5 p68-9 D 2013 Sara Martin

REVIEW: *Voice of Youth Advocates* v36 no5 p69 D 2013 Raluca Topliceanu

WEINBERGER, ELIOT.ed. The poems of Octavio Paz. See Paz, O.

WEINBERGER, ELIOT. Two American Scenes. See Davis, L.

WEINBROT, HOWARD D. Literature, religion, and the evolution of culture, 1660-1780; [by] Howard D. Weinbrot xii, 371 p. 2013 Johns Hopkins University Press

1. English literature—18th century—History and criti-

cism 2. English literature—Early modern, 1500-1700—History and criticism 3. Historical literature 4. Literature and society—Great Britain 5. Religion and literature—Great Britain
ISBN 1421405164 (hardcover : acid-free paper); 1421408600 (electronic); 9781421405162 (hardcover : acid-free paper); 9781421408606 (electronic)
LC 2012-035553

SUMMARY: "'Literature, Religion, and the Evolution of Culture, 1660-1780' chronicles changes in contentious politics and religion and their varied representations in British letters from the mid-seventeenth to the late eighteenth century. . . . Howard D. Weinbrot's broad-ranging interdisciplinary study considers sermons, satire, political and religious polemic, Anglo-French relations, biblical and theological commentary, Methodism, legal history, and the novel." (Publisher's note)

REVIEW: *Choice* v51 no3 p452 N 2013 D. L. Patey

REVIEW: *TLS* no5788 p7-8 Mr 7 2014 JONATHAN CLARK

"Literature, Religion, and the Evolution of Culture 1660-1780." "At first glance, the volume is a collection of eight rather disparate essays, loosely stitched together. . . . Examined more closely, the essays are packaged to support an argument explicitly acknowledged. . . . Here [author Howard D.] Weinbrot proposes a new organizing framework: 'progress,' conceived as a 'road' with a 'final destination.' . . . Much . . . depends on the transfer of the model of Darwinian evolution from biological organisms to society, itself identified as an organism only by the use of metaphor. Arguments from metaphor tend to be weak as soon as challenged. . . . Settling old scores, he cannot resist the temptation to revert to Samuel Johnson and to pin his new model on him."

WEINERT, FRIEDEL. The march of time; [by] Friedel Weinert 350 p. 2013 Springer

1. Cosmology 2. Philosophical literature 3. Philosophy & science 4. Philosophy of physics 5. Physics literature 6. Time—Philosophy
ISBN 9783642353468
LC 2013-930626

SUMMARY: Written by Friedel Weinert, "The aim of this interdisciplinary study is to reconstruct the evolution of our changing conceptions of time in the light of scientific discoveries. It . . . adopt[s] a new perspective and organize[s] the material around three central themes, which run through our history of time reckoning: cosmology and regularity; stasis and flux; symmetry and asymmetry. . . . This book . . . defend[s] a dynamic rather than a static view of time." (Publisher's note)

REVIEW: *Choice* v51 no2 p307 O 2013 E. Kincanon

"March of Time: Evolving Conceptions of Time in the Light of Scientific Discoveries." "This book is a historical and scientific argument against the popular view held among physicists that time is not real. [Author Friedel] Weinert . . . considers the arguments based on cosmology, stasis, and symmetry, and does an excellent job of showing that the conclusion of the existence of an atemporal world is not decisive. This is impressive for several reasons. Physicists, such as Paul Davies and Stephen Hawking, present the atemporal or block universe conclusion as almost obvious. Weinert . . . shows that the conclusions do not follow deductively or inductively. Furthermore, he argues that the temporal view of the world is actually a better match to what people know."

WEINTRAUB, STANLEY, 1929-. Young Mr. Roosevelt; FDR's introduction to war, politics and life; [by] Stanley Weintraub 288 p. 2013 Da Capo Press, A Member of the Perseus Books Group

1. Presidents—United States—Biography 2. World War, 1914-1918—United States
ISBN 9780306821189 (hardcover)
LC 2013-014328

SUMMARY: "In 'Young Mr. Roosevelt' Stanley Weintraub evokes Franklin Delano Roosevelt's political and wartime beginnings. An unpromising patrician playboy appointed assistant secretary of the Navy in 1913, Roosevelt learned quickly and rose to national visibility in World War I. Democratic vice-presidential nominee in 1920, he lost the election but not his ambitions." (Publisher's note)

REVIEW: *Choice* v51 no8 p1477-8 Ap 2014 M. J. Birkner

REVIEW: *Kirkus Rev* v81 no16 p139 Ag 15 2013

"Young Mr. Roosevelt: FDR's Introduction to War, Politics, and Life." "An account of Franklin D. Roosevelt's (1882-1945) first few years in politics. FDR began his career in the shadow of Theodore Roosevelt, America's most famous politician. By TR's death in 1919, FDR was a fairly prominent national figure and the 1920 Democratic candidate for vice president. This is where veteran historian [Stanley] Weintraub . . . ends this perceptive demi-biography of FDR's political maturation under the eyes of two other great presidents. . . . Weintraub does not ignore an unhappy Eleanor, rarely at his side, harassed with caring for six children and several large households and already suspicious of his wandering eye."

WEIR, KATHRYN. Gorilla. See Gott, T.

WEISMAN, ALAN. Countdown; Our Last, Best Hope for a Future on Earth?; [by] Alan Weisman 528 p. 2013 Little, Brown and Co.

1. HISTORY—Civilization 2. NATURE—Ecology 3. NATURE—Environmental Conservation & Protection 4. Nature—Effect of human beings on 5. Overpopulation 6. POLITICAL SCIENCE—Public Policy—Environmental Policy 7. Population ecology 8. SOCIAL SCIENCE—Future Studies 9. Social science literature 10. TECHNOLOGY & ENGINEERING—Social Aspects
ISBN 0316097756; 9780316097758
LC 2013-017113

SUMMARY: In this book, author Alan Weisman "visits an extraordinary range of the world's cultures, religions, nationalities, tribes, and political systems to learn what in their beliefs, histories, liturgies, or current circumstances might suggest that sometimes it's in their own best interest to limit their growth. [He] reveals what may be the fastest, most acceptable, practical, and affordable way of returning our planet and our presence on it to balance." (Publisher's note)

REVIEW: *Booklist* v110 no12 p19 F 15 2014 Donna Seaman

REVIEW: *Booklist* v109 no22 p10 Ag 1 2013 Donna Seaman

REVIEW: *Choice* v51 no9 p1626 My 2014 K. A. Reycraft

REVIEW: *Kirkus Rev* p32 Ag 15 2013 Fall Preview

REVIEW: *Kirkus Rev* v81 no14 p105 Jl 15 2013

REVIEW: *Libr J* v138 no7 p58 Ap 15 2013 Barbara Hoffert

REVIEW: *Libr J* v138 no14 p137 S 1 2013 David R. Conn

REVIEW: *N Y Times Book Rev* p26 O 20 2013

REVIEW: *N Y Times Book Rev* p18 O 13 2013 NATHANIEL RICH

REVIEW: *Publ Wkly* v260 no21 p45 My 27 2013

REVIEW: *Sci Am* v309 no3 p90 S 2013

"Countdown: Our Last, Best Hope for a Future on Earth." "A frenzied barnstormer of a book. From Minneapolis to Mexico, from the Holy Land to Vatican City, [Alan] Weisman presents the intermingled stories of the scientists, religious leaders and humble aid workers all striving for or against a sustainable human future. Ultimately, he finds few easy solutions. What emerges is a dismal picture of looming resource scarcities and rampant ecological destruction, brightened only by occasional success stories of countries and individuals mastering their fate. 'Countdown' is a chaotic stew of big stories, bold ideas and conflicted characters, punctuated by moments of quiet grace--just like our people-packed planet."

WEISS, KATHERINE. The plays of Samuel Beckett; [by] Katherine Weiss 2013 Bloomsbury Methuen Drama

1. Beckett, Samuel, 1906-1989 2. Dramatic criticism 3. Literary critiques 4. Literature & technology 5. Voice in literature

ISBN 9781408157305

SUMMARY: This book, by Katherine Weiss, is a critical companion to the work of playwright Samuel Beckett, "illuminating each play and Beckett's vision, and investigating his experiments with the body, voice and technology. It includes in-depth studies of the major works 'Waiting for Godot,' 'Endgame' and 'Krapp's Last Tape,' and . . . features too a series of essays by other scholars and practitioners offering different critical perspectives on Beckett in performance." (Publisher's note)

REVIEW: *TLS* no5759 p30 Ag 16 2013 JAMES MORAN

"The Plays of Samuel Beckett." "Katherine Weiss seeks to re-evaluate Beckett's play writing by showing that a concern with technology is central not only to the way we might receive these works, but also to the construction of those texts in the first place. . . . Perhaps Katherine Weiss could have extended her analysis to Beckett's Film, which is bizarrely excluded here, and it might also have been useful to know more about the original production methods, broadcasting and influence of Beckett's radio works and teleplays."

WEISSER, SUSAN OSTROV. The glass slipper; women and love stories; [by] Susan Ostrov Weisser 238 p. 2013 Rutgers University Press

1. Love in literature 2. Love stories—History and criticism 3. Social science literature 4. Women and literature 5. Women in literature

ISBN 9780813561776 (pbk. : alk. paper); 9780813561783 (hardcover : alk. paper)

LC 2012-051437

SUMMARY: This book discusses "the persistence of a familiar Anglo-American love story into the digital age. . . . Susan Ostrov Weisser relates . . . how these stories are shaped and defined by and for women, the main consumers of romantic texts. . . . Weisser shows the many ways in which nineteenth-century views of women's nature . . . have survived the feminist critique of the 1970s and continue in new and more ambiguous forms in today's media." (Publisher's note)

REVIEW: *Choice* v51 no8 p1383 Ap 2014 J. Mills

REVIEW: *N Y Times Book Rev* p30 O 6 2013 Emily Witt

"The Glass Slipper: Women and Love Stories." "[Susan Ostrov] Weisser maps these shifts through close readings beginning with Jane Austen and ending with 'The Bachelor' and 'The Rules'. These can sometimes drown in the minutiae of academic quibbles. . . . At her best, however, Weisser expresses a sarcastic exasperation with some of the more inane counsel women readily consume. Dissections of magazine headlines, like 'Your Orgasm Face: What He's Thinking When He Sees It,' are good for some laughs."

WELDON, FAY, 1931-. Kehua!; [by] Fay Weldon 325 p. 2010 Corvus

1. Families—Fiction 2. New Zealanders—England—London—Fiction 3. Speculative fiction 4. Supernatural—Fiction

ISBN 1609451376; 1848874596 (hbk.); 9781609451370; 9781848874596 (hbk.)

LC 2010-533217

SUMMARY: Written by Fay Weldon, "this tale of murder, adultery, incest, ghosts, redemption and remorse . . . takes you first to a daffodil-filled garden in Highgate, North London . . . Scarlet--a long-legged, skinny young woman of the new world order--has announced to Beverley--her aged grandmother--that she intends to leave home and husband for the glamorous actor, Jackson Wright--he of the vampire films." (Publisher's note)

REVIEW: *Booklist* v110 no4 p16 O 15 2013 Cortney Ophoff

REVIEW: *Kirkus Rev* v81 no20 p188 O 15 2013

REVIEW: *N Y Rev Books* v61 no5 p12-6 Mr 20 2014 Alison Lurie

REVIEW: *N Y Times Book Rev* p26 O 27 2013 JINCY WILLETT

"Kehua!" "The metafiction of Fay Weldon manages to charm even as it exasperates. . . . Kehua . . . aren't very bright, but they try . . . and their behavior is goofy and kind of endearing. They tie characters to plot and both to their purported author. Kehua keep the novel--and its women--running. . . . Readers unentranced by antic myths and immune to the lure of the meta will have to settle for Weldon's sly wit, which is considerable. . . . Like the real world, 'Kehua!' is overpopulated and messy, but much funnier."

WELLE, ANJA.tr. Hybrid culture. See Hybrid culture

WELLER, JOHN. The last ocean; Antarctica's Ross Sea Project; saving the most pristine ecosystem on earth; [by] John Weller 222 p. 2013 Rizzoli International Publications

ISBN 9780847841233 (hardcover : alk. paper)

LC 2013-934954

SUMMARY: Written by John Weller, this is a "collection of oceanic photography documenting the world's last pristine ocean. Due to its remoteness and harsh weather, Antarctica's Ross Sea remained free from human interference until 1996, when commercial fishing discovered it. . . . Offering a rare glimpse into life at the edge of the world--from Emperor and Adélie penguins to silverfish, seals, and minke whales--Weller takes the reader . . . above and below the ocean surface." (Publisher's note)

REVIEW: *N Y Times Book Rev* p8 D 8 2013 REBECCA PEPPER SINKLER

"Southern Light: Images From Antarctica" and "The Last Ocean: Antarctica's Ross Sea Project: Saving the Most Pristine Ecosystem on Earth." "'Southern Light' is a blast of beauty. . . . [Author] David Neilson, an Australian photographer, spreads before us myriad majestic peaks and plains in images that seem lit from within. . . . 'The Last Ocean' uses images as the hook to pull us more deeply into the science, lore and heroic history of the place and its people. [Author] John Weller is alarmed by never preachy. It helps that he is as fine a writer as he is a photographer. . . . He goes to intrepid lengths to get his underwater images."

REVIEW: *Sci Am* v310 no1 p78 Ja 2014 Lee Billings John Weller

WELLER, RICHARD.ed. Made in Australia. See Made in Australia

WELLMAN, KATHLEEN. Queens and mistresses of Renaissance France; [by] Kathleen Wellman 433 p. 2013 Yale University Press

1. Historical literature 2. Mistresses—France—Biography 3. Queens—France—Biography 4. Renaissance—France
ISBN 9780300178852 (cloth : alk. paper)
LC 2012-037490

SUMMARY: In this book, author "Kathleen Wellman argues that the role played by the queens and royal mistresses of France between 1444 and 1599 was absolutely pivotal in the development of the politics and culture of the court and far more important than has hitherto been acknowledged. . . . The book offers a series of biographies, chronologically considering the lives and legends of these prominent women." (History Today)

REVIEW: *Choice* v51 no2 p343 O 2013 J. W. McCormack

REVIEW: *Hist Today* v63 no10 p60-1 O 2013 SUZANNAH LIPSCOMB

"Queens and Mistresses of Renaissance France." "In this fascinating and lucid book Kathleen Wellman argues that the role played by the queens and royal mistresses of France between 1444 and 1599 was absolutely pivotal in the development of the politics and culture of the court and far more important than has hitherto been acknowledged. . . . The decision to deal with queens and mistresses together is instructive, for it focuses the attention on their differing sources of power and their parallel networks. . . . This scholarly, lively and absorbing narrative restores these women to the heart of any cultural or political history of France."

REVIEW: *Libr J* v138 no11 p98 Je 15 2013 Linda Frederiksen

REVIEW: *London Rev Books* v36 no2 p36-7 Ja 23 2014 Caroline Weber

WELLS, BARBARA. Daughters and granddaughters of farmworkers; emerging from the long shadow of farm labor; [by] Barbara Wells xi, 203 p. 2013 Rutgers University Press

1. Mexican American women—Social conditions—California 2. Mexican American women—Social life and customs 3. Mexican American women agricultural laborers—California 4. Social mobility 5. Social science literature
ISBN 9780813562841 (pbk.: alk. paper); 9780813562858 (hardcover: alk. paper)
LC 2013-000428

SUMMARY: This book looks at the "experiences of daughters and granddaughters of Mexican immigrant farm workers in Imperial County, California. . . . Despite Mexican American women's attempts to move up the socioeconomic ladder, most of them have not achieved an economically more stable life. . . . [Barbara] Wells argues that the structure of agriculture as well as limited local job opportunities have hindered channels of upward mobility for Mexican American women." (Choice: Current Reviews for Academic Libraries)

REVIEW: *Choice* v51 no9 p1689-90 My 2014 M. C. Cheng

"Daughters and Granddaughters of Farmworkers: Emerging From the Long Shadow of Farm Labor". "Sociologist [Barbara] Wells . . . provides a comprehensive analysis of the lived experiences of daughters and granddaughters of Mexican immigrant farm workers in Imperial County, California. . . . Wells gives a nuanced account of how Mexican American women negotiate with their work and family life; engage in farm labor and education; and develop familial ties in and attachment to the local community. . . . Overall, this is an important contribution to the study of Mexican American family lives and a great addition to the field of gender and women's studies."

WELLS, CHRISTOPHER W. Car country; an environmental history; [by] Christopher W. Wells 427 p. 2012 University of Washington Press

1. Automobiles—Environmental aspects—United States—History 2. Automobiles—Social aspects—United States—History 3. City planning—United States—History 4. Historical literature 5. Land use—United States—History 6. Transportation, Automotive—United States—History 7. Urban transportation—United States—History
ISBN 9780295992150 (hbk.: alk. paper)
LC 2012-026654

SUMMARY: In this book, Christopher W. Wells "rejects the idea that the nation's automotive status quo can be explained as a simple byproduct of an ardent love affair with the automobile. Instead, he takes readers on a . . . tour of the evolving American landscape, charting the ways that new transportation policies and land-use practices have combined to reshape nearly every element of the built environment around the easy movement of automobiles." (Publisher's note)

REVIEW: *Am Hist Rev* v119 no1 p212-3 F 2014 Michael R. Fein

"Car Country: An Environmental History". "A compelling history of America's signature car-dependent landscapes. The text is at once a deft synthesis of recent literature on motor vehicles, highways, urban planning, suburban development, and land use policy, and a persuasive reinterpretation of these histories through the lens of landscape ecology. Scholars in these fields will find it a provocative read. With lively anecdotes, effective imagery, and dozens of illustrations, the book also presents an accessible narrative that will help students visualize how Americans gradually and profoundly transformed their nation into a place 'where car dependence is woven into the basic fabric of the landscape'."

REVIEW: *J Am Hist* v100 no4 p1268-9 Mr 2014

WELLS, PETER S. How ancient Europeans saw the world; vision, patterns, and the shaping of the mind in prehistoric times; [by] Peter S. Wells 304 p. 2012 Princeton University Press

1. Antiquities, Prehistoric—Europe, Western 2. Archaeological literature 3. Bronze age—Europe, Western 4. Iron age—Europe, Western 5. Material culture—Europe, Western 6. Prehistoric peoples—Europe, Western 7. Symbolism

ISBN 0691143382 (alk. paper); 9780691143385 (alk. paper)
LC 2012-001534

SUMMARY: In this book, author "[Peter S.] Wells reconstructs how the peoples of pre-Roman Europe saw the world and their place in it. He sheds new light on how they communicated their thoughts, feelings, and visual perceptions through the everyday tools they shaped, the pottery and metal ornaments they decorated, and the arrangements of objects they made in their ritual places--and how these forms and patterns in turn shaped their experience." (Publisher's note)

REVIEW: *Choice* v50 no7 p1295 Mr 2013 R. B. Clay

REVIEW: *TLS* no5753 p7-8 Jl 5 2013 PETER THONEMANN

"The Idea of Order: The Circular Archetype in Prehistoric Europe," "Prehistoric Materialities: Becoming Material in Prehistoric Britain and Ireland" and "How Ancient Europeans Saw the World: Vision, Patterns, and the Shaping of the Mind in Prehistoric Times." "Richard Bradley argues in his absorbing new book . . . that we are dealing not solely, or even primarily, with a practical choice, but with a particular way of seeing the world. . . . representation." . . . [Andrew Meirion] Jones's 'performative' approach to material culture has a lot going for it, and it is a pity that his prose is so hard going. . . . Jones could learn a thing or two from Peter Wells, whose 'How Ancient Europeans Saw the World' covers much of the same ground (and a lot more besides) in beautifully crisp and elegant English."

WELLS, ROBISON. Blackout; [by] Robison Wells 432 p. 2013 HarperTeen

1. Ability—Fiction 2. Dystopias 3. Pandemics 4. Science fiction 5. Supernatural—Fiction 6. Teenagers—Fiction 7. Terrorism—Fiction 8. Virus diseases—Fiction 9. Young adult fiction, American

ISBN 9780062026125 (hardcover bdg.)
LC 2012-045523

SUMMARY: In this young adult novel by Robison Wells, "Laura and Alec are highly trained teenage terrorists. Jack and Aubrey are small-town high school students. There was no reason for their paths to ever cross. But now a mysterious virus is spreading throughout America, infecting teenagers with impossible superpowers--and all teens are being rounded up, dragged to government testing facilities, and drafted into the army to fight terrorism." (Publisher's note)

REVIEW: *Voice of Youth Advocates* v36 no4 p88-9 O 2013 Erika Schneider

"Black Out." "Terrorist attacks are occurring throughout the United States and the army is investigating all teenagers for a strange virus that gives them superhuman powers. . . . This fast-paced book will keep readers guessing. It is not the virus that creates superhuman powers that makes this book interesting, but rather the characters' reactions to it. Some are terrified, some delight in using their powers, and others work to manipulate it to their own ends. Readers will be kept wondering about the true intentions of many of the characters. Many readers will also enjoy the romantic element. The action, character development, and fast-paced plot will make it an appealing choice that can be enjoyed by a wide variety of young readers."

WELLS, ROSEMARY. Stella's starliner; 32 p. 2014 Candlewick Press

1. Bullying—Juvenile fiction 2. Children's stories 3. Families—Fiction 4. Mobile homes 5. Poverty

ISBN 0763614955; 9780763614959
LC 2013-943104

SUMMARY: In this children's book, by Rosemary Wells, "Stella lives in a sparkling home on wheels. . . . Her home is called the Starliner, and it has everything Stella and her mama and daddy need to be happy. Until, that is, some big weasels pop up along the road, saying mean things about the Starliner. Mama comes to soothe away the hurt, and Daddy hitches their home to a truck and drives it away to a brand-new place, where Stella meets friends who are as enchanted as she is with her shiny home." (Publisher's note)

REVIEW: *Booklist* v110 no12 p75 F 15 2014 Carolyn Phelan

REVIEW: *Bull Cent Child Books* v67 no8 p427 Ap 2014 D. S.

"Stella's Starliner". "Many kids will share Stella's love for a compact and mobile dwelling, and the book vividly depicts the joys of her cozy life; the thread of class prejudice . . . is an unusual one in picture books. The story goes off in a strange direction with Stella's mother's fantasy narrative, though, especially when it confusingly ends up in an idealized real world and concludes with a weak and unsatisfying ending. The art has that famous [Rosemary] Wells combination of adorableness and artistry."

REVIEW: *Horn Book Magazine* v90 no2 p106-7 Mr/Ap 2014 JULIE ROACH

REVIEW: *Kirkus Rev* v82 no3 p104 F 1 2014

"Stella's Starliner". "Wells' winsome animal characters are charming, as always, but her latest effort lacks coherence and depth. The casual, colloquial tone suits the simple tale beautifully. . . . Unfortunately, instead of allowing Stella to sort things out herself, Wells decides to solve her problems geographically. Stella's dad hooks up the house trailer and hauls it to another, more welcoming (and tropical) locale, where the new neighbors greet Stella and her home with awe and enthusiasm. The abrupt ending may leave listeners wondering exactly what happened."

REVIEW: *N Y Times Book Rev* p24 Ap 6 2014 SARAH HARRISON SMITH

REVIEW: *Publ Wkly* v261 no3 p54 Ja 20 2014

REVIEW: *SLJ* v60 no3 p130 Mr 2014 Tanya Boudreau

WELLS, ROSEMARY.il. Sophie's terrible twos. See Wells, R.

WELLS, ROSEMARY. Sophie's terrible twos; [by] Rosemary Wells 32 p. 2014 Viking, published by Penguin Group

1. Behavior—Fiction 2. Birthdays—Fiction 3. Children's stories 4. Family life—Fiction 5. Mice—Fiction
ISBN 0670785121; 9780670785124 (hardcover)
LC 2013-014733

SUMMARY: In this children's story, written and illustrated by Rosemary Wells, "Sophie got up on the wrong side of the crib! Nothing is right: birthday dress, birthday pancakes, or fairy wings. Then Granny and Sophie pay a visit to Zeke's Palace of Costumes. Suddenly Sophie gets a chance to become a truly terrible two." (Publisher's note)

REVIEW: *Booklist* v110 no8 p54 D 15 2013 Thom Barthelmess

REVIEW: *Bull Cent Child Books* v67 no7 p384 Mr 2014 A. A.

"Sophie's Terrible Twos." "[Rosemary] Wells captures the good, bad, and ugly of being a two-year old with accurate specifics and amusing readaloud phrasing. . . . Watercolors, ink, and gouache lend themselves well to contained but highly detailed scenes, where the personalities of central characters and mere passersby alike vividly emerge, particularly through their nuanced sartorial choices. Wells' sweet but smart drawings flesh out the well-paced text and provide additional humor. . . . The size and detail of the pictures make this a good lap read, with plenty to talk about."

REVIEW: *Horn Book Magazine* v90 no1 p81-2 Ja/F 2014 KITTY FLYNN

REVIEW: *Kirkus Rev* v82 no1 p126 Ja 1 2014

"Sophie's Terrible Twos". " It's Sophie's birthday, but nothing seems right to this headstrong 2-year-old until Granny saves the day in this rote offering from [Rosemary] Wells. . . . Mixed-media illustrations in a pastel palette showcase adept brushwork and beautiful use of pattern. However, both the narrative and illustrations miss the usual comedic beats and deftness of skill that Wells is so capable of producing. At times, the narrative seems more interested in satiric digs at modern concepts of play than in Sophie. . . . A worthy topic and a capable concept that barely miss the mark."

REVIEW: *Publ Wkly* v261 no2 p68 Ja 13 2014

REVIEW: *SLJ* v60 no1 p77 Ja 2014 Jenna Boles

WELLS, ROSEMARY.il. Stella's starliner. See Wells, R.

WELLS, STANLEY.ed. Shakespeare beyond doubt. See Shakespeare beyond doubt

WELZER, HARALD. Soldaten. See Neitzel, S.

WEN-CHIN OUYANG. Politics of Nostalgia in the Arabic Novel; Nation-state, Modernity and Tradition; [by] Wen-chin Ouyang 256 p. 2013 Edinburgh University Press

1. Arabic fiction—1801- 2. Arabic fiction—History & criticism 3. Historical literature 4. Nostalgia in literature 5. Politics & literature—History
ISBN 0748655697; 9780748655694

SUMMARY: In this book, "Wen-chin Ouyang shows how the Arabic novel has taken shape in the intercultural networks of exchange between East and West, past and present. This has created a politics of nostalgia which can be traced to discourses on aesthetics, ethics and politics that are relevant to cultural and literary transformations of the Arabic speaking world in the 19th and 20th centuries." (Publisher's note)

REVIEW: *TLS* no5781 p22 Ja 17 2014 MARILYN BOOTH

"Politics of Nostalgia in the Arabic Novel: Nation-State, Modernity and Tradition" and "Trials of Arab Modernity: Literary Affects and the New Political." "Tarek El-Ariss and Wen-chin Ouyang take nineteenth-century artistry seriously, linking writers from this period to the sweep of creative technologies and political articulations that are shaping Arabic literature today. 'Trials of Arab Modernity' and 'Politics of Nostalgia in the Arabic Novel' both offer intimate glimpses of important works from across Arab-speaking societies. . . . 'Politics of Nostalgia' is the second half of a project mapping the Arabic novel, following 'Poetics of Love in the Arabic Novel.' . . . In 'Trials of Arab Modernity,' Tarek El-Ariss traverses similar ground differently, . . . through symptom and affect."

WENRICK, RACHEL. Spirit Rising. See Kidjo, A.

WERLIN, NANCY. Unthinkable; [by] Nancy Werlin 0 Dial

1. Blessing & cursing—Fiction 2. Fairies—Fiction 3. Families—Fiction 4. Fantasy fiction 5. Young adult fiction
ISBN 9780803733732

SUMMARY: In this fantasy novel by Nancy Werlin, which was a National Book Award Finalist, "Fenella was the first Scarborough girl to be cursed, hundreds of years ago, and she has been trapped in the faerie realm ever since, forced to watch generations of daughters try to break this same faerie curse that has enslaved them all. But now Fenella's descendant, Lucy, has accomplished the impossible and broken the curse, so why is Fenella still trapped in Faerie?" (Publisher's note)

REVIEW: *Booklist* v109 no21 p41 Jl 1 2013 Michel Leber

REVIEW: *Booklist* v109 no22 p75 Ag 1 2013 Edie Ching

REVIEW: *Bull Cent Child Books* v67 no3 p188 N 2013 K. C.

"Unthinkable." "When Lucy Scarborough performed the three impossible tasks to break the centuries- old curse of the Scarborough women (in "Impossible" . . .), her ancestor, Fenella, thought she would be released to the death she has sought for four hundred years; however, it was not to be. It turns out that to reverse the life-spell cast on her, Fenella must perform three tasks of destruction to balance out the three tasks of creation in the original curse. . . . [Author Nancy] Werlin manages to create in Fenella a character both prickly and sympathetic; even though she was unable to break the curse that destroyed generation after generation of her family . . . , her backstory provides the necessary character development and motivation for readers to wish her success."

REVIEW: *Horn Book Magazine* v89 no5 p116 S/O 2013 LAUREN ADAMS

"Unthinkable." "Fenella's mission is complicated and confused by her own unexpectedly awakened desires--to learn about fascinating new technologies, to hold Lucy's child, to be with the beautiful, tender Walker Dobrez. The Faerie

Queen's brother Ryland, sent in cat form, nudges her to stay her course of destruction, and she begins her terrible tasks. Werlin, a deft storyteller and creative world-builder, weaves a twisting strand of faerie magic through the human realm, smoldering with sparks of romance and danger, just waiting to ignite."

REVIEW: *Kirkus Rev* v81 no14 p218 Jl 15 2013

REVIEW: *Publ Wkly* v260 no24 p45 Je 17 2013

REVIEW: *SLJ* v59 no8 p107 Ag 2013 Gretchen Kolderup

REVIEW: *Voice of Youth Advocates* v36 no4 p90 O 2013 Courtney Huse Wika

WERTH, BARRY. The antidote; inside the world of new pharma; [by] Barry Werth 448 p. 2014 Simon & Schuster

1. Business literature 2. Drug Industry—United States 3. Drug Industry—history—United States 4. History, 20th Century—United States 5. History, 21st Century—United States 6. Technology, Pharmaceutical—United States

ISBN 9781451655667 (hardback); 9781451655674 (trade paperback)

LC 2013-039646

SUMMARY: In this sequel to "The Billion-Dollar Molecule: One Company's Quest for the Perfect Drug," Barry Werth looks at the firm Vertex Pharmaceuticals, tracing its "transition from boutique creative group to profitable prescription drug maker. Business and science writer Werth . . . offers a blow-by-blow account of visionary Harvard chemist Joshua Boger's struggle to create a pace-setting drug company to develop breakthrough drugs for serious diseases." (Kirkus Reviews)

REVIEW: *Booklist* v110 no9/10 p27 Ja 1 2014 Mary Whaley

REVIEW: *Economist* v410 no8874 p2 F 15 2014

REVIEW: *Kirkus Rev* v82 no1 p156 Ja 1 2014

"The Antidote". "[Barry] Werth provides an inside look at the setting of priorities, the making of deals and partnerships, and the complex, high-risk challenges facing research scientists whose discoveries rarely make it to market. His molecular-level descriptions of drug making will appeal mainly to science-minded readers, but his rendering of bright, quirky individuals and their determination to make Vertex sustainable will satisfy anyone seeking an exciting biotech business story. . . . A revealing, readable book about 'some of competitive capitalism's most complicated science and most cutthroat marketing maneuvers.'"

REVIEW: *Libr J* v139 no10 p63 Je 1 2014 I. Pour-El

REVIEW: *Publ Wkly* v261 no17 p132-3 Ap 28 2014

WERTH, TIFFANY JO. The fabulous dark cloister; romance in England after the Reformation; [by] Tiffany Jo Werth ix, 234 p. 2011 Johns Hopkins University Press

1. Historical literature 2. Protestantism and literature—History—16th century 3. Reformation—England 4. Religion and literature—England—History—16th century 5. Romances, English—History and criticism 6. Romanticism—England—History—16th century

ISBN 1421403013 (hardcover : alk. paper); 9781421403014 (hardcover : alk. paper)

LC 2011-011225

SUMMARY: This book "examines 'the issues at stake in creating a new kind of literary culture built on the foundations of the old,' in this instance the continued . . . writing of romance after the Reformation." Author "Tiffany Jo Werth concentrates on canonical romances written from the 1590s to the 1620s. She argues that in works by [Philip] Sidney . . . [William] Shakespeare and Lady Mary Wroth, a process of 'reforming" romance along Protestant lines can he discerned." (Times Literary Supplement)

REVIEW: *Choice* v49 no9 p1650 My 2012 C. Baker

REVIEW: *TLS* no5747 p12 My 24 2013 HELEN MOORE

"The Fabulous Dark Cloister: Romance in England After the Reformation." "The book's main weakness lies in the fact that the author tends to use the terms 'Catholic' and 'Protestant' in a generalized, modern sense, with 'Protestant' indicating simply Western Christianity that does not submit to Rome. As a consequence, there is a certain flattening of ideological differences. . . . Also missing are the incursions into English literary culture of Continental fictions (whether romance or novella) from Italy, France and Spain. The characteristics of pre- or non-Reformation romance as it is invoked in this study are thus somewhat narrowly drawn."

WESLEY, TIMOTHY L. The politics of faith during the Civil War; [by] Timothy L. Wesley xi, 273 p. 2013 Louisiana State University Press

1. Clergy—Political activity 2. Clergy—United States—History 3. Historical literature 4. Religion and politics—United States—History—19th century

ISBN 9780807150009 (cloth: alk. paper); 9780807150016 (pdf); 9780807150023 (epub); 9780807150030 (mobi)

LC 2012-027903

SUMMARY: In this book, "Timothy L. Wesley examines the engagement of both northern and southern preachers in politics during the American Civil War, revealing an era of denominational, governmental, and public scrutiny of religious leaders. Controversial ministers risked ostracism within the local community, censure from church leaders, and arrests by provost marshals or local police." (Publisher's note)

REVIEW: *Am Hist Rev* v119 no1 p179-80 F 2014 Edward R. Crowther

"The Politics of Faith During the Civil War". "Timothy L. Wesley's splendid eight-chapter monograph joins a welter of impressive scholarship on religion and the Civil War. . . . At first glance, Wesley's focus on clerics and political preaching appears to resurrect an older approach to the writing of religious history, with its focus on male leadership. In fact, featuring preachers accurately re-creates the Civil War era, when ministers were both public intellectuals and spiritual shepherds."

REVIEW: *Choice* v51 no2 p339 O 2013 P. Harvey

REVIEW: *J Am Hist* v101 no1 p264-5 Je 2014

WEST, CHARLES. Reframing the feudal revolution; political and social transformation between Marne and Moselle, c. 800 to c. 1100; [by] Charles West 321 p. 2013 Cambridge University Press

1. Feudalism—Europe—History—To 1500 2. Historical literature 3. Political culture—Europe—History—To 1500 4. Social change—Europe—History—To 1500

ISBN 9781107028869 (hardback)

LC 2012-042957

SUMMARY: This book explores "the profound changes that took place between 800 and 1100 in the transition from Carolingian to post-Carolingian Europe." Author Charles West "shows how Carolingian reforms worked to formalise interaction across the entire social spectrum, and that the new political and social formations apparent from the later eleventh century should be seen as long-term consequence of this process." (Publisher's note)

REVIEW: *History* v99 no335 p305-7 Ap 2014 Levi Roach

REVIEW: *TLS* no5768 p22 O 18 2013 R. I. MOORE

"Reframing the Feudal Revolution: Political and Social Transformation Between Marne and Moselle, c.800-c.1100." "The case is made for specialists, but the depth and subtlety of its analysis give it much wider relevance. [Charles] West's argument is founded on close scrutiny of a wide range of materials from territory that was the core of one kingdom when he begins, at the margins of two when he ends, and at the heart of Europe ever since. It is scrupulously conducted, with more overt, and necessary, attention to method than most general readers (and too many historians) will care for, but it bears forcefully on many central issues, including the nature of feudalism and the dynamics of papal reform."

WEST, KASIE. Split second; [by] Kasie West 368 p. 2014 HarperTeen, an imprint of HarperCollinsPublishers

1. Choice (Psychology)—Fiction 2. Family life—Fiction 3. High schools—Fiction 4. Love—Fiction 5. Memory—Fiction 6. Paranormal romance stories 7. Psychic ability—Fiction 8. Schools—Fiction
ISBN 0062117386; 9780062117380 (hardcover bdg.)
LC 2013-008053

SUMMARY: In this young adult novel, by Kasie West, Addie has lost her memories, so "when Addie's dad invites her to spend her winter break with him in the Norm world, she jumps at the chance. There she meets the handsome and achingly familiar Trevor. . . . But after witnessing secrets that were supposed to stay hidden, Trevor quickly seems more suspicious of Addie than interested in her. She wants to change that." (Publisher's note)

REVIEW: *Kirkus Rev* v81 no24 p103 D 15 2013

"Split Second". "This time, [Kasie] West's dual narrative technique weaves Addie's story with Laila's viewpoint. From snooping and reading the letter Addie wrote to herself, Laila learns that in the other, lost future, she gained the ability to restore memories, and she wants to acquire it now in order to restore Addie's memory. This brings her to Connor, a handsome bad-boy who sells illegal enhancement programs and is immune to Laila's considerable natural and paranormal charms. . . . Although the climax passes a little too easily, the story effectively builds momentum that will leave readers pondering the questions it raises. A fast, smart thriller populated by lively characters."

REVIEW: *SLJ* v60 no3 p165 Mr 2014 Jeni Tahaney

REVIEW: *Voice of Youth Advocates* v36 no6 p79 F 2014 Sean Rapacki

WEST, PAIGE. From modern production to imagined primitive; the social world of coffee from Papua New Guinea; [by] Paige West xvii, 315 p. 2012 Duke University Press

1. Coffee—Social aspects—Papua New Guinea 2. Coffee industry—Papua New Guinea 3. Gimi (Papua New Guinean people) 4. Neoliberalism 5. Papua New Guinea—Social conditions 6. Social science literature
ISBN 9780822351368 (cloth : alk. paper); 9780822351504 (pbk. : alk. paper)
LC 2011-027663

SUMMARY: "In this vivid ethnography, Paige West tracks coffee as it moves from producers in Papua New Guinea to consumers around the world. She illuminates the social lives of the people who produce coffee, and those who process, distribute, market, and consume it. . . . This rich social world is disrupted by neoliberal development strategies, which impose prescriptive regimes of governmentality that are often at odds with Melanesian ways of being in, and relating to, the world." (Publisher's note)

REVIEW: *Bus Hist Rev* v87 no3 p621-3 Aut 2013 John M. Talbot

"From Modern Production to Imagined Primitive: The Social World of Coffee From Papua New Guinea." "Paige West has chosen an excellent title for this book; it nicely encapsulates the two aims that she tries to achieve. The first is to describe 'the social world of coffee from Papua New Guinea.' . . . The second aim of the book is to critique the way PNG coffee is marketed in the consuming countries. . . . Yet she ignores the richness and complexity of the specialty/ethical sector. No doubt there are cynical marketers in it, but there are also people who are deeply committed to building long-term social relationships with coffee growers. . . . Nevertheless, this book is valuable for its thick description of a relatively little-studied coffee-producing country."

WESTFAHL, GARY. William Gibson; [by] Gary Westfahl 210 p. 2013 University of Illinois Press

1. Authors, American—20th century 2. Cyberpunk fiction 3. Gibson, William, 1948- 4. Literature—History & criticism 5. Science fiction, American—20th century
ISBN 0252037804; 025207937X; 9780252037801; 9780252079375 (paperback)
LC 2013-941429

SUMMARY: This book by Gary Wesfahl looks at William Gibson's "writing career and his lasting influence in the science fiction world. Delving into numerous science fiction fanzines that the young Gibson contributed to and edited, Westfahl delivers new information about his childhood and adolescence. He describes for the first time more than eighty virtually unknown Gibson publications from his early years, including articles, reviews, poems, cartoons, letters, and a collaborative story." (Publisher's note)

REVIEW: *Choice* v51 no6 p1008 F 2014 P. J. Kurtz

REVIEW: *TLS* no5773 p26 N 22 2013 ROZ KAVENEY

"William Gibson." "One of the strengths of Gary Westfahl's study is that he sees [William] Gibson's nine solo novels, one collaboration, short stories and screenplays as being a remarkably unified body of work, in spite of the fact that Gibson has twice changed his focus. . . . Without writing a biography, Westfahl establishes enough of the crucial facts about Gibson's life and career to be able to press home the argument that it is that sense of estrangement which is crucial to the work. . . .Westfahl understands that these characters, and the culture they embody, exist at the threshold between states, which explains the significance of the Bay Bridge in his work, and why Gibson's personal explorations of London and of Japan became useful examples of a general cultural experience."

WESTON, DONNA.ed. Pop Pagans. See Pop Pagans

WESTRICK, A. B. Brotherhood; [by] A. B. Westrick 368 p. 2013 Viking Juvenile

1. American historical fiction 2. Family life—Virginia—Fiction 3. JUVENILE FICTION—Family—Siblings 4. JUVENILE FICTION—Historical—United States—Civil War Period (1850-1877) 5. JUVENILE FICTION—Social Issues—Prejudice & Racism 6. Prejudices—Fiction 7. Race relations—Fiction 8. Reconstruction (U.S. history, 1865-1877)—Fiction 9. Reconstruction (U.S. history, 1865-1877)—Juvenile fiction
ISBN 0670014397; 9780670014392 (hardback)
LC 2013-008272

SUMMARY: In this historical novel, 14-year-old Shad Weaver's "life is full of secrets. Desperate to learn to read, he begins attending a school for African-Americans. . . . He is very careful not to be seen, especially by any members of the other secret group to which he belongs, the Klan. Shad is deeply ambivalent about the brotherhood, appreciating it for the camaraderie it fosters but becoming increasingly uncomfortable with the violence it perpetuates." He must make a stand when his teacher is murdered. (Kirkus Reviews)

REVIEW: *Booklist* v110 no1 p116-9 S 1 2013 Carolyn Phelan

REVIEW: *Bull Cent Child Books* v67 no4 p243-4 D 2013 E. B.

REVIEW: *Kirkus Rev* v81 no16 p63 Ag 15 2013

"Brotherhood." "Set in Richmond, Va., in 1867, [author A. B.] Westrick's debut affords readers a look into the mind and heart of a reluctant member of the Ku Klux Klan. . . . While it becomes a bit tedious at times, Shad's inner dialogue is crucial, as it reveals his struggle against the almost overwhelming social forces seeking to shape him into an instrument of racist violence. The constant sense of danger evoked will keep readers interested, and while the resolution is not entirely satisfying, it is nonetheless realistic. From the perspective of a curious, compassionate young man caught up in Klan violence, this coming-of-age story will spark fruitful discussions about race, identity, social pressure and loyalty."

REVIEW: *Publ Wkly* v260 no31 p72 Ag 5 2013

REVIEW: *Publ Wkly* v260 no33 p32-4 Ag 19 2013 SALLY LODGE

REVIEW: *SLJ* v59 no8 p108 Ag 2013 Cary Frostick

REVIEW: *Voice of Youth Advocates* v36 no3 p70 Ag 2013 Laura Perenic

WESTSTEIJN, THIJS.ed. The making of the humanities. See The making of the humanities

WETTA, FRANK J. The long reconstruction; the post-Civil War south in history, film, and memory; [by] Frank J. Wetta xvii, 160 p. 2014 Routledge

1. Collective memory—Southern States 2. Historical literature 3. Memory—Social aspects—Southern States 4. Popular culture—Southern States—History—19th century 5. Reconstruction (U.S. history, 1865-1877)—Social aspects
ISBN 9780415894647 (hardback); 9780415894654 (pbk.)
LC 2013-010029

SUMMARY: This book by Frank J. Wett and Martin A, Novelli "addresses important issues of Reconstruction and its legacy, especially comparing the general historiography of Reconstruction with those cultural products that promulgate some of the most common myths; including films such as 'The Birth of a Nation' and 'Gone With the Wind,' as well as Flannery O'Connor and William Faulkner's stories." (Publisher's note)

REVIEW: *Choice* v51 no8 p1384 Ap 2014 C. B. Regester

"The Long Reconstruction: the Post-Civil War South in History, Film, and Memory". "Narrowly focused on the Reconstruction era, this fascinating book provides a valuable time line of the chronological developments associated with the Civil War and Reconstruction. . . . Significant literature and films are explored to critique how representations of Reconstruction have been popularized in the public imaginary. . . . The audience includes, but is not limited to, those interested in history during the Reconstruction era, particularly southern history, African American history, film studies, and cultural studies."

WEXLER, DJANGO. The forbidden library; [by] Django Wexler 384 p. 2014 Kathy Dawson Books, an imprint of Penguin Group (USA) Inc.

1. Books and reading—Fiction 2. Cats—Fiction 3. Fairies—Fiction 4. Fantasy fiction 5. Libraries—Fiction 6. Magic—Fiction 7. Orphans—Fiction 8. Wizards—Fiction
ISBN 0803739753; 9780803739758 (hardcover)
LC 2013-015285

SUMMARY: In this fantasy novel by Django Wexler, "when Alice's father goes down in a shipwreck, she is sent to live with her uncle Geryon—an uncle she's never heard of and knows nothing about. He lives in an enormous manor with a massive library that is off-limits to Alice. But then she meets a talking cat. And even for a rule-follower, when a talking cat sneaks you into a forbidden library and introduces you to an arrogant boy who dares you to open a book, it's hard to resist." (Publisher's note)

REVIEW: *Booklist* v110 no16 p51 Ap 15 2014 Krista Hutley

REVIEW: *Horn Book Magazine* v90 no2 p132-3 Mr/Ap 2014 ANITA L. BURKAM

REVIEW: *Kirkus Rev* v82 no3 p230 F 1 2014

"The Forbidden Library". "Being a Reader comes with significant challenges in this fantasy filled with ever-changing library stacks, enchanted books and talking cats. . . . Alice proves to be an active and intelligent heroine who adeptly pulls compatriot and rival Isaac out of more than one potentially fatal challenge. Vaguely reminiscent of Harry Potter, Alice's Adventures in Wonderland and Inkheart all rolled into one, it's good fun, if a tad light on character transformation and sagging a bit in the middle. Working in the grand tradition of children's fantasy, [Django] Wexler's off to a promising start."

REVIEW: *SLJ* v60 no4 p155 Ap 2014 H. Islam

REVIEW: *Voice of Youth Advocates* v37 no1 p90 Ap 2014 Katie Mitchell

WEYN, SUZANNE. The Titanic Locket; A Hauntings Novel; [by] Suzanne Weyn 208 p. 2014 Scholastic Paperbacks

1. Ghost stories 2. Lockets 3. Sisters—Fiction 4. Spirit

possession 5. Titanic (Steamship)
ISBN 0545588421; 9780545588423

SUMMARY: This book is the first in Suzanne Weyn's Haunted Museum series. "After viewing an exhibit of Titanic memorabilia at the Haunted Museum in Southampton, England, sisters Jessica and Samantha Burnett board Titanic 2, a replica liner whose maiden voyage will follow the route of the original ship. The re-enactment starts off innocently enough. . . . But soon a string of creepy incidents occur." (Publishers Weekly)

REVIEW: *Kirkus Rev* v82 no3 p321 F 1 2014

"The Titanic Locket". " Spectral voyagers practically outnumber the living ones on a re-enactment of the Titanic's cruise in this ghost-happy series opener. . . . [Suzanne] Weyn ratchets up the eeriness by pairing off several of her living characters with strangely similar dead ones and quickly builds to a stormy climax that the sisters narrowly survive thanks to timely intervention by a powerful medium. After that, it's smooth sailing—at least until the next episode. Mild goose bumps for readers who prefer their ectoplasm served up in buckets."

REVIEW: *Publ Wkly* v261 no9 p65 Mr 3 2014

WHALEY, JOHN COREY. Noggin; [by] John Corey Whaley 352 p. 2014 Atheneum Books for Young Readers

1. Death—Fiction 2. Family life—Fiction 3. Identity—Fiction 4. Interpersonal relations—Fiction 5. Science fiction 6. Transplantation of organs, tissues, etc.—Fiction
ISBN 1442458720; 9781442458727 (hardback); 9781442458734 (paperback)
LC 2013-020137

SUMMARY: In this book by John Corey Whaley, "Travis Coates has his head surgically removed and cryogenically frozen after he dies. Five years after his death, technological advances allow doctors to attach his head to a donor body that's taller and more muscular than the original." The book focuses on "Travis's comic determination to turn back the hands of time." (Publishers Weekly)

REVIEW: *Booklist* v110 no5 p60-2 N 1 2013 Michael Cart

REVIEW: *Booklist* v111 no2 p68 S 15 2014 Heather Booth

REVIEW: *Bull Cent Child Books* v67 no10 p547 Je 2014 K. C.

"Noggin". "Even in a book more focused on the emotional repercussions than the physical, the complete lack of attention to the physical readjustments of Travis' full-body transplant is odd and unimaginative, and Travis' celebrity is also unrealistically downplayed. However, it is the single-mindedness and implausibility of Travis's quest to force Kyle and Cate into acceding to his wishes that renders him oddly unsympathetic and the plot disappointing. Ultimately, the book fails to craft the conditions necessarily for reader empathy."

REVIEW: *Horn Book Magazine* v90 no2 p133 Mr/Ap 2014 JONATHAN HUNT

"Noggin". "Losing his battle to terminal cancer, sixteen-year-old Travis opts to have his head surgically removed, stored cryogenically, and restored to life at some point in the distant future when medical technology is able to attach it to a new body. That day comes sooner than anyone thinks, just five years later, but so much has changed. . . . [John Corey] Whaley's sophomore effort eschews the complicated narrative structure of 'Where Things Come Back' for a more straightforward one; and the premise isn't the most original. . . . But readers will find it easy to become invested in Travis's second coming-of-age—brimming with humor, pathos, and angst—and root for him to make peace with his new life."

REVIEW: *Kirkus Rev* v82 no3 p225 F 1 2014

REVIEW: *N Y Times Book Rev* p20 My 11 2014 A. J. JACOBS

REVIEW: *Publ Wkly* v261 no3 p58 Ja 20 2014

REVIEW: *Publ Wkly* v261 no34 p101-2 Ag 25 2014

REVIEW: *SLJ* v60 no3 p165 Mr 2014 Nancy P. Reeder

REVIEW: *SLJ* v60 no6 p69 Je 2014 Shari Fesko

REVIEW: *Voice of Youth Advocates* v36 no6 p79 F 2014 Jamie Hansen

WHAPLES, ROBERT.ed. Routledge handbook of major events in economic history. See Routledge handbook of major events in economic history

WHARTON, ROBERT M. The book publishing industry. See Milliot, J.

WHARTON, WILLIAM. A midnight clear; [by] William Wharton 241 1982 Knopf

1. Ardennes (France)—Fiction 2. Castles—Fiction 3. Military personnel—Fiction 4. War stories 5. World War, 1939-1945—Fiction
ISBN 0-394-51967-1
LC 81-2-0897

SUMMARY: In this book, "Sergeant Will Knott entered the Army in a special reserve program that drafted very intelligent youths. But by a clerical error he and his squad, all near-geniuses, have been sent into combat. By Christmas 1944 half the squad is dead. Knott and his five surviving soldiers are sent to an abandoned chateau in the Ardennes to establish an observation post." (Library Journal)For descriptive note, review excerpts and other review citations, see BRD 1982.

REVIEW: *TLS* no5757 p19-20 Ag 2 2013 D. J. TAYLOR

"A Midnight Clear" and "Shrapnel." "Written in the first-person present tense, with Wont as the raissoneur, excellent on military detail and sustained by a no-nonsense, staccato style . . . 'A Midnight Clear' bears superficial resemblances to many a celebrated war novel of the period while belonging to a class entirely of its own. Part of this is down to its keen eye for the literary tradition in which it resides. . . . Introduced as a collection of 'war stories,' which [William] Wharton had hesitated from telling his audience of admiring grandchildren, 'Shrapnel' offers a series of vignettes from the two-year period that took his conscripted teenage self from military training at Forts Benning and Jackson to the invasion of continental Europe."

WHARTON, WILLIAM. Shrapnel; a memoir; [by] William Wharton 263 p. 2013 William Morrow

1. Memoirs 2. Soldiers' writings, American 3. World War, 1914-1918—Campaigns—France 4. World War, 1939-1945—Campaigns—Germany 5. World War, 1939-1945—Personal narratives
ISBN 0062257374; 9780062257376

SUMMARY: This World War II memoir by William Wharton "offers a series of vignettes from the two-year period that took his conscripted teenage self from military training at Forts Benning and Jackson to the invasion of continental Europe. . . . Stationed in a Midlands town . . . he conducts a respectful semi-romance with a local girl named Violet. Then, on the cusp of D-Day . . . he is parachuted into the Normandy countryside with instructions to make contact with the Resistance." (Times Literary Supplement)

REVIEW: *TLS* no5757 p19-20 Ag 2 2013 D. J. TAYLOR

"A Midnight Clear" and "Shrapnel." "Written in the first-person present tense, with Wont as the raissoneur, excellent on military detail and sustained by a no-nonsense, staccato style . . . 'A Midnight Clear' bears superficial resemblances to many a celebrated war novel of the period while belonging to a class entirely of its own. Part of this is down to its keen eye for the literary tradition in which it resides. . . . Introduced as a collection of 'war stories,' which [William] Wharton had hesitated from telling his audience of admiring grandchildren, 'Shrapnel' offers a series of vignettes from the two-year period that took his conscripted teenage self from military training at Forts Benning and Jackson to the invasion of continental Europe."

WHAT IS A SUPERHERO?; 2013 Oxford University Press

1. Social science literature 2. Superhero comic books, strips, etc. 3. Superheroes 4. Supervillains 5. Women superheroes

ISBN 9780199795277

SUMMARY: This book, edited by Robin S. Rosenberg and Peter Coogan, explores the defining qualities of superheroes. It features contributors from "such fields as cultural studies, art, and psychology as well as leading comic book writers and editors. . . . Jeph Loeb, for instance, sees the desire to make the world a better place as the driving force of the superhero. Jennifer K. Stuller argues that the female superhero inspires women to stand up, be strong, support others, and . . believe in themselves." (Publisher's note)

REVIEW: *Choice* v51 no6 p997 F 2014 A. W. Austin

"Our Superheroes, Ourselves" and "What is a Superhero?" "The first half of the book asks intriguing questions . . . and sets up interesting debates. The second half of the collection compares superheroes to humans. . . . Despite a few errors in various presentations of comics history and occasionally overgeneralized analysis, this is a focused effort that advances understanding of comics from a psychological perspective. . . . In their coedited volume, [Robin S.] Rosenberg and [Peter] Coogan draw from an even wider range of perspectives in attempting to answer its titular question. Each of the 25 contributors provides at least a somewhat different answer, revealing that the question is more profound than readers new to the field might expect."

WHAT SHOULD WE BE WORRIED ABOUT?; Real Scenarios That Keep Scientists Up at Night; 528 p. 2014 HarperCollins

1. Science & civilization 2. Scientific literature 3. Social prediction 4. Social problems 5. Worry

ISBN 006229623X; 9780062296238

SUMMARY: In this book, author John Brockman "asks dozens of scientists, academics, authors and artists . . . what people should worry about. . . . The physicists tend to worry about the disastrous effect that the lack of public support for big science projects . . . is already having on future discoveries and theories. A number of neuroscientists are anxious about the effect of information technologies on the minds and language of young people. Few worry about overpopulation." (Kirkus Reviews)

REVIEW: *Booklist* v110 no7 p16 D 1 2013 Donna Seaman

REVIEW: *Kirkus Rev* v82 no2 p24 Ja 15 2014

"What Should We Be Worried About? The Hidden Threats Nobody Is Talking About". " A little of these worries goes a very long way, and reading this collection can soon oppress readers: Imagine 150 very smart people taking turns trying to outdo each other with bad scenarios no one else has thought of. Instead of reading straight through, dip in and sample the ideas of the likes of Steven Pinker, Daniel Dennett, Sam Harris, Mary Catherine Bateson, Evgeny Morozov, J. Craig Venter, Brian Eno and many more obscure but no less erudite thinkers. You will be surprised, you will learn a lot, and indeed, you will have a higher quality of things to worry about."

REVIEW: *Libr J* v139 no10 p62 Je 1 2014 Kristen L. Smith

REVIEW: *New Sci* v221 no2958 p53 Mr 1 2014 Eleanor Harris

"What Should We Be Worried About? Real Scenarios That Keep Scientists Up at Night". "WARNING: read the subtitle of this book first. Its editor, cultural impresario John Brockman, may well have you struggling to get your shut-eye as he sets out to keep us on our toes. . . . Some concerns read like dystopia mixed with moral panic, and they surface time and again. . . . Other concerns seem more surprising, some expressed by rising stars who may live to do something about them. . . Brockman's game can both confuse and entertain, as different essays put forward, dismiss and reinstate fears. . . . At the end of the exercise, Brockman's crew has left us with a net balance of new fears. But they also introduce us to some big ideas."

REVIEW: *Publ Wkly* v260 no44 p56-7 N 4 2013

WHAT'S UP WITH CATALONIA?; The causes which impel them to the separation; 224 p. 2013 Catalonia Press

1. Autonomy & independence movements 2. Catalonia (Spain)—History 3. Catalonia (Spain)—Politics & government 4. Catalonia (Spain)—Social conditions 5. Political science literature

ISBN 161150032X; 9781611500325

SUMMARY: This book, edited by Liz Castro, "an anthology of 35 articles both investigating and advocating for Catalonian independence. . . . The essays are largely written by professional academics, though a few are written by European diplomats. . . . Thematically, this is a broad and diverse assemblage of treatments evaluating the possible economic, political, cultural and educational ramifications of Catalonia's secession from Spain." (Kirkus Reviews)

REVIEW: *Kirkus Rev* p12 D 15 2013 supplemet best books 2013

"What's Up With Catalonia? The Causes Which Impel Them to the Separation". "Thematically, this is a broad and diverse assemblage of treatments evaluating the possible economic, political, cultural and educational ramifications of Catalonia's secession from Spain. . . . The essays amassed are lively, lucid and provocatively puckish, as well as edifying. While some intellectual diversity is gained by including contributions from outside Catalonia . . . , the book would have benefited from at least one or two pieces making the case against independence. This omission makes the work as a whole more activist than strictly philosophical. Also, the rhetoric hurled against the purportedly despotic Spain sometimes verges on hyperventilated."

REVIEW: *Kirkus Rev* v81 no12 p128 Je 15 2013

REVIEW: *Publ Wkly* v260 no27 p53 Jl 8 2013

WHEELER, JAN BATES. A campaign of quiet persuasion; how the College Board desegregated SAT® test centers in the deep South, 1960-1965; [by] Jan Bates Wheeler 244 p. 2013 Louisiana State University Press

1. Discrimination in education—Southern States—History 2. Education—Southern States—History 3. Historical literature 4. Law School Admission Test—History 5. SAT (Educational test)—History 6. Segregation in education—Southern States—History

ISBN 9780807152713 (cloth : alk. paper); 9780807152720 (pdf)

LC 2013-014273

SUMMARY: This book by Jan Bates Wheeler presents an "account of how a combination of bureaucratic gamesmanship and the timely intervention of the military helped to circumvent segregation. Through the efforts of Ben Cameron and others, efforts to desegregate Educational Testing Services (ETS) facilities helped African American students avoid humiliation." (Choice: Current Reviews for Academic Libraries)

REVIEW: *Choice* v51 no7 p1295-6 Mr 2014 D. R. Turner

"A Campaign of Quiet Persuasion: How the College Board Desegregated SAT Test Centers in the Deep South, 1960-1965." "This is an interesting account of how a combination of bureaucratic gamesmanship and the timely intervention of the military helped to circumvent segregation. . . . [Jan Bates] Wheeler . . . reminds readers that not all efforts were dramatic, but they were always difficult in the uncompromising atmosphere of the 1960s; no attempt, however subtle, was easy. But through the efforts of the [John F.] Kennedy administration, a small brick (though not a pillar) was taken from the house of segregation."

WHEELER, PATRICIA R. Cancer; How to Make Survival Worth Living: Coping With Long Term Effects of Cancer Treatment; [by] Patricia R. Wheeler 152 p. 2013 Createspace Independent Pub

1. Breast cancer—Treatment 2. Cancer patients 3. Cancer treatment—Complications 4. Ovarian cancer—Treatment 5. Self-help materials

ISBN 1484907701; 9781484907702

SUMMARY: This book by Patricia R. Wheeler "is the result of her personal quest to learn about life after cancer treatment. . . . She organizes the bulk of the book into 26 chapters, each related to a letter of the alphabet and each covering a specific area she wants to discuss. . . . On occasion, the author uses storytelling, references to mythological characters and excerpts from poems to add a literary flavor to her writing." (Kirkus Reviews)

REVIEW: *Kirkus Rev* v82 no2 p206 Ja 15 2014

"Cancer: How to Make Survival Worth Living: Coping With Long Term Effects of Cancer Treatment". "A heartfelt, well-crafted handbook about the effects of cancer treatments. Numerous books address the subject of living with cancer, and some discuss the side effects of cancer treatments. Few, however, tackle the challenge of living with the long-term effects of cancer treatments. . . . [Patricia R.] Wheeler pinpoints a particular challenge, symptom or issue in each short chapter and writes about it with insight and compassion. Her revealing perspective as someone who has lived through many cancer treatments combines with her research-based advice and her philosophical bent to create a personal, moving and instructive book."

WHEELER, RAMONA. Three Princes; [by] Ramona Wheeler 352 p. 2014 Tor Books

1. Alternate histories (Fiction) 2. International relations—Fiction 3. Moon—Fiction 4. Steampunk fiction

ISBN 9780765335975 (hardcover)

LC 2013-026232

SUMMARY: In this book, "Lord Scott Oken, a prince of Albion, and Professor-Prince Mikel Mabruke live in a world where the sun never set on the Egyptian Empire. In the year 1877 of Our Lord Julius Caesar, Pharaoh Djoser-George governs a sprawling realm that spans Europe, Africa, and much of Asia. When the European terrorist Otto von Bismarck touches off an international conspiracy, Scott and Mik are charged with exposing the plot against the Empire." (Publisher's note)

REVIEW: *Kirkus Rev* v81 no24 p318 D 15 2013

"Three Princes". "Julius Caesar married Queen Cleopatra, we learn, and founded the Pharoman Empire—although details of how this came about are sadly lacking. Now, in 1877, Pharaoh Djoser-George and his wife, Queen Sashetah Irene, rule much of Europe, Africa and Asia. . . . All this unfolds at a stately pace, the lavish details described with care and clarity—neither details nor characters, unfortunately, fascinate as much as the author seems to think—and the narrative, overloaded with titles and trappings, ends up (the sex scenes aside) juvenile in tone and outlook. Like static electricity: might give you a jolt but won't keep the lights on."

REVIEW: *Publ Wkly* v260 no50 p52 D 9 2013

WHEELER, SUSAN. Assorted poems; [by] Susan Wheeler 143 2009 Farrar, Straus and Giroux

1. American poetry 2. Culture in literature 3. Poems—Collections 4. Poetry—By individual authors 5. Popular culture in literature

ISBN 0-374-25861-9; 978-0-374-25861-0

LC 2008--53239

SUMMARY: This is a collection of poetry by Susan Wheeler, offering an assortment of poems from her "first three books." The "poems are a grab-bag of dime-store gewgaws alongside allusions to Lucretius, George Herbert and Michel Foucault. . . . There are recognizable fragments of family history, as well as references to consumerism, pop and high culture." (Times Literary Supplement)This is a collection of poetry by the author of Ledger and Record Palace (both 2005).

REVIEW: *TLS* no5752 p22 Je 28 2013 BEVERLEY BIE BRAHIC

"Assorted Poems." "Susan Wheeler's poems are a grab-bag of dime-store gewgaws alongside allusions to Lucretius, George Herbert and Michel Foucault. Assorted Poems, whose title trumps the expected Selected, offers work in variegated tones from Wheeler's first three books. . . . The reader who expects paraphrasable content will have to work for it: the poems are riddling. None offers a clear chain of cause and effect, narrative chronology, or tidy markers of time and space. No navigation aids. . . . What the reader will find is a love of language, from jingling brand names to Latin via acronyms, repurposed clichés and borrowings from poets as different as John Berryman and Paul Celan."

WHELAN, BERNADETTE. Reading the Irish Woman; Studies in Cultural Encounters and Exchange, 1714-1960; [by] Bernadette Whelan 272 p. 2013 Oxford University Press

1. Cultural relations 2. Historical literature 3. National characteristics, Irish 4. Women—Ireland 5. Women in literature
ISBN 1846318920; 9781846318924

SUMMARY: In this book, "the authors examine how literature, education, and cultural production and consumption redefined Irish womanhood. The impact of these cultural exchanges was not hindered by social tensions. Catholic hegemony, or insularity. Rather, the authors argue, reading and popular and consumer culture created centers of conflict, change, and adaptation in which Irish women remained active." (Choice: Current Reviews for Academic Libraries)

REVIEW: *Choice* v51 no9 p1671 My 2014 M. A. Riebe

"Reading the Irishwoman: Studies in Cultural Encounter and Exchange, 1714-1960". "This literary and cultural history examines the growing participation of contemporary Irish women in cultural activities both at home and abroad. . . . Although the cultural encounters and responding ideological tensions examined were directed at middle-class society, the authors make a point of showing how these exchanges filtered down the social ladder. A valuable contribution to cultural and women's history. . . . Highly recommended."

WHELAN, BRETT. Precision Agriculture for Grain Production Systems. See Taylor, J.

WHELAN, GLORIA. Queen Victoria's Bathing Machine; 40 p. 2014 Simon & Schuster

1. Albert, Prince Consort of Victoria, Queen of Great Britain, 1819-1861 2. Children's stories 3. Modesty 4. Swimming—Juvenile literature 5. Victoria, Queen of Great Britain, 1819-1901
ISBN 1416927530; 9781416927532

SUMMARY: In this picture book, by Gloria Whelan, "Prince Albert comes up with a royally creative solution to Queen Victoria's modesty. . . . She loves to swim, but can't quite figure out how to get to the water without her devoted subjects glimpsing her swimming suit. (Because, of course, such a sight would compromise her regal dignity.) Fortunately for the water-loving monarch, it's Prince Albert to the rescue with an invention fit for a queen!" (Publisher's note)

REVIEW: *Booklist* v110 no16 p60 Ap 15 2014 Sarah Hunter

REVIEW: *Horn Book Magazine* v90 no2 p107 Mr/Ap 2014 JOANNA RUDGE LONG

"Queen Victoria's Bathing Machine." "This entertaining story nicely encapsulates a curious bit of social history, though its glimpse of the royal family is as much fantastical as realistic, with a jaunty tall-tale tone governing a rhymed text. . . . [Nancy] Carpenter ably limns eight or so children in lively attendance. . . . The stifling frills and furbelows of Victorian dress; the loving couple's delight in each other; and jacket art of the queen frolicking underwater in her voluminous black swimming costume, a minnow in her crown--Carpenter renders each in comical detail. A concluding note features a present-day photo of the commodious vehicle. A bibliography of Victoriana for various ages is appended."

REVIEW: *Kirkus Rev* v82 no5 p58 Mr 1 2014

REVIEW: *Publ Wkly* v261 no6 p88 F 10 2014

REVIEW: *SLJ* v60 no3 p130 Mr 2014 Linda L. Walkins

WHELAN, JEAN C.ed. Routledge handbook on the global history of nursing. See Routledge handbook on the global history of nursing

WHEN ELEPHANT MET GIRAFFE; 56 p. 2013 Disney-Hyperion Books

1. Animal stories 2. Bashfulness 3. Elephants—Fiction 4. Friendship—Fiction 5. Giraffe—Fiction
ISBN 9781423163039
LC 2012-015041

SUMMARY: In this book, "three short stories depict the budding friendship between a lively elephant and a silent giraffe, beginning with their initial meeting in 'The Water Hole.' . . . In 'Pretzels,' Giraffe decides to whip up some pretzels. . . . 'The Bossy Pirate' finds Elephant so narrowly dictating the pair's pretend play that Giraffe gives up and reads a book instead, until Elephant acquiesces that each friend can choose a pretend identity." (Bulletin of the Center for Children's Books)

REVIEW: *Booklist* v110 no11 p72 F 1 2014 Ann Kelley

REVIEW: *Bull Cent Child Books* v67 no6 p313-4 F 2014 Jeannette Hulick

"When Elephant Met Giraffe." "There's a slight Daniel Pinkwater-esque flavor to this matter-of-fact yet amusingly absurd narrative, and the brevity of [Paul] Gude's text makes this accessible to young audiences while the simplicity of the vocabulary and the large, clear font also put this within range of novice readers. Shy children will particularly appreciate that Giraffe's quietness is presented as an acceptable facet of his personality rather than a problem to be fixed. Gude's childlike digital illustrations, with the blocky, rounded figures of Giraffe and Elephant outlined in black and smoothly filled with solid color, are a congenial partner to the unadorned text."

REVIEW: *Kirkus Rev* v81 no24 p129 D 15 2013

REVIEW: *Publ Wkly* v260 no48 p53 N 25 2013

REVIEW: *SLJ* v60 no2 p72 F 2014 Amy Seto Musser

WHEN PEOPLE COME FIRST; critical studies in global health; 446 p. 2013 Princeton University Press

1. MEDICAL—Public Health 2. POLITICAL SCIENCE—Globalization 3. Public health—International cooperation 4. SOCIAL SCIENCE—Anthropology—Cultural 5. Social science literature 6. World health
ISBN 9780691157382 (hardback); 9780691157399 (paperback)
LC 2012-049338

SUMMARY: Edited by João Biehl and Adriana Petryna, this book "critically assesses the expanding field of global health. It brings together an international and interdisciplinary group of scholars to address the medical, social, political, and economic dimensions of the global health enterprise through vivid case studies and bold conceptual work. The book demonstrates the crucial role of ethnography . . . in global health, arguing for a more comprehensive, people-centered approach." (Publisher's note)

REVIEW: *Choice* v51 no5 p874 Ja 2014 L. R. Barley

REVIEW: *Science* v342 no6158 p561 N 1 2013 Nicole S. Berry

"When People Come First: Critical Studies in Global Health." "A welcome examination of 'the actual impacts of [global health] initiatives on care, health systems, and governance.' . . . The authors' empirical accounts of the complexities of the global health landscape expose a litany of assumptions that drive global health and demonstrate why we must be suspicious of these. . . . 'When People Come First' shows that the issue of how people get access to the treatments they need--be those pain killers, tuberculosis drugs, or cutting-edge DNA therapies--is very much alive."

WHIPPLE, NATALIE. Transparent; [by] Natalie Whipple 368 p. 2013 HarperTeen

1. Adventure stories 2. Gangsters—Fiction 3. High schools—Fiction 4. Interpersonal relations—Fiction 5. Invisibility—Fiction 6. Psychic ability—Fiction 7. Runaways—Fiction 8. Schools—Fiction 9. Science fiction

ISBN 0062120166 (paperback); 9780062120168 (paperback)

LC 2012-038126

SUMMARY: In this novel, by Natalie Whipple, "Fiona McClean . . . has a mutation that allows her to become invisible. But her father, a Las Vegas crime lord, forces her to use her power for evil. . . . Fiona's had enough, so she escapes to a small town far from her father's reach. Happiness is hard to find . . . but Fiona manages to make some friends. And when her father finally tracks her down, Fiona discovers how far she'll go to protect everyone she's come to love." (Publisher's note)

REVIEW: *Bull Cent Child Books* v67 no1 p59-60 S 2013 K. C.

"Transparent." "When the government banned Radiasure, the criminal syndicates took over the highly profitable trade. Fiona's father, who has the power of mind control, is the head of one of the major syndicates, so when Fiona is born invisible, he sees a world of possibilities opening up to him. . . . Fiona's invisibility and her father's insistence that she join the family business against her wishes are exaggerations of common problems of the teenage years. . . . The people she meets are . . . excellent comrades and enjoyable literary company. . . . Readers looking for a romantic action/adventure with a fresh and engaging X-men-ish sci-fi twist will find it here."

REVIEW: *Kirkus Rev* v81 no8 p115 Ap 15 2013

REVIEW: *Publ Wkly* v260 no18 p62 My 6 2013

REVIEW: *Voice of Youth Advocates* v36 no3 p86 Ag 2013 Erika Schneider

WHITAKER, ALECIA. The queen of Kentucky; [by] Alecia Whitaker 375p 2011 Little, Brown

1. Children in literature 2. Dating (Social customs)—Fiction 3. Farm life—Fiction 4. Friendship—Fiction 5. Group identity 6. High school students 7. Identity (Psychology) 8. Popularity—Fiction 9. School stories 10. Teenagers

ISBN 978-0-316-12506-2; 0-316-12506-7

LC 2010-045840

SUMMARY: In this book, "Ricki Jo is determined to give herself an extreme makeover as she enters high school, . . . expanding her horizons beyond her life as a hard-working farm girl. Another new girl, Mackenzie, becomes her ally, and . . . they join up with an established group of friends who are . . . in the cool crowd. Ricki Jo, now Ericka, becomes a cheerleader, develops a crush on a much sought after boy who teases her mercilessly, experiments with alcohol, and reinvents her sense of style through magazines. Her transformation doesn't always go smoothly, and her best friend, Luke, tries his best to keep her grounded, but Ericka is determined to transform from her old self to what she considers her new and improved self." (Bulletin of the Center for Children's Books)

REVIEW: *Bull Cent Child Books* v65 no7 p378 Mr 2012 K. C.

"The Queen of Kentucky." "There are hints of authorial nostalgia in Ericka's canny and sometimes apologetic self-awareness, but her perspective remains steadfastly young teen as she argues for her right to change herself, and she never dives overboard into hyberbolic mayhem. Ericka is forthright and down-to-earth enough to be sympathetic; she clearly has her limits, even if she is willing to push them a bit, and younger readers looking to break out of an old persona into a new one will find both her complaints and her moments of triumph all too familiar. They'll just wish for their own Luke, who clearly wins all awards for best best-friend-turned-boyfriend in a tween novel."

REVIEW: *SLJ* v58 no1 p132 Ja 2012 Susan W. Hunter

WHITAKER, REG. Secret service; political policing in Canada : from the Fenians to fortress America; [by] Reg Whitaker viii, 687 p. 2012 University of Toronto Press

1. Historical literature 2. Intelligence service—Canada—History 3. Police—Aspect politique—Canada—Histoire 4. Police—Political aspects—Canada—History 5. Secret service—Canada—History 6. Service des renseignements—Canada—Histoire 7. Service secret—Canada—Histoire

ISBN 080200752X (bound : alk. paper); 080207801X (pbk. : alk. paper); 9780802007520 (bound : alk. paper); 9780802078018 (pbk. : alk. paper)

LC 2012-545006

SUMMARY: This book by Reg Whitaker, Gregory S. Kealey, and Andrew Parnaby "provides the first comprehensive history of political policing in Canada--from its beginnings in the mid-nineteenth century, through two world wars and the Cold War to the more recent 'war on terror.' This book reveals the extent, focus, and politics of government-sponsored surveillance and intelligence-gathering operations." (Publisher's note)

REVIEW: *Am Hist Rev* v118 no4 p1171-2 O 2013 Rod Macleod

"Secret Service: Political Policing in Canada From the Fenians to Fortress America." "This book brings together several decades of research on the subject of political policing in Canada by the three authors and others, mainly on the political Left. As such it is a useful compendium of information extracted with great difficulty from reluctant government agencies. It aspires to be more than that: to reveal a consistent use of police spying for 150 years on Canadian citizens as a means of propping up the (conservative) political status quo by identifying and attacking radical groups. The book does not manage to make a convincing case for that historical continuity."

WHITAKER, WILLIAM. The houses of Louis Kahn; [by] William Whitaker 269 p. 2013 Yale University Press

1. Architectural literature 2. Architecture, Domestic—History—20th century 3. Domestic architecture—Pennsylvania 4. Modern movement (Architecture)
ISBN 9780300171181 (cloth: alk. paper)
LC 2012-051171

SUMMARY: This book "is the first to look at [Louis] Kahn's nine major private houses. Beginning with his earliest encounters with Modernism in the late 1920s and continuing through his iconic work of the 1960s and 1970s, the authors trace the evolution of the architect's thinking, which began and matured through his design of houses and their interiors, a process inspired by his interactions with clients and his admiration for vernacular building traditions." (Publisher's note)

REVIEW: *Choice* v51 no9 p1581-2 My 2014 P. S. Kaufman

"The Houses of Louis Kahn". "This is a thorough, scholarly treatment of Kahn's nine private houses (all in the Philadelphia area), which until now have been relatively unnoticed, eclipsed by his well-known monumental buildings. [George H.] Marcus and [William] Whitaker explore Kahn's approach to modern architecture, and discuss his personal and professional lives and partnerships. . . . Much of the evidence and presentation for this new hook derive from e-mails, interviews, and additional archival research that yielded photographs, drawings, and previously unpublished material."

WHITE, BILL. America's fiscal constitution; its triumph and collapse; [by] Bill White 576 p. 2014 PublicAffairs

1. Budget—United States—History 2. Debts, Public—United States—History 3. Fiscal policy—United States 4. Political science literature
ISBN 1610393430; 9781610393430 (hardcover)
LC 2013-042841

SUMMARY: This book by Bill White "grounds its discussion of the United States' contemporary budget woes in a history of American fiscal policy. He demonstrates how, until very recently, a common set of ideas about why and when the federal government should go into debt kept Washington's fiscal house in order. . . . White argues for a set of reforms that he believes could win public support and restore the country's tradition of financial prudence." (Foreign Affairs)

REVIEW: *Booklist* v110 no16 p7 Ap 15 2014 Mary Whaley

REVIEW: *Kirkus Rev* v82 no3 p174 F 1 2014

"America's Fiscal Constitution: Its Triumph and Collapse". "Writing in vigorous, plain English, the author turns a few falsehoods on their heads while making his argument. . . . [Bill] White's battle is certainly uphill, given that both parties have become accustomed to staggering levels of debt that he warns are unsustainable. However, rather than merely argue in the abstract, the author undergirds his case by recommending specific steps to alleviate the crisis, including, among others, establishing solely tax-financed budgets and putting bonds up for national election. Reading between the lines, White is recommending much more—and therein lies controversy, especially when it comes to military spending. A book that deserves much attention."

REVIEW: *N Y Times Book Rev* p20 Ap 13 2014 BETHANY McLEAN

WHITE, BOYD.ed. Aesthetics, empathy and education. See Aesthetics, empathy and education

WHITE, CHRISTOPHER. The melting world; a journey across America's vanishing glaciers; [by] Christopher White 288 p. 2013 St. Martin's Press

1. Climatologists—United States—Biography 2. Ecologists—United States—Biography 3. Environmental literature 4. Glaciers—Montana—Glacier National Park 5. Glaciers—Rocky Mountains 6. Global warming—Montana—Glacier National Park 7. Global warming—Rocky Mountains
ISBN 0312546289; 9780312546281 (hardcover)
LC 2013-013453

SUMMARY: "In 'The Melting World,' Chris White travels to Montana to chronicle the work of Dan Fagre, a climate scientist and ecologist, whose work shows that alpine glaciers are vanishing rapidly close to home. For years, Fagre has monitored the ice sheets in Glacier National Park proving that they--and by extension all Rocky Mountain ice--will melt far faster than previously imagined." (Publisher's note)

REVIEW: *Booklist* v110 no2 p11 S 15 2013 Carl Hays

REVIEW: *Kirkus Rev* v81 no15 p251 Ag 1 2013

REVIEW: *N Y Times Book Rev* p26 Ja 12 2014 Coral Davenport

"The Climate Casino: Risk, Uncertainty, and Economics for a Warming World," "Fevered: Why a Hotter Planet Will Hurt Our Health--And How We Can Save Ourselves," and "The Melting World: A Journey Across America's Vanishing Glaciers." "'The Climate Casino' reads like a highly engaging college textbook. [Author William] Nordhaus's tone is conversations . . . , but too many passages bog down in technical jargon. . . . Crammed with statistics, interviews and gruesome but fund facts, 'Fevered' makes its case with plenty of hard evidence. . . . 'The Melting World' takes readers to the glacial peaks with [scientist Daniel] Fagre and his team. . . . The book would have benefited from a tighter edit. . . . Despite that, a moving story emerges."

WHITE, DONALD O.tr. The island of second sight. See Thelen, A. V.

WHITE, EDMUND, 1940-. Inside a pearl; my years in Paris; [by] Edmund White 272 p. 2014 Bloomsbury

1. Authors, American—20th century—Biography 2. Autobiography—Gay male authors 3. Memoirs
ISBN 9781608195824 (alk. paper)
LC 2013-015957

SUMMARY: This memoir describes how "when Edmund White moved to Paris in 1983, leaving New York City in the midst of the AIDS crisis, he was forty-three years old, couldn't speak French, and only knew two people in the entire city. But in middle age, he discovered the new anxieties and pleasures of mastering a new culture." (Publisher's note)

REVIEW: *Bookforum* v20 no5 p35 F/Mr 2014 ERIC BANKS

"Inside a Pearl: My Years in Paris." "It's never entirely clear what [Edmund] White expected to find in Paris. He provides several different reasons for his uprooting himself, all of which partially explain but never make completely clear such a severe life change . . . White seems to have met everyone in Paris . . . and is as generous on the page to even passing acquaintances as he is famously generous in real life. . . . Strange editing persists throughout the book.. . . All of this is irksome because White is a better writer than this, and the lapses subtract from what is fascinating about 'Inside a Pearl,' particularly its game effort at self-examination and its commitment to warts-and- all sharing about sexual aging, social activism, and the brutal sadness caused by AIDS."

REVIEW: *Booklist* v110 no7 p10 D 1 2013 Michael Autrey

REVIEW: *Economist* v410 no8877 p86-7 Mr 8 2014

"Inside a Pearl: My Years in Paris." "It is perhaps best not to think of Edmund White's latest volume of memoir as a book at all. Scattered, maddening, appealing, both bracingly candid (as Mr. White always is) and curiously elliptical, it is a monologue, divided by convenience into chapters. But hidden at its heart is a touching and profound love story, one which Mr. White, for the most part, has kept to himself until now.. . . . Much could have been pruned. . . . But the gossip and self-aggrandisement is laced with tenderness and truth."

REVIEW: *Kirkus Rev* v81 no24 p21 D 15 2013

"Inside A Pearl: My Years in Paris". "A memoir that engages on a number of levels, as a pivotal literary figure recounts his productive Parisian years. . . . The anecdotes and observations of the writer as social butterfly sustain plenty of interest, whether he's overhearing Tina Turner tell Julian Barnes how much she loves his novels or describing being in the 'historic, if tedious, company' of heiress and art patron Peggy Guggenheim. . . . Some of White's observations on rape, feminism and promiscuity continue to shock, but the writer refuses to sentimentalize or pull punches, even (or especially) when the subject is himself."

REVIEW: *N Y Times Book Rev* p26 F 16 2014

REVIEW: *N Y Times Book Rev* p19 F 9 2014 JAY PARINI

"Inside a Pearl: My Years in Paris." "The latest installment of [author Edmund] White's life story, 'Inside a Pearl,' finds the celebrating author of 'A Boy's Own Story' in Paris in 1983, just after that book had been published. . . . This narrative unfolds, for all its frenetic pleasure-seeking, in the shadow of AIDS, which also contributes to White's obvious anxiety. . . . White has a knack for meeting celebrities, and this memoir could mistakenly be read as simple gossip, with glittering names in bold face."

REVIEW: *Publ Wkly* v260 no41 p45 O 14 2013

REVIEW: *TLS* no5796 p30 My 2 2014 FRANCES WILSON

"Inside a Pearl: My Years in Paris." "'Inside a Pearl,' Edmund White's third volume of autobiography after 'My Lives' (2005) and 'City Boy: My life in New York' during the sixties and seventies (2009), begins in 1983. . . . 'Inside,' oyster-like, lies a second book whose subject is talk: table talk, idle talk, talking French, and tittle-tattle. White, whose prose style has always had an easy conversational gait, considers himself an 'archeologist of gossip,' a phrase which doesn't quite catch his memorializing of the ephemeral and the fragmentary. . . . His observations of manners are impeccable; White hears, and overhears, everything."

WHITE, HUGH. The China choice; why we should share power; [by] Hugh White 191 p. 2013 Oxford University Press

1. China—Foreign relations 2. China—Foreign relations—United States 3. China—Politics & government 4. Political science literature 5. Power (Social sciences)

ISBN 9780199684717

LC 2013-443197

SUMMARY: In this book, author Hugh White "sounds a rare note of caution about the risks of US attempts to maintain its strategic primacy in Asia. He raises the prospect of heightened and costly strategic competition, including war, between the world's greatest powers. . . . White calls for a power-sharing agreement between Beijing and Washington that would give China a role in Asia commensurate with its newfound power, while preserving strong US influence in the region." (Policy)

REVIEW: *Choice* v51 no10 p1886-7 Je 2014 M. G. Roskin

REVIEW: *N Y Rev Books* v60 no18 p59-61 N 21 2013 Ian Johnson

"Wealth and Power: China's Long March to the 21st Century," "Stumbling Giant: The Threats to China's Future," and "The China Choice: Why America Should Share Power." "[Orville] Schell and [John] Delury describe a series of eleven thinkers, activists, and leaders in their stylishly written, provocative book. . . . Identifying [wealth and power]--correctly, I think--as the dominant discourse over the past nearly two hundred years allows the authors to make several important points. . . . [Timothy] Beardson's thesis is clear and succinct. . . . Perhaps the least interesting part of the book is chapter on serious issues that need fixing, but that are not unfixable. . . . Hugh White . . . writes . . . that the United States must find a way to coexist with China. In my view, however. White constructs something of a straw man by arguing that Barack Obama's 'pivot' to Asia means the United States has chosen to confront China."

WHITE, KAREN. Return to Tradd Street; [by] Karen White 336 p. 2014 New American Library

1. FICTION—Romance—Contemporary 2. Haunted houses—Fiction 3. Historic buildings—South Carolina—Charleston—Fiction 4. Women psychics—Fiction 5. Women real estate agents—Fiction

ISBN 9780451240590 (pbk.)

LC 2013-032459

SUMMARY: In this book, part of Karen White's "Tradd Street" sereis, Realtor and psychic Melanie Middleton is facing single motherhood in a haunted house she refuses to admit she loves, but it seems her pregnancy has awakened some malevolent feelings in at least one of the ghosts who shares her home." (Kirkus Reviews)

REVIEW: *Booklist* v110 no8 p20 D 15 2013 Susan Maguire

REVIEW: *Kirkus Rev* v82 no1 p166 Ja 1 2014

"Return to Tradd Street". "In this installment of [Karen] White's Tradd Street series, there's nothing groundbreaking or surprising. White is a good writer and carries an intriguing story smoothly forward, combining a number of complex psychic, historical and romantic elements. Mellie can get tiresome (eat a doughnut, already!); the romantic he-loves-me-he-loves-me-not arc becomes annoying; and the historical mystery is somewhat convoluted, but overall, the book is an interesting, engaging read. More of the same from White and protagonist Mellie, which will please fans immensely."

WHITE, KATHRYN.ed. A north light. See A north light

WHITE, MICHAEL. Generation Dada; the Berlin Avant-Garde and the First World War; [by] Michael White 382 p. 2013 Yale University Press

1. Art and society—Germany—Berlin—History—20th century 2. Dadaism—Germany—Berlin 3. Historical literature 4. World War, 1914-1918—Art & the war 5. World War, 1914-1918—Influence

ISBN 9780300169034 (cl : alk. paper)

LC 2013-017318

SUMMARY: This book by Michael White examines the Dadaist movement in Berlin, Germany. "Studying how the Dadaists saw themselves as a new generation . . . the book sheds light on key developments and events, such as the First International Dada Fair, held in Berlin in 1920. It also offers the first serious consideration of the group's role in constructing its own legacy, even as the works were deliberately rooted in the ephemeral." (Publisher's note)

REVIEW: *Art Am* v101 no9 p64 O 2013

"Dada and Beyond," "Generation Dada: The Berlin Avant-Garde and the First World War," and "Marcel Duchamp: The Afternoon Interviews." "Paying particular attention to lesser-known Dada figures, sixteen essayists explore the movement's links to Surrealism and a host of later art developments featuring chance operations and automatism. . . . While Berlin Club Dada members such as George Grosz, John Heartfield and Raoul Hausmann espoused the topical, transitory and inane, they also worked tirelessly to spread and preserve the influence of their art. . . . These previously unreleased interviews, conducted in [Marcel] Duchamp's New York home in 1964, reveal the master at his playful, ever-provocative ease."

REVIEW: *Libr J* v139 no2 p73 F 1 2014 Marianne Laino Sade

WHITE, NICHOLAS. French divorce fiction from the Revolution to the First World War; [by] Nicholas White x, 195 p. 2013 Legenda

1. Divorce—France 2. Divorce in literature 3. Divorce law—History 4. French fiction—19th century—History and criticism 5. Historical literature

ISBN 1907975470 (hbk.); 9781907975479 (hbk.)

LC 2013-375386

SUMMARY: This book by Nicholas White "tracks the part played by novels in . . . . conflict[s] between the secular rights of individual citizens and the sanctity of the traditional family. Inspired by the sociologists Zygmunt Bauman and Anthony Giddens, White's account culminates in the first sustained analysis of the role of divorce in the refashioning of life narratives during the early decades of the Third Republic." (Publisher's note)

REVIEW: *TLS* no5765 p26 S 27 2013 ROSEMARY LLOYD

"French Divorce Fiction From the Revolution to the First World War." "[An] impeccably researched and well-written survey. . . . Here, [Nicholas] White shows particular acumen in his excavation of cultural margins, dredging up long-forgotten works to illuminate the more frequently read novels depicting love beyond and between marriage. . . . Developing White's earlier survey of the family novel . . . grounded in historical knowledge, guided by sociological readings, and underpinned by a massive amount of reading from the past two centuries, this ambitious study concludes with a meditation on contemporary images of relationships, in ways that hint at a welcome third volume of the triptych."

WHITE, PATRICK, 1912-1990. The hanging garden; [by] Patrick White 240 p. 2013 Picador

1. Historical fiction 2. Refugee children—Australia—Fiction 3. Unfinished books 4. World War, 1939-1945—Australia—Fiction

ISBN 1250028523 (paperback); 9781250028525 (paperback)

LC 2012-043260

SUMMARY: In this unfinished novel by Patrick White, "[t]wo children are brought to a wild garden on the shores of Sydney Harbour to shelter from the Second World War. The boy's mother has died in the Blitz. The girl is the daughter of a Sydney woman and a Communist executed in a Greek prison. In wartime Australia, these two children form an extraordinary bond as they negotiate the dangers of life as strangers abandoned on the far side of the world." (Publisher's note)

REVIEW: *Booklist* v109 no19/20 p31 Je 1 2013 Brendan Driscoll

REVIEW: *Kirkus Rev* v81 no7 p264 Ap 1 2013

REVIEW: *Libr J* v138 no10 p104 Je 1 2013 Patrick Sullivan

REVIEW: *N Y Rev Books* v60 no17 p89-91 N 7 2013 J. M. Coetzee

"The Hanging Garden." "Among the fruits of [David] Marr's labors we now have 'The Hanging Garden,' a 50,000-word fragment of a novel that [Patrick] White commenced early in 1981 but then, after weeks of intense and productive labor, abandoned. Marr has high praise for this resurrected fragment: 'A masterpiece in the making,' he calls it. One can see why. Although it is only a draft, the creative intelligence behind the prose is as intense and the characterization as deft as anywhere in White. There is no sign at all of failing powers. The fragment, constituting the first third of the novel, is largely self-contained. All that is lacking is a sense of where the action is leading, what all the preparation is preparatory to."

REVIEW: *N Y Times Book Rev* p1-18 My 27 2013 John Sutherland

REVIEW: *Publ Wkly* v260 no11 p56 Mr 18 2013

REVIEW: *TLS* no5698 p19 Je 15 2012 James Hopkin

REVIEW: *World Lit Today* v88 no2 p55-79 Mr/Ap 2014

WHITE, SOPHIE. Wild Frenchmen and Frenchified Indians; material culture and race in colonial Louisiana; [by] Sophie White viii, 329 p. 2012 University of Pennsylvania Press

1. Clothing and dress—Social aspects—Louisiana—History—18th century 2. French—Louisiana—History—18th century 3. Historical literature 4. Indians of North America—Louisiana—History—18th century 5. Material culture—Louisiana—History—18th century 6. Race awareness—Louisiana—History—18th century

ISBN 9780812244373 (hardcover: alk. paper)
LC 2012-014401

SUMMARY: This book by Sophie White "examines perceptions of Indians in French colonial Louisiana and demonstrates that material culture—especially dress—was central to the elaboration of discourses about race." (Publisher's note) "She argues that the ability of people to perform identities clothed in the trappings of another culture influenced the creation and evolution of racial ideas in the Americas." (American Historical Review)

REVIEW: *Am Hist Rev* v119 no1 p142-4 F 2014 James Taylor Carson

"Wild Frenchmen and Frenchified Indians: Material Culture and Race in Colonial Louisiana". "It is an important book in terms of how it brings material objects to bear on important and powerful historical and historiographical ideas about the rise of race. . . . How [Sophie] White manages cultural analysis, however, causes some problems here and there. . . . White's work challenges prevailing understandings about how ideas of race took hold. . . . Until we know more about the Canadian foundations of Louisiana, however, arguments about its existence as a French colony or about the Frenchification of its inhabitants will hover uncertainly over a human terrain that was far more complex than an imperial identity we call 'French' can ever convey."

REVIEW: *Choice* v51 no1 p150-1 S 2013 N. J. Parezo

WHITE, TEAGAN.il. Perfect ruin. See DeStefano, L.

WHITE, THEODORE H. (THEODORE HAROLD), 1915-1986. The making of the President, 1960; [by] Theodore H. (Theodore Harold) White 400 1961 Atheneum Publishers

1. Journalism 2. Kennedy, John F. (John Fitzgerald), 1960-1999 3. Nixon, Richard M. (Richard Milhous), 1913-1994 4. Political campaigns 5. Presidents—United States—Election—1960

SUMMARY: This work of political journalism by Theodore H. White won the Pulitzer Prize for general nonfiction. It tells the "story of the battle that pitted Senator John F. Kennedy against Vice-President Richard M. Nixon--from the decisive primary battles to the history-making televised debates, the first of their kind." (Publisher's note)

REVIEW: *N Y Times Book Rev* p24 O 27 2013 JILL ABRAMSON

"The Making of a President 1960," "Four Days: The Historical Record of the Death of President Kennedy," and "The Kennedy Tapes: Inside the White House During the Cuban Missile Crisis." "The classic that gave birth to the campaign book genre provides fly-on-the-wall detail about every aspect of [John F.] Kennedy's climb to the White House. Although everyone knows how the story ends, [Theodore H.] White builds considerable narrative tension. . . . This slim coffee-table book, full of arresting photographs, covers the days of national shock, from Kennedy's assassination in Dallas to his funeral cortege in Washington, with raw intensity. . . . This book of transcriptions gives readers the opportunity to sit in as history is being made by a small group of advisers, led by a stoical president."

WHITEHEAD, COLSON. The Noble Hustle; Poker, Beef Jerky, and Death; [by] Colson Whitehead 256 p. 2014 Random House Inc Doubleday

1. Gambling 2. Memoirs 3. Poker 4. Poker—Tournaments 5. Poker players 6. Texas hold 'em (Poker)
ISBN 0385537050; 9780385537056
LC 2013-031448

SUMMARY: This book, by Colson Whitehead, is the story "of an amateur player who lucked into a seat at the biggest card game in town—the World Series of Poker. In 2011 'Grantland' magazine sent award-winning novelist . . . Whitehead to brave the . . . World Series of Poker in Las Vegas. It was the assignment of a lifetime, except for one hitch—he'd never played in a casino tournament before. With just six weeks to train, our . . . narrator plunged into the gritty subculture of high-stakes Texas Hold'em." (Publisher's note)

REVIEW: *Bookforum* v21 no1 p60 Ap/My 2014 DAVE HICKEY

REVIEW: *Booklist* v111 no1 p39 S 1 2014 Bill Ott

REVIEW: *Booklist* v110 no18 p9 My 15 2014 Bill Ott

REVIEW: *Economist* v411 no8886 p81-2 My 10 2014

REVIEW: *Kirkus Rev* v82 no7 p21 Ap 1 2014

REVIEW: *Libr J* v139 no7 p84 Ap 15 2014 Mark Manivong

REVIEW: *Libr J* v138 no21 p70 D 1 2013 Barbara Hoffert

REVIEW: *N Y Times Book Rev* p28 Je 1 2014 DAVID KIRBY

REVIEW: *New York Times* v163 no56496 pC23-34 My 9 2014 DWIGHT GARNER

REVIEW: *New York Times* v163 no56496 pC23-34 My 9 2014 DWIGHT GARNER

REVIEW: *New Yorker* v90 no16 p107-1 Je 9 2014

"The Noble Hustle." "In this grimly funny account of playing in the World Series of Poker, [author Colson] Whitehead writes, 'I have a good poker face because I am half dead inside.' Preparing for the tournament, he finds a coach, works on his sitting muscles with a personal trainer, and makes midweek bus pilgrimages to Atlantic City, looking for games. . . . Yet gambling and despair make for a surprisingly buoyant narrative, and Whitehead is a companionable if misanthropic guide to the Vegas strip, where 'there are so many more disappointments to savor before dawn.'"

REVIEW: *Publ Wkly* v261 no6 p74-5 F 10 2014

WHITEHEAD, KATHY. Art from her heart: folk artist Clementine Hunter un 2008 G.P. Putnam's Sons

1. African American artists 2. Artists 3. Biography, Individual—Juvenile literature 4. Centenarians
ISBN 0-399-24219-8; 978-0-399-24219-9
LC 2006--34458

SUMMARY: This is a biography of Louisiana artist Clementine Hunter, who depicted life on a plantation. Bibliography. "Ages five to eight." (Bull Cent Child Books) "In the 1950s, segregation laws denied artist Clementine Hunter admission to the gallery that exhibited her work. . . . Hunter was not stopped by self-pity, and she did not wait for 'the perfect time to paint.' She had no canvas, so she made art with whatever she could find--window shades, glass bottles, old boards." (Booklist)

REVIEW: *Booklist* p30-5 Ja 1 2014 Supplement Henrietta Smith

"Art From Her Heart: Folk Artist Clementine Hunter,"

"Queen of the Track: Alice Coachman, Olympic High-Jump Champion," and "Daniel Hale Williams: Surgeon Who Opened Hearts and Minds." "The words and images in this moving picture-book biography show that Hunter was not stopped by self-pity, and she did not wait for 'the perfect time to paint.' . . . [Heather] Lang's descriptive text and [Floyd] Cooper's signature sepia-tone oil illustrations offer a rich, deep depiction of Coachman's determination to overcome obstacles. . . . [Mike] Venezia combines a chatty text with a mix of period photographs and playful cartoons in this history of Daniel Hale Williams, who not only performed one of the first successful open heart operations, in 1893, but also made great strides in opening up top-quality medical access to African Americans."

WHITELOCK, ANNA. The queen's bed; an intimate history of Elizabeth's court; [by] Anna Whitelock 480 p. 2014 Sarah Crichton Books, Farrar, Straus and Giroux

1. Historical literature 2. Ladies-in-waiting—England—History—16th century 3. Queens—England—Social conditions—16th century
ISBN 9780374239787 (hardcover)
LC 2013-036857

SUMMARY: "Elizabeth's private life was of public concern. . . . In 'The Queen's Bed,' the historian Anna Whitelock offers a revealing look at the Elizabethan court and the politics of intimacy. She dramatically reconstructs, for the first time, the queen's quarters and the women who patrolled them. It is a story of sex, gossip, conspiracy, and intrigue brought to life amid the colors, textures, smells, and routines of the court." (Publisher's note)

REVIEW: *Booklist* v110 no9/10 p38 Ja 1 2014 Margaret Flanagan

REVIEW: *Kirkus Rev* v81 no23 p202 D 1 2013

REVIEW: *Libr J* v139 no2 p81 F 1 2014 Kathleen McCallister

REVIEW: *N Y Times Book Rev* p10 F 9 2014 KATHRYN HARRISON

"The Queen's Bed: An Intimate History of Elizabeth's Court." "As Anna Whitelock's 'The Queen's Bed' proves, there is still a new and fascinating vantage from which to consider Elizabeth I. . . . She hastens straight to the boudoir of the queen who chose celibacy as a means of wielding power. . . . In the face of continual rumors of her 'sexual depravity,' Elizabeth maintained that she never had intercourse. Yet she never seems to have lacked for lovers. . . . Whitelock . . . demonstrates her understanding that readers are at heart voyeurs, filling her 'intimate history' with countless . . . details, both juicy and distasteful."

REVIEW: *Publ Wkly* v260 no49 p75 D 2 2013

WHITESIDE, SHAUN.tr. Red Love. See Leo, M.

WHITTEN, NATHANIEL. The Book of Extremely Common Prayer; [by] Nathaniel Whitten 128 p. 2014 Vitally Important

1. American wit & humor 2. Gratitude 3. Prayer 4. Repentance 5. Wit & humor—Religious aspects
ISBN 0977480755; 9780977480753

SUMMARY: In this book, Nathaniel Whitten "uses the language of prayer to highlight the absurdity of the modern world. . . . His subjects aren't far from those of actual prayers—prayers of thanks, confusion, repentance and mourning, among others. . . Readers get a 'Prayer for Paul McCartney to Retire Already' or . . . a mealtime prayer that expresses thanks for the food while asking for protection from the growth hormones, pesticides and preservatives that were used to help create it." (Kirkus Reviews)

REVIEW: *Kirkus Rev* v82 no5 p119 Mr 1 2014

"The Book of Extremely Common Prayer". "A humorist with an ear for social commentary uses the language of prayer to highlight the absurdity of the modern world. Veteran humorist and stylistic prankster [Nathaniel] Whitten . . . returns with a volume that is as much an experiment in style as a play for laughs. . . . At their best, these jokey conversations with God are laugh-out-loud funny; at their worst, they approach the level of an awkward stand-up routine. . . . As they try to make sense of a senseless world, these mock prayers often don't differ much from the genuine thing, which elevates Whitten's latest entry above being simply a joke book. . . . These jokey prayers are likely to resonate beyond the smiles they produce."

REVIEW: *Publ Wkly* v261 no16 p46 Ap 21 2014

WHOOLEY, OWEN. Knowledge in the time of cholera; the struggle over American medicine in the nineteenth century; [by] Owen Whooley xiii, 307 p. 2013 University of Chicago Press

1. Cholera—United States—History—19th century 2. Historical literature 3. Knowledge, Sociology of 4. Medicine—United States—History—19th century 5. Preventive medicine—History
ISBN 9780226017464 (cloth : alkaline paper); 9780226017631 (paper : alkaline paper)
LC 2012-036982

SUMMARY: "In 1832, the arrival of cholera in the United States created widespread panic throughout the country. . . . In 'Knowledge in the Time of Cholera,' Owen Whooley tells us the story of those dark days, centering his narrative on rivalries between medical and homeopathic practitioners and bringing to life the battle to control public understanding of disease, professional power, and democratic governance in nineteenth-century America." (Publisher's note)

REVIEW: *Am Hist Rev* v119 no2 p521-2 Ap 2014 Michael Willrich

REVIEW: *Choice* v51 no2 p303 O 2013 D. R. Shanklin

REVIEW: *Science* v342 no6165 p1448-9 D 20 2013 John Harley Warner

"Knowledge in the Time of Cholera: The Struggle Over American Medicine in the Nineteenth Century." "'Knowledge in the Time of Cholera' [is] a book that revisits pivotal moments in the history of cholera deploying the newer historiography of the professions and analytical methods of the sociology of knowledge. But historical sociologist Owen Whooley . . . has still larger ambitions, and he retells the familiar story of the professionalization of American medicine by placing epistemological struggle front and center. . . . 'Knowledge in the Time of Cholera' is a provocative book, sweeping in scope and valuable for bringing the interpretive insights of the sociology of knowledge to bear on 19th-century medicine."

WHYMAN, MATT. The Savages; [by] Matt Whyman 288 p. 2014 The Overlook Press

1. Cannibalism—Fiction 2. Criminal investigation—Fiction 3. Dating (Social customs)—Fiction 4. Families—Fiction 5. Humorous stories 6. JUVENILE FICTION—Family—General (see also headings under Social Issues) 7. JUVENILE FICTION—General 8. Secrets—Fiction 9. Vegetarianism—Fiction
ISBN 9781468308563 (hardback)
LC 2014-000004

SUMMARY: In this book, "sixteen-year-old Sasha Savage has a new boyfriend. Jack is a year ahead of her in school, but that's not what causes a family controversy: He's a vegetarian, and the Savages are . . . well, they're cannibals. Ever since Grandpa was in the siege of Leningrad, the family has ritualistically, on occasion, feasted on human flesh, but they are always respectful to the source and waste as little as possible." (Kirkus Reviews)

REVIEW: *Kirkus Rev* v82 no2 p130 Ja 15 2014

"The Savages". "Can Sasha introduce her controversial boyfriend to the family, and can they all keep Vernon from finding out the family's culinary peculiarity? Making fun of foodies and vegetarians alike, this is neither a laugh riot nor a page-turning thriller, but readers seeking a little grisly diversion may be entertained. [Matt] Whyman's British Addams Family of man-eaters certainly won't be to everyone's taste, but for those who like their humor very, very dry, it may just hit the spot."

REVIEW: *Publ Wkly* v261 no3 p56 Ja 20 2014

REVIEW: *SLJ* v60 no6 p132 Je 2014 Eva Mitnick

WHYNOTT, DOUGLAS. The Sugar Season; A Year in the Life of Maple Syrup, and One Family's Quest for the Sweetest Harvest; [by] Douglas Whynott 304 p. 2014 Perseus Books Group
ISBN 0306822040; 9780306822049

SUMMARY: This book by Douglas Whynott presents "an inside look at the maple syrup industry. . . . Closely following one man's year of operation, the author examines the proper weather conditions required for the sap to run, explains in detail the process of reverse osmosis, which reduces the amount of water in the sap and thereby concentrates the sugar content, and chronicles the sometimes-risky business of buying and selling sap and syrup based on projections and borrowed money." (Kirkus Reviews)

REVIEW: *Kirkus Rev* v82 no2 p208 Ja 15 2014

"The Sugar Season: A Year in the Life of Maple Syrup, and One Family's Quest for the Sweetest Harvest". "[Douglas] Whynott shows the intimate, almost reverent relationship the maple producers have with their trees. They have been handed down from generation to generation like prized family heirlooms, valued not only for their moneymaking abilities, but for their majesty and beauty. Also evident is the deep concern syrup producers have regarding climate change, as the entire industry is dependent on certain weather conditions. These conditions are in constant flux, placing a multimillion-dollar industry in possible jeopardy. Thorough research provides fascinating insight into the sweet business of maple syrup."

REVIEW: *Libr J* v139 no4 p107 Mr 1 2014 Kristi Chadwick

WICHMANN, SCOTCH. Two performance artists kidnap their boss and do things with him; [by] Scotch Wichmann 2014 Freakshow Books
1. Brainwashing—Fiction 2. Kidnapping—Fiction 3. Performance art 4. Performance artists 5. Satire
ISBN 9780991025701 (pbk.)
LC 2013-951733

SUMMARY: "Avant-garde scenesters subject a square billionaire to cultural readjustment in this . . . satire. . . . Larry Frommer and his buddy Hank, two down-on-their-luck performance artists . . . mount their most audacious piece yet: abducting Bill Gates-ian software mogul Bill Kunstler and transforming him into a 'performance art machine'. . . .The reprogramming . . . succeeds all too well, and Bill blossoms into a mystical performance savant who soon has Larry and Hank once again dancing to his tune." (Kirkus Reviews)

REVIEW: *Kirkus Rev* v81 no24 p389 D 15 2013

"Two Performance Artists Kidnap Their Boss and Do Things With Him". "Avant-garde scenesters subject a square billionaire to cultural readjustment in this raucous debut satire. . . . The reprogramming, depicted in bloody, scatological and rather disturbing detail, succeeds all too well. . . . Larry and Hank's picaresque adventures lampoon many deserving subcultures. . . . Yet there doesn't seem to be much effort put into shaping or pacing the narrative other than to pile on more craziness until the proceedings implode. As scenes of gross-out excess drag on, the novel starts to feel as exhausting as one of the haphazard performance pieces it parodies. An entertaining but overstuffed send-up that sometimes bogs down in provocations."

WICKHAM, CARRIE ROSEFSKY. The Muslim Brotherhood; evolution of an Islamist movement; [by] Carrie Rosefsky Wickham 352 p. 2013 Princeton University
1. Egypt—Politics & government 2. Islam & politics—Egypt 3. Islamic fundamentalism—History 4. Islamists 5. Political science literature
ISBN 9780691149400 (hardcover)
LC 2013-003231

SUMMARY: In this book, "Drawing on more than one hundred in-depth interviews as well as Arabic language sources not previously accessed by Western researchers, Carrie Rosefsky Wickham traces the evolution of the Muslim Brotherhood in Egypt from its founding in 1928 to the fall of Mubarak and the watershed elections of 2011-2012. . . . Wickham provides a systematic, fine-grained account of Islamist group evolution in Egypt and the wider Arab world." (Publisher's note)

REVIEW: *Libr J* v138 no11 p104 Je 15 2013 Nader Entessar

REVIEW: *London Rev Books* v35 no16 p11-2 Ag 29 2013 Charles Tripp

"The Muslim Brotherhood: Evolution of an Islamist Movement." "[Author Carrie Rosefsky Wickam's] account of the Muslim Brotherhood's political trajectory ends soon after the seeming high point of the election of its candidate to the Egyptian presidency. . . . She sets out here to understand the nature of the Brotherhood itself, its inner workings, the development of its ideology and its relationships with other political forces and with the state authorities. In particular, she assesses the effects of taking part in electoral politics on an organisation that has had to exist unofficially, unlicensed and often illegally for much of the past eighty years. . . . All these tensions are well captured in Wickham's account of the Muslim Brotherhood's trajectory."

REVIEW: *Middle East J* v68 no2 p323-4 Spr 2014 Raymond William Baker

REVIEW: *Publ Wkly* v260 no22 p48 Je 3 2013

REVIEW: *TLS* no5765 p10 S 27 2013 GERARD RUSSELL

WICOMB, ZOË. October; A Novel; [by] Zoë Wicomb 256 p. 2014 The New Press

1. Alcoholism 2. Families—Fiction 3. Home 4. Psychological fiction 5. South Africa—Fiction

ISBN 9781595589620 (hc.: alk. paper); 9781595589675 (e-book)

LC 2013-024379

SUMMARY: In this book, "Mercia Murray, a 52-year-old English teacher living in Glasgow, has recently been abandoned by her partner of two decades. Distracted from her work and daydreaming about her family back in South Africa, Mercia returns to her hometown of Kliprand, where she must face her alcoholic brother, Jake, his provincial wife, and their five-year-old son, Nicky. As she strikes up a tepid relationship with the boy, Mercia reflects on her childhood." (Publishers Weekly)

REVIEW: *Kirkus Rev* v82 no1 p296 Ja 1 2014

"October". "This novel reflects [Zoë] Wicomb's interest in bridging Europe and post-apartheid South Africa—or, more precisely, showing the extent of the gap. . . . Though the setup is dramatic, Wicomb's writing is patient and meditative. . . . At times, this story feels wan and undramatic, as Mercia continuously muses over the question of whether her true home is in Glasgow, Kliprand or Macau, where there is a potential new teaching gig. But its closing pages are genuinely affecting, intensifying the overall mood of heartbreak. A carefully crafted, if at times overly austere, study of home and loss."

REVIEW: *New Statesman* v143 no5215 p53 Je 20 2014 Neel Mukherjee

REVIEW: *New Yorker* v90 no11 p75-1 My 5 2014

"October." "Mercia Murray, the protagonist of this elegiac novel, is, like the author, a middle-aged professor living in Glasgow. She returns to her childhood home in South Africa after her partner, a poet, leaves her for a younger woman. Uprooted, stricken, childless by choice, she forces herself to confront the traumatic past of her mixed-race family, and a story of sexual abuse emerges. Wicomb adeptly navigates time, place, and the minds of various characters to illustrate the impact of apartheid on one family. She also puts motherhood on trial."

REVIEW: *Publ Wkly* v260 no48 p28 N 25 2013

REVIEW: *World Lit Today* v88 no5 p84-5 S/O 2014 Janet Mary Livesey

WIDGER, CAELI WOLFSON. Real happy family; a novel; [by] Caeli Wolfson Widger 384 p. 2014 New Harvest

1. Actresses—Fiction 2. Dysfunctional families—Fiction 3. Fame—Fiction 4. Psychological fiction 5. Reality television programs—Fiction

ISBN 0544263618; 9780544263611 (hardback)

LC 2013-033892

SUMMARY: In this novel by Caeli Wolfson Widger, "part-time actress, full-time party girl Lorelei Branch isn't famous yet, but she's perfected a Hollywood lifestyle. . . . Desperate to bring the family together again and make things right, [Lorelei's mother] Colleen hatches a plan to stage an intervention for Lorelei on the reality show Real Happy Family. Soon the entire Branch family is entangled in a mission to bring the prodigal daughter back into the fold." (Publisher's note)

REVIEW: *Booklist* v110 no12 p24-5 F 15 2014 Kristine Huntley

"Real Happy Family". "[Caeli Wolfson] Widger skewers Hollywood fame hunters in her sharply funny debut. Hollywood fame hunters in her sharply funny debut. Young would-be reality-star Lorelei Branch is mortified after her mother, Colleen, has a drunken meltdown on national TV after Lorelei loses a slot on a fashion show to a competitor. . . . When she learns Lorelei is running out of money, Colleen concocts a plan to rescue her daughter by staging a live intervention on another reality show, called Real Happy Family. . . . Widger's satirical sendup of the industry is a thoroughly enjoyable read. . . . Lorelei's ambitions and clashes with her mother will hook teens."

REVIEW: *Kirkus Rev* v82 no4 p141 F 15 2014

"Real Happy Family". "This entertaining debut novel unsparingly takes on damaged family ecosystems and the show-business machine. . . . While the locations shift per character, the real setting is Hollywood, especially the new Hollywood of reality television and its creeping reach into everyday life. [Caeli Wolfson] Widger has created a delicate suspension bridge out of her characters' relationships to one another and the world, and throughout the course of the novel, she steadily, craftily adds weight, making for compulsive reading."

WIEBE, HEATHER. Britten's unquiet pasts; sound and memory in postwar reconstruction; [by] Heather Wiebe x, 239 p. 2012 Cambridge University Press

1. Historical literature 2. Music—Great Britain—20th century—History and criticism 3. Reconstruction (1939-1951)—Great Britain 4. World War, 1939-1945—Music and the war

ISBN 9780521194679

LC 2012-015504

SUMMARY: This book on "the intersections between musical culture and a British project of reconstruction from the 1940s to the early 1960s" examines "a set of works by Benjamin Britten that engaged both with the distant musical past and with key episodes of postwar reconstruction, including the Festival of Britain, the Coronation of Elizabeth II and the rebuilding of Coventry Cathedral." (Publisher's note)

REVIEW: *Choice* v50 no9 p1636 My 2013 W. K. Kearns

REVIEW: *N Y Rev Books* v60 no13 p34-6 Ag 15 2013 Leo Carey

"Benjamin Britten: A Life in the Twentieth Century," "Letters From a Life: The Selected Letters of Benjamin Britten, 1913-1976: Volume Six, 1966-1976," and "Britten's Unquiet Pasts: Sound and Memory in Postwar Reconstruction." "An authoritative new biography by Paul Kildea and the last of six huge, exhaustively annotated volumes of Britten's selected correspondence. . . . Kildea's account improves on [Humphrey] Carpenter's in two notable ways--sketching in the social background of Britten's career and offering a surer assessment of the music. . . . Heather Wiebe's astute new monograph 'Britten's Unquiet Pasts' shows how Britten's patriotic project dovetailed both with a nostalgic turn in postwar English tastes and with the nation's more forward-looking cultural enterprises."

WIEBE, JOANNA. The unseemly education of Anne Merchant; [by] Joanna Wiebe 272 p. 2014 BenBella Books

1. Boarding schools—Fiction 2. Fantasy fiction 3. Islands—Fiction 4. JUVENILE FICTION—Fantasy & Magic 5. Schools—Fiction 6. Supernatural—Ficiton 7. Wealth—Fiction

ISBN 9781939529329 (hardback); 9781939529336 (electronic)

LC 2013-027277

SUMMARY: In this book, "from the minute sixteen-year-old Anne Merchant arrives at Cania Christy, an elite boarding school off tbe coast of Maine, she realizes there is something not quite right about the eerie, fog-ridden place. . . . Cania Christy's students are actually dead, and their grief-stricken parents pay exorbitant 'tuitions' . . . to allow their children the chance to earn a second chance at a mortal life." (Bulletin of the Center for Children's Books)

REVIEW: *Booklist* v110 no11 p66 F 1 2014 Jeanne Fredriksen

REVIEW: *Bull Cent Child Books* v67 no5 p289-90 Ja 2014 K. Q. G.

"The Unseemly Education of Anne Merchant." "Readers clued into the various allusions to Faust and the more general hints that something paranormal is going on here will find the revelation of the school's secrets not terribly surprising. [Joanna] Wiebe wisely makes Anne's discovery not the climax of the story but part of her larger experience of realizing that no one here can be trusted, but the logic gets a bit muddied when Anne realizes that she is not dead but merely in a coma and that only she has the power to put a stop to the Mephistophelean headmaster's bargaining. The evil characters . . . make this a wickedly enjoyable entertainment, while the gloomy, spooky atmosphere provides enough spine tingles to satisfy readers looking for a decent scare."

REVIEW: *Publ Wkly* v260 no45 p72-3 N 11 2013

REVIEW: *Quill Quire* v80 no1 p44 Ja/F 2014 Aya Tsintziras

"The Unseemly Education of Anne Merchant". "A page-turning supernatural story full of vividly painted characters and thrilling plot twists worthy of a good horror movie. . . . Anne is a familiar type in YA—the smart, dorky girl who clashes with a clique of mean girls. But [Joanna] Wiebe makes her distinct, giving her crazy curls and a crooked tooth, as well as a seemingly unconscious knack for questioning everything she encounters. . . . Wiebe turns the trope of the intelligent loner out of place at a new school into a moving exploration of staying true to oneself and dealing with the loss of a parent, set against the backdrop of a supernatural thriller."

REVIEW: *Voice of Youth Advocates* v36 no5 p84 D 2013 Shanna Miles

WIEGAND, WAYNE A.ed. Genreflecting. See Herald, D. T.

WIEHL, LIS. Fatal tide; [by] Lis Wiehl 336 p. 2013 Thomas Nelson

1. Conspiracies—Fiction 2. Paranormal fiction 3. Pharmaceutical industry—Fiction 4. Religious fiction, American

ISBN 9781595549464 (trade paper)

LC 2013-009865

SUMMARY: In this novel by Lis Wiehl and Pete Nelson, part of the East Salem series, "For an occult cabal in . . . Linz Pharmaceuticals, contaminating the water supply is just part of an ancient conspiracy against all of humankind. As the clouds gather, Tommy and Dani realize they must . . . stop the dissemination of Provivilan. Even then, it could take a . . . battle between angels and demons to save humanity from the supernatural evils that have been summoned to East Salem." (Publisher's note)

REVIEW: *Kirkus Rev* v81 no16 p195 Ag 15 2013

"Fatal Tide." "A plague of demons threatens humanity, and there's only a small team of the devout, backed up by some angels, to stop them. . . . Dark forces are evidently conspiring to create mayhem, and the mysterious new drug Provivilan may be on its way to achieving its creators' goal, if only Tommy and his team can find out what that is. Though usually known for memorable characters, [authors Lis] Wiehl and [Pete] Nelson lose the trail and the reader when what should be the climax of their East Salem trilogy gets bogged down describing the rules of the supernatural world and reciting the story developments since the second installment (Darkness Rising)."

REVIEW: *Libr J* v138 no15 p61 S 15 2013

WIENAND, VICKI.ed. The Tempest. See The Tempest

WIEVIORKA, MICHEL. Evil; [by] Michel Wieviorka 180 p. 2012 Polity

1. Good & evil 2. Hate 3. Social psychology 4. Social science literature 5. Violence

ISBN 9780745653938 (pbk.); 0745653936 (pbk.); 0745653928 (hbk.); 9780745653921 (hbk.)

SUMMARY: In this book, "Michel Wieviorka develops a sociological analysis of evil phenomena. His aim is to explain evil, to reveal its social, political, and cultural sources, and to clarify the processes through which the present-day forms of evil - terrorism, violence, racism, and active hatred - are constituted." (Publisher's note)

REVIEW: *Choice* v50 no5 p976 Ja 2013 P. Kivisto

REVIEW: *Contemp Sociol* v43 no1 p126-8 Ja 2014 Daniel Sullivan

"Evil". "Michel Wieviorka provides a highly suggestive (if occasionally underdeveloped) framework for thinking sociologically about evil in modernity. Drawing on empirical work produced by himself and others, Wieviorka weaves together an impressive number of themes in a relatively short space. His terminology is rich and his hypotheses are inspirational. Evil will be of interest to both theoretically- and empirically-minded investigators of the contemporary problems of victimhood, terrorism, intergroup conflict, and oppression."

WIGGINS, BETHANY. Cured; [by] Bethany Wiggins 320 p. 2014 Bloomsbury/Walker

1. Brothers and sisters—Fiction 2. Science fiction 3. Survival—Fiction 4. Twins—Fiction 5. Voyages and travels—Fiction

ISBN 0802734200; 9780802734204 (hardback)

LC 2013-024935

SUMMARY: In this book, by Bethany Wiggins, is a "reimagining of our world after an environmental catastrophe. . . . Now that Fiona Tarsis and her twin brother, Jonah, are no longer beasts, they set out to find their mother. . . . Heading for a safe settlement rumored to be in Wyoming . . . they are attacked by raiders. Luckily, they find a new ally in Kevin, who saves them and leads them to safety in his underground shelter. But the more they get to know Kevin, the more they suspect he has ties to the raiders." (Publisher's note)

REVIEW: *Kirkus Rev* v82 no1 p214 Ja 1 2014

"Cured". "Accompanied by Fo's beau, Dreyden Bowen, and Fo's emotionally and physically scarred brother, Jonah, the girls soon add another man—the sexy but enigmatic Kevin—to their group as they run into raiders, romantic entanglements and other typical teen dystopian troubles. While the Mad Max-esque raiders and zombielike beasts (children transformed into murderous monsters by their vaccines against the bee flu) seem to be standard post-apocalyptic fare, [Bethany] Wiggins poignantly raises issues of transformation and redemption. Despair and destruction are sweetened by hope and love."

WIGGINS, MICK.il. Planes fly! See Lyon, G. E.

WIGGS, SUSAN. The Apple Orchard; [by] Susan Wiggs 432 p. 2013 Harlequin Books

1. Families—Fiction 2. Inheritance & succession—Fiction 3. Love stories 4. Orchards 5. Sisters—Fiction
ISBN 0778314936 (hardcover); 9780778314936 (hardcover)

SUMMARY: In this romance novel, by Susan Wiggs, "Tess's . . . history is filled with gaps: a father she never met, a mother who spent more time traveling than with her daughter. So Tess is shocked when she discovers the grandfather she never knew is in a coma. And that she has been named in his will to inherit half of Bella Vista, a hundred-acre apple orchard in the magical Sonoma town called Archangel. . . . Tess begins to discover a world filled with the simple pleasures of food and family." (Publisher's note)

REVIEW: *Booklist* v109 no17 p62 My 1 2013 Shelley Mosley

REVIEW: *Booklist* v110 no14 p60 Mr 15 2014

"The Apple Orchard," "The Bookstore," and "A Fall of Marigolds." "Art specialist Tess has a successful professional life but is lacking in the family department. When she's named heir to one-half of an estate and discovers the other half goes to the sister she never knew she had, her life gets turned upside-down. . . . Between studying art history at Columbia University on a prestigious scholarship and a two-week fling with a magnetic, wealthy man, 23-year-old Esme Garland from England is happily settling into life in Manhattan when she discovers she's pregnant. This character-driven novel is witty and poetic. . . . The heartbreaks of two women, separated by decades, come together in the history of a scarf that holds special meaning to each woman. Christian fiction author [Susan] Meissner's first mainstream women's fiction novel hits all of the right emotional notes without overdoing the two tragedies."

REVIEW: *Kirkus Rev* p39 N 15 2013 Best Books

REVIEW: *Kirkus Rev* v81 no7 p310 Ap 1 2013

REVIEW: *Publ Wkly* v260 no19 p12 My 13 2013 Alex Crowley

WILBERDING, JAMES.ed. Neoplatonism and the philosophy of nature. See Neoplatonism and the philosophy of nature

WILD, DAVID. Everybody's brother; [by] David Wild 288 p. 2013 Grand Central Pub.

1. African American musicians—Biography 2. Autobiography 3. Gnarls Barkley (Musical group) 4. Goodie Mob (Performer) 5. Rap music—Southern States
ISBN 1455516678; 9781455516674 (hardcover); 9781619696358 (audiobk.)
LC 2013-942951

SUMMARY: Author CeeLo Green presents an autobiography. "This story begins in The Dirty South, where South Atlanta's native son transformed himself into the Abominable SHOWman. Along the way, innocence was lost; farther down the path, his parents passed on. Yet he still found family at the Dungeon with the likes of Goodie Mob, Outkast, L.A. Reid, and Lauryn Hill. Then one day he teamed up with Danger Mouse and everything went 'Crazy.' The book "is the untold story of CeeLo Green's rise from the streets of Atlanta to the top of the charts." (Publisher's note)

REVIEW: *Kirkus Rev* v81 no16 p280 Ag 15 2013

"Everybody's Brother." "An entertaining memoir that captures the voice of an artist who hasn't necessarily accomplished enough to warrant the telling of his life story. . . . He made his breakthrough as the singer of Gnarls Barkley's 'Crazy,' which he followed with the viral solo hit known to some as 'Forget You.' He then parlayed that into TV exposure on The Voice. . . . But if the ebullient entertainer born Thomas DeCarlo Burton is mainly a legend in his own mind, he seasons that legend with plenty of spice. . . . For all his grandiosity, CeeLo (who seems to be moving toward single-name status) is a funny guy with a colorful story to share, from his proto-gangster days as a petty criminal in his native Atlanta through his musical redemption."

REVIEW: *N Y Times Book Rev* p26 D 22 2013 Alan Light

"Americana: The Kinks, the Riff, the Road: The Story," "Simple Dreams: A Musical Memoir," and "Everybody's Brother." "Like some Kinks songs, 'Americana' can be overstuffed with distracting detail (especially the passages about the band's various record deals), but [author Ray] Davies is candid and honest about his personal and creative struggles. . . . In her slim, warmhearted memoir, 'Simple Dreams,' [author Linda Ronstadt] claims . . . that she is allergic to alcohol. . . . 'I am like a human lava lamp,' writer CeeLo Green in his affable autobiography, 'Everybody's Brother.' Moments like that are the highlights of the book."

REVIEW: *Publ Wkly* v260 no33 p56-7 Ag 19 2013

WILDE-MENOZZI, WALLIS. The other side of the Tiber; reflections on time in Italy; [by] Wallis Wilde-Menozzi 384 p. 2013 Farrar, Straus and Giroux

1. Americans in foreign countries 2. Italy—Description & travel 3. Memoirs 4. Parma (Italy) 5. Rome (Italy)—Description & travel
ISBN 9780374280710 (hardcover : alk. paper)
LC 2012-034571

SUMMARY: This memoir by Wallis Wilde-Menozzi "brings Italy to life in an entirely new way, treating the peninsula as a series of distinct places, subjects, histories, and geographies bound together by a shared sense of life. A multifaceted image of Italy emerges--in beautiful black-and-white photographs, many taken by Wilde-Menozzi herself-

-as does a portrait of the author." (Publisher's note)

REVIEW: *America* v209 no14 p41-3 N 11 2013 DIANA OWEN

"The Other Side of the Tiber: Reflections on Time in Italy." "Wallis Wilde-Menozzi's beautiful meditation on Italy takes the reader on a journey of discovery that transpired over three decades of a life richly lived. The work is at once a memoir, travelogue, history lesson and cultural excavation. The author's memories of life in Rome, where her journey begins, and ultimately Parma are the foundation for vignettes about the Italian people, art, language, media, religion, rituals, food and landscape. Her reflections are enlivened by liberal references to works of poetry and prose, depictions of paintings and sculpture and her own photography."

REVIEW: *Booklist* v109 no15 p17 Ap 1 2013 Elizabeth Dickie

REVIEW: *Kirkus Rev* v81 no5 p270 Mr 1 2013

REVIEW: *Libr J* v138 no10 p126 Je 1 2013 Sheila Kasperek

WILDER, APRIL. This Is Not an Accident; Stories and a novella; [by] April Wilder 224 p. 2014 Viking
ISBN 0670026042; 9780670026043
LC 2013-018401

SUMMARY: This book, by April Wilder, features "seven short stories [and] a . . . novella. . . . The stories often pivot on the upending of clichés but also focus equally on the difficult equilibrium of relationships between all sorts of people. The title story observes the inner lives of people in an odd traffic class who have become obsessed with the mechanics of driving. . . . In 'The Butcher Shop,' a divorcé, suffering through a swanky steak dinner, loses a tooth, swallowing it in a sip of wine." (Kirkus Reviews)

REVIEW: *Kirkus Rev* v82 no1 p272 Ja 1 2014

"This Is Not An Accident: Stories". "Seven short stories, a rough-and-tumble novella and a clever bit of metafiction on teaching punctuate this collection from [April] Wilder. It's very lean, this striking collection of tales that remind one less of contemporaries like Monica Drake or Sam Lipsyte and more of the darker plays of Sam Shepard. Loosely based around the western setting that surrounds California-based writer Wilder, the stories often pivot on the upending of clichés but also focus equally on the difficult equilibrium of relationships between all sorts of people. . . . Excellent meditations on the human condition, well-suited to rest alongside the likes of Denis Johnson and Richard Ford."

WILEY, DAVID C.ed. Encyclopedia of school health. See Encyclopedia of school health

WILHELM, DOUG. The Prince of Denial; [by] Doug Wilhelm 212 p. 2013 Small Pr United
1. Alcoholics—Rehabilitation 2. Children of alcoholics 3. Middle school students 4. Social work with alcoholics 5. Young adult fiction
ISBN 098578363X; 9780985783631

SUMMARY: In this book by Doug Wilhem, "At first, seventh-grader Casey refuses to play the key role in an intervention that will confront his dad's drinking and drug use, but then he begins to break through to the reality that no one in his family has faced before. . . . Casey's story demonstrates how to face the risks and discover the power of living the truth, while realistically conveying the impact on young teens of living with an alcoholic or addicted parent." (Publisher's note)

REVIEW: *Voice of Youth Advocates* v36 no4 p76 O 2013 Jonathan Ryder

"The Prince of Denial." "This is a book that has a message, and it delivers that message with the directness and repetitiveness of an intervention. Although the characters are believable and well written, there is also a sense that each has been placed in the story to fulfill a particular role. The book does a good job of conveying what it can be like to live with an alcoholic parent and gives a window into the struggles a parent faces when dealing with his/her disease. Through the telling of three separate stories of substance abuse, the author informs young readers with substance-abusing parents that they are not alone, and that they should not feel ashamed to seek help."

WILHITE, DAVID.ed. Tertullian and Paul. See Tertullian and Paul

WILK, LUCIE. The strength of bone; [by] Lucie Wilk 309 p. 2013 Biblioasis
1. Africa—Fiction 2. Canadian fiction 3. Canadians—Foreign countries 4. Malawi 5. Nurses—Fiction 6. Physicians—Fiction
ISBN 9781927428399 (pbk.)
LC 2013-432821

SUMMARY: This novel "is the story of a Western doctor, a Malawian nurse, and the crises that push both of them to the brink of collapse. With biting emotion and a pathological eye for detail, novelist and medical doctor Lucie Wilk demonstrates how, in a place where knowledge can frustrate as often as it heals, true strength requires the flexibility to let go." (Publisher's note)

REVIEW: *Quill Quire* v79 no9 p27 N 2013 Kamalal-Solaylee

"The Strength of Bone." "[Author Lucie] Wilk eschews traditional tropes, especially the romantic, and instead works with what is unspoken, hinted at, and left to the imagination. This is not to say the novel isn't deeply rooted in an historical moment or personal experience. It begins in 1995, the same year Wilk herself travelled to Malawi to practice medicine. . . . There's an occasional but unmistakable self-consciousness in the writing: the overtly literary language takes up valuable narrative space and eclipses the supporting characters. . . . The tendency toward overwriting is a typical first-novel problem in a book that otherwise is anything but typical."

WILKENS, CARRIE. Beyond addiction. See Foote, J.

WILKINSON, DAVID. Science, religion, and the search for extraterrestrial intelligence; [by] David Wilkinson xi, 227 p. 2013 Oxford University Press
1. Extraterrestrial life—Religious aspects 2. Life on other planets 3. Life on other planets—Religious aspects 4. Religion and science 5. Religious literature
ISBN 0199680205; 9780199680207 (hardback)
LC 2013-938578

SUMMARY: Written by David Wilkinson, "This book sets out the scientific arguments undergirding SETI, with particular attention to the uncertainties in arguments and the strength of the data already assembled. It assesses . . . the Fermi paradox, the origin and evolution of intelligent life, and current SETI strategies. In all of this it reflects on how these questions are shaped by history and pop culture and their relationship with religion, especially Christian theology." (Publisher's note)

REVIEW: *New Statesman* v142 no5171 p46 Ag 23 2013 Emma Crichton-Miller

REVIEW: *TLS* no5794 p26-7 Ap 18 2014 MARK VERNON

"Science, Religion, and the Search for Extraterrestrial Intelligence." "The overview of the theological terrain, ancient and modem, given by David Wilkinson (an Anglican priest and astrophysicist) is particularly useful, simply because it is infrequently summarized. . . . The book touches on the more general debates between science and religion too, and Wilkinson emphasizes examples of how faith is often placed in science, not least by enthusiasts of ETI. . . . One is, however, left wondering whether the anxieties of contact could be contained by the rational considerations that are David Wilkinson's forte."

WILL, GEORGE F., 1941-. A nice little place on the North Side; Wrigley Field at one hundred; [by] George F. Will 160 p. 2014 Crown Archetype

1. BIOGRAPHY & AUTOBIOGRAPHY—Personal Memoirs 2. SPORTS & RECREATION—Baseball—General 3. SPORTS & RECREATION—Baseball—History 4. Sports literature

ISBN 0385349319; 9780385349314 (hardback)

LC 2013-036084

SUMMARY: In this book on the Wrigley Field baseball field in Chicago, Illinois, author George Will "examines both the unforgettable stories that forged the field's legend and the larger-than-life characters . . . who brought it glory, heartbreak, and scandal. . . . Will also explores his childhood connections to the team, the Cubs' future, and what keeps long-suffering fans rooting for the home team after so many years of futility." (Publisher's note)

REVIEW: *Booklist* v110 no11 p10 F 1 2014 Wes Lukowsky

REVIEW: *Booklist* v110 no5 p4 N 1 2013 Brad Hooper

"Like A Mighty Army," "A Nice Little Place on the North Side: Wrigley Field at One Hundred," and "Uganda Be Kidding Me". "The seventh volume in the best selling Safehold series of sf novels sees the heretofore unchallenged and repressive rule of the Church of God Awaiting being threatened. . . . Conservative commentator [George] Will has always held baseball in a special place in his heart, and in his new book, he gives free rein to his passion, imparting the history of Wrigley Field, home of the Chicago Cubs. . . . In comedian and best-selling author [Chelsea] Handler's new hook, she talks about her travels."

REVIEW: *Commentary* v137 no3 p50-1 Mr 2014 RICH COHEN

REVIEW: *Kirkus Rev* v82 no2 p280 Ja 15 2014

"A Nice Little Place on the North Side: Wrigley Field at One Hundred". " Veteran conservative political pundit [George F.] Will . . . writes an affectionate birthday card to the home of his beloved Chicago Cubs. . . . This is not a traditional, chronological history but an emotional one; in fact, greedy readers will find little about the construction of the place. . . . Digressive, amusing, anecdotal, legend-shattering, self-deprecating and passionate—just what you want in a friend sitting beside you at the ballpark."

REVIEW: *Libr J* v139 no3 p112 F 15 2014 Benjamin Malczewski

REVIEW: *N Y Times Book Rev* p17 Je 29 2014 JAMES MCMANUS

REVIEW: *N Y Times Book Rev* p26 Ap 13 2014 GREGORY COWLES

REVIEW: *Publ Wkly* v261 no4 p126-30 Ja 27 2014

WILLEMS, MO.il. A big guy took my ball! See Willems, M.

WILLEMS, MO. A big guy took my ball!; [by] Mo Willems 64 p. 2013 Hyperion Books for Children

1. Animals—Fiction 2. Children's stories 3. Elephants—Fiction 4. Elephants—Juvenile fiction 5. Friendship—Fiction 6. Friendship—Juvenile fiction 7. Pigs—Fiction 8. Play—Fiction 9. Play—Juvenile fiction 10. Swine—Juvenile fiction 11. Whales—Fiction 12. Whales—Juvenile fiction

ISBN 1423174917 (reinforced); 9781423174912 (reinforced)

LC 2012-010899

SUMMARY: In this book, author and illustrator Mo "Willems observes truths about human behavior through the eyes of Gerald, an elephant, and Piggie. The premise this time is that Piggie's recently acquired ball has been snatched by some unknown creature, one so big that Piggie begs Gerald to intervene. But Gerald's perceived power and genuine desire to help his smaller friend cannot provide him with sufficient courage once he sees that he'll have to confront an enormous whale." (School Library Journal)

REVIEW: *Booklist* v109 no17 p89 My 1 2013 Daniel Kraus

REVIEW: *Bull Cent Child Books* v67 no1 p60 S 2013 K. C.

"A Big Guy Took My Ball." "[Author and illustrator Mo] Willems has once again found the sweet spot where humor and situational familiarity meet cognitive capacity; here he introduces perspective through a very familiar playground experience. Introducing comparatives through illustration, font size, and the introduction of the -er word ending, he carves out both physical and moral space in the negotiation of the way size matters. The ball and Gerald are big to Piggie, but not to the ball's owner; being big seems to hold all the advantages to our heroes, while being small has more allure for the lonely whale."

REVIEW: *Kirkus Rev* v81 no8 p115-6 Ap 15 2013

REVIEW: *SLJ* v59 no7 p74 Jl 2013 Gloria Koster

WILLEMS, MO.il. Don't pigeonhole me! See Willems, M.

WILLEMS, MO. Don't pigeonhole me!; two decades of the Mo Willems sketchbook; [by] Mo Willems 279 p. 2013 Disney Editions

1. Artists' notebooks 2. Autobiographies 3. Book illustration 4. Illustrators—United States

ISBN 1423144368; 9781423144366
LC 2012-474453

SUMMARY: In this autobiographical book by Mo Willems, "readers are given a rare glimpse into the mind of the man the 'New York Times' described as 'The biggest new talent to emerge thus far in the '00s.' Since he was a teenager, Mo has been creating characters and scribbling ideas in the pages of sketchbooks. In the early 1990s, he started self-publishing collections of his drawings, and 'The Mo Willems Sketchbook' was created." (Publisher's note)

REVIEW: *Booklist* v109 no22 p18 Ag 1 2013 Ann Kelley

REVIEW: *Bull Cent Child Books* v67 no1 p63 S 2013 K. Q. G.

"Don't Pigeonhole Me!" "With an engaging, conversational style, wisecracking [author and] illustrator Willems invites readers into the inner workings of his artistic process as he reflects upon the last twenty years of sketches, scribbles, and doodles. As a starving artist living in New York, Willems began drawing cartoons for a 'zine in 1993, eventually putting his sketches together in a special edition, the first 'Mo Willems Sketchbook'. The single-panel, editorial-like cartoons that make up that early publication and its subsequent iterations are presented here, along with more narratively structured sketches, several of which eventually led to some of Willems' best hits, including 'Don't Let the Pigeon Drive the Bus' . . . and 'Leonardo, the Terrible Monster'."

REVIEW: *Horn Book Magazine* v89 no5 p129-30 S/O 2013 CYNTHIA K. RITTER

"Don't Pigeonhole Me!: Two Decades of the Mo Willems Sketchbook." "Mostly done 'on the side' and 'just forfun,' this collection's twenty sketchbooks of humorous doodles highlight the evolution of Willems as an artist. Since each sketchbook has its own general theme, the content varies: cartoons and complete stories, gags and introspective pieces, inspiration for future picture books . . . homages to other artists, and picture book-making exercises focusing on concepts such as page turns, wordless books, and how kids learn to read. Though all these doodles contain elements of Willems's signature children's book style and humor, this volume is largely for adults to enjoy at leisure."

REVIEW: *Kirkus Rev* v81 no12 p73-4 Je 15 2013

REVIEW: *SLJ* v59 no10 p1 O 2013 Kiera Parrott

WILLIAM HAYLEY (1745-1820), SELECTED POETRY; England's Lost Laureate; 93 p. 2013 University of Chichester

1. Art—Poetry 2. English poetry 3. Odes 4. Poems—Collections 5. Sailors
ISBN 1907852204; 9781907852206

SUMMARY: "This volume of poetry, selected by Diana Barsham, is very much a taster of [William] Hayley's work, as he was a prolific writer. Extending to 96 pages, it comprises extracts from Hayley's major poems, together with several illustrations in colour--including . . . two by William Blake (Publisher's note)

REVIEW: *TLS* no5767 p22 O 11 2013 MIN WILD

"William Hayley (1745-1820): Poet, Biographer, and Libertarian: A Reassessment" and "William Hayley (1745-1820): England's Lost Laureate: Selected Poetry." "Hayley's own fatal facility has often compromised him for later audiences, and even though these two volumes contain much of use and interest, nobody's heart seems to have been in the making of them, just as Hayley's heart did not always suffuse his written words with the feeling he claimed. . . .Readers may leave these volumes grieving for two missed opportunities. One concerns production values, which are poor in both, though 'Selected Poetry' is atrocious. . . . The second missed opportunity, then, is . . . any book reassessing him needed to align itself firmly alongside current scholarly work on pre-Romantic and Romantic networks of friendship and patronage."

WILLIAMS-GARCIA, RITA. P.S. Be Eleven; [by] Rita Williams-Garcia 288 p. 2013 Harpercollins Childrens Books

1. African American families—Fiction 2. Brooklyn (New York, N.Y.)—Fiction 3. Families—Fiction 4. Historical fiction 5. Vietnam veterans—Fiction
ISBN 0061938629; 9780061938627

SUMMARY: This book is a follow-up to Rita Williams-Garcia's Newbery Honor-winning "One Crazy Summer." Here, "Delphine and her sisters return to Brooklyn from visiting their estranged mother, Cecile, a poet . . . . Change and conflict have the Gaither household in upheaval: Pa has a new girlfriend, Uncle Darnell returns from Vietnam a damaged young man, and the sixth-grade teacher Delphine hoped to get has been replaced by a man from Zambia." (Publishers Weekly)

REVIEW: *Booklist* v110 no6 p56 N 15 2013 Pam Spencer Holley

"P.S. Be Eleven." "In this follow-up to [Rita] Williams-Garcia's Newbery Honor book ('One Crazy Summer' . . .) the Gaither sisters have returned to Brooklyn after visiting their mother, Cecile, in Oakland, California. . . . [Sisi Aisha] Johnson portrays a range of characters, from the sisters' old-fashioned, proper grandmother. Big Ma, who doles out her advice in a high-pitched, somewhat scratchy voice, to the quiet, modulated tones of their father's new wife, Marva. Fern has sweet, little-girl exclamations, while Vonetta's voice matures as the story progresses. Family and school life form Delphine's days in this warmhearted tale, which has appeal for all ages."

REVIEW: *Booklist* v109 no12 p69 F 15 2013 Ann Kelley

REVIEW: *Bull Cent Child Books* v67 no1 p61 S 2013 D. S.

REVIEW: *Horn Book Magazine* v89 no3 p99 My/Je 2013 SUSAN DOVE LEMPKE

REVIEW: *Kirkus Rev* v81 no6 p173 Mr 15 2013

REVIEW: *Kirkus Rev* p85 N 15 2013 Best Books

REVIEW: *Publ Wkly* v260 no15 p63-4 Ap 15 2013

REVIEW: *Publ Wkly* p90 Children's starred review annual 2013

REVIEW: *SLJ* v59 no10 p1 O 2013 Terri Norstrom

REVIEW: *SLJ* v59 no6 p146 Je 2013 Gesse Stark-Smith

WILLIAMS, BRIAN GLYN. Afghanistan declassified; a guide to America's longest war; [by] Brian Glyn Williams xii, 248 p. 2012 University of Pennsylvania Press

1. Afghan war, 2001—Personal narratives, American 2. Afghanistan—History 3. Historical literature
ISBN 9780812244038 (hardcover : alk. paper)
LC 2011-025251

SUMMARY: This book by Brian Glyn Williams "was originally written for the US military as a guide to the country, its history and people for troops arriving there in 2007. While the book adds some of the author's travel adventures and his take on Afghan political personalities, the core stands unchanged." (Times Literary Supplement) "The author describes the bloody 1980s mujahedeen resistance followed by the vicious 1990s civil war which led to the Taliban regime." (Publishers Weekly)

REVIEW: *Middle East J* v66 no2 p391 Spr 2012 J. H.

REVIEW: *TLS* no5765 p12-3 S 27 2013 THOMAS BARFIELD

"Afghanistan Declassified: A Guide to America's Longest War," "War Comes to Garmser: Thirty Years of Conflict on the Afghan Frontier," and "Afghanistan and Pakistan: Conflict, Extremism, and Resistance to Modernity." "Brian Glyn Williams's . . . [book] was originally written for the US military as a guide to the country, its history and people for troops arriving there in 2007. . . . Much of what is presented is badly out of date. . . . Carter Malkasian's 'War Comes to Garmser,' by contrast, explores the war in Afghanistan from an explicitly provincial Afghan point of view, where foreigners (and even Kabul officials) are marginal actors rather than the centre of the story. . . . 'Afghanistan and Pakistan' . . . is a good guide by an insider familiar with the complexity of decision-making in Pakistan."

WILLIAMS, CAROL LYNCH. The haven; a novel; [by] Carol Lynch Williams 224 p. 2014 St. Martin's Griffin

1. Hospitals—Fiction 2. Insurgency—Fiction 3. JUVENILE FICTION—General 4. Science fiction 5. Sick—Fiction 6. Teenagers—Fiction
ISBN 9780312698713 (hardback)
LC 2013-032130

SUMMARY: In this book by Carol Lynch Williams, "Shiloh and the other teens living at the Haven Hospital and Halls are 'Terminals' being treated for an unknown disease that causes them to lose limbs, organs, and their memories. Those in charge at the Haven claim they want to protect the residents from the dangerous outside world and help them fight the disease, but the reality is far more sinister." (VOYA Reviews)

REVIEW: *Booklist* v110 no13 p70 Mr 1 2014 Summer Hayes

REVIEW: *Bull Cent Child Books* v67 no6 p339-40 F 2014 Alaine Martaus

REVIEW: *Horn Book Magazine* v90 no3 p101-2 My/Je 2014 DEAN SCHNEIDER

REVIEW: *Kirkus Rev* v81 no24 p290 D 15 2013

"The Haven". "Shiloh lives with her fellow Terminals in a hospital that claims to protect them from the Disease that threatens them in this creepy dystopia about a doctor who uses children as commodities. . . . [Carol Lynch] Williams, who is developing quite a varied repertoire, manages the information meted out by her deluded narrator with great skill. The simple but gripping focus on only one aspect of her dystopia sheds light on a moral question that young readers will have no difficulty answering: Are all people created equal—or not? Deliciously enigmatic."

REVIEW: *Publ Wkly* v260 no51 p61-2 D 16 2013

REVIEW: *Voice of Youth Advocates* v37 no1 p90-1 Ap 2014 Cathy Fiebelkorn

WILLIAMS, GARETH. Paralyzed With Fear; The Story of Polio; [by] Gareth Williams 336 p. 2013 Palgrave Macmillan

1. Historical literature 2. Medical research—History 3. Medical research personnel 4. Polio—History 5. Polio—Vaccination
ISBN 1137299754; 9781137299758

SUMMARY: Written by Gareth Williams, "This is the story of mankind's struggle against polio, is compelling, exciting and full of twists and paradoxes. One of the grand challenges of modern medicine, it was a battleground between good and bad science. Some research won Nobel Prizes; other work was flawed or fraudulent, holding up progress and endangering patients' lives." (Publisher's note)

REVIEW: *Choice* v51 no7 p1255 Mr 2014 R. S. Kowalczyk

REVIEW: *TLS* no5775 p28 D 6 2013 W. F. BYNUM

"Paralysed With Fear: The Story of Polio." "The polio vaccines (there were several) are inevitably the centre of any history of this disease, and [author Gareth] Williams offers an excellent account of the science behind them. Indeed, an outstanding feature of this book is the clear descriptions of how the virus works to produce its horrible damage to (mostly) young bodies. . . . There is still plenty of drama in the polio story, and Williams's skills as a writer come to the fore here. . . . Gareth Williams has mastered his material and is at his best in explaining why the science and therapeutics were good or bad, and why it has been possible to think about the global eradication of this awful disease in the first place."

WILLIAMS, GARY S. The Art of retirement; [by] Gary S. Williams 232 p. 2013 Emerson Publishing

1. Advice literature 2. Investment advisors 3. Investments 4. Michelangelo Buonarroti, 1475-1564 5. Retirement planning
LC 2013-942360

SUMMARY: This book presents "retirement planning advice using examples from the life of Michelangelo . . . devoting half his book to personal values and half to investing." Gary S. Williams "offers the idea of an 'ethical will,' a nonlegally binding document which can help people pass along their moral values to their children. The book's second half offers more traditional retirement planning advice, such as how to determine risk tolerance and build the right investment portfolio." (Kirkus Reviews)

REVIEW: *Kirkus Rev* v81 no24 p373 D 15 2013

"The Art of Retirement". " Financial planner Williams offers solid retirement planning advice using examples from the life of Michelangelo. . . . Although this premise may initially sound gimmicky, Williams has a larger concept in mind, devoting half his book to personal values and half to investing. . . . Overall, the author writes in clear, simple language, only rarely veering into jargon. Despite a few typos and occasional unnecessary preludes, his advice is easily digestible without being dumbed down. Appendices include questionnaires that will likely aid those ready to start planning. An engaging guide aimed at retirees but packed with practical advice that even 20- and 30-somethings might use."

WILLIAMS, HEATHER ANDREA. Help me to find my people; the African American search for family lost in slavery; [by] Heather Andrea Williams 251 p. 2012 University of North Carolina Press

1. African American families—History 2. Histori-

cal literature 3. Slavery—Social aspects—United States—History 4. Slavery—United States—History 5. Slaves—Family relationships—United States—History
ISBN 0807835544; 9780807835548 (cloth: alk. paper)
LC 2011-050216

SUMMARY: Author "Heather Andrea Williams uses slave narratives, letters, interviews, public records, and diaries to guide readers back to devastating moments of family separation during slavery when people were sold away from parents, siblings, spouses, and children. . . . [She tells the] stories of separation and the long, usually unsuccessful journeys toward reunification. . . . Williams follows those who were separated, chronicles their searches, and documents the rare experience of reunion." (Publisher's note)

REVIEW: *Rev Am Hist* v42 no2 p255-64 Je 2014 Kendra Field

"Help Me to Find My People: The African American Search for Family Lost in Slavery" and "Slave Breeding: Sex, Violence, and Memory in African American History." "Heather Williams' 'Help Me to Find My People' documents the 'thoughts and feelings' of enslaved people and former slaves in the midst of the forced separation of African American families that characterized Southern slavery in the United States. Gregory Smithers' 'Slave Breeding' considers the history and memory of constant interventions by white Southerners' into the sexual and reproductive lives of enslaved women and men, including the use of forced and coerced 'breeding' practices. . . . At their best, Williams and Smithers offer a complex history of chattel slavery, while locating an intellectual history of this system among slaves and former slaves."

REVIEW: *Women's Review of Books* v29 no4 p3-6 Jl/Ag 2012 Jean Humez

WILLIAMS, J. L. A. Thinker; Your Very Own Swift Kick in the Ass!: a Survival Guide for Real Estate Investment, the Stock Market, and Other People's Self-indulgence; [by] J. L. Williams 140 p. 2013 CreateSpace Independent Publishing Platform

1. Advice literature 2. Goal (Psychology) 3. Real estate investment 4. Stock exchanges 5. Success
ISBN 1483918173; 9781483918174

SUMMARY: This book by J. L. Williams is "filled with broad advice, from how to achieve dreams to how to navigate beginner investment deals. Formerly uninterested in his financial future, young entrepreneur Williams has set a goal of becoming a millionaire by June 2014. . . The author explains how to reshape bad habits by refining and prioritizing goals. He asserts the importance of conducting thorough research and provides ample resources for becoming a successful investor." (Kirkus Reviews)

REVIEW: *Kirkus Rev* v81 no24 p353 D 15 2013

"A. Thinker: Your Very Own Swift Kick in the Ass! A Survival Guide for Real Estate Investment, the Stock Market, and Other People's Self-Indulgence". "A debut filled with broad advice, from how to achieve dreams to how to navigate beginner investment deals. . . . [J. L.] Williams' research, ambition and effort inspire confidence. . . . In danger of becoming quickly dated, the book references specific websites for further information and reiterates the year 2013 as the time of its writing. It's ambitious in its range of topics but serves as an introduction rather than an in-depth study. Where it lacks depth, it succeeds in its humorous, readable approach."

WILLIAMS, JAKOBI. From the bullet to the ballot; the Illinois Chapter of the Black Panther Party and racial coalition politics in Chicago; [by] Jakobi Williams 285 p. 2013 University of North Carolina Press

1. African Americans—Civil rights—Illinois—Chicago—History—20th century 2. African Americans—Illinois—Chicago—Politics and government—20th century 3. Black power—Illinois—Chicago—History—20th century 4. Civil rights movements—Illinois—Chicago—History—20th century 5. Historical literature
ISBN 9780807838167 (cloth : alk. paper)
LC 2012-028588

SUMMARY: "In this comprehensive history of the Illinois Chapter of the Black Panther Party (ILBPP), Chicago native Jakobi Williams demonstrates that the city's Black Power movement was both a response to and an extension of the city's civil rights movement. Williams focuses on the life and violent death of Fred Hampton, a charismatic leader who served as president of the NAACP Youth Council." (Publisher's note)

REVIEW: *Am Hist Rev* v119 no1 p208-9 F 2014 Jama Lazerow

REVIEW: *Choice* v51 no1 p151 S 2013 K. Edgerton

"From the Bullet to the Ballot: The Illinois Chapter of the Black Panther Party and Racial Coalition Politics in Chicago." "During the civil rights struggles of the 1960s, long-simmering frustration and anger led many lower-class blacks to the culturally attractive, militant Black Panther Party. Thus . . . the Illinois Chapter of the Black Panther Party (ILPBB) laid much of the groundwork for nontraditional grassroots political activism. . . . Among other things, [author Jakobi] Williams . . . 'demonstrates how the ILPBB's community organizing methods . . . influenced Chicago's machine politics, grassroots organizing, racial coalitions, and political behavior.'"

WILLIAMS, JOHN.ed. Just war. See Just war

WILLIAMS, JULIE. Drama queens in the house; [by] Julie Williams 432 p. 2014 Roaring Brook Press

1. African Americans—Fiction 2. Family life—Fiction 3. Gays—Fiction 4. Gifted children—Fiction 5. Racially mixed people—Fiction 6. Theater—Fiction 7. Young adult fiction
ISBN 9781596437357 (hardback)
LC 2013-028529

SUMMARY: In this book, "sixteen-year-old Jessie Jasper Lewis doesn't remember a time in her life when she wasn't surrounded by method actors, bright spotlights, and feather boas. Her parents started the Jumble Players Theater together, and theater is the glue that holds her crazy family together. But when she discovers that her father's cheating on her mother with a man, Jessie feels like her world is toppling over." (Publisher's note)

REVIEW: *Booklist* v110 no14 p74 Mr 15 2014 Debbie Carton

REVIEW: *Bull Cent Child Books* v67 no8 p427 Ap 2014 K. C.

REVIEW: *Kirkus Rev* v82 no2 p148 Ja 15 2014

"Drama Queens in the House". "Then in a puzzling development that feels borrowed from another narrative, race, until now carrying little emotional or thematic weight, replaces sexual orientation as the catalyst for her development. Sexual orientation gets savvy, sensitive treatment, but the presentation of race is clumsy and simplistic. Previously effervescent and self-confident, Jessie now struggles with a self-limiting belief, racially nuanced, that she can't dance. Since readers know Jessie has no ambitions to act or dance, why does it matter? An initially fresh, original narrative swamped by tired tropes and conventional resolution. Pity."

REVIEW: *Publ Wkly* v260 no51 p61 D 16 2013

REVIEW: *SLJ* v60 no4 p175 Ap 2014 Krishna Grady

REVIEW: *Voice of Youth Advocates* v37 no1 p76 Ap 2014 Kristin Fletcher-Spear

WILLIAMS, KAYLA. Plenty of Time When We Get Home; Love and Recovery in the Aftermath of War; [by] Kayla Williams 288 p. 2014 W.W. Norton & Co. Inc.

1. Brain damage—Patients—Biography 2. Disabled veterans—United States—Biography 3. Iraq War, 2003-2011—Veterans—United States—Biography 4. Iraq War, 2003-2011—Women—United States—Biography 5. Memoirs 6. Military spouses—United States—Biography 7. Post-traumatic stress disorder—Patients—Biography 8. Women veterans—United States—Biography

ISBN 0393239365; 9780393239362

LC 2013-041185

SUMMARY: Iraq War veteran Kayla Williams "chronicles the . . . saga of herself and her fellow veteran husband returning to civilian life psychologically and physically wounded. . . . While in combat, she briefly met . . . Brian McGough. But . . . he suffered a severe brain injury from an explosive device. . . . Back in the United States . . . they began a romantic relationship marked by . . . violence due to his post-traumatic stress disorder and her undiagnosed psychological disabilities." (Kirkus Reviews)

REVIEW: *Booklist* v110 no7 p19 D 1 2013 June Sawyers

REVIEW: *Kirkus Rev* v81 no24 p51 D 15 2013

"Plenty of Time When We Get Home: Love and Recovery in the Aftermath of War". "An Iraq War veteran chronicles the emotionally raw, disarmingly candid saga of herself and her fellow veteran husband returning to civilian life psychologically and physically wounded. . . . In excruciating detail, [Kayla] Williams shares scenes from a marriage almost certain to explode. . . . . The memoir is certainly not a feminist tract, but Williams does examine the special adjustment problems of female combat veterans. A brave book filled with gore and trauma—and superb storytelling."

REVIEW: *Libr J* v138 no14 p87 S 1 2013

REVIEW: *Publ Wkly* v260 no45 p64 N 11 2013

WILLIAMS, MAIYA. Middle-School Cool; [by] Maiya Williams 240 p. 2014 Delacorte Press

1. Eccentrics and eccentricities—Fiction 2. Ethics—Fiction 3. Humorous stories 4. Journalism—Fiction 5. Middle schools—Fiction 6. Newspapers—Fiction 7. Schools—Fiction

ISBN 0375991158; 9780375991158 (glb); 9780385743495 (hc); 9780449816141 (ebook)

LC 2012-027816

SUMMARY: This book, by Maiya Williams, focuses on "Kaboom Academy, a new and alternative school for middle-grade kids, . . . [and] the class of Journalism 1A. These group of nine misfits are the staff of 'The Daily Dynamite,' Kaboom Academy's quarterly newspaper. As their school year kicks off with a boom, literally, the students of Journalism 1A are about to discover what really goes on at Kaboom Academy and who's really in charge of this groundbreaking school." (Publisher's note)

REVIEW: *Booklist* v110 no22 p88 Ag 1 2014 Alison O'Reilly Poage

REVIEW: *Kirkus Rev* v82 no2 p301 Ja 15 2014

"Middle-School Cool". "[Maiya] Williams weighs her episodic tale down with detailed expositions of the central cast's unhappy pasts and troubled domestic situations, as well as heavy-handed axe grinding in repeated rants against the boring, pointless, time-wasting experience of going to normal school. Nevertheless, the mix of out-and-out magic with far-fetched but logical twists creates an enjoyably surreal romp. Also, the author shows a knack for wacky inventions, from those book pills to the climactic arrival of an Invisiblimp. Middle schoolers will clamor for a transfer."

REVIEW: *SLJ* v60 no5 p119 My 2014 Emma Burkhart

WILLIAMS, MARCIA, 1945-.il. Lizzy Bennet's diary. See Williams, M.

WILLIAMS, MARCIA, 1945-. Lizzy Bennet's diary; [by] Marcia Williams 112 p. 2014 Candlewick Press

1. Bennet, Elizabeth (Fictitious character) 2. Courtship—Fiction 3. Humorous stories 4. Literature—Adaptations 5. Love stories

ISBN 9780763670306

LC 2013-944006

SUMMARY: This adaptation of Jane Austen's "Pride and Prejudice" by Marcia Williams presents an "abridgement of the novel for a young audience, fashioned as a diary given to 'Lizzy' by her father. In her diary, Lizzy offers up witty commentary on the events that transpire from the time the sisters get word of a wealthy, unattached gentleman taking up residence at nearby Netherfield to her own installment at Pemberley as the newlywed Lizzy Darcy." (Bulletin of the Center for Children's Books)

REVIEW: *Bull Cent Child Books* v67 no10 p548 Je 2014 K. C.

"Lizzy Bennet's Diary 1811-1812 Discovered by Marcia Williams". "These bits and bobs supplement the dated entries to give a feel for everyday life in 1811, while the color portraits combine authentic period detail with comic caricature to convey how Lizzy feels about each character. . . . This wry sense of humor animates the text throughout and makes the perennially popular love story not only accessible but thoroughly absorbing for young readers, who will surely be captivated by some aspect of Lizzy's tale; after all, who doesn't have an embarrassing family, or wish for true love, or find snooty people tiresome, etc., etc.? Jane Austen's early critics called her sunshine; Marcia Williams has managed to capture that feeling of light and warmth for a new generation of readers."

REVIEW: *Kirkus Rev* v82 no6 p157 Mr 15 2014

REVIEW: *SLJ* v60 no3 p150 Mr 2014 Maralita L. Freeny

WILLIAMS, MARCIA, 1945-.il. The Romans. See Williams, M.

WILLIAMS, MARCIA, 1945-. The Romans; gods, emperors, and Dormice; [by] Marcia Williams 40 p. 2013 Candlewick Press

1. Historical literature 2. Roman mythology 3. Rome—Civilization 4. Rome—History 5. Rome—Kings & rulers

ISBN 0763665819; 9780763665814
LC 2012-947731

SUMMARY: This book "introduces young readers to facts and an historical timeline of ancient Rome. Audiences will learn about the Roman Gods through a family tree and brief history, how the city was built, what life was like for the people of Rome and the demise of the great empires. In addition to the facts about the Roman Gods, Williams gives readers a history of the seven kings of Rome." (Children's Literature)

REVIEW: *Booklist* v110 no3 p50-1 O 1 2013 J. B. Petty

"The Romans: Gods, Emperors, and Dormice." "Each page receives a neoclassical border, with the page's topic heading in the pediment, a descriptive paragraph in the frieze, and the body of the comic-strip narrative inside the erstwhile building. These busy cartoons range from minuscule to full-page and always invite close inspection. . . . It's an unusual conceit pulled off quite well--by employing Dormeo as a humorous narrator, Williams is able to present atrocities imposed upon the lower classes of Roman people without overwhelming readers. Lots of information here; prepare for this book to be renewed at least once."

REVIEW: *Kirkus Rev* v81 no17 p126 S 1 2013

WILLIAMS, MARGARET S. Contagious representation; women's political representation in democracies around the world; [by] Margaret S. Williams x, 174 p. 2013 New York University Press

1. Democratization 2. Political science literature 3. Representative government and representation 4. Women—Political activity 5. Women in public life

ISBN 9780814784174 (hardback : acid-free paper); 9780814784181 (ebook); 9780814784198 (ebook)
LC 2012-028507

SUMMARY: In this book, Frank C. Thames and Margaret S. Williams "present a comprehensive analysis of how the inclusion and incorporation of women in one political institution then extends into other areas of government. They refer to this process as contagion--the influence of women's participation and political gains in one institution on others." (Choice: Current Reviews for Academic Libraries)

REVIEW: *Choice* v51 no5 p917 Ja 2014 I. Coronado

"Contagious Representation: Women's Political Representation in Democracies Around the World." "A comprehensive analysis of how the inclusion and incorporation of women in one political institution then extends into other areas of government. . . . A major strength of this book is the broad, comprehensive, original data set that includes 150 democratic countries from 1945 to 2006. . . . This is a very accessible book that provides rigorous qualitative and quantitative research methods and a theory that can be tested in other areas such as business. Highly recommended for scholars of gender and political representation and a valuable text for women's studies, research methods, and political science students."

REVIEW: *Women's Review of Books* v31 no1 p14-5 Ja/F 2014 Glenna Matthews

WILLIAMS, ROSALIND. The triumph of human empire; Verne, Morris, and Stevenson at the end of the world; [by] Rosalind Williams 432 p. 2013 University of Chicago Press

1. Fantasy fiction—19th century—History and criticism 2. Historical literature 3. Imperialism in literature 4. Literature, Modern—19th century—History and criticism

ISBN 9780226899558 (cloth : alkaline paper)
LC 2013-006682

SUMMARY: This book by Rosalind Williams "examines the ambivalence about technology felt by three famous authors--[Robert Louis] Stevenson (1850-1894), Jules Verne (1828-1905), and William Morris (1834-1896). All three embraced some innovations while bemoaning the large-scale effects of technology. . . . They also experienced technological change not as a clean break with the past, Williams writes, but as an ongoing erosion of their cherished worlds." (Times Higher Education)

REVIEW: *Choice* v51 no7 p1209 Mr 2014 A. M. Bain

"The Triumph of Human Empire: Verne, Morris, and Stevenson at the End of the World." "The book is prodigious in scope but rather unsatisfying in execution and outcomes. [Rosalind] Williams expends much space rehearsing arguments . . . that have long been accepted and worked through in the humanities and social sciences. This, plus an overload of biographical detail, leaves little room for developing substantively new arguments about how the complex aesthetics of high imperialism might inform contemporary debates over the human control of nature. Still, those interested in the cross-disciplinary potential of the history of science and technology will find this book of interest."

REVIEW: *TLS* no5768 p3-4 O 18 2013 FELIPE FERNÁNDEZ-ARMESTO

"The Triumph of Human Empire: Verne, Morris, and Stevenson at the End of the World." "[Rosalind Williams] masters literary theory and commands historical context. . . . Even more disarmingly . . . Williams is candid about the capriciousness of her choice of subject matter. . . . Williams's effort to align [Jules] Verne with [William] Morris and [Robert Louis] Stevenson as a critic of technology is unconvincing. . . . Williams's insight is grand and suggestive, and gives the author brilliantly exploited opportunities to explore Verne's, Morris's and Stevenson's worlds. I have never read anything better--more perceptive, more subtle, more closely observed--on the writings of all three. But is the argument correctly formulated?"

WILLIAMS, ROWAN, 1950-. A silent action; engagements with Thomas Merton; [by] Rowan Williams 0 Fons Vitae

1. Contemplation 2. Merton, Thomas, 1915-1968 3. Monks 4. Religious literature 5. Solitude

ISBN 9781891785788

SUMMARY: This book by Rowan Williams looks at monk and author Thomas Merton. "For Williams, the most striking aspect of Merton's work was the way his profound attention to humans as social beings, and the activism that followed from that attention, coexisted with his ongoing commitment to contemplative life and prayer. These two seemingly contradictory activities form the substance of this book." (Commonweal)

REVIEW: *Commonweal* v141 no3 p28-9 F 7 2014 Harold Isbell

"A Silent Action: Engagements With Thomas Merton". "[Rowan] Williams astutely alerts us to [Paul] Evdokimov's proposition that the vows of a religious are analogous to Christ's response to the temptations in the desert. . . . Merton was not only a man of solitude but also a man immersed in companionship. That his published work, decades after his death, should be engaged so warmly by a younger man. Rowan Williams—a man deeply rooted in a similar theological tradition and in the same conundrums of solitude and society that Merton knew so well—is indeed a graceful affirmation of such companionship."

WILLIAMS, SAM. Bunny and Bee Playtime; [by] Sam Williams 24 p. 2013 Sterling Pub Co Inc

1. Friendship—Juvenile fiction 2. Picture books for children 3. Play 4. Tree houses 5. Weather—Juvenile literature

ISBN 190796763X; 9781907967634

SUMMARY: In this children's picture book by Sam Williams, "two toddlers, one costumed as a bunny and another like a bee, are the best of friends. The duo lives in a tidy treehouse, enjoys milk and honey, and plays together in all sorts of weather. Doling out one line per page, the gentle rhyming text states: 'On sunny days, they swing in the trees. / On windy days they chase the leaves. // On rainy days they splash in the puddles. / On cold, cold days they have lots of cuddles.'" (Kirkus Reviews)

REVIEW: *Kirkus Rev* v81 no20 p315 O 15 2013

REVIEW: *Kirkus Rev* v82 no1 p44 Ja 1 2014

"Bunny and Bee Playtime". "While nothing much happens in this slice-of-life tale, toddlers will delight in the world Williams has built for the twosome. . . . Some of the double-page spreads that use a series of spot-art vignettes are difficult to make out due to the tiny size of the images. The pacing also feels rushed at times, particularly as Bunny and Bee are engaged in very active play on one page and then rushed off to bed on the next. The offering would have been better served in a larger picture-book edition with more pages to allow the delightful illustrations and the simple story room to breathe."

WILLIAMS, SEAN. Twinmaker; [by] Sean Williams 352 p. 2013 HarperCollins

1. Best friends—Fiction 2. Conspiracies—Fiction 3. Friendship—Fiction 4. Science fiction 5. Space and time—Fiction

ISBN 0062203215; 9780062203212 (hardcover bdg.)

LC 2012-043498

SUMMARY: In this book, "thanks to D-mat technology, teen Clair" and her friends "can jump around the globe in a matter of minutes simply by entering a booth. . . . They initially dismiss Improvement, a way to transform yourself through a series of jumps, but then Libby uses Improvement to remove her permanent birthmark, and as the disturbing consequences roll out, Clair digs for answers." (Booklist)

REVIEW: *Booklist* v110 no2 p67 S 15 2013 Erin Downey Howerton

"Twinmaker." "[Sean] Williams is adept at weaving together the disparate story strands: the sociopolitical implications of a giant corporation that has access to the very code to your being, and the frantic lives of teens caught in the middle of a devastating conspiracy. In the masterful hands of Williams, the technology, which has eerie parallels to contemporary life, provides a solid platform for great storytelling, and teens will revel in the drama, Clair's tenacity, and the memorable characters who discover that their utopia isn't all it's cracked up to be. Readers looking for another strong Katniss-type character to follow through a treacherous near-future will hope for a sequel."

REVIEW: *Horn Book Magazine* v89 no5 p116 S/O 2013 APRIL SPISAK

REVIEW: *Kirkus Rev* v81 no13 p233 Jl 1 2013

REVIEW: *Voice of Youth Advocates* v36 no5 p84 D 2013 Brenna Shanks

WILLIAMS, T. L. Unit 400; the assassins; 298 p. 2014 First Coast Publishers, LLC

1. Assassins—Fiction 2. Iraq War, 2003-2011—Veterans 3. Spy stories 4. Suspense fiction 5. United States. Navy. SEALs

ISBN 9780988440036

LC 2013-943666

SUMMARY: In this book, "Ex-Navy SEAL Logan Alexander . . . witnesses [his friend] Hamid getting stabbed in the chest and left for dead. He tries to help Hamid hang on, to no avail, but his friend manages to whisper to him, 'Be careful, Logan. Unit 400'—a code for the Qods Force, a dangerous Iranian assassination squad. Logan soon discovers that the weapon that killed Hamid is none other than his very own SEAL-issue knife." (Kirkus Reviews)

REVIEW: *Kirkus Rev* v81 no24 p383 D 15 2013

"Unit 400: The Assassins". " As a sequel, the story doesn't pay as much attention to character development as some readers might prefer, but those familiar with the original novel will be pleased to find the same Logan Alexander in charge. Classic elements of a modern espionage story abound: mystery, intrigue, danger, technology, and, importantly, a sense of immediacy, thanks to the global forces at play. Those with a taste for military fiction that tackles current events will find this story enticing. The author might have taken more time to explain the history of Middle Eastern conflicts, but that's hardly in the job description for a quick spy yarn. As it is, readers definitely won't feel shortchanged by this consistently exciting thriller. A worthy follow-up espionage tale."

WILLIAMS, THOMAS. The Bay Area school; Californian artists from the 1950s and 1960s; [by] Thomas Williams 240 p. 2012 Lund Humphries

1. Abstract expressionism—History 2. American art—20th century 3. Art literature 4. California—History 5. Figurative art 6. San Francisco (Calif.) art scene

ISBN 9781848221239 (hardcover : alk. paper)

LC 2012-940923

SUMMARY: This book by Thomas Williams "trac[es] the development of Abstract Expressionism and the counterblast of Figurative art on the West Coast of America" during the post-war period. "The movement had its origins in the art schools of San Francisco and Berkeley in the early 1940s and rose to prominence in the 1950s as a major challenge to the dominance of New York." Williams "argues the mutual influence of abstraction and figuration during this critical period." (Publisher's note)

REVIEW: *TLS* no5764 p30 S 20 2013 KELLY GROVIER

"The Bay Area School: Californian Artists From the 1940s,

1950s, and 1960s." "The Bay Area that [Thomas] Williams conjures is a humid glasshouse of post-traumatic experimentation uninhibited by the presence of a commercial market, demanding patrons, and a cut-throat press--realities that at once enabled and disabled the careers and imaginations of artists who headed east. . . . Part history, part catalogue of selected works indicative of the Bay Area School's anti-style style, this is a handsome, engaging and beautifully illustrated book that reminds us that Abstract Expressionism, not unlike the Beats, was always a national rather than a provincial phenomenon."

WILLIAMS, TOM. Don't start me talkin'; 250 p. 2014 Curbside Splendor Pub. Inc.
1. African Americans—Fiction 2. Blues musicians—Fiction 3. Concert tours 4. Road fiction 5. United States—Race relations
ISBN 9780988480445
LC 2013-957480

SUMMARY: This book presents "a comedic road novel about Brother Ben, the only remaining True Delta Bluesman, playing his final North American tour. Set in contemporary society, Brother Ben's protege Silent Sam Stamps narrates an episodic 'last ride,' laying bare America's complicated relationship with African American identity, music, and culture, and like his hero Sonny Boy Williamson once sang, Silent Sam promises "I'll tell everything I know."" (Publisher's note)

REVIEW: *Booklist* v110 no11 p22 F 1 2014 June Sawyers

REVIEW: *Kirkus Rev* v82 no3 p102 F 1 2014

"Don't Start Me Talkin'". "While this is a road-trip story, it's also a more profound experience—a sometimes-sardonic, sophisticated take on race in America, on fame, on mostly white artistic wannabes and acolytes co-opting black experience. . . . With allusions to cultural touchstones from Elvis to Robert Johnson, from Cosby to Oscar Wilde, Williams' metaphorical tale addresses the dualities African-Americans navigate in the American cultural maze while also dealing with the truths we all tell ourselves and the truths we let others see. Part elegy, part master-student story, part road-trip Americana, Williams riffs on the dichotomy between appearance and reality."

REVIEW: *World Lit Today* v88 no2 p8 Mr/Ap 2014

WILLIAMS, WENDY. The Story of Yelverton; A Fictional Story of the Life of the Yabbie; [by] Wendy Williams 28 p. 2013 XLIBRIS
1. Animal behavior 2. Animal stories 3. Dams 4. Habitat conservation 5. Yabbies
ISBN 1483623580; 9781483623580

SUMMARY: This book by Wendy Williams "offers young readers insight into the lives of the small crustaceans called yabbies. Yelverton is a yabbie, a shellfish that lives at the bottom of a dam, and in this book aimed at a young audience, he explains his life cycle and some of the hazards of his dangerous existence. . . . As Yelverton catalogs the dangers of his life under the dam, he shares general environmental concerns about subjects such as dirty water and humans' yabbie traps." (Kirkus Reviews)

REVIEW: *Kirkus Rev* v82 no2 p318 Ja 15 2014

"The Story of Yelverton: A Fictional Story of the Life of the Yabbie". "Yelverton is a yabbie, a shellfish that lives at the bottom of a dam, and in this book aimed at a young audience, he explains his life cycle and some of the hazards of his dangerous existence. The nature illustrations that accompany Yelverton's casual explanations give a somewhat scientific flavor to the book's early sections . . . others are uneven, particularly depictions of birds. . . . Australian audiences might be more familiar with the little crustaceans, but Americans may be baffled. Other readers may want to look up details the book leaves out, such as the region of the world in which yabbies may be found. A well-researched but lackluster children's book."

WILLIAMSON, MIKE. Dunnard's Pearl; What to do with the world when you can't get off.; [by] Mike Williamson 246 p. 2013 CreateSpace Independent Publishing Platform
1. Extraterrestrial life—Fiction 2. Friendship—Fiction 3. Satire 4. Science fiction 5. Social change
ISBN 148392081X; 9781483920818

SUMMARY: In this book, "James Justice is participating in an extracurricular Student-Teacher Action Group at school when he suddenly finds himself zapped onto a spaceship with two of his classmates. . . . Once they acclimate to their new environment, they discover that the massive ship is home to an entire alien society divided along strict class lines. James realizes that he can't allow this arrangement to go on, and so he and his fellow students decide to help the farmers take control. " (Kirkus Reviews)

REVIEW: *Kirkus Rev* v81 no24 p391 D 15 2013

"Dunnard's Pearl: What to Do With the World When You Can't Get Off". " [Mike] Williamson's novel displays a fantastic, playful sense of humor with a keen sense of the ridiculous and illogical; the characters' names are but a few examples of the book's whimsy. Overall, it's highly reminiscent of classic British humor, such as that of Lewis Carroll, Monty Python, Douglas Adams and Red Dwarf. Perhaps its most direct influence is the British sci-fi TV show Doctor Who. . . . However, the novel doesn't do nearly enough to distinguish itself, seemingly content to echo other, superior works past and present. Far too often, it meanders through its strange, not-so-new world when its wit and invention should be gaining steam. An often very funny satire, but one that has little new to say."

WILLIS, JOHN M. Unmaking north and south; cartographies of the Yemeni past, 1857-1934; [by] John M. Willis 288 p. 2012 Columbia Univ Pr
1. Historical literature
ISBN 9780231701310 (alk. paper)
LC 2012-029083

SUMMARY: This book, by John M. Willis, "revisits the Yemeni past by situating the historical construction of Yemen's north and south as bounded political, social, and moral spaces in the broader context of imperial rule, state formation, and religious reform in the Indian Ocean arena. The study is centered on the formation of the British Aden Protectorate and the Zaydi-Shiite Imamate of the Hamid al-Din family in the period between 1857and 1934." (Publisher's note)

REVIEW: *Am Hist Rev* v119 no1 p285-6 F 2014 Isa Blumi

"Unmaking North and South: Cartographies of the Yemeni Past, 1857-1934". "John M. Willis's monograph offers a welcome reflection on how state governing practices contributed to defining post-1850 Yemen. . . . If there is any enduring concern with this otherwise innovative book, it is its failure to illuminate the contours of those contested spaces of power that are still beyond the reach of the nation-state, social scientists, and American drones today. . . . More generally, Willis neglects to put events in their larger regional context. . . . Nevertheless, this is a welcome addition to the scholarship on colonial knowledge and its diverse imprints on our maps and governmental practices."

REVIEW: *Choice* v51 no1 p145-6 S 2013 N. E. Bou-Nacklie

WILLIS, SAM. In the Hour of Victory; the Royal Navy at war in the age of Nelson; [by] Sam Willis 416 p. 2013 Atlantic Books

1. Great Britain—Naval history 2. Historical literature 3. Naval battles—England 4. Naval battles—History 5. Nelson, Horatio Nelson, Viscount, 1758-1805
ISBN 9780393243147 (hardcover); 0393243141; 0857895702; 9780857895707; 9780857895738 (paperback)
LC 2013-047876

SUMMARY: This book, by Sam Willis, is a compendium of "original dispatches sent by British commanding officers to the secretary of the Admiralty. They concern eight naval victories from 1794 to 1806 and were assembled by the Lords of the Admiralty in 1859 to create an awe-inspiring record of naval success, a golden age during which the enemy lost 139 ships of the line and 229 frigates, while the British lost not a single ship of any description to the enemy." (History Today)

REVIEW: *Booklist* v110 no16 p12 Ap 15 2014 Roland Green

REVIEW: *Hist Today* v63 no5 p63 My 2013 DAVID CORDINGLY

"In the Hour of Victory: The Royal Navy at War in the Age of Nelson." "Naval historian Sam Willis recently came across a . . . massive volume containing the original dispatches sent by British commanding officers to the secretary of the Admiralty. . . . Sam Willis . . . has provided a lively and wide-ranging introduction to the dispatches. . . . In his vivid commentaries to each he manages to combine hard facts with fascinating anecdotes and pen pictures of the principal characters. He has been well served by his publishers, who have produced a handsome volume which does justice to this major contribution to a key period of maritime history."

REVIEW: *Kirkus Rev* v82 no5 p33 Mr 1 2014

REVIEW: *Publ Wkly* v261 no6 p79 F 10 2014

WILLSON-BROYLES, RACHEL.tr. Sail of stone. See Edwardson, Å.

WILLUMSON, GLENN. Iron muse; photographing the Transcontinental Railroad; [by] Glenn Willumson x, 242 p. 2013 University of California Press

1. Historical literature 2. Photography of railroads—United States—History 3. Railroads—United States—History—19th century—Sources 4. Transcontinental railroads
ISBN 0520270940 (cloth : alk. paper); 9780520270947 (cloth : alk. paper)
LC 2012-037751

SUMMARY: This book by Glenn Willumson "provides a unique look at the production, distribution, and publication of images of the transcontinental railroad: from their use as an official record by the railroad corporations, to their reproduction in the illustrated press and travel guides, and finally to their adaptation to direct sales and albums in the late nineteenth and twentieth centuries." (Publisher's note)

REVIEW: *Am Hist Rev* v119 no1 p185 F 2014 H. Roger Grant

REVIEW: *Choice* v51 no2 p251 O 2013 M. Nilsen

"Iron Muse: Photographing the Transcontinental Railroad." "Andrew Russell's photograph 'Meeting of the Rails, Promontory Point, Utah, 1869' was taken at the historic moment when thc joining of the Central Pacific and Union Pacific Railroads at Promontory, Utah, opened the first transcontinental rail line. Starting from this photograph, [author Glenn] Willumson . . . weaves a tight fabric that includes rival interests competing for the location of the line, major players in the two companies that prevailed, and the photographers hired to showcase the engineering prowess of construction. . . . With 96 illustrations, this meticulous investigation will appeal to historians of photography, of the American West, and of railroads."

WILSON, ADAM. What's Important Is Feeling; Stories; [by] Adam Wilson 224 p. 2014 HarperCollins
ISBN 0062284789; 9780062284785

SUMMARY: In this collection of short stories, by Adam Wilson, "Bankers prowl Brooklyn bars on the eve of the stock market crash. A debate over Young Elvis versus Vegas Elvis turns existential. Detoxing junkies use a live lobster to spice up their love life. . . . And in the title story, selected for The Best American Short Stories, two film school buddies working on a doomed project are left sizing up their own talent, hoping to come out on top—but fearing they won't." (Publisher's note)

REVIEW: *Kirkus Rev* v82 no3 p106 F 1 2014

"What's Important Is Feeling: Stories". "A 12-story collection detailing the existential struggles of modern youth. . . . This second tale is the only one told from a female perspective, but it's a distinction difficult to discern; male or female, the collection's young protagonists always seem mired in an existential swamp. Nevertheless, Wilson crafts artful literary phrases. . . . Wilson's stories are city stories, many seemingly set in and around Boston. . . . Wilson does yeoman work with characters. . . . . Bleak First-World angst, delivered with style."

WILSON, AMRIT. The Threat of Liberation; Imperialism and Revolution in Zanzibar; [by] Amrit Wilson 168 p. 2013 Palgrave Macmillan

1. Babu, Abdulrahman Mohamed 2. Historical literature 3. Imperialism 4. Zanzibar—History—Revolution, 1964 5. Zanzibar—Politics & government
ISBN 0745334083; 9780745334080

SUMMARY: This book by Amrit Wilson "examines the role of the Umma Party of Zanzibar and its leader, the visionary Marxist revolutionary, Abdulrahman Mohamed Babu. Drawing parallels between US paranoia about Chinese Communist influence in the 1960s with contemporary fears about Chinese influence, it looks at the new race for Africa's resources, the creation of AFRICOM and how East African politicians have bolstered US control." (Publisher's note)

REVIEW: *Choice* v51 no9 p1654-5 My 2014 R. I. Rotberg

"The Threat of Liberation: Imperialism and Revolution in Zanzibar". "This partial and incomplete book is a second effort by the author to embellish and glorify the posthumous reputation of Abdulrahman Mohamed Babu, a charming, charismatic, Marxist, Arab leader of Zanzibar. . . . The remaining two chapters very superficially attempt to bring the Zanzibar story into the present, but [Amrit] Wilson is not on top of the economic and political currents affecting Tanzania's offshore\ dependency. . . . Not recommended."

WILSON, D. W. Once you break a knuckle; stories; [by] D. W. Wilson 256 p. 2014 Bloomsbury USA

1. British Columbia—Fiction 2. Canadian short stories 3. FICTION—Short Stories (single author) 4. Kootenay Region (B.C.) 5. Working class—Fiction
ISBN 1608199940; 9781608199945 (pbk.)
LC 2013-031607

SUMMARY: Written by D. W. Wilson, these "stories reveal to us how our best intentions can be doomed to fail or injure, how our loves can fall short or mislead us, how even friendship--especially friendship--can be something dangerously temporary." It describes how "In the remote Kootenay Valley in western Canada, good people sometimes do bad things." (Publisher's note)

REVIEW: *Booklist* v110 no5 p25 N 1 2013 Mark Levine

REVIEW: *Kirkus Rev* v81 no20 p179 O 15 2013

REVIEW: *N Y Times Book Rev* p23 Mr 2 2014 KYLE MINOR

"Once You Break a Knuckle: Stories." "D. W. Wilson's 'Once You Break a Knuckle' [is a] collection in which the stories are in conversation. . . . Although the book is full of recurring characters, it finds its center in the Kootenay Valley, the rugged southeastern tip of British Columbia. . . . The stories are incessantly concerned with the question: Can you protect the ones you love. . . . The yammerer's freedom with story and time provides 'Once You Break a Knuckle' with its most emotionally powerful moments, especially at the ends of stories."

REVIEW: *New York Times* v163 no56397 pC7 Ja 30 2014 John Williams

WILSON, IVY G. Specters of democracy; blackness and the aesthetics of politics in the antebellum U.S.; [by] Ivy G. Wilson x, 237 p. 2011 Oxford University Press

1. African American authors—Political and social views 2. African Americans in literature 3. American literature—African American authors—History and criticism 4. Democracy in literature 5. Discourse analysis, Literary 6. Historical literature 7. Nationalism in literature 8. Rhetoric—Political aspects—United States—History
ISBN 0195337379 (cloth : alk. paper); 0195340353 (pbk. : alk. paper); 9780195337372 (cloth : alk. paper); 9780195340358 (pbk. : alk. paper)
LC 2010-020169

SUMMARY: This book by Ivy G. Wilson "interrogates the representational strategies that nineteenth-century Americans used in art and literature to delineate blackness as an index to the forms of U.S. citizenship. The book reveals how the difficult task of representing African Americans--both enslaved and free--in imaginative expression was part of a larger dilemma concerning representative democracy." (Publisher's note)

REVIEW: *Am Lit* v85 no3 p593-6 S 2013 Evie Shockley

"Spectacular Blackness: The Cultural Politics of the Black Power Movement and the Search for a Black Aesthetic," "Specters of Democracy: Blackness and the Aesthetics of Politics in the Antebellum United States," and "Representing the Race: A New Political History of African American Literature." "[Amy Abugo] Ongiri adds her incisive analysis of materials both familiar and little-known to the growing body of work on Black Power and the Black Arts Movement (BAM) in their most active years. . . .[Ivy G.] Wilson's book [is] . . . more densely theoretical than Ongiri's lively work, but no less readable in its eloquence. . . . [Andrew Jarrett] makes a detailed, well-researched case for the importance of distinguishing between the longstanding practice of reading creative and intellectual writing as simply informally political . . . and his scholarship, which argues that such writing . . . does formal political work."

REVIEW: *Choice* v49 no4 p680-1 D 2011 J. W. Miller

WILSON, JAMES GRAHAM. The triumph of improvisation; Gorbachev's adaptability, Reagan's engagement, and the end of the Cold War; [by] James Graham Wilson xiv, 264 p. 2014 Cornell University Press

1. Cold War—Diplomatic history 2. Historical literature
ISBN 9780801452291 (cloth: alk. paper)
LC 2013-027121

SUMMARY: "In 'The Triumph of Improvisation,' James Graham Wilson takes a long view of the end of the Cold War, from the Soviet invasion of Afghanistan in December 1979 to Operation Desert Storm in January 1991. Drawing on deep archival research and recently declassified papers, Wilson argues that adaptation, improvisation, and engagement by individuals in positions of power ended the specter of a nuclear holocaust." (Publisher's note)

REVIEW: *Hist Today* v64 no9 p64-5 S 2014 Archie Brown

REVIEW: *Natl Rev* v65 no9 p44-8 My 19 2014 STEVEN F. HAYWARD

"The Triumph of Improvisation: Gorbachev's Adaptability, Reagan's Engagement, and the End of the Cold War." "His compact narrative—just 204 pages of text—proceeds in disciplined chronological order, which restrains the sort of sweeping and dubious generalizations that often mar other treatments of the Cold War's last decade. [Author James Graham] Wilson is sparing in careful in his judgments; some are astute, others more contestable. Readers can never know whether publishers have cut down a manuscript, but we could use a longer account from Wilson, as his narrative leaves us wanting more depth on some key points and doesn't unravel some of the mysteries of Reagan."

WILSON, JASON. Boozehound; on the trail of the rare, the obscure, and the overrated in spirits; [by] Jason Wilson 240 2010 Ten Speed Press

1. Alcoholic beverages 2. Cocktails 3. Cooking (Liquors) 4. Food writing 5. Liquors
ISBN 9781580082884
LC 2010-013363

SUMMARY: This book by Jason Wilson "provide[s] historical and general information about various spirits and the author's experiences drinking them. In Leghorn, Italy, Wilson visits a distillery that makes Tuaca, a citrus-vanilla liqueur that is more popular in the United States than in Italy. Each chapter ends with associated recipes for the spirits discussed, with some standards (e.g., Sloe Gin Fizz) but more twists (e.g., Bianco Manhattan) and obscure or rare cocktails " (Library Journal)

REVIEW: *Booklist* v110 no3 p20 O 1 2013 DAVID WRIGHT

"Boozehound: On the Trail of the Rare, the Obscure, and the Overrated in Spirits," "The Hour: A Cocktail Manifesto, and "Three Sheets to the Wind: One Man's Quest for the Meaning of Beer." "Bernard DeVoto's beloved and recently reprinted 'The Hour: A Cocktail Manifesto' is perhaps ounce for ounce a purer delight, with its deft, hilarious homage to the sweet transports of drink. . . . In 'Boozehound,' spirits columnist Jason Wilson travels the globe scaring up interesting liquors. . . . Wilson's style is friendly and down to earth as he pokes fun at fads and deflates the mystical malarkey of the spirits trade. . . . Pete Brown's 'Three Sheets to the Wind' does a similar job for beer, consisting of an epic pub crawl across the globe, exploring the sociability of beer."

WILSON, KARMA. Outside the box; 176 p. 2013 Margaret K. McElderry Books

1. Animals—Poetry 2. Brothers & sisters—Juvenile literature 3. Children's poetry 4. Imagination 5. Poems—Collections

ISBN 1416980059; 9781416980056
LC 2011-049239

SUMMARY: This book, by Karma Wilson and illustrated by Diane Goode, is a "collection of more than 100 poems that touch on everything from creativity and luck to animals, siblings, and holidays. The narrator of 'My Pet Robot' stares glumly at her creation. . . . Elsewhere, a boy reflects on the duality of oatmeal . . . and a girl shouts her head off as she's about to be devoured by a monster." (Publishers Weekly)

REVIEW: *Booklist* v110 no14 p67 Mr 15 2014 Paula Willey

REVIEW: *Kirkus Rev* v82 no3 p70 F 1 2014

"Outside the Box". "A charming, gorgeously illustrated children's collection of light verse. [Karma] Wilson and [Diane] Goode here combine their comedic artistry to create an edgy and substantial collection of light verse with exquisite accompanying pen-and-ink drawings unafraid to explore childhood's darker reaches. From typographical play to concrete poems, Wilson pulls out a number of visual poetic stops in inviting readers to 'think / outside / the box' and ponder humorous cautionary tales on the perils of fibbing, snitching and sibling rivalry, alongside wildly concocted romps through the imagination. . . . At once affirming, silly, and poignant: a stunning visual and poetic compendium on growing up."

REVIEW: *Publ Wkly* v260 no45 p73 N 11 2013

REVIEW: *SLJ* v60 no2 p122 F 2014 Marie Drucker

WILSON, KEITH, 1927-.ed. The Collected Letters of Thomas Hardy. See The Collected Letters of Thomas Hardy

WILSON, S. S. Fraidy Cats; [by] S. S. Wilson 188 p. 2013 Real Deal Productions Incorporated

1. Animal stories 2. Cats—Fiction 3. Frankenstein's monster (Fictitious character) 4. Frankenstein, Victor (Fictitious character) 5. Humorous stories

ISBN 098272229X; 9780982722299

SUMMARY: This book follows "Rolf and Hermann, a pair of refined and resourceful felines who unwittingly . . . bring readers deep inside the world of Frankenstein, the maniacal, brilliant young doctor obsessed with returning life to the dead. Desperate to secure transport to a cat-worshipping island, Rolf and Hermann agree to steal Frankenstein's watch. . . . The heroes are subsequently present during all the grisly, decisive moments that form the Frankenstein mythos." (Kirkus Reviews)

REVIEW: *Kirkus Rev* v82 no3 p16 F 1 2014

"Fraidy Cats". "Two street-smart alley cats steal the spotlight from Dr. Frankenstein and his creation in this amusing, imaginative take on the classic monster tale. [S. S.] Wilson . . .-paints a rich portrait of the German village of Dunkelhaven circa 1810. . . . The novel's playful self-awareness helps buoy the action. . . . Also, despite targeting a younger demographic, this story maintains an all-ages appeal by not speaking down to its readers. Like Frankenstein, this novel creates something unique by stitching together odds and ends, then applying a few healthy doses of creative electricity."

WILSON, VICTORIA. A Life of Barbara Stanwyck; Steel-true 1907-1941; [by] Victoria Wilson 1088 p. 2013 Simon & Schuster

1. BIOGRAPHY & AUTOBIOGRAPHY—Entertainment & Performing Arts 2. BIOGRAPHY & AUTOBIOGRAPHY—Women 3. Biography (Literary form) 4. Motion picture actors and actresses—United States—Biography

ISBN 0684831686; 9780684831688
LC 2013-023244

SUMMARY: This book is the first in a two-volume biography of actress Ruby Stevens, better known as Barbara Stanwyck. "Beginning with a brief history of the Stevens family, dating back to 1740, and ending at the height of WWII with Stanwyck's work on Frank Capra's 1941 film Meet John Doe, the book offers a . . . chronological look at the actress's rise from Vaudeville chorus girl to Hollywood star." (Publishers Weekly)

REVIEW: *Bookforum* v20 no3 p24-59 S-N 2013 GEOFFREY O'BRIEN

"A Life of Barbara Stanwyck: Steel-True, 1907-1940". "A biography, particularly one of such length, must spend much of its time off camera, and by Stanwyck's clear choice there isn't that much to see. . . . But it should be noted that [Victoria] Wilson refrains throughout this book from drawing on that murky sea of innuendo and speculation so dear to most Hollywood biographers. . . . 'A Life of Barbara Stanwyck' will unquestionably remain the biography of record; beyond Wilson's excavation of so much that would otherwise have been lost, her book has a deep sensitivity to the seriousness and subtlety of Stanwyck's craft. This is the biography not of a Hollywood phenomenon but of a serious artist."

REVIEW: *Booklist* v110 no5 p21 N 1 2013 Vanessa Bush

"A Life of Barbara Stanwyck: Steel-True, 1907-1940". "[Victoria] Wilson spent 15 years exhaustively researching the life and career of an iconic actress (this is the first of two volumes). . . . Richly researched, drawing on interviews with Stanwyck's friends, family, and colleagues as well as her journals and letters, this biography offers insights into the strengths and insecurities of a woman famous for her trademark toughness and vulnerability. Photographs enhance this fabulous and expansive examination of the life of an iconic American actress."

REVIEW: *Commentary* v137 no2 p48-51 F 2014 TERRY TEACHOUT

"A Life of Barbara Stanwyck: Steel-True, 1907-1940". "Outside of her painful childhood and her failed marriages, to the vaudeville comedian Frank Fay and the film actor Robert Taylor, little of interest seems to have happened to her. . . . So why, then, is she now the subject of what will eventually become a double-decker biography? And why are so many reviewers taking 'Steel-True' seriously? It is dully and at times ineptly written, with regular descents into adolescent gush. . . . At least half of the text . . . could have been cut without disturbing the book's continuity. . . . For all its weaknesses, 'Steel-True' is scrupulously sourced and deals only in matters of verifiable fact."

REVIEW: *Kirkus Rev* v81 no21 p114 N 1 2013

REVIEW: *N Y Rev Books* v61 no4 p9-10 Mr 6 2014 Jeanine Basinger

"Ava Gardner: The Secret Conversations" and "A Life of Barbara Stanwyck: Steel-True, 1907-1940". "[Peter] Evans's book is not a complete story of Gardner's life and career, although it was originally meant to be. . . . His book is shameless but highly entertaining. He's selling everybody's idea of who Ava Gardner was—boozy and bawdy and beautiful—with a book cover that shows her in black underwear and fishnet stockings. . . . By contrast, Victoria Wilson . . . tries to find the real person. . . . In trying to lift Stanwyck out of a typical 'star image' bio, Wilson nearly goes aground, but ultimately her book succeeds in several different respects: her fresh material on Stanwyck's early years; a thorough understanding of the studio system; a deep appreciation for Stanwyck on film; and her awareness of Stanwyck's independence, which allowed her to avoid typecasting."

REVIEW: *N Y Times Book Rev* p14-5 Ja 5 2014 MOLLY HASKELL

"A Life of Barbara Stanwyck: Steel-True 1907-1940." "If ever there was an actress who was ready for prime time, it is Stanwyck, and this enormously informative tribute—juicy yet dignified, admiring yet detached—is the book to bring her to center stage. Or books . . . for . . . 'A Life of Barbara Stanwyck: Steel-True 1907-1940,' at 860 pages of text (notes, index and appendices bring it to 1,044), is only the first volume, beginning with Stanwyck's birth and ending with the films preceding World War II. [Author Victoria] Wilson stays resolutely and sometimes frustratingly within this time frame. . . . It seemed . . . especially disproportionate in the case of Stanwyck."

REVIEW: *Nation* v298 no12 p44-5 Mr 24 2014 CHARLES TAYLOR

REVIEW: *New York Times* v163 no56330 p8 N 24 2013 ALEX WILLIAMS

REVIEW: *New York Times* v163 no56330 p11 N 24 2013 CATHY HORYN

REVIEW: *New York Times* v163 no56320 pC2 N 14 2013 JANET MASLIN

:A Life of Barbara Stanwyck: Steel-True 1907-1940". "Victoria Wilson's gargantuan biography of Barbara Stanwyck manages to fill 860 glittering pages of text with only the first half of Stanwyck's story. . . . And it ends with a cliffhanger, creating eager anticipation for Ms. Wilson's concluding volume. . . . [The book] is not about the actress alone. It's bigger and splashier. Stanwyck knew the most notable directors, writers, actors, studio chiefs and Broadway impresarios of her day, and Ms. Wilson is interested in all of them."

WIMAN, CHRISTIAN. My bright abyss; meditation of a modern believer; [by] Christian Wiman 192 p. 2012 Farrar, Straus and Giroux

1. Cancer patients' writings 2. Christianity and literature 3. Faith 4. Memoirs 5. Religion and poetry
ISBN 0374216789 (hardcover); 9780374216788 (hardcover)
LC 2012-021271

SUMMARY: This book is a collection of essays that forms award-winning poet Christian Wiman's memoir. It "springboards from a much talked about 2007 essay that laid out his condition, his dark night of the soul, and his reawakening faith. Like Jacob, Wiman wrestles with that which he will not release until he is blessed--and in fact he was, his cancer apparently in remission." (Publishers Weekly)

REVIEW: *Christ Century* v131 no2 p9 Ja 22 2014 John Murawski

REVIEW: *Christ Century* v130 no13 p38-9 Je 26 2013 Lil Copan

REVIEW: *Commonweal* v140 no14 p31-2 S 13 2013 Paul Johnston

REVIEW: *Kirkus Rev* v81 no8 p71 Ap 15 2013

REVIEW: *Libr J* v137 no18 p55 N 1 2012 Barbara Hoffert

REVIEW: *N Y Times Book Rev* p16 My 27 2013 KATHLEEN NORRIS

REVIEW: *New York Times* v162 no56095 pC4 Ap 3 2013 DWIGHT GARNER

REVIEW: *New Yorker* v89 no12 p80-3 My 6 2013 Adam Kirsch

REVIEW: *Publ Wkly* v260 no6 p57-8 F 11 2013

REVIEW: *TLS* no5771 p7-8 N 8 2013 GRAEME RICHARDSON

"My Bright Abyss: Meditation of a Modern Believer." "One of the more interesting attempts in recent years to reconcile religious and poetic sensibilities. . . . 'My Bright Abyss' . . . isn't really concerned with narrative. Its meditations are more a series of remarks: on meaning, on anxiety, on consciousness, on silence and on poetry. And, as the title promises, [Christian] Wiman has no problem with paradox or inconsistency . . . 'My Bright Abyss' could function as a field guide to making atheists angry. . . . Perhaps cancer, with all its pain and boredom, gives Wiman a license here that others in religious controversy don't have. . . . Wiman the critic is more sure of his ground than Wiman the 'Modem Believer'."

REVIEW: *Va Q Rev* v89 no3 p199-202 Summ 2013 William Giraldi

WIMBUSH, VINCENT L. White men's magic; scripturalization as slavery; [by] Vincent L. Wimbush x, 294 p. 2012 Oxford University Press

1. Equiano, Olaudah, b. 1745 2. Historical literature 3. Race—Religious aspects—Christianity 4. Race relations—Religious aspects—Christianity 5. Race relations—United States 6. Religion and culture—United States 7. Sacred books
ISBN 9780199873579
LC 2012-000429

SUMMARY: "Characterizing Olaudah Equiano's eighteenth-century narrative of his life as a type of 'scriptural story' that connects the Bible with identity formation, Vincent L. Wimbush's 'White Men's Magic' probes not only how the Bible and its reading played a crucial role in the first colonial contacts between black and white persons in the North Atlantic but also the process and meaning of what he terms 'scripturalization.'" (Publisher's note)

REVIEW: *J Am Acad Relig* v81 no3 p865-8 S 2013 Margaret P. Aymer

"White Men's Magic: Scripturalization As Slavery." "Wimbush argues that 'scripturalization' functions as a kind of 'white men's magic' that, like the magic of other cultures, exercises an 'unbounded influence over the credulity and superstition of people.' The latter quote derives from the autobiography of Olaudah Equiano whose narrative serves as Wimbush's interpretative wedge of scripturalization. . . . The question is one of importance not only for historians of religion, but even, perhaps especially, for those who study the Bible, for it points to the reason why esoteric biblical studies exist, to the role of the Bible as the undergirder of the scripturalization semiosphere, both in the nineteenth century and today."

WINCHESTER, SIMON. The Men Who United the States; America's Explorers, Inventors, Eccentrics and Mavericks, and the Creation of One Nation, Indivisible; [by] Simon Winchester 480 p. 2013 HarperCollins

1. Historical literature 2. Infrastructure (Economics)—United States—History 3. United States—Discovery & exploration 4. United States—History 5. United States—Politics & government

ISBN 0062079603; 9780062079602

SUMMARY: This book by Simon Winchester "profiles a huge cast of eclectic characters who helped transform America from a cluster of colonies to a unified nation through the taming of the wilderness and the expansion of the country's infrastructure. The . . . narrative is . . . organized into five sections--each corresponds to one of the classical elements (wood, earth, water, fire, metal) and focuses on a different phase of American exploration or development." (Publishers Weekly)

REVIEW: *Booklist* v110 no1 p29 S 1 2013 Jay Freeman

REVIEW: *Booklist* v109 no19/20 p4 Je 1 2013

REVIEW: *Economist* v410 no8868 p67 Ja 4 2014

"The Men Who United the States: The Amazing Stories of the Explorers, Inventors and Mavericks Who Made America." "[Simon] Winchester uses stories to paint an unusual and personal portrait of the creation of a nation. . . . It is an unashamedly romantic sequence. . . . His style is always bright and conversational. . . . The subtitle promises readers a sackful of exciting tales--and the author delivers. This is a clever, engaging and original look at what would seem well-trodden historical paths; but Winchester, delightfully, breaks a fresh trail."

REVIEW: *Kirkus Rev* v81 no15 p246 Ag 1 2013

REVIEW: *Kirkus Rev* p32 Ag 15 2013 Fall Preview

REVIEW: *Libr J* v138 no8 p61 My 1 2013

REVIEW: *Libr J* v139 no3 p63 F 15 2014 David Faucheux

REVIEW: *N Y Times Book Rev* p45 N 10 2013 STEPHEN MIHM

"The Men Who United the States: America's Explorers, Inventors, Eccentrics, and Mavericks, and the Creation of One Nation, Indivisible." "When people are smitten, they are blind to flaws in their beloved. [Simon] Winchester is no exception, and this book is less a history than a love letter. In today's toxic political climate, the idea that Americans are united may seem laughable. But this misses Winchester's bigger and otherwise valid point: The United States endures despite its conflicts. . . . Winchester is sufficiently entertaining that it's easy to forget the holes in his arguments and enjoy the ride."

REVIEW: *New Statesman* v142 no5188 p44 12/092013 Michael Prodger Tom Gatti

REVIEW: *New Statesman* v142 no5187 p44 D 6 2013 Michael Prodger

REVIEW: *Publ Wkly* v260 no28 p155 Jl 15 2013

WINCZOREK, JAN.ed. Sociology and the unintended. See Sociology and the unintended

WINDSOR-SMITH, BARRY. Conan. See Thomas, R.

WINFREE, JASON. 15 sports myths and why they're wrong. See Fort, R.

WINKLER, HENRY, 1945-. How to scare the pants off your pets. See Oliver, L.

WINSTEAD, ROSIE. Sprout helps out; 32 p. 2013 Dial Books for Young Readers, an imprint of Penguin Group (USA) Inc.

1. Children's stories 2. Chores 3. Helpfulness—Fiction 4. Humorous stories 5. Mothers & daughters—Fiction

ISBN 0803730721; 9780803730724 (hardcover)
LC 2013-008765

SUMMARY: This children's book, by Rosie Winstead, is "about helping Mom and making a sweet, sweet mess of it. . . . Sprout's small, but she's good at helping. She makes the bed (with Mom still in it), cooks (if cooking is overflowing the cereal bowl), vacuums (up the cat—almost), and looks after her baby sister Bea (like a champ). Sure, sometimes Sprout's plans backfire, but good intentions go a long way—and make life interesting." (Publisher's note)

REVIEW: *Bull Cent Child Books* v67 no10 p549 Je 2014 J. H.

"Sprout Helps Out". "It's hard to believe that many real mothers would be quite as cheerful and understanding about Sprout's antics as her mother appears to be, but Sprout's good intentions and clueless mischief make her a winning heroine nonetheless. Illustrative details are comical and genuine. . . . The pencil, gouache, and watercolor paint pictures are thoughtfully composed but possess a casual, collage-like looseness that suits the storyline. . . . Since literature is a great way of finding perspective on one's own challenges, families with their own mess-prone 'Sprouts' are a likely audience here."

REVIEW: *Kirkus Rev* v82 no3 p63 F 1 2014

REVIEW: *Publ Wkly* v261 no2 p65 Ja 13 2014

REVIEW: *SLJ* v60 no4 p137 Ap 2014 Jenna Boles

WINSTONE, RUTH.ed. A Blaze of Autumn Sunshine. See Benn, T.

WINTER, JAY. René Cassin and human rights; from the Great War to the Universal Declaration; [by] Jay Winter xxiii, 376 p. 2013 Cambridge University Press

1. Biography (Literary form) 2. Human rights 3. Jews—France 4. Lawyers—France—Biography
ISBN 1107032563 (hardback); 1107655706 (paperback); 9781107032569 (hardback); 9781107655706 (paperback)
LC 2012-035056

SUMMARY: This book presents an "account of the life of René Cassin--advisor to de Gaulle during and after WW II, contributor to the Universal Declaration of Human Rights at the UN, and major figure in French Jewish circles. The authors' central theme is that Cassin always saw state sovereignty as limited by personal rights. In their account, Cassin's early views on law and rights were much shaped by his concern for WW I veterans." (Choice: Current Reviews for Academic Libraries)

REVIEW: *Choice* v51 no7 p1306 Mr 2014 D. P. Forsythe

"René Cassin and Human Rights: From the Great War to the Universal Declaration." "A thorough, engaging, and informative account of the life of René Cassin--advisor to [Charles] de Gaulle during and after WW II, contributor to the Universal Declaration of Human Rights at the UN, and major figure in French Jewish circles. . . . This balanced study notes that his support for Israel blinded him to the nationalistic aspirations of Palestinians and their rights. Well researched and written, this book shows why Cassin's mortal remains now rest in the Pantheon, the ultimate French honor to the country's major figures."

WINTER, JEANETTE. Henri's scissors; [by] Jeanette Winter 40 p. 2013 Beach Lane Books

1. Art literature 2. Artists—France—Biography—Juvenile literature 3. Collage 4. Picture books for children
ISBN 1442464844; 9781442464841 (hardcover); 9781442464858 (ebook)
LC 2012-033171

SUMMARY: In this children's picture book, after "quickly tracing French painter [Henri] Matisse's journey to becoming an artist ('He was happy, and his paintings made people happy') and explaining how illness left him unable to paint at the end of his life, [Jeanette] Winter . . . describes his discovery of a medium less physically demanding than painting but just as expressive: painted paper and scissors. 'Why didn't I think of it earlier?' he asks delightedly." (Publishers Weekly)

REVIEW: *Booklist* v110 no5 p65 N 1 2013 Sarah Hunter

"Brush of the Gods," "Diego Rivera: An Artist for the People," and "Henri's Scissors. "Wu Daozi is an artist with magic in his brush. As a boy in the late seventh century, Daozi was taught calligraphy, but instead of letters, worms and horsetails fall from the bristles. . . . With engaging prose that is beautifully illustrated with Rivera's paintings and murals, this spacious volume introduces the great Mexican artist to young people. . . . [Jeannette] Winter offers an elegant, accessible portrait of Matisse as an old man when, unable to paint, he begins cutting shapes from paper and dives into the art of collage."

REVIEW: *Booklist* v109 no19/20 p84 Je 1 2013 Thom Barthelmess

REVIEW: *Bull Cent Child Books* v67 no2 p125 O 2013 D. S.

REVIEW: *Horn Book Magazine* v89 no5 p124-5 S/O 2013 KATRINA HEDEEN

"Henri's Scissors." "The book's opening pages feature a simple, sedate layout: brightly colored but rather quiet acrylics showing [Henri] Matisse as a child and then creating famous early works are contained in neat square borders on café au lait pages. . . . With text that is straightforward and unflowery, [Jeanette] Winter relies, successfully, on the strength of her own art to capture the essence of Matisse's. A brief author's note explains her specific interest in this portion of the artist's oeuvre."

REVIEW: *Kirkus Rev* v81 no12 p122-3 Je 15 2013

REVIEW: *Publ Wkly* p57 Children's starred review annual 2013

REVIEW: *Publ Wkly* v260 no21 p63 My 27 2013

REVIEW: *SLJ* v59 no6 p108 Je 2013 Suzanne Myers Harold

WINTER, JEANETTE.il. Henri's scissors. See Winter, J.

WINTER, JONAH. Roberto Clemente; pride of the Pittsburgh Pirates; un 2005 Atheneum Books for Young Readers

1. Baseball—Biography 2. Baseball players 3. Biography, Individual—Juvenile literature 4. Children's literature—Works—Grades two through six 5. Children's literature—Works—Preschool through grade two 6. Puerto Ricans—Biography
ISBN 0-689-85643-1
LC 2003--25546

SUMMARY: This picture-book biography by Jonah Winter "shows how [Roberto] Clemente went from a boy with a guava tree bat, coffee-bean sack glove and soup can baseballs to a man who lifted the down-trodden Pittsburgh Pirates to victory, brought respect to Hispanic peoples, and fought to relieve his country's poverty until his death." (Children's Literature)

REVIEW: *Horn Book Magazine* v89 no5 p11-8 S/O 2013 Barbara Bader

"Ruth Law Thrills a Nation," "Charlie Parker Played Be Bop," and "Roberto Clemente: Pride of the Pittsburgh Pirates." "[Don] Brown is as much a writer as an artist. A stylist, in both cases, and a wit. . . . Chris Raschka's 'Charlie Parker Played Be Bop' . . . is less a biography than an improvisation on a personality--all juicy, exuberant cartooning, bouncy scribbles, and sweeps of color . . . with a bop-along text. For kids, a rousing performance. . . . Lives of sports heroes would stand out among picture book biographies. Jonah Winter, a professed baseball nut and a wordsmith, a poet, had something to do with this. . . . In 'Roberto Clemente' . . . the vehicle is a confiding near-verse."

WINTER, MICHAEL. Minister Without Portfolio; [by] Michael Winter 336 p. 2014 Penguin Group USA

1. Afghan War, 2001- 2. Canada—Fiction 3. Guilt—Fiction 4. Psychological fiction 5. Sublimation (Psychology)
ISBN 0143187813; 9780143187813

SUMMARY: In this book, "when Henry Hayward's life is rocked by his girlfriend breaking up with him, friends try to snap him out of his funk by getting him work with a civilian contracting crew in Afghanistan. During a routine patrol, a Taliban suicide bomber attacks the vehicle Henry and his two friends are in, killing one of them. Henry's enormous guilt . . . follows him home to Canada, where a series of bizarre accidents serves as background for Henry's further growth." (Booklist)

REVIEW: *Booklist* v110 no9/10 p43-4 Ja 1 2014 Julie Trevelyan

"Minister Without Portfolio." "This achingly resonant novel about the hidden fallout of war and every kind of human relationship packs a powerful punch with its sparse language, evocative scenes, and detailed observation of rural Newfoundland life. . . . [Henry Hayward] throws himself into restoring his dead friend's coastal family home in an earnest yet awkward attempt at personal redemption. In the process, he has a chance either to face his existential crisis and move on or to linger in it. Steer this toward readers seeking works stylistically similar to Ernest Hemingway and Raymond Carver."

REVIEW: *Kirkus Rev* v82 no4 p345 F 15 2014

REVIEW: *Quill Quire* v79 no8 p24-5 O 2013 Stephen Knight

WINTER, STEVE. Tigers Forever; Saving the World's Most Endangered Big Cat; [by] Steve Winter 224 p. 2013 Random House

1. Endangered species 2. Natural history literature 3. Photography of tigers 4. Tigers 5. Wildlife conservation
ISBN 1426212402; 9781426212406

SUMMARY: This book on endangered tigers presents photographs by Steve Winter and author Sharon Guynup. "Readers follow Winter through Myanmar's leech-infested jungles in search of tigers; into the forbidden realm of poachers in Sumatra; and witness the breathtaking intimacy between a tiger mother and her cub." (Publisher's note)

REVIEW: *Sci Am* v309 no6 p80 D 2013 Lee Billings

"Tigers Forever: Saving the World's Most Endangered Big Cat." "Drawing on a decade of tracking tigers throughout Asia, [Steve] Winter's photographs and [Sharon] Guynup's prose bring readers close--sometimes uncomfortably close--to these creatures and those who fight their extinction. 'Ricked between beautiful images of the great cats playing and bathing, we find heartbreaking photographs of slain tigers, orphaned cubs and a distressed puppy kept as bait in a poacher's snare. Poachers, the authors explain, sell tiger parts on the black market, often for use in traditional Chinese medicine. Through its portrayal of tigers struggling for survival in a hostile world, Tigers Forever is both a call to action and an indictment of human greed."

WINTERS, KAY. Voices from the Oregon Trail. See Voices from the Oregon Trail

WISDEN CRICKETERS' ALMANACK 2013; 1584 p. 2013 Wisden

1. Almanacs 2. Cricket (Sport) 3. Cricket (Sport)—Tournaments 4. Cricket players 5. Sports journalism
ISBN 1408175657; 9781408175651

SUMMARY: The 2013 edition of this almanack for cricket enthusiasts "contains coverage of every first-class game in every cricket nation, and reports and scorecards for all Tests and ODIs." (Publisher's note) Also included are several essays and obituaries on topics including "the dangers of overscheduling . . . the retiring giants of Indian batting Rahul Dravid and V. V. S. Laxman . . . [and] theAustralian Ricky Ponting." (Times Literary Supplement)

REVIEW: *New Statesman* v142 no5155 p43 Ap 26 2013 Peter Wilby

REVIEW: *TLS* no5747 p30 My 24 2013 ADRIAN TAHOURDIN

"Wisden Cricketers' Almanack 2013." "In his bracing Notes by the Editor, [Lawrence] Booth writes of the dangers of overscheduling. . . . Rupert Bates contributes an elegant pen portrait of Eric Ravilious, whose engraving of the top-batted batsman and wicketkeeper has long adorned the cover of 'Wisden'. . . . The veteran commentator from Barbados Tony Cozier writes evocatively on '50 years of touring England'. . . . The normally excellent Australian writer Gideon Haigh . . . is on disappointing form in his tribute to another retiring great, the Australian Ricky Ponting. . . . As often with 'Wisden,' the charm is in the incidental detail."

WISEMAN, ROSALIND. Masterminds and wingmen; helping your son cope with schoolyard power, locker-room tests, girlfriends, and the new rules of boy world; [by] Rosalind Wiseman 384 p. 2013 Harmony Books

1. Adolescent psychology 2. Advice literature 3. Boys—Social conditions 4. Masculinity 5. Schools—Social aspects 6. Social pressure 7. Teenage boys—Social conditions
ISBN 0307986659; 9780307986658

SUMMARY: This book offers information "for every parent--or anyone who cares about boys--to know. Collaborating with a large team of middle- and high-school-age editors, Rosalind Wiseman has created an unprecedented guide to the life your boy is actually experiencing--his on-the-ground reality. Not only does Wiseman challenge you to examine your assumptions, she offers innovative coping strategies aimed at helping your boy develop a positive, authentic, and strong sense of self." (Publisher's note)

REVIEW: *Kirkus Rev* v81 no16 p203 Ag 15 2013

"Masterminds and Wingmen: Helping Our Boys Cope With Schoolyard Power, Locker-Room Tests, Girlfriends, and the New Rules of Boy World." "Using scientific research and information gained directly from more than 150 boys, [author Rosalind] Wiseman examines the complex world of young men as they navigate school, the playground, locker room, playing fields and social arenas of modern life. Based on the concept that there are unwritten rules about how to 'Act-Like-A-Man,' which affect every male child, Wiseman unravels how these conventions stop boys from expressing their emotions and asking for help."

REVIEW: *Libr J* v139 no4 p57 Mr 1 2014 Douglas C. Lord

WISNER, GEOFF. ed. African lives. See African lives

WISSE, RUTH R. No joke; making Jewish humor; [by] Ruth R. Wisse 292 p. 2013 Princeton University Press

1. Historical literature 2. Jewish comedians 3. Jewish history 4. Jewish wit & humor 5. Jewish wit and humor—History and criticism 6. Jews—Humor—History and criticism
ISBN 0691149461; 9780691149462 (alk. paper)

LC 2012-051631

SUMMARY: In this book, Ruth R. Wisse "traces the history of Jewish humor from its first major formal appearance in the fiction of Heinrich Heine right up to material by Larry David. Wisse backtracks to the diaspora experience, contingent status of Jews throughout European history, and conflicting readings of the Talmud to underpin her analysis of themes underlying various Jewish-joke traditions." (Library Journal)

REVIEW: *Choice* v51 no2 p263-4 O 2013 S. Gittleman

"No Joke: Making Jewish Humor." "[Author Ruth R.] Wisse . . . , arguably the foremost Yiddishist in North America, has produced a jewel of a book on Jewish humor, replete with academic erudition and often side-splitting jokes. She is equally at home in the works of Heinrich Heine, Sholem Aleicheni, I. B. Singer, the Israelis, and Philip Roth, as well as among Borscht Belt comedians in the Catskills, or with Woody Allen and Mel Brooks. This slender volume is as scholarly as it is downright hilarious. . . . Inevitably, she leads into difficult discussions about self-deprecation, Freud, the horrors of the Holocaust, and how Jews manage to keep laughing in spite of the misery all around them."

REVIEW: *Christ Century* v130 no12 p41 Je 12 2013

REVIEW: *Commentary* v135 no6 p54-6 Je 2013 RICK RICHMAN

REVIEW: *Economist* v407 no8836 p87 My 18 2013

REVIEW: *Kirkus Rev* v81 no8 p71 Ap 15 2013

REVIEW: *Libr J* v138 no9 p95 My 15 2013 Scott H. Silverman

REVIEW: *N Y Times Book Rev* p38-9 Je 2 2013 ANTHONY GOTTLIEB

REVIEW: *Publ Wkly* v260 no13 p58 Ap 1 2013

WITHAM, LARRY. Piero's Light; In Search of Piero Della Francesca: a Renaissance Painter and the Revolution in Art, Religion, and Science; [by] Larry Witham 368 p. 2014 W.W. Norton & Co. Inc

1. Art & religion 2. Art & science 3. Biography (Literary form) 4. Painters—Italy—Biography 5. Piero, della Francesca, ca. 1416-1492 6. Renaissance
ISBN 1605984949; 9781605984940

SUMMARY: This book by Larry Witham is an "examination of the early Renaissance polymath Piero [della Francesca], whose life and accomplishments are used to survey 'the precipitous changes in art, religion, and science' in the painter's time and beyond. . . . Witham demonstrates how Piero's art and contributions to mathematics were absorbed over the centuries following his death, and how he participated in the evolving discourse on art interpretation, beauty, and science." (Publishers Weekly)

REVIEW: *Choice* v51 no10 p1792-3 Je 2014 K. E. Staab

REVIEW: *Kirkus Rev* v81 no24 p223 D 15 2013

"Piero's Light: In Search of Pieroo della Francesca: A Renaissance Painter and the Revolution in Art, Science, and Religion". "A wide-ranging account of the life, work and legacy of Renaissance artist Piero della Francesca. . . . Throughout, the author deals with concepts of vision, light, beauty and mind, drawing on the works and theories of numerous philosophers (from the ancient to the present world), psychologists and neuroscientists to illuminate the various debates about the nature of reality and of the mind. A thorough account of an actual 'Renaissance man'—in every way."

REVIEW: *Libr J* v139 no2 p74 F 1 2014 Nancy J. Mactague

REVIEW: *N Y Rev Books* v61 no11 p53-6 Je 19 2014 Julian Bell

REVIEW: *Publ Wkly* v260 no50 p62 D 9 2013

WITHERIDGE, JOHN. Excellent Dr Stanley; the Life of Dean Stanley of Westminster; [by] John Witheridge 416 p. 2013 Michael Russell Publishing Ltd

1. Arthur, Stanley 2. Biography (Literary form) 3. Church of England—Customs & practices 4. Church of England—Parties & movements 5. England—Church history 6. Scholars—Great Britain—Biography
ISBN 085955323X; 9780859553230

SUMMARY: This book presents a biography of scholar and Church of England official Arthur Stanley. "To him, Christianity was above all 'the love of God and man shed abroad in the human heart.' He fought hard to defend the comprehensiveness of the Church of England, and its members' freedom to hold and follow a variety of beliefs and practices. This embroiled him in the many controversies of the Victorian Church." (charterhouse.org.uk)

REVIEW: *TLS* no5770 p8 N 1 2013 A. N. WILSON

"Excellent Dr. Stanley: The Life of Dean Stanley of Westminster." "John Witheridge's timely biography of the man who first coined the 'Broad Church' label in print is not only a skilfully painted Victorian canvas, but also a bright object lesson; for Dean Stanley, surely one of the most lovable men who ever lived, calls to his Church across the ages to abandon its addiction to factionalism and hatred. . . . Witheridge paints an unforgettable portrait of Oxford in the 1840s. . . . Witheridge's gentleness makes his accounts of the footling obsessions of the Tractarians all the more devastating. . . . 'Excellent Dr Stanley' is a joyous book, celebrating a figure of sublime intelligence and grace."

WITKOWSKI, JAN.ed. The annotated and illustrated double helix. See Watson, J.

WITTCOFF, HAROLD A. Industrial organic chemicals; [by] Harold A. Wittcoff 848 p. 2012 Wiley

1. Chemical engineering 2. Chemical literature 3. Organic chemistry 4. Organic compounds 5. Organic compounds—Industrial applications 6. Technical chemistry
ISBN 9780470537435 (cloth)
LC 2011-040427

SUMMARY: This book by Harold A. Wittcoff, Bryan G. Reuben, Jeffrey S. Plotkin describes how "Products as diverse as gasoline, plastics, detergents, fibers, pesticides, tires, lipstick, shampoo, and sunscreens are based on seven raw materials derived from petroleum and natural gas. In an updated and expanded Third Edition," this book examines why each of these chemical building blocks . . . is preferred over another in the context of an environmental issue or manufacturing process." (Publisher's note)

REVIEW: *Choice* v51 no2 p297 O 2013 D. H. Stedman

"Industrial Organic Chemicals." "Readers might expect an 800-page volume discussing organic chemicals in industry to be dry and boring. This book by [Harold A.] Wittcoff . . . , [Bryan G.] Reuben . . . , and [Jeffrey S.] Plotkin . . . is a welcome exception. It is a pleasure to read because it is well written, informative, well annotated, and even, in many places, downright amusing. . . . Every organic chemist who contemplates a career in the field should read the book. Even future and active pharmaceutical researchers will need the chemical insight from this book to understand the nature of their starting materials."

WITTENSTEIN, VICKI ORANSKY. For the good of mankind?; the shameful history of human medical experimentation; [by] Vicki Oransky Wittenstein 96 p. 2014 Twenty-First Century Books

1. Historical literature 2. Human experimentation in medicine—History 3. Medical ethics 4. Medical sciences—Research—Methodology—History 5. Young adult literature

ISBN 1467706590; 9781467706599 (lib. bdg. : alk. paper)

LC 2012-043413

SUMMARY: In this book, Vicki Oransky Wittenstein "describes many cringe-inducing examples of the ways doctors have exploited the marginalized, powerless and voiceless of society as human guinea pigs over the centuries. . . . Some experiments did lead to important discoveries and breakthroughs, but readers are challenged to consider the costs of violating individual rights for the cause of advancing medical knowledge." (Kirkus Reviews)

REVIEW: *Booklist* v110 no3 p49 O 1 2013 Gail Bush

"For the Good of Mankind? The Shameful History of Human Medical Experimentation." "More than just a historical treatment of human experimentation, this title also offers an introduction to timely related issues involving biospecimens, stem cell research, and genetic enhancement. . . . Writing from a mindful, balanced perspective, [Vicki Oransky] Wittenstein keeps the essential ethical questions about rights of the individual, the advancement of science, and the evolution of informed consent in clear view. . . . [A] substantive, informative resource."

REVIEW: *Bull Cent Child Books* v67 no3 p188-9 N 2013 E. B.

REVIEW: *Kirkus Rev* v81 no18 p42 S 15 2013

REVIEW: *SLJ* v59 no9 p191 S 2013 Meaghan Darling

REVIEW: *Voice of Youth Advocates* v36 no5 p88 D 2013 Alicia Abdul

WITZEL, MORGEN.ed. The Oxford handbook of management theorists. See The Oxford handbook of management theorists

WOELFLE, GRETCHEN. Mumbet's Declaration of Independence; 32 p. 2014 Carolrhoda Books

1. African American women—Massachusetts—Biography—Juvenile literature 2. American historical fiction 3. Slavery—Massachusetts—History—18th century—Juvenile literature 4. Slaves—Massachusetts—Biography—Juvenile literature 5. Women slaves—Massachusetts—Biography—Juvenile literature

ISBN 0761365893; 9780761365891 (lib. bdg.: alk. paper)

LC 2013-018620

SUMMARY: This book, written by Gretchen Woelfle and illustrated by Alix Delinois, part of the Carolrhoda Picture Books series, describes how "the founders weren't the only ones who believed that everyone had a right to freedom. Mumbet, a Massachusetts slave, believed it too. She longed to be free, but how? Would anyone help her in her fight for freedom? Could she win against her owner, the richest man in town?" (Publisher's note)

REVIEW: *Booklist* v110 no17 p89 My 1 2014 J. B. Petty

REVIEW: *Bull Cent Child Books* v67 no9 p483-4 My 2014 D. S.

"Mumbet's Declaration of Independence". "The book incorporates historical incident, such as Mumbet's defense of her daughter against her mistress' blows, while adding an artistic (if occasionally stilted) fictionalized touch in Mumbet's recurring use of natural imagery. . . . The case is fascinating, emphasizing the destructive irony at the heart of the birth of America and making Mumbet an active and savvy architect of her own release, and this is likely to spur much discussion. . . . End matter considerably enriches the narrative."

REVIEW: *Horn Book Magazine* v90 no3 p117-8 My/Je 2014 ROBIN L. SMITH

REVIEW: *Kirkus Rev* v81 no21 p173 N 1 2013

REVIEW: *N Y Times Book Rev* p16 F 16 2014 GLENDA R. CARPIO

"Mumbet's Declaration of Independence," "Under the Same Sun," and "Knock Knock: My Dad's Dream for Me." "Gretchen Woelfle's 'Mumbet's Declaration of Independence' . . . tells the story of . . . Bett or Betty [who] successfully sued her owner . . . for her emancipation, and once liberated chose to name herself Elizabeth Freeman. . . . In 'Under the Same Sun,' Sharon Robinson, the daughter of the baseball legend Jackie Robinson, also deals with the history of slavery but folds it into a story about a modern-day family reunion. . . . [In] Daniel Beaty's 'Knock Knock: My Dad's Dream for Me,' . . . a letter from the father finally arrives explaining that he will not be coming home."

REVIEW: *Publ Wkly* v260 no49 p85 D 2 2013

REVIEW: *SLJ* v60 no1 p117 Ja 2014 Lucinda Snyder Whitehurst

WOERTZ, ECKART. Oil for food; the global food crisis and the Middle East; [by] Eckart Woertz xxiii, 319 p. 2013 Oxford University Press

1. Food industry—Export & import trade 2. Food security 3. Food supply—Middle East 4. Petroleum industry—Middle East 5. Political science literature

ISBN 0199659486 (hbk.); 9780199659487 (hbk.)

LC 2012-277645

SUMMARY: This book on the Gulf states by Eckart Woertz "outlines the food security predicament of the region, including the reliance on food imports, the limited potential for domestic food production, and the impact of the global food crisis whereby global food prices shot up in 2007/8 and 2010/11." (Middle East Journal)

REVIEW: *Choice* v51 no5 p890 Ja 2014 P. Clawson

REVIEW: *Middle East J* v68 no1 p179-80 Wint 2014 Jane Harrigan

"Oil for Food: The Global Food Crisis and the Middle East." "Although [Eckart Woertz] outlines some of the adverse effects overseas land acquisition, limited attention is given to this dimension of land acquisition. . . . In short, this is a fascinating book on the political economy of food security in the Gulf states, with an in-depth study of the so called 'land grab' phenomenon from the perspective of Gulf investors. However, it presents the practice of land acquisition in an unjustifiably rosy light, and as such is a somewhat biased study."

WOHL, ELLEN. Wide rivers crossed; the South Platte and the Illinois of the American prairie; [by] Ellen Wohl v, 344 p. 2013 University Press of Colorado

1. Natural history—Illinois—Illinois River 2. Natural history—South Platte River (Colo. and Neb.) 3. Natural history literature 4. Streamflow—Illinois—Illinois River 5. Streamflow—South Platte River (Colo. and Neb.) 6. Water use—Illinois—Illinois River 7. Water use—South Platte River Watershed (Colo. and Neb.)

ISBN 9781607322306 (hardcover : alk. paper)

LC 2013-006729

SUMMARY: This book "tells the stories of two rivers--the South Platte on the western plains and the Illinois on the eastern--to represent the environmental history and historical transformation of major rivers across the American prairie. [Ellen] Wohl begins with the rivers' natural histories . . . and follows a downstream and historical progression from the use of the rivers' resources by European immigrants through increasing population density of the twentieth century to the present day." (Publisher's note)

REVIEW: *Choice* v51 no4 p671-2 D 2013 J. H. Thorp III

"Wide Rivers Crossed: The South Platte and the Illinois of the American Prairie." "This intriguing book will quickly capture reader interest with its coverage of the natural history and ecology of shortgrass, and formerly, tallgrass prairie rivers; the effects of subtle to flagrant manipulation of riverscapes and watersheds; and future scenarios for recovery or continued degradation. Although [Ellen] Wohl . . . is a professor of fluvial geomorphology, she does not overwhelm her audience with hard science. Instead, she weaves a tale of the impacts of human manipulation of rivers."

WOHNOUTKA, MIKE.il. Moo! See LaRochelle, D.

WOLCOTT, VICTORIA W. Race, riots, and roller coasters; the struggle over segregated recreation in America; [by] Victoria W. Wolcott 310 p. 2012 University of Pennsylvania Press

1. African Americans—Civil rights—United States—History—20th century 2. African Americans—Recreation—United States—History—20th century 3. African Americans—Segregation—United States—History—20th century 4. Amusement parks—History 5. Historical literature 6. Recreation—Social aspects—United States—History—20th century

ISBN 0812244346; 9780812244342 (hardcover : alk. paper)

LC 2012-002588

SUMMARY: Author Victoria W. Wolcott presents information on the segregation of African Americans in the U.S. The book looks at "overlooked aspects of conflicts over public accommodations" and "the significance of leisure in American race relations. . . . Wolcott tells the story of this battle for access to leisure space in cities all over the United States" and how "white mobs attacked those who dared to transgress racial norms." (Publisher's note)

REVIEW: *Am Hist Rev* v118 no4 p1193-4 O 2013 Lauren Rabinovitz

"Race, Riots, and Roller Coasters: The Struggle Over Segregated Recreation in America." "Victoria M. Wolcott's new book argues that racial conflict over consumer leisure was central to shaping and expanding the modern civil rights movement. More importantly, Wolcott demonstrates that spatially segregated amusement still prevents twenty-first-century African Americans from full cultural participation. . . . Wolcott neglects any consideration of class or other factors that admitted conflict among African Americans. . . . Wolcott's work adds a much-needed chapter to both civil rights and leisure histories."

REVIEW: *Choice* v50 no6 p1124 F 2013 D. R. Jamieson

REVIEW: *J Am Hist* v100 no2 p566-7 S 2013 Julia Kirk Blackwelder

REVIEW: *Rev Am Hist* v41 no4 p710-6 D 2013 Erin D. Chapman

WOLF, ALISON. The XX factor; [by] Alison Wolf 416 p. 2013 Crown

1. Social science literature 2. Women—Employment—History 3. Women employees 4. Women executives 5. Women in the professions 6. Work and family 7. Work-life balance

ISBN 0307590402; 9780307590404

LC 2013-011785

SUMMARY: In this book, author Alison Wolf "examines why more educated women work longer hours, why having children early is a good idea, and how feminism created a less equal world. Her ideas are sure to provoke and surprise, as she challenges much of what the liberal and conservative media consider to be women's best interests." (Publisher's note)

REVIEW: *Choice* v51 no9 p1639 My 2014 B. Weston

REVIEW: *Economist* v407 no8831 p85-6 Ap 13 2013

REVIEW: *Kirkus Rev* v81 no16 p246 Ag 15 2013

REVIEW: *N Y Times Book Rev* p34 O 13 2013

REVIEW: *N Y Times Book Rev* p19 O 6 2013 KATRIN BENNHOLD

"The XX Factor: How the Rise of Working Women Has Created a Far Less Equal World." "[A] brisk, rigorously researched volume on the economic rise of (some) women. . . . [Alison] Wolf's book is a sobering reminder that as it is currently framed, the work-family debate smacks of elitism. . . . Here is where Wolf makes her most provocative but also her most problematic assertion: 'Adult female employment today isn't a common shared experience in the way that tending home and family used to be,' she writes. . . . Yet . . . women in the early 21st century still distinct hurdles based on their sex, independent of class. . . . If these passages feel old-fashioned, Wolf redeems herself by taking us on a journey across time and oceans and even DNA that is well worth traveling."

REVIEW: *Publ Wkly* v260 no31 p61-2 Ag 5 2013

REVIEW: *TLS* no5752 p3-4 Je 28 2013 PAUL SEABRIGHT

WOLF, GITA. Alone in the forest; 40 p. 2013 Tara Books

1. Agoraphobia 2. Children's stories 3. Fear in children 4. Forests & forestry—Juvenile literature 5. India—Ju-

venile literature
ISBN 8192317153; 9788192317151

SUMMARY: Author Gita Wolf features a children's picture book. "One day, Musa sets off alone to collect wood from the forest near to his home. Suddenly, he hears a deafening noise and is overcome with terror Was the sound a wild boar? A whole herd of wild boars? Or something even worse? . . . What happens to Musa and how he learns to deal with his fear is explored in this powerful yet sensitive visual story of the psychology of fear." (Publisher's note)

REVIEW: *Horn Book Magazine* v90 no1 p82 Ja/F 2014 JOANNA RUDGE LONG

"Alone in the Forest." "[Gita] Wolf . . . sets her tale of a child venturing outside his usual sphere among the forest-dwelling Gonds of central India. . . . [Bhajju] Shyam's stylized, boldly outlined forms brim with energy. The forest's dark tones convey emotion; sharp teeth and vivid red connote Musa's fear, while varied depictions of him signal his changing emotions. The source of those frightening sounds appears only in an illustration: it's a falling branch that might (ironically) have provided firewood. A simple, satisfying story, much enriched by its cultural grounding and handsome art."

REVIEW: *Kirkus Rev* v81 no16 p87 Ag 15 2013

"Alone in the Forest." "The terrifying experience of being alone in the woods is rendered through the eyes of a young Indian boy. . . . [Illustrator Bhajju Shyam], a noted Gond tribal artist, conveys the boy's experience convincingly with evocative and elegantly produced images. Patterns of lines, dots, and chains fill the figures, which are enhanced with solid blocks of colors. There is no depth to these scenes, but there is great variety. . . . A familiar story arc conveyed through traditional art captivates with its freshness and originality."

REVIEW: *Publ Wkly* v260 no31 p68-9 Ag 5 2013

REVIEW: *SLJ* v59 no9 p136 S 2013 Susan Scheps

WOLF, JENNIFER SHAW. Dead girls don't lie; [by] Jennifer Shaw Wolf 352 p. 2013 Bloomsbury/Walker

1. Best friends—Fiction 2. Dating (Social customs)—Fiction 3. Friendship—Fiction 4. Murder—Fiction 5. Mystery and detective stories 6. Secrets—Fiction 7. Single-parent families—Fiction
ISBN 0802734499; 9780802734495 (hardback)
LC 2013-012063

SUMMARY: In this murder mystery by author Jennifer Shaw Wolf "Jaycee and Rachel were best friends. But that was before . . . that terrible night at the old house. Before Rachel shut Jaycee out. Before Jaycee chose Skyler over Rachel. Then Rachel is found dead. The police blame a growing gang problem . . . but Jaycee is sure it has to do with that night at the old house. Rachel's death was no random crime, and Jaycee must figure out who to trust before she can expose the truth." (Publisher's note)

REVIEW: *Booklist* v110 no2 p68 S 15 2013 Diane Colson

REVIEW: *Bull Cent Child Books* v67 no3 p189 N 2013 K. Q. G.

"Dead Girls Don't Lie." "Six months ago, a fight over a guy officially broke up the already disintegrating friendship between sixteen-year-old Jaycee and her best friend, Rachel. Now Rachel is dead, shot through her bedroom window, a drive-by victim in a gang war that has supposedly followed the Mexican migrant workers in Jaycee's small farm town. . . . The players in Rachel's murder are all fairly obvious from the beginning, but the ways in which they are involved and the motivations behind their actions remain ambiguous until the final reveal. . . . [Author Jennifer] Shaw [Wolf] wisely stays away from any climax that brings resolution to the obviously thick and long-held racial tensions that foreground this particular crisis. . . ."

REVIEW: *Kirkus Rev* v81 no16 p41 Ag 15 2013

REVIEW: *SLJ* v59 no10 p1 O 2013 Joanna Sondheim

WOLF, ZANE ROBINSON. Exploring rituals in nursing; joining art and science; [by] Zane Robinson Wolf 224 p. 2014 Springer Pub. Co.

1. Ceremonial Behavior 2. Interpersonal Relations 3. Nursing—History 4. Nursing Process 5. Nursing literature
ISBN 9780826196620; 9780826196637 (e-book)
LC 2013-015354

SUMMARY: This book on nursing "is divided into two sections. The first section discusses interpersonal care rituals, e.g., bathing, postmortem care, and medication administration and error prevention, always emphasizing traditions and beliefs as they relate to current research. The second section discusses socialization rituals related to shift-to-shift communication between nursing staff, and transitions, celebrations, and ceremonies in the profession." (Choice: Current Reviews for Academic Libraries)

REVIEW: *Choice* v51 no6 p1045 F 2014 B. A. D'Anna

"Exploring Rituals in Nursing: Joining Art and Science." "[Zane Robinson] Wolf . . . picks up where fundamental nursing textbooks stop by merging value-based rituals with science-based knowledge, reminding nurses of their history in an effort to enhance and preserve today's nursing practice. . . . A very interesting read, this book reaffirms why and how nurses provide care and incorporate ethical values and respect for human dignity into professional practice. A useful supplemental resource for nursing curricula."

WOLFE, PETER. The theater of Terrence McNally; a critical study; [by] Peter Wolfe ix, 261 p. 2014 McFarland & Company, Inc., Publishers

1. American drama—History & criticism 2. Forgiveness in literature 3. Gay male dramatists 4. Gay men in literature 5. Theater literature
ISBN 9780786474950 (softcover: alk. paper)
LC 2013-034470

SUMMARY: "This first book-length monograph on Terrence McNally," by Peter Wolfe, "shows how McNally's decades in the theater have both deepened and refined his thoughts on subjects like growing up gay in mannish, homophobic Texas, Shakespeare's legacy in contemporary drama, and the life-giving power of forgiveness." (Publisher's note)

REVIEW: *Choice* v51 no8 p1403 Ap 2014 J. Fisher

"The Theater of Terrence McNally: A Critical Study". "[Peter] Wolfe's fine, thorough examination of McNally is woefully overdue. Wolfe . . . clearly admires McNally for his overall achievement and versatility as a playwright; as a result, the book largely celebrates him and what Wolfe identifies as McNally's recurring subjects, including gay life, music, tolerance, and forgiveness. Along with seven chapters of penetrating analysis, Wolfe provides a thorough bibliography and a full accounting of McNally's one acts, plays, musicals, screenplays, and even his undergraduate term papers at Columbia College. Thus, this book is an invaluable source on a playwright whose mission has been to capture 'what it means to be alive and human.'"

WOLFENDALE, JESSICA.ed. Fashion. See Fashion

WOLFF, ASHLEY. Baby Bear counts one; [by] Ashley Wolff 40 p. 2013 Beach Lane Books

1. Animals—Wintering—Fiction 2. Bears—Fiction 3. Children's stories 4. Counting 5. Winter—Fiction
ISBN 1442441585; 9781442441583 (hardcover); 9781442441590 (ebook)
LC 2012-020202

SUMMARY: "In this fall-themed counting book . . . Mama Bear gently answers Baby Bear's questions about who is making a noise as he counts different animals gathering food, migrating, or dashing through the woods and fields in preparation for winter. Each spread includes onomatopoeic words to suggest the animal to both children and the bear." (School Library Journal)

REVIEW: *Booklist* v110 no3 p98 O 1 2013 Ann Kelley

REVIEW: *Bull Cent Child Books* v67 no2 p125-6 O 2013 T. A.

"Baby Bear Counts One." "With each new discovery, the number of critters discovered rises, until the snow starts to fall and Baby Bear counts ten snowflakes before curling up back in the den with his mother for a long winter's nap. . . . The story progresses cozily in a pattern that quickly becomes recognizable to listeners: Baby Bear hears a noise, asks his mother who is producing it, and Mama explains which animal is preparing for snowfall. . . . The linocut illustrations tinted with watercolor are strikingly realistic and lavish in their detailed, dramatic lining and rich, earthy coloring. The comfy, easy-to-follow text and vivid pictures will make this a snug bedtime story or a feel-good selection for an autumnal storytime."

REVIEW: *Horn Book Magazine* v89 no5 p83 S/O 2013 MARTHA V. PARRAVANO

"Baby Bear Counts One." "[Ashley] Wolff's art (hand-colored linoleum blocks) is glorious, capturing the withered cornstalks, brown leaves, and fallen apples of autumn while also conveying the busyness and vibrancy of the season. Very young children may find the counting aspect too difficult, as some animals are shown only partially (and one spread strays from the pattern by featuring two species to be counted), but slightly older or more sophisticated readers may relish the challenge. And the loving bond between Baby Bear and his mama is as secure and comforting as ever."

REVIEW: *Kirkus Rev* v81 no14 p130 Jl 15 2013

REVIEW: *Publ Wkly* v260 no28 p168 Jl 15 2013

REVIEW: *SLJ* v59 no8 p93 Ag 2013 Marge Loch-Wouters

WOLFF, ASHLEY.il. Baby Bear counts one. See Wolff, A.

WOLFF, JOSHUA D. Western Union and the creation of the American corporate order, 1845-1893; [by] Joshua D. Wolff xi, 305 p. 2013 Cambridge University Press

1. Corporations—United States—History—19th century 2. Historical literature 3. Monopolies—United States—History—19th century 4. Telecommunication—United States—Management—History—19th century 5. Telegraph—United States—History—19th century
ISBN 9781107012288 (hardback)
LC 2013-000569

SUMMARY: This book by Joshua D. Wolff "chronicles the rise of Western Union Telegraph from its origins in the helter skelter ferment of antebellum capitalism to its apogee as the first corporation to monopolize an industry on a national scale. The battles that raged over Western Union's monopoly on 19th century American telecommunications . . . illuminate the fierce tensions over the rising power of corporations after the Civil War and the reshaping of American political economy." (Publisher's note)

REVIEW: *Am Hist Rev* v119 no3 p899 Je 2014 MICHAEL J. CONNOLLY

REVIEW: *Bus Hist Rev* v88 no2 p384-6 Summ 2014 Robert MacDougall

REVIEW: *Choice* v51 no8 p1458-9 Ap 2014 T. E. Sullivan

"Western Union and the Creation of the American Corporate Order, 1845-1893". "Historian [Joshua D.] Wolff has produced a worthy scholarly study that is both rich in detail and comprehensive in its interpretations about the formation, expansion and operation of Western Union Telegraph. . . . As this discerning study reveals, the actions and policies of Western Union as an unnatural monopoly can be understood on a private and micro level as well as on a macro level. . . . As a business history or as an examination of the machinations of either financial markets or the political debates around commerce in postbellum America, this is a compelling and informative study."

REVIEW: *J Am Hist* v101 no1 p278-9 Je 2014

WOLFF, LARRY. Paolina's innocence; child abuse in Casanova's Venice; [by] Larry Wolff x, 315 p. 2012 Stanford University Press

1. Child sexual abuse—Investigation—Italy—Venice—History—18th century 2. Historical literature 3. Libertinism—Italy—Venice—History—18th century 4. Sociological jurisprudence—Italy—Venice—History—18th century 5. Trials (Child sexual abuse)—Italy—Venice—History—18th century
ISBN 9780804762618 (hbk.: alk. paper); 9780804762625 (pbk.: alk. paper)
LC 2011-045204

SUMMARY: This book on the 1785 child abuse trial of Gaetano Franceschini "considers Franceschini's conduct in the context of the libertinism of Casanova and also employs other prominent contemporaries—Jean-Jacques Rousseau, Carlo Goldoni, Lorenzo Da Ponte, Cesare Beccaria, and the Marquis de Sade—as points of reference for understanding the case and broader issues of libertinism, sexual crime, childhood, and child abuse in the 18th century." (Publisher's note)

REVIEW: *Am Hist Rev* v119 no1 p267-8 F 2014 David I. Kertzer

"Paolina's Innocence: Child Abuse in Casanova's Venice". "What is most stimulating in [Larry] Wolff's book, and may be most controversial, is his examination of the tension between the portrayal of children as innocent and the generally unacknowledged tendency to view them erotically. . . . 'Paolina's Innocence' is written in a lively, accessible style and its subject is one of both historical and popular interest. . . .Confining himself here to a single court case, Wolff of course cannot offer conclusive evidence about the broad, ambitious topics he addresses. But in linking this obscure but dramatic case to broader cultural currents of the time, and in articulating his provocative thesis, Wolff offers a valuable stimulus to . . . further archival explorations."

WOLFF, PEGGY.ed. Fried walleye and cherry pie. See Fried walleye and cherry pie

WOLFSGRUBER, LINDA.il. The camel in the sun. See Ondaatje, G.

WOLLOCH, NATHANIEL. History and nature in the Enlightenment; praise of the mastery of nature in eighteenth-century historical literature; [by] Nathaniel Wolloch xviii, 290 p. 2011 Ashgate

1. Enlightenment—Europe—Historiography 2. Environmental ethics—Europe—Historiography 3. Historical literature 4. Nature—Effect of human beings on—Europe—Historiography 5. Nature—Religious aspects—Historiography 6. Philosophy of nature—Europe—Historiography 7. Progress—Social aspects—Europe—Historiography

ISBN 9781409421146 (hardcover: alk. paper); 9781409421153 (ebook)

LC 2010-043834

SUMMARY: This book by Nathaniel Wolloch examines "the mastery of nature . . . in connection with the mainstream religious, political, and philosophical elements of Enlightenment culture. It considers works by figures that include Edward Gibbon . . . Adam Smith and William Robertson. It also discusses many classical, medieval, and early modern sources which influenced Enlightenment historiography, as well as eighteenth-century attitudes toward nature." (Publisher's note)

REVIEW: *Am Hist Rev* v119 no1 p242-3 F 2014 Jan Golinski

"History and Nature in the Enlightenment: Praise of the Mastery of Nature in Eighteenth-Century Historical Literature". "The strengths of the book include valuable discussions of several lesser-known writers whom [Edward] Gibbon read, such as Robert Henry, John Pinkerton, William Robertson, and the abbé Raynal. Some very well-known authors also appear in a new light. . . . [Nathaniel] Wolloch focuses his attention firmly on the works of historians, excluding many of the works the historians themselves read. He has his furrow and he plows it thoroughly, but without raising his eyes too much to take in the wider scene. Such a decision inevitably fails to capture the richness of the intellectual landscape as it was experienced by the thinkers of the Enlightenment themselves."

WOLTERS, TIMOTHY S. Information at sea; shipboard command and control in the U.S. Navy, from Mobile Bay to Okinawa; [by] Timothy S. Wolters xii, 317 p. 2013 The Johns Hopkins University Press

1. Command and control systems—United States—History 2. Historical literature 3. Radio, Military 4. Warships—United States—History

ISBN 1421410265 (hbk.: alk. paper); 9781421410265 (hbk.: alk. paper)

LC 2012-048479

SUMMARY: This book "looks at the way commanders of U.S. Navy ships communicated vital information during battles and maneuvers from the 1860s to the 1940s." Author Timothy S. Wolters's "concern is the human system of command and control as technology progressed from messenger boats to flag signals, signal lights, radio, and finally radar." (Choice: Current Reviews for Academic Libraries)

REVIEW: *Choice* v51 no8 p1424 Ap 2014 K. D. Stephan

"Information at Sea: Shipboard Command and Control in U.S. Navy From Mobile Bay to Okinawa". "[Timothy S.] Wolters's familiarity with naval minutiae and procedures leads to a lively, highly readable narrative that also maintains scholarly depth and thoroughness. He brings to light neglected naval figures such as Samuel S. Robison, a battle fleet commander who oversaw the introduction of radio into the Navy's command system. Wolters casts doubt on the conventional view among some historians that the Navy was a hidebound lair of conservatives that adopted new technologies unwillingly, if at all. Undergraduates, graduate students, and anyone interested in this neglected aspect of Navy history will benefit from this book."

WOMEN, SEXUALITY AND THE POLITICAL POWER OF PLEASURE; sex, gender and empowerment; 2013 Palgrave Macmillan

1. Sexual excitement 2. Social science literature 3. Violence against women 4. Women—Sexual behavior 5. Women in politics

ISBN 9781780325729

SUMMARY: This book, edited by Andrea Cornwall, Susie Jolly, and Kate Hawkins, "explores the ways in which women's sexual desires are experienced by them and how this experience effects women's empowerment." According to the book, "an exploration of pleasure can have a hugely positive impact for women at the personal, social and political levels." It discusses "examples of mobilisation, programming and policy." (Publisher's note)

REVIEW: *Choice* v51 no6 p1054 F 2014 K. Y. Perry

"Women, Sexuality and the Political Power of Pleasure." "This volume makes a crucial intervention in social movement, feminist, and development theories by focusing on the political possibilities of sexual pleasure. . . . One of the most intriguing essays in the volume is Jaya Sharma's chapter, which challenges readers to critically interrogate the misuses of pleasure. This book encourages the exploration of these fresh and necessary perspectives on pleasure in gender and development work worldwide. . . . Highly recommended."

WONG, JANELLE. Asian American political participation. See Taeku Lee

WONG, NICOLE.il. Ferry tail. See Kenah, K.

WONG, NICOLE.il. No monkeys, no chocolate. See Stewart, M.

WOOD, BRADFORD.ed. Creating and contesting Carolina. See Creating and contesting Carolina

WOOD, CHRIS. Down the Drain; How We Are Failing to Protect Our Water Resources; [by] Chris Wood 304 p. 2013 Pgw

1. Environmental literature 2. Water conservation—Canada 3. Water quality 4. Water supply—Canada 5. Water use

ISBN 1926812778; 9781926812779

SUMMARY: In this book, Ralph Pentland and Chris Wood attempt to answer the question "'can Canadians be confident that [their] water is safe to drink today and secure for tomorrow?' . . . The issues they raise focus primarily on water quality—the safety of drinking water in urban and rural systems, the prevalence of pollutants of emerging concern, and how impacts of global climate change will continue to impact water sources." (Choice: Current Reviews for Academic Libraries)

REVIEW: *Choice* v51 no8 p1433-4 Ap 2014 E. S. Norman

"Down the Drain: How We Are Failing to Protect Our Water Resources". "Though their inquiry is through the lens of Canada, it is a relevant book for the entire world, considering the link between water resources and broader concerns for ecosystem and human health. . . . The authors present ample evidence to show that Canadians should be more concerned about water quality and security issues than they currently are. They conclude that the issues are too big to ignore and that how Canada, and other countries throughout the world, will fare rests largely on political will. Written in a journalistic style, the book is accessible and engaging."

REVIEW: *Quill Quire* v79 no5 p30 Je 2013 Matthew Behrens

WOOD, DAVID HOUSTON.ed. Recovering disability in early modern England. See Recovering disability in early modern England

WOOD, MARY CHRISTINA. Nature's trust : environmental law for a new ecological age; [by] Mary Christina Wood xxiii, 436 p. 2014 Cambridge University Press

1. Conservation of natural resources—Law and legislation—United States 2. Environmental law—Philosophy 3. Environmental law—United States 4. Environmental literature 5. Legal literature 6. Public trust doctrine

ISBN 9780521144117 (pbk.); 9780521195133 (hardback)

LC 2013-014274

SUMMARY: Written by Mary Christina Wood, "This book exposes what is wrong with environmental law and offers transformational change based on the public trust doctrine. An ancient and enduring principle, the trust doctrine asserts public property rights to crucial resources. Its core logic compels government, as trustee, to protect natural inheritance such as air and water for all humanity." (Publisher's note)

REVIEW: *Science* v343 no6172 p732 F 14 2014 Rena Steinzor

"Nature's Trust: Environmental Law for a New Ecological Age." "Mary Christina Wood's 'Nature's Trust' makes a discrete contribution to the search for climate change solutions by rejecting dominant paradigms out of hand. Instead Wood . . . urges the courts to pick up the isolated, tenuous threads of the 'public trust' doctrine and use them to compel the executive and legislative branches to embrace the idea that all natural resources (including Earth's atmosphere) cannot be used in any way that exacerbates climate change. . . . How a mass movement would be sustainable if fed only by Wood's idealism, without preparing for the sacrifices that are inevitable, is far from clear. . . . For anyone interested in using the legal system to prod action, Wood has made a major contribution."

WOODING, CHRIS. Silver; [by] Chris Wooding 320 p. 2014 Scholastic Press

1. Boarding school students—Juvenile fiction 2. Boarding schools—Fiction 3. Boarding schools—Juvenile fiction 4. Communicable diseases—Fiction 5. Communicable diseases—Juvenile fiction 6. Schools—Fiction 7. Science fiction 8. Survival—Fiction 9. Survival—Juvenile fiction

ISBN 0545603927; 9780545603928 (hc)

LC 2013-014037

SUMMARY: In this young adult science fiction horror novel, by Chris Wooding, "without warning, a horrifying infection will spread across the school grounds [of Mortingham Boarding Academy], and a group of students with little in common will find themselves barricaded in a classroom, fighting for their lives. Some will live. Some will die. And then it will get even worse." (Publisher's note)

REVIEW: *Booklist* v110 no13 p69 Mr 1 2014 Frances Bradburn

REVIEW: *Bull Cent Child Books* v67 no8 p428 Ap 2014 K. Q. G.

"Silver". "The focalization through four very different characters gives this end-of-the-world tale broad accessibility, but it's really the monsters, the Infected, that drive the plot forward; though they start out as mindless, shuffling creatures, they eventually transform into cunning predators with the ability to strategize and (literally) smoke the survivors out into a full-on confrontation. Though [Chris] Wooding's direct storytelling makes the most of the action sequences, it unfortunately stumbles when it comes to the emotional elements of the story, too often telling rather than showing what the characters are feeling, and the teens themselves are fairly predictable stereotypes."

REVIEW: *Kirkus Rev* v81 no24 p286 D 15 2013

"Silver". "When strange insects assault a remote boarding school in England, the kids try to save the day in this tense page-turner. . . . [Chris] Wooding deepens the narrative by developing highly distinctive characters. Caitlyn hates her supposed friend Erika, and that emotion will play a part in the later plot. Adam, the school bully, may finally find what he's really been looking for during his fight. Most importantly, however, Paul will learn that his leadership abilities trump even those of the adults on the scene. Skillfully managed subplots keep the pages flying. It looks like the end of the world is nigh. . . . It's just all kinds of white-knuckle fun."

REVIEW: *Publ Wkly* v261 no6 p91 F 10 2014

REVIEW: *SLJ* v60 no5 p120 My 2014 Vicki Reutter

REVIEW: *Voice of Youth Advocates* v37 no1 p91 Ap 2014 Erin Segreto

WOODRUFF, LIZA.il. If it's snowy and you know it, clap your paws! See Norman, K.

WOODS, GILLIAN. Shakespeare's unreformed fictions; [by] Gillian Woods ix, 239 p. 2013 Oxford University Press

1. English drama—Early modern and Elizabethan, 1500-1600—History and criticism 2. Literature—History & criticism 3. Religion & drama 4. Shakespeare, William, 1564-1616—Religion
ISBN 0199671265; 9780199671267
LC 2013-937239

SUMMARY: "In exploring the dramaturgical variety of the 'Catholic' content of Shakespeare's plays, [author] Gillian Woods argues that habits, idioms, images, and ideas lose their denominational clarity when translated into dramatic fiction: they are awkwardly 'unreformed' rather than doctrinally Catholic. . . . This book emphasises the creative function of such unreformed material, which Shakespeare uses to pose questions about the relationship between self and other." (Publisher's note)

REVIEW: *TLS* no5794 p11 Ap 18 2014 HELEN HACKETT

"Shakespeare's Unreformed Fictions" and "Eucharist and the Poetic Imagination in Early Modern England." "These new books by Gillian Woods and Sophie Read are excellent examples, and also exemplify what has been called the 'new formalism' in Renaissance studies in their use of intricate close readings and their emphasis on aesthetic questions. Woods makes clear at the outset that 'Shakespeare's Unreformed Fictions' is not about Shakespeare's personal religious position, but is unashamedly—and, as it proves, very successfully—a work of literary criticism. . . . Sophie Read has undertaken a similar project to analyse the literary effects of changing religious thinking. . . . Each chapter offers many insights."

WOODS, STUART. Standup guy; [by] Stuart Woods 320 p. 2014 G.P. Putnam's Sons

1. Barrington, Stone (Fictitious character)—Fiction 2. Crime—Fiction 3. FICTION—Action & Adventure 4. FICTION—Suspense 5. Private investigators—Fiction
ISBN 0399164154; 9780399164156 (hardback)
LC 2013-030289

SUMMARY: In this book, by Stuart Woods, "Stone Barrington's newest client does not seem the type to bring mayhem in his wake. A polite, well-deported gentleman, he comes to Stone seeking legal expertise on an unusual—and potentially lucrative—dilemma. Stone points him in the right direction and sends him on his way, but it's soon clear Stone hasn't seen the end of the case. Several people are keenly interested in this gentleman's activities and how they may relate to a long-ago crime." (Publisher's note)

REVIEW: *Booklist* v110 no1 p4 S 1 2013 Brad Hooper

REVIEW: *Booklist* v110 no5 p33 N 1 2013 Kristine Huntley

REVIEW: *Kirkus Rev* v82 no1 p54 Ja 1 2014

"Standup Guy". "New York attorney Stone Barrington . . . reaps the whirlwind after advising a walk-in client how to live safely on several million dollars in ill-gotten gains. John Fratelli is a stand-up guy. Jailed 25 years ago for armed robbery, he did his time, kept his mouth shut and patiently waited to get out. Now he's out, along with the key to a safe deposit box his cellmate, Eduardo Buono, bequeathed him. . . . The subplots lead nowhere, and the main upshot of Fratelli's little problem is some uncharacteristically salty language."

REVIEW: *Publ Wkly* v260 no41 p37 O 14 2013

WOODSON, JACQUELINE. This is the rope; a story from the Great Migration; 32 p. 2013 Nancy Paulsen Books, an imprint of Penguin Group (USA) Inc.

1. African Americans—History—Fiction 2. African Americans—History—Juvenile fiction 3. African Americans—Migrations—Fiction 4. African Americans—Migrations—Juvenile fiction 5. Families—Fiction 6. Picture books for children 7. Rope—Fiction
ISBN 0399239863 (reinforced); 9780399239861 (reinforced)
LC 2012-036569

SUMMARY: This children's story, by Jacqueline Woodson, illustrated by James Ransome, follows "one family's journey north during the Great Migration. . . . A little girl in South Carolina . . . finds a rope under a tree one summer. . . . For three generations, that rope is passed down, used for everything from jump rope games to tying suitcases onto a car for the big move north to New York City, and even for a family reunion where that first little girl is now a grandmother." (Publisher's note)

REVIEW: *Booklist* v109 no19/20 p111 Je 1 2013 Carolyn Phelan

REVIEW: *Booklist* v109 no15 p41 Ap 1 2013

REVIEW: *Bull Cent Child Books* v67 no2 p126 O 2013 H. M.

REVIEW: *Horn Book Magazine* v89 no4 p118-9 Jl/Ag 2013 KATHLEEN T. HORNING

REVIEW: *Kirkus Rev* p54 2013 Guide 20to BookExpo America Jessie Grearson

REVIEW: *Kirkus Rev* v81 no13 p92 Jl 1 2013

REVIEW: *Kirkus Rev* p57 2013 Guide 20to BookExpo America

REVIEW: *N Y Times Book Rev* p14 Ag 25 2013 VALERIE STEIKER

"Rifka Takes a Bow," "This Is the Rope: A Story From the Great Migration," and "The Blessing Cup." "It's refreshing to find three new picture books that take as their subject the stories of human families. . . . Betty Rosenberg Perlov grew up in [the world of Yiddish theater] and it's clear she knows it well. . . . Spare and evocative as a poem, [Jacqueline] Woodson's refrain winds through the book, fastening us to the comfort of memories and the strength of family ties. . . . If 'The Blessing Cup' never quite lifts off from its history lesson as do 'Rifka Takes a Bow' and 'This Is The Rope,' it nonetheless imparts a valuable message."

REVIEW: *Publ Wkly* v260 no20 p58 My 20 2013

REVIEW: *Publ Wkly* p38 Children's starred review annual 2013

REVIEW: *SLJ* v59 no7 p75 Jl 2013 Robbin E. Friedman

WOODWARD, C. VANN (COMER VANN), 1908-1999. The letters of C. Vann Woodward; 480 p. 2013 Yale University Press

1. Historians—United States 2. Historians—United States—Biography 3. Letters 4. Scholars—United States 5. United States—Intellectual life—20th century 6. Woodward, C. Vann (Comer Vann), 1908-1999

ISBN 9780300185348 (hardcover: alk. paper)
LC 2013-011897

SUMMARY: Editor Michael O'Brien describes how "C. Vann Woodward was one of the most prominent and respected American historians of the twentieth century. . . . For the first time, his sprightly, wry, sympathetic, and often funny letters are published, including those he wrote to figures as diverse as John Kennedy, David Riesman, Richard Hofstadter, and Robert Penn Warren." (Publisher's note)

REVIEW: *J Am Hist* v101 no2 p546-7 S 2014

REVIEW: *TLS* no5793 p11 Ap 11 2014 TOM F. WRIGHT
"The Letters of C. Vann Woodward." "In these letters, a number of key friendships develop with important contemporaries, including David Riesman, Richard Hofstadter and Robert Penn Warren. Perhaps the most fascinating correspondence, however, is with younger scholars, as Woodward grows into his role as editor and mentor. . . . Woodward was a consistently first-rate correspondent, and these letters offer an eloquent insight into the writing of history as an ongoing, collaborative project based around candid exchange. This is an intellectual life rich in lessons for both custodians of the present day academy and, more broadly, for modem day liberalism."

WOODWORTH, PADDY. Our once and future planet; restoring the world in the climate change century; [by] Paddy Woodworth 536 p. 2013 University of Chicago Press
1. Climatic changes 2. Environmental literature 3. Environmental quality 4. Global environmental change 5. Restoration ecology
ISBN 9780226907390 (cloth: alk. paper)
LC 2013-016605

SUMMARY: This book "provides an introduction to the relatively new discipline of ecological restoration, which describes and puts into practice means of rejuvenating the natural, and in some cases human, environment of specific locales. [Paddy] Woodworth describes . . . projects . . . ranging from forest preserve restoration in the Chicago metropolitan area and biodiversity restoration efforts across Western Australia to two separate endeavors in his native Ireland to restore forests and bogs." (Publishers Weekly)

REVIEW: *Choice* v51 no8 p1434 Ap 2014 L. Broberg
"Our Once and Future Planet: Restoring the World in the Climate Change Century". "A unique survey of restoration case studies emphasizing process and outcome. . . . A much-needed resource for those interested in the implementation and sustenance of long-term restoration efforts, the book will stimulate discussion and reassessment of restoration in multiple contexts. [Paddy] Woodworth also brings the cases together under the umbrella of restoration theory in the penultimate chapter. This title is an excellent resource for those desiring a less technical, more accessible piece examining social, cultural, political, and economic interactions with the science of restoration."

REVIEW: *Choice* v51 no8 p1434 Ap 2014 F. N. Egerton

REVIEW: *Publ Wkly* v260 no35 p48 S 2 2013

REVIEW: *Sci Am* v309 no5 p78 N 2013 Lee Billings Arielle Duhaime-Ross

REVIEW: *Science* v345 no6195 p388 Jl 25 2014 William E. Stutz

WOOLF, GREG.ed. Ancient libraries. See Ancient libraries

WOOLF, JULIA.il. Five black cats. See Hegarty, P.

WOOLF, VIRGINIA, 1882-1941. The London scene; [by] Virginia Woolf 2013 Daunt Books
1. Essay (Literary form) 2. London (England)—Description & travel 3. London (England)—Social life & customs—20th century 4. Social commentary 5. Urban life
ISBN 9781907970429 hardcover

SUMMARY: "Originally published bi-monthly in 1931 by 'Good Housekeeping,' the essays in 'The London Scene' exhibit [author] Virginia Woolf at the height of her literary powers and present [a] . . . portrait of an extraordinary metropolis—capturing the London of the 1930s and also the eternal city we recognise today." (Publisher's note)

REVIEW: *TLS* no5790 p26 Mr 21 2014 AMBER K. REGIS
"The London Scene." "'The London Scene' is a little bit seedy. First published in 'Good Housekeeping' between December 1931 and December 1932, these six essays by Virginia Woolf set out to explore the metropolis from different aspects, beginning with 'The Docks of London' and sailing into the heart of the city, via her observations of the 'Oxford Street Tide,' 'Great Men's Houses' and 'Abbeys and Cathedrals.' . . . This edition of 'The London Scene' combines a set of beautifully composed and wittily executed illustrations with an appropriately art-deco-inspired typeface, while Hermione Lee's brief introduction usefully places the essays in the context of Woolf's career and involvement in London life."

WOOLFSON, ESTHER. Field Notes from a Hidden City; an urban nature diary; [by] Esther Woolfson 368 p. 2013 Granta Books
1. Aberdeen (Scotland) 2. Human ecology 3. Scotland—Environmental conditions 4. Urban ecology (Biology) 5. Urban gardens
ISBN 1619022400; 1847082750; 9781619022409; 9781847082756

SUMMARY: This book, by Esther Woolfson," is set against the background of the . . . northeast Scottish city of Aberdeen. In it, Esther Woolfson examines the elements—geographic, atmospheric and environmental—which bring diverse life forms to live in close proximity in cities. Using the circumstances of her own life, house, garden and city, she writes of the animals who live among us. . . . Woolfson describes the seasons, the streets and the quiet places of her city over the course of a year." (Publisher's note)

REVIEW: *Booklist* v110 no6 p5 N 15 2013 Rick Roche

REVIEW: *Kirkus Rev* v82 no2 p10 Ja 15 2014
"Field Notes From a Hidden City: An Urban Nature Diary". "[Esther] Woolfson . . . offers a vivid portrait of birds, animals, insects and plants—and her place among them—in the city where she has lived for decades. . . . Taking us through a year in Aberdeen, Woolfson closely observed changes in bird life and animal visitors, soil and sky. . . . Interwoven with diarylike entries are longer meditations on spiders, pigeons, jackdaws, sparrows and the complexities of the slug, who shoots a 'love dart' as part of its mating behavior—a phenomenon, Woolfson speculates, that's pos-

sibly the origin of Cupid's arrow. Woolfson is an elegant, precise writer, and this transcendent memoir conveys exquisitely the vibrant world she inhabits."

REVIEW: *Publ Wkly* v260 no42 p40 O 21 2013

REVIEW: *TLS* no5739 p30 Mr 29 2013 JANETTE CURRIE

THE WORLD ATLAS OF STREET ART AND GRAFFITI; 400 p. 2013 Yale University Press

1. Art—Biography 2. Art literature 3. Graffiti 4. Street art 5. Street artists

ISBN 0300199422; 9780300199420

LC 2013-935855

SUMMARY: Author Rafael Schacter presents a "survey of international street art, focusing on the world's most influential urban artists and artworks. Organized geographically by country and city, more than 100 of today's most important street artists--including Espo in New York, Shepard Fairey in Los Angeles, Os Gêmeos in Brazil, and Anthony Lister in Australia--are profiled alongside key examples of their work. The evolution of street art and graffiti within each region is also chronicled." (Publisher's note)

REVIEW: *N Y Times Book Rev* p57 D 8 2013 RAILLAN BROOKS

"City As Canvas: New York City Graffiti From the Martin Wong Collection" and "The World Atlas of Street Art and Graffiti." "Dwelling int he resplendent squalor of [Martin] Wong's apartment is precisely the experience the curators Sean Corcoran and Carlo McCormick recreate in 'City as Canvas: New York City Graffiti From the Martin Wong Collection,' an accounting of Wong's huge personal trove and its in history, with reflections on the man by his artist friends. . . . 'The World Atlas of Street Art and Graffiti' is broader in scale and scope. . . . Rafael Schacter . . . has bundled into the book's 400 pages a range of styles and modes offering a rare and pleasant encounter with at in which the critic stays (mostly) out of the way."

REVIEW: *Publ Wkly* v260 no34 p62 Ag 26 2013

WORLD BANK.comp. Measuring the real size of the world's economy. See Measuring the real size of the world's economy

THE WORLD OF THE NEW TESTAMENT; cultural, social, and historical contexts; 640 p. 2013 Baker Academic

1. Church history—Primitive and early church, ca. 30-600 2. Civilization, Greco-Roman—Social aspects 3. Historical literature 4. Jews—History—586 B.C.-70 A.D 5. Jews—Palestine—Social life and customs—To 70 A.D 6. Judaism—History—Post-exilic period, 586 B.C.-210 A.D

ISBN 9780801039621 (cloth)

LC 2013-003341

SUMMARY: This book on the historical and cultural context of the New Testament "includes essays by a variety of authors . . . in five major areas: (1) the exile and Jewish history; (2) Roman Hellenism; (3) the Jewish people in the context of Roman Hellenism; (4) the literary context of early Christianity; (5) the geographical context of the New Testament." (Bible Today)

REVIEW: *Choice* v51 no6 p1026 F 2014 D. Ingolfsland

"The World of the New Testament; Cultural, Social, and Historical Contexts." "Featuring 40-plus essays written by 34 scholars, 'The World of the New Testament' is intended for general audiences. The book is divided into five sections. . . The book includes bibliographies, a glossary of terms, and indexes of ancient sources, bihlical texts, and modern authors. Its well-written essays provide an excellent resource for the historical and cultural background of the New Testament. . . . Recommended."

THE WORLD SCIENTIFIC HANDBOOK OF ENERGY; xxii, 563 p. 2013 World Scientific

1. Energy conservation 2. Energy development 3. Power resources—Handbooks, manuals, etc 4. Scientific literature 5. Transportation—Energy consumption

ISBN 9789814343510

LC 2012-034832

SUMMARY: This book presents "sets of data on energy resources and uses; it gathers in one publication a . . . description of the current state-of-the-art for a wide variety of energy resources, including data on resource availability worldwide and at different cost levels. The end use of energy in transportation, residential and industrial areas is outlined, and energy storage, conservation and the impact on the environment are included." (Publisher's note)

REVIEW: *Choice* v51 no4 p674 D 2013 B. Ransom

"The World Scientific Handbook of Energy." "This work is a compendium of chapters on standard (coal) and nonstandard (magnetic fusion, ocean energy) energy sources, each written by a different expert. Reasonable in breadth, it contains nothing that cannot be found in other reference books on the same subject. . . . Because a different person wrote each chapter, the content and presentations are uneven; some entries are purely descriptive of global trends and amounts (coal); others are equation heavy and highly technical (hydropower). . . . Although the book will expose readers to the various energy sources, it lacks the depth or engaging presentation to hold most people's attention."

WORTH, VALERIE. Pug and other animal poems. See Pug and other animal poems

WORTHEN, MOLLY. Apostles of reason; the crisis of authority in American evangelicalism; [by] Molly Worthen 376 p. 2013 Oxford University Press, USA

1. Authority 2. Culture conflict 3. Evangelicalism—United States 4. Faith & reason 5. Religious literature

ISBN 9780199896462 (hardback)

LC 2013-012871

SUMMARY: In this book, Molly Worthen "recasts American evangelicalism as a movement defined not by shared doctrines or politics, but by the problem of reconciling head knowledge and heart religion in an increasingly secular America. . . . The culture wars of the late twentieth century emerged not only from the struggle between religious conservatives and secular liberals, but also from the civil war within evangelicalism itself--a battle over how to uphold the commands of both faith and reason." (Publisher's note)

REVIEW: *Christ Century* v131 no9 p43-4 Ap 30 2014 Randall Balmer

REVIEW: *Commonweal* v141 no4 p29-31 F 21 2014

George M. Marsden

REVIEW: *Nation* v298 no8 p27-33 F 24 2014 CHRIS LEHMANN

"Apostles of Reason: The Crisis of Authority in American Evangelicalism" and "The Twilight of the American Enlightenment: The 1950s and the Crisis of Liberal Belief." "[Molly] Worthen, who is not an evangelical herself but takes the intellectual struggles of the community quite seriously as a scholar, depicts the movement in a light that is at once far more nuanced and sympathetic than what passes for serious analysis on the left, while also supplying an intellectual profile of modern evangelical thought that's at least as damning as the far more visceral secular denunciations of the religious right. . . . [George] Marsden is persuasive here--until he overreaches. . . . It's difficult, in surveying the arc of Marsden's argument, to avoid the conclusion that the author is imposing his own set of theological presuppositions on the scene before him."

WOTZKA, HANS-PETER.ed. Pastoralism in Africa. See Pastoralism in Africa

WRAGG, NATE.il. Goldi Rocks and the three bears. See Schwartz, C. R.

WRANGHAM, ELIZABETH. Ghana during the First World War; the Colonial Administration of Sir Hugh Clifford; [by] Elizabeth Wrangham xxvii, 310 p. 2013 Carolina Academic Press

1. Colonial administrators—Ghana 2. Historical literature 3. World War, 1914-1918—Economic aspects—Ghana
ISBN 9781611633603 (pbk. : alk. paper)
LC 2013-000944

SUMMARY: This book by Elizabeth Wrangham "examines a key period in the history of Ghana, then the British colony of the Gold Coast. The focus of this study is the largely neglected economic and administrative impact of global conflict on a vulnerable protectorate. Governor [Hugh] Clifford and his officials could set an agenda but they were not free agents." (Publisher's note)

REVIEW: *Choice* v51 no7 p1280 Mr 2014 J. E. Flint

"Ghana During the First World War: The Colonial Administration of Sir Hugh Clifford." "If there were a Leopold von Ranke prize for historical research revealing 'how it actually happened,' [Elizabeth] Wrangham . . . would be a prime candidate. Her study of what was then the British colony of the Gold Coast is based on a massive, and sometimes daunting, analysis of primary sources of the period that weaves together the impact of WW I on the economic, social, administrative, and political conditions and their interactions. . . . Particularly valuable is the author's analysis of the growing demands of the cocoa producers, and their influence as prime sources of government revenue. . . . Highly recommended."

WRIGHT, ALICE P.ed. Early and middle woodland landscapes of the Southeast. See Early and middle woodland landscapes of the Southeast

WRIGHT, ANGELA. Britain, France and the Gothic, 1764-1820; the import of terror; [by] Angela Wright xii, 214 p. 2013 Cambridge University Press

1. Comparative literature—English and French 2. Comparative literature—French and English 3. Gothic fiction (Literary genre), English—History and criticism 4. Gothic revival (Literature) 5. Historical literature 6. Romanticism—France 7. Romanticism—Great Britain
ISBN 9781107034068 (hardback : alk. paper)
LC 2012-043737

SUMMARY: In this book, "Angela Wright sheds new light upon the genesis of the Gothic, examining the roles translation and military conflict played in its development in Britain. The author combines contextual and literary perspectives to situate the Gothic in relation to the Seven Years' War, the French Revolution and the Treaty of Amiens." (Publisher's note)

REVIEW: *TLS* no5764 p22 S 20 2013 E. J. CLERY

"Britain, France and the Gothic 1764-1830: The Import of Terror." "The danger of this approach is that the exclusive attention to one Continental dialogue has the tendency to negate the others: German, Italian and Spanish settings and influences are demoted, at best, to code for the immediately topical and controversial entanglements of English Gothic with France. Nevertheless, Angela Wright's study importantly reinstates the French contexts for the birth and burgeoning of English Gothic, and in doing so contributes to a far more nuanced understanding of the politics of the genre."

WRIGHT, ANNABEL.il. The Lion who stole my arm. See Davies, N.

WRIGHT, DAVID.ed. Selected poems and prose. See Thomas, E.

WRIGHT, JAMES. Those who have borne the battle; America's wars and those who fought them; [by] James Wright p. cm. 2012 PublicAffairs

1. Historical literature 2. Veterans—United States 3. War and society—United States
ISBN 9781610390729 (hbk.: alk. paper); 9781610390736 (e-book)
LC 2012-004835

SUMMARY: "In 'Those Who Have Borne the Battle,' historian and marine veteran James Wright tells the story of the long, often troubled relationship between America and those who have defended her—from the Revolutionary War to today—shedding new light both on our history and on the issues our country and its armed forces face today." (Publisher's note)

REVIEW: *Choice* v50 no4 p745 D 2012 W. T. Allison

REVIEW: *Rev Am Hist* v42 no2 p379-85 Je 2014 Beth Bailey

"Veterans' Policies, Veterans' Politics: New Perspectives on Veterans in the Modern United States" and "Those Who Have Borne the Battle: A History of America's Wars and Those Who Fought Them." "[Author James] Wright calls his work a 'meditation' . . . , and the mix of autobiographical context, emotional engagement, and concrete proposals for action he offers moves his work beyond the traditional realm of historical analysis. . . . Wright's emotional commitment gives this book its power, but it also sometimes undermines its logic. . . . [Editor] Stephen R. Ortiz envisions his readers as scholars. . . . The fundamental claim of this smart, well-edited collection is historiographical: we cannot fully understand U.S. political history . . . without paying significant attention to the changing historical roles of veterans."

WRIGHT, JOHN C. The Judge of ages; [by] John C. Wright 384 p. 2014 Tor Books

1. Cryopreservation of organs, tissues, etc.—Fiction 2. FICTION—Science Fiction—General 3. Human-alien encounters—Fiction 4. Imaginary wars & battles 5. Interstellar travel—Fiction
ISBN 9780765329295 (hardback)
LC 2013-025457

SUMMARY: In this book, part of John C. Wright's "Count to a Trillion" series, "the year is 10,515 AD. The Hyades Armada, traveling at near lightspeed, will reach Earth in just four centuries to assess humanity's value as slaves. For the last 8,000 years, two opposing factions have labored to meet the alien threat in very different ways." (Publisher's note)

REVIEW: *Booklist* v110 no11 p35 F 1 2014 David Pitt

REVIEW: *Kirkus Rev* v82 no1 p276 Ja 1 2014

"The Judge of Ages". "Third part of [John C.] Wright's series . . . in which, thanks to alien technology, Texas gunslinger Menelaus Montrose transformed himself into a supergenius—and so did his rival, Ximen 'Blackie' del Azarchel. . . . With nonstop if pedestrian action, villains who chortle and strut, and Menelaus' indestructible self-confidence, it's a sequence worthy of A. E. van Vogt's spirit, though, alas, lacking van Vogt's deftness or economy of style. Weird posthumans build themselves into recognizable characters. The plot devolves into a series of revelations that make sense only to the characters or, possibly, a few readers, should any still be hanging heroically on. Dazzling, highly impressive but readable only with enormous effort."

WRIGHT, JONATHAN.tr. The corpse exhibition and other stories of Iraq. See Blasim, H.

WRIGHT, N. T. Paul and the Faithfulness of God; [by] N. T. Wright 1700 p. 2013 Augsburg Fortress Pub

1. Bible. Epistles of Paul—Theology 2. Christianity—Jewish influences 3. Jews—Doctrine of election 4. Paul, the Apostle, Saint 5. Theology—History—Early church, ca. 30-600
ISBN 0800626834; 9780800626839

SUMMARY: In this book, author N. T. "Wright carefully explores the whole context of Paul's thought and activity—Jewish, Greek and Roman, cultural, philosophical, religious, and imperial—and shows how the apostle's worldview and theology enabled him to engage with the many-sided complexities of first-century life that his churches were facing." (Publisher's note)

REVIEW: *Choice* v51 no8 p1420 Ap 2014 P. K. Moser

REVIEW: *Christ Century* v131 no22 p37-9 O 29 2014 Alexandra Brown

REVIEW: *Libr J* v139 no2 p80 F 1 2014 James R. Kuhlman

REVIEW: *Publ Wkly* v260 no40 p20 O 7 2013

REVIEW: *TLS* no5794 p9 Ap 18 2014 PAULA GOODER

"Paul and the Faithfulness of God." "Keenly awaited by scholars, 'Paul and the Faithfulness of God' is a major contribution to Pauline studies. It forms the fourth instalment of a projected six-part series, 'Christian Origins and the Question of God.' Although the author demands a vast amount of his readers on one level—the two volumes of 'Paul and the Faithfulness of God' are over a million words long—[author N. T.] Wright's style is relaxed and, for the most part, easy to follow. Anyone who is prepared to commit the amount of time necessary to read so many words can be assured that they will have a fascinating and informative companion for their journey. But the study is weakened by its repetitiveness. Tighter editing would have made these volumes more accessible."

WRIGLEY, AMANDA.ed. Louis MacNeice. See Louis MacNeice

WRIGLEY, MAGGIE.ed. The architecture of change. See The architecture of change

WU, EMILY S. Traditional Chinese medicine in the United States; in search of spiritual meaning and ultimate health; [by] Emily S. Wu v, 237 p. 2013 Lexington Books

1. Alternative medicine—History 2. Medical literature 3. Medicine, Chinese Traditional—United States 4. San Francisco Bay Area (Calif.) 5. Social medicine
ISBN 9780739173664 (cloth : alk. paper); 9780739173671 (electronic)
LC 2013-012284

SUMMARY: "This book attempts to broadly define traditional Chinese medicine (TCM). . . . It mainly emphasizes adaptations to TCM that have evolved in the US, with specific supporting details drawn from practitioners in the San Francisco area." Topics include "TCM practitioner demographics . . . environmental factors . . . [and] conceptualizations of the body." (Choice: Current Reviews for Academic Libraries)

REVIEW: *Choice* v51 no5 p874-5 Ja 2014 J. Saxton

"Traditional Chinese Medicine in the United States: In Search of Spiritual Meaning and Ultimate Health." "This book attempts to broadly define traditional Chinese medicine (TCM). . . . Weaving together cultural, historical, political, and religious views, the book illuminates this definition in the context of an increasingly globalized world. . . . Very few works address whole systems of care other than allopathic medicine, making this detailed look at TCM practice especially valuable. Faculty and researchers specializing in classical Chinese medicine or medical anthropology will find this book unique."

WU MING-YI. The man with the compound eyes; a novel; 304 p. 2014 Pantheon

1. Chinese fiction—Taiwan 2. FICTION—Literary 3. FICTION—Science Fiction—General 4. FICTION—Visionary & Metaphysical 5. Families—Fiction 6. Islands—Fiction 7. Missing persons—Fiction
ISBN 9780307907967 (hardback)
LC 2013-042177

SUMMARY: In this novel by Wu Ming-Yi, translated by Darryl Sterk, "When a tsunami sends a massive island made entirely of trash crashing into the Taiwanese coast, two very different people—an outcast from a mythical island and a woman on the verge of suicide—are united in ways they never could have imagined. Here is the English-language debut of a new and . . . award-winning voice from Taiwan." (Publisher's note)

REVIEW: *Booklist* v110 no16 p15 Ap 15 2014 Carl Hays

REVIEW: *Libr J* v139 no5 p116 Mr 15 2014 Robert E. Brown

REVIEW: *Publ Wkly* v261 no11 p61 Mr 17 2014

REVIEW: *TLS* no5775 p22 D 6 2013 LAURA PROFUMO

"The Man With Compound Eyes." "Two figures eventually collide, quite literally, when a tsunami crashes into the Haven coast, bringing with it a bewildered Atile'i and his otherworldly customs. 'The Man with Compound Eyes' is the Taiwanese writer Wu Ming-Yi's first novel to be translated into English. Reading the book, though, requires another more complex act of translation—one in which the ordinary seeps, slowly, into the bizarre. Wu shuttles between his two realms with a dizzying ease reminiscent of Haruki Murakami, twisting the dreamlike into the curiously credible. . . . The problem in this admirable novel arises when the narrative attempts to address its various environmental concerns without the mitigating sway of imagination."

WULFF, OTTO STANLEY. End Game of Terror; [by] Otto Stanley Wulff 376 p. 2013 CreateSpace Independent Publishing Platform

1. Counterterrorism—Fiction 2. Spy stories 3. Suspense fiction 4. Terrorism—Fiction 5. Victims of terrorism
ISBN 1493794248; 9781493794249

SUMMARY: This book "is the third installment in a series about Frank O'Brien, a federal agent. . . . Frank is still reeling from the success of his most recent triumph, for which he received a medal for his bravery and his success in foiling and—he believes—killing an evil mastermind who wanted to destroy much of South America. . . . When Frank learns that a suspicious-sounding charitable group intends to care for [surviving] victims, his agent's antennae rise and he insists on following the group." (Kirkus Reviews)

REVIEW: *Kirkus Rev* v82 no3 p375 F 1 2014

"End Game of Terror". "Deftly crafted with exciting twists, this action thriller has not only a compelling plot, but a likable hero whose boyish charm and humility add irony and humor to the story. The excellent pacing lends urgency to the novel, and the threat of danger remains until the last page. Cleverly devised and executed, this intriguing glimpse into the minds of killers resonates in a chilling way. A relentless ride of mystery and suspense as good battles evil for global stakes."

WUTHNOW, ROBERT. Small-town America; finding community, shaping the future; [by] Robert Wuthnow xvii, 498 p. 2013 Princeton University Press

1. Cities and towns—United States 2. Communities—United States 3. Country life 4. Popular culture—United States 5. Sociology literature
ISBN 0691157200 (hbk.: alk. paper); 9780691157207 (hbk.: alk. paper)
LC 2012-042793

SUMMARY: For this book, "over a five year period, [Robert] Wuthnow and his associates conducted hundreds of in-depth qualitative interviews to probe what it means to be a small town resident and to limn the attractions and limitations of living in small towns of under 25,000 inhabitants that are not suburbs or part of larger metropolitan areas." (America)

REVIEW: *America* v210 no4 p33-4 F 10 2014 JOHN A. COLEMAN

"Small Town America: Finding Community, Shaping the Future". "Robert Wuthnow of Princeton University is now pretty much the dean of American sociologists of religion. . . . All of Wuthnow's books show a sophisticated methodology that combines careful census and other polling data, standard questionnaires, with more nuanced open-ended interviews to yield a truly balanced view of his topic. Wuthnow is also a very gifted writer. . . . I learned a great deal about small-town America from this book. In a sense, there is no other sociological study of small-town America to equal it. It fills a significant gap in the sociological literature."

WYANT, KARL A.ed. Phosphorus, food, and our future. See Phosphorus, food, and our future

WYKE, MARIA.ed. The ancient world in silent cinema. See The ancient world in silent cinema

WYLD, EVIE. All the Birds, Singing; A Novel; [by] Evie Wyld 272 p. 2014 Pantheon

1. Country life—Fiction 2. Exiles—Fiction 3. Islands—Fiction 4. Psychological fiction 5. Shepherds
ISBN 9780307907769; 0307907767

SUMMARY: In this novel by Evie Wyld, "Jake Whyte is living on her own in an old farmhouse on a craggy British island, a place of ceaseless rain and battering wind. Her disobedient collie, Dog, and a flock of sheep are her sole companions, which is how she wants it to be. But every few nights something—or someone—picks off one of the sheep and sounds a new deep pulse of terror. There are foxes in the woods, a strange boy and a strange man, and rumors of an obscure, formidable beast." (Publisher's note)

REVIEW: *Booklist* v110 no13 p16 Mr 1 2014 Leah Strauss

REVIEW: *Harper's Magazine* v328 no1968 p80-3 My 2014 Christine Smallwood

REVIEW: *Kirkus Rev* v82 no4 p286 F 15 2014

REVIEW: *Libr J* v139 no5 p116 Mr 15 2014 Shaunna E. Hunter

REVIEW: *Libr J* v138 no18 p67 N 1 2013 Barbara Hoffert

REVIEW: *N Y Times Book Rev* p10 Je 15 2014 MAILE MELOY

REVIEW: *New Statesman* v142 no5164 p43-5 Je 28 2013 Claire Lowdon

REVIEW: *New York Times* v163 no56516 pC2 My 29 2014 John Williams

REVIEW: *New Yorker* v90 no16 p107-1 Je 9 2014

"All the Birds, Singing." "Violence takes many forms in this suspenseful and melancholy novel. Sheep die mysteriously on a farm on a lonely British island; in Australia, a school bully's nails leave scars. The protagonist, Jake Whyte, lives alone, tending to the animals on her farm and spurning all human companionship. . . . In alternating chapters, the story moves forward and backward in time—a narrative architecture that might seem gimmicky were it not for [author Evie] Wyld's masterful control. There are also surprising moments of lightness—the protagonist's dark humor, the author's unsentimental reverence for the natural world."

REVIEW: *Publ Wkly* v261 no4 p165-6 Ja 27 2014

REVIEW: *TLS* no5751 p20 Je 21 2013 SOPHIE RATCLIFFE

X

XIANGMING FANG.ed. Economics and youth violence. See Economics and youth violence

XO ORPHEUS; fifty new myths; 576 p. 2013 Penguin Books

1. Demeter (Greek deity) 2. FICTION—Anthologies (multiple authors) 3. FICTION—Fairy Tales, Folk Tales, Legends & Mythology 4. Mythology, Greek—Fiction 5. Narcissus (Greek mythology)
ISBN 0143122428; 9780143122425 (pbk.)
LC 2013-020128

SUMMARY: This book, edited by Kate Bernheimer, is a collection of "reimagined" Greek mythology. "Demeter, a divorced mom, struggles with the half-year custody of her daughter. Narcissus, a tart-tongued partier, offers lodging to a bewitching street urchin named Echo. And a Vietnam veteran, in the spirit of Daedalus, builds an emotional labyrinth for his son." (Booklist)

REVIEW: *Booklist* v110 no3 p34 O 1 2013 Carolyn Alessio

"xo Orpheus: Fifty New Myths." "[An] explosive anthology of reimagined myths. . . . In this searing yet ebullient collection, contemporary authors and one graphic artist move beyond merely updating classic myths of multiple cultures by performing gut-rehabs while maintaining the stark, terrifying moments of fate-altering choices. . . . The form is as inventive as the content. . . . Editor and award-winning author [Kate] Bernheimer describes her anthology as a necessary 'farewell' to the old world of myth and acknowledgment of a modern age in which humans are regarded as the new gods. But as these new myths attest, the frightening, timeless themes remain."

REVIEW: *N Y Times Book Rev* p34 D 1 2013 Joseph Salvatore

Y

YA-CHUNG CHUANG. Democracy on Trial; Social Movements and Cultural Politics in Postauthoritarian Taiwan; [by] Ya-Chung Chuang 292 p. 2013 Columbia University Press

1. Democracy—Taiwan 2. Political science literature 3. Social movements 4. Taiwan—Politics & government 5. Taiwan—Social conditions
ISBN 9629965461; 9789629965464

SUMMARY: This book "examines the social movements that partially laid the foundation of democracy in postauthoritarian Taiwan. . . . The author also illustrates how democracy has matured in the last five presidential races, in which different notions of community and statehood developed under the shadow of mainland China's assertion of sovereignty . . . and the manipulation of fear from politicians of both opposing parties." (Choice: Current Reviews for Academic Libraries)

REVIEW: *Choice* v51 no6 p1068 F 2014 A. Y. Lee

"Democracy on Trial: Social Movements and Cultural Politics in Postauthoritarian Taiwan." "The author's personal experience and participation in these movements as well as his professional anthropologist's vision and sensitivity bring rich ethnographic data and enlightening analysis to these trial-and-error social movements from the grass roots of the Taiwanese society. . . . In addition, the author gives a vivid description of the complex and dynamic history of the last few decades. . . . As a native Taiwanese as well as an academic anthropologist, [Ya-Chung] Chuang brings a unique academic perspective to the multiplicity, insubordination, and critical compassion pertaining to this democratic journey."

YAAKUNAH, ELI. The Woman Who Sparked the Greatest Sex Scandal of All Time; [by] Eli Yaakunah 230 p. 2013 CreateSpace Independent Publishing Platform

1. Erotic stories 2. Future, The 3. Human sexuality—Fiction 4. Journalists—Fiction 5. Missing persons—Fiction
ISBN 1481031775; 9781481031776

SUMMARY: In this erotic novel, set "in a future New York, Journalist Ishtar Benten of the News Agency is promoted from the Department of Written Chronicles to the Department of Scriptwriting. Concurrently, a man named Utu, whom she'd met in the break room for 'erotic coffee,' disappears. As she looks for him, she seeks help from Arianne, a memory thief, and Harlequin, a sad but sympathetic clown. Her investigation ultimately makes her ask herself hard questions." (Kirkus Reviews)

REVIEW: *Kirkus Rev* p57 D 15 2013 supplemet best books 2013

"The Woman Who Sparked the Greatest Sex Scandal of All Time". "This delicately intricate work provides a full dance card of themes: sex, romance, mystery and a grim peek into a devastated future. It's mainly an erotic novel, but its eroticism is complicated. For example, Ishtar envisions people she first encounters as being physically transformed during sex—strange, violent thoughts that appear to be routine for someone in her line of work. The book's text is also laced with sexual metaphors. . . . The ever-present eroticism makes the sex scenes, real and imaginary, seem less explicit; they're often lyrical and eccentric."

REVIEW: *Kirkus Rev* v81 no9 p123 My 1 2013

YANAGIHARA, HANYA. The people in the trees; [by] Hanya Yanagihara 384 p. 2013 Doubleday

1. Anthropologists—Fiction 2. Exploitation of humans 3. Immortalism—Fiction 4. Longevity 5. Micronesia 6. Speculative fiction
ISBN 0385536771; 9780385536776 (hardcover : alk. paper); 9780385536783 (ebook)
LC 2012-034034

SUMMARY: Hanya Yanagihara's novel "details the life of fictional doctor and Nobel Prize-winning scientist Dr. Abraham Norton Perina, who narrates his travels to the Micronesian islands of Ivu'ivu and U'ivu, where the secret to longevity is revealed to him. Perina learns that members of a primitive tribe who live to be 60 years old . . . are given the privilege . . . of consuming the meat of the opa'ivu'eke, a rare turtle." He discovers there is a dark side to longevity, however. (Library Journal)

REVIEW: *Booklist* v109 no22 p46 Ag 1 2013 Donna Chavez

REVIEW: *Kirkus Rev* v81 no12 p30-1 Je 15 2013

REVIEW: *Libr J* v138 no5 p90 Mr 15 2013 Barbara Hoffert

REVIEW: *Libr J* v138 no8 p76 My 1 2013 Shirley Quan

REVIEW: *N Y Times Book Rev* p13 S 29 2013 Hanya Yanagihara

"The People in the Trees." "[Hanya Yanagihara] sets her narrative dial to creepy, and challenges to the extreme the notion that a protagonist needs to be 'likable.' Yet thanks to her rich, masterly prose, it's hard to turn away from Dr. Norton Perina, her antihero. . . . In a voice at once baroque and chilly, the Nobel Prize-winning scientists tells the story of his ignominious downfall via an obsessively crafted 'memoir.' . . . Provocative and bleak, 'The People in the Trees' might leave readers conflicted. It is exhaustingly inventive and almost defiant in its refusal ot offer redemption or solace--but that is arguably one of its virtues. This is perhaps less a novel to love than to admire for its sheer audacity. As for Yanagihara, she is a writer to marvel at."

REVIEW: *New Statesman* v143 no4 p49 Ja 31 2014

REVIEW: *TLS* no5787 p20 F 28 2014 ANITA SETHI

"The People in the Trees." "Texts within texts provide the structural device for this ambitious, multi-layered novel, the bulk of which is made up of 'The Memoirs of Norton Perina' as edited by his besotted friend Dr Ronald Kubodera. The memoir is prefaced by two news clippings reporting the charging and imprisonment of Perina, a renowned immunologist accused of child sexual abuse. . . . The novel absorbingly displays the difficulties of adaptation and how former lives linger on in dreams and memories. Hanya Yanagihara compellingly explores how a place and people might be ravaged and destroyed by the voracious desire of the colonizer. . . . This thought-provoking novel was inspired by the real life of the Nobel Prize-winning virologist and anthropologist Carleton Gajdusek."

YANCEY, RICK. The final descent; [by] Rick Yancey 320 p. 2013 Simon & Schuster Books for Young Readers

1. Apprentices—Fiction 2. Horror stories 3. Monsters—Fiction 4. Orphans—Fiction 5. Supernatural—Fiction

ISBN 144245153X; 9781442451537 (hardback)

LC 2013-015811

SUMMARY: In this final installment of Rick Yancey's Monstrumologist series, "Will Henry, now 16, often drunk and colder than ever, helps Monstrumologist Pellinore Warthrop track down the T. cerrejonensis, a giant, snakelike critter that poisons its human prey then swallows them whole. At the same time, the novel also fast-forwards decades later to 1911, when Will returns to care for an elderly Warthrop and then reverts back to when he was first taken in by his employer." (Kirkus Reviews)

REVIEW: *Booklist* v111 no4 p62-3 O 15 2014 Elizabeth Nelson

REVIEW: *Booklist* v109 no22 p92 Ag 1 2013 Daniel Kraus

REVIEW: *Horn Book Magazine* v89 no6 p110 N/D 2013 JONATHAN HUNT

"The Final Descent". "In the fourth and final volume of the Monstrumologist series (a blend of gothic horror, cryptozoology, and Sherlockiana), [Rick]Yancey diverges somewhat from his successful formula. In addition to a menacing atmosphere and highly stylized nineteenth-century prose, each previous book . . . has featured a plot that pivots on an unspeakably horrible creature and the subtle and nuanced characterization of the monstrumologist and his apprentice, Will Henry. But here the plot recedes into the background . . . while the characters take center stage for their last hurrah. . . . Yancey has taken some considerable risks here. They will probably confuse casual readers, but they should thrill and horrify—in the best way possible—ardent and loyal fans."

REVIEW: *Kirkus Rev* v81 no17 p127 S 1 2013

REVIEW: *SLJ* v60 no1 p106 Ja 2014 Ryan F. Paulsen

REVIEW: *SLJ* v60 no5 p67 My 2014 Nicole Lee Martin

REVIEW: *Voice of Youth Advocates* v36 no5 p84 D 2013 Jane Murphy

YANG, ANDREW. Smart People Should Build Things; How to Restore Our Culture of Achievement, Build a Path for Entrepreneurs, and Create New Jobs in America; [by] Andrew Yang 272 p. 2014 HarperCollins

1. Business literature 2. Entrepreneurship 3. New business enterprises 4. Student loan debt 5. Youth—Employment

ISBN 0062292048; 9780062292049

SUMMARY: In this book, Andrew Yang "suggests that many young people graduate from college and seek jobs in finance, law, and medicine because it's expected of them. The downside is that many of these promising young people hit their mid-20s with tons of student debt, and realize they've been trained very narrowly, in addition to not enjoying their jobs. How much could the world be changed if these young and energetic people went to startups, rather than going corporate?" (Publishers Weekly)

REVIEW: *Kirkus Rev* v82 no2 p38 Ja 15 2014

"Smart People Should Build Things: How to Restore Our Culture of Achievement, Build a Path for Entrepreneurs, and Create New Jobs In America". "In his first book, which could be perceived as a thinly veiled promotional vehicle for his nonprofit organization, the author clearly advances the idea of new business-building rather than universities' robotically funneling top grads toward traditional high-profile arenas. . . . The author's use of business statistics and bullet-pointed lists of his own lessons learned are enlightening and frequently surprising and moves much of his pro-entrepreneurship slant from conventional wisdom into fact-based guidance. . . . A galvanizing amalgam of personal history, acquired business wisdom and mentorship."

REVIEW: *Publ Wkly* v260 no48 p47 N 25 2013

YANG, GENE LUEN, 1973-. Boxers; 328 p. 2013 First Second

1. China—Fiction 2. China—History—Boxer Rebellion, 1899-1901 3. Graphic novels 4. Historical fiction 5. Young adult fiction

ISBN 1596433590; 9781596433595 (pbk.)

LC 2013-947229

SUMMARY: This is the first volume in Gene Luen Yang's Boxers & Saints graphic novel series. Here, "life in Little Bao's peaceful rural village is disrupted when . . . a priest and his phalanx of soldiers . . . arrive." They start "smashing the village god, appropriating property, and administering vicious beatings for no reason. Little Bao and his older brothers train in kung fu and swordplay." . . . Little Bao "becomes the leader of a peasant army, eventually marching to Beijing." (School Library Journal)

REVIEW: *Booklist* v109 no22 p80 Ag 1 2013 Ian Chipman

REVIEW: *Bull Cent Child Books* v67 no3 p190-1 N 2013 E. B.

"Boxers" and "Saints." In this set of companion graphic novels, two teens struggle to discern and fulfill their destinies as foreigners intervene in China's affairs, and the Boxer Rebellion of 1900 attempts to purify the homeland of alien influence. In the volume 'Boxers', Little Bao encounters the scowling face of a girl (whom readers will later come to know as Vibiana), and instead of seeing ugliness, he sees the beautiful mask of a god in the operas he loves. . . . Vibiana's story unfolds in 'Saints' as a despised fourth daughter, left unnamed by her family, who finds her identity through the kindness and tutelage of a Christian convert . . . and she becomes convinced that apparitions of Joan of Arc signal her fate to become a female warrior for her faith. . . . The interplay of the two stories is meticulously constructed and, despite the sober subject, liberally inflected with visual and verbal humor."

REVIEW: *Horn Book Magazine* v89 no5 p117 S/O 2013 SAM BLOOM

"Boxers" and "Saints". "[Gene Luen] Yang's latest graphic novels are a 'diptych' of books set during China's Boxer Rebellion of the early twentieth century. Boxers follows Little Bao, a village boy with an affinity for opera; Saints centers on Four-Girl, an unloved and unwanted child who perfects a revolting 'devil-face' expression. . . .The inevitable showdown between the two characters leads to a surprising and bleak conclusion. While neither volume truly stands alone (making for a significant price tag for the whole story), Yang's characteristic infusions of magical realism, bursts of humor, and distinctively drawn characters are present in both books, which together make for a compelling read."

REVIEW: *Kirkus Rev* v81 no16 p55 Ag 15 2013

"Boxers & Saints." "Printz Award winner [Gene Luen] Yang's ambitious two-volume graphic novel follows the intertwined lives of two young people on opposite sides of the turn-of-the-20th-century Boxer Rebellion. . . . Scrupulously researched, the narratives make a violent conflict rarely studied in U.S. schools feel immediate, as Yang balances historical detail with humor and magical realism. . . . The restrained script often, and wisely, lets Yang's clear, clean art speak for itself. This tour de force fearlessly asks big questions about culture, faith, and identity and refuses to offer simple answers."

REVIEW: *Kirkus Rev* p59 Ag 15 2013 Fall Preview

REVIEW: *N Y Times Book Rev* p24 O 13 2013 WESLEY YANG

"Boxers" and "Saints". "The indie comic artist Gene Luen Yang . . . wrestles with the central ambiguity of colonialism throughout his remarkable set of linked graphic novels . . . recently named to the lng list for the National Book Award in young people's literature. The nuance conveyed in the dialectical design of the companion volumes counteracts the mythmaking that can result from combining history and fable in comic book form. . . . Despite the ostensibly evenhanded way Yang presents opposed perspectives, it's clear he views the Boxer Rebellion as a series of massacres conducted by xenophobes who wound up harming the very culture they had pledged to protect."

REVIEW: *New Statesman* v142 no5172 p48 Ag 30 2013 Philip Maughan

REVIEW: *Publ Wkly* p134 Children's starred review annual 2013

REVIEW: *Publ Wkly* v260 no32 p63 Ag 12 2013

REVIEW: *SLJ* v59 no7 p106 Jl 2013 Paula Willey

YANG, GENE LUEN, 1973-. Saints; 170 p. 2013 First Second

1. China—History—Boxer Rebellion, 1899-1901 2. Christians—China 3. Graphic novels 4. Historical fiction 5. Young adult fiction

ISBN 1596436891; 9781596436893 (pbk.)

LC 2013-947228

SUMMARY: This graphic novel, by Gene Luen Yang and Lark Pien, "follows a lonely girl . . . . Unwanted by her family, Four-Girl isn't even given a proper name until she converts to Catholicism and is baptized by the very same priest who bullies Little Bao's village. Four-Girl, now known as Vibiana, leaves home and finds fulfillment in service to the Church, while Little Bao roams the countryside committing acts of increasing violence as his army grows." (School Library Journal)

REVIEW: *Booklist* v109 no22 p80 Ag 1 2013 Ian Chipman

REVIEW: *Bull Cent Child Books* v67 no3 p190-1 N 2013 E. B.

"Boxers" and "Saints." In this set of companion graphic novels, two teens struggle to discern and fulfill their destinies as foreigners intervene in China's affairs, and the Boxer Rebellion of 1900 attempts to purify the homeland of alien influence. In the volume 'Boxers', Little Bao encounters the scowling face of a girl (whom readers will later come to know as Vibiana), and instead of seeing ugliness, he sees the beautiful mask of a god in the operas he loves. . . . Vibiana's story unfolds in 'Saints' as a despised fourth daughter, left unnamed by her family, who finds her identity through the kindness and tutelage of a Christian convert . . . and she becomes convinced that apparitions of Joan of Arc signal her fate to become a female warrior for her faith. . . . The interplay of the two stories is meticulously constructed and, despite the sober subject, liberally inflected with visual and verbal humor."

REVIEW: *Horn Book Magazine* v89 no5 p117 S/O 2013 SAM BLOOM

"Boxers" and "Saints". "[Gene Luen] Yang's latest graphic novels are a 'diptych' of books set during China's Boxer Rebellion of the early twentieth century. Boxers follows Little Bao, a village boy with an affinity for opera; Saints centers on Four-Girl, an unloved and unwanted child who perfects a revolting 'devil-face' expression. . . .The inevitable showdown between the two characters leads to a surprising and bleak conclusion. While neither volume truly stands alone (making for a significant price tag for the whole story), Yang's characteristic infusions of magical realism, bursts of humor, and distinctively drawn characters are present in both books, which together make for a compelling read."

REVIEW: *Kirkus Rev* p59 Ag 15 2013 Fall Preview

REVIEW: *Kirkus Rev* v81 no16 p55 Ag 15 2013

"Boxers & Saints." "Printz Award winner [Gene Luen] Yang's ambitious two-volume graphic novel follows the intertwined lives of two young people on opposite sides of the turn-of-the-20th-century Boxer Rebellion. . . . Scrupulously researched, the narratives make a violent conflict rarely studied in U.S. schools feel immediate, as Yang balances historical detail with humor and magical realism. . . . The restrained script often, and wisely, lets Yang's clear, clean art speak for itself. This tour de force fearlessly asks big questions about culture, faith, and identity and refuses to offer simple answers."

REVIEW: *N Y Times Book Rev* p24 O 13 2013 WESLEY YANG

"Boxers" and "Saints". "The indie comic artist Gene Luen Yang . . . wrestles with the central ambiguity of colonialism throughout his remarkable set of linked graphic novels . . . recently named to the lng list for the National Book Award in young people's literature. The nuance conveyed in the dialectical design of the companion volumes counteracts the mythmaking that can result from combining history and fable in comic book form. . . . Despite the ostensibly evenhanded way Yang presents opposed perspectives, it's clear he views the Boxer Rebellion as a series of massacres conducted by xenophobes who wound up harming the very culture they had pledged to protect."

REVIEW: *New Statesman* v142 no5172 p48 Ag 30 2013 Philip Maughan

REVIEW: *Publ Wkly* p134 Children's starred review annual 2013

REVIEW: *Publ Wkly* v260 no32 p63 Ag 12 2013

REVIEW: *SLJ* v59 no7 p106 Jl 2013 Paula Willey

REVIEW: *Voice of Youth Advocates* v36 no4 p76 O 2013 Rebecca Denham

YANG KEMING, 1965-. Capitalists in communist China; [by] 1965- Yang Keming xv, 211 p. 2013 Palgrave Macmillan

1. Capitalism—China 2. Capitalism—Political aspects—China 3. China—Economic policy 4. China—Politics & government 5. Politics & economics 6. Social science literature

ISBN 0230284582 (hbk.); 9780230284586 (hbk.)

LC 2012-277174

SUMMARY: "Since 1949, Chinese capitalists have experienced some dramatic shifts in their political and economic life. Keming Yang examines what such changes tell us about China's current political situation and future political development, making use of both historical and current interdisciplinary evidence." (Publisher's note)

REVIEW: *Choice* v51 no1 p141-2 S 2013 J. Li

"Capitalists in Communist China." "In this illuminating volume, sociologist [Keming] Yang . . . analyzes the political role of the new rich (capitalists) in contemporary China. The research combines statistical analyses of large samples with qualitative analyses based on the author's fieldwork and historical archives. The conclusion appears rather gloomy for those hoping for a democratic China. . . . While philosophical discussion of China's democratic future has dominated the academic discourse, this book makes a unique contribution by directing attention to a more concrete research question, and perhaps the beginning of a new academic enterprise."

YANNAI, SHMUEL.ed. Dictionary of Food Compounds With CD-ROM. See Dictionary of Food Compounds With CD-ROM

YANOFSKY, NOSON S. The outer limits of reason; what science, mathematics, and logic cannot tell us; [by] Noson S. Yanofsky xiv, 403 p. 2013 Thc MIT Press

1. Knowledge, Theory of 2. Mathematics—Philosophy 3. Philosophical literature 4. Reason 5. Science—Philosophy 6. Technology—Philosophy

ISBN 0262019353; 9780262019354 (hardcover : alk. paper)

LC 2012-050531

SUMMARY: This book, by Noson S. Yanofsky, "investigates what cannot be known. Rather than exploring the amazing facts that science, mathematics, and reason have revealed to us, this work studies what science, mathematics, and reason tell us cannot be revealed. . . . Noson Yanofsky considers what cannot be predicted, described, or known, and what will never be understood. He discusses the limitations of computers, physics, logic, and our own thought processes." (Publisher's note)

REVIEW: *Choice* v51 no9 p1615 My 2014 F. Potter

REVIEW: *New Sci* v220 no2941 p46 N 2 2013 Richard Webb

"The Outer Limits of Reason: What Science, Mathematics, and Logic Cannot Tell Us." "[Noson S.] Yanofsky provides an entertaining and informative whirlwind trip through limits on reason in language, formal logic, mathematics--and in science, the culmination of humankind's attempts to reason about the world. Themes emerge, such as the consistent sticking point of self-reference. The sentence that doesn't know whether it is true or not, [Bertrand] Russell's set that doesn't know whether it contains itself or not, or the computer that doesn't know whether it is about to loop the eternal loop: these are all entities asked to decide logically something about themselves."

YANOW, SCOTT. The great jazz guitarists; the ultimate guide; [by] Scott Yanow 237 p. 2013 Backbeat Books

1. Biographical dictionaries 2. Guitar music (Jazz)—History and criticism 3. Guitarists 4. Jazz—History 5. Jazz musicians 6. Jazz musicians—Biography

ISBN 9781617130236

LC 2012-050685

SUMMARY: Written by Scott Yanow, "With hundreds of dossiers and discographies on every major (and not so major) jazz guitar player of note, arranged in encyclopedia fashion, this is the final stop on anyone's tour of six-string wizards working the swinging side of the street." This book includes "the combination of edge, sensitivity and awe-inspiring depth of knowledge that has made author Yanow one of the most widely read and respected critics and historians in jazz history." (Publisher's note)

REVIEW: *Choice* v51 no1 p47 S 2013 J. G. Matthews

"The Great Jazz Guitarists: The Ultimate Guide." "This reference work by the prolific [Scott] Yanow exhibits the breadth and depth of knowledge and enthusiasm readers expect of his unparalleled work. . . . The guide profiles over 550 jazz guitarists and recommends standout performances by artist. Yanow divides his dazzlingly encyclopedic analysis into three sections covering the greatest jazz guitarists of all time, other contemporary jazz guitarists, and guitar players who have contributed notable performances in jazz idioms. He assesses his picks for each category by means of historical research, reviewer opinion, and in the case of living artists, a questionnaire to aid him with selection."

REVIEW: *Libr J* v138 no11 p115 Je 15 2013 Judy Quinn

YARBROUGH, JEAN M. Theodore Roosevelt and the American political tradition; [by] Jean M. Yarbrough p. cm. 2012 University Press of Kansas

1. Executive power—United States—History—20th century 2. Historical literature 3. Political culture—United States 4. Republicanism—United States—History—20th century

ISBN 9780700618866 (cloth: alk. paper)

LC 2012-019762

SUMMARY: In this book on Theodore Roosevelt, author Jean Yarbrough presents an "examination of TR's political thought, especially in relation to the ideas of Washington, Hamilton, and Lincoln-the statesmen TR claimed most to admire. Yarbrough sets out not only to explore Roosevelt's vision for America but also to consider what his political ideas have meant for republican self-government." (Publisher's note)

REVIEW: *Am Hist Rev* v119 no1 p191-2 F 2014 Bruce Miroff

"Theodore Roosevelt and the American Political Tradition". "For readers familiar with Roosevelt's life and career, the freshest part of [Jean M.] Yarbrough's book is its first two chapters. . . . Tracing his intellectual journey away from moderation and toward a militant progressivism, she offers some astute commentary on his essays and speeches. At times, she artfully skewers Roosevelt for his inflated pronouncements and conceptual muddles. However, the recurrent critical question she uses to judge Roosevelt—do his evolving ideas square with the enduring wisdom of The Federalist Papers?—is ill-conceived. . . . Anyone fascinated by Theodore Roosevelt will find much of interest in Yarbrough's work. Yet in the end, her book rests on a questionable premise."

REVIEW: *Choice* v50 no9 p1719 My 2013 J. J. Polet

REVIEW: *J Am Hist* v100 no4 p1234-5 Mr 2014

REVIEW: *Libr J* v137 no16 p88 O 1 2012 William D. Pederson

YARINGTON, ROBERT. Two lamentable tragedies. See Two lamentable tragedies

YARLETT, EMMA.il. Bear's Big Bottom. See Smallman, S.

YATES, JONATHAN. The Real Way Round; 1 Year, 1 Motorcycle, 1 Man, 6 Continents, 35 Countries, 42,000 Miles, 9 Oil Changes, 3 Sets of Tyres, and Loads More; [by] Jonathan Yates 224 p. 2013 Motorbooks Intl

1. Memoirs 2. Motorcycling 3. Motorcyclists 4. Travel—Guidebooks 5. Voyages around the world

ISBN 1845842944; 9781845842949

SUMMARY: This book by Jonathan Yates "captures one man's real of experience motorcycling around the globe—no back up teams, no spare bikes, no film crews. 42,000 miles through 35 countries, seeing amazing things, meeting fascinating people, experiencing different cultures and coping with extremely challenging conditions." It takes "a broad-brush approach covering some of the key tasks needed to plan and complete a similar trip yourself." (Publisher's note)

REVIEW: *New York Times* v163 no56344 p11 D 8 2013 CHARLES McEWEN JOSEPH SIANO JERRY GARRETT JULIA S. MAYERSOHN RICHARD S. CHANG

"Hunt vs. Lauda: The Epic 1976 Formula 1 Season," "Mustang Fifty Years: Celebrating America's Only True Pony Car," and "The Real Way Round". "This book appears to have been published to coincide with Ron Howard's movie 'Rush,' which dramatizes the battle for the 1976 Formula One drivers championship. . . . and 'rush' is what comes to mind when I think about the effort behind this book. . . . 'Mustang Fifty Years' is a voluminous book that tracks the life of a Ford that's as famous as the Model T. . . . While not exactly a beach read, the book is more digestible, even for general audiences, than its dauntingly encyclopedic appearance might suggest. . . . Libraries are full of reflective, overthought travelogues. If you prefer yours presented with all the cheer of a tale tale told in a pub and put together with the artistic élan of a family Christmas newsletter, you will strike gold with 'The Real Way Round'."

YATES, MICHAEL. A freedom budget for all Americans; recapturing the promise of the civil rights movement in the struggle for economic justice today; [by] Michael Yates 303 p. 2013 Monthly Review Press

1. Civil rights—United States—History 2. Economic security—United States—History 3. Equality—United States—History 4. Poverty—Government policy—United States 5. Social science literature

ISBN 1583673601; 9781583673607 (pbk. : alk. paper); 9781583673614 (cloth : alk. paper)

LC 2013-021619

SUMMARY: In this book, authors Paul Le Blanc and Michael D. Yates "stress that the American civil rights struggle was part of a broader fight for economic justice. . . . Social-democratic economic ideas were embodied in the 'Freedom Budget,' a 1965 document that called for the elimination of poverty by 1976 through programs to create full employment, eliminate slums, and ensure a minimum standard of living for all. . . . The book ends with a proposed updated version of the Freedom Budget." (Library Journal)

REVIEW: *Choice* v51 no7 p1272 Mr 2014 M. Perelman

"A Freedom Budget for All Americans: Recapturing the Promise of the Civil Rights Movement in the Struggle for Economic Justice Today." "[Paul] Le Blanc . . .and [Michael D.] Yates . . . do an outstanding job of recapturing the development, as well as the social and political context, of this mostly forgotten chapter of American history.. . . The authors use this historical analysis to frame a valuable overview of current social and economic deficiencies of the contemporary US, making a convincing case that the time has come to resurrect the promise of a renewed Freedom Budget. . . . It is perceptive as well as lively, accessible to typical undergraduates yet valuable for specialists in the subject."

YATES, T. M. Signal Grace; [by] T. M. Yates 216 p. 2013 T. M. Yates

1. Bereavement 2. Family violence 3. Fathers & daughters 4. Grace (Theology) 5. Memoirs

ISBN 0989223205; 9780989223201

SUMMARY: In this memoir by T. M. Yates, " a daughter

remembers her father. . . . Her family split by divorce . . . and geography, she grew up yearning for connection. . . . After her own brief marriage, while still a student Texas A&M, violently blew up, her father helped her file legal protection orders, but she still felt alone. . . . Despite the chaos . . . she began noticing hopeful signs. . . . After Michael's death in 2010, unexpected shamrock-sightings comforted her." (Kirkus Reviews)

REVIEW: *Kirkus Rev* v81 no24 p53 D 15 2013
"Signal Grace". " A daughter remembers her father as memory combines with love and forgiveness to create a touching debut memoir. [T. M.] Yates, now in her early 30s, tells it like it is. . . . Cynics might be quick to lump this life story in with the recent glut of early age memoirs, but better than most, this story achingly portrays a family severed by divorce and encourages the healing of hearts. Yates keeps a strict focus on the father-daughter dynamic, and the "signal grace" idea is only brought toward the end, so it shouldn't deter casual, irreligious readers. A well-crafted, compelling account of how one confused little girl grew up and learned to live with her past by seeing signs of God's grace."

YELLOW BIRD, MICHAEL.ed. Decolonizing social work. See Decolonizing social work

YERKES, MARA.ed. The transformation of solidarity. See The transformation of solidarity

YEZERSKI, THOMAS F.il. Pinch and Dash make soup. See Daley, M. J.

YIYUN LI. Kinder than solitude; a novel; [by] Yiyun Li 336 p. 2013 Random House
1. Accidental poisioning—Fiction 2. Chinese—United States 3. Chinese Americans—Fiction 4. Detective & mystery stories 5. Friendship—Fiction 6. Murder—Fiction
ISBN 1400068142; 9781400068142 (alk. paper)
LC 2013-017307

SUMMARY: This novel, by Yiyun Li, moves "back and forth in time, between America today and China in the 1990s. . . . [It] is the story of three people whose lives are changed by a murder one of them may have committed. . . . When Moran, Ruyu, and Boyang were young, they were involved in a mysterious 'accident' in which a friend of theirs was poisoned. Grown up, the three friends are separated by distance and personal estrangement." (Publisher's note)

REVIEW: *Atlantic* v313 no4 p42-4 My 2014 ANN HULBERT
"Kinder Than Solitude". "[Yiyun\ Li, whose pared-down prose and open-ended plots are infused with humane clarity, has predictably inspired comparison to [Anton] Chekhov. . . . Don't let the title mislead you. Her work, often leavened by a mordant humor, hasn't mellowed. . . . Still, I wasn't prepared for the bleakness of 'Kinder Than Solitude,' which revolves around a young woman's poisoning. . . . Li avoids playing up the obvious metaphor. . . . She also dances agilely around the ostensibly pressing question of who among the three younger students may bear the blame. . . . If the theme doesn't generate intense emotional suspense—and it mostly doesn't—that is Li's point, yet also her problem."

REVIEW: *Commentary* v137 no6 p77-8 Je 2014 FERNANDA MOORE

REVIEW: *Kirkus Rev* v82 no3 p38 F 1 2014
"Kinder Than Solitude". "The lives of three teenage Chinese friends, irreversibly altered by the horrible, lingering poisoning of an older girl, are the subject of the bleak yet penetrating novel from PEN/Hemingway award winner [Yiyun] Li. . . . Opening with Shaoai's death, Li tracks the three erstwhile friends, now scattered across the U.S. and China, each isolated in a different way. The whodunit is less mysterious than their interconnected fates. Li's chilly, philosophical storytelling offers layers of unsettling yet impressive insight into family legacies and cultural dynamics."

REVIEW: *Libr J* v139 no11 p52 Je 15 2014 Susan G. Baird

REVIEW: *N Y Times Book Rev* p13 Mr 9 2014 JESS ROW

REVIEW: *New Statesman* v143 no19 p46-7 My 16 2014 Megan Walsh

REVIEW: *New Yorker* v90 no2 p75-1 Mr 3 2014
"Kinder Than Solitude." "In this novel, which spans the two decades following the Tiananmen Square crackdown of 1989, a fifteen-year-old orphan named Ruyu arrives as a guest at the comparatively privileged home of Shaoai, a fiery-spirited student protester. . . . When one character is poisoned, no suspects are arrested, but every member of the victim's circle is implicated. [Author Yiyun] Li turns an intricately plotted mystery into something more profound, one that queries the meaning of crime and punishment in the moral murk of contemporary China."

REVIEW: *Publ Wkly* v260 no49 p58 D 2 2013

REVIEW: *Va Q Rev* v90 no2 p227-30 Spr 2014 Jiayang Fan

YIYUN LI. A thousand years of good prayers; stories; [by] Yiyun Li 205 2005 Random House
1. Chinese Americans 2. Short stories 3. Short stories—By individual authors
ISBN 1-4000-6312-4
LC 2004—62891

SUMMARY: This is the author's first collection of stories. "Many of the stories in 'A Thousand Years of Good Prayers' are set in the 1990's." (N Y Times Book Rev)This is the author's first collection of stories. "Many of the stories in 'A Thousand Years of Good Prayers' are set in the 1990's." (N Y Times Book Rev)

REVIEW: *Atlantic* v313 no4 p42-4 My 2014 ANN HULBERT
"Kinder Than Solitude". "[Yiyun\ Li, whose pared-down prose and open-ended plots are infused with humane clarity, has predictably inspired comparison to [Anton] Chekhov. . . . Don't let the title mislead you. Her work, often leavened by a mordant humor, hasn't mellowed. . . . Still, I wasn't prepared for the bleakness of 'Kinder Than Solitude,' which revolves around a young woman's poisoning. . . . Li avoids playing up the obvious metaphor. . . . She also dances agilely around the ostensibly pressing question of who among the three younger students may bear the blame. . . . If the theme doesn't generate intense emotional suspense—and it mostly doesn't—that is Li's point, yet also her problem."

YOMTOV, NEL. Syria; [by] Nel Yomtov 144 p. 2013 Chil-

dren's Press, an imprint of Scholastic Inc.
ISBN 053123679X; 9780531236796 (library binding)
LC 2013-000088

SUMMARY: This book, by Nel Yomtov, focuses on Syria. The "country's culture, history, and geography are explored in detail, allowing readers a chance to see how people live. . . . Sidebars highlight especially interesting people, places, and events [and] recipes give readers the opportunity to experience foreign cuisine first-hand." (Publisher's note)

REVIEW: *Booklist* v110 no9/10 p94 Ja 1 2014 Susan Dove Lempke

"Brazil," "Ireland," "North Korea." "For reliably accurate, attractively presented and well-calibrated information, the longstanding 'Enchantment of the World' series remains a superior choice. . . . Although the basic structure holds true to past versions, the updated photographs are truly eye-popping and take care to portray the countries as modern. . . . 'Brazil' . . . conveys an excitement about the country and its people as well as its plentiful animals and plants. It might not be necessary for libraries to replace 'Ireland,' since it hasn't changed radically, but this is a solid offering with updated statistics. 'North Korea' has a new author and a strong political focus, discussing life under the new leader, Kim Jong-un."

YONEZU, YUSUKE, 1982-. We Love Each Other; [by] Yusuke Yonezu 28 p. 2013 Independent Pub Group
1. Animals—Juvenile literature 2. Love 3. Picture books for children 4. Shapes—Juvenile literature 5. Toy & movable books
ISBN 9789888240562; 9888240560

SUMMARY: In this children's book, "Japanese author/illustrator [Yusuke] Yonezu marries color, animal, and shape concepts with die-cuts and a reassuring theme of love. . . . 'Birds love each other,' begins the book, while two smiling red birds appear below on separate pages; turning the page brings them together as they create a heart shape. Two blue triangular mice and brown rectangular bears create a triangle and square on subsequent pages, among other colorful animal examples." (Publisher's note)

REVIEW: *Kirkus Rev* v82 no1 p80 Ja 1 2014

"We Love Each Other". "A celebration of love and an ode to shapes for the littlest readers. The first double-page spread depicts a single, stylized red bird on each page and the text 'Birds love each other.' Thanks to cleverly placed die cuts, when the page is turned, the two birds join to form a heart on the left-hand page. . . . In a bit of an awkward transition, the back cover speaks directly to readers, with the words '. . . I love YOU too!" above a big red heart. The vibrantly colored, stylized animals are appealing, the large white shapes on bold backgrounds command attention, and the glossy, die-cut pages encourage exploration. Babies and toddlers will appreciate this playful, upbeat introduction to shapes."

REVIEW: *Kirkus Rev* v81 no22 p315 N 15 2013

REVIEW: *Publ Wkly* v260 no40 p51 O 7 2013

REVIEW: *Publ Wkly* p66-7 Children's starred review annual 2013

YONEZU, YUSUKE, 1982-.il. We Love Each Other. See Yonezu, Y.

YONGHUA LIU. Confucian rituals and Chinese villagers; ritual change and social transformation in a southeastern Chinese community, 1368-1949; [by] Yonghua Liu xv, 326 p. 2013 Brill
1. Confucianism—China, Southeast—History 2. Confucianism—China, Southeast—Rituals—History and criticism 3. Historical literature 4. Neo-confucianism—Social aspects—China, Southeast 5. Religion and sociology—China, Southeast
ISBN 9789004257245 (hardback : alk. paper); 9789004257252 (e-book)
LC 2013-024393

SUMMARY: In this book, Yonghua Liu "examines the encounter between Confucian ritual and Chinese villagers, focusing on the Sibao region from the Ming dynasty (1366-1644) through the 1949 Communist Revolution. Taking lisheng, masters of rites, as a point of departure, he reconstructs several key sociocultural processes in which Confucian rituals were introduced to the region, and discusses how local society promoted and appropriated them." (Reference & Research Book News)

REVIEW: *Choice* v51 no7 p1282-3 Mr 2014 C. Schirokauer

"Confucian Rituals and Chinese Villagers: Ritual Change and Social Transformation in a Southeastern Chinese Community, 1368-1949." "This theoretically sophisticated and meticulously researched study, based on fieldwork as well as careful analysis of a wide range of written sources, examines the complex interaction of culture and society, center and periphery in a set of villages in northwestern Fujian as lineages were formed, community compacts were adopted, and the economy expanded. . . . This thoughtful book is rich in detail . . . draws on secondary studies in English, Chinese, and Japanese, and is written in impeccable English (honed in Canada). An exemplary study that helps advance understanding of China's history. . . . Highly recommended."

YOON, PAUL. Snow hunters; a novel; [by] Paul Yoon 192 p. 2013 Simon & Schuster
1. FICTION—General 2. FICTION—Historical 3. FICTION—Literary 4. Korean War, 1950-1953—Veterans—Fiction 5. Loneliness—Fiction 6. Refugees—Korea (North)—Ficiton
ISBN 9781476714813 (hardback); 9781476714820 (trade paper)
LC 2012-048365

SUMMARY: This book tells the story of "Yohan, who defects from his country at the end of the Korean War, leaving his friends and family behind to seek a new life on the coast of Brazil. Throughout his years there, four people slip in and out of his life: Kiyoshi, the Japanese tailor for whom he works; Peixe, the groundskeeper at the town church; and two vagrant children named Santi and Bia. Yohan longs to connect with these people, but to do so he must let go of his traumatic past." (Publisher's note)

REVIEW: *Booklist* v109 no22 p32 Ag 1 2013 Leah Strauss

REVIEW: *Kirkus Rev* v81 no12 p31 Je 15 2013

REVIEW: *Libr J* v138 no4 p55 Mr 1 2013 Barbara Hoffert

REVIEW: *Libr J* v138 no10 p104 Je 1 2013 Terry Hong

REVIEW: *N Y Times Book Rev* p12 Ag 18 2013 TATJANA SOLI

"Snow Hunters." "Paul Yoon proves himself well suited to the short form. . . . War is presented here in small, exquisite slivers. . . . Despite the bleak circumstances, the pleasures of 'Snow Hunters' are many, and they begin with Yoon's prose, at once lyrical and precise. . . . The strongest parts of the book delineate the tenuous bonds of friendship between characters, especially between adults and children. . . . Inaction, like happiness, is a form of narrative stasis that is difficult to write about. No matter how strikingly rendered, a series of moments and images ultimately needs causation rather than mere accumulation to move the story forward. When his characters do have this drive, 'Snow Hunters' hits on all cylinders and roars to life."

REVIEW: *Publ Wkly* v260 no25 p46-52 Je 24 2013 MIKE HARVKEY

REVIEW: *Publ Wkly* v260 no17 p104 Ap 29 2013

YOON, SALINA. Found; [by] Salina Yoon 40 p. 2014 Walker & Co

1. Bears—Fiction 2. Children's stories 3. Lost and found possessions—Fiction 4. Moose—Fiction 5. Toys—Fiction

ISBN 0802735592; 9780802735591 (hardback); 9780802735607 (library edition)

LC 2013-029206

SUMMARY: In this children's story, written and illustrated by Salina Yoon, "when Bear finds a lost stuffed toy bunny in the forest, he begins to worry. After all, the stuffed bunny must feel lonely and want to return safely to its owner and home! But as Bear diligently searches for the bunny's owner, posting notices high and low, he begins to grow attached to his newfound friend. What will happen when the bunny's owner finally comes forward?" (Publisher's note)

REVIEW: *Booklist* v110 no16 p54 Ap 15 2014 Daniel Kraus

REVIEW: *Bull Cent Child Books* v67 no9 p484-5 My 2014 J. H.

"Found". "While some stuffed-animal lovers may not buy Moose's willingness to part with his trusty plush pal, most kids will be relieved that Bear gets to keep Floppy after all. The simplicity of the storytelling and language is nicely matched by the large sans serif font and the bright, blocky digital pictures. Heavy black outlines and flecks of black, accent the crayon-box hues of the art, and cinnamon-y brown Bear and white, patched, and aptly named 'Floppy' are as cute as can be. . . . snuggle up with a favorite stuffed pal for a cozy lap read."

REVIEW: *Kirkus Rev* v82 no5 p61 Mr 1 2014

"Found". "Bear clearly loves the toy bunny that he has found sitting up against a tree in the forest, but he wants to help it return to its home. . . . [Salina] Yoon's story is sweet without being sentimental. She uses digitized artwork in saturated colors to create a lovely little world for her animals. They are outlined in strong black lines and stand out against the yellows, blues, greens and oranges of the background. She also uses space to great effect, allowing readers to feel the emotional tug of the story. A winning tale about finding new friends."

REVIEW: *Publ Wkly* v261 no4 p191 Ja 27 2014

REVIEW: *SLJ* v60 no5 p98 My 2014 Heidi Estrin

YORIFUJI, BUNPEI. Wonderful life with the elements; the periodic table personified; [by] Bunpei Yorifuji 205 p. 2012 No Starch Press

1. COMICS & GRAPHIC NOVELS—Nonfiction 2. Chemical elements—Comic books, strips, etc 3. Chemistry textbooks 4. Periodic law—Tables—Comic books, strips, etc 5. SCIENCE—Chemistry—General 6. SCIENCE—Chemistry—Inorganic 7. SCIENCE—Chemistry—Physical & Theoretical

ISBN 1593274238 (hardcover); 9781593274238 (hardcover)

LC 2012-020784

SUMMARY: This book is a graphic book about the periodic table of elements. "The author describes the elements in terms of proportions in the Earth's crust and in seawater as well as in the immediate environment of humans in three time periods: antiquity, medieval, and current times. The periodic table is outlined and cartooned, and the groups and other categories are illustrated as human figures with differing hairstyles and garb." (Choice)

REVIEW: *Choice* v50 no7 p1306 Mr 2013 R. E. Buntrock

YORK, NEIL LONGLEY.ed. Portrait of a patriot. See Portrait of a patriot

YOUME. Mali under the night sky; a Lao story of home; 1 v 2010 Cinco Puntos Press

1. Lao (Tai people) 2. Laos—History—1975- 3. Laotian American artists—Biography—Juvenile literature 4. Refugees

ISBN 9781933693682 (alk. paper)

LC 2009-042862

SUMMARY: Written by Youme Landowne, "'Mali Under the Night Sky,' a 2011 Skipping Stones honor book, is the true story of Laotian American artist Malichansouk Kouanchao, whose family was forced by civil war to flee Laos when she was five. Before the war began, Mali lived an idyllic life in a community where she felt safe and was much loved. But the coming war caused her family to flee to another country and a life that was less than ideal." (Publisher's note)

REVIEW: *World Lit Today* v88 no2 p6 Mr/Ap 2014 J. L. Powers

"Song for Night," "Between Shades of Gray," and "Mali Under the Night Sky: A Lao Story of Home." "In this lyrical novella ['Song for Night'] narrated by a child soldier, we travel across a West African country as fifteen-year-old 'My Luck' searches for his platoon. . . . Fifteen-year-old Lina loves boys, drawing, her cousin, and her father, a professor in Soviet-occupied Lithuania. . . . [Author Ruta] Sepetys paints Lina's experiences in delicate, layered strokes, revealing the humanity of both prisoner and prison guard in unique and subtle ways. . . . In 'Mali under the Night Sky,' a true story, a young girl named Mali flees her beloved home in Laos, seeking safety on foreign soil."

YOUME.il. Mali under the night sky. See Youme

YOUNG, ALLEN. No monkeys, no chocolate. See Stewart, M.

YOUNG, CHRISTOPHER.ed. Durs Grünbein. See Durs Grünbein

YOUNG, EDWARD. Disraeli. See Hurd, D.

YOUNG, EUGENE B. The Deleuze and Guattari dictionary; [by] Eugene B. Young 384 p. 2013 Bloomsbury Academic

1. Encyclopedias & dictionaries 2. Philosophical literature 3. Philosophy—Terminology
ISBN 9780826442765 (pbk.: alk. paper); 9780826442819 (hardcover: alk. paper)
LC 2013-015415

SUMMARY: This book presents a "guide to the world of Gilles Deleuze and Felix Guattari, two of the most important and influential thinkers in twentieth-century European philosophy." It "covers all their major sole-authored and collaborative works, ideas and influences and . . . the central themes of Deleuze and Guattari's groundbreaking thought. . . . A-Z entries include . . . definitions of all the key terms used in Deleuze and Guattari's writings and . . . synopses of their key works." (Publisher's note)

REVIEW: *Choice* v51 no9 p1568 My 2014 D. W. Rothermel

"The Deleuze and Guattari Dictionary". "This is an excellent dictionary of vital use to readers interested in the work of Gilles Deleuze and Félix Guattari. . . . The authors' introductory material wisely notes the difficulties that accrue to understanding the intricate web of terminology arising in texts authored by Deleuze and Guattari. . . . Each signed entry in this alphabetically arranged dictionary begins with a sentence or two of brief explication, followed by longer quotations from relevant passages in the primary texts. Insofar as these terms carry meaning only contextually, this format of inclusion provides an immediate context for their use by Deleuze and Guattari."

YOUNG, JESSICA. My blue is happy; 32 p. 2013 Candlewick Press

1. Children—Attitudes 2. Children's stories 3. Color—Psychological aspects 4. Colors—Juvenile literature 5. Emotions (Psychology)—Juvenile literature
ISBN 0763651257; 9780763651251
LC 2012-950616

SUMMARY: In this children's picture book by Jessica Young, "a little girl realizes that not everyone feels the same about colors. Her sister sees blue as sad and associates it with lonely songs. But the protagonist sees it as happy because it reminds her of her favorite jeans and the pool on a hot day. Dad says brown is ordinary like a paper bag but chocolate syrup is the association that the child makes." (School Library Journal)

REVIEW: *Bull Cent Child Books* v67 no2 p126-7 O 2013 H. M.

"My Blue Is Happy." "This color-concept book is based on the simple premise that the same color can evoke different emotions in different people. . . . The emotional statements about colors are effectively grounded in evocative, kid-oriented similes that add substance for listeners trying to make sense of the abstract relationship between colors and feelings. [Illustrator Catia] Chien's acrylic compositions tightly correlate with the color theme of each spread. The art's dry, textural brushing, with scratchy lines overlying and outlining painted sections, is often almost crayonlike, emphasizing the child perspective."

REVIEW: *Horn Book Magazine* v89 no6 p85 N/D 2013 SUSAN DOVE LEMPKE

"My Blue Is Happy." "It's at once a celebration of the world and its colors and a book about feelings and perceptions, contrasting the differences between the way two people see the same thing. [Catia] Chien's acrylic paintings fill the pages with intense shades of the featured colors . . . while reflecting the human relationships with humor and tenderness through facial expressions and body language. Readers and young listeners can have some good conversations about their own color perceptions after sharing this warm, deceptively simple concept book."

REVIEW: *Kirkus Rev* v81 no12 p123 Je 15 2013

REVIEW: *Publ Wkly* v260 no23 p75-6 Je 10 2013

REVIEW: *SLJ* v59 no7 p75 Jl 2013 Joan Kindig

YOUNG, JOSH. Erasing death; the science that is rewriting the boundaries between life and death; [by] Josh Young 352 p. 2013 HarperOne

1. BODY, MIND & SPIRIT—Parapsychology—Near-Death Experience 2. Cardiac arrest 3. Cardiac resuscitation 4. MEDICAL—Critical Care 5. Medical literature 6. Sudden death
ISBN 0062080601; 9780062080608 (hardback)
LC 2012-041098

SUMMARY: Written by Sam Parnia with Josh Young, this book "reveals that death is not a moment in time. Death, rather, is a process--a process that can be interrupted well after it has begun. . . . What happens to human consciousness during and after death? Dr. Parnia reveals how some form of 'afterlife' may be uniquely ours, as evidenced by the continuation of the human mind and psyche after the brain stops functioning." (Publisher's note)

REVIEW: *Choice* v51 no2 p302-3 O 2013 L. K. Strodtman

"Erasing Death: The Science That Is Rewriting the Boundaries Between Life and Death." "'Erasing Death' provides compelling evidence that death is a process, not a moment. Cell death in the brain and liver can go on for hours after the heart stops. When then, does one say a person has reached the point of permanent death? . . . [Author Sam] Parnia . . . asks if bringing people back to life involves more than pushing back time boundaries, but also if future criteria for defining death should include consideration of when a person's consciousness, psyche, or soul are lost and cannot be retrieved. . . . Overall, a fascinating book, well documented with 50 pages of citation."

REVIEW: *Kirkus Rev* v81 no2 p274 Ja 15 2013

REVIEW: *Libr J* v138 no6 p97 Ap 1 2013 Aaron Klink

YOUNG, JUDY. Digger and Daisy go on a picnic; 32 p. 2014 Sleeping Bear Press

1. Brothers and sisters—Fiction 2. Children's stories 3. Dogs—Fiction 4. Picnics 5. Smell—Fiction
ISBN 9781585368433 (hard cover); 9781585368440 (paper back)
LC 2013-024892

SUMMARY: This children's book follows canine siblings Digger and Daisy. "Sometimes they agree with each other. Sometimes they disagree. But no matter the situation, one thing always stays the same—their love and concern for each other. . . . Digger and Daisy walk to the park for a picnic. On the way there Digger's keen sense of smell leads him to explore his surroundings, ending up with an encounter with a skunk." (Publisher's note)

REVIEW: *Kirkus Rev* v82 no1 p198 Ja 1 2014

"Digger and Daisy Go on a Picnic". "The words in this early reader have a nice levitating quality, even in the unlikeliest of places—"Digger likes to smell everything. He puts his nose in the hole. Digger sniffs. He sniffs dirt up his nose. Digger snuffs. He snuffs more dirt up his nose"—which make them fun to engage with. . . . . It's almost Shakespearean, until the skunk arrives on the scene, its dashing black-and-white look a fine counterpart to the waxy crayon sheen of the rest of Sullivan's artwork. A stink can come between the coziest of siblings from time to time, but rarely are they so sweet as Daisy and Digger."

REVIEW: *SLJ* v60 no3 p131 Mr 2014 Laura Scott

YOUNG, NANCY BECK.ed. Encyclopedia of the U.S. presidency. See Encyclopedia of the U.S. presidency

YOUNG, NED.il. Big rig. See Swenson, J. A.

YOUNG, STEVE. Everything's coming up profits; the golden age of industrial musicals; [by] Steve Young 251 p. 2013 Blast Books

1. Actors—United States—History—20th century 2. Conferences & conventions—History—20th century 3. Historical literature 4. Industrial musicals—History and criticism 5. Sound recordings

ISBN 9780922233441 (alk. paper)

LC 2013-020047

SUMMARY: This book by Steve Young and Sport Murphy relates how "from the 1950s to the 1980s, American corporations commissioned a vast array of lavish, Broadway-style musical shows that were only for the eyes and ears of employees. These improbable productions were meant to educate and motivate the sales force to sell cars, appliances . . . and a thousand other products." Particular focus is given to sound recordings of the musicals. (Publisher's note)

REVIEW: *New York Times* v163 no56400 p4 F 2 2014 WILLIAM GRIMES

"Everything's Coming Up Profits: The Golden Age of Industrial Musicals". "A profusely illustrated history. Mr. [Steve] Young stumbled onto the subject in the early 1990s, when he was searching out comic material for . . . a running bit in which the host played excerpts from weird albums, and he brought home 'Go Fly a Kite,' a souvenir recording from a utility executives' conference that General Electric held in Williamsburg, Va. in 1966. This, he recognized, was comic gold. . . . The new book groups by decade about a hundred industrial albums, many displaying period-snazzy cover graphics Each show is annotated."

YOUNGSTEDT, SCOTT M. Surviving with dignity; Hausa communities of Niamey, Niger; [by] Scott M. Youngstedt xv, 226 p. 2012 Lexington Books

1. Hausa (African people)—Niger—Niamey—Economic conditions 2. Hausa (African people)—Niger—Niamey—Social conditions 3. Niamey (Niger)—Social conditions 4. Rural-urban migration—Niger 5. Social science literature

ISBN 0739173502; 9780739173503 (hbk. : alk. paper); 9780739173510 (electronic)

LC 2012-040502

SUMMARY: This book, by Scott M. Youngstedt, "explores three key interconnected themes—structural violence, suffering, and surviving with dignity—through examining the lived experiences of first and second-generation migrant Hausa men in Niamey over the past two decades in the current neoliberal moment.The central goal of the book is to explain the material (migration and informal economy work) and symbolic (meaning-making) strategies that Hausa individuals and communities have deployed in their struggles . . . to survive with dignity." (Publisher's note)

REVIEW: *Choice* v51 no1 p175-6 S 2013 R. Ellovich

"Surviving With Dignity: Hausa Communities of Niamey, Niger." "[Author Scott M.] Youngstedt . . . describes the urban realities of first- and second-generation Hausa migrants in Niamey, Niger. Basing his work on over 20 years of ethnographic research, Youngstedt uses participant-observation, structured interviews, case studies, key informants, and the Internet to gather data about Hausa men in Niger, northern Nigeria, Ghana, Senegal, New York City, and Michigan. . . . By means of case studies of people he has known for a long time, the author offers important insight into the life of Niamey men."

YOUSAFZAI, MALALA, 1997-. I am Malala. See Lamb, C.

YOVANOFF, BRENNA. The Curiosities. See Stiefvater, M.

YU HUA. Boy in the twilight; stories of the hidden China; 208 p. 2014 Pantheon Books

1. China—Fiction 2. Infidelity (Couples) 3. Man-woman relationships—Fiction 4. Short story (Literary form) 5. Thieves—Fiction

ISBN 0307379361; 9780307379368

LC 2013-017450

SUMMARY: These 13 stories, by Yu Hua, "take us into the small towns and dirt roads that are home to the people who make China run. In the title story, a shopkeeper confronts a child thief and punishes him without mercy. 'Victory' shows a young couple shaken by the husband's infidelity, scrambling to stake claims to the components of their shared life. 'Sweltering Summer' centers on an awkward young man who shrewdly uses the perks of his government position to court two women at once." (Publisher's note)

REVIEW: *Booklist* v110 no4 p15 O 15 2013 Carol Haggas

REVIEW: *Economist* v410 no8869 p71 Ja 11 2014

"Boy in the Twilight: Stories of Hidden China." "A collection of short stories written between 1993 and 1998 . . . translated into English with great elegance by Allan Barr. Whereas Mr. [Yu Hua's] earlier stories were violent and bloody, in this work the brutality is mental: the cruelty of a life foreshortened; the unwarranted destruction of a marriage; the simple, horrific savagery of everyday life. . . . Even when the stories are without redemption, the vigour of Mr. Yu's storytelling and his precise, elegant prose make for a compelling, if rarely comforting, read."

REVIEW: *Kirkus Rev* v81 no21 p71 N 1 2013

REVIEW: *Publ Wkly* v260 no39 p42 S 30 2013

REVIEW: *TLS* no5796 p20 My 2 2014 REBECCA LIAO

"Boy in the Twilight: Stories of the Hidden China." "[Author] Yu [Hua]'s stories focus on the modem Chinese male and his difficult transition from a once-assured destiny as the head of the family to life as an unemployed perpetual bachelor in the wake of economic competition and a shortfall in China's female population. . . . Like much of Yu's early work, these stories are candidly violent. . . . Yu's prose is compact, unsentimental and bristling with irony. The author takes meticulous inventory of the expected male roles—father, husband, worker, son—and finds his characters wanting."

YUKI KANEKO.tr. Wait! wait! See Nakawaki, H.

Z

ZAFIRIS, ELIAS, 1970-. Foundations of relational realism. See Epperson, M.

ZAGARENSKI, PAMELA.il. What the Heart Knows. See Sidman, J.

ZAILCKAS, KOREN. Mother, mother; a novel; [by] Koren Zailckas 352 p. 2013 Crown Publishers

1. Drug abuse—Fiction 2. Dysfunctional families—Fiction 3. Mothers and daughters—Fiction 4. Narcissists—Family relationships—Fiction 5. Psychological fiction

ISBN 0385347235; 9780385347235

LC 2013-010450

SUMMARY: In this book, "Violet, the dysfunctional Hurst family's stoner middle child, cannot remember which family member slashed her 12-year-old brother Will the night she overdosed on some strange seeds. But her mother, Josephine, blames her, and has her committed to a psychiatric hospital. Violet has no idea who to turn to for help: her spineless, alcoholic father, Douglas; her runaway older sister, Rose; or Will, the home-schooled mama's boy." (Publishers Weekly)

REVIEW: *Booklist* v110 no1 p39-40 S 1 2013 Rebecca Vnuk

"Mother, Mother." "[Koren] Zailckas, known for her biting memoirs . . . turns to the (hopefully) fictional tale of a woman hell-bent on manipulating the world around her. . . To the outside world, this extremely dysfunctional family looks practically flawless, thanks to Josephine's well-plotted machinations. Josephine is a truly frightening character--realistically flawed with just the right touch of over-the-top madness-- and Zailckas crafts an intriguing mystery surrounding this family that will keep readers on edge as she slowly peels back layer after layer of deception."

REVIEW: *Kirkus Rev* v81 no9 p25-6 My 1 2013

REVIEW: *Libr J* v138 no14 p105 S 1 2013 Kate Gray

REVIEW: *Libr J* v138 no7 p56 Ap 15 2013 Barbara Hoffert

REVIEW: *Publ Wkly* v260 no28 p147 Jl 15 2013

ZAMAN, MUHAMMAD QASIM. Modern Islamic thought in a radical age; religious authority and internal criticism; [by] Muhammad Qasim Zaman ix, 363 p. 2012 Cambridge University Press

1. Historical literature 2. Intellectuals—Islamic countries 3. Islam—21st century 4. Islam—Doctrines 5. Islam—History 6. Islamic philosophy 7. Islamic sociology

ISBN 9781107096455 (hardback)

LC 2012-011716

SUMMARY: In this book by Muhammad Qasim Zaman on internal criticism in modern Islam, "Through an analysis of the work of Muhammad Rashid Rida and Yusuf al-Qaradawi in the Arab Middle East and a number of scholars belonging to the Deobandi orientation in colonial and contemporary South Asia, this book examines some of the most important issues facing the Muslim world since the late nineteenth century." (Publisher's note)

REVIEW: *Middle East J* v68 no3 p488-90 Summ 2014 John O. Voll

"Modern Islamic Thought in a Radical Age." "[Author Muhammad Qasim] Zaman begins by identifying three major individuals whose ideas provide much of the foundation for the analysis in the book, Muhammad Rashid Rida, 'Ubaidullah Sindhi, and Yusuf al-Qaradawi. . . . Zaman provides an examination of a major aspect of Muslim reform movements, the 'ulama articulation of 'internal criticism.' If one wants to go beyond the journalistic headlines, Zaman's analysis of this dimension of contemporary Muslim reform is extremely important."

ZANVILLE, HOLLY. Summer at the Z House; 40 p. 2013 CreateSpace Independent Publishing Platform

1. Books & reading—Juvenile fiction 2. Children's stories 3. Families—Juvenile fiction 4. Grandparent & child 5. Summer—Juvenile literature

ISBN 148195234X; 9781481952347

SUMMARY: In this book, "when Grandma arrives for a visit, her engaged, caring presence makes the summer days more fun for Noah, his mom, and their animals, which include a dog named Pepper and three cats. Grandma turns dinner into a special occasion by writing descriptions of her feast . . . on a menu that Noah happily reads aloud before each course. . . Grandma enjoys hearing about Noah's creative day camp endeavors. . . . She also shares the family's love for animals." (Kirkus Reviews)

REVIEW: *Kirkus Rev* v82 no5 p29 Mr 1 2014

"Summer at the Z House". "The book is the third in a series of books centered on Noah, his mom and their growing collection of pets, each with its own distinct personality. Zanville . . . offers vivid images throughout; for example, during the family's trip to an aquarium, Noah observes 'miniature jellyfish that looked like white parachutes with dangly tentacles' and 'glowed in the lights of their dark tanks so brightly—it was like looking at little stars in the sky.' There are no wacky plot twists here—just refreshingly genuine warmth and quiet observations of real-life moments among family members, be they human, canine or feline. A well-observed, colorfully illustrated book about a close-knit family's day-to-day life."

ZARATE, JUAN C. Treasury's war; the unleashing of a new era of financial warfare; [by] Juan C. Zarate 512 p. 2013 PublicAffairs

1. Commercial crimes—Prevention 2. Finance—Moral and ethical aspects—United States 3. Money launder-

ing—Prevention 4. National security—United States 5. Political science literature 6. Security, International 7. Terrorism—Finance—Prevention
ISBN 9781610391153 (hardcover)
LC 2012-051582

SUMMARY: This book by Juan Zarate describes U.S. financial warfare since September 11, 2001. "By harnessing the forces of globalization and the centrality of the American market and dollar, [the U.S.] Treasury developed a new way of undermining America's foes. Treasury and its tools soon became, and remain, critical in the most vital geopolitical challenges facing the United States, including terrorism, nuclear proliferation, and the regimes in Iran, North Korea, and Syria." (Publisher's note)

REVIEW: *Booklist* v109 no22 p14 Ag 1 2013 Mary Whaley

REVIEW: *Choice* v51 no6 p1064 F 2014 E. L. Whalen

REVIEW: *Kirkus Rev* v81 no12 p75 Je 15 2013

REVIEW: *New York Times* v162 no56246 p6 S 1 2013 BRYAN BURROUG

"Treasury's War." "A useful new book. . . . Mr. [Juan C.] Zarate . . . makes a persuasive case that a series of financial weapons developed after 9/11, and used mostly by the Treasury Department, have given the United States opportunities to weaken terrorists and rogue states as never before. . . . For those of us who start feeling drowsy at the very mention of the words 'Treasury Department,' this book is an eye-opener. . . . Fascinating stuff, I grant you, but not quite a fascinating book. Alas, some decent scene-setting aside, the author often writes like a government bureaucrat. In places, the book reads like a white paper. It also lavishes much praise on just about every official he has dealt with."

REVIEW: *Publ Wkly* v260 no30 p59 Jl 29 2013

ZARETSKY, ROBERT. A life worth living; Albert Camus and the quest for meaning; [by] Robert Zaretsky 210 p. 2013 Harvard University Press
1. Conduct of life 2. Ethics in literature 3. French authors—20th century—Biography 4. Literature—History & criticism
ISBN 9780674724761 (hardcover : alk. paper)
LC 2013-010473

SUMMARY: "Through an exploration of themes that preoccupied Camus--absurdity, silence, revolt, fidelity, and moderation--Robert Zaretsky portrays a moralist who refused to be fooled by the nobler names we assign to our actions, and who pushed himself, and those about him, to challenge the status quo. . . . For Camus, rebellion is an eternal human condition, a timeless struggle against injustice that makes life worth living." (Publisher's note)

REVIEW: *Choice* v51 no9 p1609 My 2014 L. A. Wilkinson

REVIEW: *Christ Century* v130 no23 p42 N 13 2013

REVIEW: *Publ Wkly* v260 no27 p75 Jl 8 2013

REVIEW: *TLS* no5771 p22 N 8 2013 JOHN TAYLOR

REVIEW: *World Lit Today* v88 no2 p78-9 Mr/Ap 2014 Andrew Martino

"A Life Worth Living: Albert Camus and the Quest for Meaning." "[Author Robert] Zaretsky once again gives us a concentrated, wholly enlightening and insightful study on the life of this complicated writer and man. Zaretsky's books on Camus read more like critical biographies than . . . literary criticism, and that's a good thing. Zaretsky's writing style is easy to follow yet scholarly and informed. . . . 'A Life Worth Living' examines Camus as a moralist, paying particular attention to his silence on the Algerian problem and his very public fallout with Jean-Paul Sartre. . . . This is a wonderfully written and expertly researched companion to Zaretsky's previous book on Camus. Taken together, Zaretsky has proved to be one of the most honest and thoughtful critics of Albert Camus."

ZASLOFF, BETH. Hold fast to dreams; a college guidance counselor, his students, and the vision of a life beyond poverty; [by] Beth Zasloff 320 p. 2014 The New Press
1. Academic achievement—United States 2. College choice—United States 3. Educational counseling—New York (State)—New York—Case studies 4. Educational literature 5. High school students—New York (State)—New York—Interviews 6. Minority students—Counseling of—United States 7. Student aspirations—New York (State)—New York—Case studies
ISBN 159558904X; 9781595589040 (hardcover: alk. paper); 9781595589286 (e-book)
LC 2013-043224

SUMMARY: This book, by Beth Zasloff and Joshua Steckel, "follows the lives of ten . . . students as they navigate the vast and obstacle-ridden landscape of college in America. . . . At a time when the idea of 'college for all' is alternately embraced and challenged, this . . . book uncovers . . . the many ways the American education system fails in its promise as a ladder to opportunity." (Publisher's note)

REVIEW: *Booklist* v110 no13 p5-6 Mr 1 2014 Vanessa Bush

REVIEW: *Kirkus Rev* v82 no5 p47 Mr 1 2014

"Hold Fast to Dreams: A College Guidance Counselor, His Students, and the Vision of a Life Beyond Poverty". "Inspiring account of what it takes to overcome class and ethnic barriers to gain acceptance to college. . . . [Joshua] Steckel was recruited to a new Brooklyn high school . . . from the college admissions program of a private Upper East Side school. He and his wife, [Beth] Zasloff . . . chronicle the pitfalls he faced as he helped the students navigate the college-admissions process and worked with his existing network of admissions officers and support programs to qualify candidates in innovative and unorthodox ways. A powerful story of courage and hope that should inspire others to follow trailblazers like Steckel and his students."

REVIEW: *Publ Wkly* v260 no52 p44 D 23 2013

ZAVATTARO, STACI M. Cities for sale; municipalities as public relations and marketing firms; [by] Staci M. Zavattaro xiv, 138 p. 2013 State University of New York Press
1. City promotion—United States 2. Municipal government—Public relations—United States
ISBN 9781438446813 (hardcover : alk. paper)
LC 2012-024544

SUMMARY: It was the author's intent to demonstrate that "city governments are increasingly adopting the techniques of self-promotion that businesses of all sizes have practiced for decades. . . . In competing with one another for residents, customers, investors, and tourists, they project a 'brand' that marks them as unique in the minds of their audiences. . . . Municipal employees are thereby induced to see themselves as promoters instead of service providers." (Choice: Current Reviews for Academic Libraries)

REVIEW: *Choice* v51 no5 p927-8 Ja 2014 W. C. Johnson
"Cities for Sale: Municipalities as Public Relations and Marketing Firms." "[Staci M.] Zavattaro's research spanned the spectrum from New York City to small communities in Florida. She is concerned that this image-building by cities is treating people as customers who simply consume such messages, rather than approaching them as citizens who play a vital role in their politics. Municipal employees are thereby induced to see themselves as promoters instead of service providers. This book is worthy of attention by students of public administration and the media."

ZECHEL, ELIZABETH.il. Wordbirds. See Schillinger, L.

ZEILER, THOMAS W.ed. A companion to World War II. See A companion to World War II

ZEITZ, JOSHUA. Lincoln's boys; John Hay, John Nicolay, and the war for Lincoln's image; [by] Joshua Zeitz 400 p. 2013 Viking
1. Historical literature 2. Presidents—United States—Biography 3. Presidents—United States—Staff—Biography 4. Private secretaries—United States—Biography
ISBN 0670025666; 9780670025664
LC 2013-017052

SUMMARY: This book, by Joshua Zeitz, looks at "John Hay and John Nicolay . . . [who] served as [Abraham] Lincoln's personal and presidential secretaries, witnessing Lincoln's ascent to power, his wartime trials and triumphs, and his untimely end. After his death . . . the Lincoln family gave the two men exclusive access to Lincoln's papers, and they got to work creating an official biography that put forth the interpretation of Lincoln's life that still dominates today." (Library Journal)

REVIEW: *Booklist* v110 no5 p14 N 1 2013 Jay Freeman

REVIEW: *Economist* v410 no8875 p1 F 20 2014

REVIEW: *Kirkus Rev* v81 no24 p25 D 15 2013
"Lincoln's Boys: John Hay, John Nicolay, and the War for Lincoln's Image". "[Joshua] Zeitz . . . approaches the already overloaded realm of Abraham Lincoln studies from a fresh direction. . . . Zeitz does a masterful job delineating the lives of Nicolay and Hay, explaining their roles in political contests, narrating their interactions with Lincoln and placing the Nicolay-Hay biography within the larger context of Lincoln studies. The author is mostly admiring of Nicolay and Hay, while simultaneously factoring in their biases in the service of American history. . . . Fascinating scholarship from Zeitz, who knows how to present history to an audience of nonspecialists."

REVIEW: *Libr J* v138 no8 p61 My 1 2013

REVIEW: *Libr J* v138 no18 p98 N 1 2013 Theresa McDevitt

ZELIKOW, PHILIP D.ed. The Kennedy tapes. See The Kennedy tapes

ZELLEN, BARRY SCOTT.ed. The fast-changing Arctic. See The fast-changing Arctic

ZEVIN, GABRIELLE. The storied life of A. J. Fikry; a novel; [by] Gabrielle Zevin 272 p. 2014 Algonquin Books of Chapel Hill
1. Abandoned children—Fiction 2. Booksellers—Fiction 3. Bookstores—Fiction 4. Love stories 5. Man-woman relationships—Fiction 6. Widowers—Fiction
ISBN 1616203218; 9781616203214 (alk. paper)
LC 2013-043144

SUMMARY: In this book, by Gabrielle Zevin, "A.J. Fikry, the . . . owner of Island Books, has recently endured some tough years: his wife has died, his bookstore is experiencing the worst sales in its history, and his prized possession—a rare edition of [Edgar Allan] Poe poems—has been stolen. Over time, he has given up on people. . . . Until a most unexpected occurrence gives him the chance to make his life over and see things anew." (Publisher's note)

REVIEW: *Booklist* v111 no3 p95-6 O 1 2014 Joyce Saricks

REVIEW: *Booklist* v110 no12 p28 F 15 2014 Joanne Wilkinson

REVIEW: *Kirkus Rev* v82 no4 p201 F 15 2014
"The Storied Life of A. J. Fikry". "There's a Nicholas Sparks quality to this novel about people who love books but who cannot find someone to love. With a wry appreciation for the travails of bookstore owners . . . [Gabrielle] Zevin writes characters of a type, certainly, but ones who nonetheless inspire empathy. . . . All fit the milieu perfectly in a plot that spins out as expected, bookended by tragedy. Zevin writes characters who grow and prosper, mainly A. J. and Lambiase, in a narrative that is sometimes sentimental, sometimes funny, sometimes true to life and always entertaining. A likable literary love story about selling books and finding love."

REVIEW: *Libr J* v139 no2 p69 F 1 2014 Susan Clifford Braun

REVIEW: *Libr J* v139 no9 p40 My 15 2014 Kristen L. Smith

REVIEW: *Publ Wkly* v261 no3 p28 Ja 20 2014

REVIEW: *Publ Wkly* v261 no21 p54 My 26 2014

ZHU WEN. The Matchmaker, the Apprentice, and the Football Fan; More Stories of China; 184 p. 2013 Columbia University Press
1. China—Politics & government 2. China—Social conditions 3. Murder—Fiction 4. Short stories
ISBN 9780231160902 (cloth : alk. paper)
LC 2012-043112

SUMMARY: This book by Zhu Wen presents short stories set in China. "In 'The Football Fan,' readers fall in with an intriguingly unreliable narrator who may or may not have killed his elderly neighbor for a few hundred yuan. The bemused antihero of 'Reeducation' is appalled to discover that, ten years after graduating during the pro-democracy protests of 1989, his alma mater has summoned him back for a punitive bout of political reeducation with a troublesome ex-girlfriend." (Publisher's note)

REVIEW: *N Y Times Book Rev* p30 S 1 2013 Alison McCulloch
"Through the Night," "The Matchmaker, the Apprentice, and the Football Fan," and "The Sinistra Zone." "[Stig] Saeterbakken entices the reader along some dark paths from which, in the end, there is no easy escape. . . . Even in this grim tale, Zhu [Wen] manages to inject some of the sly hu-

mor that suffuses these stories, which, unlike some of the lives he describes, are never dreary. . . . Like everything else in this cryptic novel, its main character is a bit of a mystery. . . . Adding to its perplexity is the book's structure: 15 overlapping chapters that could double as independent short stories."

REVIEW: *Publ Wkly* v260 no22 p36 Je 3 2013

REVIEW: *TLS* no5754 p21 Jl 12 2013 YIYUN LI

REVIEW: *World Lit Today* v88 no1 p79 Ja/F 2014

ZIMMER, HENRY B. The Enlightened Capitalism Manifesto; [by] Henry B. Zimmer 312 p. 2013 Henry B Zimmer

1. Capitalism 2. Financial planning 3. Political science literature 4. United States—Economic conditions 5. United States—Politics & government
ISBN 0615904793; 9780615904795

SUMMARY: In this book, author Henry B. Zimmer advocates for "enlightened capitalism—i.e., capitalism without greed or excessiveness. The direct opposite, he says, of enlightened capitalism is unbridled capitalism, the spell under which the U.S. has fallen in recent years, as the gap between the haves and have-nots widens." (Kirkus Reviews)

REVIEW: *Kirkus Rev* v82 no1 p108 Ja 1 2014

"The Enlightened Capitalism Manifesto: A Blueprint for a Revitalized America". "Drawing on both his United States citizenship and his longtime residence in Canada, Zimmer is uniquely qualified to compare and contrast the benefits and shortcomings of both countries' governments and policies. . . . Zimmer's common-sense approach and unaffected writing style make for a quick read, unburdened by complicated jargon or technical language. . . . No issue is too big or too controversial for Zimmer—he gives his views on everything from banking to gay marriage—and the sweeping political and social changes he suggests seem logical, if not logistically impossible to implement. Most useful are Zimmer's suggestions in his area of particular expertise—financial planning."

ZIMMERMAN, JEAN. Savage girl; [by] Jean Zimmerman 416 p. 2013 Viking

1. Adoption—Fiction 2. Historical fiction 3. Murder—Fiction 4. Orphans—Fiction
ISBN 0670014850; 9780670014859
LC 2013-018408

SUMMARY: This novel, by Jean Zimmerman, "tells of the dramatic events that transpire when an alluring, blazingly smart eighteen-year-old girl named Bronwyn, reputedly raised by wolves in the wilds of Nevada, is adopted in 1875 by the Delegates, an outlandishly wealthy Manhattan couple, and taken back East to be civilized and introduced into high society. . . . A series of suitors, both young and old, find her irresistible, but the willful girl's illicit lovers begin to turn up murdered." (Publisher's note)

REVIEW: *Booklist* v110 no13 p25 Mr 1 2014 Bridget Thoreson

REVIEW: *Kirkus Rev* v82 no4 p80 F 15 2014

"Savage Girl". "A formal, measured tempo only heightens the tension in Zimmerman's second historical fiction-cum-thriller. . . . Neither Hugo nor the reader is sure [of the murder's identity] right up to the satisfying if melodramatic end. [Jean] Zimmerman's dark comedy of manners is an obvious homage to Edith Wharton, a rip-roaring murder mystery more Robert Louis Stevenson than Arthur Conan Doyle and a wonderfully detailed portrait of the political, economic and philosophical issues driving post-Civil War America."

REVIEW: *Libr J* v139 no10 p61 Je 1 2014 Jason Puckett

REVIEW: *Libr J* v139 no2 p69 F 1 2014 Laurel Bliss

REVIEW: *Libr J* v138 no16 p58 O 1 2013 Barbara Hoffert

REVIEW: *N Y Times Book Rev* p23 Mr 23 2014 MARILYN STASIO

REVIEW: *Publ Wkly* v261 no2 p50 Ja 13 2014

ZIMMERMANN, SUSAN. Divide, provide, and rule; an integrative history of poverty policy, social policy, and social reform in Hungary under the Habsburg Monarchy; [by] Susan Zimmermann xii, 171 p. 2011 Central European University Press

1. Historical literature 2. Poverty—Government policy—Hungary—History—19th century 3. Public welfare—Hungary—History—19th century
ISBN 9786155053191 (hbk.)
LC 2011-037329

SUMMARY: It was the author's intent "to integrate different aspects of welfare policies in the Hungarian part of the Habsburg empire. Following the introduction, [Susan] Zimmermann investigates the poverty policy of public and private actors across the different levels of local, regional, and national administration." (Slavic Review)

REVIEW: *Am Hist Rev* v119 no1 p272-3 F 2014 Robert Nemes

"Divide, Provide, and Rule: An Integrative History of Poverty Policy, Social Policy,and Social Reform in Hungary Under the Habsburg Monarchy". "In this book, [Susan] Zimmermann offers English-language readers a concise summation of her work on Hungarian welfare and labor policies in the years around 1900. . . . This is a short but dense book. Zimmermann focuses throughout on key pieces of welfare legislation. This emphasis allows her to discuss clearly the aims, implementation, inconsistencies, and limits of different policies. Yet she does not analyze the people and institutions responsible for such measures."

ZINN, HOWARD, 1922-2010. A people's history of the United States; 1492-present; [by] Howard Zinn 729 p. 2003 HarperCollins

1. Historical revisionism 2. Minorities—United States—History 3. Social movements—United States—History 4. United States—History—Textbooks 5. Working class—United States
ISBN 0060528427 (acid-free paper)
LC 2002-032895

SUMMARY: "According to this classic of revisionist American history, narratives of national unity and progress are a smoke screen disguising the ceaseless conflict between elites and the masses whom they oppress and exploit. Historian [Howard] Zinn sides with the latter group in chronicling Indians' struggle against Europeans, blacks' struggle against racism, women's struggle against patriarchy, and workers' struggle against capitalists." (Publishers Weekly)

REVIEW: *Rev Am Hist* v42 no2 p197-206 Je 2014 Robert Cohen

"A People's History of the United States, 1492-Present." "In 'A People's History,' [author Howard] Zinn had published a powerfully written historical synthesis for a broad readership, did it solo, maintained his distinctive voice, argued with other historians in the text, took on ethical questions about the abuses of American power, aimed to be provocative rather than comprehensive, explicitly linked the present with the past, . . . and included so much inspiring protest oratory that it would later become the core for a stage production. . . . In all these ways, Zinn offered a model of successful historical writing and teaching that historians would be foolish to ignore. Successful does not mean flawless."

ZIOLKOWSKI, JAN M.ed. The Virgil encyclopedia. See The Virgil encyclopedia

ZIOLKOWSKI, THEODORE. Gilgamesh among us; modern encounters with the ancient epic; [by] Theodore Ziolkowski xiv, 226 p. 2011 Cornell University Press

1. Assyro-Babylonian epic poetry 2. Gilgamesh (Poem) 3. Intellectual life—History 4. Literature—History & criticism 5. Modern civilization

ISBN 9780801450358 (cloth : alk. paper)

LC 2011-027253

SUMMARY: "In 'Gilgamesh among Us,' Theodore Ziolkowski explores the surprising legacy of the poem and its hero, as well as the epic's continuing influence in modern letters and arts. . . . Ziolkowski sees fascination with Gilgamesh as a reflection of eternal spiritual values--love, friendship, courage, and the fear and acceptance of death. Noted writers, musicians, and artists . . . have adapted the story in ways that meet the social and artistic trends of the times." (Publisher's note)

REVIEW: *Am Lit* v85 no1 p205-11 Mr 2013

REVIEW: *Choice* v50 no5 p870-1 Ja 2013 C. Fantazzi

REVIEW: *J Am Acad Relig* v81 no3 p882-7 S 2013 Louis A. Ruprecht

"Gilgamesh Among Us: Modern Encounters With the Ancient Epic." "[Author] Theodore Ziolkowski is a prolific intellectual historian whose publications span forty years. . . . This book represents a fascinating foray--written by a scholar known for his scrupulous research, clarity of expression, subtlety and wit--into the relatively new field of reception history. It offers us a complex history of the reception of the Gilgamesh cycle, rather than an analysis of the constitutive role played by an ancient epic in the emerging modern world. . . . It is in the attempt to theorize that wealth of detail that the book seems to falter."

ZIOLKOWSKI, THEODORE. Lure of the arcane; the literature of cult and conspiracy; [by] Theodore Ziolkowski xii, 230 p. 2013 The Johns Hopkins University Press

1. Conspiracy in literature 2. Cults 3. Literature—History & criticism 4. Secrecy in literature 5. Secret societies in literature

ISBN 1421409585 (hardcover : acid-free paper); 9781421409580 (hardcover : acid-free paper)

LC 2012-041101

SUMMARY: In this book, "Theodore Ziolkowski traces the evolution of cults, orders, lodges, secret societies, and conspiracies through various literary manifestations--drama, romance, epic, novel, opera--down to the thrillers of the twenty-first century. . . . Mimicking the genre's quest driven narrative arc, the reader searches for the significance of conspiracy fiction." (Publisher's note)

REVIEW: *Choice* v51 no6 p999-1000 F 2014 E. H. Friedman

"Lure of the Arcane: The Literature of Cult and Conspiracy." "Theodore Ziolkowski's exploration of "literature of cult and conspiracy" involves a long and pleasantly vertiginous journey from classical antiquity to the present. . . . The juxtapositions in the study are impressive in a number of ways because Ziolkowski starts from the beginning, as it were, and mixes the esoteric and cultured with the popular. . . . This is a literary and cultural history for the 21st century: fascinating in scope and focus, striking in its attention to detail, solid in its continuity, and indisputably erudite."

ZIRIN, JAMES D. The mother court; tales of cases that mattered in America's greatest trial court; [by] James D. Zirin 322 p. 2014 American Bar Association

1. District courts—United States 2. Historical literature 3. Trial courts—History

ISBN 9781627223225 (print: alk. paper)

LC 2013-036466

SUMMARY: Written by James D. Zirin, "This is the first book to chronicle the history of the US District Court for the Southern District of New York, the most influential District court in the United States, from the perspective of a practicing attorney who has argued many cases before some of its most esteemed judges. It gives first-hand insight into the evolution of our justice system—where it has been, where it is now and where it is going." (Publisher's note)

REVIEW: *Economist* v411 no8893 p75 Je 28 2014

REVIEW: *Libr J* v139 no8 p90 My 1 2014 Lynne Maxwell

REVIEW: *N Y Rev Books* v61 no11 p42-3 Je 19 2014 Jed S. Rakoff

"The Mother Court: Tales of Cases That Mattered in America's Greatest Trial Court." "In 'The Mother Court,' James Zirin, a well-respected trial lawyer, deftly illustrates through anecdotes the characteristics that have led to the court's high repute, including the ingenuity of the lawyers who practice before it and the quality of its judges. . . . Zirin's fluid prose and eye for detail make 'The Mother Court' fun to read, while faithfully conveying the underlying importance of the issues at stake. . . . Another merit of Zirin's book is that it does not gloss over some of the more shameful chapters in the court's modern history, such as the execution of the Rosenbergs."

REVIEW: *New York Times* v163 no56547 p3 Je 29 2014 SAM ROBERTS

REVIEW: *TLS* no5807 p30 Jl 18 2014 MARK KAMINE

ZISSIMOPOULOS, JULIE.ed. Lifecycle events and their consequences. See Lifecycle events and their consequences

ZOEHFELD, KATHLEEN WEIDNER. Secrets of the seasons; orbiting the sun in our backyard; 40 p. 2014 Alfred A. Knopf

1. Children's stories 2. Earth (Planet)—Rotation—Juvenile literature 3. Seasons—Fiction 4. Weather—Juvenile literature

ISBN 0517709945; 9780517709948 (trade);

9780517709955 (lib. bdg.)
LC 2013-021351

SUMMARY: This book, written by Kathleen Weidner Zoehfeld and illustrated by Priscilla Lamont, is "about backyard science that explains why the seasons change. Alice and her friend Zack explore the reasons for the seasons. Alice's narrative is all about noticing the changes as fall turns into winter, spring, and then summer. She explains how the earth's yearlong journey around the sun, combined with the tilt in the earth's axis, makes the seasons happen." (Publisher's note)

REVIEW: *Horn Book Magazine* v90 no2 p148 Mr/Ap 2014 DANIELLE J. FORD

REVIEW: *Kirkus Rev* v82 no5 p79 Mr 1 2014

"Secrets of the Seasons: Orbiting the Sun in Our Backyard". "[Priscilla] Lamont's pen-and-watercolor illustrations focus on the seasonal indicators that will be familiar to most readers—tracks in the snow, leaves on the trees, robins, migrating geese, etc. Daisy and Maisy may be the comic relief, but their simple diagrams and explanations are standouts. Incorporating both a story and solid science in an engaging way, this is an accessible and welcome addition to the sometimes-confusing reasons-for-the-seasons shelf."

REVIEW: *N Y Times Book Rev* p18 My 11 2014 JOHN LITHGOW

REVIEW: *Publ Wkly* v261 no5 p54 F 3 2014

REVIEW: *SLJ* v60 no3 p178 Mr 2014 Eva Elisabeth VonAncken

ZOELLNER, TOM. Train; riding the rails that created the modern world: from the Trans-Siberian to the Southwest Chief; [by] Tom Zoellner 384 p. 2014 Viking Adult

1. Railroad travel—History 2. Railroads 3. Travelers' writings

ISBN 0670025283; 9780670025282 (hardback)
LC 2013-036816

SUMMARY: In this book, Tom Zoellner "examines both the mechanics of the rails and their engines and how they helped societies evolve. Not only do trains transport people and goods in an efficient manner, but they also reduce pollution and dependency upon oil. Zoellner also considers America's culture of ambivalence to mass transit, using the perpetually stalled line between Los Angeles and San Francisco as a case study in bureaucracy and public indifference." (Publisher's note)

REVIEW: *Booklist* v110 no7 p7 D 1 2013 Carl Hays

REVIEW: *Kirkus Rev* v81 no24 p45 D 15 2013

"Train: Riding the Rails That Created the Modern World—From the Trans-Siberian to the Southwest Chief". "A rousing around-the-world paean to the rumble of the rails by accomplished journalist [Tom] Zoellner. . . . Having train-hopped across continents, Zoellner closes his account with a cleareyed look at what needs to happen in America if trains are to have a future—it will involve considerable infusions of money and overcoming vested-interest opposition. Great for fans of Paul Theroux's railroad journeys, except that Zoellner isn't anywhere near as ill-tempered, and he has a better command of social history. A pleasure for literate travelers."

REVIEW: *Libr J* v139 no7 p50 Ap 15 2014 Susan G. Baird

REVIEW: *Libr J* v139 no2 p88 F 1 2014 Linda M. Kaufmann

REVIEW: *N Y Times Book Rev* p54 Je 1 2014 JOSHUA HAMMER

ZOLA, ÉMILE, 1840-1902. Therese Raquin; 266 p. 2014 Trafalgar Square

1. Adultery—Fiction 2. French literature—19th century 3. French literature—Translations into English 4. Human sexuality—Fiction 5. Murder—Fiction

ISBN 0099573520; 9780099573524

SUMMARY: In this novel by Émile Zola, "When Thérèse Raquin is forced to marry the sickly Camille, she sees a bare life stretching out before her. . . . Escape comes in the form of her husband's friend, Laurent, and Thérèse throws herself headlong into an affair. There seems only one obstacle to their happiness; Camille. They plot to be rid of him. . . . Adam Thorpe's unflinching translation brings Zola's dark and shocking masterwork to life." (Publisher's note)

REVIEW: *N Y Times Book Rev* p14 My 18 2014 FREDERICK BROWN

REVIEW: *TLS* no5784 p22 F 7 2014 NICHOLAS WHITE

"Thérèse Raquin." "The translator of this new edition in English, Adam Thorpe, . . . brings an unusual freshness and zip tot he task, which goes some way towards returning us to the sense of unnerving immediacy which the young Zola's novel would have given its readers in 1867. . . . If sex is notoriously difficult to write about, it is equally difficult to translate, not least across centuries as well as languages. But surely the sex between Thérèse and Laurent is a driving force in the novel's tragedy, precisely because it is resolutely sex, rather than love or romance."

ZOOB, CAROLINE. Virginia Woolf's garden; the story of the garden at Monk's house; 192 p. 2013 Jacqui Small

1. English authors—Homes & haunts 2. Gardens 3. Historical literature 4. Woolf, Leonard, 1880-1969 5. Woolf, Virginia, 1882-1941

ISBN 1909342130; 9781909342132

SUMMARY: In this book, by Caroline Zoob, "a chronological account takes the reader through the key events in the lives of Virginia and Leonard Woolf, and their deaths. This is allied to an account of the garden and its development, and the creation and development of the key areas of the garden. . . . Full-colour contemporary photographs, archive photographs, illustrated maps and planting plans take the reader through the various garden 'rooms'." (Publisher's note)

REVIEW: *Booklist* v110 no8 p17 D 15 2013 Donna Seaman

"Virginia Woolf's Garden: The Story of the Garden at Monk's House". "Striking archival photographs mix well with Caroline Arber's radiant color shots, and [Caroline] Zoob is the best possible guide, having moved into Monk's House, which is owned by the National Trust, with her husband in 2000, and tended the garden for more than a decade. Her charming and affecting chronicle grants us a new perspective on this remarkable pair of 'fantastically hard-working' and immeasurably influential writers and how profoundly they were nurtured by their gorgeously bountiful garden and refuge."

REVIEW: *Libr J* v139 no1 p1 Ja 2014

ZORKO, IRENA.tr. The master of insomnia. See Novak, B.A

ZUCKER, ALEX.tr. The Devil's Workshop. See Topol, J.

ZUCKER, RACHEL. Mothers; [by] Rachel Zucker 164 p. 2013 Counterpath
1. Early memories 2. Essay (Literary form) 3. Memoirs 4. Mothers & daughters 5. Wolkstein, Diane, 1942-2013
ISBN 9781933996431 (alk. paper)
LC 2013-027819

SUMMARY: "Part essay, part meditation, part memoir, part poem, Rachel Zucker's 'MOTHERs' defies traditional expectations of what a book should do or can be. Zucker writes about her own mother and the various surrogate mothers she has had in her life. . . . In unflinching detail, Zucker captures her extraordinarily complex relationship with her mother, acclaimed storyteller Diane Wolkstein, in terms both moving and painful." (Publisher's note)

REVIEW: *Bookforum* v21 no1 p34 Ap/My 2014 STEPHEN BURT

REVIEW: *New Yorker* v90 no15 p77-1 Je 2 2014
"The Pedestrians" and "Mothers." "Rachel Zucker is a mother of three and the author of several books of poems; her latest, 'The Pedestrians,' has just been published, along with a memoir, 'MOTHERs.' Her poems read like skin-of-your-teeth escapes from impending disaster. . . . 'MOTHERs' begins in the key of grieving (for a friend, and for a pregnancy that ended in miscarriage). Then it modulates into a reflection on memory and on Zucker's relationship with her own mother, the storyteller Diane Wolkstein, whose side of the story emerges in e-mails and iChat transcripts that Zucker has included, seemingly unedited."

ZUCKER, RACHEL. The pedestrians; [by] Rachel Zucker 160 p. 2014 Wave Books
1. American poetry—Jewish authors 2. American poetry—Women authors 3. Marriage—Poetry 4. Mothers—Poetry 5. New York (N.Y.)—Poetry
ISBN 9781933517896 (trade paperback); 9781933517902 (hardback)
LC 2013-034614

SUMMARY: Author "Rachel Zucker returns to themes of motherhood, marriage, and the life of an artist in this double collection of poems. 'Fables,' written in prose form, shows the reader different settings (mountains, ocean, Paris) of Zucker's travels and meditations on place. The 'Pedestrians' brings us back to her native New York and the daily frustrations of a woman torn by obligations." (Publisher's note)

REVIEW: *Bookforum* v21 no1 p34 Ap/My 2014 STEPHEN BURT

REVIEW: *Libr J* v139 no4 p95 Mr 1 2014 C. Diane Scharper

REVIEW: *New Yorker* v90 no15 p77-1 Je 2 2014
"The Pedestrians" and "Mothers." "Rachel Zucker is a mother of three and the author of several books of poems; her latest, 'The Pedestrians,' has just been published, along with a memoir, 'MOTHERs.' Her poems read like skin-of-your-teeth escapes from impending disaster. . . . 'MOTHERs' begins in the key of grieving (for a friend, and for a pregnancy that ended in miscarriage). Then it modulates into a reflection on memory and on Zucker's relationship with her own mother, the storyteller Diane Wolkstein, whose side of the story emerges in e-mails and iChat transcripts that Zucker has included, seemingly unedited."

REVIEW: *Publ Wkly* v261 no8 p156 F 24 2014

ZUCKERBERG, RANDI. Dot complicated; untangling our wired lives; [by] Randi Zuckerberg 256 p. 2013 HarperOne
1. BIOGRAPHY & AUTOBIOGRAPHY—General 2. FAMILY & RELATIONSHIPS—General 3. Information technology—Social aspects 4. Internet—Social aspects 5. Social science literature 6. TECHNOLOGY & ENGINEERING—Social Aspects
ISBN 9780062285140 (hardback); 9780062285157 (pbk)
LC 2013-021760

SUMMARY: In this book on social media by Randi Zuckerberg, "through first hand accounts of her time at Facebook and beyond , , , she details the opportunities and obstacles, problems and solutions, to this new online reality. In the process, she establishes rules to bring some much-needed order and clarity to our connected, complicated, and constantly changing lives online. " (Publisher's note)

REVIEW: *N Y Times Book Rev* p15 N 3 2013 JUDITH MARTIN
"Dot Complicated: Untangling Our Wired Lives" and "Dot." "What both books demonstrate, rather than state, is that social media are inherently asocial. . . . 'Dot Complicated' is written in what may be called Facebook style--every idea and opportunity is 'awesome,' 'amazing' or 'incredible'; it all blows her mind or blows her away, and we hear a great deal about how much she loves her husband and how adorable their baby is. . . . 'Don't be a jerk,' she advises. . . . But people seeking to damage others are not generally swayed by etiquette. Nor has the law figured out how to police these activities."

ZUCKERBERG, RANDI. Dot; 32 p. 2013 Harpercollins Childrens Books
1. Computers—Juvenile literature 2. Outdoor life—Fiction 3. Picture books for children 4. Play 5. Technology & children
ISBN 0062287516; 9780062287519

SUMMARY: In this children's picture book by Randi Zuckerberg, "Dot's a spunky little girl well versed in electronic devices. Dot knows a lot. She knows how to tap . . . to swipe . . . to share . . . and she pays little attention to anything else, until one day Dot sets off on an interactive adventure with the world surrounding her. Dot's tech-savvy expertise, mingled with her resourceful imagination, proves Dot really does know lots and lots." (Publisher's note)

REVIEW: *Kirkus Rev* v81 no20 p80 O 15 2013

REVIEW: *N Y Times Book Rev* p15 N 3 2013 JUDITH MARTIN
"Dot Complicated: Untangling Our Wired Lives" and "Dot." "What both books demonstrate, rather than state, is that social media are inherently asocial. . . . 'Dot Complicated' is written in what may be called Facebook style--every idea and opportunity is 'awesome,' 'amazing' or 'incredible'; it all blows her mind or blows her away, and we hear a great deal about how much she loves her husband and how adorable their baby is. . . . 'Don't be a jerk,' she advises. . . . But people seeking to damage others are not generally swayed by etiquette. Nor has the law figured out how to police these activities."

ZUCKERMAN, ETHAN. Rewire; digital cosmopolitans in the age of connection; [by] Ethan Zuckerman 288 p. 2013 W W Norton & Co Inc

1. Cosmopolitanism 2. Internet—Social aspects 3. Online social networks 4. Social media 5. Social science literature

ISBN 0393082830; 9780393082838 (hardcover)
LC 2013-007124

SUMMARY: This book is a reflection "on what it means to be a citizen of the world in the Internet age," where Ethan Zuckerman "declares that, far from aspiring to full engagement with others around the world, we seek to connect with people who share our values, nationality, gender, and race. . . . He argues that we all possess the capacity to build networks that 'rewire' our world with a better sense of interdependence." (Publishers Weekly)

REVIEW: *Bookforum* v20 no2 p54-5 Je-Ag 2013 ASTRA TAYLOR

REVIEW: *Booklist* v109 no19/20 p9 Je 1 2013 David Pitt

REVIEW: *Kirkus Rev* v81 no12 p76 Je 15 2013

REVIEW: *New Sci* v219 no2930 p46 Ag 17 2013 Sally Adee

"Rewire: Digital Cosmopolitans in the Age of Connection." "The web's ability to put information about important global topics at our fingertips makes us more likely to burrow into our Facebook friends' feed. . . . [Ethan] Zuckerman shows how foreign news coverage in most US magazines and newspapers fell precipitously between 1979 and 2009. We demand more local and less international news, and it's a tribalism that makes us bad global citizens, says Zuckerman. . . . The solution, if we wish to seek one, may lie in our allergy to shame . . . Zuckerman has several inspiring suggestions for how to rewire the internet to nudge us to more global content, including improved machine translation to help us read posts in other languages."

REVIEW: *Publ Wkly* v260 no14 p57 Ap 8 2013 David Miller

ZUCKERMAN, GREGORY. The frackers; the outrageous inside story of the new billionaire wildcatters; [by] Gregory Zuckerman 416 p. 2013 Portfolio Penguin

1. BUSINESS & ECONOMICS—Corporate & Business History 2. BUSINESS & ECONOMICS—General 3. BUSINESS & ECONOMICS—Industries—Energy Industries 4. Businesspeople—United States—Biography 5. Energy industries—United States—Biography 6. Journalism 7. Petroleum industry and trade—United States—Biography

ISBN 1591846455; 9781591846451 (hardback)
LC 2013-037926

SUMMARY: This book explores "one of America's biggest economic and scientific revolutions of recent decades: the tapping of abundant oil and natural gas reserves within our own borders using a technique called fracking. . . . Focusing on a half dozen 'wildcatters,' the ones who seek out potential drilling sites, Zuckerman takes us through their decades long drought while they refined the techniques of horizontal hydraulic drilling." (Publishers Weekly)

REVIEW: *Booklist* v110 no6 p4-5 N 15 2013 David Pitt

"The Frackers: The Outrageous Inside Story of the New Billionaire Wildcatters." "Fans of the lively, character-driven nonfiction of writers like Kurt Eichenwald and Ben Mezrich should welcome this book with open arms. . . . In [Gregory] Zuckerman's hands, the topic generates a surprisingly entertaining story about Big Men with Big Ideas. . . . Zuckerman also explores the often passionate and outspoken opposition to the drilling procedure . . . although he doesn't come down on one side or the other. He shows us the beneficial side of fracking and the potentially environmentally disastrous side, and lets us find our own ground to stand on. A lively, exciting, and definitely thought-provoking book."

REVIEW: *Kirkus Rev* v81 no20 p217 O 15 2013

REVIEW: *New York Times* v163 no56312 pC1-4 N 6 2013 DWIGHT GARNER

REVIEW: *New York Times* v163 no56309 p7 N 3 2013 BRYAN BURROUGH

"The Frackers: The Outrageous Inside Story of the New Billionaire Wildcatters." "Mr. [Gregory] Zuckerman assembles a chorus of little-heard American voices. . . . Yet despite this, 'The Frackers' doesn't' quite end up being memorable music, at least not to these ears. Much of this has to do with literary shortcomings that, while relatively minor, are the difference between this being an 'A-plus' book and the 'B-plus book it is. . . . 'The Frackers' . . . is told with care and precision and a deep understanding of finance and corporate politics as well as oil and geology. Any criticisms I have of it are akin to those aimed at a .290 hitter who ought to be hitting .335. That said, too much of 'The Frackers' reads like a very long Wall Street Journal article."

ZUPPARDI, SAM. The Nowhere box; [by] Sam Zuppardi 40 p. 2013 Candlewick Press

1. Boxes 2. Brothers—Juvenile fiction 3. Children's stories 4. Imagination 5. Imaginitive play

ISBN 0763663670; 9780763663674
LC 2012-947828

SUMMARY: In this book, by Sam Zuppardi, "George's little brothers wreck his toys and his games and trail after him wherever he goes. Try as he might, there's just no hiding from them. George has had enough! So he commandeers an empty washing machine box and goes to the one place his brothers can't follow: Nowhere. Nowhere is amazing! It's magnificent! It's also, however, free of pirates and dragons and . . . well, anyone at all." (Publisher's note)

REVIEW: *Bull Cent Child Books* v67 no5 p290-1 Ja 2014 T. A.

"The Nowhere Box." "George's plight will be familiar to kids dealing with exasperating brothers and sisters or a budding sense of introversion, and his isolationist escapism is treated both gently and enthusiastically. [Sam] Zuppardi's untidy illustrations in acrylic and pencil are kid-inspired with their scratchy, repeated outlines and thick, unevenly applied coloration. . . . Bound to appeal to a wide range of kids because of its celebration of both collaborative and solitary play, this could be used in a storytime about siblings or imagination."

REVIEW: *Kirkus Rev* v81 no19 p142 O 1 2013

REVIEW: *SLJ* v59 no10 p1 O 2013 Sara Lissa Paulson

ZWEIG, STEFAN, 1881-1942. The Collected Stories of Stefan Zweig; 2013 Pushkin Press

1. Austrian literature—20th century 2. Death—Fiction 3. Emotions (Psychology) 4. Short stories—Collections 5. Short story (Literary form)

ISBN 9781782270034

SUMMARY: This book, by Stefan Zweig, translated by Anthea Bell, presents short stories depicting "the very best and worst of human nature . . . , captured with sharp observation, understanding and vivid empathy. Ranging from love and death to faith restored and hope regained, these stories present a master at work, at the top of his form." (Publisher's note)

REVIEW: *TLS* no5787 p19 F 28 2014 JONATHAN KEATES

"The Collected Stories of Stefan Zweig." "Reading Pushkin Press's new omnibus edition of Zweig's stories, in Anthea Bell's flawlessly pitched translations, assumes the nature of a subversive act. . . . At the root of Zweig's difficulties lies his inability to sit still and accept the value of reticence and understatement. Whatever the appeal of their faded atmosphere to the many for whom Habsburg Vienna offers a narcotic escapism, these stories seldom add up to more than a gesture or performance. It is himself Zweig needs to convince, not just his readers."

ZWEIG, STEFAN, 1881-1942. Nietzsche; 104 p. 2013 Trafalgar Square

1. Biographies 2. Nietzsche, Friedrich Wilhelm, 1844-1900 3. Philosophers 4. Philosophical literature 5. Psychology & biography

ISBN 1843913836; 9781843913832

SUMMARY: In this book on the philosopher Friedrich Nietzsche, translated by Will Stone, author Stefan "Zweig eschews traditional academic discussion and focuses on Nietzsche's habits, passions, and obsessions." He "concentrat[es] on the man rather than the work, on the tragedy of his existence and his apartness from the world in which he moved in enforced isolation." (Publisher's note)

REVIEW: *TLS* no5762 p26-7 S 6 2013 LEO A. LENSING

"Nietzsche." "[Stefan] Zweig's essay is essentially an exercise in psychobiography. Will Stone, who justifiably distinguishes his own rendering from the 'summarizing technique' and 'dilution of the original text' that mar the translation by Eden and Cedar Paul reprinted last year in Pushkin Press's edition of the entire volume), proves to be an able navigator through Zweig's sea of metaphors. Where the Pauls, for example, render a description of Nietzsche propelling himself into the game of knowledge 'heart and soul'. Stone follows the German with the phrase 'heart and entrails, nerves and flesh'. .His translation brings us much closer to the rapid pulse of Zweig's original."

ZWEIGENHAFT, RICHARD L. The new CEOs. See Domhoff, G. W.

ZWERGER, LISBETH. Tales from the Brothers Grimm; selected & illustrated by Lisbeth Zwerger; 96 p. 2013 Minedition

1. Fairy tales 2. Fairy tales—Germany 3. Hansel & Gretel (Tale) 4. Illustrated books 5. Literature—Translations 6. Pied Piper of Hamelin (Legendary character)

ISBN 9789888240531 (hbk.); 9888240536 (hbk.)

SUMMARY: In this book, Lisbeth Zwerger selects and illustrates stories "from the well-known collection of fairy tales by the Brothers Grimm. Old favorites such as 'Hansel and Gretel' and 'The Bremen Town Musicians' are included as are some lesser-known stories such as 'The Seven Ravens' and 'Hans My Hedgehog.'" (Publisher's note)

REVIEW: *Booklist* v110 no5 p62 N 1 2013 Frances Bradburn

REVIEW: *Kirkus Rev* v81 no19 p129 O 1 2013

REVIEW: *N Y Times Book Rev* p24 N 10 2013 MARIA TATAR

"Tales From the Brothers Grimm," "Michael Hague's Read-To-Me Book of Fairy Tales," and "Fairy TAle Comics". "Lisbeth Zwerger's 'Tales From the Brothers Grimm' and Michael Hague's 'Read-to-me Book of Fairy Tales' draw children into nostalgic fairy-tale worlds with the seductive beauty of their illustrations. 'Fairy Tale Comics,' edited by Chris Duffy and animated by 17 cartoonists and illustrators, by contrast, refashions classic tales with bold creativity. . . . Though Zwerger's watercolors are sometimes disturbing, the decorative beauty of her work also functions as an antidote to the violent content of the tales. This dynamic is reversed in Hague's 'Read-to-Me Book of Fairy Tales'."

REVIEW: *Voice of Youth Advocates* v36 no5 p76 D 2013 Shanna Miles

ZWIRNER, LUCAS,tr. Momo. See Momo

SUBJECT AND TITLE INDEX

gineering
Animals—Government policy
Badgerlands. Barkham, P.
Animals—Great Britain
Badgerlands. Barkham, P.
Animals—Habitat *See* Habitat (Ecology)
Animals—Habits & behavior *See* Animal behavior
Animals—Identification *See* Identification of animals
Animals—Infancy *See* Animal young
Animals—Juvenile fiction
Cat says meow. Arndt, M.
Come back, Ben. Hassett, A.
Flip flap farm. Scheffler, A.
I Want Much More Than a Dinosaur. Berliner, C.
Maisy's first numbers. Cousins, L.
Pete won't eat. McCully, E. A.
The Sleepwalkers. Schwarz, V.
Animals—Juvenile life stage *See* Animal young
Animals—Juvenile literature
Ancient animals. Plant, A.
Animal opposites. Horáček, P.
Best foot forward. Arndt, I.
Frog Trouble. Boynton, S.
Herman and Rosie. Gordon, G.
I hatched!. Corace, J.
Never play music right next to the zoo. Hernandez, L.
Old Mikamba had a farm. Isadora, R.
Say hello like this. Murphy, M.
Spring. Carr, A.
Summer. Carr, A.
Animals—Juvenile literature
The Animal Book. Jenkins, S.
I say, you say feelings! Carpenter, T.
The Odd one out. Teckentrup, B.
Say hello like this. Murphy, M.
Take a Look, Buzz. Slegers, L.
We Love Each Other. Yonezu, Y.
Animals—Juvenile poetry
Poem Depot. Florian, D.
Animals—Keys *See* Identification of animals
Animals—New Mexico
New Mexico's Spanish livestock heritage. Dunmire, W. W.
Animals—Parasites *See* Parasites
Animals—Pictorial works
The trilobite book. Levi-Setti, R.
Animals—Poetry
Outside the box. Goode, D.
Animals—Population biology—Climatic factors
Narwhals. McLeish, T.
Animals—Psychology *See* Animal psychology
Animals—Reproduction *See* Animal reproduction
Animals—Songs & music
Frog Trouble. Boynton, S.
Herman and Rosie. Gordon, G.
Never play music right next to the zoo. Hernandez, L.
Animals—Sounds *See* Animal sounds
Animals—Training *See* Animal training
Animals—Treatment *See* Animal welfare
Animism
See also
Idols & images
Transmigration
People trees. Haberman, D. L.
Anitnazi movement *See* Anti-Nazi movement
Anna Carries Water. James, L.
Anna was here. Kurtz, J.
Annakin Skywalker (Fictitious character) *See* Vader, Darth (Fictitious character)
Anne Frank's chestnut tree. Sayles, E.
Anniversaries
Exeter College. Cairncross, F.
Anniversary celebrations *See* Anniversaries
The annotated and illustrated double helix. Watson, J. D.
Annuals *See* Almanacs
Annuals (Plants)
Plantiful. Green, K.
The anointed. Giberson, K. W.
The answer to the riddle is me. Maclean, D. S.
Answerable style. Galloway, A.
Ant and honey bee. McDonald, M.
Ant colonies
Ant Colony. Deforge, M.
Ant Colony. Deforge, M.
Antarctic expeditions *See* Antarctica—Discovery & exploration
Antarctic Peninsula. British Antarctic Survey (Company)
Antarctic Peninsula (Antarctica)
Antarctic Peninsula. British Antarctic Survey (Company)
A field guide to Gettysburg. Reardon, C.
The last ocean. Weller, J.
Southern Light. Neilson, D.
World's Ultimate Cycling Races. Bacon, E.
Antarctic research stations
Antarctica. Walker, G.
Empire Antarctica. Francis, G.
Antarctica. Walker, G.
Antarctica, East (Antarctica) *See* East Antarctica (Antarctica)
Antarctica—Discovery & exploration
Antarctica. Walker, G.
Empire Antarctica. Francis, G.
Antenatal care *See* Prenatal care
Anthologies
African lives. Wisner, G.
Al-mutanabbi street starts here. Shehabi, D.
Alien hearts. Howard, R.
Balthus. Rewald, S.
The big New Yorker book of cats. New Yorker Magazine Inc.
The Biteback Dictionary of Humorous Literary Quotations. Metcalf, F.
The Cambridge edition of the works of Ben Jonson. Butler, M.
The collected early poems and plays. Duncan, R.
Comparative mysticism. Katz, S. T.
The complete works of Robert Browning. Browning, R.
Feminist writings from ancient times to the modern world. Wayne, T. K.
For Who the Bell Tolls. Marsh, D.
French decadent tales. Romer, S.
Germany. Melican, B.
A Guy Davenport reader. Davenport, G.
A Heinrich Schütz reader. Johnston, G. S.
Like Sorrow or a Tune. Farjeon, E.
Lina Bo Bardi. Lima, Z. R. M. d. A.
Lina Bo Bardi. Veikos, C.
Ljubljana Tales. Coon, J. G.
Medieval English lyrics and carols. Duncan, T. G.
The Most of Nora Ephron. Ephron, N.
New Penguin Book of English Folk Songs. Bishop, J.
The Pushcart Prize Xxxviii. Henderson, B.

The winter people. McMahon, J.
Children's choruses (Musical groups) *See* Children's choirs
Children's cookbooks *See* Children's recipes & cookbooks
Children's costumes
Petunia goes wild. Schmid, P.
Children's etiquette *See* Etiquette for children & teenagers
Children's fears *See* Fear in children
Children's games *See* Games
Children's human rights *See* Children's rights
Children's illustrated books *See* Illustrated children's books
Children's literature
See also
Adventure stories for children
Children's nonfiction
Children's poetry
Children's stories
After Iris. Farrant, N.
Animal opposites. Horáček, P.
Born wicked. Spotswood, J.
Eruption!. Rusch, E.
Fire! Fuego! Brave bomberos. Elya, S. M.
Gem. Hobbie, H.
Henry's map. Elliot, D.
The house on Dirty-Third Street. Gonzalez, T.
How do you burp in space?. Goodman, S. E.
If you could be mine. Farizan, S.
Jimmy the joey. Kelly, S.
The lonely book. Bernheimer, K.
Love in the time of global warming. Block, F. L.
Magritte's marvelous hat. Johnson, D. B.
One dog and his boy. Ibbotson, E.
Prisoner 88. Miyares, D.
Rebel McKenzie. Ransom, C.
The secret tree. Standiford, N.
Stranger things. Loveridge, M.
The unseen guest. Klassen, J.
Children's literature, Swiss
Little bird. Albertine
Children's literature writers *See* Children's literature—Authorship
Children's literature—Authorship
The stories I read to the children. Sanchez Gonzalez, L.
Children's literature—Non-fiction *See* Children's nonfiction
Children's music *See* Music—Juvenile
Children's nightmares
The Sleepwalkers. Schwarz, V.
Children's nonfiction
Ancient animals. Plant, A.
Andrew Luck. O'Neal, C.
The Animal Book. Jenkins, S.
Anne Frank's chestnut tree. Kohuth, J.
Art from her heart: folk artist Clementine Hunter. Evans, S.
A baby elephant in the wild. O'Connell, C.
The beavers' busy year. Holland, M.
Becoming Babe Ruth. Tavares, M.
Beetles. Trueit, T. S.
Behold the beautiful dung beetle. Bardoe, C.
Benny Goodman & Teddy Wilson. Cline-Ransome, L.
Best foot forward. Arndt, I.
Boho fashion. Kenney, K. L.
Bone by bone. Levine, S.
The boy who loved math. Heiligman, D.
Brazil. Heinrichs, A.
Brilliant!. Mulder, M.
Bryce Harper. Bodden, V.
Buster Posey. Gagne, T.
Can people count on me?. Nelson, R.
Carrie Underwood. Bodden, V.
The Cart that carried Martin. Bunting, E.
Cat champions. Laidlaw, R.
Chasing cheetahs. Bishop, N.
Chasing the storm. Miller, R.
The CIA and FBI. Collard, S. B.
Clara and Davie. Polacco, P.
Cold, crunchy, colorful. Brocket, J.
Colin Kaepernick. Hoblin, P.
Daniel Hale Williams. Venezia, M.
Dare the wind. Fern, T.
To dare mighty things. Payne, C. F.
Dare the wind. Fern, T.
Deadly adorable animals. Higgins, N.
Deadly high-risk jobs. Landau, E.
Doctors. Meister, C.
Does my voice count?. Donovan, S.
Double victory. Mullenbach, C.
Downloading and online shopping safety and privacy. Suen, A.
Dragonflies. Bodden, V.
Electrical wizard. Dominguez, O.
The endocrine and reproductive systems. Hiti, S.
Every Day Is Malala Day. McCarney, R.
Eye to eye. Jenkins, S.
Facebook safety and privacy. Brown, T.
Farmer Will Allen and the growing table. Martin, J. B.
Feathers. Brannen, S. S.
Fleas. Bodden, V.
Flora and Ulysses. Campbell, K. G.
The fly. Gravel, É.
Fractions. Pistoia, S.
Grandfather Gandhi. Gandhi, A.
Grasshoppers. Trueit, D.
The greatest dinosaur ever. Guiberson, B. Z.
The gunsmith. Mara, W.
Handle with care. Burns, L. G.
Hands On! Math Projects. Bell, J.
He has shot the president! Brown, D.
Hippos can't swim. DiSiena, L. L.
Hipster fashion. Kenney, K. L.
Hockey counting. Weakland, M.
Hockey patterns. Weakland, M.
Hockey shapes. Weakland, M.
A Home for Mr. Emerson. Fotheringham, E.
How can I deal with bullying?. Donovan, S.
How carbon footprints work. Hunter, N.
The human body. Richards, J.
I am Abraham Lincoln. Eliopoulos, C.
I am Malala. Lamb, C.
Ick! Yuck! Eew!. Huey, L. M.
If You Were Me and Lived in ...Kenya. Roman, C. P.
Information graphics animal kingdom. Blechman, N.
Ireland. Blashfield, J. F.
The Itty Bitty Kitty Committee. Cinotto, L.
Joe Flacco. Gitlin, M.
Joe Flacco. Torres, J.
The Large Hadron Collider. Fernandes, B. J.
Lifetime the amazing numbers in animal lives. Neal, C. S.

E

G

J

1945)
Jews—Philosophy *See* Jewish philosophy
Jews—Portugal
The Mapmaker's Daughter. Corona, L.
Jews—Race identity *See* Jewish identity
Jews—Rescue, 1939-1945 *See* World War, 1939-1945—Jews—Rescue
Jews—Rites & ceremonies *See* Judaism—Customs & practices
Jews—Rituals *See* Jews—Social life & customs
Jews—Russia—Fiction
The blessing cup. Polacco, P.
Bowstring. Avagyan, S.
A hunt for optimism. Avagyan, S.
Rifka takes a bow. Cosei Kawa
Shklovsky. Richards, J.
This is the rope. Ransome, J.
Jews—Russia—History
The blessing cup. Polacco, P.
Rifka takes a bow. Cosei Kawa
This is the rope. Ransome, J.
Jews—Social life & customs
A cultural history of Jewish dress. Silverman, E.
Jews—Social life & customs—Juvenile literature
The blessing cup. Polacco, P.
Rifka takes a bow. Cosei Kawa
This is the rope. Ransome, J.
Jews—Spain—History—Expulsion, 1492
The story of the Jews. Schama, S.
Jews—United States—History
50 Children. Pressman, S.
Hanukkah in America. Ashton, D.
Jews—Zionism *See* Zionism
JFK, conservative. Stoll, I.
JFK (John Fitzgerald Kennedy), 1917-1963 *See* Kennedy, John F. (John Fitzgerald), 1917-1963
Jiang, Jieshi, 1887-1975 *See* Chiang, Kai-shek, 1887-1975
Jiddisch language *See* Yiddish language
Jihadis *See* Mujahideen
Jim Henson. Jones, B. J.
Jim Morgan and the Pirates of the Black Skull. Raney, J. M.
Jimmy the joey. Kelly, S.
Jitney buses *See* Buses
Jive music *See* Blues music
Jo Macdonald hiked in the woods. Quattlebaum, M.
Joan Eardley. Andreae, C.
Job interviewing *See* Employment interviewing
Job skills
Land your dream career. Hays, B. A.
Jobless people *See* Unemployed
Jobs, Steven, 1955-2011
Computer technology innovators. Salem Press Inc.
Internet innovators. Salem Press Inc.
Haunted Empire. Kane, Y. I.
IGods. Detweiler, C.
Joe and Sparky go to school. Remkiewicz, F.
Joe Flacco. Gitlin, M.
Joe Flacco. Torres, J.
John Brown's Raid, Harpers Ferry, W. Va., 1859 *See* Harpers Ferry (W. Va.)—History—John Brown's Raid, 1859
John Nash. Tyack, G.
John Quincy Adams. Kaplan, F.
Johns (Toilet facilities) *See* Bathrooms
Johnson and Boswell. Radner, J. B.
Johnson, Andrew, 1808-1875
He has shot the president! Brown, D.
Johnson, Ben, 1573?-1637 *See* Jonson, Ben, 1573?-1637
Johnstone, Keith
Keith Johnstone. Dudeck, T. R.
Jokes *See* Wit & humor
Jonathan Swift. Damrosch, L.
Jong-Un, Kim, 1984- *See* Kim, Chŏng-ŭn, 1984-
Jonson, Ben, 1573?-1637
The Cambridge edition of the works of Ben Jonson. Butler, M.
Joseph Conrad's critical reception. Peters, J. G.
Josephine Baker and the Rainbow Tribe. Guterl, M. P.
The Joshua Stone. Barney, J.
Joshua the odyssey of an ordinary man. Mathew, T. M.
Journal keeping *See* Journal writing
Journal (Literary form) *See* Diary (Literary form)
Journal novel *See* Diary fiction
Journal publishing *See* Periodical publishing
Journal writing
Journal your way. Diehn, G.
Journal your way. Diehn, G.
Journalism
See also
Broadcast journalism
Broadsides
Periodical publishing
Science journalism
Sports journalism
Algerian chronicles. Camus, A.
American pastimes. Okrent, D.
The assassin from Apricot City. Lloyd-Jones, A.
Badgerlands. Barkham, P.
Bargain fever. Ellwood, M.
Bending Adversity. Pilling, D.
The Boys in the Boat. Brown, D. J.
Breach of trust. Bacevich, A. J.
Breaking the line. Freedman, S. G.
Busted. Laker, B.
Caffeinated. Carpenter, M.
Can we trust the BBC?. Aitken, R.
A chance to win. Schuppe, J.
China's urban billion. Miller, T.
Citizen canine. Grimm, D.
Claire of the sea light. Danticat, E.
Cold Blood. Kerridge, R.
Color Blind. Dunkel, T.
Dogfight. Vogelstein, F.
Double Down. Halperin, M.
Enemies Within. Goldman, A.
The eternal Nazi. Kulish, N.
The everything store. Stone, B.
Extremely loud. Volcler, J.
Five billion years of solitude. Billings, L.
The frackers. Zuckerman, G.
Gülen. Hendrick, J. D.
Hatching Twitter. Bilton, N.
Homage to Catalonia. Orwell, G.
HRC. Parnes, A.
Humboldt. Brady, E.
The humor code. McGraw, P.
Hunting season. Ojito, M.
İmamin Ordusu. Sik, A.
The internet police. Anderson, N.
The island of second sight. Thelen, A. V.

M

Neurosciences & the humanities
The Domesticated Brain. Hood, B.
Neuro. Rose, N.
A skeptic's guide to the mind. Burton, R. A.
Neurosciences & the humanities
Just babies. Bloom, P.
Moral tribes. Greene, J.
Neuroscientists
Andrew's Brain. Doctorow, E. L.
Ant Colony. Deforge, M.
Starting Over. Spencer, E.
Thomas Jefferson. Kalman, M.
Neutral Buffer Zone, Korean (Korea) *See* Korean Demilitarized Zone (Korea)
Neutrino hunters. Jayawardhana, R.
Nevada—Fiction
Half lives. Grant, S.
Never ending. Bedford, M.
Never play music right next to the zoo. Lithgow, J.
Never Say Die. Nicholson, J. C.
Neverwas. Moore, K.
New Amsterdam (N.Y.) *See* New York (N.Y.)
New and selected poems. Lehman, D.
New Argentine and Brazilian cinema. Andermann, J.
New business enterprises
The Hard Thing About Hard Things. Horowitz, B.
Smart People Should Build Things. Yang, A.
The new Cambridge history of American foreign relations. Weeks, W. E.
The new CEOs. Domhoff, G. W.
New Christians (Marranos) *See* Marranos
New Dawn, Operation, 2010-2011 *See* Iraq War, 2003-2011
The new digital age. Schmidt, E. E.
New directions in conservation medicine. Aguirre, A. A.
New England witchcraft *See* Witchcraft—New England
New England—Fiction
Born wicked. Spotswood, J.
Wicked cruel. Wallace, R.
The new environmentalism? Torsello, D.
A new history of Asian America. Lee, S.
New international economic order *See* International economic relations
New journalism *See* Creative nonfiction
New kid. Green, T.
New Labour Party (Great Britain) *See* Labour Party (Great Britain)
New media (Digital media) *See* Digital media
The new medical sociology. Turner, B.
New Mexico's Spanish livestock heritage. Dunmire, W. W.
New Mexico—Environmental conditions
New Mexico's Spanish livestock heritage. Dunmire, W. W.
New money. Rosenthal, L. Z.
New natures. Pritchard, S. B.
New Negro Movement *See* Harlem Renaissance
New Netherland and the Dutch origins of American religious liberty. Haefeli, E.
New Orleans (La.)—Fiction
The Casquette Girls. Arden, A.
Elysian fields. LaFlaur, M.
New Orleans (La.)—Social life & customs
Unfathomable city, a New Orleans atlas. Solnit, R.
New Penguin Book of English Folk Songs. Bishop, J.
New realism in motion pictures *See* Realism in motion pictures
New religions *See* Cults
New religious movements *See* Cults
New Soviet gypsies. O'Keeffe, B.
New urbanism
Anglo-American Crossroads. Clapson, M.
New ventures *See* New business enterprises
New words—English *See* English language—New words
New world order *See* International organization
New World Tribe. McKay, D.
New Year
Phaedra. Livingstone, A.
New York Jets (Football team)
Collision Low Crossers. Dawidoff, N.
New York Life Insurance Co.
God Revealed. Sievert, F.
New York (N.Y.)
Mapping Manhattan. Briant, B.
The nature of urban design. Washburn, A.
The stories they tell. Greenwald, A. M.
New York (N.Y.) art scene
Art studio America. Amirsadeghi, H.
It's Not About Sex. Kalergis, D.
Murals of New York City. McHugh, J.
New York (N.Y.) art scene—History
City as canvas. McCormick, C.
The World Atlas of street art and graffiti. Schacter, R.
New York (N.Y.). Chinatown *See* Chinatown (New York, N.Y.)
New York (N.Y.). Gramercy Park *See* Gramercy Park (New York, N.Y.)
New York (N.Y.). Greenwich Village *See* Greenwich Village (New York, N.Y.)
New York (N.Y.). Metropolitan Museum of Art *See* Metropolitan Museum of Art (New York, N.Y.)
New York (N.Y.). Police Dept.
Enemies Within. Goldman, A.
New York (N.Y.). Rockaway Beach *See* Rockaway Beach (New York, N.Y.)
New York (N.Y.)—Fiction
Bleeding edge. Pynchon, T.
Burial rites. Kent, H.
Command and control. Schlosser, E.
Dissident Gardens. Lethem, J.
Doctor Sleep. King, S.
Have you seen my dragon? Light, S.
Infinite jest. Wallace, D. F.
The lowland. Lahiri, J.
New money. Rosenthal, L. Z.
The Ocean of Mrs Nagai. Ahmed, S. Z.
Shovel ready. Sternbergh, A.
The Signature of All Things. Gilbert, E.
Tales from the Sidewalks of New York. Ross, R.
The transcriptionist. Rowland, A.
Unhooking the moon. Hughes, G.
Want Not. Miles, J.
We Are Here. Marshall, M.
Year zero. Buruma, I.
New York (N.Y.)—History
In New York. Brown, M.
Tap tap boom boom. Bluemle, E.
New York (N.Y.)—History—20th century
Careless People. Churchwell, S.
Flappers. Mackrell, J.
New York (N.Y.)—Poetry
Mothers. Zucker, R.
The pedestrians. Zucker, R.
New York (N.Y.)—Social life & customs—20th century

P

Q

S

W

X

Y

Z